International Acronyms, Initialisms & Abbreviations Dictionary

Gale's publications in the acronyms and abbreviations field include:

Acronyms, Initialisms & Abbreviations Dictionary series:

Acronyms, Initialisms & Abbreviations Dictionary (Volume 1). A guide to acronyms, initialisms, abbreviations, and similar contractions, arranged alphabetically by abbreviation.

New Acronyms, Initialisms & Abbreviations (Volume 2). Two interedition supplements, in which terms are arranged alphabetically both by abbreviation and by meaning.

Reverse Acronyms, Initialisms & Abbreviations Dictionary (Volume 3). A companion to Volume 1, in which terms are arranged alphabetically by meaning of the acronym, initialism, or abbreviation.

International Acronyms, Initialisms & Abbreviations Dictionary series:

International Acronyms, Initialisms & Abbreviations Dictionary (Volume 1). A guide to foreign and international acronyms, initialisms, abbreviations, and similar contractions, arranged alphabetically by abbreviation.

New International Acronyms, Initialisms & Abbreviations (Volume 2). Two interedition supplements, in which terms are arranged alphabetically both by abbreviation and by meaning.

Reverse International Acronyms, Initialisms & Abbreviations Dictionary (Volume 3). A companion to Volume 1, in which terms are arranged alphabetically by meaning of the acronym, initialism, or abbreviation.

Periodical Title Abbreviations series:

Periodical Title Abbreviations: By Abbreviation (Volume 1). A guide to abbreviations commonly used for periodical titles, arranged alphabetically by abbreviation.

Periodical Title Abbreviations: By Title (Volume 2). A guide to abbreviations commonly used for periodical titles, arranged alphabetically by title.

New Periodical Title Abbreviations (Volume 3). Two interedition supplements, in which terms are arranged alphabetically both by abbreviation and by title.

ISSN 0743-0523

International Acronyms, Initialisms & Abbreviations Dictionary

A Guide to over 90,000 Foreign and International Acronyms, Initialisms, Abbreviations, Alphabetic Symbols, Contractions, and Similar Condensed Appellations in All Fields

Covering: Associations, Business and Trade, Communication, Correspondence, Education, Foreign and International Affairs, Government, Labor, Military, Politics, Religion, Science, Transportation, and Other Fields

FIRST EDITION

Volume 1

Ellen T. Crowley
and
Helen E. Sheppard
Editors

Julie E. Towell
Associate Editor

GALE RESEARCH COMPANY • BOOK TOWER • DETROIT, MICHIGAN 48226

Editors: Ellen T. Crowley, Helen E. Sheppard

Associate Editor: Julie E. Towell
Assistant Editors: Pamela Dear, Prindle LaBarge, Peter A. Smith
Editorial Assistant: Anthony J. Scolaro

Production Director: Carol Blanchard
Art Director: Arthur Chartow

Editorial Data Systems Director: Dennis LaBeau
Program Design: Donald G. Dillaman

Editorial Data Entry Supervisor: Doris D. Goulart
Editorial Data Entry Associate: Jean Portfolio
Senior Data Entry Assistants: Dorothy Cotter, Sue Lynch, Mildred Sherman, Joyce M. Stone, Anna Marie Woolard
Data Entry Assistants: Ann Blake, William P. Maher, Agnes T. Roland, Ann Stockham

Publisher: Frederick G. Ruffner
Executive Vice-President/Editorial: James M. Ethridge
Editorial Director: Dedria Bryfonski
Director, Indexes and Dictionaries Division: Ellen T. Crowley

ISBN 0-8103-0509-7
ISSN 0743-0523

Computerized photocomposition by
Computer Composition Corporation
Madison Heights, Michigan

Printed in the United States of America

Contents

Preface to the First Edition

Acronyms, initialisms, and abbreviations have become increasingly popular as a means of simplifying and speeding up both oral and written communication. Their use pervades not only English but nearly every other language of the world. As political, economic, and cultural interdependence among nations grows, so also does the demand for aid in deciphering abbreviated terms in languages other than English.

As a companion to the *Acronyms, Initialisms, and Abbreviations Dictionary* series, *International Acronyms, Initialisms, and Abbreviations Dictionary (IAIAD)* includes abbreviations used internationally as well as tens of thousands of terms local to specific foreign countries and, as such, not eligible for inclusion in *Acronyms, Initialisms, and Abbreviations Dictionary (AIAD)*. As a result, overlap between the two publications is minimal and is limited chiefly to certain generic terms known worldwide ("Mlle" for Mademoiselle, "eg" for Exempli Gratia) and to internationally known organization names.

This first edition of *International Acronyms, Initialisms, and Abbreviations Dictionary* includes over 90,000 abbreviated terms. It incorporates and supersedes the paperbound "preliminary edition" published in 1984.

Other Volumes in the Series

Abbreviated forms seem to proliferate as rapidly in foreign languages as in English. In order to stay abreast of the global profusion of such terms, interedition supplements *(New International Acronyms, Initialisms, and Abbreviations)* are planned. In addition, a companion volume, *Reverse International Acronyms, Initialisms, and Abbreviations Dictionary,* is available. In *RIAIAD,* terms are arranged alphabetically by the *meanings* of the abbreviations.

What Is Covered?

Our nets have been cast worldwide in collecting entries for this series. In addition to European coverage, this first edition includes numerous African, Russian, and Latin American abbreviations. There are terms from Malaysia, Cambodia, Turkey, the Middle East, Greece, Indonesia, and many other countries of the world.

Editorial concentration is focused on those countries in which English is not the major language. Beyond this, the criterion for inclusion is only that a term be clearly international in scope or be continental, regional, national, or local to a foreign area.

The range of subjects covered is virtually unlimited and includes societies, military terms, political parties, trade and commerce terms, labor unions, government units, and thousands of commonly abbreviated words in nearly two dozen languages.

Major Sources Cited

IAIAD was compiled from a variety of published sources, miscellaneous newspaper and newsmagazine references, lists provided by foreign consulates, government publications, terms provided by outside contributors, and independent research by the editorial staff. Each term from a major published source is followed by a parenthetical alphabetic code in small capitals. A key to these symbols and complete bibliographical information about the publications cited can be found in the List of Sources Cited on page 11.

Acknowledgments

For research suggestions or contributions of terms and for other courtesies during the preparation of this first edition, the editors are indebted to the embassies and/or consulate-general offices of the following nations: Austria, Colombia, Denmark, El Salvador, Finland, France, Guyana, Hungary, Italy, Nauru, the Netherlands, Poland, Sweden, Venezuela, and West Germany.

Comments and Suggestions Are Welcome

Users of *IAIAD* can make unique and important contributions to supplements and future editions by notifying the staff of subject fields or languages that are not adequately covered, by suggesting sources for covering such fields or languages, and even by sending lists of terms they feel should be included.

Editorial Policies

The rationale for compiling *International Acronyms, Initialisms, and Abbreviations Dictionary (IAIAD)* and the editorial practices followed in preparing it are much the same as those applied to *Acronyms, Initialisms, and Abbreviations Dictionary (AIAD).* These include collecting as extensively as possible in one reference the countless abbreviated terms that touch nearly every aspect of modern life worldwide; documenting and making manageable this dynamic "language"; and keeping criteria for inclusion broad enough that terms are not excluded on subtle technicalities.

Format of Entries

A typical entry would provide the foreign abbreviation, its expansion in the foreign language, an English translation, identification of the language or country of origin, and a source code. Many entries, however, do not contain all these elements; the completeness of a listing is dependent upon the information provided by the source.

Many entries are without English translations, and others consist only of the English expansion of the foreign acronym. It is felt, however, that even partial information will be helpful to a user struggling through a multilingual jungle of acronyms and abbreviations. If additional information or a translation becomes available in future research, an entry will be revised.

Capitalization, Special Characters, Transliteration

It was recognized at an early stage of compilation that complete consistency would be an elusive goal. *IAIAD* includes a multitude of languages, and sources vary in form and treatment of entries. As a result, most terms have been picked up exactly as given by the cited source.

It is common in English to write acronyms and initialisms in all-capitals and without periods, in part reflecting the limited capacity for character typesetting that marked the early days of the computer age. Periods have been eliminated from entries in *IAIAD,* but because conventions of capitalization vary widely from language to language, the capitalization of abbreviated forms has been preserved as given by the cited source. In the case of duplication, the all-capital form has been preferred.

Font limitations preclude the typesetting of diacritics, ligatures, and so forth. Where possible, however, affected letters have been altered according to accepted standards. (The German *für* became *fuer,* for example.)

Not surprisingly, various sources reflect differing systems or philosophies of transliteration. No attempt has been made to alter the original entries by applying a single system of transliteration. The potpourri of languages and sources represented makes complete consistency of treatment impossible. It is felt, however, that since *IAIAD* is aimed at a general audience rather than linguistic specialists, the simpler course will serve the needs of the general user satisfactorily.

Arrangement of Terms

Acronyms, initialisms, and abbreviations are arranged alphabetically in letter-by-letter sequence, regardless of spacing, punctuation, or capitalization. Neither ampersands, articles, conjunctions, nor prepositions are considered in the alphabetizing. If the same abbreviation has more than one meaning, the various *meanings* are then subarranged alphabetically, in word-by-word sequence. If an abbreviation uses an Arabic numeral, the term will follow other forms of the same abbreviation. (Roman numerals sort as alphabetics.)

For example:

FC ....Federacion de Comunistas [*Federation of Communists*] [*Spanish*] (WER)
F and C ......Forwarded and Charged [*International trade*]
FEOGA ......European Agricultural Guidance and Guarantee Fund [*Use EAGGF*] (WER)
FEPAC ....Federation des Patrons Catholiques [*Federation of Catholic Employees*] [*Belgian*] (WER)
fhv ....Forhenvaerende [*Former*] [*Danish*] (GPO)
fre ....Facture [*Invoice*] [*French*]
F-S ....Faire Suivre [*Please Forward*] [*French*]
FS ....Ferrovie dello Stato [*Italian State Railways*] (WER)
FS3 ....Federalni Shromazdeni 3 [*Federal Assembly, Third Level*] (CZ)
FTA.............Foreign Trade Association (EA)

List of Sources Cited

(Unless further described in an annotation, the publications listed here contain no additional information about the acronym, initialism, or abbreviation cited in *International Acronyms, Initialisms, and Abbreviations Dictionary.*)

(AF) *Reference Aid: Abbreviations in the African Press.* Arlington, Va.: Joint Publications Research Service, 1979.

(BU) *Reference Aid: Abbreviations and Acronyms Used in the Bulgarian Press.* Arlington, Va.: Joint Publications Research Service, 1978.

(CED) *Current European Directories.* 2nd ed. Ed. by G. P. Henderson. Beckenham, Kent, England: CBD Research, 1981; distributed in US by Gale Research Co., Detroit.

(CL) *Reference Aid: Abbreviations in the Cambodian and Lao Press.* Arlington, Va.: Joint Publications Research Service, 1974.

(CNC) *Codes for the Names of Countries.* National Bureau of Standards. Washington, DC: US Government Printing Office, 1977.

These standard codes, approved by the International Organization for Standardization and the American National Standards Institute, are used in the international interchange of data in many fields.

(COL) *Diccionario de Siglas y Acronismos Colombianos.* 2nd ed. By Adela Sanabria Parra. Bogota: Instituto Colombiano para el Fomento de la Educacion Superior, 1976.

(CZ) *Reference Aid: Abbreviations in the Czechoslovak Press.* Arlington, Va.: Joint Publications Research Service, 1970.

(EA) *Encyclopedia of Associations.* 1984 ed. Ed. by Denise S. Akey. Vol. 4, *International Organizations,* issue nos. 1-3. Detroit: Gale Research Co., 1983-84.

A guide to trade, professional, and other nonprofit associations that are international in scope and membership and that are headquartered outside the United States. Entries include name and address; principal foreign language name; telephone and telex number; chief official; and a description of the purpose, activities, and structure of the organization.

(EG) *Reference Aid: Glossary of Special Terms, Acronyms and Abbreviations as Used in East German and Other German Publications.* Arlington, Va.: Joint Publications Research Service, 1975.

(GC) *Reference Aid: Abbreviations, Acronyms and Special Terms in the Press of Greece and Cyprus.* Arlington, Va.: Joint Publications Research Service, 1977.

(GC1) *Reference Aid: Supplemental Abbreviations, Acronyms in the Press of Greece and Cyprus.* Arlington, Va.: Joint Publications Research Service, 1983.

(GPO) *Style Manual.* Rev. ed. Washington, DC: US Government Printing Office, 1984.

Terms are included in Chapter 24, Foreign Languages.

(HU) *Reference Aid: Abbreviations, Acronyms, and Special Terms Used in the Hungarian Press.* Arlington, Va.: Joint Publications Research Service, 1978.

(IN) *Reference Aid: Glossary of Indonesian Abbreviations and Acronyms.* Arlington, Va.: Joint Publications Research Service, 1971.

(LA) *Reference Aid: Acronyms in the Latin American Press.* Arlington, Va.: Joint Publications Research Service, 1979.

(LA1) *Reference Aid: Abbreviations and Acronyms in the Latin American Press.* Arlington, Va.: Joint Publications Research Service, 1983.

(MAR) Private collection of African abbreviations. Lawrence Marwick, late head of the Hebraic section, Library of Congress.

(ME) *Reference Aid: Administrative Structure, Military Ranks and Organization, Police, Monetary Units, and Abbreviations Related to the Middle East Press.* Arlington, Va.: Joint Publications Research Service, 1976.

(ML) *Reference Aid: A Glossary of Malaysian and English Abbreviations Appearing in the Press of Malaysia and Singapore.* Arlington, Va.: Joint Publications Research Service, 1972.

(MTD) *A French-English Military Technical Dictionary.* By Cornelis De Witt Willcox. Washington, DC: US Government Printing Office, 1917.

(NAU) *Nautical Chart Symbols and Abbreviations.* 7th ed. Washington, DC: Department of Defense, 1979.

(PD) *Political Dissent.* A Keesing's Reference Publication. Comp. by Henry W. Degenhardt. Ed. by Alan J. Day. Harlow, Essex, England: Longman Group, 1983; distributed in US by Gale Research Co., Detroit.

> "An International Guide to Dissident, Extra-Parliamentary, Guerrilla and Illegal Political Movements." Includes the history and aims of approximately 1,000 organizations, with details of their leaderships.

(POL) *Abbreviations in the Polish Press.* Translations on Eastern Europe: Political, Sociological, and Military Affairs, no. 88. Arlington, Va.: Joint Publications Research Service, 1969.

(PPE) *Political Parties of Europe.* 2 vols. Ed. by Vincent E. McHale. The Greenwood Historical Encyclopedia of the World's Political Parties. Westport, Conn.: Greenwood Press, 1983.

> One of a series of reference guides to the world's significant political parties. "Each guide provides concise histories of the political parties of a region and attempts to detail the evolution of ideology, changes in organization, membership, leadership, and each party's impact upon society."

(PPW) *Political Parties of the World.* A Keesing's Reference Publication. Comp. and ed. by Alan J. Day and Henry W. Degenhardt. Harlow, Essex, England: Longman Group, 1980; distributed in US by Gale Research Co., Detroit.

> Covers historical development, structure, leadership, membership, policy, publications, and international affiliations. For each country, an overview of the current political situation and constitutional structure is provided.

(RO) *Reference Aid: Abbreviations in the Romanian Press.* Arlington, Va.: Joint Publications Research Service, 1979.

(RU) *Glossary of Russian Abbreviations and Acronyms.* Aerospace Technology Division, Reference Department, Library of Congress. Washington, DC: US Government Printing Office, 1967.

(SJT) *Reference Aid: Glossary of Specialized Japanese Terms.* Arlington, Va.: Joint Publications Research Service, 1974.

(TU) *Reference Aid: Abbreviations, Acronyms and Special Terms in the Turkish Press of Turkey and the TFSC.* Arlington, Va.: Joint Publications Research Service, 1977.

(TVP) *Reference Aid: Glossary of Terms Used in the Vietnamese Press.* 2nd rev. Arlington, Va.: Joint Publications Research Service, 1976.

(WEN) *Reference Aid: Glossary of Acronyms, Abbreviations, and Special Terms Used in Dutch, Finnish, German (Western Europe), and Scandinavian Press.* Arlington, Va.: Joint Publications Research Service, 1977.

(WER) *Reference Aid: Glossary of Acronyms, Abbreviations, and Special Terms Used in the Western Europe Romance-Language Press.* Arlington, Va.: Joint Publications Research Service, 1977.

(YU) *Yugoslav Abbreviations: A Selective List.* 2nd ed. Washington, DC: Library of Congress, 1962.

International Acronyms, Initialisms & Abbreviations Dictionary

A

a/ A l'Acquitte [*French*]
a Aari [*or Aaria*] [*Finnish*]
a Abra [*Illustration*] (HU)
A Absolvent [*Czechoslovak*]
a Accepte [*Accepted*] [*French*] (GPO)
A Acheteur [*or Acheter*] [*Buyer*] [*French*]
A Acker [*Acre*] [*German*]
a Acte [*Act*] [*French*]
a Adjektiivi [*Adjective*] [*Finnish*]
A Advanced [*Level of General Certificate of Education*] [*Ghanaian*]
A Aerial Reconnaissance (RU)
A Aether [*Ether*] [*German*]
a Agyu [*Cannon, Gun*] (HU)
a Ajtoszam [*Room Number*] (HU)
a Akzeptiert [*Accepted*] [*German*]
a Alatt [*Under, Below*] (HU)
a Albo [*Or*] [*Polish*]
a Alias [*Alias*] [*Spanish*]
A Alimiyah [*Doctorate*] [*Moroccan*]
A Alkohol [*Alcohol*] [*German*]
A Allongement [*Lengthening*] [*French*] (MTD)
A Alm [*German*]
A Almhuette, Sennhuette [*German*]
A Alpe [*German*]
A Altesse [*Height*] [*French*] (MTD)
A Alteza [*Highness*] [*Spanish*]
A Altitude [*Altitude*] [*French*] (MTD)
a Am [*On The*] [*German*] (GPO)
A Amatol (RU)
A Ampeeri(a) [*Finnish*]
A Amper [*Polish*]
a Ampere (BU)
A Ampere [*Ampere*] (EG)
a Ampere (RU)
A Amt [*German*]
a An [*On*] [*German*] (GPO)
a An Der [*On The, At The*] [*German*] (GPO)
A Angstroem [*Angstrom*] [*German*]
a Annus [*Year*] [*Latin*] (GPO)
a Anode (BU)
A Anode (RU)
a Ante [*Before*] [*Latin*] (GPO)
A Antenna, Aerial (RU)
A Anthracite (RU)
A Aprobado [*On an examination: Passed*] [*Spanish*]
a Ar [*Are*] [*A unit of area in the metric system*] [*German*]
a Ar [*Polish*]
a Are [*Are*] [*A unit of area in the metric system*] [*French*]
a Are (RU)
a Area [*Spanish*]
A Argent [*Money*] [*French*]
A Army (RU)
A Army (BU)
A Artillerie [*Artillery*] [*On the fleuron of a bridle*] [*French*] (MTD)
A Arzt [*German*]
A Asphalt (RU)
(A) Asthuette, Vorsaess-Oder Maisaesshuette [*German*]
a Asymmetrisch [*Asymmetric*] [*German*]
A Attelee [*Said of a battery*] [*Military*] [*French*] (MTD)
A Auflage [*Edition*] [*German*]
A Aul [*Topography*] (RU)
a Aus [*Of*] [*German*]
A Ausschuss [*Committee*] (EG)
A Austria [*Austria*] [*Polish*]
A- Automobile Gasoline (RU)
A Ayer [*Stream*] [*Malay*] (NAU)
A Azimuth (RU)
A1 AKTA I [*Level of teaching license*] [*Indonesian*]
A2 AKTA II [*Level of teaching license*] [*Indonesian*]
A3 AKTA III [*Level of teaching license*] [*Indonesian*]
A4 AKTA IV [*Level of teaching license*] [*Indonesian*]
A5 AKTA V [*Level of teaching license*] [*Indonesian*]
AA Aatelissaaty [*Estate of the Nobility*] [*Finnish*] (WEN)
AA Academy of Architecture, USSR [*1934-1956*] (RU)
AA Acetylacetone (RU)
AA Acrylamide (RU)
aa Adoallomas [*Transmitting Station, Transmitter (Radio)*] (HU)
AA African Affairs [*London*] [*A publication*] (MAR)
AA Airship Association (EA)
AA Alcoholicos Anonimos [*Medellin*] (COL)
AA Altezas [*Highnesses*] [*Spanish*]
AA Anadolu Ajansi [*Anatolian (News) Agency*] (TU)
AA Anexartiti Aristera [*Independent Left*] [*Greek*] (GC)
AA Aoratoi Agonistai [*Invisible Fighters*] [*Greek*] (GC)
AA Arbeitsausschuss [*Working Committee*] (EG)
AA Arhiv za Albansku Starinu, Jezik, i Etnologiju [*Papers on Albanian Antiquities, Language, and Ethnology*] [*Belgrade*] [*A periodical*] (YU)
AA Arkhi Anadasmon [*Land Redistribution Authority*] (GC1)
AA Arkhigeion Aeroporias [*Air Force Headquarters*] (GC)
AA Army Artillery (BU)
AA Army Artillery (RU)
AA Army Aviation (RU)
AA Arsenal do Alfeite [*Alfeite Arsenal*] [*Portuguese*] (WER)
AA Artilharia Anti-Aerea [*Antiaircraft Artillery*] [*Portuguese*] (WER)
AA Asia-Africa (ML)
AA Asia Afrika [*Asia and Africa, Afro-Asian*] (IN)
AA Astrological Association (EA)
aa Auranala [*Finnish*]
AA Auswaertiges Amt [*Foreign Ministry*] [*German*] (WEN)
AA Automobile Association of Kenya (MAR)
AA Automobile Association of Zambia (MAR)
AA Autores [*Authors*] [*Spanish*]
AA Auxi-Atome [*French association*]
AA Aviatsionnaya Armiya [*Air Army*] [*USSR*]
A & A L'Afrique et l'Asie [*A publication*] (MAR)
AAA Abrasivos Americanos Asociados [*Bogota*] (COL)
AAA Agencia Autorizada Almacenes Murcia [*Barranquilla*] (COL)
AAA Alianza Anticomunista Argentina [*Argentine Anti-Communist Alliance*] (PD)
AAA Alianza Apostolica Anticomunista [*Anti-Communist Apostolic Alliance*] [*Spanish*] (PD)
AAA Allami Allattenyesztesi Allomas [*State Stockbreeding Station*] (HU)
AAA Alleanza Armata Anti-Comunista [*Anti-Communist Armed Alliance*] [*Italian*] (WER)
AAA Arab Airways Association Ltd. (MAR)
AAA Asia, Afrika, dan Amerika Latin [*Asia, Africa, and Latin America*] (IN)
AAA Association des Auditeurs et Anciens Auditeurs de l'Academie Internationale de Droit de la Haye (MAR)
AAA Auto Andes Antioquia Ltda. [*Medellin*] (COL)
AAACI American-Arab Association for Commerce and Industry, Inc. (MAR)
AAAF Association Aeronautique et Astronautique de France [*Aeronautical and Astronautical Association of France*] (WER)
AAAID Arab Authority for Agricultural Investment and Development (MAR)
AAAN Amateur Athletics Association of Nigeria (MAR)
AAAP Association d'Aide et d'Assistance a la Population [*Association for Aid and Relief to the Population*] [*Cambodian*] (CL)
AAAR Association des Amis d'Andre Rey
AAAS Association for the Advancement of Agricultural Sciences (MAR)
AAASA Association pour l'Avancement en Afrique des Sciences de l'Agriculture [*Association for the Advancement of Agricultural Sciences in Africa*] (MAR)
AAB Aerial Leaflet Bomb (RU)
AAB Akademski Aeroklub Beograd [*Academy Aero Club of Belgrade*] (YU)

AAB .... Alianca Anticomunista Brasileira [*Brazilian Anti-Communist Alliance*] (PD)
AAB .... Allied Arab Bank (MAR)
AAB .... Anti-Apartheid Bewegung (MAR)
AAB .... Arab African Bank (MAR)
AAB .... Asociacion Automotriz Boliviana [*Bolivian Automotive Association*] (LA1)
AABN .... Anti-Apartheid-Bewegung Netherland (MAR)
AAC .... Accion Anticomunista Colombiana [*Colombian Anticommunist Action*] (LA)
AAC .... African Athletics Confederation (MAR)
AAC .... All African Convention (MAR)
AAC .... Anglo American Corporation (MAR)
AAC .... Anno Ante Christum [*In the Year Before Christ*] [*Latin*] (GPO)
AAC .... Arab-African Cooperation (MAR)
AAC .... Asociaciones de Ahorro y Credito [*Savings and Loan Associations*] [*Salvadoran*] (LA1)
AAC .... Awami Action Committee [*Indian*] (PPW)
AACART ..... African-Atlantic Coast Association of Round Tables (MAR)
AACC .... Airport Associations Coordinating Council (EA)
AACC .... All-Africa Conference of Churches (AF)
AACD .... Associacao de Assistencia a Crianca Defeituosa
AACE .... Asociacion de Amistad Cubano-Espanol [*Cuban-Spanish Friendship Association*] (LA1)
AACM .... Asociacion de Amistad Cubano-Mongol [*Cuban-Mongolian Friendship Association*] (LA1)
AACMA .... All-Africa Church Music Association (MAR)
AACO .... Arab Air Carriers' Organization (ME)
AACR .... Association for the Advancement of Civil Rights [*Gibraltar*] (PPE)
AACREA ..... Asociacion Argentina de Consorcios Regionales de Experimentacion Agricola [*Argentine Association of Regional Consortiums of Agricultural Research*] (LA1)
AAD .... Afroasiatic Dialects (MAR)
AAD .... Archiwum Akt Dawnych [*Archives of Old Records*] (POL)
AADA .... Administracion Autonoma de Almacenes Aduaneros [*Autonomous Administration of Custom Warehouses*] [*Bolivian*] (LA)
AADAI .... Arab Authority for Development and Agricultural Investment (MAR)
AADFI .... Association of African Development Finance Institutions (MAR)
AADICYT .... Asociacion Argentina de Investigadores Cientificos y Tecnologicos
AAE .... Aeroporikon Arkhigeion Ellados [*Greek Air Force Command*] (GC)
AAE .... Amicale des Algeriens en Europe [*Association of Algerians in Europe*] (AF)
A Ae .... Anglo-Arabe [*French*] (MTD)
AAE .... Arkhigeion Aeroporikis Ekpaidevseos [*Air Force Training Headquarters*] (GC)
AAE .... Association d'Assistance a l'Enfance [*Association for Relief to Children*] [*Cambodian*] (CL)
AAE .... Documents of the Archaeographic Expedition [*A publication*] (RU)
AAEA .... Association Africaine de l'Education des Adultes [*African Adult Education Association*] (AF)
AAEC .... Asociacion Argentina de Educacion Comparada [*Argentine Association of Comparative Education*] (LA)
AAES .... Asociacion Azucarera de El Salvador [*Sugar Association of El Salvador*] (LA1)
AAF .... Acetylaminofluorene (RU)
AAF .... Agricultural Aids Foundation (MAR)
AAF .... Asociatia Artistilor Fotografi [*Association of Photographic Artists*] (RO)
AAFRA .... Association of African Airlines (MAR)
AAFU .... All-African Farmers' Union (MAR)
AAG .... Aerosol Generator Truck (RU)
AAG .... Armiska Artiljeriska Grupa [*Army Artillery Group*] (YU)
AAG .... Army Artillery Group (BU)
AAG .... Army Artillery Group (RU)
AAG .... Army Aviation Hospital (RU)
AAGS .... Association of African Geological Surveys (AF)
AAH .... Allami Aruhaz [*State Department Store*] (HU)
AAH .... Anyag- es Arhivatal [*Office of Materiel and Price Control*] (HU)
AAHO .... Afro-Asian Housing Organization (EA)
AAHPM .... Association des Amis de l'Hopital Preah Monivong [*Association of Friends of Preah Monivong Hospital*] [*Cambodian*] (CL)
AAI .... African-American Institute (MAR)
AAI .... Agence Africaine d'Information (MAR)
AAI .... Alleanza Anticomunista Internazionale [*International Anticommunist Alliance*] [*Italian*] (WER)
AAI .... Pulse-Height Analyzer (RU)
AAIA .... Alianza Anti-Imperialista Argentina [*Argentine Anti-Imperialist Alliance*] (LA)
AAIC .... Africa Asia Islamic Conference (MAR)
AAID .... Agence Africaine d'Information et de Documentation (MAR)
AAID .... Association des Artistes Independants Dakarois (MAR)
AAIM .... Archives of Artillery Historical Museum (RU)
AAJA .... Afro-Asian Journalists Association (AF)
AAJD .... Asociacion Argentina de Juristas Democraticos [*Argentine Association of Democratic Lawyers*] (LA)
AAJEPT .... Associacao de Jornalistas e Escritores Portugueses do Turismo [*Portuguese Association of Journalists and Writers on Tourism*] (WER)
AAK .... Acetylaspartic Acid (RU)
AAK .... Armee de l'Air Khmere [*Cambodian Air Force*] (CL)
AAK .... Aussenhandelsabrechnungskontor [*Foreign Trade Settlements Office*] (EG)
AAKC .... Association d'Amitie Khmero-Chinoise [*Cambodian-Chinese Friendship Association*] (CL)
AAL .... Afroasiatic Linguistics (MAR)
AALA .... Association d'Amitie Lao-Australienne [*Lao-Australian Friendship Association*] (CL)
AALAPSO ... Afro-Asian Latin American People's Solidarity Organization (CL)
AALC .... Afro-American Labor Center (AF)
AAM .... Amicale des Algeriens Musulmans (MAR)
AAM .... Andidiktatorikon Agrotikon Metopon [*Antidictatorial Agrarian Front*] [*Greek*] (GC)
AAM .... Anti-Apartheid Movement (MAR)
AAM .... Association des Anciens Moudjahidines [*Algerian*] (MAR)
AAMPE .... Andifasistiki Andiimperialistiki Mathitiki Parataxi Ellados [*Antifascist, Anti-Imperialist Student Faction of Greece*] (GC)
AAMRH .... International Association of Agricultural Medicine and Rural Health (EA)
AAMS .... Association of African and Malagasy States (MAR)
AAMY .... Andidiktatorikon Agrotikon Metopon Ypaithrou [*Antidictatorial Agrarian Front in the Rural Areas*] [*Greek*] (GC)
AAN .... Academy of Artillery Sciences (RU)
AAN .... Akademi Administrasi Negara [*State Administration Academy*] (IN)
AAN .... Annuaire de l'Afrique du Nord [*Moroccan*] [*A publication*] (MAR)
AAN .... Archives of the Academy of Sciences, USSR (RU)
AAN .... Archiwum Akt Nowych [*Archives of New Records*] (POL)
AAN .... Assemblee de l'Atlantique Nord [*North Atlantic Assembly*] (EA)
AAN .... Institute of Archives of the Bulgarian Academy of Sciences (BU)
AANE .... Andifasistiki Andiimperialistiki Neolaia Ellados [*Antifascist, Anti-Imperialist Youth of Greece*] (GC)
AANII .... Arctic and Antarctic Scientific Research Institute (RU)
aant .... Aantaminen [*Pronunciation*] [*Finnish*]
aant .... Aantamys [*Finnish*]
aant .... Aantyy [*Finnish*]
AAO .... Abastumani High-Mountain Astrophysical Observatory (RU)
AAO .... Adyge Autonomous Oblast (RU)
aaO .... Am [*or An*] Angefuehrten Or [*or Orte or Orten*] [*Elsewhere, In the Place Cited*] [*German*] (GPO)
aaO .... An Andern Orten [*Elsewhere, In the Place Cited*] [*German*]
aaO .... An Angegeben Orten [*Elsewhere, In the Place Cited*] [*German*]
AAO .... Assistant Agricultural Officer (MAR)
AAOC .... Amoco Algeria Oil Company (MAR)
AAONMS .... Ancient Arabic Order of the Nobles of the Mystic Shrine (MAR)
AAP .... Alianza Anticomunista Peruana [*Peruvian Anticommunist Alliance*] (LA)
AAP .... Arkhigeion Astynomias Poleon [*Cities Police Headquarters*] [*Greek*] (GC)
AAP .... Arkhigos (Stolou) Aigaiou Pelagous [*Commander, Aegean Sea (Fleet)*] (GC)
AAP .... Asociaciones de Ahorro y Prestamo [*Savings and Loan Associations*] [*Chilean*] (LA)
AAPAUNAM ... Asociaciones Autonomas de Personal Academico de la Universidad Nacional Autonoma de Mexico [*Autonomous Associations of Academic Personnel of the National University of Mexico*] (LA)
AAPC .... Africa Auxiliary Pioneer Corps (MAR)
AAPC .... All African Peoples' Conference (MAR)
AAPC .... Asociacion de Amistad Portugal-Cuba [*Cuba-Portugal Friendship Association*] (LA)
AAPO .... All African Peoples' Organization (MAR)
AAPS .... African Association of Political Science (MAR)
AAPSC .... Afro-Asian People's Solidarity Council (MAR)
AAPSO .... Afro-Asian People's Solidarity Organization (EA)
aar .... Army Artillery (BU)
AAR .... Automatic Emergency Unloading [*Electricity*] (RU)
AARCh .... Frequency-Controlled Emergency Unloading (RU)
AARDC .... Anglo-American Rhodesian Development Corporation (MAR)
AARDES ...... Association Algerienne pour la Recherche Demographique, Economique, et Sociale [*Algerian Association for Demographic, Economic, and Social Research*] (AF)
AARM .... Army Artillery Repair Shop (RU)
AARP .... Asociacion Argentina de Relaciones Publicas [*Argentine Public Relations Association*] (LA)
AARR .... Army Artillery Repair Workshop (BU)
AARRO .... Afro-Asian Rural Reconstruction Organization (AF)
AARS .... Automatic Ammonia Control Station (RU)
AARU .... Association of Arab Universities (EA)
AAS .... Academiae Americanae Socius [*Fellow of the American Academy (Academy of Arts and Sciences)*] [*Latin*] (GPO)
AAS .... Anotaton Agrotikon Symvoulion [*Supreme Agrarian Council*] (GC1)

AASA .... Associacao Africana do Sul de Angola (MAR)
AASA .... Association for the Advancement of Agricultural Sciences in Africa (MAR)
AASANA ..... Administracion de Aeropuertos y Servicios Auxiliares a la Navegacion Aerea [*Bolivian airline*]
AASANA ..... Administracion Auxiliar de Servicios Aeros de Navegacion [*Auxiliary Air Navigation Services Administration*] [*Bolivian*] (LA)
AASC .... African-American Scholars Council, Inc. (MAR)
AASFA .... Association d'Amitie et de Solidarite Franco-Algerienne (MAR)
AASM .... African Associated States and Madagascar (MAR)
AASNS .... Asian-Australasian Society of Neurological Surgeons (EA)
AASoM .... Association for the Advancement of Science of Malawi (MAR)
AASP .... Andifasistiki Andiimperialistiki Spoudastiki Parataxi [*Antifascist, Anti-Imperialist Student Faction*] [*Greek*] (GC)
AASPE .... Andiimperialistiki Andifasistiki Spoudastiki Parataxi Ellados [*Anti-Imperialist, Antifascist Student Faction of Greece*] (GC)
AASPET ...... Andiimperialistiki Andifasistiki Spoudastiki Parataxi Ergazomenon Tekhnikon [*Anti-Imperialist, Antifascist Student Faction of Working Technicians*] [*Greek*] (GC)
AASSR .... Abkhaz Autonomous Soviet Socialist Republic (RU)
AASU .... Afro-Asiatische Union (MAR)
AASU .... Atomic Aircraft Engine, Atomic Aircraft Power Plant (RU)
AAT .... Agence Arabe de Travail (MAR)
AAT .... Automobile Construction and Transportation (RU)
AAT .... United Nations Technical Assistance Administration (BU)
AATA .... Arab Air Transport Association (MAR)
AATB .... Associated Air Travel Bureau (MAR)
AATC .... Afro-Asian Travel Centre (MAR)
AATC .... American African Trading Corporation [*Moroccan*] (MAR)
AATN .... Asociacion Argentina de Tecnologia Nuclear [*Argentine Nuclear Technology Association*] (LA)
AATO .... All-Africa Teachers' Organization (MAR)
AATPO .... Association of African Trade Promotion Organisations (MAR)
AATTA .... Arab Association of Tourism and Travel Agents (MAR)
AATUC .... All-African Trade Union Congress (MAR)
AATUF .... All-African Trade Union Federation (AF)
AAUCTU ..... All-African Union of Christian Trade Unions (MAR)
AAV .... Autoalkatresz Kereskedelmi Vallalat [*Enterprise for Automobile Parts*] (HU)
AAWB .... Afro-Asian Writers Bureau (MAR)
AAWC .... All-African Women's Conference (MAR)
AAWC .... All-African Women's Congress (MAR)
AAWORD .... Association of African Women for Research and Development (MAR)
AAYe .... Air Astronomical Almanac (RU)
ab .... Abad [*Abbot*] [*Spanish*]
ab .... Abandonne [*French*]
Ab .... Abide [*Monument, Memorial*] (TU)
AB .... Adalet Bakanligi [*Ministry of Justice*] (TU)
AB .... Address Bureau (RU)
AB .... African Business (MAR)
AB .... Africana Bulletin [*Warsaw*] [*A publication*] (MAR)
AB .... Afrikaner Broederbond [*Afrikaner Brothers League*] [*South African*] (AF)
ab .... Air Base (BU)
AB .... Air Base (RU)
AB .... Air Brigade (RU)
AB .... Ak Bank (TU)
Ab .... Aktiebolag [*Joint-Stock Company*] [*Finnish*]
a-b .... Aktiebolag [*Joint-Stock Company*] [*Swedish*] (GPO)
AB .... Allami Biztosito [*State Insurance (Enterprise)*] (HU)
AB .... Andesite Basalt (RU)
AB .... Angkatan Bersendjata [*Armed Forces*] (IN)
AB .... Armiska Baza [*Army Base*] (YU)
AB .... Army Base (RU)
AB .... Artillery Brigade (RU)
AB .... Artium Baccalaureus [*Bachelor of Arts*] [*Latin*] (GPO)
AB .... Asfalt Betonu [*Asphalt Paved*] (TU)
AB .... Asociacion Bancaria [*Bank Workers Association*] [*Argentine*] (LA)
AB .... Atom Bomb (RU)
AB .... Augsburger Bekenntnis [*German*]
AB .... Ausfuehrungsbestimmungen [*Implementing Regulations*] (EG)
AB .... Leaflet Bomb (RU)
AB .... Motor Transport Battalion, Truck Battalion (RU)
AB .... Nitrogen Balance (RU)
AB .... Parti des Abanyamajambere B'I [*Burundi*] (MAR)
AB .... Reinforced Paper (RU)
ABA .... African Bar Association (MAR)
ABA .... African Business Association (MAR)
ABA .... Amateur Boxing Association of Kenya (MAR)
ABA .... Asociacion de Bibliotecarios Antioqueros [*Medellin*] (COL)
ABA .... Auxiliaire du Batiment (MAR)
ABACO .... Association Culturelle des Ressortiments du Bas Congo (MAR)
ABAKO .... Alliance des Bakongo (MAR)
ABAO .... Arbeitsschutz- und Brandschutzanordnung [*Ordinance Regarding Industrial Accident Prevention and Fire Protection*] (EG)
ABAP .... Associacao Brasileira de Agencias de Propaganda [*Brazilian Association of Advertising Agencies*] (LA)
Abat .... Abattoir [*Slaughterhouse*] [*Military map abbreviation*] [*World War I*] [*French*] (MTD)
ABATE .... Alliance des Bateke (MAR)
ABAVIA ...... Agencias Barranquilleras de Viajes [*Barranquilla*] (COL)
ABAYA .... Abutia-Teti Abeka Youth Association (MAR)
ABAZ .... Amateur Boxing Association of Zambia (MAR)
ABAZI .... Alliance des Bayanzi (MAR)
Abb .... Abbildung [*Illustration, Figure*] [*German*] (GPO)
ABB .... Allgemeine Bedingungen der Volkseigenen Bauindustrie [*General Terms of the State Construction Industry*] (EG)
ABB .... Armiska Bolnicka Baza [*Army Hospital Base*] (YU)
ABB .... Army Hospital Base (BU)
Abbe .... Abbaye [*Abbey*] [*Military map abbreviation*] [*World War I*] [*French*] (MTD)
ABC .... ABC Aruhaz [*ABC Department Store Chain*] (HU)
ABC .... Acero Beton Centrifugado [*Bogota*] (COL)
ABC .... Africa Bibliographic Centre (MAR)
ABC .... African Brotherhood Church (MAR)
ABC .... Alberto Betancourt & Compania, SA [*Venezuelan*]
ABC .... Alexandria Bridge Club [*Egypt*] (MAR)
ABC .... Alliance Biblique du Cameroun (MAR)
ABC .... American Board of Commissioners for Foreign Missions (MAR)
ABC .... Amities Belgo-Congolaises (MAR)
ABC .... [*Santo*] Andre, [*Sao*] Bernardo Do Campo, and [*Sao*] Caetano Do Sul [*Used in reference to industrial sections of these Brazilian cities*] (LA)
ABC .... Arab Banking Corporation (MAR)
ABC .... Arme Blindee et Cavalerie [*Armored Corps and Cavalry*] [*French*] (WER)
ABC .... Asociacion Bancaria de Colombia [*Colombian Banking Association*] (LA)
ABC .... Association Belgique-Chine [*Belgian-Chinese Association*] (WER)
ABC .... Association of Black Collegians (MAR)
ABC .... Audit Bureau of Circulation (MAR)
ABC .... Societe Antoine Bachour & Cie. (MAR)
ABCA .... Association des Banques Centrales Africaines [*Association of African Central Banks*] (AF)
ABCAR .... Associacao Brasileira de Credito e Assistencia Rural [*Brazilian Association of Credit and Rural Assistance*] (LA)
ABCEM .... Associacao Brasileira de Constructores de Estructuras Metalicas [*Brazilian Association of Metal Structure Manufacturers*] (LA)
ABCFM .... American Board of Commissioners for Foreign Missions (MAR)
ABCI .... Amis Belges de la Cooperation Internationale (MAR)
ABCT .... Association Belgo-Congolaise du Textile (MAR)
ABD .... Amerika Birlesik Devletleri [*United States of America*] (TU)
ABD .... Association Belge de Documentation
ABDIB .... Associacao Brasileira para o Desenvolvimento das Industrias de Base [*Brazilian Association for the Development of Basic Industries*] (LA)
Abds .... Abends [*After Noon*] [*German*]
ABE .... Association of Business Executives (MAR)
ABECAFE ... Asociacion Salvadorena de Beneficiadores y Exportadores de Cafe [*Salvadoran Association of Coffee Processors and Exporters*] (LA1)
ABECIP .... Associacao Brasileira das Empresas de Creditos Imobiliarios e Poupancas [*Brazilian Association of Building Savings and Loan Companies*] (LA)
ABEDA .... Arab Bank for Economic Development in Africa (ME)
ABEDIA ...... Arab Bank for Economic Development in Africa (MAR)
ABEO .... Altalanos Balesetelharito es Egeszsegvedo Ovorendszabaly [*General Safety Rules for Prevention of Accidents and Health Protection*] (HU)
ABERT .... Associacao Brasileira de Empresas de Radio e Televisao [*Brazilian Association of Radio and Television Companies*] (LA)
abess .... Abessiivi [*Finnish*]
ABETEX ...... Association des Bureaux d'Etudes Travaillant a l'Exportation (MAR)
Abf .... Abfahrt [*Departure*] (EG)
ABF .... African Badminton Federation (MAR)
ABF .... Arbeiter- und Bauernfakultaet [*Worker and Peasant School*] (EG)
ABF .... Arbetarnas Bildningsforbund [*Workers' Educational Association*] [*Swedish*] (WEN)
ABF .... Association des Bibliothecaires Francais
ABFM .... American Board of Foreign Missions (MAR)
ABFMS .... American Baptist Foreign Missionary Society (MAR)
Abg .... Abgeordnete [*or Abgeordneter*] [*Deputy*] (EG)
ABGB .... Allgemeines Buergerliches Gesetzbuch [*German*]
Abgedr .... Abgedruckt [*Printed, Reprinted*] [*German*]
Abges .... Abasha Hydroelectric Power Plant (RU)
Abgiz .... Abkhaz State Publishing House (RU)
Abg z NR ..... Abgeordneter zum Nationalrat [*German*]
abh .... Abhaengig [*Dependent*] [*German*]
Abh .... Abhandlungen [*Transactions*] [*German*]
ABH .... Atomsko-Biolosko-Hemisko (Oruzje, Ratovanje) [*Chemical, Biological, and Radiological (Weapons, Warfare)*] (YU)

ABI .... Abidjan Industrie (MAR)
ABI .... Agrobiological Institute of the Bulgarian Academy of Sciences (BU)
ABI .... Arbeiter- und Bauerninspektion [*Worker and Peasant Inspectorate*] (EG)
ABI .... Arnold-Bergstraesser-Institut fuer Kulturwissenschaftliche Forschung (MAR)
ABI .... Asociacion de Bienestar Infantil [*Child Welfare Association*] [*Guatemalan*] (LA)
ABI .... Associacao Brasileira de Imprensa [*Brazilian Press Association*] (LA)
ABI .... Associazione Bancaria Italiana [*Italian Bankers' Association*] (WER)
ABIBUZ .... Acta Botanica Instituti Botanici Universitatis Zagrebensis [*Papers on Botany of the Botanical Institute, University of Zagreb*] (YU)
ABICO .... Companhia de Investimentos Arabe-Brasileira [*Arab-Brazilian Investment Company*] (LA)
ABIF .... Associacao Brasileira da Industria Farmaceutica [*Brazilian Pharmaceutical Industry Association*] (LA)
ABIFFA .... Associacao Brasileira das Industrias de Fundicao de Ferro e Aco [*Brazilian Association of Iron and Steel Smelting Industries*] (LA)
ABIFT .... Arab Bank for Investment and Foreign Trade (MAR)
ABIK .... Angkatan Belia Ibukota [*Capital City Youth Forces*] (ML)
ABIMAQ .... Associacao Brasileira da Industria de Maquinas [*Brazilian Association of Machine Industries*] (LA)
ABINEE .... Associacao Brasileira da Industria Electro-Electronica [*Brazilian Electro-Electronic Industry Association*] (LA)
ab init .... Ab Initio [*From the Beginning*] [*Latin*] (GPO)
ABIQUIM .... Associacao Brasileira da Industria Quimica e de Produtos Derivados [*Brazilian Association of the Chemical and Byproducts Industry*] (LA1)
ABIRA .... Asociacion de Bancos del Interior de la Republica Argentina [*Association of Banks of the Interior of the Argentine Republic*] (LA)
ABJD .... Association Belge des Juristes Democratiques [*Belgian Association of Democratic Lawyers*] (WER)
Abk .... Abkuerzung [*Abbreviation*] [*German*] (GPO)
ABK .... Acidophilic Broth Culture (RU)
ABK .... Aerzteberatungs-Kommission [*Medical Advisory Commission*] [*West German*] (WEN)
abkh .... Abkhazian (RU)
abkhaz .... Abkhazian (RU)
ABKhZ .... Atomic, Bacteriological, and Chemical Defense (RU)
ABKK .... Amtliche Berichte aus den Koeniglichen Kunstsammlungen (MAR)
ABKO .... Societe Abou Saleh Khochen & Cie. (MAR)
abl .... Ablatiivi [*Finnish*]
abl .... Abril [*April*] [*Spanish*]
ABL .... Accra Brewery Limited (MAR)
ABM .... American Baptist Mission (MAR)
ABM .... Asociacion de Banqueros de Mexico [*Mexican Association of Bankers*] (LA)
ABM .... Associacao Brasileira de Municipios [*Brazilian Association of Municipalities*] (LA)
ABM .... Superheavy Artillery (RU)
ABMU .... American Baptist Missionary Union (MAR)
ABN .... Algemene Bank Nederland [*General Bank of the Netherlands*] (WEN)
ABN .... Arhiv Bioloskih Nauka [*Papers on Biology*] [*Belgrade*] [*A periodical*] (YU)
AbNIIK .... Abkhaz Scientific Research Institute of Regional Studies (RU)
ABNT .... Associacao Brasileira de Normas Technicas [*Brazilian national standards organization*]
ABO .... Absatz- und Bezugsorganisation [*Marketing and Purchasing Organization*] (EG)
ABOCOL .... Abonos Colombianos SA [*Cartagena*] (COL)
ABOFORT .... Allami Borforgalmi Reszvenytarsasag [*State Wine Company Limited*] (HU)
ABON .... Special-Purpose Air Brigade (RU)
ABOP .... Algemene Bond van Onderwijzend Personeel [*General Association of Teaching Personnel*] [*Dutch*] (WEN)
ABP .... Agence Benin Presse [*Benin Press Agency*] (AF)
ABP .... Agence Burundaise de Presse [*Burundi Press Agency*] (AF)
abp .... Arcybiskup [*Archbishop*] [*Polish*]
ABP .... Artiljerisko Borbeno Pravilo [*Artillery Combat Rule*] (YU)
ABP .... Associacao Brasileira de Agencias de Propaganda [*Brazilian Association of Advertising Agencies*] (LA)
abp .... Concrete Airstrip (RU)
ABPA .... African Business Promotion Association [*Rhodesian*] (AF)
ABPN .... Anggaran Belandja dan Pendapatan Negara [*Estimate of State Income and Expenditures (National budget)*] (IN)
ABQN .... Associacao Brasileira de Qualidade Nuclear [*Brazilian Association for Nuclear Quality*] (LA)
Abr .... Abreuvoir [*Watering Trough*] [*Military map abbreviation*] [*World War I*] [*French*] (MTD)
abr .... Abril [*April*] [*Portuguese*] (GPO)
ABR .... Afrique Benin Representation (MAR)
ABR .... Air-Launched Ballistic Missile (RU)
abr .... Artillery Brigade (BU)
abr .... Artillery Brigade (RU)
ABR .... Contactless Automatic Pilot, Contactless Gyropilot [*Nautical term*] (RU)
ABR .... Societe Ateliers Belges Reunies [*Engineering*] (MAR)
ABRANFE .... Associacao Brasileira de Metais Nao-Ferrosos [*Brazilian Nonferrous Metals Association*] (LA)
ABRATE .... Associacao Brasileira de Emissoras de Televisao [*Brazilian Association of Television Stations*] (LA)
ABRATES .... Associacao Brasileira de Tradutores [*Brazilian Association of Translators*]
ABRAVA .... Associacao Brasileira de Refrigeracao, Ar Condicionado, Ventilacao, e Aquecimento [*Brazil*]
ABRI .... Angkatan Bersendjata Republik Indonesia [*Armed Forces of the Republic of Indonesia*] (IN)
Abs .... Absatz [*Paragraph*] (EG)
Abs .... Absender [*Sender*] (EG)
abs .... Absolut [*Absolute*] [*German*]
abs .... Absolute (RU)
abs .... Absolutny [*Absolute*] [*Polish*]
ABS .... Asociacion Bancaria Salvadorena [*Salvadoran Banking Association*] (LA1)
ABS .... Atomska Borbena Sredstva [*Atomic Combat Equipment*] (YU)
abs .... Aux Bons Soins De [*Care Of*] [*French*]
Abschn .... Abschnitt [*Paragraph, Chapter, Section*] (EG)
abs el-magn yed .... Absolute Electromagnetic Unit (RU)
abs el st yed .... Absolute Electrostatic Unit (RU)
Abs gen .... Absolucion General [*Spanish*]
abs iur .... Absolutus Iuris [*Latin*]
abs iur .... Absolvierter Jurist [*German*]
ABSM .... Aktiebolaget Svenska Metallverken
Absol .... Absolut [*Absolute*] [*German*]
abs re .... Absente Reo [*The Defendant Being Absent*] [*Latin*] (GPO)
ABSSR .... Bashkir Autonomous Soviet Socialist Republic (RU)
abs tr .... Absolut Trocken [*Absolutely Dry*] [*German*]
abs v .... Absolute Weight (RU)
abs yed .... Absolute Unit (RU)
Abt .... Abteilung [*Department, Section*] [*German*] (GPO)
ABT .... Arbeitsstelle fuer Bibliotheks Technik
ABT .... Armored (RU)
ABT .... Automatic Bathythermograph (RU)
ABTI .... Association Bois Tropical Ivoirien (MAR)
ABTICS .... Abstract and Book Title Index Card Service [*United Kingdom*]
Abtlg .... Abteilung [*Section, Part (of a publication)*] [*German*]
ABTs .... Gasoline Tank Truck (RU)
ABTsVM .... Automatic High-Speed Digital Computer (RU)
ABTU .... Armored Troops Directorate (RU)
ABTV .... Armored Troops (RU)
ABTZ .... Armored Vehicle Spare Parts Section (RU)
ABU .... African Boxing Union (MAR)
ABU .... Ahmadu Bello University (MAR)
ABU .... Alliance Biblique Universelle (MAR)
ABU .... Armored Troops Directorate (RU)
ABU .... Asia Pacific Broadcasting Union (EA)
ABU .... Association Belge-URSS [*Belgian-Soviet Association*] (WER)
ABUS .... Ausruestung fuer Bergbau und Schwerindustrie [*Equipment for Mining and Heavy Industry*] (EG)
ABUT .... Amalgamated Bermuda Union of Teachers (LA1)
ABV .... Abschnittsbevollmaechtigter der Deutschen Volkspolizei [*Sector of the German People's Police*] (EG)
ABV .... Atom, Biologiai, Vegyi (Fegyverek) [*Atomic, Biological, Chemical (Weapons)*] (HU)
ABV .... Aviation Unit for Pest Control (RU)
ABV .... Traveling-Wave Antenna (RU)
ABVB .... Allgemeine Bedingungen der Volkseigenen Bauindustrie [*General Terms of the State Construction Industry*] (EG)
ABVP .... Automatic Vibrating Bunker-Feeding Device (RU)
ABVV .... Algemeen Belgisch Vakverbond [*Belgian General Federation of Labor*] (WEN)
ABZ .... Ameriska Bratska Zveza [*American Fraternal Union*] (YU)
ABZ .... Asphalt Concrete Plant (RU)
ABZ- .... Refueling Truck (RU)
ABZT .... Association Belgo-Zairoise du Textile (MAR)
Abzw .... Abzweigung, Strassenabzweigung [*German*]
Abzw .... Abzweigweiche [*Branch Line Switch*] (EG)
a/c .... A Cargo [*Debit Of*] [*Business and trade*] [*Spanish*]
a/c .... A Conto [*Account*] [*Italian*] (GPO)
a/c .... A Cuenta [*On Account*] [*Business and trade*] [*Spanish*]
AC .... Accion Catolica [*Catholic Action*] [*Spanish*] (WER)
AC .... Accion Comunista [*Communist Action*] [*Spanish*] (WER)
AC .... Accion Cubana [*Cuban Action*] [*Venezuelan*] (LA)
ac .... Acompte [*Payment on Account*] [*French*]
AC .... Actio Catholica [*Catholic Action*] (HU)
AC .... Acuerdo de Cartagena [*Cartagena Agreement*] [*Use Andean Group*] (LA)
AC .... Air Congo (MAR)
AC .... Amistad Combativa [*Combat Friendship*] [*Cuban military units*] (LA)
AC .... Andina de Curtidos [*Medellin*] (COL)
ac .... Annee Courante [*Current Year*] [*French*] (GPO)
ac .... Anni Currentis [*Current Year*] [*Latin*]
ac .... Anno Corrente [*Current Year*] [*Italian*] (GPO)

AC .... Ano de Cristo [*In the Year of Our Lord*] [*Spanish*]
A de C .... Ano de Cristo [*In the Year of Our Lord*] [*Spanish*]
AC .... Ante Christum [*Before Christ*] [*Latin*] (GPO)
ac .... Anul Curent [*This Year*] (RO)
ac .... Argent Comptant [*French*]
AC .... Artillerie de Corps [*Military*] [*French*] (MTD)
A de C .... Asamblea de Cataluna [*Assembly of Catalonia*] [*Spanish*] (WER)
AC .... Atleticky Club [*Athletic Club*] (CZ)
AC .... Auto-Canon [*Military*] [*French*] (MTD)
aC .... Avanti Christo [*Before Christ*] [*Italian*]
ac .... Avaries Communes [*French*]
ACA .... Accion Catolica Argentina [*Argentine Catholic Action*] (LA)
ACA .... Administration of Coloured Affairs (MAR)
ACA .... Agence Camerounaise d'Assurances (MAR)
ACA .... Agence Centrafricaine d'Assurances (MAR)
ACA .... Agence Coloniale Automobile (MAR)
ACA .... Agence Congolaise d'Assurances (MAR)
ACA .... Agricultural Credit Agency (MAR)
ACA .... Ambtelijke Commissie Automatisering [*Dutch*]
ACA .... Anti-Corruption Agency [*Malaysian*] (ML)
ACA .... Armement Cotonnec Abidjan (MAR)
ACA .... Art et Culture Negro-Africain (MAR)
ACA .... Asociacion de Cooperativas Agrarias [*Association of Agricultural Cooperatives*] (LA)
ACA .... Asociatia Crescatorilor de Albine [*Association of Beekeepers*] (RO)
ACABA .... Association Chretienne Antandroy, Bara, et Antanosy [*Antandroy, Bara, and Antanosy Christian Association*] [*Malagasy*] (AF)
ACABQ .... United Nations Advisory Committee on Administrative and Budgetary Questions (MAR)
ACAC .... African Civil Aviation Commission (MAR)
ACACED .... Asociacion Campesina de Accion Comunal Educativa y de Defensa Civil [*Cali*] (COL)
ACADITEC ... Academia de Dibujo Tecnico [*Bogota*] (COL)
ACAE .... Ateliers et Chantiers de l'Afrique Equatoriale (MAR)
ACAF .... Ateliers et Chantiers de l'Afrique Francaise (MAR)
ACAFOM ...... Association Culturelle et Amicale des Familles d'Outre-Mer (MAR)
ACAI .... Associazione Cristiana Artigiani Italiani
ACALUB ...... Academia de Ciencias, Artes, e Letras da Universidade do Brasil [*University of Brazil Academy of Sciences, Arts, and Letters*] (LA)
ACAM .... Association Culturelle Afro-Mauricienne [*Afro-Mauritian Cultural Association*] (AF)
ACAN .... Asociacion Colombiana de Administradores de Negocios [*Colombian Business Administrators Association*] (LA)
ACAP .... Agence Camerounaise de Presse [*Cameroonian Press Agency*] (AF)
ACAP .... Agence Centrafricaine de Presse [*Central African Press Agency*] (MAR)
ACAP .... Asociacion Colombiana de Agencias de Publicidad [*Colombian Advertising Agencies Association*] (LA)
ACAP .... Association Congolaise pour l'Amitie entre les Peuples [*Congolese Association for Friendship among Peoples*] (AF)
ACAR .... Associacao de Credito e Assistencia Rural [*Association of Credit and Rural Assistance*] [*Brazilian*]
ACART .... African Centre for Applied Research and Training (MAR)
ACARTSOD ... African Centre for Applied Research and Training in Social Development (MAR)
ACASA .... Autopistas de Cataluna y Aragon, Sociedad Anonima [*Superhighways of Catalonia and Aragon, Incorporated*] [*Spanish*] (WER)
ACASS .... Administratia Centrala a Actiunilor Sportive Scolare [*Central Administration for School Sports Activities*] (RO)
ACAST .... Advisory Committee on the Application of Science and Technology to Development (MAR)
ACAV .... Asociacion Colombiana de Auxiliares de Vuelo [*Bogota*] (COL)
ACB .... Association des Commercants Burundi [*Association of Burundi Merchants*] (AF)
ACC .... Academia de Ciencias de Cuba [*Academy of Sciences of Cuba*] (LA)
acc .... Acceptation [*Acceptance*] [*French*]
ACC .... Accion Catolica Colombiana [*Bogota*] (COL)
ACC .... Accra City Council [*Ghanaian*] (MAR)
ACC .... Administrative Committee on Coordination (MAR)
ACC .... African Club Championships (MAR)
ACC .... African Community Council (MAR)
ACC .... Alexandria Cricket Club [*Egypt*] (MAR)
ACC .... Alta Corte Costituzionale [*Supreme Constitutional Court*] [*Italian*] (WER)
ACC .... Anciens Combattants Coloniaux (MAR)
ACC .... Anglican Consultative Council (EA)
ACC .... Association des Cineastes du Cambodge [*Motion Picture Association of Cambodia*] (CL)
ACC .... Automovil Club de Colombia [*Bogota*] (COL)
ACCAM .... Societe des Accumulateurs du Cameroun (MAR)
ACCC .... Africa Cup of Club Champions (MAR)
ACCC .... Associated Chinese Chamber of Commerce (ML)
ACCEL .... Accelerando [*Quickening the Pace*] [*Italian*]
ACCESS ...... Arab Community Center for Economic and Social Services (MAR)
ACCF .... Agence Centrafricaine des Communications Fluviales [*Central African Agency for River Transportation*] (AF)
ACCI .... Ateliers et Chantiers de la Cote-d'Ivoire (MAR)
ACCIA .... Asociacion Chilena de Comerciantes e Importadores de Automoviles [*Chilean Association of Automobile Dealers and Importers*] (LA)
ACCO .... Algemene Classificatie-Commissie voor de Overheidsadministratie [*Dutch*]
ACCOR .... Associated Chambers of Commerce of Rhodesia (AF)
ACCT .... Agence de Cooperation Culturelle et Technique [*Agency for Cultural and Technical Cooperation*] (EA)
ACCTPF ...... Agence de Cooperation Culturelle et Technique des Pays Francophones (MAR)
ACCU .... Academisch Computer Centrum Utrecht
ACD .... Association des Capacitaires en Droit [*Lawyers Association*] [*Cambodian*] (CL)
ACD .... Automobil-Cisterna za Dekontaminaciju [*Tank Truck for Decontamination*] [*Military*] (YU)
ACD .... Societe des Ateliers et Chantiers Maritimes de Dakar [*Senegalese*] (MAR)
ACDA .... Action Concertee pour le Developpement en Afrique (MAR)
ACDA .... Agence Americaine de Controle des Armes et du Desarmement (MAR)
ACDAC .... Asociacion Colombiana de Aviadores Civiles [*Bogota*] (COL)
ACDE .... Asociacion Cristiana de Dirigentes de Empresa [*Christian Association of Business Executives*] [*Argentine*] (LA)
ACDI .... Agence Canadienne de Developpement International (MAR)
ACDI .... Agricultural Cooperative Development International (MAR)
ACDP .... Agencija Cehoslovacke Drzavne Plovidbe [*Agency of the Czechoslovak State Navigation*] [*Belgrade*] (YU)
ACDP .... Asociacion Catolica de Propagandistas [*Catholic Association of Propagandists*] [*Spanish*] (WER)
ACDRI .... Advisory Committee on the Development of Research for Industry [*South African*] (MAR)
ACE .... Accion Catolica Espanola
ACE .... Administration de Cooperation Economique [*French*]
ACE .... African Container Express (MAR)
ACE .... Alliance Cinematographique Eurafricaine (MAR)
ACE .... Arquitectos Constructores Escolares [*Bogota*] (COL)
ACE .... Association for Centrifuge Enrichment [*Made up of ten countries including Japan*] (SJT)
ACE .... Automobile Club d'Egypte (MAR)
ACEA .... Association of Cost and Executive Accountants (EA)
ACEACE ..... Asociacion Colombiana para el Avance de la Ciencia [*Bogota*] (COL)
ACEB .... Asociacion Colombiana de Empleados Bancarios [*Colombian Bank Employees Association*] (LA)
ACEBA .... Aceite y Abonos del Valle Ltda. [*Cali*] (COL)
ACEC .... Ateliers de Constructions Electriques de Charleroi [*Charleroi Electrical Engineering Shops*] [*Belgian*] (WER)
ACEGRASAS ... Aceites y Grasas Vegetales [*Cali*] (COL)
ACEGRAVE ... Fabrica de Aceites y Grasas Vegetales de la America Latina [*Barranquilla*] (COL)
ACEINEM .... Asociaciones Colombianas de Educadores de Institutos de Ensenanza Media [*Colombian Secondary School Teachers Association*] (LA)
Ac Eks .... Acik Eksilmesi [*Open Bidding*] (TU)
ACEMCI ...... Ateliers de Constructions Electro-Mecaniques de Cote-d'Ivoire (MAR)
Ac Er .... Acemi Er [*Recruit*] (TU)
ACER .... Atelier Central d'Entretien et de Renovation [*Algerian*] (MAR)
ACEREX ...... Fabrica de Articulos de Hierro y Acero Ltda. [*Barranquilla*] (COL)
ACES .... Asociacion Cafetalera de El Salvador [*Association of Salvadoran Coffee Producers*] (LA1)
ACES .... Automovil Club de El Salvador [*Automobile Club of El Salvador*]
ACEX .... Administratia de Cercetari si Exploatari Geologice [*Geological Research and Exploitation Administration*] (RO)
ACF .... Active Citizens Force (MAR)
ACF .... Air Club of France (WER)
ACF .... Americko-Ceskoslovenska Federace [*American-Czechoslovak Federation*] (CZ)
ACF .... Arap Cumhuriyetler Federasyonu [*Arab Republics Federation*] (TU)
ACF .... Automobile Club de France [*Automobile Club of France*] (WER)
ACF .... Avion de Combat Futur [*Next Generation French Combat Aircraft*] [*French*] (WER)
ACFC .... Agro-Chemical and Food Company (MAR)
ACFMO .... Association des Constructeurs Francais de Machines-Outils (MAR)
ACFRA .... Assureurs Conseils Franco-Africains (MAR)
ACG .... Assureurs Conseils Gabonais (MAR)
ACh .... Air Unit (RU)
ACh .... Aircraft Clock (RU)
a-ch .... Ampere-Hour (RU)
ach .... Ampere-Hour (BU)
ACH .... Association of Caribbean Historians (EA)

ACh .... Digital Address (RU)
ACHA .... Asociacion Costarricense de Hoteles y Afines [*Costa Rican Association of Hotels and Related Industries*] (LA1)
AChAO .... Adyge (Cherkess) Autonomous Oblast (RU)
AChDT .... Automatic Timer and Rate Unit (RU)
ACHEDO ..... Association des Chercheurs de Documents [*Document Researchers Association*] [*Cambodian*] (CL)
ACHESA ..... Asociacion Chilena de Energia Solar [*Chilean Solar Energy Association*] (LA)
ACHF .... Asociacion Colombiana de Holstein-Friesian Ltda. [*Bogota*] (COL)
AChIMESKh ... Azov-Black Sea Institute of Rural Mechanization and Electrification (RU)
AChIMSKh ... Azov-Black Sea Institute of Rural Mechanization and Electrification (RU)
AChK .... Azov-Black Sea Kray (RU)
AChK- .... Pocket [*Microfilm*] Reader (RU)
AChKh .... Amplitude-Frequency Characteristic (RU)
AChP .... Automatic Frequency Start (RU)
aChr .... Ante Christum [*Before Christ*] [*Latin*]
AChR .... Frequency-Controlled Unloading [*Device*] (RU)
aChrn .... Ante Christum Natum [*Before Christ's Birth*] [*Latin*]
AchsV .... Achsdruckverzeichnis [*Axle Pressure Index*] (EG)
ACHTR .... Advisory Committee for Humid Tropics Research (MAR)
AChU .... Air Reinforcement Unit (RU)
ACI .... Action Catholique Independante [*Independent Catholic Action*] [*French*] (WER)
ACI .... African Cultural Institute (MAR)
ACI .... Afrique Commerce Industrie (MAR)
ACI .... Agence Congolaise d'Information [*Congolese Information Agency*] (AF)
ACI .... Agencia Central de Informacion [*Central Information Agency*] [*Dominican Republic*] (LA1)
ACI .... Associacao Comercial e Industrial de Novo Hamburgo [*Commercial and Industrial Association of Novo Hamburgo*] [*Brazilian*] (LA)
ACI .... Aziono Cattolica Italiana [*Italian Catholic Action*] (WER)
ACIA .... Asociacion Colombiana de Ingenieros Agronomos [*Cali*] (COL)
ACIBU .... Association des Commercants Indigenes du Burundi [*Association of Indigenous Merchants of Burundi*]
ACIC .... Accion Coordinadora de Izquierda Cristiana [*Coordinating Activity of the Christian Left*] [*Argentine*] (LA)
ACIC .... Asociacion Colombiana de Ingenieros Contratistas [*Medellin*] (COL)
ACICAR ...... Asociacion Colombiana de Inspectores de Carreteras [*Bogota*] (COL)
ACICLISMO ... Asociacion Colombiana de Ciclismo [*Bogota*] (COL)
ACID .... Advisory Committee on Industrial Development (MAR)
ACIDER .... Fabrica de Acidos Sulfurico y Derivados [*Bogota*] (COL)
ACIEL .... Accion Coordinadora de Instituciones Empresarias Libres [*Coordinating Activity for Free Enterprise Institutions*] [*Argentine*] (LA)
ACIEL .... Accion Coordinadora de Instituciones Empresarias Libres [*Coordinating Activity for Free Enterprise Institutions*] [*Chilean*] (LA)
ACIEM .... Asociacion Colombiana de Ingenieros Electricistas y Mecanicos [*Medellin*] (COL)
ACIEM .... Asociacion Colombiana de Ingenieros Electricos y Ramas Afines [*Colombian Association of Electrical Engineers and Related Fields*] (LA)
ACIET .... Asociacion Colombiana de Institutos de Educacion Tecnologica [*Colombian Association of Institutes of Technology*] (COL)
ACIFA .... L'Auxiliaire Commerciale Immobiliere Franco-Africaine (MAR)
ACIL .... Azevedo Campos, Irmaos Lda. (MAR)
ACILOR .... Comite de Gestion Acieries Laminoirs d'Oran (MAR)
ACIM .... Association des Consommateurs de l'Ile Maurice [*Mauritius Consumers Association*] (AF)
ACIN .... Asociatia Cineastilor [*Association of Cinematographers*] (RO)
ACINDAR .... Industria Argentina de Aceros, SA [*Argentine Steel Industries, Inc.*] (LA)
ACIR .... Agencias Comerciais e Industriais Reunidas (MAR)
ACIRAM ...... Atelierul Central de Intretinere si Reparatie a Aparatelor Medicale [*Central Workshop for the Maintenance and Repair of Medical Equipment*] (RO)
ACIS .... Alto Commissariato per l'Igiene e la Sanita [*High Commissioner of Public Health*] [*Italian*] (WER)
ACIS .... Associate Chartered Institute of Secretaries (MAR)
ACISJF .... Association Catholique Internationale des Services de la Jeunesse Feminine [*International Catholic Society for Girls*] (EA)
AcIT .... Academie Internationale du Tourisme [*International Academy of Tourism*] (EA)
ACIT .... Association of Conference Interpreters of Turkey
ACJ .... Asociacion Cristiana de Jovenes [*Young People's Christian Association*] [*Spanish*] (WER)
ACJAB .... Association Culturelle des Jeunesses Africaines du Burundi (MAR)
ACJPA .... Association Culturelle de la Jeunesse Populaire Algerienne [*Cultural Association of Algerian People's Youth*] (AF)
ACJS .... Association Congolaise des Journalistes Sportifs (MAR)
ACK .... Arhiv Centralnega Komiteta (KPS) [*Archives of the Central Committee (Communist Party of Slovenia)*] (YU)
ACK .... Automobile Club du Katanga (MAR)
ACKPOM .... Akademicka Centralna Komisja Porozumiewawcza Organizacji Mlodziezy [*Central Student Consultative Commission of Youth Organizations*] (POL)
ACL .... Accion Ciudadana Liberal [*Liberal Citizens' Action*] (PPE)
ACL .... Asociacion Colombiana de Locutores [*Colombian Radio and Television Announcers Association*] (LA)
ACLALS ...... Association for Commonwealth Literature and Language Studies (EA)
ACLEN .... Asociacion Nacional del Clero [*National Association of the Clergy*] [*Nicaraguan*] (LA1)
ACLI .... Associazioni Cristiane Lavoratori Italiani [*Christian Associations of Italian Workers*] (WER)
ACLIFIM ...... Asociacion Cubana de Limitados Fisicos Motores [*Cuban Association for the Physically Handicapped*] (LA1)
ACLM .... Afro-Caribbean Liberation Movement [*Argentine*] (LA1)
ACLM .... Antigua Caribbean Liberation Movement (LA)
ACLP .... Action Committee for the Liberation of Palestine (ME)
ACLV .... Algemene Centrale der Liberale Vakbonden [*General Federation of Liberal Trade Unions*] [*Belgian*] (WEN)
ACM .... Arab Common Market (MAR)
ACM .... Asociacion de Comerciantes Mayoristas [*Wholesalers Association*] [*Nicaraguan*] (LA1)
ACM .... Ateliers et Chantiers du Mali (MAR)
ACM .... Societe Africaine de Constructions Metalliques (MAR)
ACMA .... Asociacion Colombiana de Mecanicos de Aviacion [*Bogota*] (COL)
ACMA .... Association des Classes Moyennes Angolaises (MAR)
ACMA .... Ateliers et Chantiers Maritimes d'Abidjan (MAR)
ACMAF .... Association des Classes Moyennes Africaines (MAR)
ACMB .... Association des Classes Moyennes du Burundi (MAR)
ACME .... Association of Copper Mining Employees (MAR)
ACMET .... Advisory Council on Middle East Trade (MAR)
ACMG .... Associacao Comercial de Minas Gerais [*Commercial Association of Minas Gerais*] [*Brazilian*] (LA)
ACMS .... African Centre for Monetary Studies (MAR)
ACMT .... Ateliers de Constructions Metallurgiques Tchadiens (MAR)
aCn .... Ante Christum Natum [*Before Christ's Birth*] [*Latin*]
ACN .... Ateliers et Chantiers de Nouakchott (MAR)
ACNA .... Association Cinema Negro Africaine (MAR)
ACNL .... Algemene Conferentie der Nederlandse Letteren
ACNOA .... Association des Comites Nationaux Olympiques Africains (MAR)
ACNP .... Asociacion Catolica Nacional de Propagandistas [*National Catholic Association of Propagandists*] [*Spanish*] (WER)
ACNU .... Asociacion Cubana de Naciones Unidas [*Cuban United Nations Association*] (LA)
ACNUR .... Alto Comisionado de las Naciones Unidas para los Refugiados [*United Nations High Commission for Refugees*] (LA)
ACO .... African Curriculum Organization (AF)
ACO .... Arab Communist Organisation (MAR)
ACOA .... American Committee on Africa (MAR)
ACOBE .... Asociacion Colombiana de Beisbol [*Bogota*] (COL)
ACOBOX ..... Asociacion Colombiana de Boxeo y Lucha Olimpica [*Bogota*] (COL)
ACOCERAM ... Asociacion Colombiana de Ceramistas [*Bogota*] (COL)
ACODA .... Asociacion Colombiana de Ajedrez [*Bogota*] (COL)
ACODAI ...... Asociacion Colombiana de Administracion Industrial [*Cali*] (COL)
ACODAL ..... Asociacion Colombiana de Acueductos y Alcantarillados [*Bogota*] (COL)
ACODASE ... Asociacion Colombiana de Agentes de Seguros [*Bogota*] (COL)
ACODECC ... Asociacion Colombiana de Criadores de Cerdos [*Bogota*] (COL)
ACOEXA ..... Asociacion Colombiana de Expertos Agricolas [*Bogota*] (COL)
ACOFAL ...... Asociacion Colombiana de Fabricantes de Alimentos para Animales [*Bogota*] (COL)
ACOGE .... Asociacion Costarricense de Gerentes y Empresarios [*Costa Rican Association of Managers and Businessmen*] (LA1)
ACOGES ..... Afrique Construction et Gestion (MAR)
ACOGRAFICA ... Asociacion Colombiana de Industria Grafica [*Bogota*] (COL)
ACOGRAN ... Asociacion Colombiana de Griles, Restaurantes, y Afines [*Bogota*] (COL)
ACOLECHE ... Asociacion Colombiana de Industrias de la Leche [*Bogota*] (COL)
ACOLEVE ... Asesoria en Creditos y Cobranzas [*Bogota*] (COL)
ACOLFA ...... Asociacion Colombiana de Fabricantes de Autopartes [*Colombian Association of Auto Parts Manufacturers*] (LA)
ACOLSURE ... Asociacion Colombiana de Suboficiales de las Fuerzas Militares en Retiro [*Colombian Association of Retired Armed Forces Noncommissioned Officers*] (LA)
ACOLTEX ... Asociacion Colombiana de Tecnicos de Acabados Textiles (COL)
ACOM .... Anciens Combattants Outre-Mer (MAR)
ACOMAC .... Accion Comunitaria [*Community Action*] [*Mexican*] (PPW)
ACOMINAS ... Aco Minas Gerais, SA [*Minas Gerais Steel Company*] [*Brazilian*] (LA)

ACOMOTO ... Asociacion Colombiana de Motociclistas [*Bogota*] (COL)
ACOMPAS ... Asociacion Colombiana de Musicos Profesionales [*Bogota*] (COL)
ACOPAI .... Asociaciones de Cooperativas de Productos Agropecuarios Integrados [*Associations of Cooperatives of Integrated Agricultural-Livestock Products*] [*Salvadoran*] (LA1)
ACOPECAFE ... Asociacion Colombiana de Pequenos Productores de Cafe [*Colombian Small Coffee Growers Association*] (LA)
ACOPER ..... Asociacion de Productores y Distribuidores de Cosmeticos y Perfumes [*Bogota*] (COL)
ACOPESCA ... Alianza Colombiana de Pesca Ltda. [*Cali*] (COL)
ACOPI .... Asociacion Colombiana de Pequenos Industriales [*Bogota*] (COL)
ACOPI .... Asociacion Colombiana Popular de Industrias [*Colombian Small Industries Association*] (LA)
ACOPLASTICOS ... Asociacion Colombiana de Industrias Plasticas [*Colombian Plastics Industry Association*] (LA)
ACOPROBAMA ... Asociacion de Comerciantes de Productos Basicos de Managua [*Association of Managua Merchants of Basic Goods*] [*Nicaraguan*] (LA1)
ACORBAT ... Association for Cooperation in Banana Research in the Caribbean and Tropical America (EA)
ACORD .... Asociacion Colombiana de la Prensa Deportiva [*Cali*] (COL)
ACORE .... Asociacion Colombiana de Reservistas [*Colombian Reservists Association*] (LA)
ACORP .... Asociacion Colombiana de Relaciones Publicas [*Bogota*] (COL)
ACOSA .... Aluminium Company of South Africa (MAR)
ACOSCA ..... Africa Cooperative Savings and Credit Association (AF)
ACOTA .... Asociacion Colombiana de Talleres Automotores [*Bogota*] (COL)
ACOTEL ...... Asociacion Colombiana de Hoteles [*Bogota*] (COL)
ACOTV .... Asociacion Colombiana de Tecnicos de Television [*Bogota*] (COL)
ACOTV .... Asociacion Colombiana de Television [*Colombian Television Association*] (LA)
ACOVOL ..... Agencia Coordinadora del Voluntariado de Bogota y Cundinamarca [*Bogota*] (COL)
ACP .... Accao Catolica Portuguesa [*Portuguese Catholic Action*] (WER)
ACP .... Action Congress Party [*Ghanaian*] (PPW)
ACP .... Administratia Carierelor de Piatra [*Administration of Stone Quarries*] (RO)
ACP .... African, Caribbean, and Pacific Countries [*Associated with the EEC*] (AF)
ACP .... Agence Camerounaise de Presse [*Cameroonian Press Agency*] (MAR)
ACP .... Agence Centrafricaine de Presse [*Central African Press Agency*] (MAR)
ACP .... Agence Centrale Parisienne de Presse [*Parisian Central Press Agency*] [*French*] (AF)
ACP .... Agence Centrale de Publicite [*Central Advertising Agency*] [*French*] (WER)
ACP .... Agence Comores de Presse (MAR)
ACP .... Agence Congolaise de Presse [*Congolese Press Agency*] (MAR)
ACP .... Agrupacion Comunista Proletaria [*Proletarian Communist Group*] [*Spanish*] (WER)
ACP .... Alexandria City Police [*Egypt*] (MAR)
ACP .... Arab Communist Party (MAR)
ACP .... Asociacion Colombiana de Periodistas [*Colombian Journalists Association*] (LA)
ACP .... Automovel Clube de Portugal [*Portuguese Automobile Club*] (WER)
ACPES .... Asociacion Colombiana de Profesores de Ensenanza Secundaria [*Colombian Secondary School Teachers Association*] (LA)
ACPF .... Asociacion del Congreso Panamericano de Ferrocarriles [*Pan American Railway Congress Association*] (EA)
ACPN .... Ateliers et Chantiers de Pointe-Noire (MAR)
ACPO .... Accion Cultural Popular [*Basic education organization*] [*Colombian*]
ACPS .... Arab Company for Petroleum Services (ME)
Acqt .... Acquit [*Paid in Full*] [*Business and trade*] [*French*]
ACR .... Africa Contemporary Record [*A publication*] (MAR)
ACR .... Agencia Cubana de Radio [*Cuban Radio Agency*] (LA1)
ACR .... Automobil Clubul Roman [*Romanian Automobile Club*] (RO)
ACRA .... Atelierele Centrale de Reparatii Autovehiculare [*Central Workshops for Auto Repairs*] (RO)
ACRE .... Adaptive Crop Research and Extension (MAR)
ACREFI .... Associacao das Empresas de Credito, Financiamento, e Investimento [*Association of Credit, Finance, and Investment Firms*] [*Brazilian*] (LA)
ACRM .... Anti-Corruption Revolutionary Movement [*Sierra Leonean*] (AF)
ACRN .... Ateliers de Construction et Reparation Navales (MAR)
ACROSS ..... Africa Committee for the Rehabilitation of Southern Sudan (MAR)
ACS .... African Container Service [*Nigerian*] (AF)
ACS .... Anadolu Cam Sanayii AS [*Anatolian Glass Industry Corporation*] [*Mersin*] (TU)
ACS .... Anglo-Chinese School (ML)
ACS .... Anti-Communist Society [*Belizean*] (PD)
ACS .... Association of Commonwealth Students (AF)
ACSAT .... Advisory Committee for Science and Technology (MAR)
ACSI .... Anya- es Csecsemovedelmi Intezet [*Institute for the Protection of Mothers and Infants*] (HU)
ACSI .... Anyagmozgatasi es Csomagolasi Intezet [*Material Handling and Packaging Institute*] (HU)
ACSM .... Associateship of the Camborne School of Mines (MAR)
ACSP .... Associacao Comercial de Sao Paulo [*Sao Paulo Commercial Association*] [*Brazilian*] (LA)
ACSTWU ..... African Civil Service Technical Workers' Union (MAR)
ACT .... Acordo Colectivo de Trabalho [*Collective Labor Agreement*] [*Portuguese*] (WER)
act .... Action [*French*]
ACT .... Agence pour la Cooperation Technique, Industrielle, et Economique [*Technical, Industrial, and Economic Cooperation Agency*] [*French*] (WER)
ACT .... Australian Capital Territory (PPW)
a cta .... A Cuenta [*On Account*] [*Business and trade*] [*Spanish*]
ActaIPM ...... Acta. Izdanija na Prirodnonaucniot Muzej [*Papers. Issued by the Museum of Natural Sciences*] [*Skopje*] [*A publication*] (YU)
ACTALAC ... Asociacion Civil de Tecnicos Azucareros de la America Latina y del Caribe
ACTAR .... Asian Center for Tax Administration and Research (CL)
ACTC .... Agency for Cultural and Technical Cooperation [*Use ACCT*] (LA1)
ACTE .... Asociacion Colombiana de Tecnicos Electricistas [*Bogota*] (COL)
ACTREL ...... Asociacion Colombiana de Tecnicos en Radioelectronica [*Bogota*] (COL)
ACTS .... Arab Company for Trading in Securities (MAR)
ACTT .... African Centre for the Development, Transfer, and Adaptation of Technology (MAR)
ACU .... Agrupacion Catolica Universitaria [*Catholic Group of University Students and Professionals*] (LA)
ACU .... Asociacion Colombiana de Universidades [*Bogota*] (COL)
ACU .... Association of Commonwealth Universities (EA)
ACU .... Marine Atomic Power Plant, Shipboard Nuclear Propulsion Plant (RU)
ACUABOL ... Sociedad de Acueductos y Alcantarillados de Bolivar [*Cartagena*] (COL)
ACUACALDAS ... Acueductos y Alcantarillados de Caldas [*Manizales*] (COL)
ACUACAUCA ... Sociedad de Acueductos y Alcantarillados del Cauca [*Popayan*] (COL)
ACUACORDOBA ... Sociedad de Acueductos y Alcantarillados de Cordoba [*Monteria*] (COL)
ACUAMARCA ... Acueductos y Alcantarillados de Cundinamarca [*Bogota*] (COL)
ACUAVALLE ... Acueductos y Alcantarillados del Valle SA [*Cali*] (COL)
ACUG .... Association Culturelle de Guiberoua (MAR)
ACUNI .... Asociacion de Centros de la Universidad Nacional de Ingenieria [*National Engineering University Centers Association*] [*Peruvian*] (LA)
ACUS .... Peruvian-USSR Cultural Association (LA)
ACV .... Algemeen Christelijk Vakverbond [*Confederation of Christian Trade Unions*] [*Belgian*] (WEN)
ACVAFS ...... American Council of Voluntary Agencies for Foreign Service, Inc. (MAR)
ACVG .... Anciens Combattants et Victimes de la Guerre (MAR)
ACW .... Algemeen Christelijk Werkersverbond [*Christian Labor Movement*] [*Belgian*] (WEN)
ACWW .... Associated Country Women of the World (MAR)
ACZ .... Agro-Chemisches Zentrum [*Agro-Chemical Center*] (EG)
AD .... Accion Democratica [*Democratic Action*] [*Salvadoran*] (PD)
AD .... Accion Democratica [*Democratic Action*] [*Venezuelan*] (PPW)
AD .... Action Directe [*Direct Action*] [*French*] (PD)
Ad .... Ada [*Adasi, Adacik*] [*Island, Islet*] [*Turkish*] (NAU)
Ad .... Adet [*Number*] (TU)
ad .... Admiral (BU)
AD .... Adrenaline (RU)
AD .... Africa Diary [*A publication*] (MAR)
ad .... Air Division (BU)
AD .... Air Division (RU)
AD .... Airborne (RU)
AD .... Airborne Force (RU)
AD .... Aircraft Engine (RU)
ad .... Airdrome (BU)
AD .... Akademsko Drustvo [*Academic Society*] (YU)
AD .... Akcijska Druzba [*Joint-Stock Company*] (YU)
AD .... Akcionarsko Drustvo [*Joint-Stock Company*] (YU)
AD .... Algerian Dinar (MAR)
AD .... Alianca Democratica [*Democratic Alliance*] [*Portuguese*] (PPE)
AD .... Amesos Drasis [*Immediate Action*] [*See also DTA, KAD, MMAD*] (GC1)
AD .... Amplitude Demodulator (RU)
ad .... An Der [*At The, On The*] [*German*] (GPO)
aD .... An der Donau [*On the River Danube*] [*German*] [*Austrian*] (WEN)
AD .... Andorra [*Two-letter standard code*] (CNC)

AD .... Anggaran Dasar [*Statutes, Constitution (of an organization)*] (IN)
AD .... Angkatan Darat [*Army*] (IN)
AD .... Anno Domini [*In the Year of Our Lord*] [*Latin*] (GPO)
ad .... Ante Diem [*Before the Day*] [*Latin*] (GPO)
AD .... Aptechno Delo [*Pharmaceutical Affairs*] [*A publication*] (BU)
AD .... Arab Development Journal for Science and Technology [*Tripoli*] [*A publication*] (MAR)
AD .... Archaeological Society (BU)
AD .... Armadni Divadlo [*Armed Forces Theater*] [*Prague*] (CZ)
AD .... Armadni Dum [*Armed Forces Building*] (CZ)
AD .... Arterial Pressure (RU)
AD .... Artiljerija Divizije [*Artillery of a Division*] (YU)
AD .... Artillerie Divisionnaire [*Military*] [*French*] (MTD)
AD .... Artillery Battalion (RU)
ad .... Artillery Battalion (BU)
ad .... Artillery Division (BU)
AD .... Artillery Division (RU)
AD .... Atomic Engine (RU)
aD .... Ausser Dienst [*Retired*] [*German*] (GPO)
AD- .... Automatic Dehydrator (RU)
AD .... Damped Shock Absorber (RU)
AD .... Division Artillery (RU)
AD .... Induction Motor (RU)
AD .... Joint-Stock Company (BU)
AD .... Mobile Shower Unit (RU)
ADA .... Accelerated Development Area Programme (MAR)
ADA .... Advective Dynamical Analysis (of Synoptic Processes) (RU)
ADA .... Agence Dahomeenne d'Assurances (MAR)
ADA .... Agrupacion Democratica Argentina [*Argentine Democratic Group*] (LA)
ADA .... Agrupament Democratic d'Andorra [*Andorran Democratic Association*] (PPW)
ADA .... Allgemeine Dienstanweisung [*General Service Regulations*] (EG)
ADA .... Alliance Democratique Africaine (MAR)
ADA .... Anotati Dioikisis Aeroporias [*Supreme Air Force Command*] (GC)
ADA .... Astynomiki Dievthynsis Athinon [*Athens Police Directorate*] (GC)
ADAC .... Avions aux Atterrissage et Decollage Courts [*Short Takeoff and Landing Planes*] [*Use STOL*] (CL)
ADACH .... Asociacion de Algodoneros de Chinandega [*Association of Chinandega Cotton Growers*] [*Nicaraguan*] (LA1)
ADADO .... Asociacion de Algodoneros de Oriente [*Association of Eastern Cotton Growers*] [*Nicaraguan*] (LA1)
ADAEPS ...... Association des Anciens Eleves des Peres de Scheut (MAR)
ADAF .... Arbeitskreis der Deutschen Afrika-Forschungs- und Dokumentationstellen (MAR)
ADAL .... Asociacion de Algodoneros de Leon [*Association of Leon Cotton Growers*] [*Nicaraguan*] (LA1)
ADAPC .... Associacao Democratica de Amizade Portugal-China [*Democratic Association for Portuguese-Chinese Friendship*] (WER)
adap ed .... Adapte Eden [*Which Was Adapted (From)*] (TU)
adapt .... Adaptacja [*or Adaptowal*] [*Adaptation or Adapted By*] [*Polish*]
ADAR .... Association des Amis Republicains [*Association of Republican Friends*] [*Cambodian*] (CL)
ADAS .... Administratia Asigurarilor de Stat [*State Insurance Administration*] (RO)
ADAS .... African Demonstration Centre on Sampling Agricultural Surveys (MAR)
ADAS .... Akaryakit Dagitim Anonim Sirkesi [*Fuel Distribution Corporation*] (TU)
ADAST .... Adamovske Strojirny [*Adamov Engineering Works*] (CZ)
ADATIG .... Anglo-Dutch African Textiles Investigation Group (MAR)
ADAUA .... Association pour le Developpement de l'Architecture et l'Urbanisme en Afrique (MAR)
ADB .... African Development Bank (AF)
ADB .... Agricultural Development Bank [*Trinidadian and Tobagan*] (LA1)
ADB .... Airborne Brigade (RU)
ADB .... Allgemeine Deutsche Binnen-Transport-Versicherungsbedingungen [*General German Inland Transportation Insurance Terms*] (EG)
ADB .... Asian Development Bank (ML)
ADBIENES ... Administracion de Bienes y Arrendamientos [*Medellin*] (COL)
ADBPA .... Association pour le Developpement des Bibliotheques Publiques en Afrique [*Association for the Development of Public Libraries in Africa*]
ADBV .... Allgemeiner Deutscher Blinden-Verband [*General German Association of the Blind*] (EG)
ADC .... Agricultural Development Corporation (MAR)
ADC .... Agricultural Development Council (MAR)
ADC .... Asia Development Center (CL)
ADC .... Asociacion Democratica Colombiana [*Colombian Democratic Association*] (LA)
ADCONA ..... Administradores y Contadores Asociados [*Cali*] (COL)
ADD .... Agricultural Development Division (MAR)
ADD .... Alliance Democratique Dahomeenne (MAR)
ADD .... Asociacion Dominicana de Diarios [*Dominican Association of Daily Newspapers*] [*Dominican Republic*] (LA1)
ADD .... Long-Range Artillery (RU)
ADD .... Long-Range Aviation (RU)
ADDO .... Alokasi Devisa Daerah Otomatis [*Automatic Regional Foreign-Exchange Allocation (Percentage of export earnings returned to regions by central government)*] (IN)
ADE .... Accion Democratica Ecuatoriana [*Ecuadorean Democratic Action*] (PPW)
ADE .... Asamblea Democratica Euzkadi [*Basque Democratic Assembly*] [*Spanish*] (WER)
ADE .... Asociacion Democratica de Estudiantes [*Democratic Association of Students*] [*Mexican*] (LA1)
ADE .... Asociacion Distrital de Educadores [*District Teachers Association*] [*Colombian*] (LA)
ADEA .... Asociacion de Defensores de Animales [*Animal Protection Association*] [*Uruguayan*] (LA)
ADEA .... Association Belge pour le Developpement Pacifique de l'Energie Atomique [*Belgian Association for the Peaceful Development of Atomic Energy*]
ADEAC .... Association pour le Developpement des Echanges Artistiques et Culturels (MAR)
ADEBA .... Asociacion de Bancos Argentinos [*Argentine Bank Association*] (LA)
ADEBASQUET ... Asociacion Colombiana de Basquetbol [*Bogota*] (COL)
ADEBCO ..... Association des Eglises Baptistes du Congo-Ouest (MAR)
ADEC .... Association pour le Developpement Educatif et Culturel (MAR)
ADEC .... Association des Entrepreneurs du Congo (MAR)
ADECAFEH ... Asociacion de Exportadores de Cafe de Honduras [*Association of Honduran Coffee Exporters*] (LA1)
ADECELA ... Asociacion de Celadores de Antioquia [*Medellin*] (COL)
ADECERE ... Asociacion de Empleados del Centro de Rehabilitacion [*Association of Rehabilitation Center Employees*] [*Dominican Republic*] (LA1)
ADECIF .... Associacao dos Diretores de Empresas de Credito, Investimentos, e Financiamento [*Association of Directors of Credit, Investment, and Finance Companies*] [*Brazilian*] (LA)
ADECOL ..... Asociacion de Compositores Colombianos [*Medellin*] (COL)
ADECON ..... Asociacion de Comercio Nacional Ltda. [*Bogota*] (COL)
ADECONTA ... Asociacion de Contadores del Valle del Cauca [*Cali*] (COL)
ADECRENE ... Associacao dos Diretores de Empresas de Credito, Financiamento, e Investimentos do Nordeste [*Association of Directors of Credit, Finance, and Investment Companies in the Northeast*] [*Brazilian*] (LA)
ADEDY .... Anotati Dioikousa Epitropi Dimosion Ypallilon [*Supreme Administrative Committee of Civil Servants*] [*Greek*] (GC)
ADEEP .... Association d'Entraide des Eglises de Pentecote [*Pentacostal Churches Welfare Association*] [*Burundi*] (AF)
ADEFA .... Asociacion de Fabricantes de Automotores [*Association of Motor Vehicle Manufacturers*] [*Argentine*] (LA)
ADEFUTBOL ... Asociacion Colombiana de Futbol [*Bogota*] (COL)
ADEL .... Academia de Estudios Liturgicos [*Medellin*] (COL)
ADELA .... Ayakkabi-Deri ve Lastik Sanayii AS [*Footwear, Leather, and Rubber Industry Corp.*] [*Istanbul*] (TU)
ADELCA ...... Acerias de Ecuador [*Steelworks of Ecuador*] (LA)
ADELCA ...... Administracion del Correo Aereo [*Medellin*] (COL)
ADELF .... Association des Ecrivains de Langue Francaise [*Association of French-Language Writers*] (EA)
ADEM .... Asociacion de Directores de Ensenanza Media [*Association of Mid-Level School Directors*] [*Costa Rican*] (LA1)
ADEM .... Association Democratique des Etudiants de Madagascar [*Malagasy Democratic Student Association*] (AF)
ADEMACOL ... Asociacion de Madereros Colombianos [*Bogota*] (COL)
ADENAVI .... Asociacion Nacional de Navieros [*National Shipowners Association*] [*Colombian*] (LA)
ADEOM .... Asociacion de Empleados y Obreros Municipales [*Association of Municipal Employees and Workers*] [*Uruguayan*] (LA)
ADEP .... Association pour le Developpement Economique et Pastoral [*Association for Economic and Pastoral Development*] [*Algerian*] (AF)
ADEP .... Association pour le Developpement de l'Exportation des Vins de Bordeaux
ADEP .... Ateliers de Decoupage et d'Emboutissage de Precision [*Algerian*] (MAR)
ADEPA .... Asociacion de Entidades Periodisticas Argentinas [*Argentine Newspaper Owners Association*] (LA)
ADEPA .... Asociacion de Productores de Algodon [*Association of Cotton Producers*] [*Bolivian*] (LA)
ADEPAN ...... Asociacion Nacional de Fabricantes de Pan [*Cali*] (COL)
ADEPHAR ... Association des Etudiants de Pharmacie [*Association of Pharmacy Students*] [*Cambodian*] (CL)
ADEQUA ..... Association des Entreprises de l'Equateur (MAR)
ADEQUIN .... Asociacion Quimico Industrial de Deportes [*Bogota*] (COL)
ADER .... Asociacion de Empleados de Radiodifusoras [*Association of Radiobroadcast Employees*] [*Uruguayan*] (LA)
ADER .... Association des Ecrivains Reunionnais (MAR)
ADERAL ...... Association pour le Developpement Economique et Social de la Region d'Alepe (MAR)
ADES .... Assemblee Departementale Economique et Sociale [*Algerian*] (MAR)

ADESCO ..... Amicale des Diplomes d'Etudes Superieures de Commerce (MAR)
ADESG .... Associacao dos Diplomados da Escola Superior de Guerra [*War College Graduates Association*] [*Brazilian*] (LA)
ADESKA ..... Association pour le Developpement Economique et Social de Katiola (MAR)
adess .... Adessiivi [*Finnish*]
ADET .... Asociacion de Empresas Teatrales [*Bogota*] (COL)
ADETIC .... Asociacion de Tecnicos Industriales de Colombia [*Medellin*] (COL)
ADETOM ..... Association pour le Developpement de l'Enseignement Technique d'Outre-Mer [*Association for the Development of Overseas Technical Education*] [*French*] (AF)
ADEVOCAL ... Asociacion de Empleados de Comercio del Valle [*Cali*] (COL)
ADEX .... Asociacion de Exportadores [*Exporters Association*] [*Peruvian*] (LA)
ADEZ .... Association des Entrepreneurs du Zaire [*Association of Zaire Entrepreneurs*] (AF)
ADF .... Adenosine Diphosphate (RU)
ADF .... Adenosinediphosphoric Acid (RU)
ADF .... African Defence Federation (MAR)
ADF .... African Development Fund [*or Foundation*] (AF)
ADF .... Aktion Demokratischer Fortschritt [*Action for Democratic Progress*] [*West German*] (PPE)
ADF .... All-Syrian Arab Deterrent Force (MAR)
ADF .... Arab Deterrent Force [*Palestinian*] (PD)
ADF .... Shock Absorber with Friction Damping (RU)
ADFAED .... Abu Dhabi Fund for Arab Economic Development (ME)
ad fin .... Ad Finem [*To the End*] [*Latin*] (GPO)
ADFS .... American Dentists for Foreign Service (MAR)
ADG .... Abhandlungen des Deutschen Geographentags [*A publication*] (MAR)
ADG .... African Development Group (MAR)
ADG .... Antidiuretic Hormone (RU)
ADG .... Emergency Diesel Generator (RU)
ADGB .... Allgemeiner Deutscher Gewerkschaftsbund [*General German Labor Union Federation*] (EG)
ADGB .... Amicale de Developpement du Groupement Bangoulap (MAR)
ADGK .... Guards Airborne Corps (RU)
ADGM .... Ankara Devlet Guvenlik Mahkemesi [*Ankara State Security Court*] (TU)
ad hl .... Ad Hunc Locum [*To This Place*] [*Latin*] (GPO)
AdI .... Alliance des Independants [*Independent Party*] [*Swiss*] (PPE)
ADI .... Arab Development Institute (MAR)
ADI- .... Automatic Smoke Annunciator (RU)
ADI .... Remote Measurement Equipment (RU)
ADIA .... Abu Dhabi Investment Authority (ME)
ADIA .... Asociacion Dominicana de Ingenieros Agronomos [*Dominican Association of Agronomists*] [*Dominican Republic*] (LA1)
ADIBA .... Asociacion de Industriales de Buenos Aires [*Buenos Aires Manufacturers Association*] [*Argentine*] (LA)
ADIC .... Asociacion de Industriales de Cordoba [*Association of Cordoba Industrialists*] [*Argentine*] (LA)
ADICO .... Asociacion de Ingenieros Constructores [*Cali*] (COL)
ADICT .... Agricultural Development and Industrial Company of Tanganyika [*Tanzanian*] (MAR)
ADIDAS .... Adi Dassler [*Founder of German sporting goods company; acronym used as brand name of shoes manufactured by the firm*]
A-Dienst ...... Ausrueckedienst [*Emergency Service*] [*Operational fire department unit on 24-hour service to handle emergencies*] (EG)
ADIFARCO ... Asociacion de la Industria Farmaceutica Colombiana [*Bogota*] (COL)
ADIMAGRO ... Asociacion de Distribuidores de Maquinaria Agricola [*Bogota*] (COL)
ADIMRA ...... Asociacion de Industrialistas Metalurgicos de la Republica Argentina [*Association of Metallurgic Industrialists of the Argentine Republic*] (LA1)
ADINARCO ... Asociacion de Ingenieros Arquitectos (COL)
ADINCOL .... Sociedad Industrial y Comercial Ltda. [*Bogota*] (COL)
ad inf .... Ad Infinitum [*To Infinity*] [*Latin*] (GPO)
ad init .... Ad Initium [*At the Beginning*] [*Latin*] (GPO)
ad int .... Ad Interim [*In the Meantime*] [*Latin*] (GPO)
ADIPUG .... Altin Boynuz Diriltme Projesini Uygulama Grubu [*Group for the Execution of the Golden Horn Renovation Project*] (TU)
ADIRI .... Asociatia de Drept International si Relatii Internationale [*Association for International Law and International Relations*] (RO)
ADIS .... Agence de Diffusion Industrielle et Scientifique (MAR)
ADISK .... Adesmevti Dimokratiki Syndikalistiki Kinisi [*Free Democratic Trade Union Movement*] (GC1)
ADIT .... Agencija Demokraticnega Inozemskega Tiska [*Agency of the Democratic Foreign Press*] [*Ljubljana*] (YU)
ADITECO .... Asociacion de Industriales Tecnicos Colombianos [*Bogota*] (COL)
ADITIA .... Adana Iktisadi ve Ticari Ilimler Akademisi [*Adana Academy of Economy and Commercial Science*] [*See also AITIA*] (TU)
adj .... Adjektiivi [*Adjective*] [*Finnish*]
ADJ .... Adjudan [*Adjutant, Aide*] (IN)
adj .... Adjunkt [*Adjunct*] [*Polish*]
adj .... Adjunktus [*Assistant Professor*] (HU)
ADJ .... Arheolosko Drustvo Jugoslavije [*Archaeological Society of Yugoslavia*] (YU)
ADJEN .... Adjudan Djenderal [*Adjutant General*] (IN)
ADJP .... Asociacion Democratica de Juntas Progresistas [*Democratic Association of Progressive Boards*] [*Costa Rican*] (LA)
ADK .... Absolvent Delnickeho Kursu [*Graduate of Worker's Preparatory Course (for college admission)*] (CZ)
ADK .... Adiadochokinesis (RU)
ADK .... Afrikaans-Deutsche Kulturgemeinschaft (MAR)
ADK .... Afrikaanse-Duitse Kultuurunie [*Afrikaans-German Cultural Association*] [*Namibian*] (AF)
ADK .... Arhiv Drzavne Komisije [*State Commission Archives*] (YU)
ADK .... Arkhigeion Dynameon Katadromon [*Raiding Forces Command*] [*Greek*] (GC)
ADK .... Artillery Decontamination Kit (BU)
ADK .... Artillery Decontamination Kit (RU)
ADK .... Ateliers de Kahankro (MAR)
ADKh .... Anotera Dioikisis Khorofylakis [*Supreme Gendarmery Command*] [*Greek*] (GC)
ADKM .... Antoko Demokraty Kristiana Malagasy [*Malagasy Christian Democratic Party*] (AF)
AdL .... Akademie der Landwirtschaftswissenschaften [*Academy of Agricultural Sciences*] (EG)
ad lib .... Ad Libitum [*At Pleasure*] [*Latin*] (GPO)
ad loc .... Ad Locum [*At the Place*] [*Latin*] (GPO)
ADLP .... Australian Democratic Labor Party (PPW)
ADM .... Adder Doutchi Maggia (MAR)
Adm .... Administracja [*or Administracyjny*] [*Administration or Administrative*] [*Polish*]
adm .... Administration (BU)
adm .... Administrative, Administration (RU)
adm .... Admiral [*Admiral*] [*Polish*]
adm .... Admiral (RU)
ADM .... Decontamination Truck (BU)
ADM .... Decontamination Truck (RU)
ADMA .... Abu Dhabi Marine Areas (ME)
ADMARC ..... Agricultural Development and Marketing Corporation (MAR)
ADMBAKh ... Alkyldimethylbenzylammonium Chloride (RU)
admin .... Administracja [*Administration*] (POL)
ADMK .... All-India Anna Dravida Munnetra Kazhagam (PPW)
ADMMA ...... Ankara Devlet Muhendislik ve Mimarlik Akademisi [*Ankara State Academy of Engineering and Architecture*] (TU)
admon .... Administracion [*Spanish*]
admor .... Administrador [*Spanish*]
ADMP .... Association pour Defendre la Memoire de Petain
ADMP .... Association de Droit Minier et Petrolier (MAR)
adm-terr ..... Administrative and Territorial (RU)
adm ts .... Administrative Center (RU)
ADMV .... Allgemeiner Deutscher Motorsport-Verband [*General German Motor Sports Association*] (EG)
ADN .... Accion Democratica Nacionalista [*Nationalist Democratic Action*] [*Bolivian*] (PPW)
ADN .... Acieries du Nord (MAR)
ADN .... Agentia de Presa a Republicii Democrate Germane [*Press Agency of German Democratic Republic*] (RO)
ADN .... Alianza Democratica Nacionalista [*Nationalist Democratic Alliance*] [*Bolivian*] (LA)
ADN .... Allgemeiner Deutscher Nachrichtendienst [*(GDR) German General News Service*] (EG)
adn .... Artillery Battalion (BU)
adn .... Artillery Battalion (RU)
ADN .... Asamblea Democratica Navarra [*Democratic Assembly of Navarra*] [*Spanish*] (WER)
ADN .... Automatic Remote Control Gun-Laying (RU)
ADNDC .... Abu Dhabi National Drilling Company (ME)
ADNIS .... Acik Deniz Nakliyat Iscileri Sendikasi [*Open Sea Transport Workers' Union*] (TU)
ADNOC .... Abu Dhabi National Oil Company (ME)
ADNOE .... Association pour la Direction Normale des Elections (MAR)
ADNTC .... Abu Dhabi National Tanker Company (ME)
ADO .... Agricultural Development Organization (CL)
ADO .... Airborne Detachment (RU)
adO .... An der Oder [*On the River Oder*] [*German*]
ADO .... Autodefensa Obrera [*Workers Self-Defense*] [*Formerly, MAO*] [*Colombian*] (LA1)
ADOCO .... Asociacion Nacional de Consumidores [*National Association of Consumers*] [*Dominican Republic*] (LA1)
AdoeR .... Anstalt des Oeffentlichen Rechts [*Institution Incorporated under Public Law*] (EG)
ADOEXPO ... Asociacion Dominicana de Exportadores [*Dominican Exporters Association*] [*Dominican Republic*] (LA)
ADOGEN ..... Asociacion de Oficiales Generales de los Institutos Armados [*General Officers Association of the Armed Forces Institutes*] [*Peruvian*] (LA)
ADOM .... Association pour la Documentation de l'Outre-Mer (MAR)
ADOMA .... Asociacion Dominicana de Abogados [*Dominican Bar Association*] [*Dominican Republic*] (LA)
ADORA .... Asociacion Dominicana de Radiodifusoras [*Dominican Association of Radio Broadcasters*] [*Dominican Republic*] (LA)

ADOSOM .... Association pour le Developpement des Oeuvres Sociales d'Outre-Mer [*Association for the Development of Social Welfare Projects Overseas*] [*French*] (AF)
ADP .... African Democratic Party (MAR)
ADP .... Agence Dahomeenne de Presse (MAR)
ADP .... Agence de Distribution de Presse (MAR)
ADP .... Agricultural Rural Development Pilot Programme (MAR)
ADP .... Airfield Control Tower (RU)
ADP .... Asociacion Dominicana de Profesores [*Dominican Association of Teachers*] [*Dominican Republic*] (LA1)
ADP .... Asociacion Nacional de Directores de Personal [*Bogota*] (COL)
ADP .... Australian Democratic Party (PPW)
ADP .... Automatic Long-Range Dispatcher Planning (RU)
ADP .... Azerbaijan Democratic Party [*Iranian*] (RU)
adp .... Breakthrough Artillery Division (BU)
ADP .... Breakthrough Artillery Division (RU)
ADP .... Mobile Steam Decontamination Unit (RU)
ADPC .... Abu Dhabi Petroleum Company (ME)
ADPF .... Association pour la Diffusion de la Pensee Francaise (MAR)
ADPI .... Asociacion Dominicana de Pequenas Industrias [*Dominican Association of Small Industry*] [*Dominican Republic*] (LA1)
ADPS .... Asociacion Democratica de Paz Social [*Democratic Association of Social Peace*] [*Spanish*] (WER)
adr .... Adres [*Address*] (POL)
adr .... Adress [*Address*] [*Swedish*] (GPO)
adr .... Adresse [*Address*] [*Danish*] (GPO)
adr .... Adresse [*Address*] [*Norwegian*] (GPO)
Adr .... Adresse [*Address*] [*German*] (GPO)
ADR .... Agrement Dangereuse Routier
ADR .... Ammonium Dihydrogen Phosphate (RU)
ADRAO .... Association pour le Developpment de la Riziculture en Afrique de l'Ouest [*West Africa Rice Development Association*] [*Use WARDA*] (AF)
ADRI .... Angkatan Darat Republik Indonesia [*Republic of Indonesia Army*] (IN)
ADRIPECHE ... Armement Dakarois pour le Regroupement de l'Industrie de la Peche (MAR)
Adr tel .... Adres Telegraficzny [*Telegraphic Address*] [*Polish*]
Adr tel .... Adresse Telegraphique [*Telegraphic Address*] [*French*]
adr telegr .... Adres Telegraficzny [*Telegraphic Address*] [*Polish*]
ADS .... Accao Democrato-Social [*Social Democratic Action*] [*Mozambican*] (AF)
ADS .... Accao Democrato-Social [*Social Democratic Action*] [*Portuguese*] (WER)
ADS .... Action Democratique et Sociale (MAR)
ADS .... Air Traffic Control Service (RU)
ADS .... Aircraft Engine Construction (RU)
ADS .... Airfield Control Tower Service, Airport Control Tower Service (RU)
ADS .... Anotaton Dikastikon Symvoulion [*Supreme Judicial Council*] (GC)
ADS .... Argon Arc Welding (RU)
ADS .... Armadni Delostrelecka Skupina [*Army Artillery Group*] (CZ)
ADSADLT ... Association de Defense des Societes Agricoles Depossedees par la Loi Tunisienne du 12 Mai, 1964 (MAR)
ADSB .... Allgemeine Deutsche Spediteurbedingungen [*General German Regulations for Shipping Agents*] (EG)
ADSEN .... Anotera Dimosia Skholi Emborikou Navtikou [*Higher Public Merchant Marine School*] (GC1)
ADSKh .... Anexartitos Dimokratikos Syndesmos Khanion [*Independent Democratic Association of Khania*] [*Greek*] (GC)
ADSRI .... Animal and Dairy Science Research Institute (MAR)
ADSS .... Administracoes Distritais dos Servicos de Saude [*District Health Services Administrations*] [*Portuguese*] (WER)
adsse .... Archiduchesse [*Archduchess*] [*French*] (MTD)
ADT .... Alianza del Trabajo [*Labor Alliance*] [*Spanish*] (WER)
ADT .... Aprovizionare, Desfacere, Transport [*Supply, Distribution, Transportation*] (RO)
ADTA .... Societe pour le Developpement du Tabac en Afrique (MAR)
ADTsIZO ..... Central Correspondence Training Institute in Highway Transportation (RU)
ADU .... Accion Democratica Universitaria [*University Democratic Action*] [*Guatemalan*] (LA)
ADU .... Assembleia de Delegados da Unidade [*Unit Delegate Assembly*] [*Portuguese*] (WER)
ADU .... Automatic Dewaxing Installation (RU)
ADU .... Automation of Dispatching Control (RU)
ADU .... Remote-Control Equipment (RU)
Aduc .... Archiduc [*Archduke*] [*French*] (MTD)
ADUC .... Asociacion de Universitarios de Cundinamarca [*Bogota*] (COL)
ADUTOG ..... Asociacion de Universitarios del Tolima Grande [*Ibague*] (COL)
ADV .... Active Substance (RU)
adv .... Adverbi [*Finnish*]
ADV .... Asociacion de Dirigentes de Ventas y Mercadotecnica del Peru [*Peruvian Sales and Marketing Managers Association*] (LA)
ad val .... Ad Valorem [*According to the Value*] [*Latin*] (GPO)
adw .... Adwokat [*Lawyer, Barrister*] [*Polish*]
ADW .... Aktion Dritte Welt (MAR)
ADW .... Arbeitsgemeinschaft der Waehlerinnen [*Association of Women Voters*] [*German*]
Ad/y .... Adet/Yil [*Items per Year*] (TU)
Adygnatsizdat ... Adyge National Publishing House (RU)
ADYOD .... Ankara Devrimci Yuksek Ogrenim Dernegi [*Ankara Revolutionary Organization of Higher Learning*] (TU)
ADYODD ..... Ankara Demokratik Yuksek Ogrenim Dayanisma Dernegi [*Ankara Higher Education Democratic Mutual Solidarity Association*] (TU)
Adzh .... Adzhar Autonomous Soviet Socialist Republic (RU)
AdzhASSR ... Adzhar Autonomous Soviet Socialist Republic (RU)
AE .... Abrechnungseinheit [*Accounting Unit*] [*German*] (WEN)
AE .... Accion Espanola [*Spanish Action*] (PPE)
AE .... Acetone-Ether [*Solvent*] (RU)
Ae .... Aether [*Ether*] [*German*]
AE .... Affaires Etrangeres [*Foreign Affairs*] [*French*] (WER)
AE .... [*Ministere des*] Affaires Etrangeres [*(Ministry of) Foreign Affairs*] (CL)
ae .... Air Squadron (BU)
AE .... Air Squadron (RU)
ae .... Airplane (BU)
AE .... Amme Enstrumani [*Public (Legal) Instrument*] [*Turkish Federated State of Cyprus*] (GC)
AE .... Angstromeinheit [*Angstrom Unit*] [*German*]
AE .... Anonymos Etaireia [*Joint Stock Company, Corporation*] (GC)
AE .... Anschlusseinheit [*Line Unit, Terminal*] [*Tel.*] (EG)
AE .... Arbeitseinheit [*Work Unit*] (EG)
ae .... Archives Unit (BU)
AE .... Auslandsentschaedigung [*Foreign Service (Hardship) Allowance, Foreign Service (Hardship) Differential*] (EG)
AE .... United Arab Emirates [*Two-letter standard code*] (CNC)
AEA .... Abidjan Electric Auto-Etablissements P. Weydert & Cie. (MAR)
AEA .... Agence Equatoriale d'Assurances (MAR)
AEA .... Asociacion de Estudiantes de Agronomia [*Agronomy Students Association*] [*Panamanian*] (LA)
AEA .... Attestation d'Etudes Approfondies [*French*]
AEAFM .... Association d'Entraide des Agriculteurs Francais du Maroc (MAR)
AEAM .... Association of Evangelicals of Africa and Madagascar (MAR)
AEANC .... Association des Eclaireurs de l'Armee Nationale Congolaise (MAR)
AEAS .... Asociacion de Empresarios de Autobuses Salvadorenos [*Association of Salvadoran Bus Owners*] (LA1)
AEB .... Anthopos Ethnologische Bibliothek (MAR)
AEB .... Associacao dos Exportadores Brasileiros [*Brazilian Exporters Association*] (LA)
AEB .... Association des Enseignants Burundi [*Association of Burundi Teachers*] (AF)
AEB .... Atomic Energy Board (MAR)
AEBA .... Agricultural Economics Bulletin for Africa [*Addis Ababa*] [*A publication*] (MAR)
AEBU .... Asociacion de Empleados Bancarios del Uruguay [*Association of Bank Employees of Uruguay*] (LA)
AEC .... Agence Economique des Colonies (MAR)
AEC .... All-Ewe Conference (MAR)
AEC .... Arancel Externo Comun [*Common External Tariff*] [*Andean pact*] (LA)
AEC .... Associacao de Educacao Catolica do Brasil
AEC .... Association Educative et Culturelle [*Educational and Cultural Association*] [*Algerian*] (AF)
AEC .... Association des Etudiants du Cambodge [*Association of Cambodian Students*] (CL)
AEC .... Association des Etudiants Congolais [*Association of Congolese Students*] (AF)
AECA .... Asociacion de Empresarios de Combustibles de la Argentina [*Fuel Businessmen's Association of Argentina*] (LA)
AECB .... Asociacion de Estudiantes de Ciencias Basicas [*Basic Sciences Students Association*] [*Guatemalan*] (LA)
AECB .... Association des Etudiants Congolais a Brazzaville (MAR)
AECC .... Association des Eclaireurs Catholiques du Congo (MAR)
AECE .... Asociacion Espanola de Cooperacion Europea [*Spanish Association for European Cooperation*] (WER)
AECI .... African Explosives and Chemical Industries (MAR)
AECL .... Asociatia Europeana a Comertului Liber [*European Free Trade Association*] (RO)
AECMA .... Association Europeenne des Constructeurs de Materiel Aerospatial [*European Association of Aerospace Equipment Builders*] (WER)
AED .... Africa Economic Digest [*A publication*] (MAR)
AED .... Arkhigeion Enoplon Dynameon [*Armed Forces Command*] [*Greek*] (GC)
AED .... Association for Education and Development (MAR)
AED .... Atomkernenergie-Dokumentation
AEDD .... Discrete Operation Aerodynamic Elements (RU)
AEDEN .... Asociacion de Estudios y Defensa de la Naturaleza [*Association for Studies and Protection of Nature*] [*Spanish*] (WER)
AEDEX .... Asociacion Ecuatoriana de Exportadores [*Ecuadorean Exporters Association*] (LA)
AEE .... Anotati Eforevtiki Epitropi [*Supreme Supervisory Committee*] (GC1)
AEE .... Field Emission (RU)
AEENA .... Anotati Epitropi Elengkhou Navtikon Atykhimaton [*Supreme Council for Control of Maritime Accidents*] [*Greek*] (GC)

AEERS .... Association d'Etude pour l'Expansion de la Recherche Scientifique (MAR)
AEESO .... Association des Eleves et Etudiants de la Sous-Prefecture de Ouragahis (MAR)
AEEY .... Anonymos Elliniki Etaireia Ydaton [*Greek Water Supply Company*] (GC)
AEEZ .... Association des Entreprises de l'Est du Zaire (MAR)
AEF .... Africa Evangelical Fellowship (MAR)
AEF .... Afrique Equatoriale Francaise [*French Equatorial Africa*] (AF)
AEF .... Background Equivalent Activity (RU)
AEFA .... Association des Anciens Eleves de la Faculte d'Archeologie [*Faculty of Archeology Alumni Association*] [*Cambodian*] (CL)
AEFMOM .... Association des Ecrivains d'Expression Francaise de la Mer et de l'Outre-Mer (MAR)
AEFOM .... Agence Economique de la France d'Outre-Mer (MAR)
AEG .... Allgemeine Elektrizitaets-Gesellschaft [*General Electric Company*] [*German*] (EG)
AEG .... Army Evacuation Hospital (RU)
AEGF .... Association des Etudiants Guineens en France [*Association of Guinean Students in France*] (AF)
AEH .... Allami Egyhazugyi Hivatal [*State Office of Church Affairs*] (HU)
AEI .... Alianza Electoral Independiente [*Independent Electoral Alliance*] [*Venezuelan*] (LA)
AEI .... Anotata Ekpaidevtika Idrymata [*Supreme Educational Institutions*] (GC1)
AEI .... Asesoria e Interventorias Ltda. [*Medellin*] (COL)
AEI .... Associated Electrical Industries Export Ltda. [*Bogota*] (COL)
AEI .... Associazione Elettrotecnica Italiana
aeib .... Fighter-Bomber Squadron (RU)
AEIJA .... Asociacion de Empleados del Instituto de Jubilaciones y Afines [*Association of Employees of the Pension Institute and Related Workers*] [*Uruguayan*] (LA)
AEK .... Allami Ellenorzo Kozpont [*State Control Center*] (HU)
AEK .... Atomenergikommissionen [*Atomic Energy Commission*] [*Danish*] (WEN)
AEK .... Atomik Enerjisi Komisyonu [*Atomic Energy Commission, Directorate General*] (TU)
AEK .... Avrupa Ekonomik Komisyonu [*European Economic Commission*] [*United Nations*] (TU)
AEK .... Societe Anonyme des Ets. Kritikos & Cie. (MAR)
AEKC .... Association des Etudiants Khmers au Cambodge [*Association of Cambodian Students in Cambodia*] (CL)
AEKGM .... Agaclandirma ve Erozyon Kontrol Genel Mudurlugu [*Forestation and Erosion Control Directorate General*] (TU)
AEKh .... Anomalous Hall Effect (RU)
AEKK .... Atomenergia Kutatasi Kozpont [*Atomic Energy Research Center*] (HU)
AEKN .... Association des Etudiants Khmers de Nancy [*Cambodian Students Association at Nancy*] (CL)
AEKP .... Anotati Epitropi Kratikon Promitheion [*Supreme State Supplies Committee*] [*See also YKP*] [*Greek*] (GC)
AEKS .... Association des Etudiants Khmers en Suisse [*Association of Cambodian Students in Switzerland*] (CL)
AEKS- .... Automatic Electronic Logging Station (RU)
AEL .... Agence d'Encaissement Librevilleise (MAR)
AEL .... Agricultural Enterprises Limited (MAR)
AEL .... Electroplating Unit (RU)
AELE .... Association Europeenne de Libre Echange [*European Free Trade Association*] [*Use EFTA*] [*French*] (AF)
AELF .... Association des Etudiants Lao en France [*Association of Lao Students in France*] (CL)
AELIA .... Association d'Etudes Linguistiques Interculturelles Africaines (MAR)
AELS .... Asociatia Europeana a Liberului Schimb [*European Free Trade Association*] (RO)
AELSL .... Associacao de Estudantes dos Liceos Secundarios da Luanda [*Secondary School Students Association of Luanda*] [*Angolan*] (AF)
AEM .... Allami Ellenorzes Miniszteriuma [*State Control Ministry (for Collection of Agricultural Produce)*] (HU)
AEM .... Alto Estado Mayor [*Supreme General Staff*] [*Spanish*] (WER)
AEM .... Andidiktatoriko Ergatiko Metopo [*Antidictatorial Labor Front*] [*Greek*] (GC)
AEM .... Association des Etudiants Malgaches [*Association of Malagasy Students*]
AEMCH .... Asociacion de Estudiantes de Medicina y Cirugia de Honduras [*Association of Students of Medicine and Surgery of Honduras*] (LA)
AEME .... Asociacion de Empleados del Ministerio de Educacion [*Association of Education Ministry Employees*] [*Salvadoran*] (LA1)
AEMERO ..... Africa, Eastern Mediterranean, and Europe Regional Office, UNICEF (MAR)
AEMF .... Association des Ecoles de Medecine d'Afrique [*Association of Medical Schools in Africa*] [*Use AMSA*] (AF)
AEMI .... Association Eurafricaine Miniere et Industrielle (MAR)
AEMNA .... Association des Etudiants Musulmans Nord-Africains [*North African Muslim Students Association*] (AF)
AEMO .... African Elected Members Organization (MAR)
AEMP .... Acetone Extract of Male Fern (RU)
AEMP .... Association des Etudiants en Medecine et en Pharmacie [*Association of Medical and Pharmacy Students*] [*Malagasy*] (AF)
AEMUS .... Association des Etudiants Malgaches en Union Sovietique [*Association of Malagasy Students in the Soviet Union*] (AF)
AEN .... Aerial Exposure Meter (RU)
AEN .... Alkimos Ethniki Neolaia [*Valiant National Youth*] [*Cypriot*] (GC)
AENA .... Association des Anciens Eleves et Eleves de l'Ecole Nationale d'Administration [*National School of Administration Alumni and Students Association*] [*Cambodian*] (CL)
AENF .... Association des Etudiants Nigeriens en France [*Association of Nigerien Students in France*] [*Niger*] (AF)
AENTAMUBAN ... Association Entente et Entraide Mutuelle des Ressortissants de la Region de Bangu (MAR)
AEO .... Anglo-Egyptian Oilfields (MAR)
AeO .... Arbeitsgemeinschaft Ehemaliger Offiziere [*Working Group of Former Officers*] (EG)
AEO .... Experimental Aerodynamics Department (RU)
AEOB .... Alkoholizmus Elleni Orszagos Bizottsag [*National Committee Against Alcohol Abuse*] (HU)
AEOC .... Association des Entreprises de l'Ouest du Congo (MAR)
AEOI .... Atomic Energy Organization of Iran (ME)
AEOM .... Association des Etudiants d'Origine Malgache [*Association of Students of Malagasy Origin*] (AF)
AEOS .... Ancient Egyptian Order of Scions (MAR)
AEOZ .... Association des Entreprises de l'Ouest du Zaire (MAR)
AEP .... Africa Education Project (MAR)
AEP .... Agencia Ecuatoriana de Prensa [*Ecuadorean Press Agency*] (LA)
AEP .... Agenzia Europea della Produttivita [*European Productivity Board*] [*Italian*] (WER)
AEP .... Airfield Clearing Station (RU)
AEP .... Akathariston Engkhorion Proion [*Gross National Product*] (GC)
AEP .... Amt fuer Erfindungs- und Patentwesen [*Invention and Patent Office*] (EG)
AEP .... Anelectrotonic Potential (RU)
AEP .... Anotati Epitropi Promitheion [*Supreme Supply Committee*] [*Greek*] (GC)
AEP .... Army Clearing Station (RU)
AEPA .... All Ethiopia Peasants' Association (AF)
AEPE .... Association pour l'Etude des Problemes de l'Europe [*Association for the Study of European Problems*]
AEPOM .... Association pour l'Etude des Problemes d'Outre-Mer [*Association for the Study of Overseas Problems*] [*French*] (AF)
AEPPA .... Associacao de Ex-Presos Politicos Antifascistas [*Association of Former Antifascist Political Prisoners*] [*Portuguese*] (WER)
AEPPI .... Anonymos Etaireia Prostasias tis Pnevmatikis Idioktisias [*Company for the Protection of Intellectual Property*] [*Greek*] (GC)
AEPS .... First Atomic Electric Power Plant (RU)
AEPYS .... Anotati Epitropi Promitheion Ypourgeiou Stratiotikon [*Supreme Supply Committee of the Ministry of the Army*] [*Greek*] (GC)
Aeq .... Aequivalent [*Equivalent*] [*German*]
AEQUA .... Aequatoria; Mission Catholique [*Coquilhatville*] [*A publication*] (MAR)
aer .... Aerobic (RU)
AER .... Aerostat (RU)
AER .... Airfield Maintenance Company (RU)
AER .... Asociacion Ecuatoriana de Radio [*Ecuadorean Association of Radio Broadcasters*] (LA)
AER .... Association Europeenne pour l'Etude du Probleme des Refugies (MAR)
AER .... Automatic Equipment for Optimal Power Distribution (RU)
AER- .... Ejector-Type Mining Aspirator (RU)
AEr .... Motor Transport Clearing Company (BU)
AeRCs .... Aeroklub Republiky Ceskoslovenske [*Aero Club of the Czechoslovak Republic*] (CZ)
aerd .... Aerodynamics (RU)
aerd .... Airfield, Airdrome [*Topography*] (RU)
AEREK .... Association des Etudiants de la Republique Khmere [*Cambodian Republic Students Association*] (CL)
AERIS .... Aerodynamic Test Station (RU)
AEROBECO ... Becoblohm La Guaira, CA [*Venezuelan*]
AEROCIVIL ... Empresa Colombiana de Aerodromos Informacion de Vuelos [*Formerly, ECA*] [*Bogota*] (COL)
AEROCONDOR ... Aerovias Condor de Colombia Ltda. [*Condor Airlines of Colombia Ltd.*] (LA)
aerof .... Aerial Photometry (RU)
AEROFLOT ... Aero Flotilla [*Soviet airline*]
Aeroflot .... Main Administration of the Civil Air Fleet (RU)
AEROPERU ... Linea Aerea Peruana [*Peruvian State Airlines*] (LA)
Aeroproyekt ... Central Office for the Surveying and Planning of Airlines and Airports (RU)
AEROSE ..... Societe Aeronautique du Senegal (MAR)
AEROSEA ... Servicios Especiales Aereos [*Barranquilla*] (COL)
AEROSEN ... Compagnie Aeronautique du Senegal (MAR)

AEROTUR ... Empresa de Turismo Aerea Cubana [*Cuban Air Travel Agency*] (LA)
aerp ... Airport [*Topography*] (RU)
AERP ... Assessoria Especial de Relacoes Publicas da Presidencia da Republica [*Presidential Office Special Public Relations Staff*] [*Brazilian*] (LA)
AES ... Agence Eurafricaine d'Echanges et de Services (MAR)
AES ... Agregation de l'Enseignement Superieur [*French*]
AES ... Agricultural Engineering Service (MAR)
AES ... Agrupacion de Estudios Sociales [*Social Studies Association*] [*Argentine*] (LA)
aes ... Air Liaison Squadron (BU)
AES ... Aminoethanol Sulfate (RU)
AES ... Ankara Elektrik Sanayii ve Ticaret AS [*Ankara Electric Industry and Trade Corporation*] (TU)
AES ... Anotaton Ekpaidevtikon Symvoulion [*Supreme Educational Council*] [*Greek*] (GC)
AES ... Asociacion de Estudiantes de Secundaria [*Association of Secondary School Students*] [*Salvadoran*] (LA)
AES ... Atomic Electric Power Plant (RU)
AES ... Atomnaia Elektrostantsiia (MAR)
AES ... Economic Cooperation Administration [*ECA*] (RU)
AES ... Landplane Airfield (RU)
AES ... Truck-Mounted Electric Power Plant (RU)
AESA ... Association pour l'Enseignement Social en Afrique (MAR)
AESC ... Architectural and Engineering Services Corporation (MAR)
AESC ... Association des Anciens Etudiants en Sciences Commerciales [*Association of Former Commercial Students*] [*Cambodian*] (CL)
AESLA ... Asociacion de Estudios y Solidaridad con Latinoamerica [*Association of Studies and Solidarity with Latin America*] (LA)
AESM ... All Ethiopian Socialist Movement (AF)
AESNE ... Asociacion de Empleados del Servicio Nacional de Electricidad [*Association of National Electricity Service Employees*] [*Costa Rican*] (LA1)
AESRC ... Association des Etudiants et des Sujets du Royaume du Cambodge [*Association of Students and Subjects of the Kingdom of Cambodia*] [*Used in historical material*] (CL)
AESSCR ... Asociacion de Empleados del Seguro Social de Costa Rica [*Costa Rican Social Security Employees Association*] (LA)
AET ... Aerlinte Eireann Teoranta [*Irish Air Lines*]
aet ... Aetatis [*Aged*] [*Latin*]
AET ... Allami Epitoipari Troszt [*State Trust of the Building Industry*] (HU)
AET ... Aminoethylisothiuronium (RU)
AET ... Avrupa Ekonomik Toplulugu [*European Economic Community - EEC*] (TU)
AETA ... Anotati Epitropi Teloneiakon Amfisvitiseon [*Supreme Committee for Customs Disputes*] [*Greek*] (GC)
AETA ... Societe pour l'Amenagement et l'Etude du Tourisme Algerien (MAR)
AETC ... Agricultural Extension Training Center (MAR)
AETCF ... Association pour l'Enseignement Technique et Commercial Francais au Maroc (MAR)
AETF ... Association des Etudiants Tchadiens en France [*Association of Chadian Students in France*] (AF)
AETFAT ... Association pour l'Etude Taxonomique de la Flore d'Afrique Tropicale [*Association for the Taxonomic Study of Tropical African Flora*] [*French*] (AF)
aeth ... Aetherisch [*Ethereal*] [*German*]
AETI ... Allami Epitestudomanyi es Tervezo Intezet [*State Institute of Architecture and Design*] (HU)
AETK ... Airfield Technical Crew (RU)
AETOS ... Andistasiaki Ethniki Vasiliki Organosis Ellinon [*Greek National Resistance Royalist Organization*] (GC)
AETs ... Atomic Power Plant (BU)
AETU ... All Ethiopia Trade Union (AF)
AETUO ... All-Ethiopian Trade Union Organization (MAR)
AETV ... Altalanos Epulettervezo Vallalat [*Architectural Design Enterprise*] (HU)
AEU ... Amalgamated Engineering Union [*Rhodesian*] (AF)
AEU ... Asociacion de Estudiantes Universitarios [*University Students Association*] [*Guatemalan*] (LA)
AEU ... Nuclear Propulsion Engine, Atomic Power Plant (RU)
AEUC ... Arab Economic Unity Council (MAR)
AEUCV ... Asociacion de Empleados de la Universidad Central de Venezuela [*Association of Employees of the Central University of Venezuela*] (LA)
AEUO ... Asociacion de Estudiantes Universitarios de Occidente [*Association of University Students of the West*] [*Guatemalan*] (LA)
AEV ... Allami Epitoipari Vallalat (Veszprem) [*State Construction Enterprise (Veszprem Branch)*] (HU)
AEV ... Automatic Electric Switch (RU)
AEVAL ... Anonymos Etaireia Viomikhanias Azotoukhon Lipasmaton [*Nitrogenous Fertilizers Corporation*] (GC)
AEVE ... Agrotiki Enosis Voreiou Ellados [*Agrarian Union of Northern Greece*] (GC)
AEXANDES ... Asociacion de Exalumnos de la Universidad de los Andes [*Bogota*] (COL)
af ... A Favor [*In Favor Of*] [*Business and trade*] [*Spanish*]
AF ... Action Familiale [*Family Action*] [*Mauritian*] (AF)
AF ... Afghanistan [*Two-letter standard code*] (CNC)
AF ... African Filmstrips (MAR)
af ... Air Fleet (BU)
af ... Air Squadron (BU)
AF ... Akumulacija Fondova [*Accumulation of Funds*] (YU)
AF ... Alcak Frekans [*Low Frequency*] (TU)
AF ... Alliance Francaise (MAR)
AF ... Alta Frequenza [*High Frequency*] [*Use HF*] [*Italian*] (WER)
AF ... Anbauflaeche [*Area under Cultivation*] (EG)
AF ... Ancien Franc [*Old Franc*] [*French*] (WER)
af ... Anno Futuro [*Next Year*] [*Italian*]
AF ... Antarctic Front (RU)
AF ... Arctic Front (RU)
AF ... Avala-Film [*Establishment for the production and export of motion pictures*] [*Belgrade*] (YU)
AF ... L'Afrique [*or L'Africaine*] Francaise (MAR)
AF ... Photoreconnaissance (RU)
AFA ... Aerial Camera (RU)
AFA ... Aerial Photography Equipment (BU)
AFA ... Amicale des Femmes Algeriennes [*Algerian*] (MAR)
AFA ... Archiv fuer Anthropologie [*A publication*] (MAR)
AFA ... Asociacion del Futbol Aficionado [*Bogota*] (COL)
AfA ... Ausschuss fuer Arbeitsstudien [*Committee for Labor Studies*] (EG)
AFAA ... Association of Faculties of Agriculture in Africa (MAR)
AFA-B ... Bomber Aerial Camera (RU)
AFABA ... Association des Federations Africaines de Basketball Amateur (MAR)
AFAC ... Association des Fonctionnaires et Agents de la Colonie [*Association of Civil Servants and Agents of the Colony*] [*European civil servants*] [*Congolese*]
AFA-I ... Fighter Aerial Camera (RU)
AFAL ... Association Forestiere Africaine de Libreville (MAR)
AFALI ... Association Feminine pour l'Amitie Lao Internationale [*International Lao Women's Friendship Association*] (CL)
AFAP ... Association Francaise pour l'Accroissement de la Productivite [*French Association for Increased Productivity*] (WER)
AFAR ... American Friends of the Angolan Revolution (MAR)
AFARCO ... Afro-Arab Company for Investment and International Trade (ME)
AFAS ... Afrique et l'Asie; Revue Politique, Sociale, et Economique et Bulletin des Anciens du CHEAM [*Paris*] [*A publication*] (MAR)
AFAS ... Association Francaise pour l'Avancement des Sciences [*French*] (MAR)
AFASPA ... Association Francaise d'Amitie et de Solidarite avec les Peuples d'Afrique [*French Association for Friendship and Solidarity with the Peoples of Africa*] (AF)
AFAT ... Auxiliaires Feminines de l'Armee de Terre [*Women's Army Auxiliary*] [*French*] (WER)
AFB ... Allami Fejlesztesi Bank [*State Development Bank*] (HU)
AFBS ... American and Foreign Bible Society (MAR)
AFC ... African Football Confederation (MAR)
AFC ... African Forestry Commission (MAR)
AFC ... African Fruit Company (MAR)
AFC ... Agricultural Finance Corporation (MAR)
AFC ... Alexandria Flying Club (MAR)
AFC ... All Footballers Cooperative (MAR)
AFC ... Association des Femmes Cambodgiennes [*Cambodian Women's Association*] [*Use AFK*] (CL)
AFC ... Societe Air Froid Conditionnement (MAR)
AFCA ... Association Fonciere et Commerciale Africaine [*Moroccan*] (MAR)
AFCA ... Association pour la Formation des Cadres de l'Industrie et de l'Administration (MAR)
AFCA ... Association Francaise pour la Communaute Atlantique [*French Association for the Atlantic Community*]
AFCAC ... African Civil Aviation Commission (AF)
AFCAL ... Association Francaise de Calcul
AFCC ... Arab Financial Consultants Company (MAR)
AFCC ... Armed Forces Coordinating Committee (MAR)
AFCC ... Association Francaise du Commerce des Cacaos (MAR)
AFCENT ... Allied Forces Central Europe (WEN)
AFCET ... Association Francaise pour la Cybernetique Economique et Technique [*French*]
AFCG ... Association Folklorique Culturelle Guyanaise [*Cultural Folklore Association of French Guiana*] (LA1)
AFCMO ... Association Francaise des Constructeurs de Machines Outils (MAR)
AFCO ... Agricultural Finance Corporation [*Rhodesian*] (AF)
AFCO ... American and French Company (MAR)
AFCO ... Societe Africaine de Conditionnement (MAR)
AFCODI ... Africaine Commerciale de Diffusion (MAR)
AFCODI ... Ateliers de Freinage de la Cote-d'Ivoire (MAR)
AFCOL ... Associated Furniture Companies Limited (MAR)
AFD ... African Development [*London*] [*A publication*] (MAR)
AFD ... Anexartiti Filelevthera Dimokratia [*Independent Liberal Democracy*] [*Greek*] (GC)

AFD .... Ankara Flarmoni Dernegi [*Ankara Philharmonic Association*] (TU)
AFDAC .... Association Francaise de Documentation Automatique en Chimie
AFDAMME ... Association Francaise de Documentation Automatique en Metallurgie, Materiaux, et Electrotechnique
AfDB........... African Development Bank (MAR)
AFDI .... Annuaire Francais de Droit International [*A publication*] (MAR)
AFDIN .... Association Francaise de Documentation et d'Information Nucleaires [*French Association for Nuclear Documentation and Information*] (WER)
AFDJ .... Administratia Fluviala a Dunarii de Jos [*Lower Danube River Administration*] (RO)
AFE .... Administracion de Ferrocarriles del Estado [*State Railways Administration*] [*Uruguayan*] (LA)
AfE .... Amt fuer Exportkontrolle [*Office for Export Control*] (EG)
AFE .... Ateliers et Forges de l'Ebrie (MAR)
AFEC........... Association Francophone d'Education Comparee [*French-Speaking Comparative Education Association - FSCEA*] (EA)
AFECO........ Arab-French Engine Company (MAR)
AFECTI .... Association Francaise d'Experts de la Cooperation Technique Internationale [*French Association of Experts Assigned to International Technical Cooperation*] (AF)
AFEDK .... Agrotiki Filelevtheri Enosis tou Dimokratikou Kendrou [*Liberal Agrarian Union of the Democratic Center*] [*Greek*] (GC)
AFENIC .... Asociacion de Ferreteros de Nicaragua [*Association of Nicaraguan Hardware Dealers*] (LA1)
AfEP .... Amt fuer Erfindungs- und Patentwesen [*Invention and Patent Office*] (EG)
AFER........... African Ecclesial Review [*A publication*] (MAR)
AFESD .... Arab Fund for Economic and Social Development (ME)
AFESZ......... Altalanos Fogyasztasi es Ertekesito Szovetkezetek [*General Consumer and Marketing Cooperatives*] (HU)
AFET........... Association Francaise et Togolaise (MAR)
AFETIMO .... Association Francaise pour l'Etude du Tiers Monde (MAR)
AFEX........... Societe Africaine d'Expansion et d'Equipement (MAR)
AFF............. Altalanos Fuvarozasi Feltetelek [*General Transportation Manual*] (HU)
AFF............. Societe A. et F. Fourzoli (MAR)
affmo.......... Affezionatissimo [*Most Affectionately*] [*Italian*]
Affr .... Affranchi [*Paid*] [*Business and trade*] [*French*]
AFFW .... Arab Federation of Food Workers (MAR)
afg .... Afghan (RU)
AFG............ Afghanistan [*Three-letter standard code*] (CNC)
AFGE.......... Photogeological Expedition (RU)
AFGI........... Association Fraternelle des Guineens en Cote-d'Ivoire (MAR)
AFGM......... Africa General Mission (MAR)
AFGRAD ..... African Graduate Fellowship Program (MAR)
AFH .... Afrika Heute [*Bonn*] [*A publication*] (MAR)
AFH .... Alfred Herlicq & Fils (MAR)
AFI.............. Agence Francaise d'Images [*French Photo News Agency*] (CL)
AFI.............. Amplitude-Phase Measurement (RU)
AfI.............. Amt fuer Information [*Information Office*] (EG)
AFI.............. Armement Franco-Ivoirien (MAR)
AFI.............. Association des Femmes Ivoiriennes (MAR)
AFI.............. French Territory of the Afars and Issas [*Three-letter standard code*] (CNC)
AFI.............. Institute of Agricultural Physics (RU)
AFI.............. Institute of Astrophysics (RU)
AFIA .... American Foreign Insurance Association (MAR)
AFICE.......... Association for International Cotton Emblem (EA)
AFID .... Agence Francaise d'Information et de Documentation (MAR)
AFIDA.......... Asociacion de Ferias Internacionales de America [*Association of International Trade Fairs of America*] (EA)
AFIDRO....... Asociacion de Fabricantes de Productos Farmaceuticos [*Pharmaceutical Manufacturers Association*] [*Colombian*] (LA)
AFIGAP .... Association Francophone Internationale des Groupes d'Animation de la Paraplegie [*International French-Speaking Association of Paraplegic Therapy Groups*] (EA)
AFIN .... Alianza de Fuerzas de la Izquierda Nacional [*Alliance of the National Leftist Forces*] [*Bolivian*] (LA1)
AFIN .... Asociacion Federada del Instituto Nacional [*Federated Association of the National Institute*] [*Panamanian*] (LA)
AFINCO....... L'Africaine Industrielle et Commerciale (MAR)
AFIRAN .... African-Indian Ocean Regional Air Navigation (MAR)
AFIRO.......... Association Francaise d'Informatique et de Recherche Operationnelle
AFIS .... Agence Francaise d'Informations Scientifiques [*French Scientific Information Agency*] (AF)
AFIS .... Amministrazione Fiduciaria Italiana della Somalia (MAR)
AFIT .... Autofenntarto Ipari Troszt [*Industrial Trust for Auto Maintenance*] (HU)
AFITAE........ Association Francaise des Ingenieurs et Techniciens de l'Aeronautique et de l'Espace [*French*]
AFJ............. Amt fuer Jugendfragen [*Office for Youth Affairs*] (EG)
AFJA .... Association Francaise des Journalistes Agricoles [*French*]
AFJD .... Association Francaise des Juristes Democrates [*French Association of Democratic Lawyers*] (WER)
AFK .... Adenoidal-Pharyngeal-Conjunctival [*Virus*] (RU)
AFK .... Administration and Finance Commission (RU)
AfK .... Amt fuer Kirchenfragen [*Office for Church Affairs*] (EG)
AFK .... Association des Femmes Khmeres [*Cambodian Women's Association*] (CL)
AFK .... Nitrogen-Phosphorus Combine (BU)
AFK .... Nitrogen-Phosphorus-Potassium Fertilizer (RU)
AFKh........... Amplitude-Phase Characteristic (RU)
AFL............. Armed Forces of Liberia (AF)
Afl.............. Artillerieflieger [*Artillery Spotting Pilot*] [*German*]
AFL............. Luftfahrtabteilung [*Air Force*] [*German*]
Afla............ Armeefliegerabteilung [*Army Air Force*] [*German*]
AFLNS......... Anti-Fascist League of People's Liberation (RU)
AFM............ Allami Foldmeres [*State Geodesy Office*] (HU)
AFM............ Antifasisticna Mladina [*Anti-Fascist Youth*] (YU)
AFM............ Association Africaine de Management (MAR)
afmo........... Afectisimo [*Very Affectionate*] [*Spanish*]
AFN .... Association des Femmes du Niger [*Nigerien Women's Association*] [*Niger*] (AF)
AFNE........... Astilleros y Fabricas Navales del Estado [*State Shipyards and Naval Factories*] [*Argentine*] (LA)
AFNE........... Empresa Astilleros y Fabricas Navales del Estado SA
AFNOR........ Association Francaise de Normalisation [*French Standardization Association*] (WER)
AFNRJ......... Arhiv Federativna Narodna Republika Jugoslavija [*Archives of Yugoslavia*] (YU)
AFO............ Administration and Finance Department (RU)
AFOA .... Societe Aero-Feu Ouest Afrique (MAR)
AFOD .... Arab Federation for the Organs of the Deaf (EA)
AFON .... Association for One Nigeria (MAR)
AFOR........... Asvanyolajforgalmi Vallalat [*Mineral Oils Commercial Enterprise*] (HU)
AFORT .... Asvanyolajforgalmi Vallalat [*Mineral Oils Commercial Enterprise*] (HU)
AFOSZ .... Altalanos Fogyasztasi, Termelo es Ertekesito Szovetkezet [*General Consumers' and Producers' Marketing Cooperative Enterprise*] (HU)
AFP .... Africa Pilot [*London*] [*A publication*] (MAR)
AFP .... Agence France Presse [*French Press Agency*] (CL)
AfP .... Amt fuer Presse [*Press Office*] (EG)
AFP .... Asociacion de Funcionarios Portuarios [*Association of Port Officials*] [*Uruguayan*] (LA)
AFPA........... Association pour la Formation Professionnelle des Adultes [*French*]
AFPESP ...... Associacao dos Funcionarios Publicos do Estado de Sao Paulo [*Sao Paulo State Civil Servants Association*] [*Brazilian*] (LA)
AfPU........... African Postal Union (AF)
afr.............. African (BU)
afr.............. African (RU)
afr.............. Afrikkalainen [*African*] [*Finnish*]
AfR .... Amt fuer Reparationen [*Reparations Office*] (EG)
AFR .... Distribution Function Analyzer, Amplitude Distribution Meter (RU)
AFRAA .... African Airlines Association (AF)
AFRABI .... Societe de Presse Afrique-Abidjan (MAR)
AFRAL......... Societe Europeenne pour l'Etude de l'Industrie de l'Aluminium en Afrique (MAR)
AFRASEC ... Afro-Asian Organization for Economic Cooperation (AF)
AFRAZES.... Afro-Asian Organization for Economic Cooperation (RU)
AFRC.......... Armed Forces Revolutionary Council [*Ghanaian*] (PPW)
AFRC.......... L'Afrique Francaise, Renseignements Coloniaux [*A publication*] (MAR)
AFRIC......... Agence Francaise de Representation d'Industries au Cameroun (MAR)
AFRIC......... Societe Africaine Francaise de Representations Industrielles et Commerciales (MAR)
AFRICADIS ... Societe Africaine de Distribution (MAR)
AFRICANA ... Africana Bulletin [*Warsaw*] [*A publication*] (MAR)
AFRICAP..... Societe Africaine de Diffusion d'Appareils Electriques (MAR)
AFRICAPLAST ... Industrie Africaine des Plastiques (MAR)
AFRICARE ... Societe Africaine de Reassurance [*African Reinsurance Company*] (AF)
AFRICAUTO ... Compagnie Africaine pour l'Automobile (MAR)
AFRICOL..... Africa Representacoes Industria e Comercio Lda. (MAR)
AFRIDEX..... Societe Africaine d'Importation, de Distribution, et d'Exportation (MAR)
AFRIFOS..... Societe Africaine du Phosphore (MAR)
AFRIGO...... Africaine des Frigoriferes (MAR)
AFRIGRAM ... Societe Africaine des Grandes Marques (MAR)
AFRILAIT .... Compagnie Africaine du Lait (MAR)
AFRIMA....... Afrique Materiaux (MAR)
AFRIMECA ... Societe Africaine de Mecanographie (MAR)
AFRIMEX .... Societe Africaine pour l'Importation et l'Exportation (MAR)
AFRIMEX-CI ... Africaine Import-Export - Cote-d'Ivoire (MAR)
AFRIPLAST ... Societe Africaine de Plastique (MAR)
AFRISEN..... Armement Frigorifique Senegalais (MAR)
AFRO......... African Regional Organization (MAR)
AFROSAI..... African Organisation of Supreme Audit Institutions (MAR)
AFS .... Aerial Photographic Service (RU)
AFS .... African Studies [*Johannesburg*] [*A publication*] (MAR)
afs .... Afsender [*Sender*] [*Danish*] (GPO)

AFS .... Antenna Feed System (RU)
AFS .... Autonomous Photoregistering Recorder [*Oceanography*] (RU)
AFS .... Azorubine-Binding Capacity (RU)
AFS .... Water Purification Truck (RU)
AFSAD .... Ankara Fotograf Sanatcilari Dernegi [*Ankara Photographers Society*] (TU)
AFSC .... American Friends Service Committee (MAR)
AFSEL .... Afrika Selatan [*South Africa*] (IN)
AFSK .... African Studies (Kyoto) [*A publication*] (MAR)
AFSMAS ..... Association Francophone de Spectrometrie de Masse de Solides [*French-Speaking Association of Solids Mass Spectrometry*] (EA)
AFSPEC ...... Afrika Spectrum [*Hamburg*] [*A publication*] (MAR)
AFT .... American Federation of Labor (BU)
AFT .... American Federation of Labor [*AFL*] (RU)
AFTA .... Association for Torah Advancement (MAR)
AFTAM .... Association Francaise pour l'Accueil des Travailleurs Africains et Malgaches [*Association for the Reception of African and Malagasy Workers*] (AF)
AFTC .... Assistance Forestiere, Technique, et Commerciale (MAR)
AFTE .... Arab Federation for Technical Education (EA)
AFTH .... Allami Foldmeresi es Terkepeszeti Hivatal [*State Bureau of Geodetics and Cartography*] (HU)
AFT-KIO ...... American Federation of Labor - Congress of Industrial Organizations [*AFL-CIO*] (BU)
AFT-KPP ..... American Federation of Labor and Congress of Industrial Organizations [*AFL-CIO*] (RU)
AFTN .... Aeronautical Fixed Telecommunication Network [*United Kingdom*]
afto .... Afecto [*Spanish*]
AFTP .... Association Francaise des Techniciens du Petrole
AFTPV .... Association Francaise des Techniciens des Peintures et Vernis [*French Association of Commercial Painters*] (WER)
AFTUCOT ... Societe Auxiliaire Franco-Tunisienne de Cooperation Touristique (MAR)
AFU .... Administration and Finance Office (RU)
AFU .... Aerial Camera Mount (RU)
AFU .... African Farmers' Union (MAR)
AFU .... Air Fighter Unit [*Tanzanian*] (AF)
AFU .... Amplitude-Phase Indicator (RU)
AFU .... Antenna Feed (RU)
AFUMS .... Association for the Uganda Martyrs Shrines (MAR)
AFV .... Archiv fuer Voelkerkunde (MAR)
AFVP .... Association Francaise des Volontaires du Progres [*French Association of Volunteers for Progress*] (AF)
AFZ .... Antifasisticki Front Zena [*Women's Anti-Fascist Front*] (YU)
AFZh .... Women's Anti-Fascist Front (BU)
AFZJ .... Antifasisticki Front na Zenite od Jugoslavija [*Women's Anti-Fascist Front of Yugoslavia*] (YU)
AfZKW .... Amt fuer Zoll und Kontrolle des Warenverkehrs [*Office for Customs and Control of Commodity Shipments*] (EG)
AFZM .... Antifasisticki Front na Zenite od Makedonija [*Women's Anti-Fascist Front of Macedonia*] (YU)
AG .... Action Group [*United National Independence Party Alliance of Nigeria*] (MAR)
AG .... Administrator General [*Namibian*] (AF)
ag .... Agent (RU)
AG .... Agentura [*Agency*] (YU)
Ag .... Agregacao [*Academic degree*] [*Portuguese*]
AG .... Air Group (RU)
AG .... Akademicke Gymnasium [*Secondary School (with emphasis on the humanities)*] (CZ)
AG .... Aktiengesellschaft [*Corporation, Incorporated*] [*German*] (WEN)
A/G .... Albumin-Globulin Ratio (RU)
AG .... Alcak Gerilim [*Low Tension*] (TU)
AG .... Allami Gazdasag [*State Farm*] (HU)
AG .... Anhydride (RU)
AG .... Annales de Geographie [*Paris*] [*A publication*] (MAR)
Ag .... Antigen (RU)
AG .... Antigua [*Two-letter standard code*] (CNC)
AG .... Anyaggazdalkodas [*Materiel Management Department*] (HU)
AG .... Archaeologica Geographica [*Hamburg*] [*A publication*] (MAR)
AG .... Archives of the Gambia (MAR)
AG .... Army Group (RU)
ag .... Artillery Group (BU)
AG .... Artillery Group (RU)
AG .... Artillery Gyrocompass (RU)
AG .... Assemblee Generale (MAR)
AG .... Atomgewicht [*Atomic Weight*] [*German*]
ag .... Auf Grund [*By Virtue Of, On the Basis Of*] [*German*] (WEN)
AG .... Avant-Garde [*Vanguard*] [*Military*] [*French*] (MTD)
AG .... Aviation Personnel Settlement (RU)
AG .... Aydinlik Grubu [*Enlightenment Group*] [*Leftist students*] (TU)
AG .... Etablissements Andre Gallais (MAR)
AG .... Gyro Horizon (RU)
AG .... Intelligence through Secret Agents (RU)
AGA .... Agence Gabonaise d'Assurances (MAR)
AGA .... Air Group of an Army (RU)
AGA .... Asociacion General de Agricultores [*General Association of Farmers*] [*Cuban*] (LA)
AGA .... Association Generale Automobile [*French*] (MTD)
Agac-Is .... Turkiye Agac Sanayii Isciler Birligi [*Turkish Wood Workers' Union*] (TU)
AGACOSTA ... Asociacion Ganadera de la Costa [*Barranquilla*] (COL)
AGAD .... Archiwum Glowne Akt Dawnych [*Main Archives of Old Records*] (POL)
AGADU .... Asociacion General de Autores del Uruguay [*General Association of Uruguayan Authors*] (LA)
AGANI .... Asociacion de Ganaderos de Nisibon [*Association of Nisibon Cattlemen*] [*Dominican Republic*] (LA1)
AGAO .... Asociacion de Ganaderos y Agricultores de Olancho [*Olancho Farmers and Cattlemen's Association*] [*Honduran*] (LA)
AGARD .... Advisory Group for Aerospace Research and Development [*NATO*]
AGAS .... Asociacion de Ganaderos y Agricultores de Sula [*Sula Farmers and Cattlemen's Association*] [*Honduran*] (LA)
AGAVAL ...... Agencias Varias Limitada [*Medellin*] (COL)
A/GB .... Agriculture, Great Britain [*A publication*] (MAR)
AGB .... Associacao dos Geografos Brasileiros
AGB .... Bomber Gyro Horizon (RU)
AGB .... Societe d'Alimentation Generale du Benin [*General Food Company of Benin*] (AF)
AGC .... African Groundnut Council (MAR)
AGC .... Ankara Gazeteciler Cemiyeti [*Ankara Journalists Society*] (TU)
AGC .... Asamblea General de Cataluna [*General Assembly of Catalonia*] [*Spanish*] (WER)
AGC .... Ashanti Goldfields Corporation (MAR)
AGCA .... Amicale Generale des Commercants Algeriens [*General Association of Algerian Businessmen*] [*French*] (AF)
AGCAF .... Association Generale des Cambodgiens de France [*General Association of Cambodians in France*] (CL)
AGCD .... Administration Generale de la Cooperation au Developpement (MAR)
AGChemDok ... Arbeitsgemeinschaft Chemie-Dokumentation
AGCS .... Associazione Generale delle Cooperative Somale (MAR)
AGD .... Azimuth Gyro Sensor (RU)
AgD .... Intelligence Data (RU)
AGDT .... Time-Delay Nose Fuze [*Aviation*] (RU)
AGE .... Assemblee Generale Extraordinaire [*Extraordinary General Assembly*] (CL)
AGE .... Association Generale des Etudiants [*General Students' Association*] [*French*] (WER)
AGE .... Garage Electrical Equipment (RU)
AGEA .... Association Generale des Etudiants d'Algerie (MAR)
AGEAP .... Asociacion de Graduados de la Escuela Agricola Panamericana [*Association of Graduates of the Panamerican Agriculture School*] [*Salvadoran*] (LA1)
AGECO .... Agence Generale d'Echanges Commerciaux (MAR)
AGECOOP ... Agence de Cooperation Culturelle et Technique [*Cultural and Technical Cooperation Agency*] (AF)
AGECOP ..... Agence de Cooperation Culturelle et Technique [*Cultural and Technical Cooperation Agency*] [*Use AGECOOP*] (AF)
AGEDI .... Agence Generale de Distribution (MAR)
AGEED .... Association Generale des Eleves et Etudiants du Dahomey en France (MAR)
AGEF .... Association Generale des Enseignants Francais [*Algerian*] (MAR)
AGEF .... Rede Federal de Armazens Gerais Ferroviarios [*Federal Network of General Railroad Warehouses*] [*Brazilian*] (LA)
AGEFAN ...... Association Generale des Etudiants de France en Afrique Noire [*General Association of French Students in Black Africa*]
AGEG .... Association Generale des Etudiants du Gabon [*General Association of Gabonese Students*] (AF)
AGEG .... Association Generale des Etudiants Guadeloupeens [*Guadeloupe*] (PD)
AGEK .... Association Generale des Etudiants Khmers du Cambodge [*General Association of Cambodian Students of Cambodia*] (CL)
AGEL .... Association Generale des Etudiants du Louvanium (MAR)
AGEM .... Allami Gazdasagok es Erdok Minisztere [*Minister of State Farms and Forests*] (HU)
AGEMPP ..... Association Generale des Etudiants en Medecine a Phnom Penh [*General Association of Medical Students in Phnom Penh*] [*Cambodian*] (CL)
AGENCIAUTO ... Agencia de Automoviles Ltda. [*Medellin*] (COL)
AGENEREK ... Association de la Jeunesse Nationaliste de la Republique Khmere [*Cambodian Republic Nationalist Youth Association*] [*Use AJEUNAREK*] (CL)
AGEP .... Association Generale de l'Enseignement Public [*General Association of Public School Teachers*] [*Algerian*] (AF)
AGEPOV ..... Agence Populaire de Voyage (MAR)
AGEPYM ..... Asociacion General de Empleados Publicos y Municipales [*General Association of Public and Municipal Employees*] [*Salvadoran*] (LA1)
AGER .... Association Generale des Etudiants Reunionnais [*General Association of Reunionese Students*] (AF)
AGERM .... Association Generale des Etudiants Reunionnais en Metropole [*General Association of Reunionese Students in France*] (AF)
AGERPRES ... Agentia Romana de Press [*Romanian Press Agency*] (RO)

A/GES .... Arkhigos/Genikou Epiteleiou Stratou [*Chief, Army General Staff*] [*Greek*] (GC)
AGES .... Asociacion de Ganaderos de El Salvador [*Association of Salvadoran Cattlemen*] (LA1)
AGES .... Association Generale des Etudiants Senegalais (MAR)
AGET .... Anonymos Geniki Etaireia Tsimendon [*General Cement Corporation*] [*Greek*] (GC)
AGETEX ...... Agence Generale des Textiles pour la Cote-d'Afrique (MAR)
AGEUA .... Association Generale des Etudiants de l'Universite Abidjan (MAR)
AGEUNR ..... Association Generale des Etudiants de l'Universite Nationale du Rwanda [*General Association of Students of the National University of Rwanda*] (AF)
AGEUS .... Asociacion General de Estudiantes Universitarios Salvadorenos [*General Association of Salvadoran University Students*] (LA)
AGEVACOOP ... Asociatia Generala a Vinzarilor Cooperatiste [*General Association of Romanian Engineers*] (RO)
AGF .... Allami Gazdasagok Foigazgatosaga [*Inspectorate of State Farms*] (HU)
AGFA .... Amicale Generale des Femmes Algeriennes [*General Association of Algerian Women*] [*French*] (AF)
AGFU .... Gas Fractionator-Absorber (RU)
AGG .... Arbeitsgemeinschaft Gueterbefoerderungsdienst [*Working Group for Freight Transportation Service*] (EG)
AGG .... Arhitektonsko-Gradevinarsko-Geodetski (Fakultet) [*Faculty of Architecture, Construction, and Geodesy*] [*Zagreb*] (YU)
AGG .... Arrete du Gouverneur General [*Decree of the Governor General*] [*Used in historical material*] (CL)
AGG .... Assurances Generales Gabonaises (MAR)
AGH .... Akademia Gorniczo-Hutnicza [*Academy of Mining and Metallurgy*] (POL)
AGh .... Alpengasthaus [*German*]
ag h ev .... Agostai Hitvallasu Evangelikus [*Lutheran of Augsburg Confession*] (HU)
AGHTM .... Association Generale des Hygienistes et Techniciens Municipaux
AGI .... Agence Gabonaise d'Information [*Gabonese Information Agency*] (AF)
AGI .... Agisiyo Gatolica y'Ingo (MAR)
AGI .... Allami Gazdasagok Igazgatosaga [*Directorate of State Farms*] (HU)
AGI .... Alliance Graphique Internationale (EA)
AGI .... Annee Geophysique Internationale [*International Geophysical Year*] [*French*] (WER)
agi .... Anyagi [*Financial, Economic*] (HU)
AGI .... Associazione Goliardica Italiana [*Italian Student Association*] (WER)
AGI .... Autorisation Globale d'Importation (MAR)
AGI .... Fighter Gyro Horizon (RU)
AGID .... Association of Geoscientists for International Development (EA)
AGIK .... Avrupa Guvenlik ve Isbirlik Konferansi [*European Security and Cooperation Conference*] (TU)
AGIMA .... Agence Immobiliere d'Afrique (MAR)
AGIN .... Action Group of Immigration and Nationality (MAR)
AGIP .... Agence d'Illustrations pour la Presse [*Press Illustrations Agency*] [*French*] (AF)
AGIP .... Azienda Generale Italiana Petroli [*Italian Petroleum Enterprise*] (AF)
AGIS .... Agence Generale d'Information du Sud-Est Asiatique [*Southeast Asia General Information Agency*] (CL)
agit .... Agitacio [*Agitation*] (HU)
agit .... Agitation (RU)
agit .... Agitational [*Propaganda*] (BU)
AGITAB .... Aerial Leaflet Bomb (RU)
agitgrupa .... Agitation Group [*Propaganda*] (BU)
agitprop ...... Agitacio es Propaganda [*Agitation and Propaganda*] (HU)
agitprop ...... Agitaciono-Propagandni [*Agitation and Propaganda*] (YU)
AGITPROP ... Agitacni a Propagacni Oddeleni [*Agitation and Propaganda Department*] (CZ)
agitprop ...... Agitation and Propaganda Department (RU)
agitprop ...... Agitation and Propaganda Department (BU)
agitpropchik ... Agitation and Propaganda Worker (BU)
agitpunkt .... Propaganda Center (BU)
AGJA .... Amicale Generale des Jeunes Algeriens [*General Association of Young Algerians*] (AF)
AGK .... Adenoidal-Pharyngeal-Conjunctival [*Virus*] (RU)
agk .... Adi Gecen Kaynak [*The Aforementioned Source*] (TU)
AGK .... Artiljeriska Grupa Kolona [*Artillery Column Groups*] (YU)
AGK .... Combination Gyro Horizon (RU)
AGK .... Corps Air Group (RU)
AGKS .... Automatic Gas-Logging Station [*Pet.*] (RU)
AGL .... Abteilungsgewerkschaftsleitung [*Departmental Labor Union Executive Board (Enterprise)*] (EG)
AG-L .... Aerosol Generator for Forest Pest Control (RU)
AGLINET ..... Agricultural Library Networks [*IAALD*] [*United Kingdom*]
AGLOS .... Conservational Afforestation Experimental Station (RU)
AGLR .... Army Hospital for the Slightly Wounded (RU)
agm .... Adi Gecen Makale [*The Aforementioned Article*] (TU)
AGM .... Agaclandirma ve Erozyon Kontrol Genel Mudurlugu [*Forestation and Erosion Control Directorate General*] (TU)
AGM .... Allami Gazdasagok Miniszteriuma/Minisztere [*Ministry/Minister of State Farms*] (HU)
AGM .... Altalanos Gepipari Miniszterium/Miniszter [*Ministry/Minister of Machine Industries*] (HU)
AGM .... Arts Graphiques Modernes (MAR)
AGM .... Assemblies of God Mission (MAR)
AGM .... Societe de Developpement Americaine, Greque, et Malgache (MAR)
AGMI .... Agrometeorological Institute (RU)
AGMI .... Arkhangel'sk State Medical Institute (RU)
AGMI .... Associazione Generale tra i Magistrati Italiani
AGMI .... Astrakhan' State Medical Institute Imeni A. V. Lunacharskiy (RU)
AGMI .... Bureau d'Assistance Geologique et Miniere [*Tunisian*] (MAR)
AGMS .... Agrometeorological Station (RU)
Ag Mt .... Agir Makineli Tufek [*Heavy Machine Gun*] (TU)
AGMTS .... Automatic Hydrometeorological Telemetry Station (RU)
AGO .... Angola [*Three-letter standard code*] (CNC)
AGO .... Arbeitsgerichtsordnung [*Labor Court Regulations*] (EG)
AGO .... Archives of the Geographical Society, USSR (RU)
AGO .... Automatic Geophysical Observatory (RU)
ago .... Garage Equipment Plant (RU)
AGO .... Truck Detachment (RU)
AGOK .... Allami Gazdasagok Orszagos Kozpontja [*National Center for State Farms*] (HU)
AGON .... Special-Purpose Air Group (RU)
AGOS .... Aeronautical and Seaplane Experimental Construction (RU)
AGP .... Aerogeodetic Establishment (RU)
AGP .... Agence Gabonaise de Presse [*Gabonese Press Agency*] (AF)
AGP .... Agence Guineenne de Presse [*Guinean Press Agency*] (AF)
AGP .... Arbeitsgemeinschaft der Produktionsgenossenschaften [*Working Group of (Artisan) Producer Cooperatives*] (EG)
AGP .... Automatic Field Damper, Automatic Field Damping (RU)
AGP .... Diving Gyro Horizon (RU)
AGP- .... Truck-Mounted Hydraulic Crane (RU)
AGPI .... Ashkhabad State Pedagogical Institute Imeni M. Gor'kiy (RU)
AGPI .... Azerbaydzhan State Pedagogical Institute Imeni V. I. Lenin (RU)
AGPIIYa ...... Alma-Ata State Pedagogical Institute of Foreign Languages (RU)
AGPol .... Agencja Reklamy Handlu Zagranicznego [*Advertising Agency for Foreign Trade*] [*Polish*]
AGR .... Agences Generales Reunis (MAR)
Agr .... Agrar [*German*]
agr .... Agrar [*Agrarian, Agricultural*] (HU)
agr .... Agricultural (RU)
agr .... Agronomi [*Finnish*]
Agr .... Agronomic [*or Agronomist*] (RU)
agr .... Agronomist [*or Agronomic*] (BU)
agr .... Argentine, Argentinean (RU)
AgR .... Intelligence through Secret Agents (RU)
AGRACAM ... Societe des Ateliers Graphiques du Cameroun (MAR)
AGRAL .... Asistencia Tecnica Agricola Ltda. [*Bogota*] (COL)
agrar .... Agrarian (RU)
AGREEPDDI ... General Assembly of Directors of Schools and Establishments Awarding the Engineering Diploma [*French*]
AGREPAL ... Agence de Repartition de Produits Alimentaires (MAR)
AGREX .... Elliniki Etaireia Exagogis Georgikon Proiondon [*Greek Agricultural Products Export Company*] (GC)
Agrexco ...... Agricultural Export Company [*Israeli*]
Agrfak .... School of Agronomy (BU)
AGRGK .... Air Group of the High Command Reserve (RU)
AGRH .... Association pour la Gestion et le Developpement de Resources Humaines en Cote-d'Ivoire (MAR)
AGRIFOR .... Societe Agricole et Forestiere du Mayumbe [*South African*] (MAR)
AGRILAGDO ... Societe Lagdo Agribusiness (MAR)
AGRIMECO ... Agricultural Land Development and Mechanization Corporation (MAR)
AGRINDEX ... Bibliografie van Agricultural Research Information System
AGRINTER ... Sistema Interamericana de Informacion Agricola [*Inter-American Agricultural Information System*] (LA)
AGRIPOG .... Societe Agricole de Port-Gentil (MAR)
AGRIS .... Agricultural Research Information System [*FAO*]
agrn .... Agronomus [*Agronomist*] (HU)
AGROBER ... Mezogazdasagi Tervezo es Beruhazasi Vallalat [*Agricultural Design and Investment Enterprise*] (HU)
AGROCAP .. Societe Agricole du Cap Vert [*Cape Verdean*] (MAR)
AGROCOL .. Sociedad Agricola Colombiana [*Bogota*] (COL)
agrofak .... Agricultural Division (RU)
AGROK .... Agrotika Oikistika Kendra [*Rural Housing Centers*] (GC1)
AGROKER ... Pest, Nograd, es Komarom Megyei Mezogazdasagi Ellato Vallalat [*Agricultural Supply Enterprise of Pest, Nograd, and Komarom Megyes*] (HU)
AGROMAS ... A joint Hungarian-Bulgarian foreign trade enterprise for agricultural machinery, established in 1964 (HU)

AGROMASH ... Mezhdunarodnoe Obshchestvo po Mashinam dlja Ovoshchevodstva, Sadovodstva, i Vinogradstva [*International Association for Vine, Fruit, and Vegetable-Growing Mechanization*] (EA)
AGROPEC ... Agropecuaria do Norte (MAR)
AGROPET ... Agrupacion de Orientacion Petrolera [*Oil Policy Planning Group*] [*Venezuelan*] (LA)
AGRO-PROMOTION ... Societe Agbouvillaise de Promotion de l'Habitat Urbain et Rural (MAR)
AGROSEM ... Complexul pentru Valorificarea Semintelor de Legume si Materialului Saditor Pomicol [*Complex for the Utilization of Vegetable Seeds and Fruit Tree Rootings*] (RO)
AGROT........ Agrotikon Komma [*Agrarian Party*] [*Greek*] (PPE)
AGROTERV ... Allami Gazdasagok Muszaki Tervezesi Vallalata [*Technical Planning Enterprise of the State Farms*] (HU)
AGROTERV ... Mezogazdasagi Tervezo Vallalat [*Agricultural Planning Enterprise*] (HU)
AGROTROSZT ... Mezogazdasagi Ellato Troszt [*Agricultural Supply Trust*] (HU)
AGRUMAL ... Association Inter-Professionelle Algerienne des Agrumes [*Algerian Inter-Occupational Citrus Fruit Association*] (AF)
AGRUPARE ... Agrupacion Patriotica Revolucionaria [*Revolutionary Patriotic Group*] [*Dominican Republic*] (LA1)
AGS............. Agreages Grumes et Sciages (MAR)
AGS............. Airborne Radioactivity Survey (RU)
AGS............. Weapons Announcing System [*Navy*] (RU)
AGSA.......... Anotati Geoponiki Skholi Athinon [*Supreme Agricultural School of Athens*] (GC)
AGSh........... General Staff Academy (RU)
AGSM.......... Aviation Fuels and Lubricants (RU)
A(G)SOA..... Anotaton (Gnomodotikon) Symvoulion Oikonomikis Anaptyxeos [*Supreme (Advisory) Council for Economic Development*] [*Greek*] (GC)
AGSVT........ Agence Generale Senegalaise de Voyage et de Tourisme (MAR)
AGT............. Agence Generale de Transit (MAR)
AGT............. Agence Generale de Travail (MAR)
AGT............. Assemblee Generale des Travailleurs [*Algerian*] (MAR)
AGT............. Assembleia Geral de Trabalhadores [*General Workers Conference*] [*Portuguese*] (WER)
AGT............. Territoriale Arbeitsgemeinschaften [*Regional Working Groups*] (EG)
AGT............. Truck Transport (RU)
AGTA.......... Agence Generale de Transit en Afrique (MAR)
AGTA.......... Amicale Generale des Travailleurs Algeriens [*General Association of Algerian Workers*] [*French*] (AF)
AGTI........... Agence Generale de Transports Internationaux (MAR)
AGTI........... Altalanos Geptervezo Iroda [*General Office of Machine Design*] (HU)
agto............ Agosto [*August*] [*Portuguese*] (GPO)
agto............ Agosto [*August*] [*Spanish*]
AGTs........... Anhydrite-Alumina Cement (RU)
AGTT........... Agence Generale de Transit et de Transports (MAR)
AGTU.......... Gas-Turbine Nuclear Propulsion Engine, Gas-Turbine Atomic Power Plant (RU)
AGU............. Agencia Geral do Ultramar (MAR)
AGU............. Asamblea General Universitaria [*University General Assembly*] [*Salvadoran*] (LA1)
AGU............. Azerbaydzhan State University Imeni S. M. Kirov (RU)
AGU............. Motorized Tar Spreader (RU)
AGUAPA..... Asociacion Guatemalteca de Productores de Algodon [*Guatemalan Cotton Producers Association*] (LA)
AGV-........... Automatic Gas Water Heater (RU)
AGV............. Mobile Hot-Air Decontamination Unit (RU)
AGVPS........ Asociatia Generala a Vinatorilor si Pescarilor Sportivi [*General Association of Sport Hunters and Fishermen*] (RO)
AGWU......... Artisans and General Workers Union [*Mauritian*] (AF)
AGZ............. Arhiv Grada Zagreba [*Archives of the City of Zagreb*] (YU)
AH............... Afrikaanse Handelsinstituut [*Afrikaans Institute of Trade*] [*South African*] (AF)
AH............... Akademia Handlowa [*Academy of Trade*] (POL)
AH............... Almhuette [*German*]
Ah............... Amperestunde [*Ampere-Hour*] [*German*]
Ah............... Amperogodzina [*Ampere-Hour*] [*Polish*]
AH............... Anno Hegirae [*In the Year of the Hegira, 622, the Mohammedan Era*] [*Latin*]
AH............... Arhatosag [*Price Authority (of the National Planning Office)*] (HU)
AH............... Orszagos Anyag- es Arhivatal [*National Material and Price Office*] (HU)
AHA............ Akdeniz Haber Ajansi [*Mediterranean News Agency*] [*See also AKAJANS*] (TU)
AHAC.......... Asociacion de Hombres de Accion Catolica [*Men's Catholic Action Association*] [*Argentine*] (LA)
AHAK.......... Aussenhandelsabrechnungskontor [*Foreign Trade Settlements Office*] (EG)
AHB............ Aussenhandelsbetrieb [*Foreign Trade Enterprise*] (EG)
AH-Bank..... Aussenhandelsbank [*Foreign Trade Bank*] (EG)
ahd.............. Althochdeutsch [*Old High German*] [*German*]
AHDRI......... Animal Husbandry and Dairy Research Institute (MAR)
AHEPA........ American Hellenic Educational and Progressive Association (GC1)
AHFR........... Aussenhandels-Finanzierungs-Rundschreiben [*Circular Letter on Financing of Foreign Trade*] (EG)
AHG............. Assembly of Heads of State and Government, OAU (MAR)
AHG............. Aussenhandelsgesellschaft [*Foreign Trade Company*] (EG)
AHI.............. Afrikaanse Handelsinstitut [*Afrikaans Institute of Trade*] [*South African*] (MAR)
AHI.............. Asociacion Hispano-Islamica
AHIA........... Arab Heavy Industries Ajman (ME)
AHIBA......... Asociacion Hondurena de Institutos Bancarios [*Honduran Association of Banking Institutes*] (LA1)
AHIR........... Allami Hirdeto [*State Advertising (Enterprise)*] (HU)
AHITI.......... Animal Health and Industries Training Institute (MAR)
AHK............ Abhandlungen des Hamburgischen Kolonialinstituts (MAR)
ahl.............. Ad Hunc Locum [*In This Place*] [*Latin*]
AHMSA....... Altos Hornos de Mexico, SA [*Mexican Steel Mills, Inc.*] (LA)
AHO............ Administrativni Hospodarske Oddeleni [*Administrative Management Department*] (CZ)
AHO............ Aussenhandelsorganisation [*Foreign Trade Organization*] (EG)
AHORROMET ... Ahorros Metropolitanos [*Metropolitan Savings Corp.*] [*Salvadoran*]
AHP............. Agence Haitienne de Presse [*Haitian Press Agency*] (LA1)
AHPROCAFE ... Asociacion Hondurena de Productores de Cafe [*Honduran Association of Coffee Producers*] (LA1)
AHS............. Allgemeinbildende Hoehere Schule [*German*]
AHS............. Anno Humanae Salutis [*In the Year of Human Salvation*] [*Latin*]
AHSA.......... African Heritage Studies Association (MAR)
AHT............. Allatforgalmi es Husipari Troszt [*Livestock Trading and Meat Industry Trust*] (HU)
AHU............. Arquivo Historico Ultramarina (MAR)
AHU............. Aussenhandelsunternehmen [*Foreign Trade Enterprise*] (EG)
AHZ............. Allami Hangversenyzenekar [*State Orchestra*] (HU)
AHZ............. Auto-Hrvatska, Zagreb, Trgovacko Poduzece na Veliko [*Auto-Croatia, Zagreb, Commercial Wholesale Establishment*] (YU)
AI................. Aeronautica Italiana [*Italian Air Force*] (WER)
AI................. Aerosol Inhalator (RU)
AI................. Afrique Industrie (MAR)
AI................. Alghanim Industries (MAR)
AI................. Amnesty International (EA)
AI................. Anno Inventionis [*In the Year of the Discovery*] [*Latin*] (GPO)
AI................. Archaeological Institute (BU)
AI................. Aviation Institute Imeni Sergo Ordzhonikidze (RU)
AI................. French Territory of the Afars and Issas [*Two-letter standard code*] (CNC)
AI................. Historical Documents (RU)
AI................. Institute of Archives (BU)
AI................. Pulse Analyzer (RU)
AI................. Selector [*Telephony*] (RU)
AI-5............. Acto Institucional Numero 5 [*Institutional Act Number 5*] [*Brazilian*] (LA)
AIA.............. African Information Agency (MAR)
AIA.............. Alliance Intercontinentale d'Assurances (MAR)
AIA.............. Asbestos International Association (EA)
AIA.............. Associacao Industrial de Angola (MAR)
AIA.............. Association of International Accountants (EA)
AIA.............. Association Internationale Africaine (MAR)
AIA.............. Associazione Industrie Aerospaziali [*Aerospace Industries Association*] [*Italian*] (WER)
AIAC............ Associazione Internazionale degli Agenti di Cambio [*International Stockbrokers' Association*] [*Italian*] (WER)
AIAC............ Associazione Internazionale di Archeologia Classica [*International Association for Classical Archaeology - IACA*] (EA)
AIAD............ Associazione Internazionale degli Avvocati Democratici [*International Association of Democratic Lawyers*] [*Use IADL*] [*Italian*] (WER)
AIAFD.......... Association des Institutions Africaines de Financement du Developpement (MAR)
AIAG............ Aluminium Industrie Aktiengesellschaft (MAR)
AIAM............ Asociacion de Ingenieros y Arquitectos de Mexico
AIAP............ Asociatia Internationala a Artistilor Plastici [*International Association of Plastic Artists*] (RO)
AIAP............ Association Internationale des Arts Plastiques [*International Association of Art - IAA*] (EA)
AIAT............ Association Internationale pour le Developpement Economique et l'Aide Technique [*International Association for Economic Development and Technical Aid*] [*French*] (AF)
AIB.............. Allami Ifjusagi Bizottsag [*State Youth Committee*] (HU)
AIB.............. Antiimperialistisches Informations-Bulletin [*A publication*] (MAR)
AIB.............. Army Engineer Battalion (RU)
AIB.............. Association Internationale de Bibliophile [*International Association of Bibliophiles - IAB*] (EA)
AIB.............. Associazione Italiana Biblioteche
AIB.............. Beirut International Airport (ME)
AIBA............ International Boxing Federation (BU)
AIBAN.......... Institute of Archives of the Bulgarian Academy of Sciences (BU)
AIBD............ Association of International Bond Dealers (EA)

AIBDA .... Asociacion Interamericana de Bibliotecarios y Documentalistas Agricolas [*Inter-American Association of Agricultural Librarians and Documentalists*] (EA)
AIBGA .... All-Island Banana Growers Association [*Jamaican*] (LA1)
AIBI .... Association Internationale de la Boulangerie Industrielle [*International Association of the Bread Industry*] (EA)
AIBM .... Association Internationale des Bibliotheques, Archives, et Centres de Documentation Musicaux [*International Association of Music Libraries, Archives, and Documentation Centres - IAML*] (EA)
AIBM .... Association Internationale des Bibliotheques Musicals
AIBN .... Azobis [*Isobutyronitrile*] (RU)
AIC .... Academie Internationale de la Ceramique [*International Academy of Ceramics - IAC*] (EA)
AIC .... Aeronautical Information Circular (MAR)
AIC .... African Inland Church (MAR)
AIC .... Aluminium Industries Commission (MAR)
AIC .... Arab Investment Company (MAR)
AIC .... Arquitectos, Ingenieros, Constructores Ltda. [*Cali*] (COL)
AIC .... Association Internationale des Charites de St. Vincent De Paul [*International Association of Charities of St. Vincent De Paul*] (EA)
AIC .... Association Internationale du Congo (MAR)
AIC .... Association Internationale de Cybernetique [*International Association for Cybernetics - IAC*] (EA)
AIC .... Associations d'Interet Collectif (MAR)
AICA .... African Independent Churches Association [*South African*] (AF)
AICA .... Agencia Informativa Catolica Argentina [*Argentine Catholic Information Agency*] (LA)
AICA .... Association Internationale des Critiques d'Art [*International Association of Art Critics*] (EA)
AICA .... Associazione Italiana per il Calcolo Automatico
AICB .... Association des Interets Coloniaux Belges [*Merged with AIIB into FEC*]
AICB .... Association Internationale Contre le Bruit [*International Association Against Noise*] (EA)
AICC .... Arusha International Conference Centre (MAR)
AICDT .... International Advisory Committee on Documentation and Terminology in Pure and Applied Science [*UNESCO*]
AICF .... Action Internationale Contre la Faim [*International Action Against Hunger*] (EA)
AIChPYe ...... Association for the Study of the European Quaternary (RU)
AICI .... Association Interprofessionnelle des Employeurs de la Cote-d'Ivoire (MAR)
AICL .... Association Internationale des Critiques Litteraires [*International Association of Literary Critics*] (EA)
AICMR .... Association Internationale des Constructeurs de Materiel Roulant [*International Association of Rolling Stock Builders - IARSB*] (EA)
AICN .... Agence d'Information de la Chine Nouvelle [*New China News Agency*] [*Use NCNA*] (CL)
AICO .... Asociacion Iberoamericana de Camaras de Comercio [*Ibero-American Association of Chambers of Commerce - IAACC*] (EA)
AICP .... Association Internationale des Circuits Permanents (EA)
AICR .... Association Internationale de la Croix Rouge [*International Red Cross Association*] (CL)
AICRIP .... All-India Coordinated Rice Improvement Project (MAR)
AICSA .... Aero-Industrial Colombiana SA [*Bogota*] (COL)
AICT .... Association Internationale Contre la Torture [*International Association Against Torture*] (EA)
AICV .... Accion Integral Colombo Venezolana [*Bogota*] (COL)
AID .... Agency for International Development [*A US government agency*] (CL)
AID .... Alliance Internationale de la Distribution par Fil [*International Alliance for Distribution by Wire*] (EA)
AID .... American Documentation Institute (RU)
AID .... Apparatus for Artificial Respiration (RU)
AID .... Association Internationale pour le Developpement [*International Development Association*] [*An affiliate of IBRD*] [*Use IDA*] (CL)
AID .... Association Internationale des Documentalistes
AIDA .... Asociacion Internacional de Derecho de Aguas [*International Association for Water Law - IAWL*] (EA)
AIDA .... Association Internationale de Defense des Artistes [*International Association for the Defence of Creative Workers*] (EA)
AIDA .... Association Internationale de la Distribution des Produits Alimentaires et des Produits de Grande Consommation [*International Association for the Distribution of Food Products and General Consumer Goods*] (EA)
AIDA .... Association Internationale de Droit Africain [*International African Law Association*] [*Use IALA*] (AF)
AIDA .... Associazione Italiana di Aerotecnica
AIDAA .... Associazione Italiana de Aeronautica e Astronautica
AIDAC .... Association Internationale de Developpement et d'Action Communautaires [*International Association for Community Development*] (EA)
AIDASA .... Association Internationale pour le Developpement en Afrique des Sciences Humaines Appliquees [*International Association for the Development of Applied Human Sciences in Africa*] (AF)
AIDB .... Agricultural and Industrial Development Bank [*Ethiopian*] (AF)
AIDBA .... Association Internationale pour le Developpement des Bibliotheques en Afrique [*International Association for the Development of Libraries in Africa*] (AF)
AIDC .... Association Internationale de Droit Constitutionnel [*International Association of Constitutional Law - IACL*] (EA)
AIDE .... Association Ivoirienne des Dirigeants d'Entreprise (MAR)
AIDF .... African Industrial Development Fund (MAR)
AIDHRO .... Association Internationale pour le Developpement des Hydrocolloides (MAR)
AIDLCM .... Association Internationale pour la Defense des Langues et Cultures Menacees [*International Association for the Defence of Threatened Languages and Cultures*] (EA)
AIDN .... Association International du Droit Nucleaire [*International Nuclear Law Association - INLA*] (EA)
AIDR .... Asociatia Internationala pentru Dezvoltarea Rurala [*International Association for Rural Development*] (RO)
AIDR .... Association International de Developpement Rural [*Belgian*]
AIDT .... Association Interparlementaire du Tourisme [*Interparliamentary Association for Tourism*]
AIE .... Agence Internationale de l'Energie [*International Energy Agency*] [*Use IEA*] (AF)
AIE .... Association Internationale des Entreprises d'Equipment Electrique [*International Association of Electrical Contractors - IAEC*] (EA)
AIE .... Association Internationale de l'Etancheite [*International Waterproofing Association - IWA*] (EA)
AIE .... Associazione Internazionale degli Economisti [*International Economists' Association*] [*Italian*] (WER)
AIEA .... Agence Internationale de l'Energie Atomique [*International Atomic Energy Agency*] [*Use IAEA*] (AF)
AIEA .... Agentia Internationala pentru Energia Atomica [*International Atomic Energy Agency*] (RO)
AIEA .... Association Internationale des Etudiants en Agriculture [*International Association of Agricultural Students - IAAS*] (EA)
AIEAS .... Association Internationale des Etudes de l'Asie du Sud-Est (EA)
AIEB .... Association International des Etudes Byzantines [*International Association for Byzantine Studies - IABS*] (EA)
AIECM .... Association Internationale d'Etude des Civilisations Mediterraneennes [*International Association of Studies on Mediterranean Civilizations*] (EA)
AIEE .... Association des Instituts d'Etudes Europeennes [*Association of Institutes for European Studies*]
AIEF .... Association Internationale des Etudes Francaises (EA)
AIEH .... Asociacion de Instituciones Evangelicas de Honduras
AIEJI .... Association Internationale des Educateurs de Jeunes Inadaptes [*International Association of Workers for Maladjusted Children - IAWMC*] (EA)
AIEPCI .... Association des Inspecteurs de l'Enseignement Primaire [*Association of Primary School Inspectors*] [*Ivorian*] (AF)
AIEPD .... African Institute for Economic Planning and Development (MAR)
AIERA .... Asociacion de Importadores y Exportadores de la Republica Argentina [*Importers and Exporters Association of the Argentine Republic*] (LA)
AIESEC .... Association Internationale des Etudiants en Sciences Economiques et Commerciales [*Association of International Students in Economics and Commercial Sciences*] (EA)
AIESEE .... Asociatia Internationala de Studii Sud-Est Europeene [*International Association of Southeastern European Studies*] (RO)
AIESEE .... Association Internationale d'Etudes du Sud-Est Europeen [*International Association of South-East European Studies - IASEES*] (EA)
AIESEP .... Association Internationale des Ecoles Superieures d'Education Physique [*International Association for Physical Education in Higher Education*] (EA)
AIESI .... Association Internationale des Ecoles des Sciences de l'Information [*International Association of Information Sciences Schools*] (EA)
AIF .... Alliance Internationale des Femmes [*International Alliance of Women - IAW*] (EA)
AIF .... Arbeitsgemeinschaft fuer Industrielle Forschung [*Cooperative Group for Industrial Research*] [*German*]
AIF .... Association Internationale Futuribles [*Futuribles International*] (EA)
AIFLD .... American Institute for Free Labor Development (LA)
AIFM .... Association Internationale des Femmes Medecins [*Medical Women's International Association - MWIA*] (EA)
AIFS .... African Improved Farming Scheme (MAR)
AIG .... Artiljeriske Izvidacke Grupe [*Artillery Reconnaissance Groups*] (YU)

Aigle............ Aiguille [*Needle*] [*Military map abbreviation*] [*World War I*] [*French*] (MTD)
AIH.............. Academie Internationale d'Heraldique (EA)
AIH.............. Association Internationale de l'Hotellerie (MAR)
AIHCE......... Association Internationale d'Histoire Contemporaine de l'Europe [*International Association for Contemporary History of Europe*] (EA)
AIHE............ Asociacion Interamericana de Hombres de Empresa [*Inter-American Businessmen's Association*] (LA)
AIHK............ Avrupa Insan Haklari Komisyonu [*European Human Rights Committee*] (GC)
AIHV............ Association Internationale pour l'Histoire du Verre [*International Association for the History of Glass*] (EA)
AII................ Archives of the Institute of History (of the Academy of Sciences, USSR) [*A publication*] (RU)
AII................ Associacao Interamericana de Imprensa [*Inter-American Press Association*] [*Use IAPA*] (LA)
AIIB............. Association des Interets Industriels au Congo [*Merged with AICB into FEC*]
AIIBP........... Association Internationale de l'Industrie des Bouillons et Potages [*International Association of the Manufacture of Soups and Broths*] (EA)
AIIC............. Amalgamated Industrial Investment Corporation (MAR)
AIIC............. Arab International Insurance Company (MAR)
AIIC............. Association Internationale des Interpretes de Conference [*International Association of Conference Interpreters*] [*Swiss*]
AIICO.......... American International Insurance Company (Nigeria) Ltd. (MAR)
AIISUP........ Association Internationale d'Information Scolaire, Universitaire, et Professionelle [*International Association for Educational and Vocational Information - IAEVI*] (EA)
AIJA............ Association Internationale des Jeunes Avocats [*Young Lawyers' International Association*] (EA)
AIJCFA........ All-Island Jamaica Cane Farmers Association (LA1)
AIJD............ Asociacion Internacional de Juristas Democraticos [*International Association of Democratic Lawyers*] [*Use IADL*] (LA)
AIJD............ Asociatia Internationala a Juristilor Democrati [*International Association of Democratic Jurists*] (RO)
AIJD............ Association Internationale des Juristes Democrates (MAR)
aik............... Aikaisemmin [*Earlier*] [*Finnish*]
AIK.............. Aminoimidazolecarboxamide (RU)
AIK.............. Apparatus for Artificial Blood Circulation (RU)
AIK.............. Arkhi Ilektrismou Kyprou [*Cyprus Electricity Authority*] (GC)
AIK.............. Association des Ingenieurs Khmers [*Cambodian Engineers Association*] (CL)
AIK.............. Autonomous Industrial Colony [*Kuzbas*] (RU)
AIK-............. Evaporative Condenser Unit (RU)
AIK-Kuzbass... Kuzbass Autonomous Industrial Colony (RU)
AIKM........... Ana Ikmal Merkezi [*Main Supply Center*] (TU)
AIKUP......... Association des Intellectuels Khmers pour l'Union des Peuples [*Association of Cambodian Intellectuals for the Union of Peoples*] (CL)
AIL............... Association of International Libraries
AILA............ Asociacion de Industriales Latinoamericanos [*Latin American Manufacturers Association*] (LA)
AILE............ Association Internationale des Lotteries d'Etat [*International Association of State Lotteries*] (EA)
AILg............. Association des Ingenieurs, Liege [*Association of Engineers, Liege*] [*Belgian*]
AIM.............. Africa Inland Mission (MAR)
AIM.............. Agencia de Informacao de Mocambique [*Mozambique Information Agency*] (MAR)
AIM.............. Amplitude-Impulse Modulation (BU)
AIM.............. Archaeological Bulletin of the National Museum in Sofia [*A publication*] (BU)
AIM.............. Artillery Historical Museum (RU)
AIM.............. Association Internationale de la Meunerie [*International Milling Association - IMA*] (EA)
AIM.............. Association Internationale de la Mutualite (EA)
AIM.............. Associazione Italiana di Metallurgia
AIM.............. Pulse-Amplitude Modulation (RU)
AIMA........... Association Internationale des Musees d'Agriculture [*International Association of Agricultural Museums*] (EA)
AIMBE......... Association Internationale de Medecine et de Biologie de l'Environement [*International Association of Medicine and Biology of Environment - IAMBE*] (EA)
AIMGA........ All India Mauritian Graduates Association (AF)
AIMK........... Academy of the History of Material Culture (RU)
AIML............ All-India Moslem League (MAR)
AIMM........... Africa Inter-Mennonite Mission (MAR)
AIMM........... Asociacion de Industriales Metalurgicos y Metalmecanicos [*Association of Industrial Metallurgists and Metalworkers*] [*Venezuelan*] (LA)
AIMO........... Ankara Insaat Muhendisleri Odasi [*Ankara Chamber of Construction Engineers*] (TU)
AIMO........... Service des Affaires Indigenes et de la Main-d'Oeuvre (MAR)
AIMS........... Association of International Marathons (EA)
AIMS........... Association Ivoirienne de Medecine Sportive (MAR)
AIMT........... Association Internationale de Musees de Transports [*International Association of Transport Museums - IATM*] (EA)
AIN.............. Agencia de Informacion Nacional [*National News Agency*] [*Cuban*] (LA)
AINAI........... African Integrated Network of Administrative Information [*Proposed*]
AINBN......... Association for the Introduction of New Biological Nomenclature (EA)
AINEK......... Association des Infirmiers-Infirmieres d'Etat Khmers [*Cambodian State Nurses Association*] (CL)
AINK........... Anglo-Iranian Petroleum Company (RU)
AINLF.......... Association Internationale des Navigants de Langue Francaise (EA)
AINM........... Archaeological Bulletin of the National Museum [*A publication*] (BU)
AINP........... Association Internationale des Numismates Professionnels [*International Association of Professional Numismatists - IAPN*] (EA)
ainzhb......... Army Engineer Battalion (BU)
ainzhb......... Army Engineer Battalion (RU)
AIO.............. African Insurance Organisation (MAR)
AIO.............. Agriculture et Industries des Oleagineux (MAR)
AIO.............. Arab Industries Organisation (MAR)
AIOC........... Anglo-Iranian Oil Company (ME)
AIOCC......... Association Internationale des Organisateurs de Courses Cyclistes [*International Association of Organizers of Cycle Competitions*] (EA)
AIOSP......... Association Internationale d'Orientation Scolaire et Professionnelle [*International Association for Educational and Vocational Guidance - IAEVG*] (EA)
AIOT........... Automatizalasi Informaciofeldolgozasi es Operaciokutatasi Tanacs [*Automation, Information Processing, and Operational Research Council*] (HU)
AIP.............. Aeronautical Information Publication (MAR)
AIP.............. Agence Internationale de Presse [*International Press Agency*] [*French*] (AF)
AIP.............. Agence Ivoirienne de Presse [*Ivorian Press Agency*] (AF)
AIP.............. Associacao da Imprensa de Pernambuco [*Pernambuco Press Association*] [*Brazilian*] (LA)
AIP.............. Association Internationale de Papyrologues [*International Association of Papyrologists*] (EA)
AIP.............. Association Internationale de Pediatrie [*International Pediatric Association - IPA*] (EA)
AIP.............. Automatic Integrating Pulsation Meter (RU)
AIP.............. Automatic Measuring Instrument (RU)
AIPA........... Agence d'Information Panafricaine [*Pan-African News Agency*] [*Use PAFNA*] (AF)
AIPADOKA... Societe d'Articles Injectes Padoka (MAR)
AIPC........... African Independent Pentecostal Church of Africa (MAR)
AIPCR......... Association Internationale Permanente des Congres de la Route [*Permanent International Association of Road Congresses - PIARC*] (EA)
AIPDA......... Adjun Inspektur Polisi Dua [*Assistant Police Inspector II*] (IN)
AIPE........... Association Internationale de la Presse Echiqueenne [*International Association of Chess Press*] (EA)
AIPEA......... Association Internationale pour l'Etude des Argiles [*International Association for the Study of Clays*] (EA)
AIPEHP....... Association Ivoirienne des Parents d'Enfants Handicapes Psychiques [*Ivorian Association of Parents of Psychologically Handicapped Children*] (AF)
AIPEPO....... Association Internationale de Presse pour l'Etude des Problemes d'Outre-Mer [*International Press Association for the Study of Overseas Problems*] [*French*] (AF)
AIPFO......... Automatic Integrating Pulsation Meter with a Fixed Interval of Averaging (RU)
AIPI............ Asociacion Internacional de los Profesores de Italiano [*International Association of Teachers of Italian*] (EA)
AIPK........... Anglo-Iranian Petroleum Company (BU)
AIPLF......... Association Internationale des Parlementaires de Langue Francaise [*International Association of French Language Parliamentarians*] (AF)
AIPNO......... Automatic Integrating Pulsation Meter with a Constantly Varying Interval of Averaging (RU)
AIPPh......... Association Internationale des Professeurs de Philosophie [*International Association of Teachers of Philosophy*] (EA)
AIPRTM...... Mansvetov Automatic Proportional Pulse Temperate Regulator (RU)
AIPS........... Association Internationale de la Presse Sportive [*International Sport Press Association*] (EA)
aiptap......... Army Tank-Destroyer Artillery Regiment (BU)
AIPTU......... Adjun Inspektur Polisi Satu [*Assistant Police Inspector I*] (IN)
AIR.............. Accion Independiente Revolucionaria [*Independent Revolutionary Action*] [*Venezuelan*] (LA)
AIR.............. Associacao Interamericana de Radio e Televisao [*Inter-American Radio and Television Association*] (LA)
AIR.............. Association d'Interet Rural (MAR)
AIR-............. Evaporator Control Unit (RU)
AIR.............. Observation Battalion Operations and Procedures (BU)
AIR.............. Sound-Flash Survey, Artillery Survey (RU)

AIRD............ Asociacion de Industrias de la Republica Dominicana [*Association of Dominican Industries*] [*Dominican Republic*] (LA1)
AiRE............ Automation and Radio Electronics (RU)
AIRG............ Asociacion Independiente de Radiodifusoras Guatemaltecas [*Independent Association of Guatemalan Radio Broadcasting Stations*] (LA)
AIRMEC...... Association Internationale pour la Recherche Medicale et les Echanges Culturels [*International Association for Medical Research and Cultural Exchange*] (EA)
AIRP............ Associazione Italiana Relazioni Pubbliche [*Italian Public Relations Association*]
AIRUD......... Corps Perairan dan Udara [*Air and Water Corps (Police unit)*] (IN)
AIS.............. Army Quartermaster Depot (RU)
AIS.............. Association Internationale de la Savonnerie et de la Detergence [*International Association of the Soap and Detergent Industry*] (EA)
AISA............ Association Internationale pour le Sport des Aveugles [*International Blind Sports Association - IBSA*] (EA)
AISAM......... Association Internationale des Societes d'Assurance Mutuelle [*International Association of Mutual Insurance Companies - IAMIC*] (EA)
AISB............ Association Internationale de Standardisation Biologigue [*International Association of Biological Standardization - IABS*] (EA)
AISE............ Association Internationale des Sciences Economiques [*International Economic Association - IEA*] (EA)
AISE............ Associazione Internazionale delle Scienze Economiche [*International Association of Economic Sciences*] [*Italian*] (WER)
AISF............ Association Internationale de Solidarite Francophone (MAR)
AISJ............ Association Internationale des Sciences Juridiques [*International Association of Legal Science - IALS*] (EA)
AISLF.......... Association Internationale des Sociologues de Langue Francaise [*International Association of French Language Sociologists*] (EA)
AISLLI......... Associazione Internazionale per gli Studi di Lingua e Letteratura Italiane [*International Association for the Study of the Italian Language and Literature - IASILL*] (EA)
AISM........... Armenian Scientific Research Institute of Building Materials and Structures (RU)
AISS............ Association Internationale de la Science du Sol [*International Society of Soil Science - ISSS*] (EA)
AISS............ Association Internationale de Securite Sociale (MAR)
AIT............... Alianta Interationala de Turism [*International Touring Alliance*] (RO)
AIT............... Alliance Internationale de Tourisme [*International Touring Alliance*] (EA)
AIT............... Asian Institute of Technology (CL)
AIT............... Asociacion Internacional de Trabajadores [*International Association of Workers*] [*Spanish*] (WER)
AIT............... Asociacion Internacional de Traductores [*Inter-American Association of Translators*]
AITA............ Annee Internationale du Tourisme Africain (MAR)
AITA............ Association des Ingenieurs et Techniciens Africains (MAR)
AITA............ Association Internationale des Transports Aeriens [*French*]
AITACI........ Association des Ingenieurs et Techniciens Africains de Cote-d'Ivoire (MAR)
AITC............ Association for International Technical Co-Operation (MAR)
AITC............ Association Internationale des Traducteurs de Conference [*International Association of Conference Translators*] [*Swiss*]
AITE............ Asociacion de Industriales Textiles del Ecuador [*Ecuadorean Textile Manufacturers Association*] (LA)
AITI............. Associazione Italiana Treduttori e Interpreti [*Italian Association of Translators and Interpreters*]
AITIA........... Ankara Iktisadi ve Ticari Ilimler Akademisi [*Ankara Academy of Economy and Commercial Science*] (TU)
AITIT........... Association Internationale de la Teinture et de l'Impression Textiles [*International Association of Textile Dyers and Printers - IATDP*] (EA)
AITs............. Automated Information Center (RU)
AIU.............. Asociacion Internacional de Universidades [*International Association of Universities*] [*Use IAU*] (LA)
AIU.............. Association Internationale des Urbanistes [*International Society of City and Regional Planners - ISoCaRP*] (EA)
AIUS............ Associazione Internazionale Uomo nello Spazis
AIUSSMRGW... Automatisiertes Informations- und Leitungssystem Standardization und Metrologie Rat der Gegenseitigen Wirtschaftshilfe [*Automated Information and Management System - Standardization and Metrology Council for Economic Mutual Assistance*] (EG)
AIV.............. Administratieve Informatie-Verwerking
AIVFC.......... Association Internationale des Villes Francophones de Congres [*International Association of French-Speaking Congress Towns - IAFCT*] (EA)
AIVN............ Association Internationale des Villes Nouvelles [*International New Towns Association - INTA*] (EA)
AIVPA.......... Association Internationale Veterinaire de Production Animale [*International Veterinary Association for Animal Production - IVAAP*] (EA)
AIZ............... Archaeological News and Notes [*A publication*] (RU)
AIZ............... Inventors' Association (RU)
AJ................ Auberges de Jeunesse [*Youth Hostels*] [*French*] (WER)
AJA.............. Arhiv Jugoslavenske Akademije Znanosti i Umjetnosti u Zagrebu [*Archives of the Yugoslav Academy of Sciences and Arts in Zagreb*] (YU)
AJA.............. Association des Juristes Algeriens [*Association of Algerian Jurists*] (AF)
AJAC............ Asociacion de Jovenes de Accion Catolica [*Youth Catholic Action Association*] [*Argentine*] (LA)
AJASS.......... African Jazz-Art Society and Studios (MAR)
AJBA............ Association de la Jeunesse Bakoko [*Association of Bakoko Youth*]
a de JC........ Antes de Jesucristo [*Before Christ*] [*Spanish*] (GPO)
AJC.............. Association de la Jeunesse Camerounaise [*Cameroonian Youth Association*]
AJC.............. Avant Jesus-Christ [*Before Jesus Christ*] [*French*]
AJENAKO... Association des Jeunesse Nationalistes du Kongo [*Association of Nationalist Youth of the Congo*] [*Leopoldville*]
AJES............ Association des Jeunesses Khmeres de l'Enseignement Secondaire [*Association of Cambodian Secondary Education Youth Organizations*] (CL)
AJEUNAL.... Alliance des Jeunesse Angolaise pour la Liberte (MAR)
AJEUNAREK... Association de la Jeunesse Nationaliste de la Republique Khmere [*Cambodian Republic Nationalist Youth Association*] (CL)
AJIM............ Association des Journalistes de l'Ile Maurice [*Mauritian Journalists Association*] (AF)
AJIR............. Arhiv Jadranskog Instituta u Rijeci [*Archives of the Adriatic Institute in Rijeka*] (YU)
AJM.............. Association de la Jeunesse Mauritanienne [*Mauritanian Youth Association*]
AJMK........... Jeunesse Madimbadienne du Secteur Kimuisi (MAR)
AJO.............. Arhiv Jugoslavenskog Odbora u Arhivu Jugoslavenske Akademije Znanosti i Umjetnosti u Zagrebu [*Archives of the Yugoslav Committee in the Archives of the Yugoslav Academy of Sciences and Arts in Zagreb*] (YU)
AJOM........... Association des Journalistes d'Outre-Mer (MAR)
AJP.............. Action pour la Justice et le Progress [*Somali*] (MAR)
AJPC........... Association des Journalistes Professionels du Cameroun [*Association of Professional Journalists of Cameroon*] (AF)
AJR.............. Asociacion de Jovenes Rebeldes [*Rebel Youth Association*] [*Cuban*] (LA)
AJR.............. Asociatia Juristilor Romani [*Association of Romanian Jurists*] (RO)
AJS.............. Alliance des Jeunes pour le Socialisme [*Alliance of Youth for Socialism*] [*French*] (PPE)
AJS.............. Amicale des Juristes Senegalais (MAR)
AJS.............. Association des Jeunes de Sumbe (MAR)
AJS.............. Association des Journalistes Socialistes [*Association of Socialist Reporters*] [*Senegalese*] (AF)
AJSMOC..... AJS [*Albert John Stevens*] and Matchless Owners Club (EA)
AJT.............. Association des Journalistes Tunisiens [*Tunisian Journalists Association*] (AF)
AJV.............. Arab Joint Ventures (MAR)
AJY.............. Association of Jewish Youth (MAR)
AK............... Absatzkontor [*Sales Agency*] (EG)
AK............... Adenylic Acid (RU)
AK............... Administrative Committee [*1952-1954*] (RU)
AK............... Administrativna Komisija (SIV) [*Administrative Commission*] (YU)
AK............... Advokatni Komora [*Bar Association*] (CZ)
AK............... Aero Klub [*Aero Club*] (YU)
AK............... Agoranomikos Kodix [*Marketing Code*] (GC)
AK............... Agrotikos Kodix [*Agricultural Code*] (GC)
ak................ Air Corps (BU)
AK............... Air Corps (RU)
AK............... Aircraft Compressor (RU)
AK............... Aircraft Shortwave Radio (RU)
Ak................ Akademi [*Academy*] (TU)
AK............... Akademiai Kiado [*Publishing House of the Hungarian Academy of Sciences*] (HU)
Ak................ Akademie [*or Akademisch*] [*Academy or Academic*] [*German*]
Ak................ Akra [*Akrotirion*] [*Cape*] [*Greek*] (NAU)
AK............... Alphabetic Catalog (RU)
AK............... Amino Acid (RU)
AK............... Andiproedros tis Kyverniseos [*Deputy Premier*] [*Automobile license plate designation*] [*Greek*] (GC)
AK............... Angkatan Kepolisian [*Police Force*] (IN)
AK............... Angola Kwanza (MAR)
AK............... Antenna Switch (RU)
ak................ Aranykorona [*Gold Crown (Hungarian currency before World War I, and still used to estimate real estate values)*] (HU)
AK............... Arbeitskraft [*Worker*] (EG)
AK............... Archaeographic Commission (at the Department of History of the Academy of Sciences, USSR) (RU)
AK............... Arellenorzes Orszagos Kormanybiztosa [*National Government Commissioner of Price Control*] (HU)

AK .... Armia Krajowa [*Home (Underground) Army (1942-1945)*] (POL)
ak .... Army Corps (BU)
AK .... Army Corps (RU)
AK .... Artillery Compass (RU)
AK .... Artillery Corps (RU)
AK .... Ascorbic Acid (RU)
AK .... Aspartic Acid (RU)
AK .... Astikos Kodix [*Civil Code*] (GC)
AK .... Astrocompass (RU)
AK .... Astrocorrection (RU)
AK .... Astronomical Almanac (RU)
AK .... Atleticky Klub [*Athletic Club*] (CZ)
AK .... Autoklub [*Automobile Club*] (CZ)
AK .... Automatic Control (RU)
AK .... Automatic Crane (RU)
AK .... Automobile Club (RU)
AK .... Aviation Club (RU)
AK .... Avtomat Kalishnikov [*Kalishnikov Automatic Rifle*] (CL)
AK .... Corps Artillery (RU)
AK .... Emergency Button (RU)
AK .... Instruction Address (RU)
AK .... Kalashnikov Submachine (RU)
AK .... Mechanical Pencil (RU)
AK .... Motor Convoy (RU)
AK .... Radioactive Well Logging (RU)
AK .... Subscriber's Set (RU)
AK- .... Truck-Mounted Crane (RU)
AKA .... Atom Karnkraft Avfall [*Commission for Nuclear Waste Disposal*] [*Swedish*] (WEN)
AKA .... Autonomous Finite Automaton (RU)
AKABRI .... Akademi Angkatan Bersendjata Republik Indonesia [*Republic of Indonesia Armed Forces Academy*] (IN)
akad .... Academic, Academy (RU)
akad .... Academy, Academician (BU)
Akad .... Akademia [*Academy*] (POL)
Akad .... Akademie [*Academy*] [*German*]
Akademizdat ... Publishing House of the Academy of Sciences, USSR (RU)
Akad K .... Akademiai Kiado [*Publishing House of the Hungarian Academy of Sciences*] (HU)
AKAFU .... Swinging Aerial Camera Mount (RU)
AKAJANS ... Ak Deniz Haber Ajansi [*Mediterranean News Agency*] [*See also AHA*] (TU)
AKAK .... Documents of the Caucasian Archaeographic Commission [*A publication*] (RU)
AKAKAT ..... Association Kaonde du Katanga (MAR)
AKAVA .... Akateemisammatillinen Valtuuskunta [*Academic Professional Commission*] [*Finnish*] (WEN)
AKB .... Allami Konyvesbolt [*State Book Store*] (HU)
AKBP .... Adjun Komisaris Besar Polisi [*Assistant Chief Police Commissioner*] (IN)
AKC .... Association Khmere de Confectionneurs [*Cambodian Garment Makers Association*] (CL)
AKCE .... Eskisehir Iktisadi ve Ticari Ilimler Akademisi Kulturel Calismalar ve Cevre Egitimi Enstitusu [*The Cultural Activities and Environmental Training Institute of the Eskisehir Academy of Economy and Commercial Science*] [*See also EITIA*] (TU)
AkcjaH .... Akcja Hodowli [*Pedigree Breeding Drive*] (POL)
AKD .... Agri Kultur Dernegi [*Agri/Cultural Association*] (TU)
Ak-Der .... Akhisar Halk Kultur Dernegi [*Akhisar Peoples Cultural Organization*] [*Manisa Province*] (TU)
AKDM .... Disisleri Bakanligi Akademisi Baskanligi [*Foreign Affairs Ministry Academy*] (TU)
AKDOD .... Akademicka Komisja Dzialania Organizacji Demokratycznych [*Democratic Organizations' Student Action Committee*] (POL)
AKDS .... Truck-Mounted Oxygen Station (RU)
Akdz .... Ak Deniz [*Mediterranean*] (TU)
AKE .... Agrotikon Komma Ellados [*Agrarian Party of Greece*] (GC)
AKE .... Andidiktatoriko Kinima Ellados [*Antidictatorial Movement of Greece*] (GC)
AKE .... Anexartitos Koinopolitiki Enosi [*Independent Commonwealth Union*] [*Greek*] (GC)
AKE .... Automatic Equipment for Power-Quality Maintenance (RU)
AKEL .... Anorthotiko Komma Ergazomenoy Laou [*Progressive Party of the Working People*] [*Cypriot*] (PPW)
AKF .... Abdou Karim Fall (MAR)
AKF .... Allami Kereskedelmi Felugyeloseg [*State Inspectorate of Trade*] (HU)
AKF .... Antarctic Whaling Flotilla (RU)
AKF .... Arctic Whaling Flotilla (RU)
AKFM .... Antokon'ny Kongresin'ny Fahaleovantenan'i Madagasikara [*Congress Party for Malagasy Independence*] (AF)
AKFM .... Parti du Congres de l'Independance de Madagascar [*Congress Party for Malagasy Independence*] (PPW)
AKG .... Allami Kiserleti Gazdasag [*State Experimental Farm*] (HU)
AKG .... Automatic Dew-Point Hygrometer (RU)
AKG- .... Truck-Mounted Hydraulic Crane (RU)
AKh .... Academy of Arts (RU)
AKh .... Acetylcholine (RU)
AKh .... Aerial Chemical Bomb (RU)
AKhCh .... Administrative Unit (RU)
AKhE .... Acetylcholinesterase (RU)
Akh/ha .... Arbeitskraftstunden je Hektar [*Per Hectare Man-Hours of Work*] (EG)
AKhl .... Truck for Decontaminating an Area with Chlorinated Lime (RU)
AKhL .... Agrochemical Laboratory (RU)
AKhM .... Absorption-Type Refrigeration Unit (RU)
AKhM .... Architectural and Artistic Planning Workshop (RU)
AKhO .... Administrative Department (RU)
AKhO .... Motorized Surgical Detachment (RU)
AKhR .... Association of Revolutionary Artists [*1928-1932*] (RU)
AKhRR .... Association of Artists of Revolutionary Russia [*1922-1928*] (RU)
AKhs .... Anotaton Khimikon Symvoulion [*Supreme Chemical Council*] (GC)
AKhTT .... Chemistry and Solid Fuel Processing Association (RU)
AKhU .... Administrative Office (RU)
AKI .... Agence Khmere d'Information [*Cambodian Information Agency*] (CL)
AKI .... Automatizalasi Kutato Intezet [*Automation Research Institute*] (HU)
AKI .... Magyar Tudomanyos Akademia Atommag Kutato Intezete, Debrecen [*Nuclear Science Research Institute of the Hungarian Academy of Sciences, Debrecen*] (HU)
AKII .... Azerbaydzhan "Red Banner" Industrial Institute Imeni M. Azizbekov (RU)
AKIN .... Acoustics Institute (RU)
AKJDOD ...... Akademicka Komisja Jednosci Dzialania Organizacji Demokratycznych [*Student Commission on the Unification of Activities of Democratic Organizations*] (POL)
AKK .... Administrative Committee on Coordination (RU)
akk .... Akkusatiivi [*Accusative*] [*Finnish*]
AKK .... Antifaschistischer Kampf Kaiserslautern [*Kaiserslautern Antifascist Struggle*] [*West German*] (PD)
AKK .... Arufuvarozas Kezikonyve [*Handbook on Shipping of Goods*] (HU)
AKK .... Autokozlekedesi Klub [*Automobile Transportation Club*] (HU)
AKK (Berlin) ... Amt fuer Kernforschung und Kerntechnik [*Office for Nuclear Research and Nuclear Technology*] [*Has responsibility for control, supervision, and coordination of all activities in the field of nuclear energy*] (EG)
AKKh .... Academy of Municipal Services Imeni K. D. Pamfilov (RU)
AKKK .... Amicale des Khmers du Kampuchea Krom [*Association of Friends of the Khmer Krom*] [*Literally, Association of Cambodians of Lower Cambodia*] (CL)
akkl .... Acclimatization (RU)
AKKO .... Turkish Communist Party - Marxist-Leninist (PD)
AKM .... Agazati Kapcsolatok Merlege [*Input-Output Table*] (HU)
AKM .... Astrakhan' Regional Studies Museum (RU)
AKM .... Chamber Music Association (RU)
AKMED .... Arbeiderkomiteen mot EEC og Dyrtid [*Labor Committee Against the EEC and the High Cost of Living*] [*Norwegian*] (WEN)
AKMIL .... Akademi Militer Nasional [*Indonesian*]
AKMOblast ... Autonomna Kosovo-Metohiska Oblast [*Autonomous Region of Kosovo-Metohija*] [*Serbia*] (YU)
AKMO-NRS ... Autonomna Kosovski-Metohiska Oblast - Narodna Republika Srbija [*Autonomous Region of Kosovo-Metohija, Serbia*] (YU)
AKMR .... Autonomous Kosovo-Metohija Region (YU)
AKN .... Cadmium-Nickel Plate Battery (RU)
AKNI .... Azerbaydzhan "Red Banner" Petroleum Institute Imeni M. Azizbekov (RU)
AKO .... Army Command (RU)
AKO .... Kamchatka Joint-Stock Company (RU)
AKOD .... Ankara Kibris'li Ogrenciler Dernegi [*Ankara Cypriot Students Organization*] [*Turkish Cypriot*] (GC)
AKOKD .... Ankara Kibrislilar Ogrenim ve Kultur Dernegi [*Ankara Cypriot (Students) Educational and Cultural Association*] [*Turkish Cypriot*] (GC)
akom .... Acoustic Ohm (RU)
AKOS .... Akademi Ogrenci Stajlari Merkezi [*The Academy Student Training Center*] [*of the Eskisehir Academy of Economy and Commercial Science*] [*See also EITIA*] (TU)
AKOV .... Antifasisticka Komise Osvobozenych Veznu [*Anti-Fascist Committee of Liberated (Political) Prisoners*] (CZ)
AKOV .... Autokozlekedesi Vallalat [*Automobile Transportation Enterprise*] (HU)
AKP .... Adjun Komisaris Polisi [*Assistant Police Commissioner*] (IN)
AKP .... Agence Khmere de Presse [*Cambodian Press Agency*] (CL)
AKP .... Albanian Communist Party (BU)
AKP .... Alzhirskaia Kommunisticheskaia Partia (MAR)
AKP .... American Communist Party (BU)
AKP .... Aniline Dye Industry (RU)
AKP .... Arbeidernes Kommunistiske Parti [*Workers' Communist Party*] [*Norwegian*] (PPE)
AKP .... Argentinian Communist Party (BU)
AKP .... Austrian Communist Party (BU)
AKP .... Automatic Brake Check Point [*Railroads*] (RU)
akp .... Breakthrough Artillery Corps (BU)
akp .... Breakthrough Artillery Corps (RU)

AKP(b)........ Azerbaydzhan Communist Party (of Bolsheviks) (RU)
AKP (m-l).... Arbeidernes Kommunistparti (Marxist-Leninistene) [*Workers Communist Party (Marxist-Leninist)*] [*Norwegian*] (WEN)
AKPT........... Automatic Alternating-Current Compensator (RU)
AKR............ Acetate Solvent for Leather (RU)
AKR-........... Acrylate (RU)
AKR............ Artiljeriski Komandno-Racunarski Uredaji [*Artillery Staff Computing Equipment*] (YU)
AKRA.......... Archives of the Red Army [*A publication*] (RU)
AKRCs........ Autoklub Republiky Ceskoslovenske [*Automobile Club of the Czechoslovak Republic*] (CZ)
AKRI........... Angkatan Kepolisian Republik Indonesia [*Republic of Indonesia Police Force*] (IN)
AKRP........... Mobile Motion Picture Unit and Radio Broadcasting Station (RU)
AKS............ Airfield Compressor Plant (RU)
AKS............ Akateeminen Karjala Seura [*Academic Karelia Society*] [*Finnish*] (WEN)
AKS............ Amatorski Klub Sportowy [*Amateur Sport Club*] (POL)
AKS-........... Automatic Logging Station (RU)
aks............. English Cubic Sagene (RU)
AKS............ Mobile Compressor (RU)
AKSA.......... Akrilik Kimya Sanayii AS [*Acrylic Chemical Industry Corporation*] (TU)
AKS/L-........ Laboratory of an Automatic Logging Station (RU)
AKSM.......... Anti-Fascist Committee of Soviet Youth (RU)
AKSO.......... Aksam Kiz Sanat Okulu [*Evening Trade School for Women*] (TU)
AKSSR........ Karelian Autonomous Soviet Socialist Republic (RU)
akt.............. Aktiivi(n) [*Finnish*]
AKT............ Amicale Khmere de Tourisme [*Cambodian Tourism Association*] (CL)
AKT............ Australian Trade-Union Congress (RU)
AKTG.......... Adrenocorticotrophic Hormone (RU)
Akt-Ges...... Aktiengesellschaft [*Corporation, Incorporated*] [*German*]
aktivir......... Activated (RU)
akts............ Joint-Stock (RU)
aktsd-vo...... Joint-Stock Company (BU)
akts o-vo.... Joint-Stock Company (RU)
AKTUR........ Akdeniz Tarim Urunleri Konsantre Sanayii AS [*Mediterranean Agricultural Products*] (TU)
AKTUR........ Aksiefront vir die Behoud van Turnhalle-Beginsels [*Action Front for the Preservation of Turnhalle Principles*] [*Namibian*] (AF)
Aktyubkhim ... Aktyubinsk Chemical Plant (RU)
Aktyubnefterazvedka ... Aktyubinsk Petroleum Exploration Trust (RU)
AKU............ Adiabatic Stability Constant (RU)
AKU............ Automatic Monitor (RU)
AKUKS........ Artillery Courses for Advanced Training of Command Personnel (RU)
AKV............ Academy of Communist Education Imeni N. K. Krupskaya (RU)
AKV-........... Air-Quantity Monitoring Unit [*Mine equipment*] (RU)
AKV............ Allami Konyvterjeszto Vallalat [*State Book Distributing Enterprise*] (HU)
AKV-........... Automatic Capillary Viscometer (RU)
AKV............ Automatic Humidity Regulator (RU)
AKVF.......... Amur "Red Banner" Naval Flotilla (RU)
AKVF.......... Astrakhan'-Caspian Naval Flotilla (RU)
akvo........... Anyakonyvvezeto [*Registrar of Births, Marriages, and Deaths*] (HU)
AKW............ Algemeen Kinderbijslagwet [*General Children's Allowance Act*] [*Dutch*] (WEN)
AKW............ Amt fuer Kontrolle des Warenverkehrs [*Office for the Control of Commodity Traffic*] (EG)
AKW............ Atomkraftwerk [*Nuclear Power Plant*] (EG)
AKWV.......... Algemeen Katholieke Werkgevers Vereniging [*General Catholic Employers Association*] [*Dutch*] (WEN)
AKYSDE...... Anoteron Kendron Ypiresiakou Symvouliou Dimotikis Ekpaidevseos [*Higher Center of the Public Education Service Council*] [*Greek*] (GC)
AKZS........... Truck-Mounted Oxygen-Charging Station (RU)
a/l.............. A Livraison [*On Delivery of Goods*] [*French*]
AL............... Accion Laborista [*Laborist Action*] [*Spanish*] (WER)
Al............... Alan [*Field, Clearing in a Forest*] (TU)
al............... Alanine (RU)
AL............... Albania [*Two-letter standard code*] (CNC)
Al............... Aleja [*or Aleje*] [*Avenue*] (POL)
al............... Alia [*Other Things*] [*Latin*] (GPO)
AL............... Amigos del Libro [*Publisher*] [*Bolivian*]
AL............... Angkatan Laut [*Navy*] (IN)
AL............... Armia Ludowa [*People's (Communist) Army (1944)*] (POL)
AL............... Artillerie Lourde [*Military*] [*French*] (MTD)
AL............... Artillery Observer-Pilot (RU)
AL............... Automatic Linguistics (RU)
a/l.............. Nuclear Powered Icebreaker, Atomic Icebreaker (RU)
al............... Paragraph (BU)
al............... Section (BU)
AL............... Subscriber's Line (RU)
AL-.............. Transfer Machine (RU)
ALA............ African Literature Association (MAR)
ala.............. Alakulat [*Formation, Outfit*] [*Military*] (HU)
ala.............. Alallomas [*Substation*] (HU)
ALA............ Apararea Locala Anti-Aeriana [*Local Anti-Aircraft Defense*] (RO)
ALA............ Artillerie Lourde de l'Armee [*Military*] [*French*] (MTD)
ALA............ Arussi Liberation Army [*Ethiopian*] (AF)
ALA............ Associacao Livre dos Agricultores [*Free Association of Farmers*] [*Portuguese*] (WER)
ALAC.......... Asociacion de Latinoamericanos en Cuba [*Association of Latin Americans in Cuba*] (LA)
ALACODE... Asociacion Latinoamericana de Periodistas para el Desarrollo [*Association of Latin American Journalists for Development*] (LA)
ALAD.......... Arid Lands Agricultural Development Program [*North African*] (MAR)
ALADA........ Associacao Latino-Americana de Direito Aeronautico [*Latin American Association of Aeronautical Law*] (LA)
ALADI......... Asociacion Latinoamericana de Integracion [*Latin American Integration Association*] (LA1)
ALADIN....... Automatisering Landbouwkundige Documentatie- en Informatieverspreiding [*Dutch*]
ALAF.......... Aluminium Africa Co. Ltd. (MAR)
ALAF.......... Asociacion Latinoamericana de Ferrocarriles [*Latin American Railroad Association*] (LA)
ALAICO....... Asociacion de Lineas Aereas Internacionales en Colombia [*Association of International Airlines in Colombia*] (LA)
ALAINEE..... Asociacion Latinoamericana de la Industria Electrica y Electronica [*Latin American Electric and Electronic Industry Association*] (LA)
ALAL.......... Aluminium Algerois (MAR)
ALALC........ Asociacion Latinoamericana de Libre Comercio [*Latin American Free Trade Association*] [*Use LAFTA*] (LA)
ALAMAR..... Asociacion Latinoamericana de Armadores [*Latin American Shipowners Association*] (LA)
ALAMBREC ... Alambres Galvanizados Ecuatorianos, SA [*Ecuadorean Galvanized Wires, Inc.*] (LA)
ALAMSAS... Alarko Agir Makina Sanayii Anonim Sirketi [*Alarko Heavy Machinery Industry Corporation*] (TU)
alank.......... Alankomainen [*Dutch*] [*Finnish*]
ALAP.......... Agence Litteraire et Artistique Parisienne pour les Echanges Culturels [*Parisian Literary and Artistic Agency for Cultural Exchange*] (WER)
ALAP.......... Asociacion Latinoamericana de Prensa [*Latin American Press Association*] (LA)
ALAP.......... Latin American Trade-Union Association (RU)
alapsz........ Alapszabaly [*or Alapszabalyok*] [*Statute or Statutes, Bylaws*] (HU)
ALASEI....... Agencia Latinoamericana de Servicios Especiales de Informacion [*Latin American Special Information Service Agency*] (LA)
ALAT.......... Aviation Legere de l'Armee de Terre [*Ground Forces Tactical Air Support*] [*French*] (WER)
ALATAC...... Asociacion Latinoamericana de Transportacion Automotor por Carreteras [*Latin American Automobile Highway Transport Association*] (LA)
ALB............ Albania [*Three-letter standard code*] (CNC)
alb............. Albanian (BU)
alb............. Albanian (RU)
Alb............. Albay [*Colonel (Army) or Captain (Navy)*] (TU)
ALB............ Allgemeine Leistungs- und Lieferungsbedingungen [*General Delivery and Performance Terms*] (EG)
ALB............ Antifasisticka Liga Burme [*Anti-Fascist League of Burma*] (YU)
ALB............ Arbeitsgemeinschaft Landwirtschaftliches Bauwesen [*Agricultural Construction Work Group*] (EG)
ALBA.......... Aluminum Bahrain (ME)
ALBART...... Allami Bauxit Aluminium Reszvenytarsasag [*State Bauxite Aluminum Company Limited*] (HU)
ALBRAS...... Aluminio de Brasil, SA [*Brazilian Aluminum Corporation, Inc.*] (LA)
ALBRECO... Groupement Algerie-Bretagne de Construction (MAR)
ALC............ African Lakes Company [*or Corporation*] (MAR)
ALC............ African Liberation Committee (MAR)
ALC............ Afro-American Labor Center (MAR)
ALC............ Alexandria Liaison Committee (MAR)
ALC............ Arab League Council (MAR)
ALCA.......... Artillerie Lourde de Corps d'Armee [*Military*] [*French*] (MTD)
ALCAM....... Assemblee Legislative du Cameroun (MAR)
ALCAMOR... Assemblee Legislative du Cameroun Orientale (MAR)
ALCANCALI ... Aluminio Alcan de Colombia SA [*Cali*] (COL)
ALCASA...... Aluminios del Caroni, SA [*Caroni Aluminum Company*] [*Venezuelan*] (LA)
ALCAVE...... Alambres y Cables Venezolanos, CA
alcde.......... Alcalde [*Mayor*] [*Spanish*]
ALCER........ Asociacion para la Lucha Contra las Enfermedades Renales [*Association for the Struggle Against Kidney Diseases*] [*Spanish*] (WER)
ALCIP.......... Societe Algerienne de Construction Industrielle et Petroliere [*Algerian Industrial and Petroleum Engineering Co.*] (AF)
ALCO.......... Alliance des Congolais (MAR)
ALCOMINAS ... Companhia Mineira de Aluminio [*Aluminum Company of Minas Gerais*] [*Brazilian*] (LA)

ALCONH ..... Alianza Campesina de Organizaciones Nacionales de Honduras [*Peasant Alliance of National Organizations of Honduras*] (PD)
ALCORE ...... Core Laboratories, Inc. (MAR)
ALD .... African Liberation Day (MAR)
ALD .... Agrupacion Liberal Democratica [*Democratic Liberal Group*] [*Spanish*] (WER)
ALDDH .... Argentinos por Libertades Democraticas y Derechos Humanos [*Argentines for Democratic Freedoms and Human Rights*] (LA)
ALDECA ...... Aluminio de Centroamerica, SA [*Aluminum of Central America Corp.*] [*Salvadoran*]
ALDEP .... Arable Land Development Programme (MAR)
ALDEV .... African Land Development (MAR)
ALDIM .... Societe Algerienne des Outils Diamantes [*Algerian Diamond Tool Company*] (AF)
ALEAM .... Association of Lao Employees of American Missions (CL)
alebastr .... Alabaster Quarry [*Topography*] (RU)
ALEBCI .... Asociasion Latino Americana de Escuelas de Bibliotecnomia y Ciencias de la Informacion
ALEC .... Atlas Linguistico, Etnografico de Colombia [*Bogota*] (COL)
alemp .... Alempana [*Finnish*]
ALERT .... All-African Leprosy and Rehabilitation Center (AF)
alezds .... Alezredes [*Lieutenant Colonel*] (HU)
alezr .... Alezredes [*Lieutenant Colonel*] (HU)
ALF .... Afar Liberation Front [*Ethiopian*] (PD)
alf .... Alphabetic (RU)
ALF .... Arab Liberation Forces [*or Front*] [*Palestinian*] (ME)
ALF .... Automated Laboratory of Photographic Methods (RU)
ALF .... Azania Liberation Front [*Sudanese*] (MAR)
al'fol' .... Aluminum Foil (RU)
ALFOR .... Societe Algerienne de Forage [*Algerian Drilling Company*] (AF)
ALG .... Akademia Lekarska w Gdansku [*Gdansk (Danzig) Academy of Medicine*] (POL)
alg .... Algebra [*Algebra*] (HU)
alg .... Algebra, Algebraic (RU)
ALGA .... Association of Local Government Authorities [*Jamaican*] (LA1)
ALGAK .... Association of Local Government Authorities in Kenya (MAR)
ALGEK .... Algorithmic Language for Economics Calculations (RU)
ALGEM .... Algorithmic Language for the Description of Mathematical Economics Problems (RU)
ALGEO .... Societe Algerienne de Geophysique [*Algerian Geophysical Company*] (AF)
ALGP .... Artillerie Lourde a Grande Puissance [*Military*] [*French*] (MTD)
ALHC .... African-Latin Help Committee (MAR)
alhdgy .... Alhadnagy [*Junior Lieutenant*] [*Formerly, highest rank of noncommissioned officer*] (HU)
alhgy .... Alhadnagy [*Junior Lieutenant*] [*Formerly, highest rank of noncommissioned officer*] (HU)
Ali .... Angali [*Bight, Open Bay*] [*Greek*] (NAU)
ALIANSA ..... Alimentos de Animales, SA [*Animal Food Corp.*] [*Salvadoran*]
ALIAZO .... Alianca Angolana des Originarios do Zombo (MAR)
ALICA .... Associacao Latinoamericana dos Industrias de Conservas Alimenticias [*Latin American Food Canners Association*] (LA)
ALIDE .... Asociacion Latinoamericana de Instituciones Financieras de Desarrollo [*Latin American Association of Financial Institutions for Development*] (LA)
alifatich .... Aliphatic (RU)
alig .... Aligazgato [*Deputy Director*] (HU)
alik .... Alikersantti [*Finnish*]
ALIMPORT ... Empresa Cubana Importadora de Alimentos [*Cuban Enterprise for Import of Foodstuffs*] (LA)
ALIN .... Alianza de Liberacion de la Izquierda Nacional [*National Left Liberation Alliance*] [*Bolivian*] (LA)
ALIPO .... Alianza Liberal del Pueblo [*People's Liberal Alliance*] [*Honduran*] (LA1)
ALIREC .... A corporation formed by Ito Chu with Sumitomo Metal Mining Co. Ltd., and Furukawa Co. Ltd., to continue joint uranium surveying work with AGIP of Australia (SJT)
ALISS .... Automatisiertes Leitungs- und Informationssystem Standardwerk [*Automated Management and Information System Standard Work*] (EG)
ALITALIA .... Aerolinee Italiane Internazionali [*Italian International Airline*]
alitsiklich .... Alicyclic (RU)
alk .... Alkalisch [*Alkaline*] [*German*]
alk .... Alkalmas [*Fit, Suitable*] (HU)
alk .... Alkalmazott [*Employee*] (HU)
alk .... Alkerulet [*Subdistrict*] (HU)
Alk .... Alkohol [*Alcohol*] [*German*]
Alk .... Alkotmany [*Constitution*] (HU)
alk .... Alkuaan [*Originally*] [*Finnish*]
alkal .... Alkalisch [*Alkaline*] [*German*]
alkoh .... Alkoholisch [*Alcoholic*] [*German*]
ALKON .... Productos Alkalinos SA [*Medellin*] (COL)
ALKOPROMET ... Pretprijatie za Promet so Alkoholni Pijaloci [*Establishment for Trade in Alcoholic Beverages*] [*Skopje*] (YU)
ALKSM .... Lenin Young Communist League of Azerbaydzhan (RU)
all .... Allami [*State (adjective)*] (HU)
all .... Allando [*Permanent*] (HU)
all .... Allatiivi [*Finnish*]
ALLA .... Allied Long Lines Agency (WER)
allatt .... Allattenyesztes [*Animal Husbandry*] (HU)
all eng .... Allamilag Engedelyezett, Engedelyezve [*Licensed by the State*] (HU)
allg .... Allgemein [*General or Generally*] [*German*] (GPO)
Allgmb hoh S ... Allgemeinbildende Hoehere Schule [*German*]
ALLIAMA .... Alliance du Mayombe [*Alliance of Mayombe*] [*Angolan*] (AF)
ALLIAZO ..... Alleanza delle Popolazioni di Zombo (MAR)
ALLIBAKAT ... Alliance des Bahemba du Katanga (MAR)
All Ny .... Allami Nyomda [*State Printing Office*] (HU)
Alm .... Almanca [*German*] (TU)
ALM .... Almarhum [*Deceased*] (IN)
ALM .... American Leprosy Missions, Inc. (MAR)
ALM .... Arab Liberation Movement (MAR)
ALM .... Asociacion Latinoamericana de Manufactureros [*Latin American Association of Manufacturers*] (LA)
ALM .... Conservational Afforestation (RU)
ALMA .... Anonima Libica Macchine Agricole (MAR)
ALMABANCO ... Almacenadora Grancolombiana SA [*Bogota*] (COL)
ALMACAFE ... Almacenes Generales de Deposito de Cafe [*Neiva*] (COL)
ALMACENAR ... Almacenes Generales de Deposito Mercantil SA [*Bogota*] (COL)
ALMACEROS ... Almacen de Aceros Ltda. [*Bogota*] (COL)
ALMADELCO ... Almacenes Generales de Deposito de Comercio SA [*Bogota*] (COL)
al'mag .... Aluminum-Magnesium Alloy (RU)
ALMAGRAN ... Almacenes Generales de Deposito Gran Colombia [*Bogota*] (COL)
ALMANGEL ... Almacenes Angel [*Cali*] (COL)
ALMAP .... Societe Algero-Mauritanienne de Peche (MAR)
Almetzavod ... Alaverdi Metallurgical Plant (RU)
ALMO .... African Livestock Marketing Organisation (MAR)
ALMO .... Societe Mixte Algerienne de Machines-Outils [*Algerian Joint Machine Tool Co.*] (AF)
ALN .... Alianca Libertadora Nacional [*National Liberation Alliance*] [*Brazilian*] (PD)
ALN .... Alianza de Liberacion Nacional [*National Liberation Alliance*] [*Argentino*] (LA)
ALN .... Armee de Liberation Nationale [*National Liberation Army*] [*French*] (WER)
ALN .... Armee de Liberation Nationale [*National Liberation Army*] [*Guadeloupe*] (PD)
ALN .... Armee de Liberation Nationale [*National Liberation Army*] [*Algerian*] (AF)
ALNA .... Armee de Liberation Nationale de l'Angola [*Angolan Army of National Liberation*] (AF)
ALNG .... Armee de Liberation Nacionale Guineene (MAR)
ALNK .... Armee de Liberation Nationale Kamerunaise [*Cameroonian Army of National Liberation*] (AF)
ALNS .... Anti-Fascist League of People's Liberation [*Burmese*] (RU)
ALO .... Arab Labour Organization (MAR)
ALOII .... Archives of the Leningrad Branch of the Institute of History (of the Academy of Sciences, USSR) [*A publication*] (RU)
aloszt .... Alosztaly [*Subunit*] [*Also used for army units*] (HU)
ALP .... Agence Lao Presse [*Lao Press Agency*] (CL)
ALP .... Agence Libyenne de Presse (MAR)
alp .... Alperes [*Defendant*] (HU)
ALP .... Antigua Labor Party (PPW)
ALP .... Armee de Legitimation des Pouvoirs [*Army for the Legitimation of Powers*] [*Algerian*] (AF)
ALP .... Astronomical Line of Position (RU)
ALP .... Australian Labor Party (PPW)
ALPA .... Alet ve Dayanikli Tuketim Mamulleri Pazarlama AS [*Tools and Durable Consumer Goods Marketing Corp.*] (TU)
ALPA .... Aluminio del Pacifico Ltda. [*Cali*] (COL)
ALPA .... Amiral, Porte Avions [*Aircraft Carriers and Embarked Air Squadrons*] [*French*] (WER)
ALPAIX .... Alliance pour la Paix [*Alliance for Peace*] [*Cambodian*] (CL)
ALPI-CAM ... Societe Alpi Petro & Fils, Cameroun (MAR)
alpk .... Alparancsnok [*Second in Command*] (HU)
ALPS .... Armee de Liberation du Peuple Sahraoui [*Saharan People's Liberation Army*] (AF)
ALR .... African Language Review [*Freetown*] [*A publication*] (MAR)
ALR .... Albanska Lidova Republika [*Albanian People's Republic*] (CZ)
ALRC .... Anti-Locust Research Centre (MAR)
ALREG .... Societe Algerienne de Recherches et d'Etudes Geophysiques (MAR)
ALRI .... Angkatan Laut Republik Indonesia [*Republic of Indonesia Navy*] (IN)
ALRP .... A los Reales Pies [*Spanish*]
ALS .... African Language Studies [*London*] [*A publication*] (MAR)
ALS .... Automatic Cab Signaling (RU)
ALSAML ...... Ahvenanmaan Kokoomus; Alaendsk Samling [*Aland Coalition*] [*Finnish*] (PPE)
ALSC .... African Liberation Support Committee (MAR)
ALSD .... Amerikan Lisan ve Sanaat Dersanesi [*American Language and Trade Institute*] [*Istanbul*] (TU)
ALSED .... Anthropology and Language Science in Educational Development (MAR)
ALSp .... Allgemeine Leistungsbedingungen der Spedition [*General Service Terms of Shipping Agencies*] (EG)

alsz............ Alszam [*Subheading Number*] (HU)
alt............ Altalanos [*General, Universal, Common*] (HU)
Alt............ Altesse [*Highness*] [*French*]
alt............ Altiszt [*Noncommissioned Officer*] (HU)
ALT............ Assemblee Legislative du Togo (MAR)
ALT............ Association d'Aide a la Lutte Contre la Trypanosomiase [*Anti-Trypanosomiasis Assistance Association*] [*Zairian*] (AF)
ALTACOR... Alfombras, Tapetes, Cortinas [*Bogota*] (COL)
Altaykhimles ... Altay Trust for the Production of Wood-Chemistry Raw Materials (RU)
Altaykraypromstrom ... Altay Kray Industrial Construction and Installation Trust (RU)
Altaysel'mash ... Altay Agricultural Machinery Plant (RU)
altbgy.......... Altabornagy [*Lieutenant General*] (HU)
alti............ Altiszt [*Noncommissioned Officer*] (HU)
ALTI............ Arkhangel'sk Forestry-Engineering Institute Imeni V. V. Kuybyshev (RU)
ALTOUR...... Societe Nationale Algerienne de Tourisme et d'Hotellerie (MAR)
ALTRA......... Entreprises Algeriennes de Grands Travaux (MAR)
ALTUMEC... Societe Algerienne de Tubes et de Constructions Mecaniques (MAR)
ALU............ Akademija za Likovnu Umetnost [*Academy of Representational Art*] [*Belgrade*] (YU)
ALU............ Arab Lawyers Union [*See also UAA*] (EA)
ALUAR........ Aluminio Argentino [*Argentine Aluminum Enterprise*] (LA1)
ALUAR SAIC ... Aluminio Argentino, Sociedad Anonima Industrial, y Comercial [*Argentine Aluminum, Industrial, and Commercial Enterprise*] (LA1)
ALUCAM..... Aluminium du Cameroun [*Cameroon Aluminum*] (AF)
ALUCI......... Aluminium de la Cote-d'Ivoire (MAR)
ALUCONGO ... Societe pour la Transformation de l'Aluminium et Autres Metaux au Congo (MAR)
ALUKER...... Aluminium Kereskedelmi Vallalat [*Aluminum Trade Enterprise*] (HU)
alum............ Aluminium [*Aluminum*] (HU)
ALUS............ African Land Utilization and Settlement Board (MAR)
ALUSAC...... Asociacion de Licenciados. Universidad Santiago de Cali (COL)
ALUSAF...... Aluminum Corporation of South Africa (MAR)
ALUTERV.... Aluminiumipari Tervezo Intezet [*Designing Institute for the Aluminum Industry*] (HU)
ALV............ Amsterdamsche Leesbibliotheekhouders Vereeniging
ALVF............ Artillerie Lourde sur Voie Ferree [*Military*] [*French*] (MTD)
Alvo............ Alvaro [*Spanish*]
ALWIC......... Anti-Leprosy World Information Centre (MAR)
Alyuminstroy ... Administration for the Construction of Aluminum Plants (RU)
ALZI............ Societe Algerienne du Zinc (MAR)
AM............ Acrylamide (RU)
AM............ Action Monegasque [*Monegasque Action*] (PPE)
AM............ Adetto Militare [*Military Attache*] [*Italian*] (WER)
A-M............ Aide-Memoire [*Memorandum*] [*French*] (MTD)
am............ Aircraft Engine (RU)
AM............ Aircraft Engine Designed by A. A. Mikulin (RU)
AM............ Akademia Medyczna [*Academy of Medicine*] (POL)
aM............ Am Main [*On the River Main*] [*German*]
am............ American (BU)
am............ American (RU)
Am............ Amerikanismus [*Americanism*] [*German*]
am............ Amerikkalainen [*American*] [*Finnish*]
am............ Amerykanski [*American*] [*Polish*]
am............ Amorphous (RU)
am............ Amortissable [*French*]
AM............ Amplitude Modulation (BU)
AM............ Amplitude Modulation (RU)
AM............ Anno Mundi [*In the Year of the World*] [*Latin*] (GPO)
AM............ Annus Mirabilis [*The Wonderful Year (1666)*] [*Latin*] (GPO)
am............ Annyi Mint [*That Is*] (HU)
AM............ Ansiomitali [*Finnish*]
am............ Ante Meridiano [*Before Noon*] [*Spanish*] (GPO)
AM............ Ante Meridiem [*Before Noon*] [*Latin*] (GPO)
am............ Antimeridiano [*Forenoon*] [*Italian*] (GPO)
AM............ Apostolado del Mar [*Apostleship of the Sea - AOS*] (EA)
AM............ Archipelago Mundi (EA)
AM............ Assistance Medicale (MAR)
AM............ Assurance Mutuelle [*Mutual Assurance*] [*French*]
AM............ Auto-Mitrailleuse [*Light Armored Car*] [*Military*] [*French*] (MTD)
AM............ Avant Midi [*Before Noon*] [*French*] (WER)
AM............ Aviazione Militare [*Air Force*] [*Italian*] (WER)
AM............ Avtou Makariotis [*His Beatitude*] [*Used for Patriarchs of Alexandria, Antioch, Jerusalem, Russia, Serbia, Romania, and Bulgaria; Metropolitan of Poland; and Archbishop of Cyprus*] (GC)
AM............ General, Public, Civil (ML)
Am............ Magnetic Azimuth (RU)
AM............ Naval Air Station (RU)
AMA............ American Missionary Association (MAR)
AMA............ Assistance Medicale Africaine (MAR)
AMA............ Associacao dos Mulheres de Angola (MAR)
AMA............ Ateliers Mecaniques de l'Atlantique (MAR)
AMA............ Aviation Militaire Algerienne (MAR)
AMAC......... Asociacion de Mujeres de Accion Catolica [*Women's Catholic Action Association*] [*Argentine*] (LA)
AMAC......... Assistance Medicale a l'Afrique Centrale [*Medical Assistance to Central Africa*] [*Belgian*] (AF)
AMACAM.... Assurances Mutuelles Agricoles du Cameroun (MAR)
AMACHICO ... Atlantic Machinery Company Ltda. [*Barranquilla*] (COL)
AMAD.......... Asociacion Magisterial de Accion Democratica [*Teachers Association of Democratic Action*] [*Salvadoran*] (LA1)
AMADA....... Alle Macht aan de Arbeiders [*All Power to the Workers*] [*Belgian*] (PPW)
AMADE....... Association Mondiale des Amis de l'Enfance [*World Association of Children's Friends*] (EA)
AMAF.......... American Study in Africa (MAR)
AMAFRAN... Agence Maritime France-Afrique Noire (MAR)
AMAMCO.... Agence Marocaine et Mauritanienne de Cooperation [*Moroccan-Mauritanian Cooperation Agency*] (AF)
AMANAL..... Amicale des Anciens Etudiants et Stagiaires d'Allemagne (MAR)
AMANGOLA ... Amigos do Manifesto Angolano (MAR)
AMANIC...... Agencias Maritimas y Aduaneras de Nicaragua [*Nicaraguan Shipping and Customs Agencies*] (LA1)
AMANISSA ... Entreprise Nigerienne de Batiments Travaux Publics de Constructions (MAR)
AMANO....... Association des Manianga du Nord-Luozi (MAR)
AMAP.......... Agence Malienne de Presse et de Publicite [*Malian Press and Publicity Agency*] (AF)
AMAPANAL ... Asociacion de Mutuo Auxilio de Miembros de la Policia Nacional [*Bogota*] (COL)
AMAS.......... Asociacion de Mujeres en Accion Social [*Association of Women for Social Action*] [*Uruguayan*] (LA)
AMAT.......... Associations des Musees d'Afrique Tropicale [*Museums Association of Tropical Africa*] (AF)
AMATECI.... Agence Mauritanienne de Television et de Cinema [*Mauritanian Television and Cinema Agency*] (AF)
AMAX.......... American Metal Climax (MAR)
AMAZ.......... Agence et Messageries Aeriennes Zairoises (MAR)
AMB............ Abteilung Allgemeiner Maschinenbau der Staatlichen Plankommission [*General Machine Building Department of the State Planning Commission*] (EG)
AMB............ Allami Mezogazdasagi Birtokok [*State Agricultural Properties*] (HU)
Amb............ Ambar [*Warehouse, Hold*] (TU)
amb............ Ambasador [*Ambassador*] [*Polish*]
Amb............ Ambassadeur [*Ambassador*] [*French*] (MTD)
Amb............ Ambulance [*Ambulance*] [*Military*] [*French*] (MTD)
AMB............ Asociacion Mexicana de Banqueros [*Mexican Bankers Association*] (LA)
AMB............ Ateliers Metallurgiques du Batiment (MAR)
AMB............ Group B Autochtonous Microflora (RU)
amb............ Outpatient Clinic, Dispensary [*Topography*] (RU)
amb............ Storehouse, Granary [*Topography*] (RU)
AMBAKHMER ... Ambassade [*or Ambassadeur*] Khmer [*Cambodian Embassy or Ambassador*] (CL)
Amb C (Div) ... Ambulance de Corps (Divisionnaire) [*Military*] [*French*] (MTD)
AMBES........ Aircraft Engine Designed by A. A. Mikulin and B. S. Stechkin (RU)
AMBI........... Automatisering en Mechanisering van de Bestuurlijke Informatieverwerking [*Dutch*]
AMBIB......... Ambulantna Biblioteka [*Mobile Library*] (YU)
AMBM......... American Mennonite Brethren Mission (MAR)
AMBMO...... Asociacion Mediterranea de Biologia Marina y Oceanografia (MAR)
AMC............ Agricultural Marketing Corporation [*Jamaican*] (LA1)
AMC............ Alma Mater Croatica [*Croatian University*] [*Zagreb*] (YU)
AMC............ Aparatura de Masura si Control [*Measurement and Control Apparatus*] (RO)
AMC............ Arab Mining Company (MAR)
AMC............ Archives du Ministere des Colonies (MAR)
AMCB.......... Annales du Musee du Congo Belge [*A publication*] (MAR)
AMCBME.... Annales du Musee du Congo Belge. Monographies Ethnographiques [*A publication*] (MAR)
AMCBNS..... Annales du Musee du Congo Belge. Nouvelle Serie [*A publication*] (MAR)
AMCEK....... Association des Membres du Corps Enseignant Khmer [*Association of Members of the Cambodian Teaching Corps*] (CL)
AMCI.......... Armes et Munitions de la Cote-d'Ivoire (MAR)
AMCOR....... African Metals Corporation [*South African*] (AF)
AMCOS....... Aldermaston Mechanized Cataloguing and Ordering Systems [*British*]
AMCOVIT... A & M Compania de Vigilancia Tecnica [*Bogota*] (COL)
AMCP.......... Asistenta Medicala Curativo-Profilactica [*Remedial-Prophylactic Medical Care*] (RO)
AMD............ Alliance pour Une Mauritanie Democratique [*Alliance for One Democratic Mauritania*] (PD)
AMD............ Askar Melayu Di-Raja [*Royal Malaysian Army*] (ML)
AMD............ Auto-Moto Drustvo [*Automobile and Motorcycle Club*] (YU)
AMDA.......... African Music and Drama Academy (MAR)
AMDA.......... Anglo-Malayan Defense Agreement (ML)
AMDA.......... Asociacion Medica de Antioquia [*Medellin*] (COL)

AMDAC....... Assistance aux Maternites et Dispensaires d'Afrique Centrale (MAR)
AMDET........ Administracion Municipal de Transportes [*Municipal Transportation Association*] [*Uruguayan*] (LA)
AME............ Accord Monetaire Europeen [*French*]
AMe............ Adenosylmethionine (RU)
AME............ African Methodist Episcopal Church (MAR)
AME............ Ateliers de Montage Electrique (MAR)
AMEC.......... Atelier de Mecanique et Carrosserie (MAR)
AMECA....... Ateliers de Mecanique Automobile (MAR)
AMECA....... Ateliers de Mecanique et d'Electricite du Centre-Afrique (MAR)
AMECEA..... Association of Members of the Episcopal Conference of East Africa (MAR)
AMEDCO.... American Express Middle East Development Company (ME)
AMEE.......... Agonistikon Metopon Ellinon Exoterikou [*Fighting Front of Greeks Abroad*] (GC)
AMEE.......... Apelevtherotikon Metopon Ellinon Exoterikou [*Liberation Front of Greeks Abroad*] (GC)
AMEFO........ African Media Foundation (MAR)
AMEK.......... Antifasiszta Menekulteket Ellato Kozpont [*Relief Center for Anti-Fascist Refugees*] (HU)
Amel............ Ameliyat [*Surgical Operation*] (TU)
AMELEC..... Ateliers de Mecanique et d'Electricite (MAR)
AMEM......... American Methodist Episcopal Mission (MAR)
AMEP.......... Agence Mauritanienne d'Edition et de Publicite (MAR)
amer............ American (BU)
amer............ American (RU)
amer............ Amerikkalainen [*American*] [*Finnish*]
amer............ Amerykanski [*American*] [*Polish*]
AMER.......... Societe aux Menuisiers-Ebenistes Reunis (MAR)
amerik.......... American (RU)
amer p......... American Patent (RU)
AMES.......... Association of Marine Engineering Schools (EA)
AMESU....... All-Malayan Estate Staff Union (ML)
AMEU.......... Association of Municipal Electricity Undertakings of South Africa (MAR)
AMEZ.......... African Methodist Episcopal Zion (MAR)
AMF............ Adenosine Monophosphate (RU)
AMF............ Adenylic Acid, Adenosinemonophosphoric Acid (RU)
AMF............ Arab Monetary Fund (ME)
AMF............ Militant Party for the Establishment of a Classless Society [*Malagasy*] (AF)
AMG............ Academia Militara Generala [*General Military Academy*] (RO)
AMG............ Aide Medicale Gratuite [*Free Medical Aid*] (LA1)
AMG............ Allami Mezogazdasagi Gepallomas [*or Allami Mezogazdasagi Gepkozpont or Allami Mezogazdasagi Gepuzem*] [*State Tractor Station*] (HU)
AMG............ Arzneimittelgesetz [*Drugs Act*] (EG)
AMG............ Assistance Medicale Gratuite [*Algerian*] (MAR)
AMGE.......... Association Mondiale des Guides et des Eclaireuses [*World Association of Girl Guides and Girl Scouts - WAGGGS*] (EA)
AMGECO.... African Marine General Engineering Company (MAR)
AMGI........... Atelier de Mecanique Generale Ivoirien (MAR)
AMGOT....... Allied Military Government in Occupied Territory (MAR)
AMGR.......... Ateliers de Mecanique Generale et de Rectification (MAR)
AMHC.......... All-Mauritius Hindu Congress (AF)
AMI.............. Aeronautica Militare Italiana [*Italian Air Force*] (WER)
AMI.............. Agence Maritime Internationale (MAR)
AMI.............. Agrupamento Militar de Intervencao [*Military Intervention Group*] [*Portuguese*] (WER)
AMI.............. Armement Moderne Ivoirien (MAR)
AMI.............. Association Montessori Internationale (EA)
AMI.............. Association de Murisseurs Independants [*Association of Independent Developers*] (LA1)
AMI.............. Assurance Maladie-Invalidite [*National Health Insurance Program*] [*Belgian*] (WER)
AMI.............. Ausonia Mineraria (MAR)
AMI.............. Azerbaydzhan State Medical Institute (RU)
AMICAPRO... Anciens Eleves des Missions Catholiques et Protestantes (MAR)
AMID........... Arab Military Industrial Organization (ME)
AMIEV......... Association Medicale Internationale pour l'Etudes des Conditions de Vie et de Sante [*International Medical Association for the Study of Living Conditions and Health*] (EA)
AMIF........... Societe Ausonia Miniere Francaise (MAR)
AMII............ Asociacion Mexicana de Ingenieros Industriales [*Mexican*]
AMINA......... Association Mondiale des Inventeurs [*World Association of Inventors and Researchers*] (EA)
AMINOIL..... American Independent Oil Co. (MAR)
AMINS......... Arhiv Ministarstva Inostranih dela Srbije [*Archives of the Foreign Ministry of Serbia*] (YU)
AMINTER.... Agencia Maritima Internacional Ltd. [*International Maritime Agency Ltd.*] [*Portuguese*] (WER)
AMIO........... Arab Military Industries Organisation (MAR)
AMIOAC...... Asociacion Mexicana de Investigacion de Operaciones y Administracion Cientifica [*Mexican*]
AMIPRO...... Amis des Missions Protestantes (MAR)
AMIS........... Agricultural Management Information System [*Luxembourg*]
AMIT........... Association Marocaine des Industries Textiles (MAR)
AMIT........... Intreprinderea Industriala de Stat Accesorii Mecanice pentru Industria Textila [*State Industrial Enterprise for Mechanical Accessories for the Textile Industry*] (RO)
AMJ............ Assemblee Mondiale de la Jeunesse [*World Assembly of Youth*] [*Use WAY*] (AF)
AMK............ Academie Militaire Khmere [*Cambodian Military Academy*] (CL)
AMK-.......... Amino Acid (RU)
amk............ Ammoniakalisch [*Ammoniacal*] [*German*]
AMK............ Arbeitsmittelkarten [*Machine Control Cards*] (EG)
AMK............ Archiv Mesta Kosice [*Archives of the City of Kosice*] [*A publication*] (CZ)
AMK............ Association des Medecins Khmers [*Cambodian Physicians Association*] (CL)
AMK............ Automobile and Motorcycle Club (RU)
AMK............ Avrupa Muttefik Komutanligi [*Allied European Command*] (TU)
AMK............ Methacrylic Anhydride (RU)
AML............ Amis du Manifeste et de la Liberte [*Algerian*] (MAR)
AML............ Auto Metralhadora Ligeira [*Light Machine Gun*] [*Portuguese*] (WER)
AML............ Automitrailleuse Legere [*Light Armored Car*] [*French*] (WER)
AMM............ Association Medicale Mondiale [*World Medical Association*] [*Use WMA*] (AF)
AMMD......... Ateliers de Menuiserie et de Modelage de Dakar (MAR)
AMMF......... Association Mondiale des Medecins Francophones (EA)
AMMSN....... Acta Muzei Macedonici Scientiarum Naturalum [*Papers of the Macedonian Museum of Natural Sciences*] [*Skopje*] [*A publication*] (YU)
AMN............ Academy of Medical Sciences, USSR (RU)
AMN............ Ahli Mangku Negara [*Fifth Grade of the Most Distinguished Order of Pangkuan Negara*] [*Malaysian*] (ML)
AMN............ Ansaldo Meccanico Nucleare [*Ansaldo Nuclear Machinery*] [*Italian*] (WER)
AMNCL....... Alliance des Mouvements Nationalistes Congolais-Lumumba (MAR)
AMNLAE..... Asociacion de Mujeres Nicaraguenses Luisa Amanda Espinoza [*Luisa Amanda Espinoza Association of Nicaraguan Women*] (LA1)
AMNO......... Arhiv Muzeja Narodne Osvoboditve [*Archives of the National Liberation Museum*] (YU)
A-MNR........ Alianza del Movimiento Nacionalista Revolucionario [*Bolivian*] (PPW)
AMNUT....... All-Muslim National Union of Tanganyika (MAR)
amo............ Amigo [*Friend*] [*Spanish*]
AMO............ Asian Medical Organization (CL)
AMO............ Automobile Made by the Moscow Automobile Company (RU)
AMO............ Electromachining, Sparkover-Initiated Discharge Machining (RU)
AMO............ Moscow Automobile Company (RU)
AM-OB........ Single-Sideband Amplitude Modulation (RU)
AMOCAR.... Amoniaco del Caribe [*Cartagena*] (COL)
AMOISS...... Asociacion Medical-Odontologica del Instituto Salvadoreno del Seguro Social [*Medical-Dental Association of the Salvadoran Social Security Institute*] (LA1)
AMOP.......... Association Musulmane pour l'Organisation du Pelerinage a la Mecque (MAR)
AMOR.......... Agbofi Magnans Orchestra (MAR)
AMOS.......... Agrotikai Metavatikai Oikokyriakai Skholai [*Rural Mobile Domestic Arts Schools*] (GC)
AMOSA....... Aviation Maintenance Organisation of South Africa (MAR)
Amostb....... Army Bridge Battalion (RU)
AMP............ Aerometric Station (RU)
AMP............ Agence Malgache de Presse [*Malagasy Press Agency*] (AF)
AMP............ Agence Mauritanienne de Presse [*Mauritanian Press Agency*] (AF)
AMP............ Agencia del Ministerio Publico [*Public Ministry Agency*] [*Mexican*] (LA)
AMP............ Akademickie Mistrzostwa Polski [*Polish Student Sport Championship*] (POL)
AMP............ Aminoplast (RU)
Amp............ Ampere [*Ampere*] [*German*]
amp............ Ampule (BU)
Amp............ Ampullen [*Ampoules*] (EG)
amp............ Ampuls (RU)
AMP............ Artillery Weather Post (RU)
AMP............ Asociacion de Medios Publicitarios [*Association of Advertising Media*] [*Salvadoran*] (LA1)
AMP............ Mortar Artillery Regiment (RU)
Am Pd......... Ameryka Poludniowa [*South America*] [*Polish*]
AMPERA..... Amanat Penderitaan Rakjat [*The Message of the People's Suffering*] (IN)
AMPERE..... Atomes et Molecules par Etudes Radio-Electriques [*Swiss*]
AMPICH...... Asociacion de Mediana y Pequena Industria de Chile [*Chilean Medium and Light Industry Association*] (LA)
Am Pn......... Ameryka Polnocna [*North America*] [*Polish*]
AMPP.......... Asamblea Municipal del Poder Popular [*Municipal People's Government Assembly*] [*Cuban*] (LA)
AMPRONAC... Asociacion Nacional de Mujeres ante la Problematica Nacional [*National Association of Women Concerned with the Nation's Problems*] [*Nicaraguan*] (LA)

AMPS .... Association Mondiale de Prospective Sociale [*World Social Prospects Study Association*] (EA)
AMPSA .... Association Malienne pour la Promotion Sociale des Aveugles (MAR)
AMPTC .... Arab Maritime Petroleum Transport Company (ME)
AMR .... Acetate Solvent for Furniture (RU)
AMR .... Advanced Management Research [*Arab*] (MAR)
AMR .... Alliance Marxiste Revolutionnaire [*Marxist Revolutionary Alliance*] [*French*] (WER)
AMR .... Amur Railroad (RU)
AMR .... Archives of the Museum of the Revolution, USSR [*A publication*] (RU)
AMR .... Automatic Speed Reducer (RU)
AMR .... Societe pour l'Amenagement du Milieu Rural (MAR)
AMRA .... Ancient Mediterranean Research Association (MAR)
AMRAC .... Annales du Musee Royal d'Afrique Centrale [*A publication*] (MAR)
AMRCB .... Annales du Musee Royal du Congo Belge [*A publication*] (MAR)
AMRD .... Archives of the Museum of the Revolutionary Movement [*A publication*] (BU)
AMREF .... Fondation Africaine de Recherche Medicale [*African Medical Research Foundation*] (AF)
AMRF .... African Medical and Research Foundation (MAR)
AMRFI .... African Medical and Research Foundation International (MAR)
AMRGS .... Associacao Medica do Rio Grande Do Sul [*Rio Grande Do Sul Medical Association*] [*Brazilian*] (LA)
AMRJ .... Arsenal de Marinha do Rio De Janeiro [*Rio De Janeiro Navy Yard*] [*Brazilian*] (LA1)
Amrl .... Amiral [*Admiral*] (TU)
AMROCS .... Asociacion de Militares Retirados, Obreros, y Campesinos Somocistas [*Associatio of Pro-Somoza Farmers, Workers, and Retired Military Personnel*] [*Nicaraguan*] (LA)
AMS .... Action Medico-Sociale (MAR)
AMS .... Afro-Malagasiiskii Soiuz (MAR)
AMS .... Agrometeorological Station (RU)
AMS .... Agrupacion de Militantes Socialistas [*Association of Socialist Militants*] [*Uruguayan*] (LA)
AMS .... Air Weather Service (RU)
AMS .... Air Weather Station (RU)
AMS .... American Missionary Society (MAR)
AMS .... Amme Memurlari Sendikasi [*Public Officials' Union*] [*Turkish Cypriot*] (GC)
AMS .... Annales Marocaines de Sociologie [*Rabat*] [*A publication*] (MAR)
AMS .... Arbetsmarknadsstyrelsen [*National Labor Market Board*] [*Swedish*] (WEN)
AMS .... Army Map Service (MAR)
AMS .... Army Medical Depot (RU)
AMS .... Artillery Weather Report (RU)
AMS .... Artillery Weather Service (RU)
AMS .... Ateliers Mecaniques du Sahel [*Tunisian*] (MAR)
AMS .... Auto-Moto Savez [*Automobile and Motorcycle Federation*] (YU)
AMS .... Flight Weather Report (RU)
AMS .... Light Amplitude Meter (RU)
AMS .... Robot Space Station (RU)
AMSA .... Assistance Medico-Sociale en Algerie (MAR)
AMSA .... Association of Medical Schools in Africa (AF)
AMSAC .... American Society of African Culture (MAR)
AMSD .... Advanced Management Studies Division (MAR)
AMSE .... Association Mondiale des Sciences de l'Education [*World Association for Educational Research - WAER*] (EA)
AMSEAS ..... American Overseas Petroleum Ltd. (MAR)
AMSG .... Air Weather Station of the Civil Air Fleet (RU)
AMSH .... Auto-Moto Savez Hrvatske [*Automobile and Motorcycle Federation of Croatia*] (YU)
AMSJ .... Auto-Moto Savez Jugoslavije [*Automobile and Motorcycle Federation of Yugoslavia*] (YU)
AMSKh .... Archives of the Ministry of Agriculture, USSR [*A publication*] (RU)
AMSLP .... Association Marocaine pour le Soutien a la Lutte Palestinienne [*Moroccan Association for the Support of the Palestinian Struggle*] (AF)
AMSofia ...... Archaeological Museum in Sofia (BU)
AMSS .... Auto-Moto Savez Srbije [*Automobile and Motorcycle Federation of Serbia*] (YU)
AMSSR .... Moldavian Autonomous Soviet Socialist Republic (RU)
AMStro .... Aircraft Engine Plant (RU)
amsv .... Flight Weather Report (RU)
AMT .... Assistance Militaire Technique [*Military Technical Assistance*] [*Niger*] (AF)
AMTI .... Allami Melyepitestudomanyi Intezet [*State Scientific Institute of Civil Engineering*] (HU)
Amtm .... Amtmann [*Head, Chief*] [*German*]
AMTOG .... Automation of Intersettlement Telephone Communications (BU)
AMTS .... Automatic Long Distance Telephone Exchange (RU)
AMTU .... Aviation Metallurgical Technical Specifications (RU)
AMU .... African Mine Workers' Union (MAR)
AMU .... Afrikanisch-Madegassische Union [*African and Madagascar Union*] (MAR)
AMU .... Akademie Musickych Umeni [*Academy of Fine Arts*] (CZ)
AMUR .... Automatic Control and Recording Machine (RU)
Amurknigoizdat ... Amur Book Publishing House (RU)
Amurstal' .... Amur Metallurgical Plant (RU)
Amurverf' .... Amur Repair and Shipbuilding Yard (RU)
AMUS .... Asociacion de Mujeres Universitarias Salvadorenas [*Association of Salvadoran University Women*] (LA1)
AMV .... Agencia Mocambicana de Viagens (MAR)
AMV .... Archiv Ministerstva Vnitra [*Archives of the Ministry of Interior*] [*A publication*] (CZ)
AMV .... Artillery Weather Platoon (RU)
AMV .... Association Mondiale Veterinaire [*World Veterinary Association - WVA*] (EA)
AMVA .... Asociacion Mundial Veterinaria de Avicola [*World Veterinary Poultry Association - WVPA*] (EA)
AMVC .... Archief en Museum voor het Vlaamse Cultuurleven [*Dutch*]
AMVG .... Anciens Moudjahidine et Victimes de la Guerre [*Algerian*] (MAR)
AMVHA .... Asociacion Mundial de Veterinarios Higienistas de los Alimentos [*World Association of Veterinary Food-Hygienists - WAVFH*] (EA)
AMVKD .... Arcidiecesni Mirovy Vybor Katolickeho Duchovenstva [*Archdiocesan Peace Committee of the Catholic Clergy*] (CZ)
AMVMI .... Association Mondiale des Veterinaires Microbiologistes, Immunologistes, et Specialistes des Maladies Infectieuses [*World Association of Veterinary Microbiologists, Immunologists, and Specialists in Infectious Diseases - WAVMI*] (EA)
AMVPA .... Asociacion Mundial Veterinaria de Pequenos Animales [*World Small Animal Veterinary Association - WSAVA*] (EA)
AMVT .... Agence Mauritanienne de Voyage et de Transit (MAR)
AMW .... Alubau und Metallverarbeitung (VEB) [*Aluminum Construction and Metalworking (VEB)*] (EG)
AMWU .... African Mine Workers' Union (MAR)
AMWU .... Associated Mine Workers Union [*Rhodesian*] (AF)
AMX .... Atelier de Construction d'Issy-Les-Moulineaux [*Issy-Les-Moulineaux Construction Company*] [*French*] (WER)
AMZ .... Alapayevsk Metallurgical Plant (RU)
AMZ .... Arheoloski Muzej, Zagreb [*Archaeological Museum, Zagreb*] (YU)
AMZ .... Association Mondiale de Zootechnie [*World Association for Animal Production*] [*Use WAAP*] (AF)
AMZ .... Lawyers for the Defense of the Rights of Man [*Malagasy*] (AF)
AMZ-PA ...... Archiv Ministerstva Zahranicnich Veci, Parizsky Archiv [*Paris Section of the Archives of the Ministry of Foreign Affairs*] [*A publication*] (CZ)
AMZV .... Archiv Ministerstva Zahranicnich Veci [*Archives of the Ministry of Foreign Affairs*] [*A publication*] (CZ)
AN .... Academy of Sciences (RU)
AN .... Accion Nacional [*National Action*] [*Spanish*] (PPE)
AN .... Acrylonitrile (RU)
AN .... Action Nationale [*National Action for People and Homeland*] [*Swiss*] (PPE)
an .... Adjutant (BU)
AN .... African Notes [*Ibadan*] [*A publication*] (MAR)
AN .... Afrique Nouvelle (MAR)
AN .... Aircraft Carrier (RU)
AN .... Aircraft Designed by O. K. Antonov (RU)
AN .... Akademia Nauk [*Academy of Science*] [*Polish*]
AN .... Akademija na Naukite [*Academy of Sciences*] (YU)
AN .... Alianza Nacional [*National Alliance*] [*Spanish*] (PPE)
an .... Analytic, Analytical Entry (RU)
AN .... Anangastikos Nomos [*Compulsory Law*] [*Greek*] (GC)
AN .... Anesthetic Apparatus (RU)
An .... Anmerkung [*Note*] [*German*]
an .... Anno [*In the Year*] [*Latin*] (GPO)
An .... Anonyme [*Anonymous*] [*French*]
an .... Ante [*Before*] [*Latin*] (GPO)
AN .... Automatic Equipment for Operating Reliability (RU)
AN .... National Agreement [*Paraguayan*] (PD)
AN .... Netherlands Antilles [*Two-letter standard code*] (CNC)
AN .... Observation Balloon (RU)
AN- .... Pumping Unit (RU)
AN .... Self-Contained Adjustment (RU)
ANA .... Accion Nacional Argentina [*Argentine National Action*] (LA)
ANA .... Agence Nigerienne d'Assurances (MAR)
ANA .... All-Nippon Airways (SJT)
ana .... Antifona [*Spanish*]
ANA .... Arab News Agency (MAR)
ANA .... Asociacion Nacional de Agricultores [*National Association of Farmers*] [*Salvadoran*] (LA1)
ANA .... Asociacion Narinense de Apicultores [*Pasto*] (COL)
ANAB .... Sea Marker (RU)
ANAC .... Agence Nationale pour l'Aviation Civile [*National Agency for Civil Aviation*] [*Congolese*] (AF)
anac .... Anacoreta [*Spanish*]
ANAC .... Asamblea Nacional Constituyente [*National Constituent Assembly*] [*Colombian*] (LA)
ANAC .... Asociacion Nacional Campesina [*National Association of Peasants*] [*Costa Rican*] (LA1)

ANACAFE ... Asociacion Nacional del Cafe [*National Coffee Association*] [*Guatemalan*] (LA)
ANACH .... Asociacion Nacional de Campesinos Hondurenos [*National Association of Honduran Peasants*] (PD)
ANACI .... Atelier Nationale Algerien de Confection de Drapeaux et de Travaux d'Imprimerie (MAR)
ANACIMA ... Association des Anciens Combattants Indigenes du Mayombe (MAR)
ANACON ..... Asociacion Nacional de Confeccionistas [*Barranquilla*] (COL)
ANACR .... Association Nationale des Anciens Combattants de la Resistance (MAR)
ANADE .... Asociacion de Abogados de Empresas [*Corporation Lawyers Association*] [*Mexican*] (LA)
ANADENA ... Asociacion Nacional para la Defensa de la Naturaleza [*Cali*] (COL)
ANADIM ...... Asociacion Nacional de Impresores [*Bogota*] (COL)
ANADIR .... Association Nationale des Anciens Detenus et Internes Resistants [*National Association of Former Resistance Prisoners and Internees*] [*Algerian*] (AF)
anaer .... Anaerobic (RU)
ANAF .... Anya National Armed Forces (MAR)
ANAFID .... Association Nationale de l'Amelioration Fonciere, de l'Irrigation, et du Drainage [*Moroccan*] (MAR)
ANAING ...... Asociacion Nacional de Auxiliares de Ingenieria [*Cali*] (COL)
anal .... Analityczny [*Analytic*] (POL)
anal .... Analytisch [*Analytical*] [*German*]
ANALAC ..... Asociacion Nacional de Productores Lacteos [*National Milk Producers Association*] [*Colombian*] (LA)
ANALDEX ... Asociacion Nacional de Exportadores [*National Exporters Association*] [*Colombian*] (LA)
ANALIGE ..... Accion Nacional de Liberacion de Guinea Ecuatorial (MAR)
analitich ...... Analytic (RU)
ANALJA ...... Asociacion Nacional de la Industria del Jabon [*Bogota*] (COL)
ANALPES .... Asociacion Nacional de Productores de Pasticidas [*Bogota*] (COL)
ANALTRA ... Asociacion Nacional de Transporte [*National Transportation Association*] [*Colombian*] (LA)
ANAMACO ... Anambra Motor Manufacturing Company (MAR)
ANAMMG .... Association Nationale des Anciens Moudjahidine et Mutiles de Guerre (MAR)
ANANGOLA ... Associacao dos Naturais de Angola [*Association of Angolan Natives*] (AF)
ANAP .... Asociacion Nacional de los Agricultores Pequenos [*National Association of Small Farmers*] [*Cuban*] (LA)
ANAP .... Asociacion Nicaraguense de Administracion Publica [*Nicaraguan Public Administration Association*] (LA)
ANAPCI .... Association Nationale des Artistes de Cote-d'Ivoire (MAR)
ANAPO .... Alianza Nacional Popular [*National Popular Alliance*] [*Colombian*] (PD)
ANAPOR ..... Alianza Nacional Popular Revolucionaria [*Revolutionary National Popular Alliance*] [*Colombian*] (LA)
ANAPRO ..... Accion Nacional Progresista [*National Progressive Action*] [*Venezuelan*] (LA)
ANAPROCAFE ... Asociacion Nacional de Productores de Cafe [*National Coffee Producers Association*] [*Colombian*] (LA)
ANAPROCOS ... Analisis y Pronosticos de Precios [*Price Analysis and Forecast*] [*Cuban*] (LA)
ANAPROFAR ... Asociacion Nicaraguense de Propietarios de Farmacias [*Nicaraguan Association of Pharmacy Owners*] (LA1)
ANAPS .... Asociacion Nicaraguense de Amistad con los Paises Socialistas [*Nicaraguan Association of Friendship with Socialist Countries*] (LA1)
ANAR .... Asociacion de Arroceros de Nicaragua [*Association of Nicaraguan Rice Growers*] (LA1)
ANAS .... Azienda Nazionale Autonoma delle Strade [*National Road Board*] [*Italian*] (WER)
ANASAC ..... Agricola Nacional SAC [*National Agricultural Corporation*] [*Chilean*] (LA)
ANAT .... Agence Nord-Africaine des Telephones [*Moroccan*] (MAR)
Anat .... Anatomi [*or Anatomik*] [*Anatomy or Anatomical*] (TU)
anat .... Anatomia [*Anatomy*] [*Finnish*]
anat .... Anatomical, Anatomy (RU)
anat .... Anatomy (BU)
ANATO .... Asociacion Nacional de Agencias de Turismo [*Colombian Association of Tourist Agencies*] (LA)
ANAU .... Association Nationale des Architectes et Urbanistes [*Tunisian*] (MAR)
ANAVIH .... Asociacion Nacional de Avicultores de Honduras [*National Association of Honduran Poultry Raisers*] (LA1)
ANAVZA ...... Association Nationale des Agences de Voyage du Zaire (MAR)
ANB .... Asociacion Nacional Bancaria [*National Banking Association*] [*Colombian*] (LA)
ANB .... Australian National Bibliography
ANBPE .... Association Nationale de Bienfaisance et de Protection de l'Enfance [*Moroccan*] (MAR)
ANBU .... Armee Nationale du Burundi (MAR)
ANC .... African National Congress [*South African*] (PD)
ANC .... African National Council [*Zimbabwean*] (PPW)
anc .... Ancien [*Ancient*] [*French*]
Anc .... Ancoradouro [*Roadstead*] [*Portuguese*] (NAU)
Anc .... Ancoraggio [*Anchorage*] [*Italian*] (NAU)
ANC .... Armee Nationale Congolaise (MAR)
ANC .... Asociacion Nacional de Caficultores [*National Coffeegrowers Association*] [*Honduran*] (LA)
ANCAM .... Archives Nationales du Cameroun (MAR)
ANCAM .... Assemblee Nationale du Cameroun (MAR)
ANCAP .... Administracion Nacional de Combustibles, Alcohol, y Portland [*National Fuels, Alcohol, and Cement Administration*] [*Uruguayan*] (LA)
ANCAR .... Associacao Nordestina de Credito e Assistencia Rural [*Northeastern Credit and Rural Assistance Association*] [*Brazilian*] (LA)
ANCB .... Academia Nacional de Ciencias de Bolivia
ANCHAR ..... Asociacion Nacional de Choferes de Alquiler Revolucionarios [*National Revolutionary Taxi Drivers Association*] [*Cuban*] (LA)
ANCI .... Adviescommissie Nationale Coordinatie Informatievoorzieningen [*Dutch*]
ANCI .... Asociacion Nacional de Comerciantes y Industriales
ANCI .... Associazione Nazionale Comuni Italiani [*National Association of Italian Municipalities*] (WER)
ANCI .... Ateliers Navals de Cote-d'Ivoire (MAR)
ANCIJE .... Asociacion Nacional de Cesantes y Jubilados de la Educacion [*National Association of Unemployed and Retired Educators*] [*Peruvian*] (LA)
Ancn .... Ancien [*Ancient*] [*Military map abbreviation*] [*World War I*] [*French*] (MTD)
ANCS .... Asociacion Nicaraguense de Comunidades Sumus [*Nicaraguan Association of Sumu Communities*] (LA1)
ANC-SA ...... African National Congress of South Africa (AF)
ANCVR .... Association Nationale des Combattants Volontaires de la Resistance (MAR)
ANCYL .... African National Congress Youth League [*South African*] (PD)
AND .... Algerian National Movement (RU)
AND .... Alzhirskaia Natsional'naia Dvizheniia (MAR)
AND .... Andorra [*Three-letter standard code*] (CNC)
ANDA .... Administracion Nacional de Acueductos y Alcantarillados [*National Administration of Aqueducts and Sewerages*] [*Salvadoran*]
ANDA .... Associacao Nacional para Difusao de Adubos [*National Association for Fertilizer Distribution*] [*Brazilian*] (LA)
ANDAG .... Association Nationale pour le Developpement des Antilles-Guyane [*National Association for Developing the Antilles-French Guiana*] (LA1)
ANDDOM .... Association Nationale pour le Developpement des Departements d'Outre-Mer [*National Association for Developing the Overseas Departments*] (LA1)
ANDE .... Administracion Nacional de Electricidad [*National Electric Power Administration*] [*Paraguayan*] (LA)
ANDE .... Asociacion Nacional de Educadores [*National Teachers Association*] [*Costa Rican*] (LA)
ANDEBUL ... Asociacion Nacional de Broadcasters Uruguayos [*National Association of Uruguayan Broadcasters*] (LA)
ANDECORP ... Asociacion Nacional de Rectores [*Bogota*] (COL)
ANDEL .... Asociacion Nacional de Linotipistas [*Bogota*] (COL)
ANDEMOS ... Asociacion Nacional de Importadores de Vehiculos Automotores [*National Association of Automotive Vehicle Importers*] [*Colombian*] (LA)
ANDEN .... Asociacion Nacional de Educadores de Nicaragua [*National Association of Nicaraguan Teachers*] (LA1)
ANDEPET ... Asociaciones Nacionales de Profesores de Ensenanza Tecnica [*National Associations of Technical School Teachers*] [*Colombian*] (LA)
ANDES .... Asociacion Nacional de Educadores Salvadorenos [*National Association of Salvadoran Teachers*] (PD)
ANDESE ...... Association Nationale des Docteurs es-Sciences Economiques (MAR)
ANDESS ..... Asociacion Nacional de Empleados del Seguro Social [*National Association of Social Security Employees*] [*Dominican Republic*] (LA1)
ANDI .... Asociacion Nacional de Industriales [*National Industrialists Association*] [*Colombian*] (LA)
ANDIARIOS ... Asociacion de Diarios Colombianos [*Colombian Newspapers Association*] (LA)
Andi-EFEE ... Andidiktatoriki Ethniki Foititiki Enosis Ellados [*Antidictatorial National Student Union of Greece*] (GC)
ANDIEPH ..... Asociacion Nacional de Instituciones Educativas Privadas de Honduras [*National Association of Honduran Private Education Institutes*] (LA1)
ANDIPET ..... Asociacion Nicaraguense de Distribuidores de Productos de Petroleo [*Nicaraguan Association of Petroleum Products Dealers*] (LA1)
ANDIR .... Association Nationale des Deportees et Internes de la Resistance (MAR)
ANDIVA .... Asociacion Nicaraguense de Distribuidores de Vehiculos Automotrices [*Nicaraguan Association of Motor Vehicle Dealers*] (LA1)
Andizhanirmash ... Andizhan Irrigation and Reclamation Machinery Plant (RU)
ANDR .... Alzhirskaia Narodnaia Demokraticheskaia Respublika (MAR)
ANDRE .... Asociacion Nicaraguense Democratica Revolucionaria [*Nicaraguan Democratic Revolutionary Association*] (LA1)

ANDUD........ Asamblea Nicaraguense de Unidad Democratica [*Nicaraguan Assembly of Democratic Unity*] (LA1)
ANE............ Alkimos Neolaia EOKA [*Ethniki Organosis Kyprion Agoniston] B [National Organization of Cypriot Fighters B Valiant Youth*] (GC)
ANE............ Allami Nepi Egyuttes [*State Folk Ensemble*] (HU)
ANEA.......... Asociacion Nacional de Escritores y Artistas [*National Writers and Artists Association*] [*Peruvian*] (LA)
ANEACh...... Asociacion Nacional de Empleados de Aduanas de Chile [*National Association of Customs Workers of Chile*] (LA)
ANEB.......... Asociacion Nacional de Empleados Bancarios [*National Bank Employees Association*] [*Colombian*] (LA)
ANEC.......... Asociacion Nacional de Economistas Consultores [*National Association of Consulting Economists*] [*Mexican*] (LA1)
ANEC.......... Asociacion Nacional de Economistas de Cuba [*National Association of Cuban Economists*] (LA)
ANECIP....... Asociacion Nacional de Empleados de la Cedula de Identidad Personal [*National Association of Personal Identity Document Bureau Employees*] [*Dominican Republic*] (LA1)
ANEDA........ Association Nationale d'Etudes pour la Documentation Automatique [*French*]
ANEF.......... Asociacion Nacional de Empleados Fiscales [*National Association of Government Employees*] [*Chilean*] (LA)
ANEF.......... Asociacion Nacional de Entrenadores de Futbol [*National Association of Soccer Coaches*] [*Honduran*] (LA1)
ANEI........... Asociacion Nacional de Empresas Industriales [*National Association of Industrial Firms*] [*Peruvian*] (LA)
ANEI........... Asociacion Nacional de Estudiantes Intermedios [*National Association of Intermediate-Level Students*] [*Dominican Republic*] (LA1)
ANEJ.......... Asociacion Nacional de Empleados Judiciales [*National Association of Judicial Employees*] [*Costa Rican*] (LA)
ANEL.......... Agencias Nacionais e Estrangeiras Lda. (MAR)
ANEP.......... Agence Nationale d'Edition et de Publicite [*National Publication and Advertising Agency*] [*Algerian*] (AF)
ANEP.......... Asociacion Nacional de Empleados Postales [*National Association of Postal Employees*] [*Dominican Republic*] (LA1)
ANEP.......... Asociacion Nacional de Empleados Publicos [*National Association of Public Employees*] [*Costa Rican*] (LA1)
ANEP.......... Asociacion Nacional de Empleados Publicos [*National Association of Public Employees*] [*Uruguayan*] (LA)
ANEP.......... Asociacion Nacional de la Empresa Privada [*National Association of Private Enterprise*] [*Salvadoran*] (LA1)
ANEPA........ Asociacion Nacional de Empleados Publicos Aduanales [*National Association of Customs Employees*] [*Dominican Republic*] (LA1)
ANEPA........ Asociacion Nacional para el Estudio de Problemas Actuales [*National Association for the Study of Contemporary Problems*] [*Spanish*] (WER)
ANEPEJOS... Anciens Eleves des Peres Josephites (MAR)
ANEPI......... Associacao Nacional dos Exportadores de Produtos Industriais [*National Association of Exporters of Industrial Products*] [*Brazilian*] (LA)
ANERI......... Asociacion Nacional de Empleados de Rentas Internas [*National Association of Internal Revenue Employees*] [*Dominican Republic*] (LA1)
anerk.......... Anerkannt [*Recognized*] [*German*]
ANES.......... Asociacion de Enfermeras Graduadas [*Bogota*] (COL)
ANES.......... Asociacion Nacional de Empleados Semi-Fiscales [*National Association of Semipublic Employees*] [*Chilean*] (LA)
ANES.......... Asociacion Nacional de Enfermeras Salvadorenas [*National Association of Salvadoran Nurses*] (LA1)
ANET.......... Asociacion Nacional de Empleados de Telecomunicaciones [*National Association of Telecommunications Employees*] [*Dominican Republic*] (LA1)
ANET.......... Asociacion Nacional de Empresas de Telefonos [*Bogota*] (COL)
ANEU.......... Asociacion Nacional de Estudiantes Universitarios [*National Association of University Students*] [*Dominican Republic*] (LA1)
ANEZA........ Association Nationale des Entreprises Zairoises [*National Association of Zairian Enterprises*] (AF)
ANF............ Agencia de Noticias Fides [*Fides News Agency*] [*Bolivian*] (LA)
ANF............ Anti-Fascist German Popular Front (RU)
ANF............ Arhiva Nationala de Filme [*National Films Archive*] (RO)
ANFAC........ Asociacion Colombiana de Fabricantes de Articulos de Caucho [*Bogota*] (COL)
ANFAE........ Asociacion Nacional de Funcionarios de Auxilio Escolar [*National Association of School Aid Officials*] [*Chilean*] (LA)
ANFAL........ Asociacion Nacional de Fabricantes de Alcoholes y Licores [*Alcohol and Liquor Producers National Association*] [*Guatemalan*] (LA)
ANFANOMA... Association National des Francais d'Afrique du Nord [*French*]
ANFAVEA... Associacao Nacional dos Fabricantes de Veiculos Automotores [*National Association of Autovehicle Manufacturers*] [*Brazilian*] (LA)
ANFC.......... Association Nationale des Femmes Congolaises (MAR)
ANFE.......... Asociacion Nacional de Fomento Economico [*National Economic Development Association*] [*Costa Rican*] (LA)
ANFP.......... Asociacion Nacional de Funcionarios Publicos [*National Association of Public Employees*] [*Uruguayan*] (LA)
ANFPP........ Agence Nationale de Formation et de Perfectionnement Professionnel [*National Training and Professional Improvement Agency*] [*Gabonese*] (AF)
ANFR.......... Agrupacion Nacional Femenil Revolucionaria [*National Women's Revolutionary Group*] [*Mexican*] (LA)
Anfr............ Anfrage [*Inquiry*] [*German*]
ANFRENA... Agencia Nacional de Frete e Navegacao (MAR)
ANFRIDI...... Annuaire Francais de Droit International [*Paris*] [*A publication*] (MAR)
ANG............ Agencia Noticiosa da Guine-Bissau [*Guinea-Bissau News Agency*] (AF)
ang............. Angaende [*Concerning*] [*Danish*] (GPO)
ang............. Angaende [*Concerning*] [*Norwegian*] (GPO)
ang............. Angaende [*Concerning*] [*Swedish*] (GPO)
Ang............. Angebot [*Offer*] [*German*]
Ang............. Angelegenheiten [*German*]
Ang............. Angestellte [*German*]
ang............. Angielski [*English*] (POL)
Ang............. Angirovolion [*Anchorage*] [*Greek*] (NAU)
ANG............ Angkutan [*Transport, Transportation*] (IN)
ang............. Angol [*English, Englishman*] (HU)
ang............. Anhydride (RU)
ANG............ Artiljerijska Nastava Gadanja [*Artillery Target Practice*] (YU)
ANG............ Asociacion Nacional de Ganaderos [*National Cattlemen's Association*] [*Colombian*] (LA)
ang............. Hangar, Shed [*Topography*] (RU)
ANGAD........ Angkutan Angkatan Darat [*Army Transport Corps*] (IN)
Angeb......... Angebot [*or Angeboten*] [*Offer or Offered for Sale*] [*German*]
angeb......... Angebunden [*Bound With*] [*German*]
angew......... Angewandt [*Applied*] [*German*]
ANGKASA... Angkatan Kerjasama [*Cooperative Movement*] (ML)
angl............ Anglikaaninen [*Anglican*] [*Finnish*]
angl............ English (RU)
angl............ English (BU)
angl f.......... English Pound (RU)
angl p.......... English Patent (RU)
ANGOL........ Fabrica Aga Ltda. [*Bogota*] (COL)
ANGOP........ Agencia Angola-Presse [*Angolan Press Agency*] (AF)
ANGROGRADA... Pretprijatie za Promet so Gradezen Material na Angro [*Building Materials Wholesale Establishment*] [*Skopje*] (YU)
angw........... Angewandt [*Applied*] [*German*]
Anh............. Anhang [*Appendix*] (EG)
ANI............. Agencia Nacional de Informacoes [*National Information Agency*] [*Nonexistent, see ANOP*] [*Portuguese*] (WER)
ANI............. Agencia de Noticias e de Informacoes [*News and Information Agency*] [*Portuguese*] (WER)
ANI............. All-Union Scientific Research Institute of Asbestos (RU)
ANI............. American Petroleum Institute [*API*] (RU)
ANI............. Arabe Non Identifie
ANI............. Associazione Nazionalista Italiana [*Italian Nationalist Association*] (PPE)
ANI............. Azerbaydzhan Petroleum Institute Imeni M. Azizbekov (RU)
ANIA........... Asociacion Nicaraguense de Ingenieros y Arquitectos [*Nicaraguan Association of Engineers and Architects*] (LA1)
ANIC........... Agenzia Nazionale per l'Idrogenazione dei Combustibili [*National Agency for the Hydrogenation of Fuel*] [*Italian*] (WER)
ANIDES....... Association Nationale des Infirmiers et Infirmieres Diplomes d'Etat du Senegal (MAR)
ANIE........... Associazione Nazionale Industrie Elettrotechniche ed Elettroniche [*National Association of Electrical and Electronic Industries*] [*Italian*] (WER)
ANIERM...... Asociacion Nacional de Importadores y Exportadores de la Republica Mexicana [*National Mexican Importers and Exporters Association*] (LA)
ANIF........... Asociacion Nacional de Instituciones Financieras [*National Association of Financial Institutions*] [*Colombian*] (LA)
ANIFAPE..... Association Nationale pour l'Information, la Formation, et Assistance aux Parents et Educateurs (MAR)
ANIFRMO.... Association Nationale Interprofessionnelle pour la Formation Rationelle de la Main-d'Oeuvre (MAR)
ANII............ Arctic Scientific Research Institute (RU)
ANII............ Artillery Scientific Research Institute (RU)
An Ik Mr...... Ana Ikmal Merkezi [*Main Supply Center*] (TU)
ANIL........... Asociacion Nacional de Industrias Licoreras [*Bogota*] (COL)
ANIM.......... Agence Nationale d'Information Malienne [*Malian National Information Agency*] (AF)
ANIM.......... Association Nationale Marocaine des Ingenieurs des Mines [*Moroccan National Mining Engineers Association*] (AF)
ANIMA........ Associazione Nazionale Industria Meccanica [*National Association of Mechanical Industries*] [*Italian*] (WER)
ANIMI.......... Scientific Research Institute of Naval Artillery (RU)
ANIR........... Asociacion Nacional de Innovadores y Racionalizadores [*National Association of Innovators and Efficiency Experts*] [*Cuban*] (LA)
ANIS........... Asociacion Nacional Indigena Salvadorena [*National Association of Salvadoran Indians*] (LA1)

ANISC......... Association of Indigenous Nigerian Shipping Companies (MAR)
ANITIM........ Altay Scientific Research, Planning, and Technological Institute of Machinery Manufacture (RU)
ANJS........... Association Nationale des Journalistes Senegalais [*National Association of Senegalese Reporters*] (AF)
ANJV........... Algemeen Nederlands Jeugdverbond [*General Netherlands Youth Federation*] (WEN)
ANK............. African National Congress (RU)
ANK............. Afrikaanse Nasionale Kultuurraad (MAR)
ANK............. Afrikanskii Natsional'nyi Kongress (MAR)
ANK............. Alban Nepkoztarsasag [*Albanian People's Republic*] (HU)
Ank............. Ankara [*Ankara*] (TU)
Ank............. Ankunft [*Arrival*] (EG)
ANK............. Automatic Circuit Adjustment (RU)
ANK............. Cadmium-Nickel Plate Battery (RU)
ANK............. Chinese Academy of Sciences (RU)
ANKA.......... Ankara Ajansi [*Ankara (News) Agency*] (TU)
ANKA.......... Automatic Adjustment of Circuit Amplitudes (RU)
ANKh........... Archives of the National Economy [*A publication*] (RU)
An-Kon....... Antalya Konsantre Sebze Meyve Isleme Sanayi ve Ticaret AS [*Antalya Concentrated Fruit and Vegetable Processing Industry and Trade Corp.*] (TU)
AnKT........... Annotated Labor Code (BU)
ANL............. Accademia Nazionale dei Lincei [*Lincei National Academy*] [*Italian*] (WER)
Anl.............. Anlage (im Brief) [*Enclosure (in the Letter)*] [*German*] (EG)
anl.............. Anlatan [*Explanatory*] (TU)
ANL............. Armee Nationale Laotienne [*Lao National Army*] (CL)
anm............. Anmaerkning [*Remark, Observation*] [*Danish*] (GPO)
anm............. Anmarkning [*Remark*] [*Swedish*] (GPO)
Anm............. Anmerkung [*Note*] [*German*] (GPO)
ANM............ Arab Nationalist Movement (ME)
ANM............ Associacao dos Naturais de Mocambique (MAR)
ANMADERAS... Asociacion Nacional de Industrias Forestales Madereras y Derivadas [*Bogota*] (COL)
ANMZSSR... Akademia Nauk Medycznych ZSSR [*Academy of Medical Sciences of the USSR*] (POL)
ANN............. African Newspapers of Nigeria Ltd. (MAR)
ANN............. Agencia de Noticias Nueva Nicaragua [*New Nicaraguan News Agency*] (LA1)
Ann............. Annalen [*Annals*] [*German*]
ann............. Annales [*Annals*] [*Latin*] (GPO)
ann............. Anni [*Years*] [*Latin*] (GPO)
ann............. Annotation (RU)
ANNALES... Annales; Economies, Societes, Civilisations [*Paris*] [*A publication*] (MAR)
annot.......... Annotated (RU)
annotir........ Annotated (RU)
ANO............. Armiia Natsionalnovo Osvobozhdeniia (MAR)
ANO............. Navigation Lights (RU)
ANOA........... Algerian National Liberation Army (RU)
ANOB........... Arhiv Narodnoosvobodilne Borbe [*Archives of the National Liberation Struggle*] [*A publication*] (YU)
ANOC........... Asociacion Nacional de Organizaciones Campesinas [*National Association of Peasant Organizations*] [*Chilean*] (LA)
ANOF........... Algemene Nederlandse Onderwijzers Federatie [*General Netherlands Teachers' Federation*] (WEN)
ANOK........... Akcioni Narodnooslobodilacki Komitet [*National Liberation Action Committee*] (YU)
Anon........... Anonimo [*Anonymous*] [*Spanish*]
Anon........... Anonyme [*Anonymous*] [*French*]
anon............ Anonymous (BU)
ANOP........... Agencia Noticiosa Portuguesa [*Portuguese News Agency*] (WER)
anorg.......... Anorganisch [*Inorganic*] [*German*]
anot............ Annotated (BU)
Anot............ Anotatos [*Maximum, Supreme*] [*Greek*] (GC)
ANP............. Academy of the Petroleum Industry (RU)
ANP............. Accao Nacional Popular [*National Popular Action*] [*Angolan*] (AF)
ANP............. Accao Nacional Popular [*National Popular Action*] [*Portuguese*] (PPE)
ANP............. Administracion Nacional de Puertos [*National Ports Administration*] [*Uruguayan*] (LA)
ANP............. Akademia Nauk Politycznych [*Academy of Political Sciences*] (POL)
ANP............. Algemeen Nederlands Persbureau [*General Netherlands Press Agency*] (WEN)
ANP............. Alianza Nacional Popular [*National Popular Alliance*] [*Colombian*] (LA)
ANP............. Apatite and Nepheline Rock (RU)
ANP............. Armee Nationale Populaire [*People's National Army*] [*Algerian*] (AF)
ANP............. Artillery Observation Post (RU)
ANP............. Asociacion Nacional de Periodistas [*National Journalists Association*] [*Colombian*] (LA)
ANP............. Asociacion Nacional de Periodistas [*National Journalists Association*] [*Peruvian*] (LA)
ANP............. Assemblee Nationale Populaire [*National Popular Assembly*] [*Malagasy*] (AF)
ANP............. Assembleia Nacional Popular (MAR)
ANP............. Austrian People's Party (RU)
ANP............. Direct Support Artillery (RU)
ANPA........... Armee Nationale Populaire Algerienne (MAR)
ANPA........... Asociacion Nacional de Peritos Agrarios [*National Association of Agrarian Experts*] [*Dominican Republic*] (LA)
ANPA........... Asociacion Nacional de Profesionales Agricolas [*National Association of Agricultural Professionals*] [*Dominican Republic*] (LA1)
ANPAF......... Asociacion Nacional de Padres de Familia [*National Association of Heads of Families*] [*Nicaraguan*] (LA1)
ANPE........... Anadolu Petrolleri AS [*Anatolian Petroleum Corporation*] (TU)
ANPE........... Association Nationale pour la Promotion de l'Enseignement [*National Association for the Advancement of Education*] [*Mauritian*] (AF)
ANPEC......... Associacao Nacional de Programas de Pos-Graduacao em Economia [*National Association of Economics Graduate Programs*] [*Brazilian*] (LA)
ANPEF......... Asociacion Nacional de Profesores de Educacion Fisica [*Bogota*] (COL)
ANPEF......... Asociacion Nacional de Profesores de Educacion Fisica [*National Association of Physical Education Teachers*] [*Peruvian*] (LA)
ANPEN......... Asociacion Nacional de Profesores de Educacion Normal [*National Association of Normal School Teachers*] [*Peruvian*] (LA)
ANPES......... Asociacion Nacional de Profesores de Educacion Secundaria [*National Association of Secondary Education Teachers*] [*Peruvian*] (LA)
ANPESCA... Asociacion Nacional de Industrias Pesqueras y Derivadas [*Bogota*] (COL)
ANPET......... Asociacion Nacional de Profesores de Educacion Tecnica [*National Association of Technical Education Teachers*] [*Peruvian*] (LA)
ANPG........... Asamblea Nacional Popular Galega [*People's National Assembly of Galicia*] [*Spanish*] (WER)
ANPI............ Associazione Nazionale Partigiani d'Italia [*National Association of Italian Partisans*] (WER)
ANPP........... Artillery in Direct Support of Infantry (RU)
ANPP........... Asamblea Nacional del Poder Popular [*National People's Government Assembly*] [*Cuban*] (LA)
ANPP........... Asociacion Nacional de Periodistas del Peru [*National Association of Peruvian Journalists*] (LA)
ANPP........... Asociacion Nacional de Profesionales Publicitarios [*Bogota*] (COL)
ANPROBA... Asociacion Nacional de Productores de Banano [*National Association of Banana Producers*] [*Nicaraguan*] (LA1)
ANPROCOM... Asociacion Nacional de Propietarios de Compra y Venta [*Bogota*] (COL)
ANPROS...... Asociacion Nacional de Productores de Semillas [*National Association of Seed Producers*] [*Chilean*] (LA)
ANPROSOR... Asociacion Nacional de Productores de Sorgo [*National Association of Sorghum Producers*] [*Nicaraguan*] (LA1)
ANR............. Aktion Neue Rechte [*Action New Right*] (EG)
ANR............. Assemblee Nationale Revolutionnaire [*National Revolutionary Assembly*] [*Beninese*] (AF)
ANR............. Association of Modern Directors (RU)
ANRAC......... Asociacion Nacional de Radioaficionados de Cuba [*National Association of Amateur Radio Operators of Cuba*] (LA)
ANRADIO.... Asociacion Nacional de Radio, Television, y Cine [*National Radio, Television, and Cinema Association*] [*Colombian*] (LA)
ANRD........... Alianza Nacional de Restauracion Democratica [*National Alliance for Democratic Restoration*] [*Equatorial Guinean*] (AF)
ANRH........... Arhiv Narodna Republika Hrvatska [*Archives of Croatia*] [*A publication*] (YU)
ANRPC......... Association of Natural Rubber Producing Countries (EA)
ANRS........... Assembly for Continuous Pouring of Steel (RU)
ANRT........... Association Nationale de la Recherche Technique [*National Association for Technical Research*] [*French*] (WER)
ANS............. Afrikaans-Nasionale Studentebond [*Afrikaans National Student Union*] [*South African*] (AF)
ANS............. Air Navigation Service (RU)
ans.............. An Das [*As The, To The, On The*] [*German*]
ANS............. Anotaton Navtikon Symvoulion [*Supreme Naval Council*] [*Greek*] (GC)
ANS............. Archiv Narodniho Shromazdeni [*Archives of the National Assembly*] (CZ)
ANS............. Asociacion de Ninos Sandinistas [*Association of Sandinist Children*] [*Nicaraguan*] (LA1)
ANSA........... Agenzia Nazionale Stampa Associata [*National Associated Press Agency*] [*Italian*] (WER)
ANSA........... Antibiotik ve Ilac Ham Maddeleri Sanayii AS [*Antibiotics and Medicinal Raw Materials Industry Corp.*] (TU)
ANSCO......... Asociacion Nacional de Supervisores del Cobre [*National Association of Copper Supervisors*] [*Chilean*] (LA)
ANSESAL... Salvadoran National Security Agency
ANSO/I........ Anouc Songrama I [*General mobilization unit*] [*Cambodian*] (CL)
ANSOM....... Archives Nationales, Section Outre-Mer [*A publication*] (MAR)
Anspr.......... Anspruch [*Requirement*] [*German*]

ANSSSR...... Akademija na Naukite SSSR [*Academy of Sciences of the USSR*] (YU)
Anst............ Anstalt [*German*]
ANT............ Aircraft Designed by A. N. Tupolev (RU)
Ant............ Anteil [*Part*] [*German*]
ant............ Antiikki [*Antiquity*] [*Finnish*]
ant............ Antimeridiano [*Forenoon*] [*Italian*] (GPO)
ANT............ Arme Nucleaire Tactique [*Tactical Nuclear Weapon*] [*French*] (WER)
ANT............ Armee Nationale Tchadienne [*Chadian National Army*] (AF)
ANT............ Assemblee Nationale du Togo (MAR)
ANT............ Netherlands Antilles [*Three-letter standard code*] (CNC)
ANTA.......... Agence Nationale d'Information "Taratra" [*"Taratra" National Information Agency*] [*Malagasy*] (AF)
ANTA.......... Asociacion Nacional de Trabajadores del Arte [*National Art Workers Association*] [*Peruvian*] (LA)
ANTA.......... Asociacion Nicaraguense de Talleres Automotores [*Nicaraguan Association of Auto Repair Shops*] (LA1)
ANTAFR...... Antiquites Africaines [*Paris*] [*A publication*] (MAR)
ANTBIRLIK... Antalya Tarim Satis Kooperatifleri Birligi [*Antalya Agricultural Sales Cooperatives' Union*] (TU)
ANTC.......... Asociacion Nicaraguense de Transportistas de Carga [*Nicaraguan Association of Cargo Carriers*] (LA1)
ANTCC........ Asociacion Nacional de Trabajadores Cientificos de Cuba [*National Association of Scientific Workers of Cuba*] (LA)
ANTEL......... Administracion Nacional de Telecomunicaciones [*National Administration for Telecommunications*] [*Salvadoran*] (LA1)
ANTEL......... Administracion Nacional de Telecomunicaciones [*National Telecommunications Administration*] [*Uruguayan*] (LA)
ANTH.......... Anthropologica [*Ottowa*] [*A publication*] (MAR)
anth/khos... Anthypoploiarkhos [*Lieutenant Junior Grade*] [*Navy*] (GC)
ANTI........... Associazione Nazionale Teleradio-Diffusioni Indipendenti [*National Private Radio-TV Broadcasting Network*] [*Italian*] (WER)
antich......... Antique (RU)
Antifa.......... Antifaschistisch [*Anti Fascist*] (EG)
ANTIKOR.... Preduzece za Proizvodnju, Promet, i Servisne Usluge Antikorozione Zastite [*Establishment for the Production, Trade, and Servicing of Anticorrosives*] [*Belgrade*] (YU)
ANTIKVA.... Narodni Podnik pro Vyvoz a Dovoz Starozitnosti [*National Enterprise for the Export and Import of Antiques*] (CZ)
antilog......... Antilogarithm (RU)
ANTILOPE... Antwerpse Inventaris van Lopende Periodieken
antirelig...... Antireligious (RU)
ANTO.......... Aviation Scientific and Technical Society (RU)
ANTOS........ Aviation Scientific and Technical Society of Students (RU)
antrop......... Anthropology (BU)
ANTS........... Asociacion Nacional de Trabajadores Sociales [*National Social Workers Association*] [*Costa Rican*] (LA)
ANTSCI....... Association Nationale de Travailleurs Sociaux de la Cote-d'Ivoire (MAR)
ANTUF........ All-Nigerian Trade Unions Federation (MAR)
ANU............ Anadolu Universitesi [*Anatolia University*] (TU)
ANU............ Automatic Navigation Equipment (RU)
ANUC.......... Asociacion Nacional de Usuarios Campesinos [*National Association of Consumer Peasants*] [*Colombian*] (LA)
Anude......... Asamblea Nicaraguense de Unidad Democratica [*Nicaraguan Assembly Democratic Unity*] (PD)
ANUROM.... Asociatia pentru Natiunile Unite din Romania [*Romanian Association for the United Nations*] (RO)
ANUSSCG... All-Nigerian Universities Staff Sports Clubs Games (MAR)
ANV............ Accion Nacional Vasca [*Basque National Action*] [*Spanish*] (PPE)
ANV............ Continuous Vulcanization Unit (RU)
ANVAR........ Agence Nationale pour la Valorisation de la Recherche [*French*]
Anw............ Anwalt [*or Anwaltschaft*] [*German*]
Anw............ Anwarter [*German*]
Anw............ Anwendung [*Application*] [*German*]
ANWU......... African Newspaper Workers Union (MAR)
anyagell...... Anyagellatas [*Supply of Materiel*] (HU)
anyaggazd... Anyaggazdalkodas [*Supply Management Department*] (HU)
anyagv........ Anyagvizsgalat [*Material Testing*] (HU)
ANYE.......... Anotati Navtiki Ygeionomiki Epitropi [*Supreme Naval Medical Board*] [*Greek*] (GC)
ANYOLP...... Arab Nationalist Youth Organization for the Liberation of Palestine (ME)
Anz............. Anzahl [*Number*] [*German*]
Anz............. Anzeige [*Advertisement*] [*German*]
Anz............. Anzeiger [*Announcer*] [*German*]
ANZ............. Armee Nationale du Zaire [*National Army of Zaire*] (AF)
ANZUK........ Australia, New Zealand, United Kingdom (ML)
ANZUS........ Australia, Nowa Zelandia, Stany Zjednoczone [*Australia - New Zealand - United States*] [*Polish*]
AO.............. Acridine Orange (RU)
AO.............. Administrative Department (RU)
a/o.............. Advance Report (RU)
AO.............. Aerial Fragmentation Bomb (RU)
AO.............. Air Detachment (RU)
AO.............. Air Section (RU)
AO.............. Aktivni Opatreni [*Active Measures or Covert Action*] (CZ)
AO.............. Alempi Oikenstutkinto [*Finnish*]
AO.............. Algemeen Ouderdomswet [*General Old Age Insurance Act*] [*Dutch*] (WEN)
ao.............. Allatorvos [*Veterinarian*] (HU)
ao.............. Ammattiosasto [*Finnish*]
aO.............. An der Oder [*On the River Oder*] (EG)
AO.............. Anatheoritiki Omada [*Revisionist Group*] (GC)
AO.............. Angola [*Two-letter standard code*] (CNC)
AO.............. Anonim Ortaklari [*Partnership*] [*See also TAO*] (TU)
AO.............. Anonim Ortakligi [*Joint-Stock Partnership*] [*Turkish*] (CED)
AO.............. Anordnung [*Order*] [*German*] (WEN)
AO.............. Armijska Oblast [*Army Region*] (YU)
ao.............. Army Train (BU)
AO.............. Artillery Section (BU)
ao.............. Asianomainen [*Finnish*]
AO.............. Astronomical Observatory (BU)
AO.............. Astronomical Observatory (RU)
AO.............. Athlitikos Omilos [*Athletic Club*] [*Plus initial letter of club name*] (GC)
AO.............. Atomic Orbital (RU)
AO.............. Atomic Weapons (RU)
ao.............. Ausserordentlich [*German*]
AO.............. Automatic Optimizer [*Computers*] (RU)
AO-............. Automatic Pumping Unit (RU)
AO.............. Autonomous Oblast (RU)
AO.............. Avanguardia Operaia [*Worker's Vanguard*] [*Italian*] (PPE)
AO.............. Aviation Equipment [*Aircraft maintenance*] (RU)
AO.............. Joint-Stock Company (RU)
AO.............. Operational Airfield (RU)
AOA............ African Overseas Agency (MAR)
AOA............ Antioxidant Activity (RU)
AOA............ Asociacion Odontologica Antioquera [*Medellin*] (COL)
aoabr.......... Army Gun-Artillery Brigade (BU)
AOAD.......... Arab Organisation for Agricultural Development (MAR)
AOAITM...... Asociatia Oamenilor de Arta din Institutiile Teatrale si Muzicale [*Association of Artists in Theatrical and Musical Institutions*] (RO)
AOAPC........ Association des Organisations Africaines de Promotion Commerciale [*Association of African Organizations for Trade Promotion*] (AF)
AOB............ Aerial Fragmentation Bomb (RU)
AOB............ Association des Originaires de Bandounga [*Association of Natives of Bandounga*]
AOC............ Alianca Operaria Camponesa [*Peasants and Workers Alliance*] [*Portuguese*] (PPE)
AOC............ Alvis Owners Club (EA)
AOC............ Arabian Oil Company (ME)
AOC............ Ataturk Orman Ciftligi [*Ataturk Forest Farm*] (TU)
AOD............ Aerial Sprayer (RU)
AODA.......... Ananeotiki Omada Dimokratikis Aristeras [*Restorative Group of the Democratic Left*] [*Greek*] (GC)
AOE............ Africa Occidental Espanola (MAR)
AOE............ Astronomical Observatory Imeni V. P. Engel'gardt (RU)
AOE............ Avance a l'Ouverture d'Echappement [*French*] (MTD)
AOEK.......... Avtonomos Organismos Ellinikou Kapnou [*Autonomous Greek Tobacco Organization*] (GC)
AOEK.......... Avtonomos Organismos Ergatikis Katoikias [*Autonomous Organization for Workers' Housing*] [*Greek*] (GC)
AOeR.......... Anstalt des Oeffentlichen Rechts [*Institution Incorporated under Public Law*] (EG)
AOER.......... Arab Oil and Economic Review [*Kuwait*] [*A publication*] (MAR)
AOF............ Afrique Occidentale Francaise [*French West Africa*] (AF)
AOF............ Afrique Orientale Francais [*A publication*] (MAR)
AOF............ Arbejdernes Oplysningsforbound [*Workers' Educational Association*] [*Danish*] (WEN)
AOGA.......... Arkhangel'sk Oblast State Archives [*A publication*] (RU)
AOGZ.......... Austriski Opsti Gradanski Zakonik [*Austrian General Civil Code*] (YU)
AOH............ Automatic Number Identification (RU)
AOI............. Arab Organization for Industrialization (MAR)
AOIC........... Arab Oil Investments Company (ME)
AOIEC......... Association of Iron Exporting Countries (MAR)
AOIUU......... Adyge Oblast Institute for the Advanced Training of Teachers (RU)
AOJT.......... Association of Orthodox Jewish Teachers (MAR)
AOK............ Allgemeine Ortskrankenkasse [*General Health Insurance Fund*] [*German*] (WEN)
AOK............ Armeeoberkommando [*Army High Command*] [*German*]
AOKhB........ Aerial Fragmentation Chemical Bomb (RU)
AOKosmeta... Autonomna Oblast Kosovo-Metohija [*Autonomous Region of Kosovo-Metohija*] [*Serbia*] (YU)
AOKosovometohija... Autonomna Oblast Kosovo-Metohija [*Autonomous Region of Kosovo-Metohija*] [*Serbia*] (YU)
AOKP.......... Asfalistikos Organismos Kindynon Polemou [*War Risks Insurance Organization*] (GC)
AOLGU........ Astronomical Observatory of the Leningrad State University (RU)
AOM............ Naval Operational Air Station (RU)
AOMK.......... Association des Ouvriers et Manoeuvres Khmers [*Cambodian Workers and Unskilled Laborers Association*] (CL)
AON............ Academy of Social Sciences at the TsK KPSS (RU)

AON............ Anorthotiki Organosis Neon [*Restorative Organization of Youth*] [*Cypriot*] (GC)
AON............ Special-Purpose Artillery (RU)
AON............ Special-Purpose Aviation (RU)
AONSU........ Academy of Social Sciences and Social Management (BU)
AOO............ Airfield Lighting Equipment (RU)
AOOA.......... Avtonomos Oikodomikos Organismos Axiomatikon [*Officers' Autonomous Construction Organization*] [*Greek*] (GC)
AOP............ Archives of the October Revolution [*A publication*] (RU)
AOP............ Austrian Liberation Party (RU)
AOP............ Main Astronomical Observatory in Pulkovo (RU)
AOPO.......... African Oilseed Producers' Organisation (MAR)
Ao Prof........ Ausserordentlicher Professor [*Senior Lecturer, Guest Professor, University Lecturer*] (EG)
AOR............ Administrativno-Operativni Rukovodilac [*Administrative-Operational Supervisor*] [*Military*] (YU)
AOR............ Arabskii Obshchii Rynok (MAR)
AORN.......... Automatic Optimum Load Distribution Device (RU)
AOS............ Acoustic Feedback (RU)
AOS............ Anotaton Oikonomikon Symvoulion [*Supreme Economic Council*] (GC)
AOS............ Antifasisticka Omladina Srbije [*Anti-Fascist Youth of Serbia*] (YU)
AOS............ Apostleship of the Sea [*See also AM*] (EA)
AOs............ Artiljeriski Osmatrac [*Artillery Observer*] (YU)
AOS............ Ataturk Ogrenci Sitesi [*Ataturk Student Dormitory*] [*Istanbul University*] (TU)
AOS............ Automatic Simultaneous Jettison Device [*Fuel tanks*] (RU)
AOS-........... Automatic Windshield Heater (RU)
AOSARIO.... Association des Originaires de la Seguia El Hamra et du Rio De Oro [*Association of Natives of Seguia El Hamra and Rio De Oro*] [*Saharan*] (AF)
AOSC.......... Arab Organization for Space Communications (MAR)
AOSPK........ Association des Originaires du Srok de Prey Krabas [*Association of Natives of Srok (District), Prey Krabas*] (CL)
AOT............ Asociacion Obrera Textil [*Textile Workers Association*] [*Argentine*] (LA)
AOTA.......... American Society of Travel Agents [*ASTA*] (RU)
AOU............ Air Reinforcement Detachment (RU)
AOZ............ Automobilove Opravarenske Zavody [*Automobile Repair Shops*] (CZ)
AP............... A Protester [*To Be Protested*] [*French*]
ap............... Aamupaivalla [*Before Noon*] [*Finnish*] (GPO)
AP............... Accion Popular [*Popular Action*] [*Peruvian*] (PPW)
AP............... Accion Popular [*Popular Action*] [*Spanish*] (PPE)
AP............... Accueil et la Promotion (MAR)
AP............... Adalet Partisi [*Justice Party - JP*] (TU)
AP............... Advokatski Pregled [*Lawyers' Review*] [*A publication*] (BU)
AP............... Aerolineas Peruanas [*Cali-Sucursal*] (COL)
AP............... Agen Polisi [*Policeman*] (IN)
AP............... Agonistiki Protoporeia [*Struggling Vanguard*] (GC)
ap............... Air Regiment (BU)
AP............... Air Regiment (RU)
a/p............. Airport (RU)
ap............... Alempi Palkkausluokka [*Finnish*]
AP............... Alianza Popular [*Popular Alliance*] [*Spanish*] (PPW)
AP............... Alianza Productiva [*Productive Alliance*] [*Salvadoran*] (LA1)
ap............... Allomasparancsnok [*Garrison Commander, Railroad Transport Officer*] (HU)
AP............... Amerikanisches Patent [*American Patent*] [*German*]
AP............... Aminopterin (RU)
AP............... Amsterdams Peil [*Amsterdam Ordnance Datum*] [*Dutch*] (GPO)
AP............... Analog Converter (RU)
AP............... Andhra Pradesh [*State in southeast India*]
ap............... Anno Passato [*Last Year*] [*Italian*] (GPO)
AP............... Antenna Switch, Duplexer (RU)
ap............... Aparte [*Apart, Aside*] [*Spanish*]
ap............... Apostol [*Apostle*] [*Spanish*]
Ap............... Apotheke [*or Apothaker*] [*German*]
AP............... Arkhigeion Pyrovolikou [*Artillery Command*] (GC)
AP............... Armia Polska [*Polish Army*] [*Polish*]
AP............... Artillery Park, Gun Park (RU)
AP............... Artillery Preparation (RU)
AP............... Artillery Range (RU)
ap............... Artillery Regiment (BU)
AP............... Artillery Regiment (RU)
AP............... Asociacion Proverista [*"For the Truth" Association*] [*Spanish*] (WER)
AP............... Assistance Publique [*French*]
AP............... Associative Memory (RU)
AP............... Astronomical Point (RU)
AP............... Astynomia Poleon [*City Police*] [*Greek*] (GC)
a/p............. Atmoploion [*Steamship*] (GC)
AP............... Automatic Pilot, Autopilot, Gyropilot (RU)
AP-.............. Automatic Sampler (RU)
AP............... Automatic Switch (RU)
AP............... Automatic Translation (RU)
AP............... Automatic Tuning (RU)
AP............... Automobile Industry (RU)
AP............... Automobilklub Polski [*Polish Automobile Club*] (POL)
AP............... Autonomna Pokrajina [*Autonomous Province*] (YU)
AP............... Autorisations de Programme (MAR)
AP............... Avant-Poste [*Outpost*] [*Military*] [*French*] (MTD)
ap............... Avaries Particulieres [*French*]
a/p............. Aviopoletanje [*Takeoff*] [*Aviation*] (YU)
AP............... Regimental Artillery (RU)
Ap............... Submersible Artesian Pump (RU)
AP............... Subscriber's Panel (RU)
AP............... Truck Trailer (RU)
AP............... Yielding Arch Support [*Mining*] (RU)
APA............ Abidjan Pieces Autos (MAR)
APA............ Accion Patriotica Argentina [*Argentine Patriotic Action*] (LA)
APA............ Aerovias Panama [*Bogota-Agencia*] (COL)
APA............ African Purchase Areas (MAR)
APA............ Airport Mobile Power Unit (RU)
APA............ ANCAM Political Files (MAR)
APA............ Asociacion del Personal Aeronautica [*Airline Personnel Association*] [*Argentine*] (LA)
APA............ Asociacion de Proveedores Agricolas [*Association of Agricultural Suppliers*] [*Salvadoran*] (LA1)
APA............ Astrakhan' Party Archives (RU)
APA............ Austria Presse Agentur [*Austria Press Agency*] (WEN)
APA............ Avrupa Para Anlasmasi [*European Monetary Agreement*] (TU)
APAAL........ Association Professionnelle des Artistes et Artisans d'Art Lao [*Lao Professional Artists and Artisans Association*] (CL)
APAC.......... Asociation de Profesionales de Accion Catolica [*Professionals Catholic Action Association*] [*Argentine*] (LA)
APADI......... Asosiasi Perpustakaan, Arsip dan Dokumentasi Indonesia
APAE.......... Asociacion de Productores de Aceites Esenciales [*Essential Oils Producers Association*] [*Guatemalan*] (LA)
APAEIM....... Association des Parents et Amis des Enfants Inadaptes du Maroc [*Moroccan*] (MAR)
APAK.......... Association Professionnelle Apolitique du Katanga [*Nonpolitical Professional Association of Katanga*]
APAL.......... Asociacion de Padres de Alumnos de Liceo [*Association of Parents of Secondary School Students*] [*Uruguayan*] (LA)
APAM.......... Associacao Politica do Arquipelago da Madeira [*Political Association of the Madeira Archipelago*] [*Portuguese*] (WER)
Apanc.......... Armia Pancerna [*Armoured Army*] [*Polish*]
APAP.......... Asociacion Peruana de Agencias de Publicidad [*Association of Peruvian Advertising Agencies*] (LA)
APAPHAM... Association Professionnelle des Armateurs a la Peche Hauturiere au Maroc (MAR)
APAS.......... Association of Personal Assistants and Secretaries (EA)
apat........... Apatite Mines [*Topography*] (RU)
APAU.......... Association Professionnelle de l'Administration Universitaire [*Algerian*] (MAR)
APAVIT....... Asociacion Peruana de Agencias de Viajes y Turismo [*Peruvian Association of Travel and Tourist Agencies*] (LA)
APB............ Aircraft Design Office (RU)
APB............ Association Professionnelle des Banques (MAR)
APBA.......... Asociacion de Periodistas de Buenos Aires [*Buenos Aires Newsmen's Association*] [*Argentine*] (LA)
apble.......... Apreciable [*Valued*] [*Spanish*]
APBM.......... Superheavy Artillery Regiment (RU)
APBN.......... Anggaran Pendapatan dan Belandja Negara [*Estimate of State Expenditures and Income (National budget)*] (IN)
APC............ Abadan Petrochemical Company (ME)
APC............ African Peanut Council (MAR)
APC............ Agence Presse Comores (MAR)
APC............ Alianza Popular Cristiana [*Popular Christian Alliance*] [*Ecuadorean*] (LA)
APC............ All-People's Congress [*Sierra Leonean*] (PPW)
APC............ Alliance des Pays Producteurs de Cacao [*Cocoa Producers' Alliance*] [*Use COPAL*] (AF)
apC............ Anno Post Christum [*In the Year after the Birth of Christ*] [*Latin*]
APC............ Arunachal People's Conference [*Indian*] (PPW)
APC............ Assemblee Populaire Communale [*People's Communal Assembly*] [*Algerian*] (AF)
APC............ Association des Planteurs de Caoutchouc [*Rubber Planters Association*] [*Cambodian*] (CL)
APC............ Associu di Patrioti Corsi [*Association of Corsican Patriots*] [*French*] (PPE)
APCA.......... Asociacion de Periodicos Centroamericanos [*Association of Central American Newspapers*] (LA)
APCC.......... Asian and Pacific Coconut Community (EA)
APCC.......... Asociacion Pro-Cultura China [*Pro-Chinese Culture Association*] [*Mexican*] (LA)
APCC.......... Association des Planteurs de Caoutchouc du Cambodge [*Cambodian Rubber Planters Association*] (CL)
APCCI......... Assemblee Permanente des Chambres de Commerce et d'Industrie (MAR)
apce........... Apostolice [*Spanish*]
APCE.......... Assemblee Populaire Communale Elargie [*Expanded People's Communal Assembly*] [*Algerian*] (AF)

APCET .... Association Professionnelle des Cooperants de l'Enseignement Technique [*Professional Association of Technical Studies Advisors*] [*Algerian*] (AF)
APCh .... Antifriction Porous Pig Iron (RU)
APCh .... Automatic Frequency Control (RU)
APChG .... Automatic Heterodyne Frequency Control (RU)
APCh i F ...... Automatic Frequency and Phase Control (RU)
APCJ .... Agrupacion Politica Catorce de Junio [*14 June Political Group*] [*Dominican Republic*] (LA1)
APCM .... Associated Portland Cement Manufacturers of Great Britain (MAR)
APCN .... Anno Post Christum Natum [*In the Year after the Birth of Christ*] [*Latin*]
APCO .... Application de Procedes de Construction [*Moroccan*] (MAR)
APCO .... Arab Political and Cultural Organization [*Iranian*] (PD)
APCT .... Association des Planteurs des Cultures Tropicales [*Tropical Crop Planters Association*] [*Cambodian*] (CL)
APD .... Aide Publique au Developpement (MAR)
APD .... Autoridad Portuaria Dominicana [*Dominican Port Authority*] [*Dominican Republic*] (LA1)
APD .... Data Transmission Equipment (RU)
apda .... Apreciada [*Valued*] [*Spanish*]
APDD .... Long-Range Air Regiment (RU)
APDEN .... Association pour la Protection et le Developpement de l'Economie Nationale [*Association for the Protection and Development of the National Economy*] [*Laotian*] (CL)
APDEP .... Associacao Portuguesa para o Desenvolvimento Economico Popular [*Portuguese Association for Popular Economic Development*] (WER)
APDKM .... Activist Group for Assistance to the Militia Children's Room (RU)
Apdo .... Apartado [*Post Office Box*] [*Spanish*]
APDPN .... Acetylpyridine Diphosphopyridine Nucleotide (RU)
APDR .... Long-Range Air Reconnaissance Regiment (RU)
Apdusa .... African People's Democratic Union of South Africa (PD)
APE .... Amalgamated Power Engineering (MAR)
APE .... Asociacion de Prensa Extranjera [*Foreign Press Association*] [*Chilean*] (LA)
APE .... Asociacion de Profesionales Especializados en Estados Unidos [*Bogota*] (COL)
APE .... Asociacion Proverista Espanola [*Spanish "For the Truth" Association*] (WER)
APE .... Assemblea Parlamentare Europea [*European Parliamentary Assembly*] [*Italian*] (WER)
APE .... Assemblee Parlementaire Europeenne (MAR)
APE .... Athinaikon Praktoreion Eidiseon [*Athens News Agency*] [*See also Ath Pr*] (GC)
APEA .... Association de la Presse Eurafricaine (MAR)
APEABA ...... Association pour les Echanges Bretagne - Pays Arabes (MAR)
APEC .... American Petrofina Exploration Company [*North African*] (MAR)
APEC .... Asociacion de Profesionales Electronicos de Colombia [*Bogota*] (COL)
APECA .... Asociacion de Periodistas de Centro-America [*Central American Newsmen's Association*] (LA)
APECA .... Association des Parents et Amis de l'Enseignement Catholique (MAR)
APECO .... Asociacion de Pequenos Comerciantes [*Bogota*] (COL)
APEDA .... Ananeotiki Parataxi Epangelmation Dikigoron Athinon [*Renewal Faction of Practicing Attorneys of Athens*] (GC)
APEDE .... Asociacion Panamena de Ejecutivos de Empresas [*Panamanian Business Executives Association*] (LA)
APEF .... Association des Pays Exportateurs de Mineral de Fer [*Association of Iron Ore Exporting Countries*] (EA)
APEFRAC ... Association Professionnelle des Enseignants Francais Residants au Cambodge [*Professional Association for French Teachers Living in Cambodia*] (CL)
APEGE .... Asamblea Permanente de Entidades Gremiales Empresariales [*Permanent Assembly of Union Management Organizations*] [*Argentine*] (LA)
APEH .... Asociacion de Paises Exportadores de Hierro [*Association of Iron Exporting Countries*] (LA)
APEIA .... Asociacion Profesional de Empleados Industriales Argentinos [*Professional Association of Argentine Industrial Employees*] (LA)
APEKE .... Association des Parents des Etudiants Khmers a l'Etranger [*Association of Parents of Cambodian Students Abroad*] (CL)
APEL .... Asociacion Progreso en Libertad [*Progress with Liberty Association*] [*Venezuelan*] (LA)
APEL .... Association des Parents d'Eleves de l'Enseignement Libre [*French*]
APEMA .... Association pour l'Etude des Marches d'Assurances (MAR)
APEN .... Asociacion de Periodistas y Escritores Nacionales [*National Journalists and Writers Association*] [*Honduran*] (LA)
APEP .... Agencia de Prensa Espanola Popular [*People's Spanish Press Agency*] (WER)
APEP .... Asociacion de Periodistas Escolares de Peru [*Association of Peruvian Student Journalists*] (LA)
APES .... Asociacion de Periodistas de El Salvador [*El Salvador Journalists Association*] (LA)
APES .... Asociacion de Profesores de Ensenanza Secundaria [*Secondary School Teachers Association*] [*Uruguayan*] (LA)
APES .... Association Professionnelle de l'Enseignement Superieur [*Advanced Education Professional Association*] [*Algerian*] (AF)
APESEG ...... Asociacion Peruana de Empresas de Seguros [*Peruvian Association of Insurance Companies*] (LA)
APESGE ...... Association du Personnel Enseignant et Scientifique des Grands Ecoles (MAR)
APETI .... Asociacion Profesional Espanola de Tradutores e Interpretes [*Spanish Professional Association of Translators and Interpreters*]
APEUCh ...... Asociacion de Profesores y Empleados de la Universidad de Chile [*Association of Professors and White-Collar Employees of the University of Chile*] (LA)
APEX .... Advanced Passenger Excursion (MAR)
APF .... African Peace Force (MAR)
APF .... Alianza Popular Familiar [*People's Family Alliance*] [*Spanish*] (WER)
APF .... Alianza Popular Federalista [*Popular Federalist Alliance*] [*Argentine*] (LA)
APF .... Anglican Pacifist Fellowship (EA)
APF .... Asparagine Polysaccharide Fragment (RU)
APF .... Automatic Phase Control (RU)
APF .... Phage-Inhibiting Agents (RU)
APFA .... All People's Freedom Alliance [*Liberian*] (AF)
APFRL .... Association des Professeurs Francais Residants au Laos [*Association of French Teachers Living in Laos*] (CL)
APFS .... African Peasant Farming Scheme (MAR)
APG .... Agu Pflanzungs-Gesellschaft (MAR)
APG .... Army Field Hospital (RU)
APG .... Army Mobile Hospital (RU)
APG .... Asamblea Popular Galega [*Galician People's Assembly*] [*Spanish*] (WER)
APG .... Asociacion de Periodistas de Guatemala [*Guatemalan Journalists Association*] (LA)
APGR- .... Automatic Recorder of Clay Mud Parameters (RU)
APH .... Asociacion de Prensa Hondurena [*Honduran Press Association*] (LA)
APH .... Automobilove Pohonne Hmoty [*Motor Vehicle Fuels*] (CZ)
APHLC .... All-Party Hill Leaders' Conference [*Indian*] (PPW)
API .... Accion Popular Independiente [*Independent Popular Action*] [*Chilean*] (LA)
API .... Agence Angolaise de Presse et d'Information (MAR)
API .... Agence Populaire d'Information (MAR)
API .... Agence de Presse Ivoirienne (MAR)
API .... Agence de Promotion des Investissements [*Tunisian*] (MAR)
API .... Agencja Prasowo-Informacyjna [*Press and Information Agency*] (POL)
API .... Agencja Publicystyczno-Informacyjna [*Publicity and Information Agency*] [*Polish*]
API .... Agency for Public Information [*Replaced by JIS*] [*Jamaican*] (LA1)
API .... Alianza Popular Independiente [*Independent Popular Alliance*] [*Venezuelan*] (LA)
API .... Alianza Popular Informativo [*People's Informative Alliance*] [*Spanish*] (WER)
API .... Alianza Popular de Izquierdas [*Popular Alliance of Leftists*] [*Spanish*] (WER)
API .... Allgemeiner Presse-Informationsdienst [*General Press Information Service*] (EG)
API .... American Petroleum Institute (MAR)
API .... Angkatan Pemuda Indonesia [*Indonesian Youth Corps*] (ML)
API .... Angkatan Pemuda Insaf [*Awakened Youth Corps*] (ML)
API .... Asociatia Petrolifera Internationala [*International Petroleum Association*] (RO)
API .... Associacao Paulista da Imprensa [*Sao Paulo Press Association*] [*Brazilian*] (LA)
API .... Association Pharmaceutique Interafricaine (MAR)
API .... Autorisations Prealables d'Importation [*Advance Import Authorizations*] (CL)
API .... Azerbaydzhan Pedagogical Institute Imeni V. I. Lenin (RU)
APIA .... Agence de Promotion des Investissements Agricoles [*Tunisian*] (MAR)
APIA .... Association pour la Promotion de l'Information Agricole [*French*]
APIAC .... Asociacion de Pequenos Industriales de Articulos de Cuero [*Bogota*] (COL)
APIC .... African Policy Information Center (MAR)
APIC .... Alleanza dei Patrioti Indipendenti del Congo (MAR)
APIC .... Alliance des Proletaires Independants du Congo (MAR)
APIC .... Amicale des Postiers Indigenes Congolais (MAR)
APIC .... Arab Petroleum Investment Company (ME)
APIC .... Armements des Peches Ivoiriennes Cotieres (MAR)
APIC .... Asamblea Permanent d'Intellectuals Catalans [*Permanent Assembly of Catalan Intellectuals*] [*Spanish*] (WER)
APIC .... Association des Patrons et Ingenieurs Catholiques [*Association of Catholic Employers and Engineers*] [*Belgian*] (WER)
APIC .... Association du Personnel Indigene du Congo Belge et du Rwanda-Urundi (MAR)

APICE .... Asociacion Panamericana de Instituciones de Credito Educativo [*Pan American Association of Educational Credit Institutions - PAAECI*] (EA)
APICI .... Association Professionnelle des Informaticiens de Cote-d'Ivoire (MAR)
APICOL .... Apicultura Colombiana Ltda. [*Bogota*] (COL)
APICORP .... Arab Petroleum Investment Corporation (MAR)
APID .... Agence de Production, d'Information, et de Documentation (MAR)
APIDEN .... Association Professionnelle des Inspecteurs Departementaux de l'Education Nationale [*Algerian*] (MAR)
APIE .... Administracao do Parque Imobiliaria do Estado [*Administration of State Lands and Property*] [*Mozambican*] (AF)
APIFA .... Association Professionnelle des Instituteurs Francais en Algerie [*Professional Association of French Teachers in Algeria*] (AF)
APIN .... Alianza Popular de Integracion Nacional [*Bolivian*] (PPW)
APISZ .... Allami Papiripari Szovetkezet [*State Paper Cooperative Enterprise*] (HU)
APIZ .... Alliance des Proletaires Independants du Zaire (MAR)
ap J-C .... Apres Jesus-Christ [*After Jesus Christ*] [*French*]
APK .... African Trade-Union Confederation (RU)
APK .... Afrikanskaia Profsoiuznaia Konfederatsiia (MAR)
APK .... Agen Polisi Kepala [*Senior Policeman*] (IN)
APK .... Agroindustrial Complex (BU)
APK .... Allami Pincegazdasagok Kozpontja [*State Wine Cellar Center*] (HU)
apk .... Allomasparancsnok [*Garrison Commander, Railway Transport Officer*] (HU)
APK .... Arbetarpartiet Kommunisterna [*Worker Party Communists*] [*Swedish*] (PPE)
APK .... Archives Provinciales du Katanga (MAR)
APK .... Association de la Presse Khmere [*Cambodian Press Association*] (CL)
APK .... Propionic Acid Amide (RU)
APKh .... Association of Proletarian Artists (RU)
APL .... Aircraft Preheater Lamp (RU)
APL .... Automatic Production Line (RU)
APL .... Nuclear Powered Submarine, Atomic Submarine (RU)
APLA .... Automatic Programing of Logical Algorithms (RU)
APLAN .... Agencia Journalistica do Planalto [*Planalto News Agency*] [*Brazilian*] (LA)
APLF .... Alliance of Progressive and Left-Wing Forces [*Greek*] (PPE)
APLI .... African People's League for Independence (MAR)
APLR .... Armee Populaire de Liberation Rwandaise (MAR)
APLS .... Armee Populaire de Liberation Sahraouie [*Saharan People's Liberation Army*] (AF)
APM .... Akcja Porzadkowania Miasta [*City Cleaning Drive*] (POL)
APM .... American Presbyterian Mission (MAR)
APM .... Archives of Planning Materials (RU)
APM .... Association of Proletarian Musicians (RU)
APM .... Truck-Mounted Shop (RU)
APMC .... Associated Pan Malaysia Cement (ML)
APMEPU ..... Agricultural Projects Monitoring, Evaluation, and Planning Unit (MAR)
APML .... Acao Popular Marxista-Leninista [*Marxist-Leninist Popular Action*] [*Brazilian*] (LA)
APN .... Academy of Pedagogical Sciences, RSFSR (RU)
APN .... Administracion Postal Nacional [*National Postal Administration*] [*Colombian*] (LA)
APN .... Afrikanskaia Partiia Nezavisimosti (MAR)
APN .... Armee Populaire Nationale [*National People's Army*] [*Congolese*] (AF)
APN .... Assemblee Populaire Nationale [*Algerian*] (MAR)
APN .... Association Prachea Niyum [*Humanitarian Association*] [*Cambodian*] (CL)
APN .... "Novosti" Press Agency (RU)
APN .... Submersible Artesian Pump (RU)
AP No 4 .... Association Professionnelle Numero 4 [*Professional Association Number 4*] (CL)
APNP .... Mobile Artillery Observation Post (RU)
APO .... Abteilungs-Parteiorganisation [*Department Party Organization*] (EG)
APO .... African People's Organisation (MAR)
APO .... Agitation and Propaganda Department (BU)
APO .... Agitation and Propaganda Department (RU)
Apo .... Apartado [*Post Office Box*] [*Correspondence*] [*Spanish*]
Apo .... Apoderado [*Empowered, Attorney*] [*Spanish*]
APO .... Architectural Planning Department (RU)
ApO .... Ausserparlamentarische Opposition [*Extra-Parliamentary Opposition*] [*German*] (WEN)
apof .... Apofasis [*Decision, Decree*] (GC)
apos .... Apostolica [*Spanish*]
APOSA .... Abetifi Presby Secondary School Old Students Association (MAR)
apost .... Apostol [*Apostle*] [*Spanish*]
APP .... Action Pro-Populaire [*Pro-People's Action*] [*Cambodian*] (CL)
APP .... Action Psychologique et Propagande [*Algerian*] (MAR)
APP .... African People's Party [*Kenyan*] (AF)
APP .... African Progressive Party (MAR)
APP .... Agence Parisienne de Presse [*Parisian Press Agency*] [*French*] (AF)
APP .... Alianza para el Progreso [*Bogota*] (COL)
App .... Apparat [*Extension, Apparatus*] [*German*] (WEN)
APP .... Area de Propiedad del Pueblo [*People's Ownership Sector*] [*Nicaraguan*] (LA1)
app .... Army Forwarding Station (RU)
APP .... Artillery in Support of Infantry (RU)
APP .... Asociacion de Periodistas del Peru [*Peruvian Journalists Association*] (LA)
APP .... Asociacion Politica Proverista [*"For the Truth" Political Association*] [*Spanish*] (WER)
APP .... Association of Proletarian Writers (RU)
APP .... Athinon, Peiraios, Perikhoron [*Of Athens, Piraeus, Suburbs*] (GC)
APP .... Automatic Reclosing (RU)
APP .... Breakthrough Artillery Regiment (RU)
app .... Landing Strip (RU)
APPA .... Asociacion Colombiana para Perros Pastores Alemanes [*Bogota*] (COL)
APPAN .... Asociacion de Pequenos Panaderos [*Bogota*] (COL)
APPC .... Alliance des Pays Producteurs de Cacao [*Cocoa Producers' Alliance*] [*Use COPAL*] (AF)
APPCN .... Association des Pays Producteurs de Caoutchouc Naturel [*Association of Natural Rubber-Producing Countries*] (CL)
APPMECI .... Association Professionnelle des Petites et Moyennes Entreprises de Cote-d'Ivoire (MAR)
APPO .... Anti-Fascist Secret Patriotic Organization [*1942-1945*] (RU)
APPO .... Department of Agitation, Propaganda and Press (RU)
APPP .... Asamblea Provincial del Poder Popular [*Provincial People's Government Assembly*] [*Cuban*] (LA)
Appr .... Approbiert [*German*]
approf .... Apulaisprofessori [*Finnish*]
APPS .... Alianca Portuguesa para o Progresso Social [*Portuguese Alliance for Social Progress*] [*Portuguese*] (WER)
APPSO .... Asociacion de Profesionales de la Planta Siderurgica del Orinoco [*Association of Orinoco Iron and Steel Mill Professionals*] [*Venezuelan*] (LA)
Appt .... Approvisionnement [*Victualing, Supply*] [*Military*] [*French*] (MTD)
APPU .... Asian-Pacific Postal Union (EA)
APPUG .... Carrier-Based Antisubmarine Hunter-Killer Group (RU)
apPVO .... Antiaircraft Artillery Regiment (RU)
APR .... Accion Publica del Regionalismo [*Public Regionalism Action*] [*Spanish*] (WER)
apr .... April (BU)
apr .... April [*April*] [*Danish*] (GPO)
apr .... April [*April*] [*Dutch*] (GPO)
Apr .... April [*April*] [*German*] (GPO)
apr .... April (RU)
apr .... Aprilis [*April*] (HU)
APR .... Association pour le Ravitaillement des Produits de Premiere Necessite de Phnom Penh et des Provinces [*Association for Supplying Phnom Penh and the Provinces with Necessities*] [*Cambodian*] (CL)
APR .... Automobilni Prepravni Rad [*Automobile Traffic Regulations*] (CZ)
APR .... Density Distribution Analyzer (RU)
APRA .... Alianza Popular Revolucionaria Americana [*American Revolutionary Popular Alliance*] [*Peruvian*] (PPW)
APR(AR) ..... Autodopravni Prapor (Rota) [*Truck Battalion (Company)*] (CZ)
APRC .... Anno Post Roman Conditam [*In the Year After the Building of Rome*] [*Latin*]
APRE .... Accion Popular Revolucionaria Ecuatoriana [*Ecuadorean Revolutionary Popular Action*] (LA)
APRE .... Alianza Popular Revolucionaria Ecuatoriana [*Ecuadorean Popular Revolutionary Alliance*] (PPW)
APREMA ..... Angkatan Pemuda Revolusi Malaya [*Malayan Youth Revolutionary Forces*] (ML)
APRI .... Angkatan Perang Republik Indonesia [*Combat Forces of the Republic of Indonesia*] (IN)
APRI .... Autorisations Prealables d'Importation (MAR)
APRIGA .... Agence pour la Promotion Industrielle de la Guadeloupe [*Agency for the Industrial Promotion of Guadeloupe*] (LA1)
APRIM .... Truck-Mounted Engineering Repair Shop (RU)
apr J-C .... Apres Jesus-Christ [*After Jesus Christ*] [*French*]
APRL .... Aeroklub Polskiej Rzeczypospolitej Ludowej [*Aero Club of the Polish People's Republic*] [*Polish*]
APrN .... Legal Sciences Archives [*A publication*] (BU)
APROCAL ... Asociacion de Profesores de Ensenanza Secundaria de Caldas [*Manizales*] (COL)
APROCEL ... Asociacion de Profesionales de la Comision Ejecutiva Hidroelectrica del Rio Lempa [*Professional Association of the Rio Lempa Hydroelectric Executive Commission*] [*Salvadoran*] (LA1)
APROCOLIN ... Association Professionnelle de Colons Individuels [*Professional Association of Colonials*]
APRODEBA ... Association des Progressistes et Democrates Burundi de Gitega (MAR)
APRODECO ... Association pour le Promotion de la Defense de l'Economie Congolaise (MAR)

APROFAM... Asociacion Pro Sienestar de la Familia [*Family Welfare Association*] [*Guatemalan*] (LA1)
APROLECHE ... Asociacion de Productores de Leche [*Association of Milk Producers*] [*Dominican Republic*] (LA1)
APROM .... Atelierul de Prototipuri si Serii Feromobila [*Workshop for Prototype and Mass Production of Iron Furniture*] (RO)
APROMACI ... Association des Producteurs et Manufacturiers de Caoutchouc en Cote-d'Ivoire [*Ivory Coast Rubber Producers and Manufacturers Association*] (AF)
APROMAQUINAS ... Asociacion Colombiana de Productores de Maquinas de Oficina [*Bogota*] (COL)
APROSOMA ... Association pour la Promotion Sociale de la Masse [*Association for the Social Betterment of the Masses*] [*Burundi*] (AF)
APROSOMA ... Association pour la Promotion Sociale de la Masse [*Association for the Social Betterment of the Masses*] [*Rwandan*] (AF)
APROZAR ... Aprovizionarea cu Zarzavaturi [*State Vegetable Supply Organization*] (RO)
APRP.......... All Peoples' Republican Party [*Ghanaian*] (AF)
APRSU........ All Penang Revolutionary Students Union (ML)
APRU.......... Associacao dos Portugueses Refugiados do Ultramar [*Association of Portuguese Refugees from Overseas*] (WER)
APRURD...... Asociacion de Profesores del Recinto Universitario Ruben Dario [*Ruben Dario University Professors Association*] [*Nicaraguan*] (LA)
APS .... Aborigines Protection Society [*Malaysian*] (ML)
AP-S........... Accion Popular - SOANE [*SOANE Faction of Popular Action Party*] [*Peruvian*] (LA)
APS .... Accion Popular Socialista [*Socialist Popular Action*] [*Peruvian*] (LA)
APS .... Agence de Presse Senegalaise [*Senegalese Press Agency*] (AF)
APS .... Agonistiki Parataxi Spoudaston [*Student Fighting Faction*] [*Greek*] (GC)
aps .... Air Communications Regiment (RU)
aps .... Air Regiment Liaison (BU)
APS .... Algerie Presse Service [*Algerian Press Service*] (AF)
APS .... All Africa Press Service (MAR)
APS .... Alliance pour le Progres Social [*Alliance for Social Progress*] [*Cambodian*] (CL)
APS .... Anfangspunkt der Strecke [*Starting Point of a Flight*] (EG)
APS .... Anotaton Peitharkhikon Symvoulion [*Supreme Disciplinary Council*] [*Greek*] (GC)
ApS .... Anpartsselskab [*Private Limited Company*] [*Swedish*]
APS .... Arab Press Service (MAR)
APS .... Arkhigeion Pyrosvestikou Somatos [*Fire Corps Headquarters*] [*Greek*] (GC)
aps .... Army Food Depot (RU)
APS .... Army Signal Regiment (RU)
APS .... Automatic Deicer (RU)
APS .... Automatic Signal Transmitter (RU)
APS .... Homing Station (RU)
APS .... Stechkin Automatic Pistol (RU)
APSA........... Aerolineas Peruanas [*Peruvian Airlines*] (LA)
APSA........... Aerovias Peruanas SA [*Cali-Agencia*] (COL)
APSC .... Arab Petroleum Services Company (MAR)
APSE........... Asociacion de Profesores de Segunda Ensenanza [*Secondary School Teachers Association*] [*Costa Rican*] (LA)
APSLF......... Association de Psychologie Scientifique de Langue Francaise [*French-Language Association of Scientific Psychology*] (EA)
APSM.......... Automatic Letter-Sorting Machine (RU)
APSO .... Afro-Asian People's Solidarity Organisation (MAR)
APSO .... Automatic Print Drier (RU)
APSP........... Anotati Panellinios Synomospondia Polyteknon [*Supreme Panhellenic Confederation of Parents of Large Families*] [*Greek*] (GC)
APS/RGK.... Air Communications Regiment of the High Command Reserve (RU)
APT .... African Personal Tax (MAR)
APT .... African Petroleum Terminals Ltd. (MAR)
APT .... Agence de Presse Tunisienne [*Tunisian Press Agency*] (MAR)
APT .... Albanian Labor Party (RU)
APT .... Albanian Workers' Party (BU)
apt............. Apartman [*Apartment, Flat*] [*Turkish*] (CED)
APT .... Artillery in Support of Tanks (RU)
APT .... Automatic Pictures Transmission (AF)
apt............. Pharmaceutical (BU)
apt............. Pharmacy Practice (BU)
APTAV .... Association de Pilotos y Trabajadores de la Aviacion [*Association of Pilots and Aviation Workers*] [*Venezuelan*] (LA)
APTCH .... Asociacion Postal-Telegrafica de Chile [*Postal and Telegraph Association of Chile*] (LA)
APTh........... Aristoteleion Panepistimion Thessalonikis [*Salonica Aristoteleion University*] (GC)
APTIC.......... African Pyrethrum Technical Information Centre (MAR)
APTL .... Administracion Publica de Transportes de Lima [*Lima Municipal Transportation Administration*] [*Peruvian*] (LA)
APTR........... Antitank Artillery Reserve (RU)
APTR........... Artillery Antitank Reserve (BU)
APTU........... African Postal and Telecommunications Union (AF)
APTU........... Steam-Turbine Nuclear Propulsion Engine, Steam-Turbine Atomic Power Plant (RU)
APTUN .... Association of Professional Trade Unionists of Nigeria (AF)
APU .... African Parliamentary Union (MAR)
APU .... Akademija za Pozorisnu Umetnost [*Academy of Theatrical Art*] [*Belgrade*] (YU)
APU .... Akademija Primenjenih Umetnosti [*Academy of Applied Arts*] [*Belgrade*] (YU)
APU .... Alianca Povo Unido [*United People's Alliance*] [*Portuguese*] (PPE)
APU .... Arab Postal Union (MAR)
APU .... Architectural Planning Administration (RU)
APU .... Arcidiecesni Pastoracni Ustredi [*Archdiocesan Pastoral Center*] (CZ)
APU .... Asia Parliamentary Union (CL)
APU .... Asociacion de Prensa Uruguaya [*Uruguayan Press Association*] (LA)
APU-........... Autocollimation Instrument for Checking Angular Measures (RU)
APU .... General-Purpose Truck Trailer (RU)
APUDAH ..... Agence de Publicite Dahomeene (MAR)
APUG .... Carrier-Based Hunter-Killer Group (RU)
APUK .... Apurinic Acid (RU)
apuv .... Apuverbi [*Auxiliary verb*] [*Finnish*]
APUV........... Universal Pneumatic Impact Fuze [*Aviation*] (RU)
APV .... Agence Presse Voltaique [*Voltan Press Agency*] (AF)
APV .... Automatic Reclosing (BU)
APV .... Automatic Reclosing (RU)
APV .... Autonomna Pokrajina Vojvodina [*Autonomous Province of Vojvodina*] (YU)
APV b/s....... Automatic Reclosing without Controlling Synchronism (RU)
APVN.......... Armee Populaire du Viet-Nam [*Vietnam People's Army*] [*Use VPA*] [*North Vietnamese*] (CL)
APV-NRS .... Autonomna Pokrajina Vojvodina, Narodna Republika Srbija [*Autonomous Province of Vojvodina, Serbia*] (YU)
APVO .... Army Antiaircraft Defense (BU)
APVOS .... Automatic Reclosing with Synchronism Expectation (RU)
APVRD .... Atomic Ramjet Engine (RU)
APVS.......... Automatic Reclosing with Self-Synchronization (RU)
APVT .... Actes Tenant Lieu de Proces-Verbaux et de Transaction [*Instruments Taking the Place of Proceedings and Transactions*] (CL)
APVUS .... Automatic Reclosing with Synchronism-Catch Arrangement (RU)
APW .... Assemblee Populaire des Wilayate [*Governorate Popular Assembly*] [*Algerian*] (AF)
APYSDE...... Anotera Perifereiaka Ypiresiaka Symvoulia Dimotikis Ekpaidevseos [*Higher Regional Service Councils for Elementary Education*] [*Greek*] (GC)
APZ .... Barrage Balloon (RU)
AQ .... Antarctica [*Two-letter standard code*] (CNC)
AQI .... Quartalsberichterstattung fuer Arbeitskraefte in der Industrie [*Quarterly Report on the Industrial Labor Force*] (EG)
Aque .... Aqueduc [*Aqueduct*] [*Military map abbreviation*] [*World War I*] [*French*] (MTD)
Ar .... A Retard [*Military*] [*French*] (MTD)
AR .... Academische Raad [*Dutch*]
AR .... Activated Ore (RU)
AR .... Aerial Reconnaissance (RU)
AR .... Africa Report [*A publication*] (MAR)
AR .... Agencja Reutera [*Reuters Agency*] [*Polish*]
AR .... Agencja Robotnicza [*Workers' Press Agency*] (POL)
AR .... Air Reserve (RU)
AR .... Algemeen Rijksarchief [*Dutch*]
AR .... Alger [*Algiers*] [*On cartridge bags*] [*Military*] [*French*] (MTD)
AR .... Anno Regni [*In the Year of the Reign*] [*Latin*]
ar .... Arabian, Arabic (RU)
ar .... Arabic (BU)
Ar .... Arad [*Arad*] (RO)
Ar .... Arapca [*Arabic*] (TU)
Ar .... Arapcadan [*From Arabic*] (TU)
Ar .... Arazi [*Land Surface, Terrain*] (TU)
AR .... Archeologicke Rozhledy [*Archeological Annals*] (CZ)
AR .... Argentina [*Two-letter standard code*] (CNC)
AR .... Arriere [*Home Front*] [*Military*] [*French*] (MTD)
ar .... Artillery (BU)
AR .... Artillery Reconnaissance (RU)
AR .... Asociacion Regionalista [*Regionalist Association*] [*Spanish*] (WER)
AR .... Assembleia da Republica [*Assembly of the Republic*] [*Portuguese*] (WER)
AR .... Automatic Control (RU)
AR .... Automatic Pilot, Gyropilot [*Nautical term*] (RU)
AR .... Automatic Regulator (RU)
AR .... Autonomous Recording Device (RU)
A/R.............. Avis de Reception [*Return Receipt*] [*French*]
AR .... Emergency Breaker (RU)
AR- .... Fountain Pen (RU)

AR .... Intelligence through Secret Agents (RU)
ar .... Irrigation Ditch [*Topography*] (RU)
ar .... Motor Transport Company, Truck Company (RU)
AR .... Nitrogen Equilibrium (RU)
AR .... Repair Service (BU)
ARA .... Accao Revolucionaria Armada [*Armed Revolutionary Action*] [*Portuguese*] (WER)
ARA .... Accion Revolucionaria Agraria [*Agrarian Revolutionary Action*] [*Ecuadorean*] (LA)
ARA .... Accion Revolucionaria Anticommunista [*Anticommunist Revolutionary Action*] [*Argentine*] (LA)
ARA .... Anti-Rightist Alliance (ML)
ARA .... Arab Roads Association (EA)
ARA .... Armed Revolutionary Action (MAR)
ARAAA .... Arusha Regional Amateur Athletics Association (MAR)
arab .... Arabiaa [*or Arabiaksi*] [Finnish]
arab .... Arabialainen [*Finnish*]
arab .... Arabic (BU)
arabsk .... Arabian, Arabic (RU)
arad .... Army Artillery Reconnaissance Battalion (RU)
arae .... Airplane on Artillery Mission (BU)
Aral m .... Aral Sea (RU)
ARAMCO .... Arabian-American Oil Company [*Saudi*] (ME)
ARAN-D ...... Dispatcher's Automatic Active Load Distributor (RU)
ARAN-S ...... Power Plant Automatic Active Load Distributor (RU)
aranzh .... To Arrange [*Music*] (BU)
Aras .... Arastirma [*Research*] (TU)
ARATECO ... Arabian Trading and Equipment Company [*Saudi*] (ME)
ARAVA .... Asuntorakennustuotannon Valtuuskunta [*State Housing Construction Commission*] [*Finnish*] (WEN)
ArAZ .... Aufschlagzuender [*Percussion Fuse*] [*German*]
ARB .... Africa Research Bulletin [*A publication*] (MAR)
ARB .... Air Maintenance Base (BU)
ARB .... Alianza Revolucionaria Barrientista [*Bolivian*] (PPW)
ARb .... Allgemeine Bedingungen fuer Bahnamtliche Rollfuhrbetriebe [*General Terms for Railroad Trucking Enterprises*] (EG)
Arb .... Arbeit [*or Arbeiter*] [*German*]
Arb .... Arbre [*Tree*] [*Military map abbreviation*] [*World War I*] [*French*] (MTD)
ARB .... Motor Vehicle Repair Base (RU)
ARBICA .... Arab Regional Branch of the International Council on Archives (MAR)
ARBSD .... Africa; Rivista Bimestrale di Studi e Documentazione [*Rome*] [*A publication*] (MAR)
ARC .... Action Revolutionnaire Corse [*Corsican Revolutionary Action*] (PD)
ARC .... African Representative Council (MAR)
ARC .... Alexandria Racing Club [*Egypt*] (MAR)
ARC .... Alianza Regional de Castilla y Leon [*Regional Alliance of Castille and Leon*] [*Spanish*] (WER)
ARC .... Antrepriza Romana pentru Constructii [*Romanian Construction Enterprise*] (RO)
ARC .... Autoklub Republiky Ceskoslovenske [*Automobile Club of the Czechoslovak Republic*] (CZ)
ARC .... Automatyczna Regulacja Czestotliwosci [*Automatic Frequency Control*] [*Polish*]
ARC .... Azzawiya Refinery Company [*Libyan*] (MAR)
ARC .... Societe Nationale d'Assurance du Congo (MAR)
ARCA .... Aerovias Colombianas [*Bogota*] (COL)
ARCACI ...... Association des Representants des Compagnies Aeriennes de Cote-d'Ivoire (MAR)
ARCAFA ...... Applied Research Center for Archeology and Fine Arts [*Cambodian*] (CL)
ARCAM .... Assemblee Representative du Cameroun (MAR)
ARCC .... Africa Regional Coordinating Committee (MAR)
ARCCA .... Agricultural Research Council of Central Africa (MAR)
ARCE .... Associazione per le Relazioni Culturali con l'Estero [*Association for Cultural Relations with Foreign Countries*] [*Italian*] (WER)
ARCES .... Armement Cesbron (MAR)
Arch .... Archipielago [*Archipelago*] [*Spanish*] (NAU)
Arch .... Architekt [*German*]
arch .... Architekt [*Architect*] (POL)
arch .... Architekt [*Architect*] (CZ)
Arch .... Archiv [*Archive*] [*German*]
arch .... Archivum [*Archives*] (HU)
ARCh .... Automatic Frequency Control (BU)
ARCh .... Automatic Frequency Control (RU)
ARCh .... Automatic Sensitivity Control (RU)
ARChERANUP ... Automatic Frequency Control and Economical Active Load Distribution Allowing for Network Losses (RU)
ARCHI .... Asociacion de Radiodifusoras de Chile [*Chilean Broadcasting Association*] (LA)
Archip .... Archipelag [*Archipelago*] [*Polish*]
ARChM .... Automatic Frequency and (Active) Power Control (RU)
ARCI .... Associazione Ricreativa Culturale Italiana [*Italian Cultural-Recreational Association*] (WER)
ARCI .... Atelier de Rectification de Cote-d'Ivoire (MAR)
ARCO .... Accion Revolucionaria Campesina y Obrera [*Peasant and Worker Revolutionary Action*] [*Ecuadorean*] (LA)
ARCOA .... Agence de Representation Consignation pour l'Ouest Africain (MAR)
ARCOIN ...... Arquitectura Construcciones. Ingenieria [*Medellin*] (COL)
ARCOM .... Antrepriza Romana de Constructii-Montaj [*Romanian Enterprise for Construction-Assembly*] (RO)
ARCOMA .... Atelier Regional de Construction de Materiel Agricole (MAR)
ARCOPLAN ... Arquitectura Construccion Planeamiento Ingenieria Ltda. [*Cucuta*] (COL)
ARCRAN ..... Agricultural Research Council of Rhodesia and Nyasaland (MAR)
arcybp .... Arcybiskup [*Archbishop*] [*Polish*]
arcyks .... Arcyksiaze [*Archduke*] [*Polish*]
ARD .... Accion Radical Democrata [*Democratic Radical Action*] [*Guatemalan*] (LA)
ARD .... Arbeitsgemeinschaft der Oeffentlichrechtlichen Rundfunkanstalten der Bundesrepublik Deutschland [*Working Association of the Statutory Broadcasting Corporations of the Federal Republic of Germany*] (WEN)
ard .... Artillery Reconnaissance Battalion (RU)
ARD .... Atomic Jet Engine (RU)
ARD .... Automatic Pressure Regulator (RU)
ARDA .... Agricultural and Rural Development Authority [*Rhodesian*] (AF)
ARDC .... Aswan Regional Development Centre (MAR)
ARDCES ..... Arab Regional Documentation Centre for the Economic and Social Sciences [*Proposed*]
ARDD .... Ananeotiki Kinisi Dimokratikon Dikigoron [*Restorative Movement of Democratic Lawyers*] (GC1)
ARDE .... Accion Republicana Democratica Espanola [*Spanish Democratic Republican Action*] (WER)
ARDE .... Alianza Revolucionaria Democratica [*Democratic Revolutionary Alliance*] [*Nicaraguan*] (PD)
ARDECOMAG ... Association Regionale de Developpement de la Cooperation Maritime aux Antilles-Guyane [*Regional Association for Developing Maritime Cooperation in the Antilles-French Guiana*] (LA1)
ARDES .... Accion Revolucionaria de Estudiantes de Secundaria [*Revolutionary Action of Secondary School Students*] [*Salvadoran*] (LA1)
ARDES .... Association pour la Recherche Demographique, Economique, et Sociale [*Algerian*] (MAR)
ARDF .... Association Reunion - Departement Francais (MAR)
ARDG .... Automatic Gas Pressure Regulator (RU)
ARDGT- ...... Automatic Gas Pressure Regulator for Terminal Lines (RU)
ARDIC .... Agence de Representations Directes pour la Defense des Interets Commerciaux (MAR)
ARD-L .... Algierska Republika Demokratyczno-Ludowa [*Algerian People's Democratic Republic*] [*Polish*]
Ardre .... Ardoisiere [*Slate Quarry*] [*Military map abbreviation*] [*World War I*] [*French*] (MTD)
ARDU .... Arussi Rural Development Unit (MAR)
ARE .... Accion Republicana Espanola
are .... Air Radio Squadron (BU)
ARE .... Alianza Revolucionaria Ecuatoriana [*Ecuadorean Revolutionary Alliance*] (LA)
ARE .... Alianza Revolucionaria Estudiantil [*Student Revolutionary Alliance*] [*Peruvian*] (LA)
ARE .... Arab Republic of Egypt (ME)
ARE .... Arabskaia Respublika Egipet (MAR)
ARE .... Army Air Reconnaissance Squadron (RU)
ARE .... United Arab Emirates [*Three-letter standard code*] (CNC)
AREA .... Agrupacion Reformista de Estudiantes de Agricultura [*Agriculture Students Reform Group*] [*Argentine*] (LA)
AREBO .... Association pour le Developpement de la Region de Bonoua [*Bonoua Region Development Association*] [*Ivorian*] (AF)
AREBORG ... Arens et Borgo (MAR)
AREC .... Association des Ressortissants de l'Enclave de Cabinda (MAR)
AREDI-ABIDJAN ... Africaine de Representation et Diffusion Abidjan (MAR)
AREL .... Ingenieros Electricistas [*Medellin*] (COL)
ARELAP ...... Asociacion Regional Latinoamericana de Puertos del Pacifico [*Latin American Regional Association of Pacific Coast Ports*] (LA)
AREMA .... Antoky ny Revolosiona Malagasy [*Vanguard of the Malagasy Revolution*] (PPW)
AREMA .... Avantgarde de la Revolution Malgache [*Vanguard of the Malagasy Revolution*] (PPW)
aremb .... Motor Vehicle Repair Battalion (RU)
AREMG .... Association Regionale d'Expansion Musicale de la Guyane [*Regional Association for Expanding French Guianese Music*] (LA1)
Aremkuz ..... Automobile Body Repair Plant (RU)
AREMZ .... Automobile Repair Plant (RU)
ARENA .... Alianca Renovadora Nacional [*Alliance for National Renewal*] [*Brazilian*] (PPW)
ARENA .... Nationalist Republican Alliance [*Salvadoran*]
ARENCO ..... Architects, Engineers, and Constructors [*Tunisian*] (MAR)
AREP .... Association Reunionnaise d'Education Populaire [*Reunionese Association for Populare Education*] (AF)
AREPRA ...... Asociacion de Rectores de la Ensenanza Privada de la Republica Argentina [*Association of Private School Rectors of the Argentine Republic*] (LA)

ARER.......... Asociatia de Radio Emitatori si Receptori [*Association of Radio Transmitter and Receiver Operators*] (RO)
ARER.......... Automatic Regulator of Electrical Conditions (RU)
ARES.......... Alianza Revolucionaria Estudiantil Socialista [*Socialist Students Revolutionary Alliance*] [*Dominican Republic*] (LA1)
ARESA........ Association pour le Recherche sur l'Energie Solaire en Algerie (MAR)
ARESS........ Association Reunionnaise d'Education Sanitaire et Sociale (MAR)
AREX.......... Partido de Accion Regional Extremena [*Party of Extremaduran Regional Action*] [*Spanish*] (WER)
arf.............. Arfolyam [*Current Price, Rate of Exchange, Quotation*] (HU)
ARF............ Automatic Phase Control (RU)
ARG............ Aethylen-Rohrleitungs-Gesellschaft [*West German*]
ARG............ Africa Research Group (MAR)
ARG............ Argentina [*Three-letter standard code*] (CNC)
arg.............. Arginine (RU)
Ar G............ Arriere Garde [*Rear Guard*] [*French*] (MTD)
ARG............ Artillery Reconnaissance Group (BU)
ARG............ Artillery Reconnaissance Group (RU)
ARG............ Automatic Volume Control (RU)
ARG............ Automatic Volume Regulator (RU)
arg.............. Field Artillery Group (BU)
ARGAS........ Arabian Geophysical and Surveying Company (MAR)
ARGCI......... Agence de Representation Generale en Cote-d'Ivoire (MAR)
Arged.......... Wojewodzkie Przedsiebiorstwo Hurtu Artykulow Gospodarstwa Domowego [*Voivodship Enterprise of the Wholesale Trade in Household Goods*] (POL)
argent......... Argentine, Argentinean (RU)
ARGK.......... Artillery Reserve of the High Command (RU)
ARGMM...... Agence de Representation Generale Manutention Mauritanie (MAR)
Argo............ Argo Sozu [*Argot, Slang*] (TU)
ARH............ Administracao de Recursos Hidricos [*Water Resources Administration*] [*Brazilian*] (LA)
ArhD........... Drzavni Arhiv u Dubrovniku [*State Archives in Dubrovnik*] (YU)
ArheolmS... Arheoloski Muzej u Splitu [*Archaeological Museum in Split*] (YU)
ARHIV......... Arhivatal [*Price Office*] (HU)
ArhivMP...... Arhiv Ministarstva Poljoprivrede [*Archives of the Ministry of Agriculture*] [*Belgrade*] (YU)
ArhZ............ Drzavni Arhiv u Zadru [*State Archives in Zadar*] (YU)
ARI.............. Asociacion de Relaciones Industriales [*Industrial Relations Association*] [*Peruvian*] (LA)
ARIA........... Agentia Romana de Impresariat Artistic [*Romanian Artistic Booking Agency*] (RO)
ARIANA....... Ariana-Afghan Airlines (MAR)
ARIBEV....... Association Reunionnaise Inter-Professionnelle du Betail et des Viandes [*Reunionese Interoccupational Cattle and Meat Association*] (AF)
arifm........... Arithmetic (RU)
ARIL............ Airfield Radio-Testing Laboratory (RU)
ARINFI......... Arab International Finance SA (MAR)
Ar-ls............ Turkiye Muzisyenler Sendikasi [*Turkish Musicians Union*] (TU)
ARITECSA... Arquitectura Ingenieria Tecnica Sanitaria [*Medellin*] (COL)
arithprot...... Arithmos Protokollou [*Registry Number*] (GC)
ARIV-.......... Automatic Radio Anemometer (RU)
ARIV........... Automatic Radio Information Stations of Reservoirs (RU)
arj............... Arjegyzek [*Price List, Catalog*] (HU)
arj............... Arjegyzes [*Price Quotation*] (HU)
ARK............ Aircraft Radio Compass (RU)
ARK............ Anglo-Russian Committee of Unity (RU)
ARK............ Ankara Rotary Kulubu [*Ankara Rotary Club*] (TU)
Ark.............. Arkeoloji [*Archaeology*] (TU)
ark.............. Arkikielta [*Colloquialism*] [*Finnish*]
ark.............. Arkki(a) [*Finnish*]
ark.............. Arkusz [*Sheet of Paper, Signature of a Book*] (POL)
ARK............ Association of Revolutionary Cinematography (RU)
ARK............ Automatic Radio Compass (RU)
ARK............ Ship-Based Arctic Reconnaissance Aircraft (RU)
arkeol.......... Arkeologia [*Archaeology*] [*Finnish*]
arkh............ Archaeological, Archaeology (RU)
arkh............ Archaism (RU)
arkh............ Archipelago (RU)
arkh............ Architect, Architectural, Architecture (RU)
arkh............ Architect, Architecture (BU)
arkh............ Archival (BU)
arkh............ Archival, Archives (RU)
arkhed......... Archival Unit (BU)
arkheol........ Archaeology (BU)
Arkhimpromstroy... Armenian Construction Trust of the Chemical Industry (RU)
arkhit.......... Architect, Architectural (RU)
arkhit.......... Architecture (BU)
Arkhitstroy... Administration of Urban, Rural, and Industrial Construction (RU)
Arkhiv BDZh... Archives of the Bulgarian State Railroads and Ports (BU)
Arkhmorput'... Arkhangel'sk Administration of Sea Routes (RU)
Arkh MRDB... Archives of the Museum of the Revolutionary Movement in Bulgaria (BU)
Arkh NBIV... Archives of the Ivan Vazov National Library (BU)
Arkhoblgiz... Arkhangel'sk Oblast State Publishing House (RU)
Arkhplan..... Architectural Planning Commission (RU)
Arkh PP....... Archives for Settlement Studies (BU)
arkh sb........ Archival Collection (BU)
ArkKand..... Master's Degree in Architecture [*Finnish*]
arkkit.......... Arkkitehtuuri [*Architecture*] [*Finnish*]
arkom.......... Army Commissar (RU)
ar kor.......... Arany Korona [*Gold Crown (Hungarian currency before World War I, still used to estimate real estate values)*] (HU)
arkt............. Arctic (RU)
Arktikstroy... Construction and Installation Trust of the Glavsevmorput' (RU)
arktikugol'... Trust for Coal Mining in the Arctic (RU)
ARL............ Albanska Republika Ludowa [*Albanian People's Republic*] [*Polish*]
Arl.............. Arctic Preheater Lamp (RU)
ARLO.......... Arab Regional Literacy Organization (MAR)
ARLP.......... Alliance Republicaine pour les Libertes et le Progres [*Republican Alliance for Liberties and Progress*] [*French*] (PPE)
ARLS.......... Artillery Radar Station (RU)
ARLUS........ Asociatia Romana pentru Legaturile de Prietenie cu Uniunea Sovietica [*Romanian Association for Ties of Friendship with the Soviet Union*] (RO)
ARM........... African Resistance Movement [*South African*] (PD)
ARM........... Aircraft Repair Shop (RU)
ARM........... Alliance Reformee Mondiale [*World Alliance of Reformed Churches - WARC*] (EA)
arm............ Armenian (RU)
arm............ Army (BU)
arm............ Army (RU)
ARM........... Army Repair Shop (RU)
ARM........... Artillery Repair Shop (RU)
ARM........... Automatic Power Control (RU)
ARM........... Automatic Power Regulator (RU)
ARM........... Automobile Repair Shop (RU)
Arm............ Fittings Plant [*Topography*] (RU)
ARMAPP..... Armavir Association of Proletarian Writers (RU)
ARMASAL... Armadora Maritima Salvadorena, SA [*National Association of Ship-Owners*]
Armatur...... Fittings Plant [*Topography*] (RU)
ARMAVEN.. Armas Venezolanas, CA
Armceta...... Armiska Ceta [*Army Company*] (YU)
ARME.......... Electrical Anemorhumbometer, Anemovane (RU)
ARMED....... Artileri Medan [*Field Artillery*] (IN)
Armelektro... Armenian Electromechanical Plant (RU)
Armenenergo... Armenian Regional Administration of Power System Management (RU)
ARMETAL... Artisans du Metal (MAR)
ArmFAN...... Armenian Branch of the Academy of Sciences, USSR (RU)
armgen....... Armadni General [*Army General*] [*US equivalent: General*] (CZ)
Armgiprotsvetmet... Armenian State Institute for the Planning of Establishments of Nonferrous Metallurgy (RU)
Armgiz........ State Publishing House of Armenia (RU)
Armgosizdat... State Publishing House of the Armenian SSR (RU)
ARMNIIG i M... Armenian Scientific Research Institute of Hydraulic Engineering and Reclamation (RU)
Armniikhimproyekt... Kirovakan Scientific Research and Planning Institute of Chemistry of the Council of the National Economy, Armenian SSR (RU)
ArmNIITK.... Armenian Scientific Research Institute of Industrial Crops (RU)
ArmNIIZ...... Armenian Scientific Research Institute of Agriculture (RU)
ArmNIIZhV... Armenian Scientific Research Institute of Livestock Breeding and Veterinary Science (RU)
armpod....... Army Jurisdiction (BU)
ARMS.......... Automatic Radio Meteorological Station (RU)
ARMSCOR... Armaments Development and Production Corporation (MAR)
Armset'....... State All-Union Trust for the Planning, Production, Supply of Complete Sets, and Marketing of Network Fixtures, Insulators, and Assembly Equipment for the Construction of High-Voltage Transmission Lines and Substations (RU)
ArmSSR...... Armenian Soviet Socialist Republic (RU)
ArmTAG...... Armenian News Agency (RU)
armu........... Army Medical Reinforcement Company (RU)
armuchpedgiz... Armenian State Publishing House of Textbooks and Pedagogical Literature (RU)
ArmVNITOE... Armenian Branch of the All-Union Scientific, Engineering, and Technical Society of Power Engineers (RU)
Armvodkhoz... Administration of Water Management of the Armenian SSR (RU)
armyan........ Armenian (RU)
Armzaktag... Armenian Branch of the Transcaucasian News Agency (RU)
ARN............ Accion Radical Nacionalista [*Nationalist Radical Action*] [*Guatemalan*] (LA)
Arn............. Arnavutcu [*Albanian*] (TU)
ARN............ Automatic Voltage Regulation, Automatic Voltage Regulator (RU)
ARNA.......... Arab Revolution News Agency [*Libyan*] (ME)
ARNAHIS.... Archivo Nacional de Historia [*Ecuadorean*]
ARNE.......... Accion Revolucionaria Nacionalista Ecuatoriana [*Ecuadorean Nationalist Revolutionary Action*] (LA)

ARNI............ Association des Ressortissants du Nord (MAR)
ARnl............ Association of Rhodesian Industries (AF)
aro............ Artillery Battalion (BU)
ARO............ Asian Regional Organization (RU)
ARO............ Assurance, Reassurance, Omnibranches [*Insurance, Reinsurance, Omnibranch*] [*Malagasy*] (AF)
ARO............ Automatic Cutoff Control (RU)
ARO............ Motor Vehicle Repair Section (RU)
AROF............ Association Reunionnaise d'Orientation Familiale (MAR)
ar ogn sk..... Artillery Ammunition Depot (BU)
AROL............ Anexartiti Rizospastiki Organosis Lemesou [*Independent Radical Organization of Limassol*] [*Cypriot*] (GC)
AROMAR..... Asociatia Romana de Marketing [*Romanian Marketing Association*] (RO)
aromatich ... Aromatic (RU)
AROWF....... Association of Retailer-Owned Wholesalers in Foodstuffs [*See also UGAL*] (EA)
ARP............ Agence Rwandaise de Press [*Rwandan Press Agency*] (MAR)
arp............ Air Radio Regiment (BU)
ARP............ Alliance Rurale Progressiste (MAR)
ARP............ Amur River Steamship Line (RU)
ARP............ Anti-Revolutionaire Partij - Evangelische Volkspartij [*Antirevolutionary Party*] [*Dutch*] (PPW)
ARP............ Antirassismus-Programm (MAR)
ar p............ Arany Pengo [*Gold Pengo (Hungarian currency in 1925-45, still used to estimate real estate values)*] (HU)
ARP............ Armee Revolutionnaire Populaire Ougandaise (MAR)
arp............ Artillery Park (BU)
ARP............ Automatic Radio Direction Finder (RU)
ARP............ Emergency Repair Station (RU)
ARPA............ Alianza Revolucionaria Patriotica [*Revolutionary Patriotic Alliance*] [*Venezuelan*] (LA)
ARPA............ Asociacion de Radioemisoras Privadas Argentinas [*Private Radio Stations Association of Argentina*] (LA)
ARPEL......... Associacao de Assistencia Reciproca Petroleira Latino-Americana [*Latin American Petroleum Industry Mutual Aid Association*] (LA)
ARPI............ Atelier de Reproduction de Plans Ivoiriennes (MAR)
ARPPr......... Archives for Settlement Studies (BU)
ARPS............ Aborigines Rights Protection Society (MAR)
ARPS............ Abortion Rights Protection Society (MAR)
Arq............ Arquipelago [*Archipelago*] [*Portuguese*] (NAU)
ARR............ Anno Regni Regis, or Reginae [*In the Year of the King's or Queen's Reign*] [*Latin*]
ARR............ Arab Report and Record (MAR)
Arr............ Arrecife [*Reef*] [*Spanish*] (NAU)
ARR............ Motor Vehicle Repair Company (RU)
ARRENDAVEN ... Arrendadora Industrial Venezolana, CA [*Venezuelan*]
Arr G........... Arriere-Garde [*Rear-Guard*] [*Military*] [*French*] (MTD)
ARRINSA.... Arrendamientos Industriales, Sociedad Anonima [*Industrial Leasings Corporation*] [*Salvadoran*]
ARRK.......... Association of Workers in Revolutionary Cinematography (RU)
ARRO.......... Afro-Asian Rural Reconstruction Organization (EA)
Arro............ Arroyo [*Stream*] [*Spanish*] (NAU)
ARROLIMA ... Arroceros del Tolima y del Huila [*Ibague*] (COL)
ARS............ Accion Revolucionaria Salvadorena [*Salvadoran Revolutionary Action*] (LA1)
ARS............ Accion Revolucionaria Socialista [*Socialist Revolutionary Action*] [*Peruvian*] (PPW)
ARS............ Action Republicaine et Sociale [*Republican and Social Action*] [*French*] (PPE)
ARS............ Air Communications Company (RU)
ARS............ Anodal Opening Contraction (RU)
ARS............ Archives de la Republique du Senegal [*Dakar*] [*A publication*] (MAR)
ARS............ Arrete du Resident Superieur [*Decree of the Resident Superior*] [*Used in historical material*] (CL)
Ars............ Arsiv [*Archive, File*] (TU)
ARS............ Asociacie Rusistov na Slovensku [*Association of Teachers of Russian in Slovakia*] (CZ)
ARS............ Automatic Control Rod [*Nuclear physics and engineering*] (RU)
ARS-............ Automatic Self-Adjusting Regulator (RU)
ARS............ Automatic Speed Control (RU)
ARS............ Gasoline-Filling Station (BU)
ARS-............ Stationary Aerosol Radiometer (RU)
ARS............ Truck-Mounted Spraying Unit (RU)
ARSA.......... Aeroportos de Rio De Janeiro, Sociedade Anonima [*Rio De Janeiro Airports, Incorporated*] [*Brazilian*] (LA)
ARSC.......... Academie Royale des Sciences Coloniales (MAR)
ARSC.......... African Remote Sensing Council (MAR)
ARSC.......... Association Royale Sportive Congolaise [*Congolese Royal Sporting Association*]
ARSCBS..... Academie Royale des Sciences Coloniales. Bulletin des Seances [*Brussels*] [*A publication*] (MAR)
arsh............ Arshin (RU)
Arsl............ Arsenal [*Arsenal*] [*Military map abbreviation*] [*World War I*] [*French*] (MTD)
ARSO.......... African Regional Organization for Standardization (AF)
ARSO.......... Amenagement de la Region du Sud-Ouest (MAR)
ARSO.......... Autorite pour l'Amenagement de la Region du Sud-Ouest [*Southwest Region Development Authority*] [*Ivorian*] (AF)
ARSOM....... Academie Royale des Sciences d'Outre-Mer (MAR)
ARSOM....... Mortar Detection Artillery Station (RU)
ARSOV....... Motor Delivery of Persistent Chemical Agents [*Military term*] (RU)
ARSR.......... Academia Republicii Socialiste Romania [*Academy of the Socialist Republic of Romania*] (RO)
ARSS.......... Antiquariorum Regiae Societatis Socius [*Fellow of the Royal Society of Antiquaries*] [*Latin*] (GPO)
ART............ Agency for Rural Transformation [*Grenadian*] (LA1)
ART............ Anggaran Rumah Tangga [*Bylaws*] (IN)
art............ Artel (RU)
art............ Article [*Article*] [*French*] (GPO)
art............ Articulo [*Article*] [*Spanish*]
Art............ Artikel [*Article*] [*German*] (GPO)
ART............ Artileri [*Artillery*] (IN)
Art............ Artillerie [*Artillery*] [*French*] (MTD)
art............ Artillery (BU)
art............ Artillery (RU)
art............ Artist (RU)
art............ Artykul [*Article, Item*] (POL)
art............ Artysta [*Artist*] [*Polish*]
ART............ Assemblee Representative du Togo (MAR)
ART............ Automatic Fuel Distributor (RU)
ART............ Automatic Temperature Regulator (RU)
ART............ Automobilni Registracny Trenazer [*Automobile Driver Trainer*] (CZ)
ART............ Ordnance Depot (RU)
ART............ Spray Chamber (RU)
ARTA.......... Artillery Radiotechnical Academy (RU)
ARTANES ... Aids and Research Tools in Ancient Near Eastern Studies (MAR)
ART-B......... Ammunition Depot (RU)
artbat.......... Artillery Battery (RU)
art BB.......... Short-Range Artillery (RU)
artbr........... Artillery Brigade (RU)
Art C........... Artillerie de Corps [*Military*] [*French*] (MTD)
ARTCA........ Association of Round Tables of Central Africa (MAR)
artdiv.......... Artillery Battalion (RU)
Art 1 Div...... Artillerie de la Premiere Division [*Military*] [*French*] (MTD)
ARTECOLOMBIA ... Artesanias de Colombia SA [*Bogota*] (COL)
ARTELANA ... Fabrica de Tejidos de Lana [*Bogota*] (COL)
ARTEMETAL ... Industria de Articulos Metalicos [*Bogota*] (COL)
Artemgres ... Artem State Regional Electric Power Plant (RU)
ARTEMIS.... Association de Recherche Technique pour l'Etude de la Mer Interieure Saharienne (MAR)
ARTEP......... Projet Regional Asien de Promotion de l'Emploi [*Asian Regional Project for Employment Promotion*] (CL)
ARTI............ Agricultural Research and Training Institute (MAR)
ARTIA.......... Podnik Zahranicniho Obchodu pro Dovoz a Vyvoz Kulturnich Statku [*Foreign Trade Enterprise for the Import and Export of Cultural Articles*] (CZ)
artill............ Artillery (RU)
artiller......... Artillery (RU)
art k............ Artesian Well [*Topography*] (RU)
artletnab..... Artillery Observer Pilot (RU)
art mal......... Artysta Malarz [*Painter*] [*Polish*]
Artn............ Artesien [*Artesian*] [*Military map abbreviation*] [*World War I*] [*French*] (MTD)
ARTN........... Artillery Observation (RU)
artnpp......... Artillery in Direct Support of Infantry (RU)
arto............ Articulo [*Article*] [*Spanish*]
ARTOC........ Arab European International Trading Company (ME)
ARTOP........ Arakli Toprak ve Gida Sanayii AS [*Arakli Land and Food Industry Corporation*] (TU)
artpod......... Artillery Preparation (RU)
artpp........... Artillery in Support of Infantry (RU)
art rzez........ Artysta Rzezbiarz [*Sculptor*] [*Polish*]
Art T............ Artillerie Territoriale [*Military*] [*French*] (MTD)
ARTU........... Armada Tugas [*Naval Task Force*] (IN)
artuch......... Artillery School (RU)
Artv............ Artillery Observation Tower (RU)
ARTVK........ Automatic Cabin Temperature Control (RU)
ARU............ Asociacion Rural de Uruguay [*Rural Association of Uruguay*] (LA)
ARU............ Association of Urbanist Architects (RU)
ARU............ Automatic Amplification Control (BU)
ARU............ Automatic Control Regulator (RU)
ARU............ Automatic Gain Control (RU)
ARU............ Automatic Level Control (RU)
aruatv.......... Aruatvevo [*Inspector (Standards of quality)*] (HU)
ARUC.......... Atelier de Reparatie Utilaj de Constructie [*Workshop for Repair of Construction Equipment*] (RO)
aruforg........ Aruforgalmi [*Trade (adjective)*] (HU)
ARUG.......... Atelier de Reparatie Utilaj Greu [*Workshop for Repair of Heavy Equipment*] (RO)
ARUGC....... Atelier de Reparatie Utilaj Greu de Constructie [*Workshop for Repair of Heavy Construction Equipment*] (RO)
ARUL........... Arsiv ve Ulastirma Dairesi Genel Mudurlugu [*Archives and Communications Office Directorate General*] [*of Foreign Affairs Ministry*] (TU)

ARUM.......... Atelier de Reparatie Utilaj Minier [*Workshop for Repair of Mining Equipment*] (RO)
arv.............. Arveres [*Auction*] (HU)
Arv.............. Arvoisa [*Esteemed*] [*Finnish*] (GPO)
ARV............. Automatic Excitation Control (RU)
ARV............. Automatic Humidity Regulator (RU)
ARV............. Motor Vehicle Repair Platoon (RU)
ARVB........... Army Maintenance and Recovery Battalion (RU)
ARVGK........ Artillery Reserve of the Supreme Command (RU)
ARVN.......... Armee de la Republique du Viet-Nam [*Army of the Republic of Vietnam*] [*Also, South Vietnamese Army*] (CL)
ARVP........... Automatic Internal Overvoltage Recorder (RU)
ARVR........... Motor Vehicle Repair and Reconstruction Company (RU)
ARW............ Automatyczna Regulacja Wzmocnienta [*Automatic Gain Control*] [*Polish*]
ARW............ Autoreparaturwerkstatt [*Automobile Repair Shop*] (EG)
ARYa........... Automatic Brightness Control (RU)
ARZ............. Aleksandrov Radio Plant (RU)
arz.............. Arzobispo [*Archbishop*] [*Spanish*]
ARZ............. Automatic Load Regulator (RU)
ARZ............. Automobile Repair Plant (RU)
ARZ............. Motor Vehicle Repair Plant (BU)
arzbpo......... Arzobispo [*Archbishop*] [*Spanish*]
ARZhK........ Airfield Liquid Oxygen Storage (RU)
arztl............ Aerztlich [*German*]
AS............... Ackerschlepper [*Field Tractor*] (EG)
AS............... Afrika Spectrum [*Hamburg*] [*A publication*] (MAR)
As............... Agregation de l'Enseignement Superieur [*French*]
AS............... Air Force (BU)
AS............... Aircraft Radio (RU)
AS............... Aircraft Sextant (RU)
as................ Akciova Spolecnost [*Joint-Stock Company*] (CZ)
AS............... Akoustiki Sykhnotis [*Audio Frequency*] (GC)
A/S.............. Aksjeselskap [*Joint-Stock Company*] [*Norwegian*] (GPO)
A/S.............. Aktieselskab [*Joint-Stock Company*] [*Swedish*]
A/S.............. Aktieselskab [*Joint-Stock Company*] [*Danish*] (GPO)
AS............... Alandsk Samling [*Aland Coalition (Party)*] [*Finnish*] (WEN)
AS............... Alianza Sindical [*Trade Union Alliance*] [*Spanish*] (WER)
AS............... Alkan Society (EA)
AS............... Allgemeines Sekretariat [*General Secretariat*] (EG)
AS............... American Samoa [*Two-letter standard code*] [*Postal code*] (CNC)
AS............... Amerika Serikat [*United States*] (IN)
AS............... Ammunition Depot (RU)
AS............... Ampere Stunde [*Ampere-Hour*] [*German*]
AS............... Anexartitos Syndesmos [*Independent Association*] [*Greek*] (GC)
AS............... Angiosarcoma (RU)
AS............... Anno Salutis [*In The Year of Salvation*] [*Latin*]
AS............... Anonim Sirketi [*Corporation, Joint-Stock Company*] (TU)
AS............... Arhijerejski Sabor [*Synod of Bishops*] [*Serbian Eastern Orthodox Church*] (YU)
AS............... Arkhigeion Stratou [*Army Command*] [*Greek*] (GC)
AS............... Armadni Sbor [*Army Corps*] (CZ)
as................ Army Depot (BU)
as................ Arsenal (BU)
AS............... Artillery Supply (RU)
As............... Asagi [*Lower*] (TU)
as................ Asema [*Finnish*]
AS............... Asisten [*Assistant*] (IN)
As............... Asker [*or Askeri*] [*Military*] (TU)
AS............... Asociatia Studenteasca [*Student Association*] (RO)
AS............... Assurances Sociales [*French*]
as................ Asukasta [*Finnish*]
as................ Asunto [*Finnish*]
AS............... Ausbildung und Schulung [*Training and Schooling*] (EG)
AS............... Auslieferungsschein [*Delivery Permit, Certificate of Delivery, Delivery Order*] (EG)
AS............... Austenitic Steel (RU)
AS............... Automatic Synchronization (RU)
AS............... Automatic Welding (RU)
AS............... Aviation (BU)
AS............... Landplane Airfield (RU)
AS............... Selective Lubricating Oil (RU)
ASA............. Absorption Spectral Analysis (RU)
ASA............. Accion Sindical Argentina [*Argentine Trade Union Action*] (LA)
ASA............. Aeropuertos y Servicios Auxiliares [*Airports and Auxiliary Services*] [*Mexican*] (LA)
ASA............. African Students Association [*South African*] (AF)
ASA............. African Studies Association (MAR)
ASA............. Air Ambulance Airfield (RU)
ASA............. Alianza Socialista de Andalucia [*Socialist Alliance of Andalucia*] [*Spanish*] (WER)
ASA............. Anotaton Stratiotikon Arkhigeion [*Higher Military Command*] [*Greek*] (GC)
ASA............. Anotaton Symvoulion Aeroporias [*Supreme Air Force Council*] [*Greek*] (GC)
ASA............. Anotaton Symvoulion Anasyngrotiseos [*Supreme Reconstruction Council*] [*Greek*] (GC)
ASA............. Asociacion Salvadorena de Agricultores [*Salvadoran Association of Farmers*] (LA1)
ASA............. Asociacion Sindical Antioquena [*Medellin*] (COL)
ASA............. Association of Southeast Asia (CL)
ASAC........... Assistance Sociale au Congo (MAR)
ASAC........... Association des Societes d'Assurance au Cameroun (MAR)
ASADEGA... Asociacion de Abastecedores de Ganado Mayor [*Cali*] (COL)
ASAE........... Annales du Service des Antiquites de l'Egypte [*Cairo*] [*A publication*] (MAR)
ASAFED...... Association Africaine d'Education pour le Developpement [*African Association of Education for Development*] (AF)
ASAFOP...... Association des Amis des Forets et des Peches [*Association of Friends of Forests and Fishing*] [*Cambodian*] (CL)
ASAIHL....... Association of Southeast Asia Institutions of Higher Learning (CL)
ASAL........... Asociacion Antioquena de Licenciados [*Medellin*] (COL)
ASALA........ Armenian Secret Army for the Liberation of Armenia [*Turkish*] (PD)
ASALS........ Arid and Semi-Arid Lands (MAR)
ASAM.......... Amicale des Secretaires d'Administration en Service a la Commune de Dakar (MAR)
ASAM.......... Annals of the South African Museum [*Cape Town*] [*A publication*] (MAR)
ASAMACON... Asociacion Antioquena de Constructores [*Medellin*] (COL)
ASAMANI.... Association des Agents de Marques Automobiles du Niger (MAR)
ASANESCA... Association des Anciens Eleves et Eleves de l'Ecole Superieure de Chimie Appliquee [*Association of Alumni and Students of the Higher School of Applied Chemistry*] [*Cambodian*] (CL)
ASANU........ Academic Staff Union of Nigerian Universities (MAR)
ASAO.......... Arbeitsschutzanordnung [*Accident Prevention Order*] (EG)
ASAP........... Akciova Spolecnost pro Automobilovy Prumysl [*Automobile Industry Joint-Stock Company*] (CZ)
ASAP........... All-Student Alliance Party (MAR)
ASAP........... Arab Socialist Action Party (MAR)
ASAP........... Asociacion Salvadorena de Agencias de Publicidad [*Salvadoran Association of Advertising Agencies*] (LA1)
ASAP........... Association d'Anciens Eleves des Peres Jesuites (MAR)
ASAPRA...... Asociacion Americana de Profesionales Aduaneros [*American Association of Professional Customs Employees*] (LA)
ASAPRO..... Association Africaine pour la Promotion de Main-d'Oeuvre [*African Association for Manpower Advancement*] [*French*] (AF)
ASAS.......... Academia de Stiinte Agricole si Silvice [*Academy of Agricultural and Forestry Sciences*] (RO)
ASAS 50...... Angkatan Sasterawan 1950 [*1950 Literature Generation*] (ML)
ASASA........ Action South and Southern Africa (AF)
ASASA........ African Students Association of South Africa (AF)
ASAT........... Arbeitsgemeinschaft Satellitentragersystem [*German*]
ASATA........ Association of Southern Africa Travel Agents (MAR)
ASATOM..... Association pour les Stages et l'Accueil des Techniciens d'Outre-Mer [*Association for the Reception and Instruction of Overseas Technicians*]
ASAUK........ African Studies Association of the United Kingdom (MAR)
ASAWI........ African Studies Association of the West Indies (MAR)
ASB............. Afrikaanse Studentebond [*Afrikaans Students Union*] [*South African*] (AF)
asb.............. Apostilb (RU)
ASB............. Arap Sosyalist Birligi [*Arab Socialist Union*] (TU)
asb.............. Asbestos Concentration Plant [*Topography*] (RU)
asb.............. Asbestos Mine [*Topography*] (RU)
asb.............. Asbestos Opencut Mine [*Topography*] (RU)
asb.............. Asbestos Plant [*Topography*] (RU)
Asb.............. Assubay [*Noncommissioned Officer*] (TU)
ASB............. Ateliers et Scieries de Batalimo (MAR)
asb.............. Motor Ambulance Battalion (BU)
ASB............. Special Libraries Association [*SLA*] (RU)
ASB............. Studio Equipment Unit (RU)
ASBANA..... Asociacion Bananera Nacional [*National Banana Growers Association*] [*Costa Rican*] (LA)
ASBIAPRI.... Asesores de Bibliotecas, Archivos, y Publicaciones [*Medellin*] (COL)
ASBIB......... Association of Special Libraries and Information Bureaus [*ASLIB*] (RU)
ASBL........... Association sans But Lucratif [*Nonprofit Organization*] [*French*] (WER)
ASBOLFI..... Asociacion Boliviana para el Fomento del Intercambio [*Bolivian Trade Development Association*] (LA)
ASBORA..... Asociacion Boliviana de Radiodifusoras [*Bolivian Radio Broadcasting Association*] (LA)
ASBR........... Emergency Bomb Release (RU)
ASBU.......... Arab States Broadcasting Union (MAR)
ASBw.......... Amt fuer die Sicherheit der Bundeswehr [*Office for the Security of the Armed Forces*] [*West German*] (WEN)
ASC............. Academie de Sports de Combats [*Algerian*] (MAR)
ASC............. Adult Studies Centre (MAR)
ASC............. African Settlement Convention (MAR)
ASC............. African Studies Center (MAR)
ASC............. Alexandria Sporting Club [*Egypt*] (MAR)
ASC............. Alianza Socialista de Castilla [*Socialist Alliance of Castille*] [*Spanish*] (WER)
ASC............. Arab Sports Confederation (EA)

ASC............ Arbitrajul de Stat Central [*Central State Arbitration Office*] (RO)
ASC............ Association Sportive Communale [*Algerian*] (MAR)
ASC............ Association Sportive et Culturelle (MAR)
ASCA.......... Association for Scientific Cooperation in Asia [*Association de la Cooperation Scientifique en Asie*] (CL)
ASCANIC.... Asociacion de Caneros de Nicaragua [*Nicaraguan Association of Sugar Producers*] (LA1)
ASCAR........ Centrul de Asistenta a Cardiacilor [*Care Center for Cardiac Patients*] (RO)
ASCATEP... Arab States Centre for Educational Planning and Administration (MAR)
ASCATTECK... Association Camerounaise pour le Transfert des Technologies (MAR)
ASCCOP..... Asociacion Colombiana de Cooperativas [*Bogota*] (COL)
ASCILLANOS... Asociacion de Comerciantes e Industriales de los Llanos Orientales [*Villavicencio*] (COL)
ASCIN......... Asociacion Social Cristiana de Integracion Revolucionaria [*Social Christian Association for Revolutionary Integration*] [*Guatemalan*] (LA)
ASCITRUS... Asociacion de Citricultores [*Citrus Growers Association*] [*Chilean*] (LA)
ASCODOC... Association des Commissionnaires en Douane du Cambodge [*Association of Customs Commissioners in Cambodia*] (CL)
ASCOFAM... Association Mondiale de Lutte Contre la Faim (MAR)
ASCOFAME... Asociacion Colombiana de Facultades de Medicina [*Colombian Medical Schools Association*] (LA)
ASCOIN...... Asociacion Colombiana Indigenista [*Bogota*] (COL)
ASCOLBI.... Asociacion Colombiana de Bibliotecarios [*Bogota*] (COL)
ASCOLCO.. Asociacion Colombiana de Comerciantes [*Bogota*] (COL)
ASCOLPA... Asociacion Colombiana de Cultivadores de Papa [*Bogota*] (COL)
ASCON....... Administrative Staff College of Nigeria (MAR)
ASCONA..... Asociacion Costarricense para la Conservacion de la Naturaleza [*Costa Rican Association of Nature Conservation*] (LA I)
ASCONTRY... Asesoria Contable y Tributaria [*Bogota*] (COL)
ASCOOP..... Association Cooperative [*Cooperative Association*] [*Algerian*] (AF)
ASCOP........ Association Cooperative de Recherches des Hydrocarbures (MAR)
ASCOVE..... Asociacion Colombiana de Veteranos [*Bogota*] (COL)
ASCOVEN... Asociacion de Colombianos en Venezuela [*Association of Colombians in Venezuela*] (LA)
ASCRIA....... African Society for Cultural Relations with Independent Africa [*Guyanese*] (LA)
ASCUN........ Asociacion Colombiana de Universidades [*Colombian Universities Association*] (LA)
ASCWSA.... Association of Scientific Workers of South Africa (MAR)
ASD............ Accao Social Democratica [*Social Democratic Action*] [*Portuguese*] (PPE)
ASD............ Accion Social Democrata [*Social Democratic Action*] [*Spanish*] (WER)
ASD............ Alianza Social Democrata [*Social Democratic Alliance*] [*Dominican Republic*] (LA1)
ASD............ Armadni Stredisko Dukly [*Dukla Army Sports Center*] (CZ)
ASD............ Association des Senegalais Democrates [*Association of Senegalese Democrats*] (AF)
ASD............ Association Suisse de Documentation
ASD............ Automatic Parts Counter (RU)
ASD............ Automatic Range Tracking (RU)
ASD............ Axel Springer Inlandsdienst [*Axel Springer Domestic News Service*] [*West German*] (WEN)
ASD............ Dorogov's Antiseptic Stimulant (RU)
ASDAK........ Anotati Stratiotiki Dioikisis Amynis Kyprou [*Supreme Military Command for Cyprus Defense*] (GC)
ASDAN........ Anotati Stratiotiki Dioikisis Attikis kai Nison [*Supreme Military Command of Attica and the Islands*] (GC)
ASDEN........ Anotera Stratiotiki Dioikisis Esoterikou kai Nison [*Higher Military Command for the Interior and Islands*] (GC)
ASDEP........ Anotaton Symvoulion Dioikiseos Ekpaidevtikou Prosopikou [*Supreme Administrative Council of Teachers*] (GC)
ASDER........ Asociacion Salvadorena de Radiodifusores [*Salvadoran Association of Broadcasters*] (LA1)
ASDES........ Asociacion Medica de Especialistas [*Bogota*] (COL)
ASDF........... Air Self Defense Force (SJT)
ASDI............ Associacao Social Democrata Independente [*Independent Social Democrat Association*] [*Portuguese*] (PPE)
ASDIK......... Adesmevti Syndikalistiki Dimosioypalliliki Kinisi [*Free Civil Servants Trade Union Movement*] (GC1)
ASDINARCO... Asociacion Sindical de Ingenieros y Arquitectos Colombianos [*Bogota*] (COL)
ASDINCO.... Asociacion Industrial de Ingenieros y Arquitectos Colombianos [*Bogota*] (COL)
ASDIS......... Adesmevti Syndikalistiki Dimokratiki Synergasia [*Nonaligned Democratic Trade Union Coalition*] [*Greek*] (GC)
ASDOAS..... Asociacion Odontologica Sindical [*Bogota*] (COL)
ASDT........... Timorese Social Democratic Association [*Indonesian*] (PD)
ASDU.......... Accion Social Democratica Universitaria [*Social Democratic University Action*] [*Spanish*] (WER)
ASDY.......... Anotaton Symvoulion Dimosion Ypiresion [*Supreme Council of Civil Services*] [*Greek*] (GC)
ASDZ........... Avstrijski Splosni Drzavljanski Zakonik [*Austrian General Civil Code*] (YU)
ASE............. Academia de Studii Economice [*Academy of Economic Studies*] (RO)
ASE............. Agence Spatiale Europeenne [*European Space Agency*] [*Use ESA*] [*French*] (WER)
ASE............. Alternative Sources of Energy (MAR)
ASE............. Andikommounistiki Stavroforia Elladas [*Anticommunist Crusade of Greece*] (GC)
ASE............. Anotaton Symvoulion Ergasias [*Supreme Labor Council*] [*Greek*] (GC)
Ase.............. Asile [*Asylum*] [*Military map abbreviation*] [*World War I*] [*French*] (MTD)
ASEA........... Allmanna Svenska Elektriska Aktiebolaget [*Swedish General Electric Corporation*] (WEN)
ASEA........... Anotaton Symvoulion Ethnikis Amynis [*Supreme National Defense Council*] [*Greek*] (GC)
ASEA........... Association pour la Sauvegarde de l'Enfance Africaine (MAR)
ASEACOLK... Association des Eleves et Anciens Eleves du College et du Lycee de Kompong Cham [*College and Lycee Kompong Cham Students and Alumni Association*] [*Cambodian*] (CL)
ASEAED...... Anotati Syndonistiki Epitropi Athlitismou Enoplon Dynameon [*Armed Forces Supreme Coordinating Committee for Sports*] [*Greek*] (GC)
ASEAN........ Association of South East Asian Nations (IN)
ASEAUS...... Association of Southeast Asian University Students (CL)
ASEBANCIAL... Asociacion de Empleados del Banco Comercial Antioqueno [*Medellin*] (COL)
ASEC.......... Association des Stagiaires et Etudiants Comoriens [*Association of Comoro Trainees and Students*] (AF)
ASECNA..... Agence pour la Securite de la Navigation Aerienne en Afrique et Madagascar [*Agency for Air Navigation Safety in Africa and Madagascar*] (AF)
ASECO....... Association d'Etudiants Comoriens [*Association of Comoro Students*] (AF)
ASECOL...... Asesoria Colombiana de Cultivos Tropicales [*Cali*] (COL)
ASECOLDA... Asociacion Colombiana de Companias de Seguros [*Colombian Insurance Companies Association*] (LA)
ASED.......... Andifasistikos Syndesmos Ellinon Dimosiografon [*Antifascist Union of Greek Journalists*] (GC)
ASED.......... Anotaton Symvoulion Enoplon Dynameon [*Supreme Armed Forces Council*] [*Greek*] (GC)
ASEDAMA... Seguros Tequendama SA [*Bogota*] (COL)
ASEDEC..... Asesoria Economica de Colombia [*Bogota*] (COL)
ASEEAI....... Anotati Syndonistiki Epitropi Ethnikon Agonon Ipeirou [*Supreme Coordinating Committee for the National Struggles of Ipeiros*] [*Greek*] (GC)
ASEG.......... Army Clearing Evacuation Hospital (RU)
ASEI............ Automated Epidemiological Information System (BU)
ASEIG......... Asociacion Salvadorena de Empresarius de Industrias Graficas [*Salvadoran Association of Printing Industry Owners*] (LA1)
a-sek........... Ampere-Second (RU)
ASEMOLPRO... Asociacion Nacional de Molineros de Trigo [*Bogota*] (COL)
ASEMUCH... Asociacion Nacional de Empleados Municipales de Chile [*Chilean National Association of Municipal Employees*] (LA)
ASEO.......... Anexartitai Synergazomenai Ergatoypallilikai Organoseis [*Independent Cooperating Employee Organizations*] [*Greek*] (GC)
ASEP........... Agence Senegalaise d'Edition et de Publicite (MAR)
ASEP........... Anotaton Symvoulion Ekpaidevtikou Programmatos [*Supreme Council of the Educational Program*] [*Greek*] (GC)
ASEP........... Asociacion Salvadorena de Ejecutivos de Empresas Privadas [*Salvadoran Association of Executives of Private Corporations*]
ASEP........... Association Sportive d'Entretien Physique (MAR)
ASEPAS...... Association des Exportateurs de Produits Agricoles du Senegal (MAR)
ASEQUA..... Association Senegalaise pour l'Etude du Quaternaire de l'Ouest Africain
ASER........... Asesores de Relaciones Publicas y Publicidad Ltda. [*Bogota*] (COL)
ASERJ......... Association Senegalaise d'Etudes et de Recherches Juridiques (MAR)
ASERP........ Asociacion Salvadorena de Ejecutivos de Relaciones Publicas [*Salvadoran Association of Public Relations Executives*] (LA1)
ASES........... Agency for the Economic Development of Somalia [*Italian*] (MAR)
ASES........... Asociacion Salvadorena de Empresas de Seguros [*Salvadoran Association of Insurance Companies*] (LA1)
ASETA........ Asociacion de Empresas de Telecomunicaciones Estatales Andinos [*Association of Andean State Telecommunications Enterprises*] (LA)
ASETEPEXPORT... Asociacion de Exportadores y Tecnicos en Promocion de Exportaciones [*Association of Exporters and Specialists for the Promotion of Exports*] [*Bolivian*] (LA)

ASEV .... Anangastikos Synetairismos Engeion Veltioseon [*Emergency Association of Land Reclamation*] [*Plus the initial letter of the district in which located*] [*Greek*] (GC)
ASEVALLE ... Aseguradora del Valle [*Cali*] (COL)
ASEVENTAS ... Asesoria y Ventas de Colombia [*Cali*] (COL)
ASEVIK .... Association des Etudes du Vieux Khmer [*Ancient Cambodian Studies Association*] [*Also, Samakom Niek Seksa Pheasa Khmer Boran*] (CL)
ASEWA .... Application of Sciences in Examination of Works of Art (MAR)
ASF .... Arab Sugar Federation (EA)
ASF .... Asfaleia [*Security*] [*Athens General Security Subdirectorate*] (GC)
asf .... Asphalt (RU)
asf .... Asphalt Plant [*Topography*] (RU)
ASFA .... Association pour la Solidarite Franco-Algerienne [*Association for Franco-Algerian Solidarity*] [*French*] (AF)
ASFA .... Association pour la Solidarite Franco-Arabe (MAR)
ASFAC .... Association Syndicale des Fonctionnaires et Agents du Cameroun (MAR)
ASFACO ..... Asociacion de Fabricantes de Conservas [*Canners Association*] [*Chilean*] (LA)
ASFEC .... Arab States Fundamental Education Centre (MAR)
ASFINCO .... Asociacion Financiadora Comercial [*Commercial Financing Association*] [*Chilean*] (LA)
ASFNRJ ...... Akademski Savet Federativne Narodne Republike Jugoslavije [*Academic Council of the Federal People's Republic of Yugoslavia*] (YU)
ASFO .... Association Sportive des Fonctionnaires (MAR)
ASFO .... Truck Superfilter with Sedimentation Trap (RU)
ASFOMENTO ... Asociacion de Fomento Comercial Ltda. [*Bogota*] (COL)
ASG .... Acetylsulfanilguanidine (RU)
ASG .... Akademia Sztabu Generalnego [*General Staff Academy*] (POL)
ASG .... Alekseyevskiy Student Settlement (RU)
ASG .... Armeesportgemeinschaft [*Army Sports Association*] (EG)
ASG .... Army Fuel Depot (RU)
ASG .... Ausruestungen fuer Schwerindustrie und Geraetebau (VVB) [*Equipment for Heavy Industry and Equipment Construction (VVB)*] (EG)
ASGA .... Association des Services Geologiques Africains [*Association of African Geological Services*] [*Use AAGS*] (AF)
ASGAZ .... Anadolu Sinai Gazlar Anonim Sirketi [*Anatolian Industrial Gases Corp.*] [*Izmit*] (TU)
ASGME .... Anotati Synomospondia Goneon Mathiton Ellados [*Supreme Confederation of Parents of Students of Greece*] (GC)
ASh .... Aircraft Engine Designed by A. D. Shvetsov (RU)
ASh .... Anthracite Dust (RU)
ASH .... Armadni Sportovni Hry [*Armed Forces Athletic Games*] (CZ)
ASh .... Collapsible-Whip Antenna (RU)
ASh .... Hinged Arch Support [*Mining*] (RU)
AShch .... Antenna Panel (RU)
AShchP ...... Instrument Switchboard (RU)
Ashges .... Ashkhabad Hydroelectric Power Plant (RU)
AShK .... Automatic Wrench (RU)
AShKhB ...... Ashkhabad Railroad (RU)
AShO .... Aviation School of the Osoaviakhim (RU)
AShP .... Afro-Shirazskaia Partiia [*Afro-Shirazi Party*] [*Tanzanian*] (MAR)
AShS .... Aerial Navigator's Handbook (RU)
ASI .... Agregation de l'Enseignement Secondaire Inferieur [*French*]
ASI .... Air Service Ivoirien (MAR)
ASI .... Asociacion de Sectores Industriales [*Industrial Sectors Association*] [*Salvadoran*] (LA)
ASI .... Pulse-Height Selector (RU)
ASiA .... Academy of Construction and Architecture (RU)
ASIA .... Airlines Staff International Association (EA)
ASIA .... Asociacion de Antiguos Alumnos de la Compania de Jesus [*Cali*] (COL)
ASIA .... Asociacion Salvadorena de Ingenieros y Arquitectos [*Salvadoran Association of Engineers and Architects*] (LA1)
ASIC .... Association Scientifique Internationale du Cafe [*International Scientific Association of Coffee*] (EA)
ASICH .... Asociacion Sindical de Chile [*Chilean Trade Union Association*] (LA)
ASICOL ...... Asociacion de Ingenieros Contratistas Ltda. [*Medellin*] (COL)
ASIDUOS .... Asociacion de Ingenieros de la Universidad Industrial de Santander [*Bucaramanga*] (COL)
ASIFA .... Association Internationale du Film d'Animation [*International Animated Film Association*] (EA)
ASILAC .... Asociacion de Industrias Lacteas [*Association of Dairy Industries*] [*Chilean*] (LA)
ASIMAD ...... Asociacion de Industriales Madereros [*Lumber Manufacturers Association*] [*Chilean*] (LA)
ASIMCOL .... Asociaciones de Impresores de Colombia [*Cali*] (COL)
ASIMET .... Asociacion de Industriales Metalurgicos [*Metallurgical Manufacturers Association*] [*Chilean*] (LA)
ASIN .... Accion de Sistemas de Informacion Nacional [*National Information Systems Activity*] [*Venezuelan*] (LA1)
ASIN .... Accion de Sistemas Informativos Oficiales [*Official Media Systems Action*] (LA)
ASINCAL .... Asociacion de Industriales de Calzado de Chile [*Chilean Association of Shoe Manufacturers*] (LA)
ASIO .... Australian Security Intelligence Organization (PD)
ASIP .... Agriculture Sector Implementation Project (MAR)
ASIP .... Asociatia Sindicala a Industriei Pielei [*Trade Union Association of the Leather Industry*] (RO)
ASIPA .... Asociacion Interamericana de la Propiedad Industrial [*Inter-American Association of Industrial Property - IAAIP*] (EA)
ASIS .... Agac Esya Iscileri Sendikasi [*Wood Products Workers Union*] (TU)
AS-IS .... Agac Sanayii Iscileri Birligi [*Wood Industry Workers Union*] (TU)
Asis .... Asistan [*Assistant*] (TU)
ASIS .... Socialist Art Association (RU)
asist .... Assistant (BU)
ASIT .... Asociatia Stiintifica a Inginerilor si Tehnicienilor [*Scientific Association of Engineers and Technicians*] (RO)
ASIVA .... Asociacion de Industriales de Valparaiso y Aconcagua [*Valparaiso and Aconcagua Manufacturers Association*] [*Chilean*] (LA)
Aslz .... Askeri Inzibat [*Military Police*] [*Turkish Cypriot*] (GC)
ASJ .... AB Svenska Jarnvagsverkstaderna [*Swedish Railroad Workshops*] (WEN)
ASJ .... Accion Social Juvenil [*Youth Social Action*] [*Costa Rican*] (LA)
ASJ .... Alianca Socialista de Juventude [*Socialist Youth Alliance*] [*Portuguese*] (PPE)
ASJL .... Association for the Study of Jewish Languages (EA)
ASJU .... African Sports Journalists Union (MAR)
ASK .... Adana Sinema Kultur Dernegi [*Adana Cinema Cultural Association*] (TU)
ASK .... Agricultural Society of Kenya (MAR)
ASK .... Anotati Skholi Kinimatografon [*Supreme Cinematographers' School*] [*Greek*] (GC)
ASK .... Anotaton Symvoulion Kriseos [*Supreme Rating Council*] (GC1)
ASK .... Antiimperialistische Solidaritaetskomitee fuer Afrikan, Asien, und Lateinamerika (MAR)
ASK .... Arbeitsschutzkommission [*Accident Prevention Commission*] (EG)
ASK .... Armee-Sport-Klub [*Army Sport Club*] (EG)
ASK .... Army Sports Club (RU)
Ask .... Asker [*or Askeri*] [*Soldier or Military*] (TU)
ASK- .... Reinforced Graded Bit (RU)
ASK .... Studio Equipment Complex (RU)
ASKA .... Association Khmere des Agences de Voyage et de Tourisme [*Cambodian Association of Travel and Tourism Agencies*] (CL)
ASKDF .... Amator Spor Kulupleri Dernegi Federasyonu [*Federation of Amateur Sports Clubs Associations*] (TU)
ASKF .... Amator Spor Kulupleri Federasyonu [*Federation of Amateur Sports Clubs*] (TU)
ASKhI .... Azerbaydzhan Agricultural Institute (RU)
ASKhN .... Academy of Agricultural Sciences (RU)
ASKT .... Anotati Skholi Kalon Tekhnon [*Supreme Fine Arts School*] [*Greek*] (GC)
ASKZ .... Automatic Cathodic Protection Unit (RU)
ASL .... Antistreptolysin (RU)
asl .... Transfer Machine (RU)
ASLA .... Amerikan Suomen Lainan Apurahat [*American Finnish Loan Scholarships*] (WEN)
ASLAT .... Association Senegalaise de Lutte Antituberculeuse (MAR)
ASLIB .... Association of Special Libraries and Information Bureaus [*United Kingdom*]
ASLS .... Association for Scottish Literary Studies (EA)
ASLS .... Associazione Sindacati Lavoratore della Somalia [*Workers' Trade Union Association of Somalia*]
ASM .... Academia de Stiinte Medicale [*Academy of Medical Sciences*] (RO)
ASM .... Activated Finely Porous Silica Gel (RU)
ASM .... African Service Medal (MAR)
ASM .... African Student Movement (MAR)
ASM .... Agregation de l'Enseignement Secondaire Moyen [*French*]
ASM .... American Samoa [*Three-letter standard code*] (CNC)
ASM .... Antisousmarine [*Antisubmarine*] [*French*] (WER)
ASM .... Asmara Airport (MAR)
ASM .... Avenir Sportif de la Marsa [*Tunisian*] (MAR)
ASM .... Modern Music Association (RU)
ASMAE .... Anotati Synomospondia Mikroidioktiton Avtokiniton Ellados [*Supreme Confederation of Small Vehicle Owners of Greece*] (GC)
As Mah .... Askeri Mahkeme [*Military Court, Tribunal*] (TU)
ASMAI .... Archivio Storico dell'ex Ministero dell'Africa Italiana (MAR)
ASMAR .... Astilleros y Maestranzas de la Armada [*Naval Docks and Yards*] [*Chilean*] (LA)
ASMAS .... Asbest Madencilik ve Sanayi Anonim Sirketi [*Asbestos Mining and Industry Corporation*] (TU)
ASMEDAS ... Asociacion Medica Sindical Colombiana [*Colombian Medical Union Association*] (LA)
ASMEDICA ... Asociacion Medica Odontologica [*Bogota*] (COL)
ASMIPAC .... Association des Importateurs de Pneumatiques et d'Articles en Caoutchouc Manufacture [*Moroccan*] (MAR)
ASMO .... Arab Organisation for Standardisation and Metrology (MAR)

ASMW .... Amt fuer Standardisierung Messwesen und Warenpruefung [*Standardization, Measurement, and Commodity Testing Office*] (EG)
ASN .... Agencia de Seguridad Nacional [*National Security Agency*] [*Costa Rican*] (LA)
ASN .... Association des Sourds du Niger (MAR)
ASNC .... Alexandria Shipping and Navigation Company (MAR)
ASNLH .... Association for the Study of Negro Life and History (MAR)
ASNM .... Archiv Slovenskeho Narodneho Muzea [*Archives of the Slovak National Museum*] (CZ)
ASNOCh ..... Anti-Fascist Assembly of People's Liberation of Montenegro (RU)
ASNOM .... Anti-Fascist Assembly of People's Liberation of Macedonia (RU)
ASNOM .... Antifasisticko Sobranie na Narodnoto Osloboduvanje na Makedonija [*Anti-Fascist Assembly of National Liberation of Macedonia*] (YU)
ASNOS .... Anti-Fascist Assembly of People's Liberation of Serbia (RU)
ASNOS .... Antifasisticka Skupstina Narodnog Oslobodenja Srbije [*Anti-Fascist Assembly of National Liberation of Serbia*] (YU)
ASNOVA ..... Association of Modern Architects [*1923-1932*] (RU)
ASNP .... Agricultural Societ'' of Nigeria. Proceedings [*Nsukka*] [*A publication*] (MAR)
ASNU .... Association Senegalaise pour les Nations-Unies (MAR)
ASO .... Alianza Sindical Obrera [*Workers Trade Union Alliance*] [*Spanish*] (WER)
ASO .... Anexartiti Sosialistiki Omada [*Independent Socialist Group*] (GC)
ASO .... Ankara Sanayi Odasi [*Ankara Chamber of Industry*] (TU)
ASO .... Arab Socialist Organization [*Egyptian*] (ME)
ASO .... Automatic Target Range Equipment (RU)
ASO .... Automobile Service Station (RU)
ASO .... Avtonomos Stafidikos Organismos [*Autonomous Currant Organization*] [*Greek*] (GC)
ASO .... Breakdown Rescue Department (BU)
ASOB .... Asociacion Salvadorena de Oficiales Bancarios [*Salvadoran Association of Banking Officials*] (LA1)
ASOBANC ... Asociacion Bancaria [*Bankers Association*] [*Colombian*] (LA)
ASOBANCARIA ... Asociacion Bancaria de Colombia [*Colombian Banking Association*] (COL)
ASOCAJAS ... Asociacion Nacional de Cajas de Compensacion Familiar [*National Association of Family Compensation Funds*] [*Colombian*] (LA)
ASOCAL ..... Asociacion de Oficinistas de Cali (COL)
ASOCANA ... Asociacion de Cultivadores de Cana de Azucar de Colombia [*Colombian Sugar Growers Association*] (LA)
ASOCAR ..... Asociacion Colombiana de Carreteras [*Bogota*] (COL)
ASOCHOIN ... Asociacion de Choferes Independientes [*Association of Independent Drivers*] [*Dominican Republic*] (LA1)
ASOCO .... Asociacion Colombiana de Criadores de Ganado Ovino [*Bogota*] (COL)
ASOCOPI .... Asociacion Colombiana de Profesores de Ingles. Universidad del Valle [*Cali*] (COL)
ASOCRENAL ... Asesoria de Credito Nacional Ltda. [*Cali*] (COL)
ASODAS ..... Asociacion Odontologica Sindical (COL)
ASODIRVALL ... Asociaciones de Directores de Droguerias del Valle del Cauca [*Cali*] (COL)
ASOEE .... Anotati Skholi Oikonomikon kai Emborikon Epistimon [*Supreme School of Economic and Commercial Sciences*] [*Greek*] (GC)
ASOELVA ... Asociacion de Electricistas del Valle [*Cali*] (COL)
ASOEXPORT ... Asociacion Nacional de Exportadores de Cafe [*National Association of Coffee Exporters*] [*Colombian*] (LA1)
ASOFARCO ... Asociacion Farmaceutica de Colombia [*Bogota*] (COL)
ASOFER ...... Asociacion Colombiana de Ferreteros [*Bogota*] (COL)
ASOMAR ..... Asociacion de Marineros Profesionales [*Barranquilla*] (COL)
ASOMAR ..... Asociacion de Marinos de Colombia [*Colombian Seamen's Association*] (LA)
ASOMEVA ... Asociacion de Medicos del Valle [*Cali*] (COL)
ASOMHOCOL ... Asociacion Medica Homeopata Colombiana [*Bogota*] (COL)
ASONADI .... Asociacion Nacional de Inhabilitados [*Cali*] (COL)
ASONAV ..... Asociacion Nacional de Agentes Navieros [*Bogota*] (COL)
ASOO .... Anotati Skholi Oikiakis Oikonomias [*Supreme Home Economics School*] [*Name of location usually follows name of school*] [*Greek*] (GC)
ASOPEF ...... Athinaikos Syllogos Oikogeneion Politikon Exoriston kai Fylakismenon [*Athenian Association of Families of Political Exiles and Prisoners*] (GC)
ASOQUIM ... Asociacion de Fabricantes de Productos Quimicos [*Association of Chemical Manufacturers*] [*Venezuelan*] (LA)
ASOR .... Automated System of Work Organization (RU)
ASOSCOL ... Asociacion de Simpatizantes de la Orquesta Sinfonica de Colombia [*Bogota*] (COL)
ASOTA .... Association pour le Soutien du Khet Takeo [*Association to Support Takeo Province*] [*Cambodian*] (CL)
ASOTRANCOL ... Asociacion de Transportadores de Colombia [*Colombian Transport Workers Association*] (LA)
ASOTRANSCOL ... Asociacion de Transportadores de Colombia [*Colombian Transport Workers Association*] (COL)
ASOVA .... Asociacion de Odontologos del Valle [*Cali*] (COL)
ASOVAC ..... Asociacion Venezolana para el Avance de la Ciencia [*Venezuelan Association for the Advancement of Science*] (LA)
ASOVIARO ... Asociacion de Agentes Viajeros de Occidente [*Cali*] (COL)
ASP .... Accao Socialista Portugues [*Portuguese Socialist Action*] (PPE)
ASP .... Accepte sans Protet [*Accepted without Protest*] [*Business and trade*] [*French*]
ASP .... Accion Sindical Panamena [*Panamanian Trade Union Action*] (LA)
ASP .... Accion Social Patronal [*Employers Social Welfare Association*] [*Spanish*] (WER)
ASP .... African Studies Program (MAR)
ASP .... Afro-Shirazi Party [*Tanzanian*] (AF)
ASP .... Akademia Sztuk Pieknych [*Academy of Fine Arts (1950-1957)*] (POL)
ASP .... Akademia Sztuk Plastycznych [*Academy of Plastic Arts*] (POL)
ASP .... Akcja Sanitarno-Porzadkowa [*Cleaning and Sanitation Drive*] (POL)
ASP .... Alianza Socialista Popular [*Popular Socialist Alliance*] [*Venezuelan*] (LA)
ASP .... Anotati Skholi Polemou [*Superior War School (Army)*] (GC1)
ASP .... Arab Socialist Party [*Egyptian*] (PPW)
ASP .... Arab Socialist Party [*Al Hizb al Ishtiraki al Arabi*] [*Syrian*] (PPW)
ASP .... Artillery Signal Post (RU)
asp .... Aspartic Acid (RU)
Asp .... Aspirant [*Officer Cadet (Recently candidate for a degree)*] (CZ)
ASP .... Assistant Superintendent of Police (MAR)
ASP .... Autonomous Economic Enterprise (BU)
asp .... Motor Ambulance Regiment (BU)
ASP .... Panel Station [*Aviation*] (RU)
ASP- .... Truck-Drawn Dump Trailer (RU)
ASPA .... Accion Social Patriotica [*Patriotic Social Action*] [*Colombian*] (LA)
ASPA .... Astikai Syngoinoniai Periokhis Athinon [*Athens Area Urban Communications*] (GC)
ASPAC .... Asian and Pacific Council (ML)
ASPAEN ...... Asociacion para la Ensenanza [*Bogota*] (COL)
ASPAL .... Association pour la Promotion des Artistes Lao [*Association for the Promotion of Lao Artists*] (CL)
ASPAM .... Association des Producteurs d'Agrumes du Maroc [*Association of Citrus Growers of Morocco*] (AF)
ASPAS .... Asociacion Sindical de Pilotos Aviadores Salvadorenos [*Union Association of Salvadoran Airline Pilots*] (LA)
ASPAU .... African Scholarship Program of American Universities (MAR)
ASPB .... Archiv Svazu Protifasistickych Bojovniku [*Archives of the Union of Fighters of Fascism*] (CZ)
ASPC .... Academie des Sciences, Paris, Comptes Rendus [*A publication*] (MAR)
ASPE .... Anotati Synomospondia Polemiston Ellados [*Supreme Confederation of Combatants of Greece*] (GC)
ASPE .... Association Professionnelle de l'Enseignement du Second Degre [*Algerian*] (MAR)
ASPES .... Association du Personnel de l'Enseignement Secondaire (Enseignants Francais du Maroc) [*North African*] (MAR)
ASPESCA ... Asociacion Colombiana de Pescadores [*Bogota*] (COL)
ASPIDA .... Axiomatikoi, Sosate Patrida, Idanika Dimokratias kai Axiokratia [*Officers, Save Fatherland, Ideals of Democracy, and Meritocracy*] [*Greek*] (GC)
aspir .... Aspirant (RU)
ASPL .... Arastirma ve Siyaset Planlama Dairesi Genl Mudurlugu [*Research and Political Planning Office Directorate General*] [*of Foreign Affairs Ministry*] (TU)
ASPRI .... Asisten Pribadi [*Personal Aide*] (IN)
ASPROCO ... Asesores, Proyectistas, Constructores [*Bogota*] (COL)
ASPROMEDICA ... Asociacion de Practica Medica de Grupo [*Cali*] (COL)
ASPS .... African Succulent Plant Society (MAR)
ASPS .... Azerbaydzhan Trade-Union Council (RU)
ASPTE .... Anotati Synomospondia Polemiston-Travmation Ellados [*Supreme Confederation of Wounded Combatants of Greece*] (GC)
ASPTT .... Association Sportive des Postes, Telegraphe, et Telephone (MAR)
ASPU .... Asociacion Sindical de Profesores Universitarios [*University Professors Association*] (COL)
ASPUV .... Asociacion de Profesores de la Universidad del Valle [*Cali*] (COL)
ASPYL .... Afro-Shirazi Party Youth League [*Tanzanian*] (MAR)
ASR .... Army Medical Company (RU)
asr .... Motor Ambulance Company (BU)
ASR .... Motorized Medical Company (RU)
ASRA .... Asociacion de Bacteriologos (COL)
ASRI .... Academy of Sciences Research Institute (MAR)
ASRI .... Akademi Seni Rupa Indonesia
ASRR .... Autonomiczna Socjalistyczna Republika Radziecka [*Autonomous Soviet Socialist Republic*] [*Polish*]
ASS .... African Supply Service (MAR)
ASS .... Agregation de l'Enseignement Secondaire Superieur [*French*]
ASS .... Air-Launched Cruise Missile (RU)

ASS............ Akademicke Spevacke Sdruzenie [*Student Choral Society*] (CZ)
ASS............ Akateeminen Sosialistiseura [*Academic Socialist Society*] [*Finnish*] (WEN)
ASS............ Analytic Self-Adjusting System (RU)
ASS............ Anotaton Stratiotikon Symvoulion [*Supreme Military Council*] [*Greek*] (GC)
ASS............ Anotaton Syndonistikon Symvoulion [*Supreme Coordination Council*] [*Greek*] (GC)
ASS............ Arabskii Sotsialisticheskii Soiuz (MAR)
ASS............ Asociatia Stiintifica de Studenti [*Scientific Association of Students*] (RO)
Ass............ Assistent [*German*]
ASS............ Association Sportive de Sale [*Moroccan*] (MAR)
ASS............ Avionska Signalna Stanica [*Airplane Signal Station*] [*Military*] (YU)
ASS............ Emergency Rescue Service [*Military term*] (RU)
A'SS........... Proton Soma Stratou [*First Army Corps*] [*Greek*] (GC)
ASSA.......... Adjontes Sanitaires et Sociales Auxiliaires [*Algerian*] (MAR)
ASSA.......... Astronomical Society of South Africa (MAR)
ASSABAF... Association pour l'Africanisation de la Culture Bananiere et Fruitiere (MAR)
ASSAM....... Association des Anciens Militaires et Auxiliaires Militaires [*Association of Veterans and Military Auxiliaries*] [*Cambodian*] (CL)
ASSANEF... Association des Anciens Eleves des Ecoles des Freres Chretiennes [*Association of Former Students of Catholic Schools*]
ASSB........... Anti-Secret Society Branch (ML)
Assce.......... Assurance [*Insurance*] [*Business and trade*] [*French*]
ASSCI......... Association des Scientifiques de Cote-d'Ivoire (MAR)
ASSE........... Administracion de los Seguros Sociales por Enfermedad [*Social Security Health Benefits Administration*] [*Uruguayan*] (LA)
ASSE........... Anotati Synomospondia Syndaxioukhon Ellados [*Supreme Confederation of Pensioners of Greece*] (GC)
ASSE........... Association Suisse des Syndicats Evangeliques [*Swiss Federation of Protestant Trade Unions*]
asse............ Assurance [*French*]
ASSEA........ Association Senegalaise pour la Sauvegarde de l'Enfance et de l'Adolescence (MAR)
ASSEBA...... Association des Etudiants Bahutu (MAR)
ASSECA..... Association for the Educational and Cultural Advancement of Africans [*South African*] (AF)
ASSEDIC.... Association pour l'Emploi dans l'Industrie et le Commerce [*Association for Promotion of Employment in Industry and Business*] [*French*] (WER)
ASSEDIT..... Association des Etudiants de l'Institut de Technologie Tertiaire (MAR)
ASSEKAT... Association des Entreprises du Katanga (MAR)
As-Sen........ Kibris Turk Askeri Mustahdemler Sendikasi [*Turkish Cypriot Military Employees' Union*] [*See also KTAMS*] (TU)
ass extr....... Assemblee Extraordinaire [*French*]
ASSF........... Arbetarnas och Smabrukarnas Socialdemokratiska Foerbund [*Social Democratic League of Workers and Smallholders*] [*Finnish*] (PPE)
ASSGME..... Anotati Synomospondia Syllogon Goneon Mathiton Ellados [*Supreme Confederation of Associations of Parents of Students of Greece*] (GC)
ASSh........... Automatic Glass Ball Machine (RU)
ASSINEZ..... Association pour l'Industrialisation du Nord-Est du Zaire [*Association for the Industrialization of Northeastern Zaire*] (AF)
ASSINSEL.. Association Internationale des Selectioneurs pour la Protection des Obtentions Vegetales [*International Association of Plant Breeders for the Protection of Plant Varieties*] (EA)
ASSIPORT... Association des Interets Portuaires
assist.......... Assistant (RU)
ASSNAT...... All-Union Association of Naturalists (RU)
ASSOBANCA... Associazione Bancaria Italiana [*Italian Bankers' Association*] (WER)
ASSOBELA... Association des Batetela de Lodja [*Association of Batetelas of Lodja*]
ASSOCOM... Association of Chambers of Commerce of South Africa (MAR)
ASSOFECAM... Association pour l'Emancipation de la Femme Camerounaise [*Association for the Emancipation of Cameroonian Women*]
ASSOLOMBARDA... Associazione Industriale Lombarda [*Lombardy Manufacturers' Association*] [*Italian*] (WER)
ASSOMIZO... Association Mutuelle des Ressortissants de Zombo (MAR)
ASSOMUBA... Association de Secours Mutuel de la Jeunesse Bantandu (MAR)
ASSORECO... Association des Ressortissants du Haut-Congo (MAR)
ASSOSIRACI... Association des Sinistres et Repatries de Cote-d'Ivoire [*Association of the Wounded and Repatriates of the Ivory Coast*]
assots......... Association (RU)
ASSOURMUVOIX... Association pour le Sourds-Muets et Mutiles de la Voix (MAR)
ASSP........... Academia de Stiinte Sociale si Politice [*Academy of Social and Political Sciences*] (RO)
ASSR........... Adzhar Autonomous Soviet Socialist Republic (RU)
ASSR........... Autonomna Sovjetska Socijalisticka Republika [*Autonomous Soviet Socialist Republic*] (YU)
ASSR........... Autonomni Sovetska Socialisticka Republika [*Autonomous Soviet Socialist Republic*] (CZ)
ASSR........... Autonomous Soviet Socialist Republic (RU)
ASSR........... Azerbaydzhan Soviet Socialist Republic (RU)
ASSRNP...... German Volga Autonomous Soviet Socialist Republic (RU)
ASST........... Azienda di Stato per i Servizi Telefonici [*National Telephones State Board*] [*Italian*] (WER)
ASSU.......... Association Sportive Scolaire et Universitaire [*Algerian*] (MAR)
AST............ Accion Sindical de Trabajadores [*Workers' Trade Union Action*] [*Spanish*] (WER)
AST............ Action Sociale Tchadienne (MAR)
AST............ Aerogeophysical Station (RU)
AST............ Ankara Sanat Tiyatrosu [*Ankara Theatre of Art*] (TU)
AST............ Armadni Soutez Tvorivosti [*Armed Forces Creative Activities Contest*] (CZ)
AST............ Artillery Stereoscopic Telescope (RU)
AST............ Asociatia Stiintifica de Tehnicieni [*Scientific Association of Technicians*] (RO)
AS-T........... Aspartic-Glutamic Transaminase (RU)
Ast............. Astronomi [*Astronomy*] (TU)
AST............ Aufgabenstellung (Bau) [*Project Specifications (Construction)*] (EG)
AST............ Aviation Standard (RU)
AST............ Self-Hardening Acrylate (RU)
AST............ Tank-Accompanying Artillery (RU)
AStA........... Allgemeiner Studentenausschuss [*General Student Committee (of a university)*] [*West German*] (WEN)
ASTA........... Astatic Ammeter (RU)
ASTALCO... Asociacion Colombiana de Criadores de Reses de Lidia (COL)
ASTARSA... Astilleros Argentinos Rio De La Plata, Sociedad Anonima [*Argentine River Plate Shipyards, Incorporated*] (LA)
ASTAS......... Azot Sanayii Turk Anonim Sirketi [*Turkish Nitrogen Industry Corporation*] (TU)
ASTC.......... Asociacion Sandinista de Trabajadores de la Cultura [*Sandinist Association of Cultural Workers*] [*Nicaraguan*] (LA1)
ASTECO..... Asociacion Tecnico Comercial [*Medellin*] (COL)
ASTEF......... Association pour l'Organisation des Stages de Techniciens Etrangers dans l'Industrie Francaise (MAR)
ASTELBO.... Asociacion de Tecnicos Electricitas de Bogota (COL)
ASTENG...... Asia Tenggara [*Southeast Asia*] (IN)
Aster-Is....... Askeri Tersane ve Askeri Isyerleri Sendikasi [*Military Shipyard and Military Installation Workers' Union*] (TU)
ASTI............ Arbetsstudietekniska Institutet [*Swedish*]
ASTI............ Armement Sardinier Thonier Ivoirien (MAR)
ASTI............ Association Suisse des Traducteurs et Interpretes [*Swiss Association of Translators and Interpreters*]
ASTINAVE... Astilleros Venezolanos, SA [*Venezuelan Shipyards, Inc.*] (LA)
ASTMA........ Astatic Milliammeter (RU)
ASTOK........ Astika Oikistika Kendra [*Urban Housing (Development) Centers*] (GC1)
ASTOUKIN... Association Kinoise de Tourisme (MAR)
ASTOVOCT... Association Togolaise des Volontaires Chretiens au Travail (MAR)
ASTOVOT... Association Togolaise de Volontaires du Travail [*Togolese Association of Labor Volunteers*] (AF)
A/STR......... Alor Star [*Malaysian*] (ML)
AStR............ Arbeitseinkommen-Steuerrichtlinien [*Income Tax Guidelines*] (EG)
astr............. Astronomical Point [*Topography*] (RU)
astr............. Astronomy, Astronomical (BU)
astr............. Astronomy, Astronomical (RU)
ASTRA........ Aktion Strafvollzug [*Prisoners' Union*] [*Swiss*] (WEN)
ASTRA........ Application of Science and Technology to Rural Development (MAR)
ASTRA........ Asociatia Transilvana pentru Literatura si Cultura Poporului Roman [*Transylvanian Association for the Literature and Culture of the Romanian People*] (RO)
Astrosovet... Astronomical Council (of the Academy of Sciences, USSR) (RU)
Astrybvtuz... Astrakhan' Technical Institute of the Fish Industry and Fisheries (RU)
ASTS........... Associated Scientific and Technical Societies of South Africa (MAR)
ASTs........... Automatic Target Tracking (RU)
ASTU........... Anti-Stock Theft Unit [*Kenyan*] (AF)
ASTV........... Astatic Voltmeter (RU)
AStVO......... Allgemeine Steuerverordnung [*General Tax Decree*] (EG)
ASU............ Accion Sindical Uruguaya [*Uruguayan Trade Union Action*] (LA)
ASU............ Agrupacion Socialista Universitaria [*Socialist University Group*] [*Spanish*] (WER)
ASU............ Airborne Self-Propelled Gun (RU)
ASU............ Ankara Sular Idaresi Genel Mudurlugu [*Ankara Hydraulics Administration Directorate General*] (TU)
ASU............ Arab Socialist Union [*Egyptian*] (PPW)
ASU............ Arab Socialist Union [*Libyan*] (ME)
ASU............ Arab Socialist Union [*Al Ittihad al Ishtiraki al Arabi*] [*Syrian*] (PPW)

ASU............ Atomic Power Plant (RU)
ASU............ Automated Control Systems (BU)
ASU............ Automatic Angle Tracking (RU)
ASU............ Automatic Control System (RU)
ASU............ Automatic Self-Service Information Unit (RU)
ASU............ Emergency Rescue Service at Sea (RU)
ASU............ General-Purpose Automatic Synchronizer (RU)
Asuag.......... Allgemeine Schweizerische Uhrenindustrie [*Swiss watch manufacturer*]
ASUB.......... Asociacion de Universitarios de Bucaramanga (COL)
ASUCC....... Arab Socialist Union Central Committee (MAR)
ASUG.......... Ausruestungen-Schwerindustrie und Getriebebau [*Equipment for Heavy Industry and Transmission Production*] (EG)
ASUNORTE... Asociacion de Universitarios del Norte de Santander [*Cucuta*] (COL)
ASUR.......... Association Sportive Universitaire de Rabat [*Moroccan*] (MAR)
ASUS.......... Associazione Studentesca Universitaria della Somalia [*University Students' Association of Somalia*]
ASUSA........ African Students Union of South Africa (AF)
ASUU.......... Academic Staff Union of Universities (MAR)
ASUV.......... Automatic Troop Control System (RU)
ASUVA........ Asociacion de Universitarios del Valle [*Cali*] (COL)
ASUVD........ Automated Foreign Trade Activities Management System (BU)
ASV............ Agrupacion Socialista Valencia [*Socialist Group of Valencia*] [*Spanish*] (WER)
ASV............ Arabe Standard Voyelle (MAR)
ASV............ Armadni Sokolsky Vybor [*Armed Forces Sokol Committee*] (CZ)
ASV............ Association des Scolaires Voltaiques de Dakar (MAR)
ASV............ Motorized Medical Platoon (RU)
asvb........... Army Liaison Battalion (BU)
ASVE........... Amt zum Schutze des Volkseigentums [*Office for the Protection of Public Property*] (EG)
ASVE........... Anotati Synomospondia Viotekhnon Ellados [*Supreme Confederation of Craftsmen of Greece*] (GC)
ASVG.......... Allgemeines Sozialversicherungsgesetz [*German*]
ASvNS........ Akciova Spolecnost v Narodni Sprave [*Corporation under National Administration*] (CZ)
ASW........... Akademicka Spoldzielnia Wydawnicza [*Student Publishing Cooperative*] (POL)
ASWEA....... Association for Social Work Education in Africa (MAR)
AS-YA-IS.... Ankara Askeri Yardim Isyerleri Iscileri Sendikasi [*Ankara Military Aid Employment Locations Workers Union*] (TU)
ASYD.......... Ankara Spor Yazarlari Dernegi [*Ankara Sports Writers' Association*] (TU)
ASYE.......... Anotati Stratiotiki Ygeionomiki Epitropi [*Supreme Army Medical Board*] [*Greek*] (GC)
ASYGT........ Askeri Yargitay [*Military Court of Cassation*] (TU)
ASYL.......... Afro-Shirazi Youth League [*Tanzanian*] (AF)
asym.......... Asymmetrisch [*Asymmetric*] [*German*]
asymm........ Asymmetrisch [*Asymmetric*] [*German*]
asyst.......... Asystent [*Assistant*] [*Polish*]
ASZ............ Armadni Strelecke Zavody [*Armed Forces Marksmanship Matches*] (CZ)
ASZERF...... Altalanos Szerelsi Feltetelek (Kolcsonos Gazdasagi Segitseg Tanacsa) [*General Conditions for Assembly (Council for Mutual Economic Assistance)*] (HU)
ASZF.......... Aruszallitasok Altalanos Feltetelei (Kolcsonos Gazdasagi Segitseg Tanacsa) [*General Terms for Freight Shipments (Council for Mutual Economic Assistance)*] (HU)
ASZFALTUTEP V... Aszfaltutepito Vallalat [*Asphalt Road Building Enterprise*] (HU)
ASZSZ........ Allamigazgatasi Szamitogepes Szolgalat [*State Administration Computer Service*] (HU)
ASZSZK...... Autonom Szovjet Szocialista Koztarsasag [*Autonomous Soviet Socialist Republic (ASSR)*] (HU)
AT............... Administration Territoriale (MAR)
AT............... Admission Temporaire [*French*]
AT............... Aerial Torpedo (RU)
AT............... Aerological Theodolite (RU)
AT............... Akku Triebwagen [*Battery-Operated Rail Motor Car*] (EG)
at................ Allami Tulajdon [*State Property, State-Owned*] (HU)
AT............... Altes Testament [*Old Testament*] [*German*]
AT............... Amatol with Trotyl Plug (RU)
AT............... Amplitude-Modulated Radiotelegraphy (RU)
AT............... Amtstag [*German*]
AT............... Angkatan Tugas [*Task Force*] (IN)
At................ Antibody (RU)
AT............... Arkhigeion Tethorakismenon [*Armored Command*] [*Greek*] (GC)
AT............... Army Rear Area (RU)
AT............... Army Telegraph (RU)
At................ Arret [*Halt*] [*Military map abbreviation*] [*World War I*] [*French*] (MTD)
AT............... Artillerie Territoriale [*Military*] [*French*] (MTD)
AT............... Artillerie de Tranchee [*Military*] [*French*] (MTD)
AT............... Asia Tenggara [*Southeast Asia*] (ML)
AT............... Assemblees des Travailleurs [*Workers Assemblies*] [*Algerian*] (AF)
AT............... Asynchronous Generator Tachometer (RU)
AT............... Asynchronous Transformer (RU)
At................ Atasoz [*Proverb*] (TU)
At................ Atmosphaere [*Atmosphere*] [*German*]
at................ Atoll [*Topography*] (RU)
At................ Atom [*Atom*] [*German*]
At................ Atom Prozent [*Atomic Percent*] [*German*]
at................ Atomfizika [*Nuclear Physics*] (HU)
at................ Atomic (RU)
at................ Attache [*French*]
AT............... Austria [*Two-letter standard code*] (CNC)
AT-.............. Automatic Titrimeter (RU)
AT............... Automatic Transformer Switch (RU)
AT............... Autorisation de Transferts [*French*]
AT............... Autotransformer (RU)
AT............... Aydin Tekstil [*Aydin Textile Corp.*] (TU)
AT............... Height Pattern, Isobaric Topography (RU)
AT............... Industrija Alata, Trebinje [*Tool Industry, Trebinje*] (YU)
AT............... L'Agronomie Tropicale [*Nogent-Sur-Marne*] [*A publication*] (MAR)
AT............... Motor Vehicle and Tractor Depot (RU)
AT............... Subscriber's Telegraph (RU)
at................ Technical Atmosphere (RU)
ata.............. Absolute Atmosphere (RU)
ATA............ Administrateur Territorial Assistant (MAR)
ATA............ African Travel Association (MAR)
ATA............ Agence Touristique Algerienne [*Algerian Tourist Agency*] (AF)
ATA............ Algerienne Transports Automobile (MAR)
ATA............ Antarctica [*Three-letter standard code*] (CNC)
ATA............ Anwendungstechnische Abteilung [*Department for Technical Application*] (EG)
ATA............ Arkhigeion Taktikis Aeroporias [*Tactical Air Force Command*] [*Greek*] (GC)
ATA............ Association Algerienne des Transports Automobiles [*Algerian*] (MAR)
ata.............. Atado Allomas [*Clearing Station, Relay Station*] (HU)
ata.............. Atmosphaere Absolut [*Absolute Pressure in Atmospheres*] [*German*]
ata.............. Atmospheres [*Absolute Pressure*] [*German*]
ATA............ Automatic Teleprinter Exchange (RU)
ATA............ Avtomati Timarithmiki Anaprosarmogi [*Automatic Cost of Living Readjustment*] (GC1)
ATA............ Societe Africaine de Transports Auxiliaires (MAR)
ATAC.......... Asociacion de Tecnicos Azucareros de Cuba [*Cuban Association of Sugar Technicians*] (LA)
ATACES...... Asociacion de Trabajadores Agropecuarios y Campesinos de El Salvador [*Salvadoran Association of Agricultural Workers and Peasants*] (LA)
ATAF.......... Association des Transporteurs Aeriens de la Zone Franc [*Association of Air Transporters of the Franc Zone*] (AF)
ATAGUA..... Asociacion de Tecnicos Azucareros de Guatemala [*Guatemalan Association of Sugar Technicians*] (LA)
ATALA........ Asociacion para la Transformacion Armada de America Latina [*Association for the Armed Transformation of Latin America*] [*Ecuadorean*] (LA)
ATALA........ Association pour l'Etude et le Developpement de la Traduction Automatique et de la Linguistique Appliquee
ATAP.......... Administrateur Territorial Assistant Principal (MAR)
ATAPEX...... African Timber and Plywood (MAR)
ATAQ.......... Association des Traducteurs Anglophones du Quebec [*Association of Anglophone Translators of Quebec*]
ATAS.......... Agencia de Colocacao de Trabalhadores para a Africa do Sul (MAR)
ATAS.......... Amerikan-Turk Anonim Sirketi [*American-Turkish Corporation Refinery*] [*Izmir*] (TU)
ATAS.......... Anadolu Tasfiyehanesi Anonim Sirketi [*Anatolian Refinery Corporation*] [*Mersin*] (TU)
ATASM....... Association Tunisienne d'Aide aux Sourds-Muets (MAR)
ATAVE........ Asociacion de Tecnicos Azucareros de Venezuela [*Venezuelan Association of Sugar Technicians*]
ATB............ Air Technical Base (RU)
ATB............ Allami Terv Bizottsag [*State Planning Commission*] (HU)
ATB............ Arap-Turk Bankasi [*Arab-Turkish Bank*] [*Istanbul*] (TU)
ATB............ Assistance Technique Belge (MAR)
ATB............ Association des Travailleurs du Bini (MAR)
ATB............ Motor Transport Base, Motor Pool (RU)
atb............. Motor Transport Battalion (BU)
ATB............ Motor Transport Battalion (RU)
ATBAT........ Atelier des Batisseurs [*Architectural firm founded by Le Corbusier*]
atbr............ Air Technical Brigade (RU)
ATBSA........ Aceros y Tuberias Sociedad Anonima [*Bogota*] (COL)
ATC............ African Timbers Company (MAR)
ATC............ Agence Transcongolaise des Communications [*Trans-Congolese Communications Agency*] (AF)
ATC............ Agence Transequatoriale des Communications [*Trans-Equatorial Communications Agency*] (MAR)
ATC............ Agence des Transports du Congo (MAR)
ATC............ Air Tanzania Corporation (MAR)
ATC............ Alianza de Trabajadores de la Comunidad Cubana [*Cuban Community Workers Alliance*] (LA)
ATC............ Asociacion de Trabajadores del Campo [*Agricultural Workers Association*] [*Nicaraguan*] (LA)

ATC .... Automatska Telefonska Centrala [*Automatic Telephone Exchange*] (YU)
ATCA .... Automovel e Touring Clube de Angola (MAR)
ATCAM .... Assemblee Territoriale du Cameroun (MAR)
ATCAR .... Association des Tshokwe de Congo Belge, de l'Angola, et de la Rhodesie [*Association of Belgian Congolese, Angolan, and Rhodesian Tshokwe*]
ATCAS .... African Training Centre for Agricultural Statistics (MAR)
ATCC .... Agence Telegraphique Centrale Coreenne [*Korean Central News Agency*] [*Use KCNA*] (CL)
ATCCI .... Agence de Transactions Commerciales de Cote-d'Ivoire (MAR)
ATCh .... Air Maintenance Unit (BU)
ATCT .... Association des Techniciens Congolais des Telecommunications (MAR)
atd .... Air Maintenance Division (BU)
atd .... Air Technical Division (RU)
ATD .... Anti-Tuberkulozni Dispanzer [*Antituberculosis Dispensary*] (YU)
ATD .... Archives du Territoire de Dilolo (MAR)
ATD .... Avtonomos Tourkiki Dioikisis [*Autonomous Turkish Administration*] (GC)
ATDC .... Austin Ten Drivers Club (EA)
ATDH .... Agrupacion de Tropas de Defensa de La Habana [*Havana Defense Troops*] [*Cuban*] (LA)
ATE .... Agrotiki Topiki Enosis [*Agrarian Local Union*] [*Name applied to Pan Agrarian Union of Cyprus locals*] (GC)
ATE .... Agrotiki Trapeza Ellados [*Agricultural Bank of Greece*] (GC)
ATE .... Anti-Terrorismo ETA [*Anti-ETA Terrorism*] [*Spanish*] (PPE)
ATE .... Antithrombotic Unit (RU)
ATE .... Asociacion de Trabajadores del Estado [*State Workers Association*] [*Argentine*] (LA)
ATE .... Association of Tanganyika Employers (MAR)
ATE .... Automatic Test Equipment (MAR)
ATE .... Moscow Automobile and Tractor Electrical Equipment Plant (RU)
ATEC .... Agence Transequatoriale des Communications [*Trans-Equatorial Communications Agency*] (AF)
ATEC .... Association pour le Developpement Technique des Transports de l'Envirronement et de la Circulation (MAR)
ATEF .... Asociacion de Trabajadores en Embarques de Frutas [*Association of Fruit Shipment Workers*] [*Ecuadorean*] (LA)
ATEKAD ...... Akademi Tehnik Angkatan Darat [*Indonesian*]
Atel .... Atelye [*Shop, Workshop*] (TU)
ATEM .... Association for the Teaching of English in Malawi (MAR)
ATES .... Anoteres Tekhnikes Epangelmatikes Skholes [*Higher Technical Training Schools*] [*Greek*] (GC)
ATES .... Asociacion Salvadorena de Transportistas [*Salvadoran Association of Drivers*] (LA1)
ATETA .... Anti-Terorista de ETA [*Anti-Terrorist Group of ETA*] [*Spanish*] (WER)
ATETs .... Atomic Thermal-Electric Power Plant (BU)
ATEX .... Allami Textilkiskereskedelmi Vallalat [*State Textile Retail Trade Enterprise*] (HU)
ATF .... Adenosine Triphosphate (RU)
ATF .... Adenosinetriphosphoric Acid (RU)
ATF .... French Southern and Antarctic Lands [*Three-letter standard code*] (CNC)
ATF-aza ...... Adenosinetriphosphatase (RU)
ATFS .... Association of Track and Field Statisticians (EA)
ATG .... Antigua [*Three-letter standard code*] (CNC)
ATG .... Assistance Technique Generale [*General Technical Assistance*] [*Zairian*] (AF)
At-G .... Atom Gewicht [*Atomic Weight*] [*German*]
ATG .... Autotransportgemeinschaft [*Automotive Transport Association*] (EG)
ATG .... Auxiliary Turbogenerator (RU)
ATG .... Avia Technique Gabon (MAR)
At-Gew .... Atom Gewicht [*Atomic Weight*] [*German*]
Atgm .... Astegmen [*Second Lieutenant*] (TU)
ATGW .... Anti-Tank Guided Weapon (MAR)
ATGWU .... Amalgamated Transport and General Workers Union [*Ugandan*] (AF)
ath .... Aetherisch [*Ethereal*] [*German*]
AThP .... Avtou Theiotati Panagiotis [*His (Most Divine) Holiness*] [*Used for Patriarch of Constantinople only*] (GC)
Ath Pr .... Athinaikon Praktoreion [*Athens (News) Agency*] [*See also APE*] (GC)
ATHU .... Association Tunisienne des Historiens Universitaires (MAR)
ATI .... Allami Terkepeszeti Intezet [*State Institute of Cartography*] (HU)
ATI .... Anotaton Tekhnologikon Instituton [*Supreme Technological Institute*] (GC1)
ATI .... Athinaikon Tekhnologikon Institouton [*Athens Technological Institute*] (GC)
ATI .... Automobile and Tractor Institute (RU)
ATI .... Aviation Technological Institute (RU)
ati .... Gage Atmosphere (RU)
ATI .... Industrial Asbestos Products (RU)
ATI .... Industrial Asbestos Products Plant (RU)
ATI .... Telemetry Equipment (RU)
ATIBT .... Association Technique Internationale des Bois Tropicaux [*International Technical Tropical Timber Association*] (EA)
ATIC .... Association Technique de l'Importation Charbonniere [*North African*] (MAR)
ATIE .... Associacao dos Tradutores et Interpretes do Estado do Rio De Janeiro [*Association of Translators and Interpreters of the State of Rio De Janeiro*] [*Brazilian*]
ATIGA .... Asociacion de Trabajadores de la Industria Gastronomica de Antioquia [*Medellin*] (COL)
ATILRA .... Asociacion de Trabajadores de la Industria Lechera de la Republica Argentina [*Argentine Dairy Industry Workers Association*] (LA)
ATIM .... Automatic Maximal Heat-Sensitive Alarm (RU)
ATIM .... Aviation Heat-Insulating Material (RU)
ATISS .... Asociacion de Trabajadores de la Industrial Siderurgica y Similares [*Association of Steel and Related Industry Workers*] [*Venezuelan*] (LA)
ATJ .... Association Territorial pour la Protection de la Jeunesse (MAR)
ATK .... Administrateur de Territoire de Katanga (MAR)
ATK .... Agrar-Technische Konstruction [*Technical Designing for Agriculture*] (EG)
ATK .... Air Transport Column (RU)
ATK .... Akademia Teologii Katolickiej [*Academy of Catholic Theology*] (POL)
ATK .... Amt fuer Technische Kontrolle [*Office for Technical Supervision*] (EG)
ATK .... Archives du Territoire de Katanga (MAR)
ATK .... Arkhi Tilepikoinonion Kyprou [*Cyprus Telecommunications Authority*] [*See also CYTA*] (GC)
ATK .... Armadni Telovychovny Klub [*Armed Forces Physical Education Club*] (CZ)
ATK .... Automaattinen Tietojenkasittely [*Automatic Data Processing*] [*Finnish*]
ATK .... Automobile Transportation Office (RU)
ATK .... Autotransformer of Magnetic Comparator (RU)
ATK .... Aviation Turbine Kerosene (MAR)
ATK- .... Turbocompressor Unit (RU)
ATKAT .... Association des Tshokwe du Katanga (MAR)
ATKh .... Automobile Transportation Establishment (RU)
ATL .... Akosombo Textiles Limited (MAR)
atl .... Atlas (RU)
ATLA .... American Theological Library Association (MAR)
ATLANCO ... Compagnie Atlantique de Conserves (MAR)
ATLAS .... Asociacion de Trabajadores de America Latina [*Association of Latin American Workers*] (LA)
ATLF .... Association of Literary Translators of France
ATM .... Abastecimiento Tecnico-Militar [*Military Technical Supply*] [*Cuban*] (LA)
ATM .... Angkatan Tentera Malaysia [*Malaysian Armed Forces*] (ML)
ATM .... Antifriction Heat-Conducting Material (RU)
atm .... Aprovizionare Tehnico-Materiala [*Technical-Material Supply*] (RO)
ATM .... Archiv fuer Technische Messen [*Archives for Technical Fairs*] (EG)
ATM .... Asociatia Oamenilor de Arta din Institutiile Teatrale si Muzicale [*Association of Artists in Theatrical and Musical Institutions*] (RO)
ATM .... Association of Teachers of Mathematics (EA)
Atm .... Atmosfer [*Atmosphere*] (TU)
atm .... Atmosfera [*Atmosphere Unit*] [*Polish*]
Atm .... Atmosphaere [*Atmosphere*] [*German*]
Atm .... Atmosphere [*Atmosphere*] [*French*] (MTD)
atm .... Atmospheres (BU)
atm .... Atmospheric (RU)
ATM- .... Corrosion-Resistant Heat-Conducting Material (RU)
atm .... Physical Atmosphere (RU)
ATMA .... Association Technique Maritime et Aeronautique [*French*]
Atm abs ...... Atmosphaere Absolut [*Absolute Pressure in Atmospheres*] [*German*]
ATMIL .... Atase Militer [*Military Attache*] (IN)
ATMN .... Amalgamated Tin Mines of Nigeria Ltd. (MAR)
ATMS .... Automatic Telemetry Meteorological Station (RU)
at n .... Atomic Number (RU)
ATN .... Turbine-Driven Artesian Pump (RU)
ATO .... African Timber Organisation (MAR)
ATO .... Airfield Technical Support (RU)
ATO .... Arab Telecommunications Organization (MAR)
ATO .... Arab Towns Organization (EA)
ATO .... Associated Tour Operators (MAR)
ATO .... Athinaikos Tekhnologikos Omilos [*Athens Technological Club*] (GC)
ATO .... Auto Transport de l'Ouest (MAR)
ATO .... Auto Transports Industriels de la Cote-Ouest (MAR)
ato .... Automatic Tankborne Flamethrower (RU)
ATOC .... Agence Togolaise d'Opinion Commerciale (MAR)
ATOCI .... Association de Traducteurs et Reviseurs des Organisations et Conferences Intergouvernementales
ATOF .... Almanyadaki Turk Ogrenciler Federasyonu [*Turkish Student Federation in Germany*] (TU)
ATOI .... Alliance Touristique de l'Ocean Indien (MAR)
ATOM .... Anti-Terrorist Operations in Malaya (ML)

Atomgew .... Atomgewicht [*Atomic Weight*] [*German*]
Atomizdat ... Publishing House of the State Committee of the Council of Ministers, USSR, for the Use of Atomic Energy (RU)
ATOMKI ...... Atommag Kutato Intezet [*Nuclear Research Institute*] (HU)
ATONU .... Assistance Technique de l'Organisations des Nations Unies (MAR)
ATOP .... Agence Togolaise de Presse [*Togolese Press Agency*] (AF)
ATP .... A. Trochou Petitjean & Cie. (MAR)
ATP .... African Timber and Plywood Ltd. (MAR)
ATP .... Agence Tchadienne de Presse [*Chadian Press Agency*] (AF)
ATP .... Agence Transcontinentale de Presse [*Transcontinental Press Agency*] [*French*] (AF)
ATP .... Agence Tunisienne de Publicite [*Tunisian Advertising Agency*] (AF)
ATP .... Air Technical Regiment (RU)
ATP .... Amt fuer Technisches Pruefwesen [*Office for Technical Testing*] (EG)
ATP .... Association des Tennismen Professionnels [*Tunisian*] (MAR)
ATP .... Automatic Telephone Project [*Saudi Arabian*] (ME)
ATP .... Automation of Technological Planning (RU)
ATP .... Autorisation de Transferts Prealables [*French*]
ATP .... Motor Transport Regiment (RU)
ATPF .... Action Tunisienne dans le Domaine du Planning Familial (MAR)
ATPI .... Association of Public Translators and Interpreters of Brazil
ATPLO .... Army of Tripura People's Liberation Organization [*Indian*] (PD)
ATR .... Airfield Technical Company (RU)
ATR .... Anti-Torture Research [*An association*] (EA)
atr .... Motor Transport Company (BU)
ATR .... Motor Transport Company (RU)
ATR .... Subscriber's Manually Operated Telegraph Set (RU)
ATr .... Wind Tunnel (RU)
ATRA .... Ateliers de Reparation Radiateurs (MAR)
ATRACA ..... Association des Transporteurs de Carburants, Lubrifiants, et Tous Produits Petroliers [*Association of Transporters of Motor Fuel, Lubricants, and Petroleum Products*] [*Cambodian*] (CL)
ATRACO ..... Accra Training College (MAR)
ATRCW .... African Training and Research Centre for Women (MAR)
ATRD .... Atomic Turbojet Engine (RU)
ATRIP .... International Association for the Advancement of Teaching and Research in Intellectual Property (EA)
ATRM .... Motor Vehicle and Tractor Repair Shop [*Military term*] (RU)
atro .... Absolut Trocken [*Absolutely Dry*] [*German*]
ATRS .... Association Togolaise de la Recherche Scientifique [*Togolese Scientific Research Association*] (AF)
ATRZ .... Automobile and Tractor Repair Plant (RU)
ats .... Acetone (RU)
ATS .... Active Turbulent Stratum [*Meteorology*] (BU)
ATS .... African Travel System (MAR)
ATS .... Air Technical Service (RU)
ATS .... Air Technical Supply (RU)
ATs .... Analog-to-Digital [*Converter*] (RU)
ATS .... Archives du Territoire de Sandoa (MAR)
ATS .... Armadni Telovychovny Svaz [*Armed Forces Physical Education Union*] (CZ)
ATS .... Armiska Transportna Sluzba [*Army Transport Service*] (YU)
ATS .... Artillery Medium Prime Mover (RU)
ATS .... Artillery Topographic Service (BU)
ATS .... Artillery Topographic Service (RU)
ATS .... Asiatic Territory of the USSR (RU)
ATs .... Astronomical Circular (RU)
ATS .... Automatic Telephone Exchange (RU)
ATS .... Aviotehnicka Sluzba [*Air Technical Service*] [*Air Force*] (YU)
ATs .... Cellulose Acetate (RU)
ATs .... Central Control Room (RU)
ATS .... Dial Telephone Exchange (BU)
ATS .... Telephone Subscribers' Office (RU)
ATSB .... Avrupa Turk Sosyalistler Birligi [*Union of European Turkish Socialists*] (TU)
atset ch .... Acetyl Value (RU)
Atsges .... Adzharis-Tskali Hydroelectric Power Plant (RU)
ATSh .... Albanian Telegraph Agency (BU)
ATsIIS .... Analog Cyclic Information and Measuring System (RU)
ATSK .... Crossbar-Type Telephone Exchange (RU)
ATsM- .... Modernized Tank Truck (RU)
ATsP .... Analog-to-Digital Converter (RU)
ATsP .... Asbestos Cement Production (BU)
ATsP .... Tank-Truck Trailer (RU)
ATsPu .... Alphanumeric Printer (RU)
ATSR .... Air Ambulance Company (RU)
ATsR .... Automatic Centrifugal Regulator (RU)
ATsRB .... Central Army Repair Base (RU)
ATsRM .... Central Army Repair Shop (RU)
ATsS .... Antireticular Cytotoxic Serum (RU)
ATSSR .... Tatar Autonomous Soviet Socialist Republic (RU)
ATsVM .... Analog Digital Computer (RU)
ATsVM .... Automatic Digital Computer (RU)
ATS VRS ..... Intrarayon Automatic Telephone Exchange (RU)
ATsZ .... Asbestos Cement Plant (BU)
ATsZhNG- ... Tank Truck for Transporting Liquefied Gas (RU)
ATT .... Artillery Heavy Prime Mover (RU)
ATT .... Assemblee Territoriale du Togo (MAR)
att .... Atomic Weight (BU)
Att .... Attache [*French*] (MTD)
attez .... Atomska Tezina [*Atomic Weight*] (YU)
ATTF .... African Table Tennis Association (MAR)
ATTF .... Avrupa Turk Talebe Federasyonu [*European Turkish Student Federation*] (TU)
ATTF .... Avrupa Turkiyeli Toplumcular Federasyonu [*European Turkish Socialists Federation*] (TU)
ATTJ .... Association Tunisienne: Tourisme et Jeunesse (MAR)
atto .... Atentisimo [*Very Attentive*] [*Spanish*]
attr .... Attributiivisena [*Attributive*] [*Finnish*]
attr .... Attribuutti [*Finnish*]
ATTs .... Dial Telephone Exchange (BU)
ATU .... African Telecommunications Union (MAR)
ATU .... Assemblee des Travailleurs de l'Unite [*Plant Workers Assembly*] [*Algerian*] (AF)
ATU .... Ataturk Universitesi [*Ataturk University*] (TU)
Atu .... Atmosphaere Ueberdruck [*Atmospheric Excess Pressure*] [*German*]
ATU .... Automobile Transportation Administration (RU)
ATU .... Automobile Transportation Sector (RU)
atu .... Driving School (BU)
ATU .... Standard Television Antenna (RU)
ATUC .... African Trade Union Confederation (AF)
atue .... Atmosphaeren-Ueberdruck [*Atmospheric Excess Pressure*] [*German*] (WEN)
ATUKI .... Autokozlekedesi Tudomanyos Kutato Intezet [*Scientific Research Institute for Automobile Transportation*] (HU)
ATV .... Agence de Tourisme et Voyages (MAR)
ATV .... Agence de Transit et de Voyages [*Central African*] (MAR)
ATV .... Akademiet foer de Tekniske Videnskaber [*Academy of Technical Sciences*] [*Danish*] (WEN)
at v .... Atomic Weight (RU)
atv .... Atvitel [*Balance Brought Forward*] (HU)
ATV .... Autotransportvereinigung [*Automobile Transport Association*] (EG)
ATYe .... Administrative Territorial Subdivision (RU)
at yed .... Atomic Unit (RU)
ATZ .... Altay Tractor Plant Imeni M. I. Kalinin (RU)
ATZ .... Automatische Telefonzentrale [*Automatic Telephone Exchange*] [*West German*] (WEN)
ATZ .... Nitrogen Fertilizer Plant (BU)
ATZ .... Nitrogen Fertilizer Plant (RU)
ATZ .... Refueling Truck (RU)
ATZ .... Tyumen' Battery Plant (RU)
ATZT .... Association des Techniciens Zairois des Telecommunications [*Association of Zairian Telecommunications Technicians*] (AF)
AU .... Active Carbon, Activated Carbon, Activated Charcoal (RU)
AU .... Administration of Archives (RU)
AU .... Amplitude Indicator (RU)
AU .... Angkatan Udara [*Air Force*] (IN)
AU .... Ankara Universitesi [*Ankara University*] (TU)
AU .... Arbetsutskottet [*Working Committee, Executive Committee*] [*Swedish*] (WEN)
AU .... Archelolgicky Ustav [*Institute of Archeology*] (CZ)
AU .... Arithmetic Unit [*Computers*] (RU)
AU .... Artillery Directorate (RU)
AU .... Artillery School (RU)
AU .... Associative Unit [*Computers*] (RU)
AU .... Astronomic Theodolite (RU)
AU .... Australia [*Two-letter standard code*] (CNC)
AU .... Author Index (RU)
AU .... Automatic Control (RU)
AU .... Automobilne Uciliste [*Automobile Training Center*] (CZ)
AU .... Autonomous Control (RU)
AU .... Autosaobracajno Poduzece [*Motor Transport Establishment*] (YU)
AU .... Disaster Level (of water) (RU)
AU .... Pharmaceutical Administration (BU)
AU .... Pharmaceutical Administration (RU)
AUA .... Association des Ulemas Algeriens (MAR)
AUA .... Association des Universites Africaines [*Association of African Universities*] (AF)
AUA .... Atelier d'Urbanisme et d'Architecture (MAR)
aua .... Auch under Andern [*Also among Others*] [*German*]
AUA .... Austrian Airways [*Oesterreichische Luftverkehrs AG*] (WEN)
AUB .... American University of Beirut (ME)
AUB .... Asociacion de Universidades Bolivianas [*Bolivian Universities Association*] (LA)
Aubge .... Auberge [*Inn*] [*Military map abbreviation*] [*World War I*] [*French*] (MTD)
AUBI .... Automatische Bibliofoonuitlening
AUC .... Abidjan University Club (MAR)
AUC .... American University of Cairo (ME)
AUC .... Anno Urbis Conditae [*In the Year From the Founding of the City (Rome) 753 BC*] [*Latin*] (GPO)
AUCA .... Asociacion de Universitarios del Cauca [*Popayan*] (COL)
AUCAM .... Association Universitaire Catholique d'Amitie Mondiale (MAR)
AUCh .... Arithmetic Number Unit (RU)

AUCOLDI .... Asociacion Colombiana de Autores de Obras Didacticas [*Bogota*] (COL)
AUCOS .... Autoservicios Comunitarios [*Community Self-Services*] [*Chilean*] (LA)
AUD .... Accion Universitaria Democrata de la Facultad de Derecho y Ciencias Sociales [*Democratic University Action of the School of Law and Social Services*] [*Paraguayan*] (LA)
AUD .... Aktionsgemeinschaft Unabhaengiger Deutscher [*Action Group of Independent Germans*] [*West German*] (PPE)
AUD .... Armadni Umelecke Divadlo [*Armed Forces Theater*] (CZ)
Aud .... Audiencia [*Spanish*]
aud .... Audycja [*Hearing*] [*Polish*]
AUDAVI .... Asociacion Uruguaya de Agencias Viajes [*Association of Uruguayan Travel Agencies*] (LA)
AUDEA .... Asociacion de Universitarios de Antioquia [*Medellin*] (COL)
AUDEBA ..... Asociacion de Universitarios de Barrancabermeja (COL)
AUDECAM ... Association Universitaire pour le Developpement de l'Enseignement et de la Culture en Afrique et a Madagascar [*University Association for the Development of Teaching and Culture in Africa and Madagascar*] (AF)
AUDKSC ..... Archiv Ustavu Dejin Komunisticke Strany Ceskoslovenska [*Archives of the Institute for the History of the Communist Party of Czechoslovakia*] (CZ)
AUDKSS ..... Archiv Ustavu Dejin Komunistickej Strany Slovenska [*Archives of the Institute for the History of the Communist Party of Slovakia*] (CZ)
Aufl .... Auflage [*Edition*] [*German*] (GPO)
AUFS .... American Universities Field Staff (MAR)
AUFS .... American Universities Field Staff Reports Series [*A publication*] (MAR)
Aufs .... Aufseher [*German*]
Aufs .... Aufsicht [*German*]
Aufst .... Aufstellung [*Statement*] [*German*]
aug .... August [*August*] [*Danish*] (GPO)
Aug .... August [*August*] [*German*] (GPO)
aug .... Augustus [*August*] [*Dutch*] (GPO)
aug .... Augusztus [*August*] (HU)
AUG .... Carrier-Based Attack Group (RU)
AUI .... Action d'Urgence Internationale [*International Emergency Action - IEA*] (EA)
AUJENGI ..... Association de la Jeunesse Ngidingienne (MAR)
AUK .... Aliupseerikoulu [*Finnish*]
AUK .... Aminoacetic Acid (RU)
AUL .... Agrupacion Universitaria Liberacion [*University Liberation Group*] [*Argentine*] (LA)
AUL .... Annotated Index of Literature [*A publication*] (RU)
AUL .... Artillery Training Camp (RU)
AUM .... Mantissa Arithmetic Unit [*Computers*] (RU)
AUM .... Self-Balancing Bridge (RU)
AUMA .... Association des Ulema Musulmans Algeriens (MAR)
AUN .... Afirmacion Universitaria Nacional [*National University Affirmation*] [*Spanish*] (WER)
AUN .... Agrupacion Universitaria Nacional [*National University Group*] [*Argentine*] (LA)
AUNA .... Asociacion de Universidades Nacionales y Autonomas [*Association of National and Autonomous Universities*] [*Bolivian*] (LA)
AUO .... African Unity Organisation (MAR)
AUO .... Arithmetic Remainder Unit [*Computers*] (RU)
AUOD .... Alliance Universelle des Ouvriers Diamantaires [*Universal Alliance of Diamond Workers - UADW*] (EA)
AUP .... Academy of the Coal Industry (RU)
AUP .... Agrupamentos de Unidades Producao [*Production Unit Groups*] [*Angolan*] (AF)
AUP .... Number Sequence Arithmetic Unit [*Computers*] (RU)
AUPAC .... Asociacion Universitaria para la Accion Comunal [*University Community Action Association*] [*Colombian*] (LA)
AUPELF ...... Association des Universites Partiellement ou Entierement de Langue Francaise [*Association of Universities Partially or Completely Using the French Language*] (AF)
AUR .... Administrative Expenditures (RU)
AUR .... Agence d'Urbanisme de la Reunion (MAR)
AURA .... Atelier d'Urbanisme de la Region d'Abidjan (MAR)
AURA .... Ateliers d'Usinage Mecanique et de Rectification Automobile (MAR)
AURE .... Agrupacion Universitaria Reformista [*University Reformist Association*] [*Argentine*] (LA)
AURI .... Angkatan Udara Republik Indonesia [*Republic of Indonesia Air Force*] (IN)
AURP .... Institut d'Amenagement et d'Urbanisme de la Region Parisienne (MAR)
AURS .... Guided Aircraft Rocket (RU)
AUS .... Aerodynamic Drift Angle (RU)
AuS .... Also Sundays and Holidays [*Train schedules*] (EG)
AUS .... Arbeit und Sozialfuersorge (Aemter der DDR) [*Labor and Social Welfare (GDR Government Offices)*] (EG)
AUS .... Armadni Umelecky Soubor [*Armed Forces Artistic Ensemble*] (CZ)
AUS .... Asociacion Uruguaya de Seguridad [*Uruguayan Security Association*] (LA)
aus .... Ausgeschaltet [*Eliminated*] [*German*]
AUS .... Australia [*Australia*] [*Polish*]
AUS .... Australia [*Three-letter standard code*] (CNC)
AUS .... Automatic Tracking Device (RU)
AUS .... Carrier-Based Strike Force (RU)
AUS .... Modular System Automatic Control (RU)
AUSBF .... Ankara Universitesi Siyasi Bilgiler Fakultesi [*Ankara University Faculty of Political Science*] (TU)
Ausg .... Ausgabe [*Edition*] [*German*]
ausg .... Ausgegeben [*Edited*] [*German*]
ausg .... Ausgewaehlt [*Selected*] [*German*]
ausgeb .... Ausgebessert [*Repaired*] [*Bookbinding*] [*German*]
ausgeschn ... Ausgeschnitten [*Cut Out*] [*German*]
Ausl .... Ausland [*or Auslaendisch*] [*Foreign, Export*] [*German*]
AUSS .... Andrews University Seminary Studies (MAR)
Aussch .... Ausschuss [*Committee*] [*German*]
ausschl .... Ausschliesslich [*Excluding, Exclusive*] [*German*] (EG)
Ausschn ...... Ausschnitt [*Clipping*] [*German*]
AUSSIP .... African University Student Services Internship Program (MAR)
Ausspr .... Aussprache [*German*]
austr .... Australialainen [*Australian*] [*Finnish*]
AUSVN .... Armadni Umelecky Soubor Vita Nejedleho [*Vit Nejedly Armed Forces Artistic Ensemble*] (CZ)
AUT .... Austria [*Three-letter standard code*] (CNC)
AUT .... Automatic Fuze Setter [*Artillery*] (RU)
aut .... Automatika [*or Automatikus*] [*Automatic or Automation*] (HU)
aut .... Automatyczny [*Automatic*] [*Polish*]
aut .... Autorisiert [*German*]
AUTB .... Ankara Universitesi Talebe Birligi [*Ankara University Student Union*] (TU)
AUTE .... Agrupacion de Funcionarios de la Administracion General de las Usinas Electricas y los Telefonos del Estado [*Union of UTE (General Administration of State Electric Power and Telephones) Workers*] [*Uruguayan*] (LA)
AUTEB .... Asociacion de Universitarios de la Universidad Tecnologica de Boyaca [*Tunja*] (COL)
AUTECO ..... Autotecnica Colombiana Ltda. [*Bogota*] (COL)
AUTO .... Autogestion [*Paris*] [*A publication*] (MAR)
auto .... Autoilu [*Motoring*] [*Finnish*]
AUTOCALDAS ... Automotores de Caldas Ltda. [*Manizales*] (COL)
AUTOCOL ... Automotora Colombiana Ltda. [*Medellin*] (COL)
AUTOFEM ... Autofelszereles es Femtomegcikk KSz [*Small Cooperative for Automobile Accessories and Mass-Produced Metal Articles*] (HU)
AUTOIMPORT ... Empresa Central de Abastecimiento y Venta de Equipos de Transporte Ligero [*Central Enterprise for Supply and Sales of Light Automotive Equipment*] [*Cuban*] (LA)
AUTOKER ... Auto- es Alkatreszkereskedelmi Vallalat [*Auto and Spare Parts Trade Enterprise*] (HU)
autokozl ...... Autokozlekedesi [*Automobile Transport (adjective)*] (HU)
autom .... Automatisch [*Automatic*] [*German*]
AUTOMAGDA ... Automotora del Magdalena Ltda. [*Santa Marta*] (COL)
AUTONAL ... Automotora Nacional SA [*Bogota*] (COL)
AUTOPACIFICO ... Automotriz del Pacifico Ltda. [*Cali*] (COL)
AUTOPREVOZ ... Preduzece za Automobilski Prevoz Robe i Putnika [*Establishment for Motor Transport of Goods and Passengers*] (YU)
AUTOSRBIJA ... Serbian Motor Vehicles Establishment [*Belgrade*] (YU)
Autotrans .... Auto Transport [*Rijeka*] (YU)
AUTOTURIST ... Pretprijatie za Turisticki Saobrakaj [*Establishment for Tourist Traffic*] [*Skopje*] (YU)
AUTOVILL ... Autovillamossagi Felszerelesek Gyara [*Automotive Electrical Equipment Factory*] (HU)
AUV .... Automatic Fuze Setter [*Artillery*] (RU)
AUVPS .... Army Directorate of Military Field Construction (RU)
AUXIMAD .... Societe Auxiliaire Maritime de Madagascar (MAR)
AUXITRANS ... Societe Auxiliaire Transafric (MAR)
AUZ .... Aliance Unitarskych Zen [*Alliance of Unitarian Women*] (CZ)
AUZ .... Automatic Recording Control (RU)
a/v .... A Vue [*At Sight*] [*French*]
A/V .... Ad Valorem [*According to the Value*] [*Latin*]
AV .... Aerial Bomb Fuze (RU)
AV .... Aircraft Armament [*Aircraft maintenance*] (RU)
AV .... Aircraft Carrier (RU)
AV .... Akcni Vybor [*Action Committee*] (CZ)
av .... Aknaveto [*Trench Mortar, Mine Thrower*] (HU)
AV .... Allami Vallalat [*State Enterprise*] (HU)
AV .... Allgemeiner Verkaufspreis [*General Sales Price*] (EG)
av .... Ampere-Turn (RU)
AV .... Antarctic Air (RU)
AV .... Antennenverstaerker [*Antenna Booster*] (EG)
av .... Apsolutna Visina [*Absolute Altitude*] [*Aviation*] (YU)
AV .... Arctic Air (RU)
AV .... Arheoloski Vestnik [*Review of Archaeology*] [*Ljubljana*] [*A publication*] (YU)
AV .... Aseguradora del Valle SA [*Cali*] (COL)
AV .... Attenuation Equalizer (RU)
AV .... Auslandsvertretung [*Foreign Representation*] (EG)
av .... Autovasar [*Auto Fair*] (HU)
AV .... Avant [*Military*] [*French*] (MTD)
av .... Avec [*With*] [*French*] (GPO)
Av .... Avenida [*Avenue*] [*Spanish*]

av .... Avenida [*Avenue*] [*Portuguese*] (CED)
av .... Avenue [*Avenue*] [*French*] (CED)
av .... Aviation (BU)
Av .... Avoir [*Credit*] [*French*]
av .... Avril [*April*] [*French*]
Av .... Avukat [*Attorney*] (TU)
AV .... Bus Terminal (RU)
AV .... Emergency Switch (RU)
AV .... Propeller [*Aviation*] (RU)
av .... Wave Amplitude (RU)
AVA .... Aerodynamische Versuchsanstalt [*Aerodynamic Research Institute*] (EG)
AVA .... African Voice Association (MAR)
AVA .... Agence Voltaique d'Assurances (MAR)
AVA .... Agence de Voyage Algerienne (MAR)
AVA .... Andre, Vidal & Associes (MAR)
AVA .... Assembly Vehicles Association (MAR)
AVA .... Associated Vehicle Assemblers (MAR)
avb .... Air Base (BU)
AVB .... Air Base (RU)
AVB .... Armiska Veterinarska Bolnica [*Army Veterinary Hospital*] (YU)
AVB .... Autorite pour l'Amenagement de la Vallee du Bandama [*Bandama Valley Development Authority*] [*Ivorian*] (AF)
AVB .... Truck-Mounted Drill Rig (RU)
AVBLN .... Asociacion de Vendedores de Billetes de la Loteria Nacional [*Association of National Lottery Ticket Sellers*] [*Salvadoran*] (LA1)
AVC .... Asociacion Venezolana de Cafecultores [*Venezuelan Coffee Growers Association*] (LA)
Avce .... Avance [*Advance*] [*French*]
avd .... Avdode [*Deceased*] [*Norwegian*] (GPO)
Avda .... Avenida [*Avenue*] [*Spanish*]
Avdp .... Avoirdupois [*Weight*] [*French*]
av dt .... Avec Droit [*French*]
AVE .... Asociacion Venezolana de Exportadores [*Venezuelan Exporters Association*] (LA)
Ave .... Avenida [*Avenue*] [*Spanish*]
Ave .... Avenue [*Avenue*] [*French*]
AVEC .... Asociacion Venezolana de Cooperacion Intermunicipal [*Venezuelan Association for Intermunicipal Cooperation*]
AVEC .... Asociacion Venezolana de Educadores Catolicos [*Venezuelan Association of Catholic Educators*] (LA)
AVECI .... Asociacion Venezolana de Cooperacion Intermunicipal [*Venezuelan Association for Intermunicipal Cooperation*] (LA)
AVEMECA ... Asociacion Venezolana de Medicos Catolicos [*Venezuelan Association of Catholic Physicians*] (LA)
AVENCULTA ... Asociacion Venezolana de Cultivadores de Tabaco [*Venezuelan Tobacco Growers Association*] (LA)
AVENSA ...... Aerovias Venezolanas, SA [*Venezuelan airline*]
AVEX .... Asociacion Venezolana de Exportacion [*Venezuelan Export Association*] (LA)
AVF .... Arabskii Valiutn Fond (MAR)
AVF .... Autovillamossagi Felszerelesek Gyara [*Automotive Electrical Equipment Factory*] (HU)
avg .... August (BU)
avg .... August (RU)
Av G .... Avant Garde [*Vanguard*] [*Military*] [*French*] (MTD)
AVH .... Allamvedelmi Hatosag [*State Security Authority (of the Ministry of Interior)*] (HU)
AVH .... Allamvedelmi Hivatal [*Hungarian secret police*]
AVHU .... Archiv Vojenskeho Historickeho Ustavu [*Archives of the Military Institute of History*] (CZ)
AVI .... Accion Venezolana Independiente [*Independent Venezuelan Action*] (LA)
AVI .... Arhiv Vojnoistoriskog Instituta [*Archives of the Institute of Military History*] (YU)
AVI .... Asociacion Venezolana de Inversionistas [*Venezuelan Association of Investors*] (LA)
AVI .... Association Universelle d'Aviculture Scientifique [*World's Poultry Science Association - WPSA*] (EA)
AVIACO ...... Aviacion y Comercio, SA [*Aviation and Trade Corporation*] [*Spanish airline*] (WER)
Aviadarm .... Field Directorate of Aviation and Aeronautics of Fighting Forces [*1919-1921*] (RU)
aviadiviziya ... Air Division (RU)
AVIAIMPORT ... Empresa Cubana Importadora de Aviacion [*Cuban Enterprise for Aircraft Import*] (LA)
Aviakhim .... Society for Assistance to the Aviation and Chemical Construction of the USSR [*1925-1927*] (RU)
Aviamashtekhsnab ... Moscow Technical Supply Office of the Glavsnab of the Ministry of the Aircraft Industry, USSR (RU)
aviamet .... Air Weather Station (RU)
AVIANCA .... Aerovias Nacionales de Colombia [*Colombian National Airways*] (LA)
aviap .... Air Park, Aircraft Park (RU)
aviapochta ... Air Mail (RU)
aviapribor ... Aircraft Instrument (RU)
aviaprom ..... Aircraft Industry (RU)
AVIASAN .... Aviatia Sanitara [*Health Aviation Service*] (RO)
AVIASNAB ... All-Union Office for Aviation Supply (of the Narkomtyazhprom) (RU)
AVIATECA ... Empresa Guatemalteca de Aviacion [*Guatemalan airline*]
aviats .... Aviation (BU)
Aviavnito ..... All-Union Aviation Scientific, Engineering, and Technical Society [*1932-1941*] (RU)
aviazent ...... Aviation Canvas (RU)
AVIG .... Autokozlekedesi Vezerigazgatosag [*Directorate of Automotive Transportation*] (HU)
AVINOVA .... Avicultores del Norte del Valle Ltda. [*Cartago*] (COL)
aviomarsh ... Aviators' March (BU)
AVIROM ...... Asociatia Generala a Crescatorilor de Pasari si Animale Mici din RSR [*General Association of Breeders of Fowl and Small Animals in the Socialist Republic of Romania*] (RO)
AVIRT .... Allami Villamosmuvek Reszvenytarsasag [*State Electricity Works Limited*] (HU)
AVIVALLE ... Avicultores del Valle Ltda. [*Cali*] (COL)
av J-C .... Avant Jesus-Christ [*Before Jesus Christ*] [*French*]
AVK .... Arhiv Visokog Komesarijata [*Archives of the High Commissariat*] (YU)
AVK- .... Automatic High-Frequency Concentration Meter (RU)
AVK .... Automatic Volume Control (RU)
AVk .... Continental Arctic Air (RU)
AVK .... Output Switching Devices (RU)
AVKh .... Arkhigeion Vasilikis Khorofylakis [*Royal Gendarmerie Headquarters*] [*Greek*] (GC)
AVL .... Army Veterinary Hospital (RU)
AVL .... Small Aircraft Carrier (RU)
AVM .... Analog Computer (RU)
AVM .... Aqualung (RU)
AVM .... Audio-Visuele Media
AVM .... Automatic Computer (RU)
AVm .... Maritime Arctic Air (RU)
AVMF .... Naval Aviation (RU)
AVN .... High-Voltage Equipment (RU)
AVNF .... Akcni Vybor Narodni Fronty [*Action Committee of the National Front*] (CZ)
AVNII .... Arkhangel'sk Scientific Research Institute of Algae (RU)
AVNK .... Aviation Nationale Khmere [*Cambodian National Air Force*] [*Use AVNK*] [*Formerly, AVRK*] (CL)
AVNOJ .... Antifasisticko Vece Narodnog Oslobodenja [*Anti-Fascist Council of National Liberation of Yugoslavia*] (YU)
AVNOYu ...... Anti-Fascist Popular Assembly of People's Liberation of Yugoslavia [*1942-1945*] (RU)
AVNOYU ..... Antifascist Council of the National Liberation of Yugoslavia (BU)
a-vo .... Agency (RU)
AVO .... Air Detachment (RU)
AVO .... (Magyar Allamrendorseg) Allamvedelmi Osztalya [*State Security Department (of the Hungarian State Police)*] (HU)
avometr ...... Multimeter (RU)
avost .... Alarm Stop, Emergency Stop (RU)
AVP .... Agence Voltaique de Presse (MAR)
AvP .... Air Park, Aircraft Park (RU)
AVP .... Aktionsgemeinschaft Vierte Partei [*Fourth Party Action Group*] [*West German*] (PPW)
AVP .... Allgemeiner Verkaufspreis [*General Sales Price*] (EG)
AVP .... Apparatus for Rotating Test Tubes (RU)
AVP .... Arubaanse Volks Partij [*Aruban People's Party*] [*Netherlands Antillean*] (PPW)
AVP .... Asociacion Venezolana de Periodistas [*Venezuelan Journalists Association*] (LA)
AVP .... Automatic Pilot, Autopilot, Gyropilot (RU)
Av P .... Avant-Poste [*Outpost*] [*French*] (MTD)
avp .... Aviation Park (BU)
AVP .... Foreign Policy Archives (of Russia) (RU)
AVPES .... Asociacion de Vendedores Profesionales de El Salvador [*Association of Salvadoran Professional Salesmen*] (LA1)
AVPR .... Foreign Policy Archives of Russia (RU)
AVPS .... Asociatia Vinatorilor si Pescarilor Sportivi [*Association of Sport Hunters and Fishermen*] (RO)
avr .... Air Reserve (RU)
AVR .... Arbeitsgemeinschaft Versuchsreaktor [*Test Reactor Working Group*] (EG)
AVR .... Arteriovenous Difference (RU)
AVR .... Automatic Reserve Switching (RU)
avr .... Aviation Repair Shop (BU)
AVRAC .... Agricultural and Veterinary Research Advisory Committee (MAR)
AVRDC .... Astan Vegetable Research and Development Center (MAR)
AVRK .... Aviation Royale Khmere [*Royal Cambodian Air Force*] [*Use AVRK*] [*Later, AVNK*] (CL)
AVRL .... Automatic Reserve Line Switching (RU)
AVRN .... Automatic Reserve Pump Switching (RU)
AVRO .... Algemeen Vereniging Radio Omroep [*General Broadcasting Association*] [*Dutch*] (WEN)
AVRT .... Automatic Reserve Transformer Switching (RU)
AVS .... Aeroklub Vysokoskolskeho Studentstva [*Aero Club of University Students*] (CZ)
AVS .... Anotati Viomikhaniki Skholi [*Supreme Industrial School*] [*Piraeus*] (GC)

AVS............ Anotera Viomikhaniki Skholi [*Superior Industrial School (Followed by name)*] (GC1)
AVS............ Army Clothing and Equipment Depot (RU)
avs............ Army Veterinary Depot (RU)
AVS............ Atomic Hydrogen Welding (RU)
AVS............ Nitrogen-Hydrogen Mixture (RU)
AVS............ Recording Aneroid Altimeter (RU)
AVS............ Simonov Automatic Rifle (RU)
AVSAP........ Asociatia Voluntara pentru Sprijinirea Apararii Patriei [*Voluntary Association to Support the Defense of the Fatherland*] (RO)
AVSECOM ... Aviation Security Command [*Philippine*]
AVSh.......... Attack Aircraft Fuze (RU)
avsh........... Flying School (BU)
avstr........... Austrian (RU)
avstral......... Australian (RU)
avt.............. Air Force Unit Train (BU)
AVT............ Analog Computer Engineering (RU)
AVT............ Atmospheric-Vacuum Pipe Still (RU)
avt.............. Author (BU)
avt.............. Author (RU)
avt.............. Automobile (BU)
avt.............. Automobile (RU)
avt.............. Automobile Plant [*Topography*] (RU)
avt.............. Automobilism (RU)
avt.............. Autonomous (RU)
AVT............ Large Aircraft Carrier (RU)
avtb............ Motor Transport Battalion (BU)
avtb............ Motor Transport Battalion, Truck Battalion (RU)
avtbr........... Motor Transport Brigade (BU)
avt l............ Author's Sheet [*40,000 printed characters*] (RU)
avtob.......... Autobiographical, Autobiography (RU)
avtob.......... Motor Transport Battalion (RU)
avtobat........ Motor Transport Battalion, Truck Battalion (RU)
avtobaza..... Motor Pool (RU)
avtobiogr.... Autobiographical, Autobiography (RU)
avtobiogr.... Autobiography (BU)
avt obl......... Autonomous Oblast (RU)
avtochasti... Motor Vehicle Parts (BU)
avtodispetcher ... Automatic Supervisor, Automation Dispatcher (RU)
avtodor....... Highway (RU)
Avtodor....... Society for Furthering the Development of Automobilism and Road Improvement [*1927-1935*] (RU)
avtogara...... Motor Vehicle Station (BU)
avtogr.......... Autograph (BU)
avtogr.......... Autograph (RU)
AVTOMAKEDONIJA ... Macedonian Motor Vehicle Establishment [*Skopje*] (YU)
Avtomatprom ... Rustavi Planning and Design Institute for the Automation of Production Processes (RU)
avtomob...... Automobile (RU)
avtopark..... Vehicular Depot [*for a motor vehicle fleet*] (BU)
AVTOPROMET ... Avtoprevoznisko Podjetje [*Motor transport establishment*] (YU)
avtoref......... Author's Abstract (RU)
avtoriz......... Authorized (BU)
avtoriz......... Authorized (RU)
avtostantsiya ... Automobile Station (BU)
AVTOTEK ... Automobile Transportation and Forwarding Office (RU)
avtotek........ Motor Vehicle Transport and Forwarding Office (BU)
avtotrakt..... Automobile and Tractor (RU)
Avtotransizdat ... Scientific and Technical Publishing House of Automobile Transportation Literature (RU)
Avtovneshtrans ... All-Union Office for Automobile Transportation of Export and Import Freight of the Ministry of Foreign Trade, USSR (RU)
avtozavod... Automobile Plant (BU)
avtp............ Motor Transport Regiment (BU)
avtp............ Motor Transport Regiment, Truck Regiment (RU)
AVTR.......... Motor Transport [*Military term*] (RU)
avtr............. Motor Transport Company (BU)
avtr............. Motor Transport Company, Truck Company (RU)
avtrb........... Motor Transport Battalion (BU)
AVTS.......... Allocation aux Vieux Travailleurs Salaries [*Algerian*] (MAR)
avt-sost....... Author-Compiler (RU)
avt svid....... Author's Certificate (RU)
avtur........... Automatic Level Controller (RU)
AVU............ Akademie Vytvarnych Umeni [*Academy of Creative Arts*] (CZ)
AVU............ Analog Computer (RU)
Avue........... Avenue [*Avenue*] [*Military map abbreviation*] [*World War I*] [*French*] (MTD)
AVV............ Autorite d'Amenagement des Vallees des Volta (MAR)
AVVG.......... Ausfuehrungsvorschriften zum Viehseuchengesetz [*Implementing Regulations to the Animal Diseases Law*] (EG)
avx ar.......... Avxon Arithmos [*Serial Number*] (GC)
AVYP.......... Apothiki Vaseos Ylikou Polemou [*Base Ordnance Depot*] [*Greek*] (GC)
AVZ............ Altay Railroad Car Plant (RU)
AVZ............ Sound-Reproduction Unit (RU)
AW.............. Aeroklub Warszawski [*Warsaw Aeroclub*] (POL)
aW.............. Aeussere Weite [*Outside Diameter*] [*German*]
AW.............. African World [*London*] [*A publication*] (MAR)
AW.............. Aktion Widerstand [*Resistance Action*] [*West German*] (WEN)
AW.............. Amperewindung [*Ampere Winding*] [*German*]
AW.............. Anweisung [*Directive, Instruction*] (EG)
AW.............. Archiwum Wojewodzkie [*Voivodship Archives*] (POL)
AW.............. Aussenwirtschaft [*Foreign Economic Relations*] (EG)
AWA............ Anstalt zur Wahrung der Auffuehrungsrechte auf dem Gebiet der Musik [*Institute for Protection of Musical Performance Rights*] (EG)
AWA............ Anstalt zur Wahrung der Autorenrechte [*Literary Copyrights Institute*] (EG)
AWA............ Army Wives Association (MAR)
AWACS....... Iptamenon Systima Elenkhou kai Proeidopoiiseos [*Automatic Control and Warning System*] (GC1)
AWAFC....... American West African Freight Conference (AF)
AWAM........ Association of West African Merchants (MAR)
AWB............ Afrikaner Weerstandsbeweging [*Afrikaner Resistance Movement*] [*South African*] (AF)
AWE............ Automatische Wiedereinschaltung [*Automatic Reclosing*] [*Electrical*] (EG)
AWE............ Automobilwerk Eisenach (VEB) [*Eisenach Automobile Plant (VEB)*] (EG)
Awewa........ Armeewetterwarte [*Meteorological Observatory*] [*German*]
AWF............ African Workers Federation [*Kenyan*] (AF)
AWF............ Akademia Wychowania Fizycznego [*Academy of Physical Education*] (POL)
AWF............ Ausschuss fuer Wirtschaftliche Fertigung [*Economic Production Board*] (EG)
AWFA.......... Arab Wings Flying Ambulance (Service) (MAR)
AWG............ Allgemeine Werkzeugmaschinen Gesellschaft [*General Machine-Tool Company*] (EG)
AWG............ Arbeiterwohnungsbaugenossenschaft [*Workers' Housing Construction Cooperative*] (EG)
AWG............ Aussenwirtschaftsgesetz (MAR)
AWHP.......... Archiwum Wojewodzkie Historii Partii [*Voivodship Archives of (Communist) Party History*] (POL)
AWM............ Askar Wataniah Malaysia [*Malaysian Territorial Army*] (ML)
AWP............ Akademia Wojskowo-Polityczna [*Academy of Military and Political Sciences*] (POL)
AWR............ Association for the Study of the World Refugee Problem (EA)
AWU............ Agricultural Workers Union (MAR)
AWU............ Antigua Workers Union (LA1)
AWW........... Algemeen Weduwen-en Wezenwet [*General Widows and Orphans Act*] [*Dutch*] (WEN)
AWZ............ Automobilwerk Zwickau [*Zwickau Automobile Plant*] [*Formerly, Audi Kraftfahrwerke*] (EG)
Ax................ Wytwornia Aparatow Numer X [*Number X Apparatus Plant*] (POL)
ax/kos......... Axiomatikos [*Commissioned Officer*] (GC)
AYA............. Ashanti Youth Association (MAR)
AYaM.......... Amur-Yakutsk Highway (RU)
AYaPM-....... Portable Absolute Nuclear Resonance Magnetometer (RU)
AYB............. Avrupa Yatirim Bankasi [*European Investment Bank*] (TU)
AYC............. African Youth Command [*Ghanaian*] (AF)
AYE............. Anotati Ygeionomiki Epitropi [*Supreme Medical Board*] [*Greek*] (GC)
AYe............. Antigenic Unit (RU)
AYe............. Antitoxic Unit (RU)
a ye............. Astronomical Unit (RU)
AYe............. Astronomical Yearbook (of the Academy of Sciences, USSR) [*A publication*] (RU)
AYeM.......... Atomic Mass Unit (RU)
AYFR........... Autonomist Youth Front of Reunion (MAR)
Ayk-Is.......... Antalya Yag Kurumu [*Antalya (Vegetable) Oil Industry Workers Union*] (TU)
AYKO.......... Kibris Turk Kooperatif Ayakkabi Fabrikasi [*Turkish Cypriot Cooperative Shoe Factory*] (TU)
AYLP........... African Youth Leadership Program (MAR)
AYM............ Anayasa Mahkemesi [*Constitutional Court*] (TU)
Aym upr...... Aimak Administration [*Topography*] (RU)
ayn mll........ Ayni Muellif [*The Same Author*] [*Turkish*] (GPO)
AYOD.......... Ankara Yuksek Ogrenim Dernegi [*Ankara Association of Higher Learning*] (TU)
AYOKD........ Ankara Yuksek Ogrenim Kultur Dernegi [*Ankara Higher Education Cultural Association*] (TU)
AYOTB........ Ankara Yuksek Okullar Talebe Birligi [*Ankara Advanced Schools Student Union*] (TU)
AYP............. Amerikaniki Ypiresia Plirofórion [*United States Information Service*] (GC)
AYRS........... Amateur Yacht Research Society (EA)
AYS............. Anotaton Ygeionomikon Symvoulion [*Supreme Health Council*] [*Greek*] (GC)
AYSME........ Anotaton Ypiresiakon Symvoulion Mesis Ekpaidevseos [*Supreme Administrative Council for Secondary Education*] [*Greek*] (GC)
AYSSE......... Anotaton Ypiresiakon Symvoulion Stoikheiodous Ekpaidevseos [*Supreme Administrative Council for Elementary Education*] [*Greek*] (GC)
AYTA........... Association of Yugoslav Travel Agencies (YU)
AYu............. Juridical Documents [*A publication*] (RU)

AYuB........... Documents on Juridical Practice [*A publication*] (RU)
AYuZR......... Archives of Southwestern Russia [*A publication*] (RU)
AYuZR......... Documents of Southern and Western Russia [*A publication*] (RU)
AZ................ Aerial Incendiary Bomb (RU)
AZ................ Afrika Zamani: Journal de l'Association des Historiens Africains [*A publication*] (MAR)
AZ................ Air Zaire (AF)
Az................ Aktenzeichen [*File Number*] [*German*] (WEN)
AZ................ Aktywizacja Zatrudnienia [*Activation of Employment*] (POL)
Az................ Amperozwoj [*Ampere Turn*] [*Polish*]
AZ................ Artillery Weapons Plant (RU)
Az................ Aufschlag-Zuender [*Percussion Fuse or Primer*] [*Military*] [*German*] (MTD)
AZ................ Automatic Load Control (RU)
AZ................ Automatic Start (RU)
AZ................ Automobile Plant (RU)
AZ................ Automobilove Zavody, Narodni Podnik [*Automobile Works, National Enterprise*] (CZ)
AZ................ Azerbaydzhan Railroad (RU)
az................. Azimuth (RU)
az................. Azinhaga [*Lane*] [*Portuguese*] (CED)
Az................ Azymut [*Azimuth*] [*Polish*]
AZ................ Barrage Balloon (RU)
AZ................ Core [*Nuclear physics and engineering*] (RU)
AZ................ Flight [*Air Force unit*] (RU)
AZ-.............. Localized Gasoline (RU)
AZ................ Scram System [*Nuclear physics and engineering*] (RU)
AZ................ Storage-Batteries Plant (BU)
AZA............. Antiaircraft Artillery (BU)
AZA............. Atelje za Arhitekturo [*Studio for Architecture*] [*Ljubljana*] (YU)
Aza.............. Azasi [*Member*] (TU)
AZAG.......... Army Antiaircraft Artillery Group (RU)
AZAP........... Agence Zaire-Presse [*Zairian Press Agency*] (AF)
AZAP........... Army Antiaircraft Artillery Regiment (RU)
AZAPO........ Azanian People's Organization [*South African*] (PPW)
AzAPP......... Azerbaydzhan Association of Proletarian Writers (RU)
AZASO........ Azanian Students' Organisation (MAR)
AZAT........... Association Zairoise de Tourisme [*Zairian Tourism Association*] (AF)
AZB............. Aerial Incendiary Bomb (RU)
azb.............. Alphabetic (BU)
AZC............. Archiv Zeme Ceske [*Archives of the Province of Bohemia*] (CZ)
AzcherNIRO ... Azov - Black Sea Scientific Research Institute of Sea Fisheries and Oceanography (RU)
AZDA........... Agence Zairoise de Distribution Automobile (MAR)
AZED........... Electric Motor Protective Device (RU)
AZEM........... Azinliklar ve Emlak Ofisi Genel Mudurlugu [*Minorities and Properties Office Directorate General*] [*of Foreign Affairs Ministry*] (TU)
Azenergo..... Azerbaydzhan Regional Administration of Power System Management (RU)
azerb........... Azerbaydzhan (RU)
Azeruchpedgiz ... Azerbaydzhan State Publishing House of Textbooks and Pedagogical Literature (RU)
Azervin........ Azerbaydzhan Wine-Making Trust (RU)
AzFAN.......... Azerbaydzhan Branch of the Academy of Sciences, USSR (RU)
AzFV............ Anhang zu den Fahrdienstvorschriften [*Appendix to Train Service Regulations*] (EG)
AZG............. Academisch Ziekenhuis Groningen
AzG.............. Azimut Gadanja [*Azimuth of Fire*] [*Army*] (YU)
Azgaz.......... Azerbaydzhan Gas Industry Trust (RU)
AzGIFK........ Azerbaydzhan State Institute of Physical Culture Imeni S. M. Kirov (RU)
AzGIK.......... Azerbaydzhan State Quality Inspection of Agricultural Products (RU)
Azgiprovodkhoz ... Azerbaydzhan State Institute for the Planning of Water-Management and Reclamation Construction (RU)
Azgiz........... State Publishing House of the Azerbaydzhan SSR (RU)
AzGNII......... Azerbaydzhan State Scientific Research Institute (RU)
AzGNIIP....... Azerbaydzhan State Scientific Research Institute of Pedagogy (RU)
AzGONTI..... Azerbaydzhan State United Scientific and Technical Publishing House (RU)
Azgosarkhproyekt ... Azerbaydzhan State Architectural Planning Institute (RU)
Azgospromproyekt ... Azerbaydzhan State Institute for the Planning of Industrial Establishments (RU)
Azgosstrakh ... Azerbaydzhan State Insurance Administration (RU)
Azgostekhizdat ... Azerbaydzhan State Technical Publishing House (RU)
AzGPU......... State Political Administration of the Azerbaydzhan Soviet Socialist Republic (RU)
AzGU........... Azerbaydzhan State University Imeni S. M. Kirov (RU)
AZh............. Astronomical Journal (of the Academy of Sciences, USSR) [*A publication*] (RU)
AZh............. Rigid Arch Support [*Mining*] (RU)
AZhRD......... Nuclear Liquid-Propellant Rocket Engine (RU)
AZI............... Allami Zeneiskola [*State Music School*] (HU)
aziat............ Asian, Asiatic (RU)
AZII............. Azerbaydzhan Industrial Institute Imeni M. Azizbekov (RU)
AzINEFTEKhIM ... Azerbaydzhan Institute of Petroleum and Chemistry Imeni M. Azizbekov (RU)
AzINMASh ... Azerbaydzhan Scientific Research Institute of Petroleum Machinery (RU)
AzINTI......... Azerbaydzhan Institute of Scientific and Technical Information (RU)
AzIS............ Azerbaydzhan Scientific Research Institute of Building Materials and Structures (RU)
AZJO........... All Zanzibar Journalists' Organization (MAR)
AZKG.......... Automobilove Zavody Klementa Gottwalda [*Klement Gottwald Automobile Plants*] [*Mlada Boleslav*] (CZ)
AZKMGR..... Azerbaydzhan Office of Marine Geophysical Exploration (RU)
Azkombank ... Azerbaydzhan Municipal Bank (RU)
AzKOMSTARIS ... Azerbaydzhan Committee for the Preservation of Relics of Antiquity, Art, and Nature (RU)
Azkoopinsoyuz ... Azerbaydzhan Union of Cooperative Associations of Disabled Persons (RU)
AZL............. Automobilove Zavody Letnany [*Letnany Automobile Works*] (CZ)
AZMMYO.... Ankara Zafer Muhendislik ve Mimarlik Ozel Yuksek Okulu [*Ankara Zafer (Victory) Engineering and Architectural Private Advanced School*] (TU)
Azmorput'... Azov Basin Administration of Sea Routes (RU)
Azmuzgiz.... Azerbaydzhan State Music Publishing House (RU)
Azneft'........ All-Union Trust of the Azerbaydzhan Petroleum and Gas Industry [*1934-1935*] (RU)
Azneft'........ State Association of the Azerbaydzhan Petroleum Industry (RU)
Azneftegeofizika ... Azerbaydzhan Administration of Geophysical Exploration of the Ministry of the Petroleum Industry (RU)
Aznefteizdat ... Azerbaydzhan Publishing House of Petroleum and Scientific and Technical Literature (RU)
Aznefterazvedka ... Azerbaydzhan Petroleum Geological Exploration Association (RU)
Aznefterazvedka ... Azerbaydzhan Petroleum Geological Exploration Trust [*1936-1937*] (RU)
Aznefterazvedka ... Geological Exploration Office of the Azneft' [*1933*] (RU)
Aznefterazvedka ... State All-Union Trust of the Azerbaydzhan Petroleum Exploration [*1934-1935*] (RU)
Azneftezavody ... Association of Azerbaydzhan Petroleum-Processing Plants (RU)
AZNII.......... Azerbaydzhan Scientific Research Petroleum Institute Imeni V. V. Kuybyshev (RU)
AzNIIDN...... Azerbaydzhan Scientific Research Institute for Petroleum Production (RU)
AZNIIGeofiziki ... Azerbaydzhan Scientific Research Institute of Geophysics (RU)
AzNIIGIM.... Azerbaydzhan Scientific Research Institute of Hydraulic Engineering and Reclamation (RU)
AzNIIMASh ... Azerbaydzhan Scientific Research Institute of Petroleum Machinery (RU)
AzNIIMN...... Azerbaydzhan Scientific Research Institute of Perennial Plantings (RU)
AzNIINP...... Azerbaydzhan Scientific Research Institute for Petroleum Processing Imeni V. V. Kuybyshev (RU)
AzNIIRKh.... Azov Scientific Research Institute of Fisheries (RU)
AzNIKhI...... Azerbaydzhan Scientific Research Institute of Cotton Growing (RU)
AzNIKI......... Azerbaydzhan Clinical Scientific Research Institute (RU)
AzNITON..... Azerbaydzhan Branch of the All-Union Scientific, Engineering, and Technical Society of Petroleum Workers (RU)
AzNIVI......... Azerbaydzhan Veterinary Scientific Research Institute (RU)
Aznivos....... Azerbaydzhan Scientific Research Veterinary Experimental Station (RU)
AzNKh......... Azerbaydzhan Petroleum Industry (RU)
AZNP........... Automobilove Zavody, Narodni Podnik [*Automobile Works, National Enterprise*] [*Mlada Boleslav*] (CZ)
AzNTO........ Azerbaydzhan Republic Administration of the Scientific and Technical Society (RU)
AzNTO NGP ... Azerbaydzhan Scientific and Technical Society of the Petroleum and Gas Industry (RU)
AZO............ Antiaircraft Defense (BU)
AZO............ Antiaircraft Defense (RU)
AZO............ Artillery Barrage (RU)
AZO............ Automated Zonal Observatory (RU)
AzONTI....... Azerbaydzhan United Scientific and Technical Publishing House (RU)
AzOP........... Azimut Osnovnog Pravca [*Azimuth of Main Direction*] [*Army*] (YU)
Azovstal'..... Azov Metallurgical Plant (RU)
AZP............. Antiaircraft Artillery Regiment (RU)
AZP............. Automatic Antiaircraft Sight (RU)
AZP............. Filling Station (RU)
Azpartizdat ... Party Publishing House of the Azerbaydzhan SSR (RU)
AZPB........... Andrychowskie Zaklady Przemyslu Bawelnianego [*Andrychow Cotton Mill*] (POL)
Azpoligrafizdat ... Azerbaydzhan Administration for Printing, Publishing, and the Book Trade (RU)
AZPP........... Aleksandrowskie Zaklady Przemyslu Ponczoszniczego [*Aleksandrow Hosiery Mill*] (POL)
AZR............. Documents of Western Russia (RU)

AZRI............ Arid Zone Research in Iraq (MAR)
Azryba........ Azerbaydzhan State Fish Industry Trust (RU)
AZS............ Akademicki Zwiazek Sportowy [*Student Sport Union*] (POL)
AZS............ Akademickie Zrzeszenie Sportowe [*Student Sport Association*] (POL)
AZS............ Anodal Closure Contraction (RU)
AZS............ Antiaircraft Equipment, Antiaircraft Weapons (RU)
AZS............ Arabski Zwiazek Socjalistyczny [*Arab Socialist Union*] (POL)
AZS............ Automatic Circuit Protection [*Circuit breaker*] (RU)
AZS............ Azot Sanayii Turk Anonim Sirketi [*Turkish Nitrogen Industry Corporation*] (TU)
AZS............ Battery-Charging Station (RU)
AZS............ Communications Flight [*Air Force unit*] (RU)
AZS............ Filling Station (RU)
AZS............ Students' Agrarian Union (BU)
AzSO.......... Anhang zur Signal-Ordnung [*Appendix to the Signal Regulations*] (EG)
AzSSR......... Azerbaydzhan Soviet Socialist Republic (RU)
Azstankostroy ... Azerbaydzhan Machine Tool Plant (RU)
AzTAG........ Azerbaydzhan News Agency (RU)
AZTE........... Altay Tractor Electrical Equipment Plant (RU)
AZTM.......... Alma-Ata Heavy Machinery Plant (RU)
Aztorg......... Azerbaydzhan State Retail Trade Association (RU)
AZTRA........ Azucarera Tropical Americana, SA [*American Tropical Sugar Mill, Inc.*] [*Ecuadorean*] (LA)
Az TsAU...... Azerbaydzhan Central Administration of Archives (RU)
AzTsIK........ Central Executive Committee of Azerbaydzhan SSR (RU)
AZU............ Academisch Ziekenhuis Utrecht
AZU............ Afrikanische Zahlungsunion (MAR)
AZU............ Akademija Znanosti in Umetnosti [*Academy of Sciences and Arts*] [*Slovenian Academy*] [*Ljubljana*] (YU)
AZU............ Associative Storage, Associative Memory (RU)
AZU-........... High-Speed Tin-Plating Unit (RU)
AZUCOL...... Azucarera Colombiana [*Cali*] (COL)
AZUMT........ Azerbaydzhan Administration of Local Transportation (RU)
Az m v......... Aufschlagzuender mit Verzoegerung [*Delayed-Action Fuse*] [*German*]
AZVF........... Azov Naval Flotilla (RU)
Azvin........... Azerbaydzhan State Wine-Making Trust (RU)
AZVU........... Academisch Ziekenhuis Universiteit [*Amsterdam*]
Azw............. Amperozwoj [*Ampere Turn*] [*Polish*]
AZWK.......... Amt fuer Zoll und Warenkontrolle [*Office for Customs and Commodity Control*] (EG)
AZWM......... Akademicki Zwiazek Walki Mlodych [*Student Union of the Struggle of Youth*] (POL)
AzZII........... Azerbaydzhan Industrial Correspondence Institute (RU)

B

B .... Armor, Armored (RU)
B- .... Aviation Gasoline (RU)
B .... Baai [*Bay*] [*Dutch*] (NAU)
B .... Baccalaureat [*French*]
B .... Baccalaureat en Theologie [*Fribourg*] [*French*]
B .... Baccalaureos [*Egyptian*]
B .... Bacharel [*Bachelor*] [*Portuguese*]
B .... Bacharelato [*Academic degree*] [*Portuguese*]
B .... Bachiller [*Bachelor*] [*Academic degree*] [*Spanish*]
B .... Bacillus Breslaviensis (RU)
B .... Bahia [*Bay*] [*See also Ba*] (NAU)
B .... Baia [*Bay*] [*Italian*] (NAU)
B .... Baia [*Bay*] [*Portuguese*] (NAU)
B .... Baie [*Bay*] [*French*] (NAU)
B .... Bakalaureus [*or Bakalaureat*] [*Academic degree*] [*Indonesian*]
b .... Bal [*Left*] (HU)
b .... Band [*Volume*] [*Swedish*] (GPO)
B .... Bandar [*Harbour*] [*Persian*] (NAU)
b .... Bar (RU)
B .... Baracke [*German*]
b .... Bardzo [*Very*] [*Polish*]
B .... Base (RU)
b .... Basophil, Basophile (RU)
B .... Basse [*Shoal*] [*French*] (NAU)
B .... Bati [*West*] (TU)
B .... Battery (RU)
B .... Bay [*Mister*] (TU)
b .... Bay, Cove (RU)
B .... Beacon, Buoy [*Topography*] (RU)
B .... Beato [*Blessed*] [*Spanish*]
b .... Bei [*or Beim*] [*Near, With, Care Of*] [*German*] (GPO)
b .... Bel (RU)
B .... Belgia [*Belgium*] [*Polish*]
b .... Benefice [*French*]
B .... Beobachtung [*Observation*] [*German*]
B .... Betrieb [*Operations*] [*All measures and procedures required for the assembly, operation, and breaking up of trains*] (EG)
B .... Bey [*Mister*] [*Turkish*] (GPO)
B .... Big, Large, Great (RU)
B .... Bildung [*Education*] [*German*]
b .... Billet [*French*]
B/ .... Billet a Ordre [*Promissory Note*] [*French*]
B .... Birlik [*Unit*] [*Military*] (TU)
b .... Ble [*Wheat*] [*Used in contexts having to do with flour*] [*French*] (CL)
B .... Bois [*Wood*] [*Military map abbreviation*] [*World War I*] [*French*] (MTD)
B .... Bolometer (RU)
B .... Bomber (RU)
b/ .... Bon [*Good For*] [*French*]
b .... Bonification [*French*]
B .... Bouchet [*Powder Works*] [*French*] (MTD)
B .... Brevet [*Certificate, Diploma*] [*French*]
B .... Brevete d'Etat-Major [*Of officer who has passed staff course*] [*French*] (MTD)
b .... Brigade (BU)
B .... Bucht [*Bay*] [*German*] (NAU)
B .... Bueno [*On an Examination: Good*] [*Spanish*]
B .... Bugt [*Bay, Bight*] [*Danish*] (NAU)
B .... Bukhta [*Bay, Inlet*] [*Russian*] (NAU)
B .... Bukt [*Bay, Bight*] [*Swedish*] (NAU)
B .... Bukt [*Bukta*] [*Bay, Bight*] [*Norwegian*] (NAU)
B .... Bulletin (RU)
B .... Bund [*German*]
B .... Buoy [*Topography*] (RU)
b .... Byly [*Former*] (POL)
B .... Cobblestone [*Topography*] (RU)
B .... Fast [*Nuclear physics and engineering*] (RU)
b .... Former (BU)
B .... Former (RU)
b .... Lubenter Approbatur [*Latin*]
B .... Melon Field [*Topography*] (RU)
B .... Obus a Balles [*On base of projectiles*] [*French*] (MTD)
B .... Railroad Guard's Cabin [*Topography*] (RU)
B .... Ravine, Valley [*Topography*] (RU)
°B .... Stopien Baume [*Degree Baume*] [*Polish*]
BA .... Armored Car (RU)
ba .... Author's Note (BU)
BA .... Automatic Battery [*Artillery*] (RU)
BA .... Aviation Gasoline (RU)
BA .... Baccalaureus Artium [*Bachelor of Arts*] [*Latin*] (GPO)
BA .... Bachiller Academico [*Academic degree*] [*Spanish*]
Ba .... Bag [*or Baglar*] [*Vineyard or Vineyards*] (TU)
Ba .... Bahia [*Bay*] [*See also B*] [*Spanish*] (NAU)
Ba .... Bana [*Cape, Point*] [*See also Ha*] [*Japanese*] (NAU)
BA .... Banco Agricola [*Agricultural Bank*] [*Dominican Republic*] (LA)
BA .... Banque Agreee [*Accredited Bank*] [*Cambodian*] (CL)
BA .... Banque d'Algerie (MAR)
BA .... Base Aerienne [*Air Base*] [*Cambodian*] (CL)
BA .... Bataillon d'Afrique (MAR)
BA .... Battalion Artillery (RU)
BA .... Benzoylacetone (RU)
BA .... Bergakademie Freiberg/Sachsen [*Freiberg Mining Academy*] (EG)
BA .... Berita Atjara [*Official Report or Record*] (IN)
BA .... Bevorratungsartikel [*Items for Stockpiling*] (EG)
ba .... Bez Autora [*Anonymous*] (POL)
BA .... Bibliotheca Aegyptia (MAR)
BA .... Bintara [*Noncommissioned Officer*] (IN)
BA .... Birma [*Burma*] [*Polish*]
BA .... Blocking Anticyclone (RU)
BA .... Bombardment Aviation (BU)
BA .... Bombardment Aviation (RU)
BA .... Bomber Command (BU)
BA .... Bousquet-Afrique (MAR)
BA .... Brong Ahafo (MAR)
BA .... Bureau Arabe (MAR)
BA .... Butyl Acetate (RU)
BA .... Coast Artillery (RU)
BA .... Etablissements Bruno Aduier (MAR)
BA .... Large Astrograph (RU)
BA .... Office of Automation (RU)
ba .... Submachine-Gun Battalion (RU)
BAA .... Bulletin d'Archeologie Algerienne [*A publication*] (MAR)
BAA .... Societe Biscuiterie et Alimentation Africaine (MAR)
BAAA .... Botswana Amateur Athletics Association (MAR)
BAAH .... Bureau d'Aide et d'Assistance Humanitaire [*Humanitarian Aid and Relief Office*] [*Cambodian*] (CL)
BAAI .... Bureau d'Aide et d'Assistance aux Sinistres de l'Inondation [*Office of Aid and Relief for Flood Victims*] [*Cambodian*] (CL)
BAAM .... Banque Arabe Africaine en Mauritanie [*African Arab Bank in Mauritania*] (AF)
BAAP .... Bureau d'Aide et d'Assistance a la Population [*Office of Aid and Relief for the Population*] [*Cambodian*] (CL)
BAAZ .... Begeleidings-Commissie Academische Ziekenhuizen
bab .... Air Bombardment Base (BU)
BAB .... Betriebsabrechnungsbogen [*Master Summary Sheet, Operations Sheet, Cost Control Sheet*] [*See also BB*] (EG)
BAB .... Boissons Africaines de Brazzaville (MAR)
BABA .... Botswana Amateur Boxing Association (MAR)
BAB Tarim Is ... Bati Anadolu Bolgesi Tarim Sanayii, Ziraii Arastirma, ve Orman Isletmeleri Iscileri Sendikasi [*Western Anatolian Region Agriculture Industry, Agricultural Research, and Forestry Operations Workers' Union*] (TU)
BabV .... Babiski Vestnik [*Midwife's Review*] [*Ljubljana*] [*A publication*] (YU)
Bac .... Bacac [*Mortar*] [*Military*] (YU)
BAC .... Baccalaureat [*French*]
BAC .... Bantu Affairs Commission [*South African*] (AF)
BAC .... Basutoland African Congress (MAR)
BAC .... Biblioteca Agropecuaria de Colombia [*Bogota*] (COL)

BAC............ Birlesik Arap Cumhuriyeti [*United Arab Republic - UAR*] (TU)
BAC............ Black Affairs Center (MAR)
BAC............ Bois Africains Contreplaques (MAR)
BAC............ Ghana Bauxite Company (MAR)
BAC(AG)..... Beleids Advies College (Automatisering Gezondheidszorg)
BACBRU ..... Bulletin Agricole du Congo Belge et du Ruanda-Urundi [*Brussels*] [*A publication*] (MAR)
BACCI......... Beton Arme Constructions Civiles et Industrielles (MAR)
BACh........... Number Address Unit [*Computers*] (RU)
BACI............ Banque Atlantique de Cote-d'Ivoire (MAR)
BACME .... Baza de Aprovizionare pentru Constructii si Montaje Energetice [*Supply Base for Power Plant Construction and Installation*] (RO)
bad.............. Air Bombardment Division (BU)
BAD............ Banque Africaine de Developpement [*African Development Bank*] [*Use ADB*] (AF)
BAD............ Banque Algerienne de Developpement [*Algerian Development Bank*] (AF)
BAD............ Banque Asiatique de Developpement [*Asia Development Bank*] [*Use ADB*] (CL)
BAD............ Baza de Aprovizionare si Desfacere [*Base for Supply and Distribution*] (RO)
BAD............ Bomber Division (RU)
BAD............ Bulgarian Society of Architects (BU)
BADEA........ Banque Arabe pour le Developpement Economique en Afrique [*Arab Bank for African Economic Development*] (AF)
BADEAC ..... Banque de Developpement des Etats de l'Afrique Centrale [*Development Bank of the Central African States*] (AF)
BADESP...... Banco de Desenvolvimento do Estado de Sao Paulo [*Sao Paulo State Development Bank*] [*Brazilian*] (LA)
BADOSZ ..... Banyaipari Dolgozok Szakszervezete [*Trade Union of Mine Workers*] (HU)
bae .... Air Bombardment Squadron (BU)
BAE............ Bomber Squadron (RU)
BAEE........... Ethyl Ester of Benzoylarginine (RU)
BAEMTP ..... Budget Annexe d'Exploitation du Materiel de Travaux Publics (MAR)
BAER........... Base Airfield (RU)
BA f EV........ Bundesamt fuer Eichund Vermessungswesen [*German*]
BAF............ Bananeraies Africaines (MAR)
BAF............ Benzylaminophenol (RU)
BAFED .... Basutoland Factory Estate Development Company (MAR)
BAFISUD..... Banco Financiero Sudamericano [*South American Financial Bank*] (LA)
BAFO........... Byurakan Astrophysical Observatory (RU)
BAFoeG ...... Bundesausbildungsfoerderungsgesetz [*Federal Law for the Advancement of Education*] [*German*] (WEN)
BAFS........... Beton Armat du Fibra de Sticla [*Concrete Reinforced with Glass Fibers*] (RO)
BAfW & B .... Bundesamt fuer Wehrtechnik und Beschaffung [*Federal Office for Weapons Technology and Procurement*] [*West German*] (WEN)
BAG............ Bagian [*Division, Section, Component*] (IN)
BAG............ Bloc Africain de Guinee (MAR)
BAG............ Brigadna Artiljeriska Grupa [*Brigade Artillery Group*] [*Military*] (YU)
BAG............ Bureau d'Achat du Gouvernement [*Government Purchasing Office*] [*Laotian*] (CL)
BAGES........ Baku City Electric Power Network (RU)
BAGF........... Bulletin de l'Association des Geographes Francais [*A publication*] (MAR)
BAGFAS...... Bandirma Gubre Fabrikalari Anonim Sirketi [*Bandirma Fertilizer Factories Corporation*] (TU)
Bag-Kur ...... Esnaf ve Sanatkarlar ile Bagimsiz Calisanlar Sosyal Guvenlik Kurumu [*Social Security Association Relating to Tradesmen, Artisans, and Independent Workers*] (TU)
BAGO.......... Bloque Antiguerrillero del Oriente [*Eastern Anti-Guerrilla Bloc*] [*Salvadoran*] (PD)
BAI .... Booker Agriculture International (MAR)
BAI .... Bureau des Affairs Indigenes (MAR)
BAIA............ Banca de Agricultura si Industrie Alimentara [*Bank for Agriculture and Food Industry*] (RO)
BAIBK .... Beta-Aminoisobutyric Acid (RU)
BAII .... Banque Arabe Internationale d'Investissement (MAR)
BAIMK......... Beta-Aminoisobutyric Acid (RU)
Bak .... Bakim [*Maintenance, Upkeep*] (TU)
Bak .... Bakiniz [*Look, Please Refer To, See*] (TU)
BAK............ Ballonabwehrkanone [*Antiaircraft*] [*German*]
bak .... Beacon, Buoy (RU)
BAK............ Bomber Corps (RU)
BAK............ Instruction Address Unit (RU)
BAKER........ Badan Kerdja [*Working Committee*] (IN)
BAKER........ Barisan Kemerdeka'an Rakyat Brunei [*Brunei People's Freedom Front*] (ML)
BAKIN .... Badan Koordinasi Intelidjen Negara [*State Intelligence Coordination Agency*] (IN)
Bakport....... Baku Commercial Seaport (RU)
Baksanges ... Baksan Hydroelectric Power Plant (RU)
bakt............ Bacteriological (RU)
bakt............ Bacteriologist, Bacteriology (BU)
BAKWATA ... Baraza Kuu la Waislamu [*Supreme Council of Moslems*] [*Tanzanian*] (AF)
Bal.............. Balance [*Balance*] [*Business and trade*] [*French*]
BAL .... Blok Automatique Lumineux (MAR)
BAL .... British Anti-Lewisite (RU)
bal .... Ravine, Valley [*Topography*] (RU)
BALINEX..... Banque Arabe Libyenne Nigerienne pour le Commerce Exterieur et le Developpement (MAR)
balk .... Balkanski [*Balkan*] [*Polish*]
Balkanbas... Central Balkan Basin (BU)
Balkanizdat ... Balkan Publishing House (BU)
Balkanturist ... State Economic Enterprise for Excursions and Travel (BU)
BalkPr .... Balkanski Pregled [*Balkan Review*] [*A publication*] (BU)
BALM .... Banque Arabe Libyenne-Mauritanienne [*Libyan-Mauritanian Arab Bank*] (AF)
BALM .... Banque Arabe Libyenne-Mauritanienne pour le Commerce Exterieur et le Developpement (MAR)
BALS.......... Bandas Armadas de Liberacion del Sahara [*Armed Bands for the Liberation of the Sahara*] (AF)
Balt............. Baltic (RU)
balt............. Baltycki [*Baltic*] [*Polish*]
BALTEX ...... Banque Arabe Libyenne-Togolaise du Commerce Exterieur (MAR)
Baltflot .... Baltic Fleet (RU)
Baltmorput' ... Baltic Administration of Sea Routes (RU)
BaltNIRO..... Baltic Scientific Research Institute of Sea Fisheries and Oceanography (RU)
Baltzavod.... Baltic Shipyard (RU)
BALUBAKAT ... Association des Baluba du Katanga [*Association of the Baluba of Katanga*]
BAM .... Baikal-Amur Railway [*Russian*]
BAM .... Belize Action Movement (PD)
BAM .... Brigada Antonio Maceo [*Antonio Maceo Brigade*] [*Cuban*] (LA)
BAM .... Bureau des Affaires Musulmanes (MAR)
BAMAG....... Societe Banguienne de Grands Magasins (MAR)
BAMAS .... Buyuk Anadolu Madenleri Anonim Sirketi [*Greater Anatolian Mines Corporation*] (TU)
BAMB.......... Botswana Agricultural Marketing Board (MAR)
BAMERT ..... Banyagepgyar [*Mining Machines Factory*] (HU)
BAMES........ Banque Malgache d'Escompte et de Credit [*Malagasy Discount and Credit Bank*] (AF)
BAMI .... Brothers to All Men International (EA)
BAMIN......... Banco Minero de Bolivia [*Mining Bank of Bolivia*] (LA)
BAMREL ..... Bureau Africain et Malgache de Recherches et d'Etudes Legislatives [*African and Malagasy Office for Legislative Research and Studies*] (AF)
BAMUNAS ... Badan Musjawarah Pengusaha Nasional Swasta [*Consultative Council of National Private Businessmen*] (IN)
Ban............. Banyo [*Bath*] (TU)
BAN............ Belorussian Academy of Sciences (RU)
BAN............ Bulgarian Academy of Sciences (BU)
BAN............ Bulgarian Academy of Sciences (RU)
BAN............ Bulgarska Akademija na Naukite [*Bulgarian Academy of Sciences*] [*Sofia*] (YU)
BAN............ Bulletin de l'Afrique Noire [*A publication*] (MAR)
BAN............ Library of the Academy of Sciences, USSR (RU)
BANABel..... Fundamental Library of the Academy of Sciences, Belorussian SSR (RU)
BANADE ..... Banco Nacional de Desarrollo [*National Development Bank*] [*Argentine*] (LA)
BANADESA ... Banco Nacional de Desarrollo Agricola [*National Agricultural Development Bank*] [*Honduran*] (LA1)
BANAFRIQUE ... Banque d'Afrique et d'Outre-Mer (MAR)
BANANIC.... Empresa Nicaraguense de Banano [*Nicaraguan Banana Enterprise*] (LA1)
BANAP........ Banco Nacional de Ahorro y Prestamo [*National Savings and Loan Bank*] [*Venezuelan*] (LA)
BAN-Arkheoli ... BAN [*Bulgarian Academy of Sciences*] Institute of Archaeology (BU)
BAN-ArkheolMuzey ... BAN [*Bulgarian Academy of Sciences*] Archaeological Museum (BU)
BANArm...... Central Library of the Academy of Sciences, Armenian SSR (RU)
BAN-Ashkh ... Library of the Academy of Sciences (Ashkhabad) (RU)
BANAz .... Central Library of the Academy of Sciences, Azerbaydzhan SSR (RU)
BANBel .... Fundamental Library of the Academy of Sciences, Belorussian SSR (RU)
BANBOGOTA ... Banco de Bogota [*Bogota*] Tlg. (COL)
BAN-BotGr ... BAN [*Bulgarian Academy of Sciences*] Botanical Garden (BU)
BANCA........ Banco Cafetero [*Bogota*] (COL)
BANCALDAS ... Banco de Caldas [*Manizales*] (COL)
BANCEPAC ... Bancos Centrales del Pacto Andino [*Andean Pact Central Banks*] (LA)
BANCOAMERICA ... Banco de America Latina [*Bogota*] (COL)
BANCOLOM ... Banco de Colombia [*Bogota*] (COL)
BANCOMER ... Banco Comercial [*Bank of Commerce*] [*Mexican*] (LA)
BANCOQUIA ... Banco Comercial Antioqueno [*Medellin*] Tlg. (COL)
BANCOSTA ... Banco de la Costa SA [*Barranquilla*] Tlg. (COL)
BANDAGRO ... Banco de Desarrollo Agropecuario [*Agricultural and Livestock Development Bank*] [*Venezuelan*] (LA)

BANDEGUA ... Compania de Desarrollo Bananero de Guatemala Ltda. [*Guatemalan Banana Development Company Ltd.*] (LA)
BANDELCO ... Banco del Comercio SA [*Bogota*] Tlg. (COL)
BANDESA... Banco Nacional de Desarrollo [*National Development Bank*] [*Guatemalan*] (LA)
BANDESABANA ... Banco de la Sabana [*Bogota*] Tlg. (COL)
BANEst .... Central Library of the Academy of Sciences, Estonian SSR (RU)
BANESTADO ... Banco del Estado [*Popayan*] Tlg. (COL)
BANESTES ... Banco do Estado do Espirito Santo [*Espirito Santo State Bank*] [*Brazilian*] (LA)
BAN-EtnogrMuzey ... BAN [*Bulgarian Academy of Sciences*] Ethnographic Museum (BU)
BAN-F .... Library of the Academy of Sciences (Frunze) (RU)
BANFOCO... Banco Nacional de Fomento Cooperativo [*National Cooperative Development Bank*] [*Mexican*] (LA)
BANGr......... Central Library of the Academy of Sciences, Georgian SSR (RU)
BAN-IArkh ... BAN [*Bulgarian Academy of Sciences*] Institute of Archives (BU)
BAN-IArkhit ... BAN [*Bulgarian Academy of Sciences*] Institute of Architecture (BU)
BAN-IBiol.... BAN [*Bulgarian Academy of Sciences*] Institute of Biology (BU)
BAN-IBot..... BAN [*Bulgarian Academy of Sciences*] Botanical Institute (BU)
BAN-IBulgEz ... BAN [*Bulgarian Academy of Sciences*] Institute for the Bulgarian Language (BU)
BANIC .... Banco Nicaraguense [*Nicaraguan Bank*] (LA1)
BAN-IEksKhumMed ... BAN [*Bulgarian Academy of Sciences*] Institute of Experimental Medicine (BU)
BAN-IEkspVetMed ... BAN [*Bulgarian Academy of Sciences*] Institute of Experimental Veterinary Medicine (BU)
BAN-IFilos ... BAN [*Bulgarian Academy of Sciences*] Institute of Philosophy (BU)
BAN-IFiz ..... BAN [*Bulgarian Academy of Sciences*] Institute of Physics (BU)
BAN-IGeogr ... BAN [*Bulgarian Academy of Sciences*] Geographic Institute (BU)
BAN-IGeol... BAN [*Bulgarian Academy of Sciences*] Geological Institute (BU)
BAN-IIkon ... BAN [*Bulgarian Academy of Sciences*] Institute of Economics (BU)
BAN-IIst ...... BAN [*Bulgarian Academy of Sciences*] Institute of History (BU)
BAN-IIzobrIzk ... BAN [*Bulgarian Academy of Sciences*] Institute of Representational Arts (BU)
BAN-IKhim ... BAN [*Bulgarian Academy of Sciences*] Institute of Chemistry (BU)
BAN-ILit...... BAN [*Bulgarian Academy of Sciences*] Institute of Literature (BU)
BAN-IMat.... BAN [*Bulgarian Academy of Sciences*] Institute of Mathematics (BU)
BAN-IMikrobiol ... BAN [*Bulgarian Academy of Sciences*] Institute of Microbiology (BU)
BAN-IMuz ... BAN [*Bulgarian Academy of Sciences*] Institute of Music (BU)
BAN-IPedag ... BAN [*Bulgarian Academy of Sciences*] Institute of Education (BU)
BAN-IPochv ... BAN [*Bulgarian Academy of Sciences*] Soil Institute (BU)
BAN-IPrilBiol ... BAN [*Bulgarian Academy of Sciences*] Institute of Applied Biology (BU)
BAN-IR........ Library of the Academy of Sciences (Irkutsk) (RU)
BAN-ISotsMed ... BAN [*Bulgarian Academy of Sciences*] Institute of Social Medicine (BU)
BAN-ITekhn ... BAN [*Bulgarian Academy of Sciences*] Institute of Technology (BU)
BAN-IZhiv ... BAN [*Bulgarian Academy of Sciences*] Institute of Animal Husbandry (BU)
BAN-IZool ... BAN [*Bulgarian Academy of Sciences*] Institute of Zoology (BU)
bank........... Bank (RU)
bank........... Banking (BU)
BAN-K......... Library of the Academy of Sciences (Kazan') (RU)
BANKaz ...... Central Scientific Library of the Academy of Sciences, Kazakh SSR (RU)
BAN-Kish.... Library of the Academy of Sciences (Kishinev) (RU)
BAN-Kl........ Library of the Academy of Sciences (Klyuchi) (RU)
Bankotrud... Union of Credit Institution Workers (RU)
bank sch ..... Bank Bookkeeping (BU)
Bank-Sen.... Kibris Turk Banka Iscileri Sendikasi [*Turkish Cypriot Bank Workers' Union*] (TU)
BAN-KT....... Library of the Academy of Sciences (Kurgan-Tyube) (RU)
BAN-L .... Library of the Academy of Sciences (Leningrad) (RU)
BANLat .... Fundamental Library of the Academy of Sciences, Latvian SSR (RU)
BANLit .... Library of the Academy of Sciences, Lithuanian SSR (RU)
BAN-L'v ...... Library of the Academy of Sciences, Ukrainian SSR (L'vov) (RU)
BAN-M .... Library of the Academy of Sciences (Moscow) (RU)
BAN-MK...... Library of the Academy of Sciences (Makhachkala) (RU)
BAN-Mur..... Library of the Academy of Sciences (Murgab) (RU)
BAN-N......... Library of the Academy of Sciences (Nikolayev) (RU)
BAN-Nch..... Library of the Academy of Sciences (Novocherkassk) (RU)
BAN-Ns....... Library of the Academy of Sciences (Novosibirsk) (RU)
BAN-Osh..... Library of the Academy of Sciences (Osh) (RU)
BANPOPULAR ... Banco Popular [*Bogota*] (COL)
BAN-PrirMuzey ... Bulgarian Academy of Sciences Natural History Museum (BU)
Banq........... Banque [*Bank*] [*French*]
BAN-S......... Library of the Academy of Sciences (Stalinabad) (RU)
BANSANTANDER ... Banco de Santander [*Bucaramanga*] Tlg. (COL)
BAN-Shch... Library of the Academy of Sciences (Shcherbakov) (RU)
BAN-Sim..... Library of the Academy of Sciences (Simeiz) (RU)
BAN-Simf.... Library of the Academy of Sciences (Simferopol') (RU)
BAN-Sv....... Library of the Academy of Sciences (Sverdlovsk) (RU)
BAN-Sykt.... Library of the Academy of Sciences (Syktyvkar) (RU)
BANTA........ Basutoland African National Teachers' Association (MAR)
BANU.......... State Public Library of the Academy of Sciences, Ukrainian SSR (RU)
BANU-L'v.... Library of the Academy of Sciences, Ukrainian SSR, in L'vov (RU)
BANUz .... Central Library of the Academy of Sciences, Uzbek SSR (RU)
BAN-V......... Library of the Academy of Sciences (Vladivostok) (RU)
bany........... Banyaszat [*Mining*] (HU)
BAN-Ya....... Library of the Academy of Sciences (Yakutsk) (RU)
BANYATERV ... Banyaszati Tervezo Intezet [*Planning Institute of Mining*] (HU)
Banykut ...... Banyaszati Kutato Intezet [*Mining Research Institute*] (HU)
BAN-YuS .... Library of the Academy of Sciences (Yuzhno-Sakhalinsk) (RU)
BAN-ZoolGr ... BAN [*Bulgarian Academy of Sciences*] Zoological Garden (BU)
bao............. Air Base Battalion (BU)
BAO............. Airfield Service Battalion (RU)
BAO............. Banque de l'Afrique Occidentale (MAR)
BAO............. Bayer Afrique de l'Ouest (MAR)
BAO............. Betriebs-Absatzorganisation [*Plant Sales Organization*] (EG)
BAOM.......... Bibliotheque d'Afrique et d'Outre-Mer (MAR)
Baon........... Batalion [*Battalion*] [*Polish*]
bap............. Air Bombardment Regiment (BU)
BAP .... Banco Agricola y Pecuario [*Agriculture and Livestock Bank*] [*Venezuelan*] (LA)
BAP .... Banque Agricole Paysanne [*Farmers Agricultural Bank*] [*Cambodian*] (CL)
BAP .... Billet a Payer [*Bill Payable*] [*Business and trade*] [*French*]
BAP .... Bomber Regiment (RU)
BAP .... Brevet d'Aptitude Pedagogique [*French*]
BAP .... Brigade Active du Port [*Regular Port Brigade*] [*Cambodian*] (CL)
BAP .... Brigades Attelees de Production (MAR)
BAP .... Bulgarian Agrarian Party (PPW)
BAP .... Bureau Algerien des Petroles (MAR)
Bapco.......... Bahrain Petroleum Company (ME)
BAPERDA ... Badan Perentjanaan Daerah [*Regional Planning Board*] (IN)
BAPERNAS ... Badan Perentjanaan Nasional [*National Planning Board*] (IN)
BAPINDO .... Bank Pembangunan Indonesia [*Indonesian Development Bank*] (IN)
BAPP.......... Bureau Arabe de Presse et de Publications (MAR)
BAPPENAS ... Badan Perentjanaan Pembangunan Nasional [*National Development Planning Board*] (IN)
BAPSA .... Brigade d'Assistance aux Personnes sans Abri [*French*]
BAPSC .... Badeku Agricultural Production and Supply Company (MAR)
bapt............ Baptista [*Baptist*] (HU)
BAPV.......... High-Speed Automatic Reclosing (RU)
bar.............. Barometryczny [*Barometric*] [*Polish*]
bar.............. Baron [*Baron*] [*Polish*]
Bar.............. Barrack [*Topography*] (RU)
BAR............. Berliner Aussenring [*Berlin Outer Ring*] (EG)
BAR............. Billet a Recevoir [*Bill Receivable*] [*Business and trade*] [*French*]
BAR............. Brigade Aeroportee Renforcee [*Reinforced Airborne Brigade*] [*Zairian*] (AF)
BARA .... Barisan Rakyat [*People's Front*] [*Bruneian*] (ML)
BARA .... Bureau d'Analyse et de Recherche Appliquees [*Bureau of Analysis and Applied Research*] [*French*]
BARABA ..... Narodni Podnik pro Stavbu Tunelu [*National Enterprise for the Construction of Tunnels*] (CZ)
BARC .... Berger Ardoin & Compagnie (MAR)
BARC .... Bhabha Atomic Research Centre [*Indian*]
BARC .... Bus Apartheid Resistance Committee (MAR)
Bar-Der-Is... Bagirsak ve Deri Iscilerin Sendikasi [*Animal Casings and Leather Workers Union*] (TU)
BAREM........ Bureau Algerien de Recherches et d'Exploitation Miniere (MAR)
BARIM......... Bureau d'Achat de la Republique Islamique de Mauritanie [*Islamic Republic of Mauritania Purchasing Office*] (AF)
BARJASA.... Barisan Ra'ayat Jati Sarawak [*Sarawak Indigenous People's Front*] (ML)
BARKISAN ... Bartin Kirec Sanayii AS [*Bartin Lime Industry, Inc.*] [*Zonguldak*] (TU)
BARMEL ..... Bureau Africain et Malgache de Recherches et d'Etudes Legislatives (MAR)
BARN .... Biologisch Agrarische Reactor Nederland [*Netherlands Biological Agrarian Reactor*] (WEN)
barom .... Barometer [*Barometer*] (HU)
barr .... Barrique [*French*]
BARRA .... Barisan Revolusi Rakyat [*People's Revolution Front*] (ML)
B/ART .... Bataillon d'Artillerie [*Artillery Battalion*] [*Cambodian*] (CL)

BARU .... High-Speed Automatic Gain Control (RU)
bas .... Basin, Reservoir [*Topography*] (RU)
BAS .... Bataljon Aerodromski Sluzbe [*Airport Service Battalion*] (YU)
BAS .... Befreiungsaktion fuer Suedtirol [*Liberation Group for South Tyrol*] [*Austrian*] (WEN)
BAS .... Bomber Unit (RU)
BAS .... Dry B Battery (RU)
BASA .... Bahnselbstanschlussanlage [*(GDR) Railroad Automatic Telephone System*] (EG)
BASA .... Banco da Amazonia [*Bank of Amazonia*] [*Brazilian*] (LA)
BASAF .... British and South African Forum (MAR)
BASCOL .... Bauxite Alumina Study Company Limited (MAR)
BASE .... Bureau Africain des Sciences de l'Education [*African Bureau for Science Education*] [*Zairian*] (MAR)
BASEQUA ... Bulletin de l'Association Senegalaise d'Etudes Quaternaires Africaines [*Dakar*] [*A publication*] (MAR)
BASF .... Badische Anilin- und Sodafabrik [*Baden Aniline and Soda Factory*] [*West German*] (EG)
BashASSR ... Bashkir Autonomous Soviet Socialist Republic (RU)
Bashgosizdat ... Bashkir State Publishing House (RU)
bashk .... Bashkir (RU)
BashkASSR ... Bashkir Autonomous Soviet Socialist Republic (RU)
Bashknigoizdat ... Bashkir Book Publishing House (RU)
Bashles .... Kombinat of Lumber Industry Establishments of Bashkir ASSR (RU)
BashLOS .... Bashkir Forest Experimental Station (RU)
Bashneft' .... Association of the Bashkir Petroleum Industry (RU)
BashNIINP ... Bashkir Scientific Research Institute for Petroleum Processing (RU)
BashNIIStroy ... Bashkir Scientific Research Institute for Construction (RU)
Basin-Is .... Turkiye Gazeteciler ve Basin Sanayii Iscileri Sendikasi [*Turkish Journalists and Press Industry Workers Union*] (TU)
Bas Kom .... Bas Komiser [*Chief Commissioner (of police)*] (TU)
Baskomflot ... Basin Committee of the Trade Union of Workers of the Maritime and River Fleets (RU)
Baskommor ... Basin Committee of the Marine Transportation Workers' Trade Union (RU)
Baskomrech ... Basin Committee of the River Transportation Workers' Trade Union (RU)
Bas Muf .... Bas Mufettis [*Chief Inspector*] (TU)
BASO .... Bulletin of the American Schools of Oriental Research in Jerusalem and Baghdad [*A publication*] (MAR)
Bas Ogrt .... Bas Ogretmen [*Head Teacher*] (TU)
BASOMED ... Basutoland Socio-Medical Services (MAR)
bass .... Basin, Reservoir [*Topography*] (RU)
BASSR .... Bashkir Autonomous Soviet Socialist Republic (RU)
BASSR .... Buryat Autonomous Soviet Socialist Republic (RU)
BASUCOL ... Barranquilla Supply Co. Ltda. [*Barranquilla*] (COL)
BAT .... Banque d'Algerie et de la Tunisie (MAR)
Bat .... Bataillon [*Battalion*] [*Military*] [*French*] (MTD)
Bat .... Bateau [*Boat*] [*Military map abbreviation*] [*World War I*] [*French*] (MTD)
bat .... Bateria [*Battery*] [*Polish*]
BAT .... Bois Africains Tropicaux (MAR)
BAT .... Brevet d'Aptitude Technique (MAR)
BAT .... British American Tobacco Company (MAR)
BAT .... Bureau de l'Assistance Technique (MAR)
Bata .... Batallon [*Battalion*] [*Spanish*]
BATAL .... Banque Tchado-Arabe Libyenne pour le Commerce et le Developpement [*Chadian-Libyan Arab Bank for Trade and Development*] (AF)
BATAN .... Badan Tenaga Atom Nasional [*National Atomic Energy Agency*] (IN)
BATC .... British-American Tobacco Company (MAR)
BATCO .... Bauxite and Alumina Trading Company of Jamaica (LA1)
BATELCO ... Bahamas Telecommunications Corporation (LA1)
BATI .... Bintara Tinggi [*Warrant Officer*] (IN)
BATICO .... Batiment et Construction Societe Anonyme (MAR)
Batie .... Batterie [*Battery*] [*Military map abbreviation*] [*World War I*] [*French*] (MTD)
BATIM .... Bureau Africain des Travaux d'Interet Militaire (MAR)
BATIMA .... Societe Batiments et Materiaux (MAR)
BATLSK .... British Army Training Liaison Staff, Kenya (MAR)
BATMAAGA ... Baza de Aprovizionare Tehnico-Materiala pentru Agricultura cu Ambalaje si Gospodaria Ambalajelor [*Base for Technical-Material Supply of Packaging to Agriculture and Packaging Management*] (RO)
BATMMB .... Baza de Aprovizionare Tehnico-Materiala a Municipiului Bucuresti [*Technical-Material Supply Base for Bucharest Municipality*] (RO)
bat-n .... Battalion (RU)
BATO .... Airfield Technical Support Battalion (RU)
BATO .... Britain-Africa Trade Organisation (MAR)
batr .... Artillery Battery (RU)
batr .... Battery (BU)
BATRAL .... Batiment de Transport Leger [*Light Transport Ship*] [*French*] (WER)
batr b/o .... Recoilless Gun Battery (RU)
batr b/o .... Recoilless Gun Battery (BU)
batr FR .... Photogrammetric Reconnaissance Battery (BU)
batr PTURS ... Antitank Guided Missile Battery (BU)
batr PTURS ... Antitank Guided Missile Battery (RU)
batr RTR .... Electronic Reconnaissance Battery (BU)
batr RU .... Reconnaissance Battery Command and Control (BU)
Batr SAU .... Battery of Self-Propelled Guns (RU)
batr s/o .... Battery of Self-Propelled Guns (BU)
batr s/o .... Battery of Self-Propelled Guns (RU)
batr TR .... Topographic Battery [*Artillery*] (BU)
batr ZR .... Sound Ranging Battery (BU)
batshd .... Baterie Samohybnych Del [*Battery of Self-Propelled Artillery*] (CZ)
batsr .... Artillery Ordnance Supply and Repairs Battalion (BU)
Batt .... Batterie [*Battery*] [*Military*] [*French*] (MTD)
BAUGS .... Bulletin of the All Union Geographical Society [*A publication*] (MAR)
Baumstr .... Baumeister [*German*]
BAUXIVEN ... Bauxita Venezolana, CA [*Venezuelan*] (LA)
BAV .... Barium-Aluminum-Vanadium Catalyst (RU)
BAV .... Bereit zur Arbeit und zur Verteidigung des Friedens (Sportleistungsabzeichen) [*Ready for Work and for the Defense of Peace (Sport Achievement Medal)*] (EG)
BAV .... Bizomanyi Aruhaz Vallalat [*Retail Store for Sales on Commission*] (HU)
BAV .... Boucherie Arsenique Vert (MAR)
BAV .... Bulharska Akademie Ved [*Bulgarian Academy of Sciences*] (CZ)
BAV .... Large Amphibian Truck (RU)
BAWU .... Black Allied Workers Union [*South African*] (AF)
BAYA .... Brong Ahafo Youth Association (MAR)
BAYBA .... Bayindirlik Bakanligi [*Public Works Ministry*] (TU)
Baysen-Is .... Ministry of Public Works Directorate General of Construction Activities Workers Union (TU)
BAZ .... Automobile Made by the Belorussian Automobile Plant (RU)
baz .... Basalt (RU)
BAZ .... Belorussian Automobile Plant (RU)
BAZ .... Biuro Angazowania Zalog [*Crew Hiring Office*] (POL)
BAZ .... Bogoslovsk Aluminum Plant [*Karpinsk*] (RU)
BAZ .... Character Analysis Unit (RU)
BAZA .... Banque du Zaire (MAR)
BAZIL .... Office of Automation of the Moscow Automobile Plant Imeni Likhachev (RU)
BAZIS .... Office of Automation of the Moscow Automobile Plant Imeni Stalin (RU)
bazkom .... Base Committee (RU)
bazotsentrir ... Base-Centered (RU)
BAZS .... Union of Bulgarian University Students of the Agrarian Party (BU)
BB .... Baloldali Blokk [*Coalition of the Left*] (HU)
B de B .... Banco de Bogota [*Bogota*] (COL)
BB .... Banco do Brasil [*Bank of Brazil*] (LA)
BB .... Bangsa Bersatu [*United Nations*] (ML)
BB .... Bankim Barotra [*Commerce Bank*] [*Malagasy*] (AF)
BB .... Barbados [*Two-letter standard code*] (CNC)
BB .... Battalion Base (RU)
BB .... Baugrunduntersuchung Berlin [*Office for Construction-Site Surveys in Berlin*] (EG)
BB .... Bayindirlik Bakanligi [*Public Works Ministry*] (TU)
bb .... Beacon Keeper's Cabin [*Topography*] (RU)
BB .... Beruhazasi Bank [*Investment Bank*] (HU)
BB .... Betriebsabrechnungsbogen [*Master Summary Sheet, Operations Sheet, Cost Control Sheet*] [*Also, BAB*] (EG)
BB .... Betriebsberichterstattung [*Enterprise Reporting*] (EG)
bb .... Bez Broja [*No Number*] (YU)
BB .... Billet de Bank [*Bank Note*] [*French*] (GPO)
bb .... Bojni Brod [*Battleship*] (YU)
BB .... Brasseries de Brazzaville (MAR)
BB .... Budapest Bajnoksag [*Budapest Championship*] (HU)
BB .... Bundesbahnen [*German*]
BB .... Hospital Base (BU)
BB .... Short-Range Bomber (RU)
BB .... Turret Battery (RU)
BBA .... Banco Boliviano Agropecuario [*Bolivian Farming Bank*] (LA1)
BBA .... Banque Belge d'Afrique (MAR)
BBA .... Berichterstattung zum Plan der Berufsausbildung [*Report on the Vocational Training Plan*] (EG)
BBA .... Bolnicka Baza Armije [*Army Hospital Base*] (YU)
BBA .... Botswana Bowling Association (MAR)
BBA .... Short-Range Bombardment Aviation (RU)
BBAB .... Banque Belgo-Africaine du Burundi (MAR)
BBAD .... Short-Range Bomber Division (RU)
BBAN .... Library of the Bulgarian Academy of Sciences (BU)
BBAP .... Short-Range Bomber Regiment (RU)
BBC .... Biplabi Bangla Congress [*Indian*] (PPW)
BBC .... Boxing Board of Control (MAR)
BBC .... British Broadcasting Corporation (MAR)
BBC .... Brown Boveri & Cie. [*German-Swiss builder of electrical engineering and electronic equipment, nuclear power plants, and machinery*] (EG)
BBD .... Banque Beninoise pour le Developpement [*Beninese Development Bank*] (AF)
BBD .... Buero der Betreuung der Diplomaten [*Service Office for Diplomats*] (EG)

BBE .... Short-Range Bomber Squadron (RU)
bbetr .... Concrete Construction Battalion (RU)
bbetr .... Concrete Works Battalion (BU)
BBF .... Front Hospital Base (BU)
BBG .... Biro Bantuan Guaman [*Legal Aid Bureau*] (ML)
BBG .... Bodenbearbeitungsgeraete, Leipzig [*Leipzig Agricultural Machines and Implements Plant*] (EG)
BBI .... Bereich Bezirksgeleitete Industrie [*Area or Field of Bezirk Managed Industry*] (EG)
BBI .... Bulgarian Bibliographic Institute (BU)
BBIEP .... Elin Pelin Bulgarian Bibliographic Institute (BU)
BBK .... Beroepsvereniging Beeldende Kunstenaars [*Professional Association of Plastic Artists*] [*Dutch*] (WEN)
BBK .... Bezirksbankkontor [*Bezirk Banking Office*] (EG)
BBK .... Bibliotehkarisch-Bibliographische Klassifikation
BBK .... Bolnicka Baza Korpusa [*Corps Hospital Base*] [*Military*] (YU)
BBK .... White Sea-Baltic Canal (RU)
BBL .... Banque Bruxelles Lambert [*Belgian*]
BBL .... Baubetriebsleitung [*Construction Management*] (EG)
BBME .... British Bank of the Middle East [*Moroccan*] (MAR)
BBO .... Binnenschiffs-Besetzungsordnung [*Inland Water Transport Crew Regulations*] (EG)
BBO .... Coast Defense Base (RU)
BBO .... Coast Defense Battleship (RU)
BBP .... Bagersko-Brodarsko Preduzece [*Dredging and Shipping Establishment*] (YU)
BBP .... Bechuanaland Border Police (MAR)
BBP .... Short-Range Bomber Regiment (RU)
BBR .... Babarci Buzatermelesi Rendszer [*Babarci Wheat Growing System*] (HU)
BBRU .... Bituminous Binder Research Unit (MAR)
BBS .... Betriebsberufsschule [*Plant Vocational Training School*] (EG)
BBS .... Biblioteka Beletrystyki Sportowej [*Sport Fiction Series*] (POL)
BBS .... Bioloska Borbena Sredstva [*Biological Combat Equipment*] (YU)
BBS .... Borodino Biological Station (RU)
BBS .... Short-Range Bomber Unit (RU)
BBSS .... Bielsko-Bialska Spoldzielnia Spozywcow [*Bielsko-Biala Consumers' Cooperative*] (POL)
BBT .... Barbier, Bernard, et Turenne (MAR)
BBUD .... Bornova Buyuk Ulkucu Dernegi [*Bornova Greater Idealist Association*] (TU)
BbV .... Babiski Vestnik [*Midwife's Review*] [*Ljubljana*] [*A publication*] (YU)
BBV .... Bacteriological Warfare Agent (RU)
BBWA .... Bank of British West Africa (MAR)
BBWR .... Bezpartyjny Blok Wspolpracy z Rzadem [*Non-Party Bloc of Cooperation with the Government*] [*Polish*] (PPE)
BBYP .... Birinci Bes Yillik Plani [*First Five-Year Plan*] (TU)
BBZ .... Barclays Bank of Zimbabwe (MAR)
BBZ .... Large Concrete Plant (RU)
BBZG .... Bielsko-Bialski Zaklady Gastronomiczne [*Bielsko-Biala Restaurant Enterprises*] (POL)
Bc .... Bacau [*Bacau*] (RO)
BC .... Backpackers Club (EA)
Bc .... Banc [*Bank*] [*French*] (NAU)
BC .... Bataillon des Chasseurs [*Infantry Battalion*] [*Cambodian*] (CL)
bc .... Beco [*Cul-de-Sac*] [*Portuguese*] (CED)
BC .... Bibliotheque Congo (MAR)
BC .... Brevet Commercial (MAR)
Bc .... Brzina Cilja [*Target Speed*] [*Military*] (YU)
BC .... Smokeless Powder for Field Guns [*Symbol*] [*French*] (MTD)
BCA .... Bamenda Cooperative Association (MAR)
BCA .... Banque Centrafricaine Arabe (MAR)
BCA .... Banque Centrale d'Algerie [*Central Bank of Algeria*] (AF)
BCA .... Banque Commerciale Africaine (MAR)
BCA .... Bataillon de Commandement et d'Appui [*Headquarters and Support Battalion*] [*Algerian*] (AF)
BCA .... Bouchonnerie et Capsulerie d'Algerie (MAR)
BCA .... British Central Africa (MAR)
BCA .... British Chief Administrator (MAR)
BCAET .... Bureau Central Africain d'Etudes Techniques (MAR)
BCAIF .... Agricultural, Industrial, and Mortgage Credit Bank [*Lebanese*] (ME)
BCAR .... British Council for Aid to Refugees (MAR)
BCB .... Banque Commerciale du Benin [*Benin Commercial Bank*] (AF)
BCB .... Banque de Credit de Bujumbura [*Bujumbura Credit Bank*] [*Burundi*] (AF)
BCB .... Biographie Coloniale Belge (MAR)
BCB .... Bureau Congolais des Bois (MAR)
BCC .... Banjul City Council (MAR)
BCC .... Bank of Credit and Commerce (MAR)
BCC .... Banque Commerciale Congolaise [*Congolese Commercial Bank*] (AF)
BCC .... Bataillon des Chasseurs Cambodgiens [*Cambodian Infantry Battalion*] (CL)
BCC .... Bede Cosse Chicaya (MAR)
BCC .... Botswana Christian Council (MAR)
BCC .... Brigada Coheteril Central [*Central Missile Brigade*] [*Cuban*] (LA)
BCC .... Bureau Central de Compensation [*Central Bureau of Compensation*]
BCCI .... Bank of Credit and Commerce International Holdings (AF)
BCCIA .... Banco de Credito Commercial e Industrial de Angola (MAR)
BCCO .... Bureau pour la Creation, le Controle, et l'Orientation des Entreprises et Exploitations [*Office for the Establishment, Supervision, and Guidance of Enterprises and Operations*] [*Congolese*] (AF)
BCD .... Banco de Construccion y Desarrollo [*Bogota-Agencia*] (COL)
BCD .... Banque Cambodgienne pour le Developpement [*Cambodian Development Bank*] (CL)
BCD .... Banque Camerounaise de Developpement [*Cameroonian Development Bank*] (AF)
BCDA .... Bureau Communautaire de Developpement Agricole [*Community Agricultural Development Office*] (AF)
BCDI .... Bureau Communautaire de Developpement Industriel [*Community Industrial Development Office*] (AF)
BCE .... Bloc Catala d'Estudiants [*Catalan Students Bloc*] [*Spanish*] (WER)
BCE .... British Commonwealth and Empire (MAR)
BCEAEC .... Banque Centrale des Etats de l'Afrique Equatoriale et de Cameroun [*Central Bank of the States of Equatorial Africa and Cameroon*] (AF)
BCEAO .... Banque Centrale des Etats de l'Afrique de l'Ouest [*Central Bank of the West African States*] (AF)
BCEDI .... Banque Congolaise d'Equipement et de Developpement Industriel (MAR)
BCEEOM .... Bureau Central d'Etudes pour les Equipements d'Outre-Mer [*Central Studies Office for Overseas Equipment*] [*French*] (MAR)
BCEHS .... Bulletin du Comite d'Etudes Historiques et Scientifiques de l'Afrique Occidentale Francaise [*Dakar*] [*A publication*] (MAR)
BCEN .... Banque Commerciale pour l'Europe du Nord [*Commercial Bank for North Europe*] [*French*] (WER)
BCEOM .... Bureau Central d'Etudes pour les Equipements d'Outre-Mer [*Central Study Office for Overseas Equipment*] [*French*] (AF)
BCGT .... Banque Commerciale du Ghana-Togo (MAR)
BCH .... Banco Central Hipotecario [*Central Mortgage Bank*] [*Colombian*] (LA)
BCh .... Bataliony Chlopskie [*Peasants' Battalions (1940-1944)*] (POL)
BCh .... Combat Operational Unit [*on a naval vessel*] (RU)
bch .... For the Most Part, Mostly (RU)
Bche .... Bouche [*Mouth*] [*Military map abbreviation*] [*World War I*] [*French*] (MTD)
BChF .... Frequency Filter Unit (RU)
BChK .... Bulgarian Red Cross (BU)
BChK .... Great Chu Canal (RU)
b-chka .... Small Library, Series of Small Books (RU)
BChL .... Bojove Chemicke Latky [*Chemical Warfare Agents*] (CZ)
BChS .... Baltic - Black Sea Seiner (RU)
BCI .... Banca Centrala de Investitii [*Central Investment Bank*] (RO)
BCI .... Banque Centrafricaine d'Investissement (MAR)
B-cia .... Bracia [*Brothers*] [*Polish*]
BCIB .... Bloque de Campesinos Independientes de Bolivia [*Bloc of Independent Peasants of Bolivia*] (LA)
BCIE .... Banco Centroamericano de Integracion Economica [*Central American Bank of Economic Integration*] (LA)
BCK .... Compagnie de Chemin de Fer Bas-Congo-Katanga (MAR)
BCKR .... Bulgarski Centralny Komitet Rewolucyjny [*Bulgarian Central Revolutionary Committee*] (POL)
BCL .... Bamangwato Concessions Limited (MAR)
BCL .... Bureau Central Laitier (MAR)
BCM .... Banque Centrale du Mali (MAR)
BCM .... Banque Centrale de la Mauritanie [*Central Bank of Mauritania*] (AF)
BCM .... Banque Commerciale du Maroc (MAR)
BCM .... Berendi Cement Muvek [*Berend Cement Works*] (HU)
BCM .... Black Consciousness Movement [*South African*] (MAR)
BCMSA .... Black Consciousness Movement of South Africa (AF)
BCN .... Banco Central de Nicaragua [*Central Bank of Nicaragua*] (LA1)
BCNN .... Broadcasting Company of Northern Nigeria Ltd. (MAR)
Bco .... Banco [*Bank*] [*Italian*] (NAU)
Bco .... Banco [*Bank*] [*Portuguese*] (NAU)
Bco .... Banco [*Bank*] [*Spanish*] (NAU)
BCON .... Branzowy Centralny Osrodek Normalizacyjny [*Central Standardization Point for Production Divisions*] (POL)
BCP .... Basotho Congress Party (PPW)
BCP .... Basutoland Congress Party (MAR)
BCP .... Black Community Program (MAR)
BCP .... Borneo Communist Party (ML)
BCP .... Boucherie-Charcuterie-Perigourdine (MAR)
BCP .... Bulgarian Communist Party [*Bulgarska Komunisticheska Partia*] (PPW)
BCP .... Burma Communist Party [*"White Flag" party*] (PD)
BCPE .... Bulletin du Centre Protestant d'Etudes [*A publication*] (MAR)
BCPOU .... Bahamas Communications and Public Officers Union (LA1)
BCPP .... Bureau Communautaire de Produits de la Peche (MAR)
BCR .... Banco Central de Reservas [*Central Reserve Bank*] [*Peruvian*] (LA)

BCR .... Banque Commerciale du Rwanda [*Commercial Bank of Rwanda*] (AF)
BCR .... Base Central de Reparacoes (do Estado Maior das FAPLA) [*Center for Repairs (of the FAPLA General Staff)*] [*Angolan*] (AF)
BCR .... Botswana Council of Refugees (MAR)
BCRA .... Banco Central de la Republica Argentina [*Central Bank of the Argentine Republic*] (LA)
BCRA .... Bureau Central de Renseignements et d'Action [*Free French*]
BCRG .... Banque Centrale de la Republique de Guinee [*Central Bank of the Republic of Guinea*] (AF)
BCS .... Bataillon de Commandement et des Services [*Command and Service Battalion*] [*French*] (WER)
BCS .... Bugisu Coffee Scheme (MAR)
BCSA .... Botswana Civil Servants Association (MAR)
BCSR .... Bureau de Commercialisation et de Stabilisation des Prix du Paddy et des Riz [*Rice and Paddy Marketing and Stabilization Office*] [*Malagasy*] (AF)
BCSz Kut Int ... Bor-, Cipo-, es Szormeipari Kutato Intezet [*Research Institute for the Leather, Shoe, and Fur Industries*] (HU)
BCT .... Banque Centrale de Tunisie [*Central Bank of Tunisia*] (AF)
BCT .... Bureau Central des Traitements [*Central Salary Office*] [*Zairian*] (AF)
BCT .... Bureau de Controle Technique [*Algerian*] (MAR)
BCU .... Banco Central del Uruguay [*Central Bank of Uruguay*] (LA)
BCU .... Biblioteca Centrala Universitara [*Central University Library*] (RO)
BCU .... Botswana Cooperative Union (MAR)
BCU .... Bugisu Cooperative Union Limited (MAR)
BCV .... Banco Central de Venezuela [*Central Bank of Venezuela*] (LA)
Bcvs .... Bascavus [*Master Sergeant*] (TU)
BCW .... Botswana Council of Women (MAR)
BCZ .... Banque Commerciale Zairoise [*Zairian Commercial Bank*] (AF)
b-czka .... Biblioteczka [*Little Library*] [*Often used for a series of books*] (POL)
BD .... Baccalaureat en Droit [*French*]
Bd .... Bad [*German*]
Bd .... Band [*Volume*] [*German*] (GPO)
bd .... Band [*Volume*] [*Swedish*] (GPO)
BD .... Bangladesh [*Two-letter standard code*] (CNC)
BD .... Betriebsdirektion [*Plant Management*] (EG)
bd .... Bez Daty [*Undated*] [*Polish*]
bd .... Bind [*Volume*] [*Danish*] (GPO)
BD .... Birlesik Devletler [*United States*] [*Turkish*] (GPO)
bd .... Bomber Division (RU)
bd .... Boulevard [*Boulevard*] [*French*] (CED)
bd .... Bulevardul [*Boulevard*] [*Romanian*] (CED)
BD .... Bulgarian State (BU)
BD .... Bureau Departemental [*Algerian*] (MAR)
BD .... Combat Patrol (RU)
BD .... Flank Patrol (RU)
BD .... High Pressure (RU)
BDA .... Banco de Desarrollo Agropecuario [*Agricultural and Livestock Development Bank*] (LA)
BDA .... Bibliotheek & Documentatie Akademie
bda .... Brygada [*Brigade*] [*Polish*]
BDA .... Bund Deutscher Architekten [*League of German Architects*] (EG)
BDA .... Bundesvereinigung der Deutschen Arbeitgeberverbaende [*Confederation of German Employers Associations*] [*West German*] (WEN)
BDAD .... Bibliotheek & Documentatie Akademie Deventer
BDAG .... Bibliotheek & Documentatie Akademie Groningen
BDAO .... Banque de Developpement de l'Afrique de l'Ouest (MAR)
BDAS .... Bibliotheek & Documentatie Akademie Sittard
BDAT .... Bibliotheek & Documentatie Akademie Tilburg
BDB .... Barbados Development Bank (LA1)
BDB .... High-Speed Landing Barge (RU)
BDC .... Baza pentru Desfacerea Cartii [*Base for Book Distribution*] (RO)
BDC .... Biroul de Compensatii [*Compensation Office*] (RO)
BDC .... Bloc Democratique Camerounais (MAR)
BDC .... Botswana Development Corporation (MAR)
BDCh .... Frequency Division Unit (RU)
BDD .... Banque Dahomeenne de Developpement (MAR)
BdD .... Bund der Deutschen [*League of Germans*] (WEN)
Bde .... Baende [*Volumes*] [*German*]
Bde .... Borde [*Farm*] [*Military map abbreviation*] [*World War I*] [*French*] (MTD)
Bde .... Brigade [*Brigade*] [*Military*] [*French*] (MTD)
BDE .... Bund fuer Deutschlands Erneuerung [*League for the Renewal of Germany*] (EG)
BDEAC .... Banque de Developpement des Etats de l'Afrique Centrale [*Development Bank of the Central African States*] (AF)
BDEGL .... Banque de Developpement des Etats des Grands Lacs [*Development Bank of the Great Lakes States*] [*Burundi, Rwandan, Zairian*] (AF)
BDET .... Banque de Developpement Economique de la Tunisie [*Bank for the Economic Development of Tunisia*] (AF)
BDF .... Botswana Defence Force (MAR)
Bdfu .... Bordfunker [*Radio Operator*] [*Aviation*] [*Navy*] (EG)
BDG .... Banque de Developpement du Gabon [*Development Bank of Gabon*] (AF)
BDG .... Bloc Democratique Gabonais [*Gabonese Democratic Bloc*] [*Succeeded by PDG*]
BDG .... Bloc Democratique de Gorgol (MAR)
BDG .... Bloc Democratique de Guinee-Bissau (MAR)
BDG .... Bois Deroules Gabon (MAR)
BDI .... Bundesverband der Deutschen Industrie [*Federation of German Industries*] [*West German*] (WEN)
BDI .... Bureau de Developpement Industriel [*Industrial Development Office*] [*Ivorian*] (AF)
BDI .... Burundi [*Three-letter standard code*] (CNC)
BDIC .... Bibliotheque de Documentation Internationale Contemporaine (MAR)
BDK .... Bank for Long-Term Industrial Credit (RU)
BDK .... Bezirksdirektion fuer den Kraftverkehr [*Bezirk Directorate for Automotive Traffic*] (EG)
Bdk .... Bodenkultur [*German*]
bdk .... Brigade of Landing Ships (BU)
BDK .... Bruesseler Dezimal Klassifikation
BDK .... Bulgarian State Conservatory (BU)
BDK .... Bureau for Services to the Diplomatic Corps (BU)
BDK .... Infinitely Long Cable (RU)
BDKDD .... Bingol Devrimci Kultur ve Dayanisma Dernegi [*Bingol Revolutionary Cultural and Solidarity Association*] (TU)
BDKJ .... Bund der Deutschen Katholischen Jugend [*League of German Catholic Youth*] [*West German*] (WEN)
BDkmA .... Bundesdenkmalamt [*German*]
BdkProf ...... Professor der Hochschule fuer Bodenkultur [*German*]
BDL .... Banque de Developpement du Laos [*Development Bank of Laos*] (CL)
BDL .... Bulgarian State Lottery (BU)
bdm .... Area Decontamination Battalion (BU)
BDM .... Banque de Developpement du Mali [*Development Bank of Mali*] (MAR)
BDMG .... Banco do Desenvolvimento de Minas Gerais [*Minas Gerais Development Bank*] [*Brazilian*] (LA)
BDN .... Bank Dagang Negara [*State Commerce Bank*] (IN)
BDN .... Saturation Choke Unit (RU)
BDO .... Bois Deroules de l'Ocean (MAR)
BDO .... Bund Deutscher Offiziere [*League of German Officers*] (EG)
BDOB .... Butyl Diiodohydroxybenzoate (RU)
BDP .... Bahamian Democratic Party (PPW)
BDP .... Banque du Peuple [*People's Bank*] [*Zairian*] (AF)
BDP .... Bath and Disinfection Train (RU)
BDP .... Battalion Administrative Point (BU)
BDP .... Bechuanaland Democratic Party (MAR)
BDP .... Beogradsko Dramsko Pozoriste [*Belgrade Dramatic Theatre*] (YU)
BDP .... Bophuthatswana Democratic Party (PPW)
BDP .... Botswana Democratic Party (PPW)
BDPA .... Bureau pour le Developpement de la Production Agricole [*Bureau for the Development of Agricultural Production*] [*French*] (AF)
BDPI .... Bureau de Developpement et de Promotion Industriels [*Bureau of Industrial Promotion and Development*] [*Malagasy*]
Bdr .... Bandar [*Bendar*] [*Seaport*] [*Malaysian*] (NAU)
BDRN .... Banque de Developpement de la Republique du Niger [*Development Bank of the Republic of Niger*] (AF)
BDS .... Bloc Democratique Senegalais [*Senegalese*] (PPW)
BDS .... Bulgarian State Standard (BU)
BDS .... Bund Deutscher Segler [*League of German Yachtsmen*] (EG)
BDS .... Remote Signaling Unit (RU)
BDSh .... Bulgarski Durzhavni Zheleznitsi [*Bulgarian National Railroads*] (EG)
BDSh .... Large Smoke Pot (RU)
BDT .... Banque de Developpement du Tchad [*Development Bank of Chad*] (AF)
BDTC .... Baringo Development Training Centre (MAR)
BDTM .... Bulgarian State Tobacco Monopoly (BU)
BDTRA .... Baza de Deservire Tehnica si Reparatii Aeroportuare [*Airport Technical Services and Repair Base*] (RO)
BDU .... Bromodeoxyuridine (RU)
BDU .... Bundesverband der Dolmetscher und Uebersetzer eV [*Federal Association of Interpreters and Translators*] [*West German*]
BDU .... Remote Control Unit (RU)
BDV .... Bremen Demokratische Volkspartei [*Bremen Democratic People's Party*] [*West German*] (PPE)
BDVC .... Botswana Diamond Valuing Company (MAR)
BDVP .... Bezirksbehoerde der Deutschen Volkspolizei [*Bezirk Office of the German People's Police*] (EG)
BDWi .... Bund Demokratischer Wissenschaftler [*Association of Democratic Scientists*] [*Federal Republic of Germany*] (EG)
BdZ .... Bodenzuender [*Base Percussion Fuze, Base Detonator Fuze*] (EG)
BDZ .... Bulgarski Durzhavni Zheleznitsi [*Bulgarian National Railroads*] (EG)
BDZh .... Bulgarian State Railways (BU)

BDZh .... Bulgarski Durzhavni Zheleznitsi [*Bulgarian National Railroads*] (EG)
BE .... Albumin Extract, Protein Extract (RU)
Be .... Baie [*Bay*] [*See also B*] [*French*] (NAU)
Be .... Baume [*Baume*] [*German*]
BE .... Belgium [*Two-letter standard code*] (CNC)
BE .... Berechnungsgrundlagen fuer Eisenbahnbruecken [*Basic Computation Data for Railroad Bridges*] (EG)
BE .... Brevet Elementaire (MAR)
BE .... Budapesti Eromu [*Budapest Power Plant*] (HU)
BE .... Bukti Ekspor [*Export Certificate*] (IN)
BE .... Butyl Ethyl Acetate [*Solvent*] (RU)
BE .... Electric Razor (RU)
be .... Protein Equivalent (RU)
BEA .... Banque Exterieure d'Algerie [*Algerian Foreign Bank*] (AF)
BEA .... British East Africa (MAR)
BEAAC .... British East Africa Army Corps (MAR)
BEAC .... Banque des Etats de l'Afrique Centrale [*Bank of Central African States*] (AF)
BEAC .... Budapesti Egyetemi Atletikai Club [*University Athletic Club of Budapest*] (HU)
bead .... Coast Artillery Battalion (BU)
BEAG .... Budapesti Elektroakusztikai Gyar [*Budapest Electroacoustics Factory*] (HU)
beap .... Coast Artillery Regiment (BU)
bearb .... Bearbeitet [*Edited*] [*German*]
beauftr .... Beauftragt [*German*]
BEB .... Be- und Entladebetriebe [*Loading and Unloading Enterprises*] (EG)
BEBIM .... Bulletin of Experimental Biology and Medicine [*A publication*] (RU)
BEC .... Bahamas Electricity Corporation (LA1)
BEC .... Banco do Estado do Ceara [*Ceara State Bank*] [*Brazilian*] (LA)
BEC .... Berkeley Enthusiasts Club (EA)
BEC .... Brevet d'Enseignement Commercial [*Commercial Education Certificate*] (CL)
BEC .... Brevet d'Enseignement Complementaire [*French*]
BEC .... Bureau de l'Enseignement Catholique (MAR)
BEC .... Bureau Executif Central (MAR)
BEC .... Bureau d'Execution et de Controle [*Application and Control Office*] [*Cambodian*] (CL)
BECEG .... Bureau Europeen de Controle et d'Etudes Generales (MAR)
BECI .... Bureau d'Etudes et de Controle Industriel (MAR)
BECI .... Bureau d'Etudes Techniques de Constructions Industrielles (MAR)
BECIBA .... Societes des Betons et Ciments de Bassa (MAR)
BECIP .... Bureau d'Etudes Industrielles et de Cooperation de l'Institut Francais du Petrole [*Industrial Studies and Cooperation Office of the French Petroleum Institute*] (MAR)
BECOT .... Bureau d'Etudes et de Controle Technique (MAR)
BECSP .... Bureau des Examens et Concours Scolaires et Professionnels [*Scholastic and Professional Examinations and Competitions Office*] [*Cambodian*] (CL)
Bed .... Bedeutung [*Significance*] [*German*]
BED .... Bureau Episcopal de Developpement (MAR)
BEDCO .... Basotho Enterprise Development Corporation (MAR)
BEDE .... Banco de Desarrollo del Ecuador [*Development Bank of Ecuador*] (LA1)
BEDU .... Botswana Entrepreneurs Development Unit (AF)
bed verm .... Bedeutend Vermehrt [*Much Enlarged*] [*German*]
BEEC .... Brevet d'Enseignement Economique et Commercial [*Economic and Commercial Education Certificate*] (CL)
BEEF .... British Egyptian Expeditionary Force (MAR)
BEEN .... Bureau d'Etude de l'Energie Nucleaire [*Belgian*]
bef .... Befejezes [*End, Conclusion*] (HU)
Befama .... Bydgoska Fabryka Maszyn [*Bydgoszcz Machinery Plant*] (POL)
BEFIEX .... Comissao para Concessao de Beneficios Fiscais a Programas Especiais de Exportacao [*Commission for the Concession of Fiscal Benefits to Special Export Programs*] [*Brazilian*] (LA)
BEG .... Banco do Estado da Guanabara [*Guanabara State Bank*] [*Brazilian*] (LA)
BEGA .... Bureau d'Etudes Gabonais d'Architecture (MAR)
begr .... Begruendet [*German*]
begy h .... Begyujto Hely [*Collecting Station*] (HU)
BEGYM .... Begyujtesi Miniszterium/Miniszter [*Ministry/Minister for Collection of Agricultural Produce and Livestock*] (HU)
begyujt .... Begyujtesi [*Collecting (Adjective)*] (HU)
beh .... Behandeln [*Treat, Handle*] [*German*]
Beh .... Behelfsmaessig [*Temporary*] [*In connection with railroad station capacity. It indicates that the station facilities have not been winterized and capacity cannot be maintained under winter conditions*] (EG)
Beh .... Beher [*Each*] (TU)
beh .... Behozatal [*Import, Imports*] (HU)
BEHC .... Bureau d'Etudes Henri Chomette (MAR)
BEI .... Banca Europea degli Investimenti [*European Investment Bank*] [*Use EIB*] [*Italian*] (WER)
BEI .... Banque Europeenne d'Investissements [*European Investment Bank*] [*French*] (AF)
BEI .... Brevet d'Enseignement Industriel (MAR)
BEI .... Office for Research and Experiments [*ORE*] of the International Railroad Union (RU)
BEI .... Standard-Pulse Unit (RU)
Beibl .... Beiblatt [*or Beiblaetter*] [*Supplement or Supplements (to a periodical)*] (EG)
BEICIP .... Bureau d'Etudes Industrielles et de Cooperation de l'Institut Francais du Petrole [*Industrial Studies and Cooperation Office of the French Petroleum Institute*] (AF)
beif .... Beifolgend [*Enclosed*] (EG)
beiflgd .... Beifolgend [*Enclosed*] [*German*]
beigeb .... Beigebunden [*Bound*] [*German*]
beigedr .... Beigedruckt [*Printed With*] [*German*]
Beih .... Beihefte [*Supplements*] [*German*]
beil .... Beiliegend [*Enclosed*] (EG)
Beis .... Beisitzer [*German*]
bej .... Bejarat [*Entrance*] (HU)
bej .... Bejegyzett [*Registered, Incorporated*] (HU)
BEJA .... Brigada Contra el Trafico de Estupefacientes y Juegos de Azar [*Drug Traffic and Gambling Control Squad*] [*Chilean*] (LA)
BEK .... Bakanliklararasi Ekonomik Kurul [*Inter-Ministry Economic Council*] (TU)
bek .... Bekezdes [*Paragraph*] (HU)
BEK .... Biuro Elektryfikacji Kolei [*Railroad Electrification Office*] (POL)
BEK .... Budapesti Eotvos Lorand Tudomanyegyetem Konyvtara [*Library of the Lorand Eotvos University of Budapest*] (HU)
BEK .... Bureau de l'Enseignement Kimbanguiste (MAR)
Bel .... Belediye [*Municipality*] (TU)
Bel .... Belge [*Document*] (TU)
BEL .... Belgium [*Three-letter standard code*] (CNC)
BEL .... Belorussian Railroad (RU)
BEL .... Biuro Ewidencji Ludnosci [*Population Registration Office*] (POL)
bel .... Note (BU)
bel .... White (RU)
BelAPP .... Belorussian Association of Proletarian Writers (RU)
BelAZ .... Automobile Made by the Belorussian Automobile Plant (RU)
BelAZ .... Belorussian Automobile Plant (RU)
BELC .... Bureau pour l'Enseignement de la Langage et de la Civilisation Francaises a l'Etranger [*French*]
BELC .... Buyuk Elci [*Ambassador*] (TU)
BELDE-IS .... Belediye Iscileri Sendikasi [*Municipal Workers Union*] [*Sakarya*] (TU)
belf .... Belfoldi [*Domestic, Internal*] (HU)
bel'g .... Belgian (RU)
Belgiprodor ... Belorussian State Planning Institute for the Surveying and Planning of Highways and Related Structures (RU)
Belgiprosel'stroy ... Belorussian State Institute for the Planning of Rural Construction (RU)
Belgiprotorf ... Belorussian State Institute for the Planning of Peat Establishments (RU)
Belgiz .... Belorussian State Publishing House (RU)
BELGOLAISE ... Banque Belgo-Zairoise [*Belgian-Zairian Bank*] (AF)
Belgosizdat ... Belorussian State Publishing House (RU)
Belgosproyekt ... Belorussian State Planning Institute (RU)
Belgosuniversitet ... Belorussian State University Imeni V. I. Lenin (RU)
Belgres .... Belorussian State Regional Electric Power Plant (RU)
Belinsksel'mash ... Belinskiy Agricultural Machinery Plant (RU)
BELIPECHE ... Societe Benino-Arabe Libyenne de Peche (MAR)
belker .... Belkereskedelem [*Domestic Trade*] (HU)
BELKERIG ... Belkereskedelmi Igazgatosag [*Domestic Trade Directorate*] (HU)
Belker Min ... Belkereskedelmi Miniszterium/Miniszter [*Ministry/Minister of Domestic Trade*] (HU)
BELKM .... Belkereskedelmi Miniszterium/Miniszter [*Ministry/Minister of Domestic Trade*] (HU)
Belkoopsoyuz ... Cooperative Union of the Belorussian SSR (RU)
BelNIILKh ... Belorussian Scientific Research Institute of Forestry (RU)
BelNIIMiVKh ... Belorussian Scientific Research Institute of Reclamation and Water Management (RU)
BelNITOE .... Belorussian Branch of the All-Union Scientific, Engineering, and Technical Society (RU)
BelOKS .... Belorussian Society for Cultural Relations with Foreign Countries (RU)
Belomor .... White Sea (RU)
Belomorkanal ... White Sea-Baltic Canal (RU)
Belonitomash ... Belorussian Branch of the All-Union Scientific, Engineering, and Technical Society of Machinery Manufacture (RU)
belorussk .... Belorussian (RU)
Belpromsovet ... Belorussian Council of Producers' Cooperatives (RU)
BELSPED .... Belfoldi Szallitmanyozasi Vallalat [*Domestic Transport Enterprise*] (HU)
BELT .... Belokranjska Zelezolivarna in Kovinska Tovarna [*Bela Krajina Iron and Metal Foundry*] [*Crnomelj*] (YU)
BELT .... Boloko Enterprises Limited (MAR)
BELTA .... Belorussian News Agency (RU)
BelVO .... Belorussian Military District (RU)
BEM .... Banya- es Energiaugyi Miniszterium/Miniszter [*Ministry/Minister of Mines and Power*] (HU)
Bem .... Bemerkung [*Note, Comment, Observation*] (EG)
BEM .... Borsodi Ercelokeszito Muvek [*Borsod Ore Dressing Plant*] (HU)
BEM .... Bourses d'Etudes du Mayombe (MAR)

BEM .... Brevet d'Enseignement Moyen [*French*] (MAR)
bem .... Brigade of Navy Destroyers (BU)
BEMI .... Biciklista Esperantista Movado Internacia [*International Movement of Esperantist Bicyclists - IMEB*] (EA)
BEMIS .... Besin ve Misir Sanayii AS [*Provisions and Corn Products Industry Corp.*] (TU)
BEMZ .... Baku Electromechanical Plant (RU)
Ben .... Beneficiat [*German*]
BEN .... Benin [*Three-letter standard code*] (CNC)
BEN .... Bureau d'Etudes Nucleaires [*Belgian*]
BEN .... Bureau Executif National (MAR)
BEN .... Buro Ejecutivo Nacional [*National Executive Bureau*] [*Peruvian*] (LA)
BENBO .... Bureau for Economic Research on Bantu Development [*South African*] (AF)
BENELUX.... Belgium, Netherlands, Luxembourg [*Economic Union*]
BenS .... Bibliotheek en Samenleving
BENTP .... Base-Escola de Tropas Paraquedistas [*Paratroopers School/ Base*] [*Portuguese*] (WER)
BEO .... Balesetelharito es Egeszsegvedo Ovorendszabaly [*Safety Rules for Prevention of Accidents and Health Protection*] (HU)
Beob .... Beobachter [*or Beobachtung*] [*Observer or Observation*] [*German*]
BEP .... Brevet d'Enseignement Professionnel [*French*]
BEP .... Brevet d'Etudes Professionnelles [*French*]
BEP .... Brnenska Elektrarna a Plynarna [*Brno Electric and Gas Works*] (CZ)
BEP .... Bulletin of the Electrotechnical Industry [*A publication*] (RU)
BEP .... Bureau d'Edition et de Publicite (MAR)
BEP .... Bureau de l'Enseignement Protestant (MAR)
BEP .... Bureau d'Etude et des Plans [*Study and Planning Office*] [*Cambodian*] (CL)
BEP .... Combat Echelon of Motor Park (RU)
BeP .... Flashless Powder (RU)
BEPC .... Brevet d'Etudes du Premier Cycle [*Elementary School Diploma*] [*French*] (WER)
BEPI .... Bureau d'Etudes et de Participations Industrielles [*Office of Industrial Studies and Investments*] [*Moroccan*] (AF)
BEPM .... Bureau d'Exploitation Petroliere Marocain (MAR)
BEPO .... Armored Train (RU)
BEPS .... Bund Evangelischer Pfarrer in der DDR, Schwerin [*League of Protestant Pastors in the GDR, Schwerin*] (EG)
BEPTOM ..... Bureau d'Etudes des Postes et Telecommunications d'Outre-Mer [*Overseas Postal and Telecommunications Studies Office*] [*French*] (AF)
ber .... Berechnet [*Calculated*] [*German*]
Ber .... Bericht [*Report*] [*German*]
Ber .... Berichtigung [*Settlement (of an account), Adjustment (of a bill), Correction*] (EG)
Ber .... Beruf [*German*]
ber .... Birch (RU)
BER .... Brevet Elementaire de Radio (MAR)
ber .... Coast, Shore (RU)
BER .... Roentgen Equivalent Man (RU)
BERA .... Bureau d'Etudes des Realites Africaines (MAR)
BERAMETAL ... Compania Metalurgica Bera de Colombia SA [*Cali*] (COL)
BERB .... Banque d'Emission du Rwanda et du Burundi (MAR)
BERDIKARI ... Berdiri Diatas Kaki Sendiri [*Standing on One's Own Feet (Self-sufficiency)*] (IN)
BEREG .... Bureau d'Engineering, de Recherches, et d'Etudes Generales [*Algerian*] (MAR)
berend .... Berendezes [*Equipment*] (HU)
BERES .... Bureau d'Etudes pour la Renovation de l'Enseignement Secondaire (MAR)
bergm .... Bergmaennisch [*German*]
BERI .... Bureau d'Etudes et de Realisations Industrielles [*Office of Industrial Studies and Achievements*] [*Algerian*] (AF)
BERIM .... Bureau d'Etudes et de Recherches d'Industrie Miniere [*Office of Mining Industry Studies and Exploration*] [*Algerian*] (AF)
BERJAYA.... Bersatu Rakyat Jelata Sabah [*Sabah People's Union*] [*Malaysian*] (PPW)
BERM .... Armored Evacuation and Repair Vehicle (RU)
berm .... Bermentve [*Postage Paid*] (HU)
BERNAMA ... Berita Nasional Malaysia [*Malaysian National News Agency*] (IN)
BerS .... Berufsschule [*German*]
BERU .... Bureau d'Etudes de Realisations Urbaines [*Urban Projects Studies Office*] [*Algerian*] (AF)
Bes .... Beseri [*Human, Mankind*] (TU)
Bes .... Besitzer [*German*]
bes .... Besonders [*Especially*] [*German*] (GPO)
BES .... Bipolar Electrolyte-Exchange Resin (RU)
beschn .... Beschnitten [*Cut Down*] [*German*]
BESCL .... Banco Espirito Santo e Comercial de Lisboa [*Espirito Santo Commercial Bank of Lisbon*] [*Portuguese*] (WER)
Besin-Is....... Turkiye Et, Ekmek, ve Besin Sanayii Iscileri Sendikasi [*Turkish Meat, Bread, and Food Industry Workers Union*] (TU)
BES-IS .... Bursa Elektrik ve Su Iscileri Birligi [*Bursa Municipal Electric Power and Water Workers Union*] (TU)
beskhoz ...... Ownerless Property, Property in Abeyance (RU)
BESL .... Herring-Fishing Expeditionary Base (RU)
BESM .... Bulletin Economique et Social du Maroc [*Rabat*] [*A publication*] (MAR)
BESM .... High-Speed Electronic Computer (RU)
BESONU ..... Bureau des Affaires Economiques et Sociales des Nations Unies (MAR)
besp .... Non-Party, Non-Party Man (RU)
bespl .... Free of Charge, Gratis (RU)
Best .... Bestand [*Amount*] [*German*]
Best .... Bestellung [*Order*] [*German*]
best .... Bestimmt [*Definite*] [*German*]
Best .... Bestimmung [*Determination*] [*German*]
Best Nr .... Bestellnummer [*Order Number*] (EG)
besz .... Beszerzes [*Purchase*] (HU)
BESZKART ... Budapest Szekesfovarosi Kozlekedesi Reszvenytarsasag [*Metropolitan Transit Company of Budapest*] (HU)
beszolg .... Beszolgaltatasi [*Agricultural Produce Collection*] (HU)
BET .... Board of External Trade (MAR)
BET .... Borkou-Ennedi-Tibesti [*Chadian*] (AF)
BET .... Brigadas Estudiantiles de Trabajo [*Student Labor Brigades*] [*Cuban*] (LA)
BET .... Brunauer, Emmett, and Teller [*Method*] (RU)
bet .... Concrete (RU)
bet .... Concrete Plant [*Topography*] (RU)
BETAB .... Concrete-Piercing Aerial Bomb (RU)
BETAS .... Betonarme Elemanlari Sanayi ve Ticaret Anonim Sirketi [*Reinforced Concrete Workers Industry and Trade Corporation*] (TU)
BETC .... Bureau d'Etudes Techniques de Construction (MAR)
BE-TE-HA ... Biuro Techniczno-Handlowe [*Engineering and Trade Office*] (POL)
BETEX .... Budapesti Textilnagykereskedelmi Vallalat [*Wholesale Textile Enterprise of Budapest*] (HU)
BETONPROIZVOD ... Gradsko Poduzece za Proizvodnju Betonskih Preradevina [*Municipal Establishment for Concrete Manufacture*] (YU)
BETONSAN ... Konut Sanayi ve Ticaret AS [*Reinforced Concrete Housing Industry and Trade Corp.*] (TU)
BETPA .... Bureau d'Etudes Techniques de Projets Agricoles (MAR)
betr .... Betraut [*German*]
Betr .... Betreffs [*or Betreffend*] [*Concerning*] [*German*] (GPO)
Betra .... Betriebs- und Bauanweisungen der Reichsbahn [*GDR railroad regulations for operation and construction*] (EG)
BETRACO ... Societe de Consignation et de Transit du Benin (MAR)
BETT .... Bureau d'Etudes et de Travaux Topographiques (MAR)
BEUB .... Bureau d'Etudes pour l'Urbanisme et le Batiment [*City Planning and Building Construction Studies Office*] [*Malagasy*] (AF)
beurl .... Beurlaubt [*German*]
BEV .... Banco Ecuatoriano de Vivienda [*Ecuadorean Housing Bank*] (LA)
BEV .... Banyaszati Epito Vallalat [*Mining Construction Enterprise*] (HU)
bev .... Bevetel [*Income, Proceeds*] (HU)
Bev .... Bevoelkerung [*German*]
bev .... Bevollmaechtigt [*German*]
Bev .... Billion Electron Volt (RU)
BEV .... Budapesti Elovarosi Vasut [*Budapest Suburban Railways*] (HU)
bev .... Nitrogen-Free Extractive (RU)
BEW .... Berliner Elektromotorenwerk [*Berlin Electric Motor Plant*] (EG)
BEW .... Biuro Ewidencji Wczasowiczow [*Resort Visitors' Registration Office*] (POL)
BEWAG .... Berliner Elektrizitaetswerke Aktiengesellschaft [*Berlin Electric Power Works Corporation*] (EG)
BEWAG (Ost) ... Berliner Kraft- und Licht AG (Ost) [*Berlin Power and Light Corporation (East)*] (EG)
BewaV .... Dienstvorschrift fuer den Bahnbewachungsdienst [*Service Regulations for Railroad Guards*] (EG)
Bez .... Bezhalt [*Paid, Salaried*] (EG)
bez .... Beziehungsweise [*And, And/Or, Or, Respectively*] [*German*]
Bez .... Bezirk [*One of 14 large GDR administrative units*] (EG)
bez .... Bezogen Auf [*Based On*] [*German*]
bez .... Bezueglich [*With Reference To*] (EG)
BEZ .... Bratislavske Elektrotechnicke Zavody [*Bratislava Electrical Engineering Factories*] (CZ)
BEZALKO ... Preduzece za Proizvodnju Bezalkoholnih Pica [*Establishment for Production of Nonalcoholic Beverages*] (YU)
bezFw .... Bezuegliches Fuerwort [*German*]
Bez-Ger....... Bezirksgericht [*Bezirk Court*] [*German*]
bezgw .... Beziehungsweise [*And, And/Or, Or, Respectively*] [*German*]
Bezhetsksel'mash ... Bezhetsk Agricultural Machinery Plant (RU)
bezl .... Bezueglich [*With Reference To*] [*German*]
bezl .... Impersonal (BU)
bezl .... Impersonal (RU)
Bezpieka..... Ministerstwo Bezpieczenstwa Publicznego [*Ministry of Public Security*] (POL)
bezpl .... Free of Charge (BU)
bezv .... Anhydrous, Water-Free (RU)
bezv .... Calm, Windless (RU)
Bezvodn...... Anhydrous, Water-Free (RU)
bezw .... Beziehungsweise [*And, And/Or, Or, Respectively*] [*German*] (GPO)
Bezymyanlag ... Bezymyanka Corrective Labor Camp (RU)

Bf................ Bahnhof [*Railroad Station*] (EG)
BF................ Bakelite-Phenol [*Adhesive*] (RU)
BF................ Baltic Fleet (RU)
BF................ Bassa Frequenza [*Low Frequency*] [*Use LF*] [*Italian*] (WER)
Bf................ Befehlsform [*German*]
B d F.......... Bildmeldung der Flieger [*Photgraphic Report by Aviator*] [*German*]
Bf................ Biophysics (RU)
bf................ Board Foot (RU)
BF................ Fixing Unit [*Computers*] (RU)
BF................ Small-Arm Smokeless Powder [*Symbol*] [*French*] (MTD)
BFA.............. Banco de Fomento Agropecuario [*Agricultural and Livestock Development Bank*] [*Salvadoran*] (LA)
BFA.............. Boucherie France-Afrique (MAR)
BFA.............. Bulletin of Faculty of Arts [*Cairo*] [*A publication*] (MAR)
BfA.............. Bundesstelle fuer Aussenhandelsinformation
BFAN............ Bashkir Branch of the Academy of Sciences, USSR (RU)
BFB.............. British Forces Borneo (ML)
BFC.............. Banque Francaise pour le Commerce [*French Commercial Bank*] (AF)
BFCE............ Banque Francaise du Commerce Exterieur [*French state-owned bank*]
BFD.............. Bund Freies Deutschland [*Free Germany Federation*] [*West German*] (WEN)
BFDB............ Bast Fibres Development Board (MAR)
BFdW............ Bund Freiheit der Wissenschaft [*Association for the Freedom of Science*] [*West German*] (WEN)
Bfe.............. Buero fuer Erfindungs- und Vorschlagswesen [*Office for Inventions and Suggestions*] (EG)
Bf E............ Bundesstelle fuer Entwicklungshilfe [*Federal Republic of Germany Agency for Development Aid*] (EG)
BFF.............. Bund fuer Frieden und Einheit [*League for Peace and Unity*] (EG)
BFK.............. Benzofurancarboxylic Acid (RU)
BFK.............. Great Fergana Canal (RU)
BFKhZ.......... Bulletin of Financial and Economic Legislation [*A publication*] (RU)
BFKP............ Flag Headquarters Ashore (RU)
BFL.............. Basutoland Federation of Labour (MAR)
BFL.............. Biophysical Laboratory (RU)
BFM.............. British Forces Malaya (ML)
BFN.............. Banco do Fomento Nacional (MAR)
BfN.............. Buero fuer Neurerbewegung [*Office for the Innovator Movement*] (EG)
BFNC............ Bloc Federal National Congolais (MAR)
BFO.............. Balneological and Physiotherapeutic Association (RU)
BFP.............. Basutoland Freedom Party (MAR)
BFP.............. Overflow Fixing Unit (RU)
Bfr.............. Belgian Frangi(a) [*Finnish*]
BFR.............. Combat Photoreconnaissance (RU)
BFS.............. Bromophenol Blue [*Indicator*] (RU)
BFSP............ British and Foreign State Papers [*A publication*] (MAR)
BFSz............ Bekescsabai Forgacsolo Szerszamgyar [*Cutting Tool Factory of Bekescsaba*] (HU)
BFSzIB.......... Betakaritasi es Felvasarlari Szallitasokat Intezo Bizottsag [*Committee for Collection and Purchase of Agricultural Produce*] (HU)
BFSzV.......... Baranyai Foldmuvesszovetkezetek Szolgaltato Vallalata [*Supply Enterprise of the Farmers' Cooperatives of Baranya County*] (HU)
BFT.............. Budapest Fovaros Tanacsa [*Municipal Council of Budapest*] (HU)
BFTU............ Botswana Federation of Trade Unions (MAR)
BFUS............ Control Signal Forming Unit (RU)
BFV.............. Banky Fampandrosoana ny Varotra (MAR)
BfV.............. Bundesamt fuer Verfassungsschutz [*Federal Office for the Protection of the Constitution*] [*West German*] (WEN)
BfW.............. Buero fuer Wirtschaftsfragen [*Office of Economic Affairs*] (EG)
BFW.............. Bund Freiheit der Wissenschaft [*Association for the Freedom of Science*] [*West German*] (WEN)
bg................ Ballistic Galvanometer (RU)
BG................ Baris Gucu [*Peace Force*] [*Turkish armed forces on Cyprus*] (GC)
BG................ Bela Garda [*White Guard*] [*Slovenia*] [*World War II*] (YU)
Bg................ Berg [*Mountain, Hill*] [*Norwegian*] (NAU)
Bg................ Berg [*Mountain*] [*Dutch*] (NAU)
Bg................ Berg [*Mountain*] [*German*] (NAU)
Bg................ Berg [*Mountain*] [*Swedish*] (NAU)
Bg................ Berggut [*German*]
BG................ Bezirksgericht [*Bezirk Court*] (EG)
BG................ Blocking Oscillator (RU)
bg................ Borgata [*Suburban Tenement District*] [*Italian*] (CED)
bg................ Borgo [*Village*] [*Italian*] (CED)
Bg................ Bourg [*Large Village*] [*Military map abbreviation*] [*World War I*] [*French*] (MTD)
BG................ Bulgaria [*Two-letter standard code*] (CNC)
Bg................ Bundesgymnasium [*German*]
BG................ Combat Group, Combat Team (RU)
bg................ Commanding General of a Brigade (BU)
BG................ Fuel Base (RU)
BG................ Groupe de Brigade [*Brigade Group*] [*Cambodian*] (CL)
b g.............. Next Year (RU)
Bg................ No Date [*Year of publication not given*] (RU)
bg................ No Date [*Year of publication not given*] (BU)
BG................ Oscillator Unit (RU)
BG................ Tactical Ridge [*Topography*] (RU)
BGA.............. Bulgarian Civil Aviation (BU)
BGA.............. Bulletin of Gosarbitrazh SSSR [*A publication*] (RU)
BGA.............. Bureau de Gerances d'Affaires (MAR)
BGAB............ Bolidens Gruvaktiebolag [*Boliden Mining Company*] [*Swedish*] (WEN)
BGAG............ Beteiligungsgesellschaft fuer Gemeinwirtschaft [*West German*]
B/gal............ Brigadier General [*Brigadier General*] [*Use Brig Gen*] (CL)
BGATs.......... Automatic Hump Unit Centralization [*Railroads*] (RU)
BGB.............. Bauern-, Gewerbe-, und Buergerpartei [*Farmers, Artisans, and Citizens Party*] [*Swiss*] (WEN)
BGB.............. Boulangerie de Grand Bassam (MAR)
BGB.............. Buergerliches Gesetzbuch [*Civil Code*] (EG)
bgb.............. Deep-Drilling Battalion (RU)
BGBl............ Bundesgesetzblatt [*German*]
BGC.............. Benemerita Guardia Civil [*Meritorious Civil Guard*] [*Use Civil Guard*] [*See also GC*] [*Peruvian*] (LA)
BGCE............ Banque Guineenne du Commerce Exterieur [*Guinean Bank of Foreign Commerce*] (AF)
BGD.............. Bangladesh [*Three-letter standard code*] (CNC)
BGD.............. Banque Gabonaise de Developpement [*Gabonese Development Bank*] (AF)
Bgd.............. Beograd [*Belgrade*] (YU)
Bgdr............ Brigadier [*German*]
Bge.............. Barrage [*Dam*] [*Military map abbreviation*] [*World War I*] [*French*] (MTD)
bGeg............ Bei Gegenwart [*In the Presence Of*] [*German*]
BGF.............. Benzoylglycylphenylalanine (RU)
BGG.............. Department of Biology, Geology, and Geography (BU)
BGGF............ Department of Biology, Geology, and Geography (of Sofia University) (BU)
BGG fak........ Department of Biology, Geology, and Geography (BU)
BGH.............. Turkiye Belediye Hizmetlileri Sendikasi [*Turkish Municipal Service Workers Union*] [*Istanbul*] (TU)
BGHD............ Bulletin de Geographie Historique et Descriptive [*Paris*] [*A publication*] (MAR)
BGI.............. Brasseries et Glacieres Internationales (MAR)
BGI.............. Scientific Research Institute of Biogeography (of the State University Imeni A. A. Zhdanov) (RU)
BGI.............. Societe des Brasseries et Glacieres de l'Indochine [*Indochinese Brewery and Refrigeration Plant Company*] [*French*] (CL)
BGIFK.......... Belorussian State Institute of Physical Culture (RU)
BGITIS.......... Belorussian State Institute of Theatrical Art (RU)
BGIUV.......... Belorussian State Institute for the Advanced Training of Physicians (RU)
BGK.............. Bank Gospodarstwa Krajowego [*Bank of the National Economy*] (POL)
BGKh............ Benzene Hexachloride (RU)
BGKhL.......... Biogeochemical Laboratory (of the Academy of Sciences, USSR) (RU)
BGL.............. Banque du Gabon et du Luxembourg (MAR)
BGL.............. Betriebsgewerkschaftsleitung [*Plant Labor Union Executive Board*] (EG)
Bgl.............. Bogoslovski Glasnik [*Theological Bulletin*] (YU)
Bgl.............. Burgenland [*or Burgenlaendisch*] [*German*]
BGL.............. Light Hydraulic Bulldozer (RU)
BGL.............. Societe Brasserie et Glaciere du Laos [*Lao Brewery and Refrigeration Plant Company*] (CL)
Bgld............ Burgenland [*or Burgenlaendisch*] [*German*]
Bgm.............. Buergermeister [*German*]
BGM.............. Bugesera, Gisaka, et Mikongo (MAR)
bgm.............. Without Year and Place of Publication (BU)
BGMP............ Baltic State Maritime Steamship Line (RU)
BGMP............ Hydrometeorological Forecasting Bureau (RU)
BG (OV)........ Bezirksgericht [*Bezirk Court*] [*German*]
BGPI............ Bel'tsy State Pedagogical Institute (RU)
bgr.............. Battle Group (BU)
Bgr.............. Bibliography, Bibliographic (BU)
BGR.............. Bulgaria [*Three-letter standard code*] (CNC)
BGS.............. Bank Gospodarstwa Spoldzielczego [*Bank of Cooperative Economy*] (POL)
BGS.............. Betriebsgewerkschaftsschule [*Enterprise Labor Union School*] (EG)
BGS.............. Bundesgrenzschutz [*Federal Border Police*] [*West German*] (WEN)
BGS.............. Coast and Geodetic Survey [*USCGS*] (RU)
BGSM............ Fuel and Lubricants Base (RU)
BGSO............ Be Ready for Sanitary Defense (RU)
BGSO............ Ready for Health Defense! (BU)
Bgt.............. Berget [*Mountain*] [*Swedish*] (NAU)
BGT.............. Boissons et Glacieres du Tchad (MAR)
BGT.............. Societe des Boissons Gazeuses du Tchad (MAR)
BGTO............ Be Ready for Labor and Defense (RU)
BGTO............ Ready for Labor and Defense! [*Badge slogan*] (BU)
BGTV............ Budapesti Geodeziai es Terkepeszeti Vallalat [*Budapest Geodesy and Cartography Enterprise*] (HU)

BGU............ Bashkir State University Imeni Fortieth Anniversary of the October Revolution (RU)
BGU............ Belorussian State University Imeni V. I. Lenin (RU)
Bgw............ Bergwerk [*German*]
BGW............ Bundeskammer der Gewerblichen Wirtschaft [*Federal Chamber of Commerce and Industry*] [*Austrian*] (WEN)
BGWO......... Botswana General Workers Organization (AF)
BGWU......... Bank and General Workers Union [*Grenadian*] (LA1)
Bh............... Bachelor's Degree (Honours) [*British*]
BH............... Bahrain [*Two-letter standard code*] (CNC)
BH............... Bank Handlowy [*Bank of Commerce*] (POL)
BH............... Banska a Hutni Spolecnost, Narodni Podnik [*Mining and Metallurgical Society, National Enterprise*] (CZ)
BH............... Bezirkshauptmannschaft [*German*]
BH............... Bosna i Hercegovina [*Bosnia and Hercegovina*] (YU)
BHA............. Barbados Hotel Association (LA1)
BHC............. Bank for Housing and Construction (MAR)
BHC............. Black Hebrew Community (MAR)
BHC............. Botswana Housing Corporation (AF)
BHC............. British High Commissioner (MAR)
BHC............. Societe Bois Hydraulique du Cameroun (MAR)
BHESCO..... Building, Hardware, and Electrical Supplies Company Ltd. (MAR)
BHEV........... Budapesti Helyierdeku Vasut [*Suburban Railways of Budapest*] (HU)
Bhf.............. Bahnhof [*Railroad Station*] (EG)
BHF............. Baie Hoe Frekwensie [*Very High Frequency*] [*Use VHF*] (AF)
BHG............. Baeuerliche Handelsgenossenschaft [*Peasants' Trade Cooperative*] (EG)
BHG............. Beloiannisz Hiradastechnikai Gyar [*Beloiannisz Telecommunication Factory*] (HU)
BHK............. Bezirks-Hochwasserkommission [*Bezirk Flood Control Commission*] (EG)
BHM............. Bolge Hareket Merkezi [*Regional Operations Center*] (TU)
BHMMGM... Bas Hukuk Musavirligi ve Muhakemat Genel Mudurlugu [*Chief Legal Adviser and Judgments Directorate General*] (TU)
BHNOOS..... Bosansko-Hercegovacki Narodnooslobodilacki Omladinski Savez [*Bosnian and Hercegovinian National Liberation Youth Federation*] (YU)
BHNV........... Balatoni Hajozasi Nemzeti Vallalat [*Lake Balaton National Navigation Enterprise*] (HU)
BHP............. Bezpieczenstwo i Higiena Pracy [*Industrial Safety and Hygiene*] (POL)
BHPS........... Byro Hlavni Politicke Spravy [*Bureau of the Main Political Directorate*] (CZ)
BHR............. Bahrain [*Three-letter standard code*] (CNC)
BHS............. Bahamas [*Three-letter standard code*] (CNC)
BHS............. Bane a Hute na Slovensku, Narodny Podnik [*Mines and Metallurgical Works in Slovakia, National Enterprise*] (CZ)
BHS............. Banque de l'Habitat du Senegal (MAR)
BHT............. Braunkohlen-Hochtemperaturkoks [*Brown Coal High-Temperature Coke*] (EG)
BHV............. Balatoni Hajozasi Vallalat [*Lake Balaton Navigation Enterprise*] (HU)
BHVK........... Bezirks-Havarie-Verhuetungskommission [*Bezirk Sea-Damage Prevention Commission*] (EG)
BHW............ Berliner Halbzeug-Werke [*Berlin Semi-Finished Products Factory*] (EG)
BHY............. Bursa Hava Yollari Sirketi [*Bursa Airlines Corporation*] (TU)
BHZ............. Berliner Handelszentrale [*Berlin Trade Center*] (EG)
B Hz B......... Bolge Hizmet Birligi [*Regional (or Area) Service Unit*] (TU)
Bi................ Baai [*Bay*] [*See also B*] [*Dutch*] (NAU)
BI................ Banca de Investitii [*Investment Bank*] (RO)
BI................ Banca d'Italia [*Bank of Italy*] (WER)
BI................ Bank Inwestycyjny [*Investment Bank*] (POL)
BI................ Bankin'ny Indostria [*Industrial Bank*] [*Malagasy*] (AF)
BI................ Banque de l'Indochine (MAR)
BI................ Befrienders International (EA)
BI................ Bibliographisches Institut [*Bibliographic Institute*] (EG)
BI................ Bioloski Institut [*Biological Institute*] (YU)
BI................ Bismuth Institute (EA)
BI................ Botanical Institute (BU)
BI................ Brevet Industrielle (MAR)
BI................ Brigade d'Infanterie [*Infantry Brigade*] [*Cambodian*] (CL)
B-I.............. Broz-Ivekovic, Rjecnik Hravatska Jezika [*Dictionary of the Croatian Language by Ivan Broz and Franjo Ivekovic*] (YU)
BI................ Bureau Interdepartemental [*Algerian*] (MAR)
BI................ Burundi [*Two-letter standard code*] (CNC)
Bi................ Byochi [*Anchorage*] [*Japanese*] (NAU)
BI................ Inspection Barometer (RU)
BI................ Institute of Biology of the Bulgarian Academy of Sciences (BU)
BI-.............. Integrating Unit (RU)
BIA.............. Bomber-Fighter Aviation (RU)
BiA.............. Budownictwo i Architektura [*Construction and Architecture*] [*Publisher*] (POL)
BIA.............. Bulgarian Historical Archives of the V. Kolarov State Library (BU)
BIA.............. Bureau Industriel Africain (MAR)
BIA.............. Bureau Industriel d'Algerie (MAR)
BIA.............. Bureau d'Investissements en Afrique [*Office of Investments in Africa*] [*French*] (AF)
BIA.............. Business International Assistance (MAR)
BIA.............. Union of Bulgarian Engineers and Architects (BU)
BIAD............ Bulgarian Society of Engineers and Architects (BU)
BIA-DBVK... Bulgarian Historical Archives of the V. Kolarov State Library (BU)
BIALI........... Bulletin of the Inter-African Labour Institute [*A publication*] (MAR)
BIAO............ Banque Internationale pour l'Afrique Occidentale [*International Bank for West Africa*] (AF)
BIAPE.......... Banco Interamericano de Ahorro y Prestamos [*Inter-American Savings and Loan Bank*] (LA)
BIAT............ Banque Internationale pour l'Afrique au Tchad [*International Bank for Africa in Chad*] (MAR)
BIAT............ Banque Internationale Arabe de Tunisie [*International Arab Bank of Tunisia*] (AF)
BIAZ............ Banque Internationale pour l'Afrique au Zaire [*International Bank for Africa in Zaire*] (AF)
BIB.............. Balatoni Intezo Bizottsag [*Lake Balaton Managing Committee (Tourism)*] (HU)
BIB.............. Banco de Investimento do Brasil [*Brazilian Investment Bank*] (LA)
BIB.............. Bulgarian Historical Library [*Series*] (BU)
BIB.............. Bulgarian Investment Bank (BU)
BIB.............. Bulgarian Mortgage Bank (BU)
bi banka...... Bulgarian Investment Bank (BU)
bibl.............. Biblical (BU)
Bibl.............. Bibliothek [*or Bibliothekar*] [*German*]
Bibl.............. Bibliyografya [*Bibliography*] (TU)
bibl.............. Library, Library's (BU)
bibliogr....... Bibliography, Bibliographic (BU)
bibliogr adres... Publication Data [*Library cataloging*] (BU)
bibliotech... Library (RU)
BIBM........... Bureau International du Beton Manufacture [*International Bureau for Precast Concrete*] (EA)
BIBSKI......... Buyuk Istanbul Bolgesel Su ve Kanalizasyon Idaresi Genel Mudurlugu [*Greater Istanbul Regional Water and Sewage Administration Directorate General*] (TU)
BIC.............. Banco Industrial Colombiano [*Medellin*] (COL)
BIC.............. Bantu Investment Corporation [*South African*] (AF)
BIC.............. Benefices Industriels et Commerciaux [*Industrial and Business Profits*] [*French*] (WER)
BIC.............. Boulangerie Industrielle de Cotonou (MAR)
BIC.............. Brigade d'Infanterie de Choc [*Infantry Shock Brigade*] [*Cambodian*] (CL)
BIC.............. Briqueterie Industrielle du Chari (MAR)
BIC.............. Bulletin d'Information Cooperative [*A publication*] (MAR)
BIC.............. Bureau International des Containers (EA)
BICE............ Banca Internationala de Colaborare Economica [*International Bank for Economic Cooperation*] (RO)
BICE............ Banca Internazionale per la Cooperazione Economica [*International Bank for Economic Cooperation*] [*Use IBEC*] [*Italian*] (WER)
BICELL........ Bimbresso Cellulose SA (MAR)
BICh............ Aircraft Designed by B. I. Cheranovskiy (RU)
BICI............ Banque Internationale pour le Commerce et l'Industrie [*International Bank of Commerce and Industry*] (AF)
BICIA-HV.... Banque Internationale pour le Commerce, l'Industrie, et l'Agriculture de Haute Volta [*International Bank of Commerce, Industry, and Agriculture of Upper Volta*] (AF)
BICIC.......... Banque Internationale pour le Commerce et l'Industrie du Cameroun [*International Bank of Commerce and Industry of Cameroon*] (AF)
BICIC.......... Banque Internationale pour le Commerce et l'Industrie du Congo [*International Bank of Commerce and Industry of the Congo*] (AF)
BICICI......... Banque Internationale pour le Commerce et l'Industrie de la Cote-d'Ivoire [*International Bank of Commerce and Industry of the Ivory Coast*] (MAR)
BICIG.......... Banque Internationale pour le Commerce et l'Industrie du Gabon [*International Bank of Commerce and Industry of Gabon*] (AF)
BICIS.......... Banque Internationale pour le Commerce et l'Industrie du Senegal [*International Bank of Commerce and Industry of Senegal*] (MAR)
BICIT.......... Banque Internationale pour le Commerce et l'Industrie du Tchad [*International Bank of Commerce and Industry of Chad*] (MAR)
BID.............. Banco Interamericano de Desarrollo [*Inter-American Development Bank*] [*Use IDB*] (LA)
BID.............. Banque Islamique de Developpement [*Islamic Development Bank*] [*Use IDB*] (AF)
BID.............. Buitenlandse Inlichtingendienst [*Foreign Intelligence Service*] [*Dutch*] (WEN)
BID.............. Office for Inventions (RU)
BIDC............ Bureau Interafricain de Developpement et de Cooperation [*Inter-African Development and Cooperation Office*] (AF)
BIDCO......... Bauxite Industry Development Company [*Guyanese*] (LA)
Bide............ Bastide [*Country House, Redoubt*] [*Military map abbreviation*] [*World War I*] [*French*] (MTD)
BIDECAL..... Bicicletas de Caldas [*Pereira*] (COL)

BIDI .... Banque Ivoirienne de Developpement Industriel [*Ivorian Bank for Industrial Development*] (AF)
BiDN .... Osrodek Bibliografii i Dokumentacji Naukowej [*Center of Bibliography and Scientific Documentation*] (POL)
BIDR .... Banque Internationale de Developpement et de Reconstruction (MAR)
BIDS .... Bangladesh Institute of Development Studies [*Dhaka, Bangladesh*]
Bie .... Batterie [*Battery*] [*Military*] [*French*] (MTD)
Bie .... Bergerie [*Sheepfold*] [*Military map abbreviation*] [*World War I*] [*French*] (MTD)
BIE .... Bulletin de l'Institut d'Egypte [*Cairo*] [*A publication*] (MAR)
BIE .... Bureau International d'Education [*International Bureau of Education*] [*Use IBE*] (CL)
BIE .... Bureau International des Expositions [*International Bureau of Exhibitions*] (EA)
BIE .... Bureau Ivoirien d'Engineering (MAR)
BIEC .... Bulletin de l'Institut d'Etudes Centrafricaines [*A publication*] (MAR)
BIEGT .... Bulletin d'Information et de Liaison des Instituts d'Ethno-Sociologie et de Geographie Tropicale [*Abidjan*] [*A publication*] (MAR)
BIFA .... Birlesik Alman Ilac Fabrikalari Turk Ltd. Sti. [*United German Pharmaceutical Factories*] (TU)
BIFAD .... Board for International Food and Agricultural Development (MAR)
BIFAN .... Bulletin. Institut Francais d'Afrique Noire [*Dakar*] [*A publication*] (MAR)
BIFAO .... Bulletin de l'Institut Francais d'Archeologie Orientale [*Cairo*] [*A publication*] (MAR)
BIFE .... Banco Interamericano de Fomento Economico [*Inter-American Bank for Economic Development*] (LA)
BIFEN .... Banque Internationale pour le Financement de l'Energie Nucleaire (MAR)
BIFF .... Battlefield Identification Friend or Foe (MAR)
BIFNRJ .... Bibliografski Institut FNRJ [*Federativna Narodna Republika Jugoslavija*] [*Bibliographic Institute of Yugoslavia*] (YU)
BIFOR .... Building Industry's Federation of Rhodesia (MAR)
BIFSA .... British Industries Federation of South Africa (AF)
BIG .... Bois Industriels du Gabon (MAR)
BIGRAP .... Gradezno Pretprijatie Bitola [*Bitola Construction Establishment*] (YU)
BIGWU .... Barbados Industrial and General Workers Union (LA1)
BiH .... Bosna i Hercegovina [*Bosnia and Hercegovina*] (YU)
BIH .... Budapesti Izraelita Hitkozseg [*Jewish Religious Community of Budapest*] (HU)
BIH .... Bureau International de l'Heure [*International Time Bureau*] (EA)
BIHE .... Benue Institute of Higher Education (MAR)
BII .... Banca Internationala de Investitii [*International Investment Bank*] (RO)
BIIL .... Banque Industrielle et Immobiliere de Libye (MAR)
BIIZhT .... Belorussian Institute of Railroad Transportation Engineers (RU)
BIJ .... Banque Inadana Jati [*Inadana Jati (Enn'tean Cheat; National Commerce) Bank*] [*Cambodian*] (CL)
BIK .... Basin Ilan Kuruma [*Press Advertisement Organization*] (TU)
BIK .... Bomb-Run True Heading (RU)
BIK .... Borsodvideki Ipari Kozpont [*Industrial Center of the Borsod Area*] (HU)
BIKh .... Office of Tool Supply (RU)
BIKI .... Bulletin of Foreign Commercial Information [*A publication*] (RU)
BIKSAN .... Birlesik Kablo Sanayii ve Ticaret AS [*United Cable Industry and Trade Corp.*] (TU)
BIL .... Bilangan [*Number*] (ML)
Bild .... Bildung [*Education*] [*German*]
Bildg .... Bildung [*Education*] [*German*]
bili .... Biljardipeli [*Billiards*] [*Finnish*]
b ili m .... More or Less (RU)
bilj .... Biljeska [*Note*] (YU)
Bilkokoop ... Cooperative for Medicinal Herbs (BU)
BIM .... Beriged Infanteri Malaysia [*Malaysian Infantry Brigade*] (ML)
BIM .... Bonneterie Industrielle du Maghreb (MAR)
BIM .... Brigada de Institutos Militares [*Military Institutes Brigade*] [*Colombian*] (LA)
BIM .... Large Ivanovo Textile Mill (RU)
BIMA .... Banque Internationale pour la Mauritanie [*International Bank for Mauritania*] (AF)
BIMA .... Bosques e Industrias Madereras, SA [*Timber and Lumber Industries, Inc.*] [*Chilean*] (LA)
BIMAS .... Bimbingan Massa [*Mass Guidance (Name of government-supported agricultural production projects)*] (IN)
BIMAS .... Birlesik Insaat ve Muhendislik Anonim Sirketi [*United Construction and Engineering Corporation*] (TU)
BIMCO .... Baltic and International Maritime Conference (EA)
BIMI .... Baptist International Mission (MAR)
BIMKh .... Bulletin of the Institute of World Economy [*A publication*] (RU)
BIMSA .... Bilgi Islem Merkezi Ticaret ve Sanayi AS [*Data Processing Center Trade Corp.*] (TU)
Bin .... Barin [*Military map abbreviation*] [*World War I*] [*French*] (MTD)
BIN .... Biological Institute (RU)
BIN .... Botanical Institute Imeni V. L. Komarov (of the Academy of Sciences, USSR) (RU)
BIN .... Bulgarian Institute of Standards (BU)
BINABOC .... Societe Binard et Bocconi (MAR)
Binb .... Binbasi [*Major*] (TU)
BINGI .... Batalion de Inteligencia y Contra-Inteligencia [*Intelligence and Counterintelligence Battalion*] [*Colombian*] (LA)
BINK .... Berliner Industrie- und Handelskontor [*Berlin Industrial and Commercial Office*] (EG)
BINT .... Office of Foreign Science and Technology (RU)
BIOA .... Biuro Inkasowe Oplat Abonamentowych [*Office for the Collection of Subscription Fees*] [*Post Office*] (POL)
biofak .... Biology Division (RU)
biofiz .... Biophysical, Biophysics (RU)
biogeokhim ... Biogeochemistry (RU)
biogr .... Biographic (BU)
biogr .... Biographical, Biography (RU)
biokhim .... Biochemical, Biochemistry (RU)
biol .... Biologia [*Biology*] (HU)
biol .... Biologia [*Biology*] [*Finnish*]
biol .... Biological, Biology (RU)
biol .... Biology, Biological (BU)
Biol st .... Biological Station [*Topography*] (RU)
Biomedgiz ... State Publishing House of Biological and Medical Literature (RU)
biomel .... Biological Reclamation (RU)
biomet .... Biometric, Biometry (RU)
BIOS .... Near Infrared Region of the Spectrum (RU)
BIOT .... British Indian Ocean Territory (MAR)
BIOTROP ..... Tropical Biology [*Center*] (CL)
BioV .... Bioloski Vestnik [*Biological Review*] [*Ljubljana*] [*A publication*] (YU)
BIP .... Biuro Informacji i Propagandy [*Office of Information and Propaganda*] [*World War II*] (POL)
BIP .... Borbena Izvidacka Patrola [*Combat Reconnaisance Patrol*] (YU)
BIP .... Botswana Independence Party (PPW)
BIP .... Bulletin de l'Industrie Petroliere [*A publication*] (MAR)
BIP .... Bureau International de Presse [*International Press Office*] [*French*] (AF)
BIP .... Combat Information Center (RU)
BIP .... Combat and Political Training (RU)
BIP .... Coreless Induction Furnance (RU)
BIP .... Office of Tools and Devices (RU)
BIPAC .... British Israel Public Affairs Committee (MAR)
BIPALINDO ... Biro Pengapalan Indonesia [*Indonesian Shipping Bureau*] (IN)
BIPAR .... Bureau International des Producteurs d'Assurances et de Reassurances [*International Association of Insurance and Reinsurance Intermediaries - IAIRI*] (EA)
BIPE .... Bureau d'Informations et de Previsions Economiques [*French*]
BIPG .... Banque Internationale pour le Gabon [*International Bank for Gabon*] (AF)
Biprohut ...... Biuro Projektow Urzadzen Przemyslu Hutniczego [*Metallurgical Industry Equipment Project Bureau*] (POL)
BIPT .... Banque Ivoirienne d'Epargne et de Developpement des Postes et Telecommunications [*Ivorian Postal and Telecommunications Savings and Development Bank*] (MAR)
BIR .... Banque Internationale de Reconstruction (MAR)
bir .... Birosag [*Law Court*] (HU)
BIRD .... Banca International de Reconstructie si Dezvoltare [*International Bank for Reconstruction and Development*] (RO)
BIRD .... Banco Internacional para Reconstrucao e Desenvolvimento [*International Bank for Reconstruction and Development*] [*Use IBRD*] (LA)
BIRD .... Banque Internationale pour la Reconstruction et le Developpement [*International Bank for Reconstruction and Development*] [*Use IBRD*] (AF)
BIRF .... Banco Internacional de Reconstruccion y Fomento [*International Bank for Reconstruction and Development*] [*Use IBRD*] (LA)
BIRH .... Bureau d'Inventaire des Ressources Hydrauliques (MAR)
BIRIN .... Biro Industrialisasi [*Industrialization Bureau*] (IN)
BIRKO .... Birlesik Koyunlular Ticaret ve Sanayi AS [*United Sheep Raisers Trade and Industry Corp.*] (TU)
Birl .... Birligi [*Union*] (TU)
birm .... Burmese (RU)
BIRPI .... United International Bureaus for Protection of Intellectual Property
BIRS .... Biblioteka Instrukcji i Regulaminow Sportowych [*Sport Instruction and Regulation Series*] (POL)
BIRSC .... Bulletin de l'Institut de Recherches Scientifiques du Congo [*A publication*] (MAR)
birt .... Birtokos [*Owner, Owning*] (HU)
BIS .... Bahamas Information Service (LA1)
BIS .... Bank for International Settlements (AF)
BIS .... Bataljonska Intendantska Stanica [*Battalion Quartermaster Station*] (YU)

BIS .... Bataljonsko Intendantsko Slagaliste [*Battalion Quartermaster Depot*] (YU)
BIS .... Bayraktarlik Istihbarat Teskilati [*Bayraktar Intelligence Organization*] [*Commander of Turkish forces on Cyprus*] (TU)
BIS .... Belediye Iscileri Sendikasi [*Municipal Workers Union*] [*Isparta*] (TU)
BIS .... Bois Inter Service (MAR)
BIS .... Brigade d'Infanterie Speciale [*Special Infantry Brigade*] [*Cambodian*] (CL)
BIS .... Bureau Interafricain des Sols [*Inter-African Soils Office*] (AF)
BISA .... Botswana Institutions Sports Association (MAR)
BISAN .... Bisiklet Sanayii Limited Sirketi [*Bicycle Industry Corporation*] (TU)
BISAS .... Bursa Iplik Sanayii Anonim Sirketi [*Bursa Silk Industry Corporation*] (TU)
BISER .... Bureau Interafricain des Sols et de l'Economie Rurale [*Inter-African Soils and Rural Economy Office*] (AF)
BISFA .... Bureau International pour la Standardisation de la Rayonne et des Fibres Synthetiques [*International Bureau for the Standardisation of Man-Made Fibres*] (EA)
BIS-IS .... Turkiye Devrimici Buro Iscileri Sendikasi [*Turkish Revolutionary Office Workers Union*] [*Ankara*] (TU)
BISSA .... Bulletin of the International Social Security Association [*A publication*] (MAR)
bisw .... Bisweilen [*Sometimes, Occasionally*] (EG)
BIT .... Bilateral Investment Treaty (MAR)
BIT .... Board of Internal Trade (MAR)
BIT .... Bureau International du Travail [*International Labor Office*] [*Use ILO*] (AF)
BITCO .... Biashara Transport Company Ltd. (MAR)
BITEJ .... Bureau International pour le Tourisme et les Echanges de la Jeunesse [*International Bureau for Youth Tourism and Exchanges*] (EA)
BITIA .... Bursa Iktisadi ve Ticari Ilimler Akademisi [*Bursa Academy of Economy and Commercial Science*] (TU)
Bitk .... Bitkibilim [*Botanical term*] (TU)
BITM .... Bryansk Institute of Transportation Machinery (RU)
BITPR .... Bureau d'Inspection Technique et Professionnelle, de Recherches, d'Etudes, de Documentation, et de Revue de l'Enseignement Secondaire [*Technical and Professional Inspection, Research, Study, Documentation, and Secondary Education Review Office*] [*Cambodian*] (CL)
BITS .... Bureau International du Tourisme Social [*International Bureau of Social Tourism - IBST*] (EA)
BITU .... Bustamante Industrial Trade Union [*Jamaican*] (LA1)
BIU- .... Beta-Ray Level Gauge (RU)
biul .... Biuletyn [*Bulletin*] (POL)
BIUN .... Bloque Integral de Unificacion Nacionalista [*Nationalist Integral Unification Bloc*] [*Venezuelan*] (LA)
BIV .... Banco Industrial de Venezuela [*Industrial Bank of Venezuela*] (LA)
BIV .... Banque Internationale des Voltas [*International Bank of the Voltas*] (AF)
Biv .... Bivouac [*Bivouac*] [*Military*] [*French*] (MTD)
BIV .... Budapesti Ipari Vasar [*Budapest Industrial Fair*] (HU)
BIV .... Contactless Weigher (RU)
Biw .... Biwak [*Bivouac*] (EG)
BIY .... Baska Ihtiyac Yok [*No Further Need (for someone or something)*] (TU)
Biyo .... Biyoloji [*Biology*] (TU)
Biyog .... Biyografya [*Biography*] (TU)
BIZ .... Biuro Inwentaryzacji Zabytkow [*Office of Registration of Historical Relics*] (POL)
biz .... Bizalmas [*Confidential*] (HU)
biz .... Bizottsag [*Committee*] (HU)
B i Zh .... Concrete and Reinforced Concrete (RU)
bizt .... Biztositas [*Insurance, Safety*] (HU)
BJ .... Benin [*Two-letter standard code*] (CNC)
BJ .... Biblioteka Jagiellonska [*The Jagiellonian Library*] [*Polish*]
BJATM .... Baza Judeteana de Aprovizionare Tehnico-Materiala [*County Base for Technical-Material Supply*] (RO)
BJBE .... Bulletin du Jardin Botanique de l'Etat [*Brussels*] [*A publication*] (MAR)
BJEP .... Bureau on Jewish Employment Problems (MAR)
BJIC .... Bulletin des Juridictions Indigenes et du Droit Coutumier Congolais [*Elisabethville*] [*A publication*] (MAR)
BJIDCC .... Bulletin des Juridictions Indigenes et du Droit Coutumier Congolais [*Elisabethville*] [*A publication*] (MAR)
BJK .... Besiktas Jimnastik Kulubu [*Besiktas Gymnastic Club*] [*Istanbul*] (TU)
BJMT .... Bolyai Janos Matematikai Tarsulat [*Janos Bolyai Society of Mathematics*] (HU)
BJR .... Battaillon des Jeunes Ruraux (MAR)
BJR .... Bundesjugendring [*Federal Youth Circle*] [*Austrian*] (WEN)
BJS .... British Journal of Sociology [*A publication*] (MAR)
BK .... Antiboat Battery (RU)
BK .... Bahnknoten [*Railroad Junction*] (EG)
Bk .... Bakiniz [*Look, Please Refer To, See*] (TU)
bk .... Bakken [*Side Street*] [*Norwegian*] (CED)
BK .... Balancing Network (RU)
BK .... Ballistic Cable (BU)
bk .... Bank [*Bank*] (HU)
Bk .... Bank [*Bank*] [*Dutch*] (NAU)
Bk .... Bank [*Bank*] [*Swedish*] (NAU)
BK .... Bank Komunalny [*Communal Bank*] (POL)
Bk .... Banke [*Bank*] [*Danish*] (NAU)
BK .... Banque de Kinshasa (MAR)
BK .... Banyankole Kweterana (MAR)
BK .... Belugyi Kozlony [*Gazette of the Ministry of Interior*] [*A publication*] (HU)
BK .... Benzoic Acid (RU)
BK .... Bibliotheca Kiado [*Bibliotheca Publishing House*] (HU)
BK .... Blocking Contact (RU)
Bk .... Boluk [*Company*] [*Military*] (TU)
BK .... Borclar Kanunu [*Liabilities Law*] (TU)
BK .... Budapesti Kozlony, Hivatalos Lap [*Budapest Bulletin, Official Gazette*] [*A publication*] (HU)
BK .... Bursa Beton Kiremit Ticaret ve Sanayi Ltd. Sti. [*Bursa Concrete Tile Industry and Trade Corp.*] (TU)
BK- .... Drill Carriage, Drill Truck (RU)
BK .... Firing Track (of a Tank), Bomb Run (RU)
BK .... Koch's Bacillus (RU)
BK .... Library of Congress [*United States*] (RU)
BK- .... Protein Plasma Substitute (RU)
b k .... Sentry Box [*Topography*] (RU)
BK .... Switching Unit (RU)
BK .... Tower Crane (RU)
bk .... Unit of Fire (BU)
BK .... Unit of Fire (RU)
BKA .... Armored Cutter (RU)
b-ka .... Bank (BU)
b-ka .... Bank, Shoal [*Topography*] (RU)
Bka .... Banka [*Bank*] [*Russian*] (NAU)
b-ka .... Biblioteka [*Library*] (YU)
b-ka .... Biblioteka [*Library*] [*Often used for a series of books*] (POL)
BKA .... Bundeskanzleramt [*German*]
BKA .... Bundeskriminalamt [*Federal Criminal Police Bureau*] [*West German*] (WEN)
b-ka .... Library (BU)
b-ka .... Library (RU)
BKAA .... Badan Koordinasi Amalan Agama [*Committee for the Coordination of Religious Practices*] (IN)
B/ka sv Kliment ... [*The*] Sveti Kliment Library (BU)
Bkb .... Balkan Coal Basin (BU)
BKB .... Office of Majority Committees (of the RSDRP) (RU)
BKC .... Banque Khmere pour le Commerce [*Cambodian Commercial Bank*] (CL)
BK-CK .... Bibliograficky Katalog - Ceska Kniha [*Bibliographical Catalog - The Czech Book*] (CZ)
BKD .... Bugarsko Knizovno Druzestvo [*Bulgarian Literary Society*] (YU)
BKDH .... Bupati/Kepala Daerah [*Regent/Chief of Region*] (IN)
BKF .... Balkanska Komunisticka Federacija [*Balkan Communist Federation*] (YU)
BKF .... Biblioteka Kultury Fizycznej [*Physical Culture Series*] (POL)
BKG .... Ballistocardiogram, Ballistocardiography (RU)
BKGS- .... Tower Crane for Hydraulic Engineering Construction (RU)
BKGY .... Budapesti Konzervgyar [*Budapest Cannery*] (HU)
Bkh .... Biochemistry (RU)
BKhM .... Chemical Warfare Vehicle (RU)
BKhP .... Chemical Warfare Post (RU)
bkhrr .... Chemical and Radiation Reconnaissance Battalion (BU)
bkhrr .... Chemical and Radiation Reconnaissance Battalion (RU)
BKhS .... Chemical Warfare Agent (RU)
BKhSS .... Combating the Embezzlement of Socialist Property and Speculation (RU)
BKhV .... Chemical Warfare Agent (RU)
BKhV .... Chemical Warfare Agent (BU)
bkhz .... Chemical Defense Battalion (BU)
bkhz .... Chemical Defense Battalion (RU)
Bki .... Banki [*Banks*] [*Russian*] (NAU)
BKI .... Banyaszati Kutato Intezet [*Mining Research Institute*] (HU)
BKI .... Biro Klasifikasi [*Indonesian*]
BKIA .... Balai Kesedjahteraan Ibu dan Anak [*Welfare Clinic for Mothers and Children*] (IN)
b-kite .... Libraries (BU)
BKK .... Bakanliklararasi Koordinasyon Kurullari [*Inter-Ministry Coordination Committees*] (TU)
BKK .... Braunkohlenkombinat Lauchhammer (VEB) [*Lauchhammer Brown Coal Combine (VEB)*] (EG)
BKK .... Bulgarian Constitution Clubs (BU)
BKK .... Channel Switching Unit (RU)
BKK .... Compass Heading on Bomb Run (RU)
BKKhZ .... Bagley By-Product Coke Plant (RU)
BKKI .... Badan Kongress Kebathinan Indonesia
Bkl .... Beklagter [*Defendant*] [*German*] (WEN)
BKM .... Bataljonska Komanda Mesta [*Battalion Command Post*] (YU)
Bkm .... Bekanntmachung [*Announcement*] [*German*] (WEN)
BKM .... Bel- es Kulkereskedelmi Miniszterium/Miniszter [*Ministry/Minister of Domestic and Foreign Trade*] (HU)
BKM .... Belkereskedelmi Miniszterium/Miniszter [*Ministry/Minister of Domestic Trade*] (HU)

BKME.......... Contactless Magnetic Element (RU)
BKMG.......... Biuro Konstrukcji Maszyn Gorniczych [*Mining Machinery Designing Office*] (POL)
BKMS.......... Bulgarian Communist Youth Union (BU)
BKN.......... Airborne Sky Chart (RU)
BKn.......... Bulgarski Knigopis [*Bulgarian Bibliography*] [*A periodical*] (BU)
BKNII.......... Bulletin of the Scientific Research Institute of Regional Studies (at the State Far Eastern University) [*A publication*] (RU)
BKNII.......... Buryat Complex Scientific Research Institute (RU)
BKN-Yu.......... Airborne Sky Chart of the Southern Hemisphere (RU)
BKO.......... Bezpecnostni Koordinacni Odbor [*Security Coordination Department*] (CZ)
BKO.......... Budget Control Section (BU)
bkovr.......... Naval Brigade for District Defense (BU)
BKP.......... Battalion Command Post (RU)
BKP.......... Battery Command Post (RU)
BKP.......... Belgian Communist Party (BU)
BKP.......... Belgische Kommunistische Partij [*Belgian Communist Party*] (WEN)
BKP.......... Bolgar Kommunista Part [*Bulgarian Communist Party*] (HU)
BKP.......... Bromocresol Purple [*Indicator*] (RU)
BKP.......... Bugarska Komunisticka Partija [*Bulgarian Communist Party*] (YU)
BKP.......... Bulgarian Coastal Navigation (BU)
BKP.......... Bulgarian Communist Party (RU)
BKP.......... Bulgarska Komunisticheska Partiia [*Bulgarian Communist Party*] (PPE)
BKP.......... Bulgarya Komunist Partisi [*Bulgarian Communist Party*] (TU)
BKP.......... Burmese Congress of Trade Unions (RU)
BKP.......... Lateral Command Post (RU)
BKP.......... Postal Money Order Control Office (RU)
BKP.......... Shore Command Post (RU)
BKPM.......... Biuro Konstrukcyjne Przemyslu Motoryzacyjnego [*Automotive Industry Designing Office*] (POL)
BKP(ts).......... Bulgarian Communist Party (Left Wing) (BU)
BKPZYe.......... Office of Communist Parties of Western Europe (RU)
BKR.......... Bajai Kukorica Termelesi Rendszer [*Baja Corn Growing System*] (HU)
bkr.......... Bez Kraja [*Without End*] (YU)
BKR.......... Check and Decision Unit (RU)
BKR.......... Compensation and Control Unit (RU)
BKS.......... Badan Kerdja Sama [*Cooperating Committee*] (IN)
BKS.......... Brilliant Cresyl Blue (RU)
BKS.......... Bromocresol Blue [*Indicator*] (RU)
BKS.......... Commutation and Synchronization Unit (RU)
BKS.......... Hip and Large Joints (RU)
BKSAKSI.......... Badan Kerdja Sama Antar Kotapradja Seluruh Indonesia [*All-Indonesia Inter-Municipal Cooperating Committee*] (IN)
BK-SK.......... Bibliograficky Katalog - Slovenska Kniha [*Bibliographical Catalog - The Slovak Book*] (CZ)
BKSKh-.......... Tower Crane for Agricultural Use (RU)
BKSM.......... Bulgarian Young Communist League (RU)
BKSM.......... Construction and Assembly Tower Crane (RU)
BKT.......... British Trades Union Congress [*TUC*] (RU)
BKT.......... Bulgarian Confederation of Labor (BU)
BKT.......... Communist Labor Brigade (RU)
BKTC.......... Bagimsiz Kibris Turk Cumhuriyeti [*Independent Turkish Cypriot Republic*] (TU)
BKTD.......... Bagimsiz Kibris Turk Devleti [*Independent Turkish Cypriot State*] (GC)
BKTM.......... Biuro Konstrukcyjne Taboru Morskiego [*Marine Designing Office*] (POL)
BKV.......... Betriebskollektivvertrag [*Enterprise Collective Labor Contract*] (EG)
BKV.......... Braunkohlenverwaltung [*Brown Coal Administration*] [*See BV*] (EG)
BKV.......... Budapesti Kozlekedesi Vallalat [*Budapest Transportation Enterprise*] (HU)
BKV.......... Life and Culture of the East (RU)
BKVO.......... Berufskrankheitenverordnung [*Regulation on Occupational Diseases*] [*West German*] (WEN)
BKVRD.......... Ramjet Engine (RU)
BkW.......... Bahnkraftwerk [*Railroad Power Plant*] (EG)
BKW.......... Biuro Kontroli Wojskowej [*Office of Military Control*] (POL)
BKW.......... Braunkohlenwerk [*Brown Coal Enterprise*] (EG)
BKZ.......... Barnaul Boiler Plant (RU)
BKZ.......... Lateral Logging (RU)
BL.......... Barackenlager [*German*]
BL.......... Barat Laut [*Northwest*] (ML)
bl.......... Baril [*Barrel*] [*French*]
BL.......... Base Infirmary (RU)
BL.......... Betriebsleiter [*Plant Manager*] (EG)
Bl.......... Blatt [*Newspaper, Sheet*] (EG)
bl.......... Blindage, Dugout [*Topography*] (RU)
Bl.......... Block Signal Box, Block Station [*Topography*] (RU)
Bl.......... Blockhaus [*Blockhouse*] [*Military map abbreviation*] [*World War I*] [*German*] (MTD)
bl.......... Blogoslawiony [*Blessed*] [*Polish*]
bl.......... Blok [*Block*] [*Turkish*] (CED)
Bl.......... Blok [*Block of Houses*] [*Polish*]
Bl.......... Bolge [*Region*] [*Geographical area within the country*] (TU)
Bl.......... Boluk [*Company, Squadron*] [*Military*] (TU)
bl.......... Brilliance (RU)
BL.......... Drum Winch (RU)
BL.......... Naval Base Infirmary (RU)
BL.......... State Library of the USSR Imeni V. I. Lenin (RU)
bl a.......... Bland Andra [*Among Other Things*] [*Swedish*] (GPO)
bl a.......... Bland Annat [*Among Other Things*] [*Swedish*] (GPO)
bla.......... Blandt Andet [*Among Other Things*] [*Danish*] (GPO)
bla.......... Blandt Andre [*Among Other Things*] [*Danish*] (GPO)
bl a.......... Blant Annet [*Among Others*] [*Norwegian*] (GPO)
BLA.......... Bundeslehranstalt [*German*]
BLA.......... Pilotless Aircraft (RU)
BLACT.......... Bureau de Liaison des Agents de Cooperation Technique (MAR)
BLADA.......... Bloque Latinoamericano de Actores [*Latin American Actors Group*] (LA)
BLAE.......... Banco Latinoamericano de Exportacion [*Latin American Export Bank*] (LA)
BLASZ.......... Budapesti Labdarugok Alszovetsege [*Subassociation of the Soccer Teams of Budapest*] (HU)
BLD.......... Bharatiya Lok Dal [*Indian*] (PPW)
BLD.......... Brno-Lisen Draha [*Brno-Lisen Railroad*] (CZ)
bld.......... Bulevardul [*Boulevard*] [*Romanian*] (CED)
Ble.......... Balle [*Bale*] [*Business and trade*] [*French*]
BLE.......... Buddhist League of Esperantists (EA)
BLEU.......... Belgium-Luxembourg Economic Union (PPE)
BLF.......... Baluchistan Liberation Front [*Pakistani*] (PD)
blf.......... Blaetterfoermig [*Flakes*] [*German*]
BLFAE.......... Bureau de Liaison France-Afrique-Europe (MAR)
Blg.......... Beilage [*Enclosure*] [*German*] (GPO)
BlGrO.......... Group Operations Unit (RU)
BLH.......... Bamalete Lutheran Hospital (MAR)
BLI.......... Belorussian Forestry Engineering Institute Imeni S. M. Kirov (RU)
Blinddr.......... Blinddruck [*Blind Tooling*] [*Bookbinding*] [*German*]
BLIROI.......... Bureau de Liaison de l'Information Religieuse dans l'Ocean Indien [*Indian Ocean Religious Information Liaison Office*] (AF)
blizhn.......... Near, Close, Neighboring (RU)
BLK.......... Brygada Lekkiej Kawalerii [*Light Cavalry Brigade*] (POL)
Blle.......... Bouteille [*Bottle*] [*Business and trade*] [*French*]
BLM.......... Beso la Mano [*(I Kiss Your Hand) Respectfully*] [*Spanish*]
BLN.......... Bank fuer Landwirtschaft und Nahrungsgueterwirtschaft [*Bank for Agriculture and Food Production*] (EG)
Bln.......... Berlin [*Berlin*] (EG)
BlNP.......... Short-Range Observation Post (RU)
BLNS.......... Biblioteka Laureatow Nagrod Stalinowskich [*Stalin Prize Winner Series*] (POL)
blo.......... Balloon Squad (BU)
BLOCECH.......... Bloque Campesino del Estado de Chiapas [*Peasant Bloc of Chiapas State*] [*Mexican*] (LA1)
BLOSIRH.......... Bloque de Sindicatos del Ingeniero Rio Haina [*Rio Haina Refinery Union Bloc*] [*Dominican Republic*] (LA1)
BLP.......... Bacterial Lipopolysaccharides (RU)
BLP.......... Barbados Labor Party (LA1)
BLP.......... Besa los Pies [*Kiss the Feet*] [*Spanish*]
blp.......... Blogoslawionej Pamieci [*Of Blessed Memory*] [*Polish*]
BLR.......... Bezirkslandwirtschaftsrat [*Bezirk Agricultural Council*] (EG)
BLR.......... Bolnica Lakih Ranjenika [*Hospital for the Lightly Wounded*] [*Military*] (YU)
BLR.......... Light Casualties Hospital (BU)
BLS.......... Baykal Limnological Station (RU)
BLS.......... Botswana, Lesotho, Swaziland
BLS.......... Brigade Legere de Securite [*Moroccan*] (MAR)
BLS.......... Union of Bulgarian Physicians (BU)
BLT.......... Banque Libyo-Togolaise pour le Commerce Exterieur [*Libyan-Togolese Foreign Trade Bank*] (AF)
BLT.......... Belfoldi Leveltavirat [*Domestic Night Letter (Telegram)*] (HU)
Blt.......... Blaettchen [*Leaflets*] [*German*]
BLT.......... Busola Lakog Tipa [*A Light Compass*] [*Army*] (YU)
BLTI.......... Belorussian Forestry Engineering Institute Imeni S. M. Kirov (RU)
blto.......... Air Technical Support Battalion (BU)
BluStV.......... Vorschriften fuer den Block- und Stellwerkdienst [*Regulations for Block and Control Tower Operations*] (EG)
BLV.......... Bezirkslastverteiler [*Bezirk (Electric Power) Load Distributor*] (EG)
Blvd.......... Boulevard [*Boulevard*] [*French*]
Blvd.......... Bulevard [*Boulevard*] [*Bulgarian*]
Blvd.......... Bulevard [*Boulevard*] [*Romanian*]
BLW.......... Federal Office of Agriculture [*Swiss*]
BLZ.......... Belize [*Three-letter standard code*] (CNC)
bm.......... Author's Note (BU)
Bm.......... Bahnmeisterei [*Railroad Section*] (EG)
BM.......... Banca Mondiale [*World Bank*] [*Italian*] (WER)
BM.......... Banco Mundial [*World Bank*] [*Spanish*] (LA)
BM.......... Banque Mondiale [*World Bank*] [*Use IBRD*] [*French*] (AF)
BM.......... Battalion Mortar (RU)
BM.......... Belugyminiszterium/Miniszter [*Ministry/Minister of the Interior*] (HU)
BM.......... Bermuda [*Two-letter standard code*] (CNC)

bm .... Bez Miejsca [*No Place (of publication)*] [*Polish*]
bm .... Bez Mista [*No Place (of publication)*] (CZ)
bm .... Bezny Metr [*Linear Meter*] (CZ)
BM .... Biblioteka Miejska [*Municipal Library*] (POL)
bm .... Biezacego Miesiaca [*The Current Month*] [*Polish*]
BM .... Binocular Microscope (RU)
BM .... Birlesmis Milletleri [*United Nations Organization*] (TU)
B M .... Bohr Magneton (RU)
BM .... Boundary Marker [*Beacon*] (RU)
BM .... Braca Miladinovi [*Miladinov Brothers*] (YU)
BM .... Bulgarska Misul [*Bulgarian Thought*] [*A periodical*] (BU)
BM .... Combat Vehicle (RU)
BM .... Contactless Micrometer (RU)
BM- .... Marine Bathometer (RU)
BM .... Mechanical Unit (RU)
b m .... Next Month (RU)
b m .... No Place (of Publication Given) (RU)
bm .... No Place of Publication Given (BU)
BM .... Superheavy [*Artillery*] (RU)
BMA .... Bon Marche Africain (MAR)
BMA .... Bonne Maison d'Afrique (MAR)
BMA .... British Military Administration (MAR)
BMA .... Bundesministerium fuer Auswaertige Angelegenheiten [*German*]
BMA .... Butyl Methacrylate (RU)
BMAC .... Boeing Military Airplane Company (MAR)
BMASSR .... Buryat-Mongol Autonomous Soviet Socialist Republic [*1923-1958*] (RU)
BMB .... Bois de M'Balmayo (MAR)
BMB .... Bundesministerium fuer Bauten und Technik [*German*]
BMBR .... Birlesmis Milletler ve Bogazlar Rejimi Dairesi Genel Mudurlugu [*United Nations and Straits Regime Office Directorate General*] [*of Foreign Affairs Ministry*] (TU)
BMC .... Banque de Madagascar et des Comores [*Bank of Madagascar and of the Comoro Islands*] (AF)
BMC .... Bong Mining Company [*Liberian*] (AF)
BMC .... Bosna Film, Morava Film, Croacia Film [*Bosnia and Hercegovina, Serbian, and Croatian Motion Picture Establishments*] (YU)
BMC .... Botswana Meat Commission (MAR)
BMC .... British Motor Corporation Ltd. (MAR)
BMCD .... Banque Malienne de Credits et de Depots [*Malian Credit and Deposits Bank*] (AF)
BMCE .... Banque Marocaine pour le Commerce Exterieur [*Moroccan Foreign Trade Bank*] (AF)
BMChK .... Bulgarian Junior Red Cross (BU)
BMD .... Banque Mauritanienne de Developpement [*Mauritanian Development Bank*] (AF)
BMDC .... Banque Mauritanienne pour le Developpement et le Commerce (MAR)
BMDC .... Biomedical Documentation Centre [*Swedish*]
BME .... Base Material de Estudios [*Study Materials Program*] [*Cuban*] (LA)
bme .... Bombardment Squadron (BU)
BME .... Budapesti Muszaki Egyetem [*Technical University of Budapest*] (HU)
BME .... Bueromaschinen-Export [*Office Machinery Export Foreign Trade Enterprise*] (EG)
BME .... Great Medical Encyclopedia [*A publication*] (RU)
Bment .... Batiment [*Building*] [*Military map abbreviation*] [*World War I*] [*French*] (MTD)
BMF .... Bulgarian Maritime Fleet (BU)
BMF .... Bumiputra Malaysia Finance
BMF .... Bundesministerium fuer Finanzen [*German*]
BMG .... Baader-Meinhof Group [*Revolutionary group*] [*West German*]
BMG .... Bundesministerium fuer Gesundheit und Umweltschutz [*German*]
bmg .... No Place and Year of Publication Given (BU)
BMGK .... Birlesmis Milletler Genel Kurulu [*United Nations General Assembly*] (TU)
BMH .... Berliner Metallhuetten- und Halbzeugwerke [*Berlin Metallurgical and Semifinished Products Works*] (EG)
BMH .... Bundesministerium fuer Handel, Gewerbe, und Industrie [*German*]
BMHW .... Berliner Metallhuetten- und Halbzeugwerke [*Berlin Metallurgical and Semifinished Products Works*] (EG)
BMI .... Bundesministerium fuer Inneres [*German*]
BMI .... Large Toolmaker's Microscope (RU)
BMIB .... Bank-i-Markazi-i-Iran Bulletin [*Teheran*] [*A publication*] (MAR)
b m i g .... No Place, No Date [*Bibliography*] (RU)
BMIHK .... Birlesmis Milletler Insan Haklari Komisyonu [*United Nations Human Rights Commission*] (TU)
BMin f .... Bundesminister Fuer [*German*]
BMIT .... Biological Museum Imeni K. A. Timiryazev (RU)
BMJ .... Bundesministerium fuer Justiz [*German*]
BMK .... Banque Militaire Khmere [*Cambodian Military Bank*] (CL)
BMK .... Bau und Montagekombinat [*Building and Assembly Combine*] (EG)
BMK .... Magnetic Heading on Bomb Run (RU)
BMK .... Motor Tugboat (RU)
BMKGM .... Butce ve Mali Kontrol Genel Mudurlugu [*Budget and Financial Control Directorate General*] (TU)
BMKhP .... Central Scientific and Technical Library of the Ministry of the Chemical Industry (RU)
BMKN .... Badan Meshuarat Kebudayaan Nasional [*National Cultural Council*] (ML)
BMKP .... Birlesmis Milletler Kalkinma Programi [*United Nations Development Program*] (TU)
BML .... Diodeless Magnetic Logical (Element) [*Computers*] (RU)
BML .... Magnetic-Tape Unit (RU)
BMLF .... Bundesministerium fuer Land- und Forstwirtschaft [*German*]
BMLV .... Bundesministerium fuer Landesverteidigung [*German*]
BMM .... Baptist Mid Mission (MAR)
BMM .... Burgas Copper Mines (BU)
BMM .... Buyuk Millet Meclisi [*Grand National Assembly*] [*See also TBMM*] (TU)
BMM .... V. V. Mayakovskiy Library-Museum (RU)
BMMK .... Baltic and International Maritime Conference [*BIMC*] (RU)
BMNIIK .... Buryat-Mongol Scientific Research Institute of Culture (RU)
BMNIIKE .... Buryat-Mongol Scientific Research Institute of Culture and Economics (RU)
BMNP .... Central Scientific and Technical Library of the Ministry of the Petroleum Industry (RU)
BMO .... Briqueterie Mecanique du Ouaddai (MAR)
BMO .... Bureau de Main-d'Oeuvre [*Algerian*] (MAR)
BMO .... Large Magellanic Cloud (RU)
BMOIP .... Bulletin of the Moscow Society of Naturalists [*A publication*] (RU)
BMOP .... Bureau de la Main d'Oeuvre Portaire [*Port Manpower Office*] [*Senegalese*] (AF)
Bmo Padre ... Beatisimo Padre [*Most Blessed Father*] [*Spanish*]
Bmo Pe .... Beatisimo Padre [*Most Blessed Father*] [*Spanish*]
BM OTP .... Belugyminiszterium, Orszagos Tuzrendeszeti Parancsnoksag [*Ministry of the Interior, National Fire Protection Headquarters*] (HU)
BMP .... Bank for International Settlements [*BIS*] (RU)
BMP .... Basutoland Mounted Police (MAR)
BMP .... Battalion Medical Point (BU)
BMP .... Battalion Medical Station (RU)
BMP .... Boevaya Mashina Pekhota [*Infantry Fighting Vehicle*] [*Russian*]
BMP .... Brigades Mecanisees de Production (MAR)
BMP .... Gasoline Motor Pump (RU)
BMP .... Inner Marker Beacon (RU)
BMP .... Marine Battalion (RU)
BMP .... Microprogram Unit (RU)
bmp .... Naval Infantry Battalion (BU)
BMPU .... Magnetic Bomb-Run Track Angle (RU)
bmr .... Bez Miejsca i Roku [*Place and Year of Publication Not Given*] [*Polish*]
BMR .... Contactless Magnetic Relay (RU)
BMRT .... Large Refrigerated Fishing Trawler (RU)
BMRTs .... Route Control Interlocking System (RU)
bmrw .... Bez Miejsca, Roku Wydania [*Place and Year of Publication Not Given*] [*Polish*]
BMS .... Baptist Missionary Society (MAR)
BMS .... Bloc des Masses Senegalaises [*Bloc of the Senegalese Masses*] (AF)
BMS .... Bundesministerium fuer Soziale Verwaltung [*German*]
BMS .... Fat-Free Detergent (RU)
BMSR (HV) ... [*Hauptverwaltung*] Betriebsmess-, Steuer-, und Regelungstechnik [*(Main Administration for) Industrial Measuring, Control, and Regulating Technology*] (EG)
BMSR-Technik ... Betriebsmess-, Steuer-, und Regelungstechnik [*Industrial Measuring, Control, and Regulating Technology*] (EG)
BMSS .... Beogradski Medunarodni Slavisticki Sastanak [*International Congress of Slavicists in Belgrade*] [*1955*] (YU)
BMT .... Bureau Marocain du Travail (MAR)
BMT .... Mikhaylovskiy-Turov Aiming Circle [*Artillery*] (RU)
BMT .... Small Ship-Hold Bulldozer (RU)
Bmt Anlagen ... Betriebsmaschinentechnische Anlagen [*Mechanical and Technical Railroad Installations*] (EG)
BMTK .... Office of Metal and Heat Engineering Structures (RU)
BMtkm .... Brutto Megatonnen-Kilometer [*Gross Megaton-Kilometer*] [*Metric Ton*] (EG)
BMTM .... Central Scientific and Technical Library of the Ministry of Heavy Machinery Manufacture (RU)
Bmtr .... Beamter [*German*]
BMTR .... Large Refrigerated Fish-Factory Trawler (RU)
BMTsM .... Central Library of the Ministry of Nonferrous Metallurgy (RU)
BMU .... Bermuda [*Three-letter standard code*] (CNC)
BMU .... Bundesministerium fuer Unterricht und Kunst [*German*]
BMU .... High-Speed Magnetic Amplifier (RU)
BMU .... Local-Control Unit (RU)
BMU de A .... Biblioteca Medica Universidad de Antioquia [*Medellin*] (COL)
BMV .... Bases de Multiplication et de Vulgarisation (MAR)
BMV .... Berliner Metallverarbeitung [*Berlin Metalworking Plant*] (EG)
BMV .... Bundesministerium fuer Verkehr [*German*]
BMV .... International Exhibition Bureau (RU)
BMVO .... Bulletin of the Ministry of Higher Education [*A publication*] (RU)

BMW............ Bayerische Motoren Werke [*Bavarian Motor Works*] [*German automobile manufacturer; initialism used as name of its cars*]
bmw............ Bez Miejsca Wydania [*Place of Publication Not Given*] [*Polish*]
BMW............ Bundesministerium fuer Wissenschaft und Forschung [*German*]
BMWU......... Black Municipal Workers' Union (MAR)
BMWW......... Biuro Miedzynarodowej Wymiany Wydawnictw [*International Bureau for the Exchange of Publications*] [*Polish*]
BMZ............ Berezniki Magnesium Plant (RU)
BMZ............ Bundesministerium fuer Wirtschaftliche Zusammenarbeit [*Federal Ministry for Economic Cooperation*] (EG)
bn.............. Author's Note (BU)
Bn.............. Bassin [*Basin*] [*French*] (NAU)
BN.............. Batalion [*Battalion*] (ML)
Bn.............. Bayan [*Mrs., Miss, Ms.*] (TU)
BN.............. Berita Negara [*State Journal*] (IN)
BN.............. Betriebsnummer [*Enterprise Number*] (EG)
bn.............. Bez Nakladatele [*No Publisher Given*] (CZ)
BN.............. Biblioteka Narodowa [*National Library*] (POL)
BN.............. Bibliotheque Nationale [*French*]
BN.............. Brunei [*Two-letter standard code*] (CNC)
b/n............ Brut pour Net [*French*]
BN.............. Combat Assignment, Combat Mission (RU)
BN.............. Combat Unclassified [*Gas mask*] (RU)
BN-............ Fast-Neutron Reactor, Fast Reactor (RU)
BN.............. Filament Battery [*Radio*] (RU)
BN.............. Malfunction Unit, Error Unit [*Computers*] (RU)
BN.............. Petroleum Bitumen (RU)
BN-............ Tuning Unit [*Computers*] (RU)
b/n............ Unnumbered (RU)
bn.............. Without Beginning [*Book*] (BU)
BN.............. Zero-Setting Unit (RU)
Bna............ Banchina [*Quay*] [*Italian*] (NAU)
BNA............ Banco Nacional de Angola (MAR)
BNA............ Banque Nationale Agricole [*National Agricultural Bank*] [*Tunisian*] (AF)
BNA............ Banque Nationale d'Algerie [*National Bank of Algeria*] (AF)
BNA............ Benzylnicotinamide (RU)
BNA............ Bloc Nigerienne d'Action (MAR)
BNA............ Botswana National Airways (MAR)
BNA............ Bulgarian People's Army (BU)
BNAF.......... British North Africa Force (MAR)
BNAL.......... Bundesnotaufnahmelager [*Emergency Reception Camp*] [*West German*] (EG)
BNASS........ Bureau National d'Animation du Secteur Socialiste [*National Office for the Promotion of the Socialist Sector*] [*Algerian*] (AF)
BNB............ Banco do Nordeste do Brasil [*Bank of Northeast Brazil*] (LA)
BNB............ Barbados National Bank (LA1)
Bnb............ Binbasi [*Major (Army), Lieutenant Commander (Navy)*] (TU)
BNB............ Bulgarian National Bank (BU)
BNC............ Banco Nacional de Cuba [*National Bank of Cuba*] (LA)
BNC............ Banque Nationale du Cambodge [*National Bank of Cambodia*] (CL)
BNC............ Basutoland National Council (MAR)
BNC............ Benefices des Professions Non Commerciales (MAR)
BNCC.......... Banco Nacional de Credito Cooperativo [*National Cooperative Credit Bank*] [*Brazilian*] (LA)
BNCD.......... Banque Nationale Centrafricaine de Depots (MAR)
BNCD.......... Banque Nationale Centrafricaine de Developpement [*Central African National Development Bank*] (AF)
BNCI............ Banque Nationale pour le Commerce et l'Industrie [*National Bank for Commerce and Industry*] [*French*]
BNCIA.......... Banque Nationale pour le Commerce et l'Industrie Afrique (MAR)
BND............ Banco Nacional de Desarrollo [*National Development Bank*] [*Nicaraguan*] (LA1)
BND............ Banque Nationale de Developpement [*National Development Bank*] (AF)
BND............ Banque Nationale de Developpement de la Republique Centrafricaine (MAR)
BNd............ Betriebsvorschrift fuer den Vereinfachten Nebendienst [*Traffic Regulations for Simplified Secondary Railroad Service*] (EG)
BND............ Blocul National Democrat [*National Democratic Bloc*] (RO)
BND............ Bundesnachrichtendienst [*Federal Intelligence Service*] [*West German*] (WEN)
BND............ Inertialess Nonlinear Two-Terminal Network (RU)
BNDA.......... Banque Nationale pour le Developpement Agricole [*National Agricultural Development Bank*] [*Ivorian*] (AF)
BNDC.......... Banque Nationale de Developpement du Congo [*National Development Bank of the Congo*] (AF)
BNDC.......... Bophuthatswana National Development Corporation (MAR)
BNDC.......... Bureau National de Developpement Communautaire (MAR)
BNDD.......... Banco Nacional de Deposito y Desarrollo (MAR)
BNDE.......... Banco Nacional de Desenvolvimento Economico [*National Economic Development Bank*] [*Brazilian*] (LA)
BNDE.......... Banque Nationale de Developpement Economique [*National Economic Development Bank*] [*French*] (AF)
BNDHV........ Banque Nationale de Developpement de la Haute-Volta [*National Development Bank of Upper Volta*] (AF)
BNDS.......... Banque Nationale de Developpement du Senegal [*Senegal National Development Bank*] (AF)
Bne............ Borne [*Boundary Stone*] [*Military map abbreviation*] [*World War I*] [*French*] (MTD)
BNEC.......... Banque Nationale pour l'Epargne et le Credit [*National Savings and Credit Bank*] [*Ivorian*] (AF)
BNEC.......... British National Export Council (MAR)
BNEL.......... Bureau National de l'Enseignement Libre (MAR)
BNEP.......... Biuro Nadzoru Estetyki Produkcji [*Production Aesthetics Supervisory Bureau*] (POL)
BNETD........ Bureau National d'Etudes Techniques de Developpement [*National Office for Technical Development Studies*] [*Ivorian*] (AF)
BNF............ Botswana National Front (PPW)
BNGB.......... Bloco Nacional da Guine [*National Bloc of Guinea-Bissau*] (AF)
BNH............ Banco Nacional de Habitacao [*National Housing Bank*] [*Brazilian*] (LA)
BNHSN........ Bulletin of News of the Historical Society of Nigeria [*Ibadan*] [*A publication*] (MAR)
BNI............ Bank Negara Indonesia [*Indonesian State Bank*] (IN)
BNI............ Bankin'ny Indostria [*Industrial Bank*] [*Malagasy*] (AF)
BNI............ Brodarski Naucni Institut [*Naval Scientific Institute*] (YU)
BNIB.......... Biblioteka Narodowa - Instytut Bibliograficzny [*National Library - Bibliographical Institute*] (POL)
BNIC.......... Bureau of National and International Communications [*South African*] (AF)
BNIILKh...... Belorussian Scientific Research Institute of Forestry (RU)
BNIST.......... Bureau National d'Information Scientifique et Technique [*National Bureau of Scientific and Technical Information*] [*French*] (WER)
BNK............ Bolgar Nepkoztarsasag [*Bulgarian People's Republic*] (HU)
BNK............ Bulgarian National Committee (BU)
bnk............ Without Beginning or End (BU)
BNKCPA...... Bureau National Kamerunais pour la Conference des Peuples Africains [*Cameroonian National Bureau for African Peoples Conference*]
BNKh.......... Standards Management Office (RU)
BNL............ Banque Nationale du Laos [*National Bank of Laos*] (CL)
BNL............ Base Naval de Lisboa [*Lisbon Naval Base*] [*Portuguese*] (WER)
BNL............ Borsodnadasdi Lemezgyar [*Borsodnadasd Metal Sheet Factory*] (HU)
BNLTA........ Botswana National Lawn Tennis Association (MAR)
BNM............ Bank Negara Malaysia [*Central Bank of Malaysia*] (ML)
BNM............ Banque Nationale Malgache de Developpement [*Malagasy National Development Bank*] (AF)
BNM............ Biblioteca Nacional de Mocambique (MAR)
BNM............ Black Nationalist Movement (MAR)
BNM............ Bureau de Normalisation de la Mecanique [*French*]
BNMG.......... Banco Nacional de Minas Gerais [*Minas Gerais National Bank*] [*Brazilian*] (LA)
BNML.......... League of Dutch Marxist-Leninists (WEN)
BNMO.......... Bond Nederlandse Militaire Oorlogsslachtoffers [*Federation of Dutch War Victims*] (WEN)
BNMS.......... Bulgarian National Maritime Union (BU)
BNN............ Pilot Unit for Initial Voltage (RU)
BNn............ Smokeless Powder [*Symbol*] [*French*] (MTD)
BNOC.......... Bahrain National Oil Company (ME)
BNOV.......... Bulgarian National Liberation Army (BU)
BNP............ Bangladesh National Party [*Bangladesh Jatiyabadi Dal*] (PPW)
BNP............ Banque Nationale de Paris [*National Bank of Paris*] (WER)
BNP............ Basotho National Party (PPW)
BNP............ Battery Observation Post (RU)
BNP............ Biblioteca Nationala de Programe [*National Library of Computer Programs*] (RO)
BNP............ Combat Observation Post (RU)
BNP............ Lateral Observation Post (RU)
BNPD.......... Battalion Combat Observation Post [*Artillery*] (RU)
BNPP.......... Regimental Combat Observation Post (RU)
BNPS.......... Bulgarian National Pensioners' Union (BU)
BNR............ Banque Nationale du Rwanda (MAR)
BNR............ Bibliothek der Neuesten und Wichtigsten Reisebeschreibungen (MAR)
BNR............ Botswana Notes and Records [*Gaberone*] [*A publication*] (MAR)
BNR............ Bulgarian People's Republic (BU)
BNR............ Bulgarian People's Republic (RU)
BNR............ Bureau National de Recensement [*National Census Bureau*] [*Senegalese*] (AF)
BNRSR........ Banca Nationala a Republicii Socialiste Romania [*National Bank of the Socialist Republic of Romania*] (RO)
BNS............ Dry Filament Battery [*Radio*] (RU)
BNS............ Office of Standardization (RU)
BNSC.......... Botswana National Sports Council (MAR)
BNSI.......... Barbados National Standards Institute (LA1)
BNSR.......... Bukhara People's Soviet Republic [*1920-1924*] (RU)
BNT............ Banque Nationale de Tunisie [*Tunisian National Bank*] (AF)
BNT............ Bibliotheque Nationale Togo (MAR)
BNT............ Quick-Saturation Transformer (RU)
BNTI.......... Office of Scientific and Technical Information (RU)
BNTL.......... Bibliografie van de Nederlandse Taal- en Literatuurwetenschap
BNU............ Drilling and Pumping Unit (RU)

BNV............ Budapesti Nemzetkozi Vasar [*Budapest International Fair*] (HU)
BNYE.......... Budapesti Nyomdaipari Egyesules [*Industrial Printing Syndicate of Budapest*] (HU)
Bnz............. Benzin [*Gasoline*] (TU)
bnz............. Benzine [*Solvent*] (RU)
BNZhD....... Bulgarian National Women's Association (BU)
BNZS.......... Bulgarski Naroden Zemedelski Suiuz [*Bulgarian National Agrarian Union*] (PPE)
BO.............. Bacteriological Weapons (BU)
BO.............. Bacteriological Weapons (RU)
Bo............... Bajo [*Shoal*] [*Spanish*] (NAU)
BO.............. Banco Obrero [*Workers Bank*] [*Venezuelan*] (LA)
BO.............. Bath Detachment (RU)
BO.............. Bezne Opravy [*Customary Repairs*] (CZ)
BO.............. Bocni Odrad [*Flank Screening Detachment*] (CZ)
Bo............... Bogha [*Sunken Rock*] [*Gaelic*] (NAU)
BO.............. Bolivia [*Two-letter standard code*] (CNC)
BO.............. Boracki Odred [*Combat Detachment*] (YU)
BO.............. Boulets Ogivaux [*On artillery sights*] [*French*] (MTD)
BO.............. Bulletin Officiel [*French*]
BO.............. Close Target (RU)
BO.............. Coast Defense (RU)
BO.............. Coast Guard (RU)
BO.............. Combat Organization (RU)
BO.............. Combat Security Unit, Combat Outpost (RU)
bo............... Combat Train (BU)
BO.............. Eisenbahn-Bau- und Betriebsordnung [*Railroad Construction and Traffic Regulations*] (EG)
bo............... Flamethrower Battalion (RU)
BO.............. Flank Guard (RU)
BO.............. Large Submarine Chaser (RU)
BO.............. Lateral Deviation [*Artillery*] (RU)
BO.............. [*The*] Officer's Library [*Book series*] (RU)
BO.............. Oscilloscope Unit [*Computers*] (RU)
BO.............. Recoilless Gun (BU)
BO.............. Recoilless Gun (RU)
BOA............ Boulangerie d'Armee [*Military*] [*French*] (MTD)
BOA............ Boykot Outspan Aktie (MAR)
BOA............ Butoxyanisole (RU)
BOA............ Compagnie des Bois de l'Ouest Africain (MAR)
BOAD.......... Banque Ouest-Africaine de Developpement [*West African Development Bank*] [*Use WADB*] (AF)
BOAG.......... Bureau d'Ordre et des Affaires Generales [*Appointments and General Affairs Office*] [*Cambodian*] (CL)
BOAMV....... Office for Warehouse Pest Control (RU)
BOAR.......... Biuro Obrotu Artykulami Rolniczymi [*Farm Products Sales Office*] (POL)
BOB............ Berner Oberland-Bahnen [*Bernese Overland Railways*]
BOB............ Bukhara Oblast Library (RU)
BOB............ Bureau des Organisations Benevoles (MAR)
BOBM......... Baltic Sea Coast Defense (RU)
BOC............ Border Operations Committee (ML)
BOC............ Boulangerie de Campagne [*Military*] [*French*] (MTD)
BOC............ British Overseas Citizenship (MAR)
BOC............ Brodski Operativni Centar [*Ship Operational Center*] [*Navy*] (YU)
BOChM....... Black Sea Coast Defense (RU)
boch zav..... Cooperage [*Topography*] (RU)
BOCI.......... Bloque de Obreros, Campesinos, e Intelectuales [*Bloc of Workers, Peasants, and Intellectuals*] [*Costa Rican*] (LA)
BOCO.......... Bestuurlijke Overleg Commissie voor Overheidsautomatisering [*Dutch*]
BOD............ Biskupski Ordinarijat u Dakovu [*Chancery of the Catholic Bishopric of Dakovo*] (YU)
BOD............ Data-Processing Unit (RU)
BODK.......... Bureau for Services to the Diplomatic Corps (BU)
BOE............ Boletin Oficial del Estado [*Official State Gazette*] [*Spanish*] (WER)
BOE............ Budapesti Orvostudomanyi Egyetem [*Medical University of Budapest*] (HU)
B d Oe L...... Betrieb der Oertlichen Landwirtschaft [*Local Agricultural Enterprise*] (EG)
BOeL........... Betrieb der Oertlichen Landwirtschaft [*Local Agricultural Enterprise*] (EG)
BOFF........... Biafran Organization of Freedom Fighters (MAR)
Bog............. Bogaz [*Straits, Gorge*] (TU)
Bogosl fak... School of Theology (BU)
BOK............ Bulgarian Olympic Committee (BU)
BOKhR........ Combat Security Unit, Combat Outpost (RU)
BOKN.......... Biuro Odzysku Kabli Nieeksploatowanych [*Office for the Recovery of Unused Cables*] (POL)
Bol.............. Big, Large, Great [*Topography*] (RU)
BOL............ Bojova Otravna Latka [*Chemical Warfare Agent*] (CZ)
BOL............ Bolivia [*Three-letter standard code*] (CNC)
BOL............ Bombardovace Letectvo [*Bomber Airforce*] (CZ)
Bol.............. Swamp [*Topography*] (RU)
bolg............ Bulgarian (RU)
BOLMAQ..... Bolsa de Maquinaria Industrial Ltda. [*Bogota*] (COL)
bol'n........... Hospital [*Topography*] (RU)
BOLP.......... Bydgoski Okreg Lasow Panstwowych [*Bydgoszcz State Forest District*] (POL)
BOLSAMED... Bolsa de Medellin SA (COL)
BOLSIPLAS... Fabrica de Bolsas Plasticas [*Bogota*] (COL)
BO/M.......... Bulletin Officiel (Morocco) [*Rabat*] [*A publication*] (MAR)
BOM............ Bureau d'Organisation et de Methode [*Organization and Methods Office*] [*Senegalese*] (AF)
BOMA.......... Bois et Materiaux (MAR)
BOMAS....... Bobin ve Masura Sanayi ve Ticaret Anonim Sirketi [*Bobbin and Shuttle Industry and Trade Corporation*] (TU)
BOMZh....... Without Fixed Residence (RU)
Bon............. Baron [*Baron*] [*French*] (MTD)
Bon............. Bataillon [*Battalion*] [*Military*] [*French*] (MTD)
Bon............. Buisson [*Thicket*] [*Military map abbreviation*] [*World War I*] [*French*] (MTD)
Bon............. Buron [*Cheese Factory*] [*Military map abbreviation*] [*World War I*] [*French*] (MTD)
Bona........... Ballonnachrichtenabteilung [*Balloon Communication Battalion*] [*German*]
BONA.......... Bonneterie de l'Agneby (MAR)
BONC.......... Broadcasting Organizations of Non-Aligned Countries (EA)
BO-Niger..... Societe de Promotion des Boissons Hygieniques du Niger (MAR)
Bonne.......... Baronne [*Baroness*] [*French*] (MTD)
BONOT........ Bulgarian Organization for the Scientific Organization of Labor (BU)
BONSF........ Bulgarian National Students Federation (BU)
BONSS........ Bulgarian National Students Union (BU)
BOP............ Bezpieczenstwo i Ochrona Pracy [*Industrial Safety*] (POL)
BOP............ Biuro Odbudowy Portow [*Office of Port Reconstruction*] (POL)
BOP............ Brigade de l'Ordre Publique [*Public Order Brigade*] [*Tunisian*] (AF)
BOP............ Budget, Accounting, and Enterprises (BU)
BOP............ Office of Operational Planning (RU)
BOP............ Office for the Organization of Production (RU)
BOP............ White Sea - Onega Steamship Line (RU)
BOPA.......... Botswana Press Agency (MAR)
BOPLAS...... Botellas Plasticas Ltda. [*Bogota*] (COL)
b opr.......... Bez Oprawy [*Unbound*] [*Polish*]
BOPR.......... Bulletin Officiel, Partie Reglementaire [*French*] [*A publication*] (MTD)
BOPR.......... Bureau d'Organisation des Programmes Ruraux (MAR)
BOPS.......... Bulletin Officiel, Partie Supplementaire [*French*] [*A publication*] (MTD)
BOR............ Banco de la Republica [*Bank of the Republic*] [*Colombian*] (LA)
BOR............ Budowa Osiedli Robotniczych [*Workers' Settlement Construction Office*] (POL)
BOR............ Flash-Ranging Battery (BU)
BOR............ Flash-Ranging Battery (RU)
BOR............ Recoilless Gun (RU)
BORCO....... Bahamas Oil Refining Company (LA1)
BORDOSZ... Boripari Dolgozok Szakszervezete [*Trade Union of Workers in the Leather Industry*] (HU)
Bordradist... Ship's Radio Operator (BU)
Borforg V.... Borforgalmi Vallalat [*Leather Trade Enterprise*] (HU)
BORM.......... Bulletin Officiel du Royaume du Maroc [*A publication*] (MAR)
BORO.......... Biuro Obslugi Ruchu Turystycznego [*Tourist Movement Service Bureau*] (POL)
BOR-SAN.... Boru Sanayi [*Pipe Manufacturing Industry*] [*Turkish Cypriot*] (TU)
BORTAN..... Bordeaux-Tananarive (MAR)
BORUSAN... Boru Sanayi Sirketi [*Pipe Industry Corporation*] (TU)
BOS............ Bau- und Betriebsordnung fuer Schmalspurbahnen [*Construction and Operating Regulations for Narrow-Gauge Railroads*] (EG)
BOS............ Biuro Odbudowy Stolicy [*Office for the Reconstruction of Warsaw (1945-1947)*] (POL)
BOs............ Borbeno Osiguranje [*Combat Security*] (YU)
BOS............ Burgas Oblast Court (BU)
BOS............ Coastal Convoy Detachment [*Navy*] (RU)
BOS............ Feedback Unit [*Computers*] (RU)
BOS............ Northern Coast Defense (RU)
BOS............ Silkworm Experimental Station (BU)
BOSCAM..... Bouygues Offshore Cameroon (MAR)
bosm.......... Bosman [*Boatswain*] [*Polish*]
BOSNABARIT... Bosnian Barite Mine [*Velika Kladusa, BiH*] (YU)
Bosna-Coop... Bosnian Export-Import Establishment [*Sarajevo*] (YU)
BOSNALIJEK... Preduzece za Proizvodnju Lijekova [*Bosnian Pharmaceutical Establishment*] [*Sarajevo*] (YU)
BOSNAMETAL... Bosnian Metallurgical Factory [*Sarajevo*] (YU)
BOSNATRANSPORT... Udruzenje Transportnih Preduzeca [*Bosnian Association of Transport Establishments*] [*Sarajevo*] (YU)
BOSOM....... Bogotana Sombrerera Ltda. [*Bogota*] (COL)
BOSS.......... Bureau of State Security [*South African*] (AF)
BOT............ Biuro Obslugi Turystycznej [*Tourist Service Bureau*] (POL)
BOt............ Bojni Otrovi [*Poison Gases*] [*Military*] (YU)
Bot............ Botanik [*Botany*] (TU)
bot............ Botanika [*Botany*] (HU)
bot............ Botany, Botanical (BU)
BOT............ Butoxytoluene (RU)

BOTAS........ Beynelmilel Otelcilik Turk Anonim Sirketi [*International Hotel Management Corporation*] (TU)
BOTAS........ Boru Hatlari ile Petrol Tasima Anonim Sirketi [*Pipe Lines and Petroleum Transport Corporation*] (TU)
BOTB........... British Overseas Trade Board (MAR)
BOTE........... Budapest Orvostudomany Egyetem [*Budapest Medical University*] (HU)
BOTIC......... Bankarski, Osiguravajuci, Trgovacki, i Industriski Cinovnici [*Bank, Insurance, Commercial, and Industrial Employees*] (YU)
BOTiI........... Biuro Obslugi Turystycznej i Informacji [*Tourist Service and Information Bureau*] [*Polish*]
BOTOCOL... Fabrica de Botones de Colombia [*Medellin*] (COL)
BOTOSTROJ ... Narodni Podnik pro Vyrobu Obuvnickych Stroju [*National Enterprise for the Manufacture of Shoe Machinery*] (CZ)
BOTP........... Belugyminiszterium, Orszagos Tuzrendeszeti Parancsnoksag [*Ministry of the Interior, National Fire Protection Headquarters*] (HU)
BOTU.......... Botswana Teachers Union (MAR)
BOTUB........ Office for Protection of Labor and Improvement of Living Conditions (RU)
BOU............. Hopper Directing Device (RU)
BOURP........ White Sea-Onega Administration of River Steamship Lines (RU)
BOUTM....... Biro za Organizaciju i Unapredenje Trgovinske Mreze [*Bureau for the Organization and Development of Commerce*] (YU)
bov.............. Bovitett [*Enlarged*] (HU)
BOV............. Chemical Warfare Agent (BU)
BOV............. Chemical Warfare Agent, War Gas (RU)
BOV............. "Let Us Rest Joyfully" [*Slogan*] (RU)
BOVESPA ... Bolsa de Valores de Sao Paulo [*Sao Paulo Stock Exchange*] [*Brazilian*] (LA)
BOW............ Biuro Odszkodowan Wojennych [*War Compensation Bureau*] (POL)
BOWAL....... Documentatiepool Verontreiniging Bodem, Water, en Lucht [*Dutch*]
boyepit........ Ammunition Supply (RU)
boyn............ Slaughterhouse, Abattoir [*Topography*] (RU)
Boy-szolg.... Boy-Szolgalat [*"Boy" Messenger Service*] (HU)
BOZ............. Bank of Zambia (MAR)
BP................ Action Station, Battle Station (RU)
BP................ Ammunition (RU)
BP................ Armored Train (RU)
Bp................ Bachelor's Degree (Pass) [*British*]
BP................ Bachiller Profesional [*Academic degree*] [*Spanish*]
BP................ Badan Pimpinan [*Executive Committee*] (IN)
BP................ Balai Polis [*Police Station*] (ML)
BP................ Balisticka Planseta [*Ballistic Board*] [*Army*] (YU)
BP................ Ballistic Converter (RU)
BP................ Bank Polski [*Bank of Poland*]
BP................ Bataillon Parachutiste [*Parachute Battalion*] [*Cambodian*] (CL)
BP................ Bayernpartei [*Bavarian Party*] [*West German*] (PPE)
Bp................ Bendicion Papal [*Papal Benediction*] [*Spanish*]
BP................ Bereitschaftspolizei [*Alert Police*] (EG)
BP................ Betriebspreis [*Enterprise Price*] (EG)
BP................ Bezne Prohlidky [*Customary Inspections*] (CZ)
BP................ Birlik Partisi [*Unity Party - UP*] [*See also TBP*] (TU)
bp................ Biskup [*Bishop*] [*Polish*]
BP................ Biuro Planowania [*Planning Office*] (POL)
BP................ Biuro Polityczne [*Political Bureau*] (POL)
BP................ Biuro Projektowania [*Planning Office*] (POL)
bp................ Blogoslawionej Pamieci [*Of Blessed Memory*] [*Polish*]
BP................ Boeren Partij [*Farmers' Party*] [*Dutch*] (PPE)
BP................ Boite Postale [*Post Office Box*] [*French*]
BP................ Bolsevik Part [*Bolshevik Party*] (HU)
BP................ Bomb Run [*Aviation*] (RU)
b/p.............. Borbeni Poredak [*Combat Formation*] (YU)
BP................ Britis Petrol [*British Petroleum*] (TU)
BP................ British Petroleum Co. (MAR)
BP................ Budapest [*Budapest*] (HU)
BP................ Buergerpartei [*Citizens' Party*] [*West German*] (PPE)
BP................ Bulgarian Press (BU)
Bp................ Bunteto Perrendtartas [*Code of Criminal Procedure*] (HU)
bp................ Buono Per [*Good For*] [*Italian*]
BP................ Bureau of Weather Forecasts (RU)
BP................ Burundi Populaire (MAR)
BP................ Carry Unit (RU)
BP................ Close-In Homing Radio Station (RU)
BP................ Combat Training (RU)
BP................ Drum Switch, Barrel Switch (RU)
BP................ Field Battery (RU)
BP-.............. Float Tank (RU)
BP................ High-Speed Potentiometer (RU)
BP................ Lateral Displacement [*Navy*] (RU)
bp................ Non-Party, Non-Party Man (RU)
BP................ Operation Order, Combat Order (RU)
BP................ Partai Bumiputra [*Party of Indigenous Peoples*] (ML)
BP................ Power Supply Unit, Supply Unit (RU)
BP................ Program Unit (RU)
BP................ Storage Unit, Memory Unit [*Computers*] (RU)
b/p.............. Unbound (RU)
BP................ Unconditional Transfer [*Computers*] (RU)
BP................ Weather Bureau (RU)
BPA............. Back Pain Association (EA)
BPA............. Bank Pembangunan Asia [*Asia Development Bank*] (ML)
BPA............. Betriebsplanungsausschuss [*Enterprise Planning Committee*] (EG)
BPA............. Black Parents Association (MAR)
BPA............. Bouake-Pieces d'Autos (MAR)
BPa............. Buergerpartei [*Citizens' Party*] [*West German*] (PPW)
BPA............. Bundespresse- und Informationsamt [*Federal Press and Information Office*] [*West German*] (WEN)
BPAO.......... Societe des Petroles BP d'Afrique Occidentale (MAR)
B Para......... Bataillon Parachutiste [*Parachute Battalion*] [*Cambodian*] (CL)
BPB............. Badan Perdjoangan Buruh [*Board for the Defense of Labor Interest*] [*Indonesian*]
BPB............. Balai Polis Bergerak [*Mobile Police Station*] (ML)
BPB............. Battalion Ammunition Supply Point (RU)
BPBK........... Biuro Projektow Budownictwa Komunalnego [*Communal Construction Plans Office*] (POL)
BPBM.......... Badan Pembagian Bahan Makanan [*Food Distribution Board*] (IN)
BPBM.......... Biuro Projektow Budownictwa Morskiego [*Maritime Construction Plans Office*] (POL)
BPC............. Barbados Peace Commission (LA1)
BPC............. Basic People's Congress (MAR)
BPC............. Basrah Petroleum Company (ME)
BPC............. Bataillon de Parachutistes Coloniaux (MAR)
BPC............. Black People's Convention [*South African*] (PD)
BPC............. Botswana Power Corporation (MAR)
BPC............. Brigade Parachutiste de Choc [*Algerian*] (MAR)
BPCC.......... Bamburi Portland Cement Company Ltd. (MAR)
BPCh........... Intermediate-Frequency Unit (RU)
BPCTN........ Bureau de Planification des Cadres Techniques Nationaux [*Bureau of Planning for National Technical Cadres*] [*Zairian*] (AF)
BPD............. Badan Produksi Daerah [*Regional Production Board*] (IN)
BPD............. Banco Popular do Desenvolvimento [*People's Development Bank*] [*Mozambican*] (AF)
BPD............. Bank Pembangunan Daerah [*Regional Development Bank*] (IN)
BPD............. Blocul Partidelor Democratice [*Bloc of Democratic Parties*] (RO)
BPD............. Bloque Popular Democratico [*Popular Democratic Bloc*] [*Venezuelan*] (LA)
BPD............. Data Acquisition Unit (RU)
BPD............. Program-Transducer Unit (RU)
BPDK.......... Bakanlik Planlama Danisma Kurulu [*Ministry Planning and Advisory Council*] (TU)
BPDK.......... Unit of Conversion to an Auxiliary Code (RU)
BPDO.......... Bath, Laundry, and Disinfection Service (RU)
BPDP........... Bath, Laundry, and Disinfection Train (RU)
BPE............. Bureau du Projet Education (MAR)
BPEAR........ Bureau for the Placement and Education of African Refugees (MAR)
BPERA........ Bureau de Placement et d'Education des Refugies Africains [*Bureau for the Placement and Education of African Refugees - BPEAR*] (MAR)
Bpest........... Budapest [*Budapest*] (HU)
BPF............. Bezirks-Post und Fernmeldeamt [*Bezirk Postal and Telecommunications Office*] (EG)
BPF............. Bon pour Francs [*Value in Francs*] [*French*]
BPF............. Bureau de Prospection Forestiere (MAR)
BPFP........... Bechuanaland Protectorate Federal Party (MAR)
BPG............. Balai Pendidikan Guru [*Teacher Training School*] (IN)
BPGN.......... Badan Pendjualan Gula Negara [*State Sugar Sales Board*] (IN)
BPH............. Badan Pemerintah Harian [*Government Standing Committee (DPRD executive committee)*] (IN)
BPI.............. Bank Pembangunan Indonesia [*Indonesian Development Bank*] (IN)
BPI.............. Belorussian Polytechnic Institute (RU)
BPI.............. Bernard Price Institute of Geophysical Research (MAR)
bp-i............. Budapesti [*Of Budapest*] [*Hungarian*] (GPO)
BPICA.......... Bureau Permanent International des Constructeurs d'Automobiles [*Permanent International Bureau of Motor Manufacturers*] (EA)
BPICM......... Bureau Permanent International des Constructeurs de Motocycles [*Permanent International Bureau of Motorcycle Manufacturers*] (EA)
BPID............ Bloque Parlamentario de Izquierda Democratica [*Democratic Left Parliamentary Bloc*] [*Ecuadorean*] (LA)
BPITT.......... Bureau Permanent Inter-Africain de la Tse-Tse et de la Trypanosomiase (MAR)
bpk.............. Antisubmarine Ship Brigade (BU)
BPK............. Badan Pemeriksa Keuangan [*Financial Audits Agency*] (IN)
BPK............. Barisan Pemadam Kebakaran [*Fire Department*] (IN)
BPK............. Bataljonski Partiski Komitet [*Battalion Party Committee*] (YU)
Bpk............. Beperk [*Limited*] [*South African*] (AF)
BPK............. Biochemical Oxygen Requirement (RU)
BPK............. Biological Oxygen Intake (RU)
BPK............. Boulangerie Patisserie de N'Kembo (MAR)
BPK............. Bulgarska Partia Komunistyczna [*Bulgarian Communist Party*] (POL)

BPK .... Direct-Flow Boiler Construction Office (RU)
BPK .... Office of Steam Boilers (RU)
BPKB .... Badan Pembina Kesatuan Bangsa [*Committee for the Advancement of National Unity*] (IN)
BPKBA .... Badan Penolong Korban Bentjana Alam [*Committee for Assisting Victims of Natural Disasters*] (IN)
BPKD .... Bakanlik Planlama ve Koordinasyon Dairesi [*Ministry Planning and Coordination Office*] (TU)
BPKI .... Badan Penjelidikan Karet Indonesia [*Indonesia Rubber Research Council*] (IN)
BPKK .... Bezirks-Partei-Kontroll-Kommission [*Bezirk Party Control Commission*] (EG)
BPKR .... Badan Penampungan Karet Rakjat [*Smallholders Rubber Collection Agency*] (IN)
BPL .... Baterie Proti Letadlum [*Antiaircraft Battery*] (CZ)
BPL .... Betriebsparteileitung [*Enterprise Party Management*] (EG)
BPL .... Bone Phosphate Lime (MAR)
BPL .... Budowniczy Polski Ludowej [*Builder of People's Poland (Award)*] (POL)
bpl .... Submarine Brigade (BU)
bpl .... Submarine Brigade (RU)
B-Plan .... Bahnhofs-Bedienungs Plan [*Station Service Plan*] (EG)
BPM .... Barbuda People's Movement [*Antiguan*] (PD)
BPM .... Battalion Medical Aid Station (RU)
BPM .... Biuro Pokazu Mody [*Fashion Show Office*] (POL)
BPM .... Biuro Projektow Miejskich [*Bureau of Municipal Projects*] (POL)
BpM .... Buchstaben pro Minute [*Letters per Minute*] (EG)
BPMD .... Balai Pendidikan Masjarakat Desa [*Village Community Training School*] (IN)
BPN .... Bureau Politique National [*National Political Bureau*] (AF)
BPN .... Conversion Voltage Unit (RU)
BPNC .... Ba'th Party National Command (ME)
BPNH .... Biuro Projektow Nowej Huty [*Office of Plans for Nowa Huta Metallurgical Center*] (POL)
BPO .... Bath and Laundry Detachment (RU)
BPO .... Betriebsparteiorganisation [*Plant Party Organization*] (EG)
BPP .... Bath and Laundry Train (RU)
BPP .... Battalion Small-Arms Ammunition Supply Point (RU)
BPP .... Bechuanaland People's Party (MAR)
BPP .... Black People's Party [*South African*] (PPW)
BPP .... Bojova a Politicka Priprava [*Combat and Political Training*] (CZ)
BPP .... Border Patrol Police [*Thai-Malaysia border*] (ML)
BPP .... Borge Prien Prove [*Danish intelligence test*]
BPP .... Botswana People's Party (PPW)
BPP .... Budowlane Przedsiebiorstwo Powiatowe [*County Construction Enterprise*] (POL)
BPP .... Interrupt Unit (RU)
BPP .... Office for Planning Preparation (RU)
BPP .... Variable-Conductance Unit (RU)
BPPB .... Banque de Paris et des Pays-Bas (MAR)
BPPBG .... Banque de Paris et des Pays-Bas Gabon (MAR)
BPPI .... Badan Pembangunan Perindustrian Indonesia [*Indonesian Industrial Development Board*] (IN)
BPPL .... Biuro Planow Perspektywicznych Lacznosci [*Communications Long-Range Planning Office*] (POL)
BPPOV .... Bud Pripraven k Praci a Obrane Vlasti [*Be Prepared for Work and for National Defense (Badge)*] (CZ)
BPPP .... Office for Planning the Preparation of Production (RU)
BPR .... Badan Penchegah Rasuah [*Agency to Prevent Corruption*] (ML)
BPR .... Biro za Posredovanje Rada [*Employment Agency*] (YU)
BPR .... Bloque Popular Revolucionario [*Popular Revolutionary Bloc*] [*Salvadoran*] (PD)
BPr .... Bulgarski Pregled [*Bulgarian Review*] [*A periodical*] (BU)
BPR .... Live Ammunition (BU)
BPr .... Translator's Note (BU)
BPRM .... Close-In Homing Radio Beacon (RU)
BPRS .... Badan Pembrontak Raayat Sabah [*Sabah People's Rebellion Organization*] (ML)
BPRS .... Close-In Homing Radio Station (RU)
BPRS .... Short-Range Homing Radio Station (BU)
BPS .... Banco de Prevision Social [*Social Security Bank*] [*Uruguayan*] (LA)
BPS .... Biro Pusat Statistik [*Central Bureau of Statistics*] (IN)
BPS .... Bloc Populaire Senegalais [*Senegalese*] (PPW)
BPS .... Bloc Progressiste Senegalais [*Senegalese*] (MAR)
BPS .... Bratnia Pomoc Studentow [*Students' Fraternal Aid*] (POL)
BPS .... Brigada Pohranicni Straze [*Border Guard Brigade*] (CZ)
BPS .... Brigadas Proletarias Salvadorenas [*Salvadoran Proletariat Brigades*] (LA1)
BPS .... Brygada Pracy Socjalistycznej [*Socialist Work Brigade*] [*Polish*]
BPS .... Burgas Court of Reconciliation (BU)
BPS- .... Concrete-Rolling Stand (RU)
BPS .... Gasoline Transfer-Pumping Station (RU)
BPSG .... Black Priests' Solidarity Group [*South African*] (AF)
BPSH .... Bashkimet Profesionale te Shqiperise [*Union of Albanian Trade Unions*]
BPT .... Tank-Support Battery (RU)
BPTC .... Bataljonski Protivtenkovski Cvor [*Battalion Antitank Center*] (YU)
BPTC-1 .... Bataljonski Protivtenkovski Cvor 1 Bataljona [*First Battalion Antitank Center*] (YU)
BPTs .... Bulgarian Eastern Orthodox Church (BU)
BPTU .... Battalion Antitank Strongpoint (RU)
BPU .... Badan Pimpinan Umum [*General Management Board*] (IN)
BPU .... Combat Track Angle (RU)
BPU .... Gasoline Transfer-Pumping Unit (RU)
BPU .... High-Speed Printer (RU)
BPUAO .... Coastal Battery Post for Artillery Fire Control (RU)
BPUI .... Badan Permusjawaratan Ummat Islam [*Moslem Community Consultative Council*] (IN)
BPV .... Buitenlandse Persvereniging [*Foreign Press Association*] [*Dutch*] (WEN)
bpv .... Field Water Supply Battalion (RU)
BPVCh .... High-Frequency Supply Unit (RU)
BPWA .... Business and Professional Women's Association [*Bahamian*] (LA1)
BPZ .... Bocni Pochodova Zastita [*Forward March Screening Element*] (CZ)
BPZ- .... Constant Delay Unit (RU)
BPZ .... March Flank Guard, March Flank Party (RU)
BPZB .... Bialostockie Przemyslowe Zjednoczenie Budowlane [*Bialystok Industrial Construction Association*] (POL)
BPZB .... Bielskie Przemyslowe Zjednoczenie Budowlane [*Bielsko Industrial Construction Association*] (POL)
BPZB .... Bydgoskie Przemyslowe Zjednoczenie Budowlane [*Bydgoszcz Industrial Construction Association*] (POL)
BPzH .... Bojova Pruzkumna Hl'dka [*Combat Reconnaissance Patrol*] (CZ)
BPzH .... Bojovy Pruzkum Hloubkovy [*Combat Reconnaissance in Depth*] (CZ)
BPZO .... Bud Pripraven k Zdravotnicke Obrane [*Be Prepared for Health Protection (Badge)*] (CZ)
Bque .... Banque [*Bank*] [*French*]
Bque .... Baraque [*Hut*] [*Military map abbreviation*] [*World War I*] [*French*] (MTD)
bque .... Barrique [*French*]
BR .... Armor-Piercing (RU)
Br .... Bachiller [*Bachelor*] [*Academic Degree*] [*Spanish*]
BR .... Bacteriological Warfare Reconnaissance (BU)
BR .... Balance Relay (RU)
BR .... Ballistic Missile (RU)
BR .... Bandera Roja [*Red Flag*] [*Dominican Republic*] (LA)
BR .... Bandera Roja [*Red Flag*] [*Venezuelan*] (LA)
BR .... Bank Rolny [*Agricultural Bank*] (POL)
br .... Baro [*Baron*] (HU)
BR .... Battalion Area (RU)
BR .... Battalion Radio Station (RU)
BR .... Battleship (RU)
BR .... Betriebsrat [*Workers' Council*] (EG)
br .... Bez Roku [*No Date Given*] (CZ)
br .... Bez Roku [*or Brak Roku*] [*No Date Given*] [*Polish*]
BR .... Bezpecnostni Rada [*Security Council*] [*United Nations*] (CZ)
br .... Biezacy Rok [*or Biezacego Roku*] [*The Current Year*] (POL)
BR .... Blocking Relay, Locking Relay (RU)
BR .... Boksitni Rudnici [*Bauxite Mines*] (YU)
Br .... Brat [*Bratul, Bratu*] [*Branch, Arm*] [*Romanian*] (NAU)
BR .... Brazil [*Two-letter standard code*] (CNC)
BR .... Brazylia [*Brazil*] [*Polish*]
Br .... Brdo [*Brda*] [*Mountain(s)*] [*Yugoslav*] (NAU)
Br .... Brevete d'Etat-Major [*Of officer who has passed staff course*] [*French*] (MTD)
BR .... Brigadas Revolucionarias [*Revolutionary Brigades*] [*Portuguese*] (PPE)
br .... Brigade (BU)
Br .... Brigade [*Brigade*] [*Military*] [*French*] (MTD)
br .... Brigade (RU)
BR .... Brigate Rosse [*Red Brigades*] [*Italian*] (PD)
br .... Brochure, Pamphlet (RU)
Br .... Broj [*Number*] (YU)
br .... Broschiert [*Sewn in Pamphlet Form*] [*German*]
br .... Brothers (BU)
br .... Brothers (RU)
Br .... Broussaille [*Brushwood*] [*Military map abbreviation*] [*World War I*] [*French*] (MTD)
BR .... Bulletin de Renseignements [*Military*] [*French*] (MTD)
Br .... Burun [*Cape, Headland, Promontory, Point*] (TU)
BR .... Close Reconnaissance (RU)
BR .... Combat Reconnaissance, Combat Intelligence (RU)
BR .... Contactless Relay (RU)
BR .... Deployment Base (RU)
BR .... Editor's Note (BU)
BR .... Fast Reactor (RU)
Br .... Ford [*Topography*] (RU)
Br .... Gross Weight, Gross (RU)
br .... Number (BU)
BR .... Onboard Recording Device (RU)
BR- .... Paper-Cutting Machine (RU)
BR .... Rapid Discharge Circuit (RU)

br .... Stone Blocks [*Road-paving material*] [*Topography*] (RU)
BR .... Worker's Idleness (BU)
BRA .... Base de Reparaciones de Aviacion [*Aviation Repair Base*] [*Cuban*] (LA)
BRA .... Brazil [*Three-letter standard code*] (CNC)
BRA .... Brigada Roja de Ajusticiamiento [*Red Execution Brigade*] [*Honduran*] (LA)
BRA .... Code Address Register Unit (RU)
BRAB .... Armor-Piercing Aerial Bomb (RU)
BRAB (DS) ... Armor-Piercing Aerial Bomb with Additional Velocity Component (RU)
brabr .... Coastal Artillery Rocket Brigade (BU)
BRACODI .... Societe des Brasseries de la Cote-d'Ivoire (MAR)
BRACONGO ... Brasseries du Congo (MAR)
BRADESCO ... Banco Brasileiro de Desconto [*Brazilian Discount Bank*] (LA)
bradi .... Coastal Artillery-Rocket Division (BU)
BRADUNI .... Brasseries du Niger (MAR)
BRAG .... Brigadna Artiljeriska Grupa [*Brigade Artillery Group*] (YU)
BRAL .... Bureau de Renseignements et d'Action, Londres [*Free French*]
BRALIM .... Bravarsko Limarsko Preduzece [*Locksmiths' and Plumbers' Establishment*] (YU)
BRALIMA .... Brasseries, Limonaderies, et Malteries Africaines (MAR)
BRALUP ...... Bureau of Resource Assessment and Land Use Planning (MAR)
Branc C .... Groupe de Brancardiers de Corps [*Military*] [*French*] (MTD)
BRANCOSTA ... Branco Costa & Compagnie (MAR)
BRANIGER ... Societe des Brasseries du Niger (MAR)
BRANOMA ... Societe des Brasseries du Nord-Marocain (MAR)
brap .... Coastal Artillery-Rocket Regiment (BU)
BRAS .... Bulletin of the Royal Asiatic Society [*A publication*] (MAR)
BRASPETRO ... PETROBRAS Internacional SA [*PETROBRAS International, Inc.*] [*Brazilian*] (LA)
BRASSIDER ... Empresa Brasileira de Siderurgia SA [*Brazil Steel Company, Inc.*] (LA)
BRAV .... Radioactive Warfare Contaminant (BU)
BRAVOLTA ... Brasseries de Haute-Volta (MAR)
BRAWICO ... Brandt, Willig & Co. (MAR)
brazm .... Mine-Clearing Battalion (BU)
brazm .... Mine-Clearing Battalion (RU)
BRB .... Banque de la Republique du Burundi [*Bank of the Republic of Burundi*] (AF)
BRB .... Banque du Royaume du Burundi (MAR)
BRB .... Barbados [*Three-letter standard code*] (CNC)
BRB .... Barisan Rakyat Brunei [*Brunei People's Front*] (ML)
BRBD .... Short-Range Ballistic Missile (RU)
BRC .... Bautura Racoritoare Carbonata [*Carbonated Beverage*] (RO)
BRC .... Bureau de Relations Commerciales (MAR)
BRCh .... Number Register [*Computers*] (RU)
BRD .... Bundesrepublik Deutschland [*Federal Republic of Germany*] (WEN)
BRD .... Combat Reconnaissance Patrol (RU)
BRD .... Gunpowder Rocket Engines [*Rocket shells*] (BU)
BRDD .... Long-Range Ballistic Missile (BU)
BRDD .... Long-Range Ballistic Missile (RU)
BRDE .... Banco Regional de Desenvolvimento [*Regional Development Bank*] [*Brazilian*] (LA)
Bre .... Barriere [*Barrier, Gate*] [*Military map abbreviation*] [*World War I*] [*French*] (MTD)
bre .... Roentgen Equivalent Man (RU)
Bred .... Editor's Note (BU)
BREDA .... Bureau Regional pour l'Education en Afrique [*Regional Office for Education in Africa*] (AF)
BRES .... Brigadas Revolucionarias Estudiantiles Salvadorenas [*Salvadoran Students Revolutionary Brigades*] (LA1)
BRES .... Bryansk Regional Electric Power Plant (RU)
BRES .... Bulletin of Rural Economics and Sociology [*Ibadan*] [*A publication*] (MAR)
BRESP .... Combating Enemy Radio-Electronic Equipment (BU)
BRESP .... Countermeasures Against Electronic Warfare Weapons (RU)
Brevo .... Vorschriften fuer den Bremsdienst [*Braking Regulations*] (EG)
b-reya .... Battery (RU)
BRF .... Bereich Rundfunk und Fernsehen [*Radio and Television Field*] (EG)
BRF .... Brigades Revolutionnaires Francaises [*Revolutionary French Brigades*] [*French*] (PD)
BRF .... Bulgarian River Fleet (BU)
BRF .... Physical Beryllium Reactor (RU)
BR-FAS .... Bandera Roja - Frente Americo Silva [*Red Flag - Americo Silva Front*] [*Venezuelan*] (LA1)
BRFEF .... Bureau de la Repression de Fraudes Economiques et Financieres [*Economic and Financial Crimes Repression Office*] [*Cambodian*] (CL)
BRFK .... Budapesti Rendor Fokapitanysag [*Budapest Police Headquarters*] (HU)
BRFKGTO ... Bulgarian Republic Physical Culture Program "Ready for Labor and Defense" (BU)
BRG .... Betriebsraetegesetz [*Law Concerning Workers' Councils*] (EG)
BRG .... Budapesti Radiotechnikai Gyar [*Budapest Radio Technology Factory*] (HU)
BRG-FAR .... Bases de Reparaciones Generales de las Fuerzas Armadas Revolucionarias [*Revolutionary Armed Forces General Repair Depots*] [*Cuban*] (LA)
BRGM .... Base de Reparaciones Generales de Municiones [*General Munitions Repair Base*] [*Cuban*] (LA)
BRGM .... Bureau de Recherches Geologiques et Minieres [*Bureau of Geological and Mining Exploration*] [*French*] (WER)
BRH .... Biuro Radcy Handlowego [*Trade Adviser's Bureau*] [*Polish*]
BRI .... Banca dei Regolamenti Internazionali [*Bank for International Settlements*] [*Use BIS*] [*Italian*] (WER)
BRI .... Bank Rakjat Indonesia [*People's Bank of Indonesia*] (IN)
BRI .... Bureau de Renseignements Internationaux [*International Information Bureau*] [*French*] (WER)
BRIEX .... British Railway Industry Export Group (MAR)
Brig .... Brigade [*Brigade*] [*Military*] [*French*] (MTD)
brig .... Brigade (RU)
brigadmil .... Brigade in Support of the Militia (RU)
BRIGDJEN ... Brigadir Djenderal [*Brigadier General*] (IN)
BRIGPOL ..... Brigadir Polisi [*Police Brigadier*] (IN)
BRIGPUR ..... Brigade Pertempuran [*Combat Brigade*] (IN)
BRiH .... Bank Rzemiosla i Handlu [*Bank of Handicraft Industry and Trade*] (POL)
BRIMOB ...... Brigade Mobil [*Mobile Brigade (Police)*] (IN)
br iod ist ...... Bromine and Iodine Spring [*Topography*] (RU)
BRIPDA .... Brigadir Polisi Dua [*Police Brigadier II*] (IN)
BRIPTU .... Brigadir Polisi Satu [*Police Brigadier I*] (IN)
Briqie .... Briqueterie [*Brickyard*] [*Military map abbreviation*] [*World War I*] [*French*] (MTD)
bris .... Brisures [*Broken-Grain Rice*] (CL)
BRISA .... Bienes Raices de El Salvador, SA [*Real Estate of El Salvador Corp.*]
brit .... British (RU)
britt .... Brittilainen [*British*] [*Finnish*]
BRIZ .... Office for Rationalization and Inventions (RU)
brizol .... Bitumen-Rubber Waterproofing Material (RU)
BRIZTI .... Office of Rationalization, Inventions, and Technical Information (RU)
BRK .... Betriebsfunk-Redaktionskommission [*Enterprise Radio Editorial Commission*] (EG)
BRK .... Bezirks-Revisionskommission [*Bezirk Auditing Commission*] (EG)
BrK .... Brankovo Kolo [*Sremski Karlovci*] [*A periodical*] (YU)
brk .... Brigade of Missile Warships (BU)
BRK .... Bulgarian Revolutionary Committee (BU)
br k .... Ford for Wheeled Vehicles [*Topography*] (RU)
BRK .... River Craft Squadron (RU)
brka .... Brigade of Missile Cutters (BU)
brkb .... Armored Cavalry Battalion (BU)
brkbr .... Armored Cavalry Brigade (BU)
brkhz .... Chemical Defense Brigade (BU)
BRKKV .... Algemene Bond van Rooms Katholieke Kiesverenigingen [*General League of Roman Catholic Election Societies*] [*Dutch*] (PPE)
brkp .... Armored Cavalry Regiment (BU)
BRL .... Bulgarska Republika Ludowa [*Bulgarian People's Republic*] [*Polish*]
BRM .... Banque de la Republique du Mali [*Bank of the Republic of Mali*] (AF)
BRM- .... Bimetallic Power-Control Thermostat [*Electric range*] (RU)
BRM .... Borbene Radioaktivne Materije [*Combat Radioactive Materials*] [*Military*] (YU)
BRM .... Power Control Unit (RU)
BRMA .... Bureau de Recherches Minieres de l'Algerie (MAR)
BRMD .... Short-Range Surface-to-Surface Ballistic Missile (RU)
BR-ML .... Bandera Roja - Marxista Leninista [*Red Flag - Marxist Leninist Faction*] [*Venezuelan*] (LA1)
br mog .... Common Grave [*Topography*] (RU)
BrMP .... Brigade Aid Station (BU)
BRMP .... Brigade Medical Aid Station (RU)
brmp .... Naval Infantry Brigade, Marines (BU)
BRN .... Brunei [*Three-letter standard code*] (CNC)
BRO .... Battalion Defense Area (RU)
BROC .... Brigade Rouge d'Occitanie [*Red Brigade of Occitania*] [*French*] (PD)
BRODOIMPEKS ... Preduzece za Medunarodnu Trgovinu Brodogradevnim Materijalom [*Establishment for International Trade in Shipbuilding Materials*] [*Belgrade*] (YU)
BRODOSPAS ... Preduzece za Spasavanje i Teglenje Brodova [*Shipping Salvage and Towage Establishment*] [*Split*] (YU)
BrOMO .... Brigade Medical Support Detachment (BU)
Bron .... Buron [*Cheese Factory*] [*Military map abbreviation*] [*World War I*] [*French*] (MTD)
bronkat .... Armored Cutter (RU)
BrOP .... Brigade Supply Relay Point (RU)
brosch .... Broschiert [*Sewn in Pamphlet Form*] [*German*]
brosh .... Brochure [*or Pamphlet*] (BU)
brosh der .... Abandoned Village [*Topography*] (RU)
brosz .... Broszura [*Pamphlet*] (POL)
brot .... Coastal Defense (BU)
BROTRAZ ... Brodarska Transportna Proizvodacka Zadruga [*Shipping Transport and Production Cooperative*] (YU)
BROU .... Banco de la Republica Oriental de Uruguay [*Bank of Uruguay*] (LA)
BROU .... Rapid Reduction and Cooling Unit (RU)

broz .... Brozovany [*Unbound*] (CZ)
BRP .... Brazilian Workers' Party (RU)
BRP .... Bulgarian River Navigation (BU)
BRP .... Bulgarian River Navigation Administration (BU)
BRP .... Bulgarska Rabotnicheska Partiia [*Bulgarian Workers Party*] (PPE)
BRP .... Bureau de Recherches de Petrole [*Petroleum Prospecting Office*] [*French*] (AF)
BRP .... Burmese Workers' Party (RU)
BRP .... Close-In Radio Marker Beacon (RU)
br p .... Ford for Pedestrians [*Topography*] (RU)
BRP(k) .... Bugarska Radnicka Partija (Komunisti) [*Bulgarian Workers' Party (Communists)*] (YU)
BRP (k) .... Bulgarian Workers' Party (Communist) (BU)
BRPM .... Bureau de Recherches et de Participations Minieres [*Mineral Prospecting and Investment Office*] [*Moroccan*] (AF)
BRPM .... Bureau de Recherches Petrolieres Marocain (MAR)
BRPR .... Banca Republicii Populare Romane [*Bank of the Romanian People's Republic*] (RO)
BRP (ts) ...... Bulgarian Workers' Party (Left Wing) (BU)
BRR .... Fast Breeder Reactor (RU)
BRRI .... Building and Road Research Institute [*Ghanaian*] (AF)
BRRO .... Shore-Based Radio Intelligence Detachment (RU)
BRS .... Bueromaschinenwerk Rheinmetall, Soemmerda [*Rheinmetall Office-Machine Plant, Soemmerda*] (EG)
BRS .... Bulgarian Workers' Union (BU)
BRSD .... Intermediate-Range Ballistic Missile (RU)
BRSDP .... Bulgarian Workers' Social Democratic Party (BU)
BRSDP (ts) ... Bulgarian Workers' Social Democratic Party (Left Wing) (BU)
BrSl .... Broj Sluzbeno [*Official Number*] (YU)
BRSR .... Biroul pentru Rezolvarea Sezisarilor si Reclamatiilor [*Bureau for Resolving Notifications and Complaints*] (RO)
BRST .... Botswana Roan Selection Trust (MAR)
Br st .... British Standard (RU)
BRT .... Bayrak Radyo-Televisyon [*Bayrak Radio-Television*] (TU)
BRT .... Belgische Radio en Televisie [*Belgian Radio and Television - Dutch Service*] (WEN)
BRT .... Brutto-Registertonnen [*Gross Register Tons*] (EG)
BRT .... Brutto Registrovane Tuny [*Gross Register Tons*] [*Maritime weight*] (CZ)
BRT .... Bruttoregistertonne [*Gross Ton*] [*Polish*]
brt .... Bruttorekisteritonni(a) [*Finnish*]
BRT .... Bulgarian Radio and Television (BU)
BRT .... Gross Register Ton, Gross Register Tonnage (RU)
BRT .... Large Diesel Fish-Salting Trawler (RU)
brtbr .... Armored Brigade (BU)
BrTD .... Armored Division (RU)
Br-to .... Gross Weight, Gross (RU)
brtr .... Armored Carrier (RU)
BRTR .... Electronic Reconnaissance Battery (BU)
BRTR .... Radio Reconnaissance Battery (RU)
BRTs .... Fast-Setting Expanding Cement (RU)
BRTsK .... Bulgarian Central Revolutionary Committee (BU)
BRU .... Bilharzia Research Unit (MAR)
BrU .... Bromouracil (RU)
BRU .... Building Research Unit (MAR)
BRU .... Contactless Regulating Device (RU)
BRU .... Contactless Relay (RU)
BRUC .... Bloque Revolucionario Universitario Cristiano [*Christian Revolutionary University Bloc*] [*Dominican Republic*] (LA1)
BRV .... Bezirks-Registrierverwaltung [*Bezirk Registration Administration*] (EG)
BRV .... Development and Application Base (BU)
BRV .... Gross Register Tonnage (RU)
BRV .... Radioactive Substance [*Military term*] (RU)
BRV .... Radioactive Warfare Contaminant (BU)
BRV .... Reactant Warfare Agents (BU)
BRV .... Recording and Reproduction Unit (RU)
brw .... Bez Roku Wydania [*Undated, Year of Publication Not Given*] [*Polish*]
Bryg .... Brygada [*Brigade*] [*Polish*]
bryt .... Brytyjski [*British*] [*Polish*]
BRZ .... Berdsk Radio Plant (RU)
BRZ .... Bezirksrechenzentrum [*Bezirk Computer Center*] (EG)
BS .... Adder (RU)
BS .... Armor-Piercing Projectile, Armor-Piercing Shell (RU)
BS .... Bacterial Means, Bacterial Agents (RU)
BS .... Bahamas [*Two-letter standard code*] (CNC)
BS .... Ballast Resistance (RU)
BS .... Barisan Sosialis [*Socialist Front*] (ML)
BS .... Base System (RU)
BS .... Berezin Synchronized Machine Gun [*Aviation*] (RU)
BS .... Berufsschule [*German*]
BS .... Biblioteka Sportowa [*Sport Series*] (POL)
BS .... Biochemical Society (EA)
BS .... Biuro Sprzedazy [*Sales Office*] (POL)
BS .... Blanicke Strojirny [*Blanik Engineering Works*] (CZ)
BS .... Block Station, Blocking Station (RU)
BS .... Bojove Stanoviste [*Combat Position*] (CZ)
BS .... Book Block Pasting Machine (RU)
BS .... Bookplate Society (EA)
BS .... Border Scouts (ML)
BS .... Boru Sanayii Anonim Sirketi [*Pipe Industry Corporation*] [*Istanbul*] (TU)
BS .... Combat Contact (RU)
BS .... Combat Firing (RU)
BS .... Combat Listening Post (RU)
BS .... Combat Sector (RU)
BS .... Fixed Battery [*Military term*] (RU)
BS .... Lower Beam, Passing Beam [*Vehicles*] (RU)
BS .... Reading Unit (RU)
BS .... Shift Unit [*Computers*] (RU)
BS .... Shore Station, Coast Station (RU)
BS .... Signal Battalion (RU)
BS- .... Signal Unit (RU)
BS .... Synchronization Unit [*Automation*] (RU)
BS .... White Glass (RU)
BS .... White Light [*Fluorescent lamp*] (RU)
BSA .... Botswana Softball Association (MAR)
BSA .... British South Africa Company (MAR)
BSA .... Bulletin de la Societe d'Anthropologie [*Paris*] [*A publication*] (MAR)
BSA .... Bureau Senegalaise d'Architecture et d'Etudes (MAR)
BSAB .... Bulletin de la Societe d'Anthropologie de Bruxelles [*A publication*] (MAR)
BSAC .... British South Africa Company (MAR)
BSAC .... British South Africa Corps (MAR)
BSAE .... British School of Archaeology in Egypt (MAR)
BSAM .... Great Soviet World Atlas (RU)
BSAOS .... Bulletin of the School of African and Oriental Studies [*London*] [*A publication*] (MAR)
BSAP .... British South Africa Police (MAR)
BSAT .... Vseobshchii Soiuz Alzhirskikh Trudiashchikhsia (MAR)
bsau .... Self-Propelled Gun Battalion [*Artillery*] (RU)
BSB .... Betrieb mit Staatlicher Beteiligung [*Semi-State Enterprise*] (EG)
BSB .... Border Scouts Borneo (ML)
BSB .... Bulgarska Sbirka [*Bulgarian Collection*] [*A periodical*] (BU)
BSBA .... Bulletin de la Societe Royale Belge d'Anthropologie et de Prehistoire [*A publication*] (MAR)
BSBG .... Bulletin de la Societe Royale Belge de Geographie [*A publication*] (MAR)
BSBO .... Border Special Branch Officers (ML)
BSBP .... Bataljonska Stanica Borbenih Potreba [*Battalion Combat Supply Station*] (YU)
BSc .... Baccalaureus Scientiae [*Bachelor of Science*] [*Latin*] (GPO)
BSC .... Biuro Sprzedazy Ceramiki [*Sales Office for Ceramic Wares*] (POL)
BSCh .... Bojowe Srodki Chemiczne [*Chemical Warfare Materials*] (POL)
BSch .... Read Unit (RU)
BschA .... Beschussamt [*German*]
BS CHMB .... Biuro Sprzedazy Centrali Handlowej Materialow Budowlanych [*Sales Office of the Building Materials Trade Center*] (POL)
BSD .... Banque Senegalaise de Developpement (MAR)
BSD .... Bentara Setia Di-Raja [*Medal to the Orders of Chivalry*] [*Malaysian*] (ML)
BSD .... Blutspendedienst [*Blood Donor Service*] (EG)
BSD .... Bulgarian-Soviet Society (BU)
BSDA .... Bureau Senegalais des Droits d'Auteurs [*Senegalese Copyright Office*] (AF)
BSDP .... Bulgarska Socialdemokraticheska Partiia [*Bulgarian Social Democratic Party*] (PPE)
BSDr .... Bulgaro-Suvetska Druzhba [*Bulgarian-Soviet Friendship*] [*A periodical*] (BU)
BSE .... Great Soviet Encyclopedia (RU)
BSEA .... British School of Egyptian Archaeology (MAR)
BSEC .... Brevet Superieur d'Enseignement Commercial [*Higher Commercial Education Certificate*] (CL)
BSEC .... Brevet Superieur d'Etudes Commerciales [*Algerian*] (MAR)
BSEC .... Bulletin de la Societe des Etudes Camerounaises [*A publication*] (MAR)
BSERP .... Bulletin de la Societe d'Etudes et de Recherches Prehistoriques [*Les Eyzies*] [*A publication*] (MAR)
BSFL .... Barbados Sugar Factories Limited (LA1)
BSFS .... Bulgarian Union for Physical Culture and Sports (BU)
BSG .... Betriebs-Sportgemeinschaft [*Enterprise Sports Association*] (EG)
BSGA .... Bulletin de la Societe de Geographie d'Anvers [*A publication*] (MAR)
BSGC .... Bulletin de la Societe de Geographie Commerciale [*Bordeaux*] [*A publication*] (MAR)
BSGF .... Bulletin de la Societe Geologique de France [*Paris*] [*A publication*] (MAR)
BSGH .... Bulletin de la Societe de Geographie Commerciale du Havre [*A publication*] (MAR)
BSGP .... Bulletin de la Societe de Geographie, Paris [*A publication*] (MAR)
BSGR .... Bulletin. Societatea (Reale) Geografica Romana [*A publication*] (MAR)
BSh .... Bickford Fuze, Safety Fuze (RU)
BShchP .... Battery Distribution Panel [*Telephony*] (RU)

BSHNAN ..... Bulletin de la Societe d'Histoire Naturelle d'Afrique du Nord [*A publication*] (MAR)
BShtU......... Power Unit Control Panel [*Nuclear energy*] (BU)
BSI .... Indicating Light Unit (RU)
BSI .... Pulse-Erasing Unit (RU)
BSIE .... Budget Special d'Investissement et d'Equipement [*Special Investment and Equipment Budget*] [*Ivorian*] (AF)
BSiP .... Biuro Studiow i Projektow [*Bureau for Study and Designing*] [*Polish*]
BSiPL .... Biuro Studiow i Projektow Lacznosci [*Office of Communication Research and Plans*] (POL)
BSiUS......... Biblioteka Sprzetu i Urzadzen Sportowych [*Sporting Goods and Equipment Series*] (POL)
BSK .... Banque Senegalo-Koweitienne (MAR)
Bsk .... Baskan [*or Baskanlik*] [*Chairman or Chairmanship, Chief*] (TU)
BSK .... Bereg Slovnoi Kosti (MAR)
BSK .... Berliner Stadtkontor [*Berlin Municipal Bank*] (EG)
BSK .... Braunkohlen-Schwelkoks [*Carbonized Lignite*] (EG)
BSK .... Butadiene-Styrene Rubber (RU)
BSKhA .... Belorussian Agricultural Academy (RU)
BSKhI.......... Bashkir Agricultural Institute (RU)
BSKhI.......... Belorussian Agricultural Institute (RU)
BSL .... Biblioteka Sportowo-Lekarska [*Sport and Medical Series*] (POL)
BSL .... Black Star Line (MAR)
BSL .... Bulletin de la Societe de Linguistique [*A publication*] (MAR)
BSL .... Shore Duty, Shore Service (RU)
BSM .... Barisan Sosialis Malaysia [*Malaysian Socialist Front*] (ML)
BSM .... Beso Sus Manos [*With Great Respect*] [*Spanish*]
BSM .... Biuro Spoldzielni Mieszkaniowych [*Office of Housing Cooperatives*] (POL)
BSM .... Brigade in Support of the Militia (RU)
BSMP .... Specialized Medical Aid Brigade (RU)
BSN............ Bulletin de la Societe Normande de Geographie [*A publication*] (MAR)
BSN............ Office of Standardization (RU)
BSNG .... Bulletin de la Societe Neuchateloise de Geographie [*A publication*] (MAR)
BSNKh .... Bashkir Council of the National Economy (RU)
BSO............ Baluchi Students' Organization [*Pakistani*] (PD)
BSO............ Black September Organization [*Inter-Arab*] (ME)
BSO............ Bratislavsky Symfonicky Orchester [*Bratislava Symphonic Orchestra*] (CZ)
BSO............ Equipment Monitoring Unit (RU)
BSOAS........ Bulletin. School of Oriental and African Studies. [*London*] [*A publication*] (MAR)
Bs Og .... Bas Ogretmen [*Head Teacher*] (TU)
BSOT.......... Disappearing Armored Emplacement (RU)
BSP .... Barisan Socialist Party [*Singapore*] (ML)
BSP .... Bayerische Staatspartei [*Bavarian State Party*] [*West German*] (PPW)
BSP .... Belgische Socialistische Partij [*Belgian Socialist Party*] (PPW)
BSP .... Bojowe Srodki Promieniotworcze [*Radioactive Warfare Substances*] [*Polish*]
BSP .... Overflow Signaling Unit (RU)
BSP .... Smokeless Powder for Siege and Fortress Guns [*Symbol*] [*French*] (MTD)
BSP-........... Subroutine Library [*Computers*] (RU)
BSPA.......... Barbados Sugar Producers Association (LA1)
BSPD.......... Bratsko Srpsko Potporno Drustvo [*Serbian Fraternal Welfare Society*] (YU)
BSPF .... Bulletin de la Societe Prehistorique Francaise [*Paris*] [*A publication*] (MAR)
BSPM .... Bulletin de la Societe Prehistorique du Maroc [*Rabat*] [*A publication*] (MAR)
BSPO .... Badz Sprawny do Pracy i Obrony [*Be Fit for Work and Defense (Badge)*] (POL)
BSPP........... Burma Socialist Programme Party (PPW)
BSPPG .... Bulletin de la Societe Prehistorique et Protohistorique Gabonaise [*Libreville*] [*A publication*] (MAR)
BSPSC .... Bendel State Public Service Commission (MAR)
BSR .... Brigade de Securite Republicain [*Republican Security Brigade*] [*Cambodian*] (CL)
BSR .... Brigade Speciale de Recherches (de la Gendarmerie) [*Special Investigation Brigade*] [*French*] (WER)
BSr .... Comparator (RU)
BSR .... Flash-Ranging Battery (RU)
BSRBAP...... Bulletin de la Societe Royale Belge d'Anthropologie et de Prehistoire [*Brussels*] [*A publication*] (MAR)
BSRBB .... Bulletin de la Societe Royale de Botanique de Belgique [*Brussels*] [*A publication*] (MAR)
BSRC .... Bloc Socialista Revolucionari de Catalunya [*Revolutionary Socialist Bloc of Catalonia*] [*Spanish*] (WER)
BSRC .... Bulletin de la Societe des Recherches Congolaises [*A publication*] (MAR)
BSRR.......... Bialoruska Socjalistyczna Republika Radziecka [*Belorussian Soviet Socialist Republic*] (POL)
bsrto .... Communications and Technical Support Battalion (BU)
BSS .... Ballistic Strategic Missile (RU)
BSS .... Barisan Sosialis Singapura [*Singapore Socialist Front*] (IN)
BSS .... Black Students Society (MAR)
BSS .... Brandyske Strojirny a Slevarny [*Brandys Engineering Works and Foundries*] (CZ)
BSS .... Quick-Setting Mixtures (RU)
BSS .... Union of Bulgarian Stenographers (BU)
BSSD .... Intermediate-Range Ballistic Missile (RU)
BSSR.......... Belorussian Soviet Socialist Republic (BU)
BSSR.......... Belorussian Soviet Socialist Republic (RU)
BSSR.......... Bukhara Soviet Socialist Republic [*1924*] (RU)
BST .... Bessemer Steel (RU)
BST .... Bulletin of Construction Engineering [*A publication*] (RU)
BST .... Large Stereoscopic Telescope, Large Battery Commander's Telescope (RU)
BST .... Tower Solar Telescope (RU)
Bstbp .... Bastabip [*Head Doctor*] (TU)
BSTU.......... Barbados Secondary Teachers Union (LA1)
BSTZ.......... Charging Current Stabilization Unit (RU)
BSv............ Coupling Unit (RU)
BSv............ Signal Battalion (RU)
BSW .... Badische Stahlwerke [*West German*]
BSWC.......... British Subject without Citizenship (MAR)
BSZT .... Borsodi Szenbanyaszati Troszt [*Coal Mining Trust of Borsod*] (HU)
BSZV .... Belkereskedelmi Szallitasi Vallalat [*Domestic Trade Shipping Enterprise*] (HU)
BT............... Armored (RU)
BT............... Baric Topography (RU)
Bt................ Batarya [*Battery*] [*Military*] (TU)
BT............... Bea dan Tjukai [*Duties and Customs, Customs Service*] (IN)
bt................ Bez Tiskare [*No Printing Firm Given*] (CZ)
BT............... Bhutan [*Two-letter standard code*] (CNC)
BT............... Binocular Tube (RU)
BT............... Blasnikova Tiskarna [*Blasnik Printing House*] [*Ljubljana*] (YU)
BT............... Brevet de Technicien [*French*]
bt................ Brez Tiskarne [*Without Printer's Imprint*] (YU)
bt................ Brut [*French*]
Bt................ Bukit [*Hill*] [*Indonesian*] (NAU)
Bt................ Bukit [*Hill*] [*Malay*] (NAU)
BT............... Bukit [*Hill*] (ML)
BT............... Bulgarski Turist [*Bulgarian Tourist*] [*A periodical*] (BU)
BT............... Current Unit [*Computers*] (RU)
BT............... Diesel Tug (RU)
BT............... High-Speed Tank (RU)
BT............... Labor Exchange, Employment Agency (RU)
Bt................ Transformer Vault [*Topography*] (RU)
Bta.............. A Buntetotorvenykonyv Altalanos Resze [*General Section of the Penal Code*] (HU)
BTA .... Bautechnische Abteilung [*Structural Engineering Department*] (EG)
BTA .... Bois Transformes d'Afrique (MAR)
BTA .... Bulgarian News Agency (RU)
BTA .... Bulgarian Telegraph Agency (BU)
BTAB.......... Concrete-Piercing Aerial Bomb (RU)
B-Tafel .... Stoerungstafel fuer Massnahmen des Fahrdienstleiters bei Stoerungen im Befehlstellwerk [*Table of Measures to be Taken by the Dispatcher in Case of Interruption in the Control Signaling Device*] (EG)
BTAO .... Briqueterie Tuilerie de l'Afrique Occidentale (MAR)
BTB .... Berliner Technisches Buero [*Berlin Technical Office*] (EG)
BTC .... Brigadas de Trabajadores del Campo [*Workers Brigades of the Countryside*] [*Salvadoran*] (LA1)
BTCD .... Banque Tchadienne de Credits et de Depots (MAR)
BTCF........... Bureau Technique du Chemin de Fer [*Technical Railroad Office*] [*Gabonese*] (AF)
BTCh........... Armored Unit (RU)
BTCI............ Banque Togolaise pour le Commerce et l'Industrie (MAR)
BTCI............ Bureau Technique de Conseillers Industriels (MAR)
BTD .... Brigadni Tezke Dilny [*Brigade Maintenance Shops for Heavy Equipment*] (CZ)
BTE .... Boite [*Box, Post Office Box*] [*French*]
BTE .... Boripari Tudomanyos Egyesulet [*Scientific Association of the Leather Industry*] (HU)
bte.............. Brevete [*Patent*] [*French*]
BTE .... Bureau Technique d'Etudes (MAR)
B-teczka ..... Biblioteczka [*Little Library*] [*Often used for a series of books*] [*Polish*]
BTEI .... Bulletin of Technical and Economic Information [*A publication*] (RU)
BTEI .... Office of Technical and Economic Information (RU)
BTETs .... Berezniki Heat and Electric Power Plant (RU)
Btg .... Batang [*River*] [*Malay*] (NAU)
BTGM.......... Beden Terbiyesi Genel Mudurlugu [*Directorate General of Physical Training*] (TU)
BTH .... Bureau Technique Huguet (MAR)
BTI.............. Armored Equipment (RU)
BTI.............. British Tutorial Institute (MAR)
BTI.............. Office of Technical Information (RU)
BTI.............. Office of Technical Inventory (RU)
BTiMV .... Armored and Mechanized Troops (BU)
b tit l .... No Title Page (RU)
BTJ.............. Brigadas Tecnicas Juveniles [*Youth Technical Brigades*] [*Cuban*] (LA)

BTK .... Bourse de Travail du Katanga (MAR)
BTK .... Bunteto Torvenykonyv [*Penal Code*] (HU)
btk .... Motor Torpedo Boat Brigade (RU)
BTK .... Office of Technical Control (RU)
BTK .... Office of Technical Cost Accounting (RU)
BTK .... Trapezoidal-Oscillation Unit (RU)
BTK- .... Tubular Tower Crane (RU)
btka .... Brigade of Torpedo Boats [*PT boats*] (BU)
BTL .... Bureau Technique de Liaison (MAR)
BTM .... Bankin'ny Tantsaha Mpamokatra [*National Bank for Rural Development*] [*Malagasy*] (AF)
BTM .... Batiment et Travaux du Maghreb (MAR)
BTM .... Bydgoskie Towarzystwo Muzyczne [*The Bydgoszcz Music Society*] [*Polish*]
BTM .... High-Speed Trench Excavator, High-Speed Ditching Machine (RU)
BTMot .... Biuro Turystyki Motorowej [*Motor-Touring Office*] [*Polish*]
BTN .... Bank Tabungan Negara [*State Savings Bank*] (IN)
Btn .... Bataillon [*Battalion*] [*Military*] [*French*] (MTD)
BTN .... Bhutan [*Three-letter standard code*] (CNC)
BTN .... Brussels Tariff Nomenclature (MAR)
btn .... Bruttorekisteritonni(a) [*Finnish*]
BTN .... Office of Technical Standardization (RU)
BTO .... Brussels Treaty Organization [*Western European*] (WEN)
B-to .... Gross Weight, Gross (RU)
BTP .... Bank Tabungan Pos [*Postal Savings Bank*] (IN)
BTP .... Bataljon Tim Pertempuran [*Battalion Combat Team*] (IN)
BTP .... Batiment et Travaux Publics [*Algerian*] (MAR)
BTP- .... Beta-Ray Coating Thickness Gauge (RU)
BTP .... Bulgarian Chamber of Commerce (BU)
BTP .... Technical Assistance Board of the UN [*TAB*] (RU)
BTPP .... Bulgarian Chamber of Commerce and Industry (BU)
BTPP .... Bulgarian Trade and Industrial Enterprise (BU)
BTPP .... Office of Technical Preparation of Production (RU)
BTPS .... Batiments et Travaux Publics Senegalais [*Senegalese Building Construction and Public Works*] (AF)
BTR .... Armored Personnel Carrier (BU)
BTR .... Armored Personnel Carrier (RU)
b tr .... Large Transformer (RU)
BTR- .... Stakeless Fabric Tank (RU)
BTR .... Technical Development Base (BU)
BTR .... Topographic Reconnaissance Battery (RU)
B tr .... Transformer Vault [*Topography*] (RU)
BTRGK .... Armored Reserve of the High Command (RU)
BTRIP .... Bureau for the Technology and Development of Instruments Production (BU)
BTRM .... Armored Vehicle Repair Shop (RU)
BTRR .... Armored Repair Shop (BU)
BTS .... Bible Translation Society (MAR)
BTS .... Biuro Turystyki Sportowej "Sports Tourist" [*Sport Touring Office "Sports Tourist"*] [*Polish*]
BTS .... Board of Theological Studies (MAR)
BTS .... Bois Tropicaux de Soubre (MAR)
BTs .... Bolshevist Center (of the RSDRP) (RU)
BTS .... Brevet de Technicien Superieur [*Advanced Technician's Certificate*] [*French*] (CL)
BTS .... British Troops in Sudan (MAR)
BTS .... Bromothymol Blue [*Indicator*] (RU)
BTS .... Bulgarian Tourist Union (BU)
bts .... Colorless, Achromatic (RU)
bts .... Price Not Given, No Price [*Bibliography*] (RU)
BTS .... Tactical Ballistic Missile (RU)
Bts .... Unpriced (BU)
BTs .... White Portland Cement (RU)
b-tsa .... Hospital (BU)
b-tsa .... Hospital (RU)
BTSB .... Bagimsiz Turkiye Sosyalistleri Birligi [*Union of Independent Turkish Socialists*] (TU)
BTSB .... Budapesti Testnevelesi es Sportbizottsag [*Budapest Committee for Physical Culture and Sports*] (HU)
BTsBO .... Bulgarian Central Philanthropic Society (BU)
BTsDS .... Long-Distance Communications Circuit Unit (RU)
BTSF .... Budapesti Testnevelesi es Sport Felugyeloseg [*Inspectorate of Physical Culture and Sports of Budapest*] (HU)
BTsGD .... Bicycloheptadiene (RU)
BTShch .... Coastal Minesweeper (RU)
BTSI .... Budapesti Testnevelesi es Sport Intezet [*Budapest Institute of Physical Culture and Sports*] (HU)
BTSI .... Budapesti Testnevelesi es Sportegeszsegugyi Intezet [*Budapest Institute of Physical Culture and Hygiene*] (HU)
BTSI .... Budapesti Testnevelesi es Sportorvosi Intezet [*Budapest Institute for Physical Education and Sports Physicians*] (HU)
BTsK .... Bureau of the Central Committee (RU)
BTsK .... Office of Central Cataloging (RU)
bt sk .... Powder Magazine (BU)
BTsN .... Centrifugal Gasoline Pump (RU)
BTsRK .... Bulgarian Central Revolutionary Committee (BU)
BTST .... Budapesti Testnevelesi es Sport Tanacs [*Council of Physical Culture and Sports of Budapest*] (HU)
BTsVB .... Berlin Air Safety Center (RU)
BTsVS .... Intercom Circuit Unit (RU)
BTT .... Beztrzajni Top [*Recoiless Gun*] (YU)
BTT .... Biroul de Turism pentru Tineret [*Bureau of Tourism for Young People*] (RO)
BTT .... Telephone and Telegraph Channel Unit (RU)
BTTDD .... Bati Trakya Turkleri Dayanisma Dernegi [*Association of Mutual Solidarity with the Turks of Western Thrace*] (TU)
BTTKDD .... Bati Trakya Turkleri Kultur ve Dayanisma Dernegi [*Western Thrace Turks' Culture and Mutual Solidarity Association*] (GC)
Btto .... Brutto [*Gross*] [*Business and trade*] [*German*]
BTTs .... Fast Hardening Cement (RU)
BTTsK .... Bulgarian Secret Central Committee (BU)
BTU .... Armored Troops Directorate (RU)
BTU .... Office of Technical Computation (RU)
BTU .... Remote Control Unit (RU)
BTU .... Tank Angledozer (RU)
BTV .... Armored Troops (RU)
BTVH .... Bo Tuc Van Hoa [*Supplementary Education*] (TVP)
BTW .... Belasting op Toegevoegde Waarde [*Value-Added Tax*] [*Dutch*] (WEN)
BTYe .... British Thermal Unit (RU)
BTZ .... Belorussian Tractor Plant (RU)
BTZ .... Bilimbay Pipe-Casting Plant (RU)
BTZ .... Biuro Turystyki Zagranicznej [*Bureau for Foreign Touring*] [*Polish*]
BTZU .... Remote-Control Contactless Protection Device (RU)
BU .... Accounting (RU)
BU .... Ballet School (BU)
Bu .... Batu [*Rock*] [*Malay*] (NAU)
BU .... Bau-Union (VEB) [*Construction Enterprise*] (EG)
BU .... Biblioteka Uniwersytecka [*University Library*] [*Polish*]
BU .... Biologicky Ustav [*Institute of Biology*] (CZ)
BU .... Bogazici Universitesi [*Bosporus Straits University*] [*Formerly, Robert College*] (TU)
BU .... Bollettino Ufficiale [*Official Gazette*] [*Italian*] (WER)
BU .... Brodogradiliste Uljanik [*Uljanik Shipyard*] [*Pula*] (YU)
BU .... Bromouracil (RU)
BU .... Burma [*Two-letter standard code*] (CNC)
Bu .... Buyuk [*Large, Greater*] (TU)
BU .... Combat Regulations (RU)
BU .... Combat Sector, Combat Zone (RU)
BU .... Control Unit (RU)
BU .... Drilling Rig (RU)
BU .... Gasoline-Resistant, Gasoline-Proof (RU)
BU .... Lateral Deviation, Deflection Error (RU)
BU- .... Steeping Unit [*Clothing decontamination*] (RU)
BU .... Union Bubi, Equatorial Guinea (MAR)
b/u .... Used, Not New (RU)
BUA .... Artillery Combat Regulations (RU)
Bua .... Bahnunterhaltungs-Arbeiter [*Section Hand*] (EG)
BUA .... Bibliotheques Universitaires de l'Afrique (MAR)
BUA .... Botswana Uniforms Agency (MAR)
bu alosztaly ... Bunugyi Alosztaly [*Criminal Investigation Section*] (HU)
BUB .... Bau-Union Berlin [*Berlin Construction Enterprise*] (EG)
BuB .... Buch und Bibliothek [*German*] [*A publication*]
BUBA .... Bombardment Aviation Combat Regulations (RU)
Bubel-Is .... Bursa ve Cevresi Belediye Iscileri Sendikasi [*Bursa and Environs Municipal Workers' Union*] (TU)
BUBIV .... Budapesti Butoripari Vallalat [*Budapest Furniture Industry Enterprise*] (HU)
BUBMV .... Combat Regulations of Armored and Mechanized Troops (RU)
BUC .... Banque Unie de Credit [*United Credit Bank*] [*Cameroonian*] (AF)
BUC .... Bayero University College (MAR)
Buchh .... Buchhalter [*German*]
Buchst .... Buchstabe [*Letter, Character, Type*] (EG)
BUD .... Buyuk Ulku Dernegi [*Greater Idealist Society*] (TU)
BUDAPRESS ... MTI Idegen Nyelvu Szerkesztosegenek Bulletin- es Cikkszolgalata [*Bulletin and Article Service of MTI's Foreign Language Editorial Office*] (HU)
BUDAVOX ... Budavox Hiradastechnikai Kulkereskedelmi Reszvenytarsasag [*Budavox Telecommunications Foreign Trade Company*] (HU)
Budopiec .... Budowa Piecow Przemyslowych i Kominow [*Enterprise for Industrial Furnace and Chimney Construction*] (POL)
BUDR .... Bromodeoxyuridine (RU)
BUe .... Dienstvorschrift fuer Betriebsueberwachungen von Bahnhoefen [*Service Regulations for Supervision of Railroad Station Operations*] (EG)
BUEK .... Boldog Ujevet Kivan [*or Kivanok or Kivannak*] [*Happy New Year*] (HU)
BUF .... Black United Front [*South African*] (PD)
BUFMAR ..... Bureau des Formations Medicales Agrees du Rwand (MAR)
bug .... Hillock, Knoll, Mound [*Topography*] (RU)
BUIA .... Fighter Aviation Combat Regulations (RU)
BUK .... Bratislavsky Umelecky Kabinet [*Bratislava Art Group*] (CZ)
BUK .... Tug, Tugboat (RU)
bukh .... Bay [*Topography*] (RU)
bukhg .... Bookkeeping, Bookkeeping Department (RU)
BUKOP .... Bukoba Coffee Curing Plant (MAR)

BUKS .... Cable Drilling Rig, Cable Drill (RU)
bukv .... Literally (RU)
bul .... Boulevard (BU)
bul .... Bulvar [*or Bulvari*] [*Boulevard*] [*Turkish*] (CED)
Bulasc Hst .. Bulasici Hastaliklar [*Contagious Diseases*] (TU)
BULF .... Brunei United Labor Front (ML)
Bulg .... Bulgarian (BU)
Bulg akad nauk ... Bulgarian Academy of Sciences (BU)
Bulgargeomin ... Bulgarian Specialized Organization for Geological Prospecting, Designing, and Building Mining Projects Abroad (BU)
Bulgarplodeksport ... Bulgarian Enterprise for Export of Fresh and Canned Fruit, Vegetables, and Wine (BU)
Bulgartabak ... Bulgarian Commercial Enterprise for the Export of Tobacco and Tobacco Products (BU)
Bulgartabakeksport ... Bulgarian Enterprise for Tobacco Exports (BU)
Bulg geol d-vo ... Bulgarian Geological Society (BU)
Bulg Tsurk Pregled ... Bulgarski Tsurkoven Pregled [*Bulgarian Church Review*] [*A periodical*] (BU)
Bulg Voin .... Bulgarski Voin [*Bulgarian Soldier*] [*A periodical*] (BU)
BULISR .... Brussels. Universite Libre. Institut de Sociologie. Revue [*A publication*] (MAR)
BULOGNAS ... Badan Urusan Logistik Nasional [*National Logistics Board*] (IN)
Bult .... Buletin [*Bulletin*] (TU)
BuM .... Belugyminiszterium/Miniszter [*Ministry/Minister of the Interior*] (HU)
BUM .... Booster Unit (RU)
BUM .... Combat Regulations of Mechanized Units (RU)
BUM .... Large Department Store (RU)
bum .... Paper (RU)
bum .... Paper Mill [*Topography*] (RU)
BUMA .... Bureau voor Muziek-Auteursrecht [*Dutch*]
BUMCO .... Bureau Minier Congolais (MAR)
BUMF .... Baltic Administration of the Maritime Fleet (RU)
BUMICO .... Bureau Minier Congolais [*Congolese Mining Office*] (AF)
BUMIDOM ... Bureau des Migrations d'Outre-Mer [*Overseas Migrations Office*] [*French*] (WER)
BUMIFOM ... Bureau Minier de la France d'Outre-Mer [*Mining Bureau of Overseas France*]
Bumiz .... Moscow Paper Plate and Packing Materials Factory (RU)
bum l .... Paper Sheet [*Printing*] (RU)
bumlitiz .... Molded-Pulp Insulation (RU)
Bummash ... Paper Machinery Plant (RU)
Bum pr .... Cotton-Spinning Mill [*Topography*] (RU)
BUMS .... Naval War Exercises (RU)
BUMS .... Navy Combat Regulations (RU)
BUNAP .... Borneo Utara National Party [*North Borneo National Party*] (ML)
BUND .... Bund der Deutschen Togolaender (MAR)
BUNEP .... Bureau National d'Etudes des Projets [*National Project Study Office*] [*Rwandan*] (AF)
BUO .... Bloque de Unidad Obrera [*Labor Unity Bloc*] [*Mexican*] (LA1)
BUO .... Irradiation Control Unit (RU)
BUO .... Oscilloscope-Control Unit (RU)
BUP .... Banque de l'Union Parisienne (MAR)
BUP .... Basin Administration of Waterways (RU)
BUP .... Basotho Unity Party [*South African*] (PPW)
BUP .... Bupati [*Regent*] (IN)
BUP .... Converter Control Unit (RU)
BUP .... Infantry Combat Regulations (BU)
BUP .... Infantry Field Manual (RU)
BUPO .... Firefighting Combat Regulations (RU)
BUPPIN .... Biro Urusan Perusahaan Perusahaan Industri Negara [*State Industrial Firms Bureau*] (IN)
BUPTAN .... Biro Urusan Perusahaan Tambang Negara [*State Mining Firms Bureau*] (IN)
BUR .... Bloque de Unidad Reformista [*Reformist Unity Bloc*] [*Dominican Republic*] (LA1)
Bur .... Borehole, Drill Hole [*Topography*] (RU)
BUR .... Burma [*Three-letter standard code*] (CNC)
Bur .... Burun [*Cape, Headland, Promontory, Point*] (TU)
bur .... Derrick [*Topography*] (RU)
BUR .... Disciplinary Barrack (RU)
BUR .... Fortified Coastal Area (RU)
BUR .... Safe Angle of Divergence (RU)
Bur .... Surf, Breakers [*Topography*] (RU)
BUREMI .... Bureau de Recherche et d'Exploitation Miniere [*Mining, Prospecting, and Exploitation Office*] [*Niger*] (AF)
BURGEAP ... Bureau d'Etudes de Geologie Appliquee et d'Hydrologie Souterraine (MAR)
Burgeotrest ... Drilling and Geological Exploration Trust (RU)
Burgiz .... Buryat Book Publishing House (RU)
Burgiz .... Buryat-Mongol State Publishing House (RU)
Burgosizdat ... Buryat Book Publishing House (RU)
BURIDA .... Bureau Ivoirien des Droits d'Auteurs (MAR)
Burlag .... Bureya Railroad Construction Camp [*Corrective labor camps*] (RU)
bur-mong .... Buryat-Mongol (RU)
BurMongASSR ... Buryat-Mongol Autonomous Soviet Socialist Republic [*1923-1958*] (RU)
Burmonggiz ... Buryat-Mongol State Publishing House (RU)
BURP .... Bomb-Run Drift Angle (RU)
BURP .... White Sea River Steamship Line Administration (RU)
bur skv .... Borehole, Drill Hole (RU)
burv .... Drilling Platoon (RU)
Burzh .... Bourgeois (BU)
burzh .... Bourgeois (RU)
BUS .... Bulgarian Teachers' Union (BU)
BUS .... Bureau Universitaire de Statistiques et de Documentation Scolaires et Professionnelles [*French*]
BUSDOM ..... Bureau Shell d'Outre-Mer (MAR)
Busta .... Dienstvorschrift fuer die Statistik der Bahnbetriebsunfaelle [*Service Regulations for Railroad Accident Statistics*] (EG)
BUT .... Bahamas Union of Teachers (LA1)
BUT .... Barbados Union of Teachers (LA1)
BUT .... Baza de Utilaj Transport [*Base for Transportation Equipment*] (RO)
BUT .... Biblioteka Uniwersytetu w Toruniu [*Torun University Library*] (POL)
but .... Bottle (RU)
BUTJ .... Biuro Urzadzen Techniki Jadrowej [*Nuclear Technology Equipment Bureau*] (POL)
BUTORERT ... Butorertekesito Allami Vallalat [*State Enterprise for Sale of Furniture*] (HU)
BUU .... Biro za Unapredenje Ugostiteljstva [*Bureau for Development of Hotel and Catering Trade*] (YU)
BUU .... Bursa Universitesi [*Bursa University*] (TU)
BUV .... Bactericidal Uviol Lamp (RU)
BuV .... Betrieb und Verkehr [*Operations and Traffic*] (EG)
BUV .... Budapesti Uveg- es Porcelanertekesito Vallalat [*Glass and China Commercial Enterprise of Budapest*] (HU)
BUVATEX .... Budapesti Vatta- es Textilipari Termeloszovetkezet [*Budapest Cotton and Textile Producer Cooperative*] (HU)
BUVATI .... Budapesti Varosepitesi Tervezo Vallalat [*Budapest Planning Enterprise for Urban Construction*] (HU)
BUVATI .... Budapesti Varostervezo Intezet [*City Planning Institute of Budapest*] (HU)
Buvo .... Betriebsunfall-Vorschrift [*Industrial Accident Regulations*] (EG)
BUVOGEMI ... Bureau Voltaique de la Geologie et des Mines [*Voltan Bureau of Geology and Mines*] (AF)
BUVVS .... Air Force Combat Regulations (RU)
BUW .... Biblioteka Uniwersytetu Warszawskiego [*Library of Warsaw University*] (POL)
BUW .... Biuro Urbanistyczne Warszawy [*Office for the Urban Development of Warsaw*] (POL)
BuZ .... Buchner Zahl [*Buchner Number*] [*German*]
BUZA .... Antiaircraft Artillery Combat Regulations (RU)
Buzema .... Bulgarian Farm Machinery School (BU)
bv .... Anhydrous, Water-Free (RU)
BV .... Application Base (BU)
BV .... Benzylviologen (RU)
BV .... Berliner Volksbank [*Berlin People's Bank*] (EG)
BV .... Besloten Vennootschap [*Private Limited Company*] [*Dutch*]
bv .... Bij Voorbeeld [*For Example*] [*Dutch*] (GPO)
BV .... Bosanska Vila [*Sarajevo, 1886-1914*] [*A periodical*] (YU)
BV .... Bouvetoya [*Two-letter standard code*] (CNC)
BV .... Braunkohlenverwaltung [*Brown Coal Administration*] [*See BKV*] (EG)
bv .... Brutto Vaha [*Gross Weight*] (CZ)
bv .... Buntetesvegrehajtas [*An abbreviation preceding the rank of officers of the National Penal Authority*] [*Formerly, Prison Guards*] (HU)
BV .... Convalescent Battalion (RU)
BV .... Near East (RU)
BV .... Office of Interchangeability (RU)
BV .... Recovery Unit (RU)
BVAK .... Instruction Address Unit (RU)
BVAP .... Bureau de Vulgarisation des Activites Pratiques [*Practical Activities Popularization Office*] [*Cambodian*] (CL)
BVB .... Bacterial Pathogen (RU)
BVB .... Bulgarian Foreign Trade Bank (BU)
BVCh .... High-Frequency Unit (RU)
BVD .... Binnenlandse Veiligheidsdienst [*Internal Security Service*] [*Dutch*] (WEN)
BVD .... Bond van Dienstplichtige [*League of Conscripts*] [*Dutch*] (WEN)
BvD .... Bund Vertriebener Deutschen [*Federation of German Expellees*] [*West German*] (WEN)
BVD .... Data Input Unit (RU)
bv dor .... Large Crater in Road [*Topography*] (RU)
BVdS .... Bevorzugte Versorgung der Schwerpunktbetriebe [*Procurement Priority for Key Enterprises*] (EG)
BVE .... Batallon Vasco Espanol [*Spanish Basque Battalion*] (PD)
BVE .... High-Speed Pipeless Electric Drill (RU)
BVerf .... Bundesverfassung [*German*]
BVF .... White Sea Fleet (RU)
BVG .... Bataljonska Vatrena Grupa [*Battalion Fire Group*] (YU)
BVG .... Berliner Verkehrs-Gesellschaft [*Berlin Transportation Company (West Berlin)*] (WEN)
BVH .... Betriebsvolkshochschule [*Enterprise Adult Education Institute*] (EG)

BVI .... Budapesti Vasarrendezo Iroda [*Organization Bureau of the Budapest Fair*] (HU)
BVI .... Information Selection Unit (RU)
BVI .... Military Information Bureau (BU)
bvk .... Bivouac Commandant (BU)
BVK .... Borsodi Vegyi Kombinat [*Chemical Combine of Borsod*] (HU)
BVK .... Office of Weight Checking (RU)
BVK .... Protein-Vitamin Concentrate (RU)
BVM .... Bodenverbesserungsmittel [*Soil Improvement Agent*] (EG)
BVM .... Britska Vojenska Misse [*British Military Mission*] (CZ)
BVM .... Bulgarska Voenna Misul [*Bulgarian Military Thought*] [*A periodical*] (BU)
BVM .... High-Speed Computer (RU)
BVM .... Large Computer (RU)
BVMB .... Baltic Naval Bases (RU)
BVMSiIP ...... Office of Interchangeability of the Ministry of the Machine Tool and Tool Industry (RU)
BVN .... Bund der Verfolgten des Naziregimes [*League of Persecutees of the NAZI Regime*] [*West German*] (WEN)
BVN .... Number Selection Unit (RU)
BVO .... Belorussian Military District (RU)
BVO .... Beogradska Vojna Oblast [*Belgrade Military District*] (YU)
BVO .... Beweging voor Vrijheid en Onafhankelijkheid [*Movement for Freedom and Independence*] [*Dutch*] (WEN)
BVOP .... Buntetesvegrehajtas Orszagos Parancsnoksaga [*National Penal Authority*] [*Formerly, Prison Guards*] (HU)
BVP .... Bayerische Volkspartei [*Bavarian People's Party*] [*German*] (PPE)
BVP .... Combat Air Patrol (RU)
BVPP .... Concrete Runway (RU)
BVPU .... Bath, Disinfection, and Laundry Unit (RU)
BVR .... Bloque de la Vanguardia Revolucionaria [*Bolivian*] (PPW)
BVR .... Bureaus for Reciprocal Accounts (BU)
BVR .... Clearinghouse [*Finance*] (RU)
BVS .... Bulgarian Air Routes (BU)
BVSI .... Library of the Higher Agricultural Institute (BU)
BVSL .... Bezrucova Vysoka Skola Lidova [*Bezruc People's College*] (CZ)
BVSS .... Bundesverband fuer den Selbstschutz [*Federal Self-Defense Association*] [*West German*] (WEN)
BVT .... Beke Vilagtanacs [*World Peace Council*] (HU)
BVT .... Bouvetoya [*Three-letter standard code*] (CNC)
BVT .... Budapesti Varosi Tanacs [*City Council of Budapest*] (HU)
BVTsK .... Numerical Code Delivery Unit (RU)
BVTV .... Budapesti Varosepitesi Tervezo Vallalat [*Budapest Urban Development Planning Enterprise*] (HU)
BVV .... Budapesti Villamos Vasut [*Budapest Electric Railways*] [*Formerly, BSZKRT*] (HU)
BVV .... High Explosive, Blasting Agent (RU)
BVVMI .... Library at the Higher Veterinary Medicine Institute (BU)
BVW .... Berliner Volkseigene Wohnungsverwaltung [*Berlin State Housing Administration*] (EG)
Bw .... Bahnbetriebswerk [*Locomotive Light Repair and Maintenance Shop*] (EG)
BW .... Betriebswerkstatt [*Workshop*] (EG)
bw .... Bez Wydawcy [*Name of Publisher Not Given*] [*Polish*]
Bw .... Bindewort [*German*]
bw .... Bitte Wenden [*Please Turn Page*] [*German*] (GPO)
BW .... Botswana [*Two-letter standard code*] (CNC)
B en W .... Burgemeester en Wethouders [*Mayor and Aldermen*] [*Dutch*] (WEN)
BWA .... Bank of West Africa (MAR)
BWA .... Baptist World Alliance (MAR)
BWA .... Biuro Wystaw Artystycznych [*Bureau of Art Exhibitions*] (POL)
BWA .... Botswana [*Three-letter standard code*] (CNC)
BWA .... British West Africa (MAR)
BWA .... Standard Bank of West Africa (MAR)
BWC .... Black Women's Convention (MAR)
BWCDF .... Black Women's Community Development Foundation (AF)
BWIA .... British West Indies Airways [*Trinidadian and Tobagan*] (LA1)
BWKZ .... Biuro Wspolpracy Kulturalnej z Zagranica [*Foreign Cultural Relations Bureau*] [*Polish*]
BWP .... Belgische Werkliedenpartij [*Belgian Workers' Party*] [*Later, Belgian Socialist Party*] (PPE)
BWP .... Betriebswirtschaftsplan [*Enterprise Economic Plan*] (EG)
BWP .... Biblioteka Wydawnictw Prasowych [*Press Agency Library (Series)*] (POL)
BWP .... Biblioteka Wydawnictw Prasy [*Press Agency Library*] (POL)
BWPR .... Biuro Wydawnictw Polskiego Radia [*Publications Office of the Polish Radio*] (POL)
BWR .... Boiling-Water Reactor (MAR)
BWU .... Barbados Workers Union (LA1)
BWVO .... Binnenwasserstrassen-Verkehrsordnung [*Inland Waterways Traffic Regulations*] (EG)
Bww .... Bahnbetriebswagen-Werk [*Railroad Car Maintenance Shop*] (EG)
BWW .... Biblioteka Wiedzy Wojskowej [*Military Science Library*] (POL)
Bxa .... Baixa [*Shoal*] [*Portuguese*] (NAU)
BxA .... Beaux Arts [*French*]
Bxo .... Baixo [*Shoal*] [*Portuguese*] (NAU)
B-ya .... Bulgaria (BU)
BYC .... Balatoni Yacht Club [*Balaton Yacht Club*] (HU)
BYD .... Bilimsel Yayinlar Dernegi [*Scientific Publications Society*] (TU)
b/ye .... Library Unit (RU)
b ye .... Protein Unit (RU)
BYGM .... Basin-Yayin Genel Mudurlugu [*Press and Publications Directorate General*] [*Under Office of Premier*] (TU)
BYKP .... Bes Yillik Kalkinma Plani [*Five-Year Development Plan*] (TU)
byl .... Bylina [*Bibliography*] (RU)
BYM .... Born Youth Movement (MAR)
BYTB .... Basin, Yayin, ve Turizm Bakanligi [*Ministry of Press, Broadcasting, and Tourism*] (TU)
byudzh sch ... Budget Accounting (BU)
byul .... Bulletin (RU)
Byul SPP ..... Bulletin of the Periodical Publishers Union in Bulgaria [*A publication*] (BU)
BYuP .... Office of Young Pioneers (RU)
byurobin ..... Office of Services to Foreigners (RU)
byv .... Byvaly [*Former*] (CZ)
byv .... Former [*Topography*] (RU)
byvsh ukr .... Abandoned Fortification [*Topography*] (RU)
BYYO .... Basin ve Yayin Yuksek Okulu [*Advanced School for Press and Publications*] [*Attached to Ankara University School of Political Science*] (TU)
BZ .... Antiaircraft Battery (RU)
BZ .... Bacteriological Contamination [*Warning*], Bacteriological Infection (RU)
BZ .... Banque du Zaire [*Bank of Zaire*] (AF)
BZ .... Belize [*Two-letter standard code*] (CNC)
Bz .... Benzol [*Benzene*] [*German*]
Bz .... Bestellzettel [*Order Form*] [*German*]
bz .... Bez Zmian [*Unchanged*] [*Polish*]
Bz .... Bezirk [*One of 14 large GDR administrative units*]
Bz .... Brenn-Zuender [*Time Fuse or Primer*] [*Military*] [*German*] (MTD)
BZ .... Combat Supplies on Hand, Combat Stockpile (RU)
b z .... No Title [*Bibliography*] (RU)
BZ .... Order Form, Order Blank (RU)
BZ .... Refueling Truck (RU)
BZA .... Binnenzollamt [*Inland Customs Office*] (EG)
BZAD .... Antiaircraft Artillery Battalion Battery (RU)
b zav .... Without Verification (BU)
BZB .... Bugarska Zemljoradnicka Zadruzna Banka [*Bulgarian Agricultural Cooperative Bank*] (YU)
BZB .... Bulgarian Agricultural Bank (BU)
BZC .... Bibliografia Zawartosci Czasopism [*Bibliography of Articles in Periodicals*] (POL)
BZCB .... Biuro Zbytu Ceramiki Budowlanej [*Sales Office for Building Tiles*] (POL)
BZDGM .... Bos Zamanlari Degerlendirme Genel Mudurlugu [*Directorate General for Improved Utilization of Spare Time*] (TU)
BzFstl .... Bezirksforstinspektion [*German*]
BzGK .... Bezirksgendarmeriekommando [*German*]
BZGK .... Bohuminske Zelezarny Gustava Klimenta [*Gustav Kliment Iron Works at Bohumin*] (CZ)
BZh .... Botanical Journal [*A publication*] (RU)
BZh .... Railroad Battery [*Artillery*] (RU)
BZhNS .... Bulgarian National Women's Union (BU)
BZI .... Baterija Zvukovnog Izvidanja [*Sound Reconnaissance Battery (equipped with listening apparatus)*] (YU)
BZK .... Code-Protection Unit (RU)
BZK .... Instruction Storage Unit (RU)
BZKB .... Bulgarian Agricultural and Cooperative Bank (BU)
BZKBanka ... Bulgarian Agricultural and Cooperative Bank (BU)
bzl .... Benzene [*Solvent*] (RU)
BZMAJ .... Bavlnarske Zavody Mistra Aloise Jiraska [*Alois Jirasek Cotton Mills*] (CZ)
BZmR .... Sound-Ranging Battery (RU)
Bzn .... Benzin [*Benzine*] [*German*]
bzn .... Benzine [*Solvent*] (RU)
Bzn .... Benzol [*Benzene*] [*German*]
BZN .... Biuro Zbytu Narzedzi [*Tool Sales Office*] (POL)
BZNS .... Bugarski Zemljoradnicki Narodni Savez [*National Agrarian Union of Bulgaria*] (YU)
BZNS .... Bulgarian National Agrarian Union (BU)
BZNS .... Bulgarian People's Agricultural Union (RU)
Bzo .... Brazo [*Arm (of the sea)*] [*Spanish*] (NAU)
BZO .... Correspondence Training Center (RU)
BZO .... Warhead (of Torpedo) (RU)
BZP .... Refueling Point (RU)
BZPG .... Bydgoskie Zaklady Przemyslu Gumowego [*Bydgoszcz Rubber Works*] (POL)
BZPT .... Bielskie Zaklady Przemyslu Terenowego [*Bielsko Local Industry Plant*] (POL)
BZPW .... Bialostockie Zaklady Przemyslu Welnianego [*Bialystok Wool Mill*] (POL)
BZPW .... Bytomskie Zaklady Przemyslu Weglowego [*Bytom (Beuthen) Coal Industry Plant*] (POL)
BZPW .... Bytomskie Zjednoczenie Przemyslu Weglowego [*Bytom (Beuthen) Coal Industry Association*] (POL)
BZR .... Bialostockie Zaklady Roszarnicze [*Bialystok Flax Processing Plant*] (POL)

BZR .... Office of Plant Protection (RU)
BZR .... Sound-Ranging Battery (BU)
BZR .... Sound-Ranging Battery (RU)
BZS .... Union of Bulgarian Dentists (BU)
BZT .... Armor-Piercing Incendiary Tracer Bullet (RU)
BZTM .... Biuro Zagranicznej Turystyki Mlodziezowej [*International Youth Touring Office*] [*Polish*]
BZTPMB...... Bialostockie Zjednoczenie Terenowego Przemyslu Materialow Budowlanych [*Bialystok Association of the Local Building Materials Industry*] (POL)
BZU .... Buffer Storage (RU)
BZU .... Bunkering Facilities, Bunkering Gear (RU)
BZUT.......... Bielskie Zaklady Urzadzen Technicznych [*Bielsko Technical Equipment Plant*] (POL)
bzw .... Beziehungsweise [*And, Or, And/Or, Respectively*] (EG)

C

C ... Cabo [*Cape*] [*Portuguese*] (NAU)
C ... Cabo [*Cape*] [*Spanish*] (NAU)
C ... Cadde [*Avenue, Street*] [*See also Cad, cd*] (TU)
C/ ... Caisse [*Cash*] [*French*]
C ... Calle [*Street*] [*Spanish*] (CED)
C ... Campagne [*Country*] [*French*] (MTD)
C ... Candidato a Doctor en Ciencias [*Spanish*]
C ... Candidature [*Candidature*] [*French*]
C ... Candidatus [*Academic degree*] [*Latin*]
C ... Cap [*Cape*] [*French*] (NAU)
C ... Cap [*Capul, Capu*] [*Cape*] [*Romanian*] (NAU)
C ... Capacite en Droit [*Qualification in Law*] [*French*]
c ... Capitulo [*Chapter*] [*Spanish*]
C ... Capo [*Cape*] [*Italian*] (NAU)
c ... Cas [*Hour, Given Moment or Interval of Time*] (YU)
C ... Cay [*Stream, Brook*] (TU)
C ... Celsius [*Celsius, Centigrade*] (EG)
C ... Celsius [*Celsius, Centigrade*] (HU)
C ... Celsiusta [*Finnish*]
C ... Celsjusz [*Polish*]
C ... Centavo [*Hundredth Part, Cent*] [*Spanish*]
C ... Centerpartiet [*Center Party*] [*Swedish*] (WEN)
c ... Centime [*Monetary Unit*] [*French*]
C ... Centum [*A Hundred*] [*Latin*] (GPO)
c ... Centum Milia [*One Hundred Thousand*] [*Latin*]
c ... Cesky [*or Cestina*] [*Czech or Czech Language*] (CZ)
C ... Ceta [*Platoon*] (CZ)
c ... Cikk [*or Cikkely*] [*Article or Item or Paragraph*] (HU)
C ... Cilt [*Volume*] (TU)
c ... Cim [*or Cimu*] [*Title or Entitled*] (HU)
c ... Circa [*or Circiter or Circum*] [*About (used with dates denoting approximate time)*] [*Latin*] (GPO)
c ... Cislo [*Number*] (CZ)
C ... Commandeur [*Commander*] [*of the Legion of Honor*] [*French*] (MTD)
C ... Compte [*Account*] [*French*] (GPO)
C ... Condemno [*I Condemn*] [*Latin*] (GPO)
c/ ... Contre [*French*]
c ... Corka [*Daughter*] [*Polish*]
c ... Corso [*Street*] [*Italian*] (CED)
c ... Coupon [*French*]
c ... Cours [*French*]
C ... Court [*Short*] [*Of guns*] [*French*] (MTD)
C ... Cube [*Cubic*] [*French*] (MTD)
C ... Cumhuriyet [*Republic, Republican*] (TU)
C ... Elektrische Kapazitaet [*Electrical Capacity*] [*German*]
°C ... Stopien Celsjusza [*Degree Celsius*] [*Polish*]
c^2 ... Negyzetcentimeter [*Square Centimeter*] (HU)
c^2 ... Quadratzentimeter [*Square Centimeter*] (EG)
c^3 ... Kobcentimeter [*Cubic Centimeter*] (HU)
c^3 ... Kubikzentimeter [*Cubic Centimeter*] (EG)
CA ... Cadmium Association (EA)
Ca ... Cami [*Mosque*] (TU)
CA ... Canada [*Two-letter standard code*] (CNC)
Ca ... Cay [*or Cayi*] [*Stream or River*] [*Turkish*] (NAU)
ca ... Centiare [*Centare*] [*French*] (GPO)
CA ... Central Africa (MAR)
CA ... Centro America [*Spanish*] (GPO)
CA ... Cervena Armija [*Red Army*] (YU)
ca ... Circa [*or Circiter or Circum*] [*About (used with dates denoting approximate time)*] [*Latin*]
CA ... Comites d'Action [*Action Committees*] [*French*] (WER)
Ca ... Compagnia [*Company*] [*Italian*] (GPO)
Ca ... Companhia [*Company*] [*Business and trade*] [*Portuguese*]
ca ... Compania [*Company*] [*Spanish*]
CA ... Compania Anonima [*Joint Stock Company*] [*Spanish*] (CED)
CA ... Conseil d'Administration [*Board of Directors (of a private organization, company, fund, or governmental or other financial body)*] [*Administrative Council (of a political party, university, or non-financial governmental unit)*] (CL)
CA ... Convention Africaine (MAR)
CA ... Corps d'Armee [*Army Corps*] [*Military*] [*French*] (MTD)
C/A ... Corrente Anno [*Current Year*] [*Italian*] (WER)
ca ... Corriente Alterna [*Alternating Current*] [*Spanish*]
CA ... Cruising Association (EA)
CA ... Crvena Armija [*Red Army*] (YU)
CA ... Kanada [*Canada*] [*Polish*]
CAA ... Caisse Autonome d'Amortissement (MAR)
CAA ... Central African Airways (MAR)
CAA ... Centre d'Apprentissage Agricole (MAR)
CAA ... Comitato Anti-Imperialista Antifascista [*Anti-Imperialist, Antifascist Committee*] [*Italian*] (WER)
CAA ... Commonwealth Association of Architects (EA)
CAA ... Compagnie Africaine d'Accumulateurs [*Algerian*] (MAR)
CAA ... Conseil Africaine de l'Arachide [*African Peanut Council*] (AF)
CAAC ... Civil Aviation Administration of China
CAA-CI ... Caisse Autonome d'Amortissement de la Cote-d'Ivoire [*Autonomous Sinking Fund of the Ivory Coast*] (AF)
CAADE ... Caisse Autonome d'Amortissement des Dettes de l'Etat [*Autonomous Fund for the Amortization of State Debt*] [*Central African*] (AF)
CAAKK ... Comite d'Aide et d'Assistance aux Khmers Venus du Sud Vietnam [*or Comite d'Aide et d'Assistance aux Khmers Venus du Kampuchea Krom*] [*Khmer Krom Aid and Relief Committee*] [*Cambodian*] (CL)
CAAN ... Confederacion de Asociaciones Algodoneras de Nicaragua [*Nicaraguan Cotton Associations Confederation*] (LA1)
CAAPP ... Cooperative d'Achats des Administrations Publiques et Privees [*Moroccan*] (MAR)
CAAR ... Caisse Algerienne d'Assurance et de Reassurance (MAR)
CAAR ... Compagnie Africaine des Automobiles Renault (MAR)
CAARC ... Commonwealth Advisory Aeronautical Research Council (EA)
CAARP ... Comissao de Antifascistas de Apoio aos Revolucionarios Presos [*Antifascist Committee of Support for Revolutionary Prisoners*] [*Portuguese*] (WER)
CAAS ... Canadian Association of African Studies (MAR)
CAAS ... Center for African and African-American Studies (MAR)
CAASA ... Centre Africain d'Application de Statistique Agricole (MAR)
CAASD ... Corporacion del Acueducto y Alcantarilla de Santo Domingo [*Santo Domingo Aqueduct and Sewerage Corporation*] [*Dominican Republic*] (LA1)
CAAT ... Centre Afro-Americain du Travail [*Afro-American Labor Center*] [*Use AALC*] (AF)
CAB ... Central Agricultural Board (MAR)
CAB ... Chemieanlagenbau [*Chemical Facilities Construction Enterprise*] (EG)
CAB ... Club Automobile du Burundi (MAR)
CAB ... Commonwealth Agricultural Bureaux (EA)
CAB ... Compagnie Africaine des Bois (MAR)
CABA ... Calisma Bakanligi [*Ministry of Labor*] (TU)
Cabet ... Cabaret [*Small Country Inn*] [*Military map abbreviation*] [*World War I*] [*French*] (MTD)
CABETAT ... Cabinet du Chef de l'Etat [*Office of the Chief of State*] [*Cambodian*] (CL)
CABICO ... Cabinet Comptable (MAR)
CABLAF ... Cablerie Electrique Africaine [*Algerian*] (MAR)
CABLESCO ... Cables Colombianos SA [*Bogota*] Tlg. (COL)
CABS ... Central African Broadcasting Service (MAR)
CABS ... Central African Building Society (MAR)
CABUC ... Cameroon Associated Business Corporation (MAR)
CAC ... Cairo American College (MAR)
CAC ... Camara Argentina de la Construccion [*Argentine Construction Board*] (LA1)
CAC ... Central African Council (MAR)
CAC ... Colonial Advisory Council (MAR)
CAC ... Comite Amilcar Cabral [*Amilcar Cabral Committee*] [*Angolan*] (AF)
CAC ... Cooperativa Agricola de Cotia [*Cotia Farmer Cooperative*] [*Brazilian*] (LA)
CACAM ... Caisse Algerienne de Credit Agricole Mutuel (MAR)
CACBB ... Commission Administrative Chargee du Basket-Ball [*Moroccan*] (MAR)

CACCI .... Confederation of Asian Chambers of Commerce and Industry (IN)
CACEP .... Societe Camerounaise de Commercialisation et d'Exportation de Produits (MAR)
CACEX .... Carteira de Comercio Exterior [*Foreign Trade Department*] [*Brazilian*] (LA)
CACI .... Caisse Administrative de Circonscription Indigene (MAR)
CACI .... Chaine Avion Cote-d'Ivoire (MAR)
CACI .... Civil Aviation Chaplains International (EA)
CACI .... Compagnie Agricole Commerciale Industrielle (MAR)
CACI .... Compagnie Francaise des Cafes de Cote-d'Ivoire (MAR)
CACI .... Societe Centrafricaine de Ciment (MAR)
CACIA .... Compagnie d'Agriculture, de Commerce, et d'Industrie d'Afrique (MAR)
CACIA .... Comptoirs Africains pour le Commerce, l'Industrie, et l'Agriculture (MAR)
CACM .... Central American Common Market (EG)
CACMI .... Comite Africain pour la Coordination des Moyens d'Information [*African Committee for the Coordination of Information Media*] (AF)
CACO .... Compagnie Africaine Commerciale de l'Ouest (MAR)
CACOCOM ... Cambodian Commercial Company (CL)
CACOM .... Cooperative Algeroise de Commercialisation [*Algiers Marketing Cooperative*] (AF)
CACOM .... Cooperative d'Approvisionnement et de Commercialisation [*Supply and Marketing Cooperative*] [*Algerian*] (AF)
CACOMIAF ... Comptoir de l'Automobile et du Cycle, Outillage Materiel Industriel, Agricole, et Forestier (MAR)
CACTD .... Council for the Application of Computer Technology for Development (MAR)
cad .... Cadde [*Road*] [*Turkish*] (CED)
Cad .... Caddesi [*Avenue, Street*] [*See also C, cd*] (TU)
CAD .... Caisse Algerienne de Developpement [*Algerian Development Fund*] (AF)
CAD .... Centrale Africaine de Diffusion [*Moroccan*] (MAR)
CAD .... Centres d'Assistance au Developpement (MAR)
c-a-d .... C'Est a Dire [*That Is to Say*] [*French*]
CAD .... Chinese Affairs Department (ML)
CAD .... Civil Aviation Department [*Saudi*] (ME)
CAD .... Civil Aviation Department [*Sudanese*] (MAR)
CAD .... Coloured African Department (MAR)
CAD .... Comite d'Aide au Developpement [*Committee for Developmental Aid*] (AF)
CAD .... Compagnie Africaine de Diffusion (MAR)
CAD .... Conference of African Demographers (MAR)
CAD .... Consortium Africain de Droguerie (MAR)
CAD .... Corps Adjudan Djenderal [*Adjutant General's Corps*] (IN)
CADA .... Centre d'Analyse Documentaire pour l'Archeologie
CADA .... Comision Administradora del Abasto [*Supply Management Commission*] [*Uruguayan*] (LA)
CADA .... Companhia Angolana de Agricultura [*Angolan Agricultural Company*] (AF)
CADA .... Compania Anonima Distribuidora de Alimentos [*Venezuelan*]
CADA .... Compania Antioquena de Automotores SA [*Medellin*] (COL)
CADA .... Concerted Action for Development in Africa (MAR)
CADAFE .... Compania Anonima de Administracion y Fomento Electrico [*Electrical Administration and Development Corporation*] [*Venezuelan*] (LA)
CADAN .... Centre d'Analyses Documentaires pour l'Afrique Noire (MAR)
CADAT .... Caisse Algerienne d'Amenagement du Territoire [*Algerian Territorial Development Fund*] (AF)
CADC .... Centro Academico da Democracia Crista [*Academic Center for Christian Democracy*] [*Portuguese*] (PPE)
Cade .... Cascade [*Waterfall*] [*Military map abbreviation*] [*World War I*] [*French*] (MTD)
CADE .... Conferencia Annual de Ejecutivos de Empresas [*Annual Conference of Business Executives*] [*Peruvian*] (LA)
CADE .... Conselho Administrativo de Defesa Economica [*Administrative Council for Economic Defense*] [*Brazilian*] (LA)
CADEB .... Caisse d'Epargne du Burundi [*Burundi Savings Bank*] (MAR)
CADEBU .... Caisse d'Epargne du Burundi [*Burundi Savings Bank*] (AF)
CADEG .... Consejo Anticomunista de Guatemala [*Anticommunist Council of Guatemala*] (LA)
CADEGAS ... Compania Antioquena de Gas Ltda. [*Medellin*] (COL)
CADEL .... Comite d'Action pour la Defense de la Legalite [*Committee for Legal Defense*] [*Dahomey*]
CADEM .... Societe de Ciments Artificiels de Meknes [*North African*] (MAR)
CADENALCO ... Cadena de Almacenes Colombianos SA [*Bogota*] (COL)
CADENON ... Radio Cadena del Norte Ltda. [*Cartagena*] (COL)
CADEPAN ... Camara de Defensa del Patrimonio Nacional [*Council for Conservation of National Resources*] [*Uruguayan*] (LA)
CADET .... Centrale d'Achat et de Developpement de la Region Miniere du Tafilalet [*Moroccan*] (MAR)
CADEX .... Compagnie Africaine des Explosifs [*Moroccan*] (MAR)
CADEZ .... Caisse d'Epargne du Zaire (MAR)
CADEZA .... Caisse Generale d'Epargne du Zaire [*General Savings Fund of Zaire*] (AF)
CADHU .... Comision Argentina de Derechos Humanos [*Argentine Human Rights Commission*] (LA)
CADI .... Centre Algerien de Diffusion et d'Information [*Algerian Center for Broadcasting and Information*] (AF)
CADI .... Comptoir d'Approvisionnement et de Distribution (MAR)
CADI .... Conseil Asiatique du Developpement Industriel [*Asian Council for Industrial Development*] (CL)
CADIAM .... Societe Centrafricaine Americaine de Diamants (MAR)
CADICEC .... Association des Cadres des Dirigeants Chretiens des Entreprises au Congo et au Ruanda-Urundi (MAR)
CADICI .... Consortium Africain du Disque et du Cinema (MAR)
CADIEM .... Centro Argentino de Investigacion y Ensayo de Materiales [*Argentine Center for Research and Testing of Materials*] (LA)
CADIF .... Comite National de Coordination des Associations de Deportes, Internes, et Familles des Disparus (MAR)
CADIN .... Camara de Industrias de Nicaragua [*Nicaraguan Chamber of Industries*] (LA)
CADO .... Ciments Artificieux d'Oranie [*Algerian*] (MAR)
CADP .... Centre Africain de Developpement et de Planification [*North African*] (MAR)
CADS .... Commando Anticomunista del Sur [*Southern Anticommunist Commando*] [*Guatemalan*] (PD)
CADS .... Compagnie Africaine des Docks et Silos (MAR)
CADSE .... Comision Asesora de los Delitos Socio-Economicos [*Consultation Committee on Socioeconomic Crimes*] [*Uruguayan*] (LA)
CADU .... Chilalo Agricultural Development Unit (MAR)
CADU .... Comite de Apoyo a la Democracia Universitaria [*Committee in Support of University Democracy*] [*Honduran*] (LA1)
CADYL .... Cooperativa Agropecuaria de Young Limitada [*Young Livestock Cooperative Limited*] [*Uruguayan*] (LA)
CAE .... Central African Empire (AF)
CAE .... Centro de Astroanalists Electronico [*Bogota*] (COL)
CAE .... Cobrese al Entregar [*Cash on Delivery*] [*Spanish*]
CAE .... Comision Asesora Ejecutiva [*Executive Advisory Commission*] [*Argentine*] (LA)
CAE .... Comite d'Accio d'Ensenyants [*Teachers Action Committee*] [*Spanish*] (WER)
CAE .... Comunita Agricola Europea [*European Agricultural Community*] [*Italian*] (WER)
CAE .... Consejo Andino de Exportadores [*Andean Council of Exporters*] (LA)
CAEC .... Conseil Africain de l'Enseignement de la Communication (MAR)
CAEES .... Centre Algerien d'Expansion Economique et Social (MAR)
CAEEV .... Compagnie Africaine d'Elevage et d'Exportation de Viande (MAR)
CAEGE .... Centre Algerien d'Etudes de la Gestion des Entreprises (MAR)
CAEI .... Compagnie Africaine d'Equipement Industriel (MAR)
CAEM .... Cekmece Arastirma ve Egitim Merkezi [*Cekmece Research and Training Center*] [*See also CNAEM*] (TU)
CAEM .... Centro de Altos Estudios Militares [*Center of Advanced Military Studies*] [*Peruvian*] (LA)
CAEM .... Certificat d'Aptitude a l'Enseignement Moyen [*French*]
CAEM .... Conseil d'Assistance Economique Mutuelle [*Council for Mutual Economic Assistance*] (AF)
CAEMI .... Companhia Auxiliar de Empresas de Mineracao [*Mining Enterprises Assistance Corporation*] [*Brazilian*] (LA1)
CAEP .... Certificat d'Aptitude d'Enseignement Primaire [*Primary Education Aptitude Certificate*] [*Tunisian*] (AF)
CAER .... Consiliul de Ajutor Economic Reciproc [*Council for Mutual Economic Assistance*] (RO)
CAES .... Central Agricultural Experiment Station (MAR)
CAES .... Certificat d'Aptitude a l'Enseignement Secondaire [*French*]
CAES .... Comando Anti-Extorsion y Secuestros [*Anti-Extortion and Kidnapping Command*] [*Colombian*] (LA1)
CAES .... Comissao de Aguas e Engenharia Sanitaria [*Water and Sanitary Engineering Commission*] [*Brazilian*] (LA)
CAES .... Comite Asesor Economico y Social [*Economic and Social Advisory Committee*] [*Colombian*] (LA)
CAES .... Comite de Asesoramiento Economico y Social [*Economic Social Advisory Committee*] [*Peruvian*] (LA)
CAES .... Confederacion Argentina de Estudiantes Secundarios [*Argentine Confederation of Secondary School Students*] (LA)
CAESS .... Compania de Alumbrado Electrico de San Salvador [*San Salvador Electric Power Company*] [*Salvadoran*]
CAEU .... Council for Arab Economic Unity (MAR)
CAF .... Caisse d'Allocations Familiales [*Family Allowance Office*] [*French*] (WER)
CAF .... Central African Empire [*Later, CAR*] [*Three-letter standard code*] (CNC)
CAF .... Central African Federation (MAR)
CAF .... Centralna Agencja Fotograficzna [*Central Photographic Agency*] (POL)
CAF .... Centralne Archiwum Filmowe [*Central Film Archives*] (POL)
CAF .... Club Alpin Francais [*French Alpine Club*]
CAF .... Confederation Africaine de Football (MAR)
CAF .... Convention Africaine (MAR)
CAF .... Corporacion Andina de Fomento [*Andean Development Corporation*] (LA)
CAF .... Cout, Assurance, Fret [*Cost, Insurance, Freight*] [*Use CIF*] [*French*] (CL)
CAF .... Current Affairs Films (MAR)

CAFA .... Chronique de l'Ambassade de France en Algerie [*A publication*] (MAR)
CAFA .... Compagnie Africaine Franco-Anglaise (MAR)
CAFAC .... Centrale Africaine d'Achats en Commun (MAR)
CAFAC .... Commission Africaine de l'Aviation Civile [*African Civil Aviation Commission*] [*Use AFCAC*] (AF)
CAFAL .... Compagnie Africaine Forestiere et des Allumettes (MAR)
CAFAM .... Caja de Compensacion Familiar [*Bogota*] (COL)
CAFAN .... Cooperative Africaine Forestiere et Agricole du Niari (MAR)
CAFBANGUI ... Compagnie Cafeiere du Haut Oubangui (MAR)
CAFC .... Compagnie Agricole et Forestiere du Cameroun (MAR)
CAFCO .... Compagnie Africaine de Commerce et de Commission (MAR)
CAFCO .... Compagnie Africaine de Constructions et de Travaux Publics (MAR)
CAFDA .... Commandement Aerien des Forces de Defense Aerienne [*Air Defense Forces Air Command*]
CAFE .... Cours Autodidactique de Francais Ecrit (MAR)
CAFFA .... Comissao Administrativa do Fundo de Fomento de Angola (MAR)
CAFI .... Commercial Advisory Foundation in Indonesia (IN)
CAFI .... Compania Agropecuaria Forestal Industrial [*Industrial, Forest, Agricultural, and Livestock Company*] [*Ecuadorean*] (LA)
CAFIC .... Compagnie Agricole, Forestiere, Industrielle, et Commerciale (MAR)
CAFIC .... Compagnie Algerienne de Fabrication de la Chaussure (MAR)
CAFIDEC .... Compagnie Franco-Ivoirienne d'Entreprises Commerciales (MAR)
CAFIECA .... Camara Argentina de Frigorificos Industriales y Exportadores de Carne y Afines [*Argentine Chamber of Industrial Meatpacking Houses and Exporters of Meats and Related Products*] (LA)
CAFL .... Chingola Amateur Football League (MAR)
CAFL .... Compagnie des Ateliers et Forges de la Loire (MAR)
CAFM .... Cathedral Films, Inc. (MAR)
CAFOD .... Catholic Fund for Overseas Development (MAR)
CAFOP .... Centre d'Animation et de Formation Pedagogique [*Teachers Promotion and Training Center*] (AF)
CAFOP .... Centre d'Animation et de Formation Professionnelle (MAR)
CAFR .... Renseignements Coloniaux et Documents Publiees par le Comite de l'Afrique Francaise et le Comite du Maroc 1932 (MAR)
CAFRA .... Compagnie de l'Afrique Francaise (MAR)
CAFRAD ..... Centre Africain de Formation et de Recherche Administrative pour le Developpement [*Tangiers, Morocco*]
CAFRANCO ... Compagnie de l'Afrique Francaise pour le Commerce (MAR)
CAFRICO .... Consortium Africain de Commerce (MAR)
CAFSO .... Societe de Cafe Soluble (MAR)
CAFTEX ...... Compagnie Africaine de Textile (MAR)
CAFUM .... Companhia de Fumigacoes de Mocambique (MAR)
CAG .... Comitetul Antifascist German [*German Anti-Fascist Committee*] (RO)
CAGI .... Consultative Association of Guyana Industries (LA)
CAH .... Colegio de Abogados de Honduras [*Honduran Bar Association*] (LA1)
CAH .... Compagnie Africaine d'Hotellerie (MAR)
CAHB .... Confederation Africaine de Handball (MAR)
CAHIS .... Circulo Afro-Hispano (MAR)
CAHT .... Centre Africain des Hydrocarbures et du Textile de Boumerdes [*African Center for Hydrocarbons and Textiles at Boumerdes*] [*Algerian*] (AF)
CAI .... Cairo Airport (MAR)
CAI .... Centro Aeronautico de Instrucao (MAR)
CAI .... Centro de Automatizacion Industrial [*Industrial Automation Center*] [*Cuban*] (LA)
CAI .... Club Alpino Italiano [*Italian Alpine Club*]
CAI .... Comite de Accion Internacional Sindical [*Bogota*] (COL)
CAI .... Comite Arctique International (EA)
CAI .... Comite de Asuntos Internacionales [*Committee for International Affairs*] [*Uruguayan*] (LA)
CAI .... Comites Anti-Imperialistas [*Anti-Imperialist Committees*] [*Spanish*] (WER)
CAI .... Compagnie Africaine pour le Developpement de l'Informatique (MAR)
CAI .... Comptoir d'Approvisionnement Automobile et Industriel (MAR)
CAIC .... Caribbean Association of Industry and Commerce (LA)
CAIC .... Compagnie d'Agriculture, d'Industrie, et de Commerce (MAR)
CAIC .... Companhia de Agricultura, Imigracao, e Colonizacao [*Agriculture, Immigration, and Settlement Company*] [*Brazilian*] (LA)
CAID .... Canadian Agency for International Development (MAR)
CAID .... Comptoir Africain d'Importation et de Diffusion (MAR)
CAIFOM ...... Caisse de la France d'Outre-Mer (MAR)
CAIM .... Compagnie Agricole et Industrielle de Madagascar (MAR)
CAIP .... Certificat d'Aptitude a l'Inspection Primaire (MAR)
CAIRE .... Compagnie d'Applications Industrielles de Recherches et d'Etudes (MAR)
CAIS .... Club de l'Amitie Ivoiro-Senegalaise (MAR)
CAIS .... Communautes; Archives Internationales de Sociologie de la Cooperation et du Developpement [*Paris*] [*A publication*] (MAR)
CAISA .... Compania Agricola e Industrial, Sociedad Anonima [*Agricultural and Industrial Corporation*] [*Salvadoran*]
CAITA .... Compagnie Agricole et Industrielle de Tabacs Africains [*African Tobacco Agricultural and Industrial Company*] (AF)
CAITACI ...... Compagnie Agricole et Industrielle des Tabacs de Cote-d'Ivoire (MAR)
CAJANAL .... Caja Nacional de Prevision Social [*Bogota*] (COL)
CAJL .... Central-Anzeiger fuer Juedische Literatur, Frankfurt Am Main (MAR)
CAK .... Comite des Angolais au Katanga (MAR)
CAKUR-IS ... Calisma Bakanligi Sosyal Sigortalar, Is ve Isci Bulma Kurumlari Sendikasi Federasyonu [*Labor Ministry Social Insurance, Labor and Employment Organizations' Union Federation*] (TU)
Cal .... Calata [*Wharf*] [*Italian*] (NAU)
Cal .... Caleta [*Cove*] [*See also Cta*] [*Spanish*] (NAU)
Cal .... Calibre [*Caliber*] [*French*] (MTD)
CAL .... Camara Agropecuaria Latinoamericana [*Latin American Chamber of Agriculture and Livestock*] (LA)
Cal .... Canal [*Canal*] [*Military map abbreviation*] [*World War I*] [*French*] (MTD)
CAL .... Carabine Automatique Legere (MAR)
CAL .... Centre d'Amelioration du Logement [*Center for Improved Housing Conditions*] [*French*] (WER)
CAL .... Colegio de Abogados de Lima [*Lima Bar Association*] [*Peruvian*] (LA)
CAL .... Comandos Armados de Liberacion [*Armed Liberation Commandos*] [*Puerto Rican*] (PD)
CAL .... Comision de Asesoramiento Legislativa [*Legislative Advisory Commission*] [*Argentine*] (LA)
CAL .... Comite d'Action Lyceen [*Lycee Action Committee*] [*French*] (WER)
CAL .... Confederacion Anticomunista Latinoamericana [*Latin American Anticommunist Confederation*] (LA)
Cal .... Cortal [*Military map abbreviation*] [*World War I*] [*French*] (MTD)
cal .... Gramm Calorie [*Gram Calorie*] [*German*]
Cal .... Kilogramm-Calorie [*Kilogram Calorie*] [*German*]
CALANS ..... Caribbean and Latin American News Service (LA)
CALB .... Confederation Africano-Levantine de Billard (MAR)
calc .... Calciniert [*Calcined*] [*German*]
CALECOL ... Catalogacion Legible en Computador para Colombia [*Bogota*] (COL)
CALEMPA ... Compagnie Algerienne d'Emballages en Papier (MAR)
CALEV .... Compania Anonima Luz Electrica de Venezuela [*Venezuelan Power and Light Company*] (LA)
CALFORU ... Cooperativa Agropecuaria de Sociedades de Fomento Rural [*Agricultural and Livestock Cooperative of Rural Development Associations*] (LA)
CALI .... Consortium of Arid Lands Institutions (MAR)
CALIN .... Consejo Asesor para el Licenciamiento de Instalaciones Nucleares [*Advisory Council for Licensing Nuclear Facilities*] [*Argentine*] (LA)
Calis .... Calismalar [*Efforts, Activities*] (TU)
CALNU .... Cooperativa Agropecuaria del Norte Uruguayo [*Farm Cooperative of Northern Uruguay*] (LA)
CALOM .... Comptoir Africain de Liaison Outre-Mer (MAR)
CALPA .... Cooperativa Agropecuaria Limitada de Paysandu [*Paysandu Agricultural and Livestock Cooperative, Limited*] [*Uruguayan*] (LA)
CALPC .... Centrala de Aprovizionare si Livrare Produse Chimice [*Central for the Supply and Delivery of Chemical Products*] (RO)
CALPICA .... Cooperativa Agropecuaria Limitada de Produccion e Industrializacion de Cana de Azucar [*Farm Cooperative for the Cultivation and Processing of Sugar Cane Limited*] [*Uruguayan*] (LA)
CALSAL ...... Cooperativa Agropecuaria Limitada de Salto [*Salto Agricultural and Livestock Cooperative Limited*] [*Uruguayan*] (LA)
CAM .... Cameroon Action Movement (MAR)
CAM .... Centro de Abastecimiento Medico [*Medical Supplies Center*] [*Nicaraguan*] (LA1)
CAM .... Centro Administrativo Municipal [*Cali*] (COL)
CAM .... Certificat d'Aptitude aux Fonctions de Moniteur (MAR)
CAM .... Certificat d'Aptitude Maritime (MAR)
CAM .... Comando Anticomunista de Mendoza [*Mendoza Anticommunist Command*] [*Argentine*] (LA)
CAM .... Comite d'Action Marocaine (MAR)
CAM .... Comite d'Action Musulman [*Moslem Action Committee*] [*Mauritian*] (AF)
CAM .... Commonwealth Association of Museums (EA)
CAM .... Compagnie Agricole du Mungo (MAR)
CAM .... Conference Aeronautique de la Mediterranee (MAR)
CAM .... Consejo Agrarista Mexicano [*Mexican Agrarian Council*] (LA)
CAMA .... Cartonnages Marocains (MAR)
CAMA .... Christian and Missionary Alliance (MAR)
CAMA .... Compagnie Africaine de Materiels [*Moroccan*] (MAR)
CAMAA .... Comptoir Africain de Materiel Abidjan (MAR)
CAMACOL ... Camara Colombiana de la Construccion [*Colombian Chamber of Construction (Medellin)*] (LA)
CAMACOL ... Camara de Comercio Latina [*Latin Chamber of Commerce*] (LA)

CAMAD .... Societe Camerounaise de Produits Alimentaires et Dietetiques (MAR)
CAMAG .... Societe Camerounaise des Grands Magasins (MAR)
CAMAGENCE ... Agence de Voyages H. De Suares d'Almeyda et Compagnie (MAR)
CAMAIR ...... Cameroon Airlines (MAR)
CAMAS .... Coordinador del Area Maritima del Atlantico Sur [*South Atlantic Maritime Area Coordination*] (LA)
CAMAT .... Compagnie Africaine de Materiel Europeen (MAR)
CAMAT .... Compagnie d'Assurances Maritimes Aeriennes et Terrestres (MAR)
CAMAUTO ... Cameroun Automobile (MAR)
CAMBADU ... Centro Almaceneros Minoristas, Baristas, y Afines del Uruguay [*Association of Uruguayan Retail Businessmen, Bartenders, and Related Professionals*] (LA)
CAMCOLAM ... Camara de Comercio Colombo Americana [*Bogota*] (COL)
CAMCS .... Comissao de Analise dos Meios de Comunicacao Social [*Commission for the Analysis of Mass Communication Means*] [*Portuguese*] (WER)
CAMDE .... Campanha da Mulher pela Democracia
CAMDECAF ... Compagnie Camerounaise de Decafeination (MAR)
CAMDEV ..... Cameroon Development Corporation (MAR)
CAME .... Conscripcion Agraria Militar Ecuatoriana [*Ecuadorean Agrarian Military Conscription*] (LA)
CAME .... Consejo de Asistencia Mutua Economica [*Council for Mutual Economic Assistance*] [*Use CEMA*] (LA)
CAME .... Coordinadora de Actividades Mercantiles [*Coordinating Agency for Mercantile Activities*] [*Argentine*] (LA1)
CAMEA .... Comite des Applications Militaires de l'Energie Atomique [*French*]
CAMEC .... Compagnie Africaine de Metaux et de Produits Chimiques (MAR)
CAMECA .... Compagnie d'Applications Mecaniques a l'Electronique au Cinema et a l'Atomistique [*French company that invented Scopitone, a coin-operated machine that projects musical movies in places of entertainment*]
CaMeCo ...... Catholic Media Council (EA)
CAMEL .... Compagnie Algerienne du Methane Liquide [*Algerian Liquid Methane Company*] (AF)
CAMEN .... Centro d'Applicazioni Militari dell' Energia Nucleare [*Center for Military Applications of Nuclear Energy*] [*Italian*] (WER)
CAMEN .... Centro Autonomo Militaire Energia Nucleare [*Italian*]
CAMER .... Compania Auxiliar Mercantil de Colombia SA [*Bogota*] (COL)
CAMER-INDUSTRIEL ... Compagnie Camerounaise de Representations Industrielles (MAR)
CAMES .... Conseil Africain et Malgache pour l'Enseignement Superieur [*African and Malagasy Council on Higher Education*] (AF)
CAMETANCHE ... Societe Camerounaise d'Etancheite (MAR)
CAMGAZ ..... Societe Camerounaise de Gaz Liquefies de Petrole (MAR)
CAMGOC .... Gulf Oil Company of Cameroon (MAR)
CAMI .... Cameroon Motors Industries (MAR)
CAMI .... Cercle de l'Amitie (MAR)
CAMI .... Comite Africain des Moyens d'Information (MAR)
CAMI .... Correo Aereo Militar Internacional [*International Military Air Mail*] [*Venezuelan*] (LA)
CAMIA .... Comptoir Algerien de Materiel Industriel et Agricole [*Algerian Industrial and Agricultural Equipment Office*] (AF)
CAMIA .... Correo Aereo Militar Interamericano [*Inter-American Military Air Mail*] [*Venezuelan*] (LA)
CAMICO ...... Comptoir de l'Automobile, du Materiel Industriel, du Cycle, et de l'Outillage (MAR)
CAMIK .... Club des Amis Khmers [*Cambodian Friends Club*] (CL)
CAMIMEX ... Camara Minera de Mexico
CAMINA ...... Compania Anonima Minas de Naricual [*Naricual Mines Company*] [*Venezuelan*] (LA)
CAMITEX .... Societe Camerounaise pour l'Industrie Textile (MAR)
CAMM .... Compagnie Africaine de Manutentions Mecaniques (MAR)
CAMOA .... Societe Camerounaise d'Oxygene et d'Acetylene (MAR)
CAMP .... Centre d'Assistance pour la Motorisation des Pirogues de Saint-Louis (MAR)
CAMP .... Cooperative African Microform [*or Microfilm*] Project (MAR)
CAMPA .... Comptoir d'Approvisionnements de Materiel et Produits Agricoles [*Moroccan*] (MAR)
CAMPC .... Centre Africain et Mauricien de Perfectionnement des Cadres [*African and Mauritian Center for Training Cadres*] (AF)
CAMPROMAR ... Societe Camerounaise de Produits et Marchandises (MAR)
CAMPSA ..... Compania Arrendataria del Monopolio de Petroleos, Sociedad Anonima [*Leasing Company of the Petroleum Monopoly, Incorporated*] [*Spanish*] (WER)
CAMR .... Conference Administrative Mondiale des Radiocommunications (MAR)
CAMS .... Central African Motors (MAR)
CAMS .... Chartiers Aero-Maritime de la Seine [*French*]
CAMS .... Conseil Africain et Malgache du Sucre (MAR)
Camsa Is ..... Cayirova Cam Fabrikasi Iscileri Sendikasi [*Cayirova Glass Factory Workers Union*] (TU)
CAMSHIPLINES ... Cameroon Shipping Lines (MAR)
CAMSSP ..... Caisse Militaire de Securite Sociale et de Prevoyance [*Algerian*] (MAR)
CAMSTEEL ... Cameroon Steel Products SA (MAR)
CAMSUCO ... Cameroon Sugar Company, Inc. (MAR)
CAMVAL ..... Comite d'Amenagement et de Mise en Valeur de l'Alaotra [*Malagasy*] (MAR)
CAMVOYAGES ... Agence Camerounaise de Voyages (MAR)
CAMYGIENE ... Societe Camerounaise d'Hygiene (MAR)
CAMYP .... Confederacion Argentina de Maestros y Profesores [*Argentine Confederation of Teachers and Professors*] (LA)
CAN .... Canada [*Three-letter standard code*] (CNC)
Can .... Canal [*Channel*] [*Portuguese*] (NAU)
Can .... Canal [*Channel*] [*Spanish*] (NAU)
Can .... Canale [*Channel*] [*Italian*] (NAU)
Can .... Canonikus [*German*]
CAN .... Central Autentico Nacional [*National Authentic Central*] [*Guatemalan*] (PPW)
CAN .... Centro Administrativo Nacional [*Bogota*] (COL)
CAN .... Combinado Avicola Nacional [*National Poultry Complex*] [*Cuban*] (LA)
CAN .... Comite de Accion Nacionalista [*Committee of Nationalist Action*] [*Bolivian*] (LA)
CAN .... Comite de Alto Nivel para la Reestructuracion del Mercado Comun Centroamericano [*High Level Committee for the Restructuring of the Central American Common Market*] (LA)
CAN .... Compagnie Africaine de Navigation (MAR)
CAN .... Compagnie de l'Afrique Noire (MAR)
CAN .... Consejo Agropecuario Nacional [*National Agricultural and Livestock Council*] [*Costa Rican*] (LA)
CANA .... Caribbean News Agency (LA1)
CANACINTRA ... Camara Nacional de la Industria de Transformacion [*National Association of the Processing Industry*] [*Mexican*] (LA)
CANACO ..... Camara de Comercio de la Ciudad de Mexico [*Mexico City Chamber of Commerce*] (LA1)
CANAICA .... Camara Nacional de la Industria de Calzado [*National Chamber of Shoe Industries*] [*Mexican*] (LA)
CANAIR .... Canary Islands Air (MAR)
CANAM .... Commission d'Aide aux Nord-Africains de la Metropole (MAR)
CANAPP ..... Comite Asesor Nacional de Adiestramiento Petrolero y Petroquimico [*National Advisory Committee for Petroleum and Petrochemical Training*] [*Venezuelan*] (LA)
CANAPRACOL ... Casa Nacional del Profesor Caldas [*Manizales*] (COL)
CANAPRO ... Casa Nacional del Profesor-Sociedad Cooperaria [*Bogota*] (COL)
CANAPRONAR ... Casa Nacional del Profesor Narino [*Pasto*] (COL)
CANAPROPAM ... Casa Nacional del Profesor [*Pamplona*] (COL)
CANAPROSUC ... Casa Nacional del Profesor Sucre (COL)
CANARA ..... Camara Nacional de Radio [*National Radio Council*] [*Costa Rican*] (LA1)
CANAS .... Cellule d'Analyse des Politiques Alimentaires et Nutritionnelles (MAR)
CANATUR ... Camara Nacional de Turismo [*National Tourism Board*] [*Costa Rican*] (LA1)
CANPM .... Centro Associativo dos Negros da Provincia de Mocambique [*Associative Center of the Blacks of Mozambique Province*] (AF)
CANS .... Cesko-Americke Narodni Sdruzeni [*National Czech-American Federation*] (CZ)
Cant .... Cantonnement [*Billet, Quarters*] [*Military*] [*French*] (MTD)
CANTAS ..... Cankiri Tuz Urunleri Uretim ve Dagitim Anonim Sirketi [*Cankiri Salt Products Production and Distribution Corporation*] (TU)
CANTV .... Compania Anonima Nacional de Telefonos Venezolanos [*National Telephone Company of Venezuela*] (LA)
CANU .... Caprivi African National Union (MAR)
CANU .... Convention African National Union [*Nyasaland*]
CANUC .... Campaign Against the Namibian Uranium Contract (AF)
CAO .... Campagne Anti-Outspan (MAR)
CAO .... Coalicion Aranista Organizada [*Organized Aranista Coalition*] [*Guatemalan*] (LA)
CAO .... Collectieve Arbeidsovereenkomst [*Collective Labor Agreement*] [*Dutch*] (WEN)
CAO .... Council of African Organizations (AF)
CAOMI .... Centre d'Accueil d'Observation des Mineurs Delinquants (MAR)
CAOP .... Companhia de Agricultura e Organizacoes Pecuarias [*Agricultural and Animal Husbandry Organizations Society*] [*Angolan*] (AF)
Cap .... Capacitariat [*French*]
Cap .... Capitaine [*Captain, Commander*] [*Military*] [*French*] (MTD)
cap .... Capitulo [*Chapter*] [*Spanish*]
CAP .... Central African Party (MAR)
CAP .... Central African Post (MAR)
CAP .... Centralne Archiwum Panstwowe [*Central State Archives*] (POL)
CAP .... Centre d'Analyse et de Prevision [*Center for Analysis and Forecasting*] [*French*] (WER)
CAP .... Centres d'Alevinage Principaux (MAR)
CAP .... Centres d'Approvisionnement des Planteurs (MAR)
CAP .... Certificat d'Aptitude [*French*]
CAP .... Certificat d'Aptitude Pedagogique [*For primary schoolmasters*] [*French*]
CAP .... Certificat d'Aptitude Professionnelle [*French*]

CAP............ Chaudiere Avancee Prototype [*Advanced Prototype Boiler*] [*French*] (WER)
CaP............ Church and Peace (EA)
CAP............ Comandos Armados del Pueblo [*People's Armed Commands*] [*Mexican*] (LA)
CAP............ Comite Antifascista Panameno [*Panamanian Antifascist Committee*] (LA)
CAP............ Comites de Accion Popular [*People's Action Committees*] [*Nicaraguan*] (LA1)
CAP............ Commissions d'Assistance Publique [*Commissions for Public Assistance*] [*Belgian*] (WER)
CAP............ Common Agricultural Policy (EG)
CAP............ Commonwealth Association of Planners (EA)
CAP............ Compagnie Africaine d'Armement a la Peche (MAR)
CAP............ Compagnie Africaine de Placages (MAR)
CAP............ Compania de Acero del Pacifico [*Pacific Steel Company*] [*Chilean*] (LA)
CAP............ Confederacao dos Agricultores de Portugal [*Portuguese Farmers Association*] (WER)
CAP............ Conference of African Planners (MAR)
CAP............ Consejo Argentino de la Paz [*Argentine Peace Council*] (LA)
CAP............ Consortium Africaine Pharmaceutique (MAR)
CAP............ Constructions Africaines Pontenegrines (MAR)
CAP............ Cooperativa Agraria de Produccion [*Agrarian Production Cooperative*] [*Peruvian*] (LA)
CAP............ Cooperativa Agricola de Productie [*Agricultural Production Cooperative*] (RO)
CAP............ Corporacion Argentina de Productores de Carne [*Argentine Corporation of Meat Producers*] (LA)
CAPA.......... Certificat d'Aptitude a la Profession d'Avocat [*Lawyers Professional Aptitude Certificate*] [*Moroccan*] (AF)
CAPA.......... Certificat d'Aptitude Professionnelle Agricole (MAR)
CAPA.......... Commonwealth Association of Polytechnics in Africa (EA)
CAPA.......... Compagnie d'Achat de Produits Africains (MAR)
CAPA.......... Compagnie Africaine de Produits Alimentaires (MAR)
CAPA.......... Comptoir Africain de Pieces Automobiles (MAR)
CAPAB........ Cape Performing Arts Board (MAR)
CAPAC........ Camara Panamena de la Construccion [*Panama Chamber of Construction*] (LA)
CAPAM....... Comptoir Africain de Pieces Automobiles de Meknes [*Moroccan*] (MAR)
CAPAM....... Cooperative Agricole de Production des Anciens Moudjahidine [*War Veterans Agricultural Production Cooperative*] [*Algerian*] (AF)
CAPAR........ Catalogue Partage
CAPAS........ Centre d'Assistance a la Peche Artisanale Senegalaise (MAR)
CAPC.......... Central African Power Corporation (MAR)
CAPC.......... Certificat d'Aptitude Professionnel Commercial [*Commercial Professional Aptitude Certificate*] (CL)
CAPC.......... Certificat d'Aptitude au Professorat des Colleges [*French*]
CAPCEG..... Certificat d'Aptitude au Professorat des Colleges d'Enseignement General [*French*]
CAPCI......... Compagnie Africaine de Pneumatiques et de Caoutchouc Industriel [*Moroccan*] (MAR)
CAPCO....... Capsulas Colombianas Ltda. [*Bogota*] Tlg. (COL)
CAPCO....... Central African Power Company (MAR)
CAPCS........ Cooperative Agricole Polyvalente Communale de Services [*Communal Multi-Service Agriculture Cooperative*] [*Algerian*] (AF)
CAPE........... Centre Africain de Promotion Economique (MAR)
CAPEC........ Centre Africain de Prevention et de Controle [*Moroccan*] (MAR)
CAPECO..... Camara Peruana de la Construccion [*Peruvian Chamber of Construction*] (LA)
CAPEL........ Certificat d'Aptitude Professionnelle pour l'Enseignement dans les Lycees (MAR)
CAPEM....... Certificat d'Aptitude a l'Enseignement Moyen [*Intermediate Education Aptitude Certificate*] [*Algerian*] (AF)
CAPER........ Caisse d'Accession a la Propriete et a l'Exploitation Rurales [*Algerian*] (MAR)
CAPES........ Certificat d'Aptitude Pedagogique pour l'Enseignement du Second Degre [*Secondary School Teaching Certificate*] [*French*] (WER)
CAPES........ Certificat d'Aptitude Pedagogique a l'Enseignement Secondaire [*French*]
CAPES........ Certificat d'Aptitude au Professorat de l'Enseignement Public du Second Degre [*Second Degree Public Education Teaching Aptitude Certificate*] (CL)
CAPES........ Certificat d'Aptitude au Professorat de l'Enseignement Secondaire [*French*]
CAPES........ Coordenacao para o Aperfeicoamento de Pessoal de Nivel Superior [*Coordination of Advanced Training for Higher-Level Personnel*] [*Brazilian*] (LA1)
CAPET........ Certificat d'Aptitude a l'Enseignement Technique [*Technical Education Aptitude Certificate*] (CL)
CAPET........ Certificat d'Aptitude Pedagogique a l'Enseignement Technique [*French*]
CAPET........ Certificat d'Aptitude au Professorat de l'Enseignement Technique [*French*]
CAPI........... Certificat d'Aptitude Professionnelle des Instituteurs [*French*]
CAPIM........ Consortium Africain de Produits Industriels et Menagers (MAR)
CAPISM...... Comite d'Action Politique et Sociale pour l'Independance de Madagascar [*Political and Social Committee for Malagasy Independence*]
CAPLABA... Cooperative Agricole des Planteurs Bamoun (MAR)
CAPME....... Centre d'Assistance aux Petites et Moyennes Entreprises [*Center for Aid to Small and Medium-Size Businesses*] [*Cameroonian*] (AF)
capn............ Capitan [*Captain*] [*Spanish*]
capo............ Capitulo [*Chapter*] [*Spanish*]
CAPPAP...... Commission d'Action Pro-Populaire et d'Action Psychologique [*Pro-People's Action and Psychological Action Committee*] [*Cambodian*] (CL)
cappn.......... Capellan [*Chaplain*] [*Spanish*]
CAPPO........ Cabinete de Apoio a Producao Agricola [*Office of Support to Agricultural Production*] [*Mozambican*] (AF)
CAPR.......... Centre Artisanal de Promotion Rurale (MAR)
CAPRA........ Cooperative Agricole de Production de la Revolution Agraire [*Agricultural Production Cooperative of the Agrarian Revolution*] [*Algerian*] (AF)
CAPRAL...... Compagnie Africaine de Preparations Alimentaires et Dietetiques (MAR)
CAPRE........ Comissao de Coordenacao das Atividades de Processamento Eletronico de Dados [*Electronic Data Processing Coordination Committee*] [*Brazilian*] (LA)
CAPREC..... Compagnie Equatoriale d'Equipement (MAR)
CAPRECOM... Caja de Prevision Social de Comunicaciones [*Communications Ministry Social Security Fund*] [*Colombian*] (LA)
CAPREF...... Central African Petroleum Refiners (MAR)
CAPRO........ Compagnie des Cafes et Produits Coloniaux Francais (MAR)
CAPS.......... Cesky Amatersky Plavecky Svaz [*Czech Amateur Swimming Union*] (CZ)
CAPTEAO... Conference Administrative des Postes et Telecommunications des Etats de l'Afrique de l'Ouest (MAR)
CAPU.......... Coast African Political Union (MAR)
CAR............ Central African Railway Company (MAR)
CAR............ Central African Republic (AF)
C AR........... Central Arriere [*Military*] [*French*] (MTD)
CAR............ Centre of African Studies (MAR)
CAR............ Centres d'Animation Rurale [*Rural Promotion Centers*] [*Senegalese*] (AF)
CAR............ Certificat d'Aptitude a la Recherche [*French*]
CAR............ Collectivites Autochtones Rurales (MAR)
CAR............ Comites de Accion Radical [*Radical (Party) Action Committee*] [*Chilean*] (LA)
CAR............ Commissie Automatisering Rijksdienst
CAR............ Confederation of Arab Republics (ME)
CAR............ Conference d'Action Regionale [*French*]
CAR............ Constitutional Association of Rhodesia (MAR)
CAR............ Corporacion Autonoma Regional de la Sabana de Bogota y de los Valles de Ubate y Chiquinquira [*Bogota Plain and Ubate and Chiquinquira Valleys Autonomous Regional Corporation*] [*Colombian*] (LA)
CARA.......... Club Athletique Renaissance-Aiglon (MAR)
CARA.......... Comissoes de Apoio a Reforma Agraria [*Agrarian Reform Support Committees*] [*Portuguese*] (WER)
CARA.......... Compagnie d'Applications et de Recherches Atomiques [*French*]
CARACOL... Cadena Radial Colombiana [*Bogota*] (COL)
CARAL........ Societe pour la Construction des Automobiles Renault en Algerie (MAR)
CARATOM... Compagnie d'Applications et de Recherches Atomiques [*French*]
CARBAP..... Confederacion de Asociaciones Rurales de Buenos Aires y la Pampa [*Confederation of Buenos Aires and the Pampa Rural Associations*] [*Argentine*] (LA)
CARBHOTEL... Compania del Hotel Caribe SA [*Cartagena*] Tlg. (COL)
CARBIA....... Central African Regional Branch of the International Council on Archives (MAR)
CARBOAFRIC... Societe pour l'Etude et l'Application de Combustibles et Carburants Africains (MAR)
CARBOCOL... Carbones de Colombia SA [*Colombian Coal Company, Inc.*] (LA)
CARBOEXPORT... Banska Prodejna, Narodni Podnik, Odbor pro Vyvoz Uhli [*Coal Export Section of the Mining Products Sales Office, National Enterprise*] (CZ)
CARBOMOC... Empresa Nacional de Carvao de Mocambique [*Mozambique National Coal Company*] (AF)
CARCESA... Carnes y Conservas Espanolas, Sociedad Anonima [*Spanish Meats and Canned Goods, Incorporated*] (WER)
CARCHAMAC... Exploitations Agricoles Cartier, Charvet, MacDonald (MAR)
CARCLO..... Confederacion de Asociaciones Rurales del Centro y Litoral Oeste [*Confederation of Central and Western Littoral Rural Associations*] [*Argentine*] (LA)
CARD.......... Campaign Against Racial Discrimination (MAR)
CARD.......... Center for Agricultural and Rural Development (MAR)
CARDAN..... Centre d'Analyse et de Recherche Documentaires pour l'Afrique Noire [*Documentary Analysis and Research Center for Black Africa*] [*French*] (AF)
CARDER..... Centre d'Amenagement Regional de Developpement Rural (MAR)

CARDI .... Caribbean Agricultural Research and Development Institute (LA)
cardl .... Cardenal [*Cardinal*] [*Spanish*]
CARE .... Citizens' Association for Racial Equality (MAR)
CARE .... Comision Americana de Remesas al Exterior [*Bogota-Agencia*] (COL)
CARE .... Comites de Ayuda a la Resistencia Espanola [*Spanish Resistance Support Committees*] (WER)
CARECT ..... Centre Algerien de Recherches et d'Echanges Culturels et Techniques [*Algerian Center for Cultural and Technical Research and Exchange*] (AF)
CAREF .... Centre Algerien de Recherches et Experimentations Forestieres (MAR)
CAREMOCI ... Carrelage Revetement, Mosaique de la Cote-d'Ivoire (MAR)
CARENA ..... Compagnie Abidjanaise de Reparation Navale [*Abidjan Ship Repair Company*] [*Ivorian*] (AF)
CARENA ..... Compagnie Abidjanaise de Reparations Navales et de Travaux Industriels (MAR)
CAREP .... Compagnie Algerienne de Recherche et d'Exploitation Petrolieres [*Algerian Petroleum Exploitation and Prospecting Company*] (AF)
CARFF .... Centre Africain de Recherche de Formation pour la Femme [*African Center for Research on Training for Women*] [*Niger*] (AF)
CARHB .... Comite de Coordination d'Aide aux Refugies Hutu du Burundi (MAR)
CARIBESA ... Mercantil del Caribe Ltda. [*Cartagena*] Tlg. (COL)
CARIBEX ..... Exportadora del Caribe [*Caribbean Export Enterprise*] [*Cuban*] (LA)
CARIC .... Compagnie Africaine de Representations Industrielles et Commerciales (MAR)
CARICOM ... Caribbean Community
CARIFTA ..... Caribbean Free Trade Association (LA)
CARIS .... Computerized Agricultural Research Information System [*FAO*] [*United Nations*]
CARISPLAN ... Caribbean Information System for Economic and Social Planning [*Port-Of-Spain, Trinidad and Tobago*]
CARITAS .... Coordinacion Arquidiocesana de Asistencia Social [*Cali*] (COL)
CARLDS ...... Central African Rail Link Development Survey (MAR)
CARN .... Comite de Accion para la Reconstruccion de Nicaragua [*Action Committee for the Reconstruction of Nicaragua*] (LA1)
CARNOSYMA ... Cartel National des Organizations Syndicales Malgaches [*National Coalition of Malagasy Labor Union Organizations*] (AF)
CARO .... Societe de Fabrication de Carrelages et Revetements au Cameroun (MAR)
CARP .... Casa de Ajutor Reciproc a Pensionarilor [*Pensioners Mutual Assistance Fund*] (RO)
CARPAS ..... Comision Asesora Regional de Pesca el Atlantico Sud-Occidental [*Southwest Atlantic Fishery Commission*]
CARPLE ...... Cartilla Electoral para el Plebiscito [*Colombia*]
CARP M-L ... Comite de Apoio de Reconstrucao do Partido Marxista-Leninista [*Support Committee for the Reconstruction of the Marxist-Leninist Party*] [*Portuguese*] (PPE)
Carre .... Carriere [*Quarry*] [*Military map abbreviation*] [*World War I*] [*French*] (MTD)
carref .... Carrefour [*Square*] [*In addresses*] [*French*] (CED)
Carrefr .... Carrefour [*Crossroads*] [*Military map abbreviation*] [*World War I*] [*French*] (MTD)
Cars .... Carsamba [*Wednesday*] (TU)
CARSOSYMA ... Cartel Nationale des Organisations Syndicales de Madagascar (MAR)
CARTAMOTORES ... Cartagena de Motores Ltda. [*Cartagena*] (COL)
CARTEZ ...... Confederacion de Asociaciones Rurales de la Tercera Zona [*Confederation of Rural Associations of the Third Zone*] (LA)
CARVOLT ... Societe de Cartoucherie Voltaique (MAR)
CAS .... Capricorn Africa Society (MAR)
CAS .... Casa Asigurarilor de Stat [*State Insurance Society*] (RO)
CAS .... Casablanca Airport (MAR)
Cas .... Castel [*Castello*] [*Castle*] [*Italian*] (NAU)
CAS .... Centralna Akcja Szkoleniowa [*Central Training Course*] (POL)
CAS .... Centralna Aptek Spolecznych [*Socialized Pharmacies Center*] (POL)
CAS .... Ceskoslovenska Astronomicka Spolecnost [*Czechoslovak Astronomical Society*] (CZ)
CAS .... Cesky Abstinentni Svaz [*Czech Temperance Union*] (CZ)
CAS .... Club Alpine Suisse [*Swiss Alpine Club*]
CAS .... Committee for the Assurance of Supplies (MAR)
CAS .... Conference on African Statistics (MAR)
CAS .... Confiserie Africaine de Sebikotane (MAR)
CAS .... Consorcio Agricola del Sur [*Southern Agricultural Association*] [*Chilean*] (LA)
CAS .... Council of Arab Students (MAR)
CAS .... Current Agricultural Statistics (MAR)
CASA .... Centro de Accion Social Autonoma [*Autonomous Social Action Center*] (LA)
CASA .... Centro de Assistencia Socio-Sanitaria (MAR)
CASA .... Comision Analitica del Sindicalismo Argentino [*Analytical Commission for Argentine Labor Unions*] (LA)
CASA .... Conseil Africain des Sociologues et des Anthropologues [*African Council of Sociologists and Anthropologists*] (AF)
CASA .... Construcciones Aeronauticas, Sociedad Anonima [*Spanish*]
CASA .... Cosecheros Abastecedores Sociedad Anonima [*Harvester Suppliers, Incorporated*] [*Spanish*] (WER)
CASASOL ... Caisse Saharienne de Solidarite (MAR)
CASC .... Committee on African Studies in Canada (MAR)
CASC .... Confederacion Autonoma de Sindicatos Cristianos [*Autonomous Confederation of Christian Trade Unions*] [*Dominican Republic*] (LA1)
CASCOM .... Casa de Asigurari Sociale si Pensii din Cooperatia Mestesugareasca [*Social Security and Pension Fund in the Artisan Cooperatives*] (RO)
CASE .... Comision Administradora de los Servicios de Estiba [*Administrative Commission of Wood Compressing Services*] [*Uruguayan*] (LA)
CASHA .... Centre Africain des Sciences Humaines Appliquees [*African Center for Applied Human Sciences*] [*French*] (AF)
CASL .... Confederation Africaine des Syndicats Libres [*African Federation of Free Trade Unions*] (AF)
CASL .... Cooperativa Algodonera Salvadorena Limitada [*Salvadoran Cotton Cooperative Limited*] (LA1)
CASLE .... Commonwealth Association of Surveying and Land Economy (EA)
CASL(-FO) ... Confederation Africaine des Syndicats Libres (-Force Ouvriere) (MAR)
CASLHV ...... Confederation Africaine des Syndicats Libres de la Haute Volta (MAR)
CASMU .... Centro de Asistencia del Sindicato Medico del Uruguay [*Assistance Center of the Medical Union of Uruguay*] (LA)
Casne .... Caserne [*Barracks*] [*Military map abbreviation*] [*World War I*] [*French*] (MTD)
CASNO .... Crnogorska Antifasisticka Skupstina Narodnog Oslobodenja [*Montenegrin Anti-Fascist Assembly of National Liberation*] (YU)
CASOC .... California Arabian Standard Oil Company (MAR)
CASORAL ... Caisse Sociale de la Region d'Alger (MAR)
CASORAN .. Caisse Sociale de la Region d'Oran [*North African*] (MAR)
CASP .... Compagnie Africaine de Services Publics (MAR)
CASS .... Centrul de Astronomie si Stiinte Spatiale [*Center for Astronomy and Space Sciences*] (RO)
CASSU .... Comites d'Arondissement du Sport Scolaire et Universitaire (MAR)
CAST .... Centre d'Actualisation Scientifique et Technique
CAST .... Consolidated African Selection Trust [*Sierra Leonean*] (AF)
CASTARAB ... Conference des Ministres Arabes pour l'Application de la Science et de la Technologie pour le Developpement (MAR)
CASTME ..... Commonwealth Association of Science, Technology, and Mathematics Educators (EA)
CASWIG ...... Council for the Affairs and Status of Women in Guyana (LA1)
CAT .... Cameroun Air Transport (MAR)
CAT .... Capsule Ariane Technologique [*Ariane Technological Capsule*] [*French*] (WER)
CAT .... Centro de Asistencia Tecnica [*Technical Assistance Center*] [*Cuban*] (LA)
CAT .... Certificado de Abono Tributario [*Tax Credit Certificate*] [*Colombian*] (LA)
CAT .... Certificado de Abono Tributario [*Export Tax Rebate Certificate*] [*Uruguayan*] (LA)
CAT .... Chahada 'Amma fi al Tarbiya [*Academic qualification*] [*Syrian*]
c at .... Ciezar Atomowy [*Atomic Weight*] [*Polish*]
CAT .... Coffee Authority of Tanzania (MAR)
CAT .... Comando Aereo Tattico [*Tactical Air Command*] [*Use TAC*] [*Italian*] (WER)
CAT .... Comando de Apoyo Tupamaro [*Tupamaro Support Command*] [*Uruguayan*] (LA)
CAT .... Comisaria de Abastecimientos y Transportes [*Commissariat for Supplies and Transportation*] [*Spanish*] (WER)
CAT .... Comite de l'Assistance Technique de l'Organisation des Nations Unies (MAR)
CAT .... Compagnie Abidjanaise des Techniques (MAR)
CAT .... Compagnie d'Achat du Togo (MAR)
CAT .... Compagnie Africaine de Transports (MAR)
CAT .... Compagnie Algerienne de Transports (MAR)
CAT .... Comptoir Africain des Textiles (MAR)
CAT .... Confederation Autonome de Travail [*Autonomous Confederation of Labor*]
CAT .... Conseil Africain de la Teledetection (MAR)
CAT .... Continental African Travels (MAR)
CATA .... Cashew-Nut Authority of Tanzania (MAR)
CATA .... Centre d'Assistance Technique Artisanal [*Handicrafts Technical Assistance Center*] [*Algerian*] (AF)
CATA .... Commonwealth Association of Tax Administrators (EA)
CATA .... Compagnie Africaine de Transports Automobiles (MAR)
CATA .... Compania Amazonia Textil de Aniagem [*Commercial firm*] [*Brazilian*]
CATC .... Central African Trading Company (MAR)
CATC .... Commonwealth Air Transport Council (EA)
CATC .... Compagnie Africaine de Tissage et de Confection (MAR)

CATC .... Confederation Africaine des Travailleurs Croyants [*African Confederation of Believing Workers*] (AF)
CATCI .... Compagnie Africaine de Transports Cote-d'Ivoire (MAR)
CATCM .... Centre Administratif des Troupes Coloniales en Metropole (MAR)
CATCO .... Central African Transport Company (MAR)
CATD .... Confederacion Autentica de Trabajadores Democraticos [*Authentic Confederation of Democratic Workers*] [*Costa Rican*] (LA1)
CATE .... College for Advanced Technical Education (MAR)
CATECO .... Societe Camerounaise d'Automobile, de Technique, et du Commerce [*Cameroonian Automobile, Technological, and Trading Company*] (AF)
CATEES .... Conference Africaine pour les Techniques d'Exploitation des Eaux Sousterraines [*African Conference for Subterranean Waters Exploitation Techniques*] (AF)
CATEL .... Compagnie Africaine de Television (MAR)
CATES .... Centres d'Appui Technique et Social (MAR)
CATESA .... Casas y Terrenos, Sociedad Anonima [*Houses and Lands, Incorporated*] [*Costa Rican*] (LA1)
CATEX .... Societe Centrafricaine des Textiles pour l'Exportation (MAR)
CATG .... Compagnie pour l'Application des Techniques Geophysiques (MAR)
Cathle .... Cathedrale [*Cathedral*] [*Military map abbreviation*] [*World War I*] [*French*] (MTD)
CATI .... Confederacion Argentina de Trabajadores Independientes [*Argentine Confederation of Independent Workers*] (LA)
CATIE .... Centro Agronomico Tropical de Investigacion y Ensenanza [*Costa Rican*]
CATK .... Cesko-Americka Tiskova Kancelar [*Czech-American Press Bureau*] (CZ)
CATO .... Compania Colombo Americana de Tornillos Ltda. [*Barranquilla*] (COL)
CATOSON .... Compagnie Allemande et Togolaise pour le Sondage (MAR)
CATP .... Compagnie Africaine de Travaux Publics (MAR)
CATRA .... Compagnie Africaine de Travaux (MAR)
CATRF .... Central Africa Tea Research Foundation (MAR)
CATT .... Confederacion Argentina de Trabajadores del Transporte [*Argentine Confederation of Transport Workers*] (LA)
c att .... Coupon Attache [*French*]
CATU .... Confederation of Arab Trade Unions (ME)
CAU .... Commis Auxiliaire (MAR)
CAUCHAMA .... Cauchos del Amazonas Ltda. [*Bogota*] (COL)
CAUCHOSOL .... Compania Colombiana de Caucho el Sol SA [*Bogota*] (COL)
CAUNC .... Comite de Accao da Uniao Nacional de Cabinda [*Action Committee of the Cabindan National Union*] [*Angolan*] (MAR)
CAUNC .... Comite d'Action de l'Union Nationale Cabindaise [*Action Committee of the Cabindan National Union*] [*Angolan*] (AF)
CAUS .... Central de Accion de Unificacion Sindical [*Central Organization of Trade Union Action and Unity*] [*Nicaraguan*] (LA1)
CAUSA .... Compania Aeronautics Uruguaya, Sociedad Anonima
CAUTOR .... Central Automotor Ltda. [*Cali*] Tlg. (COL)
Cav .... Cavalerie [*Cavalry*] [*Military*] [*French*] (MTD)
C AV .... Central Avant [*Military*] [*French*] (MTD)
CAV .... Ceska Akademie Ved [*Czech Academy of Sciences*] (CZ)
CAV .... Ceskoslovensti Amateri Vysilaci [*Czechoslovak Amateur Radio Operators*] (CZ)
CAV .... Comando Anticastrista de Venezuela [*Venezuelan Anti-Castroite Commando*] (LA)
CAV .... Corporacion de Ahorro y Vivienda [*Bogota*] (COL)
CAVASA .... Corporacion de Abastecimiento del Valle del Cauca [*Cali*] (COL)
CAVE .... Comptoir Africain de Vente (MAR)
CAVEIS .... Comite de Accion de Viviendas y Edificaciones de Interes Social [*Public Housing and Building Action Committee*] [*Uruguayan*] (LA)
CAVELBA .... Cavendes, Lansberg, Brunet & Alcantara, CA [*Venezuelan*]
CAVENBA .... Consortium d'Achats et de Ventes des Bois Africains (MAR)
CAVIC .... Corporacion Agroeconomica Vinicola Industrial y Comercial [*Wine Manufacturing and Sales Agricultural-Economic Corporation*] [*Argentine*] (LA)
CAVIM .... Compania Anonima Venezolana de Industrias Militares [*Military Industries Company*] [*Venezuelan*] (LA)
CAVINEX .... Societe Camerounaise d'Exploitation Vinicole (MAR)
CAVIS .... Caisse Assurance-Viellesse (MAR)
CAVN .... Comite d'Amenagement de la Vallee du Niari (MAR)
CAVN .... Compania Anonima Venezolana de Navegacion [*Venezuelan Navigation Company*] (LA)
Cav T .... Cavalerie Territoriale [*Military*] [*French*] (MTD)
CAVU .... Ceska Akademie Ved a Umeni [*Czech Academy of Sciences and Arts*] (CZ)
CAVUB .... Commissie Algemene Vraagstukken Universitair Bibliotheekwezen [*'s-Gravenhage*]
CAW .... Centralne Archiwum Wojskowe [*Central Military Archives*] (POL)
CAYKUR .... Cay Kurumu [*Tea Producers Organization*] [*Limited economic state enterprise*] (TU)
Cayr .... Cayolar [*Military map abbreviation*] [*World War I*] [*French*] (MTD)
CAZ .... Ceska Akademie Zemedelska [*Czech Agricultural Academy (Since 1969)*] (CZ)
CAZ .... Ceskoslovenska Akademie Zemedelska [*Czechoslovak Academy of Agriculture (Until 1969)*] (CZ)
CAZ .... Ceskoslovenske Automobilove Zavody Praha [*Czechoslovak Automobile Works, Prague*] (CZ)
CAZ .... Cycling Association of Zambia (MAR)
CAZACRUZ .... Compania Azucarera Santa Cruz [*Cartagena*] (COL)
CAZF .... Comite des Agences de la Zone Franc [*North African*] (MAR)
CAZRI .... Central Arid Zone Research Institute (MAR)
CB .... Comptabilite Budgetaire (MAR)
CB .... Kongo Belgijskie [*Belgian Congo*] [*Polish*]
CB-21 .... Comite Benque 21 de Septiembre [*21 September Benqueno Committee*] (LA1)
CBA .... Chef de Bureau Adjoint (MAR)
CBA .... College of Business Administration (MAR)
CBA .... Comite Brasileiro pela Anistia [*Brazilian Amnesty Committee*] (LA)
CBA .... Commercial Bank of Africa (MAR)
CBA .... Commonwealth Broadcasting Association (EA)
CBA .... Consortium des Bois Africains (MAR)
CBA .... De Colonne Beaufaict, A., Azande (MAR)
CBAE .... Commonwealth Board of Architectural Education (EA)
CBAS .... Complexe de Bois Alger Sahel (MAR)
CBBMG .... Centralne Biuro Budowy Maszyn Gorniczych [*Central Office of Mining Machinery Construction*] (POL)
CBC .... Carrieres de Basalte du Cayor (MAR)
CBC .... Chad Basin Commission (MAR)
CBC .... Consumer Buying Corporation of Zambia Ltd. (MAR)
CBC .... Societe Commerciale des Bois du Cameroun (MAR)
cbcm .... Kubikzentimeter [*Cubic Centimeter*] [*German*]
CBD .... Centrale Bibliotheek Dienst
CBD .... Coffee Berry Disease (MAR)
CBDA .... Chad Basin Development Authority (MAR)
CBDD .... Cografya Bakimindan Dezavantajli Devletler [*Geographically Disadvantaged Nations*] (TU)
cbdo .... Co Bylo do Okazania [*or Okreslenia*] [*Which Was to Be Proved*] [*Polish*]
CBDT .... Citizenship of British Dependent Territories (MAR)
CBE .... Commander of the British Empire (ML)
CBE .... Commercial Bank of Ethiopia (AF)
CBECI .... Centre Belge des Echanges Culturels Internationaux (MAR)
CBEMR .... Commercial Bank of Ethiopia. Market Report [*Addis Ababa*] [*A publication*] (MAR)
CBF .... Corporacion Boliviana de Fomento [*Bolivian Development Corporation*] (LA)
CBG .... Compagnie de Bauxites de Guinee [*Guinea Bauxite Company*] (AF)
CBI .... Caribbean Basin Initiative (LA1)
CBI .... Central Bank of Iran (ME)
CBJO .... Co-Ordinating Board of Jewish Organizations for Consultation with the Economic and Social Council of the United Nations (MAR)
CBK .... Centralne Biuro Konstrukcyjne [*Central Designing Office*] (POL)
CBKK .... Centralne Biuro Konstrukcji Kotlow [*Central Boiler Design Office*] (POL)
CBKM .... Centralne Biuro Konstrukcji Maszynowych [*Central Machinery Designing Office*] (POL)
CBKMiUO .... Centralne Biuro Konstrukcyjne Maszyn i Urzadzen Odlewniczych [*Central Machineryand Foundry Equipment Designing Office*] (POL)
CBKN .... Centralne Biuro Konstrukcyjne Narzedzi [*Central Tool Designing Office*] (POL)
CBKO .... Centralne Biuro Konstrukcji Okretowych [*Central Ship Designing Office*] (POL)
CBKO .... Centralne Biuro Konstrukcyjne Obrabiarek [*Central Machine Tool Design Office*] (POL)
CBKO .... Centralne Biuro Kulturalno-Oswiatowe [*Central Office of Culture and Education*] (POL)
CBKT .... Centralne Biuro Konstrukcji Teletechnizcnych [*Central Telecommunication Installation Designing Office*] (POL)
CBKT .... Centralne Biuro Konstrukcyjne Telekomunikacji [*Central Telecommunication Designing Office*] (POL)
CBKUB .... Centralne Biuro Konstrukcji Urzadzen Budowlanych [*Central Building Equipment Designing Office*] (POL)
CBKW .... Centralne Biuro Konstrukcji Wagonow [*Central Office for Railroad Car Design*] (POL)
CBLT .... Centralne Biuro Lozysk Tocznych [*Central Ball Bearings Office*] (POL)
CBLT .... Commission du Bassin du Lac Tchad [*Lake Chad Basin Commission*] [*Cameroonian*] (AF)
CBM .... Congo Balolo Mission (MAR)
cbm .... Kubikmeter [*Cubic Meter*] (EG)
CBMM .... Companhia Brasileira de Metalurgia e Mineracao [*Brazilian Mining and Metallurgy Company*] (LA)
CBN .... Central Bank of Nigeria (MAR)
CBN .... Comision Bancaria Nacional [*National Banking Commission*] [*Panamanian*] (LA)
CBO .... Comite de Bases Obreras [*Workers Base Committee*] [*Salvadoran*] (LA1)

CBO .... Commissie Bibliografisch Onderzoek
CBOA .... Comite des Bons Offices Angolais [*Angolan Good Offices Committee*] (AF)
CBOAR .... Centralne Biuro Obrotu Artykulami Rolnymi [*Central Agricultural Products Sales Office*] (POL)
CBOM .... Centralne Biuro Obrotu Maszynami [*Central Machinery Sales Office*] (POL)
CBOR .... Centrala Budowy Osiedli Robotniczych [*Polish*]
CBP .... Caribbean Basin Program (LA1)
CBP .... Centar Bateriskog Polozaja [*Center of Battery Position*] (YU)
CBP .... Centralne Biuro Planowania [*Central Planning Office*] (POL)
CBP .... Centralni Biro za Projektiranje [*Central Bureau for Designs (Naval Architecture)*] [*Brodogradnja*] (YU)
CBPBM .... Centralne Biuro Projektow Budownictwa Miejskiego [*Central Office of Urban Construction Plans*] (POL)
CBPBW .... Centralne Biuro Projektow Budownictwa Wiejskiego [*Central Office of Rural Construction Plans*] (POL)
CBPF .... Centro Brasileiro de Pesquisas Fisicas [*Brazilian Center for Physics Research*]
CBPiSBP .... Centralne Biuro Projektow i Studiow Budownictwo Przemyslowego [*Central Office of Plans and Research in Industrial Construction*] (POL)
CBPP .... Centralne Biuro Projektow Przemyslu [*Central Office of Plans in the Industry*] (POL)
CBPPW .... Centralne Biuro Projektow Przemyslu Weglowego [*Central Office of Plans in the Coal Industry*] (POL)
CBRPW .... Centralne Biuro Rozliczen Przemyslu Weglowego [*Central Clearing Office of the Coal Industry*] (POL)
CBS .... Centraal Bureau voor de Statistiek [*Dutch*]
CBS .... Cesky Bruslarsky Svaz [*Czechoslovak Skating Association*] (CZ)
CBS .... Comite de Barrio Sandinista [*Sandinist Neighborhood Committee*] [*Nicaraguan*] (LA1)
CBSE .... Commonwealth Board of Surveying Education (EA)
CBSiPKol .... Centralne Biuro Studiow i Projektow Kolejowych [*Central Office of Railroad Research and Plans*] (POL)
CBSiPTD .... Centralne Biuro Studiow i Projektow Transportu Drogowego [*Central Office of Research and Plans for Road Transportation*] (POL)
CBSiPTDL .... Centralne Biuro Studiow i Projektow Transportu Drogowego i Lotniczego [*Central Office of Research and Plans for Road and Air Transportation*] (POL)
CBSKol .... Centralne Biuro Statystyki Kolejowej [*Central Railroad Statistics Office*] (POL)
CBSPPKP .... Centralne Biuro Statystyki Przewozow Polskich Kolei Panstwowych [*Central Office of Statistics on Polish State Railroad Shipments*] (POL)
CBTIP .... Chambre Belge des Traducteurs, Interpretes, et Philologues [*Belgian Chamber of Translators, Interpreters, and Philologists*]
CBTN .... Companhia Brasileira de Tecnologia Nuclear [*Brazilian Nuclear Technology Company*] (LA)
CBU .... Caribbean Broadcasting Union (LA1)
CBV .... Christliche Bayerische Volkspartei - Bayerische Patriotenbewegung [*Christian Bavarian People's Party - Movement of Bavarian Patriots*] [*West German*] (PPW)
CBW .... Centralne Biblioteka Wojskowa [*Central Military Library*] (POL)
CBW .... Centralne Biuro Wystaw [*Central Exhibitions Office*] (POL)
CBWA .... Centralne Biuro Wystaw Artystycznych [*Central Art Exhibitions Office*] (POL)
cc .... Calcada [*Street*] [*Portuguese*] (CED)
CC .... Camara de la Construccion [*Chamber of Construction*] [*Nicaraguan*] (LA1)
CC .... Carabinieri [*Italian National Military Police*] (WER)
C de C .... Carton de Colombia [*Cali*] (COL)
cc .... Celni Cent [*Customs Quintal (About 50 kilograms)*] (CZ)
CC .... Centrale Catalogus [*KB*] [*'s-Gravenhage*]
CC .... Chancellor College (MAR)
CC .... Cobres de Colombia SA [*Urbanizacion Industrial Acopi-Menga Cali*] (COL)
CC .... Cocos [*Keeling*] Islands [*Two-letter standard code*] (CNC)
cc .... Combustibil Conventional [*Conventional Fuel*] (RO)
CC .... Comisiones Campesinos [*Rural Workers Commissions*] [*Spanish*] (WER)
CC .... Comitato Centrale [*Central Committee*] [*Italian*] (WER)
CC .... Comite Central (MAR)
CC/ .... Comite Central De [*Central Committee Of*] [*Cambodian*] (CL)
CC .... Comitetul Central [*Central Committee*] (RO)
CC .... Commanders Call [*Meeting of KODAM commanders*] (IN)
c/c .... Compte Courant [*Current Account*] [*French*]
CC .... Consiliul Central [*Central Council*] (RO)
CC .... Constituency Committee [*Mauritian*] (AF)
c/c .... Conto Corrente [*Current Account*] [*Italian*]
CC .... Coordination Committee for the Transfer of Powers (MAR)
CC .... Corps de Cavalerie [*Military*] [*French*] (MTD)
CC .... Corps Consulaire [*French*]
cc .... Corriente Continua [*Direct Current*] [*Spanish*]
cc .... Cours de Compensation [*French*]
CC .... Cours Complementaire [*French*]
CC .... Crevettes du Cameroun (MAR)
CC .... Crossword Club (EA)
CC .... Cultural Colombiana Ltda. [*Bogota*] (COL)
CCA .... Caise Congolaise d'Amortisation [*Congolese Sinking Fund*] (AF)
CCA .... Caribbean Conservation Association (LA1)
CCA .... Centre Commercial Africain (MAR)
cca .... Circa [*About, Approximately*] [*Latin*]
CCA .... Clubul Central al Armatei [*Central Army Club*] (RO)
CCA .... Comites Communistes pour l'Autogestion [*Communist Committees for Self-Management*] [*French*] (PPW)
CCA .... Commission Centrale des Arbitres de Football (MAR)
CCA .... Compagnie Commerciale Africaine (MAR)
CCA .... Companhia de Culturas de Angodre (MAR)
CCA .... Comptoirs Commerciaux Africains (MAR)
CCAA .... Caribbean-Central American Action (LA1)
CCAC .... Compagnie Commerciale de l'Afrique Centrale (MAR)
CCACU .... Central Coordinating Allocation Committee for University Project Research (MAR)
CCAF .... Compagnie Commerciale Agricole et Forestiere (MAR)
CCAF .... Consejo Central de Asignaciones Familiares [*Family Aid Council*] [*Uruguayan*] (LA)
CCAI .... Chambre de Commerce, Agriculture, et Industrie [*Chamber of Commerce, Agriculture, and Industry*] (AF)
CCAJ .... Consiliul Central al Asociatiei Juristilor [*Central Council of the Association of Jurists*] (RO)
CCAM .... Centre de Conjoncture Africaine et Malgache (MAR)
CCAP .... Caja Central de Ahorros y Prestamos [*Central Savings and Loan Bank*] [*Chilean*] (LA)
CCAP .... Church of Central Africa Presbyterian (MAR)
CCAR .... Compagnie Camerounaise d'Assurances et de Reassurances (MAR)
CCAS .... Consiliul de Cultura si Arta Socialista [*Council of Socialist Culture and Arts*] (RO)
CCAST .... Cameroon College of Arts, Science, and Technology (MAR)
CCAT .... Comptoir Commercial des Alfas Tunisie (MAR)
CCAT .... Control de Conmutaciones Automaticas [*Telex-Automatic Switching Control*] [*Cuban*] (LA)
CCB .... Centrala Industriei Confectiilor Bucuresti [*Bucharest Central for the Clothing Industry*] (RO)
CCB .... Centre Commercial du Benin (MAR)
CCB .... Colegio Colombiano de Bibliotecarios [*Medellin*] [*Formerly, CBC*] (COL)
CCB .... Comite de Comercio de Bogota (COL)
CCB .... Commercial Crimes Bureau [*Hong Kong*]
CCB .... Compagnie Camerounaise de Boissons (MAR)
CCB .... Compagnie Commerciale du Betsileo (MAR)
CCB .... Comunidades Cristianas de Base [*Christian Base Communities*] [*Spanish*] (WER)
CCB .... Concorde des Citoyens du Burundi (MAR)
CCB .... Cooperatieve Centrale Boerenleebank (MAR)
CCB .... Cooperatives des Commercants du Burundi (MAR)
CCBN .... Compagnie des Cultures Bananieres du Nieky (MAR)
CCBP .... Certificat de Capacite au Bornage et a la Peche (MAR)
CCC .... Camara Chilena de la Construccion [*Chilean Construction Council*] (LA)
CCC .... Camara de Comercio de la Republica de Cuba [*Chamber of Commerce of the Republic of Cuba*] (LA)
CCC .... Cameroon Cultural Centre (MAR)
CCC .... Caribbean Council of Churches (LA)
CCC .... Central Classification Committee [*FID*] [*'s-Gravenhage*]
CCC .... Chinese Chamber of Commerce (ML)
CCC .... Chlorcholinchlorid [*Trimethyl Ammonium Chloride*] (EG)
CCC .... Club des Clubs de Casablanca (MAR)
CCC .... Comando de Caca aos Communistas [*Communist Hunters Command*] [*Brazilian*] (LA)
CCC .... Commissione Centrale di Controllo [*Central Control Commission*] [*Italian*] (WER)
CCC .... Compagnie Commerciale Cypriote (MAR)
CCC .... Compagnie de Cultures Cacayeres (MAR)
CCC .... Complexe Chimique Camerounais (MAR)
CCC .... Confederacion de Camara de Comercio [*Chamber of Commerce Confederation*] [*Nicaraguan*] (LA1)
CCC .... Confederacion Nacional de Colegio Catolicos [*Bogota*] (COL)
CCC .... Customs Co-Operation Council [*See also CCD*] (EA)
CCC .... Societe de Commission, de Consignation, et de Courtage de l'Ocean Indien (MAR)
CCC .... Vanguarda de Comando de Caca aos Comunistas [*Vanguard of the Commando for Hunting Communists*] [*Brazilian*] (PD)
CCCA .... Centre de Cooperation et de Coordination Agricole (MAR)
CCCAM .... Caisse Centrale de Credit Artisanal et Maritime (MAR)
CCCB .... Cooperative Casamancaise de Construction de Batiments (MAR)
CCCE .... Caisse Centrale de Cooperation Economique [*Central Fund for Economic Cooperation*] [*French*] (AF)
CCCE .... Centre Congolais du Commerce Exterieur (MAR)
CCCHV .... Cooperative Centrale de Consommation de la Haute-Volta (MAR)
CCCI .... Compagnie du Congo pour le Commerce et l'Industrie [*Congo Commerce and Industry Company*]
CCCMAES .... Consiliul Central de Control Muncitoresc al Activitatilor Economico-Sociale [*Central Council of Worker Control of Socioeconomic Activities*] (RO)

CCCN.......... Customs Co-Operation Council Nomenclature (MAR)
CCCOE....... Comision Coordinadora de las Comisiones de Euzkadi Obreras [*Coordinating Commission for the Basque Workers Commissions*] [*Spanish*] (WER)
CCCP.......... Caisse Central du Credit Populaire [*People's Central Credit Fund*] [*Algerian*] (AF)
CCCP.......... Union of Soviet Socialist Republics [*Initialism represents Russian phrase*]
CCD........... Camara de Comercio de la Dorada (COL)
CCD........... Certificat de Capacite en Droit [*French*]
CCD........... Comissao Civica Democratica (MAR)
CCD........... Commission Centrale de Discipline [*Tunisian*] (MAR)
CCD........... Confederazione dei Coltivatori Diretti [*Confederation of Small Farmers*] [*Italian*] (WER)
CCD........... Conference of the Committee on Disarmament (MAR)
CCD........... Conseil de Cooperation Douaniere [*Customs Co-Operation Council - CCC*] (EA)
CCDC.......... Capital City Development Corporation (MAR)
CCDEE........ Compagnie Centrale de Distribution d'Energie Electrique (MAR)
CCDEE........ Compagnie Coloniale de Distribution d'Energie Electrique (MAR)
CCDG.......... Compagnie Commerciale du Gabon (MAR)
CCDL.......... Camera Confederale del Lavoro [*Confederal Chamber of Labor*] [*Trieste, Italy*]
CCDN.......... Comite Contra la Dependencia y el Neo-Colonialismo [*Committee Against Dependence and Neocolonialism*] [*Venezuelan*] (LA)
CCDP.......... Compagnie Camerounaise de Depots Petroliers (MAR)
CCDR.......... Compagnie Camerounaise de Developpement Regional (MAR)
CCDVT........ Caisse Centrale de Depots et Vriements de Titres
CCE............ Centre for Civic Education (MAR)
CCE............ Comite de Coordination et d'Execution [*Algerian*] (MAR)
CCE............ Compagnie Commerciale d'Electronique (MAR)
CCE............ Consejo Central de Elecciones [*Central Elections Council*] [*Salvadoran*] (LA)
CCE............ Consejo Coordinador Empresarial [*Coordinating Business Council*] [*Mexican*] (LA)
CCE............ Conselho dos Comissariados de Estado (MAR)
CCE............ Coordinating Committee Executive (MAR)
CCEA.......... Center for Climate and Environmental Assessment (MAR)
CCEA.......... Commonwealth Council for Education Administration (EA)
CCEAE........ Conference des Chefs d'Etat de d'Afrique Equatoriale [*Conference of Heads of State of Equatorial Africa*] (AF)
CCEE.......... Commission de Cooperation Economique Europeenne [*French*]
CCEHO....... Compagnie Centrafricaine d'Exploitation Hoteliere (MAR)
CCEI........... Conference sur la Cooperation Economique Internationale (MAR)
CCEN.......... Comision Chilena de Energia Nuclear [*Chilean Nuclear Energy Commission*] (LA1)
CCEP.......... Commission Consultative des Etudes Postales [*de l'Union Postale Universelle*]
CCEPL........ Consejo Central Ejecutivo del Partido Liberal [*Central Executive Council of the Liberal Party*] [*Honduran*] (LA1)
CCEPTI....... Centrul de Cercetari Economice pentru Promovarea Turismului International [*Economic Research Center for the Promotion of International Tourism*] (RO)
CCER.......... Centre de Coordination et d'Exploitation des Renseignements [*Center for Coordinating and Utilizing Intelligence*] [*Chadian*] (AF)
CCES.......... Centrala Industriei Poligrafice [*Central for the Printing Industry*] (RO)
CCES.......... Consiliul Culturii si Educatiei Socialiste [*Council for Socialist Culture and Education*] (RO)
CCETI......... Commission Consultative des Employes et des Travailleurs Intellectuels [*de l'OIT*]
CCF............ Centre Culturel Francais (MAR)
CCF............ Centrul de Chimie Fizica [*Center for Physical Chemistry*] (RO)
CCF............ Cesky Casopis Filologicky [*Czech Journal of Philology*] [*A publication*] (CZ)
CCF............ Christian Children's Fund (MAR)
CCF............ Co-Operative Commonwealth Federation [*Canadian*] (PPW)
CCF............ Comando do Corpo de Fuzileiros [*Marine Corps Command*] [*Portuguese*] (WER)
CCFA.......... Caribbean Cane Farmers' Association (EA)
CCFA.......... Comando Conjunto de la Fuerza Armada [*Joint Command of the Armed Forces*] [*Peruvian*] (LA)
CCFA.......... Comptoir Commercial Francais d'Approvisionnement (MAR)
CCFA.......... Comptoir Commercial Franco-Africain [*Franco-African Trade Office*] [*Guinean*] (AF)
CCFAN........ Conseil de Commandement des Forces Armees du Nord [*Northern Armed Forces Command Council*] [*Chadian*] (AF)
CCFC.......... Corporacion Colombiana de Fomento de la Construccion [*Bogota*] (COL)
CCFOM....... Caisse Centrale de la France d'Outre-Mer (MAR)
CCFOM....... Comite Central Francais pour l'Outre-Mer [*French Central Committee for Overseas Affairs*] (AF)
CCFPC........ Comision Coordinadora de Fuerzas Politicas de Cataluna [*Coordinating Commission for Political Forces of Catalonia*] [*Spanish*] (WER)
CCFS.......... Comitetul de Cultura Fizica si Sporturi [*Committee for Physical Education and Sports*] (RO)
CCFS.......... Compagnie Commerciale Franco-Scandinave [*Senegalese*] (MAR)
CCG........... Conseil de Cooperation du Golfe [*Moroccan*] (MAR)
CCGA.......... Compagnie de Constructions Generales en Afrique [*Company for General Construction in Africa*] [*French*] (AF)
CCGC.......... Cooperative Centrale des Grandes Cultures [*North African*] (MAR)
CCGEU........ Confederation of Central Government Employees' Unions [*Indian*]
CCh............ Ceskoslovenske Chemicke Zavody, Narodny Podnik [*Czechoslovak Chemical Plants, National Enterprise*] (CZ)
CCH............ Ceskoslovensky Casopis Historicky [*Czechoslovak Historical Journal*] [*A publication*] (CZ)
CCH............ Combinatul de Celuloza si Hirtie [*Cellulose and Paper Combine*] (RO)
CCHA.......... Compagnie Commerciale Hollando-Africaine (MAR)
CCHC.......... Camara de Comercio Hispano Colombiana [*Bogota*] (COL)
CCHFA........ Combinatul de Celuloza, Hirtie, si Fibre Artificiale [*Cellulose, Paper, and Artificial Fibers Combine*] (RO)
CChZ.......... Ceskoslovenske Chemicke Zavody [*Czechoslovak Chemical Plants*] (CZ)
CCI............ Camera di Commercio Internazionale [*International Chamber of Commerce*] [*Use ICC*] [*Italian*] (WER)
CCI............ Canadian Crossroads International (MAR)
CCI............ Central Campesina Independiente [*Independent Peasants Federation*] [*Mexican*] (LA)
CCI............ Chambre de Commerce et d'Industrie [*Chamber of Commerce and Industry*] (AF)
CCI............ Chambre de Commerce et d'Industrie [*Chamber of Commerce and Industry*] [*Guadeloupe*] (LA1)
CCI............ Chambre de Commerce Internationale [*International Chamber of Commerce - ICC*] (EA)
CCI............ Comites Consultatifs Internationaux (MAR)
CCI............ Compagnie Camerounaise Industrielle (MAR)
CCI............ Compagnie Commerciale Ivoirienne (MAR)
CCI............ Compagnie de Construction Internationale [*French*]
CCI............ Compagnie de Cultures de la Cote-d'Ivoire (MAR)
CCI............ Credit de la Cote-d'Ivoire (MAR)
CCIA.......... Comite de Cooperacion para el Istmo Centroamericano [*Cooperation Committee for the Central American Isthmus*] (LA)
CCIA.......... Comptoir Commercial et Industriel Afrique (MAR)
CCIA.......... Consejo Coordinador de la Industria de Autopartes [*Auto Parts Industry Coordinating Council*] [*Argentine*] (LA1)
CCIC-MAROC... Compagnie Centrale Industrielle et Commerciale [*Moroccan*] (MAR)
CCIES......... Camara de Comercio e Industria de El Salvador [*Chamber of Commerce and Industry of El Salvador*] (LA1)
CCIG.......... Chambre de Commerce et d'Industrie de Guyane [*Chamber of Commerce and Industry of French Guiana*] (LA1)
CCIM.......... Chamber of Commerce and Industry of Malawi (AF)
CCIR........... Comite Consultatif International des Radiocommunications (MAR)
CCIS........... Compagnie Commerciale Industrielle du Senegal [*Tunisian*] (MAR)
CCITAC....... Centrul de Cercetare si Inginerie Tehnologica pentru Articole Casnice [*Research and Technical Engineering Center for Household Articles*] (RO)
CCITT......... Comite Consultatif International Telephonique et Telegraphique [*International Consultative Commission for Telephone and Telegraph*] (WEN)
CCITT......... Comite Consultivo de la Internacional de Telefonos y Telegrafos [*International Telephone and Telegraph Consultative Committee*] (LA)
CCIZ........... Centre de Commerce International du Zaire [*International Trade Center of Zaire*] (AF)
CCJP........... Catholic Commission for Justice and Peace (MAR)
CCK............ Centrale Catalogus Kartografie [*Utrecht*]
CCK............ Ceskoslovensky Cerveny Kriz [*Czechoslovak Red Cross*] (CZ)
CCK............ Cocos [*Keeling*] Islands [*Three-letter standard code*] (CNC)
CCL............ Caribbean Congress of Labor (LA1)
CCL............ Centre de la Construction et du Logement (MAR)
CCL............ Comite Clandestino Local [*Local Clandestine Committee*] [*Guatemalan*] (LA1)
CCL............ Commonwealth Countries' League (EA)
CCL............ Communications Consultants Limited (MAR)
CCLAMG..... Chicago Committee for the Liberation of Angola, Mozambique, and Guinea (MAR)
CCLU.......... Confederation of Citizens Labor Union [*Philippine*]
CCM............ Caribbean Common Market (LA)
CCM............ Casopis Ceskeho Musea [*Journal of the Czech Museum*] [*A publication*] (CZ)
CCM............ Central Cigarette Manufacturers (MAR)
CCM............ Centro Comercial de Mocambique (MAR)
CCM............ Chama Cha Mapinduzi [*Revolutionary Party*] [*Tanzanian*] (PPW)
CCM............ Chama Cha Mapinduzi [*Revolutionary Party*] [*Ugandan*] (AF)
ccm............ Kubikzentimeter [*Cubic Centimeter*] (EG)

CCMB .... Centrala de Constructii-Montaj Bucuresti [*Bucharest Central for Constructions-Installations*] (RO)
CCMCC .... Continuing Committee on Muslim-Christian Cooperation (MAR)
CCMEE .... Comite Consultatif Maghrebin de l'Education et de l'Enseignement (MAR)
CCMM .... Compagnie Camerounaise de Mobilier Metallique (MAR)
CCMRC .... Caribbean Medical Research Council (LA)
CCMRP .... Centrul de Cercetari pentru Metale Rare si Pure [*Research Center for Rare and Pure Metals*] (RO)
CCN .... Christian Council of Nigeria (MAR)
CCN .... Comissao Coordenadora Nacional [*National Coordinating Commission*] [*Portuguese*] (WER)
CCN .... Compagnie Camerounaise du N'Goko (MAR)
CCN .... Compagnie Commerciale du Niger (MAR)
CCN .... Compania Cervecera de Nicaragua [*Nicaraguan Brewery Company*] (LA1)
CCN .... Comunidad de Compensacion Minera [*Mining Compensation Community*] [*Peruvian*] (LA)
CCN .... Consulta di i Cumitati Nationalisti [*Corsican*] (PD)
CCN .... Cruzada Civica Nacionalista [*Nationalist Civic Crusade*] [*Venezuelan*] (PPW)
CCNEO .... Compagnie de Commerce et de Navigation d'Extreme Orient (MAR)
CCNN .... Cement Company of Northern Nigeria (MAR)
CCNPBC ..... Comite Consultatif National pour la Protection des Biens Culturels [*National Advisory Committee for the Protection of Cultural Property*] [*Cambodian*] (CL)
CCNR .... Conseil Consultatif National pour le Renouveau [*National Consultative Council for the Renewal*] [*Upper Voltan*] (AF)
CCO .... Chief of Combined Operations (MAR)
CCO .... Clandestine Communist Organization (ML)
CCO .... Cours Complementaires Officiels (MAR)
CCODP .... Canadian Catholic Organisation for Development and Peace (MAR)
CCOJB .... Comite de Coordination des Organisations Juives de Belgique [*Coordinating Committee for Jewish Organizations in Belgium*] (WER)
CCOM .... Caisse Centrale de la France d'Outre-Mer (MAR)
CCOO .... Comisiones Obreras [*Workers' Commissions*] [*Spanish*] (WER)
CCOP .... Comite Coordinador de Organizaciones Populares [*Popular Organizations Coordinating Committee*] [*Peruvian*] (LA)
CCOSA .... Christian College of Southern Africa (MAR)
CCOV .... Comite de Coordination de l'Opposition Voltaique [*Coordination Committee of the Voltan Opposition*] (AF)
CCP .... Camara de Comercio de Pereira (COL)
CCP .... Centrale Catalogus van Periodieken [*KB*] [*'s-Gravenhage*]
CCP .... Centre de Cheques Postaux [*French*]
CCP .... Centro Catolico Portugues [*Portuguese Catholic Center*] (PPE)
CCP .... Cercle Culture et Progres [*Culture and Progress Club*] [*Beninese*] (AF)
CCP .... Chinese Communist Party (PD)
CCP .... Commissao Coordenadora do Programa [*Program Coordinating Commission*] [*Mozambican*] (AF)
CCP .... Compagnie des Caoutchoucs de Pakidie (MAR)
CCP .... Compagnie de Commerce et de Plantations (MAR)
CCP .... Compte Courant Postal (MAR)
CCP .... Comptes Cheques Postaux [*French*]
CCP .... Confederacion de Campesinos del Peru [*Peasants Confederation of Peru*] (LA)
CCP .... Conference Chretienne pour la Paix [*Christian Peace Conference - CPC*] (EA)
CCP .... Conferenza Cristiana della Pace [*Christian Peace Conference*] [*Use CPC*] [*Italian*] (WER)
CCPCE .... Comissao de Coordenacao da Politica da Compras no Exterior [*Commission for the Coordination of a Policy for Purchases Abroad*] [*Brazilian*] (LA)
CCPCI .... Cuirs, Caoutchoucs, Plastiques de Cote-d'Ivoire (MAR)
CCPDF .... Committee for the Co-Ordination of Patriotic and Democracy-Loving Forces [*Thai*] (PD)
CCPFCI .... Caisse de Compensation des Prestations Familiales de la Cote-d'Ivoire (MAR)
CCPKI .... Central Comite Partai Komunis Indonesia [*Central Committee of the Indonesian Communist Party*] (IN)
CCPM .... Comite Consultatif Permanent Maghrebin [*Maghreb Permanent Consultative Committee*] [*North African*] (AF)
CCPM .... Comite de Coordination pour la Prospection en Mer [*Ocean Prospecting Coordination Committee*] [*Cambodian*] (CL)
CCPMFS ..... Centrul de Cercetari si Proiectari Mecanica Fina si Scule [*Research and Design Center for Precision Machinery and Tools*] (RO)
CCPO .... Comite Central Permanent de l'Opium
CCPP .... Centrul de Cercetari si Proiectari Pompe [*Center for Pump Research and Design*] (RO)
CCPT .... Centrul de Cercetari in Problemele Tineretului [*Center for Research into Youth Problems*] (RO)
CCPTF .... Centrul de Cercetare si Proiectare Tehnologia pentru Fabricatie [*Technological Research and Design Center for Manufacturing*] (RO)
CCR .... Centrul de Control al Radiocomunicatiilor [*Center for the Control of Radiocommunications*] (RO)
CCR .... Christian Council of Rhodesia (MAR)
CCR .... Comites Communaux de la Revolution [*Communal Committees of the Revolution*] [*Beninese*] (AF)
CCR .... Commission Centrale de Reglements [*Tunisian*] (MAR)
CCR .... Conseil de Commandement de la Revolution [*Revolution Command Council*] [*Chadian*] (AF)
CCR .... Conseil de Commandement Revolutionnaire [*Revolutionary Command Council*] [*Use RCC*] (AF)
CCR .... Conseil Communal de la Revolution [*Communal Council of the Revolution*] [*Beninese*] (AF)
CCRA .... Centre Cooperatif de la Reforme Agraire [*Agrarian Reform Cooperative Center*] [*Algerian*] (AF)
CCRA .... Comptoir Commercial de Representations Africaines (MAR)
CCRAO .... Communaute Chretienne Rurale de l'Afrique Orientale [*Christian Rural Fellowship of East Africa*] [*Use CRFEA*] (AF)
CCRE .... Comptoir Commercial de Radio-Electricite Radiodisc (MAR)
CCRM .... Comite Clandestin des Resistants Metro [*Metro Clandestine Committee of Resisters*] [*Guadeloupe*] (PD)
CCR M-L ..... Comites Comunistas Revolucionarios, Marxistas-Leninistas [*Marxist-Leninist Revolutionary Communist Committees*] [*Portuguese*] (PPE)
CCROI .... Comptoir de Commerce et de Representation pour l'Ocean Indien (MAR)
CCRP .... Commission Centrale des Reserves et Penalites (MAR)
CCS .... Cahier des Charges Speciales [*List of Special Charges*] [*Cambodian*] (CL)
CCS .... Centro de Campesinos Salvadorenos [*Salvadoran Peasants Center*] (LA1)
CCS .... Cirkev Ceskoslovenska [*Czechoslovak Church*] (CZ)
CCS .... Co-Operative Credit Scheme (MAR)
CCS .... Comite Coordinador de Sindicatos [*Trade Union Coordinating Committee*] [*Salvadoran*] (LA1)
CCS .... Commemorative Collectors Society (EA)
CCS .... Compagnie de Commandement et des Services [*Command and Service Company*] [*French*] (WER)
CCS .... Comptoir Commercial du Senegal (MAR)
CCS .... Consiliul Central al Sindicatelor [*Central Council of Trade Unions*] (RO)
CCSA .... Christian Concern for Southern Africa (AF)
CCSA .... Comite Chretien de Service en Algerie (MAR)
CCSATU ..... Coordinating Council of South African Trade Unions (AF)
CCSC .... Confederation Camerounaise des Syndicats Croyants [*Cameroonian Confederation of Believing Workers Unions*] (AF)
CCSFA .... Comissao Coordenadora de Sargentos da Forca Aerea [*Air Force Sergeants' Coordinating Committee*] [*Portuguese*] (WER)
CCSFB .... Centrul de Calculatii pentru Sistemul Financiar-Bancar [*Computation Center for the Financial and Banking System*] (RO)
CCSM .... Centrul de Cercetare pentru Securitate Miniera [*Research Center for Mine Safety*] (RO)
CCSM .... Comite de Coordination des Syndicats du Mali [*Coordinating Committee of the Trade Unions of Mali*] (AF)
CCSM .... Confederation Chretienne des Syndicats Malgaches [*Christian Federation of Malagasy Trade Unions*] (AF)
CCSO .... Compagnie Commerciale Sangha-Oubangui (MAR)
CCSS .... Caja Costarricense de Seguro Social [*Costa Rican Social Security Institute*] (LA)
CCSV .... Comite Central Socialista Vasca [*Basque Socialist Central Committee*] [*Spanish*] (WER)
Cct .... Centi-Stoc [*Centistoke*] (TVP)
CCT .... Centrale Kranten en Tijdschriften Catalogus [*Van West-Vlaanderen*]
CCT .... Christian Council of Tanzania (AF)
CCT .... Comissao Coordenadora de Trabalhadores [*Workers' Coordinating Commission*] [*Portuguese*] (WER)
CCT .... Commission Centrale Technique [*Tunisian*] (MAR)
CCT .... Compagnie Cherifienne de Transit (MAR)
CCT .... Compagnie de Circulation et des Transports (MAR)
CCT .... Confederacion Centroamericana de Trabajadores [*Central American Workers Confederation*] (LA)
CCT .... Confederacion Cristiana de Trabajadores [*Christian Confederation of Workers*] [*Paraguayan*] (LA)
CCTA .... Commission de Cooperation Technique en Afrique (MAR)
CCTC .... Centro Cultural de Trabajadores del Callao [*Workers Cultural Center of Callao*] [*Peruvian*] (LA)
CCTD .... Confederacion Costarricense de Trabajadores Democraticos [*Costa Rican Confederation of Democratic Workers*] (LA)
CCTP .... Compagnie de Construction et de Travaux Publics (MAR)
CCTT .... Congres des Chefs Traditionnels du Togo (MAR)
CCU .... Centro de Calculos Universitario [*University Computer Center*] [*Cuban*] (LA)
CCU .... Comision para la Carga Unitaria [*Container Cargo Committee*] [*Cuban*] (LA)
CCU .... Croatian Catholic Union [*Hrvatski Katolicki Savez*] (YU)
CCUA .... Casopis Ceskoslovenskych Ustavu Astronomickych [*Journal of the Czechoslovak Astronomical Institutes*] [*A publication*] (CZ)

CCULES...... Comite de Coordinacion y Unificacion de las Luchas Estudiantiles Secundarias [*Committee to Coordinate the Struggles of Secondary School Students*] [*Peruvian*] (LA)
CCUMES..... Comite Coordinador y Unificador del Movimiento Estudiantil Secundario [*Committee to Coordinate and Unify the Secondary School Student Movement*] [*Peruvian*] (LA)
CCUP.......... Commission Consultative Universitaire de Pedagogie [*Belgian*]
CCV............ Societe Cotonniere du Cap-Vert (MAR)
CCVAR........ Chrui Changvar [*Cambodian*] (CL)
CCWM......... Congregational Council for World Missions (MAR)
CCWU......... Clerical and Commercial Workers Union [*Guyanese*] (LA)
CCZ............ Christian Council of Zambia (MAR)
c cz............ Ciezar Czasteczkowy [*Molecular Mass*] [*Polish*]
cd............... Caddesi [*Avenue, Street*] [*See also C, Cad*] (TU)
CD.............. Cambio Democratico [*Democratic Change*] [*Spanish*] (WER)
CD.............. Centre Democratique [*Democratic Center*] [*Later, Center of Social Democrats*] [*French*] (PPE)
CD.............. Centrum-Demokraterne [*Center Democrats*] [*Danish*] (PPE)
CD.............. Ceskoslovenske Doly, Narodni Podnik [*Czechoslovak Mines, National Enterprise*] (CZ)
CD.............. Cevljarska Delavnica [*Shoemaker's Shop*] (YU)
cd............... Ciag Dalszy [*Continued*] [*Polish*]
CD.............. Coalicion Democratica [*Democratic Coalition*] [*Spanish*] (PPE)
CD.............. Commission du Danube [*Danube Commission*]
CD.............. Conseil de Direction [*Algerian*] (MAR)
CD.............. Convergencia Democratica [*Democratic Convergence*] [*Spanish*] (WER)
CD.............. Cooperation et Developpement, Paris (MAR)
CD.............. Coordinacion Democratica [*Democratic Coordination*] [*Spanish*] (PPE)
CD.............. Corps Diplomatik [*Diplomatic Corps*] (IN)
CD.............. Corps Diplomatique [*Diplomatic Corps*] [*French*]
C & D.......... Cultures et Developpement, Louvain (MAR)
cd............... Kandela [*Candela*] [*Polish*]
CD.............. Societe Claud Delmotte & Cie. (MAR)
CDA............ Capital Development Authority (MAR)
CDA............ Christen Democratisch Appel [*Christian Democratic Appeal*] [*Dutch*] (PPW)
CDA............ Corporacion Dominicana de Aviacion [*Dominican Aviation Corporation*] [*Dominican Republic airline*] (LA)
CDAG.......... Confederacion Deportiva Autonoma de Guatemala [*Autonomous Athletic Confederation of Guatemala*] (LA)
CDAHS........ Compagnie Diamantifere et Aurifere de la Haute-Sangha (MAR)
CDAP.......... Centro para el Desarrollo de la Administracion [*Public Administration Development Center*] [*Guatemalan*] (LA)
CDB............ Cameroon Development Bank (MAR)
CDB............ Caribbean Development Bank (LA)
CDB............ Cattle Development Board (MAR)
CDB............ Caves de Bordeaux (MAR)
CDB............ Centro de Documentacion y Bibliografia. Universidad Industrial de Santander [*Bucaramanga*] (COL)
CDB............ Comite de Liaison des Producteurs de Bois Divers (MAR)
CDB............ Comptoirs de Bordeaux (MAR)
CDC............ Caisse des Depots et Consignations (MAR)
CDC............ Cameroon Development Corporation (AF)
CDC............ Caribbean Documentation Centre [*Port-Of-Spain, Trinidad and Tobago*]
CDC............ Church Development Commission [*Ethiopian*] (AF)
CDC............ Club Discomano Colombiano [*Bogota*] (COL)
CDC............ Colonial Development Corporation (MAR)
CDC............ Coloured Development Corporation (MAR)
CDC............ Commonwealth Development Corporation (ML)
CDC............ Commonwealth Development Corporation [*Dominican*] (LA1)
CDC............ Compagnie Generale des Produits Dubonnet, Cinzano, Byrrh (MAR)
CDC............ Constitution Drafting Committee (MAR)
CDC............ Convergencia Democratica de Catalunya [*Democratic Convergence of Catalonia*] [*Spanish*] (PPE)
CDCAS....... Centrul de Documentare pentru Constructii, Arhitectura, si Sistematizare [*Documentation Center for Constructions, Architecture, and Systematization*] (RO)
CDCB.......... Caisse des Depots et Consignations du Benin [*Depot and Storage Office of Benin*] (AF)
CDCC.......... Caribbean Development and Cooperation Committee [*Port-Of-Spain, Trinidad and Tobago*]
CDCC.......... Comite de Desarrollo y Cooperacion del Caribe [*Committee for Development and Cooperation in the Caribbean*] (LA)
CDCM.......... Centrale Data Communicatie Machine
CDCN.......... Commonwealth Development Corporation Nigeria (MAR)
CDD............ Centralny Dom Dziecka [*Central Children's Home*] [*Department store*] (POL)
CDD............ Classification Decimale de Dewey [*French*] [*A publication*]
CDD............ Committee in Defense of Democracy [*Guyanese*] (LA)
CDD............ Comptoir Dahomeen de Distribution (MAR)
CDDC.......... Central District Development Committee (MAR)
CDDCA....... Comite de Defense des Droits Culturels en Algerie (MAR)
CDDN.......... Comite de Defensa de la Democracia en Nicaragua [*Committee for the Defense of Democracy in Nicaragua*] (LA1)
CDDPH........ Conselho de Defesa dos Direitos da Pessoa Humana [*Human Rights Defense Council*] [*Brazilian*] (LA)
CDDPW....... Centrala Dostaw Drzewnych dla Przemyslu Weglowego [*Central Lumber Supply Office of the Coal Industry*] (POL)
c/de............ Casa De [*Care Of*] [*Spanish*]
CDE............ Centro de Desarrollo de la Educacion (MAR)
CDE............ Centrul de Documentare Energetica [*Center for Energy Documentation*] (RO)
CDE............ Comissao Democratica Eleitoral [*Democratic Electoral Committee*] [*Portuguese*] (PPE)
CDE............ Comitetul Democratic Evreiesc [*Jewish Democratic Committee*] (RO)
CDE............ Compagnie Dolisienne d'Entreprises (MAR)
CDE............ Congo Diesel Electric (MAR)
CDE............ Conselho de Desenvolvimento Economico [*Economic Development Council*] [*Brazilian*] (LA)
CDE............ Conselho de Desenvolvimento do Estado [*Brazilian*]
CDE............ Consortium d'Entreprises (MAR)
CDE............ Croix des Evades [*Belgian military decoration*]
CDEA.......... Centro de Dinamizacao e Esclarecimento da Armada [*Navy Dynamization and Enlightenment Center*] [*Portuguese*] (WER)
CDEA.......... Comite Deportivo de los Ejercitos Amigos [*Friendly Armies Sports Committee*] [*Cuban*] (LA)
CDEI........... Club des Exportateurs Ivoiriens (MAR)
CDEN.......... Caisse de Developpement de l'Elevage du Nord (MAR)
CDEPS........ Centre Departemental d'Education Populaire et Sportive (MAR)
CDF............ Caribbean Development Facility (LA)
CDF............ Centralni Devisni Fond [*Central Foreign Exchange Fund*] (YU)
CDF............ Community Development Foundation, Inc. (MAR)
CDFC.......... Commonwealth Development Finance Company Ltd. (MAR)
CDG............ Caisse de Depot et de Gestion [*Moroccan*] (MAR)
CDG............ Cellulose du Gabon (MAR)
CDG............ Centres Departmentaux de Gestion (MAR)
CDG............ Croix de Guerre [*French military decoration*]
CDI............. Centro de Desarrollo Infantil [*Child Development Center*] [*Nicaraguan*] (LA1)
CDI............. Conselho de Desenvolvimento Industrial [*Industrial Development Council*] [*Brazilian*] (LA)
CDICP......... Centrul de Documentare al Industriei Chimice si Petroliere [*Documentation Center for the Chemical and Petroleum Industry*] (RO)
CDIE........... Centre de Documentation, d'Etudes, et d'Information [*Documentation, Studies, and Information Center*] [*Algerian*] (AF)
CDIL........... Centrul de Documentare pentru Industria Lemnului [*Documentation Center for the Wood Industry*] (RO)
CDIN........... Comite pour la Defense des Interets Nationaux [*Committee for the Defense of National Interests*] [*Use CDNI*] [*Replaced by NMDF*] [*Laotian*] (CL)
CDJ............ Comandos 18 de Julio [*18 July Commandos*] [*Spanish*] (WER)
CDJA.......... Centralni dom Jugoslovenske Armije [*Central House of the Yugoslav Army*] (YU)
CDJA.......... Circulos Doctrinales Jose Antonio [*Jose Antonio Doctrinal Circles*] [*Spanish*] (WER)
CDK............ Centralny Dom Ksiazki [*Central Publishing House*] (POL)
CDK............ Centralny Dom Kultury [*Central House of Culture*] (POL)
CdL............ Camera del Lavoro [*Chamber of Labor*] [*Italian*] (WER)
CDL............ Comissao para a Defesa de Liberdade [*Committee for Defense of Liberty*] [*Portuguese*] (WER)
CDLDM....... Comite de Defense des Libertes Democratiques au Mali [*Committee for the Defense of Democratic Liberties in Mali*] (PD)
CDLP.......... Centre de Diffusion du Livre et de la Presse [*Center for Book and Press Dissemination*] [*French*] (WER)
CDM............ Centralny Dom Mlodziezy [*Central Youth House*] (POL)
CDM............ Centro Democratico de Macau [*Macao Democratic Center*] (PPW)
CDM............ Centrul de Documentare Medicala [*Medical Documentation Center*] (RO)
CDM............ Consolidated Diamond Mines (Proprietary) Ltd. (AF)
CDM............ Convergencia Democrata de Mocambique [*Democratic Convergence of Mozambique*] (AF)
CDM............ Corps Dokter Militer [*Army Medical Corps*] (IN)
CDMB.......... Corporacion de Defensa de la Meseta de Bucaramanga (COL)
cdn.............. Ciag Dalszy Nastapi [*To Be Continued*] [*Polish*]
CDN............ Comitato di Difesa Nazionale [*National Defense Committee*] [*Italian*] (WER)
CDN............ Commission de Defense Nationale (MAR)
CDNI........... Committee for the Defense of National Interests [*Replaced by NMDF*] [*Laotian*] (CL)
CDOS.......... Conseils Departementaux Olympiques et Sportifs (MAR)
CDP............ Centre pour Democratie et Progres [*Center for Democracy and Progress*] [*Later, Center of Social Democrats*] [*French*] (PPE)
CDP............ Christian Democratic Party [*Namibian*] (AF)
CDP............ Christian Democratic Party [*Jamaican*] (LA1)
CDP............ Club Democratie et Progres [*Democracy and Progress Club*] [*Senegalese*] (AF)
CDP............ Compagnie Camerounaise de Depots Petroliers (MAR)
CDP............ Conselho de Desenvolvimento Politico [*Political Development Council*] [*Brazilian*] (LA)

CDPN .... Centrul de Documentare si Publicatii Nucleare [*Center for Nuclear Documentation and Publications*] (RO)
CDPNRH ..... Centar za Naucnu i Tehnicku Dokumentaciju i Produktivnost Narodna Republika Hrvatska [*Center for Scientific and Technical Documentation and Productivity of Croatia*] (YU)
CDPP .... Centrala de Desfacere a Produselor Petroliere [*Central for the Sale of Petroleum Products*] (RO)
CDPT .... Centrul de Documentare si Publicatii Tehnice [*Center for Technical Publications and Documentation*] (RO)
CDPT .... Conseil de Defense du Pacte de Tripoli [*North African*] (MAR)
CDR .... Comitato per la Difesa della Repubblica [*Committee for the Defense of the Republic*] [*Sanmarinese*] (PPW)
CDR .... Comite d'Action pour la Defense de la Republique [*Action Committee for the Defense of the Republic*] [*French*] (WER)
CDR .... Comite de Defensa de la Revolucion [*Committee for the Defense of the Revolution*] [*Cuban*] (LA)
CDR .... Comite de Defense de la Revolution [*Committee for the Defense of the Revolution*] [*Beninese*] (AF)
CDR .... Comite de Defense de la Revolution [*Committee for the Defense of the Revolution*] [*Congolese*] (AF)
CDR .... Comite Directivo Regional [*Regional Directive Committee*] [*Nicaraguan*] (LA1)
CDR .... Comites para la Defensa de la Revolucion [*Committees for the Defense of the Revolution*] [*Peruvian*] (LA)
CDR .... Comites para a Defesa da Revolucao [*Committees for the Defense of the Revolution*] [*Portuguese*] (WER)
CDR .... Commission des Reparations [*Reparation Commission*]
CDR .... Conseil Democratique Revolutionnaire [*Democratic Revolutionary Council*] [*Chadian*] (PD)
CDRC .... Curriculum Development and Research Centre (MAR)
CDRI .... Central Drug Research Institute [*Indian*]
CDRN .... Comite de Defense de la Race Negre (MAR)
CDRO .... Comite de Desarrollo del Oriente [*Committee for the Development of Eastern Peru*] (LA)
CDS .... Central Department of Statistics [*Saudi*] (ME)
CDS .... Centre des Democrates Sociaux [*Center of Social Democrats*] [*French*] (PPW)
CDS .... Centro Democratico y Social [*Democratic and Social Center*] [*Spanish*] (PPE)
CDS .... Chief of Defence Staff (MAR)
CDS .... Comite de Defensa Sandinista [*Sandinist Defense Committee*] [*Nicaraguan*] (LA)
CDS .... Comite de Defense et de Securite [*Committee for Defense and Security*] [*Chadian*] (AF)
CDS .... Community Development Service (MAR)
CDS .... Conseil de Defense et de Securite (MAR)
CDS .... Conserveries du Senegal (MAR)
CDS .... Partido do Centro Democratico Social [*Party of the Social Democratic Center*] [*Portuguese*] (PPE)
CDSS .... Comision de Deportes de la Seccion Sindical [*Local Union Sports Committee*] [*Cuban*] (LA)
CDSSU .... Comites Departementaux du Sport Scolaire et Universitaire (MAR)
CDT .... Centralna Dyrekcja Teatrow [*Central Administration of Theatres*] (POL)
CDT .... Centralny Dom Towarowy [*Central Department Store*] (POL)
CDT .... Centrul de Documentatie Tehnica [*Center for Technical Documentation*] (RO)
CDT .... Comites de Defensa de los Trabajadores [*Committees for the Defense of Workers*] [*Nicaraguan*] (LA1)
Cdt .... Commandant [*Commander*] [*Military*] [*French*] (MTD)
CDT .... Confederation Democratique du Travail [*Democratic Labor Confederation*] [*Moroccan*] (AF)
CDTL .... Centralny Dom Teatrow Ludowych [*Central House of People's Theaters*] (POL)
CDTL .... Centralny Dom Tworczosci Ludowej [*Central House of People's Art*] (POL)
CDTN .... Centro de Desenvolvimento de Tecnologia Nuclear [*Nuclear Technology Development Center*] [*Brazilian*] (LA)
CDTOF .... Centralna Dyrekcja Teatrow, Oper, i Filharmonii [*Central Administration of Theares, Opera Houses, and Philharmonic Orchestras*] (POL)
CDU .... Christelijk-Democratische Unie [*Christian Democratic Union*] [*Dutch*] (PPE)
CDU .... Christlich-Demokratische Union [*Christian Democratic Union*] [*West German*] (PPW)
CDU .... Christlich-Demokratische Union Deutschlands [*Christian Democratic Union of Germany*] [*East German*] (PPW)
CDU .... Classification Decimale Universelle
CDU .... Cocoa Development Unit (MAR)
CDU .... Convergencia Democratica en Uruguay [*Democratic Convergence in Uruguay*] (PD)
CDU/CSU ... Christlich Demokratische Union/Christlich Soziale Union [*Christian Democratic Union/Christian Social Union*] [*West German*] (PPE)
CDV .... Compagnie Delmas Vieljeux (MAR)
CDVM .... Centrale Data Verwerkende Machine
CDW .... Colonial Development and Welfare (MAR)
CDWA .... Colonial Development and Welfare Act (MAR)
CDZ .... Ceskoslovenske Drevarske Zavody, Narodni Podnik [*Czechoslovak Lumber Industries, National Enterprise*] (CZ)
CE .... Centar Eksplosije [*Center of Explosion*] (YU)
CE .... Comercio Exterior, Mexico (MAR)
CE .... Comite Executive [*Executive Committee*] [*Malagasy*] (AF)
CE .... Communaute Europeenne [*European Community*] [*Use EC*] (AF)
CE .... Communidades Europeas [*European Communities*] [*Use EC*] (LA)
CE .... Complexe d'Emballages [*Algerian*] (MAR)
CE .... Cours Elementaire [*North African*] (MAR)
CE- .... Electronic Frequency Counter (RU)
CEA .... Cahiers d'Etudes Africaines [*Paris*] [*A publication*] (MAR)
CEA .... Centres d'Enseignement Agricole [*Algerian*] (MAR)
CEA .... Centro de Estudios y Accion [*Action and Studies Center*] [*Argentine*] (LA1)
CEA .... Centro de Estudios Agrarios [*Agrarian Studies Center*] [*Chilean*] (LA)
CEA .... College d'Enseignement Agricole [*North African*] (MAR)
CEA .... Commissariat a l'Energie Atomique [*Atomic Energy Commission*] [*Use AEC*] [*French*] (WER)
CEA .... Commission Economique (des Nations Unies) pour l'Afrique [*(United Nations) Economic Commission for Africa*] [*Use ECA*] (AF)
CEA .... Commonwealth Education Association (MAR)
CEA .... Communaute Est-Africain [*East African Community*] [*Use EAC*] (AF)
CEA .... Compagnie d'Exploitation Automobile (MAR)
CEA .... Compania Ecuatoriana de Aviacion [*Ecuadorean Aviation Company*] (LA)
CEA .... Confederacion de Educadores Americanos [*Confederation of Latin American Educators*] (LA)
CEA .... Consejo Empresario Argentino [*Argentine Business Council*] (LA1)
CEA .... Consejo Estatal de Azucar [*State Sugar Council*] [*Formerly, Dominican Sugar Corp.*] [*Dominican Republic*] (LA)
CEA .... Consultores de Empresas Asociados [*Bogota*] (COL)
CEAA .... West Africa Economic Community (MAR)
CEAC .... Colonial Economic Advisory Committee (MAR)
CEAC .... Compagnie Euro-Africaine de Commerce (MAR)
CEAC .... Compagnie d'Exploitation Automobile au Cameroun (MAR)
CEAC .... Compagnie d'Exploitation d'Automobile et de Camions (MAR)
CEAE .... Circulo Espanol de Amigos de Europa [*Spanish Circle of Friends of Europe*] (WER)
CEAEO .... Commission Economique pour l'Asie et l'Extreme-Orient [*Economic Commission for Asia and the Far East*] [*Use ECAFE*] (CL)
CEAEX .... Comite Empresarial de Apoio as Exportacoes [*Export Promotion Business Committee*] [*Brazilian*] (LA1)
CEAF .... Publications du Comite d'Etudes Historiques et Scientifiques de l'Afrique Occidentale Francaise (MAR)
CEAGESP ... Companhia de Entrepostos e Armazens Gerais do Estado de Sao Paulo [*State of Sao Paulo General Warehouse and Supply Station Company*] [*Brazilian*] (LA)
CEAGRI ...... Conselho Estadual de Agricultura [*Brazilian*]
CEAI .... Centre d'Etude et d'Action Internationales (MAR)
CEAL .... Centro de Estudio de Accion Liberal [*Cali*] (COL)
CEAM .... Centre d'Experiences Aeriennes Militaires [*Military Air-Experimentation Center*] [*French*] (WER)
CEAM .... Certificat d'Etudes d'Administration Municipal [*Certificate in Municipal Administration*] [*French Guiana*] (LA1)
CEAM .... Confederation des Employeurs et Artisans de Mauritanie (MAR)
CEAMP .... Centrale d'Equipement Agricole et de Modernisation du Paysannat (MAR)
CEAMSE ..... Cinturon Ecologico del Area Metropolitana, Sociedad del Estado [*State Ecological Belt of the Metropolitan Area*] [*Argentine*] (LA)
CEAN .... Centre d'Etude d'Afrique Noire [*Center for the Study of Black Africa*] [*French*] (AF)
CEAN .... Centre d'Etudes pour les Applications de l'Energie Nucleaire [*Belgian*]
CEAN .... Centro de Estudios y Afirmaciones Nacionales [*National Reaffirmation and Studies Center*] [*Argentine*] (LA)
CEAO .... Communaute Economique de l'Afrique de l'Ouest [*West African Economic Community*] (AF)
CEAO .... Confederation des Etudiants d'Afrique Occidentale [*West African Students Confederation*] [*Use WASC*] (AF)
CEAP .... Certificat Elementaire d'Aptitude Pedagogique (MAR)
CEAP .... Comite d'Entente et d'Action Politique [*Committee for Understanding and Political Action*]
CEAP .... Comite d'Etat d'Administration de la Province [*State Committee for Province Administration*] [*Beninese*] (AF)
CEAS .... Cukurova Elektrik Anonim Sirketi [*Cukurova Electric (Power) Corporation*] (TU)
CEASA .... Centro Estadual de Abastecimento Sociedade Anonima [*State Supplies Center, Incorporated*] [*Brazilian*] (LA)
CEAT .... Cycle d'Enseignement d'Agriculture Tropicale (MAR)

CEATM .... Comite Estatal de Abastecimiento Tecnico-Material [*State Committee for Technical and Material Supply*] [*Cuban*] (LA)
Ceaux .... Faisceaux [*Pile (of arms)*] [*Used in commands*] [*French*] (MTD)
CEAV .... Centro de Ensino Audio-Visual (MAR)
CEAVG .... Comite d'Entr'aide et d'Assistance des Victimes de Guerre [*Committee for Welfare and Relief to War Victims*] [*Cambodian*] (CL)
CEB .... Central Electricity Board [*Mauritian*] (AF)
CEB .... Comite Electrotechnique Belge
CEB .... Communaute Electrique du Benin (MAR)
CEB .... Compagnie Equatoriale des Bois (MAR)
CEB .... Comunitatea Evreieasca din Bucuresti [*Bucharest Jewish Community*] (RO)
CEB .... Conferencia Episcopal Boliviana [*Bolivian Episcopal Conference*] (LA1)
CEB .... Construction Engineers and Builders (MAR)
CEBAC .... Comision Economica Brasileira-Argentina de Comercio [*Argentine-Brazilian Economic Commission on Trade*] (LA)
CEBAC .... Comissao Especial Brasileira-Argentina de Coordenacao [*Special Brazilian-Argentine Coordination Commission*] (LA)
CEBE .... Compagnie d'Exploitation des Bois Exotiques (MAR)
CEBEC .... Conseil des Eglises Baptiste et Evangelique du Cameroun (MAR)
CEBES .... Centro Boliviano de Estudios Sociales [*Bolivian Social Studies Center*] (LA)
CEBEVITO ... Laduree & Cie., Entreprise de Beton Vibre Togolais (MAR)
CEBI .... Comite Europeen des Bureaux d'Ingenerie (MAR)
Cebiloz .... Centralne Biuro Lozysk Tocznych "Cebiloz" [*Central Ball Bearings Office "Cebiloz"*] (POL)
CEBKN .... Compagnie d'Exploitation des Bois du Kouilou Niari (MAR)
CEBLANCO ... Cemento Blanco de Colombia SA [*Puerto Berrio*] (COL)
CEBRAP ...... Centro Brasileiro de Analise e Planejamento [*Brazilian Analysis and Planning Center*] (LA)
CEBs .... Comunidades Eclesiasticas de Base [*Ecclesiastic Base Communities*] [*Brazilian*] (LA1)
CEBTP .... Centre Experimental de Recherches et d'Etudes du Batiment et des Travaux Publics [*Algerian*] (MAR)
CEBV .... Communaute Economique du Betail et de la Viande [*Economic Community for Livestock and Meat*] (AF)
CEBWU .... Central Electricity Board Workers Union [*Mauritian*] (AF)
CEC .... Caribbean Employers Conference (LA1)
CEC .... Case de Economii si Consemnatiuni [*Savings and Loan Bank*] (RO)
CEC .... Centrale Examen Commissie [*GO*] [*'s-Gravenhage*]
CEC .... Centre Extra-Coutumier (MAR)
CEC .... Centro de Estudios Colombianos [*Colombian Studies Center*] (LA)
CEC .... China-Export-Corporation [*China Export Corporation*] (EG)
CEC .... Circulo Estudiantil de Comercio [*Business Students Club*] [*Panamanian*] (LA)
CEC .... Commonwealth Economic Committee (MAR)
CEC .... Commonwealth Education Cooperation (MAR)
CEC .... Commonwealth Engineers Council (EA)
CEC .... Consiglio Economica Corporativa (MAR)
CECA .... Carbonisation et Charbons Actifs (MAR)
CECA .... Centro de Estudios Catolicos Argentinos [*Argentine Catholic Studies Center*] (LA)
CECA .... Communaute Europeenne du Charbon et de l'Acier [*European Coal and Steel Community*] [*French*]
CECA .... Compagnie d'Exploitations de Carriere (MAR)
CECA .... Compagnie d'Exploitations Commerciales Africaines (MAR)
CECA .... Comunidad Europea del Carbon y del Acero [*European Coal and Steel Community*] [*Use ECSC*] (LA)
CECA .... Comunita Europea del Carbone e dell'Acciaio [*European Coal and Steel Community*] [*Use ECSC*] [*Italian*] (WER)
CECACI ...... Compagnie d'Explorations Commerciales et Automobiles en Cote-d'Ivoire (MAR)
CECAFA ..... Confederation of East and Central African Football Associations (MAR)
CECA-GADIS ... Compagnie d'Exploitations Commerciales Africaines - Societe Gabonaise de Distribution (MAR)
CECALGERIE ... Carbonisation et Charbon Actif d'Algerie (MAR)
CECARA ..... Centro de Capacitacion en Reforma Agraria [*Agrarian Reform Training Center*] [*Dominican Republic*] (LA1)
CECAS .... Conference of East and Central African States (MAR)
CECAT .... Committee for the Eastern Central Atlantic (MAR)
CECAUF ..... Comptoir d'Echanges Commerciaux avec l'Union Francaise (MAR)
CECC .... Compagnie d'Elevage et de Cultures du Cameroun (MAR)
CECDV .... Centro de Estudio y Control del Desarrollo de la Vivienda [*Housing Development Study and Control Center*] [*Cuban*] (LA)
CECE .... Comite Estatal de Colaboracion Economica [*State Committee for Economic Cooperation*] [*Cuban*] (LA)
CECHA .... Confederacion de Entidades de Comercio de Hidrocarburos y Afines [*Confederation of Retailers of Hydrocarbons and Related Products*] [*Argentine*] (LA)
CECI .... Centre Europeen de Cooperation Internationale (MAR)
CECLA .... Comision Especial de Coordinacion Latinoamericana [*Special Latin American Coordinating Commission*] (LA)
CECMA .... Compagnie pour l'Exploitation de Centraux Mecanographiques en Afrique (MAR)
CECO .... Commission d'Enquete pour le Crime Organise [*Organized Crime Investigating Commission*] [*Canadian, French*] (WER)
CECO .... Coordinadora de Euzkadi de Comisiones Obreras [*Basque Coordinating Staff of Workers Commissions*] [*Spanish*] (WER)
CECOAAP ... Central de Cooperativas Agrarias de Produccion Azucarera del Peru [*Peruvian Central of Agrarian Sugar Production Cooperatives*] (LA)
CECOF .... Cabinet d'Entreprise Comptable et Fiscale (MAR)
CECOJEF .... Cabinet d'Etudes Comptables, Juridiques, et Fiscales (MAR)
CECOMA .... Centre Commercial du Maroc Alimentation (MAR)
CECOME .... Centro par le Cooperazione Mediterranea (MAR)
CECON .... Comision Especial de Consulta y Negociacion [*Special Commission for Consultation and Negotiation*] (LA)
CECONA ..... Centrala de Contractari Achizitii [*Central for Contract Purchases*] (RO)
CECONDEVI ... Centro de Estudio y Control del Desarrollo de la Vivienda [*Center for the Study and Control of Housing Development*] [*Cuban*] (LA)
CECOPANE ... Centre de Commercialisation des Produits Agricoles du Nord-Est [*Marketing Center for Agricultural Products of the Northeast*] [*Zairian*] (AF)
CECORA ..... Central de Cooperativas de la Reforma Agraria [*Agrarian Reform Cooperatives Headquarters*] [*Colombian*] (LA)
CECOT .... Centro de Estudos e Consultas Tecnicas Lda. (MAR)
CECOTRET ... Centre de Cooperation Technique et de Recherche de Suisse (MAR)
CECP .... Club Egyptien de Chasse et de Peche (MAR)
CECP .... European Communist Parties (WER)
CECSA .... Compania de Electronica y Comunicaciones, Sociedad Anonima [*Spanish*]
CECSFM ..... Commission d'Enquete et de Controle de la Situation Financiere et Materielle [*Commission for Investigation and Control of the Financial and Material Situation*] [*Chadian*] (AF)
CECT .... Comite Estatal de la Ciencia y Tecnologia [*State Committee for Science and Technology*] [*Cuban*] (LA)
CECTAL ...... Centro para a Aplicacao da Ciencia e da Tecnologia ao Desenvolvimento da America Latina [*Center for the Application of Science and Technology to the Development of Latin America*] [*Brazilian*] (LA)
CED .... Centro de Esploro kaj Dokumentado pri la Monda Lingvo-Problemo [*Center for Research and Documentation on International Language Problems*] (EA)
CED .... Centro de Estudiantes de Derecho [*Law Students Center*] [*Panamanian*] (LA)
CED .... Communaute Europeenne de Defense [*European Defense Community*] [*French*]
CED .... Comunita Europea di Difesa [*European Defense Community*] [*Use EDC*] [*Italian*] (WER)
CED .... Corporation for Economic Development [*South African*] (AF)
CEDA .... Caisse d'Equipement pour le Developpement de l'Algerie [*Equipment Fund for the Development of Algeria*] (AF)
CEDA .... Centre for Economic Development and Administration [*Katmandu, Nepal*]
CEDA .... Centre d'Edition et de Diffusion Africaines (MAR)
CEDA .... Centre d'Etudes et de Developpement du Cafe Arabusta (MAR)
CEDA .... Centro de Desarrollo Agropecuario [*Center for Agricultural Development*] [*Salvadoran*] (LA1)
CEDA .... Confederacion Espanola de Derechas Autonomas [*Spanish Confederation of Autonomous Rightist Forces*] (PPE)
CEDAC .... Commissao de Estudos de Desenvolvimento da Aviacao Civil [*Study Commission for Civil Aviation Development*] (AF)
CEDADE ..... Circulo Espanol de Amigos de Europa [*Spanish Circle of Friends of Europe*] (PD)
CEDADEC ... Centre National de Developpement des Entreprises Cooperatives (MAR)
CEDAF .... Centre d'Etude et de Documentation Africaine (MAR)
CEDAG .... Companhia Estadual de Aguas da Guanabara [*Guanabara State Water Company*] [*Brazilian*] (LA)
CEDAOM .... Centre d'Etudes et de Documentation sur l'Afrique et l'Outre-Mer [*Studies and Documentation Center for Africa and Overseas Areas*] [*French*] (AF)
CEDATOS ... Compania Ecuatoriana de Datos [*Ecuadorean Data Company*] (LA)
CEDCA .... Centre d'Etudes de Droit Compare Africain (MAR)
CEDCA .... Centro de Estudios Dirigidos de Ciencias Agropecuarias [*Supervised Studies Center for Agricultural and Animal Sciences*] [*Cuban*] (LA)
CEDE .... Centro de Estudio sobre Desarrollo Economico, Universidad de los Andes [*Bogota*] (COL)
CEDEAO ..... Communaute Economique des Etats de l'Afrique de l'Ouest [*Economic Community of West African States*] [*Use ECOWAS*] (AF)
CEDEC .... Coordenacao da Defesa Civil [*Civil Defense Administration*] [*Brazilian*] (LA)

CEDECAL ... Compania Explotadora de Cal SA [*Guasca-Cundi*] (COL)
CEDED .... Centro de Documentacion Educativa. Universidad de Antioquia [*Medellin*] (COL)
CEDEGE ..... Comision de Estudios para el Desarrollo de la Cuenca de Guayas [*Study Commission for the Development of the Guayas Basin*] [*Ecuadorean*] (LA)
CEDEICO .... Centro de Especializacion Tecnica e Intensiva de Contabilidad [*Bogota*] (COL)
CEDELA ...... Cercle pour le Developpement Economique et Social de la Prefecture de Lakota (MAR)
CEDELCA ... Centrales Electricas del Cauca [*Electric Power Plants of Cauca*] [*Colombian*] (LA)
CEDEM .... Centro de Estudios Demograficos [*Center for Demographic Studies*] [*Cuban*] (LA)
CEDEN .... Comite Evangelico de Desarrollo y Emergencia Nacional [*Evangelical Committee of Development and National Emergency*] [*Honduran*] (LA1)
CEDEPAL .... Colombiana de Papeles Limitada [*Cali*] (COL)
CEDES .... Centros de Estudios para una Democracia Social [*Study Centers for a Social Democracy*] [*Argentine*] (LA)
CEDES .... Corps Europeen de Developpement Economique et Social [*European Corps for Economic and Social Development*] [*Belgian*] (AF)
CEDESA ..... Centre de Documentation Economique et Sociale Africaine (MAR)
CEDETIM .... Centre Socialiste de Documentation et d'Etudes sur les Problemes du Tiers-Monde [*North African*] (MAR)
CEDETRAN ... Compania Especial de Transportes SA [*Bogota*] (COL)
CEDEV .... Centre d'Etudes des Problemes des Pays en Developpement [*Center for the Study of Problems of Developing Countries*] [*Belgian*] (AF)
CEDEX .... Courrier d'Entreprise a Distribution Exceptionnelle [*French*]
CEDI .... Centro Ecumenico de Documentacao e Informacao [*Ecumenical Center of Documents and Information*] [*Brazilian*] (LA)
CEDIC .... Centro de Desarrollo Integral Canero [*Center for the Integral Development of the Sugar Industry*] (LA)
CEDIC .... Centro Ecuatoriano de Organizaciones Clasistas [*Ecuadorean Center for Class Organizations*] (LA)
CEDICON .... Centro de Diseno y Contruccion Ltda. [*Cali*] (COL)
CEDIES .... Socio-Economic Research and Information Center [*Malagasy*] (AF)
CEDIM .... Compania Explotadora de Industrias Metalicas Ltda. [*Bogota*] (COL)
CEDIMEX .... Societe Centrafricaine de Distribution-Importation-Exportation (MAR)
CEDIMO ...... Centro Nacional de Documentacao e Informacao de Mocambique (MAR)
CEDIMOM ... Centre Europeen pour le Developpement Industriel et la Mise en Valeur de l'Outre-Mer [*European Center for Overseas Industrialization and Development*] (AF)
CEDIN .... Centre de Documentation et d'Information du Commerce Exterieur (MAR)
CEDIT .... Centro Didattico Telefonico [*Telephone Teaching Center*] [*Italian*]
CEDITEX ..... Centrale de Diffusion de Textile (MAR)
CEDLA .... Centre d'Etudes et de Documentation Legislatives Africaines [*African Legislative Studies and Documentation Center*] (AF)
CEDO .... Centre for Educational Development Overseas (MAR)
CEDOC .... Central Ecuatoriana de Organizaciones Clasistas [*Ecuadorean Central of Classist Organizations*] (LA)
CEDOC .... Centre de Documentation [*Documentation Center*] [*Gabonese*] (AF)
CEDOC .... Confederacion Ecuatoriana de Obreros Catolicos [*Ecuadorean Confederation of Catholic Workers*] (LA)
Cedok .... Ceskoslovenska Dopravni Kancelar [*Czechoslovak Travel Bureau*] (CZ)
CEDOPEX ... Centro Dominicano de Promocion de Exportaciones [*Dominican Center for Export Development*] (LA)
CEDOR .... Centrul Demografic ONU. Romania [*UN Demographic Center in Romania*] (RO)
CEDRO .... Comite de Desarrollo del Oriente [*Committee on Development of the East*] [*Peruvian*] (LA)
CEE .... Caisses Enregistreuses Electroniques (MAR)
CEE .... Cercle Egyptien d'Escrime et de Tir (MAR)
CEE .... Comite Estatal de Estadisticas [*State Committee for Statistics*] [*Cuban*] (LA)
CEE .... Commission Economique pour l'Europe [*French*]
CEE .... Communaute Economique Europeenne [*European Economic Community*] [*Use EEC*] [*French*]
CEE .... Comunidad Economica Europea [*European Economic Community*] [*Use EEC*] (LA)
CEE .... Comunita Economica Europea [*European Economic Community*] [*Use EEC*] [*Italian*] (WER)
CEE .... Comunitatea Economica Europeana [*European Economic Community*] [*Use EEC*] (RO)
CEE .... Corporacion de Empresas Estatales [*State Enterprise Corporation*] [*See also CORDE*] [*Dominican Republic*] (LA)
CEEA .... Comision Ecuatoriana de Energia Atomica [*Ecuadorean Atomic Energy Commission*] (LA)
CEEA .... Commissione Europea per l'Energia Atomica [*European Atomic Energy Commission*] [*Use EURATOM*] [*Italian*] (WER)
CEEA .... Communaute Europeenne de l'Energie Atomique [*French*]
CEECSN ..... Comissao Especial de Estudo das Condicoes Sociais do Nordeste [*Special Commission for Studies of Social Conditions in the Northeast*] [*Brazilian*] (LA)
CEEE .... Comissao Estadual Energia Electrica [*State Electric Power Commission*] [*Brazilian*] (LA)
CEEG .... Certificat d'Etudes Economiques Generales [*French*]
CEEMA .... Centre d'Experimentation et d'Enseignement du Machinisme Agricole, Division du Machinisme Agricole du Genie Rural [*Malian*]
CEEMAT ..... Centre d'Etudes et d'Experimentation du Machinisme Agricole et Tropicale [*French*]
CEEN .... Centre d'Etude de l'Energie Nucleaire [*Also known as NERC or SCK*] [*Belgian*]
CEEO .... Centro de Estudios Sobre Europa Occidental [*Center for West European Studies*] [*Cuban*] (LA)
CEES .... Centro de Estudios de Estado y Sociedad [*State and Society Studies Center*] [*Argentine*] (LA1)
CEES .... Conferencia Episcopal de El Salvador [*Episcopal Conference of El Salvador*] (LA1)
CEESP .... Centro de Estudios Economicos del Sector Privado [*Private Sector Center for Economic Studies*] [*Mexican*] (LA)
CEESTEM ... Centro de Estudios Economicos y Sociales del Tercer Mundo [*Center for Third World Economic and Social Studies*] [*Mexican*] (LA1)
CEET .... Compagnie Energie Electrique du Togo (MAR)
CEF .... Caixa Economica Federal [*Federal Savings Bank*] [*Brazilian*] (LA)
CEF .... Comite Estatal de Finanzas [*State Committee for Finance*] [*Cuban*] (LA)
CEF .... Consejo Ejecutivo Federal [*Federal Executive Council*] [*Panamanian*] (LA)
CEFA .... Centro Educacional Femenino de Antioquia [*Medellin*] (COL)
CEFA .... Centro de Ensenanza de las Fuerzas Armadas [*Armed Forces Training Center*] [*Dominican Republic*] (LA)
CEFA .... Centro de Estudios de las Fuerzas Armadas [*Armed Forces Studies Center*] [*Salvadoran*] (LA)
CEFA .... Compagnie d'Exploitations Forestieres Africaines (MAR)
CEFAG .... Centre d'Etudes et de Formation Agricole de Gagnoa (MAR)
CEFAM .... Centre de Formation pour l'Administration Municipale a Buea (MAR)
CEFDI .... Compagnie d'Exploitation Forestiere de Divo (MAR)
CEFEB .... Centre d'Etudes Financieres, Economiques, et Bancaires [*Financial, Economic, and Banking Study Center*] [*French*] (AF)
CEFEB .... Controle des Etudes de Fin d'Enseignement de Base [*Basic Education End Studies Control*] [*Beninese*] (AF)
CEFEM .... Compagnie Francaise du Methane (MAR)
CEFEN .... Certificat de Fin d'Etudes Normales [*Certificate of Completion of Normal School*] [*French*] (WER)
CEFHB .... Centre d'Etudes Economiques, Financieres, et Bancaires [*Economic, Financial, and Banking Studies Center*] [*French*] (CL)
CEFI .... Comision Interministerial de Exposiciones y Ferias Internacionales [*Interministerial Commission for International Fairs and Expositions*] [*Uruguayan*] (LA)
Cefis .... Ceskoslovenska Filmova Spolecnost [*Czechoslovak Motion Picture Company*] (CZ)
CEFOE .... Curso Especial de Formacion de Oficiales del Ejercito [*Special Army Officer Training Course*] [*Venezuelan*] (LA)
CEFRACOR ... Centre Francais de la Corrosion
CEFRI .... Centrais de Estocagem Frigorificada [*Cold Storage Plants*] [*Brazilian*] (LA)
CEFS .... Comite Europeen des Fabricants de Sucre [*European Committee of Sugar Manufacturers*] [*Common Market*]
CEG .... Certificate d'Education Generale [*General Education Certificate*] [*Algerian*] (AF)
CEG .... College d'Enseignement General [*Secondary General Education School*] [*French*] (AF)
CEGB .... Central Electricity Generating Board (MAR)
CEGD .... Centre d'Etudes Geologiques et de Developpement [*Geological and Development Studies Center*] [*Djibouti*] (AF)
CEGEDA ..... Compagnie Generale de Distribution et d'Approvisionnement (MAR)
CEGEDUR ... Compagnie Generale de Duralumin et de Cuivre (MAR)
CEGEPAR ... Compagnie Generale de Participations et d'Entreprises (MAR)
CEGERS ..... Centre Guyanais d'Etudes et de Reflexions sur la Sante [*French Guianese Center for Health Studies and Research*] (LA1)
CEGET .... Centre d'Etudes de Geographie Tropicale (MAR)
CEGET .... Compagnie Gabonaise d'Entreprise (MAR)
CEGEX .... Centre d'Etudes de Gestion et d'Expansion (MAR)
CEGI .... Compagnie d'Etudes Economiques et de Gestion Industrielle (MAR)
CEGIR .... Centre d'Etudes de Gestion d'Information et de Recherches (MAR)
CEGOS .... Commission d'Etudes Generales de l'Organisation Scientifique (MAR)

CEGOS .... Commission Generale d'Organisation Scientifique [*General Commission on Scientific Organization*] [*French*] (WER)
CEGP .... Centro de Estudos da Guine Portuguesa (MAR)
CEGS .... Comptoir d'Electricite Generale du Senegal (MAR)
CEGUI .... Compania Espanola del Golfo de Guinea (MAR)
cegv .... Cegvezeto [*Manager*] (HU)
CEHC .... Comite d'Etudes du Haut-Congo (MAR)
CEHMP .... Centro de Estudios Historicos Militares del Peru [*Peruvian Military History Studies Center*] (LA)
CEHO .... Compagnie Centrafricaine d'Exploitation Hoteliere (MAR)
CEI .... Centre d'Etudes Industrielles du Maghreb (MAR)
CEI .... Chambre d'Etudes Industrielles [*North African*] (MAR)
CEI .... Comisia de Electronica Internationala [*International Electronics Commission*] (RO)
CEI .... Comitato Elettrotechnico Italiano
CEI .... Comite Economique Interministeriel [*Interministerial Economic Committee*] [*Cambodian*] (CL)
CEI .... Commission Electrotechnique Internationale [*International Electrotechnical Commission - IEC*] (EA)
CEI .... Compagnia Edizioni Internazionali SPA
CEI .... Congreso Eucaristico Internacional [*Bogota*] (COL)
CEI .... Constructions et Entreprises Industrielles [*Industrial Construction and Enterprise Company*] [*Belgian*] (WER)
CEI .... Cuerpo del Ejercito Independiente de Pinar Del Rio [*Pinar Del Rio Independent Army Corps*] [*Cuban*] (LA)
CEIA............ Centre Economique Ital-Afrique (MAR)
CEIA............ Centre d'Entr'aide Intellectuelle Africaine (MAR)
CEIA............ Centro Economico Italia Africa [*Italian-African Economic Center*] (AF)
CEIA............ Comunidad de Espanoles con Intereses en Africa (MAR)
CEIB............ Centre d'Exploitation Industrielle du Betail [*Center for the Industrial Exploitation of Livestock*] [*Ivorian*] (AF)
CEIC............ Confederacion de Empleados de Industria y Comercio [*Industrial and Business Employees Confederation*] [*Chilean*] (LA)
CEIE .... Cuerpo de Ejercito Independiente del Este [*Independent Army Corps of the East*] [*Cuban*] (LA)
CEIGA .... Comite de Empresarios Industriales del Grupo Andino [*Committee of Andean Industrialists*] [*Ecuadorean*] (LA)
CEIL .... Combinat pentru Exploatarea si Industrializarea Lemnului [*Combine for the Exploitation and Industrialization of Wood*] (RO)
CEIM .... Centre d'Etudes Industrielles du Maghreb [*North African*] (MAR)
CEIMA......... Centro de Estudios de Investigacion sobre Mercadeo Agropecuario. Universidad JTL [*Bogota*] (COL)
CEIO............ Catholic International Education Office [*See also OIEC*] (EA)
CEIO............ Cuerpo Ejercito Independiente del Oeste [*Independent Army Corps of the West*] [*Cuban*] (LA)
CEIR............ Centre d'Etudes et d'Initiative Revolutionnaire [*Center for Revolutionary Studies and Initiative*] [*French*] (WER)
CEIS............ Centro de Estudios de Ingenieria de Sistemas [*Systems Engineering Study Center*] [*Cuban*] (LA)
CEJG........... Certificat d'Etudes Juridiques Generales [*French*]
CEK............. Cocuk Esirgeme Kurumu [*Child Protection Association*] [*See also TCEK*] (TU)
CEL .... Centre d'Essais des Landes (de Biscarosse) [*Landes Testing Center*] [*French*] (WER)
Cel.............. Colonel [*Colonel*] [*Military*] [*French*] (MTD)
CEL .... Comision Ejecutiva Hidroelectrica del Rio Lempa [*Lempa River Hydroelectric Executive Commission*] [*Salvadoran*] (LA1)
CEL .... Comite Executif de la Lutte [*Executive Struggle Committee*] [*Guinean*] (AF)
CEL .... Conselho Executivo da Luta (MAR)
CELA........... Comision Economica para la America Latina [*Economic Commission for Latin America*] (LA1)
CELADE...... Centro Latinoamericano de Demografia [*Latin American Center on Demography*] [*Santiago, Chile*] (LA)
CELAM........ Conferencia Episcopal Latinoamericana [*Latin American Bishops Conference*] (LA)
CELAM........ Consejo Episcopal Latinoamericano [*Latin American Bishops Council*] (LA)
CELB........... Companhia Electrica do Lobito et Benguela [*Angolan*] (MAR)
CELCAIRO ... Cementos el Cairo SA [*Medellin*] (COL)
CELCIT .... Centro Latinoamericano de Creacion e Investigacion Teatral [*Latin American Center for Theatrical Production and Research*] (LA)
CELCO........ Controles Electricos Colombianos [*Cali*] (COL)
CELEDESCO ... Cooperativa Industrial Lechera de Colombia [*Barranquilla*] (COL)
CELEF......... Centre d'Etude des Litteratures d'Expression Francaise (MAR)
CELEG .... Centre d'Etude des Litteratures d'Expression Graphique
CELEMA ..... Central Lechera de Manizales (COL)
CELG........... Centrais Eletricas de Goias
CELG........... Certificat d'Etudes Litteraires Generales [*French*]
CELHTO...... Centre d'Etude Linguistique par Tradition Orale (MAR)
CELIF .... Centrala de Exploatare a Lucrarilor de Imbunatatiri Funciare [*Central for the Execution of Land Improvement Work*] (RO)
CELLUCAM ... Societe de Cellulose du Cameroun (MAR)
CELLUNAF ... Compagnie Nord Africaine de Cellulose (MAR)
CELNA .... Compania Electrica Nacional Ltda. [*Itagui-Antioquia*] (COL)
CELP........... Centro de Estudios Laborales del Peru [*Labor Study Center of Peru*] (LA)
CELPA .... Centrais Electricas do Para, SA [*Para Electric Powerplants, Inc.*] [*Brazilian*] (LA)
CELPA .... Centro de Experimentacion y Lanzamiento de Proyectiles Autopropulsados [*Rocket Testing and Launching Center*] [*Argentine*] (LA)
CELRA .... Conference of Latin Bishops of Arab Regions (EA)
CELRIA .... Centre des Litteratures Romanes d'Inspiration Africaine (MAR)
CELU........... Confederation of Ethiopian Labor Unions (AF)
CELZA .... Cultures et Elevage du Zaire (MAR)
Cem .... Cemiyeti [*Society, Association*] (TU)
CEM .... Center for Entrepreneurship and Management [*Ethiopian*] (AF)
CEM .... Centre d'Essais de la Mediterranee [*Mediterranean Test Center*] [*French*] (WER)
CEM .... Centres d'Etudes Marxistes [*Centers for Marxist Studies*] [*French*] (WER)
CEM .... Centro Electromecanico [*Bogota*] (COL)
CEM .... Centro de Ensenanza Militar [*Military Training Center*] [*Cuban*] (LA)
CEM .... Chefe do Estado Maior [*Chief of Staff*] [*Portuguese*] (WER)
CEM .... College d'Enseignement Moyen [*College of Intermediate Studies*] [*Algerian*] (AF)
CEM .... Comissao Eleitoral Monarquica [*Monarchy Electoral Committee*] [*Portuguese*] (PPE)
CEM .... Compagnie Electro-Mecanique [*Electromechanical Equipment Company*] [*French*] (WER)
CEM .... Compagnie Electromecanique [*Swiss-German electrical equipment company*]
CEM .... Compagnie Equatoriale des Mines (MAR)
CEM .... Compagnie des Experts Maritimes et en Transports (MAR)
CEM .... Congo Evangelistic Mission (MAR)
CEMA.......... Centrale Marketing-Gesellschaft der Deutschen Agrarwirtschaft [*German Agriculture Central Marketing Association*] [*West German*] (WEN)
CEMA.......... Centres d'Education aux Methodes Actives [*Centers for Training in Methods of Action*] [*French*] (WER)
CEMA.......... Centro de Estudios Macroeconomicos de Argentina [*Macroeconomics Studies Center of Argentina*] (LA1)
CEMA.......... Centros Maternales [*Mothers Centers*] [*Chilean*] (LA)
CEMA.......... Chefe de Estado Maior da Armada [*Navy Chief of Staff*] [*Portuguese*] (WER)
CEMA.......... Consejo de Ayuda Mutua Economica [*Council for Mutual Economic Assistance*] [*Cuban*] (LA)
CEMA.......... Council for Mutual Economic Assistance (LA)
CEMAC .... Comptoir Electro-Mecanique du Maroc (MAR)
CEMACC .... Centro de Matematica Aplicada y Computacion de la Construccion [*Applied Mathematics and Computation Center for Construction*] [*Cuban*] (LA)
CEMACO .... Central Distribuidora de Materiales de Construccion [*Cali*] (COL)
CEMAN .... Centro de Estudios Audiovisuales. Universidad Nacional [*Bogota*] (COL)
CEMAT .... Centro Mesoamericano de Estudios sobre Tecnologia Apropiada [*Guatemalan*]
CEMB.......... Compagnie des Experts Maritimes du Benin (MAR)
CEMBRAL... Compania Elaboradora de Metales Barbosa Limitada [*Bogota*] (COL)
CEMCI......... Compagnie des Experts Maritimes de Cote-d'Ivoire (MAR)
CEMD.......... Compagnie des Experts Maritimes du Dahomey (MAR)
CEME.......... Central de Medicamentos [*Central Enterprise for Medicines*] [*Brazilian*] (LA)
CEME.......... Commisao Estadual de Material Excedente [*State Surplus Materials Commission*] [*Brazilian*] (LA)
CEME.......... Construcora Colombiana de Maquinaria Ltda. [*Medellin*] (COL)
CEMEA .... Centre d'Entrainement aux Methodes d'Education Active (MAR)
CEMEACI.... Centre d'Entrainement aux Methodes d'Education Active de Cote-d'Ivoire (MAR)
CEMEC .... Cementos Ecuatorianos [*Ecuadorean Cement Enterprise*] (LA)
CEMEDOM ... Centre Medical d'Interentreprises d'Outre-Mer (MAR)
CEMENCO ... Liberian Cement Corporation (MAR)
CEMGFA..... Chefe do Estado Maior General das Forcas Armadas [*Armed Forces Chief of Staff*] [*Portuguese*] (WER)
CEMIG .... Central Eletrica de Minas Gerais, SA [*Minas Gerais Electric Power Plant, Inc.*] [*Brazilian*] (LA)
CEMJA........ Centre d'Entrainement des Moniteurs de la Jeunesse d'Algerie (MAR)
CEMLA........ Centro de Estudios Monetarios Latinoamericanos [*Centre for Latin American Monetary Studies*] (EA)
CEMM .... Compagnie des Experts Maritimes de Madagascar (MAR)
CEMN.......... Comite d'Entente des Mouvements Nationaux (MAR)
CEMN.......... Compagnie des Experts Maritimes du Niger (MAR)
CEMPEX ..... Comissao de Emprestimos Externos [*Foreign Loans Commission*] [*Brazilian*] (LA)
CEMPN .... Centre d'Expertise Medicale du Personnel Navigant [*North African*] (MAR)
CEMS.......... Compagnie des Experts Maritimes du Senegal (MAR)
CEMS.......... Constructions Electro-Mecaniques de Sologne [*French*] (MAR)

CEMSA .... Centro de Mejoramiento de Semillas Agamicas [*Agamic Seeds Improvement Center*] [*Cuban*] (LA)
CEMSZOV ... Cementaru- es Mukoipari KTSZ [*Kisipari Termeloszovetkezet*] [*Artisans Cooperative of Cement Products and Artificial Stone Industry*] (HU)
CEMT .... Compagnie des Experts Maritimes du Togo (MAR)
CEMTAS ..... Celik Makina Sanayi ve Ticaret Anonim Sirketi [*Steel Machinery Industry and Trade Corporation*] (TU)
CEMUBAC ... Centre Scientifique et Medical de l'Universite de Bruxelles en Afrique Centrale [*Scientific and Medical Center of the University of Brussels in Central Africa*] [*Belgian*] (AF)
CEN .... Central Electronuclear [*Thermonuclear Power Plant*] [*Cuban*] (LA)
CEN .... Centre d'Etude de l'Energie Nucleaire [*Nuclear Energy Research Center*] [*Belgian*] (WER)
CEN .... Centro Nacionalista [*Nationalist Center*] [*Bolivian*] (PPW)
CEN .... Centro di Studi dell'Energia Nucleare [*Nuclear Energy Research Center*] [*Italian*] (WER)
Cen .... Cenup [*South*] (TU)
CEN .... Comando Estrategico Nacionalista [*Nationalist Strategic Command*] [*Argentine*] (LA)
CEN .... Comision de Energia Nuclear [*National Nuclear Energy Commission*] [*Mexican*] (LA)
CEN .... Comision Estatuaria Nacional [*National Statutes Commission*] [*Peruvian*] (LA)
CEN .... Comite Ejecutivo Nacional [*National Executive Committee (of the Institutional Revolutionary Party)*] [*Mexican*] (LA)
CEN .... Comite Ejecutivo Nacional (de Accion Democratica) [*National Executive Committee (of Democratic Action)*] [*Venezuelan*] (LA)
CEN .... Comite Estatal de Normacion [*State Committee for Standardization*] [*Cuban*] (LA)
CEN .... Commission pour l'Etude des Nuages [*OMI*]
CEN .... Commission Executive Nationale [*National Executive Commission*] [*Algerian*] (AF)
CEN .... Conseil Executif National [*National Executive Committee*] [*Zairian*] (AF)
CEN .... Consejo Nacional de Economia [*National Council on Economy*] [*Venezuelan*] (LA)
CEN .... Consiliul Energetic National [*National Energy Council*] (RO)
CEN .... Corporacion de Empresas Nacionales [*National Business Corporation*] [*Argentine*] (LA)
CENA .... Centre d'Etudes Nord-Africaines (MAR)
CENA .... Centro de Energia Nuclear na Agricultura [*Center for Use of Nuclear Energy in Agriculture*] [*Brazilian*] (LA)
CENACE ..... Cercle National Chretien d'Education [*National Christian Educational Club*] [*Malagasy*] (AF)
CENADEC... Centre National de Developpement des Entreprises Cooperatives (MAR)
CENADI....... Central Nacional de Distribucion [*National Distribution Headquarters*] [*Chilean*] (LA)
CENAFOP ... Centre National de Formation Professionnelle Continuee (MAR)
CENAL .... Comissao Executiva Nacional do Alcool [*National Alcohol Executive Commission*] [*Brazilian*] (LA1)
CENALC ..... Centro Educacional y de Capacitacion Comercial [*Cali*] (COL)
CENAM .... Centre National de l'Artisanat Malagasy [*Malagasy National Handicraft Center*] (AF)
CENAP .... Centre d'Apprentissage Professionnel [*Vocational Apprenticeship Center*] [*Cambodian*] (CL)
CENAP .... Centro Nacional de Productividad [*National Productivity Center*] [*Salvadoran*] (LA)
CENAP .... Corriente Estudiantil Nacionalista Popular [*Popular Nationalist Student Current*] [*Argentine*] (LA)
CENAPEC ... Centre National de Promotion des Entreprises Cooperatives (MAR)
CENAPER ... Centro Nacional de Perfeccionamiento Educativo [*Bogota*] (COL)
CENAPHI .... Centre de Formation Professionnelle pour les Handicapes et Invalides Physiques [*Vocational Training Center for Invalids and the Physically Handicapped*] [*Zairian*] (AF)
CENAPLANF ... Centro Nacional de Planificacion Natural de la Familia [*National Center for Natural Family Planning*] [*Uruguayan*] (LA)
CENARESO ... Centro Nacional de Reeducacion Social [*National Social Reeducation Center*] [*Argentine*] (LA)
CENAT .... Comissao Executiva do Sistema Tiete-Parana [*Tiete-Parana System Executive Commission*] [*Brazilian*] (LA)
CENATRIN ... Centre National de Traitement de l'Information (MAR)
CENAZUCA ... Centrales Azucareros [*Sugar Refineries*] [*Venezuelan*] (LA)
CENC .... Centre d'Etudes Nucleaires de Cadarache [*French*]
CENCAFOR ... Centro de Capacitacion y Experimentacion Forestal [*Training and Forestry Experiment Center*] [*Ecuadorean*] (LA)
CENCIRA .... Centro Nacional de Capacitacion e Investigacion de la Reforma Agraria [*National Center for Agrarian Reform Training and Research*] [*Peruvian*] (LA)
CENCOA..... Central de Cooperativas Agrarias de Occidente [*Cali*] (COL)
CENCOP ..... Centro de Control Pecuario [*Livestock Control Center*] [*Cuban*] (LA)
CENCOS..... Centro Nacional de Communicacion Social [*National Mass Media Center*] [*Mexican*] (LA)
CENDA........ Centro de Desarrollo Agropecuario [*Agricultural Development Center*] [*Dominican Republic*] (LA1)
CENDA........ Centro Nacional de Derechos de Autor [*National Center of Authors Rights*] [*Cuban*] (LA)
CENDEC ..... Centro de Treinamento e Pesquisa para o Desenvolvimento Economico [*Training and Research Center for Economic Development*] [*Brazilian*] (LA)
CENDES ..... Centro de Desarrollo Industrial del Ecuador [*Industrial Development Center of Ecuador*] (LA)
CENDES ..... Centro de Estudios del Desarrollo [*Development Studies Center*] [*Venezuelan*] (LA)
CENDES ..... Centro de Estudios para el Desarrollo Social de Colombia [*Center of Studies for the Social Development of Colombia*] (LA)
CENDIP....... Centro Nacional de Documentacion e Informacion Pedagogica [*Bogota*] (COL)
CENDIT....... Centre for Development of Industrial Technology [*New Delhi, India*]
CENDOPU... Centro de Documentacion y Publicaciones. Universidad del Valle [*Cali*] (COL)
CENE .... Centro de Energia Nuclear del Ecuador [*Nuclear Energy Center of Ecuador*] (LA)
CENED........ Centro Nacional de Educadores [*National Educators Center*] [*Colombian*] (LA)
CENEEMA .. Centre National d'Etude et d'Experimentation des Machines Agricoles (MAR)
CENET .... Centro Nacional de Electronica y Telecomunicaciones [*National Electronics and Telecommunications Center*] [*Chilean*] (LA)
CENFOCAT ... Centre de Formation des Cadres Techniques [*Technical Employee Training Center*] [*Since 1972, CENFOCATAP*] [*Cambodian*] (CL)
CENFOCATAP ... Centre pour la Formation des Cadres Techniques et pour l'Accroissement de la Productivite [*Center for Technical Employee Training and for Increased Productivity*] [*Before 1972, CENFOCAT*] [*Cambodian*] (CL)
CENG .... Centre d'Etudes Nucleaires de Grenoble [*Grenoble Nuclear Research Center*] [*French*] (WER)
CENIC .... Centro Nacional de Investigaciones Cientificas [*National Scientific Research Center*] [*Cuban*] (LA)
CENICANA ... Centro de Investigaciones de la Cana [*Center for Sugarcane Research*] [*Colombian*] (LA1)
CENIMAR.... Centro de Informacoes da Marinha [*Naval Intelligence Center*] [*Brazilian*] (LA)
CENIP .... Centro Nacional de Incremento a la Produccion [*National Central of Production Increase*] [*Peruvian*] (LA)
CENIT .... Centro Nicaraguense de Informacion Tecnologica [*Nicaraguan Center for Technological Information*] (LA)
CENITAL..... Centro Nacional de Inseminacion Artificial [*Bogota*] (COL)
CENOPROM ... Centres Operationnels de Programmation Multinationale [*Multinational Programing Operational Centers*] (AF)
Cenosid ...... Genocide (TU)
CENPES...... Centro de Pesquisas e Desenvolvimento [*Research and Development Center*] [*Brazilian*] (LA)
CENPRO ..... Centro Nacional de Formacion y Promocion [*Bogota*] (COL)
CENPRO ..... Centro de Promocion de Inversiones y Exportaciones [*Investment and Exports Promotion Center*] [*Costa Rican*] (LA)
CENRADERU ... Centre National de la Recherche Appliquee au Developpement Rural (MAR)
CENS .... Centre d'Etudes Nucleaires de Saclay [*French*]
CENSA........ Centro Nacional de Salud Animal [*National Animal Health Center*] [*Cuban*] (LA)
CENSAV ..... Centro de Sanidad Vegetal [*Plant Health Center*] [*Cuban*] (LA)
CENSERI..... Centro de Servicios Rurales Integrados [*Center for Integrated Rural Services*] [*Dominican Republic*] (LA1)
CENSOCULCO ... Centro Social y Cultural de Comercio (COL)
CENSUPE... Centro Superior de Estudios Penales [*Barranquilla*] (COL)
cent .... Centime [*Monetary unit*] [*French*]
CENT........... Centre Nucleaire Trico [*Trico Nuclear Center*] [*Zairian*] (AF)
cent .... Centum [*A Hundred*] [*Latin*] (GPO)
CENTA .... Centro Nacional de Tecnologia [*National Center for Technology*] [*Salvadoran*] (LA1)
CENTI .... Centre pour le Traitement de l'Information
CENTO........ Central Treaty Organization (MAR)
centr .... Centralny [*Central*] (POL)
CENTRABOIS ... Societe Centrafricaine de Travaux du Bois (MAR)
CENTRACO ... Societe Centrafricaine pour le Commerce et l'Industrie (MAR)
CENTRACUIRS ... Societe Centrafricaine des Cuirs (MAR)
CENTRAG... Societe Centrafricano-Arabe d'Agriculture (MAR)
CENTRA-HYDRO ... Societe Centrafricaine des Hydrocarbures (MAR)
CENTRALCO ... Central Colombiana Autoagricola Ltda. [*Bogota*] (COL)
CENTRAMINES ... Compagnie Centrafricaine des Mines (MAR)
CENTRANSPORT ... Societe Centrafricaine-Arabe de Transports (MAR)
CentrbC...... Centralna Biblioteka u Cetinju [*Central Library in Cetinje*] [*Montenegro*] (YU)
CENTRIFAN ... Centre d'Institut Francais d'Afrique Noire (MAR)
CENTROCOOP ... Uniunea Centrala a Cooperativelor de Consum [*Central Union of Consumer Cooperatives*] (RO)
Centrofarm ... Centrala Handlu Farmaceutycznego [*Pharmaceutical Sales Center*] (POL)

CENTROFARM ... Oficiul Central Farmaceutic [*Central Pharmaceutical Office*] (RO)
CENTROKOMISE ... Podnik Zahranicniho Obchodu pro Dovoz a Vyvoz Potravin [*Foreign Trade Enterprise for the Import and Export of Foodstuffs*] (CZ)
CENTROMIN ... Empresa Minera del Centro del Peru [*Central Peruvian Mining Enterprise*] (LA)
CENTROMINPERU ... Empresa Minera del Centro del Peru [*Central Peruvian Mining Enterprise*] (LA)
Centrosan... Centrala Handlowa Farmaceutyczno-Sanitarna [*Pharmaceutical and Sanitary Goods Sales Center*] (POL)
CENTROSPED ... Medunarodna Spedicija i Transporti [*International Shipment and Transport Center*] (YU)
Centrosprzet ... Centrala Sprzetu Lekarsko-Sanitarnego [*Medical and Health Protection Supply Center*] (POL)
CENTROTEKSTIL ... Preduzece za Izvoz i Uvoz Tekstila [*Establishment for Import and Export of Textiles*] (YU)
CENTROTEX ... Podnik Zahranicniho Obchodu pro Dovoz a Vyvoz Textilniho a Kozeneho Zbozi [*Foreign Trade Enterprise for the Import and Export of Textiles and Leather Goods*] (CZ)
CENTROVITAL ... Central Colombiana de Vittalium [*Bogota*] Tlg. (COL)
Centrowet... Centrala Zaopatrzenia Weterynaryjno-Zootechniczna [*Veterinary and Animal Husbandry Supply Center*] (POL)
cents.......... Centimos [*Spanish*]
CENTSCO... Centro Tecnico Superior de la Construccion [*Higher Technical Center for Construction*] [*Cuban*] (LA)
CEO............ Centre d'Etudes et d'Organisation (MAR)
CEO............ Chief Education Officer (MAR)
CEON.......... Centro de Estudios y Orientacion Nacional [*Center of Studies and National Orientation*] [*Bolivian*] (LA)
CEOSL........ Confederacion Ecuatoriana de Organizaciones Sindicales Libres [*Ecuadorean Confederation of Free Union Organizations*] (LA)
CEOT .... Centre d'Education Ouvriere du Togo [*Workers Education Center of Togo*] (AF)
CEP............ Centraal Economisch Plan [*Dutch*]
CEP............ Centre d'Etudes de Prevention (MAR)
CEP............ Centro de Estudos do Pessoal [*Personnel Studies Center*] [*Brazilian*] (LA)
CEP............ Centro de Estudos de Planeamento [*Center for Planning Studies*] [*Portuguese*] (WER)
CEP............ Centros de Educacion Popular [*Popular Education Centers*] [*Nicaraguan*] (LA1)
CEP............ Certificat d'Etudes Primaires [*Primary Studies Certificate*] (CL)
CEP............ Comite Estatal de Precios [*State Committee for Prices*] [*Cuban*] (LA)
CEP............ Comite Estudiantil Peruano [*Peruvian Student Committee*] (LA)
CEP............ Commission d'Enquete Parlementaire (MAR)
CEP............ Compagnie d'Encouragement a la Peche (MAR)
CEP............ Compagnie Equatoriale de Peintures (MAR)
CEP............ Compagnie Europeenne de Publication [*French*]
CEP............ Compagnie d'Exploration Petroliere [*Petroleum Exploration Company*] [*Algerian*] (AF)
CEP............ Comptoir d'Exportation du Poisson (MAR)
CEPA.......... Centro de Educacion y Promocion Agraria [*Agrarian Education and Promotion Center*] [*Nicaraguan*] (LA1)
CEPA.......... Centro Experimental de Produccion Agropecuaria [*Center for Agricultural-Livestock Experimental Production*] [*Nicaraguan*] (LA1)
CEPA.......... Comision Ejecutiva Portuaria Autonoma [*Autonomous Executive Port Commission*] [*Salvadoran*] (LA1)
CEPA.......... Commission Economique pour l'Afrique (MAR)
CEPAD........ Comite Evangelico pro Ayuda al Desarrollo [*Evangelical Committee for Development Aid*] [*Nicaraguan*] (LA1)
CEPAL .... Comision Economica para America Latina [*Economic Commission for Latin America*] [*Use ECLA*] [*Santiago, Chile*] (LA)
CEPAS........ Centre d'Etudes pour l'Action Sociale (MAR)
CEPC .... Certificat d'Etudes Primaires Complementaires de l'Enseignement National [*National Education Further Primary Studies Certificate*] [*Laotian*] (CL)
CEPCEO ..... Comite d'Etude des Producteurs de Charbon d'Europe Occidentale [*West European Coal Producers' Association*]
CEPCh .... Confederacion de Empleados Particulares de Chile [*Chilean Confederation of Private Sector Employees*] (LA)
CEPE.......... Centre d'Etudes Phytosociologiques et Ecologiques [*Center for Phytosociological and Ecological Studies*] [*Under the CNRS*] [*French*] (WER)
CEPE.......... Centre d'Etudes des Programmes Economiques (MAR)
CEPE.......... Certificat d'Etudes Primaires et Elementaires [*Primary and Elementary Studies Certificate*] [*Malagasy*] (AF)
CEPE.......... Corporacion Estatal Petrolera Ecuatoriana [*Ecuadorean State Petroleum Corporation*] (LA)
CEPEB .... Centre d'Etudes et de Promotion des Entreprises Beninoises (MAR)
CEPECA...... Centrul de Perfectionare a Pregatirii Cadrelor de Conducere din Intreprinderi [*Center for Advanced Training of Management Personnel in Enterprises*] (RO)
CEPECOM ... Centrul de Perfectionare a Lucrarilor din Comert [*Center for Improving Work in Trade*] (RO)
CEPECOOP ... Centrul de Perfectionare a Cadrelor din Cooperatia de Consum [*Center for Advanced Training of Personnel in the Consumer Cooperative System*] (RO)
Cepede .... Centrala Importowo-Eksportowa Przemyslu Drzewnego [*Central Import-Export Office of the Lumber Industry*] (POL)
CEPEIT .... Centrul pentru Perfectionarea Personalului Didactic din Invatamintul Profesional si Tehnic [*Center for the Advanced Training of Teaching Cadres in Vocational and Technical Education*] (RO)
CEPEM........ Centro de Preparacion de Especialistas Menores [*Training Center for Junior Specialists*] [*Cuban*] (LA)
CEPEN .... Centro de Preparacion de Especialistas Navales [*Naval Specialists Training Center*] [*Cuban*] (LA)
CEPES .... Centro de Estudios Politicos, Economicos, y Sociales [*Center for Political, Economic, and Social Studies (of the PRI)*] [*Mexican*] (LA1)
CEPES .... Comitato Europeo per il Progresso Economico e Sociale [*European Committee for Economic and Social Development*] [*Italian*] (WER)
CEPEX .... Centre de Promotion des Exportations [*Tunisian*] (MAR)
CEPGL .... Communaute Economique des Pays des Grands Lacs [*Economic Community of the Countries of the Great Lakes*] (AF)
CEPI........... Centre d'Etudes de Prevention Ivoirien (MAR)
CEPI........... Convenios de Especificaciones de Productos Internos [*Agreements on Specifications for Domestic Products*] [*Cuban*] (LA)
CEPIA .... Caisse d'Encouragement a la Peche (MAR)
CEPIC .... Centre Politique des Independants et Cadres Chretiens [*Political Center of Christian Independents and Cadres*] [*Belgian, French*] (WER)
CEPLAC...... Comissao Executiva do Plano da Lavoura Cacaueira [*Executive Commission for the Cocoa Production Plan*] [*Brazilian*] (LA)
CEPMAE..... Centre d'Edition et de Production Manuels et d'Auxiliaires de l'Enseignement (MAR)
CePO.......... Centrala Poszukiwan Osob [*Central Office of Missing Persons*] (POL)
CEPOM .... Centre d'Etudes des Problemes d'Outre-Mer [*Center for the Study of Overseas Problems*] [*French*] (AF)
CEPr........... Centre d'Essais des Propulseurs [*Aircraft Motor Testing Center*] [*French*] (WER)
CEPR.......... Cercle des Etudiants Progressistes Rwandais [*Rwandan Progressive Students Club*] (AF)
CEPRA .... Cooperative d'Elevage Pastorale de la Revolution Agraire [*Stock Breeding Cooperative of the Agrarian Revolution*] [*Algerian*] (AF)
CEPRO........ Centre d'Etudes des Problemes Humains du Travail (MAR)
CEPSA........ Compania Espanola de Petroleos, Sociedad Anonima [*Spanish Petroleum Company*] (WER)
CEPSC........ Centre d'Etudes des Problemes Sociaux Congolais (MAR)
CEPSI.......... Bulletin Trimestriel du Centre d'Etude des Problemes Sociaux Indigenes [*A publication*] (MAR)
CEPSI.......... Centre d'Etude des Problemes Sociaux Indigenes [*Center for the Study of Indigenous Social Problems*] [*Zairian*] (AF)
CEPT.......... Conference Europeenne des Postes et des Telecommunications
CEPYRDE ... Cuerpo Especial de Prevencion y Represion de Delitos Economicos [*Special Force for the Prevention and Repression of Economic Crimes*] [*Uruguayan*] (LA)
CER............ Centre for Economic Research (MAR)
CER............ Centres d'Enseignement Revolutionnaire [*Revolutionary Education Centers*] [*Guinean*] (AF)
CER............ Centres d'Expansion Rurale [*Rural Expansion Centers*] [*Senegalese*] (AF)
Cer .... Cerrahiye [*Surgical Ward, Surgery*] (TU)
CER............ College d'Enseignement Rural (MAR)
CER............ Comissao de Estudos Rodoviarios [*Road Studies Commission*] [*Mozambican*] (AF)
CER............ Comite d'Expansion Regional [*French*]
CER............ Commission d'Etudes et de Recherches [*Study and Research Commission*] [*Cambodian*] (CL)
CERA .... Centre d'Etudes et de Recherches en Automatisme [*Study and Research Center on Automation*] [*French*] (WER)
CERA .... Centre d'Etudes des Religions Africaines [*Studies Center for African Religions*] [*Zairian*] (AF)
CERA .... Centros de Reforma Agraria [*Agrarian Reform Centers*] [*Chilean*] (LA)
CERA .... Comptoirs d'Equipements et de Reparations Automobiles (MAR)
CERAG........ Centre d'Etudes et de Recherches Agricoles [*Algerian*] (MAR)
CERAR........ Centre d'Education Rurale et Artisanale au Rwanda (MAR)
CERBH........ Cycle d'Etude et de Recherche en Biologie Humaine [*French*]
CERCA........ Centre de Recherches pour Combustibles Atomiques [*French*]
CERCA........ Compagnie pour l'Etude et la Realisation de Combustible Atomique [*Company for the Study and Manufacture of Atomic Fuel*] [*French*] (WER)
CERCHAR... Centre d'Etudes et Recherches des Charbonnages de France [*Center for Studies and Research on French Coal Mines*] [*French*] (WER)

CERCON..... Cerramientos de Construccion [*Cali*] (COL)
CERCOVINS ... Centrale Regionale de Conditionnement et de Commercialisation de Vins et Spiritueux (MAR)
CERDAS ..... Centre de Coordination des Recherches et de la Documentation en Science Sociale Desservant l'Afrique Sud-Saharienne [*Center for Coordination of Social Science Research and Documentation for Sub-Saharan Africa*] (AF)
CERDIC....... Centre de Recherche et de Documentation des Institution Chretiennes
CERDOC..... Centre d'Etudes et de Recherches Documentaires [*French*]
CERDOTOLA ... Centre Regional de Documentation sur les Traditions Orales et les Langues Africaines [*Regional Center for Documentation on Oral Traditions and African Languages*] (AF)
CERDS........ Charter of Economic Rights and Duties of States (WER)
CEREA........ Centre de Regroupement Africain [*Algerian*] (MAR)
CEREMADE ... Centre de Recherche de Mathematiques de Decision (MAR)
CEREQ........ Centre d'Etudes et de Recherches sur les Enseignements et les Qualifications [*French*]
CERES........ Centre d'Etude, de Recherche, et d'Education Socialistes [*Center for Socialist Study, Research, and Education*] [*Senegalese*] (AF)
CERES........ Centre d'Etudes et de Recherches Economiques et Sociales [*Economic and Social Research and Studies Center*] [*French*] (AF)
CERES........ Comite d'Etudes Regionales Economiques et Sociales
CERESD...... Center of Social Democratic Studies and Thought [*Portuguese*] (WER)
CERESIS..... Centro Regional de Sismologia para America del Sur [*Regional Seismology Center for South America*] (LA)
CERF........... Centre d'Experimentation, de Recherche, et de Formation [*North African*] (MAR)
CERF........... Comptoir Electro Radio-Froid [*Moroccan*] (MAR)
CERFA........ Compagnie des Experts Reunis France Afrique (MAR)
CERFER...... Centre de Formation pour Entretien Routier (MAR)
CERI........... Centre d'Etudes et de Recherches en Informatique [*Computer Study and Research Center*] [*Algerian*] (AF)
CERI........... Centre d'Etudes et de Recherches Internationales (MAR)
CERIC......... Consortium d'Etudes et de Realisations Industrielles et Commerciales (MAR)
CERICAM.... Societe Ceramique Industrielle du Cameroun (MAR)
CERILH....... Centre d'Etudes et de Recherches de l'Industrie des Liants Hydrauliques (MAR)
CERINECA ... Centre International d'Etudes et de Recherches sur l'Integration Economique de l'Afrique [*International Center for Studies and Research on the Economic Integration of Africa*] (AF)
CERIS......... Centro de Estatisticas Religiosas e Investigacao Social [*Religious Statistics and Social Research Center*] [*Brazilian*] (LA)
CERK.......... Centre d'Etudes et de Recherches de Kara (MAR)
CERM.......... Centre d'Etudes et de Recherches Marxistes [*Center for Marxist Study and Research*] [*French*] (WER)
CERMA....... Centre d'Etudes et de Recherches de Medecine Aeronautique [*French*]
CERMAC..... Centre de Recherches sur le Monde Arabe Contemporain (MAR)
CERMACOM ... Compagnie pour l'Exploitation des Ressources Maritimes et le Commerce (MAR)
CERN.......... Conseil Europeen pour la Recherche Nucleaire [*European Council for Nuclear Research*] [*Geneva, Switzerland*]
CERN.......... Consiglio Europeo per le Ricerche Nucleari [*European Council for Nuclear Research*] [*Use ECNR*] [*Italian*] (WER)
CERNE........ Companhia de Eletrificacao Rural do Nordeste [*Northeast Rural Electrification Company*] [*Brazilian*] (LA)
CERP........... Centre d'Etudes des Reformes Politiques [*Center for the Study of Political Reforms*] [*Belgian*] (WER)
CERP........... Centre Europeen des Relations Publiques
CERP........... Centro de Estudios de Relaciones Publicas [*Public Relations Studies Center*] [*Colombian*] (LA)
CERPA........ Centro de Estudios y de Investigaciones Peruanas y Andinas [*Center for Peruvian and Andean Studies and Research*] (LA)
CERPER...... Empresa Publica de Certificaciones Pesqueras [*Public Enterprise for Fishing Certificates*] [*Peruvian*] (LA)
CERPHOS... Centre d'Etudes et de Recherches des Phosphates Mineraux (MAR)
CERRACOL ... Cerraduras de Colombia SA [*Bogota*] (COL)
CERRAMETAL ... Cerraduras Metalicas Medellin (COL)
CERT........... Compagnie d'Etudes et de Realisations de Travaux (MAR)
CERTEX...... Certificados de Exportacion [*Export Certificates*] [*Peruvian*] (LA)
CERUR........ Centro de Estudios Regionales Urbanos Rurales [*Center for Regional Urban and Rural Studies*] [*Dominican Republic*] (LA1)
Cervarm...... Cervena Armija [*Red Army*] (YU)
CERVECOL ... Cerveceria Colombo Alemana SA [*Bogota*] (COL)
CERVUNION ... Cerveceria Union [*Medellin*] (COL)
CES............ Cahiers Economiques et Sociaux [*Kinshasa*] [*A publication*] (MAR)
ces............ Centimes [*French*] (GPO)
CES............ Centre d'Etudes Sociales [*Belgian*]
CES............ Centre d'Etudes Sociologiques (MAR)
CES............ Centre d'Etudes Superieurs (MAR)
CES............ Centro de Estudios Politicos y Sociales [*Political and Social Studies Center*] [*Uruguayan*] (LA)
CES............ Certificat d'Etudes Secondaires (MAR)
CES............ Certificat d'Etudes Superieures [*Certificate of Higher Studies*] [*French*]
CES............ College d'Enseignement Secondaire [*French*]
CES............ Comando Estrategico de Sabotaje [*Strategic Sabotage Command*] [*Venezuelan*] (LA)
CES............ Comites de Estudiantes Socialistas [*Socialist Student Committees*] [*Spanish*] (WER)
CES............ Commission d'Etudes Salariales (MAR)
CES............ Confederazione Europea dei Sindacati [*European Trade Union Confederation*] [*Use ETUC*] [*Italian*] (WER)
CES............ Conseil Economique et Social (MAR)
CES............ Conservation des Eaux et des Sols (MAR)
CES............ Cuerpo Especial de Seguridad [*Special Security Corps*] [*Honduran*] (LA)
CESA.......... Centre d'Enseignement Superieur des Affaires (MAR)
CESA.......... Centre d'Etudes Sociales Africaines (MAR)
CESAH........ Comite Ecumenico Salvadoreno de Ayuda Humanitaria [*Salvadoran Ecumenical Committee for Humanitarian Aid*] (LA1)
CESAO........ Centre d'Etudes Economiques et Sociales de l'Afrique Occidentale [*West African Economic and Social Studies Center*] (AF)
CESB.......... Confederacion de Estudiantes de Secundaria de Bolivia [*Bolivian Confederation of Secondary Schools*] (LA)
CESC.......... Certificat d'Etudes Superieures Commerciales [*Commercial Advanced Studies Certificate*] (CL)
CESCA........ Comunidad Economica y Social Centroamericana [*Central American Socioeconomic Community*] (LA)
CESD.......... Centre Europeen de Formation des Statisticiens Economistes des Pays en Voie de Developpement [*European Center for Training Statisticians and Economists from Developing Countries*] (CL)
CESDE........ Centro de Estudios Superiores para el Desarrollo [*Center of Higher Studies for Development*] [*Colombian*] (LA)
CESEDEN... Centro Superior de Estudios de la Defensa Nacional [*Highest National Defense Studies Center*] [*Spanish*] (WER)
CESES........ Centro Studio Economico e Sociale [*Studies Center for Economic and Social Affairs*] [*Of the PCI*] [*Italian*] (WER)
CESETA...... Centro de Servicios Tecnicos Automotrices [*Automotive Technical Services Center*] [*Cuban*] (LA)
CESI........... Centre for Economic and Social Information (MAR)
CESI........... Centre d'Etudes Superieures Industrielles (MAR)
CESID......... Centro Superior de Informacion de la Defensa [*Spanish*]
CESITRADO ... Central Sindical de Trabajadores Dominicanos [*Dominican Workers Federation*] [*Dominican Republic*] (LA1)
CESL........... Confederacion Ecuatoriana de Sindicatos Libres [*Ecuadorean Confederation of Free Trade Unions*] (LA)
CESMAD..... Sdruzeni Ceskoslovenskych Mezinarodnich Automobilovych Dopravcu [*Association of Czechoslovak International Truckers*] (CZ)
CESMAT..... Centre d'Etudes Superieures des Matieres Premieres (MAR)
CESME........ Centro de Servicios Metalurgicos [*Metallurgical Services Center*] [*Chilean*] (LA)
CESNAV..... Centro de Estudios Superiores Navales [*Naval War College*] [*Mexican*] (LA)
CESNEF...... Centro di Studi Nucleari Enrico Fermi [*Italian*]
CESO.......... Centro de Estudios Socioeconomicos [*Socioeconomic Studies Center*] [*Chilean*] (LA)
CESOM....... Confederacao Europeia dos Espoliados do Ultramar [*European Confederation of Persons Exploited Overseas*] [*Portuguese*] (WER)
CESP........... Centrais Eletricas de Sao Paulo, SA [*Sao Paulo Electric Powerplants, Inc.*] [*Brazilian*] (LA1)
CESP........... Centre d'Etudes des Supports de Publicite [*Center for the Study of Advertising Support*] [*French*]
CESP........... Companhia Energetica de Sao Paulo [*Sao Paulo Electric Company*] [*Brazilian*] (LA)
CESPASD... Comite Charge d'Etudier et de Suivre les Problemes de Prix, d'Approvisionnement, de Stockage, et de Distribution [*Committee in Charge of Studying and Following Price, Supply, Stocking, and Distribution Problems*] [*Cambodian*] (CL)
CESPE........ Centro Studi di Politica Economica [*Center for Studies in Economic Policy*] [*Of the PCI*] [*Italian*] (WER)
CESSA........ Cemento de El Salvador, Sociedad Anonima [*Cement of El Salvador Corporation*]
CESSID....... Centre d'Etudes Superieures de la Siderurgie [*Center for Advanced Steel Research*] [*French*] (WER)
CESTI......... Centre d'Etudes des Sciences et Techniques de l'Information [*Center for the Study of Information Sciences and Techniques*] [*Senegalese*] (AF)
CESU.......... Consejo de Estudiantes Secundarios Uruguayos [*Council of Uruguayan Secondary School Students*] (LA)
CESUP........ Centre d'Enseignement Superieur (MAR)

CESUP .... Centre d'Etudes Superieures (MAR)
CET .... Centrala Energie Termala [*Thermoelectric Power Plant*] (RO)
CET .... Certificat d'Etudes Techniques (MAR)
Cet .... Cetar [*Sergeant*] (CZ)
Cet .... Cetvel [*Table*] [*As a statistical table*] (TU)
CET .... Club Europeen du Tourisme (MAR)
CET .... College d'Enseignement Technique [*French*]
CET .... Common External Tariff (MAR)
CETA .... Centre Economique et Technique de l'Artisanat [*Economic and Technical Crafts Center*] [*Malagasy*] (AF)
CETA .... Centre d'Entrainement des Troupes Aeroportees [*Airborne Troops Training Center*] [*Zairian*] (AF)
CETA .... Compagnie Equatoriale des Tabacs et Allumettes (MAR)
CETA .... Conference des Eglises de Toute l'Afrique [*All Africa Conference of Churches*] [*Use AACC*] (AF)
CETAL .... Confederacion de Trabajadores de America Latina [*Latin American Workers Confederation*] (LA)
Cetasp .... Cetar Aspirant [*Sergeant Cadet*] (CZ)
CETAUTO ... Centro Tecnico Automovel (MAR)
CETE .... Centre d'Etudes Techniques de l'Equipement [*Equipment Technical Studies Center*] [*French*] (WER)
CETEL .... Companhia Estadual de Telefonos da Guanabara [*Guanabara State Telephone Company*] [*Brazilian*] (LA)
CETEM .... Centre d'Enseignement Technique d'Etudes Municipales [*Center for Technical Education in Municipal Administration*] [*French Guiana*] (LA1)
CETEM .... Centre d'Etudes des Techniques Economiques Modernes (MAR)
CETEMA ..... Centre d'Etudes Techniques et Economiques des Matieres Grasses (MAR)
CETESB ...... Companhia de Tecnologia de Saneamento Basico [*Basic Sanitation Technology Company*] [*Brazilian*] (LA)
CETI .... Centre d'Etude et de Traitement de l'Informatique (MAR)
CETI .... Comissao de Estudos Tributarios e Internacionais [*Tax and International Studies Commission*] [*Brazilian*] (LA)
CETIC .... College d'Enseignement Technique, Industriel, et Commercial (MAR)
CETIS .... European Atomic Energy Community Scientific Data-Processing Centre [*Luxembourg*]
CETLANTIC ... Ceramica Atlantico [*Barranquilla*] (COL)
CETRA .... Compagnie Equatoriale des Travaux (MAR)
CETRAC ..... Centrale de Transports en Commun (MAR)
CETRAMET-Congo ... Compagnie Equatoriale pour la Transformation des Metaux au Congo (MAR)
CETREMFA ... Centro de Treinamento e Desenvolvimento do Pessoal do Ministerio da Fazenda [*Center for the Training and Development of Finance Ministry Personnel*] [*Brazilian*] (LA)
CETRIC .... Consortium d'Etudes Techniques et de Realisations Industrielles du Cameroun (MAR)
CETSS .... Comite Estatal de el Trabajo y Seguro Social [*State Committee for Labor and Social Security*] [*Cuban*] (LA)
CETURIS ..... Corporacion Ecuatoriana del Turismo [*Ecuadorean Corporation for Tourism*] (LA)
CEU .... Centro de Estudiantes Universitarios [*University Students Center*] (LA)
CEUC .... Confederation de Estudiantes Universitarios de Colombia [*Confederation of University Students of Colombia*] (LA)
CEUCA .... Centros de Estudios Universitarios Colombo Americano [*Bogota*] (COL)
CEUCA .... Confederacion de Estudiantes Universitarios de Centroamerica [*Confederation of University Students of Central America*] (LA)
CEUD .... Comissao Eleitoral para a Unidade Democratico [*Electoral Committee for Democratic Unity*] [*Portuguese*] (PPE)
CEUD .... Comite Eleitoral de Unidade Democratica [*Democratic Unity Electoral Committee*] [*Portuguese*] (WER)
CEV .... Centre d'Essais en Vol [*In-Flight Testing Center*] [*French*] (WER)
CEV .... Ceskoslovenske Energeticke Vyrobny [*Czechoslovak Electric Power Producing Enterprises*] (CZ)
Cev .... Ceviri [*or Ceviren*] [*Translation or Translator*] (TU)
CEVA .... Cementarny a Vapenky [*Cement and Lime Works*] (CZ)
CEVAL .... Cementos del Valle SA [*Cali*] (COL)
CEVER .... Centro de Educacion Vocacional Evangelico y Reformado [*Honduran*]
CEVOI .... Comptoir d'Exportation de Vanille de l'Ocean Indien (MAR)
CEW .... Commissions Electorales de Wilaya [*Governorate Electoral Commissions*] [*Algerian*] (AF)
CEWA .... Central Water and Electricity Administration [*Sudanese*] (MAR)
CEWAL .... Central West Africa Lines (AF)
CEXIM .... Carteira de Exportacao e Importacao [*Export and Import Department*] [*Brazilian*] (LA)
CEZ .... Centrale des Enseignants Zairois (MAR)
CEZ .... Ceskoslovenske Energeticke Zavody, Narodni Podnik [*Czechoslovak Power Plants, National Enterprise*] (CZ)
CEZAC .... Centre Zairois de Commerce Exterieur [*Zairian Foreign Trade Center*] (AF)
CEZAREP .... Centre Zairois des Relations Publiques [*Zairian Public Relations Center*] (AF)
CEZAS .... Centrala Zaopatrzenia Szkol [*Central Supply Office for Schools*] (POL)
CF .... Capitaine de Fregate [*French*] (MTD)
CF .... Central African Empire [*Later, CAR*] [*Two-letter standard code*] (CNC)
CF .... Ceska Filharmonie [*Czech Philharmonic Orchestra*] (CZ)
C d f .... Chemin de Fer [*Railway*] [*French*] (MTD)
CF .... Communaute Francaise
cf .... Confer [*Compare*] [*Latin*] (GPO)
Cf .... Conferez [*French*]
cf .... Confesor [*Confessor*] [*Spanish*]
cf .... Confirma [*In old documents*] [*Spanish*]
CF .... Cout-Fret [*French*]
CF .... Les Colonies Francaises (MAR)
CFA .... Caminho de Ferro de Amboim [*Amboim Railroad*] [*Angolan*] (AF)
CFA .... Centre de Formation Administrative [*Algerian*] (MAR)
CFA .... Chemins de Fer Algeriens (MAR)
CFA .... Colonies Francaises d'Afrique (MAR)
CFA .... Commonwealth Forestry Association (EA)
CFA .... Communaute Financiere Africaine [*African Financial Community*] (AF)
CFA .... Communaute Francaise d'Afrique [*French*]
CFA .... Compagnie Financiere Africaine (MAR)
CFA .... Compagnie Forestiere Africaine (MAR)
CFA .... Compagnie Forestiere d'Azingo (MAR)
CFA .... Compagnie France-Amerique [*Ivorian*] (MAR)
CFA .... Compagnie Franco-Africaine (MAR)
CFA .... Conference des Femmes Africaines [*Conference of African Women*] (AF)
CFA .... Conseils Associes en Afrique (MAR)
CFA .... Cote Francaise d'Afrique (MAR)
CFA .... Credit Foncier d'Afrique (MAR)
CFAA .... Coloured Film Artists' Association (MAR)
CFAA .... Compagnie Commerciale Franco-Africaine et Antillaise (MAR)
CFAD .... Centre de Formation d'Auto-Defense [*Algerian*] (MAR)
CFAE .... Centre de Formation en Aerodynamique Experimentale
CFAE .... Chemins de Fer Algeriens de l'Etat (MAR)
CFAE .... Compagnie Francaise de l'Afrique Equatoriale (MAR)
CFAF .... Credit Foncier de l'Afrique Francaise (MAR)
CFAF .... Francs de la Communaute Financiere Africaine (MAR)
CFAO .... Compagnie Francaise de l'Afrique Occidentale [*French Company of West Africa*] (AF)
CFAPAL .... Compagnie Franco-Africaine de Produits Alimentaires (MAR)
CFAR .... Centres de Formation d'Animateurs Ruraux (MAR)
CFAT .... Centre de Sidi-Fredj de Formation en Art Traditionnel (MAR)
CFAT .... Credit Foncier d'Algerie et de Tunisie (MAR)
CFB .... Caminho de Ferro de Benguela [*Benguela Railroad*] [*Angolan*] (AF)
CFB .... Commercial Farmers Bureau (MAR)
CFB .... Compagnie Forestiere de Bika (MAR)
CFBN .... Chemin de Fer Benin-Niger [*Benin-Niger Railroad*] (AF)
CFC .... Caribbean Food Corporation (LA)
CFC .... Centres de Formation de Cadres (MAR)
CFC .... Chemins de Fer du Cambodge [*Cambodian Railroads*] [*Replaced CFRC*] (CL)
CFC .... Compagnie Forestiere du Congo (MAR)
CFC .... Corporacion Financiera Colombiana [*Colombian Financial Corporation*] (LA)
CFC .... Credit Foncier du Cameroun (MAR)
CFCB .... Compagnie Francaise de Credit et de Banque [*North African*] (MAR)
CFCCA .... Centre de Formation des Cadres pour Cooperatives Agricoles (MAR)
CFCD .... Compagnie Fonciere et Commerciale de Distribution (MAR)
CFCD .... Compagnie Francaise des Charbonnages de Dakar (MAR)
CFCD .... Compagnons du Feu, Fernand Cronel (MAR)
CFCE .... Centre Francais du Commerce Exterieur (MAR)
CFCE .... Conseil des Federations Commerciales d'Europe [*Council of Commercial Federations of Europe*] (AF)
CFCG .... Compagnie Forestiere et Commerciale du Gabon (MAR)
CFCI .... Compagnie Francaise de la Cote-d'Ivoire (MAR)
CFCIM .... Chambre Francaise de Commerce et de l'Industrie du Maroc [*French Chamber of Commerce and Industry in Morocco*] (AF)
CFCO .... Chemin de Fer Congo-Ocean [*Congo-Ocean Railroad*] (AF)
CFCP .... Compagnie Francaise de Cultures et de Participation (MAR)
CFCS .... Caribbean Food Crops Society (EA)
CFD .... Christlicher Friedensdienst [*Christian Peace Service*] (EG)
CFD .... Comite Francais de Documentation
CFD .... Comitetul Femeilor Democratice [*Committee of Democratic Women*] (RO)
CFD .... Compagnie Forestiere Dolisienne (MAR)
CFDC .... Compagnie Forestiere du Cameroun (MAR)
CFDP .... Compagnie Forestiere Durecu Pontabry (MAR)
CFDPA .... Compagnie Francaise de Distribution des Petroles en Afrique (MAR)
CFDT .... Compagnie Francaise pour le Developpement des Fibres Textiles [*French Company for the Development of Textile Fibers*] (AF)
CFDT .... Compagnie Francaise pour la Diffusion des Techniques (MAR)

CFDT.......... Confederation Francaise et Democratique du Travail [*French Democratic Confederation of Labor*] (WER)
CFDV.......... Compagnie Financiere Delmas-Vieljeux (MAR)
CFE............ Comision Federal de Electricidad [*Federal Electricity Commission*] [*Mexican*] (LA)
CFE............ Compagnie du Chemin de Fer Franco-Ethiopien [*Franco-Ethiopian Railroad Company*] (AF)
CFE............ Compagnie Forestiere d'Eseka (MAR)
CFE............ Conselho Federal de Educacao [*Federal Education Council*] [*Brazilian*] (LA)
CFEA.......... Comptoir Fournitures Electriques Automobiles Ets. Weydert (MAR)
CFEN.......... Certificat de Fin d'Etudes Normales (MAR)
CFEP.......... Certificat de Fin d'Etudes Pedagogiques (MAR)
CFF............ Cooperative Financing Facility [*Zambian*] (AF)
CFF............ Croatian Franciscan Fathers [*Chicago*] (YU)
CFFA.......... Credit Foncier et Financier d'Afrique (MAR)
CFFV.......... Cooperative Forestiere du Fernan-Vaz (MAR)
CFG............ Chemins de Fer du Gabon [*Gabonese Railroad*] (AF)
CFG............ Chemins de Fer de Guinee [*Guinea Railroad*] (AF)
CFG............ Compagnie Forestiere du Gabon [*Gabonese Forestry Company*] (AF)
CFG............ Compagnie Francaise du Gabon (MAR)
CFG............ Comunn Forbairt na Gaidhealtachd [*Highland Development League*] [*Scottish*]
CFGG.......... Compagnie Forestiere du Golfe de Guinee (MAR)
CFHBC........ Compagnie Francaise du Haut et Bas Congo (MAR)
CFHC.......... Compagnie Francaise du Haut-Congo (MAR)
CFHP.......... Compagnie Fermiere des Huileries de Palme (MAR)
CFHTA........ Centre de Formation Hoteliere et Touristique d'Abidjan (MAR)
cfi............... Caile Ferate Inguste [*Narrow-Gauge Railroads*] (RO)
CFI............. Clothing and Footwear Institute (EA)
CFI............. Compagnie Forestiere de l'Indenie (MAR)
CFI............. Control Financial Intern [*Internal Financial Control*] (RO)
CFI............. Corporacion de Fomento Industrial [*Industrial Development Corporation*] [*Dominican Republic*] (LA)
CFI............. Credit Foncier et Immobilier (MAR)
CFI............. Societe Cafeiere Franco-Ivoirienne (MAR)
CFIC........... Compagnie Fonciere et Immobiliere du Cameroun (MAR)
CFIEX......... Compagnie Francaise d'Importation et d'Exportation (MAR)
CFK............ Christliche Friedenskonferenz [*Christian Conference for Peace*] (EG)
CFK............ Compagnie Forestiere de Kango (MAR)
CFK............ Credit Foncier Khmer [*Cambodian Real Estate Bank*] (CL)
CFKR.......... Comite des Femmes Khmeres Republicaines [*Cambodian Republican Women's Committee*] (CL)
CFL............ Caminho de Ferro de Luanda [*Luanda Railroad*] [*Angolan*] (AF)
CFL............ Chemins de Fer des Grands Lacs [*Great Lakes Railroad Company*] [*Zairian*] (AF)
CFL............ Club Francais du Livre [*French Book Club*]
CFL............ Compagnie des Chemins de Fer du Congo Superieur et des Grands Lacs (MAR)
CFLN.......... Comite Francais de Liberation Nationale [*Algerian*] (MAR)
CFM............ Caminhos de Ferro do Mocambique [*Mozambique Railroad*] (AF)
CFM............ Centre de Formation Maritime (MAR)
CFM............ Chemin de Fer de Mayumbe (MAR)
CFM............ Committee for a Free Mozambique (MAR)
CFM............ Compagnie Francaise du Methane [*French Methane Company*] (WER)
CFM............ Consortium Forestier et Maritime [*Forestry and Maritime Consortium*] [*French*] (WER)
CFM............ Council of Foreign Ministers (MAR)
CFM............ Ports, Railways, and Transport Services [*Moroccan*] (AF)
CFMB.......... Compagnie Forestiere Michel Brouillet (MAR)
CFME.......... Compagnie Franco-Malgache d'Entreprises (MAR)
CFMK.......... Chemin de Fer Matadi-Kinshasa (MAR)
CFML.......... Chemin de Fer de Matadi-Leopoldville (MAR)
CFMR.......... Centre de Formation de Monitrices Rurales (MAR)
CFMU.......... Compagnie Francaise des Minerais d'Uranium [*French Uranium Ores Company*] (AF)
CFN............ Commission du Fleuve Niger [*Niger River Commission*] (AF)
CFN............ Compagnie Forestiere du Niari [*Niary Forestry Company*] [*Congolese*] (AF)
CFN............ Compagnie Forestiere du Nombo (MAR)
CFN............ Corporacion Financiera Nacional [*Bogota*] (COL)
CFN............ Corporacion Financiera Nacional [*National Financing Corporation*] [*Ecuadorean*] (LA)
CFNI........... Caribbean Food and Nutrition Institute (LA)
CFNIS......... Consolidated Food and Nutrition Information System (MAR)
CFNR.......... Compagnie Francaise de Navigation Rhenane (MAR)
CFOA.......... Credit Foncier de l'Ouest Africain (MAR)
CFOM.......... Centre de Formation des Officiers de Marine (MAR)
CFP............ Centre de Formation Professionnelle de la Police (MAR)
CFP............ Centrul de Fizica Pamintului [*Center for Earth Physics*] (RO)
CFP............ Combinatul Fondului Plastic [*Combine of the Plastics Fund*] (RO)
CFP............ Comissao de Financiamento da Producao [*Production Financing Commission*] [*Brazilian*] (LA)
CFP............ Compagnie Francaise des Petroles [*French Petroleum Company*] (AF)
CFP............ Comptoirs Francais du Pacifique
CFP............ Concentracion de Fuerzas Populares [*Concentration of Popular Forces*] [*Ecuadorean*] (PPW)
CFP............ Concentration des Forces Populaires (MAR)
CFPA.......... Centre de Formation et de Perfectionnement Administratif (MAR)
CFPA.......... Centre de Formation Professionelle des Adultes [*Adult Vocational Training Center*] [*Algerian*] (AF)
CFPA.......... Centre de Formation Professionnelle Agricole [*North African*] (MAR)
CFP-A......... Compagnie Francaise des Petroles - Algerie [*French Petroleum Company - Algeria*] (AF)
CFPC.......... Consell de Forces Politicas de Catalunya [*Council of Political Forces of Catalonia*] [*Spanish*] (WER)
CFPFAO...... Centre Forestier Pilote de la FAO (MAR)
CFPG.......... Consello de Forzas Politicas Galegas [*Galician Political Forces Council*] [*Spanish*] (WER)
CFPI........... Centro de Fomento y Productividad Industrial [*Industrial Productivity and Development Center*] [*Guatemalan*] (LA)
CFPL.......... Centro Federado de Periodistas de Lima [*Federated Center of Journalists of Lima*] [*Peruvian*] (LA)
CFPM.......... Centro de Formacao de Pilots Militares [*Military Pilots Training Center*] [*Brazilian*] (LA)
CFPO.......... Commission des Forets pour le Proche-Orient (MAR)
CFPPU........ Comite de Familiares de Presos Politicos Uruguayos [*Relatives' Committee for Uruguayan Political Prisoners*] (EA)
CFPR.......... Centre de Formation Professionnelle Rapide (MAR)
CFPS.......... Compagnie Francaise de Prospection Sismique [*North African*] (MAR)
CFR............ Caile Ferate Romane [*Romanian Railroads*] (RO)
CFR............ Comite des Femmes Revolutionnaires [*Committee of Revolutionary Women*] [*Beninese*] (AF)
CFR............ Commander of the Order of the Federal Republic (MAR)
CFR............ Compagnie Francaise de Raffinage
CFRC.......... Chemins de Fer Royaux du Cambodge [*Royal Cambodian Railroads*] [*Replaced by CRC*] (CL)
CFRO.......... Centre Francais de Recherche Operationnelle (MAR)
CFRZ.......... Centre Federal de Recherches Zootechniques (MAR)
CFS............ Ceskoslovenska Filmova Spolecnost [*Czechoslovak Motion Picture Company*] (CZ)
CFS............ Compagnie Financiere de Suez (MAR)
CFS............ Compagnie Forestiere de Sangatanga (MAR)
CFS............ Compagnie Forestiere de Sassandra (MAR)
CFSG.......... Compagnie Forestiere du Sud-Gabon (MAR)
CFSI........... Centre de Formation de Specialistes de l'Information [*Information Media Specialists Training Center*] [*Malagasy*] (AF)
CFSI........... Confederation Francaise des Syndicats Independents [*French Confederation of Independent Unions*]
CFSO.......... Compagnie Forestiere Sangha-Oubangui (MAR)
CFT............ Centrul de Fizica Tehnica [*Center for Technical Physics*] (RO)
CFT............ Chemin de Fer du Togo (MAR)
Cft.............. Cift [*Pair (Of)*] (TU)
CFT............ Compagnie Forestiere Tere (MAR)
CFT............ Compagnie Forestiere Tropicale (MAR)
CFT............ Confederation Francaise du Travail [*French Confederation of Labor*] (WER)
CFT............ Corporacion Financiera del Transporte [*Transport Financial Corporation*] [*Colombian*] (LA)
CFTC.......... Commonwealth Fund for Technical Cooperation (MAR)
CFTC.......... Confederation Francaise des Travailleurs Chretiens [*French Confederation of Christian Workers*] (WER)
CFTH.......... Compagnie Francaise Thomson Houston
CFTI........... Centre de Formation aux Techniques de l'Information (MAR)
CFTP.......... Compagnie Franco-Tunisienne de Petrole [*Franco-Tunisian Petroleum Company*] (AF)
CFTTP........ Centre de Formation des Techniciens des Travaux Publics [*Public Works Technician Training Center*] [*Laotian*] (CL)
CFU............ Ceskoslovensky Filmovy Ustav [*Czechoslovak Motion Picture Institute*] (CZ)
CFU............ Commercial Farmers Union (MAR)
CFVA.......... Centre de Formation et de Vulgarisation Agricoles de Kaedi [*Mauritanian*] (MAR)
CFVU.......... Cesky Fond Vytvarnych Umelcu [*Czech Creative Artists' Fund*] (CZ)
Cg............... Caglayan [*Waterfall*] (TU)
cg............... Centigramm [*Centigram*] (HU)
cg............... Centigramme [*Centigram*] [*French*]
cg............... Centigramo [*Centigram*] [*Spanish*]
CG.............. Chemische Gesellschaft [*Chemical Society*] (EG)
CG.............. Congo [*Two-letter standard code*] (CNC)
CG.............. Connradh na Gaedhilge [*Gaelic League*] [*Founded 1893*]
CG.............. Conseil General [*General Council*] (LA1)
CG.............. Consul General [*French*] (MTD)
CG.............. Crna Gora [*Montenegro*] (YU)
C de G........ Croix de Guerre [*French military decoration*]
cg............... Senttigramma(a) [*Finnish*]
cg............... Zentigramm [*Centigram*] [*German*]
CGA............ Clove Growers' Association (MAR)
CGA............ Comandacia General de Aeronautica [*Peru*]
CGA............ Compagnie Gaziere d'Afrique (MAR)

CGA .... Compagnie Generale Africaine (MAR)
CGA .... Comptoir General d'Approvisionnement (MAR)
CGA .... Confederation Generale de l'Agriculture [*General Confederation of Agriculture*] [*French*] (WER)
CGADIP .... Compagnie Gaziere d'Afrique et de Distribution de Primagaz (MAR)
CGAE .... Compagnie Generale Africaine d'Electricite (MAR)
CGAF .... Confederation Generale de l'Artisanat Francais
CGAGC .... Cyprus Geographical Association. Geographical Chronicles, Nicosia [*A publication*] (MAR)
CGB .... Christlicher Gewerkschaftsbund Deutschlands [*Christian Trade Union Federation of Germany*] [*West German*] (WEN)
CGC .... Compagnie Generale de Carrelages (MAR)
CGC .... Compagnie Generale de la Chaussure [*North African*] (MAR)
CGC .... Confederation Generale des Cadres [*General Confederation of Managerial Personnel*] [*French*] (WER)
CGCCET ..... Comisia Guvernamentala pentru Colaborare si Cooperare Economica si Tehnica [*Governmental Commission for Economic and Technical Collaboration and Cooperation*] (RO)
CGCE .... Comptoir Guineen du Commerce Exterieur [*Guinean Foreign Trade Agency*]
CGCED .... Caribbean Group for Cooperation in Economic Development (LA)
CGCP .... Confederacion General de Campesinos del Peru [*General Confederation of Peasants of Peru*] (LA)
CGCT .... Compagnie Generale de Constructions Telephoniques (MAR)
CGCTP .... Compagnie Gabonaise de Construction et Travaux Publics (MAR)
CGD .... Commissariat General au Developpement [*General Development Commission*] [*Niger*] (AF)
CGDORIS .... Compagnie Generale pour les Developpements Operationnels de Richesses Sous-Marines (MAR)
CGE .... Compagnie Generale d'Electricite [*Moroccan*] (MAR)
CGE .... Confederacion General Economica [*General Economic Confederation*] [*Argentine*] (LA)
CGEA .... Centre de Gestion des Exploitations Agricoles [*North African*] (MAR)
CGEA .... Commissariat General de l'Energie Atomique [*General Atomic Energy Commission*] [*Zairian*] (AF)
CGEA .... Confederation Generale Economique Algerienne [*Algerian General Economic Confederation*] (AF)
CGEC .... Confederacion General de Empleados de Comercio [*General Confederation of Business Employees*] [*Argentine*] (LA)
CGECI .... Compagnie Generale d'Electricite de Cote-d'Ivoire (MAR)
CGEE .... Compagnie Generale de l'Equipement Electrique [*General Electrical Equipment Company*] [*French*] (WER)
CGEEOM .... Compagnie Generale des Eaux pour l'Etranges et l'Outre-Mer (MAR)
CGEM .... Confederation Generale Economique Marocaine [*Moroccan General Economic Federation*] (AF)
CGERA .... Confederacion General de Educadores de la Republica Argentina [*General Teachers Confederation of the Argentine Republic*] (LA)
CGES .... Compagnie Generale des Eaux du Senegal (MAR)
CGF .... Commonwealth Games Federation (EA)
CGG .... Compagnie Generale de Geophysique [*North African*] (MAR)
CGGE .... Compagnie Generale Guineenne d'Electricite (MAR)
CGH .... Castle of Good Hope Decoration (MAR)
CGI .... Comissao Geral de Investigacoes [*General Investigations Committee*] [*Brazilian*] (LA)
CGI .... Compagnie Generale Immobiliere [*North African*] (MAR)
CGI .... Confederacion General de la Industria [*General Confederation of Industry*] [*Argentine*] (LA)
CGIAR .... Consultative Group on International Agricultural Research (MAR)
CGICA .... Credit Guarantee Insurance Corporation of Africa (MAR)
CGIL .... Confederazione Generale Italiana del Lavoro [*Italian General Confederation of Labor*] (WER)
CGIOR .... Centro General de Instruccion de Oficiales de Reserva [*General Training Center for Reserve Officers*] [*Uruguayan*] (LA)
CGIS .... Comisaria General de Investigacion Social [*General Headquarters of Social Studies*] [*Spanish*] (WER)
CGK .... Cihelny Gustava Klimenta [*Gustav Kliment Brick Works*] (CZ)
CGKT .... Confederation Generale Kamerunaise du Travail [*Cameroonian General Confederation of Labor*] (AF)
CGLS .... Confederazione Generale dei Lavoratori della Somalia [*General Confederation of Somali Workers*] (AF)
CGM .... Compagnie Generale de Madagascar (MAR)
CGM .... Compagnie Generale Maritime (MAR)
CGM .... Compagnie Generale des Moteurs (MAR)
CGM .... Confederatia Generala a Muncii [*General Confederation of Labor*] (RO)
CGM .... Congo Gospel Mission (MAR)
CGN .... Compagnie Generale du Niger (MAR)
CGO .... Compagnie Generale d'Organisation (MAR)
CGOT .... Compagnie Generale des Oleagineux Tropicaux (MAR)
CGP .... Centre Gabonais de Prevention (MAR)
CGP .... Commando de Guerra Popular [*Popular War Command*] [*Venezuelan*] (LA)
CGP .... Confederacion General de Profesionales [*General Confederation of Professionals*] [*Argentine*] (LA)
CGP .... Conseil de la Guerre Politique [*Political Warfare Council*] [*Cambodian*] (CL)
CGP .... Cuerpo General de Policia [*General Police Corps*] [*Spanish*] (WER)
CGP .... Cumhuriyet Guvenlik Partisi [*Republican Reliance Party*] (TU)
CGPF .... Confederation Generale du Patronat Francais [*General Confederation of French Employers*] [*Now CNPF*] (WER)
CGPIF .... Compagnie Generale de Participation Industrielle et Financiere (MAR)
CGPM .... Conseil General des Peches pour la Mediterranee (MAR)
CGPPO .... Compagnie Generale des Plantations et Palmeraies de l'Ogooue [*Gabonese*] (MAR)
CGPS .... Caisse Gabonaise de Prevoyance Sociale (MAR)
cgr .... Centigrade [*Centigrade*] [*French*]
CGR .... Compagnie Generale de Radiologie (MAR)
CGR .... Contraloria General de la Republica [*National General Accounting Office*] [*Colombian*] (LA)
CGS .... Centymetr-Gram-Sekunda [*Centimeter-Gram-Second*] [*Polish*]
CGS .... Confederacion General de Sindicatos [*General Confederation of Trade Unions*] [*Salvadoran*] (LA)
CGS .... Confederation Generale des Syndicats [*General Confederation of Trade Unions*] [*French*]
CGSI .... Confederation Generale des Syndicats Independents [*General Confederation of Independent Unions*] [*Algerian*]
CGSL .... Compagnie Generale Sangha-Likouala (MAR)
CGSL .... Confederazione Generale Somala dei Lavoratori [*Somali General Workers Confederation*] (AF)
CGSLB .... Centrale Generale des Syndicats Liberaux de Belgique [*General Organization of Belgian Liberal Labor Unions*] (WER)
CGT .... Central General de Trabajadores [*General Workers Federation*] [*Honduran*] (LA)
CGT .... Comando Geral dos Trabalhadores [*Union Headquarters*] [*Brazilian*] (LA)
CGT .... Compagnie Generale des Constructions Telephoniques [*General Telephone Construction Company*] [*French*] (WER)
CGT .... Compagnie Generale Transatlantique [*General Transatlantic Shipping Company*] [*French*] (WER)
CGT .... Compagnie Generale de Transports Aeriens (MAR)
CGT .... Confederacao Geral de Trabalho [*General Confederation of Labor*] [*Portuguese*] (WER)
CGT .... Confederacion General de Trabajadores [*General Confederation of Workers*] [*Salvadoran*] (LA1)
CGT .... Confederacion General del Trabajo [*General Labor Confederation*] [*Colombian*] (LA)
CGT .... Confederacion General del Trabajo [*General Labor Confederation*] [*Dominican Republic*] (LA)
CGT .... Confederacion General del Trabajo [*General Labor Confederation*] [*Nicaraguan*] (LA)
CGT .... Confederacion General del Trabajo [*General Confederation of Labor*] [*Argentine*] (PD)
CGT .... Confederation Generale du Travail [*General Confederation of Labor*] [*Luxembourg*] (WER)
CGT .... Confederation Generale du Travail [*General Confederation of Labor*] [*Martiniquais*] (PPW)
CGT .... Confederation Generale du Travail [*General Confederation of Labor*] [*French*] (PPE)
CGT .... Confederation Generale des Travailleurs [*South Vietnamese*]
CGTA .... Confederation Generale des Travailleurs Africains (MAR)
CGTA .... Confederation Generale des Travailleurs de l'Angola [*General Confederation of Workers of Angola*] (AF)
CGTAE .... Compagnie Generale de Transports en Afrique Equatoriale [*Equatorial Africa General Transport Company*] [*Congolese*] (AF)
CGTAP .... Compagnie Generale de Transports en Afrique et de Participations (MAR)
CGTB .... Confederation Generale du Travail du Burundi [*General Confederation of Labor of Burundi*] (AF)
CGTC .... Confederacion General de Trabajadores Costarricenses [*General Confederation of Costa Rican Workers*] (LA)
CGTC .... Confederation Generale des Travailleurs Congolais (MAR)
CGTDS .... Confederation Generale des Travailleurs Democrates du Senegal [*General Confederation of Democratic Workers of Senegal*] (AF)
CGTFB .... Confederacion General de Trabajadores Fabriles de Bolivia [*General Confederation of Bolivian Factory Workers*] (LA)
CGT-FO ...... Confederation Generale du Travail - Force Ouvriere [*General Confederation of Labor - Workers' Force*] [*French*] (AF)
CGTG .... Confederacion General de Trabajadores de Guatemala [*General Confederation of Workers of Guatemala*] (LA)
CGTK .... Confederation Generale du Travail du Kamerun (MAR)
CGTP .... Confederacion General de Trabajadores del Peru [*General Confederation of Workers of Peru*] (LA)
CGTP .... Construction Generale et Travaux Publics (MAR)
CGTR .... Confederation Generale du Travail de la Reunion [*General Confederation of Labor of Reunion*] (AF)
CGTR .... Confederation Generale du Travail du Ruanda (MAR)
CGTRA .... Compagnie Gabonaise de Transport et de Reparation Automobile (MAR)

CGTS .... Confederacion General de Trabajadores Salvadorenos [*General Confederation of Salvadoran Workers*] (LA)
CGTS .... Confederation Generale du Travail du Senegal [*General Confederation of Labor of Senegal*] (AF)
CGTU .... Confederacion General de Trabajadores del Uruguay [*General Confederation of Uruguayan Workers*] (LA)
CGTU .... General Confederation of Trade Unions [*Syrian*] (ME)
CGU .... Ceremonial Guard Unit [*Singapore*] (ML)
CGU .... Cesky Geologicky Urad [*Czech Geological Office*] (CZ)
CGUP .... Comite Guatemalteco de Unidad Patriotica [*Guatemalan Committee of Patriotic Unity*] (PD)
CGWU .... Commercial and General Workers' Union [*Rhodesia and Nyasaland*]
CH .... Centrala Handlowa [*Sales Center*] (POL)
CH .... Ceskoslovenske Hute, Narodni Podnik [*Czechoslovak Metallurgical Works, National Enterprise*] (CZ)
ch .... Chapitre [*Chapter*] [*French*]
ch .... Chaussee [*Road*] [*French*] (CED)
Ch/ .... Chef De [*Chief Of*] [*Cambodian*] (CL)
Ch .... Chemie [*Chemistry*] [*German*]
ch .... Chervonets [*Monetary unit; 1922-1947*] (RU)
Ch .... Chevaux [*Horses*] [*Military*] [*French*] (MTD)
Ch .... Chitalishte [*Library*] [*A periodical*] (BU)
ch .... Date (BU)
Ch .... H-Hour [*Military term*] (RU)
Ch .... H-Hour, Time of Attack (BU)
ch .... Hour (BU)
ch .... Hour (RU)
Ch .... Library (BU)
ch .... Man, Men (RU)
ch .... Number (BU)
ch .... Number, Date (RU)
ch .... Part, Section (BU)
ch .... Part, Unit (RU)
ch .... Pure (RU)
CH .... Switzerland [*Two-letter standard code*] (CNC)
ch .... Via (RU)
CHA .... Centrale van Hogere Ambtenaren
ChA .... Red Army (BU)
CHACONA ... Chantier des Constructions Navales [*Naval Shipyard*] [*Congolese*] (AF)
CHADA .... Societe Chimique et Industrielle Africaine du Dahomey (MAR)
CHADECJA ... Stronnictwo Chrzescijanskiej Demokracji [*Christian Democratic Party*] [*Polish*] (PPE)
Ch d'aff .... Charge d'Affaires [*French*] (MTD)
CHAIDIS .... Chaine Africaine d'Importation, de Distribution, et d'Exportation [*Senegalese*] (MAR)
CHAKA .... Chama Cha Kiswahili Africa (MAR)
CHALLPESCA ... Empresa Mixta Pesquera Peruano-Japonesa [*Peru-Japan Mixed Fisheries Enterprise*] (LA)
CHAMA .... Chama Cha Mapinduzi [*Revolutionary Party*] [*Tanzanian*] (AF)
Chamb .... Chambellan [*Chamberlain*] [*French*] (MTD)
CHANETA ... Tanzania Amateur Netball Association (MAR)
CHANIC .... Chantier Naval et Industriel du Congo (MAR)
ChAO .... Chuvash Autonomous Oblast [*1920-1925*] (RU)
ChAO .... Quaternary Ammonium Compound (RU)
ChAP .... Automatic Frequency Control (RU)
Chap .... Chapelle [*Chapel*] [*French*] (NAU)
chap .... Chapitre [*Chapter*] [*French*]
ChARS .... Automatic Reader with a Shift Register (RU)
CHAS .... Centrala Handlu Artykulami Sportowymi [*Sports Goods Trade Center*] (POL)
Chas .... Chapel [*Topography*] (RU)
chasprom ... Watchmaking Industry (RU)
CHASS .... Conference of Heads of Assisted Secondary Schools (MAR)
Chat .... Chateau [*Castle*] [*French*] (NAU)
CHATO .... Societe Chimique et Industrielle Africaine du Togo (MAR)
Chau .... Chateau [*Castle, Country House*] [*Military map abbreviation*] [*World War I*] [*French*] (MTD)
chayn .... Tea Factory [*Topography*] (RU)
chayn .... Tea Sovkhoz [*Topography*] (RU)
ChAZ .... Chelyabinsk Abrasives Plant (RU)
CHB .... Central Housing Board (MAR)
CHB .... Commonwealth Heraldry Board (EA)
CHB .... Corps Perhubungan [*Signal Corps*] (IN)
ChBm .... Church of the Brethren Mission (MAR)
ChBT .... Black and White Television (System) (RU)
ChBT- .... Pulse Frequency Towed Thermograph [*Oceanography*] (RU)
ChBVP .... Black Sea - Baltic Sea Waterway (RU)
CHC .... Centrala Handlowa [*or Handlu*] Ceramiki [*Ceramic Products Sales Center*] (POL)
CHC .... Societe Cameroon Hotels Corporation (MAR)
chch .... Parts, Units (RU)
CHD .... Cagdas Hukukcular Dernegi [*Contemporary Jurists' Organization*] (TU)
ChD .... Frequency Discriminator (RU)
ChD .... Point of Advance Guard (BU)
ChD .... Rate of Respiration (RU)
chda .... Analytically Pure (RU)
CHE .... Centrala Hidroelectrica [*Hydroelectric Power Plant*] (RO)
CHE .... Christian Higher Education (MAR)
ChE .... Number Equivalent (RU)
ChE .... Sensitive Element (RU)
CHE .... Switzerland [*Three-letter standard code*] (CNC)
CHEAM .... Centre des Hautes Etudes Administratives sur l'Afrique et l'Asie Modernes [*Center for Advanced Administrative Studies on Modern Africa and Asia*] [*French*] (AF)
CHEC .... Central Hidroelectrica de Caldas [*Manizales*] (COL)
CHEC .... Commonwealth Human Ecology Council (EA)
Chechengosizdat ... Chechen-Ingush State Publishing House (RU)
Chechoblizdat ... Chechen-Ingush Oblast Publishing House (RU)
Chee .... Chaussee [*Road*] [*Military map abbreviation*] [*World War I*] [*French*] (MTD)
Cheka .... Extraordinary Commission for Combating Counterrevolution and Sabotage [*1918-1922*] (RU)
chekhosl ..... Czechoslovak (RU)
chel .... Man, Men (RU)
chel-ch .... Man-Hour (RU)
Chem .... Chemie [*or Chemiker*] [*Chemistry or Chemist*] [*German*]
chem .... Chemisch [*Chemical*] [*German*]
CHEMAK ..... Zjednoczenie Przemyslu Budowy Aparatury Chemicznej [*Association of Chemical Equipment Construction Industry*] (POL)
CHEMAPOL ... Podnik Zahranicniho Obchodu pro Dovoz a Vyvoz Chemickych Vyrobku a Surovin [*Foreign Trade Enterprise for the Import and Export of Chemical Products and Raw Materials*] (CZ)
Chemifa .... Chemie- und Pharmazie-GmbH [*Chemical and Pharmaceutical Co.*] (EG)
CHEMODROGA ... Narodni Podnik pro Prodej Drog a Kosmetickych Vyrobku [*National Enterprise for the Retail Sale of Drugs and Cosmetic Products*] (CZ)
CHEMOKOMPLEX ... CHEMOKOMPLEX Vegyipari Gep es Berendezes Export-Import Vallalat [*CHEMOKOMPLEX Export-Import Enterprise for Chemical Industry Machinery and Equipment*] (HU)
CHEMOLIMPEX ... CHEMOLIMPEX Magyar Vegyiaru Kulkereskedelmi Vallalat [*CHEMOLIMPEX Foreign Trade Enterprise for Hungarian Chemical Products*] (HU)
ChEMZ .... Cheboksary Electromechanical Plant (RU)
ChEMZ .... Frequency Electromagnetic Sounding (RU)
Chen .... Chenal [*Channel*] [*French*] (NAU)
ChENIS .... Black Sea Experimental Scientific Research Station (RU)
cherep .... Tile Factory [*Topography*] (RU)
Chern m .... Black Sea (RU)
Chernomorneft' ... Association of the Black Sea Region Petroleum Industry (RU)
Cheroblnatsizdat ... Cherkess Oblast National Publishing House (RU)
Cherpen .... Cherita Pendek [*Short Story*] (ML)
chert .... Drawing, Diagram (RU)
chert .... Sketch, Drawing (BU)
cherv .... Chervonets [*Monetary unit; 1922-1947*] (RU)
CHESF .... Companhia Hidroeletrica do Sao Francisco [*Sao Francisco Hydroelectric Company*] [*Brazilian*] (LA)
chesh .... Czech (BU)
chesh .... Czech (RU)
Chet .... Chalet [*Swiss Cottage*] [*Military map abbreviation*] [*World War I*] [*French*] (MTD)
chet .... Even (RU)
Cheteka .... Czechoslovak Telegraph Agency (BU)
Chev .... Chevalier [*French*] (MTD)
CHEVAP .... Companhia Hidroeletrica do Vale do Paraiba [*Paraiba Valley Hydroelectric Company*] [*Brazilian*] (LA)
ChF .... Black Sea Fleet (RU)
ch f .... Change Fixe [*French*]
ch de f .... Chemin de Fer [*Railway*] [*French*] (GPO)
Ch d f .... Chemin de Fer [*Railway*] [*French*] (MTD)
chf .... Pair (BU)
ChFAP .... Automatic Frequency - Phase Control (RU)
ChFZh .... Czechoslovak Physics Journal [*A publication*] (RU)
Chg .... Chiang [*River, Shoal, Harbour, Inlet, Channel, Sound*] [*Chinese*] (NAU)
CHG .... Compagnie de la Haute Gambie (MAR)
ChGK .... Extraordinary State Commission for the Determination and Investigation of Crimes Committed by the German Fascist Aggressors (RU)
ChGMP .... Black Sea State Steamship Line (RU)
ChGPI .... Cherkassy State Pedagogical Institute (RU)
ChGS .... Black Sea Hydrophysical Station (RU)
ChGU .... Chernovtsy State University (RU)
Ch-H .... Chemiehandel [*Trade in Chemicals*] (EG)
CHH .... Commission d'Histoire de l'Historiographie [*Commission of the History of Historiography*] (EA)
ChIASSR ..... Chechen-Ingush Autonomous Soviet Socialist Republic (RU)
ChIK .... Number-Pulse Code (RU)
CHILECTRA ... Compania Chilena de Electricidad Ltda. [*Chilean Electric Company Ltd.*] (LA)
ChIM .... Pulse Frequency Modulation (RU)
CHIMAF .... Societe Gabonaise de Produits Chimiques et Industriels (MAR)
ChIMESKh ... Chelyabinsk Institute of Rural Mechanization and Electrification (RU)

CHIMI-KHMER ... Societe Khmere d'Industrie Chimique [*Cambodian Chemical Industries Company*] (CL)
Chin .... Chemin [*Way, Road*] [*Military map abbreviation*] [*World War I*] [*French*] (MTD)
CHIPRODAL ... Compania Chilena de Productos Alimenticios [*Chilean Food Products Company*] (LA)
Chir .... Chirurg [*German*]
CHIRANA .... Narodni Podnik pro Vyrobu Lekarskych Stroju a Nastroju [*National Enterprise for the Production of Medical Appliances and Surgical Instruments*] (CZ)
Chirchiksel'mash ... Chirchik Agricultural Machinery Plant (RU)
ChIS .... Pulse Frequency System (RU)
chisl .... Numeral (BU)
chisl .... Numeral [*Grammar*] (RU)
chisl kolich ... Cardinal Number (RU)
chisl por ...... Ordinal Number (RU)
chisl sobir ... Collective Numeral (RU)
ChISS .... Frequency Selection Seismic Station (RU)
Chitkoop ..... Library Cooperative (BU)
Chitkori .... Chitalishtni Korespondenti [*Library Correspondents*] [*A periodical*] (BU)
ChIZ .... Chelyabinsk Measuring Instruments Plant (RU)
ChK .... Extraordinary Commission for Combating Counter-Revolution and Sabotage [*1918-1922*] (RU)
ChKKh .... Frequency-Contrast Characteristic (RU)
ChKLB .... Extraordinary Commission for the Liquidation of Illiteracy (RU)
ChKP .... Czechoslovak Communist Party (BU)
ChKZ .... Chelyabinsk Kirov Plant (RU)
ChKZ .... Member of the College of Attorneys (RU)
chl .... Article [*Grammar*] (BU)
chl .... Article [*Legal document*] (BU)
CHL .... Chile [*Three-letter standard code*] (CNC)
chl .... Member [*of a society*] (BU)
chl .... Member (RU)
ch-l .... Something, Anything, Whatever (RU)
chl chl .... Articles [*Legal document*] (BU)
chl chl .... Members [*of a society*] (BU)
chl koll zashch ... Member of the College of Attorneys (RU)
chl-kor .... Corresponding Member (RU)
Chlle .... Chapelle [*Chapel*] [*Military map abbreviation*] [*World War I*] [*French*] (MTD)
ChLTs .... Iron Foundry Shop (RU)
ChLZ .... Cast Iron Foundry (BU)
chl zor .... Corresponding Member (BU)
CHM .... Centre d'Hebergement des Misereux [*Indigent Shelter Center*] [*Cambodian*] (CL)
Chm .... Chemie [*Chemistry*] [*German*]
ChM .... Clockwork (RU)
ChM .... Extremely Soft (RU)
ChM .... Ferrous Metallurgy (BU)
ChM .... Ferrous Metallurgy (RU)
ChM .... Frequency-Modulated, Frequency Modulation (RU)
ChM .... Frequency Modulation (BU)
ChM .... Sensitive Manometer (RU)
chm .... Triannual Publication (BU)
CHMB .... Centrala Handlowa Materialow Budowlanych [*Building Materials Sales Center*] (POL)
ChM/ChM ... Frequency-Modulated Carrier/Frequency-Modulated Subcarrier Type System [*FM/FM*] (RU)
ch met .... Ferrous Metallurgy Plant [*Topography*] (RU)
ChMG .... Auxiliary-Heterodyne Frequency Modulation (RU)
ChMG .... Frequency Modulation Generator (RU)
CHMN .... Centrala Handlowa Metali Niezelaznych [*Non-Ferrous Metals Sales Center*] (POL)
ChMN .... Cranial Nerve (RU)
ChMOIDR .... Lectures of the Moscow Society of Russian History and Antiquities at the Moscow University [*A publication*] (RU)
ChMS- .... High-Speed Combing Machine (RU)
ChMT .... Black Sea Trawler (RU)
ChMTU .... Technical Specifications for Ferrous Metallurgy (RU)
ChMZ .... Chelyabinsk Metallurgical Plant (RU)
ChMZ .... Cherepovets Metallurgical Plant (RU)
ChMZAP ..... Chelyabinsk Machinery Plant for Motor Vehicle and Tractor Trailers (RU)
ChN .... Chemicky Nacelnik [*Chief of Chemical Service*] (CZ)
CHN .... China [*Three-letter standard code*] (CNC)
ChN .... Chirurgicka Nemocnice [*Surgical Hospital*] (CZ)
Chne .... Chaine [*Military map abbreviation*] [*World War I*] [*French*] (MTD)
Chnee .... Cheminee [*Chimney*] [*Military map abbreviation*] [*World War I*] [*French*] (MTD)
ChNII .... Cherkess Scientific Research Institute of Language, Literature, and History (RU)
ChNIIGD ...... Chelyabinsk Scientific Research Institute of Mining (RU)
ChNN .... Peak-Load Hour [*Telephony*] (RU)
ChNP .... Low-Pressure Component (RU)
ChO .... Advance Detachment (BU)
CHO .... Centrala Handlu Opalem [*Fuel Sales Center*] (POL)
ChOA .... Chkalov Oblast Archives (RU)
CHOCOCAM ... Chocolaterie et Confiserie Camerounaise (MAR)
CHOCODI ... Chocolaterie et Confiserie de Cote-d'Ivoire (MAR)
CHOGM .... Commonwealth Heads of Government Meeting (MAR)
ChOIDR .... Lectures at the Society of History and Russian Antiquities [*A publication*] (RU)
CHOiW .... Centrala Handlu Owocami i Warzywami [*Fruit and Vegetable Sales Center*] (POL)
ChOKPROD ... Extraordinary Oblast Food and Supply Committee (RU)
ChOMGI ...... Black Sea Branch of the Marine Hydro-Physical Institute (RU)
ChON .... Chasti Osobogo Naznacheniia [*Elements of Special Designation*] [*Political police units attached to the armed forces (1918-1924)*] [*USSR*]
chor .... Chorazy [*Ensign*] [*Polish*]
Chovnitovt ... Black Sea Branch of the All-Union Scientific, Engineering, and Technical Society of Water Transportation (RU)
ChP .... Black Sea Steamship Line (RU)
CHP .... Centrala Handlowa Przemyslu [*Industry Sales Center*] (POL)
CHP .... Cumhuriyet Halk Partisi [*Republican Peoples' Party - RPP*] (TU)
ChP .... Drawing Instrument (RU)
ChP .... Extraordinary Event (RU)
ChP .... Magnifying Projector for Watch Parts (RU)
ChP .... Pulse Rate (RU)
CHPC .... Centrala Handlowa Przemyslu Ceramicznego [*Ceramic Industry Sales Center*] (POL)
CHPCh .... Centrala Handlowa Przemyslu Chemicznego [*Chemical Industry Sales Center*] (POL)
CHPD .... Centrala Handlowa Przemyslu Drzewnego [*Lumber Industry Sales Center*] (POL)
CHPE .... Centrala Handlowa Przemyslu Elektrotechnicznego [*Electric Engineering Industry Sales Center*] (POL)
CHPH .... Centrala Handlowa Przemyslu Hutniczego [*Metallurgical Industry Sales Center*] (POL)
ChPI .... Chelyabinsk Polytechnic Institute (RU)
ChPI .... Repetition Rate (RU)
ChPK .... Black Sea Coast of the Caucasus (RU)
CHPM .... Centrala Handlowa Przemyslu Metalowego [*Metal Industry Sales Center*] (POL)
CHPM .... Centrala Handlowa Przemyslu Muzycznego [*Commercial Center for Music Industry*] [*Polish*]
CHPO .... Centrala Handlowa Przemyslu Odziezowego [*Clothing Industry Sales Center*] (POL)
CHPP .... Centrala Handlowa Przemyslu Papierniczego [*Paper Industry Sales Center*] (POL)
CHPS .... Centrala Handlowa Przemyslu Skorzanego [*Leather Industry Sales Center*] (POL)
ChPV .... Preignition Number (RU)
ChPZ .... Advance Party (BU)
Chq .... Cheque [*Check*] [*French*]
CHR .... Chronique [*French*]
ChR .... Czechoslovak Republic (BU)
chr .... Partly Soluble (RU)
Chrezpolpred ... Plenipotentiary Extraordinary (RU)
chrezv .... Extraordinary, Special (RU)
ChRF .... Partial Recursive Function (RU)
ChRL .... Chinska Republika Ludowa [*Chinese People's Republic*] (POL)
CHRONOR ... Narodni Podnik pro Tuzemskou Distribuci Hodin a Zlatnickeho Zbozi [*National Enterprise for Domestic Distribution of Watches and Jewelry Products*] (CZ)
ChRTS .... Private Manual Exchange (RU)
chrv .... Net Register Tonnage (RU)
ChS .... Carrier Telegraphy (RU)
CHS .... Centralni Hospodarske Skladiste [*Central Warehouse*] (CZ)
CHS .... Centre for Human Settlements (MAR)
ChS .... Chemicky Spolek, Narodni Podnik [*Chemical Society, National Enterprise*] (CZ)
ch s .... Private Collection (RU)
ChSA .... Human Serum Albumin (RU)
ChSAN .... Czechoslovak Academy of Sciences (RU)
ChSD .... Medium-Pressure Component (RU)
chshch .... Calyx (RU)
chshl .... Sepal (RU)
ch-shte .... Library (BU)
ChSM .... Czechoslovak Youth League (RU)
ch sp .... Pure Alcohol (RU)
ChSR .... Czechoslovak Republic (RU)
CHSS .... Centrala Handlowa Sprzetu Sportowego [*Sport Equipment Sales Center*] (POL)
ChSSR .... Czechoslovak Socialist Republic (BU)
ChSSR .... Czechoslovak Socialist Republic (RU)
CHSSS .... Centrala Handlowa Sprzetu Sportowego i Szkutniczego [*Sport and Boating Equipment Sales Center*] (POL)
ChT .... Carrier Telegraphy (RU)
CHT .... Centrala Handlowo-Techniczna [*Technical Trade Center*] (POL)
cht .... Chetvert [*Measures*] (RU)
ChT .... Extremely Hard (RU)
Cht .... Read, Reading [*Computers*] (RU)
cht .... Thursday (RU)
ChTA .... Czechoslovak News Agency (RU)
ChTPD .... Chlopskie Towarzystwo Przyjaciol Dzieci [*Peasants' Society of Children's Friends*] (POL)
ChTPZ .... Chelyabinsk Pipe-Rolling Plant (RU)

ChTR........... Chervena Tribuna [*Red Tribune*] [*A periodical*] (BU)
ChTs........... Number of Centers [*of Recrystallization*] (RU)
ChTS........... Technical Supply Unit (RU)
ChTT........... Number of Theoretical Plates (RU)
chtv........... Thursday (RU)
ChTZ........... Chelyabinsk Tractor Plant (RU)
ChTZ........... Specific Technical Task (RU)
CHU........... Centre Hospitalier Universitaire [*University Hospital Center*] [*French*] (WER)
ChU........... Chemicky Ustav [*Chemical Institute*] (CZ)
CHU........... Christelijk-Historische Unie [*Christian-Historical Union*] [*Dutch*] (PPW)
ChU........... Reader, Reading Device [*Computers*] (RU)
chug........... Iron Foundry [*Topography*] (RU)
chuk........... Chukchi, Chuckchee (RU)
ChUSTO...... Extraordinary Plenipotentiary of the Council of Labor and Defense (RU)
chuv........... Chuvash (RU)
ChuvAO...... Chuvash Autonomous Oblast [*1920-1925*] (RU)
Chuvashgiz... Chuvash State Publishing House (RU)
Chuvashgosizdat... Chuvash State Publishing House (RU)
ChuvASSR... Chuvash Autonomous Soviet Socialist Republic (RU)
ch-v........... Cheval Vapeur [*Horse Power*] [*French*]
chv-ch......... Man-Hour (RU)
ChVD........... High-Pressure Component (RU)
chv-d........... Man-Day (RU)
ChVO........... Military Guard Unit (RU)
ChVS........... Member of the Military Council (RU)
ChVSK........ Extraordinary Military Medical Commission (RU)
chx........... Chevaux [*Horsepower*] [*French*] (MTD)
CHZ........... Centrala Handlu Zagranicznego [*Commercial Center for Foreign Trade*] [*Polish*]
CHZ........... Centralni Higijenski Zavod [*Central Institute of Hygiene*] (YU)
ChZ........... Chemicka Zaloha [*Chemical Reserve*] (CZ)
ChZ........... Chemicke Zavody [*Chemical Works*] (CZ)
Chz........... Cihaz [*Device, Instrument*] (TU)
ChZ........... Light Dimming, Dimout [*In blackout*] (RU)
chz........... Reading Room (RU)
CHZFuzine... Crpna Hidroelektrana Fuzine [*Fuzine Pumped Storage Hydroelectric Station*] (YU)
CHZiS......... Centrala Handlowa Zelasa i Stali [*Iron and Steel Sales Center*] (POL)
ChZJD......... Chemicke Zavody Juraja Dimitrova [*Juraj Dimitrov Chemical Works*] (CZ)
ChZPW........ Chorzowskie Zaklady Przemyslu Weglowego [*Chorzow Coal Enterprises*] (POL)
ChZS........... Chemicke Zavody na Slovensku, Narodny Podnik [*Chemical Plants in Slovakia, National Enterprise*] (CZ)
ChZWP........ Chemicke Zavody Wilhelma Piecka [*Wilhelm Pieck Chemical Works*] (CZ)
CI........... Caritas Internationalis [*International Confederation of Catholic Organizations for Charitable and Social Action*] (EA)
CI........... Carte d'Identite [*Identification Card*] (CL)
CI........... Carte d'Importation [*Import License*] [*Cambodian*] (CL)
CI........... Centre d'Instruction [*Instruction Center*] [*Cambodian*] (CL)
CI........... Christian Institute (MAR)
CI........... Circonscription Indigene (MAR)
CI........... Comite Interimaire [*Provisional Committee*] [*Chadian*] (AF)
CI........... Conselho de Imprensa [*Press Council*] [*Portuguese*] (WER)
CI........... Consiliul Intercooperatist [*Intercooperative Council*] (RO)
CI........... Corps Intendans [*Quartermaster Corps*] (IN)
CI........... Crux Iberica [*Iberian Cross*] [*Spanish*] (WER)
CI........... Ivory Coast [*Two-letter standard code*] (CNC)
CIA........... Centrala a Industriei Alimentare [*Food Industry Central*] (RO)
CIA........... Centro de Investigaciones Agrarias [*Agricultural Research Center*] [*Mexican*] (LA)
CIA........... Centro de Investigaciones Agrarias [*Agricultural Research Center*] [*Venezuelan*] (LA1)
CIA........... Centro de Investigaciones Aplicadas. Universidad del Cauca [*Popayan*] (COL)
CIA........... Comite International d'Auschwitz (MAR)
CIA........... Compagnie Immobiliere Algerienne [*Algerian Real Estate Company*] (AF)
cia........... Compania [*Company, Society*] [*Spanish*]
CIA........... Conseil International des Archives
CIA........... Construccion, Ingenieria, Arquitectura [*Bogota*] (COL)
CIA........... Construccion e Inversiones Astoria [*Cali*] (COL)
CIA........... Credit Insurance Association (MAR)
CIAA........... Comptoir Industriel et Agricole Abidjan (MAR)
CIAAU......... Comptoir Ivoirien d'Accessoires Automobiles (MAR)
CIABA......... Compagnie Immobiliere de l'Avenue Barthe (MAR)
CIABRA....... Centro Integrado de Abastecimento de Brasilia [*Brasilia Integrated Supply Center*] [*Brazilian*] (LA)
CIAC........... Centrala Industriei Articolelor Casnice [*Central for the Household Articles Industry*] (RO)
CIAC........... Comision Interamericana de Arbitraje Comercial [*Inter-American Commercial Arbitration Commission*] (LA)
CIAC........... Compagnie Industrielle et Agricole au Cameroun (MAR)
CIAC........... Compagnie des Industries Africaines du Caoutchouc (MAR)
CIAC........... Corporacion de la Industria Aeronautica Colombiana [*Bogota*] (COL)
CIACAM...... Compagnie Industrielle d'Automobiles au Cameroun (MAR)
CIACUT....... Centrala Industriei Articolelor Casnice si Utilajelor Tehnologice [*Central for the Household Articles and Technical Equipment Industry*] (RO)
CIADFOR.... Centre Inter-Africain pour le Developpement de la Formation Professionnelle [*Inter-African Center for the Development of Professional Training*] (AF)
CIAE........... Compania Italo Argentina de Electricidad [*Italo-Argentine Electric Power Company*] (LA)
CI-AEA........ Certificat d'Importation sur l'Aide Economique Americaine [*Import Certificate on American Economic Aid*] [*Cambodian*] (CL)
CIAEF......... Comision Intersectorial de Asuntos Economicos y Financieros [*Intersectorial Committee on Economic and Financial Affairs*] [*Peruvian*] (LA)
CIAF........... Centro Interamericano de Fotointerpretacion [*Bogota*] (COL)
CIAGA......... Confederacion Interamericana de Ganaderos [*Inter-American Cattlemen's Confederation*] (LA)
CIAGE......... Centro Internacional de Agencias, Lda. (MAR)
CIAGO......... Chemische Industrie AKU [*Algemene Kunstzidie Unie*]-Goodrich [*Belgian*]
CIALA......... Inter-Faculty Centre for African Anthropology and Linguistics (MAR)
CIAN........... Fabrica de Monturas para Anteojos [*Bogota*] (COL)
CIANA......... Comision Ibero-Americano de Navigacion Aerea [*Spanish*]
CIANS......... Collegium Internationale Activitatis Nervosae Superioris (EA)
CIAO........... Compagnie Industrielle et Agricole Oubangui (MAR)
CIAO........... Conference Internationale des Africanistes de l'Ouest (MAR)
CIAP........... Comite Interamericano de la Alianza para el Progreso [*Inter-American Committee on the Alliance for Progress*] [*Use ICAP*] (LA)
CIAP........... Compagnie Ivoirienne d'Armement a la Peche (MAR)
CIAPG......... Confederation Internationale des Anciens Prisonniers de Guerre [*International Confederation of Former Prisoners of War*] (EA)
CIAPT......... Centre d'Instruction et d'Application de Police de Tchibanga (MAR)
CIARA......... Conference Internationale sur l'Assistance aux Refugies d'Afrique (MAR)
CIARCO...... Colombiana de Ingenieros Arquitectos Constructores Ltda. [*Bogota*] (COL)
CIARD......... Comite Francais des Concours d'Inventions et Innovations Adaptees aux Regions en Developpement [*French Committee for Competitions Relating to Inventions and Innovations Suitable for Use in Third World Areas*] (AF)
CIAS........... Centro de Investigacion y Accion Social [*Bogota*] (COL)
CIAS........... Centro de Investigacion y Accion Social [*Social Research and Action Center*] [*Argentine*] (LA)
CIAS........... Centro de Investigaciones y Accion Social [*Center of Social Research and Action*] [*Peruvian*] (LA)
CIAS........... Comitato Interministeriale per Ricerche Spaziale [*Interministerial Committee for Space Research*] [*Italian*] (WER)
CIAS........... Conference of Independent African States (MAR)
CIASI.......... Comite Interministeriel d'Amenagement des Structures Industrielles [*Interministerial Committee for Planning Industrial Structures*] [*Guadeloupe*] (LA1)
CIAT........... Centrala Industriei de Autovehicule si Transport [*Central of the Motor Vehicle and Transportation Industry*] (RO)
CIAT........... Centro Interamericano de Administracion del Trabajo [*Inter-American Centre for Labour Administration*] (EA)
CIAT........... Centro Interamericano Administradores Tributarios [*Inter-American Center of Tax Administrators*] (EA)
CIAT........... Centro Internacional de Agricultura Tropical [*International Center for Tropical Agriculture*] (LA)
CIAT........... Comision Interamericana del Atun Tropical [*Inter-American Tropical Tuna Commission*] (LA)
CIAT........... Comite Interministeriel de l'Amenagement du Territoire [*Moroccan*] (MAR)
CIAT........... Compagnia Italiana Autoservizi Turistici
CIAT........... Comptoir Immobilier de l'Afrique Tropicale (MAR)
CIATF......... Comite International des Associations Techniques de Fonderie [*International Committee of Foundry Technical Associations*] (EA)
CIATI.......... Centre Inter-Administratif de Traitement de l'Information [*Inter-Administrative Center for Information Processing*] [*Tunisian*] (AF)
CIB........... Capital Investments Board (MAR)
CIB........... Ceramique Industrielle du Benin (MAR)
CIB........... Classification Internationale des Brevets
CIB........... Comite Interprofessionel du Bourgogne [*French*]
CIB........... Comite Interprofessionnel Bananier (MAR)
CIB........... Communaute International Baha'ie (MAR)
CIB........... Compagnie Ivoirienne de Boissons (MAR)
CIB........... Conseil International du Batiment pour la Recherche, l'Etude, et la Documentation [*International Council for Building Research, Studies, and Documentation*] (EA)
CIB........... Conseil International du Ble [*International Wheat Council - IWC*] (EA)
CIB........... Societe Congolaise Industrielle des Bois (MAR)
CIBC........... Commonwealth Institute of Biological Control (MAR)

CIBE .... Confederation Internationale des Betteraviers Europeens [*International Confederation of European Sugar Beet Growers*] [*Common Market*]
CIBER .... Centre Interafricain d'Information et de Liaison sur le Bien-Etre Rural (MAR)
CIBESTAL... Societe de Constructions Industrielles de Batiment de l'Est-Algerien (MAR)
CIBOAF....... Compagnie d'Importation des Bois Africains (MAR)
CIBPU .... Comissao Interestadual da Bacia Parana-Uruguai [*Interstate Commission on Parana-Uruguay Basin*] [*Brazilian*] (LA)
CIBRASCEX ... Companhia Brasileira de Comercio Exterior [*Brazilian Foreign Trade Company*] (LA)
CIBRAZEM ... Companhia Brasileira de Armazenamento [*Brazilian Warehousing Company*] (LA)
CIBV.......... Consejo Internacional de Buena Vecindad, AC [*International Good Neighbor Council - IGNC*] (EA)
CIC .... Cala Izba Cywilna [*The Full Civil Chamber of the Supreme Court*] (POL)
CIC .... Capital Issues Commission (MAR)
CIC .... Caribbean Investment Corporation (LA)
CIC .... Central Incentives Committee [*Guyanese*] (LA)
CIC .... Central de Inversion y Credito, SA [*Investment and Credit Center, Inc.*] [*Spanish*] (WER)
CIC .... Centres d'Initiative Communiste [*Centers of Communist Initiative*] [*French*] (WER)
CIC .... Centro de Informaciones y Control [*Information and Control Center*] [*Bolivian*] (LA)
CIC .... Centro de Informaciones y Control [*Information and Control Center*] [*Chilean*] (LA)
CIC .... Centro de Investigacion y Capacitacion [*Research and Training Center*] [*Peruvian*] (LA)
CIC .... Combinat de Ingrasaminte Chimice [*Chemical Fertilizer Combine*] (RO)
CIC .... Comite International de Coordination pour l'Initiation a la Science et le Developpement des Activites Scientifiques Extra-Scolaires [*International Coordinating Committee for the Presentation of Science and the Development of Out-of-School Scientific Activities - ICC*] (EA)
CIC .... Commission Internationale de Supervision et de Controle [*International Supervisory and Control Commission*] [*Use ISCC*] (CL)
CIC .... Compagnie Immobiliere du Congo (MAR)
CIC .... Compagnie Internationale de Commerce (MAR)
CIC .... Compania de Industrias Chilenas [*Chilean Industries Company*] (LA)
CIC .... Confederation Internationale des Cadres (EA)
CIC .... Conseil International de la Chasse et de la Conservation du Gibier [*International Council for Game and Wildlife Conservation*] (EA)
CIC .... Conseil Ivoirien des Chargeurs (MAR)
CIC .... Consejo Internacional del Cafe [*International Coffee Council*] (LA)
CIC .... Corporation des Instituteurs et Institutrices Catholiques du Quebec
CIC .... Credit Industriel et Commercial [*French*]
CICA .... Centro de Investigacao Cientifica Algodoeira (MAR)
CICA .... Circulo Colombiano de Artistas [*Bogota*] (COL)
CICA .... Compagnie Industrielle de Conserves Alimentaires (MAR)
CICA .... Confederation of International Contractors' Associations (EA)
CICA .... Confederation Internationale du Credit Agricole [*International Confederation of Agricultural Credit*] (EA)
CICA .... Conference Internationale des Controles d'Assurances des Etats Africains, Francais, et Malgache [*International Conference of African, French, and Malagasy States on Insurance Supervision*] (AF)
CICA .... Societe Commerciale et Industrielle de la Cote-d'Afrique (MAR)
CICAF .... Caisse Inter-Professionnelle de Compensation des Allocations Familiales [*Interoccupational Family Allowance Compensation Fund*] [*Cambodian*] (CL)
CICAF .... Compagnie Industrielle de Combustibles Atomiques Frittes [*French*]
CICALIM ..... Compagnie Industrielle et Commerciale d'Alimentation [*Moroccan*] (MAR)
CICAM .... Societe Cotonniere Industrielle du Cameroun (MAR)
CICC .... Compagnie Immobiliere et Commerciale du Cameroun (MAR)
CICD .... Collegium Internationale Chirurgiae Digestivae (EA)
CICE.......... Centre Ivoirien du Commerce Exterieur [*Ivorian Center for Foreign Trade*] (AF)
CICE.......... Comite de Informacion y Contacto Externo para Empresarios Privados [*Committee on Information and External Contacts for Private Business Owners*] [*Ecuadorean*] (LA)
CICE.......... Corriente Izquierdista en las Ciencias Economicas [*Leftist Trend Economic Sciences*] [*Argentine*] (LA)
CICEPLA..... Confederacion Industrial de Celulosa y Papel Latinoamericana [*Latin American Cellulose and Paper Industrial Confederation*] (LA)
CICER .... Companhia Industrial de Cervejas e Refrigerantes da Guine [*The Brewery Company of Guinea-Bissau*] (AF)
CICF .... Chambre des Ingenieurs - Conseils de France
CICH .... Comite International de la Culture du Houblon [*International Hop Growers Convention - IHGC*] (EA)
CICHE .... Committee for International Co-Operation in Higher Education (MAR)
CICI .... Centre Industriel Centrafricano-Israelien (MAR)
CICI .... Consortium Ivoirien de Commerce et d'Industrie (MAR)
CICIAMS..... Comite International Catholique des Infirmieres et Assistantes Medico-Sociales [*International Committee of Catholic Nurses - ICCN*] (EA)
CICLA .... Corporacion de Integracion Cultural Latinoamericana [*Latin American Cultural Integration Corporation*] [*Chilean*] (LA)
CICM.......... Centro de Investigaciones de Ciencias Marinas [*Cartagena*] (COL)
CICM.......... Commission Internationale Catholique pour les Migrations [*International Catholic Migration Commission - ICMC*] (EA)
CICO .... Conference of International Catholic Organizations (EA)
CICODEC.... Compania Colombiana de Calzado [*Medellin*] (COL)
CICOL .... Compania Comercial Ltda. [*Popayan*] (COL)
CICOLAC.... Compania Colombiana de Alimentos Lacteos [*Bogota*] (COL)
CICOLPAGRO ... Compania Comercial de Productos Agropecuarios [*Bogota*] (COL)
CICOLPLAS ... Compania Colombiana de Plasticos [*Bogota*] (COL)
CICOMO ..... Companhia Industrial de Cordoarias de Mocambique (MAR)
CICOOP ...... Centrul de Calcul si Informatica al Cooperativelor de Consum [*Computation and Data Processing Center of the Consumer Cooperatives*] (RO)
CICOTP....... Compagnie Ivoirienne de Construction des Travaux Publics (MAR)
CICP.......... Comite Internacional para la Cooperacion de los Periodistas [*International Committee for Cooperation of Journalists*] [*Use ICCJ*] (LA)
CICP.......... Confederation Internationale du Credit Populaire [*International Confederation of Popular Credit - ICPC*] (EA)
CICPLB .... Comite International pour le Controle de la Productivite Laitiere du Betail [*International Committee for Recording the Productivity of Milk Animals - ICRPMA*] (EA)
CICR.......... Comitato Interministeriale per il Credito e Risparmio [*Interministerial Committee for Credit and Savings*] [*Italian*] (WER)
CICR.......... Comite International Contre la Repression [*International Committee Against Repression*] (EA)
CICR.......... Comite International de la Croix-Rouge [*International Committee of the Red Cross*] [*French*] (WER)
CICRED....... Comite International de Cooperation dans les Recherches Nationales en Demographie [*Committee for International Cooperation in National Research in Demography*] (EA)
CICRODEPORTES ... Circulo de Cronistas Deportivos de Antioquia [*Medellin*] (COL)
CICSA .... Centro de Informacion y Computo Sociedad Anonima [*Cali*] (COL)
CICTM........ Combinatul de Ingrasaminte Chimice Turnu Magurele [*Chemical Fertilizer Combine of Turnu Magurele*] (RO)
CICYP .... Consejo Interamericano de Comercio y Produccion [*Inter-American Council of Commerce and Production*] [*Use IACCP*] (LA)
CID .... Center for Industrial Development [*Barbadian*] (LA1)
CID .... Centre d'Information et de Documentation [*EG*] [*Luxembourg*]
CID .... Centre d'Information et de Documentation du Congo et du Ruanda-Urundi (MAR)
CID .... Centre International pour le Developpement [*International Center for Development*] [*French*] (AF)
CID .... Centro de Informacion y Documentacion [*Information and Documentation Center*] [*Argentine*] (LA)
CID .... Centro de Integracion y Desarrollo [*Integration and Development Center*] [*Bolivian*] (LA)
CID .... Centro de Investigacion Documentaria [*Buenos Aires, Argentina*]
CID .... Centro de Investigaciones Digitales [*Computer Research Center*] [*Cuban*] (LA)
CID .... Coalicion Institucionalista Democratica [*Democratic Institutional Coalition*] [*Ecuadorean*] (PPW)
CID .... Comite International du Dachau (MAR)
CID .... Consortium for International Development (MAR)
CID .... Criminal Investigation Department (MAR)
CID .... Criminal Investigation Directorate (MAR)
CID .... Criminal Investigation Division [*Mauritian*] (AF)
CID .... Czechoslovak Industrial Design (CZ)
CIDA.......... Canadian International Development Agency (AF)
CIDA.......... Centre International de Documentation Arachnologique [*International Centre for Arachnological Documentation*] (EA)
CIDA.......... Comision Interprofesional de Antioquia [*Antioquia Interprofessional Commission*] [*Colombian*] (LA)
CIDA.......... Comite Interamericano de Desarrollo Agricola [*Inter-American Committee for Agricultural Development*] (LA)
CIDA.......... Comite Intergouvernemental du Droit d'Auteur [*Intergovernmental Copyright Committee - IGC*] [*UNESCO*] (EA)
CIDAC .... Centro de Informacao e Documentacao Anticolonial [*Anticolonial Information and Documentation Center*] [*Portuguese*] (WER)

CIDAECA.... Comite International pour le Developpement des Activities Educatives et Culturelles en Afrique (MAR)
CIDAK......... Centre d'Information de Dakar (MAR)
CIDALC....... Comite International pour la Diffusion des Arts et des Lettres par le Cinema [*International Committee for the Diffusion of Arts and Literature through the Cinema*] (EA)
CIDAN......... Compagnie Immobiliere d'Afrique Noire (MAR)
CIDAPA....... Comptoir International d'Automobiles, Pieces Detachees et Accessoires [*Moroccan*] (MAR)
CIDAS......... Centro Italiano Documentazione Azione Studi [*Italian Center for Documentation, Action, and Studies*] (WER)
CIDAS......... Centrul de Informare si Documentare pentru Agricultura si Silvicultura [*Information and Documentation Center for Agriculture and Silviculture*] (RO)
CIDAS......... Conference on Industrial Development in Arab States (MAR)
CIDB............ Chemie-Information und Dokumentation Berlin [*Chemical Information and Documentation-Berlin*] [*Information service*] [*German*]
CIDC............ Consortium Interafricain de Distribution Cinematographique [*Inter-African Moving Picture Distribution Consortium*] (AF)
CIDE............ Centro de Investigaciones de Desarrollo Economico. Universidad del Valle [*Cali*] (COL)
CIDE............ Comision de Inversiones y Desarrollo Economico [*Uruguayan*]
CIDEC......... Conseil International pour le Developpement du Cuivre [*International Copper Development Council*] (AF)
CIDEF.......... Commonwealth Industrial Development Fund (MAR)
CIDELCA.... Compania Importadora del Caribe [*Bogota*] (COL)
CIDELTRA... Compania Industrial del Transporte Ltda. [*Neiva*] (COL)
CIDEMA...... Compania Importadora de Materiales Ltda. [*Cartagena-Bogota*] (COL)
CIDEP......... Centre Interdisciplinaire pour le Developpement et l'Education Permanente [*Interdisciplinary Center for Development and Permanent Education*] [*Zairian*] (AF)
CIDESA....... Centre International de Documentation Economique et Sociale Africaine [*International Center for African Economic and Social Documentation*] (AF)
CIDET......... Cooperation Internationale en Matiere de Documentation sur l'Economie des Transports
CIDEX......... Compagnie Commerciale d'Importation et d'Exportation (MAR)
CIDH............ Centrul de Informare si Documentare Hidrotehnica [*Center for Hydrotechnology Information and Documentation*] (RO)
CIDI............. Centre Internationale de Documentation et d'Information
CIDI............. Centro de Investigaciones para el Desarrollo Integral. Universidad Bolivariana [*Medellin*] (COL)
CIDI............. Centrul de Informare si Documentare a Invatamintului [*Information and Documentation Center for Education*] (RO)
CIDI............. Cote Ivoirienne d'Importation et de Distribution (MAR)
CIDMA........ Centro de Investigaciones y Desarrollo de la Maquinaria Agropecuaria [*Agricultural Machinery Research and Development Center*] [*Cuban*] (LA)
CIDNET....... Consortium for International Development Information Network (MAR)
CIDNT......... Centralny Instytut Dokumentacji Naukowo-Technicznej [*Central Institute of Scientific and Technical Documentation*] (POL)
CIDOLOU.... Cimenterie Domaniale de Loutete (MAR)
CIDR............ Comite Infantil de Defensa de la Revolucion [*Children's Committee for Defense of the Revolution*] [*Cuban*] (LA)
CIDR............ Compagnie Internationale de Developpement Rural [*International Rural Development Company*] [*French*] (AF)
CIDRA......... Comercial Industrial de Automotores SA [*Bogota*] (COL)
CIDSP......... Centrul de Informare si Documentare in Stiintele Sociale si Politice [*Information and Documentation Center for the Social and Political Sciences*] (RO)
CIDSS......... Comite International pour la Documentation des Sciences Sociales
CIDST......... Comite d'Information et de Documentation Scientifique et Techniques [*EEG*] [*Belgian*]
CIDT............ Compagnie Ivoirienne pour le Developpement des Textiles (MAR)
CIDUNATI... Comite d'Information et de Defense de l'Union Nationale des Artisans et Travailleurs Independants [*French*]
CIE.............. Centre International de l'Enfance [*International Children's Centre*] (EA)
CIE.............. Centro de Informacao do Exercito [*Army Intelligence Center*] [*Brazilian*] (LA)
CIE.............. Centro de Investigaciones Economicas [*Economic Research Center*] [*Argentine*] (LA1)
CIE.............. Centro de Investigaciones Economicas. Universidad de Antioquia [*Medellin*] (COL)
CIE.............. Centro de Investigaciones Espaciales [*Space Research Center*] [*Argentine*] (LA)
Cie............... Compagnie [*Company*] [*French*] (MTD)
CIE.............. Compagnie Ivoirienne des Etiquettes (MAR)
CIE.............. Compagnie Ivoirienne d'Etudes (MAR)
CIE.............. Compania Industrial de Estructuras Ltda. [*Barranquilla*] (COL)
CIE.............. Conseil International de l'Etain [*International Tin Council - ITC*] (EA)
CIE.............. Consejo Interamericano do Escultismo [*Inter-American Scout Committee - IASC*] (EA)
CIE.............. Consejo Internacional de Estano [*International Tin Council - ITC*] (LA)
CIE.............. Consorcio de Ingenieria Electromecanica [*Electromechanical Engineering Consortium*] [*Paraguayan*] (LA)
Cie............... Kompanie [*Company*] (EG)
CIEA........... Centrala Industriala de Electronica si Automatizare [*Industrial Central for Electronics and Automation*] (RO)
CIEBA......... Compagnie Industrielle d'Exploitation des Bois Africains (MAR)
CIEC........... Commission Internationale de l'Etat Civil [*International Commission on Civil Status - ICCS*] (EA)
CIEC........... Confederacion Interamericana de Educacion Catolica [*Bogota*] (COL)
CIEC........... Conference on International Economic Cooperation (AF)
CIEC........... Consejo de Iglesias Evangelicas de Cuba [*Council of Evangelical Churches of Cuba*] (LA)
CIECA......... Comptoir Import-Export Casablancais (MAR)
CIECC......... Comite Interamericano para la Educacion, la Ciencia, y la Cultura [*Inter-American Educational, Scientific, and Cultural Committee*] [*OAS*] (LA)
CIECH......... Centrala Importowo-Eksportowa Chemikalii i Aparatury Chemicznej [*Import-Export Center for Chemicals and Chemical Equipment*] (POL)
CIECMM..... Comision Internacional para la Exploracion Cientifica del Mar Mediterraneo (MAR)
CIED........... Centre International ?'Echanges de Dakar (MAR)
CIED........... Compagnie Industrielle des Entrepots de Dakar (MAR)
CIEE........... Council on International Educational Exchange (MAR)
CIEES......... Centre Interarmees d'Essais d'Engins Speciaux (de Colomb-Bechar) [*Inter-Service Center for Testing Special Devices (At Colomb-Bechar)*] [*French*] (WER)
CIEET......... Centrala Industriala a Energiei Electrice si Termice [*Industrial Central for Thermal and Electric Power*] (RO)
CIEF........... Centro de Investigaciones y Estudios Familiares [*Family Research and Study Center*] [*Uruguayan*] (LA)
CIEF........... Commission Importation Exportation Francaise (MAR)
CIEH........... Comite Inter-Africain d'Etudes Hydrauliques [*Inter-African Committee for Hydraulic Studies*] (AF)
CIEI............ Centro de Investigaciones en Economia Internacional [*Center for Research in International Economics*] [*Cuban*] (LA)
CIEI............ Comision Investigadora Contra el Enriquecimiento Ilicito de Funcionarios y Empleados Publicos [*Committee Investigating the Illegal Use of Public Funds by Public Officials and Employees*] [*Venezuelan*] (LA)
CIEL........... Centre International d'Etudes du Lindane [*International Research Centre on Lindane - IRCL*] (EA)
CIEL........... Constructions Installations Electriques du Littoral (MAR)
CIEL........... Construtora e Incorporadora Eldorado
CIELDA....... Construcciones y Estudios Electricos Ltda. [*Cali*] (COL)
CIEM........... Centre de Recherches et de Production pour l'Information et l'Education des Masses (MAR)
CIEM........... Comision Intergremial de Educadores de Montevideo [*Interunion Commission of Montevideo Educators*] [*Uruguayan*] (LA)
CIEM........... Compagnie Ivoirienne d'Elevage Marin (MAR)
CIEMA......... Centre International des Etudes de la Musique Ancienne (MAR)
CIEMA......... Comptoir d'Importation et d'Exportation de Materiel Automobile (MAR)
CIEMA......... Constructions Industrielle Electro Mecanique d'Algerie (MAR)
CIEN........... Comision Interamericana de Energia Nuclear [*Inter-American Nuclear Energy Commission*] [*Use IANEC*] (LA)
CIEN........... Commissione Italiana per l'Europa Nucleare [*Italian Committee for Nuclear Europe*] (WER)
CIENES....... Centro Interamericano de Ensenanza Estadistica [*Inter-American Statistical Training Institute*] (LA)
CIEP........... Commission Internationale de l'Enseignement de la Physique [*International Commission on Physics Education - ICPE*] (EA)
CIEP........... Council of International Economic Policy (EG)
CIEPA......... Centro de Investigacion Economica para la Accion [*Center for Action-Oriented Economic Research*] [*Peruvian*] (LA)
CIEPS......... Centre International pour l'Enregistrement des Publications en Serie
CIER........... Conseil International des Economies Regionales [*International Council for Local Development*] (EA)
CIERA......... Club Ivoirien d'Etudes et de Recherche Appliquee (MAR)
CIERIE........ Compagnie Ivoirienne d'Etudes et de Realisations Informatiques et Economiques (MAR)
CIERO......... Centre Interafricain d'Etudes en Radio Rurale [*Inter-African Rural Radio Studies Center*] (AF)
CIERP......... Centre Intersyndical d'Etudes et de Recherches de Productivite (MAR)
CIERSES..... Centre International d'Etudes et de Recherches en Socio-Economie de la Sante [*International Health Centre of Socioeconomics, Researches and Studies - IHCSERS*] (EA)
CIES........... Consejo Interamericano Economico y Social [*Inter-American Economic and Social Council*] [*Use IA-ESOSOC*] (LA)
CIESM......... Commission Internationale pour l'Exploration Scientifique de la Mer Mediterrannee [*International Commission for the Scientific Exploration of the Mediterranean Sea - ICSEM*] (EA)

CIESM......... Commission Internationale d'Exploration Sous-Marine dans la Mer Mediterranee (MAR)
CIESMM...... Commission Internationale d'Exploration Sous-Marine dans la Mer Mediterranee (MAR)
CIESP.......... Centro das Industrias do Estado de Sao Paulo [*Sao Paulo State Industry Center*] [*Brazilian*] (LA)
CIESPAL..... Centro Internacional de Estudios Superiores de Periodismo de America Latina [*International Center of Higher Journalism Studies for Latin America*] (LA)
CIESS .... Centro Interamericano de Estudios de Seguridad Social [*Inter-American Center of Social Security Studies*] (LA)
CIEST.......... Centre International des Etudes Superieures de Tourisme [*International Center of Advanced Tourism Studies*] [*Use ICATS*] (CL)
CIET............ Centre d'Instruction et d'Etudes Techniques [*Technical Studies and Instruction Center*] [*French*] (CL)
CIETA.......... Centrala Industriala de Echipamente de Telecomunicatii si Automatizari [*Industrial Central for Telecommunications and Automation Equipment*] (RO)
CIETC .... Centrala Industriala de Electronica si Tehnica de Calcul [*Industrial Central for Electronics and Computer Technology*] (RO)
CIEx .... Centro de Informacoes do Exercito [*Army Intelligence Center*] [*Brazilian*] (LA)
ciez .... Ciezar [*Weight*] [*Polish*]
CIF .... Camara de la Industria Frigorifica [*Chamber of the Meatpacking Industry*] [*Uruguayan*] (LA)
CIF .... Cameroon Industrial Forest (MAR)
Cif .... Ciftlik [*Farm, Ranch*] (TU)
CIF .... Comptoir d'Importations Francaises [*Moroccan*] (MAR)
CIF .... Cost, Insurance, Freight [*Appears thus in Turkish economic articles*] (TU)
CIFA............ Committee for Inland Fisheries of Africa (MAR)
CIFA............ Companhia Industrial de Fibras Artificiais [*Industrial Company of Artificial Fibers*] [*Portuguese*] (WER)
CIFARA....... Camara de Industriales Fabricantes de Repuestos Automotrices [*Chamber of Auto Parts Manufacturers*] [*Argentine*] (LA)
CIFAS.......... Franco-German Consortium for Symphonie Satellite (WER)
CIFAVE .... Camara de la Industria Farmaceutica [*Chamber of Pharmaceutical Industry*] [*Venezuelan*] (LA)
CIFE .... Compagnie Industrielle et Financiere d'Entreprises (MAR)
CIFEL.......... Companhia Industrial de Fundicao e Laminagem (MAR)
CIFEN.......... Compania Industrial Financiera Empresa Nacional [*National Industrial Financial Company Enterprise*] [*Argentine*] (LA)
CIFFCH .... Centrala Industriala de Fire si Fibre Chemice Savinesti [*Industrial Central for Chemical Yarns and Fibers in Savinesti*] (RO)
CIFI .... Centres Interentreprises de Formation Industrielle (MAR)
CIFIM .... Compagnie Ivoirienne de Financement de l'Immobilier (MAR)
CIFOS .... Compagnie Immobiliere et Fonciere du Senegal (MAR)
CIFP .... Comite International pour le Fair Play [*International Fair Play Committee*] (EA)
CIFPSE .... Catholic International Federation for Physical and Sports Education [*See also FICEP*] (EA)
CIG.............. Centre d'Information Generale (MAR)
CIG.............. Conference Internationale du Goudron [*International Tar Conference - ITC*] (EA)
CIG.............. Credit Immobilier du Gabon [*Gabon Real Estate Credit Bank*] (AF)
CIGA .... Compagnia Italiana del Grandi Alberghi [*Italian hotel chain*]
CIGB .... Commission Internationale des Grands Barrages [*International Commission on Large Dams - ICOLD*] (EA)
CIGE............ Centre Ivoirien de Gestion des Entreprises (MAR)
CIGH .... Confederation Internationale de Genealogie et d'Heraldique [*International Confederation of Genealogy and Heraldry - ICGH*] (EA)
CIGM........... Centrala Industriala de Gaz Metan [*Industrial Central for Methane Gas*] (RO)
CIGR............ Commission Internationale du Genie Rural [*International Commission on Agricultural Engineering*] (EA)
CIGS .... Curso Intensivo de Guerrilla nas Selvas [*Intensive Guerrilla Jungle Training Course*] [*Brazilian*] (LA)
CIGTRG....... Centre d'Instruction du Groupement de Transport de Reserves Generales [*Algerian*] (MAR)
CIH .... Credit Immobilier et Hotelier [*Moroccan*] (MAR)
CIHEAM ...... Centre International des Hautes Etudes Agronomiques Mediterraneennes (MAR)
CIHM .... Commission Internationale d'Histoire Militaire [*International Commission of Military History*] (EA)
CIHV............ Centre International Humanae Vitae [*International Centre Humanae Vitae*] (EA)
CII................ Compagnie Internationale pour l'Informatique [*French*]
CIIA .... Commission Internationale des Industries Agricoles et Alimentaires [*International Commission for Food Industries*] (EA)
CIIB .... Cooerdinatiecommissie Internationale Informatie-Betrekkingen [*Dutch*]
CIID .... Commission Internationale des Irrigations et du Drainage [*International Commission on Irrigation and Drainage - ICID*] (EA)
CIIP .... Centro de Informacion de la Industria Petrolera [*Bogota*] (COL)
CIIR .... Catholic Institute for International Relations (EA)
CIIS .... Comitato Interministeriale per le Informazioni e la Sicurezza [*Interministerial Committee on Intelligence and Security*] [*Italian*] (WER)
CIJ............... Cour Internationale de Justice [*International Court of Justice*] [*North African*] (MAR)
CIJ............... Curtea Internationala de Justitie [*International Court of Justice*] (RO)
CIJL............. Centre for the Independence of Judges and Lawyers [*See also CIMA*] (EA)
CIJM............ Comite Internationale des Jeux Mediterraneens [*North African*] (MAR)
CIK .... Centralny Instytut Kultury [*Central Institute of Culture*] (POL)
CIK .... Cestovna Informacna Kancelaria [*Travel Information Bureau*] (CZ)
CIL............... Centro de Investigaciones Literarias [*Center of Literary Studies*] [*Cuban*] (LA)
CIL............... Combinatul de Industrializare a Lemnului [*Combine for the Industrialization of Wood*] (RO)
CIL............... Compagnie Ivoirienne Lamoulere (MAR)
CILA .... Consortium International des Librairies d'Afrique (MAR)
CILAM .... Compagnie Ivoirienne de Location Automobile et de Materiel (MAR)
CILAS.......... Compagnie Industrielle des Lasers (MAR)
CILC .... Confederation Internationale du Lin et du Chanvre [*International Linen and Hemp Confederation*] (EA)
CILECT .... Centre International de Liaison des Ecoles de Cinema et de Television [*International Liaison Centre for Film and Television Schools*] (EA)
CILEDCO .... Cooperativa Industrial Lechera de Colombia Ltda. [*Barranquilla*] (COL)
CILF .... Conseil International de la Langue Francaise [*International Council of the French Language - ICFL*] (EA)
CILNET .... Consortium for International Development Information Network (MAR)
CILO............ Comites de Industrias Locales [*Local Industry Committees*] [*Cuban*] (LA)
CILO............ Cooerdinatiegroep Informatiesystemen Lopend Onderzoek [*Dutch*]
CILOP.......... Conversion-in-Lieu-of-Production Pirating (MAR)
CILSS.......... Comite Permanent Inter-Etats de Lutte Contre la Secheresse dans le Sahel [*Inter-State Committee to Fight the Drought in the Sahel*] (AF)
CIM.............. Centrala Industriei Matasii [*Silk Industry Central*] (RO)
CIM.............. Centre d'Instruction Militaire [*Military Training Center*] [*French*] (WER)
CIM.............. Centro de Instruccion de la Marina [*Naval Training Center*] [*Uruguayan*] (LA)
CIM.............. Comision Interamericana de Mujeres [*Inter-American Women's Commission*] (LA)
CIM.............. Comite Intergouvernmental pour les Migrations (MAR)
CIM.............. Companhia Industrial de Matols (MAR)
CIM.............. Convention Internationale Concernant le Transport des Merchandises par Chemins de Fer [*North African*] (MAR)
CIM.............. Convention Internationale des Marchandises [*French*]
CIM.............. Cooperative Investigations in the Mediterranean [*IOC*] (MAR)
CIMA .... Centrala Industriala de Masini Agricole [*Industrial Central for Agricultural Machinery*] (RO)
CIMA .... Centre pour l'Independence des Magistrats et des Avocats [*Centre for the Independence of Judges and Lawyers - CIJL*] (EA)
CIMA .... Comision Interministerial del Medio Ambiente [*Interministerial Commission on the Environment*] [*Spanish*] (WER)
CIMA .... Comite Intergovernamental para as Migracoes Europeias [*Intergovernmental Committee for European Migrations*] [*Portuguese*] (WER)
CIMA .... Compagnie Industrielle de Miroiterie en Afrique (MAR)
CIMA .... Companhia Industrial das Mahotas Lda. (MAR)
CIMA .... Comptoir Ivoirien de Materiel (MAR)
CIMAC .... Conseil International des Machines a Combustion [*International Council on Combustion Engines*] (EA)
CIMACO...... Compania Industrial de Materiales para Construccion [*Cartagena*] (COL)
CIMAFRIC... Societe Africaine des Ciments (MAR)
CIMAG .... Societe des Grands Magasins de la Cote-d'Ivoire (MAR)
CIMA-IS ...... Ege Bolgesi Civa, Izole Maden Arama Iscileri Sendikasi [*Aegean Region Mercury, Insulation Ore Exploration Workers' Union*] [*Izmir*] (TU)
CIMAL......... Centre d'Information Mondiales Antilepre (MAR)
CIMALOR.... Societe des Ciments de l'Algerie Orientale (MAR)
CIMAO .... Societe des Ciments de l'Afrique de l'Ouest [*Cement Company of West Africa*] (AF)
CIMAP......... Commission Internationale des Methodes d'Analyses des Pesticides [*Collaborative International Pesticides Analytic Council - CIPAC*] (EA)
CIMAR......... Compagnie Industrielle des Petroles du Maroc (MAR)
CIMARA ...... Camara de Instituciones Medicas de la Republica Argentina [*Chamber of Medical Institutions of the Argentine Republic*] (LA1)

CIMASA ...... Construcoes e Industria Metalurgica Amazonia SA [*Amazon Metal Industry and Construction, Inc.*] [*Brazilian*] (LA)
CIMATAO-YS ... Compagnie Malienne de Montage et d'Exploitation Automobiles (MAR)
CIMATEC .... Cote Ivoirienne de Materiels Techniques (MAR)
CIMCCL ...... Centrala Industriala de Medicamente, Cosmetice, Coloranti, si Lacuri [*Industrial Central for Drugs, Cosmetics, Dyes, and Lacquers*] (RO)
CIMCO .... Compagnie des Ciments du Congo Francais (MAR)
CIME .... Comitato Internazionale per le Migrazioni Europee [*International Committee for European Migrations*] [*Italian*] (WER)
CIME .... Comite Intergubernamental para la Migracion Europea [*Intergovernmental Committee for European Migration*] [*Use ICEM*] (LA)
CIMEA .... Comite International des Mouvements d'Enfants et d'Adolescents [*International Committee of Children's and Adolescents' Movements*] (EA)
CIMELTA .... Constructions Mecaniques et Electriques de Tananarive (MAR)
CIMENCAM ... Cimenterie du Cameroun [*Cameroon Cement Plant*] (AF)
CIMENCO ... Societe de la Cimenterie du Congo (MAR)
CIMENTAL ... Cimenteries d'Albertville (MAR)
CIMEX .... Control de Creditos Importacion y Exportacion [*Cucuta*] (COL)
CIMI .... Conselho Indigenista Missionario [*Native Missionary Council*] [*Brazilian*] (LA)
CIMJI .... Committee for Inquiry of Missing Japanese in Indochina (CL)
CIMMYT ...... Centro Internacional de Mejoramiento de Maiz y Trigo [*International Maize and Wheat Improvement Center*] (EA)
CIMNR .... Centrala Industriala pentru Metale Neferoase si Rare [*Industrial Central for Nonferrous and Rare Metals*] (RO)
CIMO .... Commission des Instruments et des Methodes d'Observation [*Commission for Instruments and Methods of Observation*] [*OMI*]
CIMP .... Centro de Instruccion Militar de Peru [*Military Training Center of Peru*] (LA)
CIMPEC ...... Centro Interamericano de Produccion de Material Educativo y Cientifico para la Prensa [*Inter-American Center for the Production of Press Information on Educational and Scientific Matters*] (LA)
Cimre .... Cimetiere [*Cemetery*] [*Military map abbreviation*] [*World War I*] [*French*] (MTD)
CIMS .... Centro de Investigaciones Multidisciplinarias de Sistemas de Bienestar Social [*Bogota*] (COL)
CIMS .... Consociatio Internationalis Musicae Sacrae (EA)
Cimse-Is ..... Turkiye Cimento, Seramik, ve Toprak Sanayii Iscileri Sendikasi [*Turkish Cement, Ceramics, and Earthenware Industry Workers' Union*] (TU)
CIMTOGO ... Societe des Ciments du Togo (MAR)
CIMTP .... Congres Internationaux de Medecine Tropicale et de Paludisme (MAR)
CIMU .... Centrala Industriala de Masini Unelte [*Industrial Central for Machine Tools*] (RO)
CIMUIU .... Centrala Industriala de Masini si Utilaje pentru Industria Usoara [*Industrial Central for Machines and Equipment for Light Industry*] (RO)
CIMUMFS ... Centrala Industriala de Masini Unelte, Mecanica Fina, si Scule [*Industrial Central for Machine Tools, Precision Machinery, and Tools*] (RO)
CIMUR .... Comite d'Information pour le Developpement des Facades Legeres et Cloisons Industrialisees (MAR)
CIN .... Centro de Informacoes Nucleares [*Nuclear Information Center*] [*Brazilian*] (LA)
CIN .... Centro de Integracion Nacional [*National Integration Center*] [*Bolivian*] (LA)
CIN .... Centro de Investigaciones Nucleares [*Nuclear Research Center*] [*Uruguayan*] (LA)
CINAG .... Centro de Informatica Nacional Aplicada a la Gestion [*National Applied Data Processing Center*] [*Cuban*] (LA)
CINAM .... Compagnie d'Etudes Industrielles et d'Amenagement du Territoire (MAR)
CINAN .... Centro de Informacion Aplicada a la Normalizacion [*Applied Standardization Data Center*] [*Cuban*] (LA)
CINAREMA ... Comite Inter-Sindical Nacional de Radioelectricidad, Metalurgica, y Afines [*National Inter-Union Committee of Radioengineering and Metallurgical Workers*] [*Uruguayan*] (LA)
CINAT .... Cimenterie Nationale [*National Cement Plant*] [*Zairian*] (AF)
CINAV .... Commission Internationale de la Nomenclature Anatomique Veterinaire [*International Committee on Veterinary Anatomical Nomenclature - ICVAN*] (EA)
CINCMEAF ... Commander-in-Chief, Middle East Air Forces (MAR)
CINCMED ... Commander-in-Chief, British Naval Forces in the Mediterranean (MAR)
CINCMELF ... Commander-in-Chief, Middle East Land Forces (MAR)
CINCNELM ... Commander-in-Chief, US Naval Forces, Eastern Atlantic and Mediterranean (MAR)
CINCO .... Compania de Ingenieros Contratistas Ltda. [*Bogota*] (COL)
CINCOL .... Compania Industrial y Comercial Ltda. [*Bogota*] (COL)
CINDACOL ... Consorcio Industrial Aleman para Colombia [*Bogota*] (COL)
CINDACTA ... Centro Integrado de Defesa Aerea e de Controle de Trafico Aereo [*Combined Air Safety and Air Traffic Control Center*] [*Brazilian*] (LA)
CINDESTRUC ... Compania Industrial Aleman para Colombia Ltda. [*Barranquilla*] (COL)
CINECO ...... Cine Colombia SA [*Medellin*] (COL)
CINE-PERU ... Empresa de Cinematografia del Peru [*Peruvian Motion Picture Enterprise*] (LA)
CINGRA ...... Coordenacao de Assuntos Internacionais da Agricultura [*Coordination of International Agricultural Issues*] [*Brazilian*] (LA)
Cin-Kur .... Cinko-Kursun Fabrikasi [*Zinc-Lead Factory*] [*Kayseri*] (TU)
CIN-KUR ..... Cinko-Kursun Metal Sanayii AS [*Zinc and Lead Metal Industry Corp.*] [*Ankara*] (TU)
CINOR .... Centrul de Informatica si Organizare [*Center for Data Processing and Organization*] (RO)
CINP .... Comite International de Liaison pour la Navigation de Plaisance [*Pleasure Navigation International Joint Committee - PNIC*] (EA)
CINPEC .... Comite Interdiocesain des Pelerinages Catholiques (MAR)
CINPEXAM ... Centre d'Information pour l'Expansion Africaine, Malgache, et Mauricienne [*Information Center for African, Malagasy, and Mauritian Development*] (AF)
CINTERFOR ... Centro Interamericano de Investigacion y Documentacion sobre Formacion Profesional [*Inter-American Centre for Research and Documentation on Vocational Training - IACRDVT*] (EA)
CINTRACINTEL ... Sindicato de Trabajadores de Cine [*Medellin*] (COL)
CINU .... Centro de Informacion e las Naciones Unidas para Colombia, Ecuador, y Venezuela [*UN Information Center for Colombia, Ecuador, and Venezuela*] (LA)
CIO .... Comite International Olympique [*North African*] (MAR)
CIO .... Commission Internationale d'Optique [*International Commission for Optics - ICO*] (EA)
CIO .... Compania Industrial de Occidente [*Cali*] (COL)
CIO .... Congress of Industrial Organizations (MAR)
CIOAC .... Central Independiente de Obreros Agricolas y Campesinos [*Independent Central Organization of Agricultural Workers and Peasants*] [*Mexican*] (LA1)
cion .... Commission [*French*]
CIOP .... Centralny Instytut Ochrony Pracy [*Central Institute of Labor Safety*] (POL)
CIOP .... Commissie Informatie-Opleiding [*Dutch*]
CIOR .... Confederation Interalliee des Officers de Reserve [*Interallied Confederation of Reserve Officers - ICRO*] (EA)
CIOS .... Comisia pentru Incercarea si Omologarea Soiurilor [*Commission for the Testing and Approval of Seed Varieties*] (RO)
CIOS .... Comitato Internazionale Organizzazione Scientifica [*International Committee for Scientific Organization*] [*Italian*] (WER)
CIOS .... Conseil Internationale pour l'Organisation Scientifique
CIOSL .... Conferencia Internacional de Organizaciones Sindicales Libres [*International Conference of Free Trade Union Organizations*] [*Use ICFTUO*] (LA)
CIOT .... Commerce et Industrie de l'Oubangui et du Tchad (MAR)
CIOT .... Compagnie Industrielle d'Ouvrages en Textiles (MAR)
CIOVNI .... Centro de Investigacion de Objetos Voladores No Identificados [*Unidentified Flying Objects Research Center*] [*Uruguayan*] (LA)
CIP .... Centre d'Information de Presse [*Press agency*] [*Belgian*]
CIP .... Centre d'Instruction des Parachutistes [*Paratroop Training Center*] [*Zairian*] (AF)
CIP .... Centro Internacional de la Papa [*International Potato Center*] [*Peruvian*]
CIP .... Centro de Investigaciones Pesqueras [*Fishing Research Center*] [*Cuban*] (LA)
CIP .... Collection de l'Institut Pasteur [*French*]
CIP .... Comandos Incontrolados Patrioticos [*Patriotic Autonomous Commandos*] [*Spanish*] (WER)
CIP .... Comitato Interministeriale Prezzi [*Interministerial Price Committee*] [*Italian*] (WER)
CIP .... Comite Inter-Etats Permanent (MAR)
CIP .... Comite Internacional Preparatorio [*International Preparatory Committee*] [*Cuban*] (LA)
CIP .... Companhia Industrial de Plasticos (MAR)
CIP .... Comptoir Ivoirien des Papiers (MAR)
CIP .... Confederacao da Industria Portuguesa [*Portuguese Industry Confederation*] (WER)
CIP .... Conselho Interministerial de Precos [*Interministerial Price Council*] [*Brazilian*] (LA)
CIP .... Cook Islands Party (PPW)
CIP .... Coordinadora Internacional Publicitaria [*Bogota*] (COL)
CIP .... Cote-d'Ivoire Plastique (MAR)
CIPA .... Centrul de Instruirea Personalului Aeronautic [*Center for the Instruction of Aeronautical Personnel*] (RO)
CIPA .... Comite International de Photogrammetrie Architecturale [*International Committee of Architectural Photogrammetry*] (EA)
CIPA .... Comite International de Plastiques en Agriculture [*International Committee of Plastics in Agriculture*] (EA)

CIPA........... Compagnie Ivoirienne de Produits Alimentaires (MAR)
CIPAC......... Collaborative International Pesticides Analytic Council [*See also CIMAP*] (EA)
CIPAL.......... Centro de Informaciones para la America Latina [*Latin American Information Center*] (LA)
CIPAL.......... Companhia Industrial de Produtos Alimentares, SARL (MAR)
CIPAL.......... Compania Industrial de Productos de Acero [*Bogota*] (COL)
CIPAO......... Compagnie Industrielle des Petroles de l'Afrique Occidentale [*Petroleum Industry Company of West Africa*] [*Senegalese*] (AF)
CIPAR......... Centro de Investigaciones Parasicologicas [*Medellin*] (COL)
CIPAS......... Cimento Pazarlama Anonim Sirketi [*Cement Marketing Corporation*] (TU)
CIPASE....... Commission Internationale des Peches de l'Atlantique Sud-Est [*International Commission for the Southeast Atlantic Fisheries - ICSAF*] (EA)
CIPC........... Centre d'Instruction Para-Commando (MAR)
CIPC........... Centrul de Investitii Proiectari si Constructii [*Center for Construction and Design Investments*] (RO)
CIPC........... Compagnie Ivoirienne de Plomberie et Chaudronnerie (MAR)
CIPCMP...... Centrala Industriala de Prelucrare Cauciuc si Mase Plastice [*Industrial Central for the Processing of Rubber and Plastic*] (RO)
CIPCO......... Compagnie Ivoirienne de Poisson Congele (MAR)
CIPDEM...... Comite Internacional pro Defensa de la Democracia [*International Committee for the Defense of Democracy*] [*Venezuelan*] (LA)
CIPE........... Centro Interamericano de Promocion de Exportaciones [*Inter-American Export Promotion Center*] (LA)
CIPE........... Comitato Interministeriale per la Programmazione Economica [*Interministerial Committee for Economic Planning*] [*Italian*] (WER)
CIPEA......... Centre Internationale pour l'Elevage en Afrique (MAR)
CIPEC......... Compagnie Camerounaise des Instruments de Pesage et des Coffres-Forts (MAR)
CIPEC......... Conseil Intergouvernemental des Pays Exportateurs de Cuivre [*Intergovernmental Council of Copper-Exporting Countries*] [*Use ICCEC*] (EA)
CIPEC......... Consejo Intergubernamental de Paises Exportadores de Cobre [*Intergovernmental Council of Copper Exporting Countries*] (LA)
CIPEET....... Centrala Industriala pentru Productia Energiei Electrice si Termice [*Industrial Central for the Production of Electric and Thermal Power*] (RO)
CIPEL.......... Compagnie Industrielle des Piles Electriques (MAR)
CIPEM......... Comite International pour les Etudes Myceniennes [*Standing International Committee for Mycenaean Studies*] (EA)
CIPEXI........ Compagnie Ivoirienne de Promotion pour l'Exportation et l'Importation (MAR)
CIPH........... Comite International des Pharmaciens Homeopathiques [*International Committee of Homeopathic Pharmacists*] (EA)
CIPI............ Comitato Interministeriale per la Politica Industriale [*Interministerial Committee for Industrial Policy Coordination*] [*Italian*] (WER)
CIPI............ Compagnie Ivoirienne de Peche Industrielle (MAR)
CIPIK........... Compagnie Industrielle de Pikine (MAR)
CIPIMM....... Centro de Investigaciones para la Industria Minera-Metalurgica [*Research Center for the Mining-Metallurgical Industry*] [*Cuban*] (LA)
CIPL........... Comite International Permanent des Linguistes [*Permanent International Committee of Linguists*] (EA)
CIPLA.......... Confederacion Industrial Papelera Latinoamericana [*Latin American Paper Industry Confederation*] [*Mexican*] (LA)
CIPM.......... Centrala Industriala de Prelucrari Metalurgice [*Industrial Central for Metallurgical Processing*] (RO)
CIPP........... Conseil Indo-Pacifique des Peches [*Indo-Pacific Fisheries Council*] [*Use IPFC*] (CL)
CIPPAS....... Comite International Provisoire de Prevention Acridienne au Soudan Francais (MAR)
CIPRA......... Camara de Industrias de Procesos de la Republica Argentina [*Processing Industries Association of the Argentine Republic*] (LA)
CIPRA......... Commission Internationale pour la Protection des Regions Alpines [*International Commission for the Protection of Alpine Regions*] (EA)
CIPRES....... Centre Ivoirien de Reparation a la Promotion Renault Saviem (MAR)
CIPRO......... Compagnie Ivoirienne de Produits (MAR)
CIPROFILMS... Centre Interafricain de Production de Films [*Inter-African Film Production Center*] (AF)
CIPSA......... Compania Iberica de Prospeccion, Sociedad Anonima (MAR)
CIPSEP....... Comptoir Ivoirien de Prestation de Services et d'Electricite et de Plomberie (MAR)
CIPT........... Comite International des Telecommunications de Presse [*International Press Telecommunications Council - IPTC*] (EA)
CIR............. Centralny Instytut Rolniczy [*Central Agricultural Institute*] (POL)
CIR............. Centros de Instrucao Revolucionaria [*Centers for Revolutionary Instruction*] (AF)
CIR............. Circulos de Instruccion Revolucionaria [*Revolutionary Training Circles*] [*Cuban*] (LA)
cir.............. Cirilica [*Cyrillic Alphabet*] (YU)
CIR............. Comite de Innovadores y Racionalizadores [*Innovators and Efficiency Experts Committee*] [*Cuban*] (LA)
CIR............. Comite Integracionista Revolucionario [*Revolutionary Integration Committee*] [*Venezuelan*] (LA)
CIR............. Comite Intergouvernemental pour les Refugies (MAR)
CIR............. Commission Internationale du Riz [*International Rice Commission*] [*Use IRC*] (CL)
CIR............. Conference Internationale des Reparations (MAR)
CIR............. Convention des Institutions Republicaines [*Convention of Republican Institutions*] [*French*] (PPE)
CIRA........... Centrala Industriala de Reparatii Auto [*Industrial Central for Auto Repairs*] (RO)
CIRA........... Centre International de Recherches sur l'Anarchisme [*International Research Centre on Anarchism*] (EA)
CIRA........... Centro Interamericano de Reforma Agraria [*Bogota*] (COL)
CIRA........... Commission Internationale pour la Reglementation des Ascenseurs et Monte-Charge [*International Committee for Lift Regulations - ICLR*] (EA)
CIRA........... Consejo Inter-Sindical Renovador Argentino [*Argentina Inter-Union Reform Council*] (LA)
CIRA........... Cooperativa Integral de Reforma Agraria [*Integral Land Reform Cooperative*] [*Brazilian*] (LA)
CIRB........... Companhia Industrial de Rochas Betuminosas [*Shale Oil Company*] [*Brazilian*] (LA)
circ............ Circa, Circiter, or Circum [*About (Used with dates denoting approximate time)*] [*Latin*]
CIRD........... Compagnie Internationale de Riz et de Denrees (MAR)
CIRDA......... Centre for Integrated Rural Development for Africa (MAR)
CIRDAFRICA... Centre for Integrated Rural Development for Africa (MAR)
CIRDI.......... Centre International pour le Reglement des Differends Relatifs aux Investissements (MAR)
CIRE........... Caisse Israelite de Relevement Economique [*Moroccan*] (MAR)
CIRES......... Centre Ivoirien de Recherches Economiques et Sociales [*Ivorian Economic and Social Research Center*] (AF)
CIRFS......... Comite International de la Rayonne et des Fibres Synthetiques [*International Rayon and Synthetic Fibres Committee - IRSFC*] (EA)
CIRIEC........ International Centre of Research and Information on Public and Co-Operative Economy (EA)
ciril............ Cirilica [*Cyrillic Alphabet*] (YU)
CIRIP.......... Centre d'Instruction du Renseignement et d'Interpretation Photographique [*Center for Intelligence Training and Photo Interpretation*] [*French*] (WER)
CIRM.......... Comissao Interministerial de Recursos do Mar [*Interministerial Commission for Ocean Resources*] [*Brazilian*] (LA1)
CIRM.......... Comite International Radio Maritime [*International Maritime Radio Association*] (EA)
CIRMF......... Centre International de Recherches Medicales de Franceville (MAR)
CIRN........... Comite de l'Industrie et des Ressources Naturelles [*Committee on Industry and Natural Resources*] [*Cambodian*] (CL)
CIRO........... Centre Interarmees de Recherche Operationnelle [*Inter-Service Operational Research Center*] [*French*] (WER)
CIRP........... Central de Instituciones Regionales del Peru [*Center for Peruvian Regional Institutions*] (LA)
CIRP........... College International pour l'Etude Scientifique des Techniques de Production Mecanique [*International Institute for Production Engineering Research*] (EA)
CIRT........... Compagnie Industrielle de Radio et de Television (MAR)
CIRTEF........ Conseil International des Radios-Televisions d'Expression Francaise [*International Council of French-Speaking Radio and Television*] (EA)
cirvall.......... Circonvallazione [*Outer Circle*] [*In addresses*] [*Italian*] (CED)
CIS............. Caribbean Information System [*Proposed*]
CIS............. Catalogiseren In Samenwerking
CIS............. Centrala Industriala Siderurgica [*Industrial Central for Iron and Steel*] (RO)
CIS............. Centralny Inspektorat Standaryzacji [*Central Inspectorate for Standardization of Imports and Exports*] (POL)
CIS............. Centre International des Stages (MAR)
CIS............. Centro de Industriales Siderurgicos [*Iron and Steel Industrialists Center*] [*Argentine*] (LA)
CIS............. Centro de Investigaciones Sociales [*Social Research Center*] [*Colombian*]
CIS............. Centro de Investigaciones Submarinas [*Underseas Research Center*] [*Chilean*] (LA)
CIS............. Cestovni Informacni Sluzba [*Travel Information Service*] [*Prague*] (CZ)
CIS............. Cetna Intendantska Stanica [*Company Quartermaster Station*] (YU)
CIS............. Comitato Internazionale degli Scambi Presso la Camera Internazionale di Commercio [*International Trade Committee of the International Chamber of Commerce*] [*Italian*] (WER)
CIS............. Comite Inter-Sindical [*Inter-Trade Union Committee*] [*Salvadoran*] (LA1)
CIS............. Communications and Information Service (MAR)
CIS............. Compagnie Ivoirienne de Sciages (MAR)

CIS .... Constructeurs Inga-Shaba [*Inga-Shaba Engineers*] [*Zairian*] (AF)
CIS .... Credit Information Service [*Iranian*] (ME)
CIS .... Credito Industriale Sardo [*Sardinian*]
CIS .... Criminal Investigation Service [*Philippine*]
CISA .... Centro de Informacion sobre el Alcoholismo [*Bogota*] (COL)
CISA .... Centro de Informacoes e Seguranca da Aeronautica [*Air Force Intelligence and Security Center*] [*Brazilian*] (LA)
CISA .... Confederation Internationale des Syndicats Arabes [*International Confederation of Arab Trade Unions*] [*Use ICATU*] (AF)
CISAF .... Conseil International des Services d'Aide Familiale [*International Council of Homehelp Services - ICHS*] (EA)
Cisalp .... Centre Internationale de Secours Alpins
CISAN .... Turkiye Cimento Sanayii TAS [*Turkish Cement Industry Corporation*] (TU)
CISB .... Centrala Industriala Siderurgica Bucuresti [*Bucharest Industrial Central for Iron and Steel*] (RO)
CISB .... Copper Industry Service Bureau (MAR)
CISC .... Comite International de Sociologie [*International Committee on Clinical Sociology - ICCS*] (EA)
CISC .... Commission Internationale de Supervision et de Controle [*International Supervisory and Control Commission*] [*Use ISCC*] (CL)
CISC .... Confederacion Internacional de Sindicatos Cristianos [*International Federation of Christian Trade Unions*] [*Use IFCTU*] (LA)
CISC .... Confederation Internationale des Syndicats Chretiens [*International Federation of Christian Trade Unions*] [*Use IFCTU*] (AF)
CISCF .... Centrala Industriei Sticlei si Ceramicii Fine [*Central of the Glass and Fine Ceramics Industry*] (RO)
CISCL .... Commission Internationale de Supervision et de Controle au Laos [*International Supervisory and Control Commission for Laos*] [*Use ISCC for Laos*] (CL)
CISCO .... Compagnie Industrielle et Commerciale du Sud-Ouest (MAR)
CISCOP .... Centre d'Investigation sur le Colonialisme Portugais
CISCS .... Centre International Scolaire de Correspondance Sonore Solidarite avec la Jeunesse Algerienne (MAR)
CISE .... Cuerpo Internacional de Servicios Ejecutivos [*International Executives Service Corps*] [*Salvadoran*]
CISL .... Confederatia Internationala a Sindicatelor Libere [*International Confederation of Free Trade Unions*] (RO)
CISL .... Confederation Internationale des Syndicats Libres [*International Confederation of Free Trade Unions*] [*Use ICFTU*] (WER)
CISL .... Confederazione Italiana Sindacati Lavoratori [*Italian Confederation of Labor Unions*] (WER)
CISL .... Confederazione Italiana di Sindacati Liberi [*Italian Confederation of Free Workers*]
CISL .... Italian Confederation of Free Trade Unions (PPE)
CISLB .... Comite International pour la Sauveguard de la Langue Bretonne [*International Committee for the Defense of the Breton Language - ICDBL*] (EA)
CISM .... Conseil International du Sport Militaire [*North African*] (MAR)
CISNAL .... Confederazione Italiana dei Sindacati Nazionali Lavoratori [*Italian Confederation of National Labor Unions*] (WER)
CISNU .... Confederation of Iranian Students [*West German*] (PD)
CISP .... Comitato Interministeriale per gli Studi dei Problemi Spaziali [*Interministerial Committee for Space Research*] [*Italian*] (WER)
CISPEL .... Confederazione Italiana dei Servizi Pubblici degli Enti Locali [*Italian Confederation of Public Services of Local Government*] (WER)
CISPR .... Comite International Special des Perturbations Radioelectriques [*International Special Committee on Radio Interference*] (EA)
CISS .... Conferencia Interamericana de Seguridad Social [*Inter-American Conference on Social Security - IACSS*] (EA)
CISS .... Conseil International des Sciences Sociales [*International Social Science Council - ISSC*] (EA)
CISSL .... Comissoes Integradoras dos Servicos de Saude Locais [*Local Health Services Coordinating Commissions*] [*Portuguese*] (WER)
CISTOD .... Confederation of International Scientific and Technological Organizations for Development (EA)
CISTT .... Centre d'Information Scientifique et Technique et de Transfer Technologique (MAR)
CISV .... Children's International Summer Villages International Association (EA)
CIT .... Center for International Trade (MAR)
CIT .... Central Istmena de Trabajadores [*Isthmian Workers Federation*] [*Panamanian*] (LA)
CIT .... Centre Internationale de Transit (MAR)
CIT .... Centro de Informacao e Turismo [*Information and Tourist Center*] [*Mozambican*] (AF)
Cit .... Citation [*Mention in Dispatches*] [*Military*] [*French*] (MTD)
CIT .... Comite International des Transports par Chemins de Fer [*International Rail Transport Committee*] (EA)
CIT .... Compagnie Ivoirienne de Transports (MAR)
CIT .... Confection Industrielle Tchadienne (MAR)
CIT .... Confederacion Interamericana de Trabajadores [*Inter-American Workers Confederation*] [*Later, ORIT*] (LA)
CIT .... Confederation Internationale du Travail [*North African*] (MAR)
CIT .... Conseil International des Tanneurs [*International Council of Tanners - ICT*] (EA)
CIT .... Cooperative Ivoirienne des Transporteurs (MAR)
CITA .... Centre d'Information et de Tourisme d'Angola [*French*] (MAR)
CITA .... Centro de Informacao e Turismo de Angola [*Portuguese*] (MAR)
CITA .... Comite International de l'Inspection Technique Automobile [*International Motor Vehicle Inspection Committee*] (EA)
CITA .... Confederacion Interamericana de Transporte Aero [*Inter-American Air Transport Confederation*] (LA)
CITA .... Conference Internationale des Trains Speciaux d'Agencies de Voyages [*International Conference on Special Trains for Travel Agencies*] (EA)
CITAB .... Compagnie Industrielle des Tabacs de Madagascar (MAR)
CITC .... Christian Industrial Training Centre (MAR)
CITDEE .... Centrala Industriala pentru Transportul si Distributia Energiei Electrice [*Industrial Central for the Transportation and Distribution of Electric Power*] (RO)
CITE .... Centre d'Information Technique et Economique [*Technical and Economic Information Center*] [*Malagasy*] (AF)
CITE .... Centro de Instruccion de Tropas Especiales [*Special Forces Training Center*] [*Bolivian*] (LA)
Cite .... Citerne [*Cistern, Well*] [*Military map abbreviation*] [*World War I*] [*French*] (MTD)
CITE .... Compagnie d'Ingenieurs et Techniciens d'Etudes (MAR)
CITE .... Compagnie Ivoirienne de Travaux et d'Entreprises (MAR)
CITEC .... Compagnie de l'Industrie Textile Cotonniere (MAR)
CITEC-huilerie ... Societe des Huiles et Savons de Haute-Volta (MAR)
CITEFA .... Centro de Investigaciones Cientificas y Tecnicas de las Fuerzas Armadas [*Armed Forces Scientific and Technical Research Center*] [*Argentine*] (LA)
CITEP .... Centro de Investigacion y Tecnicas Politicas [*Center for Political Research and Techniques*] [*Spanish*] (WER)
CITHA .... Confederation of International Trading Houses Associations (EA)
CITIES .... Convention on Trade in Endangered Species of Wild Fauna and Flora (MAR)
Citlle .... Citadelle [*Citadel*] [*Military map abbreviation*] [*World War I*] [*French*] (MTD)
CITM .... Compagnie Ivoirienne de Transit et de Manutention (MAR)
CITMA .... Centrala Industriala de Tractoare si Masini Agricole [*Industrial Central for Tractors and Agricultural Machinery*] (RO)
CITO .... Groupement Interprofessional des Entrepris du Togo (MAR)
CITR .... Compagnie Ivoirienne de Transports Routiers (MAR)
CITRA .... Compagnie Industrielle de Travaux [*Moroccan*] (MAR)
CITRAM .... Compagnie Industrielle de Travaux du Maroc [*Moroccan*] (MAR)
CITROA .... Compagnie Internationale de Terrassements Routes et Ouvrages d'Art (MAR)
CITS .... China International Travel Service
CITS .... Commission Internationale Technique de Sucrerie [*International Commission of Sugar Technology*] (EA)
CITTA .... Confederation Internationale des Fabricants de Tapis et de Tissus d'Ameublement [*International Confederation of Manufacturers of Carpets and Furnishing Fabrics*] (EA)
CiU .... Convergencia i Unio [*Convergence and Union*] [*Spanish*] (PPE)
CIUDCO .... Comision Permanente Inter-Universitaria de Desarrollo de la Comunidad [*Bogota*] (COL)
CIUEMC .... Centrala Industriala de Utilaj Energetic, Metalurgic, si pentru Constructii [*Industrial Central for Power, Metallurgical, and Construction Equipment*] (RO)
CIUEMMR ... Centrala Industriala de Utilaj Energetic, Metalurgic, si Masini de Ridicat [*Industrial Central for Power and Metallurgical Equipment, and for Hoisting Machines*] (RO)
CIUL .... Congress of Industrial Unions of Liberia (AF)
CIUR .... Comite Interministeriel d'Intervention d'Urgence des Secours aux Refugies [*Interministerial Committee for Urgent Provision of Aid to Refugees*] [*Cambodian*] (CL)
CIUS .... Consiglio Internazionale delle Unioni Scientifiche [*International Council of Scientific Unions*] [*Use ICSU*] [*Italian*] (WER)
CIUSS .... Catholic International Union for Social Service (MAR)
CIUTCPM .... Centrala Industriala de Utilaj Tehnologic, Chimic, Petrolier, si Minier [*Industrial Central for Technological, Chemical, Petroleum, and Mining Equipment*] (RO)
CIUTI .... Conference Internationale Permanente de Directeurs d'Instituts Universitaires pour la Formation de Traducteurs et d'Interpretes [*Standing International Conference of the Directors of University Institutes for the Training of Translators and Interpreters*] (EA)
CIUTMR .... Centrala Industriala de Utilaj Tehnologic si Material Rulant [*Industrial Central for Technological Equipment and Rolling Stock*] (RO)
CIV .... Civilisations [*Brussels*] [*A publication*] (MAR)
CIV .... Colegio de Ingenieros de Venezuela [*Venezuelan Engineers Association*] (LA)
CIV .... Commerce Industrie Voltaique (MAR)
CIV .... Commission Internationale du Verre [*International Commission on Glass - ICG*] (EA)

CIV .... Convention Internationale Concernant le Transport des Voyageurs et des Baggages par Chemins de Fer (MAR)
CIV .... Ivory Coast [*Three-letter standard code*] (CNC)
CIVACC ...... Comercio e Industria de Vidros e Acabamentos de Construcao Civil Lda. (MAR)
CIVB........... Conseil Interprofessionel du Vin de Bordeaux [*French*]
CIVEM......... Constructions Ivoiriennes Electro-Mecaniques (MAR)
CIVEXIM ..... Compagnie Ivoirienne d'Exportation et d'Importation (MAR)
CIVI .... Centraal Instituut voor Industrie-Ontwikkeling [*Dutch*]
CIVILCO...... Construcciones Civiles Ltda. [*Cartagena*] (COL)
CIVINEX...... Compagnie Ivoirienne d'Exploitation Vinicole (MAR)
CIWF .... Centralny Instytut Wychowania Fizycznego [*Central Institute of Physical Education*] (POL)
CIWU.......... Commercial and Industrial Workers Union [*Grenadian*] (LA1)
CJ............... Chief Judge (MAR)
cj .... Cislo Jednaci [*File Number*] (CZ)
CJ............... Comision de Jornaleros [*Commission of Day Laborers*] [*In Andalusia; dominated by the Labor Party and the ORT*] [*Spanish*] (WER)
C de J......... Compania de Jesus [*Society of Jesus*] [*Spanish*]
c/j............... Courts Jours [*French*]
CJA .... Commonwealth Journalists Association (EA)
CJA .... Conseil de la Jeunesse Africaine [*African Youth Council*] [*Senegalese*] (AF)
CJAS.......... Canadian Journal of African Studies [*Montreal*] [*A publication*] (MAR)
CJD .... Centrala Jajczarsko-Drobiarska [*Egg and Poultry Center*] (POL)
CJEFS........ Consiliul Judetean al Educatiei Fizice si al Sportului [*County Council for Physical Education and Sports*] (RO)
CJG .... Council of Jews from Germany (EA)
CJI.............. Comissao Juridica Interamericana [*Inter-American Juridical Committee*] [*Portuguese*] (LA)
CJI.............. Comite Juridico Interamericano [*Inter-American Juridical Committee*] [*Spanish*] (LA)
CJIT............ Consiliul Judetean al Inginerilor si Tehnicienilor [*County Council of Engineers and Technicians*] (RO)
CJKZ.......... Casopis za Slovenski Jezik, Knjizevnost, in Zgodovino [*Journal on the Slovenian Language, Literature, and History*] [*Ljubljana*] [*A publication*] (YU)
CJM............ Code de Justice Militaire [*Military Law*] [*Military*] [*French*] (MTD)
CJM............ Confederacion de la Juventud Mexicana [*Mexican Youth Confederation*] (LA)
CJP............ Centre de Jeunes Patrons [*Young Employers' Center*] [*French*] (WER)
CJR .... Circulos de Jovenes Revolucionarios [*Revolutionary Youth Circles*] [*Spanish*] (WER)
CJS .... Confederation des Jeunesses Socialistes [*Confederation of Socialist Youth*] [*Belgian*] (WER)
CJV .... Christelike Jongeliedevereniging (MAR)
CK .... Centralna Komisja [*Central Board*] [*Polish*]
CK .... Centralni Komitet [*Central Committee*] (YU)
CK .... Centralny Komitet [*Central Committee*] (POL)
CK .... Cerveny Kriz [*Red Cross*] (CZ)
ck .... Cesarsko-Krolewski [*Polish*]
CK .... Channel Bay (RU)
CK .... Chawangan Khas [*Special Branch*] (ML)
Ck............... Cikmaz [*Dead-End Street, Impasse*] (TU)
ck .... Cisarsky Kralovsky [*Imperial Royal (In reference to the Austro-Hungarian Empire)*] (CZ)
CK .... Compagnie du Kasai (MAR)
CK .... Cook Islands [*Two-letter standard code*] (CNC)
CK .... Corvina Kiadovallalat [*Corvina Publishing Enterprise*] (HU)
CK .... Crven Krst [*Red Cross*] (YU)
CK .... Cyklisticky Klub [*Cycling Club*] (CZ)
CKBA .... Centralna Komisja Brakowania Akt [*Central Commission for the Destruction of Records*] (POL)
CKBKP........ Centralni Komitet Bugarske Komunisticke Partije [*Central Committee of the Bulgarian Communist Party*] (YU)
CKBRP(komunisti) ... Centralni Komitet Bugarske Radnicke Partije (Komunisti) [*Central Committee of the Bulgarian Workers' Party (Communists)*] (YU)
CKC .... Cesky Klub Cyklistu [*Czech Cycling Club*] (CZ)
CKC .... Samozaryadnyy Karabin Simonov [*Simonov Semi-Automatic Carbine*] [*Use SKS*] (CL)
CKCh .... Ceska Katolicka Charita [*Czech Catholic Charity Society*] (CZ)
CKD............ Ceskomoravska - Kolben - Danek, Narodni Podnik [*Ceskomoravska - Kolben - Danek, National Enterprise*] [*Heavy machinery plants*] (CZ)
CKG .... Centralni Komitet Grcke [*Central Committee of Greece*] (YU)
CKH............ Centrale Kamer voor Handelsbevordering [*Dutch*]
CKH............ Corps Kehakiman [*Military Justice Corps*] (IN)
CKIOAB ...... Caglayan Kucukler Ilkokulu Okul Aile Birligi [*Caglayan Kucukler Elementary School Family Union*] [*Turkish Cypriot*] (GC)
CKK............ Centralna Komisja Kwalifikacyjna [*Central Qualification Commission*] (POL)
CKK............ Cesky Klub Kanoistu [*Czech Canoe Club*] (CZ)
CKKP .... Centralna Komisja Kontroli Partyjnej [*Central Party Control Commission*] (POL)
CKKP .... Centralni Komitet Komunisticke Partije [*Central Committee of the Communist Party*] (YU)
CKKPA........ Centralni Komitet Komunisticke Partije Albanije [*Central Committee of the Communist Party of Albania*] (YU)
CKKPB........ Centralni Komitet Komunisticke Partije Bugarske [*Central Committee of the Communist Party of Bulgaria*] (YU)
CKKPBiH .... Centralni Komitet Komunisticke Partije Bosne i Hercegovine [*Central Committee of the Communist Party of Bosnia and Hercegovina*] (YU)
CKKPC........ Centralni Komitet Komunisticke Partije Cehoslovacke [*Central Committee of the Communist Party of Czechoslovakia*] (YU)
CKKPCG..... Centralni Komitet Komunisticke Partije Crne Gore [*Central Committee of the Communist Party of Montenegro*] (YU)
CKKPG........ Centralni Komitet Komunisticke Partije Grcke [*Central Committee of the Communist Party of Greece*] (YU)
CKKPH........ Centralni Komitet Komunisticke Partije Hrvatske [*Central Committee of the Communist Party of Croatia*] (YU)
CKKPJ .... Centralni Komitet Komunisticke Partije Jugoslavije [*Central Committee of the Communist Party of Yugoslavia*] (YU)
CKKPM .... Centralni Komitet Komunisticke Partije Makedonije [*Central Committee of the Communist Party of Macedonia*] (YU)
CKKPP........ Centralni Komitet Komunisticke Partije Poljske [*Central Committee of the Communist Party of Poland*] (YU)
CKKPS........ Centralni Komite Komunisticne Partije Slovenije [*Central Committee of the Communist Party of Slovenia*] (YU)
CKKPS........ Centralni Komitet Komunisticke Partije Srbije [*Central Committee of the Communist Party of Serbia*] (YU)
CKKPSS ..... Centralni Komitet Komunisticke Partije Sovjetskog Saveza [*Central Committee of the Communist Party of the Soviet Union*] (YU)
CKKPSZ...... Centralni Komite Komunisticne Partije Sovjetske Zveze [*Central Committee of the Communist Party of the Soviet Union*] (YU)
CKL .... Centralny Komitet Ludowy [*Central People's Committee*] (POL)
CKLMJ .... Centralni Komite Ljudske Mladine Yugoslavije [*Central Committee of the People's Youth of Yugoslavia*] (YU)
CKLMS .... Centralni Komite Ljudske Mladine Slovenije [*Central Committee of the People's Youth of Slovenia*] (YU)
CKM .... Chawangan Keselamatan Medan [*Field Security Branch*] (ML)
CKM .... Ciezki Karabin Maszynowy [*Heavy Machine Gun*] (POL)
CKMP.......... Cumhuriyet Koylu Millet Partisi [*Republican Peasants Nation Party - RPNP*] [*See also MHP*] (TU)
CKMPT .... Centralni Komitet Madarske Partije Trudbenika [*Central Committee of the Hungarian Workers' Party*] (YU)
CKNMM ...... Centralni Komitet na Narodnata Mladina na Makedonija [*Central Committee of the People's Youth of Macedonia*] (YU)
CKNO.......... Centralni Komitet Narodne Omladine [*Central Committee of the People's Youth*] (YU)
CKO .... Centralna Komisja Odwolawcza [*Central Appeals Commission*] (POL)
CKO .... Cesky Komorni Orchestr [*Czech Chamber Music Ensemble*] (CZ)
CKOM .... Communaute Khmere d'Outre Mer [*Overseas Cambodian Community*] (CL)
CKOS.......... Centralny Komitet Opieki Spolecznej [*Central Committee on Social Welfare*] (POL)
CKP............ Centrala Kolportazu Prasy [*Center for Press Circulation*] (POL)
CKP............ Cinli Komunist Partisi [*Chinese Communist Party*] (TU)
CKPiW Ruch ... Centrala Kolportazu Periodykow i Wydawnictw "Ruch" [*"Ruch" Center for Circulation of Periodicals and Publications*] (POL)
CK PZPR..... Centralny Komitet Polskiej Zjednoczonej Partii Robotnicznej [*Polish United Workers' Party Central Committee*] (POL)
CKR............ Centralna Komisja Rewizyjna [*Central Review Commission*] (POL)
CKRRP .... Centralni Komitet Rumunske Radnicke Partije [*Central Committee of the Romanian Labor Party*] (YU)
CKRSDRP ... Centralni Komitet Ruske Socijal-Demokratske Radnicke Partije [*Central Committee of the Russian Social-Democratic Workers' Party*] (YU)
CKS............ Ceska Kardiologicka Spolecnost [*Czech Cardiological Society*] (CZ)
CK SD .... Centralny Komitet Stronnictwa Demokratycznego [*Central Committe of the Democratic Party*] (POL)
CKSE .... Centralna Komisja Slownictwa Elektrycznego [*Central Commission on Electric Terminology*] (POL)
CKSKBiH .... Centralni Komitet Saveza Komunista Bosne i Hercegovine [*Central Committee of the League of Communists of Bosnia and Hercegovina*] (YU)
CKSKJ .... Centralni Komitet Saveza Komunista Jugoslavije [*Central Committee of the League of Communists of Yugoslavia*] (YU)
CKSKM .... Centralni Komitet Saveza Komunista Makedonije [*Central Committee of the League of Communists of Macedonia*] (YU)
CKSKMJ ..... Centralni Komitet na Sojuzot na Komunistickata Mladina na Jugoslavija [*Central Committee of the Union of Communist Youth of Yugoslavia*] (YU)

CKSKOJ...... Centralni Komitet Saveza Komunisticke Omladine Yugoslavije [*Central Committee of the Union of Communist Youth of Yugoslavia*] (YU)
CKSKP(b)... Centralni Komitet Sovjetske Komunisticke Partije (Boljsevika) [*Central Committee of the Soviet Communist Party (Bolsheviks)*] (YU)
CKSKP(b)... Centralni Komitet Svesavezne Komunisticke Partije (Boljsevika) [*Central Committee of the All-Union Communist Party (Bolsheviks)*] (YU)
CKSKS....... Centralni Komitet Saveza Komunista Srbije [*Central Committee of the League of Communists of Serbia*] (YU)
CKSS.......... Ceskoslovenska Keramicka a Sklarska Spolecnost [*Czechoslovak Ceramics and Glass Company*] (CZ)
CKSW......... Centrala Krajowych Surowcow Wlokienniczych [*Domestic Textile Materials Center*] (POL)
CKT............ Chahada Khassa fi al Tarbiya [*Academic qualification*] [*Syrian*]
CKT............ Compagnie Khmere de Tabacs [*Cambodian Tobacco Company*] (CL)
CKTP.......... Cumhuriyet Kibris Turkiye Partisi [*Turkish Cypriot Republican Party*] (TU)
CKU............ Corps Keuangan [*Finance Corps*] (IN)
CKUAP........ Centralna Komisja Usprawnienia Administracji Publicznej [*Central Commission for the Improvement of Public Administration*] (POL)
CKV............ Cesky Klub Velocipedistu [*Czech Cycling Club*] (CZ)
CKV............ Cesky Klub Veslaru [*Czech Rowing Club*] (CZ)
CKVKP(b)... Centralni Komite Vsezvezne Komunisticne Partije (Boljsevikov) [*Central Committee of the All-Union Communist Party (Bolsheviks)*] (YU)
CKVMRO.... Centralni Komitet Unutrasnje Makedonske Revolucionarne Organizacije [*Central Committee of the Internal Macedonian Revolutionary Organization*] (YU)
CKVO......... Ceskoslovensky Komitet pro Vedeckou Organisaci [*Czechoslovak Committee for the Organization of Scientific Work*] (CZ)
CKVR......... Ceskoslovensky Komitet pro Vedecke Rizeni [*Czechoslovak Committee for Scientific Management*] (CZ)
CKW........... Centralny Komitet Wykonawczy [*Central Executive Committee*] (POL)
CKW PPS.... Centralny Komitet Wykonawczy Polskiej Partii Socjalistycznej [*Central Executive Committee of the Polish Socialist Party*] (POL)
CKZ............ Ceskoslovenske Keramicke Zavody, Narodni Podnik [*Czechoslovak Ceramic Works, National Enterprise*] (CZ)
CKZKMJ..... Centralni Komite Zvezekomunisticne Mladine Jugoslavije [*Central Committee of the Union of Communist Youth of Yugoslavia*] (YU)
CKZKS....... Centralni Komite Zveze Komunistov Slovenije [*Central Committee of the League of Communists of Slovenia*] (YU)
CKZP.......... Centralny Komitet Zydow w Polsce [*Central Committee of Jews in Poland*] (POL)
CKZZ.......... Centralny Komitet Zwiazkow Zawodowych [*Central Committee of Trade Unions*] (POL)
CL............... Celtic League (EA)
cl................ Centiliter [*Centiliter*] (HU)
cl................ Centilitre [*Centiliter*] [*French*]
cl................ Centilitro [*Centiliter*] [*Spanish*]
cl................ Centylitr [*Centiliter*] [*Polish*]
CL............... Chawangan Laut [*Marine Branch*] (ML)
CL............... Chile [*Two-letter standard code*] (CNC)
CL............... Cirkevne Listy [*Church News*] [*A periodical*] (CZ)
cl................ Clanek [*Article*] (CZ)
CL............... Council for Libya (MAR)
cl................ Cum Laude Approbatur [*Latin*]
c/l............... Curso Legal [*Legal Procedure*] [*Spanish*]
cl................ Senttilitra(a) [*Finnish*]
CLA............ Central Legislative Assembly (MAR)
CLA............ Commonwealth Lawyers' Association (EA)
CLA............ Conselho de Libertacao de Angola (MAR)
CLAA.......... Centre Lyonnais d'Applications Atomiques [*French*]
CLAC.......... Caisettes de Livres de l'Association Albert Camus (MAR)
CLAC.......... Centre de Loisirs et d'Animation Culturelle (MAR)
CLAC.......... Comites Lutadoras Anticolonista [*Anticolonial Struggle Committees*] [*Portuguese*] (WER)
CLAD.......... Centre de Linguistique Appliquee de Dakar (MAR)
CLAD.......... Centro Latinoamericano de Administracion para el Desarrollo [*Caracas, Venezuela*]
CLADE........ Conferencia Latinoamericana de Ejecutivos [*Latin American Executives Conference*] (LA)
CLADES...... Centro Latinoamericano de Documentacion Economica y Social [*Santiago, Chile*]
CLAE.......... Congreso Latino Americano de Estudiantes [*Latin American Students Congress*] (LA)
CLAF.......... Centro Latinoamericano de Fisica [*Latin American Center for Physics*] [*Cuban*] (LA)
CLAIM........ Christian Literature Association in Malawi (MAR)
CLAM.......... Comite de Liaison de l'Agrumiculture Mediterraneenne [*Liaison Committee for Mediterranean Citrus Fruit Culture - LCMCFC*] (EA)
CLAMPI....... Confederacion Latinoamericana de Pequena y Mediana Industria [*Latin American Confederation of Small and Medium Industries*] (LA)
CLAN.......... Comision Liberal de Accion Nacional [*Liberal National Action Commission*] [*Colombian*] (LA)
CLAPU........ Confederacion Latinoamericana de Profesionales Universitarios [*Latin American Conference of University Professionals*] (LA)
CLAR........... Conferencia Latinoamericana de Religiosas [*Latin American Conference of Religious Women*] (LA)
CLARA........ China's Liberated Areas Rehabilitation Administration
CLAS........... Confederacion Latino Americana de Sindicatos [*Latin American Confederation of Trade Unions*] (LA)
CLASC........ Confederacao Latino-Americana dos Sindicalistas Cristaos [*Latin American Federation of Christian Trade Unionists*] [*Portuguese*] (LA)
CLASC........ Confederacion Latinoamericana de Sindicalistas Cristianos [*Latin American Federation of Christian Trade Unionists*] [*Spanish*] (LA)
CLAT........... Central Latinoamericana de Trabajadores [*Latin American Workers Federation*] (LA)
CLATE........ Confederacion Latino Americana de Trabajadores Estatales [*Latin American Confederation of Government Employees*] (LA)
CLAUPAE... Comite de Lineas Aereas de la Union Postal de las Americas y Espana [*Air Lines Committee of the Postal Union of the Americas and Spain*] (LA)
CLAVE........ Centro Latinoamericano de Venezuela
CLB............ Commissie Literatuurdocumentatie Bouwwezen
CLC............ Capitaine au Long Cours (MAR)
CLC............ Centrale Landbouwcatalogus [*LHS*] [*Wageningen*]
CLC............ Chinese Liaison Committee (ML)
CLC............ Conseil pour la Liberation du Congo (MAR)
CLC............ Conseil pour la Liberation du Congo-Kinshasa [*Council for the Liberation of the Congo-Kinshasa*] [*Zairian*] (PD)
CLCCR........ Comite de Liaison de la Construction de Carrosseries et de Remorques [*Liaison Committee of Coachwork and Trailer Builders*] (EA)
CLCF........... Centro Linguistico Colombo Frances [*Bogota*] (COL)
CLCI............ Comptoir Lorrain de la Cote-d'Ivoire (MAR)
CLDC.......... Centru de Librarii si Distributie de Carti [*Center for Bookstores and Book Distribution*] (RO)
CLE............ Centre de Litterature Evangelique (MAR)
CLE............ Comando de Lucha Estudiantil [*Student Struggle Command*] [*Ecuadorean*] (LA)
CLE............ Committee of Liberal Exiles (EA)
CLEA.......... Commonwealth Legal Education Association (EA)
CLEF.......... Club des Lecteurs d'Expression Francaise
CLEPA........ Comite de Liaison de la Construction d'Equipements et de Pieces d'Automobiles [*Liaison Committee of Manufacturers of Motor Vehicle Parts and Equipment*] (EA)
Cler............ Clocher [*Steeple*] [*Military map abbreviation*] [*World War I*] [*French*] (MTD)
CLER........... Comite de Liaison des Etudiants Revolutionnaires [*Revolutionary Students Liaison Committee*] [*French*] (WER)
CLER........... Comites de Luchas de Estudiantes Revolucionarios [*Struggle Committees of Revolutionary Students*] [*Venezuelan*] (LA)
CLERES...... Centre de Liaison des Etudes et Recherches Economiques et Sociales [*French*]
CLF............ Cooperative League Fund (MAR)
clg.............. Kologarytm [*Cologarithm*] [*Polish*]
CLI............. Corps Legers d'Intervention (MAR)
CLII............ Centrul de Lupta Impotriva Intoxicantiilor [*Poison Control Center*] (RO)
CLINIMED... Societe des Cliniques Medicales (MAR)
CLIS........... Comite de Liberation des Iles Sao Tome et Principe [*Committee for the Liberation of the Islands of Sao Tome and Principe*] (AF)
CLITAM....... Chadian Livestock Tanning and Manufacturing Industries (MAR)
Clj.............. Cluj [*Cluj*] (RO)
clkor.......... Clen Korespondent [*Corresponding Member*] (CZ)
CLL............ Confederation of Lebanese Labor (ME)
CLLA.......... Comite Laboral Latinoamericano [*Latin American Labor Committee*] [*Mexican*] (LA)
cllo............ Cuartillo [*A unit of measure*] [*Spanish*]
CLM........... Compagnie Lyonnaise de Madagascar (MAR)
CLN........... Committee of National Liberation: Italian All-Party Coordinating Organization for Resistance (MAR)
CLN........... Conseil Legislatif National [*National Legislative Council*] [*Zairian*] (AF)
CLN........... Conseil de Liberation Nationale (MAR)
CLNAI........ Comitato de Liberazione Nazionale per l'Alta Italia [*Committee of National Liberation for Upper Italy*]
CLO........... Centralne Laboratorium Optyki [*Central Optical Laboratory*] (POL)
CLO........... Centrum voor Literatuuronderzoekers ['*s-Gravenhage*]
CLOCCI...... Comite de Liaison des Organismes Chretiens de Cooperation Internationale (EA)

CLODO........ Comite Liquidant ou Detournant les Ordinateurs [*Committee to Liquidate or Neutralize Computers*] [*French*] (PD)
clog............ Kologarytm [*Cologarithm*] [*Polish*]
CLOTI.......... Comite de Liaison des Organisations de Travailleurs Immigrants [*Liaison Committee of the Immigrant Workers Organization*] [*French*] (WER)
CLP............ Centre de Liaison Politique [*Center for Political Liaison*] [*French*] (WER)
CLP............ Comite de Luchas Populares [*Popular Struggle Committee*] [*Venezuelan*] (LA1)
CLP............ Congress Liberation Party (MAR)
CLPD.......... Centralne Laboratorium Przemyslu Drzewnego [*Central Laboratory of the Lumber Industry*] (POL)
CLPG.......... Chretiens pour la Liberation du Peuple Guadeloupeen [*Guadeloupe*] (PD)
CLPO.......... Centralne Laboratorium Przemyslu Odziezowego [*Central Laboratory of the Clothing Industry*] (POL)
CLPS.......... Centralne Laboratorium Przemyslu Szklarskiego [*Central Laboratory of the Glass Industry*] (POL)
CLR............ Cinska Lidova Republika [*Chinese People's Republic*] (CZ)
CLS............ Caribbean Labor Solidarity Organization (LA1)
CLS............ Ceska Logopedicka Spolecnost [*Czech Logopedic Society*] (CZ)
CLS............ Ceskoslovenska Letecka Spolecnost [*Czechoslovak Airlines*] (CZ)
CLS............ Comites de Lucha Sindical [*Union Struggle Committees*] [*Nicaraguan*] (LA1)
CLSC.......... Confederation Luxembourgeoise des Syndicats Chretiens [*Confederation of Christian Trade Unions of Luxembourg*]
CLSM.......... Caribbean Labor Solidarity Movement (LA1)
CLSS.......... Club Leopold Sedar Senghor (MAR)
CLSTP........ Comite de Liberation de Sao Tome e Principe [*Liberation Committee of Sao Tome and Principe*] (AF)
CLSUM....... Chinese Language Society of the University of Malaya (ML)
CLT............ Centrale Laitiere de Tananarive (MAR)
CLT............ Comite de Lucha de los Trabajadores [*Workers Struggle Committee*] [*Nicaraguan*] (LA1)
CLT............ Compagnie Libanaise de Television [*Lebanese Television Company*] (MAR)
CLT............ Consolidacao das Leis Trabalho [*Consolidated Labor Laws*] [*Brazilian*] (LA)
CLTADP...... Comite de Libertacao dos Territorios Africanos Sub o Dominio Portugues (MAR)
CLTC.......... Congreso Latinoamericano de Trabajadores de Comunicaciones [*Latin American Congress of Communications Workers*] (LA)
CLTK.......... Cesky Lawn-Tennisovy Klub [*Czech Lawn Tennis Club*] (CZ)
CLUP.......... Comites de Lucha Universidad Popular [*Committees of Popular University Struggle*] [*Spanish*] (WER)
CLUSA........ Cooperative League of the USA (MAR)
CLZ............ Ceske Lnarske Zavody [*Czech Flax Mills*] (CZ)
CLZ............ Conseil de Liberation du Zimbabwe (MAR)
CM.............. Cameroon [*Two-letter standard code*] (CNC)
CM.............. Cechy-Morava [*Bohemia-Moravia*] (CZ)
Cm.............. Centimetre [*Centimeter*] [*French*] (MTD)
cm.............. Centimetro [*Centimeter*] [*Portuguese*] (GPO)
CM.............. Centrala Miniera [*Mining Central*] (RO)
cm.............. Centymetr [*Centimeter*] [*Polish*]
cm.............. Cesko-Moravsky [*Czech-Moravian*] (CZ)
CM.............. Ceskoslovenske Mlyny [*Czechoslovak Flour Mills*] (CZ)
CM.............. Chirurgiae Magister [*Master of Surgery*] [*Latin*] (GPO)
CM.............. Compagnie de Mitrailleuses [*Military*] [*French*] (MTD)
CM.............. Conseil des Ministres [*Cabinet*] [*Cambodian*] (CL)
CM.............. Conselho de Ministros [*Council of Ministers*] [*Portuguese*] (WER)
cm.............. Corrente Mese [*Instant*] [*Italian*] (GPO)
CM.............. Council of Ministers (MAR)
c/m............ Cours Moyen [*French*]
CM.............. Crna Metalurgija [*Iron and Steel Industry*] (YU)
CM.............. Cyrilo-Metodejska (Bohoslovecka Fakulta) [*Cyril and Methodius (School of Divinity)*] (CZ)
cm.............. Senttimetri(a) [*Finnish*]
Cm.............. Zentimeter [*Centimeter*] (EG)
Cm²............ Centimetre Carre [*Square Centimeter*] [*French*] (MTD)
cm²............ Centymetr Kwadratowy [*Square Centimeter*] [*Polish*]
cm²............ Neliosenttimetri(a) [*Finnish*]
Cm³............ Centimetre Cube [*Cubic Centimeter*] [*French*] (MTD)
cm³............ Centymetr Szescienny [*Cubic Centimeter*] [*Polish*]
cm³............ Kuutiosenttimetri(a) [*Finnish*]
CMA............ Christian and Missionary Alliance (MAR)
CMA............ Commonwealth Magistrates' Association (EA)
CMA............ Commonwealth Medical Association (EA)
CMA............ Compania Mexicana de Aviacion [*Mexican Aviation Company*] (LA)
CMA............ Confection Moderne Africaine (MAR)
CMA............ Corporacion de Mercadeo Agricola [*Venezuelan*]
CMA............ Egyptian Capital Market Authority (MAR)
CMA............ Societe de Carrosserie Moderne Artisanale (MAR)
CMAP.......... Commission Mondiale d'Action Professionnelle [*World Committee for Trade Action - WCTA*] (EA)
CMAR.......... Comite Maghrebin d'Assurances et de Reassurances (MAR)
CMAS.......... Confederation Mondiale des Activities Subaquatiques [*World Underwater Federation*] (EA)
CMATA........ Compagnie Maritime et Aerienne de Transports et d'Affretement [*Moroccan*] (MAR)
CMB............ Centrala Materialow Budowlanych [*Building Materials Center*] (POL)
CMB............ Cocoa Marketing Board (MAR)
CMB............ Compagnie Maritime Belge
CMB............ Confederation des Metalurgistes Belges [*Confederation of Belgian Metallurgists*] (WER)
CMB............ Cuyas Manos Beso [*Very Respectfully*] [*Formal correspondence*] [*Spanish*]
CMBEFS..... Consuliul Municipal Bucuresti pentru Educatie Fizica si Sport [*Bucharest Municipality Council for Physical Education and Sports*] (RO)
CMBU.......... Confederation of Metal and Building Unions [*South African*] (AF)
CMC............ Centrala Materialelor de Constructie [*Central for Construction Materials*] (RO)
CMC............ Compagnie Malgache de Cabotage (MAR)
CMC............ Compagnie Miniere de Conakry [*Conakry Mining Company*] [*Guinean*] (AF)
CMC............ Cooper Motor Corporation Limited (MAR)
CMCA.......... Commission of Mediation, Conciliation, and Arbitration (MAR)
CMCA.......... Constructions Metallurgiques de Centrafrique (MAR)
CMCAT........ Caisse Mutuelle de Credit Agricole de Tunisie (MAR)
CMCE.......... Centre Malien du Commerce Exterieur (MAR)
CMCES........ Comite Ministeriel de Coordination Economique et Sociale [*Ministerial Committee for Economic and Social Coordination*] [*Belgian*] (WER)
CMCF.......... Comite Mondial Contre le Faim [*World Committee to Combat Hunger*] [*French*] (CL)
CMCH.......... Campana Mundial Contra el Hambre [*World Committee to Combat Hunger*] [*Spanish*] (MAR)
CMCI........... Centrala de Mecanizare pentru Constructii Industriale [*Mechanization Central for Industrial Constructions*] (RO)
CMCO.......... Chinese Malayan Communist Organization (ML)
CMCO.......... Complexe de Materiaux de Construction d'Oran [*Algerian*] (MAR)
CMCP.......... Compagnie Marocaine des Cartons et Papiers (MAR)
CMCPT........ Comite Maghrebin de Coordination des Postes et Telecommunications (MAR)
CMCR.......... Compagnie Maritime des Chargeurs Reunis (MAR)
CMCRI........ Comptoir Malgache de Courtage, de Representation, et d'Importation (MAR)
CMD............ Centrala Maszyn Drogowych [*Road Building Machinery Center*] (POL)
CMD............ Ceskomoravske Statni Drahy [*Czech-Moravian State Railroads*] (CZ)
CMD............ Comite Militaire pour le Developpement [*Military Development Committee*] [*Malagasy*] (AF)
CMD............ Comite de Mujeres Democraticas [*Committee of Democratic Women*] [*Colombian*] (LA)
CMD............ Compagnie Marocaine de Distribution (MAR)
CMDC.......... Consejo Metropolitano del Distrito Central [*Central District Metropolitan Council*] [*Honduran*] (LA1)
CMDLRS..... Cirilmetodijsko Drustvo Katoliskih Duhovnikov Ljudska Republika Slovenija [*Cyril and Methodius Society of the Catholic Priests of Slovenia*] (YU)
CMDM.......... Compagnie Malgache de Manutention (MAR)
CMDPA........ Centrul de Material Didactic si Propaganda Agricola [*Center for Teaching Materials and Agricultural Propaganda*] (RO)
CMDT.......... Compagnie Malienne pour le Developpement des Textiles (MAR)
CME............ Comite Mixte Economique [*Joint Economic Committee*] [*Cambodian*] (CL)
CME............ Compagnie Mauritanienne d'Entreprises (MAR)
CME............ Conference Mondiale de l'Energie [*World Energy Conference - WEC*] (EA)
CMEA.......... Council for Mutual Economic Assistance (LA1)
CMEF.......... Centro Mexicano de Estudios de Farmacodependencia [*Mexican Center for Studies of Drug Addiction*] (LA)
CMELTA..... Constructions Mecaniques et Electriques de Tananarive (MAR)
CMEM.......... Centros Militares de Ensenanza Media [*Military Centers for Secondary Education*] [*Cuban*] (LA)
CMERA........ Centre Maghrebin d'Etudes et de Recherches Administratives (MAR)
CMET.......... Comite Maghrebin de l'Emploi et du Travail [*North African*] (MAR)
CMET.......... Council on Middle East Trade (MAR)
CMF............ Casopis pro Moderni Filologii [*Journal of Modern Philology*] [*A publication*] (CZ)
CMF............ Cordis Mariae Filius (Misioneros Hijos del Corazon de Maria) [*Bogota*] (COL)
Cmg............ Candidatus Magisterii [*Academic degree*] [*Latin*]
CMG............ Comite Mixte Gabonaise [*Gabonese Joint Committee*] (AF)
CMG............ Constructions Mecaniques Generales (MAR)
CMG............ Constructions Metalliques Generales (MAR)
Cmh Rs....... Cumhur Reisi [*President*] [*of Republic*] (TU)
CMHV.......... Communaute Musulmane de Haute-Volta [*Upper Volta Moslem Community*] (AF)

CMI.............. Comite Maritime International [*International Maritime Committee*] (EA)
CMI.............. Compagnies Mobiles d'Intervention [*Mobile Intervention Companies*] [*Moroccan*] (AF)
CMI.............. Conference of African Ministers of Industry (MAR)
CMIAP......... Comite Militaire Inter-Armee Provisoire [*Provisional Joint Military Committee*] [*Chadian*] (AF)
CMID........... Ceskomoravska Impregnace Dreva [*Czech-Moravian Wood Impregnating Enterprise*] (CZ)
CMIDOM..... Centre Militaire d'Information et de Documentation sur l'Outre-Mer [*Military Center for Overseas Information and Documentation*] [*French*] (AF)
CMIEB......... Centre Mondial d'Information sur l'Education Bilingue [*World Information Centre for Bilingual Education - WICBE*] (EA)
CMIM.......... Constructions Metalliques et Industrielles Mecaniques (MAR)
CMJP.......... Centre Marocain des Jeunes Patrons (MAR)
CMKD......... Consortium Marocain-Kuwaitien de Developpement [*Moroccan-Kuwaiti Development Consortium*] (AF)
CML............ Camara Municipal de Lisboa [*Lisbon City Hall*] [*Portuguese*] (WER)
CML............ Comite Marxista Leninista (MAR)
CML............ Companhia Mineira de Lobito (MAR)
CMLN.......... Comite Militaire de Liberation Nationale [*Military National Liberation Committee*] [*Malian*] (AF)
CM-LP......... Comite Marxista-Leninista Portugues [*Portuguese Marxist-Leninist Committee (1975-)*] (PPE)
CM-LP......... Comite Marxista-Leninista Portuguesa [*Portuguese Marxist-Leninist Committee (1964-1970s ?)*] (PPE)
CMM........... Casopis Matice Moravske [*Journal of the Moravian Foundation (A Moravian cultural organization)*] [*A publication*] (CZ)
CMM........... Comissao de Marinha Mercante [*Merchant Marine Commission*] [*Brazilian*] (LA)
CMM........... Comite du Cahier Medical de Madagascar (MAR)
CMM........... Compagnie Marseillaise de Madagascar (MAR)
CMM........... Compagnie des Messageries Maritimes (MAR)
CMM........... Compagnie Metallurgique et Miniere (MAR)
CMM........... Compagnie Miniere de la Moufumbi (MAR)
CMM........... Constructions Metalliques de Mauritanie (MAR)
CMMI.......... Council of Mining and Metallurgical Institutions (EA)
CMML......... Christian Missions in Many Lands (MAR)
CMMN......... Centrala Minereurilor si Metalurgiei Neferoase [*Central for Nonferrous Ores and Metallurgy*] (RO)
CMMR......... Centrala Mecanica de Material Rulant [*Machine Central for Rolling Stock*] (RO)
CMN............ Compagnie Malgache de Navigation (MAR)
CMN............ Compagnie Malienne de Navigation (MAR)
CMN............ Conselho Monetario Nacional [*National Monetary Council*] [*Brazilian*] (LA)
CMNR.......... Comite Militaire de Redressement National [*Military Committee for National Recovery*] [*Use CMRN*] [*Mauritanian*] (AF)
CMNT.......... Comissao Mista Nacional de Telecomunicacoes [*National Mixed Commission of Telecommunications*] [*Portuguese*] (WER)
CMO............ Chemin de Fer du Maroc Oriental (MAR)
CMOO......... Compagnie Miniere de l'Oubangi Oriental (MAR)
CMOPE....... Confederation Mondiale des Organisations de la Profession Enseignante [*World Confederation of Organizations of the Teaching Profession*] [*Use WCOTP*] (AF)
CMOT.......... Confederation Maghrebine des Operateurs de Tourisme [*North African*] (MAR)
CMP............ Comite Militaire du Parti (MAR)
CMP............ Comite Militaire du PCT [*PCT Military Committee*] [*Congolese*] (AF)
CMP............ Compagnie Malgache des Petroles (MAR)
CMP............ Conseil Mondial de la Paix [*World Peace Council*] [*Use WPC*] [*French*] (AF)
CMP............ Consejo Mundial de Paz [*World Peace Council*] [*Use WPC*] [*Spanish*] (LA)
CMP............ Consiglio Mondiale della Pace [*World Peace Council*] [*Use WPC*] [*Italian*] (WER)
CMPC.......... Compania Manufacturera de Papeles y Cartones [*Paper and Cardboard Manufacturing Company*] [*Chilean*] (LA)
CMPD.......... Comite Militaire pour le Developpement [*Military Development Committee*] [*Use CMD*] (AF)
CMPFE........ Centre Malagasy de Production de Films Educatifs [*Malagasy Center for Production of Educational Films*] (AF)
CMPP.......... Comite Maghrebin des Produits Pharmaceutiques [*North African*] (MAR)
CMPR.......... Centre Militaire de Preformation de la Reunion [*Basic Military Training Center of Reunion*] (AF)
CMPR.......... Comptoir Malgache de Pieces de Rechange (MAR)
CMPS.......... Combined Military Planning Staff (MAR)
CMR............ Cameroon [*Three-letter standard code*] (CNC)
CMR............ Cape Mounted Rifles (MAR)
CMR............ Centrul Metodologic de Reumatologie [*Methodology Center for Rheumatology*] (RO)
CMR............ Comite Militaire de la Revolution [*Military Committee of the Revolution*] [*Beninese*] (AF)
CMR............ Comites Militares Regionales [*Regional Military Committees*] [*Cuban*] (LA)
CMRN.......... Comite Militaire de Redressement National [*Military Committee for National Recovery*] [*Mauritanian*] (AF)
CMRN.......... Military Committee for National Recovery [*Central African*] (PD)
CMRP.......... Cesky a Moravsky Rudny Pruzkum [*Mineral Prospecting in Bohemia and Moravia*] (CZ)
CMRPN....... Comite Militaire de Redressement pour le Progres National [*Military Committee for Redress and National Progress*] (MAR)
C-M-S......... Cechy - Morava - Slovensko [*Bohemia - Moravia - Slovakia*] (CZ)
CMS............ Central Medical Stores (MAR)
CMS............ Centrul de Mecanica a Solidelor [*Center for the Mechanics of Solids*] (RO)
cm/s............ Centymetr na Sekunde [*Centimeter per Second*] [*Polish*]
CMS............ Ceska Matice Skolska [*Czech Educational Foundation*] (CZ)
CMS............ Ceskomoravske Sklarny, Narodni Podnik [*Czech-Moravian Glass Factories, National Enterprise*] (CZ)
CMS............ Ceskoslovenska Mykologicka Spolecnost [*Czechoslovak Mycological Society*] (CZ)
CMS............ Church Missionary School (MAR)
CMS............ Church Missionary Society (MAR)
CMS............ Comite Maghrebin des Sports (MAR)
CMS............ Conseil Militaire Supreme [*Supreme Military Council*] [*Niger*] (AF)
CMSC......... Council of Moslem School Proprietors (MAR)
CMSL-FO.... Confederation Malgache des Syndicats Libre - Force Ouvriere (MAR)
CMSN.......... Comite Militaire de Salut National [*Military Committee for National Salvation*] [*Mauritanian*] (AF)
CMSP.......... Confederacion de Militares en Servicio Pasivo [*Federation of Retired Servicemen*] [*Ecuadorean*] (LA)
CMSS.......... Caisse Mutuelle de Securite Sociale [*Moroccan*] (MAR)
CMSSp....... Casopis Muzealnej Slovenskej Spolocnosti [*Journal of the Slovak Museum Society*] [*A publication*] (CZ)
CMT............ Centros de Mantenimiento de Transmision [*Transmission Maintenance Centers*] [*Cuban*] (LA)
CMT............ Ceska Matice Technicka [*Czech Foundation for Advancement of Technology*] (CZ)
CMT............ Comite Maghrebin du Tourisme (MAR)
CMT............ Confederacion Multigremial del Trabajo [*Confederation of Business and Professional Associations*] [*Chilean*] (LA)
CMT............ Confederation Mondiale du Travail [*World Confederation of Labour - WCL*] (EA)
CMT............ Construction Metallique Tropicale (MAR)
CMTA.......... Comite Maghrebin des Transports Aeriens (MAR)
CMTM......... Comite Maghrebin des Transports Maritimes (MAR)
CMTR.......... Comite Maghrebin des Transports Routiers (MAR)
CMTR.......... Compagnie Malienne des Transports Routiers (MAR)
CMTT.......... Consortium Marocain de Transit et de Transports (MAR)
CMU............ Ceza Mahkemeleri (Kanunu) Usul [*Criminal Courts' Procedural Law*] (TU)
CMU............ Commandement Militaire Unifie [*Unified Military Command*] [*Angolan*] (AF)
CMU............ Cumhuriyet Muddei Umumisi [*Public Prosecutor*] (TU)
CMUF.......... Compagnie Miniere de l'Uranium de Franceville (MAR)
CMUK.......... Ceza Mahkemeleri Usul Kanunu [*Criminal Courts' Procedural Law*] (TU)
CMV............ Celostatni Mirovy Vybor [*All-State Peace Committee*] (CZ)
CMV............ Comite Militaire de Vigilance [*Military Vigilance Committee*] [*Beninese*] (AF)
CMVKD....... Celostatni Mirovy Vybor Katolickeho Duchovenstva [*All-State Peace Committee of the Catholic Clergy*] (CZ)
CMZ............ Compagnie Maritime Zairoise [*Zairian Shipping Company*] (AF)
Cn............... Black Powder [*Symbol*] [*French*] (MTD)
CN............... China [*Two-letter standard code*] (CNC)
CN............... Cirkevne Nakladatelstvo [*Religious Literature Publishing House*] (CZ)
c/n.............. Compte Nouveau [*French*]
CN............... Conselho Nacional (MAR)
c/n.............. Cours Nul [*French*]
CN............... Credit National [*National Credit Bank*] [*Guinean*] (AF)
CN............... Credit du Niger (MAR)
CNA............. Cartel dos Nationalistas Angolanos (MAR)
CNA............. Central News Agency Ltd. (MAR)
CNA............. Centrale Nucleaire des Ardennes
CNA............. Centre National d'Agriculture [*National Agricultural Center*] [*Senegalese*] (AF)
CNA............. Centre National d'Alphabetisation [*Algerian*] (MAR)
CNA............. Cesky Narodni Aeroklub [*Czech National Aero Club*] (CZ)
CNA............. Charbonnages Nord-Africains [*Moroccan*] (MAR)
CNA............. Code de la Nationalite Algerienne (MAR)
CNA............. Colegio Nacional de Arquitectos de Cuba [*National Association of Cuban Architects*] (LA)
CNA............. Comissao Nacional do Alcool [*National Alcohol Commission*] [*Brazilian*] (LA)
CNA............. Comite Nacional de Abastos [*National Supply Committee*] [*Nicaraguan*] (LA1)
CNA............. Confederacao Nacional da Agricultura [*National Agriculture Confederation*] [*Brazilian*] (LA)

CNA............ Confederacion Nacional Agraria [*National Agrarian Confederation*] [*Peruvian*] (LA)
CNA............ Conseil National de l'Aeronautique (MAR)
CNA............ Consejo Nacional Agrario [*National Agrarian Council*] [*Honduran*] (LA)
CNA............ Consiliul National de Agricultura [*National Council for Agriculture*] (RO)
CNA............ Consiliul National al Apelor [*National Water Council*] (RO)
CNAAC....... Comite National d'Aide et d'Assistance aux Combattants [*National Aid and Relief Committee for Combattants*] [*Cambodian*] (CL)
CNAC......... Comision Nacional de la Academia de Ciencias [*National Commission of the Academy of Sciences*] [*Cuban*] (LA)
CNAC......... Comision Nacional de Accion Conservadora [*Conservative National Action Commission*] [*Colombian*] (LA)
CNAC......... Compagnie Nationale d'Assurances du Cambodge [*National Insurance Company of Cambodia*] (CL)
CNAE......... Campanha Nacional de Alimentacao Escolar [*National School Lunch Drive*] [*Brazilian*] (LA)
CNAE......... Comissao Nacional de Atividades Espaciais [*National Space Activities Commission*] [*Later, INPE*] [*Brazilian*] (LA)
CNAEE....... Conselho Nacional de Aguas e Energia Eletrica [*National Council on Water and Electric Power*] [*Brazilian*] (LA)
CNAEM....... Cekmece Nucleer Arastirma ve Egitim Merkezi [*Cekmese Nuclear Research and Training Center*] (TU)
CNAFAT...... Caisse Nationale d'Allocations Familiales et des Accidents du Travail [*National Welfare and Workmen's Compensation Fund*] [*Malagasy*] (AF)
CNAFM....... Conseil National des Associations des Femmes de Madagascar [*National Council of Women's Associations of Madagascar*] (AF)
CNAG......... Comite National d'Assainissement General [*National General Cleanup Committee*] [*Cambodian*] (CL)
CNAM......... Congreso Nacional Africano de Mocambique (MAR)
CNAN......... Compagnie Nationale Algerienne de Navigation [*Algerian National Shipping Company*] (AF)
CNAO......... Comite Nacional de Auscultacion y Organizacion [*National Committee for Auscultation and Organization*] [*Mexican*] (LA)
CNAP......... Centre National Anti-Pollution [*National Antipollution Center*] [*Gabonese*] (AF)
CNAP......... Comitetul National pentru Apararea Pacii [*National Committee for the Defense of Peace*] (RO)
CNAPC........ Comite National d'Action pour la Paix et la Concorde [*National Action Committee for Peace and Concord*] [*Cambodian*] (CL)
CNAPCM.... Comite National d'Action pour la Paix et la Concorde [*National Action Committee for Peace and Concord*] [*Use CNAPC*] [*Cambodian*] (CL)
CNAPD........ Comite National d'Action pour la Paix et le Developpement [*National Action Committee for Peace and Development*] [*Belgian*] (WER)
CNAPS........ Caisse Nationale de Prevoyance Sociale [*National Social Welfare Fund*] [*Malagasy*] (AF)
CNAR.......... Compagnie Nationale d'Assurances et de Reassurances [*Ivorian*] (MAR)
CNAT.......... Comissao Nacional de Assistencia Tecnica [*National Technical Assistance Commission*] [*Brazilian*] (LA)
CNAT.......... Commission Nationale pour l'Amenagement du Territoire [*French*]
CNAVS........ Cesky Narodni Aeroklub Vysokoskolskeho Studentstva [*Czech National Aero Club of University Students*] (CZ)
CNB............ Centrale Nucleaire Belge [*Nuclear reactor*] [*Belgian*]
CNB............ Coordinador Nacional de Bases [*National Coordination of Bases*] [*Colombian*] (PD)
CNBB.......... Conferencia Nacional dos Bispos do Brasil [*National Conference of Brazilian Bishops*] (LA)
CNBF.......... Centre National des Bureaux de Fret (MAR)
CNBU.......... Commission Nationale du Burundi pour l'UNESCO (MAR)
CNBV.......... Comissao Nacional de Bolsas de Valores [*National Stock Exchange Commission*] [*Brazilian*] (LA)
CNC............ Camara Nicaraguense de la Construccion [*Nicaraguan Chamber of Construction*] (LA)
CNC............ Capitaine de Navigation Cotiere (MAR)
CNC............ Centre National du Cinema [*National Motion Picture Center*] [*Upper Voltan*] (AF)
CNC............ Centre National Cinematographique [*National Cinematographic Center*] [*Algerian*] (AF)
CNC............ Centrul National de Chimie [*National Center for Chemistry*] (RO)
CNC............ Comite National de la Consommation [*French*]
CNC............ Comite National de Coordination (MAR)
CNC............ Compagnie Nouvelle de Cadres [*Moroccan*] (MAR)
CNC............ Confederacao Nacional do Comercio [*National Confederation of Commerce*] [*Brazilian*] (LA)
CNC............ Confederacion Nacional Campesina [*National Peasant Confederation*] [*Chilean*] (LA)
CNC............ Confederacion Nacional Campesina [*National Peasant Confederation*] [*Mexican*] (LA)
CNC............ Confederation Nationale des Cadres [*National Confederation of Cadres*] [*Trade union*] [*Belgian*] (WER)
CNC............ Conseil National Consultatif [*National Advisory Committee*] [*Mauritanian*] (AF)
CNC............ Consejo Nacional de Campesinos [*National Council of Peasants*] [*Chilean*] (LA1)
CNC............ Consejo Nacional de Cultura [*National Council of Culture*] [*Cuban*] (LA)
CNC............ Consell Nacional Catala [*National Council of Catalonia*] [*Spanish*] (WER)
CNCA.......... Caisse Nationale de Credit Agricole [*National Agricultural Credit Bank*] [*Ivorian*] (AF)
CNCA.......... Caisse Nationale de Credit Agricole [*National Agricultural Credit Bank*] [*Moroccan*] (AF)
CNCA.......... Caisse Nationale de Credit Agricole [*National Fund for Agricultural Credits*] [*Togolese*] (AF)
CNCA.......... Caisse Nationale de Credit Agricole [*National Agricultural Credit Bank*] [*Beninese*] (AF)
CNCA.......... Centre National du Cinema Algerien [*Algerian National Motion Picture Center*] (AF)
CNCA.......... Centre National de la Cooperation Agricole (MAR)
CNCA.......... Compagnie Nationale de Credit Agricole [*North African*] (MAR)
CNCACI...... Caisse Nationale de Credit Agricole de la Cote-d'Ivoire (MAR)
CNCC.......... Conseil National des Chargeurs du Cameroun (MAR)
CNCE.......... Centre National du Commerce Exterieur [*National Center for Foreign Trade*] [*French*] (AF)
CNCE.......... Comite Nationale de Coordination des Eleves [*National Student Coordination Committee*] [*Malagasy*] (AF)
CNCE.......... Consejo Nacional de Comercio Exterior [*National Foreign Trade Council*] [*Venezuelan*] (LA)
CNCECT..... Comision Nacional de Colaboracion Economica y Cientifico-Tecnica [*National Commission for Economic, Scientific, and Technical Cooperation*] [*Cuban*] (LA)
CNCI........... Confederacion Nacional de Comunas Industriales [*National Confederation of Industrial Communes*] [*Peruvian*] (LA)
CNCI........... Societe Commerciale du Nord de la Cote-d'Ivoire (MAR)
CNCK.......... Comite National de Coordination du Karate (MAR)
CNCMA....... Centre National de la Cooperation et de la Mutualite Agricoles (MAR)
CNCO.......... Compagnie Nantaise des Chargeurs de l'Ouest (MAR)
CNCO.......... Coordinadora Nacional de Comisiones Obreras [*National Coordinator of Workers Commissions*] [*Spanish*] (WER)
CNCS.......... Consiliul National de Cercetari Stiintifice [*National Council for Scientific Research*] (RO)
CNCT.......... Consejo Nacional de Ciencia y Tecnologia [*National Council on Science and Technology*] [*Cuban*] (LA)
CNCU.......... Comision Nacional Cubana de la UNESCO [*Cuban National UNESCO Commission*] (LA)
CNCU.......... Commission Nationale Congolaise pour l'UNESCO (MAR)
CNCV.......... Confederacion Nacional Campesina de Venezuela [*Venezuelan National Peasant Confederation*] (LA)
CND............ Centre National de Documentation [*National Documentation Center*] [*Laotian*] (CL)
CND............ Centre National de Documentation [*National Documentation Center*] [*Zairian*] (AF)
CND............ Ceskoslovenske Naftove Doly [*Czechoslovak Petroleum Fields*] (CZ)
CND............ Club Nation et Developpement [*Nation and Development Club*] [*Senegalese*] (AF)
CND............ Club Nautique de Dakar (MAR)
CND............ Comisia Nationala de Demografie [*National Commission for Demography*] (RO)
CND............ Comision Nacional de Desarrollo [*Commission for National Development*] [*Dominican Republic*] (LA1)
CND............ Comptoir National du Diamant (MAR)
CND............ Confrerie de Notre-Dame (MAR)
CND............ Conseil National du Developpement [*National Development Council*] [*Niger*] (AF)
CND............ Conseil National de Discipline [*National Discipline Council*] [*Cambodian*] (CL)
CNDACLMG... Comite National de Direction des Actions Communes de Lutte dans le Cadre de la Mobilisation Generale [*National Committee for Directing Joint Campaigns for General Mobilization*] [*Cambodian*] (CL)
CNDC.......... Ciskei National Development Corporation (MAR)
CNDC.......... Corps National de Defense Civile [*National Civil Defense Corps*] [*Congolese*] (AF)
CNDEP........ Comite Nacional para la Defensa de la Economia Popular [*National Committee for Defending the Popular Economy*] [*Mexican*] (LA1)
CNDF.......... Compagnie de Navigation Denis Freres (MAR)
CNDFA........ Conseil National Democratique des Forces Armees [*National Democratic Council of Armed Forces*] [*Algerian*] (AF)
CNDH.......... Comision Nacional de Derechos Humanos [*National Commission of Human Rights*] [*Paraguayan*] (LA)
CNDI........... Caisse Nationale des Depots et des Investissements [*National Deposits and Investments Fund*] [*Upper Voltan*] (AF)
CNDPK........ Centre National de Peche a Kinkole [*National Fishing Center at Kinkole*] [*Zairian*] (AF)
CNDR.......... Comite Nationale de Defense de la Revolution [*National Committee for the Defense of the Revolution*] [*Algerian*] (AF)

CNDR .... Comite Nationale de Defense de la Revolution [*National Committee for the Defense of the Revolution*] [*Malian*] (AF)
CNDR .... Consiglio Nazionale delle Ricerche [*National Research Council*] [*Italian*]
CNDST .... Centre National de Documentation Scientifique et Technique [*French*]
Cne .... Cabane [*Cabin*] [*Military map abbreviation*] [*World War I*] [*French*] (MTD)
CNE .... Caisse Nationale d'Epargne [*National Savings Bank*] [*Upper Voltan*] (AF)
CNE .... Caisse Nationale d'Equipement [*National Equipment Bank*] [*Cambodian*] (CL)
CNE .... Centrala Nucleara de Energie [*Nuclear Power Plant*] (RO)
CNE .... Centrale Nationale des Employes [*Employees' National Center*] [*Belgian*] (WER)
CNE .... Chantier Naval de l'Estuaire (MAR)
CNE .... Christian National Education (MAR)
CNE .... Comision Nacional de Emulacion [*National Emulation Committee*] [*Cuban*] (LA)
CNE .... Comision Naval de Energia [*Naval Commission for Energy*] [*Chilean*] (LA1)
CNE .... Comissao Nacional Eleitoral [*National Electoral Commission*] [*Portuguese*] (WER)
CNE .... Comissao Nacional de Energia [*National Energy Commission*] [*Brazilian*] (LA)
CNE .... Comissao Nacional Executivo (MAR)
CNE .... Comite Nacional de Emergencia [*National Emergency Committee*] [*Salvadoran*] (LA)
CNE .... Comite Nacional de Emergencia [*National Emergency Committee*] [*Nicaraguan*] (LA)
CNE .... Comite National d'Entr'aide [*National Welfare Committee*] [*Cambodian*] (CL)
CNE .... Consejo Nacional de Educacion [*National Education Council*] [*Cuban*] (LA)
CNE .... Conselho Nacional de Economia [*National Economic Council*] [*Brazilian*] (LA)
CNE .... Constructions Nautiques Eburneennes (MAR)
CNEA .... Centre National d'Etudes Agricoles (MAR)
CNEA .... Comision Nacional de Energia Atomica [*National Atomic Energy Commission*] [*Mexican*]
CNEA .... Comision Nacional de Energia Atomica [*National Atomic Energy Commission*] [*Uruguayan*] (LA)
CNEA .... Comision Nacional de Energia Atomica [*National Atomic Energy Commission*] [*Argentine*] (LA)
CNEC .... Centre National d'Enseignement par Correspondance [*National Center for Instruction by Correspondence*] [*Algerian*] (AF)
CNEC .... Confederacion Nacional de Ex Combatientes [*National Confederation of Veterans*] [*Spanish*] (WER)
CNEC .... Conseil National de l'Education et de la Culture [*National Education and Culture Council*] [*Cambodian*] (CL)
CNECA .... Comision Nacional de Estudio de la Cana y del Azucar [*National Commission for Studying Sugar and Sugarcane*] [*Bolivian*] (LA1)
CNECI .... Caisse Nationale d'Epargne et de Credit Immobiliere [*National Savings and Real Estate Credit Fund*] [*Zairian*] (AF)
CNED .... Confederacion Nacional de Estudiantes Democraticos [*National Confederation of Democratic Students*] [*Mexican*] (LA)
CNEDES ..... Centre National d'Etudes et de Documentation Economique et Sociale (MAR)
CNEE .... Comision Nacional del Espacio Exterior [*National Commission for Outer Space*] [*Mexican*]
CNEFS .... Consiliul National pentru Educatie Fizica si Sport [*National Council for Physical Education and Sports*] (RO)
CNEG .... Centre National d'Enseignement Generalise (MAR)
CNEI .... Centre Nationale d'Etudes Industrielles [*National Industrial Studies Center*] [*Tunisian*] (AF)
CNEJ .... Conseil National de l'Education et de la Jeunesse [*National Education and Youth Council*] [*Malagasy*] (AF)
CNEL .... Caisse Nationale d'Epargne Logement [*Tunisian*] (MAR)
CNEL .... Consiglio Nazionale dell'Economia e del Lavoro [*National Council for Economy and Labor*] [*Italian*] (WER)
CNELAJ ...... Centre National d'Etudes et de Liaison des Associations de Jeunesse (MAR)
CNEN .... Comision Nacional de Energia Nuclear [*National Commission for Nuclear Energy*] [*Mexican*]
CNEN .... Comissao Nacional de Energia Nuclear [*National Nuclear Energy Commission*] [*Brazilian*] (LA)
CNEN .... Comitato Nazionale per l'Energia Nucleare [*National Nuclear Energy Commission*] [*Italian*] (WER)
CNEOT .... Centre National d'Education Ouvriere du Togo [*National Workers Education Center of Togo*] (AF)
CNEP .... Caisse Nationale Algerienne d'Epargne et de Prevoyance [*Algerian National Savings and Insurance Bank*] (AF)
CNEP .... Caisse Nationale d'Epargne et de Prevoyance [*North African*] (MAR)
CNEP .... Comptoir National d'Escompte de Paris (MAR)
CNEPCE ..... Consejo Nacional de Evaluacion, Programacion, y Capacitacion Educativa [*National Council of Educational Evaluation, Programming, and Training*] [*Nicaraguan*] (LA1)
CNEPS .... Centre National d'Education Physique et Sportive [*Algerian*] (MAR)
CNERAT ...... Centre National d'Etudes et de Recherches en Amenagement du Territoire [*Algerian*] (MAR)
CNERNA ..... Centre National de Coordination des Etudes et Recherches sur la Nutrition et l'Alimentation (MAR)
CNERTP ...... Centre National d'Essais et de Recherches des Travaux Publics [*National Public Works Test and Research Center*] [*Beninese*] (AF)
CNERV .... Centre National de l'Elevage et de la Recherche Veterinaire (MAR)
CNES .... Centre National d'Etudes Scientifiques [*National Center for Scientific Studies*] [*French*]
CNES .... Centre National d'Etudes Spatiales [*National Center for Space Studies*] [*French*] (WER)
CNES .... Conseil National Economique et Social [*National Economic and Social Council*] [*Algerian*] (AF)
CNES .... Consejo Nacional de Educacion Superior [*National Council of Higher Education*] [*Bolivian*] (LA)
CNES .... Consejo Nacional de Educacion Superior [*National Council of Higher Education*] [*Nicaraguan*] (LA1)
CNES .... Consejo Nacional de Ensenanza Secundaria [*National Council of Secondary Education*] [*Uruguayan*] (LA)
CNET .... Centre National d'Etudes des Telecommunications [*National Center for Telecommunications Studies*] [*French*] (WER)
CNEUPEN ... Commission Nationale pour l'Etude de l'Utilisation Pacifique de l'Energie Nucleaire [*Belgian*]
CNEV .... Conseil National des Entreprises Voltaiques [*National Council of Voltan Enterprises*] (AF)
CNEXCA ..... Confederacion Nacional de Ex Cautivos [*National Confederation of Ex-Prisoners*] [*Spanish*] (WER)
CNEXO .... Centre National pour l'Exploitation des Oceans [*National Center for Exploitation of the Oceans*] [*French*] (WER)
CNF .... Cameroon's National Federation (MAR)
CNF .... Centre Nationale de Floristique (MAR)
CNF .... Code de la Nationalite Francaise [*North African*] (MAR)
CNF .... Commonwealth Nurses Federation (EA)
CNF .... Compagnie du Niger Francais (MAR)
CNF .... Consiliul National al Femeilor [*National Council of Women*] (RO)
CNFA .... Centre National de Formation Administrative [*National Administration Training Center*] [*Malagasy*] (AF)
CNFB .... Conseil National des Femmes Belges [*Belgian Women's National Council*] (WER)
CNFC .... Centre National de Formation Cooperative (MAR)
CNFI .... Caribbean Food and Nutrition Institute (LA1)
CNFUS .... Consiliul National al Frontului Unitatii Socialiste [*National Council of the Socialist Unity Front*] (RO)
CNG .... Christlichnationaler Gewerkschaftsbund [*Christian-National Trade Union Federation*] [*Swiss*] (WEN)
CNG .... Comite National des Guerrillas [*National Committee of Guerrillas*] [*Guinean*] (AF)
CNG .... Compagnie de Navigation Gabonaise (MAR)
CNG .... Consejo Nacional de Gobierno [*National Council of Government*] [*Uruguayan*] (LA)
CNGSE .... Commission Nationale pour la Gestion Socialiste des Entreprises [*National Commission for the Socialist Management of Businesses*] [*Algerian*] (AF)
CNGU .... Commission Nationale Gabonaise pour l'UNESCO (MAR)
CNH .... Centre National Hospitalier de Tokoin (MAR)
CNH .... Concours National d'Habilitation [*French*]
CNHE .... Consejo Nacional de Hombres de Empresa [*National Council of Businessmen*] [*Dominican Republic*] (LA1)
CNI .... Centrale Nucleaire Interescaut [*A nuclear power station*] [*Belgian*]
CNI .... Centre National des Independants [*National Center of Independents*] [*French*] (PPE)
CNI .... Centro Nacional de Informaciones [*National Information Center*] [*Supersedes DINA*] [*Chilean*]
CNI .... Comision Nacional Intersindical [*National Interunion Commission*] [*Argentine*] (LA)
CNI .... Comision Nacional Intersindical [*National Inter-Trade Union Commission*] [*Nicaraguan*] (LA1)
CNI .... Commissariat National a l'Informatique [*National Data-Processing Commission*] [*Algerian*] (AF)
CNI .... Commission Nationale d'Investissements [*National Investment Committee*] [*Algerian*] (AF)
CNI .... Compagnie Nationale Interieure (MAR)
CNI .... Confederacao Nacional de Industrias [*National Confederation of Industries*] [*Brazilian*] (LA)
CNI .... Consejo Nacional de Investigacion [*National Research Council*] [*Peruvian*] (LA)
CNI .... Conselho Nacional de Imigracao [*National Council for Immigration*] [*Brazilian*] (LA1)
CNI .... Construction Navale Ivoirienne (MAR)
CNI .... National Information Center [*Chilean military intelligence body*] (PD)
CNIA .... Compagnie Nordafricaine et Intercontinentale d'Assurances [*Moroccan*] (MAR)
CNIA .... Compagnie Nosybeenne d'Industries Agricoles (MAR)
CNIC .... Centre National de l'Information Chimique

CNIC .... Centro Nacional para la Investigacion Cientifica [*National Scientific Research Center*] [*Cuban*] (LA)
CNIC .... Confederacion Nacional de la Industria de la Construccion [*National Construction Workers Confederation*] [*Uruguayan*] (LA)
CNICT .... Consejo Nacional para la Investigacion Cientifica del Trabajo [*National Scientific Labor Research Council*] [*Cuban*] (LA)
CNICT .... Consejo Nacional de Investigaciones Cientificas y Tecnicas [*National Council for Scientific and Technical Research*] [*Argentine*] (LA)
CNIE .... Comision Nacional de Investigaciones Espaciales [*National Commission for Space Research*] [*Argentine*] (LA)
CNIM .... Centre Naturaliste International de la Mediterranee (MAR)
CNIM .... Confederation Nationale des Instituteurs Malgaches [*National Confederation of Malagasy Teachers*]
CNIM .... Constructions Navales et Industrielles de la Mediterranee [*North African*] (MAR)
CNIP .... Centre National des Independants et Paysans [*National Center of Independents and Peasants*] [*French*] (PPW)
CNIPT .... Centre National d'Instruction des Postes, Telegraphes, et Telephones [*National PTT Training Center*] [*Niger*] (AF)
CNIT .... Centre National des Industries et Techniques [*French*]
CNIT .... Confederation Nationale Independante des Travailleurs [*National Independent Confederation for Workers*] [*Belgian*]
CNIT .... Consiliul National al Inginerilor si Tehnicienilor [*National Council of Engineers and Technicians*] (RO)
CNIZA .... Centro Nacional de Investigacion para el Desarrollo de Zonas Aridas (MAR)
CNJ .... Conseil National de la Jeunesse [*National Youth Council*] [*Congolese*] (AF)
CNJ .... Conseil National de la Jeunesse [*National Youth Council*] [*Zairian*] (AF)
CNJ .... Consejo Nacional de Justicia [*National Justice Council*] [*Peruvian*] (LA)
CNJA .... Centre National des Jeunes Agriculteurs [*National Young Farmers Center*] [*French*] (WER)
CNJD .... Confederacion Nacional de Jovenes Democraticos [*National Confederation of Democratic Youths*] [*Mexican*] (LA)
CNJM .... Conseil National de la Jeunesse Mauricienne [*National Mauritian Youth Council*] (AF)
CNJS .... Conseil National de la Jeunesse et des Sports [*Moroccan*] (MAR)
CNK .... Confederation of Khmer Nationalists [*Kampuchean*] (PD)
CNKi .... Comite National de Kivu (MAR)
CNL .... Colodense Nigeria Limited (MAR)
CNL .... Comite National de Liberation [*National Liberation Committee*] [*Zairian*] (AF)
CNL .... Commission Nationale de Linguistique [*National Linguistics Commission*] [*Beninese*] (AF)
CNL .... Conferentie der Nederlandse Letteren
CNL .... Conseil National de Liberation (MAR)
CNL .... Conselho Nacional de Libertacao (MAR)
CNLGE .... Cruzada Nacional de Liberacion de la Guinea Ecuatorial (MAR)
CNLM .... Comite National Lao du Mekong [*Lao National Mekong Committee*] (CL)
CNLP .... Caribbean National Labor Party [*Trinidadian and Tobagan*] (LA)
CNM .... Caribbean Nationalist Movement (LA1)
CNM .... Casopis Narodniho Musea [*Journal of the National Museum*] [*A publication*] (CZ)
CNM .... Compagnie de Navigation Mixte (MAR)
CNM .... Conseil National des Moudjahidines [*National War Veterans Council*] [*Algerian*] (AF)
CNMA .... Caisse Nationale de Mutualite Agricole [*National Farmers Mutual Bank*] [*Algerian*] (AF)
CNME .... Caisse National des Marches et l'Etat (MAR)
CNME .... Comite National de la Meanerie d'Exportation (MAR)
CNMI .... Commissie Nucleaire en Metallurgische Informatieverzorging [*Dutch*]
CNMP .... Comite National Malgache pour la Paix [*Malagasy National Peace Committee*] (AF)
CNMU .... Commission Nationale Marocaine pour l'UNESCO (MAR)
CNN .... Chantiers Navals de Nianing (MAR)
CNO .... Christelijke Nasionale Onderwys (MAR)
CNO .... Comite Nationale d'Organisation (MAR)
CNO .... Comites Nationaux Olympiques (MAR)
CNO .... Commission Nationale Operationelle [*National Operational Commission*] [*Algerian*] (AF)
CNO .... Crnogorska Narodna Omladina [*People's Youth of Montenegro*] (YU)
CNO .... Crnogorski Narodni Odbor [*People's Committee of Montenegro*] (YU)
CNOF .... Comite National de l'Organisation Francaise (MAR)
CNOis .... Centrala Nasiennictwa Ogrodniczego i Szkolkarstwa [*Garden and Nursery Seeds Center*] (POL)
CNOM .... Consiliul National al Oamenilor Muncii [*National Council of Workers*] (RO)
CNOP .... Confederacion Nacional de Organizaciones Populares [*National Confederation of Popular Organizations*] [*Mexican*] (LA)
CNOP .... Consiliul National al Organizatiei Pionierilor [*National Council of the Organization of Pioneers*] (RO)
CNOPU .... Crnogorsko Narodnooslobodilacki Partizanski Udarni [*Montenegrin National Liberation Partisan Shock Detachment*] (YU)
CNOT .... Comite National Olympique Togolais (MAR)
CNOU .... Centre National des Oeuvres Universitaires (MAR)
CNOUS .... Centre National des Oeuvres Universitaires et Scolaires [*French*]
CNP .... Caisse Nationale d'Epargne de Paris
CNP .... Centre National Pilote [*National Pilot Center*] [*Zairian*] (AF)
CNP .... Centre National de Pret
CNP .... Colegio Nacional de Periodistas [*National Journalists Association*] [*Colombian*] (LA)
CNP .... Comissao Nacional do Plano [*National Planning Commission*] (AF)
CNP .... Commissariat National du Parti [*National Party Commission*] [*Algerian*] (AF)
CNP .... Compagnie Navale des Petroles (MAR)
CNP .... Compagnie de Navigation Paquet (MAR)
CNP .... Companhia Nacional de Petroquimica [*National Petrochemical Company*] [*Portuguese*] (WER)
CNP .... Comptoir National de Peche [*North African*] (MAR)
CNP .... Consejo Nacional de Produccion [*National Council for Production*] [*Costa Rican*] (LA1)
CNP .... Conselho Nacional de Petroleo [*National Petroleum Council*] [*Brazilian*] (LA)
CNPA .... Coordinadora Nacional Plan de Ayala [*National Coordinating Board for the Ayala Plan*] [*Mexican*] (LA1)
CNPC .... Centre National de Production Cinematographique [*National Moving Picture Production Center*] [*Malian*] (AF)
CNPC .... Centrul National pentru Promovarea Prieteniei si Colaborarii cu Alte Popoare [*National Center for the Promotion of Friendship and Cooperation with Other Peoples*] (RO)
CNPC .... Comite National de la Production et de la Commercialisation Agricoles [*National Committee for Agricultural Production and Marketing*] [*Beninese*] (AF)
CNPD .... Conseil National de la Paix et le Developpement [*National Council for Peace and Development*] [*Beninese*] (AF)
CNPD .... Conseil National Populaire du Developpement [*People's National Development Council*] [*Malagasy*] (AF)
CNPF .... Conseil National du Patronat Francais [*National Council of French Employers*] (WER)
CNPI .... Conselho Nacional de Protecao aos Indios [*National Council for Protecting the Indians*] [*Brazilian*] (LA)
CNPPA .... Comite Nacional de la Pequena Produccion Agropecuaria [*National Committee of Small Agricultural-Livestock Producers*] [*Nicaraguan*] (LA1)
CNPPME .... Centre National de Promotion des Petites et Moyennes Entreprises (MAR)
CNPq .... Conselho Nacional de Desenvolvimento Cientifico e Tecnologico [*National Scientific and Technological Development Council*] [*Brazilian*] (LA)
CNPq .... Conselho Nacional de Pesquisas [*Brazilian*]
CNPS .... Caisse Nationale de Prevoyance Sociale (MAR)
CNPS .... Caja Nacional de Prevision Social [*National Social Security Fund*] [*Colombian*] (LA)
CNPS .... Club Nautique de Port-Said (MAR)
CNPS .... Conselho Nacional de Politica Salarial [*National Wage Policy Council*] [*Brazilian*] (LA)
CNPU .... Comissao Nacional de Politica Urbana [*National Urban Policy Commission*] [*Brazilian*] (LA)
CNPV .... Colegio Nacional de Periodistas de Venezuela [*National Association of Venezuelan Journalists*] (LA)
CNR .... Caisse Nationale de Reassurances SA (MAR)
CNR .... Cantieri Navali Riunti (MAR)
CNR .... Ceska Narodni Rada [*Czech National Council*] (CZ)
CNR .... Conseil National de la Resistance [*National Council of the Resistance*] [*French*] (WER)
CNR .... Conseil National de la Revolution [*National Council of the Revolution*] [*Beninese*] (AF)
CNR .... Conseil National de la Revolution [*National Council of the Revolution*] [*Congolese*] (AF)
CNR .... Conseil National de la Revolution [*National Council of the Revolution*] [*Guinean*] (AF)
CNR .... Consejo Nacional de Rectores [*Bogota*] (COL)
CNR .... Consiglio Nazionale delle Ricerche [*National Research Council*] [*Italian*] (WER)
CNRA .... Centre National de Recherches Agronomiques [*National Agronomic Research Center*] [*Niger*] (AF)
CNRA .... Commission Nationale de la Revolution Agraire [*National Commission of the Agrarian Revolution*] [*Algerian*] (AF)
CNRA .... Conseil National de la Revolution Algerienne [*National Council of the Algerian Revolution*] (AF)
CNRB .... Ceskoslovenska Narodni Rada Badatelska [*Czechoslovak National Research Council*] (CZ)
CNREF .... Centre National de Recherche et d'Experimentation Forestiere (MAR)
CNRET .... Centre for Natural Resources, Energy, and Transport (MAR)
CNRF .... Centre National de Recherches Forestieres (MAR)

CNRG.......... Conseil National de la Revolution de la Guinee Dite Portugaise [*National Revolutionary Council of So-Called Portuguese Guinea*]
CNRHVU..... Commission Nationale de la Republique de Haute-Volta pour l'UNESCO (MAR)
CNRI............ National Research and Investigations Center [*Zairian*] (PD)
CNRIR......... Comite National pour la Renovation des Institutions Republicaines [*National Committee for the Restoration of Republican Institutions*] [*Malagasy*] (AF)
CNRM.......... Centre National de Recherches Metallurgiques [*Belgian*]
CNRM.......... Comite National de Reforme et de Modernisation (MAR)
CNRM.......... Commission Nationale de la Republique Malgache (MAR)
CNRN.......... Comitato Nazionale per le Ricerche Nucleari [*National Committee for Nuclear Research*] [*Later, CNEN*] [*Italian*] (WER)
CNRN.......... Comite National pour une Republique Nouvelle [*National Committee for a New Republic*] [*Malagasy*] (AF)
CNRPM....... Centre National de Recherches Pharmaceutiques de Madagascar [*National Pharmaceutical Research Center of Madagascar*] (AF)
CNRPS........ Caisse Nationale de Retraite et de Prevoyance Sociale [*Tunisian*] (MAR)
CNRS.......... Centre de Documentation Graphique et Geographique (MAR)
CNRS.......... Centre National de la Recherche Scientifique [*National Center for Scientific Research*] [*French*] (WER)
CNRS.......... Centre National des Republicains Sociaux [*National Center of Social Republicans*] [*French*] (PPE)
CNRS.......... Centre Nationale de la Recherche Scientifique [*French*]
CNRSH........ Centre Nigerien de Recherches en Sciences Humaines [*Nigerien Center for Research in the Social Sciences*] [*Niger*] (AF)
CNRST........ Comite National de la Recherche Scientifique et Technique [*National Scientific and Technical Research Committee*] [*Malagasy*] (AF)
CNRZ.......... Centre National de Recherche Zootechnique [*Algerian*] (MAR)
CNS............ Central Nacional Sindical [*National Labor Union Federation*] [*Spanish*] (WER)
CNS............ Centralno Narodno Sveucilište [*Central People's University*] [*Zagreb*] (YU)
CNS............ Centre National des Sports [*Algerian*] (MAR)
CNS............ Co-Ordinadora Nacional Sindical [*National Trade Union Co-Ordinating Body*] [*Chilean*] (PD)
CNS............ Compagnies Nationales de Securite [*National Security Companies*] [*Algerian*] (AF)
CNS............ Complexe National Sportif [*National Sports Complex*] [*Cambodian*] (CL)
CNS............ Conseil National de Securite [*National Security Council*] [*Algerian*] (AF)
CNS............ Conseil National des Sports (MAR)
CNS............ Coordinadora Nacional de Sindicatos [*National Coordinating Board of Trade Unions*] [*Costa Rican*] (LA1)
CNSC.......... Confederacion Nacional Sindical Campesina [*National Peasant Trade Union Confederation*] [*Chilean*] (LA)
CNSM.......... Comision Nacional de los Salarios Minimos [*National Commission on Minimum Wages*] [*Mexican*] (LA1)
CNSM.......... Confederation Nationale des Syndicats du Mali [*National Confederation of Malian Unions*]
CNSP.......... Comite Nicaraguense de Solidaridad con los Pueblos [*Nicaraguan Committee of Solidarity with Peoples*] (LA1)
CNSS.......... Caisse Nationale de Securite Sociale [*Moroccan*] (MAR)
CNSS.......... Caja Nacional de Seguro Social [*National Social Security Fund*] [*Bolivian*] (LA)
CNSS.......... Comite National de Solidarite Sociale [*National Committee for Social Solidarity*] [*Tunisian*] (AF)
CNST.......... Consiliul National pentru Stiinta si Tehnologie [*National Council for Science and Technology*] (RO)
CNT............ Central Nacional de Trabajadores [*National Central Organization of Workers*] [*Salvadoran*] (LA1)
CNT............ Code de la Nationalite Tunisienne (MAR)
CNT............ Comision Nacional del Trabajo [*National Commission of Workers*] [*Argentine*] (PD)
CNT............ Compagnie Nigerienne de Television (MAR)
CNT............ Confederacion Nacional de Trabajadores [*National Confederation of Workers*] [*Colombian*] (LA)
CNT............ Confederacion Nacional de Trabajadores [*National Confederation of Workers*] [*Peruvian*] (LA)
CNT............ Confederacion Nacional del Trabajo [*National Confederation of Labor*] [*Spanish*] (PPE)
CNT............ Confederation Nationale du Travail [*National Labor Confederation*] [*French*] (WER)
CNT............ Confederation Nationale du Travail [*National Confederation of Labor*] [*Zairian*] (AF)
CNT............ Conselho Nacional do Trabalho [*Brazilian*]
CNT............ Convencion Nacional de Trabajadores [*National Convention of Workers*] [*Uruguayan*] (LA)
CNT............ Corporacion Nacional de Turismo [*Bogota*] (COL)
CNT............ Corporation Nationale du Transport (MAR)
CNTC.......... Confederacao Nacional dos Trabalhadores no Comercio [*National Confederation of Commercial Workers*] [*Brazilian*] (LA)
CNTC.......... Confederation Nationale des Travailleurs du Centrafrique (MAR)
CNTC.......... Confederation Nationale des Travailleurs Croyants du Senegal [*National Confederation of Believing Workers of Senegal*]
CNTCB........ Confederacion Nacional de Trabajadores Campesinos de Bolivia [*Bolivian National Peasant Workers Confederation*] (LA)
CNTCCI...... Centrale Nationale des Travailleurs Croyants de Cote-d'Ivoire [*National Union of Believing Workers of the Ivory Coast*] (AF)
CNTCS........ Confederation Nationale des Travailleurs Croyants du Senegal [*National Confederation of Believing Workers of Senegal*] (AF)
CNTD.......... Confederacion Nacionalista de Trabajadores Democraticos [*National Confederation of Democratic Workers*] [*Nicaraguan*] (LA)
CNTE........... Central Nacional de Trabajadores de Euzkadi [*National Federation of Basque Workers*] [*Spanish*] (WER)
CNTE........... Coordinadora Nacional de Trabajadores de la Educacion [*National Coordinating Board of Education Workers*] [*Mexican*] (LA1)
CNTEEC...... Confederacao Nacional dos Trabalhadores em Estabelecimentos de Educacao e Cultura [*National Confederation of Education and Cultural Workers*] [*Brazilian*] (LA)
CNTG.......... Confederation Nationale des Travailleurs Gabonais [*National Confederation of Gabonese Workers*] (AF)
CNTG.......... Confederation Nationale des Travailleurs de Guinee [*National Confederation of Guinean Workers*] (AF)
CNTI............ Confederacao Nacional dos Trabalhadores na Industria [*National Confederation of Industrial Workers*] [*Brazilian*] (LA)
CNTMAF..... Confederacao Nacional dos Trabalhadores Maritimos, Aereos, e Fluviais [*National Confederation of Maritime, Air, and River Transport Workers*] [*Brazilian*] (LA)
CNTP........... Central Nacional de Trabajadores Panamenos [*National Central of Panamanian Workers*] (LA)
CNTR.......... Compagnie Nationale des Transports Routiers (MAR)
CNTS.......... Centre National de Transfusion Sanguine [*National Blood Transfusion Center*] [*Cambodian*] (CL)
CNTS.......... Confederation Nationale des Travailleurs du Senegal [*National Confederation of Senegalese Workers*] (AF)
CNTT........... Confederation Nationale des Travailleurs du Togo [*National Confederation of Togolese Workers*] (AF)
CNTTT........ Confederacao Nacional dos Trabalhadores em Transporte Terrestres [*National Confederation of Land Transport Workers*] [*Brazilian*] (LA)
CNTU.......... Commission Nationale Tunisienne pour l'UNESCO (MAR)
CNTur......... Conselho Nacional de Turismo [*National Tourism Council*] [*Brazilian*] (LA)
CNTV.......... Confederation Nationale des Travailleurs Voltaiques [*National Confederation of Voltan Workers*] (AF)
CNTYPI....... Centro Nacional de Tecnologia y Productividad Industrial [*National Center for Industrial Productivity and Technology*] [*Uruguayan*] (LA)
CNU............ Cameroon National Union (MAR)
CNU............ Clubul Nautic Universitar [*University Sailing Club*] (RO)
CNU............ Comando Nacional Urbano [*National Urban Command*] [*Venezuelan*] (LA)
CNU............ Comando Nacionalista Universitario [*Nationalist University Command*] [*Ecuadorean*] (LA)
CNU............ Concentracion Nacional Universitaria [*National University Concentration*] [*Argentine*] (LA)
CNU............ Conseil National d'Union [*National Council of Unity*] [*Chadian*] (AF)
CNU............ Consiglio Nazionale Universitario [*National University Council*] [*Italian*] (WER)
CNUCED..... Conference des Nations Unies sur le Commerce et le Developpement [*United Nations Conference on Trade and Development*] [*Use UNCTAD*] [*French*] (WER)
CNUP.......... Consejo Nacional Provisorio de Universidades [*National Provisional Council of Universities*] [*Venezuelan*] (LA)
CNUPEA..... Comision Nacional para el Uso Pacifico de la Energia Atomica [*National Commission for the Peaceful Use of Atomic Energy*] [*Cuban*] (LA)
CNUS.......... Comite Nacional de Unidad Sindical [*National Committee of Trade Union Unity*] [*Guatemalan*] (LA1)
CNUS.......... Comite National de l'Unite Syndicale (MAR)
CNUTS........ Central Nacional Unificada de Trabajadores de la Salud [*National Federation of Health Workers*] [*Peruvian*] (LA)
CNV............ Christelijk Nationaal Vakverbond in Nederland [*National Federation of Christian Workers in the Netherlands*] (WEN)
CNV............ Comision Nacional de Valores [*National Securities Commission*] [*Panamanian*] (LA)
CNV............ Comite National Vietnam [*National Vietnam Committee*] [*French*] (WER)
CNVE.......... Conseil National des Volontaires Etudiants [*National Council of Student Volunteers*] [*Algerian*] (AF)
CNVS.......... Comite Nacional de Vanguardia Socialista [*National Committee of Socialist Vanguard*] [*Colombian*] (LA)
CNZ............ Casova Norma Zasob [*Supply Schedule*] (CZ)

CNZ............ Ceskoslovenske Naftove Zavody, Narodni Podnik [*Czechoslovak Petroleum Industries, National Enterprise*] (CZ)
CO.............. Centrala Odziezowa [*Clothing Center*] (POL)
CO.............. Centrala Ogrodnicza [*Horticultural Center*] (POL)
CO.............. Centralne Ogrzewanie [*Central Heating*] [*Polish*]
CO.............. Centralni Odbor [*Central Committee*] (YU)
CO.............. Cerkvena Obcina [*Parish*] (YU)
Co.............. Cerro [*Hill*] [*Spanish*] (NAU)
CO.............. Civilni Obrana [*Civil Defense*] (CZ)
CO.............. Colombia [*Two-letter standard code*] (CNC)
CO.............. Colonial Office (MAR)
CO.............. Comites Obreros [*Workers' Committees*] [*Spanish*] (WER)
Co.............. Compagnie [*French*]
co.............. Compagno [*Partner*] [*Italian*]
c/o............. Compte Ouvert [*Open Account*] [*French*]
CO.............. Kolumbia [*Colombia*] [*Polish*]
Co.............. Kompanie [*Company*] (EG)
COA............ Centre Operationnel des Armees [*Armed Forces Operations Center*] [*French*] (WER)
COA............ Comite Obrero Antipolitico [*Antipolitical Workers Committee*] [*Of "Bunkerist" tendency*] [*Spanish*] (WER)
COA............ Commis et Ouvriers d'Administration [*Military*] [*French*] (MTD)
COA............ Confederacion Obrera Argentina [*Argentine Worker Confederation*] (LA)
COA............ Cote Occidentale d'Afrique (MAR)
COA............ Operational Command in Angola (MAR)
COAF.......... La Commerciale de l'Afrique Francaise (MAR)
COAKA....... Coalition Kasaienne (MAR)
COAM......... Colegio Oficial de Arquitectos de Madrid [*Official Association of Architects of Madrid*] [*Spanish*] (WER)
COAMA....... Coordenacao da Amazonia [*Amazon Basin Administration*] [*Brazilian*] (LA)
COAP.......... Comissao de Abastecimento e Precos [*Supply and Price Commission*] [*Brazilian*] (LA)
COAP.......... Comite de Asesoramiento de la Presidencia de la Republica [*Advisory Committee of the Presidency*] [*Peruvian*] (LA)
COAR.......... Comando Obrero de Accion Revolucionaria [*Workers Commando of Revolutionary Action*] [*Spanish*] (WER)
COARPIMAR ... Compania de Artifices en Piedra y Marmol [*Bogota*] (COL)
COAV.......... Comisiones Obreras Anticapitalistas de Valencia [*Anticapitalist Workers Commissions of Valencia*] [*Spanish*] (WER)
COB............ Central Obrera Boliviana [*Bolivian Labor Federation*] (LA)
COB............ Comisiones Obreras de Barrio [*Workers City District Commissions*] [*Spanish*] (WER)
COB............ Commission des Operations de Bourse [*French*]
COB............ Confederation of Business [*Rhodesian*] (AF)
COBAE........ Comissao Brasileira de Actividades Espaciais [*Brazilian Space Activities Commission*] [*Brazilian*] (LA)
COBAFRUIT ... Cooperative Bananiere et Fruitiere de la Cote-d'Ivoire (MAR)
COBAG....... Cooperative Bananiere Guineenne (MAR)
COBAKWA ... Abako Cooperative (MAR)
COBAL........ Companhia Brasileira de Alimentos [*Brazilian Foods Company*] (LA)
COBAM....... Confection-Bonneterie Africaine et Malgache (MAR)
COBAP........ Comissao da Bacia do Plata [*River Plate Basin Commission*] [*Brazilian*] (LA)
COBAUTOS ... Cooperativa Boyacense de Autos Ltda. [*Tunja*] (COL)
COBEC........ Companhia Brasileira de Entrepostos e Comercio [*Brazilian Warehouses and Trade Company*] (LA)
COBELMIN ... Compagnie Belge d'Entreprise Minieres (MAR)
COBELTO ... Consortium Belge pour le Togo (MAR)
COBEMAG ... Cooperative Beninoise de Materiel Agricole [*Benin Cooperative for Agricultural Supplies*] (AF)
COBENAM ... Compagnie Beninoise de Navigation Maritime [*Beninese Shipping Company*] (AF)
COBIDOC.... Commissie voor Bibliografie en Documentatie [*Dutch*]
COBISCAL ... Complexe de l'Industrie de la Biscuiterie et de la Chocolaterie [*North African*] (MAR)
COBLSA..... Committee to Oppose Bank Loans to South Africa (MAR)
COBOEN..... Comision Boliviana de Energia Nuclear [*Bolivian Nuclear Energy Commission*] (LA)
COBOLIVAR ... Compania de Seguros Bolivar [*Bogota*] (COL)
COBOMA.... Compagnie des Bois du Mayumba (MAR)
COBOPAL... Boulangerie, Patisserie, et Alimentation [*Tunisian*] (MAR)
COBRA........ Computadores e Sistemas Brasileiros SA [*Brazilian Computers and Systems, Inc.*] (LA)
COBRAZIL ... Companhia de Mineracao e Metalurgia Brasil [*Brazil Mining and Metallurgy Company*] (LA)
COBRECAF ... Compagnie Bretonne de Cargos Frigorifiques (MAR)
COBSA........ Computer Service Bureaux Association [*British*]
COC............ Central Obrera Colombiana [*Colombian Workers Federation*] (LA)
COC............ Centro do Operaciones Conjuntas [*Joint Operations Center*] [*Venezuelan*] (LA)
COC............ Circulos Obreros Comunistas [*Communist Workers Circles*] [*Spanish*] (WER)
COC............ Comisia pentru Organizarea Cooperativelor [*Commission for Organizing Cooperatives*] (RO)
COC............ Comite Olimpico Colombiano [*Colombian Olympic Committee*] [*Bogota*] (COL)
COC............ Comite Olimpico Cubano [*Cuban Olympic Committee*] (LA)
COC............ Compagnie Ouest-Cameroun (MAR)
COCADA..... Compagnie des Commercants Africains du Dahomey (MAR)
COCADAC SA ... Compagnie Camerounaise Danoise de Construction SA (MAR)
COCAP....... Comissao de Coordenacao da Alianca para o Progresso [*Alliance for Progress Coordinating Commission*] [*Brazilian*] (LA)
COCARZI.... Comite d'Organisation pour le Carnaval de la Ville de Ziguinchor (MAR)
COCC......... Centrul de Organizare si Cibernetica in Constructii [*Center for Organization and Cybernetics in Constructions*] (RO)
COCC......... Confederacion de Obreros y Campesinos Cristianos [*Christian Workers and Peasants Confederation*] [*Costa Rican*] (LA)
COCE......... Coalicion Obrera-Campesina-Estudiantil [*Worker-Peasant-Student Coalition*] [*Mexican*] (LA)
COCEA....... Companhia Central de Abastecimento do Estado da Guanabara [*Central Supply Company of the State of Guanabara*] [*Brazilian*] (LA)
COCEI........ Coalicion Obrera, Campesina, Estudiantil del Istmo [*Labor, Peasant, Student Coalition of the Isthmus*] [*Mexican*] (LA1)
COCEI........ Compagnie Central d'Etudes Industrielles [*Central Industrial Research Company*] [*French*] (WER)
COCEI........ Compagnie Centrale d'Etudes Industrielles (MAR)
coch........... Cochlear [*Spoonful*] [*Latin*] (GPO)
coch amp.... Cochlear Amplum [*Tablespoon*] [*Latin*] (GPO)
COCHEPA... Compagnie Cherifienne d'Emballages en Papier (MAR)
COCHEREX ... Compagnie Cherifienne d'Explosifs (MAR)
coch mag.... Cochlear Magnum [*Large Spoonful*] [*Latin*] (GPO)
coch med.... Cochlear Medium [*Dessert Spoonful*] [*Latin*] (GPO)
COCHOSAM ... Cooperativa de Choferes de Taxis de Santa Marta Ltda. (COL)
coch parv.... Cochlear Parvum [*Teaspoonful*] [*Latin*] (GPO)
COCI.......... Consortium des Agrumes et Plantes a Parfum de Cote-d'Ivoire (MAR)
COCI.......... Consortium on Chemical Information [*United Kingdom*]
COCIDEPRO ... Comite Civico de Desarrollo y Progreso [*Civic Committee for Development and Progress*] [*Bolivian*] (LA)
COCITAM ... Compagnie Cote-d'Ivoirienne pour Tous Appareillages Mecaniques (MAR)
COCITEX.... Compagnie Camerounaise d'Importation d'Articles Textiles (MAR)
COCITRA.... Compagnie Ivoirienne de Transports (MAR)
COCLA........ Coordinating Committee for the Liberation of Africa (MAR)
COCOCAM ... Comite de Coordination Camerounaise [*Committee for Cameroonese Coordination*]
COCODI...... Compagnie de Commerce de la Cote-d'Ivoire (MAR)
COCOES..... Comite de Coordination des Etudes Statistiques [*Statistical Research Coordination Committee*] [*Moroccan*] (AF)
COCOMBO ... Comptoir Commercial de M'Boss (MAR)
COCOMI..... Comunidad de Compensacion Minera [*Community for Mining Compensation*] [*Peruvian*] (LA)
COCONEX ... Commission Confederal Executive [*Executive Committee of the CSC*] [*Congolese*] (AF)
COCOP....... Comite de Organizaciones Populares [*Committee of People's Organizations*] [*Peruvian*] (LA)
COCPCIA.... Centrul de Organizare Calcul si Perfectionarea Cadrelor pentru Industria Alimentara [*Center for the Computer Organization and Advanced Training of Cadres for the Food Industry*] (RO)
COD........... Central Obrera Departamental [*Department Labor Federation*] [*Bolivian*] (LA)
COD........... Centro de Orientacion Docente [*Bogota*] (COL)
COD........... Comites de Distritos [*District Committees*] [*Spanish*] (WER)
COD........... Congress of Democrats (MAR)
CODACERO ... Compania de Productos de Acero Ltda. [*Bogota*] (COL)
CODAL........ Comptoir Industriel de Produits Alimentaires [*Malagasy*] (MAR)
CODAM....... Companhia de Destroncas e Aluguer de Maquinas (MAR)
CODAP........ Compagnie Dakaroise de Peches (MAR)
CODAPAG ... Compagnie Dakaroise de Produits Agricoles (MAR)
CODAR....... Codage Arabe (MAR)
CODARTE... Compania Nacional de Artefactos Electricos [*Cali*] (COL)
CODARU..... Codage Arabe Unifie (MAR)
CODATA..... Committee on Data for Science and Technology
CODATAL.... Compagnie Daho-Togolaise des Allumettes (MAR)
CODATU..... Conference de Dakar sur les Transports Urbains (MAR)
CODAUTO ... Companhia Distribuidora de Automoveis (MAR)
CODDETREISA ... Compania de Desarrollo Turistico, Residencial, e Industrial, Sociedad Anonima [*Dominican Republic resort development company*]
CODEBRAS ... Coordenacao do Desenvolvimento de Brasilia [*Brasilia Development Coordination*] [*Brazilian*] (LA)
CODECARGA ... Corporacion del Transporte Automotor [*Medellin*] (COL)
CODECOP ... Comite de Defensa de Comensales en los Comedores Populares [*Committee to Defend Eaters in Relief Canteens*] [*Peruvian*] (LA)
CODECOS ... Colombiana de Construccion [*Medellin*] (COL)
CODEJU...... Comision Nacional pro Derechos Juveniles [*National Commission for Children's Rights*] [*Chilean*] (LA1)

CODEL........ Compania Colombiana de Elementos Electricos [*Medellin*] (COL)
CODEL........ Coordination for Development, Inc. (MAR)
CODELAM ... Comite de Desarrollo Departamental [*Departmental Development Committee*] [*Peruvian*] (LA)
CODELCA... Compania Odontologica del Caribe [*Barranquilla*] (COL)
CODELCO... Corporacion del Cobre [*Copper Corporation*] [*Chilean*] (LA)
CODELSINA ... Coalicion del Sindicalismo Nacional [*National Labor Coalition*] [*Argentine*] (LA)
CODEMACO ... Compania Colombiana de Maderas Compensadas [*Cali*] (COL)
CODEMY..... Comite de Developpement Auto-Centre de l'Arrondissement de Massangam, Annexe de Yaounde (MAR)
CODEN .... Colombiana de Negocios Ltda. [*Bogota*] (COL)
CODENAL... Confederacion pro Defensa Nacional [*Confederation for National Defense*] [*Bolivian*] (LA)
CODENAL... Corporacion de Accion Comunal [*Cali*] (COL)
CODENO..... Conselho de Desenvolvimento do Nordeste [*Northeast Development Council*] [*Brazilian*] (LA)
CODEP........ Compania Distribuidora de Equipos Petroleros Ltda. [*Bogota*] (COL)
CODEPALE ... Ley Organica para la Ensenanza Secundaria [*Organic Law for Secondary Education*] [*Uruguayan*] (LA)
CODEPAR... Companhia de Desenvolvimento Economico do Parana [*Parana Economic Development Company*] [*Brazilian*] (LA)
CODER........ Commission de Developpement Economique Regional [*Regional Economic Development Commission*] [*French*] (WER)
CODERA..... Comite de Desarrollo de la Reforma Agraria [*Agrarian Reform Development Committee*] [*Chilean*] (LA)
CODERESA ... Colombiana de Repuestos Ltda. [*Cali*] (COL)
CODERESA ... Conseil pour le Developpement de la Recherche Economique et Sociale en Afrique [*Council for the Development of Economic and Social Research in Africa*] (AF)
CODESA..... Centro Operacional del Desarrollo [*Operational Center for Development*] [*Colombian*]
CODESA..... Comite de Sindicatos Autonomos [*Committee of Autonomous Unions*] [*Venezuelan*] (LA)
CODESA..... Corporacion de Desarrollo, SA [*Development Corporation, Inc.*] [*Costa Rican*] (LA)
CODESARROLLO ... Corporacion Social de Desarrollo y Bienestar [*Medellin*] (COL)
CODESCO ... Convention des Democrates Socialistes (MAR)
CODESRIA ... Council for the Development of Economic and Social Research in Africa (EA)
CODESUL... Conselho de Desenvolvimento do Extremo Sul [*Council for Development of the Far South*] [*Brazilian*] (LA)
CODESUR... Comision para el Desarrollo del Sur [*Committee for the Development of the South*] [*Venezuelan*] (LA)
CODETAF-CI ... Compagnie d'Etancheite Africaine en Cote-d'Ivoire (MAR)
CODETAR... Comite de Obras Publicas y Desarrollo de Tarija [*Public Works and Development Committee of Tarija*] [*Bolivian*] (LA)
CODETRAN ... Compania Especial de Transportes SA [*Bogota*] (COL)
CODEV........ Commerce et Developpement (MAR)
CODEV........ Communications for Development Foundation [*Rome, Italy*]
CODEVASF ... Companhia de Desenvolvimento do Vale do Sao Francisco [*Sao Francisco Valley Development Company*] [*Brazilian*] (LA)
CODI .... Centro de Operacoes de Defesa Interna [*Internal Defense Operations Center*] [*Brazilian*] (LA)
CODI .... Colombianos Distribuidores de Combustibles SA [*Cali*] (COL)
CODIA......... Colegio de Ingenieros Agronomos [*Agronomic Engineers Association*] [*Dominican Republic*] (LA)
CODIA......... Comite pour l'Organisation et le Developpement des Investissements Intellectuels en Afrique et a Madagascar (MAR)
CODIAM...... Comite pour le Developpement des Activities Intellectuelles en Afrique et Madagascar [*Committee for the Development of Intellectual Activities in Africa and Madagascar*] [*French*] (AF)
CODICA...... Compania Distribuidora de Calzado Ltda. [*Medellin*] (COL)
CODICE...... Comissao Dinamizadora Central [*Central Dynamization Commission*] [*Portuguese*] (WER)
CODIF......... Societe Commerciale de Diffusion (MAR)
CODIL......... Colombiana de Importadores Ltda. [*Cali*] (COL)
CODILOL.... Colombiana Distribuidora de Loterias Ltda. [*Bogota*] (COL)
CODIM........ Cooerdinatiegroep Documentatie en Informatie Milieu-Hygieene Nederland
CODIMA...... Union Commerciale de Diffusion de Marques en Cote-d'Ivoire (MAR)
CODIMCO... Compania Distribuidora de Materiales de Construccion Ltda. (COL)
CODINA...... Compania Distribuidora Nacional [*National Distributing Company*] [*Chilean*] (LA)
CODINP...... Confederacion de Investigadores Profesionales [*Bogota*] (COL)
CODIP......... Compagnie de Distribution Internationale de Periodiques [*International Periodical Distribution Company*] [*Mauritian*] (AF)
CODIPETROLEOS ... Colombianos Distribuidores de Combustibles SA [*Bucaramanga*] (COL)
CODIPRAL ... Compagnie de Distribution de Produits Alimentaires (MAR)
CODIS......... Continentale de Distribution (MAR)
CODISCOS ... Compania Colombiana de Discos Ltda. [*Medellin*] (COL)
CODITEX.... Compania Distribuidora Textil Ltda. [*Cali*] (COL)
CODIVAL.... Compagnie Ivoirienne de Securite (MAR)
CODKO....... Centralny Osrodek Doskonalenia Kadr Oswiatowych [*Central Institute for the Improvement of Teaching Personnel*] (POL)
CODUL........ Companhia de Desenvolvimento Urbano Lda. (MAR)
COE............ Comisiones Obreras de Empresa [*Workers Commissions of Enterprises*] [*Spanish*] (WER)
COE............ Conseil Oecumenique des Eglises [*World Council of Churches*] [*Use WCC*] (AF)
COELBA...... Companhia de Eletricidade do Estado da Bahia
COEMA....... Confederacion de Obreros y Empleados Municipales de la Argentina [*Confederation of Municipal Workers and Employees of Argentina*] (LA)
COEMAR..... Commission on Ecumenical Mission and Relations (MAR)
COEMPAQUES ... Compania Andina de Empaques Ltda. [*Cali*] (COL)
COEMSAVAL ... Cooperativa de Ahorro y Credito. Empleados de Salud del Valle [*Cali*] (COL)
COEN.......... Comision Boliviana de Energia Nuclear [*Bolivian Nuclear Energy Commission*] (LA)
COES.......... Centro Obrero de Estudios Sociales [*Worker Center for Social Studies*] [*Nicaraguan*] (LA1)
COES.......... Comite Organizador de Estudiantes Secundarios [*Secondary School Students Organizing Committee*] [*Peruvian*] (LA)
COES.......... Consiliul Organizarii Economico-Sociale [*Council for Socioeconomic Organization*] (RO)
COES.......... Cooperativa Estudiantil de Ahorro y Credito. Universidad del Valle [*Cali*] (COL)
COEXPORT ... Comite de Exportadores de El Salvador [*Committee of Exporters of El Salvador*]
COF............ Comites d'Organisation des Femmes [*Women's Organization Committees*] [*Beninese*] (AF)
COFA.......... Compagnie Francaise pour l'Afrique Equatoriale (MAR)
COFACE..... Compagnie Francaise d'Assurance pour le Commerce Exterieur [*French Insurance Company for Foreign Trade*] (AF)
COFACICO ... Compagnie Financieres Africaine Cinematographiques et Commerciales [*Congolese*] (MAR)
COFADENA ... Corporacion de las Fuerzas Armadas para el Desarrollo Nacional [*Armed Forces National Development Corporation*] [*Bolivian*] (LA)
COFAMA..... Comptoirs Franco-Africains de Materiaux (MAR)
COFAMILIAR ... Cooperativa Familar de Medellin (COL)
COFAP........ Comissao Federal de Abastecimento e Precos [*Federal Supply and Price Commission*] [*Brazilian*] (LA)
COFAPEFIRE ... Comptoir Familial Pere et Fils Reunis (MAR)
COFARMA ... Consorcio Farmaceutico Colombiano Ltda. [*Barranquilla*] (COL)
COFARMA ... Cooperation Pharmaceutique Malgache (MAR)
COFCE........ Comite pour l'Orientation et la Formation des Cadres de l'Economie [*Committee for the Guidance and Training of Economic Cadres*] [*Belgian*] (AF)
COFE.......... Confederacion de Organizaciones de Funcionarios de Estado [*State Civil Service Organizations Confederation*] [*Uruguayan*] (LA)
COFE.......... Confederacion de Organizaciones de Funcionarios de Estado [*Confederation of State Civil Service Organizations*] [*Venezuelan*] (LA1)
COFEB........ Centre Ouest-Africain de Formation et d'Etudes Bancaires (MAR)
COFEBA...... Compagnie Francaise d'Engineering Barets (MAR)
COFEGES... Conseil Federal des Groupements Economiques du Senegal [*Federal Council of Economic Groups of Senegal*] (AF)
COFEL........ Cooperative des Fruits et Legumes [*Fruit and Vegetable Cooperative*] [*Algerian*] (AF)
COFELI....... Comite Femenino de Liberacion [*Women's Committee for Liberation*] [*Honduran*] (LA)
COFIAGRO ... Corporacion Financiera de Fomento Agropecuario y Exportaciones [*Agriculture and Livestock Development and Exports Financing Corporation*] [*Colombian*] (LA)
COFIBOIS ... Compagnie Forestiere et Industrielle du Bois (MAR)
COFICA....... Comptoir Francais des Industries de la Conserverie Alimentaire [*French Agency for Food Canning Industries*] (WER)
COFICOM ... Compagnie Financiere pour le Commerce [*Financial Trading Company*] [*Guinean*] (AF)
COFICOMEX ... Compagnie Financiere pour le Commerce Exterieur [*Financial Foreign Trade Company*] [*French*] (AF)
COFIDE....... Corporacion Financiera de Desarrollo [*Financial Development Corporation*] [*Peruvian*] (LA)
COFIEC....... Compania Financiera Ecuatoriana [*Ecuadorean Finance Company*] (LA)
COFIFA....... Compagnie Financiere France-Afrique (MAR)
COFIGEST ... Compagnie Financiere d'Information et de Gestion (MAR)
COFILLA..... Corporacion Financiera de los Llanos [*Financial Corporation of the Plains*] [*Venezuelan*] (LA)
COFIMER.... Compagnie Financiere pour l'Outre-Mer [*Overseas Finance Company*] [*French*] (AF)
COFIMPAC ... Compagnie Francaise Industrielle et Miniere du Pacifique [*French commercial firm*]

COFINA....... Corporacion Financiera Nacional [*National Financial Corporation*] [*Panamanian*] (LA)
COFINANCIERA ... Corporacion Financiera Colombiana de Desarrollo Industrial [*Bogota*] (COL)
COFINATOME ... Compagnie de Financement de l'Industrie Atomique [*French*]
COFINCI ..... Compagnie Financiere de la Cote-d'Ivoire (MAR)
COFINDE .... Conferencia para el Financiamiento y el Desarrollo de America Latina y el Caribe [*Conference for the Financing and Development of Latin America and the Caribbean*] (LA)
COFININDUS ... Compagnie Financiere et Industrielle (MAR)
COFINORTE ... Corporacion Financiera del Norte [*Barranquilla*] (COL)
COFI PECHE ... Compagnie Industrielle Ivoirienne de Filets de Peche (MAR)
COFIREP..... Compagnie Financiere de Recherches Petrolieres (MAR)
COFITEX..... Compagnie Marocaine de Filature et de Textiles [*Saharan*] (MAR)
COFITOUR ... Compagnie Financiere et Touristique [*Tunisian*] (MAR)
COFLONORTE ... Cooperativa de Flota Norte Ltda. [*Quintana-Boyaca*] (COL)
COFLUMA... Compagnie Fluviale et Maritime de l'Ouest Africain (MAR)
COFOCI ...... Compagnie Forestiere de la Cote-d'Ivoire (MAR)
COFOR........ Compagnie Generale de Forages (MAR)
COFORGA ... Compagnie Forestiere Gabonaise (MAR)
COFORIC.... Compagnie Forestiere et Industrielle du Congo (MAR)
COFRAL...... Compagnie du Froid Alimentaire (MAR)
COFRAMET ... Compagnie Franco-Americaine des Metaux et des Minerals (MAR)
COFRAPAL ... Compagnie Franco-Africaine de Produits Alimentaires (MAR)
COFRASED ... Comite France-Asie pour la Sante et le Developpement [*France-Asia Committee for Health and Development*] (CL)
COFREM..... Compagnie pour la Fabrication d'Elements Mecaniques (MAR)
COFROI....... Comptoir Franco-Ivoirien (MAR)
COFROR ..... Compagnie Francaise d'Organisation (MAR)
COFRUBA... Comptoir de Fruits et Bananes [*Moroccan*] (MAR)
COFRUCI .... Cooperative Agricole de Production Bananiere et Fruitiere de Cote-d'Ivoire [*Ivory Coast Agricultural Cooperative for Banana and Fruit Production*] (AF)
COFRUIT..... Compagnie des Fruits et Legumes du Senegal (MAR)
COFRUMAD ... Cooperative Fruitiere de Madagascar [*Malagasy Fruit Cooperative*] (AF)
COFUPA ..... Comptoir de Fumage de Produits Alimentaires (MAR)
Cog .... Cografya [*Geography*] (TU)
COG .... Confederacion Obrera de Guayas [*Guayas Labor Confederation*] [*Ecuadorean*] (LA)
COG .... Congo [*Three-letter standard code*] (CNC)
COGAL........ Consul General [*Consul General*] [*Cambodian*] (CL)
COGEAC..... Compagnie Generale de l'Afrique Centrale (MAR)
COGECAM ... Constructions Generales Camerounaise (MAR)
COGEDA..... Compagnie Generale de Distribution et d'Approvisionnement (MAR)
COGEDEP... Association pour la Cogestion des Deplacements a But Educatif de Jeunes (MAR)
COGEDRO ... Comptoirs Generaux Reunis de Droguerie Produits Chimiques, Peintures, Colorants (MAR)
COGEFAR... Costruzioni Generali Farsura (MAR)
COGEFIC.... Compagnie Generale de Financement et de Credit (MAR)
COGEGA..... Comptoirs Generaux du Gabon (MAR)
COGEI......... Compagnie de Gestion d'Investissements Internationaux (MAR)
COGEL........ Comptoir General Commercial [*Moroccan*] (MAR)
COGEMA.... Compagnie Generale des Matieres Nucleaires (MAR)
COGEMAC ... Compagnie Generale Marocaine (MAR)
COGEODATA ... Commission on Storage, Automatic Processing, and Retrieval of Geological Data (EA)
COGER........ Compagnie Gabon ELF [*Essences et Lubrifiants de France*] de Raffinage (MAR)
COGERA..... Compagnie Generale d'Etudes Economiques et de Recherches Appliquees (MAR)
COGERAF... Compagnie Generale d'Etudes et Recherches pour l'Afrique [*General Company for African Studies and Research*] [*French*] (AF)
COGERAN ... Societe de Courtage et de Gerance (MAR)
COGERCO ... Comite de Gerance de la Caisse des Reserves Cotonnieres (MAR)
COGEREC... Comptoir General de Representation Commerciale [*Moroccan*] (MAR)
COGERIM ... Societe de Commerce General en Republique Islamique de Mauritanie (MAR)
COGETA..... Cooperative Generale de Takeo [*General Cooperative of Takeo Province*] [*Cambodian*] (CL)
COGETEXIM ... Compagnie Generale Togolaise d'Export Import (MAR)
COGETRANS ... Compagnie Generale de Transit et de Transport (MAR)
COGETRO... Compagnie Generale des Transports Routiers (MAR)
COGEX........ Comptoirs Generaux d'Exploitations (MAR)
COGICOM... Consortium General Industriel et Commercial (MAR)
COGIMEX ... Comptoir General d'Importation et d'Exportation (MAR)
COGIP......... Compagnie Generale Ivoirienne de Piles Electriques (MAR)
COGIR......... Compagnie Petroliere ELF [*Essences et Lubrifiants de France*] - Gabon (MAR)
COGISA ...... Compagnie Generale Immobiliere (MAR)
Coglu .... Cagaloglu [*Quarter of Istanbul*] (TU)
COGRA .... Compania Colombiana de Grasas [*Bogota*] (COL)
COGUISA.... Colonizadora de la Guinea Continental, SA (MAR)
COHAB .... Companhia de Habitacao Popular [*Low-Cost Housing Company*] [*Brazilian*] (LA)
COHACA..... Compagnie Havraise Camerounaise (MAR)
COHBANA ... Corporacion Hondurena del Banano [*Honduran Banana Corporation*] (LA)
COHDEFOR ... Corporacion Hondurena de Desarrollo Forestal [*Honduran Corporation for Forest Development*] (LA)
COHEP........ Consejo Hondureno de la Empresa Privada [*Honduran Private Enterprise Council*] (LA)
COI.............. Comision de Orientacion Ideologica [*Ideological Orientation Commission*] [*Cuban*] (LA)
COI.............. Commission Oceanographique Intergouvernementale [*Intergovernmental Oceanographic Commission - IOC*] (EA)
COI.............. Conseil Oleicole International [*International Olive Oil Council - IOOC*] (EA)
COIDIEA ..... Conseil des Organisations Internationales Directement Interessees a l'Enfance et a l'Adolescence [*Council of International Organizations Directly Interested in Children and Youth*] (EA)
COIE........... Continentale d'Import Export (MAR)
COIN .... Construcciones Industriales Ltda. [*Bogota*] (COL)
COIN .... Counterinsurgency (MAR)
COINDUSTRIAL ... Control e Instrumentacion Industrial Ltda. [*Medellin*] (COL)
COINTRASUR ... Cooperativa de Transportadores del Sur del Tolima Ltda. [*Chaparral-Tolima*] (COL)
COIP........... Corporacion Industrial del Pueblo [*People's Industrial Corporation*] [*Nicaraguan*] (LA1)
COJ .... Comites d'Organisation des Jeunes [*Youth Organization Committees*] [*Beninese*] (AF)
COJCK .... Centralni Odbor Jugoslovenskog Crvenog Krsta [*Central Committee of the Yugoslav Red Cross*] (YU)
COJE........... Comite d'Organisation des Jeux Africains d'Alger (MAR)
COJM.......... Comite d'Organisation des Jeux Mediterraneens [*Algerian*] (MAR)
COK .... Ceskoslovenska Obchodni Komora [*Czechoslovak Chamber of Commerce*] (CZ)
COK .... Cook Islands [*Three-letter standard code*] (CNC)
COL............. Ceskoslovenska Obec Legionarska [*Czechoslovak Legion*] (CZ)
COL............. Colombia [*Three-letter standard code*] (CNC)
Col.............. Colonel [*Colonel*] [*French*] (MTD)
col .... Colonia [*Spanish*]
col .... Columna [*Column*] [*Spanish*]
cola .... Colonia [*Spanish*]
cola .... Columna [*Column*] [*Spanish*]
COLACEROS ... Compania Colombiana de Aceros SA [*Bucaramanga*] (COL)
COLADIN.... Commissie voor Landbouwdocumentatie en Informatie TNO
COLAF .... Colombiana Asesora y Financiera Ltda. [*Bogota*] (COL)
COLAR........ Compania Colombiana de Arrabio [*Colombian Pig Iron Company*] (LA)
COLAROMA ... Colombiana de Aromaticos Ltda. [*Cali*] (COL)
COLBIENES ... Colombiana de Bienes [*Medellin*] (COL)
COLC .... Comite de Liaison et de Coordination du Travail et de la Mobilisation Generale [*Liaison and Coordination Committee for Labor and General Mobilization*] [*Cambodian*] (CL)
COLCADENAS ... Industria Colombiana de Cadenas Ltda. [*Cali*] (COL)
COLCAFE... Industria Colombiana de Cafe [*Bogota*] (COL)
COLCAR ..... Colombiana de Carrocerias Ltda. [*Bogota*] (COL)
COLCEMENTO ... Colombiana de Cementos SA [*Bogota*] (COL)
COLCERRAM ... Colombiana de Cerraduras Metalicas [*Medellin*] (COL)
COLCIENCIAS ... Centro Colombiano de Investigaciones Cientificas y Proyectos Especiales Francisco Jose De Caldas (COL)
COLCITRICOS ... Compania Colombiana de Citricos [*Bogota*] (COL)
COLCREDITOS ... Compania Colombiana de Creditos y Cobranzas Ltda. [*Cali*] (COL)
COLCULTURA ... Instituto Colombiano de Cultura [*Colombian Cultural Institute*] (LA)
COLDAMPAROS ... Cooperativa Colombiana de Prevision y Amparos Ltda. [*Bucaramanga*] (COL)
COLDEINAR ... Colombiana de Inseminacion Artificial [*Medellin*] (COL)
COLDEMAR ... Compania Colombiana de Navegacion Maritima [*Bogota*] (COL)
COLDEPORTES ... Instituto Colombiano de la Juventud y el Deportes [*Colombian Institute for Youth and Sports*] (LA)
COLDESA... Compania Colombiana de Desarrollo Agricola SA [*Bogota*] (COL)
COLDESIVOS ... Colombiana de Adhesivos Ltda. [*Cali*] (COL)
COLDEST ... Colombiana de Servicios Tecnicos [*Bucaramanga*] (COL)
COLDEX...... Colombiana de Exportaciones Ltda. [*Bogota*] (COL)
COLDICON ... Compania Colombiana de Inversiones y Construcciones [*Bogota*] (COL)
COLDIGRASAS ... Sociedad Colombiana de Industriales de Grasas Vegetales [*Bogota*] (COL)
COLEACP... Comite de Liaison des Fruits Tropicaux et Legumes de Contresaison Originaires des Etats ACP (MAR)

COLECHE ... Cooperativa de Leches de Santander [*Bucaramanga*] (COL)
COLECHERA ... Cooperativa de Productos de Leche del Atlantico [*Barranquilla*] (COL)
COLEGAS ... Colegio Antioqueno de Abogados [*Medellin*] (COL)
COLENCERA ... Compania Colombiana de Encerados SA [*Medellin*] (COL)
COLESAL ... Compania Lechera de la Sabana SA [*Bogota*] (COL)
COLESTE .... Grupo de Coordenacao do Comercio com os Paises Socialistas da Europa Oriental [*Coordinating Group for Trade with the Socialist Countries of Eastern Europe*] [*Brazilian*] (LA)
COLFECAR ... Confederacion de Transporte de Carga [*Confederation of Cargo Transport Workers*] [*Colombian*] (LA)
COLFICOM ... Colombiana de Fomento Industrial y Comercial Ltda. [*Bogota*] (COL)
COLFIM .... Compania Colombiana de Financiamientos [*Bogota*] (COL)
COLFINANZAS ... Compania Colombiana de Finanzas y Creditors [*Bogota*] (COL)
COLFRA ...... Societe du Fruit Colonial Francais (MAR)
COLGAS ..... Compania Colombiana de Gas SA (COL)
COLIM .... Colombiana de Limas Ltda. [*Manizales*] (COL)
COLINAL ..... Compania Litografica Nacional Ltda. [*Medellin*] (COL)
COLINAV .... Conference des Lignes de Navigation (MAR)
COLINDA .... Colombiana de Industrias y Agencias Ltda. [*Bogota*] (COL)
COLINDUC ... Compania Colombiana para Industria y Comercio Ltda. [*Bogota*] (COL)
COLIPED ..... Liaison Committee of Manufacturers of Parts and Equipment for Two-Wheeled Vehicles (EA)
COLISE .... Comptoir de Literie du Senegal (MAR)
COLMALLAS ... Colombiana de Mallas [*Bogota*] (COL)
COLMAQUINAS ... Industria Colombiana de Maquinaria Ltda. [*Bogota*] (COL)
COLMEDICAL ... Colombian Medical Industrial Equipment Ltda. [*Bogota*] (COL)
COLMENA ... Consorcio Metalurgico Nacional SA [*Bogota*] (COL)
COLMETAL ... Compania Colombiana de Metales Ltda. [*Medellin*] (COL)
COLMIL .... Colegio Militar [*Military College*] [*Bolivian*] (LA1)
COLMINERA ... Corporacion Minera Colombiana SA [*Bogota*] (COL)
COLMOTORES ... Fabrica Colombiana de Automotores [*Bogota*] (COL)
COLMOVIL ... Colombiana de Automotores Ltda. [*Cali*] (COL)
COLMUEBLES ... Compania Colombiana de Muebles [*Bogota*] (COL)
COLNEON ... Compania Colombiana de Neon Ltda. [*Medellin*] (COL)
COLO .... Comisiones Obreras de Loita Obreira [*Workers' Commissions of Loita Obreira*] [*Spanish*] (WER)
COLOMBATES ... Compania Colombiana de Empaques Bates SA [*Bogota*] (COL)
COLOMBEX ... Compania Colombiana de Comercio Exterior [*Bogota*] (COL)
Colombr ...... Colombier [*Dovecote*] [*Military map abbreviation*] [*World War I*] [*French*] (MTD)
COLPA .... Colombiana de Publicidad Ltda. [*Bogota*] (COL)
COLPAEF .... Comite de Liaison du Patronat de l'AEF (MAR)
COLPAPELES ... Compania Industrial de Papeles [*Medellin*] (COL)
COLPATRIA ... Compania Colombiana de Capitalizacion y Seguros Patria [*Cali*] (COL)
COLPET ...... Colombiana de Petroleos [*Bogoto*] (COL)
COLPETROL ... Colombian Petroleum Company SA [*Cucuta*] (COL)
COLPIELES ... Compania Colombiana de Pieles [*Cali*] (COL)
COLPIN .... Colombiana de Pinturas Ltda. [*Medellin*] (COL)
COLPOZOS ... Colombiana Perforadora de Pozos [*Cali*] (COL)
COLPPOSUMAH ... Colegio Profesional de Subimiento Magisterio Hondureno [*Professional Association for the Improvement of Teaching in Honduras*] (LA)
COLPUERTOS ... Empresa Puertos de Colombia [*Colombian Ports Enterprise*] (LA)
COLQUIMICA ... Compania Colombiana de Productos Quimicos [*Medellin*] (COL)
COLRESIN ... Colombiana de Resinas [*Medellin*] (COL)
COLSEGUROS ... Compania Colombiana de Seguros [*Bogota*] (COL)
COLTABACO ... Compania Colombiana de Tabaco [*Colombian Tobacco Company*] (LA1)
COLTEJER ... Compania Colombiana de Tejidos [*Colombian Textile Company*] (LA)
COLTEPUNTO ... Compania Colombiana de Tejidos de Punto [*Medellin*] (COL)
COLTEXCO ... Colombiana de Textiles y Confecciones Ltda. [*Bogota*] (COL)
COLTOLIMA ... Compania Automotora del Tolima Ltda. [*Ibague*] (COL)
COLTRADA ... Compania General Transportadora Ltda. [*Bogota*] (COL)
COLTRAP ... Compania Colombiana de Trabajos Publicos [*Bogota*] (COL)
COLTUBOS ... Colombiana de Tubos [*Medellin*] (COL)
COLTUR ...... Colombiana de Turismo [*Bogota*] (COL)
COLUCHO ... Comite de Lucha Choferil [*Drivers Struggle Committee*] [*Dominican Republic*] (LA)
COLVAPORES ... Colombiana Internacional de Vapores [*Bogota*] (COL)
COLVENTAS ... Compra y Venta de Propiedad Raiz [*Medellin*] (COL)
COLVEX ...... Conservas California Ltda. [*Barranquilla*] (COL)
COLVIDRIOS ... Compania Colombiana de Vidrios [*Cali*] (COL)
COLVINOS ... Compania Colombiana de Vinos Ltda. [*Bogota*] (COL)
COLVIVIENDAS ... Compania Colombiana de Viviendas [*Cali*] (COL)
COLYMAD ... Comptoir Lyon-Madagascar [*Lyon-Madagascar Bank*] (AF)
COM .... Cahiers d'Outre-Mer [*A publication*] (MAR)
COM .... Centrala Obrotu Maszynami [*Machinery Sales Center*] (POL)
COM .... Centralny Osrodek Metodyczny [*Central Methodological Institute*] (POL)
COM .... Comoros [*Three-letter standard code*] (CNC)
COM .... Confederacion Obrera de Mexico [*Mexican Labor Confederation*] (LA)
COM .... Consiliul Oamenilor Muncii [*Council of Workers*] (RO)
COMABU .... Cooperative des Maraichers de Bugarama (MAR)
COMACERO ... Compania Manufacturera de Muebles Colombiana [*Barranquilla*] (COL)
COMACh .... Confederacion Maritima de Chile [*Chilean Maritime Confederation*] (LA)
COMACI ...... Comptoir Marocain Commercial et Industrial (MAR)
COMACI ...... Confection Masculine de Cote-d'Ivoire (MAR)
COMACI ...... Societe de Commission et d'Approvisionnement de la Cote-d'Ivoire (MAR)
COMACO .... Compagnie de Manutention et de Chalandage d'Owendo (MAR)
COMACO .... Compagnie Maritime et Commerciale [*Moroccan*] (MAR)
COMADAN ... Corporacion de Mercado Agricola de Antioquia [*Medellin*] (COL)
COMADEV ... Consortium Maghrebin de Developpement Economique [*Maghreb Economic Development Consortium*] [*North African*] (AF)
COMADIEX ... Comptoir Abidjanais d'Import-Export (MAR)
COMAF .... Commercial Sud-Est Afrique (MAR)
COMAFAK ... Compagnie Malienne des Ets. Fakhry (MAR)
COMAFCI ... Compagnie Maritime Africaine (MAR)
COMAFRA ... Comptoir Africain d'Assurances (MAR)
COMAFRIQUE ... Societe Ivoirienne d'Expansion Commerciale (MAR)
COMAFRUTA ... Companhia de Amadurecimento de Frutas Lda. (MAR)
COMAF-SENEGAL ... Compagnie Maritime Africaine (MAR)
COMAG .... Societe Malgache de Constructions Metalliques et du Materiel Agricole (MAR)
COMAGRI ... Compagnie Marocaine de Gestion des Exploitations Agricoles [*Moroccan*] (MAR)
COMAHA .... Cooperative Marocaine des Huileries Alimentaires [*Moroccan Cooperative for Edible Oils*] (MAR)
COMAIA ...... Comptoir Automobile Industriel et Agricole (MAR)
COMAL .... Compagnie Commerciale Camerounaise de l'Alumine et de l'Aluminium (MAR)
COMALFA ... Comptoir Maghrebin de l'Alfa [*Maghreb Alfa Agency*] [*North African*] (AF)
COMANAN ... Compagnie Marocaine de Navigation (MAR)
COMANAV ... Compagnie Malienne de Navigation (MAR)
COMANAV ... Compagnie Marocaine de Navigation [*North African*] (MAR)
COMANAV ... Compagnie Nationale Algerienne de Navigation (MAR)
COMAP .... Comite Maghrebin des Agrumes et Primeurs [*North African*] (MAR)
COMAPAN ... Cooperativa de Maestros Panaderos [*Cooperative of Master Bakers*] [*Salvadoran*] (LA1)
COMAPEG ... Compagnie Malgache de Participations et de Gestion (MAR)
COMAPIC ... Compagnie Mauritanienne pour l'Armement, la Peche, l'Industrie, et le Commerce (MAR)
COMAPOCO ... Comando de Accion Politica-Conservadora [*Conservative Political Action Command*] [*Colombian*] (LA)
COMAPOPE ... Compagnie Mauritanienne Portugaise des Peches (MAR)
COMAPRA ... Compagnie Marocaine de Commercialisation et de Produits Agricoles (MAR)
COMAR .... Compagnie Mauritanienne des Armements (MAR)
COMAR .... Companhia Mocambicana de Ar Condicionado Lda. (MAR)
COMAR .... Compania Maritima Internacional [*Medellin*] (COL)
COMARAN ... Compagnie Maritime de l'Afrique Noire (MAR)
COMARNA ... Comision Nacional para la Proteccion del Ambiente y Conservacion de los Recursos Naturales [*National Committee for Environmental Protection and Conservation of Natural Resources*] [*Cuban*] (LA)
COMASE ..... Companhia Agricola de Sergipe [*Brazilian*]
COMATAM ... Compagnie Malienne pour Tous Appareillages Mecaniques (MAR)
COMATEX ... Compagnie Malienne de Textiles (MAR)
COMATRANSIT ... Compagnie Malienne de Transit (MAR)
COMAUNAM ... Compagnie Mauritanienne de Navigation Maritime [*Mauritanian Shipping Company*] (AF)
COMAUR .... Societe des Commercants de Mauritanie (MAR)
COMAURAL ... Comptoir Mauritano Algerien (MAR)
COMB .... Cahiers d'Outre-Mer. Revue de Geographie de Bordeaux et de l'Atlantique, Bordeaux [*A publication*] (MAR)
COMCABI ... Comunidade Cabindense (MAR)
ComCES ..... Comitetul pentru Cultura si Educatie Socialista [*Committee for Socialist Culture and Education*] (RO)
COMCORDE ... Comision Coordinadora para el Desarrollo Economico [*Coordinating Committee for Economic Development*] [*Uruguayan*] (LA)
COMDAC .... Comite d'Action en France
COMDEV ..... Commonwealth Development Corporation (MAR)
COMEBA ..... Cooperatives des Menuisiers Burundi (MAR)
COMECAFCO ... Commerciale Europeenne de Cafes et Cacaos (MAR)
COMECON ... Comite d'Entraide Economique [*North African*] (MAR)
COMECON ... Council for Economic Mutual Assistance (CEMA) (WEN)

COMEDOR ... Comite Permanent d'Etudes de Developpement, d'Organisation, et d'Amenagement de l'Agglomeration d'Alger [*Permanent Committee for Development, Organization, and Planning Studies for the Algiers Metropolitan Area*] (AF)
COMEFA ..... Constructions Metalliques Ferronnerie d'Art (MAR)
COMEL .... Consorcio de Maquinas e Electricidade Lda. (MAR)
COMELEC ... Comite Maghrebin de l'Energie Electrique [*North African Electric Power Committee*] (AF)
COMELEC ... Compagnie Malienne d'Electricite et d'Equipement (MAR)
COMEMA .... Comite d'Expansion Economique de Marovoay (MAR)
COMEPLAST ... Compagnie Malgache de Produits Metallurgiques et Plastiques (MAR)
COMERAL .. Comercial de Alimentos [*Cali*] (COL)
COMERCO ... Compagnie Commerciale Congolaise (MAR)
COMERCOL ... Comercial Colombia [*Medellin*] (COL)
COMERGAN ... Compania de Comercializacion del Ganado [*Bogota*] (COL)
COMERWA ... Cooperative de Manuiserie du Rwanda (MAR)
COMES .... Cooperation Mediterraneenne pour l'Energie Solaire (MAR)
COMES .... Cooperativa de Ahorro y Credito Maizena y Empresas Similares [*Cali*] (COL)
COMES .... Societe Commerciale du Methane Saharien [*Saharan Methane Trading Company*] [*Algerian*] (AF)
COMESTRA ... Comissao Especial de Estudo de Reforma Administrativa [*Special Commission for Studies of Administrative Reform*] [*Brazilian*] (LA)
COMET .... Council on Middle East Trade (MAR)
COMETAL... Complexe Metallurgique Algerois (MAR)
COMETAL... Talleres de Construcciones Metalicas [*Barranquilla*] (COL)
COMETE ..... Compagnie Mauritanienne des Etudes Techniques et Economiques (MAR)
COMETEC-GAZ ... Comite d'Etudes Economiques de l'Industrie du Gaz [*Economic Research Committee of the Gas Industry*]
COMETRA ... Compagnie Financiere et de Gestion pour l'Etranger (MAR)
COMETRAP ... Cooperativa Metropolitana del Transporte [*Metropolitan Transport Cooperative*] [*Panamanian*] (LA)
COMEX .... Compagnie Maritime d'Expertise [*Maritime Appraisal Company*] [*French*] (WER)
COMEX .... Compagnie Mauritanienne d'Explosifs (MAR)
COMEX .... Compania Colombiana de Comercio Exterior [*Colombian Foreign Trade Company*] (LA)
COMEXPO ... Commerciale d'Exploitation et d'Importation (MAR)
COMEXPORT ... Comercio de Exportadores Metalurgicos SA [*Bogota*] (COL)
COMFENALCO ... Caja de Compensacion Familiar de Fenalco [*Cucuta*] (COL)
COMFER ..... Comite Federal de Radiodifusion [*Federal Committee for Broadcasting*] [*Argentine*] (LA1)
COMGAR .... Comando Geral do Ar [*Brazilian Air Force*]
COMHOTEB ... Compagnie Hoteliere de Bouake (MAR)
COMIAO ...... Compagnie Commerciale et Industrielle de l'Afrique de l'Ouest (MAR)
COMIBERLANT ... Commander, Iberian-Atlantic Area [*Portuguese*] (WER)
COMIBOL .... Corporacion Minera de Bolivia [*Mining Corporation of Bolivia*] (LA)
COMIEX ..... Compagnie Ivoirienne d'Import-Export (MAR)
COMIEXCO ... Compania Minera Exportadora de Colombia Ltda. [*Cali*] (COL)
COMIGAL ... Commissariat General [*General Commissariat*] [*Cambodian*] (CL)
COMIGEM... Combinat Industriel de Gemens (MAR)
COMIL .... Compagnie Marocaine par l'Industrie du Liege (MAR)
COMIL .... Compostos Quimicos Industriais Lda. (MAR)
COMILOG ... Compagnie Miniere de l'Ogooue [*Ogooue Mining Company*] [*Gabonese*] (AF)
COMIMPRA ... Compagnie Mauritanienne d'Importation de Produits Alimentaires (MAR)
COMINA ...... Compagnie Miniere d'Andriamena (MAR)
COMINAK ... Compagnie Miniere d'Akouta [*Akouta Mining Company*] [*Niger*] (AF)
COMINARMAR ... Compagnie Internationale d'Armement Maritime, Industriel, et Commercial (MAR)
COMINES ... Comptoir des Mines Ivoiriennes (MAR)
COMINIERE ... Societe Commerciale et Miniere du Congo (MAR)
COMINIF ..... Irano-France Investment Company (ME)
COMIN KHMER ... Compagnie Industrielle du Cambodge [*Cambodian Industrial Company*] (CL)
COMIN KHMERE ... Compagnie Industrielle du Cambodge [*Cambodian Industrial Company*] [*Use COMIN KHMER*] (CL)
COMINO ...... Nouvelle Societe Commerciale et l'Immobiliere (MAR)
COMINOA ... Comptoir des Mines et des Grands Travaux de l'Ouest Africain (MAR)
COMINOR ... Complexe Minier du Nord [*Mining Complex of the North*] [*French*] (WER)
COMINPRA ... Compagnie Mauritanienne de Produits Alimentaires (MAR)
Comintern ... Communist International (PPE)
COMIP .... Comision Mixta del Rio Parana [*Parana River Joint Commission*] [*Argentine, Brazilian, Paraguayan*] (LA)
COMIP .... Compagnie Mauritanienne des Industries de Peches (MAR)
COMIPAL .... Comision Mixta de Palmar [*Palmar Joint Commission*] [*Uruguayan*] (LA)
COMIPEZ .... Comisariato-Industria Pescados y Mariscos Congelados Ltda. [*Barranquilla*] (COL)
COMIPHOS ... Compagnie Miniere et Phosphatiere (MAR)
COMIPLAN ... Commissariat General du Plan [*General Commissariat for Planning*] [*Cambodian*] (CL)
COMIPOL .... Comision Militar Politica [*Political Military Commission*] [*Argentine*] (LA1)
COMIR .... Compagnie Marocaine d'Equipements Industriels et Routiers (MAR)
Comis .... Comisario [*Commissioner*] [*Spanish*]
COMISIREK ... Comite Charge de Suivre l'Evolution de l'Esprit et de l'Idee de la Republique [*Committee to Oversee the Evolution of the Spirit and the Concept of the Republic*] [*Cambodian*] (CL)
comiso .... Comisario [*Spanish*]
COMITRA .... Comite des Transporteurs au Congo (MAR)
COMIVAL .... Cooperativa de Militares en Retiro del Valle del Cauca Ltda. [*Cali*] (COL)
COMIVOIRE ... La Commerciale Ivoirienne (MAR)
COMIZA ...... Communaute Islamique au Zaire [*Islamic Community of Zaire*] (AF)
Comm .... Commandeur [*or Commandant*] [*Commander*] [*French*] (MTD)
COMMIGAL ... Commissariat General [*General Commissariat*] [*Cambodian*] (CL)
COMMIGAL MOBIGALE ... Commissariat General de Mobilisation Generale [*General Commissariat for General Mobilization*] [*Cambodian*] (CL)
COMNOMET ... Corporacion Nicaraguense de Minerales No Metalicos [*Nicaraguan Corporation of Nonmetallic Minerals*] (LA1)
COMO .... Comptoir du Mono (MAR)
COMODHOR ... Comptoir Moderne d'Horlogerie (MAR)
COMOROCLANT ... Commander, Maritime Forces, Morocco (MAR)
COMOUNA ... Compagnie Commerciale de l'Ouhame-Nana (MAR)
COMP .... Groupement Outre-Mer Pharmaceutique (MAR)
COMPA .... College Moderne Prive d'Adzope (MAR)
compa .... Compania [*Company, Society*] [*Spanish*]
COMPAS ..... Comite por la Paz, el Anti-Imperialismo, y la Solidaridad entre los Pueblos [*Mexican Committee for Peace, Anti-Imperialism, and Solidarity among Nations*] (LA)
COMPAU .... Comision Tecnica Mixta del Puente entre Argentina y Uruguay [*Joint Technical Commission for the Argentina-Uruguay Bridge*] (LA)
COMPER ..... Companhia de Desenvolvimento de Pernambuco [*Pernambuco Development Company*] [*Brazilian*] (LA)
COMPLES ... Cooperation Mediterraneenne pour l'Energie Solaire (MAR)
COMPROBA ... Compania de Produccion Bananera [*Banana Production Company*] [*Ecuadorean*] (LA)
comps .... Companeros [*Companions*] [*Spanish*]
compt .... Comptabilite [*Accountancy*] [*French*]
Comptes Rend ... Comptes Rendus [*Proceedings*] [*French*]
COMR .... Comite Organizador del Movimiento de la Revolucion [*Organizing Committee of the Revolutionary Movement*] [*Peruvian*] (LA)
COMSAT ..... Union Internationale des Communications par Satellites [*North African*] (MAR)
COMSTSELMAREA ... Commander, Military Sea Transportation Service, Eastern Atlantic and Mediterranean Area (MAR)
COMSUBCOMNELM ... Commander, Subordinate Command, United States Naval Forces, Eastern Atlantic and Mediterranean (MAR)
COMSUBMED ... Commander, Submarines Mediterranean (MAR)
COMSUBMEDNOREAST ... Commander, Submarines Northeast Mediterranean (MAR)
Comt .... Commandant [*Commander*] [*French*] (MTD)
COMTEC ..... Compagnia Tecnica di Progettazione (MAR)
COMTOVAL ... Le Comptoir du Valo [*Senegalese*] (MAR)
COMUF .... Compagnie des Mines d'Uranium de Franceville [*Franceville Uranium Mining Company*] [*Gabonese*] (AF)
CON .... Commander of the Order of the Niger (MAR)
Con .... Commission [*Commission*] [*Business and trade*] [*French*]
con .... Coniunx [*Wife*] [*Latin*] (GPO)
con .... Contra [*Against*] [*Latin*] (GPO)
Con .... Coron [*Miner's House*] [*Military map abbreviation*] [*World War I*] [*French*] (MTD)
CONAC .... Confederacion Nacional de Asentamientos Campesinos [*National Confederation of Peasant Settlements*] [*Panamanian*] (LA)
CONAC .... Consejo Nacional de la Cultura [*National Culture Council*] [*Venezuelan*] (LA)
CONAC .... Societe la Continentale Agricole du Cameroun (MAR)
CONACA ..... Comision Nacional de Aqueductos y Alcantarillado [*National Waterworks and Sewerage Commission*] [*Cuban*] (LA)
CONACE ..... Comite Nacional pro Construccion de Escuelas [*National Committee for School Construction*] [*Guatemalan*] (LA1)
CONACED ... Confederacion Nacional de Centros Docentes [*Bogota*] (COL)
CONACI ...... Confederacion Nacional de Comunidades Industriales [*National Confederation of Industrial Communities*] [*Peruvian*] (LA)
CONACIONAL ... Compania Nacional de Fosforos Ltda. [*Manizales*] (COL)
CONACO .... Confederacion Nacional de Comerciantes [*National Confederation of Merchants*] [*Peruvian*] (LA)
CONACO .... Confederation Nationale des Associations Congolaises (MAR)
CONACO .... Convention Nationale Congolaise [*Congolese National Convention*] (MAR)

CONACYT... Consejo Nacional de Ciencia y Tecnologia [*National Council for Science and Technology*] [*Argentine*] (LA)
CONACYT... Consejo Nacional de Ciencia y Tecnologia [*National Council for Science and Technology*] [*Mexican*] (LA1)
CONADE..... Comite Nacional de Defensa de la Democracia [*National Committee for Defending Democracy*] [*Bolivian*] (LA1)
CONADE..... Consejo Nacional de Desarrollo [*National Development Council*] [*Argentine*] (LA)
CONADE..... Corporacion Nacional de Desarrollo [*National Development Corporation*] [*Honduran*] (LA)
CONADEF... Comite Nacional de Desarrollo Fronterizo [*National Committee for Border Development*] [*Honduran*] (LA1)
CONADEP... Conseil National de Planification [*National Planning Council*] [*Haitian*] (LA)
CONADESE ... Consejo Nacional de Desarrollo y Seguridad [*National Development and Security Council*] [*Argentine*] (LA)
CONADESOPAZ ... Comite Nacional de Defensa de la Soberania y la Paz [*National Committee for the Defense of Sovereignty and Peace*] [*Panamanian*] (LA)
CONADIN.... Corporacion Nacional de Inversiones [*National Investment Corporation*] [*Honduran*] (LA)
CONADIS.... Compania Nacional de Distribucion Ltda. [*Cali*] (COL)
CONAE........ Consejo Nacional de Educacion [*National Education Council*] [*Uruguayan*] (LA)
CONAE........ Convocatoria Nacional Empresaria [*National Business Assembly*] [*Argentine*] (LA1)
CONAES..... Colegio Nicaraguense de Administradores de Empresa [*Nicaraguan College of Business Managers*] (LA1)
CONAI......... Comision Nacional de Asuntos Indigenas [*National Commission for Indian Affairs*] [*Costa Rican*] (LA)
CONAIM...... Comision Nacional de la Industria del Maiz [*National Commission of the Corn Industry*] [*Mexican*] (LA1)
CONAIN ...... Comision Nacional del Ano Internacional del Nino [*National Commission for the International Year of the Child*] [*Peruvian*] (LA)
CONAKAT .. Confederation des Associations du Katanga [*Confederation of Katangan Associations*]
CONAL........ Comision Nacional de Algodon [*National Cotton Commission*] [*Nicaraguan*] (LA)
CONAL........ Comite Nacional de Asesoramiento y Legislacion [*National Legislative Advisory Committee*] [*Bolivian*] (LA1)
CONALALC ... Comision Nacional de Asociacion Latinoamericana de Libre Comercio [*Latin American Free Trade Association National Commission*] [*Venezuelan*] (LA)
CONALBO... Corporacion Colegio Nacional de Abogados [*National Bar Association*] [*Colombian*] (LA)
CONALBOS ... Corporacion Colegio Nacional de Abogados [*National Bar Association*] [*Colombian*] (COL)
CONALBUSES ... Corporacion Nacional de Buses [*National Bus Corporation*] [*Colombian*] (LA)
CONALCO ... Cooperativa Nacional de Consumo Ltda. [*Bogota*] (COL)
CONALFE ... Confederacion Nacional Femenina [*National Confederation of Women*] [*Colombian*] (LA)
CONALPES ... Coonacional los Alpes Ltda. [*Bogota*] (COL)
CONALPRUN ... Cooperativa Nacional de Profesionales Unidos Ltda. [*Bogota*] (COL)
CONALTRA ... Corporacion Nacional de Transportes Ltda. (COL)
CONALVIDRIOS ... Compania Nacional de Vidrios [*Cali*] (COL)
CONAM....... Confederacion Nacional de Municipalidades [*National Confederation of Municipalities*] [*Chilean*] (LA)
CONAMAR ... Consejo Nacional Maritimo [*National Maritime Council*] [*Bolivian*] (LA)
CONAMCOS ... Consejo Nacional de Comunicacion Social [*National Mass Media Council*] [*Peruvian*] (LA)
CONAME .... Consejo Nacional de Menores [*National Advisory Board for Minors*] [*Bolivian*] (LA)
CONAN .... Consejo Nacional para el Desarrollo de la Industria Nuclear [*National Council for Development of the Nuclear Industry*] [*Venezuelan*] (LA)
CONANCRA ... Comite National Contre le Racisme et l'Apartheid [*National Committee Against Racism and Apartheid*] [*Malagasy*] (AF)
CONANI ...... Consejo Nacional para la Ninez [*National Council for Children*] [*Dominican Republic*] (LA1)
CONAP........ Consejo Nacional de la Publicidad [*National Council for Publicity*] [*Guatemalan*] (LA1)
CONAPLAN ... Consejo Nacional de Planificacion y Coordinacion Economica [*National Economic Planning and Coordination Council*] [*Salvadoran*] (LA)
CONAPOL... Consejo Nacional Politico y Social [*National Council for Political and Social Affairs*] [*Bolivian*] (LA1)
CONAPRO ... Comite National Provisoire (MAR)
CONAPRO ... Confederacion Nacional de Asociaciones Profesionales [*National Confederation of Professional Associations*] [*Nicaraguan*] (LA1)
CONAPROLE ... Cooperativa Nacional de Productores de Leche [*National Milk Producers Cooperative*] [*Uruguayan*] (LA)
CONAPS..... Comision Nacional de Propiedad Social [*National Social Property Commission*] [*Peruvian*] (LA)
CONARA..... Comision Nacional de Reformas Administrativas [*National Administrative Reform Commission*] [*Chilean*] (LA)
CONARA..... Concilio Nacional de la Reconstrucion Administrativa [*National Council for Administrative Reconstruction*] [*Argentine*] (LA)
CONARCA ... Comision Nacional de Renovacion de Cafetales [*National Committee for Renovating Coffee Lands*] [*Nicaraguan*] (LA1)
CONARE ..... Consejo Nacional de Reformas [*National Council for Structural Reforms*] [*Bolivian*] (LA)
CONAREPA ... Comision Nacional de Recuperacion Patrimonial [*National Commission for Patrimonial Recovery*] [*Argentine*] (LA1)
CONAREX... Consortium Africain de Realisation et d'Exploitation (MAR)
CONART ..... Consejo Nacional de Radiodifusion y Television [*National Radiobroadcasting and Television Council*] [*Argentine*] (LA)
CONASE ..... Consejo Nacional de Seguridad [*National Security Council*] [*Argentine*] (LA)
CONASEV... Comision Nacional Supervisora de Empresas y Valores [*National Enterprises and Securities Supervisory Commission*] [*Peruvian*] (LA)
CONASUPO ... Compania Nacional de Subsistencias Populares [*Government Basic Commodities Company*] [*Mexican*] (LA)
CONATON ... Comision Nacional de Toxicomania y Narcoticos [*National Commission on Addiction and Narcotics*] [*Argentine*] (LA)
CONATRAP ... Coordinadora Nacional de Trabajadores de Prensa [*National Coordinating Board of Press Workers*] [*Argentine*] (LA1)
CONAVAL... Astilleros Construcciones Navales Ltda. [*Cartagena*] (COL)
CONAVE ..... Compania Nacional de Ventas Ltda. [*Bogota*] (COL)
CONAVI ...... Consejo Nacional de Vivienda [*National Housing Council*] [*Bolivian*] (LA)
CONAZU ..... Confederacion Nacional de Azucareros [*National Sugar Producers Confederation*] [*Chilean*] (LA)
CONC.......... Comision Obrera Nacional de Catalunya [*Catalonia National Workers Commission*] [*Spanish*] (WER)
CONCAB..... Conseil du Cabinet [*Cabinet*] [*Cambodian*] (CL)
CONCACAF ... Confederacion Norte-Centro America y del Caribe de Futbol [*North and Central American and Caribbean Soccer Confederation*] (LA)
CONCAMIN ... Confederacion de Camaras Industriales [*Confederation of Industrial Chambers*] [*Mexican*] (LA)
CONCANACO ... Confederacion de Camaras Nacionales de Comercio [*Confederation of National Chambers of Commerce*] [*Mexican*] (LA)
CONCAP..... Confederacion de Campesinos Peruanos [*Confederation of Peruvian Peasants*] (LA)
CONCENTRAL ... Cooperativa Central de Distribucion [*Bogota*] (COL)
CONCERN ... Congregational Outreach Network Concerned with Elderly Residents of Nursing Homes (MAR)
CONCERTA ... Concessionaire de la Route Tahoua-Arlit (MAR)
CONCEX..... Conselho Nacional de Comercio Exterior [*National Council on Foreign Trade*] [*Brazilian*] (LA)
CONCIVILES ... Construcciones Civiles Ltda. [*Cali*] (COL)
CONCLAP... Conselho Superior das Classes Produtoras [*Higher Board of Producer Groups*] [*Brazilian*] (LA)
CONCLAT... Conferencia Nacional das Classes Trabalhadores [*National Conference of the Working Classes*] [*Brazilian*] (LA1)
CONCORDE ... Consejo de Coordinacion para el Desarrollo [*Coordinating Council for Development*] [*Honduran*] (LA)
CONCP .... Conference des Organisations Nationalistes des Colonies Portugaises [*Conference of National Organizations of Portuguese Colonies*] (LA)
CONCP .... Conferencia de Organizacoes Nacionalistas das Colonias Portuguesas [*Moroccan*] (MAR)
CONCRENAL ... Control Nacional de Credito [*Bogota*] (COL)
CONCUERO ... Confecciones de Cuero Ltda. [*Medellin*] (COL)
Con De........ Canon Declasse [*Military*] [*French*] (MTD)
CONDECA ... Consejo de Defensa Centroamericano [*Central American Defense Council*] (LA)
CONDEMINA ... Corporacion Nicaraguense de Minas [*Nicaraguan Corporation of Mines*] (LA1)
CONDEP ..... Conselho de Desenvolvimento da Pecuaria [*Livestock Development Council*] [*Brazilian*] (LA)
CONDEPALE ... Ley Organica para la Ensenanza Secundaria [*Organic Law for Secondary Education*] [*Uruguayan*] (LA1)
CONDESE... Conselho de Desenvolvimento Economico de Sergipe [*Brazilian*]
CONE .... Comision Obrera Nacional de Euzkadi [*Basque National Workers Commissions*] [*Spanish*] (WER)
CONEE........ Comision Nacional del Espacio Exterior [*National Outer Space Committee*] [*Mexican*] (LA)
CONEFO ..... Conference of the New Emerging Forces (IN)
CONELCA... Conductores Electricos de Centroamerica, SA [*Electric Conductors of Central America Corp.*] [*Salvadoran*]
CONEMPA ... Consorcio de Empresas Constructoras Paraguayas [*Consortium of Paraguayan Construction Companies*] (LA)
CONEP........ Comissao Nacional de Estimulos e Estabilizacao de Precos [*National Commission for Incentives and Price Stabilization*] [*Brazilian*] (LA)
CONEP........ Consejo Nacional de la Empresa Privada [*National Council of Private Enterprise*] [*Panamanian*] (LA)
CONEPLAN ... Consejo Nacional de Economia y Planificacion [*National Economic and Planning Council*] [*Bolivian*] (LA)

CONES........ Consejo Nacional Economico y Social [*National Economic and Social Council*] [*Argentine*] (LA)
CONESTUDIOS ... Construcciones y Estudios Ltda. [*Cali*] (COL)
CONET........ Consejo Nacional de Educacion Tecnica [*National Technical Education Council*] [*Argentine*] (LA)
CONEXITO ... Concentrados Exitos Ltda. [*Cali*] (COL)
CONFECAMARAS ... Confederacion de Camaras de Comercio [*Confederation of Chambers of Commerce*] [*Colombian*] (LA)
CONFEJES ... Conference des Ministres de la Jeunesse et des Sports des Pays d'Expression Francaise (MAR)
CONFENACOOP ... Confederacion Nacional de Cooperativas [*National Confederation of Cooperatives*] [*Peruvian*] (LA)
CONFER...... Confederacion Nicaraguense de Escuelas Catolicas [*Nicaraguan Confederation of Catholic Schools*] (LA1)
CONFER...... Consejo Federal de Radiodifusion [*Federal Broadcasting Council*] [*Argentine*] (LA)
CONFIGI ..... Confiturerie de Gihindamuyaga (MAR)
CONGOBOIS ... Compagnie Congolaise des Bois (MAR)
CONGO-MECA ... Societe Congolaise de Mecanographie (MAR)
CONGOMER ... Societe Congolaise de Commerce (MAR)
CONGONA ... Compagnie Congolaise de Navigation (MAR)
CONIBIR ..... Corporacion Nicaraguense de Bienes Raices [*Nicaraguan Corporation of Real Estate*] (LA1)
CONICET.... Consejo Nacional de Investigaciones Cientificas y Tecnologicas [*National Scientific and Technical Research Council*] [*Argentine*] (LA)
CONICIT ..... Consejo Nacional de Investigaciones Cientificas y Tecnologicas [*National Council for Scientific and Technological Research*] [*Venezuelan*] (LA)
CONICYT.... Comision Nacional de Investigacion Cientifica y Tecnologica [*National Commission for Scientific and Technological Research*] [*Chilean*] (LA)
CONIE......... Comision Nacional de Investigacion del Espacio [*Spanish space commission*]
CONIEL....... Compagnia Imprese Elettriche dell'Eritrea (MAR)
CONIEXCO ... Compagnie Nigerienne d'Expansion Commerciale (MAR)
CONIF......... Corporacion Nacional de Investigaciones Foretales [*National Corporation for Forestry Research*] [*Colombian*] (LA)
CONINAGRO ... La Confederacion Intercooperativa Agropecuaria [*Agricultural and Livestock Intercooperative Confederation*] [*Argentine*] (LA)
CONISTO.... Comite National Inter-Syndical du Togo [*Inter-Union National Committee of Togo*] (AF)
CONITE....... Comision Nacional de Inversiones y Tecnologia Extranjeras [*National Commission for Foreign Investments and Technology*] [*Peruvian*] (LA)
CONITO ...... Comite National Intersyndical du Togo (MAR)
CONLAC..... Empresa Consolidada de Industrias Lacteas [*Consolidated Enterprise of Dairy Industries*] [*Cuban*] (LA)
CONLARDEPE ... Confederacion Latinoamericana de Expendedores de Derivados del Petroleo [*Latin American Confederation of Oil Derivative Merchants*] (LA)
CONMETAL ... Construcciones Metalicas SA [*Bucaramanga*] (COL)
CONOBRAS ... Compania Constructora de Obras de Ingenieria Ltda. [*Cartagena*] (COL)
CONOCA .... Consejo Centroamericano de Organizaciones Campesinas [*Central American Council of Peasant Organizations*] (LA)
CONOCO .... Continental Oil Company (MAR)
CONOTON ... Centro Nacional de Narcoticos y Sustancias Peligrosas [*National Center for Narcotics and Dangerous Drugs*] [*Argentine*] (LA1)
CONPANCOL ... Compania Consultante Panamericana de Colombia Ltda. [*Cali*] (COL)
CONPES ..... Consejo Nacional de Politica Economica y Social [*National Economic and Social Policy Council*] [*Colombian*] (LA)
CON-PLAC ... Contreplacages, Placages Camerounais (MAR)
CONRUB..... Comision Nacional de Reordenamiento de la Universidad Boliviana [*National Council for Restructuring the Bolivian University*] (LA1)
CONS.......... Central Obrera Nacional Sindicalista [*National Workers Trade Union Confederation*] [*Of Hedillist tendency*] [*Spanish*] (WER)
Cons........... Consejo [*Council*] [*Spanish*]
CONSAFRIQUE ... Consortium Europeen pour le Developpement des Ressources Naturelles de l'Afrique (MAR)
CONSANE... Conselho Nacional de Saneamento Basico [*National Basic Sanitation Council*] [*Brazilian*] (LA)
CONSCARIBE ... Compania Constructora del Caribe Ltda. [*Cartagena*] (COL)
CONSEMACh ... Confederacion de Sindicatos de Empleadores Agricolas de Chile [*Confederation of Unions of Agriculture Employers*] (LA)
CONSEPP... Confederacion de Servidores Publicos del Peru [*Confederation of Civil Servants of Peru*] (LA)
CONSFA ..... Consejo Superior de Fomento Agropecuario [*Higher Council for Agricultural and Livestock Development*] [*Chilean*] (LA)
CONSICOL ... Confederacion Sindical de Colombia [*Trade Union Confederation of Colombia*] (LA)
CONSIDER ... Conselho Nacional de Nao-Ferrosos e Siderurgia [*National Nonferrous Metals and Steel Council*] [*Brazilian*] (LA)
CONSIGUA ... Confederacion Sindical de Guatemala [*Guatemalan Trade Union Confederation*] (LA)
CONSINTRA ... Conselho Sindical dos Trabalhadores [*Labor Union Council*] [*Brazilian*] (LA)
CONSISAL ... Consejo Sindical Salvadoreno [*Salvadoran Trade Union Council*] (LA1)
conso .... Consejo [*Spanish*]
CONSOB..... Commissione Nazionale per le Societa e la Borsa [*National Commission for Companies and the Stock Exchange*] [*Italian counterpart of the American Sècurities and Exchange Commission*] (WER)
CONSPLAN ... Conselho do Planejamento [*Planning Council*] [*Brazilian*] (LA)
CONSTRAL ... Construtores Associados Lda. (MAR)
CONSTRUIMPORT ... Empresa Cubana Importadora de Maquinarias y Equipos de Construccion [*Cuban Enterprise for the Import of Construction Machinery and Equipment*] (LA)
CONSTRUNAVES ... Constructores Navales Espanoles
CONSUCASA ... Constructora de Casas Consucasa Ltda. [*Medellin*] (COL)
CONSULTECA ... Consultora Tecnico Administrativa Ltda. [*Bogota*] (COL)
CONSUMIMPORT ... Empresa Cubana Importadora de Articulos de Consumo General [*Cuban Enterprise for the Import of General Consumer Goods*] (LA)
CONSURCO ... Cooperativa Surcolombiana Ltda. [*Bogota*] (COL)
CONSUSENA ... Consejo Superior de Seguridad Nacional [*National Security Council*] [*Chilean*] (LA)
CONT .... Centralni Odbor Narodne Tehnike [*Central Committee of the People's Technology Society*] (YU)
CONTAG..... Confederacao Nacional dos Trabalhadores na Agricultura [*National Farmworkers Confederation*] [*Brazilian*] (LA)
CONTAP ..... Conselho de Cooperacao Tecnica da Alianca para o Progresso [*Alliance for Progress Technical Cooperation Council*] [*Brazilian*] (LA)
CONTEC ..... Confederacao Nacional dos Trabalhadores nas Empresas de Credito [*National Confederation of Credit Institution Workers*] [*Brazilian*] (LA)
CONTEC ..... Confederacion de Trabajadores Establecimientos Bancarios y Credito [*Confederation of Workers of Banks and Credit Firms*] [*Uruguayan*] (LA)
CONTEF...... Consultoria Tecnica de Assuntos Economicos e Financeiros [*Technical Office for Economic and Financial Affairs*] [*Brazilian*] (LA1)
CONTEL...... Conselho Nacional de Telecomunicacoes [*National Telecommunications Council*] [*Brazilian*] (LA)
CONTINENTAL-SENEGAL ... Continental Oil Company of Senegal (MAR)
CONTRAGUA ... Confederacion de Trabajadores de Guatemala [*Confederation of Guatemalan Workers*] (LA)
CONTRAN... Conselho Nacional Transito [*National Traffic Council*] [*Brazilian*] (LA)
CONTRANAL ... Cooperativa de Transportes Nacionales de Pamplona Ltda. (COL)
CONUAR..... Combustibles Nucleares Argentinos, SA [*Argentine Nuclear Fuel Corporation, Inc.*] (LA1)
CONUB .... Conferencia de la Universidad Boliviana [*Conference of the Bolivian University*]
CONUP........ Consejo Nacional de la Universidad Peruana [*National Council of Peruvian Universities*] (LA)
CONUPIA .... Confederacion Nacional Unica de la Pequena Industria y el Artesanado [*National Single Confederation of Small Industry and Crafts*] [*Chilean*] (LA)
CONUPRO ... Consejo Nacional Provisorio de Universidades [*National Provisional Council of Universities*] [*Venezuelan*] (LA)
CONURBANAS ... Compania Colombiana de Construcciones Urbanas SA [*Cali*] (COL)
CONUTEC... Consultores Uruguayos en Tecnologia Avanzada [*Uruguayan Advanced Technology Consultants*] (LA)
conv .... Converti [*Converted*] [*French*]
conv .... Convex [*Convex*] (HU)
convte......... Conveniente [*Convenient*] [*Spanish*]
COOCHOTAS ... Empresa de Transporte de la Cooperativa de Taxis del Atlantico [*Barranquilla*] (COL)
COOD.......... Centralny Osrodek Oswiaty Doroslych [*Adult Education Center*] (POL)
COOEMSAVAL ... Cooperativa de Ahorro y Credito de Empleado de Salud del Valle [*Cali*] (COL)
COOFAVA... Cooperativa Quimica Farmaceutica del Valle del Cauca [*Cali*] (COL)
COOGRANCOL ... Cooperativa Grancolombiana de Credito Ltda. [*Bogota*] (COL)
COOHACREDITO ... Cooperativa de Habitaciones y Credito Ltda. [*Bogota*] (COL)
COOMEVA ... Cooperativa de Ahorro y Credito Medico del Valle [*Cali*] (COL)
COOMPOR ... Cooperativa de Mao-de-Obra do Pessoal de Trafego Portuario [*Port Traffic Employees Labor Cooperative*] [*Portuguese*] (WER)
COONORTE ... Cooperativa Nortena de Transportes [*Medellin*] (COL)
COOP.......... Comite de Organizaciones Populares [*Committee for Popular Organizations*] [*Peruvian*] (LA)
COOP.......... Cooperativa, Preduzece za Uvoz i Izvoz Poljoprivrednih Proizvoda i Stocne Hrane [*Cooperative for Import and Export of Agricultural Products and Fodder*] (YU)
COOPAHA ... Cooperative Agricole de Houin-Agame (MAR)

COOPANCOL ... Cooperativa de Panificadores de Colombia [*Bogota*] (COL)
COOPANKAM ... Cooperative Agricole des Planteurs du Nkam (MAR)
COOPEINDUMA ... Cooperativa de Trabajadores de la Industria de la Madera Ltda. [*Cali*] (COL)
COOPEMAD ... Cooperatives de Moudjahidine et Ayants-Droit (MAR)
COOPENAL ... Cooperativa Nacional de Creditos y Servicios Especiales Ltda. [*Cali*] (COL)
COOPENORTE ... Cooperativa de Transportes del Norte de Santander [*Cucuta*] (COL)
COOPERADIAL ... Cooperativa Radial Colombiana Ltda. [*Bogota*] (COL)
COOPERMAROC ... Societe Marocaine de Cooperation Pharmaceutique (MAR)
COOPERTOLCA ... Cooperativa de Transportadores y Transportes del Norte del Tolima y Oriente de Caldas Ltda. (COL)
COOPESA... Cooperative de la Solidarite Africaine (MAR)
COOPETRA ... Cooperative de Travaux Publics et Particuliers du Cameroun (MAR)
COOPETRABAN ... Cooperativa de Trabajadores de Antioquia Ltda. [*Medellin*] (COL)
COOPHARMA ... Cooperation Pharmaceutique Khmere [*Cambodian Pharmaceutical Cooperative*] (CL)
COOPI......... Cooperative Ouvriere Publication Impression [*Tunisian*] (MAR)
COOPILLANTAS ... Cooperativa de Trabajadores de Icollantas [*Bogota*] (COL)
CO-OPPLABAM ... Cooperative des Planteurs Bamilike (MAR)
COOPTRANSCART ... Cooperativa Especializada de Transportes de Carga [*Bogota*] (COL)
COORBUQUIN ... Cooperativa de Buses Urbanos del Quindio Ltda. [*Armenian*] (COL)
COORCOM ... Comite de Coordination des Hauts Fonctionnaires des Pays du Sud-Est Asiatique sur les Transports et Communications [*Southeast Asian High-Level Government Employees Coordination Committee on Transportation and Communication*] [*Use COORDCOM*] (CL)
COORDCOM ... Comite de Coordination des Hauts Fonctionnaires des Pays du Sud-Est Asiatique sur les Transports et Communications [*Southeast Asian High-Level Government Employees Coordination Committee on Transportation and Communication*] (CL)
COOTRAINGASCOL ... Cooperativa de Ahorro y Credito de Trabajadores de la Industria Gaseosa de Colombia [*Cali*] (COL)
COOTRANSAL ... Cooperativa de Transportadores de Saldana Ltda. (COL)
COOTRANSHUILA ... Cooperativa de Transportes de Huila [*Neiva*] (COL)
COOTRANSO ... Cooperativa de Transportadores de Soacha [*Bogota*] (COL)
COOTRANSPAL ... Cooperativa Integral de Transportadores Palmeras Ltda. [*Palmira*] (COL)
COOTRANSUCOL ... Cooperativa de Transportadores Unidos de Colombia Ltda. [*Cali*] (COL)
COOTRAVAL ... Cooperativa de Trabajadores del Valle Ltda. [*Cali*] (COL)
COP............ Central Optique Photo (MAR)
COP............ Centralny Okreg Przemyslowy [*Central Industrial District*] (POL)
COP............ Centre d'Orientation Pratique [*Practical Work Orientation Center*] [*Malian*] (AF)
COP............ Comite Olimpico Peruano [*Peruvian Olympics Committee*] (LA)
COP............ Commissie Ontwikkelings-Plan [*NOBIN*]
COP............ Commissie Opvoering Produktiviteit [*SER*] [*Dutch*]
COP............ Companias de Orden Publico [*Public Order Companies*] [*Panamanian*] (LA)
COPAC .... Committee for the Promotion of Aid to Cooperatives (EA)
COPACE ..... Comite des Peches pour l'Atlantique Centre-Est [*North African*] (MAR)
COPACI ...... Cooperative des Planteurs d'Ananas de la Cote-d'Ivoire (MAR)
COPACO..... Comision de Pesca para el Atlantico Centro Occidental [*West Central Atlantic Fisheries Commission*] [*Use WECAFC*] (LA)
COPAL........ Agencia Comercial de Porto Amelia (MAR)
COPAL........ Cocoa Producers Alliance (AF)
COPAL........ Comision de Industrias de Productos Alimenticios, de Bebidas, y Afines [*Commission of Foods, Drinks, and Related Products*] [*Argentine*] (LA1)
COPAM....... Companhia Portuguesa de Amidos [*Portuguese Amide Company*] (WER)
COPAN........ Consejo por la Paz y Amistad con Nicaragua [*Council for Peace and Friendship with Nicaragua*] [*Honduran*] (LA1)
COPANT ..... Comision Panamericana de Normas Tecnicas [*Pan American Standards Commission - PASC*] (EA)
COPAP........ Commission Permanente de l'Administration Publique [*Permanent Public Administration Commission*] [*Zairian*] (AF)
COPAR........ Comite Parisien des Oeuvres Scolaires et Universitaires [*Parisian Committee for Assistance to Universities and Schools*] (WER)
COPAREX... Compagnies de Participations, de Recherches, et d'Exploitations Petrolieres [*Petroleum Investments, Research, and Exploitation Company*] [*Algerian*] (AF)
COPARMEX ... Confederacion Patronal de la Republica Mexicana [*Employers Confederation of the Mexican Republic*] (LA)
COPASCO ... Confecciones de Papel Shellmar de Colombia SA [*Bogota*] (COL)
COPASOPRI ... Comite Panameno de Solidaridad con Puerto Rico [*Panamanian Committee of Solidarity with Puerto Rico*] (LA)
COPAT........ Comite pro Autodeterminacion Tecnologica [*Committee for Technological Self-Determination*] [*Venezuelan*] (LA)
COPATRA... Cooperativa Antioquena de Transportadores Ltda. (COL)
COPAVIO.... Cooperativa de Agentes Viajeros [*Cali*] (COL)
COPCIA ...... Centrul de Organizare Calcul, si Perfectionare a Cadrelor pentru Industria Alimentara [*Center for the Computer Organization and Advanced Training of Cadres for the Food Industry*] (RO)
COPCON..... Comando de Operacoes do Continente [*Continental Operations Command*] [*Portuguese*] (WER)
COPE .... Compagnie Orientale des Petrole d'Egypte [*Egyptian-Italian Oil Company*]
COPEBUSES ... Cooperativa de Transportes Medellin-Bello Ltda. (COL)
COPEC........ Compania de Petroleos de Chile [*Chilean Oil Company*] (LA)
COPECI....... Conserveries et Pecheries de la Cote-d'Ivoire (MAR)
COPECODECA ... Comision Permanente del Consejo de Defensa Centroamericano [*Permanent Commission of the Central American Defense Council*] (LA)
COPECOL... Cooperativa Colombiana de Transportes [*Bogota*] (COL)
COPEDESMEL ... Comision Permanente de Planeamiento del Desarrollo de los Metales Livianos [*Permanent Commission for Planning the Development of Light Metals*] [*Argentine*] (LA)
COPEFA...... Compagnie des Petroles France-Afrique [*France-Africa Petroleum Company*] [*Algerian*] (AF)
COPEFA...... Consejo Permanente de la Fuerza Armada [*Permanent Council of the Armed Forces*] [*Salvadoran*] (LA1)
COPEG........ Companhia Progresso do Estado da Guanabara [*Guanabara State Progress Company*] [*Brazilian*] (LA)
COPEGAN... Cooperativa de Transportadores de Ganado [*Villavicencio-Bogota*] (COL)
COPEI .... Comite de Organizacion Politica Electoral Independiente [*Committee of Independent Political Electoral Organization*] [*Use Social Christian Party*] [*Venezuelan*] (LA)
COPEL .... Spanish Prisoners' Trade Union (PD)
COPEMA..... Compagnie Eburneenne des Peches Maritimes (MAR)
COPEMACO ... Corporacion Civil de Medianos y Pequenos Agricultores de Colombia [*Bogota*] (COL)
COPEMAR ... Cooperative des Pecheurs Maritimes [*Maritime Fishermen's Cooperative*] [*Cambodian*] (CL)
COPEMH..... Colegio de Profesores de Educacion Media de Honduras [*Professional Association of High School Teachers of Honduras*] (LA)
COPEN........ Comite Permanente de Emergencia Nacional [*Permanent National Emergency Committee*] [*Honduran*] (LA)
COPENAL ... Cooperativa Nacional de Choferes [*Bogota*] (COL)
COPERSUCAR ... Cooperativa dos Produtores de Acucar e do Alcool do Estado de Sao Paulo [*Sao Paulo Cooperative of Sugar and Alcohol Producers*] [*Brazilian*] (LA)
COPESA ..... Consorcio Periodistico de Chile, SA [*Chilean Newsmen's Association, Inc.*] (LA)
COPESA ..... Corporacion Pesquera Ecuatoriana [*Ecuadorean Fishing Corporation*] (LA)
COPESCA... Proyecto Integrado de Turismo [*Integrated Tourism Project*] [*Peruvian*] (LA)
COPESVAL ... Compania Pesquera del Valle [*Cali*] (COL)
COPETAO... Compagnie des Petroles Total Afrique Ouest (MAR)
COPETRAN ... Cooperativa Santandereana de Transportes Ltda. [*Cali*] (COL)
COPIA .... Centrala Obslugi Przedsiebiorstw i Instytucji Artystycznych [*Center of Services to Art Enterprises and Agencies*] (POL)
COPIME ...... Cooperativa de Pequenos Industriales Metalarios [*Bogota*] (COL)
COPIMETAL ... Cooperativa de Industrias Metalurgicas del Valle [*Cali*] (COL)
COPITEX..... Compania Distribuidora Textil Ltda. [*Cali*] (COL)
COPIZ .... Conseil Permanent de l'Informatique au Zaire [*Permanent Data Processing Council in Zaire*] (AF)
COPLAMAR ... Coordinacion General del Plan Nacional de Zonas Deprimidas y Grupos Marginados [*General Coordinating Board of the National Plan for Depressed Areas and Marginal Groups*] [*Mexican*] (LA1)
COPLAN ..... Comissao de Planejamento Nacional [*National Planning Commission*] [*Brazilian*] (LA)
COPLANAR ... Construccion, Planificacion, Arquitectura [*Medellin*] (COL)
COPLANARH ... Comision del Plan Nacional de Aprovechamiento de los Recursos Hidraulicos [*Commission for the National Plan of Water Resources Development*] [*Venezuelan*] (LA)
COPLASTIC ... Compagnie Generale Industrielle de Plastiques [*Moroccan*] (MAR)
COPNEU ..... Compagnie Industrielle et Commerciale du Pneumatique (MAR)
COPO .... Centralny Osrodek Przygotowan Olimpijskich [*Olympic Games Arrangements Center*] [*Polish*]
COPORTCHAD ... Cooperative des Transporteurs Tchadiens (MAR)
COPPAL...... Conferencia Permanente de Partidos Politicos de America Latina [*Permanent Conference of Latin American Political Parties*] (LA1)

COPPE........ Coordenacao dos Programas de Pos-Graduacao em Engenharia [*Coordination of Postgraduate Programs in Engineering*] [*Brazilian*] (LA)

COPR.......... Centre for Overseas Pest Research (MAR)

COPRA........ Comision Permanente para la Racionalizacion Administrativa [*Permanent Commission for Administrative Efficiency*] [*Argentine*] (LA)

COPRACAM ... Societe Industrielle du Coprah Camerounais (MAR)

COPRAF...... Compagnie des Produits d'Afrique (MAR)

COPREFA ... Comite de Prensa de las Fuerzas Armadas [*Press Committee of the Armed Forces*] [*Salvadoran*] (LA1)

COPRO........ Societe Nationale de Commerce et de Production (MAR)

COPROA..... Comptoir des Produits Africains (MAR)

COPROARTE ... Cooperativa Nacional de Profesiones, Artes, Oficios, e Industrias Ltda. [*Bogota*] (COL)

COPROBIC ... Comite National pour la Protection des Biens Culturels en Cas de Conflit Arme [*National Committee for the Protection of Cultural Property in Case of Armed Conflict*] [*Cambodian*] (CL)

COPROCI.... Compagnie des Produits de la Cote-d'Ivoire (MAR)

COPRODUITS ... Groupement Cooperatif de Ventes Internationales des Produits de Haute (MAR)

COPROMA ... Compagnie des Produits du Mali (MAR)

COPRON..... Comissao de Coordenacao da Protecao ao Programa Nuclear Brasileiro [*Coordinating Commission for Protecting the Brazilian Nuclear Program*] (LA1)

COPRONA ... Compania Productora Nacional de Aceites [*National Production Company of Edible Oils*] [*Chilean*] (LA)

COPRO-Niger ... Societe Nationale de Commerce et de Production du Niger [*National Trade and Production Company of Niger*] (AF)

COPRORIBU ... Cooperative des Producteurs du Riz au Burundi (MAR)

COPSA........ Compania Oleaginosa del Peru SA [*State Vegetable Oil Company of Peru, Inc.*] (LA)

COPVIDU.... Conferencia Permanente Centroamericana de Vivienda y Desarrollo Urbano [*Permanent Conference on Central American Housing and Urban Development*] (LA1)

COPWE....... Commission for Organizing the Party of the Working People of Ethiopia (PD)

COPYME..... Corporacion de la Pequena y la Mediana Empresa [*Small and Medium Enterprise Corporation*] [*Argentine*] (LA)

COR............ Calabar-Ogoja-Rivers (MAR)

COR............ Comite de Organizaciones Revolucionarias [*Committee of Revolutionary Organizations*] [*Peruvian*] (LA)

COR............ Confederacion Obrera Revolucionaria [*Revolutionary Labor Confederation*] [*Mexican*] (LA1)

COR............ Corona [*London*] [*A publication*] (MAR)

COR............ Departamento de Orientacion Revolucionaria [*Revolutionary Orientation Department*] [*See DOR*] [*Cuban*] (LA)

CORA.......... Cooperatives de Reforme Agraire [*Agrarian Reform Cooperatives*] [*Algerian*] (AF)

CORA.......... Corporacion de Reforma Agraria [*Agrarian Reform Corporation*] [*Chilean*] (LA)

CORACREVI ... Corporacion de Ahorro y Credito para la Vivienda [*Housing Savings and Loan Corporation*] [*Venezuelan*] (LA)

CORAD .... Construtora Radio Electrica Lda. (MAR)

CORADEP... Corporacion de Radiodifusion del Pueblo [*People's Radio Broadcasting Corporation*] [*Nicaraguan*] (LA1)

CORAL........ Colombian Oil Refiners Additives Ltda. [*Bogota*] (COL)

CORAL........ Consorcio Geral de Comercio Lda. (MAR)

CORAL........ Corporacion Algodonera del Litoral [*Cotton Corporation of the Coast*] [*Colombian*] (LA)

CORAM....... Colles et Resines Adhesives du Midi [*French*]

CORAUTO... Corporacion Automotora Ltda. [*Bogota*] (COL)

CORCOP..... Corporacion Comercial del Pueblo [*People's Commercial Corporation*] [*Nicaraguan*] (LA1)

CORDAC..... Corporation Radiodiffusion de l'Afrique Centrale (MAR)

CORDE........ Corporacion de Empresas Estatales [*Dominican Corporation of State Enterprises*] [*Dominican Republic*] (LA)

CORDECO ... Corporacion de Desarrollo de Cochabamba [*Development Corporation of Cochabamba*] [*Bolivian*] (LA)

CORDECRUZ ... Corporacion Regional de Desarrollo de Santa Cruz [*Bolivian*]

CORDENTAL ... Corporacion Dental Ltda. [*Bogota*] (COL)

CORDEPAZ ... Corporacion de Desarrollo de La Paz [*La Paz Development Corporation*] [*Bolivian*] (LA)

CORDINA.... Coordinadora Industrial [*Bogota*] (COL)

CORDIPLAN ... Oficina de Coordinacion y Planificacion [*Office of Coordination and Planning*] [*Venezuelan*] (LA)

CORDIVENTAS ... Coordinadora de Ventas Ltda. [*Cali*] (COL)

CORE .... Centre for Operation Research and Econometrics (MAR)

CORE .... Committee on Racial Equality (MAR)

CORE .... Confederation of Rhodesian Employers (MAR)

CORE .... Congress of Racial Equality (MAR)

CORE .... CSIR Committee on Research Expenditure (MAR)

COREB........ Conference des Ordinaires du Rwanda et du Burundi (MAR)

CORECA..... Comite pour la Reunification du Camaroon [*Committee for the Reunification of the Cameroons*]

COREDIF .... Compagnie de Realisations d'Usines de Diffusion Gazeuse [*Gaseous Diffusion-Factory Construction Company*] [*French*] (WER)

COREDIF .... Compagnie de Recherche et d'Etude sur la Diffusion Gazeuse [*Gaseous Diffusion Research Company*] [*French*] (WER)

COREDO..... Commercants Reunis de Diedieng (MAR)

COREG........ Compagnie de Recherches Geophysiques [*North African*] (MAR)

COREGA..... Constructions et Realisations au Gabon (MAR)

CORELCA... Corporacion Electrica de la Costa Atlantica [*Electric Corporation of the Atlantic Coast*] [*Colombian*] (LA)

COREM .... Compagnie Rwandaise d'Exploitation Miniere (MAR)

COREMA..... Corporacion de Repuestos y Maquinaria Ltda. [*Bogota*] (COL)

COREMO .... Comite Revolutionnaire du Mocambique [*Mozambique Revolutionary Committee*] (AF)

COREN........ Combustibili per Reattori Nucleari [*A nuclear power company*] [*Italian*]

COREN........ Council of Registered Engineers of Nigeria (MAR)

CORES........ Coal Ore Reserves Evaluation System (MAR)

CORESTA... Centre de Cooperation pour les Recherches Scientifiques Relatives au Tabac [*Cooperation Center for Scientific Research Relative to Tobacco*] [*French*]

COREZI....... Comite pour la Renovation de la Ville de Ziguinchor (MAR)

CORFACO .. Comptoir Franco-Comorien (MAR)

CORFIN....... Corporacion Financiera de Nicaragua [*Nicaraguan Financial Corporation*] (LA1)

CORFINA .... Corporacion Financiera Nacional [*National Financial Corporation*] [*Guatemalan*] (LA)

CORFINANSA ... Corporacion Financiera de Santander [*Bucaramanga*] (COL)

CORFO........ Corporacion de Fomento de la Produccion [*Production Development Corporation*] [*Chilean*] (LA)

CORFODEC ... Corporacion de Fomento del Centro [*Central Development Corporation*] [*Ecuadorean*] (LA)

CORFONOR ... Corporacion de Fomento del Norte [*Northern Development Corporation*] [*Ecuadorean*] (LA)

CORFOP ..... Corporacion Forestal del Pueblo [*People's Forestry Corporation*] [*Nicaraguan*] (LA1)

CORFUCI .... Cooperative Agricole de Production Bananiere et Fruitiere de Cote-d'Ivoire (MAR)

CORHABIT ... Corporacion de Servicios Habitacionales [*Housing Services Corporation*] [*Chilean*] (LA)

CORI........... Compagnia Ricerche Idrocarburi [*or Idrocarburanti*] (MAR)

CORICAFRIC ... Comptoir de Representation Industrielle et Commerciale en Afrique (MAR)

CORINA-CARACAS ... Corredores Internacionales Asociados Caracas, CA [*Venezuelan*]

CORINCA.... Corporacion Industrial Centroamericana, SA [*Industrial Corporation of Central America*] [*Salvadoran*]

CORMA .... Corporacion Chilena de Madera [*Chilean Lumber Corporation*] (LA)

CORMU .... Corporacion de Mejoramiento Urbano [*Urban Renewal Corporation*] [*Chilean*] (LA)

CORNICAL ... Corporacion Nacional de Industriales del Calzado [*Bogota*] (COL)

COROI......... Comptoir de Commerce et de Representation pour l'Ocean Indien [*Bank of Commerce and Representation for the Indian Ocean*] [*Malagasy*] (AF)

CORPA........ Corporacion Publicitaria Nacional [*Venezuelan*]

CORPAC ..... Corporacion de Aeropuertos y Aviacion Comercial [*Airports and Commercial Aviation Corporation*] [*Peruvian*] (LA)

CORPACERO ... Corporacion del Acero [*Bogota*] (COL)

CORPAL...... Corporacion Proveedora de Instituciones de Asistencia Social [*Bogota*] (COL)

CORPE........ Comite de la Revolucion Peruana [*Committee of the Peruvian Revolution*] (LA)

CORPECOM ... Corporacion Colombiana de Pequenos Comerciantes [*Colombian Small Businessmen's Association*] (LA)

CORPESCA ... Corporacion de Pesca [*Fishing Corporation*] [*Chilean*] (LA)

CORPOANDES ... Corporacion de los Andes [*Andes Corporation*] [*Venezuelan*] (LA)

CORPOBUSES ... Corporacion de Buses Urbanos del Departamento del Valle [*Cali*] (COL)

CORPO-INDUSTRIA ... Corporacion para el Desarrollo de la Pequena y Mediana Industria [*Venezuelan*]

CORPO-TURISMO ... Corporacion de Turismo de Venezuela

CORPOVEN ... [*A*] Subsidiary of PETROVEN (LA)

CORPOZULIA ... Corporacion de Desarrollo de la Region del Zulia

CORPRAGRO ... Corporacion Agricola del Valle del Cauca [*Cali*] (COL)

CORPROCOM ... Cooperativa de Produccion y Consumo de Cali Ltda. (COL)

CORPUNO ... Corporacion de Fomento y Desarrollo de Puno [*Puno Promotion and Development Corporation*] [*Peruvian*] (LA)

corr .... Corrigiert [*Corrected*] [*German*]

corrte.......... Corriente [*Current*] [*Spanish*]

CORSM .... Calabar-Ogoja-Rivers State Movement (MAR)

CORTURISMO ... Corporacion Nacional de Turismo [*National Tourism Corporation*] [*Colombian*] (LA)

CORU .... Consejo de Organizaciones Revolucionarias Unidas [*Council of United Revolutionary Organizations*] [*Exiles*] [*Cuban*] (LA)

CORVI .... Corporacion de la Vivienda [*Housing Corporation*] [*Chilean*] (LA)

COS............ Ceska Obec Strelecka [*Czech Rifleman Organization*] (CZ)

COS............ Ceskoslovenska Obec Sokolska [*Czechoslovak Sokol (An athletic and gymnastic organization)*] (CZ)

COS............ Ceskoslovenska Obilni Spolecnost [*Czechoslovak Grain Company*] (CZ)
COS............ Comite de Coordination Speciale [*Special Coordination Committee*] [*Cambodian*] (CL)
COS............ Coordinadora de Organizaciones Sindicales [*Coordinating Body of Trade Union Organizations*] [*Spanish*] (WER)
Cos.............. Kosinus [*Cosine*] [*German*]
COSA.......... Christian Brothers Council on the Overseas Apostolate (MAR)
COSA.......... Conseils Olympiques et Sportifs d'Arrondissement (MAR)
COSAGRA ... Compania Santandereana de Grasas Ltda. [*Bucaramanga*] (COL)
COSANDI.... Compania Santandereana de Importaciones Ltda. [*Bucaramanga*] (COL)
COSAS........ Congress of South African Students (MAR)
COSATA..... Cooperative Supply Association of Tanzania (MAR)
COSBERG... Compagnie Shell de Recherche et d'Exploitation au Gabon (MAR)
COSC.......... Cambridge Overseas School Certificate (MAR)
COSC.......... Club Olympique et Sportif des Cooperants (MAR)
COSC.......... Commandement Operationnel Sud-Casamance [*Southern Casamance Operational Command*] [*Senegalese*] (AF)
COSCV .... Comissao Organizadora dos Sindicatos Caboverdianos [*Commission to Establish Cape Verdian Trade Unions*] (AF)
COSDEGUA ... Confederacion de Sacerdotes Diocesanos de Guatemala [*Confederation of Guatemalan Diocesan Priests*] (LA)
COSDO .... Consejo Sindical de Obreros [*Trades Union Council of Workers*] [*Salvadoran*] (LA1)
COSEAB ..... Compagnie Senegalaise d'Exploitation d'Arachides de Bouche (MAR)
COSEC........ Companhia de Seguro e Creditos [*Credit Insurance Company*] [*Portuguese*] (WER)
COSECA..... Compagnie Senegalaise de Construction Automobile (MAR)
COSEH........ Comite de Secours aux Hopitaux [*Hospital Aid Committee*] [*Cambodian*] (CL)
COSEM .... Cooperative de Semence de Tunisie [*Tunisian Seed Cooperative*] (AF)
COSEMA..... Comptoirs des Secheries de Mauritanie (MAR)
COSENA..... Compagnie Senegalaise de Navigation (MAR)
COSENA..... Consejo de Seguridad Nacional [*National Security Council*] [*Uruguayan*] (LA)
COSENAM ... Compagnie Senegalaise de Navigation Maritime (MAR)
COSENEGALAIS ... Commerce Senegalais (MAR)
COSEP........ Consejo Superior de la Empresa Privada [*Higher Council of Private Enterprise*] [*Nicaraguan*] (LA)
COSERCOL ... Corporacion de Servicios Colectivos Ltda. [*Cali*] (COL)
COSERU ..... Comite Secreto da Restauracao da Udenamo (MAR)
COSETAM ... Compagnie Senegalaise pour Tous Appareillages Mecaniques (MAR)
COSG.......... Centralni Odbor Sindikata Graficara [*Central Committee of the Trade-Union of Workers in the Graphic Trades*] (YU)
COSICA ...... Comptoir Senegalais de l'Industrie des Conserves Alimentaires (MAR)
COSIGUA.... Companhia Siderurgica da Guanabara [*Guanabara Iron and Steel Company*] [*Brazilian*] (LA)
COSIMEX.... Compagnie Senegalaise d'Importation et d'Exportation (MAR)
COSIPA....... Companhia Siderurgica Paulista [*Sao Paulo Iron and Steel Company*] [*Brazilian*] (LA)
COSLITAM ... Confederation des Syndicats Libres des Travailleurs de Madagascar [*Confederation of Malagasy Workers Free Labor Unions*] (AF)
COSMIVOIRE ... Omnium Chimique et Cosmetique (MAR)
COSMOGRAFICAS ... Cooperativa Integral de Artes Graficas Cosmos Ltda. [*Cali*] (COL)
COSO.......... Central Obrera Sindical de Occidente [*Trade Union Workers Central Organization of the West*] [*Salvadoran*] (LA1)
COSOB .... Comite de Organizacion Socialista Obrera de Bogota [*Socialist Workers Organization Committee of Bogota*] [*Colombian*] (LA)
COSOMA .... Comite de Solidarite de Madagascar [*Solidarity Committee of Madagascar*] (AF)
COSONAV ... Cooperativa de Suboficiales Navales Ltda. [*Bogota*] (COL)
COSOUP..... Cooperative Sfaxienne Ouvriere de Production [*Sfax Worker Production Cooperative*] [*Tunisian*] (AF)
COSPAR ..... Committee on Space Research [*Under ICSU*] (SJT)
COSPE........ Comite Peruano de Solidaridad con los Patriotas Espanoles [*Peruvian Committee of Solidarity with Spanish Patriots*] (LA)
COSP PZPR ... Centralny Osrodek Szkolenia Partyjnego Polskiej Zjednoczonej Partii Robotniczej [*Central Institute for Party Training of the Polish United Workers Party*] (POL)
COSREG ..... Compagnie Shell de Recherche et d'Exploration au Gabon (MAR)
COSS .... Centralny Osrodek Szkolenia Sportowego [*Central Institute of Sport Training*] (POL)
COSS .... Ceskoslovensky Odborny Spolek Slevarensky [*Czechoslovak Foundry Specialists Association*] (CZ)
COSS .... Committee to Organize Support for a Settlement (MAR)
COSSH........ Centralni Odbor Saveza Sindikata Hrvatske [*Central Committee of the Council of Trade-Unions of Croatia*] (YU)
COSSJ .... Centralni Odbor Saveza Sindikata Jugoslavije [*Central Committee of the Council of Trade-Unions of Yugoslavia*] (YU)
COSSMIL.... Corporacion del Seguro Social Militar [*Corporation for Military Social Security*] [*Bolivian*] (LA1)
COST .... Cooperation Europeenne Scientifique et Technique [*EEG*] [*Belgian*]
COSTED ..... Committee on Science and Technology in Developing Countries (MAR)
COSU .... Coordination de l'Opposition Senegalaise Unie [*Coordination of the United Senegalese Opposition*] (AF)
COSU .... Correspondence and Open Studies Unit (MAR)
COSUF........ Conseil des Organisations Syndicales de l'Union Francaise [*Council of Labor Unions of the French Union*] (MAR)
COSUFFAA ... Consejo Superior de las Fuerzas Armadas [*Senior Council of the Armed Forces*] [*Honduran*] (LA1)
COSUKO..... Compagnie Sucriere de Koumassi (MAR)
COSUMA .... Compagnie Sucriere Marocaine (MAR)
COSUMAR ... Compagnie Sucriere Marocaine et de Raffinage (MAR)
COSUPEBAN ... Consejo Superior de Estudiantes de Bachillerato Nocturno [*Bogota*] (COL)
COSUPENSA ... Consejo Superior de Seguridad Nacional [*Superior Council for National Security*] [*Chilean*] (LA)
COSUR........ Cooperative de Surveillance des Produits Exportes [*Export Products Supervisory Cooperative*] [*Cambodian*] (CL)
COSVN........ Central Office for South Vietnam (CL)
COSYGA..... Confederation Syndicale Gabonaise [*Gabonese Trade Union Confederation*] (AF)
COSZ .... Centralny Osrodek Szkolenia Zadowowego [*Chief Vocational Training Center*] (POL)
COT............. Central Obrera Tucumana [*Tucuman Workers Union*] [*Argentine*] (LA)
COT............. Ceskoslovenska Obec Turisticka [*Czechoslovak Tourist Association*] (CZ)
COT............. Club Olympique des Transports [*Tunisian*] (MAR)
COT............. Compagnie Oubangui Transports (MAR)
COT............. Congreso Obrero Textil [*Congress of Textile Workers*] [*Uruguayan*] (LA)
COTAL .... Confederacion de Organizaciones Turisticas de la America Latina [*Confederation of Latin American Tourist Organizations*] (LA)
COTAL .... Confederation des Organisations Touristiques d'Amerique Latine [*Moroccan*] (MAR)
COTAM .... Commandement du Transport Aerien Militaire (MAR)
COTEBU ..... Complexe Textile de Bujumbura (MAR)
COTEC........ Centre de Cooperation Technique (MAR)
COTEF .... Complexe Textile de Fes [*Moroccan*] (MAR)
COTEF .... Consultoria Tecnica de Assuntos Economicos e Financeiros [*Technical Office for Economic and Financial Affairs*] [*Brazilian*] (LA)
COTELCO... Corporacion Hotelera de Colombia [*Colombian Hotels Corporation*] (LA)
COTEMA..... Compagnie Technique Mauritanienne (MAR)
COTEQ........ Comptoir Tunisien d'Equipement Industriel [*Tunisian*] (MAR)
COTEVO ..... Compagnie de Textiles de la Volta (MAR)
COTIMIP ..... Comite Technique Interministerial pour l'Industrie Miniere et Petroliere [*Interministerial Technical Committee for the Mining and Petroleum Industry*] [*Niger*] (AF)
COTIV .... Compagnie de Transports Ivoiriens (MAR)
COTIVO....... La Cotonniere Ivoirienne (MAR)
CO/TNO...... Centrale Organisatie [*Toegepast Natuurwetenschappelijk Onderzoek*] [*Dutch*]
COTOA .... Compagnie Textile de l'Ouest Africain (MAR)
COTODICACS ... Compagnie Togolaise de Diffusion le Coprah Dacomsons (MAR)
COTOMET ... Compagnie Togolaise des Metaux (MAR)
COTOMIB ... Compagnie Togolaise des Mines du Benin (MAR)
COTONA..... Cotonniere d'Antsirabe [*Antsirabe Cotton Industry*] [*Malagasy*] (AF)
COTONAF... Societe Francaise des Cotons Africains (MAR)
COTONANG ... Companhia Geral dos Algodoes de Angola (MAR)
COTONCO ... Compagnie Cotonniere Congolaise (MAR)
COTONFRAN ... Societe Cotonniere Franco-Tchadienne (MAR)
COTONTCHAD ... Societe Cotonniere du Tchad (MAR)
COTOUBANGUI ... Societe Cotonniere du Haut-Oubangui (MAR)
COTOUNA ... Compagnie Cotonniere de l'Ouhame-Nana (MAR)
COTRA........ Compagnie des Transports [*Transport Company*] [*Guinean*] (AF)
COTRABOIS ... Compagnie de Transports de Bois (MAR)
COTRACAIME ... Cooperativa de Transportes de Cajamarca y Amaime Ltda. [*Cajamarca-Tolima*] (COL)
COTRACOLDA ... Cooperativa de Transportadores de Colombia Ltda. [*Bogota*] (COL)
COTRAGAB ... Compagnie des Traverses Gabonaises [*Gabonese Railroad Tie Company*] (AF)
COTRANAL ... Cooperativa de Transportes Nacionales [*Cucuta*] (COL)
COTRANS... Cooperativa Auto-Transporte Ltda. [*Malaga-Santander*] (COL)
COTRASANA ... Cooperativa de Transportes de San Antonio Ltda. [*Bogota*] (COL)
COTRATLANTICO ... Cooperativa Transportadora del Atlantico Ltda. [*Barranquilla*] (COL)

COTRAULTOL ... Transportes del Servicio Urbano del Tolima Ltda. [*Ibague*] (COL)
COTRAVAUX ... Association de Cogestion pour le Travail Volontaire des Jeunes (MAR)
COTRICO .... Societe Camerounaise de Tricotage et de Confection Industrielle (MAR)
COTSOM .... Compagnie de Travaux Sous-Marins du Cameroun (MAR)
COTT .... Central Organisation for Trade Testing (MAR)
COTTIA .... Complexe Telegraphique et Telex International Automatique d'Abidjan (MAR)
COTU .... Central Organization of Trade Unions [*Kenyan*] (AF)
COTUK .... Central Organization of Trade Unions [*Kenyan*] (MAR)
COTUSAL ... Compagnie Generale des Salines de Tunisie [*Tunisian*] (MAR)
COU .... Centrala Odpadkow Uzytkowych [*Usable Waste Materials Center*] (POL)
COU .... Comites Obreros Unitarios [*Unitary Workers Committees*] [*Spanish*] (WER)
COU .... Corporation de Obras Urbanas [*Urban Works Corporation*] [*Chilean*] (LA)
COU .... Curso de Orientacion Universitaria [*Spanish*]
coup .... Coupon [*French*]
coup arr ...... Coupon Arriere [*French*]
cour .... Courant [*Of the Current Month*] [*French*]
Couvt .... Couvent [*Convent*] [*Military map abbreviation*] [*World War I*] [*French*] (MTD)
COV .... Ceskoslovensky Olympijsky Vybor [*Czechoslovak Olympic Committee*] (CZ)
COVAM .... Centraal Overleg Voorlichting Audio-Visuele Media [*Dutch*]
COVAP .... Comissao do Vale do Paraiba do Sul [*Paraiba do Sul Valley Commission*] [*Brazilian*] (LA)
COVAS .... Cooperatieve Vereniging voor de Afzet van Suikerbieten (MAR)
COVATRANS ... Cooperativa Vallecaucana de Transportadores Ltda. [*Cali*] (COL)
COVE .... Coalition Opposed to Violence and Extremism (MAR)
COVECO ..... Centrale Organisatie van Veeafzeten en Vleesverwerkings-Cooperaties (MAR)
COVEMI ...... Compagnie Voltaique d'Exploitation Miniere (MAR)
COVIAJES ... Corporacion de Viajes [*Bogota*] (COL)
COVICA ...... Compania Colombiana de Vivienda Ltda. [*Bogota*] (COL)
COVIEMCALI ... Cooperativa de Vivienda de Emcali Ltda. [*Cali*] (COL)
COVIM .... Societe des Concentres de Viande de Madagascar (MAR)
COVIMA ...... Compagnie de Commercialisation des Viandes de Mauritanie (MAR)
COVIMER .... Compagnie Vinicole Meridionale (MAR)
COVINA ...... Compagnie Vinicole de l'Ouest Africain (MAR)
COVINCA .... Corporacion Venezolana para el Desarrollo de la Industria Naval [*Venezuelan Corporation for Development of the Shipbuilding Industry*] (LA)
COVINEX .... Societe Congolaise d'Exploitation Vinicole (MAR)
COVINOC .... Compania de Vigilancia Nacional de Credito [*Bogota*] (COL)
COVKS(b) .. Centralni Odbor Vsezvezne Komunisticne Stranke (Boljsevikov) [*Central Committee of the All-Union Communist Party (Bolsheviks)*] (YU)
COVODIAM ... Compagnie Voltaique de Distribution Automobile et de Materiel (MAR)
COVOLCO ... Comptoir Voltaique pour le Commerce (MAR)
COVOLCO ... Cooperativa Santandereana de Volquetas de Colombia [*Bucaramanga*] (COL)
COVOS .... Comite d'Etudes des Consequences des Vols Stratospheriques
COVOTEX ... Comptoir Voltaique des Textiles (MAR)
COW .... Centralny Osrodek Werbunkowy [*Recruiting Center*] (POL)
COW .... Committee of the Whole (MAR)
COWAC ...... Continental West Africa Conference (AF)
COWAD .... Corps Wanita Angkatan Darat [*Women's Army Corps*] (IN)
COZH .... Centrala Obrotu Zwierzetami Hodowlanymi [*Pedigreed Animals Sales Center*] (POL)
COZS .... Ceskoslovensky Ovocnarsky a Zahradkarsky Svaz [*Czechoslovak Fruit and Garden Union*] (CZ)
cp .... Cai Putere [*Horse Power*] (RO)
CP .... Caixa Postal [*Post Office Box*] [*Portuguese*]
CP .... Caja Postale [*Post Office Box*] [*Spanish*]
CP .... Cape Province (MAR)
CP .... Carinski Pregled [*Customs Inspection*] (YU)
CP .... Case Postale [*Post Office Box*] [*French*] (WER)
CP .... Casetta Postale [*Post Office Box*] [*Italian*]
CP .... Centerpartiet [*Center Party*] [*Finnish*] (PPE)
CP .... Centerpartiet [*Center Party*] [*Swedish*] (PPE)
CP .... Centre Party (MAR)
CP .... Ceskoslovenska Posta [*Czechoslovak Postal Service*] (CZ)
cp .... Charte-Partie [*French*]
CP .... Chawangan Penyiasatan [*Investigation Department*] (ML)
cp .... Cislo Popisne [*House Number*] (CZ)
CP .... Commonwealth Party [*Gibraltar*] (PPE)
CP .... Compagnie Portee [*Algerian*] (MAR)
CP .... Companhia dos Caminhos de Ferro Portugueses [*Portuguese Railroad Company*] (WER)
CP .... Confederate Party (MAR)
CP .... Constitutionalist Party [*Maltese*] (PPE)
CP .... Cours Preparatoire (MAR)
CP .... Credits de Paiement (MAR)
CP .... Cumhuriyetci Partisi [*Republican Party*] (TU)
CPA .... Calico Printers Association (MAR)
CPA .... Celula Parlamentaria Aprista [*Aprista Parliamentary Bloc*] [*Peruvian*] (LA)
CPA .... Central Personnel Agency [*Ethiopian*] (AF)
CPA .... Centrala Przemyslu Artystycznego [*Central Office of Art Crafts*] (POL)
CPA .... Centrale Persoons Administratie [*Dutch*]
CPA .... Centre de Perfectionnement dans l'Administration des Affaires (MAR)
CPA .... Cocoa Producers Alliance (MAR)
CPA .... Commissione Pontificia di Assistenza [*Pontifical Commission of Assistance*] [*Italian*] (WER)
CPA .... Commonwealth Parliamentary Association (EA)
CPA .... Commonwealth Pharmaceutical Association (EA)
CPA .... Compagnie de Petrole d'Algerie [*Algerian Petroleum Company*] (AF)
CPA .... Conseil du Peuple Angolais (MAR)
CPA .... Conselho do Povo Angolano [*Angolan People's Council*] (AF)
CPA .... Conselho de Promocoes da Armada [*Navy Promotions Board*] [*Portuguese*] (WER)
CPA .... Consumer Protective Association (MAR)
CPA .... Cooperativa de Produccion Agropecuaria [*Agricultural and Livestock Cooperative*] [*Cuban*] (LA)
CPAC .... Comision Permanente de la Asamblea de Cataluna [*Permanent Commission of the Catalonian Assembly*] [*Spanish*] (WER)
CPAD .... Comite Preparatorio do Accao Directa (MAR)
CPAL .... Comitetul pentru Problemele Administratiei Locale [*Committee for Problems of Local Administration*] (RO)
c par .... Cieplo Parowania [*Heat of Evaporation*] [*Polish*]
CPAS .... Centre Publique d'Aide Sociale [*Public Center for Social Aid*] [*Belgian*] (WER)
CPASL .... Ceskoslovenska Plarba Akciova Spolecnost Labska [*Czechoslovak Elbe River Navigation Joint-Stock Company*] (CZ)
CPB .... Centraal Planbureau
CPB .... Centralni Projektanski Biro [*Central Industrial Design Bureau*] (YU)
CPB .... Circulo de Periodistas de Bogota [*Bogota Press Club*] [*Colombian*] (LA)
CPB .... Comissao Popular de Bairro [*People's Neighborhood Commission*] [*Angolan*] (AF)
CPB .... Cuyos Pies Beso [*Very Respectfully*] [*Formal correspondence*] [*Spanish*]
CPBA .... Caribbean Press and Broadcasting Association (LA1)
CPBCA .... Cooperative des Planteurs Bamoun du Cafe Arabica (MAR)
CPBG .... Compagnie des Placages en Bois Gabonais (MAR)
CPC .... Caisse des Pensions Civiles [*Civilian Pension Fund*] [*Cambodian*] (CL)
CPC .... Centros Populares de Cultura [*People's Cultural Centers*] [*Nicaraguan*] (LA1)
CPC .... Ceskoslovensky Prumysl Cukrovarnicky, Narodni Podnik [*Czechoslovak Sugar Industry, National Enterprise*] (CZ)
CPC .... Christian Peace Conference [*See also CCP*] (EA)
CPC .... Clouterie Pointerie Camerounaise (MAR)
CPC .... Communist Party of China [*Chung-Kuo Kung-Ch'an Tang*] [*Taiwanese*] (PPW)
CPC .... Communist Party of Colombia (PPW)
CPC .... Compagnie des Phosphates du Congo (MAR)
CPC .... Compagnie des Potasses du Congo (MAR)
CPC .... Comptoir Pharmaceutique du Cambodge [*Cambodian Pharmaceutical Warehouse*] (CL)
CPC .... Congolese Protestant Council (MAR)
CPC .... Consejo Provincial de Cultura [*Provincial Council of Culture*] [*Cuban*] (LA)
CPC .... Construcciones y Prefabricados Colombianos [*Bogota*] (COL)
CPC .... Copperbelt Power Company (MAR)
CPCAB .... Cooperative des Planteurs de Cafe Arabica de Bafoussam (MAR)
CPCAN .... Comissao do Plano do Carvao Nacional [*Commission of the National Coal Plan*] [*Brazilian*] (LA)
CPCAT .... Centre de Perfectionnement des Cadres de l'Administration du Travail [*Labor Administration Cadre Retraining Center*] [*Cameroonian*] (AF)
CPCD .... Comissoes Provinciais dos Conselhos de Producao [*Provincial Commissions of the Production Councils*] [*Mozambican*] (AF)
CPCDM .... Centrala de Prelucrarea si Colectarea Deseurilor Metalice [*Central for Processing and Collecting Metallic Waste*] (RO)
CPCDMR ..... Centrala de Prelucrarea si Colectarea Deseurilor Metalice si Refractare [*Central for Processing and Collecting Metallic and Refractory Waste*] (RO)
CPCE .... Comite des Patriotes Cambodgiens d'Europe [*Committee of Cambodian Patriots in Europe*] (CL)
CPCIP .... Commission Permanente de la Convention Internationale des Peches [*Permanent Commission of the International Fisheries Convention*]
CPCL .... Caisse de Prets aux Collectivites Locales (MAR)
CPCM .... Comite Permanent Consultatif du Maghreb [*Maghreb Permanent Consultative Committee*] [*North African*] (AF)
CPCMU .... Central Province Cooperative Marketing Union (MAR)

CPCP .... Comite Preparatoire du Congres Populaire Angolais [*Preparatory Committee for the People's Congress of Angola*] (AF)
CPCPM .... Comisia pentru Controlul Polutiei Mediului [*Commission for Control of Environmental Pollution*] (RO)
CPCS .... Caithness Paperweight Collectors Society (EA)
CPCT .... Caisse de Prets aux Collectivites Territoriales (MAR)
CPD .... Ceskoslovenska Plavba Dunajska [*Czechoslovak Danube River Navigation Lines*] (CZ)
CPD .... Comite de Planification du Developpement (MAR)
CPD .... Convention a Paiement Differe [*Deferred Payment Agreement*] [*French*] (WER)
CPD .... Popular Democratic Coalition [*Ecuadorean*] (PPW)
CPDCET ...... Centre de Perfectionnement pour le Developpement et la Cooperation Economique et Technique [*French*]
CPDT .... Centre de Preparation Documentarie a la Traduction [*French*]
CPE .... Campaign for Promotion of Education [*Grenadian*] (LA1)
CPE .... Center for Popular Education [*Grenadian*] (LA1)
CPE .... Centrally Planned Economy [*Arab*] (MAR)
CPE .... Centre de Protection a l'Enfance [*Children's Protection Center*] [*Cambodian*] (CL)
CPE .... Comite de Politique Economique [*OCDE*]
CPE .... Comite de Prospective et d'Evaluation [*Research and Evaluation Committee*] [*French*] (WER)
CPE .... Committees for Popular Education [*Grenadian*] (LA1)
CPE .... Contribution Personnelle d'Etat [*Tunisian*] (MAR)
CPEM .... Centro de Preparacion de Especialistas Menores [*Junior Specialists Training Center*] [*Cuban*] (LA)
CPEM .... Certificat Preparatoire aux Etudes Medicales [*Medical Studies Preparatory Certificate*] (CL)
CPEMA .... Comite de Prospective et d'Evaluation du Ministere des Armees [*Committee on Forecasting and Evaluation of the Ministry of the Armies*] [*French*] (WER)
CPEMPN ..... Centre Principal d'Expertise Medicale du Personnel Navigant [*Main Center for Medical Expertise for Navigation Personnel*] (WER)
CPEN .... Centro de Preparacion de Especialistas Navales [*Naval Specialists Training Center*] [*Cuban*] (LA)
CPES .... Centre de Preparation aux Enseignements Superieurs (MAR)
CPES .... Centres Preparatoires aux Etudes Superieurs [*North African*] (MAR)
CPF .... Central Provident Fund [*Singapore*]
CPF .... Centre de Promotion Feminine [*Women's Advancement Center*] [*Guinean*] (AF)
CPF .... Centre de Protection Familiale [*Family Protection Center*] [*Zairian*] (AF)
CPF .... Comissao de Politica Florestal [*Forestry Policy Commission*] [*Brazilian*] (LA)
CPF .... Compagnie du Polyisoprene Francais
CPFC .... Comision de Proteccion Fitosanitaria para el Caribe [*Caribbean Plant Protection Commission - CPPC*] (EA)
CPG .... Compagnie des Phosphates de Gafsa [*Tunisian*] (MAR)
CPGB .... Communist Party of Great Britain (MAR)
CPH .... Census Population and Housing (MAR)
CPH .... Communistische Partij Holland [*Communist Party of Holland*] [*Dutch*] (PPE)
CPHEA .... Cooperative des Produits de l'Huilerie d'Etat d'Alokoegbe (MAR)
CPI .... Central Personnel Institution [*Namibian*] (AF)
CPI .... Comissao Parlamentar de Inquerito [*Congressional Investigating Committee*] [*Brazilian*] (LA)
CPI .... Commission Permanente Internationale Europeenne des Gaz Industriels et du Carbure de Calcium [*Permanent International European Committee on Industrial Gases and Calcium Carbide*] (EA)
CPI .... Commission Phytosanitaire Interafricaine (MAR)
CPI .... Communist Party of India (PPW)
CPI .... Communist Party of Indonesia (PD)
CPI .... Communist Party of Iraq (ME)
CPI .... Communist Party of Ireland (PPW)
CPI .... Continuous Printing Industry (MAR)
CPIB .... Corrupt Practices Investigation Bureau [*Singapore*] (ML)
CPIC .... Communist Party of Indo-China (PPW)
CPIH .... Compagnie de Participation et d'Investissement Holding SA (MAR)
CPI(M) .... Communist Party of India (Marxist) (PPW)
CPI(ML) ...... Communist Party of India (Marxist-Leninist) (PD)
CPISRA .... Cerebral Palsy International Sports and Recreation Association (EA)
CPJ .... Communist Party of Jamaica (LA1)
CPK .... Ceskoslovenska Presidlovaci Komise [*Czechoslovak Commission for Population Resettlement*] (CZ)
CPK .... Cesky Plavecky Klub [*Czech Swimming Club*] (CZ)
CPK .... Chawangan Penyiasatan Khas [*Special Investigation Branch*] (ML)
CPK .... Communist Party of Kampuchea (PD)
CPL .... Ceskoslovenska Plavba Labska [*Czechoslovak Elbe River Navigation Lines*] (CZ)
CPL .... Ceskoslovenske Podniky Lihovarnicke, Narodni Podnik [*Czechoslovak Alcohol Distilling Industries, National Enterprise*] (CZ)
CPL .... Chawangan Polis Laut [*Marine Police Branch*] (ML)
CPL .... Combinatul de Prelucrarea Lemnului [*Wood Processing Combine*] (RO)
CPL .... Communist Party of Lebanon (ME)
CPL .... Communist Party of Lesotho (PD)
CPL .... Conference Europeenne des Pouvoirs Locaux (MAR)
CPL .... Corps Peralatan [*Ordnance Corps*] (IN)
CPLCM .... Centrul de Proiectare pentru Lucrari de Constructii-Montaj [*Design Center for Construction-Installation Projects*] (RO)
CPLiA .... Centrala Przemyslu Ludowego i Artystycznego [*Central Office of Folk and Art Crafts*] (POL)
CPLIM .... Centrul de Perfectionare a Lucratorilor din Industria Metalurgica [*Center for Advanced Training of Workers in the Metallurgical Industry*] (RO)
CPLO .... Ceskoslovenska Plavba Labskooderska [*Czechoslovak Elbe-Oder River Navigation Lines*] (CZ)
CPLO .... Consortium Photo Lunetterie Optique (MAR)
CPLS .... Centrul de Proiectari pentru Lucrari Speciale de Constructii Montaj in Constructiile de Masini [*Design Center for Special Construction Installation Projects in Machine Building*] (RO)
CPM .... Communist Party of Malaya [*Malaysian*] (PD)
CPM .... Communist Party of Malaya [*Singapore*] (PD)
CPM .... Coordinadora Politico-Militar [*Political-Military Coordinator*] [*Salvadoran*] (LA1)
CPM .... Corpo de Policia do Mocambique [*Mozambique Police Corps*] (AF)
CPM .... Corps Polisi Militer [*Military Police Corps*] (IN)
CPM .... Cour Permanente des Mandats (MAR)
CPMB .... Consiliul Popular al Municipiului Bucuresti [*People's Council of Bucharest Municipality*] (RO)
CPMCT .... Comite Provincial Malgache Contre le Tuberculose (MAR)
CPMG .... Carrosserie Parisienne-Mecanique Generale (MAR)
CPMJO .... Conference of Presidents of Major Jewish Organizations (MAR)
CPM-ML ...... Communist Party of Malaya - Marxist-Leninist [*Malaysian*] (PD)
CPMOAC ..... Comite Permanent de Mise en Oeuvre des Aides Commercialisees [*Permanent Committee for the Application of Commercialized Aid*] [*Cambodian*] (CL)
CPMP .... Comissariado Provincial da Mocidade Portuguesa (MAR)
CPM-RF ...... Communist Party of Malaya - Revolutionary Faction [*Malaysian*] (PD)
CPN .... Centrala Produktow Naftowych [*Petroleum Products Center*] (POL)
CPN .... Centrala Przemyslu Naftowego [*Petroleum Industry Center*] (POL)
CPN .... Comissao de Politica Nacional [*National Policy Committee*] [*Portuguese*] (WER)
CPN .... Comite Politico Nacional [*National Political Committee (of Accion Democratica)*] [*Venezuelan*] (LA)
CPN .... Communistische Partij Nederland [*Communist Party of the Netherlands*] (PPE)
CPN .... Consejo Politico Nacionalista [*Nationalist Political Council*] [*Bolivian*] (LA)
CPNC .... Cameroon People's National Convention (AF)
CPNK .... Communist Party of North Kalimantan (ML)
CPNLAF ...... Cambodian People's National Liberation Armed Forces (CL)
CPNU .... Conference des Plenipotentiaires
CPO .... Ceskoslovenska Plavba Oderska [*Czechoslovak Oder River Navigation Lines*] (CZ)
CPO .... Chief Personnel Officer [*Trinidadian-Tobagan*] (LA1)
CPO .... Civilna Protiletecka Obrana [*Civil Air Defense*] (CZ)
CPOIR .... Commission Permanente de l'Organisation Internationale pour les Refugies (MAR)
CPOR .... Centro de Preparacao de Oficiais da Reserva [*Reserve Officers Training Center*] [*Brazilian*] (LA)
CPP .... Centralna Poradnia Przeciwgruzlicza [*Central Anti-Tuberculosis Counseling Office*] (POL)
CPP .... Christian People's Party [*Norwegian*]
CPP .... Code de Procedure en Matiere Penale [*Penal Procedure Code*] [*Cambodian*] (CL)
CPP .... Convention Peoples' Party [*Ghanaian*] (AF)
CPP .... Cornwall People's Party [*Jamaican*] (LA1)
CPPA .... Corpo de Policia Popular de Angola [*Angolan People's Police Corps*] (AF)
CPPC .... Carribbean Plant Protection Commission [*See also CPFC*] (EA)
CPPC .... Centrul de Productie, Prestari, si Constructii [*Center for Production, Service, and Constructions*] (RO)
CPPCh .... Centrala Prywatnego Przemyslu Chemicznego [*Central Office of the Privately-Owned Chemical Industry*] (POL)
CPPS .... Centrala Prywatnego Przemyslu Spozywczego [*Central Office of the Privately-Owned Food Industry*] (POL)
CPR .... Centre du Perfectionnement et de Recyclage [*Training and Retraining Center*] [*Cambodian*] (CL)
CPR .... Centres Pedagogiques Regionaux [*Regional Teacher Training Centers*] [*Cambodian*] (CL)
CPR .... Chantiers Populaires de Reboisement [*Popular Projects for Reforestation*] [*Algerian*] (AF)
CPR .... Conseil Populaire de Redemption (MAR)
CPR .... Conseil Provincial de la Revolution [*Provincial Council of the Revolution*] [*Beninese*] (AF)
CPr .... Preparatory Classes [*French*]

CPRAD .... Corps Pemeliharaan Rochani Angkatan Darat [*Army Chaplains Corps*] (IN)
CPRC .... Coloured Persons' Representative Council [*South African*] (PPW)
CPRI .... Central Power Research Institute [*Indian*]
CPRM .... Companhia de Pesquisas de Recursos Minerais (MINEROBRAS) [*Mineral Resources Prospecting Company*] [*Brazilian*] (LA)
CPRU .... Colonial Pesticides Research Unit (MAR)
CPS .... Celostatni Plachtarske Zavody [*All-State Glider Contest*] (CZ)
CPS .... Centrul de Proiectare si Scularie [*Center for Design and Tooling*] (RO)
CPS .... Ceska Protifasisticka Spolecnost [*Czech Anti-Fascist Society*] (CZ)
CPS .... Ceskoslovenske Pivovary a Sladovny, Narodni Podnik [*Czechoslovak Breweries and Malt Factories, National Enterprise*] (CZ)
CPS .... Cesky Pevecky Sbor [*Czech Choral Society*] (CZ)
CPS .... Communist Party of Syria (ME)
cps .... Companeros [*Companions*] [*Spanish*]
CPS .... Credit Populaire du Senegal (MAR)
CPS .... Cristianos por el Socialismo [*Christians for Socialism*] [*Spanish*] (WER)
CPS .... Custos Privati Sigilli [*Keeper of the Privy Seal*] [*Latin*] (GPO)
CPSA .... Communist Party of South Africa (PD)
CPSA .... Compromiso Politico, SA [*Political Compromise, Inc.*] [*Spanish*] (WER)
CPSA .... Consiliul Politic Superior al Armatei [*Higher Political Council of the Army*] (RO)
CPSASA ..... Clay Pigeon Shooting Association of Southern Africa (MAR)
CPSCDN ..... Centrul pentru Specializarea Cadrelor in Domeniul Nuclear [*Center for Specialization of Personnel in the Nuclear Field*] (RO)
CPSD .... Club de Peche Sportive de Dakar (MAR)
CPSDHRK ... Commission Parlementaire Speciale pour la Defense de l'Honneur de la Republique Khmere [*Special Parliamentary Committee to Defend the Honor of the Khmer Republic*] [*Cambodian*] (CL)
CPSL .... Ceskoslovenska Paroplavebni Spolecnost Labska [*Czechoslovak Elbe River Lines*] (CZ)
CPSP .... Caisse de Perequation et de Stabilisation des Prix (MAR)
CPSU .... Communist Party of the Soviet Union [*Kommunisticheskaya Partiya Sovetskovo Soyuza*] (PPW)
CPT .... Comissao Pastoral da Terra [*Pastoral Land Commission*] [*Brazilian*] (LA1)
CPT .... Communist Party of Thailand (PD)
CPT .... Communist Party of Turkey (PD)
cpt .... Comptant [*Cash*] [*French*]
CPT .... Confederacion Paraguaya de Trabajadores [*Paraguayan Workers Federation*] (LA)
cpte .... Compte [*Account*] [*French*]
cpte ct .... Compte Courant [*Current Account*] [*French*]
CPTL .... Compagnie des Petroles Total Libye (MAR)
CPTR .... Cetni Protivtenkovski Reon [*Company Antitank Sector*] (YU)
CPTT .... Central Panamena de Trabajadores del Transporte [*Federation of Panamanian Transport Workers*] (LA)
CPTU .... Council of Progressive Trade Unions [*Trinidadian and Tobagan*] (LA1)
CPU .... Ceskoslovensky Plavebni Ustav [*Czechoslovak Institute for Navigation*] (CZ)
CPU .... Comite Patriotico Unificado [*United Patriotic Committee*] [*Dominican Republic*] (LA1)
CPU .... Commonwealth Press Union (EA)
CPU .... Complexe Polytechnique Universitaire (MAR)
CPUN .... Comite pour la Paix et l'Unite Nationale (MAR)
CPUSTAL .... Congreso Permanente de Unidad Sindical de Trabajadores de America Latina [*Latin American Workers Permanent Congress for Trade Union Unity*] (LA)
CPV .... Consorcio de Publicidad y Ventas [*Bogota*] (COL)
CPV .... Corporacion Peruana de Vapores [*Peruvian Shipping Corporation*] (LA)
CPV .... Republic of Cape Verde [*Three-letter standard code*] (CNC)
CPVZ .... Celostatne Patranie po Vojenskom Zbehovi [*National Search for Military Deserters*] (CZ)
CPWOA .... Cape Peninsula Welfare Organization of the Aged (MAR)
CPY .... Communist Party of Yugoslavia (MAR)
CPZ .... Celni Pochodova Zastita [*Forward March Screening Element*] (CZ)
CQ .... Chef de Quart (MAR)
CQFD .... Ce Qu'il Fallait Demontrer [*The Thing to Be Proved*] [*French*]
CQG .... Compagnie de Quartier General (MAR)
CR .... Centrala Rybna [*Fish Center*] (POL)
CR .... Ceskoslovensky Rozhlas [*Czechoslovak Broadcasting*] (CZ)
CR .... Chargeurs Reunis (MAR)
CR .... Comandos de la Resistencia [*Commandos of the Resistance*] [*Dominican Republic*] (LA)
CR .... Compagnons de la Revolution (MAR)
CR .... Conselho da Revolucao [*Council of the Revolution*] [*Portuguese*] (WER)
CR .... Costa Rica [*Two-letter standard code*] (CNC)
cr .... Credit [*or Crediteur*] [*Creditor*] [*French*]
CR .... Cuadernos Rojos [*Red Notebooks*] [*Spanish*] (WER)
CRA .... Centre de Recherche Africaine (MAR)
CRA .... Centre de la Recherche Appliquee (MAR)
CRA .... Centro Richerche Aerospaziali [*Italian*]
CRA .... Centros de Reforma Agraria [*Agrarian Reform Centers*] [*Chilean*] (LA)
CRA .... Commission Permanente du Controle et de la Repression de la Circulation des Automobiles [*Permanent Automobile Traffic Control Commission*] [*Cambodian*] (CL)
CRA .... Confederaciones Rurales Argentinas [*Argentine Rural Confederations*] (LA)
CRA .... Croissant Rouge Algerien [*Algerian Red Crescent*] (AF)
CRAC .... Centre Reunionnais d'Action Culturelle (MAR)
CRAC .... Centro de Rehabilitacion para Adultos y Ciegos [*Bogota*] (COL)
CRAC .... Comite Regional Africain de Coordination (pour l'Integration de la Femme au Developpement) [*African Regional Committee for Coordination (for the Integration of Women in Development)*] (AF)
CRAC .... Community Renewal and Action Council (MAR)
CRACCUS ... Comite Regional de l'Afrique Centrale et l'Utilisation du Sol (MAR)
CRAD .... Centre de Recherches Appliques du Dahomey (MAR)
CRAD .... Centres Regionaux d'Assistance Technique pour le Developpement [*Regional Centers for Technical Development Assistance*] [*Senegalese*] (AF)
CRAD .... Comite Revolutionnaire d'Administration du District [*Revolutionary Committee for District Administration*] [*Beninese*] (AF)
CRADAT ..... Centre Regional Africain d'Administration du Travail [*African Regional Labor Administration Center*] (AF)
CRADS .... Comite Republicain d'Action Democratique et Sociale [*Republican Committee for Democratic and Social Action*] [*Reunionese*] (AF)
CRADY .... Compania Radial de Yarumal Ltda. [*Yarumal-Antioquia*] (COL)
CRAF .... Comptoir de Representation et d'Agences de Fabriques (MAR)
CRAF .... Comptoirs Reunis d'Afrique (MAR)
CRAL .... Comando Revolucionario para America Latina [*Revolutionary Command for Latin America*] (LA)
CRAM .... Centre de Recherches sur l'Afrique Mediterraneene [*North African*] (MAR)
CRAM .... Centre de Renovation de l'Agriculture Malgache (MAR)
CRAM .... Centro Revolucionario d'Aplicacao Militar (MAR)
CRAM .... Collectivites Rurales Autochones Modernisees a Madagascar (MAR)
CRAN .... Cadena Radial Andina [*Medellin*] (COL)
CRAOCA ..... Cercle Royal des Anciens Officiers des Campagnes d'Afrique (MAR)
CRAOCUS ... Comite Regional de l'Afrique Occidentale pour la Conservation et l'Utilisation du Sol (MAR)
CRAP .... Centre de la Recherche en Anthropologie Prehistorique [*Prehistoric Anthropology Research Center*] [*Algerian*] (AF)
CRAP .... Centres Regionaux d'Action Pedagogique [*French*]
CRARA .... Comissao Revolucionaria de Apoio a Reforma Agraria [*Revolutionary Commission for Support to the Agrarian Reform*] [*Portuguese*] (WER)
CRAS .... Centro Regional de Aguas Subterraneas [*Regional Center for Underground Water*] [*Argentine*] (LA)
CRAS .... Comisia Romana pentru Activitati Spatiale [*Romanian Commission for Space Activities*] (RO)
CRAS .... Comptes Rendus des Seances de l'Academie des Sciences [*A publication*] (MAR)
CRAS .... Comunas Revolucionarias de Accion Socialista [*Revolutionary Communes of Socialist Action*] [*Spanish*] (WER)
CRAU .... Centre de Recherches Appliquee pour l'Architecture et Urbanisme [*French*] (MAR)
CRC .... Cairo River Club [*Egyptian*] (MAR)
CRC .... Civilian Rule Committee [*Sierra Leonean*] (AF)
CRC .... Colored Persons Representative Council [*South African*] (AF)
CRC .... Comite Revolutionnaire Cabindais (MAR)
CRC .... Comptoirs Reunis du Cameroun (MAR)
CRC .... Conseil de la Revolution Centrafricaine [*Council of the Central African Revolution*] (AF)
CRC .... Cooperative Regionale de Commerce [*Tunisian*] (MAR)
CRC .... Cruz Roja Colombiana [*Colombian Red Cross*] (LA)
CRCA .... Caisse Reunionnaise de Credit Agricole [*Reunion Agricultural Credit Bank*] (AF)
CRCAM .... Caisse Regionale de Credit Agricole Mutuel [*Regional Fund for Mutual Agricultural Credit*] [*Beninese*] (AF)
CRCB .... Comissao Reguladora do Comercio de Bacalhau [*Codfish Trade Regulatory Commission*] [*Portuguese*] (WER)
CRCP .... Conference of Rivers Chiefs and Peoples (MAR)
CRD .... Commission Regionale de Developpement [*Regional Development Commission*] [*Senegalese*] (AF)
CRD .... Conseil Revolutionnaire de District [*District Revolutionary Council*] [*Beninese*] (AF)
CRD .... Cruz Roja Dominicana [*Dominican Red Cross*] [*Dominican Republic*] (LA)
CRDA .... Christian Relief and Development Association (MAR)
CRDI .... Centre de Recherche pour le Developpement International (MAR)

CRDP .... Central Rangelands Development Project (MAR)
CRDS .... Centre de Recherches et de Documentation du Senegal [*Research and Documentation Center of Senegal*] (AF)
CRDTO .... Centre de Recherche et de Documentation pour la Tradition Orale [*Research and Documentation Center for Oral Tradition*] [*Niger*] (AF)
CRE .... Caisse de Retraites des Expatries (MAR)
Cre .... Calvaire [*Calvary, Wayside Cross*] [*Military map abbreviation*] [*World War I*] [*French*] (MTD)
CREA .... Centre de Recherches Economiques Appliquees [*Algerian*] (MAR)
CREA .... Centros Regionales de Experimentacion [*Regional Experimentation Centers*] [*Uruguayan*] (LA)
CREAI .... Carteira de Credito Agricola e Industrial do Banco do Brasil [*Agricultural and Industrial Credit Department of the Bank of Brazil*] (LA)
CREAM .... Centre Regional d'Enseignement et d'Apprentissage Maritime (MAR)
CREC .... Centre Rural d'Education Communautaire [*Rural Community Education Center*] [*Laotian*] (CL)
CREC .... Comissao Revolucionaria do Enclave de Cabinda [*Revolutionary Committee of the Cabinda Enclave*] [*Angolan*] (AF)
CRECI .... Comptoir Radiophonique et Electricite de la Cote-d'Ivoire (MAR)
CRECINCO ... Fondo de Crecimiento Industrial Colombiano [*Bogota*] (COL)
CRECINCO ... Fondo de Inversiones Industriales y Comerciales [*Industrial and Commercial Investment Fund*] [*Chilean*] (LA)
crecte .... Creciente [*Spanish*]
CRED .... Center for Research on Economic Development (MAR)
CREDES .... Centre de Recherches et d'Etudes du Developpement Economique et Social (MAR)
CREDIBANCO ... Credito Bancario [*Bogota*] (COL)
CREDICODI ... Credit de la Cote-d'Ivoire (MAR)
CREDIF .... Centre de Recherche et d'Etude pour la Diffusion du Francais [*French*]
CREDILA ..... Centre de Recherches d'Etudes et de Documentation sur les Institutions et la Legislation Africaines (MAR)
CREDISA .... Credito Inmobiliario, SA [*Real Estate Loans Corp.*] [*Salvadoran*]
CREDITARIO ... Caja de Credito Agrario Industrial y Minero [*Bogota*] (COL)
CREDOC ..... Centre de Recherche, d'Etude, et de Documentation sur la Consommation [*French*]
CREDOC ..... Centrum voor Rechts-Documentatie [*Dutch*]
CREE .... Centro de Recursos para la Ensenanza. Universidad del Valle [*Cali*] (COL)
CREGCI .... Comptoir Radiophonique et d'Electricite Generale de la Cote-d'Ivoire (MAR)
CREIA .... Concours de Recrutement des Eleves-Inspecteurs Adjoints (MAR)
CREM .... Centre Congolaise de Recyclage des Professeurs en Mathematiques Modernes (MAR)
CREN .... Centre Regional d'Etudes Nucleaires (MAR)
CRENK .... Centre Regional d'Etudes Nucleaires de Kinshasa [*Kinshasa Regional Nuclear Studies Center*] [*Zairian*] (AF)
CREPLA ...... Centre Regional de Promotion du Livre en Afrique (MAR)
CREPS .... Compagnie de Recherches et d'Exploitation de Petrole au Sahara [*Saharan Petroleum Exploration and Exploitation Company*] [*Algerian*] (AF)
CRESEX ...... Camara de Representantes de Casas Extranjeras [*Chamber of Representatives of Foreign Enterprises*] [*Costa Rican*] (LA)
CRESS .... Center for Research in Social Systems (MAR)
CREST .... Comite de Recherche Scientifique et Technique [*EG*]
CRESU .... Consejo Representativo del Sistema Universitario [*Representative Council of the University System*] [*Peruvian*] (LA)
CRETE .... Association des Correspondants des Radios et Televisions Etrangeres a Paris [*Association of Foreign Radio and Television Correspondents in Paris*] [*French*] (AF)
CRETRINA ... Comite de Reception des Aides Etrangeres [*Foreign Aid Receiving Committee*] [*Cambodian*] (CL)
CREVICO .... Credito de Viajes Populares [*Bogota*] (COL)
CRF .... Centrala Rozpowszechniania Filmow [*Center for Film Distribution*] (POL)
CRF .... Comite pour la Renaissance de France [*Algerian*] (MAR)
CRF .... Conseil Presidentiel de la Federation (MAR)
CRF .... Croix-Rouge Francaise [*French Red Cross*] (WER)
CRFA .... Chongwe River Farmers Associations (MAR)
CRFA .... Conseil Revolutionnaire des Forces Armees (MAR)
CRFEA .... Christian Rural Fellowship of East Africa (AF)
CRFER .... Centre Regional de Formation pour Entretien Routier (MAR)
CRFP .... Centre National de Recherches Forestieres et Piscicoles (MAR)
CRFS .... Comites Revolutionnaires des Forces de Securite [*Revolutionary Committees of the Security Forces*] [*Beninese*] (AF)
CRG .... Comites Revolutionnaires de Garnison [*Garrison Revolutionary Committees*] [*Beninese*] (AF)
CRG .... Compagnie Reynolds de Geophysique (MAR)
CRG .... Comptoir de Representations Generales (MAR)
CRGE .... Companhias Reunidas de Gas e Electricidade [*Unified Gas and Electricity Companies*] [*Portuguese*] (WER)
CRI .... Centre de Recherches et d'Irradiations [*French*]
CRI .... Centre Regional d'Instruction [*Regional Instruction Center*] [*Cambodian*] (CL)
CRI .... Children's Relief International (MAR)
CRI .... Commando Regional Independiente [*Independent Regional Command*] [*Venezuelan*] (LA)
CRI .... Commission Regionale d'Investissements [*Regional Investment Commission*] [*Algerian*] (AF)
CRI .... Costa Rica [*Three-letter standard code*] (CNC)
CRI .... Croix-Rouge Internationale [*International Red Cross*] (CL)
CRI .... Crops Research Institute [*Ghanaian*] (AF)
CRIAC .... Centre des Recherches Industrielles en Afrique Centrale [*Industrial Research Center in Central Africa*] (AF)
CRIAMS ...... Comite Regional Intersectorial de Apoyo a la Movilizacion Social [*Intersectoral Regional Committee for Support of Social Mobilization*] [*Peruvian*] (LA)
CRIBUCA .... Comite Regional de Integracion de Bibliotecas Universitarias de la Costa Atlantica [*Cordoba*] (COL)
CRIC .... Centre de Reflexion et d'Information sur la Cooperation Internationale avec le Tiers Monde (MAR)
CRIDE .... Centre de Recherches Interdisciplinaires pour le Developpement de l'Education (MAR)
CRIE .... Comision de Represion de Ilicitos Economicos [*Committee for Repression of Economic Crimes*] [*Uruguayan*] (LA)
CRIF .... Conseil Representatif des Institutions Juives en France
CRIFRI .... Comitato Interministeriale per il Risanamento Finanziario e la Rinascita Industriale [*Interministerial Committee for Financial Recovery and Industrial Rebirth*] [*Italian*] (WER)
CRIG .... Cocoa Research Institute of Ghana (MAR)
CRIK .... Centre de Regroupement pour les Interets du Kwango (MAR)
CRIM .... Comite Regional Intersyndical de Montreal [*Montreal Regional Inter-Trade Union Committee*] [*Canadian*] (WER)
CRIN .... Cocoa Research Institute of Nigeria (MAR)
CRI/RUL ...... Centraal Rekeninstituut [*Rijksuniversiteit, Leiden*]
CRISP .... Centre de Recherche et d'Information Socio-Politiques [*Center for Socio-Political Research and Information*] [*Belgian*] (WER)
CRIT .... Coordinating Centre for Regional Information Training (MAR)
CRIVA .... Commissie Reken- en Informatieverwerkende Apparatuur
CRJT .... Centre Reunionnais d'Information, d'Etudes, et d'Action Sociale pour les Jeunes Travailleurs [*Reunionese Information, Study, and Social Action Center for Young Workers*] (AF)
CRK .... Croix-Rouge Khmere [*Cambodian Red Cross*] (CL)
CRL .... Centralni Rizeni Letounu [*Central Aircraft Control*] (CZ)
CRL .... Conseil Revolutionnaire Local pour les Villages et Quartiers de Villes [*Local Revolutionary Council for Villages and City Districts*] [*Beninese*] (AF)
CRM .... Charles Rennie Mackintosh Society (EA)
CRM .... Comite Revolucionario de Mozambique (MAR)
CRM .... Compagnie Radio Maritime (MAR)
CRM .... Comptoir Radio le "Mono" (MAR)
CRM .... Coordinacion Revolucionaria de las Masas [*Revolutionary Coordination of the Masses*] [*Salvadoran*] (PD)
CRM .... Croissant Rouge Maroc (MAR)
CRM .... Cultuur, Recreatien, Maatschappelijk Werk [*Ministry of Culture, Recreation, and Social Work*] [*Dutch*] (WEN)
CRMK .... Confederation Royale Marocaine de Karate (MAR)
CRMM .... Centre de Reeducation Motrice de Madagascar [*Musculo-Skeletal Reeducation Center*] [*Malagasy*] (AF)
CRMP .... Comite Revolutionnaire de Milice Populaire [*Revolutionary Committee of the Popular Militia*] [*Guinean*] (AF)
CRMSA .... Caisse Regionale de Mutualite Sociale Agricole [*Regional Agricultural and Social Mutual Fund*] [*Algerian*] (AF)
CRN .... Comite de Reconciliation Nationale (MAR)
CRN .... Comite de Reconstruccion Nacional [*National Reconstruction Committee*] [*Guatemalan*] (LA)
CRN .... Comite de Renovation Nationale [*National Renewal Committee*] [*Beninese*] (AF)
CRN .... Constructions Reparations Navales (MAR)
CRNA .... Comite da Revolucao Nacional de Angola (MAR)
CRO .... Central Records Office [*Sudanese*] (MAR)
CRO .... Centre de Recherches Oceanographiques (MAR)
CRO .... Commissie voor Rassenonderzoek van Groenvoedergewassen (MAR)
CRO .... Commonwealth Relations Office (MAR)
CROATIAFILM ... Croatian Film Establishment [*Zagreb*] (YU)
CROATIAPETROL ... Croatian Petrol Derivatives Establishment [*Zagreb*] (YU)
CROC .... Confederacion Revolucionaria de Obreros y Campesinos [*Revolutionary Confederation of Workers and Peasants*] [*Mexican*] (LA)
CRODT .... Centre de Recherches Oceanographiques de Dakar-Thiaroye (MAR)
CROMACOL ... Cromados Colombia y Cia. Ltda. [*Medellin*] (COL)
CROS .... Ceska Rada Odborovych Svazu [*Czech Council of Trade Unions*] (CZ)

CROUS........ Centre Regional des Oeuvres Universitaires et Scolaires [*Regional Center for Assistance to Universities and Schools*] [*French*] (WER)
CRP............. Centre Regional de Planification et l'Administration de l'Education pour les Pays Arabes [*North African*] (MAR)
CRP............. Cetna Ranjenicka Prihvatnica [*Company First Aid Station*] (YU)
CRP............. Comando de Resistencia Popular Javier Carrera [*Javier Carrera Popular Resistance Commando*] [*Chilean*] (PD)
CRP............. Comite Regional Provisoire (MAR)
CRPA.......... Centro Regional da Reforma Agraria [*Regional Agrarian Reform Center*] [*Portuguese*] (WER)
CRPAO........ Comision Regional de Pesca para el Africa Occidental (MAR)
CRPB.......... Comite de Relevement du Peuple Bassa [*Committee for the Aid of the Bassa People*]
CRPLF......... Communaute Radiophonique des Programmes de Langue Francaise [*Community of French-Language Radio Programmes*] (EA)
CRPTA........ College Royal Preparatoire aux Technique Aeronautiques [*Moroccan*] (MAR)
CRR............ Centre de Recherches Routieres [*Belgian*]
CRRG.......... Comisia Republicana de Rezerve Geologice [*National Commission of Geological Reserves*] (RO)
CRRS.......... Central Rainlands Research Station [*Sudanese*] (MAR)
Crrta........... Carretera [*Highway*] [*Spanish*] (CED)
CRRU.......... Cosmic Rays Research Unit (MAR)
Crs.............. Carsi [*Market*] (TU)
CRS............. Catholic Relief Services (CL)
CRS............. Centrala Rolnicza Spoldzielni [*Agricultural Cooperative Center*] (POL)
CRS............. Centrala Rolnicza Spoldzielni "Samopomoc Chlopska" [*Agricultural Centre of the Co-Operative "Peasants' Self-Help"*] [*Polish*]
CRS............. Centralna Rada Spoldzielcza [*Central Cooperative Council*] (POL)
CRS............. Cesky Rohovnicky Svaz [*Czech Boxing Association*] (CZ)
CRS............. Circulo Radial Santandereano [*Bucaramanga*] (COL)
CRS............. Compagnies Republicaines de la Securite [*Republican Security Companies*] [*French*] (AF)
CRS............. Compagnies Republicaines de Securite [*Republican Security Companies*] [*State Mobile Police*] [*French*] (WER)
CRS............. Consiglio Rivoluzionario Supremo [*Supreme Revolutionary Council*] [*Use SRC*] [*Somali*] (AF)
CRS............. Czechoslowacka Republika Socjalistyczna [*Polish*]
CRSI............ Calisma, Rehabilitasyon, ve Sosyal Isler Bakanligi [*Ministry of Labor, Rehabilitation, and Social Affairs of the Turkish Cypriot Federated State*] (GC)
CRSSCh...... Centrala Rolnicza Spoldzielni "Samopomoc Chlopska" [*Agricultural Cooperative Center of the "Peasant's Mutual Aid"*] (POL)
CRSSGF...... Comptes Rendus des Seances de la Societe Geologique de France (MAR)
CRT............. Central Regional de Trabajadores [*Regional Labor Federation*] [*Venezuelan*] (LA)
CRT............. Centre de Recherches Tchadienne (MAR)
CRT............. Confederacion Revolucionaria de Trabajadores [*Revolutionary Confederation of Workers*] [*Mexican*] (LA1)
CRT............. Conselho Revolucionario dos Trabalhadores [*Revolutionary Workers' Councils*] [*Portuguese*] (WER)
CRT............. Croix Rouge Togolaise [*Togolese Red Cross*] (AF)
CRTA.......... Centre de Recherches sur les Trypanosomiases Animales (MAR)
CRTCI......... Caisse de Retraite des Travailleurs Salaries de Cote-d'Ivoire (MAR)
CRTO.......... Centre Regional de Teledetection [*Regional Center for Remote-Sensing*] [*Upper Voltan*] (AF)
CRTSM........ Secretariado Nacional Pro-Conselhos Revolucionarios de Trabalhadores, Soldados, e Marinheiros [*National Secretariat for Revolutionary Councils of Workers, Soldiers, and Sailors*] [*Portuguese*] (WER)
CRU............. Collective Reserve Unit (MAR)
CRU............. Commodities Research Unit (MAR)
CRUA.......... Comite Revolutionnaire pour l'Unite et l'Action [*Algerian*] (MAR)
CRUA.......... Conference des Recteurs des Universites Africaines (MAR)
CRUEA........ Centre de Recherche sur l'Utilisation des Energies Alternatives [*Burundi*]
CRUEI......... Centre Italien pour les Relations Universitaires avec l'Etranger [*Italian*]
CRUESI....... Centre de Recherches pour l'Utilisation de l'Eau Salee en Irrigation (MAR)
CRUP.......... Consejo de Rectores de Universidades Privadas [*Council of Private Universities Rectors*] [*Argentine*] (LA)
CRUTAC..... Centro Rural Universitario de Treinamento e de Acao Comunitaria [*University Rural Center for Training and Community Action*] [*Brazilian*] (LA)
Crvarm........ Crvena Armija [*Red Army*] (YU)
Crvkr........... Crveni Krst [*Red Cross*] (YU)
Crx.............. Croix [*Cross*] [*Military map abbreviation*] [*World War I*] [*French*] (MTD)
CRYF.......... Corporacion de Reconstruccion y Fomento [*Reconstruction and Development Corporation*] [*Peruvian*] (LA)
CRYRZA...... Comision de Reconstruccion y Rehabilitiacion de la Zona Afectada [*Commission for the Reconstruction and Rehabilitation of the Affected Zone*] [*Peruvian*] (LA)
CRZ............. Centre de Recherches Zootechniques (MAR)
CRZA.......... Centre de Recherches sur les Zones Africaines [*Algerian*] (MAR)
CRZZ........... Centralna Rada Zwiazkow Zawodowych [*Central Council of Trade Unions*] (POL)
CS............... Celostatni Spartakiada [*All-State Spartakiad*] [*National sport and athletic competition*] (CZ)
cs................ Centimos [*Spanish*]
CS............... Centrala Spozywcow [*Consumer's Center*] (POL)
CS............... Centralna Szkola [*Central School*] (POL)
CS............... Ceskoslovensko [*or Ceskoslovensky*] [*Czechoslovakia or Czechoslovak*] (CZ)
CS............... Ceskoslovensky Spisovatel [*The Czechoslovak Writer*] [*A publishing house*] (CZ)
Cs................ Cesme [*Spring*] (TU)
CS............... Chawangan Siasatan [*Investigation Branch*] (ML)
CS............... Commonwealth Secretariat (EA)
CS............... Concrete Society (EA)
CS............... Confederacion Socialista [*Socialist Confederation*] [*Spanish*] (WER)
CS............... Corriente Socialista [*Socialist Current*] [*Mexican*] (LA1)
Cs................ Cottbus [*Cottbus*] [*One of the eight GDR reichsbahn directorates*] (EG)
cs................ Cours [*French*]
CS............... Cran Sonar [*Medellin*] (COL)
CS............... Cristianos por el Socialismo [*Christians for Socialism*] [*Spanish*] (WER)
CS............... Crkveni Sud [*Ecclesiastical Court*] (YU)
cs................ Csapat [*Troop, Company, Detachment, Squadron*] (HU)
cs................ Cuartos [*Rooms*] [*Spanish*]
CS............... Cumhuriyet Senatosu [*Republican Senate*] (TU)
CS............... Custos Sigilli [*Keeper of the Seal*] [*Latin*] (GPO)
CS............... Czechoslovakia [*Two-letter standard code*] (CNC)
CS............... Czechoslowacja [*Czechoslovakia*] [*Polish*]
CSA............. Central South Africa Railway (MAR)
CSA............. Centrale Syndicale Angolaise (MAR)
CSA............. Ceskoslovenska Armada [*Czechoslovak Army*] (CZ)
CSA............. Ceskoslovenske Aerolinie [*Czechoslovak Airlines*] (CZ)
CSA............. Ceskoslovenske Spolky v Americe [*Czechoslovak Organizations in America*] (CZ)
CSA............. Cesky Severozapadni Aeroklub [*Czech Northwestern Aero Club*] (CZ)
CSA............. Channel Swimming Association (EA)
CSA............. Christliche-Sozialistiche Arbeitsgemeinschaft [*Christian Social-Workers' Community*] [*Lithuanian*] (PPE)
CSA............. Civil Service Association [*St. Lucian*] (LA1)
CSA............. Club Sportif d'Atakpame (MAR)
CSA............. Comite de Soutien de l'Angola (MAR)
CSA............. Comite Superieur Arabe [*North African*] (MAR)
CSA............. Comitetul de Stat al Apelor [*State Water Committee*] (RO)
CSA............. Commission Federale pour la Securite des Installations Atomiques [*Atomic Installations Safety Commission*] [*French*] (WER)
CSA............. Confederacion Socialista Argentina [*Socialist Confederation of Argentina*] (LA)
CSA............. Confederation Syndicale Africaine [*African Trade Union Confederation*] [*Use ATUC*] (AF)
CSA............. Conseil Scientifique pour l'Afrique [*Scientific Council for Africa*] (AF)
Cs A............ Csepeli Autogyar [*Automobile Factory of Csepel*] (HU)
CSAD.......... Ceskoslovenska Automobilova Doprava [*Czechoslovak Automobile Transportation*] (CZ)
CSAD.......... Ceskoslovenska Statni Automobilova Doprava [*Czechoslovak State Automobile Transportation*] (CZ)
CSAF........... Ceskoslovenska Asociace Footballova [*Czechoslovak Soccer Association*] (CZ)
CSAK.......... Ceskoslovensky Aeroklub [*Czechoslovak Aero Club*] (CZ)
CSAL........... Club Sportif Automobile du Littoral (MAR)
CSAO.......... Ceskoslovenske Automobilove Opravny [*Czechoslovak Automobile Repair Shops*] (CZ)
csap............ Csapat [*Troop, Company, Detachment, Squadron*] (HU)
CSAPS........ Ceskoslovensky Amatersky Plavecky Svaz [*Czechoslovak Amateur Swimming Association*] (CZ)
CSAR.......... Central South Africa Railway (MAR)
CSAR.......... Compagnie Senegalaise d'Assurance et de Reassurances (MAR)
csatl............ Csatlakozas [*Connection*] (HU)
CSAV.......... Ceskoslovenska Akademie Ved [*Czechoslovak Academy of Sciences*] (CZ)
CSAZ.......... Ceskoslovenska Akademie Zemedelstvi [*Czechoslovak Agricultural Academy*] (CZ)
CSAZV........ Ceskoslovenska Akademie Zemedelskych Ved [*Czechoslovak Academy of Agricultural Sciences*] (CZ)
CSB............. Centrala Sprzetu Budownictwa [*Building Equipment Center*] (POL)
CSB............. Centro Simon Bolivar [*Venezuelan*]
CSB............. Christliche Sozialbewegung der Schweiz [*Swiss Christian Social Movement*] (WEN)

CSB............ Comite Solidarite-Burundi (MAR)
csb............ Csapatbajnoksag [*Team Championship*] (HU)
CSBP.......... Cetna Stanica Borbenih Potreba [*Company Combat Supply Station*] (YU)
CSBr.......... Crkveni Sud Broj [*Ecclesiastical Court Number*] (YU)
CSBS.......... Ceskoslovensky Basketballovy Svaz [*Czechoslovak Basketball Association*] (CZ)
CSBZ.......... Cold Storage Board of Zambia (MAR)
CSc............ Candidatus Scientiae [*Candidate for Doctor of Science*] (CZ)
CSC............ Cartel des Syndicats Caledoniens [*Federation of New Caledonian Trade Unions*]
CSC............ Central Standardization Committee (MAR)
CSC............ Cold Storage Commission (MAR)
CSC............ Comite Syndical de Coordination (MAR)
CSC............ Commonwealth Science Council (EA)
CSC............ Confederacion Sindical de Colombia [*Bogota*] (COL)
CSC............ Confederation Syndicale Congolaise [*Congolese Trade Union Confederation*] (AF)
CSC............ Confederation des Syndicats Chretiens [*Confederation of Christian Trade Unions*] [*Belgian*] (WER)
CSC............ Convergencia Socialista Cataluna [*Socialist Convergence of Catalonia*] [*Spanish*] (WER)
CSCAS........ Comitetul de Stat pentru Constructii, Arhitectura, si Sistematizare [*State Committee for Constructions, Architecture, and Systematization*] (RO)
CSCB.......... Confederacion Sindical de Choferes de Bolivia [*Trade Union Confederation of Bolivian Drivers*] (LA1)
CSCC.......... Confederation des Syndicats Chretiens du Congo [*Confederation of Christian Syndicates of the Congo*] [*Leopoldville*]
CSCD.......... Committee on Studies for Cooperation in Development [*Colombo, Sri Lanka*]
CSCE.......... Conference on Security and Cooperation in Europe (PD)
CSCF.......... Curtea Superioara de Control Financiar [*Higher Court for Financial Control*] (RO)
CSCG.......... Centre Socio-Culturel Guyanais [*French Guianese Socio-Cultural Center*] (LA1)
CSCH.......... Ceskoslovensky Casopis Historicky [*Czechoslovak Historical Journal*] [*A publication*] (CZ)
CSCITM...... Centrul de Studii si Cercetari de Istorie si Teorie Militara [*Center for Studies and Research in Military History and Theory*] (RO)
CSCK.......... Ceskoslovensky Cerveny Kriz [*Czechoslovak Red Cross*] (CZ)
CSCO.......... Caisse de Stabilisation Cotonniere [*Cotton Stabilization Fund*] [*Zairian*] (AF)
CSCPA........ Comitetul de Stat pentru Colectarea Produselor Agricole [*State Committee for the Collection of Agricultural Products*] (RO)
CSCS.......... Commonwealth Students' Children's Society (MAR)
CSCSGY..... Csepeli Csogyar [*Pipe Factory of Csepel*] (HU)
CSCSU........ Common Service Civil Servants Union [*Ugandan*] (AF)
CSCZ.......... Ceskoslovenske Cihlarske Zavody [*Czechoslovak Brick Works*] (CZ)
CSD............ Centralised Services Division (MAR)
CSD............ Ceskoslovenska Socialni Demokracie [*Czechoslovak Social-Democratic Party*] (CZ)
CSD............ Ceskoslovenske Statni Drahy [*Czechoslovak State Railroads*] (CZ)
CSD............ Commissione Suprema di Difesa [*Supreme Defense Board*] [*Italian*] (WER)
CSD............ Consejo Superior de la Defensa [*Superior Defense Council*] [*Honduran*] (LA)
CSD............ Czechoslovak Railroads (EG)
CSDES........ Consiliul Suprem al Dezvoltarii Economice si Sociale [*Supreme Council for Economic and Social Development*] (RO)
CSDP.......... Ceskoslovenske Dopravni Podniky [*Czechoslovak Transportation Enterprises*] (CZ)
CSDS.......... Ceskoslovenska Demograficka Spolecnost [*Czechoslovak Demographic Society*] (CZ)
CSE............ Archives de la Congregation du Saint Esprit [*Paris*] [*A publication*] (MAR)
Cse............ Cense [*Farm*] [*Military map abbreviation*] [*World War I*] [*French*] (MTD)
CSE............ Centre de Sante Elementaire (MAR)
CSE............ Compagnie Senegalaise d'Entreprises (MAR)
CSE............ Consejo Supremo Electoral [*Venezuelan*]
CSEAL........ Comitetul de Stat pentru Economie si Administratie Locala [*State Committee for Local Economy and Administration*] (RO)
CSEERI....... Comite Scientifique pour l'Etude des Effets des Radiations Ionisantes
CSEHMADOK... Csehszlovakiai Magyar Dolgozok Kulturegylete [*Cultural Association of Hungarian Workers in Czechoslovakia*] (HU)
c/sek.......... Cykl na Sekunde [*Cycle per Second*] [*Polish*]
CSELT......... Centro Studi e Laboratori Telecomunicazioni [*Telecommunications Research and Study Center*] [*Italian*] (WER)
CSEMADOK... Csehslovakiat Magyar Dolgozok Kulturegyesulete [*Culture Society of Hungarian Workers in Czechoslovakia*] (CZ)
CSEMADOK... Csehszlovakai Magyarok Kulturalis-Tarsadalmi Szovetsege [*Cultural-Social Association of Hungarians in Czechoslovakia*] (HU)
CSEMKER... Orszagos Csemegekereskedelmi Vallalat [*National Delicatessen Enterprise*] (HU)
CSEN.......... Comite Sindical de Emergencia Nacional [*National Labor Emergency Committee*] [*Salvadoran*] (LA)
CSEN.......... Comitetul de Stat pentru Energia Nucleara [*State Committee for Nuclear Energy*] (RO)
CSEN.......... Conseil Superieur de l'Education Nationale [*Higher Council of National Education*] [*Guinean*] (AF)
CSEPP........ Central Sindical de Empleados Particulares del Peru [*Peruvian Trade Union Federation of Workers in Private Enterprise*] (LA)
CSES.......... Comite de Solidaridad con El Salvador [*Committee of Solidarity with El Salvador*] [*Costa Rican*] (LA1)
CSF............ Cesky Svaz Footballovy [*Czech Soccer Association*] (CZ)
CSF............ Commonwealth Schoolbook Fund (MAR)
CSF............ Community Systems Foundation (MAR)
CSF............ Compagnie Generale de Telegraphie sans Fil [*General Radio Company*] [*French*] (WER)
CSF-B......... Ceskoslovensky Film Bratislava [*Czechoslovak Film Bratislava*] (CZ)
csfk............ Csoportfonok [*Chief/Commander of Group, Troop Detachment, or Special Task Force*] (HU)
CSFM.......... Csepeli Femmu [*Csepel Metal Factory*] (HU)
CSFN.......... Ceskoslovenske Filmove Nakladatelstvi [*Czechoslovak Motion Picture Publishing House*] (CZ)
CSG............ Centar Sektora Gadanja [*Center of Firing Sector*] [*Military*] (YU)
CSG............ Centre Spatial Guyanais [*Guyana Space Center*] [*French*] (WER)
CSG............ Combinatul Siderurgic Galati [*Galati Iron and Steel Combine*] (RO)
CSG............ Comitetul de Stat pentru Geologie [*State Committee for Geology*] (RO)
CSG............ Confederacion Sindical Guatemalteca [*Guatemalan Labor Union Federation*] (LA)
CSG............ Consejo Sindical de Guatemala [*Union Council of Guatemala*] (LA)
CSGS.......... Ceskoslovensky Golfovy Svaz [*Czechoslovak Golf Association*] (CZ)
CSH............ Centralna Skladnica Harcerska [*Scouts' Central Store*] [*Polish*]
CSH............ Ceskoslovenske Hute [*Czechoslovak Metallurgical Enterprises*] (CZ)
CSH............ Cesky Svaz Hazene [*Czech Volleyball Association*] (CZ)
CSH............ Combina Siderurgica Hunedoara [*Hunedoara Iron and Steel Combine*] (RO)
CSH............ Compagnie de Services et d'Hotellerie (MAR)
CSHL.......... Club Sportif d'Hammam-Lif [*Tunisian*] (MAR)
CSHP.......... Conference of Societies for the History of Pharmacy (EA)
CSI............ Centrala Spoldzielni Inwalidow [*Disabled Persons' Cooperatives Center*] (POL)
CSI............ Centro Social Independente [*Independent Social Center*] [*Portuguese*] (WER)
CSI............ Ceskoslovensko-Sovietsky Institut [*Czechoslovak-Soviet Institute*] [*Bratislava*] (CZ)
CSI............ Christian Solidarity International (EA)
CSI............ Commission Sericole Internationale [*International Sericultural Commission - ISC*] (EA)
CSI............ Conferencia Socialista Iberica [*Iberian Socialist Conference*] [*Spanish*] (WER)
CSI............ Conseil Superieur des Institutions [*Higher Council of Institutions*] [*Malagasy*] (AF)
CSI............ Consejo de Sindicatos Independientes [*Council of Independent Trade Unions*] [*Salvadoran*] (LA1)
CSIB.......... Cartel des Syndicats Independants de Belgique [*Cartel of Independent Unions of Belgium*] (WER)
CSIC.......... Camara Salvadorena de la Industria de Construccion [*Salvadoran Chamber of the Construction Industry*] (LA1)
CSIC.......... Consejo Superior de Investigaciones Cientificas [*Higher Council for Scientific Research*] [*Spanish*] (WER)
csill............ Csillagaszat [*Astronomy*] (HU)
CSIO.......... Centrul de Sudura si Incercari la Oboseala [*Center for Welding and Fatigue Testing*] (RO)
CSIR.......... Council for Scientific and Industrial Research [*Ghanaian*] (AF)
CSIR.......... Council for Scientific and Industrial Research [*South African*] (AF)
CSIR.......... Council for Scientific and Industrial Research [*Indian*]
CSIRO........ Commonwealth Scientific and Industrial Research Organisation (MAR)
CSIRT......... Comite Scientifique International de Recherches sur les Trypanosomiases
CSIS.......... Center of Strategic International Studies (MAR)
CSIS.......... Comitetul de Stat pentru Invatamintul Superior [*State Committee for Higher Education*] (RO)
CSITSL....... Comite Syndical International du Tourisme Social et des Loisirs [*International Trade Unions Committee of Social Tourism and Leisure - ITUCSTL*] (EA)
CSJ............ Comisiones Sindicales Juveniles [*Youth Trade Union Committees*] [*Cuban*] (LA)

CSJ .... Conseil Superieur des Jeunes [*Higher Youth Council*] [*Mauritanian*] (AF)
CSJ .... Corte Suprema de Justicia [*Supreme Court*] [*Colombian*] (LA)
CSJKZ......... Casopis za Slovenski Jezik, Knijizevnost in Zgodovino [*Journal of Slovenian Language, Literature, and History*] [*Ljubljana*] [*A publication*] (YU)
CSJS........... Ceskoslovensky Jezdecky Svaz [*Czechoslovak Riding Association*] (CZ)
CSK............ Cesky Sermirsky Klub [*Czech Fencing Club*] (CZ)
CSK............ Cesky Svaz Kanoistu [*Czech Canoe Association*] (CZ)
CSK............ Chawangan Siasatan Khas [*Special Investigation Branch*] (ML)
CSK............ Comite Special du Katanga (MAR)
CSK............ Compagnie Special du Kongo (MAR)
csk .... Cseh Korona [*Czechoslovak Crown*] (HU)
CSK............ Csehszlovak Koztarsasag [*Czechoslovak Republic*] (HU)
CSK............ Czechoslovakia [*Three-letter standard code*] (CNC)
CSKF........... Centralna Szkola Kultury Fizycznej [*Central School of Physical Education*] (POL)
cs es kir ...... Csaszari es Kiralyi [*Imperial and Royal*] (HU)
CSKM.......... Ceskoslovensky Klub Motoristu [*Czechoslovak Motoring Club*] (CZ)
CSKP .... Csehszlovakia Kommunista Partja [*Communist Party of Czechoslovakia*] (HU)
csl .... Cerkvena Slovanscina [*Church Slavonic*] [*Language*] (YU)
CSL .... Ceskoslovenska Statni Loterie [*Czechoslovak State Lottery*] (CZ)
CSL .... Ceskoslovenska Strana Lidova [*Czechoslovak People's Party*] (PPE)
CSL .... Ceskoslovenske Statni Lesy [*Czechoslovak State Forests*] (CZ)
csl .... Ceskoslovensky [*Czechoslovak*] (CZ)
CSL .... Cesky Svaz Lukostrelecky [*Czech Archery Association*] (CZ)
CSL .... Compagnie Senegalaise de Lubrifiants (MAR)
CSL .... Confederazione Somala dei Lavoratori [*Somali Confederation of Labor*] (AF)
CSL .... Conseil Superieur de la Lutte [*Supreme Struggle Committee*] [*Guinean*] (AF)
CSLA.......... Confederation des Syndicats Libres Angolais [*Confederation of Angolan Free Trade Unions*] (AF)
CSLA.......... Conferencia Sindical Latinoamericana [*Latin American Trade Union Conference*] (LA)
CSLC .... Confederation des Syndicales Libres du Congo (MAR)
CSLCCA ..... Comite de Soutien a la Lutte Contre le Colonialisme et l'Apartheid [*Committee for Supporting the Struggle Against Colonialism and Apartheid*] [*French*] (WER)
Cslt............ Consulat [*Consulate*] [*French*] (MTD)
CSLTA .... Ceskoslovenska Lawn-Tennisova Asociace [*Czechoslovak Lawn Tennis Association*] (CZ)
Cslt G.......... Consulat-General [*Consulate-General*] [*French*] (MTD)
CSLUS .... Confederazione Sindicale Lavoratori Uniti della Somalia [*Confederation of United Trade Unions of Somalia*] (AF)
CSLUT .... Celostatni Soutez Lidove Umelecke Tvorivosti [*Folk Arts Contest*] (CZ)
CSM .... Centrala Spoldzielni Mieszkaniowych [*Central Office of Housing Cooperatives*] (POL)
CSM .... Centre Superieur Militaire [*Advanced Military Training Center*] [*Zairian*] (AF)
CSM .... Ceskoslovensky Svaz Mladeze [*Czechoslovak Union of Youth*] (CZ)
CSM .... Church of Scotland Mission (MAR)
CSM .... Comite de Solidarite de Madagascar [*Solidarity Committee of Madagascar*] (AF)
CSM .... Compagnie Saliniere du Maroc (MAR)
CSM .... Compagnie Senegalaise de Metallurgie (MAR)
CSM .... Conseil Superieur Militaire [*Supreme Military Council*] [*Chadian*] (AF)
CSM .... Convergencia Socialista de Madrid [*Socialist Convergence of Madrid*] [*Spanish*] (WER)
CSME.......... Confederation Syndicale Mondiale des Enseignants [*World Confederation of Teachers - WCT*] (EA)
CSMJ .... Centrala Spoldzielni Mleczarsko-Jajczarskich [*Dairy and Egg Cooperatives Center*] (POL)
CSMJ .... Ceskoslovenska Myslivecka Jednota [*Czechoslovak Hunting Association*] (CZ)
CSMS.......... Ceskoslovenska Spolecnost pro Mezinarodni Styky (CZ)
CSMS.......... Ceskoslovensky Myslivecky Svaz [*Czechoslovak Game Keepers Union*] (CZ)
CSMSK .... Ceskoslovensko-Madarska Smiesana Komisia [*Czechoslovak-Hungarian Joint Commission*] (CZ)
CSN............ Ceskoslovenska Spolecnost Normalisacni [*Czechoslovak Society for Standardization*] (CZ)
CSN............ Ceskoslovenske Normy [*Czechoslovak Standards*] (CZ)
CSN............ Ceskoslovenske Statni Normy [*Czechoslovak State Standards*] (CZ)
CSN............ Comision Sindical Nacional [*National Trade Union Commission*] [*Argentine*] (LA)
CSN............ Commissariat of Nuclear Sciences [*French*] (MAR)
CSN............ Companhia Siderurgica Nacional [*National Iron and Steel Company*] [*Brazilian*] (LA)
CSN............ Conselho de Seguranca Nacional [*National Security Council*] [*Brazilian*] (LA)
CSN............ Coordinadora Sindical Nacional [*National Trade Union Coordinating Board*] [*Nicaraguan*] (LA1)
CSNA .... Compagnie Senegalaise de Negoce Alimentaire (MAR)
CSNH .... Ceska Spolecnost Narodohospodarska [*Czech Economic Society*] (CZ)
CSNL........... Centre for the Study of Nigerian Languages (MAR)
CSNPT .... Ceskoslovensky Soubor Narodnich Pisni a Tancu [*Czechoslovak National Song and Dance Ensemble*] (CZ)
CSNR .... Ceskoslovenska Narodni Rada [*Czechoslovak National Council*] (CZ)
CSNRB........ Ceskoslovenska Narodni Rada Badatelska [*Czechoslovak National Research Council*] (CZ)
CSNRD........ Consortium for the Study of Nigerian Rural Development (MAR)
CSNS .... Ceskoslovenska Strana Narodnesocialisticka [*Czechoslovak National Socialist Party*] (CZ)
CSNYV........ Csongradi Nyomda Vallalat [*Csongrad Printing Enterprise*] (HU)
CSO............ Central Selling Organisation (MAR)
CSO............ Central Statistical Office [*Ethiopian*] (AF)
CSO............ Centralna Spoldzielnia Ogrodnicza [*Central Gardening Cooperative*] (POL)
CSO............ Ceskoslovensky Orel [*An athletic and gymnastic organization*] (CZ)
CSO............ Cesky Symfonicky Orchestr [*Czech Symphony Orchestra*] (CZ)
CSO............ Circulo Social Obrero [*Workers Social Circle*] [*Cuban*] (LA)
CSO............ Confederacion Sindical Obrera [*Workers Trade Union Confederation*] [*Spanish*] (WER)
CSO............ Consejo Sindical de Oriente [*Trade Union Council of the East*] [*Salvadoran*] (LA1)
CSO............ Crkveno Skolska Opstina [*Parish School District*] (YU)
cso .... Csendor [*Gendarme*] (HU)
CSO............ Cumhurbaskani Senfoni Orkestrasi [*Presidential Symphony Orchestra*] (TU)
CSOB .... Ceskoslovenska Obchodni Banka [*Czechoslovak Commerce Bank*] (CZ)
CSOK .... Ceskoslovenska Obchodni Komora [*Czechoslovak Chamber of Commerce*] (CZ)
CSOL .... Ceskoslovenska Obec Legionarska [*Czechoslovak Legion*] (CZ)
csom .... Csomag [*Parcel*] (HU)
CSOP .... Centralna Szkola Oficerow Politycznych [*Central School for Political Army Officers*] (POL)
CSOP .... Csoport [*Group, Section, Troop Detachment, Special Task Force*] (HU)
CSOS .... Ceskoslovenska Obec Sokolska [*Czechoslovak Sokol (An athletic and gymnastic organization)*] (CZ)
CSOV .... Ceskoslovensky Olympijsky Vybor [*Czechoslovak Olympic Committee*] (CZ)
CSP............ Centrala Spoldzielni Pracy [*Labor Cooperatives Center*] (POL)
CSP............ Centralna Szkola Partyjna [*Central Party School*] (POL)
CSP............ Ceskoslovenska Posta [*Czechoslovak Postal Service*] (CZ)
CSP............ Christlich Soziale Partei [*Christian Social Party*] [*Liechtenstein*] (PPW)
CSP............ Club Soliman Pacha [*Egyptian*] (MAR)
CSP............ Code du Statut Personnel [*Tunisian*] (MAR)
CSP............ Comitetul de Stat al Planificarii [*State Planning Committee*] (RO)
CSP............ Comitetul de Stat pentru Preturi [*State Committee for Prices*] (RO)
CSP............ Compagnie Saharienne Portee (MAR)
CSP............ Conseil du Salut du Peuple [*People's Salvation Council*] [*Upper Voltan*] (PD)
CSP............ Conseil Superieur du Pays (MAR)
CSP............ Conseil Superieur du Plan [*Higher Planning Council*] [*Cambodian*] (CL)
CSPAA........ Conseil de Solidarite des Pays Afro-Asiatiques (MAR)
CSPB.......... Confederacao dos Servidores Publicos do Brasil [*Confederation of Public Employees of Brazil*] (LA)
CSPC .... Caisse de Stabilisation des Prix du Coton (MAR)
CSPC .... Centrul Special de Perfectionare a Cadrelor [*Special Center for the Advanced Training of Personnel*] (RO)
CSPD .... Ceskoslovenska Plavba Dunajska [*Czechoslovak Danube River Navigation Lines*] (CZ)
CSPH .... Cesky Svaz Pozemniho [*Czech Field Hockey Association*] (CZ)
CSPiR.......... Centrala Spoldzielni Przemyslowych i Rzemieslniczych [*Industrial and Handicraft Industry Cooperatives Center*] (POL)
CSPL........... Ceskoslovenska Statni Plavba Labska [*Czechoslovak State Elbe River Navigation Lines*] (CZ)
CSPL........... Compagnie Saharienne Portee Legere (MAR)
CSPLE......... Compagnie Saharienne Portee de la Legion Etrangere (MAR)
CSPLO .... Ceskoslovenska Plavebni Spolecnost Labsko-Oderska [*Czechoslovak Elbe-Oder River Navigation Lines*] (CZ)
CSPMS .... Comitetul de Stat pentru Probleme de Munca si Salarii [*State Committee for Labor and Wage Problems*] (RO)
CSPNP .... Conseil Superieur de la Promotion Nationale et du Plan [*Higher Council for National Promotion and Planning*] [*Moroccan*] (AF)
CSPO .... Ceskoslovenska Statni Plavba Oderska [*Czechoslovakia State Oder River Navigation Lines*] (CZ)

CSPO .... Ceskoslovensky Svaz Pozarni Ochrany [*Czechoslovak Fire Fighting Union*] (CZ)
CSPOCP ..... Conference of Speakers and Presiding Officers of Commonwealth Parliaments (EA)
CSPP........... Ceskoslovenska Polni Posta [*Czechoslovak Field Postal Service*] (CZ)
CSPP........... Ceskoslovenske Paroplavebni Podniky [*Czechoslovak Steamship Lines*] (CZ)
CSPP........... Ceskoslovenske Plynarenske Podniky [*Czechoslovak Gas Works*] (CZ)
CSPPA........ Caisse de Stabilisation des Prix des Produits Agricoles (MAR)
CSPPN........ Caisse de Stabilisation des Prix des Produits du Niger (MAR)
CSPT........... Compagnie Senegalaise des Phosphates de Taiba (MAR)
CSPU .... Ceskoslovensky Plavebni Ustav [*Czechoslovak Institute for Navigation*] (CZ)
CSPV........... Convergencia Socialista del Pais Valencia [*Socialist Convergence of the Valencian Country*] [*Spanish*] (WER)
CS PZPR ..... Centralna Szkola Polskiej Zjednoczonej Partii Robotniczej [*Central School of the Polish United Workers Party*] (POL)
CSR............. Centrala Spoldzielni Rolniczych [*Agricultural Cooperatives Center*] (POL)
CSR............. Ceska Socialisticka Republika [*Czech Socialist Republic (since 1969)*] (CZ)
CSR............. Ceskoslovenska Republika [*Czechoslovak Republic (until 1960)*] (CZ)
CSR............. Club Sportif de Redeyef [*Tunisian*] (MAR)
CSR............. Combinatul Siderurgic Resita [*Resita Iron and Steel Combine*] (RO)
CSR............. Congress for the Second Republic (MAR)
CSR............. Conseil Supreme de la Republique (MAR)
CSR............. Conseil Supreme de la Revolution [*Supreme Revolutionary Council*] [*Malagasy*] (AF)
CSR............. Czesko-Slowacka Republika [*Czechoslovak Republic*] (POL)
CSRA .... Comite Scientifique pour les Recherches Antarctiques [*Scientific Committee on Antarctic Research*]
CSRO .... Comite Scientifique pour les Recherches Oceaniques [*Scientific Committee on Oceanic Research*]
CSRS .... Centre Suisse de Recherches Scientifiques en Cote-d'Ivoire (MAR)
CSRS .... Ceskoslovensky Rybarsky Svaz [*Czechoslovak Fishing Union*] (CZ)
CSRS .... Czecho-Slowacka Republika Socjalistyczna [*Czechoslovak Socialist Republic*] (POL)
CSRSA........ Comite Secreto Revolucionario do Sul de Angola (MAR)
CSRV .... Comite de Soutien a la Republique de Vietnam [*Committee for Supporting the Republic of Vietnam*] [*French*] (WER)
CSS............. Centrala Sprzetu Samochodowego [*Automobile Equipment Center*] (POL)
CSS............. Ceskoslovenska Silnicni Sluzba [*Czechoslovak Road Service*] (CZ)
CSS............. Ceskoslovenska Strana Socialisticka [*Czechoslovak Socialist Party*] (PPE)
CSS............. Ceskoslovensky Svaz Studentstva [*Czechoslovak Student Union*] (CZ)
CSS............. Cesky Sermirsky Svaz [*Czech Fencing Association*] (CZ)
CSS............. Club Sportif Sfaxien [*Tunisian*] (MAR)
CSS............. Compagnie Sucriere Senegalaise (MAR)
CSS............. Consiglio Superiore di Sanita [*Higher Health Council*] [*Italian*] (WER)
CSS............. Consiliul Superior al Sanatatii [*Higher Council for Health*] (RO)
CSSA .... Conseil Superieur du Sport en Afrique [*Higher Sports Council in Africa*] (AF)
CSSD .... Ceskoslovenska Socialnedemokraticka Strana Delnicka [*Czechoslovak Social Democratic Workers' Party*] (PPE)
Csse............ Caisse [*Cash*] [*French*]
CSSE .... Compagnie Senegalaise du Sud-Est (MAR)
CSSF........... Ceskoslovenske Statni Filmy [*Czechoslovak State Film Studios*] (CZ)
CSSiS .... Centrala Sprzetu Sportowego i Szkutniczego [*Sport and Boating Equipment Center*] (POL)
CSSL........... Ceskoslovenske Statni Lesy [*Czechoslovak State Forests*] (CZ)
CSSLD .... Ceskoslovenska Smiesana Letecka Divizia [*Czechoslovak Combined Air Division*] [*World War II*] (CZ)
CSSL'L........ Ceskoslovensky Svaz L'udoveho Letectva [*Czechoslovak Civil Aviation League*] (CZ)
CSSM.......... Ceskoslovenske Statne Majetky [*Czechoslovak State Farms*] (CZ)
CSS Motozbyt ... Centrala Sprzetu Samochodowego "Motozbyt" [*"Motozbyt" (Motor Sales) Automotive Equipment Center*] (POL)
CSSMW ...... Centrum Szkolenia Specjalistow Marynarki Wojennej [*Navy Specialists Training Center*] (POL)
CSSO .... Cursos Secundarios de Superacion Obrera [*Workers Secondary Improvement Courses*] [*Cuban*] (LA)
CSSPPA...... Caisse de Stabilisation et de Soutien des Prix des Productions Agricoles (MAR)
CSSPT .... Ceskoslovensky Statni Soubor Pisni a Tancu [*Czechoslovak State Song and Dance Ensemble*] (CZ)
CSSPVZ...... Ceskoslovenska Spolecnost pro Sireni Politickych a Vedeckych Znalosti [*Czechoslovak Society for the Dissemination of Political and Scientific Knowledge*] (CZ)
CSSR .... Ceskoslovenska Socialisticka Republika [*Czechoslovak Socialist Republic*] (CZ)
CSSR .... Ceskoslovensky Svaz Rugby [*Czechoslovak Rugby Association*] (CZ)
CSSR .... Tschechoslowakische Sozialistische Republik [*Czechoslovak Socialist Republic*] (EG)
CSSS .... Ceskoslovenske Statni Statky [*Czechoslovak State Farms*] (CZ)
CSS Spolem ... Centrala Spoldzielni Spozywcow "Spolem" [*"Spolem" Consumers' Cooperatives Center*] (POL)
CSST........... Cesky Svaz Stolniho Tennisu [*Czech Ping-Pong Association*] (CZ)
CSSV .... Ceskoslovensky Svaz Vcelaru [*Czechoslovak Beekeepers Union*] (CZ)
CSSZ........... Ceskoslovenska Spolecnost Zemepisna [*Czechoslovak Geographical Society*] (CZ)
CSSZ........... Ceskoslovenske Stavebni Zavody [*Czechoslovak Construction Plants*] (CZ)
CSSZ........... Ceskoslovensky Svaz Zen [*Czechoslovak Union of Women*] (CZ)
cs sz........... Csekk-Szamla [*Bank Account, Checking Account*] (HU)
CSSZK .... Csehszlovak Szocialista Koztarsasag [*Czechoslovak Socialist Republic*] (HU)
CST............. Central Sandinista de Trabajadores [*Sandinist Workers Federation*] [*Nicaraguan*] (LA)
CST............. Centrala Spoldzielni Transportu [*Transportation Cooperatives Center*] (POL)
CST............. Confederation Senegalaise du Travail [*Senegalese Labor Confederation*] (AF)
CST............. Consortium on Soils of the Tropics (MAR)
CST............. Cooperation Scientifique et Technique (MAR)
CSTA .... Cesky Svaz Tezke Atletiky [*Czech Athletic Association*] (CZ)
CSTA .... Chinese Schoolteachers' Association (ML)
CSTA .... Commandant Superieur des Troupes en Algerie (MAR)
CSTA .... Consejo Sindical de Trabajadores Andinos [*Trade Union Council of Andean Workers*] (LA)
CSTAL .... Confederacion Sindical de los Trabajadores de America Latina [*Trade Union Confederation of Latin American Workers*] (LA)
CSTB........... Centre Scientifique et Technique du Batiment [*Building research*] [*French*]
CSTC .... Compagnie Senegalaise de Transports en Commun (MAR)
CSTC .... Confederacion Sindical de Trabajadores de Colombia [*Colombian Workers Trade Union Confederation*] (LA)
CSTCB........ Confederacion Sindical de Trabajadores de Construccion de Bolivia [*Bolivian Construction Workers Union*] (LA)
CSTI........... Csepeli Tervezo Intezet [*Csepel Planning Institute*] (HU)
CsTI............ Csomagolastechnikai Intezet [*Institute of Packaging Technology*] (HU)
CSTM.......... Compagnie Senegalaise pour la Transformation des Metaux (MAR)
CSTN .... Centre des Sciences et de la Technologie Nucleaire [*Algerian*] (MAR)
CSTP........... Ceskoslovensky Tabakovy Prumysl [*Czechoslovak Tobacco Industry*] (CZ)
CSTR........... Ceskoslovenska Tabakova Rezie [*Czechoslovak Tobacco Monopoly*] (CZ)
CSTR........... Commission Scientifique, Technique, et de la Recherche (de l'OUA) [*Scientific, Technical, and Research Commission (of the OAU)*] [*Use STRC*] (AF)
CSTS........... Ceskoslovensky Telovychovny Svaz [*Czechoslovak Physical Education Association*] (CZ)
CSTT........... Confederation Syndicale des Travailleurs Togolais [*Trade Union Confederation of Togolese Workers*] (AF)
CSTTA .... Ceskoslovenska Table-Tennisova Asociace [*Czechoslovak Ping-Pong Association*] (CZ)
CSTV........... Ceskoslovensky Svaz Telesne Vychovy [*Czechoslovak Union of Physical Training*] (CZ)
CSTV........... Confederation des Syndicats des Travailleurs du Viet-Nam [*Confederation of Workers' Trade Unions of Viet-Nam*] [*South Vietnamese*]
CSU............. Cesky Statisticky Urad [*Czech Statistical Office*] (CZ)
CSU............. Christian Students' Union of South Africa (MAR)
CSU............. Christlich-Soziale Union [*Christian Social Union*] [*Bavarian Affiliate of the CDU*] [*West German*] (WEN)
CSU............. Confederacion Sindical del Uruguay [*Confederation of Uruguayan Trade Unions*] (LA)
CSU............. Consejo Superior Universitario [*University Higher Council*] [*Guatemalan*] (LA)
CSU............. Consejo Superior Universitario [*University Higher Council*] [*Salvadoran*] (LA1)
CSUA .... Ceskoslovenske Ustavy Astronomicke [*Astronomical Institutes of Czechoslovakia*] (CZ)
CSUC .... Ceskoslovenske Ustredi Cyklistu [*Czechoslovak Central Organization of Cyclists*] (CZ)
CSUCA .... Consejo Superior Universitario Centroamericano [*Higher Council of the Central American University*] (LA1)
CSUP .... Ceskoslovensky Urad Pamatkovy [*Czechoslovak Office for the Preservation of Historical Monuments*] (CZ)
CSUP .... Ceskoslovensky Ustav Prace [*Czechoslovak Labor Institute*] (CZ)

CSUR .... Conseil Superieur des Universites Royales [*Higher Royal University Council*] [*Cambodian*] (CL)
CSUT .... Confederacion de Sindicatos Unitarios de Trabajadores [*Confederation of Unitary Trade Unions of Workers*] [*Spanish*] (WER)
csut .... Csutortok [*Thursday*] (HU)
CSUTHD ..... Ceskoslovensky Ustav pro Technickou a Hospodarskou Dokumentaci [*Czechoslovak Institute for Technical and Economic Documentation*] (CZ)
CSUZ .... Civil Service Union of Zambia (MAR)
CSV .... Chreschtlech-Sozial Vollekspartei [*Christian Social Party*] [*Luxembourg*] (PPW)
CSV .... Confederation Syndicale Voltaique [*Voltan Trade Union Confederation*] (AF)
CSVA .... Csepeli Vas- es Acelontodek [*Iron and Steel Foundries of Csepel*] (HU)
CSVD .... Cesky Svaz Vyrobnich Druzstev [*Czech Union of Production Cooperatives*] (CZ)
CSVF .... Csepeli Vas- es Femmuvek [*Iron and Steel Works of Csepel*] (HU)
CSVOD .... Ceskoslovensky Vybor na Ochranu Deti [*Czechoslovak Committee for the Protection of Children*] (CZ)
CSVOM .... Ceskoslovensky Vybor Obrancu Miru [*Czechoslovak Committee of the Defenders of Peace*] (CZ)
CSVPA .... Comitetul de Stat pentru Valorificarea Produselor Agricole [*State Committee for the Exploitation of Agricultural Products*] (RO)
CSVS .... Ceskoslovensky Volleyballovy Svaz [*Czechoslovak Volleyball Association*] (CZ)
CSVTS .... Ceskoslovenska Vedecka Technicka Spolecnost [*Czechoslovak Scientific and Technological Society*] (CZ)
CSVV .... Ceskoslovensky Vsesportovni Vybor [*Czechoslovak Athletic Committee*] (CZ)
CSWiK .... Centrala Spoldzielni Wydawniczych i Ksiegarskich [*Central Office of Publishing and Bookselling Cooperatives*] (POL)
CSW Solidarnosc ... Centrala Spoldzielni Wytworczych "Solidarnosc" [*Central Office of the "Solidarnosc" (Solidarity) Production Cooperatives*] (POL)
CSWV .... Centraal Sociaal Werkgeversverbond [*Central Social Employers' Association*] [*Defunct*] [*Dutch*] (WEN)
CSZ .... Ceskoslovensky Svaz Zen [*Czechoslovak Union of Women*] (CZ)
CSZP .... Ceskoslovenske Zavody Papirenske [*Czechoslovak Paper Mills*] (CZ)
CSZPS .... Ceskoslovenske Zavody Presneho Strojirenstvi [*Czechoslovak Precision Machinery Factories*] (CZ)
CSZS .... Ceskoslovenska Zemepisna Spolecnost [*Czechoslovak Geographical Society*] (CZ)
CT .... Cameroon Tribune [*A publication*] (MAR)
CT .... Canton [*Canton, District, Section*] [*Military map abbreviation*] [*World War I*] [*French*] (MTD)
CT .... Canton and Enderbury Islands [*Two-letter standard code*] (CNC)
CT .... Carbonique de Tanger (MAR)
CT .... Celjska Tiskarna [*Celje Printing House*] (YU)
CT .... Centrala Tekstylna [*Textile Center*] (POL)
CT .... Ceskoslovenska Televise [*Czechoslovak Television*] (CZ)
CT .... Comissao de Trabalhadores [*Workers Committee*] [*Portuguese*] (WER)
CT .... Comunion Tradicionalista [*Traditionalist Communion*] [*Spanish*] (WER)
CT .... Congreso del Trabajo [*Labor Congress*] [*Mexican*] (LA1)
CT .... Congresul Taranimii [*Congress of the Peasantry*] (RO)
ct .... Courant [*Of the Current Month*] [*French*]
CT .... Credit du Togo [*Credit Bank of Togo*] (AF)
Cta .... Caleta [*Cove*] [*See also Cal*] [*Spanish*] (NAU)
CTA .... Central de Trabajadores del Estado Aragua [*Federation of Workers of Aragua State*] [*Venezuelan*] (LA)
CTA .... Centrala Teatrow Amatorskich [*Central Office of Amateur Theatres*] (POL)
CTA .... Centrala de Transporturi Auto [*Automotive Transportation Central*] (RO)
CTA .... Centro Tecnologico da Aeronautica [*Aerospace Technology Center*] [*Brazilian*] (LA)
CTA .... Commission Technique des Achats [*Technical Purchasing Committee*] [*Cambodian*] (CL)
CTA .... Consorcio Tecnico de Aeronautica (MAR)
Cta .... Constanta [*Constanta*] (RO)
cta .... Cuenta [*Count*] [*Spanish*]
Cta crrte ..... Cuenta Corriente [*Account Current*] [*Spanish*] [*Business and trade*]
CTAL .... Confederacion de Trabajadores de America Latina [*Confederation of Latin American Workers*] (LA)
Ctal .... Cortal [*Shepherd's Hut*] [*Military map abbreviation*] [*World War I*] [*French*] (MTD)
CTAMA .... Caisse Tunisienne d'Assurances Mutuelles Agricoles [*Tunisian Agricultural Insurance Fund*] (AF)
CTAT .... Centre Technique d'Agriculture Tropicale (MAR)
CTB .... Central de Trabajadores Bolivianos [*Federation of Bolivian Workers*] (LA)
CTB .... Companhia Telefonica Brasileira [*A telecommunications company*] [*Brazilian*]
Ctb .... Cottbus [*Cottbus*] [*One of the eight reichsbahn directorates*] (EG)
CTBA .... Complexe de Transports Bel Abbesiens (MAR)
CTC .... Central de Trabajadores de Cuba [*Central Organization of Cuban Trade Unions*] (LA)
CTC .... Centrale Technische Catalogus [*Dutch*]
CTC .... Centro de Teatro Colombiano [*Cali*] (COL)
CTC .... Comando Territorial Central [*Central Territorial Command*] [*Mozambican*] (AF)
CTC .... Compagnie Tchadienne de Construction (MAR)
CTC .... Compagnie de Transactions Commerciales (MAR)
CTC .... Compagnie de Transport et de Commerce (MAR)
CTC .... Comptoir Togolais du Commerce (MAR)
CTC .... Confederacion de Trabajadores del Cobre [*Copper Workers Confederation*] [*Chilean*] (LA)
CTC .... Confederacion de Trabajadores de Colombia [*Colombian Confederation of Workers*] (LA)
CTC .... Container Terminal Company (MAR)
CTC .... Control Tehnic de Calitate [*Technical Quality Control*] (RO)
CTC .... Controle Technique de la Construction [*Algerian*] (MAR)
CTCA .... Confederacion de Trabajadores de Centroamerica [*Confederation of Central American Workers*] (LA)
CTCA .... Cooperative des Tailleurs et Couturieres d'Abidjan (MAR)
CTCASS ..... Commission for Technical Co-Operation in Africa South of the Sahara (MAR)
CTCE .... Centru Teritorial de Calcul Electronic [*Territorial Center for Electronic Data Processing*] (RO)
CTCh .... Confederacion de Trabajadores de Chile [*Chilean Workers Confederation*] (LA)
CTCI .... Confederacion de Trabajadores Colombianos Independientes [*Independent Colombian Workers Confederation*] (LA)
CTCIA .... Compagnie Togolaise de Commerce, d'Industrie, et d'Agriculture (MAR)
CTCS .... Centre Technique de la Canne et du Sucre [*Technical Center for Cane and Sugar*] [*French Guiana*] (LA1)
CTCS .... Comisia Tehnica de Colaboratie Stiintifica [*Technical Commission for Scientific Collaboration*] (RO)
CTD .... Comhluchd Tuathanach Duthchail [*National Farmers' Union*] [*Scottish*]
CTE .... Canton and Enderbury Islands [*Three-letter standard code*] (CNC)
CTE .... Centrala Termoelectrica [*Thermoelectric Power Plant*] (RO)
CTE .... Compagnie de Traitement des Eaux [*Water Treatment Company*] (CL)
Cte .... Compte [*Account*] [*French*] (GPO)
Cte .... Comte [*Count*] [*French*]
CTE .... Confederacion de Trabajadores Ecuatorianos [*Confederation of Ecuadorean Workers*] (LA)
CTEEV .... Compagnie Tchadienne d'Elevage et d'Exportation de Viande (MAR)
CTEP .... Societe Cooperative de Transports de Fret et Personnel de Fort - Archambault (MAR)
CTERA .... Confederacion de Trabajadores de la Educacion de la Republica [*Confederation of Education Workers of the Argentine Republic*] (LA)
CTESE .... Cengiz Topel Erkek Sanaat Enstitusu [*Cengiz Topel Men's Trade Institute*] [*Turkish Cypriot*] (GC)
Ctesse .... Comtesse [*Countess*] [*French*]
CTETOC ..... Council for Technical Education and Training for Overseas Countries (MAR)
CTF .... Central de Trabajadores Federados [*Confederation of Federated Workers*] [*Guatemalan*] (LA)
CTFM .... Comite des Transports Ferroviaires du Maghreb [*Moroccan*] (MAR)
CTFT .... Centre Technique Forestier Tropical [*Technical Center for Tropical Forestry*] [*French*] (AF)
CTG .... Cabinet de Topographie et Geometrie (MAR)
CTG .... Compagnie des Transports Gabonais (MAR)
ctg .... Courtage [*Brokerage, Commission*] [*French*]
CTgS .... Centralna Telegrafska Stanica [*Central Telegraph Station*] [*Military*] (YU)
CTH .... Commerce et Transport du Hodh (MAR)
CTH .... Confederacion de Trabajadores Hondurenos [*Confederation of Honduran Workers*] (LA)
CTI .... Centre Telex International (MAR)
CTI .... Centre de Transit International [*International Transit Center*] [*Cameroonian*] (AF)
CTIF .... Comite Technique International de Prevention et d'Extinction du Feu [*International Technical Committee for the Prevention and Extinction of Fire*] (EA)
CTIP .... Compagnia Tecnica Industrie Petroli [*Technical Petroleum Industries Company*] [*Italian*] (WER)
CTK .... Ceskoslovenska Tiskova Kancelar [*Czechoslovak Press Bureau*] (CZ)
CTK .... Ceskoslovenska Tlacova Kancelaria [*Czechoslovak Press Bureau*] (CZ)
CTK .... Tschechoslowakische Nachrichten-Agentur [*Czechoslovak News Agency*] (EG)
ctkm .... Cisty Tunkilometr [*Net Ton-Kilometer*] (CZ)

CTL .... Ceske Tovarny na Lahve [*Czech Bottle Factories*] (CZ)
CTLA .... Central Transport Licensing Authority (MAR)
CTM .... Carrieres et Transports de la Mondah (MAR)
CTM .... Centro Tecnologico Mineral [*Mineral Technology Center*] [*Brazilian*] (LA)
CTM .... Ceske Technicke Museum [*Czech Museum of Technology*] (CZ)
CTM .... Ceskoslovensky Tabakovy Monopol [*Czechoslovak Tobacco Monopoly*] (CZ)
CTM .... Comision Tecnica Mixta Argentina-Uruguaya de Salto Grande [*Argentine-Uruguayan Joint Commission of Salto Grande*] (LA)
CTM .... Compagnie Auxiliaire de Transports au Maroc (MAR)
CTM .... Compagnie de Transports Maritimes (MAR)
CTM .... Compagnie de Transports Marocains (MAR)
CTM .... Confederacion de Trabajadores Mexicanos [*Confederation of Mexican Workers*] (LA)
CTMB .... Compagnie Togolaise des Mines du Benin [*Togolese Mining Company of Benin*] (AF)
CTMC .... Centre de Tannage et de Manufacture des Cuirs (MAR)
CTMC .... Compagnie pour la Transformation des Metaux au Cameroun (MAR)
CTMLN .... Compagnie de Transports au Maroc "Lignes Nationales" (MAR)
ctmo .... Centesimo [*Hundredth*] [*Spanish*]
ctmo .... Centimo [*Centime*] [*Spanish*]
CTN .... Central de Trabajadores de Nicaragua [*Federation of Nicaraguan Workers*] (LA)
CTN .... Compagnie Tunisienne de Navigation (MAR)
CTN .... Corps Tjadangan Nasional [*National Reserve Corps*] (IN)
CTNC .... Code of Conduct for Transnational Corporations (MAR)
CTNE .... Compania Telefonica Nacional de Espana [*National Telephone Company of Spain*] (WER)
CTO .... Central Transport Organisation (MAR)
CTO .... Communist Terrorist Organization (ML)
cto .... Cuarto [*Room*] [*Spanish*]
CTOS .... Central de Trabajadores Organizados de El Salvador [*Central Organization of Salvadoran Organized Workers*] (LA1)
CTOSSU ..... Comite Tunisien d'Organisation des Sports Scolaires et Universitaires (MAR)
CTP .... Confederacion de Trabajadores del Peru [*Confederation of Workers of Peru*] (LA)
CTP .... Cumhuriyetci Turk Partisi [*Republican Turkish Party*] [*Turkish Cypriot*] (PPE)
Ctr .... Centner [*100 Kilograms*] [*Business and trade*] [*German*]
CTR .... Court Tir Rapide [*Military*] [*French*] (MTD)
Ctra .... Carretera [*Highway*] [*Spanish*] (CED)
CTRI .... Central Tobacco Research Institute (MAR)
CTRIN .... Comercializacao do Trigo Nacional [*National Wheat Marketing Enterprise*] [*Brazilian*] (LA)
CTRJ .... Commission Technique Regionale des Jeunes (MAR)
CTRM .... Compagnie de Transports Routiers et de Messageries (MAR)
CTRO .... Compagnie des Transports Routiers de l'Oubangui (MAR)
CTRP .... Central de Trabajadores de la Revolucion Peruana [*Federation of Workers of the Peruvian Revolution*] (LA)
CTRP .... Confederacion de Trabajadores de la Republica de Panama [*Confederation of Workers of the Republic of Panama*] (LA)
CTRPD .... Comite Technique Regional du Plan et du Developpement [*Regional Technical Planning and Development Committee*] [*Malagasy*] (AF)
CTRS .... Cooperative des Transporteurs Routiers du Senegal (MAR)
CTRU .... Colonial Termite Research Unit (MAR)
CTS .... Cambodia Travel Service (CL)
cts .... Centimos [*Spanish*]
CTS .... Central de Trabajadores Salvadorenos [*Central Organization of Salvadoran Workers*] (LA1)
CTS .... Centralna Telefonska Sluzba [*Central Telephone Service*] [*Military*] (YU)
CTS .... Centralna Telefonska Stanica [*Central Telephone Station*] [*Military*] (YU)
CTS .... Cesky Tennisovy Svaz [*Czech Tennis Association*] (CZ)
CTS .... Comando Territorial do Sul [*Southern Territorial Command*] [*Mozambican*] (AF)
CTS .... Compagnie de Transports Senegalais (MAR)
CTS .... Compagnies Tchadiennes de Securite [*Chadian Security Companies*] (AF)
CTS .... Container-Transport-System (EG)
cts .... Cuartos [*Rooms*] [*Spanish*]
CTSK .... Cetinkaya Turk Spor Klubu [*Cetinkaya Turkish Sports Club*] [*Turkish Cypriot*] (TU)
CTT .... Administracao-Geral dos Correios, Telegrafos, e Telefones [*General Administration of Post Offices, Telegraphs, and Telephones*] [*Portuguese*] (WER)
CTT .... Central de Trabajadores Textiles [*Federation of Textile Workers*] [*Venezuelan*] (LA)
CTT .... Compagnie de Tifnout Tiranimine [*Moroccan*] (MAR)
CTT .... Confederacion de Transporte Terrestre [*Automotive Transportation Confederation*] [*Chilean*] (LA)
CTT .... Cooperative des Transports Tchadiens (MAR)
CTTA .... Compagnie de Transports et de Travaux Aeriens (MAR)
CTTC .... Centrale Togolaise des Travailleurs Croyants [*Togolese Federation of Believing Workers*] (AF)
CTTM .... Cok Tarafli Ticaret Muzekereleri [*Multilateral Trade Negotiations*] (TU)
CTTT .... Compagnie Tunisienne de Tourisme et de Thermalisme (MAR)
CTU .... Central de Trabajadores del Uruguay [*Uruguayan Workers Federation*] (LA)
CTUC .... Commonwealth Trade Union Council (EA)
CTV .... Comites Toupeiras Vermelhas [*Red Youth Committees*] [*Portuguese*] (WER)
CTV .... Confederacion de Trabajadores de Venezuela [*Confederation of Venezuelan Workers*] (LA)
CTVM .... Centre for Tropical Veterinary Medicine (MAR)
ctvo .... Centavo [*Cent*] [*Spanish*]
CTZ .... Ceskoslovenske Textilni Zavody, Narodni Podnik [*Czechoslovak Textile Factories, National Enterprise*] (CZ)
CTZ .... Ceskoslovenske Tukove Zavody [*Czechoslovak Fats Rendering Plants*] (CZ)
c/u .... Cada Uno [*Every One, Each*] [*Spanish*]
CU .... Centralny Urzad [*Central Administration, Agency, Office*] (POL)
CU .... Charge Utile [*French*]
CU .... Cirkevna Ustava [*Church Statutes*] (CZ)
CU .... Cuba [*Two-letter standard code*] (CNC)
CU .... Cukurova Universitesi [*Cukurova University*] (TU)
CU .... Cumhuriyet Universitesi [*Republic University*] [*Sivas*] (TU)
CUA .... Columbia University Contributions to Anthropology [*A publication*] (MAR)
CUACSA ..... Comite de Unidade de Accao e de Goordinacao Sindical de Angola (MAR)
CUAG .... Centre Universitaire des Antilles-Guyane [*Antilles-French Guiana University Center*] (LA1)
CUAN .... Centro Urbano Antonio Narino [*Bogota*] (COL)
CUAP .... Comision Uruguaya de la Alianza para el Progreso [*Uruguayan Commission for the Alliance for Progress*] (LA)
CUARIC ...... Centrala de Automatizare de Utilaje si Reparatii pentru Industria Chimica [*Central for the Automation of Equipment and Repairs for the Chemical Industry*] (RO)
CUAS .... Comite de Unidad de Accion Sindical [*Committee for Unity of Labor Union Action*] [*Colombian*] (LA)
CUASS .... Comite de Unidad de Accion y Solidaridad Sindical [*Committee for Unity of Trade Union Action and Solidarity*] [*Colombian*] (LA)
CUAVES ..... Comunidad Urbana Autogestionaria de Villa El Salvador [*Urban Self-Management Community of Villa El Salvador*] [*Peruvian*] (LA)
CUB .... Centralna Uprava Brodogradnje [*Central Administration of Shipbuilding*] (YU)
CUB .... Comitato Unitario di Base [*Local Unitary Committee*] [*Italian*] (WER)
CUB .... Confederacion Universitaria Boliviana [*Bolivian University Confederation*] (LA)
CUB .... Cuba [*Three-letter standard code*] (CNC)
CUBACONTROL ... Empresa Cubana de Control [*Cuban Control Enterprise*] (LA)
CUBAEXPORT ... Empresa Cubana Exportadora de Alimentos y Productos Varios [*Cuban Enterprise for the Export of Foodstuffs and Various Products*] (LA)
CUBAFRUTAS ... Empresa Cubana Exportadora de Frutas Tropicales [*Cuban Tropical Fruit Exporting Enterprise*] (LA)
CUBAINDUSTRIA ... Empresa Exportadora de Productos Industriales [*Industrial Products Exporting Enterprise*] [*Cuban*] (LA)
CUBAINDUSTRIAL ... Empresa Cubana Importadora de Plantas Completas [*Cuban Complete Plant Importing Enterprise*] (LA)
CUBAMETALES ... Empresa Importadora de Metales [*Cuban Enterprise for the Import of Metals*] (LA)
CUBANIQUEL ... Empresa Cubana Exportadora de Minerales y Metales [*Cuban Enterprise for the Export of Minerals and Metals*] (LA)
CUBAPESCA ... Empresa Importadora de Buques y Equipos de Pesca [*Cuban Enterprise for the Import of Fishing Ships and Fishing Equipment*] (LA)
CUBARTIMPEX ... Empresa Cubana Exportadora e Importadora de Articulos de Arte y Cultura [*Cuban Enterprise for Export and Import of Items of Art and Culture*] (LA)
CUBATABACO ... Empresa Cubana de Tabaco [*Cuban Tobacco Enterprise*] (LA)
CUBATEX ... Empresa Cubana Importadora de Fibras, Tejidos, Cueros, y Sus Productos [*Cuban Enterprise for the Import of Fibers, Fabrics, Leathers, and Their By-Products*] (LA)
CUBATUR ... Empresa de Turismo Nacional e Internacional [*National and International Tourist Enterprise*] [*Cuban*] (LA)
CUBAZUCAR ... Empresa Cubana Exportadora de Azucar y Sus Derivados [*Cuban Enterprise for Export of Sugar and Sugar By-Products*] (LA)
CUBEPAL ... Coordinadora de Unidades Basicas de Emigrados Peronistas en America Latina [*Coordinator of Basic Units of Peronist Emigres in Latin America*] (LA)
CUBI .... Centro Nazionale per il Catalogo Unico delle Biblioteche Italiane [*Italian*]
CUC .... Cameroon United Congress (AF)
CUC .... Committee of Peasant Unity [*Guatemalan*] (PD)

CUCA.......... Cercle Universitaire "Connaissance de l'Afrique" (MAR)
CUCMS....... Compagnie Universelle du Canal Maritime de Suez (MAR)
CUCO.......... Comite de Unidad Civica Organizado [*Organized Civic Unity Committee*] [*Guatemalan*] (LA)
CUCODEP... Credit Union of Community Development Personnel [*Cambodian*] (CL)
CUD............ Comite de l'Union Douaniere [*Customs Union Committee*] [*Ivorian*] (AF)
CUD............ Comite de l'Union Douaniere [*Customs Union Committee*] [*Upper Voltan*] (AF)
CUDAG....... Comite Unificador Docente de Accion Gremial [*Teachers Unification Committee for Union Action*] [*Argentine*] (LA)
CUDMER..... Comite Unificador del Movimiento Estudiantil Revolucionario [*Unifying Committee of the Revolutionary Student Movement*] [*Peruvian*] (LA)
CUDW......... Centralny Urzad Drobnej Wytworczosci [*Central Administration of Small Scale Industry*] (POL)
CUED.......... Certificat Universitaire d'Etudes de Droit [*French*]
CUEE.......... Certificat Universitaire d'Etudes Economiques [*French*]
CUEG.......... Centro Universitario de Estudios Generales [*University General Studies Center*] [*Dominican Republic*] (LA)
CUEL........... Certificat Universitaire d'Etudes Litteraires [*French*]
CUES.......... Certificat Universitaire d'Etudes Scientifiques [*French*]
CUF............ Companhia Uniao Fabril [*United Manufacturers' Company*] [*Portuguese*] (AF)
CUFEC........ Curso de Formacion Estadistica del Caribe [*Barranquilla*] (COL)
CUFF........... Comando Unico Frente de Liberacion Nacional - Fuerzas Armadas de Liberacion Nacional [*Single Command of the National Liberation Front - Armed Forces of National Liberation*] [*Venezuelan*] (LA)
CUFLET...... Empresa Cubana de Fletes [*Cuban Freight Enterprise*] (LA)
CUFOP........ Centre Universitaire de Formation Permanente (MAR)
CUG............ Centralny Urzad Geologii [*Central Office of Geology*] (POL)
CUG............ Computer Utilization Group [*OECD*]
CUGCO....... Confederation of Unions in Government Corporations and Offices [*Philippine*]
CUGiK......... Centralny Urzad Geodezji i Kartografii [*Central Administration of Geodesy and Cartography*] (POL)
CUGK.......... Cesky Urad Geodeticky a Kartograficky [*Czech Geodetic and Cartographic Office*] (CZ)
CUGM......... Centralny Urzad Gospodarki Materialowej [*Central Administration of the Management of Materials*] (POL)
CUGW......... Centralny Urzad Gospodarki Wodnej [*Central Office for Water Management*] (POL)
CUIP........... Comite Universitario de Investigaciones de Poblacion, Universidad del Valle [*Cali*] (COL)
CUJAE........ Ciudad Universitaria Jose Antonio Echeverria [*Jose Antonio Echeverria University City*] [*Cuban*] (LA)
CUJiM......... Centralny Urzad Jokosci i Miar [*Central Quality and Measure Office*] (POL)
CUK............ Centralny Urzad Kinematografii [*Central Administration of Motion Pictures*] (POL)
CUKB.......... Cairo University Khartoum Branch (MAR)
CUKC.......... Citizens of the United Kingdom and Commonwealth (MAR)
CUKK.......... Ceskoslovenske Ustredi Knizni Kultury [*Czechoslovak Book Culture Center*] (CZ)
CUKOBIRLIK ... Cukurova Pamuk ve Narenciye Tarim Satis Kooperatifleri Birligi [*Cukurova Cotton and Citrus Fruit Agricultural Sales Cooperatives Union*] [*Adana*] (TU)
CUKOSEN... Cukurova Pamuk Taris Satis Kooperatifi Sendikasi [*Cukurova Cotton Agricultural Sales Cooperative Union*] [*Adana*] (TU)
CUKREX..... Akciova Spolecnost pro Obchod s Cukrem [*Sugar Trading Joint-Stock Company*] (CZ)
CUKROHURT ... Nadmorska Hurtownia Wyrobow Cukierniczych [*Coastal Confectionary Wholesale House*] (POL)
CUM........... Chinese Unity Movement (ML)
cum............ Cumulatif [*French*]
CUMA......... Cooperative d'Utilisation du Materiel Agricole en Commun (MAR)
Cumh.......... Cumhuriyet [*Republic*] (TU)
CUN............ Consiglio Universitario Nazionale [*National University Council*] [*Italian*]
CUNA.......... Central Unica Agraria [*Single Agrarian Federation*] [*Peruvian*] (LA)
CUNA.......... Centro Universitario de Alajuela [*Alajuela University Center*] [*Costa Rican*] (LA1)
CUNA.......... Co-Operative Union National Association, Inc. (MAR)
CUNA.......... Comite de l'Unite Nationale Angolaise [*Angolan National Unity Committee*] (AF)
CUNC.......... Comite d'Union Nationale des Cabindais [*Cabindan Committee of National Union*] [*Angolan*] (AF)
CUOP.......... Ceskoslovensky Urad Ochrany Prace [*Czechoslovak Office for Labor Protection*] (CZ)
CUP............ Centralny Urzad Planowania [*Central Planning Administration*] (POL)
CUP............ Ceskoslovensky Ustav Prace [*Czechoslovak Labor Institute*] (CZ)
CUP............ Comites de Unidad Popular [*Committees of Popular Unity*] [*Spanish*] (WER)
CUPASAN... Cukurova Plastik Ambalaj Sanayi ve Ticaret AS [*Cukurova Plastics Packaging Industry and Trade Corp.*] (TU)
CUPROCH... Confederacion Unica de Profesionales y Tecnicos de Chile [*Single Confederation of Chilean Professionals and Technicians*] (LA)
CUPS.......... Centrala pentru Utilaje si Piese de Schimb [*Central for Equipment and Spare Parts*] (RO)
CUPSIC....... Centrala de Utilaje si Piese de Schimb pentru Industria Chimica [*Central for Equipment and Spare Parts for the Chemical Industry*] (RO)
CUR............ Centralny Urzad Radiofonii [*Central Administration of the Radio Loudspeaker Network*] (POL)
CUR............ Centre Universitaire Regional (MAR)
CUR............ Comite de Unidad Revolucionaria [*Committee of Revolutionary Unity*] [*Venezuelan*] (LA)
CURC.......... Cairo University Rowing Club (MAR)
CURE.......... Citizens United for Racial Equality (MAR)
CURE.......... Comite Unico Regional de Estudiantes [*Single Regional Student Committee*] [*Venezuelan*] (LA)
CURE.......... Comite Unificado Regional de Estudiantes [*Unified Regional Student Committee*] [*Venezuelan*] (LA)
CUREM....... Centre Universitaire Regional d'Etudes Municipales [*Regional University Center for Municipal Studies*] [*French Guiana*] (LA1)
CURER........ Centre Universitaire de Recherches, d'Etudes, et de Realisations [*Algerian*] (MAR)
CURN.......... Centro Universitario Regional del Norte [*Regional University Center of the North*] [*Honduran*] (LA1)
CURS.......... Centre Universitaire de Recherche Scientifique [*North African*] (MAR)
CUS............ Ceskoslovenska Unitarska Spolecnost [*Czechoslovak Unitarian Society*] (CZ)
CUS............ Cok Uluslu Sirketler [*Multinational Corporations*] (TU)
CUS............ Comite de Unidad Sindical [*Committee for Labor Unity*] [*Costa Rican*] (LA)
CUS............ Comite de Unidad Sindical del Salvador [*Committee for Salvadoran Trade Union Unity*] (LA1)
CUS............ Comite de l'Unite Syndicale (MAR)
CUS............ Confederacion de Unificacion Sindical [*Confederation for Trade Union Unity*] [*Nicaraguan*] (LA1)
CUSAF........ Commercial Union Assurance Company of South Africa (MAR)
CUSC.......... Coastal Union Sports Club (MAR)
CUSC.......... Colegio Universitario del Sagrado Corazon [*Valle del Lily-Cali*] (COL)
CUSCA........ Comite de Unidad Sindical de Centroamerica, Belice, y Panama [*Committee for Trade Union Unity in Central America, Belize, and Panama*] [*Costa Rican*] (LA1)
CUSEGO..... Cuellar Serrano Gomez & Cia. Ltda. [*Bogota*] (COL)
CUSK.......... Centralny Urzad Skupu i Kontraktacji [*Central Procurement and Contracting Office*] (POL)
CUSO.......... Canadian University Service Overseas [*Jamaican*] (LA1)
CUSS.......... Centre Universitaire des Sciences Sanitaires [*University Center for Health Sciences*] [*Cameroonian*] (AF)
CUSS.......... Centre Universitaire des Sciences de la Sante [*University Center for Health Sciences*] [*Upper Voltan*] (AF)
CUSZ.......... Centralny Urzad Szkolenia Zawodowego [*Central Vocational Training Agency*] (POL)
CUT............ Central Unica de Trabajadores [*Single Federation of Workers*] [*Ecuadorean*] (LA)
CUT............ Central Unica dos Trabalhadores [*Single Federation of Workers*] [*Brazilian*] (LA)
CUT............ Comite de l'Unite Togolaise [*Committee for Togolese Unity*] [*Defunct*]
CUT............ Confederacion Unitaria de Trabajadores [*United Confederation of Workers*] [*Costa Rican*] (LA1)
CUT............ Cooperative Union of Tanganyika (MAR)
CUTA.......... Conduccion Unica de los Trabajadores Argentinos [*United Leadership of Argentinian Workers*] (PD)
CUTAL........ Central Unica de Trabajadores de America Latina [*Single Federation of Latin American Workers*] (LA)
CUTCh........ Central Unica de Trabajadores de Chile [*Chilean Trade Union Federation*] (LA)
CUTCSA..... Compania Uruguaya de Transportes Colectivos, Sociedad Anonima [*Uruguayan Bus Company, Incorporated*] (LA)
CUTE........... Cooperativa Usinas Electricas y Telefonos del Estado [*Uruguayan Electric and Telephone Cooperative*] (LA)
CUTEC........ Central Unica de Trabajadores del Estado Carabobo [*Single Federation of Workers of Carabobo State*] [*Venezuelan*] (LA)
CUTEM....... Central Unitaria de Trabajadores del Estado Monagas [*Single Federation of Workers of Monagas State*] (LA)
CUTI............ Cesky Urad pro Tisk a Informace [*Czech Office for Press and Information*] (CZ)
CUTMA....... Consejo Colombiano de Usuarios del Transporte Maritimo y Aereo [*Colombian Council of Users of Maritime and Air Transport*] (LA)
CUTS.......... Confederacion Unitaria de Trabajadores Salvadorenos [*United Confederation of Salvadoran Workers*] (LA1)
CUTT........... Confederacion Uruguaya de Trabajadores del Transporte [*Uruguayan Confederation of Transport Workers*] (LA)

CUTV .... Central Unitaria de Trabajadores de Venezuela [*Single Federation of Workers of Venezuela*] (LA)
CUU .... Club de Unidad Universitaria [*University Unity Club*] [*Guatemalan*] (LA)
CUUN .... Centro Universitario de la Universidad Nacional Autonoma de Nicaragua [*University Center of the Autonomous National University of Nicaragua*] (LA)
CUUS .... Comitetul Uniunii Uniunilor de Sanatate [*Committee of the Union of Health Unions*] (RO)
CUV .... Centar Uprave Vatrom [*Firing Control Center*] [*Military*] (YU)
CUV .... Ciudad Universitaria del Valle [*Cali*] (COL)
CUVb .... Centar Uprave Vatrom Bataljona [*Firing Control Center of Battalion*] (YU)
CUVISA .... Companias Unidas Vitarte, Victoria, Inca, SA [*The United Companies of Vitarte, Victoria, Inca, Inc.*] [*Peruvian*] (LA)
CUVS .... Comite Universitario de Vanguardia Socialista [*Socialist Vanguard University Committee*] [*Colombian*] (LA)
CUW .... Centralny Urzad Wydawniczy [*Central Publishing Administration*] (POL)
CUWPGiK ... Centralny Urzad Wydawnictw, Przemyslu Graficznego, i Ksiegarstwa [*Central Administration of Publications, the Printing Industry, and Bookselling*] (POL)
CUWPPiK .... Centralny Urzad Wydawnictw, Przemyslu Poligraficznego, i Ksiegarstwa [*Central Administration of Publications, the Printing Industry, and Bookselling*] (POL)
CUZ .... Ceskoslovensky Ustav Zahranicni [*Czechoslovak Foreign Institute*] (CZ)
CV .... Capitaine de Vaisseau [*French*] (MTD)
cv .... Cas Vysazeni [*Airdrop Time*] (CZ)
CV .... Celozavodni Vybor [*All-Factory Committee (of the Communist Party of Czechoslovakia)*] (CZ)
CV .... Centar Veze [*Communications Center*] [*Military*] (YU)
CV .... Centrale Vereniging voor Openbare Bibliotheken [*Later, NBLC*] [*Dutch*]
CV .... Centralno Vece [*Central Council*] (YU)
CV .... Cheval Vapeur [*Horse Power*] [*French*]
cv .... Cista Vaha [*Net Weight*] (CZ)
CV .... Commanditaire Vennootschap [*Limited Partnership*] [*Dutch*]
cv .... Compte Vieux [*Old Account*] [*French*]
CV .... Convoi Automobile [*Military*] [*French*] (MTD)
Cv .... Craiova [*Craiova*] (RO)
CV .... Republic of Cape Verde [*Two-letter standard code*] (CNC)
CVA .... Comite de Vigilance et d'Action [*Vigilance and Action Committee*] [*Algerian*] (AF)
CVAAR .... Corpo Voluntario Angolano de Assistencia aos Refugiados (MAR)
CVAD .... Convoi Administratif d'Armee [*Military*] [*French*] (MTD)
CVAX .... Convoi Auxiliaire [*Military*] [*French*] (MTD)
CVB .... Centralna Vojna Bolnica [*Central Military Hospital*] (YU)
CVC .... Chemins de Fer Vicinaux du Congo (MAR)
CVC .... Cooperative Viviere Camerounaise (MAR)
CVC .... Corporacion Autonoma Regional del Valle del Cauca [*Autonomous Regional Corporation of the Cauca Valley*] [*Colombian*] (LA)
CVCI .... Comptoir de Vente de Cote-d'Ivoire (MAR)
CVD .... Cercle de la Voile de Dakar (MAR)
CVD .... Consejo Voluntario Deportivo [*Volunteer Sports Council*] [*Cuban*] (LA)
CVE .... Cape Verde Escudo (MAR)
CVF .... Corporacion Venezolana de Fomento [*Venezuelan Development Corporation*] (LA)
CVG .... Corporacion Venezolana de Guayana [*Venezuelan Corporation of Guayana*] (LA)
CVIAA .... Comite des Volontaires Internationales d'Aide et d'Assistance aux Refugies [*Committee of International Women Volunteers for Aid and Relief to Refugees*] [*Cambodian*] (CL)
CVK .... Ceske Valcovny Kovu, Narodni Podnik [*Czech Metal Rolling Mills, National Enterprise*] (CZ)
CVK .... Cetnicka Vrhovna Komanda [*Chetnik Supreme Command*] [*World War II*] (YU)
CVKPL .... Ceta Velkoraznich Kulometu Protiletadlovych [*Platoon of Heavy Antiaircraft Machine-Guns*] (CZ)
CVL .... Comite Vietnam Lycee [*Lycee Vietnam Committee*] [*French*] (WER)
CVL .... Corps of Volunteers for Liberty (MAR)
CVM .... Comissao de Valores Mobiliarios [*Equity Shares Commission*] [*Brazilian*] (LA)
CVM .... Corporacion Autonoma de los Valles del Magdalena y del Sinu [*Barranquilla*] (COL)
CVMS .... Centralna Vazduhoplovna Modelarska Skola [*Central Air Force Model School*] (YU)
CVN .... Consejo Venezolano del Nino
CVO .... Cislo Vojenske Odbornosti [*Military Occupation Specialty Number*] (CZ)
CVP .... Celorocni Vyrobni Plan [*One Year Production Plan*] (CZ)
CVP .... Christelijke Volkspartij [*Christian People's Party*] [*Belgian*] (PPW)
CVP .... Christlichdemokratische Volkspartei der Schweiz [*Christian Democratic Party of Switzerland*] (PPE)
CVP .... Christliche Volkspartei [*Christian People's Party*] [*West German*] (PPE)
CVP .... Christliche Volkspartei [*Christian People's Party*] [*Pre-1945*] [*German*] (PPE)
CVP .... Corporacion Venezolana del Petroleo [*Venezuelan Petroleum Corporation*] (LA)
CVR .... Corps des Volontaires de la Republique (MAR)
CVRA .... Comites de Volontariat de la Revolution Agraire (MAR)
CVRD .... Companhia Vale do Rio Doce [*Rio Doce Valley Company*] [*Brazilian*] (LA)
CVRFA .... Comissao da Vigilancia Revolucionaria das Forcas Armadas [*Armed Forces Revolutionary Vigilance Committee*] [*Portuguese*] (WER)
CVRS .... Centre Voltaique de la Recherche Scientifique (MAR)
Cvs .... Cavus [*Sergeant*] (TU)
CVS .... Cesky Veslarsky Svaz [*Czech Rowing Association*] (CZ)
CVSF .... Comissao do Vale do Sao Francisco [*Sao Francisco Valley Commission*] [*Brazilian*] (LA)
CVSMOL ..... Casopis Vlasteneckeho Spolku Musejniho v Olomouci [*Journal of the Patriotic Museum Society in Olomouc*] [*A publication*] (CZ)
CVSSJ .... Centralno Vece Saveza Sindikata Jugoslavije [*Central Assembly of the Council of Trade-Unions of Yugoslavia*] (YU)
CVT .... Centrale de Vente Textiles (MAR)
CVT .... [*A*] Collection of Voyages and Travels [*London*] [*A publication*] (MAR)
CVTC .... Confederation Vietnamienne du Travail Chretien [*Vietnamese Confederation of Christian Labor*] [*South Vietnamese*]
CVTM .... Compagnie Voltaique pour la Transformation des Metaux (MAR)
CVU .... Conference Vehicles Unit (MAR)
CVUT .... Ceske Vysoke Uceni Technicke [*Czech Institute of Technology*] [*Prague*] (CZ)
CVUT .... Ceskoslovensky Vojensky Ustav Technicky [*Czechoslovak Military Institute of Technology*] (CZ)
CVUV .... Ceskoslovensky Vedecky Ustav Vojensky [*Czechoslovak Institute of Military Science*] (CZ)
CVV .... Cesky Vsesportovni Vybor [*Czech Athletic Committee*] (CZ)
CVZ .... Ceske Vlnarske Zavody, Narodni Podnik [*Czech Woolen Mills, National Enterprise*] [*Liberec*] (CZ)
CVZ .... Societe des Chemins de Fer Vicinaux du Zaire (MAR)
CWC .... Cairo Women's Club (MAR)
CWD .... Centrala Wydawnicza Drukow [*Central Publishing Office*] (POL)
CWDF .... Colonial Welfare and Development Fund (MAR)
CWE .... Centralne Warsztaty Elektryczne [*Central Electrical Workshops*] (POL)
CWF .... Centrala Wynajmu Filmow [*Central Rental Office for Films*] (POL)
CWF .... Commonwealth Weightlifting Federation (EA)
CWGC .... Commonwealth War Graves Commission (EA)
CWI .... Chilanga Women's Institute (MAR)
CWI .... Clean World International (EA)
CWISz .... Centrum Wyszkolenia Instruktorow Szybowcowych [*Center for Training Glider Instructors*] (POL)
CWK .... Centralne Warsztaty Koksochemiczne [*Central Coke Chemical Plants*] (POL)
CWKS .... Centralny Wojskowy Klub Sportowy [*Central Military Sport Club*] (POL)
CWL .... Centrala Wyszkolenia Lotniczego [*Aeronautical Training Center*] (POL)
cwl .... Ciezar Wlasciwy [*Specific Weight*] [*Polish*]
CWM .... Communist Workers' Movement [*British*] (PPW)
CWP .... Centrum Wyszkolenia Piechoty [*Infantry Training Center*] (POL)
CWP .... Christian Workers Party [*Maltese*] (PPE)
CWP .... Committee of Women for Progress [*Jamaican*] (LA1)
CWS .... Centralne Warsztaty Samochodowe [*Central Automotive Shops*] (POL)
CWS .... Centrum Wyszkolenia Sanitarnego [*Medical (Military) Training Center*] (POL)
CWS .... Charles Williams Society (EA)
CWS .... Church World Service (MAR)
CWSC .... Ghana Water and Sewerage Corporation (MAR)
cwt .... Centum Weight [*Hundredweight*] [*Latin*] (GPO)
CWU .... Christliche Waehlerunion Bayern [*Christian Voters' Union of Bavaria*] [*West German*] (PPW)
CWU .... Communications Workers Union [*Trinidadian and Tobagan*] (LA1)
CWWA .... Coloured Workers Welfare Association (MAR)
CX .... Christmas Island [*Two-letter standard code*] (CNC)
CXR .... Christmas Island [*Three-letter standard code*] (CNC)
Cy .... Csakeyhtioe [*Joint Stock Company*] [*Finnish*] (CED)
CY .... Cypr [*Cyprus*] [*Polish*]
CY .... Cyprus [*Two-letter standard code*] (CNC)
CYA .... Ceska Yachetni Asociace [*Czech Yacht Association*] (CZ)
CYA .... Concretos y Agregados Ltda. (COL)
CYC .... Cairo Yacht Club [*Egyptian*] (MAR)
CYC .... Central Youth Club [*Mauritian*] (AF)
CYCLOTCHAD ... Industrie Tchadienne du Cycle et du Motocycle (MAR)
CYDA .... Confederation of Yemen Development Associations (ME)

CYK............ Cowethas an Yeth Kernewek [*Cornish Language Society*]
CYL............ Cameroon's Youth League (MAR)
CYL............ City Youth League (MAR)
CYL............ Congress Youth League (MAR)
CYM............ Cayman Islands [*Three-letter standard code*] (CNC)
CYO............ Catholic Youth Organization (MAR)
CYO............ Committee for Youth Organisation (MAR)
CYP............ Commonwealth Youth Programme (MAR)
CYP............ Cyprus [*Three-letter standard code*] (CNC)
Cypfruvex... Kibris Sebze, Meyve Isletmeleri Ltd. [*Cyprus Vegetable and Fruit Processing and Exporting Corp. Ltd.*] (TU)
Cypruvex.... Kibris Sebze, Meyve Isletmeleri Ltd. [*Cyprus Vegetable and Fruit Processing and Exporting Corp. Ltd.*] (GC)
cyt............ Cytat [*or Cytowany*] [*Quotation or Quoted*] [*Polish*]
CYTA.......... Cyprus Telecommunications Authority [*See also ATK*] (GC)
CYUK.......... Ceza Yargilamalari Usulu Kanunu [*Criminal Suits Procedural Law*] [*See also CYUY*] (TU)
CYUY.......... Ceza Yargilamalari Usulu Yasasi [*Criminal Trials Procedural Law*] [*See also CYUK*] (TU)
CZ............ Cankarjeva Zalozba [*Cankar Publishing House*] [*Ljubljana*] (YU)
CZ............ Centrala Zbytu [*Sales Center*] (POL)
CZ............ Centralny Zarzad [*Central Administration*] (POL)
CZ............ Centralny Zwiazek [*Central Union*] [*Polish*]
CZ............ Cervena Zastava [*Red Flag*] (YU)
CZ............ Ceska Zbrojovka [*Czechoslovak Munitions Plants, National Enterprise*] (CZ)
CZ............ Ceskoslovenska Zbrojovka, Narodni Podnik [*Czechoslovak Munitions Plants, National Enterprise*] (CZ)
CZ............ Civilna Zastita [*Civilian Defense*] (YU)
CZ............ Corps Zeni [*Corps of Engineers*] (IN)
CZ............ Crvena Zastava [*Red Flag*] (YU)
cz............ Czesc [*Part*] (POL)
cz............ Czyli [*That Is*] [*Polish*]
Cz............ "Czytelnik" Spoldzielnia Wydawniczo-Oswiatowa [*"Czytelnik" (The Reader)*] [*Cooperative Educational Publishing House*] (POL)
Cz............ Senozoyik [*Cenozoic*] (TU)
CZA............ Centralny Zarzad Aptek [*Central Administration of Pharmacies*] (POL)
CZA............ Ceskoslovensky Zemedelsky Archiv [*Czechoslovak Agricultural Archives*] (CZ)
CZAL.......... Ceskoslovenske Zavody Avia [*Czechoslovak Avia Aircraft Plant*] [*Letnany*] (CZ)
CZAT.......... Centrala Zbytu Artykulow Technicznych [*Technical Goods Sales Center*] (POL)
CZA WP...... Centralny Zespol Artystyczny Wojska Polskiego [*Central Art Team, Polish Army*] (POL)
CZB............ Centralny Zarzad Bibliotek [*Central Administration of Libraries*] (POL)
CZB............ Clubul Ziaristilor din Bucuresti [*Bucharest Newspapermen's Club*] (RO)
CZBDiM...... Centralny Zarzad Budowy Drog i Mostow [*Central Administration of Road and Bridge Construction*] (POL)
CZBL.......... Centralny Zarzad Budownictwa Lacznosci [*Central Administration of Communication Construction*] (POL)
CZBM.......... Centralny Zarzad Budownictwa Miejskiego [*Central Administration of Urban Construction*] (POL)
CZBM.......... Centralny Zarzad Budownictwa Mieszkaniowego [*Central Administration of Residential Construction*] (POL)
CZBM.......... Centralny Zarzad Budynkow Mieszkalnych [*Central Administration of Residential Buildings*] (POL)
CZBMC....... Centralny Zarzad Budowy Maszyn Ciezkich [*Central Administration of Heavy Machinery Construction*] (POL)
CZBME........ Centralny Zarzad Budowy Maszyn Elektrycznych [*Central Administration of Electric Machine Building*] (POL)
CZBMG....... Centralny Zarzad Budowy Maszyn Gorniczych [*Central Administration of Mining Machinery Construction*] (POL)
CZBMiO...... Centralny Zarzad Budowy Miast i Osiedli [*Central Administration of City and Settlement Construction*] (POL)
CZBP.......... Centralny Zarzad Budownictwa Przemyslowego [*Central Administration of Industrial Construction*] (POL)
CZBPBM..... Centralny Zarzad Biur Projektowych Budownictwa Miejskiego [*Central Administration of Offices of Plans in Municipal Construction*] (POL)
CZBWI......... Centralny Zarzad Budownictwa Wodno-Inzynieryjnego [*Central Administration of Hydraulic Engineering Construction*] (POL)
CZC............ Centralny Zarzad Cel (Ministerstwa Handlu Zagranicznego) [*Central Customs Administration (Ministry of Foreign Trade)*] (POL)
CZCB.......... Centralny Zarzad Ceramiki Budowlanej [*Central Administration of Building Tiles*] (POL)
CZCC.......... Centralny Zarzad Ceramiki Czerwonej [*Central Administration of Red Ceramics*] (POL)
CZCE.......... Centre Zalrols du Commerce Exterleur (MAR)
CZD............ Centralny Zarzad Dyspozytorski [*Central Managerial Administration*] (POL)
CZD............ Centrum Zdrowia Dziecka [*Children's Health Center*] (POL)
CZD............ Ceskoslovenske Zavody Drevozpracujici [*Czechoslovak Lumber Industries, National Enterprise*] (CZ)
CZD............ Ceskoslovenske Zavody na Zpracovani Dreva, Narodni Podnik [*Czechoslovak Lumber Industries, National Enterprise*] (CZ)
CZDP.......... Centralny Zarzad Drog Publicznych [*Central Administration of Public Roads*] (POL)
CZDWS....... Centralny Zarzad Drog Wodnych Srodladowych [*Central Administration of Inland Waterways*] (POL)
CZE............ Centralny Zarzad Energetyki [*Central Power Administration*] (POL)
CZE............ Ceskoslovenske Zavody Energeticke [*Czechoslovak Power Plants*] (CZ)
CZER.......... Centralny Zarzad Elektryfikacji Rolnictwa [*Central Administration of Rural Electrification*] (POL)
CZF............ Canal Zone Forces [*Egyptian*] (MAR)
CZGM.......... Centralny Zarzad Gospodarki Maszynami [*Central Administration of the Allocation of Machinery*] (POL)
CZGP.......... Ceskoslovenske Zavody Gumarenske a Plastikarske [*Czechoslovak Rubber and Plastics Works*] (CZ)
CZGZ.......... Centralny Zarzad Gospodarki Zlomem [*Central Administration of the Utilization of Scrap Metal*] (POL)
CZH............ Centralny Zarzad Handlu [*Central Trade Administration*] (POL)
CZHAGD..... Centralny Zarzad Hurtu Artykulow Gospodarstwa Domowego [*Central Administration of Wholesale Trade in Household Goods*] (POL)
CZHAKid..... Centralny Zarzad Handlu Artykulami Kolonialnymi i Delikatesami [*Central Administration of the Grocery and Delicatessen Trade*] (POL)
CZHG.......... Centralny Zarzad Handlu Galanteryjnego [*Central Administration of the Haberdashery Trade*] (POL)
CZHG.......... Centralny Zarzad Hurtu Galanteryjnego [*Central Administration of the Haberdashery Wholesale Trade*] (POL)
CZHiPJ........ Centralny Zarzad Handlu i Przemyslu Jubilerskiego [*Central Administration of the Jewelry Trade and Industry*] (POL)
CZHM.......... Centralny Zarzad Handlu Miesem [*Central Administration of the Meat Trade*] (POL)
CZHOiMB.... Centralny Zarzad Handlu Opalem i Materialami Budowlanymi [*Central Administration of the Fuel and Building Materials Trade*] (POL)
CZHOiW...... Centralny Zarzad Handlu Owocami i Warzywami [*Central Administration of the Fruit and Vegetable Trade*] (POL)
CZHOW....... Centralny Zarzad Hurtu Owocarsko-Warzywnego [*Central Administration of the Fruit and Vegetable Wholesale Trade*] (POL)
CZHS.......... Centralny Zarzad Hurtu Spozywczego [*Central Administration of the Wholesale Food Trade*] (POL)
CZHU.......... Centralny Zarzad Handlu w Uzdrowiskach [*Central Administration of Trade in Health Resorts*] (POL)
CZHwU........ Centralny Zarzad Handlu w Uzdrowiskach [*Central Administration of Trade in Health Resorts*] (POL)
CZI............ Confederation of Zimbabwe Industries (MAR)
CZIP.......... Centralny Zarzad Instalacji Przemyslowych [*Central Administration of Industrial Installations*] (POL)
CZISP.......... Centralny Zarzad Instytucji Sztuk Plastycznych [*Central Administration of Institutions of Plastic Arts*] (POL)
CZIUS.......... Centrala Zaopatrywania Instytucji Ubezpieczen Spolecznych [*Central Supply Office for Social Security Institutions*] (POL)
CZJD.......... Centralny Zarzad Jajczarsko-Drobiarski [*Central Eggs and Poultry Administration*] (POL)
CZK............ Centralny Zarzad Kinematografii [*Central Administration of Motion Pictures*] (POL)
CZK............ Centralny Zarzad Ksiegarstwa [*Central Administration of Bookselling*] (POL)
CZKG.......... Ceskoslovenske Zavody Kovodelne a Gumarenske, Narodni Podnik [*Czechoslovak Leather and Rubber Plants, National Enterprise*] (CZ)
CZKHP........ Centralna Zydowska Komisja Historyczna w Polsce [*Central Jewish Historical Commission in Poland*] (POL)
CZKiKD....... Centralny Zarzad Kamieniolomow i Klinkierni Drogowych [*Central Administration of Quarries and Road Gravel*] (POL)
CZKR.......... Centralny Zwiazek Kolek Rolniczych [*Central Union of Agricultural Cooperatives*] [*Polish*]
CZKRZ........ Centralny Zarzad Kopalnictwa Rud Zelaznych [*Central Administration of Iron Ore Mining*] (POL)
CZKS.......... Centralny Zarzad Konstrukcji Stalowych [*Central Administration of Steel Construction Designing*] (POL)
CZKS.......... Ceskoslovenske Zavody Kovodelne a Strojirenske, Narodni Podnik [*Czechoslovak Metalworking and Machine Building Plants, National Enterprise*] (CZ)
CZKZP........ Centralny Zarzad Kolejowych Zakladow Produkcyjnych [*Central Administration of Railway Equipment Plants*] (POL)
CZLK.......... Ceskoslovenske Zavody Lehkeho Kovoprumyslu [*Czechoslovak (Light) Metal Industry Plants*] (CZ)
CZLMiK....... Centralny Zarzad Linii Miedzymiastowych i Kabli [*Central Administration of Inter-Urban and Cable Lines*] (POL)
CZLP.......... Centralny Zarzad Lasow Panstwowych [*Central Administration of State Forests*] (POL)
CZM............ Centrala Zaopatrzenia Materialowego [*Central Material Supply Office*] (POL)

CZM .... Centralny Zarzad Muzeow [*Central Administration of Museums*] (POL)
CZM .... Ceske Zavody Motocyklove [*Czech Motorcycle Works*] (CZ)
CZMHD .... Centralny Zarzad Miejskiego Handlu Detalicznego [*Central Administration of the Municipal Retail Trade*] (POL)
CZMHM .... Centralny Zarzad Miejskiego Handlu Miesem [*Central Administration of the Municipal Meat Trade*] (POL)
CZMN .... Centralny Zarzad Metali Niezelaznych [*Central Administration of Non-Ferrous Metals*] (POL)
CZMO .... Czestochowskie Zaklady Materialow Ogniotrwalych [*Czestochowa Fireproof Material Plants*] (POL)
CZMP .... Centralny Zarzad Mechaniki Precyzyjnej [*Central Administration of Precision Instruments*] (POL)
CZMPW .... Centrala Zaopatrzenia Materialowego Przemyslu Weglowego [*Central Material Supply Office of the Coal Industry*] (POL)
CZMPW .... Centrala Zaopatrzenia Materialowego Przemyslu Wlokienniczego [*Central Material Supply Office of the Textile Industry*] (POL)
CZMUE .... Centralny Zarzad Montazu Urzadzen Elektrycznych [*Central Administration of Assembly of Electrical Equipment*] (POL)
CZN .... Casopis za Zgodovino in Narodopisje [*Journal of History and Ethnography*] [*Ljubljana*] [*A publication*] (YU)
CZOBM .... Centralny Zarzad Ogolnego Budownictwa Maszynowego [*Central Administration of the General Machine Construction Industry*] (POL)
CZOFIM ...... Centralny Zarzad Oper, Filharmonii, i Instytucji Muzycznych [*Central Administraion of Opera Houses, Philharmonic Orchestras, and Musical Institutions*] (POL)
CZOOW .... Centralny Zarzad Obrotu Owocami i Warzywami [*Central Administration of Fruit and Vegetable Sales*] (POL)
CZOZ Rz ..... Centralny Zarzad Obrotu Zwierzetami Rzeznymi [*Center Sales Agency for Slaughter Animals*] (POL)
CZP .... Centrala Zaopatrywania Przemyslu [*Industry Supply Center*] (POL)
CZP .... Centralny Zarzad Poczty (Ministerstwa Lacznosci) [*Central Post Office Administration (of the Ministry of Communication)*] (POL)
CZP .... Centralny Zarzad Przemyslu [*Central Administration of the Industry*] (POL)
CZPAE .... Centralny Zarzad Przemyslu Artykulow Elektrotechnicznych [*Central Administration of the Electric Equipment Industry*] (POL)
CZPB .... Centralny Zarzad Przemyslu Bawelnianego [*Central Administration of the Cotton Industry*] (POL)
CZPC .... Centralny Zarzad Przemyslu Ceramicznego [*Central Administration of the Ceramics Industry*] (POL)
CZPC .... Centralny Zarzad Przemyslu Cukrowniczego [*Central Administration of the Sugar Industry*] (POL)
CZPC .... Ceskoslovenske Zavody na Papir a Celulosu, Narodni Podnik [*Czechoslovak Paper and Cellulose Factories, National Enterprise*] (CZ)
CZPCh .... Centrala Zbytu Przemyslu Chemicznego [*Chemical Industry Sales Center*] (POL)
CZPCh .... Centralny Zarzad Przemyslu Chemicznego [*Central Administration of the Chemical Industry*] (POL)
CZPD .... Centralny Zarzad Przemyslu Drzewnego [*Central Administration of the Lumber Industry*] (POL)
CZPDT .... Centralny Zarzad Powszechnych Domow Towarowych [*Central Administration of Department Stores*] (POL)
CZPEI .... Centralny Zarzad Przemyslu Elektrotechnicznego [*Central Administration of the Electric Industry*] (POL)
CZPF .... Centralny Zarzad Przemyslu Farmaceutycznego [*Central Administration of the Pharmaceutical Industry*] (POL)
CZPG .... Centralny Zarzad Przemyslu Garbarskiego [*Central Administration of the Tanning Industry*] (POL)
CZPG .... Centralny Zarzad Przemyslu Gastronomicznego [*Central Administration of the Restaurant Industry*] (POL)
CZPG .... Centralny Zarzad Przemyslu Gorniczego [*Central Administration of the Mining Industry*] (POL)
CZPGG .... Centralny Zarzad Przemyslu Guzikarsko-Galanteryjnego [*Central Administration of the Haberdashery Goods Industry*] (POL)
CZPGR .... Centralny Zarzad Panstwowych Gospodarstw Rolnych [*Central Administration of State Farms*] (POL)
CZPH .... Centralny Zarzad Przemyslu Hutniczego [*Central Administration of the Metallurgical Industry*] (POL)
CZPiUK .... Centralny Zarzad Przedsiebiorstw i Urzadzen Komunalnych [*Central Administration of Communal Enterprises and Establishments*] (POL)
CZPJD .... Centralny Zarzad Przemyslu Jajczarsko-Drobiarskiego [*Central Administration of the Egg and Poultry Industry*] (POL)
CZPK .... Centralny Zarzad Przemyslu Kablowego [*Central Administration of the Cable Industry*] (POL)
CZPK .... Centralny Zarzad Przemyslu Kosmetycznego [*Central Administration of the Cosmetics Industry*] (POL)
CZPKons .... Centralny Zarzad Przemyslu Konserwowego [*Central Administration of the Canning Industry*] (POL)
CZPKS .... Centralny Zarzad Panstwowej Komunikacji Samochodowej [*Central Administration of State Motor Transport*] (POL)
CZPL .... Centralny Zarzad Przemyslu Lesnego [*Central Administration of Forestry*] (POL)
CZPM .... Centralny Zarzad Przemyslu Meblarskiego [*Central Administration of the Furniture Industry*] (POL)
CZPM .... Centralny Zarzad Przemyslu Metalowego [*Central Administration of the Metal Industry*] (POL)
CZPM .... Centralny Zarzad Przemyslu Miesnego [*Central Administration of the Meat Industry*] (POL)
CZPM .... Centralny Zarzad Przemyslu Mleczarskiego [*Central Administration of the Dairy Industry*] (POL)
CZPME .... Centralny Zarzad Przemyslu Maszyn Elektrycznych [*Central Administration of the Electric Machinery Industry*] (POL)
CZPMH .... Centralny Zarzad Polskiej Marynarki Handlowej [*Central Administration of the Polish Merchant Marine*] (POL)
CZPMH .... Centralny Zarzad Przewozow Morskich Handlowych [*Central Administration of Maritime Trade Transportation*] (POL)
CZP Mies .... Centralny Zarzad Przemyslu Miesnego [*Central Administration of the Meat Industry*] (POL)
CZP Mlecz ... Centralny Zarzad Przemyslu Mleczarskiego [*Central Administration of the Dairy Industry*] (POL)
CZP Mlyn .... Centralny Zarzad Przemyslu Mlynarskiego [*Central Administration of the Flour Industry*] (POL)
CZP Mot ..... Centralny Zarzad Przemyslu Motoryzacyjnego [*Central Administration of the Automotive Industry*] (POL)
CZPMR .... Centralny Zarzad Przemyslu Maszyn Rolniczych [*Central Administration of the Agricultural Machine Industry*] (POL)
CZPN .... Centralny Zarzad Przemyslu Naftowego [*Central Administration of the Petroleum Industry*] (POL)
CZPO .... Centralny Zarzad Przemyslu Odziezowego [*Central Administration of the Clothing Industry*] (POL)
CZPO .... Centralny Zarzad Przemyslu Okretowego [*Central Administration of the Shipbuilding Industry*] (POL)
CZPOM .... Centralny Zarzad Panstwowych Osrodkow Maszynowych [*Central Administration of State Agricultural Machine Stations*] (POL)
CZPOW .... Centralny Zarzad Przemyslu Owocowo-Warzywnego [*Central Administration of the Fruit and Vegetable Industry*] (POL)
CZPOZiR ..... Centralny Zarzad Przetworstwa Odpadkow Zwierzecych i Roslinnych [*Central Administration of the Utilization of Animal and Vegetable By-Products*] (POL)
CZPP .... Centrala Zbytu Produktow Przemyslu [*Polish*]
CZPP .... Centralny Zarzad Produkcji Pomocniczej [*Central Administration of Auxiliary Industry*] (POL)
CZPP .... Centralny Zarzad Produktow Przemyslu [*Central Administration of Industry Products*] (POL)
CZPP .... Centralny Zarzad Przemyslu Papierniczego [*Central Administration of the Paper Industry*] (POL)
CZPPB .... Centralny Zarzad Panstwowych Przedsiebiorstw Budowlanych [*Central Administration of State Construction Enterprises*] (POL)
CZPPP .... Centralny Zarzad Przemyslu Paliw Plynnych [*Central Administration of the Liquid Fuel Industry*] (POL)
CZPPW .... Centrala Zbytu Produktow Przemyslu Weglowego [*Sales Center for the Coal Industry*] (POL)
CZPR .... Centralny Zarzad Przemyslu Rolnego [*Central Administration of the Agricultural Industry*] (POL)
CZPR .... Centralny Zarzad Przemyslu Roszarniczego [*Central Administration of the Flax Industry*] (POL)
CZPR .... Centralny Zarzad Przemyslu Rybnego [*Central Administration of the Fish Industry*] (POL)
CZPRK .... Centralny Zarzad Przedsiebiorstw Robot Komunikacyjnych [*Central Administration of Transportation Work Enterprises*] (POL)
CZPS .... Centrala Zbytu Przemyslu Skorzanego [*Leather Industry Sales Center*] (POL)
CZPS .... Ceskoslovenske Zavody Presneho Strojirenstvi [*Czechoslovak Precision Machinery Factories*] (CZ)
CZPSp .... Centralny Zarzad Przemyslu Spozywczego [*Central Administration of the Food Industry*] (POL)
CZPSS .... Centralny Zarzad Przemyslu Stali Specjalnej [*Central Administration of the Special Steel Industry*] (POL)
CZPT .... Centralny Zarzad Przemyslu Teletechnicznego [*Central Administration of the Communications Supply Industry*] (POL)
CZPT .... Centralny Zarzad Przemyslu Tytoniowego [*Central Administration of the Tobacco Industry*] (POL)
CZPUK .... Centralny Zarzad Przedsiebiorstw i Urzadzen Komunalnych [*Central Administration of Communal Enterprises and Establishments*] (POL)
CZPU Orbis ... Centralny Zarzad Przedsiebiorstw Uslugowych "Orbis" [*Central Administration of the "Orbis" Travel Service Enterprises*] (POL)
CZPW .... Centralny Zarzad Przemyslu Weglowego [*Central Administration of the Coal Industry*] (POL)
CZPW .... Centralny Zarzad Przemyslu Welnianego [*Central Administration of the Wool Industry*] (POL)
CZPW .... Czestochowskie Zaklady Przemyslu Welnianego [*Czestochowa Wool Plant*] (POL)
CZPWB .... Centralny Zarzad Przemyslu Wyrobow Blaszanych [*Central Administration of the Tin Products Industry*] (POL)
CZPWl Lykowych ... Centralny Zarzad Przemyslu Wlokien Lykowych [*Central Administration of the Bast Fiber Industry*] (POL)

CZPWM....... Centralny Zarzad Przemyslu Wyrobow Metalowych [*Central Administration of the Metal Products Industry*] (POL)
CZPWP........ Centralny Zarzad Przemyslu Wyrobow Precyzyjnych [*Central Administration of the Precision Instrument Industry*] (POL)
CZR............ Central Zambia Railways (MAR)
CZR............ Centrala Zaopatrzenia Rolnictwa [*Agriculture Supply Center*] (POL)
CZR............ Centralny Zarzad Rybactwa [*Central Administration of Fisheries*] (POL)
CZRK.......... Centralny Zarzad Radiofonizacji Kraju [*Central Administration of Country-Wide Radio Installation*] (POL)
CZRM.......... Centralny Zarzad Rybolowstwa Morskiego [*Central Administration of Deep Sea Fisheries*] (POL)
CZRMB........ Centralny Zarzad Remontow Maszyn Budowlanych [*Central Administration of Building Machinery Repairs*] (POL)
CZS............ Centrala Zaopatrzenia Szkol [*School Supply Center*] (POL)
CZS............ Centrala Zwalczania Szkodnikow [*Center for Control of Agricultural Pests*] (POL)
CZS............ Centrala Zwiazkow Spoldzielni [*Central Office of Cooperative Unions*] (POL)
CZS............ Centralny Zwiazek Spoldzielni [*Central Union of Cooperatives*] (POL)
CZS............ Ceskoslovenske Zavody Sklarske [*Czechoslovak Glass Factories*] (CZ)
CZSA.......... Centralny Zarzad Szkolnictwa Artystycznego [*Central Administration of Art Education*] (POL)
CZSBM....... Centralny Zwiazek Spoldzielni Budownictwa Mieszkaniowego [*Central Housing Construction Cooperative Union*] (POL)
CZSK.......... Centralny Zarzad Szkolenia Kadr [*Central Administration of Personnel Training*] (POL)
CZSP.......... Centralny Zwiazek Spoldzielni Pracy [*Central Union of Labor Cooperatives*] (POL)
CZSPB........ Centralny Zarzad Spolecznych Przedsiebiorstw Budowlanych [*Central Administration of Local Construction Enterprises*] (POL)
CZSPB........ Centralny Zarzad Stolecznego Przedsiebiorstwa Budowlanego [*Central Administration of the Warsaw Construction Enterprise*] (POL)
CZSS.......... Centralny Zarzad Sprzetu Samochodowego [*Central Administration of Automobile Equipment*] (POL)
CZSSWiS.... Centralny Zarzad Skupu Surowcow Wlokienniczych i Skorzanych [*Central Administration of the Purchase of Textile and Leather Raw Materials*] (POL)
CZSZ.......... Centralny Zarzad Szkolenia Zawodowego [*Central Vocational Training Board*] (POL)
CZSZb-M.... Centrala Zwalczania Szkodnikow Zbozowo-Macznych [*Grain and Flour Pest Control Center*] (POL)
CZT............ Centralny Zarzad Teatrow [*Central Administration of Theatres*] (POL)
CZT............ Ceskoslovenske Zavody Tukove [*Czechoslovak Fats Rendering Plants*] (CZ)
CZT............ Ceskoslovenske Zavody na Umele Jedle Tuky, Narodni Podnik [*Czechoslovak Vegetable Oil Plants*] (CZ)
CZTiT.......... Centralny Zarzad Telefonii i Telegrafii [*Central Telephone and Telegraph Administration*] (POL)
CZTOiF....... Centralny Zarzad Teatrow, Oper, i Filharmonii [*Central Administration of Theatres, Opera Houses, and Philharmonic Orchestras*] (POL)
CZTOR........ Centralny Zarzad Technicznej Obslugi Rolnictwa [*Central Administration of Engineering Service for Agriculture*] (POL)
CZTP.......... Centralny Zarzad Tuczu Przemyslowego [*Central Administration of the Animal Fattening Industry*] (POL)
CZTS.......... Ceskoslovenske Zavody Tezkeho Strojirenstvi [*Czechoslovak Heavy Machine Building Plants*] (CZ)
CZU............ Ceske Zemske Ustredi Obci, Mest, a Okresu [*Organization of Communities, Towns, and Districts in the Province of Bohemia*] (CZ)
CZU............ Ceskoslovensky Zahranicni Ustav [*Czechoslovak Foreign Institute*] (CZ)
CZU............ Ceskoslovensky Zuctovaci Ustav [*Czechoslovak Accounting Institute*] (CZ)
CZUK.......... Centralny Zarzad Urzadzen Kolejowych [*Central Administration of Railroad Equipment*] (POL)
CZUR.......... Centralny Zarzad Urzadzen Rolnych [*Central Administration of Agricultural Establishments*] (POL)
CZW............ Centrala Zbytu Wegla [*Coal Sales Center*] (POL)
CZW............ Centralny Zarzad Wagonow [*Central Railroad Car Administration*] (POL)
CZW............ Centralny Zarzad Weterynarii [*Central Veterinary Administration*] (POL)
CZWM.......... Centralny Zarzad Wodnych Melioracji [*Central Administration of Land Reclamation*] (POL)
CZW-PMG... Centrala Zbytu Wegla - Przeladunki Morskie Gdansk [*Gdansk (Danzig) Center for Sales and Maritime Shipments of Coal*] (POL)
CZWS.......... Centralny Zarzad Warsztatow Szkolnych [*Central Administration of School Workshops*] (POL)
czyt............ Czytaj [*Read*] [*Polish*]
CZZ............ Centralny Zarzad Zaopatrzenia [*Central Supply Administration*] (POL)
CZZ............ Centralny Zarzad Zbytu [*Central Sales Administration Of*] (POL)
CZZBMiO.... Centralny Zarzad Zaopatrzenia Budownictwa Miast i Osiedli [*Central Supply Administration of City and Settlement Construction*] (POL)
Cz ZG.......... Czestochowskie Zaklady Gastronomiczne [*Czestochowa Restaurant Establishments*] (POL)
CZZH.......... Centralny Zarzad Zaopatrzenia Handlu [*Central Administration of Trade Supplies*] (POL)
CZZL.......... Centralny Zarzad Zaopatrzenia Lacznosci [*Central Administration of Communication Supplies*] (POL)
CZZMT........ Centralny Zarzad Zaopatrzenia Materialowo-Technicznego [*Central Administration of Engineering Material Supply*] (POL)
CZZP.......... Centralny Zarzad Zakladow Prefabrykacji [*Central Administration of Prefabrication Plants*] (POL)
Cz ZPB........ Czestochowskie Zaklady Przemyslu Bawelnianego [*Czestochowa Cotton Mill*] (POL)
CZZPM........ Centralny Zarzad Zbytu Przemyslu Metalowego [*Central Sales Administration of the Metal Industry*] (POL)
CZZZ PZZ... Centralny Zarzad Zakladow Zbozowych "Panstwowe Zaklady Zbozowe" [*Central Administration of Grain Storage "State Grain Storage"*] (POL)

D

/D A Titre Definitif [*Permanent Rank*] [*Used following a military rank in French*] (CL)
d Act, Action (BU)
d Act, Deed, Lawsuit, Affairs (BU)
d Action (RU)
D Battalion [*Artillery*], Divisional (RU)
D D-Day, Day of Commencement of Operations [*Military*] (RU)
d Da [*Give*] [*Latin*] (GPO)
D Dag [*Mountain*] (TU)
D Daire [*Room, Office*] (TU)
d Dakika [*Minute*] (TU)
d Das [*German*]
D Dative [*Case*] (RU)
D Day of Operation (BU)
d De [*Of*] [*Business and trade*] [*Spanish*]
D Debit [*French*]
d Docretum [*Decree*] [*Latin*] (GPO)
D Del [*South*] [*Hungarian*] (GPO)
d Dem [*German*]
d Demande [*Request, Claim*] [*French*]
d Den [*German*]
d Denarius [*Penny*] [*Latin*] (GPO)
D Deport [*French*]
d Der [*The*] [*German*]
D Dere [*Stream*] (TU)
d Des [*German*]
D Desaleux [*Type of projectile having a sharp ogive and truncated base*] [*Military*] [*French*] (MTD)
d Despoinis [*Miss*] (GC)
D Deus [*God*] [*Latin*] (GPO)
d Dias [*Day*] [*Business and trade*] [*Spanish*]
D Dichte [*Density, Specific Gravity*] [*German*]
D Didaktorikon [*Greek*]
d Die [*German*]
D Dienst [*German*]
D Diesel (RU)
D Dinar Tunisien (MAR)
D Diopter (RU)
D Diplome [*French*]
D Distance, Range (RU)
d Division (BU)
D Docteur en Medecine [*Notation that appears after the name of a pharmacist in the Annuaire de l'armee*] [*French*] (MTD)
D Doctoraat [*Academic degree*] [*Dutch*]
D Doctorado [*Doctorate*] [*Spanish*]
D Doctorat [*Doctorate*] [*French*]
D Doctorat d'Etat [*French*]
D Doctori [*Doctor of Medicine*] [*Afghan*]
d Dod [*Dead*] [*Danish*] (GPO)
d Dod [*Dead*] [*Swedish*] (GPO)
D Dogu [*East*] (TU)
D Doit [*French*]
D Doivent [*Owing, Due*] [*French*]
D Doktor [*Czechoslovak*]
D Doktor [*Norwegian*]
D Doktor [*Polish*]
D Doktor [*Russian*]
D Doktor [*Swedish*]
D Doktor na Naukite [*Doctorate of Science*] [*Bulgarian*]
D Doktora [*Academic qualification*] [*Turkish*]
D Doktora [*Egyptian*]
D Doktorat [*Doctorate*] [*Austrian*]
D Doktorgrad [*Danish*]
D Doktorsprof [*Academic examination*] [*Icelandic*]
D Dom [*Sir*] [*Portuguese*] (GPO)
D Dominant [*Biology*] (RU)
D Dominus [*Lord*] [*Latin*] (GPO)
D Don [*Spanish*] (GPO)
D Dona [*Lady*] [*Portuguese*] (GPO)
D Dorf (Geschlossener Ort) [*German*]
D Doutorado [*Doctorate*] [*Portuguese*]
D Doutoramento [*Academic degree*] [*Portuguese*]
d Dulo [*Balk between strips of cultivated land, farm road*] (HU)
D Duna [*Danube*] (HU)
D "Dynamo" [*Sports society*] (RU)
D Dysis [*or Dytikos*] [*West, Western, or Westerly*] (GC)
d File, Dossier, [*Legal*] Case (RU)
D Girl [*In Questionnaires*] (RU)
d Hitno [*Urgent*] [*Military code*] (YU)
D House (RU)
d Inch (RU)
D Kat Prosty [*Right Angle*] [*Polish*]
D Line-of-Sight Distance (RU)
d Longitude (RU)
D Niemcy [*Germany*] [*Polish*]
d Part (BU)
d Persons [*Number of people*] (BU)
d Persons [*Statistics*] (RU)
D Quingenti [*Five Hundred*] [*Polish*]
d Rechtsdrehend [*Clockwise*] [*German*]
d Road (RU)
D- Road Machine (RU)
D Transmitter, Transducer, Pickup (RU)
D Village [*Topography*] (RU)
D1 Diploma I [*Indonesian*]
D2 Diploma II [*Indonesian*]
D3 Diploma III [*Indonesian*]
D^{16} Spezifisches Gewicht bei 16° [*Specific Weight at 16°*] [*German*]
D-66 Democraten '66 [*Democrats '66*] [*Dutch*] (PPW)
D_4^{20} Spezifisches Gewicht bei 20° Bezogen auf Wasser von 4° [*Specific Weight at 20° with Reference to Water at 4°*] [*German*]
DA Arctic Diesel (Fuel) (RU)
DA Auxiliary Attenuator (RU)
Da Dag [*Dagi*] [*Mountain*] [*Turkish*] (NAU)
DA Degtyarev Aircraft (Machine Gun) (RU)
DA Delnicka Akademie [*Academy of Labor*] (CZ)
d:a Den Aldre [*Senior*] [*Swedish*] (GPO)
dA Der Aeltere [*Senior*] [*Title*] [*German*] (GPO)
d:a Det Ar [*That Is*] [*Swedish*] (GPO)
da Dette Ar [*This Year*] [*Danish*] (GPO)
da Dette Ar [*This Year*] [*Norwegian*] (GPO)
DA Deutsche Aussenpolitik [*Berlin*] [*A publication*] (MAR)
DA Dienstanweisung [*Service Regulation*] [*West German*] (WEN)
DA Diethnis Amnistia [*Amnesty International*] (GC)
DA Dievthynsis Allodapon [*Aliens Directorate*] [*Greek*] (GC)
DA Dimokratiki Allagi [*Democratic Change*] [*Greek*] (GC)
DA Dimokratiki Amyna [*Democratic Defense*] [*Greek*] (GC)
DA Dimokratikos Agonas [*Democratic Struggle*] [*Greek*] (GC)
DA Dimos Athinaion [*Municipality of Athens*] [*License plate designation*] (GC)
DA Dinar Algerien (MAR)
DA Directeur Administratif [*Managing Director*] [*Cambodian*] (CL)
DA Direction de l'Armee [*Directorate of the Army*] [*Cambodian*] (CL)
DA Direction de l'Arriere [*Military*] [*French*] (MTD)
DA Dissociated Ammonia (RU)
DA Division Artillery (BU)
DA Division Artillery (RU)
DA Documents Contre Acceptation [*French*]
DA Dom Akademicki [*Student House*] (POL)
Da Dona [*Lady*] [*Spanish*]
DA Dopamine (RU)
DA Doppelachse [*Two-Axle Freight Car*] [*Unit of freight volume equivalent to that carried by a two-axle freight car*] (EG)
DA Drzavna Arhiva [*State Archives*] (YU)
DA Long-Range Aviation (BU)
DA Long-Range Aviation (RU)
DA Smoke-Generating Apparatus (RU)
DAA Defense Anti-Aerienne (MAR)
daa Division of Automatic Aerostats (BU)

DAAC .... Direccion Administrativa de Aeronautica Civil [*Civil Aeronautics Administrative Directorate*] [*Colombian*] (LA)
DAAD .... Deutscher Akademischer Austauschdienst [*German Academic Exchange Service*]
DAAF .... Direction des Affaires Administratives et Financieres (MAR)
DAAFAR ...... Defensa Antiaerea y Fuerza Aerea Revolucionaria [*Antiaircraft Defense and Revolutionary Air Force*] [*Cuban*] (LA)
DAALPS ...... Detachement d'Armee des Alpes
DAATL .... Detachement d'Armee de l'Atlantique
DAAyC .... Departamento de Asuntos Agrarios y de Colonizacion [*Department of Agrarian Affairs and Colonization*] [*Mexican*] (LA)
DAB .... Aerial Smoke Bomb (RU)
DAB .... Deutsches Arzneibuch [*German Pharmacopoeia*] [*West German*] (WEN)
DAB .... Dimethylaminoazobenzene (RU)
DAB .... Dimethylaminobenzene (RU)
DAB .... Domestic Appliances & Bicycles Co. Ltd. (MAR)
DABA .... Deutsche Aussenhandelsbank [*German Foreign Trade Bank*] (EG)
DABCO .... Domestic Appliances & Bicycles Company Ltd. (MAR)
DAC .... Democratic Action Congress [*Trinidadian and Tobagan*] (PPW)
DAC .... Demokratik Almanya Cumhuriyeti [*German Democratic Republic - GDR*] (TU)
DAC .... Departamento de Accion Comunal [*Federal District Community Action Department*] [*Colombian*] (LA)
DAC .... Development Assistance Committee [*OECD*] (WEN)
DAC .... Direccion de Aviacion Civil [*Office of Civil Aviation*] [*Ecuadorean*] (LA)
DAC .... Direccion de Aviacion Comercial y Civil [*Peruvian*]
DAC .... Directoria de Aeronautica Civil [*Civil Aeronautics Directorate*] [*Brazilian*] (LA)
DAC .... Drzavni Arhiv Cetinje [*State Archives in Cetinje*] (YU)
DAD .... Department Administratiewe Dienste (MAR)
DAD .... Drzavni Arhiv u Dubrovniku [*State Archives in Dubrovnik*] (YU)
DADA .... Dar Es Salaam Regional Darts Association (MAR)
DA-DE .... Dimokratikos Agonas - Dimokratiki Enotita [*Democratic Struggle - Democratic Unity*] (GC1)
dad gek .... Dadurch Gekennzeichnet [*Thereby Characterized*] [*German*]
DAdK .... Deutsche Akademie der Kuenste [*German Academy of the Arts*] (EG)
DADMAKh ... Dialkyldimethylammonium Chloride (RU)
DAdW .... Deutsche Akademie der Wissenschaften (zu Berlin) [*German Academy of Sciences (in Berlin)*] (EG)
DAE .... Departamento de Aguas e Esgotos [*Water and Sewer Department*] [*Brazilian*] (LA)
DAE .... Diethnis Andikarkiniki Enosis [*International Cancer Union*] (GC)
DAE .... Diethnis Astronavtiki Etaireia [*International Astronautical Society*] (GC)
DAE .... Dikastirion Aeroporikon Epitaxeon [*Air Force Requisitions Court*] [*Greek*] (GC)
DAE .... Direction des Achats a l'Etranger [*Office of Foreign Purchases*] [*Cambodian*] (CL)
DAEC .... Direction de l'Action Exterieure et de la Cooperation (MAR)
DAEE .... Departamento de Aguas e Energia Eletrica [*Water and Electric Power Department*] [*Brazilian*] (LA)
DAF .... Daniel Ancel & Fils, Tamatave (MAR)
DAF .... Dansk Arbejdsgiverforening [*Danish Employers' Association*] (WEN)
DAF .... Dansk Astronautisk Forening [*Danish Astronautical Society*]
DAF .... Desert Air Force (MAR)
DAF .... Deutsche Arbeitsfront [*German Workers Front*] [*Post-World War II*]
DAF .... Diaminophenol (RU)
DAF .... Diammonium Phosphate (RU)
DAFA .... Direction pour l'Administration des Forces Armees [*Directorate of Administration of the Armed Forces*] [*Malagasy*] (AF)
DAFAR .... Defensa Antiaerea y Fuerza Aerea Revolucionaria [*Revolutionary Air Force and Antiaircraft Defense*] [*Cuban*] (LA)
DAFFO .... Dansk Forening til Fremme af Opfindelser [*Danish Society for Furthering Inventions*]
DAFNRJ ...... Drzavna Arhiva Federativna Narodna Republika Jugoslavija [*State Archives of Yugoslavia*] (YU)
DAFRIC .... La Demeure Africaine (MAR)
DAG .... Aerial Grenade Rack (RU)
dag .... Dagestan (RU)
dag .... Decagramme [*Dekagram*] [*French*] (GPO)
DAG .... Deutsch-Arabische Gesellschaft [*German-Arab Society*] (EG)
DAG .... Deutsche Afrika Gesellschaft (MAR)
DAG .... Deutsche Agrarwissenschaftliche Gesellschaft, Kuehlungsborn [*German Society of Agricultural Sciences, Kuehlungsborn*] (EG)
DAG .... Deutsche Angestellten-Gewerkschaft [*German Salaried Employees' Union*] [*West German*] (WEN)
DAG .... Division Artillery Group (RU)
DAG .... Diviziska Artiljeriska Grupa [*Artillery Group in a Division*] (YU)
DagASSR .... Dagestan Autonomous Soviet Socialist Republic (RU)
Daggiz .... Dagestan State Publishing House (RU)
Dagknigoizdat ... Dagestan Book Publishing House (RU)
Daguchpedgiz ... Dagestan State Publishing House of Textbooks and Pedagogical Literature (RU)
Dah .... Dahili [*Internal, Local (Phone call)*] [*Turkish Cypriot*] (GC)
DAH .... Drustvo Arhitekta Hrvatske [*Society of Architects of Croatia*] (YU)
DAHOTEX ... Societe Dahomey-Texas du Petrole (MAR)
DAHW .... Deutsche Aussaetziges Hilfswerk (MAR)
DAI .... Departamento Administrativo de Inquilinato [*Tenancy Administration Department*] [*Honduran*] (LA1)
DAI .... Direction des Affaires Internationales [*International Affairs Directorate*] (WER)
DAI .... State Motor Vehicles Inspectorate (BU)
DAIA .... Delegacion de Asociaciones Israelitas Argentinas [*Delegation of Argentine Jewish Associations*] (LA)
DAIC .... Departamento Administrativo de Intendencias y Comisarias [*Administrative Department for Police Headquarters and Intendencies*] [*Colombian*] (LA)
DAIC .... Dominica Association of Industry and Commerce [*Dominican*] (LA1)
DAIR .... Observation Battalion [*Artillery*] (RU)
DAK .... Address-Code Selector [*Computers*] (RU)
Dak .... Daktilo [*Typing, Typist*] (TU)
DAK .... Dehydroascorbic Acid (RU)
DAK .... Demokratisch Aktie-Komite (Vlaanderen) [*Democratic Action Committee (Flanders)*] [*Belgian*] (WEN)
DAK .... Deutsche Atomkommission [*German*]
DAK .... Deutsches Afrika Korps (MAR)
DAK .... Dimokratiki Andifasistiki Kinisi [*Democratic Antifascist Movement*] [*Greek*] (GC)
DAK .... Dnepr Aluminum Kombinat (RU)
DAK .... Documents of the Archaeological Commission (RU)
DAK .... Remote-Reading Astrocompass (RU)
DAKARMARINE ... Societe pour le Developpement de l'Infrastructure de Chantiers Maritimes du Port de Dakar (MAR)
DAK-B .... Remote-Reading Astrocompass of a Bomber (RU)
DAK-DB ...... Remote-Reading Astrocompass of a Long-Range Bomber (RU)
DAK-I .... Remote-Reading Astrocompass of a Fighter (RU)
DAKO .... Compagnie Dakaroises de Conserves (MAR)
dal .... Decaliter (RU)
dal .... Decalitre [*Decaliter*] [*French*]
DAL .... Deutsche Akademie der Landwirtschaftswissenschaften [*German Academy of Agricultural Sciences*] (EG)
DALCAN ..... Societe Aluminium Alcan du Dahomey (MAR)
DALEKOVOD ... Preduzece za Izgradnju Dalekovoda i Trafostanica [*Enterprise for the Manufacture of Long-Distance Transmission Lines and Transformer Stations*] (YU)
Dal'giz .... Far Eastern State Publishing House (RU)
DALIT .... Ljevaonica Zeljeza i Tvornica Strojeva Daruvar [*Daruvar Iron Foundry and Machinery Factory*] (YU)
DALMACIJABILJE ... Poduzece Ljekovitog Bilja [*Dalmatian Medicinal Plants Establishment*] [*Dubrovnik*] (YU)
DALMACIJACEMENT ... Dalmatian Cement Export-Import Establishment (YU)
DALMACIJATEKSTIL ... Dalmatian Wholesale Textile Establishment (YU)
dal'n .... Distant, Far (RU)
Dal'neft' ...... Association of the Far Eastern Petroleum Industry (RU)
Dal'NIILKh ... Far Eastern Scientific Research Institute of Forestry (RU)
Dal'NIVI .... Far Eastern Scientific Research Veterinary Institute (RU)
DALRO .... Dramatic, Artistic, and Literary Rights Organisation Ltd. (MAR)
Dal'rybvtuz ... Far Eastern Technical Institute of the Fish Industry and Fisheries (RU)
Dal'sel'mash ... Far Eastern Agricultural Machinery Plant (RU)
Dal'stroy ..... Main Construction Administration of the Far North (RU)
Dal'TA .... Far Eastern News Agency (RU)
Dal'yevtsib ... Far Eastern Jewish Central Information Office (RU)
DAM .... Daerah Militer [*Military Region (KODAM)*] (IN)
dam .... Decameter (RU)
dam .... Decametre [*Decameter*] [*French*]
DAM .... Denrees Africaines Manufacturees (MAR)
DAM .... Diacetylmonoxime (RU)
DAM .... Diplome d'Assistant Medical [*French*]
DAM .... Distribuidora de Articulos Metalicos Ltda. [*Bogota*] (COL)
DAM .... Djaksa Agung Muda [*Deputy Attorney General*] (IN)
DAM .... Drzaven Arhiv na Makedonija [*State Archives of Macedonia*] (YU)
DAMAG .... Societe Dakaroise de Grands Magasins "Printania" (MAR)
Dam-E .... Damasteinband [*Damask Binding*] [*German*]
dAMF .... Deoxyadenosine Monophosphate (RU)
DAMFK .... Diisoamyl Ester of Methylphosphinic Acid (RU)
DAMG .... Deutsches Amt fuer Masse und Gewichte [*German Office for Weights and Measures*] (EG)
DAMISTOR ... Societe Dahomeenne de Transistors (MAR)
DAMK .... Diakheirisis Andalaximon Mousoulmanikon Ktimaton [*Administration for Exchangeable Moslem Properties*] [*Greek*] (GC)
DAMS .... State Arbitration of the Council of Ministers (BU)
DAMW .... Deutsches Amt fuer Messwesen und Warenpruefung [*German Office for Measurement and Commodity Testing*] (EG)
DAN .... Defensa Armada Nacional [*National Armed Defense*] [*Uruguayan*] (LA)

DAN .... Dimokratiki Andistasis Neon [*Democratic Youth Resistance*] [*Greek*] (GC)
dan .... Doctor of Architectural Sciences (RU)
DAN .... Dvizheniia Arabskikh Natsionalistov (MAR)
DAN .... Komandan [*Commanding Officer*] (IN)
DAN .... Reports of the Academy of Sciences, USSR [*A publication*] (RU)
DANBIF .... Danske Boghandleres Importrfrening [*Danish Booksellers Import Association*]
DANDAM .... Komandan Daerah Militer [*Military Region Commander*] (IN)
DANDJEN .... Komandan Djenderal [*Commanding General*] (IN)
DANE .... Departamento Administrativo Nacional de Estadistica [*National Administrative Department of Statistics*] [*Colombian*] (LA)
DANI .... Dimokratia-Anexartisia Nomou Imathias [*Democracy-Independence of Imathia Nome*] (GC)
DANIDA .... Danish International Development Agency (MAR)
DANJON .... Komandan Bataljon [*Battalion Commander*] (IN)
DANRH .... Drzavni Arhiv Narodne Republike Hrvatske [*State Archives of Croatia*] (YU)
DANRS .... Drzavni Arhiv Narodne Republike Srbije [*State Archives of Serbia*] (YU)
DAO .... State Pharmaceutical Trust (BU)
DAOS .... Dolgoprudnyy Agrochemical Experimental Station Imeni D. N. Pryanishnikov (RU)
DAP .... Aircraft Reciprocating Engine (RU)
DAP .... Aircraft Smoke Generator (RU)
DAP .... Democratic Action Party [*Malaysian*] (PPW)
DAP .... Democratic Action Party [*Maltese*] (PPE)
DAP .... Departamento Administrativo de Planeacion Distrital [*Federal District Administrative Department for Planning*] [*Colombian*] (LA)
DAP .... Desarrollo Agropecuario del Pais [*National Agriculture and Livestock Development Agency*] [*Cuban*] (LA)
DAP .... Diakheirisis Andallaximou Periousias [*Management of Exchangeable Estates*] [*Greek*] (GC)
DAP .... Diazopyruvic Acid (RU)
DAP .... Dimokratiki Ananeotiki Protoporeia [*Democratic Renewal Vanguard*] [*Greek*] (GC)
DAP .... Division Aeroportee [*Airborne Division*] [*Zairian*] (AF)
DAP .... House of Antireligious Education (RU)
DAP .... State Motor Vehicle Enterprise (BU)
DAP .... State Motor Vehicle Transportation (BU)
DAP .... State Pharmaceutical Enterprise (BU)
DAPCEG .... Diplome d'Aptitude Pedagogique au Professorat des Colleges d'Enseignement General [*French*]
DAPE .... Diffusion Affichage Publicite Edition (MAR)
DAPERA .... Dana Pembangunan Daerah [*Regional Development Fund*] (IN)
DAPIB .... Dana Pembangunan Irian Barat [*West Irian Development Fund*] (IN)
DAPPS .... Drzavno Avtobusno in Prevoznisko Podjetje Slovenije [*State Autobus and Transport Establishment of Slovenia*] (YU)
DAR .... Diphenylamine Reaction (RU)
dar .... Division Artillery (BU)
DAR .... Divisione Affari Riservati [*Secret Affairs Division*] [*Italian*] (WER)
DAR .... Drzavni Arhiv u Rijeci [*State Archives in Rijeka*] [*Fiume*] (YU)
DAR .... Long-Range Arctic Reconnaissance Aircraft (RU)
DARA .... Deutsche Arbeitgemeinschaft fuer Rechen-Anlagen [*A data processing association*]
DARA .... Development and Reconstruction of the African Land Areas (MAR)
DARAG .... Deutsche Auslands- und Rueckversicherungs-AG [*German Foreign Insurance and Reinsurance Corporation*] (EG)
DARE .... Data Retrieval [*System for documentation in the social and human sciences*] [*UNESCO*]
DAREX .... Organisace pro Tuzemsky Prodej Exportniho Zbozi za Valuty v Drobnem a Darkovy Vyvoz [*Organization for the Domestic Retail Sale of Export Goods for Foreign Currencies and for the Export of Gifts*] (CZ)
DARH .... Drustvo Arhitekta Republike Hrvatske [*Society of Architects of Croatia*] (YU)
DARM .... Division Aircraft Repair Shop (RU)
DARM .... Division Artillery Repair Shop (RU)
DARM .... Division Motor Vehicle Repair Shop (RU)
DARM .... Drifting Automatic Radiometeorological Station (RU)
DARMS .... Drifting Automatic Radiometeorological Station (RU)
DARNDR .... Departement de l'Agriculture, des Ressources Naturelles, et du Developpement Rural [*Department of Agriculture, Natural Resources, and Rural Development*] [*Haitian*] (LA)
DARR .... Division Ordnance Repair Shop (BU)
Darst .... Darstellung [*Description, Explanation*] [*German*]
DARTEL .... Distribuidora de Artigos Electricos Lda. (MAR)
DAS .... Departamento Administrativo de Seguridad [*Administrative Department of Security*] [*Colombian*] (LA)
DAS .... Directia Asistentei de Sanatate [*Health Care Directorate*] (RO)
DAS .... Discrete Automatic System (RU)
DAS .... Division Ammunition Depot (RU)
DAS .... Division Artillery Dump (BU)
DAS .... Divizisko Artiljerisko Skladiste [*Division Ordnance Depot*] (YU)
DAS .... Drustvo Arhitektov Slovenije [*Society of Architects of Slovenia*] (YU)
DAS .... Drzavni Arhiv Narodna Republika Bosne i Hercegovine, Sarajevo [*State Archives of Bosnia and Hercegovina in Sarajevo*] (YU)
DAS .... Long-Distance Automatic Service, Long-Distance Dial Service [*Telephony*] (RU)
DAS .... Motor Vehicle Transportation Directorate (BU)
DAS .... State Court of Arbitration (BU)
DAS-114 .... Dimokratiki Andistasis Spoudaston [*Democratic Resistance of Students*] [*Greek*] (GC)
DASA .... Dagitim ve Satis AS [*Distribution and Sales Corp.*] [*Istanbul*] (TU)
DASA .... Dental Association of South Africa (MAR)
DASA .... Dimokratiki Andistasis Spoudaston Athinon [*Democratic Resistance of Athens Students*] (GC)
DASA .... Direccion de Abastecimientos y Servicios Auxiliares [*Board of Logistics and Support Services*] [*Peruvian*] (LA)
DASC .... Departamento Administrativo de Servicio Civil [*Civil Service Administrative Department*] [*Colombian*] (LA)
DASC .... Department of Agriculture, Southern Cameroons (MAR)
DASIP .... Diplomatski Arhiv Sekretarijata Inostranih Poslova [*Diplomatic Archives of the Secretariat for Foreign Affairs*] (YU)
DASK .... Dimokratiki Avtonomi Syndikalistiki Kinisi [*Democratic Autonomous Trade Union Movement*] (GC)
DASP .... Departamento Administrativo do Servico Publico [*Public Service Administrative Department*] [*Brazilian*] (LA)
DASP .... Drzavno Autobusno Saobracajno Preduzece [*State Autobus Transport Establishment*] [*Serbia*] (YU)
DASP .... State Autonomous Economic Enterprise (BU)
DASPE .... Dimokratiki Aristeri Syndikalistiki Parataxi Elladas [*Democratic Left Labor Faction of Greece*] (GC)
DASR .... Deutsche Akademie fuer Staats- und Rechtswissenschaften "Walter Ulbricht" [*"Walter Ulbricht" German Academy of Political Science and Jurisprudence*] (EG)
DASSR .... Dagestan Autonomous Soviet Socialist Republic (RU)
dast .... Decastere [*Dekastere*] [*French*] (GPO)
DAST .... Division Administrativa de Servicios de Transporte [*Administrative Division of Transportation Services*] [*Nicaraguan*] (LA1)
DASTA .... Daerah Istimewa [*Special Region (Jogjakarta and Atjeh)*] (IN)
DASTTTR .... Direction des Affaires Sociales, de Travail, du Tourisme, de Transport, et des Refugies [*Directorate of Social Affairs, Labor, Tourism, Transport, and Refugees*] [*Cambodian*] (CL)
DASWATI I .... Daerah Swatantra Tingkat I [*First Level Autonomous Region (Former province)*] (IN)
DASWATI II .... Daerah Swatantra Tingkat II [*Second Level Autonomous Region (Former regency)*] (IN)
dat .... Danish (RU)
dat .... Dative [*Case*] (BU)
dat .... Dative [*Case*] (RU)
DAT .... Delmagyarorszagi Aramtermelo Vallalat [*Electric Power Producing Enterprise of Southern Hungary*] (HU)
DAT .... Den, Aoyama, and Takemake [*Early investors in automobile manufacturer Nissan*] [*Initials used in creating automobile name DATSUN*] [*Japanese*]
DAT .... Depot a Terme [*Time Deposit*] (CL)
DAT .... State Motor Vehicle Transportation (BU)
DATAPREV .... Empresa de Processamento de Dados da Previdencia Social [*Social Security Data Processing Enterprise*] [*Brazilian*] (LA)
DATAR .... Delegation a l'Amenagement du Territoire et a l'Action Regionale [*Delegation for Territorial Development and Regional Action*] [*French*] (WER)
dATF .... Deoxyadenosine Triphosphate (RU)
DATINSAC .... Empresa Integral de Sistemas y Tecnica de Computacion [*Systems and Computation Techniques Integral Enterprise*] [*Cuban*] (LA)
DATT .... Departamento Administrativo de Transito y Transporte [*Administrative Department of Traffic and Transportation*] [*Colombian*] (LA)
DAU .... Automatic Remote Control (RU)
DAU .... Departamento de Assuntos Universitarios [*Department of University Affairs*] [*Brazilian*] (LA)
DAU .... Development Administration Unit [*Malaysian*] (ML)
DAV .... Decolare si Aterizare Verticale [*Vertical Takeoff and Landing*] (RO)
DAV .... Delmagyarorszagi Aramszolgaltato Vallalat [*Electric Power Service Enterprise of Southern Hungary*] (HU)
DAV .... Dunantuli Aramszolgaltato Vallalat [*Electric Power Service Enterprise of Transdanubia*] (HU)
DAVIBO .... Societe Dakaroise des Vins et Autres Boissons (MAR)
davl .... Pressure (RU)
DAW .... Deutsche Akademie der Wissenschaften [*German Academy of Sciences*] (EG)
DAWU .... Dominica Amalgamated Workers Union [*Dominican*] (LA1)
DAZ .... Dnepr Aluminum Plant Imeni S. M. Kirov (RU)
DAZ .... Dnepropetrovsk Automobile Plant (RU)
DAZ .... Drzavni Arhiv Zadra [*State Archives in Zadar*] (YU)
DAZ .... Drzavni Arhiv u Zagrebu [*State Archives in Zagreb*] (YU)
DAZ .... State Motor Vehicles Repair Plant (BU)
Db .... Battery Range (RU)

DB .... Biovular Twins (RU)
DB .... Daljina Baterije [*Battery Range*] (YU)
db .... Darab [*Piece*] [*Hungarian*] (GPO)
db .... Decibel (RU)
Db .... Decibel (BU)
DB .... Delostrelecka Baterie [*Artillery Battery*] (CZ)
DB .... Denizcilik Bank [*Maritime Bank of Turkey*] (TU)
DB .... Deutsche Bundesbahn [*German Federal Railways*] [*Since 1949*] [*West German*] (WEN)
DB .... Deutscher Beamtenbund [*German Civil Servants' League*] (EG)
dB .... Dezibel [*Decibel*] (EG)
DB .... Diakjoleti Bizottsag [*Student Relief Committee*] (HU)
DB .... Diesel Ram, Diesel Pile Hammer (RU)
DB .... Differentiator (RU)
DB .... Dinitrobenzene (RU)
DB .... Disisleri Bakanligi [*Foreign Affairs Ministry*] (TU)
DB .... Dispatcher's Office, Control Office (RU)
DB .... Division Blindee [*French*]
Db .... Diviziska Baza [*Division Base*] (YU)
DB .... Donets Basin (RU)
DB .... Dunya Bankasi [*World Bank*] (TU)
DB .... Durch Boten [*By Messenger*] [*Business and trade*] [*German*]
DB .... Durchfuehrungsbestimmung [*Implementing Regulation*] [*West German*] (WEN)
DB .... Duta Besar [*Ambassador*] (IN)
DB .... Far Eastern Office (RU)
db .... Good Quality, Soundness (RU)
DB .... Long-Range Bomber (RU)
db .... Probably, It Must Be (RU)
DB .... Smoke Bomb (RU)
DB .... Twin-Engine Bomber (RU)
DB .... Weighing Batcher, Weighing Batchbox (RU)
DBA .... Deutsche Bauakademie [*German Architectural Academy*] (EG)
DBA .... Dibutyl Azelate (RU)
DBA .... Long-Range Artillery (RU)
DBA .... Long-Range Bombardment Aviation (RU)
DBAD .... Long-Range Bomber Division (RU)
DBAE .... Long-Range Bomber Squadron (RU)
DBAP .... Long-Range Bomber Regiment (RU)
DBAT .... Delostrelecka Baterie [*Artillery Battery*] (CZ)
DBB .... Deutsche Bauernbank [*German Peasant Bank*] (EG)
DBB .... Deutsche Bundesbahn [*German Federal Railway*] [*Since 1949*] [*West German*]
DBB .... Deutscher Beamtenbund [*Federation of German Civil Servants*] [*West German*] (WEN)
DBBM .... DeBeers Botswana Mining (MAR)
DBC .... Development Bank of the Caribbean (LA)
DBC .... Devrimci Birlesik Cephesi [*Revolutionary United Front*] (TU)
DBD .... Demokratische Bauernpartei Deutschlands [*Democratic Farmers' Party of Germany*] [*East German*] (PPW)
DBE .... Development Bank of Ethiopia (AF)
DBED .... Dibenzylethylenediamine (RU)
DBF .... Dibromophenol (RU)
DBF .... Dibutyl Phosphate (RU)
DBF .... Dibutyl Phthalate (RU)
DBGA .... Dominica Banana Growers Association [*Dominican*] (LA1)
DBI .... Deutsche Bibliotheks Institut
DBIV .... Ivan Vazov State Library (BU)
DBK .... Debreceni Boripari Kisipari Tsz [*Leather Industry Production Cooperative of Debrecen*] (HU)
DBK .... Depoh Besar Kelengkapan [*Central Ordnance Depot*] (ML)
Dbk .... Dubrovnik (YU)
DBL .... Development Bank of Laos (CL)
d Bl .... Dieses Blattes [*Of This Paper*] [*German*]
dbm .... Decibel at the One-Milliwatt Level (RU)
DBM .... Dibenzoylmethane (RU)
DBM .... Dyrekcja Budowy Miasta [*Administration of Municipal Construction*] (POL)
dbn .... Doctor of Biological Sciences (RU)
DBO .... Dzielnicowe Biura Opalowe [*City Section Fuel Offices*] (POL)
DBOR .... Dyrekcja Budowy Osiedli Robotniczych [*Administration of the Construction of Workers' Settlements*] (POL)
DBP .... Deutsche Bundespost [*Federal German Postal Service*] [*West German*] (EG)
DBP .... Dewan Bahasa dan Pustaka [*Language and Literature Council*] (ML)
DBP .... Drzavno Bagersko Preduzece [*State Dredging Establishment*] (YU)
DBPC .... Demi-Brigade Parachutiste de Choc [*Algerian*] (MAR)
DB Pd .... State Library, Plovdiv (BU)
DBR .... Direckcija Broj [*Direction Number*] [*Railroads*] (YU)
dbr .... Road Brigade (RU)
DBRS .... Long-Range Ballistic Missile (RU)
DBS .... Departamento de Bienestar Social [*Federal District Social Welfare Department*] [*Colombian*] (LA)
DBS .... Long-Range Ballistic Missile (RU)
DBS .... Long-Range Bomber Unit (RU)
DBSV .... Deutscher Billiard-Sport-Verband [*German Billiard Association*] (EG)
DBTD .... Dibenzothiazyl Disulfide (RU)
DBU .... Dnepr Basin Administration (RU)
DBV .... Deutscher Boxer-Verband [*German Boxing Association*] (EG)
DBVK .... Vasil Kolarov State Library (BU)
DBVK BIA .... Vasil Kolarov State Library, Bulgarian Historical Archives (BU)
DBW .... Deutsche Babcock Wilcox Werke
DBYKP .... Dorduncu Bes Yil Kalkinma Plan [*Fourth Five-Year Development Plan*] (TU)
DBYP .... Dorduncu Bes Yillik Plani [*Fourth Five-Year Plan*] (TU)
DBZ .... Development Bank of Zambia (MAR)
dc .... Da Capo [*Again*] [*Italian*]
DC .... Decision Conjointe [*Joint Decision*] [*French*] (CL)
DC .... Defensa Civil [*Bogota*] (COL)
DC .... Democracia Cristiana [*Christian Democratic Party*] [*Colombian*] (PPW)
DC .... Democracia Cristiana [*Christian Democratic Party*] [*Paraguayan*] (PD)
DC .... Democrats Camerounais (MAR)
DC .... Democrazia Cristiana [*Christian Democratic Party*] [*Italian*] (WER)
DC .... Developpement Communautaire [*Community Development*] [*Cambodian*] (CL)
DC .... Direkcija za Ceste [*Department of Roads*] (YU)
D & C .... Discusion y Convivencia [*Discussion and Coexistence*] [*Spanish*] (WER)
DC .... District Commissioner (MAR)
DC .... District Council (MAR)
DC .... Division de Cavalerie [*Military*] [*French*] (MTD)
DC .... Djujijeva Klasifikacija [*Dewey Classification*] (YU)
Dc .... Doctor Docent in Stiinte [*Academic degree*] [*Romanian*]
dC .... Dopo Cristo [*After Christ*] [*Italian*] (GPO)
DC .... Partito Democrazia Cristiano [*Christian Democratic Party*] [*Italian*] (PPW)
DC .... Turkiye Demir ve Celik Isletmeleri [*Turkish Iron and Steel Enterprise*] (TU)
D3C .... Diplome de Troisieme Cycle [*French*]
DCA .... Dar Es Salaam Cricket Association (MAR)
DCA .... Defense Contre Avions [*or Aeronefs*] [*Antiaircraft*] [*French*]
DCA .... Democratic Congress Alliance [*Gambian*] (AF)
DCA .... Department of Civil Aviation [*Rhodesian*] (AF)
DCA .... Directorate of Civil Aviation (MAR)
DCA .... Divadlo Ceskoslovenske Armady [*Czechoslovak Armed Forces Theater*] (CZ)
DCA .... Documentatie Centrum Atoomkernenergie [*Documentation Center for Nuclear Energy*] [*Dutch*] (WEN)
dca .... Dowodca [*Chief, Commander*] [*Polish*]
DCAN .... Direction des Constructions et Armes Navales [*Naval Construction and Weapons Directorate*] [*French*] (AF)
dcbel .... Decybel [*Decibel*] [*Polish*]
DCC .... Defensa Civil Colombiana [*Colombian Civil Defense*] (LA)
DCCA .... Direccion Central de Construccion y Alojamiento [*Central Directorate for Construction and Housing*] [*Cuban*] (LA)
DCCAN .... Direction Centrale des Constructions et Armes Navales [*Central Directorate for Naval Weapons and Shipbuilding*] [*French*] (WER)
DCCM .... Direccion Central de Construcciones Militares [*Central Directorate for Military Construction*] [*Cuban*] (LA)
DCCM .... Disciples of Christ Congo Mission (MAR)
DCD .... Department of Community Development (MAR)
DCE .... Direction du Commerce Exterieur [*Directorate of Foreign Trade*] [*Cambodian*] (CL)
DCEM .... Deuxieme Cycle d'Etudes Medicales [*French*]
DCF .... Democratie Chretienne Francaise [*French Christian Democracy*] (PPE)
DCF .... Direccion de Coordinacion Federal [*Directorate of Federal Coordination*] [*Argentine*] (LA)
DCF .... Directeur des Chemins de Fer [*Military*] [*French*] (MTD)
DCF .... Discounted Cash Flow (MAR)
dcg .... Decygram [*Polish*]
DCG .... Democracia Cristiana Guatemalteca [*Guatemalan Christian Democracy*] (LA)
DCH .... Direction Centrale d'Hydraulique (MAR)
DCh .... Doppler Frequency (RU)
dch .... Durch [*Through, By*] [*German*]
DCh .... Frequency Divider (RU)
DCh .... Unit on Duty, Alert Unit (RU)
DChA .... State Watch Repair Shop (BU)
DChD .... Net Income Tax (BU)
d chl .... Full Member (RU)
DChM .... Double Frequency Modulation (RU)
Dcho .... Derecho [*Right*] [*Spanish*]
DChT .... Double Frequency Telegraphy, Two-Channel Frequency Telegraphy (RU)
DCI .... Daerah Chusus Ibukota [*Special Capital Region (Djakarta)*] (IN)
DCI .... Demir ve Celik Isletmesi [*Iron and Steel Enterprise*] [*See also TDCI*] (TU)
DCI .... Developpement et Civilisations [*Paris*] [*A publication*] (MAR)
dcl .... Decylitr [*Polish*]
DCL .... Dental Colombiana Ltda. [*Medellin*] (COL)
Dcm .... Decimetre [*Decimeter*] [*French*] (MTD)
dcm .... Decymetr [*Decimeter*] (POL)
DCM .... Direction Centrale des Marches (MAR)
DCM .... Dovize Cevrilebilir Mevduat [*Convertible Lira Account*]

DCM .... Dunai Cement Muvek [*Danube Cement Works*] (HU)
Dcm² .... Decimetre Carre [*Square Decimeter*] [*French*] (MTD)
Dcm³ .... Decimetre Cube [*Cubic Decimeter*] [*French*] (MTD)
DCMP .... Depot Central Medico-Pharmaceutique (MAR)
dcn .... Dalszy Ciag Nastapi [*To Be Continued*] [*Polish*]
DCO .... Divisao Centro-Oeste [*Center-West Division*] [*of the National Indian Foundations*] [*Brazilian*] (LA)
DCO .... Dominion Colonial and Overseas (MAR)
DCOS .... Directia Caselor de Odihna si Sanatorii [*Directorate of Rest Homes and Sanatoriums*] (RO)
DCP .... Democratic Congress Party (MAR)
DCPEP .... Diplome de Conseiller Pedagogique de l'Enseignement Primaire [*French*]
DCS .... Democrazia Cristiana Sanmarinese [*Christian Democratic Party of San Marino*] [*Italian*] (WER)
DCS .... Diosgyori Csapagygyar [*Bearing Factory of Diosgyor*] (HU)
DCS .... Directia Centrala de Statistica [*Central Directorate of Statistics*] (RO)
DCSA .... Divadlo Ceskoslovenske Armady [*Czechoslovak Armed Forces Theater*] (CZ)
DCsCK .... Dorost Ceskoslovenskeho Cerveneho Krize [*Czechoslovak Junior Red Cross*] (CZ)
DCSV .... Direccion de Circulacion y Seguridad Vial [*Directorate for Traffic and Highway Safety*] [*Peruvian*] (LA)
DCT .... Departamento de Correios e Telegrafos [*Postal and Telegraph Department*] [*Brazilian*] (LA)
DCTF .... Dil, Cografya, ve Tarih Fakultesi [*Faculty of Language, Geography, and History*] [*of Ankara University*] (TU)
DCV .... Druzstvo Cestujici Verejnosti [*Public Travel Cooperative*] (CZ)
DCVP .... Druzina Ceskoslovenskych Valecnych Poskozencu [*Society of Czechoslovak War Victims*] (CZ)
dd .... Dags Dato [*The Date of the Day*] [*Danish*] (GPO)
d/d .... Daily Ration (BU)
DD .... Dampfdichte [*Vapor Density*] [*German*]
DD .... Damping Diode (RU)
d d .... Dandar [*Brigade*] (HU)
dd .... De Dato [*From Date*] [*Business and trade*] [*German*]
DD .... Dedinske Divadlo [*Village Theater*] (CZ)
DD .... Defense Democratique (MAR)
DD .... Delostrelecka Divize [*Artillery Division*] (CZ)
DD .... Diastolic Pressure (RU)
DD .... Dienst fuer Deutschland [*Service for Germany*] [*See also DfD*] (EG)
DD .... Diesel Engine (RU)
DD .... Differential Range Finder (RU)
DD .... Diode Decoder (RU)
DD .... Dionicko Drustvo [*Joint-Stock Company*] (YU)
DD .... Divinitatis Doctor [*Doctor of Divinity*] [*Latin*] (GPO)
DD .... Doctores [*Doctors*] [*Spanish*]
DD .... Donnees pour le Developpement [*Data for Development International Association - DFD*] (EA)
DD .... German Democratic Republic [*East Germany*] [*Two-letter standard code*] (CNC)
DD .... Long-Range [*Military term*] (RU)
DD .... Road Distance (RU)
dd .... Villages (RU)
DD .... Vrlo Hitno [*Very Urgent*] [*Military code*] (YU)
DDA .... Direction Departementale de l'Agriculture (MAR)
DDA .... Dominica Democratic Alliance (PPW)
DDA .... Truck-Mounted Disinfection and Shower Unit (RU)
DDA .... Two-Arm Sprinkler Apparatus (RU)
DDAP .... Deutsche Demokratische Arbeiterpartei [*German Democratic Workers' Party*] [*West German*] (PPW)
DDAR .... Differential Diphenylamine Reaction (RU)
DDC .... Dar Es Salaam Development Corporation (MAR)
DDC .... District Development Committee [*Malawian*] (AF)
DDC .... District Development Corporation [*Tanzanian*] (AF)
DDC .... Divisional Development Committee (MAR)
DDD .... Dichlorodiphenyldichloroethane (RU)
DDD .... Diffusion Pressure Deficit (RU)
DDD .... Discagem Direta a Distancia [*Direct Long-Distance Dialing*] [*Brazilian*] (LA)
DDD .... Izvanredno Vazno [*Extremely Important*] [*Military code*] (YU)
DDDD .... Devterovathmion Dioikitikon Diaititikon Dikastirion [*Second Degree Administrative and Arbitration Court*] [*Greek*] (GC)
DDE .... Dichlorobis(dichlorophenyl)ethylene (RU)
DDE .... Direction Departementale d'Equipement [*Departmental Equipment Bureau*] [*French*] (WER)
DDETsA .... Dvizhenie Demokraticheskoi Evoliutsii Tsentral'noi Afriki (MAR)
DDF .... Departamento del Distrito Federal [*Federal District Department*] [*Mexican*] (LA)
DDF .... Dimokratikes Dynameis Foititon [*Student Democratic Forces*] [*Greek*] (GC)
DDGF .... Dunya Demokratik Genclik Federasyonu [*World Federation of Democratic Youth*] (TU)
DDGRES .... Dneprodzerzhinsk State Regional Electric Power Plant (RU)
DDI .... Diamond Distributors, Incorporated (MAR)
DDI .... Discagem Direta Internacional [*International Direct Dialing*] [*Brazilian*] (LA)
DDI .... Double-Image Range Finder (RU)
DDK .... Children's Book House (RU)
ddk .... Del-Delkelet [*South-Southeast*] (HU)
DDK .... Dimethyldithiocarbamate (RU)
ddk .... Division of Landing Boats (BU)
DDK .... Dzielnicowy Dom Kultury [*City Section House of Culture*] (POL)
ddk .... Landing Ship Division (RU)
DDKD .... Devrimci Demokratik Kultur Dernegi [*Revolutionary Democratic Cultural Association*] (TU)
DDKD .... Devrimci Dogu Kultur Dernegi [*Revolutionary Eastern Cultural Organization*] (TU)
DDKO .... Devrimci Dogu Kultur Ocaklari [*Revolutionary Eastern Cultural Hearths*] [*Clubs*] (TU)
DDL .... Disegno di Legge [*Draft Bill*] [*Italian*] (WER)
Ddm .... Diplome de Docteur en Medecine [*French*]
DDMV .... Demokraticheskaia Dvizheniia za Malagasiiskoe Vozrozhdenie (MAR)
DDN .... Departemen Dalam Negeri [*Department of Internal Affairs*] (IN)
DDN- .... Normal Disk Diaphragm (RU)
d d ny .... Del-Delnyugat [*South-Southwest*] (HU)
DDP .... Denni Davka Potravin [*Daily Food Ration*] (CZ)
DDP .... Departamento de Diversoes Publicas [*Public Recreation Department*] [*Brazilian*] (LA)
DDP .... Derecha Democratica Espanola [*Spanish Right-Wing Democratic Party*] (PPW)
DDP .... Deutsche Demokratische Partei [*German Democratic Party*] (PPE)
DDP .... Double Diode-Pentode (RU)
DDP .... Duodioda-Pentoda [*Duodiode-Pentode (Radio tube)*] (HU)
DDP .... Trailer-Mounted Disinfection and Shower Unit (RU)
DDP .... Wooden Landing-Craft Park [*for river crossing*] (RU)
DDR .... Deutsche Demokratische Republik [*German Democratic Republic (East Germany)*]
DDR .... Direction du Developpement Regional (MAR)
DDR .... Divadelni a Dramaturgicka Rada [*Theater and Drama Council*] (CZ)
DDS .... Dimethyldichlorosilane (RU)
DDS .... Divizni Delostrelecka Skupina [*Division Artillery Group*] (CZ)
DDSE .... Dioikitikon Dikastirion Stratiotikon Epitaxeon [*Army Requisitions Administrative Court*] [*Greek*] (GC)
DDSG .... Donau-Dampfschiffahrtsgesellschaft [*Danube Steamship Company*] (EG)
DDT .... Dichlorodiphenyltrichloroethane (RU)
DDT .... Double Diode-Triode (RU)
DDT .... Duodioda-Trioda [*Duodiode-Triode (Radio tube)*] (HU)
DDTK .... Diethyldithiocarbamate (RU)
DDUSCP .... Depozitul de Dotare a Unitatilor Sanitare Curativo-Profilactice [*Supply Warehouse for Remedial-Prophylactic Health Units*] (RO)
DDV .... Dienstdauervorschriften [*Permanent Service Regulations*] (EG)
DDY .... Devlet Demiryollari [*State Railways*] [*See also TCDD*] (TU)
DDZ .... Timber Extracting and Processing Plant (BU)
DE .... Arc-Suppression Element (RU)
De .... Dake [*Mountain, Hill*] [*See also Te*] [*Japanese*] (NAU)
de .... Delelott [*Morning, Midmorning*] (HU)
DE .... Demokratiki Enosis [*Democratic Union*] [*Greek*] (PPE)
DE .... Deputy (IN)
De .... Dere [*Deresi*] [*Valley, Stream*] [*Turkish*] (NAU)
de .... Det Er [*This Is*] [*Norwegian*] (GPO)
DE .... Dielektrizitaetskonstante [*Dielectric Constant*] [*German*]
d/e .... Diesel-Electric Ship (RU)
DE .... Dimokratiki Enosis [*Democratic Union*] [*Cypriot*] (GC)
DE .... Dioikitiki Epitropi [*Administrative Committee*] (GC)
DE .... Direction des Etapes [*Military*] [*French*] (MTD)
DE .... Dizel-Elektricni Pogon [*Diesel-Electric Power*] (YU)
DE .... Dizelelektrane [*Diesel-Powered Electric Plants*] (YU)
De .... Doctorat d'Etat [*French*]
DE .... Drustvena Evidencija [*Budgetary Records*] (YU)
DE .... Drustvo Ekonomista [*Society of Economists*] (YU)
De .... Durchgangs-Eilgueterzug [*Through Express Freight Train*] (EG)
DE .... Federal Republic of Germany [*Two-letter standard code*] (CNC)
DE .... Other Type of Energy (BU)
DEA .... Departement Economique Appliquee [*Applied Economics Department*] [*French*] (WER)
DEA .... Deutsche Erdoel AG (MAR)
DEA .... Diffusione Edizioni Anglo-Americane [*Distributors of English and American Publications*] [*Italian*]
DEA .... Dimoiria Eidikis Apostolis [*Special Mission Platoon*] (GC1)
DEA .... Dimokratiki Epitropi Andistaseos [*Democratic Resistance Committee*] [*Greek*] (GC)
DEA .... Diplome d'Etudes Approfondies [*Advanced Study Diploma*] [*French*] (CL)
DEA .... Distribution d'Equipement Automobile pour la Region du Centre (MAR)
DEAC .... Debreceni Egyetemi Atletikai Club [*University Athletic Club of Debrecen*] (HU)
DEAETs .... Diethylaminoethyl Cellulose (RU)
DEAG .... Deutsche Einfuhr- und Ausfuhrgesellschaft [*German Import and Export Company*] (EG)
DEAM .... Diplome d'Etudes d'Administration Municipale [*Diploma in Municipal Administration*] [*French Guiana*] (LA1)

DEAN .... Diethnis Epitropi Aeronavtilias [*International Air Navigation Commission*] (GC)
deb .... Debit [*French*]
DEB .... Distrito Especial de Bogota [*Bogota Federal District*] [*Colombian*] (LA)
DEB .... Road Maintenance Battalion (RU)
DEBA .... Direccion de la Energia de Buenos Aires [*Buenos Aires Power Administration*] [*Argentine*] (LA)
debit .... Debiteur [*Debtor*] [*French*]
Debr .... Debrecen [*Debrecen*] (HU)
Debre .... Debarcadere [*Station, Platform*] [*Military map abbreviation*] [*World War I*] [*French*] (MTD)
dec .... Decede [*Deceased*] [*French*]
dec .... December [*December*] [*Danish*] (GPO)
dec .... December [*December*] [*Dutch*] (GPO)
dec .... December [*December*] [*Hungarian*] (GPO)
dec .... Decembre [*December*] [*French*]
Dec .... Decort [*Deduct*] [*Business and trade*] [*German*]
DEC .... Depenses d'Equipement Communal [*Algerian*] (MAR)
DEC .... Developing Economies [*Tokyo*] [*A publication*] (MAR)
DEC .... Diplome d'Etudes Complementaires [*Further Studies Diploma*] (CL)
DEC .... Direccion de Estadistica y Censos [*Bureau of Statistics and Census*] [*Chilean*] (LA)
DEC .... Direction des Echanges Commerciaux (MAR)
DEC .... Drzavna Elektricna Centrala [*State Electric Station*] (YU)
DECARP .... Desert Encroachment Control and Rehabilitation Programme [*Sudanese*] (MAR)
Dech .... Dechant [*German*]
DECO .... Delegacion Exterior de Comisiones Obreras [*Foreign Delegation of Workers Commissions*] [*Spanish*] (WER)
DECORATONY ... Decoracion por Tony Ltda. [*Medellin*] (COL)
DECS .... Diplome d'Etudes Comptables Superieurs (MAR)
DED .... Depenses d'Equipement Departementaux (MAR)
DED .... Deutscher Entwicklungsdienst [*German Development Service (Peace Corps)*] [*West German*] (WEN)
DED .... Developpement Economique Departemental (MAR)
DEDASZ .... Deldunantuli Aramszolgaltato Vallalat [*Electric Power Service Enterprise of Southern Transdanubia*] (HU)
DEE .... Diethnes Emborikon Epimelitirion [*International Chamber of Commerce*] (GC)
DEE .... Dioikisis Exoterikou Emboriou [*Foreign Trade Administration*] [*Greek*] (GC)
DEE .... Distribucija Elektricne Energije [*Distribution of Electric Power*] (YU)
DEEAS .... Dievthynsis Epopteias kai Elengkhou Aktoploikon Syngoinonion [*Directorate for Supervision and Control of Coastal Shipping Communications*] [*Greek*] (GC)
DEES .... Diethnis Epitropi Erythrou Stavrou [*International Red Cross Committee*] (GC)
DEF .... Delegations Economiques et Financieres (MAR)
DEF .... Diethnis Enosis Foititon [*International Union of Students*] (GC)
DEF .... Differential Figure Elements [*Cybernetics*] (RU)
DEF .... Diplomes d'Etudes Fondamentales (MAR)
def .... Imperfect, Defective (RU)
DEFA .... Deutsche Film Aktiengesellschaft [*German Film Corporation*] (EG)
DEFA .... Dimotiki Epikheirisis Fotaeriou Athinon [*Athens Public Gas Corporation*] (GC)
Defe .... Defile [*Defile*] [*Military map abbreviation*] [*World War I*] [*French*] (MTD)
DEFE .... Destacamento Escuela de Fuerzas Especiales [*Special Forces School Detachment*] [*Ecuadorean*] (LA)
def ekz .... Defective Copy, Defective Item (BU)
DEFOSZ .... Dolgozo Parasztok es Foldmunkasok Orszagos Szovetsege [*National Association of Working Peasants and Laborers*] (HU)
DEFP .... Departamento de Educacao e Formacao Professional [*Department of Education and Vocational Training*] [*Mozambican*] (AF)
DEFPA .... Direction de l'Enseignement et de la Formation Professionnelle Agricole (MAR)
DEG .... Derechos Especiales de Giro [*Special Drawing Rights*] [*Argentine*] (LA)
DEG .... Deutsche Entwicklungsgesellschaft [*German Development Company*] (EG)
DEG .... Deutsche Gesellschaft fuer Wirtschaftliche Zusammenarbeit (Entwicklungsgesellschaft) mbH (MAR)
DEG .... Direction des Etudes Generales [*Moroccan*] (MAR)
DEGM .... Din Egitimi Genel Mudurlugu [*Religious Education Directorate General*] (TU)
DEGT .... Deutscher Eisenbahnguetertarif [*German Railway Freight Tariff*] (EG)
DEGU .... Diesel-Electric Drive [*Nautical term*] (RU)
DEGUFA .... Deutsche Gummifabrik [*German Rubber Factory*] (EG)
DEGUSSA .... Deutsche Gold- und Silberscheide-Anstalt [*German Gold and Silver Separation Installation*] [*West German*] (WEN)
DEH .... Departement Etranger Hachette
DEH .... Drustvo Ekonomista Hrvatske [*Society of Economists of Croatia*] (YU)
DEHOGA .... Deutscher Hotel- und Gaststaettenverband [*German Hotel and Catering Trade Association*] [*West German*] (EG)
DEI .... Dimosia Epikheirisis Ilektrismou [*Public Power Corporation*] [*Greek*] (GC)
DEI .... State Electric Power Installation (BU)
DEIC .... Departamento de Investigacoes Criminais [*Criminal Investigations Department*] [*Brazilian*] (LA)
DEIP .... Dewan Ekonomi Indonesia Pusat [*Central Economic Council of Indonesia*] (IN)
DEJ .... Drustvo Ekonomista Jugoslavije [*Society of Economists of Yugoslavia*] (YU)
DEJG .... Diplome d'Etudes Juridiques Generales [*French*]
dek .... Dean (RU)
DEK .... Debreceni Kossuth Lajos Tudomanyegyetem Konyvtara [*Library of the Louis Kossuth University of Debrecen*] (HU)
dek .... Decare (BU)
dek .... December (BU)
dek .... December (RU)
Dek .... Dekanat [*German*]
DEK .... Demokratiki Enosis Kyprou [*Democratic Union of Cyprus*] [*Greek Cypriot*] (PPE)
DEK .... Dimokratiki Enosis Kendrou [*Democratic Center Union*] [*Greek*] (GC)
DEK .... Dimokratikon Enotikon Komma [*Democratic Union Party*] [*Cypriot*] (GC)
DEK .... Dimokratikon Ethnikon Komma [*Democratic National Party*] [*Cypriot*] (GC)
DEKA .... Dimokratikon Ethnikon Kinima Andistaseos [*Democratic National Resistance Movement*] [*Greek*] (GC)
DEKAGE .... Deutsche Kamerun GmbH (MAR)
DEKAS .... Deputy Kepala Staf [*Deputy Chief of Staff*] (IN)
DEKE .... Dimokratiki Ergatikon Kinima Ellados [*Democratic Labor Movement of Greece*] (GC)
DEKFA .... Dimokratiki Enosis Kyprion Foititon Athinas [*Democratic Union of Cypriot Students of Athens*] [*Greek*] (GC)
DEKO .... Demokratiko Komma [*Democratic Party*] [*Greek Cypriot*] (PPE)
Deko .... Deutsch- Europaeische Transportgesellschaft (VEB) [*German-European Transport Company (VEB)*] (EG)
DEKO .... Dominikanska Edice Krystal, Olomouc [*Dominican "Krystal" Publishing House, Olomouc*] (CZ)
DEKOR .... Kirakatrendezo es Reklamkivitelezo KTSz [*Producers' Cooperative of Window Dressers and Advertising Designers Enterprise*] (HU)
dekr .... Decree, Statute (RU)
del .... Delineat [*Drawn By*] [*Latin*]
Del .... Delostrelectvo [*Artillery*] (CZ)
DEL .... Depenses d'Equipement Local [*Algerian*] (MAR)
DEL .... Developpement Economique Local (MAR)
del .... Fission [*Nuclear physics and engineering*] (RU)
del .... Plot, Parcel [*of land*] (RU)
Delbat .... Delostrelecka Baterie [*Artillery Battery*] (CZ)
DELCO .... Sierra Leone Development Company (MAR)
DELDAV .... Deldunantuli Aramszolgaltato Vallalat [*Electric Power Service Enterprise of Southern Transdanubia*] (HU)
DELG .... Diplome d'Etudes Litteraires Generales [*French*]
DELIMA .... Fundicion de Metales de Lima [*Barranquilla*] (COL)
DELIMCO .... Deutsche Liberian Mining Company (MAR)
DELITBANG ... Dewan Penelitian dan Pembangunan [*Research and Development Council*] (IN)
DELK .... Deutsche Evangelisch-Lutheranische Kirche in Suedwestafrika (MAR)
delker .... Delkeruleti [*Southern District (Adjective)*] (HU)
DELMAIZ .... Derivados del Maiz, SA [*Medellin*] (COL)
Delodd .... Delostrelecky Oddil [*Artillery Battalion*] (CZ)
DELPCO .... Delta Petroleum Company (MAR)
Delpluk .... Delostrelecky Pluk [*Artillery Regiment*] (CZ)
delyuv .... Diluvial (RU)
dem .... Deminutiivi [*Finnish*]
dem .... Demokraatti(nen) [*Finnish*]
dem .... Demokrata [*or Demokratikus*] [*Democrat or Democratic*] (HU)
DEM .... Departamento de Exploracao Mineral [*Minerals Exploration Department*] [*Brazilian*] (LA)
DEM .... Dievthynsis Enaerion Metaforon [*Air Transport Directorate*] [*Greek*] (GC)
DEM .... Dievthynsis Ergon Mikhanikou [*Engineering Projects Directorate*] [*Greek*] (GC)
DEMA .... Dewan Mahasiswa [*Student Council*] (IN)
DEMAK .... Demir-Makina Sanayi ve Ticaret AS [*Iron-Machinery Industry and Trading Corporation*] (TU)
DEMASZ .... Del-Magyarorszagi Aramszolgaltato Vallalat [*Electric Power Service Enterprise of Southern Hungary*] (HU)
DEMBA .... Demerara Bauxite Company Ltd. [*Guyanese*] (LA)
DEMCOP .... Democratic Cooperative Development Party (MAR)
DEMD .... Devlet Emlak ve Malzeme Dairesi Mudurlugu [*State Properties and Equipment Office Directorate*] [*Turkish Cypriot*] (GC)
DEME .... Diakyvernitiki Epitropi Metanastevseos ex Evropis [*Intergovernmental Committee for European Emigration*] (GC)
demilit .... Demilitarized (RU)

DEMISAS.... Dokum Emaye Mamulleri Sanayi Anonim Sirketi [*Enamelled Cast Iron Products Industry Corporation*] (TU)
dem pron.... Demonstratiivipronomini [*Demonstrative Pronoun*] [*Finnish*]
dem red...... Demandes Reduites [*French*]
DEn............ Delavska Enotnost [*Workers Unity*] [*A newspaper*] (YU)
den............ Denaturalt [*Denatured*] (HU)
DEN............ Detasemen [*Detachment*] (IN)
DEN............ Directia Energiei Nationale [*National Power Directorate*] (RO)
den............ Doctor of Economic Sciences (RU)
dendr.......... Dendrological (RU)
DENEK........ Dimokratiki Enosis Neolaias Kyprou [*Democratic Union of Cypriot Youth*] (GC)
DENG.......... Dimokratiki Enosi Neon Gynaikon [*Democratic Union of Young Women*] [*Greek*] (GC)
DENI........... Departamento Nacional de Investigacion [*National Department of Investigation*] [*Panamanian*] (LA)
DENI........... Departamento Nacional de Investigaciones [*National Department of Investigations*] [*Chilean*] (LA)
Deniz.......... Denizci [*or Denizcilik*] [*Sailor or Maritime*] (TU)
Deniz Ulas-Is... Istanbul Deniz Ulas-Is Sendikasi [*Istanbul Maritime Transport Workers' Union*] (TU)
DENKA........ Diakommatiki Epitropi Neolaion Kypriakou Agonos [*Interparty Committee of Youth for the Cypriot Struggle*] [*Greek*] (GC)
DENMA....... Detasemen Markas [*Headquarters Detachment*] (IN)
DENTEL...... Departamento Nacional de Telecomunicacoes [*National Telecommunications Department*] [*Brazilian*] (LA)
DEO............ District Education Officer (MAR)
DEO............ Divisional Executive Officer (MAR)
DEOK.......... Dimokratiki Ergatiki Omospondia Kyprou [*Democratic Labor Federation of Cyprus*] (GC)
DEON.......... Dioikitiki Epitropi Oikou Navtou [*Sailors' Home Administrative Committee*] (GC)
DEOPS........ Departamento Estadual de Ordem Politica e Social [*State Department of Political and Social Order*] [*Brazilian*] (LA)
DEP............ Departamento de Educacao Politica [*Department of Political Education*] [*Angolan*] (AF)
dep............ Departement [*Department*] [*French*]
dep............ Deposited (BU)
dep............ Deputy, Representative (RU)
DEP............ Diesel-Electric Drive (RU)
DEP............ Dimosia Epikheirisis Petrelaiou [*Public Petroleum Corporation*] [*Greek*] (GC)
DEP............ Diplome d'Etat de Pharmacien [*French*]
DEP............ Direccion de Educacion Profesional [*Directorate of Professional Education*] [*Cuban*] (LA)
DEP............ Distributivno Elektricno Pretprijatie [*Electric Power Distribution Establishment*] (YU)
DEP............ Road Maintenance Regiment (RU)
DEP............ State Electric Power Enterprise (BU)
DEPA.......... Diplome d'Etudes Pratiques d'Anglaise (MAR)
DEPAD........ Departemen Angkatan Darat [*Department of the Army*] (IN)
DEPAG........ Departemen Agama [*Department of Religious Affairs*] (IN)
DEPAL........ Departemen Angkatan Laut [*Department of the Navy*] (IN)
DEPARI....... Dewan Parawisata Indonesia [*Indonesia Tourism Council*] (IN)
DEPARLU.... Departemen Luar Negeri [*Department of Foreign Affairs*] (IN)
DEPAS........ Denizli Boru ve Profil Sanayii ve Ticaret Anonim Sirketi [*Denizli Pipe and Construction Steelwork Industry Corporation*] (TU)
DEPAU........ Departemen Angkatan Udara [*Department of the Air Force*] (IN)
DEPDAG..... Departemen Perdagangan [*Department of Commerce*] (IN)
DEPDAGRI... Departemen Dalam Negeri [*Department of Internal Affairs*] (IN)
DEPE.......... Diakheiristiki Epitropi Ploion ex Epanorthoseon [*Administrative Committee of Ships Obtained from Reparations*] [*Greek*] (GC)
DEPE.......... Division de Ejecucion de Proyectos Educativos [*Division for the Implementation of Educational Projects*] [*Nicaraguan*] (LA1)
DEPED........ Departamento de Pesquisas e Desenvolvimento [*Research and Development Department*] [*Brazilian*] (LA)
DEPERDAG... Departemen Perdagangan [*Department of Commerce*] (IN)
DEPERHUB... Departemen Perhubungan [*Department of Communications*] (IN)
DEPERIN..... Departemen Perindustrian [*Department of Industry*] (IN)
DEPERTAM... Departemen Pertambangan [*Department of Mining*] (IN)
DEPERTAN... Departemen Pertanian [*Department of Agriculture*] (IN)
DEPES........ Diplome d'Etudes Pratiques de l'Enseignement Secondaire (MAR)
DEPGAKER... Departemen Tenaga Kerdja [*Department of Manpower*] (IN)
DEPGAM..... Departemen Agama [*Department of Religious Affairs*] (IN)
DEPHAK...... Departemen Kehakiman [*Department of Justice*] (IN)
DEPHANKAM... Departemen Pertahanan dan Keamanan [*Department of Defense and Security*] (IN)
DEPKEH...... Departemen Kehakiman [*Department of Justice*] (IN)
DEPKES...... Departemen Kesehatan [*Department of Health*] (IN)
DEPKEU...... Departemen Keuangan [*Department of Finance*] (IN)
DEPLADIS.. Development Planning Documents Information System for ESCAP Countries [*Proposed*]
Deple.......... Departementale [*Departmental*] [*Military map abbreviation*] [*World War I*] [*French*] (MTD)
DEPLU......... Departemen Luar Negeri [*Department of Foreign Affairs*] (IN)
DEPNAKER... Departemen Tenaga Kerdja [*Department of Manpower*] (IN)
DEPOS........ Dimosia Epikheirisis Poleodomiseos, Oikismou, kai Stegaseos [*Public Enterprise for Town Planning, Housing, and Shelter*] [*Greek*] (GC)
DEPP.......... Societe Dahomeenne d'Entreposage de Produits Petroliers (MAR)
DEPPEN...... Departemen Penerangan [*Department of Information*] (IN)
DEPPERHUB... Departemen Perhubungan [*Department of Communications*] (IN)
DEPPERIN... Departemen Perindustrian [*Department of Industry*] (IN)
DEPPERTAM... Departemen Pertambangan [*Department of Mining*] (IN)
DEPPI......... Angola's Political, Educational, Propaganda, and Information Department (MAR)
Dep prov..... Deputato Provinciale [*Member of the Provincial Parliament*] [*Italian*] (GPO)
DEPPU........ Departemen Pekerdjaan Umum [*Department of Public Works*] (IN)
DEPRIN....... Departemen Perindustrian [*Department of Industry*] (IN)
DEPRONAS... Dewan Produksi Nasion [*National Production Council*] (IN)
DEPS.......... Diplome d'Etudes Primaires Superieures [*Advanced Primary Studies Diploma*] (CL)
DEPSOS...... Departemen Sosial [*Department of Social Affairs*] (IN)
DEPT.......... Direction d'Entreaide et de Promotion des Travailleurs [*Algerian*] (MAR)
DEPTAM..... Departemen Pertambangan [*Department of Mining*] (IN)
DEPTAN...... Departemen Pertanian [*Department of Agriculture*] (IN)
DEPTRANSKOP... Departemen Transmigrasi dan Koperasi [*Department of Resettlement and Cooperatives*] (IN)
DEPU.......... Departemen Keuangan [*Department of Finance*] (IN)
DER............ Departamento de Estradas de Rodagem [*Highway Department*] [*Brazilian*] (LA)
DER............ Depenses d'Equipement Rural [*Rural Equipment Expenditures*] [*Algerian*] (AF)
Der............ Derinlik [*Depth*] [*As in meters*] (TU)
Der............ Derivat [*Derivative*] [*German*]
DER............ Deutsches Reisebuero [*German Travel Agency*] (EG)
DER............ Developpement Economique Rural [*Rural Economic Development*] [*Moroccan*] (AF)
Der............ Dokter [*Academic degree*] [*Indonesian*]
Der............ Village (RU)
Der............ Wooden [*Bridge, sluice, dam*] [*Topography*] (RU)
DERAP........ Development Economics Research and Advisory Project [*Kenyan*] (MAR)
DERBH........ Diplome d'Etudes et de Recherches en Biologie Humaine [*French*]
Derg.......... Dergi [*or Dergisi*] [*Review*] [*As a publication*] (TU)
dergl.......... Dergleichen [*Similar*] [*German*]
Deri-Is........ Turkiye Deri, Debbag, Kundura ve Saraciye Iscileri Sendikasi [*Turkish Leather and Shoe Industry Workers Union*] (TU)
Deriv.......... Derivat [*Derivative*] [*German*]
derm.......... Dermatology, Dermatologist (BU)
DERRO........ Projet de Developpement Economique et Rural du Rif Occidental [*Economic and Rural Development of the Western Rif*] (MAR)
ders............ Derselbe [*The Same*] [*German*] (GPO)
DERTS........ Departement d'Etudes et de Recherches en Technologie Spatiale
DERUTRA... Deutsch-Russische Transport AG [*GDR-Soviet Transport Corp.*] (EG)
DES............ Arc Welding (RU)
des............ Decimal (RU)
DES............ Defektni Sluhom [*Persons with Defective Hearing*] [*Labor*] (YU)
des............ Desatnik [*Corporal*] (CZ)
DES............ Diesel Electric Power Plant (RU)
DES............ Diethnis Erythros Stavros [*International Red Cross*] (GC)
DES............ Dimosia Emboriki Skholi [*Public Commercial School*] (GC)
DES............ Diploma de Estudos Superiores [*Polytechnical Higher Studies*] [*Portuguese*]
DES............ Diplome d'Etudes Superieures [*Advanced Studies Diploma*] [*French*] (WER)
DES............ Diplome d'Etudes Superieures Bancaires (MAR)
DES............ Direction des Etapes et Services [*Obsolete*] [*Military*] [*French*] (MTD)
DES............ Drustvo Ekonomista Srbije [*Society of Economists of Serbia*] (YU)
DES............ Landing Force (RU)
DESA.......... Demir, Kazan, ve Makina Sanayii AS [*Iron, Boilers, and Machinery Industry, Inc.*] [*Subsidiary of Yesar Holding*] (TU)
DESA.......... Desarrollo de Edificaciones Sociales y Agropecuarias [*Farm and Social Building Development Agency*] [*Cuban*] (LA)
DESAL........ Centro para el Desarrollo Economico y Social de America Latina [*Latin American Center for Socioeconomic Development*] (LA)
DESAL........ Desenvolvimiento Economic e Social da America Latina [*Latin American Center for Socioeconomic Development*] (LA)
DESAM........ Diplome d'Etudes Superieures Administratives Municipale [*Diploma in Advanced Municipal Administration Studies*] [*French Guiana*] (LA1)

DESAS........ Dioikousa Epitropi Syllogon Anoteron Skholon [*Administrative Committee of Associations of Higher Schools*] [*Greek*] (GC)
desasp........ Desatnik Aspirant [*Cadet Corporal*] (CZ)
DESAUR ChM... Decentralized Automatic Frequency and Active Power Control System (RU)
DESCON..... Desertification Control (AF)
DESCTC..... Dewaniya State Cotton Textile Company [*Iraqi*] (MAR)
DESG.......... Diplome d'Etudes Scientifiques Generales [*French*]
desgl........... Desgleichen [*Similar*] [*German*]
DESIYAB..... Devlet Sanayi ve Isci Yatirim Bankasi [*State Industry and Worker Investment Bank*] (TU)
DESK.......... Dimokratiki Enotita Syndikalistikon Kiniseon [*Democratic Union of Trade Union Movements*] [*Greek*] (GC)
DESO.......... Landing Detachment (RU)
DESP........... Departamento Estadual de Seguranca Publica [*State Department of Public Security*] [*Brazilian*] (LA)
DESP........... Destacamento Especial de Selva Petrolifera [*Oil Jungle Special Detachment*] [*For security work in Santa Cecilia region*] [*Ecuadorean*] (LA)
DESP........... Dimokratiki Enotiki Syndikalistiki Parataxi [*Democratic Unifying Trade Union Faction*] (GC)
DESP........... Diplome de l'Ecole Superieure de Pali [*Pali Higher School Diploma*] (CL)
DESP........... Diplome d'Etudes Scientifiques Preparatoires [*French*]
DESPA........ Dimokratiki Enotiki Syndikalistiki Parataxi Athinon [*Democratic Unifying Trade Union Faction of Athens*] (GC)
DESPA........ Dioikousa Epitropi Syllogon Panepistimiou Athinon [*Administrative Committee of Athens University Associations*] (GC)
despb.......... Assault Troop Crossing Battalion (BU)
despb.......... River Crossing Assault Battalion (RU)
DESPC........ Diplome d'Etudes Secondaires du Premier Cycle [*First Cycle Secondary Studies Diploma*] (CL)
despr........... River Crossing Assault Company (RU)
Despred...... State Shipping Enterprise (BU)
DESS........... Diplome d'Etudes Superieures Specialisees [*Advanced Specialized Studies Diploma*] [*French*] (WER)
dest............ Destillation [*Distillation*] [*German*]
DESTI.......... Direction des Etudes Statistiques et du Traitement de l'Information (MAR)
DESY........... Deutsches Elektronen-Synchrotron [*German Electron-Synchrotron*] (EG)
des zn......... Decimal Point (RU)
det.............. Children's Word (BU)
det.............. Child's, Children's (RU)
det.............. Detache [*French*]
DET............ Detasemen [*Detachment*] (IN)
DET............ Diesel-Electric Tractor (RU)
DET............ Diethnis Enosis Tilepikoinion [*International Telecommunications Union*] (GC)
DET............ Diethnis Enosis Tourismou [*International Touring Alliance*] (GC)
DET............ Diffuse Emission Nebula (RU)
DET............ Division de Desarrollo Tecnologico [*Colombian*]
det.............. Part, Element (RU)
DETA.......... Direccao de Exploracao dos Transportes Aereos [*Air Transport Exploitation Directorate*] [*Mozambican*] (AF)
det d........... Children's Home [*Topography*] (RU)
DETEC........ Detectivismo Tecnico Particular [*Medellin*] (COL)
De-Te-Ha.... Dom Techniczno-Handlowy [*Engineering Trade House*] (POL)
determ pron... Determinatiivipronomini [*Determinative Pronoun*] [*Finnish*]
DETERT...... Duna-Tenger Hajozasi Reszvenytarsasag [*Danube-Ocean Navigation Company Limited*] (HU)
DETGIZ....... State Publishing House of Children's Literature (RU)
DETh.......... Diethnis Ekthesis Thessalonikis [*Salonica International Fair*] (GC)
Detizdat...... Publishing House of Children's Literature (RU)
Detizdat...... State Publishing House for Children's Books (BU)
Det kol........ Children's Colony [*Topography*] (RU)
det kom....... Children's Town [*Topography*] (RU)
Detkom....... Commission for the Improvement of Children's Living Conditions (RU)
Detmag....... Children's Store (BU)
DETN.......... Departement des Etudes et des Travaux Neufs (MAR)
DETRA........ Societe de Distribution et d'Equipement pour l'Industrie et les Transports (MAR)
Detran......... Departamento de Transito [*Traffic Department*] [*Brazilian*] (LA)
DETs........... Diesel Electric Power Plant (BU)
det san........ Children's Sanatorium [*Topography*] (RU)
detszagotovka... Decentralized Procurement, Local Procurement (RU)
Dett............ Detachement [*Detachment*] [*Military*] [*French*] (MTD)
DETT........... Length of Apparatus Equivalent to a Theoretical Plate (RU)
det tub san... Children's Tuberculosis Sanatorium [*Topography*] (RU)
Detyunizdat... State Publishing House of Children's and Young People's Literature (RU)
DEU............ Federal Republic of Germany [*Three-letter standard code*] (CNC)
DEU............ Road Maintenance Section (RU)
DEUG.......... Diplome d'Etudes Universitaires Generales [*French*]
DEUP........... Diplome d'Etudes Universitaires Pedagogiques [*French*]
deut............ Deutsch [*German*]
dev.............. Deviza [*Foreign Exchange*] (HU)
deva............ Field Forces (BU)
DEVCO........ Development Corporation (MAR)
DEV GENC... Turkiye Devrimci Genclik Federasyonu [*Turkish Revolutionary Youth Federation*] [*See also TDGF*] (TU)
DEV-IS........ Devrimci Isci Sendikalari Federasyonu [*Federation of Revolutionary Workers' Unions*] [*Turkish Cypriot*] (GC)
Dev-Lis........ Devrimci Liseciler Birligi [*Union of Revolutionary Lycee Students*] (TU)
Dev Maden-Sen... Devrimci Maden Arama ve Isletme Iscileri Sendikasi [*Revolutionary Mineral Research and Exploitation Workers' Union*] [*Belongs to DISK*] (TU)
DEV-MEM... Devrimci Memurlar Dernegi [*Revolutionary Public Officials Organization*] [*Reformist*] (TU)
DEVNET...... Development Information Network [*Proposed*]
DEVREKTAS... Devrek Insaat Elemanlari Sanayi ve Ticaret Anonim Sirketi [*Devrek Construction Elements Industry and Trade Corporation*] (TU)
DEW........... Deutsche Edelstahlwerke Aktiengesellschaft [*German High-Grade Steel Works*] [*West German*]
DEWAG....... Deutsche Werbe- und Anzeigengesellschaft [*German Promotion and Ad Company*] (EG)
dex.............. Dexamenoploion [*Tanker*] [*See also D/P*] (GC)
DEY............ Diethnis Ethelondiki Ypiresia [*International Volunteer Service*] (GC)
DEY............ Dievthynsis Englimatologikon Ypiresion [*Criminal Services Directorate*] [*Greek*] (GC)
deyeprich... Verbal Adverb (RU)
DEYF-Is....... Demiryollari Isci Sendikalari Federasyonu [*Federation of Railway Worker Unions*] (TU)
deystv......... Active (BU)
deystv......... Active (Voice) (RU)
deystv......... Actual (BU)
deystv chlen... Active Member (RU)
Dez............. Dezember [*December*] [*German*] (GPO)
dez.............. Dezembro [*December*] [*Portuguese*] (GPO)
DEZ............ State Lighting Fixtures Plant (BU)
deza........... Misleading Information, Deception [*Military term*] (RU)
dezh........... Duty Officer, Man on Duty, Officer of the Day (RU)
dezhkom..... Duty Commandant (RU)
dezhoperot... Operations Duty Officer (RU)
Dezinstitut... Central Scientific Research Institute of Disinfection (RU)
DE-ZZU....... Diesel-Electric Suction Dredge (RU)
DF............... Deutscher Forschungsrat [*German Research Council*] (EG)
df................ Dias Fecha [*Days from Date*] [*Spanish*]
DF............... Dias Freres (MAR)
DF............... Distrito Federal [*Federal District*] [*Spanish*] (GPO)
DF............... Djakarta Fair (IN)
DF............... Dnepr Flotilla (RU)
d/f.............. Slide Film, Film Strip, Strip Positive (RU)
DFA............ Diphenylamine (RU)
DFAI........... Department of Foreign Affairs and Information [*South African*]
DFB............ Demokratischer Frauenbund Deutschlands [*Democratic Women's League of Germany*] (EG)
DFB............ Deutsche Frauenbewegung [*German Women's Movement*] [*West German*] (PPW)
DFB............ South African Deciduous Fruit Board (MAR)
DFBD.......... Demokratischer Frauenbund Deutschlands [*Democratic Women's League of Germany*] (EG)
DFCK.......... Development Finance Company of Kenya Ltd. (MAR)
DFCU.......... Development Finance Company of Uganda Ltd. (MAR)
DFD............ Data for Development International Association [*See also DD*] (EA)
DFD............ Demokratischer Frauenbund Deutschlands [*Democratic Women's League of Germany*] (EG)
DFD............ Devterovathmion Forologikon Dikastirion [*Tax Court of the Second Instance*] [*Greek*] (GC)
DfD............ Dienst fuer Deutschland [*Service for Germany*] [*See also DD*] (EG)
DFE-............ Photoelectric Densitometer (RU)
DFEPC........ Diplome de Fin d'Etudes du Premier Cycle [*French*]
DFF............ Deutsche Friedensgesellschaft [*German Peace Society*] (EG)
DFF............ Deutscher Fernsehfunk [*German Television*] (EG)
DFF............ Diisopropylfluorophosphate (RU)
DFFF........... Demokratiska Foerbundet av Finlands Folk [*Finnish People's Democratic League*] (PPE)
DFFG.......... De Forenade FNL-Grupperna [*The United National Liberation Front Groups*] [*Swedish*] (WEN)
DFG............ Deutsche Forschungsgemeinschaft [*German Research Association*] [*West German*] (WEN)
dfg.............. Dienstfaehig [*Fit for Duty*] (EG)
DFG............ Diphenylguanidine (RU)
DFJ............ Demokratska Federativna Jugoslavija [*Democratic Federative Yugoslavia*] (YU)
DFK............ Differential Photoelectric Calorimeter (RU)
DFK............ Dolnoslaska Fabryka Krosien [*Lower Silesia Loom Factory*] (POL)
DFK............ House of Physical Culture (RU)
DFK............ State Fodder Combine (BU)
DFK............ State Leather Factory (BU)

DFLP .... Democratic Front for the Liberation of Palestine (PD)
DFLR .... Deutsche Forschungsanstalt fuer Luft- und Raumfahrt [*West German*]
DFM .... Direccion de Fabricaciones Militares [*Military Construction Administration*] [*Argentine*] (LA)
DFMDFJ ...... Demokratska Federalna Makedonija vo Demokratska Federativna Jugoslavija [*Democratic Federative Macedonia in Democratic Federal Yugoslavia*] (YU)
d f-m n .... Doctor of Physical and Mathematical Sciences (RU)
DFMV .... Debreceni Finommechanikai Vallalat [*Precision Machine Enterprise of Debrecen*] (HU)
DFN .... Diphosphopyridine Nucleotide (RU)
dfn .... Doctor of Pharmaceutical Sciences (RU)
dfn .... Doctor of Philological Sciences (RU)
dfn .... Doctor of Philosophical Sciences (RU)
DFOM .... Departements Francais d'Outre-Mer (MAR)
DFP .... Demokratische Fortschrittliche Partei [*Democratic Progressive Party*] [*Austrian*] (PPE)
DFP .... Dominica Freedom Party (PPW)
DFPJ .... Dolnoslaska Fabryka Przemyslu Jedwabniczego [*Lower Silesia Silk Factory*] (POL)
DFPS .... Direction de la Formation Professionnelle et des Stages (MAR)
DFRH .... Drustvo Filmskih Radnika Hrvatske [*Society of Motion Picture Workers of Croatia*] (YU)
DFS .... Direccion Federal de Seguridad [*Federal Security Office*] [*Mexican*] (LA)
DFS-904 ...... Deutscher Freiheitssender 904 [*German Freedom Station 904 (Communist Radio)*] [*West German*] (WEN)
DFSI .... Demokraticna Fronta Slovencev v Italiji [*Slovenian Democratic Front in Italy*] (YU)
DFSP .... Departamento Federal de Seguranca Publica [*Federal Department of Public Security*] [*Brazilian*] (LA)
DFSS .... Democratic Front for the Salvation of Somalia (PD)
DFU .... Deutsche Friedens-Union [*German Peace Union*] [*West German*] (WEN)
DFU .... Dominica Farmers Union [*Dominican*] (LA1)
DFV .... Deutscher Fussball-Verband [*German Soccer League*] (EG)
DFVLR .... Deutsche Forschungs- und Versuchsanstalt fuer Luft- und Raumfahrt [*German Research and Development Institute for Air and Space Travel*] (EG)
DFZ .... State Fodder Plant (BU)
DG .... Arc Converter (RU)
Dg .... Dag [*Mountain, Mount*] (TU)
DG .... Dalasi Gambia (MAR)
Dg .... Daljina Gadanja [*Firing Range*] [*Military*] (YU)
DG .... Damping Gyro (RU)
Dg .... Decagramo [*Decagram*] [*Spanish*]
dg .... Decigram (RU)
dg .... Decigramme [*Decigram*] [*French*]
dg .... Decigramo [*Decigram*] [*Spanish*]
Dg .... Degirmen [*Mill*] (TU)
DG .... Dehydrogenase (RU)
DG .... Dei Gratia [*By the Grace of God*] [*Latin*] (GPO)
dg .... Dekagramm [*Decagram*] (HU)
DG .... Deo Gratias [*Thanks to God*] [*Latin*] (GPO)
DG .... Deoxy-D-Glucose (RU)
dg .... Dergleichen [*Similar*] [*German*]
dG .... Des Generalstabs [*or Generalstabsdienstes*] [*German*]
dg .... Desigramma(a) [*Finnish*]
DG .... Deutsche Gemeinschaft [*German Union*] (EG)
dg .... Dezigramm [*Decigram*] [*German*]
DG .... Diesel Generator (BU)
DG .... Diesel Generator (RU)
DG .... Differentiating Gyro (RU)
DG .... Diplome de Docteur Ingenieur [*French*]
DG .... Division Hospital (RU)
dG .... Durch Guete [*Kindness Of*] [*German*]
Dg .... Durchgangsgueterzug [*Through Freight Train*] (EG)
DG .... For Long-Range Shell [*Sight scale*] (RU)
dg .... General Commanding a Division (BU)
Dg .... Horizontal Range (RU)
DG .... State Forests (BU)
DGA .... Directia Generala a Agriculturii [*General Directorate of Agriculture*] (RO)
DGAD .... Directia Generala de Aprovizionare si Desfacere [*General Directorate for Supply and Sales*] (RO)
DGAFA .... Deposito Geral de Adidos da Forca Aerea [*General Register of Air Force Attaches*] [*Portuguese*] (WER)
DGAS .... Direction Generale des Affaires Sociales [*Directorate General of Social Affairs*] [*Cambodian*] (CL)
DGB .... Deutsche Geographische Blaetter (MAR)
DGB .... Deutscher Gewerkschaftsbund (fuer das Gebiete der Bundesrepublik Deutschland und Berlin) [*German Trade Union Federation (for the Area of the Federal Republic and Berlin)*] [*West German*]
DGB .... Devrimci Genclik Birligi [*Revolutionary Youth Union*] (TU)
DGCMB .... Directia Generala Comerciala pentru Municipiul Bucuresti [*General Trade Directorate for Bucharest Municipality*] (RO)
DGD .... Demokratik Genclik Dernegi [*Democratic Youth Organization*] [*Turkish Cypriot*] (GC)
DGD .... Deutsche Gesellschaft fuer Dokumentation
DGD .... Devrimci Genclik Dernegi [*Revolutionary Youth Association*] [*Turkish Cypriot*] (GC)
DGD .... Direccao Geral dos Desportos [*General Directorate of Sports*] [*Portuguese*] (WER)
DGDAL .... Directia Generala pentru Dezvoltarea Constructiilor de Locuinte Social Culturale si Administratie Locativa [*General Directorate for the Construction of Socio-Cultural Housing and Housing Administration*] (RO)
DGDC .... Departamento Geral de Defesa Civil [*General Department of Civil Defense*] [*Brazilian*] (LA1)
DGE .... Diethnes Grafeion Ergasias [*International Labor Office*] (GC)
DGE .... Direccion General de Estadistica [*General Office of Statistics*] [*Venezuelan*] (LA)
DGEA .... Dehydroepiandrosterone (RU)
DGEA .... Direccion General de Economia Agropecuario [*General Directorate of Agricultural Economy*] [*Salvadoran*] (LA1)
DGEC .... Direccion General de Estadisticas y Censos [*General Statistics and Census Bureau*] [*Uruguayan*] (LA)
DGED .... Direction Generale d'Etudes et de Documentation [*Directorate General of Studies and Documentation*] [*Moroccan*] (AF)
DGEP .... Direccao Geral de Educacao Permanente [*General Directorate of Permanent Education*] [*Portuguese*] (WER)
DGEP .... Direccion General de Establecimientos Penales [*General Directorate of Penal Institutions*] [*Peruvian*] (LA)
DGER .... Direction Generale des Enquetes et Recherches [*French*]
DGES .... Deutsche Gesellschaft fuer Eingeborenenschutz (MAR)
DGES .... Dnepr Hydroelectric Power Plant (RU)
DGF .... State Forestry Resources (BU)
DGFFC .... Directia Generala de Fond Funciar si Cadastru [*General Directorate of Land Resources and Cadastres*] (RO)
DGFI .... Deutsches Geodaetisches Forschungsinstitut [*Munich, West Germany*]
DGFK .... Deutsche Gesellschaft fuer Friedens- und Konfliktforschung (MAR)
DGFM .... Direccion General de Fabricaciones Militares [*General Directorate of Military Construction*] [*Argentine*] (LA1)
DGGC .... Direccion General de la Guardia Civil [*Civil Guard General Directorate*] [*Spanish*] (WER)
DGGC .... Directia Generala de Gospodarie Comunala [*General Directorate for the Communal Economy*] (RO)
DGH .... Directia Generala de Hidrometeorologie [*General Directorate of Hydrometeorology*] (RO)
DGHR .... Directia Generala a Hotelurilor si Restaurantelor [*General Directorate of Hotels and Restaurants*] (RO)
DGI .... Denatured Histone (RU)
DGI .... Direccion General Impositiva [*General Directorate of Taxation*] [*Argentine*] (LA)
DGI .... Direccion General de Inteligencia [*General Directorate of Intelligence*] [*Cuban*] (LA)
DGI .... Direccion General de Investigaciones [*General Directorate of Investigations*] [*Chilean*] (LA)
DGI .... Directia Generala a Industriei [*General Directorate of Industry*] (RO)
DGI .... Director Geral de Informacao [*General Director of Information*] [*Portuguese*] (WER)
DGI .... Dnepropetrovsk Mining Institute Imeni Artem (RU)
DGI .... Donets Mining Institute (RU)
DGIAC .... Direccion General de Investigaciones Aplicadas a la Construccion [*General Directorate for Construction Research*] (LA)
DGID .... Direction Generale d'Information et de Documentation [*Directorate General of Information and Documentation*] [*Malagasy*] (AF)
DGIE .... Departamento Geral de Investigacoes Especiais [*General Department of Special Investigations*] [*Brazilian*] (LA1)
DGIE .... Direccion General de Inmigracion y Extranjeria [*General Directorate of Immigration and Alien Affairs*] [*Venezuelan*] (LA)
DGIET .... Directia Generala a Intreprinderilor Electrotehnice [*General Directorate of Electrotechnical Enterprises*] (RO)
DGIM .... Drustvo na Gradeznite Inzeneri na Makedonija [*Society of Construction Engineers of Macedonia*] (YU)
DGIS .... Devrimci Genel Is Sendikasi [*Revolutionary (Reformist) General Workers' Union*] (TU)
DGITH .... Drustvo Gradevinskih Inzinjera i Tehnicara Hrvatske [*Society of Construction Engineers and Technicians of Croatia*] (YU)
DGITLRS ..... Drustvo Gradbenih Inzenirjev in Tehnikov Ljudska Republika Slovenija [*Society of Construction Engineers and Technicians of Slovenia*] (YU)
DGIT na NRM ... Drustvo na Gradeznite Inzeneri i Tehnicari na Narodna Republika Makedonija [*Society of Construction Engineers and Technicians of Macedonia*] (YU)
DGK .... Deutsche Gastspiel- und Konzert-Direktion [*German Play and Concert Management*] (EG)
DGKC .... Deutsche Gesellschaft fuer Klinischen Chemie
DGKP .... Dyrekcja Generalna Kolei Panstwowych [*General Administration of State Railroads*] (POL)
DGL .... Denatured Gliadin (RU)
dgl .... Dergelijke [*Such*] [*Dutch*] (GPO)
dgl .... Dergleichen [*The Like, Of That Kind*] [*German*] (GPO)

DGLI........... Directia Generala a Liniilor si Instalatilor [*General Directorate of Lines and Installations*] (RO)
DGLR........... Deutsche Gesellschaft fuer Luft- und Raumfahrt [*West German*]
DGM........... Devlet Guvenlik Mahkemesi [*State Security Court*] (TU)
DGM........... Directia Generala de Metrologie [*General Directorate of Metrology*] (RO)
DGM........... Direction de la Geologie et des Mines (MAR)
DGM........... Divisao de Geologia e Mineralogia [*Brazilian*]
DGM........... Duncan, Gilbey, and Matheson (MAR)
DGM........... Dynamic Magnetic Loudspeaker (RU)
DGMA........... Deutsche Gesellschaft fuer Messtechnik und Automatisierung [*German Society for Measuring Technology and Automation*] (EG)
dGMF........... Deoxyguanosine Monophosphate (RU)
DGMG........... Deposito Geral de Material de Guerra [*General War Material Depot*] [*Portuguese*] (WER)
DGMK........... Remote-Reading Gyromagnetic Compass (RU)
dg-mn........... Doctor of Geological and Mineralogical Sciences (RU)
DGMR........... Directia Generala a Materialelor Refractare [*General Directorate of Refractory Materials*] (RO)
DGMR........... Directorate General of Mineral Resources (MAR)
DGN........... Direccion General de Normas [*National Standards Organization*] [*Mexican*]
dgn........... Doctor of Geographical Sciences (RU)
DGO........... Deutsche Gemeindeordnung [*German Municipal Regulations*] (EG)
DGON........... Deutsche Gesellschaft fuer Ortung und Navigation [*West German*]
DGOP........... Direccion General de Orden Publico [*General Directorate of Public Order*] [*Cuban*] (LA)
DGOR........... Direccion General de Obras de Riego [*General Directorate of Irrigation Workers*] [*Salvadoran*] (LA1)
DGP........... Deutsche Grenzpolizei [*German Border Police*] (EG)
DGP........... Direccion General del Presupuesto [*General Budget Office*] [*Venezuelan*] (LA)
DGP........... Dunya Gida Programi [*World Food Program*] (TU)
DGPEI........... Direccion General de Prevencion y Extincion de Incendios [*General Directorate of Fire Fighting and Prevention*] [*Cuban*] (LA)
DGPH........... Deutsche Gesellschaft fuer Photographie [*West German*]
DGPI........... Dagestan State Pedagogical Institute Imeni S. Stal'skiy (RU)
DGPM........... Direction de la Geologie et de la Prospection Miniere (MAR)
DGPP........... State Forestry Industrial Enterprise (BU)
DGPS........... State Forestry Industrial Farm (BU)
DGPT........... Direccion General de Policia y Transito [*General Directorate of Police and Traffic*] [*Mexican*] (LA)
DGPT........... Directia Generala a Presei si Tipariturilor [*General Directorate of the Press and Printing*] (RO)
DGPTC........... Directia Generala a Postelor si Telecomunicatiilor [*General Directorate of Posts and Telecommunications*] (RO)
DGPYT........... Direccion General de Policia y Transito [*General Directorate of Police and Traffic*] [*Mexican*] (LA)
dgr........... Decigrade [*French*]
DGRAS........... Direction Generale du Renseignement et de l'Action Social (MAR)
DGRCST........... Direction Generale des Relations Culturelles, Scientifiques, et Techniques [*French*]
DGRM........... Directia Generala a Rezervelor Muncitoresti [*General Directorate of Labor Reserves*] (RO)
DGRR........... Deutsche Gesellschaft fuer Raketentechnik und Raumfahrt [*German Society for Rocketry and Astronautics*] (EG)
DGRS........... Directia Generala a Rezervelor de Stat [*General Directorate of State Reserves*] (RO)
DGRST........... Delegation Generale a la Recherche Scientifique et Technique [*General Delegation for Scientific and Technical Research*] [*French*] (WER)
DGS........... Direccao Geral de Seguranca [*Directorate General for Security*] [*Portuguese*] (AF)
DGS........... Direccion General de Seguridad [*General Directorate of Security*] [*Spanish*] (WER)
DGS........... State Forestry Farm (BU)
DGSA........... Devlet Guzel Sanatlar Akademisi [*State Fine Arts Academy*] [*See also GSA*] (TU)
DGSE........... Direccion General de la Seguridad del Estado [*General Directorate of State Security*] [*Nicaraguan*] (LA1)
DGSE........... Direction Generale de la Securite Exterieure [*French*]
DGSN........... Direction General de la Surete Nationale [*Directorate General of National Security*] [*Algerian*] (AF)
DGSN........... Direction Generale de Surete Nationale [*National Surete Directorate General*] [*Moroccan*] (AF)
DGSP........... Direccion General de Seguridad Personal [*General Directorate for Personal Safety*] [*Cuban*] (LA)
DGSP........... Direccion General de Seguridad Politica [*General Board for Political Security*] [*Ecuadorean*] (LA)
DGSP........... State Forestry Economic Enterprise (BU)
DGSS........... Directia Generala a Securitatii Statului [*General Directorate of State Security*] (RO)
DGST........... Direction Generale pour le Surveillance du Territoire [*Directorate General for Surveillance of the Territory*] [*Moroccan*] (AF)
DGSTF........... Direction Generale des Services Techniques et de Fabrications [*National Directorate of Technical Services and Manufacturing*] [*Central African*] (AF)
DGT........... Directia Generala a Transporturilor [*General Directorate of Transportation*] (RO)
DGT........... Duna Gozhajozasi Tarsasag [*Danube Steamship Company*] (HU)
dGTF........... Deoxyguanosine Triphosphate (RU)
DGTF........... Directia Generala a Transporturilor Feroviare [*General Directorate of Railway Transportation*] (RO)
DGTF........... Don State Tobacco Factory Imeni Rosa Luxemburg (RU)
DGTI........... Direccion General Tecnica de Investigaciones [*Technical General Directorate of Investigations*] [*Cuban*] (LA)
Dgt Nok........... Dagitim Noktasi [*Distribution Point*] (TU)
DGTS........... Conference Call, Conference Circuit, Round Call (RU)
DGTs........... Germanium-Cesium Diode (RU)
DGU........... Dnepropetrovsk State University Imeni Tercentenary of the Reunification of the Ukraine with Russia (RU)
DGU........... Far Eastern State University (RU)
DGVG........... Directeur General Charge des Victimes de Guerre [*Director General for War Victims*] [*Cambodian*] (CL)
DGVR........... Direction Generale Chargee des Victimes de Guerre et des Refugies [*Directorate General for War Victims and Refugees*] [*Cambodian*] (CL)
dh........... Das Heisst [*That Is, Namely*] [*German*] (GPO)
dH........... Deutsche Haerte [*German Hardness*] [*Degrees of hardness of water. Parts of calcium oxide per 100,000 parts of water. Locomotive boiler water is good if its hardness is less than 6°dH and still usable up to a hardness of 12°dH*] (EG)
DH........... Dewan Harian [*Standing Committee*] (IN)
DH........... Dirham (MAR)
DH........... Dolgoz Hibatlanul [*Work without Mistakes (A movement)*] (HU)
dha........... Dicha [*Spanish*]
Dhab........... Doktor Habilitowany [*Senior Doctor*] [*Polish*]
DHB........... Deutsche Handelsbank [*German Commercial Bank*] (EG)
DHEL........... Departamento de Helicopteros de Mozambique [*Mozambique Helicopter Department*] (AF)
DHF........... Dis Hekimligi Fakultesi [*School of Dentistry*] [*of Diyabakir University*] (TU)
DHfK........... Deutsche Hochschule fuer Koerperkultur [*German Advanced School of Physical Culture*] (EG)
DHG........... Deutsche Handelsgesellschaft [*German Trading Company*] (EG)
DHI........... Deutsches Hydrographisches Institut [*Hamburg, West Germany*]
DHJ........... Difaa Hassani Jadidi [*Moroccan*] (MAR)
DHK........... Drustvo Hrvatskih Knjizevnika [*Society of Croatian Writers*] [*Zagreb*] (YU)
DHKD........... Devrimci Halk Kultur Dernegi [*Revolutionary People's Cultural Association*] (TU)
dhmD........... Des Hoeheren Militaerischen Dienstes [*German*]
DHMI........... Devlet Havayollari Meydanlari Isletmesi [*State Airlines Airfields Operations*] (TU)
dhmtD........... Des Hoeheren Militaertechnischen Dienstes [*German*]
DHN........... Directoria de Hidrografia e Navegacao [*Bureau of Hydrography and Navigation*] [*Brazilian*] (LA)
DHO........... Deniz Harb Okul [*Naval Academy*] (TU)
dho........... Dicho [*Spanish*]
DHP........... Demokratik Halk Partisi [*Democratic People's Party*] [*Turkish Cypriot*] (PPE)
DHP........... Deutsche Hannover Partei [*German Hanover Party*] (PPE)
DHP........... Dyrekcja Hoteli Pracowniczych [*Administration of Workers' Hotels*] (POL)
DHPV........... Druzstvo pre Hospodarenie Pol'-nohospodarskymi Vyrobkami [*Agricultural Produce Cooperative*] (CZ)
DHQ........... Defence Headquarters (MAR)
DHS........... Daughters of the Holy Spirit [*Cameroonian*] (MAR)
DHS........... Dodavaci Hospodarske Smlouvy [*Economic Delivery Contracts*] (CZ)
DHV........... Deutscher Handball-Verband [*German Handball League*] (EG)
DHV........... Deutscher Handels- und Industrieangestellten-Verband [*Association of Clerical Employees of Germany*] [*West German*]
DHZ........... Deutsche Handelszentrale [*German Trade Center*] (EG)
Di........... Calculated Range (RU)
DI........... Daerah Istimewa [*Special Region (Jogjakarta and Atjeh)*] (IN)
DI........... Darul Islam [*Organization of Moslem Dissidents*] (IN)
di........... Das Ist [*That Is, Namely*] [*German*] (GPO)
di........... Dat Is [*That Is, Namely*] [*Dutch*] (GPO)
DI........... Declaration d'Importation [*Bill of Entry*] [*Cambodian*] (CL)
DI........... Depot Intermediaire [*Military*] [*French*] (MTD)
DI........... Deutsches Industrieninstitut [*Institute of German Industry*] [*West German*] (WEN)
DI........... Devizni Inspektorat (DSPF) [*Foreign Exchange Inspectorate*] (YU)
Di........... Diplom [*German*]
Di........... Diplom [*Norwegian*]
Di........... Diplom [*Russian*]
DI........... Diplom-Ingenieur [*Diploma Engineer, Engineer*] (EG)
Di........... Diplom za Zavarseno Visse Obrazovanie [*Diploma of Higher Education*] [*Bulgarian*]

Di ... Diploma [*Portuguese*]
Di ... Diplomasi [*Turkish*]
Di ... Diplome [*Diploma*] [*French*]
Di ... Diplome d'Etudes Universitaires Pratiques en Economie et en Droit [*French*]
DI ... Diplome d'Ingenieur [*French*]
DI ... Diplomi-Insinoori [*Finnish*]
DI ... Direkcija za Ishranu (DSPRP) [*Directorate of Supply*] (YU)
DI ... Division Engineer [*Military term*] (RU)
DI ... Division d'Infanterie [*French*] (MTD)
DI ... Dopravni Inspektorat [*Office of the Transportation Inspector*] (CZ)
DI ... Inductive Pickup, Inductive Transducer (RU)
Di ... Primary Teacher's Diploma [*Greek*]
DI ... State Publishing House (BU)
Di ... Technician's Diploma [*Egyptian*]
DI ... Two-Seater Fighter (RU)
DIA ... Daerah Istimewa Atjeh [*Atjeh Special Region*] (IN)
DIA ... Dehydroisoandrosterone (RU)
DIA ... Departamento de Investigaciones Agropecuarias Vease Ademas Ica (COL)
DIA ... Deutscher Innen- und Aussenhandel [*Inner-German and Foreign Trade*] (EG)
DIA ... Dievthynsis Iatrikis Andilipseos [*Directorate of Medical Assistance*] [*Greek*] (GC)
Dia ... Diplome d'Ingenieur Agronome [*French*]
DIA ... Documentation et Information Africaines [*African Documentation and Information*] [*Vatican*] (AF)
DIAC ... Diffusion Industrielle et Automobile par le Credit (MAR)
DIACEMENTO ... Cementos Diamante SA [*Bogota*] (COL)
DIACOS ... Diario de la Costa [*Cartagena*] (COL)
DIAF ... Deutsches Institut fuer Afrika Forschung [*A publication*] (MAR)
DIAFUTBOL ... Division Aficionada del Futbol Colombiano [*Bogota*] (COL)
DIAGONAL ... Distribuidora de Algodon Nacional [*Medellin*] (COL)
diagr ... Diagram (BU)
diagr ... Diagram, Drawing, Figure (RU)
DIALEC ... Distribuidora de Equipos Agricolas y Electricos [*Bogota*] (COL)
diam ... Diameter (RU)
DIAMANG ... Companhia de Diamantes de Angola [*Angola Diamond Company*] (AF)
diamat ... Dialectic Materialism (RU)
diamat ... Dialectical Materialism (BU)
DIAMAT ... Dialektischer Materialismus [*Dialectical Materialism*] (EG)
DIANCA ... Diques y Astilleros Nacionales, Compania Anonima [*National Docks and Shipyards, Incorporated*] [*Venezuelan*] (LA)
DIASFALTOS ... Distribuidora de Asfaltos Ltda. [*Bogota*] (COL)
DIAUTOS ... Distribuidora Antioquera de Automotores SA [*Medellin*] (COL)
DIA/VEHDIA ... Deutscher Innen- und Aussenhandel/Volkseigenes Handelsunternehmen [*Inner-German and Foreign Trade/State-Owned Commercial Enterprise*] (EG)
DIB ... Dana Irian Barat [*West Irian Fund*] (IN)
DIB ... Departamento de Instrumentacion Electronica [*Electronic Instrumentation Department*] (LA)
DIB ... Deutsche Investitionsbank [*German Investment Bank*] (EG)
DIB ... Deutsches Institut fuer Berufsausbildung [*German Vocational Training Institute*] (EG)
DIB ... Dis Isleri Bakanligi [*Foreign Affairs Ministry*] (TU)
DIB ... Drogowy Instytut Badawczy [*Road Research Institute*] (POL)
DIB ... Drzavna Investicijska Banka [*State Investment Bank*] (YU)
DIBAG ... Diisobutylaluminum Hydride (RU)
DIBI ... Development and Investment Bank of Iran (ME)
DIC ... Dairy Industry Corporation (MAR)
DIC ... Departamento de Investigacion Criminal [*Criminal Investigation Department*] [*Bolivian*] (LA)
dic ... Dicembre [*December*] [*German*]
DIC ... Direccion de Instruccion de Cuadros [*Directorate for Training and Cadres*] [*Cuban*] (LA)
DIC ... Doubleday International Communications Films Division (MAR)
DICA ... Direccion de Instrumentacion y Control Automatico [*Directorate of Automated Control and Instrumentation*] [*Cuban*] (LA)
DICARWS ... Division of Inter-Church Aid: Refugees and World Service (MAR)
dice ... Diciembre [*December*] [*Spanish*]
dicht ... Dichterisch [*German*]
DICMA ... Division de Capacitacion del Magisterio [*Bogota*] (COL)
DICOCALI ... Distribuidora de Combustibles [*Cali*] (COL)
DICOFILMS ... Distribuidora Colombiana de Films Mundiales [*Bogota*] (COL)
DICOL ... Distribuidora Colombiana de Libros [*Bogota*] (COL)
DICOLSA ... Distribuidora Comercial de Cigarrillos SA [*Bogota*] (COL)
DICOMA ... Distribuidora Colombiana de Manufacturas [*Bogota*] (COL)
DICONAL ... Distribuidora Nacional de Confecciones Ltda. [*Pereira*] (COL)
DICOPA ... Societe de Distribution de Cosmetiques et Parfumerie (MAR)
DICOPAL ... Distribuidora de Combustibles Palmira (COL)
DICOR ... Diamond Corporation (MAR)
DICORTOT ... Societe Diamond Corporation Cote-d'Ivoire Ltd. (MAR)
DICORWAF ... Diamond Corporation of West Africa (MAR)
DICOVE ... Distribuidora Colombo Venezolana Ltda. [*Cucuta*] (COL)
DICTMA ... Delegation Italienne de Cooperation Technique Militaire Aeronautique (MAR)
DID ... Direccion Departamental de Investigacion [*Departmental Directorate of Investigation*] [*Bolivian*] (LA1)
DIDACEROS ... Distribuidora de Hierros y Aceros [*Cali*] (COL)
DIDAR ... Direccion de Investigacion de Delitos Aduaneros y de la Renta [*Department for the Investigation of Customs and Tax Crimes*] [*Bolivian*] (LA)
DIDEA ... Distribuidora de Automoviles, SA [*Automobile Distributor Corp.*] [*Salvadoran*]
DIDECO ... Direccion de Desarrollo Comunal [*Directorate of Communal Development*] [*Salvadoran*] (LA1)
didodekaedr ... Diploid, Didodecahedral (RU)
DIDULCES ... Fabrica de Dulces la Colombiana SA [*Bogota*] (COL)
DIE ... Departamento de Investigaciones Economicas [*Economic Research Department*] [*Bolivian*] (LA1)
DIE ... Devlet Istatistik Enstitusu [*State Statistical Institute*] (TU)
DIE ... Diethnis Ilektrologiki Epitropi [*International Electrological Committee*] (GC1)
DiE ... Diplome d'Etat [*French*]
DIE ... Direccion de Inteligencia del Estado [*State Intelligence Directorate*] [*Bolivian*] (LA1)
DIEC ... Department of International Economic Cooperation (MAR)
DIEESE ... Departamento Intersindical de Estatistica e Estudos Socio-Economicos [*Interunion Department of Statistics and Socioeconomic Studies*] [*Brazilian*] (LA)
DIEKA ... Sodium Diethyldithiocarbamate (RU)
DIELCI ... Diffusion Electrique de la Cote-d'Ivoire (MAR)
DiENS ... Diplome des Ecoles Normales Superieures [*French*]
DIEPE ... Direccion de Investigacion, Experimentacion, y Perfeccionamiento Educativo [*Directorate of Research, Experimentation, and Educational Improvement*] [*Argentine*] (LA)
DIEST ... Parti de la Defense des Interets Economiques et Sociaux du Territoire (MAR)
dif ... Differential (RU)
DIF ... Diiodofluorescein (RU)
DIF ... Diisopropyl Phosphate (RU)
DIF ... Sistema para el Desarrollo Integral de la Familia [*System for Complete Family Development*] [*Mexican*] (LA)
DIFANAL ... Distribuidora de Fabricas Nacionales Ltda. [*Bogota*] (COL)
diff ... Differe [*French*]
DIFF ... Diisopropyl Fluophosphate (RU)
differ ... Differential (RU)
DIFK ... Del-Vietnami Ideiglenes Forradalmi Kormany [*Provisional Revolutionary Government of South Vietnam*] (HU)
DIFMAD ... Diffusion Industrielle de Madagascar (MAR)
DIFOR ... Dibamba Forestiere (MAR)
DIfR ... Deutsches Institut fuer Berufsausbildung [*German Vocational Training Institute*] (EG)
DIFSTL ... State Publishing House for Physical Culture and Sports Publications (BU)
DIFU ... Diphenylacetic Acid (RU)
Dig ... Digue [*Dam*] [*Military map abbreviation*] [*World War I*] [*French*] (MTD)
DIGEDECOM ... Direccion General para el Desarrollo de la Comunidad [*General Directorate for Community Development*] [*Panamanian*] (LA)
DIGEP ... Diosgyori Gepgyar [*Diosgyor Machine Factory*] (HU)
DIGEPOL ... Direccion General de Policias [*General Directorate of Police*] [*Venezuelan*] (LA)
DIGESA ... Direccion General de Servicios Agricolas [*General Directorate of Agricultural Services*] [*Guatemalan*] (LA1)
DIGESEPE ... Direccion General de Servicios Pecuarios [*General Directorate of Livestock Services*] [*Guatemalan*] (LA1)
DIHT ... Deutscher Industrie- und Handelstag [*Federation of Chambers of German Industry and Commerce*] [*West German*] (WEN)
DII ... Direccion de Informacion e Inteligencia [*Office of Intelligence and Information*] [*Uruguayan*] (LA)
DII ... Donets Industrial Institute (RU)
DIIT ... Dnepropetrovsk Institute of Railroad Transportation Engineers (RU)
DIJ ... Daerah Istimewa Jogjakarta [*Jogjakarta Special Region*] (IN)
dijszab ... Dijszabalyzat [*Price Register*] (HU)
DIK ... Drvno Industriski Kombinat [*Industrial Combine for Wood Products*] (YU)
DIK ... Remote-Reading Induction Compass (RU)
DIK ... State Industrial Combine (BU)
DIKEP ... Dimokratiki Kinisi Epistimonon [*Democratic Movement of Professionals*] [*Greek*] (GC)
DIKIF ... Dimokratiki Kinisi Foititon [*Democratic Student Movement*] [*Greek*] (GC)
DI KO ... Dimokratiko Komma [*Democratic Party*] [*Cypriot*] (GC)
dikovr ... Division of Ships for Defense of a Waterway Area (BU)
dikr ... Cruiser Division (RU)
DIKS ... Discrete Measurement Correlation System (RU)
DIKS ... State Goods Quality Inspectorate (BU)
DIL ... Depenses d'Interet Local [*Algerian*] (MAR)
DIL ... Directia Industriei Locale [*Local Industry Directorate*] (RO)
DILAPSA ... Distribuidora Latinoamericana de Publicaciones SA [*Latin American Publications Distributor, Inc.*] [*Chilean*] (LA)

DILFA .... Direccion de Lucha Contra la Fiebre Aftosa [*Office for the Prevention of Foot-and-Mouth Disease*] [*Uruguayan*] (LA)
DILIA .... Ceskoslovensky Divadelni a Literarni Jednatelstvi [*Czechoslovak Theater and Literary Agency*] (CZ)
DILKUR .... Turkiye Dil Kurumu [*Turkish Linguistic Association*] (TU)
DIM .... Dardo de Investigacion Meteorologica [*Argentine*]
DIM .... Deportivo Independiente Medellin [*Medellin*] (COL)
DIM .... Deutsches Institut fuer Marktforschung [*German Institute for Market Research*] [*West German*] (WEN)
DIM .... Direccion de Inteligencia Militar [*Military Intelligency Directorate*] [*Cuban*] (LA)
DIM .... Distrik Militer [*Military District (KODIM)*] (IN)
DIM .... Division d'Infanterie Marocaine (MAR)
DIM .... Dnepropetrovsk Scientific Research Institute of Metals (RU)
DIM .... Pulse-Duration Modulation (RU)
DIMA .... Distribuidora de Maquinas, SARL (MAR)
DIMA .... Societe de Developpement Industriel Mecanique et Agricole (MAR)
DIMAC .... Distribuidora de Materiales de Construccion [*Bogota*] (COL)
DIMAFRIC ... Societe de Distribution de Materiel en Afrique (MAR)
DIMAK .... Dimokratiki Mathitiki Kinisi [*Democratic Student Movement*] [*Greek*] (GC)
DIMATIT ...... Societe Nord-Africaine de l'Amiante - Ciment Dimatit (MAR)
DIMAVAG ... Diosgyori Vas-, Acel-, es Gepgyar [*Diosgyor Iron, Steel, and Machine Factory*] (HU)
DIMAYOR .... Direccion Mayor de Futbol Colombiano [*Bogota*] (COL)
DIMDI .... Deutsches Institut fuer Medizinische Dokumentation und Information
DIMENTAL ... Distribuidora Mercantil Nacional [*Bogota*] (COL)
DIMENTALES ... Distribuidora de Metales [*Bogota*] (COL)
DIMES .... Distribution de Materiel Electrique au Senegal (MAR)
DIMINCO ..... National Diamond Mining Company (MAR)
DIMINT .... Division de Inteligencia del Ministerio del Interior [*Intelligence Division of the Interior Ministry*] (LA)
DIMONIKA ... Societe Miniere de Dimonika (MAR)
DIMP .... Induced Magnetic Dipole Surveying (RU)
dimp .... Marine Division (RU)
DIN .... Demographic Institute (of the Academy of Sciences, USSR) (RU)
DIN .... Departamento de Impuestos Nacionales [*National Tax Department*] [*Colombian*] (LA)
DIN .... Departamento de Investigacion Nacional [*Department of National Investigation*] [*Honduran*] (LA)
DIN .... Deutsche Industrie-Norm [*German Industrial Standard*] [*West German*] (WEN)
DIN .... Deutsches Institut fuer Normung [*German Standards Institute*] [*Formerly, DNA*]
Din .... Dinar [*Monetary unit of Yugoslavia*] (YU)
Din .... Dinbilgisi [*Religion*] (TU)
DIN .... Direccion de Impuestos Nacionales [*Bogota*] (COL)
din .... Doctor of Art Studies (RU)
din .... Doctor of Historical Sciences (RU)
din .... Dyne (RU)
DINA .... Departamento de Inteligencia Nacional [*National Intelligence Department*] [*Chilean secret police*] [*Superseded by CNI*] (LA)
DINA .... Diesel Nacional [*National Diesel*] [*Mexican*] (LA)
DINA .... Distribuidora Nacional de Repuestos para Automotores SA [*Bogota*] (COL)
DINA .... Division d'Infanterie Nord-Africaine (MAR)
DINAC .... Empresa Nacional de Comercializacion y Distribucion, SA [*National Marketing and Distribution Enterprise*] [*Chilean*] (LA)
DINACOPRIN ... Direccion Nacional de Costes, Precios, e Ingresos [*National Costs, Price, and Income Bureau*] [*Uruguayan*] (LA)
DINADECO ... Direccion Nacional de Desarrollo de la Comunidad [*National Community Development Directorate*] [*Costa Rican*] (LA)
DINAGECA ... Direccao Nacional de Geografia e Cadastro [*National Directorate for Geography and Survey*] [*Mozambican*] (AF)
DINALCREDITOS ... Directorio Nacional de Creditos (COL)
DINALIADAS ... Distribuciones Internacionales Aliadas Ltda. [*Bogota*] (COL)
DINAME ...... Direccion Nacional de Mecanizacion [*National Mechanization Directorate*] [*Cuban*] (LA)
DINAPROPE ... Distribuidora Nacional de Produtos Pecuarios [*National Cattle Products Distributing Company*] [*Angolan*] (AF)
DINARO .... Distribuidora Nacional de Rodamientos [*Bogota*] (COL)
DINARP .... Direccion Nacional de Relaciones Publicas [*National Public Relations Bureau*] [*Uruguayan*] (LA)
DINASEM .... Direccion Nacional de Semillas [*National Seed Directorate*] [*Cuban*] (LA)
DINAVI .... Direccion Nacional de Vivienda [*National Office of Housing*] [*Uruguayan*] (LA)
DINCOL .... Distribuidora Industrial de Colombia Ltda. [*Cali*] (COL)
DINE .... Direccion de Industrias del Ejercito [*Army Industries Board*] [*Ecuadorean*] (LA)
DINEA .... Direccion Nacional de Education de Adultos [*Bogota*] (COL)
DINES .... Direccion Nacional de Emergencias Sociales [*National Social Emergencies Directorate*] [*Argentine*] (LA)
Ding .... Docteur-Ingenieur [*French*]
DINIKA .... Civil Engineering Study Enterprise [*Malagasy*] [*Use EEGC*] (AF)
DINOK .... Dinitro-Ortho-Cresol (RU)
DINOPROC ... Direccao Nacional da Organizacao da Producao Colectiva [*National Directorate for the Organization of Collective Production*] [*Mozambican*] (AF)
DINTEL .... Distribuidora Nacional de Telas Ltda. [*Cali*] (COL)
DIO .... State Industrial Trust (BU)
DIOF .... Frontline Disinfection Instruction Detachment (RU)
DIOM .... Dievthynsis Organoseos kai Methodon [*Organization and Methods Directorate*] [*Greek*] (GC)
Dion .... Direktion [*German*]
DIOO .... State Social Insurance Institute (BU)
diovr .... Harbor Defense Division (RU)
DIP .... Departamento de Imprensa e Propaganda [*Press and Propaganda Department*] [*Brazilian*] (LA)
DIP .... Departamento de Informacao e Propaganda [*Department of Information and Propaganda*] [*Mozambican*] (AF)
dip .... Diplomatic (RU)
DiP .... Diplome de Professeur de l'Enseignement Secondaire [*French*]
DIP .... Divisiones de Infanteria Permanente [*Regular Infantry Divisions*] [*Cuban*] (LA)
DIP .... Drvno Industrijsko Preduzece [*Industrial Enterprise in Wood Products*] (YU)
DIP .... State Industrial Enterprise (BU)
DIP .... Supplementary Spark Gap (RU)
DIP .... "To Overtake and Surpass" [*Slogan*] (RU)
DIPA .... Societe Distilleries de la M'Passa (MAR)
DIPAKFA ..... Dimokratiki Parataxi Kyprion Foititon Athinon [*Democratic Faction of Cypriot Students in Athens*] (GC)
DIPD .... Departamento de Inteligencia de la Policia Distrital [*Federal District Police Intelligence Department*] [*Mexican*] (LA)
DIP-FAR ...... Direccion Politica de las FAR [*Political Directorate of the Revolutionary Armed Forces*] [*Cuban*] (LA)
DIP Fokhar ... State Industrial Enterprise for Photographic and X-Ray Paper (BU)
dipiramid .... Dipyramidal (RU)
dipk .... Division of Antisubmarine Ships (BU)
dipl .... Diploid (RU)
Dipl .... Diplom [*or Diplomiert*] [*German*]
dipl .... Diploma [*Diploma*] (HU)
dipl .... Diplomacy (RU)
dipl .... Diplomacy, Diplomatic (BU)
dipl .... Submarine Division (BU)
dipl .... Submarine Division (RU)
DIPLAN .... Diretriz Basica de Planejamento [*Basic Planning Directorate*] [*Brazilian*] (LA)
Dipl-Dolm ... Diplom-Dolmetsch [*German*]
Dipl-HdlL .... Diplom-Handelslehrer [*German*]
DIPLIN .... Distribuidora de Plasticos Industriales [*Barranquilla*] (COL)
Dipl-Ing .... Diplom Ingenieur [*Graduate Engineer*] [*German*]
diplins .... Diplomi-Insinoori [*Finnish*]
Diplinz .... Diplomovany Inzenyr [*Certified Engineer*] (CZ)
Dipl-Kfm ..... Diplom-Kaufmann [*German*]
Dipl rer pol ... Diplomatus Rerum Politicarum [*Political Science Diplomate*] (EG)
Dipl-TA .... Diplom-Tierarzt [*German*]
Dipl-Vw .... Diplom-Volkswirt [*German*]
DIPP .... Distribution Ivoirienne de Produits Petroliers (MAR)
DIPPSA .... Distribuidora de Productos de Petroleo [*Petroleum Products Distributor Corporation*] [*Salvadoran*] (LA1)
DIPRE .... Division de Informacion de la Prefectura Naval [*Navy Headquarters Information Division*] [*Uruguayan*] (LA)
DIPROCO .... Distribuidora de Productos Colombianos Ltda. [*Aguachica-Magdalena*] (COL)
DIPROGAS ... Distribuidora Provincial de Gas [*Ocana*] (COL)
DIPS .... Document Information Search System (RU)
DIPSEA .... Dievthynsis Politikis Skhediaseos Ektaktou Anangis [*Emergency Policy Planning Directorate*] [*Greek*] (GC)
DIR .... Dimbokro Rangers (MAR)
DIR .... Directeur [*or Direction*] [*Director or Directorate*] [*Used as a prefix*] [*Cambodian*] (CL)
dir .... Director, Directorate (BU)
dir .... Director, Manager (RU)
Dir .... Direktor [*German*]
DIR .... Direktur [*Director*] (IN)
dir .... Orchestra Conductor (BU)
DIRCAB .... Directeur de Cabinet [*Frequently followed by the abbreviation for a ministry*] (CL)
DIRCABETAT ... Directeur de Cabinet du Chef de l'Etat [*Cambodian*] (CL)
DIRCEN .... Direction des Centres d'Experimentation Nucleaire [*Nuclear Experimentation Centers Directorate*] [*French*] (WER)
DIRCENGENIE ... Direction Centrale du Genie [*Central Directorate of Engineering*] [*Cambodian*] (CL)
Dircenmat ... Direction Centrale du Materiel [*Central Equipment Directorate*] [*Cambodian*] (CL)
Dircensante ... Direction Centrale de Sante [*Central Health Directorate*] [*Cambodian*] (CL)
Dircentrans ... Direction Centrale du Transport [*Central Transportation Directorate*] [*Cambodian*] (CL)
DIRDJEN ..... Direktur Djenderal [*Director General*] (IN)
DIRECO .... Groupe de Defense des Interets de la Region Cotiere (MAR)

DIRESSENCE ... Direction d'Essence [*Gasoline Directorate*] [*Cambodian*] (CL)
DIREVE .... Directorio Revolucionario Venezolano [*Venezuelan Revolutionary Directorate*] (LA)
Dirgale .... Direction Generale [*Directorate General*] (CL)
Dirgenie ...... Direction de la Genie [*Engineering Directorate*] [*Cambodian*] (CL)
Dirgeo .... Direction Geographique [*Geographic Directorate*] [*Cambodian*] (CL)
Dir geol i min prouchv ... Geological and Mining Surveys Directorate (BU)
DIRINCO ..... Direccion de Industria y Comercio [*Industry and Trade Directorate*] [*Chilean*] (LA)
Dirintendance ... Direction de l'Intendance [*Quartermaster Corps Directorate*] [*Cambodian*] (CL)
DIRIVENTAS ... Asociacion de Dirigentes de Ventas [*Medellin*] (COL)
dirizh........... Conductor (RU)
dirk.............. Division of Missile Ships (BU)
Dir Mu .... Direkt Muhabere [*Direct Communication*] (TU)
dir-or........... Director, Manager (RU)
Dir pech ...... Press Directorate (BU)
DIRPOLICE ... Direction de la Police d'Immigration [*(Immigration) Police Directorate*] [*Cambodian*] (CL)
Dir PTT........ Post, Telegraph, and Telephone Directorate (BU)
DIRRELATIONS ... Direction des Relations (Publiques) [*Directorate of (Public) Relations*] [*Cambodian*] (CL)
Dir Tls Mu ... Direkt Telsiz Muhabere [*Direct Radio Communication*] (TU)
Dirtrans....... Direction du Transport [*Transportation Directorate*] [*Cambodian*] (CL)
DIRUT.......... Direktur Utama [*Director in Chief*] (IN)
DIS .... Defense Intelligence Service [*Danish*] (WEN)
DIS .... Deontische Informations System
DIS .... Diarkis Iera Synodos [*Standing Holy Synod*] [*Greek*] (GC)
DIS .... Dinas [*Service, Office*] (IN)
DiS .... Diplome de Specialisation [*French*]
Dis............... Dissertation (BU)
DIS .... Division Intendantske Stanice [*Divisional Quartermaster Station*] (YU)
DIS .... Druzstevni Informacni Sluzba [*Cooperative Information Service*] (CZ)
DIS .... Station Duty Engineer [*Telephony*] (RU)
DISA............ Directorate of Information and Security of Angola (MAR)
DISA............ Distribuciones SA [*Cali*] (COL)
DISB............ Disisleri Bakanligi [*Ministry of Foreign Affairs*] (TU)
DISCA .... Division de Investigaciones Sobre Contaminacion Ambiental [*Division of Research on Environmental Pollution*] [*Venezuelan*] (LA)
DISCAL....... Distribuidora Comercial [*Cali*] (COL)
DISCARTONES ... Distribuidora Nacional de Papeles y Cartones [*Cali*] (COL)
DISCENPOL ... Distribuidora Central de Polietileno [*Cali*] (COL)
DISCOLANA ... Distribuidora Colombiana de Lanas Ltda. [*Bogota*] (COL)
DISDROCOL ... Distribuidora de Drogas Alianza [*Bogota*] (COL)
DISEXTRAS ... Distribuidora de Loterias Extras Ltda. [*Cali*] (COL)
DISFABRILES ... Distribuidora Fabriles Ltda. [*Cali*] (COL)
DISFANAL ... Distribuidor de Fabricas Nacionales [*Medellin*] (COL)
DISFOR....... Distribuidora de Repuestos Ford [*Bogota*] (COL)
DISFUENTES ... Fabrica de Discos Fuentes Ltda. [*Medellin*] (COL)
Dishek......... Dishekimligi [*Dental, Dentistry*] (TU)
DISI .... Dnepropetrovsk Construction Engineering Institute (RU)
DISIP........... Direccion de Servicios de Inteligencia y Prevencion [*Directorate of Intelligence and Prevention Services*] [*Venezuelan*] (LA)
DISIP........... Directorate for Services of Intelligence and Prevention [*Jamaican*] (LA1)
DISK............ Confederation of Revolutionary Trade Unions of Turkey (PD)
DISK............ Devrimci Isci Sendikalar Konfederasyonu [*Confederation of Revolutionary Worker Unions*] (TU)
DISKES....... Dinas Kesehatan [*Health Service*] (IN)
d isk n .... Doctor of Art Studies (RU)
diskus .... Discussion (RU)
DISMACOL ... Distribuidora de Materiales para Construccion Ltda. [*Bogota*] (COL)
DISMETAL ... Distribuidora Metalurgica de Occidents Ltda. [*Cali*] (COL)
DISMOTORES ... Distribuidora de Motores Ltda. [*Cali*] (COL)
DISMUSICAL ... Distribuidora Colombiana de Musica Funcional [*Bogota*] (COL)
DISNEGO.... Distribuciones Negocios Generales [*Bogota*] (COL)
DISNEL .... Distribuidora Nacional de Elementos Electricos [*Medellin*] (COL)
disp............. Dispensa [*Number*] [*Italian*] (GPO)
disp............. Disponible [*Available*] [*French*]
DISPA .... Diethnis Synandisis Perifereiakis Anaptyxeos [*International Meeting on Area Development*] [*Greek*] (GC)
DISPAPELES ... Distribuidora de Papeles Ltda. [*Cali*] (COL)
DISPIELES ... Distribuidora de Pieles Ltda. [*Cali*] (COL)
DISPINTURAS ... Distribuidora de Pinturas Ltda. [*Cali*] (COL)
DISPO .... Dis Politika Yazar ve Muhabirleri Birligi [*Union of Foreign Political Writers and Correspondents*] (TU)
DISPROCAL ... Distribucion Pro-Capilar Ltda. [*Cali*] (COL)
DISPROIM... Distribuidora de Propaganda Impresa Ltda. [*Cali*] (COL)
DISPROMECO ... Distribuidora de Productos Farmaceuticos [*Medellin*] (COL)
DISPRON .... Distribucion de Propaganda Ltda. [*Cali*] (COL)
DISPROQUIL ... Distribuidora de Productos Quimicos [*Medellin*] (COL)
DISS............ Diethnes Instituton Stratigikon Spoudon [*International Institute of Strategic Services*] (GC1)
Diss............. Dissertation [*Dissertation*] [*German*]
diss .... Dissertation (RU)
DISS............ Doppler Speed-and-Drift Meter (RU)
dissud .... Disciplinary Court (RU)
dist.............. Distilled (RU)
DISTA.......... Daerah Istimewa Atjeh [*Atjeh Special Region*] (IN)
DISTAPAS ... Distribuidora de Tapas y Productos Metalicos Ltda. [*Bogota*] (COL)
Distie........... Distillerie [*Distillery*] [*Military map abbreviation*] [*World War I*] [*French*] (MTD)
distill........... Distilled (RU)
DISTINTAS ... Distribucion de Tintas Ltda. [*Cali*] (COL)
DISTRACOL ... Distribuidora Colombiana Ltda. [*Bogota*] (COL)
DISTRAL..... Distribuidora Industrial Ltda. [*Bogota*] (COL)
DISTRICENTRO ... Distribuidora Central de Confecciones Ltda. (COL)
DISTRICON ... Distribuidora de Confecciones Ltda. [*Bogota*] (COL)
DISTRIPHARM ... Societe de Distribution Pharmaceutique (MAR)
dists .... Disciplinary (RU)
DISUDA....... Distribuidora Sudamericana [*Cali*] (COL)
DISY............ Dimokratikos Synagermos [*Democratic Rally*] [*Cypriot*] (GC1)
DISYA .... Dimokratiko Syndikalistiko Kinima [*Democratic Trade Union Movement*] [*Greek*] (GC)
DISZ............ Dolgozo Ifjusag Szovetsege [*Federation of Working Youth*] (HU)
DIT .... Direktorat [*Directorate*] (IN)
DIT .... Drustvo Inzenirjev in Tehnikov [*Society of Engineers and Technicians*] (YU)
DIT .... Drustvo Inzenirjev in Tehnikov Gozdarstva in Lesne Industrije Ljudska Republika Slovenija [*Society of Engineers and Technicians of Forestry and Wood Industry of Slovenia*] (YU)
DITDIKDAS ... Direktorat Pendidikan Dasar [*Directorate of Basic Education*] (IN)
DITEX-CA ... Societe de Gerance et de Diffusion Textile pour le Centre-Afrique (MAR)
DITh .... Diethnis Institouton Theatrou [*International Institute of the Theater*] (GC)
DITH .... Drustvo Inzinjera i Tehnicara Hrvatske [*Society of Engineers and Technicians of Croatia*] (YU)
DITH .... Societe du Domain Industriel de Thies (MAR)
DI/TII........... Darul Islam/Tentara Islam Indonesia [*State of Islam/Islamic Army of Indonesia*] (IN)
DITJ............. Drustvo Inzinjera i Tehnicara Jugoslavije [*Society of Engineers and Technicians of Yugoslavia*] (YU)
DITR .... House of Engineers and Technicians (RU)
DITRAC .... Division des Troupes Aeroportees et de Choc [*Airborne and Shock Troops Division*] [*Zairian*] (AF)
ditrig .... Ditrigonal (RU)
DITT .... Drustvo Inzinjera i Tehnicara Tekstilaca [*Society of Textile Engineers and Technicians*] (YU)
DITTH.......... Drustvo Inzinjera i Tehnicara Tekstilaca Hrvatske [*Society of Textile Engineers and Technicians of Croatia*] (YU)
DITTNRS..... Drustvo Inzenjera i Tehnicara Tekstilaca Narodna Republika Srbija [*Society of Textile Engineers and Technicians of Serbia*] (YU)
DIU .... Dispositif Intra-Uterin (MAR)
div .... Battalion [*Artillery*], Division [*Navy*], Divisional (RU)
DIV .... Delpesti Ipari Vizmu [*Industrial Water Works of South Budapest*] (HU)
Div............... Diverse [*Various*] [*Business and trade*] [*German*]
div .... Dividende [*Dividend*] [*French*]
DIV .... Divisi [*Division*] (IN)
Div............... Division [*Division*] [*Military*] [*French*] (MTD)
Div............... Division d'Infanterie [*Military*] [*French*] (MTD)
div .... Divisioona [*Finnish*]
DIVATERV ... Dinamikus Vallalasi Terszamitasi Modell [*Dynamic Enterprise Plan Computing Model*] (HU)
DI-VB........... Dopravni Inspectorat Verejne Bezpecnosti [*Transportation Inspectorate, Public Security*] (CZ)
DIVERMA.... Societe Nationale d'Importation de Marchandises Diverses (MAR)
divesmintsev ... Destroyer Division (RU)
DIVETIN ...... Dnepropetrovsk Scientific Research Institute for Rehabilitation and Determination of Work Fitness of Disabled Persons (RU)
divinzh .... Division Engineer [*Military term*] (RU)
DIVIVIENDA ... Direccion Colombiana de Ahorro y Vivienda [*Colombian Savings and Housing Association*] (LA)
div-n............ Battalion [*Artillery*], Division [*Navy*] (RU)
DIVSZ.......... Demokratikus Ifjusagi Vilagszovetseg [*World Federation of Democratic Youth*] (HU)
divtr............. Division Transport (RU)
DIW .... Deutsches Institut fuer Wirtschaftsforschung [*German Institute for Economic Research*] [*West German*] (WEN)
Diyan........... Diyanet [*Religious*] (TU)
DiyB .... Diyanet Isleri Baskanligi [*Religious Affairs Chairmanship (under Office of Premier)*] (TU)
Diyetprodukt ... All-Union Office for the Dietetic Foods Trade (RU)

DIZ .... Deutsches Institut fuer Zeitgeschichte [*German Institute for Contemporary History*] (EG)
diz .... Diesel (RU)
DIZ .... State Tool Plant (BU)
Dizel'montazh ... Assembly and Repair Office of the Glavlokomobil'dizel' (RU)
diz ind .... Diesel Index (RU)
dJ .... Der Juengere [*Junior*] [*German*] (GPO)
dJ .... Dieses Jahres [*Of This Year*] [*German*] (GPO)
Dj .... Djebel [*Mountain, Hill*] [*Arabic*] (NAU)
DJA .... Dotations aux Jeunes Agriculteurs [*Endowments for Young Farmers*] [*Guadeloupe*] (LA1)
DJABAR .... Djawa Barat [*West Java*] (IN)
DJAGUNG ... Djaksa Agung [*Attorney General*] (IN)
DJAPEN .... Djawatan Penerangan [*Information Office*] (IN)
DJATENG .... Djawa Tengah [*Central Java*] (IN)
DJATI .... Djaksa Tinggi [*District Attorney*] (IN)
DJATIM .... Djawa Timur [*East Java*] (IN)
DJAYA .... Djakarta Raya [*Greater Djakarta*] (IN)
DJB .... Drustvo Jugoslovenskih Bibliotekara [*Society of Yugoslav Librarians*] (YU)
DJC .... Desantni Jurisni Camac [*Landing Attack Boat*] (YU)
d de JC .... Despues de Jesucristo [*After Jesus Christ*] [*Spanish*] (GPO)
DjelaJA .... Djela, Izdanje Jazu [*Works. Publication of the Yugoslav Academy of Sciences and Arts*] (YU)
DJEN .... Djenderal [*General (Rank)*] (IN)
DJERBAR .... Djerman Barat [*West Germany*] (IN)
DJERTIM .... Djerman Timur [*East Germany*] (IN)
DJL .... Djalan [*Street*] (IN)
DJO .... Deutsche Jugend des Ostens [*German Youth of the East*] [*West German organization*] (EG)
DJR .... Deutscher Jugendring [*German Youth Ring*] (EG)
DJS .... District Jungle Squads (ML)
DJU .... Deutsche Journalisten-Union [*Union of German Journalists*] [*West German*] (WEN)
DJUBIR .... Djurubitjara [*Spokesman*] (IN)
DJZ .... Direkcija Jugoslovenskih Zeleznica [*Administration of Yugoslav Railroads*] (YU)
DK .... Association Committee (BU)
DK- .... Bell-Type Differential Manometer (RU)
DK .... Dania [*Denmark*] [*Polish*]
dk .... Decare (BU)
DK .... Decimal Classification (RU)
DK .... Decimalna Klasifikacija [*Decimal Classification*] (YU)
DK .... Decontamination Kit (RU)
DK .... Decontamination Rooms (BU)
DK .... Dedictvi Komenskeho [*Comenius Heritage*] [*A publishing house*] (CZ)
DK .... Delkelet [*Southeast*] [*Hungarian*] (GPO)
DK .... Denmark [*Three-letter standard code*] (CNC)
DK .... Depoh Kelengkapan [*Ordnance Depot*] (ML)
DK .... Deutsche Kennziffer [*German Index Number (For standards)*] (EG)
DK .... Deutscher Kulturbund [*German Cultural Federation*] [*East German*] (PPE)
DK .... Dewan Keamanan [*Security Council (UN)*] (IN)
DK .... Dezimal Klassifikation
DK .... Diaplanitiko Komma [*Interplanetary Party*] [*Greek*] (GC)
DK .... Diesel Compressor (RU)
DK .... Diesel Crane (RU)
DK .... Diesel-Kraftstoff [*Diesel Fuel*] (EG)
DK .... Dimokratiko Komma [*Democratic Party*] [*See also DIKO*] (GC1)
DK .... Dispatching, Dispatcher Control (RU)
D K .... Division Cavalry (BU)
DK .... Dlouhodobe Kursy [*Long-Term Courses*] (CZ)
DK .... Dom Ksiazki [*Book Store*] [*Polish*]
DK .... Dom Kultury [*House of Culture*] (POL)
DK .... Drvni Kombinat [*Wood Combine*] (YU)
DK .... Drzavna Komisija [*State Commission*] (YU)
DK .... Dukhovna Kultura [*Spiritual Culture*] [*A periodical*] (BU)
dk .... Good Quality, Soundness (RU)
DK .... House of Culture (RU)
DK .... House of the Peasant (RU)
DK- .... Indicating Pocket Dosimeter (RU)
DK .... Landing Ship (RU)
DK .... Palace of Culture (RU)
DK .... Respiratory Quotient (RU)
DK .... State Combine (BU)
DK .... State Control (BU)
DK .... Throttle Valve, Butterfly Valve (RU)
d-k .... Transmitter, Transducer, Pickup (RU)
dka .... Decares (BU)
DKA .... House of the Red Army (RU)
DKB .... Deutscher Kulturbund [*German Cultural League*] (EG)
DKB .... Dzielnicowy Komitet Blokowy [*City Section Block Committee*] (POL)
DKB .... Road Commandant Battalion (RU)
dkbr .... Road Commandant Brigade (RU)
DKC .... Delnicky Klub Cyklistu [*Workers' Cycling Club*] (CZ)
DKCM .... Delnicky Klub Cyklistu a Motoristu [*Workers' Cycling and Motoring Club*] (CZ)
DKD .... Dewey Decimal Classification (RU)
DKD .... Dogu Karadeniz Kultur Dernegi [*Eastern Black Sea Cultural Association*] (TU)
DK na DSNM ... Association Committee of the Dimitrov People's Youth Union (BU)
DKEL .... Demokratikon Komma Ergazomenou Laou [*Democratic Party of Working People*] [*Greek*] (PPE)
DKF .... Dicalcium Phosphate (RU)
DKF .... Dimokratiki Kinisi Foititon [*Democratic Movement of Students*] [*Greek*] (GC)
DKF .... Dyskusyjny Klub Filmowy [*Film Discussion Club*] (POL)
DKF .... House of the Red Navy (RU)
DKF .... State Cannery (BU)
DKF .... State Paper Factory (BU)
DKfm .... Diplom-Kaufmann [*German*]
dkg .... Decagram (RU)
dkg .... Dekagram [*Decagram*] (POL)
dkg .... Dekagramm [*Decagram*] (EG)
dkg .... Dekagramm [*Decagram*] (HU)
dkg .... Dekagramma(a) [*Finnish*]
DKG .... Deutsche Kolonialgesellschaft (MAR)
DKG .... Dunantuli Koolajipari Gepgyar [*Transdanubian Petroleum Industry Machine Factory*] (HU)
DKGF .... House of Culture of the Humanities Divisions of MGU (RU)
DKGMK .... Cutter Remote-Reading Gyrocompass (RU)
DKh .... Dimosia Khrisis [*Public Vehicle, Vehicle for Hire*] [*Automobile license plate designation*] (GC)
DKh .... Dynamic Characteristic, Load Characteristic (RU)
DKhB .... Bulgarian Painters' Union (BU)
DKhE .... Dichloroethane (RU)
DKhFK .... State Chemical-Pharmaceutical Plant (BU)
DKhGPI .... State Art Gallery in Plovdiv (BU)
DKhK .... State Chemical Combine (BU)
DKhM .... Dichloral Urea (RU)
dkhn .... Doctor of Chemical Sciences (RU)
DKhVD .... House of Children's Art Education (RU)
DKhZ .... State Chemical Plant (BU)
DKhZ .... State Refrigeration Systems Plant (BU)
DKK .... Dengan Kawan-Kawannja [*And His Friends, With His Colleagues*] (IN)
DKK .... Deniz Kuvvetleri Komutanligi [*Naval Forces Command*] (TU)
DKK .... Dimotikos kai Koinotikos Kodix [*Municipal and Communal Code*] [*Greek*] (GC)
DKK .... State Canning Combine (BU)
DKK .... State Ready-Made Clothing Combine (BU)
DKK .... State Rubber Products Combine (BU)
DKKF .... Dzielnicowy Komitet Kultury Fizycznej [*City Section Committee on Physical Culture*] (POL)
DKKFiT .... Dzielnicowy Komitet Kultury Fizycznej i Turystyki [*District Committee for Physical Culture and Tourism*] [*Polish*]
DKL .... Das Kommando des Luftschutzes [*Air Defense Command*] (EG)
dkl .... Decaliter (RU)
dkl .... Dekalitr [*Decaliter*] [*Polish*]
dkl .... Dekalitra(a) [*Finnish*]
Dkl .... Dekovil [*Narrow Gauge Railway*] (TU)
DKL .... Gunboat Division (RU)
dkm .... Decameter (RU)
dkm .... Dekametr [*Decameter*] [*Polish*]
dkm .... Dekametri(a) [*Finnish*]
DKM .... Divizisko Komandno Mesto [*Divisional Command Post*] (YU)
DKM .... House of Culture of the Metrostroy (RU)
DKM .... Karjah Kerabat Di-Raja Malaysia [*Royal Order - Malaysia*] (ML)
DKMEI .... House of Culture of the Moscow Power Engineering Institute (RU)
DKmEn .... Delavsko Kmecka Enotnost [*Workers' and Peasants' Unity*] [*A periodical*] (YU)
DKMS .... Dimitrov Communist Youth Union (BU)
DKMS .... Dimitrovski Komunisticheski Mladezhki Suiuz [*Bulgarian*]
DKMZ .... State Cardboard and Pasteboard Plant (BU)
DKN .... Dom Kultury Nauczyciela [*Teacher's House of Culture*] (POL)
DKN .... House of Culture and Science (RU)
DKNGL .... Dimokratiko Kinima Neolaias Grigoriou Lambraki [*Grigorios Lambrakis Youth Democratic Movement*] (GC1)
DKO .... Children's Communist Organization (RU)
DKOV .... Deutscher Kriegsopfer Verband [*League of German War Victims*] (EG)
DKP .... Alternate Command Post (RU)
DKP .... Command Post of the Division Commander (RU)
DKP .... Communist Party of Denmark (BU)
DKP .... Dania Kommunista Partja [*Communist Party of Denmark*] (HU)
DKP .... Danmarks Kommunistiske Parti [*Communist Party of Denmark*] (PPW)
DKP .... Depoh Kelengkapan Pangkalan [*Base Ordnance Depot*] (ML)
DKP .... Deutsche Kommunistische Partei [*German Communist Party*] [*West German*] (PPE)
DKP .... Dispatcher Control Points (BU)
DKP .... Dopravni Komunalni Podnik [*Municipal Transport Enterprise*] [*Prague*] (CZ)
DKP .... Drobne a Kratkodobe Predmety [*Small and Short Term Items*] (CZ)

DKP .... Mobile Disinfection Chamber (RU)
DKP .... State Book Printing Enterprise (BU)
DKP .... State Committee for Planning (BU)
DKPG .... Democratic Peasants' Party of Germany (RU)
Dkr .... Dan Korona [*Danish Crown*] (HU)
DKR .... Dynamic Demagnetization Curve (RU)
DKR .... Road Commandant Company (RU)
DKR .... Road Commandant District (RU)
DKRMP .... House of Culture of Local Industry Workers (RU)
DKS .... Deutsches Kontor fuer Seefrachten [*German Sea Freight Office*] (EG)
DKS .... House of Culture of Construction Workers (RU)
DKS .... Road Commandant Service (RU)
DKSA .... State Committee for Construction and Architecture (BU)
DKSM .... Dimitrov Young Communist League [*Bulgarian People's Republic*] (RU)
DkSt .... Dekontaminacione Stanice [*Decontamination Stations*] (YU)
DKSV .... Deutscher Kanusport-Verband [*German Canoeing League*] (EG)
DKT .... Deutscher Kraftwagentarif [*German Motor Vehicle License Fee*] (EG)
DKT .... Dominican Confederation of Labor (RU)
DKT .... Dzial Kontroli Technicznej [*Technical Control Department*] (POL)
DKTNRH ..... Drustvo Kemicara-Tehnologa Narodne Republike Hrvatske [*Society of Chemical Technologists of Croatia*] (YU)
DKTs .... Shop Dispatcher's Switchboard (RU)
DKU .... Danmarks Kommunistisk Ungdom [*Danish Communist Youth*] (WEN)
DKU .... Diosgyori Kohaszati Uzem [*Metalworks of Diosgyor*] (HU)
DKU .... Road Commandant Section (RU)
DKV .... Deutscher Kohlen-Verkauf [*German Coal Sales Office*] (EG)
DKV .... Deutscher Kraftverkehr [*German Motor Vehicle Transport*] (EG)
DKV .... Dunai Koolajipari Vallalat [*Danubian Petroleum Industry Enterprise*] (HU)
DKVD .... House of Children's Communist Education (RU)
DKW .... Deutsche Kraftfahrzeugwerke [*German Motor Vehicle Plants*] (EG)
DKZ .... Koloinalzeitung (MAR)
DKZ .... Plant Dispatcher's Switchboard (RU)
DKZ .... State Boilers Plant (BU)
DKZ .... State Commission on Reserves [*Military*] (BU)
DKZ .... State Rubber Products Plant (BU)
DKZh .... House of Culture of Railroad Workers (RU)
DK ZIL .... Palace of Culture of the Automobile Plant Imeni I. A. Likhachev (RU)
Dl .... Decalitro [*Decaliter*] [*Spanish*]
dl .... Deciliter [*Deciliter*] (HU)
dl .... Deciliter (RU)
dl .... Decilitre [*Deciliter*] [*French*]
dl .... Decilitro [*Deciliter*] [*Spanish*]
dl .... Deel [*Part*] [*Dutch*] (GPO)
DL .... Demarkationslinie [*Line of Demarcation*] (EG)
DL .... Demokratische Linke [*Democratic Left Party*] [*West German*] (EG)
DL .... Derecha Liberal [*Liberal Right*] [*Spanish*] (WER)
dl .... Desilitra(a) [*Finnish*]
DL .... Deutsche Literaturzeitung (MAR)
DL .... Deutscher Landwirtschaftsverlag [*German Agricultural Publishing House*] (EG)
DL .... Dinar Libyen [*Monetary unit*] (MAR)
DL .... Division Infirmary (RU)
dl .... Dlugosc [*Length*] (POL)
DL .... Dopravni Letectvo [*Transport Air Force Units*] (CZ)
DL .... Landing Boat (RU)
dl .... Length (RU)
DL .... Summer Diesel (Fuel) (RU)
DLA .... Dievthynsis Limenikis Astynomias [*Port Police Directorate*] [*Greek*] (GC)
DLA .... Douala Airport (MAR)
d lar .... Long-Range Artillery (BU)
d lch .... Division Field Hospital (BU)
DLCO-EA .... Desert Locust Control Organization for Eastern Africa (AF)
DLDS .... Detachement Local de Defense en Surface [*Local Surface Defense Detachment*] [*Cambodian*] (CL)
D lesn .... Forester's House [*Topography*] (RU)
DLF .... Development Loan Fund (MAR)
DLfM .... Deutsche Liga fuer Menschenrechte [*German League for Human Rights*] (EG)
DLG .... Deutsche Landwirtschaftsgesellschaft [*German Agricultural Society*] (EG)
dl geogr ...... Dlugosc Geograficzna [*Longitude*] [*Polish*]
DLH .... Demiryollari, Limanlar, ve Hava Meydanlara Insaat Genel Mudurlugu [*Railways, Harbors, and Airfields Construction Directorate General*] [*Under Public Works Ministry*] (TU)
DLH .... Deutsche Lufthansa [*German Lufthansa*] [*Airline*] (EG)
dlhrfilm .... Dlouhy Hrany Film [*Full Length Film*] (CZ)
DLI .... Far Eastern Forestry Engineering Institute (RU)
DLIS .... Desert Locust Information Service (MAR)
DLK .... Dienstleistungskombinat [*Services Combine*] [*Valet-Shop Services*] (EG)
dlM .... Des Laufenden Monats [*Of the Current Month*] [*German*]
DLM .... Differential Lift Manometer (RU)
DLMA .... Dominican Liberation Movement Alliance [*Dominican*] (LA1)
DLN .... Directorio Liberal Nacional [*National Liberal Directorate*] [*Colombian*] (LA)
DLO .... Detachement de Liaison et d'Observation (MAR)
DLP .... Democratic Labor Party [*Trinidadian and Tobagan*] (PPW)
DLP .... Democratic Labor Party [*Barbadian*] (PPW)
DLP .... Democratic Labor Party [*Dominican*] (LA1)
DLP .... Demokraattinen Lehtipalvelu [*Democratic Press Service (Communist SKDL)*] [*Finnish*] (WEN)
DLP .... Dominica Labor Party (PPW)
DLP .... Double Refraction, Birefringence (RU)
DLP .... Light Wooden Park [*Pontoons, bridges*] (RU)
DLS .... House of Detention, Prison (RU)
DLSU .... De La Salle University [*Philippine*]
DLT .... House of Leningrad Trade [*Department store*] (RU)
D lu .... Dogumlu Yil [*Year of Birth*] (TU)
DLUM .... Drustvo na Likovnite Umetnici na Makedonija [*Macedonian Society of Representational Artists*] (YU)
DLV .... Deutscher Landwirtschaftsverlag (VEB), Berlin [*German Agricultural Publishing House (VEB), Berlin*] (EG)
DM .... Amphibious Force (RU)
DM .... Children's World [*Department store*] (RU)
DM .... D-Markka (Saksan Markka) [*Finnish*]
DM .... Darlow & Moule [*Historical catalogue*] (MAR)
Dm .... Decametro [*Decameter*] [*Spanish*]
dm .... Decimeter (BU)
dm .... Decimeter (RU)
dm .... Decimetre [*Decimeter*] [*French*]
dm .... Decimetro [*Decimeter*] [*Spanish*]
DM .... Decoder Matrix (RU)
Dm .... Dekameter [*Decameter*] (EG)
DM .... Delta-Modulation (RU)
DM .... Demodulator (RU)
dm .... Denne Maned [*This Month*] [*Danish*] (GPO)
dm .... Desimetri(a) [*Finnish*]
DM .... Deutsche Mark [*German Mark*] [*Monetary unit*] (EG)
dm .... Dezimeter [*Decimeter*] (EG)
dM .... Dieses Monats [*Of This Month, Instant*] (EG)
DM .... Differential Manometer (BU)
DM .... Differential Manometer (RU)
DM .... Disk Magnet [*Weld inspection device*] (RU)
DM .... Doctorat en Medecine [*French*]
DM .... Dominica [*Two-letter standard code*] (CNC)
DM .... Draza Mihailovic [*A Yugoslav General*] (YU)
Dm .... Durchmesser [*Diameter*] [*German*]
DM .... Electric Oil-Pump Motor (RU)
DM .... Ground Position (of an aircraft) (RU)
dm .... Inch (RU)
DM .... Machine Parts (RU)
DM .... Outer Radio Marker Beacon (RU)
DM .... Patrol Vehicle (RU)
DM .... Range Finder (RU)
DM .... Road Mine (RU)
DM .... Smoke Generator (RU)
DM .... Smoke Pot (RU)
DM .... Smoke Screening (RU)
DM- .... Sprinkler, Sprinkling Machine (RU)
DM .... State Mines (BU)
dm .... Supply Officer (BU)
DM .... Wooden Bridge (RU)
dm^2 .... Square Decimeter (BU)
DMA .... Centre d'Experimentation et d'Enseignement du Machinisme Agricole, Division du Machinisme Agricole du Genie Rural [*Malian*]
DMA .... Delegation Ministerielle a l'Armement [*French*]
DMA .... Dimethylaniline (RU)
DMA .... Dominica [*Three-letter standard code*] (CNC)
DMA-DTE .... Direction Ministerielle pour l'Armement-Direction Technique des Engins [*Ministerial Directorate for Armaments-Missile Technology Directorate*] [*French*] (WER)
DMAMYu ..... Documents of the Moscow Archives of the Ministry of Justice (RU)
DMB .... Departamento de Material Belico [*War Materiel Department*] [*Brazilian*] (LA1)
DMB .... State Mineral Water Bath (BU)
DMBA .... Dimethylbenzanthracene (RU)
DMC .... Diviziski Medicinski Centar [*Divisional Medical Center*] [*Military*] (YU)
DME .... Dimethoxyethane (RU)
DME .... Distant Measuring Equipment (AF)
DMEA .... Dimosyndiritoi Monades Ethnofylakis Amynis [*State-Supported National Guard Defense Units*] [*Greek*] (GC)
D mel'n .... Miller's House [*Topography*] (RU)
DMETI .... Dnepropetrovsk Metallurgical Institute (RU)
DMF .... Dimethyl Phthalate (RU)
DMF .... Dimethylformamide (RU)
DMFA .... Dimethylformamide (RU)

DMFKhS ..... Dimethylphenylchlorosilane (RU)
DMG .... Direction des Mines et de la Geologie (MAR)
DMG .... Dom Mlodego Gornika [*House of the Young Miner*] (POL)
DMG .... Dynamograph (RU)
DMGS .... Dennis Memorial Grammar School (MAR)
DMH .... Dom Mlodego Hutnika [*House of the Young Metallurgist*] (POL)
DMI .... Dar al Mal al Islami [*Islamic financial institution*]
DMI .... Directia Monumentelor Istorice [*Directorate of Historic Monuments*] (RO)
DMI .... Dnepropetrovsk Metallurgical Institute (RU)
D M i Kh ...... Doctor of Medicine and Surgery (RU)
DMK .... Dimokratikon Metarrythmistikon Komma [*Democratic Reform Party*] (GC)
DMK .... Dravida Munnetra Kazhagam [*Indian*] (PPW)
DMK .... State Meat Combine (BU)
DMKP .... State Mining and Coke Producing Enterprise (BU)
DMKRNRH ... Drustvo Muzejsko-Konservatorskih Radnika Narodne Republike Hrvatske [*Society of Workers in Museums of Croatia*] (YU)
DML .... Dieselmotorenwerk Leipzig (VEB) [*Leipzig Diesel Motor Works (VEB)*] (EG)
DML .... Dvizheniia Molodezhi Lagosa (MAR)
DMM .... Dimethylurea (RU)
DMM .... Drustvo na Muzicarite na Makedonija [*Society of Musicians of Macedonia*] (YU)
DMMA .... Devlet Mimarlik ve Muhendislik Akademisi [*State Academy of Architecture and Engineering*] (TU)
DMN .... Darjah Utama Seri Mahkota Negara [*Most Exalted Order of the Crown*] (ML)
dmn .... Doctor of Medical Sciences (RU)
DMN .... Dom Mlodego Naukowca [*House of the Young Scholar*] (POL)
DMNA .... Dimethylnitrosoamine (RU)
dmo .... Decare [*In plowing standard units*] (BU)
DMO .... Devlet Malzeme Ofisi Genel Mudurlugu [*State Equipment Office Directorate General*] [*Under Finance Ministry*] (TU)
DMO .... Dimethyloxazolidinedione (RU)
DMO .... Machine/Work Days (BU)
DMO .... State Mining Trust (BU)
dmob .... Service Train [*Military*] (BU)
DMO-IS .... Devlet Malzeme Ofisi Iscileri Sendikasi [*State Equipment Office Workers' Union*] (TU)
DMP .... Deutsche Mittelstandspartei [*German Middle Class Party*] [*West German*] (PPW)
DMP .... Division Medical Station (RU)
DMP .... Diviziski Medicinski Punkt [*Divisional Medical Point*] (YU)
dmp .... Male Persons [*Statistics*] (RU)
DMP .... Outer Marker Beacon (RU)
DMP .... State Assembly Enterprise (BU)
DMP .... State Mining Enterprise (BU)
DMP .... Wooden-Bridge Park [*Military term*] (RU)
DMPA .... Dimercaptopropylamine (RU)
DMPP .... State Mining and Processing Enterprise (BU)
DMPS .... State Motor Transportation Vehicles (BU)
DMR .... Detachement Mobile de Reparation [*Mobile Repair Detachment*] [*Malagasy*] (AF)
DMR .... Dieselmotorenwerk Rostock (VEB) [*Rostock Diesel Motor Works (VEB)*] (EG)
DMR .... Dom Mlodego Robotnika [*House of the Young Worker*] (POL)
DMR .... Dom Mlodziezy Robotniczej [*House of Working Youth*] (POL)
DMRK .... State Ore Mining Combine (BU)
DMS .... Meteorological Station with Distant-Recording Instruments (RU)
DMSh .... State Music School (BU)
dm sl .... Administrative Duty [*Military*] (BU)
DMSO .... State Mining Construction Trust (BU)
DMSP .... Domaines de la Motte-Saint-Pierre & Cie. (MAR)
DMSP .... State Mine Salt Extraction Enterprise (BU)
DMSZ .... State Mine Salt Extraction Plant (BU)
dmt .... Bottom Dead Center (BU)
DMT .... Dimethyl Terephthalate (RU)
DMT .... Dimethyl Triphthalate (RU)
DMT .... Donja Mrtva Tacka [*Lower Dead Center*] [*Engine*] (YU)
DMTII .... Directorate of Music Composition and Performance (BU)
DMTN .... Direction du Materiel et des Travaux Neufs [*Directorate of Equipment and New Construction*] [*Cambodian*] (CL)
DMTS .... Machine-Tractor Stations Directorate (BU)
DMU .... Grid Magnetic Azimuth (RU)
DMU .... Magnetic Choke-Coupled Amplifier (RU)
DMU .... State Installations Administration (BU)
DMU PROMMONTAZH ... State Installations Administration for Industrial Installations (BU)
DMuzA .... State Academy of Music (BU)
DMV .... Decimeter Waves (BU)
DMV .... Decimetric Waves (RU)
DMV .... Diecesni Mirovy Vybor Katolickeho Duchovenstva [*Diocesan Peace Comittee of the Catholic Clergy*] (CZ)
DMWU .... Dockers and Marine Workers Union [*Jamaican*] (LA1)
Dmy .... Demiryol [*Railway*] (TU)
DMY-IS .... Demiryollari Iscileri Sendikasi [*Railway Workers' Union*] (TU)
DMZ .... Dnepr Magnesium Plant (RU)
DMZ .... Magnetic Door Fastening (RU)
DMZ .... State Machine-Building Plant (BU)
DMZ .... State Metallurgical Plant (BU)
DMZ .... Wood Pulp Plant (RU)
dn .... Active Principle [*Chemistry*] (RU)
dn .... Battalion [*Artillery*], Division [*Navy*] (RU)
DN .... Chemin de Fer Dakar-Niger (MAR)
DN .... Daily Nation [*Nairobi*] [*A publication*] (MAR)
DN .... Defense Nationale [*National Defense*] [*Cambodian*] (CL)
DN .... Democrazia Nazionale [*National Democratic Party*] [*Italian*] (WER)
DN .... Democrazia Nazionale-Constituente di Destra [*National Democracy-Right Constituent*] [*Italian*] (PPE)
DN .... Destra Nazionale [*National Right*] [*Italian*] (PPE)
DN .... Deutsche Notenbank [*German Bank of Issue*] (EG)
DN .... Developing Nation (AF)
DN .... Dewan Nasional [*National (Operations) Council*] (ML)
dn .... Diary, Journal (RU)
DN .... Dimokratiki Neolaia [*Democratic Youth*] (GC1)
dn .... Dnia [*Day*] (POL)
dn .... Dokonczenie Nastapi [*To Be Concluded*] [*Polish*]
DN .... Dominus Noster [*Our Lord*] [*Latin*] (GPO)
Dn .... Don [*Spanish*]
DN .... Drustvo Naroda [*League of Nations*] (YU)
dn .... Dyne (BU)
dn .... Dyne (RU)
DN .... Dyrekcja Naczelna [*Chief Administration*] (POL)
Dn .... Observation Range (RU)
DN .... Saturation Choke (RU)
DN .... Saturation Pressure (RU)
DN .... Section Chief [*Railroads*] (RU)
dn .... Today, Today's (BU)
DN .... Voltage Divider (RU)
DNA .... Det Norske Arbeiderparti [*Norwegian Labor Party*] (PPE)
DNA .... Deutscher Normenausschuss [*German Standards Committee*] [*Later, DIN*] (EG)
DNA .... People's Army Club (BU)
DNAEE .... Departamento Nacional de Aguas e Energia Eletrica [*National Water and Electrical Power Department*] [*Brazilian*] (LA)
DNB .... Deutsche Notenbank [*German Bank of Issue*] (EG)
DNB .... Direccion Nacional del Banano y Frutas Tropicales [*National Banana and Tropical Fruit Office*] [*Ecuadorean*] (LA)
DnC .... Den Norske Creditbank [*Norwegian*]
DNC .... Departamento Nacional do Cafe [*Brazilian*]
DNC .... Direction Nationale de la Construction [*Algerian*] (MAR)
DNC .... Direction Nationale des Cooperatives [*Algerian*] (MAR)
DNC .... Directorate of National Coordination [*Laotian*] (CL)
DNC .... Directorio Nacional Conservador [*Conservative National Directorate*] [*Colombian*] (LA)
DNCSP .... Directorio Nacional para el Control de Sustancias Peligrosas [*National Directorate for Controlling Dangerous Substances*] [*Bolivian*] (LA1)
DND .... Parti des Nationalistes du Dahomey (MAR)
D/ndis .... Dievthyndis [*Manager, Director*] (GC)
DN/DMR/ST ... Defense Nationale, Direction de Mobilisation et de Recruitement, Bureau des Stages [*National Defense, Directorate of Mobilization and Recruiting, Training Office*] [*Cambodian*] (CL)
DNE .... Department of National Education (MAR)
DNE .... Diethnis Navtikon Epimelitirion [*International Maritime Chamber*] (GC)
DNE .... Dinitroethane (RU)
dne .... Douane [*Customs, Duty*] [*French*]
DNEC .... Direccion Nacional de Energia y Combustibles [*National Fuels and Energy Board*] [*Argentine*] (LA)
DNEE .... Direccao Nacional de Energia Electrica [*National Administration for Electric Energy*] [*Angolan*] (AF)
DNEF .... Departamento Nacional de Estradas de Ferro [*National Railways Department*] [*Brazilian*] (LA)
Dneproenergo ... State Administration of the Dnepropetrovsk Oblast Power System Management (RU)
Dneproges ... Dnepr Hydroelectric Power Plant Imeni V. I. Lenin (RU)
Dneprostroy ... State Dnepr Construction Project (RU)
DNER .... Departamento Nacional de Estradas de Rodagem [*National Highway Department*] [*Brazilian*] (LA)
DNERU .... Departamento Nacional de Endemias Rurais [*National Rural Endemic Disease Department*] [*Brazilian*] (LA)
DNF .... Det Nye Folkepartiet [*New People's Party*] [*Norwegian*] (PPE)
DNF .... Dinitrophenol (RU)
DNF .... Directia de Navigatie Fluviala [*Directorate of River Navigation*] (RO)
DNF .... Disjunctive Normal Form (RU)
DNF .... People's Navy Club (BU)
DNFA .... Ammonium Dinitrophenolate (RU)
DNFF .... Del-Vietnami Nemzeti Felszabaditasi Front [*National Front for the Liberation of South Vietnam*] (HU)
DNFG .... Dinitrophenyl Hydrazone (RU)
DNFG .... Dinitrophenylhydrazine (RU)
DNFYuK ...... Democratic People's Front in South Korea (BU)
DNGTs .... Dinitroglycerol (RU)
DNI .... Departamento Nacional de Investigaciones [*National Department of Investigations*] [*Nicaraguan*] (LA1)

DNI .... Direccion Nacional de Impuestos [*National Tax Office*] [*Colombian*] (LA)
DNI .... Direccion Nacional de Investigaciones [*National Investigations Directorate*] [*Dominican Republic*] (LA)
DNI .... Documento Nacional de Identidad [*National Identity Document*] [*Spanish*] (WER)
DNIGL .... Dubovskaya Hydrological Scientific Research Laboratory (RU)
DNIGRI .... Dnepropetrovsk Scientific Research Institute of Ore Mining (RU)
DNII .... Direccion Nacional de Inteligencia e Informacion [*National Intelligence and Information Bureau*] [*Uruguayan*] (LA)
DNIS .... Deniz Nakliyat Iscileri Sendikasi [*Maritime Transport Workers' Union*] (TU)
DNIT .... Direction Nationale de l'Infrastructure des Transports [*Malian*] (MAR)
DNK .... Denmark [*Three-letter standard code*] (CNC)
DNK .... Deoxyribonucleic Acid (RU)
DNKaza .... Deoxyribonuclease (RU)
DNL .... Dimokratiki Neolaia Lambraki [*Lambrakis Democratic Youth*] [*Greek*] (GC)
DNL .... Direccion Nacional Liberal [*Liberal National Directorate*] [*Colombian*] (LA1)
DNL .... Pneumatic Landing Boat (RU)
DNLE .... Dimokratiki Neolaia Lambraki Ellados [*Lambrakis Democratic Youth of Greece*] (GC)
DNLP .... Direccion Nacional del Liberalismo Popular [*National Directorate of the Popular Liberal Party*] [*Colombian*] (LA)
DNLRS .... Drustvo Novinarjev Ljudske Republike Slovenije [*Journalists' Society of Slovenia*] (YU)
DNM .... Directia de Navigatie Maritima [*Directorate of Maritime Navigation*] (RO)
DNM .... Dvizheniia Nigeriiskoi Molodezhi (MAR)
DNM .... People's Militia Directorate (BU)
DNM .... State People's Militia (BU)
DNMG .... Direction Nationale de la Geologie et des Mines (MAR)
DNMO .... Departamento Nacional de Mao-de-Obra [*National Manpower Department*] [*Brazilian*] (LA)
DNNH .... Dyrekcja Naczelna Nowej Huty [*Main Administration of Nowa Huta*] [*Metallurgical center*] (POL)
DNO .... Division of People's Militia (RU)
DNOCS .... Departamento Nacional de Obras Contra as Secas [*National Drought Control Department*] [*Brazilian*] (LA)
DNOE .... Direccao Nacional de Obras de Engenharia (MAR)
DNOS .... Departamento Nacional de Obras e Saneamento [*National Department of Works and Sanitation*] [*Brazilian*] (LA)
DNOS .... State Irrigation and Drainage Systems (BU)
DNP .... Alternate Observation Post (RU)
DNP .... Democratic Nationalist Party [*1959-1966*] [*Maltese*] (PPE)
DNP .... Demokrata Neppart [*Democratic People's Party*] (HU)
DNP .... Deoxyribonucleoprotamine (RU)
DNP .... Deoxyribonucleoprotein (RU)
DNP .... Departamento Nacional de Planeacion [*National Planning Department*] [*Colombian*] (LA)
DNP .... State Economic Plan (BU)
DNPM .... Departamento Nacional da Producao Mineral [*National Department of Mineral Production*] [*Brazilian*] (LA)
DNPP .... Direccao Nacional de Propaganda e Publicidade (MAR)
DNPS .... Departamento Nacional da Previdencia Social [*National Social Welfare Department*] [*Brazilian*] (LA)
dn PTURS ... Antitank Guided Missile Battalion (BU)
DNPVN .... Departamento Nacional de Portos e Vias Navegaveis [*National Department of Ports and Waterways*] [*Brazilian*] (LA)
DNR .... Direccion Nacional de la Resistencia [*National Directorate of Resistance*] [*Bolivian*] (LA1)
DNS .... Daily News [*Tanzania*] [*A publication*] (MAR)
DNS .... Departamento Nacional de Salario [*National Wage Department*] [*Brazilian*] (LA)
DNS .... Department of National Security [*South African*] (AF)
DNS .... Direccion Nacional de Seguridad [*National Directorate of Security*] [*Dominican Republic*] (LA1)
DNS .... Docasne Narodne Shromazdenie [*Provisional National Assembly*] (CZ)
DNS .... Doppler Navigation System (RU)
DNSAP .... Danmarks Nationalsocialistisk Arbejdersparti [*National Socialist Worker's Party of Denmark (or Danish Nazi Party)*] (PPE)
dn SAU .... Self-Propelled Artillery Battalion (BU)
DNSEP .... Diplome National Superieur d'Expression Plastique [*French*]
DNSO .... Diakyvernitikos Navtiliakos Symvoulevtikos Organismos [*Intergovernmental Maritime Consultation Organization*] (GC)
DNSP .... Departamento Nacional de Saude Publica [*Brazilian*]
DNT .... Danistay [*Council of State*] (TU)
DNT .... Departamento Nacional do Trabalho [*National Department of Labor*] [*Brazilian*] (LA)
DNT .... Diethnes Nomismatikon Tameion [*International Monetary Fund*] (GC)
DNT .... Dinitrotoluene (RU)
DNT .... Direccao Nacional de Trabalho [*National Administration of Labor*] (AF)
DNT .... Dni Novej Techniky [*Promotion (Days) of New Technology*] (CZ)
DNT .... Drustvo Narodne Tehnike [*People's Technology Society*] (YU)
DNT .... House of Folk Art (RU)
DNTP .... House of Scientific and Technical Propaganda (RU)
DNU .... Department of National Unity (ML)
DNU .... Low-Level Discriminator [*Computers*] (RU)
DNVP .... Deutschnationale Volkspartei [*German National People's Party*] (EG)
D Ny .... Delnyugat [*Southwest*] (HU)
DNZ .... Public Health Directorate (BU)
DNZ .... State Petroleum Refinery (BU)
DO .... Delostrelecky Oddil [*Artillery Battalion*]. (CZ)
dO .... Der (Die, Das) Obige [*The Above Mentioned*] (EG)
DO .... Diakotthon [*Student Home*] (HU)
DO .... Diamine Oxidase (RU)
DO .... Dilci Organisace [*Branch Organization*] [*Communist Party*] (CZ)
DO .... Dioxane (RU)
d:o .... Dito [*Ditto*] [*Swedish*] (GPO)
do .... Dito [*French*]
do .... Ditto [*The Same*] [*German*] (GPO)
DO .... Dominican Republic [*Two-letter standard code*] (CNC)
Do .... Dopunske Odredbe [*Supplementary Regulations*] (YU)
DO .... Dum Osvety [*House of Culture*] (CZ)
DO .... Dyrekcja Okregowa [*District Administration*] (POL)
DO .... House of Officers (RU)
DO .... Landing Detachment (RU)
DO .... Landing Operation (RU)
DO .... Long-Range Fire (RU)
DO .... Operational Decoder (RU)
DO .... Patrol Detachment (RU)
DO .... Rest Home, Rest Center (RU)
DO .... Road Detachment (RU)
DO .... State Trusts (BU)
DO .... Turnover Tax (BU)
DOA .... Demokraticheskaia Ob'edineni Afriki (MAR)
DOA .... Deutsch-Ostafrika (MAR)
DOA .... Diethnis Olymbiaki Akadimia [*International Olympic Academy*] (GC)
DOA .... Diethnis Omospondia Andistasiakon [*International Resistance Federation*] (GC)
DOA .... Directie Overheidsorganisatie- en Automatisering [*'s-Gravenhage*]
DOAE .... Department of Oriental Antiquities and Ethnology (MAR)
DOAE .... Diethnis Organismos Atomikis Energeias [*International Atomic Energy Agency*] (GC)
DOAF .... Dihydroxyaceto Phosphate (RU)
DOAG .... Deutsch Ostafrikanische Gesellschaft (MAR)
DOAP .... Diethnis Organismos Apokatastaseos Prosfygon (GC)
DOAT .... Diethnis Omospondia Athlitikou Typou [*International Federation of Sports Publications*] (GC)
DOAV .... Deutscher Oesterreichischer Alpen Verein [*Austro-German Alpine Federation*]
dob .... Addition [*or Supplement*] (BU)
dob .... Additional, Supplementary (RU)
DOB .... Devrimci Ogrenci Birligi [*Revolutionary Student Union*] (TU)
dob .... Division Ammunition Train (BU)
dob .... Supplement, Appendix (RU)
DOB .... Turkiye Devrimci Ogretmenler Birligi [*Union of Turkish Revolutionary Teachers*] (TU)
DOBGM .... Devlet Opera ve Balesi Genel Mudurlugu [*State Opera and Ballet Directorate General*] (TU)
DOBOPS ..... Director Borneo Ops (ML)
dobr .... Good Quality, Soundness (RU)
Dobrarmiya ... Volunteer Army [*1917-1920*] (RU)
Dobroflot .... Volunteer Fleet [*1870-1922*] (RU)
Dobrokhim ... Voluntary Society for Furthering the Construction of the Chemical Industry [*1924-1925*] (RU)
Dobrolet ...... All-Union Society of the Volunteer Air Fleet [*1923-1930*] (RU)
dobr o-vo .... Voluntary Society (RU)
DOC .... Depots Ocean Congo (MAR)
doc .... Docent [*Assistant Professor*] [*Polish*]
Doc .... Docent [*Lecturer*] (CZ)
Doc .... Docent [*Docent, Assistant Professor*] (TU)
DOCA .... Section Documentation Automatique [*CETIS*] [*Luxembourg*]
DOCPAL ..... Sistema de Documentacion sobre Poblacion en America Latina [*Santiago, Chile*]
Doct .... Doctor [*Doctor*] [*Spanish*]
documto ..... Documento [*Document*] [*Spanish*]
DOD .... Devrimci Ogretmenleri Dernegi [*Revolutionary Teachers' Organization*] [*See also TDOD*] (TU)
DOD .... Diethnis Omospondia Dimosiografon [*International Federation of Journalists*] (GC)
dod .... Dodatek [*Supplement, Appendix*] [*Polish*]
DOD .... Gross Income Tax (BU)
DOE .... Departamento de Operaciones Especiales [*Department of Special Operations*] [*Uruguayan*] (LA)
DOE .... Didaskaliki Omospondia Ellados [*Teachers Federation of Greece*] (GC)
DOE .... Diethnis Oikonomiki Epitropi [*International Economic Committee*] (GC)

DOE .... Diethnis Oikonomikos Elengkhos [*International Economic Control*] (GC)
DOE .... Diethnis Organosis Ergasias [*International Labor Organization*] (GC)
DOE .... Direccion de Operaciones Especiales [*Directorate of Special Operations*] [*Cuban*] (LA)
DOEM .... Diethnis Omospondia Ergaton Metaforas [*International Transport Workers Federation*] (GC)
DOES .... Diethnis Omospondia ton Ergatikon Syndikaton [*International Federation of Trade Unions*] (GC)
DOF .... Dioctyl Phthalate (RU)
DOF .... House of Fleet Officers (RU)
DOFA .... Dihydroxyphenylalanine (RU)
DOFSP .... Departamento de Obras e Fiscalizacao dos Servicos Publicos [*Public Services Works and Control Department*] [*Brazilian*] (LA)
DOG .... Deoxyglucose (RU)
DOG .... Deutsche Orient-Gesellschaft (MAR)
Dog .... Dogum Yili [*Year of Birth*] (TU)
Dog .... Dogumevi [*Maternity Ward*] (TU)
DOI .... Departamento de Operacoes Internas [*Department of Domestic Operations*] [*Brazilian*] (LA)
DOI .... Dispozitive Optice Integrate [*Integrated Optical Devices*] (RO)
DOI .... State Publishing Houses Trust (BU)
DOK .... Deoxycorticosterone (RU)
dok .... Documents (BU)
dok .... Dokonczenie [*Conclusion*] [*Polish*]
dok .... Dokumentacio [*Documentation*] (HU)
DOK .... Dowodztwo Okregu Korpusu [*District Corps Headquarters*] (POL)
DOK .... Dozer Kolovy [*Wheeled Dozer*] (CZ)
DOK .... Woodworking Kombinat (RU)
DOKA .... Deoxycorticosterone Acetate (RU)
dok csop ..... Dokumentacios Csoport [*Documentation Group*] (HU)
DOKD .... Department Oswiaty i Kultury Doroslych [*Department of Adult Education and Culture*] (POL)
DOKDI .... Dokumentationsdienst der Schweizerischen Akademie der Medizinischen Wissenschaften [*Bern*]
Dok Gemi-Is ... Turkiye Liman, Dok, ve Gemi Sanayii Iscileri Sendikasi [*Turkish Harbor, Dock, and Ship Industry Workers Union*] (TU)
DOKh .... Deoxycholate (RU)
DOKhES ...... Diethnis Omospondia ton Khristianikon Ergatikon Syndikaton [*International Federation of Christian Trade Unions*] (GC)
doki .... Doktor [*Doctor or Doc (Slang)*] (HU)
DOKiP .... Dni Oswiaty, Ksiazki i Prasy [*Education, Book and Press Days*] (POL)
dokl .... Report (RU)
dok nast ...... Dokonczenie Nastapi [*To Be Concluded*] [*Polish*]
DOKP .... Dni Oswiaty, Ksiazki i Prasy [*Education, Book and Press Days*] (POL)
DOKP .... Dyrekcja Okregowa Kolei Panstwowych [*District Directorate of State Railroads*] (POL)
DOKSA .... Deoxycorticosterone Acetate (RU)
dokt .... Doctoral (RU)
DOKTAS ..... Dokumculuk Ticaret ve Sanayi Anonim Sirketi [*Weaving Trade and Industry, Incorporated*] [*Bursa*] (TU)
dokt fiz mat n ... Doctor of Physical and Mathematical Sciences (RU)
dokum .... Document, Deed, Record (RU)
dol .... Dolar [*Dollar*] [*Polish*]
dol .... Dollar (RU)
Dol .... Dollarion [*Dollar*] (GC)
D-O-L .... Plavebni Cesta Dunaj-Odra-Labe [*Danube-Oder-Elbe Waterway*] (CZ)
Dol .... Valley [*Topography*] (RU)
dolg .... Dolgozo [*or Dolgozok*] [*Working or Workers*] (HU)
dolg .... Longitude (RU)
DOLITAC .... US Department of Labor, International Technical Assistance Corps (MAR)
doll .... Dollar [*Dollar*] [*French*]
doll .... Dollari(a) [*Finnish*]
Doll .... Dollaria [*Dollars*] (GC)
dolm .... Dolmen [*Topography*] (RU)
DOM .... Debreceni Orvosi Muszergyar [*Medical Instrument Factory of Debrecen*] (HU)
DOM .... Departement d'Outre-Mer [*Overseas Department*] [*French*] (WER)
DOM .... Devizno Obracunsko Mesto [*Foreign Exchange Clearinghouse*] (YU)
DOM .... Diethneis Odikes Metafores [*International Road Transportations*] (GC1)
DOM .... Direccao das Organizacoes de Massa [*Directorate for the Organization of the Masses*] [*Angolan*] (AF)
Dom .... Domingo [*Sunday*] [*Spanish*]
DOM .... Dominican Republic [*Three-letter standard code*] (CNC)
dom .... Domyslnie [*To Be Understood*] [*Polish*]
DOM .... Republika Dominikanska [*Dominican Republic*] [*Polish*]
DOMA .... Deep Ocean Minerals Association (MAR)
DomD .... Knjiznica Samostana Dominikanaca u Dubrovniku [*Library of the Dominican Monastery in Dubrovnik*] (YU)
Dome .... Domaine [*Military map abbreviation*] [*World War I*] [*French*] (MTD)
DOMENG .... Direccion de Organizacion del Estado Mayor General [*Directorate for Organization and Mobilization of the General Staff*] [*Cuban*] (LA)
Domh .... Domherr [*German*]
DOMK .... Dihydroxymaleic Acid (RU)
domkom ..... Apartment House Committee (RU)
Domnz .... Dom Narodnog Zdravlja [*Public Health Center*] (YU)
domo .... Domingo [*Sunday*] [*Spanish*]
domostr ...... House-Building Kombinat [*Topography*] (RU)
domostr ...... House-Building Plant [*Topography*] (RU)
domouprav ... House Manager (RU)
Domprosvet ... House of Education (RU)
DOMSAT ..... Domestic Satellite System [*Guyanese*] (LA)
DOM-TOM .. Departements et Territoires d'Outre-Mer (MAR)
domzak .... House of Confinement, Prison (RU)
don .... Donem [*Session, Period*] [*As of assembly*] (TU)
DON .... Donets Railroad (RU)
DON .... Long-Range Fire, Distant Concentration (BU)
DON .... Long-Range Harassing Fire, Long-Range Attack [*Artillery*] (RU)
Donbass ...... Donets Coal Basin (RU)
Donbassenergo ... Donbass Power System (RU)
do ne .... Before Christ (RU)
Dongres ...... Northern Donets State Regional Electric Power Plant (RU)
DONL .... Dimokratiki Omada Navtilias Londinou [*Democratic Seamen's Group of London*] (GC)
DONNII .... Donets Scientific Research Institute of Pithead Construction (RU)
Donobsoyuz ... Don Oblast Union of Consumers' Societies (RU)
Donsoda ..... Northern Donets Soda Plant (RU)
DONUGI ...... Donets Scientific Research Institute of Coal (RU)
DOO .... State Social Insurance (BU)
DOO .... Voluntary Hunting Society (RU)
DOOR .... Dyrekcja Okregowa Osiedli Robotniczych [*District Housing Administration of Workers' Settlements*] (POL)
dop .... Additional, Complementary, Enlarged, Supplementary, Supplemented (RU)
dop .... Correspondence [*Press*] (BU)
DOP .... Departamento del Orden Publico [*Department of Public Order*] [*Cuban*] (LA)
DOP .... Depot Pusat [*Central Depot*] (IN)
DOP .... Detachement Operationnel de Protection [*Algerian*] (MAR)
DOP .... Division Supply Relay Point (RU)
DOP .... Dolnoslaski Okreg Przemyslowy [*Lower-Silesian Industrial District*] [*Polish*]
dop .... Dopoledne [*Morning*] (CZ)
dop .... Enlarged, Expanded [*Edition*] (BU)
dop .... Supplement, Addition, Complement (RU)
DOPA .... Diethnis Organismos Politikis Aeroporias [*International Civil Aviation Organization*] (GC)
DOPA .... Dimosthenikos Omilos Politistikis Anaptyxeos [*Demosthenes Group for Cultural Development*] [*Greek*] (GC)
DOP art ...... Division Artillery Supply Relay Point (RU)
DOPCO .... Dashtestan Offshore Petroleum Company (ME)
DOPEM .... Director Operations East Malaysia (ML)
dopl .... Doplyw [*Affluent*] [*Polish*]
DOPMA .... Defense Officer Personnel Management Act (MAR)
dop otkl ...... Permissible Variation, Tolerance (RU)
doppayek .... Supplementary Ration, Extra Ration (RU)
DOPR .... Pretrial House of Detention (RU)
DOPR .... Workhouse (RU)
DOPS .... Departamento de Ordem Politica e Social [*Department of Political and Social Order*] [*Brazilian*] (LA)
DOPS .... Halo and Sun Tracking Probe (RU)
DOPT .... Dyrekcja Okregowa Poczt i Telekomunikacji [*District Post and Telecommunication Administration*] (POL)
dop tir .... Additional Printing [*of a publication*] (BU)
dop tit l .... Supplementary Title Page (RU)
dopushch .... Admitted, Authorized (RU)
DOR .... Departamento de Orientacao Revolucionaria [*Department of Revolutionary Orientation*] [*Angolan*] (AF)
DOR .... Departamento de Orientacion Revolucionaria [*Revolutionary Orientation Department*] [*Cuban*] (LA)
Dor .... Doktor [*Academic degree*] [*Indonesian*]
DOR .... Dyrekcja Osiedli Robotniczych [*Administration of Workers' Settlements*] (POL)
dor .... Road (RU)
DORAA .... Direccao da Organizacao Regional do Alentejo-Algrave [*Alentejo-Algrave Region Organization Directorate*] [*Portuguese*] (WER)
DORB .... Direccao da Organizacao Regional das Beiras [*Beiras Region Organization Directorate*] [*Portuguese*] (WER)
DORBRAS ... Companhia Brasileira de Dormentes [*Brazilian Railway Tie Company*] (LA)
dorChK .... Railroad Extraordinary Commission for Combating Counterrevolution and Sabotage (RU)
doreb .... Road Maintenance Battalion (RU)
dorev .... Prerevolutionary (RU)
DORG .... Departamento de Reconstruccao Nacional [*Department of National Reconstruction*] [*Angolan*] (AF)

Dorgan........ Spoldzielnia Pracy Doradcow Organizacyjnych [*Labor Cooperative of Consultants on Organization*] (POL)
Dorizdat...... Publishing House of Road Construction Literature (RU)
dorizul......... Railroad Office of Inventions and Improvements (RU)
DORK.......... Dyrekcja Okregowa Radiofonizacji Kraju [*District Administration for Country-Wide Radio Installation*] (POL)
Dorkhimzavod ... Dorogomilovskiy Chemical Plant Imeni M. V. Frunze (RU)
DORKTEK... Railroad Office for Container Shipments and Transportation and Forwarding Operations (RU)
DORL........... Direccao da Organizacao Regional de Lisboa [*Lisbon Region Organization Directorate*] [*Portuguese*] (WER)
DORM.......... Direccao da Organizacao Regional do Minho [*Minho Region Organization Directorate*] [*Portuguese*] (WER)
DORMA....... Departamento de Organizacion y Masas [*Department of Organization and the Masses*] [*Nicaraguan*] (LA1)
Dormash..... Road Machinery Repair Plant (RU)
Dormashina ... Road Machinery Plant (RU)
Dormost...... Road and Bridge Administration (RU)
Dormostmekhanizatsiya ... Trust of the Road and Bridge Construction Administration of the Glavmosstroy (RU)
Dormostproyekt ... Institute for the Planning of Roads, Bridges, and Embankments (RU)
Dormoststroy ... Republic Trust of Road and Bridge Construction [*RSFSR*] (RU)
Dormoststroymaterialy ... Trust of the Road and Bridge Construction Administration of thn Glavmosstroy (RU)
DORN.......... Direccao da Organizacao Regional do Norte [*Northern Region Organization Directorate*] [*Portuguese*] (WER)
DORNII........ Scientific Research Institute of Roads (RU)
DorNITO...... Scientific, Engineering, and Technical Society of Railroad Transportation (RU)
dorNTO....... Railroad Administration of the Scientific and Technical Society of Railroad Transportation (RU)
DOROR........ Direccao da Organizacao Regional do Oeste e Ribatejo [*West and Ribatejo Region Organization Directorate*] [*Portuguese*] (WER)
Dorprofsozh ... Railroad Committee of the Railroad Transportation Workers' Trade (RU)
dorr............ Road Company (RU)
dorsanupr... Railroad Medical Administration (RU)
dorsb.......... Road-Building Battalion (RU)
Dorstroy...... Road-Building Trust (RU)
DORTEK...... Railroad Transportation and Forwarding Office (RU)
DORURS..... Road Administration of Workers' Supply (RU)
dorv............ Road Platoon (RU)
Dorzdrav..... Railroad Department of Public Health (RU)
DOS............ Dioikisis Oikonomikis Synergasias (GC)
DOS............ Direccion de Obras Sanitarias [*Sanitary Public Works Department*] [*Chilean*] (LA)
DOS............ Directorate of Overseas Surveys (MAR)
dos............. Dosentti [*Finnish*]
DOS............ Duvanska Ogledna Stanica [*Tobacco Experimental Station*] (YU)
DOS............ House of Officer Personnel (RU)
dos............. Permanent Emplacement (RU)
DOS............ Permanent Emplacement, Fighting Pillbox (BU)
DOSA.......... House of Soviet Army Officers (RU)
DOSAAF..... All-Union Voluntary Society for Assistance to the Army, Air Force, and Navy of the USSR (RU)
DOSAAF..... Dobrovol'noye Obshchestvo Sodeystviya Armii, Aviatsii, i Floty SSSR [*Voluntary Society for Assistance to the Army, Air Force, and Navy of the USSR*] (CZ)
DOSARM..... All-Union Voluntary Society for Assistance to the Army of the USSR [*1948-1951*] (RU)
DOSAV........ All-Union Voluntary Society for Assistance to the Air Force of the USSR [*1948-1951*] (RU)
DOSFLOT ... All-Union Voluntary Society for Assistance to the Navy of the USSR [*1948-1951*] (RU)
doshk.......... Preschool (RU)
DOSK.......... Docasna Okresna Spravna Komisia [*Provisional District Administrative Commission*] (CZ)
dosl............ Doslownie [*Literally*] (POL)
dosl............ Doslowny [*Literal*] (POL)
DOSO.......... Voluntary Civil Defense Organization (BU)
DOSO.......... Voluntary Society for Assistance to Landscaping (RU)
DOSOM....... Voluntary Society for Assisting the Landscaping of the City of Moscow (RU)
DOS-(VEB) ... Deutsche Oder-Schiffahrt [*German Oder Shipping Enterprise (VEB)*] (EG)
DOSZ.......... Dyrekcja Okregowa Szkolenia Zawodowego [*District Administration of Vocational Training*] (POL)
DOT............ Doswiadczalny Osrodek Telewizyjny [*Experimental Television Center*] (POL)
dot.............. Dotyczy [*or Dotyczacy*] [*Refers To, Concerning*] [*Polish*]
DOT............ Operational Detachment of Ships of the Baltic Fleet [*1919*] (RU)
DOT............ Permanent Emplacement (RU)
DOT............ Reinforced Concrete Pillbox (BU)
DOTE.......... Debreceni Orvostudomanyi Egyetem [*Medical University of Debrecen*] (HU)
DOTS.......... Associate Professor (BU)
dots............ Docent (BU)
dots............ Docent, Lecturer (RU)
DOTs........... Woodworking Shop (RU)
douz........... Douzaine [*Dozen*] [*French*]
DOV............ Doplnovaci Okresni Velitelstvi [*Military District Command for Records and Reserves*] (CZ)
DOV............ Supplementary Excitation Winding (RU)
dov rub........ Prewar Ruble (RU)
DOW........... Dowodztwo Okregow Wojskowych [*Military District Headquarters*] (POL)
DOW........... Dowodztwo Okregu Wojskowego [*Military District Headquarters*] (POL)
Doz.............. Dozent [*German*]
DOZ............ Drzaven Osiguritelen Zavod [*State Insurance Institute*] (YU)
DOZ............ Patrol (RU)
DOZ............ State Shoe Manufacturing Plant (BU)
DOZ............ Woodworking Plant (RU)
DOZAB........ Dopravne Zavody v Bratislave [*Transportation Enterprises in Bratislava*] (CZ)
dozavuch.... School for Pre-Plant Training (RU)
DOZK.......... Ship Patrol (RU)
DOZPL........ Submarine Patrol (RU)
DOZV.......... Air Patrol Detachment (RU)
DP............... Arc Furnace (RU)
DP............... Breathing Apparatus (RU)
DP............... Center-Line Plane, Fore-and-Aft Line (of a Ship) (RU)
DP............... Child's Gas Mask (RU)
DP............... Circular Saw (RU)
DP............... Dacha Settlement (RU)
DP............... Decontamination Apparatus (RU)
DP............... Decontamination Area (RU)
DP............... Decontamination Station [*Military*] (BU)
DP............... Decontamination Station (RU)
DP............... Defense Passive [*French*]
DP............... Degtyarev Infantry (Machine Gun) (RU)
DP............... Delostrelecky Pluk [*Artillery Regiment*] (CZ)
DP............... Democracia Popular [*Popular Democracy Party*] [*Ecuadorean*] (LA)
DP............... Democratic Party [*Ugandan*] (PD)
DP............... Democratic Party [*Cook Islander*] (PPW)
DP............... Democratic Party [*Stronnictwo Demokratyczne*] [*Polish*] (PPW)
DP............... Democratic Party (RU)
DP............... Democratische Partij - Bovenwinden [*Democratic Party - Windward Islands*] [*Netherlands Antillean*] (PPW)
DP............... Democratische Partij van Curacao [*Democratic Party*] [*Netherlands Antillean*] (PPW)
DP............... Democrazia Proletaria [*Proletarian Democracy*] [*Italian*] (PPE)
DP............... Demokrat Partisi [*Democratic Party*] (TU)
DP............... Demokratesch Partei [*Democratic Party*] [*Luxembourg*] (PPE)
DP............... Demokraticheska Partiia [*Democratic Party*] [*Bulgarian*] (PPE)
DP............... Demokratiki Parataksis [*Democratic Front*] [*Greek*] (PPE)
DP............... Departamento de Pesca [*Fisheries Department*] [*Mexican*] (LA)
DP............... Deutsche Partei [*German Party*] [*West German*] (PPE)
DP............... Deutsche Post [*German Post Office*] (EG)
DP............... Dewan Pimpinan [*Executive Council*] (IN)
D/P............. Dexamenoploion [*Tanker*] [*See also dex*] (GC)
DP............... Diagnostic Subroutine (RU)
DP............... Dielectric Constant (RU)
DP............... Differential Gear (RU)
DP............... Dimokratiki Parataxi [*Democratic Front*] [*Cypriot*] (GC)
DP............... Dimokratiki Poreia [*Democratic Path*] [*Greek*] (GC)
DP............... Direction des Poudres [*Weapons Powder Directorate*] [*French*] (WER)
DP............... Direkcija za Patista [*Department of Roads*] (YU)
DP............... Dispatcher's Console (RU)
DP............... Dispatcher's Station, Control Post, Dispatch Office (RU)
DP............... Displacement Pickup (RU)
DP............... Distance-Finding Station [*Navy*] (RU)
DP............... Documents Contre Paiement [*French*]
DP............... Domaine de Pechpeyrou (MAR)
DP............... Dominion Party (MAR)
DP............... Dopravni Podniky Hlavniho Mesta Prahy [*Transportation Enterprises of the Capital Prague*] (CZ)
DP............... Dopravoprojekt-Statni Ustav pro Projektovani Dopravnich Staveb [*State Planning Institute for Transport Construction*] (CZ)
DP............... Dosimeter (RU)
DP............... Drustveni Plan [*Economic Plan*] (YU)
DP............... Drzavno Posestvo [*State Agricultural Estate*] (YU)
Dp............... Duga Plovidba [*Ocean Shipping*] (YU)
DP............... Duplex Device (RU)
DP............... Dynamic Party (MAR)
DP............... Dywizja Pancerna [*Armored Division*] (POL)
DP............... Enemy Documents (BU)
DP............... Flight Range (RU)
DP............... Hoisting Motor (RU)
DP............... House of Pioneers (RU)
DP............... Long-Range Homing Radio Station (RU)
DP............... Obus a Double Paroi [*Type of shell*] [*Military*] [*French*] (MTD)
DP............... Piston Engine (RU)

DP .... Popular Democracy [*Ecuadorean*] (PD)
DP .... Press Directorate (BU)
DP .... Regimental Duty Officer (RU)
DP .... Remote-Indicating Instrument, Remote-Reading Instrument (RU)
DP .... Remote Transmission (RU)
DP .... State Enterprise (BU)
DP .... State Printing Press (BU)
DP .... Yeast Peptone (RU)
DPA .... Averkiyev Breathing Apparatus (RU)
DPA .... Children's Preventive Clinic (RU)
DPA .... Demokraticheskaia Partiia Angoly (MAR)
DPa .... Deutsche Patentanmeldung [*German Patent Application*] [*German*]
DPA .... Deutsche Presse Agentur [*German Press Agency*] [*West German*] (WEN)
DPA .... Deutscher Personalausweis [*German Identity Card*] (EG)
DPa .... Deutsches Patent Angemeldet [*German Patent Pending*] (EG)
DPA .... Dewan Pertimbangan Agung [*Supreme Advisory Council*] (IN)
DPA .... Direccion Provincial de Acueductos [*Provincial Waterworks Office*] [*Cuban*] (LA)
DPA .... Direccion del Proyecto CN Asco [*Asco Nuclear Power Station Project Bureau*] [*Spanish*] (WER)
DPA .... Division Politicoadministrativa [*Political Administrative Division*] [*Cuban*] (LA)
DPA .... House of Party Activists (RU)
DPB .... Dairy Produce Board (MAR)
DPB .... Obus a Double Paroi et a Balles [*Type of shell*] [*Military*] [*French*] (MTD)
DPBG .... Democratic Party for British Gibraltar (PPW)
DPBZ .... Dukelske Preteky Brannej Zdatnosti [*Dukla Military Fitness Contest*] (CZ)
DPC .... Democratic People's Congress (MAR)
DPC .... Direccion de Preparacion Combativa [*Directorate of Combat Training*] [*Cuban*] (LA)
DPC .... Dubai Petroleum Company (ME)
DPD .... Delnicke Potravni Druzstvo [*Workers' Consumer Cooperative*] (CZ)
DPD .... Devlet Personel Dairesi [*State Personnel Office*] [*Under Prime Ministry*] (TU)
DPD .... Diretoria de Pesquisas e Desenvolvimento [*Bureau of Research and Development*] [*Brazilian*] (LA)
DPD .... Division Decontamination Unit (RU)
DPD .... Dobrovolno Protivpozarno Drustvo [*Society of Volunteer Firemen*] (YU)
DPD .... Drzavno Poljoprivredno Dobro [*State Agricultural Estate*] (YU)
DPD .... Volunteer Fire Brigade (RU)
DPD"Svoboda" ... Delavsko Prosvetno Drustvo "Svoboda" [*"Svoboda," Workers' Educational Society*] (YU)
Dp E .... Depot d'Eclopes [*Military*] [*French*] (MTD)
DPEI .... Departamento de Prevencion y Extincion de Incendios [*Department of Fire Fighting and Prevention*] [*Cuban*] (LA)
DPES .... Mobile Diesel Electric Power Plant (RU)
DPF .... Darfur Progress Front (MAR)
DPF .... Departamento da Policia Federal [*Federal Police Department*] [*Brazilian*] (LA)
DPF .... Devlet Planlama Fonu [*State Planning Fund*] (TU)
DPF .... State Land Fund (BU)
DPFF .... State Pasture and Forage Fund (BU)
DPG .... Democratic Party of Guinea (RU)
DPG .... Demokraticheskaia Partiia Guinei (MAR)
DPgem .... Deutsches Patent Angemeldet [*German Patent Pending*] (EG)
DPH .... Dewan Pimpinan Harian [*Standing Executive Committee*] (IN)
DPI .... Department of Public Information (MAR)
DPI .... Disabled People's International (EA)
DPI .... Don Polytechnic Institute (RU)
DPICG .... Destacamento Pedagogico Internacionalista "Che" Guevara [*Che Guevara Internationalist Teachers Detachment*] [*Cuban*] (LA)
DPIT .... Drustvo Poljoprivrednih Inzenjera i Tehnicara [*Society of Agricultural Engineers and Technicians*] (YU)
DPJ .... Direction Active de la Police Judiciaire [*Directorate of Criminal Investigation Police*] [*French*] (WER)
DPK .... Container Position Probe (RU)
DPK .... Democratic Party of Kurdistan [*Al-Hizb ad-Dimuqraati al-Kurid*] [*Iraqi*] (PPW)
DPK .... Dimokratiki Panepistimiaki Kinisi [*Democratic University Movement*] [*Greek*] (GC)
DPK .... Divadlo 5 Kvetna [*May 5th Theater*] (CZ)
DPK .... Pneumatic Telecompass (RU)
DPK .... Ship Decontamination Apparatus (RU)
DPK .... State Planning Commission (BU)
DPK .... State Printing Combine (BU)
DPKh .... Division Field Bakery (RU)
DPKK .... Dimokratikon Proodevtikon Komma Kyprou [*Democratic Progressive Party of Cyprus*] (GC)
DPL .... Delostrelectvo Proti Letadlum [*Antiaircraft Artillery*] (CZ)
DPL .... Division Field Infirmary (RU)
DPL .... Dopravni Pluk Letecky [*Air Force Transport Regiment*] (CZ)
DPL .... Floating Dock (RU)
DPl .... Planned Idleness [*Machine placed in temporary reserve*] (BU)
DPL .... Submarine Division (RU)
DPLG .... Diplome par le Gouvernement [*French*]
DPlKom .... State Planning Commission (BU)
DPLRS .... Drustvo Pravnikov Ljudska Republika Slovenija [*Slovenian Lawyers' Society*] (YU)
DPM .... Dewan Perniagaan Melayu [*Malayan Commercial Council*] (ML)
DPM .... Diplomatoukhos Politikos Mikhanikos [*Certified (Graduate) Civil Engineer*] (GC)
DPM .... Directia Porturilor Maritime [*Directorate of Maritime Ports*] (RO)
DPM .... Dorazna Pomoc Medyczna [*Medical First Aid*] (POL)
DPM .... First-Aid Medical Station (RU)
DPM .... Modernized Degtyarev Infantry (Machine Gun) (RU)
DPMC .... Diviziska Pekarsko-Mesarska Ceta [*Divisional Bakers' and Butchers' Company*] (YU)
DPMJ .... Dewan Perniagaan Melayu Johor [*Johor Malayan Commercial Council*] (ML)
DPMP .... Dewan Persuratan Melayu Pahang [*Pahang Malayan Literature Council*] (ML)
DPMS .... Data Processing and Maintenance Services Limited (MAR)
DPN .... Diphosphopyridine Nucleotide (RU)
dpn .... Doctor of Pedagogical Sciences (RU)
DPNC .... Democratic Party of Nigeria and the Cameroons (MAR)
DPO .... Demokratische Partei Oesterreichs [*Democratic Party of Austria*] (PPE)
DPO .... Dimitrov Pioneer Organization (BU)
DPO .... Direct-Current Motor with Printed-Coil Armature (RU)
DPO .... Division Dressing Detachment (RU)
DPO .... Divisional Police Officer (MAR)
DPO .... Divisional Prosecutions Officer (MAR)
DPO .... House of Party Education (RU)
DPO .... State Printing and Publishing Trust (BU)
DPO .... Voluntary Consumers' Society [*1921-1924*] (RU)
DPO .... Volunteer Fire Society (RU)
DPolitekh .... State Polytechnical School (BU)
DPolitekhn-IFotogrTopogr ... State Polytechnical School, Institute of Photogrammetry and Topography (BU)
DPolitekhn-IGrad ... State Polytechnical School, Institute of City Planning (BU)
DPolitekhn-IInzhGeol ... State Polytechnical School, Institute of Geological Engineering (BU)
DPolitekhn-IKadZemeustr ... State Polytechnical School, Institute of Cadastral Study and Land Organization (BU)
DPolitekhn-IMel ... State Polytechnical School, Institute of Reclamation (BU)
DPolitekhn-IMelPochv ... State Polytechnical Institute of Soil Reclamation (BU)
DPolitekhn-INeorKhimTekhnol ... State Polytechnical Institute of Inorganic Chemical Technology (BU)
DPolitekhn-IOrKhimTekhnol ... State Polytechnical Institute of Organic Chemical Technology (BU)
DPolitekhn-IPrilElektrotekhn ... State Polytechnical Institute of Applied Electrical Engineering (BU)
DPolitekhn-IPrilGeol ... State Polytechnical Institute of Applied Geodesy (BU)
DPolitekhn-IRudNakh ... State Polytechnical School, Institute of Ore Deposits (BU)
DPolitekhn-ITekhnBot ... State Polytechnical School, Institute of Industrial Botany (BU)
DPolitekhn-ITekhnMekh ... State Polytechnical School, Institute of Applied Mechanics (BU)
DPolitekhn-ITopTekhnTekhTerm ... State Polytechnical School, Institute of Heat Engineering and Technical Thermodynamics (BU)
DPolitekhn-IVodkan ... State Polytechnical School, Institute of Water Supply and Sewage (BU)
DPOS .... "Septemvriyche" Dimitrov Pioneer Organization (BU)
DPOZ .... Dopravna Protiletecka Ochrana Zeleznic [*Mobile Anti-Aircraft Defense of Railroads*] (CZ)
DPP .... Democratic Progressive Party [*Transkei*] (PPW)
DPP .... Demokratikus Polgari Part [*Democratic Citizens' Party*] (HU)
DPP .... Dewan Perniagaan dan Perindustrian [*Chamber of Commerce and Industry*] (IN)
DPP .... Dewan Pimpinan Pusat [*Central Executive Council*] (IN)
DPP .... Director of Public Prosecutions [*Jamaican*] (LA1)
DPP .... Division Dressing Station (RU)
DPP .... Division Reloading Point, Division Load Transfer Point (RU)
DPP .... House of Party Education (RU)
DPP .... Long-Range Infantry Support (RU)
DPP .... Long-Range Weather Forecast (RU)
DPP .... State Industrial Enterprise (BU)
DPPNRBiH ... Direkcija za Planinske Pasnjake Narodne Republike Bosne i Hercegovine [*Department for Mountain Pastures of Bosnia and Hercegovina*] (YU)
DPPS .... Divisao da Policia Politica e Social [*Political and Social Police Division*] [*Brazilian*] (LA)
DPPS .... Voluntary Fire Fighting Service (BU)
DPPU .... Voluntary Fire Fighting School (BU)
DPR .... Dewan Perwakilan Rakjat [*Parliament*] (IN)
dpr .... River Crossing Assault Company (RU)
DPR .... State Livestock Breeding Farm (BU)
DPR .... Workhouse (RU)
DPRA .... Democratic People's Republic of Angola (MAR)

DPRD.......... Dewan Perwakilan Rakjat Daerah [*Regional Legislature*] (IN)
DPRD-GR.... Dewan Perwakilan Rakjat Daerah - Gotong Rojong [*Regional Legislature*] (IN)
DPR-GR....... Dewan Perwakilan Rakjat - Gotong Rojong [*Parliament*] (IN)
DPRK.......... Democratic People's Republic of Korea [*Also known as North Korea*] (CL)
DPRM.......... Long-Range Homing Radio Beacon (RU)
DPRM.......... Outer Marker Beacon (RU)
DPRS.......... Long-Range Homing Radio Station (BU)
DPRS.......... Long-Range Homing Radio Station (RU)
DPRZ.......... Dnepropetrovsk Locomotive Repair Plant (RU)
D Pr Zak...... Pretrial House of Detention (RU)
DPS............ Demokratische Partei Saar [*Democratic Party of the Saar*] [*West German*] (PPE)
DPS............ Detaliczny Punkt Sprzedazy [*Retail Sales Center*] (POL)
DPS............ Dische-Positive Substances (RU)
DPS............ Division Advanced Depot (RU)
DPS............ Division Food Depot (RU)
DPS............ Double Flip-Flop Circuit (RU)
DPS............ Dzielnica Przemyslowo-Skladowa [*Industrial and warehouse city section*] (POL)
DPS............ Message Center Duty Officer (RU)
dps............ Semiweekly (BU)
DPSP........... Control Tower for Instrument Landing (RU)
DPT............ Devlet Planlama Teskilati [*State Planning Organization*] (TU)
DPT............ Dewan Pimpinan Tjabang [*Branch Executive Council*] (IN)
DPT............ Direct-Current Motor (RU)
DPT............ Division Message Code (RU)
DPT............ Domy Pracy Tworczej [*Houses of Artistic Creation*] (POL)
DPT............ State Tourism Enterprise (BU)
DPTE.......... Directoria de Pesquisa e Ensino Tecnico do Exercito [*Army Directorate of Technical Research and Training*] [*Brazilian*] (LA)
DPTK.......... State Cotton Weaving Combine (BU)
DPTR.......... Diviziske Protivtenkovski Rezerve [*Divisional Antitank Reserves*] (YU)
D -pu.......... Deli-Palyaudvar [*Deli (South) Station (in Budapest)*] (HU)
DPU............ Dispatcher's Control Post (RU)
DP-UDC...... Democracia Popular - Union Democrata Cristiana [*People's Democracy - Christian Democratic Union*] [*Ecuadorean*] (PPW)
DPUT.......... Departemen Pekerdjaan Umum dan Tenaga [*Department of Public Works and Power*] (IN)
DPUV.......... Delostrelectvo Proti Utocne Vozbe [*Anti-Tank Artillery*] (CZ)
DPV............ Democracia Popular Venezolana [*Venezuelan Popular Democratic Movement*] (LA)
DPV............ Dievthinsis Polemikis Viomikhanias [*War Industry Directorate*] (GC1)
dPVO.......... Antiaircraft Defense Division (BU)
DPVRD........ Subsonic Ramjet Engine (RU)
DPYa.......... Dynamic Polarization of a Nucleus (RU)
DPz............ Delostrelecky Pruzkum [*Artillery Reconnaissance*] (CZ)
DPZ............ Pretrial House of Detention (RU)
DPzH.......... Dustojnicke Pruzkumne Hlidky [*Officer Reconnaissance Patrols*] (CZ)
DPZI........... Deutsches Paedagogisches Zentral-Institut [*German Central Teachers' Institute*] (EG)
DPZKh......... State Grain Foods Enterprise (BU)
DPZL.......... Divizni Prostredky Zabezpeceni Letectva [*Aviation Support by Division Resources*] (CZ)
DPzL........... Divizni Pruzkumne Letectvo [*Division Reconnaissance Air Force Units*] (CZ)
DPzLP......... Delostrelecky Pruzkumny Letecky Pluk [*Air Reconnaissance Artillery Regiment*] (CZ)
Dr.............. Choke (RU)
DR.............. Company Duty Officer (RU)
dr............... Comrade (BU)
DR.............. Danmarks Retsforbund [*Justice Party of Denmark*] (PPE)
dr............... Debiteur [*Debtor*] [*French*]
DR.............. Delnicka Rada [*Workers' Council*] (CZ)
dR.............. Der Reserve [*Reserve*] (EG)
dr............... Dernier [*Last*] [*French*]
dR.............. Des Ruhestandes [*German*]
DR.............. Deutsche Reichsbahn [*German State Railways*] (WEN)
DR.............. Deutsche Reichspartei [*German Reich Party*] [*West German*] (PPE)
DR.............. Dilenska Rada [*Shop Council*] (CZ)
d-r.............. Director, Manager (RU)
DR.............. Division de Reserve [*Military*] [*French*] (MTD)
DR.............. Division Reserve (RU)
Dr.............. Docteur [*Doctor*] [*French*] (MTD)
d-r.............. Doctor (BU)
Dr.............. Doctor [*Doctor*] [*Spanish*]
d-r.............. Doctor (RU)
Dr.............. Doktor [*Doctor*] [*German*]
dr............... Doktor [*Doctor*] (HU)
dr............... Doktor [*Doctor*] (POL)
dr............... Doktor [*Doctor*] [*Danish*] (GPO)
d:r.............. Doktor [*Doctor*] [*Swedish*] (GPO)
Dr.............. Doktorat [*German*]
D & R.......... Douanes et Regies [*Customs*] (CL)
DR.............. Double Socket (RU)
Dr.............. Doutor [*Doctor*] [*Portuguese*] (GPO)
dr............... Drive [*Formerly*] (CZ)
dr............... Droit de Souscription [*French*]
dr............... Druk [*Printed Matter*] [*Polish*]
Dr.............. Druzhba [*Friendship*] [*A periodical*] (BU)
dr............... Druzstvo [*Squad (Military); Cooperative (Economic)*] (CZ)
DR.............. Duty Radio Operator, Duty Radioman (RU)
dr............... Fraction (RU)
dr............... Others (RU)
dr............... Others (BU)
DR.............. Radio Broadcasting Directorate (BU)
dra............. Derecha [*Right*] [*Spanish*]
DRA............ Diplome de Recherches Approfondies [*French*]
DRA............ Direction a la Recherche Agronomique (MAR)
Dra............. Doctora [*Doctor (Feminine)*] [*Spanish*] (GPO)
DRA............ Doctoranda [*Doctoral Candidate - Female*] (ML)
d-ra............ Doktora [*Doctor (Feminine)*] (POL)
DRA............ Doktoranda [*Academic title held by women*] (IN)
Dra............. Doutora [*Doctor (Feminine)*] [*Portuguese*] (GPO)
DRA............ Etablissements Devanlay Recoing Afrique (MAR)
DRAE.......... Long-Range Air Reconnaissance Squadron (RU)
Drag........... Dragees [*Dragees*] (EG)
dram........... Dramatic (BU)
dram........... Dramatic (RU)
Dramkruzhok... Drama Circle (BU)
DRAP.......... Decret Portant Reglement d'Administration Publique [*North African*] (MAR)
DRAP.......... Long-Range Air Reconnaissance Regiment (RU)
drb............. Darab [*Piece*] (HU)
DRB............ Deutsche Reichsbahn [*German State Railways*] [*Pre-1945*] [*East German*]
DRB............ Drzavno Recno Brodarstvo [*State River Shipping*] (YU)
DrBdk.......... Doktor der Bodenkultur [*German*]
Drc............. Derece [*Degree, Grade*] (TU)
dr c............ Dernier Cours [*French*]
DRC............ Dutch Reformed Church (MAR)
DRCDF........ Directia Retelei Cinematografice si Difuzarii Filmelor [*Directorate of the Movie Network and Film Distribution*] (RO)
Drchfb......... Durchfuehrungsbestimmung [*Implementing Regulation*] (EG)
DRCM.......... Dutch Reformed Church Mission (MAR)
DRE............ Direction des Relations Exterieures (MAR)
Dre............. Dresden [*One of the eight GDR Reichsbahn directorates*] (EG)
DRE............ Long-Range Reconnaissance Squadron (RU)
DREE.......... Direction des Relations Economiques Exterieures [*French*]
DREF.......... Directia Regionala a Economiei Forestiere [*Regional Directorate of the Forest Economy*] (RO)
DREGRAP... Drzavno Recno-Gradevinsko Preduzece [*State River Construction Establishment*] (YU)
Drehko........ Drehkondensator [*Variable Condenser*] (EG)
drev........... Woodworking Industry Plant [*Topography*] (RU)
DREVAP...... Drzavno Recno Preduzece za Vadenje Potopljenih Objekata [*State River Establishment for Salvage of Submerged Objects*] (YU)
drevn ukr.... Ancient Fortification [*Topography*] (RU)
DRG............ Direction Active des Renseignements Generaux [*Directorate of General Information*] [*French*] (WER)
DRGB.......... German Law Code
drgl............ Dergleichen [*Similar*] [*German*]
DRGM.......... Deutsches-Reichsgebrauchsmuster [*German-Registered Design*]
dr-gr........... Ancient Greek (RU)
dr-grech...... Ancient Greek (RU)
DRH............ Daerah [*Region*] (IN)
DRHA.......... Dar Es Salaam Regional Hockey Association (MAR)
Dr habil....... Doktor (Habilitiert) [*Doctor (Usually Professor)*] (EG)
Dr hc.......... Doctor Honoris Causa [*Honorary Doctor*]
DRI............. Disaster Research Institute (EA)
DRI............. House of Workers in the Arts (RU)
DRI............. Programa de Desarrollo Rural Integrado [*Integrated Rural Development Program*] [*Colombian*] (LA)
DRIA........... Direction Regionale de l'Industrie [*Regional Industrial Directorate*] [*Algerian*] (AF)
DRIL........... Directorio Revolucionario Iberico de Liberta [*Revolutionary Directorate for Iberian Liberation*]
Dr-Ing......... Doktor der Ingenieurwissenschaften [*Doctor of Engineering*] (EG)
DRIPAE....... Direction des Relations Inter-Gouvernementales pour les Aides Exterieures [*Directorate of Intergovernmental Relations for Foreign Aid*] [*Cambodian*] (CL)
Dr iur.......... Doctor Iuris [*Latin*]
Dr iur can.... Doctor Iuris Canonici [*Latin*]
Dr jur.......... Doktor der Rechte [*Doctor of Laws (LLD)*] (EG)
Dr jur utr..... Doktor Beider Rechte [*Doctor of Laws (LLD)*] (EG)
DRK............ Deutsches Rotes Kreuz [*German Red Cross*] [*West German*] (WEN)
DRK............ Far Eastern Revolutionary Committee (RU)
drka............ Battalion of Rocket Boats (BU)
DRKhR........ Radiation and Chemical Reconnaissance Patrol (RU)
DRM............ Deborah Relief Memorial Hospital (MAR)

DRM .... Dewan Revolusioner Malaya [*Malayan Revolutionary Council*] (ML)
DRME .... Direction des Recherches et Moyens d'Essais [*Research and Test Methods Directorate*] [*French*] (WER)
dr med .... Doktor Medycyny [*Doctor of Medicine*] [*Polish*]
Drmeduniv ... Doctor Medicinae Universae [*Latin*]
Dr med vet ... Doctor Medicinae Veterinariae [*Latin*]
Dr mont .... Doctor Rerum Montanarum [*Latin*]
DRN .... Departamento de Recursos Naturais [*Natural Resources Department*] [*Brazilian*] (LA)
DRN .... Dzielnicowa Rada Narodowa [*City Section People's Council*] (POL)
Drnattechn ... Doctor Rerum Naturalium Technicarum [*Latin*]
drn bv .... Duty Officer in Bivouac Area (BU)
DRNK .... Deoxyribonucleic Acid (RU)
drn k .... Officer of the Day (BU)
DRNM .... Directia Regionala a Navigatiei Maritime [*Regional Directorate of Maritime Navigation*] (RO)
DRNT .... Long-Range Radio Navigation Point (RU)
dro .... Derecho [*Right*] [*Spanish*]
DRO .... Dobrudzha Revolutionary Organization (BU)
dro .... Druzstvo s Rucenim Omezenym [*Limited Liability Cooperative*] (CZ)
DRO .... Grinding and Crushing Equipment (RU)
DRO .... Supplementary Workers' Education (RU)
drob fabr ..... Stone Crusher Plant [*Topography*] (RU)
DROM .... Druzstvo pre Obchod Mliekom a Mliecnymi Vyrobkami [*Cooperative for Marketing Milk and Milk Products*] (CZ)
DROT .... Departamento de Relacoes com os Organismos de Trabalho [*Department of Relations with Labor Organizations*] [*Portuguese*] (WER)
drov .... Firewood Yard [*Topography*] (RU)
drozh .... Yeast Plant [*Topography*] (RU)
drp .... And Others, Et Cetera (BU)
DRP .... Democratic Republican Party [*Minchu Kong Hwa Dang*] [*South Korean*] (PPW)
DRP .... Deutsche Rechtspartei [*German Party of the Right*] [*West German*] (PPE)
DRP .... Deutsches Reichs-Patent [*German State Patent*]
DRP .... Dnepr River Steamship Line (RU)
DRP .... Hand-Operated Dynamo (RU)
DRP .... House of Education Workers (RU)
DRP .... Road Repair Station (RU)
Drpaed .... Doctor Paedogogikae [*Doctor of Pedagogy*] (CZ)
Dr pharm ...... Doctor Pharmaciae [*Latin*]
Dr phil .... Doctor Philosophiae [*Latin*]
Dr phil fac theol ... Doctor Philosophiae Facultatis Theologicae [*Latin*]
DRPLC .... Departement des Recherches des Plantations Lever au Congo (MAR)
Dr rer agr .... Doktor der Bodenkultur [*Doctor of Agriculture*] (EG)
Dr rer comm ... Doctor Rerum Commercialium [*Latin*]
Dr rer nat .... Doctor Rerum Naturalium [*Latin*]
Dr rer nat .... Doktor der Naturwissenschaften [*Doctor of Science (DSc, ScD)*] (EG)
Dr rer oec .... Doktor der Wirtschaftswissenschaften [*Doctor of Economic Science*] (EG)
Dr rer pol .... Doctor Rerum Politicarum [*Doctor of Political Science*] [*Latin*]
Dr rer soc oec ... Doctor Rerum Socialium Oeconomicarumque [*Latin*]
DRRS .... Radio Relay Communications Duty Officer (RU)
DRRS .... State Fishing and Fish Breeding Farm (BU)
DRRSM .... Mantissa Sum Register Supplemental Digit (RU)
DRS .... Democratic Republic of the Sudan (MAR)
DRS .... Direction de la Restauration des Sols [*Soil Reclamation Directorate*] [*Algerian*] (AF)
DRS .... Direkcija Recnog Saobracaja [*Administration of River Transport*] (YU)
DRS .... Divisao Regional de Saude [*Regional Health Division*] [*Brazilian*] (LA)
Drs .... Doctorandus [*Academic qualification*]
DRS .... Doktorandus [*Academic title held by men*] (IN)
DRS .... Duty Radioman (RU)
DRS .... Old Russian Dictionary [*A publication*] (RU)
DRS .... Speed Regulator Motor (RU)
DRS .... State Fish Breeding Farm (BU)
DrSc .... Doctor Scientiae [*Doctor of Science*] (CZ)
DRT .... Delegacia [*or Divisao*] Regional do Trabalho [*Regional Labor Headquarters*] [*Brazilian*] (LA)
DRT .... Direction de Recherches Techniques [*Directorate of Technological Research*] [*French*] (WER)
Dr techn ...... Doctor Technicae [*Latin*]
d-r tekhn nauk ... Doctor of Technical Sciences (RU)
Dr theol .... Doctor Theologiae [*Latin*]
DRTS .... Management of a Radio Wire Broadcasting Network (RU)
DR Tv-BUC ... Directia de Radio si Televiziune Bucuresti [*Bucharest Directorate for Radio and Television*] (RO)
DRU .... Direccion Revolucionaria Unificada [*Unified Revolutionary Directorate*] [*Honduran*] (LA1)
DRU .... Direccion Revolucionaria Unificada [*Unified Revolutionary Directorate*] [*Salvadoran*] (LA1)
Druckf-V ..... Druckfehlerverzeichnis [*Table of Errata*] [*German*]
DRUJAT ...... Druzstvo Jatecnich Delniku [*Stockyard Workers' Cooperative*] (CZ)
druk .... Drukarnia [*Printing Shop*] (POL)
druk .... Drukarski [*Printing*] (POL)
druk .... Drukarz [*Printer*] [*Polish*]
druk .... Drukowano [*Printed*] (POL)
DRUKAR ..... Druzstvo Mistru Kartacnickych a Stetkarskych [*Brushmakers' Cooperative*] (CZ)
DRUKOL ..... Druzstvo Kolaru [*Wheelwrights' Cooperative*] (CZ)
DRUO .... Dyrekcja Radiowych Urzadzen Odbiorczych [*Administration of Radio Receiving Installations*] (POL)
DRUPEKA ... Druzstvo Pekaren [*Bakers' Cooperative*] (CZ)
DRV .... Democratic Republic of Vietnam (CL)
DRV .... Dunantuli Rostkikeszito Vallalat [*Fiber Processing Enterprise of Dunantul*] (HU)
DRVN .... Democratic Republic of Vietnam [*Use DRV*] (CL)
dr-vo .... Society, Association, Company (BU)
Dr u Vrl .... Druck und Verlag [*Publisher, Printed and Published By*] [*German*]
DRVV .... Dunantuli Regionalis Vizmu es Vizgazdalkodasi Vallalat [*Transdanubian Regional Water Works and Water Conservation Enterprise*] (HU)
DRW .... Democratic Revolutionary Welfare (MAR)
DRW .... Demokratyczna Republika Wietnamu [*Democratic Republic of Viet-Nam*] [*Polish*]
dRW .... Deutsche Reichswaehrung [*German*]
DRX .... Drachma [*Monetary unit in Greece*]
dr yevr .... Hebrew, Hebraic (RU)
DRZ .... Dienstvorschrift Ueber das Rangierzettelverfahren [*Service Regulations on the Shunting Ticket System*] (EG)
Drzh .... State (BU)
DrzknigNRM ... Drzavno Knigoizdatelstvo na Narodna Republika Makedonija [*Government Publishing House of Macedonia*] (YU)
DS .... Additional Resistance (RU)
DS .... Binary Counter, Binary Scaler (RU)
DS .... Dansk Samling [*Danish Union*] (PPE)
ds .... Das Sind [*That Is, Namely*] [*German*]
DS .... Daylight (RU)
DS .... Daylight (Fluorescent Lamp) (RU)
DS .... Decontamination Station (RU)
DS .... Delavski Svet [*Workers' Council*] (YU)
DS .... Demokraticheska Sgovor [*Democratic Alliance*] [*Bulgarian*] (PPE)
DS .... Demokraticka Strana [*Democratic Party*] [*Czechoslovak*] (PPE)
DS .... Demokratikos Sinaspismos [*Democratic Coalition*] [*Greek*] (PPE)
DS .... Demokratikos Synagermos [*Democratic Rally*] [*Greek Cypriot*] (PPE)
DS .... Demokratischer Sektor [*Democratic Sector*] (EG)
DS .... Differential Selsyn (RU)
DS .... Differential System (RU)
DS .... Dimokratiki Synergasia [*Democratic Cooperation*] (GC)
DS .... Dioikitikon Symvoulion [*Administrative Council*] (GC)
DS .... Diploma de Stat [*Professional qualification*] [*Romanian*]
DS .... Direkcija za Sirovine [*Administration of Raw Materials*] (YU)
Ds .... Disari [*Outside*] (TU)
DS .... Divadelni Soubor [*Theater Ensemble*] (CZ)
ds .... Do Spraw [*For Affairs*] [*Polish*]
Ds .... Doctorat de Specialite [*French*]
DS .... Doctorat de Specialite de Troisieme Cycle [*French*]
Ds .... Doktoratus [*Hungarian*]
DS .... Dom Studencki [*Student's Home*] [*Polish*]
DS .... Dozorci pro Spojeni [*Communications Duty Officer*] (CZ)
DS .... Dry Dock (RU)
DS .... Duty Communications Officer (RU)
DS .... Duty Signal Officer (BU)
DS .... Duty Signalman, Duty Communications Man (RU)
DS .... Far North (RU)
DS .... High Beam [*Vehicles*] (RU)
DS .... House of Soviets (RU)
DS .... Permanent Emplacement, Permanent Installation (RU)
DS .... Signal Transmitter, Signaler (RU)
DS .... Soviet Detergent (RU)
DS .... Special Diesel (Fuel) (RU)
DS .... State Security (BU)
DS .... Synchronous Motor (RU)
DS .... Telecommunication, Long-Distance Traffic (RU)
DS-70 .... Democratische Socialisten [*Democratic Socialist Party*] [*Right-wing party, formed in 1970*] [*Dutch*] (WEN)
DSA .... Career Army Service (BU)
DSA .... Democracia Socialista Asturiana [*Asturian Socialist Democracy*] [*Spanish*] (WER)
DSA .... Deutscher Sport-Ausschuss [*German Sports Committee*] (EG)
DSA .... Die Stimme Afrikas [*Cologne*] [*A publication*] (MAR)
DSA .... Dievthynsis Stratiotikou Arkheiou [*Military Archives Directorate*] [*Greek*] (GC)
DSA .... Dikigorikos Syllogos Athinon [*Athens Bar Association*] (GC)
DSA .... Dimokratiki Syndikalistiki Allagi [*Democratic Labor Change*] [*Greek*] (GC)
DSA .... Diplome Superieur d'Aptitude [*French*]
DSA .... Duplex Synchronous Telegraph (RU)

DSA .... House of the Soviet Army (RU)
DSAA .... Defense Secretary Assistance Agency (MAR)
DSAG .... Deutsch-Suedafrikanische Gesellschaft (MAR)
DSAG Wismut ... Deutsch-Sowjetische Aktiengesellschaft Wismut [*German-Soviet Wismut Corporation*] (EG)
DS-AIK .... Demokratiske Sosialister-Arbeidernes Informasjon Kommitte [*Democratic Socialists-Workers' Information Committee*] [*Norwegian*] (PPE)
DSAP .... State Medical and Pharmaceutical Enterprise (BU)
DSAPC .... Directia de Sistematizare, Arhitectura, si Proiectare a Constructiilor [*Directorate for Systematization, Architecture, and Construction Design*] (RO)
DSAR .... Deutsch-Suedafrikanische Reisebuero (MAR)
dsau .... Battalion of Self-Propelled Guns (RU)
DSB .... Danske Stats Baner [*Danish State Railways*] (WEN)
DSB .... Deutscher Sportbund [*German Sports Association*] (EG)
DSB .... Road-Building Battalion (RU)
DSB .... Wooden Dry-Cargo Barge (RU)
DSBE .... Direkcija za Suzbijanje Bujica i Erozija [*Administration of Flood and Erosion Control*] (YU)
DSBS .... Diviziona Stanica Borbenih Sredstava [*Divisional Station of Combat Supplies*] (YU)
DSC .... Democracia Social Cristiana [*Social Christian Democracy*] [*Spanish*] (WER)
D Sc .... Doctor Scientiae [*Doctor of Science*] [*Latin*] (GPO)
DSCh .... Random Numbers Transducer (RU)
DSD .... Dedinske Spotrebne Druzstvo [*Rural Consumer Cooperative*] (CZ)
DSD- .... Differential Pressure Warning Device (RU)
DSD .... Division Medical Battalion (BU)
Dsdn .... Dresden (EG)
DSDP .... Deep Sea Drilling Project (MAR)
DSDP .... Division Sanitary and Decontamination Station (RU)
DSDR .... State Supply and State Reserve (BU)
DSe .... Absolutely Lethal Dose (RU)
DSE .... Departamento de Seguridad del Estado [*Department of State Security*] [*Cuban*] (LA)
DSE .... Deutsche Stiftung fuer Entwicklungslaender [*German Foundation for Developing Countries*] (EG)
DSE .... Dimokratikos Stratos Ellados [*Democratic Army of Greece*] (GC)
DSEChA ...... Dvizhenie Sotsialnoi Evoliutsii Chernoi Afriki (MAR)
DSEES .... Diethnis Synomospondia Elevtheron Ergatikon Syndikaton [*International Confederation of Free Trade Unions*] (GC)
DSEN .... Dimosios Skholi Emborikou Navtikou [*Public School for the Merchant Marine*] [*Greek*] (GC)
DSEN .... Directia Sistemului de Energie Natonal [*Directorate of the National Power System*] (RO)
DSER .... Road Construction and Maintenance District (RU)
DSF .... Crushing and Sorting Factory (RU)
DSF .... Danske Studerendes Faellesrad [*National Union of Danish Students*] (WEN)
DSF .... [*Gesellschaft fuer*] Deutsch-Sowjetische Freundscraft [*German-Soviet Friendship Society*] (EG)
DSFN .... Democratic Union of the Finnish People (BU)
DSG .... Democratie Socialiste de Guinee (MAR)
DSG .... Deutsche Saatzuchtgesellschaft [*German Seed Growing Company*] (EG)
DSG .... Deutscher Saatgut-Handelsbetrieb [*German Seed Trading Enterprise*] (EG)
DSG .... Diplome Superieur de Gestion [*French*]
DSG .... Division Fuel Depot (RU)
dsgl .... Desgleichen [*Similar*] [*German*]
DSh .... Decoder, Selector (RU)
DSh .... Detonating Cord (BU)
DSh .... Detonating Fuze (RU)
DSH .... Direktion des Seeverkehrs und der Hafenwirtschaft [*Ocean-Going Traffic and Port Management Directorate*] (EG)
DSh .... Staff Duty Officer (RU)
DShI .... Two-Motion Selector [*Telephony*] (RU)
DShK .... Instruction Decoder (RU)
DShS .... Two-Motion System [*Telephony*] (RU)
DShtK .... State Personnel Commission (BU)
DShZ .... Dnepropetrovsk Tire Plant (RU)
DSI .... Children's Social Inspection (RU)
DSI .... Devlet Su Isleri Genel Mudurlugu [*State Hydraulic Affairs Directorate General*] [*Under Ministry of Energy and Natural Resources*] (TU)
DSI .... Diffusion Selective de l'Information [*Selective Distribution of Information*]
DSI .... Difuzare Selectiva a Informatiilor [*Selective Distribution of Information*] (RO)
DSI .... Diplome en Soins Infirmiers [*French*]
DSI .... Directia de Statistica Industriala [*Directorate of Industrial Statistics*] (RO)
DSI .... State Medical Inspectorate (BU)
DSI .... State Stenographic Institute (BU)
DSIP .... Drzavni Sekretarijat za Inostrane Poslove [*State Secretariat for Foreign Affairs*] (YU)
DSIR .... Department of Scientific and Industrial Research [*United Kingdom*]
DSITJ .... Drustvo Sumarskih Inzenjera i Tehnicara Jugoslavije [*Society of Forestry Engineers and Technicians of Yugoslavia*] (YU)
DSIYB .... Devlet Sanayi ve Isci Yatirim Bankasi [*State Industry and Worker Investment Bank*] (TU)
DSJ .... Dunav Sava Jadran [*Danube Sava Adriatic*] (YU)
DSK .... Dacha-Building Cooperative (RU)
DSK .... Demokratikon Sosialistikon Komma [*Democratic Socialist Party*] [*Greek*] (PPE)
DSK .... Diak Sport Kozpont [*Students' Sport Center*] (HU)
DSK .... Dimokratikon Syndikalistikon Kinima [*Democratic Labor Movement*] [*Greek*] (GC)
DSK .... Dokumentacni Stredisko Ceskoslovenskych Zavodu Kovodelnych a Strojirenskych [*Documentation Center of the Czechoslovak Metalworking and Machine-Building Plants*] (CZ)
DSK .... Drustvo Slovenskih Knjizevnikov [*Society of Slovenian Writers*] (YU)
DSK .... House-Building Kombinat (RU)
DSK .... House of Sanitary Culture (RU)
DSK .... State Savings Bank (BU)
d s-kh n .... Doctor of Agricultural Sciences (RU)
DSL .... Collapsible Landing Boat (RU)
dsl .... Deleslouzici [*Reenlistee*] (CZ)
DSM .... Dar Es Salaam [*Tanzania*] (MAR)
DSM .... Dimokratikon Syndikalistikon Metopon [*Democratic Labor Front*] (GC)
DSM .... Direction de la Securite Militaire [*Directorate of Military Security*] [*French*] (WER)
DSM .... State Alcohol Monopoly (BU)
DSM .... Ten-Key Adding Machine (RU)
DSMA .... Desarrollo del Sur de Monagas y Anzoategui [*Development of South Monagas and Anzoategui*] [*Venezuelan*] (LA1)
DSMK .... Democratic Youth League of Korea [*North Korean*] (RU)
DSML .... Delft Soil Mechanics Laboratory (MAR)
DSMO .... State Construction and Installation Trust (BU)
DSN .... Division First Aid Kit (RU)
DSN .... Dodecyl Sodium Sulfate (RU)
DSNED .... Dimokratikos Syndesmos Neon Epistimonon kai Dianooumenon [*Democratic Association of Young Professionals and Intellectuals*] [*Greek*] (GC)
DSNF .... Democratic Union of the People of Finland (RU)
DSNF .... Disjunctive Perfect Normal Form (RU)
DSNKh .... Don Council of the National Economy (RU)
DSNM .... Dimitrov People's Youth League [*Bulgarian People's Republic*] (RU)
DSNM .... Dimitrovski Suiuz na Narodnata Mladesh [*Dimitrov Union of People's Youth*] [*Bulgarian*]
DSNO .... Diakyvernitikos Symvoulevtikos Navtiliakos Organismos [*Intergovernmental Maritime Consultative Organization*] (GC)
DSNO .... Drzavni Sekretarijat Narodne Odbrane [*State Secretariat for National Defense*] (YU)
DSNT .... Demokraticheskii Soiuz Naseleniia Togo (MAR)
DSO .... Democratic Students' Organization (MAR)
DSO .... Diakyvernitikos Symvoulevtikos Organismos [*Intergovernmental Maritime Consultative Organization*] (GC)
DSO .... Differential System with Amplitude Limiter (RU)
DSO .... Dunya Saglik Orgutu [*World Health Organization*] (TU)
DSO .... Road-Building Department (RU)
DSO .... State Construction Trust (BU)
DSO .... State Economic Trust (BU)
DSO .... State Sports Organization (BU)
DSO .... State Symphony Orchestra (BU)
DSO .... Voluntary Civil Defense (BU)
DSO .... Voluntary Sports Organization (BU)
DSO .... Voluntary Sports Society (RU)
DSOMS .... State Construction Trusts of the Ministry of Construction (BU)
DSO Sokol ... Dobrovolna Sportovni Organisace Sokol [*Sokol Athletic Organization*] (CZ)
DSP .... Control Panel of the Station Master on Duty [*Railroads*] (RU)
dsp .... Decessit sine Prole [*Died without Issue*] [*Latin*] (GPO)
DSP .... Democratic Socialist Party [*Minshushakaito*] [*Japanese*] (PPW)
DSP .... Dimokratiki Sosialistiki Parataxi [*Democratic Socialist Faction*] (GC)
DSP .... Direccion de Seguridad Personal [*Directorate of Personal Security*] [*Cuban*] (LA)
DSP .... Direction Active de la Securite Publique [*Directorate of Public Security*] [*French*] (WER)
DSp .... Doctorat Special [*French*]
DSP .... Dom Slowa Polskiego [*Polish Publication and Press Institute*] [*Polish*]
DSP .... Druzstevna Skola Prace [*Agricultural Training School*] (CZ)
DSP .... Duty Station Master [*Railroads*] (RU)
DSP .... Duty Switchman [*Railroads*] (RU)
DSP .... For Official Use (RU)
DSP .... Individual Decontamination Kit (RU)
DSP .... State Construction Enterprise (BU)
DSP .... State Economic Enterprise (BU)
DSP .... State Supply Enterprise (BU)
DSP .... Wood Laminate (RU)

DSPF.......... Drzavni Sekretarijat za Poslove Finansija [*State Secretariat for Finance*] (YU)
DSPNO........ Drzavni Sekretarijat za Poslove Narodne Odbrane [*State Secretariat for National Defense*] (YU)
DSPNOUIJNA ... Drzavni Sekretarijat za Poslove Narodne Odbrane, Uprava Inzenjerije, Jugoslovenska Narodna Armija [*State Secretariat for National Defense, Administration of Engineer Corps, Yugoslav People's Army*] (YU)
DSPRP .... Drzavni Sekretarijat za Poslove Robnog Prometa [*State Secretariat for Trade*] (YU)
DSPU.......... Drzavni Sekretarijat za Pravosodno Upravo [*State Secretariat for the Judiciary*] (YU)
DSPULRS.... Drzavni Sekretarijat za Pravosodno Upravo Ljudska Republika Slovenija [*State Secretariat for the Judiciary of Slovenia*] (YU)
DSPV.......... Division Prisoner-of-War Collecting Point (RU)
DSP "Zemsnab" ... State Economic Enterprise for Compulsory Grain Delivery (BU)
DSQ............ Diplome de Specialiste Qualifie [*French*]
DSR............ Deutsche Seereederei Rostock [*German Maritime Shipping Company, Rostock*] (EG)
DSR............ Road-Building District (RU)
DSRC .... Development Studies and Research Centre (MAR)
DSRF.......... Drzaven Sekretarijat za Raboti na Finansite [*State Secretariat for Finance*] (YU)
DSRK .... DDR [*Deutsche Demokratische Republik*] Schiffsrevision und - Klassifikation [*GDR Ship Inspection and Classification Agency*] (EG)
DSRV.......... Deep Submergence Rescue Vehicle (MAR)
DSS............ Drustvo Slovenskih Skladateljev [*Society of Slovenian Composers*] (YU)
DSS............ Drustvo Srpske Slovesnosti [*Society of Serbian Literature*] (YU)
DSS............ Druzyna Sluzby Socjalistycznej [*Socialist Service Team*] (POL)
DSS............ State Seed Growing Farm (BU)
Dsse............ Duchesse [*Duchess*] [*French*] (MTD)
DSSh.......... Children's Sports School (RU)
DSSO .... Voluntary Rural Sports Society (RU)
DSSV.......... Deutscher Schwimmsport-Verband [*German Swimming League*] (EG)
DST............ Day Construction Technicum (RU)
dst............ Decistere [*Decistere*] [*French*] (GPO)
DST............ Departement des Statistiques de Transport [*Transportation Statistics Department*] [*of the SAEI*] [*French*] (WER)
DST............ Devrimci Sanat Tiyatrosu [*Revolutionary Fine Arts Theatre*] [*Turkish Federated State of Cyprus*] (GC)
DST............ Diethylstilbestrol (RU)
DST............ Direction de la Surveillance du Territoire [*Directorate of Territorial Surveillance*] [*French*] (WER)
DST............ Diretoria dos Servicos de Transito [*Traffic Services Administration*] [*Brazilian*] (LA)
DST............ Dom Srodowisk Tworczych [*House of Creative Art Associations*] (POL)
Dstg............ Dienstgutzug [*Local Service Freight Train*] (EG)
DST I.......... Daerah Swatantra Tingkat I [*See DASWATI I*] (IN)
DST II.......... Daerah Swatantra Tingkat II [*See DASWATI II*] (IN)
Dstp............ Dienstpersonen-Zug [*Service Personnel Train*] (EG)
DSTU.......... Drzavno Sredno Tehnicko Uciliste [*State Secondary Technical School*] (YU)
DSU............ Children's Self-Government (RU)
DSU............ Danmarks Social-Demokratisk Ungdom [*Denmark's Social Democratic Youth*] (WEN)
DSU............ Deutsche Soziale Union [*German Social Union*] [*West German*] (PPW)
DSU............ Deutscher Schiffahrts- und Umschlagbetrieb [*German Water Transport and Transshipping Enterprise*] (EG)
DSU............ Diagnostic Scintillation Unit (RU)
DSU............ Differentiating Smoothing Device (RU)
DSU............ Druzstvo Spojenych Umelcu Divadelnich a Filmovych [*Joint Association of Theater and Motion Picture Artists*] (CZ)
DSU............ Drzavni Statisticki Ured [*State Statistical Office*] (YU)
DSU............ State Construction Administration (BU)
DSUPFNRJ ... Drzavni Sekretarijat za Unutrasnje Poslove Federativna Narodna Republika Jugoslavija [*State Secretariat for Internal Affairs of Yugoslavia*] (YU)
DSUPNRBiH ... Drzavni Sekretarijat za Unutrasnje Poslove Narodne Republike Bosne i Hercegovine [*State Secretariat for Internal Affairs of the People's Republic of Bosnia and Hercegovina*] (YU)
DSV............ Deutscher Schriftstellerverband [*German Writers' Union*] (EG)
DSV............ Deutscher Sportverband [*German Sports Union*] (EG)
DSV............ Duty Communication Officer [*or Noncommissioned Officer*] (BU)
DSVR.......... Drzaven Sekretarijat za Vnutrasnji Raboti [*State Secretariat for Internal Affairs*] (YU)
DSVTI.......... Division Materiel Depot (RU)
DSW............ Deutsche Solvay-Werke [*German Solvay Works*] (EG)
DSW............ Dom Sprzedazy Wysylkowej [*Mail Order House (Lodz)*] (POL)
DSZ............ House of Socialist Agriculture (RU)
DSZAI.......... Demokraticheskii Soiuz Zashchity Afrikanskikh Interesov (MAR)
DSZE.......... Dunantuli Szojatermelesi Egyutt-Mukodes [*Transdanubian Soya Bean Growing Cooperation*] (HU)
DSZPNP...... Drzavni Sekretarijat za Poslove Narodne Privrede [*State Secretariat for National Economic Affairs*] (YU)
DSZT.......... Dorogi Szenbanyaszati Troszst [*Coal Mining Trust of Dorog*] (HU)
DSZTP........ Delavski Svet, Zeleznisko Transportno Podjetje [*Workers' Council, Railroad Transport Establishment*] (YU)
DT............... Daily Times [*Lagos*] [*A publication*] (MAR)
Dt .... Dato (ML)
Dt .... Debit [*or Debiteur*] [*Debit or Debtor*]
D-t.............. Debit (RU)
DT............... Degtyarev Tank (Machine Gun) (RU)
DT............... Delovodski Tehnikum [*Technology for Foremen*] (YU)
Dt .... Dentist [*German*]
DT............... Deputies of the Working People (BU)
dt............... Derleme Tarihi [*Date Assembled or Collected*] (TU)
DT............... Desetinne Trideni [*Decimal Classification System*] (CZ)
dt............... Deutsch [*German*]
Dt .... Dezitonne [*Deciton*] [*100 kilograms (of grain)*] (EG)
DT............... Diesel Fuel, Diesel Tractor (RU)
DT............... Dinar Tunisien (MAR)
DT............... Diplomatic Corps (BU)
DT............... Diplome Technique [*French*]
DT............... Direktni Teretni Vlak [*Direct Freight Train*] (YU)
Dt .... Dis Tabibi [*Dentist*] (TU)
dt............... Doit [*French*]
DT............... Droit de Timbre [*Stamp Duty*] [*Cambodian*] (CL)
DT............... Fuel-Supply Motor (RU)
dt............... Gas-Expansion Machine (RU)
DT............... Hybrid Transformer, Hybrid Coil [*Telephony*] (RU)
DT............... Labor Directorate (BU)
DT............... Temperature Transmitter, Temperature Gauge, Temperature-Sensing Element (RU)
DTA............ Demokratiese Turnhalle Alliansie [*Democratic Turnhalle Alliance*] [*Namibian*] (AF)
DTA............ Diethnis Tameion Anaptyxeos [*International Development Fund*] (GC)
DTA............ Diethnis Trapeza Anasyngrotiseos [*International Bank for Reconstruction and Development*] [*See also DTAA*] (GC)
DTA............ Differential Thermal Analysis (BU)
DTA............ Differential Thermal Analysis (RU)
DTA............ Diploma in Tropical Agriculture [*British*]
DTA............ Direccao dos Transportes Aereos [*Air Transport Directorate*] [*Angolan*] (AF)
DTA............ Divisao de Transportes Aereos (MAR)
DTA............ Drzavna Trgovacka Akademija [*State Commercial Academy*] (YU)
DTA............ Dynameis Takheias Anaptyxeos [*Rapid Deployment Forces*] [*See also KAD, MMAD*] (GC1)
DTAA .... Diethnis Trapeza Anasyngrotiseos kai Anaptyxeos [*International Bank for Reconstruction and Development*] [*See also DTA*] (GC)
DTB............ Danmarks Tekniske Bibliotek
DTB............ Dogan Turk Birligi [*Arising Turkish Union*] [*Soccer team*] [*Turkish Cypriot*] (GC)
DTC............ Development Technology Center [*Indonesian*]
DTC............ Diplome de Technicien de Laboratoire [*French*]
DTCA.......... Direction Technique des Constructions Aeronautiques [*Directorate for Technical Aeronautical Construction*] [*French*] (WER)
DTCF.......... Ankara Universitesi Dil ve Tarih-Cografya Fakultesi [*Faculty of Language and History-Geography of Ankara University*] (TU)
DTCh.......... Two-Tone Frequency Telegraphy (RU)
DTCN .... Direction Technique de Construction Navale [*Technical Directorate for Naval Construction*] [*French*] (WER)
DTD............ Dekorasie voor Trouwe Dienst (MAR)
dtD .... Des Technischen Dienstes [*German*]
DTD............ Dunav-Tisa-Dunav (Kanal) [*Danube-Tisza-Danube (Canal)*] [*Vojvodina*] (YU)
D-T-D .... Money-Commodity-Money (RU)
DTE .... Departamento de Trabajadores Estatales [*Department of Government Workers*] [*Uruguayan*] (LA)
DTE .... Direction Technique des Engins [*Missile Technology Directorate*] [*French*] (WER)
DTEVT......... Department of Technical Education and Vocational Training [*Zambian*] (AF)
DTF .... Dessolo Traore Freres (MAR)
DTG............ Deutsche Togo Gesellschaft (MAR)
DTGM.......... Devlet Tiyatrosu Genel Mudurlugu [*State Theatre Directorate General*] (TU)
DTH............ Dom Techniczno-Handlowy [*Engineering Trade House*] (POL)
DTH Ith........ Dis Ticaret Hacmi ve Ithalat [*Foreign Trade Volume and Imports*] (TU)
DThKM........ Dievthynsis Thalassion Kratikon Metaforon [*State Maritime Transport Directorate*] [*Greek*] (GC)
DThM .... Dievthynsis Thalassion Metaforon [*Maritime Transport Administration*] [*Greek*] (GC)
DTI .... Departamento Tecnico de Investigaciones [*Technical Investigation Department*] [*Cuban*] (LA)

DTI .... State Trade Inspectorate (BU)
DTIA .... Direction Technique et Industrielle de l'Aeronautique [*Aeronautics Technical-Industrial Directorate*] [*French*] (WER)
DTIH .... Deutsche Togolandische Industrie und Handelgesellschaft GmbH (MAR)
DTIP .... Departamento do Trabalho Ideologico do Partido [*Department of Party Ideological Propaganda*] [*Mozambican*] (AF)
DTJ .... Delnicka Telocvicna Jednota [*Workers' Gymnastic Association*] (CZ)
DTK .... Motor Torpedo Boat Division (RU)
DTK .... State Textile Combine (BU)
DTK .... State Tobacco Combine (BU)
DTK .... State Weaving Combine (BU)
DTKA .... Battalion of Torpedo Boats [*PT boats*] (BU)
dtka .... Motor Torpedo Boat Division (RU)
DTLS .... Diode-Transformer Logical Circuit (RU)
DTM .... Diploma in Tropical Medicine (MAR)
DTM .... Ditolylmethane (RU)
DTM .... Druhotne Tezebni Metody [*Secondary Mining Methods*] (CZ)
DTM .... Duplex Morse Telegraphy (RU)
DTM .... State Tobacco Monopoly (BU)
dtn .... Desitonni(a) [*Finnish*]
dtn .... Doctor of Technical Sciences (RU)
DTO .... Drustvo za Telesni Odgoj [*Physical Education Society*] (YU)
DTO .... Road Transportation Department (RU)
DTO .... State Commercial Trust (BU)
DTO .... Streetcars and Lighting Directorate (BU)
DTP .... State Commercial Enterprise (BU)
DTPA .... Diethylenetriaminopentaacetic Acid (RU)
DTPK .... Diethylenetriaminopentaacetic Acid (RU)
DTP Narmag ... "People's Store" State Commercial Enterprise (BU)
DTPP .... State Tourist Passenger Shipping Administration (BU)
DTR .... Domaca Tvornica Rublja [*Underclothing Manufacturer*] [*Zagreb*] (YU)
DTR .... Druzina Tipografskih Radenika [*Society of Typographers*] (YU)
DTR .... Long-Distance Tropospheric Propagation (RU)
DTRD .... Ducted-Fan Turbine Engine, Turbo-Fan (RU)
DTRT .... Duna-Tenger Hajozasi Reszvenytarsasag [*Danube-Ocean Navigation Company Limited (Prewar)*] (HU)
DTs .... Cement Batcher (RU)
DTs .... Deoxycytidine (RU)
DTs .... Differentiating Circuit (RU)
DTS .... Diplome de Technicien Superieur [*French*]
DTS .... Direction des Travaux et Services [*North African*] (MAR)
DTs .... Dispatcher Center (BU)
DTs .... Dispatcher Controlled Signals, Central Traffic Control, Centralized Dispatching Control [*Railroads*] (RU)
DTS .... Divadlo Tesinskeho Slezska [*Silesian (Tesin Area) Theater*] (CZ)
DTS .... Diviziska Triazna Stanica [*Divisional Discarding Station*] [*Military*] (YU)
DTS .... Droits de Tirage Special [*Special Drawing Rights*] [*Use SDR*] (AF)
DTS .... Road Transportation Council (RU)
DTS .... Road Transportation Service (RU)
DTS- .... Twin-Arc Welding Tractor (RU)
DTSB .... Deutscher Turn- und Sportbund [*German Gymnastics and Sports Federation*] (EG)
dt(sch) .... Deutsch [*German*] (EG)
DTsDA .... Dicyandiamide, Dicyanodiamide (RU)
DTS GK .... [*A*] Mixture of Three Parts of Calcium Hypochlorite and Two Parts of Calcium Hydroxide [*Decontaminant*] (RU)
DTSh .... State Theater School (BU)
DTShch .... Minesweeper Division (RU)
DTsIK .... Central Executive Committee of Dagestan ASSR (RU)
DTsK .... State Cement Combine (BU)
D-ts/ka .... Debit Account (BU)
DTSS .... Diplome de Technicien Superieur de la Sante [*French*]
DTsV .... Decimetric Waves (RU)
DTsZ .... State Cement Plant (BU)
DTTV .... Deutscher Tischtennis-Verband [*German Table-Tennis League*] (EG)
DTU .... Road Transportation Administration (RU)
DTuV .... Deutscher Turn-Verband [*German Gymnastics League*] (EG)
DTV .... Deutsche Treuhand-Verwaltung [*German Trusteeship Administration*] (EG)
DTV .... Drustvo za Telesno Vaspitanje [*Physical Education Society*] (YU)
DTVF .... Danmarks Teknisk-Videnskabelige Forskningsrad [*Danish Council for Technical and Scientific Research*] (WEN)
DTVS .... Dny Telesne Vychovy a Sportu [*Physical Education and Sport Days*] (CZ)
dt v sl .... Active Military Service (BU)
DTYN .... Dievthynsis Tekhnikis Ypiresias Nomou [*Directorate of the Technical Services of the Nome*] [*Plus initial letter of the nome*] (GC)
DTZ .... Drustvo Tehnike Zavarivanja [*Society of Welding Technology*] (YU)
Dtz .... Dutzend [*Dozen*] (EG)
Dtzd .... Dutzend [*Dozen*] [*German*] (GPO)
DU .... Additional Amplifier, Booster (RU)
DU .... Decoder (RU)
DU .... Defensa Universitaria [*University Defense*] [*Spanish*] (WER)
DU .... Delostrelecke Uciliste [*Artillery Training Center*] (CZ)
du .... Delutan [*After Noon*] [*Hungarian*] (GPO)
DU .... Demokratisk Ungdom [*Democratic Youth*] [*Swedish*] (WEN)
DU .... Deutsche Union [*German Union*] [*West German*] (EG)
DU .... Differential Amplifier (RU)
DU .... Direccion Unificada [*Unified Directorate*] [*Salvadoran*] (LA1)
DU .... Disciplinary Regulations (of the Armed Forces of the USSR) (RU)
DU .... Dispatch Control Unit (RU)
DU .... Dispatcher Control [*Railroads*] (RU)
DU .... Diyarbakir Universitesi [*Diyarbakir University*] (TU)
DU .... Dozorci Utvaru [*Regimental Duty Officer*] (CZ)
du .... Dulout [*Farm Road*] (HU)
DU .... Dum Umelcu [*House of Artists*] [*Prague*] (CZ)
Du .... Durak [*Railroad Stop*] (TU)
DU .... Dzielnica Urzedowa [*Government Building City District*] (POL)
DU .... House Installation, Home Wiring [*Telephony*] (RU)
DU- .... Level Transmitter (RU)
DU .... Remote Control, Remote Handling (RU)
DU .... Remote Indicator (RU)
DU .... Road Administration (RU)
DU .... Road Section (RU)
DUAA .... Dakar Universite Faculte de Droit et des Sciences Economiques Annales Africaines [*Paris*] [*A publication*] (MAR)
DUBAL .... Dubai Aluminum Company (ME)
DUBES .... Duta Besar [*Ambassador*] (IN)
dubl .... Duplicate (BU)
DUC .... Dakar University Club (MAR)
DUC .... Devlet Uretme Ciftligi Genel Mudurlugu [*State Stud Farm Directorate General*] (TU)
DUC .... Devlet Uretme Ciftlikleri Genel Mudurlugu [*State Stud Farms Directorate General*] [*Turkish Cypriot*] (TU)
DuchFAN .... State Higher School for Financial and Administrative Studies (BU)
DUEB .... Diplome Universitaire d'Etudes Biologiques [*French*]
DUEE .... Diplome Universitaire d'Etudes Economiques [*French*]
DUEG .... Diplome Universitaire d'Etudes Generales [*French*]
DUEG .... Diplome Universitaire d'Etudes de Gestion [*French*]
DUEJ .... Diplome Universitaire d'Etudes Juridiques [*French*]
DUEL .... Diplome Universitaire d'Etudes Litteraires [*University Literary Studies Diploma*] [*French*] (CL)
DUEPS .... Diplome Universitaire d'Education Physique et Sportive [*French*]
DUES .... Diplome Universitaire d'Etudes Scientifiques [*University Scientific Studies Diploma*] [*French*] (CL)
DUES .... Diplome Universitaire d'Etudes Superieures [*French*] (MAR)
DUET .... Diplome Universitaire d'Etudes Technologiques [*French*]
DUF .... Dansk Ungdoms Faellesrad [*Joint Council of Danish Youth*] (WEN)
DUI .... State Information Administration (BU)
Duk .... Dukkan [*Shop, Store*] (TU)
DUKhI .... Donets Institute of Coal Chemistry (RU)
DULMO .... Diplome Universitaire de Lettres Modernes [*French*]
DUMA .... Dubai Marine Areas Ltd. (ME)
DUN .... Dockworkers Union of Nigeria (MAR)
Dunantul .... Transdanubia (HU)
DUNATIM .... Dunavolgyi Timfold Ipar (Magyar-Szovjet Bauxit-Aluminium Reszvenytarsasag) [*Danube Valley Bauxite Industry (Hungarian-Soviet Bauxite-Aluminum Limited)*] (HU)
DUND .... Drzavna Uprava Narodnih Dobara [*State Administration of National Property*] (YU)
DUP .... Delnicke Ustredni Podniky [*Central Workers' Enterprises*] (CZ)
DUP .... Democratic Unification Party [*Minjutongil Dang*] [*South Korean*] (PPW)
DUP .... Democratic Unionist Party [*Sudanese*] (PD)
DUP .... Remote Perforator Control (RU)
DUP .... Ulster Democratic Unionist Party [*Northern Ireland*] (PPW)
Dupdo .... Duplicado [*Duplicate*] [*Spanish*]
durchschn ... Durchschnittlich [*On the Average*] [*German*]
DURICAM ... Durisotti Cameroun (MAR)
DURP .... Dnepr River Steamship Line Administration (RU)
DURT .... Dnepr Administration of River Transportation (RU)
Durzh izd .... State Publication (BU)
Durzh k-vo ... State Publishing House (BU)
Durzh pech ... Government Printing Office (BU)
Durzh v .... Durzhaven Vestnik [*State Gazette*] (BU)
Durzh v-k br ... State Gazette Issue Number (BU)
Durzh voen izd ... State Military Publishing House (BU)
DUS .... Defense de l'Unite Senegalaise (MAR)
DUS .... Diplome Universitaire de Sciences [*French*]
DUS .... Droit Unique de Sortie (MAR)
DUS .... Spin-Rate Meter (RU)
DUS .... Supplementary Drift Angle (RU)
DUSJEG .... Diplome Universitaire de Sciences Juridiques, Economiques, et de Gestion [*French*]
DUSO .... Dar Es Salaam University Student Organization [*Tanzanian*] (AF)
dust .... Dustojnik [*Officer*] [*Military*] (CZ)

DUSvK .... Sv. Kiril Slavyanobulgarski State University in Varna (BU)
DUT .... Diplome Universitaire de Technologie [*French*]
Dutz .... Dutzend [*Dozen*] [*German*]
DUV .... Demokratisk Ungdoms Varldsfederation [*World Federation of Democratic Youth*] [*Swedish*] (WEN)
DUV .... Dunai Vasmu [*Danube Iron Works*] (HU)
duv .... Duverne [*Confidential*] [*Document Classification*] (CZ)
duv .... Duvernik [*Trustee*] (CZ)
Duz .... Duzelten [*Corrected*] (TU)
DUZN .... Drustvo na Umetnicite, Zurnalistite, i Naucnicite [*Society of Artists, Journalists, and Scientists*] (YU)
DUZSAN ..... Duzce Birlik Orman Urunleri Sanayi ve Ticaret AS [*Duzce (of Bolu Province) United Forest Products Industry and Trade Corp.*] (TU)
DV .... Airborne Force (RU)
dv .... Binary, Double, Dual (Number), Twin (RU)
DV .... Dalekovod [*Long-Distance Transmission Line*] (YU)
DV .... Decontaminating Agents [*Military*] (BU)
dv .... Den Yngre [*Junior*] [*Swedish*] (GPO)
DV .... Deo Volente [*God Willing*] [*Latin*] (GPO)
d/v .... Dias Vista [*Days Sight*] [*Spanish*]
Dv .... Dienstvorschriften [*Service Regulations*] [*Railroad police*] (EG)
DV .... Dilensky Vybor [*Factory Shop Committee*] (CZ)
Dv .... Direct Fire Range, Point-Blank Range (RU)
Dv .... Division [*Military*] (BU)
Dv .... Doktor Ved [*Czechoslovak*]
DV .... Domaci Vysetrovani [*House Arrest*] (CZ)
DV .... Domovy Vychovy [*Reform Schools*] (CZ)
DV .... Druzstevni Vestnik [*Cooperative Bulletin*] (CZ)
DV .... Dunai Vasmu [*Danube Iron Works*] (HU)
DV .... Durchfuehrungsverordnung [*Implementing Regulation*] (EG)
DV .... Durzhaven Vestnik [*State Gazette*] (BU)
DV .... Far East (RU)
Dv .... Farm [*Topography*] (RU)
DV .... Long Waves (BU)
DV .... Long Waves (RU)
DV .... Smoke Agent, Toxic Smoke Agent (RU)
DV .... Smoke Agents [*Military*] (BU)
DV .... Vibration Transducer, Vibration Pickup (RU)
DVA .... Deutsche Versicherungs-Anstalt [*German Insurance Institute*] (EG)
DVA .... Deutsche Verwaltungsakademie [*German Management Academy*] (EG)
DVA .... Distribuidora Venezolana de Azucares [*Venezuelan Sugar Distributing Enterprise*] (LA)
DVA .... Divinylacetylene (RU)
DVB .... Divinylbenzene (RU)
DVB .... Divinylbutyral (RU)
DVB .... Diviziska Veterinarska Bolnica [*Divisional Veterinary Hospital*] (YU)
Dvbr .... State Gazette Number (BU)
DV-CENTRO ... Delegacia de Vigilancia-Centro [*Vigilance Center Headquarters*] [*Brazilian*] (LA)
DVD .... Deutscher Veranstaltungsdienst [*German Service for Organized Events*] (EG)
DVD .... Dobrovoljno Vatrogasno Drustvo [*Society of Volunteer Firemen*] (YU)
DVD .... Dytiko-Voreio-Dytikos [*West-Northwest*] (GC)
dVerf .... Der Verfasser [*The Author*] (EG)
DVF .... Dnepr Naval Flotilla (RU)
DVF .... Far Eastern Branch of the Academy of Sciences, USSR (RU)
DVF .... Far Eastern Front [*1945*] (RU)
DVFAN .... Far Eastern Branch of the Academy of Sciences, USSR (RU)
dvg .... Internal Combustion Engine (BU)
DVGI .... Far Eastern Mining Institute (RU)
DVGU .... Far Eastern State University (RU)
DVGW .... Deutscher Verein Gas- und Wasserfachmaenner [*German Society of Gas and Water Technologists*] [*German*]
DVI .... Standard Time-Interval Pulse-Generating Unit (RU)
DVI .... State Air Navigation Inspectorate (BU)
DVI .... State Military Publishing House (BU)
DVIEV .... Far Eastern Institute of Experimental Veterinary Science (RU)
DVJ .... Dobrovoljacka Vojska Jugoslavije [*Volunteer Army of Yugoslavia*] [*World War II*] (YU)
DVK .... Druckerei- und Verlagskontor [*Printing and Publishing Office*] (EG)
DVK .... Far Eastern Kray (RU)
dv kh .... Double Stroke (RU)
DVKhL .... Long-Wave Chlorophyll (RU)
DVKNII .... Far Eastern Kray Scientific Research Institute (RU)
DVL .... Delostrelecke Vyzbrojovani Letectva [*Artillery Arming of Aviation (or Aircraft)*] (CZ)
DVL .... Deutsche Versuchsanstalt fuer Luft- und Raumfahrt [*German Air and Space Travel Research Institute*] [*West German*] (WEN)
Dvlt Mues .... Devlet Muessese [*Government Agency*] (TU)
DVM .... Domovy Vychovy Mladeze [*Reform Schools*] (CZ)
dvn .... Doctor of Military Sciences (RU)
dvn .... Doctor of Veterinary Sciences (RU)
DVN .... Two-Rotor Vacuum Pump (RU)
DVNIGMI ..... Far Eastern Hydrometeorological Scientific Research Institute (RU)
DVNIISKh .... Far Eastern Scientific Research Institute of Agriculture (RU)
DVO .... Air-Cooled Engine (RU)
d-vo .... Association, Society, Company (BU)
d-vo .... Drustvo [*Society*] (YU)
DVO .... Durchfuehrungsverordnung [*Implementing Decree*] (EG)
DVO .... Far Eastern Military District (RU)
DVO .... Far Eastern Oblast (RU)
DVO .... Far Eastern Review [*A publication*] (RU)
DVO .... House of Extramural Education (RU)
DVOS .... Far Eastern Railroad (RU)
DVP .... Demokratische Volkspartei [*Democratic People's Party*] [*West German*] (PPE)
DVP .... Deutsche Volkspartei [*German People's Party (1919-1933)*] (PPE)
DVP .... Deutsche Volkspolizei [*German People's Police*] (EG)
DVP .... Druzstevni Vinarske Podniky [*Cooperative Wine Enterprises*] (CZ)
DVP .... Wood Fiber Slabs (RU)
DVPI .... Far Eastern Polytechnic Institute Imeni V. V. Kuybyshev (RU)
dv pl .... Twinning Plane (RU)
DVR .... Far Eastern Republic [*1920-1922*] (RU)
DVR .... Van Riebeeck Decoration (MAR)
DVRP .... Two-Channel Visual Radio Direction Finder (RU)
dvs .... Det Vil Si [*That Is*] [*Norwegian*] (GPO)
dvs .... Det Vil Sige [*That Is*] [*Danish*] (GPO)
dvs .... Det Vill Saga [*That Is*] [*Swedish*] (GPO)
DVS .... Division Clothing and Equipment Depot (RU)
DVS .... House of Veterans of the Stage Imeni M. G. Savina (RU)
DVS .... Internal Combustion Engine (RU)
DVSSh- .... Self-Propelled Chassis with an Air-Cooled Diesel (RU)
Dvst .... Dienstvorsteher [*Stationmaster*] (EG)
DvstV .... Dienstvorsteher Vertreter [*Deputy Stationmaster*] (EG)
Dvt .... Deadweight (RU)
DVTeatrU .... State Higher Theater School (BU)
DVTK .... State Wool Weaving Combine (BU)
DVTK .... State Woolen Textiles Combine (BU)
DVTLRS ...... Drustvo za Varilno Tehniko Ljudska Republika Slovenija [*Slovenian Society for Welding Technology*] [*Ljubljana*] (YU)
DVTU .... Far Eastern Territorial Administration (RU)
DVTU .... State Higher Theater School (BU)
DVU .... Deutsche Volksunion [*German People's Union*] [*West German*] (PD)
DVU .... Drevarsky Vyskumny Ustav [*Lumber Research Institute*] (CZ)
DVU .... Far Eastern University (RU)
DVU .... High-Level Discriminator (RU)
DVUFAN ...... State Higher School of Finance and Administration (BU)
dvukhned .... Fortnightly, Two-Week (RU)
Dvumes .... Bimonthly (BU)
dvupr .... Birefringence (RU)
DVV .... Debreceni Villamosvasut Vallalat [*Electric Railroad Enterprise of Debrecen*] (HU)
DVV .... Dvojni Vatreni Val [*Dual Firing Wave*] [*Military*] (YU)
DVV .... High Explosive, Blasting Agent (RU)
DVW .... Deutscher Verlag fuer Wissenschaften [*German Scientific Publishing House*] (EG)
DVZ .... State Railroad Car Plant (BU)
DW .... Deutsche Welle [*Deutsche Welle (Overseas Radio)*] [*West German*] (WEN)
DW .... Doktor der Wissenschaften [*German*]
Dw .... Dworzec [*Railway Station*] [*Polish*]
DWA .... Deutsche Waren-Abnahme Gesellschaft [*German Commodity Acceptance Company*] (EG)
DWB .... Deutsch West-Afrikanische Bank (MAR)
DWBV .... Deutscher Wanderer- und Bergsteigerverband [*German Hiking and Mountain-Climbing League*] (EG)
DWC .... Development Works Corporation [*Mauritian*] (AF)
DWD .... De Wet Decoration (MAR)
DWD .... Dom Wczasow Dzieciecych [*Children's Vacation House*] (POL)
DWHG .... Deutsch-Westafrikanische Handelsgesellschaft (MAR)
DWI .... Deutsches Wirtschaftsinstitut [*German Economics Institute*] (EG)
dWiD .... Des Wirtschaftsdienstes [*German*]
DWIKORA ... Dwi Komando Rakjat [*Two Commands of the People (Refers to confrontation with Malaysia)*] (IN)
DWK .... Deutsche Wirtschaftskommission [*German Economic Commission*] (EG)
DWLot .... Dowodztwo Wojsk Lotniczych [*Air Force Command*] [*Polish*]
DWM .... Deutsche Waffen- und Munitionsfabriken [*Name of German armament company*] [*World War II*]
DWME .... Division of World Mission and Evangelism (MAR)
DWP .... Deutsches Wirtschaftspatent [*German Industrial Patent*] (EG)
DWP .... Dom Wojska Polskiego [*House of the Polish Army*] (POL)
DWS .... Diplomatic Wives Society [*Sudanese*] (MAR)
DWStK .... Deutsche Waffen Stillstandkommission [*German Armistice Commission, in France*] [*World War II*]
DWT .... Ded Wate Tonluk [*Dead Weight Tons*] [*As in rail or maritime transport*] (TU)
dwt .... Denarius Weight [*Pennyweight*] [*Latin*] (GPO)

dwumies ..... Dwumiesiecznik [*Bimonthly Publication*] [*Polish*]
DWUN .... Dock Workers Union of Nigeria (MAR)
dwustr......... Dwustronny [*Two-Sided*] [*Polish*]
dwuszp .... Dwuszpaltowy [*Two-Column*] [*Polish*]
dwutyg .... Dwutygodnik [*Fortnightly Publication*] [*Polish*]
DWV .... Deutsche Warenvertriebsgesellschaft [*German Commodity Trading Company*] (EG)
DY .... Dimosia Ypiresia [*Civil Service*] (GC)
DY .... Dimosios Ypallilos [*Civil Servant*] (GC)
DYaER......... Electron-Nuclear Double Paramagnetic Resonance (RU)
DYB .... Devlet Yatirim Bankasi [*State Investment Bank*] (TU)
DYDM.......... Devlet Yayinlari Dokumantasyon Merkezi [*State Publications Documentation Center*] [*Under Ministry of Culture*] (TU)
DYe .... Capacity Transducer, Capacity Pickup (RU)
DYeP .... Transfer Unit Length (RU)
DYF-Is .... Turkiye Demiryollari Isci Sendikalar Federasyonu [*Federation of Turkish Railway Worker Unions*] [*See also DYI-Is*] (TU)
DYI-Is .... Demiryollari Isci Sendikalari Federasyonu [*Federation of Railway Worker Unions*] [*See also DYF-Is*] (TU)
DYK .... Dynameis Ypovrykhion Katastrofon [*Underwater Demolition Forces*] [*Greek*] (GC)
DYKFE .... Dimokratiki Yperkommatiki Kinisi Foititon Ellados [*Democratic Supra-Party Movement of Greek Students*] (GC)
DYKO .... Dievthinsis Ypiresion Koinovoulevtikis Omados [*Directorate of Parliamentary Group Services (Parliamentary liaison to the premier)*] (GC1)
DYMD.......... Demiryolu Memurlari Dernegi [*Railway Employees Organization*] (TU)
DYMM .... Dulian Yang Maha Mulia [*His Majesty*] (ML)
dympribor... Smoke Generator (RU)
dymzavesa ... Smoke Screen (RU)
DYO............. Durmus Yasar ve Ogullari [*Durmus Yasar and Sons Paint Company*] [*Subsidiary of Yasar Holding Corp.*] (TU)
dyon .... Dywizjon [*Unit or Wing*] [*Polish*]
DYOO .... Deneme Yuksek Ogretmen Okulu [*Experimental Advanced Normal (Teacher's) School*] (TU)
dypl .... Dyplomacja [*or Dyplomatyczny*] [*Diplomacy or Diplomatic*] [*Polish*]
dypl .... Dyplomowany [*Certified*] [*Polish*]
dyr............... Dyrekcja [*Administration, Directorate*] (POL)
dyr............... Dyrektor [*Director*] (POL)
DYuBKh ...... South Bulgarian Painters' Union (BU)
dyun .... Doctor of Laws (RU)
dyuzh .... Dozen (RU)
DZ................ Algeria [*Two-letter standard code*] (CNC)
DZ................ Delavska Zdruzenja [*Workers' Association*] (YU)
Dz .... Deniz [*Sea, Navy*] (TU)
d-z............... Diagnosis (RU)
DZ................ Dipole Sounding (RU)
DZ................ Direkcija Jugoslovenskih Zeleznica [*Administration of Yugoslav Railroads*] (YU)
DZ................ Divadelni Zatva [*Theatrical Harvest Festival*] (CZ)
DZ................ Divisional, Division (BU)
dz .... Doppelzentner [*100 Kilograms*] (EG)
Dz .... Drustveni Zivot [*Social Life*] [*Sarajevo*] [*A periodical*] (YU)
DZ................ Drzavne Zeleznice [*State Railroads*] (YU)
DZ................ Dusanov Zakonik [*Code of the Emperor Dusan*] (YU)
Dz .... Duzine [*Dozen*] (TU)
Dz .... Dywizja Zmechanizowana [*Mechanized Division*] (POL)
dz .... Dzien [*The Day*] [*Polish*]
dz .... Dziennie [*A Day*] [*Polish*]
dz .... Dziennik [*Daily*] (POL)
DZ................ Shutter Motor (RU)
DZ................ Smoke Screen (BU)
DZ................ Smoke Screen (RU)
DZ................ Winter Diesel (Fuel) (RU)
DZA .... Algeria [*Three-letter standard code*] (CNC)
Dza .... Denizalti [*Submarine*] (TU)
DZA .... Deutsches Zentralinstitut fuer Arbeitsmedizin [*German Central Institute for Labor Medicine*] (EG)
DZAG .... Division Antiaircraft Artillery Group (RU)
Dz Alb .... Deniz Albay [*Navy Captain*] (TU)
Dzauges...... Dzaudzhikau Hydroelectric Power Plant (RU)
DZB .... Dzial Zaopatrzenia Bibliotek [*Department of Library Supply*] (POL)
DZBANK ..... Denizcilik Bankasi Turk Anonim Ortakligi [*Turkish Maritime Bank Corporation*] (TU)
DZBM .... Dzielnicowy Zarzad Budynkow Mieszkalnych [*City Section Administration of Apartment Houses*] (POL)
DZBMPW .... Dolnoslaskie Zaklady Budowlano-Montazowe Przemyslu Weglowego [*Lower Silesia Construction and Assembly Establishments of the Coal Industry*] (POL)
DZBUP .... Dolnoslaskie Zaklady Budowy Urzadzen Przemyslowych [*Lower Silesia Industrial Equipment Construction Plant*] (POL)
DZBZ........... Dukelske Zavody Branne Zdatnosti [*Dukla Military Fitness Contest*] (CZ)
Dzd.............. Dutzend [*Dozen*] [*German*]
DZD .... State Cattle Farm (BU)
DZF .... Deutsche Zentrale fuer Filmforschung [*German Center for Film Research*] (EG)
DZFS........... Dmitrov Milling Machine Plant (RU)
DZGI............ Donets Mining Correspondence Institute (RU)
DZh .... Dirigible, Airship (RU)
dzh .... Joule (RU)
DZh .... Liquid Decontaminating Agent (RU)
DZhD........... Children's Railway (RU)
DZHEZKAZGANGIPROTSVETMET ... Dzhezkazgan State Institute for the Planning of Establishments of Nonferrous Metallurgy (RU)
dzhp............ Female Persons [*Statistics*] (RU)
DZhS .... Democratic Women's Union of Germany (RU)
DZhSG .... Democratic Women's Union of Germany (RU)
dzhut........... Jute Plant [*Topography*] (RU)
DZI .... State Insurance Institute (BU)
dziek .... Dziekan [*Dean*] [*Polish*]
dzien .... Dziennik [*Daily*] [*Polish*]
DZII .... Donets Industrial Correspondence Institute (RU)
DZK .... Monitoring Dosimeter (RU)
DZK .... State Sugar Combine (BU)
Dz KK.......... Deniz Kuvvetler Komutanligi [*Naval Forces Command*] (TU)
Dz Kuv .... Deniz Kuvvetleri [*Naval Forces*] (TU)
DZL .... Differential Line Protection (RU)
DZM .... Dolnoslaskie Zaklady Metalowe [*Lower Silesia Metal Plant*] (POL)
DZMO.......... Dnepropetrovsk Metallurgical Equipment Plant (RU)
DZNAK .... Deniz Bank Deniz Nakliyat Turk Anonim Sirketi [*Turkish Maritime Bank's Maritime Transport Corporation or Turkish Maritime Transport Corporation*] (TU)
dzne .... Douzaine [*Dozen*] [*French*]
DZNIS .... State Agricultural Scientific Research Station (BU)
DZOS .... Earth and Timber Weapon Emplacement (BU)
DZOS .... Log Emplacement (RU)
DZOT........... Earth and Timber Pillbox (BU)
DZOT........... Log Emplacement (RU)
DZOT........... Permanent Ground Gun Emplacement (BU)
DZPD........... Dolnoslaskie Zaklady Przemyslu Drzewnego [*Lower Silesia Wood-Working Plant*] (POL)
DZPJ .... Dolnoslaskie Zaklady Przemyslu Jedwabnego [*Lower Silesia Silk Mill*] (POL)
DZPW.......... Dabrowskie Zaklady Przemyslu Weglowego [*Dabrowa Basin Coal Enterprise*] (POL)
DZPW.......... Dabrowskie Zjednoczenie Przemyslu Weglowego [*Dabrowa Basin Coal Industry Association*] (POL)
DZPW.......... Dolnoslaskie Zaklady Przemyslu Weglowego [*Lower Silesia Coal Plant*] (POL)
DZRCh .... State Spare Parts Plant (BU)
DZS .... Direkcija na Zeleznite Skopje [*Railroad Administration, Skopje*] (YU)
DZS .... Drevarske Zavody na Slovensku, Narodny Podnik [*Lumber Mills in Slovakia, National Enterprise*] (CZ)
DZS .... Drzavna Zalozba Slovenije [*Government Publishing House of Slovenia*] [*Ljubljana*] (YU)
DZS .... Drzavno Zemjodelsko Stopanstvo [*State Farm*] (YU)
DZS .... State Farm (BU)
DZS .... State Soda Plant (BU)
dzt .... Derzeit [*German*]
DZTs .... State Cellulose Plant (BU)
DZU .... Diode Storage, Diode Memory (RU)
Dz U............. Dziennik Urzedowy [*Regulations Gazette*] [*Polish*]
Dz U............. Dziennik Ustaw [*Government Regulations and Laws Gazette*] [*Polish*]
DZU .... Permanent Storage, Permanent Memory (RU)
D-Zug.......... Durchgangs-Zug [*A Through Train*] [*German*]
Dz UMBMiO ... Dziennik Urzedowy Ministerstwa Budowy Miast i Osiedli [*Official Gazette of the Ministry of City and Settlement Construction*] [*A publication*] (POL)
Dz UMS....... Dziennik Urzedowy Ministerstwa Sprawiedliwosci [*Official Gazette of the Ministry of Justice*] [*A publication*] (POL)
Dz U PRL..... Dziennik Ustaw Polskiej Rzeczypospolitej Ludowej [*Government Gazette of the Polish People's Republic*] [*Polish*] [*A publication*]
Dz URP........ Dziennik Urzedowy Rzeczpospolitej Polskiej [*Journal of Laws of the Polish Republic*] [*A publication*] (POL)
Dz Urz Min Osw ... Dziennik Urzedowy Ministerstwa Oswiaty [*Official Gazette of the Ministry of Education*] [*A publication*] (POL)
DZV .... Air Smoke Screen (RU)
DZV .... Deutscher Zentralverlag [*German Central Publishing House*] (EG)
DZWME....... Dolnoslaskie Zaklady Wytworcze Maszyn Elektrycznych [*Lower Silesia Electric Machinery Plant*] (POL)
DZWUR .... Dolnoslaskie Zaklady Wytworcze Urzadzen Radiowych [*Lower Silesia Radio Equipment Plant*] (POL)
DZZ .... Ground Smoke Screen (RU)
DZZ .... State Sugar Refinery (BU)
DZZSO .... Drzavni Zavod za Socijalno Osiguranje [*State Institute for Social Insurance*] (YU)

E

E .... Eau [*Water*] [*Military map abbreviation*] [*World War I*] [*French*] (MTD)
E .... Ehren [*German*]
E .... Eilean [*Island(s)*] [*Gaelic*] (NAU)
E .... Eilzug [*Fast Train*] (EG)
E .... Einschicht [*German*]
E .... Einwohner [*German*]
E .... Eisenbahn [*German*]
E .... Electric Steel (RU)
e .... Electron (RU)
E .... Elektromotorische Kraft [*Electromotive Force*] [*German*]
e .... Elott [*Prior To, In Front Of*] (HU)
E .... Emekli [*Retired*] (TU)
E .... Epreuve [*Surmounted by a crown, and stamped on gun barrels after firing test*] [*French*] (MTD)
E .... Equivalent (RU)
E .... Erkekler [*Men*] (TU)
e .... Erkezik [*Arrives*] (HU)
E .... Erstarrungspunkt [*Freezing Point*] [*German*]
e .... Erzbischoeflich [*German*]
E .... Especialidad [*Spanish*]
E .... Est [*East*] [*French*] (MTD)
E .... Este [*East*] [*Spanish*]
e .... Este [*Evening*] (HU)
e .... Estrada [*Road*] [*Portuguese*] (CED)
E .... Eszak [*North*] [*Hungarian*] (GPO)
e .... Ether, Ester (RU)
e .... Ev [*Year*] (HU)
E- .... Evacuation Tag [*Anti-aircraft and atomic defense*] (RU)
e .... Evenkent [*Annually*] (HU)
E .... Examen [*Swedish*]
E- .... Excavator (RU)
e .... Ezer [*Thousand*] (HU)
e .... Ezred [*Regiment*] (HU)
e .... Ezred [*or Evezred*] [*Thousand Years or Millenium*] (HU)
e .... Oersted (RU)
E .... Screen Grid (BU)
E .... Squadron [*Navy*] (RU)
°E .... Stopien Englera [*Engler Degree*] [*Polish*]
EA .... East African Airways (MAR)
EA .... Efedros Axiomatikos [*Reserve Officer*] (GC)
EA .... Egyptian Army (MAR)
ea .... Eloado [*Consultant*] (HU)
e a. .... En Apostrateia [*Retired*] [*Military*] (GC)
EA .... Enomeni Aristera [*United Left*] [*Greek*] (GC)
EA .... Enosi Agoton [*Farmers' Union*] (GC1)
EA .... Ethniki Allilengyi [*National Solidarity*] [*Greek*] (GC)
EA .... Ethyl Acetate (RU)
EA .... Exportauftrag [*Export Order*] (EG)
EAA .... East African Airways (AF)
EAA .... East African Artillery (MAR)
EAA .... Ecole d'Aviation d'Algerie [*Algerian Aviation School*] (AF)
EAA .... Elliniki Aeroporiki Astynomia [*Later, Aeronomia*] [*Greek Air Police*] (GC)
EAA .... Etaireia Anaptyxeos Alieias [*Association for the Development of Fishing*] [*Greek*] (GC)
EAA .... Ethnikon Asteroskopeion Athinon [*Athens National Observatory*] (GC1)
EAAC .... East African Airways Corporation (MAR)
EAAEC .... East African Army Education Corps (MAR)
EAAEI .... Epitropi Adeias Askiseos tou Epangelmatos tou Ithopiou [*Actors' Licensing Committee*] [*Greek*] (GC)
EAAFRO .... East African Agriculture and Forestry Research Organization (AF)
EAAJ .... East African Agricultural and Forestry Journal [*Nairobi*] [*A publication*] (MAR)
EAAVA .... Enosis Apostraton Axiomatikon Vasilikis Aeroporias [*Union of Retired Royal Air Force Officers*] (GC)
EAAVE .... Epitropi Agonos Avtokinitiston Voreiou Ellados [*Struggle Committee of Drivers of Northern Greece*] (GC)
EAB .... East African Breweries (MAR)
EAB .... Elektro-Apparatebau, Koenigs Wusterhausen [*Koenigs Wusterhausen Electrical Equipment Plant*] (EG)
EAB .... Epitoipari Allando Bizottsag [*Standing Committee of the Construction Industry (CEMA)*] (HU)
EABC .... European American Banking Corporation (MAR)
EABL .... East African Breweries Limited (MAR)
EAC .... East African Command (MAR)
EAC .... East African Community (AF)
EAC .... Economic Advisory Council (MAR)
EAC .... Entreprise Artisanale de Cocobeach (MAR)
EAC .... Exploitations Agricoles Ceppo (MAR)
EACA .... East African Court of Appeal (MAR)
EACAT .... Euro-Arab Centre for Appropriate Technology (MAR)
EACB .... East African Currency Board (MAR)
EACC .... East African Cricket Conference (MAR)
EACE .... East African Certificate of Education (MAR)
EACH .... East African Command Headquarters (MAR)
EACI .... Electricite Automobile de Cote-d'Ivoire (MAR)
EACM .... East African Common Market (MAR)
EACM .... Ecole de l'Aviation Civile et de la Meteorologie (MAR)
EACROTANAL ... Eastern African Centre for Research on Oral Traditions and African National Languages (MAR)
EACSA .... East African Common Services Authority (MAR)
EACSO .... East African Common Services Organization (AF)
EAD .... Ekonomik Arastirma Dernegi [*Economic Research Association*] (TU)
EADA .... East African Dental Association (MAR)
EADB .... East African Development Bank (AF)
EADCA .... East African Directorate of Civil Aviation (MAR)
EADE .... Epitropi Apokatastaseos tis Dimokratias eis tin Ellada [*Committee for the Restoration of Democracy in Greece*] (GC)
EADE .... Ethniki Andidiktatoriki Dimokratiki Enotis [*National Antidictatorial Democratic Unity*] (GC)
EADI .... European Association of Development Research and Training Institutes (MAR)
EAE .... East African Engineers (MAR)
EAE .... Elliniki Andikarkiniki Etaireia [*Greek Cancer Society*] (GC)
EAE .... Elliniki Astronavtiki Etaireia [*Greek Astronautical Society*] (GC)
EAE .... Empresa Agropecuaria Estatal [*Agricultural and Livestock Enterprise*] [*Cuban*] (LA)
EAEC .... East African Economic Community (MAR)
EAEC .... East African Extract Corporation (MAR)
EAEC .... Egyptian Atomic Energy Commission (MAR)
EAEE .... Ellinikai Andidiktatorikai Epitropai Exoterikou [*Greek Antidictatorial Committees Abroad*] (GC)
EAEME .... East African Electrical and Mechanical Engineers (MAR)
EAEN .... Escuela de Altos Estudios Nacionales [*National War College*] [*Bolivian*] (LA1)
EAER .... Eastern Africa Economic Review [*Nairobi*] [*A publication*] (MAR)
EAF .... East African Federation (MAR)
EAF .... East African Forces (MAR)
EAF .... Egyptian Air Force (MAR)
EAFFRO .... East African Freshwater Fisheries Research Organisation (MAR)
EAFIT .... Escuela de Administracion y Finanzas e Instituto Tecnologico [*Medellin*] (COL)
EAFORD .... International Organisation for the Elimination of All Forms of Racial Discrimination (EA)
EAFRO .... East African Fisheries Research Organization (MAR)
EAG .... Ecole d'Application du Genie [*North African*] (MAR)
EAG .... Economists Advisory Group (MAR)
EAG .... Elektroakusztikai Gyar [*Electroacoustical Factory*] (HU)
EAG .... Etablissements Andre Gallais (MAR)
EAGC .... East African Governors' Conference (MAR)
EAGE .... Ethniki Akadimia Grammaton kai Epistimon [*National Academy of Letters and Sciences*] (GC1)
EAGE .... Ethniki Akadimia Grammaton kai Tekhnon [*National Academy of Arts and Letters*] (GC1)
EAGLEPEN ... Eagle Pencil de Colombia SA [*Bogota*] (COL)

EAGR .... East African Geographical Review [*Kampala*] [*A publication*] (MAR)
EAHC .... East African Harbours Corporation (MAR)
EAHC .... East African High Commission [*or Commissioner*] (MAR)
EAHRA .... East African Railways and Harbours Administration (MAR)
EAHTRC ...... East African Human Trypanosomiasis Research Centre (MAR)
EAI .... East African Industries (MAR)
EAI .... Ecole d'Application de l'Infrastructure [*Algerian*] (MAR)
EAI .... Ellinikon Andikarkinikon Institouton (Agiou Savva) [*Greek Cancer Institute (Ag. Savvas)*] (GC)
EAIMB .... East African Industries Management Board (MAR)
EAIMR .... East African Institute for Medical Research (MAR)
EAIMTR .... East African Institute of Meteorological Training and Research (MAR)
EAIMVD ...... East African Institute of Malaria and Vector-Borne Diseases (MAR)
EAINC .... East African Indian National Congress (MAR)
EAIRB .... East African Industrial Research Board (MAR)
EAIRO .... East Africa Industrial Research Organization (MAR)
EAISR .... East African Institute of Social Research (MAR)
EAJRD .... East African Journal of Rural Development [*Kampala*] [*A publication*] (MAR)
EAK .... Egyesult Arab Koztarsasag [*United Arab Republic*] (HU)
EAK .... Enosis Agroton Kyprou [*Union of Cypriot Farmers*] (GC)
EAK .... Ethnikon Agronomikon Komma [*National Agrarian Party*] (GC)
EAK .... Ethnikon Agrotikon Komma [*National Agrarian Party*] [*Greek*] (GC)
EAK .... Europai Atommagkutatasi Kozpont [*European Nuclear Science Research Center*] (HU)
EAK .... Evropaiki Amyntiki Koinotis [*European Defense Community*] (GC)
EAKKI .... Epitoanyagipari Kozponti Kutato Intezet [*Central Research Institute of the Building Materials Industry*] (HU)
EAKN .... Ethnikon Athlitikon Kendron Neotitos (Agiou Kosma) [*National Youth Athletic Center (Ag. Kosmas)*] [*Greek*] (GC)
EAL .... Elektro-Akustisches Laboratorium [*Electro-Acoustic Laboratory*] (EG)
EAL .... Enosis Agoniston Levkosias [*Union of Nicosia Fighters*] (GC)
EAL .... Ethiopian Airlines Share Co. (AF)
EAL .... Europe Africa Line (MAR)
EALA .... East African Legislative Assembly (MAR)
EALA .... East African Library Association (MAR)
EALB .... East Africa Literature Bureau (MAR)
EALJ .... East African Law Journal [*Nairobi*] [*A publication*] (MAR)
EALR .... East Africa Protectorate Law Reports (MAR)
EALR .... East African Law Review [*A publication*] (MAR)
EALRC .... East African Leprosy Research Centre (MAR)
EALS .... East African Literature Service (MAR)
EAM .... Elektronische Analogmaschine [*Electronic Analog Computer*] (EG)
EAM .... ELF [*Essences et Lubrifiants de France*] Aquitaine Maroc (MAR)
EAM .... Eniaion Armenikon Metopon [*Armenian United Front*] (GC)
Ea M .... Epitoanyagipari Miniszterium/Miniszter [*Ministry/Minister of the Building Materials Industry*] (HU)
EAM .... Escolas de Aprendizes-Marinheiros [*Schools For Apprentice Seamen*] [*Brazilian*] (LA1)
EAM .... Ethnikon Apelephtherotikon Metopon [*National Liberation Front*] [*Greek*] (PPE)
EAMA .... Etats Africains et Malgache Associes [*Afro-Malagasy States Associated (with the EEC)*] (AF)
EAMAC .... Ecole Africaine de la Meteorologie et de l'Aviation Civile (MAR)
EAMB .... Exploitation Agricole Mecanisee de Battambang [*Battambang Mechanized Agricultural Enterprise*] [*Cambodian*] (CL)
EAMC .... Entreprise Africaine de Menuiserie et de Construction (MAR)
EAMD .... East African Meteorological Department (MAR)
EAME .... European, African, Middle East Theaters of Operations (MAR)
EAMEAACS ... Europe, Africa, and Middle East Airways and Communication Service (MAR)
EAMECM .... European-African-Middle Eastern Campaign Medal (MAR)
EAMFO .... East African Marine Fisheries Organisation (MAR)
EAMFRO ..... East African Marine Fisheries Research Organisation (MAR)
EAMJ .... East African Management Journal [*A publication*] (MAR)
EAMO .... United Antifascist Youth Organization (BU)
EAMRC .... East African Medical Research Council (MAR)
EAMRDC ..... East African Mineral Resources Development Centre (MAR)
EAMU .... East Africa Malaria Unit (MAR)
EAMWS .... East African Muslim Welfare Society (MAR)
EAN .... Effective Atomic Number (RU)
EAN .... Elliniki Andidiktatoriki Neolaia [*Greek Antidictatorial Youth*] (GC)
EANDC .... European American Nuclear Data Committee [*ENEA*] [*France*]
EANE .... Ethniki Andikommounistiki Neolaia Ellados [*National Anticommunist Youth of Greece*] (GC)
EANHS .... East Africa Natural History Society (MAR)
EANHS .... East African National Health Service (MAR)
EANHSJ ...... East African Natural History Society Journal [*Nairobi*] [*A publication*] (MAR)
EANSL .... East African National Shipping Lines (MAR)
EAO .... Egyptian Agricultural Organization (MAR)
EAO .... Entreprise Africaine Ortal (MAR)
EAO .... Ethnikai Andartikai Omades [*National Guerrilla Groups*] [*Greek*] (GC)
EAOK .... Ethnikai Andikommounistikai Omades Kynigon [*National Anticommunist Hunters' Groups*] (GC)
EAP .... East Africa Protectorate (MAR)
eap .... Effet a Payer [*Bill Payable*] [*French*]
EAP .... Electrical Autopilot (RU)
EAP .... Electronic Acoustic Converter (RU)
EAP .... Epitropi Analyseos kai Programatismou [*Analysis and Planning Committee*] (GC1)
EAP .... Epitropi Apokatastaseos Prosfygon [*Refugee Resettlement Committee*] [*Greek*] (GC)
EAP .... Europaeische Arbeiterpartei [*European Workers' Party*] [*West German*] (PPE)
EAPDTh ...... Epitropi dia tin Apokatastasin kai Prostasian Dimokratikon Thesmon [*Committee for the Restoration and Protection of Democratic Institutions*] [*Greek*] (GC)
EAPH .... East African Publishing House (MAR)
EAPL .... East African Power and Lighting Company Ltd. (MAR)
EAPL .... Eastern Africa Publications Limited (MAR)
EAP & T .... East African Posts and Telecommunications Administration (MAR)
EAPTC .... East Arab Posts and Telecommunications Corporation (MAR)
EAR .... East Africa and Rhodesia [*London*] [*A publication*] (MAR)
EAR .... East African Railways [*Kenyan*] (AF)
ear .... Effet a Recevoir [*Bill Receivable*] [*French*]
EAR .... Elliniki Anatoliki Roumeli [*Greek Eastern Roumelia*] (GC)
EARC .... East Africa Royal Commission (MAR)
EARC .... East African Railways Corporation (MAR)
EARCCUS ... East African Regional Committee for the Conservation and Utilisation of the Soil (MAR)
EARCR .... East African Royal Commission Report 1953-1955 [*A publication*] (MAR)
EARH .... East African Railways and Harbours Authority (MAR)
EARIC .... East African Research Information Centre (MAR)
EAROPH ...... East Asia Regional Organization for Planning and Housing (ML)
EARPC .... East African Royal Pioneer Corps (MAR)
EAs .... East African Shilling (MAR)
EAS .... East African Standard [*Nairobi*] (MAR)
EAS .... Ebonit ve Akumulator Sanayii AS [*Ebonite and Battery Industry Corporation*] (TU)
EAS .... Ellinikos Andiapoikiakos Syndesmos [*Greek Anti-Colonialist League*] (GC)
EAS .... Empresa Antillana de Salvamentos [*West Indian Salvage Company*] (LA)
EAS .... Ethnikos Andidiktatorikos Stratos [*National Antidictatorial Army*] [*Greek*] (GC)
EAS .... Ethnikos Apelevtherotikos Stratos [*National Liberation Army*] [*Greek*] (GC)
EAS .... Ethnikos Apelevtherotikos Synaspismos [*National Liberation Alliance*] [*Cypriot*] (GC)
EAS .... Rapid Analyzer of Ultra-Sound Velocity (RU)
EASA .... Engineers' Association of South Africa (MAR)
EASA .... Ethniki Akadimia Somatikis Agogis [*National Physical Education Academy*] (GC)
EASB .... East African Settlement Board (MAR)
EASC .... East African School Certificate (MAR)
EASC .... East African Service Corps (MAR)
EASCO .... East African Common Services Organisation (MAR)
EASE .... Ethnikon Andifasistikon Symvoulion Ergazomenon [*National Antifascist Council of Workers*] [*Greek*] (GC)
EASIT .... Integrated Automated System for Control and Processing of Transport Information (BU)
EASK .... Enosis Athlitikon Syndakton Kyprou [*Cypriot Sports Writers Union*] (GC)
EASKEN ...... Eniaia Andidiktatoriki Syndikalistiki Kinisi Ellinon Navtergaton [*United Antidictatorial Labor Movement of Greek Seamen*] [*Organized in Hamburg, Federal Republic of Germany, in July 1967*] [*Also, AESKEN*] (GC)
EASL .... Eastern African Shipping Lines (MAR)
EASO .... Egyptian Arab Socialist Organization (MAR)
EASP .... Egyptian Arab Socialist Party (MAR)
EASTLANTMEDCOM ... Eastern Atlantic and Mediterranean Command (MAR)
EAT .... East African Time (MAR)
EAT .... Eidikon Anakritikon Tmima [*Special Investigating Section (of ESA)*] (GC1)
EAT .... ELF [*Essences et Lubrifiants de France*] Aquitaine Tunisie (MAR)
EAT .... Entreprise Africaine de Travaux (MAR)
EAT's .... East African Troops (MAR)
EATC .... East African Training Centre (MAR)
EATEC .... East African Tanning Extract Company (MAR)
EATITU .... East African Tractor and Implement Testing Unit (MAR)
EATOP .... Epitropi Avtodioikiseos kai Topikon Provlimaton [*Committee for Local Self-Government and Local Problems*] (GC1)
EATRO .... East African Trypanosomiasis Research Organisation (MAR)
EATS .... Electronic Automatic Telephone Exchange (RU)
EATSO .... Egyptian-American Transport and Services Corporation (MAR)

EATTA .... East Africa Tourist Travel Association (MAR)
EATTRRO ... East African Tsetse and Trypanosomiasis Research and Reclamation Organization (MAR)
EATZ .... Elektronische Automatische Telefonzentrale [*Electronic Automatic Telephone Exchange*] (EG)
EAU .... Emirats Arabes Unis (MAR)
EAUDRL ...... Egyptian Authority for Utilization and Development of Reclaimed Lands (MAR)
EAUS .... Unified Electronic Subassembly System (RU)
EAV .... Elliniki Aeroporiki Viomikhania [*Greek Aircraft Industry*] (GC1)
EAV .... Eszak-Magyarorszagi Aramszolgaltato Vallalat [*Electric Power Enterprise of Northern Hungary*] (HU)
EAV .... Evangelische Afrika Verein (MAR)
EAVRI .... East African Virus Research Institute (MAR)
EAVRO .... East African Veterinary Research Organisation (MAR)
EAW .... Eisenbahnausbesserungswerk [*Railroad Repair Yard*] (EG)
EAW .... Elektro-Apparatewerk [*Electrical Apparatus Plant*] (EG)
EB .... Butyl Ethyl Acetate [*Solvent*] (RU)
EB .... Efficiency Beurs [*Dutch*]
EB .... Egyezteto Bizottsag (Uzem) [*(Plant) Arbitration Committee*] (HU)
EB .... Ekonomski Biro [*Economic Bureau*] (YU)
EB .... Energiebezirk [*Power District*] (EG)
EB .... Entwurfsbuero [*Design Office*] (EG)
EB .... Ere Bouddhique [*Buddhist Era*] [*Cambodian*] (CL)
EB .... Eskortni Brodovi [*Escort Ships*] [*Navy*] (YU)
EB .... Ethiopian Birr (MAR)
EB .... Europa Bajnoksag [*European Championships*] (HU)
EB .... Evacuation Hospital (BU)
EB .... Evako-Bolnice [*Evacuation Hospitals*] [*Military*] (YU)
EBA .... Ekonomik Basin Ajansi [*Economic Press Agency*] (TU)
EBAD .... Ecole des Bibliothecaires Archivistes et Documentalistes (MAR)
EBAM .... Empresa Brasileira Comercial e Industrial de Alem Mar [*Brazilian Overseas Commercial and Industrial Company*] (LA)
EBAP .... Escola Brasileira de Administracao Publica [*Brazilian School of Public Administration*] (LA)
EBB .... Endoskopbau, Berlin [*Berlin Endoscope Plant*] (EG)
EBB .... Evakuaciska Bolnicka Baza [*Evacuation Hospital Base*] [*Military*] (YU)
EBC .... Evakuacioni Bolnicki Centar [*Evacuation Hospital Center*] [*Military*] (YU)
ebd .... Ebenda [*In the Same Place*] (EG)
ebd .... Ebendaselbst [*In the Same Place*] [*German*]
EBE .... Exportation des Bois Exotiques (MAR)
EBG .... Economic Bulletin of Ghana [*A publication*] (MAR)
EBGM .... Eti Bank Genel Mudurlugu [*Eti Bank Directorate General*] (TU)
EBI .... Electricite-Batiment-Industrie (MAR)
EBIC .... European Banks International Company (MAR)
E(B)IR .... Escuela (Basica) de Instruccion Revolucionaria [*(Basic) Revolutionary Training School*] [*Cuban*] (LA)
EBK .... Elektroenergie-Bezugskarte [*Electric Power Consumption Permit*] (EG)
EBK .... Et ve Balik Kurumu Genel Mudurlugu [*Meat and Fish Association Directorate General*] [*Under Ministry of Commerce*] (TU)
EBM .... Eisen-, Blech-, und Metallwaren [*Iron, Sheetmetal, and Metalware*] (EG)
EBM .... Empreendimentos Brasileiros de Mineracao [*Brazilian Mining Enterprises*] (LA)
EB Mitte ...... Energiebezirk Mitte [*Central Energy District*] (EG)
EBN .... Elektroenergie-Bezugsnachweis [*Electric Power Consumption Voucher*] (EG)
EBN .... Empresa Brasileira de Noticias [*Brazilian News Agency*] (LA)
EB Nord ...... Energiebezirk Nord [*North Energy District*] (EG)
EBO .... Jadrova Elektraren Jaslovske Bohunice [*Nuclear Power Plant Jaslovske Bohunice*] (CZ)
EBR .... Electric Drill (RU)
EBR .... Engin Blinde de Reconnaissance [*Armored Reconnaissance Vehicle*] [*French*] (WER)
Ebr .... Eparhija Broj [*Eparchy Number*] [*Diocese of Orthodox Eastern Church, Serbian*] (YU)
EBS .... Ethiopian Broadcasting System (MAR)
EBS .... European Book Service [*Netherlands*]
EB Sued ...... Energiebezirk Sued [*South Energy District*] (EG)
EBTU .... Empresa Brasileira de Transportes Urbanos [*Brazilian Urban Transport Company*] (LA)
EBTZ .... Electrical Bathythermograph (RU)
EB West ...... Energiebezirk West [*West Energy District*] (EG)
EBY .... Entidad Binacional Yacyreta [*Yacyreta Binational Agency*] [*Argentine*] (LA)
EC .... Echanges Compenses [*Compensated Exchange*] [*Cambodian*] (CL)
EC .... Economic Council, Arab League (MAR)
EC .... Ecuador [*Two-letter standard code*] (CNC)
EC .... Electricna Centrala [*Electrical Station*] (YU)
EC .... Esquerra Catalana [*Catalan Left*] [*Spanish*] (WER)
EC .... Estat Catala [*Catalan State*] [*Spanish*] (WER)
EC .... Ethiopian Calendar (MAR)
EC .... Etudes Camerounaises (MAR)
EC .... European Communities (WEN)
ec .... Exempli Causa [*For Example*] [*Latin*]
ECA .... Empire Centrafricain [*Central African Empire*] [*Use CAE*] (AF)
ECA .... Empresa Colombiana de Aerodromos [*Colombian Airport Corporation*] (LA)
ECA .... Empresa de Comercio Agricola [*Agricultural Commerce Enterprise*] [*Chilean*] (LA)
ECA .... Empresa Consolidada de Azucar [*Consolidated Sugar Enterprise*] [*Cuban*] (LA)
ECA .... Empresa Cubana de Artistas [*Cuban Artists Enterprise*] (LA)
ECA .... Entreprise du Centre Afrique (MAR)
ECA .... Entreprise de Conditionnement d'Air [*Algerian*] (MAR)
ECA .... Exercit Catala d'Alliberament [*Catalonian Liberation Army*] [*Spanish*] (WER)
ECA .... Societe Eburneenne de Courtage et d'Assurances (MAR)
ECA .... United Nations Economic Commission for Africa (AF)
ECAFE .... Economic Commission for Asia and the Far East (IN)
ECAM .... Employers' Consultative Association of Malawi (MAR)
ECAM .... Entreprise de Construction d'Automobiles Malgaches (MAR)
ECAM .... Escuela de Cadetes Interarmas General Antonio Maceo [*General Antonio Maceo Interservice School*] [*Cuban*] (LA)
ECAP .... Empresa Consolidada de Almacenes de Ferreteria [*Consolidated Enterprise of Hardware Warehouses*] [*Cuban*] (LA)
ECAR .... Empresa Consolidada de Aguas Minerales y Refrescos [*Consolidated Mineral Water and Soft Drinks Enterprise*] [*Cuban*] (LA)
ECARBICA ... East and Central African Regional Branch, International Council of Archives (MAR)
ECAS .... East and Central African States (MAR)
ECAT .... Ecole Coloniale d'Agriculture de Tunis (MAR)
ECB .... Encyclopedie du Congo Belge [*Brussels*] [*A publication*] (MAR)
ECB .... Entreprise Camerounaise de Batiments (MAR)
ECBS .... East Central Broadcasting System (MAR)
ecc .... Eccetera [*And So On*] [*Italian*] (GPO)
ECC .... Emergency Cleansing Corps [*Singapore*] (ML)
ECCA .... Eastern Caribbean Currency Authority (LA)
ecca .... Eclesiastica [*Spanish*]
ECCI .... Empresa de Construcoes Civis e Industriais Lda. (MAR)
ECCM .... Empresa Consolidada de Consignatarias Mambisas [*Mambisas Cuban Ship's Agent Enterprise*] (LA)
ecco .... Eclesiastico [*Spanish*]
ECCR-Afrique ... Etudes, Couritage, Commerce, Representation en Afrique (MAR)
ECDA .... Empresa Colombiana de Anuncios Ltda. [*Medellin*] (COL)
ECE .... Economic Commission for Europe [*United Nations*]
ECE .... Economische Commissie voor Europa [*Economic Commission for Europe*] [*United Nations*] [*Dutch*]
ECE .... Empresa Consolidada de Electricidad [*Consolidated Electric Power Enterprise*] [*Cuban*] (LA)
ECEA .... Economic Community of Eastern Africa (MAR)
ECEA .... Empresa de Construccion de Equipos Agricolas [*Agricultural Equipment Manufacturing Enterprise*] [*Cuban*] (LA)
ECEM .... Ecole de Commandement et d'Etat-Major [*Command and Staff School*] [*Zairian*] (AF)
ECEMAR ...... Escola de Comando e Estado-Maior da Aeronautica [*Air Force Command and General Staff School*] [*Brazilian*] (LA)
ECEME .... Escola de Comando e Estado-Maior do Exercito [*Army Command and General Staff School*] [*Brazilian*] (LA)
ECEX .... Empresa de Engenharia e Construcoes Especiais [*Engineering and Special Construction Enterprise*] [*Brazilian*] (LA)
ECF .... Empresa Cubana de Fletes [*Cuban Freight Enterprise*] (LA)
ECG .... Electricity Corporation of Ghana (MAR)
ECGC .... Empire Cotton Growing Corporation (MAR)
ECGD .... British Export Credit Guarantee Department (MAR)
ech .... Echantillon [*Sample*] [*Business and trade*] [*French*]
ECh .... Elementary Particles (RU)
ECH .... Empresa Consolidada de la Harina [*Consolidated Flour Enterprise*] [*Cuban*] (LA)
ECHAP .... Empresa Publica de la Comercializacion de Harina y Aceite de Pescado [*Public Agency for Marketing Fishmeal and Fish Oil*] [*Peruvian*] (LA)
EChP .... Screened Four-Tube Receiver (RU)
ECI .... Equipos y Controles Industriales [*Bogota*] (COL)
ECI .... World Federation of Trade Unions for Energy, Chemical, and Miscellaneous Industries (EA)
ECIC .... Export Credit Insurance Corporation (MAR)
Ecie .... Ecurie [*Stable*] [*Military map abbreviation*] [*World War I*] [*French*] (MTD)
ECIL .... Empresa Consolidada de la Industria Lactea [*Dairy Industry Consolidated Enterprise*] [*Cuban*] (LA)
ECIMACT .... Empresa Comercial para Industria de Materiales, Construccion, y Turismo [*Commercial Enterprise for Construction Materials, Building, and Tourism*] [*Cuban*] (LA)
ECIMETAL ... Empresa Comercial de la Industria Metalurgica y Metal-Mecanica [*Commercial Enterprise for the Metallurgical and Metalworking Industry*] [*Cuban*] (LA)
ECIQUIM ..... Empresa Comercial de Industrias Quimicas [*Chemical Industries Commercial Enterprise*] [*Cuban*] (LA)
ECIT .... Escuelas Cubanas de Instruccion Tecnica [*Cuban Technical Training Schools*] (LA)

ECK............ Elektrochemisches Kombinat [*Electrochemical Combine*] (EG)
ECL............ Egyptian Confederation of Labor (MAR)
ECL............ Enterprise Container Lines (MAR)
ECLA.......... Economic Commission for Latin America [*See also CEPAL*]
ECLP.......... Egyptian Communist Labour Party (MAR)
ECM............ Empresa Consignatoria Mambisa [*Mambisa Steamship Enterprise*] [*Cuban*] (LA)
ECM............ European Common Market (MAR)
ECMES....... Societe d'Entreprise de Construction, d'Ebenisterie et de Menuiserie du Senegal (MAR)
ECMM......... Extracts from China Mainland Magazines [*A publication*] (MAR)
ECN............ Electricity Corporation of Nigeria (MAR)
ECN............ Energie Centrum Nederland
ECNAMP..... Eastern Caribbean Natural Area Management Program (LA1)
ECO............ Economic Cooperation Office (MAR)
ECO............ Entreprise Commerciale de l'Ouest Africain (MAR)
ECOA.......... Empresa Constructora de Obras de Arquitectura [*Architectural Projects Construction Enterprise*] [*Cuban*] (LA)
ECOCARBON... Empresa Colombiana del Carbon [*National Coal Enterprise*] [*Colombian*] (LA)
ECODES..... Empresa Consolidada de Servicio Electrodomestica [*Consolidated Enterprise for Electric Household Appliance Service*] [*Cuban*] (LA)
ECOI............ Empresa Constructora de Obras de Ingenieria [*Engineering Projects Construction Enterprise*] [*Cuban*] (LA1)
ECOL........... Empresa Colombiana Ltda. [*Bogota*] (COL)
ECOMA....... Entreprise Commerciale d'Arrondissement [*District Trading Enterprise*] [*Guinean*] (AF)
ECOMOL..... Empresa Construtora Mocambicana Lda. (MAR)
ECON.......... Economist [*London*] [*A publication*] (MAR)
ECONA........ Economistas Asociados [*Barranquilla*] (COL)
ECONEC..... Entreprise de Construction Economique (MAR)
ECONOMINAS... Empresa Colombiana de Minas [*Colombian Mining Enterprise*] (LA)
ECOPAL...... Empresa Colombiana de Pavimentos Ltda. [*Bogota*] (COL)
ECOPETROL... Empresa Colombiana de Petroleos [*Colombian Petroleum Enterprise*] (LA)
ECOPLAS... Empresa Colombiana de Plasticos Ltda. [*Bogota*] (COL)
ECOPREFIL... Empresa de Correos, Prensa, y Filatelia [*Post, Press, and Philately Enterprise*] [*Cuban*] (LA1)
ECOSOC..... Economic and Social Council of the United Nations
ECOTEC..... Bureau National d'Etudes Economiques et Techniques [*National Office for Economic and Technical Studies*] [*Algerian*] (AF)
ECOWAS.... Economic Community of West African States (AF)
ECP............ Congolese Progressive Students [*Zairian*] (PD)
ECP............ Ecole Centrale de Pyrotechnie [*French*] (MTD)
ECP............ Egyptian Communist Party (PD)
ECP............ Entreprise de Canalisation et de Plomberie (MAR)
ECP............ Ethiopian Communist Party (PD)
ECPA.......... Empresa Constructora de Pozos y Acueductos Ltda. [*Barranquilla*] (COL)
ECPC.......... Egyptian Company for Prestressed Concrete (MAR)
ECPTT......... Ecole Centrale des Postes et Telecommunications [*Algerian*] (MAR)
ECR............ Ecoles des Cadets de la Revolution [*Algerian*] (MAR)
ECS............ Echantillons Commerciaux [*French*]
ECS............ Episcopal Church of the Sudan (MAR)
ECS............ Escadron de Commandement et de Service [*Command and Service Squadron*] [*French*] (WER)
ECS............ European Space Conference (SJT)
ECSC.......... European Coal and Steel Community (EG)
Ecse........... Ecluse [*Lock, Flood Gate*] [*Military map abbreviation*] [*World War I*] [*French*] (MTD)
ECT............ Empresa de Correios e Telegrafos [*Postal and Telegraph Company*] [*Brazilian*] (LA)
ECT............ Esquerra Catalana dels Treballadors [*Workers Leftist Movement of Catalonia*] [*Spanish*] (WER)
ECT............ Intreprinderea Electroceramica Turda [*Turda Electroceramics Plant*] (RO)
ECTCI......... Entreprise Commerciale et de Transports en Cote-d'Ivoire (MAR)
ECTH........... Entreprise de Construction et de Travaux Hydrauliques (MAR)
ECTI............ Echanges et Consultations Techniques Internationaux (MAR)
ECTV........... Empresa Consolidada de Tiendas de Viveres [*Consolidated Enterprise of Grocery Stores*] [*Cuban*] (LA)
ECU............ Ecuador [*Three-letter standard code*] (CNC)
ECU............ Egyptian Cultural Union (MAR)
ECU............ European Currency Unit (AF)
ECUASIDER... Ecuatoriana de Siderurgia [*Ecuadorean Iron and Steel*] (LA)
ECV............ Esperantist Club of Veterans [*See also VEK*] (EA)
ECWA.......... Economic Commission for Western Asia [*United Nations*] [*Arab*] (MAR)
ECWA.......... Economic Community of West Africa (MAR)
ECWP.......... Egyptian Communist Workers' Party (PD)
Ecz............. Eczaci [*or Eczahane*] [*Pharmacist or Pharmacy*] (TU)
ECZ............ Eglise du Christ au Zaire (MAR)
ECZ............ Elektricna Cestna Zeleznica [*Electric Streetcar*] (YU)
ED.............. Airship Shed (RU)
ed............... Edafion [*Paragraph, Verse (of the Bible)*] (GC)
Ed............... Edebiyat [*Literature*] (TU)
ed............... Edella [*or Edellinen*] [*Preceding or Previous*] [*Finnish*] (GPO)
ed............... Edistyspuolue [*Finnish*]
ed............... Edition [*Edition, Issue, Publication*] [*French*]
Ed............... Editore [*Editor*] [*Italian*] (GPO)
Ed............... Edizione [*Edition*] [*Italian*] (GPO)
ed............... Edustaja [*Finnish*]
ED.............. Efficiency Decoration (MAR)
ED.............. Electric Detonator (RU)
ED.............. Electric Differential (RU)
ED.............. Electric Motor (RU)
ED.............. Electrode Pickup (RU)
ED.............. Electrodynamic (Apparatus) (RU)
ED.............. Electronic Differentiator (RU)
ED.............. Esquerra Democratica [*Democratic Left*] [*Spanish*] (PPE)
ED.............. Units (BU)
EDA............ Electronic Differential Analyzer (RU)
EDA............ Eniaia Dimokratiki Aristera [*United Democratic Left*] [*Greek*] (GC)
EDA............ Entreprise Decoration et Ameublement [*Algerian*] (MAR)
EDA............ Epitropai Dimosias Asfaleias [*Public Security Committees*] [*Greek*] (GC)
EDAF.......... Escuela de Administracion y Finanzas [*School of Administration and Finances*] [*Colombian*] (LA)
EDAH.......... Etudes Dahomeennes [*Porto-Novo*] [*A publication*] (MAR)
EDAI........... Empresa de Automatizacion Industrial [*Industrial Automation Enterprise*] [*Cuban*] (LA)
EDAN.......... Epitropi Dimosias Asfaleias Nomou [*Nome Public Security Committee*] [*Greek*] (GC)
EDAP.......... Enosis Dikaiomaton Anthropou kai Politou [*Union of Rights of Man and Citizen*] [*Greek*] (GC)
EDAP.......... Epitropi Diakheiriseos Andallaximou Periousias [*Committee for the Administration of Exchangeable Estates*] [*Greek*] (GC)
EDASZ........ Eszak-Dunantuli Aramszolgaltato Vallalat [*Electric Power Service Enterprise of Northern Transdanubia*] (HU)
EDB............ Einkaufs- und Dienstleistungsbetrieb [*Purchasing and Service Enterprise*] (EG)
EDB............ Electrodynamic Unit (RU)
EDC............ Economic Development Commission (MAR)
EDC............ Education Development Centre (MAR)
EDC............ Educational and Cultural Commission (MAR)
EDC............ Electricite du Cambodge [*Cambodian Power Company*] [*Replaced Energie du Cambodge*] (CL)
EDC............ Electricite du Cameroun [*Cameroon Electric Company*] (AF)
EDC............ Energie du Cambodge [*Cambodian Power Company*] [*Replaced by Electricite du Cambodge*] (CL)
EDC............ Esquerra Democratica de Catalunya [*Democratic Left of Catalonia*] [*Spanish*] (WER)
EDC............ European Defense Community (WEN)
EDC............ Exploration Data Consultants (MAR)
EDCEE........ Equipo Democrata Cristiano del Estado Espanol [*Christian Democratic Team of the Spanish State*] (WER)
ed ch.......... Singular [*Grammar*] (BU)
ed cit.......... Editio Citata [*Edition Cited*] [*Latin*]
edd............. Ediderunt; Haben (es) Herausgegeben [*Published By*] (EG)
EDDE.......... Enosis Dimokratikon Dikigoron Ellados [*Union of Democratic Lawyers of Greece*] (GC)
EDE............ Demokratiki Enosis [*National Democratic Union*] [*Greek*] (PPW)
EDE............ Elliniki Diethnistiki Enosi [*Greek Internationalist Union*] (GC)
EDE............ Ergatiki Diethnikistiki Enosi (Trotskyite) [*Workers Internationalist Union*] [*Greek*] (GC)
EDE............ Esquerda Democratica Estudantil [*Democratic Student Left*] [*Portuguese*] (PPE)
EDE............ Ethniki Dimokratiki Enosis [*National Democratic Union*] [*Greek*] (GC)
Edeb........... Edebiyat [*Literature*] (TU)
EDEE........... Enosis Diafimistikon Epikheiriseon Ellados [*Union of Greek Advertising Enterprises*] (GC)
EDEK........... Elevthero Dimokratiko Ergatiko Kinima [*Free Democratic Labor Movement*] [*Greek*] (GC)
EDEK........... Eniaia Dimokratiki Enosis Kendrou [*United Democratic Union of the Center*] [*Cypriot*] (GC)
EDEK........... Socialist Party of Cyprus (PD)
EDELCA....... Electrificacion del Caroni [*Caroni River Electrification Project*] [*Venezuelan*] (LA)
EDELVIVES... Editorial Luis Vives (COL)
EDEMED..... Etaireia Diakheiriseos Eidon Monopolion tou Ellinikou Dimosiou [*Company for the Administration of Commodities Sold by Greek Public Monopolies*] (GC)
EDEN........... Eniaia Dimokratiki Enosis Neon [*United Democratic Union of Youth*] [*Cypriot*] (GC)
EDES........... Ellinikos Dimokratikos Ethnikos Syndesmos [*Greek Democratic National League*] (GC)
EDES........... Ethnikos Demokratikos Ellinikos Stratos [*National Democratic Greek Army*] (PPE)
EDESA......... Economic Development for Equatorial and Southern Africa (MAR)
EDF............ Electricite de France [*French Electric Company*] (WER)
EdF............ Enroles de Force [*Forced Conscripts*] [*Luxembourg*] (PPE)
EDF............ European Development Fund (MAR)
EDFO.......... Economic Development Financing Organization (MAR)

EDG............ Emigracion Democratica Guatemalteca [*Guatemalan Democratic Emigration*] (LA)
EDHK.......... Enose Demokratikou Hellinikou Kendrou [*Union of the Greek Democratic Center*] (PPE)
EDI............. Economic Development Institute (MAR)
e-d-i............ Eszak-Deli [*North-South (Adjective)*] (HU)
EDI............. Societe Electricite Domestique et Industrielle (MAR)
EDIC........... Etablissements Dumarest pour l'Industrie et le Commerce (MAR)
EDICO......... Entreprise de Distribution Congolaise (MAR)
EDIK........... Enosi Dimokratikou Kendrou [*Democratic Center Union*] [*Formerly, EK-ND*] [*Greek*] (GC)
EDIL........... Empresa Distribuidora Livreria [*Angolan*] (MAR)
EDIM.......... Edition Imprimerie du Mali (MAR)
EDIMEC...... Empresa de Diseno Mecanico [*Mechanical Design Enterprise*] [*Cuban*] (LA)
EDIMEL....... Empresa Regional de Acquisicao, Producao, Distribuicao de Equipamento e Material Escolar e Didactico [*Regional Enterprise for Acquisition, Production, and Distribution of Educational and Teaching Equipment*] [*Angolan*] (AF)
EDIN........... Elliniki Dimokratiki Neolaia [*Greek Democratic Youth*] [*Also, ELDIN*] [*Greek*] (GC)
EDI-PERU... Empresa de Ediciones del Peru [*Peruvian Publishing Enterprise*] (LA)
EDIS........... Empresa Distrital de Servicios [*Bogota*] (COL)
EDISA......... Eletronica Digital SA [*Digital Electronics, Inc.*] [*Brazilian*] (LA)
edit............ Edition [*Edition, Issue, Publication*] [*French*]
EDITABECE... Editorial ABC [*Bogota*] (COL)
EDITOGO.... Etablissement National des Editions du Togo (MAR)
Editora........ Empresa Editora del Estado [*State Publishing Enterprise*] [*Peruvian*] (LA)
ediz............ Edizione [*Edition*] [*Italian*]
EDJABA....... Edjaan Baru [*New Spelling (of the Indonesian and Malay languages)*] (IN)
EDK............ Eisenbahndrehkran [*Rotary Railroad Crane*] (EG)
EDK............ Ekonomik Danisma Kurulu [*Economic Advisory Board*] [*Turkish Federated State of Cyprus*] (GC)
EDK............ Ellinikon Dimokratikon Kinima [*Greek Democratic Movement*] (GC)
EDKD.......... Epitropi Dimosion Kipon kai Dendrostoikheion [*Committee of Public Gardens and Tree Plantings*] (GC)
EDKE........... Enosis Dimon kai Koinotiton Ellados [*Union of Municipalities and Communes of Greece*] (GC)
EDKh........... Encyclopedia of Housekeeping (RU)
EDL............ Electricite du Laos [*Lao Power Company*] (CL)
EDM............ Societe Energie du Mali [*Electric Power Company of Mali*] (AF)
EDMA.......... Eniaion Dimokratikon Metopon Anadimiourgias [*United Democratic Regeneration Front*] [*Cypriot*] (GC)
EDMA.......... Ethyldimethacrylamide (RU)
EDME.......... Endolodokhos Diakheiriseos Mikhanikou Exoplismou [*Administrative Agent for Mechanical Equipment*] [*Greek*] (GC)
EDMMA....... Elazig Devlet Muhendislik ve Mimarlik Akademisi [*Elazig State Engineering and Architecture Academy*] (TU)
edn............. Ednina [*Singular*] (YU)
EDNE........... Enosis Dimokratikis Neolaias Ellados [*United Democratic Youth of Greece*] (GC)
EDNLA......... Elliniki Dimokratiki Neolaia Lambraki Avstralias [*Greek Democratic Lambrakis Youth of Australia*] (GC)
EDO............ Economic Development Organization [*Egyptian*] (MAR)
EDOC.......... Estudios y Documentacion del Caribe [*Caribbean Studies and Documentation*] [*Dominican Republic*] (LA1)
EDOEAP...... Eniaios Dimosiografikos Organismos Epikourikis Asfaliseos kai Perithalpseos [*United Journalistic Organization of Auxiliary Insurance and Relief*] [*Greek*] (GC)
EDOF........... United Democratic Fatherland Front (BU)
EDON.......... Eniaia Dimokratiki Organosis Neon [*or Eniaia Dimokratiki Organosis Neolaias*] [*United Democratic Youth Organization*] [*Cypriot*] (GC)
EDOSZ........ Elelmezesipari Dolgozok Szakszervezete [*Trade Union of Food Industry Workers*] (HU)
EDOSZ........ Epitoipari Dolgozok Szakszervezete [*Construction Workers' Trade Union*] (HU)
EDP............ Ellinika Diylistiria Petrelaiou [*Greek Oil Refineries*] (GC)
EDP............ Emergency Development Plan (MAR)
EDP............ Epikourikon Didaktikon Prosopikon [*Auxiliary Teaching Personnel*] (GC1)
EDR............ Entwurfsbuero der Reichsbahn [*(GDR) Railroad Design Office*] (EG)
EDS............ Eisenbahndienstsache [*Official Railroad Service Document*] (EG)
EDS............ Electromotive Force (BU)
EDS............ Electromotive Force (RU)
EDS............ Societe d'Etat Electricite du Senegal (MAR)
EDSECGEN... Education Secretaries General (MAR)
EDSSA........ Evreia Dimokratiki Syndikalistiki Synergasia Athinon [*Broad Democratic Labor Collaboration of Athens*] (GC)
EDSSP........ Evreia Dimokratiki Syndikalistiki Synergasia Peiraios [*Broad Democratic Labor Collaboration of Piraeus*] (GC)
EDT............ Ethylenediamine Tartrate (RU)
EDTA.......... Entreprise Durieux de Transports Automobiles (MAR)
EDTA.......... Ethylenediaminetetra-Acetate (RU)
EDTK.......... Ethylenediaminetetra-Acetic Acid (RU)
EDTPL........ Entreprise de Dragage et de Travaux Publics de la Lowe (MAR)
EDU............ Eidgenoessische Demokratische Union [*Federal Democratic Union*] [*Swiss*] (WEN)
EDU............ Ethiopian Democratic Union (PD)
EDU............ European Democratic Union (PPE)
EDUCA........ Editorial Universitaria Centroamericana [*Central American University Publishing House*] [*Nicaraguan*] (LA1)
edul............ Entgegengesetzt dem Urzeiger Laufend [*Counterclockwise*] [*German*]
EDV............ Double-Range Shielded Wattmeter (RU)
EDV............ Elektronische Datenverarbeitung [*Electronic Data Processing (EDP)*] [*West German*] (WEN)
EDV............ Ethylenediamine Tartrate (RU)
EDVA.......... Elektronische Datenverarbeitungsanlage [*Electronic Data-Processing Equipment*] (EG)
EDYP.......... Etaireia Diakheiriseos Ypengyon Prosodon [*Company for the Administration of Accountable Revenues*] [*Greek*] (GC)
EDYTh......... Enosis Dimosion Ypallilon Thessalonikis [*Salonica Civil Servants Union*] (GC1)
ED-ZD......... Delayed Action Electric Detonator (RU)
EE............... Egitim Enstitusu [*Training Institute*] (TU)
EE............... Ektelestiki Epitropi [*Executive Committee*] (GC)
EE............... Elengtiki Epitropi [*Control Committee*] (GC)
EE............... Elevtheroi Ellines [*Free Greeks*] (GC)
e e.............. Enestotos Etous [*Of This Year, Of the Current Year*] (GC)
EE............... Entropieeinheit [*Entropy Unit*] [*German*]
Ee............... Envoye Extraordinaire [*French*] (MTD)
EE............... Eparkhiaki Epitropi [*District Committee*] [*Cypriot*] (GC)
EE............... Epitropi Epilogis [*Selection Committee*] (GC)
EE............... Ergatiki Estia [*Labor Hearth*] [*Greek*] (GC)
e e.............. Eterorrythmos Etaireia [*Limited or Registered Partnership*] (GC)
EE............... Ethniki Enosis [*National Unity Party*] [*Greek*] (PPE)
EE............... Euzkadiko Ezkerra [*Basque Left*] [*Spanish*] (PPE)
EEA............ Egyptian Electricity Authority (MAR)
EEA............ Enosi Efimeridopolon Athinon [*Union of Athens Newspaper Vendors*] (GC)
EEA............ Enosis Efedron Axiomatikon [*Union of Reserve Officers*] (GC)
EEA............ Epangelmatikon Epimelitirion Athinon [*Athens Chamber of Commerce*] (GC)
EEAA.......... Enosis Ellinon Apostraton Axiomatikon [*Union of Retired Greek Officers*] (GC)
EEAE.......... Elliniki Epitropi Atomikis Energeias [*Greek Atomic Energy Committee*] (GC)
EEAKh........ Elliniki Epitropi Allilengyis gia tin Khili [*Greek Committee of Solidarity for Chile*] (GC)
EEAM.......... Ellinikon Epanastatikon Apelevtherotikon Metopon [*Greek Revolutionary Liberation Front*] (GC)
EEAM.......... Ergatikon Ethnikon Apelevtherotikon Metopon [*Workers National Liberation Front*] [*Greek*] (GC)
EEASTh....... Enosis Ergatoypallilon Astikis Syngoinonias Thessalonikis [*Union of Workers of Salonica Urban Transport*] (GC)
EEAU.......... Etat des Emirates Arabes Unis (MAR)
EEBI........... Escuela de Entrenamiento Basico de Infanteria [*Infantry Basic Training School*] [*Nicaraguan*] (LA1)
EEC............ Commission of the European Communities
EEC............ European Economic Community [*Common Market*] (AF)
EEC............ Ewe Evangelical Church (MAR)
EECA.......... Empresa Estatal de Comercializacion de Alimentos [*State Food Marketing Enterprise*] [*Peruvian*] (LA)
EEC-ACP.... European Economic Community - African, Caribbean, and Pacific Countries (AF)
EECI........... Energie Electrique de Cote-d'Ivoire [*Ivory Coast Electric Power Company*] (AF)
EED............ Ellinikai Enoploi Dynameis [*Greek Armed Forces*] (GC)
EEDA.......... Elliniki Epitropi Dikaiomaton tou Anthropou [*Greek Human Rights Committee*] (GC)
EEDA.......... Enosis Epangelmation Dikigoron Athinon [*Union of Professional Attorneys of Athens*] (GC)
EEDAP........ Elliniki Enosis Yper ton Dikaiomaton tou Anthropou kai tou Politou [*Greek Union for the Rights of Man and Citizen*] (GC)
EEDDA........ Elliniki Epitropi Diethnous Dimokratikis Allilengiis [*Greek Committee for International Democratic Solidarity*] (GC1)
EEDE.......... Elliniki Etaireia Dioikiseos Epikheiriseon [*Greek Association for Business Management*] (GC)
EEDE.......... Enosis Ellinon Dikaston kai Eisangeleon [*Union of Greek Judges and Prosecutors*] (GC)
EEDI........... Entreprise d'Electricite Domestique et Industrielle (MAR)
EEDK.......... Eniaion Ethnikon Dimokratikon Komma [*United National Democratic Party*] [*See also EK*] [*Cypriot*] (GC)
EEDYE........ Elliniki Epitropi dia tin Diethni Yfesin kai Eirinin [*Greek Committee for an International Detente and Peace*] (GC)
EEE............ Elliniki Epitropi Eirinis [*Greek Peace Committee*] (GC)
EEE............ Enosi Ellinon Ethnikiston [*Union of Greek Nationalists*] (GC)
EEE............ Enosis Ellinon Efopliston [*Union of Greek Shipowners*] (GC)
EEE............ Ethniki Enosis Ellinon [*National Union of Greece*] (GC)

EEEDEE ...... Ethniki Elliniki Epitropi Diethnous Emborikou Epimelitiriou [*National Greek Committee of the International Chamber of Commerce*] (GC)

EEEE .... Ektelestiki Epitropi Exoterikou Emboriou [*Foreign Trade Executive Committee*] [*Greek*] (GC)

EE-EE .... Ellines Ethnikistai - Ethnikistai Ellines [*Greek Nationalists - National Greeks*] (GC)

EEEE .... Evropaiki Enosis Elevtherou Emboriou [*European Free Trade Association*] (GC)

EEEF .... Elliniki Ethniki Enosis Kata tis Fimatioseos [*Greek National Anti-Tuberculosis Association*] (GC1)

EEEL .... Ethniki Etaireia Ellinon Logotekhnon [*National Association of Greek Writers*] (GC)

EEEP .... Enosis Efopliston Epivatikon Ploion [*Union of Passenger Ship Owners*] (GC1)

EEEV .... Elevtheroi Ellines Epanaferoun Vasilea [*Free Greeks Reinstate King*] (GC)

EEF .... Etaireia Ellinon Filologon [*Association of Greek Philologists*] (GC)

EEG .... Electroencephalogram, Electroencephalography (RU)

EEG .... Europese Economische Gemeenschap

EEGC .... Entreprise d'Etudes de Genie Civil [*Civil Engineering Study Enterprise*] [*Malagasy*] (AF)

EEK .... Elevtheron Ergatikon Kendron [*Free Labor Center*] [*Abbreviation usually followed by initial of town in which located*] [*Cypriot*] (GC)

EEK .... Epitropi tis Evropaikis Koinotitos [*European Community Commission*] (GC1)

eek .... Eszak-Eszakkelet [*North-Northwest*] (HU)

EEK .... Ethnikon Enotikon Komma [*National Unifying Party*] [*Greek*] (GC)

EEK .... Evropska Ekonomska Komisija [*Economic Commission for Europe*] [*United Nations*] (YU)

EEKA .... Ethniki Epitropi Kypriakou Agonos [*National Committee for the Cypriot Struggle*] [*Greek*] (GC)

EEKETP ...... Elliniki Etaireia tis Kosmiteias Ethnikou Topeiou kai Poleon [*Greek Society for National Landscape and Cities Beautification*] (GC)

EEKh .... Enosis Ellinon Khimikon [*Union of Greek Chemists*] (GC)

EEKhPL ...... Elliniki Etaireia Khimikon Proiondon kai Lipasmaton [*Greek Chemical Products and Fertilizer Company*] (GC)

EEL .... Enosis Ellinon Logotekhnon [*Association of Greek Writers*] (GC)

EELA .... Equipamentos de Escritorio (Beira) Lda. (MAR)

EELAP .... Enosis Eispraktoron Leoforeion Athinon-Peiraios [*Union of Athens-Piraeus Bus Collectors*] (GC)

EELPA .... Ethiopian Electric Light and Power Authority (AF)

EEM .... Electricite et Eaux de Madagascar [*Electric Power and Water Company of Madagascar*] (AF)

EEM .... Emission Electron Microscope (RU)

EEM .... Energie Electrique de Madagascar (MAR)

EEM .... Enosis Ellinon Mousourgon [*Greek Composers Union*] (GC)

EEM .... Ethniki Etaireia Meleton [*National Research Society*] [*Greek*] (GC)

EEMGM ...... Eski Eserler ve Muzeler Genel Mudurlugu [*Antiquities and Museums Directorate General*] [*Under Ministry of Culture*] (TU)

EEMOS ...... Egtim Enstitusu Mezunu Oretmenler Sendikasi [*Training Institute Graduate Teachers Union*] (TU)

Ee et M pl .... Envoye Extraordinaire et Ministre Plenipotentiaire [*French*] (MTD)

EENA .... Enosis Ellinon Neon Axiomatikon [*Union of Young Greek Officers*] (GC)

EENSL .... Elliniki Epitropi Navtiliakis Synergasias Londinou [*Greek Committee of London for Maritime Cooperation*] [*See also ENEL*] (GC)

e e ny .... Eszak-Eszaknyugat [*North-Northwest*] (HU)

EEO .... Compagnie des Eaux et Electricite de l'Ouest Africain (MAR)

EEO .... Enosis Eisagogeon Osprion [*Union of Legume Importers*] (GC)

EEO .... Ethniki Ergatiki Omospondia [*National Labor Federation*] [*Cypriot*] (GC)

EEOA .... Compagnie des Eaux et Electricite de l'Ouest Africain (MAR)

EEOE .... Elliniki Etaireia Okeanografikon Erevnon [*Greek Oceanographic Research Society*] (GC)

EEOE .... Enotiki Epitropi ton Oikodomon Ellados [*Unifying Committee of Builders of Greece*] (GC)

EEOO .... Elliniki Etaireia Oinon kai Oinopnevmaton [*Greek Wines and Spirits Association*] (GC)

EEOPO .... Ergatiki Epitropi Organotikis Protovoulias Oikodomon [*Labor Committee for the Organizational Initiative of Construction Workers*] [*Greek*] (GC)

EEOTh .... Enosis Ergatotekhniton Oikodomon Thessalonikis [*Union of Construction Technicians of Salonica*] (GC)

EEP .... Epangelmatikon Epimelitirion Peiraios [*Piraeus Chamber of Commerce*] (GC)

EEP .... Evropaiki Enosis Pliromon [*European Payments Union*] (GC)

EEPAP .... Elliniki Etaireia Prostasias Anapiron Paidon [*Greek Association for the Protection of Handicapped Children*] (GC)

EEPDE .... Enosis Ellinon Panepistimiakon Dytikis Evropis [*Union of Greek Universitarians of Western Europe*] (GC)

EEPE .... Elliniki Epitropi Pyrinikis Energeias [*Greek Nuclear Energy Commission*] (GC1)

EEPF .... Elliniki Etaireia Prostasias tis Fyseos [*Greek Society for the Protection of Nature*] (GC)

EEPK .... Etaireia Ellinikou Pyritidopoieiou kai Kalykopoieiou [*Greek Gunpowder and Cartridge Manufacturing Company*] (GC)

EEPMK .... Etaireia Epistimonikon kai Politistikon Meleton Kyprou [*Scientific and Cultural Research Company of Cyprus*] (GC)

EEPOIE ...... Ekpaidevtikos, Epistimonikos, kai Politistikos Organismos ton Inomenon Ethnon [*United Nations Educational, Scientific, and Cultural Organization*] (GC)

EEPP .... Epitropi Epanapatrismou Politikon Prosfygon [*Committee for the Repatriation of Political Refugees*] [*Greek*] (GC)

EEPsPs ...... Elliniki Etaireia Psykhoanalytikis Psykhotherapeias [*Greek Society for Psychoanalytic Psychotherapy*] (GC1)

EER .... Electronic Optimalizing Control (RU)

EERA .... Epitropi Elengkhou Rypanseos tis Atmosfairas [*Air Pollution Control Committee*] [*Greek*] (GC)

EES .... Egypt Exploration Society (MAR)

EES .... Electric Power System (BU)

EES .... Electric Power System (RU)

EES .... Elektricky Energeticky System [*Electric Power System*] (CZ)

EES .... Elevtheron Ergatikon Somateion [*Free Labor Union*] [*Used in reference to Confederation of Cypriot Workers unions*] [*Cypriot*] (GC)

EES .... Ellinikos Erythros Stavros [*Greek Red Cross*] (GC)

EES .... Etaireia Ellinikon Spoudon [*Association of Greek Studies*] (GC)

EES .... Ethniki ton Ellinon Sotiria [*National Salvation of Greeks*] (GC)

EESAK ...... Elliniki Epitropi Seismologias kai Andiseismikon Kataskevon [*Greek Committee for Seismology and Earthquake-Proof Construction*] (GC)

EESV .... Ethniki Enosi Stemmatos Voreioelladiton [*National Union of Northern Greeks for the Crown*] (GC)

EET .... Eglise Evangelique du Togo (MAR)

EETA .... Enosis Ergaton Typou Athinon [*Athens Press Workers Union*] (GC)

EETE .... Epitropi Elengkhou Timologiou Exagogon [*Export Price Control Committee*] [*Greek*] (GC)

EEThS .... Etaireia Ellinon Theatrikon Syngrafeon [*Greek Playwrights Association*] (GC)

EEUU .... Estados Unidos de America [*United States of America*] [*Spanish*]

EE UU da A ... Estados Unidos da America [*United States of America*] [*Portuguese*] (GPO)

EEV .... Enosis Epangelmaton kai Viotekhnon [*Union of Tradesmen and Craftsmen*] [*Plus initial letter of district*] [*Greek*] (GC)

EEVaSS ...... Elliniki Epitropi gia tin Valkaniki Synennoisi kai Synergasia [*Greek Committee for Balkan Understanding and Cooperation*] (GC)

EEVP .... Ektelestiki Epitropi Vasilikis Pronoias [*Royal Welfare Executive Committee*] (GC)

EEVS .... Elliniki Epitropi gia tin Valkaniki Synergasia [*Greek Committee for Balkan Cooperation*] (GC)

EEVVE .... Ethniki Enosi Vasilofronon Voreiou Ellados [*National Union of Northern Greek Royalists*] (GC)

EEY .... Elliniki Etaireia Ydaton [*Greek Water Company*] (GC)

EEY .... Epitropi Ekpaidevtikis Ypiresias [*Educational Services Committee*] (GC)

EEYDAP ...... Elliniki Epitropi Yper ton Dikaiomaton tou Anthropou kai Politou [*Greek Committee for the Rights of Man and Citizen*] (GC)

EEYEE .... Elliniki Etaireia Ydravlikon kai Exygiantikon Ergon [*Greek Association for Water and Sanitation Projects*] (GC)

EEYkaiE ...... Elliniki Epitropi gia Yfesi kai Eirini [*Greek Committee for Detente and Peace*] (GC)

EEZ .... Evropska Ekonomska Zajednica [*European Economic Community (EEC)*] (YU)

EEZ .... Exclusive Economic Zone (MAR)

EF .... Eleftherofronon [*Free Opinion Party*] [*Greek*] (PPE)

EF .... Elektricna Filijala [*Electrical Substation*] (YU)

EF .... Ethniki Froura [*National Guard*] [*Cypriot*] (GC)

EF .... Ethnikon Fos [*National Light*] (GC)

EFA .... Ecole des Forces Aeriennes de Bouake (MAR)

EFA .... Ecole des Forces Armees [*Armed Forces School*] [*Ivorian*] (AF)

EFA .... Empresa Ferrocarriles Argentinos [*Argentine Railway Enterprise*] (LA)

EFA .... Empresa de Fumigacion Aerea [*Bogota*] (COL)

EFA .... Etablissements France-Atlantic (MAR)

EFA .... Exploitations Forestieres de l'Afema (MAR)

EFAC .... Echanges Francs d'Avarie Commune [*Exchange Free from General Average*] (CL)

EFAC .... Entreprises Franco-Africains de Constructions (MAR)

EFAc .... Exportations, Frais, Accessoires (Comptes) [*Exports, Expenses, and Accessories (Accounts)*] (CL)

EFACI .... Exploitations Forestieres et Agricoles de la Cote-d'Ivoire (MAR)

EFAK .... Enosis Filon tou Aravikou Kosmou [*Association of Friends of the Arab World*] [*Greek*] (GC)

EFB .... Societe d'Exploitation Forestiere de la Bembai (MAR)

EFBA .... Entreprise Forestiere des Bois Africains (MAR)

EFBACA ...... Entreprise Forestiere des Bois Africains Centrafrique (MAR)

EFC .... Entreprise Forestiere Camerounaise (MAR)

EFCA.......... Ecole de Formation des Cadres Auxiliaires (MAR)
EFCSA........ Establecimientos Frigorificos del Cerro SA [*Cerro Packing Plants, Inc.*] [*Uruguayan*] (LA)
EFE............ Agencia Efe [*Efe Agency*] [*Press Association*] [*Spanish*] (WER)
EFE............ Educational Film Enterprises, Inc. (MAR)
EFE............ Elliniki Filoteliki Etaireia [*Greek Philatelic Society*] (GC)
EFE............ Elliniki Fotografiki Etaireia [*Greek Photographic Society*] (GC)
EFE............ Ethniki Froura Elladas [*National Guard of Greece*] (GC)
EFEDOSZ.... Epito-, Fa-, es Epitoanyagipari Dolgozok Szakszervezete [*Trade Union of Workers of the Construction, Woodworking, and Building Material Industries*] (HU)
EFEE.......... Ethniki Foititiki Enosis Ellados [*National Student Union of Greece*] (GC)
EFEK.......... Ethniki Foititiki Enosis Kyprou [*National Union of Cypriot Students*] (GC)
EFEM.......... Entwicklung und Fabrikation Elektrischer Messinstrumente [*Development and Production of Electrical Measuring Instruments*] (EG)
EFEO.......... Ecole Francaise d'Extreme-Orient [*French School of the Far East*] (CL)
EFEX.......... Ypiresia Efodion ek tou Exoterikou [*Foreign Supplies Office*] (GC)
eff............... Effektiv [*Effective*] [*Business and trade*] [*German*]
effekt.......... Effective, Efficient (RU)
eff Mossb.... Mossbauer Effect (RU)
Eff a P.......... Effet a Payer [*Bill Payable*] [*Business and trade*] [*French*]
Eff a R.......... Effet a Recevoir [*Bill Receivable*] [*Business and trade*] [*French*]
EFH............ Entwurfsbuero fuer Hochbau [*Design Office for Above-Ground Construction*] (EG)
EFI.............. Eje Fluvial Industrial [*Industrial River Axis*] [*Argentine*] (LA)
EFI.............. Elektrisitetsforsyningens Forskninginstitutt [*Research Institute of Electricity Supply*] [*Norwegian*]
EfI.............. Entwurfsbuero fuer Industriebau (VEB) [*Design Office for Industrial Construction (VEB)*] (EG)
EFIAP.......... Enosis Fymatikon Isfalismenon Athinon-Peiraios [*Athens-Piraeus Union of Insured Tuberculars*] (GC)
EFIK............ Evkaf Finansman ve Inkisaf Korperasyonu Ltd. [*Religious Endowments' Financing and Development Corporation Ltd.*] [*Turkish Cypriot*] (GC)
EFIM............ Ente Partecipazioni e Finanziamento Industria Manifatturiera [*Manufacturing Industry Holding and Financial Company*] [*Italian*] (WER)
EFKI............ Elektronikai es Finommechanikai Kutato Intezet [*Electronics and Precision Mechanics Research Institute*] (HU)
EFL.............. Egyptian Federation of Labor (MAR)
EFL.............. Exploitation Forestiere de la Lobo (MAR)
EFLA............ Entreprise Force Lumiere Africaine (MAR)
ef-masl........ Essential Oil Culture Sovkhoz [*Topography*] (RU)
ef-masl........ Essential Oil Plant [*Topography*] (RU)
EfmoR.......... Erntefestmeter ohne Rinde [*Crop-Yield in Cubic Meters Not Including the Bark*] (EG)
EFMP.......... Escuela Formadora de Maestros de Primaria [*Primary Teachers Training School*] [*Cuban*] (LA)
EFO............ Ecole de Formation d'Officiers [*Officers Training School*] [*Zairian*] (AF)
EFOA.......... Elliniki Filathlos Omospondia Andisfairiseos [*Greek Lawn Tennis Athletic Federation*] (GC)
EFOEA........ Elliniki Filathlos Omospondia Epitrapeziou Andisfairiseos [*Greek Table Tennis Athletic Federation*] (GC)
EFORTOM... Ecole de Formation des Officiers de Reserve des Territoires d'Outre-Mer [*Overseas Territories Reserve Officers Training School*] [*French*] (AF)
EFP............ Epitropi Physikou Perivallondos [*Committee for Natural Environment*] [*See also EKEP*] (GC1)
EFP............ Europaeische Foederalistische Partei [*European Federalist Party*] [*Austrian*] (PPE)
EFPA.......... Enosis Foititon Panepistimiou Athinon [*Union of Athens University Students*] (GC)
EFr............ Energetische Futtereinheit [*Energy Feed Unit*] (EG)
EFRL.......... Exploitation Forestiere Robert Lamoulie (MAR)
EFSA.......... Ecole Federale Superieure d'Agriculture (MAR)
EFSA.......... Epistimonikos kai Filologikos Syllogos Ammokhostou [*Famagusta Professional and Literary Association*] (GC)
EFSD.......... Exploitations Forestieres et Scieries de Divo (MAR)
EFSEE........ Ethniki Foititiki Spoudastiki Enosis Ellados [*National Union of Students of Greece*] (GC)
EFSO-GD.... Exploitation Forestiere du Sud-Ouest-GD (MAR)
EFT............ Einheitliche Traegerfrequenz Fernsprecheinrichtung [*Uniform Carrier Frequency Telephone Installation*] (EG)
Eft.............. Erfurt (EG)
EFT............ Exploitation Forestiere et Agricole de la Tanoe (MAR)
EFTA.......... European Free Trade Association (WER)
EFTAL........ Ecole de Formation Technique et Administrative de la Logistique [*Algerian*] (MAR)
Eftf............ Etterfoelger [*Successors*] [*Norwegian*] (CED)
Eftf............ Successors [*Danish*]
Eftf............ Successors [*Swedish*]
EFUK.......... Elblaska Fabryka Urzadzen Kuziennych [*Elblag (Elbing) Forging Equipment Factory*] (POL)
eg.............. Eerstgenoemde [*The Former*] [*Dutch*] (GPO)
Eg.............. Egypt (BU)
EG.............. Egypt [*Two-letter standard code*] (CNC)
EG.............. Eingetragene Genossenschaft [*Registered Cooperative*] (EG)
Eg.............. Eisessig [*Glacial Acetic Acid*] [*German*]
EG.............. Ektelestikon Grafeion [*Executive Office*] (GC)
EG.............. Electrogram (RU)
EG.............. Eparkhiakon Grafeion [*District Office*] [*Cypriot*] (GC)
EG.............. Eparkhiakos Grammatevs [*District Secretary*] [*Cypriot*] (GC)
EG.............. Epitelikon Grafeion [*Staff Office*] (GC)
EG.............. Etudes Guineennes [*A publication*] (MAR)
EG.............. Europese Gemeenschappen [*Luxembourg*]
EG.............. Evacuation Hospital (BU)
EG.............. Evacuation Hospital (RU)
eg.............. Exempli Gratia [*For Example*] [*Latin*] (GPO)
EG.............. Natural Science and Geography (BU)
EGA............ Electricite et Gaz d'Algerie (MAR)
EGA............ Entreprise Generale Atlantique (MAR)
EGAE.......... Etaireia Genikon Apothikon Ellados [*General Warehouses Company of Greece*] (GC)
EGAM.......... Ente di Gestione per le Aziende Minerarie e Metallurgiche [*Agency for the Management of Mineral and Metallurgical Concerns*] [*Italian*] (WER)
EGAP.......... Entreprise Generale Africaine de Peinture (MAR)
EGART........ Energiagazdalkodasi Reszvenytarsasag Vallalat [*Power Engineering Enterprise Ltd.*] (HU)
EGATP........ Entreprise Generale Africaine de Travaux Publics (MAR)
EGB............ Elektrogeraetebau [*Electrical Equipment Plant*] (EG)
EGB............ Entreprise Generale de Batiments (MAR)
EGB............ Europaeischer Gewerkschaftsbund [*European Trade Union Confederation*] (EG)
EGB............ Europai Gazdasagi Bizottsag [*European Economic Commission*] (HU)
EGBTP........ Entreprise Generale de Batiments et de Travaux Publics (MAR)
EGC............ Ecole de Gardes-Cotes (MAR)
EGC............ Entreprise Generale de Chaudonnerie (MAR)
EGC............ Entreprise Generale de Construction (MAR)
EGC............ Ethiopian Grain Corporation (MAR)
EGCAP........ Entreprise Generale du Cap Vert de Travaux Publics et Particuliers (MAR)
EGCM.......... Entreprise Gabonaise de Constructions Metalliques (MAR)
EGCT.......... Entreprise Generale de Construction et de Topographie (MAR)
EGD............ Ethylhexanediol (RU)
EGDA.......... Electrohydrodynamic Analogy [*Research method in hydraulics*] (RU)
EGE............ Enosis Gynaikon Ellados [*Union of Greek Women*] (GC)
EGE............ Entreprise Generale d'Electricite (MAR)
EGE............ Equatorial Guinea Ekuele (MAR)
EGEA.......... Eidikon Grafeion Exypiretiseos Aeroskafon [*Special Aircraft Services Office*] (GC)
EGEA.......... Etablissement General des Entreprises Anani (MAR)
EGEB.......... Entreprise Generale Entretien Batiment (MAR)
EGEC.......... Egyptian General Electricity Corporation (ME)
EGEC.......... Etablissements Guerin & Cie. (MAR)
EGED.......... Entreprise Nationale Guineenne d'Exploitation du Diamant (MAR)
EGEMAC..... Egyptian-German Electrical Manufacturing Company (MAR)
EGEMAK..... Ege Makina ve Ticaret AS [*Aegean Machinery and Trade Corporation*] (TU)
EGEPPVE.... Eidikon Grafeion Epanepikismou Paramethorion Periokhon Voreiou Ellados [*Special Office for the Resettlement of Frontier Areas of Northern Greece*] (GC)
EGERT........ Entreprise Generale d'Electricite et Radio du Tchad (MAR)
Egeszs K..... Egeszsegugyi Kiado [*Public Health Publishing House*] (HU)
EGETRAV... Entreprise Generale de Travaux (MAR)
EGEV.......... Entreprise Generale des Espaces Verts [*Algerian*] (MAR)
EGF............ Electricite-Gaz de France [*French Electric and Gas Company*] (WER)
EGF............ Emprestimos do Governo Federal [*Federal Government Loans*] [*Brazilian*] (LA1)
EGFGB........ Einfuehrungsgesetz zum Familiengesetzbuch [*Introductory Law to the Family Code*] (EG)
EGG............ Electrogastrogram (RU)
EGHA.......... Ege Haber Ajansi [*Aegean News Agency*] [*Izmir*] (TU)
EGI.............. Energia Gazdalkodasi Intezet [*Institute of Energy Economy*] (HU)
EGI.............. Entreprise Generale d'Installations Electriques J. Sanchez et A. Martinez (MAR)
egip............ Egyptian (BU)
Egit............ Egitim [*Education*] (TU)
EGITIM-IS... Turkiye Egitim Iscileri Sendikasi [*Turkish Educational Workers Union*] [*Istanbul*] (TU)
EGK............ Electric Gas Valve (RU)
EGK............ Electrohydraulic Valve (RU)
EGK............ Europai Gazdasagi Kozosseg [*European Economic Community, Common Market*] (HU)
EGL............ Electrification de la Region des Grands Lacs [*Electrification of the Great Lakes Region*] (AF)
EGLI............ Esperantista Go-Ligo Internacia (EA)
EGM............ Egypt General Mission (MAR)
EGM............ Emniyet Genel Mudurlugu [*Directorate General of Security*] [*Under Interior Ministry*] (TU)
EGM............ Entreprise Generale de Menuiserie (MAR)

EGM .... Etibank Genel Mudurlugu [*Eti Bank Directorate General*] [*Under Ministry of Energy and Natural Resources*] (TU)
eGmbH .... Eingetragene Genossenschaft mit Beschraenkter Haftpflicht [*Registered Cooperative with Limited Liability*] (EG)
eGmbH .... Eingetragene Gesellschaft mit Beschraenkter Haftung [*Registered Company with Limited Liability*] (EG)
Egmp .... Eilgueterzug mit Personenbefoerderung [*Express Freight Train with Passenger Facilities*] (EG)
EGN .... Ecole de la Garde Nationale [*National Guard School*] [*Tunisian*] (AF)
EGN .... Escola de Guerra Naval [*Naval War College*] [*Brazilian*] (LA)
EGNK .... Egipetskaia Generalnaia Neftianaia Korporatsiia (MAR)
EGNY .... Ellinika Grafeia Navtikon Ypiresion [*Greek Maritime Services Offices*] (GC)
EGO .... Eichgebuehren-Ordnung [*Regulations on Calibration Fees*] (EG)
EGO .... Elektrik, Havagaz, ve Otobus Isletme Muessesi [*Electric Power, Gas, and Bus Administration*] (TU)
EGO- .... Experimental Gamma-Irradiator (RU)
EGO-BURO-IS ... Ankara Elektrik, Havagazi, ve Otobus Isletme Muessesi Buro Iscileri Sendikasi [*Ankara Electric, Gas, and Bus Administration Office Workers Union*] (TU)
Eg Og H .... Egitim ve Ogretim Hizmetleri [*Teaching and Training Duties*] (TU)
EGOTH .... Egyptian General Organisation for Tourism and Hotels (MAR)
EGP .... Ejercito Guerrillero de los Pobres [*Poor People's Guerrilla Army*] [*Guatemalan*] (LA1)
EGP .... Electrohydraulic Converter (RU)
EGP .... Electrohydraulic Drive (RU)
EGP .... Energoprojekt [*Power Development Project*] (CZ)
EGP .... Entreprise Generale de Peinture (MAR)
EGP .... Entreprise Guineenne de Prefabrication (MAR)
EGPA .... Egyptian National Petroleum Authority (MAR)
EGPC .... Egyptian General Petroleum Corporation (ME)
EGR .... Electrohydraulic Speed Regulator of Hydraulic Turbines (RU)
EGRA .... Extractora de Grasas [*Bogota*] (COL)
EGREM .... Empresa de Grabaciones y Emisiones Musicales [*Musical Recording and Publishing Enterprise*] [*Cuban*] (LA)
EGS .... Electrogastrograph (RU)
EGS .... Enosis Georgikon Synetairismon [*Union of Farm Cooperatives*] [*Followed by initial letter of district name*] (GC)
EGS .... Eparkhiaki Geniki Synelevsis [*Metropolitan General Assembly*] [*Orthodox Church of Greece*] (GC)
EGS .... Ethnikos Gymnastikos Syllogos [*National Gymnastic Club*] (GC)
EGSAThPE ... Ethniki Geniki Synomospondia Anapiron kai Thymaton Polemou Ellados [*Greek National General Confederation of Handicapped and Victims of War*] (GC)
Egse .... Eglise [*Church*] [*Military map abbreviation*] [*World War I*] [*French*] (MTD)
EGSI .... Enosis Georgikon Synetairismon Irakleiou [*Union of Irakleion Agricultural Cooperatives*] (GC)
EGSKP .... Ethnikon Gnomodotikon Symvoulion Koinonikis Politikis [*National Advisory Council for Social Policy*] (GC)
EGSM .... Electric Gas Welding Machine (RU)
EGSZI .... Epitesgazdasagi es Szervezesi Intezet [*Institute of Construction Management and Organization*] (HU)
EGT .... Einheitsgebuehrentarif [*Uniform Rates*] (EG)
EGT .... Energotrust [*Power Trust*] (CZ)
EGT .... Entreprise Generale de Transports (MAR)
EGT .... Entreprise Generale de Travaux (MAR)
EGTA .... Entreprise Generale de Travaux en Afrique (MAR)
EGTB .... Entreprise Generale du Travail du Bois (MAR)
EGTB .... Entreprise Guineenne de Travaux de Batiments (MAR)
EGTBL .... Energotrust Bratislava, Rozvodove Zavody Elektrickej Energie [*Bratislava Power Trust, Electric Power Distributing Plants*] (CZ)
EGTH .... Entreprise de Grands Travaux Hydrauliques (MAR)
EGTP .... Entreprise Generale des Travaux Publics (MAR)
EGTR .... Societe Anonyme d'Entreprise Generale de Travaux Routiers (MAR)
EGU .... Energeticky Ustav Pruzkumu [*Power Research Institute*] (CZ)
EGU .... Engineering and General Union [*Bahamian*] (LA1)
EGV .... Energovod [*Electrical Engineering Enterprise*] (CZ)
egy .... Egyetem [*University*] (HU)
EGY .... Egypt [*Three-letter standard code*] (CNC)
EGY BE .... Egeszsegugyi Berendezeseket Karbantarto es Javito KSZ [*Cooperative for Maintenance and Repair of Sanitation Equipment*] (HU)
egyes .... Egyesulet [*Association, Club*] (HU)
egyes .... Egyesult [*United*] (HU)
egyet .... Egyetem [*University*] (HU)
egyet .... Egyetemes [*Universal*] (HU)
egyet m tanar ... Egyetemi Magantanar [*Honorary Lecturer at the University*] (HU)
egyezm .... Egyezmenyes [*Customary, By Agreement*] (HU)
egyh .... Egyhaz [*Church, Religious Community*] (HU)
egy hallg ..... Egyetemi Hallgato [*University Student*] (HU)
egy ny rk tanar ... Egyetemi Nyilvanos Rendkivuli Tanar [*Associate Professor*] (HU)
egy ny r tanar ... Egyetemi Nyilvanos Rendes Tanar [*Full Professor*] (HU)
egys .... Egyseg [*Unity*] (HU)
EGYT .... Egyesult Gyogyszer- es Tapszergyar [*United Pharmaceutical and Nutriment Factory*] (HU)
egz .... Egzemplarz(e) [*Copy, Copies*] (POL)
eh .... E Helyett [*Instead Of, In Place Of*] (HU)
eh .... Ehrenhalber [*Honorary (of a degree)*] [*German*] (WEN)
EH .... Ethiopoan Herald [*A publication*] (MAR)
EH .... Western Sahara [*Two-letter standard code*] (CNC)
EHAS .... Euzko Harriak Alderdi Sozialista [*Socialist Party of the Basque People*] [*Spanish*] (WER)
EHB .... Elektronik Hesap Bilimleri Enstitusu [*Electronic Accounting Science Institute*] [*of Istanbul Technical University*] [*See also ITUEHB*] (TU)
EHE .... Every Home Evangelism [*Tanzania*] (MAR)
ehem .... Ehemals [*or Ehemalig*] [*Former or Formerly*] (EG)
EHEP .... Ecole des Hautes Etudes Pratiques (MAR)
EHESS .... Ecole des Hautes Etudes des Sciences Sociales [*School of Higher Studies in Social Sciences*] [*French*] (MAR)
EheVerfO .... Eheverfahrensordnung [*Marriage Rules of Procedure*] (EG)
EHK .... Eisenhuettenkombinat [*Metallurgical Combine*] [*See also EKO*] (EG)
EHK .... Evropska Hospodarska Komise [*Economic Commission for Europe*] [*United Nations*] (CZ)
Ehm .... Ehemals [*Formerly*] (EG)
EHO .... Elektrarna Hodonin [*Electric Power Plant Hodonin*] (CZ)
EHP .... Einzelhandelspreis [*Retail Price*] (EG)
EHS .... Einzelhandelsspanne [*Retail Markup*] (EG)
EHS .... Evropske Hospodarske Spolecenstvi [*European Economic Community*] (CZ)
EHStG .... Entwicklungshilfe- Steuergesetz (MAR)
EHW .... Eisenhuettenwerk [*Metallurgical Works*] (EG)
EI .... Ekonomski Institut [*Economic Institute*] (YU)
EI .... Electric Impulse Generator (RU)
EI .... Electric Integrator (RU)
EI .... Electric Power Installations (BU)
EI .... Elektrogenetski Inspektorat [*Electric Power Inspectorate*] (YU)
EI .... Elektroinstallationen [*Electrical Installations*] (EG)
EI .... Elettro-Nucleare Italiana [*Italian Nuclear Electric Industry*] (WER)
EI .... Entrepreneurs Individuels (MAR)
EI .... Epilepsy International (EA)
EI .... Express Information (RU)
EI .... Power Engineering Institute (of the Siberian Department of the Academy of Sciences, USSR) (RU)
EIA .... Basque Revolutionary Party [*Spanish*] (PPW)
EIAA .... Ethnikon Idryma Apokatastaseos Anapiron [*National Foundation for Rehabilitation of Handicapped Persons*] [*Greek*] (GC)
EIB .... Entreprise et Industrie du Bois (MAR)
EIB .... Escuela Interamericana de Bibliotecologia [*Medellin*] (COL)
EIB .... European Investment Bank (AF)
EIBCV .... Entreprise Industrielle des Bois de Construction Voltaique (MAR)
EIC .... Entreprise Ivoirienne de Constructions (MAR)
EIC .... Etat Independant du Congo (MAR)
EICOGE .... Entreprise Industrielle pour la Construction Generale (MAR)
EID- .... Electronic Deformation Meter (RU)
EIDAD .... Ellinikon Institouton Diethnous kai Allodapou Dikaiou [*Greek Institute of International and Foreign Law*] (GC)
EIDE .... Escuela de Iniciacion Deportiva Escolar [*School for Sports Beginners*] [*Cuban*] (LA)
EIDE .... Especialidad Industrial de Estampacion [*Bogota*] (COL)
EIDSZSZ ..... Elelmezesi Ipari Dolgozok Szabad Szakszervezete [*Free Union of Food Industry Workers*] (HU)
EIE .... Elektrik Isleri Enstitusu [*Electric Affairs Institute*] (TU)
EIE .... Elliniki Ilektriki Etaireia [*Greek Electric Company*] (GC)
EIE .... Ethnikon Idryma Erevnon [*National Research Foundation*] [*Greek*] (GC)
EIEI .... Elektrik Isleri Etud Idaresi [*Electric Affairs Study Administration*] (TU)
EIER .... Ecole Inter-Etats d'Ingenieurs de l'Equipement Rural (MAR)
EIET .... Enosis Idioktiton Eparkhiakou Typou [*Union of Provincial Press Owners*] [*Greek*] (GC)
EIFC .... Etablissement International de Financement et de Credit (MAR)
eig .... Eigene [*or Eigener*] [*Own*] (EG)
eig .... Eigentlich [*Properly*] (EG)
Eigg .... Eigenschaften [*Properties*] [*German*]
Eigsch .... Eigenschaft [*Property*] [*German*]
EIGT .... Ellinikon Institouton Grafikon Tekhnon [*Greek Institute of Graphic Arts*] (GC)
eigtl .... Eigentlich [*Properly*] (EG)
EIIEA .... Enosis Idioktiton Imerision Efimeridon Athinon [*Union of Athens Daily Newspaper Owners*] (GC)
EIIEE .... Enosis Idioktiton Imerision Eparkhiakon Efimeridon [*Union of Daily Provincial Newspaper Owners*] [*Greek*] (GC)
EIKA .... Encyclopedia of Measurements, Control, and Automation [*A publication*] (RU)
Eil .... Eiland [*Island*] [*Dutch*] (NAU)
EIL .... Experiment in International Living (MAR)
Eiln .... Eilanden [*Islands*] [*Dutch*] (NAU)

EIM .... Computer (BU)
EIM .... Elelmiszeripari Miniszterium/Miniszter [*Ministry/Minister of the Food Industry*] (HU)
EIM .... Ellinikon Institouton Modas [*Greek Fashion Institute*] (GC)
EIM .... Ente Italiano della Moda
EIM .... Experimental Data Processor (RU)
EIN .... European Information Network
EIN .... Power Engineering Institute (RU)
EINAP .... Enosis Iatron Nosokomeion Athinon-Peiraios [*Union of Doctors of Athens-Piraeus Hospitals*] (GC)
Einfl .... Einfluss [*Influence*] [*German*]
Einl .... Einliegend [*Enclosed*] [*Correspondence*] [*German*]
einschl .... Einschliesslich [*Including, Inclusive*] (EG)
Einw .... Einwirkung [*Effect*] [*German*]
Einzbl .... Einzelblatt [*Single Sheet*] [*German*]
EIO .... Egyptian Investment Office (MAR)
EIO .... Elliniki Istioploiki Omospondia [*Greek Sailing Federation*] (GC)
EIO .... Ellinikos Ippikos Omilos [*Greek Riding Club*] (GC)
EIOC .... Egyptian Independent Oil Co. SAE (MAR)
EIP .... Association Mondiale pour l'Ecole Instrument de Paix [*World Association for the School as an Instrument of Peace*] (EA)
EIP .... Ellinikon Institouton Paster [*Greek Pasteur Institute*] (GC)
EIPA .... Enosis Iptamenon Politikis Aeroporias [*Union of Civil Aviation Flying Personnel*] (GC)
EIPEP .... Ethnikon Idryma Prostasias Ergazomenou Paidiou [*National Foundation for the Protection of the Working Child*] (GC)
EIPT .... Enosis Idioktiton Periodikou Typou [*Union of Owners of the Periodical Press*] [*Greek*] (GC)
EIR .... Eidgenoessisches Institut fuer Reaktorforschung [*Swiss Federal Institute for Reactor Research*] (WEN)
EIR .... Escuela de Instruccion Revolucionaria [*Revolutionary Training School*] [*Cuban*] (LA)
EIR .... Ethnikon Idryma Radiofonias [*National Radio Institute*] [*Later, EIRT*] [*Greek*] (GC)
EIRMA .... European Industrial Research Management Association
EIRT .... Ethnikon Idryma Radiofonias-Tileoraseos [*National Radio-Television Institute*] [*Later, ERT*] [*Greek*] (GC)
EIS .... Electrotechnical Institute of Communications (RU)
EIS .... Ellinikoi Ilektrikoi Sidirodromoi [*Greek Electric Railways*] (GC)
EIS .... Etaireia Ilektrikon Sidirodromon [*Later, ISP*] [*Greek Electric Railways*] (GC)
EIS .... Export Intelligence Service (MAR)
EI-S .... Special Electric Integrator (RU)
EIT .... Computer Technology (BU)
EIT .... Ecole d'Interpretes et Traducteurs de la Chambre de Commerce de Paris [*School of Interpreters and Translators of the Chamber of Commerce of Paris*]
EIT .... Economisch Instituut Tilburg
EITC .... Entreprise d'Installations Techniques et de Constructions (MAR)
EITIA .... Eskisehir Iktisat ve Ticari Ilimler Akademisi [*Eskisehir Academy of Economics and Commercial Science*] [*See also IITIA*] (TU)
EITs .... Computer Center (BU)
EIU .... Economic Intelligence Unit [*Jamaican*] (LA1)
EI-VP .... Ethnikon Idryma-Vasilevs Pavlos [*King Paul National Foundation*] [*Greek*] (GC)
EIVRT .... Egyesult Izzolampa es Villamossagi Reszvenytarsasag [*United Incandescent Lamp and Electrical Company*] (HU)
EJ .... Enciklopedija Jugoslavije [*Encyclopedia of Yugoslavia*] (YU)
EJ .... Estradni Jednatelstvi [*Theatrical Agency (of the Center of Music Performers and Entertainers)*] (CZ)
EJEA .... Empire Journal of Experimental Agriculture [*Oxford*] [*A publication*] (MAR)
EJF .... Elektricke Zavody Julia Fucika [*Julius Fucik Electric Power Plants*] [*Brno*] (CZ)
EJK .... Elhagyott Javak Kormanybiztosa [*Commissioner for Abandoned Property*] (HU)
EJL .... Entreprise Jean Lefebvre (MAR)
EJLCI .... Entreprise Jean Lefebvre Cote-d'Ivoire (MAR)
EJPD .... Eidgenoessisches Justiz- und Polizeidepartement [*Federal Justice and Police Department*] [*Swiss*] (WEN)
EJT .... Association "Edro de la Jeunesse du Togo" (MAR)
EJT .... Echo de la Jeunesse Togolaise (MAR)
EJT .... Ejercito Juvenil del Trabajo [*Youth Labor Army*] [*Cuban*] (LA)
EK .... Commission of Experts (RU)
ek .... Economic, Economical, Economics (RU)
EK .... Economics Study Center (of the Academy of Sciences, USSR) (RU)
EK .... Efimeris tis Kyverniseos [*Government Gazette*] [*Greek*] [*A publication*] (GC)
EK .... Eisernes Kreuz [*Iron Cross*] (EG)
EK .... Electric Boiler, Electric Caldron (RU)
EK- .... Electric Heater (RU)
EK .... Electrochemical Corrosion (RU)
EK .... Electrolytic Core Sampling (Method) (RU)
EK .... Electronic Commutator (RU)
EK .... Electronic Contact (RU)
EK .... Electropneumatic Valve (RU)
EK .... Energiekonzentration [*Energy Concentration*] (EG)
EK .... Energy Factor (RU)
EK .... Eniaion Komma [*United Party*] [*Cypriot*] (GC)
EK .... Enosis Kendrou [*Center Union (Party)*] [*Greek*] (GC)
EK .... Ergatikon Kendron [*Labor Center*] (GC)
e k .... Eszakkelet [*Northeast*] (HU)
eK .... Etter Kristi [*After Christ*] [*Norwegian*] (GPO)
E K .... Europa Kiado [*Europa Publishing House*] (HU)
EK .... Europa Kupa [*Europe Cup (Sports)*] (HU)
ek .... Ezred Kozvetlen [*Directly Subordinate to the Regiment Commander*] (HU)
e K .... Kerr Effect (RU)
EK .... Power Kombinat (RU)
EK .... Power System [*Maritime term*] (RU)
EKA .... Ekonomicheskaia Komissiia dlia Afriki (MAR)
EKA .... Elektromos Keszulekek es Anyagok Gyara [*Factory of Electric Appliances and Materials*] (HU)
EKA .... Enosis Klostoyfandourgon Athinon [*Athens Textile Workers Union*] (GC)
EKA .... Enosis Kyprion Agroton [*Union of Cypriot Farmers*] (GC)
EKA .... Enosis Kyprion Anglias [*Union of Cypriots in England*] (GC)
EKA .... Entwicklung und Konstruction fuer Apparatebau [*Development and Design Office for Apparatus Building*] (EG)
EKA .... Ergatikon Kendron Athinon [*Athens Labor Center*] (GC)
EKA .... Ergatikon Kinima Allagis [*Labor Movement for a Change*] [*Greek*] (GC)
EKA .... Etaireia Kypriakon Aerogrammon [*Cyprus Airways*] (GC)
EKA .... Evropaiki Koini Agora [*European Common Market*] (GC)
EKA .... United Nations Economic Commission for Africa [*ECA*] (RU)
EKADV .... United Nations Economic Commission for Asia and the Far East [*ECAFE*] (RU)
EKAE .... Ergatiki Kinisis dia ton Afoplismon kai tin Eirinin [*Labor Movement for Disarmament and Peace*] [*Greek*] (GC)
EKAE .... Evropaiki Koinotis Atomikis Energeias [*European Atomic Energy Community*] (GC)
EKAKh .... Evropaiki Koinopraxia Anthrakos kai Khalyvos [*European Coal and Steel Community*] (GC)
EKAS .... Ellino-Kypriakos Apelevtherotikos Stratos [*Greek-Cypriot Liberation Army*] [*See also KRKO*] [*EKAS is preferred*] (GC)
EKATE .... Epimelitirion Kalon Tekhnon [*Chamber of Fine Arts*] (GC)
EKB .... Elektrochemisches Kombinat Bitterfeld (VEB) [*Bitterfeld Electrochemical Combine (VEB)*] (EG)
EKB .... Experimental Design Office (RU)
EKD .... Elektryczna Kolej Dojazdowa [*Suburban Electric Railroad*] (POL)
EKD .... Evangelische Kirche Deutschlands [*Evangelical Church of Germany*] [*West German*] (WEN)
EKDITh .... Ellinikon Kendron Diethnous Institoutou Theatrou [*Greek Center of the International Institute of the Theater*] (GC)
EKDYE .... Ergatiki Kinisis dia tin Diethni Yfesin kai Eirinin [*Labor Movement for an International Detente and Peace*] [*Greek*] (GC)
EKE .... Elliniki Ktiniatriki Etaireia [*Greek Veterinary Association*] (GC1)
EKE .... Ellinikos Kodix Epangelmaton [*Greek Job Classification Code*] (GC)
EKE .... Energie- und Kraftanlagen Export, Berlin (VEB) [*Berlin Energy and Power Plant Export (VEB)*] (EG)
EKE .... Ethniki Kinisi Ellinon [*National Movement of Greeks*] (GC)
EKE .... Ethnikon Komma Ellados [*National Party of Greece*] (GC)
EKEES .... Eidiki Koinovoulevtiki Epitropi Epexergasias tou Syndagmatos [*Special Parliamentary Committee for Elaboration of the Constitution*] [*Greek*] (GC)
EKEkaiP ...... Elliniko Kinima Eirinis kai Politismou [*Greek Committee for Peace and Civilization*] (GC)
EKEKh .... Ekpaidevtikon Kendron Efedron Kheiriston [*Reserve Pilots' Training Center*] (GC)
EKEL .... Eniaia Kinisi Ekmetallevomenou Laou [*United Movement of Exploited People*] [*Greek*] (GC)
EKEOP .... Eidikon Kendron Ekpaidevseos Oreivatikou Pyrovolikou [*Special Mountain Artillery Training Center*] [*Greek*] (GC)
EKEP .... Eniaion Komma Ethnikofronou Parataxeos [*Unified Nationalist Alignment Party*] [*Cypriot*] (GC)
EKEP .... Ethnikon Kendron Perivallondos [*National Center for Environment*] [*See also EKP*] (GC1)
EKES .... Enotiki Kinisi Elevtheron Syndikaliston [*Unifying Movement of Free Trade Unionists*] [*Cypriot*] (GC)
EKF .... Enosis Kyprion Foititon (Londinou) [*Cypriot Student Union (London)*] (GC)
EKFSE .... Enosis Kyprion Foititon (Sovietikis Enoseos) [*Cypriot Student Union (Soviet Union)*] (GC)
EKG .... Electrocardiogram (BU)
EKG .... Electrocardiogram, Electrocardiography (RU)
Ekg .... Elektrokardiagram [*Electrocardiogram*] (EG)
EKG .... Elektrokardiogram [*Electrocardiogram*] [*Polish*]
EKG .... Europejska Komisja Gospodarcza [*European Economic Commission*] (POL)
EKG .... Open-Pit Caterpillar Excavator (RU)
EKGG .... Electrocardiogastrogram (RU)
Ekgiz .... State Economics Publishing House (RU)
EKGV .... Elelmiszeripari Kozponti Gepjavito Vallalat [*Central Machine Repair Shop of the Food Industry*] (HU)

EKGY .... Elektromos Keszulekek Gyara [*Electrical Apparatus Factory*] (HU)
EKh .... Ethniki Khorofylaki [*National Gendarmery*] (GC)
EKhDEVDG ... Elliniki Khristianiki Dimokratiki Enosi Vasilofronon Dytikis Germanias [*Greek Christian Democratic Union of Royalists of West Germany*] (GC)
EKhE .... Elliniki Khristianokoinoniki Enosis [*Greek Christian Socialist Union*] (GC)
EKhEE .... Enosis Kheirourgikon Etaireion Ellados [*Union of Greek Surgical Societies*] (GC1)
EKhG .... Electrochemical Automatic Gas Analyzer (RU)
EKhG .... Electrochordogram (RU)
EKhG .... Ethylene Chlorohydrin (RU)
EKhKE .... Ethniko Khristianodimokratikon Komma Ellados [*National Christian Democratic Party of Greece*] (GC)
EKhO .... Electrochemical Water Desalting (RU)
EKhPA .... Enosis Kheiriston Politikis Aeroporias [*Civil Aviation Pilots Association*] [*Greek*] (GC)
EKhPL .... Etaireia Khorikon Proiondon kai Lipasmaton [*Domestic Products and Fertilizers Company*] [*Greek*] (GC)
EKhS .... Ethniko Khorotaxiko Symvoulio [*National Zoning Council*] (GC1)
EkhV .... Electrochemical Fuze (RU)
EKI .... Electrokymogram (RU)
EKI .... Eregli Komur [*or Komurleri*] Isletmesi [*The Eregli Coal Works*] (TU)
EKI .... Erjedesipari Kutato Intezet [*Fermentation Research Institute*] (HU)
EKI .... Exekutiva Komunisticke Internacionaly [*Executive Committee of the Communist International*] (CZ)
EKIKhIMMASh ... Experimental Institute of Chemical Machinery (RU)
EKISZ .... Egyenruhazati Kisipari Szovetkezet [*Uniforms Producers' Cooperative Enterprise*] (HU)
EKJ .... Estradni a Koncertni Jednatelstvi [*Theatrical and Concert Agency (of the Center of Music Performers and Entertainers)*] (CZ)
EKK .... Enopoiitiki Kinisi Kentrou [*Unification Movement of the Center*] (GC1)
EKK .... Epanastatiko Kommounistiko Komma [*Revolutionary Communist Party*] [*Greek*] (GC)
EKKA .... Ethniki kai Koinoniki Apelevtherosis [*National and Social Liberation (Organization)*] [*Greek*] (GC)
EKKE .... Epanastatiko Kommounistiko Kinima Elladas [*Revolutionary Communist Movement of Greece (Maoist)*] (GC)
EKKE .... Epanastatiko Kommounistiko Komma Ellados [*Revolutionary Communist Party of Greece*] (PPW)
EKKE .... Ethniko Kommounistiko Komma Ellados [*National Communist Party of Greece*] (GC)
EKKE .... Ethnikon Kendron Koinonikon Erevnon [*National Center for Social Research*] [*Greek*] (GC)
EKKI .... Epitoanyagipari Kozponti Kutato Intezet [*Central Research Institute of the Building Materials Industry*] (HU)
EKKU .... Ekonomi dan Keuangan [*Economic and Financial Affairs*] (IN)
EKLA .... United Nations Economic Commission for Latin America [*ECLA*] (RU)
EKLIP .... Entreprise Khmere de Librairie, d'Imprimerie, et de Papeterie, SARL [*Cambodian Book, Printing, and Paper Company, Inc.*] (CL)
EKM .... Electric Contact Pressure Gauge (RU)
EKM .... Elektromos Keszulekek es Meromuszerek Gyara [*Factory of Electric Apparatus and Measuring Instruments*] (HU)
EkM .... Energie- und Kraftmaschinen [*Energy Generators and Engines*] (EG)
EKM .... Epites- es Kosmunkaugyi Miniszter [*Minister of Construction and Public Works*] (HU)
EKM .... Square Meter Equivalent (RU)
EKM .... Warenzeichen der Volkseigenen Betriebe des Energie- und Kraftmaschinenbaus [*Trademark to Designate a Product of the State Enterprises of the Energy Generating and Engine Construction Branch*] (EG)
EKME .... Epitoipari es Kozlekedesi Muszaki Egyetem [*Technical University of Construction and Transportation*] (HU)
EK-ND .... Enosis Kendrou-Neai Dynameis [*Center Union - New Forces*] [*Later, EDIK*] (GC)
EKNE .... El'brus Complex High-Altitute Scientific Expedition (RU)
EKO .... Economics Department (RU)
EKO .... Eisenhuettenkombinat Ost [*East Metallurgical Combine (Eisenhuettenstadt)*] (EG)
EKO .... Ekonomik Konut Organizasyonu ve Insaat AS [*Economic Housing Organization and Construction Corp.*] (TU)
EKO .... Elliniki Kopilatiki Omospondia [*Greek Rowing Federation*] (GC)
EKO .... Evreiskoe Kolonizatsionnoe Obshchestvo [*Jewish Colonization Association*]
EKOF .... Elliniki Kolymvitiki Omospondia Filathlon [*Greek Swimming Federation (of Sportsmen)*] (GC)
EKOF .... Ethniki Koinoniki Organosis Foititon [*National Social Organization of Students*] [*Greek*] (GC)
EKOFNS ...... Elliniki Kopilatiki Omospondia Filathlon Navtikon Somateion [*Greek Rowing Federation of Sportsmen of Boating Clubs*] (GC)
EKoG .... Electrocorticogram, Electrocorticography (RU)
ekol .... Ecologic, Ecological, Ecology (RU)
ekon .... Economic, Economical (RU)
ekon .... Ekonomi [*Finnish*]
EKON .... Elliniki Kommounistiki Neolaia "Rigas Feraios" [*Greek Communist Youth "Rigas Feraios"*] [*Formerly, RIGAS*] (GC)
Ekonomizdat ... Publishing House of Economic Literature (RU)
Ekoso .... Economic Conference [*1920-1936*] (RU)
EKOSOS ..... United Nations Economic and Social Council [*ECOSOC*] (RU)
EKOTE .... Enosis Kataskevaston Oikodomikon-Tekhnikon Ergon [*Union of Construction and Technical Projects Builders*] [*Greek*] (GC)
EKP .... Einkaufspreis [*Purchase Price*] (EG)
EKP .... Epitropi Kratikon Promitheion [*State Supplies Committee*] [*Greek*] (GC)
EKP .... Ergatikon Kendron Patron [*Patras Labor Center*] (GC)
EKP .... Ergatikon Kendron Peiraios [*Piraeus Labor Center*] (GC)
EKP .... Ethnikon Kendron Perivallondos [*National Center for Environment*] [*See also EKEP*] (GC1)
EKP .... Etsiva Keskuspoliisi [*Central Detective Police*] [*Finnish*] (WEN)
EKPAS .... Ekleme Parcalari Ticaret Anonim Sirketi [*Pipe Fittings Trade Corporation*] (TU)
EKPE .... Evropaikon Kendron Pyrinikon Erevnon [*European Nuclear Research Center*] (GC)
EKPOU .... Uniform Enterprise, Organization, and Establishment Classifier (BU)
Ekprav .... Economics and Law Department (RU)
EKR .... Elektronski Komandni Racunar [*Electronic Command Computer*] [*Military*] (YU)
eKr .... Ennen Kristuksen Syntymaa [*Finnish*]
EKRF .... Einheitskontenrahmen der Forstwirtschaft [*Standard Accounts for Forestry*] (EG)
EKRG .... Electrocorticogram (RU)
EKRI .... Einheitskontenrahmen der Industrie [*Standard Accounts for Industry*] (EG)
EKRL .... Einheitskontenrahmen der Landwirtschaft [*Standard Accounts for Agriculture*] (EG)
eks .... Eksempel [*Example*] [*Danish*] (GPO)
EKS .... Ekspedisi [*Expediting, Forwarding, Shipping*] (IN)
Eks .... Ekspresi [*Express*] (TU)
EKS .... Epanastatikos Kommounistikos Syndesmos [*Revolutionary Communist League*] [*Greek*] (GC)
EKS .... Ermittlungsbogen fuer Kostensenkungen, Beziehungsweise Kostensteigerungen [*Form for Determining Cost Decreases or Increases*] (EG)
EKSE .... Ekstratevtikon Soma Ellados [*Greek Expeditionary Force*] (GC)
EKSK .... Elliniki Koinotiki Synelevsis Kyprou [*Greek Communal Chamber*] [*Cypriot*] (GC)
Ekskavatorzapchast' ... Technical Office for the Production of Excavator Spare Parts (RU)
eksp .... Expedition, Expeditionary (RU)
Eksportkhleb ... All-Union Association of the Ministry of Foreign Trade, USSR (RU)
Eksportles ... All-Union Export-Import Association of the Ministry of Foreign Trade, USSR (RU)
Eksportobuv' ... Export Footwear Factory (RU)
ekspr .... Express (RU)
EKSR .... Electrical Signal Flare Container (RU)
ekstr .... Extract (RU)
EKTE .... Ellinikos Kodix Epangelmaton [*Greek Job Classification Code*] (GC)
EKTE .... Ethniki Ktimatiki Trapeza tis Ellados [*National Land Bank of Greece*] (GC)
EKTEK .... Ekonomi dan Teknik [*Economic and Technical Affairs*] (IN)
EKTEL .... Enopoiimenon Koinon Tameion Eispraxeon Leoforeion [*United Joint Bus Collections Fund*] [*Greek*] (GC)
EKTENOL ... Ethnoktimatiki Energou Poleodomias [*National Land Company for Active City Development*] (GC1)
EKU .... Economic Administration (RU)
EKU .... Evangelische Kirche der Union [*Evangelical Church of the Union*] [*West German*] (WEN)
EKUIN .... Ekonomi, Keuangan, dan Industri [*Economic, Financial, and Industrial Affairs*] (IN)
EKVS .... Elliniki Kinisis dia tin Valkanikin Synennoisin [*Greek Movement for a Balkan Understanding*] (GC)
ekv vl .... Moisture Equivalent (RU)
EKW .... Eisenhuettenkombinat West [*West Metallurgical Combine*] (EG)
ekw .... Ekwiwalent [*Equivalent*] [*Polish*]
EKYe .... United Nations Economic Commission for Europe [*ECE*] (RU)
EKYSY .... Enosis Kyprion Syndaxioukhon [*Cypriot Pensioners' Union*] (GC)
ekz .... Copy (BU)
ekz .... Copy (RU)
EKZ .... Forklift Trucks Plant (BU)
EL .... Einheits-Lack [*Unit Lacquer*] [*German*]
el .... Elaintiede [*Zoology*] [*Finnish*]
el .... Electric, Electrical (RU)
El .... Electric Power (BU)
el .... Electrical Engineering (BU)
EL .... Electroluminescence (RU)

EL............... Electron Tube (RU)
el................. Elektrisch [*Electric*] [*German*]
el................. Elektromos [*Electric*] (HU)
el................. Eller [*Or*] [*Norwegian*] (GPO)
EL................ Sounding Device (RU)
ELA............ Ellinikos Laikos Agonas [*Greek Popular Struggle*] (GC1)
ELA............ Enomenos Laikos Agonas [*United People's Struggle*] [*Greek*] (GC)
ELA............ Epanastatikos Laikos Agonas [*Revolutionary Popular Struggle*] (GC1)
ELA............ Estado Libre Asociado [*Commonwealth*] [*Puerto Rican*] (LA)
ELA............ Exercito de Libertacao de Angola (MAR)
ELABOSEDAS... Sociedad Elaborada de Articulos de Seda Ltda. [*Bogota*] (COL)
ELAF.......... Electrification Africaine (MAR)
elag............ Elagazas [*Junction*] (HU)
elainl.......... Elainlaaketiede [*Veterinary Medicine*] [*Finnish*]
ELAN.......... Ethnikon Laikon Apelevtherotikon Navtikon [*National People's Liberation Navy*] [*Greek*] (GC)
ELANA........ Elaboradores de Lana SA [*Yumbo-Valle*] (COL)
ELAR.......... Egyseges Lakossag Adatfelveteli Rendszer [*Uniform Population Survey System*] (HU)
ELAS.......... Ellenikos Laikos Apeleutherotikos Stratos [*Hellenic People's Army of Liberation*] [*Military arm of EAM*] [*Greek*]
ELAS.......... Ethnikos Laikos Apelevtherotikos Stratos [*National People's Liberation Army*] [*Greek*] (GC)
ELASA........ Empresa Ladrillera de Soacha [*Bogota*] (COL)
ELAT.......... Ecole de Lutte Anti-Tse-Tse (MAR)
elat............ Elatiivi [*Finnish*]
ELC............ Estudiantes Libertarios de Cataluna [*Anarchist Students of Catalonia*] [*Spanish*] (WER)
ELC............ Evangelical Lutheran Church (MAR)
ELCT.......... Evangelical Lutheran Church of Tanzania (MAR)
ELD............ Enosis Laikis Dimokratias [*Popular Democratic Union*] [*Greek*] (GC)
ELDO.......... European Launcher Development Organization [*Later, ESA*]
ELDYK........ Ellinikai Dynameis Kyprou [*Greek Forces of Cyprus*] (GC)
Ele.............. Ecole [*School*] [*Military map abbreviation*] [*World War I*] [*French*] (MTD)
ELE............ Ethniki Laiki Enotis [*National Popular Unity*] (GC1)
ELECAM..... Electricite Canalisations du Maroc (MAR)
ELECTA...... Electricidad Tecnica Colombiana Ltda. [*Bogota*] (COL)
ELECTRA.... Electrical, Electronic, and Nucleonic Trade Fair (MAR)
ELECTRAGUAS... Instituto de Aprovechamiento de Aguas y Fomento Electrico [*Institute for the Utilization of Waters and Electric Power Development*] [*Colombian*] (LA)
ELECTRICOL... Electromecanica Industrial Ltda. [*Bogota*] (COL)
ELECTROGAZ... Establissement Public de Production, de Transport, et de Distribution d'Electricite, d'Eau, et de Gaz [*Public Electricity, Water, and Gas Production, Transport, and Distribution Company*] [*Rwandan*] (AF)
ELECTROPERU... Electricidad del Peru [*Peruvian State Electric Power Enterprise*] (LA)
ELEK.......... Elliniko Leninistiko Epanastatiko Kinima [*Greek Leninist Revolutionary Struggle*] (GC)
Elekt........... Elektrizitaet [*Electricity*] [*German*]
ELEKTHERMAX... Villamos Hokeszulekek Gyara, Papa [*Thermoelectric Equipment Factory, Papa*] (HU)
elektr.......... Electrical (BU)
elektr.......... Electronics (RU)
Elektr.......... Elektrizitaet [*German*]
elektr.......... Elektromos [*Electric*] (HU)
elektr.......... Elektromossag [*Electricity*] (HU)
ELEKTRIK-IS... Turkiye Elektrik Istihsali, Nakli, ve Tevzi Isci Sendikarlari Federasyonu [*Turkish Electric Power Production, Transmission, and Distribution Worker Unions' Federation*] (TU)
Elektrobank... Bank for Electrification of the USSR (RU)
ELEKTROBOSNA... Bosnian Electrochemical Industry [*Jacje*] (YU)
Elektrochasofikatsiya... State Repair Planning and Installation Office of the Glavchasprom (RU)
ELEKTRODISTRIBUCIJA... Establishment for Electric Power Distribution (YU)
ELEKTROIMPEX... ELEKTROIMPEX Hiradastechnikai es Finommechanikai Kulkereskedelmi Vallalat [*ELEKTROIMPEX Foreign Trade Enterprise for Telecommunication and Precision Products*] (HU)
Elektrokomplekt... Trust for the Supply of Complete Sets of Electrical Equipment (RU)
ELEKTROKOVINA... Tovarna Elektrokovinskih Izdelkov [*Electric and Metal Products Factory*] [*Maribor-Tezno*] (YU)
elektrol....... Elektrolytisch [*Electrolytic*] [*German*]
ELEKTROMATERIJAL... Electric Equipment Establishment (YU)
ELEKTROMEDICINA... Establishment for Trade in Electric Medical Apparatus (YU)
Elektromontazhkonstruktsiya... Trust of the Glavelektromontazh of the Glavmontazhspetsstroy SSSR (RU)
Elektropromremont... Industrial Establishment for the Repair of the Industrial Electrical Equipment of the Administration of the Chief Mechanical and Power Engineer (RU)
ELEKTRORAD... Elektro Instalaterska Radnja [*Electrical Installation Shop*] (YU)
ELEKTROSRBIJA... Serbian Electric Power Establishment [*Belgrade*] (YU)
ELEKTROSREM... Otsek za Elektrifikaciju Srema [*Section for the Electrification of Srem*] [*Zemun*] (YU)
Elektrotochpribor... Precision Electrical Instruments Plant (RU)
Elektrotsink... Electrolytic Zinc Plant (RU)
Elektrotyazhmash... Heavy Electrical Machinery Plant (RU)
ELEKTROVODA... Komunalno Preduzece za Distribuciju Elektricne Energije i Vode [*Communal Establishment for the Distribution of Electricity and Water*] (YU)
Elektrozem... Rural Electrification Department (RU)
elelm.......... Elelmezes [*Food Supply*] (HU)
Elemko........ Electric Enameling Cooperative (BU)
ELES.......... Elektrogospodarska Skupnost Slovenije [*Electric Management Corporation of Slovenia*] [*Ljubljana*] (YU)
ELETROBRAS... Centrais Eletricas Brasileiras SA [*Brazilian Electric Power Companies, Inc.*] (LA)
ELETROSUL... Centrais Eletricas do Sul [*Southern Electric Power Plants*] [*Brazilian*] (LA)
elev............ Grain Elevator [*Topography*] (RU)
ELEVME...... Elliniki Etaireia Viomikhanikon kai Metallevtikon Ependiseon [*Greek Industrial and Mining Investments Company*] (GC)
ELF............. Eritrean Liberation Front [*Ethiopian*] (PD)
ELF............. Esperanto-Ligo Filatelista [*Philatelic Esperanto League - PEL*] (EA)
ELF............. Essences et Lubrifiants de France [*Gasoline and Lubricants Company of France*] (AF)
ELF-ERAP... Essences et Lubrifiants de France - Entreprise de Recherches et d'Activites Petrolieres (MAR)
ELF-PLF...... Eritrean Liberation Front - Popular Liberation Forces [*Ethiopian*] (PD)
ELF-RC....... Eritrean Liberation Front - Revolutionary Command [*Ethiopian*] (PD)
ELF-SEREPCA... Societe ELF [*Essences et Lubrifiants de France*] de Recherches et d'Exploitation des Petroles du Cameroun (MAR)
ELF-SPAFE... Societe ELF [*Essences et Lubrifiants de France*] des Petroles d'Afrique Equatoriale [*ELF-Petroleum Company of Equatorial Africa*] [*Gabonese*] (AF)
ELFT........... Eotvos Lorand Fizikai Tarsulat [*Lorand Eotvos Physics Society*] (HU)
ELG............ Einkaufs- und Liefergenossenschaft [*Purchase and Delivery Cooperative (for artisans)*] (EG)
elg.............. Ellenseg [*or Ellenseges*] [*Enemy*] (HU)
ELGEP......... Elelmiszeripari Gepgyar es Szerelo Vallalat [*Food Industry Machine Factory and Assembly Enterprise*] (HU)
ELGH.......... Einkaufs- und Liefergenossenschaft des Handwerks [*Purchase and Delivery Cooperative for Artisans*] (EG)
el-grafich.... Electron Diffraction (RU)
ELI.............. Electron Tube Integrator (RU)
ELINAMO.... Exercito de Libertacao Nacional de Monomotapa (MAR)
ELIP............ Elektro-Industrisko Preduzece [*Industrial Electrical Establishment*] [*Zemun*] (YU)
elip............. Elelmiszeripar [*Food Industry*] (HU)
Elip M......... Elelmiszeripari Miniszterium/Miniszter [*Ministry/Minister of the Food Industry*] (HU)
ELITOSA..... Empresa Litografica Sociedad Anonima [*Barranquilla*] (COL)
ELIZOMAT... Fabrika na Elektro Izolacioni Materiali [*Electric Insulating Materials Plant*] [*Prilep*] (YU)
elj............... Eljaras [*Procedure, Process, Proceedings*] (HU)
ELK............ Ellinikon Laikon Kinima [*Greek Popular Movement*] (GC)
ELK............ Enosis Laikou Kommatos [*Union of Populist Parties*] [*Greek*] (PPE)
ELK............ Ethniko Laiko Komma [*National Populist Party*] [*Greek*] (PPE)
ELK............ Evangelisch-Lutherische Kirche [*Evangelical Lutheran Church*] [*Namibian*] (AF)
Elka............ Elektrokarren [*Electric Carts*] (EG)
ELKA.......... Elyafli Plaka Sanayii TAS [*Fiber Record Industry Corporation*] (TU)
ELKA.......... Tvornica Elektricnih Kabela [*Electric Cable Works*] [*Zagreb*] (YU)
ELKAD........ Eidikos Logariasmos Koinonikon Asfaliseon Dodekanisou [*Dodecanese Social Insurance Special Account*] [*Greek*] (GC)
elkall.......... Elkallodott [*Missing*] (HU)
ELKAR........ Electrocardiograph (RU)
El Ke Pa...... Ellinikon Kendron Paragogikotitos [*Greek Productivity Center*] (GC)
el-khim....... Electrochemistry (RU)
Elkhima....... Electrochemical and Technical Cooperative (BU)
ELKI........... Ellinikon Laikon Kinima [*Greek Popular Movement*] (GC)
ELKO.......... Tvornica Elektrokovinskih Proizvodov [*Electrical Equipment Plant*] [*Maribor*] (YU)
elkolt.......... Elkoltozott [*Departed, Moved*] (HU)
ELKOOP...... Producers Cooperative for Electric Appliances (BU)
ell............... Ellato [*or Ellatas*] [*Supplying or Supply*] (HU)
ell............... Ellenor [*Controller, Inspector*] (HU)
ell............... Eller [*Or*] [*Swedish*] (GPO)
ello............. Ellato Osztaly [*Supply Department*] (HU)
ELM............ Cathode-Ray Minimizer (RU)

elm .... Elelmezes [*or Elelmezesi*] [*Food Supply, Supplying, Catering*] (HU)
ELM .... Ethiopian Liberation Movement (MAR)
ELMA .... Empresa Lineas Maritimas Argentinas [*Argentine Shipping Lines*] (LA)
ELMA .... Tovarna Elektroinstalacijskega Materiala [*Electrical Installation Works*] [*Crnuce*] (YU)
ELMAF .... Societe des Emballages Legers Metalliques Africains (MAR)
el-magn .... Electromagnetic (RU)
el magn yed ... Electromagnetic Unit (RU)
ELME .... Enosis Leitourgon Mesis Ekpaidevseos [*Union of Intermediate School Teachers*] [*Greek*] (GC)
EL-MEK .... Elektro Mekanik Cihazlar Sanayii [*Electromechanical Instruments Industry*] (TU)
ELMES .... Ellinikai Mesogeiakai Grammai [*Greek Mediterranean Lines*] (GC)
ELMEX .... Elementos Electronics Mexicanos SA [*Mexican*]
el-mikroskopich ... Electron-Microscopic (RU)
EIMK .... Elelmezesugyi Miniszterium Kollegiuma [*Council of the Ministry of Food Supply*] (HU)
ELMO .... Elektromotorenwerk (VEB) [*Electric Motor Plant (VEB)*] (EG)
elmo .... Elelmezesi Osztaly [*Food Provisioning Department, Quartermaster Corps Unit*] (HU)
ELMOK .... Ellinikon Monarkhikon Kinima [*Greek Monarchist Movement*] (GC)
ELMP .... Experimental Machine-Translation Laboratory (RU)
ELMS .... Eskisehir Lokomotif ve Motor Sanayii [*Eskisehir Locomotive and Motor Industry*] (TU)
ELN .... Ejercito de Liberacion Nacional [*National Liberation Army*] [*Argentine*] (LA)
ELN .... Ejercito de Liberacion Nacional [*National Liberation Army*] [*Chilean*] (LA)
ELN .... Ejercito de Liberacion Nacional [*National Liberation Army*] [*Bolivian*] (PD)
ELN .... Ejercito de Liberacion Nacional [*National Liberation Army*] [*Colombian*] (PD)
ELN .... Ejercito de Liberacion Nacional [*National Liberation Army*] [*Peruvian*] (PD)
ELN .... Ejercito de Liberacion Nicaraguense [*Nicaraguan Liberation Army*] (LA1)
ELN .... Ejercito Liberador Nacional [*National Liberating Army*] [*Argentine*] (LA)
eln .... Elnok [*President*] (HU)
ELN .... Erzeugnis- und Leistungsnomenklatur [*Product and Performance Nomenclature*] (EG)
ELNA .... Exercito de Libertacao Nacional de Angola (MAR)
EINII .... Scientific Research Institute for Electric Locomotive Building (RU)
ELO .... Ecole Speciale des Langues Orientales Vivantes (MAR)
el-od .... Electrode (RU)
elof .... Elofizeto [*Subscriber*] (HU)
ELOK .... Elektricna Lokomotiva [*Electric Locomotive*] (YU)
elok .... Elokuva [*Film, Cinema*] [*Finnish*]
ELOK .... Evangelisch-Lutheranische Ovambokavangokirche [*Evangelical-Lutheran Ovambo-Kavango Church*] [*Namibian*] (MAR)
el-optich .... Electron-Optical (RU)
ELOSPINA ... Hijos de Eleazar Ospina & Cia. Ltda. [*Medellin*] (COL)
ELOU .... Electric Desalination Unit (RU)
ELOV .... Ecole Speciale des Langues Orientales Vivantes (MAR)
ELP .... Exercito de Libertacao Portugues [*Portuguese Liberation Army*] (WER)
ELPA .... Elliniki Leskhi Periigiseon kai Avtokinitou [*Greek Automobile and Touring Club*] (GC)
ELPEC .... Entreprise Lao de Promotion et d'Exploitation Cinematographique [*Lao Motion Picture Promotion and Exploitation Company*] (CL)
el podst .... Electric Substation (RU)
ELPOH .... Elektricno Poduzece Hrvatske [*Electrical Establishment of Croatia*] (YU)
ELPROM .... Electric Power Industry Enterprise (BU)
ELRU .... Electronic Recorder (RU)
els .... Effective Horsepower (RU)
ELS .... Elliniki Lyriki Skini [*Greek Lyric Theater*] (GC)
ELSA .... End Loans to South Africa (MAR)
ELSASSER ... Elsaess-Lothringen Partei [*Alsace-Lorraine Party*] [*German*] (PPE)
ELSE .... Elliniki Synomospondia Ergasias [*Greek Labor Confederation*] (GC)
EL-SEN .... Kibris Turk Elektrik Mustahdemleri Sendikasi [*Turkish Cypriot Electric Power Employees Union*] (TU)
el-st .... Electric Power Plant [*Topography*] (RU)
el-st yed .... Electrostatic Unit (RU)
ELT .... Cathode-Ray Tube (RU)
ELTA .... Ellinika Takhydromeia [*Greek Posts*] (GC)
ELTE .... Eotvos Lorand Tudomanyegyetem [*Lorand Eotvos University of Arts and Sciences*] (HU)
ELTEK .... Elektronik Teknoloji AS [*Electronic Technology Corp.*] (TU)
El-term .... Electrothermics (RU)
ELTERV .... Elelmezesipari Tervezo Vallalat [*Food Industry Planning Enterprise*] (HU)
ELTSA .... End Loans to South Africa (MAR)
ELTV .... Eternal Love Television (MAR)
ELV .... Elektrovod [*Electrical Engineering Enterprise*] (CZ)
elv .... Elvalt [*Divorced*] (HU)
ELV .... Etaireia Laikis Vasis [*Public Base Company*] (GC1)
ELVIL .... Elliniki Viomikhania Lipasmaton [*Greek Fertilizer Industry (of Kavala, OTE)*] (GC1)
elvt .... Elvtars [*Comrade*] (HU)
ELWA .... Eternal Love Winning Africa (MAR)
ELWE .... Elektromotorenwerk Wernigerode [*Wernigerode Electric Motor Plant*] (EG)
ELYPAL .... Elliniki Yperpondios Alieia [*Greek Overseas Fishing*] (GC)
elyuv .... Eluvial, Eluvium (RU)
ELZ .... Electric Bulb Plant (RU)
ELZ .... Enciklopedija Leksikografskog Zavoda [*Encyclopedia of the Lexicographic Institute*] [*Zagreb*] [*A publication*] (YU)
elzagr .... Electrified Wire Obstacle Company (RU)
el zhd .... Electric Railroad (RU)
ELZI .... Electroluminescent Character Indicator (RU)
EM .... Destroyer [*Navy*] (RU)
EM .... East Malaysia (ML)
em .... Edella Mainittu [*Finnish*]
EM .... Efficiency Medal (MAR)
EM- .... Electromagnet (RU)
EM .... Electromagnetic (Instrument) (RU)
EM .... Electron Microscope, Electron Microscopy (RU)
Em .... Emekli [*Retired*] (TU)
em .... Emelet [*Floor*] (HU)
em .... Emeritiert [*German*]
em .... Emerytowany [*Retired*] [*Polish*]
EM .... Emmanuel Mission (MAR)
em .... Emulsion (RU)
em .... Ennen Mainittu [*Finnish*]
EM .... Entente Mauritanienne (MAR)
EM .... Entfernungsmesser [*Range Finder*] (EG)
EM .... Epitesugyi Miniszterium/Miniszter [*Ministry/Minister of Construction*] (HU)
EM .... Escuadron de la Muerte [*Death Squadron*] [*Salvadoran*] (LA1)
EM .... Estado Maior [*General Staff*] [*Portuguese*] (WER)
EM .... Estado Mayor [*Spanish*]
E-M .... Etat-Major [*Headquarters*] [*French*]
EM .... Ethnikon Metopon [*National Front*] [*Cypriot*] (GC)
EM .... Etudes Mauritaniennes [*A publication*] (MAR)
EM .... Euroopan Mestaruus [*Finnish*]
EM .... Excerpta Medica [*Amsterdam*]
EM .... Exploatatie Miniera [*Mining Exploitation*] (RO)
EM .... Magnetic Clutch (RU)
EM- .... Multibucket Excavator (RU)
EMA .... Ecole Marocaine d'Administration (MAR)
EMA .... Ecole Militaire d'Administration [*Algerian*] (MAR)
EMA .... Einwohnermeldeamt [*Resident Registration Office*] (EG)
EMA .... Electro Mecanique Abidjan (MAR)
EMA .... Electromagnetic Analyzer (RU)
EMA .... Elliniki Mousiki Akadimia [*Greek Music Academy*] (GC)
Ema .... Eminencia [*Eminence*] [*Spanish*]
EMA .... Estado Maior da Armada [*Navy General Staff*] [*Brazilian*] (LA)
EMA .... Etat-Major de l'Armee [*Military*] [*French*] (MTD)
EMA .... Ethyl Methacrylamide (RU)
EMA .... Medical Electric Equipment (Plant) (RU)
EMAB .... Entreprise Malienne du Bois (MAR)
EMAC .... Empresa Mocambicana de Aviacao Comercial (MAR)
EMAC .... Equipamentos e Materiais de Construcao Lda. (MAR)
EMACI .... Entrepots Miliens en Cote-d'Ivoire (MAR)
EMAD .... Efippa Mikta Apospasmata Dioxeos [*Mounted Joint Pursuit Detachments*] [*Greek*] (GC)
EMADI .... Empresa Administradora de Inmuebles [*Buildings Administrative Enterprise*] [*Peruvian*] (LA)
EMAer .... Estado Maior da Aeronautica [*Air Force General Staff*] [*Brazilian*] (LA)
EMAG .... Elso Magyar Gazdasagi Gepgyar [*First Hungarian Agricultural Machine Factory*] (HU)
EMAK .... Ethnikon Metopon Agoniston Kyprou [*National Front of Fighters*] [*Cypriot*] (GC)
EMALEDH ... Union of Ethiopian Marxist-Leninist Organizations (AF)
EMAS .... "El Mouggar" Art et Spectacle (MAR)
EMASA .... Equipos y Maquinarias, Sociedad Anonima [*Equipment and Machinery, Inc.*] [*Chilean*] (LA)
EMASZ .... Eszak-Magyarorszagi Aramszolgaltato Vallalat [*Electric Power Enterprise of Northern Hungary*] (HU)
EMATEC .... Entreprise Nationale d'Importation de Materiel Technique (MAR)
EMB .... Editio Musica Budapest (Budapesti Zenemukiado Vallalat) [*"Editio Musica" (Music Publishing Company, Budapest)*] (HU)
EMB .... Electromagnetic Blocking (RU)
EMBAL .... Embalagens de Madeiras de Mocambique Lda. (MAR)
EMBALLAF ... Societe "L'Emballage Africain" [*North African*] (MAR)
EMBOSA .... Empresa Metalurgica Boliviana, Sociedad Anonima [*Bolivian Metallurgical Enterprise, Inc.*] (LA)
EMBOSALVA ... Embotelladora Salvadorena, SA [*Salvadoran Bottling Corp.*]
embr .... Embryology (RU)

EMBRAER... Empresa Brasileira Aeronautica [*Brazilian Aeronautics Company*] (LA)
EMBRAFILME ... Empresa Brasileira de Filmes [*Brazilian Film Company*] (LA)
EMBRAMED ... Empresa Brasileira de Medicamentos [*Brazilian Pharmaceutical Companmy*] (LA)
EMBRAPA... Empresa Brasileira de Pesquisa Agropecuaria [*Brazilian Agriculture and Livestock Research Enterprise*] (LA)
EMBRASID ... Empresa Brasileira de Sistemas de Defensa [*Brazilian Defense Systems Enterprise*] (LA1)
EMBRATEL ... Empresa Brasileira de Telecomunicacoes [*Brazilian Telecommunications Company*] (LA)
EMBRATER ... Empresa Brasileira de Assistencia Tecnica e Extensao Rural [*Brazilian Rural Extension and Technical Assistance Enterprise*] (LA)
EMBRATUR ... Empresa Brasileira de Turismo [*Brazilian Tourism Company*] (LA)
Embre .... Embarcadere [*Pier*] [*Military map abbreviation*] [*World War I*] [*French*] (MTD)
Embriol .... Embryology, Embryological (BU)
Embure .... Embouchure [*Mouth*] [*Military map abbreviation*] [*World War I*] [*French*] (MTD)
EMC .... Elektroniczna Maszyna Cyfrowa [*Digital Computer*] (POL)
EMC .... Elso Magyar Cernagyar [*First Hungarian Yarn Factory*] (HU)
EMC .... Empresa Metalurgica Colombiana SA [*Bucaramanga*] (COL)
EMC .... Entreprise Miniere et Chimique [*French*] (MAR)
EMC .... Estado Mayor Conjunto [*Joint General Staff*] [*Salvadoran*] (LA1)
EMCC.......... Escuelas Militares Camilo Cienfuegos [*Camilo Cienfuegos Military Schools*] [*Cuban*] (LA)
EMC/JS ...... Etat-Major Central de la Jeunesse Sauvetage [*Salvation Youth Central Headquarters*] [*Cambodian*] (CL)
EMCO......... Empresa de Produccion de Medios Tecnicos de Computacion [*Enterprise for the Production of Technical Means of Computation*] [*Cuban*] (LA)
EMCOCABLES ... Empresa Colombiana de Cables SA [*Bogota*] (COL)
EMCOLDROMOS ... Empresa Colombiana de Aerodromos [*Bogota*] (COL)
EMCTCU..... European-Middle East Channel and Traffic Control Unit (MAR)
EMD .... Eidgenoessisches Militaerdepartement [*Swiss Military Department*] (WEN)
EMD .... Electronique Marcel Dassault [*Marcel Dassault Electronics*] [*French*] (WER)
EMDAI......... Enosis Mousoulmanon Didaskalon Apofoiton ton Ierospoudastirion [*Union of Moslem Teacher Graduates of the Religious Schools*] (GC)
EMDP......... Etaireia Metaforas kai Diyliseos Petrelaion [*Petroleum Transport and Refining Company*] (GC)
EMDY......... Enosis Mikhanikon Dimosion Ypallilon [*Union of Civil Service Engineers*] [*Greek*] (GC)
EME............ Elektrarna Melnik [*Electric Power Plant Melnik*] (CZ)
EME............ Elliniki Mathimatiki Etaireia [*Greek Mathematics Society*] (GC)
EME............ Elliniki Metallevtiki Etaireia [*Hellenic Mines Corporation*] [*Cypriot*] (GC)
EME............ Empirical Matrix Element (RU)
EME............ Empresa Mocambicana de Empreitadas (MAR)
EME............ Enosis Mousoulmanon Ellados [*Union of Moslems of Greece*] (GC)
EME............ Estado Maior do Exercito [*Army General Staff*] [*Portuguese*] (WER)
EME............ Ethnikon Metopon Ellados [*National Front of Greece*] (GC)
EMEA.......... Etaireia Meleton Ethnikis Amynis [*Association for National Defense Studies*] [*Greek*] (GC)
EMEC.......... Empresa Estatal de Construcao [*State Construction Company*] [*Cape Verdean*] (AF)
EMEC.......... Estado Mayor del Ejercito del Centro [*Staff of the Central Army*] [*Cuban*] (LA)
EMEK.......... Ethniki Mathitiki Enosis Kyprou [*National Student Union of Cyprus*] (GC)
EMEKEL...... Eniaion Metopon Ergaton kai Ergazomenou Laou [*United Front of Workers and Working People*] [*Greek*] (GC)
EMELEC ..... Empresa Electrica Ecuatoriana [*Ecuadorean Electric Power Enterprise*] (LA)
EMEO......... Esoteriki Makedoniki Epanastatiki Organosis [*Internal Macedonian Revolutionary Organization*] (GC)
EMEP......... Etaireia Meletis Ellinikon Provlimaton [*Society for the Study of Greek Problems*] (GC)
EMEPS........ Ecole Militaire d'EPS [*Enseignements Primaire et Secondaire*] (MAR)
EMERGE ..... Magyar Ruggyantagyar Reszvenytarsasag [*Hungarian Rubber Processing Factory*] (HU)
EMF............ Etablissements Martre Freres (MAR)
EMF............ Ethyl Mercury Phosphate (RU)
EMFA.......... Estado Maior das Forcas Armadas [*Armed Forces General Staff*] [*Brazilian*] (LA)
EMG............ Electromyogram, Electromyography (RU)
EMG............ Elektronikus Merokeszulekek Gyara [*Factory for Electronic Measuring Instruments*] (HU)
EMG............ Estado Mayor General [*General Staff*] (LA1)
EMG............ Etablissements Metalliques du Gabon (MAR)
EMG............ Etat-Major General [*General Staff*] (CL)
EMGDO....... Evangelische Mission Gesellschaft fuer Deutsch-Ostafrika (MAR)
EMGE.......... Estado Mayor General del Ejercito [*Army General Staff*] [*Cuban*] (LA)
Emgekali..... Magnesiumhaltiges Kali [*Magnesium-Bearing Potash*] (EG)
EMGFA........ Estado-Maior General das Forcas Armadas [*General Staff of the Armed Forces*] [*Portuguese*] (WER)
EMGy .... Elektronikus Merokeszulekek Gyara [*Factory for Electronic Measuring Instruments*] (HU)
emhaka/MHK ... Munkara Harcra Kesz [*Ready for Work and Combat (Organization)*] (HU)
EMI............. Empresa de Montajes Industriales [*Industrial Installations Enterprise*] [*Cuban*] (LA)
EMI............. Epitesugyi Minosito Intezet [*Construction Qualification Institute*] (HU)
EMI............. Etat-Major Interarmes [*Algerian*] (MAR)
EMIA.......... Ecole Militaire Interarmes [*Military Inter-Service School*] [*Algerian*] (AF)
EMIAC......... Ecole Militaire Interarmes Camerounaise [*Cameroonian Military Inter-Service School*] (AF)
EMIC........... Entreprise Marocaine d'Irrigation et de Canalisation (MAR)
EMID........... Electromagnetic Inductive Flaw Detector (RU)
EMIDICT ..... Empresa Especializada Importadora y Distribuidora para la Ciencia y la Tecnica [*Enterprise Specialized in Importing and Distributing Science and Technology*] [*Cuban*] (LA1)
E Min.......... Eau Minerale [*Military map abbreviation*] [*World War I*] [*French*] (MTD)
EMINSA ...... Empressa Sahara Minera [*Sahara Mining Enterprise*] (AF)
EMINSU ...... Emekli Subaylar [*Retired Officers Association*] (TU)
EMIRTEL..... Emirates Telecommunications Corporation (MAR)
EMIS .... Ege Bolgesi Maden Iscileri Sendikasi [*Aegean Regional Mine Workers' Union*] [*Zonguldak*] (TU)
EMIT........... Electromagnetic Instrument for Measuring Sea Currents (RU)
EMIZ........... Electromechanical Tool Plant (RU)
EMK .... Electromagnetic Compensator (RU)
EMK .... Electromagnetic Corrector (RU)
EMK .... Electromagnetic Valve (RU)
EMK .... Elektrik, Makine, Kablo [*Electric Power, Machinery, and Cable Directorate*] [*Turkish Cypriot*] (GC)
EMK .... Elektromotorische Kraft [*Electromotive Force*] (EG)
EMK .... Epitok Muszaki Klubja [*Engineers Club*] (HU)
EMKA.......... Ettehadiyye Markazi Kargarane Iran Central Federation of Trade Unions of Workers and Peasants of Iran (MAR)
EMKE.......... Ethnikon Metarrythmistikon Komma Ellados [*National Reformation Party of Greece*] (GC)
EMKh.......... Ethyl Mercury Chloride (RU)
EMKIE......... Ellinikon Morfotikon Kendron Inomenon Ethnon [*United Nations Educational Center of Greece*] (GC)
EMKL.......... Ekspedisi Muatan Kapal Laut [*Maritime Cargo Handling Association*] (IN)
EMKS.......... Electronic Crossbar Switch (RU)
EMLKB........ Turkiye Emlak Kredi Bankasi TAS [*Turkish Real Estate Credit Bank Corp.*] (TU)
EMM........... Mathematical Methods in Economics (RU)
EMMA .... Empresa Mocambicana de Malhas (MAR)
EMMHO....... Ecole Militaire pour les Metiers d'Hotellerie [*Algerian*] (MAR)
EMMIU .... Empresa Metropolitana de Mantenimiento de Inmuebles Urbanos [*Metropolitan Enterprise for Maintenance of Urban Property*] [*Cuban*] (LA)
Emmo .... Eminentisimo [*Most Eminent*] [*Spanish*]
Emn............ Emniyet [*Security*] (TU)
EMN .... Escuadron de la Muerte Nuevo [*New Death Squad*] [*Salvadoran*] (PD)
EMO .... Elektrarna Mesta Opavy, Narodni Podnik [*Electric Power Works of the City of Opava, National Enterprise*] (CZ)
EMO .... Elektrik Muhendisleri Odasi [*Chamber of Electrical Engineers*] (TU)
EMO .... United Youth Organization (BU)
EM/OP .... Etat Major Operationnel [*Operational Staff*] (CL)
EMOS.......... High School Students Youth Union (BU)
EMOSE .... Empresa Mocambicana de Seguros (MAR)
EMP............ Electric Installation Train (RU)
EMP............ Electromechanical Production (of Mosgoraptekoupravleniye) (RU)
EMP............ Electromechanical Transducer (RU)
EMP............ Electromechanical Transmission (RU)
EMP............ Elektro-Mehanicko Pretprijatie [*Electro-Mechanical Establishment*] [*Skopje*] (YU)
EMP............ Elektrotehnicko i Masinsko Preduzece [*Electrical Engineering and Machinery Establishment*] (YU)
EMP............ Ellinikon Metsovion Polytekhneion [*Greek Metsovion Polytechnic School*] [*Also referred to as National Technical University of Athens*] (GC)
EMPA.......... Empresa Publica de Abastecimentos [*Public Enterprise for Supply*] [*Cape Verdean*] (AF)
EMPACO..... Empaques del Pacifico Ltda. [*Cali*] (COL)
EMPACOL... Empaquetadora de Colombia Ltda. [*Cali*] (COL)
EMPE .... Extra Mural Penal Employment (MAR)
EMPI........... Empresa de Promocion Integral [*Integral Promotion Enterprise*] [*Cuban*] (LA)
EMPI........... Ship Electric Centrifugal Firefighting Pump (RU)

engl .... Englantia [*or Englanniksi*] [*Finnish*]
engl .... Englantilainen [*English*] [*Finnish*]
engl .... Englisch [*English*] [*German*]
englj .... Englanninjalka [*Finnish*]
ENH .... Elektrik Nakliyat Hatti [*Electric Power Transmission Line*] (TU)
ENHER .... Empresa Nacional Hidroelectrica de Ribagorza [*Ribagorza National Hydroelectric Enterprise*] [*Spanish*] (WER)
ENI .... Ecole Nationale d'Ingenieurs (MAR)
ENI .... Ecole Normale d'Infirmiers (MAR)
ENI .... Ecole Normale d'Instituteurs [*French*]
ENI .... Ente Nazionale Idrocarburi [*National Hydrocarbons Agency*] [*Italian*] (WER)
ENI .... Ethiopian Nutrition Institute (MAR)
ENIA .... Ecole des Ingenieurs Agricoles [*Agricultural Engineers School*] [*Moroccan*] (AF)
ENIA .... Empresa Nicaraguense de Insumos Agropecuarios [*Nicaraguan Enterprise for Agricultural-Livestock Investments*] (LA1)
ENIB .... Entreprise Nationale de l'Industrie du Bois [*Algerian*] (MAR)
ENICAB .... Empresa Nicaraguense de Cabotaje [*Nicaraguan Enterprise for Coastal Shipping*] (LA1)
ENICAS .... Ecole Nationale des Infirmiers Certifies et de l'Action Sociale (MAR)
ENIIZiM .... Estonian Scientific Research Institute of Agriculture and Reclamation (RU)
ENIKMASh ... Experimental Scientific Research Institute of Forging-and-Pressing Machinery (RU)
ENIM .... Ecole Nationale de l'Industrie Minerale (MAR)
ENIM .... Entreprise Nationale de l'Industrie Metallique [*Algerian*] (MAR)
enimm .... Enimmakseen [*Mostly*] [*Finnish*]
ENIMPORT ... Empresa Nicaraguense de Importaciones [*Nicaraguan Imports Enterprise*] (LA1)
ENIMS .... Experimental Scientific Research Institute of Metal-Cutting Machine Tools (RU)
ENIN .... Power Engineering Institute Imeni G. M. Krzhizhanovskiy (RU)
ENIP .... Entreprise Nationale de l'Industrie de Prefabrication [*Algerian*] (MAR)
ENIPREX ..... Empresa Nicaraguense de Exportaciones [*Nicaraguan Exports Enterprise*] (LA1)
ENIR .... Escuela Nacional de Instruccion Revolucionaria [*National Revolutionary Training School*] [*Cuban*] (LA)
ENIT .... Ecole Nationale des Ingenieurs Tunisiens (MAR)
ENIT .... Ente Nazionale Italiano per il Turismo [*Italian*]
ENITA .... Ecole Nationale des Ingenieurs et de Techniciens de Bordj-El-Bahri (MAR)
ENITRA .... Entreprise Nationale des Travaux [*Algerian*] (MAR)
ENJC .... Ecole Normale Jacques Cartier
ENJEP .... Ecole Nationale de la Jeunesse et de l'Education Populaire [*National School of Youth and People's Education*] [*Malagasy*] (AF)
ENL .... Ejercito Nacional de Liberacion [*National Liberation Army*] [*Nicaraguan*] (PD)
ENLF .... Ethiopian National Liberation Front (MAR)
ENLO .... Ecole Nationale des Langues Orientales (MAR)
ENLOV .... Ecole Nationale des Langues Orientales Vivantes (MAR)
ENM .... Electric Oil Heater (RU)
ENM .... Empresa de Navegacion Mambisa [*Mambisa Navigation Enterprise*] [*Cuban*] (LA)
ENM .... Empresa Nuclear de Mendoza [*Mendoza Nuclear Enterprise*] [*Argentine*] (LA)
ENM .... Escuela Nacional de Maestros [*National Teachers College*] [*Mexican*] (LA)
ENM .... Evropaiki Nomismatiki Monas [*European Monetary Unit*] (GC1)
ENMISA ...... Empresa Nacional Mineral del Sahara [*Corporation owned by the Spanish government*] [*Later, Fosfatos de Bucraa*]
ENMIU .... Empresa Nacional de Mantenimiento de Inmuebles Urbanos [*National Enterprise for Maintenance of Urban Real Estate*] [*Cuban*] (LA)
ENNET .... Ecole Normale d'Enseignement Technique de Tananarive (MAR)
ENNICO ...... Entreprise Nigerienne de Confiserie (MAR)
ENO .... Electric Pump Irrigation (RU)
ENO .... Elektrarne Novaky [*Electric Power Plants Novaky*] (CZ)
eno .... Enero [*January*] [*Spanish*]
ENOF .... United People's Liberation Front (BU)
ENOK .... Ekonomiese Ontwikkelingskorporasie [*First National Development Corporation*] [*Namibian*] (AF)
ENOPO .... United People's Social and Political Organization (BU)
ENOPOOF ... United People's Social and Political Organization of the Fatherland Front (BU)
ENP .... Empresa Nacional Portuaria [*National Port Enterprise*] [*Honduran*] (LA1)
ENP .... Equivalent Neutral Density (RU)
ENP .... Escuela Nacional de Policia [*National Police School*] [*Costa Rican*] (LA1)
ENPA .... Ecole Normale des Professeurs Adjoints [*North African*] (MAR)
ENPAS .... Ente Nazionale di Previdenza e Assistenza per i Dipendenti Statali [*National Board of Social Security and Welfare for Civil Servants*] [*Italian*] (WER)
ENPI .... Ente Nazionale di Prevenire Infortuni [*National Agency for the Prevention of Accidents*] [*Italian*] (WER)
ENPROVIT ... Empresa Nacional de Productos Vitales [*National Enterprise for Vital Products*] [*Ecuadorean*] (LA)
ENPS .... Ecole Nationale Promotion Sociale (MAR)
ENPT .... Ecole Nationale des Postes et Telecommunications [*National Posts and Telecommunications School*] [*Zairian*] (AF)
ENR .... Uniform Norms and Rates (BU)
ENRAD-PERU ... Empresa Nacional de Radiodifusion [*National Radio Broadcasting Enterprise*] [*Peruvian*] (LA)
ENROK .... Maquinaria y Envases Rock Ltda. [*Bogota*] (COL)
ENS .... Ecole Nationale de Secretariat (MAR)
ENS .... Ecole Normale Superieure [*French teacher-training institution*] (WER)
ENS .... Enosi Neon Sosialiston [*Union of Young Socialists*] [*Greek*] (GC)
Ens .... Enseada [*Bay, Creek*] [*Portuguese*] (NAU)
Ens .... Ensenada [*Bay, Creek*] [*Spanish*] (NAU)
ens .... Ensimmainen [*Finnish*]
Ens .... Enstitusu [*Institute*] (TU)
ENSA .... Ecole Nationale de Ski et d'Alpinisme
ENSA .... Empresa Nacional de Seguros [*National Insurance Company*] [*Angolan*] (AF)
ENSAC .... Ecole Normale Superieure de l'Afrique Centrale [*Higher Teachers Training School of Central Africa*] [*Congolese*] (AF)
ENSAE .... Ecole Nationale de la Statistique Appliquee a l'Economie [*National School for Statistics Applied to Economics*] [*French*] (WER)
ENSAT .... Ecole Nationale Superieure d'Agriculture Tunisienne [*Tunisian National Higher Institute of Agriculture*] (AF)
ENSEME ..... Entreprise Senegalaise des Mousses et Plastiques (MAR)
ENSEP .... Ecole Normale Superieure d'Enseignement Polytechnique [*Algerian*] (MAR)
ENSEPORT ... Empresa Nacional de Servicios Portuarios [*National Port Services Enterprise*] [*Chilean*] (LA)
ENSET .... Advanced Teacher-Training College for Technical Studies [*French*]
ENSG .... Ecole Nationale des Sciences Geodesiques [*Algerian*] (MAR)
ENSG .... Ecole Nationale des Sciences Geographiques [*National School of Geographic Sciences*] [*French*] (WER)
ENSI .... Ecole Nationale Superieure d'Ingenieurs [*Higher Schools of Engineering*] [*French*]
ENSI .... Energia Nucleare Sud Italia [*Italian nuclear power plant project*]
ENSIA .... Ecole Nationale Superieure d'Ingenieurs d'Abidjan (MAR)
ENSIDESA ... Empresa Nacional Siderurgica, Sociedad Anonima [*National Iron and Steel Enterprise, Incorporated*] [*Spanish*] (WER)
ENSIL .... National School of Engineering [*French*]
ENSJ .... Ecole Nationale Superieure de Journalisme a Alger (MAR)
ENSP .... Ecole Nationale de Sante Publique (MAR)
ENSP .... Ecole Nationale Superieure de Police (MAR)
ENSP .... Ecole Normale Superieure Polytechnique [*Higher Polytechnic Teachers Training School*] [*Algerian*] (AF)
ENS-System ... Einheitsnebenstellensystem [*Standard Extension System*] (EG)
ENSTI .... European Network Scientific and Technical Information
ENSTP .... Ecole Nationale Superieure des Travaux Publics [*Public Works National Staff College*] [*Ivorian*] (AF)
ENSUME ..... Empresa Cubana Importadora de Equipos-Medicos [*Cuban Enterprise for the Import of Medical Equipment*] (LA)
EN(SVU) ..... Ekonomicky Namestnik (Stavebni Vyrobni Usek) [*Deputy Economist (Construction and Production Sector)*] (CZ)
ENSz .... Egyesult Nemzetek Szovetsege [*United Nations Organization*] (HU)
ENT .... Ecole Nationale des Telecommunications [*National Telecommunications School*] [*Algerian*] (AF)
ent .... Entinen [*Former, Earlier*] [*Finnish*] (GPO)
ent .... Entomology (RU)
ENT .... Evropaikon Nomismatikon Tameion [*European Monetary Fund*] (GC)
ENTA .... Entreprise Nationale de Tabacs et de Cigarettes (MAR)
ENTA .... Entreprise Nouvelle de Transports [*Moroccan*] (MAR)
ENTARA ...... Entreprise Mauritanienne de Travaux Publics, d'Etudes et d'Impression (MAR)
ENTAS .... Entas Nakliyat ve Turizm Anonim Sirketi [*Entas Transport and Tourism Corporation*] (TU)
ENTECOL ... Convenuto Telegrafico dell'Ente Colonizzazione della Libia (MAR)
ENTEL .... Empresa Nacional de Telecomunicaciones [*National Telecommunications Company*] (LA)
ENTELPERU ... Empresa Nacional de Telecomunicaciones del Peru [*National Telecommunications Enterprise of Peru*] (LA)
enth .... Enthaltend [*Containing*] [*German*]
ENTP .... Entreprise Nantaise de Travaux Publics (MAR)
ENTP .... Entreprise Nigerienne de Travaux Publics (MAR)
entr .... Entropy (RU)
ENTRACO ... Entreprise Artisanale de Cocobeach (MAR)
ENTRAT ...... Entreprise Nationale de Transports Routiers, d'Acconage, de Transit, et de Consignation Maritime (MAR)
ENTRELCO ... Societe d'Entreprises Electriques au Congo (MAR)
ENTRELEC ... Compagnie d'Entreprises Electriques [*Cameroonian*] (MAR)
ENTREU ...... Entreprises Reunionnaises [*Reunionese Enterprises*] (AF)
entspr .... Entsprechend [*Corresponding*] [*German*] (GPO)

Ents sl .... Encyclopedic Dictionary [*A publication*] (RU)
Ents slov ..... Encyclopedic Dictionary [*A publication*] (RU)
Entsteh .... Entstehung [*Origin*] [*German*]
ENTTAS ...... Entreprise Togolaise des Techniciens Associes (MAR)
ENTUPERU ... Empresa Nacional de Turismo [*Peruvian National Tourist Enterprise*] (LA)
entw .... Entweder [*Either*] [*German*]
entw .... Entwickelt [*or Entwickelung*] [*Developed or Development*] [*German*]
ENUSA .... Empresa Nacional del Uranio, Sociedad Anonima [*National Uranium Enterprise, Incorporated*] [*Spanish*] (WER)
ENV .... Ecole Nationale Veterinaire [*National Veterinary School*] [*Algerian*] (AF)
ENV .... Electric Water Heater (RU)
en v .... En Ville [*Locally*] [*Correspondence*] [*French*]
env .... Environ [*About, Nearly, Approximately*] [*French*]
ENVAC .... Envases Colombianos SA [*Barranquilla*] (COL)
ENVAFLEX ... Envasamientos Flexibles [*Cali*] (COL)
ENVI .... Division of Environmental Engineering [*Thai*]
E Ny .... Eszaknyugat [*Northwest*] (HU)
ENYVA .... Enosis Ypallilon Vrettanikon Arkhon [*Union of British Authorities Employees*] [*Cypriot*] (GC)
enz .... En Zo Voort [*And So Forth*] [*Dutch*] (GPO)
en Zn .... En Zoon [*And Son*] [*Dutch*] (CED)
EO .... Cathode-Ray Oscillograph (RU)
EO .... Daily Service of Motor Vehicles (BU)
EO .... Egeszsegugyi Osztaly [*Health Department*] (HU)
EO .... Ekonomski Otsek [*Economic Section*] (YU)
EO .... Elementary Operator [*Computers*] (RU)
eo .... Eloors [*Reconnaissance Group, Outpost*] (HU)
EO .... Ethnographic Review [*A publication*] (RU)
EO .... Evacuation Detachment (RU)
EO .... Evacuation Section (RU)
EO .... L'Equippe Ouvriere (MAR)
EO .... Oscillograph Screen (RU)
EOA .... Ente Opera Assistenziali Presso le Federazioni Fasciste della Libia (MAR)
EOA .... Epitropi Olymbiakon Agonon [*Olympic Games Committee*] (GC)
EOA .... Ethniki Organosis Axiomatikon [*National Organization of Officers*] (GC)
EOAAYL ...... Enosis Odigon Avtokiniton Astikon kai Yperastikon Leoforeion [*Union of Drivers of Urban and Suburban Buses*] [*Greek*] (GC)
EOAC .... Etats Ouest Africains de la Communaute (MAR)
EOAS .... Eleves Officiers d'Active du Service de Sante [*Regular Medical Service Officer Candidates*] [*Cambodian*] (CL)
EOAVB .... Evakuaciono Odeljenje Armiske Veterinarske Bolnice [*Evacuation Sector of the Army Veterinary Hospital*] (YU)
EOAVE .... Enosis Odigon Avtokiniton Voreiou Ellados [*Drivers' Union of Northern Greece*] (GC)
EOB .... Ethiopia Observer [*Addis Ababa*] [*A publication*] (MAR)
EOC .... Educacion Obrero-Campesina [*Workers and Peasants Education*] [*Cuban*] (LA)
EOC .... Elva Owners Club (EA)
EODVL .... Evacuation Section of a Division Veterinary Hospital (RU)
EODYL .... Elevthera Organosis Dimotikon Ypallilon Levkosias [*Free Organization of Nicosia Civil Servants*] (GC)
EOEA .... Elliniki Omospondia Erasitekhnon Alieias [*Greek Federation of Amateur Fishermen*] (GC)
EOEA .... Ethnikai Omades Ellinon Andarton [*National Groups of Greek Guerrillas (Zervas-led)*] (GC)
EOED .... Epistimonikos Omilos Erevnon Diastimatos [*Scientific Association for Space Research*] [*Greek*] (GC)
EOEE .... Epitropi Oikonomikou Elengkhou Endypon [*Committee for Financial Audit of Publications*] (GC)
EOEKh .... Ethnikos Organismos Ellinikis Kheirotekhnias [*National Organization of Greek Handicrafts*] (GC)
EOEP .... Ethnikos Organismos Ellinon Patrioton [*National Organization of Greek Patriots*] (GC)
EOF .... Elementary Evaluative Function (RU)
EOFAP .... Escuela de Oficials de la Fuerza Aerea del Peru [*Peruvian Air Force Academy*] (LA)
EOGM .... Egitim ve Ogretim Genel Mudurlugu [*Education and Teaching Directorate General*] (TU)
EOH .... Egitim Ozel Hizmetleri [*Special Educational Duties*] (TU)
EOI .... Edition de l'Ocean Indien (MAR)
EOK .... Ethnikos Organismos Kapnou [*National Tobacco Organization*] [*Greek*] (GC)
EOK .... Ethnikos Organismos Katoikias [*National Housing Organization*] [*Greek*] (GC)
EOK .... Evropaiki Oikonomiki Koinotis [*European Economic Community*] (GC)
EOK .... Ostravsko-Karvinske Elektrarny [*Ostrava-Karvin Electric Power Plants*] (CZ)
EOKA .... Ethniki Organosis Kyprion Agoniston [*or Ethniki Organosis Kypriakou Agonos*] [*National Organization of Cypriot Fighters*] (GC)
EOKhA .... Ethnikos Organismos Khristianikis Allilengyis [*National Christian Solidarity Organization*] [*Greek*] (GC)
EOMA .... Epikourikos Organismos Metaforon di'Avtokinitou [*Auxiliary Vehicular Transport Organization*] [*Greek*] (GC)
EOMMEHh ... Ellinikos Organismos Mikromesaion Epikheiriseon kai Kheirotekhnias [*Hellenic Organization of Medium and Small-Size Enterprises and Handicrafts*] (GC1)
EOMS .... Engel's Experimental Reclamation Station (RU)
EOMTA .... Enosis Oikogeneion Makhomenon Travmation, Anapiron [*Union of Families of Injured and Disabled Fighters*] [*Greek*] (GC)
EON .... Ethniki Organosis Neolaias [*National Youth Organization*] [*Greek*] (GC)
eooe .... Erreur ou Omission Exceptee [*Errors or Omissions Excepted*] [*French*]
EOP .... Elektrarna Opatovice [*Opatovice Electric Power Plant*] (CZ)
EOP .... Elementary Machining Surfaces (RU)
EOP .... Elliniki Omospondia Pygmakhias [*Greek Boxing Federation*] (GC)
EOP .... Ethnikos Organismos Pronoias [*National Welfare Organization*] [*Greek*] (GC)
EOP .... Evropaikos Organismos Paragogikotitos [*European Productivity Organization*] (GC)
EOP .... Evropska Organizacija za Produktivnost [*Organization for European Economic Cooperation (OEEC)*] (YU)
EOP .... Image Converter Tube (RU)
EOPAE .... Ethniki Omospondia Prosopikou Avtokiniton Ellados [*National Federation of Automotive Personnel of Greece*] (GC)
EOPO .... United Social and Political Organization (BU)
EO POM ...... Ekspozytury Organizacyjne Panstwowych Osrodkow Maszynowych [*Organizational Branches of the State (Agricultural) Machine Stations*] (POL)
EOPSA .... Ellinikos Organismos Pnevmatikis kai Somatikis Agogis [*Greek Organization for Mental and Physical Health*] (GC)
EOPTR .... Expeditionary Detachment for Underwater Technical Operations (RU)
EOR .... Eleve Officier de Reserve [*Reserve Officer Cadet*] [*French*] (WER)
EOS .... Egyptian Organisation for Standardization (MAR)
EOS .... Ellinikos Oreivatikos Syndesmos [*Greek Mountaineering League*] (GC)
EOS .... Erweiterte Oberschule [*Expanded Secondary School*] (EG)
EOS .... Ethnikos Organismos Syndaxeon [*National Pensions Organization*] (GC1)
EOS .... Evropske Obranne Spolecenstvi [*European Defense Community*] (CZ)
EOSI .... Ethniki Omospondia Syndaxioukhon Idryma Koinonikon Asfaliseon [*National Federation of Social Insurance Foundation Pensioners*] [*Greek*] (GC)
EOT .... Ellinikos Organismos Tourismou [*Greek Tourist Organization*] (GC)
EOTE .... Eleves Officiers Techniciens des Essences [*Fuel Technician Officer Candidates*] [*Cambodian*] (CL)
EOUV .... Ekonomicko-Organizacni Ustav Vlnarskeho Prumyslu [*Economic-Organizational Institute of the Wool Industry*] (CZ)
EOVS .... Ekonomski Otsek Vrhovnog Staba [*Economic Section of the Supreme Headquarters*] (YU)
EOWU .... Electrical and Other Workers Union [*Mauritian*] (AF)
EOY .... Epitropi Oikonomikon Ypotheseon [*Economic Affairs Committee*] [*Greek*] (GC)
EOYESK ...... Eniaia Organosis Ypallilon Epitropis Sitiron [*United Organization of Wheat Board Employees*] [*Cypriot*] (GC)
EP .... Clearing Station (RU)
ep .... Diocese (BU)
EP .... Eastern Province (MAR)
EP .... Economic Planning; Journal for Agriculture and Related Industries [*Montreal*] [*A publication*] (MAR)
e a p .... Effet a Payer [*French*]
EP .... Egyseg Partja [*Party of Unity*] [*Hungarian*] (PPE)
EP .... Ejercito Peruano [*Peruvian Army*] (LA)
EP .... Electric Heater (RU)
EP .... Electric Range (RU)
EP .... Electric Saw (RU)
EP .... Electric Transmission (RU)
EP .... Electricke Podniky Hlavniho Mesta Prahy [*Prague Capital Electric Enterprises*] (CZ)
EP .... Electron Flow (RU)
EP .... Electron Gun (RU)
EP .... Elektricno Poduzece [*Electrical Establishment*] (YU)
EP .... Elektro-Praga Jablonec Nad Nisou [*Electrical Engineering Enterprise, Jablonec Nad Nisou*] (CZ)
EP .... Energieprojektierung (VEB) [*Project Planning Office for Electric Power (VEB)*] (EG)
EP .... Englisches Patent [*English Patent*] [*German*]
EP .... Enotiki Parataxis [*Unifying (Pro-Enosis) Faction*] [*Cypriot*] (GC)
EP .... Epitropi Poleos [*City Committee*] (GC)
EP .... Ergatiki Pali [*Worker Struggle*] (GC)
EP .... Erweichungspunkt [*Softening Point*] [*German*]
EP .... Ethniki Parataxi [*National Array*] (GC)
EP .... Evacuation Center (BU)
E-P .... Evaporacija-Padavine [*Evaporation of Precipitation*] [*Meteorology*] (YU)

ERK .... Ethniko Rizospastiko Komma [*National Radical Party*] GK (PPE)
erkl .... Erklaert [*Explained, Illustrated*] [*German*]
ERL .... Environmental Research Laboratory [*Zambian*]
Erl .... Erlaeuterung [*Explanation, (Explanatory) Note*] (EG)
ERM .... Ecole Royale de Medecine [*Royal School of Medicine*] [*Laotian*] (CL)
ermit .... Ermitano [*Spanish*]
ERMP .... Empresa para la Recuperacion de Materias Primas [*Enterprise for the Recovery of Raw Materials*] [*Cuban*] (LA)
ERN .... Emissora Regional do Norte [*Northern Regional Radio*] [*Portuguese*] (WER)
ERO .... Operation and Repair Department (RU)
EROTERV .... Eromuveket Tervezo Vallalat [*Designing Enterprise for Electric Power Plants*] (HU)
ERP .... Effective Radiative Power (EG)
ERP .... Ejercito Revolucionario del Pueblo [*People's Revolutionary Army*] [*Argentine*] (PD)
ERP .... Ejercito Revolucionario del Pueblo [*People's Revolutionary Army*] [*Salvadoran*] (PD)
ERP .... European Recovery Program (WEN)
ERPDB .... Eastern Regional Production Development Board (MAR)
ERPT .... Etablissements Ruraux des Postes et Telecommunications [*Rural Posts and Telecommunications Offices*] [*Cambodian*] (CL)
err .... Errata [*Errata*] [*Latin*]
err .... Errichtet [*German*]
ERS .... Economic Research Service (MAR)
ERS- .... Electrical Exploration Station (RU)
ERS .... Emissora Regional do Sul [*Southern Regional Radio*] [*Portuguese*] (WER)
ERShR- .... Walking Rail Mounted Wheel Excavator (RU)
ERSK .... Uniform Republic Sports Classification (BU)
ERSPO .... Estonian Republic Union of Consumers' Societies (RU)
erst .... Oersted (RU)
Erst P .... Erstarrungspunkt [*Freezing Point*] [*German*]
ERT .... Elliniki Radiofonia kai Tileorasis [*Greek Radio and Television*] (GC)
ERT .... Ertekesito [*Selling or Sale*] (HU)
ert .... Ertekezes [*Treatise*] (HU)
ert .... Ertekezlet [*Meeting*] (HU)
ert .... Ertelmeben [*or Ertelemben*] [*In Accordance With*] (HU)
ert .... Ertesites [*Notification*] (HU)
ERT .... Union Explosivos Rio Tinto, SA [*Name of company*] [*Spanish*] (WER)
ERTEC .... Societe Anonyme d'Etudes et de Realisations Techniques (MAR)
ERTI .... Erdeszeti Tudomanyos Intezet [*Scientific Institute of Forestry*] (HU)
ERTS .... Earth Resources Technology Satellite (MAR)
ERTS-GEOBOL ... Earth Resources Technology Satellite - Bolivian Geological Service (LA)
ERU- .... Cathode-Ray Recorder (RU)
ERU .... Electronic Resolver [*Computers*] (RU)
ERU .... Environmental Review Unit (MAR)
ERU .... Exponential Amplification Control (RU)
ERV .... Electronic Timing Relay (RU)
erw .... Erwaehnt [*German*]
erw .... Erwaermt [*Heated*] [*German*]
ERYEA .... Elliniki Etaireia Erevnis Elengkhou Rypanseos Ydaton Edafous Aeros [*Greek Research Association for the Control of Water, Land, and Air Pollution*] (GC)
ERZ .... Electric Locomotive Repair Plant (RU)
ES .... Air Squadron (RU)
ES .... Destroyer (RU)
ES .... Economic Conference (RU)
ES .... Economic Council (RU)
ES .... Egyesules [*Joint Enterprise, Association*] (HU)
ES .... Ektakton Symvoulion [*Emergency Council*] [*Greek*] (GC)
ES .... Ektelestikon Symvoulion [*Executive Council*] (GC)
ES .... Electric Power Plant (RU)
ES .... Electric Power System (RU)
ES- .... Electric Salinometer (RU)
ES .... Electrostatic Instrument (RU)
ES .... Elektrosrbija [*An establishment for planning, construction, and production of electrical equipment*] [*Belgrade*] (YU)
ES .... Elet es Irodalom [*Life and Literature*] [*Title of a publication*] (HU)
ES .... Ellinikos Stratos [*Greek Army*] (GC)
ES .... Ellinikos Synagermos [*Greek Rally*] (GC)
ES .... Empresa de Semillas [*Seed Enterprise*] [*Cuban*] (LA)
ES .... Encyclopedic Reference Book (RU)
ES .... Energeticka Sluzba [*Electric Power Supply Service*] [*Civil defense*] (CZ)
ES .... Enseignement Secondaire [*Secondary Education*] [*Cambodian*] (CL)
ES .... Epanastatikoi Sosialistes [*Revolutionary Socialists*] [*Greek*] (GC)
ES .... Epitropi Sitiron [*Wheat Board*] [*Cypriot*] (GC)
ES .... Ernteschaetzung [*Crop Estimate*] (EG)
es .... Esempio [*Example*] [*Italian*] (GPO)
Es .... Eski [*Old, Ancient*] (TU)
ES .... Ethniki Sotiria [*National Salvation*] [*Greek*] (GC)
ES .... Euzko Socialista [*Basque Socialist Party*] [*Spanish*] (WER)
e/s .... Expedition Vessel (RU)
ES .... Screen Grid (RU)
ES .... Spain [*Two-letter standard code*] (CNC)
ES- .... Synchronization Element (RU)
ES .... Uniform System (BU)
ESA .... Department of Economic and Social Affairs (MAR)
ESA .... Eastern and Southern African Countries (MAR)
ESA .... Ecole Superieure d'Agriculture
ESA .... Ejercito Salvadoreno Anticomunista [*Salvadoran Anti-Communist Army*] (PD)
ESA .... Ejercito Secreto Anti-Comunista [*Secret Anticommunist Army*] [*Salvadoran*] (LA1)
ESA .... Ejercito Segredo Anti-Comunista [*Secret Anti-Communist Army*] [*Guatemalan*] (PD)
ESA .... Electric Equipment for Aircraft and Automobiles (RU)
ESA .... Elliniki Stratiotiki Astynomia [*Greek Military Police*] (GC)
ESA .... Emborikos Syllogos Athinon [*Commercial Chamber of Athens*] (GC)
ESA .... European Space Agency [*Formerly, ESRO*]
ESAAT .... Ecole Superieure d'Application d'Agriculture Tropicale (MAR)
ESACC .... Ecole Superieure Africaine des Cadres du Chemin de Fer (MAR)
ESACTA ...... Ente Specializzato Aerofotogrammetria, Cartografia, Topografia, Aerofotogeologia, [*Specialized Agency for Aerophotogrammetry, Cartography, Topography, and Aerophotogeology*] [*Italian*] (AF)
ESAD .... Ege Bolgesi Seyahat Acenteleri Dernegi [*Aegean Region Travel Agents' Organization*] (TU)
ESADE .... Escuela Superior de Administracion y Direccion de Empresas
ESAK .... Ellinikon Stratiotikon Apospasma Kyprou [*Greek Army Contingent on Cyprus*] (GC)
ESAK .... Eniaia Syndikalistiki Andidiktatoriki Kinisi [*United Antidictatorial Labor Movement*] [*Greek*] (GC)
ESAK-S .... Eniaia Syndikalistiki Andidiktatoriki Kinisi - Synergazomenoi [*United Antidictatorial Labor Movement - Cooperating*] (GC1)
ESAL .... Empresa de Saneamiento de Lima [*Lima Sanitation Enterprise*] [*Peruvian*] (LA)
ESAM .... Evangelization Society of African Missions (MAR)
ESAN .... Escuela de Administracion de Negocios [*School of Business Administration*] [*Peruvian*] (LA)
ESAO .... Escola de Aperfeicoamento de Oficiais [*Officer Training School*] [*Brazilian*] (LA)
ESAP .... Egyptian Society of Animal Production (MAR)
ESAP .... Escuela Superior de Administracion Publica [*Advanced School for Public Administration*] [*Colombian*] (LA)
ESAP .... Escuela Superior de Administracion Publica del Peru [*Advanced School for Public Administration*] [*Peruvian*] (LA)
ESAP .... Ethniko Symvoulio Anotatis Ekpaidevseos [*National Council of Supreme Education*] (GC1)
ESAP .... Ethnikos Syndesmos Anapiron Polemou [*National League of Persons Disabled by War*] [*Greek*] (GC)
ESAPAC ...... Escuela Superior de Administracion Publica America Central [*Costa Rican*]
ESAPE .... Ethnikon Symvoulion Anotatis Paideias kai Erevnon [*National Council of Higher Education and Research*] [*Greek*] (GC)
ESAS .... Elektrometallurji Sanayii Anonim Sirketi [*Electrometallurgy Industry Corporation*] (TU)
ESAT .... Ecole Superieure d'Agriculture Tropicale (MAR)
ESAT .... Enosis Syndakton Athinaikou Typou [*Union of Athens Newspaper Editors*] (GC)
ESB .... Einheitssystem Bau [*Standard Construction System*] (EG)
ESB .... Energeticke Strojirny [*Electrical Engineering Enterprises*] (CZ)
ESB .... Escuela Secundaria Basica [*Basic Secondary School*] [*Cuban*] (LA)
ESBEC .... Escuela Secundaria Basica en el Campo [*Basic Secondary Farm School*] [*Cuban*] (LA)
ESBEEC ...... Escuela Secundaria Basica en el Campo [*Basic Secondary Farm School*] [*Cuban*] (LA)
ESBR .... Electrical Bomb-Release Mechanism (RU)
ESBR .... Escuela Secundaria Basica Rural [*Rural Basic Secondary School*] [*Cuban*] (LA)
ESBUR .... Escuela Secundaria Basica Urbana [*Urban Basic Secondary School*] [*Cuban*] (LA)
ESBUWU ..... Elementary School Building Unit Workers Union (MAR)
ESBV .... Escuela Secundaria Basica Vocacional [*Vocational Basic Secondary School*] [*Cuban*] (LA)
ESC .... Electricity Supply Commission (MAR)
ESC .... Elektrarensky Svaz Ceskoslovensky [*Union of Czechoslovak Power Plants*] (CZ)
ESC .... Elektrotechnicky Svaz Ceskoslovensky [*Czechoslovak Electrical Engineering Association*] (CZ)
Esc .... Escadron [*Squadron*] [*Military*] [*French*] (MTD)
esc .... Escompte [*Discount, Rebate*] [*French*]
Esc .... Escudo (MAR)
ESCA .... Ecole Superieure de Commerce d'Abidjan (MAR)
ESCA .... Ecole Superieure de Commerce d'Alger (MAR)

Esca .... Escadrille d'Avions [*Air Squadron*] [*Military*] [*French*] (MTD)
ESCAMA ..... Escadrille Malgache [*Malagasy Air Squadron*] (AF)
ESCAP .... United Nations Economic and Social Commission for Asia and the Pacific [*Bangkok, Thailand*]
ESCHC .... Educational, Scientific, Cultural, and Health Commission (MAR)
esco .... Escudo [*Spanish*]
ESCOLOMBIAS ... Escuelas Colombianas de Alto Comercio y Finanzas [*Bogota*] (COL)
ESCOM .... Electricity Supply Commission [*South African*] (AF)
ESCOMO .... Escuela de Comercio Moderno [*Bogota*] (COL)
ESCOPREFIL ... Empresa de Correos, Prensa, y Filatelia [*Post, Press, and Postal Stamps Enterprise*] [*Cuban*] (LA)
escs .... Escudos [*Spanish*]
escte .... Escompte [*Discount, Rebate*] [*French*]
ESD .... Elektroschaltgeraete Dresden (VEB) [*Dresden Electric Switch Plant (VEB)*] (EG)
ESDAC .... European Space Data Centre
ESDE .... Elevtheri Sosialistiki Dimokratiki Enosis [*Free Socialist Democratic Union*] [*Greek*] (GC)
ESDE/AM/S ... Elliniki Sosialistiki Dimokratiki Enosis/Apelevtherotiko Metopo/"Spartakos" [*Greek Socialist Democratic Union/Liberation Front/"Spartakos"*] (GC)
ESDIN .... Elliniki Sosialistiki Dimokratiki Neolaia [*Greek Socialist Democratic Youth*] (GC)
ESDON .... Elliniki Sosialdimokratiki Organosi Neon [*Greek Social Democratic Youth Organization*] (GC)
ESDY .... Enosi Syndaxioukhon Dimosion Ypallilon [*Civil Service Pensioners' Union*] [*Cypriot*] (GC)
ESE .... Est Sud Est [*East Southeast*] [*French*] (MTD)
ESE .... Estesudeste [*East Southeast*] [*Spanish*]
ESE .... Estimate of Supplementary Expenditure [*Mauritian*] (AF)
ESE .... Ethniki Sosialistiki Enosis [*National Socialist Union*] [*Cypriot*] (GC)
ESE .... Ethnikon Symvoulion Energeias [*National Energy Council*] [*Greek*] (GC)
ESE .... Ethnikon Symvoulion Erevnon [*National Research Council*] [*Greek*] (GC)
ESE .... Ethnikos Synagermos Ellinon [*National Rally of Greeks*] (GC)
ESEA .... Enosis Sympolemiston Ethnikou Agonos [*Union of Fellow-Combatants in the National Struggle*] [*Cypriot*] (GC)
ESEA .... Epitropi Syndonismou tou Enotikou Agonos [*Coordinating Committee for the Enosis Struggle*] [*Cypriot*] (GC)
ESEA .... Ethnikos Syndesmos Ellinon Axiomatikon [*National League of Greek Officers*] (GC)
ESEADE ...... Escuela Superior de Economia y Administracion de Empresas [*School of Economy and Business Administration*] [*Argentine*] (LA)
ESEAK .... Enosis Syllogon Ellinon Apofoiton Kyprou [*Union of Greek Alumni Associations of Cyprus*] (GC)
ESEC .... Escuela Secundaria en el Campo [*Secondary Farm School*] [*Cuban*] (LA)
ESEDENA ... Escuela de Seguridad y Defensa Nacional [*National Security and Defense School*] [*Uruguayan*] (LA)
ESEDES ...... Elliniki Synomospondia Elevtheron Dimokratikon Ergatikon Syndikaton [*Greek Federation of Free Democratic Labor Unions*] (GC)
ESEE .... Ethniki Sosialistiki Enosi Ellados [*National Socialist Union of Greece*] (GC)
ESEEA .... Ethnikon Symvoulion Epistimonikis Erevnis kai Anaptyxeos [*National Council for Scientific Research and Development*] [*Greek*] (GC)
ESEEC .... Escuela Secundaria en el Campo [*Secondary Farm School*] [*Cuban*] (LA)
ESEF .... Escuela Superior de Educacion Fisica [*Higher School of Physical Education*] [*Cuban*] (LA)
ESEKA .... Elliniki Syndonistiki Epitropi Kypriakou Agonas [*Greek Coordinating Committee of the Cyprus Struggle*] [*Greek*] (GC)
ESEN .... Ekklisiastikon Symvoulion Enoriakou Naou [*Church Parish Council*] [*Greek*] (GC)
ESEP .... Escuelas Superiores de Educacion Profesional [*Higher Schools for Professional Education*] (LA)
ESEPAS ...... Empresa de Servicios Petroleros Asociados [*Associated Petroleum Services Enterprise*] [*Ecuadorean*] (LA)
ESEPP .... Enosis Syngenon Ellinon Politikon Prosfygon [*Union of Relatives of Political Refugees*] [*Greek*] (GC)
ESER .... Einheitliches System der Elektronischen Rechentechnik [*Uniform Electronic Data Processing System*] [*CEMA*] (EG)
ESETC .... Empresa de Servicios Tecnicos de Computacion de Holguin [*Enterprise for Technical Computation Services of Holguin*] [*Cuban*] (LA)
ESETTM ...... Ecole Superieure d'Economie et de Technique des Transports Maritimes (MAR)
ESF .... Economic Support Fund (MAR)
ESF .... European Social Fund (EG)
ESF .... Exchange Support Fund [*Cambodian*] (CL)
ESFC .... Epidemiological Study of Female Circumcision [*Sudanese*] (MAR)
ESFINCO .... Estudios, Financieros, y Contables [*Bogota*] (COL)
ESFOA .... L'Ecole Speciale de Formation des Officiers d'Active (MAR)
ESG .... Ecole Superieure de Guerre [*Armed Forces War College*] [*French*] (WER)
ESG .... Electrostatic Generator (RU)
ESG .... Escola Superior de Guerra [*War College*] [*Brazilian*] (LA)
ESGM .... TC Emekli Sandigi Genel Mudurlugu [*Retirement Fund Directorate General of Republic of Turkey*] (TU)
ESGP .... Epitropi gia to Syndonismo Georgikis Paragogis [*Committee for the Coordination of Agricultural Production*] (GC1)
ESGRAON ... Integrated Civil Registration and Administrative Population Services System (BU)
esh .... Echelon (RU)
ESh .... Stark Effect (RU)
ESh .... Walking Excavator, Dragline (RU)
ESH .... Western Sahara [*Three-letter standard code*] (CNC)
EShD .... Electric Step-by-Step Motor (RU)
EShP .... Electrical Tie Tamper [*Railroads*] (RU)
ESIAC .... Estructuras. Ingenieria, Arquitectura, y Construcciones [*Cali*] (COL)
ESIALA .... Eastern States Interim Assets and Liabilities Agency [*Nigerian*] (AF)
ESI-ANDINA ... Empresa de Servicios Informativos Andina [*Andean Information Services Enterprise*] (LA)
ESIC .... Ecole Superieure Internationale de la Cooperation [*Higher International School for Cooperation*] [*French*] (AF)
ESIC .... Emirates Sudan Investment Company (MAR)
ESICUBA .... Empresa de Seguros Internacionales de Cuba [*Cuban Enterprise for International Insurance*] (LA)
ESIEA .... Enosis Syndakton Imerision Efimeridon Athinon [*Union of Athens Daily Newspaper Editors*] (GC)
ESIGA .... Entretien Service Immobilier Gabonais (MAR)
ESIJY .... Ecole Superieure Internationale de Journalisme de Yaounde [*International Higher School of Journalism of Yaounde*] [*Cameroonian*] (AF)
ESIL .... Egyptian Society of International Law (MAR)
esim .... Esimerkiksi [*For Example*] [*Finnish*] (GPO)
esim .... Esimerkkeja [*Finnish*]
ESIN .... Esin Uluslararasi Nakliyat ve Ticaret Anonim Sirketi [*The Esin International Transport and Trade Corp.*] [*Istanbul*] (TU)
ESINA .... Exercito Secreto de Intervencao Nacionale de Angola [*Secret Army of National Intervention of Angola*] (AF)
ESI-PERU .... Empresa de Servicios de Informacion del Peru [*Peruvian Information Services Enterprise*] (LA)
ESIT .... Ecole Superieure d'Interpretation et Traduction [*School of Interpretation and Translation, University of Paris*]
ESJ .... Enotni Sindikati Jugoslavije [*United Trade-Unions of Yugoslavia*] (YU)
ESJL .... Entreprise Senegalaise Jean Lefebvre (MAR)
ESK .... Electronic Pointer Compensator (RU)
ESK .... Enosis Syndakton Kyprou [*Union of Cypriot Editors*] (GC)
ESK .... Epanastatikos Kommounistikos Syndesmos [*Revolutionary Communist Association*] [*Greek*] (GC)
ESK .... Evropaiki Sosialistiki Kinisi [*European Socialist Movement*] (GC)
ESK .... Squadron [*Navy*] (RU)
ESKA .... Enotiki Syndikalistiki Kinisi Athinon [*Unifying Labor Movement of Athens*] (GC)
ESKE .... Eniaion Sosialistikon Komma Ellados [*United Socialist Party of Greece*] (GC)
ESKE .... Eniaion Syndikalistikon Kinima Ellados [*United Labor Movement of Greece*] (GC)
ESKE .... Ergatikon Syndekhniakon Komma Ellados [*Worker Labor Union Party of Greece*] (GC)
ESKI .... Ettehadiyye Sendikayee Kargarene Iran Federation of Iranian Workers' Unions (MAR)
eskim .... Eskimo (RU)
esk-l'ya .... Squadron [*Aviation*] (RU)
Es-Koop ...... Eskisehir Koy Kooperatifler Birligi [*Eskisehir Village Cooperatives' Union*] (TU)
ESKP .... Crystal Field Stabilization Energy (RU)
ESKP .... Ethniko Symvoulio Khorotaxias kai Perivallondos [*National Zoning and Environment Council*] (GC1)
ESKP .... Ethnikon Symvoulion Koinonikis Pronoias [*National Social Welfare Council*] [*Greek*] (GC)
eskpl .... Submarine Squadron (BU)
eskpl .... Submarine Squadron (RU)
ESKS .... Enosis Stafidergostasiarkhon Korinthiakis Stafidas [*Union of Corinthian Currant Processing Plant Owners*] [*Greek*] (GC)
ESL .... Ethiopian Shipping Lines (MAR)
ESL .... Vltavska Elektrarna [*Vltava Electric Power Plant*] (CZ)
ESLCE .... Ethiopian School-Leaving Certificate Examination
ESLOV .... Ecole Speciale de Langues Orientales Vivantes (MAR)
ESM .... Ecole Superieure Militaire (MAR)
ESM .... Electric Spreading Machine [*Peat industry*] (RU)
ESM .... Encyclopedic Handbook "Machinery Manufacture" [*A publication*] (RU)
ESM .... Entreprise Senegalaise du Mobilier (MAR)
ESM .... Estrecho Su Mano [*I Press Your Hand*] [*Spanish*]
ESM .... Etudiants Socialistes Malgaches [*Malagasy Socialist Students*] (AF)

ETO .... Ellinikos Tapitourgikos Organismos [*Greek Carpet Manufacturers Organization*] (GC)
ETO .... Ethiopian Tourist Organization (MAR)
ETP .... Ecole des Travaux Publics (MAR)
ETP .... Electrotechnical Industry (RU)
ETP .... Electrotonic Potential (RU)
ETP .... Entreprise Travaux Publics (MAR)
ETP .... Semiconductor Soil Electrical Thermometer (RU)
ETPD .... Entreprise des Travaux pour l'Extension et l'Amenagement du Part de Dakar (MAR)
ETPM .... Entreprise-GTM pour les Travaux Petroliers Maritimes (MAR)
ETPO .... Entreprise de Travaux Publics de l'Ouest (MAR)
ETR .... Etudes Rurales; Revue Trimestrielle d'Histoire, Geographie, Sociologie, et Economie des Campagnes [*The Hague*] [*A publication*] (MAR)
ETR .... Etudes Techniques et Realisations (MAR)
ETR .... Technical Operations Area (RU)
ETR- .... Wheel Trench Excavator (RU)
ETRA .... Empresa de Trabajos Agricolas Ltda. [*Cali*] (COL)
ETs .... Electrical Centralization of Switches and Signals [*Railroads*] (RU)
ETS .... Entreprise de Transports Senegalais (MAR)
Ets .... Etablissements [*Establishment*] [*French*] (CED)
Ets .... Ethylcellulose (RU)
ETS .... Etudes Senegalaises (MAR)
ETS .... Excursion and Tourist Station (RU)
ETS .... Integrated Transportation System (BU)
ETSA .... Ecole Technique Secondaire Agricole [*Secondary Agricultural Technical School*] [*Zairian*] (AF)
ETSA .... Empresa de Transportes y Servicio Aereos [*Air Transportation and Service Enterprise*] [*Nicaraguan*] (LA1)
ETSAB .... Escuela Tecnica y Superior de Arquitectura de Barcelona [*Spanish*]
ETsBG .... Electrocerebellogram (RU)
ETSEC .... Etablissements Simon et Cie. (MAR)
et seq .... Et Sequens [*or Et Sequentes, Et Sequentia*] [*And the Following*] [*Latin*]
EtsG .... Electrocerebrogram (RU)
ETShch .... Ocean Mine Sweeper (RU)
ETSHOS ...... Ecole Technique Superieure des Hostesses et Secretaires (MAR)
ETsM .... Electronic Digital Computer (RU)
ETsN .... Electrical Centrifugal Pump (RU)
ETs NPK po biologiya ... Consolidated Center for Scientific Training of Cadres in Biology (BU)
ETsNPKMM ... Consolidated Center for the Scientific Training of Cadres in Mathematics and Mechanics (BU)
ETsO .... United Zionist Organization (BU)
ETsR .... Electronic Digital Recorder (RU)
ETsUM .... Electronic Digital Control Computer (RU)
ETsVM .... Electronic Digital Computer (RU)
ETsVP- .... Electronic Digital Recording Voltmeter (RU)
ETT .... Egeszsegugyi Tudomanyos Tanacs [*Scientific Council of Health*] (HU)
ETT .... Einheitlicher Transittarif [*Uniform Transit Tariff*] (EG)
ETT .... Electric Skidding Tractor (RU)
ETT .... Entreprise Travaux-Togo (MAR)
ETT .... Uniform Transit Rates (BU)
Ette .... Baionnette [*Bayonet*] [*French*] (MTD)
ETTE .... Ethiopian Tourist Trading Enterprise (MAR)
Ettf .... Etterfoelger [*Successors*] [*Norwegian*] (CED)
ETU .... Technical Operations Administration (RU)
ETU .... Technical Specifications for Export (RU)
ETU .... Universal Electric Tractor (RU)
ETU .... Universal Trench Excavator (RU)
ETUC .... European Trade Union Confederation [*Western Europe*] (WER)
Etud .... Etudler [*Studies*] (TU)
ETUDIS .... Etudes et Distributions (MAR)
ETUP .... Egypto-Tripolitanian Union Party (MAR)
et ux .... Et Uxor [*And Wife*] [*Latin*] (GPO)
ETV .... Eskisehir TV Enstitusu [*Eskisehir TV Institute*] (TU)
ETVA .... Elliniki Trapeza Viomikhanikis Anaptyxeos [*Hellenic Industrial Development Bank*] (GC)
ETVKYA ...... Enosis Tekhniton-Voithon Kalorifer-Ydravlikon Athinon [*Union of Athens Heating and Plumbing Technicians and Helpers*] (GC)
ETW .... Ernst Thaelmann Werke [*Ernst Thaelmann Works*] (EG)
etw .... Etwas [*Something*] [*German*]
ETY .... Enosis Trapezitikon Ypallilon [*Union of Bank Employees*] [*Greek*] (GC)
ETYAP .... Epikourikon Tameion Ypallilon Astynomias Poleon [*City Police Employees Auxiliary Fund*] [*Greek*] (GC)
ETYK .... Conference on Security and Cooperation in Europe [*Use CSCE*] [*Finnish*] (WEN)
ETYK .... Enosis Trapezitikon Ypallilon Kyprou [*Union of Cyprus Bank Employees*] (GC)
ETYOO .... Erkek Teknik Yuksek Ogretmen Okulu [*Men's Advanced Teachers School*] [*Ankara*] (TU)
ETYPS .... Eidikon Tameion Ypallilon Pyrosvestikou Somatos [*Special Fund for Employees of the Fire Corps*] [*Greek*] (GC)
ETZ .... Electric Hoists Plant (BU)
ETZ- .... Electrical Grain Thermometer (RU)
EU .... Ege Universitesi [*Aegean University*] [*Izmir*] (TU)
EU .... Einzelhandelsumsatz [*Retail Turnover*] (EG)
EU .... Ekonomicky Ustav [*Institute of Economics (of the Czechoslovak Academy of Sciences)*] (CZ)
EU .... Electronic Amplifier (RU)
EU .... Energeticky Ustav [*Power Research Institute*] (CZ)
EU .... Estados Unidos de America [*United States of America*] [*Spanish*]
E-U .... Etats-Unis [*United States*] [*French*]
EU .... Etats-Unis d'Amerique [*United States of America*] (MAR)
EU .... Power Plant [*Maritime term*] (RU)
EUA .... Estados Unidos da America [*United States of America*] [*Portuguese*] (GPO)
EUA .... Estados Unidos Americanos [*United States of America*] [*Spanish*]
EUA .... European Unit of Account (MAR)
EUA .... Ewe Unionist Association (MAR)
EUBM .... Egba United Board of Management (MAR)
Eu Cs .... Egeszsegugyi Csoport [*Health Group, Sanitary Group*] (HU)
EUDISED ..... European Documentation and Information System for Education
EufR .... Knjiznica Samostana Sveti Eufemije na Rabu [*Library of the St. Eufemija Monastery on the Island of Rab*] (YU)
EUITBF .... Ege Universitesi Iktisadi ve Ticari Bilimler Fakultesi [*Aegean University Faculty of Economy and Commercial Science*] (TU)
Eu M .... Egeszsegugyi Miniszterium/Miniszter [*Ministry/Minister of Health*] (HU)
EUM .... Electronic Control Machine (RU)
EUM .... Entraide Universitaire Mondiale [*World University Service - WUS*] (EA)
EUM- .... Teletypewriter (RU)
EUP .... Electrical Turn Indicator (RU)
EUR .... Esposizione Universale di Roma [*Universal Exposition of Rome*] [*Also suburb of Rome*] [*Italian*] (WER)
EURA .... Europa-Afrika-Union (MAR)
EURAFREP ... Societe de Recherches et d'Exploitation du Petrole (MAR)
EURAGRIS ... European Agricultural Research Information System
EURATEX .... Societe Eurafricaine Textiles (MAR)
EURATOM .. European Atomic Energy Community (SJT)
EUROBANK ... Common designation and telegraphic address of the BCEN [*Banque Commerciale pour l'Europe du Nord*] [*French*] (WER)
EUROBOIS ... Entreprise Europeenne de Courtage des Bois (MAR)
EUROCAM ... Societe Europ-Cameroun (MAR)
Eurochemic ... Europese Maatschappij voor de Chemische Bewerking van Bestraalte Reactor Splijtstoffen [*European Company for the Chemical Processing of Irradiated Fuels*] [*Dutch*] (WEN)
EUROCOPI ... European Computer Program Information Centre
EURODIF ..... European Diffusion Agency [*France, Spain, Italy, Belgium*] (WER)
EUROGRAM ... Societe Europeenne d'Etudes, de Calcul et de Programmation (MAR)
EURONET ... European On-Line Information Network [*Brussels, Belgium*]
EUROVALUTA ... European Foreign Exchange (WEN)
EURTRAG ... Groupement Europeen d'Entreprises pour le Transgabonais (MAR)
EUS .... European User Service
EUSIDIC ...... European Association of Scientific Information Dissemination Centres [*'s-Gravenhage*]
EUTB .... Ege Universitesi Talebe Birligi [*Aegean University Student Union*] (TU)
EUU .... Optimalizing Control Device (RU)
EUWS .... Egyptian University Students' Welfare Society (MAR)
ev .... Eerstvolgende [*The Following*] [*Dutch*] (GPO)
eV .... Eingetragener Verein [*Registered Association*] [*German*] (WEN)
EV .... Electric Fan (RU)
EV .... Electromagnetic Valve (RU)
ev .... Electron Volt (RU)
EV .... Electronic Calculator (RU)
eV .... Elektronenvolt [*Electron Volt*] [*German*] (WEN)
eV .... Elektronowolt [*Electron Volt*] [*Polish*]
EV .... Elektrotehniski Vestnik [*Electrical Engineering Review*] [*Ljubljana*] [*A publication*] (YU)
EV .... Elektrovojvodina [*Establishment for production, transport, and distribution of electric power*] [*Novi Sad*] (YU)
eV .... Emotionelle Verarbeitung [*Emotional Working Up*] [*German*]
EV .... Empfangsverstaerker [*Receiving Amplifier (RAD)*] (EG)
EV .... En Ville [*Local*] [*French*]
EV .... Endverzweiger [*Distribution Terminal (Telephone cables)*] (EG)
EV .... Enosis Viotekhnon [*Union of Craftsmen*] [*Greek*] (GC)
EV .... Equatorial Air (RU)
Ev .... Ev Adresi [*Home Address*] (TU)
ev .... Evangelicky [*Protestant*] (CZ)
ev .... Evangelisch [*Protestant*] [*German*] (GPO)
ev .... Evente [*Yearly*] (HU)
ev .... Eventuell [*Eventual*] [*German*]
ev .... Eversti [*Finnish*]

EV............... Oriental Epigraphy (RU)
EVA............ Einkaufs- und Verkaufsabteilung [*Purchasing and Sales Department*] (EG)
EVA............ Elliniki Vasiliki Aeroporia [*Royal Greek Air Force*] (GC)
EVA............ Empresa de Viacao e Comercio de Angola, SARL (MAR)
evak............ Evacuation, Clearing (RU)
Evakkom..... Evacuation Commission (RU)
Evakom....... Evacuation Commission (RU)
Evakopunkt ... Evacuation Center (BU)
Evakpriyemnik ... Clearing Station (RU)
evang.......... Evangelikus [*Lutheran*] (HU)
evang.......... Evangelisch [*Protestant*] [*German*]
EVAY........... Ethniki Viomikhania Aeroporikou Ylikou [*National Aircraft Equipment Industry*] [*Greek*] (GC)
EVB............ Energieversorgungsbetrieb [*Energy Supply Plant*] (EG)
EVC............ Eenheidsvakcentrale [*Unity Trade Union Federation*] [*Dutch*] (WEN)
EVCh.......... Sympathetic Electric Clock (RU)
evcis........... Evidencni Cislo [*Registration Number*] (CZ)
EVD............ Economische Voorlichtingsdienst [*'s-Gravenhage*]
EVDA.......... Engage Volontaire par Devancement d'Appel [*Person who volunteers prior to induction*] [*French*]
EVDR.......... Entwurfs- und Vermessungsbueros der Deutschen Reichsbahn [*GDR Railroad Design and Surveying Office*] (EG)
EVE............ Elliniki Vasiliki Enosis [*Greek Royalist Union*] (GC)
EVE............ Emborikon kai Viomikhanikon Epimelitirion [*Chamber of Commerce and Industry*] [*Followed by initial letter of city name*] (GC)
EVED.......... Eidgenoessisches Verkehrs- und Energiewirtschafts-Department [*Transportation, Communications, and Energy Department*] [*Swiss*] (WEN)
event.......... Eventuell [*Eventual*] [*German*]
EVEV.......... Ethniki Vasiliki Enosi Voreioelladiton [*National Royalist Union of Northern Greeks*] (GC)
evf.............. Euphemistic (RU)
evf.............. Evfolyam [*Year of Publication*] [*Hungarian*] (GPO)
EVG............ Egyesult Villamosgepgyar [*United Electrical Machine Factory*] (HU)
EVG............ Europaische Verteidigungsgemeinschaft [*European Defense Community (EDC)*] (EG)
Evg............. Evangel [*Gospel*] [*German*]
EVG-........... Stripping Caterpillar Excavator (RU)
EVGY.......... Epito-Vegyianyagokat Gyarto Vallalat [*Construction Chemical Materials Manufacturing Enterprise*] (HU)
Evidst.......... Evidencna Stevilka [*Registration Number*] (YU)
EVIG........... Egyesult Villamosgepgyar [*United Electrical Machine Factory*] (HU)
EVITERV..... Elektromos es Villanyhalozatokat Tervezo Vallalat [*Electric Networks Designing Enterprise*] (HU)
EVITERV..... Szereloipari Tervezo Vallalat [*Fixture Installation Planning Enterprise*] (HU)
EVK............ Eisenbahnverkehrskasse [*Railroad Cashier's Office*] (EG)
EVK............ Europai Vedelmi Kozosseg [*European Defense Community*] (HU)
evk............. Evkonyv [*Yearbook*] (HU)
EVK............ Large-Panel Interior Structures (BU)
Evkaf.......... Evkaf Idaresi [*Religious Foundations (Trusts) Administration*] (TU)
Evkaf.......... Religious Foundations [*Trusts*] Administration [*Turkish Cypriot*] (GC)
EVKh.......... Elliniki Vasiliki Khorofylaki [*Greek Royal Gendarmery*] (GC)
EVKOM....... Elektrisiteitsvoorsieningskommissie [*Electricity Supply Commission*] [*Use ESCOM*] (AF)
EVKXV........ Enosis Viotekhnon Katergasias Xylou Volou [*Volos Union of Wood Craftsmen*] (GC)
evltn........... Everstiluutnantti [*Finnish*]
evlut........... Evankelis-Luterilainen [*Finnish*]
evluutn........ Everstiluutnantti [*Finnish*]
EVM............ Egyesult Vegyimuvek [*United Chemical Works*] (HU)
EVM............ Electronic Computer (RU)
EVM............ Epitesugyi es Varosfejlesztesi Miniszterium [*Ministry of Construction and Urban Development*] (HU)
EVMCC....... Escuela Vocacional Militar Camilo Cienfuegos [*Camilo Cienfuegos Military Vocational School*] [*Cuban*] (LA)
EVN............ Energie Verbrauchsnorm(en) [*Energy Consumption Norm(s)*] (EG)
EVO............ Eisenbahnverkehrsordnung [*Railroad Traffic Regulations*] (EG)
EVO............ Elliniki Viotekhnia Oplon [*Greek Arms Industry*] (GC1)
EVOC.......... Edoevor Vegetable Oil Company (MAR)
EVON.......... Ethniki Vasiliki Organosi Neon [*National Royalist Youth Organization*] [*Greek*] (GC)
EVP............ Einzelhandelsverkaufspreis [*Retail Selling Price*] (EG)
EVP............ Electron Device, Vacuum Tube (RU)
evp............. Erossa Vakinaisesta Palveluksesta [*Finnish*]
EVP............ Evangelische Volkspartei [*Protestant People's Party*] [*Swiss*] (WEN)
EVPE.......... Epitropi Voitheias Prosfygon en Elladi [*Refugees Service Committee for Greece*] (GC)
evr.............. Jewish (BU)
evrop.......... European (BU)
Evr Tur....... European Turkey (BU)
EVS............ Elliniki Viomikhania Sakkhareos [*Greek Sugar Industry*] [*Greek*] (GC)
EVS............ Epitropi gia tin Valkanikin Synennoisin [*Committee for a Balkan Understanding*] [*Greek*] (GC)
EVS............ Epitropi Viomikhanikon Skheseon [*Industrial Relations Committee*] [*Cypriot*] (GC)
EVS............ Etaireia Vyzandinon Spoudon [*Society of Byzantine Studies*] [*Greek*] (GC)
EVSA.......... Enosis Viotekhnikon Somateion Athinon [*Union of Craft Associations of Athens*] (GC)
evsz............ Evszam [*Date*] (HU)
evtl............. Eventuell [*Perhaps, Possibly*] [*German*] (GPO)
EVTsM........ Electronic Digital Computer (RU)
EVU............ Energeticky Vyzkumny Ustav [*Power Research Institute*] (CZ)
EVW............ Erdoelverarbeitungswerk Schwedt [*Schwedt Oil Refinery*] (EG)
Ew.............. Eigenschaftswort [*German*]
EW.............. Eingetragenes Warenzeichen [*Registered Trademark*] [*German*]
EW.............. Einheitswert [*Standard Value*] (EG)
Ew.............. Einwohner [*German*]
EW.............. Eisenwerke West [*West Iron Works*] [*See also EKW*] (EG)
EW.............. Elektrowaerme [*Electrical Heating Equipment Plant*] (EG)
Ew.............. Euer [*Your*] [*German*]
ew.............. Ewentualnie [*Or, Otherwise*] [*Polish*]
EWBS.......... Exportwarenbegleitschein [*Export Bill of Lading*] (EG)
ewent.......... Ewentualnie [*Or, Otherwise*] [*Polish*]
EWG........... Europaeische Wirtschaftsgemeinschaft [*European Economic Community (EEC)*] [*German*] (WEN)
EWG........... European Work Group (MAR)
EWG........... Europejska Wspolnota Gospodarcza [*European Economic Community*] (POL)
EWk............ Elektrizitaetswerk [*German*]
EWT............ Elektrizitaetswerkstelefonie [*Power Plant Telephone System*] (EG)
e Wu........... Emotionelles Werturteil [*Emotional Evaluation*] [*German*]
EWW........... Eisenwerke West (VEB) [*West Ironworks (VEB)*] (EG)
EWWA......... Ethiopian Women's Welfare Association (AF)
ex............... Exempel [*Example*] [*Swedish*] (GPO)
ex............... Exercice [*French*]
ex c............ Ex-Coupon [*French*]
Exca........... Excelencia [*Excellence*] [*Spanish*]
EXCAF........ Expo Carrefour Afrique (MAR)
EXCARBON ... Explotaciones Carboniferas SA [*Medellin*] (COL)
EXCHEM...... Explosives and Chemicals Ltd. (MAR)
Excma......... Excelentisima [*Most Excellent*] [*Spanish*]
Excmo......... Excelentisimo [*Most Excellent*] [*Spanish*]
EXCOMEX.. Explotaciones. Comercio Exterior Ltda. [*Cali*] (COL)
ExcPrv........ Excurrendoprovisor [*German*]
EXCUARSO ... Explotaciones de Cuarso Ltda. [*Medellin*] (COL)
ex d............ Ex-Dividende [*French*]
ex dr........... Ex-Droits [*French*]
EXE............ Enosis Xenodokheion Ellados [*Hotel Union of Greece*] (GC)
EXECO........ Societe d'Expansion Economique et Commerciale (MAR)
exempl........ Exemplaire [*Copy (of a printed work)*] [*French*]
EXFORKA ... Exploitation Forestiere du Kiangi (MAR)
EXh............ Mixture of Tetraethyl-Lead and Organic Chlorides and Bromides (RU)
exhdb.......... Railroad Operation Battalion (RU)
exhdp.......... Railroad Operation Regiment (RU)
EXIM........... Expor Impor [*Export-Import*] (IN)
EXIM........... Export-Import Bank (MAR)
EXIMAR...... Exportaciones e Importaciones Marinas [*Cali*] (COL)
EXIMBANK ... Export-Import Bank [*Tunisian*] (MAR)
EXIMCOOP ... Intreprindere de Comert Exterior a Cooperativei de Consum [*Foreign Trade Enterprise of the Consumer Cooperatives*] (RO)
EXIMPO....... Export- und Importgesellschaft [*Export and Import Company*] (EG)
Exkl............ Exklusiv [*Except(ed), Not Included*] (EG)
EXMIBAL.... Exploraciones y Explotaciones Mineras Izabal SA [*Izabal Mining Exploration and Exploitation, Inc.*] [*Guatemalan*] (LA)
Exmo.......... Excelentissimo [*or Excellentissimo*] [*Excellency*] [*Portuguese*] (GPO)
ExMun........ Exerziermunition [*Dummy Ammunition, Blank Ammunition*] (EG)
EXOBOIS.... Bois Exotiques Ouvrages (MAR)
Exp............ Expedie [*Shipped*] [*Business and trade*] [*French*]
exp............ Experimentell [*Experimental*] [*German*]
Exp............ Expositur [*German*]
EXPASA...... Compania Exportadora Panamericana Sociedad Anonima [*Cali*] (COL)
ExPatr......... Exerzierpatrone [*Dummy Cartridge, Blank*] (EG)
EXPEDICUBA ... Empresa Cubana Expedidora de Mercancias de Importacion y Exportacion [*Cuban Import and Export Merchandise Expediting Enterprise*] (LA)
EXPEDIPORT ... Empresa Expedidora Portuaria [*Port Expediting Enterprise*] [*Cuban*] (LA)
Expl........... Exemplar [*Copy*] (EG)
EXPLACO ... Explanaciones Colombia Ltda. [*Medellin*] (COL)
EXPLANICAS ... Explanaciones Mecanicas SA [*Medellin*] (COL)
EXPLANOBRAS ... Explanaciones y Obras Ltda. [*Medellin*] (COL)

FACCP........ Frente Africana Contra o Colonialismo Portugues (MAR)
FACE........... Federacion Argentina de Comercio Exterior [*Argentine Foreign Trade Federation*] (LA)
FACE........... International Federation of Associations of Computer Users in Engineering Architecture and Related Fields (EA)
FACEJ......... Forges et Ateliers de Constructions Electriques de Jeumont (MAR)
FACELA...... Fabrica Centroamericana de Lapices, SA [*Pencils of Central America Corp.*] [*Salvadoran*]
FACh........... Fuerza Aerea de Chile [*Chilean Air Force*] (LA)
FachS.......... Fachschule [*German*]
FACI............ Federacao Angolana de Ciclismo (MAR)
FACOBO..... Fabrica Colombiana de Botones [*Cali*] (COL)
FACOBOL... Fabrica Colonial de Borracha Lda. (MAR)
FACOENVASES... Fabrica Colombiana de Envases Ltda. [*Barranquilla*] (COL)
FACOL........ Fabricas Colombianas [*Bogota*] (COL)
FACOLAMP... Fabrica Colombiana de Lamparas [*Bogota*] (COL)
FACOLTA... Fabrica Colombiana de Tapas [*Medellin*] (COL)
FACOMEC... Fabrica Colombiana de Materiales Electricos SA [*Cali*] (COL)
FACONOL... Fabrica de Conos Linero [*Bogota*] (COL)
FACP........... Front d'Action Commune Provisoire (MAR)
FACP........... Front Provisionnel pour Action Commune [*Provisional Front for Joint Action*] [*Chadian*] (AF)
FACT........... Front d'Action Civique du Tchad (MAR)
FACUR........ Federacion de Asociaciones y Comunidades Urbanas [*Federation of Urban Associations and Communities*] [*Venezuelan*] (LA)
FAD............. Flavine-Adenine Dinucleotide (RU)
FAD............. Fonds Africain de Developpement [*African Development Fund*] [*Use ADF*] (AF)
FAD............. Force Arabe de Dissuasion (MAR)
FAD............. Frente Amplio de la Izquierda [*Ecuadorean*] (PD)
FAD............. Front d'Action Democratique [*Democratic Action Front*] [*Beninese*] (AF)
FAD............. Front d'Algerie Democratique (MAR)
FAD............. Fuerza Aerea Dominicana [*Dominican Air Force*] [*Dominican Republic*] (LA)
FAD............. Fuerzas Armadas Democraticas [*Democratic Armed Forces*] [*Nicaraguan*] (PD)
FAD............. International Fund for Agricultural Development (AF)
FADA........... Fuerzas de Accion Armada [*Armed Action Forces*] [*Guatemalan*] (PD)
FADALTEC... Fabrica de Alambres Tecnicos [*Bogota*] (COL)
FADEFA...... Fundacion Argentina de Erradicacion de la Fiebre Aftosa [*Argentine Foundation for the Eradication of Foot-and-Mouth Disease*] (LA)
FADEMA..... Fabrica de Articulos de Madera [*Bogota*] (COL)
FADEMPA... Fabrica de Bolsas de Papel [*Bogota*] (COL)
FADEPSA.... Fonds d'Aide au Developpement de l'Education Physique et du Sport en Afrique (MAR)
FADES........ Fonds Arabe pour le Developpement Economic et Social [*Arab Economic and Social Development Fund*] (AF)
FADETEX.... Fabrica de Accesorios Textiles [*Barranquilla*] (COL)
FADEXCO... Fiduciaire Africaine d'Expansion Commerciale (MAR)
FADI............ Frente Amplio de la Izquierda [*Broad Front of the Left*] [*Ecuadorean*] (LA1)
FADP........... Funtua Agricultural Development Project (MAR)
FAE............. Federation of Arab Engineers (MAR)
FAE............. Federation Autonome de l'Enseignement (MAR)
FAE............. Frente Anti-Comunista Espanol [*Spanish Anti-Communist Front*] (WER)
FAE............. Fuerza Aerea Ecuatoriana [*Ecuadorean Air Force*] (LA)
FAEC........... Federation Algerienne de l'Education et de la Culture (MAR)
FAEC........... France Afrique d'Expertise Comptable (MAR)
FAEC........... Societe Anonyme Fiduciaire d'Assistance and d'Expertise Comptable (MAR)
FAEDA........ Federacion Argentina de Entidades Democraticas Anticomunistas [*Argentine Federation of Democratic Anticommunist Organizations*] (LA)
FAEM.......... Federation des Associations d'Etudiants de Madagascar [*Federation of Malagasy Student Associations*] (AF)
FAEMG........ Federacao da Agricultura do Estado de Minas Gerais [*Minas Gerais State Agricultural Federation*] [*Brazilian*] (LA1)
FAERT......... Fureszaru es Epuletfa Ertekesito Vallalat [*Wood and Lumber Trade Enterprise*] (HU)
FAES........... Fabrica de Equipos Estereofonicos [*Bogota*] (COL)
FAESP......... Federacao de Agricultura do Estado de Sao Paulo [*Sao Paulo State Agricultural Federation*] [*Brazilian*] (LA)
FAF.............. Facile a Fabriquer (MAR)
FAF.............. Facile a Financer (MAR)
FAF.............. Faellesrepraesentationen foer Danske Arbejdsleder-Ogtekniske Funktionaerforeninger [*Joint Representation of Danish Foremen's and Technical Employees' Association*] (WEN)
FAF.............. Force Aerienne Francaise [*French Air Force*] (WER)
FAF.............. Front de l'Algerie Francaise (MAR)
FAFILE........ Faculdade de Filosofia e Letras [*Brazilian*]
FAFS........... Federation des Associations Feminines (MAR)
FAG............. Federacao Angolana de Ginastica (MAR)
FAG............. Fliegerabwurfgondel (Einsatzmittel) [*(Aerial Drop) Container (Vector)*] (EG)
FAGA.......... Forces Aeriennes Gabonaises [*Gabonese Air Force*] (AF)
FAGANIC.... Federacion de Asociaciones Ganaderas de Nicaragua [*Federation of Nicaraguan Cattlemen's Associations*] (LA1)
FAGE........... Federacion de Agrupaciones Gremiales de Educadores [*Federation of Educators Union Associations*] (LA)
FAGG.......... Fakultet za Arhitekturo, Gradnjo, in Geodezijo [*Faculty of Architecture, Construction, and Geodesy*] [*Ljubljana*] (YU)
FAGI........... Federazione Anarchica Giovanile Italiana [*Italian Anarchist Youth Federation*] (WER)
FAGICTMAT... Ferme Agro-Industrielle et Commerciale des Tabacs et du Mais du Togo (MAR)
FAGRAM..... Fabrika Gradevinskih Masina [*Construction Machinery Works*] [*Smederevo*] (YU)
FAGRAVE... Fabrica Unida de Aceites y Grasas Vegetales (COL)
FAGRIN....... Fundo de Desenvolvimento Agricola e Industrial [*Agricultural and Industrial Development Fund*] [*Brazilian*] (LA)
FAGS........... Federation of Astronomical and Geophysical Data Analysis Services (EA)
fah.............. Frei aus Hier [*Free at Factory, Free from Here*] [*Business and trade*] [*German*]
FAHILOS..... Fabrica de Hilos Cordobes y Rey Ltda. [*Medellin*] (COL)
FAHUILA..... Fumigacion Aerea del Huila Ltda. [*Neiva*] (COL)
FAI.............. All-Union Scientific Research Institute of Agricultural Physics (RU)
FAI.............. Federacion Anarquista Iberica [*Iberian Anarchist Federation*] [*Spanish*] (WER)
FAI.............. Federation Aeronautique Internationale [*French*] (MTD)
FAI.............. Federazione Anarchica Italiana [*Italian Anarchist Federation*] (WER)
FAI.............. Federazione Autonoma Indossatrici [*Autonomous Federation of Models*] [*Italy*]
FAICO......... Fabrica Italo Colombiana de Baterias (COL)
FAIM........... Friends Africa Industrial Mission (MAR)
faip............. Faipari [*Lumber, Woodworking (Adjective)*] (HU)
FAIPA......... Front for the Independence of the Azores [*Portuguese*] (WER)
FAIR........... Federation of Afro-Asian Insurers and Reinsurers (MAR)
FAJ............. Fabrika Azotnih Jedinjenja [*Nitrogen Compounds Factory*] [*Gorazde*] (YU)
FAJ............. Fundiciones Artisticas de Joyas [*Cali*] (COL)
FAJARCOL... Fajardo y Compania Ltda. [*Cali*] (COL)
FAJDA......... Federation Algerienne de Judo et de Disciplines Assimilees (MAR)
FAJE........... Federation Algerienne des Jeux d'Echecs [*Algerian*] (MAR)
FAJURE....... Frente de Accion de la Juventud Reformista [*Reformist Youth Action Front*] [*Dominican Republic*] (LA1)
fak.............. Division (RU)
fak.............. Fakulta [*Faculty*] (CZ)
Fak............. Fakultaet [*German*]
FAK............. Fakultas, Fakultet [*Faculty (School, Department)*] (IN)
Fak............. Fakulte [*Faculty*] (TU)
FAK............. Federasie van Afrikaanse Kultuurvereniginge [*Federation of Afrikaner Cultural Associations*] [*South African*] (AF)
FAK............. Freight All Kinds (MAR)
fak.............. University Department [*or School*] (BU)
FAKEM........ Fabrique Khmere d'Emballages Metalliques [*Cambodian Metal Container Factory*] (CL)
FAKNLP...... Forces Armees Khmeres Nationales de Liberation Populaire [*Cambodian People's National Liberation Armed Forces*] [*Use CPNLAF*] (CL)
FAKO.......... Fachkommission [*Technical Commission*] [*See also FK*] (EG)
faks............ Facsimile (BU)
faks............ Facsimile (RU)
Fak za stop i sots nauki... School of Economic and Social Sciences (BU)
fak-t........... Division (RU)
Fakt............ Faktura [*Invoice*] [*German*] [*Business and trade*]
FAL............. Facilitation du Transport Aerien [*Air Transportation Facilities*] [*Rwandan*] (AF)
FAL............. Food and Agriculture Legislation [*Rome*] [*A publication*] (MAR)
FAL............. Forces Armees Laotiannes [*Federated Army of Laos*]
FAL............. Frente Argentino de Liberacion [*Argentine Liberation Front*] (LA)
FAL............. Fuerzas Armadas de Liberacion [*Armed Forces of Liberation*] [*Argentine*] (LA)
FAL............. Fuerzas Armadas de Liberacion [*Armed Forces of Liberation*] [*Colombian*] (LA)
FAL............. Fuerzas Armadas de Liberacion [*Armed Forces of Liberation*] [*Salvadoran*] (LA1)
FAL............. Fusil Automatique Leger (MAR)
fal.............. Phenylalanine (RU)
FALA.......... Federation Algerienne de Lutte Amateur (MAR)
FALA.......... Forcas Armadas de Libertacao de Angola (MAR)
FALANGE... Frente Anticomunista de Liberacion-Guerra de Eliminacion [*Anticommunist Front of Liberation-War of Elimination*] [*Salvadoran*] (LA1)
FALANGE... Fuerzas Armadas de Liberacion Anticomunistas y Guerra de Eliminacion [*Armed Forces for Anticommunist Liberation and War of Elimination*] [*Salvadoran*] (LA)
FALC.......... Armed Forces for the Liberation of Cabinda [*Angolan*] (PD)

FALCA .... Frente Anticomunista para la Liberacion de Centro America [*Anticommunist Front for the Liberation of Central America*] [*Salvadoran*] (LA1)
Fallsch .... Fallschirm [*Parachute*] (EG)
FALN .... Frente Angolana de Libertacao Nacional (MAR)
FALN .... Fuerzas Armadas de Liberacion Nacional [*Armed Forces of National Liberation*] [*Mexican*] (LA)
FALN .... Fuerzas Armadas de Liberacion Nacional [*Armed Forces of National Liberation*] [*Puerto Rican*] (PD)
FALN .... Fuerzas Armadas de Liberacion Nacional [*Armed Forces of National Liberation*] [*Venezuelan*] (LA)
FAM .... Fabricas de Artefatos Metalicos SA [*Metallic Devices Manufacturing Ltd.*] [*Brazilian*] (LA1)
FAM .... Fabrika Masina [*Machinery Works*] [*Novi Sad*] (YU)
FAM .... Fabrique Africaine de Meubles (MAR)
Fam .... Familie [*Family*] [*German*]
FAM .... Football Association of Malaya (ML)
FAM .... Frente Amplio de Masas [*Broad Front of the Masses*] [*Honduran*] (LA)
FAM .... Frente Anti-Macias [*Anti-Macias Front*] [*Equatorial Guinean*] (AF)
FAMA .... Federal Agricultural Marketing Association (ML)
FAMA .... Fondation pour l'Assistance Mutuelle en Afrique au Sud du Sahara [*Foundation for Mutual Aid in Africa South of the Sahara*] (AF)
FAMACO ..... Entreprise de Materiaux de Construction (MAR)
FAMAE .... Fabricas y Maestranzas del Ejercito [*Army Ordnance*] [*Chilean*] (LA)
Fa Ma L .... Fabryka Maszyn Lniarskich [*Flax Machine Factory*] (POL)
FAMAQUIN ... Fabrica de Maquinaria Industrial [*Cali*] (COL)
FAMAR .... Federacion Maritima Argentina [*Argentine Maritime Federation*] (LA)
FAMBEL ...... Fabrica de Malas de Beira Lda. (MAR)
FAMECHAS ... Fabrica de Mechas Ltda. [*Manizales*] (COL)
FAMECOL ... Fabrica de Articulos Metalicos de Colombia [*Bogota*] (COL)
FAMETAL ... Fabrica de Muebles Metalicos [*Medellin*] (COL)
FAMOLAC ... Fabrica de Molinos y Accesorios [*Cali*] (COL)
FAMOS .... Fabrika Motora Sarajevo [*Motor Works, Sarajevo*] (YU)
FAMOS .... Fantasias Modernas Ltda. [*Cali*] (COL)
FAMOUS ..... French-American Mid-Oceanic Underseas Survey (WER)
FAMP .... Frontier Armed and Mounted Police [*of the Cape Colony*] (MAR)
FAMSA .... Federation of African Medical Students Associations (MAR)
FAMSCO ..... Farm Services Company (MAR)
FAN .... Branch of the Academy of Sciences, USSR (RU)
FAN .... Fabrica de Aparatura Nucleara [*Nuclear Instrumentation Plant*] (RO)
FAN .... Fiduciaire de l'Afrique Noire (MAR)
FAN .... Fondo Aeronautico Nacional [*National Aeronautics Fund*] [*Colombian*] (LA)
FAN .... Forces Armees Neutralistes [*Neutralist Armed Forces*] [*Laotian*] (CL)
FAN .... Forces Armees Nigeriennes [*Niger Armed Forces*] (AF)
FAN .... Forces Armees du Nord [*Northern Armed Forces*] [*Chadian*] (AF)
FAN .... Frente Amplio Nacional [*Broad National Front*] [*Salvadoran*] (LA1)
FAN .... Frente Anticomunista Nacional [*National Anticommunist Front*] [*Salvadoran*] (LA1)
FAN .... Frente de Avance Nacional [*National Advancement Front*] [*Guatemalan*] (LA)
FAN .... Fuerzas Armadas Nacionales [*National Armed Forces*] [*Venezuelan*] (LA)
fan .... Plywood (RU)
FANABRA ... Fabrica Nacional de Abrasivos [*Bogota*] (COL)
FANABRO ... Fabrica Nacional de Brochas [*Bogota*] (COL)
FANAC .... Fabrica Nacional de Accesorios [*Bogota*] (COL)
FANAL .... Federacion Agraria Nacional [*National Farmers Federation*] [*Colombian*] (LA)
FANALRES ... Fabrica Nacional de Resortes [*Medellin*] (COL)
FANALSO ... Fabrica Nacional de Sombreros [*Medellin*] (COL)
FANASYCOA ... Federation Nationale des Syndicats du Commerce Ouest Africain (MAR)
FANATRAM ... Fabrica Nacional de Tractores y Motores [*National Factory for the Manufacture of Tractors and Motors*] [*Bolivian*] (LA)
FANAVE ...... Fabrica Nacional de Carrocerias para Vehiculos [*Bogota*] (COL)
FANCI .... Forces Armees Nationales de la Cote-d'Ivoire [*National Armed Forces School of the Ivory Coast*] (AF)
FANE .... Federation d'Action Nationale et Europeene [*Federation of National and European Action*] [*French*] (PPE)
FANEL .... Federacion de Asociaciones Nacionales de Estudiantes Latinoamericanos [*Federation of National Associations of Latin American Students*] (LA)
FANEON ..... Fabrica de Avisos de Gas Neon Ltda. [*Manizales*] (COL)
fanern .... Plywood Factory [*Topography*] (RU)
FANK .... Automatic Circuit Phase Adjustment (RU)
FANK .... Forces Armees Nationales Khmeres [*Cambodian National Armed Forces*] [*Replaced Royal Cambodian Armed Forces*] (CL)
FANO .... Fabrica Nacional de Oxigeno [*Medellin*] (COL)
FANO .... Frente Anticomunista del Nororiente [*Northeastern Anticommunist Front*] [*Guatemalan*] (PD)
FANO .... Frente Aranista Nacional Obrero [*National Pro-Arana Workers Front*] [*Guatemalan*] (LA)
FANT .... Forces Armees Nationales Tchadiennes [*Chadian*] (PD)
FANUS .... Federazione fra le Associazioni Nazionali Ufficiali e Sottufficiali in Congedo Provenienti dal Servizio Effettivo [*Federation of National Associations for Discharged Career Officers and Petty Officers*] [*Italian*]
FAO .... Compagnie Francaise de l'Afrique Occidentale-Mali (MAR)
FAO .... Food and Agriculture Organization [*United Nations*] (WEN)
FAO .... Forces Armees Occidentales [*Western Armed Forces*] [*Chadian*] (AF)
FAO .... Frente Amplio de Oposicion [*Broad Opposition Front*] [*Nicaraguan*] (LA)
FAO/APS .... FAO [*Food and Agriculture Organization of the United Nations*] Association of Professional Staff (EA)
FAP .... Fabrika Automobila Pionir [*"Pioneer" Automobile Factory*] (YU)
FAP .... Fabrika Automobila, Priboj [*Automobile Factory, Priboj*] (YU)
FAP .... Fabrique d'Articles en Plastique (MAR)
FAP .... Federacion Argentina de Periodistas [*Argentine Newsmen's Federation*] (LA)
FAP .... Forca Aerea Portuguesa [*Portuguese Air Force*] (WER)
FAP .... Forces Armees Populaires [*People's Armed Forces*] [*Beninese*] (AF)
FAP .... Forces Armees Populaires [*People's Armed Forces*] [*Chadian*] (AF)
FAP .... Forces Armees Populaires [*People's Armed Forces*] [*Malagasy*] (AF)
FAP .... Forces Armees Populaires [*People's Armed Forces*] [*Zairian*] (AF)
FAP .... Foros Akinitou Periousias [*Real Estate Tax*] (GC1)
fap .... Franc d'Avarie Particuliere [*French*]
FAP .... Frente de Accao Popular [*Popular Action Front*] [*Portuguese*] (WER)
FAP .... Frente Accion Progresista [*Progressive Action Front*] [*Honduran*] (LA)
FAP .... Front d'Action Patriotique (MAR)
FAP .... Fuerza Aerea del Peru [*Peruvian Air Force*] (LA)
FAP .... Fuerza Armada de la Paz [*Inter-American Peace Force*] [*Use IAPF*] [*Dominican Republic*] (LA)
FAP .... Fuerzas Armadas Peruanas [*Peruvian Armed Forces*] (LA)
FAPA .... Fermes Agro-Pastorales d'Arrondissement [*Agro-Pastoral District Farms*] [*Guinean*] (AF)
FAPA .... Ferro Alloys Producers Association (MAR)
FAPA .... Force Aerienne Populaire d'Angola (MAR)
FAPC .... Food and Agriculture Planning Committee (MAR)
FAPCO .... Fayoum Petroleum Company (MAR)
FAPI .... Federazione Artisti e Professionisti Italiani [*Italian Federation of the Arts and Professions*]
FAPI .... Fonds Allemand pour les Perimetres Irrigues [*Tunisian*] (MAR)
FAPIG .... [*The*] First Atomic Power Industry Group (SJT)
FAPL .... Forces Armees Populaires de Liberation [*People's Liberation Armed Forces*] [*Use PLAF*] [*South Vietnamese*] (CL)
FAPLA .... Forcas Armadas Populares da Liberacao de Angola [*People's Armed Forces for the Liberation of Angola*] (AF)
FAPLE .... Frente Anti-Totalitario dos Portugueses Libres Exilados (MAR)
FAPLK .... Forces Armees Populaires de Liberation Khmere [*Cambodian People's National Liberation Armed Forces*] [*Use CPNLAF*] (CL)
FAPLNC ...... Forces Armees Populaires de Liberation Nationale du Cambodge [*Cambodian People's National Liberation Armed Forces*] [*Use CPNLAF*] (CL)
FAPRA .... Federation of African Public Relations Association (MAR)
FAPS .... Fakulta Architektury a Pozemniho Stavitelstvi [*Department of Architecture and Civil Engineering (of the Czech Institute of Technology in Prague)*] (CZ)
FAPU .... Federacion de Asociaciones de Profesores Universitarios [*Federation of Associations of University Professors*] [*Venezuelan*] (LA)
FAPU .... Frente de Accion Popular Unida [*United Popular Action Front*] [*Salvadoran*] (LA)
FAQ .... Fair Average Quality (MAR)
Far .... Farsca [*Persian*] (TU)
FAR .... Federal Department of Agricultural Research (MAR)
FAR .... Federation of Arab Republics (MAR)
FAR .... Football Association of Rhodesia (MAR)
FAR .... Forces Armees Royales [*Royal Armed Forces*] [*Laotian*] (CL)
FAR .... Forces Armees Royales [*Royal Armed Forces*] [*Moroccan*] (AF)
FAR .... Foreign Affairs Research Documentation Center (MAR)
FAR .... Fuerza Armada Revolucionaria Peruana [*Peruvian Revolutionary Armed Forces*] (LA)
FAR .... Fuerzas Armadas Rebeldes [*Rebel Armed Forces*] [*Guatemalan*] (PD)
FAR .... Fuerzas Armadas Revolucionarias [*Revolutionary Armed Forces*] [*Argentine*] (LA)
FAR .... Fuerzas Armadas Revolucionarias [*Revolutionary Armed Forces*] [*Bolivian*] (LA)
FAR .... Fuerzas Armadas Revolucionarias [*Revolutionary Armed Forces*] [*Cuban*] (LA)

FD............... Fernschnellzug [*Long-Distance Express Passenger Train (Including Sleepers)*] (EG)
FD............... Fiskulturno Drustvo [*Physical Culture Society*] (YU)
fd............... For Detta [*Formerly*] [*Swedish*] (GPO)
FD............... Fovgh-e Diplome [*Academic qualification*] [*Iranian*]
FD............... Franc Djibouti [*Monetary unit*] (MAR)
FD............... Frente Democratico [*Democratic Front*] [*Salvadoran*] (LA1)
FD............... Phase Deflector (RU)
FD............... Phase Discriminator (RU)
FD............... Photodiode (RU)
FDA............ Fundacja Domow Akademickich [*Students' House Fund*] (POL)
FDA............ Phenylenediamine (RU)
FDAE.......... Fundo de Desenvolvimento de Areas Estrategicas [*Strategic Areas Development Fund*] [*Brazilian*] (LA)
FDAF.......... Forologikon Dikastirion Amesou Forologias [*Tax Court for Direct Taxes*] [*Greek*] (GC)
FDAR.......... Fonds de Developpement et d'Action Rurale (MAR)
FDB............ Faellesforeninger foer Danmarks Brugsforeninger [*Danish Cooperative Wholesale Society*] (WEN)
FDC............ Federacion Democrata Cristiana [*Christian Democratic Federation*] [*Spanish*] (PPE)
FDC............ Fisheries Development Corporation (MAR)
FDC............ Fonds de Developpement Communal [*Communal Development Fund*] [*Rwandan*] (AF)
FDC............ Food Distribution Corporation (MAR)
FDC............ Foodcrop Development Committee [*Mauritian*] (AF)
FDC............ Front Democratique Congolais (MAR)
FDD............ Federacion Dominicana de Desarrollo [*Dominican Development Federation*] [*Dominican Republic*] (LA1)
FDD............ Fondation Documentaire Dentaire
FDD............ Frente Democrata Docente [*Teachers Democratic Front*] [*Bolivian*] (LA)
FDE............ Fondo Dominicano de Educacion [*Dominican Education Fund*] [*Dominican Republic*] (LA1)
FDE............ Frente Democratico Eleitoral [*Democratic Electoral Front*] [*Portuguese*] (PPE)
F a DE......... Fusee a Double Effet [*Military*] [*French*] (MTD)
FDES.......... Fonds de Developpement Economique et Sociale [*Economic and Social Development Funds*] [*Guadeloupe*] (LA1)
FDF............ Front Democratique des Francophones [*Francophone Democratic Front*] [*Belgian*] (PPW)
FDF............ Fructose Diphosphate (RU)
FDG............ Frente Democratico Guatemalteco [*Guatemalan Democratic Front*] (LA)
FDG-............ Gas Filter-Throttle (RU)
FDGB.......... Freier Deutscher Gewerkschaftsbund [*Free German Trade Union Federation*] [*East German*] (PPE)
FDGP.......... Front Democratique de la Gauche Progressiste [*Democratic Front of the Progressive Left*] [*Malagasy*] (AF)
FDHKC........ Filistin Demokratik Halk Kurtulus Cephesi [*Palestine Democratic Peoples Liberation Front*] (TU)
FDI............... Frente Democratico de Izquierdas [*Democratic Front of Leftist Forces*] [*Spanish*] (WER)
f/di............. Frondidi [*Care Of*] (GC)
FDI............... Fundacion para el Desarrollo Industrial [*Cali*] (COL)
FDIC............ Front pour la Defense des Institutions Constitutionnelles (MAR)
FDID............ Federazione Democratica Internazionale delle Donne [*Women's International Democratic Federation - WIDF*] (WER)
FDIF............ Federation Democratique Internationale des Femmes [*Women's International Democratic Federation - WIDF*] (EA)
FDIM........... Federacion Democratica Internacional de Mujeres [*Women's International Democratic Federation - WIDF*] (LA)
FDj............... Franc Djibouti [*Monetary unit*] (MAR)
FDJ.............. Freie Deutsche Jugend [*Free German Youth*] (PPE)
FDK............. Filelevtheron Dimokratikon Kendron [*Liberal Democratic Center*] [*Greek*] (GC)
FDK............. Long-Term Credit Fund (RU)
Fdl............... Fahrdienstleiter [*Dispatcher*] (EG)
f dl.............. Fale Dlugie [*Long Waves*] [*Polish*]
FDL.............. Ferndauerlinie [*Permanent Long-Distance Telephone Line*] (EG)
FDLA........... Frente Democratica para a Libertacao de Angola [*Democratic Front for the Liberation of Angola*] (MAR)
FDLA........... Front Democratique pour la Liberation de l'Angola [*Democratic Front for the Liberation of Angola*] (AF)
FDLD........... Front Democratique pour la Liberation de Djibouti [*Democratic Front for the Liberation of Djibouti*] (MAR)
FDLUQ........ Fronte Democratica Liberale dell'Uomo Qualunque [*Liberal Democratic Front of the Common Man*] [*Italian*] (PPE)
FDM............. Phenyldimethylurea (RU)
FDMM.......... Democratic Association of Students of Madagascar (AF)
FDMS.......... Additional Material Incentive Fund (BU)
FDN............. Frente Democratica Nacional [*National Democratic Front*] [*Portuguese*] (WER)
FDN............. Frente Democratico Nacionalista [*Nationalist Democratic Front*] [*Salvadoran*] (LA1)
FDN............. Front Democratique National [*National Democratic Front*] [*Senegalese*] (AF)
FDN............. Fuerza Democratica Nicaraguense [*Nicaraguan Democratic Force*] (PD)
FDNB........... Fluorodinitrobenzene (RU)
FDNR........... Frente Democratico Nacional Revolucionario [*National Revolutionary Democratic Front*] [*Spanish*] (WER)
FDP............. Federal Dominion Party (MAR)
FDP............. Freie Demokratische Partei [*Free Democratic Party*] [*West German*] (WEN)
FDP............. Freisinnig-Demokratische Partei der Schweiz [*Radical Democratic Party of Switzerland*] (PPW)
FDP............. Frente Democratico Popular [*Popular Democratic Front*] [*Peruvian*] (LA)
FDP............. Front Democratique de la Patrie (MAR)
FDP............. Frontul Democratic Popular [*Democratic Popular Front*] [*Romanian*] (PPE)
FDP............. Fuerza Democratica Popular [*Popular Democratic Force*] [*Venezuelan*] (LA)
FDR............. Frente Democratico Contra la Represion [*Democratic Front Against Repression*] [*Guatemalan*] (PD)
FDR............. Frente Democratico Revolucionario [*Revolutionary Democratic Front*] [*Salvadoran*] (LA1)
F-Draht....... Fe-Ni Wire [*Iron-nickel alloy*] (EG)
FDRP........... Frente de Defensa de la Revolucion Peruana [*Front for the Defense of the Peruvian Revolution*] (LA)
FDS............. Falusi Dolgozok Spartakiadja [*Village "Spartakiads"*] (HU)
FDSA........... Front Democratique et Social Algerien [*Algerian Democratic and Social Front*] (AF)
FDT............. Forca Democratica do Trabalho [*Labor Democratic Force*] [*Portuguese*] (WER)
FDT............. Frente Democratico de Trabajadores [*Democratic Workers Front*] [*Costa Rican*] (LA1)
FDT............. Frente Democratico de Trabajadores [*Democratic Workers Front*] [*Ecuadorean*] (LA)
FDTA........... Federacion Departamental de Trabajadores de Arequipa [*Arequipa Departmental Workers Federation*] [*Peruvian*] (LA)
FDTh........... Foros Dimosion Theamaton [*Public Entertainment Tax*] [*Greek*] (GC)
FDTJ............ Federace Delnickych Telocvicnych Jednot [*Federation of Workers' Athletic and Gymnastic Organizations*] (CZ)
FDTN........... Fabrication et Diffusion des Textiles du Nord (MAR)
FDU............. Fernando Democratic Union (MAR)
FDU............. Frente Democratica Unida [*United Democratic Front*] [*Portuguese*] (WER)
FDVR........... Federal Department of Veterinary Research (MAR)
FDYa........... Ferrodiode Cell (RU)
FD(-ZUG).... Fernschnellzug [*Long-Distance Express Train*] (EG)
FE............... Falange Espanola [*Spanish Falange*] (WER)
Fe............... Ferme [*Farm*] [*Military map abbreviation*] [*World War I*] [*French*] (MTD)
FE............... Filiki Etaireia [*Society of Friends*] [*Greek*] (GC)
fe............... Folyo Evi [*Of the Current Year*] [*Hungarian*] (GPO)
FE............... Fuerza Emancipadora [*Emancipating Force*] [*Venezuelan*] (LA)
FE............... Photoelectric Cell (RU)
FE............... Physical Electrotonus (RU)
FEA............. Fabrica de Elemente pentru Automatizare [*Factory for Automation Elements*] (RO)
FEA............. Falange Espanola Autentica [*Authentic Spanish Falange*] (WER)
FEA............. Filodasiki Enosi Athinon [*Athens Friends of the Forest Association*] (GC)
FEA............. Fratsuzskaia Ekvatorialnaia Afrika (MAR)
FEA............. French Equatorial Africa (MAR)
FEAF........... Far East Air Force (ML)
FEAK........... Foititiki Epitropi Allilengyis pros tous Kyprious [*Student Committee of Solidarity for the Cypriots*] [*Greek*] (GC)
FEAKA........ Foititiki Epitropi Allilengyis dia ton Kypriakon Agona [*Student Solidarity Committee for the Cypriot Struggle*] [*Greek*] (GC)
FEAMAR..... Fundacao de Estudos do Mar [*Sea Studies Foundation*] [*Brazilian*] (LA)
FEAN........... Federation des Enseignants de l'Afrique Noire [*Federation of Teachers of Black Africa*] (AF)
FEANF......... Federation des Etudiants de l'Afrique Noire en France [*Federation of Students from Black Africa in France*] (AF)
FEAPTh....... Foititiki Enosis Aristoteleiou Panepistimiou Thessalonikis [*University of Salonica Student Union*] (GC)
FEARALAT... Federacion Arabe de America Latina [*Arab Federation of Latin America*] (LA)
Feb............. Febrero [*February*] [*Spanish*]
feb............. Februar [*February*] [*Danish*] (GPO)
Feb............. Februar [*February*] [*German*] (GPO)
feb............. Februar [*February*] [*Hungarian*] (GPO)
feb............. Februari [*February*] [*Dutch*] (GPO)
FEB............. Federacion de Empleados Bancarios del Peru [*Peruvian Bank Employees Federation*] (LA)
FEB............. Federation des Entreprises de Belgique [*Federation of Belgian Enterprises*] (WER)
FEB............. Finance and Economics Office (RU)
FEB............. Forca Expedicionaria Brasileira [*Brazilian Expeditionary Force, 1944-1955*]
FEBACAM... Federation Bananiere du Cameroun (MAR)
febb........... Febbraio [*February*] [*Italian*]

FEBEL .... Ferrageira da Beira Lda. (MAR)
FEBEM .... Federacao Estadual do Bem Estar do Menor [*State Child Welfare Foundation*] [*Brazilian*] (LA)
febo .... Febrero [*February*] [*Spanish*]
febr .... Februar [*February*] (HU)
FEC .... Fabrica de Elementos Combustiveis [*Fuel Elements Factory*] [*Brazilian*] (LA1)
FEC .... Far East Command (ML)
FEC .... Federal Electoral College (MAR)
FEC .... Federal Electoral Commission (MAR)
FEC .... Federation des Entreprises au Congo [*Merger of AIIB and AICB*]
FEC .... Fianarantsoa-East Coast (MAR)
FEC .... Fonds d'Equipement Communal (MAR)
FEC .... Forestiere Equatoriale du Cameroun (MAR)
FECABA ...... Federation of East and Central African Amateur Boxing Associations (MAR)
FECAFOOT ... Federation Camerounaise de Football [*Cameroon Football Federation*] (MAR)
FECAICA .... Federacion de Camaras y Asociaciones Industriales Centroamericanas [*Federation of Central American Industrial Chambers and Associations*] (LA)
FECAMCO ... Federacion de Camaras de Comercio del Istmo Centroamericano [*Federation of Chambers of Commerce of the Central American Isthmus*] [*Salvadoran*] (LA)
FECAMU ..... Federacion Centroamericana de Mujeres Universitarias [*Central American Federation of University Women*] (LA1)
FECANAT ... Federations Camerounaises de Natation (MAR)
FECANIC .... Federacion de Cooperativas de Ahorro y Credito [*Federation of Savings and Loan Cooperatives*] [*Nicaraguan*] (LA1)
FECARIBE .. Corporacion Financiera del Caribe [*Bogota*] (COL)
FECCAS ...... Federacion de Campesinos Cristianos Salvadorenos [*Salvadoran Christian Peasants' Federation*] (LA)
FECCI .... Frente Estudiantil Critico, Combativo, e Independente [*Critical, Combative, and Independent Student Front*] [*Panamanian*] (LA)
FECEE .... Federacio d'Entitats Catalanes a l'Exilo i a l'Emigracio [*Federation of Catalan Exile and Emigre Organizations*] [*Spanish*] (WER)
FECESITLIH ... Federacion Central de Sindicatos de Trabajadores Libres de Honduras [*Central Federation of Unions of Free Honduran Workers*] (LA)
FECETRAG ... Federacion Central de Trabajadores de Guatemala [*Central Federation of Guatemalan Workers*] (LA)
FECEU .... Federacion Centroamericana de Estudiantes Universitarios [*Central American Federation of University Students*] (LA)
FECh .... Federacion de Estudiantes de Chile [*Student Federation of Chile*] (LA)
FECIA .... Federacion de Empleados de Comercio e Industria de Arequipa [*Federation of Commercial and Industrial Employees of Arequipa*] [*Peruvian*] (LA)
FEC/ML ...... Frente Eleitoral de Comunistas/Marxista-Leninista [*Electoral Front of Communists/Marxist-Leninist*] [*Portuguese*] (WER)
FECN .... Fabrica de Elementos Combustibles Nucleares [*Nuclear Fuel Elements Enterprise*] [*Argentine*] (LA1)
FECO .... Fundacion de Estudios para la Comunidad Organizada [*Studies Foundation for the Organized Community*] [*Argentine*] (LA1)
FECOAC ..... Federacion Nacional de Cooperativas de Ahorro y Credito [*National Federation of Savings and Loan Cooperatives*] [*Ecuadorean*] (LA)
FECODE ...... Federacion Colombiana de Educadores [*Colombian Teachers Federation*] (LA)
FeCoFoot .... Federation Congolaise de Football (MAR)
FECOLDROGAS ... Federacion Colombiana de Droguistas [*Bogota*] (COL)
FECOONIC ... Federacion de Cooperativas de Nicaragua [*Federation of Nicaraguan Cooperatives*] (LA1)
FECOPAM ... Federacion Nacional de Cooperativas de Produccion Agricola y Mercadeo [*National Federation of Cooperatives for Agricultural Production and Marketing*] [*Ecuadorean*] (LA)
FECORAH ... Federacion de Cooperativas de Reforma Agraria de Honduras [*Federation of Honduran Agrarian Reform Cooperatives*] (LA)
FECOSA ...... Ferrocarriles de Costa Rica [*Costa Rican Railways*] (LA1)
FECOTRIGO ... Federacao das Cooperativas Brasileiras de Trigo e Soja [*Federation of Brazilian Wheat and Soybean Cooperatives*] (LA)
FECSA .... Fuerzas Electricas de Cataluna, Sociedad Anonima [*Electric Power of Catalonia, Incorporated*] [*Spanish*] (WER)
FECSITLIH ... Federacion Central de Sindicatos de Trabajadores Libres de Honduras [*Central Federation of Unions of Free Honduran Workers*] (LA)
FECUIMPORT ... Empresa Cubana Importadora de Ferrocarriles [*Cuban Enterprise for Import of Rolling Stock*] (LA)
FED .... F. E. Dzerzhinskiy [*Camera type*] (RU)
FED .... Federacion de Estudiantes Dominicanos [*Federation of Dominican Students*] [*Dominican Republic*] (LA)
FED .... Fondo Especial de Desarrollo [*Special Development Fund*] [*Nicaraguan*] (LA1)
FED .... Fonds Europeen de Developpement [*European Development Fund*] [*Use EDF*] (AF)
FEDAGRI ..... Federacion Agricola de Chile [*Chilean Agricultural Federation*] (LA)
FEDAN .... Federacion Educativa para el Desarrollo Agricola [*Educational Federation for Agricultural Development*] [*Colombian*] (LA)
FEDAN .... Frente Estudiantil de Accion Nacional [*Student National Action Front*] [*Ecuadorean*] (LA)
FEDAP .... Federacion de Asociaciones de Padres y Apoderados [*Federation of Parents and Guardians Associations*] [*Chilean*] (LA)
FEDASEC ... Federation Dahomeene des Syndicats de l'Education et de la Culture (MAR)
FEDCO .... Federmann Entreprises Overseas Ltd. (MAR)
FEDE .... Federacion Estudiantil [*Student Federation*] [*Argentine*] (LA)
FEDE .... Frente Estudiantil de Economia [*Economy Students Front*] [*Panamanian*] (LA)
FEDEACh .... Federacion de Estudiantes Agricolas de Chile [*Federation of Chilean Agricultural Students*] (LA)
FEDEAGRO ... Federacion Nacional de Productores Agropecuarios [*National Federation of Agricultural and Livestock Producers*] [*Venezuelan*] (LA)
FEDEARROZ ... Federacion Nacional de Arroceros [*Bogota*] (COL)
FEDEAU ...... Federation pour le Developpement de l'Artisanat Utilitaire [*Federation for the Development of Utilitarian Crafts*] (EA)
FEDEBAT .... Federation des Bateke (MAR)
FEDEBATE ... Federation des Batetela (MAR)
FEDEBOL .... Federacion del Futbol Colombiano [*Bogota*] (COL)
FEDEC .... Federacion Democratica de Estudiantes Colombianos [*Democratic Federation of Colombian Students*] (LA)
FEDECACES ... Federacion de Cooperativas de Ahorro y Credito de El Salvador [*Federation of Savings and Loan Cooperatives of El Salvador*] (LA1)
FEDECAFE ... Federacion Nacional de Cafeteros [*National Federation of Coffee Growers*] [*Colombian*] (LA)
FEDECAMARAS ... Federacion Venezolana de Camaras y Asociaciones de Comercio y Produccion [*Association of the Chambers of Commerce and Industry*] [*Venezuelan*] (LA)
FEDECAME ... Federacao Cafeeira de America [*Federation of Coffee Growers of America*] (LA)
FEDECAME ... Federacion Cafetalera de America [*Federation of Coffee Growers of America*] (LA)
FEDECAP ... Federacion Centroamericana de Periodistas [*Central American Federation of Journalists*] [*Honduran*] (LA)
FEDECARBON ... Federacion Nacional de Carboneros [*National Federation of Coal Miners*] [*Colombian*] (LA)
FEDECh ...... Federacion de Educadores de Chile [*Chilean Teachers Federation*] (LA)
FEDECINE ... Federacion Nacional de Exhibidores de Cine [*Bogota*] (COL)
FEDECO ...... Federal Electoral Commission [*Nigerian*]
FEDECONTA ... Federacion de Contadores de Antioquia [*Medellin*] (COL)
FEDEGAN ... Federacion Colombiana de Ganaderos [*Colombian Cattlemen's Association*] (LA)
FEDEGAS ... Federacion Colombiana de Gas [*Bogota*] (COL)
FEDEIEC ..... Federacion Unitaria de Trabajadores de la Industria Electrica del Ecuador [*Single Federation of the Ecuadorean Workers of the Electrical Industry*] (LA)
FEDEKA ...... Federation des Associations Tribales des Originaires du Kasai [*Federation of Associations of Kasai Tribes*]
FEDELAC .... Federacion Dominicana de Ligas Agrarias Cristianas [*Dominican Federation of Christian Agrarian Leagues*] [*Dominican Republic*] (LA1)
FEDELCO ... Federacion de Loterias de Colombia [*Bogota*] (COL)
FEDEM .... Federacion de Estudiantes Democratas de Ensenanza Media [*Federation of Democratic Secondary School Students*] [*Spanish*] (WER)
FEDEMETAL ... Federacion Colombiana de Industrias Metalicas [*Colombian Metals Industries Federation*] (LA)
FEDEMETAL ... Federacion Metalurgica Colombiana [*Colombian Metallurgical Federation*] (LA)
FEDEMI .... Federacion de Mineros de Cundinamarca [*Cundinamarca Miners Federation*] [*Colombian*] (LA)
FEDEMOL ... Federacion Nacional de Molineros de Trigo [*Bogota*] (COL)
FEDEMRIFAS ... Federacion Nacional de Empresarios de Rifas Autorizadas [*Bogota*] (COL)
FEDENAGRIC ... Federacion Nacional de Trabajadores Agricolas de Colombia [*National Federation of Agricultural Workers of Colombia*] (LA)
FEDEPAS .... Federacion Nacional de Fabricantes de Pastas Alimenticias [*Bogota*] (COL)
FEDEPETROL ... Federacion Colombiana de Petroleos [*Bogota*] (COL)
FEDEPETROL ... Federacion de Trabajadores Petroleros [*Petroleum Workers Federation*] [*Venezuelan*] (LA)
FEDEPROCOL ... Federacion de Profesionales Colombianos [*Colombian Professionals Federation*] (LA)
FEDERADIO ... Federacion Colombiana de Radiodifusion [*Bogota*] (COL)
FEDERAL .... Federacion de Alimentos Concentrados para Animales [*Bogota*] (COL)
FEDERBAN ... Federation Bananiere et Fruitiere de la Cote-d'Ivoire (MAR)
FEDERMAR ... Federation Maritime de la Cote-d'Ivoire (MAR)

fenyk .... Fenykep [*or Fenykepesz*] [*Photograph or Photographer*] (HU)
FENYSZOV ... Fenykepesz KSZ [*Cooperative of Photographers*] (HU)
fenyt .... Fenytan [*Optics*] (HU)
feod .... Feudal (BU)
FEODET ...... Federacion de Empleados y Obreros de Telecomunicaciones [*Federation of Telecommunications Employees and Workers*] [*Uruguayan*] (LA)
FEOF .... Foreign Exchange Operations Fund [*Laotian*] (CL)
feog .... Felderitoosztag [*Reconnaissance Group, Detachment*] (HU)
FEOGA .... European Agricultural Guidance and Guarantee Fund [*Italian*] (WER)
FEOIC .... Federacion de Estudiantes de Odontologia del Istmo Centroamericano [*Dentistry Students Federation of the Central American Isthmus*] (LA)
FEOP .... Foititiki Epitropi Organotikis Protovoulias [*Student Committee for Organizational Initiative*] [*Greek*] (GC)
FEOR .... Foglalkozasok Egyseges Osztalyozasi Rendszere [*Unified Classification System for Occupations*] (HU)
FEOU .... Photoelectrooptic Amplifier (RU)
FeOv .... Fernsprech-Ortsverkehr [*Local Telephone Traffic*] (EG)
FEP .... Federacion de Estudiantes Panamenos [*Federation of Panamanian Students*] (LA)
FEP .... Federacion de Estudiantes del Peru [*Peruvian Students Federation*] (LA)
FEP .... Forward Medical and Evacuation Facility (BU)
FEP .... Front des Etudiants Progressistes [*Progressive Students Front*] [*Moroccan*] (AF)
FEP .... Frontline Evacuation Station (RU)
FEP .... Photoelectric Pyrometer (RU)
FEPA .... Frente Patriotico Antifascista [*Patriotic Antifascist Front*] [*Chilean*] (LA)
FEPAC .... Federation des Patrons Catholiques [*Federation of Catholic Employers*] [*Belgian*] (WER)
FEPACI .... Federation Panafricaine de Cineastes [*Pan-African Motion Picture Federation*] (AF)
FEPAFEM ... Federacion Panamericana de Asociacions de Facultades de Medicina [*Pan American Federation of Associations of Medical Schools - PAFAMS*] (EA)
FEPASA ...... Ferroviaria Paulista Sociedade Anonima [*Sao Paulo Railroad, Incorporated*] [*Brazilian*] (LA)
FEPICOL ..... Federacion de Pequenos Industriales Colombianos [*Medellin*] (COL)
FEPICOL ..... Federacion Propulsora de Industrias Colombianas [*Federation for the Promotion of Colombian Industries*] (LA)
FEPLAS .... Fabrica de Estuches Plasticos [*Bogota*] (COL)
FEPNS .... Fabrika Elektroporcelana Novi Sad [*Insulating Porcelain Factory, Novi Sad*] (YU)
FEPRANAL ... Federacion Nacional del Sector Privado para la Accion Comunal [*Bogota*] (COL)
FEPRO .... Federacion de Asociaciones de Profesionales [*Federation of Associations of Professionals*] [*Salvadoran*]
FEPRODEI ... Foro Permanente para la Promocion y Defensa de las Exportaciones Militares [*Permanent Body for the Defense and Promotion of Military Exports*] [*Argentine*] (LA)
FEPROSICS ... Federacion Provincial de Sindicatos Cristianos de Santiago [*Santiago Provincial Federation of Christian Trade Unions*] [*Dominican Republic*] (LA1)
FEPU .... Frente Eleitoral do Povo Unido [*United People's Electoral Front*] [*Portuguese*] (PPE)
Fer .... Farm [*Topography*] (RU)
FER .... Federacion de Estudiantes Revolucionarios [*Federation of Revolutionary Students*] [*Uruguayan*] (PD)
FER .... Federacion de Estudiantes Revolucionarios [*Federation of Revolutionary Students*] [*Panamanian*] (LA)
FER .... Federation des Etudiants Revolutionaires [*Federation of Revolutionary Students*] [*French*]
FER .... Fondo Educativo Regional [*Cali*] (COL)
FER .... Fonds d'Entretien Routier (MAR)
FER .... Fonds d'Extension et de Renouvellement pour le Developpement de la Culture du Palmier a Huile (MAR)
FER .... Frente Estudiantil Revolucionario [*Revolutionary Student Front*] [*Mexican*] (LA)
FER .... Frente Estudiantil Revolucionario [*Revolutionary Student Front*] [*Nicaraguan*] (LA)
FER .... Frente Estudiantil Revolucionario [*Revolutionary Student Front*] [*Panamanian*] (LA)
FER .... Frente Estudiantil Revolucionario [*Revolutionary Student Front*] [*Peruvian*] (LA)
FER .... Frente Estudiantil Revolucionario [*Revolutionary Student Front*] [*Uruguayan*] (LA)
FER .... Roentgen Equivalent Physical (RU)
FERA .... Federacion Ecuatoriana de Radioaficionados [*Ecuadorean Federation of Radio Hams*] (LA)
FERBUBLANC ... Fernandinos-Bubi-Blancos (MAR)
FERCAMPANA ... Ferreteria la Campana [*Cali*] (COL)
FERDES ...... Fonds d'Equipements Ruraux et de Developpement Economique et Social (MAR)
FERE .... Fondation Egyptologique Reine Elisabeth (MAR)
FEREP .... Federation Executive Recruitment and Education Program (MAR)
FERIAUTO ... Sociedad de Ferias de Automotores [*Bogota*] (COL)
ferj .... Ferjezett [*Married Woman*] (HU)
Ferm .... Farm [*Topography*] (RU)
FERMAC ..... Ferramentas, Maquinas, e Acessorios Lda. (MAR)
ferr .... Ferrovia [*Railroad*] [*Italian*] (GPO)
FERRAL ...... Ferragens e Acessorios Lda. (MAR)
FERRIL .... Compania de Ferrocarriles de Cucuta SA [*Cucuta*] (COL)
FERRIMPORT ... Empresa Cubana Importadora de Articulos de Ferreteria [*Cuban Enterprise for Hardware Import*] (LA)
FERROCOL ... Ferrometalurgica de Colombia Ltda. [*Bogota*] (COL)
FERROMET ... Podnik Zahranicniho Obchodu pro Vyvoz a Dovoz Hutnickych Vyrobku [*Foreign Trade Enterprise for the Export and Import of Metallurgical Products*] (CZ)
FERRONAL ... Ferrocarriles Nacionales [*Santa Marta*] (COL)
FERSICRISPP ... Federacion Regional de Sindicatos Cristianos de Puerto Plata [*Puerto Plata Regional Federation of Christian Trade Unions*] [*Dominican Republic*] (LA1)
fert .... Fertotlenito [*Antiseptic*] (HU)
fert .... Fertozo [*Contagious*] (HU)
FERTICA ..... Fertilizantes de Centro America, SA [*Central American Fertilizers, Inc.*] [*Mexican, Salvadoran*] (LA)
FERTIMA ..... Societe Marocaine des Fertilisants (MAR)
FERTIPERU ... Empresa de Fertilizantes [*State Fertilizer Enterprise*] [*Peruvian*] (LA)
FERTIZA ..... Fertilizantes del Ecuador [*Ecuadorean Fertilizer Enterprise*] (LA)
FERTRIN ..... Fertilizers of Trinidad and Tobago (LA1)
FES .... Encyclopedic Dictionary of Physics (RU)
FES .... Falange Espanola Sindicalista [*Spanish Trade Union Falange*] (WER)
FES .... Federacion de Estudiantes de Secundaria [*Federation of Secondary School Students*] [*Bolivian*] (LA)
FES .... Federacion de Estudiantes de Secundaria [*Federation of Secondary School Students*] [*Honduran*] (LA)
FES .... Frente de Estudiantes Secundarios [*Secondary School Students Front*] [*Peruvian*] (LA)
FES .... Frente de Estudios Sociales [*Social Studies Front*] [*Colombian*] (LA)
FES .... Fundacion para la Educacion Superior. Universidad del Valle [*Cali*] (COL)
FESAC .... Fondation pour l'Enseignement Superieur en Afrique Centrale [*Foundation for Higher Education in Central Africa*] (AF)
FESC .... Frente Estudiantil Social Cristiano [*Social Christian Student Front*] [*Guatemalan*] (LA)
FESCRIDINA ... Federacion de Sindicatos Cristianos del Distrito Nacional [*National District Federation of Christian Trade Unions*] [*Dominican Republic*] (LA1)
FESE .... Federacion de Estudiantes Secundarios del Ecuador [*Ecuadorean Federation of Secondary Students*] (LA)
FESEB .... Federacion Sindical de Empleados Bancarios de Guatemala [*Trade Union Federation of Bank Employees of Guatemala*] (LA)
FESECh ...... Federacion de Estudiantes Secundarios de Chile [*Chilean Federation of Secondary Students*] (LA)
FESES .... Federacion de Estudiantes Secundarios de Santiago [*Santiago Federation of Secondary Students*] [*Chilean*] (LA)
FESGAS ...... Fuerzas Especiales de Guerillas Anticomunistas [*Special Forces of Anticommunist Guerrillas*] [*Nicaraguan*] (LA1)
FESIATHONEMB ... Federation des Syndicats des Industries Alimentaires, Tourisme, Hotellerie, Employees de Maison du Benin [*Federation of Unions of Food Industries, Tourism, Hotel, and Housework Employees of Benin*] (AF)
FESINCONSTRANS ... Federacion de Sindicatos de la Industria de la Construccion, Transporte, y Similares [*Federation of Labor Unions of the Construction, Transportation, and Allied Industries*] [*Salvadoran*] (LA)
FESINOVAL ... Federacion de Sindicatos de Obreros del Valle del Cauca [*Cali*] (COL)
FESINTEXIS ... Federacion de Sindicatos Textiles, Similares, y Conexos [*Federation of Textile, Similar, and Related Unions*] [*Salvadoran*] (LA)
FESINTRABS ... Federacion de Sindicatos de Trabajadores de Alimentos, Bebidas, y Similares [*Federation of Labor Unions of the Food, Beverage, and Allied Industries*] [*Salvadoran*] (LA)
FESINTRANH ... Federacion Sindical de Trabajadores Nortenos de Honduras [*Union Federation of Northern Honduras Workers*] (LA)
FESITRISEVA ... Federacion de Sindicatos de Trabajadores en Industrias y Servicios Varios [*Federation of Workers of Unions in Various Industries and Services*] [*Salvadoran*] (LA)
FESNATEP ... Federacion Sindical Nacional de Telecomunicaciones y Postales [*National Labor Federation of Telecommunication and Postal Workers*] [*Bolivian*] (LA)
FESNESCUB ... Federation des Syndicats Nationaux des Enseignants de la Science et de la Culture du Benin [*Federation of National Unions of Teachers of Science and Culture of Benin*] (AF)
FESOMENIC ... Federacion de Sociedades Medicas de Nicaragua [*Federation of Nicaragua Medical Societies*] (LA1)
FESPACO ... Festival Pan-Africain du Cinema de Ouagadougou [*Ouagadougou Pan-African Cinema Festival*] (AF)
FESS .... Photoelectric Monitoring System [*Chemical engineering*] (RU)
FEST .... Foundation for Education, Science, and Technology (MAR)
FEST .... Funkempfangsstelle [*Radio Receiving Station*] (EG)

FESTAC ...... Festival of Arts and Culture [*Nigerian*] (AF)
FESTBRA.... Federacion Departamental de Trabajadores Bancarios y Ramas Afines de La Paz [*La Paz Departmental Federation of Bank Employees and Related Branches*] [*Bolivian*] (LA1)
FESTIAVTSCES ... Federacion Nacional de Sindicatos de Trabajadores de la Industria del Alimento, Vestido, Textil, Similares y Conexos de El Salvador [*Salvadoran National Trade Union Federation of Workers of the Food, Clothing, Textile, and Related Industries*] (LA1)
FESTRA ...... Federacion de Trabajadores de Santander [*Federation of Workers of Santander*] [*Colombian*] (LA)
FESTRAC.... Federacion Sindical de Cundinamarca [*Trade Union Federation of Cundinamarca*] [*Colombian*] (LA)
FESTRACOL ... Federacion Sindical de Trabajadores Agrarios de Colombia [*Trade Union Federation of Colombian Agricultural Workers*] (LA)
FESTRAL .... Federacion Sindical de Trabajadores del Atlantico [*Trade Union Federation of Atlantico Workers*] [*Colombian*] (LA)
FESTRALVA ... Federacion Sindical de Trabajadores Libres del Valle [*Cali*] (COL)
FESTRAN.... Federacion Sindical de Trabajadores de Antioquia [*Trade Union Federation of Antioquia Workers*] [*Colombian*] (LA)
FESTRAS.... Federacion Sindical de Trabajadores Salvadorenos [*Trade Union Federation of Salvadoran Workers*] (LA1)
FESU .... Farm Economic Survey Unit (MAR)
FESYGA...... Federation Syndicale Gabonaise [*Gabonese Trade Union Federation*] (AF)
FESYSFEB ... Federation des Syndicats des Services Financiers et Economiques du Benin [*Federation of Unions of Financial and Economic Services of Benin*] (AF)
FET.............. Division of Electrical Engineering (RU)
FET.............. Falange Espanola Tradicionalista [*Traditionalist Spanish Falange*] (WER)
FET.............. Fiainana Eokaristian' ny Tanora (MAR)
FETAG .... Federacao dos Trabalhadores na Agricultura [*Farm Workers Federation*] [*Brazilian*] (LA)
FETAL .... Federacion de Trabajadores Agricolas del Litoral [*Federation of Coastal Farm Workers*] [*Ecuadorean*] (LA)
FETAP......... Federacion de Trabajadores de la Administracion Publica [*Federation of Workers of Public Administration of the UGT*] [*Spanish*] (WER)
FETE .... Federacion de Trabajadores de Ensenanza [*Federation of Educational Workers*] [*Spanish*] (WER)
FETICEV ..... Federacion de Trabajadores de la Industria Cervecera [*Brewery Workers Federation*] [*Peruvian*] (LA)
FETIE .... Federacion Ecuatoriana de Trabajadores de la Industria Electrica [*Ecuadorean Federation of Workers of the Electric Power Industry*] (LA)
FETIM .... Societe N. V. Fijnhout en Triplex Import (MAR)
FETIMP .... Federacion de Trabajadores de la Industria Metalurgica [*Metallurgical Industry Workers Federation*] [*Peruvian*] (LA)
FET de las JONS ... Falange Espanola Tradicionalista y de las Juntas de Ofensiva Nacional Sindicalista [*Traditionalist Spanish Falange of the Syndicalist Juntas of the National Offensive*] (PPE)
FETLIG........ Federacion Ecuatoriana de Trabajadores Libres del Guayas [*Ecuadorean Federation of Free Workers of Guayas*] (LA)
FETO........... Federation Togolaise des Orchestres (MAR)
FETPAL....... Federacion de Trabajadores Limonenses [*Federation of Limon Workers*] [*Costa Rican*] (LA1)
FETPQS ...... Federacion Ecuatoriana de Trabajadores del Petroleo, Quimicos, y Similares [*Ecuadorean Federation of Workers of the Petroleum, Chemical, and Allied Industries*] (LA)
FETRABARINAS ... Federacion de Trabajadores del Estado Barinas [*Barinas State Workers Federation*] [*Venezuelan*] (LA)
FETRACID ... Federation des Travailleurs du Commerce et de l'Industrie du Dahomey (MAR)
FETRACUN ... Federacion de Trabajo de Cundinamarca [*Labor Federation of Cundinamarca*] [*Colombian*] (LA)
FETRAELEC ... Federacion de Trabajadores de la Industria Electrica [*Federation of Electrical Industry Workers*] [*Venezuelan*] (LA)
FETRAES.... Federacion de Trabajadores de la Educacion Superior [*Federation of Higher Education Workers*] [*Costa Rican*] (LA1)
Fetrahidrocarburos ... Federacion de Trabajadores de la Industria de Hidrocarburos y Sus Derivados [*Federation of Workers of the Industry of Hydrocarbons and Derivatives*] [*Venezuelan*] (LA)
FETRAMECOL ... Federacion de Trabajadores de las Industrias Metalurgicas [*Bogota*] (COL)
FETRAMETAL ... Federacion de Trabajadores Metalurgicos [*Federation of Metalworkers*] [*Venezuelan*] (LA)
FETRAPEP ... Federacion de Trabajadores Pesqueros del Peru [*Federation of Fishery Workers of Peru*] (LA)
FETRIKAT... Federation Generale des Tribes du Haut Katanga [*General Federation of Tribes of North Katanga*]
FETSALUD ... Federacion de Trabajadores de la Salud [*Federation of Health Workers*] [*Nicaraguan*] (LA1)
FEU .... Amplifier for Photoelectric Cell (RU)
FEU .... Federacion de Estudiantes Universitarios [*Federation of University Students*] [*Costa Rican*] (LA)
FEU .... Federacion de Estudiantes Universitarios [*Federation of University Students*] [*Cuban*] (LA)
FEU .... Federacion Estudiantil Universitario [*University Student Federation*] [*Dominican Republic*] (LA1)
FEU .... Frente Estudiantil Universitario [*University Student Front*] [*Venezuelan*] (LA)
FEU .... Photomultiplier (RU)
FEUB........... Federacao dos Estudantes da Universidade de Brasilia [*Brasilia University Students Federation*] [*Brazilian*] (LA)
FEUC........... Federacion de Estudiantes de la Universidad Catolica [*Catholic University Student Federation*] [*Chilean*] (LA)
FEUC........... Federacion de Estudiantes Universitarios de Cuba [*Federation of University Students of Cuba*] (LA)
FEUCA .... Federacion Estudiantil Universitaria Centroamericana [*Federation of Central American University Students*] (LA)
FEUCE .... Federacion de Estudiantes de Universidades Catolicas del Ecuador [*Federation of Students of Catholic Universities of Ecuador*] (LA)
FEUCP .... Federacion de Estudiantes de la Universidad Catolica del Paraguay [*Federation of Students of the Catholic University of Paraguay*] (LA)
FEUCR .... Federacion de Estudiantes Universitarios de Costa Rica [*Federation of University Students of Costa Rica*] (LA)
FEUE........... Federacion de Estudiantes Universitarios del Ecuador [*Federation of Ecuadorean University Students*] (LA)
FEUH........... Federacion de Estudiantes Universitarios de Honduras [*Honduran University Students Federation*] (LA)
FEUNA .... Federacion de Estudiantes de la Universidad Nacional [*Federation of National University Students*] [*Costa Rican*] (LA1)
FEUTE......... Federacion de Estudiantes de la Universidad Tecnica del Estado [*Student Federation of the State Technical University*] [*Chilean*] (LA)
FEUTH......... Federacion Unitaria de Trabajadores de Honduras [*United Federation of Honduran Workers*] (LA1)
FEUU........... Federacion de Estudiantes Universitarios de Uruguay [*Federation of University Students of Uruguay*] (LA)
FEUV........... Federacion de Estudiantes de la Universidad del Valle [*Cali*] (COL)
FEUV........... Federacion de Estudiantes Universitarios del Valle [*Federation of University Students of Valle*] [*Colombian*] (LA)
FEV .... Federacion de Estudiantes Venezolanos [*Federation of Venezuelan Students*] (LA)
fev .... Fevereiro [*February*] [*Portuguese*] (GPO)
fev .... Fevrier [*February*] [*French*]
FEV .... Forschungs- und Entwicklungswerk des Verkehrswesens [*Research and Development Works for Transportation*] (EG)
FEV .... Fuszer- es Edessegkereskedelmi Vallalat [*Spices and Confectionery Enterprise*] (HU)
FEVBE......... Fovarosi es Videki Belyeggyujtok Egyesulete [*Philatelists' Association*] (HU)
FEVE .... Ferro-Carriles Espanoles de Via Estrecha [*Spanish Narrow-Gauge Railroads*] (WER)
FEVINAL ..... Federacion Avicola Nacional [*Bogota*] (COL)
fevr............. February (BU)
fevr............. February (RU)
FEW........... Forschungs- und Entwicklungswerk [*Research and Development Works*] (EG)
FEWAC .... Far East West African Conference (MAR)
FEWO......... Federatie van Werknemers Organisaties [*Federation of Employee Organizations*] [*Dutch*] (WEN)
FEX............. Ceskoslovensky Filmexport [*Czechoslovak Film Export*] (CZ)
FEZ............. Federation d'Entreprises du Zaire (MAR)
FeZaFA .... Federation Zairoise de Football Association (MAR)
FF .... Department of Philology (BU)
FF .... Department of Philosophy (BU)
FF .... Fehlerfreies Arbeiten [*Error-Free Work*] (EG)
FF .... Fianna Fail [*Warriors of Destiny*] [*Irish political party*]
FF .... Filozofski Fakultet [*Faculty of Philosophy*] (YU)
ff................. Folgende [*The Following*] [*Danish*] (GPO)
ff................. Folgende (Seiten) [*Following (pages)*] [*German*] (GPO)
ff................. Folio [*On the Following Pages*] [*Latin*]
Ff................. Fortsetzung Folgt [*To Be Continued*] [*German*] (GPO)
FF .... Francs Francais [*French Francs*] (CL)
FF .... Fredspolitisk Folkeparti [*People's Peace Policy Party*] [*Danish*] (PPE)
FF .... Freiwillige Feuerwehr [*Volunteer Fire Department*] (EG)
FF .... Frie Folkevalgte [*Freely Elected Representatives*] [*Norwegian*] (PPE)
ff................. Funds (RU)
FF .... Phenolphthalein (RU)
Ff................. Sehr Fein [*Extra Fine*] (EG)
ff................. Und Folgende [*And Following*] [*German*]
FFA............. Forces Francaises en Allemagne [*French Forces in Germany*]
FF AA .... Forze Armate [*Armed Forces*] [*Italian*] (WER)
FFAA........... Fuerzas Armadas [*Bogota*] (COL)
FFAB........... Funk- und Fernmelde-Anlagenbau (VEB) [*Construction of Radio and Telecommunication Installations (VEB)*] (EG)

FIDOM......... Fonds d'Investissements pour les Departements d'Outre-Mer [*Overseas Departments Investment Fund*] [*French*] (AF)
FID/RI.......... Federation Internationale de Documentation/Research on Theoretical Basis of Information
FID/SRC ..... Federation Internationale de Documentation/Subject-Field Reference Code
FID/TM........ Federation Internationale de Documentation/Theory of Machine Techniques and Systems
FIDU............ Federacion Internacional Deportiva Universitaria [*International University Sports Federation*] (LA1)
FIDUCOM.... Fiduciaire Marocaine Comptable et Fiscale (MAR)
FIDUJID....... Fiduciaire Marocaine Juridique et Fiscale (MAR)
FIDUMAC.... Fiduciaire Marocaine de Controle (MAR)
FIDUSEN..... Fiduciaire Senegalaise (MAR)
FIDUTEC..... Fiduciaire Marocaine d'Editions Techniques (MAR)
FIE............... Frente Izquierdista Ecuatoriano [*Ecuadorean Leftist Front*] (LA)
FIEA .... Federation Internationale des Experts en Automobiles (EA)
FIEF............. Federation Internationale pour l'Economie Familiale [*International Federation for Home Economics - IFHE*] (EA)
FIEGA.......... Federacao das Industrias do Estado da Guanabara [*Guanabara State Federation of Industries*] [*Brazilian*] (LA)
FIEJ............. Federation Internationale des Editeurs de Journaux [*International Federation of Newspaper Publishers*] (EA)
FIEL............. Fundacion de Investigaciones Economicas Latinoamericanas [*Latin American Economic Research Foundation*] [*Argentine*] (LA)
FIELTROSA ... Fabrica de Sombreros de Fieltro Ltda. [*Medellin*] (COL)
FIEMC......... Federacion Industrial de la Construccion [*Industrial Construction Federation*] [*Chilean*] (LA)
FIEMG......... Federacao das Industrias do Estado de Minas Gerais [*Minas Gerais Federation of Industries*] [*Brazilian*] (LA)
FIEN .... Forum Italiano dell'Energia Nucleare
FIEP............. Federacao das Industrias de Pernambuco [*Pernambuco Federation of Industries*] [*Brazilian*] (LA1)
FIEP............. Federation Internationale pour l'Education des Parents [*International Federation for Parent Education - IFPE*] (EA)
FIEP............. Federation Internationale d'Education Physique [*International Federation for Physical Education*] (EA)
FIERGS .... Federacao das Industrias do Estado do Rio Grande Do Sul [*Rio Grande Do Sul Federation of Industries*] [*Brazilian*] (LA)
FIESP .... Federacao das Industrias do Estado de Sao Paulo [*Sao Paulo State Federation of Industries*] [*Brazilian*] (LA)
FIET............. Facultad de Ingenieria Electrica y Telecomunicaciones. Universidad del Cauca [*Popayan*] (COL)
FIET............. Federacion Internacional de Empleados y Tecnicos [*International Federation of Employees and Technicians*] (LA)
FIET............. Federation Internationale des Employes, Techniciens, et Cadres [*International Federation of Commercial, Clerical, Professional, and Technical Employees*] (EA)
FIEU .... Fonds International d'Echanges Universitaires (MAR)
FIF .... Department of Philosophy and History (BU)
FIF .... Federation Ivoirienne de Football (MAR)
FIF .... Feria Internacional de la Frontera [*Cucuta*] (COL)
FIF .... Fundacion Institucional Federalista [*Federalist Institutional Center*] [*Argentine*] (LA)
FIFA .... Federacion International del Futbol Aficionado [*Bogota-Filial*] (COL)
FIFARMA .... Federacion Interamericana de la Industria Quimica Farmaceutica [*Bogota*] (COL)
FIFATO........ Fikambanana Fampandrosoana an'i Toliara [*Development Company of Tulear Region*] [*Malagasy*] (AF)
FIFCh .... Federacion Industrial Ferroviaria de Chile [*Chilean Industrial Railways Federation*] (LA)
FIFD .... Federatia Internationala a Femeilor Democratice [*International Federation of Democratic Women*] (RO)
FIFE............. Federation Internationale des Associations de Fabricants de Produits d'Entretien [*International Federation of Associations of Manufacturers of Household Products*] (EA)
FIFSP .... Federation Internationale des Fonctionnaires Superieurs de Police [*International Federation of Senior Police Officers*] (AF)
FIG .... Federation Internationale des Geometres [*International Federation of Surveyors - IFS*] (EA)
FIG .... Federation Internationale de Gymnastique [*International Gymnastic Federation - IGF*] (EA)
fig................ Figur [*Figure*] [*Danish*] (GPO)
Fig............... Figur [*Figure*] [*German*]
fig................ Figure [*Figure*] [*French*]
fig................ Figure, Illustration, Diagram [*Bibliography*] (RU)
fig................ Figures (BU)
FIG .... Forestiere Ivoirienne du GO (MAR)
FIGA............ Iberian Federation of Anarchist Groups [*Spanish*] (PD)
FIGADI .... Financiere Gabonaise de Developpement Immobilier (MAR)
FIGIEFA ...... Federation Internationale des Grossistes, Importateurs, et Exportateurs en Fournitures Automobiles [*International Federation of Wholesalers, Importers, and Exporters in Automobile Fittings*] (EA)
FIGIJ........... Federation Internationale de Gynecologie Infantile et Juvenile [*International Federation of Infantile and Juvenile Gynecology - IFIJG*] (EA)
FIGO........... Federation Internationale de Gynecologie et d'Obstetrique [*International Federation of Gynecology and Obstetrics*] (EA)
FIHC .... Federation Internationale des Hommes Catholiques [*International Council of Catholic Men - ICCM*] (EA)
FIIC .... Federacion Interamericana de la Industria de la Construccion [*Inter-American Federation of the Construction Industry - IAFCI*] (EA)
FIIM .... Federation Internationale de l'Industrie du Medicament [*International Federation of Pharmaceutical Manufacturers Associations - IFPMA*] (EA)
FIIM .... Federation Internationale des Ingenieurs Municipaux [*International Federation of Municipal Engineers - IFME*] (EA)
FIIR............. Federal Institute of Industrial Research (MAR)
FIJ .... Federation Internationale des Journalistes [*International Federation of Journalists - IFJ*] (EA)
FIJ .... Frente Independiente de Juventudes [*Independent Youth Front*] [*Peruvian*] (LA)
FIJDA .... Federation Ivoirienne de Judo et Disciplines Associees (MAR)
FIJL .... Federacion Iberica de Juventudes Libertarias [*Iberian Federation of Anarchist Youth*] [*Spanish*] (WER)
fijor............. Figyelojaror [*Patrol*] (HU)
FIJU............ Federation Internationale des Producteurs de Jus de Fruits [*International Federation of Fruit Juice Producers - IFFJP*] (EA)
FIK.............. Fakultas Ilmu Kedokteran [*School of Medicine*] (IN)
FIK.............. Fovarosi Ingatlanforgalmi Kozpont [*Capital Real Estate Center*] (HU)
FIKI............. Faipari Kutato Intezet [*Lumber Industrial Research Institute*] (HU)
FIKIE .... Fakultas Ilmu Keguruan Ilmu Eksakta [*School of Education and Exact Sciences*] (IN)
FIKIN........... Foire Internationale de Kinshasa [*International Fair in Kinshasa*] [*Zairian*] (AF)
FiKP .... Finn Kommunista Part [*Finnish Communist Party*] (HU)
fikt zagl....... Fictitious Title (BU)
fil .... Branch (RU)
FIL............... Federation Internationale de Laiterie [*International Dairy Federation - IDF*] (EA)
FIL .... Federazione Italiana del Lavoro [*Italian Federation of Labor*]
FIL............... Feira Internacional de Lisboa [*Lisbon International Fair*] [*Portuguese*] (WER)
fil .... Filialka [*Branch*] (CZ)
fil .... Filosofia [*Finnish*]
FIL............... Fish Industries Limited (MAR)
FIL............... Frente de Integracion Liberal [*Liberal Integration Front*] [*Colombian*] (LA)
fil .... Philosophy (BU)
FIL .... Pulse Phototube (RU)
FILA............ Federation Internationale de Lutte Amateur (EA)
FILA............ Federazione Italiana Lavoratori Abbigliamento [*Italian Federation of Garment Workers*]
FILAI .... Federazione Italiana Lavoratori Ausiliari dell'Impiego [*Italian Federation of Auxiliary Services*]
FILAM .... Federazione Italiana Lavoratori Albergo Mensa e Termali [*National Union of Hotel and Restaurant Workers*] [*Italian*]
filat.............. Filatelia [*Philalely*] [*Finnish*]
FIL-BA......... Club Filatelico de Barranquilla (COL)
FILC .... Federazione Italiana Lavoratori Chimici [*Italian Federation of Chemical Workers*]
FILCA.......... Federazione Italiana Lavoratori Costruzioni e Affini [*Italian Federation of Construction and Related Workers*]
FILCAM....... Nylon Fils Cameroun (MAR)
FILCAMS .... Federazione Italiana Lavoratori Commercio Albergo Mensa e Servizi
FILCEA........ Federazione Italiana Lavoratori Commercio e Aggregati [*Italian Federation of Commercial and Associated Workers*]
FILCOTEX... Societe Industrielle de Filature, Confection, et Textiles (MAR)
FILDA.......... Federazione Italiana Lavoratori degli Acquedotti [*Italian Federation of Aqueduct Workers*]
FILEF........... Federazione Italiana Lavoratori Emigrati e Famiglie [*Italian Federation of Italian Emigrants and Their Families*] (WER)
filfak........... Division of Philology (RU)
FILFP........... Forum International de Liaison des Forces de la Paix [*International Liaison Forum of Peace Forces - ILF*] (EA)
FILIA .... Federazione Italiana Lavoratori Industrie Alimentari [*Italian Federation of Food Processing Workers*]
FILIE............ Federazione Italiana Lavoratori Industrie Estrattive [*Italian Federation of Workers in Mining Industries*]
Filintern ...... Philatelic International (RU)
FilK.............. Filosofian Kandidaatti [*Master's Degree in Philosophy*] [*Finnish*]
filkand......... Filosofian Kandidaatti [*Master's Degree in Philosophy*] [*Finnish*]
fill .... Filler [*Filler*] (HU)
FILLBAV...... Federazione Italiana Lavoratori Legno-Boschivi - Artistiche e Varie [*National Federation of Carpenters, Lumbermen, and Cabinetmakers*] [*Italian*]

FILLEA .... Federazione Italiana Lavoratori del Legno, dell'Edilizia e Industrie Affini [*Italian Federation of Workers in Carpentry, Construction, and Related Industries*]

fillis .... Filosofian Lisensiaatti [*Finnish*]

FILLM .... Federation Internationale des Langues et Litteratures Modernes [*International Federation for Modern Languages and Literatures*] (EA)

FILM .... Federazione Italiana Lavoratori del Mare [*Italian Federation of Merchant Seamen*]

FilM .... Filosofian Maisteri [*Finnish*]

filmaist .... Filosofian Maisteri [*Finnish*]

FILM-IS .... Turkiye Film Iscileri Sendikasi [*Turkish Film Workers Union*] [*Istanbul*] (TU)

filol .... Philologic, Philology (RU)

Filol fak .... Department of Philology (BU)

filos .... Filosofia [*Philosophy*] [*Finnish*]

filos .... Philosophical, Philosophy (RU)

Filos-ist fak ... Department of Philosophy and History (BU)

filosof .... Philosophical (RU)

FILP .... Federazione Italiana Lavoratori dei Porti [*Italian Federation of Longshoremen*]

FILPC .... Federazione Italiana Lavoratori Poligrafici e Cartai [*Italian Federation of Printers and Paperworkers*]

FILS .... Federazione Italiana Lavoratori dello Spettacolo [*Italian Federation of Entertainment Workers*]

FILS .... Federazione Italiana Lavoratori Statali [*Italian Federation of Government Employees*]

FILSA .... Federazione Italiana Lavoratori Sanatoriali [*Italian Federation of Public Health Workers - Hospital and Sanatorium Employees*]

FILSTA .... Federazione Italiana Lavoratori Servizi Tributari e Assicuratori [*Italian Federation of Tax Workers*]

FILTA .... Filature et Teinturerie de l'Atlas [*Moroccan*] (MAR)

FILTAT .... Federazione Italiana Transporti ed Ausiliari del Traffico [*Italian Federation of Transportation and Auxiliary Services*]

FILTISAC .... Filature, Tissages, Sacs, Cote-d'Ivoire (MAR)

filtri .... Filosofian Tohtori [*Finnish*]

FIM .... Federation Internationale des Mineurs [*Miners' International Federation - MIF*] (EA)

FIM .... Federation Internationale Motocycliste [*International Motorcycle Federation*] (EA)

FIM .... Federation Internationale des Musiciens [*International Federation of Musicians*] (EA)

FIM .... Federazione Italiana Metal-Meccanici [*Italian Metal Mechanic Workers' Federation*]

FIM .... Pulse-Phase Modulation (RU)

FIMA .... Food Industries of Malaysia (ML)

FIMADOMIA ... Pro-Military Government Peasant's Association [*Malagasy*] (AF)

FIMCAP .... Federation Internationale de Communautes de Jeunesse Catholique Paroissiales [*International Federation of Catholic Parochial Youth Communities*] (EA)

FIME .... Factoria e Industrias Metalicas [*Cali*] (COL)

FIMITIC .... Federation Internationale des Mutiles et Invalides du Travail et des Invalides Civils [*International Federation of Disabled Workmen and Civilian Cripples*] (EA)

FIMM .... Federation Internationale de Medicine Manuelle [*International Federation of Manual Medicine*] (EA)

FIMMEMA ... Fikambanan' Ny Mpanoratra Sy Mpamoron-Kira Ary Editora Malagasy [*Malagasy Republic*]

FIMPAMA .... Fivondronan'ny Mpandraharaha Malagasy [*Association of Malagasy Businessmen*] (AF)

FIMPATEMA ... Association des Enseignants de la Langue Malagasy [*Malagasy Language Teachers Association*] (AF)

FIMTM .... Federation des Industries Mecaniques et Transformatrices des Metaux (MAR)

fin .... Financial (BU)

fin .... Financial (RU)

Fin .... Finanz [*German*]

FIN .... Finland [*Three-letter standard code*] (CNC)

fin .... Finnish (RU)

FIN .... Fraternidad Independiente Nacionalista [*Nationalist Independent Fraternity*] [*Honduran*] (LA1)

FIN .... Physiological Institute (RU)

FINADEICO ... Finanzas Administracion y Contabilidad [*Bogota*] (COL)

FINAME .... Fundo de Financiamento de Maquinas e Equipamentos [*Fund for the Financing of Machinery and Equipment*] [*Brazilian*] (LA)

FINAPRI ...... Financiera de Preinversion [*Preinvestment Financing Enterprise*] [*Nicaraguan*] (LA1)

FINAREP ..... Societe Financiere des Petroles [*Petroleum Finance Company*] [*Algerian*] (AF)

FINARTOIS ... Societe Financiere et Industrielle de l'Artois (MAR)

FINAT .... Federation Internationale des Fabricants et Transformateurs d'Adhesifs et Thermocollants sur Papiers et Autres Supports [*International Federation of Manufacturers and Converters of Pressure-Sensitive and Heatseals on Paper and Other Base Materials*] (EA)

FINAUTOS ... Financiadora de Autos [*Bogota*] (COL)

FINAVI .... Financiera Nacional de Viviendas [*National Housing Finance Company*] [*Honduran*] (LA1)

FINCA .... Fabrica Industrial de Concentrados Alimenticios [*Bogota*] (COL)

FINCh .... Low-Pass Measuring Filter (RU)

FINCOL .... Compania Colombiana de Financiamientos [*Bogota*] (COL)

FINDECO .... Financial Development Corporation [*Zambian*] (AF)

FINDES .... Fedetracao das Industrias do Estado do Espirito Santo

FINEK .... Finansiil dan Ekonomi [*Financial and Economic Affairs*] (IN)

FINEK .... Preduzece za Finansiske i Ekonomske Usluge [*Financial and Economic Services Enterprise*] (YU)

FINEP .... Financiadora de Estudos e Projetos [*Funding Authority for Studies and Projects*] [*Brazilian*] (LA)

FINEX .... Fundo de Financiamento e Exportacao [*Financing and Export Fund*] [*Brazilian*] (LA)

FINGUINEA ... Sociedad Financiera de Guinea (MAR)

FINIWAX ..... Societe de Finition de Tissus Wax (MAR)

finl .... Finnish (RU)

FINOR .... Fundo de Investimentos do Nordeste [*Northeast Investments Fund*] [*Brazilian*] (LA)

finotdel .... Financial Department (BU)

FINSIDER .... Societa Finanziaria Siderurgica (MAR)

FINSZ .... Fakutato Intezetek Nemzetkozi Szovetsege [*International Union of Forestry Research Organizations*] (HU)

FINUL .... Force des Nations Unies au Liban (MAR)

FINUMA ...... Fabrique Ivoirienne de Nuoc-Mam [*Ivorian Nuoc-Mam Plant*] (AF)

Finupr .... Finance Administration (RU)

FIO .... Last Name, First Name, and Patronymic (RU)

FIODS .... Federation Internationale des Organisations de Donneurs de Sang Benevoles [*International Federation of Blood Donor Organizations - IFBDO*] (EA)

FIOM .... Federation Internationale des Organisations de Travailleurs de la Metallurgie [*International Metalworkers Federation - IMF*] (EA)

FIOM .... Federazione Impiegati e Operai Metallurgici [*Federation of Those Employed in Metallurgical Industries*] [*Italian*] (WER)

FIOPM .... Federation Internationale des Organismes de Psychologie Medicale [*International Federation of Psychological-Medical Organizations - IFPMO*] (EA)

FIOPP .... Federacion Interamericana de Organizaciones de Periodistas Profesionales [*Inter-American Federation of Working Newspapermen's Organizations*] [*Use IAFWNO*] (LA)

FIOSS .... Federation Internationale des Organisations de Sciences Sociales [*International Federation of Social Science Organizations - IFSSO*] (EA)

FIOST .... Federation Internationale des Organisations Syndicales du Personnel des Transporte [*International Federation of Trade Unions of Transport Workers - IFTUTW*] (EA)

FIOT .... Federazione Impiegati Operai Tessili [*Federation of Textile Workers*] [*Italian*]

FIP .... Fabrica de Implementos, SA [*Mexican*]

FIP .... Federacion Internacional de Periodistas [*International Federation of Journalists*] [*Use IFJ*] (LA)

FIP .... Federation Internationale Pharmaceutique [*International Pharmaceutical Federation*] (EA)

FIP .... Federation Internationale de la Precontrainte [*International Federation of Prestressed Concrete*] (EA)

FIP .... Federazione Italiana Pensionati [*Italian Federation of Pensioners*]

FIP .... Federazione Italiana Postelegrafonici [*Italian Federation of Postal, Telegraph, and Telephone Workers*]

FIP .... Fondo de Inversiones Privadas (COL)

FIP .... Frente Independiente Parlamentario [*Independent Parliamentary Front*] [*Venezuelan*] (LA)

FIP .... Fuerzas Interamericanas de la Paz [*Inter-American Peace Force*] [*Use IAPF*] (LA)

FIPA .... Federation Internationale des Producteurs d'Agrumes [*North African*] (MAR)

FIPAD .... Fondation Internationale pour un Autre Developpement [*International Foundation for Development Alternatives - IFDA*] (EA)

FIPAGO .... Federation Internationale des Fabricants de Papiers Gommes [*International Federation of Manufacturers of Gummed Paper*] (EA)

FIPC .... Federation Internationale des Pharmaciens Catholiques [*International Federation of Catholic Pharmacists*] (EA)

FIPEME .... Fundo de Financiamento as Pequenas e Medias Empresas [*Fund for Financing Small and Medium-Size Businesses*] [*Brazilian*] (LA)

FIPESO .... Federation Internationale des Professeurs de l'Enseignement Secondaire Officiel [*International Federation of Secondary Teachers*] (EA)

FIPF .... Federation Internationale pour la Planification Familiale (MAR)

FIPF .... Federation Internationale des Professeurs de Francais [*International Federation of Teachers of French - IFTF*] (EA)

FIPIA .... Fakultas Ilmu Pasti dan Ilmu Alam [*Department of Mathematics and Physics*] (IN)

FIPIMA .... Fivondronam-Pirenena Malagasy [*Malagasy National Union*] (AF)

FIPJP .... Federation Internationale de Petanque et Jeu Provencal (EA)

FLAMA........ Frente de Libertacao do Arquipelago da Madeira [*Front for Liberation of the Madeira Islands*] [*Portuguese*] (WER)
FLAMK........ Flugzeugabwehrmaschinenkanone [*Antiaircraft Machine Gun*] (EG)
FLAP........... Federacion Latinoamericana de Periodistas [*Latin American Federation of Journalists*] (LA)
FLASCO...... Facultad Latinoamericana de Ciencias Sociales [*Latin American School of Social Sciences*] (LA)
FLASOG...... Federacion Latinoamericana de Sociedades de Obstetricia y Ginecologia [*Latin American Federation of Obstetrics and Gynecology Societies*] (LA)
FLAWP........ French-Language Association of Work Psychology (EA)
FLB.............. Front de Liberation de la Bretagne [*Brittany Liberation Front*] [*French*] (WER)
FLB-ARB..... Front de Liberation de la Bretagne - Armee Republicaine Bretonne [*Liberation Front of Brittany - Breton Republican Army*] [*French*] (PD)
FLB-LNS..... Front de Liberation de la Bretagne pour la Liberation Nationale et le Socialisme [*Liberation Front of Brittany for National Liberation and Socialism*] [*French*] (PD)
FLC.............. Fives Lille Cail [*North African*] (MAR)
FLC.............. Front de Liberation Centrafrique (MAR)
FLCB............ Front de Liberation du Congo-Brazzaville (MAR)
FLCS............ Front de Liberation de la Cote des Somalis [*Somali Coast Liberation Front*] [*Djibouti*] (AF)
FLDA............ Federal Land Development Agency (ML)
FLDP............ Federation of Liberal and Democratic Parties (PPE)
FLE.............. Front de Liberation Erythreenne [*Eritrean Liberation Front*] [*Use ELF*] [*Ethiopian*] (AF)
FLE.............. Fronte di Liberazione Eritreo (MAR)
FLEC............ Frente de Libertacao do Enclave de Cabinda [*Front for the Liberation of the Cabinda Enclave*] [*Angolan*] (PD)
FLEC............ Front de Liberation de l'Enclave de Cabinda [*Front for the Liberation of the Cabinda Enclave*] [*Angolan*] (AF)
flek.............. Fleet Crew (RU)
FLEPSA....... Fabrica de Ladrillos el Progreso SA [*Bogota*] (COL)
FLERD......... Front de Liberation et de Rehabilitation de Dahomey (MAR)
FLG.............. Federal Libyan Government (MAR)
Fl G.............. Flanc Garde [*Flank Guard*] [*French*] (MTD)
FLG.............. Frente de Libertacao da Guine (MAR)
FLGC............ Frente de Libertacao da Guine Portuguesa e Cabo Verde (MAR)
Fl h.............. Dutch Florin, Guilder [*Business and trade*] [*German*]
FLI................ Federation Lainiere Internationale [*International Wool Textile Organization - IWTO*] (EA)
FLID............. Front de la Lutte pour l'Independence du Dahomey (MAR)
FLIN............. Frente de Liberacion Nacional [*National Liberation Front*] [*Bolivian*] (LA)
FLING.......... Frente para a Libertacao e Independencia da Guine Portuguesa [*Front for the Liberation and Independence of Portuguese Guinea*] (MAR)
FLING.......... Frente da Luta pela Independencia Nacional da Guine "Portuguesa" [*Front for the Fight for Guinea-Bissau's National Independence*] (PD)
FLIPG.......... Front for the Liberation and Independence of Portuguese Guinea (MAR)
FLIPPG........ French-Language Infant Pneumology and Phthisiology Group (EA)
FLIRT.......... Free Language Information Retrieval Tool [*IWIS/TNO*] [*'s-Gravenhage*]
FLK.............. Falkland Islands [*Three-letter standard code*] (CNC)
FLKK........... Front du Lutte des Khmers du Kampuchea Krom [*Front for the Struggle of the Khmer Krom*] [*Cambodian*] (CL)
Fll................ Fluessigkeiten [*Liquids, Fluids*] [*German*]
FLLA............ Front for the Liberation of Lebanon from Aliens (MAR)
Flli............... Fratelli [*Brothers*] [*Italian*] (GPO)
FLM.............. Federation Lutherienne Mondiale [*Lutheran World Foundation - LWF*] (EA)
FLM.............. Federazione dei Lavoratori Metalmeccanici [*Federation of Metalworkers*] [*Italian*] (WER)
FLM.............. Fiangonana Loterana Malagasy (MAR)
FLM.............. Fotometrischer Leistungsmesser [*Photometric Capacity Meter*] (EG)
FLN.............. Frente de Liberacion Nacional [*National Liberation Front*] [*Venezuelan*] (PD)
FLN.............. Frente de Liberacion Nacional [*National Liberation Front*] [*Chilean*] (LA)
FLN.............. Frente de Liberacion Nacional [*National Liberation Front*] [*Peruvian*] (LA)
FLN.............. Frente de Liberacion Nacional [*National Liberation Front*] [*Salvadoran*] (LA1)
FLN.............. Frente de Libertacao Nacional [*National Liberation Front*] [*Portuguese*] (WER)
FLN.............. Frente de Libertacao Nacional [*National Liberation Front*] [*Brazilian*] (LA)
FLN.............. Front de Liberation Nationale [*National Liberation Front*] [*French*]
FLN.............. Front de Liberation Nationale [*National Liberation Front*] [*Algerian*] (PPW)
FLN.............. Front de Liberation Nationale [*National Liberation Front*] [*South Vietnamese*] [*Use NFLSV*] (CL)
FLNA............ Front de Liberation Nationale de l'Angola (MAR)
FLNC............ Front de Liberation Nationale Congolais [*Congolese National Liberation Front*] [*Zairian*] (PD)
FLNC............ Front de Liberation Nationale de la Corse [*Corsican National Liberation Front*] (PD)
Flne............. Fluane [*or Fluene*] [*Sunken Rocks*] [*Norwegian*] (NAU)
FLNF............ Front de Liberation Nationale Francaise [*French National Liberation Front*] (PD)
FLNG............ Front de Liberation Nationale de Guinee [*Guinean National Liberation Front*] (AF)
FLNK............ Force de Liberation Nationale Kamerunaise [*National Cameroonian Liberation Force*]
FLNR............ Front de Liberation Nationale de la Reunion [*National Liberation Front of Reunion*] (AF)
flo................ Felugyelo [*Inspector, Supervisor*] (HU)
FLO.............. Front de Liberation des Oubanguiens [*Ubangi People's Liberation Front*] [*Central African*] (AF)
FLOARCA... Flotilla y Arrendamientos Compania Anonima [*Venezuelan*]
FLOMERCA... Flota Mercante Gran Centroamericana [*Greater Central American Merchant Fleet*] [*Guatemalan*] (LA)
FLOPEC...... Flota Petrolera Ecuatoriana [*Ecuadorean Oil Tanker Fleet*] (LA)
FLOPETROL... Societe Auxiliaire des Producteurs de Petrole (MAR)
flor.............. Floren [*or Floreny*] [*Florin or Florins*] [*Polish*]
FLOSY......... Front for the Liberation of Occupied South Yemen (PD)
FLP.............. Federacion Latinoamericana de Periodistas [*Latin American Federation of Journalists*] (LA)
FLP.............. Finlands Landsbygdsparti [*Finnish Rural Party*] (PPE)
FLP.............. Frente de Liberacion de los Pobres [*Liberation Front of the Poor*] [*Ecuadorean*] (PD)
FLP.............. Frente de Liberacion Popular [*Peoples' Liberation Front*] [*Spanish*] (WER)
FLP.............. Phytolipopolysaccharide (RU)
FLPC............ Front de Liberation du Peuple Centrafricain [*Central African People's Liberation Front*] (AF)
Flpkt............ Flammpunkt [*Flash Point*] (EG)
FLPP............ Front de Lutte Populaire Palestinien (MAR)
FLRD............ Front de Liberation et de Rehabilitation du Dahomey [*Dahomey Liberation and Rehabilitation Front*] [*Beninese*] (PD)
FLRJ............ Federacyjna Ludowa Republika Jugoslowianska [*Federated People's Republic of Yugoslavia*] (POL)
FLRJ............ Federativna Ljudska Republika Jugoslavija [*Federated People's Republic of Yugoslavia*] (YU)
FLRJ............ Federativni Lidova Republika Jihoslovenska [*Federated People's Republic of Yugoslavia*] (CZ)
FLRS............ Federativna Ljudska Republika Slovenija [*Federated People's Republic of Slovenia*] (YU)
FLRS............ Federativna Ljudska Republika Srbija [*Federated People's Republic of Serbia*] (YU)
FLS.............. Federazione Lavoratori Somali [*Somali Labor Federation*]
FLS.............. Fremde Legion Suedtirol [*South Tyrolean Foreign Legion*] [*Austrian*] (WEN)
FLS.............. Frente de Liberacion Social [*Social Liberation Front*] [*Panamanian*] (LA)
FLS.............. Front de Liberation de Seguia [*Seguia Liberation Front*] [*Saharan*] (AF)
FLSC............ Front for the Liberation of the Somali Coast [*Djibouti*] (AF)
FLSO............ Front de Liberation de Somalie Occidentale [*Western Somalia Liberation Front*] [*Use WSLF*] (AF)
FLT.............. Front de Liberation Tchadien [*Chadian Liberation Front*] (AF)
FLTP............ Federacion Latinoamericana de Trabajadores de Plantaciones [*Latin American Federation of Plantation Workers*] (LA)
FLU.............. Federation of Labor Unions [*Lebanon*] (MAR)
FLU.............. Field Laborers Union [*Mauritian*] (AF)
FLU.............. Frente de Libertacao e da Unidade [*Front for Liberation and Unity*] [*Portuguese*] (WER)
FLU.............. Front de Liberation et d'Union [*Front for Liberation and Unity*] [*Saharan*] (AF)
FLU.............. Front pour la Liberation et l'Unite [*Front for Liberation and Unity*] [*Moroccan*] (AF)
FLUNA......... Front de Liberation Unifie de la Nouvelle Algerie [*United Liberation Front for a New Algeria*] (AF)
FLUT............ Festival Lidove Umelecke Tvorivosti [*Folk Arts Festival*] (CZ)
FM................ Federation of Malaya (ML)
FM................ Feld Marechal [*Field Marshal*] [*French*] (MTD)
FM................ Feldmarschall [*German*]
Fm................ Fernmelde [*German*]
FM................ Ferromanganese (RU)
Fm................ Festmeter [*Cubic Meter*] (EG)
fm................ Field Marshal (BU)
FM................ Filosofian Maisteri [*Finnish*]
fm................ Finn Marka [*Finnish Mark*] (HU)
FM................ Fluorometer (RU)
fm................ Foldmuveles [*Agriculture*] (HU)
FM................ Foldmuvelesugyi Miniszterium/Miniszter [*Ministry/Minister of Agriculture*] (HU)
fm................ Foldmuves [*Farmer*] (HU)
Fm................ Forstmeister [*German*]
FM................ Franc Malien (MAR)
FM................ Franchise Militaire [*French*]
FM................ Free Morocco (MAR)
FM................ Fusil Mitrailleur [*Military*] [*French*] (MTD)

FM .... Invoice Machine (RU)
FM .... Phase Modulation (RU)
FM- .... Photomagnetic Amplifier (RU)
FM .... Photometer (RU)
FM .... Physics and Mathematics (BU)
FM .... Physics and Mathematics (Division) (RU)
FMA .... Ammonium Phosphomolybdate (RU)
FMA .... Fernmeldeamt [*Telephone and Telegraph Office*] (EG)
FMA .... Fonds Monetaire Arabe (MAR)
FMA .... Frederik Muller Akademie [*Amsterdam*]
FMA .... French Military Administration (MAR)
FMA .... Phenylmercuric Acetate (RU)
FMAC .... Federation Mondiale des Anciens Combattants [*World Veterans Federation - WVF*] (EA)
FMAM .... Federation Mondiale des Amis de Musees [*World Federation of Friends of Museums - WFFM*] (EA)
FMANU .... Federatia Mondiala a Asociatiilor pentru Natiunile Unite [*World Federation of United Nations Associations*] (RO)
FMATH .... Federation Mondiale de Travailleurs des Industries Alimentaires, du Tabac, et de l'Hotellerie [*World Federation of Workers in Food, Tobacco, and Hotel Industries - WFFTH*] (EA)
FMB .... Fast Missile Boat (MAR)
FMBI .... Engineer's Library of Physics and Mathematics (RU)
FMBN .... Federal Mortgage Bank of Nigeria (MAR)
FMC .... Federacion de Mujeres Cubanas [*Federation of Cuban Women*] (LA)
FMC .... Fire Mark Circle (EA)
FMC .... Flotte Marchande Centrafricaine (MAR)
FMC .... Fondo Monetario Centroamericano [*Central American Monetary Fund*] (LA)
FMCA .... Fermetures Mischler du Cameroun (MAR)
FMCA .... Flotte Marchande Centrafricaine (MAR)
FMCE .... Federation of Malaya Certificate of Education (ML)
FMCI .... Fermetures Mischler de la Cote-d'Ivoire (MAR)
FMCVC .... Federation Mondiale des Communautes de Vie Chretienne [*World Federation of Christian Life Communities - WFCLC*] (EA)
FMD .... Feinmess, Dresden [*Dresden Precision Measuring Equipment Plant*] (EG)
FMD .... Fermetures Mischler Dakar (MAR)
FMD .... Front Militant Departmentaliste [*Militant Departmentalist Front*] [*Reunionese*] (PD)
FMDP .... Fuggetlen Magyar Demokrata Part [*Independent Hungarian Democratic Party*] (HU)
FMDR .... Federacion de Mujeres Dominicanas Revolucionarias [*Federation of Revolutionary Dominican Women*] [*Dominican Republic*] (LA)
FMDR .... Fonds Mutualiste de Developpement Rural (MAR)
Fme .... Ferme [*Farm*] [*Military map abbreviation*] [*World War I*] [*French*] (MTD)
FME .... Photoelectromagnetic Effect (RU)
FMF .... Federalni Ministerstvo Financi [*Federal Finance Ministry*] (CZ)
FM fakultet ... Department of Physics and Mathematics (BU)
FMG .... Federacion Magisterial Guatemalteca [*Federation of Guatemalan Teachers*] (LA)
FMG .... Federal Military Government (MAR)
FMG .... Fermetures Mischler du Golfe de Guinee (MAR)
FMG .... Franc Malgache [*Malagasy Franc*] (AF)
FMGD .... Federazione Mondiale della Gioventu Democratica [*World Federation of Democratic Youth - WFDY*] [*Italian*] (WER)
FMGM .... Free Methodist Church General Missionary Board (MAR)
fmh .... Felteteles Megallohely [*Stops on Signal*] (HU)
FMI .... Family Misery Index (MAR)
FMI .... Fondo Monetario Internacional [*International Monetary Fund - IMF*] (LA)
FMI .... Fondo Monetario Internazionale [*International Monetary Fund - IMF*] [*Italian*] (WER)
FMI .... Fonds Monetaire International [*International Monetary Fund - IMF*] [*French*] (WER)
FMI .... Fondul Monetar International [*International Monetary Fund - IMF*] (RO)
FMI .... Institute of Physics and Mathematics (of the Academy of Sciences, USSR) (RU)
FMJ .... Financial Mail, Johannesburg [*A publication*] (MAR)
FMJC .... Federation Mondiale de Jeunesse Catholique [*World Federation of Catholic Youth*] [*Use WFCY*] (AF)
FMJC .... Front de Mouvements des Jeunesse du Congo (MAR)
FMJD .... Federacion Mundial de la Juventud Democratica [*World Federation of Democratic Youth - WFDY*] (LA)
FMJD .... Federation Mondiale du Jeu de Dames [*World Draughts (Checkers) Federation - WDF*] (EA)
FMJD .... Federation Mondiale de la Jeunesse Democratique [*World Federation of Democratic Youth - WFDY*] (EA)
FMK .... Ferromagnetic Compensator (RU)
FMK .... Flugmedizinische Kommission [*Commission for Flight Medicine (A GST pilot training unit)*] (EG)
FMKT .... Fiatal Muszakiak es Kozgazdaszok Tanacsa [*Council of Young Technologists and Economists*] (HU)
FML .... Feldmarschalleutnant [*German*]
FMLN .... Frente Farabundo Marti de Liberacion Nacional [*Farabundo Marti National Liberation Front*] [*Salvadoran*] (LA1)
FMLN .... Frente Morazanista de Liberacion Nacional [*Morazanista National Liberation Front*] [*Honduran*] (PD)
FMLS .... Federazione Mondiale dei Lavoratori Scientifici [*World Federation of Scientific Workers - WFSW*] [*Italian*] (WER)
FMM .... Fivondronam Ben'ny Mpiasa Malagasy [*Malagasy Workers Federation*] (AF)
FMM .... French Military Mission (CL)
FMM .... Physics of Metals and Metal Science (RU)
FMME .... Fund for Multinational Management Education (AF)
FMMTP .... Federacion de Mineros y Trabajadores Metalurgicos del Peru [*Federation of Miners and Metalworkers of Peru*] (LA)
FMN .... Flavine Mononucleotide (RU)
FMN .... Frente Nacional Magisterial [*National Teachers Front*] [*Guatemalan*] (LA1)
FMO .... Department of Physics and Mathematics (RU)
FMO .... Fabryka Maszyn Odlewniczych [*Foundry Machinery Factory*] (POL)
FMO .... Nederlandse Financiering Maatschappij voor Ontwikkelingslanden (MAR)
FMP .... Fabryka Maszyn Papierniczych [*Paper Machinery Factory*] (POL)
FMP .... Federalni Ministerstvo Planovani [*Federal Ministry of Planning*] (CZ)
FMPA .... Federation Mondiale pour la Protection des Animaux [*World Federation for the Protection of Animals*] [*Use WFPA*] (AF)
FMPO- .... Photometer for Measuring Underwater Light Intensity (RU)
FMPSV .... Federalni Ministerstvo Prace a Socialnich Veci [*Federal Ministry of Labor and Social Affairs*] (CZ)
FMPU .... Actual Magnetic Track Angle (RU)
FMRI .... Fondo de Modernizacao e Reorganizacao Industrial [*Industrial Modernization and Reorganization Fund*] [*Brazilian*] (LA)
FMS .... Federacion Magisterial Salvadorena [*Salvadoran Teachers Federation*] (LA)
FMS .... Federated Malay States (ML)
FMS .... Federatia Mondiala a Sindicatelor [*World Federation of Trade Unions*] (RO)
FMS .... Foreign Military Sales (MAR)
FMS .... Franko-Malagasiiskii Soiuz (MAR)
FMS .... Frontline Medical Depot (RU)
FMS .... Funkmessstation [*RADAR Station*] (EG)
FMS .... Machine-Calculating Center (RU)
FMS .... Phenazine Methyl Sulfate (RU)
FMSM .... Federation Mondiale pour la Sante Mentale [*World Federation for Mental Health*] [*Use WFMH*] (AF)
FMSNP .... Fysiolatrikos Morfotikos Syllogos Neon Peramatos Peiraios [*The Perama, Piraeus Nature Lovers and Cultural Youth Club*] (GC)
FMSp .... Fiziko-Matematichesko Spisanie [*Journal of Physics and Mathematics*] [*A publication*] (BU)
FMSR .... Federation des Mouvements Socialistes Regionalistes de la Reunion [*Federation of Socialist Regionalist Movements of Reunion*] (PPW)
FMSVR .... Federated Malay States Volunteer Reserve (ML)
fmsz .... Foldmuves Szovetkezet [*Farmers' Cooperative*] (HU)
FMT .... Fabryka Maszyn Tytoniowych [*Tobacco Processing Machine Factory*] (POL)
FMTA .... Federation Mondiale de Travailleurs Agricoles [*World Federation of Agricultural Workers - WFAW*] (EA)
FMTC .... Federacion Mundial de Trabajadores Cientificos [*World Federation of Scientific Workers*] [*Use WFSW*] (LA1)
FMTD .... Federatia Mondiala a Tineretului Democrat [*World Federation of Democratic Youth*] (RO)
FMTNM .... Federation Mondiale des Travailleurs Non-Manuels [*World Federation of Trade Unions of Non-Manual Workers - WFNMW*] (EA)
FMTS .... Federation Mondiale des Travailleurs Scientifiques [*World Federation of Scientific Workers - WFSW*] (EA)
FMTZ .... Association for the Youth Liberation Struggle [*Malagasy*] (AF)
FMU .... Federation of Mining Unions [*South African*] (AF)
FMU .... Frente Militar Unica [*Single Military Front*] [*Portuguese*] (WER)
FMU .... Machine Accounting and Computing Office (RU)
FMUA .... Fabrica de Masini Unelte si Agregate [*Factory for Machine Tools and Aggregates*] (RO)
FMV .... Fakulta Mezinarodnich Vztahu [*Department of International Relations*] [*Charles University*] (CZ)
FMV .... Federacion Medica de Venezuela [*Medical Federation of Venezuela*] (LA)
FMV .... Federalni Ministerstvo Vnitra [*Federal Ministry of the Interior*] (CZ)
FMV .... Finommechanikai Vallalat [*Precision Mechanics Enterprise*] (HU)
FMV .... Fredrikstad Mekaniske Verksted [*Norwegian*]
FMV .... Szekesfehervari Finommechanikai Vallalat [*Precision Mechanics Enterprise of Szekesfehervar*] (HU)
FMVJ .... Federation Mondiale des Villes Jumelees [*World Federation of Sister Cities*] (LA1)
FMVJ .... Federation Mondiale des Villes Jumelees - Cities Unies [*United Towns Organisation - UTO*] (EA)
FMW .... Fernmeldewerk [*Telecommunications Equipment Plant*] (EG)

FMWA .... Farm Machineries West Africa, Ltd. (MAR)
FMZ .... Fabryka Maszyn Zniwnych [*Harvesting Machine Factory*] (POL)
FMZE .... Fondo Monetario de Zona do Escudo (MAR)
FN .... Fabrique Nationale (d'Armes de Guerre, Societe Anonyme)
FN .... Filharmonia Narodowa [*National Philharmonic Society*] [*Polish*]
FN .... Filmske Novosti [*Newsreel*] (YU)
FN .... Forenta Nationerna [*United Nations - UN*] [*Swedish*] (WEN)
FN .... Frente Nacional [*Bogota*] (COL)
FN .... Front Narodowy [*People's Front*] (POL)
FN .... Front Nasional [*National Front*] (IN)
FN .... Front National [*National Front*] [*French*] (PPW)
FN .... Fuerza Nueva [*New Force*] [*Spanish*] (WER)
Fn .... Fusant [*Military*] [*French*] (MTD)
Fn .... Smokeless Powder [*Symbol*] [*French*] (MTD)
FNA .... Fachnormenausschuss [*Committee on Technical Standards and Specifications*] (EG)
FNA .... Federacion Nacional Agraria [*National Agrarian Federation*] [*Peruvian*] (LA)
FNA .... Filature Nord Africaine [*North African*] (MAR)
FNA .... Fondo Nacional de Ahorro [*National Savings Fund*] [*Colombian*] (LA)
FNA .... Fonds National de l'Assainissement (MAR)
FNA .... Frente Nacional Angolana (MAR)
FNA .... Front National Angolais (MAR)
FNACE .... Federation Nationale des Agents sous Contract de l'Etat (MAR)
FNACEM ..... Federation Nationale des Associations de Culture et de Musique [*National Federation of Cultural and Musical Associations*] [*French Guiana*] (LA1)
FNAET .... Fonds National d'Achat et d'Equipement de Terrain [*Moroccan*] (MAR)
FNAGE .... Federation Nationale d'Association des Eleves des Grandes Ecoles [*National Federation of the "Grandes Ecoles" Student Association*] [*French*] (WER)
FNAL .... Frente Nacional de Alianza Libre [*National Front of Free Alliance*] [*Spanish*] (WER)
FNAMCI ...... Federation Nationale des Associations des Movements des Jeunes de Cote-d'Ivoire [*National Federation of Ivorian Youth Movement Associations*] (AF)
FNAT .... Fundacao Nacional para Alegria no Trabalho [*National Foundation of Joy through Work*] [*Portuguese*] (WER)
FNB .... Federacion Nacional de Bananeros [*National Federation of Banana Growers*] [*Ecuadorean*] (LA)
FNBIV .... Poor Harvest, Natural Calamities, and Economic Assistance Fund (BU)
FNC .... Frente Nacional Constitucionalista [*National Constitutionalist Front*] [*Ecuadorean*] (PPW)
FNC .... Frente Nacional Constitucionalista [*National Constitutionalist Front*] [*Dominican Republic*] (LA1)
FNC .... Frente Nacional Opositora [*National Opposition Front*] [*Panamanian*] (PPW)
FNC .... Front Nacional Catala [*Catalan National Front*] [*Spanish*] (WER)
FNC .... Front National des Combattants [*Algerian*] (MAR)
FNCA .... Fonds National de Credit Agricole et Artisanal [*National Farming and Crafts Credit Fund*] [*Zairian*] (AF)
FNCAO .... Federation Nationale des Comites d'Alliance Ouvriere [*National Federation of the Committees of Workers' Alliance*] [*French*] (WER)
FNCC .... Federation Nationale des Cheminots du Cameroun [*National Federation of Railroad Employees of Cameroon*] (AF)
FNCE .... Fabricacion Nacional de Colorantes, SA
FNCh .... Low-Pass Filter (RU)
FNCI .... Fondo Nacional de Credito Industrial [*National Industrial Credit Fund*] [*Venezuelan*] (LA)
FNCPME ..... Federation Nationale des Chefs des Petites et Moyennes Entreprises [*National Federation of Heads of Small and Medium Sized Enterprises*] [*Ivorian*] (AF)
FNCR .... Frente Nacional Contra la Represion [*National Front Against Repression*] [*Mexican*] (LA1)
FNCS .... Federation Nationale des Cheminots du Senegal [*National Federation of Railroad Workers of Senegal*] (AF)
FND .... Frente Nacional Democratico [*Democratic National Front*] [*Guatemalan*] (LA)
FND .... Frente Nacional Democratico [*Democratic National Front*] [*Venezuelan*] (LA)
FND .... Front National Democratique [*Democratic National Front*] [*Central African*] (AF)
FND .... Frontul National Democratic [*National Democratic Front*] [*Romanian*] (PPE)
FND .... Fundo Nacional de Desenvolvimento [*National Development Fund*] [*Brazilian*] (LA)
FNDCT .... Fundo Nacional de Desenvolvimento Cientifico e Tecnologico [*National Scientific and Technological Development Fund*] [*Brazilian*] (LA)
FNDE .... Fondo Nacional de Desarrollo Economico [*National Fund for Economic Development*] [*Peruvian*] (LA)
FNDE .... Fonds National de Developpement et d'Equipement [*National Development and Equipment Fund*] [*Malagasy*] (AF)
FNDE .... Fundo Nacional de Desenvolvimento da Educacao [*National Educational Development Fund*] [*Brazilian*] (LA1)
FNDEL .... Federazione Nazionale Dipendenti Enti Locali [*National Federation of Local Government*] [*Italian*]
FNDF .... Federal National Democratic Front [*Burmese*] (PD)
FNDIRP .... Federation Nationale des Deportes, Internes, Resistants, et Patriotes (MAR)
FNDP .... First National Development Plan (MAR)
FNDP .... Frente Nacional Democratico Popular [*Popular National Democratic Front*] [*Mexican*] (PD)
FNDR .... Front National pour la Defense de la Revolution [*National Front for the Defense of the Revolution*] [*Malagasy*] (AF)
FNDRESS ... Federation Nationale des Deportes, Refugies, Expulses, Sinistres, et Spolies (MAR)
FNDS .... Federazione Nazionale degli Statali [*Italian Federation of Government Employees*]
FNDSCAC ... Frente Nacional de Defensa del Salario y Contra la Austeridad y la Carestia [*National Front for Defense of Salaries and Against Austerity and the High Cost of Living*] [*Mexican*] (LA1)
FNE .... Faisceaux Nationalistes Europeens [*European Nationalist Alliances*] [*French*] (PD)
FNE .... Federation National de l'Enseignement [*National Front for the Defense of the Revolution*] [*Moroccan*] (AF)
Fne .... Fontaine [*Fountain, Spring*] [*Military map abbreviation*] [*World War I*] [*French*] (MTD)
FNE .... Frente Nacional Espanol [*Spanish National Front*] (WER)
FNEB .... Fovarosi Nepi Ellenorzo Bizottsag [*Capital City People's Control Committee*] (HU)
FNEC .... Federacion Nacional de Estudiantes Catalanes [*National Federation of Catalan Students*] [*Spanish*] (WER)
FNECC .... Federation Nationale des Employes Commerciaux et Cadres (MAR)
FNED .... Federation Nationale des Etudiants Destouriens [*National Federation of Destourian Students*] [*Tunisian*] (AF)
FNEEGA ...... Federation Nationale de l'Energie Electrique et du Gaz d'Algerie [*Algerian National Electric Power and Gas Federation*] (AF)
FNEF .... Federation Nationale des Etudiants de France [*National Federation of Students of France*] (WER)
FNEL .... Federation Nationale des Etudiants au Laos [*National Federation of Students in Laos*] (CL)
FNEN .... Federacion Nacional de Empresarios Nacionalistas [*National Federation of Nationalist Entrepreneurs*] [*Mexican*] (LA)
FNES .... Federation Nationale des Enseignants du Senegal [*National Federation of Teachers of Senegal*] (AF)
FNET .... Federacion Nacional de Empleados y Tecnicos [*National Federation of Office Workers and Technicians*] [*Uruguayan*] (LA)
FNF .... Federacao Nacional dos Ferroviarios [*National Federation of Railway Workers*] [*Brazilian*] (LA)
FNFA .... Fundo Nacional de Financiamento para Abastecimento de Agua [*National Fund for the Financing of Water Supply*] [*Brazilian*] (LA)
FNFL .... Forces Navales Francaises Libres [*Free French Naval Forces*] [*World War II*]
FNFPM .... Federation National de la Fonction Publique de Madagascar [*National Civil Service Federation of Madagascar*] (AF)
FNFPZ .... Federation Nationale des Femmes Protestantes du Zaire [*Zairian National Federation of Protestant Women*] (AF)
FNG .... Federacion Nacional de Ganaderos [*National Cattlemen's Federation*] [*Venezuelan*] (LA)
FNGP .... Federation Nationale des Gaullistes de Progres [*National Federation of Progressive Gaullists*] [*French*] (PPW)
FNH .... Fonds National de l'Hydraulique (MAR)
FNI .... Fonds National d'Investissement [*National Investment Fund*] [*Moroccan*] (AF)
FNJ .... Federatie van Nederlandse Journalisten [*Netherlands Journalists' Union*] (WEN)
FNJ .... Frente Nacional de la Juventud [*National Youth Front*] [*Spanish*] (WER)
FNJ .... Front National de la Jeunesse [*National Youth Front*] [*French*] (PD)
FNK .... Fovarosi Nepmuvelesi Kozpont [*Capital Center of Popular Education*] (HU)
FNKh .... Phosphonitril Chloride (RU)
FNL .... Front National de Liberation [*National Front for the Liberation of South Vietnam*] [*Use NFLSV*] (CL)
FNLA .... Frente Nacional de Libertacao de Angola [*Angolan National Liberation Front*] (AF)
FNLA .... Front National de Liberation de l'Angola [*Angolan National Liberation Front*] (PD)
FNLB .... Front National de Liberation de Bretagne [*National Liberation Front of Brittany*] [*French*] (PD)
FNLC .... Front Nationale de Liberation Congolaise [*Congolese National Liberation Front*] [*Zairian*] (AF)
FNLG .... Front National de Liberation Guyanais [*Guiana National Liberation Front*] [*French Guiana*] (PD)
FNLO .... Front National de Liberation d'Ouganda [*Ugandan National Liberation Front*] [*Use UNLF*] (AF)
FNM .... Ferrocarriles Nacionales de Mexico [*National Railways of Mexico*]
FNM .... Free National Movement [*Bahamian*] (PPW)

FNM .... Frente Nacional Magisterial [*National Teachers Front*] [*Guatemalan*] (LA)
FNMA .... Front National Martiniquais pour l'Autonomie [*Martinique National Front for Autonomy*] (PPW)
FNMAJ .... Federation Nationale des Mouvements et Associations de Jeunesse [*National Federation of Youth Movements and Associations*] [*Ivorian*] (AF)
FNMAJCI .... Federation Nationale des Mouvements et Associations de Jeunesse de Cote d'Ivoire (MAR)
FNMAL .... Fabrica Nacional de Municoes de Armas Ligeiras [*National Light Weapons Ammunition Factory*] [*Portuguese*] (WER)
FNMM .... Federacion Nacional de Mineros y Metalurgicos [*National Miners and Metalworkers Federation*] [*Peruvian*] (LA)
FNO .... Fond Narodni Obnovy [*National Reconstruction Fund*] (CZ)
FNO .... Frente Nacional de Oposicion [*National Opposition Front*] [*Venezuelan*] (LA)
FNO .... Front Natsional'novo Osvobozhdeniia (MAR)
FNO .... People's Liberation Front (RU)
FNOA .... Federation Nationale des Ouvriers Angolais [*National Federation of Angolan Workers*] (AF)
FNOI .... Frente Nacional Obrero Intelectual [*National Front of Workers and Intellectuals*] [*Colombian*] (LA)
FNOS .... Fundo Nacional de Obras de Saneamento [*National Sanitation Works Fund*] [*Brazilian*] (LA)
FNOSS .... Federation Nationale des Organismes de Securite Sociale [*National Federation of Social Security Agencies*] [*Malagasy*] (AF)
FNP .... Federation Nationale des Patronages de Belgique
FNP .... Fijian Nationalist Party (PPW)
FNP .... Frente Nacional de Panama [*Panamanian National Front*] (PD)
FNP .... Fuerza Nacional Progresista [*Progressive National Force*] [*Bolivian*] (LA1)
FNPC .... Federacion Nacional de Patronatos Comunales [*National Federation of Community Boards*] [*Honduran*] (LA)
FNPG .... Fashoda National Provisional Government [*Sudanese*] (MAR)
FNPG .... Federation Nationale du Petrole et du Gaz [*National Petroleum and Gas Federation*] [*Algerian*] (AF)
FNPL .... Forces Neutralistes Patriotiques Laotiennes [*Lao Patriotic Neutralist Forces*] (CL)
FNPLT .... Front Nationaliste pour la Liberation de la Tunisie [*Nationalist Front for the Liberation of Tunisia*] (AF)
FNPLT .... Front Nationaliste Progressiste pour la Liberation de la Tunisie [*Progressive Nationalist Front for the Liberation of Tunisia*] (PD)
FNPS .... Federation Nationale du Personnel de la Sante (MAR)
FNPS .... Fonds National de Promotion et de Service Social [*National Fund for Social Advancement and Service*] [*Zairian*] (AF)
FNPT .... Fondo Nacional de Proteccion al Trabajo [*National Fund for the Protection of Labor*] [*Spanish*] (WER)
FNR .... Federative People's Republic (BU)
FNR .... Frente Nacional de Redemocratizacao [*National Redemocratization Front*] [*Brazilian*] (LA)
FNR .... Frente Nacional Revolucionario [*National Revolutionary Front*] [*Argentine*] (LA)
FNR .... Fundo Nacional de Refinanciamento [*National Refinancing Fund*] [*Brazilian*] (LA)
FNRBiH .... Federativna Narodna Republika Bosna i Hercegovina [*Federated People's Republic of Bosnia and Hercegovina*] (YU)
FNRCG .... Federativna Narodna Republika Crna Gora [*Federated People's Republic of Montenegro*] (YU)
FNRH .... Federativna Narodna Republika Hrvatska [*Federated People's Republic of Croatia*] (YU)
FNRI .... Federation Nationale des Republicains Independants [*National Federation of Independent Republicans*] [*French*] (PPW)
FNRJ .... Federativna Narodna Republika Jugoslavija [*Federal People's Republic of Yugoslavia*] (YU)
FNRM .... Federativna Narodna Republika Makedonija [*Federated People's Republic of Macedonia*] (YU)
FNRS .... Federativna Narodna Republika Slovenija [*Federated People's Republic of Slovenia*] (YU)
FNRS .... Federativna Narodna Republika Srbija [*Federated People's Republic of Serbia*] (YU)
FNRS .... Fonds National de la Recherche Scientifique [*Belgian*]
FNRYu .... Federal People's Republic of Yugoslavia (BU)
FNRYu .... Federal People's Republic of Yugoslavia (RU)
FNS .... Forces Nucleaires Strategiques [*Strategic Nuclear Forces*] [*French*] (WER)
FNS .... Front National Senegalais (MAR)
FNSA .... Federation Nationale des Syndicats Agricoles [*National Federation of Farmers Unions*] [*French*] (WER)
FNSA .... Frente Nacional Socialista Argentino [*Argentinian National Socialist Front*] (PD)
FNSC .... Federation pour une Nouvelle Societe Caledonienne [*Federation for a New Caledonian Society*] (PPW)
FNSEA .... Federation Nationale des Syndicats d'Exploitants Agricoles [*National Federation of Unions of Farm Operators*] [*French*] (WER)
FNSI .... Federacion Nacional de Sindicatos Independientes [*National Federation of Independent Trade Unions*] [*Mexican*] (LA1)
FNSI .... Federazione Nazionale della Stampa Italiana [*National Federation of the Italian Press*] (WER)
FNSP .... Federation Nationale des Services Publics (MAR)
FNSP-CERI ... Fondation Nationale des Sciences Politiques Centre d'Etudes des Relations Internationales (MAR)
FNSRA .... Fonds National de Solidarite de la Revolution Agraire [*National Fund for Solidarity with the Agrarian Revolution*] [*Algerian*] (AF)
fn st .... Pound Sterling (RU)
FNT .... Federacion Nacional de Trabajadores [*National Federation of Workers*] [*Dominican Republic*] (LA)
FNT .... Federation Nationale du Theatre (MAR)
FNTA .... Federacion Nacional de Trabajadores Azucareros [*National Federation of Sugar Workers*] [*Uruguayan*] (LA)
FNTC .... Frente Nacional de Trabajadores y Campesinos [*National Workers' and Peasants' Front*] [*Peruvian*] (PPW)
FNTM .... Federation Nationale des Travailleurs de la Metallurgie [*National Metallurgy Workers Federation*] [*Algerian*] (AF)
FNTME .... Federacion Nacional de Trabajadores Municipales del Ecuador [*National Federation of Municipal Workers of Ecuador*] (LA)
FNTPGA ...... Federation Nationale des Travailleurs du Petrole, Gas, et Assimiles [*National Federation of Petroleum, Gas, and Related Industry Workers*] [*Algerian*] (AF)
FNTR .... Federation Nationale des Travailleurs du Rail [*National Federation of Railroad Workers*] [*Moroccan*] (AF)
FNTT .... Federation Nationale des Travailleurs de Terre [*National Federation of Farm Workers*] [*Algerian*] (AF)
FNTTR .... Federacion Nacional de Trabajadores Textiles Revolucionarios [*National Federation of Revolutionary Textile Workers*] [*Peruvian*] (LA)
FNTUP .... Federacion Nacional de Trabajadores de la Universidad Peruana [*National Federation of Peruvian University Workers*] (LA)
FNU .... Front National Uni [*National United Front*] [*Comoran*] (AF)
FNUAP .... Fondo de las Naciones Unidas para Actividades de Poblacion [*United Nations Population Activities Fund*] (LA)
FNUAP .... Fonds des Nations Unies pour les Activites en Matiere de Population [*United Nations Fund for Population Activities*] [*Use UNFPA*] (AF)
FNUDI .... Fonds des Nations Unies pour le Developpement Industriel (MAR)
FNUI .... Fondo de las Naciones Unidas para la Infancia [*United Nations Children's Fund*] [*Use UNICEF*] (LA)
FNUK .... Front National Uni des Komores [*National United Front of the Comoros*] (PD)
FNUOD .... Force de Desengagement de l'ONU entre Syriens et Israeliens (MAR)
FNUR .... Fonds des Nations Unies pour les Refugies (MAR)
FNV .... Fabrica Nacional de Vagoes [*National Railway Car Factory*] [*Brazilian*] (LA)
FNV .... Federatie Nederlandse Vakbeweging [*Netherlands Trade Unions Federation*] (WEN)
FNV .... Financiera Nacional de la Vivienda [*Salvadoran*]
FNV .... Partido Federacion Nacional Velasquista [*National Velasquista Federation*] [*Ecuadorean*] (PPW)
FNVCA .... Federazione Nazionale Vetro e Ceramica [*National Federation of Glass and Pottery Workers*] [*Italian*]
FO .... Faroe Islands [*Two-letter standard code*] (CNC)
FO .... Fasistiki Organosis [*Fascist Organization*] (GC)
FO .... Finance Department (RU)
FO .... Fizicki Odgoj [*Physical Education*] (YU)
fo .... Folio [*Folio*] [*French*]
fo .... Folio [*Folio*] [*Correspondence*] [*Spanish*]
fo .... For Ovrigt [*Besides*] [*Swedish*] (GPO)
FO .... Force Ouvriere [*Workers Force*] [*French*] (WER)
FO .... Foreign Office (MAR)
FO .... Frente Obrero [*Workers' Front*] [*of the Carlists in the Workers Commissions*] [*Spanish*] (WER)
FO .... Frente Obrero [*Workers' Front*] [*Nicaraguan*] (PD)
FO .... Fucikuv Odznak [*Fucik Badge*] (CZ)
FOA .... Forsvarets Forskningsanstalt [*Defense Research Institute*] [*Swedish*] (WEN)
FOB .... Filmugyek Orszagos Bizottsaga [*National Committee on Motion Pictures*] (HU)
FOB .... Free on Board (MAR)
FOBER .... Fovarosi Epitoipari Beruhazasi Vallalat [*Investment Enterprise of the Capital City Construction Industry*] (HU)
FOBID .... Federatie van Organisaties op het Gebied van het Bibliotheek-Informatie- en Documentatiebestel [*Dutch*]
Fobiz .... Fobizottsag [*Main Committee*] (HU)
FOC .... Facultad Obrera y Campesina [*Workers and Peasants Faculty*] [*Cuban*] (LA)
FOC .... Federacion Obrera Capitalina [*Capital Labor Federation*] [*Costa Rican*] (LA)
FOC .... Flag of Convenience (MAR)
FOC .... Fonds des Operations de Changes [*Foreign Exchange Operations Fund*] [*Use FEOF*] [*Laotian*] (CL)
FOC .... Force Ouvriere du Congo (MAR)
FOC .... Front Obrer Catala [*Catalan Workers Front*] [*Spanish*] (WER)

FOCAPE...... Fonds d'Aide et de Garantie de Credits aux Petites et Moyennes Entreprises (MAR)
FOCCO .... Fomento y Cooperacion Comunal con Esfuerzo Propio y Ayuda Mutua [*Self-Help and Mutual Aid Communal Development and Cooperation Program*] [*Salvadoran*] (LA1)
FOCE .... Frente Obrero Campesino Estudiantil [*Worker-Peasant Student Front*] [*Ecuadorean*] (LA)
FOCEP .... Frente Obrero Campesino Estudiantil Popular [*Worker-Peasant-Student Popular Front*] [*Peruvian*] (LA)
FOCSAT...... Fovarosi Csatornazasi Muvek [*Capital Sewage Plant*] (HU)
FOD............ Filmowy Osrodek Doswiadczalny [*Film Experimental Center*] (POL)
FOD............ Foersoeks- och Demonstrationsskolan [*Swedish*]
FOD............ Frydlant nad Ostravici-Bila Draha [*Frydlant nad Ostravici-Bila Railroad*] (CZ)
FOdD........... Fabryka Obrabiarek do Drewna (Bydgoszcz) [*Woodworking Machine Tool Plant (Bydgoszcz)*] (POL)
FODECO ..... Frente de Organizaciones Democratas Constitucionalistas [*Constitutionalist Democratic Organizations Front*] [*Dominican Republic*] (LA1)
FODELICO ... Forces Democratiques de Liberation du Congo (MAR)
FODERCO... Front de Resistance Congolais [*Congolese Resistance Front*] (AF)
FODERUMA ... Fondo de Desarrollo Rural Marginal [*Marginal Rural Area Development Fund*] [*Ecuadorean*] (LA)
FODIC .... Fonds pour le Developpement de l'Industrie Cinematographique (MAR)
foea .... Foeloado [*Chief Consultant*] (HU)
FOEB........... Federacion de Obreros y Empleados de la Bebida [*Beverage Workers Federation*] [*Uruguayan*] (LA)
FOECYT...... Federacion de Obreros y Empleados de Correos y Telecomunicaciones [*Federation of Postal and Telecommunications Workers*] [*Argentine*] (LA)
FOEIMYA.... Federacion de Obreros y Empleados Molineros y Afines [*Flour Mill Workers Federation*] [*Uruguayan*] (LA)
FOeJ........... Freie Oesterreichische Jugend [*Free Austrian Youth*] (WEN)
foell............ Foellenor [*General Inspector*] (HU)
FOETRA...... Federacion de Obreros y Empleados Telefonicos de la Republica Argentina [*Federation of Telephone Workers and Employees of the Argentine Republic*] (LA)
FOEVA .... Federacion de Obreros y Empleados Vitivinicolas y Afines [*Federation of Vineyard and Wine Industry Workers and Employees*] [*Argentine*] (LA)
FOFATUSA ... Federation of Free African Trade Unions of South Africa (MAR)
FOFIPA .... Foibe Filankevitry ny Mpampianatra (MAR)
foflo............ Fofelugyelo [*General Inspector*] (HU)
FOG............ Feinoptisches Werk, Goerlitz [*Goerlitz Precision Optics Plant*] (EG)
fog.............. Fogaszat [*Dentistry*] (HU)
FOG............ Fougasse Flamethrower (RU)
FOGAPE...... Fonds d'Aide et de Garantie des Credits aux Petites et Moyennes Entreprises (Cameroonaises) [*Fund for Aid and Loan Guarantees for (Cameroonian) Small and Medium-Size Businesses*] (AF)
FOGEBA ..... Fournitures Generales pour le Batiment (MAR)
fogl............. Foglalkozas [*Occupation, Profession*] (HU)
FOGU .... Federacion Obrera Gastronomica de Uruguay [*Federation of Food Workers of Uruguay*] (LA)
fogy............ Fogyasztas [*Consumption*] (HU)
fohdgy......... Fohadnagy [*First Lieutenant*] (HU)
fohg............. Foherceg [*Archduke*] (HU)
FOI .... Fruit of Islam (MAR)
foig.............. Foigazgato [*Inspector of Schools, Director*] (HU)
FOINSA....... Fomenta de Inversiones, Sociedad Anonima [*Investments Promotion Corp.*] [*Salvadoran*]
foint............ Fointezo [*General Manager*] (HU)
FOIQ........... Federacion Obrera de la Industria Quimica [*Chemical Workers Federation*] [*Uruguayan*] (LA)
foisk .... Foiskola [*College, Academy*] (HU)
foisk .... Foiskolai [*Collegiate, Academic*] (HU)
FOITAF........ Federacion Obrera de la Industria Tabaquera de Filipinas [*Workers' Federation of the Tobacco Industry of the Philippines*]
FOK............ Cutting Trench Digger (RU)
fok.............. Fokonyvelo [*Head Bookkeeper*] (HU)
FOK............ Foldmivesszovetkezetek Orszagos Kozpontja [*National Center of Farmers' Cooperatives*] (HU)
FOK............ Photocolorimeter (RU)
FOK............ Symfonicky Orchestr Hlavni Mesta Prahy FOK [*Prague Symphony Orchestra FOK (Film, Opera, Concert)*] (CZ)
FOKA .... Folyamszabalyozo es Kavicskotro Vallalat [*River Control and Dredging Enterprise*] (HU)
FOL .... Federacion de Obreros en Lana [*Wool Workers Federation*] [*Uruguayan*] (LA)
fol................ Folio [*Spanish*]
FOL .... Frente Obrero de Liberacion [*Workers' Liberation Front*] [*Netherlands Antillean*] (PPW)
foldgazd...... Foldgazdasag [*Agricultural Economics*] (HU)
foldr .... Foldrajz [*Geography*] (HU)
FOLDSZOV ... Foldmuvesszovetkezet [*Farmers' Cooperative*] (HU)
FOLDSZOVARU ... Foldmuvesszovetkezetek Arubeszerzo es Ertekesito Vallalata [*Buying and Selling Enterprise of Farmers' Cooperatives*] (HU)
foldt............ Foldtan [*Geology*] (HU)
FOLG.......... Federation des Oeuvres Laiques de La Guyane [*Federation of Lay Works of Guiana*] [*French Guiana*] (LA1)
folg .... Folgend [*Following*] [*German*]
folyt .... Folytatas [*Continuation, Continued*] (HU)
folyt kov ...... Folytatasa Kovetkezik [*To Be Continued*] (HU)
FOM .... Archives de la Ministere de la France d'Outre-Mer [*Paris*] (MAR)
FOM .... Federation of Malaya (ML)
FoM .... Felsooktatasi Miniszterium/Miniszter [*Ministry/Minister of Higher Education*] (HU)
FoM .... Felsooktatasugyi Miniszter [*Minister of Higher Education*] (HU)
FOM .... Filterie et Ouate du Maroc (MAR)
FOM .... Force Ouvriere Mauricienne [*Mauritian Labor Force*] (AF)
FOM .... Forces Ouvrieres Marocaines [*Moroccan Labor Forces*] (AF)
FOM .... Formation d'Officier-Marinier (MAR)
fom.............. Fra Og Med [*From and With*] [*Norwegian*] (GPO)
FOM .... Free Officers' Movement [*Egyptian*] (MAR)
FOM .... Stichting voor Fundamenteel Onderzoek de Materie [*Foundation of Fundamental Research on Matter*] [*Dutch*] (WEN)
FOMAV .... Foldmuvelesugyi Miniszterium Anyagellato Vallalata [*Supply Enterprise of the Ministry of Agriculture*] (HU)
FOMETRO... Fonds Medical Tropical [*Tropical Medicine Fund*] (AF)
FOMEX........ Fondo para el Fomento de Exportaciones de Productos Manufacturados [*Fund for the Promotion of Exports of Manufactured Products*] [*Mexican*] (LA)
FOMGOMIAM ... Pro-Military Government Community Economic Advancement Association of Ambandrika [*Malagasy*] (AF)
FOMI .... Foldmeresi Intezet [*Institute of Geodesy*] (HU)
FOMIZ......... Federation des Ouvriers des Mines du Zaire (MAR)
FOMO.......... Direccion de Formacion de Mano de Obra [*Directorate for the Training of Labor*] [*Bolivian*] (LA)
FOMODA..... Fonds de Modernisation et de Developpement de l'Artisanat [*French*]
FOMTI .... Budapest Fovarosi Tanacs Melyepito Tervezo Vallalat [*Budapest City Council, Designing Unit in Structural Engineering*] (HU)
FOMULAC... Fondation Medicale de l'Universite de Louvain au Congo (MAR)
FON............ Division of Social Sciences (RU)
fon.............. Fonetiikka [*Phonetics*] [*Finnish*]
fon.............. Fonok [*Manager, Head*] (HU)
FON............ Frente Opositor Nacional [*National Opposition Front*] [*Nicaraguan*] (LA)
fon.............. Phonetic, Phonetics (RU)
fon.............. Phonetics (BU)
FON............ Special Division (RU)
FONADE ..... Fondo Nacional de Proyectos de Desarrollo [*National Development Projects Fund*] [*Colombian*] (LA)
FONADER ... Fonds National de Developpement Rural [*National Rural Development Fund*] [*Cameroonian*] (AF)
FONAFE...... Fondo Nacional de Fomento Ejidal [*National Ejido Development Fund*] [*Mexican*] (LA)
FONAMES... Fonds National Medico-Social [*National Medical and Social Fund*] [*Zairian*] (AF)
FONAPRE ... Fondo Nacional de Preinversion [*National Investment Feasibility Study Fund*] [*Ecuadorean*] (LA)
FONASBA... Federation of National Associations of Shipbrokers and Agents (EA)
FONAVI....... Fondo Nacional de la Vivienda [*National Housing Fund*] [*Argentine*] (LA)
Fond........... Fondeadero [*Anchorage*] [*Spanish*] (NAU)
fond............ Foundation (BU)
fond............ Part de Fondateur [*French*]
FONDILAC ... Fondo de Desarrollo de la Industria Lactea [*Dairy Industry Development Fund*] [*Nicaraguan*] (LA1)
fondkom ..... Fund Committee (RU)
FONDOUTCHAD ... Fondation de l'Ouvrier Tchadien [*Chadian Worker Foundation*] (AF)
Fondre .... Fondriere [*Quagmire, Slough*] [*Military map abbreviation*] [*World War I*] [*French*] (MTD)
FONDUR ...... Fondo Nacional de Desarrollo Urbano [*National Urban Development Fund*] [*Venezuelan*] (LA)
FONINVES ... Fondo de Investigaciones Petroleras [*Petroleum Research Fund*] [*Venezuelan*] (LA)
FONIVA....... Federacion Obrera Nacional de la Industria del Vestido y Afines [*National Garment Workers Federation*] [*Argentine*] (LA)
Fontne......... Fontaine [*Fountain, Spring*] [*Military map abbreviation*] [*World War I*] [*French*] (MTD)
FONTTCYV ... Federacion Obrera Nacional de Trabajadores Textiles, del Cuero, y del Vestuario [*National Textile, Leather, and Garment Workers Federation*] [*Uruguayan*] (LA)
FONY.......... Federation of Nigerian Youth (AF)
foo .... Fee [*Business and trade*] [*German*]
foorv........... Foorvos [*Chief Surgeon*] (HU)
fooszt .... Foosztaly [*Main Department*] (HU)
FOPA DESC ... Pan-African Foundation for Economic, Social, and Cultural Development (MAR)

FOPERDA ... Fondation Pere Damien pour la Lutte Contre la Lepre (MAR)
FOPEX .... Fondo de Promocion de Exportaciones No Tradicionales [*Fund for the Promotion of Non-Traditional Exports*] [*Lima, Peru*]
FOP-PT .... Front Oubangais Patriotique - Parti du Travail [*Oubangian Patriotic Front - Party of Labor*] [*Central African*] (PD)
FOPRODI .... Fonds de Promotion et de Decentralisation Industrielles (MAR)
FOR .... Fundusz Oszczednosci [*or Oszczednosciowy*] Rolnictwa [*Agricultural Savings Fund*] (POL)
FORA .... Federacion Obrera Regional Argentina [*Argentine Regional Workers Federation*] (LA)
FORANGA ... Societe Forestiere de la Nyanga (MAR)
FORCES ...... Societe des Forces Hydroelectriques du Bas-Congo (MAR)
ford .... Forditas [*Translation*] (HU)
ford .... fordito [*Translator*] (HU)
ford .... Forditotta [*Translated By*] [*Hungarian*] (GPO)
ford .... Fordits [*Please Turn Page*] (HU)
FOREAMI .... Fonds Reine Elisabeth pour l'Assistance Medicale aux Indigenes [*Queen Elisabeth Funds for Medical Assistance to the Natives*] [*Belgian*]
FORENCO ... Compagnie Nouvelle de Forages Petroliers (MAR)
FOREX .... Forages et Exploitations Petrolieres [*Petroleum Drilling and Exploitation Company*] [*French*] (AF)
FOREXI .... Societe pour la Realisation des Forages d'Exploitation en Cote-d'Ivoire (MAR)
forf .... Forfattare [*Author*] [*Swedish*] (GPO)
forf .... Forfattarinna [*Authoress*] [*Swedish*] (GPO)
forf .... Forfatter [*Author*] [*Danish*] (GPO)
FORINDI ...... Societe Forestiere d'Irindi (MAR)
FORIS .... Forschungs Informations System
FORLAF ...... Societe Force et Lumiere Afrique (MAR)
form .... Format [*Size*] (POL)
form .... Format, Size (RU)
FORMA .... Fonds d'Orientation et de Regularisation des Marches Agricoles [*Fund for the Organization and Regulation of Agricultural Markets*] [*French*] (WER)
FORMINIERE ... Societe Internationale Forestiere et Miniere du Congo [*International Forestry and Mining Company of the Congo*] (MAR)
FORMINIERE ... Societe Internationale Forestiere et Miniere du Zaire [*International Forestry and Mining Company of Zaire*] (AF)
forp .... Outpost (RU)
FORSZ .... Forgacsolo Szerszamok Gyara [*Cutting Tools Factory*] (HU)
fort .... Fortepian [*Piano*] [*Polish*]
Fortif .... Fortification [*Fortification*] [*Military map abbreviation*] [*World War I*] [*French*] (MTD)
Forts .... Fortsetzung [*Continuation*] [*German*] (GPO)
FORU .... Federacion Obrera Regional Uruguaya [*Uruguayan Regional Workers Federation*] (LA)
FOS .... Focusing-Deflecting System (RU)
FOS .... Frauenoberschule [*German*]
FOS .... Fuel Oil Surcharge (MAR)
FOS .... Fundusz Odbudowy Szkol [*School Reconstruction Fund*] (POL)
FOS .... Organophosphorus Compound (RU)
FOSAP-HD ... Forestiere de San Pedro-HD (MAR)
FOSATU ...... Federation of South African Trade Unions (AF)
FOSDA .... Fonds Special de Developpement Agricole [*Special Agricultural Development Fund*] [*Tunisian*] (AF)
fosf .... Phosphorite Factory [*Topography*] (RU)
fosf .... Phosphorite Mine [*Topography*] (RU)
FOSFATOTUK ... Association of Plants and Mines of the Phosphate Fertilizers Industry (RU)
FOSIDEC .... Fonds de Solidarite et d'Intervention pour le Developpement de la Communaute Economique de l'Afrique de l'Ouest (MAR)
FOSKh .... Federation of Soviet Artists' Associations [*1930-1932*] (RU)
FOSKOR ..... Phosphate Development Corporation (MAR)
FOSONAM ... Foyer de la Solidarite Nationale Mobutu [*Mobutu National Solidarity Center*] [*Zairian*] (AF)
FOSP .... Federation of Soviet Writers' Associations [*1926-1932*] (RU)
FOSPED ...... Fovarosi Szallitasi Vallalat [*Capital Transport Enterprise*] (HU)
FOST .... Force Oceanique Strategique [*Strategic Naval Force*] [*French*] (WER)
FOT .... Federacion Obrera del Transporte [*Transport Workers Federation*] [*Uruguayan*] (LA)
fot .... Fotografia [*Photograph*] (POL)
fot .... Fotografia [*Photography*] (HU)
fot .... Fotografowal [*Photoghraphed By*] (POL)
fot .... Photograph, Photographic, Photography (RU)
fot .... Photography (BU)
FOTAB .... Fotografske Aviobombe [*Photographic (Phosphorous) Air Bombs*] (YU)
FOTAB .... Photoflash Bomb (RU)
fotan .... Fotanacsos [*Chief Councilor (of a council) or Chief Counselor*] (HU)
FOTAV .... Fovarosi Tavfuto Muvek [*Capital City District Heating Works*] (HU)
FOTEM .... Folklor Temsilcilik [*Folklore Presentation Organization*] (TU)
FOTI .... Fovarosi Tervezo Intezet [*Capital Planning Institute*] (HU)
FOTIA .... Federacion Obrera Tucumana de la Industria del Azucar [*Tucuman Sugar Industry Workers Federation*] [*Argentine*] (LA)
fotisztv .... Fotisztviselo [*Senior Civil Servant*] (HU)
fotitk .... Fotitkar [*General Secretary*] (HU)
fotobatr .... Photogrammetric Battery (BU)
fotobatr .... Photogrammetric Battery [*Military term*] (RU)
FOTOCOL ... Industria Fotografica Colombiana Ltda. [*Medellin*] (COL)
fotogr .... Photography (BU)
fotokhromolitogr ... Photochromolithography (RU)
foto kop .... Photographic Copy (BU)
fotokor .... Press Photographer (RU)
fotom .... Fotomontaz [*Trick Picture*] [*Polish*]
fotorep .... Fotoreportaz [*Camera-Report*] [*Polish*]
fototip .... Phototype (RU)
fot pl .... Photographic Plate (RU)
FOTRA .... Federacion de Obreros del Tabaco de la Republica Argentina [*Federation of Tobacco Workers of the Argentine Republic*] (LA)
FOU .... Frente Obrero Unido [*United Workers Front*] [*In Alicante*] [*Spanish*] (WER)
FOUPSA ...... Frente Obrero Unificado Pro-Sindicatos Autonomos [*Autonomous United Pro-Union Workers Front*] [*Dominican Republic*] (LA1)
fov .... Fovaros [*or Fovarosi*] [*Metropolis, Capital or Metropolitan, Of the Capital*] (HU)
fov .... Fovezerseg [*Supreme Command, General Headquarters*] (HU)
FOV .... Phosphoric Chemical Agent (BU)
FOV .... Phosphororganic War Gas (RU)
FOVIZ .... Fovarosi Vizmuvek [*Capital Water Works*] (HU)
Fov K .... Fovarosi Kiado [*Capital Publishing Company*] (HU)
Fov Kvtar .... Fovarosi Konyvtar [*Metropolitan Library, Municipal Library of Budapest*] (HU)
FOZ .... Fucikuv Odznak Zdatnosti [*Fucik Badge of Bravery*] (CZ)
FOZA .... Nabavljacka Zadruga Fotografskih Obrtnika [*Supply Cooperative for Photographers*] (YU)
FP .... Absorption Filter (RU)
FP .... Family Planning (MAR)
FP .... Federal Party [*Namibian*] (PPW)
FP .... Federal Party [*South African*] (AF)
FP .... Ferrite Storage, Ferrite Memory (RU)
FP .... Filharmonie Pracujicich [*Workers' Philharmonic Orchestra*] (CZ)
FP .... Film Polski [*Polish Motion Pictures*] (POL)
FP .... Filmovy Prumysl [*Film Industry*] (CZ)
FP .... Fiskulturno Popodne [*Physical Culture Afternoons*] [*Military*] (YU)
FP .... Flavoprotein (RU)
FP .... Flota de la Plataforma [*Insular Shelf Fishing Fleet*] [*Cuban*] (LA)
FP .... Folkpartiet [*Liberal Party*] [*Swedish*] (WEN)
FP .... Fonction de Production (MAR)
FP .... Fonction Publique [*North African*] (MAR)
FP .... Franzoesisches Patent [*French Patent*] [*German*]
FP .... Fremskridtspartiet [*Progressive Party*] [*Danish*] (WEN)
FP .... Fremskrittspartiet [*Progress Party*] [*Norwegian*] (PPE)
FP .... Fuerzas Populares [*Popular Forces*] [*Peruvian*] (LA)
FP .... Function Converter (RU)
FP .... Fundusz Posmiertny [*Death Benefit Fund*] (POL)
FP .... Fusee Percutante [*Percussion-Fuse*] [*French*] (MTD)
FP .... Petryanov Filter (RU)
FP .... Phosphoprotein (RU)
FP .... Photopyrometer (RU)
f-p .... Piano (RU)
FP-25 .... People's Forces of 25 April [*Portuguese*] (PD)
FP-31 .... Frente Popular 31 de Enero [*31st January Popular Front*] [*Guatemalan*] (PD)
FPA .... Fabrique de Peintures en Afrique (MAR)
FPA .... Forest Products Association [*Guyanese*] (LA)
FPA .... Formation Professionnelle des Adultes [*Adult Vocational Training*] [*French*] (AF)
FPA .... Fovarosi Penzalap [*Capital Monetary Fund*] (HU)
FPA .... Frente Politico Anticomunista [*Anticommunist Political Front*] [*Salvadoran*] (LA)
FPA .... Petryanov Analytical Filter (RU)
FPAK .... Family Planning Association of Kenya (MAR)
FPC .... Farsi Petroleum Company [*Iranian*] (ME)
FPC .... Food Production Corporation (MAR)
FPC .... Frente Popular Costarricense [*Costa Rican Popular Front*] (PPW)
FPCCB .... Fabrica de Preparate si Conserve de Carne Bucuresti [*Bucharest Factory for Canned and Preserved Meat*] (RO)
FPCR .... Fronte Popolare Comunista Rivoluzionario [*Revolutionary Communist Popular Front*] [*Italian*] (WER)
FPD .... Federacion Popular Democratica [*Popular Democratic Federation*] [*Spanish*] (PPE)
FPDA .... Five Power Defense Arrangement (ML)
FPDL .... Federacion de Partidos Democraticas y Liberales [*Federation of Democratic and Liberal Parties*] [*Spanish*] (PPE)
FPEP .... Foititiki Pnevmatiki Estia Peiraios [*Piraeus Spiritual Home for Students*] (GC)
FPF .... Federacion Peruana de Futbol [*Peruvian Soccer Federation*] (LA)
FPG .... Absorption Filter (RU)
FPG .... Fabrique de Peintures au Gabon (MAR)

FPG .... Fischerei-Produktionsgenossenschaft [*Fishing Production Cooperative*] (EG)

FPG .... Fundusz Pomocy Gospodarczej [*Economic Aid Fund*] (POL)

FPH .... Frente Patriotico Hondureno [*Honduran Patriotic Front*] (PD)

FPI .... Forest Products Institute (MAR)

FPI .... Fraccion Popular Independiente [*People's Independent Faction*] [*Venezuelan*] (LA)

FPIA .... Family Planning International Assistance (MAR)

FPIKP .... Frente Patriotica para a Independencia do Kongo Portugues (MAR)

FPIKP .... Front Patriotique pour l'Independance du Kongo Dit Portugais (MAR)

FPIP .... Federation Professionnelle Independante de la Police Nationale [*French*]

FPiU .... Fabryka Przyrzadow i Uchwytow [*Tool and Fixture Factory*] (POL)

FPJ .... Front Patriotique de la Jeunesse (MAR)

FPK .... Francuska Partia Komunistyczna [*French Communist Party*] (POL)

FPK .... Phosphopyruvic Acid (RU)

FPL .... Forces Populaires de Liberation [*People's Liberation Forces*] [*Chadian*] (AF)

FPL .... Frente Portugal Livre (MAR)

FPL .... Fuerzas Populares de Liberacion [*Popular Liberation Forces*] [*Salvadoran*] (LA)

FPL .... Fuerzas Populares de Liberacion Farabundo Marti [*Farabundo Marti Popular Liberation Forces*] [*Salvadoran*] (PD)

FPLD .... Popular Front for the Liberation of Djibouti (AF)

FPLE .... Front Populaire de Liberation de l'Erythree [*Eritrean People's Liberation Front*] [*Use EPLF*] [*Ethiopian*] (AF)

FPLE .... Fronte Popolare di Liberazione Eritreo (MAR)

FPLGAO ...... Front Populaire pour la Liberation du Golfe Arabe Occupe (MAR)

FPLM .... Forcas Populares para a Libertacao do Mocambique [*Popular Forces for the Liberation of Mozambique*] (AF)

FPLN .... Frente Patriotica de Libertacao Nacional [*Patriotic Front of National Liberation*] [*Portuguese*] (WER)

FPLN .... Frente Patriotico de Liberacion Nacional [*National Liberation Patriotic Front*] [*Colombian*] (LA)

FPLN .... Frente Portuguesa de Libertacao Nacional (MAR)

Fplo .... Fahrplananordnungen [*Train Schedule Orders*] (EG)

FPLP .... Frente Patriotico de Libertacao de Portugal [*Patriotic Front for the Liberation of Portugal*] (PPE)

FPLP .... Front Populaire pour la Liberation de la Palestine [*Popular Front for the Liberation of Palestine*] [*French*] (WER)

FPLT .... Front Populaire de Liberation du Tchad [*Popular Front for the Liberation of Chad*] (AF)

FPLT .... Front Populaire de Liberation du Tigre [*Tigre People's Liberation Front*] [*Use TPLF*] (AF)

FPM- .... Photo- and Transparency Meter (RU)

FPMA .... Fiangonana Protestanta Malagasy aty Andafy [*Malagasy Protestant Church in France*] (AF)

FPMPI .... French Education Museum in Plovdiv (BU)

FPN .... Falange Patria Nova [*New Fatherland Phalange*] [*Brazilian*] (PD)

FPN .... Forces de Police Nationale (MAR)

FPN .... Frente Patriotico Nacional [*National Patriotic Front*] [*Nicaraguan*] (PPW)

FPN .... Frente Popular Nacionalista [*Nationalist Popular Front*] [*Bolivian*] (LA)

FPNR .... Photosynthetic Pyridine Nucleotide Reductase (RU)

FPO .... Financne Planovaci Odbor [*Budget Planning Branch*] (CZ)

FPO .... Freiheitliche Partei Oesterreichs [*Liberal Party of Austria (or Austrian Freedom Party)*] (PPW)

FPO .... Front Patriotique Oubanguien [*Ubangi People's Patriotic Front*] [*Central African*] (AF)

FPOe .... Freiheitliche Partei Oesterreichs [*Liberal Party of Austria (or Austrian Freedom Party)*] (WEN)

FPOLISARIO ... Frente Popular para la Liberacion de Saguia El Hamra y Rio De Oro [*Popular Front for the Liberation of Saguia El Hamra and Rio De Oro*] [*Use POLISARIO Front*] (AF)

FPOS .... Federacja Polskich Organizacji Studenckich [*Federation of Polish Students' Organizations*] (POL)

FPP .... Federacion de Periodistas de Peru [*Peruvian Federation of Journalists*] (LA)

FPPS .... Front Progressiste du Peuple Seychellois [*Seychelles People's Progressive Front*] [*Use SPPF*] (AF)

FPr .... Filosofski Pregled [*Philosophy Review*] [*A periodical*] (BU)

FPR .... Fonds Projets Ruraux (MAR)

FPR .... Frente Patriotico Revolucionario [*Revolutionary Patriotic Front*] [*Nicaraguan*] (LA1)

FPR .... Frente Popular Contra la Represion [*Popular Front Against Repression*] [*Honduran*] (PD)

FPR .... Fuerzas Populares Revolucionarias Lorenzo Zelaya [*Lorenzo Zelaya Popular Revolutionary Forces*] [*Honduran*] (PD)

FPRI .... Forest Products Research Institute [*Ghanaian*] (AF)

FPS .... Federacion de Partidos Socialistas [*Federation of Socialist Parties*] [*Spanish*] (WER)

FPS .... Filmovy Poradni Sbor [*Motion Picture Advisory Board*] (CZ)

FPS .... Front Populaire Soudanais (MAR)

FPS- .... Photoelectric Device for the Measuring of Scattering of Light (RU)

FPS .... Underwater Sports Federation (RU)

FPSC .... Federal Public Service Commission (MAR)

FPSZ .... Fovarosi Pedagogiai Szeminarium [*Capital Seminary for Advanced Teacher Training*] (HU)

FPT .... Federace Proletarske Telovychovy [*Proletarian Physical Education Federation*] (CZ)

FPT .... Fondo de Promocion Turistica [*Tourism Promotion Fund*] [*Peruvian*] (LA)

FPT .... Fundusz Postepu Technicznego [*Fund for the Advancement of Technology*] [*Polish*]

FPTG .... Federacion Provincial de Trabajadores de Guayas [*Guayas Provincial Workers Federation*] [*Ecuadorean*] (LA)

FPTM .... Federatsiia Profsoiuzov Trudiashchikhsia Madagaskara (MAR)

FPTU .... Federation of Progressive Trade Unions [*Tanzanian*] (AF)

FPTUL .... Federation of Petroleum Trade Unions in Lebanon (ME)

FPU .... Actual Track Angle (RU)

FPU .... Folkpartiets Ungdomsforbund [*Liberal Youth Association*] [*Swedish*] (WEN)

FPU .... Small Size Absorption Filter (RU)

FPUP .... Front Populaire pour l'Unite et la Paix (MAR)

FPV .... Federation of Vietnamese Trade Unions [*North Vietnamese*] (RU)

FPV .... Front Populaire Voltaique (MAR)

FPV .... Front Progressiste Voltaique [*Upper Volta Progressive Front*] (PPW)

FQ .... French Southern and Antarctic Lands [*Two-letter standard code*] (CNC)

Fque .... Fabrique [*Factory*] [*Business and trade*] [*French*]

Fr .... Fee [*Business and trade*] [*German*]

fr .... Folio Recto [*Right-Hand Page*] [*Latin*] (GPO)

fr .... Forager (BU)

FR .... Forstrat [*German*]

Fr .... Four [*Furnace*] [*Military map abbreviation*] [*World War I*] [*French*] (MTD)

fr .... Franc [*French*] (GPO)

fr .... Franc (RU)

FR .... Franc du Ruanda (MAR)

FR .... France [*Two-letter standard code*] (CNC)

fr .... Francia [*French*] (HU)

fr .... Frangi [*or Frangia*] [*Finnish*]

Fr .... Frank [*or Franki*] [*Franc or Francs*] [*Polish*]

fr .... Franko [*Postpaid*] [*German*]

Fr .... Fransizca [*French*] (TU)

Fr .... Frau [*Mrs.*] [*German*]

Fr .... Fray [*or Frey*] [*Friar*] [*Spanish*]

fr .... Frei [*Free*] [*German*]

fr .... French (BU)

fr .... French (RU)

f-r .... Medical Assistant (RU)

FR .... Physical Workers (BU)

FRA .... Fabrika Rezanog Alata [*Cutting Tools Factory*] [*Cacak*] (YU)

fra .... Factura [*Invoice of Merchandise*] [*Spanish*]

FRA .... Faculte de Resiliation Annuelle [*French*]

FRA .... Federation des Republiques Arabes [*North African*] (MAR)

FRA .... Fondo de Refinanciamiento Agropecuario [*Agricultural and Livestock Refinancing Fund*] [*Bolivian*] (LA)

FRA .... Forces Royales Air (MAR)

FRA .... France [*Three-letter standard code*] (CNC)

FRA .... Frente Radical Alfarista [*Radical Alfarista Front*] [*Ecuadorean*] (PPW)

FRA .... Front de Resistance d'Angola [*Angola Resistance Front*] (AF)

FRAB .... Banque Franco-Arabe d'Investissements Internationaux [*Inter-Arab*] (ME)

FRAC .... Formation Rationnelle Acceleree de Chauffeurs [*Algerian*] (MAR)

fragm .... Fragment [*Fragment*] [*Polish*]

FRAIN .... Front Revolutionnaire Africain pour l'Independance Nationale des Colonies Portugaises [*African Revolutionary Front for the National Independence of the Portuguese Colonies*] (AF)

frakt .... Fraktioniert [*Fractionated*] [*German*]

F es R alapok ... Fejlesztesi es Reszesedesi Alapok [*Development and Profit Sharing Fund*] (HU)

FRAM .... Fraternite Franco-Africaine et Malgache (MAR)

FRAMATOME ... Societe Franco Americaine de Constructions Atomiques [*Franco-American Atomic Construction Co.*] [*French*] (WER)

FRAMPO ..... Frente Amplio Popular [*Broad Popular Front*] [*Panamanian*] (PPW)

FRAN .... Frente Renovador de Accion Nacional [*National Action Renovating Front*] [*Ecuadorean*] (LA)

franc .... Francuski [*French*] (POL)

FRANCAREP ... Compagnie Franco-Africaine de Recherches Petrolieres (MAR)

FRANCEVIN ... Societe les Bons Vins de France (MAR)

FRANTIR ..... France Explosifs (MAR)

FRAP .... Frente Revolucionaria Anti-Facista e Patriota [*Revolutionary Antifascist and Patriotic Front*] [*Portuguese*] (WER)

FRAP .... Frente Revolucionario de Accion Popular [*People's Action Revolutionary Front*] [*Spanish*] (WER)
FRAP .... Frente Revolucionario Antifascista y Patriota [*Anti-Fascist and Patriotic Revolutionary Front*] [*Spanish*] (WER)
FRAP .... Fuerzas Revolucionarias Armadas Populares [*People's Revolutionary Armed Forces*] [*Mexican*] (PD)
FRAP .... Fuerzas Revolucionarias Armadas Populares [*People's Revolutionary Armed Forces*] [*Salvadoran*] (LA1)
FRAPAR ...... Front Anticolonialiste pour l'Autodetermination de la Reunion [*Anti-Colonialist Front for the Self-Determination of Reunion*] (AF)
FRAR .... Fonds Regional d'Amenagement Rural [*Regional Rural Development Fund*] (AF)
FRAS .... Fuerzas Revolucionarias Antiimperialistas por el Socialismo [*Anti-Imperialist Revolutionary Forces for Socialism*] [*Peruvian*] (LA)
Frat .... Fratello [*Brother*] [*Italian*]
FRAT .... Tanzania Football Referee Association (MAR)
FRAUL .... Movimento Nacional de Fraternidade Ultramarina [*National Movement of Overseas Fraternity*] [*Portuguese*] (WER)
fraz .... Frazione [*Ward*] [*In addresses*] [*Italian*] (CED)
fr b .... Belga Frank [*Belgian Franc*] (HU)
FRB .... Fuerza Revolucionaria Barrientista [*Barrientist Revolutionary Force*] [*Bolivian*] (LA)
frbl .... Farblos [*Colorless*] [*German*]
FRCN .... Federal Radio Corporation of Nigeria (MAR)
FRD .... Frente de Resistencia Democratica [*Democratic Resistance Front*] [*Costa Rican*] (LA)
FRD .... Frente Revolucionario Democratico [*Democratic Revolutionary Front*] [*Salvadoran*] (LA1)
FRD .... Photon Jet Engine (RU)
FRD .... Record of All Workers' Activities during a Working Day (RU)
FrDF .... Fructose Diphosphate (RU)
Frdl .... Freundlich [*Kind, Kindly*] (EG)
FRDMO .... Federalni Rada Detskych a Mladeznickych Organizaci [*Federal Council of Children's and Youth Organizations*] (CZ)
fre .... Facture [*Invoice*] [*French*]
FRE .... Frente Revolucionario Estudiantil [*Revolutionary Student Front*] [*Guatemalan*] (LA)
FREC .... Forestry Research and Education Centre [*Sudanese*] (MAR)
FRECILINA ... Frente Civico de Liberacion Nacional [*Civic Front for National Liberation*] [*Argentine*] (LA1)
FRECOMO ... Frente Comun de Mocambique (MAR)
FRECSA ...... Frigorifica Ecuatoriana [*Ecuadorean Packing Plant*] (LA)
FRED .... Frente Revolucionario Estudiantil Democratico [*Democratic Student Revolutionary Front*] [*Venezuelan*] (LA)
FREE .... Fondation Republicaine pour les Etudes a l'Etranger [*Republican Foundation for Study Abroad*] [*Cambodian*] (CL)
Freibl .... Freibleibend [*Optional*] [*Business and trade*] [*German*]
FREJULI ...... Frente Justicialista de Liberacion [*Justicialista Liberation Front*] [*Argentine*] (LA)
FRELIFER ... Front de Liberation de Fernando Poo [*Fernando Poo Liberation Front*] [*Equatorial Guinean*] (AF)
FRELIGE ..... Frente de Liberacion de Guinea Ecuatorial (MAR)
FRELIMO ..... Frente da Libertacao de Mocambique [*Mozambique Liberation Front*] (PPW)
FRELINA ..... Frente de Liberacion Nacional [*National Liberation Front*] [*Bolivian*] (LA1)
FRELINAGE ... Front for the Liberation of the Equatorial Guinean People (AF)
FRELIP .... Frente de Libertacao de Portugal [*Liberation Front of Portugal*] (WER)
FREN .... Frente Revolucionario Estudiantil [*Student Revolutionary Front*] [*Dominican Republic*] (LA1)
FRENA .... Frente de Reivindicacion Nacionalista [*Nationalist Revindication Front*] [*Honduran*] (LA1)
FRENACAIN ... Frente Nacional de Campesinos Independientes [*National Front of Independent Peasants*] [*Honduran*] (LA1)
FRENACAINH ... Frente Nacional de Campesinos Independientes de Honduras [*National Front of Honduran Independent Peasants*] (LA1)
FRENACHODEP ... Frente Nacional de Choferes Revolucionarios, Democraticos, y Progresistas [*National Front of Revolutionary, Democratic, and Progressive Drivers*] [*Dominican Republic*] (LA1)
FRENAP ...... Frente Nacional del Area Privada [*Private Sector National Front*] [*Chilean*] (LA)
FRENAPO ... Frente Nacional y Popular de Liberacion de Guinea Ecuatorial (MAR)
FRENATRACA ... Frente Nacional de Trabajadores y Campesinos [*National Workers and Peasants Front*] [*Peruvian*] (LA)
Frenatraca ... National Front of Workers and Peasants [*Peruvian*] (PD)
FRENU .... Frente Nacional de Unidad [*National Unity Front*] [*Guatemalan*] (PPW)
FREP .... Federacao Revolucionaria dos Estudantes Portugueses [*Revolutionary Federation of Portuguese Students*] (WER)
FREP .... Frente Reformista de Educadores Panamenos [*Reformist Front of Panamanian Educators*] (LA)
FREPA .... Frente Patriotico Anticomunista [*Anticommunist Patriotic Front*] [*Guatemalan*] (LA1)
FRES .... Frente Revolucionario Estudiantil [*Student Revolutionary Front*] [*Colombian*] (LA)
Fres .... Freres [*Brothers*] [*Business and trade*] [*French*]
FRESC .... Frente Revolucionario Estudiantil Social Cristiano [*Christian Social Student Revolutionary Front*] [*Honduran*] (LA)
FRESERH .... Fondation pour la Recherche en Endocrinologie Sexuelle et l'Etude de la Reproduction Humaine
FRETILIN .... Frente Revolucionaria de Timor Leste Independente [*Revolutionary Front for East Timor Independence*] [*Indonesian*] (AF)
FREU .... Frente Revolucionario Estudiantil Universitario [*University Student Revolutionary Front*] [*Guatemalan*] (LA)
FREUCV ...... Frente de Reorganizacion Estudiantil de la Universidad Central de Venezuela [*Student Reorganization Front of the Central University of Venezuela*] (LA)
fr ez .... French Language (BU)
FRF .... Fundusz Rozbudowy Floty [*Fund for the Development of the Fleet*] [*Polish*]
frfr .... Francia Frank [*French Franc*] (HU)
FRG .... Federal Republic of Germany (RU)
FRG .... Fonds de Reconstitution des Gisements [*North African*] (MAR)
FRH .... Federation for Respect for Man and Humanity (MAR)
Frh .... Freiherr [*Baron*] [*German*]
Frhr .... Freiherr [*Baron*] [*German*]
FRI .... Fondo de Refinanciamento Industrial [*Industrial Refinancing Fund*] [*Bolivian*] (LA)
FRI .... Fondo de Rehabilitacion Industrial [*Industrial Rehabilitation Fund*] [*Bolivian*] (LA)
FRI .... Forest Research Institute [*New Zealand*]
FRI .... Frente Revolucionaria de Izquierda [*Left Revolutionary Front*] [*Bolivian*] (PPW)
FRIA .... Compagnie Internationale pour la Fabrication de l'Aluminium (MAR)
FRIB .... Frontline Repair Engineer Base (RU)
FRIBAL .... Frigorifik Balik Ihracat ve Ticaret AS [*Refrigerated Fish Export and Trade Corp*] (TU)
FRIDA .... Fonds de Recherche d'Investissement pour le Developpement de l'Afrique [*Fund for Research and Investment for the Development of Africa*] (AF)
Frie .... Fonderie [*Foundry*] [*Military map abbreviation*] [*World War I*] [*French*] (MTD)
FRIE .... Fondo Rotazione Iniziative Economiche [*Revolving Fund for Economic Initiatives*] [*Italian*] (WER)
FRIGOCA .... Frigorifico de Cartagena [*Cartagena*] (COL)
FRIGOMA .... Societe d'Etudes de Frigorifiques de Mauritanie (MAR)
FRIPUR .... Frigorifico Pesquero Uruguayo [*Uruguayan Fish Cold Storage Company*] (LA)
FRISA .... Fire Research Institute of South Africa (MAR)
FRISA .... Fuel Research Institute of South Africa (MAR)
FRIU .... Frente Revolucionario de la Izquierda Universitaria [*University Leftist Revolutionary Front*] [*Ecuadorean*] (LA)
frk .... Froken [*Miss*] [*Danish*] (GPO)
Frk .... Froken [*Miss*] [*Norwegian*] (GPO)
frk .... Froken [*Miss*] [*Swedish*] (GPO)
Frl .... Fraeulein [*Miss*] [*Title*] [*German*] (GPO)
fr lux .... Luxemburgi Frank [*Luxembourg Franc*] (HU)
FRMAJ .... Federation Royale Marocaine des Auberges de la Jeunesse (MAR)
FRMF .... Federation Royale Marocaine de Football [*Moroccan*] (MAR)
FRMG .... Fundusz Remontow Mlynow Gospodarczych [*Repair Fund for State Mills*] (POL)
FRN .... Federativnaia Respublika Nigeriia (MAR)
FRN .... Frontul Renasterii Nationala [*Front of National Rebirth*] [*Romanian*] (PPE)
FRO .... Faroe Islands [*Three-letter standard code*] (CNC)
FROE .... Fractional Investigation of the Precipitation Test of Erythrocites (RU)
FROLINA ..... Nationale Tchadienne [*Chadian National Liberation Front*] (MAR)
FROLINAT ... Front de Liberation Nationale Tchadienne [*Chadian National Liberation Front*] (AF)
FROLIZI .... Front for the Liberation of Zimbabwe [*Rhodesian*] (AF)
FRONAPE ... Fronta Nacional de Petroleiros [*National Tanker Fleet*] [*Brazilian*] (LA)
FRONASA ... Front for National Salvation [*Ugandan*] (AF)
front .... Frontispiece (RU)
FRP .... Federation des Republicains de Progres [*Federation of Progressive Republicans*] [*French*] (PPW)
FrP .... Franzoesisches Patent [*French Patent*] [*German*]
FRR .... Fundusz Rozwoju Rolnictwa [*Agricultural Development Fund*] (POL)
FRS .... Forces Republicaines de Securite [*Republican Security Forces*] [*Malagasy*] (AF)
frs .... Francs [*French*] (GPO)
FRS .... Fraternitatis Regiae Socius [*Fellow of the Royal Society*] [*Latin*] (GPO)
FRS .... Frente Republicana Socialista [*Republican and Socialist Front*] [*Portuguese*] (PPE)
FRS .... Frente Revolucionario Sandino [*Sandino Revolutionary Front*] [*Nicaraguan*] (LA1)
fr s .... Svajci Frank [*Swiss Franc*] (HU)

FRSKGD...... Fauna Research Section of the Kenya Game Department (MAR)
FRSM.......... Fonds de la Recherche Scientifique Medicale [*Belgian*]
FRT............ Federacion Revolucionaria de Trabajadores [*Revolutionary Workers Federation*] [*Uruguayan*] (LA)
FRTJ........... Federovane Robotnicke Telocyicne Jednotky [*Federated Workers' Athletic and Gymnastic Organizations*] (CZ)
FRTM.......... Filim-Radyo-Televisyon ile Egitim Merkezi [*Film, Radio, Television Training Center*] [*of Education Ministry*] (TU)
FRTP........... Frente Revolucionario de Trabajadores de la Educacion [*Revolutionary Front of Education Workers*] [*Panamanian*] (LA)
FRTU........... Development and Technical Advancement Fund (BU)
FRTU........... Federation of Revolutionary Trade Unions [*Tanzanian*] (AF)
FRU............ Frente de Reforma Universitaria [*University Reform Front*] [*Honduran*] (LA)
FRU............ Frente de Reforma Universitaria [*University Reform Front*] [*Panamanian*] (LA)
FRU............ Frente Revolucionario Universitario [*University Revolutionary Front*] [*Guatemalan*] (LA)
FRUCO........ Frutera Colombiana Ltda. [*Bogota*] (COL)
FRUMF........ Ministry of Finance Financial Auditing Administration (BU)
FRUN.......... Frente Revolucionario Universitario Nacionalista [*Nationalist University Revolutionary Front*] [*Dominican Republic*] (LA1)
FRUS........... Frente Universitario de Estudiantes Socialistas [*Socialist Students University Front*] [*Dominican Republic*] (LA1)
Frw.............. Franc Rwandais (MAR)
fr-yag.......... Fruit and Berry Orchard [*Topography*] (RU)
Frz............... Franzoesisch [*French*] (EG)
FRZ.............. Wage Fund (BU)
FS................ Aircraft Landing Light (RU)
FS................ Faire Suivre [*Please Forward*] [*French*]
fs................. Fajsuly [*Specific Gravity*] (HU)
FS................ Federalni Shromazdeni [*Federal Assembly*] (CZ)
FS................ Fernschreiber [*German*]
FS................ Ferrovie dello Stato [*Italian State Railways*] (WER)
FS................ Filoproodos Syllogos Anthoupoleos - Neas Ionias [*Anthoupolis - Nea Ionia Progressive Association*] [*Greek*] (GC)
FS................ Financni Sprava [*Finance Directorate*] (CZ)
FS................ Financni Straz [*Customs Guards*] (CZ)
FS................ Foyers Sportifs (MAR)
FS................ Funkstelle [*Radio Station, Wireless Station, Sending Station (Radio)*] (EG)
FS................ Glass Light Filter, Violet (RU)
FS................ Resistance Photocell (RU)
FS................ Violet Glass (RU)
FSA............. Fernsehamt [*Television Office*] (EG)
FSA............. Fonds de Solidarite Africain (MAR)
FSA............. Force Syndicale Africaine [*African Trade Union Force*] [*Zairian*] (AF)
FSA............. Front Socialiste Africain (MAR)
FS (Abteilung)... Fernseh-Abteilung [*Television Department*] (EG)
FSAC........... Folia Scientifica Africae Centralis (MAR)
FSAR........... Fonds Special d'Action Rural (MAR)
FSAS........... Food Security Assistance Scheme (MAR)
FSB............. Falange Socialista Boliviana [*Bolivian Socialist Falange*] (PPW)
FSB............. Filmove Studio Barrandov [*Barrandov Film Studios*] (CZ)
FSBI............ Falange Socialista Boliviana de Izquierda [*Bolivian Socialist Falange of the Left*] (PPW)
FSBKM........ Social Services and Cultural Measures Fund (BU)
FSBTI.......... Frontline Armored Equipment Depot (RU)
FSC............. Fabryka Samochodow Ciezarowych [*Truck Factory*] (POL)
FSC............. Faculte des Sciences Commerciales [*Faculty of Commercial Sciences*] [*Cambodian*] (CL)
FSC............. Federacion Socialista de Cataluna [*Socialist Federation of Catalonia*] [*Spanish*] (WER)
FSC............. Federation Socialiste Caledonienne [*Caledonian Socialist Federation*] (PPW)
FSC............. Federation Syndicale du Cameroun [*Trade Union Federation of Cameroon*] (AF)
FSC............. Fonds de Soutien des Changes [*Exchange Support Fund*] [*Use ESF*] [*Cambodian*] (CL)
FSCAI.......... Fonds Special de Credit Agricole Indigene (MAR)
FSCC........... Faisal Siddiq Cricket Club (MAR)
FSCEA........ French-Speaking Comparative Education Association [*See also AFEC*] (EA)
FSD............. Federacion Social-Democrata [*Social Democratic Federation*] [*Spanish*] (WER)
FSD............. Federation des Socialistes Democrates [*Federation of Democratic Socialists*] [*French*] (PPE)
FSD............. Mixed Action Filter [*Nuclear energy*] (BU)
FSDVP......... Freiheitlich Soziale Deutsche Volkspartei [*Liberal Social German People's Party*] [*West German*] (PPW)
Fse.............. Fosse [*Ditch*] [*Military map abbreviation*] [*World War I*] [*French*] (MTD)
f-sek............ Phot-Second (RU)
FSEL........... Frontline Sanitary and Epidemiological Laboratory (RU)
FSF............. Federation Senegalaise de Football (MAR)
FSG............. Federacion Socialista Gallega [*Socialist Federation of Galicia*] [*Spanish*] (WER)
FSG............. Federation Syndicale du Gabon [*Gabonese Trade Union Federation*] (AF)
FSG............. Follicle-Stimulating Hormone (RU)
FSG............. Frontline Fuel Depot (RU)
fsh............... Medical Practitioner (BU)
FShM........... Youth Soccer School (RU)
FSI.............. Federacion Social Independiente [*Independent Social Federation*] [*Spanish*] (WER)
FSI.............. Federation Syndicale Internationale [*French*]
FSI.............. Forces de Securite Interieures [*Lebanese*] (MAR)
FSI.............. Internal Security Forces [*Lebanese*] (ME)
FSJ.............. Fiskulturni Savez Jugoslavije [*Physical Culture Union of Yugoslavia*] (YU)
FSL.............. Shaped Castings Shop (RU)
FSLC........... First School Leaving Certificate Examination (MAR)
FSLN........... Frente Sandinista de Liberacion Nacional [*Sandinista National Liberation Front*] [*Nicaraguan*] (PPW)
FSLUS......... Federazione dei Sindacati Lavoratori Uniti della Somalia [*Somali Federation of United Trade Unions*]
FSM............. Federacion Sindical de Managua [*Trade Union Federation of Managua*] [*Nicaraguan*] (LA1)
FSM............. Federacion Sindical Mundial [*World Federation of Trade Unions - WFTU*] (LA)
FSM............. Federatia Sindicala Mondiala [*World Federation of Trade Unions - WFTU*] (RO)
FSM............. Federation Sephardite Mondiale [*World Sephardi Federation - WSF*] (EA)
FSM............. Federation Syndicale Mondiale [*World Federation of Trade Unions - WFTU*] [*French*] (EA)
FSM............. Federazione Sindacale Mondiale [*World Federation of Trade Unions - WFTU*] [*Italian*] (WER)
FSM............. Fiskulturni Sojuz na Makedonija [*Physical Culture Union of Macedonia*] (YU)
FSMF........... Federation des Syndicats des Travailleurs de la Sante [*Federation of Health Workers' Unions*] [*Malagasy*] (AF)
FSN............. Forestiere et Scierie du Nord (MAR)
FSN............. Funksjonaersambandet i Norge [*Confederation of Salaried Employees of Norway*] (WEN)
FSNP........... Foititikos Syllogos Nikaias Peiraios [*Nikaia, Piraeus Student Club*] (GC)
FSNS........... French-Speaking Neuropsychological Society (EA)
FSO............. Fabryka Samochodow Osbowych [*Automobile Factory*] (POL)
FSO............. Finance and Bookkeeping Department (BU)
FSO............. Funksjonaerenes Sentralorganisasjoh [*Central Organization of Salaried Employees*] [*Norwegian*]
FSOD........... Fakultetsko Sumsko Ogledno Dobro [*College Forestry Experimental Station*] [*Igman*] (YU)
FSODC......... Federacion de Sindicatos de Obreros Democraticos de Colon [*Federation of Unions of Democratic Workers of Colon*] [*Panamanian*] (LA)
FSP............. Free Socialist Party [*Egyptian*] (MAR)
FSP............. Freie Sozialistische Partei [*Free Socialist Party (Pro-Chicom)*] [*West German*] (WEN)
FSP............. Frente Social Progresista [*Progressive Social Front*] [*Ecuadorean*] (PPW)
FSP............. Frente Socialista Popular [*Popular Socialist Front*] [*Portuguese*] (WER)
FSR............. Falange Social Revolucionaria [*Revolutionary Social Falange*] [*Spanish*] (WER)
f sr.............. Fale Srednie [*Medium Waves*] [*Radio*] [*Polish*]
FSR............. Farming Systems Research (MAR)
FSR............. Federacion Sindical Revolucionaria [*Revolutionary Trade Union Federation*] [*Salvadoran*] (LA1)
FSR............. Fotografske Svetlece Rakete [*Photographic Illuminating Rockets*] (YU)
FSR............. Fraccion Socialista Revolucionaria [*Revolutionary Socialist Faction*] [*Panamanian*] (LA)
FSR............. Frente Socialista Revolucionario [*Revolutionary Socialist Front*] [*Venezuelan*] (LA)
FSRA........... Fonds de Soutien de la Revolution Agraire [*Agrarian Revolution Support Fund*] (AF)
FSS............. Fabrique Suisse d'Explosifs
FSS............. Front Sotsialisticheskikh Sil (MAR)
FSSC........... Federation des Syndicats du Service Civile [*Federation of Civil Service Unions*] [*Use FCSU*] [*Mauritian*] (AF)
FSSC........... Federazione Svizzera dei Sindicati Cristiani [*Swiss Federation of National-Christian Trade Unions*]
FSSCN......... Federation Suisse des Syndicats Chretiens-Nationaux [*Swiss Federation of National-Christian Trade Unions*]
FSSP........... Federation des Salaries du Secteur Prive [*South Vietnamese*]
FST............. Federacion Sindical de Trabajadores [*Workers Trade Union Federation*] [*Spanish*] (WER)
Fst.............. Forst [*German*]
f st.............. Pound Sterling (RU)
FSTA........... Food Science and Technology Abstracts [*IFIS*] [*United Kingdom*]
FSTIV.......... Frente de Sindicalistas y Trabajadores Independientes de Venezuela [*Venezuelan Independent Workers and Trade Unionists Front*] (LA)
FSTMB........ Federacion Sindical de Trabajadores Mineros de Bolivia [*Mineworkers Federation of Bolivia*] (LA)

Fstr.............. Foerster [*German*]
FSTSE......... Federacion de Sindicatos de Trabajadores al Servicio del Estado [*Federation of Government Workers Unions*] [*Mexican*] (LA)
FSTT........... Federation Senegalaise des Travailleurs du Transport [*Senegalese Federation of Transportation Workers*] (AF)
FSTU........... Federacion Sindical de Trabajadores Universitarios [*Federation of University Workers*] [*Mexican*] (LA)
FstW............ Forstwirtschaft [*German*]
FSU............. Federalni Statisticky Urad [*Federal Office of Statistics*] (CZ)
FSU............. Freie Soziale Union [*Free Social Union*] [*West German*] (WEN)
FSU............. Freisoziale Union - Demokratische Mitte [*Free Social Union - Democratic Center*] [*West German*] (PPW)
FSU-........... Photoelectric Reader (RU)
FSUJ........... Friedrich-Schiller-Universitaet Jena [*Friedrich Schiller University, Jena*] (EG)
FSV............. Aircraft Telescopic Landing Light (RU)
FSVCI.......... Federation Voltaique du Commerce et de l'Industrie (MAR)
FSVV........... Frontline Engineer Ammunition and Explosives Depot (RU)
FSWU.......... Federation of Sudanese Workers' Unions (MAR)
fsz.............. Foldszint [*Ground Floor*] (HU)
f sz............. Folyo Szam [*Consecutive Number*] (HU)
FSzEK......... Fovarosi Szabo Ervin Konyvtar [*Ervin Szabo Municipal Library (Budapest)*] (HU)
f szla........... Folyo Szamla [*Current Account*] (HU)
fszmstr........ Foszallasmester [*Quartermaster General*] (HU)
fszt............. Foldszint [*Ground Floor*] (HU)
f szt............ Funt Szterling [*or Funty Szterlingi*] [*Pound Sterling*] [*Polish*]
FT............... Filosofian Tohtori [*Finnish*]
FT............... Fondstraeger [*Authorized Funds Investor*] (EG)
FT............... Food Technology (MAR)
Ft................ Foret [*Forest*] [*Military map abbreviation*] [*World War I*] [*French*] (MTD)
Ft................ Forint [*Florin*] [*Hungarian*] (GPO)
Ft................ Fort [*Fort*] [*French*] (NAU)
ft................. Fotanacsos [*Chief Councilor (of a council) or Chief Counselor*] (HU)
ft................. Fotisztelendo [*Right Reverend (Catholic)*] (HU)
ft................. Fountain [*Topography*] (RU)
FT............... Fovarosi Tanacs [*Capital City Council*] (HU)
F de T......... Fulano de Tal [*John Doe*] [*Spanish*]
FT............... Funkentelegraphie [*Radio-Telegraphy*] (EG)
FT............... Technical Photographic Film (RU)
f-t............... University Department or School (BU)
FTA............. Facsimile Equipment, Phototelegraphic Apparatus (RU)
FTA............. Fiches Typologiques Africaines
FTA............. Foreign Trade Association (EA)
FTA............. Free Trade Area (MAR)
FTA............. Phenyltrifluoroacetone (RU)
FTAE........... Fonds Territorial d'Action Economique (MAR)
FTAI............ French Territory of Afars and Issas [*Djibouti*] (AF)
FTB............. Fabrica de Tigari Bucuresti [*Bucharest Cigarette Factory*] (RO)
FTB............. Federation des Travailleurs Burundi [*Federation of Burundi Workers*] (AF)
FTB............. Federation Tunisienne de Boxe (MAR)
FTBB........... Federation Tunisienne de Basketball (MAR)
FTC............. Federacion de Trabajadores del Campo [*Federation of Farm Workers*] [*Salvadoran*] (LA1)
FTC............. Ferencvarosi Torna Club [*Athletic Club of Ferencvaros*] (HU)
FTC............. Foreign Transactions Company [*Iranian*] (ME)
FTC............. Frente de Trabajadores Copeyanos [*Social Christian Workers Front*] [*Venezuelan*] (LA)
FTC............. Frente de Trabajadores de la Cultura [*Cultural Workers Front*] [*Panamanian*] (LA)
FTCCP......... Federacion de Trabajadores en Construccion Civil del Peru [*Peruvian Federation of Civil Construction Workers*] (LA)
FTCV........... Federacion de Trabajadores de Comunicaciones de Venezuela [*Federation of Venezuelan Communication Workers*] (LA)
FTD............. Ferrite-Transistor Levels (RU)
FTD............. Fobeo Timoien Domini [*Fomento el Temor de Dios*] (COL)
FTD............. Foreign Trade Department (MAR)
FTD............. Freve Theofan Diogene [*Hermano Teofano Diogenes*] (COL)
FTD............. Front de Travailleurs du Dahomey (MAR)
FTDF........... Federacion de Trabajadores del Distrito Federal [*Federation of Federal District Workers*] [*Mexican*] (LA1)
FTDM.......... Fikambanany Tanora Demokratikan' i Madagasikara [*Association of Malagasy Democratic Youth*] (AF)
Fte............... Forte [*Fort*] [*Italian*] (NAU)
Fte............... Forte [*Fort*] [*Portuguese*] (NAU)
Fte............... Fuerte [*Fort*] [*Spanish*] (NAU)
FTEC........... Federation des Travailleurs de l'Enseignement et de la Culture [*Federation of Educational and Cultural Workers*] [*Algerian*] (AF)
FTEC........... Federation des Travailleurs des Mines et Carrieres [*Algerian*] (MAR)
FTF............. Faeliesradet for Danske Tjenestemands- og Funktionaerorganisationer [*Joint Council of Civil Servants' and Salaried Employees' Organizations*] [*Danish*] (WEN)
FTF............. Federation Tunisienne de Football (MAR)
FTF............. Funksjonser og Tjeneste Mannsorganisasjonenes Fellesutvalg [*Central Committee of Salaried Employees and Public Servants*] [*Norwegian*] (WEN)
FTG............. Federation of Guatemalan Workers (PD)
FTHB........... Federation Togolaise de Hand-Ball (MAR)
FTHB........... Federation Tunisienne de Handball (MAR)
FThS........... Foititikos Theologikos Syndesmos [*Theological Association of Students*] [*Greek*] (GC)
FTI.............. Foldmero es Talajvizsgalo Iroda [*Surveying and Soil Testing Office*] (HU)
FTI.............. Foreningen Teknisk Information [*Swedish Society on Technical Communication*]
FTI.............. Fundacao de Tecnologia Industrial [*Brazilian*]
FTI.............. Institute of Physiotherapy (RU)
FTI.............. Physicotechnical Institute (RU)
FTIM........... Federacion de Trabajadores de la Industria Metalurgica [*Federation of Metallurgical Industry Workers*] [*Peruvian*] (LA)
FTIP............ Federacion de Trabajadores de la Industria Pesquera [*Federation of Fishing Industry Workers*] [*Venezuelan*] (LA)
FTK............. Filmova Tiskova Korespondence [*Motion Picture Information Bureau*] (CZ)
FTL............. Federal Territory of Lagos (MAR)
FTM............ Confederation des Travailleurs Malgaches (MAR)
FTM............ Federacion de Trabajadores de Managua [*Managua Workers Federation*] [*Nicaraguan*] (LA)
FTM............ Federacion de Trabajadores del Metal [*Metalworkers Federation*] [*Venezuelan*] (LA)
FTM............ Foiben-Taosarintanin'i Madagasikara (MAR)
FTM............ Fondations et Travaux Miniers (MAR)
FTM............ Front des Technicians Malgaches [*Malagasy Technicians Front*] (AF)
FTMMC....... Federacion de Trabajadores Mineros y Metalurgicos del Centro [*Federation of Miners and Metalworkers of the Central Zone*] [*Peruvian*] (LA)
FTMP.......... Federacion de Trabajadores Maritimos de Panama [*Federation of Maritime Workers of Panama*] (LA)
FTMTK........ Fivondronan'ny Tanora Malagasy Tantsaha Katolika [*Movement of Malagasy Catholic Rural Youth*] (AF)
FTN............ Federation Tunisienne de Natation (MAR)
FTN............ Forces Terrestres et Navales (MAR)
FTN............ Frente de Transformacion Nacional [*Bogota*] (COL)
FTNS.......... Frente de Trabajadores Nacional Sindicalista [*National Trade Union Workers Front*] [*Spanish*] (WER)
FTOO.......... Fovarosi Tanacs Oktatasi Osztalya [*Education Department of the Capital City Council*] (HU)
ftorm........... Fotorzsormester [*Master Sergeant*] (HU)
FTP............ Faraday Dark Space (RU)
FTP............ Federacion de Trabajadores Pesqueros [*Fishing Industry Workers Federation*] [*Venezuelan*] (LA)
FTP............ Federacion de Trabajadores Petroleros [*Oil Workers Federation*] [*Venezuelan*] (LA)
FTP............ Federacion de Trabajadores de Pichincha [*Pichincha Workers Federation*] [*Ecuadorean*] (LA)
FTP............ Francs-Tireurs et Partisans [*Guerrillas and Partisans*] [*French*]
FTPB.......... Federacion de Trabajadores de la Prensa [*Bolivian Press Federation of Newspaper Workers*] (LA)
FTPC.......... Francs-Tireurs et Partisans Corses [*Corsican Guerrillas and Partisans*] (PD)
FTPF.......... Francs-Tireurs et Partisans Francais [*French Guerrillas and Partisans*]
FTPP.......... Festiwal Teatrow Polski Polnocnej [*North Poland Theatre Festival*] (POL)
FTR............ Federacion de Trabajadores Revolucionarios [*Revolutionary Workers' Federation*] [*Salvadoran*] (PD)
FTR............ Frente de Trabajadores Revolucionarios [*Revolutionary Workers Front*] [*Chilean*] (LA)
FTRP.......... Federacion de Trabajadores de la Revolucion Peruana [*Federation of Workers of the Peruvian Revolution*] (LA)
FTs............ (Pulse-) Shaping Circuit (RU)
FTsGIA....... Branch of the Central State Historical Archives (RU)
FTsGVIA..... Branch of the Central State Archives of Military History (RU)
f-tsiya......... Function [*Mathematics*] (RU)
FTSKB........ Findik Tarim Satis Kooperatifleri Birligi [*Hazel Nut Agricultural Sales Cooperatives Union*] (TU)
FTsTA......... Branch of Central Technical Archives (RU)
FTT............ Federation Tunisienne de Tennis (MAR)
FTT............ Solid State Physics (RU)
FTU............ Federation des Travailleurs Unis [*United Workers Federation*] [*Mauritian*] (AF)
ftu............. Fotiszteletu [*Right Reverend*] (HU)
FTV............ Filmtechnikai Vallalat [*Phototechnical Enterprise*] (HU)
FTV............ Fovarosi Takarito Vallalat [*Capital Cleaning Enterprise*] (HU)
FTV............ Wage Fund (BU)
FTYa.......... Ferrite-Transistor Cell (RU)
FTYa.......... Ferrite-Triode Cell (RU)
FTZ............ Fernmeldetechnisches Zentralamt [*Telecommunications Central Exchange*] (EG)
Ftza........... Fortaleza [*Fortress*] [*Portuguese*] (NAU)
FU............. Faglige Ungdom [*Trade Union Youth*] [*Danish*] (WEN)

FU........ Filmovy Ustav [*Film Institute*] (CZ)
FU........ Finance Administration (RU)
FU........ Firat Universitei [*Euphrates University*] (TU)
FU........ Foederalistische Union [*Federal Union*] [*West German*] (PPE)
FU........ Freie Union in Niedersachsen [*Free Union in Lower Saxony*] [*West German*] (PPW)
FU........ Freie Universitaet (Berlin) [*Free University (Berlin)*] [*West German*] (WEN)
Fu........ Funk [*Radio*] (EG)
Fu........ Funker [*Radio Operator*] (EG)
FU........ Fysikalni Ustav [*Institute of Physics (of the Czechoslovak Academy of Sciences)*] (CZ)
FU........ Shaping Device (RU)
FUA........ Federacion Universitaria Argentina [*Argentine University Federation*] (LA)
FUA........ Frente Unida Angolana [*Angolan United Front*] (AF)
FUA........ Fund Units of Account (MAR)
FUAAV........ Federation Universelle des Associations d'Agences de Voyages [*Universal Federation of Travel Agents' Associations - UFTAA*] (EA)
FUACE........ Federation Universelle des Associations Chretiennes d'Etudiants [*World Student Christian Federation*] [*Use WSCF*] (AF)
FUAF........ Federation of Uganda African Farmers (MAR)
FUAI........ Front Uni pour l'Autonomie Interne [*United Front for Internal Autonomy*] [*French Polynesian*] (PPW)
FUAJ........ Federation Unie des Auberges de Jeunesse [*United Federation of Youth Hostels*] [*French*] (WER)
FUAN........ Fronte Universitario di Azione Nazionale [*University Front of National Action*] [*Italian*] (WER)
FUAR........ Frente Unido de Accion Revolucionaria [*United Front for Revolutionary Action*] [*Colombian*] (LA)
FUB........ Federacion Universitaria Boliviana [*Bolivian University Students Federation*] (LA)
FUB........ Front de l'Unite Bangala (MAR)
FUBA........ Federacion Universitaria de Buenos Aires [*Buenos Aires University Federation*] [*Argentine*] (LA)
FUC........ Federacion Universitaria de Cordoba [*Cordoba University Federation*] [*Argentine*] (LA)
FUC........ Frente Unico Constitucionalista [*Single Constitutionalist Front*] [*Ecuadorean*] (LA)
FUC........ Frente de Unidad Campesina [*Peasant Unity Front*] [*Honduran*] (LA)
FUC........ Frente de Unidad Clasista [*Class Unity Front*] [*Ecuadorean*] (LA)
FUCA........ Federacion Uruguaya de Cooperativas Agropecuarias [*Uruguayan Federation of Farm Cooperatives*] (LA)
FUCAC........ Federacion Uruguaya de Cooperativas de Ahorro y Credito [*Uruguayan Federation of Savings and Loan Cooperatives*] (LA)
FUCODES... Fundacion Costarricense de Desarrollo [*Costa Rican Development Foundation*] (LA1)
FUCREA........ Federacion Uruguaya de Centros Regionales de Experimentacion Agropecuaria [*Uruguayan Federation of Regional Agricultural and Livestock Experimentation Centers*] (LA)
FUCU........ Fundacion Cultural Universal [*Bogota*] (COL)
FUD........ Frente Voluntario de Defensa [*Voluntary Defense Front*] [*Guatemalan*] (PD)
FUDA........ Frente Unido de Agronomia [*United Front of Agronomy*] [*Panamanian*] (LA)
FUDC........ Frente Universitario Democrata Cristiano [*Christian Democratic University Front*] [*Bolivian*] (LA)
FUDE........ Federacion Universitaria Democratica Espanola [*Spanish Democratic University Federation*] (WER)
FUDECO........ Fundacion para el Desarrollo de la Region Centro Occidental [*Foundation for the Development of the Middle Western Region*] [*Venezuelan*] (LA)
FUDEM........ Federacion Uruguaya de Musicos [*Uruguayan Federation of Musicians*] (LA)
FUDEPA........ Frente Unico de Defensa de la Economia Popular de Arequipa [*United Front for the Defense of the People's Economy of Arequipa*] [*Peruvian*] (LA)
FUDI........ Frente Unido Democratico Independiente [*United Independent Democratic Front*] [*Salvadoran*] (LA)
FUDIC........ Frente Unico de Defensa de los Intereses del Departamento de Cuzco [*United Front for the Defense of the Interests of Cuzco Department*] [*Peruvian*] (LA)
FUDM........ Frente Unida Democratica de Mocambique [*United Democratic Front of Mozambique*] (AF)
FUDP........ Frente de Union Democratica Popular [*Popular Democratic Union Front*] [*Bolivian*] (LA)
FUDUT........ Federacion Uruguaya de Docentes de la Universidad de Trabajo [*Uruguayan Teachers Federation of the Labor University*] (LA)
FUEA........ Frente de Unidad Estudiantil Abelista [*Abelista Student Unity Front*] [*Panamanian*] (LA)
FUECI........ Federacion Uruguaya de Empleados de Comercio e Industria [*Uruguayan Federation of Employees of Commerce and Industry*] (LA)
FUEGO........ Frente Unido del Estudiantado Guatemalteco [*United Front of Guatemalan Students*] (LA)
FUEL........ Flacq United Estates Limited (MAR)
FUEN........ Federal Union of European Nationalities (PPW)
FUEP........ Frente Universitario Estudiantil Progresista [*Progressive University Student Front*] [*Guatemalan*] (LA)
FUER........ Federacion Universitaria de Estudiantes Revolucionarios [*Federation of Revolutionary University Students*] [*Dominican Republic*] (LA1)
FUFEPA........ Fuerza Federalista Popular [*Popular Federalist Force*] [*Argentine*] (LA)
FUFEPO........ Fuerzas Federalistas Populares [*Popular Federalist Forces*] [*Argentine*] (LA)
FUG........ Felderito Uszo Gepkocsi [*Amphibious Reconnaissance Vehicle*] [*Military*] (HU)
FUH........ Fondazione Universale Hallesint [*Italian*]
FUI........ Division for the Advanced Training of Engineers (RU)
FUICO........ Frente Unida para a Independencia dentro la Comunidade (MAR)
FUILA........ Federazione Unitaria Italiana Lavoratori Abbigliamento [*Italian Amalgamated Federation of Garment Workers*]
FUJA........ Frente Unida da Juventude de Angola (MAR)
FUK........ Fabryka Urzadzen Kuziennych [*Forge Equipment Factory*] (POL)
FUK........ Fachunterkommission [*Technical Subcommittee*] (EG)
FUL........ Federacion Universitaria Local [*Local University Federation*] [*Bolivian*] (LA)
FUL........ Frente Unida de Libertacao (MAR)
FUL........ Frente Unido de Liberacion [*United Liberation Front*] [*Colombian*] (LA)
FUL........ Frente Universitario Laboral [*University Labor Front*] [*Chilean*] (LA)
FUL........ Front Uni de Liberation de la Guinee et du Cap Vert (MAR)
FULA........ Frente Unida para a Libertacao de Angola (MAR)
FULC........ Federazione Unitaria Lavoratori Chimici [*Italian union*]
FULN........ Frente Unido de Liberacion Nacional [*United Front of National Liberation*] [*Dominican Republic*] (LA1)
FULNA........ Frente Unido de Liberacion Nacional [*United Front of National Liberation*] [*Paraguayan*] (LA)
FULPARA.... Frente Unitario de Lucha para la Aplicacion de la Reforma Agraria [*Single Front of Struggle for the Enforcement of the Agrarian Reform*] [*Ecuadorean*] (LA)
FULPIA........ Federazione Unitaria Lavoratori Prodotti Industrie Alimentari e dello Zucchero e dell'Alcool [*Amalgamated Federation of Food Processing, Sugar and Liquor Industries' Workers*] [*Italian*]
FULREAC.... Fondation de l'Universite de Liege pour les Recherches Scientifiques en Afrique Centrale [*Foundation of Liege University for Scientific Research in Central Africa*] [*Belgian*] (AF)
FULREAC.... Fondation de l'Universite de Liege pour les Recherches Scientifiques au Congo Belge et au Raunda-Urundi (MAR)
FULRO........ Front Unifie de Lutte des Races Opprimees [*United Front of the Battle for Oppressed Races*] (CL)
FULS........ Federazione Unitaria Lavoratori dello Spettacolo [*Amalgamated Federation of Entertainment Workers*] [*Italian*]
FULZ........ Federacion Universitaria de Lomas De Zamora [*University Federation of Lomas De Zamora*] [*Argentine*] (LA)
FUM........ Fabryka Urzadzen Mechanicznych [*Mechanical Equipment Factory*] (POL)
FUM........ Federacion Uruguaya del Magisterio [*Uruguayan Federation of Primary Teachers*] (LA)
FuM........ Foldmuvelesugyi Miniszterium/Miniszter [*Ministry/Minister of Agriculture*] (HU)
FUM........ Frente de Unidad Magisterial [*Teachers Unity Front*] [*Honduran*] (LA1)
FUM........ Frontul Unic Muncitoresc [*United Workers Front*] (RO)
FUME........ Frente Unido de Mujeres del Ecuador [*United Front of Ecuadorean Women*] (LA)
FUMICOL.... Fumigaciones Colombia Ltda. [*Bogota*] (COL)
FUMN........ Frente Unido del Magisterio Nacional [*National Teachers United Front*] [*Guatemalan*] (LA)
FUMO........ Frente Unida de Mocambique [*Mozambique United Front*] (AF)
FUMOA........ Societe des Futs Metalliques de l'Ouest Africain (MAR)
FUN........ Federacion Universitaria Nacional [*National University Federation*] [*Colombian*] (LA)
FUN........ Fondo Universitario Nacional [*Later, ICFES*] [*Bogota*] (COL)
FUN........ Frente de Unidad Nacional [*National Unity Front*] [*Guatemalan*] (PPW)
FUN........ Frente de Unidad Nacional [*National Unity Front*] [*Venezuelan*] (LA)
FUN........ Frente Unido Nacionalista [*Nationalist United Front*] [*Venezuelan*] (PPW)
FUN........ Frente Unido Nacionalista [*Nationalist United Front*] [*Guatemalan*] (LA)
FUN........ Frente de Universitarios Nacionalistas [*National University Students Front*] [*Bolivian*] (LA)
FUNA........ Frente Unido Nacional Anticomunista [*Anticommunist National United Front*] [*Guatemalan*] (LA)

FUNA.......... Front d'Union Nationale de l'Angola [*National Union Front of Angola*] (AF)
FUNABEM... Fundacao Nacional do Bienestar do Menor [*National Child Welfare Foundation*] [*Brazilian*] (LA)
FUNACAMP ... Frente de Unidad Nacional de Campesinos de Honduras [*National Unity Front of Honduran Peasants*] (LA1)
FUNAGRI .... Fundo Geral para Agricultura e Industria [*General Fund for Agriculture and Industry*] [*Brazilian*] (LA)
FUNAI.......... Fundacao Nacional do Indio [*National Indian Foundation*] [*Brazilian*] (LA)
FUNAI.......... Fundo Nacional de Investimentos [*National Investment Fund*] [*Brazilian*] (LA)
FUNAPER.... Fundicion Andina del Peru, SA [*Peruvian Andean Foundry Enterprise, Inc.*] (LA)
FUNC .... Force de l'Union National Cambodge [*Cambodian*]
FUNCINPEC ... National United Front for an Independent National, Peaceful, and Cooperative Kampuchea (PD)
fund............ Fundador [*Spanish*]
Fund............ Fundeadouro [*Anchorage*] [*Portuguese*] (NAU)
FUNDACOMUN ... Fundacion para el Desarrollo de la Comunidad y Fomento Municipal [*Foundation for Community and Municipal Development*] [*Venezuelan*] (LA)
FUNDAG ..... Fundo de Desenvolvimento Agricola [*Agricultural Development Fund*] [*Brazilian*] (LA)
FUNDAGRO ... Fundo de Desenvolvimento Agropecuario [*Fund for Agriculture and Livestock Development*] [*Brazilian*] (LA)
Fundamentproyekt ... State Institute for the Planning of Foundations and Substructures (RU)
FUNDAPOL ... Fundacion para la Asistencia Social del Policia [*Venezuelan*]
FUNDASE ... Fundo Especial para o Desenvolvimento do Programa Habitacional do Instituto de Previdencia e Assistencia dos Servidores do Estado [*Special Fund for the Development of a Housing Program for the State Employees Social Welfare and Assistance Institute*] [*Brazilian*] (LA)
FUNDE .... Fundacion Nicaraguense de Desarrollo [*Nicaraguan Development Foundation*] (LA1)
FUNDEA...... Fundacion para la Extension Agropecuaria [*Agriculture and Livestock Extension Service*] [*Argentine*] (LA)
FUNDECE ... Fundo de Democratizacao do Capital das Empresas [*Fund for the Democratization of Enterprise Capital*] [*Brazilian*] (LA)
FUNDEFE.... Fundo de Desenvolvimento do Distrito Federal [*Fund for Development of the Federal District*] [*Brazilian*] (LA)
FUNDEPRO ... Fundo de Desenvolvimento da Produtividade [*Fund for Productivity Development*] [*Brazilian*] (LA)
FUNDES...... Fundacion Nacional para el Desarrollo Social [*National Foundation for Social Development*] [*Colombian*] (LA)
FUNDINOR ... Fundo de Desenvolvimento do Nordeste [*Northeast Development Fund*] [*Brazilian*] (LA)
FUNDWI ...... United Nations Fund for West Irian (IN)
FUNFERTIL ... Fundo de Estimulo Financeiro ao Uso de Fertilizantes e Suplementos Minerais [*Fund for Financially Encouraging the Use of Fertilizers and Mineral Supplements*] [*Brazilian*] (LA)
FUNGIRO .... Fundo Especial para o Financiamento de Capital de Giro [*Special Fund to Finance Working Capital*] [*Brazilian*] (LA)
FUNIMAQ.... Fundiciones y Maquinaria SA [*Bucaramanga*] (COL)
FUNINSO .... Fundo de Investimentos Sociais [*Social Investments Fund*] [*Brazilian*] (LA)
FUNIPAMO ... Frente Unida Anti-Imperialista Popular Africana de Mocambique (MAR)
FUNK.......... Front Uni National du Kampuchea [*National United Front of Cambodia*] (CL)
FUNKSN...... Frente de Union Nacional de Kampuchea para la Salvacion Nacional [*Kampuchean National Union Front for National Salvation*] [*Use KNUFNS*] (LA)
FUNOF .... Fundacion para la Orientacion Familiar [*Cali*] (COL)
FUNPROCOP ... Fundacion Promotora de Cooperativas [*Cooperatives Promotion Foundation*] [*Salvadoran*] (LA1)
FUNRES...... Fundo de Recuperacao Economica do Espirito Santo [*Espirito Santo Economic Recovery Fund*] [*Brazilian*] (LA)
FUNRURAL ... Fundo de Assistencia e Previdencia ao Trabalhador Rural [*Fund for Social Assistance and Welfare for the Rural Worker*] [*Brazilian*] (LA)
FUNSA .... Fabrica Uruguaya de Neumaticos, SA [*Uruguayan Tire Plant, Inc.*] (LA)
FUNTAC...... Federacion Unitaria Nacional de Trabajadores Agricolas y Campesinos [*United Agricultural Workers and Peasants Federation*] [*Costa Rican*] (LA)
FUNTEC...... Fundo de Desenvolvimento Tecnico-Cientifico [*Scientific-Technical Development Fund*] [*Brazilian*] (LA)
FUNTEL ...... Fundo Nacional de Telecomunicacoes [*National Telecommunications Fund*] [*Brazilian*] (LA)
FUNTEVE.... Fundo de Financiamento da Televisao Educativa [*Fund for Financing Educational Television*] [*Brazilian*] (LA)
FUNTP......... Frente Unico Nacional de Trabajadores de Prensa del Peru [*Single National Front of Peruvian Press Workers*] (LA)
FUNTRAC ... Federacion Unitaria Nacional de Trabajadores Agricolas y Campesinos [*National Unified Federation of Agricultural Workers and Peasants*] [*Costa Rican*] (LA)
FUNU.......... Forces d'Urgence des Nations-Unies (MAR)
FUP .... Federacion Universitaria del Paraguay [*University Federation of Paraguay*] (LA)
FUP .... Frente de Unidad Popular [*People's Unity Front*] [*Honduran*] (LA1)
FUP .... Frente por la Unidad del Pueblo [*United Popular Front*] [*Colombian*] (PPW)
FUP .... Front de l'Union Populaire [*Peoples Union Front*] [*Moroccan*] (AF)
FUPAC .... Frente Universitaria Privada de America Central [*Central American Private University Front*] [*Nicaraguan*] (LA)
FUPI .... Federacion Universitaria Pro-Independencia de Puerto Rico [*University Federation for Puerto Rican Independence*] (LA)
FUPIT .... Fundo de Pesquisas Industriais e Tecnicas [*Industrial and Technical Research Fund*] [*Brazilian*] (LA)
FUPS........... Fabrica de Utilaje si Piese de Schimb [*Factory for Equipment and Spare Parts*] (RO)
FUR .... Frente Unico de Resistencia [*Single Resistance Front*] [*Chilean*] (LA)
FUR .... Frente Unico Revolucionario [*Single Revolutionary Front*] [*Bolivian*] (LA)
FUR .... Frente de Unidade Revolucionaria [*Front of Revolutionary Unity*] [*Portuguese*] (WER)
FUR .... Frente Unido de la Revolucion [*United Revolutionary Front*] [*Guatemalan*] (PPW)
FUR .... Frente Universitario Revolucionario [*Revolutionary University Front*] [*Honduran*] (LA1)
FUR-30 .... Frente Universitario Revolucionario [*University Revolutionary Front*] [*Salvadoran*] (PD)
FUR-30 .... Frente Universitario Revolucionario 30 de Julio [*30 July Revolutionary University Front*] [*Salvadoran*] (LA1)
FURD.......... Frente Unido Revolucionario Democratico [*United Revolutionary Democratic Front*] [*Guatemalan*] (LA)
FURE.......... Frente Universitario Reformista Ecuatoriano [*Ecuadorean University Reformist Front*] (LA)
FURF .... Federation des Unions Royalistes de France [*Federation of Royalist Unions of France*] (PPW)
FURFA......... Fureszaru es Faanyag Nagykereskedelmi Vallalat [*Wood and Lumber Wholesale Trade Enterprise*] (HU)
FURR.......... Frente Universitario Radical Revolucionario [*Revolutionary Radical University Front*] [*Dominican Republic*] (LA1)
FUS .... Fakultni Umelecky Soubor [*Faculty Art Ensemble*] (CZ)
FUS .... Federacion Uruguaya de Sanitarios [*Federation of Uruguayan Sanitary Workers*] (LA)
FUS .... Filmovy Umelecky Sbor [*Motion Picture Artistic Ensemble*] (CZ)
FUS .... Fondo Unido de Solidaridad [*United Solidarity Front*] [*Spanish*] (WER)
FUS .... Frente de Unidad Sindical [*United Labor Front*] [*Bolivian*] (LA)
FUS .... Front Uni du Sud [*Southern United Front*] [*Chadian*] (AF)
FUS .... Frontul Unitatii Socialiste [*Front of Socialist Unity*] [*Romanian*] (PPE)
FUSD.......... Frente Universitario Socialista Democratico [*Socialist Democratic University Front*] [*Dominican Republic*] (LA1)
FUSE.......... Frente Unido Socialista Espanol [*Spanish Socialist United Front*] (WER)
FUSEP......... Fuerza de Seguridad Publica [*Public Security Force*] [*Honduran*] (LA1)
FuSf .... Fortsetzung und Schluss Folgen [*To Be Continued and Concluded*] [*German*]
FUSM .... Federacion Universitaria de San Marcos [*San Marcos University Students Federation*] [*Peruvian*] (LA)
FUSNA .... Fusileros Navales [*Naval Riflemen Corps*] [*Uruguayan*] (LA)
FUSS .... Federacion Unitaria de Sindicatos Salvadorenos [*Single Federation of Salvadoran Trade Unions*] (LA)
FUSZERT .... Fuszer Ertekesito Allami Vallalat [*State Retail Grocery Enterprise*] (HU)
FUT .... Fabryka Urzadzen Technicznych [*Technical Equipment Factory*] (POL)
FUT .... Federacion Unificada de Trabajadores [*Unified Federation of Workers*] [*Venezuelan*] (LA)
FUT .... Frente Unitario de Trabajadores [*Single Workers Front*] [*Ecuadorean*] (LA)
fut.............. Futeral [*Case*] [*For a Book*] (POL)
FUTC.......... Federacion Unica de Trabajadores Campesinos [*Single Federation of Peasant Workers*] [*Bolivian*] (PD)
FUTE .... Frente Unico de Trabajadores y Estudiantes [*Single Front of Workers and Students*] [*Peruvian*] (LA)
FUTEUNI..... Frente Unico de Trabajadores y Estudiantes de la Universidad Nacional de Ingenieria [*Single Front of UNI Workers and Students*] [*Peruvian*] (LA)
FUTH.......... United Workers' Front of Honduras (PD)
FUTI .... Fovarosi Epitoipari Uzemgazdasagi es Ugyviteli Iroda [*Capital Construction Industry Business Administration and Management Office*] (HU)
Futt............. Futteral [*Case*] [*German*]
FUTU.......... Federation of Uganda Trade Unions (AF)
FUU .... Federacion de Universitarios de Uruguay [*Federation of University Students of Uruguay*] (PD)
FUUD.......... Frente Unido Universitario Democratico [*United University Students Democratic Front*] [*Honduran*] (LA)

fuv .... Fuvarozas [*Transport*] (HU)
FUVA .... Federacion Unica de Viajantes de la Republica Argentina [*Single Federation of Traveling Salesmen of Argentina*] (LA)
FuW .... Funkwerk [*Radio Communications Equipment Plant*] (EG)
fuz .... Fuzet [*Issue, Number (Periodicals), or Fascicle*] (HU)
fuz .... Fuzott [*or Fuzve*] [*Paperbound*] (HU)
FUZ .... Street Public Address System Feeder Lines (RU)
FV .... Fahrdienstvorschriften [*Train Service Regulations*] (EG)
FV .... Farmacevtski Vestnik [*Pharmaceutical Review*] [*Ljubljana*] (YU)
Fv .... Farni Vestnik [*Parish Bulletin*] (CZ)
fv .... Felelos Vezeto [*Chief, Manager*] (HU)
fv .... Folio Verso [*On the Back of the Leaf*] [*Latin*] (GPO)
FV .... Phase Equalizer (RU)
FVA .... Filter-Ventilation System (BU)
FVA .... Filtration and Ventilation Unit (RU)
FVB .... Federale Volksbeleggings [*Federal People's Investment*] [*South African*] (AF)
FVB .... Foiskolai Vilagbajnoksag [*World Championships of University Students*] (HU)
FVCh .... High-Pass Filter (RU)
FVD .... Federalni Vybor pro Dopravu [*Federal Committee for Transportation*] (CZ)
fvda .... Favorecida [*Esteemed*] [*Spanish*]
FVerfO .... Familienrechtsverfahrensordnung [*Code of Family Law Procedure*] (EG)
FVJ .... Federation Mondiale des Villes Jumelees [*North African*] (MAR)
FVK .... Filter-Ventilation Chamber [*Air-raid shelter*] (BU)
FVK .... Filter-Ventilation Set (BU)
FVK .... Filtration and Ventilation Chamber (RU)
Fvk .... Flugverkehr [*German*]
FVK .... Photographic Vertical Circle (RU)
FVK .... Searched Channel [*Navy*] (RU)
FVL .... Frontline Veterinary Hospital (RU)
FVM .... Farm for Raising Young Animals (RU)
FVM .... Federacion Venezolana de Maestros [*Venezuelan Teachers Federation*] (LA)
FVM .... Fovarosi Vizmuvek [*Capital Water Works*] (HU)
FVM .... Viet-Nam Youth Federation [*North Vietnamese*] (RU)
FVP .... Federalni Vybor pro Prumysl [*Federal Committee for Industry*] (CZ)
FVP .... Freie Volkspartei [*Free People's Party*] [*West German*] (PPE)
FVPT .... Federalni Vybor pro Posty a Telekomunikace [*Federal Committee for Postal Affairs and Telecommunications*] (CZ)
FVR .... Federal Department of Veterinary Research (MAR)
FVS .... Frontline Clothing and Equipment Depot (RU)
FVTIR .... Federalni Vybor pro Technicky a Investicni Rozvoj [*Federal Committee for Technical and Investment Development*] (CZ)
FVV .... Fovarosi Vasutepito Vallalat [*Capital Railway Construction Enterprise*] (HU)
FVV .... Fovarosi Villamos Vasut [*Capital Electric Railways*] (HU)
FVVA .... Femmes, Voiture, Villa, Argent (MAR)
FVYa .... Division of Oriental Languages (RU)
FVZV .... Federalni Vybor pro Zemedelstvi a Vyzivu [*Federal Committee for Agriculture and Food*] (CZ)
Fw .... Fermeldewerkstatt [*Communications Shop*] (EG)
FW .... Front Walfougui [*Walfougui Front*] [*Mauritanian*] (AF)
Fw .... Fuerwort [*German*]
FWACP .... Fellowship Examinations of the West African College of Physicians (MAR)
FWCC .... Federation of West African Chambers of Commerce (MAR)
FWCC .... Friends World Committee for Consultation (EA)
FWI .... Federation of Women's Institutes (MAR)
FWK .... Funkwerk Koepenick VEB [*Koepenick Radio Factory VEB*] (EG)
FWP .... Fundusz Wczasow Pracowniczych [*Workers' Vacation Fund*] (POL)
FWVO .... Finanzwirtschafts-Verordnung [*Fiscal Regulations*] (EG)
FYa .... Formalized Language (RU)
FYDEP .... Empresa Nacional de Fomento y Desarrollo Economico del Peten [*National Agency for the Economic Promotion and Development of El Peten*] [*Guatemalan*] (LA)
FYeBO .... Federation of European Biochemical Societies (RU)
fys .... Fysiikka [*Physics*] [*Finnish*]
fysiol .... Fysiologia [*Physiology*] [*Finnish*]
f-z .... Factory (RU)
FZ .... Filmove Zpravodajstvi [*Motion Picture Information Service*] (CZ)
FZ .... Fundusz Ziemi [*Land Fund*] (POL)
FZA .... Fratsuzkaia Zapadnaia Afrika (MAR)
FZAG .... Frontline Antiaircraft Artillery Group (RU)
FZH .... Fond Znarodneneho Hospodarstvi [*Fund of the Nationalized Economy*] (CZ)
FZhP .... Animal Protein Factor (BU)
FZhYeL .... Forced Vital Capacity (RU)
FZK .... Factory Committee (RU)
FZKI .... Front Zashchity Konstitutsionnykh-Institutov (MAR)
FZM .... Feldzeugmeister [*German*]
FZO .... Factory Training (RU)
FZR .... Fundusz Zasilkow Rodzinnych [*Family Allowance Fund*] (POL)
FZS .... Factory-Plant Construction (BU)
FZS .... Factory Seven-Year (School) (RU)
FZSh .... Factory-Plant Course (BU)
FZSZ .... Fovarosi Zeneiskola Szervezet [*Capital Music Education Institute*] (HU)
FZT .... Photographic Zenith Telescope (RU)
FZTs .... Factory-Plant Prices (BU)
FZU .... Factory-Plant School (BU)
FZU .... Factory Training (RU)
FZU .... Factory Training School (RU)
FZZ .... Health Insurance Fund (BU)

G

g .... Annual Issue [*Periodicals and newspapers*] (BU)
G................. Bitter Water [*Topography*] (RU)
G................. Gakushi [*Japanese*]
g .... Gaseous, Gasiform (RU)
G................. Gasse [*German*]
g .... Gatan [*Street*] [*Swedish*] (CED)
g .... Gate [*Street*] [*Norwegian*] (CED)
G................. Gavan' [*Harbour, Basin*] [*Russian*] (NAU)
G................. Gebel [*Mountain, Hill*] [*See also Geb*] [*Arabic*] (NAU)
G................. Gedeckter Gueterwagen [*Covered Freight Car (Usually a boxcar)*] (EG)
G................. Gegensatz [*German*]
G................. Gendarm [*or Gendarmerie*] [*German*]
G................. Genie [*French*] (MTD)
G................. Gesellschaft [*Company*] [*German*]
g .... Godina [*Year*] (YU)
g .... Godzina [*or Godziny*] [*Hour or Hours*] [*Polish*]
g .... Goetu [*Gate, Street*] [*Icelandic*] (CED)
G................. Gol [*Lake*] (TU)
G................. Golf [*Gulf*] [*Dutch*] (NAU)
G................. Golfe [*Gulf*] [*French*] (NAU)
G................. Golfo [*Gulf*] [*Italian*] (NAU)
G................. Golfo [*Gulf*] [*Portuguese*] (NAU)
G................. Golfo [*Gulf*] [*Spanish*] (NAU)
G................. Gora [*Mountain*] [*Polish*]
G................. Gora [*Mountain, Hill*] [*Russian*] (NAU)
G................. Gracia [*Favor*] [*Spanish*]
G................. Grado [*Academic degree*] [*Spanish*]
G................. Graduat [*French*]
G................. Gram (BU)
g .... Gram [*Gram*] (POL)
g .... Gram (RU)
G................. Gramm [*Gram*] (EG)
g .... Gramm [*Gram*] (HU)
g .... Gramma [*or Grammaa*] [*Finnish*]
g .... Gramme [*Gram*] [*French*]
g .... Gramo [*Gram*] [*Spanish*]
g .... Group (BU)
g .... Guberniya [*1708-1929*] (RU)
G................. Gueterzuglokomotive [*Freight Train Locomotive*] (EG)
G................. Guney [*South*] (TU)
G................. Gwatemala [*Guatemala*] [*Polish*]
g .... Mister (RU)
G................. Mountain [*Topography*] (RU)
g .... Mrs., Madame (RU)
G................. Town, City (RU)
g .... Year (BU)
g .... Year (RU)
GA .... City Archives (BU)
GA .... Civil Aviation (RU)
GA .... Gabon [*Two-letter standard code*] (CNC)
Ga .... Gawa [*River*] [*See also Ka*] [*Japanese*] (NAU)
GA .... General Assembly of the United Nations (MAR)
GA .... Geografiska Annaler [*Stockholm*] [*A publication*] (MAR)
GA .... Geomagnetism and Aeronomy (RU)
ga .... Gepagyu [*Automatic Gun*] (HU)
GA .... Gesellschaft fuer Arsneipflanzenforschung [*Society for Medicinal Plant Research*] (EA)
GA .... Glucosamine (RU)
GA .... Groupe d'Armees [*Military*] [*French*] (MTD)
GA .... Grundaufbauplan [*Basic Development Plan*] (EG)
GA .... Grupo Andino [*Andean Group*] (LA)
Ga .... Guba [*Bay, Inlet, Creek*] [*Russian*] (NAU)
Ga .... Gueterabfertigung [*Freight Office*] (EG)
GA- .... Gyro Assembly (RU)
ga .... Hectare (RU)
GA .... Howitzer Artillery (RU)
GA .... Mountain Artillery (RU)
GA .... State Archives (RU)
GAA .... Groupement Aeronautique et Automobile (MAR)
GAA .... Groupement Atomique Alsacienne Atlantique [*French*]
GAAAU .... Ghana Association of Alumni of American Universities (MAR)
GAAF .... Grupo de Accao Antifascista [*Antifascist Action Group*] [*Portuguese*] (WER)
GAAO .... Gorno-Altay Autonomous Oblast (RU)
GAArkh obl ... State Archives of the Arkhangel'sk Oblast (RU)
GAAstr obl ... State Archives of the Astrakhan' Oblast (RU)
GAB .... Gabon [*Three-letter standard code*] (CNC)
GAB .... Gabungan [*Association, Group, Joint (Staff), Combined (Operations)*] (IN)
GAB .... Gaestelijk Arbeidsbureau [*Regional Labor Bureau*] [*Dutch*] (WEN)
GAB .... Gepipari Allando Bizottsag [*Standing Committee for the Machine Industry (CEMA)*] (HU)
GAB .... Gesellschaft fuer Ausland Beteiligungen (MAR)
GAB .... Gewestelijk Arbeids Bureau [*Dutch*]
GABAL .... Societe Anonyme Immobiliere du Gabon (MAR)
GABELEC ... Gabonaise d'Electricite (MAR)
GABEXFO ... Gabonaise d'Exploitation Forestiere (MAR)
GABHOTELS ... Grands Hotels du Gabon (MAR)
GABIDOC.... Gespreksgroep Archief, Bibliotheek, Documentatie [*Dutch*]
GABIM .... La Gabonaise Immobiliere (MAR)
GABMIT ...... Gabungan Minjak Tanah [*Petroleum Association*] (IN)
GABOA .... Societe Gabonaise d'Oxygene et d'Acetylene (MAR)
GABOMA .... Societe Gabonaise de Grands Magasins (MAR)
GABONAP... Societe Gabonaise de Diffusion d'Appareils Electriques (MAR)
GABONEX... Societe Gabonaise d'Exploitation Vinicole (MAR)
GABOSEP ... Societe Gabonaise de Sepulture (MAR)
gabr............ Howitzer Artillery Brigade (BU)
GABr .... Howitzer Artillery Brigade (RU)
GABT .... State Academic Large Theater of the USSR [*The Bol'shoy*] (RU)
GABTRANS ... Societe Gabonaise de Transports Internationaux (MAR)
GABTU .... Main Directorate of the Armored Troops (RU)
GAC .... Groupe d'Armees du Centre [*Military*] [*French*] (MTD)
GAC .... Grupo de Accion Catala [*Catalan Action Group*] [*Spanish*] (WER)
GAC .... Grupo Anti-Comunista [*Anticommunist Group*] [*Brazilian*] (LA)
GAC .... Guyana Airways Corporation (LA1)
GACO .... La Gabonaise de Construction (MAR)
GAD .... Groupes d'Auto Defense [*Algerian*] (MAR)
GADASE ..... Gazete Dagiticilari Sendikasi [*Newspaper Distributors Union*] (TU)
GADC .... Gulf Agriculture Development Company (MAR)
GAD-IS .... Gaziantep Dikim Isciler Sendikasi [*Gaziantep Millinery (Thread) Workers Union*] (TU)
GADIS .... Societe Gabonaise de Distribution (MAR)
GADIT .... Groupement Algerien des Industries Textiles (MAR)
GADNA .... Youth Battalions [*Israeli*] (ME)
GAE .... Grupo Anticomunista Espanol [*Spanish Anti-Communist Group*] (WER)
GAE .... Grupos Armados Espanoles [*Armed Spanish Groups*] (PD)
GAEC .... Groupement Agricole d'Exploitation en Commun [*French*]
GAES .... Pumped-Storage Electric Power Plant (RU)
GAF .... State Archives Fund (RU)
GAFCICO .... Societe Generale Africaine de Genie Civil et de Constructions (MAR)
GAFI .... State Astrophysical Institute (RU)
GAFIC .... Ghana All Forces Inner Council (MAR)
GAFKE .... State Archives of the Age of Feudalism and Serfdom (RU)
GAFOR .... Societe Gabonaise de Forage (MAR)
GAFS .... Civilian Aerial Photography (RU)
GAG .... Azimuth Gyro Horizon (RU)
GAG .... Ganzzug [*Through-Freight Train with Specific Load with One or Few Points of Origin and One or Few Points of Destination*] (EG)
GAGI .... State Institute of Obstetrics and Gynecology (RU)
GAGO .... Gor'kiy Astronomical and Geodetic Society (RU)
GAG obl ...... State Archives of the Gor'kiy Oblast (RU)
GAGP .... Generale Africaine du Genie et de la Promotion (MAR)
GAHAL .... Right-Wing Combination of Herut Movement and Liberal Party [*Israeli*] (ME)

GAI .... City Automobile Inspection (RU)
GAI .... Grupos Autonomos de Intervencion [*Autonomous Interventionist Groups*] [*Spanish*] (WER)
GAI .... State Automobile Inspection (RU)
GAIBANK .... Guyana Agricultural and Industrial Development Bank (LA1)
GAID .... Ghana Agricultural and Industrial Development Ltd. (MAR)
GAIF .... General Arab Insurance Federation (MAR)
GAIL .... Guyana Agricultural Industries Limited (LA)
GAIM .... Greek-Arab Investment Meeting (MAR)
GAIMK .... State Academy of the History of Material Culture (RU)
GAIRLAC .... Groupement d'Achat, d'Importation, et de Repartition des Laits de Conserves (MAR)
GAIS .... State Academy for the Study of Art (RU)
GAISh .... State Astronomical Institute Imeni P. K. Shternberg (RU)
GAIT .... Guatemalan Association of Interpreters and Translators
GAIZ .... State Antireligious Publishing House (RU)
GAIZ .... State Astronomical Publishing House (RU)
GAK .... Astatic Quartz Gravimeter (RU)
GAK .... Gendarmerieabteilungskommando [*German*]
GAKalinin obl ... State Archives of the Kalinin Oblast (RU)
GAKAS .... Gabungan Kepala Staf [*Joint Chiefs of Staff*] (IN)
GAKhN .... State Academy of Arts (RU)
GAKhO .... State Archives of Khar'kov Oblast (RU)
GAKK .... State Archives of Krasnodar Kray (RU)
GAKursk obl ... State Archives of the Kursk Oblast (RU)
GAKuyb obl ... State Archives of the Kuybyshev Oblast (RU)
gal .... Galerie [*French*] (CED)
gal .... Galon [*Gallon*] [*Polish*]
GAL .... Gdynia-Ameryka Linia [*Gdynia-America Line*] (POL)
Gal .... General [*General*] [*French*] (MTD)
GAL .... Gibraltar Airways Limited (MAR)
GAL .... Gioventu Araba del Littorio (MAR)
GAL .... Gravimeter of the Aerogravimetric Laboratory (RU)
GAL .... Grupos Armados Libertarios [*Armed Libertarian Groups*] [*Spanish*] (PD)
gal .... Notions Industry Factory [*Topography*] (RU)
GALA .... Guyana Association of Local Authorities (LA)
GALF .... Groupement des Acousticiens de Langue Francaise [*Group of French-Speaking Acousticians*] (EA)
GALIAF .... Societe Gaz Liquefies de l'Afrique (MAR)
Galie .... Galerie [*Gallery*] [*Military map abbreviation*] [*World War I*] [*French*] (MTD)
galkul'tpromsoyuz ... Union of Producers' Cooperatives of the Notions Industry and Goods for Cultural Purposes (RU)
gall .... Galleria [*Italian*] (CED)
Gall Prak ..... Gallikon Praktoreion [*French Press Agency*] (GC)
GAM .... Garnizonowa Administracja Mieszkaniowa [*Garrison Housing Administration*] (POL)
GAM .... Groupe d'Action Municipale [*French*]
GAM .... Guyana Association of Musicians (LA)
GAM .... State Antireligious Museum [*Leningrad*] (RU)
GAMA .... Gadjah Mada [*University in Jogjakarta*] (IN)
Gama .... Gdanska Agencja Morska i Asekuracyjna [*Gdansk (Danzig) Maritime and Insurance Agency*] (POL)
GAMag obl ... State Archives of the Magadan Oblast (RU)
GAMD .... Generale Aeronautique Marcel Dassault [*Swiss*]
GAMEDA ..... Gazete-Mecmua Dagitim Ltd. Sti. [*Newspaper and Periodicals Distribution Corp.*] (TU)
GAMEFA ..... Ghana-American Friendship Association (MAR)
GAMK .... Gamma-Aminobutyric Acid (RU)
GAMKI .... Gerakan Angkatan Muda Keristen Indonesia [*Indonesian Christian Youth Movement*] (IN)
GAML .... City Model Aircraft Laboratory (RU)
GAMO .... Groupement Administratif Mobile [*Mobile Administrative Unit*] [*Cambodian*] (CL)
GAMS .... Civil Air Weather Station (RU)
GAMS .... Groupement pour l'Avancement des Methodes Spectroscopiques et Physicochimiques d'Analyse [*French*]
GAMS .... Main Air Weather Station (RU)
GAMSEN ..... Turkiye Garanti Bankasi AS Mensuplari Sendikasi [*Turkish Guarantee Bank Corp. Employees Union*] (TU)
GAMT .... State Academic Small Theater (RU)
GAMTs .... Main Air Weather Center (RU)
GAN .... Generalauftragnehmer [*General Contractor*] (EG)
GAN .... Georgian Academy of Sciences (RU)
GAN .... German Academy of Sciences [*East German*] (BU)
GAN .... Groupe d'Armees du Nord [*Military*] [*French*] (MTD)
GANC .... Groupe d'Action Nationale Camerounaise [*Cameroonian National Action Group*]
GANEFO ..... Games of the New Emerging Forces (CL)
GANIDE .... Gestion-Animation-Developpement (MAR)
GANO .... Grupos de Accion Nacionalista Oriental [*Groups for Uruguayan Nationalist Action*] (LA)
GANUPT ..... Groupe d'Assistance Militaire et Civile des Nations Unies pour la Periode de Transition (MAR)
GAO .... Main Astronomical Observatory (of the Academy of Sciences, USSR) (RU)
GAOCMAO ... Gulf Area Oil Company Mutual Aid Organization (MAR)
GAOR .... General Assembly Official Records (MAR)
GAOR .... State Archives of the October Revolution (RU)
GAOreno obl ... State Archives of the Orenburg Oblast (RU)
GAOR LO .... State Archives of the October Revolution and of the Building of Socialism of the Leningrad Oblast (RU)
GAOR MO ... State Archives of the October Revolution and of the Building of Socialism of the Moscow Oblast (RU)
GAORSS ..... State Archives of the October Revolution and of the Building of Socialism (RU)
GAP .... Grosshandelsabgabepreis [*Wholesale Price*] (EG)
GAP .... Groupement d'Action Populaire [*People's Action Group*] [*Upper Voltan*] (AF)
GAP .... Groupement d'Action Progressiste [*Progressive Action Group*] [*Belgian*] (WER)
GAP .... Groupement des Aides Privees (MAR)
GAP .... Groupement Associe de Producteurs (MAR)
GAP .... Grupo de Amigos Personales [*Group of Personal Friends*] [*Chilean*] (LA)
GAP .... Grupo de Auto-Defensa [*Self-Defense Group*] [*Uruguayan*] (PD)
GAP .... Gruppo d'Azione Partigiana [*Partisan Action Group*] [*Italian*] (WER)
GAP .... Guards Air Regiment (RU)
GAP .... Howitzer Artillery Regiment (BU)
GAP .... Howitzer Artillery Regiment (RU)
GAP .... Main Administration of the Aniline Dye Industry (RU)
GAP .... "Pravda" Newspaper Plant (RU)
GAPA .... Guyana Agricultural Producers Association (LA)
GAPBM .... Heavy Howitzer Artillery Regiment (RU)
GAPE .... Guyana Association of Professional Engineers (LA)
GAPEI .... Gabungan Pengusaha Ekspor Indonesia [*Association of Indonesian Exporters*] (IN)
GAPENI .... Gabungan Pengusaha Nasional Indonesia [*Indonesian National Businessmen's Association*] (IN)
GAPEX .... General Agricultural Products Export Corporation [*Tanzanian*] (AF)
GAPHI .... Guyana Association of Public Health Inspectors (LA)
GAPI .... Societe Gabonaise d'Armement et de Peche Industrielle (MAR)
gapl .... Haploid (RU)
GAPS .... Grupo Autonomo do Partido Socialista [*Autonomous Group of the Socialist Party*] [*Portuguese*] (WER)
GAPU .... Main Architectural and Planning Administration (RU)
GAPU .... Main Pharmaceutical Administration (RU)
gar .... Garage [*Topography*] (RU)
gar .... General [*Artillery*] (BU)
GAR .... Grand Axe Routier (MAR)
GAR .... Grupos de Accion Revolucionaria [*Revolutionary Action Groups*] [*Venezuelan*] (LA)
GAR .... Grupos de Accion Revolucionaria [*Revolutionary Action Groups*] [*Spanish*] (WER)
GAR .... Gruppi Armati Radicali per il Comunismo [*Armed Radical Groups for Communism*] [*Italian*] (PD)
Gar .... Gueteraussenring [*Outer Freight Ring*] [*Berlin*] (EG)
GARI .... Groupe d'Action Revolutionnaire Internationaliste [*Group of International Revolutionary Action*] [*French*] (PD)
GARI .... Grupo de Accion Revolucionaria Internacional [*International Revolutionary Action Group*] [*Spanish*] (WER)
GARIM .... Groupe Militaire Aerien de la Republique Islamique de Mauritanie [*Military Air Group of the Islamic Republic of Mauritania*] (AF)
GARKI .... Gabungan Remilling Karet Indonesia [*Indonesian Rubber Remilling Association*] (IN)
Garkreba ..... Garantie- und Kreditbank [*Guarantee and Credit Bank*] (EG)
GARNOCI .... Groupement d'Amenagement des Routes du Nord-Ouest de la Cote-d'Ivoire (MAR)
GARO .... Garage Equipment Plant (RU)
GARO .... Trust for the Manufacture of Garage Equipment (RU)
GARost obl ... State Archives of the Rostov Oblast (RU)
GAROZ .... State Artillery Weapons Factory (RU)
GARP .... Global Atmospheric Research Program (AF)
GARS .... Main Ammunition Depot (RU)
GARyaz obl ... State Archives of the Ryazan' Oblast (RU)
GARZ .... State Automobile Repair Plant (RU)
GAS .... Advanced Air Depot (RU)
GAS .... Advanced Ammunition Depot (RU)
GAS .... Autonomous Anarchist Groups [*Spanish*] (PD)
GAS .... Gabinete da Area de Sines [*Sines Area Council*] [*Portuguese*] (WER)
GAS .... Geological Association of Students (MAR)
GAS .... Ghana Academy of Sciences (MAR)
GAS .... Groupement Aerien Senegalais (MAR)
GAS .... Groupement des Aviculteurs du Senegal (MAR)
GAS .... Grupo de Accion Sindicalista [*Trade Union Action Group*] [*Spanish*] (WER)
GAS .... Hydroxylamine Sulfate (RU)
GAS .... Main Air Depot (RU)
GAS .... Main Ammunition Depot (RU)
GAS .... State Administrative Council [*Chinese People's Republic*] (RU)
GASBIINDO ... Gabungan Serikat Buruh Islam Indonesia [*Indonesian Moslem Labor Union Federation*] (IN)
GASC .... Grupo al Servicio de Cataluna [*Catalan Service Group*] [*Spanish*] (WER)
GASCARB ... Productora de Gas Carbonico [*Venezuelan*]
GASCO .... Gasolinera Colombiana [*Bogota*] (COL)

GASCOL ..... Gaseosas Colombianas SA [*Bogota*] (COL)
Gasentw ...... Gasentwicklung [*Evolution of Gas*] [*German*]
GASK .... State Architectural and Construction Control (RU)
GASKhN ..... Georgian Academy of Agricultural Sciences (RU)
GASP .... Gas and Oil Separation Plant [*Arab*] (MAR)
GASPEKRI ... Gabungan Serikat Pekerdja Keristen [*Federation of Christian Labor Unions*] (IN)
GASSOMEL ... Groupement des Associations Mutuelles de l'Empire Lunda (MAR)
GASSR .... Mountain Autonomous Soviet Socialist Republic [*1921-1924*] (RU)
GAST .... Grenzaufsichtsstelle [*Border Control Point*] (EG)
Gastrol'byuro ... Theatrical Tour Office (RU)
GasV .... Gasilski Vestnik [*Fire Prevention Review*] [*Ljubljana*] [*A publication*] (YU)
GAT .... Address-Current Generator [*Computers*] (RU)
gat .... Gatunek [*Sort*] [*Polish*]
GAT .... Gefechtsaufklaerungstruppe [*Combat Reconnaissance Unit*] (EG)
g-at .... Gram Atom (RU)
GAT .... Groupe des Assurances de Tunisie (MAR)
GAT .... Groupement Africain de Travaux (MAR)
GAT .... Hypersonic Wind Tunnel (RU)
GAT .... State Academic Theater (RU)
GATA .... Gabinete de Agencias e Trabalhos de Agrimensura (MAR)
GATA .... Gulhane Askeri Tip Akademisi [*Gulhane Academy of Military Medicine*] [*Ankara*] (TU)
GATE .... Gambia Association of Teachers of English (MAR)
GATE .... German Appropriate Technology Exchange [*West German*]
GATE .... Global Atlantic Experiment (AF)
GAT-ELS ..... Gas Turbine Electric Power Plant (RU)
GATKh .... Trucking Establishment (RU)
GATOB .... Leningrad State Academic Theater of Opera and Ballet Imeni S. M. Kirov (RU)
g-atom .... Gram Atom (RU)
g-atom .... Gramoatom [*Gram Atom*] [*Polish*]
GATRA .... Gabungan Sasterawan Sedar [*Association of Enlightened Writers*] (ML)
GATRAC ..... Garages et Transports Commerciaux (MAR)
GATRAMAR ... Societe Gabonaise de Transports Maritimes (MAR)
GATs .... Automatic Centralized Switching Control [*Railroads*] (RU)
GATS .... City Automatic Telephone Exchange (RU)
GATT .... General Agreement on Tariffs and Trade
GATTA .... Ghana Association of Travel and Tourist Agents (MAR)
GAU .... Groesster Anzunehmender Unfall [*Worst Conceivable (Nuclear) Accident*] [*West German*] (WEN)
GAU .... Groupement d'Architecture et d'Urbanisme (MAR)
GAU .... Grupos de Accion Unificadora [*Groups for Unified Action*] [*Uruguayan*] (PD)
GAU .... Main Archives Administration (RU)
GAU .... Main Artillery Directorate (RU)
gaub .... Howitzer (BU)
gaub .... Howitzer (RU)
Gaux .... Generaux [*Generals*] [*French*]
GAV .... Gabor Aron Vasontode es Gepgyar [*Aron Gabor Iron Foundry and Machine Factory*] (HU)
gav .... Harbor [*Topography*] (RU)
GAVB .... Main Air Base (RU)
GAVlad obl ... State Archives of the Vladimir Oblast (RU)
GAVolog obl ... State Archives of the Vologda Oblast (RU)
GAVTU .... Main Automobile Administration (RU)
GAWI .... Deutsche Foerderungsgesellschaft fuer Entwicklungslaender (MAR)
GAWU .... Guyana Agricultural and General Workers Union (LA)
GAY .... Guyana Assembly of Youth (LA)
GAYaPEY .... Group of Algorithmic Languages for the Processing of Economic Information (RU)
GAYE .... Gemicilik, Armatorluk, ve Yapim Endustrisi Sanayi ve Ticaret Limited Sirketi [*Shipbuilding, Shipowner, and Construction Industry and Trade Corp.*] (TU)
GAZ .... Automobile Made by the Gor'kiy Automobile Plant (RU)
Gaz .... Gas Plant [*Topography*] (RU)
gaz .... Gas Well [*Topography*] (RU)
GAZ .... Gor'kiy Automobile Plant (RU)
GAZ .... Gruene Aktion Zukunft [*Green Action for the Future*] [*West German*] (PPW)
gaz .... Newspaper (RU)
GAZ .... State Aircraft Plant (RU)
gazd .... Gazdasag [*Agriculture, Economy*] (HU)
gazd .... Gazdasagi [*Agricultural, Economic*] (HU)
GAZDEP ...... Kozepmagyarorszagi Epitesi Vallalat [*Central Hungarian Construction Enterprise*] (HU)
Gazete .... Gazetesi [*Newspaper*] (TU)
gazg .... Gasholder, Gas Tank [*Topography*] (RU)
gazoobr .... Gaseous, Gasiform (RU)
Gazoochistka ... All-Union Trust of Electrical, Chemical, and Mechanical Gas Purification (RU)
gazopr .... Gas Pipeline [*Topography*] (RU)
GAZT .... Gemeinsamer Aussenzolltarif [*Common External Tariff*] (EG)
GB .... Gazdasagi Bizottsag [*Economic Committee*] (HU)
GB .... Gencler Birligi [*Youth Union*] [*Soccer team*] [*Cypriot*] (TU)
GB .... Genossenschaftlicher Betrieb [*Cooperative Enterprise*] (EG)
gb .... Gilbert (RU)
GB .... Great Britain [*United Kingdom*] [*Two-letter standard code*] (CNC)
GB .... Grosses Balles [*Boite a mitraille*] [*Military*] [*French*] (MTD)
gb .... Gulf, Bay (RU)
GB .... Main Base (RU)
GB .... State Library (RU)
GB .... State Security (RU)
GBA .... Army Hospital Base (RU)
GBA .... Generalbundesanwalt [*Chief Federal Prosecutor*] [*West German*] (WEN)
GBA .... Gesetzbuch der Arbeit [*Labor Code*] (EG)
GBAE .... Ghanaian Bulletin of Agricultural Economics [*Accra*] [*A publication*] (MAR)
GBAO .... Gorno-Badakhshan Autonomous Oblast (RU)
gbar .... Howitzer Artillery (BU)
GBB .... Gerakan Buruh Bahari [*Maritime Workers Movement*] (IN)
GBB .... Guild of British Butlers (EA)
GB/BHE ...... Gesamtdeutscher Block/Bund der Heimatvertriebenen und Entrechteten [*All-German Bloc/Association of Homeless and Disenfranchised*] (PPE)
GBBI .... Annals of the Bulgarian Bibliographic Institute [*A publication*] (BU)
GBC .... General Border Committee (Thai-Malaysian) (ML)
GBC .... Ghana Broadcasting Corporation (MAR)
GBC .... Groupe de Brancardiers de Corps [*Military*] [*French*] (MTD)
GBC .... Gulf Boycott Coalition (MAR)
GBC .... Guyana Broadcasting Corporation (LA)
GbD .... Gradska Biblioteka u Dubrovniku [*City Library in Dubrovnik*] (YU)
GBD .... Groupe de Brancardiers Divisionnaires [*Military*] [*French*] (MTD)
gbdn .... Gebunden [*Bound*] [*German*]
GBDT .... Leningrad State Large Dramatic Theater Imeni M. Gor'kiy (RU)
GBF .... Frontline Hospital Base (RU)
Gbf .... Gueterbahnhof [*Railroad Freight Station*] [*German*] (WEN)
GBG .... Grande Boulangerie du Gabon (MAR)
GBGPGS ..... Groupe Bakounine-Gdansk-Paris-Guatemala-Salvador [*Bakunin-Gdansk-Paris-Guatemala-Salvador Group*] [*French*] (PD)
Gbh .... Geburtshilfe [*German*]
GBH .... Gesellschaft fuer Betriebsberatung des Handels [*Society for Commercial Management Consultants*] (EG)
GBI .... Godisnjak Balkanoloskog Instituta [*Yearbook of the Balkan Institute*] [*Sarajevo*] (YU)
GBI .... Gridlays Bank International Zambia Ltd. (MAR)
GBI .... Groupement des Bois Ivoiriens (MAR)
GBI .... Groupement Brigade d'Infanterie [*Infantry Brigade Group*] [*Cambodian*] (CL)
GBI .... State Library Institute (RU)
GBIAD .... Annals of the Bulgarian Society of Engineers and Architects [*A publication*] (BU)
GBIL .... State Library of the USSR Imeni V. I. Lenin (RU)
GBK .... Grenzbrigade Kueste [*Coastal Border Brigade (Part of border command)*] (EG)
GBl .... Gesetzblatt [*Legal Gazette*] (EG)
GBL .... State Library Imeni V. I. Lenin (RU)
GBMM .... State Library-Museum of V. V. Mayakovskiy (RU)
GBNO .... State Library for Public Education Imeni K. D. Ushinskiy (RU)
gbor .... Howitzer (BU)
GBP .... Baltic State Steamship Line (RU)
GBP .... Groupement Brigade Parachutiste [*Parachute Brigade Group*] [*Cambodian*] (CL)
GBP .... Guinea-Bissau Peso (MAR)
GBP .... Ponomarev Hydraulic Swab [*Artillery*] (RU)
GBPA .... Grand Bahama Port Authority (LA1)
GBPDP .... Garrison Bath, Laundry, and Disinfection Station (RU)
gbr .... Gebraeuchlich [*Used Commonly*] [*German*]
gbr .... Gebraeunt [*Burned*] [*German*]
GBR .... Gibberellin (RU)
GBR .... Godolloi Buzatermelesi Rendszer [*Godollo Wheat Growing System*] (HU)
GBR .... Grupo Bandera Roja [*Red Flag Group*] [*Dominican Republic*] (LA)
GBR .... United Kingdom [*Three-letter standard code*] (CNC)
GBS .... Gokkusagi Boya Sanayii [*Gokkusagi Paint Industry*] [*A subsidiary of Sanayi Holding*] [*Turkish Cypriot*] (GC)
GbS .... Gradska Biblioteka u Splitu [*City Library in Split*] (YU)
GBS .... Guyana Broadcasting Service (LA)
GBS .... Main Botanical Garden (of the Academy of Sciences, USSR) (RU)
GBS .... Sofia City Library (BU)
GBSU .... Guyana Bauxite Supervisors Union (LA1)
GBTU .... Main Directorate of Armored Forces (RU)
GBV .... Gueter-Befoerderungs-Vorschriften [*Freight Transportation Regulations*] (EG)
GC .... General Command (MAR)
GC .... Gloria Combativa [*Combat Glory (Cuban military units)*] (LA)
GC .... Grand Champ [*Broad Field*] [*French*] (WER)
GC .... Grand-Croix [*Awarded by the Legion of Honor*] [*French*] (MTD)

GC .... Guardia Civil [*Civil Guard*] [*Peruvian*] (LA)
GCA .... Global Citizens Association (EA)
GCA .... Grenada Cocoa Association (LA1)
GCA .... Groupe des Confiseurs Africains (MAR)
GCA .... Guyana Consumers Association (LA)
GCADC .... Grupo Coheteril Antiaereo de la Defensa de la Capital [*Antiaircraft Missile Group for the Defense of the Capital*] [*Cuban*] (LA)
Gcal .... Gigakalorien [*Gigacalories*] (EG)
GCB .... Ghana Commercial Bank (MAR)
GCC .... Gulf Cooperation Council [*Arabian*] (MAR)
GCD .... Ghana Consolidated Diamonds Ltd. (MAR)
GCE .... General Certificate of Education (MAR)
GCE .... General Certificate Examination (MAR)
GCEI .... Gemeentelijk Centrum voor Elektronische Informatieverwerking [*Amsterdam*]
GCFA .... Groupement Commercial Franco-Africain (MAR)
GCFA .... Guyana Cane Farmers Association (LA1)
GCFI .... Comptoir d'Exportation du Groupement des Commercants Francais Independants (MAR)
GCFL .... Garde Cotiere, Fluviale, et Lacustre [*Coast, River, and Lake Guard*] [*Zairian*] (AF)
GCHC .... Ghana Cargo Handling Company (MAR)
GChZ .... State Clock Plant (RU)
GCI .... Genie Climatique International (EA)
GCIB .... Grenada Cocoa Industry Board (LA1)
GCIC .... Groupement Cinematographique International de Conciliation (EA)
GCIRC .... Groupe Consultatif International de Recherches sur le Colza [*International Consultative Research Group on Rape - ICRGR*] (EA)
GCL .... General Confederation of Labor in Lebanon (MAR)
GCLW .... General Confederation of Lebanese Workers (MAR)
GCM .... Grande Confiserie du Mali (MAR)
GCMB .... Ghana Cocoa Marketing Board (MAR)
GCNA .... Grenada Cooperative Nutmeg Association (LA1)
GCP .... Gambia Congress Party (MAR)
GCP .... Ghana Congress Party (MAR)
GCR .... Gruppi Comunisti Rivoluzionari [*Communist Revolutionary Groups*] [*Italian*] (WER)
GCR .... Guerrilleros de Cristo Rey [*Guerrillas of Christ the King*] [*Spanish*] (WER)
GCRAI .... Groupe Consultatif de la Recherche Agricole Internationale (MAR)
GCRG .... Groupe de Compagnies de Reserve du Genie [*Algerian*] (MAR)
GCSA .... Government Clerical Service Association [*Mauritian*] (AF)
GCSI .... Societe d'Importation-Exportation du Groupement des Commercants Senegalais Independants (MAR)
GCTA .... Groupe de Canevas de Tir des Armees [*Military*] [*French*] (MTD)
GCU .... Guyana Cooperative Union (LA1)
GCV .... Glavni Centar Veze [*Chief Communications Center*] [*Military*] (YU)
GD .... Advance Party Point (RU)
GD .... Airtight Door (RU)
GD .... Dynamic Loudspeaker (RU)
GD .... Freight Yard (RU)
GD .... Gambia Dalasi (MAR)
gd .... Gazdasagi (Hivatal) [*Paymaster's Office*] [*Military*] (HU)
Gd .... General Der [*German*]
GD .... Generaldirektion [*General Directorate, General Manager's Office*] (EG)
GD .... Geografsko Drustvo [*Geographic Society*] [*Belgrade*] (YU)
GD .... Germanium Diode (RU)
GD .... Gordulocsapagygyar, Debrecen [*Roller Bearing Plant, Debrecen*] (HU)
Gd .... Grand [*Large*] [*Military map abbreviation*] [*World War I*] [*French*] (MTD)
GD .... Grenada [*Two-letter standard code*] (CNC)
GD .... Grossdimension [*Large Size, Oversize*] (EG)
Gd .... Grund [*Shoal*] [*See also Grd*] [*Danish*] (NAU)
Gd .... Grund [*Shoal*] [*See also Grd*] [*German*] (NAU)
Gd .... Grund [*Shoal*] [*See also Grd*] [*Swedish*] (NAU)
GD .... Horizontal Range (RU)
GD .... Main Marine Engine (RU)
GD .... Mining [*Encyclopedic Handbook*] [*A publication*] (RU)
GD .... Motor-Generator Set (RU)
GD's .... Grupas Dinamizadores (MAR)
gda .... Garda [*Guards, Bodyguard*] (HU)
G-da .... Gentlemen (BU)
g-da .... Gospoda [*Mrs.*] (YU)
g-da .... Messieurs [*Plural of Mister*] (RU)
GDACI .... Grupo de Deteccao, Alerta, e Conduta de Intercepcao [*Detection, Alert, and Interception Group*] [*Portuguese*] (WER)
GDB .... Gabonskii Demokraticheskii Blok (MAR)
GDB .... Glavna Direkcija Brodogradnje [*General Administration of Shipbuilding*] (YU)
Gdb .... Grundbesitzer [*German*]
GDBH .... Gesellschaft Deutscher Berg- und Huettenleute [*Society of German Miners and Metallurgists*] (EG)
GDC .... Groupe des Democrates Camerounais [*Cameroonian Democratic Group*]
GDCh .... Gesellschaft Deutscher Chemiker
GDCI .... Gaz de Cote-d'Ivoire (MAR)
GDCP .... Glavna Direkcija Cestnega Prometa [*General Administration of Road Transport*] (YU)
GDD .... Geniki Dioikisis Dodekanisou [*General Administration of the Dodecanese*] (GC)
GDD .... Gocmen Dayanisma Dernegi [*Immigrant's Solidarity Association*] (TU)
GDDA .... General Desert Development Authority [*Egyptian*] (MAR)
GDDD .... Geniki Dievthynsis Dimosias Dioikiseos [*General Directorate of Public Administration*] [*Greek*] (GC)
GDE .... Gabinete de Dinamizacao do Exercito [*Army Morale Office*] [*Portuguese*] (WER)
Gde .... Gemeinde [*German*]
gde .... Guarde [*Spanish*]
GDE .... Main Directorate of Electrification (BU)
GDEA .... Geniki Dievthynsis Ethnikis Asfaleias [*Later, YPEA*] [*General Directorate of National Security*] [*Greek*] (GC)
GDELRS ...... Generalna Direkcija za Elektrogospodarstvo Ljudska Republika Slovenija [*General Administration of the Electrical Industries of Slovenia*] (YU)
GDEZ .... Generalna Direkcija za Eksploatacijo Zeleznic [*General Administration for the Utilization of Railroads*] (YU)
GDEZ .... Glavna Direkcija Eksploatacije Zeleznica [*General Administration for the Utilization of Railroads*] (YU)
GDF .... Gaz de France [*French Gas Company*] (WER)
GDF .... Geniki Dievthynsis Forologias [*General Directorate of Taxation*] [*Greek*] (GC)
GDF .... Guanosine Diphosphate (RU)
GDF .... Guyana Defense Force (LA)
GDFG .... Guanosine Diphosphate Glucose (RU)
GdF(S) .... Gesellschaft der Freunde der Sowjetunion [*Society of Friends of the Soviet Union*] (EG)
Gdg .... Grossgueterwagenzug [*Train Consisting of Large Freight Cars*] (EG)
GDH .... Gesellschaft Deutscher Huettenleute [*Society of German Metallurgists*] (EG)
GDIPPTPP ... Main Directorate of Publishing Houses, the Printing Industry, and Trade in Printed Matter (BU)
GDJDRS ...... Glavna Direkcija Jugoslovenskog Drzavnog Recnog Saobracaja [*General Administration of Yugoslav State River Traffic*] (YU)
GDJZ .... Generalna Direkcija Jugoslovanskih Zeleznic [*General Administration of Yugoslav Railroads*] (YU)
GDK .... Group Decontamination Kit (RU)
GDKh .... Main Food Supply Directorate (BU)
GDKP .... Geniki Dievthynsis Kyvernitikis Politikis [*General Directorate of Government Policy*] [*Greek*] (GC)
GDL .... Gas Dynamics Laboratory [*1928-1934*] (RU)
GDM .... Gdanska Dzielnica Mieszkaniowa [*Gdansk (Danzig) Residential District*] (POL)
GDM .... Gibraltar Democratic Movement (PPE)
GDM .... Grunwaldzka Dzielnica Mieszkaniowa [*Grunwald Residential District*] (POL)
GDM .... Lead Vehicle of an Advance Party (RU)
GDO .... Gdanska Dyrekcja Odbudowy [*Gdansk (Danzig) Administration of Reconstruction*] (POL)
GDO .... Government Diamond Office (MAR)
GDOIFK .... State Twice Decorated Institute of Physical Culture Imeni P. F. Lesgaft (RU)
GDP .... Generalna Direkcija Posta [*General Administration of the Postal Service*] (YU)
GDP .... Geniki Dievthynsis Programmatismou [*General Directorate of Planning*] [*Greek*] (GC)
GDP .... Gesamtdeutsche Partei [*All-German Party*] [*West German*] (PPE)
GDP .... Ghana Democratic Party (AF)
GDP .... Grafeion Dimosion Plirofórion [*Public Information Office*] [*Greek*] (GC)
GDP .... Gross Development Product (MAR)
GDP .... Main Dispatcher's Station (RU)
GDPA .... Geniki Dievthynsis Politikis Amynis [*Civil Defense General Directorate*] [*Greek*] (GC)
GDPB .... General Department of Publications and Broadcasting (MAR)
GDPTT .... Generalna Direkcija Posta, Telegrafa, i Telefona [*General Administration of Postal, Telegraph, and Telephone Service*] (YU)
GDR .... Generaldirektion der Reichsbahn [*General Directorate of the GDR Railroad*] (EG)
GDR .... German Democratic Republic (BU)
GDR .... German Democratic Republic (RU)
GDRI .... Main Directorate of Radio Information (BU)
GDRS .... Glavna Direkcija Recnog Saobracaja [*General Administration of River Traffic*] (YU)
GDRZ .... State House of Broadcasting and Sound Recording (RU)
GDS .... City Disinfection Station (RU)
GDS .... Generaldirektion Schiffahrt [*General Directorate for Navigation*] (EG)
GDS .... Main Directorate of Construction (BU)

GDS............ Main Statistical Directorate (BU)
GDSF.......... Gesellschaft fuer Deutsch-Sowjetische Freundschaft [*German-Soviet Friendship Society*] (EG)
GDSh.......... Large Smoke Pot [*Military*] (BU)
GDSP.......... Guardia Distrital de Seguridad Publica [*District Police Force*] [*Bolivian*] (LA)
GDSS.......... Gabonskii Demokraticheskii i Sotsialnyi Soiuz (MAR)
GDSSI......... General Department for State Security Investigations [*Egyptian*] (ME)
GDT............ Geniki Dievthynsis Takhydromeion [*General Directorate of Post Offices*] [*Greek*] (GC)
GDTA.......... Groupement pour le Developpement de la Teledetection Aerospatiale [*Group for Development of Aerospace Teledetection*] [*French*] (WER)
GDTP.......... Geniki Dievthynsis Typou kai Pliroforion [*General Directorate of Press and Information*] [*Greek*] (GC)
GDU............ Gas-Arc Unit (RU)
GDU............ Grupos de Delegados de Unidade [*Unit Delegates' Group*] [*Portuguese*] (WER)
GDU............ State Far Eastern University (RU)
GDUP.......... Generalna Direkcija Unutrasnje Plovidbe [*General Administration of Inland Navigation*] (YU)
GDUP.......... Grupos de Dinamizacao e Unidade Popular [*Popular Unity Activation Groups*] [*Portuguese*] (WER)
Gduz........... Geografska Duzina [*Geographic Longitude*] (YU)
GDVE.......... Geniki Dioikisis Voreiou Ellados [*General Administration of Northern Greece*] (GC)
GdVP........... Grossdeutsche Volkspartei [*Pan-German People's Party*] [*Austrian*] (PPE)
GDVUFAN... Annals of the Higher State School of Finance and Administration [*A publication*] (BU)
GDZ............ Hydrodynamic Component (RU)
GDZ............ State House of Sound Recording (RU)
Gdzh........... Gigajoule (RU)
GE.............. Getreideeinheit [*Grain Unit*] (EG)
GE.............. Gewichtseinheit [*Unit of Weight*] [*German*]
GE.............. Gilbert Islands [*Two-letter standard code*] (CNC)
GE.............. Grafeio Eparkhion [*Office of the Provinces*] [*Greek*] (GC)
GE.............. Grupo Especial [*Special Group*] [*Mozambican*] (AF)
GE.............. Mining Electromechanics (RU)
GE.............. Publishing House of the State Hermitage (RU)
GE.............. State Hermitage (RU)
GEA............ Gambia Employers' Association (MAR)
GEA............ Genikon Epiteleion Aeroporias [*Air Force General Staff*] [*Greek*] (GC)
GEAC.......... German East Africa Company (MAR)
GEACAP..... Grupo Especial para Assuntos de Calamidade Publica [*Special Group for Handling Public Disasters*] [*Brazilian*] (LA)
GEAR.......... Generacion de Empleo en el Ambito Rural [*Generation of Employment in Rural Areas*] [*Peruvian*] (LA)
GEAST........ Groupe d'Etude et d'Action Socialiste Tunisien (MAR)
Geb............ Gebel [*Mountain, Hill*] [*See also G*] [*Arab*] (NAU)
geb............ Gebildet [*Educated*] [*German*]
geb............ Gebonden [*Bound*] [*Dutch*] (GPO)
geb............ Geboren [*Born*] [*Dutch*] (GPO)
geb............ Geboren [*Born*] [*German*] (GPO)
Geb............ Gebrueder [*Brothers*] [*German*]
geb............ Gebunden [*Bound*] [*German*] (GPO)
GEB............ Hemato-Encephalic Barrier, Blood-Brain Barrier (RU)
gebr........... Gebraucht [*Used, Secondhand*] [*German*]
Gebr........... Gebroeders [*Brothers*] [*Dutch*] (GPO)
Gebr........... Gebrueder [*Brothers*] [*German*] (GPO)
Gec............ Gecici [*Temporary*] (TU)
GEC............ Gradska Elektricna Centrala [*City Electric Power Plant*] (YU)
GEC............ Groupes d'Etudes Communistes (MAR)
GEC............ Guyana Electricity Corporation (LA)
GECACI...... Generale Cafeiere et Cacaoyere de Cote-d'Ivoire (MAR)
GECAM....... Gerencia de Operacoes de Cambio (do Banco Central) [*Exchange Operations Directorate*] [*Brazilian*] (LA)
GECAMINES... Generale des Carrieres et des Mines [*General Quarries and Mines Company*] [*Zairian*] (AF)
GECAN........ Grupo Executivo do Carvao Nacional [*National Coal Executive Group*] [*Brazilian*] (LA)
GECh.......... Standard-Frequency Pulse Generator (RU)
GECICAM... Entreprise de Genie Civil et Construction au Cameroun [*Cameroon Civil Engineering and Construction Company*] (AF)
GECOMA.... Groupement d'Action Economique Malgache [*Malagasy Economic Action Group*] (AF)
GECOMIN... Generale Congolaise des Minerais [*Congolese*]
GECRI......... Gerencia de Coordenacao do Credito Rural e Industrial [*Management of Rural and Industrial Credit Coordination*] [*Brazilian*] (LA)
GED............ Electric Paddle-Wheel Engine (RU)
GED............ Guanidoethyldisulfide (RU)
GEDC.......... Groupement d'Etudes pour le Developpement du Cameroun (MAR)
GEDEO........ Groupement d'Equipement et d'Outillage [*Central African*] (MAR)
GEDM.......... Groupement d'Etude pour le Developpement de la Mauritanie (MAR)
GEDPA........ Genikon Epiteleion Dioikiseos Politikis Amynis [*Civil Defense General Administrative Staff*] [*Cypriot*] (GC)
GeDPA/Khoras... Geniki Dievthynsis Politikis Amynis tis Khoras [*General Directorate of National Civil Defense*] [*Greek*] (GC)
GEE............ Gazi Egitim Enstitusu [*The Gazi Training Institute*] [*Ankara*] (TU)
GEE............ Gaziantep Egitim Enstitusu [*Gaziantep Training Institute*] (TU)
GEE............ Geotekhnikon Epimelitirion Ellados [*Geotechnical Chamber of Greece*] (GC1)
GEE............ Grafeion Evreseos Ergasias [*Employment Office*] (GC)
GEEF.......... Genikon Epiteleion Ethnikis Frouras [*National Guard General Staff*] [*Cypriot*] (GC)
GEEI........... State Experimental Electrotechnical Institute (RU)
GEERS........ Groupe d'Etudes Europeen des Recherches Spatiales
GEES.......... Gulf Energy and Environmental Systems (MAR)
GEEThA...... Genikon Epiteleion Ethnikis Amynis [*National Defense General Staff*] [*Greek*] (GC)
gef............ Gefaelligst [*Kindly*] [*German*] (GPO)
Gef............ Gefaells [*German*]
Gef............ Gefechts [*Fighting, Engagement, Combat, Battle*] (EG)
gef............ Gefunden [*Found*] [*German*]
GEFAR........ Groupement d'Interets Economiques d'Exportateurs (MAR)
GEFFA........ Gesellschaft fuer Forstliche Arbeitswissenschaft
gefl........... Gefalligst [*Kindly, Please*] [*Correspondence*] [*German*]
GEFLI......... Groupement d'Etudes Francais en Libye (MAR)
GEFO.......... Gesellschaft fuer die Foerderung des Ost-West Handels [*Society for the Advancement of East-West Trade*] (EG)
Gef P.......... Gefrierpunkt [*Freezing Point*] [*German*]
geg............ Gegen [*Against*] [*German*]
Gegenw...... Gegenwart [*Presence*] [*German*]
gegr........... Gegruendet [*Founded*] [*German*] (GPO)
geh............ Geheftet [*Stitched*] (EG)
GehKaem.... Geheimkaemmerer [*German*]
GEI............ Gosudorstvenuse Energeticheskoe Izdatel'stvo
GEI............ State Economic Publishing House (RU)
GEI............ State Scientific and Technical Power Engineering Publishing House (RU)
GEICINE...... Grupo Executivo da Industria Cinematografica [*Executive Group of the Motion-Picture Industry*] [*Brazilian*] (LA)
GEII........... Geographic and Economic Research Institute (RU)
GEIMA........ Grupo Executivo da Industria da Mecanica Aeronautica [*Executive Group of the Aviation Mechanics Industry*] [*Brazilian*] (LA)
GEIMAC...... Grupo Executivo da Industria de Materias de Construcao Civil [*Executive Group of the Building Materials Industry*] [*Brazilian*] (LA)
GEIME........ Grupo Executivo da Industria de Mineracao [*Executive Group of the Mining Industry*] [*Brazilian*] (LA)
GEIMEC...... Grupo Executivo das Industrias Mecanicas [*Executive Group of the Mechanical Industries*] [*Brazilian*] (LA)
GEIMET...... Grupo Executivo da Industria Metalurgica [*Executive Group of the Metallurgical Industry*] [*Brazilian*] (LA)
GEIMOT...... Grupo Executivo da Industria Automotora [*Executive Group of the Automotive Industry*] [*Brazilian*] (LA)
GEINEE....... Grupo Executivo das Industrias Eletrica e Eletronica [*Executive Group of the Electrical and Electronics Industry*] [*Brazilian*] (LA)
GEIPAG....... Grupo Executivo da Industria do Papel e Artes Graficas [*Executive Group of Paper and Graphic Arts Industry*] [*Brazilian*] (LA)
GEIPAL....... Grupo Executivo da Industria de Produtos Alimentares [*Executive Group of the Food Industry*] [*Brazilian*] (LA)
GEIPOT....... Grupo Executivo de Estudos de Integracao da Politica de Transportes [*Executive Group for Study of Transportation Integration Policy*] [*Brazilian*] (LA)
GEIQUIM..... Grupo Executivo da Industria Quimica [*Executive Group of the Chemical Industry*] [*Brazilian*] (LA)
GEIS........... State Experimental Institute of Silicates (RU)
GEITEX....... Grupo Executivo das Industrias de Fiacao e Tecelagem [*Executive Group of the Spinning and Textile Industries*] [*Brazilian*] (LA)
GEITs.......... Main Computer Center (BU)
gek............ Gekocht [*Boiled*] [*German*]
gek............ Gekuerzt [*Abridged, Abbreviated*] (EG)
GEK............ Geniki Epitropi Katanomon [*General Apportionment Committee*] (GC)
GEKMOA.... Grafeion Elengkhou Kataskevon Monimon Odostromaton Athinon [*Office for the Control of Construction of Athens Permanent Road Pavement*] (GC)
GEKO.......... Grafeion Elengkhou Kataskevis Odon [*Road Construction Control Office*] [*Followed by initial letter of district name*] [*Greek*] (GC)
geksag........ Hexagonal (RU)
geksagon.... Hexagonal (RU)
geksag s..... Hexagonal Syngony (RU)
geksatetraedr... Hexatetrahedral (RU)
geksoktaedr... Hexoctahedral (RU)
GEKTEMAS... State Experimental Theatrical Workshops (RU)
g-ekv.......... Gram Equivalent (RU)
GEL............ Gabinete Electrotecnico Lda. (MAR)
gel............ Geloest [*Dissolved*] [*German*]

GEL .... General Enterprise Limited (MAR)
GEL .... Gilbert Islands [*Three-letter standard code*] (CNC)
GEL .... Grafeion Ergasias Limenos [*Labor Office of the Port Of*] [*Followed by district name*] (GC)
GEL .... Guerrilla del Ejercito Libertador [*Liberation Army Guerrillas*] [*Argentine*] (LA)
GELAN .... Laboratory of Helminthology of the Academy of Sciences, USSR (RU)
gelat .... Gelatinoes [*Gelatinous*] [*German*]
GELKA .... Gepipari Elektromos Karbantarto Vallalat [*Electrical Maintenance Enterprise of the Machine Industry*] (HU)
GELNA .... Groupe d'Etudes sur la Litterature Neo-Africaine (MAR)
GELP .... Groupement d'Exploitation de Laboratoire Photo-Cinema (MAR)
gem .... Gemahlen [*Powdered*] [*German*]
Gem .... Gemeinde [*German*]
gem .... Gemischt [*Mixed*] [*German*]
GEM .... Glasnik Etnografskog Muzeja [*Bulletin of the Ethnographic Museum*] [*Belgrade*] [*A publication*] (YU)
GEM .... Gnomodotiki Epitropi Meleton [*Advisory Committee on Studies*] (GC1)
GEM .... Groupe d'Etudes Meroitiques de Paris (MAR)
GEM .... Groupes Evangile et Mission [*Institute of the Heart of Jesus - IHJ*] (EA)
GEM .... Groupeurs d'Export du Maroc (MAR)
GEMA .... Gerakan Mahasiswa [*College Student Movement*] (IN)
GEMA .... Gesellschaft fuer Musikalische Auffuehrungs- und Mechanische Vervielfaeltigungsrechte [*Society for Musical Performance Rights and Rights of Mechanical Reproduction*] (EG)
GEMA .... Gikuyu-Emba-Meru Association [*Kenyan*] (AF)
GEMADA ..... Groupement des Entreprises de Manutention du Dahomey (MAR)
GEMAS .... Genel Muhendislik ve Mimarlik Anonim Sirketi [*General Engineering and Architecture Corporation*] [*Ankara*] (TU)
GEME .... Geniki Etaireia Meleton kai Ekmetallevseon [*General Research and Mining Company*] (GC)
GEMEE .... Geniki Etaireia Metallevtikon Erevnon kai Ekmetallevseon [*General Company for Mineral Prospecting and Exploitation*] [*Greek*] (GC)
Gem-Geb .... Gemeindegebiet [*German*]
GEMICO ...... Societe Geologique et Miniere du Congo (MAR)
GEMMKA .... Grammateia tis Gnomodotikis Epitropis Mitroou Meletiton kai Kanonismou Anatheseos [*Advisory Committee Secretariat of the Researcher Registry and (Contract) Assignment Regulations*] [*Greek*] (GC)
GEMPPS ..... Groupe d'Etudes Mathematiques de Problemes Politiques et Strategiques [*French*]
GEMS .... Gilevi Exploration and Mining Syndicate (MAR)
GEMS .... Global Environment Monitoring System (MAR)
GEMZ .... Harmonic Electromagnetic Sounding (RU)
GEMZ .... State Experimental Machine Plant (RU)
gen .... Genannt [*Alias*] (EG)
Gen .... General (BU)
Gen .... General [*General*] [*German*]
Gen .... General [*General*] [*Spanish*]
gen .... General [*General*] (POL)
Gen .... General [*General*] [*French*] (MTD)
Gen .... General [*General*] (TU)
gen .... General (RU)
gen .... Generalny [*General*] (POL)
gen .... Genetic [*Genetics*] (RU)
gen .... Genetiivi [*Genitive*] [*Finnish*]
GEN .... Genie [*Engineering*] [*French*] (CL)
GEN .... Genikon Epiteleion Navtikou [*Naval General Staff*] [*Greek*] (GC)
Gen .... Genossenschaft [*German*]
gen-ad .... Adjutant General (RU)
GENAREP ... Compagnie Generale de Recherches Petrolieres [*General Petroleum Prospecting Company*] [*Algerian*] (AF)
gen bryg ...... General Brygady [*Brigadier-General*] [*Polish*]
GENCO .... Societe Generale de Construction au Cameroun (MAR)
Gencor .... General Mining Corporation [*South African*]
Gend .... Gendarmerie [*Gendarmery*] [*Military*] [*French*] (MTD)
gendir .... General Manager, General Director (RU)
gen dyw ...... General Dywizji [*Lieutenant-General*] [*Polish*]
GENE .... Grafeion Evreseos Navtikis Ergasias [*Merchant Seamen Employment Office*] [*Greek*] (GC)
GENELEC ... Generale Electronique SA (MAR)
Genel-Is ...... Turkiye Genel Hizmetler Iscileri Sendikasi [*Public Services Employees Union of Turkey*] (TU)
gen g .... General of the Army (RU)
gengazmotor ... Gas Engine Fueled by Producer Gas (RU)
GENICIAT ... Genie Civil en Afrique Tropicale (MAR)
GENII .... Scientific Research Institute of Economic Geography (RU)
genisl .... Genisletilmis [*Expanded*] (TU)
gen-l .... Lieutenant General (RU)
gen-leyt .... Lieutenant General (RU)
gen-m .... Major General (RU)
genmaj .... General Major [*Major General*] (YU)
genmaj .... General Major [*Major General*] (CZ)
Genmor .... Naval General Staff (RU)
genn .... Gennaio [*January*] [*Italian*]
GENOTO ..... General Otomotiv Sanayi ve Ticaret AS [*General Automotive Industry and Trading Corp.*] (TU)
gen-p .... Colonel General (RU)
genplk .... General Plukovnik [*Colonel General*] (CZ)
genpor .... General Porucik [*Lieutenant General*] (CZ)
Genred .... Generalni Reditel [*Director General*] (CZ)
gensek .... Secretary General (RU)
Gen-Sekr .... Generalsekretaer [*German*]
gen shtab .... General Staff (RU)
GENSI .... Gabungan Etjeran Indonesia [*Indonesian Retailers Association*] (IN)
GENSORU ... Genel Soru [*General Questioning, Interpellation*] (TU)
Genst .... Generalni Stab [*General Staff*] (CZ)
Gen T .... Genie Territorial [*French*] (MTD)
GENTAS ...... Genel Metal Sanayii ve Ticaret Anonim Sirketi [*General Metal Industry and Trading Corporation*] (TU)
Gentma Dottssa ... Gentilissima Dottoressa [*Honorable Doctor*] [*Title used to address a woman who has a doctorate*] [*Italian*]
GEOBIRO .... Biro za Geodetske Radove u Zagrebu [*Geodetic Operations Bureau in Zagreb*] (YU)
GEOBOL ..... Servicio Geologico de Bolivia [*Bolivian Geological Service*] (LA)
geod .... Geodesic, Geodesy, Geodetic (RU)
geod .... Geodesy (BU)
geod .... Geodezia [*Geodesy*] (HU)
GEODEZIZDAT ... Publishing House of Geodetic and Cartographic Literature (RU)
geofak .... Division of Geography (RU)
GEOFIAN .... Geophysical Institute of the Academy of Sciences, USSR (RU)
geofiz .... Geophysical, Geophysics (RU)
GEOGN .... Geography (Nanking) [*A publication*] (MAR)
geogr .... Geographic (BU)
geogr .... Geographic, Geographical, Geography (RU)
Geografgiz ... State Publishing House of Geographical Literature (RU)
Geografizdat ... State Publishing House of Geographical Literature (RU)
Geogrduz .... Geografska Duzina [*Geographic Longitude*] (YU)
GEOIMPRO ... Geological and Mining Surveys (BU)
GEOISTRAGE ... Preduzece za Geoloske Istrazne Radove [*Geological Research Establishment*] [*Sarajevo*] (YU)
GEOKARTA ... Geographic Maps Institute [*Belgrade*] (YU)
Geokartproekt ... Geological Cartographic Design Organization (BU)
GEOKhI .... Institute of Geochemistry and Analytical Chemistry Imeni V. I. Vernadskiy (of the Academy of Sciences, USSR) (RU)
geokhim ...... Geochemical, Geochemistry (RU)
geol .... Geologia [*Geology*] (HU)
geol .... Geologia [*Geology*] [*Finnish*]
geol .... Geological, Geology (RU)
Geol .... Geologist, Geology (BU)
Geol Geograf i Khim I-t pri BAN ... Institute of Geology, Geography, and Chemistry of the Bulgarian Academy of Sciences (BU)
Geolgiz .... Geological State Publishing House (RU)
Geoli-tutnaBAN ... Geological Institute of the Bulgarian Academy of Sciences (BU)
Geolkom ..... Geological Committee (RU)
Geol i min ... Geological and Mineralogical (BU)
Geolnerudstrom ... Trust for Exploration for Nonmetallic Minerals and Building Materials of the Central Regions (of the Main Administration of Geology and Conservation of Mineral Resources of the Council of Ministers, RSFSR) (RU)
geolog .... Geologisch [*Geological*] [*German*]
geol-razv ..... Geological-Exploration (RU)
geol-razved ... Geological-Exploration (RU)
Geolstromtrest ... Republic Geological Exploration Trust of the Ministry of the Building Materials Industry, RSFSR (RU)
Geom .... Geometer [*German*]
Geom .... Geometri [*Geometry*] (TU)
geom .... Geometria [*Geometry*] [*Finnish*]
geom .... Geometria [*Geometry*] (HU)
geom .... Geometric (BU)
geom .... Geometric, Geometry (RU)
GEOMIN ...... Geomorphological Institute (of the Academy of Sciences, USSR) (RU)
GEOMIN ...... Institute of Geology and Mineralogy (RU)
GEOMINCO ... GEOMINCO Reszvenytarsasag [*GEOMINCO Company (Handles export of geological and mining know-how)*] (HU)
GEOMINES ... Compagnie Geologique et Miniere des Ingenieurs Industriels Belges [*Geological and Mining Company of Belgian Industrial Engineers*] [*Zairian*] (AF)
GEOPETROLE ... Societe Geotechnique pour la Production Petrole (MAR)
Geoplanproekt ... Geological Planning and Designing Organization (BU)
GEP .... Advance Echelon of Motor Park (RU)
GEP .... Advanced Evacuation Station (RU)
GEP .... Grosshandels-Einkaufspreis [*Wholesale Purchasing Price*] (EG)
GEP .... Groupement des Exploitants Petroliers (MAR)
GEP .... Grupo Especial Paraquedista [*Special Paratroop Group*] [*Portuguese*] (WER)
GEP .... Main Evacuation Station (RU)
Gepa .... Gepaeckabfertigung [*Baggage Dispatching Room*] (EG)
gepalkr .... Gepalkatresz [*Machine Part*] (HU)

GEPATA...... Groupe d'Etude des Problemes de l'Automatisme dans les Travaux Administratifs
GEPEXI....... Koho es Gepipari Miniszterium Gepipari Export Irodaja [*Machine Industry Export Office of the Ministry of Metallurgy and Machine Industry*] (HU)
GEPI........... Societa Gestione e Partecipazioni Industriali [*Industrial Participations and Management Company*] [*Italian*] (WER)
gepk........... Gepkocsi [*Motor Vehicle*] (HU)
GEPLACEA... Grupo de Paises Latinoamericanos y del Caribe Exportadores de Azucar [*Group of Latin American and Caribbean Sugar Exporting Countries - GLACSEC*] (EA)
gept............ Geptan [*Mechanics*] (HU)
Ger............. Gericht [*German*]
GER............ Gerisen [*Garrison*] (ML)
GER............ Grups d'Estudiants Revolucionaris [*Revolutionary Student Groups*] [*Spanish*] (WER)
GERA.......... Geological Exploration and Resources Appraisal (MAR)
GERA.......... Grupo Executivo da Reforma Agraria [*Executive Group for Land Reform*] [*Brazilian*] (LA)
GERAKAN... Parti Gerakan Rakyat Malaysia [*People's Action Party of Malaysia*] (ML)
GERAL........ Gerland Algerie (MAR)
GERALCO... Geral de Comercio e Industria Lda. (MAR)
GERAN........ Grupo Executivo de Racionalizacao da Agro-Industria Canavieira do Nordeste [*Executive Group for Rationalizing the Northeast Sugarcane Industry*] [*Brazilian*] (LA)
GERBUMI.... Gerakan Buruh Muslimin Indonesia [*Indonesian Moslem Workers Movement*] (IN)
GERC.......... Groupe d'Etudes sur les Ressources du Cambodge [*Cambodian Resources Study Group*] (CL)
GERDAT...... Groupement d'Etudes et de Recherches d'Agronomie Tropicale [*Studies and Research Group for Tropical Agriculture Development*] [*French*] (AF)
GERE........... Gewerkschaft Erdoel-Raffinerie Emsland [*West German*]
GEREC........ Groupe d'Etudes et de Recherches en Espace Creolophone [*Study and Research Group in Creole-Speaking Areas*] (LA1)
Geref........... Gereformeerde [*Reformed*] [*Calvinist*] [*Dutch*] (GPO)
GERES........ Grupo Executivo de Recuperacao Economica do Espirito Santo [*Executive Group for Espirito Santo Economic Recovery*] [*Brazilian*] (LA)
GERGU........ Grupo de Exploracion y Reconocimiento Geografico del Uruguay [*Exploration and Geographical Survey Group of Uruguay*] (LA)
GERI............ Groupement d'Etude des Routes et de l'Infrastructure [*Road and Infrastructure Study Group*] [*Gabonese*] (AF)
germ........... Germaaninen [*Finnish*]
germ........... German (BU)
germ........... German (RU)
GERMAHII... Gerakan Mahasiswa Islam Indonesia [*Indonesian Moslem College Students Movement*] (IN)
GERME....... Groupe d'Etudes et de Recherches en Microscopie Electronique (MAR)
GERMINDO... Gerakan Mahasiswa Indonesia [*Indonesian College Students Movement*] (IN)
germ p........ German Patent (RU)
GEROVE..... Gesellschaft fuer Rohstoffgewinnung und Verfahrenstechnik [*Raw Material Extraction and Processing Technology Company*] (EG)
GERPII........ Gerakan Pemuda Islam Indonesia [*Indonesian Moslem Youth Movement*] (IN)
GERPOL...... Gerilja Politik [*Guerrilla Politics (Subversive political activity)*] (IN)
GERS.......... Groupe d'Etude et Recherches Sous-Marin
GERWASI.... Gerakan Wanita Sosialis Indonesia [*Indonesian Socialist Women's Movement*] (IN)
GERWASII... Gerakan Wanita Serikat Islam Indonesia [*Indonesian Islamic Alliance Women's Movement*] (IN)
GES............ Gaz, Elektrik, ve Su Tesisleri [*Gas, Electric Power, and Hydraulic Installations*] (TU)
GES............ Gemi Kaptanlari Sendikasi [*Ship Captains' Union*] (TU)
GES............ Genikon Epiteleion Stratou [*Army General Staff*] [*Greek*] (GC)
GES............ Genikos Epitheoritis Stratou [*Army Inspector General*] [*Greek*] (GC)
ges............. Gesaettigt [*Saturated*] [*German*]
ges............. Gesammelte [*Collected, Compiled*] [*German*]
ges............. Gesamt [*Complete, Total*] [*German*]
Ges............ Gesandter [*German*]
Ges............ Gesellschaft [*Association, Company, Society*] (EG)
Ges............ Gesetzlich [*Registered (Trademark)*] (EG)
ges............. Gesucht [*In Demand*] [*German*]
GES............ Ghana Education Service (MAR)
GES............ Groupements Economiques du Senegal [*Economic Groups of Senegal*] (AF)
GES............ Hydroelectric Power Plant (RU)
GES............ State Electric Power Plant (RU)
GESAMP..... Joint Group of Experts on the Scientific Aspects of Marine Pollution (EA)
GESASE...... Geniki Synomospondia Agrotikon Syllogon Ellados [*General Confederation of Greek Agricultural Unions*] [*See also GSAS*] (GC1)
gesatt.......... Gesaettigt [*Saturated*] [*German*]
Gesch.......... Geschichte [*History*] [*German*]
gesch.......... Geschieden [*Divorced*] (EG)
Geschlw...... Geschlechtswort [*German*]
geschm....... Geschmolzen [*Molten, Melted*] [*German*]
Geschw....... Geschwindigkeit [*Speed*] (EG)
Geschw....... Geschwister [*Brother(s) and Sister(s)*] (EG)
gesch Wm... Geschuetzte Warenmarke [*German*]
GESCO....... Groupement d'Entreprises Suisses de Construction (MAR)
ges gesch... Gesetzlich Geschuetzt [*Registered Trademark, Patented*] [*German*] (GPO)
Ges-Is......... Turkiye DSI Enerji, Su, ve Gaz Iscileri Sendikasi [*State Irrigation, Energy, Water, and Gas Workers Union*] (TU)
GESM.......... Groupement des Ecoles Superieures Militaires [*Advanced Military Training Schools Group*] [*Zairian*] (AF)
GESP........... German Socialist Unity Party (BU)
gest............ Gestochen [*Engraved*] [*German*]
Gest........... Gestorben [*Deceased*] (EG)
GESTAPU... Gerakan September Tiga Puluh [*30 September Movement (G-30-S)*] (IN)
GESTAS...... Genel Sinai Tesisleri ve Ticaret Anonim Sirketi [*General Industrial Installations and Trade Corporation*] [*Ankara*] (TU)
GESTOK..... Gerakan Satu Oktober [*1 October Movement (Another name for G-30-S)*] (IN)
GESY.......... Geniki Ekklisiastiki Synelevsis [*General Ecclesiastical Assembly*] [*Greek*] (GC)
GESyN........ Groupement d'Etude du Synchrotron National [*French*]
GET............ State Electrotechnical Trust (RU)
GETAX........ Intreprinderea de Transport Bucuresti, Gospodaria Camioane Taximetre [*Bucharest Transportation Enterprise, Truck and Taxi Management*] (RO)
GETEPE...... Grupo Executivo de Trabalhos, Estudos, e Projetos Espaciais [*Executive Group for Space Projects, Studies, and Work*] [*Brazilian*] (LA)
geterog....... Heterogeneous (RU)
GETF.......... Hexaethyl Tetraphosphate (RU)
GETI........... Gepipari Tervezo Intezet [*Design Institute of the Machine Industry*] (HU)
getr............ Getrennt [*German*]
GEU............ Electrical Propeller Drive [*Nautical term*] (RU)
GEU............ Electronically Controlled Generator (RU)
GEU............ Main Economic Administration (RU)
GeV............ Giga-Elektronenvolt [*Giga Electron Volts (One billion electron volts)*] (EG)
Gev............ Gigaelectron-Volt (RU)
GEVEV........ Geniki Etaireia Viomikhanikon Epikheiriseon Volou [*General Association of Volos Industrial Enterprises*] (GC)
Gew............ Gewerbe [*or Gewerblich*] [*German*]
GEW............ Gewerkschaft Erziehung und Wissenschaft [*Education and Science Labor Union*] [*West German*] (WEN)
Gew............ Gewicht [*Weight, Gravity*] [*German*]
gew............ Gewoehnlich [*Usual, Ordinary*] [*German*]
GewO.......... Gewerbeordnung [*German*]
GewS.......... Gewerbeschule [*German*]
Gew-T......... Gewichtsteil [*Part by Weight*] [*German*]
gew Temp... Gewoehnliche Temperatur [*General Temperature*] [*German*]
Gez............ Gezeichnet [*Signed (Before signatures)*] (EG)
GEZAMINES... Societe Generale Zairoise des Minerais [*Zaire Ores Company*] (AF)
GF.............. Comb Filter (RU)
GF.............. French Guiana [*Two-letter standard code*] (CNC)
GF.............. Gazdasagi Fotanacs [*Supreme Economic Council*] (HU)
GF.............. Glucose Phosphate (RU)
GF.............. Grumes Flottees (MAR)
GF.............. Guarda Fiscal [*Customs Guard*] [*Portuguese*] (WER)
GF.............. Gubernium Fiuminense [*Province of Fiume*] [*Rijeka*] (YU)
GF.............. Gustav Fischer Verlag (VEB) [*Gustav Fischer Publishing House (VEB)*] (EG)
GF.............. State Pharmacopoeia (RU)
GFA............ General Football Association [*Sudanese*] (MAR)
GFA............ Groupement Foncier Africain (MAR)
GFA............ Groupement Francais d'Assurances (MAR)
G-f-aza........ Glucose Phosphatase (RU)
GFB............ Hexafluorobutadiene (RU)
GFCh.......... Fixed-Frequency Generator (RU)
GFCI........... Groupement Foncier de Cote-d'Ivoire [*Ivory Coast Real Estate Group*] (AF)
GFCM.......... General Fisheries Council for the Mediterranean (MAR)
GFD............ Groupement Foncier Dakar (MAR)
GFDC.......... Ghana Food Distribution Corporation (MAR)
GfdWd........ Gesellschaft fuer die Wiedervereinigung Deutschlands [*Society for the Reunification of Germany*] (EG)
gfi.............. Geographic Institute (BU)
GFI............. Geophysical Institute (of the Academy of Sciences, USSR) (RU)
GFI............. State Financial Publishing House (RU)
GFIF........... Annals of the School of Philosophy and History of Sofia University [*A publication*] (BU)
GfK............ Gesellschaft fuer Kernforschung (MAR)
GFK............ Gewerkschaftsgruppe fuer Kleinbetriebe [*Small-Plant Trade Union Group*] (EG)

GFK .... Glycerophosphoric Acid (RU)
GFK .... Main Philatelic Office (RU)
GFLU .... General Federation of Labour Unions [*Iraqi*] (MAR)
GFO .... Main Physical Observatory (RU)
GFP .... Glasfaserverstaerkte Plaste [*Glass-Fiber-Reinforced Plastics*] (EG)
GFPA .... Gambia Family Planning Association (MAR)
GFPD .... Groupement Forestier de la Pointe-Denis (MAR)
GFPS .... General Federation of Peasant Societies [*Iraqi*] (MAR)
GFR .... Federal Republic of Germany (BU)
GFR .... German Federal Republic (RU)
GFS .... General Fund Services (MAR)
GFSA .... Gold Fields of South Africa (MAR)
GFSTU .... General Federation of Somali Trade Unions (AF)
GFT .... Gazdasagi Fotanacs [*Supreme Economic Council*] (HU)
GFT .... Glasfaserverstaerkte Thermoplasten [*Glass-Fiber-Reinforced Thermoplastics*] (EG)
GFTI .... Gor'kiy Physicotechnical Institute (RU)
GFTRI .... State Physicotechnical Institute of Roentgenology (RU)
GFTU .... General Federation of Trade Unions [*Iraqi*] (ME)
GFTU .... General Federation of Trade Unions [*Syrian*] (MAR)
GFTUL .... General Federation of Trade Unions - Libya (MAR)
GfU .... Geofysikalni Ustav [*Institute of Geophysics (of the Czechoslovak Academy of Sciences)*] (CZ)
GFV .... Gyori Festekipari Vallalat [*Paint Manufacturing Enterprise of Gyor*] (HU)
GfW .... Gesellschaft fuer Weltraumforschung [*Space Research Society*] (EG)
gg .... Cities (RU)
GG- .... Deep-Water Hydrostat (RU)
GG .... Gas Generator (RU)
GG .... Gasgewinde [*Gas Thread*] [*German*]
GG .... Gedeckter Gueterwagen [*Boxcar*] (EG)
gg .... Gegen [*Against*] [*German*]
GG .... Genclik Gucu [*Youth Strength Soccer Team*] [*Turkish Cypriot*] (GC)
GG .... Genikos Grammatevs [*Secretary General*] (GC)
GG .... Giorni [*Days*] [*Italian*]
Gg .... Gosong [*or Gosung, Gusong*] [*Shoal, Reef, Islet*] [*Indonesian*] (NAU)
Gg .... Gosong [*or Gosung, Gusong*] [*Shoal, Reef, Islet*] [*Malaysian*] (NAU)
gg .... Gospoda [*Plural of Mister*] (YU)
GG .... Gouvernement General [*North African*] (MAR)
GG .... Gozdno Gospodarstvo [*Forestry Management*] (YU)
Gg .... Gunong [*Mountain*] [*Malaysian*] (NAU)
Gg .... Gunong [*Mountain*] [*Indonesian*] (NAU)
GG .... Gyro Horizon (RU)
GG .... Harmonic Oscillator (RU)
gg .... Hectogram (RU)
GG .... Main Generator (RU)
gg .... Messieurs [*Plural of Mister*] (RU)
GG .... Producer Gas (RU)
gg .... Years (RU)
gg .... Years (BU)
GGA .... Gas-Hydraulic Analogy (RU)
GGA .... Geniki Grammateia Athlitismou [*General Secretariat of Athletics*] (GC)
GGAB .... Ghana Geographical Association Bulletin [*Legon*] [*A publication*] (MAR)
GGAO .... Main State Astronomical Observatory (RU)
GGB .... Histohematic Barrier (RU)
GGC .... Graduates' General Congress (MAR)
GGC .... Grand Garage du Chari (MAR)
GGE .... Gazette Geographique et l'Exploration [*A publication*] (MAR)
Gge .... Gorge [*Pass, Gorge*] [*Military map abbreviation*] [*World War I*] [*French*] (MTD)
Gge .... Grange [*Barn*] [*Military map abbreviation*] [*World War I*] [*French*] (MTD)
GGEA .... Geniki Grammateia Exoskholikou Athlitismou [*General Secretariat of Extracurricular Athletics*] [*Greek*] (GC)
GGES .... Gas Generator Electric Power Plant (RU)
ggf .... Gegebenenfalls [*If Necessary, If the Occasion Arises*] (EG)
GGf .... Geology and Geophysics (RU)
GGFI .... State Geophysical Institute (RU)
GGG .... Gesetz ueber die Gesellschaftlichen Gerichte [*Law on Social Courts*] (EG)
GGH .... Gran Guarnicion de La Habana [*Main Havana Garrison*] [*Cuban*] (LA)
GGI .... Main Pulse Generator (RU)
GGI .... Mining and Geological Institute (RU)
GGI .... State Hydrological Institute (RU)
GGIUFAN .... Mining and Geological Institute of the Ural Branch of the Academy of Sciences, USSR (RU)
GGK .... Gamma-Gamma Logging (RU)
GGK .... Gehaltsgruppenkatalog [*Salary Grade Schedule*] (EG)
GGK .... Horizontal Gyrocompass [*Nautical term*] (RU)
GGK .... State Geodetic Committee (RU)
GGl .... Geografski Glasnik [*Geographic Bulletin*] [*Zagreb*] [*A publication*] (YU)
GGM .... Gamma-Gamma Method (RU)
GGMI .... Gor'kiy State Medical Institute Imeni S. M. Kirov (RU)
GGN .... Department of the State Geological Inspection (RU)
GGO .... Gamma-Gamma Testing (RU)
GGO .... Main Geophysical Observatory Imeni A. I. Voyeykov (RU)
GGP .... Gas Gathering Pipelines (MAR)
GGR .... Gas-Cooled Graphite-Moderated Reactor (RU)
GGRU .... Main Administration of Geological Exploration (RU)
GGR-Up ...... Gas-Cooled Graphite-Moderated Natural Uranium Reactor (RU)
GGSI .... Main State Sanitary Inspection, USSR (RU)
GGT .... Hydrostatic Ground Pipe (RU)
GGT .... State Geophysical Trust (RU)
GGU .... Geodetska Glavna Uprava [*Central Geodetic Administration*] (YU)
GGU .... Gor'kiy State University Imeni N. I. Lobachevskiy (RU)
GGU .... Main Geodetic Administration (RU)
GGV .... Ground-Water Level (RU)
Ggw .... Gegenwart [*Presence*] [*German*]
GGZ .... Government Gazette (Zambia) [*A publication*] (MAR)
Gh .... Gasthaus [*German*]
GH .... Gazdasagi Hivatal [*Accounting Office*] (HU)
GH .... Gerakan Hutan [*Jungle Operation*] (ML)
GH .... Ghana [*Ghana*] [*Polish*]
GH .... Ghana [*Two-letter standard code*] (CNC)
GHA .... Ghana [*Three-letter standard code*] (CNC)
GHA .... Societe du Grand Hotel Restaurant d'Abidjan (MAR)
GHAC .... Groupement des Hommes d'Affaires Camerounais (MAR)
GHACIMS .... Ghana Co-Operative of Indigenous Musicians (MAR)
GHANASO ... Ghana National Student Organization (AF)
GHASEL ...... Ghana Sugar Estates Limited (MAR)
GHD .... Genc Hukukcular Dernegi [*Young Jurists Association*] (TU)
GHE .... Girne Halk Evi [*Kyrenia Peoples' House*] (TU)
GHG .... Grosshandelsgenossenschaft [*Wholesale Trade Cooperative*] (EG)
GHH .... Gutehoffnungshuette [*West German engineering group*]
GHK .... Grosshandelskontor [*Wholesale Trade Office*] (EG)
GHM .... Groupe de Haute Montagne [*Mountaineering association*]
GHPD .... Glasnik Hrvatskog Prirodoslovnog Drustva [*Bulletin of the Croatian Natural Sciences Society*] [*Zagreb, 1886-1940*] [*A publication*] (YU)
GHS .... Grosshandelsspanne [*Wholesale Markup*] (EG)
GHU .... Guyana Headmen's Union (LA)
GI .... General Intelligence [*Egyptian*] (ME)
GI .... Geografski Institut [*Geographic Institute*] (YU)
GI .... Gibraltar [*Two-letter standard code*] (CNC)
GI .... Gradevinski Inspektorat [*Building Inspectorate*] (YU)
GI .... Group Selector (RU)
GI .... Institute of Geology (BU)
GI .... Main Pulse (RU)
GI .... Pulse Generator, Impulse Generator (RU)
gi .... Year of Publication (RU)
GIA .... Garuda Indonesian Airways (IN)
GIA .... Ghana Institute of Architects (MAR)
GIA .... Groupement des Independants Africains [*Independent Africans Group*]
GIA .... Groupement Interprofessionnel de l'Automobile (MAR)
GIA .... Groupement Ivoirien d'Assurances (MAR)
GIA .... Main Historical Archives (RU)
GIA .... State Scientific Research Institute of Nitrogen (RU)
GIAB .... Grupo Independente de Aviacao de Bombardeamento [*Portuguese*]
GIAC .... Groupement d'Importation Algerien de la Chaussure (MAR)
GIALO .... Leningrad Oblast State Historical Archives (RU)
GIAMO .... Moscow Oblast State Historical Archives (RU)
GIAN .... Institute of Geology of the Academy of Sciences, USSR (RU)
GIAP .... Guards Fighter Air Regiment (RU)
GIAP .... State Scientific Research and Planning Institute of the Nitrogen Industry and Products of Organic Synthesis (RU)
GIAT .... Groupement Interprofessionnel de l'Afrique Tropicale [*Interprofessional Group of Tropical Africa*] (AF)
GIATO .... Tambov Oblast State Historical Archives (RU)
GIB .... Gibraltar [*Three-letter standard code*] (CNC)
GIBAIR .... Gibraltar Airways Ltd. (MAR)
GIBCA .... General International Business Contracting Associates [*Arab*] (MAR)
GIBER .... Giraschi, Bernadi, et Compagnie (MAR)
GIBMED ...... Gibraltar Mediterranean Command (MAR)
gibr .... Hybridization (RU)
GIC .... Gabonaise Industrielle de Construction (MAR)
GIC .... Groupement d'Impregnateurs Camerounais (MAR)
GIC .... Groupement de l'Industrie Chimique [*French*]
GIC .... Grupos Pro-Independencia de Cataluna [*Pro-Independence Groups of Catalonia*] [*Spanish*] (WER)
GIC .... Guilde Internationale des Cooperatrices
GIC .... Gulf International Company [*Sudanese*] (MAR)
GICA .... Groupement Intersyndical de la Communication Audiovisuelle
GICAF .... Groupement des Industries de la Conserve Africaine (MAR)
GICAM .... Groupement Interprofessionnel pour l'Etude et la Coordination des Interets Economiques au Cameroun [*Interoccupational Group for the Study and Coordination of Cameroon's Economic Interests*] (AF)

GICE........... Groupement d'Ingenieurs Conseils en Expertise Interessant le Batiment et les Travaux Publics (MAR)
GICEX......... Groupement Interbancaire pour les Operations de Credits a l'Exportation [*French*]
GICP........... Groupement Professionnel d'Importation des Cuires et Peaux [*Algerian*] (MAR)
GID............. Gesellschaft fuer Information und Dokumentation
GID............. Glasnik Istoriskog Drustva [*Bulletin of the Historical Society*] [*Novi Sad*] [*A publication*] (YU)
GID............. Grande Imprimerie Dahomeenne (MAR)
GID-............ Hydroacoustic Bottom Indicator (RU)
GIDA........... Groupement Interprofessionnel des Entreprises du Dahomey (MAR)
Gida Is......... Turkiye Gida Sanayii Iscileri Sendikasi [*Turkish Food Industry Workers' Union*] (TU)
GIDAS......... Association for Hydraulics, Hydraulic Engineering, and Wind Power (RU)
GIDA-SEN... Kibris Turk Gida, Tutun, ve Muskirat Iscileri Sendikasi [*Turkish Cypriot Foodstuffs, Tobacco, and Intoxicants Workers' Union*] (TU)
GIDC........... Ghana Industrial Development Corporation (MAR)
GIDEC......... Grupo de Informacion y Documentacion Economica [*Bogota*] (COL)
GIDEP......... All-Union State Planning Institute Gidroenergoproyekt [*Planning hydroelectric power plants*] (RU)
GIDET......... Groupement International pour le Developpement Economique et Technique (MAR)
GIDNT......... Glowny Instytut Dokumentacji Naukowo-Technicznej [*Main Institute of Scientific and Technical Documentation*] (POL)
GIDOR......... Gemeenschappelijk Informatie- en Documentatiecentrum voor Organisatiewerk in Rijksdienst [*'s-Gravenhage*]
gidr k-t'....... Hydrolytic Acidity (RU)
gidroizol...... Waterproofing Material (RU)
gidrokhim... Hydrochemical, Hydrochemistry (RU)
Gidromashkomplekt ... Trust for the Supply of Complete Sets of Compressor Pumps and Fittings of the Glavkomplektooborudovaniye (RU)
Gidromekhanizatsiya ... State All-Union Trust for the Planning and Execution of Hydraulic Excavation Work (RU)
gidromet..... Hydrometeorological, Hydrometeorology (RU)
GIDROMETEOIZDAT ... State Scientific and Technical Hydrometeorological Publishing House (RU)
Gidrometsluzhba ... Main Administration of the Hydrometeorological Service at the Council of Ministers, USSR (RU)
Gidromontazh ... State All-Union Construction and Installation Trust of Glavgidroenergostroy (RU)
Gidropostavka ... Technical Office for the Supply of Hydroelectric-Power and Hydromechanical Equipment (RU)
gidro-p/p.... Seaplane Landing Area (RU)
Gidroproyekt ... All-Union Planning, Surveying, and Scientific Research Institute Imeni S. Ya. Zhuk (RU)
gidrorazryv ... Hydraulic Fracturing (RU)
Gidrorybproyekt ... State Institute for the Planning of Hydraulic-Engineering, Fishery-Improvement, and Pond Structures (RU)
Gidrospetsstroy ... State All-Union Trust for the Reinforcement of Foundations and Structures of the Glavgidroenergostroy (RU)
gidrotekh.... Hydraulic Engineering (RU)
Gidr st......... Hydrological Station [*Topography*] (RU)
GIDUV......... State Institute for the Advanced Training of Physicians (RU)
Gi E............ Gite d'Etapes [*Road-Post*] [*Military*] [*French*] (MTD)
GIE............. Glowny Instytut Elektrotechniki [*Main Institute of Electric Engineering*] (POL)
GIE............. Groupement d'Interet Economique [*Economic Interest Group*] [*Western European*] (WER)
GIE............. Grupo de Interesse Economico [*Economic Interest Group*] (MAR)
GIE............. Gruppo Industrie Elettromeccaniche per Impianti all'Estero (MAR)
GIEFCA....... Groupement d'Interet Economique pour Favoriser le Developpement du Credit Automobile et Industriel en Afrique (MAR)
GIEKI........... State Scientific Research Electroceramic Institute (RU)
GI EI............ Glowny Instytut Elektrotechniki [*Main Institute of Electric Engineering*] (POL)
GIEM........... Groupement des Importateurs et Exportateurs Mauritaniens (MAR)
GIES........... Hydraulic Engineering Surveys of Electric Power Plants (RU)
GIEV........... State Institute of Experimental Veterinary Science (RU)
GIF............. State Scientific Research Institute of Physiotherapy (RU)
GIFAP.......... Groupement International des Associations Nationales de Fabricants de Produits Agrochimiques [*International Group of National Associations of Agrochemical Manufacturers*] (EA)
GIFATOME ... Groupement pour l'Industrie Nucleaire [*Nuclear Industries Group*] [*French*] (WER)
GIFF........... State Institute of Physiotherapy and Physical Culture (RU)
GIFK........... State Institute of Physical Culture Imeni P. F. Lesgaft (RU)
GIFML......... State Publishing House of Physical and Mathematical Literature (RU)
GIFO........... State Institute of Physiatrics and Orthopedics (RU)
GIFON......... Belorussian State Institute of Physiatrics, Orthopedics, and Neurology (RU)
GIFTI........... Gor'kiy Research Physicotechnical Institute (RU)
GIG............. Glowny Instytut Gornictwa [*Main Institute of Mining*] (POL)
GIG-............ Hydroacoustic Depth Indicator (RU)
GIGC........... Grupul Intreprindelor de Gospodarie Comunala [*Group of Communal Economy Enterprises*] (RO)
GIGK........... State Scientific Research Institute of Geodesy and Cartography (RU)
GIGKhS....... State Scientific Research Institute of Chemical Raw Materials Obtained by Mining (RU)
GIGMS......... Chief Engineer of the Hydrometeorological Service (RU)
gigrosk........ Hygroscopic, Hygroscopy (RU)
GIH............. Genel Idari Hizmetleri [*General Administrative Duties*] (TU)
GIHOC......... Ghana Industrial Holding Company (AF)
GII.............. Georgian Industrial Institute Imeni S. M. Kirov (RU)
GII.............. Gor'kiy Industrial Institute (RU)
GIII............. State Institute of Art History (RU)
GIIL............ Grupul Intreprindelor de Industrie Locala [*Group of Local Industry Enterprises*] (RO)
GIIL............ State Publishing House of Foreign Literature (RU)
GIINS.......... State Publishing House of Foreign and National Dictionaries (RU)
GIIS............ State Institute of Art Studies (RU)
GIIVT........... Gor'kiy Institute of Water Transportation Engineers (RU)
GIJ.............. Geoloski Institut Jugoslavije [*Yugoslav Geological Institute*] [*Belgrade*] (YU)
GIJ.............. Ghana Institute of Journalism (MAR)
GIJNA.......... Geografski Institut Jugoslovenske Narodne Armije [*Geographic Institute of the Yugoslav People's Army*] (YU)
GIK............. Check Pulse Generator (RU)
GIK............. City Executive Committee (RU)
GIK............. Gyro Induction Compass (RU)
GIK............. State Institute of Cinematography (RU)
GIK............. State Quality Inspection (RU)
GIKhL.......... State Publishing House of Belles Lettres (RU)
GIKI............ State Scientific Research Institute of Ceramics (RU)
GIKTorf....... State Quality Inspection of Peat (RU)
GIL............. General Instrument Lusitana [*Portuguese*] (WER)
GIL............. Glowny Instytut Lotnictwa [*Main Institute of Aeronautics*] (POL)
GiL............. Gore in Ljudje [*Mountains and Men*] [*Ljubljana*] [*A periodical*] (YU)
GIL............. Groupement Interprofessionnel de Legumes [*North African*] (MAR)
GILS i A....... State Publishing House of Literature on Construction and Architecture (RU)
GIM............. Glowny Instytut Mechaniki [*Main Institute of Mechanical Engineering*] (POL)
GIM............. Glowny Instytut Metalurgii [*Main Institute of Metallurgy*] (POL)
GIM............. Grupo de Intervencao Militar [*Military Intervention Group*] [*Portuguese*] (WER)
GIM............. Gruppe Internationale Marxisten [*International Marxist Group*] [*West German*] (PPW)
gim.............. High School (BU)
GIM............. Hydraulic Servomotor, Hydraulic Control Motor (RU)
GIM............. Long-Distance Group Selector (RU)
GIM............. State Historical Museum [*Moscow*] (RU)
GIM............. State Institute of Makhorka Culture (RU)
GIMA........... Gida ve Ihtiyac Maddeleri TAS [*Foodstuffs and Necessary Articles Corporation*] [*Chain store*] (TU)
GIMA........... Groupement des Importateurs de Mauritanie (MAR)
GIMAS......... Gida ve Ihtiyac Maddeleri Subesi [*Foodstuff and Necessities Branch*] [*A subsidiary of Industry, Commerce, and Manufacturing Enterprises Ltd.*] [*Turkish Cypriot*] (GC)
GIMCI.......... Groupement des Industries de la Metallurgie en Cote-d'Ivoire (MAR)
GIME........... Georgian Scientific Research Institute of Rural Mechanization and Electrification (RU)
GIMEE......... Groupement Syndical des Industries de Materiel d'Equipement Electrique (MAR)
GIMEIN........ Hydrometeorological Institute (RU)
GIMEIN........ Hydrometeorological Scientific Research Institute (RU)
GIMet.......... Glowny Instytut Metalurgii [*Main Institute of Metallurgy*] (POL)
GIMIZ.......... Hydrometeorological Publishing House (RU)
GIMMOM..... Groupement des Industries Minieres et Metallurgiques d'Outre-Mer [*Overseas Mining and Metal Industries Group*] (AF)
gimn........... Gimnazium [*High School, Secondary School*] (HU)
GIMN.......... State Institute of Musical Science (RU)
gimn u-l...... High School Teacher (BU)
GIMOI......... Groupe d'Information Madagascar Ocean Indien [*Madagascar-Indian Ocean Information Group*] (AF)
GIM-OPI...... State Historical Museum, Department of Written Sources (RU)
Gimp........... State Institute of Musical Education (RU)
GIMP........... State Scientific Research Society for the Study of Musical Occupations (RU)
GIMPA......... Ghana Institute of Management and Public Administration (AF)
GIMPEX....... Guyana Import-Export Company Ltd. (LA)
GIM RO....... State Historical Museum, Manuscript and Incunabula Department (RU)
GIMZ........... State Institute of Medical Sciences [*1919-1930*] (RU)
GIN............. Global Information Network [*Proposed*]

GIN .... Glowny Instytut Naftowy [*Main Petroleum Institute*] (POL)
GIN .... Guinea [*Three-letter standard code*] (CNC)
gin .... Gynecology, Gynecologist (BU)
GIN .... Individual Carrier Generator (RU)
GIN .... Institute of Geology (of the Academy of Sciences, USSR) (RU)
GIN .... Last Name Unknown (BU)
GIN .... Pulse Voltage Generator (RU)
GINA .... Gaufretterie Industrielle Africaine (MAR)
GINAN .... Institute of Geology of the Academy of Sciences, USSR (RU)
GINB .... Geodezyjny Instytut Naukowo-Badawczy [*Geodetic Scientific Research Institute*] (POL)
GINI .... State Scientific Research Institute of Petroleum (RU)
GINK .... Isonicotinic Acid Hydrazide, Isoniazid (RU)
GINMASh .... State Scientific Research Institute of Petroleum Equipment and Machinery (RU)
GINP .... State Institute of Scientific Pedagogy (RU)
Ginplastmass ... State Scientific Research Institute of Plastics and Synthetic Resins (RU)
GINSI .... Gabungan Importir Nasional Seluruh Indonesia [*All-Indonesia National Importers Association*] (IN)
GINTsVETMET ... State Scientific Research Institute of Nonferrous Metals (RU)
GINZ .... State Scientific Institute of Public Health [*1918-1930*] (RU)
Ginzoloto .... State Scientific Research Institute of Gold (RU)
GIO .... City Election District (RU)
GIO .... Glavni Izvrsni Odbor [*Central Executive Committee*] (YU)
GIO .... Operations Research Group (RU)
GIOA .... State Institute of Experimental Agronomy (RU)
GIOAPV .... Gradski Izvrsni Odbor Autonomne Pokrajine Vojvodine [*City Executive Committee of the Autonomous Province of Vojvodina*] (YU)
g-ion .... Gram Ion (RU)
GIONSAPV ... Glavni Izvrsni Odbor Narodne Skupstine Autonomne Provincije Vojvodine [*Central Executive Committee of the People's Assembly of Vojvodina*] (YU)
GIOP .... Glowny Inspektorat Ochrony Pracy [*Chief Inspectorate for the Protection of Labor*] [*Polish*]
GIOV .... Hospital for Veterans of World War II (RU)
GIP .... Forestry Industrial Enterprise (BU)
GIP .... Glowny Instytut Pracy [*Main Institute of Labor*] (POL)
GIP .... State Scientific Research Institute of Psychiatry (RU)
GIPI .... State Research and Planning Institute (RU)
GIPKh .... State Institute of Applied Chemistry (RU)
GIPKKh .... Gor'kiy Institute for Improving the Qualifications of Managerial Personnel (RU)
GIPL .... State Publishing House of Political Literature (RU)
GIPMA .... Main Testing Range for Naval Artillery (RU)
GIPN .... Glowny Instytut Paliw Naturalnych [*Main Institute of Natural Fuels*] (POL)
Gipredmet ... State Scientific Research and Planning Institute of the Rare Metals Industry (RU)
GIPRiS .... Glowny Instytut Przemyslu Rolnego i Spozywczego [*Main Institute of the Agriculture and Food Industries*] (POL)
Giproalyuminiy ... State Institute for the Planning of Aluminum, Magnesium, and Electrode Plants (RU)
Giproanilkraska ... State Planning Institute of the Aniline Dye Industry (RU)
Giproarktika ... State Institute for Planning and Exploration in the Arctic and the Far North (RU)
Giproaviaprom ... State Institute for the Planning of Aircraft Industry Plants (RU)
Giproavtoprom ... State Institute for the Planning of Automobile Industry Plants (RU)
Giproavtotraktoroprom ... State Institute for the Planning of Establishments of the Automobile and Tractor Industry (RU)
Giproavtotraktorprom ... State Institute for the Planning of Automobile and Tractor Industry Plants (RU)
Giproavtotrans ... State Institute for the Planning of Automobile Repair and Transportation Establishments and Structures (RU)
Giproazotmash ... State Institute for the Planning of Nitrogen Machinery Manufacture (RU)
Giprobum ... State Institute for the Planning of Establishments of the Pulp, Paper, and Hydrolysis Industries (RU)
GIPROBYTPROM ... State Institute for the Planning of Personal-Service Establishments, Bakeries, Local Industries in the Rayons, and of Art Craft Industries (RU)
Giprodor ..... State Institute of Road Planning (RU)
Giprodortrans ... State Institute for the Planning of Roads, Transportation Establishments, and Structures (RU)
Giprodrev ... State Institute for the Planning of Sawmilling, Woodworking, and Lumber-Hauling Establishments of the Lumber Industry (RU)
Giprodrevprom ... State Institute for the Planning of Establishments of the Woodworking Industry (RU)
Giproenergoprom ... State Institute for the Planning of the Power Industry [*Khar'kov*] (RU)
Giproenergoprom ... State Planning Institute of the Electrotechnical Industry [*Moscow*] (RU)
Giproesprom ... State Institute for the Planning of Plants of the Electrical Communications Industry (RU)
Giprogazoochistka ... State Institute for the Planning of Gas-Purifying Installations (RU)
Giprogaztopprom ... State All-Union Institute for the Planning of Synthetic Liquid Fuel and Gas Plants (RU)
Giprogidroliz ... State Institute for the Planning of Hydrolysis Industry Establishments (RU)
Giprogor ..... State Institute for the Planning of Cities (RU)
Giprograd ... State Institute for the Planning of Cities (RU)
Giprogrozneft' ... State Institute for the Planning of Establishments of the Petroleum Industry [*in the Groznyy Region*] (RU)
Giproiv .... State Institute for the Planning of Synthetic Fiber Establishments (RU)
Giprokauchuk ... State Planning and Scientific Research Institute of the Synthetic Rubber Industry (RU)
Giprokhim ... State Institute for the Planning of Plants of the Basic Chemical Industry (RU)
GIPROKhIMMASh ... State Institute for the Planning of Chemical Machinery Plants (RU)
Giprokholod ... State Institute for the Planning of Cold Storage Plants, Ice-Cream Factories, and Dry Ice, Ice, and Liquid Carbon Dioxide Plants (RU)
Giprokinopoligraf ... State Planning Institute (for the Planning of Motion-Picture and Printing-Industry Establishments) (RU)
Giprokislorod ... State Institute for the Planning of Oxygen Industry Establishments (RU)
Giprokoks ... State Institute for the Planning of Establishments of the By-Product Coke Industry (RU)
Giprokommundortrans ... State Institute for the Planning of Municipal Road Transportation Structures (RU)
Giprokommunenergo ... State [*RSFSR*] Republic Planning Institute of the Municipal Power System Management (RU)
Giprokommunstroy ... State [*RSFSR*] Republic Institute for the Planning of Municipal Construction (RU)
Giprokommunvodokanal ... State Republic Institute for the Planning and Surveying of the Municipal Water Supply and Sewer System (RU)
GIPROLEGPROM ... State Institute for the Planning of Light Industry Establishments (RU)
Giproleskhim ... State Institute for the Planning of Establishments of the Wood-Chemistry Industry (RU)
Giprolesmash ... State Institute for the Planning of New Machines for Logging and Rafting (RU)
Giprolesprom ... State Institute for the Planning of Establishments of the Woodworking Industry (RU)
Giprolestrans ... State Institute for the Planning of Logging, Rafting, and Woodworking Establishments and Lumber Transportation (RU)
Gipromash ... State Institute for the Planning of Machinery Plants (RU)
Gipromashpribor ... State Institute for the Planning of Machinery and Instrument Plants (RU)
Gipromedprom ... State Planning Institute for the Planning of the Medical Equipment Industry (RU)
Gipromesttop ... State Institute for the Exploration of Coal and Peat Deposits and the Planning of Fuel Industry Establishments (RU)
Giprometiz ... State Institute for the Planning of Metalware Plants (RU)
Gipromez .... State All-Union Institute for the Planning of Metallurgical Plants (RU)
Gipromoloko ... State Institute for the Planning of Dairy Industry Establishments (RU)
Gipromolprom ... State Institute for the Planning of Dairy Industry Establishments (RU)
Gipromorneft' ... State Scientific Research and Planning Institute of Offshore Oil (RU)
Gipromyaso ... State Institute for the Planning of Meat Industry Establishments (RU)
Gipromyasomolprom ... State Institute for the Planning of Establishments of the Meat and Dairy Industry (RU)
Giproneftemash ... State Scientific Research and Planning Institute of Petroleum Machinery Manufacture (RU)
Giproneftezavod ... State Institute for the Planning of Petroleum-Processing Plants (RU)
Gipronemetrud ... State Institute for the Planning of Establishments Extracting and Processing Nonmetallic Building Materials (RU)
GIPRONII ..... All-Union State Institute for the Planning of Scientific Research Institutes and Laboratories of the Academy of Sciences, USSR, and the Academies of Sciences of the Union Republics (RU)
Gipronikel' ... State Institute for the Planning of Nickel Industry Establishments (RU)
GIPRONISEL'KhOZ ... All-Union Planning and Scientific Research Institute for the Planning of Standard and Experimental Agricultural Production Centers and Establishments for Storing and Processing of Grain (RU)
Gipronisslyuda ... State Scientific Research and Planning Institute of Mica (RU)
Giproobshchmash ... State Institute for the Planning of General Machinery Plants (RU)
Giproogneupor ... All-Union State Institute for the Planning of Plants and Quarries of the Refractory Industry (RU)
Giproorgkhim ... State Institute for the Planning of Establishments Producing Organic Intermediates, Dyestuffs, and Reagents (RU)

GIPROORGSEL'STROY ... State Planning Institute for the Organization of Rural Construction and the Rendering of Technical Assistance (RU)
Giproorgstroy ... State Institute for Planning the Organization and the Carrying-Out of Construction Work (RU)
Gipropishcheprom ... State Planning Institute for the Planning of Food Industry Establishments (RU)
Giproplast... State Institute for the Planning of Establishments Producing Plastics and Semifinished Products (RU)
Giptopribor ... State Institute for the Planning of Instrument Plants (RU)
GIPROPROM ... State Planning Institute for the Planning of Industrial Establishments (RU)
Gipropromtransstroy ... State Planning and Surveying Institute of the State Industrial Committee for Transportation Construction, USSR (RU)
Gipropros ... Republic Planning Institute of the Ministry of Education, RSFSR (RU)
Giproraszhirmaslo ... All-Union State Institute for the Planning of Establishments of the Vegetable Oils and Fats Industry (RU)
Giprorechtrans ... State Institute for Planning in River Transportation (RU)
Giproruda... State All-Union Institute for the Planning of Establishments of the Ore-Mining Industry (RU)
Giprorybflot ... State Planning Institute of the Fishing Fleet (RU)
Giprorybprom ... State Institute for the Planning of Fish Industry Establishments (RU)
Giprosakhar ... State Institute for the Planning of Sugar Industry Establishments (RU)
Giprosel'elektro ... All-Union State Institute for the Planning of Rural Electrification (RU)
Giprosel'khoz ... All-Union State Institute for the Planning of Industrial Buildings and Structures for Agriculture (RU)
Giprosel'stroy ... State Planning Institute for Rural Housing and Civil Engineering Construction (RU)
Giproshakht ... State Institute for the Planning of Mines (RU)
Giproshaktostroymash ... State Planning, Design, and Scientific Research Institute for the Development of New Machines and Mechanisms for Shaft-Sinking Operations (RU)
Giprosovkhozstroy ... All-Union State Institute for the Planning of Sovkhoz Construction (RU)
Giprosovkhozvodstroy ... All-Union State Institute for the Planning of Water-Management Construction of the Ministry of Sovkhozes, USSR (RU)
Giprospetsneft' ... State Institute for the Planning of Special Structures in the Petroleum Industry (RU)
Giprospetspromstroy ... State Institute for the Planning of Special Structures in Industrial Construction (RU)
GIPROSPIRTVINO ... State Institute for the Planning of Establishments of Wine-Making, Beer, Soft Drink, Alcohol, Liquor, and Vodka, Tobacco, Enzyme, Starch, and Syrup Industries (RU)
Giprosport ... State Institute for the Planning of Sports Structures (RU)
Giprostal'.... State Scientific Research and Planning Institute of the Metallurgical Industry (RU)
Giprostandartdom ... State Institute for the Planning of 3-4 Story Prefabricated Houses (RU)
Giprostanok ... State Institute for the Planning of Machine Tool, Tool, and Abrasives Plants and Forging-and-Pressing Machinery Plants [*Moscow*] (RU)
Giprostanok ... State Planning Institute of the Machine Tool Industry [*Kiev*] (RU)
GIPROSTROM ... State All-Union Institute for the Planning of Establishments of the Building Materials Industry (RU)
Giprostrommash ... All-Union State Planning and Design Institute of the Giprostroyindustriya (RU)
Giprostrommekhanizatsiya ... State All-Union Planning Institute for the Mechanization of Production of Building Materials (RU)
Giprostroydormash ... State Institute for the Planning of Construction and Road Machinery Plants (RU)
Giprostroyindustriya ... All-Union State Planning and Design Institute for the Planning of Establishments of the Construction Industry (RU)
Giprostroymaterialy ... State Institute for the Planning of Establishments of the Building Materials Industry (RU)
Giprosvyaz' ... State Institute for the Surveying and Planning of Communications Installations (RU)
Giproteatr... State Institute for the Planning of Theatrical and Entertainment Establishments (RU)
GIPROTIS ... State Institute for Standard Experimental Planning and Technical Research (RU)
Giprotopprom ... State Institute for the Exploration of Coal and Peat Deposits and Wood Raw-Material Bases and for the Planning of Fuel Industry Establishments (RU)
Giprotorf..... State Planning Institute for the Multipurpose Use of Peat in the National Economy (RU)
Giprotorfrazvedka ... State Planning and Surveying Institute for the Exploration of Peat (RU)
Giprotorg.... State All-Union Institute for the Planning of Trade Establishments and Public Eating Facilities (RU)
Giprotraktorosel'khozmash ... State Institute for the Planning of the Tractor Industry and Agricultural Machinery Manufacture (RU)
Giprotranskar'yer ... State Institute for Geological Exploration and the Planning of Gravel Plants and Quarries of the State Industrial Committee for Transportation Construction, USSR (RU)
Giprotransmost ... State Planning and Surveying Institute for the Survey and Planning of Large Bridges (RU)
Giprotransneft' ... State Institute for the Planning of Transportation Structures and Storage for Petroleum Products (RU)
Giprotranssignalsvyaz' ... State Planning and Surveying Institute for the Planning of Signalization, Centralization, Communications, and Radio in Railroad Transportation (RU)
Giprotranstei ... State Institute for the Technical and Economic Investigation and Planning of Railroad Transportation (RU)
Giprotruboprovod ... State Institute for the Planning of Main Pipelines (RU)
Giprotsement ... All-Union State Scientific Research and Planning Institute of the Cement Industry (RU)
GIPROTsMO ... State Scientific Research and Planning Institute of Alloys and the Working of Nonferrous Metals (RU)
Giprotsvetmet ... State Institute for the Planning of Establishments of Nonferrous Metallurgy (RU)
Giprotsvetmetobrabotka ... State Scientific Research and Planning Institute of Alloys and Nonferrous Metal Processing (RU)
Giprotsvetmetzoloto ... Institute for the Planning of Establishments of Nonferrous Metallurgy and Gold (RU)
Giprotyazhmash ... State Institute for the Planning of Heavy Machinery Plants (RU)
Giprougleavtomatizatsiya ... State Planning and Design, and Scientific Research Institute for the Automation of Operations in the Coal Industry (RU)
Giprouglemash ... State Planning, Design, and Experimental Institute of Coal Machinery Manufacture (RU)
Giprovino.... State Scientific Research Institute for the Planning of the Wine-Making Industry (RU)
Giprovodkhoz ... All-Union State Planning, Surveying, and Scientific Research Institute of Water Management Construction (RU)
Giprovodokanalproyekt ... State Institute for the Planning and Surveying of the Urban Water Supply and Sewer Systems (RU)
Giprovodtrans ... State Institute for Planning and Research in Water Transportation (RU)
Giprovostokneft' ... State Institute for Planning and Research in the Petroleum Production Industry (RU)
Giprovuz..... State All-Union Institute for the Planning of Higher Educational Institutions with Scientific Research and Exploration Departments (RU)
Giprozdrav ... State Planning Institute for the Planning of Establishments for Medical and Preventive Treatment (RU)
Giprozhir .... State Institute for the Planning of the Oil-Extracting, Fats, Soap-Making, Perfumery, and Margarine Industries (RU)
GIPS............ Groupement Industriel des Plastiques Senegalais (MAR)
Gipzoloto.... State Scientific Research Institute for Gold and Its Accessory Minerals (RU)
GIR.............. Groupement Independant de Reflexion et d'Action Politique, Economique, Culturelle, et Sociale (MAR)
GIR.............. State Scientific Research Institute of Rheumatism (RU)
GIRA............ Groupe d'Information Revolution Africaine [*African Revolution Information Group*] [*French*] (WER)
GIRA............ Groupement Independant de Reflexion et d'Action [*Independent Grouping of Reflection and Action*] [*Central African*] (PD)
GIRC............ Groupement d'Importation et de Repartition du Coton (MAR)
GIRCA......... Groupement Interprofessionnel pour l'Etude et le Developpement de l'Economie Centrafricaine [*Interprofessional Group for the Study and Development of the Central African Economy*] (AF)
GIRCUIL...... Grupul de Intreprinderi de Reparatii si Constructii Utilaje pentru Industria Lemnului [*Group of Enterprises for the Repair and Construction of Equipment for the Wood Industry*] (RO)
GIRD............ Group for the Study of Jet Propulsion [*1932-1934*] (RU)
GIRedmet ... State Scientific Research and Planning Institute of the Rare Metals Industry (RU)
GIRK............ State Institute of Cultivation of Speech (RU)
GIRT............ Groupe des Independants Ruraux Tchadiens [*Chadian Independent Rural Group*]
GIS .... City Statistical Inspectorate (BU)
GIS .... Glowny Inspektorat Sanitarny [*Chief Sanitary Inspectorate*] [*Polish*]
GIS .... Government Information Service [*Dominican*] (LA1)
GIS .... Gozdarski Institut Slovenije [*Forestry Institute of Slovenia*] (YU)
GIS .... Grupo de Intervencao Socialista [*Socialist Intervention Group*] [*Portuguese*] (WER)
gis .... Histidine (RU)
GIS .... Hospital Inhalator Station (RU)
GIS .... Main Pulse Shifted by Half-Period (RU)
GIS .... State Institute of Literary Readings (RU)
GIS .... State Publishing House of Foreign and National Dictionaries (RU)
GIS .... State Scientific Research Institute of Glass (RU)
GISAN......... Geografski Institut Srpska Akademija Nauka [*Geographic Institute of the Serbian Academy of Sciences*] (YU)

GISE .... "Soviet Encyclopedía" State Institute (RU)
GISECA .... Groupement Ivoirien des Societes d'Exportation et Cooperatives Agricoles (MAR)
GISh .... Master-Pulse Bus (RU)
GISI .... Gor'kiy Construction Engineering Institute Imeni V. P. Chkalov (RU)
GISM .... State Planning, Design, and Experimental Institute of Glass Machinery (RU)
GISO .... State Institute of Stomatology and Odontology (RU)
Gisogneupor ... State Quality and Service Life Inspection of Refractories (RU)
gist .... Histological (RU)
GISU .... Hydrographic Ship (RU)
GIT .... Group Inclusive Tour (MAR)
GIT .... Grupo Independiente de Trabajo [*Independent Labor Group*] [*Spanish*] (WER)
GIT .... Pulse Current Generator (RU)
GITA .... Gremio dos Industriais de Transportes em Automoveis [*Association of Automobile Transportation Industrialists*] [*Portuguese*] (WER)
GITEXAL ..... Groupement d'Importation des Textiles en Algerie [*Algerian Textile Imports Group*] (AF)
GITIS .... State Institute of Theatrical Art Imeni A. V. Lunacharskiy (RU)
GITO .... Groupement Interprofessionnel des Entreprises du Togo (MAR)
GIU- .... Gamma-Ray Level Gauge (RU)
GIU .... Main Engineer Directorate (RU)
GIU .... State Publishing House of the Ukraine (RU)
GIU .... Universal Group Selector (RU)
Giun .... Giuniore [*Junior*] [*Italian*] (GPO)
GIV- .... Hydraulic Weight Indicator (RU)
GIV .... Pulse Generator (RU)
GIV .... State Veterinary Inspection (RU)
GIVA .... Chief Engineer of an Air Army (RU)
GIVD .... State Chemical Scientific Research Institute of High Pressures (RU)
GIVD .... State Institute of Veterinary Dermatology (RU)
GIVT .... Gor'kiy Institute of Water Transportation Engineers (RU)
GiW .... Gebethner i Wolff [*Gebethner and Wolff*] [*Publisher*] (POL)
GIWB .... Glowny Inspektorat Wyszkolenia Bojowego [*Main Inspectorate of Combat Training*] (POL)
Giy-Sen .... Giyim Iscileri Sendikasi [*Wearing Apparel Workers Union*] [*Turkish Cypriot*] (GC)
GIZ .... State Institute of Dentistry (RU)
GIZ .... State Publishing House (RU)
GIZBel .... State Publishing House of Belorussia (RU)
GIZh .... State Institute of Journalism (RU)
Gizlegprom ... State Scientific and Technical Publishing House of Light Industry (RU)
Gizmestprom ... State Publishing House of Local Industry (RU)
GIZO .... State Institute for the Study of Arid Regions (RU)
GIZU .... State Publishing House of Ukrainian SSR (RU)
GJ .... Geographical Journal [*A publication*] (MAR)
GJA .... Ghana Journalists Association (AF)
GJED .... Glasnik Jugoslovenskog Entomoloskog Drustva [*Bulletin of the Yugoslav Entomological Society*] [*Belgrade*] [*A publication*] (YU)
GJK .... Grupa Jurisnih Korpusa [*Group of Assault Corps*] [*Military*] (YU)
GJL .... Geographical Journal (London) [*A publication*] (MAR)
gjmu .... Gepjarmu [*Motor Vehicle*] (HU)
GJS .... Ghana Journal of Sociology [*Accra*] [*A publication*] (MAR)
GK .... Calcium Hypochlorite (RU)
GK .... Citizens Committee (BU)
GK .... City Committee (BU)
GK .... City Committee (RU)
GK .... Civil Code (RU)
GK .... Compensating Signal Generator (RU)
GK .... Foam Rubber (RU)
GK .... Gallic Acid (RU)
GK .... Gamma-Ray Logging (RU)
GK .... Gas Compressor (RU)
GK .... Gas-Engine Compressor (RU)
GK .... Genclik Kol [*Youth Auxiliary*] [*As of a political party*] (TU)
gk .... General [*Cavalry*] (BU)
GK .... Geological Committee (RU)
gk .... Gepkocsi [*Motor Vehicle*] (HU)
GK .... Gereformeerde Kerk [*Reformed Church*] [*South African*] (AF)
GK .... Giant Cell (RU)
GK .... Gibberellic Acid (RU)
GK .... Glavni Kolodvor [*Central Railroad Station*] [*Croatian*] (YU)
GK .... Glowna Kwatera [*Headquarters*] [*Polish*]
GK .... Glowny Komitet [*Chief Committee*] [*Polish*]
GK .... Glutamic Acid (RU)
GK .... Gondolat Kiado [*Gondolat Publishing House*] (HU)
GK .... Gottwaldovy Knihovny [*Gottwald Libraries*] (CZ)
GK .... Gradska Klanica [*City Slaughterhouse*] (YU)
GK .... Guvenlik Konseyi [*Security Council*] [*United Nations*] (TU)
GK .... Gyrocompass (RU)
GK .... Hexokinase (RU)
GK .... High Command (RU)
GK .... Hydrolized Blood (RU)
GK .... Hypophyseal Cell (RU)
Gk .... Pebble and Crushed Stone [*Topography*] (RU)
GK .... Pressurized Cabin (RU)
GK .... Primary Caliber [*Artillery*] (RU)
GK .... Quartz-Crystal Oscillator (RU)
GKA .... Annular Astatic Gravimeter (RU)
GKA .... Gebrauchswert-Kostenanalyse [*Utility Value Cost Analysis*] (EG)
GKA .... Glowna Komisja Arbitrazowa [*Main Arbitration Commission*] (POL)
GKAE .... State Committee for the Use of Atomic Energy (RU)
Gkal .... Gigacalorie (RU)
g kat .... Gorog Katolikus [*Greek Catholic, Uniate*] (HU)
GKB .... Chief Design Office (RU)
GKB .... Garantie- und Kreditbank [*Guaranty and Credit Bank*] (EG)
GK na BKP ... City Committee of the Bulgarian Communist Party (BU)
GKBS .... Urgent [*Military code*] (YU)
GKBZHwP ... Glowna Komisja Badania Zbrodni Hitlerowskich w Polsce [*Main Commission for the Investigation of NAZI Crimes in Poland*] (POL)
GKCh .... Pilot-Frequency Generator (RU)
GKCh .... Wobbulator, Sweep Generator, Frequency-Sweep Generator (RU)
GKD .... Gonyeli Kultur Dernegi [*Gonyeli (or Geunyeli) Cultural Association*] [*Turkish Cypriot*] (GC)
GKD .... Gornoslaska Kolej Dojazdowa [*Upper Silesia Suburban Railroad*] (POL)
GKDH .... Gubernur/Kepala Daerah [*Governor/Chief of Region*] (IN)
GKDP .... Main Control Tower [*Aviation*] (RU)
GKE .... Geodeziai es Kartografiai Egyesulet [*Association of Geodesy and Cartography*] (HU)
g kel .... Gorog Keleti [*Greek Orthodox*] (HU)
GKES .... State Committee of the Council of Ministers, USSR, on Foreign Economic Relations (RU)
GKFN .... Gminny Komitet Frontu Narodowego [*Rural Commune Committee of the People's Front*] (POL)
GKFS .... City Committee for Physical Culture and Sports (BU)
g/kh .... Gas-Powered Boat (RU)
GKhA .... Hexachloroacetone (RU)
GKhB .... Hexachlorobenzene (RU)
GKhCh .... Human Chorionic Gonadotrophin (RU)
GKhI .... State Grain Inspection (RU)
GKhI .... State Scientific and Technical Publishing House of Chemical Literature (RU)
GKhK .... Genikon Khimeion Kratous [*State General Chemical Laboratory*] [*Greek*] (GC)
GKhK .... Main Cotton Committee [*1921-1931*] (RU)
GKhP .... Main Administration of the Basic Chemical Industry (RU)
g khr .... Mountain Chain (RU)
GKhTsG ...... Hexachlorocyclohexane (RU)
GKhTsPD .... Hexachlorocyclopentadiene (RU)
GKI .... Channel Pulse Generator (RU)
GKI .... Code Pulse Generator (RU)
GKI .... Geodeziai es Kartografiai Intezet [*Institute of Geodesy and Cartography*] (HU)
GKI .... Standard-Pulse Generator (RU)
GKI .... State Control Institute of Medical Biological Preparations Imeni L. A. Tarasevich (RU)
GKI .... State Quarantine Inspection (RU)
GKISV .... State Control Institute of Serums and Vaccines Imeni L. A. Tarasevich (RU)
GKK .... City Control Commission (RU)
GKK .... Civil Board of Appeals of the Supreme Court (RU)
GKK .... Glowna Komisja Kontrolna [*Main Control Commission*] (POL)
GKK .... Glowna Komisja Ksiezy [*Main Commission of the Clergy*] (POL)
GKK .... Main Committee on Concessions (RU)
GKK .... Pilot-Channel Generator (RU)
GKKF .... Glowny Komitet Kultury Fizycznej [*Main Committee on Physical Culture*] (POL)
GKKFiT .... Glowny Komitet Kultury Fizycznej i Turystyki [*Main Committee for Physical Culture and Tourism*] (POL)
GKKh .... City Municipal Services (RU)
GKL .... Guzelyurt Kurtulus Lisesi [*Guzelyurt Liberation Lycee*] [*Turkish Cypriot*] (GC)
GKL .... State Control Laboratory (RU)
GKM .... Glavno Komandno Mesto [*Central Command Post*] (YU)
GKM .... Horizontal Forging Machine (RU)
GKMTAP ..... Guards Red Banner Mine and Torpedo Air Regiment (RU)
GKN .... Gorlickie Kopalnictwo Naftowe [*Gorlice Oil Wells*] (POL)
GKN .... Helium Condensation Pump (RU)
GK NII VVS ... State Red Banner Scientific Testing Institute of the Air Force (RU)
GKO .... Garnizonowy Klub Oficerski [*Garrison Officers Club*] (POL)
GKO .... State Defense Committee [*1941-1945*] (RU)
GKOE .... Grafeio Kommatikon Organoseon Exoterikou [*Office of Party Organization Abroad*] [*Greek Communist Party*] [*Greek*] (GC)
GKOPI .... Glowna Komisja Opiniowania Projektow Inwestycyjnych [*Main Commission on the Evaluation of Investment Plans*] (POL)
GKP .... Commanding Officer's Battle Station [*Navy*], Main Command Post, Primary Command Post (RU)

GKP............ Disastrous Flood Level (RU)
GKP............ German Communist Party (BU)
GKP............ Glowny Komitet Przeciwpowodziowy [*Main Committee on Flood Control*] (POL)
GKP............ Gradsko Komunalno Preduzece [*City Communal Establishment*] (YU)
GKP............ Greek Communist Party (BU)
GKP............ Main Administration of the Oxygen Industry (RU)
GKP............ Main Control Post, Primary Control Post (RU)
GK po KNIR ... State Committee of the Council of Ministers, USSR, for Coordination of Scientific Research (RU)
GKpoM....... State Committee on Machinery Manufacture (RU)
GKR............ Generalna Konfederacija Rada [*General Confederation of Labor*] (YU)
GKRAM....... Group of Cambodian Residents in America (CL)
GKRE .... State Committee of the Council of Ministers, USSR, for Radio Electronics (RU)
GKrS .... Glavna Kurirska Stanica [*Central Courier Station*] [*Military*] (YU)
GKRT .... State Committee of the Council of Ministers, USSR, on Radio Broadcasting and Television (RU)
GKS............ City Cooperative Union (BU)
GKS............ Gabungan Kepala Staf [*Joint Chiefs of Staff*] (IN)
GKS............ Gas-Logging Station [*Pet.*] (RU)
GKS............ Gminna Kasa Spoldzielcza [*Rural Commune Cooperative Bank*] (POL)
GKS............ Gorniczy Klub Sportowy [*Miners' Sports and Athletics Club*] [*Polish*]
GKs............ Hypoxanthine (RU)
GKSNRM..... Glaven Kooperativen Sojuz na Narodnata Republika Makedonija [*Central Cooperative Union of Macedonia*] (YU)
GKSS .... Gesellschaft fuer Kernenergieverwertung in Schiffbau und Schiffahrt [*Nuclear energy*] [*German*]
GKT............ Annual Temperature Fluctuation (RU)
GKT............ Gueter-Kraftverkehrs-Tarif [*Truck Freight Rate Schedule*] (EG)
GKTP.......... Main Administration of the Boiler and Turbine Industry (RU)
GKTSz......... Gepszakmai Kisipari Termelo Szovetkezet [*Cooperative for Machine Production*] (HU)
GKU............ Main Health Resort Administration (RU)
gkvez .... Gepkocsivezeto [*Chauffeur*] (HU)
GKW............ Geraer Kompressorenwerk (VEB) [*Gera Compressor Factory (VEB)*] (EG)
GKW............ Gesellschaft fuer Klaranlagen und Wasserversorgung [*Mannheim*] (MAR)
GKW............ Gminny Komitet Wykonawczy [*Rural Commune Executive Committee*] (POL)
GKWP .... Glowny Komitet Wspolzawodnictwa Pracy [*Main Committee on Labor Competition*] (POL)
GKWR .... Glowna Komisja Wynalazczosci i Racjonalizacji [*Chief Committee for Inventiveness and Rationalization*] (POL)
GKWZSL..... Glowny Komitet Wykonawczy Zjednoczonego Stronnictwa Ludowego [*Main Executive Committee of the United Peasant Party*] (POL)
GKZ............ State Commission on Mineral Resources (RU)
GKZ............ State Stud Farm (RU)
GKZh.......... Sealed Cabin for an Animal (RU)
GKZh.......... Waterproofing Organo-Silicon Fluid (RU)
GK ZSL .... Gromadzki Komitet Zjednoczonego Stronnictwa Ludowego [*Village Committee of the United Peasants' Party*] [*Polish*]
gl................ Chapter (BU)
gl................ Chapter (RU)
Gl................ Clay, Clay Pit [*Topography*] (RU)
gl................ Depth (RU)
gl................ Gammel [*Old*] [*Danish*] (GPO)
GL................ Gas Discharge Lamp (RU)
gl................ General (BU)
gl................ Glava [*Chapter*] (YU)
gl................ Glebokosc [*Depth*] [*Polish*]
GL................ Gledaliski List [*Theatrical Bulletin*] [*A publication*] (YU)
Gl................ Gleichung [*Equation*] [*German*]
gl................ Glownie [*Mainly*] (POL)
gl................ Glowny [*Main, Chief*] (POL)
GL................ Glutamine (RU)
GL................ Greenland [*Two-letter standard code*] (CNC)
GL................ Gwardia Ludowa [*People's Guard (1942-1943)*] (POL)
gl................ Hectoliter (RU)
gl................ Lieutenant General (BU)
Gl................ Main, Chief, Primary (RU)
gl................ See (BU)
gl................ Verb (RU)
gl................ Verb (BU)
GLA............ Groupe de Liberation Armee [*Armed Liberation Group*] [*Guadeloupe*] (PD)
GLACSEC... Group of Latin American and Caribbean Sugar Exporting Countries [*See also GEPLACEA*] (EA)
GLAG .... Groupe de Liberation Armee de la Guadeloupe [*Armed Liberation Group of Guadeloupe*] (LA1)
Glag............ Verb (RU)
GLA-Martinique ... Groupe de Liberation Armee de la Martinique [*Armed Liberation Group of Martinique*] (PD)
Gl AO.......... Main Astronomical Observatory (RU)
GlasSKA ..... Glas Srpske Kraljevske Akademije [*Organ of the Serbian Royal Academy*] [*Belgrade*] [*A publication*] (YU)
Glav............ Glaven [*Chief, Main*] (YU)
glav .... Main, Chief, Primary (RU)
Glavabraziv ... Main Administration of the Abrasives Industry (RU)
Glavalyuminiy ... Main Administration of the Aluminum Industry (RU)
Glavanilkraska ... Main Administration of the Aniline Dye Industry (RU)
Glavanilprom ... Main Administration of the Aniline Dye Industry (RU)
Glavantibioprom ... Main Administration of the Antibiotics Industry (RU)
GlavAPU ..... Main Architectural Planning Administration of the City of Moscow (RU)
Glavarkhiv ... Main Administration of Archives (RU)
Glavasbest ... Main Administration of the Asbestos Industry (RU)
Glavasboshifer ... Main Administration of the Asbestos and Shale Industry (RU)
Glavatom .... Main Administration for the Use of Atomic Energy (RU)
Glavatomenergo ... Main Administration for the Use of Atomic Energy (RU)
Glavaviaprom ... Main Administration of the Aircraft Industry (RU)
Glavaviastroy ... Main Administration of Aircraft Construction (RU)
Glavavtoagregat ... Main Administration of Plants for Automobile Assemblies (RU)
Glavavtogen ... Main Administration of the Gas-Welding Industry (RU)
Glavavtopribor ... Main Administration for the Manufacture of Automobile Instruments and Equipment (RU)
Glavavtoprom ... Main Administration of the Automobile Industry (RU)
Glavavtoremont ... Main Administration of Automobile Repair Plants and Stations (RU)
Glavavtotraktorosbyt ... Main Administration for the Marketing of Tractors, Agricultural Machinery, and Spare Parts for Automobiles and Tractors (RU)
Glavavtozavodov ... Main Administration of Automobile Plants (RU)
Glavazcherrybprom ... Main Administration of the Fish Industry of the Azov - Black Sea Basin (RU)
Glavazot...... Main Administration of the Nitrogen Industry (RU)
Glavbakaleya ... Main Administration of Wholesale Trade in Sugar, Confectionery, Canned Goods, Tobacco, Salt, and Other Groceries (RU)
Glavblagoustroystva ... Main Administration of Urban Improvement and Municipal Services Establishments (RU)
GLAVBUM... Main Administration of State Establishments of the Paper Industry (RU)
Glavbumdrevstroy ... Main Administration for the Construction of Establishments of the Pulp, Paper, and Woodworking Industries (RU)
Glavbumprom ... Main Administration of the Paper Industry (RU)
Glavbumsbyt ... Main Administration for Marketing Paper Industry Products (RU)
Glavbumsbyt ... Main Administration for Marketing Wood-Chemical, Pulp, and Paper Industries Products (RU)
Glavchasprom ... Main Administration of the Watch Industry (RU)
Glavchay..... Main Administration of the Tea Industry (RU)
Glavdal'stroy ... Main Administration for the Construction of Industrial Establishments in the Regions of the Far East (RU)
Glavdal'vostokrybprom ... Main Administration of the Fish Industry of the Far East (RU)
Glavdizel'.... Main Administration of Diesel Building (RU)
Glavdormash ... Main Administration of Road Machinery Manufacture (RU)
Glavdorrestoran ... Main Administration of Railroad Restaurants (RU)
Glavdorstroy ... Main Administration for the Construction of All-Union Highways (RU)
Glavdortrans ... Main Administration of Highways, Dirt Roads, and Automobile Transportation (RU)
Glavdorupr ... Main Administration of Construction and Operation of Republic and Local Roads (RU)
Glavdorupr ... Main Administration of Republic and Local Highways (RU)
Glavdrevlitmash ... Main Administration of Woodworking and Foundry Machinery (RU)
Glavekskavator ... Main Administration for the Manufacture of Excavators and Cranes (RU)
Glavelektro ... Main Administration of the Electrotechnical Industry (RU)
Glavelektromontazh ... Main Administration for Installation of Electrical Equipment of Electric Power Plants and Substations (USSR) (RU)
Glavelektromontazh ... Main Administration for Planning and Performing Electrical Installation Work (RSFSR) (RU)
Glavelektrosbyt ... Main Administration for the Marketing of Electrotechnical Products (RU)
Glavelektroset'stroy ... Main Administration for the Construction of Substations and Electric Power Networks (RU)
Glavelektrotochpribor ... Main Administration of Electrical Precision Instruments (RU)
Glavelevator ... Main Administration of Elevators (RU)
Glavelevatorspetsstroy ... Main Administration for the Construction of Elevators and Other Specialized Reinforced Concrete Structures (RU)
Glavenergo ... Main Power Supply Administration (RU)
Glavenergoizdat ... Main State Publishing House of Literature on Power Engineering (RU)

Glavenergokomplekt ... Main Administration for Ensuring the Supply of Complete Sets of Power Engineering Equipment of Electric Power Plants, Substations, and Networks (RU)
Glavenergoproyekt ... Main Administration for the Planning of Electric Power Plants, Substations, and Networks (RU)
Glavenergoremont ... Main Administration for the Repair of Electric Power Plant Equipment (RU)
Glavenergostroy ... Main Administration for Construction and Installation of Thermal Electric Power Plants (RU)
Glavenergostroymekhanizatsiya ... Main Administration for Construction Mechanization of the State Industrial Committee for Power Engineering and Electrification, USSR (RU)
Glavenergostroymontazh ... Main Administration for Construction and Installation of Hydroelectric Power Plants (RU)
Glavenergostroyprom ... Main Administration of Establishments for the Manufacture of Structural Parts and Building Materials of the Ministry of Electric Power Plant Construction, USSR (RU)
Glavesprom ... Main Administration of the Electrical Communications Industry (RU)
Glavfanerspichprom ... Main Administration of the Plywood and Match Industries (RU)
Glavfanspichprom ... Main Administration of the Plywood and Match Industries (RU)
Glavfarfor.... Main Administration of the Porcelain and Faience Industry (RU)
Glavflot .... Main Administration of the Dry Cargo Fleet (RU)
Glavflot .... Main Administration of Shipping and of Ship-Repair Establishments (of the Ministry of the River Fleet, RSFSR) (RU)
Glavgalantereya ... Main Administration of the Wholesale Trade in Notions, Perfume, Cosmetics, and Toilet Soap (RU)
Glavgastronom ... Main Administration of Delicatessen and Grocery Stores (RU)
Glavgaz....... Main Administration of the Gas Industry [*USSR*] (RU)
Glavgaz....... Main Administration of the Gas Supply System [*RSFSR*] (RU)
Glavgeologiya ... Main Administration of Geology and Conservation of Mineral Resources (at the Council of Ministers, RSFSR) (RU)
Glavgeologiya ... Main Geological Exploration Administration (of the Ministry of the Building Materials Industry, USSR) (RU)
Glavgidroenergostroy ... Main Administration for the Construction and Installation of Hydroelectric Power Plants in the Central and Southern Regions (RU)
Glavgidrolizprom ... Main Administration of the Hydrolysis Industry (RU)
Glavgidromash ... Main Administration for the Manufacture of Pumps, Fittings, and Hydraulic Turbines of the Ministry of Machinery Manufacture, USSR (RU)
Glavgidrostroy ... Main Administration of Hydraulic Engineering Construction (RU)
Glavgimet... Main Administration of the Hydrometeorological Service (RU)
Glavgips...... Main Administration of the Gypsum Industry (RU)
Glavgorkhimprom ... Main Administration of the Chemical Raw Materials Mining Industry (RU)
Glavgormash ... Main Administration of Mining and Fuel Machinery Manufacture (RU)
Glavgortop ... Main Mineral Fuel Administration (RU)
Glavgosrybvod ... Main State Inspection for Fish Conservation (RU)
Glavgramplastprom ... Main Administration of the Phonograph Record Industry (RU)
Glavinstrument ... Main Administration of the Tool Industry (RU)
glavinzh ...... Chief Engineer (RU)
Glaviskozh ... Main Administration of the Artificial Leather and Industrial Fabric Industry (RU)
Glaviskusstvo ... Main Administration of Art (RU)
Glavizdat .... Main Administration of Publishing Houses, the Printing Industry, and the Book Trade [*USSR*] (RU)
Glavizo........ Main Administration of Fine Arts (RU)
glavk .... Main Administration, Main Directorate [*Military term*] (RU)
Glavkabel'... Main Administration of the Cable Industry (RU)
Glavkauchuk ... Main Administration of the Synthetic Rubber Industry (RU)
Glavkhimfarmprom ... Main Administration of the Chemical and Pharmaceutical Industry (RU)
Glavkhimmash ... Main Administration of Chemical Machinery Manufacture (RU)
Glavkhimprom ... Main Administration of the Basic Chemical Industry (RU)
Glavkhimpromstroy ... Main Administration for Construction and Installation of Chemical Industry Establishments (RU)
Glavkhimsbyt ... Main Administration of Marketing of Chemical Industry Products (RU)
Glavkhimsnab ... Main Administration of Supply of the Chemical Industry (RU)
Glavkholod ... Main Administration of Cold Storage Plants (RU)
Glavkhoztorg ... Main Administration of Wholesale Trade in Household Goods (RU)
Glavkinofikatsiya ... Main Administration for the Development of Motion-Picture Facilities and for Motion-Picture Distribution (RU)
Glavkinoprokat ... Main Administration of Motion-Picture Distribution (RU)
Glavkinosnab ... Main Supply Administration of the Ministry of Cinematography, USSR (RU)
Glavkirpich ... Main Administration of the Brick Industry (RU)
Glavkislorod ... Main Administration of the Oxygen Industry (RU)
Glavkislorodmash ... Main Administration of Oxygen Machinery (RU)
Glavkiyevstroy ... Main Administration for Housing and Civil Engineering Construction of the Kiev Gorispolkom (RU)
Glavknigtorg ... Main Administration of the Book Trade (RU)
Glavknizhtorg ... Main Administration of the Book Trade (RU)
Glavkoks..... Main Administration of the By-Product Coke Industry (RU)
Glavkolkhozstroy ... Main Administration for Construction in Kolkhozes (RU)
Glavkombaynprom ... Main Administration of the Combine Industry and Harvesting Machines (RU)
Glavkomplekt ... Main Administration of Supply of Equipment in Complete Sets (RU)
Glavkomplektooborudovaniye ... Main Administration of Supply of Metallurgical, Power-Engineering, and Petrochemical Equipment in Complete Sets (RU)
Glavkonditer ... Main Administration of the Confectionery Industry (RU)
Glavkonserv ... Main Administration of the Canning and Food Concentrates Industry (RU)
Glavkontsesskom ... Main Committee on Concessions (RU)
Glavkoopbakaleytorg ... Main Administration for the Grocery Trade (of the Tsentrosoyuz) (RU)
Glavkoopgalantereytorg ... Main Administration for the Notions and Perfumery Trade (of the Tsentrosoyuz) (RU)
Glavkoopkhoztorg ... Main Administration for Trade in Metalware and Household Goods (of the Tsentrosoyuz) (RU)
Glavkoopkul'ttorg ... Main Administration for Trade in Goods for Cultural Purposes (of the Tsentrosoyuz) (RU)
Glavkooplektekhsyr'ye ... Main Administration for the Procurement, Processing, and Marketing of Raw Materials for the Drug Industry, Wild Plants and Berries, and Beekeeping Products (of the Tsentrosoyuz) (RU)
Glavkoopmetiztorg ... Main Administration for Trade in Metalware and Silicate Products (of the Tsentrosoyuz) (RU)
Glavkoopplodoovoshch ... Main Administration for the Procurement, Processing, and Marketing of Produce (of the Tsentrosoyuz) (RU)
Glavkoopsnab ... Main Administration for Equipment Manufacture and Materials and Equipment Supply (of the Tsentrosoyuz) (RU)
Glavkoopsyr'ye ... Main Administration for Procurement, Processing, and Marketing of Raw Materials, Scrap Metal, and Utility Waste (of the Tsentrosoyuz) (RU)
Glavkoopzhivsyr'ye ... Main Administration for the Procurement, Processing, and Marketing of Livestock Products, Raw Materials, and Fur (of the Tsentrosoyuz) (RU)
Glavkord ..... Main Administration of the Cord Industry (RU)
Glavkotloprom ... Main Administration of the Boiler Industry (RU)
Glavkozh..... Main Administration of the Leather and Tanning Extract Industry (RU)
Glavkozhsyr'ye ... Main Administration for the Primary Processing of Leather and Fur Raw Materials and the Manufacture of Tanning Extracts (RU)
Glavkraska ... Main Administration of the Paint Industry (RU)
Glavkul'tprosvet ... Main Administration of Cultural and Educational Institutions (RU)
Glavkul'tsnabsbyt ... Main Supply and Marketing Administration of the Ministry of Culture, USSR (RU)
Glavkul'ttorg ... Main Administration of Wholesale Trade in Goods for Cultural Purposes and Sports (RU)
Glavkurorttorg ... Main Administration for Trade in Health Resorts (RU)
Glavkursanupr ... Main Administration of Health Resorts, Sanatoriums, and Rest Homes (RU)
Glavkurupr ... Main Administration of Health Resorts (RU)
Glavkustprom ... Main Administration of Cottage Industry (RU)
Glavlegmash ... Main Administration of Light Machinery Manufacture (RU)
Glavlegsbytsyr'ye ... Main Administration for the Marketing of Raw Materials of Textile and Light Industries (RU)
Glavleningradstroy ... Main Administration for the Housing, Civil Engineering, and Industrial Construction of the Leningrad Gorispolkom (RU)
Glavlenstroymaterialy ... Main Leningrad Administration of the Building Materials and Parts Industry (RU)
Glavles........ Main Administration for Logging and Woodworking (RU)
Glavleskhim ... Main Administration of the Wood-Chemistry Industry (RU)
Glavleskhoz ... Main Administration of Forestry and Forest Conservation (RU)
Glavleskom ... Main Committee of the Lumber Industry (RU)
Glavlesosbyt ... Main Administration for the Marketing of Products of the Logging, Sawmilling, and Woodworking Industry (RU)
Glavlesosplav ... Main Administration for Log Rafting (RU)
Glavlesstroytorg ... Main Administration of the Lumber and Building Materials Trade (RU)
Glavleszapchast' ... Main Administration for the Manufacture of Spare Parts, the Repair of Equipment, and the Manufacture of Mechanical Devices for the Lumber Industry (RU)
Glavleszheldorstroy ... Main Administration for the Construction of Lumber-Hauling Railroads (RU)
Glavlit .... Main Administration for the Safeguarding of Military and State Secrets in the Press (RU)
Glavl'nopen'koprom ... Main Administration of the Flax and Hemp Industry (RU)
Glavl'noprom ... Main Administration of the Flax Industry (RU)

Glavlokomibil'dizel' ... Main Administration of Locomobile and Diesel Machinery Manufacture (RU)
Glavmashdetal' ... Main Administration of Machine Parts Manufacture (RU)
Glavmashfurnitura ... Main Administration of Machine Parts Manufacture and Accessories (RU)
Glavmashmet ... Main Administration of Machinery Plants of the Ministry of Ferrous Metallurgy, USSR (RU)
Glavmashsbyt ... Main Administration for the Marketing of Machinery (RU)
Glavmaslosyrprom ... Main Administration of the Butter and Cheese Industry (RU)
Glavmebel'prom ... Main Administration of the Furniture Industry (RU)
Glavmedinstrumentprom ... Main Administration of the Medical Instrument Industry (RU)
Glavmedsnabsbyt ... Main Administration of Interrepublic Medical Supply and Marketing (RU)
Glavmekh ... Main Administration of the Fur Industry (RU)
Glavmekhanomontazh ... Main Administration of Machine-Assembling Operations (RU)
Glavmekhprom ... Main Administration of the Fur Industry (RU)
Glavmerves ... Main Administration of Measures and Weights (RU)
Glavmestpromsbyt ... Main Marketing Administration of the Ministry of Local Industry, RSFSR (RU)
Glavmestpromsnab ... Main Administration of Materials and Equipment Supply of the Ministry of Local Industry, RSFSR (RU)
GLAVMETALL ... Main Administration of the Metals Industry (RU)
Glavmetalloizdeliy ... Main Administration of the Metalware Industry (RU)
Glavmetallosbyt ... Main Administration for the Marketing of Ferrous Metals and Metalware (of the Ministry of Ferrous Metallurgy, USSR) (RU)
Glavmetallosbyt ... Main Administration for the Marketing of Ferrous Metals, Metalware, Ore, Refractories, and By-Product Coke Products (at the Gosplan SSSR) (RU)
Glavmetallurgmontazh ... Main Administration for the Installation of Metallurgical Establishments (RU)
Glavmetiz ... Main Administration of the Metalware Industry (RU)
Glavmezhavtotrans ... Main Administration of Intercity and International Automobile Transportation (RU)
Glavmoloko ... Main Administration of the Dairy Industry (RU)
Glavmolprom ... Main Administration of the Dairy Industry (RU)
Glavmontazhstroy ... Main Administration for Installation Work (RU)
Glavmorrechstroy ... Main Administration for the Construction of Maritime and River Structures (RU)
Glavmorrevizor ... Administration of the Chief Inspector for Safety at Sea (RU)
Glavmorstroy ... Main Administration for the Construction of Maritime Structures (RU)
Glavmosavtotrans ... Main Administration of Automobile Transportation of the Mosgorispolkom (RU)
Glavmoskhlopprom ... Main Administration of the Cotton Industry of Moscow Oblast (RU)
Glavmosoblmestprom ... Main Administration of Local Industry of the Mosoblispolkom (RU)
Glavmosoblstroy ... Main Administration for Construction in Moscow Oblast (RU)
Glavmosoblstroymaterialy ... Main Administration of the Building Materials and Structural Parts Industry of the Mosoblispolkom (RU)
Glavmospromstroymaterialy ... Main Administration of the Building Materials and Structural Parts Industry of the Mosgorispolkom (RU)
Glavmossovkhozov ... Main Administration of Sovkhozes of the Moscow Area (RU)
Glavmosstroy ... Main Administration for Housing and Civil Engineering Construction in Moscow City (RU)
Glavmosstroymaterialy ... Main Administration of the Building Materials Industry of the Mosgorispolkom (RU)
Glavmostostroy ... Main Administration for Bridge Construction (RU)
Glavmoszhelezobeton ... Main Administration of Establishments of Reinforced Concrete Structures and Large Building Blocks of the Mosgorispolkom (RU)
Glavmotoveloprom ... Main Administration of the Motorcycle and Bicycle Industry (RU)
GlavMRS..... Main Administration of Motorized Fishing Stations (RU)
Glavmuzinstrument ... Main Administration of the Musical Instruments Industry (RU)
Glavmyasomolmash ... Main Administration for the Manufacture of Machinery and of Packing Materials of the Ministry of the Meat and Dairy Products Industry, USSR (RU)
Glavmyasomolsnab ... Main Administration of Materials and Equipment Supply of the Ministry of the Meat and Dairy Products Industry, USSR (RU)
Glavmyasorybtorg ... Main Administration of Cold Storage Plants and Wholesale Meat, Butter, and Fish Trade (RU)
Glavnauka... Main Administration of Scientific Institutions, Museums, and Science and Art Establishments (RU)
Glavneft'..... Main Administration of the Petroleum Industry (RU)
Glavneftedorvodstroy ... Main Administration of Hydraulic-Engineering, Water-Supply, Sewer-System, and Road Construction of the Ministry of Construction of Petroleum Industry Establishments, USSR (RU)
Glavneftegaz ... Main Administration of the Petroleum and Gas Industry (RU)
Glavneftemash ... Main Administration of Petroleum Machinery Manufacture (RU)
Glavneftemontazh ... Main Administration of Installation Operations of the Ministry of Construction of Petroleum Industry Establishments, USSR (RU)
Glavneftemontazh ... Main Administration for Installation of Petroleum-Processing and Petroleum-Producing Establishments [*RSFSR*] (RU)
Glavneftepererabotka ... Main Administration for Petroleum Processing (RU)
Glavneftepromstroy ... Main Administration of Oil Field Construction (RU)
Glavnefteprovodstroy ... Main Administration for Pipeline Construction of the Ministry of Construction of Petroleum Industry Establishments, USSR (RU)
Glavnefteproyekt ... Main Planning Administration of the Ministry of the Petroleum Industry, USSR (RU)
Glavneftesbyt ... Main Administration for the Marketing and Transportation of Petroleum and Petroleum Products (RU)
Glavneftesnab ... Main Administration for the Transportation and Supply of Petroleum and Petroleum Products (RU)
Glavneftestroymekhanizatsiya ... Main Administration for the Mechanization of Construction of the Ministry of Construction of Petroleum Industry Establishments, USSR (RU)
Glavneftestroysnab ... Main Administration of Materials and Equipment Supply of the Ministry of Construction of Petroleum Industry Establishments, USSR (RU)
Glavnefteurs ... Main Administration of Workers' Supply of the Ministry of the Petroleum Industry, USSR (RU)
Glavneftezavodstroy ... Main Administration of Petroleum Plant Construction (RU)
Glavnerud... Main Administration of the Nonmetallic Mineral Industry (of the Ministry of the Building Materials Industry, USSR) (RU)
Glavnerud... Main Administration of Nonmetallic Mineral Materials (of the Ministry of the Building Materials Industry, RSFSR) (RU)
Glavniiproyekt SSSR ... Main Administration of Scientific Research and Planning Organizations, USSR (RU)
Glavnit .... Main Administration for Petroleum Processing and the Manufacture of Synthetic Liquid Fuel (RU)
Glavoboz..... Main Administration of Cart and Sledge Making (RU)
Glavobuv'torg ... Main Administration of the Wholesale Footwear Trade (RU)
Glavogneupor ... Main Administration of the Refractory Industry (RU)
Glavokhota ... Main Administration of Hunting and Game Preserves (RU)
Glavparovoz ... Main Administration of Locomotive Building (RU)
Glavpereselenorgnabor ... Main Administration of Resettlement and Organized Recruitment of Workers (RU)
Glavpochvomash ... Main Administration of Cultivators and Seeding Machines (RU)
Glavpodshipnik ... Main Administration of the Bearing Industry (RU)
Glavpodzemgaz ... Main Administration of Underground Coal Gasification (RU)
Glavpogruztransupr ... Main Freight and Transportation Administration (RU)
Glavpoligrafizdat ... Main Administration of Publishing Houses, the Printing Industry, and the Book Trade (RU)
Glavpoligrafprom ... Main Administration of the Printing Industry (RU)
GLAVPOLITPROSVET ... Main Political Education Committee of the Narkompros RSFSR [*1920-1930*] (RU)
Glav polit upravlenie ... Main Political Administration (BU)
Glavport...... Main Administration of Port Management and Sea Routes (RU)
Glavpribor ... Main Administration of Instrument Making (RU)
Glavpriborsbyt ... Main Administration for the Marketing of Instruments (RU)
Glavprimorrybprom ... Main Administration of the Primor'ye Fish Industry (RU)
Glavprodmash ... Main Administration of Food Machinery Manufacture (RU)
Glavproekt ... Main Designing Organization (BU)
Glavproizvodfil'm ... Main Administration for the Production of Films (RU)
Glavpromenergomontazh ... Main Administration for the Installation of Power Engineering Equipment of Industrial Electric Power Plants (RU)
Glavpromstrom ... Main Administration of the Building Materials Industry (RU)
Glavpromtekhsnab ... Main Administration of Materials and Equipment Supply of the Rospromsovet (RU)
Glavprotez ... Main Administration of the Prosthetics Industry (RU)
Glavproyekt ... Main Administration for the Planning of Ferrous Metallurgy Establishments (RU)
Glavproyekt ... Main Administration of Planning Organizations (RU)
Glavproyektmontazhavtomatika ... Main Administration for the Planning and Installation of Automation Systems (RU)
GlavPU........ Main Political Directorate of the Soviet Army and the Navy (RU)
GlavPURKKA ... Main Political Directorate of the Workers' and Peasants' Red Army (RU)
GlavPU SA i VMF ... Main Political Directorate of the Soviet Army and the Navy (RU)
Glavradiosbyt ... Main Administration for the Marketing of Radiotechnical Products (RU)
Glavraszhirmaslo ... Main Administration of the Vegetable Oils and Fats Industry (RU)
Glavrechstroy ... Main Administration for the Construction of River Structures (RU)
Glavrechtrans ... Main Administration for the Transportation Development and Use of Small Rivers (RU)

Glavredmet ... Main Administration of the Rare Metals Industry (RU)
Glavrepertkom ... Main Committee for Control of Entertainment and Repertoires (RU)
Glavrestoran ... Main Administration of Restaurants (RU)
glavrezh ...... Chief Director, Chief Producer (RU)
Glavrezina ... Main Administration of the Rubber, Asbestos, and Industrial Fabric Industries (RU)
Glavrezina ... Main Administration of the Rubber Industry (RU)
Glavrezinprom ... Main Administration of the Industrial Rubber Goods and Rubber Footwear Industry (RU)
Glavrosgosstrakh ... Main Administration of State Insurance, RSFSR (RU)
Glavrossovkhozsnab ... Main Administration of Materials and Equipment Supply of the Ministry of Sovkhozes, RSFSR (RU)
Glavruda ..... Main Administration of the Ore Industry (RU)
Glavsakhalinbumprom ... Main Administration of the Sakhalin Paper Industry (RU)
Glavsakhalinlesprom ... Main Administration of the Sakhalin Lumber Industry (RU)
Glavsakhar ... Main Administration of the Sugar Industry (RU)
Glavsantekhmontazh ... Main Administration for Sanitary Engineering and Installation (of the Ministry of Construction of Establishments of the Metallurgical and Chemical Industries, USSR) (RU)
Glavsantekhmontazh ... Main Administration for Ventilation and Sanitary Engineering [*RSFSR*] (RU)
Glavsantekhprom ... Main Administration of the Sanitary Engineering Industry (RU)
Glavsanupr ... Main Medical and Sanitary Administration (RU)
Glavsel'elektro ... Main Administration of Rural Electrification (RU)
Glavsel'elektrostroy ... Main Administration for the Construction of Rural Electric Power Plants and Electric Power Networks (RU)
Glavsel'khoztrans ... Main Administration for the Organization of Transportation of Agricultural Freight (RU)
Glavsel'mash ... Main Administration of Agricultural Machinery Manufacture (RU)
Glavsel'stroy ... Main Administration of Rural Construction (RU)
Glavsel'stroyproyekt ... Main Administration for the Planning of Rural Buildings and Structures at the State Committee for Construction, USSR (RU)
Glavseverotorg ... Main Administration for Planning and for Ahead-of-Time Delivery of Goods to the Far Northern Regions and Similar Remote Areas (RU)
Glavsevlesprom ... Main Administration of the Lumber Industry in the Northern Regions (RU)
Glavsevmorput' ... Main Administration of the Northern Sea Route (RU)
Glavsevmorputi ... Main Administration of the Northern Sea Route (RU)
Glavsevuralstroy ... Main Administration of Construction of Industrial Establishments in the Northern Ural Regions (RU)
Glavsevzapenergo ... Main Administration of Electric Power Plants and Networks of the North and West (RU)
Glavsevzapstroy ... Main Administration of Construction of the Northwestern Regions (RU)
Glavshakhtoles ... Main Administration for Supplying Mines with Lumber (RU)
Glavshakhtoproyekt ... Main Administration for the Planning of Mines (RU)
Glavshakhtostroymash ... Main Administration of Mine Construction Machinery Manufacture (RU)
Glavshelk.... Main Administration of Sericulture (of the Ministry of Industrial Crops, USSR) (RU)
Glavshelk.... Main Administration of the Silk Industry (of the Ministry of the Textile Industry) (RU)
Glavshelkprom ... Main Administration of the Silk Industry (RU)
Glavsherst' ... Main Administration of the Wool Industry (RU)
Glavshinprom ... Main Administration of the Tire Industry (RU)
Glavshveyprom ... Main Administration of the Garment Industry (RU)
Glavsibdal'stroy ... Main Administration for the Construction of Industrial Establishments in Siberian and Far Eastern Regions (RU)
Glavsibstroy ... Main Administration for the Construction of Industrial Establishments in Siberian Regions (RU)
Glavsilikatvyazhprom ... Main Administration of the Silicate and Binding-Material Industries (RU)
Glavslanets ... Main Administration of the Shale Industry (RU)
Glavsnab..... Main Supply Administration (RU)
Glavsnabpros ... Main Administration for Supply of and Trade in Educational Visual Aids, Equipment, Materials, and Other Educational and Housekeeping Requirements (of the Ministry of Education, RSFSR) (RU)
Glavsnabsbyt ... Main Administration of Materials and Equipment Supply and Marketing (RU)
Glavsnabsbyt ... Main Administration of Supply and Marketing (RU)
Glavsnabsvyaz' ... Main Administration of Materials and Equipment Supply (of the Ministry of Communications, USSR) (RU)
GLAVSOTsSTRAKH ... Main Administration of Social Insurance (RU)
GLAVSOTsVOS ... Main Administration of Children's Social Upbringing and Polytechnical Education of the Narkompros RSFSR [*1921-1933*] (RU)
GLAVSOVKhOZ ... Main Administration of Sovkhozes (RU)
Glavspetspromstroy ... Main Administration for Special Types of Construction and Installation (RU)
Glavspetsstroy ... Main Administration of Specialized Operations of the Ministry of Construction of Establishments of the Metallurgical and Chemical Industries, USSR (RU)
Glavspetsstroy ... Main Administration of Specialized Trusts of the Ministry of Urban and Rural Construction, RSFSR (RU)
Glavsporttorg ... Main Administration for Trade in Sport Goods (RU)
Glavstal'konstruksiya ... Main Administration for the Manufacture and Installation of Steel and Complex Reinforced Concrete Structures (RU)
Glavstandartdom ... Main Administration of Standard Housing Construction (RU)
Glavstankoinstrumentsbyt ... Main Marketing Administration of the Machine Tool and Tool Industry (RU)
Glavstankoprom ... Main Administration of the Machine Tool Industry (RU)
Glavsteklo .. Main Administration of the Glass Industry (RU)
Glavstrommashina ... Main Administration for the Manufacture of Machinery for the Building Materials Industry (RU)
Glavstromsnab ... Main Administration of Materials and Equipment Supply of the Ministry of the Building Materials Industry, RSFSR (RU)
Glavstrotsnab ... Main Administration of Materials and Equipment Supply (of the Ministry of Urban and Rural Construction, RSFSR) (RU)
Glavstroy .... Main Construction Administration (RU)
Glavstroykeramika ... Main Administration of Building Ceramics (RU)
Glavstroyleszag ... Main Administration for Logging of the Ministry of Construction, USSR (RU)
Glavstroymash ... Main Administration for the Manufacture of Construction Machinery (RU)
Glavstroymekhanizatsiya ... Main Administration of Mechanization of Construction Work (RU)
Glavstroyprom ... Main Administration of the Construction Industry (RU)
Glavstroyprom ... Main Administration for the Manufacture of Structural Parts and Units (RU)
Glavstroyproyekt ... Main Administration of Planning Organizations at the State Committee for Construction, USSR (RU)
Glavstroysbyt ... Main Administration for the Marketing of Building Materials (RU)
Glavstroysnab ... Main Administration of Materials and Equipment Supply (of the Ministry of Construction, RSFSR) (RU)
Glavstroysnab ... Main Supply Administration (of the Ministry of Construction of Establishments of the Metallurgical and Chemical Industries, USSR) (RU)
Glavstroysteklo ... Main Administration of Structural Glass (RU)
Glavsudkhoz ... Main Administration of the Shipping Industry and Ship Repair Yards (RU)
Glavsudomekh ... Main Administration of the Technical Operation of the Fleet and of Ship Repair Yards (RU)
Glavsvyaz'stroy ... Main Administration for the Construction of Communications Installations (RU)
Glavtekhmontazh ... Main Administration for the Assembly of Technological Equipment and for Installation Operations [*USSR*] (RU)
Glavtekhmontazh ... Main Administration for Installation in Chemical and Machinery Establishments [*RSFSR*] (RU)
Glavtekhremont ... Main Administration for the Organization of Maintenance and Repair of Machines and Mechanical Devices (RU)
Glavtekstil'torg ... Main Administration of the Wholesale Textile Trade (RU)
Glavteploenergomontazh ... Main Administration for the Installation of Heat and Power Engineering Equipment in Electric Power Plants (RU)
Glavteplomontazh ... Main Administration of Heat Engineering and Heat Insulation (RU)
Glavteplostroy ... Main Administration of Heat Engineering and Heat Insulation of the Ministry of Construction of Establishments of the Metallurgical and Chemical Industries, USSR (RU)
Glavtochmash ... Main Administration of Precision Machinery Manufacture (RU)
Glavtonnel'metrostroy ... Main Administration for the Construction of Tunnels and Subways (RU)
Glavtop .... Main Administration of the Fuel Industry (RU)
GLAVTOP ... Main Fuel Committee (RU)
Glavtorf....... Main Administration of the Peat Industry (RU)
Glavtorf....... Main Peat Committee (RU)
Glavtorffond ... Main Administration of Peat Reserves (RU)
Glavtorg...... Main Administration of Trade (RU)
Glavtorgmash ... Main Administration for Trade in Automobiles, Tractors, Agricultural Machinery, and Other Producer Goods (RU)
Glavtorgmortrans ... Main Administration of Trade and Provisioning of the Fleet (of the Ministry of the Maritime Fleet, USSR) (RU)
Glavtorgoborudovaniye ... Main Administration of Commercial Equipment (RU)
Glavtorgodezhda ... Main Administration of the Wholesale Clothing Trade (RU)
Glavtraktoroprom ... Main Administration of the Tractor Industry (RU)
Glavtramnay ... Main Administration of Streetcars and Trolleybuses (RU)
Glavtranselektromontazh ... Main Administration for the Electrification of Railroads of the Ministry of Transportation Construction, USSR (RU)
Glavtransproyekt ... Main Administration of Planning and Surveying of the State Industrial Committee for Transportation Construction, USSR (RU)

Glavtsellyuloza ... Main Administration of the Pulp Industry (RU)
Glavtsentrelektroset'stroy ... Main Administration for the Construction of High-Voltage Electric Power Networks and Substations of the Central and Southern Regions (RU)
Glavtsentrenergo ... Main Administration of Electric Power Plants and Networks of the Central Region (RU)
Glavtsentrenergostroy ... Main Administration for Construction of Thermal Electric Power Plants of the Central and Southern Regions (RU)
Glavtsentroelektroset'stroy ... Main Administration for the Construction and Installation of High-Voltage Electric Power Networks and Substations of the Central and Southern Regions (RU)
Glavtsentroenergostroy ... Main Administration for the Construction and Installation of Thermal Electric Power Plants of the Central and Southern Regions (RU)
Glavtsentrokhlopprom ... Main Administration of the Cotton Industry of the Central Regions (RU)
Glavtsentroshakhtostroy ... Main Administration for Construction of Coal Mines and Establishments of the Central Region (RU)
Glavtsentrostroy ... Main Administration for Construction in the Central Regions (of the Ministry of Construction, USSR) (RU)
Glavtsentrostroy ... Main Administration for Construction in the Moscow Economic Region (RU)
Glavtsentrostroy ... Main Construction Administration in the Central Regions (of the Ministry of Construction of Establishments of the Metallurgical and Chemical Industries, USSR) (RU)
Glavtsvetmetsbyt ... Main Administration for the Marketing of Products of Nonferrous Metallurgy (RU)
Glavturboprom ... Main Administration of the Turbine Industry (RU)
Glavuborochkhlopkomash ... Main Administration for the Manufacture of Cotton-Picking Machinery (RU)
Glavuchtekhprom ... Main Administration of Technical Education Aids Industry (RU)
Glavuglemash ... Main Administration of Coal Machinery Manufacture (RU)
Glavuglesbyt ... Main Administration for the Marketing of Coal (RU)
Glavuglesnab ... Main Administration of Materials and Equipment Supply of the Ministry of the Coal Industry, USSR (RU)
Glavunivermag ... Main Administration of Department Stores Selling Manufactured Goods (RU)
glavupr........ Chief Director, Head Manager (RU)
glavupr........ Main Administration (RU)
glavupr........ Main Directorate [*Military term*] (RU)
Glavuralenergo ... Main Administration of Electric Power Plants and Electric Power Networks of the Urals (RU)
Glavurallesprom ... Main Administration of the Ural Lumber Industry (RU)
Glavuralshakhtostroy ... Main Administration for the Construction of Mines in the Urals and Central Asia (RU)
Glavuralstroy ... Main Administration for the Construction of Industrial Establishments in the Ural Regions (RU)
Glavurs .... Main Administration of Workers' Supply (RU)
Glavurstorg ... Main Administration of Workers' Supply and Trade (RU)
Glavvagon... Main Administration of Railroad-Car Building (RU)
Glavvetupr ... Main Veterinary Administration (RU)
Glavvino...... Main Administration of the Wine Industry (RU)
Glavvitaminprom ... Main Administration of the Vitamin Industry (RU)
Glavvodkhoz ... Main Administration of Water Management (RU)
Glavvodokanal ... Main Administration of the Water Supply and Sewer Systems (RU)
Glavvodput' ... Main Administration of Waterways and Hydraulic Engineering Structures (RU)
Glavvostbumprom ... Main Administration of the Paper Industry of the Eastern Regions (RU)
Glavvostdrev ... Main Administration for Sawmilling and Woodworking in the Eastern Regions (RU)
Glavvostok ... Main Administration of the Industry of the Regions of Siberia and the Far East (RU)
Glavvostokelektroset'stroy ... Main Administration for Construction and Installation of High-Voltage Electric Power Networks and Substation in the Urals and Siberia (RU)
Glavvostokenergo ... Main Administration of Electric Power Plants and Networks of the East (RU)
Glavvostokenergostroy ... Main Administration for Construction and Installation of Thermal Electric Power Plants in the Urals and Siberia (RU)
Glavvostokgidroenergostroy ... Main Administration for Construction and Installation of Hydroelectric Power Plants of the East (RU)
Glavvostokneftedobycha ... Main Administration for Petroleum Production in the Eastern Regions (RU)
Glavvostokrybosudostroy ... Main Administration of Shipbuilding and Ship Repair in the East of the Ministry of the Fish Industry, USSR (RU)
Glavvostokrybprom ... Main Administration of the Fish Industry of the East (RU)
Glavvostokshakhtstroy ... Main Administration for the Construction of Mines in Eastern Siberia, the Far East, and the Pechora Basin (RU)
Glavvostoktsement ... Main Administration of the Cement Industry of the Eastern Regions (RU)
Glavvostokzoloto ... Main Administration of the Gold and Platinum Industry of the Far East and Eastern Siberia (RU)
Glavvoyenprom ... Main Administration of War Industry (RU)
Glavvoyenpromstroy ... Main Administration of War Industry Construction (RU)
Glavvoyentorg ... Main Administration of Trade Establishments for Military Personnel (RU)
Glavvtorchermet ... Main Administration for the Procurement, Processing, and Marketing of Secondary Ferrous Metals (RU)
Glavvtormet ... Main Administration for the Procurement, Processing, and Marketing of Secondary Ferrous and Nonferrous Metals (RU)
Glavvtorsyr'ye ... Main Administration for the Procurement and Processing of Secondary Raw Material (RU)
Glavvtortsvetmet ... Main Administration for the Procurement, Processing, and Marketing of Secondary Nonferrous Metals (RU)
Glavyugstroy ... Main Administration for the Construction of Industrial Establishments in the Regions of the South (of the Ministry of Construction of Establishments of the Metallurgical and Chemical Industries, USSR) (RU)
Glavyugstroy ... Main Administration for the Construction of Industrial Establishments in the Southern Regions (of the Ministry of Construction, USSR) (RU)
Glavyugstroy ... Main Administration for Construction in the Southern Regions (of the Ministry of Urban and Rural Construction, RSFSR) (RU)
Glavyuvelirtorg ... Main Administration of the Jewelry Trade (RU)
Glavyuzhenergo ... Main Administration of Southern Power Systems (RU)
Glavyuzhenergostroy ... Main Administration for Construction and Installation of Thermal Electric Power Plants of the Central and Southern Regions (RU)
Glavyuzhgrazhdanstroy ... Main Construction Administration of the Southern Regions of the Ministry of Housing and Civil-Engineering Construction, RSFSR (RU)
Glavyuzhuralstroy ... Main Administration for Construction in the South Ural Economic Region (RU)
Glavzagotkhlopprom ... Main Administration of Cotton Procurement and the Ginning Industry (RU)
Glavzagotstroy ... Main Construction Administration of the Ministry of Procurement, USSR (RU)
Glavzapadneftedobycha ... Main Administration for Petroleum Production in the Southern and Western Regions (RU)
Glavzapadneftestroy ... Main Administration for Construction in the Western Regions of the Ministry of the Petroleum Industry, USSR (RU)
Glavzapadtsement ... Main Administration of the Cement Industry of the Western Regions (RU)
Glavzapadzoloto ... Main Administration of the Gold and Platinum Industry of Western Siberia, the Urals, and Kazakhstan (RU)
Glavzapdrev ... Main Administration of Sawmilling and Woodworking in the Western Regions (RU)
Glavzarubezhkomplekt ... Main Administration for Supplying in Complete Sets Equipment and Materials for Establishments Being Built Abroad (RU)
Glavzheldorstroy ... Main Administration of Railroad Construction (RU)
Glavzheldorstroymekhanizatsiya ... Main Administration for the Mechanization of Construction Work in Railroad Transportation (RU)
Glavzhelezobeton ... Main Administration for the Manufacture of Reinforced Concrete Parts and Structures (RU)
Glavzhilupr ... Main Housing Administration (RU)
Glavzhilupravleniye ... Main Housing Administration (RU)
Glavzhivupr ... Main Administration of Livestock Breeding (RU)
Glavzverovod ... Main Administration of Fur-Farming Sovkhozes (RU)
GLB .... Depth Charge (RU)
GLBI .... State Publishing House of the Lumber and Paper Industries (RU)
glbp............ Pigeon Communication Service (BU)
GlBZBU .... Glasnik Botanickog Zavoda i Baste Univerziteta u Beogradu [*Bulletin of the Botanical Institute and University Garden in Belgrade*] (YU)
GLC............ Guyana Liquor Corporation (LA)
GLD............ Germaniki Laiki Dimokratia [*German Democratic Republic*] (GC)
Gldir .... Main Directorate (BU)
GlDirGeolMProuchv ... Main Directorate of Geological and Mining Surveys (BU)
Gl dir kin ..... Main Directorate of Cinematography (BU)
Gl dir ptt ..... Main Directorate of Post, Telegraph, and Telephone (BU)
Gl dir radio ... Main Directorate of Radio Broadcasting (BU)
Gl dir statist ... Main Statistical Directorate (BU)
Gl dirz zhel i prist ... Main Directorate of Railways and Harbors (BU)
glDSSI......... Glasnik Drustva Srpske Slovesnosti [*Bulletin of the Society of Serbian Literature*] [*Belgrade*] (YU)
GLECS........ Groupe Linguistique d'Etudes Chamito-Semitiques (MAR)
GlEM .... Glasnik Etnografskog Muzeja [*Bulletin of the Ethnographic Museum*] [*Belgrade*] [*A publication*] (YU)
Gler .... Glacier [*Glacier*] [*Military map abbreviation*] [*World War I*] [*French*] (MTD)
GLGA .... Guyana Local Government Association (LA)
GlGD .... Glasnik Geografskog Drustva [*Bulletin of the Geographic Society*] [*Belgrade*] (YU)
GLI .... Garp Linyitler Isletmesi [*Western Lignites Operation*] (TU)
GLI .... State Meadow Institute (RU)

GIID .... Glasnik Istoriskog Drustva [*Bulletin of the Historical Society*] [*Novi Sad*] (YU)
Glin .... Clay Pit [*Topography*] (RU)
gl in .... Quartermaster General, Quartermaster General's Department (BU)
glinoz .... Alumina, Aluminum Oxide [*Topography*] (RU)
GLINT .... Gospel Literature International [*A publication*] (MAR)
GLINT .... Gospel Literature in National Tongues [*A publication*] (MAR)
Gl IPN .... Glowny Instytut Paliw Naturalnych [*Main Institute of Natural Fuels*] (POL)
glits .... Glycine (RU)
GlJPD .... Glasnik Jugoslovenskog Profesorskog Drustva [*Bulletin of the Yugoslav Society of Professors*] [*A publication*] (YU)
glk .... Commander in Chief (BU)
GLK .... Genikon Logistirion Kratous [*General State Accounting Office*] [*Greek*] (GC)
GLK .... Glucokinase (RU)
GLK .... Main Lumber Industry Committee (RU)
gl kpl .... Eye Drops (RU)
GLM .... State Literary Museum (RU)
GlMdzS .... Glasnik Muzejskega Drustva za Slovenijo [*Bulletin of the Museum Society of Slovenia*] [*A publication*] (YU)
GlMP .... Glasnik Ministarstva Poljoprivrede [*Bulletin of the Ministry of Agriculture*] [*Belgrade*] [*A publication*] (YU)
GLN .... Linear-Buildup Voltage Generator (RU)
gl obr .... Chiefly, Mostly, For the Most Part (RU)
GLP .... Gasolina Liquido de Petroleo [*Liquefied Petroleum Gas*] [*Use LPG*] (LA)
GLP .... Gor'kiy Steamship Line (RU)
GLP .... Guadeloupe [*Three-letter standard code*] (CNC)
GLP .... Linear Sawtooth Generator (RU)
GLP .... State Forest Nursery (RU)
GLP-AACR ... Gibraltar Labour Party - Association for the Advancement of Civil Rights (PPW)
GlPC .... Glasnik Pravoslavne Crkve [*Bulletin of the Eastern Orthodox Church*] (YU)
GlPMSZ .... Glasnik Prirodnjackog Muzeja Srpske Zemlje [*Bulletin of the Museum of Natural Sciences of Serbia*] (YU)
GLPN .... Generator of Linearly Decreasing Voltage (RU)
GLR .... Group Line Relay (RU)
GLR .... Hospital for the Slightly Wounded (RU)
GLRE .... Geniki Laiki Rizospastiki Enosis [*General Union of Populists and Radicals*] [*Greek*] (PPE)
GLRN .... Generator of Linearly Increasing Voltage (RU)
GLS .... Sonar (RU)
GlSAN .... Glasnik Srpske Akademije Nauka [*Bulletin of the Serbian Academy of Sciences*] [*Belgrade*] [*A publication*] (YU)
gl sch .... Main Accounting Office (BU)
gl schet .... Chief Accountant (BU)
GLSF .... Societe Georges Lesieur & Ses Fils (MAR)
GLSFNRJ .... Glavni Lovacki Savez Federativna Narodna Republika Jugoslavija [*Central Association of Yugoslav Riflemen*] (YU)
GlSGD .... Glasnik Srpskog Geografskog Drustva [*Bulletin of the Serbian Geographic Society*] [*Belgrade*] [*A publication*] (YU)
gls-ka .... Main Account (BU)
GlSPC .... Glasnik Srpske Pravoslavne Crkve [*Bulletin of the Serbian Orthodox Church*] [*A publication*] (YU)
GlStHrv .... Glavni Stab Hrvatske [*Supreme Headquarters of Croatia*] [*World War II*] (YU)
GlSUD .... Glasnik Srpskog Ucenog Drustva [*Bulletin of the Serbian Learned Society*] [*Belgrade*] [*A publication*] (YU)
glts .... Glycerol, Glycerin (RU)
GLU .... Gambia Labour Union (MAR)
GLU .... Gruene Liste Umweltschutz [*Green List Ecology*] [*West German*] (PPE)
GLU .... Guyana Labor Union (LA1)
Gl upr .... Main Administration, Main Directorate (RU)
GlVIS .... Glasnik Vrhovnog Islamskog Starjesinstva u Federativna Narodna Republika Jugoslavija [*Bulletin of the Supreme Islamic Authority in Yugoslavia*] [*A publication*] (YU)
glvp .... Judge Advocate General (BU)
GLZ .... Grubenlampenwerk, Zwickau (VEB) [*Zwickau Mine Lamp Plant (VEB)*] (EG)
GLZ .... Lyubertsy State Agricultural Machinery Plant (RU)
GlZMBH .... Glasnik Zemaljskog Muzeja u Bosni i Hercegovini [*Bulletin of the National Museum of Bosnia and Hercegovina*] [*Sarajevo*] [*A publication*] (YU)
GM .... Cigarette-Wrapping Machine (RU)
GM .... Gambia [*Two-letter standard code*] (CNC)
GM .... Gamma Method (RU)
GM .... Geheimer Mitarbeiter [*Secret Collaborator*] (EG)
G-M .... Geiger-Mueller Counter (RU)
GM .... Genel Muduru [*Director General*] (TU)
GM .... General Major [*Major General*] (YU)
GM .... General Motor [*Bogota-Otras Ciudades*] (COL)
GM .... Genie Mobilier [*Military*] [*French*] (MTD)
GM .... Genio Militare [*Corps of Engineers*] [*Italian*] (WER)
GM .... Geographic Position (RU)
GM .... Geographical Magazine [*London*] [*A publication*] (MAR)
gm .... Gmina [*Rural Commune*] (POL)
GM .... Goldmark [*Gold Marks*] [*German*]
GM .... Guvenlik Mahkemesi [*Security Court*] (TU)
GM .... Gyro Pendulum (RU)
gm .... Hectometer (RU)
Gm .... Homogeneous [*Nuclear physics and engineering*] (RU)
gm .... Major General (BU)
g-m .... Major General (RU)
GM .... Maleic Acid Hydrazide (RU)
GM .... Mining Machinery (RU)
GMA .... Gazdasagi es Muszaki Akademia [*Academy of Economics and Technology*] (HU)
GMA .... Ghana Manufacturers Association (MAR)
GMA .... Gospel Music Association (MAR)
GMA .... Grands Moulins d'Abidjan (MAR)
GMA .... Guyana Manufacturers Association (LA)
GMB .... Gambia [*Three-letter standard code*] (CNC)
GMB .... Goerlitzer Maschinenbau (VEB) [*Goerlitz Machine Construction Plant (VEB)*] (EG)
GMB .... Grain Marketing Board [*Rhodesian*] (AF)
GMB .... Grands Moulins du Benin (MAR)
GMB .... Hydrometeorological Office (RU)
GmbH .... Gesellschaft mit Beschraenkter Haftung [*Cooperative with Limited Liability*] [*German*] (WEN)
GMC .... Gambia Muslim Congress (MAR)
GMC .... Generale des Matieres Colorantes (MAR)
GMC .... Grands Moulins du Cameroun (MAR)
GMC .... Grands Moulins du Congo [*Great Mills of the Congo*] (AF)
GMC .... Guyana Marketing Corporation (LA)
GMCh .... Guards Mortar Unit (RU)
GMCh .... Motorized Howitzer Unit (RU)
GMD .... Gemeenschappelijke Medische Dienst [*Community Medical Service*] [*Dutch*] (WEN)
GMD .... Grands Moulins de Dakar (MAR)
GMD .... Guards Mortar Battalion (RU)
GMDITs .... Hexamethylene Diisocyanate (RU)
GMDOA .... Government Medical and Dental Officers Association [*Mauritian*] (AF)
GME .... State Museum of Ethnography (RU)
GMEL .... Groupement des Mathematiciens d'Expression Latine [*Group of Mathematicians of Romance Languages - GMRL*] (EA)
GMF .... Guanosine Monophosphate (RU)
GMF .... Guanosine Monophosphoric Acid (RU)
GMF .... State Museum Fund (RU)
GMFN .... Sodium Hexametaphosphate (RU)
GMG .... State Museum of Georgia (RU)
GMI .... Gor'kiy Medical Institute Imeni S. M. Kirov (RU)
GMI .... State Meat Inspection (RU)
GMII .... State Museum of Fine Arts Imeni A. S. Pushkin (RU)
GMIL .... State Museum of the History of Leningrad (RU)
GMIP .... Depth Manometer Recording Absorption Intensity (RU)
GMIZ .... Gor'kiy Medical Instrument Plant Imeni M. Gor'kiy (RU)
GMK .... Generator of Mechanical Oscillations (RU)
GMK .... Guards Mechanized Corps (RU)
GMK .... Gyro Magnetic Compass (RU)
GMK .... Hydrometeorological Committee (RU)
GMK .... International Geological Congress (RU)
GMK .... Maleic Hydrazide (RU)
GMKI .... Gerakan Mahasiswa Keristen Indonesia [*Indonesian Christian College Students Movement*] (IN)
GMM .... Gerakan Mahasiswa Marhaen [*Marhaenist College Students Movement*] (IN)
GMMTA .... Groupement des Moyens Militaires de Transport Aerien [*French*]
GMN .... Grands Moulins de Nouakchott (MAR)
GMN .... Monitor, Hydraulic Excavator (RU)
GMNI .... Gerakan Mahasiswa Nasional Indonesia [*Indonesian National College Students Movement*] (IN)
GMNII .... Mining and Metallurgical Scientific Research Institute (RU)
GMO .... Dead Storage Level [*of a reservoir*] (RU)
GMO .... Hydrometeorological Observatory (RU)
GMO ChAM ... Hydrometeorological Observatory of the Black and Azov Seas (RU)
g-mol' .... Gram Molecule (RU)
g-Mol .... Grammolekuel [*Gram Molecule*] [*German*]
GmOR .... Homogeneous Research Reactor (RU)
GMP .... Grands Moulins de Paris (MAR)
GMP .... Groupe Motopropulseur [*Military*] [*French*] (MTD)
GMP .... Groupements Mutualistes du Progres (MAR)
GMP .... Guards Mortar Regiment (RU)
Gmp .... Gueterzug mit Personenbefoerderung [*Freight Train with Passenger Transportation Facilities*] (EG)
GMP .... Hydromechanical Gear, Hydromechanical Transmission (RU)
GMP .... Hydrometeorological Station (RU)
GMP .... Main Medical Aid Station (RU)
GMPI .... Groupe Mobile de Premiere Intervention [*Mobile First Intervention Group*] [*Algerian*] (AF)
GMPI .... State Music Pedagogical Institute Imeni Gnesiny (RU)
GMPO .... Annals of Plovdiv Okrug Museums (BU)
GMPR .... Groupes Mobiles de Protection Rurale [*Algerian*] (MAR)
GMR .... Gouvernement Militaire Revolutionnaire [*Military Revolutionary Government*] [*Beninese*] (AF)

GMR .... Grupo Marxista Revolucionario [*Marxist Revolutionary Group*] [*Portuguese*] (PPE)
GMRL .... Group of Mathematicians of Romance Languages [*See also GMEL*] (EA)
GMS .... Erasing Magnetic Head (RU)
GMS .... Geographic Position of a Heavenly Body (RU)
GMS .... George MacDonald Society (EA)
GMS .... Glasnik Muzejskega Drustva za Slovenijo [*Bulletin of the Museum Society of Slovenia*] (YU)
GMS .... Groupement de Missiles Strategiques [*Strategic Missiles Group*] [*French*] (WER)
GMS .... Hydrometeorological Service (RU)
GMS .... Hydrometeorological Station (RU)
GMSOS .... Gerakan Mahasiswa Sosialis [*Socialist College Students Movement*] (IN)
gm st .... Hydrometeorological Station [*Topography*] (RU)
GMT .... Gornja Mrtva Tacka [*Upper Dead Center*] [*Engine*] (YU)
GMT .... Grands Moulins du Tchad (MAR)
GMT .... Hexamethylenetetramine (RU)
GMT .... Locus, Geometric Locus of Points (RU)
GMT .... Methane Gas Detector (RU)
GMT .... Societe Generale du Mecanique et Thermique [*Tunisian*] (MAR)
GMT .... Societe des Generale des Moulins du Togo (MAR)
gmt .... Top Dead Center [*Military*] (BU)
GMU .... Gadjah Mada University [*Indonesian*]
GMU .... Gospel Missionary Union (MAR)
GMV .... Grands Moulins Voltaiques (MAR)
GMV .... Low-Water Line, Low-Water Level (RU)
GMV .... Meter-Wave Generator (RU)
GMV- .... Reproducing Magnetic Head (RU)
GMWU .... Guyana Mine Workers Union (LA)
GMZ .... Gor'kiy Metallurgical Plant (RU)
GMZ .... Gor'kiy Motorcycle Plant (RU)
GMZ .... Gorlovka Machinery Plant (RU)
GMZ .... Gur'yev Machine Plant (RU)
GMZ .... Hydromechanical Lock (RU)
GMZ .... Mine-Laying and Obstacle Group (RU)
GMZS .... Glasnik Muzejskega Drustva za Slovenijo [*Bulletin of the Museum Society of Slovenia*] (YU)
GN .... Directional Gyro (RU)
GN .... Gas Detector for Command Personnel (RU)
GN .... Gas Heat Exchanger [*Nuclear physics and engineering*] (RU)
GN .... Gendarmerie Nationale [*National Gendarmerie*] [*Replaced GRK*] [*Cambodian*] (CL)
Gn .... Genel [*General*] [*Turkish*] (GPO)
Gn .... Gradevinarstvo [*Building Industry*] (YU)
GN .... Gradevinske Norme [*Building Standards*] (YU)
gn .... Grenade (BU)
GN .... Guinea [*Two-letter standard code*] (CNC)
gn .... Henry (RU)
GN .... Hydraulic Pump (RU)
g-n .... Mister (BU)
gn .... Mister (RU)
GNA .... Ghana National Archives (MAR)
GNA .... Ghana News Agency (AF)
GNA .... Grupos No-Alineados [*Non-Aligned Groups*] [*Spanish*] (WER)
GNA .... Gulf News Agency (MAR)
GNA .... Guyana News Agency (LA1)
GNA .... Guyana Nurses Association (LA)
GNaIPZR ..... Annals of the Scientific Institute for Improvement of Agricultural Crops (BU)
GNAMPI ...... Annals of the National Archaeological Museum in Plovdiv (BU)
GNAT .... Ghana National Association of Teachers (MAR)
GNB .... Gambia News Bulletin (MAR)
GNB .... Guinea-Bissau [*Three-letter standard code*] (CNC)
GNB .... State Scientific Library (RU)
GNB .... State Scientific and Technical Library (RU)
GNBMPI ...... Annals of the National Library and Museum in Plovdiv (BU)
GNBPI .... Annals of the National Library and Museum in Plovdiv (BU)
GNBS .... Annals of the National Library in Sofia (BU)
GNC .... Gambia National Congress (MAR)
GNC .... Godisnjak Nikole Cupica [*Nikola Cupic Yearbook*] [*Belgrade*] [*A periodical*] (YU)
GNCB .... Guyana National Cooperative Bank (LA)
GNCh .... Carrier-Frequency Generator, Low-Frequency Generator (RU)
GNEC .... Guyana National Engineering Corporation (LA)
GNFU .... Ghana National Farmers Union (MAR)
GNG .... Grupe za Neposredno Gadanje [*Groups for Direct Firing*] [*Military*] (YU)
GNI .... Gross National Income (MAR)
GNI .... Groznyy Petroleum Institute (RU)
GNIGI .... State Scientific Research Institute of Geophysics (RU)
GNIGK .... State Scientific Research Institute of Geodesy and Cartography (RU)
GNII .... State Scientific Research Institute (RU)
GNIIGlaz ..... State Scientific Research Institute of Eye Diseases Imeni Gel'mgol'ts (RU)
GNIIKhP ...... State Scientific Research Institute of the Chemical Industry (RU)
GNIIS .... State Scientific Research Institute of Glass (RU)
GNIISM .... State Scientific Research Institute of Forensic Medicine (RU)
GNIIT .... State Scientific Research Institute of Tuberculosis (RU)
GNIIVitamin ... State Scientific Research Institute of Vitaminology (RU)
GNILICOM ... Le Comptoir de Gnilil [*Senegalese*] (MAR)
GNIOM .... State Scientific Institute of Mother and Child Welfare (RU)
GNIOMM ..... State Scientific Institute of Mother and Child Welfare (RU)
GNIRRI .... State Scientific Research Institute of Roentgenology and Radiology (RU)
GNISE .... "Soviet Encyclopedia" State Scientific Institute (RU)
GNISI .... State Scientific Research Institute of Sanitation Imeni F. F. Erisman (RU)
GNIU .... State Scientific Institute of Coal (RU)
GNK .... Gamma-Neutron Logging (RU)
GnKh .... Genel Karargah [*General Headquarters*] (TU)
GNKI .... State Control Scientific Research Institute of Veterinary Preparations (RU)
GNKUR .... Genel Kurmay [*General Staff*] (TU)
GNKURB ..... Genel Kurmay Baskanligi [*Chief of the General Staff*] (TU)
GNL .... Gaz Naturel Liquefie [*Liquified Natural Gas*] [*Use LNG*] (AF)
Gnl .... General [*General*] (TU)
GNL .... Low Ice-Floe Level (RU)
Gnlk .... Gunluk [*Daily*] (TU)
GNM .... Annals of the National Archaeological Museum in Sofia (BU)
GNM .... Annals of the National Museum in Sofia (BU)
GNM .... Gamma-Neutron Method (RU)
GNMB .... State Scientific Medical Library (RU)
GNMC .... Ghana National Manganese Corporation (MAR)
GNMPI .... Annals of the National Archaeological Museum in Plovdiv (BU)
GNNCh .... Low-Frequency Voltage Generator (RU)
GNNE .... Guild of Nigerian Newspaper Editors (AF)
GNO .... Gradski Narodni Odbor [*City People's Committee*] (YU)
GNOE .... Gabinete Nacionale de Organizacao de Eleicoes [*National Election Office*] [*Mozambican*] (AF)
GNP .... Close Support Party [*Military*] (BU)
GNP .... Grenada National Party (PPW)
GNPA .... Ghana National Procurement Agency (MAR)
GNPP .... Great Nigeria People's Party (PPW)
GNQ .... Equatorial Guinea [*Three-letter standard code*] (CNC)
GNR .... Guarda Nacional Republicana [*Republican National Guard*] [*Portuguese*] (WER)
GNR .... Sodium-Graphite Reactor (RU)
GNRC .... Ghana National Reconstruction Corps (MAR)
GNRC .... Guyana National Relief Committee (LA)
GNRR .... Guineiskaia Narodnaia Revoliutsionnaia Respublika (MAR)
GNS .... City People's Council (BU)
GNS .... Gas Filling Station (RU)
GNS .... Guyana National Service (LA)
GNS .... Gyro Navigation System (RU)
GNSDT .... City People's Council of Workers' Deputies (BU)
GNSP .... Guardia Nacional de Seguridad Publica [*National Guard for Public Security*] [*Bolivian*] (LA)
GNTB .... State Scientific and Technical Library (RU)
GNTC .... Ghana National Trading Corporation (MAR)
GNTI .... State Scientific and Technical Publishing House (RU)
GNTIU .... State Scientific and Technical Publishing House of the Ukraine (RU)
GNTK .... State Scientific and Technical Committee (RU)
GNU .... Underground Heaters [*Pet.*] (RU)
GNV .... Downstream Water Line, Downstream Water Level, Level of Tail Water, Low-Water Level (RU)
GNV .... Gesellschaft fuer Nukleare Verfahrenstechnik [*Commercial firm*]
GNV .... Grupos de No-Violentos [*Non-Violent Groups*] [*Spanish*] (WER)
GNWA .... Gwelo Native Welfare Association (MAR)
GNYC .... Ghana National Youth Council (MAR)
GO .... Advance Detachment (RU)
GO .... Archives of the Geographic Society of the USSR (RU)
GO .... City Branch Office [*Communications*] (RU)
GO .... Civil Defense (RU)
GO .... Course Reading (RU)
GO .... Gemeenschappelijke Opleiding voor Archief, Bibliotheek, Documentatie- en Informatiebewerking [*'s-Gravenhage*]
GO .... Generalni Oprava [*General Repair*] (CZ)
GO .... Geographic Society (RU)
GO .... Gerilski Odredi [*Guerrilla Detachments*] [*World War II*] (YU)
GO .... Glavni Odbor [*Central Committee*] (YU)
GO .... Grand-Officier [*of the Legion of Honor*] [*French*] (MTD)
GO .... Grundorganisation [*Basic Organization*] (EG)
GO .... Main Winding (RU)
GOA .... Gebuehrenordnung fuer Architekten [*Scale of Fees for Architects*] (EG)
GOA .... Grupos Obreros Autonomos [*Autonomous Workers Groups*] [*Spanish*] (WER)
GOA .... Optical and Acoustical Gas Analyzer (RU)
GOAFZM ..... Glaven Odbor na Antifasistickiot Front na Zenite od Makedonija [*Central Committee of the Women's Anti-Fascist Front of Macedonia*] (YU)
GOB .... Government of Botswana (MAR)
GOB .... Hemato-Ophthalmic Barrier (RU)
GOBLL .... Glowny Osrodek Badan Lotniczo-Lekarskich [*Main Center of Aviation Medicine Research*] (POL)
Gobno .... Gobierno [*Government*] [*Spanish*]

Gobo .... Gobierno [*Government*] [*Business and trade*] [*Spanish*]
g-obr .... Gaseous, Gasiform (RU)
Gobr .... Gobernador [*Governor*] [*Spanish*]
GOBSIINDO ... Gabungan Organisasi Buruh Serikat Islam Indonesia [*Federation of Indonesian Islamic Alliance Labor Organizations*] [*Also known as GOBSII*] (IN)
GOCM .... Groupe Ophtalmologique Chirurgical Mobile (MAR)
GOCNAE ..... Grupo de Organizacao da Comissao Nacional de Atividades Espaciais [*Organizing Group of the National Commission on Space Activities*] [*Brazilian*] (LA)
GOCR .... Groupe Operationnel de la Croix-Rouge pour l'Indochine [*Red Cross Operational Group for Indochina*] (CL)
GOCS .... Gordulocsapagy Gyar, Debrecen [*Roller Bearing Plant of Debrecen*] (HU)
God .... Annals [*Annual Publication*] (BU)
god .... Anniversary (BU)
god .... Godina [*Year*] (YU)
god .... Year (BU)
God agr f-t ... Annals of Sofia University, School of Agronomy (BU)
GODCA .... Gabinete de Organizacao e Desenvolvimento das Cooperativas Agricolas [*Department for the Organization and Development of Agricultural Cooperatives*] [*Mozambican*] (AF)
God na Dir za geol i minni prouchvaniya ... Annals of the Directorate for Geological and Mining Surveys (BU)
God na Dir za GMP ... Annals of the Directorate for Geological and Mining Surveys (BU)
GODE .... Gulf Organisation for the Development of Egypt (MAR)
GodisnikSNOI ... Godisnik. Sumarsko Naucno Opiten Institut [*Yearbook of the Forestry Research Institute*] [*Skopje*] (YU)
GodisnjakBI ... Godisnjak Bioloskog Instituta u Sarajevu [*Yearbook of the Biological Institute in Sarajevo*] (YU)
GODOS .... Geniki Dievthinsis Diethnon Oikonomikon Skheseon [*General Directorate of International Economic Relations*] (GC1)
GODSA .... Gabinete de Orientacion y Documentacion, SA [*Documentation and Orientation Office, Inc.*] [*Spanish*] (WER)
GodSAN ...... Godisnjak Srpske Kraljevske Akademije Nauka [*Yearbook of the Serbian Royal Academy of Sciences*] [*Belgrade*] (YU)
God na Sof u-tet ... Annals of Sofia University (BU)
GodSU .... Annals of Sofia State University (BU)
God vet-med f-t ... Annals of the School of Veterinary Medicine (BU)
godz .... Godzin [*Hours*] (POL)
godz .... Godzina [*O'Clock, Hour*] (POL)
GODZS .... Godisnjak Zaduzbine Save i Vase Stojanovica Mostarca [*Yearbook of the Foundation of Sava i Vasa Stojanovic of Mostar*] [*Belgrade*] (YU)
GOE .... Gare Origine d'Etapes [*Military*] [*French*] (MTD)
GOELRO ..... State Commission for the Electrification of Russia [*1920*] (RU)
GOES .... Grupo de Operaciones Especiales [*Special Operations Group*] [*Colombian*] (LA1)
GOEV .... Genikos Organismos Engeion Veltioseon [*General Organization for Land Reclamation*] [*Greek*] (GC)
GoeV .... Gesetz ueber die Oertlichen Volksvertretungen [*Law on Local People's Representations*] (EG)
GOFAT .... Groupe des Officiers des Forces Armees Tchadiennes [*Officers Group of the Chadian Armed Forces*] (AF)
GOFSM .... Glaven Odbor na Fiskulturniot Savez na Makedonija [*Central Committee of the Physical Culture Union of Macedonia*] (YU)
GOGRES ..... Gor'kiy State Regional Electric Power Plant (RU)
GOI .... Gebuehrenordnung fuer Ingenieure [*Scale of Fees for Engineers*] (EG)
GOI .... Government of Iran (MAR)
GOI .... Government of Israel (MAR)
GOI .... Single-Pulse Generator (RU)
GOI .... State Institute of Optics Imeni S. I. Vavilov (RU)
GOI .... State Scientific Research Institute of Oncology Imeni P. A. Gertsen (RU)
GOIC .... Government of Ivory Coast (MAR)
GOIC .... Gulf Organization for Industrial Consulting (EA)
GOICEM ...... General Officer in Command East Malaysia (ML)
GOICWM ..... General Officer in Command West Malaysia (ML)
GOIFE .... Government of Israel Furnished Equipment (MAR)
GOIN .... State Institute of Oceanography (RU)
GOK .... Genikos Oikodomikos Kanonismos Kratous [*General State Building Regulations*] [*Greek*] (GC)
GOK .... Mining and Concentration Kombinat (RU)
GOKhl .... State Agricultural Publishing House (RU)
GOKhP .... Main Administration of the Basic Chemical Industry (RU)
GOkhR .... Gas-Cooled Reactor (RU)
Gokhran ...... State Repository for Precious Metals (RU)
GOKO .... State Defense Committee [*1941-1945*] (RU)
GOL .... Deepwater Oceanographic Winch (RU)
gol .... Dutch (RU)
GOL .... Government of Liberia (MAR)
GOL .... Grundorganisationsleitung [*Management of Basic Organizations*] (EG)
Goldschn .... Goldschnitt [*Gilt Edges*] [*Bookbinding*] [*German*]
GOLE .... Groupement Operationnel de la Legion Etrangere [*Operational Group of the Foreign Legion*] [*French*] (WER)
golf .... Golfpeli [*Golf*] [*Finnish*]
GOLKAR ..... Golongan Karya [*Functional Group*] [*Technically, a group in Parliament whose members represent the armed services, occupational groups, labor unions, and other nonpolitical sectors, but actually a political party in its own right*] (IN)
GOLKAR ..... Sekber Golongan Karya [*Joint Secretariat of Functional Groups*] [*Indonesian*] (PPW)
goll .... Dutch (RU)
GOLPOL ...... Golongan Politik [*Political group (The members of Parliament who represent political parties, as opposed to GOLKAR)*] (IN)
GOLS .... Carrier Pigeon Station (RU)
GOM .... City Militia Station (RU)
GOM .... Gminny Osrodek Maszynowy [*Rural Commune Machinery Station*] (POL)
GOM .... Government of Malawi (MAR)
GOM .... Government of Mauritania (MAR)
GOM .... Government of Mauritius (MAR)
GOMB .... Gambia Oilseeds Marketing Board (AF)
GOMB-TEX ... Gomb- es Textilfeldolgozo Haziipari Termelo Szovetkezet [*Cooperative for Home Production of Buttons and Clothing Accessories*] (HU)
Gomel'sel'mash ... Gomel' Agricultural Machinery Plant (RU)
GOMETs ..... State Music, Stage, and Circus Association (RU)
gomog .... Homogeneous (RU)
GOMP .... Groupement d'Outre-Mer Pharmaceutique (MAR)
GOMPCI ...... Groupement Pharmaceutique de Cote-d'Ivoire (MAR)
GOMPLA ..... Industria Gomez Plata Ltda. [*Barranquilla*] (COL)
Gomsel'mash ... Gomel' Agricultural Machinery Plant (RU)
GOMT .... General Organisation for Maritime Transport [*Libyan*] (MAR)
GOMZ .... State Optical Instrument Plant (RU)
GOMZ .... State United Machinery Plants (RU)
GOMZA .... State United Machinery Plants (RU)
GOMZY .... State United Machinery Plants (RU)
Gon .... Gonderen [*Sender*] [*of a letter*] (TU)
GON .... Gorska Odznaka Narciarska [*Mountain Ski Badge*] (POL)
GON .... Government of Niger (MAR)
gon .... Pottery Plant [*Topography*] (RU)
GON .... Reference Voltage Generator (RU)
gonch .... Pottery Plant [*Topography*] (RU)
gond .... Gondozo [*Caretaker*] (HU)
gondn .... Gondnok [*Guardian, Curator*] (HU)
GONFM .... Glaven Odbor na Narodniot Front na Makedonija [*Central Committee of the National Front of Macedonia*] (YU)
GONG .... Groupe d'Organisation Nationale Guadeloupeenne [*Guadeloupe*] (PD)
GONMM ...... Glaven Odbor na Narodnata Mladina na Makedonija [*Central Committee of the People's Youth of Macedonia*] (YU)
GONTI .... State Joint Scientific and Technical Publishing House (RU)
GOP .... Gabinet Ochrony Pracy [*Office of Labor Safety*] (POL)
GOP .... Genetically Homogeneous Surface (RU)
GOP .... Gornoslaski Okreg Przemyslowy [*Upper Silesia Industrial District*] (POL)
GOP .... Gorski Okreg Przemyslowy [*Mountain Industrial District*] (POL)
GOP .... Gromadzka Organizacja Partyjna [*Gromada Party Organization*] (POL)
GOPA .... Gesellschaft fuer Organisation, Planning, und Ausbildung (MAR)
GOPDEI .... Geniki Omospondia Prosopikou Dimosias Epikheiriseos Ilektrismou [*General Federation of Public Power Corporation Personnel*] (GC)
GOPEC .... Group Operationnel d'Etudes et de Concertation (MAR)
GOPEP .... Advanced Section of a Field Evacuation Station (RU)
GOPERNAS ... Gabungan Organisasi Perusahaan Nasional Swasta [*Federation of Private National Business Firms*] (IN)
GOPR .... Gorskie Ochotnicze Pogotowie Ratunkowe [*Volunteer Mountain Rescue Service*] (POL)
gor .... City, Municipal, Town, Urban (RU)
GOR .... Gas-Cooled Reactor (RU)
GOR .... Gor'kiy Railroad (RU)
gor .... Gorog [*Greek*] (HU)
GOR .... Groupe Ouvrier Revolutionnaire [*Revolutionary Workers Group*] [*Senegalese*] (AF)
GOR .... Gulf Olympic Ranges (MAR)
gor .... Horizon (RU)
gor .... Hot (RU)
gor .... Hot Spring [*Topography*] (RU)
gor .... Mountainous, Mining (RU)
gor ad .... Mountain Artillery Battalion (RU)
gor ap .... Mountain Artillery Regiment (RU)
Gorbytpromsoyuz ... City General Services Producers' Union (RU)
Gordezbyuro ... City Disinfection and Deratization Office (RU)
Gordorekspluatatsiya ... Moscow City Trust for the Operation of Roads and Drainage Systems of the Administration of the Operation of the Road and Bridge System of the Ispolkom of the Mosgorsovet (RU)
Gordormekhanizatsiya ... City Trust for Road Operation and Mechanization (RU)
Gordorremont ... Trust of the Administration for the Operation of the Road and Bridge System of the Mosgorispolkom (RU)
gorekskursbyuro ... City Excursion Office (RU)
gorem .... Advance Repair Train (RU)

Gorenergo ... City Power System Administration Management (RU)
gorfo .... City Finance Department (RU)
Gorgeonefteizdat ... State Scientific and Technical Publishing House of Mining, Geological, and Petroleum Literature (RU)
Gorgeos'yemka ... State Trust for the Geodetic Survey of Cities (RU)
GORINKhU ... City Inspection of the Statistical Survey of the National Economy (RU)
gor inzh....... Mining Engineer (RU)
Gorkhimpromsoyuz ... City Chemical Producers' Union (RU)
Gorkhimpromstroy ... All-Union Trust for the Construction of Chemical Raw Materials Mining Establishments (RU)
Gorkhudozhpromsoyuz ... City Producers' Union of Artels of Art Crafts (RU)
gorkomkhoz ... City Department of Municipal Services (RU)
gorkommunotdel ... City Department of Municipal Services (RU)
Gorkoopinsoyuz ... City Union of Disabled Persons' Cooperative Artels (RU)
gorkooptorg ... City Cooperative Trade Organization (RU)
Gorkozhpromsoyuz ... City Union of Leather Producers' Cooperatives (RU)
GORKTEK ... City Office for Container Shipments and Transportation and Forwarding Operations (RU)
Gormashuchet ... State Office for the Rationalization and Mechanization of Accounting (RU)
Gormebpromsoyuz ... City Furniture Producers' Union (RU)
Gormesttopprom ... City Administration of Local and Fuel Industries (RU)
gormetallopromsoyuz ... City Metal Producers' Union (RU)
Gormetpromsoyuz ... City Metal Producers' Union (RU)
Gormnogopromsoyuz ... City Multitrade Producers' Union (RU)
gorn............. Mountain, Mountainous, Mining (RU)
gornadompromsoyuz ... City Home-Working Producers' Union (RU)
gornarobraz ... City Department of Public Education (RU)
GorONO ...... City Department of Public Education (RU)
Gorpechat'promsoyuz ... City Union of Producers' Cooperatives of the Printing Industry (RU)
gorpishchetorg ... City Trade Organization for Trade in Food Products (RU)
gorplan .... City Planning Commission (RU)
gorpo .... City Consumers' Cooperatives (RU)
gorpo .... City Consumers' Society (RU)
gorpotrebsoyuz ... City Union of Consumers' Societies (RU)
gor prkh ...... Mountain Pass [*Topography*] (RU)
Gorprom ..... Forestry Industrial Enterprise (BU)
gorpromsovet ... City Council of Producers' Cooperatives (RU)
gorpromtorg ... City Establishment for Trade in Manufactured Goods (RU)
gorpromuch ... School of Mining Apprenticeship (RU)
gorproyekt ... City Soviet Planning Department (RU)
gorraykom ... City Rayon Committee of the KPSS (RU)
gorremstroytrest ... City Repair and Construction Trust (RU)
Gorrybkoop ... City Union of Fisheries Consumers' Cooperatives (RU)
gorsanepidstantsiya ... City Sanitary and Epidemiological Station (RU)
Gor-Sen ...... Kamu Gorevlileri Sendikasi [*Civil Servants' Union*] (TU)
GOR-SEN.... Kibris Turk Kamu Gorevlileri Sendikasi [*Turkish Cypriot Civil Servants' Union*] [*Later, KAMU-SEN*] (TU)
gorSES........ City Sanitary and Epidemiological Station (RU)
Gorshveypromsoyuz ... City Garment Producers' Union (RU)
gorsobes...... City Department of Social Security (RU)
gor solen..... Bitter Salt Mud [*Topography*] (RU)
gorsportsoyuz ... City Council of the Union of Sports Societies and Organizations (RU)
GorSt .... Gorsko Stopanstvo [*Forestry Resources*] [*A periodical*] (BU)
gorstroy ...... Administration of Urban Construction (RU)
Gorstroy...... Forestry Construction Administration (BU)
Gorstroyproyekt ... State Planning Institute of Urban Construction (RU)
GORTEK ..... City Transportation and Forwarding Office (RU)
gortekhnadzor ... Mining Engineering Inspection (RU)
Gortekstil'promsoyuz ... City Textile Producers' Union (RU)
gortop .... City Fuel Department (RU)
gortop .... City Fuel Trust (RU)
Gortorg .... City Trade Administration (RU)
gortorg........ City Trade Department (RU)
GORUBSO ... Bulgarian-Soviet Ore Mining Company (BU)
goruprmestprom ... City Administration of Local Industry (RU)
Gorvodkanalstroy ... State Trust for the Survey and Planning of Urban Water Supply and Sewer Systems (RU)
gorVTEK ..... City Medical Commission for Determination of Disability (RU)
gorzags....... City Civil Registry Office (RU)
gorzags....... City Department of the Civil Registry (RU)
gorzdrav ..... City Department of Public Health (RU)
Gorzelenkhoz ... City Landscape Management Trust (RU)
Gor zh d ...... Gor'kiy Railroad (RU)
gorzo........... City Land Department (RU)
GOS .... Government of Senegal (MAR)
GOS .... Government of Sudan (MAR)
GOS .... Hospital Ship (RU)
GOS .... Variable Feedback (RU)
Gosakteatr ... State Academic Theater (RU)
GOSAP........ Grupo de Organizacao de Sessoes da Assembleia Popular [*Group for the Organization of People's Assembly Sessions*] [*Mozambican*] (AF)
Gosarbitrazh ... State Arbitration Commission (RU)
Gosarkhstroykontrol' ... State Architectural and Construction Control (RU)
Gosatomizdat ... State Publishing House of Literature in the Field of Atomic Science and Technology (RU)
Gosavtoinspektsiya ... State Automobile Inspection (RU)
GOSBEZ ..... State Security (RU)
Gosbumizdat ... State Scientific and Technical Publishing House of the Ministry of the Pulp and Paper Industry, USSR (RU)
gosdepartament ... US Department of State (RU)
GOSEK........ State Economic Commission of the Council of Ministers, USSR, for Current Planning of the National Economy (RU)
Gosekonomkomissiya ... State Economic Commission of the Council of Ministers, USSR, for Current Planning of the National Economy (RU)
Gosekonomsovet ... State Scientific and Economic Council of the Council of Ministers, USSR (RU)
GOSENERGOIZDAT ... State Scientific and Technical Power-Engineering Publishing House (RU)
Gosenergonadzor ... State Inspection for Industrial Power Engineering and for Power Engineering Supervision (RU)
GOSET........ State Jewish Theater (RU)
Gosfil........... State Philharmonic (RU)
GOSFINIZDAT ... State Financial Publishing House (RU)
GOSFIZKhIM ... State Physicochemical Institute Imeni L. Ya. Karpov (RU)
Gosgeolizdat ... State Publishing House of Geological Literature (RU)
GOSGEOLTEKHIZDAT ... State Scientific and Technical Publishing House of Literature on Geology, Geodesy, and Conservation of Mineral Resources (RU)
Gosgeonadzor ... Department of the State Geological Inspection (RU)
Gosgeotekhizdat ... State Publishing House of Geological and Technical Literature (RU)
Gosgorgeolnefteizdat ... State Scientific and Technical Publishing House for Petroleum Mining and Geology (RU)
Gosgorizdat ... State Mining Publishing House (RU)
Gosgorkhimproyekt ... State All-Union Institute for the Planning of Establishments of the Chemical Raw Materials Mining Industry (RU)
GOSGORTEKhIZDAT ... State Scientific and Technical Publishing House of Literature on Mining (RU)
GOSGORTEKHNADZOR ... State Committee of the Council of Ministers for Supervision of Industrial Safety and for Mining Inspection [*RSFSR*] (RU)
GOSI .... General Organization for Social Insurance (MAR)
Gosinoizdat ... State Publishing House of Foreign Literature (RU)
Gosinsilikat ... State Experimental Institute of Silicates (RU)
GOSINTI...... State Scientific Research Institute of Scientific and Technical Information (RU)
Gosinzhgorproyekt ... State Trust for the Planning of Units of Municipal Housing Construction (RU)
GOSIZDAT ... State Publishing House (RU)
GOSKAP ..... Caspian State Steamship Line (RU)
GOSKhIMIZDAT ... State Scientific and Technical Publishing House of Chemical Literature (RU)
Goskhimproyekt ... State All-Union Institute for the Planning of Special Structures, Buildings, and Sanitary-Engineering and Power Installations for Chemical Industry Establishments (RU)
Goskhimtekhizdat ... State Scientific and Technical Publishing House of Chemical Literature (RU)
GOSKINO.... Central State Photography and Motion-Picture Establishment of the Narkompros (RU)
Goskinoizdat ... State Publishing House of Cinematographic Literature (RU)
Goskinoizdat ... State Publishing House of Literature on Motion-Picture Problems (RU)
Goskontrol' ... State Control Commission of the Council of Ministers (RU)
Goskontsert ... State Concert Association of the USSR (RU)
Goskul'tprosvetizdat ... State Publishing House of Cultural and Educational Literature (RU)
Goslegpromizdat ... State Scientific and Technical Publishing House of the Ministry of the Consumers' Goods Industry, USSR (RU)
Goslesbumizdat ... State Publishing House of the Lumber, Paper, and Woodworking Industries (RU)
Goslestekhizdat ... State Publishing House of Forestry Engineering (RU)
GOSLITIZDAT ... State Publishing House of Belles Lettres (RU)
Gosmanopo ... State Visual Aids Workshops (RU)
Gosmashmetizdat ... State Publishing House for Machinery Manufacture, Metalworking, and Ferrous Metallurgy (RU)
Gosmedizdat ... State Publishing House of Medical Literature (of the UkrSSR) (RU)
Gosmestprom ... State Committee of the Council of Ministers, RSFSR, for Local Industry and Art Crafts (RU)
Gosmestpromizdat ... State Publishing House of Local Industry and Art Crafts, RSFSR (RU)
Gosmetallurgizdat ... State Publishing House of Metallurgical Literature (RU)
Gosmontazhspetsstroy ... State Industrial Committee for the Installation and Specialized Construction Operations, USSR (RU)
Gosmuzizdat ... State Music Publishing House (RU)
Gosnardom ... State People's House Imeni Karl Liebknecht and Rosa Luxemburg (RU)
Gosnauchtekhizdat ... State Scientific and Technical Publishing House (RU)
GosNII .... State Scientific Research Institute (RU)
GosNIIGA.... State Scientific Research Institute of Civil Aviation (RU)
GosNII GVF ... State Scientific Research Institute of the Civil Air Fleet, USSR (RU)
GosNIORKh ... State Scientific Research Institute of Lake and River Fisheries (RU)

GOSNITI...... State All-Union Scientific Research Technological Institute for Repair and Operation of Machine and Tractor Fleets (RU)
Gosp .... Hospital [*Topography*] (RU)
GOSPLAN... State Planning Commission (RU)
GOSPLAN... State Planning Committee, USSR (RU)
GOSPLANIZDAT ... State Publishing House of Literature on Economic Planning (RU)
Gospolitizdat ... State Publishing House of Political Literature (RU)
Gospolitnauchizdat ... State Publishing House of Political and Scientific Literature (RU)
Gospozhnadzor ... State Fire Inspection (RU)
Gosprodsnab ... State Committee of the Council of Ministers, USSR, for the Supply of Foodstuffs and Industrial Goods (RU)
Gosradioizdat ... State Radio Publishing House (RU)
Gosrybflotinspektsiya ... State Inspection for Safety at Sea and Port Supervision of the Fish Industry Fleet (RU)
gosrybnadzor ... State Fishing Inspection (RU)
Gossaninspektsiya ... State Sanitary Inspection (RU)
GOSSEL'KHOZIZDAT ... State Publishing House of Agricultural Literature [*UkrSSR*] (RU)
Gossel'sindikat ... State Russian Agricultural Syndicate (RU)
GOSSH........ Glavni Odbor Saveza Sindikata Hrvatske [*Central Committee, Council of Trade-Unions of Croatia*] (YU)
gossortouchastok ... State Crop-Testing Station, State Strain Trial Station (RU)
gossortsemfond ... State Fund of Selected Seeds (RU)
GOSSTATIZDAT ... State Statistical Publishing House (RU)
Gosstrakh... Main Administration of State Insurance (RU)
Gosstroy ..... All-Russian Central State Construction Office [*RSFSR*] (RU)
Gosstroy ..... State Committee for Construction [*USSR*] (RU)
GOSSTROYIZDAT ... State Publishing House of Literature on Construction, Architecture, and Building Materials (RU)
GOSSTROYIZDAT USSR ... State Publishing House of Literature on Construction and Architecture, UkrSSR (RU)
GOSSTROY SSSR ... State Committee of the Council of Ministers, USSR, for Construction (RU)
Gosstroytrest ... State Construction Trust of the Glavmosstroy (RU)
GOST .... All-Union State Standard (RU)
Gost .... Hotel [*Topography*] (RU)
GOST .... Soviet State Standards [*USSR*] (WEN)
Gosteasvet ... State Electromechanical Plant for the Manufacture of Theatrical Equipment (RU)
Gostekhgornadzor ... State Inspection for Technical and Mining Supervision (RU)
Gostekhizdat ... State Publishing House of Technical and Theoretical Literature (RU)
Gostekhnika ... State Committee of the Council of Ministers, USSR, for New Technology (RU)
Gostekhteoretizdat ... State Publishing House of Technical and Theoretical Literature (RU)
GosTIM .... State Theater Imeni V. E. Meyerkhol'd (RU)
Gostopizdat ... State Publishing House of Literature on the Fuel Industry (RU)
GOSTOPTEKhIZDAT ... State Scientific and Technical Publishing House of Petroleum and Mineral Fuel Literature (RU)
GOSTORG ... State Import-Export Trade Office (RU)
Gostorginspektsiya ... Main Administration of State Quality Inspection of Goods and State Trade Inspection (RU)
GOSTORGIZDAT ... State Publishing House of Literature on Trade (RU)
Gostransizdat ... State Transportation Publishing House (RU)
Gostrudizdat ... State Publishing House for Labor Problems (RU)
gostrudsberkassa ... State Workers' Savings Bank (RU)
Gostsentyuz ... State Central Theater for the Young Spectator (RU)
gos-vo......... State (RU)
Gosvodkhoz ... State Committee of the Council of Ministers for Water Management (RU)
Gosvoyenizdat ... State Military Publishing House (RU)
GOSYuRIZDAT ... State Publishing House of Legal Literature (RU)
GOSZ .... Gepeszek Orszagos Szovetsege [*National Association of Mechanics*] (HU)
Goszdravproyekt ... State Planning Office of the Ministry of Public Health, USSR (RU)
Goszelenkhoz ... State Landscape Management Trust (RU)
Goszemvodkhoz SSSR ... State Industrial Committee for the Irrigation Farming and Water Management, USSR (RU)
GOSZHELDORIZDAT ... State Railroad Publishing House (RU)
GOT............ Gorska Odznaka Turystyczna [*Mountain-Climbing Tourist Badge*] (POL)
got.............. Gotisch [*German*]
GOT............ Government of Tanzania (MAR)
GOT............ Reference Current Generator (RU)
GOTA .... Gasdotti Oleodotti Transcontinentali Afro-Europi SPA (MAR)
GotdMGP.... Annals of the Geological and Mining Surveys Department (BU)
GOTEDR ..... State Dramatic Theater (RU)
GOTOB........ State Theater of Opera and Ballet (RU)
GOU .... Grupo de Oficiales Unidos [*Group of United Officers*] [*Argentine*] (LA)
Gouville....... Gouvernement de la Ville [*City or Municipal Government*] (CL)
GOVPF .... Groupement Obligatoire des Viticulteurs et Producteurs de Fruits [*Tunisian*] (MAR)
GOZ............ State Optical Plant (RU)
GOZB .... Glavni Odbor Zveze Borcev [*Central Committee of the Union of Veterans*] (YU)
GOZBNOV Slovenije ... Glavni Odbor Zveze Borcev Narodnoosvobodilne Vojske Slovenije [*Central Committee of the Slovenian Union of Veterans of the National Liberation War*] (YU)
Goznak........ State Bank Note Factory (RU)
GOZNAK..... State Bank Notes, Coins, and Medals Administration (RU)
GOZZD........ Glavni Odbor Zveze Zenskih Drustev [*Central Committee of the Federation of Women's Clubs*] (YU)
GP .... Breakthrough Group (RU)
GP .... Caterpillar Trailer (RU)
GP .... City Enterprise (BU)
GP .... Civilian Gas Mask (RU)
GP .... Gas Main, Gas Pipeline (RU)
GP .... Gas Producers Ltd. (MAR)
gp............... General of the Infantry (BU)
GP .... General Porucnik [*Lieutenant General*] (YU)
GP .... Generalni Prokurator [*Prosecutor General*] (CZ)
GP .... Geologicky Pruzkum [*Geological Research*] (CZ)
gp............... Geppuska [*Heavy Machine Gun*] (HU)
GP .... Gozo Party [*Maltese*] (PPE)
GP .... Gradevinsko Preduzece [*Building Establishment*] (YU)
GP .... Gradska Plinara [*City Gas Plant*] (YU)
GP .... Grafeion Periokhis [*Regional Office*] [*Greek*] (GC)
GP .... Grafeion Programmatismou [*Planning Office*] (GC1)
GP .... Group Converter (RU)
GP .... Grupos Profesionales [*Professional Groups*] [*Spanish*] (WER)
GP .... Guadeloupe [*Two-letter standard code*] (CNC)
GP .... Guard Regiment (BU)
GP .... Guven Partisi [*Reliance Party - RP*] (TU)
GP .... Heterodyne Conversion Transducer (RU)
GP-............. Hexagonal Close-Packed (Lattice) (RU)
GP .... Hyaloplasm (RU)
g/p .... Load-Carrying Capacity, Tonnage (RU)
GP .... Pulse-Train Generator (RU)
GP .... Sawtooth Voltage Generator (RU)
GPA............ Gerakan Pemuda Ansor [*Ansor Youth Movement*] (IN)
GPA............ Grafeion Poleodomias Athinon [*Athens City Planning Office*] (GC)
GPA............ Grand Parc d'Armee [*Military*] [*French*] (MTD)
G PA........... Grand Parc d'Artillerie [*Military*] [*French*] (MTD)
GPA............ Groupement des Pharmaciens d'Afrique (MAR)
GPA............ Guyana Press Association (LA)
GPAA .... Hydrolyzed Polyacrylamide (RU)
GPAE .... Gouvernement Provisoire Algerien en Exil [*Algerian Provisional Government in Exile*] (AF)
GPB............ Gazdasagpolitikai Bizottsag [*Economic Policy Committee (of the MSZMP CC)*] (HU)
GPB............ State Public Library Imeni M. Ye. Saltykov-Shchedrin (RU)
GPBN.......... Groupement Pharmaceutique Benin-Niger (MAR)
GPBSShch ... State Public Library Imeni M. Ye. Saltykov-Shchedrin (RU)
GPC............ Compagnie Generale de la Petite Cote (MAR)
GPC............ General People's Congress [*Libyan*] (PPW)
GPC............ General Petroleum Company [*Equatorial Guinean*] (MAR)
GPC............ Ghana Publishing Corporation (MAR)
GPC............ Grenada Peace Council (LA1)
GPC............ Groupe des Progressistes du Cameroun (MAR)
GPC............ Guyana Petroleum Corporation (LA)
GPC............ Guyana Pharmaceutical Corporation (LA)
GPD............ Generals for Peace and Disarmament (EA)
GPD............ Grupe Podvodnih Diverzanata [*Groups of Underwater Saboteurs*] [*Military*] (YU)
GPECC........ Groupement Professionnel des Exportateurs de Cafe et de Cacao (MAR)
GPEG .... Advanced Field Evacuation Hospital (RU)
GPEIS.......... Gabungan Pengusaha Ekspor Indonesia Sementara [*Provisional Association of Indonesian Exporters*] (IN)
GPEP........... Advanced Field Evacuation Station (RU)
GPF .... Gibraltar Police Force (MAR)
GPF .... Group Band Filter (RU)
GPG............ Gaertnerische Produktions-Genossenschaft [*Horticultural Producer Cooperative*] (EG)
GP GUSMP ... Hydrographic Establishment of the Glavsevmorput' (RU)
GPH............ Grenzpolizeihaelfer [*Border Police Assistant*] (EG)
GPI .... Georgian Polytechnic Institute Imeni V. I. Lenin (RU)
gpi.............. Geppisztoly [*Machine Pistol, Submachine Gun*] (HU)
GPI .... Gesellschaft fuer Programmierte Instruktion
GPI .... Gor'kiy Polytechnic Institute Imeni A. A. Zhdanov (RU)
GPI .... Graphique et Papeterie Ivoirienne (MAR)
GPI .... Grupe za Podvodno Izvidanje [*Groups for Underwater Reconnaissance*] [*Military*] (YU)
GPI .... Grupo Parlamentario Independiente [*Independent Parliamentary Group*] [*Spanish*] (WER)
GPI .... Guinnes Peat International [*Sudanese*] (MAR)
GPI-............ Hydraulic Soil Evaporator (RU)
GPI .... State Pedagogical Institute (RU)
GPI .... State Planning Institute (RU)
GPI .... Underwater Exploration Group (RU)
GPIB............ State Public Historical Library, RSFSR (RU)
GPII .... Gabungan Pengusaha Impor Indonesia [*Indonesia Importers Association*] (IN)

GPIIYa......... Gor'kiy Pedagogical Institute of Foreign Languages (RU)
GPIIYa......... State Pedagogical Institute of Foreign Languages (RU)
GPIN........... Groupement Professionnel de l'Industrie Nucleaire [*Also known as NIC*] [*Belgian*]
GPK............ City Consumers' Cooperative (BU)
GPK............ City Fire Brigade (RU)
GPK............ City Industrial Kombinat (RU)
GPK............ City Party Committee (RU)
GPK............ City Post Office (RU)
GPK............ Civil Procedure Code (BU)
GPK............ Code of Civil Procedure (RU)
GPK............ Cumene Hydroperoxide (RU)
GPK............ Direction Indicator (RU)
GPK............ Geological Survey Branch (BU)
GPK............ Gradanski Procesualni Kodeks [*Civil Procedure Code*] (YU)
GPK............ Main Check Point (RU)
GPK............ Main Compass [*Aviation*] (RU)
GPK............ State Pedigree Stock Book, State Breeding Register (RU)
GPK............ State Pedigree Stud Farm (RU)
GPKhO......... Ready for Chemical Defense (RU)
GPL............ Gaz et Petrole Liquefies [*Algerian*] (MAR)
GPL............ Societe Gabonaise de Peintures et Laques (MAR)
GPlAM......... Annals of the Plovdiv Archaeological Museum (BU)
GPLS........... Groupement Professionnel des Commercants et Industriels Libanais du Senegal (MAR)
GPM............ Gerakan Papua Merdeka [*Free Papua Movement*] (IN)
GPM............ Grupe za Podvodno Miniranje [*Groups for Underwater Mine-Laying*] [*Military*] (YU)
GPM............ Guyana People's Militia (LA)
GPM............ Main Medical Aid Station (RU)
GPMB.......... Gambia Produce Marketing Board (MAR)
GPMI........... Grupo Permanente de Mobilizacao Industrial [*Permanent Industrial Mobilization Group*] [*Brazilian*] (LA)
GPMS.......... Gabongan Pelajar Melayu Semenanjong [*Malay Peninsula Students Association*] (ML)
GPMV.......... Groupements Pre-Cooperatifs de Mise en Valeur (MAR)
GPN............ Constant-Potential Generator (RU)
GPN............ Sawtooth Voltage Generator (RU)
GPN............ State Fire Inspection (RU)
GPNB.......... Annals of the Plovdiv National Library (BU)
GPNBM........ Annals of the Plovdiv National Library and Museum (BU)
GPNRB........ Prosecutor General's Office of the Bulgarian People's Republic (BU)
GPNS.......... Advanced Observation and Communication Post (RU)
GPNTB........ State Public Scientific and Technical Library, USSR (RU)
GPO............ La Grande Pecherie de l'Ouest (MAR)
GPO............ Main Defense Zone (BU)
GPO............ State Border Guard (RU)
GPP............ Border Guard Infantry Regiment (BU)
GPP............ City Industrial Enterprise (BU)
GPP............ Forestry Industrial Enterprise (BU)
GPP............ Gambia People's Party (AF)
GPP............ Geological Surveys Enterprise (BU)
GPP............ Grafeion Pliforion kai Paraponon [*Information and Complaints Office*] [*Greek*] (GC)
GPP............ Groupement Professionnel du Petrole (MAR)
GPP............ Main Dressing Station (RU)
GPP............ Main Political Education Committee of the Narkompros, RSFSR (RU)
GPP............ Main Step-Down Sub-Station (RU)
GPP............ Mountain Infantry Regiment (RU)
GPP............ Production Preparation Group (RU)
GPP............ State Fruit Nursery (RU)
GPPL........... Gdanskie Przedsiebiorstwo Produkcji Lesnej "LAS" [*Gdansk Forest Production Enterprise "LAS"*] (POL)
GPPP........... Hydrologic Receiving-Sending Post (RU)
GPr............ Geografski Pregled [*Geographic Review*] [*A periodical*] (BU)
GPR............ Grupe za Podvodno Rusenje [*Groups for Underwater Demolition*] [*Military*] (YU)
GPR............ Main Starting Relay (RU)
GPR............ Mountain Infantry Company (RU)
g pr............ Mountain Pass [*Topography*] (RU)
GPR............ State Pedigree Cattle Breeding Farm (RU)
GPRA.......... Gouvernement Provisoire de la Republique Algerienne [*Provisional Government of the Algerian Republic*] (AF)
GPRB.......... Government of the People's Republic of Benin (AF)
GPRFE........ Gouvernement Provisoire des Revolutionnaires Fiotes en Exil (MAR)
GPrIzpD...... Annals of the Bulgarian Society of Natural History (BU)
GPRz.......... Grupe za Podvodno Razminiranje [*Groups for Underwater Mine Removal*] [*Military*] (YU)
GPS............ Bandwidth Shift Generator (RU)
GPS............ Forestry Industrial Farm (BU)
GPSA.......... Gava Property & Sales Agencies Ltd. (MAR)
GPSD.......... Main Message Center (RU)
GPSU.......... Guyana Public Service Union (LA)
GPSYF........ Grand Port-Savanne Youth Federation [*Mauritian*] (AF)
GPT............ Amphibian Tracked Personnel Carrier (RU)
GPT............ Direct-Current Generator (RU)
GPT............ Glutamic Pyruvic Transaminase (RU)
GPT............ Graduated Personal Tax (MAR)
GPT............ Labor Party of Guatemala (RU)
GPTC.......... Groupe Politique des Travailleurs Chretiens [*Christian Workers' Political Group*] [*Belgian*] (WER)
GPTI........... Georgian Polytechnic Institute (RU)
GPTU.......... Gas and Steam Turbine Power Plant (RU)
GPU............ State Political Administration [*1922*] (RU)
gpuaz.......... Hectopoise (RU)
GPV............ Gereformeerd Politiek Verbond [*Reformed Political League*] [*Dutch*] (PPE)
GPVNaR...... Main Air Observation and Reconnaissance Post (RU)
GPVNOS..... Main Aircraft-Warning Service Post (RU)
GPVO.......... Ready for Antiaircraft Defense (RU)
GPZ............ Advance Party (RU)
gpz............ Hectopieze (RU)
gpz............ Hectopoise (RU)
GPZ............ State Bearing Plant (RU)
GPZB.......... Gdanskie Przemyslowe Zjednoczenie Budowlane [*Gdansk (Danzig) Industrial Construction Association*] (POL)
GPZU.......... Hump Program-Setting Device [*Railroads*] (RU)
GQ............. Equatorial Guinea [*Two-letter standard code*] (CNC)
GQG........... Grand Quartier General [*General Headquarters*] [*French*]
gr.............. Citizen, Civic, Civil, Civilian (RU)
gr.............. City (BU)
gr.............. Column (BU)
gr.............. Column (RU)
gr.............. Degree (RU)
GR-............ Gamma Relay (RU)
GR............. Gare Regulatrice [*Military*] [*French*] (MTD)
GR............. Gemeinderat [*German*]
GR............. Gendarmerie Royale [*Royal Gendarmerie*] [*Use GRK*] [*Cambodian*] (CL)
GR............. Generalne Riaditelstvo [*General Directorate*] (CZ)
GR............. Generalreparaturplan [*General Overhaul Plan*] (EG)
g-r............. Generator, Oscillator (RU)
GR............. Gospodarsko Razstavisce [*Economic Exhibit*] [*Ljubljana*] (YU)
GR............. Gotong Rojong [*Mutual Cooperation*] (IN)
Gr.............. Graben [*Ditch, Trench*] (EG)
gr.............. Gracht [*Canal*] [*Dutch*] (CED)
gr.............. Gram (BU)
g-r............. Gram Roentgen (RU)
gr.............. Gramm [*Gram*] (EG)
gr.............. Gramm [*Gram*] (HU)
gr.............. Grammar (RU)
Gr.............. Gramme [*Gram*] [*French*] (MTD)
gr.............. Gramo [*Gram*] [*Spanish*]
gr.............. Granat [*or Granatos*] [*Grenade, Shell, Grenade Thrower*] (HU)
Gr.............. Granate [*Shell, Grenade*] (EG)
Gr.............. Gravel [*Topography*] (RU)
Gr.............. Greben [*or Grebeni*] [*Rock, Reef, Cliff, Ridge*] [*Yugoslav*] (NAU)
GR............. Grecia [*Greece*] [*Polish*]
GR............. Greece [*Two-letter standard code*] (CNC)
gr.............. Greek (BU)
gr.............. Greek, Grecian (RU)
GR............. Green Revolution (MAR)
gr.............. Greenwich Time (RU)
Gr.............. Greenwichista [*Finnish*]
Gr.............. Grenz [*German*]
Gr.............. Gros [*Gross*] [*Business and trade*] [*German*]
gr.............. Grosha [*Old monetary unit*] (BU)
gr.............. Grosz [*A coin, Hundredth part of a zloty*] (POL)
gr.............. Group (RU)
Gr.............. Groupe [*Group, Division, Unit*] [*Military*] [*French*] (MTD)
GR............. Groupe Revolution [*Revolution Group*] [*French*] (WER)
GR............. Growth Hormone (RU)
Gr.............. Grubu [*Group*] (TU)
Gr.............. Grunn [*or Grunnen, Grunnane*] [*Shoal or Shoals*] [*Norwegian*] (NAU)
Gr.............. Grunn [*Shoal*] [*Icelandic*] (NAU)
Gr.............. Gruppe [*German*]
GR............. Guardia Republicana del Peru [*Republican Guard of Peru*] (LA)
GR............. Gurkha Rifles (ML)
G-R............ Hertzsprung-Russell (Diagram) (RU)
Gr.............. Load Capacity, Load-Lifting Capacity, Carrying Capacity (RU)
Gr.............. Loudspeaker (RU)
GR............. Mercury Fulminate (RU)
GR............. Sweep Generator (RU)
Gr.............. Tomb [*Topography*] (RU)
gr.............. Urban (BU)
gr.............. Year of Birth (RU)
GRACETALES... Grasas y Aceites Vegetales Ltda. [*Barranquilla*] (COL)
grad............ Degree (RU)
Grad............ Gradevinarstvo [*Building Industry*] (YU)
GRADAPROMET... Poduzece za Promet Gradevinskim Materijalom [*Enterprise for Trade in Building Materials*] (YU)
grad ekv...... Degree of Equator (RU)
GRADEP...... Gradevinsko Preduzece [*Building Establishment*] (YU)
grad mer..... Degree of Meridian (RU)
GRADSPED... Gradsko Preduzece za Transport i Spediciju [*City Establishment for Transport and Shipment*] [*Rijeka*] (YU)
GRAE.......... Gouvernement Revolutionnaire de l'Angola en Exil [*Revolutionary Angolan Government-in-Exile*] (MAR)

GRAE .... Governo Revolucionario de Angola no Exilio [*Revolutionary Angolan Government-in-Exile*] (PD)
graf .... Graficzny [*Printing*] (POL)
graf .... Graphite [*Topography*] (RU)
Gral .... General [*General*] [*Spanish*] (GPO)
gram .... Grammar (RU)
gram .... Grammar, Grammatical (BU)
Gram .... Grammateia [*Secretariat*] (GC)
GRAMAG .... Gradski Magacin [*City Department Store*] (YU)
GRAMAR ..... Granitos y Marmoles SA [*Bogota*] (COL)
GRAMAT ..... Poduzece za Promet Gradevinskim Materijalom i Tehnickom Robom [*Establishment for Trade in Building and Technical Materials*] [*Zagreb*] (YU)
Gramcheka ... Extraordinary Commission for the Elimination of Illiteracy (RU)
GRAMETAL ... Metalurgica Grancolombiana [*Pacho-Cundinamarca*] (COL)
gramm .... Grammar (RU)
GRAMOA .... Grands Magasins de l'Ouest Africain (MAR)
GRAN .... Grupo Regional Andino [*Andean Regional Group*] [*Peruvian*] (LA)
GRANAP ..... Gradsko Narodno Preduzece [*City Department Store*] (YU)
granetsentrir ... Face-Centered (RU)
GRANUPHOS ... Tunisian Granular Phosphate Co. (AF)
GRANVIVIENDA ... Grancolombiana de Vivienda [*Cali*] (COL)
GRAPO .... Grupo de Resistencia Armada Primero Octubre [*First of October Armed Revolutionary Group*] [*Spanish*] (WER)
GRAPO .... Grupos de Resistencia Anti-Fascista Primero de Octubre [*October First Antifascist Resistance Groups*] [*Spanish*] (PPE)
GRARR MADGAR ... Goddard Range and Range Rate Station, Madagascar (MAR)
GRASCO ..... Grasas y Aceites Vegetales [*Cali*] (COL)
GRATEKS ... Gradsko Trgovinsko Preduzece za Promet Tekstilom [*City Establishment for Trade in Textiles*] (YU)
GRATPRED ... Gradsko Trgovinsko Preduzece [*City Commercial Establishment*] (YU)
grav .... Cut, Engraved, Engraving, Print (RU)
grav .... Engraved [*or Engraving*] (BU)
G Rav .... Gare de Ravitaillement [*Military*] [*French*] (MTD)
grav .... Gravel Pit [*Topography*] (RU)
GRAVETAL ... Grasas Vegetales de Antioquia Ltda. (COL)
gravitats ...... Gravitational, Gravity (RU)
grazh .... Civilian, Civil, Civic (RU)
grazhd .... Citizen, Civic, Civil, Civilian (RU)
GRB .... Advance Repair Crew (RU)
GrB .... City Library (BU)
GRB .... Glavna Recna Baza [*Main River Base*] [*Navy*] (YU)
GRB .... Guyana Rice Board (LA)
GRC .... Greece [*Three-letter standard code*] (CNC)
gr coup .... Grosses Coupures [*French*]
GRCS .... Ghana Red Cross Society (MAR)
gr d .... Dirt Road [*Topography*] (RU)
Grd .... Grand [*Large*] [*Military map abbreviation*] [*World War I*] [*French*] (MTD)
GRD .... Grenada [*Three-letter standard code*] (CNC)
Grd .... Grund [*Shoal*] [*See also Gd*] [*Danish*] (NAU)
Grd .... Grund [*Shoal*] [*See also Gd*] [*German*] (NAU)
Grd .... Grund [*Shoal*] [*See also Gd*] [*Swedish*] (NAU)
GRD .... Hybrid Rocket Engine, Hydrojet (RU)
gr dal .... Grade Decalitri [*Degrees Decaliters*] (RO)
GRDCh .... Harmonic Relaxation Frequency Divider (RU)
GRDO .... Gambia River Development Organisation (MAR)
gr dor .... Dirt Road [*Topography*] (RU)
GRE .... Generalreparatur [*General Overhaul*] (EG)
GREA .... Groupements pour la Recherche et l'Exploitation Aurifere [*Groups for Gold Prospecting and Exploitation*] [*Malagasy*] (AF)
GREACAM ... Guardian Royal Exchange Assurance du Cameroun (MAR)
GREAEM ..... Gabinete Regional de Estudos das Associacoes Economicas de Mocambique (MAR)
GRECE .... Groupement de Recherche et d'Etudes pour la Civilisation Europeenne [*Research and Study Group for European Civilization*] [*French*] (PD)
grech .... Greek, Grecian (RU)
GREI .... Grupo para la Racionalizacion de la Energia Industrial [*Group for Industrial Energy Efficiency*] [*Uruguayan*] (LA)
GREL .... Ghana Rubber Estates Limited (MAR)
GREO .... Mining Electrical Equipment (RU)
GREPOS .... Grenzpolizei [*Border Guards*] (EG)
GRES .... State Regional Electric Power Plant (RU)
GRESEL .... Groupement pour l'Exportation des Systemes Electroniques (MAR)
GRET .... Group Relations Educational Trust (MAR)
GRETI .... Groupe Romand pour l'Etude des Techniques d'Instruction [*Swiss*]
Grge .... Gorge [*Pass, Gorge*] [*Military map abbreviation*] [*World War I*] [*French*] (MTD)
GRI .... Gospel Recordings Incorporated (MAR)
GRI .... State Radium Institute (RU)
GRII .... Trust for Geodetic Operations and Engineering Surveys (RU)
GRINACO .... Grupo de Investigaciones Nacional Aplicadas a la Construccion [*Group for Applied Research in Construction*] [*Cuban*] (LA)
Gr k .... Civil Code (RU)
GRK .... Gendarmerie Royale Khmere [*Royal Cambodian Gendarmerie*] [*Replaced by National Gendarmerie*] (CL)
GRK .... Main Committee for Control of Entertainment and Repertoires (RU)
gr k .... Pile of Stones, Cairn [*Topography*] (RU)
gr-ka .... Citizen (RU)
gr-kath .... Griechisch-Katholisch [*German*]
Gr Kod .... Civil Code (RU)
gr k-t .... City Committee (BU)
GRKU .... Gerilja Rakjat Kalimantan Utara [*North Kalimantan People's Guerrilla Force*] (IN)
GRL .... Gendarmerie Royale Lao [*Royal Lao Gendarmerie*] (CL)
GRL .... Greenland [*Three-letter standard code*] (CNC)
GRM .... Gemeinschaft Revolutionaerer Marxisten [*League of Revolutionary Marxists*] [*Austrian*] (WEN)
GRM .... Geology of Ore Deposits (RU)
GRM .... Glide Beacon (RU)
GRM .... Gruppe Revolutionaerer Marxisten [*Group of Revolutionary Marxists*] [*Austrian*] (PPE)
GRM .... State Russian Museum (RU)
gr-n .... Citizen (RU)
GRN .... Gminna Rada Narodowa [*Rural Commune People's Council*] (POL)
GRN .... Gouvernement de Redressement National (MAR)
GRN .... Gouvernement de Renouveau National [*National Renewal Government*] [*Upper Voltan*] (AF)
GRN .... Gromadzka Rada Narodowa [*Gromada People's Council*] (POL)
gr-ne .... Citizens (RU)
Grne .... Grunn [*or Grunnen, Grunnane*] [*Shoal or Shoals*] [*Norwegian*] (NAU)
grn lz .... Station Hospital (BU)
Gr NR .... Sodium-Graphite Reactor (RU)
GRNSK .... Grafeion Nomikou Symvoulou Kratous [*State Legal Council Office*] [*Greek*] (GC)
gro .... Gromada [*Village, Group of villages*] (POL)
GROCAF ..... Groupement des Commercants de Kao-Lack [*Senegalese*] (MAR)
GROCOMAF ... Groupement Commercial Africain (MAR)
GROKO .... Groupement Commercial de Kossi (MAR)
gr-or .... Griechisch-Orientalisch [*German*]
Gros .... Generos [*Goods*] [*Business and trade*] [*Spanish*]
GROUPAGRI ... Groupement des Syndicats et Enterprises Agricoles de Madagascar (MAR)
GROZNII .... Groznyy Petroleum Scientific Research Institute (RU)
GRP .... Design Flood Level (RU)
GRP .... Gambia and the Rio Pongas (MAR)
GRP .... Gas-Distributing Point (RU)
GRP .... Gas-Pickup Point (RU)
GRP .... Gas-Regulating Point (RU)
GRP .... Glass Reinforced Plastic Pipes (MAR)
GRP .... Gouvernement Revolutionnaire Provisoire (de la Republique du Sud Viet Nam) [*Provisional Revolutionary Government (of the Republic of South Vietnam)*] [*Use PRGRSV*] (CL)
GRP .... Hydraulic Fracturing [*Pet.*] (RU)
GRP .... Project Starting Management Group (BU)
GRPL .... Grupo Revolucionario Portugues de Libertacao [*Portuguese Revolutionary Liberation Group*] (WER)
GRPP .... Advance Company Small Arms Ammunition Point (RU)
GRPP .... Gradanski Parnicni Postupak [*Civil Code of Procedure*] (YU)
Gr prots kod ... Code of Civil Procedure (RU)
GRPSM .... Groupement Rural de Production et de Secours Mutuel (MAR)
GRRRI .... State Roentgenology, Radiology, and Cancer Institute (RU)
GRRTSN ...... Groupement de Realisation de la Route Transsaharienne du Service National [*North African*] (MAR)
GRS .... Gas-Distributing Station (RU)
GRS .... Glavni Radnicki Savez [*Central Workers' Council*] (YU)
GRS .... Gminna Rada Spoldzielcza [*Rural Commune Cooperative Council*] (POL)
GRS .... Gorska Resevalna Sluzba [*Mountain Rescue Service*] (YU)
GRShch .... Main Switchboard (RU)
Grssgdb ...... Grossgrundbesitzer [*German*]
Grsshdlr ...... Grosshaendler [*German*]
Grssind .... Grossindustrieller [*German*]
GRT .... Gambia River Transport (AF)
Grte .... Grotte [*Grotto*] [*Military map abbreviation*] [*World War I*] [*French*] (MTD)
GRTS .... City Manual Telephone Exchange (RU)
GRTS .... City Radio Wire Broadcasting Network (RU)
GRTs .... Generator of Equally Probable Digits (RU)
grts .... Greek (BU)
GRU .... Geographische Rundschau; Zeitschrift fuer Schulgeographie [*Braunschweig*] [*A publication*] (MAR)
GrU .... Grosshandelsumsatz [*Wholesale Turnover*] (EG)
GRU .... Main Distributing Installation (RU)
GRU .... Main Radio Administration (RU)
GRU .... Regional Administration of Geological Exploration (RU)

GRUAS........ Grupo Universitario Artistico Surcolombiano [*Neiva*] (COL)
grub............ Grubosc [*Thickness*] [*Polish*]
GRULA........ Grupo Regional Latinoamericano [*Latin American Regional Group*] (LA1)
GRUMCAM ... Grumes du Cameroun (MAR)
grundl......... Gruendlich [*Entirely*] [*German*]
GRUNK........ Gouvernement Royal d'Union Nationale du Kampuchea [*Royal Government of National Union of Cambodia*] (CL)
Gruporg...... Group Organizer (BU)
gruz............ Georgian (RU)
Gruzenergo ... Georgian Power System (RU)
GruzFAN..... Georgian Branch of the Academy of Sciences, USSR (RU)
Gruzgiprovodkhoz ... Georgian State Institute for the Planning of Water Management (RU)
Gruzgosplan ... State Planning Commission at the Council of Ministers, Georgian SSR (RU)
Gruzmedgiz ... Georgian State Publishing House of Medical Literature (RU)
Gruzneft'..... Georgian Oil Field Administration (RU)
GruzNIIGiM ... Georgian Scientific Research Institute of Hydraulic Engineering and Reclamation (RU)
GruzNIIGM ... Georgian Scientific Research Institute of Hydraulic Engineering and Reclamation (RU)
GruzNIIVKh ... Georgian Scientific Research Institute of Water Management (RU)
GruzNITO.... Georgian Scientific Research and Technical Society (RU)
GruzNITOLes ... Georgian Scientific and Technical Society of the Lumber Industry and Forestry (RU)
GruzSSR..... Georgian Soviet Socialist Republic (RU)
GruzTAG..... Georgian News Agency (RU)
Grv.............. Gorev [*Duty, Mission*] (TU)
grv.............. Granatveto [*Grenade Thrower*] (HU)
Gr v............ Grande Vitesse [*High Speed, Express*] [*French*]
GRVC.......... Groupement Revolutionnaire a Vocation Cooperative [*Revolutionary Cooperative Group*] [*Beninese*] (AF)
GRV-K......... Graficheski Vestnik [*Graphics Newspaper*] [*A periodical*] (BU)
Gr VR.......... Water-Cooled Graphite Reactor (RU)
Gr VRD........ Pressurized-Tube Water-Cooled Graphite Reactor (RU)
Gr VRK........ Boiling-Water Graphite Reactor (RU)
Gr VRK-P.... Boiling-Water Graphite Reactor with Nuclear Superheat (RU)
GRW........... Geraete- und Reglerwerke (VEB) [*Appliance and Regulator Works (VEB)*] [*Teltow*] (EG)
gryaz.......... Mud Volcano, Muddy Spring [*Topography*] (RU)
gryaz lech... Mud-Bath Clinic [*Topography*] (RU)
GRZ............ Government of the Republic of Zambia (MAR)
g/s.............. Advanced Station (RU)
GS.............. Aircraft Generator (RU)
GS.............. Chief Referee [*Sports*] (RU)
GS.............. City Council (BU)
GS.............. Civil Procedure [*Law*] (BU)
GS.............. Draw-Off Level (RU)
GS.............. Erase Head, Erasing Head (RU)
GS.............. Galatasaray Lisesi [*Galatasaray Lycee*] [*Istanbul*] (TU)
Gs.............. Gaus [*Gauss*] [*Polish*]
gs.............. Gauss (BU)
gs.............. Gauss (RU)
GS.............. Gefechtsstand [*Headquarters, Command Post*] (EG)
GS.............. Gefechtsstation [*Battle Station*] (EG)
GS.............. Genikon Symvoulion [*General Council*] (GC)
GS.............. Glavni Stab [*General Headquarters*] [*Military*] (YU)
GS.............. Gminna Spoldzielnia [*Rural Commune Cooperative*] (POL)
GS.............. Gorsko Stopanstvo [*Forestry Resources*] [*A periodical*] (BU)
GS.............. Gradska Stamparija [*City Printing Office*] (YU)
gs.............. Gram Force (RU)
GS-............. Gravimetric Station (RU)
GS.............. Group for Support [*to border troops*] (BU)
GS.............. Grupo Socialista [*Socialist Group*] [*Portuguese*] (PPE)
GS.............. Guild of Surveyors (EA)
GS.............. Guinea Syli (MAR)
GS.............. Gymnastikos Syllogos [*Gymnastics Club*] (GC)
GS.............. Gyro Stabilizer (RU)
GS.............. Hospital Ship (RU)
GS.............. Hydraulic Engineering Construction (RU)
GS.............. Main Forces, Main Body (RU)
GS-............. Second Goniometer (RU)
GS.............. Self-Defense Group (RU)
GS.............. Signal Generator (RU)
GS.............. Signal Oscillator (BU)
G-30-S......... Gerakan 30 September [*30 September Movement (1965)*] (IN)
GSA............ General Series in Anthropology (MAR)
GSA............ Groupe Scolaire d'Astrida (MAR)
GSA............ Guzel Sanatlar Akademisi [*Fine Arts Academy*] [*See also DGSA, IDGSA*] (TU)
GSAE.......... Geniki Synomospondia Avtokiniston Ellados [*General Confederation of Motorists of Greece*] (GC)
GSAS.......... Geniki Synomospondia Agrotikon Syllogon Ellados [*General Confederation of Greek Agricultural Unions*] [*See also GESASE*] (GC1)
GSAThP...... Geniki Synomospondia Anapiron kai Thymaton [*General Confederation of Handicapped and Victims*] [*Greek*] (GC)
GSAVE........ Geniki Synomospondia Avtokiniston Voreiou Ellados [*General Confederation of Drivers of Northern Greece*] (GC)
GSB............ Genc Sosyal Devrimciler Birligi [*Young Socialists' Organization*] (TU)
GSB............ Genclik ve Spor Bakanligi [*Youth and Sports Ministry*] (TU)
GSB............ Grumes et Sciages du Bini (MAR)
GS na BChK ... City Council of the Bulgarian Red Cross (BU)
GSBI........... Gabungan Serikat Buruh Indonesia [*Indonesian Labor Union Federation*] (IN)
GSC............ Gezira Sporting Club [*Egyptian*] (MAR)
GSC............ Ghana Students' Congress (MAR)
GSCh.......... Stable-Frequency Generator (RU)
GSCI........... Grupul de Santiere Constructii Instalatii [*Group of Construction and Installation Worksites*] (RO)
GSCR.......... Grupul de Santiere Constructii si Reparatii [*Group of Construction and Repair Worksites*] (RO)
GSD............ Genc Sosyalistler Dernegi [*Young Socialists' Organization*] (TU)
GSD............ Mountain Rifle Division (RU)
GSDF.......... Ground Self Defense Force (SJT)
GSDP.......... German Social Democratic Party (BU)
Gsdtr.......... Gesandter [*German*]
Gsdtsch...... Gesandtschaft [*German*]
GSE............ Gestion Socialiste des Entreprises [*Socialist Management of Businesses*] [*Algerian*] (AF)
GSEAE........ Geniki Synomospondia Epangelmation Avtokiniston Ellados [*General Confederation of Professional Drivers of Greece*] (GC)
GSEE.......... Geniki Synomospondia Ergaton Ellados [*Greek General Confederation of Labor*] (GC)
GSEI........... "Soviet Encyclopedia" State Dictionary and Encyclopedia Publishing House (RU)
GSEM.......... Grupul de Santiere Electromontaj [*Group of Electroassembly Worksites*] (RO)
GSEU.......... Main Sanitary and Epidemiological Administration (RU)
GSEVE........ Geniki Synomospondia Epangelmation kai Viotekhnon Ellados [*General Confederation of Tradesmen and Craftsmen of Greece*] (GC)
GSF............ State Strain Seed Fund (RU)
GSFC.......... Ghana State Farm Corporation (MAR)
GSFK.......... City Council of Physical Culture (RU)
GSG............ Advanced Fuel Depot (RU)
GSGM.......... Guzel Sanatlar Genel Mudurlugu [*Fine Arts Directorate General*] [*Under Ministry of Culture*] (TU)
GSGS.......... Geographical Section, General Staff (MAR)
GSh............ Flapping Hinge (RU)
GSh............ General Staff (RU)
GSH............ Glavni Stab Hrvatske [*General Headquarters of Croatia*] [*World War II*] (YU)
GSH............ Glowna Szkola Handlowa [*Polish*]
GShchT....... Glutamic Oxaloacetic Transaminase (RU)
GShchU...... Main Control Board, Main Control Panel (RU)
GShI........... Wide Pulse Generator (RU)
GShK.......... State Permanent Staff Commission (RU)
GShN.......... Low-Frequency Noise Generator (RU)
GSHR.......... Generalni Sekretariat Hospodarske Rady [*Office of the Secretary General of the Economic Council*] (CZ)
GSHR.......... Gremium Statni Hospodarske Rady [*Board of the State Economic Council*] (CZ)
GShS.......... Noise-Spectrum Generator (RU)
GShSA........ General Staff of the Soviet Army (RU)
GShSI......... Wide Strobe-Pulse Generator (RU)
gsht........... General Staff (BU)
GSI............ Gate Generator, Strobe-Pulse Generator (RU)
GSI............ General Service Industrials (MAR)
GSI............ Gesellschaft fuer Schwerionenforschung [*Nuclear laboratory*]
GSI............ Grupul de Supraveghere a Investitiilor [*Investments Supervision Group*] (RO)
GSI............ Main Sanitary Inspection (RU)
GSI............ Standard-Pulse Generator (RU)
GSI............ State Sanitary Inspection (RU)
GSI............ Timing-Pulse Generator [*Computers*] (RU)
GSIK.......... Interstitial Cell Stimulating Hormone (RU)
GSJ............ Gimnasticki Savez Jugoslavije [*Yugoslav Gymnastic Federation*] (YU)
GSK............ Combined-Signal Generator (RU)
GSK............ Main Board of Referees [*Sports*] (RU)
GSKB.......... State Special Design Office (RU)
GSKBD........ State Special Design Office for Engines (RU)
GSKD.......... Genclik, Spor, ve Kultur Isleri Dairesi [*Youth, Sports, and Cultural Affairs Office*] [*Turkish Cypriot*] (TU)
GSKhOS..... State Agricultural Experimental Station (RU)
GSL............ Georgikos Syllogos Lysis [*Agricultural Society of Lysi*] [*Cypriot*] (GC)
GSL............ Greater Somalia League (MAR)
GSLA.......... Grupul de Santiere Lucrari Hidrotehnice Galati [*Group of Hydrotechnical Projects Worksites in Galati*] (RO)
GSLP.......... Gibraltar Socialist Labour Party (PPW)
GSM............ Fuel and Lubricants (RU)
GSM............ Fuel and Lubricants (BU)
GSMH.......... Gayri Safi Milli Hasili [*Gross National Product*] (TU)
GSMP.......... Glowna Skladnica Materialow Pocztowych [*Main Warehouse for Postal Materials*] (POL)

GSMP .... Specialized Medical Aid Group (RU)
GSMT .... Glowna Skladnica Materialow Teletechnicznych [*Main Warehouse for Communications Materials*] (POL)
GSN .... Genikon Stratiotikon Nosokomeion [*Army General Hospital*] (GC)
GSN .... House Supplies Generator [*Power plant*] (BU)
GSND .... Glasnik Skopskog Naucnog Drustva [*Bulletin of the Skopje Learned Society*] (YU)
GSNI .... Gerakan Siswa Nasional Indonesia [*Indonesian National Student Movement*] (IN)
GSNOPOJ ... Glavni Stab Narodnooslobodilackih Partizanskih Odreda Jugoslavije [*General Headquarters of the National Liberation Partisan Detachments of Yugoslavia*] [*World War II*] (YU)
GSNOV .... Glavni Stab Narodnooslobodilacke Vojske [*General Headquarters of the National Liberation Army*] [*World War II*] (YU)
GSNOVM .... Glavni Stab Narodnooslobodilacke Vojske Makedonije [*General Headquarters of the National Liberation Army of Macedonia*] [*World War II*] (YU)
GSNOVPOM ... Glavni Stab na Narodnoosloboditelnata Vojna i Partizanskite Odredi na Makedonija [*General Headquarters of the National Liberation Army and Partisan Detachments of Macedonia*] (YU)
GSO .... City Economic Enterprise (BU)
GSO .... Ready for Medical Defense (BU)
GSO .... Ready for Sanitary Defense (RU)
GSOEA .... Government Servants and Other Employees Association [*Mauritian*] (AF)
g-sol .... Bitter-Salt Water [*Topography*] (RU)
GSOON .... Generalno Sobranie na Organizacijata na Obedinenite Narodi [*General Assembly of the United Nations Organization*] (YU)
GS/OPS .... Generalni Stab, Operacni Planovaci Sprava [*Operations Planning Directorate, General Staff*] (CZ)
GSORB .... Glavni Stab Omladinskih Radnih Brigada [*General Headquarters of Youth Work Brigades*] (YU)
GSOS .... Generalni Sekretariat Obrany Statu [*National Defense General Secretariat*] (CZ)
GS/OS .... Generalni Stab, Operacni Sprava [*Operations Directorate, General Staff*] (CZ)
GSOV .... Group of Soviet Occupation Troops (RU)
GSOVG .... Group of Soviet Occupation Troops in Germany (RU)
GSP .... Generalised Scheme of Preferences [*Arabian*] (MAR)
GSP .... Glasnik za Sumske Pokuse [*Bulletin on Forestry Research*] [*Zagreb, 1926-1941*] (YU)
GSP .... Grafeion Skhediou Poleos [*City Plan Office*] [*Greek*] (GC)
GSP .... Gyro-Stabilized Platform (RU)
GSP .... Hospital (RU)
GSP .... Mountain Rifle Regiment (RU)
GSP .... Royal Geographical Society. Proceedings [*A publication*] (MAR)
GSP .... Special City Postal Service [*Bulk mail*] (RU)
GSP .... State Instrument System (RU)
GSP .... Tracked Self-Propelled Ferry (RU)
GSPE .... Geniki Synomospondia Polemiston Ellados [*General Confederation of Greek Combatants*] (GC)
GSPEU .... Main Epidemic Control Administration (RU)
GSPI .... State All-Union Planning Institute (RU)
GSPKB .... State Special Planning and Design Office (RU)
GSPKI .... State Special Planning and Design Institute (RU)
GSPM .... Groupement des Sapeurs Pompiers Militaires (MAR)
GSPPE .... Geniki Synomospondia Palaion Polemiston Ellados [*General Confederation of Greek Veterans*] (GC)
GSPS .... Guberniya Council of Trade Unions (RU)
GSPZNRH ... Glavni Savez Poljoprivrednih Zadruga Narodne Republike Hrvatske [*Central Union of Agricultural Cooperatives of Croatia*] (YU)
GSPZNRS ... Glavni Savez Poljoprivrednih Zadruga Narodne Republike Srbije [*Central Union of Agricultural Cooperatives of Serbia*] (YU)
GSRP .... Gambian Socialist Revolutionary Party (PD)
GSS .... Advance Signal Depot (RU)
GSS .... General Superintendence Society (MAR)
GSS .... Glavni Stab Slovenije [*General Headquarters of Slovenia*] [*World War II*] (YU)
GSS .... Glavni Stab Srbije [*General Headquarters of Serbia*] [*World War II*] (YU)
GSS .... Gradovi Van Sastava Sreza [*Towns Outside District Limits*] (YU)
GSS .... Hero of the Soviet Union (RU)
GSS .... Random-Signal Generator, Standard-Signal Generator (RU)
GSS .... Standard Signal Oscillator (BU)
GSS .... State Selection Station [*Agriculture*] (RU)
GSSD .... Gruppe Sowjetischer Streitkraefte in Deutschland [*Group of Soviet Forces in Germany (GSFG)*] (EG)
GSSEE .... Geniki Synomospondia Syndaxioukhon Ergatoypallilon Ellados [*General Confederation of Pensioned Workers of Greece*] (GC)
GSSFPS .... General Council of the World Federation of Trade Unions (BU)
GSSI .... Glavni Stab Slovenije [*General Headquarters of Slovenia*] (YU)
GS/SP .... Generalni Stab, Souhrnny Plan [*Master Plan, General Staff*] (CZ)
GSSR .... Georgian Soviet Socialist Republic (RU)
GSSSD .... State Service for Standard Information Data (RU)
GST .... City Telephone Exchange (RU)
GST .... Erasing-Current Oscillator (RU)
GSt .... Gefechtsstand [*Command Post*] (EG)
Gst .... Generalni Stab [*General Staff*] (CZ)
GST .... Gesellschaft fuer Sport und Technik [*Society for Sport and Technology*] (EG)
GSTB .... Geographic Reference and Transcription Office (RU)
GStbOffz .... Generalstabsoffizier [*German*]
GSTC .... Gambia Tourist and Shipping Company (MAR)
GSTC .... Ghana State Tourist Corporation (MAR)
GSTD .... Gruppe Sowjetischer Truppen in Deutschland [*Group of Soviet Forces in Germany (GSFG)*] (EG)
Gstl .... Geistlich [*German*]
Gstozer .... Glavni Stozer [*General Headquarters*] [*Croatian*] [*World War II*] (YU)
GS/TS .... Generalni Stab, Technicka Sprava [*Technical Directorate, General Staff*] (CZ)
GSTS .... Geodetska Srednja Tehnicka Skola [*Geodetic Technical Secondary School*] (YU)
GSTS .... Stair-Step Generator (RU)
GSTT .... General Agreement on Tariffs and Trade [*GATT*] (RU)
Gstw .... Gastwirt [*German*]
GSU .... Annals of Sofia University [*A publication*] (BU)
GSU .... General Service Unit (MAR)
GSU .... Main Construction Administration (RU)
GSU .... Main Statistical Administration (RU)
GSU .... State Strain-Testing Plot, State Strain-Testing Station (RU)
GSUalf .... GSU [*Annals of Sofia University*] School of Agronomy and Forestry (BU)
GSUBF .... GSU [*Annals of Sofia University*] School of Theology (BU)
GSUbogf .... GSU [*Annals of Sofia University*] School of Theology (BU)
GSUFF .... GSU [*Annals of Sofia University*] Department of Philology (BU)
GSUFIF .... GSU [*Annals of Sofia University*] Department of Philosophy and History (BU)
GSUFMF .... GSU [*Annals of Sofia University*] School of Physics and Mathematics (BU)
GSUIFF .... GSU [*Annals of Sofia University*] Department of History and Philology (BU)
GSUmedf .... GSU [*Annals of Sofia University*] School of Medicine (BU)
GSUPrMF .... GSU [*Annals of Sofia University*] School of Mathematics and Natural Science (BU)
GSUvmedf ... GSU [*Annals of Sofia University*] School of Veterinary Medicine (BU)
GSUVMF .... GSU [*Annals of Sofia University*] School of Veterinary Medicine (BU)
GSUYuF .... GSU [*Annals of Sofia University*] School of Law (BU)
GSV .... Army General Staff (BU)
GSv .... Geodisnjak Hrvatskog Sveucilista [*Yearbook of the Croatian University*] (YU)
GSV .... Greenwich Mean Time (RU)
GSVCh .... Super-High-Frequency Generator (RU)
GSVG .... Group of Soviet Troops in Germany (RU)
GSvobU-t .... Annals of the Free University (BU)
GS/VSV .... Generalni Stab, Velitelstvi Spojovaciho Vojska [*Communications Troop Headquarters, General Staff*] (CZ)
GSYIH .... Gayrisafi Yurtici Hasila [*Gross Domestic Revenue*] (TU)
GSYIM .... Gayrisafi Yurtici Mamulati [*Gross Domestic Product*] (TU)
GSZ .... Deep Seismic Sounding (RU)
gsz .... Golyoszoro [*Light Machine Gun*] (HU)
GSZT .... Gazdaszati Szakoktatasi Tanacs [*National Council of Agricultural Education*] (HU)
GSZZNRM ... Glaven Sojuz na Zemjodelskite Zadrugi na Narodnata Republika Makedonija [*Central Union of Agricultural Cooperatives of Macedonia*] (YU)
GSZZNRS ... Glavni Savez Zemljoradnickih Zadruga Narodne Republike Srbije [*Central Union of Agricultural Cooperatives of Serbia*] (YU)
GT .... Gas Turbine (RU)
gt .... Gazdaszati (Tiszt) [*Paymaster*] [*Military*] (HU)
gt .... Generator, Oscillator (RU)
G/T .... Georgtown [*Penang, Malaysia*] (ML)
GT .... Ghanaian Times [*A publication*] (MAR)
GT .... Goldberger Textil Muvek [*Goldberger Textile Mills*] (HU)
GT .... Gradska Tiskarna [*City Printers*] (YU)
GT .... Guatemala [*Two-letter standard code*] (CNC)
Gt .... Gueterzugtenderlokomotive [*Freight Train Tender Locomotive*] (EG)
GT .... Gugus Tugas [*Task Force*] (IN)
GT .... Gutta-Percha (RU)
GT .... Gyroscopic Tachometer (RU)
Gt .... Heterogeneous [*Nuclear physics and engineering*] (RU)
GT .... Hydraulic Turbine (RU)
GT .... Industrial Hygiene (RU)
GT .... Trinitrotoluene Nose Fuze (RU)
GTA .... Globe Travel Agency (MAR)
GTA .... Gospel Truth Association (MAR)

GTA .... Groupement Togolais d'Assurance (MAR)
GTA .... Guyana Teachers Association (LA)
GTA .... Gyrotachoaccelerometer (RU)
GTAP .... Heavy Howitzer Artillery Regiment (RU)
GTB .... Gumruk ve Tekel Bakanligi [*Ministry of Customs and Monopolies*] (TU)
GTBTP .... Groupement Tchadien des Entreprises du Batiment, Travaux Publics, et Industries Connexes (MAR)
GTC .... Ghana Tobacco Company Ltd. (MAR)
GTD .... Gas Turbine Engine (RU)
GTD .... Grands Travaux de Distribution (MAR)
GTDC .... Ghana Tourist Development Company Ltd. (MAR)
GTDD .... Double-Action Turbojet Engine (RU)
GTDN .... Grupo de Trabalho para o Desenvolvimento do Nordeste [*Working Group for Development of the Northeast*] [*Brazilian*] (LA)
GTE .... Gepipari Tudomanyos Egyesulet [*Scientific Association for Machine Building*] (HU)
Gte .... Gerente [*Manager*] [*Spanish*] [*Business and trade*]
GTE .... Grands Travaux de l'Est [*Algerian*] (MAR)
GTE .... State Technical Examination (RU)
GTEB .... Guyana Timber and Export Board (LA)
GTES .... Geothermal Electric Power Station (RU)
GTF .... Guanosine Triphosphate (RU)
GTF .... Hydraulic Engineering Division (RU)
GTFT .... Groupement du Theatre et du Folklore Togolais (MAR)
GTG .... Gas Turbogenerator (RU)
GTG .... Gonadotrophic Hormone (RU)
GTG .... Ground Training Group (MAR)
GTG .... State Tret'yakov Gallery (RU)
GTHB .... Gida-Tarim ve Hayvancilik Bakanligi [*Ministry of Food, Agriculture, and Animal Husbandry*] (TU)
GTI .... Gepipari Technologiai Intezet [*Technological Institute of the Machine Industries*] (HU)
GTI .... Halogen Leak Detector (RU)
GTI .... Mining Engineering Inspection (RU)
GTI .... State Scientific Institute of Tuberculosis (RU)
GTI .... State Technical Publishing House (RU)
GTIZ .... State Trust of Construction Engineering Surveying (RU)
GTK .... Geological and Technical Commission (RU)
GTL .... Grosstanklager [*Tank Farm*] (EG)
GTL .... Rubber Conveyor Belts (BU)
GTM .... Grands Travaux de Marseille (MAR)
GTM .... Guatemala [*Three-letter standard code*] (CNC)
GTM .... State Theatrical Museum Imeni A. A. Bakhrushin (RU)
GTMB .... Ghana Timber Marketing Board (MAR)
GTML .... State Theatrical Museum in Leningrad (RU)
GTN .... Technical Standardization Group (RU)
GTN .... Voice-Frequency Dialing Generator (RU)
GTO .... Grands Travaux de l'Ouest (MAR)
GTO .... Group Technological Operations (RU)
GTO .... "Ready for Labor and the Defense of the USSR" [*Slogan and badge*] (RU)
GTO .... Ready for Work and Defense [*Program*] (BU)
GTP .... City Trade Enterprise (BU)
GTP .... Ghana Textiles Printing (MAR)
GTP .... Glutamine-Pyruvic Transaminase (RU)
GTP .... Grands Travaux Petroliers [*Algerian*] (MAR)
GTP .... Magnetizing Current Oscillator (RU)
GTP .... Retarding-Field Oscillator (RU)
GTPE .... Technical Assistance and Recovery Group (RU)
GTRD .... Gas Turbine Jet Engine (RU)
GTS .... City Telephone Communications (RU)
GTS .... City Telephone Exchange (RU)
GTS .... City Telephone Network (RU)
GTS .... City Trust of Eating Places (RU)
GTS .... City Wire Broadcasting Network (RU)
GTS .... Groupement Technique et Financier pour le Sahara (MAR)
GTS .... Groupement des Transporteurs du Senegal (MAR)
G/Ts .... Guanine-Cytosine Ratio (RU)
gts .... Hertz, Cycle per Second (RU)
g-tsa .... Hotel (RU)
g-tsa .... Miss [*Title*] (BU)
Gtsb .... Gutsbesitzer [*German*]
GTsD .... Hepatocerebral Dystrophy (RU)
GTsK .... Face-Centered Cubic [*Lattice*] (RU)
GTSKiGK .... Administration of State Workers' Savings Banks and State Credit (RU)
GTsKP .... State Central Book Chamber (RU)
GTsN .... Primary Circulating Pump, Main Circulating Pump [*Nuclear physics and engineering*] (RU)
GTsNMB ..... State Central Scientific Medical Library (RU)
GTsNPK ...... Primary-Loop Circulating Pump (RU)
GTsOLIFK ... State Central "Order of Lenin" Institute of Physical Culture (RU)
GTsP .... Bar Generator, Color Bar Generator (RU)
GTsP .... Main Circulation Pump (BU)
GT-SPGG .... Free-Piston Gas Turbine (RU)
GTsTB .... State Central Theatrical Library (RU)
GTsTK .... State Central Puppet Theater (RU)
Gtsvwltr ..... Gutsverwalter [*German*]
GTTA .... General Table Tennis Association [*Sudanese*] (MAR)
GTTA .... Ghana Table Tennis Association (MAR)
GTTI .... State Publishing House of Technical and Theoretical Literature (RU)
GTU .... Gas Turbine Engine, Gas Turbine Power Plant (RU)
GTU .... Government Teachers Union [*Mauritian*] (AF)
GTU .... Main Customs Administration (RU)
GTUC .... Ghana Trade Union Congress (AF)
GTU-SPGG ... Free-Piston Gas Turbine Power Plant (RU)
GTV .... Voice-Frequency Ringing Generator (RU)
GTVD .... Turboprop Engine (RU)
GTVU .... Voice-Frequency-Ringing and Control Generator (RU)
GTYD .... Girne Taksiciler Yardimlasma Dernegi [*Kyrenia Taxi Drivers' Mutual Aid Association*] (GC)
GTZ .... Deutsche Gesellschaft fuer Technische Zusammenarbeit [*West German*]
GTZ .... Inhibitor-Current Generator [*Computers*] (RU)
GU .... Dating-Pulse Generator, Ultrasonic Generator (RU)
GU .... Galvanometric Amplifier (RU)
GU .... Geodetska Uprava [*Geodetic Administration*] (YU)
GU .... Group Amplifier (RU)
GU .... Guam [*Two-letter standard code*] [*Postal code*] (CNC)
GU .... Gyro Device (RU)
GU .... Hydraulic Amplifier (RU)
GU .... Hydraulic Shock (RU)
GU .... Hydroelectric Development (RU)
GU .... Hydrographic Administration (RU)
GU .... Main Administration (BU)
GU .... Main Center [*Telephony*] (RU)
GU .... Reinforcement Group [*Military term*] (RU)
GU .... State University (RU)
GU .... Unpaved Section of Road (RU)
GUAD .... Main Administration of Archives (RU)
GUADS .... Main Administration of the Automobile Transportation and Road Service (RU)
GUAME .... Grupul de Uzine pentru Aparataj si Masini Electrice [*Group of Plants for Electrical Machinery and Instruments*] (RO)
GUAP .... Main Administration of the Aircraft Industry (RU)
GUAP .... Main Administration of the Nitrogen Industry (RU)
Guard .... Guardian [*German*]
GUASS .... Main Administration of Special Machine Tool Units (RU)
GUATEL ...... Empresa Guatemalteca de Telecomunicaciones [*Guatemalan Telecommunications Enterprise*] (LA)
GUATP .... Main Administration of the Automobile and Tractor Industry (RU)
GUAU .... Grupo de Unificacion de Admisiones Universitarias. Universidad del Valle [*Cali*] (COL)
gub .... Governor [*1708-1917*] (RU)
gub .... Guberniya [*1708-1929*] (RU)
GUB .... Gubernur [*Governor*] (IN)
GUC .... Gambia Utilities Corporation (MAR)
GUC .... Glowny Urzad Cel [*Head Office of Tariffs*] [*Polish*]
GUC .... Groupe d'Union Camerounaise (MAR)
GUCh .... Controlled-Frequency Generator (RU)
GUD .... Main Administration of Traffic (RU)
GUDS .... Geologicky Ustav Dionyza Stura [*Dionyz Stur Geological Institute*] (CZ)
gue .... Guarde [*Spanish*]
GUES .... State Administration of Electric Power Plants (RU)
GUF .... French Guiana [*Three-letter standard code*] (CNC)
GUGB .... Main Administration of State Security (RU)
GUGGN .... Main Administration of State Mining Inspection (RU)
GUGiK .... Glowny Urzad Geodezji i Kartografii [*Head Office of Land-Surveying and Cartography*] [*Polish*]
GUGK .... Main Administration of Geodesy and Cartography (BU)
GUGK .... Main Administration of Geodesy and Cartography (RU)
GUGMP .... Main Administration for Geological and Mining Surveys (BU)
GUGMR .... Main Administration of State Material Reserves (RU)
GUGMS .... Main Administration of the Hydrometeorological Service (RU)
GUGSh .... Main Directorate of the General Staff (RU)
GUGSK .... Main Administration of State Surveying and Cartography (RU)
GUGSO .... Main Administration of Civil Legal Bodies (RU)
GUGVF .... Main Administration of the Civil Air Fleet (RU)
GUI .... Master Oscillator, Pilot Oscillator (RU)
GUIAS .... Main Directorate of the Aviation Engineering Service (RU)
GUIMAG ...... Societe Guineenne de Grands Magasins (MAR)
GUINELEC ... Societe Guineenne d'Installations Electriques (MAR)
GUINEXPORT ... Enterprise Nationale d'Exportation de Produits Guineens (MAR)
GUITK .... Main Administration of Corrective Labor Colonies (RU)
GUIV .... Main Administration of Synthetic Fiber (RU)
GUKES .... Main Administration for Ensuring the Supply of Complete Sets of Power Engineering Equipment to Electric Power Plants, Substations, and Networks (RU)
GUKF .... Glowny Urzad Kultury Fizycznej [*Main Office of Physical Culture*] (POL)
GUKF .... Main Administration of the Motion-Picture and Photography Industry (RU)
GUKKh .... Main Administration of the Municipal Economy (RU)
GUKMASh ... Main Administration of Forging and Pressing Machinery Manufacture (RU)

GUKO......... Main Administration of Municipal Equipment (RU)
GUKOP........ Main Administration of the Leather and Footwear Industry (RU)
GUK(PP)..... Glowny Urzad Kontroli Prasy, Publikacji, i Widowisk [*Main Office of the Control of the Press, Publishing, and Public Performances*] [*Polish*]
GUKPPiW.... Glowny Urzad Kontroli Prasy, Publikacji, i Widowisk [*Main Office of the Control of the Press, Publishing, and Public Performances*] (POL)
GUKR.......... Main Directorate of Counterintelligence (RU)
GUKS.......... Main Administration of Capital Construction (RU)
GUKV.......... Main Directorate of Convoy Troops (RU)
GULAG........ Glavnoe Upravlenie Ispravitel'no-Trudovykh Lagerei [*Main Administration of Corrective Labor Camps*] [*USSR*]
GULP........... Grenada United Labour Party (PPW)
GULP........... Main Administration of Light Industry (RU)
GULP........... Main Administration of the Lumber Industry (RU)
GULZhDS.... Main Administration of Railroad Construction Camps (RU)
GUM............ City Administration of Militia (RU)
GUM............ Gdanski Urzad Morski [*Gdansk (Danzig) Maritime Office*] (POL)
GUM............ Gewaesser- und Meliorationsbetriebe, Frankfurt-Oder (VEB) [*Frankfurt-Oder Waterways and Amelioration Enterprises (VEB)*] (EG)
GUM............ Glowny Urzad Miar [*Main Office of Measures*] (POL)
GUM............ Glowny Urzad Morski [*Main Maritime Office*] (POL)
GUM............ Gosudarstvennyi Universal'nyi Magazin [*Government Department Store*] [*Moscow*]
GUM............ Guam [*Three-letter standard code*] (CNC)
Gum............ Gumruk [*Customs*] (TU)
GUM............ Main Administration of Militia (RU)
GUm............ Umschalter fuer Gemeinschaftsanschluesse [*Commutator Switch for (Telephone) Party Lines*] (EG)
GUM............ United Mozambique Group (MAR)
GUMD.......... Main Administration of Machine Parts Manufacture (RU)
GUMMASh... Main Administration of Metallurgical Machinery Manufacture (RU)
GUMO......... Grupo Unido de Mocambique [*United Group of Mozambique*] (AF)
GUMP.......... Glavna Uprava Medicinske Proizvodnje [*Central Administration of Pharmaceutical Production*] (YU)
GUMP.......... Main Administration of the Metallurgical Industry (RU)
GUMP.......... Main Administration of the Metals Industry (RU)
GUMTO....... Main Administration of Materials and Equipment Supply (RU)
GUMTTS..... Main Administration of Long-Distance Telegraph and Telephone Communications (RU)
GUMUZ....... Main Administration of Medical Educational Institutions (RU)
GUMZ.......... Main Administration of Prisons (RU)
GUNA.......... Ghana United Nations Association (AF)
GUNEYDOGUBIRLIK... Guneydogu Uzum ve Mamulleri Tarim Satis Kooperatifleri Birligi [*Southeastern Grape and Products' Agricultural Sales Cooperatives' Union*] (TU)
GUNRAL..... Glavna Uprava za Nabavku i Raspodelu Lekova [*Central Administration for Supply and Distribution of Medicines*] (YU)
GUNRBiH.... Geodetska Uprava Narodne Republike Bosne i Hercegovine [*Geodetic Administration of Bosnia and Hercegovina*] (YU)
GUNRS........ Geodetska Uprava Narodna Republike Srbije [*Geodetic Administration of Serbia*] (YU)
GUNT.......... Gouvernement d'Union Nationale Transitionnel [*Transitional National Union Government*] [*Chadian*] (AF)
GUNT.......... Government of National Unity [*Chadian*] (PD)
GUO............ Gespreksgroep Universitair Onderzoek [*Dutch*]
GUOS.......... Main Directorate of Defense Construction (RU)
GUP............ Glavna Uprava Prometa [*Central Administration of Transportation*] (YU)
GUP............ Industrial Gamma-Ray Source, Mobile Gamma-Ray Source (RU)
GUP............ Main Administration of Roads (BU)
GUPAC........ Gulf Permanent Assistance Committee (MAR)
GUPCO........ Gulf of Suez Petroleum Company (ME)
GUPer......... Group Repeater (RU)
GUPK.......... Glowny Urzad Pomiarow Kraju [*Main Office of Country-Wide Surveying*] (POL)
GUPKO i BG... Main Administration of Municipal Services Establishments and Urban Improvement (RU)
GUP-LRS.... Glavna Uprava Prometa Ljudske Republike Slovenije [*Central Administration of Transportation of the People's Republic of Slovenia*] (YU)
GUPO.......... Main Administration of Fire Prevention (RU)
GUPP.......... Glowny Urzad Planowania Przestrzennego [*Main Administration of Area Planning*] (POL)
GUPP.......... Main Administration of Industrial Establishments (RU)
GUPP.......... Main Administration of Manufacturing Establishments (RU)
GUPS.......... Glavna Uprava za Promet Slovenije [*Central Administration of Transportation of Slovenia*] (YU)
GUPS.......... Main Postal Administration (RU)
GUPSM....... Main Administration of the Building Materials Industry (RU)
GUPTMASh... Main Administration of Hoisting and Conveying Machinery Manufacture (RU)
GUPU.......... Main Administration of Teacher Training (RU)
GUPV.......... Main Directorate of Border Troops (RU)
GURETS...... Main Administration for Development of Radio Facilities, for Intrarayon Telecommunications, and for the Television Receiving Network (RU)
GURP.......... Main Administration for the Distribution of Publications (RU)
GURS.......... Glavna Uprava Recnog Saobracaja [*Central Administration of River Traffic*] (YU)
GUS............ Glavni Ustaski Stan [*Ustashi General Headquarters*] [*World War II*] (YU)
GUS............ Glowny Urzad Statystyczny [*Central Office of Statistics*] (POL)
GUS............ Guss- und Schmiedeerzeugnisse [*Cast and Forged Products*] (EG)
GUS............ State Scientific Council [*1919-1933*] (RU)
GUSH.......... Bloc [*Israeli*] (ME)
Gushosdor... Main Administration of Highways (RU)
GUShP........ Main Administration of the Silk Industry (RU)
GUSI........... Narrow Strobe-Pulse Generator (RU)
GUSKO....... Gida Maddeleri Uretim ve Satis Kooperatifi [*Foodstuff Articles Production and Sales Cooperative*] (TU)
GUSMP....... Main Administration of the Northern Sea Route (RU)
GUSP.......... Main Administration of the Shipbuilding Industry (RU)
GUSRIC....... Grupul de Utilaje Speciale si Reparatii in Industria Chimica [*Group for Special Equipment and Repairs in the Chemical Industry*] (RO)
GUSS.......... Gradovi u Sastavu Sreza [*Towns within District Limits*] (YU)
GUSV.......... Main Administration of Construction Troops (BU)
GUT............ Genc Ulkuculer Teskilati [*Young Idealists Organization*] (TU)
GUT............ Main Administration for Fuel (RU)
GUT............ Main Directorate of the Rear Area (RU)
GUT............ Therapeutic Gamma-Ray Source (RU)
GUTM.......... Glowny Urzad Telekomunikacji Miedzymiastowei [*Head Office of Interurban Telecommunication*] [*Polish*]
GUT MO...... Main Directorate of Trade of the Ministry of Defense, USSR (RU)
GUTP.......... Main Administration of the Compulsory Labor Service (BU)
GUTR.......... Main Administration of Labor Reserves (BU)
GUTR.......... Main Administration of Labor Reserves (RU)
GUTsl......... State School of Circus Art (RU)
GUTSK........ Main Administration of State Workers' Savings Banks and State Credit (RU)
GUTSKiGK... Main Administration of State Workers' Savings Banks and State Credit, USSR (RU)
guttat.......... Guttatim [*By Drops*] [*Latin*] (GPO)
GUUM......... Grupul de Uzine pentru Utilajul Minier [*Group of Mining Equipment Plants*] (RO)
GUUZ.......... Main Administration of Educational Institutions (RU)
GUVECO...... Platerias Colombianas de E. Gutierrez Vega SA [*Bogota*] (COL)
GUVP.......... Main Administration of War Industry (RU)
GUVPS........ Main Administration of War Industry Construction (RU)
GuV-Rechnung... Gewinn-und-Verlust-Rechnung [*Profit and Loss Statement*] (EG)
GUVS.......... Main Directorate of Military Supply (RU)
GUVT.......... Main Directorate of Military Tribunals (RU)
Guvuz.......... Main Administration of Higher Educational and Secondary Pedagogical Institutions [*RSFSR*] (RU)
GUVUZ........ Main Administration of Military Educational Institutions (RU)
GUVV.......... Main Directorate of Internal Troops (RU)
GUVVO........ Main Directorate of Universal Military Training (RU)
GUWiM........ Glowny Urzad Wag i Miar [*Main Office of Weights and Measures*] (POL)
GUY............ Guyana [*Three-letter standard code*] (CNC)
GUYBAU..... Guyana Bauxite Co. (LA)
GUYINTEL... Guyana International Telecommunications Corporation (LA)
GUYMINE.... Guyana Mining Enterprises Ltd. (LA)
GUYNEC..... Guyana National Engineering Corporation (LA)
GUYOIL...... Guyana Oil Co. (LA)
GUYSTAC... Guyana State Corporation (LA)
GUYSUCO... Guyana Sugar Corporation (LA)
GUYWA....... Guyana Water Authority (LA)
GUZ............ Glavna Uprava Zeleznica [*Central Administration of Railroads*] (YU)
GUZh.......... Main Administration of Railways (BU)
GV.............. Disturbance Function Generator (RU)
GV.............. Gasverteilung [*Gas Distribution*] (EG)
GV.............. Gazdasagi Vasutak [*or Gazdasagi Vasut*] [*Narrow Gauge Rail Carrier System*] (HU)
GV.............. Geografski Vestnik [*Geographic Review*] [*Ljubljana*] (YU)
GV.............. Geographical Herald [*A publication*] (RU)
GV.............. Gozdarski Vestnik [*Forestry Review*] (YU)
GV.............. Grande Vitesse [*French*]
GV.............. Gravimeter-Altimeter (RU)
GV.............. Greenwich Time (RU)
GV.............. Guard, Guards (RU)
Gv.............. Guverte [*Deck*] [*Navy rating*] (TU)
GV.............. Reproducing Head (RU)
GV.............. Vertical-Flight Gyroscope (RU)
GV.............. Water Level (RU)
GvA............ Genootschap voor Automatisering [*Amsterdam*]
gvamp......... Guards Artillery Mortar Regiment (RU)
gv ap.......... Guards Artillery Regiment (RU)
GVB............ Upper-Water Level, Upstream Water Level (RU)
GVC............ Garde des Voies et Communication [*Military*] [*French*] (MTD)

GVC............ Groupements a Vocation Cooperative (MAR)
GVCh.......... High-Frequency Oscillator (RU)
GVChM....... Main Administration for the Procurement, Processing, and Marketing of Secondary Ferrous Metals (RU)
gvdbr.......... Guards Airborne Brigade (RU)
gvdp........... Guards Airborne Regiment (RU)
GVE............ Grossvieh-Einheiten [*Live Weight Unit of Cattle*] [*Equal to 500 kilograms*] (EG)
GVF............ Civil Air Fleet, USSR (RU)
GVF............ Experimental Water-Cooled Graphite (Reactor) (RU)
GVFU.......... Main Military Finance Directorate (RU)
GVG............ Garrison Hospital (RU)
GVG............ Gerichtsverfassungsgesetz [*Judiciary Act*] (EG)
gvgabr........ Guards Howitzer Artillery Brigade (RU)
GVGGU....... Ganz Vagon es Gepgyar [*Ganz Railroad Car and Machine Factory*] (HU)
GVI............. State Institute of Venereal Diseases (RU)
GVI............. Time Interval Generator (RU)
GVII............ Main Military Engineering Inspection (RU)
GVIS........... Main Military Engineer Depot (RU)
GVIU........... Main Military Engineering Directorate (RU)
GVIZ........... State Military Publishing House (RU)
GVK............ City Military Commissariat (RU)
GVK............ Mountain Pack Kitchen (RU)
GVKhU....... Main Directorate of Logistics (RU)
GVL............ High Ice-Floe Level (RU)
GVL............ Load Line, Load Waterline (RU)
GVL............ Main Waterline (RU)
GVMB.......... Main Naval Base (RU)
GVMU.......... Main Military Medical Directorate (RU)
GVOBL........ Gesetz- und Verordnungsblatt [*Law and Ordinance Gazette*] [*A publication*] (EG)
gvozd.......... Nail Plant [*Topography*] (RU)
GVP............ Auxiliary Industries Group (RU)
GVP............ Generalni Vojensky Prokurator [*Judge Advocate General*] (CZ)
GVP............ Gesamtdeutsche Volkspartei [*All-German People's Party*] [*West German*] (PPE)
GVP............ Glasfaserverstaerkte Plasten [*Glass-Fiber Reinforced Plastics*] (EG)
GVP............ Grupos de Vigilancia Popular [*People's Vigilance Groups*] [*Mozambican*] (AF)
GVP............ Main Naval Port (RU)
GVP............ Veterinary Aid Group [*Civil defense*] (RU)
GVPM.......... Mountain Pack Regimental Mortar (RU)
GVR............ Groupement Vigilance et Reconciliation (MAR)
GVR............ Water-Cooled Graphite Reactor (RU)
GVS............ Geheime Verschlusssache [*Secret Material (to be locked in safe)*] (EG)
GV-SOLAS ... Gesellschaft fuer Versuchstierkunde - Society of Laboratory Animal Science (EA)
GVSU.......... Main Court-Martial Directorate (RU)
GVSU.......... Main Medical and Sanitary Administration (RU)
GVSU.......... Main Military Construction Directorate (RU)
GVSU.......... Main Military Medical Directorate (RU)
Gvt............. Gigawatt (RU)
gvt............. Hectowatt (RU)
gvt-ch......... Hectowatt-Hour (RU)
GVTU.......... Main Military Technical Directorate (RU)
GVTUch Svishtov ... Annals of the Higher Commerce School, Svishtov (BU)
GVU............ Main Veterinary Administration (RU)
GVUchSSNa ... Annals of the Higher School of Economic and Social Sciences (BU)
GVV............ High-Water Level (RU)
gvvdd.......... Guards Airborne Division (RU)
GVVG.......... Gebietsvereinigung Volkseigener Gueter [*Regional Federation of State Farms*] (EG)
GVYRM....... State Higher Theatrical Directors' Workshops (RU)
GVYTM....... State Higher Theatrical Workshops (RU)
Gw.............. Gegenwart [*German*]
GW.............. Guinea-Bissau [*Two-letter standard code*] (CNC)
Gwd............ Greifswald [*Railroad abbreviation*] (EG)
GWF............ Gambia Women Federation (MAR)
GWF............ General Workers Federation [*Mauritian*] (AF)
Gwf............. Geraetewerk Friedrichshagen [*Friedrichshagen Equipment Plant*] (EG)
GWG............ Gemeinnuetzige Wohnungsbaugenossenschaft [*Nonprofit Housing Construction Cooperative*] (EG)
GWH............ Gigawatt Hours [*Giga Vatlik Saat*] (TU)
GWh............ Gigawattstunden [*Gigawatt Hours*] [*German*] (WEN)
Gwl............. Gueterwagenleitstelle [*Freight Car Routing Office*] (EG)
GWN............ Grosswaehlnebenstellenanlage [*Large Extension Switchboard Equipped for Dial System*] (EG)
GwN............ Gruppenwaehler-Nebenanschluss [*Extension Switchboard*] (EG)
GWOA......... Guerilla Warfare Operational Area (MAR)
GWSC......... Ghana Water and Sewerage Corporation (MAR)
GWU............ Gambia Workers Union (AF)
GWV............ Gueterwagenvorschriften [*Freight Car Regulations*] (EG)
GWW........... Gesellschaftswissenschaftliche Weiterbildung [*Advanced Social Science Training*] (EG)
GY............... Genikai Ypiresiai [*General Services*] (GC)
GY............... Guyana [*Two-letter standard code*] (CNC)
gy............... Gyalogos [*Infantryman*] (HU)
gy............... Gyalogsag [*Infantry*] (HU)
gy............... Gyar [*Factory*] (HU)
gyak........... Gyakorlati [*Practical*] (HU)
gyak........... Gyakorlo [*Practicing*] (HU)
gyal............ Gyalogos [*Infantryman*] (HU)
gyartm........ Gyartmany [*Product*] (HU)
GYC............ Gibraltar Yacht Club (MAR)
GYCSE........ Gyori Csonakazo Egyesulet [*Boating Club of Gyor*] (HU)
GYES.......... Gyermekgondozasi Segely [*Childcare Benefits*] (HU)
GYeSS......... State Unified System of Stenography (RU)
GYM........... Gelisme Yolundaki Memleketler [*Underdeveloped Countries*] (TU)
GYMGV....... Gyori Mezogazdasagi Gepjavito Vallalat [*Agricultural Machine Repair Shop of Gyor*] (HU)
Gymn.......... Gymnasium [*German*]
Gyn............. Gynaekologie [*or Gynaekologisch*] [*German*]
GYNI........... Gyogypedagogiai Nevelo Intezet [*Institute for Retarded Children*] (HU)
GYO............ Gandhi Youth Organization [*Guyanese*] (LA1)
gyogysz....... Gyogyszer [*Medicine, Drug*] (HU)
gyogysz....... Gyogyszeresz [*Druggist*] (HU)
GYOSZ........ Gyariparosok Orszagos Szovetsege [*National Association of Manufacturers*] (HU)
GYP............ Ghana Young Pioneers (MAR)
GYS............ Geografiki Ypiresia Stratou [*Army Geographic Service*] [*Greek*] (GC)
GYSEV........ Gyor- Sopron- Eberfurthi Vasut [*Gyor-Sopron-Eberfurth Railroad*] (HU)
GyT............. Gyori Textilmuvek [*Textile Mill of Gyor*] (HU)
GYUBER...... Kulonleges Villamos Gyujtoberendezesek KTSz [*Production Cooperative for Special Ignition Equipment Enterprise*] (HU)
GYuF........... Annals of the School of Law [*A publication*] (BU)
gyujt........... Gyujtemeny [*Collection*] (HU)
gyujt........... Gyujtotte [*Collected By*] (HU)
GYUMERT... Zoldseg- es Gyumolcs Ertekesito Vallalat [*Vegetable and Fruit Marketing Enterprise*] (HU)
gyv............. Gyorsvonat [*Express Train*] (HU)
GYVGY........ Gyori Vagongyar [*Railroad Car Factories of Gyor*] (HU)
GZ............... Blocking Party [*Military term*] (RU)
Gz............... Gazete [*Newspaper*] (TU)
Gz............... Gefuehlszustand [*Disposition*] [*German*]
GZ............... Geodetska Zveza [*Geodetic Association*] (YU)
GZ............... Geoloski Zavod [*Geological Institute*] [*Zagreb*] (YU)
GZ............... Geschaeftszeichen [*(Business) Reference Number*] (EG)
GZ............... Gostinska Zbornica [*Chamber of Hotel and Restaurant Trade*] (YU)
GZ............... Gradanski Zakonik [*Civil Code*] (YU)
GZ............... Grain Boundary (RU)
GZ............... Gramofonove Zavody [*Phonograph Enterprises*] (CZ)
GZ............... Recording Head [*Computers*] (RU)
GZ-............. Sound Generator (RU)
GZB............ Gemerske Zelezorudne Bane [*Gemer Iron Ore Mines*] (CZ)
GZbFF......... Godisen Zbornik na Filozofskiot Fakultet vo Skopje [*Yearbook of the Faculty of Philosophy in Skopje*] (YU)
GZbZSF(S) ... Godisen Zbornik na Zemjodelsko-Sumarskiot Fakultet na Univerzitetot - Skopje [*Yearbook of the Faculty of Agriculture and Forestry, Skopje University. Forestry*] (YU)
GZCh........... Audio-Frequency Oscillator (RU)
gzd............. Chemical Depot (BU)
GZFFUS...... Godisen Zbornik na Filozofskiot Fakultet - Univerzitet Skopje [*Yearbook of the Faculty of Philosophy, University of Skopje*] (YU)
GZFS........... Gor'kiy Milling-Machine Plant (RU)
GZG............ Gdanskie Zaklady Gastronomiczne [*Gdansk (Danzig) Restaurant Enterprises*] (POL)
GZH............ Gornoslaskie Zaklady Hutnicze [*Upper Silesia Metallurgical Plant*] (POL)
GZH............ Graficki Zavod Hrvatske [*Graphic Institute of Croatia*] (YU)
GZh............ Mining Journal [*A publication*] (RU)
G-zha.......... Mrs. (BU)
g-zha.......... Mrs., Madame (RU)
GZhD........... City Railroad (RU)
GZhK........... Gas-Liquid Contact (RU)
GZI............. Glowny Zarzad Informacji [*Main Information Directorate*] (POL)
GZI............. State Land Holdings (RU)
GZIP........... Gdanskie Zjednoczenie Instalacji Przemyslowych [*Gdansk (Danzig) Industrial Installation Association*] (POL)
GZK............ State Stud Farm (RU)
GZM............ Glasnik Zemaljskog Muzeja [*Bulletin of the National Museum*] [*Sarajevo*] [*A publication*] (YU)
GZMBH....... Glasnik Zemaljskog Muzeja u Bosni i Hercegovini [*Bulletin of the National Museum of Bosnia and Hercegovina*] [*A publication*] (YU)
GZME.......... Gdanskie Zaklady Maszyn Elektrycznych [*Gdansk (Danzig) Electric Machinery Plant*] (POL)
GZMS.......... Glasnik Zemaljskog Muzeja Sarajevo [*Bulletin of the National Museum in Sarajevo*] (YU)
GZO............ City Land Department (RU)

gzo .... Gas Officer (BU)
GZOS .... Central State Correspondence Courses in Stenography (RU)
GZP .... Glowny Zarzad Polityczny [*Main Political Directorate*] (POL)
GZPB .... Giebultowskie Zaklady Przemyslu Bawelnianego [*Giebultow (Gebhardsdorf) Cotton Mill*] (POL)
GZPG .... Grudziadzkie Zaklady Przemyslu Gumowego [*Grudziadz Rubber Works*] (POL)
GZPI .... State Correspondence Pedagogical Institute (RU)
gzpo .... Gas Sergeant (BU)
GZPT .... Gubinskie Zaklady Przemyslu Terenowego [*Gubin (Guben) Local Industry Plant*] (POL)
GZP WP .... Glowny Zarzad Polityczny Wojska Polskiego [*Main Political Directorate, Polish Army*] (POL)
GZR .... Gdanskie Zaklady Rybne [*Gdansk Fish Industry Enterprise*] (POL)
GZRW .... Gdynskie Zjednoczenie Robot Wiertniczych [*Gdynia Drilling Work Association*] (POL)
GZS .... Geoloski Zavod Slovenije [*Geological Institute of Slovenia*] (YU)
GZS .... Glavni Zdravstveni Savet (SIV) [*General Health Council*] (YU)
GZSFNRJ .... Glaven Zadruzen Sojuz na Federativna Narodna Republika Jugoslavija [*Central Cooperative Union of Yugoslavia*] (YU)
gzsl .... Chemical Warfare Service (BU)
gzsn .... Gas Projectile (BU)
GZSnaNRM ... Glaven Zadruzen Sojuz na Narodna Republika Makedonija [*Central Cooperative Union of Macedonia*] (YU)
GZSNRBiH ... Glavni Zadruzni Savez Narodne Republike Bosne i Hercegovine [*Central Cooperative Union of Bosnia and Hercegovina*] (YU)
GZSNRCG... Glavni Zadruzni Savez Narodne Republike Crne Gore [*Central Cooperative Union of Montenegro*] (YU)
GZTrst......... Gregorciceva Zalozba, Trst [*Gregorcic Publishing House, Trieste*] (YU)
GZU .... City Land Administration (RU)
GZU .... Hydraulic Ash Removal (RU)
GZU .... Lightning Protector, Lightning Arrester (RU)
GZUT .... Gliwickie Zaklady Urzadzen Technicznych [*Gliwice (Gleiwitz) Technical Equipment Plant*] (POL)
GZV .... Glavna Zaprecna Vatra [*Main Barrage Fire*] (YU)
GZV .... Gueterzugbildungsvorschriften [*Regulations for Freight Train Formation*] (EG)
GZZ .... Gradska Zeljeznica Zagreb [*Zagreb City Railroad*] (YU)
GZZ .... Main Blocking Valve (BU)
GZZLRS ...... Glavna Zadruzna Zveza Ljudske Republike Slovenije [*Central Cooperative Union of Slovenia*] (YU)
GZZS .... Glavna Zadruzna Zveza Slovenije [*Central Cooperative Union of Slovenia*] (YU)

H

H Einzelhaus [*German*]

H Haerte [*Hardness*] [*German*]

H Hakkinda [*Concerning, Regarding*] [*In legal documents*] (TU)

H Hakushi [*Japanese*]

h Han [*Commercial Building*] [*Turkish*] (CED)

H Haupt [*German*]

H Haus [*German*]

H Hauteur [*French*] (MTD)

H Heft [*Number or Part (of a Publication)*] [*German*]

h Heiss [*Hot*] [*German*]

H Heizwert [*Calorific Value*] [*German*]

h Helyett [*Instead, For*] (HU)

h Helyettes [*Deputy*] (HU)

H Helyi Ipar [*Local Industry*] (HU)

H Henry [*Henry (Symbol for unit of inductance)*] [*German*]

H Hetfo [*Monday*] (HU)

h Heure [*Hour*] [*French*] (GPO)

H Hicri [*The Hejira Era*] (TU)

h Hier [*Yesterday*] [*French*]

h Hoch [*High*] [*German*]

H Hoehe [*Altitude*] [*German*]

h Hoeherer [*German*]

H Hoek [*Cape, Hook*] [*Dutch*] (NAU)

H Hof [*German*]

(H) Holzknechthuette [*German*]

H Hommes [*Men*] [*Military*] [*French*] (MTD)

h Honap [*Month*] (HU)

H Hora [*Hour*] [*Latin*] (GPO)

H Hoyre [*Conservative Party*] [*Norwegian*] (PPE)

H Huette [*German*]

h Hus [*House*] [*Norwegian*] (CED)

h Tunti [*Finnish*]

H Wegry [*Hungary*] [*Polish*]

HA Haber Ajansi [*Haber Agency*] [*News agency*] [*See also HHA*] (TU)

ha Hajoallomas [*Quay, Pier*] (HU)

Ha Hana [*Cape, Point*] [*See also Ba*] [*Japanese*] (NAU)

HA Handelsabgabe [*Commercial Tax*] (EG)

HA Harb Akademileri [*Military Academies*] (TU)

HA Hauptabteilung [*Main Department*] [*German*] (WEN)

ha Hectare [*Hectare*] [*French*]

ha Hehtaari [*or Hehtaaria*] [*Finnish*]

ha Hektar [*Hectare*] (EG)

ha Hektar [*Hectare*] (POL)

ha Hektar [*Hectare*] (HU)

HA Hektar [*Hectare*] (IN)

Ha Hektar [*Hectare*] (TU)

HA Historical Association (EA)

HA Hlas Ameriky [*Voice of America*] (CZ)

ha Hoc Anno [*In This Year*] [*Latin*] (GPO)

ha Huius Anni [*Of This Year*] [*Latin*] (GPO)

HAAZ Hoofden Automatisering Academische Ziekenhuizen [*Dutch*]

HAB Hamburg Afrika Bank [*Hamburg Africa Bank*] (AF)

Habaemfa Hallesche Baeckereimaschinenfabrik [*Halle Bakery Machine Plant*] (EG)

hab corp Habeas Corpus [*Have the Body (A writ)*] [*Latin*] (GPO)

Haber-Is Turkiye Posta, Telgraf, Telefon, Radyo, ve Televizyon Iscileri Sendikasi [*Turkish Postal, Telegraph, Telephone, Radio, and Television Workers Union*] (TU)

HABITAT Human Settlements Information System [*Nairobi, Kenya*]

Habt Habert [*Cowhouse*] [*Military map abbreviation*] [*World War I*] [*French*] (MTD)

HAC Hlavni Armadni Cesta [*Main Army Route*] (CZ)

Hac U Hacettepe Universitesi [*Hacettepe University*] [*Ankara*] (TU)

HAD Hanseatische Afrika-Dienst (MAR)

HAD Hrvatsko Arheolosko Drustvo [*Croatian Archaeological Society*] (YU)

hadmtk Hadmernok Torzskar [*Engineer Corps*] (HU)

hadoszt Hadosztaly [*Division*] [*Military*] (HU)

haeors Harci Eloors [*Tactical Outpost*] (HU)

HAER Hydraulique et de l'Amenagement de l'Espace Rural (MAR)

HAFE Hajtomu- es Felvonogyar [*Driving Mechanism and Elevator Factory*] (HU)

HAFMED Headquarters, Allied Forces Mediterranean (MAR)

HAGE Hajdusagi Agroipari Egyesules [*Agro-Industrial Association of Hajdusag*] (HU)

HAGY Hiradastechnikai Anyagok Gyara [*Telecommunication Materials Factory*] (HU)

HAIB Hukumet ve Askeri Isci Birlikleri [*Government and Military Worker Unions*] [*Turkish Cypriot*] (GC)

HAk Handelsakademie [*German*]

HAK Historical Association of Kenya (MAR)

H Akcja (Akcja) Hodowli [*Pedigree Breeding Drive*] (POL)

Hak-Is Turkiye Hak-Iscileri Ozyol-Is [*Turkish Moral Rights Workers' Trade Union*] [*Konya*] (TU)

HAKS Hopital de l'Amitie Khmero-Sovietique [*Cambodian-Soviet Friendship Hospital*] (CL)

hakus Hakusana [*Catchword*] [*Finnish*]

HAL Haftarbeitslager [*Penal Labor Camp*] (EG)

Hal Halogen [*Halogen*] [*German*]

hal Halozat [*Network, System*] (HU)

HAL Handarbeitslehrerin [*German*]

HAL Handbook of African Languages (MAR)

Hal Hopital [*Hospital*] [*Military map abbreviation*] [*World War I*] [*French*] (MTD)

halbst Halbstaatlich [*Semistate*] (EG)

HALCO Harvey Aluminium Company (MAR)

HALE Helping All Live Equally (MAR)

HALERT Halertekesito Vallalat [*Fish Market*] (HU)

Halk-Is Halk ve Isci Sirketleri Sendikasi [*Peoples and Workers Companies Labor Union*] [*Related to labor in West Germany*] (TU)

hallg Hallgato [*Student, Listener*] (HU)

halv Halventavasti [*Disparagingly*] [*Finnish*]

HAM Heart of Africa Mission (MAR)

HAMAL-IS Turkiye Hamallari ve Yukculeri Sendikasi [*Turkish Porters and Freight Carriers Union*] [*Istanbul*] (TU)

hammasl Hammaslaaketiede [*Dentistry*] [*Finnish*]

hammaslkand Hammaslaaketieteen Kandidaatti [*Finnish*]

hammasllis Hammaslaaketieteen Lisensiaatti [*Finnish*]

hammasltri Hammaslaaketieteen Tohtori [*Finnish*]

HAN Hauptauftragnehmer [*Main Contractor*] (EG)

HANAO Hrvatska Nacionalisticka Omladina [*Croatian Nationalist Youth*] (YU)

HANDICO Tanzania Handicrafts Corporation (MAR)

HANKAM Departemen Pertahanan dan Keamanan [*Department of Defense and Security*] (IN)

HANKAMNAS Pertahanan dan Keamanan Nasional [*National Defense and Security*] (IN)

HANKAMRATA Pertahanan dan Keamanan Rakjat Semesta [*Total People's Defense and Security*] (IN)

HANSIP Pertahanan Sipil [*Civil Defense Organization*] (IN)

HANUDAD Pertahanan Udara Angkatan Darat [*Army Air Defense*] (IN)

HAO Handelns Arbetsgivare-Organisation [*Commercial Employers Association*] [*Swedish*] (WEN)

hao Hataror [*Border Guard*] (HU)

hap Harcallaspont [*Command Post, Command Observation Post*] (HU)

HAP Hersteller-Abgabepreis [*Producer Sales Price*] (EG)

Hapeko Hutnicze Przedsiebiorstwo Kompletacji Dostaw Maszyn i Urzadzen [*Enterprise for the Supplementing of Deliveries of Metallurgical Machinery and Equipment*] (POL)

Har Harabe [*Ruins*] (TU)

Har Harici [*Long Distance (Telephone call)*] (GC)

Har Harita [*Map, Chart*] (TU)

HARB-IS Turk Harb Sanayii ve Yardimci Isci Sendikalari Federasyonu [*Turkish War Industry and Allied Workers Unions Federation*] (TU)

HARP High Altitude Research Project (MAR)

HART Halt All Racist Tours (MAR)

harv Harvinainen [*Rare*] [*Finnish*]

harv Harvoin [*Rare*] [*Finnish*]

HASAS........ Hali Sanayii ve Pazarlama Anonim Sirketi [*Rug Industry and Marketing Corporation*] (TU)
HASIDA....... Handicrafts and Small-Scale Industries Development Agency [*Ethiopian*] (AF)
HAS-IS........ Turkiye Hastane Iscileri Sendikasi [*Turkish Hospital Workers' Union*] (TU)
Hast............. Hastahane [*Hospital*] (TU)
HASTAS...... Halk Sektoru Turk Anonim Sirketleri [*Turkish Public Sector Corporations*] [*A community of sixteen companies*] (TU)
hat............... Hatarozat [*Decision, Resolution, Provision*] (HU)
hat............... Hatosag [*Public Authority*] (HU)
hatabl.......... Harcallomanytabla [*Listing of the Active Military Strength*] (HU)
HATAS........ Hastahane Tesisleri Ticaret ve Sanayii Anonim Sirketi [*Hospital Equipment Trade and Industry, Incorporated*] (TU)
HATERV...... Villamos Halozati Fejleszto es Tervezo Vallalat [*Electric Power Network Development and Designing Enterprise*] (HU)
Hau.............. Hameau [*Small Village, Hamlet*] [*Military map abbreviation*] [*World War I*] [*French*] (MTD)
HAU............. Hebrew Actors Union (MAR)
HAU............. Hudebni a Artisticka Ustredna [*Center of Music Performers and Entertainers*] (CZ)
Hauptwrk.... Hauptwirkung [*Main Action*] [*German*]
HauswS....... Hauswirtschaftsschule [*German*]
hav.............. Havonkent [*Monthly*] (HU)
Hav.............. Havuz [*Basin, Pond*] (TU)
Hava-Is........ Turkiye Sivil Havacilik Sendikasi [*Turkish Civil Aviation Workers Union*] (TU)
HAVO.......... Hoger Algemeen Vormend Onderwijs [*Dutch*]
HAW............ Hochspannungsarmaturenwerk, Radebeul (VEB) [*Radebeul High Voltage Armature Factory (VEB)*] (EG)
HAWS.......... Harcerska Akademia Wiedzy Spolecznej [*Scouting Academy of Social Sciences*] (POL)
Haz.............. Hazirlayan [*The Individual Who Prepared (article or work)*] (TU)
HAZ............. Historical Association of Zambia (MAR)
hazt............. Haztartas [*or Haztartasi*] [*Household or Of the Household*] (HU)
hazt............. Haztartasbeli [*Housekeeper, Servant*] (HU)
HAZU........... Hrvatska Akademija Znanosti i Umjetnosti [*Croatian Academy of Sciences and Arts*] [*JAZU*] (YU)
HB............... Halk Bankasi [*Peoples Bank of Turkey*] [*See also THB*] (TU)
HB............... Handelsbeziehungen [*Trade Relations*] (EG)
Hb................ Harabe [*Ruins*] (TU)
HB............... Haztartasi Bolt [*Household Goods Stores*] (HU)
HB............... Helvetisches Bekenntnis [*German*]
HB............... Herri Batazuna [*Union of the People*] [*Spanish*] (PPE)
HB............... Hesap Birimi [*Unit of Calculation*] [*As kg, liters, etc.*] (TU)
HB............... Honvedelmi Bizottmany [*Defense Committee*] (HU)
HB............... Hrazeni Bystrin [*Flood Control*] (CZ)
HBC............. Heliopolis Bridge Club [*Egyptian*] (MAR)
HBD............. Haupteisenbahndirektion [*Main Railroad Directorate*] (EG)
Hbd.............. Holzboden-Flaeche [*Lumber-Producing Area*] (EG)
Hbf............... Hauptbahnhof [*Main Railroad Station*] [*German*] (WEN)
Hbg.............. Hamburg [*Hamburg*] (EG)
HBKL........... Hayvan Besleyicileri Kooperatif Limited [*Animal Raisers' Cooperative Limited*] [*Turkish Cypriot*] (GC)
HBM............. Habitations Bon Marche [*North African*] (MAR)
Hbm.............. Hochbaumeisterei [*Office (Section or Shop) for Above-Ground Structures*] (EG)
HBNC........... Houilleres du Bassin Nord Pas de Calais [*Tunisian*] (MAR)
HBO............. Hoger Beroeps Onderwijs [*Dutch*]
hbs.............. Hadbiztos [*Quartermaster Officer*] (HU)
HBS............. Havergal Brian Society (EA)
HBS............. Hemiska Borbena Sredstva [*Chemical Combat Equipment*] (YU)
HBUB........... Hayvan Yetistirici ve Besleyicileri Birligi [*Livestock Raisers and Breeders' Union*] (TU)
HBV............. Handel, Banken, und Versicherungen [*Trade, Banks, and Insurance (Trade Union)*] [*West German*] (WEN)
HBV............. Hromadna Bytova Vystavba [*Mass Housing Construction*] (CZ)
HC............... Hidroelektricna Centrala [*Hydroelectric Power Station*] (YU)
HC............... High Commission (MAR)
HC............... Hodoninske Cihelny [*Hodonin Brick Works*] (CZ)
hc................ Honoris Causa [*For the Sake of Honor*] [*Latin*]
HC............... Honoris Crux (MAR)
HC............... Hors Cadre [*French*] (MTD)
HC............... Hors Concours [*Not Competing*] [*French*]
HC............... Hydrocentrala [*Hydroelectric Plant*] (CZ)
HC............... Societe Hatton & Cookson (MAR)
HCA............. Hunting-Clan Air Transport Ltd. (MAR)
HCAI............ Haut Comite Administratif pour l'Ivoirisation (MAR)
HCAR........... Higher Committee for Agrarian Reform [*Egyptian*] (MAR)
HCB............. Hidroelectrica de Cabora Bassa (MAR)
HCB............. Huileries du Congo Belge (MAR)
HCD............. Honoris Crux Diamond (MAR)
HCG............. Honoris Crux Gold (MAR)
HCL............. Hospitais Civis de Lisboa [*Lisbon Civilian Hospitals*] [*Portuguese*] (WER)
HCM............. Hejocsabai Cement Muvek [*Hejocsaba Cement Works*] (HU)
HCM............. Hotarirea Consiliului de Ministri [*Decision of the Council of Ministers*] (RO)
h cn............. Hier, Cours Nul [*French*]
HCP............. H. Cegielski, Poznan [*H. Cegielski Works, Poznan*] (POL)
HCPRN........ Haut-Commissariat au Plan et a la Reconstruction Nationale [*Zairian*] (MAR)
HCPRU........ Hot Climate Physiological Research Unit (MAR)
HCS............. Honoris Crux Silver (MAR)
HCS............. Hurtownia Centrali Spozywczych [*Wholesale House for Central Food Stores*] (POL)
HCT............. Huilerie Centrale de Tananarive (MAR)
HCTR........... Heki Cukorrepa Termelesi Rendszer [*Sugar Beet Production System of Hek*] (HU)
HCUSA........ High Commissioner for the Union of South Africa (MAR)
HCWU......... Hotel and Catering Workers Union (MAR)
hd................ Halk Dili [*Peoples' Language, Vulgarism*] (TU)
HD............... Handelsvidenskabelig Diplomprove [*Danish*]
HD............... Hnedouhelne Doly [*Lignite (Brown Coal) Mines*] (CZ)
HD............... Hochdruck [*High Pressure*] [*German*]
HD............... Hospodarske Druzstvo [*Agricultural Cooperative*] (CZ)
Hd................ Hoved [*Headland*] [*Danish*] (NAU)
HD............... Hrvatsko Domobranstvo [*Croatian Home-Guard*] [*World War II*] (YU)
HD............... Hudebni Soubor [*Music Ensemble*] (CZ)
Hd................ Hudut [*Border, Boundary*] (TU)
Hd................ Huvud [*Headland*] [*Swedish*] (NAU)
hdb.............. Hadbiro [*Judge Advocate, Military Prosecutor*] (HU)
HdB............. Handwerkskammer des Bezirks [*Bezirk Artisan Chamber*] (EG)
HDBS........... Hnedouhelne Doly a Briketarny v Sokolove [*Lignite (Brown Coal) Mines and Briquette Plants in Sokolov*] (CZ)
hdc.............. Hier Dernier Cours
HDD............. Halkci Devrimci Dernegi [*Populist Revolutionary Organization*] (TU)
HDD............. Handlowy Dom Dziecka [*Children's Articles Trade Center*] (POL)
HDG............. Hauptverwaltung Deutsche Grenzpolizei [*Main Administration of the German Border Police*] (EG)
HDGB........... Halk Devrimci Genclik Birligi [*Peoples' Revolutionary Youth Union*] (TU)
HDGF........... Halkci Devrimci Genclik Federasyonu [*Populist Revolutionary Youth Federation*] (TU)
HDGO........... Halkci Devrimci Genclik Orgutu [*Populist Revolutionary Youth Organization*] (TU)
hdgy............. Hadnagy [*Lieutenant*] (HU)
Hdl............... Handel [*German*]
Hdl............... Hauptdispatcherleitung [*Main Dispatcher Office*] (EG)
Hdlg............. Handlung [*Store, Trading*] [*Business and trade*] [*German*]
Hdlr............. Haendler [*German*]
hdm.............. Hadmuvelet [*or Hadmuveleti*] [*Military Operation or Operational*] (HU)
HDM............. Hermandad del Maestrazgo [*Brotherhood of Teachers*] [*Spanish*] (WER)
HDMS........... Hisbia Dastouri Mustaquil (MAR)
HDMS........... Hizbia Digil-Mirifle Somali (MAR)
HDog............ Directive on Contracts (BU)
HDP............. Houfnicovy Delostrelecky Pluk [*Howitzer Artillery Regiment*] (CZ)
HDP............. Statni Ustav pro Projektovani Vodohospodarskych Staveb - Hydroprojekt [*State Planning Institute for Water Construction*] (CZ)
HDr.............. Doktor der Handelswissenschaften [*German*]
HDRA........... Henry Doubleday Research Association (EA)
HDRU........... Human Development and Research Unit (MAR)
hds.............. Hadsereg [*Army*] (HU)
Hds.............. Handschrift [*Manuscript*] [*German*]
HDS............. Hnedouhelne Doly, Sokolov [*Lignite (Brown Coal) Mines in Sokolov*] (CZ)
HDS............. Hospodarske Dokumentacni Stredisko [*Economic Documentation Center*] (CZ)
HDS............. Hospodarske Druzstvo Skladistni [*Warehouse Cooperative*] (CZ)
HDS............. Hrvatski Drzavni Sabor [*Croatian Diet*] (YU)
Hds M.......... Hendes Majestaet [*Her Majesty*] [*Danish*] (GPO)
Hds Maj....... Hennes Majestet [*Her Majesty*] [*Norwegian*] (GPO)
HDSV........... Hospodarske Druzstvo Skladistni a Vyrobni [*Warehouse and Production Cooperative*] (CZ)
hdt............... Hadtest [*Army Corps*] (HU)
HDW............ Hebdrehwaehler [*Two-Motion Selector, Vertical Selector Switch*] (EG)
HdwStDB.... Handwerkssteuer-Durchfuehrungsbestimmung [*Implementing Regulation to the Artisan Tax*] (EG)
HdWStVo.... Handwerkssteuerverordnung [*Artisan Tax Decree*] (EG)
HDZ............. Hrvatski Dijalektoloski Zbornik [*Croatian Dialect Papers*] (YU)
HE................ Halk Evleri [*Peoples' Houses Organization*] [*A very old educational institution, mostly in rural areas*] (TU)
He................ Halte [*Halt*] [*Military map abbreviation*] [*World War I*] [*French*] (MTD)
he................ Hic Est [*This Is*] [*Latin*] (GPO)
HE................ Hidro Elektrik [*Hydroelectric*] (TU)
HE................ Hidroelektrana [*Hydroelectric Power Plant*] (YU)
he................ Hoc Est [*That Is*] [*Latin*] (GPO)
heb............... Heber [*Hebrew*] (HU)
HEB.............. Heinemann Educational Books (MAR)
HEBERMA... Societe Anonyme d'Hebergement en Mauritanie (MAR)

HEC............ Hautes Etudes Commerciales [*School for Advanced Business Studies*] [*French*] (WER)
HEC............ Hidroelektricna Centrala [*Hydroelectric Power Station*] (YU)
HEC............ High Executive Council [*Sudanese*] (MAR)
HECA......... Cepillos Heca Ltda. [*Barranquilla*] (COL)
hect............ Hectare [*Hectare*] [*Portuguese*] (GPO)
hect............ Hectarea [*Hectare*] [*Spanish*]
HEE............ Hydro-Electric Energy (MAR)
Hek............ Hekimlik [*Medical Science, Medicine*] (TU)
Hekt............ Hektoliter [*Hectoliter*] [*German*]
Hel............ Hotel [*Hotel*] [*Military map abbreviation*] [*World War I*] [*French*] (MTD)
HELIBRAS.... Helicopteros de Brasil, SA [*Brazilian Helicopters, Inc.*] (LA)
HELICOL..... Helicopteros Nacionales de Colombia SA [*Buga*] (COL)
HELN.......... Hubungan Ekonomi Luar Negeri [*Foreign Economic Relations*] (IN)
helyk.......... Helyi Kirendeltseg [*Local Branch Office*] (HU)
HEMA.......... Hidrolik Makina Sanayii ve Ticaret AS [*Hydraulic Machinery Industry and Trade Corp.*] (TU)
HEMPRO..... Hemizacija Poljoprivrede [*Agricultural Chemistry*] (YU)
henk........... Henkilosta [*About a Person*] [*Finnish*]
H Entw....... H-Entwicklung [*Hydrogen*] [*German*]
heo............ Helyorseg [*Garrison*] (HU)
HEO............ Hirurski Epidemoloski Odred [*Surgical Epidemic Detachment*] [*Military*] (YU)
HEPAL......... Helicopteros Portugal Africa Limitada (MAR)
HEPND........ Hnuti Exulantu pro Navrat Domu [*Exiles' Movement for the Return Home*] (CZ)
hepr............ Hepreaa [*or Hepreaksi*] [*Finnish*]
hepr............ Heprealainen [*Finnish*]
her............. Heraldiikka [*Heraldry*] [*Finnish*]
HER............ Hydraulique et Equipement Rural (MAR)
Herb........... Herbege [*German*]
HERCEGKOOPERATIVA ... Hercegovina Cooperative Establishment [*Mostar*] (YU)
herg............ Hergestellt [*Produced*] [*German*]
Hermge....... Hermitage [*Hermitage*] [*Military map abbreviation*] [*World War I*] [*French*] (MTD)
HERRAGRO ... Herramientas Agricolas SA [*Manizales*] (COL)
Herst........... Herstellung [*Production*] [*German*]
HES............ Hidro-Elektrik Santral [*Hydroelectric Power Plant*] (TU)
HES............ Hidro-Elektrik Sema [*Hydroelectric (Power) Diagram or Plan*] (TU)
HES............ Hygienicko-Epidemicke Stanice [*Public Health and Epidemiology Stations*] (CZ)
HEV............ Budapesti Helyierdeku Vasut [*Budapest Suburban Railway System*] (HU)
HeV............ Hermlin Verlag [*Hermlin Publishing House*] (EG)
HEVECAM.. Hevea Camerounais [*Cameroonian Rubber Company*] (AF)
Hey............ Heyet [*Committee, Board*] (TU)
Heyk........... Heykeltraslik [*Sculpture*] (TU)
HEZ............ Higijensko Epidemoloski Zavod [*Institute of Hygiene and Epidemiology*] (YU)
Hf............... Einzelhof [*German*]
HF.............. Hlutafelag [*Joint-Stock Company*] [*Icelandic*] (CED)
HF.............. Hochfrequenz [*High Frequency*] (EG)
hf............... Holland Forint [*Dutch Guilder*] (HU)
Hf............... Meierhof [*German*]
HfA............ Hauptverwaltung fuer Aufklaerung [*Main Administration for Intelligence Collection (within Ministry of State Security)*] (EG)
HfBL........... Hochschule fuer Bauwesen Leipzig [*Leipzig Advanced School for Architecture*] (EG)
HFCK.......... Housing Finance Company of Kenya (MAR)
HFD............ Hrvatsko Filolosko Drustvo [*Croatian Philological Society*] (YU)
HFF............ Hazai Fesusfono Reszvenytarsasag [*Domestic Worsted Mills Ltd.*] (HU)
Hfl.............. Hollannin Floriini [*or Hollannin Floriinia*] [*Finnish*]
HFPP........... Habe Fulami People's Party (MAR)
Hfst............ Hoofdstuk [*Chapter*] [*Dutch*] (GPO)
Hft.............. Heft [*Part*] [*German*]
HfV............ Hochschule fuer Verkehrswesen "Friedrich List" [*"Friedrich List" Advanced School for Transportation*] (EG)
HFVO.......... Hochfrequenzverordnung [*High Frequency Regulations*] (EG)
hg............... Hectogramme [*Hectogram*] [*French*]
Hg............... Hectogramo [*Hectogram*] [*Spanish*]
H G............ Hegyseg [*Mountain, Mountain Range*] (HU)
hg............... Hehtogramma [*or Hehtogrammaa*] [*Finnish*]
hg............... Hektogram [*Hectogram*] [*Polish*]
Hg............... Herausgeber [*German*]
hg............... Herausgegeben [*German*]
HG.............. Hlinkova Garda [*Hlinka Guards*] (CZ)
HGB............ Handelsgesetzbuch [*Commercial Code*] [*German*] (WEN)
HGer........... Handelsgericht [*German*]
HGF............ Holy Ghost Fathers (MAR)
HGG............ Hrvatski Geografski Glasnik [*Croatian Geographic Bulletin*] [*Zagreb*] [*A publication*] (YU)
HGL............ Hauptgesellschaftsleitung [*Main Company Management*] (EG)
HGL............ Hausgemeinschaftsleitung [*Housing Community Leadership*] (EG)
HGL............ Hochschulgewerkschaftsleitung [*Advanced School Labor Union Leadership*] (EG)
HGM............ Harita Genel Mudurlugu [*Cartography Directorate General*] [*Under Defense Ministry*] (TU)
HGP............ Hidrogradevinsko Preduzece [*Hydraulic Construction Establishment*] (YU)
HGr............. Haeusergruppe [*German*]
HGS............ Hauptgefechtsstand [*Main Battle Station*] [*Navy*] (EG)
HGUB.......... Historisch Genootschap te Utrecht, Bijdragen en Mededeelingen (MAR)
hgv............. Hangverseny [*Concert*] (HU)
hgvkozv...... Hangversenykozvetites [*Concert Broadcast*] (HU)
hgy............. Hegyi [*Mountain (Adjective)*] (HU)
HGZ............ Hrvatska Gradanska Zastita [*Croatian Civil Defense*] (YU)
Hgz............. Hrvatski Glazbeni Zavod [*Croatian Music Institute*] (YU)
hh.............. Hojas [*Leaves*] [*Spanish*]
HHA............ Haushaltsaufschlaege [*Budget Surtaxes*] (EG)
HHA............ Hurriyet Haber Ajansi [*Hurriyet News Agency*] [*Formerly, HA*] (TU)
HHS............ Haushaltungsschule [*German*]
HHW........... Hoechstes Hochwasser [*Maximum Known Water Level*] (EG)
Hhz............. Hochdruckdampfheizung [*High Pressure Steam Heating System*] (EG)
HI............... Haditechnikai Intezet [*Institute of Military Technology*] (HU)
Hi............... Hakuchi [*Roadstead*] [*Japanese*] (NAU)
HI............... Hemiska Industrija [*Chemical Industry*] (YU)
HI............... Hostesses Internationales [*French dating service*]
HI............... Hotel Indonesia (IN)
HIAG........... Hilfsgemeinschaft auf Gegenseitigkeit der Soldaten der Ehemaligen Waffen-SS [*Mutual Aid Society of the Former Waffen-SS Soldiers*] [*West German*] (WEN)
hibabej........ Hibabejelento [*Repair Center (of telephone company)*] (HU)
HIBV........... Hlavni Inspektorat Branne Vychovy [*Main Inspectorate for Military Training*] (CZ)
HIC............. Habitat International Council (EA)
Hic.............. Hicri Yil [*The Moslem Year*] (TU)
HIDECA....... Hidrocarburos y Derivados, Compania Anonima [*Hydrocarbons and Derivatives, Inc.*] [*Venezuelan*] (LA)
Hidro........... Hidrografi [*Hydrography*] (TU)
HIDROCIVILES ... Ingenieria Civil Hidraulica Sanitaria y de Estructuras Ltda. [*Bogota*] (COL)
HIDRONOR ... Hidroelectrica Norpatagonica [*North Patagonia Hydroelectric Company*] [*Argentine*] (LA)
HIDROSAN ... Ingenieria Civil Hidraulica Sanitaria [*Bogota*] (COL)
Hie.............. Haie [*Hedge*] [*Military map abbreviation*] [*World War I*] [*French*] (MTD)
HIERROPERU ... Empresa Minera de Hierro del Peru [*Peruvian Iron Mines Enterprise*] (LA)
Hifz............ Hifzissiha [*Hygiene*] (TU)
hig.............. Helyettes Igazgato [*Deputy Director*] (HU)
HIG............. Helyi Ipar Igazgatosaga [*Directorate for Local Industry*] (HU)
HIGIETEX.... Industrias Higienicas Textiles [*Medellin*] (COL)
HIJRM......... Hidrografski Institut Jugoslovenske Ratne Mornarice [*Hydrographic Institute of the Yugoslav Navy*] (YU)
Hik.............. Hildebrand-Knorr Bremse [*Hildebrand-Knorr Brake*] (EG)
HIKI............ Hiradastechnikai Ipari Kutato Intezet [*Research Institute of the Telecommunication Industry*] (HU)
HI L............ Hadtortenelmi Intezet Leveltara [*Archives of the Institute of Military History*] (HU)
HIL............. Hlavni Inzenyr Letectva [*Chief Aviation Engineer*] (CZ)
HiL............. Huta Imienia Lenina [*Polish*]
HILACOL..... Hilaturas de Colombia [*Bogota*] (COL)
HILANZA..... Hiladerias del Fonce SA [*Bucaramanga*] (COL)
HILASAL..... Hilanderia Salvadorena, SA [*Salvadoran Spinning Corp.*]
HIM............. Helyiipari Miniszterium/Miniszter [*Ministry/Minister of Local Industry*] (HU)
HIM............. His Imperial Majesty (MAR)
hinterl........ Hinterlassen [*Posthumous*] [*German*]
HINTTAS..... Hitit Ziraat ve Nebati Yag Sanayii Anonim Sirketi [*Hittite Agriculture and Vegetable Oil Industry, Incorporated*] (TU)
hinw Fw...... Hinweisendes Fuerwort [*German*]
HIP............. Hlavni Inzenyr Projektu [*Project Chief Engineer*] (CZ)
HIPISI......... Himpunan Pengusaha Islam Indonesia [*Indonesian Moslem Businessmen's Association*] (IN)
HIPO........... Hlavni Inspekce Pozarni Ochrany [*Main Inspectorate for Fire Prevention*] (CZ)
hird............ Hirdetes [*Advertisement*] (HU)
hird............ Hirdetmeny [*Announcement*] (HU)
HIRIMEX...... Societe Hiridjee Import Export (MAR)
hirl............. Hirlap [*Newspaper*] (HU)
hirod.......... Hirursko Odeljenje [*Surgical Department*] [*Military*] (YU)
HiS............. Hilfsschule [*German*]
HIS............. Hochschul Informations System
HISPANOBRAS ... Companhia Hispano-Brasileira de Mineracao [*Spanish-Brazilian Mining Company*] (LA)
HISSBI........ Himpunan Serikat-Serikat Buruh Indonesia [*Federation of Indonesian Labor Unions*] (IN)
hist............. Historia [*History*] [*Finnish*]
hist............. Historisch [*German*]
hist............. Historyczny [*Historical*] (POL)
HISTOMAT ... Historischer Materialismus [*Historical Materialism*] (EG)

HISZ .... Haziipari Szovetkezet [*Home Production Cooperative Enterprise*] (HU)
HISZ .... Helyiipari Szovetkezet [*Local Industrial Cooperative Enterprise*] (HU)
HISZOV .... Haziipari Szovetkezetek Orszagos Kozpontja [*National Center of Home Production Cooperative Enterprises*] (HU)
HIT .... Haupt-Investitions-Traeger [*Main Authorized Investor*] (EG)
hit .... Hiteles [*Authentic, Genuine*] (HU)
hit .... Hites [*Certified Expert*] (HU)
Hitig .... Hiteligazgatosag (Nemzeti Bank) [*Credit Management (National Bank)*] (HU)
hitk .... Hitkozseg [*Religious Community, Parish*] (HU)
hittud .... Hittudomany [*Theology*] (HU)
hiv .... Hivatal [*or Hivatalos*] [*Office or Official*] (HU)
hiv .... Hivatasos [*Vocational, Professional*] (HU)
HIVDOSZ .... Helyiipari es Varosgazdasagi Dolgozok Szakszervezete [*Trade Union of Workers in Municipal Administration*] (HU)
Hiz .... Hizmet [*Service*] (TU)
HK .... Hallinto-Opin, Hallintotieteiden Kandidaatti [*Finnish*]
hk .... Harckocsi [*Tank, Armored Car*] (HU)
HK .... Hefner-Kerze [*Hefner Candle*] [*German*]
HK .... Holzkontore der Bezirke [*Bezirk Lumber Marketing Agency*] (EG)
HK .... Hong Kong [*Type of rice*] [*Cambodian*] (CL)
HK .... Hong Kong [*Two-letter standard code*] (CNC)
HK .... Honvedelmi Kozlony [*Defense Gazette (A journal of the Ministry of Defense)*] [*A publication*] (HU)
HK .... Hviezdoslavova Kniznica [*Hviezdoslav Library*] (CZ)
HKA .... Hospodarska Komise Organisace Spojenych Narodu pro Afriku [*United Nations Economic Commission for Africa*] (CZ)
HKCE .... Hongkong Commodities Exchange
HKD .... Hrvatsko Kemijsko Drustvo [*Croatian Chemical Society*] (YU)
HKG .... Hong Kong [*Three-letter standard code*] (CNC)
HKGV .... Hava Kuvvetleri Guclendirme Vakfi [*Air Force Strengthening Fund*] (TU)
HKH .... Hans Kongelige Hojhed [*His Royal Highness*] [*Norwegian*] (GPO)
Hki .... Helsinki [*Finnish*]
HKI .... Hiradastechnikai Ipari Kutato Intezet [*Research Institute of the Telecommunication Industry*] (HU)
HKJ .... Hashemite Kingdom of Jordan (ME)
HKK .... Hava Kuvvetleri Komutanligi [*Air Forces Command*] (TU)
HKKA .... Hoogstudenten Verband voor Katholieke Actie [*Secondary Students Catholic Action Federation*] [*Belgian*] (WEN)
hkm .... Hectokilometre [*Metric System*] [*French*] (GPO)
HKN .... Harcerski Klub Narciarski [*Scout Ski Club*] (POL)
HKP .... Hostitelsky Komunalny Podnik [*Community Hotel Establishment*] (CZ)
HKS .... Harcerski Klub Sportowy [*Scout Sports Club*] (POL)
HKS .... Hlavni Kadrova Sprava [*Main Personnel Directorate*] (CZ)
HKS .... Hospodarska Kontrolni Sluzba [*Economic Control Service*] (CZ)
HKW .... Heizkraftwerk [*Heat and Electric Power Plant*] (EG)
HKZ .... Hornobrizske Kaolinove Zavody [*Horni Briza Kaolin Works*] (CZ)
HKZ .... Hrvatska Katolicka Zajednica [*Croatian Catholic Union*] [*Lemont, IL*] (YU)
HK-ZUN .... Handelskontor fuer Zucht- und Nutzvieh [*Marketing Office for Breeding and Productive Livestock*] (EG)
Hl .... Halbleder [*Half Leather*] [*German*]
Hl .... Halle [*Halle (Abbreviation used in railroading)*] (EG)
H-L .... Hamalainen-Laatunen [*Hamalainen-Laatunen Trade-Union Agreement*] [*Finnish*] (WEN)
Hl .... Hameen Laani [*Finnish*]
Hl .... Hauptlehrer [*German*]
hl .... Hectolitre [*Hectoliter*] [*French*]
Hl .... Hectolitro [*Hectoliter*] [*Spanish*]
hl .... Hehtolitra [*or Hehtolitraa*] [*Finnish*]
Hl .... Heilig [*Holy*] (EG)
hl .... Hektoliter [*Hectoliter*] (HU)
Hl .... Hektoliter [*Hectoliter*] (EG)
hl .... Hektolitr [*Hectoliter*] [*Polish*]
hl .... Hlavni [*Principal, Main, Chief*] (CZ)
hl .... Hoyrylaiva [*Finnish*]
Hlg .... Halogen [*Halogen*] [*German*]
HLK .... Hammaslaaketieteen Kandidaatti [*Finnish*]
HLL .... Hammaslaaketieteen Lisensiaatti [*Finnish*]
HLM .... Habitations a Loyer Moderee [*Low-Cost Housing Program*] [*French*] (WER)
HLMP .... Hlavni Mesto Praha [*Capital City Prague*] (CZ)
hlmPraha .... Hlavni Mesto Praha [*Capital City Prague*] (CZ)
Hlnw .... Halbleinwand [*German*]
HLO .... Handelsleitendes Organ [*Trade Managing Agency*] (EG)
hlred .... Hlavni Redaktor [*Chief Editor*] (CZ)
HLSRS .... High-Level Sisal Research Station (MAR)
Hlst .... Hlavni Stab [*Main Staff*] (CZ)
HLT .... Hammaslaaketieteen Tohtori [*Finnish*]
HLV .... Hauptlastverteilung [*Main Load Distribution Station*] (EG)
Hlw .... Halbleinwand [*Half Cloth*] [*German*]
Hlwnd .... Halbleinwand [*Half Cloth*] [*German*]
Hlz .... Holzband [*German*]
HM .... Hallitusmuoto [*Finnish*]
H M .... Hans Majestaet [*His Majesty*] [*Danish*] (GPO)
HM .... Hans Majestat [*His Majesty*] [*Swedish*] (GPO)
HM .... Hans Majestet [*His Majesty*] [*Norwegian*] (GPO)
HM .... Hare Majesteit [*Her Majesty*] [*Dutch*] (GPO)
HM .... Heard Island and McDonald Islands [*Two-letter standard code*] (CNC)
hm .... Hectometre [*Hectometer*] [*French*] (GPO)
Hm .... Hectometro [*Hectometer*] [*Spanish*]
hm .... Hehtometri [*or Hehtometria*] [*Finnish*]
hm .... Hektometr [*Hectometer*] [*Polish*]
hm .... Helyi Megbizott [*Local Representative*] (HU)
HM .... Higijenska Mobilna [*Mobile Sanitary Service*] [*Military*] (YU)
HM .... Hiradastechnikai Muszerkeszito KTSz [*Production Cooperative for Telecommunication Equipment*] (HU)
hm .... Hoc Mense [*In This Month*] [*Latin*] (GPO)
Hm .... Holm [*or Holmen*] [*Islet*] [*Norwegian*] (NAU)
Hm .... Holm [*or Holmen*] [*Islet*] [*Swedish*] (NAU)
Hm .... Holm [*Islet*] [*Danish*] (NAU)
HM .... Honvedelmi Miniszterium/Miniszter [*Ministry/Minister of Defense*] (HU)
HM .... Hudebni Matice [*Society for the Promotion of Music*] (CZ)
HM .... Hudebni Mladez [*Young Music Fans*] (CZ)
hm .... Huius Mensis [*Of This Month*] [*Latin*] (GPO)
HMA .... Huileries Modernes d'Algerie (MAR)
HMB .... Hatarugyi Muszaki Bizottsag [*Technical Committee on Surveying*] (HU)
HMBA .... Hebrew Master Bakers Association (MAR)
HMC .... Historical Monuments Commission (MAR)
HMC .... Hospital Militar Central [*Central Military Hospital*] [*Colombian*] (LA)
HMD .... Heard Island and McDonald Islands [*Three-letter standard code*] (CNC)
HME .... Higijenska Mobilna Ekipa [*Mobile Sanitary Team*] [*Military*] (YU)
HMEZAD .... Zadruzno Trgovinsko Podjetje za Izvoz Hmelja [*Commercial Cooperative for Export of Hops*] (YU)
HMG .... His Majesty's Government (MAR)
HMI .... Hahn-Meitner-Institut fuer Kernforschung [*West German*]
HMI .... Himpunan Mahasiswa Islam [*Moslem College Students Association*] (IN)
HML .... Hellenic Mediterranean Lines (MAR)
HMLS .... Helsingin Marxilais-Leninilais Seura [*Helsinki Marxist-Leninist Society*] [*Finnish*] (WEN)
HMO .... Hidrometeoroloski Observatorij [*Hydrometeorological Observatory*] [*Split*] (YU)
HMOCS .... His Majesty's Colonial Service (MAR)
HMP .... Hlavni Mesto Praha [*Capital City Prague*] (CZ)
HMS .... Hind Mazdoor Sabha [*Indian*]
HMS .... Historical Metallurgy Society (EA)
HMS .... Hrvatska Meteoroloska Sluzba [*Croatian Meteorological Service*] (YU)
HMSO .... His [*or Her*] Majesty's Stationery Office (MAR)
HMU .... Hydrometeorologicky Ustav [*Hydrometeorological Institute*] (CZ)
HMUK .... Hukuk Muhakemeleri Usulu Kanunu [*Legal Trials Procedural Law*] (TU)
HMV .... Hungaria Muanyagfeldolgozo Vallalat [*Hungaria Plastics Processing Enterprise*] (HU)
HMZ .... Hidrometeoroloski Zavod [*Hydrometeorological Institute*] (YU)
Hn .... Hafen [*Harbor*] [*German*] (NAU)
Hn .... Hamn [*or Hamnen*] [*Harbor*] [*Swedish*] (NAU)
Hn .... Hamn [*or Havn*] [*Harbor*] [*Norwegian*] (NAU)
HN .... Handelsniederlassung [*Commercial Branch*] (EG)
Hn .... Havn [*or Havnen*] [*Harbor*] [*Danish*] (NAU)
HN .... Hazafias Nepfront [*Patriotic People's Front*] (HU)
hn .... Hely Nelkul [*No Place of Publication Given*] (HU)
HN .... Honduras [*Two-letter standard code*] (CNC)
HN .... Hutni Normy [*Production Standards in Metallurgy*] (CZ)
HNB .... Hrvatska Narodna Banka [*Croatian National Bank*] (YU)
HNC .... Hermandad Nacional de Combatientes [*National Brotherhood of Fighters*] [*Spanish*] (WER)
HND .... Higher National Diploma (MAR)
HND .... Honduras [*Three-letter standard code*] (CNC)
Hne .... Holmane [*Islets*] [*Norwegian*] (NAU)
Hne .... Holmene [*Islets*] [*Danish*] (NAU)
HNF .... Hazafias Nepfront [*Patriotic People's Front (PPF)*] (HU)
HNK .... Hrvatsko Narodno Kazaliste [*Croatian National Theater*] (YU)
HNM .... Hermandad Nacional del Maestrazgo [*National Brotherhood of Teachers*] [*Spanish*] (WER)
HNO .... Hrvatski Narodni Odbor [*Croatian National Resistance*] [*Yugoslav*] (PD)
Hnos .... Hermanos [*Brothers*] [*Spanish*] (GPO)
HNP .... Herstigte Nasionale Party [*Reconstituted National Party*] [*South African*] (PPW)
HNP .... Herstigte Nasionale Party [*Reconstituted National Party*] [*Namibian*] (PPW)
ho .... Hadosztaly [*Army Division*] (HU)
HO .... Handelsorganisation [*State Trade Organization*] (EG)
HO .... Harb Okul [*Military Academy*] (TU)
ho .... Hataror [*or Hatarorseg*] [*Border Guard or Border Guards*] (HU)

HO .... Hemisko Obezbedenje [*Chemical Defense*] [*Military*] (YU)
Ho............... Hirursko Odeljenje [*Surgical Department*] [*Military*] (YU)
HO .... Hochofen [*Blast Furnace*] (EG)
HO .... Hovioikeus [*Court of Appeals*] [*Finnish*] (WEN)
HOA............ Huileries de l'Ouest Africain [*Senegalese*] (MAR)
HOAC .... Hermandad Obrera de Accion Catolica [*Workers Brotherhood of Catholic Action*] [*Spanish*] (WER)
HOACF........ Hermandad Obrera de Accion Catolica Femenina [*Women Workers Brotherhood of Catholic Action*] [*Spanish*] (WER)
HOC .... Hillman Owners Club (EA)
hod............. Hodina [*Hour*] (CZ)
HOE............ Hopital d'Evacuation [*Clearing Hospital*] [*Military*] [*French*] (MTD)
Hoefl........... Hoeflich [*Respectfully*] [*Correspondence*] [*German*]
HOG .... Gaststaette der Handelsorganisation [*State Trade Organization Restaurant*] (EG)
HOKI........... Hotechnikai Kutato Intezet [*Research Institute in Thermodynamic Engineering*] (HU)
HOKS .... Hind Oil Kamger Sabha [*Indian*]
holl .... Hollantia [*or Hollanniksi*] [*Finnish*]
holl .... Hollantilainen [*Dutch*] [*Finnish*]
hom............. Homerseklet [*Temperature*] (HU)
HOMA .... Holzmessanweisung [*Wood Measuring Regulations*] (EG)
HOMA .... Iran National Airways (ME)
HOMS.......... Homme et la Societe [*Paris*] [*A publication*] (MAR)
HOMT.......... Houston Oil Mineral of Tunisia (MAR)
HOMYKD .... Harb Okulu Mezunlari Yardimlasma ve Kultur Dernegi [*Military Academy Graduates' Mutual Aid and Cultural Association*] (TU)
Hon.............. Honorar [*German*]
hon .... Honorowy [*Honorary*] [*Polish*]
HON............. Hydraulicky Otocny Nakladac, Typ 051 [*Hydraulic Rotary Loader, Type 051*] (CZ)
HONDUTEL ... Empresa Hondurena de Telecomunicaciones [*Honduran Telecommunications Enterprise*] (LA1)
honv .... Honved [*Private Soldier, Army, Military*] (HU)
hop.............. Hadosztalyparancsnok [*Division Commander*] (HU)
HOP............. Hrvatski Oslobodilacki Pokret [*Croatian Liberation Movement*] (YU)
HOP............. Verkaufspreis bei der Handelsorganisation [*State Trade Organization Sales Price*] (EG)
HOPE........... Healthcare Organization with Poor Economy (MAR)
HOPOKO..... Hochschulpolitisches Kollektiv [*FRG student organization*] (EG)
Hor .... Hataror [*Border Guard*] (HU)
HORAN........ Hommes et Organisations d'Afrique Noire (MAR)
HO-RE-CA ... Federation Internationale des Organisations d'Hoteliers, Restaurateurs, et Cafetiers [*International Organization of Hotel and Restaurant Associations*] (EA)
HOS............. Hrvatski Orlovski Savez [*Croatian Eagles Federation*] (YU)
Hosp............ Hospice [*Asylum*] [*Military map abbreviation*] [*World War I*] [*French*] (MTD)
hosp............ Hospodarsky [*Economic*] (CZ)
hot............... Hotan [*Thermodynamics*] (HU)
HOTAFRIC ... Societe pour le Developpement Hotelier et Touristique de l'Afrique de l'Ouest [*West African Hotel Industry and Tourism Development Company*] (AF)
HOTELIM .... Societe Hoteliere et Immobiliere de Guinee (MAR)
HP................ Halkci Partisi [*Populist Party*] [*Turkish people's party of Cyprus*] (TU)
HP................ Hauptprodukt [*Main Product*] (EG)
hp .... Hazaspar [*Married Couple*] (HU)
HP................ Hidroelecktricno Preduzece [*Hydroelectric Establishment*] (YU)
HP................ Hidrogradevinsko Preduzece [*Hydraulic Construction Establishment*] (YU)
HP................ Hogerpartiet [*Conservative Party*] [*Swedish*] (WEN)
HP................ Homeland Party (MAR)
hp .... Hoyrypursi [*Finnish*]
HP................ Hranicni Pasmo [*Border Zone*] (CZ)
HP................ Hromadna Palba [*Mass Barrage*] (CZ)
HP................ Hrvatski Planinar [*Croatian Mountaineer*] [*Zagreb*] [*A periodical*] (YU)
HP................ Hutni Projekt [*Metallurgical Project*] (CZ)
HPA............. Handelspolitische Abteilung [*Trade Policy Department*] (EG)
HPA............. Hurlingham Polo Association (EA)
HPB .... Hirurska Poljska Bolnica [*Surgical Field Hospital*] [*Military*] (YU)
HPB-1.......... Hirurska Poljska Bolnica Prve Linije [*First Line Surgical Field Hospital*] (YU)
HPC............. Higher Petroleum Council [*Saudi*] (ME)
HPC............. Higher Press Council [*Egyptian*] (MAR)
HPCPAL...... Higher Political Committee for Palestinian Affairs in Lebanon (ME)
HPD .... Hrvatsko Pjevacko Drustvo [*Croatian Singing Society*] (YU)
HPD .... Hrvatsko Prirodoslovno Drustvo [*Croatian Natural Science Society*] (YU)
HPD .... Hrvatsko Prosvjetno Drustvo [*Croatian Cultural Society*] (YU)
HPE .... Inomeni Parataksis Ethnikofronon [*United Front of Nationalists*] (PPE)
HPG............. Handwerkerproduktionsgenossenschaft [*Artisan Producer Cooperative*] (EG)
HPK .... Hutna Projekcna Kancelaria [*Bureau of Metallurgical Projects*] (CZ)
HPKM.......... Hopital Preah Ket Mealea [*Preah Ket Mealea Hospital*] [*Cambodian*] (CL)
HPL .... Hochschulparteileitung [*Advanced-School Party Management*] (EG)
HPM .... Hopital Preah Monivong [*Preah Monivong Hospital*] [*Cambodian*] (CL)
HPO............. Hochschulparteiorganisation [*Advanced-School Party Organization*] (EG)
HPP .... Hernieuwde Progressieve Partij [*Renewed Progressive Party*] [*Surinamese*] (PPW)
HPPB........... Hirurska Pukovska Poljska Bolnica [*Regimental Surgical Field Hospital*] [*Military*] (YU)
HPR .... Halden Reaktor Prosjekt [*Norwegian*]
HPR .... Hutnicze Przedsiebiorstwo Remontowe [*Metallurgical Establishment Repair Enterprise*] (POL)
HPS .... Hazai Pamut Szovogyar [*Domestic Cotton Mill*] (HU)
HPS .... Hlavni Politicka Sprava [*Metallurgical Sales Depot*] (CZ)
HPSS........... Hrvatska Pucka Seljacka Stranka [*Croatian People's Peasant Party*] [*Yugoslav*] (PPE)
Hpt .... Haupt- [*Main*] [*German*]
HPT .... Hauptplantraeger (bei Investitionen) [*Principal Enterprise (or Body) (for Investments)*] (EG)
Hptm .... Hauptmann [*German*]
hpz .... Hektopieza [*Polish*]
hq................ Hoc Quaere [*Look for This*] [*Latin*] (GPO)
hr................. Hadirokkant [*War Invalid*] (HU)
HR .... Hauptreferent [*Main Expert, Main Reporter, Main Desk Chief*] (EG)
hr................. Herr [*Sir, Mister*] [*Danish*] (GPO)
Hr .... Herr [*Mister*] [*Norwegian*] (GPO)
hr................. Herr [*Mister*] [*Swedish*] (GPO)
HR .... Hessischer Rundfunk [*Radio network*] [*West German*]
HR .... Hospodarska Rada [*Economic Council*] (CZ)
hr................. Hrabia [*Count*] [*Polish*]
Hr .... Hrid [*or Hridi*] [*Rock*] [*Yugoslav*] (NAU)
HR .... Humber Register (EA)
Hra .... Herra [*Mister, Sir*] [*Finnish*] (GPO)
HRAF........... Human Relations Area Files (MAR)
HRB............. Croatian Revolutionary Brotherhood [*Yugoslav*] (PD)
HRB............. Hockey Rules Board (EA)
HRC............. Heliopolis Racing Club [*Egyptian*] (MAR)
HRC............. Human Rights Commission (MAR)
HRDU .... Housing Research and Development Unit (MAR)
HREU........... Hotels and Restaurants Employees Union [*Mauritian*] (AF)
HRG............. Human Rights Group (EA)
HRIBROD .... Hrvatsko Rijecno Brodarstvo [*Croatian River Shipping*] [*NDH*] (YU)
HRIP .... Hic Requiescat in Pace [*Here Rests in Peace*] [*Latin*] (GPO)
HrJ............... Hrvatski Jezik [*Croatian Language*] [*Zagreb*] [*A periodical*] (YU)
HROT .... Huileries et Rizeries de l'Oubangui et du Tchad (MAR)
Hrp .... Harp [*War, Warfare*] (TU)
Hrp Gm .... Harp Gemisi [*Warship*] (TU)
HRRC .... Human Rights Resource Center (EA)
HRS............. Hrvatska Republikanska Stranka [*Croatian Republican Party*] (YU)
HRS............. Hrvatski Radnicki Savez [*Croatian Workers' Union*] (YU)
Hrsg .... Herausgeber [*Publisher*] (EG)
hrsg............. Herausgegeben [*Edited or Published*] [*German*] (GPO)
HRSS........... Hrvatska Republikanska Seljacka Stranka [*Croatian Republican Peasant Party*] [*Yugoslav*] (PPE)
hrsz .... Helyrajzi Szam [*Lot Number (Real estate)*] (HU)
hrtkm .... Hruby Tunkilometr [*Gross Ton-Kilometer*] (CZ)
HS .... Hakluyt Society (MAR)
HS .... Handelsschule [*German*]
Hs .... Handschrift [*Manuscript*] [*German*]
HS .... Hauptschule [*German*]
HS .... Hic Sepultus [*Here Is Buried*] [*Latin*] (GPO)
HS .... Hic Situs [*Here Lies*] [*Latin*] (GPO)
HS .... Hlasna Sluzba (Ceskoslovenske Armady) [*(Czechoslovak Army) Observation Service*] (CZ)
HS .... Hlavni Sprava [*Main Administration, Main Directorate*] (CZ)
HS .... Hoc Sensu [*In This Sense*] [*Latin*] (GPO)
HS .... Hochschule [*Advanced School*] (EG)
HS .... Hors Service [*French*] (MTD)
HS .... Horska Sluzba [*Mountain Service (subordinate to SUTVS)*] (CZ)
HS .... Hospodarska Sekce [*Economic Section*] (CZ)
HS .... Hospodarska Skupina [*Economic Group*] (CZ)
HS .... Hospodarska Sprava [*Economic Administration*] (CZ)
HS .... Hundertschaftssanitaeter [*Detachment Medical Aide (Workers Militia)*] (EG)
HSA............. Hilfsfond Sudliches Afrika (MAR)
HSAP........... Hospodarska Skupina Ambulantnich Podnikani [*Economic Group of Itinerant Enterprises*] (CZ)
HSA-TRANSIT ... Societe Camerounaise de Transit Henri de Suares d'Almeyda & Compagnie (MAR)

Hsb............ Hausbesitzer [*German*]
HSB............ Hospodarska Skupina Banskeho Prumyslu [*Economic Group of the Mining Industry*] (CZ)
HSC............ Heliopolis Sporting Club (MAR)
HSCh.......... Hospodarska Skupina Chemickeho Prumyslu [*Economic Group of the Chemical Industry*] (CZ)
HSchG......... Handelsschutzgesetz [*Trade Protection Law*] (EG)
HSChP........ Hospodarska Skupina Chemickeho Prumyslu [*Economic Group of the Chemical Industry*] (CZ)
HSD............ Halk Sagligi Dernegi [*Peoples Health Association*] (TU)
HSD............ Hospodarska Skupina Drevozpracujiciho Prumyslu [*Economic Group of the Lumber Industry*] (CZ)
HSD............ Hrvatsko Stenografsko Drustvo [*Croatian Stenographic Society*] (YU)
HSE............ Hlavni Sprava Elektraren [*Main Administration of Electric Power Stations*] (CZ)
HSE............ Hospodarska Skupina Energetickeho Prumyslu [*Economic Group of the Power Industry*] (CZ)
HSF............ Havadan Satha Fuze [*Air-to-Surface Missile*] (TU)
HSG............ Heinemann Student's Guide (MAR)
HSGL.......... Hochschulgruppenleitung (FDJ) [*Advanced-School Group Management*] (EG)
HSGM.......... Hudud ve Sahiller Saglik Genel Mudurlugu [*Borders and Coasts Health Directorate General*] (TU)
HSGP.......... Hlavni Sprava Geologickeho Pruzkumu [*Main Administration for Geological Prospecting (of the Ministry of Metallurgy and Ore Mines)*] (CZ)
Hshlt........... Haushalt [*German*]
HSHZ.......... Hospodarska Skupina Hostinskych Zivnosti [*Economic Group of the Catering Business*] (CZ)
HSI............. Hauptsicherheitsinspektion [*Main Safety Inspection Office*] (EG)
HSIU........... Haile Selassie I University [*Ethiopian*] (AF)
HSK............ Hrvatsko-Srpska Koalicija [*Croatian-Serbian Coalition*] (YU)
HSk............. Husova Skola [*Hus School*] (CZ)
HSKA.......... Hospodarska Skupina Kamene, Zemin, a Keramickeho Prumyslu [*Economic Group of the Stoneware, Earthenware, and Ceramics Industries*] (CZ)
HSKO.......... Hospodarska Skupina Kozedelneho Prumyslu [*Economic Group of the Leather Industry*] (CZ)
HSKZ.......... Hrvatska Sveucilisna Knjiznica u Zagrebu [*Croatian University Library in Zagreb*] (YU)
HSL............ Hospodarska Skupina Lihovarskeho Prumyslu [*Economic Group of the Distilling Industry*] (CZ)
HSL............ Household Subsistence Level (MAR)
HSL............ Huilerie et Savonnerie des Lagunes Blohorn et Fils (MAR)
HSL............ Schluesselnummer des Binnenhandels [*Domestic Trade Index*] (EG)
HSL'S.......... Hlinkova Slovenska l'Udova Strana [*Hlinka's Slovak People's Party*] [*Also, SL'S*] (PPE)
HSLS.......... Hospodarska Skupina Lazni a Sportovnich Mist [*Economic Group of Health Resorts and Athletics Establishments*] (CZ)
Hs M........... Hans Majestaet [*His Majesty*] [*Danish*] (GPO)
HSM............ Havadan Satha Mermi [*Air-to-Surface Missile*] (TU)
HSM............ Hospodarska Skupina Maloobchodu [*Economic Group of the Retail Business*] (CZ)
HSMP.......... Hospodarska Skupina Mlynarskeho Prumyslu [*Economic Group of the Flour Milling Industry*] (CZ)
HSMY.......... Havagazi Sayaclari Ayar ve Muayene Yonetmeligi [*Gas Meter Calibration and Inspection Administration*] [*Under Ministry of Commerce*] (TU)
HSMZ.......... Hlavni Sprava Ministerstva Zemedelstvi [*Main Administration of the Ministry of Agriculture*] (CZ)
HSNC.......... Health, Sanitation, and Nutrition Commission (MAR)
HSNO.......... Hrvatsko-Srpska Napredna Omladina [*Croatian-Serbian Progressive Youth*] (YU)
HSO............ Hlavni Sprava Odbytu [*Main Distribution Department (of the Ministry of Metallurgy)*] (CZ)
HSOA.......... Huileries Savonneries de l'Ouest Africain (MAR)
HSP............ Hlavni Sprava Prumyslu [*Main Administration for Industry (of the Ministry of National Defense)*] (CZ)
HSP............ Hospodarska Skupina Prumyslu Papiru [*Economic Group of the Paper Industry*] (CZ)
HSP............ Hrvatska Stranka Prava [*Croatian Party of Rights*] [*Yugoslav*] (PPE)
HSP............ Hurtownia Spozywczo-Przemyslowa [*Wholesale House for the Food Industry*] (POL)
HSPDP........ Hill State People's Democratic Party [*Indian*] (PPW)
HSPi........... Hospodarska Skupina Prumyslu Pil [*Economic Group of Sawmills*] (CZ)
HSPP.......... Hospodarska Skupina Potravinarskeho Prumyslu [*Economic Group of the Food Industry*] (CZ)
Hsprael....... Hauspraelat [*German*]
HSPS.......... Hospodarska Skupina Pivovarskeho a Sladarskeho Prumyslu [*Economic Group of the Brewing and Malting Industries*] (CZ)
HSR............ Hospodarsko-Socialni Rada [*Economic and Social Council*] [*United Nations*] (CZ)
HSRC.......... Human Sciences Research Council [*South African*] (AF)
Hss............. Handschriften [*Manuscripts*] [*German*]
HSS............ Heraldry Society of Scotland (EA)
HSS............ Historiae Societatis Socius [*Fellow of the Historical Society*] [*Latin*] (GPO)
HSS............ Hospodarska Skupina Sklarskeho Prumyslu [*Economic Group of the Glass Industry*] (CZ)
HSS............ Hrvatska Samostalna Stranka [*Croatian Independent Party*] (YU)
HSS............ Hrvatska Seljacka Stranka [*Croatian Peasant Party*] [*Yugoslav*] (PPE)
HSSGM....... Hudut ve Sahiller Saglik Genel Mudurlugu [*Border and Coastal Health Directorate General*] [*Under Ministry of Health*] (TU)
HSSL.......... Hospodarska Spravni Sluzba [*Economic Administration Service*] (CZ)
HSSP.......... Hlavni Sprava Statni Pojistovny [*Main Administration of the State Insurance Institute*] (CZ)
HSSP.......... Hlavni Sprava Statnich Sporitelen [*Central Administration of State Savings Banks*] (CZ)
HSSP.......... Hospodarska Skupina Stavebniho Prumyslu [*Economic Group of the Building Industry*] (CZ)
Hst............. Hastane [*Hospital*] (TU)
HSt............. Hlavni Stab [*Main Staff*] (CZ)
HST............ Hospodarska Skupina Tisku [*Economic Group of the Press*] (CZ)
HST............ Hrvatska Seljacka Tiskarna [*Croatian Rural Printers*] (YU)
HSTBK........ Hlavni Sprava Tezby Barevnych Kovu [*Main Administration of the Mining of Nonferrous Metals*] (CZ)
HSTO.......... Hospodarska Skupina Textilniho a Odevniho Prumyslu [*Economic Group of the Textile and Clothing Industries*] (CZ)
HSV............ Hlavni Sprava Vydavatelstev, Tiskaren, a Knizniho Obchodu [*Main Administration of Publishing, Printing, and the Book Trade*] (CZ)
HSV............ Hlavni Stavebni Vyroba [*Main Section for Building Production (of the Advisory Board for the Mechanization of the Building Industry)*] (CZ)
HSVO.......... Hlavni Sprava Vojenske Osvety [*Main Directorate for Cultural Activities (of the Ministry of National Defense)*] (CZ)
HSVO.......... Hlavni Sprava Vychovy a Osvety [*Main Directorate of Education and Culture (of the Ministry of National Defense)*] (CZ)
HSVUP........ Hlavni Sprava pro Vystavbu Uhelneho Prumyslu [*Main Administration for Coal Industry Development*] (CZ)
HSVZ.......... Hospodarska Skupina Prumyslu Vyrabejiciho Zelezo [*Economic Group of the Iron Industry*] (CZ)
HSVZ(O)..... Hospodarska Skupina Velkoobchodu a Zahranicniho Obchodu [*Economic Group of Wholesale Trade and Foreign Trade*] (CZ)
HsW............ Hoechster Schiffbarer Wasserstand [*Maximum Navigable Water Level*] (EG)
HSWP.......... Hungarian Socialist Workers' Party (PPW)
HSZ............ Hasznaltcikk Szovetkezet [*Cooperative for Second-Hand Items*] (HU)
hsz............. Haziipari Szovetkezet [*Home Production Cooperative Enterprise*] (HU)
HSZ............ Hospodarska Skupina Zprostredkovatelu [*Economic Group of Commission Business Firms*] (CZ)
HSZD.......... Hlavni Sprava Zeleznych Dolu [*Main Administration of Iron Ore Mines*] (CZ)
HSZK.......... Hospodarska Skupina Prumyslu Zeleza a Kovu [*Economic Group of the Iron and Steel Industries*] (CZ)
HSZV.......... Hushasznu Szarvasmarhatenyeszto Kozos Vallalkozas [*Joint Enterprise for Raising Beef Cattle*] (HU)
HT.............. Haiti [*Two-letter standard code*] (CNC)
HT.............. Hatarozatok Tara [*Collection of Decisions*] (HU)
Ht............... Haut [*Height*] [*Military map abbreviation*] [*World War I*] [*French*] (MTD)
ht............... Helyi Tanacs [*Local Council*] (HU)
HT.............. Hermandades de Trabajo [*Labor Brotherhoods*] [*Spanish*] (WER)
HT.............. Hesperis Tamuda [*Rabat*] [*A publication*] (MAR)
ht............... Hivatasos [*Professional*] (HU)
HT.............. Hlavni Tyl [*Main Rear Services*] (CZ)
ht............... Hoc Tempore [*At This Time*] [*Latin*] (GPO)
ht............... Hoc Titulo [*In or Under This Title*] [*Latin*] (GPO)
HT.............. Hradecke Tiskarny [*Hradec Printing Plants*] (CZ)
Hta............. Hasta [*Until*] [*Business and trade*] [*Spanish*]
htap........... Hadtap [*War Materiel*] (HU)
HTE............ Hiradestechnikai Tudomanyos Egyesulet [*Scientific Association of Telecommunications*] (HU)
Ht fd.......... Haut Fond [*Shoal*] [*French*] (NAU)
HTGGY....... Hiradastechnikai Gepgyar [*Telecommunication Machine Factory*] (HU)
HTI............. Haiti [*Three-letter standard code*] (CNC)
HTK............ Humanististen Tieteiden Kandidaatti [*Finnish*]
HTM............ Hyvaksytty Tilimies [*Finnish*]
Hts............. Hauts [*Heights*] [*Military map abbreviation*] [*World War I*] [*French*] (MTD)
HTS............ Hochschulring Tubinger Studenten (MAR)
HTS............ Hoger Technische School
HTS............ Hunting Technical Services (MAR)

htsz .... Haziipari Termelo Szovetkezet [*Home Production Cooperative Enterprise*] (HU)
htt .... Helyett [*For, Instead*] (HU)
HTUP .... Hospodarsko-Technicke Upravy Pozemkov [*Economic and Technical Soil Improvement*] (CZ)
HTUP .... Hospodarsko-Technicke Upravy Puiy [*Economic and Technical Soil Improvement*] (CZ)
HTV .... Hiradotechnikai Vallalat [*Communication Technology Enterprise*] (HU)
HTX .... Hop Tac Xa [*Cooperative*] (TVP)
HTZ .... Hemisko-Tehnicka Zastita [*Chemical-Technical Defense*] (YU)
HTZ .... Hmotne-Technicke Zasobovani [*Materiel Provisioning*] (CZ)
HU .... Hacettepe Universitesi [*Hacettepe University*] [*Ankara*] (TU)
HU .... Historicky Ustav [*Historical Institute (of the Czechoslovak Academy of Sciences)*] (CZ)
HU .... Hungary [*Two-letter standard code*] (CNC)
hu .... Huszar [*Hussar, Cavalryman*] (HU)
HUB .... Humboldt-Universitaet Berlin [*Humboldt University, Berlin*] (EG)
HUBAD .... Perhubungan Angkatan Darat [*Army Communications*] (IN)
HUBESZ .... Mezogazdasagi Ipari Tudomanyos Egyesulet Hus-, Baromfi-, es Hutoipari Szakosztalya [*Scientific Association of Agricultural Industries - Department of Meat, Poultry, and Refrigeration*] (HU)
HUBMAS .... Hubungan Masjarakat [*Public Relations*] (IN)
HUD .... Hornicky Ucnovsky Domov [*Hostel for Mining Apprentices*] (CZ)
HUDCO .... Housing and Urban Development Corporation (MAR)
HUeP .... Handelsueblicher Preis [*Market Price*] (EG)
HUILIVOIRE ... Societe pour la Realisation des Huileries de Graines de Cote-d'Ivoire (MAR)
HUILKA .... Huilerie de Nkavi (MAR)
Huk .... Hukuk [*Law, Legal*] (TU)
Huk .... Hukum [*Law, Decree*] (TU)
Huk .... Hukumet [*Government*] (TU)
HuK .... Humanist. Kandidaatti [*Bachelor's Degree in Humanities*] [*Finnish*]
HuKand .... Humanist. Kandidaatti [*Bachelor's Degree in Humanities*] [*Finnish*]
HUKK .... Turk Hukuk Kurumu [*Turkish Law Association*] (TU)
HUKO .... Hutny Kombinat, Kosice [*Metallurgical Works at Kosice*] (CZ)
HUMAN .... Oltoanyagtermelo es Kutato Intezet [*Vaccine Production and Research Institute*] (HU)
HUMK .... Hukumet Umumi Medeni Kanunu [*Government General Civil Law*] (TU)
humkand .... Humanististen Tieteiden Kandidaatti [*Finnish*]
HUMUCI .... Humus-Cote-d'Ivoire (MAR)
HUN .... Hungary [*Three-letter standard code*] (CNC)
HUNAP .... Hotelsko Ugostitelsko Narodno Pretprijatie [*National Enterprise for Hotel and Catering Trade*] (YU)
HUNAS .... Human Needs and Services Committee (MAR)
HUNGAROCAMION ... HUNGAROCAMION Nemzetkozi Autokozlekedesi Vallalat [*HUNGAROCAMION International Automotive Transport Enterprise*] (HU)
HUNGAROFILM ... Film Export Import Vallalat [*Motion Picture Export-Import Enterprise*] (HU)
HUNGAROFLOR ... HUNGAROFLOR Disznoveny Export-Import Ertekesito Iroda [*HUNGAROFLOR Export-Import Marketing Office for Ornamental Plants*] (HU)
HUNGAROFRUCT ... Zoldseg-Gyumolcs Szovetkezeti Export Vallalat [*Cooperative Export Enterprise for Vegetables and Fruit*] (HU)
HUNGAROTEX ... HUNGAROTEX Textilkulkereskedelmi Vallalat [*HUNGAROTEX Foreign Trade Enterprise for Textile Goods*] (HU)
HUNGAROTURIST ... Orszagos Udulovendeglato Vallalat [*National Tourist Service Enterprise*] (HU)
HUNGAROVOX ... Sajto, Radio, es Televizio Tudosito Iroda [*Press, Radio, and Television News Agency*] (HU)
HUNOSA .... Empresa Nacional Hulleras del Norte, SA [*National Northern Coal Enterprise*] [*Spanish*] (WER)
huom! .... Huomaa! [*Finnish*]
huom .... Huomautus [*Finnish*]
HUPZ .... Hornicke Uciliste Pracovnich Zaloh [*Mining School for Labor Reserves*] (CZ)
HURACA .... Societe Huilerie-Raffinerie du Cameroun (MAR)
Hur Cam-Is ... Turkish Window Glass, Fiberglass, Mosaic, Glass, Bottle, and Glass Industries Workers Union (TU)
HURIDOCS ... Human Rights International Documentation System (EA)
HURPRO .... Huileries et Raffineries de la Province Orientale (MAR)
HUS .... Human Settlements (MAR)
HUSAMI .... Himpunan Usahawan Muslimin Indonesia
HUSPZ .... Hornicke Uciliste Statnich Pracovnich Zaloh [*Mining School for State Labor Reserves*] (CZ)
HUT .... Hari Ulang Tahun [*Anniversary*] (IN)
Hutmen .... Zaklady Hutniczo-Przetworcze Metali Niezelaznych we Wroclawiu [*Non-Ferrous Metals Smelter and Processing Plant in Wroclaw*] (POL)
HuV .... Handel und Versorgung [*Trade and Supply*] (EG)
HUYAS .... Hukuk Yayinlari Anonim Sirketi [*Legal Publications Corporation*] [*Istanbul*] (TU)
hv .... Hatarvedo [*or Hatarvedelmi*] [*Frontier Guard or Of the Frontier Guards*] (HU)
HV .... Hauptverwaltung [*Main Administration For*] (EG)
Hv .... Hava [*Air*] (TU)
Hv .... Havacilik [*Aviation*] (TU)
HV .... Heimevernel [*Home Guard*] [*Norwegian*] (WEN)
HV .... Henschel-Verlag [*Henschel Publishing House*] (EG)
hv .... Hevosvoima [*or Hevosvoimaa*] [*Finnish*]
hv .... Hivatasos [*Professional*] (HU)
HV .... Hlavni Velitel [*Commander-in-Chief*] (CZ)
HV .... Hlavni Velitelstvi [*Main Command*] (CZ)
H V .... Hyva Veli [*Finnish*]
HV .... Upper Volta [*Two-letter standard code*] (CNC)
HVA .... Handels Vereniging Amsterdam (MAR)
HVA .... Hauptverwaltung Aufklaerung [*Main Administration for Intelligence Collection*] (EG)
HVA .... Hauptverwaltung fuer Ausbildung [*Main Administration for Training (People's Police)*] (EG)
HVDGP .... Hauptverwaltung Deutsche Grenzpolizei [*Main Administration of the German Border Police*] (EG)
HVDSZ .... Helyiipari es Varosgazdasagi Dolgozok Szakszervezete [*Trade Union of Municipal and Local Economy Workers*] (HU)
HVDVP .... Hauptverwaltung Deutsche Volkspolizei [*Main Administration of the German People's Police*] (EG)
HVE .... Hauptverwaltung Elektromaschinenbau [*Main Administration for Electrical Machine Production*] (EG)
HVF .... Hauptverwaltung Fernmeldewesen [*Main Administration for Telecommunications*] (EG)
HVIA .... Hauptverwaltung Innen- und Aussenhandel [*Main Administration for Inner-German and Foreign Trade*] (EG)
HVK .... Havarieverhuetungskommission [*Sea-Damage Prevention Commission*] (EG)
Hv KK Ted Bsk ... Hava Kuvvetleri Komutanligi Tedarik Baskanligi [*Air Force Command Procurement Chief*] (TU)
Hv Kuv .... Hava Kuvvetler [*Air Force*] (TU)
HVL .... Hauptverwaltung Luftpolizei [*Main Administration for the Air Police*] (EG)
HVLM .... Hauptverwaltung Leichtmaschinenbau [*Main Administration for Light Machine Building*] (EG)
HVM .... Hauptverwaltung fuer Maschinenwirtschaft [*Main Administration for Machine Management*] (EG)
Hv Mey .... Hava Meydani [*Airfield*] (TU)
HVO .... Upper Volta [*Three-letter standard code*] (CNC)
HVRC .... Honneur Vous Rendre Compte [*For Your Information*] (CL)
HVS .... Hauptverwaltung fuer Schulung [*Main Administration for Training*] (EG)
HVS .... Hauptverwaltung Seepolizei [*Main Administration for the Maritime Police*] (EG)
HVS .... Hlavni Vozatajsky Sklad [*Main Supply Depot*] (CZ)
HVTS .... Hospodarska a Vedeckotechnicka Spoluprace [*Economic and Scientific Technical Cooperation*] (CZ)
HVU .... Hasicska Vyzbrojni Ustredna [*Central Fire-Fighting Equipment Depot*] (CZ)
HVV .... Hlavni Vojenske Velitelstvi [*Supreme Military Command*] (CZ)
Hw .... Hauptwort [*German*]
HWF .... Halbleiterwerk Frankfurt/Oder (VEB) [*Frankfurt-Oder Semiconductor Plant (VEB)*] (EG)
HWP .... Hungarian Workers' Party (PPW)
HwSt .... Handwerkssteuer [*Handicraft Tax*] (EG)
HWWA .... Hamburgisches Weltwirtschaftsarchiv (MAR)
HY .... Helsingin Yliopisto [*University of Helsinki*] [*Finnish*]
Hydr .... Hydraulique [*Hydraulic*] [*Military map abbreviation*] [*World War I*] [*French*] (MTD)
Hydroprojekt ... Statni Ustav pro Projektovani Vodnich Staveb [*State Institute for the Design of Hydraulic Constructions*] (CZ)
hyp .... Hypothecaire [*On Mortgage*] [*French*]
hyp .... Hypotheque [*Mortgage*] [*French*]
Hyt .... Heyet [*Committee, Commission*] (TU)
Hz .... Haubitze-Zuender [*Howitzer Fuse*] [*Military*] [*German*] (MTD)
Hz .... Hazretleri [*His Excellency*] [*Turkish*] (GPO)
HZ .... Hemiska Zastita [*Chemical Defense*] (YU)
Hz .... Herc [*Hertz*] [*Polish*]
Hz .... Hertz [*Hertz*] (EG)
HZ .... Hidrometeoroloski Zavod [*Hydrometeorological Institute*] (YU)
Hz .... Hizmet [*or Hizmetler*] [*Service or Services*] (TU)
HZ .... Hospodarska Zmluva [*Economic Contract*] (CZ)
HZ .... Hurtownia Zbytu [*Wholesale Outlets*] (POL)
HZA .... Hauptzollamt [*Main Customs Office*] (EG)
Hzg .... Herzog [*German*]
HZMLJ .... Hriscanska Zajednica Mladih Ljudi [*Young Men's Christian Association (YMCA)*] (YU)
HZZO .... Hlavni Zavody pro Zeleninu a Ovoce [*Central Vegetable and Fruit Enterprise*] (CZ)

I

I .... East (BU)
I .... Elektrische Stromstaerke [*Strength of Electrical Current*] [*German*]
I- .... Fighter Airplane (RU)
I .... Hospital for Contagious Diseases (RU)
i .... Id [*That*] [*Latin*] (GPO)
I .... Idus [*The Ides*] [*Latin*] (GPO)
I- .... Ignitron (RU)
I .... Ihr [*Your*] [*German*]
I .... Ile [*Island*] [*French*] (NAU)
I .... Ile [*Island*] [*Military map abbreviation*] [*World War I*] [*French*] (MTD)
I .... Ilha [*Island*] [*Portuguese*] (NAU)
I .... Ilheu [*or Ilhota*] [*Islet*] [*Portuguese*] (NAU)
i .... Illalla [*Finnish*]
I .... Ilot [*Islet*] [*French*] (NAU)
i .... Im [*or In*] [*In or In The*] (EG)
i .... Immortalis [*Immortal*] [*Latin*] (GPO)
i .... Improbatur [*Latin*]
i .... Indul [*Departing*] (HU)
I .... Ingenieur [*Engineer*] [*French*]
I .... Inginer [*Romanian*]
I .... Instantanee [*Instantaneous*] [*Military*] [*French*] (MTD)
I- .... Instruction, Directive (RU)
I .... Insula [*Island*] [*Romanian*] (NAU)
I .... Internatura [*Advanced medical studies*] [*Russian*]
I .... Inzynier [*Professional title*] [*Polish*]
I .... Isla [*Island*] [*Spanish*] (NAU)
I .... Islote [*Islet*] [*Spanish*] (NAU)
I .... Isola [*or Isole*] [*Island or Islands*] [*Italian*] (NAU)
I .... Isolotto [*or Isolotti*] [*Islet or Islets*] [*Italian*] (NAU)
I .... Istok [*East*] (YU)
i .... Iv [*Sheet*] (HU)
I .... Izgrev [*Sunrise*] [*A periodical*] (BU)
I .... Nominative [*Case*] (RU)
I .... Set of Tools, Set of Instruments (RU)
I .... Wlochy [*Italy*] [*Polish*]
Ia .... Army Inspector (BU)
IA .... Fighter Aviation (BU)
IA .... Fighter Aviation (RU)
IA .... Historical Archives (RU)
ia .... Im Allgemeinen [*In General*] [*German*]
iA .... Im Auftrage [*For, By Order, Under Instruction*] [*German*] (WEN)
iA .... In Absenz [*In Absentia*] [*German*]
IA .... Ingenieur Agronome [*French*]
IA .... Inspector of Artillery (RU)
IA .... Instantanee Allongee [*Military*] [*French*] (MTD)
IA .... Institute of Archaeology (RU)
IA .... Instituto de Angola (MAR)
IA .... Interciencia Association [*Latin American*] (EA)
IA .... Intermediaire Agree [*Accredited Intermediary*] [*Refers to banks*] [*Cambodian*] (CL)
IA .... Intreprinderea de Autocamioane [*Truck Enterprise*] (RO)
IA .... True Azimuth (RU)
IAA .... Institute of Administrative Accountants (EA)
IAA .... Instituto do Acucar e do Alcool [*Sugar and Alcohol Institute*] [*Brazilian*] (LA)
IAA .... International Aerosol Association (EA)
IAA .... International African Association (MAR)
IAA .... International Association of Art [*See also AIAP*] (EA)
IAAC .... International Association for Analogue Computation [*Belgian*]
IAACC .... Ibero-American Association of Chambers of Commerce [*See also AICO*] (EA)
IAAE .... Institute of Anthropology, Archaeology, and Ethnography (RU)
IAAE .... International Association of Agricultural Economists (MAR)
IAAF .... International Amateur Athletic Federation [*See also FIAA*] (EA)
IAAFE .... Instituto Autonomo Administracion Ferrocarriles del Estado [*Venezuelan*]
IAAIP .... Inter-American Association of Industrial Property [*See also ASIPA*] (EA)
IAALD .... International Association for Agricultural Librarians and Documentalists [*United Kingdom*]
IAAS .... Institute of African and Asian Studies (MAR)
IAAS .... International Association of Agricultural Students [*See also AIEA*] (EA)
IAB .... Engineer Aviation Battalion (RU)
iab .... Fighter Air Base (BU)
IAB .... Fighter Air Brigade (RU)
IAB .... International Association of Bibliophiles [*See also AIB*] (EA)
IAB .... Internationale Akademie fuer Bader-, Sport-, und Freizeitheitbau [*International Board for Aquatic, Sports, and Recreation Facilities*] (EA)
IABA .... International Association of Aircraft Brokers and Agents (EA)
IABAR .... Inter-African Bureau for Animal Resources (MAR)
IABC .... International Association of Building Companions [*See also IBO*] (EA)
IABE .... Ibero-American Bureau of Education [*See also OEI*] (EA)
IABG .... International Association of Buying Groups [*See also IVE*] (EA)
IABM .... International Association of Broadcasting Manufacturers (EA)
IABO .... International Association of Biblicists and Orientalists (EA)
IABS .... International Association of Biological Standardization [*See also AISB*] (EA)
IABS .... International Association for Byzantine Studies [*See also AIEB*] (EA)
IAC .... Indefinite Arrival Confirmed (MAR)
IAC .... Institut d'Aviation Civile (MAR)
IAC .... Institute of Administration and Commerce of South Africa (MAR)
IAC .... Insurance Advisory Council [*Mauritian*] (AF)
IAC .... Inter-Afrique Charters (MAR)
IAC .... International Academy of Ceramics [*See also AIC*] (EA)
IAC .... International Artists' Cooperation (EA)
IAC .... International Association for Cybernetics [*See also AIC*] (EA)
IAC .... Intreprinderea de Aprovizionare pentru Constructii [*Enterprise for Construction Supply*] (RO)
IACA .... International Air Carrier Association (EA)
IACA .... International Association for Classical Archaeology [*See also AIAC*] (EA)
IACAHP .... Inter-African Advisory Committee for Animal Health and Production (MAR)
IACC .... Instituto de Aeronautica Civil de Cuba [*Cuban Civil Aeronautics Institute*] (LA)
IACCE .... Inter-American Confederation for Catholic Education (EA)
IACDOCTER ... International Advisory Committee on Documentation and Terminology [*UNESCO*]
IACED .... Inter-African Advisory Committee on Epizootic Diseases (MAR)
IACI .... Iran Aircraft Industries (ME)
IACL .... International Association of Constitutional Law [*See also AIDC*] (EA)
IACME .... Intreprinderea de Aprovizionare pentru Constructii si Montaje Energetice [*Supply Enterprise for Power Constructions and Installations*] (RO)
IACO .... Inter-African Coffee Organization (AF)
IACOD .... International Agency for Cooperation and Development (MAR)
IACODLA ..... International Advisory Committee on Documentation, Libraries, and Archives [*UNESCO*]
IACR .... International Association of Cancer Registries (EA)
IACRDVT ..... Inter-American Centre for Research and Documentation on Vocational Training [*See also CINTERFOR*] (EA)
IACRE .... Intreprinderea de Aprovizionare pentru Centrale si Retele Electrice [*Supply Enterprise for Electric Plants and Networks*] (RO)
IACSS .... Inter-American Conference on Social Security [*See also CISS*] (EA)
IACT .... Inter-Association Commission on Tsunami (EA)
IAD .... Bulletin of the Archeological Society [*A publication*] (BU)
IAD .... Fighter Air Division (BU)
IAD .... Fighter Air Division (RU)
IAD .... Inomeni Araviki Dimokratia [*United Arab Republic*] (GC)
IAD .... Instituto Agrario Dominicano [*Dominican Agrarian Institute*] [*Dominican Republic*] (LA)

IAD .... Internationale Arbeitsgemeinschaft Donauforschung [*International Working Association for Danube Research*] (EA)
IADB .... Inter-American Defense Board (LA)
IA-DBVK ..... Historical Archives at the Vasil Kolarov State Library (BU)
IADC .... International Agricultural Development Centre [*Arab*] (MAR)
IADC .... International Association of Dentistry for Children (EA)
IAdEM .... Internacia Asocio de Esperantistaj Matematikistoj [*International Association of Esperantist Mathematicians*] (EA)
IADH .... International Association of Dentistry for the Handicapped (EA)
IADIZA .... Instituto Argentino de Investigaciones de la Zona Arida [*Argentine Arid Zone Research Institute*] (LA)
IADMFR .... International Association of Dento-Maxillo-Facial Radiology (EA)
IADP .... Integrated Agricultural Development Project (MAR)
IADSL .... Instituto Americano para el Desarrollo del Sindicalismo Libre [*American Institute for Free Labor Development*] [*Use AIFLD*] (LA)
IAE .... Fighter Air Squadron (RU)
IAE .... Institute of Anthropology, Archaeology, and Ethnography (RU)
IAE .... Institute of Anthropology and Ethnography (of the Academy of Sciences, USSR) (RU)
IAE .... Institute of Atomic Energy Imeni I. V. Kurchatov (of the Academy of Sciences, USSR) (RU)
IAE .... Institute of Automation and Electrometry (RU)
IAE .... Instituto de Atividades Espaciais [*Space Activities Institute*] [*Brazilian*] (LA)
IAEA .... Institute of Asian Economic Affairs (MAR)
IAEA .... International Association of Empirical Aesthetics (EA)
IAEA .... International Atomic Energy Agency (WEN)
IAEAC .... International Association of Environmental Analytical Chemistry (EA)
IAEC .... International Association of Electrical Contractors [*See also AIE*] (EA)
IAEC .... Intreprinderea de Aparataje Electrice pentru Constructii [*Enterprise for Electrical Equipment for Constructions*] (RO)
IAEC .... Iran Atomic Energy Commission (ME)
IAEDEN .... Instituto de Altos Estudios para la Defensa Nacional [*Institute of Higher Studies for National Defense*] [*Venezuelan*] (LA)
IAEE .... International Association for Earthquake Engineering (EA)
IAEE .... International Association of Energy Economists [*Arab*] (MAR)
IAEL .... International Association of Entertainment Lawyers (EA)
IAEM .... Instituto de Altos Estudos Militares [*Institute of Advanced Military Studies*] [*Portuguese*] (WER)
IAEMS .... International Association of Environmental Mutagen Societies (EA)
IAEN .... Instituto de Altos Estudios Nacionales [*Institute for Higher National Studies*] [*Ecuadorean*] (LA)
IAESTE .... International Association for the Exchange of Students for Technical Experience (MAR)
IAEVG .... International Association for Educational and Vocational Guidance [*See also AIOSP*] (EA)
IAEVI .... International Association for Educational and Vocational Information [*See also AISUP*] (EA)
IAF .... Fundacion Interamericana [*Inter-American Foundation*] (LA1)
IAF .... Inter-African Force (AF)
IAF .... International Aikido Federation (EA)
IAF .... International Apparel Federation (EA)
IAF .... International Astronautical Federation (SJT)
IAF .... Internationales Afrika Forum [*A publication*] (MAR)
IAF .... Israel Air Force (ME)
IAF .... Societe Interafricaine de Financement (MAR)
IAFA .... International African Friends of Abyssinia (MAR)
IAFCI .... Inter-American Federation of the Construction Industry [*See also FIIC*] (EA)
IAFCT .... International Association of French-Speaking Congress Towns [*See also AIVFC*] (EA)
IAFES .... International Association for the Economics of Self-Management (EA)
IAFMM .... International Association of Fish Meal Manufacturers (EA)
IAG .... IFIP [*International Federation for Information Processing*] Administrative Data Processing Group [*Dutch*]
IAG .... Instituto de Adminstracion General de la Escuela de Administracion Publica [*Bogota*] (COL)
IAG .... International Association of Geodesy (EA)
IAG .... Investitionsauftraggeber [*Capital Investment Contractor (Enterprise or organization responsible for planning and carrying out an investment project)*] (EG)
IAGESA .... Istanbul-Anadoluhisari Genclik ve Spor Akademisi [*Istanbul-Anadoluhisari Youth and Sports Academy*] (TU)
IAGLL .... International Association of Germanic Languages and Literatures [*See also IVG*] (EA)
IAGOD .... International Association of the Genesis of Ore Deposits (EA)
IAGSC .... Intreprinderea de Administrare a Grupurilor Sociale si Cantinelor [*Enterprise for the Management of Social Groups and Canteens*] (RO)
IAH .... Internationales Arbeiter-Hilfswerk [*International Workers Aid*] (EA)
IAHB .... International Association of Human Biologists (EA)
IAHI .... International Association of Hail Insurers (EA)
IAHM .... International Academy of the History of Medicine (EA)
IAHP .... International Academy of the History of Pharmacy (EA)
IAHR .... International Association for the History of Religions (EA)
IAHRC .... Inter-American Human Rights Commission (LA)
IAI .... Bulletin of the Archaeological Institute [*A publication*] (BU)
IAI .... Historical and Archaeographical Institute (of the Academy of Sciences, USSR) (RU)
IAI .... Institut Africain d'Informatique [*African Data Processing Institute*] (AF)
IAI .... International African Institute (AF)
IAI .... Investigaciones Agro-Industriales [*Agroindustrial Research*] [*Peruvian*] (LA)
IAI .... Israel Aircraft Industries (ME)
IAI .... Moscow State Institute of Historical Archives (RU)
IAIALAR ...... Ibero-American Institute of Agrarian Law and Agrarian Reform [*See also IIDARA*] (EA)
IAIE .... International Association for Integrative Education (EA)
IAIN .... Institut Agama Islam Negeri [*State Islamic Institute*] (IN)
IAIN .... International Association of Institutes of Navigation (EA)
IAI RANION ... Institute of Archaeology and Art Studies of the Russian Association of Scientific Research Institutes (RU)
IAIRI .... International Association of Insurance and Reinsurance Intermediaries [*See also BIPAR*] (EA)
IAJ .... International Association of Judges (EA)
IAK .... Chamber of Engineers and Architects (BU)
iak .... Fighter Air Corps (BU)
IAK .... Fighter Air Corps (RU)
IAK .... Internationales Auschwitz-Komitee [*International Auschwitz Committee*] (EA)
IAK .... News of the Archaeological Commission [*A publication*] (RU)
IAKh .... Idiais avtou Khersi [*(To Be Delivered) to the Addressee in Person or to the Addressee Only*] (GC)
IAKS .... Internationaler Arbeitskreis Sport- und Freizeiteninrichtungen [*International Working Group for the Construction of Sports and Leisure Facilities*] (EA)
IAL .... International Affairs (London) [*A publication*] (MAR)
IAL .... Intreprinderea de Administratie Locativa [*Enterprise for Housing Administration*] (RO)
IALA .... International African Law Association (AF)
IALA .... Islamic Alliance for the Liberation of Afghanistan (PD)
IALB .... Institut fuer Auslaendische Landwirtschaft (Berlin) [*A publication*] (MAR)
IALHI .... International Association of Labour History Institutions (EA)
IALL .... International Association of Law Libraries
I allg .... Im Allgemeinen [*In General, Generally Speaking*] (EG)
IALS .... International Association of Legal Science [*See also AISJ*] (EA)
IAM .... Institute of Aircraft Engines (RU)
IAM .... Institute of Aviation Medicine (RU)
IAM .... Intreprinderea de Aprovizionare cu Materiale [*Materials Supply Enterprise*] (RO)
IAM .... Pulse-Amplitude Modulation (RU)
IAMA .... International Abstaining Motorists' Association (EA)
IAMANEH .... International Association for Maternal and Neonatal Health (EA)
IAMB .... Intreprinderea de Aprovizionare a Municipiului Bucuresti [*Supply Enterprise for Bucharest Municipality*] (RO)
IAMBE .... International Association of Medicine and Biology of Environment [*See also AIMBE*] (EA)
IAMC .... Intreprinderea de Aparate de Masura si Control [*Enterprise for Measurement and Control Instruments*] (RO)
IAMCR .... International Association for Mass Communication Research (MAR)
IAMFS .... International Association for Maxillo-Facial Surgery (EA)
IAMHIST ..... International Association of Audio-Visual Media in Historical Research and Education (EA)
IAMIC .... International Association of Mutual Insurance Companies [*See also AISAM*] (EA)
IAML .... International Association of Music Libraries, Archives, and Documentation Centres [*See also AIBM*] (EA)
IAMMM .... International Association of Margaret Morris Method (EA)
IAMO .... Interafrikanisch-Madegassische Organisation [*Inter-African and Malagasy Organization*] (MAR)
IAMS .... International Association for Mission Studies (EA)
IAMSLIC ..... International Association of Marine Science Libraries and Information Centers
IAMSO .... Inter-African and Malagasy State Organisation (MAR)
IAMVVS ...... Institute of Aviation Medicine of the Air Force (RU)
IAMY .... International Assembly of Muslim Youth (MAR)
IAN .... Institutions d'Afrique Noire Annuaire de la Documentation Africaine (MAR)
IAN .... Instituto Agrario Nacional [*National Agrarian Institute*] [*Venezuelan*] (LA)
IAN .... Instituto de Asuntos Nucleares [*Nuclear Affairs Institute*] [*Colombian*] (LA)
IAN .... News of the Academy of Sciences [*A publication*] (RU)
IANA .... Inter-African News Agency (AF)
IANB .... Institutul Agronomic N. Balcescu [*N. Balcescu Agronomic Institute*] (RO)
IANC .... International Anatomical Nomenclature Committee (EA)
IANEC .... Inter-American Nuclear Energy Commission (LA)
IANLS .... International Association for Neo-Latin Studies (EA)

IANSA .... Industria Azucarera Nacional [*National Sugar Industry*] [*Chilean*] (LA)
IAO .... News of the Archaeological Society [*A publication*] (RU)
IAOMO .... International Association of Olympic Medical Officers (EA)
IAOS .... International Association of Oral Surgeons (EA)
IAP .... Fighter Air Regiment (RU)
IAP .... Industrial Arbitration Panel (MAR)
IAP .... Industrie-Abgabepreis [*Industrial Sales Price*] (EG)
IAP .... Institut Algerien de Petrole [*Algerian Petroleum Institute*] (AF)
IAP .... Institute for African Prehistory (MAR)
IAP .... Instituto de Aposentadoria e Pensoes [*Retirement and Pension Institute*] [*Brazilian*] (LA)
IAP .... Institutul de Anatomie Patologica [*Institute for Pathological Anatomy*] (RO)
IAPA .... Inter-American Press Association (LA)
IAPAS .... Instituto de Administracao da Previdencia e Assistencia Social [*Institute for the Administration of Social Assistance and Welfare*] [*Brazilian*] (LA)
IAPB .... Inter-African Phytosanitary Bureau [*OAU*] (MAR)
IAPB .... International Agency for the Prevention of Blindness (EA)
IAPC .... Instituto de Aposentadoria e Pensoes dos Comerciarios [*Brazilian*]
IAPCO .... International Association of Professional Congress Organizers (EA)
IAPF .... Inter-American Peace Force (LA)
IAPG .... International Association of Psychoanalytic Gerontology (EA)
IAPKE .... Istatistik, Arastirma-Planlama, Koordinasyon, ve Egitim Dairesi Reisligi [*Statistics, Research-Planning, Coordination, and Education Office*] [*Under Provinces Bank of Turkey*] (TU)
IAPL .... International Association of Penal Law (EA)
IAPL .... Intreprinderea de Alimentatie Publica Locala [*Local Public Food Service Enterprise*] (RO)
IAPN .... International Association of Professional Numismatists [*See also AINP*] (EA)
IAPP .... International Association for Plant Physiology (EA)
IAPS .... Institutos de Aposentadoria e Previdencia Social [*Retirement and Social Welfare Institutes*] [*Brazilian*] (LA)
IAPS .... Inter-American Press Society (LA)
IAPSC .... Inter-African Phytosanitary Commission (MAR)
IAPSIA .... Intreprinderea de Ambalaje si Piese de Schimb pentru Industria Alimentara [*Enterprise for Packaging and Spare Parts for the Food Industry*] (RO)
IAPTV .... Instituto Autonomo Postal y Telegrafico de Venezuela [*Autonomous Postal and Telegraph Institute of Venezuela*] (LA)
IAPUP .... International Association on the Political Use of Psychiatry (EA)
IAPUZV ...... Intreprinderea pentru Aprovizionarea cu Produse de Uz Zooveterinar [*Supply Enterprise for Products of Zooveterinary Usage*] (RO)
IAPVO .... Air Defense Fighter Aviation (RU)
IAPZ .... Irbit Automobile Trailer Plant (RU)
IAQ .... International Academy for Quality (EA)
IAR .... Expanding Interval Arithmetic (RU)
IAR .... Iemenskaia Arabskaia Respublika (MAR)
IAR .... Industria Aeronautica Romana [*Romanian Aeronautical Industry*] (RO)
i ar .... Inspector General of Artillery (BU)
IAR .... Institute of Agricultural Research (MAR)
IARC .... International Agency for Research on Cancer (EA)
IARD .... International Association for Rural Development (MAR)
IARI .... Indian Agricultural Research Institute (MAR)
IARIW .... International Association for Research on Income and Wealth (HU)
IARN .... Instituto de Apoio ao Retorno de Nacionais [*Institute of Assistance for Returnees*] [*Portuguese*] (WER)
IARR .... International Association for Radiation Research (EA)
IARSB .... International Association of Rolling Stock Builders [*See also AICMR*] (EA)
IARSEP .... Institut Africain de Recherches Sociales et Economiques pour l'Education Populaire [*African Institute of Social and Economic Research for Popular Education*] (AF)
IART .... Intreprinderea Auto Reparatii si Transporturi [*Auto Repair and Transportation Enterprise*] (RO)
IARU .... Internacionalna Amaterska Radio Unija [*International Amateur Radio Union*] (YU)
IAS .... Automatic Pulse System, Automatic Sampled-Data System (RU)
IAS .... Contracting Interval Arithmetic (RU)
IAS .... Engineer Aviation Service (RU)
IAS .... Fighter Air Unit (RU)
IAS .... Impot sur les Affaires et Services (MAR)
IAS .... Institute of African Studies (MAR)
IAS .... Institute of Earthquake-Proof Construction (of the Academy of Sciences, Turkmen SSR) (RU)
IAS .... Institutiile Administrative de Stat [*State Administrative Institutions*] (RO)
IAS- .... Integrating Air Sextant (RU)
IAS .... Interafricaine Socialiste (MAR)
IAS .... International Advertising Service [*Bogota*] (COL)
IAS .... International Atherosclerosis Society (EA)
IAS .... Intreprinderea Agricola de Stat [*State Agricultural Enterprise*] (RO)
IAS .... Intreprinderile Agricole Socialiste [*Socialist Agricultural Enterprises*] (RO)
IAS .... Isobaric Analog State (RU)
IAS .... Istoriski Arhiv Srbije [*Historical Archives of Serbia*] (YU)
IASA .... International Association of Sound Archives (EA)
IASAIL .... International Association for the Study of Anglo-Irish Literature (EA)
IASAJ .... International Association of Supreme Administration Jurisdictions (EA)
IASB .... Inter-African Soils Bureau [*OAU*] (MAR)
IASB .... International African Service Bureau (MAR)
IASB .... Intreprinderea de Articole de Sticlarie Bucuresti [*Bucharest Glassware Enterprise*] (RO)
IASC .... Inter-American Scout Committee [*See also CIE*] (EA)
IASC .... International Accounting Standards Committee (EA)
IASC .... International Association of Seed Crushers (EA)
IASEES .... International Association of South-East European Studies [*See also AIESEE*] (EA)
IASILL .... International Association for the Study of the Italian Language and Literature [*See also AISLLI*] (EA)
IASL .... International Association for the Study of the Liver (EA)
IASLIC .... Indian Association of Special Libraries and Information Centres
IASMF .... Instituto Argentino de la Soberania de los Espacios Maritimos y Fluviales [*Argentine Institute for Sovereignty over Maritime and Fluvial Areas*] (LA)
IASPEI .... International Association of Seismology and Physics of the Earth's Interior (EA)
IASPM .... International Association for the Study of Popular Music (EA)
IASRR .... Institute of African Studies. Research Review [*Legon*] [*A publication*] (MAR)
IASS .... International Association of Sanskrit Studies (EA)
IASS .... International Association for Scandinavian Studies (EA)
IASSW .... International Association of Schools of Social Work (MAR)
IAST .... Institute of Applied Science and Technology [*Guyanese*]
IASTED .... International Association of Science and Technology for Development (EA)
IAT .... Ivoire Aero-Technique (MAR)
IATA .... Institut Algerien de Technologie Agricole [*Algerian Agricultural Technology Institute*] (AF)
IATA .... International Air Transport Association (SJT)
IATASA .... Ingenieria y Asistencia Tecnica Argentina, Sociedad Anonima [*Argentine Engineering and Technical Assistance, Incorporated*] (LA1)
IATC .... Institutul de Arta Teatrala si Cinematografica [*Institute for Theater and Film Arts*] (RO)
IATc .... Intreprindere de Aparataj pentru Telecomunicatii [*Enterprise for Telecommunications Apparatus*] (RO)
IATDP .... International Association of Textile Dyers and Printers [*See also AITIT*] (EA)
IATEFL .... International Association of Teachers of English as a Foreign Language (EA)
IATG .... International Association of Teachers of German [*See also IDV*] (EA)
IATL .... International Association of Theological Libraries [*IFLA*]
IATM .... International Association of Transport Museums [*See also AIMT*] (EA)
IATM .... Intreprinderea de Aprovizionare Tehnico-Materiala [*Enterprise for Technical Material Supply*] (RO)
IATSA .... Intreprinderea de Asistenta Tehnica si Service pentru Autoturisme Dacia [*Enterprise for Technical Assistance and Service to Dacia Automobiles*] (RO)
IATSS .... International Association of Traffic and Safety Sciences (EA)
IATT .... Inter-Africaine de Transit et de Transport (MAR)
IAT (TK) ...... Institute of Automation and Remote Control (Engineering Cybernetics) (RU)
IATUL .... International Association of Technical University Libraries [*Delft*]
IAU .... International Association of Universities
IAUPS .... Intreprinderea de Aprovizionare cu Utilaje si Piese de Schimb [*Enterprise for Equipment and Spare Parts Supply*] (RO)
IAUTM .... Ingiliz Askeri Uslerinde Turk Memurlar [*Turkish Workers of the British Military Bases*] [*Turkish Cypriot*] (GC)
IAV .... Instituto de Auxilios y Viviendas [*Institute for Help in Housing*] [*Dominican Republic*]
IAVA .... Instituto Alfredo Vasquez Acevedo [*Alfredo Vasquez Acevedo Institute*] [*Uruguayan*] (LA)
IAVS .... International Association for Vegetation Science [*See also IVV*] (EA)
IAvS .... Intreprinderea Avicola de Stat [*State Poultry Raising Enterprise*] (RO)
IAVSD .... International Association for Vehicle Systems Dynamics (EA)
IAW .... International Alliance of Women [*See also AIF*] (EA)
IAWE .... International Association for Wind Engineering (EA)
IAWL .... International Association for Water Law [*See also AIDA*] (EA)
IAWMC .... International Association of Workers for Maladjusted Children [*See also AIEJI*] (EA)
IAWP .... International Association of Women Philosophers (EA)
IAWR .... International Working Community of Waterworks in the Rhine River Basin [*Western European*] (WEN)

IAZ.............. Inspectoratul Agro-Zootehnic [*Agrozootechnical Inspectorate*] (RO)
IB................ Actuating Unit (RU)
IB................ Communicable Diseases Hospital (BU)
ib................ Engineer Battalion (RU)
IB................ Executive Bureau (BU)
ib................ Ibidem [*In the Same Place*] [*Latin*] (GPO)
ib................ Im Besonderen [*In Particular*] (EG)
IB................ Instituuts Bibliotheken
IB................ Instytut Bibliograficzny [*Bibliographical Institute*] (POL)
IB................ Investicni Banka [*Investment Bank*] (CZ)
IB................ Irian Barat [*West Irian*] (IN)
IB................ Istanbul Belediyesi [*Istanbul Municipality*] (TU)
IB................ Test Unit (RU)
IBA.............. Fighter-Bomber Aviation (RU)
IBA.............. Industrie Bois Africains (MAR)
IBA.............. International Bartenders Association (EA)
IBA.............. International Bauxite Association (LA)
IBA.............. International Biliary Association (EA)
IBA.............. Israel Broadcasting Authority (MAR)
ibab............ Fighter-Bomber Air Base (BU)
IBAC............ Instituto de Bachillerato, Administracion, y Contaduria [*Bogota*] (COL)
IBAD............ Bulletin of the Bulgarian Archaeological Society [*A publication*] (BU)
ibad............ Fighter-Bomber Aviation Division (BU)
ibad............ Fighter-Bomber Division (RU)
IBADAN....... Ibadan; A Journal Published at University College [*Ibadan*] [*A publication*] (MAR)
IBAH............ Inter-African Bureau for Animal Health (AF)
IBAHP.......... Inter-African Bureau for Animal Health and Protection (MAR)
IBAI............ Bulletin of the Bulgarian Archaeological Institute [*A publication*] (BU)
ibak............ Fighter-Bomber Air Wing (BU)
ibap............ Fighter-Bomber Regiment (RU)
IBAR............ Inter-African Bureau for Animal Resources (AF)
IBASECON ... Compania Administradora de Inversion Finibec SA (COL)
IBATE.......... Instituto Brasileiro de Analise Tecnica e Estatistica [*Brazilian Institute of Technical and Statistical Analysis*] (LA1)
i B auf.......... In Berechnung Auf [*Calculated on the Basis Of*] [*German*]
IBB.............. Instytut Badawczy Budownictwa [*Construction Research Institute*] (POL)
IBBA............ Instituto Boliviano de Biologia de la Altura [*Bolivian Institute of Biology of the Highland*] (LA1)
IBBD............ Bulletin of the Bulgarian Botanical Society [*A publication*] (BU)
IBBD............ Instituto Brasileiro de Bibliografia e Documentacao [*Brazilian Institute of Bibliography and Documentation*] (LA)
IBC.............. Instituto Brasileiro do Cafe [*Brazilian Coffee Institute*] (LA)
IBC.............. Instituto Brasileiro do Comercio [*Brazilian Commerce Institute*] (LA)
IBCC............ International Building Classification Committee [*Rotterdam*]
IBD.............. Instytut Bodowy Drog [*Road Construction Institute*] (POL)
IBDF............ Instituto Brasileiro de Desenvolvimento Florestal [*Brazilian Forestry Development Institute*] (LA)
IBE.............. History of the Bulgarian Language (BU)
IBE.............. International Bureau for Epilepsy (EA)
IBEA............ Imperial British East Africa Co. (MAR)
IBEA............ Instituto Brasileiro de Estudos Antarticos [*Brazilian Institute for Antarctic Studies*] (LA)
IBEAC.......... Imperial British East Africa Company (MAR)
IBEC............ International Basic Economy Corporation [*Venezuelan*] (MAR)
IBECC.......... Instituto Brasileiro de Educacao, Ciencia, e Cultura [*Brazilian Education, Science, and Culture Institute*] (LA)
IBED............ Interafrican Bureau for Epizootic Diseases (MAR)
IBEE............ Instituto Boliviano de Estudios Economicos [*Bolivian Institute for Economic Research*] (LA1)
IBEI.............. Iktisadi Iliskiler Dairesi Genel Mudurlugu [*Economic Affairs Office Directorate General*] [*of Foreign Affairs Ministry*] (TU)
IBEL............ Instituto Brasileiro de Estudos Literarios [*Brazilian Literary Studies Institute*] (LA)
IBELCO....... Institut Belge de Cooperation Technique [*Belgian Institute for Technical Cooperation*] (AF)
IBERSOM.... Institute Belge pour l'Encouragement de la Recherche Scientifique Outre-Mer (MAR)
IBERTO....... Societe Industrielle et Commerciale Ibero-Togolaise (MAR)
IBES............ Instituto Boliviano de Estudios Sociologicos [*Bolivian Institute of Social Studies*] (LA)
IBETEX........ Industrie Beninoise des Textiles [*Beninese Textile Industry*] (AF)
ibf................ Fighter-Bomber Squadron (BU)
IBF.............. Institute of Biophysics (of the Academy of Sciences, USSR) (RU)
IBF.............. Institutul de Balneologie si Fizioterapie [*Institute for Balneology and Physiotherapy*] (RO)
IBF.............. International Badminton Federation (EA)
IBF.............. International Balint Federation (EA)
IBF.............. International Balut Federation (EA)
IBF.............. International Bandy Federation (EA)
IBFAN.......... International Baby Food Action Network (MAR)
IBFG............ Internationaler Bund Freier Gewerkschaften [*International Confederation of Free Trade Unions (ICFTU)*] (WEN)
IBG.............. Incorporated Brewers' Guild (EA)
IBG.............. Industriebaukombinat [*Industrial Construction Combine*] (EG)
IBGE............ Instituto Brasileiro de Geografia e Estatistica [*Brazilian Institute of Geography and Statistics*] (LA)
IBGT............ Institute of British Geographers. Transactions and Papers [*London*] [*A publication*] (MAR)
IBHASA....... Industria Boliviana del Hierro y Acero, Sociedad Anonima [*Bolivian Iron and Steel Company, Incorporated*] (LA)
IBI................ Industria Biancheria Intima-Italia [*Italian*] (MAR)
IBI................ Intergovernmental Bureau for Informatics (EA)
IBI-BAN....... Institute of Bulgarian History of the Bulgarian Academy of Sciences (BU)
IBIC............ Industria de Bisuteria Contemporanea [*Bogota*] (COL)
IBICT.......... Instituto Brasileiro de Informacao en Ciencia e Tecnologia [*Rio De Janerio and Brasilia, Brazil*]
IBID............ Bulletin of the Bulgarian Historical Society [*A publication*] (BU)
ibid.............. Ibidem [*In the Same Place*] [*Latin*] (GPO)
IBIS............ Integrated On-Line Bibliotheks-System
IBJ.............. Instytut Badan Jadrowych [*Institute of Nuclear Research*] (POL)
IBK.............. Industrial Bank of Kuwait (ME)
IBK.............. Institut fuer Bekleidungskultur [*Institute of Clothing Design*] (EG)
IBKA............ Ikatan Buruh Kereta Api [*Railway Workers Association*] (IN)
IBKB............ Ikatan Buruh Kendaraan Bermotor [*Motor Vehicle Workers Association*] (IN)
IBKGiC........ Instytut Badania Koniunktur Gospodarczych i Cen [*Research Institute on Economics and Prices*] (POL)
IBL.............. Instructions on Issuing Medical Certificates for Temporary Disability (BU)
IBL.............. Instytut Badan Literackich [*Literary Research Institute*] (POL)
IBL.............. Instytut Badawczy Lesnictwa [*Forestry Research Institute*] (POL)
IBLA............ Institut des Belles-Lettres Arabes [*Tunisian*] (MAR)
IBM.............. Instytut Budownictwa Mieszkaniowego [*Housing Construction Institute*] (POL)
IBM.............. Intreprinderile Banatiene Metalurgice [*Banat Metallurgical Enterprises*] (RO)
IBMP............ Institute for Emergency Medical Aid (BU)
IBN.............. High-Voltage Indicator (RU)
IBN.............. Institut Belge de Normalisation [*Belgian*]
IBN.............. Voltage Test Unit (RU)
IBO.............. Instituto Batlle y Ordonez [*Batlle-Ordonez Institute*] [*Uruguayan*] (LA)
IBO.............. International Baccalaureate Office [*See also OBI*] (EA)
IBO.............. Internationale Bouworde [*International Association of Building Companions - IABC*] (EA)
IBOCO......... Industrie du Bois Congolais [*Congolese Lumber Industry*] (AF)
IBOOI.......... Hospital for Particularly Dangerous Communicable Diseases (BU)
IBOPE.......... Instituto Brasileiro de Opiniao Publica e Estatistica [*Brazilian Public Opinion and Statistics Institute*] (LA)
IBP.............. International Biological Programme (MAR)
IBPC............ Institutul de Biologie si Patologie Celulara [*Institute for Biology and Cell Pathology*] (RO)
IBPD............ Bulletin of the Bulgarian Speleological Society [*A publication*] (BU)
IBPT............ Instituto de Biologia e Pesquisas Tecnologicas [*Biology and Technological Research Institute*] [*Brazilian*] (LA)
ibpu............ Engineer Battalion Organization of the Command Post (BU)
IBQN............ Instituto Brasileiro da Qualidade Nuclear [*Brazilian Nuclear Quality Institute*] (LA)
IBR.............. Fast-Neutron Pulsed Reactor (RU)
Ibr................ Ibraniceden [*Hebrew*] (TU)
IBRA............ Instituto Brasileiro de Reforma Agraria [*Brazilian Agrarian Reform Institute*] (LA)
IBRA............ International Bible Reading Association (EA)
IBRADES..... Instituto Brasileiro de Desenvolvimento [*Brazilian Development Institute*] (LA)
IBRD............ International Bank for Reconstruction and Development [*Also known as World Bank*]
IBS.............. Incorporated Bronte Society (EA)
IBS.............. Instituto Brasileiro de Siderurgia [*Brazilian Iron and Steel Institute*] (LA)
IBS.............. Instruction on Budget Accounts (BU)
IBS.............. International Boundary Studies [*A publication*] (MAR)
IBS.............. Islamic Broadcasting Services (ME)
IBSA............ International Blind Sports Association [*See also AISA*] (EA)
IBSS............ Instituto Boliviano de Seguro Social [*Bolivian Social Security Institute*] (LA)
IBST............ International Bureau of Social Tourism [*See also BITS*] (EA)
IBTA............ Instituto Boliviano de Tecnologia Agropecuaria [*Bolivian Institute of Agricultural-Livestock Technology*] (LA1)
IBTE............ Imperial Board of Telecommunications in Ethiopia (AF)
IBTK............ Iranian-Bulgarian Transportation Company (BU)
IBU.............. Ikatan Belia Utama [*Association of Outstanding Youth*] (ML)
IBUSZ.......... Idegenforgalmi, Beszerzesi, Utazasi, es Szallitasi Reszvenytarsasag [*Touring, Money Changing, Traveling, and Shipping Co. Ltd.*] (HU)

IBV .... Institute of the Biology of Water Reservoirs (RU)
IBW .... Instytut Budownictwa Wodnego [*Institute of Hydrotechnics*] [*Polish*]
IBWA .... International Bank for West Africa (AF)
IBWZ .... Internationale Bank fuer Wirtschaftliche Zusammenarbeit [*International Bank for Economic Cooperation*] (EG)
IBYKP .... Ikinci Bes Yillik Kalkinma Programi [*Second Five-Year Development Program*] [*See also UBYKP*] (TU)
IBYS .... Instituto de Biologia y Sueroterapia, SA [*Institute of Biology and Serum Therapy, Inc.*] [*Spanish*] (WER)
IC .... Infracrveni [*Infrared*] (YU)
IC .... Ingenieur de Conception [*French*]
IC .... Institute of Ceramics (EA)
IC .... Islamic Congress (MAR)
IC .... Istoriski Casopis [*Historical Journal*] [*Belgrade*] [*A publication*] (YU)
IC .... Izquierda Cristiana [*Christian Left*] [*Chilean*] (LA)
ICA .... Imprimerie Centrale d'Afrique [*Central Printing Office of Africa*] [*Central African*] (AF)
ICA .... Ingenieros Civiles Asociados [*Associated Civil Engineers*] [*Mexican*] (LA)
ICA .... Institut Culturel Africain [*African Cultural Institute*] (AF)
ICA .... Instituto de Ciencia Animal [*Institute of Animal Science*] [*Cuban*] (LA)
ICA .... Instituto Colombiano Agropecuario [*Colombian Agricultural and Animal Sciences Institute*] (LA)
ICA .... Instituto de Credito Agricola [*Institute of Agricultural Credit*] [*Venezuelan*] (LA)
ICA .... Institutul de Cercetari Alimentare [*Food Research Institute*] (RO)
ICA .... Institutul de Cercetari pentru Apicultura [*Apiculture Research Institute*] (RO)
ICA .... International Co-Operative Alliance (MAR)
ICA .... International Cocoa Agreement (MAR)
ICA .... International Commission on Acoustics (EA)
ICA .... International Commodity Agreements (MAR)
ICA .... International Congress of Africanists (EA)
ICA .... International Cooperation Administration [*USA*] (MAR)
ICA .... International Council on Archives
ICA .... Israel Consumers' Association (MAR)
ICAA .... International Civil Airports Association (EA)
ICAA .... International Council on Alcohol and Addictions (WEN)
ICAB .... Intreprinderea de Canal Apa Bucuresti [*Bucharest Canal Water Enterprise*] (RO)
ICAB .... Societe Industrie Camerounaise des Annexes du Batiment (MAR)
ICACCP .... International Commission Against Concentration Camp Practices (EA)
ICAD .... Societe Israelo-Centrafricaine de Diamants (MAR)
ICAE .... International Council for Adult Education (EA)
ICAED .... Interafrican Advisory Committee on Epizootic Diseases (MAR)
ICAES .... International Congress of Anthropological and Ethnological Sciences (MAR)
ICAF .... International Committee on Aeronautical Fatigue (EA)
ICAI .... International Commission for Agricultural and Food Industries (MAR)
ICA/IADF .... International Council on Archives/Archival Development Fund
ICAIC .... Instituto Cubano de Arte e Industria Cinematografica [*Cuban Institute of Cinematographic Arts and Industry*] (LA)
ICAITI .... Central American Research Institute for Industry [*Guatemalan*]
ICAITI .... Instituto Centroamericano de Investigacion y Tecnologia Industrial [*Central American Industrial Research Institute*] (LA)
ICALU .... International Confederation of Arab Labour Unions (MAR)
ICAM .... Imprimerie Commerciale et Administrative de Mauritanie (MAR)
ICAM .... Institut Culturel Africain et Mauricien (MAR)
ICAM .... International Confederation of Architectural Museums (EA)
ICAMI .... International Committee Against Mental Illness (MAR)
ICAN .... Institute of Chartered Accountants of Nigeria (MAR)
ICAO .... International Civil Aviation Organization (WER)
ICAP .... Instituto Centroamericano de Administracion Publica [*Central America Institute of Business Administration*] [*San Jose, Costa Rica*] (LA1)
ICAP .... Instituto de Credito Agricola y Pecuario [*Venezuelan*]
ICAP .... Instituto Cubano de Amistad con los Pueblos [*Cuban Institute for Friendship with Peoples*] (LA)
ICAR .... Indian Council for Agricultural Research (MAR)
ICAR .... Information Caraibe [*Caribbean Information*] (LA1)
ICAR .... Institutul de Cercetari Agronomice Roman [*Romanian Institute of Agronomic Research*] (RO)
ICAR .... Intreprinderea pentru Constructii Aeronautice Romane [*Enterprise for Romanian Aeronautical Constructions*] (RO)
ICARE .... Instituto Chileno de Administracion Racional de Empresas [*Chilean Institute for Efficient Administration of Industries*] (LA)
ICARIS .... International Campaign Against Racism in Sport (MAR)
ICAS .... Institutul de Cercetari si Amenajari Silvice [*Institute for Forestry Research*] (RO)
ICAS .... Intreprinderile de Canalizare, Apa, si Salubritate [*Sewage, Water, and Sanitary Engineering Enterprises*] (RO)
ICASA .... Industria Colombiana de Artefactos [*Bogota*] (COL)
ICASALS .... International Center for Arid and Semi-Arid Land Studies (MAR)
ICASC .... International Contraception Abortion and Sterilization Campaign (EA)
ICASE .... Instituto Centroamericano de Administracion y Supervision de la Educacion
ICAT .... Industrie Centrafricaine de Textile [*Central African Textile Industry*] (AF)
ICAT .... International Committee for the Coordination of Clinical Application and Teaching of Autogenic Therapy (EA)
ICATO .... Iranian Civil Aviation Training Organization (MAR)
ICATU .... International Confederation of Arab Trade Unions (ME)
ICAZ .... Intreprinderea de Constructii Agro-Zootehnice [*Enterprise for Agrozootechnical Construction*] (RO)
ICB .... Icisleri Bakanligi [*Ministry of Internal Affairs*] (TU)
ICB .... Industrial Credit Bank [*Iranian*] (ME)
ICB .... Intercontinentale des Bois (MAR)
ICB .... International Council for Building Research, Studies, and Documentation [*Rotterdam*]
ICBD .... International Council of Ballroom Dancing (EA)
ICBF .... Instituto Colombiano de Bienestar Familiar [*Colombian Family Welfare Institute (Bogota)*] (LA)
ICBP .... International Council for Bird Preservation (EA)
ICBUL .... Industrias de Ceramica e Betao do Ultramar (MAR)
ICC .... Imprimerie Commerciale du Cameroun (MAR)
ICC .... Indice de Construcao Civil [*Civil Construction Index*] [*Brazilian*] (LA)
ICC .... Ingenieria de Consulta y de Control [*Cali*] (COL)
ICC .... Institutul Central de Chimie [*Central Institute for Chemistry*] (RO)
ICC .... Institutul de Cercetari Chimice [*Chemical Research Institute*] (RO)
ICC .... Institutul de Cercetari Comerciale [*Trade Research Institute*] (RO)
ICC .... Institutul de Cercetari pentru Constructie [*Construction Research Institute*] (RO)
ICC .... International Association for Cereal Chemistry (EA)
ICC .... International Cello Centre (EA)
ICC .... International Chamber of Commerce [*See also CCI*] (EA)
ICC .... International Coffee Council (MAR)
ICC .... International Computation Center [*UNESCO*]
ICC .... International Computing Centre [*Geneva, Switzerland*]
ICC .... International Coordinating Committee for the Presentation of Science and the Development of Out-of-School Scientific Activities [*See also CIC*] (EA)
ICC .... International Corrosion Council (EA)
ICC .... International Supervisory and Control Commission [*Use ISCC*] (CL)
ICC .... Inuit Circumpolar Conference (EA)
ICC .... Iran Carbon Company (ME)
ICC .... Iran Communications Company (ME)
ICCA .... Industrie Cotonniere Centrafricaine [*Central African Cotton Industry*] (AF)
ICCA .... Institutul Central de Cercetari Agricole [*Central Institute for Agricultural Research*] (RO)
ICCA .... International Corrugated Case Association (EA)
ICCA .... International Council for Commercial Arbitration (EA)
ICCAS .... Intreprinderea de Conditionare, Conservare, si Ambalare a Semintelor [*Enterprise for the Treatment, Preservation, and Packaging of Seeds*] (RO)
ICCAT .... International Commission for the Conservation of the Atlantic Thonids (MAR)
ICCATCI .... International Committee to Coordinate Activities of Technical Groups in Coatings Industry (EA)
ICCC .... Institutul Central pentru Cercetari Chimice [*Central Institute for Chemical Research*] (RO)
ICCC .... International Concentration Camp Committee (EA)
ICCE .... Instituto Colombiano de Comercio Exterior [*Colombian Foreign Trade Institute (Bogota)*] [*Formerly, OAPEC*] (LA)
ICCE .... Instituto Colombiano de Construcciones Escolares [*Colombian Schools Construction Institute*] (LA)
ICCE .... Institutul Central de Cercetari Economice [*Central Institute for Economic Research*] (RO)
ICCE .... Institutul Central pentru Cercetari Energetice [*Central Institute for Energy Research*] (RO)
ICCE .... Institutul de Cercetari pentru Componente Electronice [*Research Institute for Electronic Components*] (RO)
ICCEC .... Intergovernmental Council of Copper Exporting Countries (AF)
ICCF .... Institutul de Cercetari Chimico-Farmaceutice [*Pharmaceutical-Chemical Research Institute*] (RO)
ICCJ .... International Council of Christians and Jews (EA)
ICCM .... International Committee for the Conservation of Mosaics (EA)
ICCM .... International Council of Catholic Men [*See also FIHC*] (EA)
ICCN .... International Committee of Catholic Nurses [*See also CICIAMS*] (EA)
ICCO .... International Carpet Classification Organization (EA)
ICCO .... International Cocoa Organization (EA)

ICCP............ Institutul de Cercetari pentru Cultura Porumbului [*Research Institute for Corn Growing*] (RO)
ICCP............ International Committee for Coal Petrology (EA)
ICCPDC ...... Institutul Central de Cercetare, Proiectare, si Directivare in Constructii [*Central Institute for Construction Research, Design, and Direction*] (RO)
ICCPT .... Institutul de Cercetari pentru Cereale si Plante Tehnice [*Research Institute for Grains and Technical Crops*] (RO)
ICCR............ Interfaith Center for Corporate Responsibility (MAR)
ICCR............ International Committee for Coal Research (EA)
ICCROM...... Centre International d'Etudes pour la Conservation et la Restauration des Biens Culturels [*International Centre for the Study of the Preservation and the Restoration of Cultural Property*] (EA)
ICCS............ International Commission on Civil Status [*See also CIEC*] (EA)
ICCS............ International Committee on Clinical Sociology [*See also CISC*] (EA)
ICCS............ International Committee of Creole Studies (EA)
ICD .... Institute of Civil Defence (EA)
ICD .... International Centre for Development (MAR)
ICD .... Intreprinderea Chimica Dudesti [*Dudesti Chemical Enterprise*] (RO)
ICD .... Intreprinderea de Constructii Drumuri [*Road Building Enterprise*] (RO)
ICDA............ International Coalition for Development Action (MAR)
ICDBL.......... International Committee for the Defense of the Breton Language [*See also CISLB*] (EA)
ICDC .... Industrial and Commercial Development Corporation (MAR)
ICDE............ International Council for Distance Education (EA)
ICDI .... Instituto Cubano de la Demanda Interna [*Cuban Domestic Consumer Demand Institute*] (LA)
ICDIQ .... Instituto Cubano para el Desarrollo de la Industria Quimica [*Cuban Institute for Development of the Chemical Industry*] (LA)
ICDM........... Instituto Cubano de Desarrollo de Maquinaria [*Cuban Institute for Machinery Development*] (LA)
ICDT............ Institutul Central de Documentare Tehnica [*Central Institute for Technical Documentation*] (RO)
ICE .... Instituto de Comercio Exterior [*Foreign Trade Institute*] [*Venezuelan*] (LA)
ICE .... Instituto Costarricense de Electricidad [*Costa Rican Electricity Institute*] (LA)
ICE .... Institutul de Cercetari Economice [*Economic Research Institute*] (RO)
ICE .... Institutul de Cercetari Electronice [*Electronic Research Institute*] (RO)
ICE .... Institutul de Cercetari Energetice [*Institute for Energy Research*] (RO)
ICE .... International Council on Electrocardiology (EA)
ICE .... Intreprinderea de Calculatoare Electronice [*Electronic Computer Enterprise*] (RO)
ICE .... Intreprinderea de Comert Exterior [*Foreign Trade Enterprise*] (RO)
ICE .... Istituto per il Commercio Estero [*Foreign Trade Institute*] [*Italian*] (WER)
ICEA............ Instituto Cubano de Estabilizacion del Azucar [*Cuban Sugar Stabilization Institute*] (LA)
ICEA............ Institutul de Cercetari pentru Economie Agrara [*Research Institute for the Agrarian Economy*] (RO)
ICEAM......... International Committee on Economic and Applied Microbiology (EA)
ICEAOIAS ... Institutul de Cercetari pentru Economie Agrara si Organizarea Intreprinderilor Agricole Socialiste [*Research Institute for the Agrarian Economy and the Organization of Socialist Agricultural Enterprises*] (RO)
ICEC............ Instituto Cultural Ecuatoriano [*Ecuadorean Cultural Institute*] (LA)
ICEC............ Institutul de Cercetari pentru Carbune [*Coal Research Institute*] (RO)
ICECHIM..... Institutul Central de Cercetari Chimice [*Central Institute for Chemical Research*] (RO)
ICECU .... Instituto Centroamericano de Extension de la Cultura [*Central American Institute of Culture Extension*] [*Costa Rican*] (LA)
ICED............ International Council for Educational Development (MAR)
ICED............ Intreprinderea de Constructii Edilitare si Drumuri [*Enterprise for Municipal and Road Construction*] (RO)
ICEFIZ......... Institutul Central de Fizica [*Central Physics Institute*] (RO)
ICEI .... Instituto Colombiano de Estudios Internacionales de la Escuela de Administracion Publica [*Bogota*] (COL)
ICEI .... Instituto de Comercio Exterior e Integracion [*Institute for Foreign Trade and Integration*] [*Ecuadorean*] (LA)
ICEIL .... Institutul de Cercetari pentru Industria Lemnului si Hirtiei [*Research Institute for the Wood and Paper Industry*] (RO)
ICEIN........... Ingenieros, Constructores, e Interventores Ltda. [*Bogota*] (COL)
ICEL .... Instituto Colombiano de Energia Electrica [*Colombian Electrical Power Institute*] (LA)
ICEL .... International Committee for Ethnic Liberty [*See also IKEL*] (EA)
ICEM .... Institutul de Cercetari Metalurgice [*Institute for Metallurgical Research*] (RO)
ICEM .... Institutul de Constructii si Exploatari Miniere [*Institute for Mine Constructions and Exploitation*] (RO)
ICEM .... Intergovernmental Committee for European Migration (MAR)
ICEMENERG ... Institutul de Cercetari si Modernizari Energetice [*Institute for Power Research and Modernization*] (RO)
ICEMET....... Institutul de Cercetari Metalurgice a Minereurilor [*Institute for the Metallurgical Research of Ores*] (RO)
ICEMIN........ Institutul de Cercetari Miniere [*Mining Research Institute*] (RO)
ICENERG .... Institutul de Cercetari Electroenergetice si pentru Termoficare [*Electric and Thermal Power Research Institute*] (RO)
ICEPROM.... Institutul de Cercetari si Proiectari Miniere si Metalurgice [*Institute for Mining and Metallurgy Research and Design*] (RO)
ICEPRONAV ... Institutul de Cercetari si Proiectari Navale [*Institute for Naval Research and Design*] (RO)
ICEPS.......... Institutul pentru Cercetare, Experimentare, si Productie Semi-Industriala [*Institute for Semi-Industrial Research, Experiments, and Production*] (RO)
ICEPS.......... Istituto per la Cooperazione con i Paesi in Via di Sviluppo [*Institute for Cooperation with Developing Countries*] [*Italian*] (AF)
ICES............ Institut Congolais d'Enseignement Social (MAR)
ICES............ Institutul de Cercetari Silvice [*Institute for Silvicultural Research*] (RO)
ICET .... Institutul de Cercetari Electrotehnice [*Electrotechnical Research Institute*] (RO)
ICET .... Institutul de Cercetari pentru Telecomunicatii [*Institute for Telecommunications Research*] (RO)
ICET .... International Centre for Earth Tides (EA)
ICETEX .... Instituto Colombiano de Credito Educativo y Estudios Tecnicos en el Exterior [*Colombian Educational Credits and Overseas Technical Studies Institute*] (LA)
ICEVH .... International Council for Education of the Visually Handicapped (EA)
ICF .... Institutul Central de Fizica [*Central Physics Institute*] (RO)
ICF .... Institutul de Cercetari Forestiere [*Institute for Forestry Research*] (RO)
ICF .... Institutul Clinic de Ftiziologie [*Clinical Institute for Phthisiology*] (RO)
ICF .... International Canoe Federation [*See also FIC*] (EA)
ICF .... International Casting Federation (EA)
ICF .... International Christian Fellowship (MAR)
ICF .... International Communication Films (MAR)
ICF .... International Congress on Fracture (EA)
ICF .... Intreprinderea Cailor Ferate [*Railways Enterprise*] (RO)
ICF .... Islamic Charter Front [*Sudanese*] (MAR)
ICFA............ Industria Colombo Francesa de Aluminio [*Bogota*] (COL)
ICFCM......... Institutul de Cercetari Farmaceutice si Controlul Medicamentelor [*Institute for Pharmaceutical Research and Control of Drugs*] (RO)
ICFE .... Institutul de Cercetari pentru Foraj si Extractie [*Research Institute for Drilling and Extraction*] (RO)
ICFES.......... Instituto Colombiano para el Fomento de la Educacion Superior [*Formerly, FUN*] [*Colombian Institute for Promotion of Higher Education*] (LA)
ICFL .... International Council of the French Language [*See also CILF*] (EA)
ICFMH......... International Committee on Food Microbiology and Hygiene (EA)
ICFTU.......... International Confederation of Free Trade Unions (MAR)
ICG.............. Institutul de Cercetari Geografice [*Geographic Research Institute*] (RO)
ICG.............. International Commission on Glass [*See also CIV*] (EA)
ICGC .... Instituto Cubano de Geodesia y Cartografia [*Cuban Institute of Geodesy and Cartography*] (LA)
ICGEB .... International Center of Genetic Engineering and Biotechnology
ICGH .... International Confederation of Genealogy and Heraldry [*See also CIGH*] (EA)
ICGI............. Impuestos de Compensacion de Gravamenes Interiores [*Domestic Assessment Compensation Taxes*] [*Spanish*] (WER)
ICh .... Frequency Meter (RU)
ICH .... Instituto Cubano de Hidrografia [*Cuban Institute of Hydrography*] (LA)
ICH .... Institutul de Cercetari Hidrotehnice [*Hydrotechnical Research Institute*] (RO)
ICH .... Intreprinderea de Constructii Hidroenergetice [*Enterprise for Hydroelectric Power Constructions*] (RO)
ich .... Iodine Number (RU)
ICh .... Selective Quadripole (RU)
ICHA............ Instituto Chileno del Acero [*Chilean Steel Institute*] (LA)
ICHDA .... International Cooperative Housing Development Association (MAR)
IChF .... Instytut Chemii Fizycznej [*Institute of Physical Chemistry*] [*Polish*]
ICHF .... Intreprinderea de Constructii Hidrotehnice si Foraje [*Enterprise for Hydrotechnical Constructions and Drilling*] (RO)
IChKh.......... Frequency-Response Characteristic Meter (RU)
ICHLM......... International Conference of Historians of the Labour Movement (EA)

IChN............ Instytut Chemii Nieorganicznej [*Institute of Inorganic Chemistry*] [*Polish*]
I Ch O.......... Instytut Chemii Ogolnej [*Institute of General Chemistry*] (POL)
I Ch O.......... Instytut Chemii Organicznej [*Institute of Organic Chemistry*] (POL)
I Ch P.......... Instytut Chemii Przemyslowej [*Institute of Industrial Chemistry*] (POL)
IChPW.......... Instytut Chemicznej Przerobki Wegla [*Institute for Chemical Processing of Coal*] [*Polish*]
ICHR............ Inter-American Commission on Human Rights [*OAS*] (PD)
ICHRPI........ International Commission for the History of Representative and Parliamentary Institutions (EA)
IChS............ Foreign Students Institute (BU)
ICHS............ Interafrican Committee for Hydraulic Studies (MAR)
ICHS............ International Council of Homehelp Services [*See also CISAF*] (EA)
IChSAN....... Publishing House of the Czechoslovak Academy of Sciences (RU)
ICHSMSS.... International Commission for the History of Social Movements and Social Structures (EA)
ICHV............ Institutul de Cercetari Hortiviticole [*Horticultural and Viticultural Research Institute*] (RO)
ICI................ Industria Carnii Ilfov [*Ilfov Meat Industry*] (RO)
ICI................ Institut de Cooperation Internationale (MAR)
ICI................ Institutul Central de Informatica [*Central Institute for Data Processing*] (RO)
ICIA.............. Intergovernmental Council for Information in Africa (AF)
ICIA.............. International Center of Information on Antibiotics (EA)
ICIA.............. International Credit Insurance Association (EA)
ICICA........... Institutul de Cercetari pentru Industrie si Chimie Alimentara [*Research Institute for Food Chemistry and Industry*] (RO)
ICID.............. Instituto Central de Investigacion Digital [*Central Institute for Digital Research*] [*Cuban*] (LA)
ICID.............. International Commission on Irrigation and Drainage [*See also CIID*] (EA)
ICIDA........... Instituto Cubano de Investigaciones de Derivados del Azucar [*Cuban Institute for Sugar Byproducts Research*] (LA)
ICIEP............ Institutul de Creatie Industriala si Estetica a Productiei [*Institute for Industrial Creativity and Production Aesthetics*] (RO)
ICIF.............. International Cooperative Insurance Federation (EA)
ICIFI............. International Council of Infant Food Industries (MAR)
ICIL.............. Intreprinderea de Colectare si Industrializare a Laptelui [*Enterprise for Milk Collection and Industrialization*] (RO)
ICIMC........... Institutul de Cercetari si Incercari a Materialelor de Constructii [*Institute for Research and Testing of Construction Materials*] (RO)
ICIMM.......... Instituto Cubano de Investigaciones Minero-Metalurgicas [*Cuban Institute of Mining and Metallurgical Research*] (LA)
ICINAZ......... Instituto Cubano de Investigaciones Azucareras [*Cuban Sugar Research Institute*] (LA)
ICIODI.......... Instituto Cubano de Investigaciones y Orientacion e la Demanda Interna [*Cuban Institute of Research and Orientation on Consumer Demand*] (LA)
ICIP.............. Intreprinderea de Constructii Instalatii Petroliere [*Enterprise for the Construction of Petroleum Installations*] (RO)
ICIPE............ International Centre of Insect Physiology and Ecology (EA)
ICIRA............ Instituto de Capacitacion e Investigacion sobre Reforma Agraria [*Agrarian Reform Training and Research Institute*] [*Chilean*] (LA)
ICIREPAT.... Committee for International Cooperation on Information Retrieval among Examining Patent Offices [*Swiss*]
ICIS.............. Independientes con Inclinacion Socialista [*Independents with Socialist Inclination*] [*Spanish*] (WER)
ICIT.............. Instituto Cubano de Investigaciones Tecnologicas [*Cuban Institute for Technical Research*] (LA)
ICITO/GATT... Interim Commission for the International Trade Organization/General Agreement on Tariffs and Trade [*Swiss*]
ICJ................ Institutul de Cercetari Juridice [*Institute for Juridical Research*] (RO)
ICJ................ International Commission of Jurists (MAR)
ICJ................ International Court of Justice (MAR)
ICJC............. International Council of Jews from Czechoslovakia (EA)
ICL................ International Computers Limited (MAR)
ICL................ Intreprinderea Comerciala Locala [*Local Trade Enterprise*] (RO)
I Cl................ Prima Classe [*First Class*] [*Italian*] (GPO)
ICLAM.......... International Committee for Life Assurance Medicine (EA)
ICLARM....... International Center for Living Aquatic Resources Management (EA)
ICLC............. International Centre for Local Credit (EA)
ICLF............. Institutul de Cercetari pentru Legumicultura si Floricultura [*Research Institute for Vegetable and Flower Growing*] (RO)
ICLR............. International Committee for Lift Regulations [*See also CIRA*] (EA)
ICM............... Imposto sobre a Circulacao de Mercadorias [*Tax on Movement of Merchandise*] [*Brazilian*] (LA)
ICM............... Independent Citizens' Movement [*US Virgin Islands*] (PPW)
ICM............... Industries Chimiques Maghrebines [*Maghreb Chemical Industries*] [*Tunisian*] (AF)
ICM............... Intergovernmental Committee for Migration (MAR)
ICM............... International Confederation of Midwives (EA)
ICM............... Intreprinderea pentru Colectarea Materialelor [*Enterprise for the Collection of Materials*] (RO)
ICM............... Intreprinderea de Constructii-Montaj [*Constructions and Installations Enterprise*] (RO)
ICMA............ Institutul de Cercetari pentru Mecanizarea Agriculturii [*Research Institute for Agricultural Mechanization*] (RO)
ICMA............ International Christian Maritime Association (EA)
ICMA............ International City Management Association (MAR)
ICMA............ Intreprinderea de Constructii Metalice si Aparataje [*Enterprise for Metal Constructions and Equipment*] (RO)
ICMB............ Intreprinderea Cinematografica a Municipiului Bucuresti [*Bucharest Municipality Film Enterprise*] (RO)
ICMB............ Intreprinderea de Constructii-Montaj Bucuresti [*Bucharest Constructions and Installations Enterprise*] (RO)
ICMC............ Institutul de Cercetari pentru Materiale de Constructii [*Research Institute for Construction Materials*] (RO)
ICMC............ International Catholic Migration Commission [*See also CICM*] (EA)
ICME............ Intreprinderea de Cabluri si Materiale Electroizolante [*Enterprise for Cables and Electrical Insulation Materials*] (RO)
ICMEA.......... Institutul de Cercetari pentru Mecanizarea si Electrificarea Agriculturii [*Research Institute for the Mechanization and Electrification of Agriculture*] (RO)
ICMICA........ Pax Romana, International Catholic Movement for Intellectual and Cultural Affairs [*See also MIIC*] (EA)
ICML............ Intreprinderea de Constructii Metalice si Lemn [*Enterprise for Metal and Wood Constructions*] (RO)
ICMM............ Intreprinderea de Constructii si Montaje Metalurgice [*Enterprise for Metallurgical Constructions and Installations*] (RO)
ICMMR......... Intreprinderea de Constructii si Montaje Metalurgice Resita [*Resita Metallurgical Construction and Installation Enterprise*] (RO)
IC MON........ Instytucje Centralne Ministerstwa Obrony Narodowej [*Ministry of National Defense Central Institutions*] (POL)
ICMP............ Intreprinderea de Constructii Metalice si Prefabricate [*Enterprise for Metallic and Prefabricated Constructions*] (RO)
ICMPC.......... Intreprinderea Constructii-Montaj si Prestarea in Constructii [*Enterprise for Construction-Installation and Construction Services*] (RO)
ICMR............ Intreprinderea Constructoare de Masini Resita [*Resita Machine Building Enterprise*] (RO)
ICMS............ International Council of Military Sports (MAR)
ICMS............ Iran Center for Management Studies (ME)
ICMSG.......... Intreprinderea de Constructii si Montaje Siderurgice Galati [*Galati Enterprise for Iron and Steel Construction and Installation*] (RO)
ICN.............. International Communes Network (EA)
ICN.............. International Computers Nederland [*'s-Gravenhage*]
ICNAF.......... International Commission on Northeast Atlantic Fisheries (WER)
ICNEM......... International Center of the Neutral Esperanto Movement (EA)
ICNMCC...... Instituto Cubano de Normalizacion, Metrologia, y Control de Calidad [*Cuban Institute of Standardization, Metrology, and Quality Control*] (LA)
ICNT............ Informal Composite Negotiating Text (MAR)
ICO.............. International Carbohydrate Organization (EA)
ICO.............. International Cocoa Organization (MAR)
ICO.............. International Coffee Organisation (MAR)
ICO.............. International Commission for Optics [*See also CIO*] (EA)
ICO.............. Islamic Conference Organisation (MAR)
ICOBAL........ Industria Colombiana de Balones [*Bogota*] (COL)
ICOBAN....... Industria Colombiana de Bandas Ltda. [*Cali*] (COL)
ICOBORDADO... Industria Colombiana de Bordados Ltda. [*Bogota*] (COL)
ICOCIVIL..... Ingenieria y Construcciones Civiles [*Neiva*] (COL)
ICODA.......... Industrie Cotonniere du Dahomey (MAR)
ICODEMA... Industria Colombiana de Maderas [*Medellin*] (COL)
ICODEMPA... Industria Colombiana de Empaques [*Bogota*] (COL)
ICODES........ Instituto Colombiano de Desarrollo Social [*Colombian Social Development Institute*] (LA)
ICODI........... Societe des Impressions sur Tissus de Cote-d'Ivoire (MAR)
ICODIETETICOS... Industria Colombiana de Dieteticos Ltda. [*Bogota*] (COL)
ICOFIELTROS... Industria Colombiana de Fieltros (COL)
ICOFOS......... Industria Colombiana de Fosforos [*Bogota*] (COL)
ICOGRASA... Industria Colombiana de Aceites y Grasas Vegetales [*Bogota*] (COL)
ICOGRAV.... Industria de Grabado y Decoracion en Vidrio [*Bogota*] (COL)
ICOLAPIZ.... Industria Colombiana de Lapices [*Cali*] (COL)
ICOLD.......... International Commission on Large Dams [*See also CIGB*] (EA)
ICOLLANTAS... Industria Colombiana de Llantas [*Bogota*] (COL)
ICOLPAR..... Industria de Partes para Motores [*Bogota*] (COL)
ICOLTA........ Industria Colombiana de Tarjetas para Sistematizacion de Datos [*Bogota*] (COL)
ICOM............ International Council of Museums (CL)
ICOM............ Intreprinderea de Confectii Metalice [*Metal Products Enterprise*] (RO)
ICOME......... International Committee on Microbial Ecology (EA)

ICOMI.......... Industria e Commercio de Mineros, SA
ICOMOS...... Conseil International des Monuments et des Sites (MAR)
ICON........... Investment Company of Nigeria Ltd. (MAR)
ICONA......... Instituto Nacional para la Conservacion de la Naturaleza [*National Institute for the Preservation of Nature*] [*Spanish*] (WER)
ICONTAS.... Ingenieros Contratistas Asociados Ltda. [*Bucaramanga*] (COL)
ICONTEC.... Instituto Colombiano de Normas Tecnicas [*Bogota*] (COL)
ICOO........... Iraqi Company for Oil Operations (ME)
ICOPESCA... Industria Colombiana de Pesca [*Bogota*] (COL)
ICOPLAST... Industria Colombiana de Articulos Plasticos [*Barranquilla*] (COL)
ICOPLATA... Industria Colombiana de Articulos de Plata [*Cali*] (COL)
ICOPLAX..... Industria Colombiana de Articulos Plasticos [*Barranquilla*] (COL)
ICOPTERAP... Instituto Colombo Terapeutico Ltda. [*Bogota*] (COL)
ICOPULPA... Industria Colombiana de Pulpa [*Bogota*] (COL)
ICOS........... Industria Constructora de Obras [*Bogota*] (COL)
ICOSER....... Industria Costurera Americana Ltda. [*Bogota*] (COL)
ICOSIM....... Industrie Cotonniere Senegalaise d'Impression (MAR)
ICOT............ Industrie Cotonniere de l'Oubangui et du Tchad (MAR)
ICOT............ Interprovincial Coordinating Committee on Road Traffic (MAR)
ICOTAF....... Industrie Cotonniere Africaine [*African Cotton Industry*] [*Senegalese*] (AF)
ICOTAL....... Industrie Cotonniere Algerienne (MAR)
ICOTUERCAS... Industria Colombiana de Tuercas Ltda. [*Bogota*] (COL)
ICOZ............ Industrie Cotonniere d'Oued Zem [*Moroccan*] (MAR)
ICP.............. Instituto Cubano del Petroleo [*Cuban Petroleum Institute*] (LA)
ICP.............. Institutul de Cercetari Petrolifere [*Petroleum Research Institute*] (RO)
ICP.............. Institutul de Cercetari Piscicole [*Piscicultural Research Institute*] (RO)
ICP.............. Institutul de Cercetari si Proiectari [*Research and Design Institute*] (RO)
ICP.............. Instytut Celulozowo-Papierniczy [*Pulp and Paper Institute*] (POL)
ICP.............. International Comparison Project (MAR)
ICP.............. Iraqi Communist Party (PPW)
ICPA............ Institutul de Cercetari si Proiectari Alimentare [*Institute for Food Research and Planning*] (RO)
ICPA............ Institutul de Cercetari si Proiectari Automatizari [*Institute for Automation Research and Design*] (RO)
ICPAC......... Instituto Coreano-Panameno de Amistad y Cultura [*Korean-Panamanian Institute of Friendship and Culture*] (LA)
ICPAT.......... Institutul de Cercetari si Proiectari Automotive si Tractoare [*Institute for Automotive and Tractor Research and Design*] (RO)
ICPBB......... Intreprinderea de Constructii din Prefabricate de Beton Bucuresti [*Bucharest Enterprise for Prefabricated Concrete Constructions*] (RO)
ICPC............ Institutul de Cercetari Pielarie Cauciuc [*Institute for Leather and Rubber Research*] (RO)
ICPC............ International Cable Protection Committee (EA)
ICPC............ International Confederation of Popular Credit [*See also CICP*] (EA)
ICPCH......... Institutul de Cercetari si Proiectari pentru Industria de Celuloza si Hirtie [*Research and Design Institute for the Cellulose and Paper Industry*] (RO)
ICPCI........... Intreprinderea Comunala de Prestari si Constructii Ilfov [*Ilfov Communal Enterprise for Services and Constructions*] (RO)
ICPCMP...... Institutul de Cercetari Piele, Cauciuc, si Mase Plastice [*Research Institute for Leather, Rubber, and Plastics*] (RO)
ICPCSH....... Institutul de Cercetari si Proiectari pentru Celuloza, Stuf, si Hirtie [*Research and Design Institute for Cellulose, Reeds, and Paper*] (RO)
ICPDIL......... Institutul de Cercetare, Proiectare, si Documentare pentru Industria Lemnului [*Institute for Research, Design, and Documentation for the Wood Industry*] (RO)
ICPDILA...... Institutul de Cercetare, Proiectare, si Documentare pentru Industria Liantilor si Azbocimentului [*Institute for Research, Design, and Documentation for the Binder and Asbestos Cement Industry*] (RO)
ICPDS......... Institutul de Cercetare, Proiectare, si Documentare Silvica [*Institute for Research, Design, and Documentation in Silviculture*] (RO)
ICPE............ Institutul de Cercetare si Proiectare pentru Industria Electrotehnica [*Research and Design Institute for the Electrotechnical Industry*] (RO)
ICPE............ International Center for Public Enterprises in Developing Countries (EA)
ICPE............ International Commission on Physics Education [*See also CIEP*] (EA)
ICPEA......... Institutul de Cercetari pentru Economie Agrara [*Research Institute for the Agrarian Economy*] (RO)
ICPEHR....... Institutul de Cercetari si Proiectari pentru Echipamente Hidroenergetice din Resita [*Resita Research and Design Institute for Hydropower Equipment*] (RO)
ICPEMC...... International Commission for Protection Against Environmental Mutagens and Carcinogens (EA)
ICPET.......... Institutul de Cercetare si Proiectare Echipamente Termoenergetice [*Institute for Research and Design of Thermal Power Equipment*] (RO)
ICPET.......... Institutul de Cercetari si Proiectari Electrotehnice [*Institute for Electrotechnical Research and Design*] (RO)
ICPGA......... Institutul de Cercetari si Proiectari pentru Gospodarirea Apelor [*Research and Design Institute for Water Management*] (RO)
ICPIETG...... Institutul de Cercetari si Proiectari pentru Industria Extractiva de Titei si Gaz [*Research and Design Institute for the Crude Oil and Gas Extractive Industry*] (RO)
ICPIL........... Institutul de Cercetari si Proiectari pentru Industria Lemnului [*Research and Design Institute for the Wood Industry*] (RO)
ICPILA......... Institutul de Cercetari si Proiectari pentru Industria Liantilor si Azbocimentului [*Research and Design Institute for the Binder and Asbestos Cement Industry*] (RO)
ICPIPCM..... Institutul de Cercetari si Proiectari pentru Industria de Prelucrare Cauciuc si Mase Plastice [*Research and Design Institute for the Rubber and Plastics Processing Industry*] (RO)
ICPLF.......... Institutul de Cercetari Stiintifice si Proiectari privind Pastrarea si Valorificarea Legumelor si Fructelor [*Institute for Scientific Research and Design for the Preservation and Utilization of Vegetables and Fruits*] (RO)
ICPM........... Institutul de Cercetari si Proiectari Miniere [*Institute for Mining Research and Design*] (RO)
ICPMA......... Institutul de Cercetari si Proiectari de Masini Agricole [*Research and Design Institute for Agricultural Machinery*] (RO)
ICPMC......... Institutul de Cercetari si Proiectari pentru Industria Materialelor de Constructii [*Research and Design Institute for the Construction Materials Industry*] (RO)
ICPMFS....... Institutul de Cercetari si Proiectari Mecanica Fina si Scule [*Research and Design Institute for Precision Mechanics and Tools*] (RO)
ICPMMN...... Institutul de Cercetari si Proiectari Miniere si Metalurgice Neferoase [*Research and Design Institute for Nonferrous Mining and Metallurgy*] (RO)
ICPMS......... International Council of Prison Medical Services (EA)
ICPMTR....... Institutul de Cercetari si Proiectari pentru Masini de Transport si Ridicat [*Research and Design Institute for Transportation and Hoisting Machines*] (RO)
ICPMUA...... Institutul de Cercetare si Proiectare Masini Unelte si Agregate [*Institute for Research and Design of Machine Tools and Aggregates*] (RO)
ICPO............ Investment Cooperative Program Office [*Arab*] (MAR)
ICPP............ Institutul de Cercetari pentru Protectia Plantelor [*Research Institute for the Protection of Plants*] (RO)
ICPPD......... Institutul Central de Perfectionare a Personalului Didactic [*Central Institute for Advanced Training of Teaching Personnel*] (RO)
ICPPG......... Institutul de Cercetari si Proiectari pentru Petrol si Gaze [*Research and Design Institute for Oil and Gas Technology*] (RO)
ICPR............ Institutul di Cercetari si Proiectari Rafinarii [*Institute for Refinery Research and Design*] (RO)
ICPRAP....... International Commission for the Protection of the Rhine Against Pollution [*See also IKSR*] (EA)
ICPRP.......... Institutul de Cercetari si Proiectari Tehnologice pentru Rafinarii si Instalatii Petrochimice [*Institute for Technological Research and Design of Refineries and Petrochemical Installations*] (RO)
ICPS............ International Cerebral Palsy Society (EA)
ICPSH......... Institutul de Studii, Experimentari, si Proiectari pentru Stuf si Hirtie [*Institute for Studies, Experiments, and Design for Reeds and Paper*] (RO)
ICPSOR....... Institutul Central pentru Proiectarea si Sistematizarea Oraselor si Regiunilor [*Central Institute for Urban and Regional Design and Systematization*] (RO)
ICPT............ Institutul de Cercetare pentru Prelucrarea Titeiului [*Research Institute for Crude Oil Processing*] (RO)
ICPTANA.... Institutul de Cercetari si Proiectari in Transporturile Auto, Navale, si Aeriene [*Institute for Research and Design in Automotive, Naval, and Air Transportation*] (RO)
ICPTC......... Institutul de Cercetari si Proiectari pentru Tehnica de Calcul [*Research and Design Institute for Computer Technology*] (RO)
ICPTc.......... Institutul de Cercetari si Proiectari Telecomunicatii [*Research and Design Institute for Telecommunications*] (RO)
ICPTCM...... Institutul de Cercetari si Proiectari Tehnologice pentru Industria Constructiilor de Masini [*Research and Design Institute for the Machine Building Industry*] (RO)
ICPTSC....... Institutul de Cercetari si Proiectari Tehnologice pentru Sectoare Calde [*Technological Research and Design Institute for Hot Sectors*] (RO)
ICPTSCF..... Institutul de Cercetari si Proiectari Tehnologii Sticla si Ceramica Fina [*Research and Design Institute for the Technology of Glass and Fine Ceramics*] (RO)

ICPTT.......... Institutul de Cercetari si Proiectari Tehnologice in Transporturi [*Institute for Technological Research and Design for Transportation*] (RO)
ICPTUR....... International Conference for Promoting Technical Uniformity on Railways (EA)
ICPUCR....... Institutul de Cercetare si Proiectare Utilaj Chimic si Rafinarii [*Research and Design Institute for Chemical Equipment and Refineries*] (RO)
ICPUEC....... Institutul de Cercetari si Proiectari pentru Utilaje Electronice de Calcul [*Research and Design Institute for Electronic Computer Equipment*] (RO)
ICPUP.......... Institutul de Cercetari si Proiectari pentru Utilaj Petrolier [*Research and Design Institute for Petroleum Equipment*] (RO)
ICPUPS....... Institutul de Cercetari si Proiectari pentru Utilaje si Piese de Schimb [*Research and Design Institute for Equipment and Spare Parts*] (RO)
ICR.............. Indian Cooperative Review [*New Delhi*] [*A publication*] (MAR)
ICR.............. International Council for Reprography
ICR.............. Intreprinderea de Constructii si Reparatii [*Enterprise for Construction and Repair*] (RO)
ICR.............. Societe Tessieres Commerciale et Representation (MAR)
ICRA............ Intreprinderea Comertului cu Ridicata pentru Produse Alimentare [*Wholesale Trade Enterprise for Food Products*] (RO)
ICRAF.......... International Council for Research in Agroforestry (EA)
ICRAL.......... Intreprinderea de Constructii, Reparatii, si Administratie Locativa [*Enterprise for Housing Construction, Repair, and Administration*] (RO)
ICRB............ International Co-Operative Reinsurance Bureau (EA)
ICRC............ International Committee of the Red Cross (EA)
ICREP.......... Instituto Chileno de Relaciones Publicas [*Chilean Public Relations Institute*] (LA)
ICRET.......... Intreprinderea de Constructii si Reparatii Echipamente de Telecomunicatii [*Enterprise for the Construction and Repair of Telecommunications Equipment*] (RO)
ICRGR......... International Consultative Research Group on Rape [*See also GCIRC*] (EA)
ICRISAT...... International Crops Research Institute on Agriculture in Semi-Arid Tropics [*North African*] (MAR)
ICRM........... Instituto Cubano de Recursos Minerales [*Cuban Institute for Mineral Resources*] (LA)
ICRM........... Intreprinderea Comertului cu Ridicata pentru Produse Metalo-Chimice [*Wholesale Trade Enterprise for Metal-Chemical Products*] (RO)
ICRMA......... Intreprinderea de Constructii si Reparatii Materiale Aeronautice [*Enterprise for the Construction and Repair of Aeronautical Materials*] (RO)
ICRO............ Interallied Confederation of Reserve Officers [*See also CIOR*] (EA)
ICRO............ International Cell Research Organization (EA)
ICRP............ International Commission on Radiological Protection (SJT)
ICRPMA...... International Committee for Recording the Productivity of Milk Animals [*See also CICPLB*] (EA)
ICRT............ Instituto Cubano de Radio y Television [*Cuban Institute of Radio and Television*] (LA)
ICRTI........... Intreprinderea Comertului cu Ridicata pentru Textile si Incaltaminte [*Wholesale Trade Enterprise for Textiles and Footwear*] (RO)
ICRTv.......... Intreprinderea de Casete Radio si Televisoare [*Enterprise for Radio and Television Cabinets*] (RO)
ICRW........... International Center for Research on Women (MAR)
ICS.............. Industries Chimiques du Senegal [*Chemical Industries of Senegal*] (MAR)
ICS.............. Inspectia Comerciala de Stat [*State Trade Inspectorate*] (RO)
ICS.............. Institutul de Cercetari si Studii [*Institute for Research and Studies*] (RO)
ICS.............. International Camellia Society (EA)
ICS.............. International Chamber of Shipping (EA)
ICS.............. International Committee on Sarcoidosis (EA)
ICS.............. International Committee of Slavists (EA)
ICS.............. Intreprinderea Comerciala de Stat [*State Trade Enterprise*] (RO)
ICS.............. Prvni Celostatni Spartakiada [*First All-State Athletic Games*] (CZ)
ICSA............ Interim Common Services Agency (MAR)
ICSA............ International Committee Against Apartheid, Racism, and Colonialism in Southern Africa (EA)
ICSAF.......... International Commission for the Southeast Atlantic Fisheries [*See also CIPASE*] (EA)
ICSC............ Institutul de Cercetari Stiintifice pentru Constructii [*Scientific Research Institute for Constructions*] (RO)
ICSCF.......... Institutul de Cercetari Sticla si Ceramica Fina [*Research Institute for Glass and Fine Ceramics*] (RO)
ICSCMA...... Institutul Central pentru Sisteme de Conducere cu Mijloace de Automatizare [*Central Institute for Automated Management Systems*] (RO)
ICSEAF....... International Convention for South-East Atlantic Fisheries (MAR)
ICSEM......... International Commission for the Scientific Exploration of the Mediterranean Sea [*See also CIESM*] (EA)
ICSH............ International Committee for Standardization in Haematology (EA)
ICSH............ Intreprinderea de Constructii Siderurgice Hunedoara [*Hunedoara Enterprise for Iron and Steel Constructions*] (RO)
ICSID........... International Centre for the Settlement of Investment Disputes (MAR)
ICSIM.......... Intreprinderea de Constructii Speciale Industriale si Montaj [*Enterprise for Special Industrial Constructions and Installations*] (RO)
ICSL............ International Catalogue of Scientific Literature
ICSMCF...... Institutul pentru Controlul de Stat al Medicamentului si Cercetari Farmaceutice [*Institute for State Control of Drugs and Pharmaceutical Research*] (RO)
ICSMJ......... Institutul de Cercetari Stiintifice Medico-Judiciare [*Institute for Legal Medicine Scientific Research*] (RO)
ICSOR......... Institutul Central de Sistematizare a Oraselor si Regiunilor [*Central Institute for Urban and Regional Systematization*] (RO)
ICSPM......... Institutul de Cercetari Stiintifice pentru Protectia Muncii [*Scientific Research Institute for Labor Safety*] (RO)
ICSPS......... Institutul de Cercetari, Studii, si Proiectari Silvice [*Institute for Silvicultural Research, Studies, and Design*] (RO)
ICSRE......... International Centre for Studies in Religious Education (EA)
ICSS............ Instituto Colombiano de los Seguros Sociales [*Colombian Social Security Institute (Bogota)*] (LA)
ICSSD......... International Committee for Social Sciences Documentation [*French*]
ICSSVM...... International Commission for Small Scale Vegetation Maps (EA)
ICST............ Intreprinderea Constructii si Lucrari Speciale Transporturi [*Enterprise for Transportation Constructions and Special Projects*] (RO)
ICSTI........... International Center for Scientific and Technical Information (EA)
ICSTT.......... Institutul de Cercetari Stiintifice de Transporturi si Telecomunicatii [*Scientific Research Institute for Transportation and Telecommunications*] (RO)
ICSU............ International Council of Scientific Unions (SJT)
ICSU/AB..... International Council of Scientific Unions/Abstracting Board
ICSU-CTS... Committee on the Teaching of Science of the International Council of Scientific Unions (EA)
ICSW........... International Council of Social Welfare (MAR)
ICT.............. Ida College of Technology (MAR)
ICT.............. Institut fuer Chemie der Treibstoffe [*West German*]
ICT.............. Institute of Circuit Technology (EA)
ICT.............. Instituto Costarricense de Turismo [*Costa Rican Tourism Institute*] (LA)
ICT.............. Instituto de Credito Territorial [*Institute of Territorial Credit*] [*Colombian*] (LA)
ICT.............. Institutul de Cercetari Textile [*Textiles Research Institute*] (RO)
ICT.............. Institutul de Cercetari Transporturi [*Transportation Research Institute*] (RO)
ICT.............. International Council of Tanners [*See also CIT*] (EA)
ICTA............ Instituto de Ciencia y Tecnologia Agricola [*Agriculture Science and Technology Institute*] [*Guatemalan*] (LA1)
ICTA............ Ivory Coast Travel Agency (MAR)
ICTAA......... Imperial College of Tropical Agriculture Association (MAR)
ICTB............ Intreprinderea de Confectii si Tricotaje Bucuresti [*Bucharest Clothing and Knitwear Enterprise*] (RO)
ICTC............ Institutul de Cercetari pentru Tehnica de Calcul [*Research Institute for Computer Technology*] (RO)
ICTc............ Institutul de Cercetari Telecomunicatii [*Institute for Telecommunications Research*] (RO)
ICTCM......... Institutul de Cercetari Tehnologice pentru Constructii de Masini [*Technological Research Institute for Machine Construction*] (RO)
ICTMM........ International Congress on Tropical Medicine and Malaria (MAR)
ICTO............ Industrie Cotonniere de l'Oubangui et du Tchad (MAR)
ICTPIC........ Intreprinderea de Colectare si Transportul Paielor pentru Industria de Celuloza [*Enterprise for the Collection and Transportation of Straw and Cellulose Industry*] (RO)
ICTT............ Institutul de Cercetari pentru Transporturi si Telecomunicatii [*Research Institute for Transportation and Telecommunications*] (RO)
ICTV............ International Committee on Taxonomy of Viruses (EA)
ICU.............. Industrial and Commercial Workers' Union (MAR)
ICUAE......... International Congress of University Adult Education (EA)
ICUAER....... International Committee on Urgent Anthropological and Ethnological Research (EA)
ICUMSA...... International Commission for Uniform Methods of Sugar Analysis (EA)
ICUPECH.... Instituto Cultural Peruano-Chino [*Peru-China Cultural Institute*] (LA)
ICUS............ International Committee on Urgent Surgery (EA)
ICV.............. Indice do Custo de Vida [*Cost of Living Index*] [*Brazilian*] (LA1)
ICV.............. Istaknuti Centar Veze [*Advanced Communication Center*] [*Military*] (YU)
ICVA............ International Council of Voluntary Agencies [*Sudanese*] (MAR)

ICVA........... Intreprinderea Centrala pentru Valorificarea Ambalajelor [*Central Enterprise for Packaging Utilization*] (RO)
ICVAN......... International Committee on Veterinary Anatomical Nomenclature [*See also CINAV*] (EA)
ICVB........... Institutul de Cercetari Veterinare si Biopreparate [*Institute for Veterinary Research and Biological Preparations*] (RO)
ICVL........... Intreprinderea pentru Construirea si Vinzarea Locuintelor [*Enterprise for the Construction and Sale of Houses*] (RO)
ICVPA......... Intreprinderea Centrala pentru Valorificarea Produselor Animale [*Central Enterprise for the Utilization of Animal Products*] (RO)
ICVS........... Instituto Cultural Venezolano Sovietico [*Venezuelan-Soviet Cultural Institute*] (LA)
ICVSR......... Instituto Cubano-Venezolano de Solidaridad con la Revolucion [*Cuban-Venezuelan Institute for Solidarity with the Revolution*] (LA)
ICVT........... Institut de Cultures Vivrieres et Textiles (MAR)
ICW............ International Council of Women (MAR)
ICWA.......... Indian Council of World Affairs [*New Delhi*]
ICWB.......... Interministerieele Commissie voor Wetenschaps Beleid
ICWU.......... Industrial and Commercial Workers' Union (MAR)
ICYYLM....... International Commission on Yeasts and Yeast-Like Microorganisms (EA)
ICZ............. Infracrveni Zraci [*Infrared Rays*] (YU)
ICZ............. Institutul de Cercetari Zootehnice [*Institute for Zootechnical Research*] (RO)
ICZN........... International Commission on Zoological Nomenclature (EA)
i d............... Acting (BU)
id................ Acting (RU)
ID................ Actuating Motor (RU)
ID................ Engineering Sector [*Railroads*] (RU)
Id................ Idare [*Administration*] (TU)
id................ Ideiglenes [*Temporary, Provisional*] (HU)
id................ Idem [*The Same*] [*Spanish*]
id................ Idem [*The Same*] [*Latin*] (GPO)
id................ Idezes [*Summons, Writ*] (HU)
id................ Idezett [*The Passage Quoted*] (HU)
id................ Idosb [*or Idosebb*] [*Senior*] (HU)
ID................ Ikatan Dinas [*Service Contract*] (IN)
ID................ Imerisia Diatagi [*Order of the Day*] (GC)
ID................ Imerisia Diataxis [*Daily Agenda*] (GC)
ID................ Indonesia [*Two-letter standard code*] (CNC)
ID................ Inspektorat Dela [*Labor Inspectorate*] (YU)
ID................ Institute of Documentation (RU)
ID................ Institute of Rainmaking (RU)
ID................ Integrating Motor (RU)
ID................ Islamic Dinar (MAR)
ID................ Izin Devisen [*Foreign Exchange Permit*] (IN)
ID................ Izquierda Democratica [*Democratic Left*] [*Ecuadorean*] (PPW)
ID................ Pressure Gauge (RU)
ID................ Test Engine (RU)
Ida.............. Idare [*Administration*] (TU)
IDA............. Injection-Type Decontamination Device (RU)
IDA............. Institute for Development Anthropology, Inc. (MAR)
IDA............. Instituto de Desarrollo Agrario [*Agrarian Development Institute*] [*Costa Rican*] (LA1)
IDA............. International Development Agency [*North African*] (MAR)
IDA............. International Development Association (AF)
IDA............. International Dispensary Association [*Acronym is used as association name*] (EA)
IDAAN......... Instituto de Acueductos y Alcantarillados Nacionales [*National Water and Sanitation Institute*] [*Panamanian*] (LA)
IDAF........... International Defence and Aid Fund for Southern Africa (EA)
IDAI............ Institut du Developpement Agricole et Industriel [*Agricultural and Industrial Development Institute*] [*Haitian*] (LA)
IDAMF......... Interdenominational African Ministers' Federation (MAR)
IDATEX....... Industrie Dahomeenne du Textile (MAR)
IDB............. Industrial Development Bank (MAR)
IDB............. Insurance Development Bureau (EA)
IDB............. Inter-American Development Bank (WEN)
IDB............. Islamic Development Bank (ME)
IDBG........... Industries des Bois du Gabon (MAR)
IDBiH.......... Istorisko Drustvo Bosne i Hercegovine [*Historical Society of Bosnia and Hercegovina*] (YU)
IDBRA......... International Drivers' Behaviour Research Association (EA)
IDBS........... Intercollegiate Department of Black Studies (MAR)
IDC............. Industrial Development Corporation (MAR)
IDC............. Infection Disease Clinic (MAR)
IDC............. International Diamond Council (EA)
IDC............. International Documentation Centre
IDC............. Intreprinderea de Difuzarea Cartii [*Enterprise for the Distribution of Books*] (RO)
IDC............. Izquierda Democrata-Cristiana [*Christian-Democratic Left*] [*Spanish*] (WER)
IDC............. Izquierda Democratica Cristiana [*Christian Democratic Left Party*] [*Peruvian*] (LA)
IDCA........... International Development Cooperation Administration (MAR)
IDCA........... International Dragon Class Association (EA)
IDCAS......... Industrial Development Centre for the Arab States (MAR)
IDCh-.......... Frequency-Deviation Meter (RU)
IDDD........... Intreprinderea de Dezinfectie, Deratizare, si Dezinsectie [*Enterprise for Disinfection and Extermination of Rats and Insects*] (RO)
IDDKD......... Istanbul Devrimci Demokratik Kultur Dernegi [*Istanbul Revolutionary Democratic Cultural Organization*] (TU)
IDE............. Industrial Development Enterprise [*Cuban*] (LA)
IDE............. Institouton Dasikon Erevnon [*Forestry Research Institute*] [*Greek*] (GC)
IDEA........... Ieros Desmos Ellinon Andikommouniston [*Sacred Bond of Greek Anticommunists*] (GC)
IDEA........... Ieros Desmos Ellinon Axiomatikon [*Sacred Bond of Greek Officers*] (GC)
IDEA........... Instituto para el Desarrollo de Ejecutivos en la Argentina [*Institute for the Development of Executives in Argentina*] (LA)
IDEA........... Instituto de Estudios Africanos [*Institute of African Studies*] [*Spanish*] (AF)
IDEA........... Instituto de Estudios Argentinos [*Institute of Argentine Studies*] (LA)
IDEAL......... Instituto de Adaptacion Laboral [*Bogota*] (COL)
IDEASE....... Industria de Aceros [*Bogota*] (COL)
IDEB........... Intreprinderea de Distributie a Energiei Electrice Bucuresti [*Bucharest Enterprise for Electrical Power Distribution*] (RO)
IDEC........... Instituto Diverisificado de Educacion Comprensiva [*Cali*] (COL)
IDECEL....... Ingenieria de Construccion y Estudios [*Bogota*] (COL)
IDECOOP.... Instituto de Desarrollo y Credito Cooperativo [*Institute of Development and Cooperative Credit*] [*Dominican Republic*] (LA)
IDEF........... Institut International de Droit d'Expression Francaise [*International Institute of Law of the French Speaking Countries - IILFSC*] (EA)
ideigl.......... Ideiglenes [*Temporary*] (HU)
IDEL........... Industria de Lavado [*Bogota*] (COL)
IDELAC....... Instituto de la Construccion. Universidad del Valle [*Cali*] (COL)
IDELBO....... Industria de Leches de Boyaca [*Bogota*] (COL)
IDEM........... Instituto para el Desarrollo de la Empresa Moderna [*Institute for the Development of Modern Enterprise*] [*Argentine*] (LA)
IDEMA......... Industria de Maquinas y Mallas [*Cali*] (COL)
IDEMA......... Instituto de Mercadeo Agropecuario [*Agricultural and Livestock Marketing Institute (Bogota)*] [*Formerly, INA*] [*Colombian*] (LA)
IDEMPA...... Industrial de Empaque [*Cali*] (COL)
IDEN........... Inspecteur Departemental de l'Education Nationale [*French*]
IDEN........... Instituto de Engenharia Nuclear [*Brazilian*]
IDEO........... Industria de Equipos de Oficina Ltda. [*Bogota*] (COL)
IDEP........... Institut Africain de Developpement Economique et de Planification [*African Institute for Economic Development and Planning*] [*French*] (AF)
IDEP........... Instituto de Estudios Politicos (MAR)
IDEPA......... Industria de Bolsas de Papel Ltda. [*Bogota*] (COL)
IDEPAN....... Industria de Panaderos Nacionales [*Bogota*] (COL)
IDEPROM.... Industria de Productos Metalicos [*Bogota*] (COL)
IDEPTEX..... Industrias Deportivas Textiles Ltda. [*Medellin*] (COL)
IDERPC....... Institut de Developpement Economique de la Republique Populaire du Congo (MAR)
IDERT......... Institut d'Enseignement et de Recherches Tropicales (MAR)
IDES........... Instituto de Doctrina y Estudios Sociales [*Bogota*] (COL)
IDESCO....... Ingenieros de Estudios y Construcciones Ltda. [*Bogota*] (COL)
IDESSA....... Institut des Savanes (MAR)
IDET........... Institut de Developpement Economique et Technique [*Institute for Economic and Technical Development*] [*French*] (AF)
IDEX........... Instituto de Extension. Universidad del Valle [*Cali*] (COL)
IDEX........... Societe Ivoirienne de Distribution et d'Exportation (MAR)
IDF............. Inosinediphosphate (RU)
IDF............. Inosinediphosphoric Acid (RU)
IDF............. International Dairy Federation [*See also FIL*] (EA)
IDF............. Israel Defense Forces (ME)
IDFA........... Ilala District Football Association (MAR)
IDFF........... Internationale Demokratische Frauenfoederation [*Women's International Democratic Federation (WIDF)*] [*West German*] (WEN)
IDG............. Institutional Development Grant (MAR)
IDGB........... Intreprinderea de Distribuire a Gazului Metan Bucuresti [*Bucharest Enterprise for the Distribution of Methane Gas*] (RO)
IDGM.......... Istanbul Devlet Guvenlik Mahkemesi [*Istanbul State Security Court*] (TU)
IDGSA......... Istanbul Devlet Guzel Sanatlar Akademisi [*Istanbul State Fine Arts Academy*] [*See also DGSA, GSA*] (TU)
IDH............. Innerdeutscher Handel [*Inner-German Trade*] [*West German*] (WEN)
IDH............. Instituto para el Desarrollo Hondureno [*Honduran Development Institute*] (LA1)
IDHEC......... Institut des Hautes Etudes Cinematographiques [*Institute of Advanced Cinematographic Studies*] [*French*] (WER)
IDI.............. Ikatan Dokter Indonesia [*Indonesian Physicians Association*] (IN)
IDI.............. Instituto de la Demanda Interna [*Domestic Consumer Demand Institute*] [*Cuban*] (LA)

IDIA Instituto de Desarrollo Integral y Armonico [*Harmonious and Integral Development Institute*] [*Paraguayan*] (LA)

IDICT Instituto de Documentacion e Informacion Cientifica y Tecnica [*Scientific and Technical Documentation and Information Institute*] [*Cuban*] (LA)

IDID Idare Isleri Dairesi Genel Mudurlugu [*Administrative Affairs Office Directorate General*] [*of Foreign Affairs Ministry*] (TU)

IDII Institut za Drvno-Industriska Istrazivanja [*Research Institute on Industrial Utilization of Wood*] (YU)

IDIS Industrial Drip Irrigation System (MAR)

idJ In Diesem Jahr [*In This Year*] [*Correspondence*] [*German*]

IDJEN Inspektur Djenderal [*Inspector General*] (IN)

IDK Iktisadi Devlet Kurulus [*Economic State Enterprise*] (TU)

IDK Individual Decontamination Kit (RU)

IdK Internationale der Kriegsdienstgegner [*Conscientious Objectors' International*] [*Swiss*] (WEN)

IDK Irodalomtorteneti Dokumentacios Kozpont [*Documentation Center for Literary History*] (HU)

IDKD Istanbul Demokratik Kultur Dernegi [*Istanbul Democratic Cultural Organization*] (TU)

IDM Institute of Development Management (MAR)

IDMMA Istanbul Devlet Mimarlik ve Muhendislik Akademisi [*Istanbul State Academy of Architecture and Engineering*] [*See also DMMA*] (TU)

IDMS Industrie de Matieres Synthetiques (MAR)

IDMS Intreprinderea de Difuzare a Materialelor Sportive [*Enterprise for the Dissemination of Sports Equipment*] (RO)

IDN Indonesia [*Three-letter standard code*] (CNC)

IDNS Istorisko Drustvo u Novom Sadu [*Historical Society of Novi Sad*] (YU)

IDO Degradation Failure Rate (RU)

IDO Societe Industrie des Oleagineux (MAR)

idorb Engineer Road Battalion (RU)

idorbr Engineer Road Brigade (RU)

idorp Engineer Road Regiment (RU)

idorr Engineer Road Company (RU)

IDORT Instituto de Organizacao Racional do Trabalho [*Institute for the Efficient Organization of Labor*] [*Brazilian*] (LA)

idorv Engineer Road Platoon (RU)

IDP Individual Decontamination Kit (RU)

IDP Institut pour le Developpement et le Progres [*Institute for Development and Progress*] [*Mauritian*] (AF)

IDP Institute of Data Processing [*United Kingdom*]

IDP Italian Democratic Party (RU)

IDPB Intreprinderea de Drumuri si Poduri Bucuresti [*Bucharest Enterprise for Roads and Bridges*] (RO)

IDPC Intreprinderea de Desfacere a Produselor Chimice [*Enterprise for the Sale of Chemical Products*] (RO)

IDPJI Intreprinderea de Drumuri si Poduri a Judetului Ilfov [*Ilfov County Enterprise for Roads and Bridges*] (RO)

i dr And Others (BU)

i dr And Others, The Rest (RU)

IDR Institut du Developpement Rural (MAR)

IDR Institute of Development Research (MAR)

IDRC International Development Research Centre

IDREM Institut de Documentation de Recherches et d'Etudes Maritimes (MAR)

Idr Ilm Fak Idare Ilimler Fakultesi [*Administrative Science Faculty of METU*] [*Ankara*] (TU)

IDRO Industrial Development and Renovation Organization [*Iranian*] (ME)

IDRP Irrigation and Drainage Research Project (MAR)

i dr pod Et Cetera (BU)

i dr t Et Cetera (BU)

IDS Dispersing Power Index (RU)

IDS Identifikacni Skupina [*Identification Group*] (CZ)

IDS Institute for Development Studies of the University of Nairobi (MAR)

IDS Instituto de Desarrollo de Salud [*Institute for Health Development*] [*Cuban*] (LA)

IDS International Development Services, Inc. (MAR)

IDS International Development Strategy (MAR)

IDS International Diabetes Federation [*See also FID*] (EA)

IDSA Instituto Dominicano de Servicios Agrarios [*Dominican Institute of Agrarian Services*] [*Dominican Republic*] (LA)

IDSO Istanbul Devlet Senfoni Orkestrasi [*Istanbul State Symphony Orchestra*] (TU)

IDSS Instituto Dominicana de Seguros Sociales [*Dominican Social Security Institute*] [*Dominican Republic*] (LA)

IDT Corrective Labor Home (RU)

IDT Iktisadi Devlet Tesekkulleri [*Economic State Enterprises*] (TU)

IDT Imprimerie du Tchad (MAR)

IDT Institutul de Documentare Tehnica [*Institute for Technical Documentation*] (RO)

IDTF International Documents Task Force

IDTs Radar Moving-Target Indicator (RU)

IDU Igala Divisional Union (MAR)

IDU Instituto de Desarrollo Urbano [*Urban Development Institute*] [*Colombian*] (LA)

iDurchschn Im Durchschnitt [*On the Average*] (EG)

IDUSCOA Societe Industrielle de Conservation Agricole [*Moroccan*] (MAR)

IDV Integrierte Datenverarbeitung [*Integrated Data Processing*] (EG)

IDV Internationaler Deutschlehrerverband [*International Association of Teachers of German - IATG*] (EA)

IDV Istorisko Drustvo Vojvodine [*Historical Society of Vojvodina*] (YU)

IdV Bank Innerdeutsche Verrechnungsbank [*Inner-German Clearing Bank*] (EG)

IDW Institut fuer Dokumentationswesen [*German*]

IDWSSD International Drinking Water Supply and Sanitation Decade (MAR)

Id Yp Idiaitera Ypiresia [*Special Service*] [*In datelines*] (GC)

IDZA Interdepartementale Documentatiezaken [*Ministerie Binnenlandse Zaken, 's-Gravenhage*]

IE Electric Welding Institute (RU)

IE Fighter Squadron (RU)

ie Id Est [*That Is*] [*Latin*] (GPO)

ie Idoszamitasunk Elott [*Before Christ*] (HU)

IE Industrie-Entwurf [*Industrial Designing Office*] (EG)

IE Institut Egyptien (MAR)

IE Institute of Economics (of the Academy of Sciences, USSR) (RU)

IE Institute of Ethnography Imeni N. N. Miklukho-Maklay (of the Academy of Sciences, USSR) (RU)

IE International Units (BU)

IE Ireland [*Two-letter standard code*] (CNC)

IE Measuring Element (RU)

IE Pulse Element (RU)

IEA Industrias Electricas Asociadas [*Medellin*] (COL)

IEA Ingenieria Electronica Aplicada [*Bogota*] (COL)

IEA Institut de l'Enseignement pour Adultes (MAR)

IEA Instituto de Economia Agricola [*Agricultural Economy Institute*] [*Brazilian*] (LA)

IEA Instituto de Energia Atomica [*Atomic Energy Institute*] [*Brazilian*] (LA)

IEA International Economic Association [*See also AISE*] (EA)

IEA International Emergency Action [*See also AUI*] (EA)

IEA International Energy Agency (AF)

IEA Internationale Energieagentur [*International Energy Agency*] [*West German*] (WEN)

IEA Intreprinderea de Elemente pentru Automatizari [*Enterprise for Automation Elements*] (RO)

IEAA Institut d'Etudes Administratives Africaines [*Institute of African Administrative Studies*] (AF)

IEABS Intreprinderea Economica de Administrare a Bazelor Sportive [*Economic Enterprise for the Administraton of Sports Installations*] (RO)

IEAF Imperial Ethiopian Air Force (AF)

IEAJ Internacia Esperanto-Asocio de Juristoj [*International Esperanto-Association of Jurists*] (EA)

IEAP Ilektriki Etaireia Athinon-Peiraios [*Athens-Piraeus Electric Company*] (GC)

IEAR Instituto de Energia Atomica Reactor [*Brazilian*]

IEAT Institute of Electronics, Automation, and Remote Control (of the Academy of Sciences, Georgian SSR) (RU)

IEB Institute of Experimental Biology (RU)

IEB Intreprinderea Electrocentrale Bucuresti [*Bucharest Electric Power Enterprise*] (RO)

IEBiM Institute of Experimental Biology and Medicine (of the Siberian Department of the Academy of Sciences, USSR) (RU)

IEBS Intreprinderea de Exploatare a Bazelor Sportive [*Enterprise for the Utilization of Sports Installations*] (RO)

IEC Institut d'Etudes Centrafricaines (MAR)

IEC International Egg Commission (EA)

IEC International Electrotechnical Commission [*See also CEI*] (EA)

IECAMA Imperial Ethiopian College of Agriculture and Mechanical Arts (MAR)

IECCF Intreprinderea de Electrificare si Centralizare Cai Ferate [*Enterprise for the Electrification and Centralization of Railways*] (RO)

IECE Instituto Ecuatoriano de Credito Educativo [*Ecuadorean Institute of Educational Credit*] (LA)

IECMGM Intreprinderea de Exploatare a Conductelor Magistrale de Gaz Metan [*Enterprise for the Exploitation of Main Pipelines for Methane Gas*] (RO)

IED Ilektroenergetiki Dynamis [*Electromotive Force*] (GC)

IEDA Institut d'Etudes du Developpement Africain (MAR)

IEDC International Energy Development Corporation (MAR)

IEDES Institut d'Etude du Developpement Economique et Social [*Institute for the Study of Economic and Social Development*] [*French*] (WER)

IEDI Instituto Ecuatoriano de Derecho Internacional [*Ecuadorean Institute of International Law*] (LA)

IEDOM Institut d'Emissions des Departements d'Outre-Mer [*Overseas Departments Institute for Broadcasting*] [*French Guianese*] (LA1)

IEE Institution of Electrical Engineers [*United Kingdom*]

IEEE Istoriki kai Ethnologiki Etaireia tis Ellados [*Greek Historical and Ethnological Society*] (GC)

IEF.............. Institute of Evolutionary Physiology Imeni I. M. Sechenov (of the Academy of Sciences, USSR) (RU)
IEF.............. Izmir Enternasyonal Fuari (MAR)
IEFAEP........ Instituto de Ejecutivos Financieros y Administrativos de Empresas Publicas [*Public Enterprise Executives Institute*] [*Peruvian*] (LA)
IEFM........... Intreprinderea de Exploatare a Flotei Maritime [*Enterprise for the Operation of the Maritime Fleet*] (RO)
IEFR........... International Emergency Food Reserve (MAR)
IEFS........... Institutul de Educatie Fizica si Sport [*Institute for Physical Education and Sports*] (RO)
IEGF........... Imperial Ethiopian Ground Forces (AF)
IEGR........... Imperial Ethiopian Government Railways (AF)
IEI.............. Institut d'Etudes Islamiques [*Institute for Islamic Studies*] (AF)
IEI.............. Institute of Engineering Economics Imeni Sergo Ordzhonikidze (RU)
IEI.............. International Enamellers Institute (EA)
IEI.............. International Esperanto Institute (EA)
IEI.............. Ivanovo Power Engineering Institute Imeni V. I. Lenin (RU)
IEILIF.......... Intreprinderea de Exploatare a Lucrarilor de Imbunatatiri Funciare [*Enterprise for the Execution of Land Improvement Projects*] (RO)
IEILIFGA..... Intreprinderea de Exploatare si Intretinere a Lucrarilor de Imbunatatiri Funciare si Gospodarirea Apelor [*Enterprise for the Exploitation and Maintenance of Land Improvement Projects and Water Management*] (RO)
IEIM............ Bulletin of the Ethnographic Institute with Museum [*A publication*] (BU)
IEiOP.......... Instytut Ekonomiki i Organizacji Przemyslu [*Institute of Industrial Economics and Organizations*] (POL)
IEKA........... Internacia Esperanto Klubo Automobilista [*International Automobile Esperanto Club*] (EA)
IEL.............. Istanbul Erkek Lisesi [*Istanbul Men's Lycee*] (TU)
IELAN.......... Institute of Electrochemistry of the Academy of Sciences, USSR (RU)
IEM............. Bulletin of the Ethnographic Museum [*A publication*] (BU)
IEM............. Ilektriki Etaireia Metaforon [*Electric Transport Company Ltd.*] [*Greek*] (GC)
IEM............. Infectious Encephalomyelitis (of Horses) (RU)
IEM............. Institut de l'Enseignement Medical [*Medical Teaching Institute*] [*Zairian*] (AF)
IEM............. Institute of Electromechanics (RU)
IEM............. Institute of Epidemiology and Microbiology (RU)
IEM............. Institute of Evolutionary Morphology Imeni Academician A. N. Severtsov (RU)
IEM............. Institute of Experimental Medicine (of the Academy of Medical Sciences, USSR) (RU)
IEM............. Institute of Experimental Morphogenesis (RU)
IEMAC......... Israeli-Egyptian Mixed Armistice Commission (MAR)
IEMBAL....... Instituto de Envase y Embalaje [*Canning and Packing Institute*] [*Ecuadorean*] (LA)
IEMC........... Imperial Ethiopian Marine Corps (AF)
IEMF........... Imperial Ethiopian Military Forces (AF)
IEMG........... Scientific Research Institute of Epidemiology, Microbiology, and Hygiene (RU)
IEMI............ Intreprinderea de Aparate Electronice de Masura si Industriale [*Enterprise for Electronic Measurement and Industrial Instruments*] (RO)
IEMS........... Institute of Extra-Mural Studies (MAR)
IEMSS......... Institute of Economics of the World Socialist System (of the Academy of Sciences, USSR) (RU)
IEMVPT....... Institut d'Elevage et de Medecine Veterinaire des Pays Tropicaux [*Institute for Livestock and Veterinary Medicine for Tropical Countries*] [*French*] (AF)
IEMVT......... Institut d'Elevage et de Medecine Veterinaire des Pays Tropicaux (MAR)
IEN............. Imperial Ethiopian Navy (AF)
ien.............. Inainte de Era Noastra [*Before Our Era*] [*Before Christ*] (RO)
IEN............. Instituto Ecuatoriano de Normalizacion [*Ecuadorean Institute of Standardization*] (LA)
IEN............. Instituto de Engenharia Nuclear [*Nuclear Engineering Institute*] [*Brazilian*] (LA)
IEN............. Istituto Elettrotecnico Nazionale [*Torino, Italy*]
IENTh.......... Institouton Erevnis Nosimaton Thorakos [*Thoracic Diseases Research Institute*] (GC)
IEOC........... International Egyptian Oil Company (ME)
IEON........... International Esperantist Organization of Naturalists [*See also INOE*] (EA)
IEOP........... Instytut Ekonomiki i Organizacji Przemyslu [*Institute of Industrial Economics and Organizations*] (POL)
IEP.............. Imperial Ethiopian Police (AF)
IEP.............. Institut d'Ethnologie de l'Universite de Paris (MAR)
IEP.............. Institut d'Etudes Politiques [*Institute of Political Studies*] [*French*] (WER)
IEP.............. Instituto de Ensaios e Padroes [*Tests and Standards Institute*] [*Brazilian*] (LA)
IEP.............. Intreprinderea de Exploatare Portuara [*Port Operation Enterprise*] (RO)
IEPER.......... Intreprinderea de Echipamente Periferice [*Enterprise for Peripheral Equipment*] (RO)
IEPES.......... Instituto de Estudios Politicos, Economicos, y Sociales [*Institute for Political, Economic, and Social Studies*] [*Mexican*] (LA1)
IEPES.......... Instituto de Estudos Politicos, Economicos, e Sociais [*Institute of Political, Economic, and Social Studies*] [*Brazilian*] (LA)
IER.............. Industria Electrica Romana [*Romanian Electric Industry*] (RO)
IER.............. Institut d'Economie Rural (MAR)
IER.............. Instituto de Educacion Rural [*Rural Education Institute*] [*Chilean*] (LA)
IER.............. Instytut Ekonomiki Rolnej [*Institute of Agricultural Economy*] (POL)
IER.............. Instytut Ekonomiki Rolnictwa [*Institute of the Economy of Agriculture*] (POL)
IER.............. Organization for International Economic Relations (EA)
IERAC......... Instituto Ecuatoriano de Reforma Agraria y Colonizacion [*Ecuadorean Institute for Agrarian Reform and Settlement*] (LA)
IERCM......... Institutul de Expertiza Medicala si Recuperare a Capacitatii de Munca [*Institute for Medical Evaluation and Recovery of the Ability to Work*] (RO)
IEREGEM.... Institut Equatorial de Recherches et d'Etudes Geologiques et Minieres
IERM........... Institut d'Economie Rurale du Mali (MAR)
IES.............. Electric Welding Institute Imeni Ye. O. Paton (of the Academy of Sciences, Ukrainian SSR) (RU)
IES.............. Institute of Ethiopian Studies (MAR)
IES.............. Instituto de Engenharia Sanitaria [*Institute of Sanitation Engineering*] [*Brazilian*] (LA)
IES.............. Instituto de Estudios Superiores [*Institute of Higher Studies*] [*Dominican Republic*] (LA1)
IES.............. Institutul de Economie Socialista [*Socialist Economics Institute*] (RO)
IESA........... Institut d'Enseignement Secondaire Angolais (MAR)
IESA........... Instituto de Educacion Superior de Administracion [*Institute of Higher Education for Administration*] [*Venezuelan*] (LA)
IESC........... International Execution Service Corps [*North African*] (MAR)
IESE........... Institut d'Etudes Sociales de l'Etat [*State Institute for Social Studies*] [*Zairian*] (AF)
IESE........... Instituto de Estudios Sociales y Economicos [*Institute of Social and Economic Studies*] [*Bolivian*] (LA1)
IESE........... Instituto de Estudios Sociales y Economicos [*Institute of Social and Economic Studies*] [*Colombian*] (LA)
IESP........... Instituto de Engenharia, Sao Paulo [*Brazilian*]
IESS........... Instituto Ecuatoriano de Seguridad Social [*Ecuadorean Social Security Institute*] (LA)
IESSA......... Institute of Education and Social Services of Angola (AF)
IEST........... News of the Electrical Communications Industry [*A publication*] (RU)
IESUA......... Institut de l'Energie Solaire de l'Universite d'Alger (MAR)
IET.............. Institut d'Ecologie Tropicale (MAR)
IET.............. Isoelectric Point (RU)
IETEL.......... Instituto Ecuatoriano de Telecomunicaciones [*Ecuadorean Telecommunications Institute*] (LA)
IETT........... Istanbul Elektrik, Tunel, ve Tramvay Idaresi [*Istanbul Electric Power, Subway, and Tramway Administration*] [*See also IETTI*] (TU)
IETTI.......... Istanbul Elektrik, Tunel, ve Tramvay Idaresi [*Istanbul Electric Power, Subway, and Tramway Administration*] [*See also IETT*] (TU)
IEUM........... Institute of Electronic Control Machines (RU)
IEV.............. Istocno Evropsko Vreme [*Eastern European Time*] (YU)
IEVKh.......... Institute of Power Engineering and Water Management (RU)
IEVZAC....... Institut d'Enseignement Zootechnique et Veterinaire d'Afrique Centrale (MAR)
IEW............. Ingenieurschule fuer Eisenbahnwesen [*Railroad Engineering School*] (EG)
IEZ.............. Institut za Elektrozveze [*Institute of Telecommunications*] [*Ljubljana*] (YU)
IF................ Dummy Fougasse, Dummy Mine (RU)
if................. Fighter Group [*Aviation*] (BU)
If................. Ifalos [*or Ifaloi*] [*Reef or Reefs*] [*Greek*] (NAU)
if................. Ifolge [*According To*] [*Danish*] (GPO)
IF................ Infanteri [*Infantry*] (IN)
IF................ Inositol Phosphate (RU)
IF................ Instalatie de Foraj [*Drilling Installation*] (RO)
IF................ Institute of Philosophy (RU)
IF................ Institute of Physiology Imeni I. P. Pavlov (RU)
IF................ Instytut Filmowy [*Motion Picture Institute*] (POL)
IF................ Interference Light Filter (RU)
IF................ Interfrigo [*Council for Economic Mutual Assistance*] (BU)
IF................ Investicioni Fond [*Investment Fund*] (YU)
i/f............... Istioforon [*Sailing Ship*] (GC)
IFA.............. Ibadan Football Association (MAR)
IFA.............. Industrie et Forets Africaines (MAR)
IFA.............. Industrievereinigung Fahrzeugbau [*Trademark of State Vehicle Accessories Works*] [*Formerly, Industrial Association for Motor Vehicle Construction*] (EG)
IFA.............. Institute of Physics of the Atmosphere (of the Academy of Sciences, USSR) (RU)
IFA.............. Instituto de Fomento Algodonero [*Armero-Tolima*] (COL)

IFA.............. Institutt for Atomenergi [*Institute for Atomic Energy*] [*Norwegian*] (WEN)
IFA.............. Institutul de Fizica Atomica [*Atomic Physics Institute*] (RO)
IFA.............. International Federation of Airworthiness (EA)
IFA.............. International Fertilizer Industry Association (EA)
IFA.............. International Finn Association (EA)
IFA.............. International Fiscal Association (EA)
IFAA.............. International Federation of Associations of Anatomists (EA)
IFAAW.............. International Federation of Agricultural and Allied Workers (MAR)
IFABC.............. International Federation of Audit Bureaux of Circulations (EA)
IFAC.............. Institut Francais d'Action Cooperative [*French Institute for Cooperative Action*] (AF)
IFAC.............. Institut Francais de Recherches Fruitieres d'Outre-Mer [*French Institute for Overseas Fruit Research*] (AF)
IFAC.............. Institution dun Centre de Formation d'Animateurs Culturels et de Comediens (MAR)
IFAC.............. International Federation of Automatic Control [*German*]
IFAD.............. International Fund for Agricultural Development (MAR)
IFAL.............. Istituto Fascista per l'Artigianato della Libia (MAR)
IFALPA.............. International Federation of Air Line Pilots Associations (EA)
IFAM.............. Institut fuer Allgemeine Mikrobiologie [*University of Kiel*] [*West German*]
IFAM.............. Instituto de Fomento y Asesoria Municipal [*Municipal Development and Counseling Institute*] [*Costa Rican*] (LA1)
IFAN.............. Institut Fondamental d'Afrique Noire [*Basic Institute of Black Africa*] [*Senegalese*] (AF)
IFAN.............. International Foderation der Ausschusse Normenpraxis [*International Federation for the Application of Standards*] (EA)
IFAO.............. Institut Francais d'Archeologie Orientale du Caire (MAR)
IFAP.............. Industrie Africaine de Filets de Pedre (MAR)
IFAP.............. International Federation of Agricultural Producers (MAR)
IFAPAO.............. International Federation of Asian and Pacific Associations of Optometry (EA)
IFARC.............. Institut pour la Formation Agronomique et Rurale en Regions Chaudes (MAR)
IFA-RCA.............. Industries et Forets Africaines Centrafrique (MAR)
IFARHU.............. Instituto para Formacion y Adiestramiento de Recursos Humanos [*Human Resources Education and Training Institute*] [*Panamanian*] (LA)
IFATCA.............. International Federation of Air Traffic Controllers' Associations (EA)
IFATSEA.............. International Federation of Air Traffic Safety Electronic Associations (EA)
IFATU.............. International Federation of Arab Trade Unions (MAR)
IFAWPCA.............. International Federation of Asian and Western Pacific Contractors' Associations (EA)
IFB.............. Independent Forward Bloc [*Mauritian*] (AF)
IfB.............. Institut fuer Bedarfsforschung [*Institute for Market Research*] [*West German*] (WEN)
IFBDO.............. International Federation of Blood Donor Organizations [*See also FIODS*] (EA)
IFC.............. Instituto de Investigacion y Formacion Cooperativista [*Institute for Cooperative Research and Training*] [*Honduran*] (LA1)
IFC.............. Instytut Fryderyka Chopina [*Frederick Chopin Institute*] (POL)
IFC.............. Interfaith Conference (MAR)
IFC.............. International Federation of Master-Craftsmen [*See also IFH*] (EA)
IFC.............. International Finance Corporation (AF)
IFC.............. Iran Fertilizer Company (ME)
IFCB.............. International Federation of Cell Biology (EA)
IFCC.............. Institut Francais du Cafe, du Cacao, et Autres Plantes Stimulantes [*French Institute of Coffee, Cocoa, and Other Stimulating Plants*] (AF)
IFCCS.............. Intreprinderea pentru Fabricarea Celulozei si Cartoanelor din Stuf [*Enterprise for the Manufacture of Cellulose and Cardboard from Reeds*] (RO)
IFCh.............. Instytut Fryderyka Chopina [*Frederick Chopin Institute*] (POL)
IFCP.............. International Federation of the Cinematographic Press [*See also FIPRESCI*] (EA)
IFCPC.............. International Federation of Cervical Pathology and Colposcopy (EA)
IFCS.............. Institut de Formation Coloniale et Social (MAR)
IFCT.............. Institut Francais de Cooperation Technique [*French Institute for Technical Cooperation*] (AF)
IFCTU.............. International Federation of Christian Trade Unions (AF)
IFCU.............. International Federation of Catholic Universities [*See also FIUC*] (EA)
IFD.............. Internationalen Foderation des Dachdeckerhandwerks [*International Federation of Roofing Contractors - IFRC*] (EA)
IFDA.............. International Foundation for Development Alternatives [*See also FIPAD*] (EA)
IFDAS.............. International Federation of Dental Anesthesiology Societies (EA)
IFDCO.............. International Flying Dutchmen Class Organization (EA)
IFDO.............. International Federation of Data Organizations for the Social Sciences (EA)
IFE.............. Industria la Fuente Electrica [*Bogota*] (COL)
IfE.............. Inspekteur fuer Elektrizitaet [*Electricity Inspector*] (EG)
IFE.............. Instituto de Fomento Economico [*Economic Development Institute*] [*Bogota*] (LA)
IFEAT.............. International Federation of Essential Oils and Aroma Trades (EA)
IFED.............. Iraq Fund for External Development (ME)
IFEDEC.............. Instituto de Formacion Democrata Cristiana [*Institute for Christian Democratic Training*] [*Venezuelan*] (LA)
IFEF.............. Internacia Fervojista Esperanto Federacio [*International Federation of Esperantist Railwaymen*] (EA)
IFELPA.............. Industria de Felpa de Lana y Pelo [*Bogota*] (COL)
IFEN.............. Industria Forniture Elettriche Navali (MAR)
IFER.............. International Federation of Engine Reconditioners [*See also FIRM*] (EA)
IFERT.............. Iskolai Felszereleseket Ertekesito Vallalat [*School Supplies Retail Enterprise*] (HU)
IFES.............. International Fellowship of Evangelical Students (MAR)
IFET.............. Intreprinderile Forestiere de Exploatare si Transport [*Forestry Enterprises for Exploitation and Transportation*] (RO)
IFF.............. Department of History and Philology (BU)
IFF.............. Identification Friend or Foe (MAR)
IfF.............. Institut fuer Festkoerperphysik [*Institute for Solid State Physics*] (EG)
IFFJP.............. International Federation of Fruit Juice Producers [*See also FIJU*] (EA)
IFFTU.............. International Federation of Free Teachers' Unions [*See also SPIE*] (EA)
IfG.............. Institut fuer Gasentladungsphysik [*Institute for Gas Discharge Physics*] (EG)
IfG.............. Institut fuer Geraetebau [*Institute for Apparatus Construction*] (EG)
IFG.............. Institute of Physical Geography (RU)
IFGA.............. International Federation of Grocers' Associations [*See also IVLD*] (EA)
IFGHIE.............. Istanbul Universitesi Iktisat Fakultesi Gazetecilik ve Halkla Iliskiler Enstitusu [*The Institute of Journalism and Public Relations of the Istanbul University's Faculty of Economics*] (TU)
IFH.............. Internationale Foderation des Handwerks [*International Federation of Master-Craftsmen - IFC*] (EA)
IFHE.............. International Federation for Home Economics [*See also FIEF*] (EA)
IFHFC.............. Irano-France Hotel Financing Company (ME)
IFHOH.............. International Federation of the Hard of Hearing (EA)
IFHPM.............. International Federation of Hydraulic Platform Manufacturers (EA)
IFHRO.............. International Federation of Health Records Organizations (EA)
IFI.............. Engineering Physics Institute (RU)
IFI.............. Instituto de Fomento e Coordenacao Industrial [*Industrial Coordination and Promotion Institute*] [*Brazilian*] (LA)
IFI.............. Instituto de Fomento Industrial [*Industrial Development Institute*] [*Bogota*] (COL)
IFI.............. International Federation of Interior Architects Interior Designers (EA)
IFIA.............. International Federation of Inventors' Associations (EA)
IFIA.............. International Federation of Ironmongers and Iron Merchants Associations [*See also FIDAQ*] (EA)
IFIAS.............. International Federation of Institutes for Advanced Study (EA)
IFICOOP.............. Instituto Financiario Cooperativo [*Institute of Cooperative Financing*] [*Chilean*] (LA)
IFIFR.............. International Federation of International Furniture Removers [*See also FIDI*] (EA)
IFIJG.............. International Federation of Infantile and Juvenile Gynecology [*See also FIGIJ*] (EA)
IFIL.............. Intreprinderile Forestiere si de Industria Lemnului [*Forestry and Wood Industry Enterprises*] (RO)
IFIN.............. Institutul de Fizica si Inginerie Nucleara [*Institute for Nuclear Physics and Engineering*] (RO)
IFIP.............. International Federation for Information Processing [*Amsterdam*]
IFIS.............. International Food Information Service [*United Kingdom*]
IFIVNED.............. Institute of Physiology and Pathology of Higher Nervous Activity (RU)
IFIWA.............. International Federation of Importers and Wholesale Grocers Associations (EA)
ifj.............. Ifjabb [*Junior*] (HU)
ifj.............. Ifjusag [*or Ifjusagi*] [*Youth*] (HU)
IFJ.............. Instytut Fizyki Jadrowej [*Institute of Nuclear Physics*] [*Polish*]
IFJ.............. International Federation of Journalists [*See also FIJ*] (EA)
Ifj K.............. Ifjusagi Kiado [*Youth Publishing House*] (HU)
IFK.............. Film-Badge Personnel Monitoring (RU)
IFK.............. Institut Franco-Khmer [*French-Cambodian Institute*] (CL)
IFK.............. Institute of Physical Culture (RU)
IFK.............. Isopropyl Ester of Phenylcarbamic Acid (RU)
IFK.............. Isopropyl Phenyl Carbamate (RU)
IFKh.............. Institute of Physical Chemistry (of the Academy of Sciences, USSR) (RU)
IFKhA.............. Institute of Physicochemical Analysis [*1918-1934*] (RU)
IFKhI.............. Institute of Physical and Chemical Research (RU)
IFKN.............. Film-Badge Personnel Monitoring of Neutrons (RU)

IFKT .... International Federation of Knitting Technologists [*See also FITB*] (EA)
IFKU .... Improved Film-Badge Personnel Monitoring (RU)
ifl .... Ifolge [*According To*] [*Norwegian*] (GPO)
IfL .... Institut fuer Landtechnik [*Institute for Agricultural Technology*] (EG)
IfL .... Institut fuer Leichtbau [*Institute for Light Construction*] (EG)
IFLA .... International Federation of Landscape Architects (EA)
IFLA .... International Federation of Library Associations ['*s-Gravenhage*]
IFLASC .... International Federation of Latin American Study Centers (EA)
IFLB .... Islamic Front for the Liberation of Bahrain (PD)
IFLGS .... Intreprinderea de Foraj si Lucrari Geologice Speciale [*Enterprise for Drilling and Special Geological Projects*] (RO)
IFLI .... Institute of Philosophy, Literature, and History (RU)
IFM .... Industrial Fasteners Manufacturers (MAR)
IfM .... Institut fuer Marktforschung [*Institute for Market Research*] [*West German*] (WEN)
IFM .... Institute of Finance Management (MAR)
IFM .... Institute of Physics of Metals (RU)
IFMA .... International Farm Management Association (EA)
IFMA .... International Federation of Margarine Associations (EA)
IFMA .... Intreprinderea de Fabricatie si Montaj Ascensoare [*Enterprise for Elevator Manufacture and Installation*] (RO)
IFME .... International Federation of Municipal Engineers [*See also FIIM*] (EA)
IFMES .... Institut de Formation aux Metiers Educatifs, Sanitaires, et Sociaux [*Training Institute for Educational, Sanitary, and Social Occupations*] (LA1)
IFMP .... International Federation of Maritime Philately (EA)
IFMP .... International Federation for Medical Psychotherapy [*See also IGAP*] (EA)
IFMS .... International Federation of Magical Societies [*See also FISM*] (EA)
IFMSA .... International Federation of Medical Students Associations [*See also FIAEM*] (EA)
IFMSO .... Institute of Finance Management Students' Organisation (MAR)
IFMSS .... International Federation of Multiple Sclerosis Societies (EA)
IFN .... International Friends of Nature [*See also NFI*] (EA)
IFNA .... International Federation of Netball Associations (EA)
IFNSA .... International Federation of the National Standardizing Associations
IFOCAF .... Institut de Formation des Cadres Paysans Francais (MAR)
IFONA .... Instituto Forestal Nacional [*National Forestry Institute*] [*Argentine*] (LA1)
IFOP .... Institut Francais de l'Opinion Publique [*French Public Opinion Institute*] (AF)
IFOP .... Instituto de Fomento Pesquero [*Fishing Promotion Institute*] [*Chilean*] (LA)
IFOP-ETMAR ... Institut Francais de l'Opinion Publique - Institut pour l'Etude des Marches en France et a l'Etranger (MAR)
IFORD .... Institut de Formation et de Recherches en Demographie [*Institute for Demographic Training and Research*] [*Cameroonian*] (AF)
IFORS .... International Federation of Operational Research Societies (EA)
IFOS .... International Federation of Oto-Rhino-Laryngological Societies (EA)
IFOSOM ...... Industria Manufacturera de Forros para Sombreros Ltda. [*Bogota*] (COL)
IFP .... Institut Francais du Petrole [*French Petroleum Institute*] (AF)
IFP .... Institute of Physical Problems Imeni S. I. Vavilov (of the Academy of Sciences, USSR) (RU)
IFPA .... International Federation of Psoriasis (EA)
IFPAAW .... International Federation of Plantation, Agricultural and Allied Workers (MAR)
IFPE .... International Federation for Parent Education [*See also FIEP*] (EA)
IFPED .... Institut de Formation de Perfectionnement et d'Etudes [*Improvement and Studies Training Institute*] [*Upper Voltan*] (AF)
IFPI .... International Federation of Phonogram and Videogram Producers (EA)
IFPM .... Instituto de Formacion Profesional del Magisterio [*Teacher Training Institute*] [*Costa Rican*] (LA)
IFPMA .... International Federation of Pharmaceutical Manufacturers Associations [*See also FIIM*] (EA)
IFPMM .... International Federation of Purchasing and Materials Management (EA)
IFPMO .... International Federation of Psychological-Medical Organizations [*See also FIOPM*] (EA)
IFPRA .... International Federation of Park and Recreation Administration (EA)
IFPRI .... International Food Policy and Research Institute (MAR)
IFPS .... Instructeur de Formation Professionnelle Specialisee (MAR)
IFPS .... International Federation of Philosophical Societies [*See also FISP*] (EA)
IFPTO .... International Federation of Popular Travel Organisations (EA)
IFPWKA ...... International Federation of Public Warehouse Keepers Associations (EA)
IFR .... Impot Forfaitaire sur le Revenu (MAR)
IfR .... Institut fuer Regelungstechnik [*Institute for Control Technology*] (EG)
IFR .... Institute of Plant Physiology Imeni K. A. Timiryazev (of the Academy of Sciences, USSR) (RU)
IFRA .... International Fragrance Association (EA)
IFRC .... International Federation of Roofing Contractors [*See also IFD*] (EA)
IFRD .... International Federation of Retail Distributors (EA)
IFRED .... Institut International de Recherches et de Formation en Vue de Developpement Harmonise [*Lebanese*] (MAR)
IFRP .... International Fertility Research Program (MAR)
IFRZ .... Instruction for the Wage Fund (BU)
IFS .... Impot Forfaitaire sur les Salaires (MAR)
IFS .... Inspectia Financiara de Stat [*State Financial Inspectorate*] (RO)
IfS .... Institut fuer Schienenfahrzeuge [*Institute for Rail Vehicles*] (EG)
IFS .... International Federation of Surveyors [*See also FIG*] (EA)
IFS .... International Fertilizer Supply Scheme [*North African*] (MAR)
IFS .... International Foundation for Science [*See also FIS*] (EA)
IFSA .... Industrias Farmaceuticas SA [*Valle*] (COL)
IFSA .... International Federation of Sports Acrobatics (EA)
IFSC .... Instituto de Formacao Social e Corporativa [*Portuguese*]
IFSC .... International Federation of Surgical Colleges (EA)
IFSC .... Iran Financial Services Company (ME)
IFSCC .... International Federation of Societies of Cosmetic Chemists (EA)
IFSDP .... International Federation of the Socialist and Democratic Press (EA)
IFSHC .... International Federation of Societies for Histochemistry and Cytochemistry (EA)
IFSMA .... International Federation of Shipmasters Associations (EA)
IFSSO .... International Federation of Social Science Organizations [*See also FIOSS*] (EA)
IFSTAD .... Islamic Foundation for Science, Technology, and Development
IFSW .... International Federation of Social Workers (MAR)
IFT .... International Federation of Translators [*See also FIT*] (EA)
IFT .... Italian Federation of Labor (RU)
IFTA .... International Federation of Teachers' Associations [*See also FIAI*] (EA)
IFTA .... International Federation of Television Archives [*See also FIAT*] (EA)
IFTAR .... Institutul de Fizica si Tehnologia Aparatelor cu Radiatii [*Institute for the Physics and Technology of Radiation Instruments*] (RO)
IFTF .... International Federation of Teachers of French [*See also FIPF*] (EA)
IFTF .... International Fur Trade Federation (EA)
IFTM .... Institutul de Fizica si Tehnologia Materialelor [*Institute for the Physics and Technology of Materials*] (RO)
IFTO .... International Federation of Tour Operators (EA)
IFToMM .... International Federation for the Theory of Machines and Mechanisms (EA)
IFTs .... Price Equalization Fund (BU)
IFTU .... International Federation of Trade Unions (SJT)
IFTUTW .... International Federation of Trade Unions of Transport Workers [*See also FIOST*] (EA)
IfV .... Institut fuer Verkehrsforschung [*Institute for Transport Research*] (EG)
IFVD .... Institute of Physics of High Pressures (RU)
IFVTCC .... Internationale Foderation der Vereine der Textilchemiker und Coloristen [*International Federation of Associations of Textile Chemists and Colourists*] (EA)
IFVUKh .... Institute for Physical Education and School Hygiene (BU)
IfW .... Institut fuer Werkzeugmaschinen [*Machine Tool Institute*] (EG)
IFWEA .... International Federation of Workers' Educational Associations [*See also IVB*] (EA)
IFZ .... Institute of Physics of the Earth Imeni O. Yu. Shmidt (of the Academy of Sciences, USSR) (RU)
IG .... Hospital for Contagious Diseases (RU)
ig .... Igazgatas [*or Igazgatasi*] [*Administration or Administrative*] (HU)
ig .... Igazgato [*or Igazgatosag*] [*Director or Directorate*] (HU)
iG .... Im Generalstab [*Attached to the General Staff (appended to, or preceding army rank)*] (EG)
IG .... Industriegewerkschaft [*Industrial Labor Union*] [*West German*] (WEN)
IG .... Institut za Geoloska Istrazivanja [*Geological Research Institute*] (YU)
IG .... Institute of Geography (of the Academy of Sciences, USSR) (RU)
IG .... Institutul de Geriatrie [*Geriatrics Institute*] (RO)
IG .... Instytut Geografii [*Institute of Geography*] (POL)
IG .... Instytut Geologiczny [*Institute of Geology*] [*Polish*]
IG .... Interessengemeinschaft [*Business Pool, Trust*] [*West German*] (WEN)
IG .... Interessengemeinschaft Deutschsprachiger Suedwester [*Interest Society of German-Speaking Southwesterners*] [*Namibian*] (AF)

IG .... Interessengruppe [*Interest Group (Society for the protection of interests of the German-speaking population)*] [*Namibian*] (AF)
IG .... Istoriski Glasnik [*Historical Bulletin*] [*Belgrade*] [*A publication*] (YU)
IG .... Izvidacka Grupa [*Reconnaissance Group*] [*Military*] (YU)
IG .... Measuring Head (RU)
IG .... Signal Generator (RU)
IG .... Spark Generator (RU)
IGA .... Instituto de Geofisica y Astronomia [*Institute of Geophysics and Astronomy*] [*Cuban*] (LA)
IGA .... International Gartenbauausstellung [*International Horticultural Exhibition*] (EG)
IGA .... International Gay Association - International Association of Lesbians/Gay Women and Gay Men (EA)
IGAC .... Instituto Geografico "Agustin Codazzi" [*Agustin Codazzi Geographic Institute*] [*Colombian*] (LA)
IGAeM .... Internationale Gesellschaft fuer Aerosole in der Medizin [*International Society for Aerosols in Medicine - ISAeM*] (EA)
IGAIMK .... News of the State Academy of the History of Material Culture [*A publication*] (RU)
IGAME .... Inspecteur General de l'Administration en Mission Extraordinaire [*Inspector General of Administration on Extraordinary Mission*] [*Algerian*] (AF)
IGAN .... Institute of Geography of the Academy of Sciences, USSR (RU)
IGAP .... Internationale Gesellschaft fuer Arztliche Psychotherapie [*International Federation for Medical Psychotherapy - IFMP*] (EA)
IGASK .... Inspection of the State Architectural and Construction Control (RU)
IGAT .... Iranian Gas Trunkline (ME)
IGB .... Ihtilalci Gencler Birligi [*Revolutionary Youth Union*] (TU)
IGB .... International Gravimetric Bureau (EA)
IGB .... Ipargazdasagi Bizottsag [*Committee of Industrial Economy*] (HU)
IGBE .... Institute of State Certified Accountants (RU)
ig biz .... Igazolo Bizottsag [*Screening Committee*] (HU)
IGC .... Intergovernmental Copyright Committee [*See also CIDA*] (EA)
IGC .... International Guides' Club (EA)
IGCB .... Institut Geographique du Congo Belge (MAR)
IGCMC .... Israel Government Coins and Medals Corporation (MAR)
IGCP .... International Geological Correlation Programme [*See also PICG*] (EA)
IGD .... Bulletin of the Bulgarian Geographic Society [*A publication*] (BU)
IGD .... Ilerici Gencler Dernegi [*Progressive Youth Association*] (TU)
IGD .... Institute of Hydrodynamics (of the Siberian Department of the Academy of Sciences, USSR) (RU)
IGD .... Mining Institute (RU)
IGDO .... International Guild of Dispensing Opticians (EA)
IGE .... Imposta Generale sull'Entrata [*Income Tax*] [*Italian*] (WER)
IGE .... Institouton Geoponikon Epistimon [*Agricultural Sciences Institute*] (GC)
IGECO .... Inspection Generale pour la Cooperation Hors Metropole [*General Inspectorate for Overseas Cooperation*] [*French*] (WER)
IGEM .... Ihracat Gelistirme Etud Merkezi [*Export Development Studies Center*] [*See also IGEME*] (TU)
IGEM .... Institute of Geology of Ore Deposits, Petrography, Mineralogy, and Geochemistry (of the Academy of Sciences, USSR) (RU)
IGEME .... Ihracati Gelistirme Etud Merkezi [*Center for Export Development Studies*] [*See also IGEM*] (TU)
IGEN .... Inspecteur General de l'Education Nationale [*French*]
IGEN .... Institute of Genetics (of the Academy of Sciences, USSR) (RU)
IGERGI .... Institute of Geology and Development of Mineral Fuels (RU)
IGEX .... Intreprinderea Geologica de Explorari [*Geological Enterprise for Explorations*] (RO)
IGEY .... Institouton Geologias kai Erevnon Ypedafous [*Geology and Subsoil Research Institute*] [*EthIGME is preferred*] (GC)
IGF .... Institut za Geodeziju i Fotogrametriju [*Institute of Geodesy and Photogrammetry*] (YU)
IGF .... International Foundation for the Conservation of Game (EA)
IGF .... International Graphical Federation [*See also FGI*] (EA)
IGF .... International Gymnastic Federation [*See also FIG*] (EA)
I G Farben ... Interessengemeinschaft der Farbenindustrie [*German Dye Trust*]
IGFCOT .... Institutul de Geodezie, Fotogrametrie, Cartografie, si Organizarea Teritoriului [*Institute for Geodesy, Photogrammetry, Cartography, and Territorial Organization*] (RO)
IGFFA .... Immobiliere Gabonaise Fiduciaire France Afrique (MAR)
IGG .... Institute of Geology and Geophysics (of the Siberian Department of the Academy of Sciences, USSR) (RU)
IGG .... Institute of Hydrology and Hydraulic Engineering (of the Academy of Sciences, Ukrainian SSR) (RU)
IGG .... Institutul de Geologie si Geofizica [*Institute for Geology and Geophysics*] (RO)
IGGI .... Inter-Governmental Group on Indonesia (IN)
IGGO .... News of the State Geographic Society [*A publication*] (RU)
IGGRU .... News of the Main Administration of Geological Exploration [*A publication*] (RU)
IGI .... Institute of Civil Engineers (RU)
IGI .... Institute of Mineral Fuels (RU)
IGI .... News of the Institute of Geography [*A publication*] (RU)
IGiG .... Institute of Geology and Geophysics (of the Siberian Department of the Academy of Sciences, USSR) (RU)
IGiG .... Institute of Hydrology and Hydraulic Engineering (of the Academy of Sciences, Ukrainian SSR) (RU)
IGiK .... Institute of Geodesy and Cartography (RU)
IGiK .... Instytut Geodezji i Kartografji [*Institute of Land-Surveying and Cartography*] [*Polish*]
IGiO .... Instytut Gluchoniemych i Ociemnialych [*Institute for the Deaf-Mute and the Blind*] [*Polish*]
IGIP .... Internationale Gesellschaft fuer Ingenieurpadogogik [*International Society for Engineering Education*] (EA)
IGiRGI .... Institute of Geology and Development of Mineral Fuels (RU)
IGK .... Il [*or Ilce*] Genclik Kolu [*Provincial (or District) Youth Branch*] [*of a political organization*] (TU)
IGK .... Institute of Geodesy and Cartography (RU)
IGK .... Instytut Gospodarki Komunalnej [*Institute of Municipal Economy*] (POL)
IGK .... News of the Geological Committee [*A publication*] (RU)
IGL .... Intreprinderile Gospodariei Locale [*Enterprises of the Local Economy*] (RO)
igla .... Iglesia [*Church*] [*Spanish*]
IGLL .... Inspectia Generala de Locuinte si Locale [*General Inspectorate for Housing and Public Buildings*] (RO)
IGM .... Institouton Georgikis Mikhanologias [*Agricultural Engineering Institute*] (GC)
IGM .... Institute of Mining Mechanics (RU)
IGM .... Internationale Gesellschaft fuer Menschenrechte [*International Society for Human Rights - ISHR*] (EA)
IGM .... Istituto Geografico Militare (Florence) [*Military Geographic Institute*] [*Italian*] (WER)
IGM .... Izcilik Genel Mudurlugu [*Scouting Directorate General*] (TU)
IGME .... Idryma Geologikon kai Metallevtikon Epevnon [*Institute for Geological and Mineral Research*] (GC)
IG Metall ..... Industriegewerkschaft Metall [*Metalworkers Union*] [*West German*] (EG)
IG/MG .... Inspecteur General/Mobilisation Generale [*or Inspection Generale/Mobilisation Generale*] [*Inspector General, General Mobilization or Inspectorate General, General Mobilization*] [*Cambodian*] (CL)
IGMI .... Irkutsk State Medical Institute (RU)
IGMI .... Ivanovo State Medical Institute (RU)
Ig Min .... Igazsagugyminiszterium/Miniszter [*Ministry/Minister of Justice*] (HU)
IGN .... Institut Geographique National [*National Geographic Institute*] [*French*] (WER)
IGN .... Institute of Geological Sciences (RU)
IGN .... Instytut Gospodarki Narodowej [*Institute of the National Economy*] (POL)
IGN .... Societe de l'Imprimerie Generale du Niger (MAR)
IGNC .... International Good Neighbor Council [*See also CIBV*] (EA)
IGO .... Hospital for Highly Contagious Diseases (RU)
IGO .... International Governmental Organisation (MAR)
IGO .... News of the Geographic Society [*A publication*] (RU)
IGP .... Indice Geral de Precos [*General Price Index*] [*Brazilian*] (LA)
IGP .... Inspector-General of Police (MAR)
IGP .... Institut de Gestion du Portefeuille (MAR)
IGPAN .... Institute of Government and Law of the Academy of Sciences, USSR (RU)
IG PAN .... Instytut Geografii Polskiej Akademii Nauk [*Polish Academy of Sciences Institute of Geography*] (POL)
IGPSMS .... Intreprinderea Geologica de Prospectiuni pentru Substante Minerale Solide [*Geologic Prospecting Enterprise for Solid Mineral Substances*] (RO)
IGR .... Graphite Pulse Reactor (RU)
IGR .... Impot General sur le Revenu [*General Income Tax*] [*Belgian, French*] (WER)
IGR .... Institute of Geomantic Research (EA)
IGR .... Instytut Genetyki Roslin [*Institute of Plant Genetics*] [*Polish*]
IGRA .... Instituto Gaucho de Reforma Agraria [*Rio Grande Do Sul Institute of Agrarian Reform*] [*Brazilian*] (LA)
IGS .... Impot General sur les Salaires (MAR)
IGS .... Instytut Gospodarstwa Spolecznego [*Institute of the Nation's Economy*] (POL)
IGS .... Istanbul Giyim Sanayii ve Ticaret AS [*Istanbul Wearing Apparel Industry and Trade Corp.*] (TU)
IGSA .... Istanbul Devlet Guzel Sanatlar Akademisi [*Istanbul State Fine Arts Academy*] (TU)
IGSAS .... Istanbul Gubre Sanayii Anonim Sirketi [*Istanbul Fertilizer Industry Corporation*] (TU)
IGSCCP .... Inspectoratul General de Stat pentru Controlul Calitatii Produselor [*State General Inspectorate for Product Quality Control*] (RO)
IGSCCPE .... Inspectoratul General de Stat pentru Controlul Calitatii Produselor de Export [*State General Inspectorate for Quality Control of Exported Products*] (RO)

IGSP............ Inspection Generale des Services de la Police Nationale [*Inspectorate General for National Police Services*] [*Cambodian*] (CL)
IGSS............ Instituto Guatemalteco de Seguridad Social [*Guatemalan Social Security Institute*] (LA)
IGT.............. Igala Tribal Union (MAR)
IGT.............. Imprimerie Graphique Tananarive (MAR)
IGTPZ.......... Institute of Labor Hygiene and Occupational Diseases (RU)
IGTYF.......... International Good Templar Youth Federation (EA)
IGU.............. International Gas Union [*See also UIIG*] (EA)
IGU.............. Irkutsk State University Imeni A. A. Zhdanov (RU)
IGUL............ Instytut Geograficzny Uniwersytetu Lodzkiego [*Lodz University Institute of Geography*] (POL)
IGUSZI........ Ipargazdasagi es Uzemszervezesi Intezet [*Institute of Industrial Economy and Business Organization (of the Ministry of Heavy Industry)*] (HU)
IGUW........... Instytut Geograficzny Uniwersytetu Warszawskiego [*Warsaw University Institute of Geography*] (POL)
IGV.............. Irodagepipari es Finommechanikai Vallalat [*Business Machine and Precision Mechanics Enterprise*] (HU)
IGVF............ Institute of the Civil Air Fleet (RU)
IGW............. Instytut Gospodarki Wodnej [*Institute for Water Control and Exploitation*] [*Polish*]
IGZ.............. Is Guclugu Zammi [*Labor Hardship Increase*] (TU)
IH................ Idegenforgalmi Hivatal [*Tourist Bureau*] (HU)
IH................ Instytut Historii [*Institute of History*] [*Polish*]
IHA.............. Imperial Highway Authority [*Ethiopian*] (AF)
IHAR............ Instytut Hodowli i Aklimatyzacji Roslin [*Institute of Plant Cultivation and Acclimatization*] (POL)
IHB.............. Industrie- und Handelsbank [*Industry and Commerce Bank*] (EG)
IHC.............. Intercontinental Hotels Corporation (MAR)
IHC.............. Israel Histadrut Campaign (MAR)
IHCSERS..... International Health Centre of Socio-Economics Researches and Studies [*See also CIERSES*] (EA)
IHD.............. Institut Henry-Dunant [*Henry Dunant Institute*] (EA)
IHD.............. International Hydrological Decade (MAR)
IHEDN.......... Institut des Hautes Etudes de Defense Nationale [*Institute for High National Defense Studies*] [*French*] (WER)
IHEOM......... Institut des Hautes Etudes d'Outre-Mer [*Overseas Institute of Higher Learning*] [*French*] (AF)
IHF.............. International Health Foundation (EA)
IHGC........... International Hop Growers Convention [*See also CICH*] (EA)
IHJ.............. Institute of the Heart of Jesus [*See also GEM*] (EA)
IHK.............. Industrie- und Handelskammer [*Chamber of Industry and Commerce*] (EG)
IHKM........... Instytut Historii Kultury Materialnej [*Institute of the History of Material Culture*] (POL)
IHMA........... Instituto Hondureno de Mercadeo Agricola [*Honduran Agricultural Marketing Institute*] (LA1)
IHMAT......... Instituto de Hidrologia, Meteorologia, y Adecuacion de Tierras [*Hydrology, Meteorology, and Soil Preparation Institute*] [*Colombian*] (LA)
IHO.............. International Hydrographic Organisation (MAR)
IHPCADE.... Institut Haitien de Promotion du Cafe et des Denrees d'Exportation [*Haitian Institute for the Promotion of Coffee and Export Commodities*] (LA)
IHR.............. Intreprinderile de Hoteluri si Restaurante [*Hotel and Restaurant Enterprises*] (RO)
IHSS............ Instituto Hondureno de Seguridad Social [*Honduran Social Security Institute*] (LA1)
IHSSA......... Industrie Horlogere Suisse [*Swiss watch manufacturer*]
IHT.............. Istanbul Halk Tiyatrosu [*Istanbul Peoples' Theatre*] (TU)
IHV.............. Internationale Hegel-Vereinigung (EA)
IHW............. Instytut Handlu Wewnetrznego [*Institute of Domestic Trade*] (POL)
IHZ.............. Instytut Handlu i Zywienia [*Institute of Trade and Catering*] (POL)
IHZZ............ Instytut Handlu i Zywienia Zbiorowego [*Institute of Trade and Communal Catering*] (POL)
i i................. I Inni [*And Others*] (POL)
II.................. Institute of Economics (BU)
II.................. Institute of History (of the Academy of Sciences, USSR) (RU)
II.................. Instituto de la Infancia [*Children's Institute*] [*Cuban*] (LA)
II.................. Istoriski Institut [*Historical Institute*] (YU)
IIA................ Institut International Africain [*International African Institute*] [*Use IAI*] (AF)
IIA................ Institut International d'Anthropologie [*International Institute of Anthropology*] (EA)
IIA................ Instituto de Investigaciones Agroindustriales [*Institute of Agroindustrial Research*] [*Peruvian*] (LA)
IIAA............ Imperial Iranian Army Aviation Corps (ME)
IIAA............ Instituto de Investigacao Agronomica de Angola (MAR)
IIAE............ Instituto de Investigaciones Aeronauticas y Espaciales [*Aeronautics and Space Research Institute*] [*Argentine*] (LA)
IIAF............ Imperial Iranian Air Force (ME)
IIALC.......... International Institute of African Languages and Culture (MAR)
IIALM......... International Institute for Adult Literacy Methods (EA)
IIAM........... Institut de la Recherche Agronomique Mozambique (MAR)
IIAN............ Institute of History of the Academy of Sciences, USSR (RU)
IIAP............ Institut International d'Administration Publique [*International Institute of Public Administration*] [*French*] (AF)
IIAS............ Inter-Island Air Services (LA1)
IIAS............ International Institute for the Administrative Sciences [*Brussels, Belgium*]
IIASA.......... Institut International d'Analyse de Systemes Appliquee (MAR)
IIB................ Ic Isleri Bakanligi [*Interior Ministry*] (TU)
IIB................ Imar ve Iskan Bakanligi [*Reconstruction and Settlement Ministry*] (TU)
IIB................ Institut International des Brevets [*Rijswijk*]
IIB................ Instituto de Investigaciones Bibliograficas [*Mexican*]
IIB................ Intreprinderea Instalatii Bucuresti [*Bucharest Enterprise for Installations*] (RO)
IIB................ Ionospharen-Institut Breisach [*West German*]
IIBE............. Bulletin of the Bulgarian Language Institute [*A publication*] (BU)
IIBH............ International Institute of Biological Husbandry (EA)
IIBI.............. Bulletin of the Institute of Bulgarian History [*A publication*] (BU)
IIBK............ Is ve Isci Bulma Kurumu Genel Mudurlugu [*Labor and Employment Organization Directorate General*] (TU)
IIC................ Intreprinderea pentru Industrializarea Carnii [*Enterprise for the Industrialization of Meat*] (RO)
IIC................ Iran Investment Company (ME)
IIC................ Islamic Investment Company (MAR)
IICA............ Instituto Interamericano de Ciencias Agricolas (de la OEA) [*Inter-American Institute of Agricultural Sciences (of the Organization of American States)*] [*Costa Rican*] (LA)
IICA............ Instituto Internacional de Ciencias Administrativas [*International Institute of Administrative Sciences*] [*Use IIAS*] (LA)
IICA............ Instituto de Investigacao Cientifica de Angola (MAR)
IICC............ Industrial Investment Credit Corporation (MAR)
IICC............ International Institute for Commercial Competition (EA)
IICE............ Institut International des Caisses d'Epargne [*International Savings Banks Institute - ISBI*] (EA)
IICE............ Instituto de Investigaciones en Ciencias Economicas [*Economic Science Research Institute*] [*Costa Rican*] (LA1)
IICG............ Istoriski Institut Crne Gore [*Historical Institute of Montenegro*] (YU)
IICHG.......... Institute of the International Conference on the Holocaust and Genocide (EA)
IICM............ Instituto de Investigacao Cientifica de Mocambique (MAR)
IICM............ Intreprinderea pentru Intretinerea Cladirii Ministerului Transporturilor si Telecomunicatiilor [*Building Maintenance Enterprise for the Ministry of Transportation and Telecommunications*] (RO)
IICM............ Junta de Investigacoes do Ultramar (MAR)
IICMRPS..... Intreprindere Intercooperatista de Constructii, Montaj, Reparatii, si Prestari de Servicii [*Intercooperative Enterprise for Constructions, Installations, Repairs, and Services*] (RO)
IICY............ International Independent Christian Youth [*See also JICI*] (EA)
IID................ Bulletin of the Historical Society [*A publication*] (BU)
IID................ Institut International de Documentation
IID................ True Motion Indicator (RU)
IIDA............ Instituto Interamericano de Direito de Autor [*Interamerican Copyright Institute*] (EA)
IIDARA........ Instituto Iberoamericano de Derecho Agrario y Reforma Agraria [*Ibero-American Institute of Agrarian Law and Agrarian Reform - IAIALAR*] (EA)
IIDH............ Institut International de Droit Humanitaire [*International Institute of Humanitarian Law - IIHL*] (EA)
IIDS............ Instituto Interamericano de Derechos Humanos [*Inter-American Institute of Human Rights - IIHR*] (EA)
IID-vo.......... Bulletin of the Historical Society [*A publication*] (BU)
IIe................ Deuxieme [*Second*] [*French*] (GPO)
IIE................ Institute of International Education (CL)
IIEFC.......... Iran International Exhibitions and Fairs Corporation (ME)
IIEO............ International Islamic Economic Organization (MAR)
IIES............ Institut International d'Etudes Sociales (MAR)
IIES............ Instituto de Investigaciones Economicas y Sociales [*Institute of Economic and Social Research*] [*Guatemalan*] (LA1)
IIF................ Institute of History and Philosophy (RU)
IIF................ Internationales Institut fuer den Frieden [*International Peace Institute*] (EG)
IIFMC.......... Istanbul Iktisat Fakultesi Mezunlar Cemiyeti [*Istanbul Faculty of Economics' Alumni Society*] (TU)
IIFSO.......... International Islamic Federation of Student Organizations (EA)
IIG................ Institute of Gas Utilization (RU)
IIGF............ Imperial Iranian Ground Forces (ME)
IIHL............ International Institute of Humanitarian Law [*See also IIDH*] (EA)
IIHR............ Inter-American Institute of Human Rights [*See also IIDS*] (EA)
IIHR............ International Institute of Human Rights (EA)
III................ Institute of Art History (of the Academy of Sciences, USSR) (RU)
IIIAN.......... Institute of Art History of the Academy of Sciences, USSR (RU)
IIIC............ International Institute for Intellectual Cooperation [*UNESCO*]
IIK................ Icra ve Iflas Kanunu [*Executor and Bankruptcy Law*] (TU)
IIkonSS....... Institute of Agricultural Economics (BU)

IIL .... Intreprinderea de Industrie Locala [*Local Industry Enterprise*] (RO)
IIL .... Publishing House of Foreign Literature (RU)
IILA .... Istituto Italo-Latino-Americano [*Italian-Latin American Institute*] (WER)
IILFSC .... International Institute of Law of the French Speaking Countries [*See also IDEF*] (EA)
IIM .... Bulletin of the Institute of Morphology [*A publication*] (BU)
IIM .... File Computer (BU)
IIM .... Intreprindere de Instalatii si Montaje [*Enterprise for Installations and Assemblies*] (RO)
IIMA .... Instituto de Investigacao Medica de Angola (MAR)
IIMF .... Odessa Institute of Engineers of the Maritime Fleet (RU)
IIMI .... Intreprindere Instalatii, Montaj, si Izolatii [*Enterprise for Installation, Assembly, and Insulation*] (RO)
IIMK .... Institute of the History of Material Culture [*1937-1959*] (RU)
IIMLIF .... Intreprinderea de Instalatii si Montaje pentru Lucrari de Imbunatatiri Funciare [*Enterprise for Installations and Assembly for Land Improvement Projects*] (RO)
IIMM .... Instituto de Investigacao Medica de Mocambique (MAR)
IIMM .... Instituto de Investigaciones Minero-Metalurgicas [*Mining and Metallurgical Research Institute*] [*Bolivian*] (LA)
IIMO .... Istanbul Insaat Muhendisleri Odasi [*Istanbul Chamber of Construction Engineers*] (TU)
i in .... I Inni [*And Others*] (POL)
IIN .... Imperial Iranian Navy (ME)
IINA .... International Islamic News Agency [*North African*] (EA)
IINIT .... Institute of the History of Science and Technology (of the Academy of Sciences, USSR) (RU)
IINITAN .... Institute of the History of Science and Technology of the Academy of Sciences, USSR (RU)
i inzh v .... Inspector General of Engineering Troops (BU)
IIOP .... Institut Ivoirien d'Opinion Publique [*Ivorian Institute of Public Opinion*] (AF)
IIP .... Institut International de la Presse [*International Press Institute*] [*Use IPI*] (CL)
IIP .... Institute of the History of the Party (RU)
IIP .... Instituto Internacional de la Prensa [*International Press Institute*] [*Use IPI*] (LA)
IIP .... International Institute of Philosophy (EA)
IIP .... Istituto Internazionale per la Pace [*International Institute for Peace*] [*Italian*] (WER)
IIPA .... Instituto das Industrias de Pesca em Angola (MAR)
IIPC .... Intreprinderea Industriala de Produse pentru Constructii [*Industrial Enterprise for Construction Products*] (RO)
IIPCCPMR ... Institutul de Istorie al Partidului pe Linga Comitetul Central al Partidului Muncitoresc Roman [*Institute for Party History of the Central Committee of the Romanian Workers' Party*] (RO)
IIPF .... International Institute of Public Finance (EA)
IIPM .... Institutul de Igiena si Protectia Muncii [*Institute for Hygiene and Labor Safety*] (RO)
IIPP .... International Institute for Promotion and Prestige (EA)
IIPS .... Institute of Transportation Engineers (RU)
IIRP .... Institut za Izucavanje Radnickog Pokreta [*Institute for the Study of the Labor Movement*] (YU)
IIRR .... International Institute of Rural Reconstruction (MAR)
IIRSA .... Institut International de Recherche Scientifique d'Adiopodoume (MAR)
IIRUC .... Intreprinderea pentru Intretinerea si Repararea Utilajelor de Calcul [*Enterprise for Maintenance and Repair of Computer Equipment*] (RO)
IIS .... Institut International de la Soudure [*International Institute of Welding - IIW*] (EA)
IIS .... Intreprinderea Industriala de Stat [*State Industrial Enterprise*] (RO)
IIS .... Measuring Information System (RU)
IISE .... International Institute of Social Economics (EA)
IISEC .... Instituto de Investigaciones Socioeconomicas [*Socioeconomic Research Institute*] [*Bolivian*] (LA1)
IISK .... Institute of Art History (RU)
IISKDOO ..... Instruction for the Election of Councils and Commissions on State Social Insurance (BU)
IISL .... International Institute of Space Law (EA)
IISN .... Institut Interuniversitaire des Sciences Nucleaires [*Interuniversity Institute of Nuclear Sciences*] [*Belgian*] (WER)
IISP .... Institutul de Igiena si Sanatate Publica [*Institute for Hygiene and Public Health*] (RO)
IISS .... Institute of Agricultural Economics (BU)
IISS .... International Institute for the Science of Sintering (EA)
IISS .... International Institute for Strategic Studies (MAR)
IISV .... Instituto de Investigaciones de Sanidad Vegetal [*Plant Health Research Institute*] [*Cuban*] (LA1)
IIT .... Institut Interafricain du Travail (MAR)
IIT .... Institut International du Theatre [*International Theater Institute*] [*Use ITI*] (CL)
IIT .... Technicum of Industrial Instructors (RU)
IIT .... Technion Israel Institute of Technology
IITA .... International Institute of Tropical Agriculture (EA)
IITF .... Imperial Iranian Task Force (ME)
IITIA .... Istanbul Iktisadi ve Ticari Ilimler Akademisi [*Istanbul Academy of Economy and Commercial Science*] [*See also ITIA*] (TU)
IITR .... Inspection of Corrective Labor (RU)
IITT-IITW ..... Institut International du Travail Temporaire - International Institute for Temporary Work (EA)
IIVKh .... Institute of Hydraulic Engineers Imeni V. R. Vil'yams (RU)
IIW .... International Institute of Welding [*See also IIS*] (EA)
IIYeSTEKh ... Institute of History of Natural Sciences and Technology (of the Academy of Sciences, USSR) (RU)
IIYeT .... Institute of History of Natural Sciences and Technology (RU)
IIZhT .... Institute of Railroad Transporation Engineers (RU)
ij .... Idojaras Jelentes [*Weather Forecast*] (HU)
iJ .... Im Jahre [*In the Year*] [*German*]
IJ .... [*Banque*] Inadana Jati [*National Commerce (Bank)*] [*Cambodian*] (CL)
IJA .... Institut des Jeunes Aveugles de Faladie (MAR)
IJAE .... Indian Journal of Agricultural Economics [*Bombay*] [*A publication*] (MAR)
IJAHS .... International Journal of African Historical Studies [*A publication*] (MAR)
iJdW .... Im Jahre der Welt [*In the Year of the World*] [*German*]
IJI .... Istok Jugo-Istok [*East South-East*] (YU)
IJLFI .... Intreprinderea Judeteana pentru Legume si Fructe Ilfov [*Ilfov County Enterprise for Vegetables and Fruit*] (RO)
IJMB .... Interim Joint Matriculation Board (MAR)
IJO .... International Juridical Organization (EA)
IJPC .... Iran-Japan Petrochemical Company (ME)
IK .... Artificial Leather (RU)
IK .... Executive Committee (BU)
IK .... Executive Committee (RU)
IK .... Igazsagugyi Kozlony [*Ministry of Justice Gazette*] [*A publication*] (HU)
Ik .... Iktisat [*Economy*] (TU)
IK .... Indeks Kupovne Snage [*Purchasing Power Index*] (YU)
IK .... Infrared (RU)
IK .... Initiatwkreis Freiheit fuer Angola, Guinea-Bissau, und Mocambique (MAR)
i k .... Inspector General of Cavalry (BU)
IK .... Inspekter Kanan [*Senior Inspector*] (ML)
IK .... Institute of Crystallography (of the Academy of Sciences, USSR) (RU)
IK .... Institute of Sinology (RU)
IK .... Integrating Circuit (RU)
IK .... Invalidska Komisija [*Commission for the Disabled*] (YU)
IK .... Ionization Chamber (RU)
IK .... Izvrsni Komitet [*Executive Committee*] (YU)
IK .... Publishing Commission (RU)
IK .... Test Set (RU)
IK .... Tool Stock Room (RU)
IK .... True Course (RU)
IKA .... Idryma Koinonikon Asfaliseon [*Social Insurance Foundation*] [*Greek*] (GC)
IKA .... Installation Kabel und Apparate [*Now trademark of enterprises in the electrical household equipment and installations, automobile electric fittings, and infrared lamp production branch*] (EG)
IKA .... Publishing House of the Communist Academy (RU)
IKA .... Vereinigung Internationaler Kulturaustausch (MAR)
IKAG .... Internationale Konfoederation Arabischer Gewerkschaften [*International Confederation of Arab Trade Unions*] (EG)
IKAHI .... Ikatan Hakim Indonesia [*Indonesian Jurists Association*] (IN)
IKAPEL .... Ikatan Pelaut [*Seamen's Association*] (IN)
IKAPI .... Ikatan Penerbit Indonesia [*Indonesian Publishers Association*] (IN)
IKAR .... Internationale Kommission fur Alpines Rettungswesen [*International Commission for Alpine Rescue*] (EA)
IKB .... Internationale Kommunistenbond [*International Communist League*] [*Dutch*] (PPW)
IKB .... Isolierstoff- und Kondensatorenwerk, Berlin (VEB) [*Berlin Insulator and Condenser Plant (VEB)*] (EG)
IKC .... Ilustrowany Kurier Codzienny [*Polish*]
IKCh .... Pilot-Frequency Indicator (RU)
IKD .... All Pacific and Asian Dockworkers' Corresponding Committee [*DCC*] (RU)
IKD .... Ilerici Kadinlar Dernegi [*Progressive Women's Organization*] (TU)
IKDP .... Institute of Books, Documents, and Letters (RU)
IKE .... United Nations Economic Commission for Europe (BU)
IKEL .... Internacia Komitato por Etnaj Liberecoj [*International Committee for Ethnic Liberty - ICEL*] (EA)
IKF .... Etablissements I. Karim Freres (MAR)
IKF .... Institouton Kalliterevseos Fyton [*Plant Improvement Institute*] [*Greek*] (GC)
IKFM .... Italian Communist Youth Federation (RU)
IKG .... Institute of Kinetics and Combustion (of the Siberian Department of the Academy of Sciences, USSR) (RU)
IKh .... Idiotikis Khriseos [*(For) Private Use*] [*Automobile license plate designation*] (GC)
IKH .... Ihre Koenigliche Hoheit [*Her Royal Highness*] [*German*]
IKhF .... Institute of Chemical Physics (of the Academy of Sciences, USSR) (RU)

IKhFK.......... Isopropyl Ester of Trichlorophenylcarbamic Acid (RU)
IKhFK.......... Isopropylchlorophenyl Carbamate (RU)
IKhN.......... Scientific Research Institute of Surgical Neuropathology (RU)
IKhPS.......... Institute of the Chemistry of Naturally Occuring Compounds (of the Academy of Sciences, USSR) (RU)
IKhR.......... Institute of Chemical Reagents (RU)
IKhS.......... Institute of the Chemistry of Silicates (of the Academy of Sciences, USSR) (RU)
IKhTI.......... Ivanovo Institute of Chemical Technology (RU)
IKI.......... Cosmic Radiation Intensity (RU)
IKI.......... Industrija Kovinskih Izdelkov [*Metal Products Industry*] [*Maribor*] (YU)
IKIP.......... Institut Keguruan dan Ilmu Pendidikan [*Teacher Training Institute*] (IN)
IKK.......... International Control Commission (RU)
IKKA.......... Kulfoldi Kereskedelmi Akcio [*Foreign Trade Enterprise*] (HU)
IKKh.......... Institute of Potato Growing (RU)
IKKI.......... Executive Committee of the Communist International [*1919-1943*] (BU)
IKKI.......... Executive Committee of the Communist International [*1919-1943*] (RU)
IKKIM.......... Executive Committee of the Communist Youth International (RU)
IKKN.......... Instytut Ksztalcenia Kadr Naukowych [*Institute for Training Scientific Personnel*] (POL)
IKKP.......... Indochinese Communist Party (RU)
IKL.......... Industrija Kotrljajucih Lezaja [*Roller Bearing Industry*] [*Belgrade*] (YU)
IKL.......... Infrared Rays (RU)
IKL.......... Isaenmaallinen Kansanliike [*Patriotic People's Movement*] [*Finnish*] (PPE)
IKM.......... Ikatan Karyawan Muhammadijah [*Muhammadijah Workers Association*] (IN)
Ikm.......... Ikmal [*Completion (of a project or job), Supplies*] (TU)
IKM.......... Pulse-Code Modulation (RU)
IKMNP.......... Ministry of Education Official Assignments Bulletin [*A publication*] (BU)
IKMVO.......... Electoral Committee of Moscow Military District (RU)
IKNPT.......... Italian Confederation of National Trade Unions (RU)
IKO.......... Catastrophic Failure Rate (RU)
IKO.......... Instituut voor Kernphysisch Onderzoek [*Institute for Research in Nuclear Physics*] [*Dutch*] (WEN)
IKO.......... Plan-Position Indicator (BU)
IKO.......... Plan Position Indicator (RU)
IKOA.......... Institouton Koinonikis kai Oikonomikis Anasyngrotiseos [*Social and Economic Reconstruction Institute*] (GC)
IKOKD.......... Istanbul Kibrislilar Ogrenim ve Kultur Dernegi [*Istanbul Cypriots' Educational and Cultural Association*] (GC)
IKOM.......... Industriska Kovnica "Oreskovic Marko" [*"Marko Oreskovic" Industrial Plant*] [*Zagreb*] (YU)
IKOM pri BAN... Institute of Clinical and Social Medicine of the Bulgarian Academy of Sciences (BU)
ikon.......... Economics [*or Economic*] (BU)
IKOPZ.......... Testing Commission of the Okhta Gunpowder Plant (RU)
IKOSZ.......... Informaciofeldolgozasi, Kibernetikai, es Operaciokutatasi Kozponti Szakosztaly [*Central Department for Information Processing, Cybernetics, and Operations Research*] (HU)
IKP.......... Indiai Kommunista Part [*Communist Party of India*] (HU)
IKP.......... Indian Communist Party (BU)
IKP.......... Indonesian Communist Party (BU)
IKP.......... Institute of the Red Professoriat (RU)
IKP.......... Irakskaia Kommunisticheskaia Partiia [*Iraqi Communist Party*] (MAR)
IKP.......... Iranian Communist Party (BU)
IKP.......... Iraqi Communist Party (BU)
IKP.......... Iraqi Communist Party (RU)
IKP.......... Irish Communist Party (BU)
IKP.......... Israeli Communist Party (BU)
IKP.......... Italian Communist Party (BU)
IKP.......... Italian Communist Party (RU)
IKPT.......... Italian Confederation of Trade Unions (RU)
IKR.......... Iparszeru Kukoricatermelesi Rendszer [*Industry-Type Corn Production System*] (HU)
IKR.......... Izba Kontroli Rachunkowej [*Account Auditing Bureau*] (POL)
IKRPiT.......... Izba Kontroli Rachunkowej Poczty i Telekomunikacji [*Account Auditing Bureau of Posts and Telecommunications*] (POL)
IKrS.......... Istaknuta Kurirska Stanica [*Advanced Courier Station*] [*Military*] (YU)
IKS.......... Indicirana Konjska Snaga [*Indicated Horsepower*] (YU)
IKS.......... Infrared Glass (RU)
IKS.......... Inspektorat Kontroli Skarbowej [*Polish*]
IKS.......... Institute of Kolkhoz Construction (RU)
IKS.......... International Kolping Society [*See also IKW*] (EA)
IKSA.......... Measuring, Checking, and Counting Equipment (RU)
IKSM.......... Institute of Clinical and Social Medicine (BU)
IKSR.......... Internationale Kommission zum Schutze des Rheins Gegen Verunreinigung [*International Commission for the Protection of the Rhine Against Pollution - ICPRAP*] (EA)
Ikt.......... Iktisadi [*Economy, Economic*] (TU)
IKT.......... Infrared Engineering (RU)
IKT.......... Isolier- und Kaeltetechnik [*Insulation and Refrigeration Equipment Works*] (EG)
IKTC.......... Ingiltere Kibris Turk Cemiyeti [*Turkish Cypriot Society of Great Britain*] (GC)
IKTP.......... Institute of Complex Transportation Problems (RU)
IKTTC.......... Istanbul Kibris Turkler Talebe Cemiyeti [*Istanbul Turkish Cypriot Student Society*] (GC)
IKU.......... Ivanovo Communist University (RU)
IKV.......... Boiler Water Evaporator (RU)
IKV.......... Iktisadi Kalkinma Vakfi [*Economic Development Fund Directorate General*] (TU)
IKV.......... Ingatlankezelo Vallalat [*Real Estate Management Enterprise*] (HU)
IKV.......... Institute of Communist Education (RU)
IKW.......... Internationales Kolpingwerk [*International Kolping Society - IKS*] (EA)
IKY.......... Idryma Kratikon Ypotrofion [*State Scholarships Institute*] [*Greek*] (GC)
IKZh.......... All-Union Scientific Research Institute of Farm Animal Feeding (RU)
IL.......... Aircraft Designed by S. V. Il'yushin (RU)
IL.......... Foreign Literature (RU)
il.......... Illustrated By, Illustrated (BU)
il.......... Ilman Lisamaksuvelvollisuutta [*Finnish*]
il.......... Ilustrace [*or Ilustrator*] [*Illustration or Illustrator*] (CZ)
Il.......... Ilustre [*Illustrious*] [*Correspondence*] [*Spanish*]
iL.......... In Liquidation [*In Liquidation*] (EG)
IL.......... Indicator Lamp (RU)
IL.......... Industrielaeden [*Industrial Sales Outlets (in production enterprises)*] (EG)
IL.......... Instituto del Libro [*Book Institute*] [*Cuban*] (LA)
IL.......... Instytut Lacznosci [*Communication Institute*] (POL)
IL.......... Israel [*Two-letter standard code*] (CNC)
IL.......... Izrael [*Israel*] [*Polish*]
IL.......... Lenin Institute (RU)
IL.......... Measuring Line (RU)
IL.......... Publishing House of Foreign Literature (RU)
ILA.......... Impresa Libica Asfalti (MAR)
ILA.......... Institute of Latin American Studies (RU)
ILA.......... International Leprosy Association (MAR)
ILA.......... Italo Libica Agricola (MAR)
ILAB.......... International League of Antiquarian Booksellers [*See also LILA*] (EA)
ILAFA.......... Instituto Latinoamericano del Fierro y Acero [*Latin American Iron and Steel Institute*] (LA)
ILAN.......... Forest Institute of the Academy of Sciences, USSR (RU)
ILAP.......... Instituto Latinoamericano del Plastico
ILAR.......... Ilmi Istisare ve Arastirmalar Kurulu [*Council of Scientific Consultation and Research*] [*National Defense Ministry*] (TU)
ILARI.......... Instituto Latinoamericano de Relaciones Internacionales [*Latin American Institute of International Relations*] (LA)
ILASE.......... International League of Agricultural Specialists-Esperantists (EA)
ilb.......... Engineer Airdrome Battalion (BU)
ILB.......... Institut fuer Landmaschinenbau [*Institute for Agricultural Machine Production*] (EG)
ILBANK.......... Iller Bankasi [*Provinces Bank*] (TU)
ILBE.......... International League of Blind Esperantists [*See also LIBE*] (EA)
ILC.......... International Law Commission (CL)
ILC.......... International Lifeboat Conference (EA)
ILCA.......... Industria Lechera de Caldas [*Armenia*] (COL)
ILCA.......... Instituto Linguistico Colombo Americano [*Bogota*] (COL)
ILCA.......... International Livestock Center for Africa (AF)
ILCCG.......... International Laity and Christian Community Group [*See also LAEEC*] (EA)
ILDIS.......... Instituto Latinoamericano de Investigaciones Sociales [*Latin American Social Research Institute*] (LA)
ILDS.......... International League of Dermatological Societies (EA)
ILDU.......... Industrias Laneras del Uruguay [*Wool Industries of Uruguay*] (LA)
Ile.......... Ilustre [*Illustrious*] [*Spanish*]
ILEF.......... Internacia Ligo de Esperantistaj Foto-Kino-Magnetofon-Amatoroj [*International League of Esperantist Amateur Photographers, Cinephotographers, and Tape-Recording*] (EA)
ILEI.......... Internacia Ligo de Esperantistaj Instruistoj [*International League of Esperantist Teachers*] (EA)
ILEI.......... Ligue Internationale des Enseignants Esperantistes [*International League of Teachers of Esperanto*] (AF)
ILek.......... Instytut Lekow [*Institute of Pharmacy*] [*Polish*]
ILERA.......... International League of Esperantist Radio Amateurs (EA)
ILEXIM.......... Intreprinderea de Stat pentru Comert Exterior [*State Enterprise for Foreign Trade*] (RO)
Il F.......... Ilahiyet Fakultesi [*School of Divinity*] [*Ankara University*] (TU)
ILF.......... International Liaison Forum of Peace Forces [*See also FILFP*] (EA)
ILFJIMB.......... Intreprinderea Legume Fructe Judet Ilfov Municipiul Bucuresti [*Ilfov County Bucharest Municipality Enterprise for Vegetables and Fruits*] (RO)

ILFMB.......... Intreprinderea pentru Legume si Fructe Municipiul Bucuresti [*Bucharest Municipality Enterprise for Vegetables and Fruits*] (RO)
ILGAZ.......... Institute of Local Government Association of Zambia (MAR)
ILGU........... Publishing House of the Leningrad State University (RU)
Ilh............... Ilahiri [*Etcetera*] (TU)
ILHS............ Intreprinderea de Lucrari Hidrotehnice Speciale [*Enterprise for Special Hydrotechnical Projects*] (RO)
ILI............... Institute of Flight-Testing (RU)
ILI............... Institute of History and Linguistics (RU)
ILIC............ Intreprinderile Locale Industriale din Cluj [*Local Industrial Enterprises of Cluj*] (RO)
ILIS............ Integriertes Leitungs- und Informationssystem [*Integrated Control and Data System*] (EG)
ILIS............ International Labour Information System [*Proposed*]
ILIYaZV....... Institute of Literature, Art, and Language of the East (RU)
ILJAK.......... Il Jandarma Alay Komutani [*Provincial Gendarmery Regimental Command*] (TU)
Ilk-Der......... Ilkokul Ogretmenleri Dernegi [*Elementary School Teachers' Association*] (TU)
Ilk Sen......... Istanbul Ilkokul Ogretmenleri Sendikasi [*Istanbul Elementary School Teachers' Union*] (TU)
ill................ Illatiivi [*Finnish*]
ill................ Illetekes [*Authoritative*] (HU)
ill................ Illustrated [*Business and trade*] [*German*]
ill................ Illustrated, Illustration, Illustrator (RU)
ill................ Illusztracio [*Illustration*] (HU)
ILL.............. Institut [*Max Von*] Lave - [*Paul*] Langevin [*Grenoble, France*]
ILL.............. Intreprinderea de Locuinte si Locale [*Housing and Public Buildings Enterprise*] (RO)
Il(l)mo......... Il(l)ustrissimo [*Illustrious*] [*Portuguese*] (GPO)
Illmo............ Illustrissimo [*Most Illustrious*] [*Italian*] (GPO)
ILLS............. Institutul de Limbi si Literaturi Straine [*Institute for Foreign Languages and Literatures*] (RO)
Illustr........... Illustrissime [*Most Illustrious*] [*French*] (MTD)
ilm............... Ilmailu [*Aeronautics*] [*Finnish*]
ilm............... Ilmaisee [*or Ilmauksessa*] [*Express or Expression*] [*Finnish*]
ilm............... Ilmaista [*Finnish*]
ilm............... Ilmestynyt [*Finnish*]
ilm............... Ilmoittaa [*Finnish*]
ilm............... Ilmoitus [*Finnish*]
ILM.............. Information Logical Machine (RU)
Ilma............. Ilustrisima [*Most Illustrious*] [*Spanish*]
ILMA............ Instituto Latinoamericano de Mercadeo Agricola [*Bogota*] (COL)
ILMAC......... Israeli-Lebanese Mixed Armistice Commission (ME)
Ilmo............. Ilustrisimo [*Most Illustrious*] [*Spanish*]
ILO.............. International Labor Office (CL)
ILO.............. International Labor Organization (LA1)
ILOSU.......... International Labor Organization Staff Union (EA)
ILot............. Instytut Lotnictwa [*Institute of Aircraft*] [*Polish*]
ILP.............. Independent Labor Party [*Trinidadian and Tobagan*] (LA)
ILP.............. Industria Lopez Pallomaro [*Cali*] (COL)
ILP.............. Institut Libyen du Petrole (MAR)
ILPA............ Industria e Laboracao de Produtos Agricolas [*Labor and Industry of Agricultural Products*] [*Portuguese*] (WER)
ILPAP.......... Ilektrokinita Leoforeia Periokhis Athinon-Peiraios [*Electric-Powered Buses of the Athens-Piraeus Area*] (GC)
ILPE............ Industria Lobera y Pesquera del Estado [*National Seal and Fishing Industry*] [*Uruguayan*] (LA)
ILPES.......... Instituto Latinoamericano de Planificacion Economica y Social [*Latin American Social and Economic Planning Institute*] [*Santiago, Chile*] (LA)
ILPiKhD....... Institute of Forestry Problems and Wood Chemistry (of the Academy of Sciences, Latvian SSR) (RU)
ILPNR.......... International League for the Protection of Native Races (MAR)
ILR.............. International Labour Review [*Geneva*] [*A publication*] (MAR)
ILRLP.......... International League for the Rights and Liberation of Peoples (EA)
ILRLSC........ Information on Land Reform, Land Settlement, and Cooperatives [*Rome*] [*A publication*] (MAR)
ILRS............ International League of Religious Socialists (EA)
ILR Zeleznik... Ivo Lola Ribar Zeleznik [*Ivo Lola Ribar Machine Factory in Zeleznik*] (YU)
ils................ Indicated Horsepower (RU)
ILS.............. Information Logical System (RU)
ILS.............. Institut fuer Lichtempfindliche Stoffe [*Institute for Light-Sensitive Materials*] (EG)
ILS.............. Instrument Landing System (AF)
ILS.............. Inzenyrsko Letecka Sluzba [*Aviation Engineer Service*] (CZ)
ILS.............. Societe Ivoirienne Leroy-Somer (MAR)
ILSAN.......... Ilac ve Ham Maddeleri Sanayii AS [*Medicine and Raw Materials Industry Corporation*] (TU)
ILTAS.......... Ilac Sanayii ve Ticaret Anonim Sirketi [*Medicinal Industry and Trade Corporation*] (TU)
ILTE............ Industria Libraria Tipografica Editrice
ILTE............ Ioniki kai Laiki Trapeza tis Ellados [*Ionian and People's Bank of Greece*] (GC)
ilustr........... Ilustracja [*Figure, Illustration*] (POL)
ilustr........... Ilustrowal [*Illustrated By*] (POL)
ilv............... Ilave [*Supplement*] [*Turkish*] (GPO)
ILV.............. Instituto Linguistico de Verano [*Summer Institute of Linguistics*] (LA)
IlVj............. Ilustrirani Vjesnik [*Illustrated Review*] [*Zagreb*] [*A publication*] (YU)
Ilv Rev......... Ilaveler ve Revisyonlar [*Additions and Revisions, as to a document*] (TU)
ILYa............ Information Logical Language (RU)
ILYaZV........ Scientific Research Institute of Comparative History of Literatures and Languages of the West and East (RU)
IM................ Actuating Mechanism (RU)
IM................ Data Processor, Data-Processing Machine (RU)
im................ Idezett Mu [*Opus Citatum*] (HU)
IM................ Igazsagugyminiszter [*Minister of Justice*] (HU)
im................ Imeni [*Named For*] (RU)
im................ Imienia [*Named For*] (POL)
IM................ Immanuel Mission (MAR)
im................ In Margine [*On the Margin*] [*Latin*]
IM................ Industriemeldung [*Industrial Statistics*] (EG)
IM................ Information for Mariners (RU)
IM................ Institute of Mathematics (of the Siberian Department of the Academy of Sciences, USSR) (RU)
IM................ Instytut Metalurgii [*Institute of Metallurgy*] (POL)
IM................ Intreprinderea Miniera [*Mining Enterprise*] (RO)
IM................ Measuring Device (RU)
IM................ Multiseater Fighter (RU)
im................ Nominal (BU)
im................ Nominative [*Case*] (RU)
IM................ Performing Mechanism (BU)
IM................ Power Meter (RU)
IM................ Pulse Modulation (RU)
IM................ Research Method (RU)
Im-.............. Testing Machine (RU)
IMA.............. Industria de Articulos de Madera [*Bogota*] (COL)
IMA.............. Industria Metalica para Automotores [*Cali*] (COL)
IMA.............. Institute of Mediterranean Affairs (MAR)
IMA.............. Institute of the Science of Machines and Automation (of the Academy of Sciences, Ukrainian SSR) (RU)
IMA.............. International Milling Association [*See also AIM*] (EA)
IMA.............. International Mycological Association (EA)
IMA.............. Intreprinderea pentru Mecanizarea Agriculturii [*Enterprise for the Mechanization of Agriculture*] (RO)
IMA.............. Tagged-Atom Rate Meter (RU)
IMACASA... Implementos Agricolas Centroamericanos, SA [*Agricultural Implements Corp.*] [*Salvadoran*]
IMACC........ Instituto de Matematica, Cibernetica, y Computacion [*Institute of Mathematics, Cybernetics, and Computation*] [*Cuban*] (LA)
IMACY......... Industrie Malienne de Cycles et Cyclomoteurs (MAR)
IMADA......... Ikatan Mahasiswa Djakarta [*Djakarta College Student Association*] (IN)
IMADUNI..... Impuesto Aduanero Unico a las Importaciones [*Single Import Customs Tax*] [*Uruguayan*] (LA)
IMAGIS........ Igazsagugyi Muszaki-Gazdasagi Szakertok (Kozponti Bizottsag) [*(Central Committee of) Judicial Scientific-Economic Experts*] (HU)
IMAIA.......... Intreprinderea Mecanica a Agriculturii si Industriei Alimentare [*Machine Enterprise for Agriculture and the Food Industry*] (RO)
IMAL............ Industrias Metalicas Asociadas Ltda. [*Bogota*] (COL)
IMALCO...... Muebles Metalicos de Aluminio [*Cali*] (COL)
IMAPEC...... Industries Mauritaniennes de Peche [*Mauritanian Fishing Industries*] (AF)
IMARPE....... Instituto del Mar de Peru [*The Sea Institute of Peru*] (LA)
IMART......... International Medical Association for Radio and Television (EA)
IMAS........... Industrial and Management Services Ltd. (MAR)
IMAS........... Industrie Marbriere Senegalaise [*Senegalese Marble Industry*] (AF)
IMAS........... Instituto Mixto de Ayuda Social [*Mixed Institute for Social Aid*] [*Costa Rican*] (LA1)
IMASh......... Institute of the Science of Machines (RU)
imaskb........ Engineer Camouflage Battalion (RU)
imaskr......... Engineer Camouflage Company (RU)
IMASLA....... International Muslim Academy of Sciences, Letters, and Arts (MAR)
IMASOIE..... Industrie Marocaine de Soieries [*Moroccan Silk Industry*] (AF)
IMB............. Industria Metalurgica Banateana [*Banat Metallurgical Industry*] (RO)
IMB............. Institutul Meteorologic Bucuresti [*Bucharest Meteorological Institute*] (RO)
IMB............. Intreprinderea de Montaje Bucuresti [*Bucharest Assembly Enterprise*] (RO)
IMBEL......... Industria de Material Belico [*Ordnance Industry*] [*Brazilian*] (LA)
IMC............. Industria Materialelor de Constructii [*Construction Materials Industry*] (RO)
IMC............. Industria de Materiales de la Construccion [*Construction Materials Industry*] [*Cuban*] (LA)
IMC............. Ingenieria Mecanica Colombiana [*Bogota*] (COL)
IMC............. Instituto Mexicano del Cafe [*Mexican Coffee Institute*] (LA)
IMC............. International Micrographic Congress

IMC............ Intreprinderea de Materiale de Constructie [*Construction Materials Enterprise*] (RO)
IMC............ Preparatory Committee for the International Medical Commission for Health and Human Rights (EA)
IMCARY...... International Movement of Catholic Agricultural and Rural Youth [*See also MIJARC*] (EA)
IMCC.......... International Medical Co-Operation Committee (MAR)
IMCE.......... Instituto Mexicano de Comercio Exterior [*Mexican Foreign Trade Institute*] (LA)
IMCE.......... International Meeting of Cataloguing Experts
IMCES........ Industrias Mecanicas Colombo Espanolas [*Bogota*] (COL)
IMCh.......... Testing Machine for Pig Iron (RU)
IMCI........... Industries Metallurgiques de la Cote-d'Ivoire (MAR)
IMCIC......... Instituto Mexicano-Cubano de Intercambio Cultural [*Mexican-Cuban Cultural Exchange Institute*] (LA)
IMCM......... Intreprinderea de Montaje Conducte Magistrale [*Enterprise for the Installation of Main Pipelines*] (RO)
IMCO.......... Industrial Merchandising Company (MAR)
IMCO.......... Intergovernmental Maritime Consultative Organization (WEN)
IMCOLEMN... Intreprinderea de Stat pentru Constructii si Montaje Lemn [*State Enterprise for Wood Constructions and Assemblies*] (RO)
IMCOMA..... Immobiliere Construction du Maroc (MAR)
IMCS.......... Industrias Metalicas Colombo Espanolas [*Bogota*] (COL)
IMCS.......... Pax Romana, International Movement of Catholic Students [*See also MIEC*] (EA)
IMD............ Institute of Music and Drama [*Sudanese*] (MAR)
IMD............ Instytut Medycyny Doswiadczalnej [*Institute for Experimental Medicine*] [*Polish*]
IMD............ Intreprinderea de Material Didactic [*Teaching Materials Enterprise*] (RO)
IMD............ Intreprinderile Metalurgice Dunariene [*Danube Metallurgical Enterprises*] (RO)
IMD............ Iron and Minerals Development (MAR)
IMDB.......... Intreprinderea de Material Didactic Bucuresti [*Bucharest Teaching Materials Enterprise*] (RO)
IMDBI......... Industrial and Mining Development Bank of Iran (ME)
IMDEQUI..... Industrias Mecanicas del Quindio [*Armenia*] (COL)
IMDER........ Investigaciones Multidisciplinarias para el Desarrollo Rural. Universidad del Valle [*Cali*] (COL)
IMDICOL..... Importadora y Distribuidora Colombiana de Licores [*Bogota*] (COL)
IME............ Ideiglenes Muszaki Eloirasok [*Temporary Technical Directives*] (HU)
IME............ Industrias Mecanicas del Estado [*State Mechanical Industries*] [*Argentine*] (LA)
IME............ Instituto Militar de Engenharia [*Military Engineering Institute*] [*Brazilian*] (LA)
IME............ Manual for Assembly and Operation (RU)
IME............ Marx and Engels Institute [*1920-1931*] (RU)
IMEB.......... Institute of Microbiology, Epidemiology, and Bacteriophage (RU)
IMEB.......... International Movement of Esperantist Bicyclists [*See also BEMI*] (EA)
IMEB.......... Intreprinderea pentru Mecanizarea Evidentei Bucuresti [*Bucharest Enterprise for the Mechanization of Records*] (RO)
IMEC.......... Industria de Materiales Electricos Colombianos [*Cali*] (COL)
IMEC.......... Intreprinderea de Microproductie si Lucrari Experimentale de Constructii [*Enterprise for Microproduction and Experimental Construction Projects*] (RO)
IMECO........ Intreprinderea de Comert Exterior [*Foreign Trade Enterprise*] (RO)
IMEDE......... Institut pour l'Etude des Methodes de Direction de l'Enterprise [*A management development institute*] [*Lausanne, Switzerland*]
IMEG.......... Iranian Management Engineering Group (MAR)
IMEI........... Ipari Minoseg Ellenorzo Intezet [*Quality Control Institute for Industry*] (HU)
IMEKh......... Institute of Mechanics (of the Academy of Sciences, USSR) (RU)
IMEKO......... Internationale Messtechnische Konfoderation [*International Measurement Confederation*] (EA)
IMEKO......... Miedzynarodowa Federacja Pomiarow i Budowy Przyrzadow Precyzyjnych [*International Measurement and Precision Instrument Construction Federation*] (POL)
IMEL........... Marx-Engels-Lenin Institute at the TsK KPSS (RU)
IMELCA....... Ingenieria Electrica y Mecanica Ltda. [*Barranquilla*] (COL)
IMELPA....... Industrias Metalicas de Palmira (COL)
IMELS......... Marx-Engels-Lenin-Stalin Institute (RU)
IMEMO........ Institute of World Economics and International Relations (of the Academy of Sciences, USSR) (RU)
IMER........... Instytut Mechanizacji i Elektryfikacji Rolnictwa [*Institute for Mechanization and Electrification of Agriculture*] (POL)
IMES........... Industrias Metalicas Escobar [*Cali*] (COL)
IMES........... Instituto Militar de Estudios Superiores [*Military Institute of Advanced Studies*] [*Uruguayan*] (LA)
IMESCO...... Industrias Metalicas y Esmaltes de Colombia Ltda. [*Bogota*] (COL)
IMESKO...... Izmir Madeni Esya Sanayii Anonim Sirketi [*Izmir Metal Products Industry Corporation*] (TU)
IMESS......... Institute for the Mechanization and Electrification of Agriculture (BU)
IMET........... Institute of Metallurgy Imeni A. A. Baykov (RU)
IMETAL....... Industria de Metales [*Cali*] (COL)
IMETRA....... Institut de Medecine Tropicale Reine Astrid (MAR)
IME UDC..... International Medium Edition of the Universele Decimale Classificatie
IMEVALLE... Industrias Metalicas del Valle [*Cali*] (COL)
IMEWACO... Industrias Metalicas Waco [*Barranquilla*] (COL)
IMEXCO...... Importaciones Exportaciones Comerciales [*Medellin*] (COL)
IMEXIN........ Empresa Importadora y Exportadora de Infraestructura [*Enterprise for Import and Export of Infrastructure*] [*Cuban*] (LA)
IMEXPAL..... Empresa Importadora y Exportadora de Plantas Alimentarias, Sus Implementos, y Derivados [*Import and Exports Enterprise for Food Processing Plants and Related Accessories*] [*Cuban*] (LA)
IMF............. Inosinemonophosphoric Acid, Inosinic Acid (RU)
IMF............. Institute of Physics of Metals (RU)
IMF............. Institutul de Medicina si Farmacie [*Institute for Medicine and Pharmacy*] (RO)
IMF............. Institutul Medico-Farmaceutic [*Medico-Pharmaceutical Institute*] (RO)
IMF............. International Marketing Federation (EA)
IMF............. International Metalworkers Federation [*See also FIOM*] (EA)
IMF............. International Monetary Fund (SJT)
IMFBRM...... Institutul de Medicina Fizica, Balneoclimatologie, si Recuperare Medicala [*Institute for Physical Medicine, Balneo-Climatology, and Medical Recovery*] (RO)
IMFCA......... Institutul de Mecanica Fluidelor si Constructii Aerospatiale [*Institute for Fluid Mechanics and Aerospace Constructions*] (RO)
IMF-JC........ International Metal Workers' Federation Japan Council (SJT)
IMG............ Instytut Mechanizacji Gornictwa [*Institute of Mining Mechanization*] (POL)
IMG............ International Marxist Group [*British*] (PPW)
IMG............ Ivoirienne du Marbre et du Granit (MAR)
IMG............ Societe Commerciale d'Importation de Marchandises Generales (MAR)
IMGB.......... Intreprinderea de Masini Grele din Bucuresti [*Bucharest Heavy Machinery Enterprise*] (RO)
IMGE.......... Idryma Metallevtikon kai Geologikon Epevnon [*Institute for Mineral and Geological Research*] [*See also IGME*] (GC1)
IMGO.......... Sailing Instructions of Fleet Hydrographic Departments (RU)
IMGRE........ Institute of Mineralogy, Geochemistry, and Crystallochemistry of Rare Elements (of the Academy of Sciences, USSR) (RU)
IMGU.......... Publishing House of the Moscow State University Imeni M. V. Lomonosov (RU)
IMH............ Instytut Ministerstwa Hutnictwa [*Institute of the Ministry of Metallurgy*] (POL)
IMH............ Island Maternity Hospital (MAR)
IMI............. Instituto de Medicina Industrial Ltda. [*Cali*] (COL)
IMI............. International Marketing Institute (MAR)
IMI............. Irkutsk Medical Institute (RU)
IMI............. Istituto Mobiliare Italiano [*Italian Credit Institute*] (WER)
IMI............. Izhevsk Mechanical Engineering Institute (RU)
IMIA........... International Machinery Insurers Association (EA)
IMIA........... International Medical Informatics Association (EA)
IMIA........... Intreprinderea Montaj Instalatii Automatizare [*Enterprise for Automation Assemblies and Installations*] (RO)
IMIC........... Industria Mecanica Italo-Colombiana [*Cali*] (COL)
IMiD........... Instytut Matki i Dziecka [*Mother and Child Institute*] [*Polish*]
IMID........... News of the Ministry of Foreign Affairs [*A publication*] (RU)
IMIF............ International Maritime Industries Forum (EA)
IMINOCO.... Iranian Marine International Oil Company (ME)
IMIO........... Marine Research and Oceanographic Institute (BU)
IMIQ........... Instituto Mexicano de Ingenieros Quimicos [*Mexican Institute of Chemical Engineers*] (LA)
Imit............. Imitation [*Imitation*] [*German*]
IMJ............ Institut za Makedonski Jezik [*Macedonian Language Institute*] (YU)
IMK............ Institut Makanda Kabobi [*Makanda Kabobi Institute*] [*Zairian*] (AF)
IMK............ Institute of Material Culture (RU)
IMK............ Izvestja Muzejskega Drustva za Kranjsko [*Report of the Museum Society for Carniola*] [*A publication*] (YU)
IMKh.......... Institute of World Economy and World Politics [*1925-1947*] (RU)
IMKhA........ Idryma Meleton tis Khersonisou tou Aimou [*Aimos Peninsula Studies Foundation*] [*A Macedonian studies society in Salonica*] (GC)
IMKhiMP..... Institute of World Economy and World Politics (RU)
IML............ Industrias Metalicas Lisasa [*Cali*] (COL)
IML............ Institut fuer Marxismus-Leninismus (Beim ZK der SED) [*Institute for Marxism-Leninism (A part of the SED Central Committee)*] (EG)
IML............ Institute of Marxism-Leninism at the TsK KPSS (RU)
IML............ Institutul de Medicina Legala [*Institute of Legal Medicine*] (RO)
IMLI........... Institute of World Literature Imeni A. M. Gor'kiy (of the Academy of Sciences, USSR) (RU)

IMM .... Ilektromagnitikai Monades [*Electromagnetic Units*] (GC)
imm .... Immune (RU)
IMM .... Institute of Metal Science and Metallurgy (RU)
IMM .... Instytut Maszyn Matematycznych [*Computer Institute*] [*Polish*]
IMM .... Instytut Medycyny Morskiej [*Institute for Marine Medicine*] [*Polish*]
IMM .... International Money Market (MAR)
IMM .... Intreprinderea Metalurgica de Morarit [*Metallurgical Milling Enterprise*] (RO)
IMMB .... Inspectoratul de Militie a Municipiului Bucuresti [*Militia Inspectorate of the Bucharest Municipality*] (RO)
IMMOAF ...... Societe Immobiliere et Hypothecaire Africaine [*African Real Estate and Mortgage Company*] [*Zairian*] (AF)
IMMOAFRIC ... Societe Immobiliere Afrique (MAR)
IMMP .... Institute of Malaria and Medical Parasitology (BU)
i mn dr .... And Many Others (BU)
IMNL .... International Messengers Nigerian Limited (MAR)
IMNR .... Institutul de Proiectari si Cercetari pentru Industria Metalelor Neferoase si Rare [*Design and Research Institute for the Nonferrous and Rare Metals Industry*] (RO)
IMO .... Insaat Muhendisleri Odasi [*Chamber of Construction Engineers*] (TU)
IMO .... Institute of International Relations (RU)
IMO .... Institute of Teaching Methods (of the Academy of Pedagogical Sciences, RSFSR) (RU)
IMO .... Instytut Materialow Ogniotrwalych [*Institute of Fireproof Materials*] [*Polish*]
IMO .... International Maritime Organization [*See also OMI*] (EA)
IMO .... International Meteorological Organization [*Replaced by World Meteorological Organization in December 1951*] (SJT)
IMO .... Young People's Art (RU)
IMOP .... Instituto Mexicano de Opinion Publica [*Mexican Public Opinion Institute*] (LA)
IMOPI .... Institute for the Mechanical Processing of Minerals (RU)
imostb .... Engineer Bridge-Building Battalion (BU)
imostb .... Engineer Bridge Construction Battalion (RU)
imostr .... Engineer Bridge-Building Company (BU)
imostr .... Engineer Bridge Construction Company (RU)
imostv .... Engineer Bridge Construction Platoon (RU)
imp .... Emperor (RU)
imp .... Impaye [*French*]
Imp .... Imprenta [*Spanish*]
imp .... Imprimatur [*Let It Be Printed*] [*Latin*] (GPO)
IMP .... Independence of Malaya Party (ML)
IMP .... Industrias Metalicas de Palmira (COL)
IMP .... Instituto Mexicano del Petroleo [*Mexican Petroleum Institute*] (LA)
IMP .... Instytut Mechaniki Precyzyjnej [*Institute of Precision Mechanics*] (POL)
IMP .... Instytut Medycyny Pracy [*Institute of Industrial Medicine*] (POL)
imp .... Pulse, Impulse (RU)
IMPA .... Industrias Metalurgicas del Pacifico Ltda. [*Palmira*] (COL)
Impa .... Industrija Metalnih Proizvoda [*Metal Products Industry*] [*Zemun*] (YU)
IMPA .... Instituto de Matematica Pura e Aplicada [*Institute of Pure and Applied Mathematics*] [*Brazilian*] (LA)
imp a .... Pulse Analyzer (RU)
IMPADOC ... Impalpables de Occidente Ltda. [*Cali*] (COL)
IMPAS .... Insaat Malzemeleri Pazarlama Subesi [*Construction Materials' Marketing Branch*] [*A subsidiary of Industry, Commerce, and Manufacturing Enterprises Ltd.*] [*Turkish Cypriot*] (GC)
IMPCO .... Iran Milk Producers Cooperative Organization (ME)
IMPE .... Institutul de Microbiologie, Parazitologie, si Epidemiologie [*Institute for Microbiology, Parasitology, and Epidemiology*] (RO)
imperat .... Imperatiivi [*Imperative*] [*Finnish*]
IMPERCOL ... Impermeabilizaciones Colombia [*Medellin*] (COL)
impf .... Imperfekti [*Past Tense*] [*Finnish*]
IMPG .... Institut de Meteorologie et de Physique du Globe [*Algerian*] (MAR)
IMPGA .... Institut de Meteorologie et de Physique du Globe d'Algerie (MAR)
IMPI .... Societe Independante Maritime de Peche Ivoirienne (MAR)
IMPiHW .... Instytut Medycyny Pracy i Higieny Wsi [*Institute of Industrial Medicine and Rural Hygiene*] [*Polish*]
IMPITM .... Institute of Medical Parasitology and Tropical Medicine Imeni Ye. I. Martsinovskiy (RU)
IMPOREXCO ... Importaciones, Exportaciones, Representaciones Comerciales [*San Andres*] (COL)
IMPORGA .... Societe Gabonaise pour l'Importation et l'Exportation (MAR)
IMPORTTEX ... Textilbehozatali Vallalat [*Textile Import Enterprise*] (HU)
IMPOS .... Instituto Mexicano de Planeacion y Operacion de Sistemas
IMPP .... Institut za Medunarodnu Politiku i Privredu [*Institute for International Politics and Economics*] (YU)
IMPR .... International of Seamen and Port Workers (RU)
IMPRE .... Instituto de Medicina Preventiva para Ejecutivos [*Cali*] (COL)
IMPRECO .... Societe Impression de Textiles de la Republique Populaire du Congo (MAR)
IMPRIGA ..... Imprimerie Gabonaise (MAR)
IMPRIKIN .... Imprimeries de Kinshasa [*Kinshasa Press*] [*Zairian*] (AF)
IMPRIM .... Imprimerie Mauritanienne (MAR)
IMPROME ... Impuesto Minimo a la Produccion Media [*Minimum Tax on Average Production*] [*Uruguayan*] (LA)
IMPROME ... Impuesto a la Produccion Minima de las Explotaciones Agro [*Tax on Minimum Crop Yields*] [*Uruguayan*] (LA)
IMPROMER ... Societe Ivoirienne d'Importation des Produits de la Mer (MAR)
IMR .... Industrija Motora Rakovica [*Rakovica Motor Industry*] (YU)
IMR .... Institut fuer Metallphysik und Reinstmetalle [*Institute for Metal Physics and High-Purity Metals*] (EG)
IMR .... Institute for Mideast Research (MAR)
IMRO .... Internal Macedonian Revolutionary Organization [*Bulgarian*] (PPE)
IMS .... Industrias Mecanicas Sistematizadas [*Mechanical Systems Industry*] [*Brazilian*] (LA)
IMS .... Ingenieria Mecanica Sanitaria [*Bogota*] (COL)
IMS .... Inspectia Metrologiei de Stat [*State Inspectorate for Metrology*] (RO)
IMS .... Institute of Mineral Raw Materials (RU)
IMS .... Instituto de Materiales de Servia [*Serbian Materials Institute*] [*Cuban*] (LA)
IMS .... International Magnetic System (SJT)
IMS .... Intreprinderea Metalurgica de Stat [*State Metallurgical Enterprise*] (RO)
IMSA .... Industrias Metalicas Sudamericanas Ltda. [*Medellin*] (COL)
IMSA .... Ingenieros Mecanicos Siderurgicos Asociados [*Cali*] (COL)
IMSA .... Istanbul Mesrubat Sanayii Anonim Sirketi [*Istanbul Non-Alcoholic Drink Industry Corporation*] (TU)
IMShR .... Institute of School Work Methods (RU)
IMSKh .... Institute of Agricultural Mechanization (RU)
ImSND .... Imikiniton Nosokomeion Diakomidis [*Semimobile Evacuation Hospital*] (GC)
IMSS .... Institute of Powder Metallurgy and Special Alloys (of the Academy of Sciences, Ukrainian SSR) (RU)
IMSS .... Instituto Mexicano de Seguridad Social [*Mexican Social Security Institute*] (LA)
IMST .... Institut de Mecanique Statistique de la Turbulence [*French*]
IMT .... Institute of Management and Training (MAR)
IMTA .... Institut de Medicine Tropicale Appliquee [*Institute of Applied Tropical Medicine*] (AF)
IMTACO ...... Impermeabilizacion Tecnica Colombiana [*Medellin*] (COL)
IMTAS .... Ittihadi Milli Turk Anonim Sigorta Sirketi [*United National Turkish Insurance Corporation*] (TU)
IMTEC .... International Movements toward Educational Change (EA)
IMTG .... Internationale Moor und Torf-Gesellschaft [*International Peat Society - IPS*] (EA)
IMTP .... Mining Research Institute (BU)
IMTPA .... Institut de Medecine Tropicale Princesse Astrid (MAR)
IMU .... Internacionalna Matematicka Unija [*International Mathematical Union*] (YU)
IMU .... International Mathematical Union [*See also UMI*] (EA)
IMU .... International Metal Union (EA)
IMU .... Intreprinderea Metalurgica de Utilaj [*Metallurgical Equipment Enterprise*] (RO)
IMUA .... Intreprinderea de Masini Unelte si Agregate [*Machine Tools and Aggregates Enterprise*] (RO)
IMUAB .... Intreprinderea de Masini Unelte si Agregate Bucuresti [*Bucharest Machine Tool and Aggregates Enterprise*] (RO)
IMUC .... Intreprinderea Mecanica de Utilaj Chimic [*Machine Enterprise for Chemical Equipment*] (RO)
IMUDel .... Control Pulse from Local Division Control [*Computers*] (RU)
IMUJ .... Instytut Matematyczny Uniwersytetu Jagiellonskiego [*Jagiellonian University Institute of Mathematics*] (POL)
IMUM .... Industriile Metalurgice de Unelte si Masini [*Metallurgical Tools and Machines Industries*] (RO)
IMUSA .... Industrias Metalurgicas Unidas SA [*Medellin*] (COL)
IMUZ .... Instytut Melioracji i Uzytkow Zielonych [*Institute of Reclamation and Use of Pasture Lands*] (POL)
IMV .... International Federation of Meat Traders' Associations (EA)
IMVR .... Institute of Extra-Scholastic Work Methods (RU)
IMVTs .... Institute of Mathematics with Computation Center (of the Academy of Sciences, Moldavian SSR) (RU)
IMWA .... International Mine Water Association (EA)
im wl .... Imie Wlasne [*Proper Name*] [*Polish*]
IMwO .... Instytut Mazurski w Olsztynie [*Masurian Institute in Olsztyn (Allenstein)*] (POL)
IMYeN .... News of Mathematical and Natural Sciences [*A publication*] (RU)
IMZ .... Instytut Metalurgii Zelaza [*Institute for Metallurgy of the Ferrous Metals*] [*Polish*]
IMZ .... Internationales Musikzentrum [*International Music Centre*] (EA)
IMZ .... Irbit Motorcycle Plant (RU)
IMZh .... Institute of Animal Morphology Imeni A. N. Severtsov (of the Academy of Sciences, USSR) (RU)
IMZO .... Institute for Mass Correspondence Training of Party Activists at the TsK VKP(b) (RU)
In .... Commissariat (BU)
IN .... Direction Finder (RU)
in .... Foreign (RU)
in .... Inaczej [*Or, Also*] [*Polish*]
IN .... India [*Two-letter standard code*] (CNC)

IN- .... Indicator Lamp (RU)
in .... Inny [*or Inni*] [*Other or Others*] [*Polish*]
in .... Inspector (RU)
IN .... Institute of Nationalities (RU)
IN .... Instytut Naftowy [*Petroleum Institute*] (POL)
IN .... Petroleum Institute (of the Academy of Sciences, USSR) (RU)
in .... Quartermaster, Supply Officer (BU)
IN .... Voltage Source (RU)
in-4° .... In-Quarto [*Quarto*] [*French*]
in-8° .... In-Octavo [*Octavo*] [*French*]
INA .... Industria Nacional de Armas [*National Weapons Industry*] [*Brazilian*] (LA)
INA .... Institut National Agronomique [*National Agronomic Institute*] [*French*] (AF)
INA .... Institut National des Arts [*National Art Institute*] [*Zairian*] (AF)
INA .... Institute of the Peoples of Asia (of the Academy of Sciences, USSR) (RU)
INA .... Instituto Nacional de Abastecimientos [*National Supply Institute*] [*Later, IDEMA*] [*Bogota, Colombia*] (LA)
INA .... Instituto Nacional Agrario [*National Agrarian Institute*] [*Honduran*] (LA)
INA .... Instituto Nacional de Aprendizaje [*National Apprenticeship Institute*] [*Costa Rican*] (LA)
INA .... International Newsreel and News Film Association (EA)
INA .... Iraqi News Agency (ME)
INA .... Isolants Nord Africain [*North African*] (MAR)
INA .... Istituto Nazionale delle Assicurazioni [*National Insurance Institute*] [*Italian*] (WER)
INAA .... Instituto Nicaraguense de Acueductos y Alcantarillados [*Nicaraguan Water and Sewage Institute*] (LA1)
INAC .... Instituto Nacional de la Carne [*National Meat Institute*] [*Uruguayan*] (LA)
INAC .... Instituto Nacional de Cultura [*National Culture Institute*] [*Panamanian*] (LA)
INACAP .... Instituto Nacional de Capacitacion Profesional [*National Professional Training Institute*] [*Chilean*] (LA)
INACESA .... Industria Nacional de Cemento Sociedad Anonima [*National Cement Industry, Incorporated*] [*Chilean*] (LA)
INACh .... Instituto Antartico Chileno [*Chilean Antarctic Institute*] (LA)
INACOP .... Instituto Nacional de Cooperativas [*National Institute of Cooperatives*] [*Salvadoran*] (LA1)
INACRE .... Industria Nacional de Cremalleras [*Bogota*] (COL)
INAD .... Instituto Nacional de Administracion para el Desarrollo [*National Institute of Administration for Development*] [*Guatemalan*] (LA)
INADEPAL ... Instituto Americano de Eficiencia Personal [*Bogota*] (COL)
INADES .... Institut Africain pour le Developpement Economique et Social [*African Institute for Economic and Social Development*] [*Ivorian*] (AF)
INAE .... Instituto de Altos Estudios [*Institute for Higher Studies*] [*Peruvian*] (LA)
INAFOR .... Instituto Nacional Forestal [*National Forestry Service*] [*Guatemalan*] (LA)
INAGRARIO ... Almacenes Generales de Deposito Organizado por INA y por la Caja de Credito Agrario [*Bogota*] (COL)
INAGRICO ... Industria Agricultura e Comercio Lda. (MAR)
INAH .... Instituto Nacional de Antropologia e Historia [*Mexican*]
INAIL .... Istituto Nazionale Assicurazione Contro gli Infortuni sul Lavoro [*National Work Accident Insurance Institute*] [*Italian*] (WER)
inakt .... Inaktiv [*Inactive*] [*German*]
INALPRE ..... Instituto Nacional de Preinversion [*National Investment Feasibility Studies Institute*] [*Bolivian*] (LA)
INALPRO ..... Instituto Nacional de Provisiones [*Bogota*] (COL)
INALTRA ..... Industria Nacional de Troqueles [*Bogota*] (COL)
INALWA ...... International Airlift West Africa (MAR)
INAM .... Istituto Nazionale Assicurazione Contro le Malattie [*National Health Insurance Institute*] [*Italian*] (WER)
INAMHI .... Instituto Nacional de Meteorologia e Hidrologia [*National Meteorology and Hydrology Institute*] [*Ecuadorean*] (LA)
INAMI .... Institut National d'Assurance Maladie-Invalidite [*National Institute for Illness and Disability Insurance*] [*Belgian*] (WER)
INAMM .... Institut National des Mass Media [*National Institute of Mass Media*] [*Zairian*] (AF)
INAMPS ...... Instituto Nacional de Assistencia Medica da Previdencia Social [*National Institute for Social Security Medical Assistance*] [*Brazilian*] (LA)
INAN .... Infectious Anemia of Horses (RU)
INAN .... Instituto Nacional de Alimentacao e Nutricao [*National Food and Nutrition Institute*] [*Brazilian*] (LA)
INANDINA ... Industria Quimica Andina Ltda. [*Bogota*] (COL)
INANK .... Petroleum Institute of the Chinese Academy of Sciences (RU)
INANTIC ...... Instituto Nacional de Normas Tecnicas y Certificacion [*National Institute of Technical Standards and Certification*] [*Peruvian*] (LA)
INAP .... Instituto Nacional de Administracion Publica [*National Public Administration Institute*] [*Peruvian*] (LA)
INAP .... Instituto Nicaraguense de Administracion Publica [*Nicaraguan Public Administration Institute*] (LA1)
INAPA .... Instituto Nacional de Aguas Potables y Alcantarillados [*National Institute of Waterworks and Sewage*] [*Dominican Republic*] (LA)
INAPE .... Instituto Nacional de Pesca [*National Fishing Institute*] [*Uruguayan*] (LA)
INAPET .... Instituto de Adiestramiento Petrolero y Petroquimico [*Petroleum and Petrochemical Training Institute*] [*Venezuelan*] (LA)
INAPI .... Instituto Nacional de Prevencion Contra Incendios [*National Institute of Fire Prevention*] [*Nicaraguan*] (LA1)
INAPROMEF ... Instituto Nacional de Promocion del Menor y la Familia [*National Institute for the Aid and Advancement of Minors and the Family*] [*Peruvian*] (LA)
INAR .... Comercial de Ingenieros y Arquitectos de Caldas [*Manizales*] (COL)
INARC .... Institut Nord-Africain de Recherches Cottonieres (MAR)
INARCON .... Ingenieria, Arquitectura, Construcciones [*Cali*] (COL)
INAS .... Institut National d'Animation Sociale [*National Institute for Social Promotion*] [*Zairian*] (AF)
INAS .... Institut National des Assurances Sociales [*North African*] (MAR)
INASEN .... International Assembly of Non-Governmental Organizations Concerned with Environment (MAR)
INASOL .... Instituto Aleman de Soldadura [*Bogota*] (COL)
INAVI .... Instituto Nacional de la Vivienda [*National Housing Institute*] [*Venezuelan*] (LA)
INB .... Inspekcja Nadzoru Budowlanego [*Inspectorate of Construction Control*] (POL)
INB .... Instytut Naukowo-Badawczy [*Scientific Research Institute*] (POL)
INBEC .... Instituto Nacional de Becas y Credito Educativo [*National Scholarship and Educational Credit Institute*] [*Peruvian*] (LA)
INBEL .... Institut Belge d'Information et de Documentation [*Belgian Institute of Information and Documentation*] (WER)
INBELSA ..... Industria Brasileira de Eletricidade SA [*Brazilian Electric Power Industry, Inc.*] (LA)
INBI .... Institute of Biochemistry Imeni A. N. Bakh (of the Academy of Sciences, USSR) (RU)
INBK .... Instytut Naukowo-Badawczy Kolejnictwa [*Railroad Scientific Research Institute*] (POL)
INBOLPEX ... Instituto Boliviano de Promocion a las Exportaciones [*Bolivian Institute for the Promotion of Exports*] (LA)
INBPW .... Instytut Naukowo-Badawczy Przemyslu Weglowego [*Coal Industry Scientific Research Institute*] (POL)
INBTP .... Institut National du Batiment et des Travaux Publics [*National Institute of the Building Trades and Public Works*] [*Zairian*] (AF)
INBWL .... Instytut Naukowo-Badawczy Wojsk Lotniczych [*Air Force Scientific Research Institute*] (POL)
INC .... Institut National de Cartographie [*National Cartography Institute*] [*Algerian*] (AF)
INC .... Institut National de Cartographie [*National Cartography Institute*] [*Beninese*] (AF)
INC .... Instituto Nacional de Canalizaciones [*Venezuelan*]
INC .... Instituto Nacional de Cinema [*National Motion-Picture Institute*] [*Brazilian*] (LA)
INC .... Instituto Nacional de Colonizacion [*National Settlement Institute*] [*Uruguayan*] (LA)
INC .... Instituto Nacional de Colonizacion [*National Settlement Institute*] [*Bolivian*] (LA1)
INCA .... Instituto de Ciencia Agricola [*Institute of Agricultural Sciences*] [*Cuban*] (LA)
INCA .... Instituto Nacional de Cirugia y Anestesiologia [*National Institute of Surgery and Anesthesiology*] [*Cuban*] (LA)
INCADELMA ... Instituto de Capacitacion y Perfeccionamiento del Magisterio [*Bogota*] (COL)
INCAE .... Instituto Centroamericano de Administracion de Empresas [*Central American Institute of Business Administration*] (LA)
INCAME ...... Industria Nacional de Repuestos [*Cali*] (COL)
INCAP .... Instituto de Nutricion de Centroamerica y Panama [*Nutrition Institute of Central America and Panama*] (LA)
INCAR .... Industrias Metalicas Carbonell [*Ibague*] (COL)
INCARIBE ... Ingenieria del Caribe Ltda. [*Barranquilla*] (COL)
INCAS .... Ingenieros Constructores Arquitectos Asociados Ltda. [*Bogota*] (COL)
INCATEL ..... Instituto Centroamericano de Telecomunicaciones [*Central American Telecommunications Institute*] (LA1)
INCAUCA .... Ingenio del Cauca SA [*Cali*] (COL)
INCAUCHO ... Industria de Caucho de Medellin (COL)
INCB .... International Narcotics Control Board (CL)
INCC .... International Nuclear Credit Corporation (SJT)
INCCA .... Instituto Colombiano de Ciencias Administrativas [*Colombian Institute of Administrative Sciences*] (LA)
INCE .... Industria Nacional de Conductores Electricos [*Cali*] (COL)
INCE .... Instituto Nacional de Cooperacion Educativa [*National Institute of Cooperative Education*] [*Bogota*] (COL)
INCE .... Instituto Nacional de Cooperacion Educativa [*National Institute of Cooperative Education*] [*Venezuelan*] (LA)

INCEF......... Institutul de Cercetari Forestiere [*Forestry Research Institute*] (RO)
INCEI........... Instituto Nacional de Comercio Exterior e Interior [*National Institute of Foreign and Domestic Trade*] [*Nicaraguan*] (LA)
INCERC....... Institutul de Cercetari in Constructii si Economia Constructoriilor [*Research Institute for Constructions and the Construction Economy*] (RO)
INCERDA.... Industria Colombiana de Cerdas [*Medellin*] (COL)
INCERG....... Institutul de Cercetari Electroenergetice si pentru Termoficare [*Institute for Electrical and Thermal Power Research*] (RO)
INCH........... Institute for Contemporary History (MAR)
INCI............ Instituto Nacional de Ciegos [*Bogota*] (COL)
INCIBA........ Instituto Nacional de Cultura y Bellas Artes [*National Institute of Culture and Fine Arts*] [*Venezuelan*] (LA)
INCIDI......... Institut International des Civilisations Differentes (MAR)
INCITEMI.... Instituto Cientifico y Tecnologico Minero [*Scientific and Technological Mining Institute*] [*Peruvian*] (LA)
INCLAS....... Ingenieros Civiles Asociados Ltda. [*Cali*] (COL)
INCLINIC..... Instituto Clinico Ltda. [*Bogota*] (COL)
INCN........... Institut National pour la Conservation de la Nature (MAR)
INCO........... Industria de Congreto Centrifugado Ltda. [*Bogota*] (COL)
INCO........... Industrias Consolidadas, SA [*Consolidated Industries Corp.*] [*Salvadoran*]
INCOA......... Ingenieros Constructores Asociados [*Cali*] (COL)
INCOAGRO... Inversiones Comerciales y Agropecuarios Ltda. [*Barranquilla*] (COL)
INCOAL....... Industria de Cobre y Aluminio Ltda. [*Medellin*] (COL)
INCOBOL.... Industria Colombiana de Bolos Ltda. [*Palmira*] (COL)
INCOBRA.... Instituto Cientifico Colombo Brasilero Ltda. [*Barranquilla*] (COL)
INCOCEGA... Industrie et Commerce General Gabonais [*Gabonese Industry and General Trade*] (AF)
INCOCOL.... Internacional Colombiana [*Medellin*] (COL)
INCODENTAL... Industrias Colombianas Dentales [*Medellin*] (COL)
INCOFRAN... Ingenieria Colombo Francesa [*Cali*] (COL)
INCOGEGA... Industrie et Commerce General Gabonais (MAR)
INCOHORMAS... Industria Colombiana de Hormas Ltda. [*Bogota*] (COL)
INCOIN........ Ingenieros Constructores Industriales [*Medellin*] (COL)
INCOLANA (EPS)... Empresa de Explotacion de Lana de Vicuna [*Vicuna Wool Production Enterprise*] [*Peruvian*] (LA)
INCOLCA.... Industria Colombiana de Cauchos [*Cali*] (COL)
INCOLDA.... Instituto Colombiano de Administracion [*Colombian Institute of Administration*] [*Bogota*] (LA)
INCOLDER... Industria Colombiana de Troqueles [*Bogota*] (COL)
INCOLDEX... Industria Colombiana de Extinguidores [*Bogota*] (COL)
INCOLFRENOS... Industria Colombiana de Liquidos para Frenos Gardiol [*Cali*] (COL)
INCOLGRASOS... Industria Colombiana de Derivados Grasos SA [*Medellin*] (COL)
INCOLMA.... Industria Colombo Alemana de Machetes [*Manizales*] (COL)
INCOLQUIPO... Industria Colombiana de Equipos de Oficina [*Bogota*] (COL)
INCOLTRA... Industria Colombiana de Transformadores Ltda. [*Bogota*] (COL)
INCOM........ Internacional Comercial Lda. (MAR)
INCOMAL.... Industria Comercial y de Alimentos [*Bogota*] (COL)
INCOMEX.... Instituto Colombiano de Comercio Exterior [*Colombian Foreign Trade Institute*] [*Bogota*] (LA)
INCOMEX.... Instituto de Comercio Exterior [*Foreign Trade Institute*] [*Colombian*] (LA)
INCOMEX.... Instituto Mexicano de Comercio Exterior [*Mexican Foreign Trade Institute*] (LA)
INCOMINDIOS... International Committee for the Indians of the Americas (EA)
INCON......... Industrias Consolidadas Ltda. [*Barranquilla*] (COL)
INCONAV.... Industria e Comercio Naval [*Shipbuilding Industry and Commerce*] [*Brazilian*] (LA)
INCONAVE... Industria de Construcao Naval [*Shipbuilding Industry*] [*Brazilian*] (LA)
INCOPE....... Industria Colombiana de Productos Electricos [*Bogota*] (COL)
INCOPLAN... Instituto Colombiano de Planeacion Integral [*Medellin*] (COL)
INCOPLAS... Industria Colombiana de Plastico [*Bogota*] (COL)
INCOPORE... Internationales Kommittee der Politischen Fluechtlinge und Verschleppten Personen in Deutschland [*International Committee for Political Refugees and Displaced Persons in Germany*] (EG)
INCOPP....... Instituto Costarricense de Puertos del Pacifico [*Costa Rican Pacific Ports Institute*] (LA)
INCOR......... Israeli National Committee for Oceanographic Research (MAR)
INCORA...... Instituto Colombiano de Reforma Agraria [*Colombian Agrarian Reform Institute*] (LA)
INCORSA.... Industria Colombiana de Refrigeracion SA [*Manizales*] (COL)
INCOSAR.... Ingenieros Constructores Arquitectos Ltda. [*Bogota*] (COL)
INCOSEM.... Instituto Costarricense del Sector Empresarial [*Costa Rican Institute of the Business Sector*] (LA1)
INCOSUR.... Industria del Cono Sur [*Southern Cone Industries*] [*Peruvian*] (LA)
INCOVIAS... Ingenieria de Construcciones y Vias [*Bogota*] (COL)
INCP............ Instituto Nacional de Contadores Publicos [*Bogota*] (COL)
INCRA......... Instituto Nacional de Colonizacao e Reforma Agraria [*National Land Reform and Settlement Institute*] [*Brazilian*] (LA)
INCREDIAL... Instituto de Credito Territorial [*Territorial Credit Institute*] [*Colombian*] (LA)
INCREST..... Institutul pentru Creatie Stiintifica si Tehnica [*Institute for Scientific and Technical Creativity*] (RO)
INCRET....... Instituto para Capacitacion y Recreacion de los Trabajadores [*Workers Training and Recreation Institute*] [*Venezuelan*] (LA)
INCS............ Iran National Cancer Society (ME)
INCSAS....... Ingenieros Civiles y Sanitarios Asociados Ltda. [*Bogota*] (COL)
INCUBAR.... Asociacion Colombiana de Incubadoras [*Bogota*] (COL)
INCURSABA... Industria de Curtidos Sabaneta Ltda. [*Medellin*] (COL)
IND.............. In Nomine Dei [*In the Name of God*] [*Latin*] (GPO)
ind............... Index, Indicator (BU)
IND.............. India [*Three-letter standard code*] (CNC)
ind............... Indian (BU)
ind............... Indian (RU)
ind............... Indikatiivi [*Indicative Mood*] [*Finnish*]
Ind............... Indirme [*Debarkation*] (TU)
ind............... Indulas [*Departure*] (HU)
Ind............... Industrie [*Industry*] [*German*]
IND.............. Instituto Nacional de Deportes [*National Institute of Sports*] [*Venezuelan*]
IND.............. Instituto Nacional de Deportes [*National Institute of Sports*] [*Nicaraguan*] (LA1)
ind............... Megindult [*First Published*] (HU)
INDA............ Industrias de Aluminio [*Medellin*] (COL)
INDA............ Instituto Nacional de Alimentacion [*National Nutrition Institute*] [*Uruguayan*] (LA)
INDA............ Instituto Nacional de Desenvolvimento Agricola [*National Institute of Agricultural Development*] [*Brazilian*] (LA)
INDACOM... Bureau d'Etudes Industrielles Agricoles et Commerciales (MAR)
INDACY....... Industrie Dahomeenne du Cycle (MAR)
INDAER-PERU... Empresa Publica de la Industria Aeronautica [*Aeronautics Industry State Enterprise*] [*Peruvian*] (LA)
INDAF......... Instituto Nacional de Desarrollo y Aprovechamiento Forestales [*National Institute of Forestry Development and Exploitation*] [*Cuban*] (LA)
INDAG......... Industrial and Agricultural Co. Ltd. (MAR)
INDAL.......... Fabrica Nacional de Aluminio [*Bogota*] (COL)
INDAP......... Instituto de Desarrollo Agropecuario [*Agriculture and Livestock Development Institute*] [*Chilean*] (LA)
INDAR......... Industria Artesanal Colombiana [*Bogota*] (COL)
INDBCY....... Industrie Beninoise du Cycle (MAR)
INDCA......... Industria de Caucho [*Bogota*] (COL)
INDCAM...... Societe Indocamerounaise (MAR)
INDE............ Instituto Nacional de Electrificacion [*National Electrification Institute*] [*Guatemalan*] (LA)
INDE............ Instituto Nicaraguense de Desarrollo [*Nicaraguan Institute of Development*] (LA1)
INDEA......... Industria Nacional de Ingenieria Automotriz [*Cali*] (COL)
INDEASE..... Industria de Acero Ltda. [*Medellin*] (COL)
INDEBANK... Investment and Development Bank [*Malawian*] (MAR)
INDEC......... Instituto Nacional de Estadisticas y Censo [*National Statistics and Census Industry*] [*Argentine*] (LA)
INDECA....... Instituto Nacional de Comercializacion Agricola [*National Institute of Agricultural Marketing*] [*Guatemalan*] (LA1)
INDECAM.... Independants Camerounais (MAR)
INDECO...... Industrial Development Corporation [*Zambian*] (AF)
INDECO...... Instituto Nacional para el Desarrollo de la Comunidad Rural y la Vivienda Popular [*National Institute for the Development of the Rural Community and Low-Cost Housing*] [*Mexican*] (LA)
INDECON.... Inspectores de Construccion Ltda. [*Medellin*] (COL)
indef........... Indefiniittinen [*Finnish*]
INDEF.......... Instituto de Financiamiento [*Financing Institute*] [*Bolivian*] (LA)
indef pron... Indefiniittipronomini [*Indefinite Pronoun*] [*Finnish*]
INDEGA....... Industria de Gaseosas SA [*Medellin*] (COL)
INDEICOOP... Instituto Nacional de Estudios e Investigaciones Cooperativas [*National Institute of Studies and Cooperative Research*] [*Peruvian*] (LA)
INDELCAR... Industrias Electronicas del Caribe Ltda. [*Medellin*] (COL)
INDELCO.... Industrias Electrometalicas Colombia Ltda. [*Medellin*] (COL)
INDELVA..... Industrias Electronicas del Valle [*Cali*] (COL)
INDEMA...... Instituto de Mercado Agropecuario [*Agricultural and Livestock Marketing Institute*] [*Colombian*] (LA)
INDEP.......... Instituto Nacional de Desenvolvimento da Educacao e Pesquisa [*National Institute for Promoting Education and Research*] [*Brazilian*] (LA)
INDEPAC.... Industria de Papel Carbon y Cintas para Maquina [*Bogota*] (COL)
INDEPORT... Industria Deportiva [*Cali*] (COL)
INDER......... Instituto Nacional de Deportes, Educacion Fisica, y Recreacion [*National Institute for Sports, Physical Education, and Recreation*] [*Cuban*] (LA)
INDER......... Instituto Nacional de Reaseguros [*National Institute of Reinsurance*] [*Argentine*] (LA)
INDERENA... Instituto de Desarrollo de los Recursos Naturales Renovables [*Institute for Development of Renewable Natural Resources*] [*Colombian*] (LA)

INDES .... Instituto Nacional de los Deportes de El Salvador [*National Sports Institute of El Salvador*] (LA1)
INDESCO .... Unidad de Docencia [*Bogota*] (COL)
INDETRO .... Industria Nacional de Troqueles Ltda. [*Bogota*] (COL)
INDEVA .... Industrias Fotograficas Eva y Compania Ltda. [*Barranquilla*] (COL)
INDICOL ...... Importadora y Distribuidora Colombiana de Licores [*Bogota*] (COL)
indik .... Indicator (RU)
INDISA .... Indega de Inversiones SA [*Medellin*] (COL)
INDITECNOR ... Instituto Nacional de Investigaciones Tecnicas y Normalizacion [*National Institute of Technical Research and Standards*] [*Chilean*] (LA)
INDNAGA .... Industrias Naga [*Bogota*] (COL)
INDOCAS .... Instituto Dominicano de Capacitacion Sindical [*Dominican Institute of Trade Union Training*] [*Dominican Republic*] (LA1)
INDOELECTRA ... Industrias Electromecanicas [*Bogota*] (COL)
INDOL .... Industrias Oleiferas SA [*Medellin*] (COL)
indonez .... Indonesian (RU)
INDOS .... Industrija Obdelovalnih Strojev [*Agricultural Machinery Industry*] [*Ljubljana*] (YU)
Indproekt .... Industrial Design (BU)
INDRAP .... Institut National de Recherches et Application Pedagogique (MAR)
INDRHI .... Instituto Nacional de Recursos Hidraulicos [*Institute of Water Resources*] [*Dominican Republic*] (LA)
INDSCO ...... Industrial Development Corporation (MAR)
INDUACERO ... Industrias Centrales de Acero [*Bogota*] (COL)
INDUACOPLES ... Industria de Acoples Flexibles [*Bogota*] (COL)
INDUAGRO ... Industrias Agricolas Ltda. [*Bogota*] (COL)
INDUBOLCES ... Industria Nacional de Boceles [*Bogota*] (COL)
INDUCARTON ... Cartoneria Industrial Ltda. [*Bogota*] (COL)
INDUCERAMICA ... Ceramica Industrial Pegaso Ltda. [*Medellin*] (COL)
INDUCERRA ... Industria de Cerraduras Metalicas [*Medellin*] (COL)
INDUCO ...... Industrial de Confecciones Carlos Restrepo Olano & Compania Ltda. [*Medellin*] (COL)
INDUCON .... Industria de Concreto Ltda. [*Cali*] (COL)
INDUCOR .... Industria Cordelera Ltda. [*Manizales*] (COL)
INDUCUIR ... Societe Industrielle du Cuir (MAR)
INDUDECOL ... Industria Colombiana de Colas [*Bogota*] (COL)
INDUFARMA ... Industria de Farmacia Franco-Colombiana Ltda. [*Bogota*] (COL)
INDUFULL ... Industrias Full Ltda. [*Bogota*] (COL)
INDUGAN .... Industria Ganadera Colombiana SA [*Bogota*] (COL)
INDUGAS .... Industria Colombiana de Gas (COL)
INDULAMP ... Industria de Lamparas Ltda. [*Barranquilla*] (COL)
INDULECHE ... Industrial de Leches [*Medellin*] (COL)
Indulg plen ... Indulgencia Plenaria [*Plenary Indulgence*] [*Spanish*]
INDULLERA ... Industrial Hullera SA [*Medellin*] (COL)
INDUMA ...... Industrias Manizales (COL)
INDUMALLAS ... Industria de Mallas [*Bogota*] (COL)
INDUMEC .... Industrias Mecanicas Ltda. [*Bogota*] (COL)
INDUMEL .... Industrias Mel Ltda. [*Medellin*] (COL)
INDUMIL-PERU ... Industrias Militares del Peru [*Military Industries of Peru*] (LA)
INDUMODE ... Industrias Modernas [*Bogota*] (COL)
INDUMOL .... Industrias Molineras Ltda. [*Cali*] (COL)
INDUPALMA ... Industrial Agraria la Palma SA [*Bogota*] (COL)
INDUPAN .... Industria Panificadora Nacional [*Cali*] (COL)
INDUPERU ... Industrias del Peru [*Peruvian State Industries*] (LA)
INDUPLANO ... Industrial de Vidrio Plano [*Medellin*] (COL)
INDUPLAS ... Industrias Plasticas Ltda. (COL)
INDUPLATI ... Industrija Platnenih Izdelkov [*Linen Products Industry*] [*Jarse*] (YU)
INDUPOL ..... Industria Nacional de Poleas [*Manizales*] (COL)
INDUPOMO ... Industria de Pomos Ltda. [*Cali*] (COL)
INDURACE ... Industria Purace SA [*Cauca*] (COL)
INDURRAJES ... Industria de Herrajes Ltda. [*Medellin*] (COL)
INDUSGUAN ... Industrias de Guantes de Cuero [*Barranquilla*] (COL)
INDUSPANAM ... Industrializacion Panamericana Ltda. [*Bogota*] (COL)
Industroy .... All-Union Construction and Installation Trust of the Ministry of Construction of the Metallurgical and Chemical Industries, USSR (RU)
Industroyproyekt ... Planning and Design Office of the State Committee for the Building Materials Industry of the Gosstroy SSSR (RU)
INDUTEC .... Industrias Tecnoquimicas de la Costa [*Barranquilla*] (COL)
INDUTRENZ ... Industria Colombiana de Trenzados Ltda. [*Barranquilla*] (COL)
INDUVAR .... Industrias Varias [*Medellin*] (COL)
INDUVIC ...... Industrias Victoria [*Cali*] (COL)
IndV .... Industrijski Vestnik [*Industrial Review*] [*A publication*] (YU)
INE .... Institut National d'Education [*National Education Institute*] [*Upper Voltan*] (AF)
INE .... Instituto Nacional de Energia [*National Energy Institute*] [*Ecuadorean*] (LA)
INE .... Instituto Nacional de Estadisticas [*National Statistics Institute*] [*Bolivian*] (LA1)
INE .... Instituto Nacional de Estadisticas [*National Statistics Institute*] [*Chilean*] (LA)
INE .... Instituto Nacional de Estatistica [*National Statistics Institute*] [*Portuguese*] (WER)
INE .... Instituto Nicaraguense de Energia [*Nicaraguan Institute of Energy*] (LA1)
INE .... Istituto Nazionale Esportazioni [*National Institute for the Promotion of Export Trade*] [*Italian*] (WER)
INEA .... Institut National de l'Enseignement pour Adultes [*National Institute for Adult Education*] [*Tunisian*] (AF)
INEAC .... Institut National pour l'Etude Agronomique au Congo Belge (MAR)
INEC .... Instituto Nicaraguense de Estadistica y Censos [*Nicaraguan Institute of Statistics and Census*] (LA1)
INECEL .... Instituto Ecuatoriano de Electrificacion [*Ecuadorean Electrification Institute*] (LA)
ined .... Inedit [*Unpublished*] [*French*]
INED .... Institut National d'Etudes Demographiques [*French*]
INEEP .... Institut National d'Education et d'Etudes Politiques [*National Institute for Political Education and Studies*] [*Mauritanian*] (AF)
INEF .... Instituto Nacional de Educacao Fisica [*National Physical Education Institute*] [*Portuguese*] (WER)
INEFTI .... Petroleum Institute (RU)
InEG .... Institute of Power Engineering and Hydraulics (of the Academy of Sciences, Armenian SSR) (RU)
Ineksbio ...... Institute of Experimental Biology (RU)
INELCA .... Industrias Electronicas Colombo Alemanas Ltda. [*Bogota*] (COL)
INELGO .... Institut za Elektrisko Gospodarstvo [*Institute of Electrical Power*] [*Ljubljana*] (YU)
INEM .... Bulletin of the National Ethnographic Museum [*A publication*] (BU)
INEM .... Instituto Nacional de Ensenanza Media Diversificada [*National Institute for Diversified Medium-Level Education*] [*Colombian*] (LA)
INEM .... Institutos Nacionales de Educacion Media [*Bogota*] (COL)
INEN .... Instituto Nacional de Energia Nuclear [*National Nuclear Energy Institute*] [*Guatemalan*] (LA)
INEN .... Instituto Nacional de Energia Nuclear [*National Nuclear Energy Institute*] [*Mexican*] (LA)
INEOS .... Institute of Hetero-Organic Compounds (of the Academy of Sciences, USSR) (RU)
INEP .... Institut National d'Etudes Politiques [*National Institute for Political Studies*] [*Zairian*] (AF)
INEP .... Instituto Nacional de Estabilizacion de Precios [*National Institute for Price Stabilization*] [*Venezuelan*] (LA)
INEP .... Instituto Nacional de Estudos Pedagogicos [*National Institute of Educational Research*] [*Brazilian*] (LA)
INEPS .... Institut National de l'Education Physique et Sportive [*National Institute of Physical and Sports Education*] [*Cambodian*] (CL)
INERA .... Institut National pour les Etudes et des Recherches Agronomiques [*National Institute for Agronomic Study and Research*] [*Zairian*] (AF)
INERGON .... Industrial Electrica Ergon Ltda. [*Bogota*] (COL)
INERHI .... Instituto Ecuatoriano de Recursos Hidraulicos [*Ecuadorean Institute for Water Resources*] (LA)
INES .... Instituto Nacional de Estudios Sindicales [*National Labor Studies Institute*] [*Venezuelan*] (LA)
INESCO .... Ingenieria Estudios Construcciones [*Medellin*] (COL)
INESPRE ..... Instituto Nacional de Estabilizacion de Precios [*National Price Stabilization Institute*] [*Dominican Republic*] (LA)
iness .... Inessiivi [*Finnish*]
INETER .... Instituto Nicaraguense de Estudios Territoriales [*Nicaraguan Institute of Territorial Studies*] (LA1)
INEUM .... Institute of Electronic Control Machines (of the Academy of Sciences, USSR) (RU)
INEX .... Industrieanlagen-Export (VEB) [*Industrial Facilities Exports (VEB)*] (EG)
INEXTRA ..... Industrias Extractivas [*Medellin*] (COL)
in f .... In Fine [*At the End*] [*Latin*] (GPO)
in-f .... In-Folio [*Folio*] [*French*]
Inf .... Infanterie [*Infantry*] [*Military*] [*French*] (MTD)
inf .... Infinitiivi [*Infinitive*] [*Finnish*]
inf .... Infinitive (RU)
inf .... Informacio [*Information*] (HU)
inf .... Infra [*Below*] [*Latin*] (GPO)
INF .... Institute of Physiology Imeni I. P. Pavlov (RU)
INF .... Iranian National Front (PPW)
INFA .... International Federation of Aestheticians (EA)
INFACT .... Infant Formula Action Coalition (MAR)
infak .... Division of Foreign Languages (RU)
INFAS .... Institute for Applied Social Science [*Bad Godesberg, West Germany*] (WEN)
INFAS .... Instituto Nacional de Formacion Agraria y Sindical [*National Institute of Agrarian and Labor Training*] [*Dominican Republic*] (LA1)
INFAVA .... Industria Farmaceutica del Valle [*Cali*] (COL)
InfBPZLRS ... Informativni Bilten Protiletalske Zascite Ljudska Republika Slovenija [*Information Bulletin of the Antiaircraft Defense of Slovenia*] [*Ljubljana*] [*A publication*] (YU)

INFC........... Institut National de Formation de Cadres [*National Institute for the Training of Cadres*] [*Zairian*] (AF)
INFCE.......... International Nuclear Fuel Cycle Evaluation (MAR)
INFEDOP..... International Federation of Employees in Public Service (EA)
INFELOR..... Informacio Feldolgozo Laboratorium [*Information Processing Laboratory*] (HU)
INFICO........ Industria Fiquera de la Costa Ltda. [*Barranquilla*] (COL)
INFIND........ Bureau de l'Information pour l'Indigenes (MAR)
INFIZKUL'T... Institute of Physical Culture (RU)
INFLI........... Institut pour la Formation Litteraire [*Institute of Literary Training*] [*Cambodian*] (CL)
Inflot........... Maritime Agency for Servicing Foreign Ships in Soviet Ports (RU)
INFLTEC..... Instalaciones Electricas Tecnicas [*Bogota*] (COL)
INFN........... Istituto Nazionale di Fisica Nucleare [*National Institute for Nuclear Physics*] [*Italian*] (WER)
INFO........... Information Department (RU)
INFOCO...... Industrial Forestal Colombiana Ltda. [*Tumaco*] (COL)
INFOCOOP... Instituto Nacional de Fomento Cooperativo [*National Cooperatives Development Institute*] [*Costa Rican*] (LA)
INFOGE....... Instituto de Fomento de Guinea Ecuatorial (MAR)
INFOM......... Instituto de Fomento Municipal [*Municipal Development Institute*] [*Guatemalan*] (LA)
INFONAC.... Instituto de Fomento Nacional [*National Development Institute*] [*Nicaraguan*] (LA)
INFONAVIT... Instituto del Fondo Nacional de la Vivienda para los Trabajadores [*Institute of the National Fund for Workers Housing*] [*Mexican*] (LA)
INFOP......... Instituto de Fomento de la Produccion [*Production Development Institute*] [*Guatemalan*] (LA)
INFOP......... Instituto Nacional de Formacion Profesional [*National Institute of Professional Training*] [*Honduran*] (LA1)
INFOPLAN... Latin American Planning Information Network [*Santiago, Chile*]
INFORAMA... Information et Radiodiffusion de Mauritius (MAR)
INFORCONGO... Office de l'Information et des Relations Publiques pour le Congo Belge et le Ruanda-Urundi (MAR)
inform......... Information (RU)
inform......... Informational (BU)
Informbyuro... Information Bureau (BU)
Informbyuro... Information Office of Communist and Workers' Parties [*1947-1956*] (RU)
informot...... Information Department (RU)
informupr.... Information Administration (RU)
INFORSA..... Industrias Forestales, SA [*Forestry Industries, Inc.*] [*Chilean*] (LA)
INFOSEC.... Institut de Formation Sociale, Economique, et Civique [*Institute for Social, Economic, and Civic Training*] [*Beninese*] (AF)
INFOTEC..... Servicio de Informacion Tecnica [*Technical Information Service*] [*Mexican*] (LA)
INFOTEP..... Instituto Nacional de Formacion Tecnico-Profesional [*National Institute of Technical-Professional Training*] [*Dominican Republic*] (LA1)
INFOTERM... International Information Centre for Terminology
INFOTERRA... International Referral System for Sources of Environmental Information [*Nairobi, Kenya*]
INFRA.......... Industrias el Fraile [*Cali*] (COL)
INFRAERO... Empresa Brasileira de Infraestrutura Aeroportuaria [*Brazilian Airport Support Enterprise*] (LA)
Inf T............ Infanterie Territoriale [*Military*] [*French*] (MTD)
Ing.............. Engineer [*Czechoslovak*]
ING.............. Ingegnere [*Engineer*] [*Italian*]
ING.............. Ingeniero [*Engineer*] [*Spanish*]
ING.............. Ingenieur [*Engineer*] [*French*]
Ing.............. Ingenieur [*Engineer*] [*German*] (GPO)
Ing.............. Ingilizce [*English*] (TU)
ING.............. Institut National de Gestion [*National Management Institute*] [*Niger*] (AF)
Ing.............. Inzenyr [*Engineer (Academic degree)*] (CZ)
INGACOL..... Industria Galvanotecnica Colombiana Ltda. [*Bogota*] (COL)
ingatl........... Ingatlan [*Real Estate*] (HU)
IngC............ Kandidat Inzenyrstvi [*Candidate for Engineering Degree*] (CZ)
IngCom....... Komercni Inzenyr [*Business School Graduate*] (CZ)
INGELCO.... Ingenieros Electricistas Contratistas Ltda. [*Bogota*] (COL)
INGELCO.... Instalaciones Electricas [*Cali*] (COL)
INGEMAR.... Cooperativa de Ingenieros y Oficiales Marinos Ltda. [*Bogota*] (COL)
INGEMETAL... Industria General de Metales [*Medellin*] (COL)
INGEOMINAS... Instituto de Investigaciones Geologico-Mineras [*Geological and Mining Research Institute*] [*Colombian*] (LA)
INGESCOL... Ingenieros Civiles [*Medellin*] (COL)
INGESISTEMAS... Ingenieria de Sistemas Ltda. [*Medellin*] (COL)
INGETEC.... Ingenieros Consultores Civiles y Electricos Ltda. [*Bogota*] (COL)
INGI............ Institute of Civil Engineers (RU)
INGOMPLA... Industria Gomez Plata de Oriente Ltda. [*Bucaramanga*] (COL)
INGRA......... Industrisko Gradevna Exportna Zajednica [*Industrial Building Export Association*] (YU)
INGUAT....... Instituto Guatemalteco de Turismo [*Guatemalan Institute of Tourism*] (LA1)
INGY........... Ideiglenes Nemzetgyules [*Temporary National Assembly*] (HU)
Inh.............. Inhaber [*Proprietor*] (EG)
Inh.............. Inhalt [*Contents*] (EG)
INH.............. Instituto Nacional de Hipodromos [*Venezuelan*]
INHELIOS.... Industrias Graficas Helios Ltda. [*Bogota*] (COL)
INHIGEO..... International Commission on the History of the Geological Sciences (EA)
INI............... Institut za Nacionalnu Istoriju [*National History Institute*] (YU)
INI............... Institut National de l'Industrie (MAR)
INI............... Institute of Scientific Information (RU)
INI............... Instituto Nacional de Identificacao [*National Identification Institute*] [*Brazilian*] (LA)
INI............... Instituto Nacional de Industria [*National Institute of Industry*] [*Spanish*] (WER)
INI............... Instituto Nacional de Inversiones [*National Investment Institute*] [*Bolivian*] (LA)
INI-............. Nonlinear Distortion Meter (RU)
INIA............ Instituto Nacional de Investigacao Agraria [*National Institute for Agrarian Studies*] [*Portuguese*] (WER)
INIA............ Instituto Nacional de Investigacion Agraria [*National Institute for Agrarian Research*] [*Peruvian*] (LA)
INIA............ Instituto Nacional de Investigaciones Agricolas [*National Institute for Agricultural Research*] [*Mexican*] (LA)
INIAP........... Instituto Nacional de Investigaciones Agropecuarias [*National Agricultural and Livestock Research Institute*] [*Ecuadorean*] (LA)
INIC............ Instituto Nacional de Imigracao e Colonizacao [*National Immigration and Settlement Institute*] [*Brazilian*] (LA)
INIC............ Instituto Nacional de Investigacion y Capacitacion [*National Research and Training Institute*] [*Peruvian*] (LA)
INIC............ Instituto Nacional de Investigaciones Cientificas [*National Institute for Scientific Research*] [*Mexican*] (LA)
INID............ Institutul National de Informare si Documentare Stiintifica si Tehnica [*National Institute for Scientific and Technical Information and Documentation*] (RO)
INIDEP......... Instituto Nacional de Investigacion y Desarrollo de la Industria Pesquera [*National Institute for the Development and Research of the Fishing Industry*] [*Argentine*] (LA1)
INIE............ Instituto Nacional de Investigaciones Energeticas [*National Energy Research Institute*] [*Peruvian*] (LA)
INIFAT......... Instituto de Investigaciones Fundamentales en Agricultura Tropical [*Institute for Basic Research in Tropical Agriculture*] [*Cuban*] (LA)
INIL............. Institut National des Industries Legeres [*Algerian*] (MAR)
ININ............ Instituto Nacional de Investigaciones Nucleares [*National Institute for Nuclear Research*] [*Cuban*] (LA)
ININ............ Instituto Nacional de Investigaciones Nucleares [*National Institute for Nuclear Research*] [*Mexican*] (LA1)
ININTEC...... Instituto de Investigacion Tecnologica Industrial y de Normas Tecnicas [*Industrial Technology and Standards Research Institute*] [*Peruvian*] (LA)
ININTEF...... Instituto de Investigacion Tecnica Fundamental [*Institute for Basic Technical Research*] [*Cuban*] (LA)
INIS............ International Nuclear Information System [*Vienna, Austria*]
INISER......... Instituto Nicaraguense de Seguros [*Nicaraguan Institute of Insurance*] (LA1)
init.............. Initio [*In the Beginning*] [*Latin*] (GPO)
INITDI......... Institute of Scientific and Technical Documentation and Information (RU)
INITO.......... Societe Initiative Togolaise (MAR)
Inja............. Inadana Jati [*National Commerce (Bank)*] [*Cambodian*] (CL)
INJM........... Instituto Nacional de la Juventud Mexicana [*National Institute of Mexican Youth*] (LA)
INJS............ Institut National de la Jeunesse et des Sports (MAR)
INJUPEM..... Instituto de Jubilaciones y Pensiones del Magisterio [*Teachers Retirement and Pension Institute*] [*Honduran*] (LA1)
INJUVE....... Instituto Nacional de la Juventud Mexicana [*National Institute of Mexican Youth*] (LA)
INK............. Ideiglenes Nemzeti Kormany [*Temporary National Government*] (HU)
INK............. Indian National Congress (RU)
INKA........... Institouton Prostasias Katanaloton [*Consumer Protection Institute*] [*Greek*] (GC)
INKh........... Institute of Inorganic Chemistry (of the Siberian Department of the Academy of Sciences, USSR) (RU)
INKh........... Moscow Institute of National Economy Imeni G. V. Plekhanov (RU)
INKhP......... Institute of New Chemical Problems (RU)
INKhP......... Institute of Petrochemical Processes (RU)
INKhS......... Institute of Petrochemical Synthesis Imeni A. V. Topchiyev (of the Academy of Sciences, USSR) (RU)
INKhUK....... Institute of Art Culture (RU)
inkl............. Inklusive [*Inclusive, Included*] [*German*] (GPO)
INKOPAD.... Induk Koperasi Angkatan Darat [*Main Army Cooperative*] (IN)
INKP........... Indian National Trade-Union Congress (RU)
INL............. Instituto Nacional do Livro [*National Book Institute*] [*Brazilian*] (LA)
INLA........... International Nuclear Law Association [*See also AIDN*] (EA)
INLASA....... Industria Nacional Laminadora SA [*National Sheet Steel Industry, Inc.*] [*Uruguayan*] (LA)
INLES......... Forest Institute (of the Academy of Sciences, USSR) (RU)
INLI............ Institute of Literature (RU)
INLICO........ Industrias Livinas de Colombia [*Cali*] (COL)

in lim .... In Limine [*On the Threshold*] [*Latin*] (GPO)
Inlit .... Moulding and Casting Equipment Plant (RU)
in loc .... In Loc [*In Place*] [*Latin*] (GPO)
in loc cit ...... In Loco Citato [*In the Place Cited*] [*Latin*] (GPO)
INM .... Imbokodvo National Movement [*Swazi*] (PPW)
INM .... Imprimerie Nationale du Mali (MAR)
INM .... Institut National des Mines [*National Mines Institute*] [*Zairian*] (AF)
INMA .... Quarry Materials (BU)
INMALLAS ... Industria de Mallas Ltda. [*Cali*] (COL)
INMARCO ... Industria de Marmoles y Cementos del Nare SA [*Medellin*] (COL)
INMARSAT ... Organisation Internationale de Satellite Maritime [*International Maritime Satellite Organization*] (LA1)
INMB .... Institutul National de Metrologie Bucuresti [*National Institute for Metrology in Bucharest*] (RO)
INM Burgas ... Bulletin of the National Museum in Burgas [*A publication*] (BU)
INMC .... Iraq National Minerals Company (ME)
INME .... Industrias Metalicas Ltda. [*Bogota*] (COL)
INMEC .... Industrias Metalicas Ltda. [*Bogota*] (COL)
INMECA ...... Industria Metalurgica [*Bogota*] (COL)
INMECAFE ... Instituto Mexicano del Cafe [*Mexican Coffee Institute*] (LA)
INMECOL .... Ingenieria Metalurgica Colombiana [*Bogota*] (COL)
INMERO ...... Institute of Permafrost Study Imeni V. A. Obruchev (RU)
INMES .... Institut National Medico-Social [*National Medical-Social Institute*] [*Beninese*] (AF)
INMETAL .... Industria de Metales Preciosos Ltda. [*Medellin*] (COL)
INMI .... Institute of Microbiology (of the Academy of Sciences, USSR) (RU)
INMINEH ..... Instituto Nicaraguense de Minas e Hidrocarburos [*Nicaraguan Institute of Mines and Hydrocarbons*] (LA1)
INMV .... Instituto Nacional de Medicina Veterinaria [*National Institute of Veterinary Medicine*] [*Cuban*] (LA)
INN .... Instituto Nacional de Nutricion [*National Nutrition Institute*] [*Bogota*] (COL)
INN .... Instituto Nacional de Nutricion [*National Nutrition Institute*] [*Venezuelan*] (LA)
INN .... Low-Voltage Indicator (RU)
INNICA .... Instituto Nicaraguense de la Costa Atlantica [*Nicaraguan Institute of the Atlantic Coast*] (LA1)
INNK .... Iranian National Petroleum Company (RU)
INNK .... Pulsed Neutron-Neutron Logging (RU)
INNK-t .... Pulsed Neutron-Neutron Logging with Thermal Neutron Recording (RU)
INNOTECH ... Innovation et Technologie de l'Education [*Educational Innovation and Technology*] (CL)
InNPI .... Instruction for Applying the Directive on Payments (BU)
INNRLNT ..... Instruction for Applying the Directive on the Work of the Bureaus of Registration and Direction of Manpower and for Job Placement of People with Reduced Working Capacity (BU)
INO .... Foreign Department (RU)
INO .... Institute of Public Education (RU)
INO .... Instruction for the Application of the Directive on Workers' and Employees' Leaves (BU)
INOC .... Iraq National Oil Company (ME)
INOCO .... Compagnie Nationale des Petroles (MAR)
INODEP .... Institut Oecumenique pour le Developpement des Peuples [*Ecumenical Institute for the Development of Peoples*] (EA)
INOE .... Internacia Naturist Organizo Esperantista [*International Esperantist Organization of Naturalists - IEON*] (EA)
INOGIZ .... State Publishing House of Foreign Language Literature (RU)
INOiK .... Instytut Naukowy Organizacji i Kierownictwa [*Scientific Institute of Organization and Management*] (POL)
INOIZDAT ... Publishing House of Foreign Literature (RU)
INOMGA ...... L'Industrie des Objets Moule's au Gabon (MAR)
INORCA ...... Industrias Nortecaucanas [*Cali*] (COL)
INOROSTA ... Foreign Department of the Russian News Agency (RU)
INOS .... Instituto Nacional de Obras Sanitarias [*National Institute of Sanitation Works*] [*Venezuelan*] (LA)
INOS .... Instituto Nacional de Obras Sociales [*National Institute for Social Works*] [*Argentine*] (LA)
Inoslovizdat ... State Publishing House of Foreign Dictionaries (RU)
INOT .... Institute of Scientific Organization of Labor (RU)
INOTEX .... Industrie Nouvelle Textile (MAR)
INOX .... Industrias Inoxidables [*Medellin*] (COL)
INP .... Engineer Observation Point (BU)
INP .... Engineer Observation Post (RU)
INP .... Field-Strength Meter (RU)
INP .... Institut National des Prix [*National Price Institute*] [*Algerian*] (AF)
INP .... Institute of National Planning [*Egyptian*] (MAR)
INP .... Instituto Nacional de Pesca [*National Fishing Institute*] [*Cuban*] (LA)
INP .... Instituto Nacional de Planificacion [*National Planning Institute*] [*Peruvian*] (LA)
INP .... Instituto Nacional de Prevision [*National Institute of Social Security*] [*Spanish*] (WER)
INP .... Instituto Nacional de Puertos [*National Institute of Ports*] [*Venezuelan*] (LA)
INP .... Israeli National Police (ME)
INPA .... Industria Nacional de Productos Alimenticios [*Bogota*] (COL)
INPA .... Instituto Nacional de Pesquisas da Amazonia [*National Institute for Amazon Region Research*] [*Brazilian*] (LA)
INPADOC .... International Patent Documentation
INPC .... Indice Nacional de Precos ao Consumidor [*National Consumer Price Index*] [*Brazilian*] (LA1)
INPC .... Iran-Nippon Petrochemical Company (ME)
INPE .... Instituto Nacional Pastoral Ecuatoriano [*Ecuadorean National Pastoral Institute*] (LA)
INPE .... Instituto Nacional de Perfeccionamiento Estomatologico [*National Dental Training Institute*] [*Cuban*] (LA)
INPE .... Instituto Nacional de Pesquisas Espaciais [*National Space Research Institute*] [*Brazilian*] (LA)
INPE .... Instituto de Pesquisas Espaciais [*Formerly, CNAE*] [*Brazilian*]
INPED .... Institut National de Production et de Developpement [*North African*] (MAR)
INPED .... Institut National de la Productivite et du Developpement Industriel [*National Productivity and Industrial Development Institute*] [*Algerian*] (AF)
INPELCA ..... Industria de Productos Electricos Centroamericana, SA [*Electric Products Corp.*] [*Salvadoran*]
INPEP .... Instituto Nacional de Pensiones de los Empleados Publicos [*National Government Employee Pension Institute*] [*Salvadoran*] (LA)
INPES .... Instituto Nacional de Pesquisa [*National Research Institute*] [*Brazilian*] (LA)
INPES .... Instituto Nacional para Programas Especiales de Salud [*Bogota*] (COL)
INPESCA .... Instituto Nicaraguense de Pesca [*Nicaraguan Institute of Fisheries*] (LA1)
INPGE .... Institut National de Productivite et de Gestion des Entreprises [*National Institute for Enterprises Productivity and Management*] [*Tunisian*] (AF)
INPI .... Institute of Proletarian Fine Arts (RU)
INPI .... Instituto Nacional de Promocion Industrial [*National Industrial Promotion Institute*] [*Peruvian*] (LA)
INPI .... Instituto Nacional da Propriedade Industrial [*National Institute of Industrial Property*] [*Brazilian*] (LA)
INPI .... Instituto Nacional de Proteccion de la Infancia [*National Institute for Infant Protection*] [*Mexican*] (LA)
INPIBOL ...... Instituto Promotor de Inversiones en Bolivia
INPM .... Institute of Normal and Pathological Morphology (of the Academy of Medical Sciences, USSR) (RU)
INPM .... Instituto Nacional de Pesos e Medidas [*National Institute of Weights and Measures*] [*Brazilian*] (LA)
Inposhiv ...... Custom Sewing and Repair of Clothing (RU)
INPP .... Institut National du Perfectionnement Permanent (MAR)
INPP .... Institut National de Preparation Professionnelle [*National Institute for Vocational Preparation*] [*Zairian*] (AF)
in pr .... In Principio [*In the Beginning*] [*Latin*] (GPO)
INPRAV .... Institute of Government and Law (RU)
INPRECC .... Industria de Prefabricados de Concreto [*Bogota*] (COL)
INPRES .... Instituto Nacional para Prevenciones Sismicas [*National Institute for Seismic Prevention*] [*Argentine*] (LA1)
INPRHU .... Instituto de Promocion Humana [*Institute for Human Development*] [*Nicaraguan*] (LA1)
IN-PRO .... Instituto Salvadoreno de Productividad [*Salvadoran Institute of Productivity*] (LA1)
INPRO .... Instituto Venezolano de Productividad
inprs .... Inspector of Wire Communications (RU)
INPS .... Institut National de Prevoyance Sociale (MAR)
INPS .... Instituto Nacional de Previdencia Social [*National Social Security Institute*] [*Brazilian*] (LA)
INPS .... Istituto Nazionale della Previdenza Sociale [*National Social Security Institute*] [*Italian*] (WER)
INPT .... Institut National des Postes et Telecommunications [*National Institute of Posts and Telecommunications*] [*Malagasy*] (AF)
INPUD .... Industrias Nacionales de Productos y Utensilios Domesticos [*National Industries for Domestic Products and Utensils*] [*Cuban*] (LA)
INPZ .... Irkutsk Petroleum-Processing Plant (RU)
inqor .... Inquisidor [*Spanish*]
INQUA .... International Association for Quaternal Research (MAR)
INQUIFAR ... Instituto Quimico Farmaceutico [*Barranquilla*] (COL)
INQUINAL ... Industria Quimica Nacional Ltda. [*Yumbo-Valle*] (COL)
INR .... Institut National de Radiodiffusion [*Belgian*]
INR .... Institute of Natural Resources [*Fijian*]
INRA .... Industria Nacional de Repuestos y Accesorios SA [*Bogota*] (COL)
INRA .... Institut National de Recherche Agronomique [*French National Institute of Agronomic Research*] (AF)
INRA .... Institute for Rationalizations (BU)
INRA .... Instituto Nacional de la Reforma Agraria [*National Institute for Agrarian Reform*] [*Cuban*] (LA)
INRA .... Instituto Nacional de la Reforma Agraria [*National Institute for Agrarian Reform*] [*Nicaraguan*] (LA1)

INRAA .... Institut National de la Recherche Agronomique de l'Algerie (MAR)
INRAF .... Institut National de la Recherche Agronomique Francaise [*North African*] (MAR)
INRAM .... Institut de Recherches Agronomiques a Madagascar [*Agronomic Research Institute of Madagascar*] (AF)
INRAT .... Institut National de la Recherche Agronomique de Tunisie (MAR)
INRAVISION ... Instituto Nacional de Radio y Television [*National Radio and Television Institute*] [*Colombian*] (LA)
INRDG .... Institut National de Recherches et Documentation de la Guinee [*Guinean National Institute of Research and Documentation*] (AF)
INRED .... Instituto Nacional de Recreacion, Educacion Fisica, y Deportes [*National Institute for Recreation, Physical Education, and Sports*] [*Peruvian*] (LA)
INRENA .... Instituto Nacional de Recursos Naturales [*National Institute of Natural Resources*] [*Nicaraguan*] (LA)
INRESA .... Industrias Reunidas Sociedad Anonima [*United Industries, Incorporated*] [*Peruvian*] (LA)
INRH .... Instituto Nacional de Recursos Hidraulicos [*National Institute for Water Resources*] [*Cuban*] (LA)
INRO .... International Natural Rubber Organization (EA)
INRS .... Institut National de la Recherche Scientifique [*National Institute of Scientific Research*] [*French*] (WER)
Ins .... Insaat [*Construction*] (TU)
ins .... Insinoori [*Finnish*]
INS .... Inspector of Communications (RU)
INS .... Institut National de la Sante [*North African*] (MAR)
INS .... Institut National des Sports [*French*]
INS .... Institut National de la Statistique [*Tunisian*] (MAR)
INS .... Institute of the North (RU)
INS .... Instituto Nacional de Seguros [*National Insurance Institute*] [*Portuguese*] (WER)
INS .... Instytut Nauk Spolecznych [*Institute of Social Sciences*] (POL)
INSA .... Industria Nacional de Neumaticos [*National Tire Industry*] [*Chilean*] (LA)
INSA .... Industrija Satova [*Watch Industry*] [*Zemun*] (YU)
INSA .... Instituts Nationaux de Sciences Appliquees [*National Institutes of Applied Sciences*] [*French*]
INSA .... International Shipowners' Association (EA)
INSA .... Istanbul Naylon Sanayii Anonim Sirketi [*Istanbul Nylon Industry Corporation*] (TU)
INSAC .... Instituto Nacional de Sistemas Automatizados y Tecnicas de Computacion [*National Institute of Automated Systems and Computer Technology*] [*Cuban*] (LA)
INSAFI .... Instituto Salvadoreno de Fomento Industrial [*Salvadoran Institute for Industrial Development*] (LA)
INSAFOCOOP ... Instituto Salvadoreno de Fomento Cooperativo [*Salvadoran Institute of Cooperative Development*] (LA1)
INSAFOP ..... Instituto Salvadoreno de Fomento de la Produccion [*Salvadoran Production Promotion Institute*] (LA)
INSATC .... Instituto Nacional de Sistemas Automatizados y Tecnicas de Computacion [*National Institute of Automated Systems and Computer Technology*] [*Cuban*] (LA)
INSATEC ..... Instalaciones Sanitarias y Tecnicas [*Bogota*] (COL)
insb .... Insbesondere [*In Particular*] [*German*] (GPO)
INSCIN .... Institutul pentru Studierea Conjuncturii Economice Internationale [*Institute for the Study of the International Economic Situation*] (RO)
INSCOL .... Instituto Psicologico Colombiano [*Bogota*] (COL)
INSCOMO ... Instituto Comercial Moderno [*Cali*] (COL)
INSCREDIAL ... Instituto de Credito Territorial [*Territorial Credit Institute*] [*Colombian*] (LA)
INSE .... Institut National des Sciences de l'Education (MAR)
INSE .... Instituto Superior de Educacion [*Bogota*] (COL)
INSE .... National Institute for Education [*French*]
INSEA .... Institut National de Statistique et d'Economie Applique [*National Institute of Statistics and Applied Economics*] [*Moroccan*] (AF)
INSEA .... International Society for Education through the Arts (MAR)
INSEE .... Institut National de Statistique et d'Etudes Economiques [*National Institute of Statistics and Economic Studies*] [*French*] (WER)
INSERE .... Institut National de la Statistique et des Recherches Economiques [*National Economic Research and Statistics Institute*] [*Cambodian*] (CL)
INSERM .... Institut National de la Sante et de la Recherche Medicale [*National Institute of Health and Medical Research*] [*French*] (AF)
INSESO .... Instituto Nacional de Seguridad Social (MAR)
INSET .... Institut National Superieur de l'Enseignement Technique (MAR)
INSFOPAL ... Instituto de Fomento Municipal [*Institute for Municipal Development*] [*Colombian*] (LA)
INSH .... Institut National des Sciences Humaines (MAR)
INSI .... Institut za Naucna Sumarska Istrazivanja [*Forestry Research Institute*] (YU)
INSINCA ..... Industrias Sinteticas de Centro America, SA [*Synthetic Industries of Central America Corp.*] [*Salvadoran*]
INSIVUMEH ... Instituto Nacional de Sismologia, Vulcanologia, Meteorologia, e Hidrologia [*National Institute of Seismology, Vulcanology, Meteorology, and Hydrology*] [*Guatemalan*] (LA)
inskapoch ... Postal Service Inspector Attached to the Chief Signal Officer of the Red Army (RU)
Inskoksugol' ... Coking Coal Inspection (RU)
INSMAK ...... Yol ve Insaat Makinalari Sanayii AS [*Highway and Construction Machinery Industry Corp.*] [*Izmir*] (TU)
INSMET .... Instituto de Meteorologia [*Institute of Meteorology*] [*Cuban*] (LA)
INSNA .... International Network for Social Network Analysis (EA)
INSORA .... Instituto de Organizacion y Administracion de Empresas [*Institute for Company Organization and Administration*] [*Chilean*] (LA)
Insp .... Inspektion [*German*]
Insp .... Inspektor [*Inspector*] (CZ)
INSP .... Inspektur [*Inspector*] (IN)
INSP .... Institut National de Sante Publique (MAR)
insparm ...... Inspector of the Army (RU)
INSPART ..... Inspector of Artillery (RU)
inspartarm ... Inspector of Army Artillery (RU)
INSPAT .... Institute of Comparative Pathology (RU)
INSPEC .... Information Service of Physics, Electrotechnology, and Control [*IEE*] [*United Kingdom*]
inspekh .... Inspector of Infantry (RU)
inspets .... Foreign Specialist (RU)
Inspiz .... Inspizient [*German*]
insposvedupr ... Inspection and Information Department of the Political Administration of a Republic (RU)
Inspred .... State Enterprise for International Transport (BU)
inspvozdukh ... Inspector of the Air Force (RU)
INSRE .... Institut National de la Statistique et de la Recherche Economique [*National Institute for Statistics and Economic Research*] [*Malagasy*] (AF)
INSRFP .... Institut National Superieur de Recherches et de Formation Pedagogique (MAR)
INSS .... Institut National de Securite Sociale [*National Social Security Institute*] [*Zairian*] (AF)
INSS .... Instituto Nicaraguense de Seguridad Social [*Nicaraguan Institute of Social Security*] (LA1)
inst .... Instans [*The Current Month*] [*Latin*]
Inst .... Institut [*Institute*] [*German*]
Inst .... Institut [*Institute*] (CZ)
inst .... Institute (BU)
inst .... Institute [*Topography*] (RU)
Inst .... Instytut [*Institute*] [*Polish*]
insta .... Instancia [*Spanish*]
INSTMC ...... Institute of Measurement and Control (EA)
INSTN .... Institut National des Sciences et Techniques Nucleaires [*French*]
INSTOP .... Institut National Scientifique et Technique d'Oceanographie et de Peche [*Tunisian*] (MAR)
InstOP .... Instruction for the Application of the Directive for Payment for Responsible Care of Property (BU)
Instorf .... Scientific Experimental Institute of Peat (RU)
instr .... Instructor (RU)
instr .... Instruktiivi [*Finnish*]
instr .... Orchestrated (BU)
INSTRUEQUIPO ... Instrumental y Equipos Cientificos [*Bogota*] (COL)
INSUPAV ..... Ingenieria de Suelos y Pavimentos [*Bogota*] (COL)
INSz .... Instytut Nawozow Sztucznych [*Institute of Artificial Fertilizers*] [*Polish*]
INT .... Institut fuer Nachrichtentechnik [*Communications Engineering Institute (in Berlin-Oberschoeneweide)*] (EG)
INT .... Institut Nikola Tesla [*Nikola Tesla Institute*] (YU)
in-t .... Institute (BU)
in-t .... Institute (RU)
INT .... Instituto Nacional de Tecnologia [*National Institute of Technology*] [*Brazilian*] (LA)
INT .... Instituto Nacional del Trabajo [*National Labor Institute*] [*Uruguayan*] (LA)
INT .... Instituto Nacional de Turismo [*National Institute of Tourism*] [*Cuban*] (LA)
int .... Integral (RU)
Int .... Intendant [*or Intendent*] [*German*]
Int .... Intendant [*Administrative Officer*] [*Military*] [*French*] (MTD)
int .... Interet [*French*]
INT .... Intergovernmental Negotiating Team (MAR)
int .... Intern [*German*]
int .... Intezet [*Institute*] (HU)
int .... Intezo [*Manager, Steward*] (HU)
int .... Intialainen [*Indian*] [*Finnish*]
int .... Quartermaster (RU)
int .... Quartermaster Section (RU)
Int .... Quartermaster Service (RU)
INTA .... Institut National de Techniques Administratives [*National Institute for Administrative Procedures*] [*Burundi*] (AF)
INTA .... Instituto Nacional de Tecnica Aeroespacial [*National Institute for Aerospace Research*] [*Spanish*] (WER)

INTA .... Instituto Nacional de Tecnologia Agropecuaria [*National Institute of Agricultural and Livestock Technology*] [*Argentine*] (LA)
INTA .... Instituto Nacional de Tecnologia Agropecuaria [*National Institute of Agricultural and Livestock Technology*] [*Nicaraguan*] (LA)
INTA .... Instituto Nacional de Transformacion Agraria [*National Agrarian Transformation Institute*] [*Guatemalan*] (LA)
INTA .... International New Towns Association [*See also AIVN*] (EA)
INTAD .... Intendans Angkatan Darat [*Army Quartermaster*] (IN)
INTAE .... Instituto Tecnologico de Administracion de Empresas [*Technological Institute for Enterprise Administration*] [*Honduran*] (LA1)
INTAL .... Instituto para la Integracion de America Latina [*Institute for the Integration of Latin America*] [*Argentine*] (LA)
INTALPEL ... Fabrica de Bolsas y Rollos de Papel [*Bogota*] (COL)
INTAMIC ..... International Microcircuit Card Association (EA)
INTAS .... Insaatcilar Sosyal Sehircilik Sanayi ve Ticaret Anonim Sirketi [*Constructors Social City Planning Industry and Trade Corporation*] (TU)
INTASAT ..... INTA [*Instituto Nacional de Tecnica Aeroespacial*] Satellite [*Spanish*]
Int Brig .... Internationale Brigade [*International Brigade*] (EG)
INTD .... Institut National des Techniques de la Documentation [*French*]
INTE .... Instituto Nacional de Teleducacion [*National Television Education Institute*] [*Peruvian*] (LA)
INTEBIS ...... Industrias Texteis de Beiriz (MAR)
INTEC .... Industrie Textile Centrafricaine (MAR)
INTEC .... Instituto Tecnologico de Chile [*Chilean Technological Institute*] (LA)
INTEC .... Instituto Tecnologico de Santo Domingo [*Technological Institute of Santo Domingo*] [*Dominican Republic*] (LA1)
INTECAP ..... Instituto Tecnico de Capacitacion y Productividad [*Technical Institute for Training and Productivity*] [*Guatemalan*] (LA1)
INTECMAR ... Instituto de Tecnologia y Ciencias Marinas [*Marine Sciences and Technology Institute*] [*Venezuelan*] (LA)
INTECO .... Industrias Tecnicas Colombianas Ltda. [*Barranquilla*] (COL)
INTECOF ..... International Economic Functions Co. (MAR)
INTECOL ..... International Association for Ecology (EA)
INTECON .... Ingenieria y Tecnica de Construccion Ltda. [*Bogota*] (COL)
integr .... Integral (RU)
INTEL .... Instituto Nacional de Telecomunicaciones [*National Telecommunications Institute*] [*Panamanian*] (LA)
INTELCAM ... Societe des Telecommunications Internationales du Cameroun [*International Telecommunications Company of Cameroon*] (AF)
INTELCI ...... Telecommunications Internationales de la Cote-d'Ivoire [*International Telecommunications of the Ivory Coast*] (AF)
INTELCO ..... Office des Telecommunications Internationales du Congo [*International Telecommunications Office of the Congo*] (AF)
INTELCUBA ... Telecomunicaciones Internacionales [*International Telecommunications*] [*Cuban*] (LA)
INTELEC ..... Instalaciones Electricas Ltda. [*Cali*] (COL)
INTELSAT ... International Telecommunications Satellite Consortium
INTEMA .... Industrielle Textile du Maroc (MAR)
intendte ...... Intendente [*Spanish*]
intenokr ...... Quartermaster Directorate of a Military District (RU)
INTERALUMINIO ... Internacional de Aluminio Ltda. [*Cali*] (COL)
INTERASMA ... Asociacion Internacional de Asmologia [*International Association of Asthmology*] (EA)
INTERATOM ... Internationale Atomreactorbau [*German*]
INTERBASE ... Empresa Cabo-Verdiana das Infraestruturas de Pesca [*Cape Verdean Fishing Infrastructures Company*] (AF)
INTERBOR ... Union Internationale des Techniciens Orthopedistes [*International Association of Orthotists and Prosthetists*] (EA)
INTERBRAS ... PETROBRAS Comercio Internacional SA [*PETROBRAS International Trade, Inc.*] [*Brazilian*] (LA)
INTERCA ..... Societe Commerciale Intercamerounaise (MAR)
INTERCAM ... Internacional de Caucho Manufacturado [*Bogota*] (COL)
INTERCARGO ... International Association of Dry Cargo Shipowners (EA)
INTERCO .... International Council on Jewish Social and Welfare Services (EA)
INTERCOL ... International Petroleum Colombia Limited [*Dorada-Caldas*] (COL)
INTERCOMEX ... Intermediaria en las Operaciones de Compensaciones y Trueques [*Export Trade Handling Enterprise*] [*Cuban*] (LA)
INTERCOMSA ... Intercontinental de Comunicaciones por Satelite, SA [*Intercontinental of Communications via Satellite, Inc.*] [*Panamanian*] (LA)
INTERCON ... Interventoria de Construcciones Ltda. [*Medellin*] (COL)
INTERCOOPERATION ... INTERCOOPERATION Kereskedelemfejlesztesi Reszvenytarsasag [*INTERCOOPERATION Company for the Development of Trade*] (HU)
INTEREG ..... International Institute for Ethnic Group Rights and Regionalism (EA)
INTERFILM ... International Inter-Church Film Center (EA)
INTERFLUG ... Internationale Fluggesellschaft mbH [*Name of GDR airline*] (EG)
INTERFORM ... Societe Internationale de Formation (MAR)
INTERGU ..... Internationale Gesellschaft fuer Urheberrecht [*International Copyright Society*] (EA)
interj .... Interjektio [*Interjection*] [*Finnish*]
INTERMARC ... International Machine Readable Cataloguing
INTERMEC ... Industria Termico Mecanica [*Bogota*] (COL)
INTERMETAL ... Internal Trade Corporation for Metals and Construction Materials [*Syrian*] (ME)
intern .... International [*German*]
intern .... International (RU)
INTERNACO ... Representaciones Internacionales Ltda. [*Medellin*] (COL)
INTEROM .... L'Intermediaire Outre-Mer (MAR)
INTERPAG ... International Problem Area Group (MAR)
INTERPHIL ... International Standing Conference on Philanthropy (EA)
INTERPLAX ... Industria Tecnica de Plasticos [*Bogota*] (COL)
INTERPOL ... International Criminal Police Organization (CL)
INTERPUBLIC ... Izdavacki Institut i Agencija za Unutrasnju i Spoljnu Trgovacku Propagandu, Publicitet, i Organizaciju [*Publishing Institute and Agency for Domestic and Foreign Commercial Propaganda, Publicity, and Organization*] (YU)
interr pron ... Interrogatiivipronomini [*Interrogative Pronoun*] [*Finnish*]
INTERSAPA ... Inter-Southern African Philatelic Agency (MAR)
INTERSPUTNIK ... International Organization of Space Communications (EA)
INTERSTENO ... Federation Internationale de Stenographie et de Dactylographie [*International Federation of Shorthand and Typewriting*] (EA)
INTERTANKO ... International Association of Independent Tanker Owners (EA)
INTERWOOLABS ... International Association of Wool and Textile Laboratories (EA)
INTEVEP ..... Instituto de Tecnologia Venezolana del Petroleo [*Venezuelan Institute of Petroleum Technology*] (LA)
INTEX .... Industria Textil de Mocambique Lda. (MAR)
INTEXTIL .... Industria Nacional de Textiles [*Bogota*] (COL)
INTEYCO ..... Ingenieria Tecnica y Comercial Ltda. [*Medellin*] (COL)
intezm .... Intezmeny [*Institution*] (HU)
inth ed .... Intihap Eden [*Selected, Chosen*] (TU)
INTI .... Institute of Scientific and Technical Information (RU)
INTI .... Instituto Nacional de Tecnologia Industrial [*National Institute of Industrial Technology*] [*Argentine*] (LA)
INTIiP .... Institute of Scientific and Technical Information and Propaganda (RU)
intk .... Intezkedes [*Order, Command, Arrangement, Directive*] (HU)
INTOC .... Industria Tornillera Colombiana [*Bogota*] (COL)
INTOPLAN ... Ingenieria Topografica-Planeacion [*Medellin*] (COL)
Intourist ...... Sowjetisches Reiseburo Internationale Touristik [*Soviet Travel Bureau for International Tourism*] (EG)
INTP .... Institut National des Telecommunications et des Postes [*National Institute of Telecommunications and Postal Services*] [*Malagasy*] (AF)
INTP .... Instituto Nacional do Trabalho e Previdencia [*National Institute of Labor and Social Welfare*] [*Portuguese*] (WER)
intr .... Intransitiivinen [*Finnish*]
INTRA .... Instituto Nacional de Transporte [*National Transport Institute*] [*Colombian*] (LA)
INTRACO .... International Trading Corporation [*Singapore State trading company*] (ML)
INTRADEP ... Cabinet Interafricain d'Etudes, de Pilotage, et de Promotion de Travaux (MAR)
INTRAMETAL ... Industrie et Travaux Metalliques [*Metallurgical Industry and Works*] [*Congolese*] (AF)
INTRAMETALES ... Industria Transformadora de Metales Ltda. [*Bogota*] (COL)
in trans .... In Transitu [*On the Way*] [*Latin*] (GPO)
INTRATA ..... International Trading and Credit Company of Tanganyika Ltd. (MAR)
INTRATEX ... Industria de Transformacion Textil Ltda. [*Medellin*] (COL)
INTROPLAS ... Industria de Troqueles y Moldes para Plasticos [*Bogota*] (COL)
INTRUSCO ... International Trust Company of Liberia (MAR)
INTs .... Cycle-Start Pulse (RU)
INTSH .... Institut National Tchadien pour les Sciences Humaines (MAR)
INTSHU .... Institut Togolais des Sciences Humaines (MAR)
INTSOY .... International Soybean Program (MAR)
INTUG .... International Telecommunications Users Group (EA)
INTUMEL .... Industria de Tubos Metalicos [*Bogota*] (COL)
INTUR .... Instituto Nacional de Turismo [*National Tourist Institute*] [*Cuban*] (LA)
Inturist .... All-Union Joint-Stock Company for Foreign Tourism in the USSR (RU)
INTUSA .... Industrias Turisticas, Sociedad Anonima [*Tourist Industries, Incorporated*] [*Spanish*] (WER)
INU .... Foreign Directorate [*MVD*] (RU)
INU .... History of the Peoples of Uzbekistan (RU)
INU .... Initial Setting Pulse [*Of converter*] (RU)
INU .... Inonu Universitesi [*Inonu University*] (TU)
INU .... Institut za Narodnu Umjetnost [*Institute of Folk Arts*] [*Zagreb*] (YU)
INU .... Institut za Nuklearne Nauke [*Institute of Nuclear Sciences*] [*Vinca*] (YU)

INUR............ Instituto Nacional de Urbanismo [*National Institute of City Planning*] [*Spanish*] (WER)
INUTOM...... Institut Universitaire des Territoires d'Outre-Mer (MAR)
inv.............. Inventorial (BU)
inv.............. Inventorial (RU)
INVAP.......... Instituto de Investigacion Aplicada [*Applied Research Institute*] [*Argentine*] (LA1)
INVARSA.... Inversiones Industriales y Comerciales [*Medellin*] (COL)
INVARSAL... Administracion e Inversiones Ltda. [*Medellin*] (COL)
INVASA....... Industrias Varias, Sociedad Anonima [*Miscellaneous Industries, Incorporated*] [*Chilean*] (LA)
INVATEX..... Industria de Derivados Textiles Ltda. [*Medellin*] (COL)
INVE............ Instituto Nacional de Viviendas Economicas [*National Institute of Low-Cost Housing*] [*Uruguayan*] (LA)
INVE............ Investitionen [*Investments*] (EG)
INVEPET..... Instituto Venezolano de Petroquimica [*Venezuelan Petrochemical Industry*] (LA)
INVERCOL... Inversiones Colombia [*Bogota*] (COL)
INVESCO.... Investigaciones Comerciales Ltda. [*Bogota*] (COL)
INVESTA..... Akciova Spolecnost pro Dovoz a Vyvoz Vyrobku Tezkeho Strojirenstvi [*Import and Export Joint-Stock Company for Heavy Machinery*] (CZ)
INVI............. Instituto Nacional de Vivienda [*National Institute of Housing*] [*Guatemalan*] (LA)
INVI............. Instituto Nacional de Vivienda [*National Institute of Housing*] [*Dominican Republic*] (LA1)
INVICALI..... Instituto de Vivienda de Cali (COL)
inv kniga..... Inventory Book (BU)
inv op.......... Inventory (RU)
INVU............ Instituto Nacional de Vivienda y Urbanismo [*National Institute of Housing and City Planning*] [*Costa Rican*] (LA)
INWACOL... Industria Wayne de Colombia [*Bogota*] (COL)
INWRL......... Instytut Naukowy Wydawnictw Rolniczych i Lesnych [*Scientific Publishing Institute for Agriculture and Forestry*] (POL)
IN-YaZ......... Institute of Foreign Languages (RU)
IN-YaZ......... State Central Courses for Correspondence Training in Foreign Languages (RU)
Inyurkollegiya... College of Foreign Law at the Moscow City Bar Association (RU)
Inz............... Inzenyr [*Engineer (Academic degree)*] (CZ)
inz............... Inzynier [*Engineer (Academic degree)*] (POL)
INZ.............. Public Health Institute (BU)
inza............. Tool Plant (RU)
inz agr......... Inzynier Agronomii [*Agricultural Engineer*] [*Polish*]
inz arch....... Inzynier Architektury [*Architectural Engineer*] [*Polish*]
INZAV.......... Investicni Zavod [*Investment Enterprise*] (CZ)
inz chem..... Inzynier Chemii [*Chemical Engineer*] [*Polish*]
INZEL.......... Industrias Zeus de Elementos Electronicos Ltda. [*Cali*] (COL)
inz elektr..... Inzynier Elektrotechnik [*Electrical Engineer*] [*Polish*]
inz gor......... Inzynier Gornik [*Mining Engineer*] [*Polish*]
inzh............. Engineer (BU)
inzh............. Engineer, Engineering (RU)
Inzh............. Engineer Troops (RU)
inzhb........... Engineer Battalion (BU)
inzhb........... Engineer Battalion (RU)
inzhbat........ Engineer Battalion (RU)
inzhbr.......... Engineer Brigade (RU)
INZhEKIN.... Leningrad Institute of Engineering Economics (RU)
inzh-mekh... Mechanical Engineer (RU)
inzh ob........ Engineer Train (BU)
inzh p.......... Engineer Mobile Depot (BU)
inzhp........... Engineer Park (RU)
inzhp........... Engineer Regiment (RU)
Inzhrez........ Engineer Reserve (RU)
inzh s.......... Engineer Depot (BU)
Inzhstroy..... Engineering Construction Administration (BU)
inzh-tekhnol... Engineer-Technologist (RU)
inzhtekhot... Engineering and Technical Department (RU)
inzhtr.......... Engineer Tank Company (RU)
inz hut......... Inzynier Hutnik [*Metallurgic Engineer*] [*Polish*]
inzh v.......... Corps of Engineers (BU)
inz inz......... Inzynierowie [*Engineers*] [*Polish*]
inz lesn....... Inzynier Lesnik [*Forestry Engineer*] [*Polish*]
inz mech..... Inzynier Mechanik [*Mechanical Engineer*] [*Polish*]
IO................ Acting (RU)
IO................ Actuating Element (RU)
IO................ British Indian Ocean Territory [*Two-letter standard code*] (CNC)
IO................ Election District (RU)
IO................ Institute of Oceanology (of the Academy of Sciences, USSR) (RU)
IO................ Isa'dan Once [*Before Christ*] (TU)
IO................ Izvidacki Organi [*Reconnaissance Units*] (YU)
IO................ Izvrsilni Odbor [*Executive Committee*] (YU)
IO................ Quartermaster Section (RU)
IO................ Test Sample (RU)
IO................ Tools Section (BU)
IOA.............. International Orthoptic Association (EA)
IOAIE.......... News of the Society of Archaeology, History, and Ethnography (at the Kazan' University) [*A publication*] (RU)
IOAIEKU...... News of the Society of Archaeology, History, and Ethnography at the Kazan' University [*A publication*] (RU)
IOAKMO...... Izvrsni Odbor Autonomne Kosovo-Metohija Oblasti [*Executive Committee of the Autonomous Region of Kosovo-Metohija*] (YU)
IOAN........... Institute of Oceanology of the Academy of Sciences, USSR (RU)
IOB.............. Institute of Bankers (EA)
IOB.............. Inter-Organization Board for Information Systems and Related Activities [*Swiss*]
IOBC........... International Organization for Biological Control of Noxious Animals and Plants [*See also OILB*] (EA)
IOC.............. Intergovernmental Oceanographic Commission [*See also COI*] (EA)
IOC.............. Internationales Olympisches Komitee [*International Olympic Committee*] (EG)
IOC.............. Iran Ocean Company (ME)
IOCC........... International Office of Cocoa and Chocolate (EA)
IOCHC......... International Organization for Cooperation in Health Care [*See also MMI*] (EA)
IOCO........... Izvrsni Odbor Centralnog Odbora [*Executive Committee of the Central Committee*] (YU)
IOCOL......... Industria Ortopedica Colombiana [*Cali*] (COL)
IOD.............. Open Door International [*For the Economic Emancipation of the Woman Worker*] (RU)
IOE.............. International Organization of Experts (EA)
IOEPCO....... Iranian Oil Exploration and Producing Company (ME)
IOF.............. Imposto sobre Operacoes Financeiras [*Financial Operations Tax*] [*Brazilian*] (LA1)
IOF.............. Ion-Exchange Filter (RU)
IOFI............. International Organization of the Flavor Industry (EA)
IOGM.......... Ilk Ogretim Genel Mudurlugu [*Elementary Education Directorate General*] (TU)
IOGT........... International Organization of Good Templars (EA)
IOI............... International Ocean Institute (EA)
IOI............... International Ombudsman Institute (EA)
IOIMK.......... News of the Society for the Study of Manchurian Region [*A publication*] (RU)
IOJ............... International Organization of Journalists [*See also OIJ*] (EA)
IOJ............... Internationale Journalistenorganisation [*International Organization of Journalists*] (EG)
IOJD............ International Organization for Justice and Development (EA)
IOK.............. Ipartestuletek Orszagos Kospontja [*National Center of Craftsmen's Associations*] (HU)
IOKAE......... Institouton Okeanografikon kai Alievtikon Meleton [*Institute of Oceanographic and Fishing Studies*] [*Greek*] (GC)
IOKG........... Institute of General and Municipal Hygiene (RU)
IOKh............ Institute of Organic Chemistry Imeni N. D. Zelinskiy (of the Academy of Sciences, USSR) (RU)
IOKSZ......... Iparosok Orszagos Kozponti Szovetkezete [*Central Handicraft Cooperative*] (HU)
IOL.............. Footwear-Testing Laboratory (RU)
IOL.............. Institute of Librarians [*Indian*]
IOLO........... Izvrsni Odbor Ljudskega Odbora [*Executive Committee of the People's Committee*] (YU)
IOLPS.......... Izvrsni Odbor Ljudske Prosvete Slovenije [*Executive Committee, People's Education of Slovenia*] (YU)
IOM............. Independants d'Outre-Mer [*Overseas Independents*] [*Upper Voltan*] (AF)
IOM............. Instituto de Organizacion y Metodos [*Bogota*] (COL)
IOMB........... Instytut Organizacji i Mechanizacji Budownictwa [*Institute of Organization and Mechanization of Construction*] (POL)
IOMTR......... International Organization for Motor Trades and Repairs (EA)
ION-............ Indicator of Dangerous Voltages (RU)
IOnk............ Instytut Onkologii [*Institute of Oncology*] [*Polish*]
ion k............ Ionization Chamber (RU)
IONKh......... Institute of General and Inorganic Chemistry Imeni N. S. Kurnakov (of the Academy of Sciences, USSR) (RU)
IONO........... Izvrsni Odbor Narodnog Odbora [*Executive Committee of the People's Committee*] (YU)
IOO.............. Social Insurance Institute (BU)
IOOC........... International Olive Oil Council [*See also COI*] (EA)
IOOF........... Izvrsni Odbor Osvobodilne Fronte [*Executive Committee of the Liberation Front*] (YU)
IOOL........... International Optometric and Optical League (EA)
IOOS........... Instytut Obrabiarek i Obrobki Skrawaniem [*Institute of Machine Tools and Machining by Cutting*] (POL)
IOP.............. Ibero-American Organization of Pilots [*See also OIP*] (EA)
IOP.............. International Organization of Psychophysiology [*See also IPO*] (EA)
IOP.............. Iran Oil Participants (ME)
IOP.............. Istioploikos Omilos Peiraios [*Piraeus Sailing Club*] [*Greek*] (GC)
IOP.............. True Reciprocal Bearing (RU)
IOPM........... Instytut Organizacji Przemyslu Maszynowego [*Machinery Industry Institute on Organization*] (POL)
IOPS........... Relative Network [*Load*] Increase Meter (RU)
IOR.............. Instituto per le Opere di Religione [*Institute for Religious Works*] [*The Vatican bank*]
IOR.............. Instytut Ochrony Roslin [*Institute of Plant Protection*] (POL)

IOR .... Inter-Organizacoes dos Refugiados [*Interorganizations of Refugees*] [*Portuguese*] (WER)
IORD............ International Organization for Rural Development (MAR)
IORLO .... Izvrsni Odbor, Rajonski Ljudski Odbor [*Executive Committee, District People's Committee*] (YU)
IORN............ Instruction for Annulling Decisions of Conciliation Commissions by Central Committees of Trade Unions through Supervision (BU)
IORYaS .... News of the Department of Russian Language and Literature of the Academy of Sciences [*1852-1927*] [*A publication*] (RU)
IOS .... Instituto de Organizacion y Sistemas [*Bogota*] (COL)
IOS .... International Organization for Succulent Plant Study (EA)
IOS .... Investor Overseas Service [*Barranquilla*] (COL)
IOSA............ Integrated Optic Spectrum Analyser (MAR)
IOSE............ Instituto de Obra Social del Ejercito [*Army Social Benefits Institute*] [*Argentine*] (LA)
IOSEWR ...... International Organization for the Study of the Endurance of Wire Ropes (EA)
IOSMTS ...... Instruction for Organizing Machine-Tractor Stations Accounting (BU)
IOSOT .... International Organisation for the Study of the Old Testament (MAR)
IOSS............ Imperial Organization for Social Services [*Iranian*] (ME)
IOSTA .... Comission Internationale de l'Organisation Scientifique du Travail [*International Committee of Work Study and Labour Management in Agriculture*] (EA)
IOSZ............ Ifjumunkasok Orszagos Szovetsege [*National Federation of Working Youth*] (HU)
IOT .... British Indian Ocean Territory [*Three-letter standard code*] (CNC)
IOT .... Institute of Work Safety (RU)
IOTA............ Institut d'Ophthalmologie Tropicale de l'Afrique [*Tropical Ophthalmological Institute of Africa*] (AF)
IOTC............ Iraqi Oil Tankers Company (ME)
IOTO............ Industrie des Oleagineux du Togo (MAR)
IOV .... Disabled Veterans of World War II (RU)
IOVE............ Institouto Oikonomikon kai Viomikhanikon Erevnon [*Institute of Economic and Industrial Research*] (GC1)
IOVE............ Institouton Viomikhanikon Erevnon [*Industrial Research Institute*] [*Greek*] (GC)
IOW .... Interdepartementaal Overleg Wetenschapsbeleid [*Dutch*]
IOZPK .... Institute for Improving the Qualifications of Engineering and Technical Personnel through Resident and Correspondence Training (RU)
IP............ Actuating Station (RU)
ip............ And the Like (BU)
IP............ Cannon-Armed Fighter (RU)
ip............ Iltapaivalla [*Afternoon*] [*Finnish*] (GPO)
IP............ Independence Party (MAR)
IP............ Induction Electric Furnace (RU)
IP............ Indulgencia Plenaria [*Plenary Indulgence*] [*Spanish*]
IP............ Industrias Pallomaro [*Cali*] (COL)
IP............ Initial Point (RU)
IP............ Initial Position, Assault Position, Forming-Up Place (RU)
IP............ Injector Preheater (RU)
IP............ Inspector Polis [*Police Inspector*] (ML)
IP............ Inspektur Polisi [*Police Inspector*] (IN)
IP............ Institute of Nutrition (RU)
IP............ Institute of Semiconductors (of the Academy of Sciences, USSR) (RU)
IP............ Institute of Soil Science Imeni V. V. Dokuchayev (RU)
IP............ Instruccion Programada (COL)
IP............ Instruction Station (RU)
IP............ Instytut Pracy [*Institute of Labor*] [*Polish*]
IP............ Interpretative Routine (RU)
ip............ Ipar [*Indusry*] (HU)
ip............ Iparos [*Craftsman*] (HU)
IP............ Isomeric Transition (RU)
IP............ Istoricheski Pregled [*Historical Review*] [*A periodical*] (BU)
IP............ Izvidacka Patrola [*Reconnaissance Patrol*] (YU)
IP............ Izvrsni Postupak [*Executive Procedure*] (YU)
IP............ Law Institute (of the Academy of Sciences, USSR) (RU)
IP............ Measuring Plate (RU)
IP............ Needle Bearing (RU)
IP............ Oxygen-Breathing Gas Mask (BU)
IP............ Portable Inhaler (RU)
IP............ Power Supply (RU)
IP............ Predicate Calculus (RU)
IP............ Roads Institute (BU)
IP............ Spark Gap (RU)
IP............ Stratum Tester (RU)
IP............ Summary Puncher (RU)
IP............ True Bearing (RU)
IPA .... Indice de Precos no Atacado [*Wholesale Price Index*] [*Brazilian*] (LA)
IPA .... Information Processing Association [*Israeli*]
IPA .... Inomenai Politeiai Amerikis [*United States of America*] (GC)
IPA .... Institouto Perifereiakis Anaptyxeos [*Regional Development Institute*] (GC)
IPA .... Institut Pedagogique Africain [*African Pedagogical Institute*] [*French*] (AF)
IPA .... International Pediatric Association [*See also AIP*] (EA)
IPA .... International Police Association (EA)
IPA .... International Press Agency (MAR)
IPA .... International Psycho-Analytical Association (EA)
IPA .... International Publishers Association [*See also UIE*] (EA)
IPAC............ Industria Papelera Andina Colombiana [*Bogota*] (COL)
IPAC............ Industria Pecuaria, Agricultura, e Comercio Lda. (MAR)
IPAC............ Institut Polytechnique de l'Afrique Centrale (MAR)
IPAC............ Iran Pan American Oil Company (ME)
IPAE .... Instituto Peruano de Administracion de Empresas [*Peruvian Institute of Business Administration*] (LA)
IPAFRIC ...... Inter-Peches-Afrique (MAR)
IPAG............ Instituto de Pedagogia Autoactiva de Grupo [*Cali*] (COL)
IPAI .... International Primary Aluminium Institute (EA)
IPALMO....... Istituto per le Relazioni tra l'Italia e i Paesi dell' Africa, America Latina, e Medio Oriente [*Institute for Italy's Relations with Africa, Latin America, and the Middle East*] (WER)
IPAM .... Institut Pedagogique Africain et Malgache (MAR)
IPAN............ Institute of Semiconductors of the Academy of Sciences, USSR (RU)
IPAP .... Idryma Prostasias Aprosarmoston Paidon [*Institute for the Protection of Handicapped Children*] (GC)
IPARDES..... Instituto Paranaense de Desenvolvimento Economico e Social [*Parana Economic and Social Development Institute*] [*Brazilian*] (LA)
IPARTERV... Ipari es Mezogazdasagi Tervezo Vallalat [*Architectural Designing Enterprise for Industry and Agriculture*] (HU)
IPAS .... Independants et Paysans d'Action Sociale [*Independents and Peasants of Social Action*] [*French*] (PPE)
IPASA.......... Inversiones, Promociones, y Administracion [*Bogota*] (COL)
IPASE.......... Instituto de Previdencia e Assistencia dos Servidores do Estado [*Welfare and Aid Institute for Civil Servants*] [*Brazilian*] (LA)
IPASME....... Instituto de Prevision y Asistencia Social del Ministerio de Educacion [*Institute of Social Welfare and Aid of the Ministry of Education*] [*Venezuelan*] (LA)
IPAT .... Instituto Panameno de Turismo [*Panamanian Tourist Institute*] (LA)
ipb............ Engineer Road Battalion (BU)
IPB............ Institut Pasteur de Brazzaville (MAR)
IPB............ Interna Poljska Bolnica [*Field Hospital for Internal Medicine*] [*Military*] (YU)
ipbr .... Engineer Pontoon Brigade (RU)
ipbr .... Engineer Road Brigade (BU)
IPC .... Indice de Precios al Consumidor [*Consumer Price Index*] [*Use CPI*] (LA)
IPC .... Industrie des Papiers et Carbones (MAR)
IPC .... Institut Politique Congolais [*Congolese Political Institute*]
IPC .... Institut de Promotion Commerciale [*Institute for Trade Promotion*] [*Guadeloupe*] (LA1)
IPC .... Instytut Przemyslu Cukrowniczego [*Institute of Sugar Industry*] [*Polish*]
IPC .... Integrated Program for Commodities (MAR)
IPC .... Inter-African Phytosanitary Commission (MAR)
IPC .... International Petroleum Company [*Peruvian*] (LA)
IPC .... International Photosynthesis Committee (EA)
IPC .... Iraq Petroleum Company (ME)
IPCCC .... International Peace, Communication, and Coordination Center (EA)
IPCh .... Gas Tube Frequency Converter (RU)
IPCORN....... Industrial Promotion Corporation of Rhodesia and Nyasaland Ltd. (MAR)
IPCS............ Institutul de Proiectari de Constructii Speciale [*Design Institute for Special Constructions*] (RO)
IPCT .... Institutul de Proiectari a Constructiilor Tip [*Design Institute for Model Constructions*] (RO)
IPCUP.......... Institutul de Proiectari si Cercetari pentru Utilaj Petrolier [*Design and Research Institute for Petroleum Equipment*] (RO)
I pd .... In Podobno [*And the Like*] (YU)
IPD .... Industrial Plantation Department (MAR)
IPD .... Institut Panafricain pour le Developpement [*Pan-African Institute for Development*] (AF)
IPD .... Institute for Planning and Development [*Israeli*] (MAR)
IPD .... Instituto de Pesquisas e Desenvolvimento [*Research and Development Institute*] [*Brazilian*] (LA)
IPDE .... Invesfissements Prives Directs Etrangers (MAR)
IPDiR .... Instytut Przemyslu Drobnego i Rzemiosla [*Institute of Light Industries and Handicraft*] [*Polish*]
IPDiRz .... Instytut Przemyslu Drobnego i Rzemiosla [*Institute of Light Industries and Handicraft*] [*Polish*]
IPDR .... Institut Pratique de Developpement Rural (MAR)
IPE............ Informacion de Prensa Especial [*Special Press Information*] [*Bolivian*] (LA)
IPE............ Instituto de Investigaciones y Planeacion Educacionales. Universidad del Valle [*Cali*] (COL)
IPEA .... Instituto de Pesquisa Economico-Social Aplicada [*Applied Economic-Social Research Institute*] [*Brazilian*] (LA)
IPEA .... Instituto de Planejamento Economico e Social [*Institute of Economic and Social Planning*] [*Brazilian*] (LA1)

IPEAC......... Instituto de Pesquisas, Estudos, e Assessoria do Congresso [*Congressional Research, Study, and Advisory Institute*] [*Brazilian*] (LA)
IPEAN......... Instituto de Pesquisas e Experimentacao Agropecuarias do Norte [*Northern Institute for Agricultural and Livestock Research and Experiment*] [*Brazilian*] (LA)
IPEDA......... Iuran Pembangunan Daerah [*Regional Development Tax*] (IN)
IPEE......... Instituto de Pesquisas e Estudos Economicos [*Brazilian*]
IPEI......... Institute of Industrial and Economic Research (RU)
IPEIL......... Intreprinderile pentru Exploatarea si Industrializarea Lemnului [*Enterprises for the Exploitation and Industrialization of Wood*] (RO)
IPEN......... Instituto Peruano de Energia Nuclear [*Peruvian Nuclear Energy Institute*] (LA)
IPEN......... Instituto de Pesquisas Energeticas e Nucleares [*Nuclear and Energy Research Institute*] [*Brazilian*] (LA)
IPES......... Institut de Preparation aux Enseignements du Second Degre [*French*]
IPES......... Instituto de Pesquisas e Estudos Sociais [*Research and Social Studies Institute*] [*Brazilian*] (LA)
IPES......... Instituto de Planejamento Economico e Social [*Institute of Economic and Social Planning*] [*Brazilian*] (LA1)
IPESA......... Instituto de Pesquisa Economico-Social Aplicada [*Institute of Applied Economic-Social Research*] [*Brazilian*] (LA1)
IPESAN......... Institut de Promotion Economique et Sociale de l'Afrique Noire [*Institute for the Economic and Social Promotion of Black Africa*] (AF)
IPETB......... Institutul de Proiectare a Uzinelor si Instalatiilor pentru Industria Electrotehnica Bucuresti [*Bucharest Institute for the Design of Plants and Installations for the Electrotechnical Industry*] (RO)
IPF......... Indicative Planning Figures (MAR)
IPF......... Institut fuer Post und Fernmeldewesen [*Institute for Postal Affairs and Telecommunications*] (EG)
IPF......... Institut za Proucavanje Folklora [*Institute of Folklore Research*] [*Sarajevo*] (YU)
IPF......... Institute of Applied Physics (RU)
IPF......... Institutul de Proiectari Forestiere [*Forestry Design Institute*] (RO)
IPF......... International Powerlifting Federation (EA)
IPF......... Polarizing Interference Filter (RU)
IPFE......... Institutul de Proiectare pentru Forajul Sondelor si Extragerea Titeiului si Gazelor [*Design Institute for Well Drilling and Extraction of Crude Oil and Gas*] (RO)
Ip Fel......... Iparfelugyeloseg [*Industrial Inspectorate*] (HU)
IPFK......... Isopropyl Phenyl Carbamate (RU)
IPG......... Information Policy Group [*OECD*]
IPG......... Institute of Applied Geophysics (of the Academy of Sciences, USSR) (RU)
IPG......... Institutul de Petrol si Gaze [*Petroleum and Gas Institute*] (RO)
IPG......... Instytut Przemyslu Gumowego [*Institute of Rubber Industry*] [*Polish*]
IPG......... Interparlamentarische Gruppe [*Interparliamentary Group*] (EG)
IPGAN......... Institut Polytechnique Gamal Abdel Nasser [*Gamal Abdel Nasser Polytechnic Institute*] [*Guinean*] (AF)
IPGC......... Institutul de Proiectare a Constructiilor si Instalatiilor de Gospodarie Comunala [*Design Institute for Communal Economy Constructions and Installations*] (RO)
IPGC......... Institutul de Proiectari de Geniu Civil [*Civil Engineering Design Institute*] (RO)
IPGE......... Idea Popular de la Guinea Ecuatorial (MAR)
IPGG......... Institutul de Petrol, Gaze, si Geologie [*Institute for Petroleum, Gases, and Geology*] (RO)
IPGGH......... Intreprinderea de Prospectiuni Geologice si Geofizice pentru Hidrocarburi [*Enterprise for Geological and Geophysical Prospecting for Hydrocarbons*] (RO)
IPGI......... Institute on Pluralism and Group Identity (MAR)
IPGum......... Instytut Przemyslu Gumowego [*Institute of Rubber Industry*] [*Polish*]
IPH......... International Association of Paper Historians (MAR)
IPH......... Izba Przemyslowo-Handlowa [*Chamber of Industry and Trade*] (POL)
IPHA......... Instituto Peruano del Hierro y del Acero [*Peruvian Iron and Steel Institute*] (LA)
IPHAN......... Instituto do Patrimonio Historico e Artistico Nacional [*National Historic and Artistic Heritage Institute*] [*Brazilian*] (LA)
IPI......... Imposto sobre Produtos Industrializados [*Finished Goods Tax*] [*Brazilian*] (LA)
IPI......... Institute of Production Innovation (MAR)
IPI......... Institutul de Proiectari Ilfov [*Ilfov Design Institute*] (RO)
IPI......... Institutul de Proiectari Industriale [*Industrial Design Institute*] (RO)
IPI......... International Potash Institute (EA)
IPI......... International Press Institute (AF)
IPIA......... Institutul de Patologie si Igiena Animala [*Institute for Animal Pathology and Hygiene*] (RO)
IPIA......... Institutul de Proiectari al Industriei Alimentare [*Design Institute for the Food Industry*] (RO)
IPIAPS......... Intreprinderea de Productie Industriala Autoutilare si Prestari Servicii [*Enterprise for Industrial Production, Self-Equipping, and Services*] (RO)
IPIB......... Industrial Projects Implementation Bureau [*Arab*] (MAR)
IPIBC......... Institutul de Proiectari al Industriei Bunurilor de Consum [*Design Institute for the Consumer Goods Industry*] (RO)
IPIECA......... International Petroleum Industry Environmental Conservation Association (EA)
IPIK......... Institute for the Training of Party Cadres (RU)
IPIL......... Institutul de Proiectari al Industriei Lemnului [*Design Institute for the Wood Industry*] (RO)
IPILF......... Intreprinderea pentru Producerea si Industrializarea Legumelor si Fructelor [*Enterprise for the Production and Industrialization of Vegetables and Fruit*] (RO)
IPIMC......... Institutul de Proiectari pentru Industria Materialelor de Constructii [*Design Institute for the Construction Materials Industry*] (RO)
IPIN......... Institute for the Study of Nationalities of the USSR (RU)
IPIP......... Institutul de Proiectari pentru Instalatii Petroliere [*Design Institute for Petroleum Installations*] (RO)
IPIU......... Institutul de Proiectari al Industriei Usoare [*Design Institute for Light Industry*] (RO)
IPK......... Ilektroniko Pliroforiako Kentro [*Computerized Information Center*] (GC1)
IPK......... Inspektorat Parnih Kotlova [*Steam Boilers Inspectorate*] (YU)
IPK......... Institut Polytechnique de Kankan [*Kankan Polytechnic Institute*] [*Guinean*] (AF)
IPK......... Institut za Proucavanje Knjizevnost [*Institute of Literary Studies*] (YU)
IPK......... Institute of Blood Transfusion (RU)
IPK......... Institute of Consumers' Cooperatives (RU)
IPK......... Institute for the Improvement of Qualifications (RU)
ipkh......... Inspector General of Infantry (BU)
IPKh......... Transfer-Characteristic Meter (RU)
IPKI......... Ikatan Pendukung Kemerdekaan Indonesia [*Association of Supporters of Indonesian Independence*] (IN)
IPKITR......... Institute for Improving the Qualifications of Engineering and Technical Personnel (RU)
IPKKNO......... Institute for Improving the Qualifications of Public Education Personnel (RU)
IPKP......... Institute for Improving the Qualifications of Teachers (RU)
IPKPON......... Institute for Improving the Qualifications of Instructors in Social Sciences (RU)
IPKRK......... Institute for Improving the Qualifications of Supervisory Personnel (RU)
IPKVOD......... Institute for Improving the Qualifications of Water Transportation Workers (RU)
IPL......... Ibu Pejabat Laut [*Navy Headquarters*] (ML)
IPL......... Institutul pentru Proiectari de Laminoare [*Institute for Rolling Mill Design*] (RO)
IPL......... Ivoirienne de Peinture et Laques (MAR)
IPLA......... Instituto Pastoral Latino Americano [*Latin American Pastoral Institute*] (LA)
IPLC......... Intreprinderea de Produse din Lemn pentru Constructii [*Enterprise for Wood Products for Constructions*] (RO)
IPLM......... Intreprinderea Produse Lemn Mobila [*Enterprise for Furniture Wood Products*] (RO)
IPLT......... Iuran Pembangunan Lima Tahun [*5-Year Development Tax*] (IN)
IPM......... Flight Departure Point (BU)
IPM......... Inquerito Policial-Militar [*Police-Military Inquiry*] [*Brazilian*] (LA)
IPM......... Institut fuer Polygraphische Maschinen [*Institute for Printing Machines*] (EG)
IPM......... Institute of Applied Mineralogy (RU)
IPM......... Institute of the Problems of Mechanics (RU)
IPM......... Institutul de Proiectari Metalurgice [*Metallurgical Design Institute*] (RO)
IPM......... Institutul de Proiectari Miniere [*Institute for Mining Design*] (RO)
IPM......... Institutul de Protectie a Muncii [*Labor Safety Institute*] (RO)
IPM......... Instytut Prawa Miedzynarodowego [*Institute of the International Law*] [*Polish*]
IPM......... Instytut Przemyslu Miesnego [*Institute of the Meat Industry*] [*Polish*]
IPM......... Instytut Przemyslu Mleczarskiego [*Institute of the Dairy Industry*] [*Polish*]
Ip M......... Iparugyi Minisztérium/Miniszter [*Ministry/Minister of Industry*] (HU)
IPM......... Point of Departure [*Aviation*] (RU)
IPMA......... Intreprinderea de Proiectari si Prototipuri pentru Masini Agricole [*Enterprise for Agricultural Machine Design and Prototypes*] (RO)
IPMM......... Institute of Applied Mineralogy and Metallurgy (RU)
IPMP......... Institut za Proucavanje Medunarodnih Pitanja [*Institute of International Studies*] [*Belgrade*] (YU)
IPMP......... Intreprinderea de Prelucrarea Mase Plastice [*Enterprise for Processing Plastics*] (RO)
IPMPB......... Intreprinderea de Poduri Metalice si Prefabricate din Beton [*Enterprise for Metallic and Prefabricated Concrete Bridges*] (RO)
IPMS......... Izdavacko Preduzece Matice Srpske ["*Matica Srpska" Publishing House*] [*Novi Sad*] (YU)

IPMUPaFNRJ ... Izdavacko Preduzece Ministarstva Unutrasnjih Poslova Federativna Narodna Republika Jugoslavija [*Publishing House of the Yugoslav Ministry of Internal Affairs*] (YU)
IPN .... Initial Aiming Point [*Artillery*], Initial Guidance Point [*To an objective*] (BU)
IPN .... Institut Pedagogique National [*National Pedagogic Institute*] [*French*]
IPN .... Instituto Politecnico Nacional [*National Polytechnic Institute*] [*Mexican*] (LA)
IPN .... Instytut Pamieci Narodowej [*Institute of National Memorabilia*] (POL)
IPNA .... International Pediatric Nephrology Association (EA)
IPNCB .... Institut des Parcs Nationaux du Congo Belge (MAR)
IPNETP........ Institut Pedagogique National de l'Enseignement Technique et Professionnel (MAR)
IPNRK .... Institut des Parcs Nationaux et des Reserves Naturelles de Katanga (MAR)
IPNS .... Izvestiya na Prezidiuma na Narodnoto Subranie [*Journal of the Presidium of the National Assembly*] [*A publication*] (BU)
IPO .... Inter-Provinciaal Overleg [*Dutch*]
IPO .... International Progress Organization (EA)
IPO .... Istituto per l'Oriente (MAR)
IPO .... Ivanovo Industrial Region (RU)
IPO .... True Check Point Bearing (RU)
ipod............ And So Forth (BU)
i pod........... Et Cetera, And So Forth (RU)
IPOD........... International Phase of Ocean Drilling (MAR)
IPOL .... Institute of Semiconductors (of the Academy of Sciences, USSR) (RU)
IPOL .... Point of Departure of Return Flight (RU)
IPOP .... Instruction for the Procedure for Granting, Paying, and Accounting Financial Indemnities and Aids (BU)
ipozb........... Engineer Positional Battalion (BU)
ipozb........... Fortification Battalion (RU)
ipozbr.......... Engineer Positional Brigade (BU)
ipozbr.......... Fortification Brigade (RU)
ipozr........... Engineer Positional Company (BU)
ipozr........... Fortification Company (RU)
IPP.............. Flight Instructions (RU)
IPP.............. Gas Casualty First Aid Kit (RU)
IPP.............. Indice de Precos do Produtor [*Producer Price Index*] [*Brazilian*] (LA1)
IPP.............. Institute for Plasma Physics [*West German*]
IPP.............. Institute for Study and Design (BU)
IPP.............. Quarantine Clearing Station (RU)
IPP.............. Surgical Dressing Kit (RU)
IPPB .... Interna Pukovska Poljska Bolnica [*Regimental Field Hospital for Internal Medicine*] (YU)
IPPB .... Mobile Communicable Diseases Hospital (BU)
IPPEC.......... Inventaire Permanent des Periodiques Etrangers en Cours
IPPF............ International Penal and Penitentiary Foundation [*See also FIPP*] (EA)
IPPF............ International Planned Parenthood Federation (MAR)
IPPG........... Mobile Communicable Diseases Hospital (BU)
IPPG........... Mobile Field Hospital for Contagious Diseases (RU)
IPPI............. Institute of Information Transmission Problems (of the Academy of Sciences, USSR) (RU)
IPPI............. Instituto Nacional para el Progreso [*Bogota*] (COL)
IPPK .... Infectious Pleuropneumonia of Goats (RU)
ipr............... And So On (BU)
i pr............. Et Cetera, And So Forth (RU)
IPR.............. Industriepreisreform [*Industrial Price Reform*] (EG)
IPR.............. Instituto de Pesquisas Radioativas [*Radioactive Research Institute*] [*Brazilian*] (LA)
IPR.............. Instituto de Pesquisas Rodoviarias [*Highway Research Institute*] [*Brazilian*] (LA)
IPr............... Istoricheski Pregled [*Historical Review*] [*A periodical*] (BU)
IPR.............. True Bearing of a Radio Station (RU)
IPRA .... Ivoirienne Pieces de Rechange Automobile (MAR)
IPRALCOOP ... Intreprinderea de Produse Alimentare a Cooperatiei de Consum [*Consumer Cooperative Food Products Enterprise*] (RO)
IPRAN.......... Institutul de Proiectari Tehnologice pentru Industria Chimica Anorganica si Ingrasaminte [*Technological Design Institute for the Inorganic Chemicals and Fertilizer Industry*] (RO)
IPRAO .... Institution de Prevoyance et de Retraites de l'Afrique Occidentale [*West African Institute of Welfare and Retirement*] [*Togolese*] (AF)
IPRAS.......... Istanbul Petrol Rafinerisi Anonim Sirketi [*Istanbul Petroleum Refinery Corporation*] (TU)
IPREC.......... Intreprinderea de Prestatii, Reclama, si Expozitii [*Enterprise for Services, Advertising, and Exhibits*] (RO)
IPRI............. Instituto Peruano de Relaciones Internacionales [*Peruvian International Relations Institute*] (LA)
IPRiS .... Instytut Przemyslu Rolnego i Spozywczego [*Institute of the Agriculture and Food Industry*] (POL)
IPROC .... Institutul de Proiectari Carbonifere [*Institute for Coal Design*] (RO)
IPROCHIM... Institutul de Proiectari pentru Industria Chimica Organica de Baza si Petrochimica [*Design Institute for the Basic Organic Chemical and Petrochemical Industry*] (RO)
IPROCIL ...... Institutul de Proiectari Cercetari Stiintifice pentru Industria Lemnului [*Scientific Research and Design Institute for the Wood Industry*] (RO)
IPROCOM ... Institutul de Cercetari si Proiectari pentru Comert [*Research and Design Institute for Trade*] (RO)
IPROED .... Institutul de Proiectari Edilitare [*Municipal Design Institute*] (RO)
IPROFIL....... Institutul de Proiectari Forestiere si pentru Industria Lemnului [*Design Institute for Forestry and the Wood Industry*] (RO)
IPROFIL....... Intreprinderile de Produse Finite din Lemn [*Enterprises for Finished Wood Products*] (RO)
IPROIL......... Institutul de Proiectari din Industria Lemnului [*Design Institute for the Wood Industry*] (RO)
IPROLAM .... Institutul de Proiectare Tehnologica pentru Laminoare [*Technological Design Institute for Rolling Mills*] (RO)
IPROM......... Institutul de Proiectari de Masini [*Machinery Design Institute*] (RO)
IPROMET .... Institutul de Proiectari de Uzine si Instalatii Metalurgice [*Design Institute for Metallurgical Plants and Installations*] (RO)
IPROMIN ..... Institutul de Proiectari si Tehnica Miniera [*Institute for Mining Design and Technology*] (RO)
IPRONAV .... Institutul pentru Proiectarea Constructiilor Navale [*Naval Construction Design Institute*] (RO)
IPROSCO .... Instituto de Promocion Industrial Suizo-Colombiano [*Swiss-Colombian Institute for Industrial Promotion*] (LA)
IPROSIN...... Institutul de Proiectari pentru Industria Chimica Organica de Sinteza Medicamente si Fibre Sintetice [*Design Institute for the Organic Chemical Industry for Drug Syntheses and Synthetic Fibers*] (RO)
IPROUP .... Institutul de Proiectari Utilaj Petrolifer [*Design Institute for Petroleum Equipment*] (RO)
IPROYAZ..... Instituto de Projectos de la Industria Azucarera [*Sugar Industry Planning Institute*] [*Cuban*] (LA)
IPRS .... International Confederation for Plastic and Reconstructive Surgery (EA)
IPRS .... Intreprinderea de Piese Radio si Semiconductori Baneasa [*Baneasa Enterprise for Radio Parts and Semiconductors*] (RO)
IPS.............. East African Industrial Promotion Services (MAR)
IPS.............. Ibero-American Philosophical Society (EA)
IPS.............. Inaltimea Prea Sfinta [*Most High Holiness*] (RO)
IPS.............. Incubator Poultry-Raising Station (RU)
IPS.............. Industrial Promotion Services Ltd. (MAR)
IPS.............. Information Retrieval System (RU)
IPS.............. Institute for Planned Economy (BU)
IPS.............. Institute of Professional Studies (MAR)
IPS.............. Institute of Purchasing and Supply (MAR)
IPS.............. Institutul de Proiectari Schele [*Derrick Design Institute*] (RO)
IPS.............. Inter-Press Service [*Arab*] (MAR)
IPS.............. Inter/Press Service - Third World News (EA)
IPS.............. International Peat Society [*See also IMTG*] (EA)
IPS.............. International Political Surveys (MAR)
IPS.............. International of Proletarian Freethinkers (RU)
IPS.............. Intreprinderea Prestari Servicii [*Services Enterprise*] (RO)
IPS.............. Isopropyl Alcohol (RU)
IPS.............. True Bearing of an Aircraft (RU)
IPSA .... International Professional Security Association (EA)
IPSCI.......... Industrial Promotion Services Cote-d'Ivoire (MAR)
IPSEJES...... Institut de Planification, de Statistique et d'Etudes Juridiques, Economiques, et Sociales [*Tunisian*] (MAR)
IPSF .... International Pharmaceutical Students' Federation (EA)
IPSFA .... Instituto de Prevision Social de las Fuerzas Armadas [*Venezuelan*]
IPSFAN .... Instituto de Prevision Social de las Fuerzas Armadas Nacionales [*National Armed Forces Social Insurance Institute*] [*Venezuelan*] (LA)
IPSI............. Institut de Presse et des Sciences de l'Information [*Tunisian*] (MAR)
IPSI............. Institut de Presse et des Sciences de l'Information [*Algerian*] (MAR)
IPSiC .... Instytut Przemyslu Szkla i Ceramiki [*Institute of the Glass and Ceramics Industry*] (POL)
IPSMF .... Institutul de Perfectionare si Specializare a Medicilor si Farmacistilor [*Institute for the Advanced Training and Specialization of Physicians and Pharmacists*] (RO)
IPSO .... Instituut voor Politiek en Sociaal Onderzoek [*Institute for Political and Social Research*] [*Dutch*] (WEN)
IPSS .... Instituto Peruano de Seguridad Social [*Peruvian Institute of Social Security*] (LA1)
IPST .... Institut de Promotion Superieure du Travail [*Institute for the Advancement of Labor*] [*Algerian*] (AF)
IPSTAS .... Izmir Plastik Sunger Sanayi ve Ticaret Anonim Sirketi [*Izmir Plastic Sponge Industry and Trading Corporation*] (TU)
IPS TsIChM ... Institute of Precision Alloys of the Central Institute of Ferrous Metallurgy (RU)
IPT.............. Instituto de Pesquisas Tecnologicas [*Technological Research Institute*] [*Brazilian*] (LA)
IPT.............. Instituto Postal Telegrafico [*Telegraph and Postal Institute*] [*Venezuelan*] (LA)
IPT.............. Ipelske Tehelne [*Ipel Brick Works*] (CZ)
IPTA .... Antitank Artillery (RU)

iptab........... Antitank Artillery Battery (RU)
iptabr.......... Antitank Artillery Brigade (RU)
iptabr.......... Tank-Destroyer Artillery Brigade (BU)
IPTAD.......... Antitank Artillery Battalion (RU)
iptadn.......... Tank-Destroyer Artillery Battalion (BU)
IPTAP.......... Antitank Artillery Regiment (RU)
iptap........... Tank-Destroyer Regiment (BU)
iptb............. Antitank Battery (RU)
iptbat.......... Antitank Battery (RU)
iptbatr........ Antitank Battery (RU)
IPTC............ Institutul de Proiectari Telecomunicatii [*Telecommunications Design Institute*] (RO)
IPTC............ International Press Telecommunications [*See also CIPT*] (EA)
IPTD............ Antitank Battalion (RU)
iptd............. Tank-Destroyer Battalion (BU)
IPTEA.......... Internacia Postista kaj Telekomunikista Esperanto-Asocio [*International Esperanto Association of Post and Telecommunication Workers*] (EA)
IPTP............ Antitank Regiment (RU)
IPTs............ Moving-Target Indicator (RU)
IPTT............ Internationale du Personnel des Postes, Telegraphes, et Telephones [*Postal, Telegraph, and Telephone International - PTTI*] (EA)
IPTTc.......... Institutul de Proiectari Transporturi si Telecomunicatii [*Institute for Transportation and Telecommunications Design*] (RO)
IPU.............. Igala Progressive Union (MAR)
IPU.............. Igbirra Progressive Union (MAR)
IPU.............. Interparlamentarische Union [*Interparliamentary Union*] (EG)
IPU.............. Sparking Prevention Device (RU)
IPU.............. True Track Angle (RU)
IPUC............ Institutul de Proiectari de Uzine Chimice [*Institute for Chemical Plant Design*] (RO)
IPUEC......... Instituto Preuniversitario en el Campo [*Pre-University Farming and Academic Institute*] [*Cuban*] (LA)
IPUP............ Intreprinderea de Plase si Unelte Pescaresti [*Enterprise for Fishing Nets and Equipment*] (RO)
ipv............... In Plaats Van [*Instead Of*] [*Dutch*] (GPO)
IPVP............ Support for Military Reasons (BU)
IPVS............ International Pig Veterinary Society (EA)
IPWL........... Instytut Przemyslu Wlokien Lykowych [*Institute of the Bast Fiber Industry*] (POL)
IPYa............ Information Retrieval Language (RU)
IPZ.............. Crosstalk Attenuation Meter (RU)
IPZ.............. Instytut Przemyslu Zielarskiego [*Institute of the Herbal Industry*] [*Polish*]
IPZ.............. Inzinjersko Projektni Zavod [*Engineering Planning Institute*] (YU)
iq................. Idem Quod [*The Same As*] [*Latin*] (GPO)
IQ................ Iraq [*Two-letter standard code*] (CNC)
iqed............. Id Quod Erat Demonstrandum [*What Was to Be Proved*] [*Latin*] (GPO)
IQSA............ Industrias Quimicas, Sociedad Anonima [*Chemical Industries Corporation*] [*Salvadorean*]
IR................. Engineer Reconnaissance (BU)
IR................. Engineer Reconnaissance (RU)
ir.................. Idezett Resz [*Section Cited*] (HU)
iR................. Im Ruhestand [*Retired*] (EG)
IR................. Impulse Relay (RU)
iR................. In Ruhe [*German*]
IR-............... Induction Flow Meter (RU)
Ir.................. Ingenieur [*Academic degree*] [*Dutch*]
IR................. Insinjur [*Engineer*] (IN)
i-r................. Inspector (BU)
IR................. Inspektorat Rada [*Labor Inspectorate*] (YU)
IR................. Inspektur [*Inspector*] (IN)
IR................. Institut Rizeni [*Management Institute*] (CZ)
IR................. Institute of Rationalizations (BU)
IR................. International Relations [*Prague*] [*A publication*] (MAR)
IR................. Iran [*Iran*] [*Polish*]
IR................. Iran [*Two-letter standard code*] (CNC)
ir.................. Iranyito [*Leading*] [*Military*] (HU)
Ir.................. Irmak [*River, Large Stream*] (TU)
ir.................. Iroda [*Office*] (HU)
ir.................. Ivret [*Folio*] (HU)
IR................. Izquierda Republicana [*Republican Left*] [*Spanish*] (PPE)
IR................. Lockout Relay (RU)
IR................. Manual Injector (RU)
IR................. Proportional-Plus-Integral Controller (RU)
IRA.............. Industrial Relations Act [*Mauritian*] (AF)
IRA.............. Industries et Representations en Afrique (MAR)
IRA.............. Institut des Recherches Agronomiques (MAR)
IRA.............. Instituto Regulador de Abastecimientos [*Supply Regulation Institute*] [*Salvadoran*] (LA)
IRA.............. Instituto de Reorganizacao Agraria [*Agrarian Reorganization Institute*] [*Portuguese*] (WER)
IRA.............. International Rubber Association (EA)
IRA.............. Intreprinderile de Reparatie Auto [*Automotive Repair Enterprises*] (RO)
IRA.............. Islamic Research Association (MAR)
IRAIK........... Bulletin of the Russian Archeological Institute in Constantinople [*A publication*] (BU)
IRAIMK........ News of the Russian Academy of the History of Material Culture [*A publication*] (RU)
IRALCOOP... Intreprinderea de Produse Alimentare a Cooperativei de Consum [*Food Products Enterprise for the Consumer Cooperatives*] (RO)
IRAM............ Institut de Recherche et d'Applications de Methodes de Developpement [*Institute for Research and Applications of Methods of Development*] [*French*] (AF)
IRAM............ Institut de Recherches Agronomiques a Madagascar [*Madagascar Agronomic Research Institute*] (AF)
IRAN............ Industries Reunies de l'Afrique Noire (MAR)
IRAN............ News of the Russian Academy of Sciences [*A publication*] (RU)
IRANDOC.... Iranian Documentation Centre (MAR)
IRANSENCO... Iran-Senegal Company (ME)
IRAO............ News of the Russian Archaeological Society [*A publication*] (RU)
IRAS............ Institute on Religion in an Age of Science (MAR)
IRASENCO... Societe Irano-Senegalaise des Petroles et des Mines (MAR)
IRAT............ Institut de Recherches Agronomiques Tropicales et des Cultures Vivrieres [*Institute of Tropical Agronomic Research and Food Crops*] [*French*] (AF)
IRB.............. Instituto de Resseguros do Brasil [*Brazilian Reinsurance Institute*] (LA)
IRBAR.......... Irian Barat [*West Irian*] (IN)
IRBB............ Institut Royal Colonial Belge, Bulletin des Seances [*A publication*] (MAR)
IRBM............ Institut Royal Colonial Belge, Memoires [*A publication*] (MAR)
IRC.............. Institutul Roman de Consulting [*Romanian Consulting Institute*] (RO)
IRC.............. Integrated Research Center [*Philippine*]
IRC.............. International Red Cross (MAR)
IRC.............. International Rescue Committee (MAR)
IRC.............. International Rice Commission (MAR)
IRC.............. Islamic Revival Committee [*Sudanese*] (MAR)
IRCA............ Institut de Recherches sur le Cafe (MAR)
IRCA............ Institut de Recherches sur le Caoutchouc en Afrique [*Institute for Rubber Research in Africa*] [*French*] (AF)
IRCAFEX..... Institution de Retraites des Cadres et Assimiles de France et de l'Exterieur (MAR)
IRCAM......... Institut de Recherche et de Coordination Acoustique/Musique [*Institute for Research and Coordination Acoustics/Music*] [*French*]
IRCAM......... Institut de Recherches Scientifiques du Cameroun (MAR)
IRCAU......... Instituto de Relaciones Culturales entre Argentina y la URSS [*Argentine-USSR Cultural Relations Institute*] (LA)
IRCB............ Institut Royal Colonial Belge (MAR)
IRCC............ Institut de Recherches sur le Caoutchouc au Cambodge [*Cambodian Rubber Research Institute*] (CL)
IRCE............ Istituto per le Relazioni Culturali con l'Estero [*Institute for Cultural Relations with Foreign Countries*] [*Italian*] (WER)
IRCh............ Frequency-Difference Relay (RU)
IRC-L.......... Instituto Regional Castellano-Leones [*Castille-Leon Regional Institute*] [*Spanish*] (WER)
IRCL............ International Research Centre on Lindane [*See also CIEL*] (EA)
IRCM............ Institutul Romanesc de Cercetari Marine [*Romanian Institute for Marine Research*] (RO)
IRCOBI........ International Research Committee on the Biokinetics of Impacts (EA)
IRCOSA....... International Radio Corporation Societe Anonyme (MAR)
IRCOTEX..... Institut de Recherches du Coton et des Textiles Exotiques [*Research Institute for Cotton and Exotic Textiles*] [*French*] (MAR)
IRCT............ Institut Recherche Coloniale Tropicale (MAR)
IRCTE.......... Institut de Recherches du Coton et des Textiles Exotiques [*Research Institute for Cotton and Exotic Textiles*] [*French*] (AF)
IRD.............. Engineer Reconnaissance Patrol (RU)
IRD.............. Instituto de Radioprotecao e Dosimetria [*Radio-Protection and Dosimetry Institute*] [*Brazilian*] (LA)
IRD.............. Integrated Rural Development (MAR)
IRDA............ Institut Royal de Droit et l'Administration [*Royal Institute of Law and Administration*] [*Laotian*] (CL)
IRDJENAU... Inspektur Djemderal Angkat Udara [*Air Force Inspector General*] (IN)
IRDP............ Integrated Rural Development Programme (MAR)
IRE.............. Institute of Radio Engineering and Electronics (of the Academy of Sciences, USSR) (RU)
IRE.............. Intreprinderea Regionala de Electricitate [*Regional Electricity Enterprise*] (RO)
IREA............ All-Union Scientific Research Institute of Chemical Reagents and Ultrapure Chemical Substances (RU)
IREB............ Intreprinderea Regionala de Electricitate Bucuresti [*Bucharest Regional Electricity Enterprise*] (RO)
IREB............ Intreprinderea de Retele Electrice Bucuresti [*Bucharest Enterprise for Electricity Networks*] (RO)
IRED............ Innovations et Reseaux pour le Developpement [*Development Innovations and Networks*] (EA)
IREDA.......... Iuran Rehabilitasi Daerah [*Regional Rehabilitation Tax*] (IN)
IREM............ Institut de Recherche pour l'Enseignement des Mathematiques [*Institute for Research in the Teaching of Mathematics*] [*Malagasy*] (AF)

iremb .... Engineer Maintenance Battalion (RU)
IREMIL .... Impresa Rappresentanze e Mediazioni in Libia (MAR)
IREMOAS.... Intreprinderea de Radiatoare, Echipament Metalic, Obiecte, si Armaturi Sanitare [*Enterprise for Radiators, Metal Equipment, and Sanitary Articles and Fittings*] (RO)
iremr .... Engineer Maintenance Company (RU)
iremvb........ Engineer Maintenance and Recovery Battalion (RU)
IREN .... Institut de Recherche pour les Energies Douces de l'Universite (MAR)
IREN .... Institut de Recherche sur les Energies Nouvelles [*Ivorian*]
IRENA .... Instituto de Recursos Naturales [*Institute of Natural Resources*] [*Nicaraguan*] (LA1)
irer .... Engineer Maintenance and Recovery Company (RU)
IRES .... Institut de Recherches Economiques et Sociales [*Institute of Economic and Social Research*] [*Zairian*] (AF)
IRES .... Integrated Refinery Engineering Services (MAR)
IRES .... Intreprinderea Regionala de Electricitate din Sibiu [*Sibiu Regional Electricity Enterprise*] (RO)
IRESA.......... Institut des Recherches Economiques et Sociales [*Algerian*] (MAR)
IRF............... Institut de Recherches Fruitieres (MAR)
IRF............... International Road Federation (MAR)
IRFA .... Imprimerie Reliure Franco Africaine (MAR)
IRFA .... Institut de Recherches sur les Fruits et Agrumes (MAR)
IRFB .... International Resources and Finance Bank SA (MAR)
IRFE .... Ispettorato Generale per i Rapporti Finanziari con l'Estero [*General Inspectorate for Financial Relations with Foreign Countries*] [*Italian*] (WER)
IRFED.......... Institut International de Recherches et de Formation en Vue du Developpement Harmonise [*International Institute for Research and Training for Standardized Development*] [*French*] (AF)
IRFED.......... Institut de Recherche et de Formation en Vue du Developpement Harmonise [*French*]
IRFKhB........ Institute of Radiation and Physicochemical Biology (of the Academy of Sciences, USSR) (RU)
IRG .... Engineer Reconnaissance Group (RU)
IRG .... International Research Group on Wood Preservation (EA)
IRG .... Intreprinderea Regionala de Constructii [*Regional Constructions Enterprise*] (RO)
IRG .... Ipari Robbanoanyaggyar [*Industrial Explosives Factory*] (HU)
IRGA............ Instituto Riograndense do Arroz [*Rio Grande Do Sul Rice Institute*] [*Brazilian*] (LA)
IRGCVD....... International Research Group on Colour Vision Deficiencies (EA)
IRGIREDMET ... Irkutsk Scientific Research Institute of Rare Metals (RU)
IRGK............ Engineer Reserve of the High Command (RU)
IRGO .... News of the Russian Geographic Society [*A publication*] (RU)
IRHO............ Institut de Recherches pour les Huiles et Oleagineux [*Institute for Research on Edible Oils and Oleaginous Products*] [*French*] (AF)
IRI................ Institut des Relations Internationales [*Institute of International Relations*] [*Zairian*] (AF)
IRI................ Istituto per la Ricostruzione Industriale [*Industrial Reconstruction Institute*] [*Italian*] (WER)
IRIA .... Institut de Recherche d'Informatique et d'Automatique [*French*]
IRIC .... Institut des Relations Internationales du Cameroun (MAR)
IRICASE...... Institution de Retraite Interprofessionnelle des Cadres Superieurs d'Enterprises (MAR)
IRICS........... Israel Research Institute of Contemporary Society
IRIRC........... International Refugee Integration Resource Centre (EA)
IRIS .... Iwo Recreational, Intellectual, and Social Club (MAR)
IRITUN......... Instituto Regional de Investigaciones Tecnologicas de la Universidad del Norte [*Regional Institute for Technological Research of the University of the North*] [*Chilean*] (LA)
IRK .... Tool-Distributing Stock Room (RU)
IRKAZ.......... Irkutsk Aluminum Plant (RU)
IRKIVA .... News of the Russian Committee for the Study of Central and East Asia [*A publication*] (RU)
IRKTD.......... Instruction for the Registration of Collective Labor Contracts (BU)
IRL............... Information Retrieval Limited [*United Kingdom*]
IRL............... Ireland [*Three-letter standard code*] (CNC)
irl................. Irish (RU)
irl................. Irlantilainen [*Irish*] [*Finnish*]
IRLA .... International Religious Liberty Association (MAR)
irland........... Irish (RU)
IRLCOSA .... International Red Locust Control Organisation for Central and Southern Africa (MAR)
IRLCS.......... International Red Locust Control Service (MAR)
IRLI.............. Institute of Russian Literature (of the Academy of Sciences, USSR) (RU)
IRM.............. Industrial Workers of the World [*IWW*] (RU)
IRM.............. Islamskaia Respublika Mauritaniia (MAR)
IRMA .... Intreprinderea de Reparat Material Aeronautic [*Enterprise for the Repair of Aeronautical Material*] (RO)
IRME .... Intreprinderea pentru Rationalizarea si Modernizarea Instalatiilor Energetice [*Enterprise for the Rationalization and Modernization of Power Installations*] (RO)
IRMS .... Institute of Rationalization of the Council of Ministers (BU)
IRN .... Iran [*Three-letter standard code*] (CNC)
IRN .... Source of Regulated Voltage (RU)
IRNE .... Institutul de Reactori Nucleari Energetici [*Institute for Nuclear Power Reactors*] (RO)
IRNR .... Instituto de Recursos Naturales Renovables [*Institute for Renewable Natural Resources*] [*Ecuadorean*] (LA)
IRNRTR .... Instruction for Assignment and Job Placement of Labor Reserves (BU)
IRO .... Institut de Recherches sur l'Onchocerose [*Institute for Research on Onchocerosis*] (AF)
IRO .... Intensity of X-Ray Reflections (RU)
irod............. Irodalom [*Literature*] (HU)
IRO-FIET ..... Interamerican Regional Organization of the International Federation of Commercial, Clerical, Professional, and Technical Employees (EA)
iron............. Ironic (BU)
Iron............. Ironisesti [*Ironically*] [*Finnish*]
IROPCO....... Iranian Offshore Petroleum Company (ME)
IRP.............. Indian Reform Party [*South African*] (AF)
IRP.............. Individual Jet Exhaust Nozzle (RU)
IRP.............. International of Education Workers [*1920-1939*] (RU)
IRP.............. Islahat Refah Partisi [*Reformation and Welfare Party*] [*Turkish Cypriot*] (PPE)
IRP.............. Islamic Republican Party [*Iranian*] (PPW)
IRP.............. Italian Republican Party (RU)
IRP.............. True Radio Bearing (RU)
IRPA .... All-Union Scientific Research Institute of Radio Broadcasting Reception and Acoustics (RU)
IRPA .... Instituto de la Reforma y Promocion Agrarias [*Agrarian Reform and Development Institute*] [*Peruvian*] (LA)
IRPA .... International Radiation Protection Association (EA)
IRPGR......... Inspektorat Rejonowy Panstwowych Gospodarstw Rybackich [*District Inspectorate of State Fish Farms*] (POL)
IRPM........... Impot sur le Revenue des Personnes Morales (MAR)
IRPP .... Impot sur le Revenue des Personnes Physiques (MAR)
irpu............. Engineer Company for Preparation of Command Posts (BU)
IRQ .... Irak [*Iraq*] [*Polish*]
IRQ .... Iraq [*Three-letter standard code*] (CNC)
irr .... Engineer Reconnaissance Company (RU)
IRR.............. Institute of Race Relations (EA)
IRRC........... Investor Responsibility Research Center (MAR)
IRRCS .... Institutul Romanesc pentru Relatii Culturale cu Strainatatea [*Romanian Institute for Cultural Relations with Foreign Countries*] (RO)
IRRDB......... International Rubber Research and Development Board (EA)
IRRI .... International Rice Research Institute (MAR)
Irrig .... Irrigation [*Irrigation*] [*Military map abbreviation*] [*World War I*] [*French*] (MTD)
IRS .... Institut de Recherche Scientifique [*Scientific Research Institute*] [*Zairian*] (AF)
IRS .... Institut de Recherches Sahariennes (MAR)
IRS .... Institutul Romanesc de Standarde [*Romanian Institute of Standards*] (RO)
IRS .... Instytut Rybactwa Srodladowego (Olsztyn) [*Institute of Inland Fisheries (Olsztyn)*] (POL)
IRS .... Reactivity Index (RU)
IRSA........... International Rural Sociology Association (EA)
IRSAC .... Institut pour la Recherche Scientifique en Afrique Centrale [*Institute for Scientific Research in Central Africa*] [*Zairian*] (AF)
IRSC........... Institut de Recherches Scientifiques au Congo (MAR)
IRSFC......... International Rayon and Synthetic Fibres Committee [*See also CIRFS*] (EA)
IRSG........... International Rubber Study Group (EA)
IRSH........... Institut de Recherche en Sciences Humaines [*Institute for Research in Human Sciences*] [*Niger*] (AF)
IRSIA.......... Institut pour l'Encouragement de la Recherche Scientifique dans l'Industrie et l'Agriculture [*Institute for the Promotion of Scientific Research in Industry and Agriculture*] [*Belgian*] (WER)
IRSID.......... Institut de Recherches de la Siderurgie [*Institute of Siderurgical Research*] [*French*] (WER)
IRSM .... Institut de Recherches Scientifiques de Madagascar (MAR)
IRSM .... Institut de Recherches Scientifiques du Mali (MAR)
Irstroypromsoyuz ... Irkutsk Special Producers' Union for the Manufacture of Building Materials (RU)
IRT.............. Institut de Recherche des Transports [*Transportation Research Institute*] [*French*] (WER)
IRT.............. Instituto Nacional de Radio y Television [*Bogota*] (COL)
Irt................ Irtibat [*Liaison, Communication*] (TU)
IRTA .... Intreprinderile Regionale Transport Auto [*Regional Automotive Transportation Enterprises*] (RO)
Irtf .... Irtifa [*Altitude*] (TU)
IRTO........... Institut de Recherches Scientifiques du Togo (MAR)
IRU .... International Raiffeisen Union (EA)
IRU .... International Road Transport Union (EA)
IRUC........... Intreprinderea de Reparatii Utilajelor de Calcul [*Enterprise for the Repair of Computer Equipment*] (RO)
IRUM .... Intreprinderea de Reparatii, Utilaje, si Montaj [*Enterprise for Repairs, Equipment, and Assembly*] (RO)
IRUSTAT..... Institut Rundi des Statistiques (MAR)
irv.............. Engineer Reconnaissance Platoon (RU)

IRVM .... Impot sur le Revenu des Valeurs Mobilieres [*Tunisian*] (MAR)
IRYa .... Institute of Russian Language (of the Academy of Sciences, USSR) (RU)
IRYaZ .... Institute of Russian Language (of the Academy of Sciences, USSR) (RU)
IRZ .... Institut de Recherches Zootechniques Pastorales et Veterinaires (MAR)
IRZ .... Is Riski Zammi [*Labor Risk Premium*] (TU)
IS .... Artificial Satellite (RU)
IS .... Extraordinary Session (BU)
Is .... Iasi [*Iasi*] (RO)
IS .... Iceland [*Two-letter standard code*] (CNC)
iS .... Im Sinne [*In the Meaning*] (EG)
IS .... Informacni Sluzba [*Information Service*] (CZ)
IS .... Inspektorat za Sumarstvo [*Forestry Inspectorate*] (YU)
IS .... Institute of Slavic Studies (of the Academy of Sciences, USSR) (RU)
IS .... Institute of Speech (RU)
IS .... Instytut Sztuki [*Institute of Fine Arts*] [*Polish*]
IS .... International Standard [*ISO*]
IS .... Internazionale Socialista [*Socialist International*] [*Italian*] (WER)
IS .... Interpretive System (RU)
IS .... Intreprindere de Stat [*State Enterprise*] (RO)
Is .... Is Adresi [*Business Address*] (TU)
IS .... Isa'dan Sonra [*After Christ*] (TU)
IS .... Iskrcne Stanice [*Unloading Stations*] [*Military*] (YU)
IS .... Islandia [*Iceland*] [*Polish*]
is .... Islenmis [*Processed, Fabricated, Made Up*] (TU)
IS .... Izvrsni Svet [*Executive Council*] (YU)
IS .... Pulse Counter (RU)
IS .... Quartermaster Service (RU)
IS .... Reset Pulse (RU)
ISA .... Iatrikos Syllogos Athinon [*Athens Medical Association*] (GC)
ISA .... Ingenieros Sanitarios Asociados Ltda. [*Cali*] (COL)
ISA .... Institut Superieur des Arts Plastiques (MAR)
ISA .... Interconexion Electrica SA [*Bogota*] (COL)
ISA .... International Security Affairs (MAR)
ISA .... International Service Association (MAR)
ISA .... International Soling Association (EA)
ISA .... International Strabismological Association (EA)
ISA .... International Studies Association
ISA .... International Sugar Agreement (LA)
ISA .... International Surfing Association (EA)
ISAA .... Institute of South African Architects (MAR)
ISAA .... Intreprinderile de Stat pentru Gospodarirea Apelor din Agricultura [*State Enterprises for Water Management in Agriculture*] (RO)
ISABR .... International Society for Animal Blood Group Research (EA)
ISABU .... Institut des Sciences Agronomiques du Burundi [*Institute of Agronomic Studies of Burundi*] (AF)
ISACMETU ... International Secretariat of Arts, Communications Media, and Entertainment Trade Unions (EA)
ISADA .... Industries et Savonneries du Dahomey (MAR)
ISAeM .... International Society for Aerosols in Medicine [*See also IGAeM*] (EA)
ISAF .... Intreprinderea de Semnalizari si Automatizari Feroviare [*Enterprise for Railways Signals and Automation*] (RO)
ISAIV .... Integriertes System der Automatisierten Informationsverarbeitung [*Integrated System of Automated Information Processing*] (EG)
ISAL-Bolivia ... Iglesia y Sociedad para America Latina - Seccion Boliviana [*Church and Society for Latin America - Bolivian Section*] (LA)
ISAP .... Ilektrikoi Sidirodromoi Athinon-Peiraias Anonymos Etaireia [*Athens-Piraeus Electric Railways*] (GC)
ISAP .... Institut Superieur des Arts Plastiques (MAR)
ISAP .... Instituto Sudamericano de Petroleo [*South American Petroleum Institute*] (LA)
ISAP .... Instituto Superior de Administracion Publica [*Advanced Institute for Public Administration*] [*Bolivian*] (LA)
ISAP .... Instituto Superior de Capacitacion Azucarera [*Higher Institute for Sugar Technology Training*] [*Cuban*] (LA)
isapb .... Engineer Battalion (RU)
isapp .... Engineer Regiment (RU)
isapr .... Engineer Company (RU)
isapv .... Engineer Platoon (RU)
ISAPVS .... Intreprinderea de Stat pentru Asigurarea Producerii si Valorificarii Semintelor [*State Enterprise to Ensure the Production and Utilization of Seeds*] (RO)
ISAR .... Institut des Sciences Agronomiques du Rwanda [*Institute of Agronomic Sciences of Rwanda*] (AF)
ISART .... Institutul de Studii, Cercetari, si Proiectari pentru Sistematizare, Arhitectura, si Tipizare [*Studies, Research, and Design Institute for Systematization, Architecture, and Standardization*] (RO)
ISAS .... Institute of Space and Aeronautical Science [*Under Tokyo University*] (SJT)
ISAT .... International Society of Analytical Trilogy [*See also SITA*] (EA)
ISATA .... Israel-South Africa Trade Association (MAR)
isb .... Combat Engineer Battalion (BU)
ISB .... Engineer Battalion (RU)
isb .... Engineer Construction Battalion (RU)
ISB .... Institut Sumarstva - Beograd [*Belgrade Forestry Institute*] (YU)
ISB .... International Society of Biometeorology (EA)
ISB .... Internationaler Studentenbund [*International Union of Students, IUS*] (EG)
ISB .... Intreprinderea de Salubritate Bucuresti [*Bucharest Sanitation Enterprise*] (RO)
ISBC .... Intreprinderile de Statiuni Balneo-Climaterice [*Health Spa Enterprises*] (RO)
ISBD(M) .... International Standard Bibliographic Description for Monographs
ISBD(S) .... International Standard Bibliographic Description for Serials
ISBI .... International Savings Banks Institute [*See also IICE*] (EA)
ISBN .... International Standard Book Number
ISBO .... Islamic States Broadcasting Organization (EA)
isbr .... Combat Engineer Brigade (BU)
ISBr .... Engineer Brigade (RU)
ISC .... Institut Scientifique Cherifien [*Moroccan*] (MAR)
ISC .... Inter-American Society of Cardiology (EA)
ISC .... International Seismological Centre (EA)
ISC .... International Sericultural Commission [*See also CSI*] (EA)
ISC .... International Society of Chemotherapy (EA)
ISC .... International Society of Cryosurgery (EA)
ISCA .... Instituto Superior de Ciencias Agropecuarias [*Advanced Institute of Agricultural and Animal Sciences*] [*Cuban*] (LA)
ISCA .... International Sailing Craft Association (EA)
ISCAB .... Instituto Superior de Ciencias Agropecuarias de Bayamo [*Bayamo Higher Institute of Agricultural-Livestock Sciences*] [*Cuban*] (LA1)
ISCAE .... Institut Superieur de Commerce et Administration des Entreprises a Casablanca [*Moroccan*] (MAR)
ISCAH .... Instituto Superior de Ciencias Agropecuarias de La Habana [*Higher Institute of Agricultural and Animal Sciences of Havana*] [*Cuban*] (LA)
ISCAM .... Institut Superieur des Cadres Militaires [*Higher Institute for Military Cadres*] [*Burundi*] (AF)
ISCAP .... Instituto Superior de Ciencias Agropecuarias de Bayamo [*Higher Institute of Agricultural and Animal Sciences of Bayamo*] [*Cuban*] (LA)
ISCAS .... Institutul Central de Studii, Cercetari Stiintifice, si Proiectari in Constructii, Arhitectura, si Sistematizare [*Central Institute for Studies, Scientific Research, and Design in Constructions, Architecture, and Systematization*] (RO)
ISCAS .... Institutul de Studii si Proiectare pentru Constructii, Arhitectura, si Sistematizare [*Studies and Design Institute for Constructions, Architecture, and Systematization*] (RO)
ISCAY .... International Solidarity Committee with Algerian Youth (MAR)
ISCB .... International Society for Classical Bibliography (EA)
ISCC .... International Supervisory and Control Commission (CL)
ISCC .... International System and Control Corporation (MAR)
ISCD .... International Society for Community Development (MAR)
ISCE .... Instituto Salvadoreno de Comercio Exterior [*Salvadoran Foreign Trade Institute*] (LA)
ISCE .... International Society for Clinical Enzymology (EA)
ISCE .... Intreprinderile de Stat pentru Comertul Exterior [*State Enterprises for Foreign Trade*] (RO)
ISCED .... International Society of Continuing Education in Dentistry [*See also SIECD*] (EA)
ISCED .... International Standard Classification of Education
ISCEI .... Institutul pentru Studierea Conjuncturii Economice Internationale [*Institute for the Study of the International Economic Situation*] (RO)
ISCFD .... Instituto Superior de Cultura Fisica y Deportes [*Higher Institute for Physical Education and Sports*] [*Cuban*] (LA)
ISCH .... Institutul de Studii si Cercetari Hidrotehnice [*Institute for Hydrotechnical Studies and Research*] (RO)
ISCIF .... Institutul de Studii si Cercetari pentru Imbunatatiri Funciare [*Studies and Research Institute for Land Improvement*] (RO)
ISCIFGA .... Institutul de Studii si Cercetari pentru Imbunatatiri Funciare si Gospodarirea Apelor [*Studies and Research Institute for Land Improvement and Water Management*] (RO)
ISCIP .... Intreprindere de Stat pentru Cresterea si Ingrasarea Porcilor [*State Enterprise for the Raising and Fattening of Hogs*] (RO)
ISCIR .... Inspectoratul de Stat pentru Cazane si Instalatii de Ridicat [*State Inspectorate for Pressure Vessels and Hoisting Installations*] (RO)
ISCM .... Instituto Superior de Ciencias Medicas [*Higher Institute of Medical Sciences*] [*Cuban*] (LA)
ISCM .... Intreprinderea de Stat pentru Materiale de Constructii [*State Enterprise for Construction Materials*] (RO)
ISCO .... Istituto per la Congiuntura [*Institute for the Study of Economic Trends*] [*Italian*] (WER)
ISCOR .... South African Iron and Steel Corporation (AF)
ISCOS .... Inter-Governmental Standing Committee on Shipping (AF)
ISCOTT .... Iron and Steel Company of Trinidad and Tobago (LA1)
ISCP .... Institutul de Studii si Cercetari Pedologice [*Pedological Studies and Research Institute*] (RO)

ISCPA .... Institutul de Studii, Cercetari, si Proiectari pentru Constructii si pentru Organizarea Productiei Agricole [*Studies, Research, and Design Institute for Constructions and for the Organization of Agricultural Production*] (RO)
ISCPCH .... Institutul de Studii, Cercetari, si Proiectari pentru Constructii Hortiviticole [*Studies, Research, and Design Institute for Horticultural and Viticultural Constructions*] (RO)
ISCPCZ .... Institutul de Studii, Cercetari, si Proiectari pentru Constructii Zootehnice [*Studies, Research, and Design Institute for Zootechnical Constructions*] (RO)
ISCPGA .... Institutul de Studii, Cercetari, si Proiectari pentru Gospodarirea Apelor [*Studies, Research, and Design Institute for Water Management*] (RO)
ISCR .... Institut Superieur de Culture Religieuse (MAR)
ISCSP .... Instituto Superior de Ciencias Sociais e Politicas [*Institute of Higher Social and Political Studies*] [*Portuguese*] (WER)
ISCSPU .... Instituto Superior de Ciencias Sociais e Politicas Ultramarina (MAR)
ISCTR .... International Scientific Committee for Trypanosomiasis Research (MAR)
ISD .... Institute of the Building Industry (RU)
ISD .... Internal Security Department [*Singapore*] (ML)
ISD .... Internal Security Division [*Bahamian*] (LA1)
ISDE .... International Society for Diseases of the Esophagus (EA)
ISDE .... Izquierda Social Democrata Espanola [*Spanish Social Democratic Left*] (WER)
ISDEMIR ..... Iskenderun Demir-Celik Isletmeleri Muessese [*Iskenderun Iron and Steel Works Enterprise*] (TU)
ISDP .... Italian Social Democratic Party (RU)
ISDS .... International Serials Data System [*UNESCO/UNISIST*] (EA)
ISDS .... International Sheep Dog Society (EA)
ISE .... Instituto de Superacion Educacional [*Educational Advancement Institute*] [*Cuban*] (LA)
ISE .... Institutos Superiores de Educacion [*Higher Institutes of Education*] [*Spanish*]
ISEA .... Institut de Science Economique Appliquee [*French*]
ISEA .... Institut Superieur d'Etudes Agronomiques [*Higher Institute of Agronomic Studies*] [*Zairian*] (AF)
ISEAAN ...... Institut de Science Economique Appliquee. Centre d'Afrique du Nord [*North African*] (MAR)
ISEAC .... Institut de Science Economique Appliquee. Cahiers [*Paris*] [*A publication*] (MAR)
ISEB .... Instituto Superior de Estudos Brasileiros [*Advanced Institute of Brazilian Studies*] (LA)
ISEC .... Iran Solar Energy Company (ME)
ISECAAN .... Institut des Sciences Economiques et Commerciales Appliquees a l'Afrique Noire (MAR)
ISECS .... International Society for Eighteenth-Century Studies [*See also SIEDS*] (EA)
ISEM .... International Society for Ecological Modelling (EA)
ISEM .... Intreprinderile de Servicii Edilitare si Montaj [*Municipal Services and Installations Enterprises*] (RO)
ISENCY .... Industrie Senegalaise du Cycle (MAR)
ISEP .... Instituto Superior de Estudios Policiales [*Higher Institute for Police Studies*] [*Costa Rican*] (LA1)
ISEP .... Institutul de Stiinte Economice si Planificare [*Institute for Economic Sciences and Planning*] (RO)
ISEP .... International Society of Esperantist-Philologists [*See also IUEFI*] (EA)
ISER .... Instituto Superior de Educacion Rural [*Pamplona*] (COL)
ISERST .... Institut Superieur d'Etudes et de Recherches Scientifiques et Techniques [*Advanced Institute for Scientific and Technical Research and Study*] [*Djibouti*] (AF)
ISES .... International Ship Electric Service Association (EA)
ISES .... International Solar Energy Society (EA)
ISETI .... Institut Superieur de l'Etat de Traducteurs et Interpretes [*State Higher Institute of Translators and Interpreters*] [*Belgian*]
ISF .... International Shipping Federation (EA)
ISFC .... International Society and Federation of Cardiology (EA)
ISFI .... Institute of Students and Faculty on Israel (MAR)
ISFL .... International Society of Family Law (EA)
ISFP .... Institut Superieur de Formation Pedagogique (MAR)
ISGD .... International Study Group of Diabetes in Children and Adolescents (EA)
ISGE .... Institut Superieur de Gestion des Entreprises [*Higher Business Management Institute*] [*Tunisian*] (AF)
ISGO .... International Society of Geographic Ophthalmology (EA)
ISGR .... Inzinierske Stavitelstvo, Generalne Riaditelstvo [*Engineering Construction, General Directorate*] (CZ)
ISGSH .... International Study Group for Steroid Hormones (EA)
ISH .... International Society of Hypertension (EA)
ISh .... Measuring Disk (RU)
ISHIBRAS .... Ishikawajima do Brasil Estaleiros SA [*Ishikawajima Shipyards of Brazil, Inc.*] (LA)
Ishimbayneft' ... Ishimbay Petroleum Industry Trust (RU)
IShK .... Outgoing Cord Assembly (RU)
ISHM .... Institut des Sciences Humaines du Mali (MAR)
ISHR .... International Society for Human Rights [*See also IGM*] (EA)
ISHS .... International Society for Horticultural Science [*See also SISH*] (EA)
ISI .... Construction Engineering Institute (RU)
ISI .... Engineering Construction Institute (BU)
ISI .... Iera Synodos tis Ierarkhias [*Holy Synod of the Hierarchy*] [*Greek*] (GC)
ISI .... Ikatan Sardjana Indonesia [*Indonesian College Graduates Association*] (IN)
ISI .... Institut za Sumarska Istrazivanja [*Forestry Research institute*] (YU)
ISI .... Institute for Economic Research (BU)
ISI .... Istanbul Sular Idaresi [*Istanbul Water Works Administration*] (TU)
ISI .... Istok Severo-Istok [*East North-East*] (YU)
ISIAP .... Intreprinderea de Stat pentru Imprimate si Administratia Publicatiilor [*State Enterprise for Printing and Administration of Publications*] (RO)
ISIC .... Instituto Salvadoreno de Investigaciones del Cafe [*Salvadoran Institute of Coffee Research*] (LA1)
ISIC .... International Standard Industrial Classification (MAR)
ISIF .... Instituto Superior de Idiomas y Finanzas [*Bogota*] (COL)
ISIG .... Institute of Standards and Industrial Research [*Ghanaian*] (MAR)
ISIM .... Institutul de Sudura si Incercari de Materiale [*Institute for Welding and Testing Materials*] (RO)
ISIMA .... Industrie Sisaliere du Maroc [*North African*] (MAR)
ISIMC .... International Study Institution of the Middle Classes (EA)
ISIRI .... Institute of Standards and Industrial Research of Iran (ME)
ISIS .... Institutul de Studii Istorice si Social-Politice [*Institute for Historical and Sociopolitical Studies*] (RO)
ISISP .... Instituto Superior de Investigaciones Sociales y Politicas [*Advanced Institute for Social and Political Research*] [*Ecuadorean*] (LA)
ISISSAPORCI ... International Section of ISSA [*International Social Security Association*] on the Prevention of Occupational Risks in the Construction Industry (EA)
ISJ .... Inspectoratul Scolar Judetean [*County School Inspectorate*] (RO)
ISK .... Historical Commission (RU)
ISK .... Institute for Construction Cybernetics (BU)
Isk .... Iskele [*Landing Place, Wharf*] (TU)
isk .... Iskola [*School*] (HU)
ISKD .... Izmir Sinema Kultur Dernegi [*Izmir Cinema Cultural Association*] (TU)
ISKh .... Institute of Agriculture (RU)
ISKhI .... Irkutsk Agricultural Institute (RU)
ISKhI .... Izhevsk Agricultural Institute (RU)
iskh r-zh ...... Line of Departure (RU)
ISKLP .... Institute for Medical Treatment and Rest at Health Resorts (BU)
Iskolastrel ... Executive Committee of Latvian Riflemen (RU)
Iskolat .... Executive Committee of the Soviet of Workers', Soldiers', and Peasants' Deputies of Latvia (RU)
ISKOMOF .... Executive Committee of the Soviet of Officers' Deputies (RU)
ISKOMZAP ... Executive Committee of the Soviet of Soldiers' Deputies of the Western Front (RU)
ISKORAD .... Executive Committee of the Soviet of Workers' Deputies (RU)
ISKORASOL ... Executive Committee of the Soviet of Workers' and Soldiers' Deputies (RU)
ISKOSOL .... Executive Committee of the Soviet of Soldiers' Deputies (RU)
ISKOSOVDEP ... Executive Committee of the Soviet of Deputies (RU)
Iskozh .... Artificial Leather Plant (RU)
Iskozh .... Kalinin Artificial Leather Kombinat (RU)
Iskozh .... Kazan' Artificial Leather Factory (RU)
Iskozh .... Leningrad Artificial Leather Factory (RU)
ISKUR .... Isci, Isadami, Kimya Sanayii Kuruluslari AS [*Worker, Businessmen, Chemical Industry Organizations, Corporation*] [*Bandirma fertilizer factory*] (TU)
iskusstv ...... Artificial, Synthetic (RU)
ISL .... Artificial Moon Satellite (RU)
isl .... I Slicno [*And the Like*] (YU)
ISL .... Iceland [*Three-letter standard code*] (CNC)
isl .... Icelandic (RU)
ISL .... Institut Franco-Allemand de Recherches de Saint-Louis [*Franco-German Research Institute at Saint-Louis*] [*French*] (WER)
ISL .... Institut fuer Stahlbau und Leichtmetallbau [*Institute for Steel and Light-Metal Construction*] (EG)
ISl .... Instytut Slaski [*Silesian Institute*] (POL)
ISL .... International Society of Literature (EA)
ISL .... International Society of Lymphology (EA)
isl .... Islantia [*or Islanniksi*] [*Finnish*]
isl .... Islantilainen [*Finnish*]
Isl .... Islavca [*Slavic*] (TU)
island .... Icelandic (RU)
ISLGC .... Institutul de Cercetari si Proiectari pentru Sistematizare Locuinte si Gospodarie Comunala [*Research and Design Institute for Systematization of Housing and Communal Administration*] (RO)
ISLIC .... Israel Society Libraries and Information Centers
ISLIF .... Intreprinderea de Stat pentru Lucrari si Imbunatatiri Funciare [*State Enterprise for Land Projects and Improvements*] (RO)
ISLIMA .... Industrie Senegalaise de Linge de Maison (MAR)

ISLRS.......... Izvrsni Svet Ljudska Republika Slovenija [*Executive Council of Slovenia*] (YU)
ISLSCB....... Intreprinderea Santier de Lucrari Speciale in Constructii Bucuresti [*Bucharest Worksite Enterprise for Special Construction Projects*] (RO)
ISM.............. Artificial and Synthetic Materials (RU)
ISM.............. Ilektrostatikai Monades [*Electrostatic Units*] (GC)
ISM.............. Institut Scientifique de Madagascar (MAR)
ISM.............. Institute of Structural Mechanics (of the Academy of Sciences, USSR) (RU)
ism.............. Ismeretlen [*Unknown*] (HU)
ism.............. Ismertetes [*or Ismerteti*] [*Review or Reviewed By*] (HU)
ism.............. Ismetles [*Repeat*] (HU)
ISMA........... Industrie Senegalaise des Marbres et Agglomeres (MAR)
ISMA........... Institute for the Study of Man in Africa (MAR)
ISMA........... International Superphosphate and Compound Manufacturers' Association (MAR)
ISMAC......... Israeli-Syrian Mixed Armistice Commission (ME)
ISMAK......... Istif Makinalari Sanayi ve Ticaret AS [*Loading and Unloading Machinery Industry and Trade Corp.*] (TU)
ISMB........... International Society of Mathematical Biology (EA)
ISMEO......... Istituto Italiano per il Medio ed Estremo Oriente [*Italian Institute for the Middle and Far East*] (WER)
ISMiS.......... Institute of Building Materials and Structures (RU)
ISML............ Instituto Sperimentale dei Metalli Leggeri
ISMM........... International Society of Mini- and Micro-Computers (EA)
ISMN........... International Standard Music Number
ISN.............. Instituto Social Nicaraguense [*Nicaraguan Social Institute*] (LA)
ISNN............ Measurement of Night Sky Luminescence (RU)
ISNT............ Informal Single Negotiating Text (MAR)
ISO.............. Engineer Construction Section (RU)
ISO.............. Engineering Economic Organization (BU)
ISO.............. International Organization for Standardization
ISO.............. International Shopfitting Organization (EA)
ISO.............. International Standards Organisation [*Swiss*]
ISO.............. International Sugar Organization [*See also OIA*] (EA)
ISO.............. Istanbul Sanayi Odasi [*Istanbul Chamber of Industry*] (TU)
ISO.............. Lime-Sulfur Solution (RU)
ISOCAR....... ISO Colombiana Ltda. [*Bogota*] (COL)
ISoCaRP..... International Society of City and Regional Planners [*See also AIU*] (EA)
ISOD............ Istanbul Sanayii Odasi Dergisi [*Istanbul Chamber of Industry Review*] [*A publication*] (TU)
ISORID........ International Information System on Research in Documentation [*UNESCO*]
ISOSC......... International Society for Soilless Culture (EA)
ISOTAL....... Isolamentos Termicos e Acusticos Lda. (MAR)
isp.............. Combat Engineer Regiment (BU)
isp.............. Engineer Regiment (RU)
ISP.............. Ilektrikoi Sidirodromoi Protevousis [*Capital Electrical Railways*] [*Formerly, EIS*] [*Greek*] (GC)
ISP.............. Industrija Stakla, Pancevo [*Glass Industry, Pancevo*] (YU)
ISP.............. Institut Superieur Pedagogique (MAR)
ISP.............. Institut Superieur Polytechnique (MAR)
ISP.............. Institute of Hygiene Education (RU)
ISP.............. Instituto Superior Pedagogico [*Advanced Institute of Teaching*] [*Cuban*] (LA)
ISP.............. Institutul de Stiinte Pedagogice [*Institute for Pedagogical Sciences*] (RO)
ISP.............. Institutul de Studii si Proiectari [*Institute for Studies and Design*] (RO)
ISP.............. Internacional de Servidores Publicos [*Public Services International*] [*Use PSI*] (LA)
ISP.............. International Society of Postmasters (EA)
ISP.............. Internationale des Service Publics [*Public Service International - PSI*] (EA)
Isp.............. Ispanyolca [*Spanish*] (TU)
ISP.............. Italian Socialist Party (RU)
ISP.............. Izdavacko Stamparsko Preduzece [*Publishing and Printing Establishment*] (YU)
ISP-............ Network Power Supply (RU)
isp.............. Spanish (BU)
isp.............. Spanish (RU)
ISPACAIA... Institutul de Studii si Proiectari de Constructii pentru Agricultura si Industrie Alimentara [*Institute for Studies and Designs of Constructions for Agriculture and the Food Industry*] (RO)
ispan.......... Spanish (RU)
ISPC........... Industrial Survey and Promotion Center (MAR)
ISPC........... Institut Superieur de Pastorale Catechetique de Paris
ISPCMCF.... Institutul de Stat pentru Controlul Medicamentelor si Cercetari Farmaceutice [*State Institute for Drug Control and Pharmaceutical Research*] (RO)
ISPE........... Institutul de Studii si Proiectari Energetice [*Institute for Power Studies and Design*] (RO)
ISPE........... Istituto Studi Programmazione Economica [*Institute for Studies in Economic Planning*] [*Italian*] (WER)
ISPEA......... Institut de Statistique, de Planification, et d'Economie Appliquee (MAR)
ISPF........... Institutul de Studii si Proiectari al Ministerului Economiei Forestiere [*Studies and Design Institute of the Ministry of the Forestry Economy*] (RO)
ISPGC......... Institutul de Studii si Proiectari pentru Constructii si Instalatii de Gospodarie Comunala [*Studies and Design Institute for Constructions and Installations of the Communal Economy*] (RO)
ISPH........... Institut Superieur de Pedagogie du Hainaut [*Belgian*]
ISPH........... Institutul de Studii si Proiectari Hidroenergetice [*Hydroelectric Power Studies and Design Institute*] (RO)
ISPI............ Istituto per gli Studi di Politica Internazionale [*Institute for International Policy Studies*] [*Italian*] (WER)
ISPIF.......... Institutul de Studii si Proiectari pentru Imbunatatiri Funciare [*Studies and Design Institute for Land Improvements*] (RO)
ISPIFGA...... Institutul de Studii si Proiectari pentru Imbunatatiri Funciare si Gospodarirea Apelor [*Studies and Design Institute for Land Improvements and Water Management*] (RO)
ISPJAE........ Instituto Superior Politecnico Jose Antonio Echeverria [*Jose Antonio Echeverria Higher Polytechnic Institute*] [*Cuban*] (LA)
ISPL........... Intreprinderea de Stat pentru Produse Lactate [*State Enterprise for Dairy Products*] (RO)
ISPM........... International Society of Plant Morphologists (EA)
ISPO........... International Society for Prosthetics and Orthotics (EA)
ISPOTA....... Institutul de Studii si Proiectari pentru Organizarea Teritoriului Agricol [*Studies and Design Institute for the Organization of Agricultural Land*] (RO)
ISPP........... International Society for Plant Pathology (EA)
ISPP........... Internationale Studiengemeinschaft fuer Pranatale Psychologie [*International Society for the Study of Prenatal Psychology*] (EA)
ispr............ Corrected, Correction, Revised, Revision (RU)
ispravdom... Corrective Labor Home (RU)
ISPS........... Intreprinderea de Sirma si Produse de Sirma [*Enterprise for Wire and Wire Products*] (RO)
ISPSPN....... Institutul de Stiinte Politice si de Studiere a Problemei Nationale [*Institute for Political Sciences and for the Study of the National Question*] (RO)
ISPU........... Investment Servicing and Promotion Unit (MAR)
ISPWP........ International Society for the Prevention of Water Pollution (EA)
isr.............. Engineer Company (RU)
ISR............. Israel [*Three-letter standard code*] (CNC)
ISRA........... International Seabed Resource Authority (AF)
ISRC........... International Standard Recording Code
ISRCA......... Institute for Scientific Research in Central Africa (MAR)
ISRD........... International Society for Rehabilitation of the Disabled (MAR)
ISRF........... International Squash Rackets Federation (EA)
ISRHAI........ International Secretariat for Research on the History of Agricultural Implements (EA)
ISRN........... International Standard Record Number
ISRP........... Spanish Socialist Workers' Party (RU)
ISRS........... Institutul de Studii Roman-Sovietic [*Romanian-Soviet Institute for Studies*] (RO)
ISRT........... Istituto Storico della Resistenza in Toscana [*Italian*]
ISS............. Economic and Social Council (BU)
ISS............. Information Reference System (RU)
ISS............. Institute of Social Studies (MAR)
ISS............. Instituto Superiore di Sanita [*Italian*]
ISS............. International Scotist Society [*See also SIS*] (EA)
ISS............. International Self-Service Organization (EA)
ISS............. International Social Service [*See also SSI*] (EA)
ISSA........... Informationsstelle Sudliches Afrika eV (MAR)
ISSARA....... Instituto de Servicios Sociales para las Actividades Rurales y Afines [*Institute of Social Services for Rural and Related Activities*] [*Argentine*] (LA)
ISSBD......... International Society for the Study of Behavioural Development (EA)
ISSC........... International Social Science Council [*See also CISS*] (EA)
ISSD........... International Society for Social Defence [*See also SIDS*] (EA)
ISSE........... Instituto Superior del Servicio en el Extranjero [*Higher Institute of the Foreign Service*] [*Cuban*] (LA)
ISSER......... Institute of Statistical Social and Economic Research [*Legon*] (MAR)
ISSK........... International Society for the Sociology of Knowledge (EA)
issl............ Research, Investigation, Analysis (RU)
issled......... Research, Investigation, Analysis (RU)
ISSMB........ Inspectoratul Sanitar de Stat al Municipiului Bucuresti [*State Health Inspectorate of Bucharest Municipality*] (RO)
ISSMFE....... International Society for Soil Mechanics and Foundation Engineering (EA)
ISSN........... International Standard Serial Number
ISSS........... Instituto Salvadoreno de Seguro Social [*Salvadoran Institute of Social Security*] (LA)
ISSS........... International Society of Soil Science [*See also AISS*] (EA)
ISSSTE....... Instituto de Seguridad y Servicios Sociales de Trabajadores Estatales [*Institute of Social Security and Services for Government Workers*] [*Mexican*] (LA)
ist.............. Historical (BU)
ist.............. Historical (RU)
IST............. Information Scientifique et Technique (MAR)

IST............. Institut za Spoljnu Trgovinu [*Institute of Foreign Trade*] (YU)
IST............. Instituto Superior Tecnico [*Higher Technical Institute*] [*Portuguese*] (WER)
Ist............. Istanbul [*Istanbul*] (TU)
Ist............. Istasyon [*Station*] (TU)
ISt............. Iststaerke [*Actual Strength*] [*Military*] (EG)
IST............. Italian Labor Union (RU)
ist............. Spring [*Topography*] (RU)
ISTA........... Indian Scientific Translators Association
ISTA........... Institut Superieur des Techniques Appliques [*Advanced Institute of Applied Techniques*] [*Zairian*] (AF)
ISTA........... Instituto Salvadoreno de Transformacion Agraria [*Salvadoran Institute of Agrarian Transformation*] (LA)
ISTA........... Instituto Superior Tecnico Azucarero [*Higher Institute of Sugar Technology*] [*Cuban*] (LA)
ISTA........... International Seed Testing Association (MAR)
ISTA........... Istanbul Ajansi [*Istanbul Agency*] [*News agency*] (TU)
ISTARKh..... Historical Archives (RU)
ISTAT......... Istituto Centrale di Statistica [*Central Statistics Institute*] [*Italian*] (WER)
ISTC........... International Student Travel Conference (EA)
ISTEI.......... Intreprinderea de Stat pentru Transporturi si Expedieri Internationale [*State Enterprise for International Transportation and Shipments*] (RO)
Istekhkozh... Leningrad Industrial Artificial Leather Plant (RU)
i st f............ I Stallet For [*In Place Of*] [*Swedish*] (GPO)
ISTF........... International Social Travel Federation [*See also FITS*] (EA)
istfak.......... History Division (RU)
Ist-fil fak...... Department of History and Philosophy (BU)
ISTI............. Institut des Sciences et Techniques de l'Information [*Institute of Media Sciences and Techniques*] [*Zairian*] (AF)
Istih............ Istihsal [*Production*] [*See also Ur*] (TU)
ISTIMARBIRKO... Istanbul ve Marmara Bolge Koy Kalkinma ve Diger Tarimsal Amacli Kooperatifler Birligi [*Union of Istanbul and Marmara Region Village Development Cooperatives and Other Agriculturally Inclined Cooperatives*] (TU)
ISTIS........... International Scientific and Technical Information System (EA)
ISTIUAPS.... Intreprinderea de Servicii Tehnice pentru Instalatii, Utilaje, Aparate, si Piese de Schimb [*Technical Services Enterprise for Installations, Equipment, Instruments, and Spare Parts*] (RO)
ISTLC.......... Intreprinderea de Servicii Tehnice pentru Lucrari Capitale si Livrari de Instalatii Complexe in Industria Materialelor de Constructii [*Technical Services Enterprise for Capital Projects and Deliveries of Complex Installations in the Construction Materials Industry*] (RO)
ISTM........... Instituto Superior Tecnico-Militar [*Advanced Institute of Military Technology*] [*Cuban*] (LA)
Istmat.......... Historical Materialism (RU)
istmat.......... Historical Materialism (BU)
Istmol.......... Commission for the Study of the History of the Komsomol (RU)
ISTORA....... Istana Olah Raga [*Sports Stadium*] (IN)
Istpart......... Commission for Collection and Study of Materials on the History of the October Revolution and the History of the Communist Party (RU)
istpart......... History of the Communist Party (RU)
ISTPM......... Institut Scientifique et Technique pour la Peche Maritime [*Scientific and Technical Institute for Ocean Fishing*] [*French*] (WER)
ISTPM......... Institut Scientifique et Technique des Peches Maritimes (MAR)
IstPr........... Istoricheski Pregled [*Historical Review*] [*A periodical*] (BU)
ISTPROF..... Commission for the Study of the History of Trade Unionism (RU)
istprof......... History of Trade Unionism (RU)
ISTPROFLOSPS... Department for the Study of the History of Trade Unionism of the Leningrad Oblast Council of Trade Unions (RU)
ISTRACEMENT... Istrian Cement Factory (YU)
ISTRATEKSTIL... Istrian Textile Trade [*Rijeka*] (YU)
istraviaotryad... Fighter Detachment (RU)
ISTRAVINO... Istrian Wine and Alcoholic Beverage Trade [*Rijeka*] (YU)
istrb............ Engineer Construction Battalion (BU)
istrbr........... Engineer Construction Brigade (BU)
ISTRO......... International Soil Tillage Research Organization (EA)
ISTU........... Instituto Salvadoreno de Turismo [*Salvadoran Institute of Tourism*] (LA1)
ist vr........... Apparent Time, True Time (RU)
ISU............. Idoma State Union (MAR)
ISU............. Internal Security Unit (MAR)
ISU............. International Skating Union [*See also UIP*] (EA)
ISU............. International Society of Urology [*See also SIU*] (EA)
ISUL........... Institute for Specialization and Advanced Study of Physicians (BU)
ISV............. Informacni Sluzba Vystrizkova [*Clipping Information Service*] (CZ)
ISV............. Iparszeru Sertestarto Termeloszovetkezetek [*Cooperatives for Hog Raising on an Industrial Scale*] (HU)
ISVBM........ International Society of Violin and Bow Makers (EA)
ISVE........... Istituto Studi Sviluppo Economico [*Institute for Economic Development Studies*] [*Italian*] (AF)
ISVEIMER... Istituto per lo Sviluppo Economico dell'Italia Meridionale [*Institute for the Economic Development of Southern Italy*] (WER)
ISW............. Institut fuer Schiffbautechnik Wolgast [*Wolgast Institute for Naval Engineering*] (EG)
ISW............. Institut fuer Steuerungstechnik der Werkzeugmaschinen
ISYa........... Information Reference Language (RU)
ISZ............. Artificial Earth Satellite (RU)
ISZ............. Artificial Earth Satellite (BU)
isz.............. Idoszamitasunk Szerinti [*In the Year of Our Lord*] [*Hungarian*] (GPO)
ISz............. Instytut Sztuki [*Institute of Fine Arts*] [*Polish*]
ISZOT......... Ipari Szovetkezetek Orszagos Tanacsa [*National Council of Industrial Cooperatives*] (HU)
ISZP........... Indiai Szocialista Part [*Socialist Party of India*] (HU)
ISZSZI......... Ipargazdasagi, Szervezesi, es Szamitastechnikai Intezet [*Institute of Industrial Management, Organization, and Computer Technology*] (HU)
IT............... Current Source (RU)
IT............... Inalta Tensiune [*High Voltage*] (RO)
IT............... Indeks Troskova Zivota [*Cost of Living Index*] (YU)
IT............... Indonesia Timur [*East Indonesia (Sulawesi, Maluku, Nusatenggara, Irian Barat)*] (IN)
IT............... Ingenieur de Travaux [*French*]
IT............... Inspektorat [*Inspectorate*] (IN)
IT............... Inspektorat na Trudot [*Labor Inspectorate*] (YU)
IT............... Institut de Technologie [*North African*] (MAR)
i-t.............. Institute (BU)
IT............... Institute of Tuberculosis (of the Academy of Medical Sciences, USSR) (RU)
IT............... Instituto de Texteis [*Textile Institute*] [*Portuguese*] (WER)
IT............... Instytut Torfowy [*Peat Institute*] (POL)
IT............... Inzenjeri i Tehnicari [*Engineers and Technicians*] (YU)
it............... Itainen [*Finnish*]
it............... Italian (RU)
IT............... Italy [*Two-letter standard code*] (CNC)
it............... Item [*Spanish*]
IT............... Pulse Transformer (RU)
IT............... Technical School of Economics (BU)
IT............... Testing Telephone (RU)
IT-.............. Thickness Gauge (RU)
IT............... Three-Phase Induction Meter (RU)
ITA............. Individual Telephone (RU)
ITA............. Industrie Technologique Alimentaire de Dakar (MAR)
ita............... Initial Teaching Alphabet (MAR)
ITA............. Institut de Technologie Agricole [*Institute of Agricultural Technology*] [*Algerian*] (AF)
ITA............. Institut de Technologie Alimentaire de Dakar (MAR)
ITA............. Institute of Theoretical Astronomy (of the Academy of Sciences, USSR) (RU)
ITA............. Instituto Tecnico Americano [*Bogota*] (COL)
ITA............. Instituto Tecnologico de Aeronautica [*Technical Aeronautics Institute*] [*Brazilian*] (LA)
ITA............. Instituto Tecnologico Agricola. Universidad de Narino [*Pasto*] (COL)
ITA............. International Tin Agreement (MAR)
ITA............. International Trans-Aerea [*Bogota*] (COL)
ITA............. International Tube Association (EA)
ITA............. Intreprinderea de Transport Auto [*Automotive Transportation Enterprise*] (RO)
ITA............. Italy [*Three-letter standard code*] (CNC)
Ita.............. Italyanca [*Italian*] (TU)
ITA............. Technical Institutes of Agriculture [*Spanish*]
ITAB........... Institut Technique Agricole du Burundi (MAR)
ITABRASCO... Companhia Italo-Brasileira de Mineracao [*Italian-Brazilian Mining Company*] (LA)
ITAC........... Intreprinderea de Transporturi Auto Comerciale [*Enterprise for Automotive Transportation in Trade*] (RO)
ITAE........... Institut de Technologie d'Agriculture et d'Elevage [*Algerian*] (MAR)
ITAE........... Instituto Tecnologico de Administracion y Economia [*Technological Institute of Administration and Economy*] [*Colombian*] (LA)
ITAER......... Instituto Tecnologico de la Alimentacion "Ejercito Rebelde" [*Ejercito Rebelde Food Technology Institute*] [*Cuban*] (LA)
IT AIUS SM... Internationaler Thesaurus Standardisierung und Metrologie [*International Thesaurus for Standardization and Metrology*] [*A publication*] (EG)
ITAK........... Illankai Tamil Arasu Kadchi [*Federal Party*] [*Sri Lankan*] (PPW)
ITAL........... Instituto Tecnico Agricola de Lorica (COL)
ITAL........... Instituut voor Toepassing van Atoomenergie in de Landbouw [*Institute for the Application of Nuclear Energy to Agriculture*] [*Dutch*] (WEN)
ital.............. Italiaa [*or Italiaksi*] [*Finnish*]
ital.............. Italialainen [*Finnish*]
ital.............. Italian (BU)
ital.............. Italian (RU)
ITALCEL..... Industria Italo-Colombiana de Conductores Electricos Ltda. [*Cali*] (COL)
ITALJUG..... Italijansko-Jugoslovenska Komora u Rimu [*Italo-Yugoslav Chamber in Rome*] (YU)

ITALPIANTI ... Societa Italiana Impianti [*Italian Industrial Plant Company*] (WER)
ITALTOGO ... Societe Italo-Togolaise (MAR)
ITAM .... Instituto Tecnologico Autonomo de Mexico [*Mexico City*]
ITB.............. Industrial Training Board [*Iranian*] (ME)
ITB.............. Institut Tehnologi Bandung [*Bandung Technological Institute*] (IN)
ITB.............. Instytut Techniki Budowlanej [*or Budownictwa*] [*Institute of Civil Engineering*] (POL)
ITB.............. Intreprinderea de Transport Bucuresti [*Bucharest Transportation Enterprise*] (RO)
ITBA........... Industries Tunisiennes de Broderie Automatique (MAR)
ITBF .... Iktisadi ve Ticari Bilimler Fakultesi [*Faculty of Economy and Commercial Science*] [*Aegean University*] (TU)
ITBM........... Institut du Batiment et des Travaux Publics [*Moroccan*] (MAR)
ITC .... Compagnia Italiana dei Cavi Telegrafici Sottomarini [*Italian Underwater Telegraph Cable Company*] (WER)
ITC .... Ingenieurs, Techniciens, et Cadres [*Engineers, Technicians, and Middle Management People*] [*French*] (WER)
ITC .... Institutul de Cercetari pentru Tehnica de Calcul [*Research Institute for Computer Technology*] (RO)
ITC .... Instytut Techniki Cieplnej [*Institute of Thermal Technics*] [*Polish*]
ITC .... International Tar Conference [*See also CIG*] (EA)
ITC .... International Tea Committee (EA)
ITC .... International Tin Council [*See also CIE*] (EA)
ITC .... International Trade Centre (MAR)
ITC .... International Translations Centre
ITC .... Intreprinderile de Transporturi Comerciale [*Enterprises for Commercial Transportation*] (RO)
ITC .... Ivoirienne de Transactions Commerciales (MAR)
ITCME......... Institutul de Studii si Cercetari Tehnologice pentru Industria Constructiilor de Masini si Electrotehnica [*Technological Studies and Research Institute for the Electrotechnical and Machine Building Industry*] (RO)
ITCO........... Instituto de Tierras y Colonizacion [*Institute of Lands and Settlement*] [*Costa Rican*] (LA)
ITCR........... Instituto Tecnologico de Costa Rica [*Technological Institute of Costa Rica*] (LA1)
ITCZ........... Intertropical Convergence Zone (MAR)
i td............. And So On, And So Forth (RU)
ITD .... Corrective Labor House (RU)
itd............... I Tak Dalej [*And So On*] (POL)
itd............... I Tako Dalje [*Et Cetera*] (YU)
ITD .... Information et Traitement des Donnees [*Information and Data Processing*] (AF)
ITD .... Instytut Technologii Drewna [*Institute of Lumber Technology*] (POL)
ITdelT......... Instituto Tecnologico del Tabaco [*Technological Tobacco Institute*] [*Cuban*] (LA)
ITDG........... Intermediate Technology Development Group (EA)
ITDJEN....... Inspektorat Djenderal [*Inspectorate General*] (IN)
ITEA .... Instituto Tecnico Administrativo [*Administrative Technical Institute*] [*Colombian*] (LA)
ITEBA......... Institut Technique du Batiment et des Travaux Publics d'Algerie [*Technical Institute for Building Trade and Public Works of Algeria*] (AF)
ITEC .... Ingenieria Termodinamica Ltda. [*Medellin*] (COL)
ITEC .... International Total Energy Congress (MAR)
ITEC .... International Transport Exposition and Conference (MAR)
ITECIF........ Institut de Technologie des Cultures Industrielles et Fourrageres [*Algerian*] (MAR)
ITECMO ...... Instituto Tecnico Comercial [*Cali*] (COL)
ITECS.......... Instituto Tecnologico de Educacion Superior [*Cali*] (COL)
ITEF............ Institut de Technologie Forestiere [*Forest Technology Institute*] [*Algerian*] (AF)
ITEF............ Institute of Theoretical and Experimental Physics (RU)
ITEGA .... Industrie Textile Gabonaise (MAR)
ITEIN.......... Institute of Technical and Economic Information (RU)
itekhr .... Engineer Equipment Company (RU)
ITEMA......... Societe Industrie Textile du Mali (MAR)
ITESNIC...... Instituto Tecnologico Nicaraguense [*Nicaraguan Technological Institute*] (LA1)
ITF.............. Industrial Training Fund [*Niger*] (AF)
ITF.............. Inosinetriphosphoric Acid (RU)
ITF.............. Institute of Theoretical Physics (RU)
ITF.............. Institute of Thermophysics (of the Siberian Department of the Academy of Sciences, USSR) (RU)
ITF.............. International Trade and Finance Division (MAR)
ITF.............. International Transport Workers' Federation (EA)
ITFCA......... International Track and Field Coaches Association (EA)
ITG .... Institute of Theoretical Geophysics (of the Academy of Sciences, USSR) (RU)
ITGLWF....... International Textile, Garment, and Leather Workers' Federation [*See also FITTHC*] (EA)
ITGY........... Iskolai Taneszkozok Gyara [*School Epuipment Manufacturers*] (HU)
ITH.............. Institut des Techniques Hotelieres [*North African*] (MAR)
ITHR .... Intreprinderea de Turism, Hoteluri, si Restaurante [*Enterprise for Tourism, Hotels, and Restaurants*] (RO)
ITHT .... Institut des Techniques Hotelieres et Touristiques [*North African*] (MAR)
ITI .... Institute of Technical Information (RU)
ITI .... International Theatre Institute (EA)
ITI .... News of the Institute of Heat Engineering [*A publication*] (RU)
ITIA .... Iktisat ve Ticari Ilimler Akademisi [*The Academy of Economics and Commercial Science*] [*Eskisehir*] [*See also IITIA*] (TU)
ITIA .... Intreprinderea pentru Turism International Automobilistic [*Enterprise for International Automobile Tourism*] (RO)
ITIEINEFTEGAZ ... Institute of Technical Information and Economic Research (of the State Committee of the Council of Ministers, USSR, for the Fuel Industry) (RU)
ITIM............ Institutul de Tehnologie Isotopica si Moleculara [*Institute for Isotopic and Molecular Technology*] (RO)
ITIM............ News Agency of Associated Israel Press Limited (ME)
ITINTEC ...... Instituto de Investigacion Tecnologica, Industrial, y de Normas Tecnicas [*Peruvian*]
ITIOP.......... Institute of Trade and Public Eating Facilities (RU)
ITIPAT........ Institut pour la Technologie et l'Industrialisation des Produits Agricoles Tropicaux [*Ivorian*] (MAR)
ITIS............ Institute for Standard Designing and Industrialization of Construction (BU)
ITIS............ Intermediate Technology Industrial Services (MAR)
ITJ .... Instytut Techniki Jadrowej [*Institute of Nuclear Technics*] [*Polish*]
ITJ .... Inzenjeri i Tehnicari Jugoslavije [*Engineers and Technicians of Yugoslavia*] (YU)
ITJ .... Ipari Termekek Jegyzeke [*Industrial Products Register*] (HU)
ITK .... Corrective Labor Code (RU)
ITK .... Corrective Labor Colony (RU)
ITK .... Idegennyelvu Tovabbkepzo Kozpont [*Center for Continuing Education in Foreign Languages*] (HU)
ITK .... Instytut Technologii Krzemianow [*Institute of Silicate Technology*] (POL)
ITK .... Technical Control Inspection (RU)
ITK .... True Boiling Point (RU)
ITK .... True Boiling Temperature (RU)
ITKUM......... Inspektorat Hukum [*Inspectorate of Legal Affairs*] (IN)
ITL.............. Corrective Labor Camp (RU)
ITLPP .... Intreprinderea Transpoarte si Livrari Produse Petroliere [*Enterprise for the Transportation and Delivery of Petroleum Products*] (RO)
ITM............. Industria Tehnico-Medicala [*Medical Technology Industry*] (RO)
ITM............. Industrija Traktora i Masina [*Tractors and Machines Industry*] [*Belgrade*] (YU)
ITM............. Industry and Trade Ministry (MAR)
ITM............. Institut Teknoloji MARA [*MARA Technology Institute*] (ML)
ITM............. Institute of Transportation Machinery (RU)
ITM............. Instituto Tecnico Militar [*Institute of Military Technology*] [*Cuban*] (LA)
ITMA .... Institut de Technologie Moyens Agricoles [*Agricultural Implements Institute of Technology*] [*Algerian*] (AF)
ITMA .... International Textile Machinery Association
ITM i VT...... Institute of Precision Mechanics and Computer Engineering (RU)
itn............... And So On (BU)
itn............... I Taka Natamu [*Et Cetera*] (YU)
ITN .... Initial Aiming Point [*Artillery*], Initial Guidance Point [*To an objective*] (BU)
ITN .... Institutul de Tehnologie Nucleara [*Nuclear Technology Institute*] (RO)
ITO .... Institut der Technologie und Organisation [*Institute of Technology and Organization*] (EG)
ITO .... Institute of Technical Training (RU)
ITO .... Istanbul Tabibler Odasi [*Istanbul Chamber of Physicians*] (TU)
ITO .... Istanbul Ticaret Odasi [*Istanbul Chamber of Commerce*] (TU)
ITOChMEKh ... Institute of Precision Mechanics and Computer Engineering (RU)
ITOCY .... Industrie Togolaise du Cycle et du Cyclomoteur (MAR)
ITOF .... Ingiltere Turk Ogrenci Federasyonu [*Turkish Student Federation of Great Britain*] [*Turkish Cypriot*] (GC)
ITOMKKh.... Institute of Technical Training of the Ministry of the Municipal Economy, RSFSR (RU)
ITOPF.......... International Tanker Owners Pollution Federation (EA)
ITOV........... Ipari Tanfolyamok Orszagos Vezetosege [*National Headquarters of Industrial Training Courses*] (HU)
ITOV .... Ipartestuletek Orszagos Vezetosege [*National Office of Craftsmen's Associations*] (HU)
ITP.............. Engineering and Technical Personnel (RU)
i tp.............. Et Cetera, And So Forth (RU)
itp............... I Tym Podobne [*And the Like*] (POL)
ITP.............. Impozitele si Taxele de la Populatie [*Public Taxes and Fees*] (RO)
ITP.............. Industrija Tepiha "Proleter" [*The "Proleter" Rug Factory*] [*Zrenjanin*] (YU)
ITP.............. Ingenieurtechnisches Personal [*Engineering and Technical Personnel*] (EG)
ITP.............. Inzenyrsko-Technicti Pracovnici [*Engineering and Technical Specialists*] (CZ)
itp............... Itaista Pituutta [*Finnish*]

ITP .... Ittihat ve Terakki Partisi [*Union and Progress Party*] [*Historic*] (TU)
ITPA .... International Tea Promotion Association (EA)
ITPAS .... Instituto do Trabalho, Previdencia, e Accao Social [*Institute of Labor, Welfare, and Social Security*] [*Mozambican*] (AF)
itpbatr .... Tank-Destroyer Battery (BU)
ITPEA .... Institut des Techniques de Planification et d'Economie Appliquee [*Algerian*] (MAR)
ITPM .... Institute of Theoretical and Applied Mechanics (of the Siberian Department of the Academy of Sciences, USSR) (RU)
ITPP .... Ilorin Talaka Parapo Party (MAR)
ITPT .... News of the Textile Industry and Trade [*A publication*] (RU)
i-tr .... Corrective Labor (RU)
itr .... Engineer Equipment Company (RU)
ITR .... Engineering and Technical Personnel (RU)
ITR .... Engineering and Technical Workers (BU)
ITR .... Instytut Tele- i Radiotechniczny [*Institute of Telecommunications*] (POL)
itralb .... Engineer Mine-Sweeping Battalion (RU)
itralr .... Engineer Mine-Sweeping Company (RU)
ITRC .... International Tin Research Council (EA)
ITS .... Engineering and Technical Convention (RU)
ITS .... Engineering and Technical Council (RU)
ITS .... Engineering and Technical Section (RU)
ITS .... Engineering and Technical Service (RU)
its .... Engineering and Technical Staff (RU)
ITS .... Engineering and Technical Union (RU)
ITS .... Impot sur les Traitements et Salaires (MAR)
ITS .... Industrial Training Service (MAR)
ITS .... Instalaciones Tecnicas Sanitarias Hidraulicas y Mecanicas [*Bogota*] (COL)
ITS .... Instytut Transportu Samochodowego [*Institute of Motor Transport*] (POL)
ITS .... Instytut Tworzyw Sztucznych [*Institute of Plastics*] [*Polish*]
ITS .... International Tracing Service (EA)
ITS .... International Trade Secretariat [*Portuguese*] (WER)
ITS .... Inzenjerska Tehnicka Sluzba [*Engineering Technical Service*] [*Military*] (YU)
ITS .... Inzenjersko Tehnicko Snabdevanje [*Engineering and Technical Supplying*] [*Military*] (YU)
ITS .... Technical Information Collection (RU)
ITSAKS .... Institut Technique Superieur de l'Amitie Khmero-Sovietique [*Cambodian-Soviet Friendship Higher Technological Institute*] (CL)
itsen .... Itsenainen [*Used as a Noun, Substantively*] [*Finnish*]
ITsG .... Institute of Cytology and Genetics (of the Siberian Department of the Academy of Sciences, USSR) (RU)
itsl .... I Tome Slicno [*And the Like*] (YU)
ITSR .... Indo-Pacific Fisheries Council [*IPFC*] (RU)
ITsYeZhD .... Information Center of the European Railways [*ICER*] (RU)
ITT .... Industrie Textile Togolaise (MAR)
ITT .... Instituto Tecnologico del Tabaco [*Technological Institute for Tobacco*] [*Cuban*] (LA1)
ITTA .... Intreprinderea de Transporturi Turistice Auto [*Enterprise for Tourism Automotive Transportation*] (RO)
ITTF .... International Table Tennis Federation (MAR)
ITTTA .... International Technical Tropical Timber Association (MAR)
ITTU .... Intermediate Technology Transfer Units (MAR)
ITU .... Corrective Labor Establishment (RU)
ITU .... Igbirra Tribal Union (MAR)
ITU .... Individual Telephone Amplifier (RU)
ITU .... Institute of Managerial Techniques (RU)
ITU .... Institutul Teologic Universitar [*University Theological Institute*] (RO)
ITU .... Intendanska Uprava [*Quartermaster Administration*] (YU)
ITU .... International Telecommunication Union (MAR)
ITU .... Istanbul Teknik Universitesi [*Istanbul Technical University*] (TU)
ITUAK .... News of the Tavricheskaya Scientific Archaeological Commission [*A publication*] (RU)
ITUCNW .... International Trade Union Committee of Negro Workers (MAR)
ITUCSTL .... International Trade Unions Committee of Social Tourism and Leisure [*See also CSITSL*] (EA)
ITUEHB .... Istanbul Teknik Universitesi Elektronik Hesap Bilimleri Enstitusu [*Electronic Accounting Science Institute of Istanbul Technical University*] [*See also EHB*] (TU)
ITUMMF .... Istanbul Teknik Universitesi Mimarlik ve Muhendislik Fakultesi [*Istanbul Technical University Faculty of Architecture and Engineering*] (TU)
ITUOB .... Istanbul Teknik Universitesi Ogrenci Birligi [*Istanbul Technical University Student Union*] [*See also ITUTB*] (TU)
ITUSCO .... Instituto Universitario Surcolombiano [*Neiva*] (COL)
ITUTB .... Istanbul Teknik Universitesi Talebe Birligi [*Istanbul Technical University Student Union*] [*See also ITUOB*] (TU)
ITUTOTB .... Istanbul Teknik Universitesi Teknik Okulu Talebe Birligi [*Istanbul Technical University's Technical School Student Union*] (TU)
ITV .... Industrijska Televizija [*Industrial Television*] (YU)
ITV .... Instructional Television (MAR)
ITV .... Irodageptechnika Vallalat [*Enterprise of Business Machine Technology*] (HU)
ITVS .... Institut Telesne Vychovy a Sportu [*Institute of Physical Education and Sports*] (CZ)
ITWL .... Instytut Techniczny Wojsk Lotniczych [*Air Force Institute of Technology*] (POL)
ITWP .... Independent True Whig Party (MAR)
ITX .... Individual Tour Excursion (MAR)
ITZU .... Installation of Technical Establishments and Equipment (BU)
IU .... Actuating Amplifier (RU)
IU .... Actuating Device (RU)
IU .... Engineering Administration (RU)
iu .... Idoszamitasunk Kezdete Utan [*Of Our Era, Anno Domini*] (HU)
iu .... Igazsagugy [*Justice, Judiciary*] (HU)
IU .... Integrating Amplifier (RU)
iU .... Intellektuelle Unterlage [*Intellectual Base*] [*German*]
IU .... Izquierda Unida [*United Left*] [*Peruvian*] (LA1)
IU- .... Level Gauge (RU)
IU .... Measuring Device (RU)
IU .... Needle Filter Installation (RU)
IU .... Quartermaster Directorate (RU)
IUA .... Instytut Urbanistyki i Architektury [*Institute of City Planning and Architecture*] (POL)
IUAES .... International Union of Anthropological and Ethnological Sciences [*See also UISAE*] (EA)
IUAI .... International Union of Aviation Insurers (EA)
IUAKP .... Iuzhno-Afrikanskaia Kommunisticheskaia Partiia (MAR)
IUAPPA .... International Union of Air Pollution Prevention Associations (EA)
IUAR .... Iuzhno-Afrikanskaia Respublika (MAR)
IUAS .... Iuzhno-Afrikanskii Soiuz (MAR)
IUAT .... International Union Against Tuberculosis [*See also UICT*] (EA)
IUC .... Inter-University Council (MAR)
IUC .... Intreprinderea de Utilaj Chimic [*Chemical Equipment Enterprise*] (RO)
IUCADC .... Inter-Union Commission of Advice to Developing Countries (EA)
IUCN .... International Union for the Conservation of Nature (MAR)
IUCT .... Intreprinderea de Utilaje Constructii Transport [*Enterprise for Transportation Equipment and Constructions*] (RO)
IUCW .... International Union for Child Welfare (MAR)
IUDOP .... Instituto Uruguayo de la Opinion Publica [*Public Opinion Institute of Uruguay*] (LA)
IUDP .... Intreprinderea Utilaje Drumuri si Poduri [*Enterprise for Road and Bridge Equipment*] (RO)
IuD-Programm ... Information und Dokumentation Programm
IUEF .... Internacia Unuigo de la Esperantistoj-Filologoj [*International Society of Esperantist-Philologists - ISEP*] (EA)
IUEF .... International University Exchange Fund (MAR)
IUEGS .... International Union of European Guides and Scouts [*See also UIGSE*] (EA)
IUES .... Instituto Uruguayo de Educacion Sindical [*Uruguayan Institute for Labor Union Education*] (LA)
IUF .... International Union of Food and Allied Workers Associations [*See also IUL*] (EA)
IUFLJP .... International Union of French-Language Journalists and Press [*See also UIJPLF*] (EA)
IUFO .... International Union of Family Organizations (AF)
IUFoST .... International Union of Food Science and Technology (EA)
IUFRO .... International Union of Forestry Research Organizations (EA)
IUG .... Intreprinderea de Utilaj Greu [*Heavy Equipment Enterprise*] (RO)
IUGB .... International Union of Game Biologists (EA)
IUGRI .... International Union of Graphic Reproduction Industries (EA)
IUHE .... International Union of Health Education [*See also UIES*] (EA)
IUHF .... Istanbul Universitesi Hukuk Fakultesi [*Istanbul University Faculty of Law*] (TU)
IUiA .... Instytut Urbanistyki i Architektury [*Institute of City Planning and Architecture*] (POL)
IUIkF .... Istanbul Universitesi Iktisat Fakultesi [*Istanbul University Faculty of Economics*] (TU)
IUK .... Indolylacetic Acid (RU)
IUL .... Institute of Ukrainian Literature Imeni T. G. Shevchenko (RU)
IUL .... Internationale Union der Lebens- und Genussmittelarbeiter-Gewerkschaften [*International Union of Food and Allied Workers Associations - IUF*] (EA)
IULCLG .... Imposto Unico sobre Lubrificantes e Combustiveis Liquidos e Gasosos [*Single Tax on Lubricants and Liquid or Gaseous Fuels*] [*Brazilian*] (LA)
IULVTFT .... International Union for Land Value Taxation and Free Trade (EA)
IUMP .... International Union of Master Painters [*See also UNIEP*] (EA)
IUMSBD .... IUMS [*International Union of Microbiological Societies*] Bacteriology Division (EA)
IUNG .... Instytut Uprawy, Nawozenia, i Gleboznawstwa [*Institute of Cultivation, Fertilization, and Soil Science*] (POL)
IUOTO .... International Union of Official Travel Organizations (CL)
IUP .... University Polytechnical Institute [*Spanish*]
IUPAC .... International Union for Pure and Applied Chemistry (MAR)
IUPESM .... International Union for Physical and Engineering Sciences in Medicine (EA)
IUPIP .... International Union for the Protection of Industrial Property

IUPPS.......... International Union of Prehistoric and Protohistoric Sciences (EA)
IUPS........... Intreprinderea de Utilaje si Piese de Schimb [*Enterprise for Equipment and Spare Parts*] (RO)
IUPSMB....... Intreprinderea de Utilaje si Piese de Schimb a Municipiului Bucuresti [*Bucharest Municipality Enterprise for Equipment and Spare Parts*] (RO)
IUR-............ Level Indicator (RU)
IURC........... International Union for Research of Communication (EA)
IURN........... Institut Unifie de Recherches Nucleaires
IURP........... International Union of Roofing and Plumbing (EA)
IUS.............. Information Index of Standards (RU)
IUS.............. International Union of Speleology [*See also UIS*] (EA)
IUS.............. International Union of Students [*See also UIE*] (EA)
IUSA........... Industrias Unidas, Sociedad Anonima [*United Industries Corporation*] [*Salvadoran*]
IUSAMH...... International Union of Societies for the Aid of Mental Health (EA)
IUSE........... Institut Universitaire des Sciences de l'Education (MAR)
IUSF........... International Union of Societies of Foresters [*See also UISIF*] (EA)
IUSIT.......... Institute for the Advanced Training of Specialists, Engineers, and Technicians (BU)
IUSP........... Internationale Union fuer Wissenschaftliche Psychologie [*International Union for Scientific Psychology*] (EG)
IUSSP......... International Union for the Scientific Study of Population (MAR)
IUSTI.......... Institut Universitaire des Sciences et Techniques de l'Information [*University Institute for Information Sciences and Techniques*] [*Zairian*] (AF)
IUSUHM...... International Union of School and University Health and Medicine [*See also UIHMSU*] (EA)
IUSY........... International Union of Socialist Youth (AF)
IUT.............. Institut Universitaire de Technologie [*University Institute of Technology*] [*French*] (WER)
IUT.............. Instituto Universitario de Tecnologia [*University Technological Institute*] [*Bogota*] (COL)
IUT.............. International Union of Tenants (EA)
IUT.............. Intreprinderea Utilaje Transport [*Enterprise for Transportation Equipment*] (RO)
IUTB........... Istanbul Universitesi Talebe Birligi [*Istanbul University Student Union*] (TU)
IUTCA......... International Union of Technical Cinematograph Associations [*See also UNIATEC*] (EA)
IUU............. Institute for the Advanced Training of Teachers (BU)
IUU............. Institute for the Advanced Training of Teachers (RU)
IUV............. Industrija Usnja, Vrhnika [*Vrhnika Leather Industry*] (YU)
IUV............. Institute for the Advanced Training of Physicians (RU)
IUVSTA....... International Union for Vacuum Science, Technique and Applications [*See also UISTAV*] (EA)
IUWA.......... International Union of Women Architects [*See also UIFA*] (EA)
IUZA........... Iugo-Zapadnaia Afrika (MAR)
IUZSSKh..... Institute for the Advanced Training of Agricultural Specialists Imeni Academician V. R. Vil'yams (RU)
IV................ Call Finder (RU)
IV................ Gas Tube Rectifier (RU)
iV................ Im Vakuum [*In a Vacuum*] [*German*]
iV................ Im Vorjahre [*Last Year*] (EG)
iV................ In Vertretung [*By Proxy, By Order, On Behalf Of*] (EG)
IV................ Institute of Oriental Studies (of the Academy of Sciences, USSR) (RU)
IV................ Izvrsno Vece [*Executive Council*] (YU)
IV................ Output Meter (RU)
IV................ Propositional Calculus (RU)
IV................ Viscosity Index (RU)
IV................ Visibility Meter (RU)
IVA............. Imposta sul Valore Aggiunto [*Value-Added Tax*] [*Italian*] (WER)
IVA............. Impuesto al Valor Agregado [*Value Added Tax*] [*Use VAT*] (LA)
IVA............. Ingeniorsveten-Skapsakademien [*Academy of Engineering Sciences*] [*Swedish*] (WEN)
IVA............. Instituut voor Automatisering [*Rotterdam*]
IVA............. Intendanska Vojna Akademija [*Quartermaster Military Academy*] (YU)
IVAAP......... International Veterinary Association for Animal Production [*See also AIVPA*] (EA)
IVAC........... Instituto Venezolano de Accion Comunitaria [*Venezuelan Institute for Community Action*] (LA)
IVAD........... Bulletin of the Varna Archeological Society [*A publication*] (BU)
IVAK........... News of the Eastern Archaeological Committee [*A publication*] (RU)
IVAN........... Institute of Oriental Studies of the Academy of Sciences, USSR (RU)
IVB............. Internationaler Verband fuer Arbeiterbildung [*International Federation of Workers' Educational Associations - IFWEA*] (EA)
IVBiH.......... Izvrsno Vijece Bosne i Hercegovine [*Executive Council of Bosnia and Hercegovina*] (YU)
IVC............. Instituto Venezolano del Consumo [*Venezuelan Consumer Institute*] (LA)
IVCA........... Instituto Venezolano-Cubano de Amistad [*Venezuelan-Cuban Friendship Institute*] (LA)
IVCPT......... Intreprinderea de Valorificare a Cerealelor si Plantelor Tehnice [*Enterprise for the Utilization of Grains and Technical Crops*] (RO)
IVD............. Height-Range Indicator (RU)
IVDJ........... Internationale Vereinigung Demokratischer Juristen [*International Union of Democratic Jurists*] (EG)
IVDZ........... Institouton Veltioseos kai Diatrofis Zoon [*Animal Husbandry Institute*] [*Greek*] (GC)
IVE............. Instituto Vallecaucano de Estadistica [*Cali*] (COL)
IVE............. Internationale Vereinigung von Einkaufsverbanden [*International Association of Buying Groups - IABG*] (EA)
IVECOM...... Ivoirienne d'Echanges Commerciaux (MAR)
IVEPO......... Venezuelan Institute of Popular Education
IVF............. Institutet fuer Verkstadsteknisk Forskning [*Institute for Production Engineering Research*] [*Swedish*]
IVG............. Internationale Vereinigung fuer Germanische Sprach - und Literaturwissenschaft [*International Association of Germanic Languages and Literatures - IAGLL*] (EA)
IVG............. Internationale Vereinigung der Gewerkschaften [*International Union of Trade Unions*] (EG)
Ivgiz........... Ivanovo State Publishing House (RU)
IVGO.......... News of the All-Union Geographic Society [*A publication*] (RU)
Ivgres......... Ivanovo State Regional Electric Power Plant (RU)
IVGRO........ News of the All-Union Geological Exploration Association [*A publication*] (RU)
IVIC............ Instituto Venezolano de Investigaciones Cientificas [*Venezuelan Institute of Scientific Research*] (LA)
IVIETA........ Instituto de Vuelo por Instrumentos y Escuela de Tierra [*Bogota*] (COL)
IvIOT.......... All-Union Scientific Research Institute of Work Safety of the VTsSPS [*Ivanovo*] (RU)
IVITA.......... Instituto Veterinario de Investigaciones Tropicales y de Altura [*The Veterinary Institute for Tropical and Altitude Research*] [*Peruvian*] (LA)
IVK............. Institute of Medical Cosmetology (RU)
IVK............. Invalidska Vrhovna Komisija [*Supreme Commission for the Disabled*] (YU)
IVKh........... Institute of Restorative Surgery (RU)
IVKh........... Institute of Water Management (RU)
IVKT........... Italian General Confederation of Labor (RU)
IVL............. Publishing House of Oriental Literature (RU)
IVLD........... Internationale Vereinigung der Organisationen von Lebensmittel-Detaillisten [*International Federation of Grocers' Associations - IFGA*] (EA)
iVm............ In Verbindung Mit [*In Conjunction With, In Association With*] (EG)
IVM............ Institut fuer Verbrennungsmotoren und Kraftfahrwesen [*Institute for Internal Combustion Engines and Motor Vehicles*] (EG)
IVN............. High-Voltage Source (RU)
IVN............. Institute of High Voltages (of the Siberian Department of the Academy of Sciences, USSR) (RU)
IVN............. Internationale Vereniging voor Neerlandistiek [*International Association of Dutch Studies*] (EA)
IVND........... Institute of Higher Nervous Activity (RU)
IVNDiNF..... Institute of Higher Nervous Activity and Neurophysiology (of the Academy of Sciences, USSR) (RU)
IVNIOT....... Ivanovo Scientific Research Institute of Work Safety and Occupational Diseases (RU)
IVNITI......... Ivanovo Scientific Research Textile Institute (RU)
IVOBRA....... Ivoirienne de Brasserie (MAR)
IVOIRAGRI... Societe Ivoirienne d'Exploitation Agricole, Industrielle, Commerciale et de Transports (MAR)
IVOIRAL...... Compagnie Ivoirienne de l'Aluminium (MAR)
IVOIRAUTO... Cote-d'Ivoire Automobile (MAR)
IVOIRLAIT... Societe Ivoirienne de Produits Laitiers (MAR)
IVOLCY....... Industrie Voltaique du Cycle et Cyclomoteur (MAR)
IVOSEP....... Societe Ivoirienne de Sepultures et Transports Speciaux (MAR)
IVOSEPSASEP... Societe Ivoirienne de Sepultures et Transports Speciaux (MAR)
IVOTEX....... Societe Ivoirienne de Textiles (MAR)
IVP............. Institute of Water Problems (RU)
IVP............. Instituto Venezolano de Petroquimica [*Venezuelan Petrochemical Institute*] (LA)
IVP............. Soil Moisture Meter (RU)
IVPI............ Ivanovo-Voznesensk Polytechnic Institute Imeni M. V. Frunze (RU)
IVPP........... Surfaced Runway (RU)
IVR............. Internationale Vereinigung fur Rechts- und Sozialphilosophie [*International Association for Philosophy of Law and Social Philosophy*] (EA)
IVS............. Institute of Macromolecular Compounds (of the Academy of Sciences, USSR) (RU)
IVS............. Institute of Vaccines and Serums (RU)
IVS............. International Voluntary Service (CL)
IVS............. Isturena Veterinarska Stanica [*Advanced Veterinary Station*] [*Military*] (YU)
IVSA........... International Veterinary Students Association (EA)
IVSS........... Instituto Venezolano de Seguros Sociales [*Venezuelan Social Security Institute*] (LA)
IVSS........... Internationale Vereinigung fuer Soziale Sicherheit (MAR)

IVSZ .... Szakszervezeti Iskolat Vegzettek Szovetsege [*Association of Graduates of Trade Union Schools*] (HU)
IVT.............. Institute of Air Transport (RU)
IVT.............. Institute of Foreign Trade (RU)
IVTE .... Institute for Medical Determination of Disability (RU)
Ivtekmash... Ivanovo Textile Machinery Plant (RU)
Ivtorfmash ... Ivanovo Peat Machinery Plant (RU)
IVTs............ Information and Computation Center (RU)
IVU .... Instituto de Vivienda Urbana [*Urban Housing Institute*] [*Salvadoran*] (LA)
IVU .... Instituto de Vivienda y Urbanismo [*Institute of Housing and City Planning*] [*Panamanian*] (LA)
IVUz............ Institute of Oriental Studies (of the Academy of Sciences, Uzbek SSR) (RU)
IVV.............. Initiator [*Expl.*] (RU)
IVV.............. Internationale Vereinigung fuer Vegetationskunde [*International Association for Vegetation Science - IAVS*] (EA)
IVVS .... Air Force Inspection (RU)
IVYa............ Institut Vostochnykh Yazykov (MAR)
IVYa............ Institute of Oriental Languages (RU)
IVZ.............. Islamska Vjerska Zajednica [*Islamic Religious Community*] [*Bosnia and Hercegovina*] (YU)
iW .... In Worten [*In Words*] (EG)
IW .... Industriewerk [*Industrial Plant*] (EG)
IW .... Innere Weite [*Inside Diameter*] [*German*]
IW .... Instytut Weglowy [*Coal Institute*] (POL)
IW .... Instytut Wlokiennictwa [*Textile Institute*] (POL)
IW .... Israelitische Wochenschrift, Breslau/Magdeburg (MAR)
IWA .... International Waterproofing Association [*See also AIE*] (EA)
IWA .... International Workers of Africa (MAR)
IWBP .... Integration with Britain Party [*Gibraltar*] (PPE)
IWBS .... Importwarenbegleitschein [*Import Bill of Lading*] (EG)
IWC .... International Wheat Council [*See also CIB*] (EA)
IWCC........... International Women's Cricket Council (EA)
IWCC........... International Wrought Copper Council (EA)
IWD .... Inland Waterways Department (MAR)
IWEVO......... Informatiespecialisten Werkgroep voor Voedingsmiddelen [*Dutch*]
IWF............. International Weightlifting Federation [*See also FHI*] (EA)
IWF............. Internationale Wahrungsfond (MAR)
IWFS .... International Wine and Food Society (EA)
IWGIA.......... International Work Group for Indigenous Affairs (EA)
IWIS/TNO ... Instituut voor Wiskunde, Informatieverwerking, en Statistiek/ Toegepast Natuurwetenschappelijk Onderzoek [*'s-Gravenhage*]
IWMA .... International Wire and Machinery Association (EA)
IWO .... Iran Women's Organization (ME)
IWO .... Iran Workers' Organization (ME)
IWP............. Indicative World Plan (MAR)
IWP............. Instytut Wzornictwa Przemyslowego [*Industrial Pattern Institute*] (POL)
IWP............. Irish Workers' Party (PPW)
IWRB .... International Waterfowl Research Bureau (EA)
IWSA........... International Water Supply Association (EA)
IWSAW........ Institute for Women's Studies in the Arab World (EA)
IWSG........... International Wool Study Group (EA)
IWSS .... Instytut Wlokien Sztucznych i Syntetycznych [*Institute of Artificial and Synthetic Fibers*] [*Polish*]
IWTO........... International Wool Textile Organization [*See also FLI*] (EA)
IWv............. Im Werte Von [*Amounting To*] [*German*]
IXbre........... Novembre [*November*] [*French*]
IXbre .... Noviembre [*November*] [*Spanish*]
IYa.............. Information Language (RU)
IYA .... Ismailia Youth Association [*North African*] (MAR)
IYaIMK .... Institute of Language, History, and Material Culture (RU)
IYaIYaE .... Institute for Nuclear Research and Nuclear Power Industry (BU)
IYAK............ Isci Yardimlasma Kurumu [*Workers Mutual Aid Organization*] [*See also IYK*] (TU)
IYaL............ Institute of Language and Literature (RU)
IYaLI........... Institute of Language, Literature, and History (RU)
IYaM........... Institute of Language and Thought Imeni N. Ya. Marr (Academy of Sciences, USSR) (RU)
IYaORGO .... News of the Yakutsk Branch of the Russian Geographic Society [*A publication*] (RU)
IYaP............ Institute of Nuclear Problems (RU)
IYaSh .... Foreign Languages in the School (RU)
IYaZ............ Institute of Linguistics (of the Academy of Sciences, USSR) (RU)
IYC .... International Year of the Child [*1979*] [*United Nations*] (MAR)
IYC .... International Youth Conference (EG)
IYDP .... International Year for Disabled Persons (MAR)
IYe............. Immunizing Unit (RU)
IYE.............. Institouto Ypotropikon kai Elaias [*Institute for Sub-Tropical Plants and Olive Trees*] (GC1)
IYe.............. International Unit (RU)
IYeSTEKh ... Institute of History of Natural Sciences and Technology (of the Academy of Sciences, USSR) (RU)
IYHF .... International Youth Hostel Federation [*See also FAIJ*] (EA)
IYK .... Isci Yardimlasma Kurumu [*Workers Mutual Aid Society*] [*See also IYAK*] (TU)
IYOD........... Istanbul Yuksek Ogrenim Dernegi [*Istanbul Higher Education Association*] (TU)
IYOKD......... Istanbul Yuksek Ogrenim Kultur Dernegi [*Istanbul Higher Education Cultural Association*] (TU)
IYOKD .... Izmir Yuksek Ogrenim Kultur Dernegi [*Izmir Higher Education Cultural Association*] (TU)
IYOTB.......... Istanbul Yuksek Okullar Talebe Birligi [*Istanbul Advanced Schools Student Union*] (TU)
IYTOTB .... Istanbul Yuksek Teknik Okulu Talebe Birligi [*Istanbul Advanced Technical School Student Union*] (TU)
IYuF............ News of the Law Division [*A publication*] (RU)
IZ................ East, West (BU)
IZ................ Electoral Law (BU)
IZ................ Historical Records (of the Academy of Sciences, USSR) [*A publication*] (RU)
IZ................ Industriezweig [*Industrial Branch*] (EG)
IZ................ Instalacni Zavody [*Installation Enterprises*] [*Prague*] (CZ)
IZ................ Instruments Plant (BU)
IZ................ Instytut Zachodni [*Institute of the Western Territories*] (POL)
IZ................ Instytut Zootechniki [*Institute of Animal Husbandry*] (POL)
i-z............... Istok-Zapad [*East-West*] (YU)
iz .... Izquierda, Izquierdo [*Left*] [*Spanish*]
IZ................ Trigger Pulse (RU)
IZB.............. Inspektorat za Zastitu Bilja [*Plant Protection Inspectorate*] (YU)
izbr............. Elected (BU)
izd .... Edition, Publication, Issue (RU)
izd .... Izdanje [*Edition*] (YU)
izd .... Publication, Publisher, Publishing House (BU)
izd .... Publisher (RU)
izd .... Publishing House (RU)
Izdatinlit...... Publishing House of Foreign Literature (RU)
izd avt .... Published by the Author (BU)
izdinlit......... Publishing House of Foreign Literature (RU)
izd-vo.......... Publishing House (RU)
IZGRADNJA ... Gradevinsko Preduzece [*Building Establishment*] (YU)
IZh.............. Engineering Journal [*A publication*] (RU)
izh .... Izhaja [*Published*] (YU)
IZh.............. Izhevsk Motorcycle Plant (RU)
IZh.............. Motorcycle Made by the Izhevsk Motorcycle Plant (RU)
IZhB .... Izhevsk Hammerless Gun (RU)
IZhS .... Housing Constructions Institute (BU)
IZhSA.......... Institute of Painting, Sculpture, and Architecture Imeni I. Ye. Repin (of the Academy of Arts, USSR) (RU)
IZhT............ Synthetic Liquid Fuel (RU)
IZIGIZ......... State Publishing House of Fine Arts (RU)
IZiZ............. Instytut Zywnosci i Zywienia [*Institute of Food and Feeding*] [*Polish*]
IZJA............ Izdavacki Zavod Jugoslavenske Akademije [*Publishing Institute of the Yugoslav Academy*] [*Zagreb*] (YU)
izk .... Art (BU)
izkh .... Output [*Electricity*] (BU)
izl .... Exposition, Statement (BU)
izl .... Fracture, Fissure (RU)
IZL.............. Industriezweigleitung [*Industrial Branch Management*] (EG)
IZLC .... Izvestaj Zaduzbine Luke Celovica [*Report of the Luka Celovic Foundation*] [*Belgrade*] (YU)
izm .... Change (RU)
izm .... Changed, Amended, Modified, Change (BU)
IZM-............ Measuring Machine (RU)
izmerit......... Measuring (RU)
IZMIRAN ..... Institute of Terrestrial Magnetism, the Ionosphere, and Radio Wave Propagation of the Academy of Sciences, USSR (RU)
IZO .... Fine Arts (RU)
IZO .... Fine Arts Department (RU)
IZO .... Quarantine Clearing Station (RU)
Izogiz .... State Publishing House of Fine Arts (RU)
izokruzhok ... Fine Arts Group (RU)
izol .... Isoleucine (RU)
Izolit........... Moscow Insulation Plant (RU)
Izomuzgiz ... State Publishing House of Fine Arts and Music Literature [*UkrSSR*] (RU)
Izoplit.......... Insulation Tile Plant (RU)
Izopropunkt ... Quarantine Clearing Station (RU)
IZORAM ...... Fine Arts Group of Working Youth (RU)
IZOS............ Inicijativni Zadruzni Odbor za Slovenijo [*Initiatory Cooperative Committee for Slovenia*] (YU)
IZOS............ Lzyum Optical Glass Plant Imeni F. E. Dzerzhinskiy (RU)
Izostat......... Scientific Research Institute for the Graphic Presentation of Statistics on Soviet Construction and Economy (RU)
IZOTUM ...... Izolasyon Maddeleri Sanayii ve Ticaret Ltd. Sirketi [*Insulation Materials Industry and Marketing Corp. Ltd.*] (TU)
Izpulkom..... Executive Committee (BU)
Izq .... Izquierda [*Left*] [*Correspondence*] [*Spanish*]
izqa .... Izquierda [*Left*] [*Spanish*]
izqda .... Izquierda [*Left*] [*Spanish*]
izqdo .... Izquierdo [*Left*] [*Spanish*]
izqo .... Izquierdo [*Left*] [*Spanish*]
IZR.............. Institute fcr the Protection of Plants (RU)
iz-r.............. Insulator (RU)
izr .... Israeli (RU)

izr .... Izraelita [*Jew or Jewish*] (HU)
izr .... Sentence [*Grammar*] (BU)
izrab .... Prepared, Completed, Earned (BU)
IZSK .... Institut za Zastitu Spomenika Kulture [*Institute for the Protection of Cultural Monuments*] (YU)
Izsled .... Research (BU)
IZSORGO .... News of the West Siberian Branch of the Russian Geographic Society [*A publication*] (RU)
izt .... East, Eastern (BU)
izt .... Sources (BU)
iz tekh .... Computer Equipment (BU)
IZTM............ Irkutsk Heavy Machinery Plant Imeni V. V. Kuybyshev (RU)
IZTO .... Correspondence Institute of Technical Education (RU)
IZU............... Office of Inventions and Improvements (RU)
IZUL .... Office of Inventions and Improvements of Transportation Technology (RU)
izumr........... Emerald Mines [*Topography*] (RU)
izv................ Bulletin, Information (BU)
Izv................ Extraordinary (BU)
IZV............... Industriezweigverband [*Industrial Branch Association*] (EG)
izv................ Izvadak [*Excerpts*] (YU)
Izv................ Izvestiya na Prezidiuma na Narodnoto Subranie [*Journal of the Presidium of the National Assembly*] (BU)
izv................ Lime Plant [*Topography*] (RU)
izv................ Lime Quarry [*Topography*] (RU)
Izv................ News (RU)
IzvBAI.......... Bulletin of the Bulgarian Archeological Institute (BU)
Izv BIAD ...... Bulletin of the Bulgarian Society of Engineers and Architects [*A publication*] (BU)
IzvBIstD ...... Bulletin of the Bulgarian Historical Society [*A publication*] (BU)
Izv Bulg geogr d-vo ... Bulletin of the Bulgarian Geographic Society [*A publication*] (BU)
Izv na Geol geogr i khim i-ti pri BAN ... Bulletin of the Geological, Geographic, and Chemical Institutes of the Bulgarian Academy of Sciences [*A publication*] (BU)
Izv Geol i-t BAN ... Bulletin of the Geological Institute of the Bulgarian Academy of Sciences [*A publication*] (BU)
Izv Inst muzika ... Bulletin of the Institute of Music [*A publication*] (BU)
IzvjescaBIU ... Izvjesca Botanickog Instituta Universiteta u Zagrebu [*Report of the Botanical Institute of the University in Zagreb*] (YU)
Izv KNK .... Bulletin of the Chamber of National Culture [*A publication*] (BU)
izvlech .... Abstract (RU)
izvlech .... Extract, Excerpt (BU)
Izv Mikrobiol inst BAN ... Bulletin of the Microbiological Institute of the Bulgarian Academy of Sciences [*A publication*] (BU)
IzvMNZdr .... Bulletin of the Ministry of Public Health [*A publication*] (BU)
izv p............. Lime Kiln [*Topography*] (RU)

J

J .... Das Joule [*Joule*] (EG)
J .... Jabal [*or Jabel or Jebel*] [*See also Jl*] [*Mountain, Hill*] [*Arabic*] (NAU)
J .... Jahr [*Year*] [*German*]
J .... Jahrbuch [*Journal, Annual Report*] [*German*]
J .... Jahresbericht [*Journal, Annual Report*] [*German*]
j .... Jalka [*Finnish*]
J .... Jandarma [*Gendarme, Gendarmery*] (TU)
j .... Jaras [*District*] (HU)
j .... Jarat [*Line, Route (Bus line)*] (HU)
J .... Jezioro [*Lake*] [*Polish*]
j .... Jih [*South*] (CZ)
j .... Jobb [*On the Right Side*] (HU)
j .... Jour [*Day*] [*French*] (MTD)
J .... Journal [*Journal, Annual Report*] [*German*]
j .... Journal [*Newspaper*] [*French*]
J .... Judex [*Judge*] [*Latin*] (GPO)
J .... Jug [*South*] (YU)
J .... Justiz [*German*]
JA .... Jeune Afrique [*Tunis*] [*A publication*] (MAR)
JA .... Jeux Africains (MAR)
Ja .... Jima [*Island*] [*See also Sa*] [*Japanese*] (NAU)
JA .... Journal Asiatique [*A publication*] (MAR)
JA .... Jugoslavenska Akademija Znanosti i Umjetnosti [*Yugoslav Academy of Sciences and Arts*] [*Zagreb*] (YU)
JA .... Jugoslovenska Armija [*Yugoslav Army*] (YU)
JAA .... Jordan Arab Army (ME)
JAA .... Journal of African Administration [*London*] [*A publication*] (MAR)
JAA .... Jugoslovenska Autorska Agencija [*Yugoslav Authors' Agency*] (YU)
JAAC .... Juventude Africana Amilcar Cabral (MAR)
JAAS .... Journal of Asian and African Studies [*Leiden*] [*A publication*] (MAR)
Jab .... Jabal [*Mountain, Hill*] [*See also J, Jl*] [*Arabic*] (NAU)
Jab .... Jabal [*Mountain, Hill*] [*Persian*] (NAU)
JAB .... Joint Africa Board (MAR)
JABLONEX ... Podnik Zahranicniho Obchodu pro Vyvoz Jabloneckeho Zbozi [*Foreign Trade Enterprise for the Export of Jablonec Glassware*] (CZ)
JAC .... Jeunesse Agricole Catholique [*Catholic Farm Youth*] [*Cameroonian*] (AF)
JAC .... Jeunesse Agricole Catholique [*Catholic Farm Youth*] [*Congolese*] (AF)
JAC .... Jeunesse Agricole Chretienne [*French*] (MAR)
JAC .... Junta de Aeronautica Civil [*Civil Aeronautics Board*] [*Chilean*] (LA)
JAC .... Junta de Aeronautica Civil [*Civil Aeronautics Board*] [*Argentine*] (LA)
JAC .... Juventud de Accion Catolica [*Catholic Action Youth*] [*Argentine*] (LA)
JACFA .... Jamaican-Cuban Friendship Association (LA1)
JADRANSPORT ... Adriatic Shipbuilding [*Pula*] (YU)
Jadrolinija ... Jadranska Linijska Plovidba [*The Adriatic Shipping Line*] [*Rijeka*] (YU)
JAE .... Journal of Agricultural Economics [*Reading*] [*A publication*] (MAR)
JAEA .... Junta Autonoma de Estradas de Angola (MAR)
Jaehrl .... Jaehrlich [*Annual*] [*German*] [*Business and trade*]
JAERI .... Japan Atomic Energy Research Institute (SJT)
JAF .... Jordanian Armed Forces (ME)
JAFC .... Jamaica Association for Friendship with China (LA1)
JAFI .... Jarmufejlesztesi Intezet [*Institute of Transportation Development*] (HU)
JAG .... Etablissements Jean Abile Gal, SA [*South African*] (MAR)
Jagerspr ..... Jaegersprache [*German*]
JAGO .... Jugendarrestgeschaeftsordnung [*Germany*]
JAH .... Journal of African History [*A publication*] (MAR)
JAH .... Wilajah [*Territory, Region, Area*] (IN)
Jahrg .... Jahrgang [*Annual Set*] [*German*]
JAI .... Journal of the (Royal) Anthropological Institute [*A publication*] (MAR)
JAIC .... Joint Arab Investment Company (MAR)
JAICORP ..... Joint Arab Investment Corporation (MAR)
JAIF .... Japan Atomic Industrial Forum (SJT)
JAK .... Jugoslovenski Akademski Klub [*Yugoslav Academic Club*] (YU)
JAL .... Japan Air Lines (SJT)
JAL .... Jordanian Air Line (ME)
JAL .... Journal of African Languages [*Hertford*] [*A publication*] (MAR)
JAL .... Journal of African Law [*London*] [*A publication*] (MAR)
JALGO .... Jamaica Association of Local Government Officers (LA1)
jalk .... Jalkeen [*After*] [*Finnish*]
jalkap .... Jalkapallo [*Football*] [*Finnish*]
JAM .... Jamaica [*Three-letter standard code*] (CNC)
JAM .... Jednotne Analyticke Metody [*Standard Analytical Processes*] (CZ)
JAMA .... Moslem People's Revolutionary Movement [*Iranian*] (PPW)
JAMAL .... Jamaican Movement for the Advancement of Literacy (LA)
JAMALCO ... Jamaica Alumina Company (LA1)
JAMB .... Joint Admissions and Matriculation Board [*Nigerian*] (AF)
JAMINTEL ... Jamaica International Telecommunications Ltd. (LA1)
JAMU .... Janackova Akademie Musickych Umeni [*Janacek Academy of the Fine Arts*] (CZ)
jan .... Janeiro [*January*] [*Portuguese*] (GPO)
jan .... Januar [*January*] [*Danish*] (GPO)
Jan .... Januar [*January*] [*German*] (GPO)
jan .... Januar [*January*] [*Hungarian*] (GPO)
jan .... Januari [*January*] [*Dutch*] (GPO)
JAN .... Junta de Asistencia Nacional [*National Assistance Board*] [*Peruvian*] (LA)
JANA .... Jamahiriyah News Agency (MAR)
JANU .... Jugoslovenska Akademija na Naukite i Umetnosta [*Yugoslav Academy of Sciences and Arts (JAZU)*] [*Zagreb*] (YU)
janv .... Janvier [*January*] [*French*]
JAO .... Journal of Administration Overseas [*London*] [*A publication*] (MAR)
jap .... Japania [*or Japaniksi*] [*Finnish*]
jap .... Japanilainen [*Finnish*]
JAP .... Junta de Abastecimientos y Precios [*Supply and Price Board*] [*Chilean*] (LA)
JAP .... Juntas de Accao Patriotica [*Patriotic Action Boards*] [*Portuguese*] (PPE)
JAP .... Juventud Aprista Peruana [*Peruvian Aprista Youth*] (LA)
JAP .... Juventudes de Accion Popular [*Spanish*] (PPE)
JAPAC .... [*The*] Japan Atomic Power Company (SJT)
JAPDEVA .... Junta de Administracion Portuaria para el Desarrollo Economico de la Vertiente Atlantica [*Port Administration Board for the Economic Development of the Atlantic Coast*] [*Costa Rican*] (LA)
JAPI .... Jajasan Pensiaran Islam [*Foundation for the Propagation of Islam*] (IN)
JAPINDA ..... Japan-Indonesia Association (IN)
JAPIS .... Jajasan Pendidikan Islam [*Islamic Educational Institute*] (IN)
jar .... Jaras [*District*] (HU)
Jarhg .... Jahrgang [*Year's Set*] [*German*]
JAS .... Jane Austen Society (EA)
JAS .... Javen Avto-Soobrakaj [*Public Motor Transport*] (YU)
JAS .... Journal of the African Society [*A publication*] (MAR)
JAS .... Juventud Argentina por la Soberania [*Argentine Youth for Sovereignty*] (LA)
JAS .... Narodni Podnik pro Prodej Kozeneho Zbozi a Obuvi [*National Sales Enterprise of Leather Goods and Footwear*] (CZ)
JASPA .... Jobs and Skills Programme for Africa (MAR)
JASTA .... Junta de Assistencia e Trabalho de Angola [*Angolan Labor and Welfare Board*] (AF)
JASZOV ...... Jarasi Foldmuves Szovetkezet [*District Farmers' Cooperative*] (HU)
JAT .... Jugoslovenski Aerotransport [*Yugoslav Air Transport*]
JATBA .... Journal d'Agronomie Tropicale et de Botanique Appliquee [*A publication*] (MAR)

JATE .... Jozsef Attila Tudomanyegyetem [*Attila Jozsef University of Sciences*] (HU)
JATELCO .... Jamaica Telephone Company (LA1)
jatk .... Jatketaan [*Finnish*]
jatk .... Jatkoa [*Finnish*]
jatk .... Jatkuu [*Finnish*]
jav .... Javara [*For the Benefit Of, In Favor Of*] (HU)
JAWA .... Janecek-Wanderer, Narodni Podnik [*Janecek-Wanderer, National Enterprise*] [*Automobile works*] (CZ)
Jazh .... Jazireh [*Island, Peninsula*] [*Persian*] (NAU)
Jazt .... Jazirat [*Island, Peninsula*] [*Arabic*] (NAU)
JAZU .... Jugoslavenska Akademija Znanosti i Umjetnosti [*Yugoslav Academy of Sciences and Arts*] [*Zagreb*] (YU)
JB .... Etablissements Jean Bergounioux (MAR)
Jb .... Jahrbuch [*Annual, Yearbook*] (EG)
j b .... Jarasi Bizottsag [*District Committee*] (HU)
JBH .... Jarasi Begyujtesi Hivatal [*District Collection Committee*] (HU)
JBI .... Jamaica Bauxite Institute (LA1)
JBR .... Journal of Bible and Religion [*A publication*] (MAR)
JBST .... Jugoslovenska Banka za Spoljnu Trgovinu [*Yugoslav Bank for Foreign Trade*] (YU)
JC .... Jesucristo [*Jesus Christ*] [*Spanish*]
J-C .... Jesus-Christ [*Jesus Christ*] [*French*] (GPO)
JC .... Jeunesse Communiste [*Communist Youth*] [*French*] (WER)
JC .... Junta de Comandantes [*Junta of Commanders*] [*Spanish*] (WER)
JC .... Juventud Comunista [*Communist Youth*] [*Spanish*] (WER)
JC .... Juventudes Carlistas [*Carlist Youth*] [*Spanish*] (WER)
JCA .... Judo Club d'Abidjan (MAR)
JCA .... Juventude Crista de Angola (MAR)
JCAD .... Joint Committee on Agricultural Development (MAR)
JCAFU .... Joint Committee of the Autonomous Federations and Unions [*Comite d'Entente des Federations et Syndicats Autonomes d'Algerie*] [*Algeria*]
JCAN .... Junta Coordinadora de Afirmacion Nacional [*Coordinating Junta of National Affirmation*] [*Spanish*] (WER)
J can Dr .... Doktor des Kanonischen Rechtes [*German*]
JCAP .... Junta Central de Accao Patriotica (MAR)
JCB .... Jeunesse Communiste de Belgique [*Communist Youth of Belgium*] (WER)
JCB .... Juventud Comunista de Bolivia [*Bolivian Communist Youth*] (LA)
JCC .... Jeunesse Cotiere Cabindienne (MAR)
JCC .... Jihoceske Cihelny [*South Bohemian Brick Works*] (CZ)
JCC .... Judo Club de Cocody (MAR)
JCC .... Juventud Comunista de Colombia [*Communist Youth of Colombia*] (LA)
JCD .... John Chard Decoration (MAR)
JCD .... Juris Civilis Doctor [*Doctor of Civil Law*] [*Latin*] (GPO)
JCD .... Juventud Costarricense Democratica [*Democratic Costa Rican Youth*] (LA)
JCE .... Jeunes Chambres Economiques [*Youth Economic Chambers*] (LA1)
JCE .... Jihoceske Elektrarny, Narodni Podnik [*South Bohemian Electric Power Plants, National Enterprise*] (CZ)
JCE .... Jockey Club of Egypt (MAR)
jce .... Jouissance [*French*]
JCE .... Judo Club Eburneen (MAR)
JCE .... Junta Central Electoral [*Central Electoral Board*] [*Dominican Republic*] (LA)
JCE .... Juventud Comunista Ecuatoriana [*Ecuadorean Communist Youth*] (LA)
JCEA .... Junta de Control de Energia Atomica [*Atomic Energy Control Board*] [*Peruvian*] (LA)
JCEHV .... Jeune Chambre Economique de Haute Volta [*Junior Economic Chamber of Upper Volta*] (AF)
JCEM .... Jeune Chambre Economique Marocaine (MAR)
JCE (M-L) .... Juventud Comunista de Espana (Marxista-Leninista) [*Communist Youth of Spain*] (Marxist-Leninist) (WER)
JCF .... Jamaica Constabulary Force (LA1)
JCF .... Jeunesse Communiste Francaise [*French Communist Youth*] (WER)
JCH .... Joint Control Headquarters [*Singapore*] (ML)
Jchtbd .... Juchtenband [*Russia Leather Binding*] [*German*]
Jchtn .... Juchtenband [*Russia Leather Binding*] [*German*]
Jchtnb .... Juchtenband [*Russia Leather Binding*] [*German*]
JCI .... Johannesburg Consolidated Investment Co. Ltd. (MAR)
JCIA .... Japan Chemical Industry Association
JCK .... Jugoslovenski Crveni Krst [*Yugoslav Red Cross*] (YU)
JCKGOM .... Jugoslovenski Crven Krst, Glaven Odbor za Makedonija [*Yugoslav Red Cross, Central Committee of Macedonia*] (YU)
JCLIL .... Journal of Comparative Legislation and International Law [*London*] [*A publication*] (MAR)
JCM .... Jego Cesarska Mosc [*His Imperial Majesty*] [*Polish*]
JCM .... Jeunesse Chretienne Malgache [*Malagasy Christian Youth*] (AF)
JCM .... John Chard Medal (MAR)
JCM .... Juventud Comunista de Mexico [*Mexican Communist Youth*] (LA)
JCMF .... Jednota Ceskych Matematiku a Fysiku [*Association of Czech Mathematicians and Physicists*] (CZ)
JCN .... Junta Civica Nacional [*National Civic Board*] [*Ecuadorean*] (LA)
JCP .... Japan Communist Party [*Nikon Kyosanto*] (PPW)
JCP .... Jordanian Communist Party (PD)
JCP .... Juventud Comunista Peruana [*Peruvian Communist Youth*] (LA)
JCR .... Jeunesse Communiste Revolutionnaire [*Revolutionary Communist Youth*] [*Student group*] [*French*] (WER)
JCR .... Junta Coordenativa Revolucionaria [*Revolutionary Coordinating Junta*] [*Portuguese*] (WER)
JCR .... Junta de Coordinacion Revolucionaria [*Revolutionary Coordinating Junta*] [*Argentine*] (LA)
JCS .... Juventud Comunista de El Salvador [*Salvadoran Communist Youth*] (LA)
JCSA .... Jamaica Civil Service Association (LA1)
JCSP .... Jednota Ceskoslovenskych Pravniku [*Union of Czechoslovak Lawyers*] (CZ)
JCSZ .... Jednota Ceskoslovenskych Zemedelcu [*Czechoslovak Farmers' Association*] (CZ)
JCTND .... Jugoslovenski Centar za Tehnicku i Naucnu Dokumentaciju [*Yugoslav Center of Technical and Scientific Documentation*] (YU)
JCV .... Juventud Comunista Venezolana [*Venezuelan Communist Youth*] (LA)
JCW .... Jego Cesarska Wysokosc [*His Imperial Highness*] [*Polish*]
JCWI .... Joint Council for the Welfare of Immigrants (MAR)
JD .... Jandarma [*Gendarme, Gendarmery*] (TU)
JD .... Jeunesse Democratique [*Democratic Youth*] [*Luxembourg*] (WER)
j/d .... Jours de Date [*French*]
JD .... Junta Democratica [*Democratic Junta*] [*Spanish*] (PPE)
JD .... Jurum Doctor [*Doctor of Laws*] [*Latin*] (GPO)
JD .... Justizdienst [*Legal Service or Judge Advocate's Office*] [*Military*] (EG)
JD .... Juventudes Democraticas [*Democratic Youth*] [*Spanish*] (WER)
JDA .... Juventude Democratica de Angola [*Angolan Democratic Youth*] (AF)
JDBTHI .... Jajasan Dana Bantuanuntuk Tjalon Hadji Indonesia [*Aid Foundation for Prospective Indonesian Pilgrims to Mecca*] (IN)
JDC .... Jeunesse Democratique Camerounaise (MAR)
JDC .... Juventud Democrata Cristiana [*Christian Democratic Youth*] [*Chilean*] (LA)
JDC .... Juventud Democrata Cristiana [*Christian Democratic Youth*] [*Paraguayan*] (LA)
JDC .... Juventud Democrata Cristiana [*Christian Democratic Youth*] [*Salvadoran*] (LA1)
JDCB .... Juventud del Partido Democrata Cristiano [*Christian Democratic Party Youth*] [*Bolivian*] (LA)
jdk .... Joidenkuiden [*Finnish*]
JDr .... Doktor der Rechte [*German*]
JDRB .... Jugoslovensko Drzavno Recno Brodarstvo [*Yugoslav State River Transport*] (YU)
JDS .... Jamhuuriyadda Dimoqraadiga ee Soomaliya [*Somali Democratic Republic*] [*Use SDR*] (AF)
JDS .... Jugoslovenska Demokratska Stranka [*Yugoslav Democratic Party*] (PPE)
JDT .... Jednotny Dunajsky Tarif [*Standard Danube Tariff*] (CZ)
JDT .... Jeunesse Democratique du Togo (MAR)
JDU .... Jednota Duchovnich a Ucitelu Nabozenstvi Cirkve Ceskoslovenske [*Association of Clergyman and Teachers of Religion of the Czechoslovak Church*] (CZ)
JDZ .... Jugoslovanske Drzavne Zeleznice [*Yugoslav State Railroads*] (YU)
JE .... Jego Ekscelencia [*His Excellency*] [*Polish*]
JEA .... Jamaica Exporters Association (LA1)
JEAfrSC .... Journal of the East African Swahili Committee [*Kampala*] [*A publication*] (MAR)
JEARD .... Journal of Eastern African Research and Development [*A publication*] (MAR)
JEASC .... Journal of the East African Swahili Committee [*Kampala*] [*A publication*] (MAR)
Jeb .... Jebel [*Mountain, Hill*] [*See also J, Jl*] [*Arabic*] (NAU)
JEC .... Jeunesse Etudiante Catholique Internationale [*International Young Catholic Students*] (EA)
JEC .... Jeunesse Etudiante Chretienne [*French*]
JEC .... Joint Economic Committee (MAR)
JEC .... Junta de Exportacao do Cafe (MAR)
JEC .... Juventud Estudiantes Catolicos [*Catholic Student Youth*] [*Argentine*] (LA)
JEC .... Juventud Estudiantil Catolica [*Catholic Student Youth*] [*Paraguayan*] (LA)
JECC .... Joint Egyptian Cotton Committee (MAR)
JECS .... Job Evaluation and Classification Scheme [*Sudanese*] (MAR)
JED .... Jugoslovensko Entomolosko Drustvo [*Yugoslav Entomological Society*] [*Belgrade*] (YU)
jedn .... Jednostka [*Unit*] [*Polish*]
Jee .... Jetee [*Pier, Jetty, Mole*] [*Military map abbreviation*] [*World War I*] [*French*] (MTD)

JEF .... Jamaica Employers Federation (LA1)
JEF .... Jeunesses Europeennes Federalistes
jegyz .... Jegyzet [*Note, Footnote*] [*Hungarian*] (GPO)
JEK .... Jugoslovenska Elektrotehnicka Komisija [*Yugoslav Electrotechnical Commission*] (YU)
jel .... Jelenet [*Scene (Theater)*] (HU)
jel .... Jelentes [*Report*] (HU)
JELI .... Junta Revolucionaria de Libertacao Iberica (MAR)
j em .... Jednostka Elektromagnetyczna [*Electromagnetic Unit*] [*Polish*]
JEN .... Junta de Energia Nuclear [*Nuclear Energy Board*] [*Spanish*] (WER)
JENAKAT .... Jeunesse Nationale Katangaise [*Katangan National Youth*] (MAR)
Jeod .... Jeodetik [*Geodetic*] (TU)
Jeol .... Jeoloji [*Geology*] (TU)
JEPM .... Junta de Exportacao da Provincia de Mocambique (MAR)
JEPPT .... Jeunesse du Parti Progressiste du Tchad [*Youth of the Progressive Party of Chad*] (AF)
jes .... Jednostka Elektrostatyczna [*Electrostatic Unit*] [*Polish*]
JES .... Young European Students' Union [*Pro-OeVP*] [*Austrian*] (WEN)
JESAME .... Journal of the Ethiopian Students Association of the Middle East [*A publication*] (MAR)
JET .... J. E. Thiebaut & Cie. [*Malagasy*] (MAR)
JET .... Jewish Effectiveness Training (MAR)
JET .... Junta de Estudiantes Tradicionalistas [*Junta of Traditionalist Students*] [*Spanish*] (WER)
JETCO .... Jamaica Export Trading Company (LA1)
JETRO .... Japan External Trade Organization (SJT)
JETRO .... Japanese External Trade Office (MAR)
JETS .... Junior Engineers, Technicians, Scientists (MAR)
JEUBAKAT .... Jeunesses Balubakat (MAR)
JEUCAFRA .... Jeunesse Camerounaise Francaise (MAR)
JEWEL .... Joint Endeavour for Welfare, Education, and Liberation [*In name of Grenadian political party, the New Jewel Movement, which governed from 1979 until ousted by a coup in 1983. Maurice Bishop, a founder of the party and prime minister under it, was killed during the overthrow*]
JEYESCO .... Justice Eyeson Memorial College (MAR)
Jez .... Jezioro [*Lake*] [*Polish*] (NAU)
Jez .... Jezirat [*Island, Peninsula*] [*Arabic*] (NAU)
jez .... Jezyk [*Language*] (POL)
jez oryg .... Jezyk Oryginalu [*Original Language*] [*Polish*]
jf .... Javnfor [*Compare*] [*Danish*] (GPO)
JF .... Juznoslovenski Filolog [*South Slavic Philologist*] [*Belgrade*] [*A periodical*] (YU)
JFC .... Jungle Force Companies (ML)
JFL .... Jamaica Freedom League (LA1)
JFLN .... Jeunesse du Front de Liberation Nationale [*National Liberation Front Youth*] [*Algerian*] (AF)
JFM .... Jeunesses Federalistes Mondiales
JFM .... Junkers Flugzeug-und-Motorenwerk [*Junkers Aircraft and Engines Plant*] (EG)
JFNDR .... Jeunesse du Front National pour la Defense de la Revolution [*Youth of the National Front for the Defense of the Revolution*] [*Malagasy*] (AF)
JFNLA .... Juventude da Frente Nacional de Libertacao de Angola [*Youth of the Angolan National Liberation Front*] (AF)
JFP .... Jednotny Fond Pracujicich [*Workers United Fund*] (CZ)
JFPLN .... Juventude da Frente Patriotica de Libertacao Nacional (MAR)
jfr .... Jamfor [*Compare*] [*Swedish*] (GPO)
jfr .... Javnfor [*Compare*] [*Danish*] (GPO)
JFRO .... Joint Fisheries Research Organization of Northern Rhodesia and Nyassaland (MAR)
JFSP .... Juventude da Frente Socialista Popular [*Socialist Popular Youth Front*] [*Portuguese*] (WER)
JFTU .... Jordanian Federation of Trade Unions (MAR)
Jg .... Jahrgang [*Year's Set*] [*German*]
Jgdhbg .... Jugendherberge [*German*]
JGE .... Junta de Generales del Ejercito [*Army Council of Generals*] [*Uruguayan*] (LA)
JGG .... Jugendgerichtsgesetz [*Juvenile Court Law*] (EG)
JGK .... Jandarma Genel Komutanligi [*Gendarmery General Command*] [*Interior Ministry*] (TU)
JGR .... Joven Guardia Roja [*Young Red Guard*] [*Spanish*] (WER)
JGRN .... Junta de Gobierno de Reconstruccion Nacional [*Junta of the Government of National Reconstruction*] [*Nicaraguan*] (LA1)
JGS .... Jeunes Gardes Socialistes [*Young Socialist Guards*] [*Belgian*] (WER)
jgyz .... Jegyzek [*List, Catalog, Memorandum*] (HU)
Jh .... Jahrhundert [*German*]
JH .... Jugendherberge [*German*]
JHC .... Joint High Command (MAR)
Jhdte .... Jahrhunderte [*German*]
JHDV .... Jewish Historical Documentation Centre, Vienna (MAR)
jhk .... Johonkin [*Finnish*]
jhk .... Johonkuhun [*Finnish*]
JHK .... Jugendhilfekommission [*Youth Aid Commission*] (EG)
JHR .... Jednotlive Hospodarici Rolnici [*Individual Farmers*] (CZ)
JHS .... Journal Historique du Sokoto [*A publication*] (MAR)
JHSN .... Journal of the Historical Society of Nigeria [*Ibadan*] [*A publication*] (MAR)
JHVO .... Jugendhilfeverordnung [*Youth Aid Decree*] (EG)
JI .... Jugoistok [*Southeast*] (YU)
JIB .... Djibouti Airport (MAR)
JIB .... Journal of the Institute of Bankers [*A publication*] (MAR)
JIB .... Jugoslovenska Investiciona Banka [*Yugoslav Investment Bank*] (YU)
JIC .... Jugoslovenski Istoriski Casopis [*Yugoslav Historical Journal*] (YU)
JICANA .... Joint Intelligence Collecting Agency, North Africa (MAR)
JICI .... Jeunesse Independante Chretienne Internationale [*International Independent Christian Youth - IICY*] (EA)
JICST .... Japan Information Centre of Science and Technology
JID .... Junta Inter-Americana de Defensa [*Inter-American Defense Board*] [*Use IADB*] (LA)
JIDC .... Jamaica Industrial Development Corporation (LA1)
JIDC .... Junta Inter-Americana de Defensa Continental [*Inter-American Board for Continental Defense*] (LA)
JIF .... Journees Ivoiriennes du Froid (MAR)
JIM .... Jamaica Institute of Management (LA1)
Jin .... Jardin [*Garden*] [*Military map abbreviation*] [*World War I*] [*French*] (MTD)
JIN .... Junta de Inteligencia Nacional [*National Intelligence Board*] [*Colombian*] (LA)
JIPDC .... Japan-Iraq Petroleum Development Corporation (SJT)
JIR .... Jeunes Instituteurs Revolutionnaires [*Young Revolutionary School Teachers*] [*Beninese*] (AF)
JIRA .... Journal. International Relations Association. University of Dar Es Salaam [*A publication*] (MAR)
JIRAMA .... Societe Jiro sy Rano Malagasy [*Malagasy Electricity and Water Company*] (AF)
JIS .... Jamaica Information Service [*Formerly, API*] (LA1)
JIS .... Japanese Industrial Standards (SJT)
JIT .... Jamiat-i-Talaba [*Pakistani*] (PD)
JITK .... Jugoslovensko-Italijanska Trgovinska Komora [*Yugoslav-Italian Chamber of Commerce*] [*Belgrade*] (YU)
JIU .... Joint Inspection Unit (MAR)
jj .... Juoksujalka(a) [*Finnish*]
JJCC .... Juventudes Comunistas [*Communist Youth*] [*Spanish*] (WER)
JJI .... Jug Jugo-Istok [*South Southeast*] (YU)
JJLL .... Juventudes Libertarias [*Anarchist Youth*] [*Spanish*] (WER)
JJP .... Jatiya Janata Party [*National People's Party*] [*Bangladesh*] (PPW)
JJSS .... Juventudes Socialistas [*Socialist Youth*] [*Spanish*] (WER)
jjv .... Jiho-Jihovychod [*South-Southeast*] (CZ)
JJV .... Jug Jugovzhod [*South-Southeast*] (YU)
jjz .... Jiho-Jihozapad [*South-Southwest*] (CZ)
JJZ .... Jug Jugo-Zapad [*South-Southwest*] (YU)
JK .... Jalkikirjoitus [*Finnish*]
jk .... Jegyzek [*List, Catalog, Memorandum*] (HU)
jk .... Jokin [*Finnish*]
jk .... Joku [*Finnish*]
JKACI .... Jeunes Khmers Anti-Communistes Indochinois [*Young Cambodians Against Indochinese Communism*] (CL)
jkh .... Johonkuhun [*Finnish*]
JKI .... Jugoslovenska Krznarska Industrija [*Yugoslav Fur Industry*] [*Indija*] (YU)
JKIA .... Jajasan Kesedjahteraan Ibu dan Anak [*Welfare Foundation for Mothers and Children*] (IN)
jklla .... Jollakulla [*Finnish*]
jklle .... Jollekulle [*Finnish*]
jklta .... Joltakulta [*Finnish*]
JKM .... Jego Krolewska Mosc [*His Royal Majesty*] [*Polish*]
JKMci .... Jego Krolewskiej Mosci [*His Royal Majesty's*] [*Polish*]
JKMosci .... Jego Krolewskiej Mosci [*His Royal Majesty's*] [*Polish*]
jkn .... Jonkun [*Finnish*]
jkna .... Jonakuna [*Finnish*]
JKNC .... Jammu and Kashmir National Conference [*Indian*] (PPW)
JKol .... Jadranski Koledar [*Adriatic Almanac*] [*A periodical*] (YU)
JKP .... Jawatankuasa Perhubungan [*Public Relations Committee*] (ML)
JKPN .... Jabatan Kuasa Kerja Perang Negeri [*State War Executive Committee*] (ML)
JKR .... Jabatan Kerja Raya [*Public Works Department*] (ML)
jKr .... Jalkeen Kristuksen Syntyman [*Finnish*]
jksk .... Joksikin [*Finnish*]
jksk .... Joksikuksi [*Finnish*]
jkssa .... Jossakussa [*Finnish*]
jksta .... Jostakusta [*Finnish*]
JKT .... National Development Army [*Tanzanian*] (AF)
jkta .... Jotakuta [*Finnish*]
JKU .... Jeshi la Kujenga Uchumi (MAR)
JKU .... Youth Contact for International Solidarity and Exchange [*Dutch*] (WEN)
jkv .... Jegyzokonyv [*Minutes*] (HU)
jkvo .... Jegyzokonyvvezeto [*Recording Secretary*] (HU)
jkvv .... Jegyzokonyvvezeto [*Recording Secretary*] (HU)
JKW .... Jego Krolewska Wysokosc [*His Royal Highness*] [*Polish*]

Jl .... Jabal [*Jabel, Jebel*] [*Mountain, Hill*] [*See also J*] [*Arabic*] (NAU)
JL .... Jabatan Laut [*Navy Department*] (ML)
Jl .... Jalan [*Street*]
jl .... Jongstleden [*Last*] [*Dutch*] (GPO)
JLA .... Jamaica Livestock Association (LA1)
JLA .... Jugoslovanska Ljudska Armija [*Yugoslav People's Army*] (YU)
JLAO .... Journal of Local Administration Overseas [*A publication*] (MAR)
JLJM .... Jurutera Letrik dan Jentera Malaysia [*Malaysian Electrical and Mechanical Engineers*] (ML)
jllak .... Jollakin [*Finnish*]
jllak .... Jollakulla [*Finnish*]
jllek .... Jollekin [*Finnish*]
jllek .... Jollekulle [*Finnish*]
jllk .... Jollekin [*Finnish*]
JLP .... Jamaica Labour Party (PPW)
JLPC .... Johannesburg Light Plane Club (MAR)
JLR .... Junta Local de Reconstruccion [*Local Reconstruction Board*] [*Nicaraguan*] (LA1)
jltk .... Joltakin [*Finnish*]
jltk .... Joltakulta [*Finnish*]
JM .... Jamaica [*Two-letter standard code*] (CNC)
JM .... Jang Mulia [*The Honorable, His Excellency, Your Excellency*] (IN)
j M .... Jednostka Macke'a [*Macke Unit*] [*Polish*]
jm .... Jednostka Masy Magnetycznej [*Magnetic Unit*] [*Polish*]
JM .... Jego Magnificencja [*Rector's title*] [*Polish*]
JM .... Jeho Magnificence [*Academic title of the president of a university*] (CZ)
JM .... Jeunesse Militante [*Militant Youth*] [*Mauritian*] (AF)
jm .... Jmeno [*Name*] (CZ)
JM .... Journal Militaire [*French*] (MTD)
JMA .... Jamaica Manufacturers Association (LA1)
JMAE .... Junta Militar Angolano no Exilio (MAR)
JMAS .... Journal of Modern African Studies [*Cambridge*] [*A publication*] (MAR)
JMB .... Jeunesse Musulmane de Bardo [*Tunisian*] (MAR)
JMB .... Joint Matriculation Board (MAR)
JMci .... Jego Mosci [*The Honorable Gentleman's*] [*Polish*]
JMD .... Jeoloji ve Maden Dairesi [*Geology and Mining Department (Office)*] [*Turkish Cypriot*] (GC)
JMD .... Jihomoravske Doly [*South Moravian Mines*] (CZ)
JME .... Jihomoravske Energeticke Zavody [*South-Moravian Electrical Power Plants*] (CZ)
JMF .... Jeunesses Musicales de France [*Young People's Musical Association of France*] (WER)
JMGK .... Juznomoravska Grupa Korpusa [*Southern Moravia Group of Corps*] [*World War II*] (YU)
J-MIR .... Juventud-Movimiento de la Izquierda Revolucionaria [*Youth Movement of the Revolutionary Left*] [*Venezuelan*] (LA)
JML .... Jihomoravske Lignitove Doly [*South Moravian Lignite Mines*] (CZ)
JML .... Jihomoravsky Lignitovy Revir [*South Moravian Lignite Basin*] (CZ)
JMN .... Johan Mangku Negara [*Third Grade of the Most Distinguished Order of Pangkuan Negara*] [*Malaysian*] (ML)
JMNA .... Juventude Movimento Nacional de Angola [*Youth of the Angolan National Movement*] (AF)
JMNCL .... Jeunesse du Mouvement National Congolaise-Lumumba (MAR)
JMNR .... Jeunesse du Mouvement National de la Revolution (MAR)
JMNS .... Jednota Mladych Narodnich Socialistu [*Youth Association of the National Socialist Party*] (CZ)
JMO .... Jugoslovenska Muslimanska Organizacija [*Yugoslav Moslem Organization*] (PPE)
JMPLA .... Juventude Movimento Popular de Libertacao de Angola [*Youth of the Popular Movement for the Liberation of Angola*] (AF)
JMPR .... Jeunesse du Mouvement Populaire de la Revolution [*Youth of the Popular Movement of the Revolution*] [*Zairian*] (AF)
JMPS .... Jeunesse Marocaine pour le Progres et le Socialisme [*Moroccan Youth for Progress and Socialism*] (AF)
JMPST PW ... Jaworznicko-Mikolowskie Przedsiebiorstwo Spedycyjno-Transportowe Przemyslu Weglowego [*Jaworznik-Mikolow Coal Industry Forwarding and Transport Enterprise*] (POL)
JMRL .... Juventudes del Movimiento Revolucionario Liberal [*Youth of the Liberal Revolutionary Movement*] [*Colombian*] (LA)
jms .... Ja Muuta Sellaista [*Finnish*]
jms .... Ja Muuta Semmoista [*Finnish*]
JMTR .... Japan-Made Material Testing Reactor (SJT)
jn .... Jak Nizej [*As Below*] [*Polish*]
JN .... Jeunesse Nationaliste (MAR)
JN .... Jugoslavenska Njiva [*Zagreb*] [*A periodical*] (YU)
JNA .... Jordanian News Agency (ME)
JNA .... Jugoslovenska Narodna Armija [*Yugoslav People's Army*] (YU)
jnak .... Jonakin [*Finnish*]
jnak .... Jonakuna [*Finnish*]
JNB .... Jugoslovenska Narodna Banka [*Yugoslav National Bank*] (YU)
JNC .... Jeunesse Nationale Camerounaise [*Cameroonian National Youth*] (AF)
JND .... Jihoceske Narodni Divadlo [*South Bohemian National Theater*] (CZ)
JNDA .... Junta Nacional de Distribucion de los Abastecimientos [*National Board for Distribution of Supplies*] [*Cuban*] (LA)
jne .... Ja Niin Edelleen [*Et Cetera, And So On*] [*Finnish*]
jne .... Ja Niin Edespain [*And So On*] [*Finnish*] (GPO)
Jne .... Jeune [*Junior*] [*Business and trade*] [*French*]
JNE .... Jurado Nacional de Elecciones [*National Election Jury*] [*Peruvian*] (LA)
JNEC .... Jamaica National Export Corporation (LA1)
JNF .... Japan Nuclear Fuel Co. Ltd. [*A joint entity set up by Toshiba, Hitachi, and US General Electric*] (SJT)
JNF .... Jewish National Fund [*Israeli*] (ME)
JNG .... Junta Nacional de Granos [*National Grain Board*] [*Argentine*] (LA)
jni .... Juoksumetria [*Finnish*]
JNIC .... Jamaica National Investment Company (LA1)
JNIP .... Jamaica National Investment Promotions (LA1)
JNj .... Jugoslavenska Njiva [*Zagreb*] [*A periodical*] (YU)
JNK .... Jeunesse Nationale Katangaise (MAR)
jnk .... Jonkin [*Finnish*]
jnk .... Jonkun [*Finnish*]
JNKFAO ...... Jugoslovenska Nacionalna Komisija za Saradnju sa FAO [*Yugoslav National Commission for Cooperation with FAO*] (YU)
JNKMOR ..... Jugoslovenska Nacionalna Komisija za Medunarodnu Organizaciju Rada [*Yugoslav National Commission for the International Labor Organization*] (YU)
JNKUNESKO ... Jugoslovenska Nacionalna Komisija za UNESKO [*Yugoslav National Commission for UNESCO*] (YU)
JNL .... Jeunesse Nationale Lumumbiste (MAR)
jnnk .... Jonnekin [*Finnish*]
JNO .... Jugoslovenski Narodni Odbor [*Yugoslav National Committee*] (YU)
JNOF .... Jedinstveni Narodno Oslobodilacki Front [*United National Liberation Front*] (YU)
JNOF .... Jugoslovenski Narodnooslobodilacki Front [*Yugoslav National Liberation Front*] (YU)
JNP .... Juventud Nacionalista Popular [*Nationalist Popular Youth*] [*Colombian*] (LA)
JNPN .... Jeunesse Nationale Pierre Ngendenduniwe (MAR)
JNPP .... Junta Nacional dos Produtos Pecuarios [*National Beef Products Board*] [*Portuguese*] (WER)
JNR .... Jeunesse Nationaliste Rwagasore [*Rwagasore Nationalist Youth*] [*Burundi*] (AF)
JNRC .... Jeunesse Nationaliste Rurale du Congo (MAR)
JNS .... Jugoslovenska Nacionalna Stranka [*Yugoslav National Party*] (PPE)
JNV .... Jednotny Narodni Vybor [*United National Committee*] (CZ)
JNV .... Junta Nacional do Vinho [*National Wine Board*] [*Portuguese*] (WER)
JO .... Jasnie Oswiecony [*His Highness, His Grace*] [*Polish*]
JO .... Jeux Olympiques [*Olympic Games*] [*French*] (WER)
JO .... Jilemnickeho Odznak [*Jilemnicky Badge*] (CZ)
JO .... Jordan [*Two-letter standard code*] (CNC)
JO .... Journal Officiel [*Official Bulletin*] [*French*] (WER)
JO .... Jugoslovenski Odbor [*Yugoslav Committee*] (YU)
JOA .... Jawatankuasa Olimpik Antarabangsa [*International Olympic Committee*] (ML)
JOAC .... Juventud Obrera de Accion Catolica [*Catholic Action Worker Youth*] [*Spanish*] (WER)
JOAEF .... Journal Officiel, Afrique Equatoriale Francaise [*A publication*] (MAR)
JOAOF .... Journal Officiel, Afrique Occidentale Francaise [*A publication*] (MAR)
JOC .... Jeunesse Ouvriere Catholique [*Young Catholic Workers*] [*Belgian*] (WER)
JOC .... Jeunesse Ouvriere Catholique [*Young Catholic Workers*] [*Rwandan*] (AF)
JOC .... Jeunesse Ouvriere Chretienne [*Christian Workers Youth Organization*] [*Belgian*] (WER)
JOC .... Jeunesse Ouvriere Chretienne [*Christian Workers Youth Organization*] [*Reunionese*] (AF)
JOC .... Jeunesse Ouvriere Congolaise (MAR)
JOC .... Juventud Obrera Catolica [*Young Catholic Workers*] [*Spanish*] (WER)
JOC .... Juventude Operaria Catolica [*Catholic Labor Youth*] [*Portuguese*] (WER)
JOCF .... Juventud Obrera Catolica Femenina [*Catholic Young Women Workers*] [*Spanish*] (WER)
JOCI .... Juventud Obrera Catolica Internacional [*International Catholic Worker Youth*] (LA)
JOCV .... Japanese Overseas Co-Operation Volunteers (MAR)
JOEA .... Journal Officiel de l'Etat Algerien [*A publication*] (MAR)
JOESCO ...... Jovenes Escritores Colombianos [*Cali*] (COL)
JOF .... Juntas de Oposicion Falangistas [*Falangist Opposition Juntas*] [*Spanish*] (WER)
JOFA .... Jukwa, Okumaning, Fosu, and Akwansrem (MAR)
JOG .... Junta de Oficiales Generales [*Council of General Officers*] [*Uruguayan*] (LA)
jogsz .... Jogszabaly [*Legal Provision*] (HU)

jogtan......... Jogtanacsos [*Legal Counselor*] (HU)
JOH............ Johore (ML)
joht............ Johtaja [*Finnish*]
JOIDES....... Joint Oceanographic Institute for Deep Earth Sampling (MAR)
JOKA.......... People's Democratic Students of Jyvaskyla [*Finnish*] (WEN)
JOKs.......... Jasnie Oswiecony Ksiaze [*His Highness Duke Of ____*] [*Polish*]
JOL............ Jeunesse Ouvriere Luxembourgeoise [*Luxembourg Working Youth*] (WER)
JOM............ Jeunesse Ouvriere Marocaine [*Moroccan Working Youth*] (AF)
JONLINUD... Bataljon Lintas Udara [*Airborne Battalion*] (IN)
JONS.......... Juntas de Ofensiva Nacional Sindicalista [*Syndicalist Juntas of the National Offensive*] [*Spanish*] (PPE)
JOPA.......... Juventud Organizada del Pueblo en Armas [*Armed People's Organized Youth*] [*Guatemalan*] (PD)
JOPP.......... Jednotna Organisace Podnikoveho Pocetnictvi [*Standard Organization of Management Accounting*] (CZ)
jor.............. Jaror [*Patrol*] (HU)
JOR............ Jordan [*Three-letter standard code*] (CNC)
JORA.......... Journal Officiel de la Republique Algerienne [*A publication*] (MAR)
JORDM........ Journal. Republique Democratique de Madagascar [*A publication*] (MAR)
JORF.......... Journal Officiel de la Republique Francaise [*A publication*] (MAR)
JORT.......... Journal Officiel de la Republique Tunisienne [*A publication*] (MAR)
JOS............ Jeunesse Ouvriere du Senegal (MAR)
josk............ Joskus [*Sometimes*] [*Finnish*]
JOSP.......... Jezdecky Odbor Sokola Prazskeho [*Equestrian Division of the Sokol (Athletic and Gymnastic Association) in Prague*] (CZ)
JOT............ Journal Officiel Tunisien [*A publication*] (MAR)
jov.............. Jovedelem [*Income*] (HU)
JOZ............ Jugoslovanska Orlovska Zveza [*Yugoslav Union of Eagles*] [*Slovenia*] (YU)
JP.............. Jabatan Polis [*Police Department*] (ML)
JP.............. Janata Party [*Indian*] (PPW)
JP.............. Japan [*Two-letter standard code*] (CNC)
JP.............. Jasnie Pan [*His Lordship*] [*Polish*]
JP.............. Jasnie Pani [*Her Ladyship*] [*Polish*]
JP.............. Javno Paravobranilstvo [*Body of Government Attorneys*] (YU)
JP.............. Jones Party [*Maltese*] (PPE)
JP.............. Jugoplastika [*Manufacturer of plastic articles*] [*Split*] (YU)
JP.............. Junge Pioniere [*Young Pioneers*] (EG)
JP.............. Junta de Planeamento [*Planning Council*] [*Portuguese*] (WER)
JP.............. Justice Party [*Ghanaian*] (AF)
JP.............. Justice Party [*See also AP*] (TU)
JPA............ Jeunesse Pionniere Agricole [*Young Agricultural Pioneers*] [*Togolese*] (AF)
JPAT.......... Jeunesse Pionniere Agricole Togolaise [*Togolese Agricultural Pioneer Youth*] (AF)
JPC............ [*The*] Japan Productivity Center (SJT)
JPC............ Jeunesse pour Christ [*Youth for Christ International - YFCI*] (EA)
JPC............ Jeunesse Pionniere Camerounaise [*Cameroonian Pioneer Youth*] (AF)
JPC............ Jeunesse Progressiste Casamancaise (MAR)
JPC............ Joint Provincial Council (MAR)
JPD............ Jednotne Polnohospodarske Druzstvo [*United Agricultural Cooperative*] (CZ)
JPD............ Jeunesse Progressiste Dahomeenne (MAR)
JPD............ Jugoslovensko Profesorsko Drustvo [*Yugoslav Professors' Society*] (YU)
JPDA.......... Juventude do Partido Democratico Angolano [*Youth of the Angolan Democratic Party*] (AF)
JPDC.......... Jeunesse du Parti Democrate Congolais (MAR)
JPDP.......... Juventud del Partido del Pueblo [*People's Party Youth*] [*Panamanian*] (LA)
JPDR.......... Japan Power Development Reactor (SJT)
JPFNRJ....... Javno Pravobraniostvo Federativna Narodna Republika Jugoslavija [*Body of Government Attorneys of Yugoslavia*] (YU)
JPJ............ Jabatan Penyiasatan Jenayat [*Criminal Investigation Department*] (ML)
JPK............ Jabatan Pemereksa Kapal [*Shipping Survey Department*] (ML)
JPK............ Jednolity Plan Kont [*Unified Accountancy Scheme*] [*Polish*]
JPL............ Jeunesse Progressiste Luxembourgeoise [*Luxembourg Progressive Youth*] (WER)
JPMAP........ Jednota Pratel Masarykovy Akademie Prace [*Association of Friends of the Masaryk Academy of Labor*] (CZ)
JPN............ Japan [*Three-letter standard code*] (CNC)
JPN............ Jeunesse Pionniere Nationale [*National Pioneer Youth*] [*Central African*] (AF)
JPN............ Jeunesse Pionniere Nationale [*National Pioneer Youth*] [*Zairian*] (AF)
JPN............ Jeunesse Pionniere Nigerienne [*Nigerien Pioneer Youth*] [*Niger*] (AF)
JPN............ Junta Patriotica Nacional [*National Patriotic Board*] [*Ecuadorean*] (LA)
JPO-SS....... Jugoslovanski Pomozni Odbor, Slovenska Sekcija [*Yugoslav Welfare Committee, Slovenian Section*] (YU)
jpp.............. Jalkeen Puolenpaivan [*Afternoon*] [*Finnish*] (GPO)
JPP............ Jasa Perkasa Persekutuan [*Federation Gallantry Decorations*] [*Malaysian*] (ML)
JPP............ Jasnie Panowie [*The Honourables*] [*Polish*]
JPPA.......... Junta Provincial de Povoamento de Angola (MAR)
JPPM.......... Jeunesse du Parti du Peuple Mauritanien [*Youth of the Mauritanian People's Party*] (AF)
JPPM.......... Junta Provincial de Povoamento de Mocambique (MAR)
JPR............ Jeunes Professeurs Revolutionnaires [*Young Revolutionary Professors*] [*Beninese*] (AF)
JPS............ Jamaica Public Service Co. (LA1)
JPS............ Jeunesse Populaire Senegalaise (MAR)
JPS............ Juventud Popular Socialista [*Socialist Popular Youth*] [*Mexican*] (LA)
JPT............ Jednota Proletarske Telovychovy [*Proletarian Physical Education Association*] (CZ)
JPT............ Juventud del Partido de Trabajo [*Labor Party Youth*] [*Guatemalan*] (LA)
JPTT.......... Jugoslovenske Poste, Telegrafi, i Telefoni [*Yugoslav Post, Telegraph, and Telephone Services*] (YU)
JR.............. El Jarida Ar-Rasmiya [*Libyan*] [*A publication*] (MAR)
jr................ Jaar [*Year*] [*Dutch*] (GPO)
JR.............. Jonkheer [*Dutch*]
jr................ Jour [*Day*] [*French*]
JR.............. Jugoslovenski Radio [*Yugoslav Radio*] (YU)
jr................ Jungere [*Junior*] [*Business and trade*] [*German*]
Jr................ Junior [*Junior*] [*Dutch*] (GPO)
jr................ Junior [*Finnish*]
JR.............. Junta Revolucionaria [*Revolutionary Junta*] [*Peruvian*] (LA)
JR.............. Juventud Radical [*Radical Youth*] [*Chilean*] (LA)
JRAI............ Journal of the Royal Anthropological Institute of Great Britain and Ireland [*A publication*] (MAR)
JRAS.......... Journal of the Royal Asiatic Society of Great Britain and Ireland [*A publication*] (MAR)
JRB............ Jugoslovenski Registar Brodova [*Yugoslav Ship Register*] (YU)
JRB............ Jugoslovensko Recno Brodarstvo [*Yugoslav River Shipping*] (YU)
JRC............ Jamaica Railway Corporation (LA1)
JRC............ Jeunesse Rurale Catholique [*Catholic Rural Youth*] [*Belgian*] (WER)
JRC............ Juventud Revolucionaria Copeyana [*COPEI Revolutionary Youth*] [*Venezuelan*] (LA)
JRC............ Juventud Revolucionaria Cristiana [*Christian Revolutionary Youth*] [*Dominican Republic*] (LA1)
JRC............ Juventudes Revolucionarias Catalanas [*Catalan Revolutionary Youth*] [*Spanish*] (WER)
JRD............ Jednotne Riadeni Dopravy [*Unified Control Over Transportation*] (CZ)
JRD............ Jednotne Rolnicke Druzstvo [*United Agricultural Cooperative in Slovakia*] (CZ)
JRDA.......... Jeunesse du Rassemblement Democratique Africain (MAR)
JRDA.......... Jeunesse de la Revolution Democratique Africaine [*Youth of the African Democratic Revolution*] [*Guinean*] (AF)
JRDACI....... Jeunesse de RDA de la Cote-d'Ivoire [*Youth of the RDA in Ivory Coast*] (AF)
JRDS.......... Jugoslovenska Republikanska Demokratska Stranka [*Yugoslav Republican Democratic Party*] (YU)
JRF............ Juventud Revolucionaria Febrerista [*Revolutionary Febrerist Youth*] [*Paraguayan*] (LA)
JRG............ Junta Revolucionaria de Gobierno [*Revolutionary Governing Junta*] [*Salvadoran*] (LA1)
JRK............ Jeunesse de la Republique Khmere [*Cambodian Republic Youth*] (CL)
JRK............ Jugoslovanski Rdeci Kriz [*Yugoslav Red Cross*] (YU)
JRLI............ Junta Revolucionaria de Libertacao Iberica (MAR)
JRM............ Jugoslovenska Ratna Mornarica [*Yugoslav Navy*] (YU)
JRN............ Junta de Reconstruccion Nacional [*Junta of National Reconstruction*] [*Nicaraguan*] (LA1)
JRO............ Jugoslovenska Ravnogorska Omladina [*Yugoslav Ravna Gora Youth*] [*World War II*] (YU)
JRP............ Juventud Revolucionaria del Peru [*Peruvian Revolutionary Youth*] (LA)
Jrprok......... Jednaci Rad Prokuratur [*Regulations for Public Prosecutors*] (CZ)
JRPT.......... Jeunesse du Rassemblement du Peuple Togolais [*Youth of the Rally of the Togolese People*] (AF)
JRR............ Japan Research Reactor (SJT)
JRR............ Jeunesse Revolutionnaire Rwagasore [*Rwagasore Revolutionary Youth*] [*Burundi*] (AF)
JRRP.......... Junta Reguladora de Remuneraciones y Precios [*Wage and Price Control Board*] [*Chilean*] (LA)
Jrs.............. Jednaci Rad Soudni [*Court Rules*] (CZ)
JRS............ Jugoslovenska Radnicka Stranka [*Yugoslav Workers' Party*] (YU)
JRUV.......... Juventud Revolucionaria. Universidad del Valle [*Cali*] (COL)
JRV............ Jugoslovensko Ratno Vazduhoplovstvo [*Yugoslav Air Force*] (YU)
JRZ............ Jugoslovenska Radikalna Zajednica [*Yugoslav Radical Union*] (PPE)

JS .... Jeunes Socialistes [*Young Socialists*] [*Belgian*] (WER)
JS .... Jeunesse de Sauvetage [*Salvation Youth*] [*Cambodian*] (CL)
JS .... Jugoslavenska Suma [*Yugoslav Forest*] [*Belgrade, Zagreb*] [*A periodical*] (YU)
JS .... Jugoslovanski Sokol [*The Yugoslav Hawk*] [*An organization for physical culture and sport*] (YU)
JS .... Juventud Socialista [*Socialist Youth*] [*Chilean*] (LA)
JS .... Juventud Socialista [*Socialist Youth*] [*Nicaraguan*] (LA)
JS .... Juventude Socialista [*Socialist Youth*] [*Portuguese*] (WER)
JS .... Juzna Sirina [*Southern Latitude*] (YU)
JSA .... Jeunesse pour la Solidarite Africaine (MAR)
JSA .... Journal de la Societe des Africanistes [*Paris*] [*A publication*] (MAR)
JSC .... Jamaica School Certificate (LA1)
JSC .... Juventud Socialista Costarricense [*Costa Rican Socialist Youth*] (LA)
JSCF .... Jamaica Special Constabulary Force (LA1)
JSCs .... Jezdecky Svaz Ceskoslovensky [*Czechoslovak Equestrian Association*] (CZ)
JSCZ .... Jednotny Svaz Ceskych Zemedelcu [*Central Union of Czech Farmers*] (CZ)
JSD .... Jatiya Samajtantrik Dal [*National Socialist Party*] [*Bangladesh*] (PPW)
JSD .... Jeunesse Sociale Democrate [*Social Democratic Youth*] [*Malagasy*] (AF)
JSD .... Johan Setia Di-Raja [*Second Grade of the Most Honorable Order of Setia Di-Raja*] [*Malaysian*] (ML)
JSD .... Jugoslovensko Statisticko Drustvo [*Yugoslav Statistical Society*] (YU)
JSD .... Juventude Social-Democratica [*Social Democratic Youth*] [*Portuguese*] (WER)
JSE .... Johannesburg Stock Exchange (MAR)
JS/IWAL ..... Jeco Shipping/Interwave West Africa Line (MAR)
JSJ .... Jabatan Siasatan Jenayat [*Criminal Investigation Department*] (ML)
JS 19 J .... Juventud Sandinista 19 de Julio [*19 July Sandinist Youth*] [*Nicaraguan*] (LA1)
JSK .... Jeunesse Sportive Kairouanaise (MAR)
JSK .... Jeunesse du Sud-Kasai
JSL .... Jeunesse Socialiste Luxembourgeoise [*Luxembourg Socialist Youth*] (WER)
JSM .... Johan Setia Mahkota [*Third Grade of Darjah Yarg*] (ML)
JSMIR .... Juventud Socialista Movimiento de la Izquierda Revolucionaria [*Movement of the Revolutionary Left Socialist Youth*] [*Venezuelan*] (LA)
JSN .... Junta de Salvacao Nacional [*Junta of National Salvation*] [*Portuguese*] (WER)
JSN .... Juventud Socialista Nicaraguense [*Nicaraguan Socialist Youth*] (LA)
JSP .... Japan Socialist Party [*Nikon Shakaito*] (PPW)
JSP .... Jugoslovensko Stamparsko Preduzece [*Yugoslav Printing Establishment*] [*Belgrade*] (YU)
JSP .... Juventud Social Progresista [*Progressive Social Youth*] [*Peruvian*] (LA)
JSPP .... Joint Council of Swaziland Political Parties (MAR)
JSR .... Juventudes Socialistas Revolucionarias [*Revolutionary Socialist Youth*] [*Spanish*] (WER)
JSRK .... Jeunesse Socialiste Royale Khmere [*Royal Cambodian Socialist Youth*] (CL)
JSS .... Jednota Spolecenstev Stavitelu [*Association of Builders' Cooperatives*] (CZ)
JSS .... Jednotna Stredni Skola [*Uniform Secondary School*] (CZ)
jssk .... Jossakin [*Finnish*]
jssk .... Jossakussa [*Finnish*]
JSSP .... Jednolity System Stenografii Polskiej [*Standardized System of Polish Stenography*] (POL)
JSSR .... Jednotny Svaz Slovenskych Rolnikov [*Central Association of Slovak Farmers*] (CZ)
jstk .... Jostakin [*Finnish*]
jstk .... Jostakusta [*Finnish*]
JSU .... Juventudes Socialistas Unificadas [*Unified Socialist Youth*] [*Ecuadorean*] (LA)
JSZ .... Jednota Slovanskych Zen [*Association of Slavic Women*] (CZ)
jt .... Jarasi Tanacs [*District Council*] (HU)
JT .... Jatekvezetok Testulete [*Association of Sports Referees*] (HU)
JT .... Javno Tozilstvo [*Public Prosecutors*] (YU)
JT .... Johnston Atoll [*Two-letter standard code*] (CNC)
JTA .... Jabatan Pertahan Awam [*Public (or Civil) Defense Department*] (ML)
JTA .... Jamaica Teachers Association (LA1)
JTB .... Jamaica Tourist Board (LA1)
JTC .... Jamaica Telephone Company (LA1)
JTC .... Jurong Town Corporation [*Singapore*] (ML)
JTC .... Juventud Trabajadora Colombiana [*Colombian Worker Youth*] (LA)
JTFLRJ .... Javno Tozilstvo Federativna Ljudska Republika Jugoslavija [*Public Prosecutors of Yugoslavia*] (YU)
JTFNRJ .... Javno Tuziostvo Federativna Narodna Republika Jugoslavija [*Public Prosecutors of Yugoslavia*] (YU)
jtk .... Jotakin [*Finnish*]
jtk .... Jotakuta [*Finnish*]
JTK .... Jugoslovenska Trgovinska Komora [*Yugoslav Chamber of Commerce*] (YU)
JTL .... Juapong Textiles Limited (MAR)
JTM .... Jeunes Travailleurs Marocains (MAR)
JTN .... Johnston Atoll [*Three-letter standard code*] (CNC)
JTO .... Jeunesse Travailleuse Oubanguienne (MAR)
JTS .... Japan Tobacco and Salt Public Corp.
JTT .... Jednotny Transitni Tarif [*Standard Transit Tariff*] (CZ)
JTURDC ...... Joint Trade Unions Research Development Center [*Jamaican*] (LA1)
jtv .... Jarasi Tanacs ala Rendelt Varos [*Town Administered by a District Council*] (HU)
JU .... Jeunesse Universelle
JUBM .... Jajasan Urusan Bahan Makanan [*Food Affairs Board*] (IN)
JUC .... Jabatan Urusan China [*Chinese Affairs Department*] (ML)
JUC .... Juventud Universitaria Catolica [*Catholic University Youth*] [*Argentine*] (LA)
JUC .... Kandidat Prav (Iuris Utriusque Candidatus) [*Candidate for a Law Degree*] (CZ)
JUCEI .... Junta de Coordinacion, Ejecucion, e Inspeccion [*Coordination, Execution, and Inspection Board*] [*Cuban*] (LA)
JUCEPLAN ... Junta Central de la Planificacion [*Central Planning Board*] [*Cuban*] (LA)
JUCO .... Juventud Comunista [*Communist Youth*] [*Colombian*] (LA)
JUD .... Jeunesse d'Union Dahomeenne (MAR)
JUD .... Juris Utriusque Doctor [*Doctor of Both Civil and Canon Law*] [*Latin*] (GPO)
JUDECA ...... Juventud Democrata Cristiana de America [*Christian Democratic Youth of America*] (LA)
JUDr .... Doctor of Law [*Czechoslovak*]
JUDr .... Doktor Prav (Iuris Utriusque Doctor) [*Doctor of Law*] (CZ)
JUDRAL ...... Juventudes Democraticas Revolucionarias de America Latina [*Revolutionary Democratic Youth of Latin America*] (LA)
JUDY .... Jamaica Union of Democratic Youth (LA1)
juev .... Jueves [*Thursday*] [*Spanish*]
JUF .... Jamaica United Front (LA1)
JUFI .... Jugoslovenska Filatelisticka Izlozba [*Yugoslav Philatelic Exhibit*] (YU)
JUGEL .... Jugoslovenska Elektroprivreda [*Yugoslav Electrical Industries*] (YU)
JUGELEKSPORT ... Eksport Elektricne Energije iz Jugoslavije [*Electric Power Export from Yugoslavia*] (YU)
JUGOAGENCIJA ... Jugoslovenska Pomorska Agencija [*Yugoslav Maritime Agency*] [*Belgrade*] (YU)
JUGOAGENT ... Jugoslovenska Pomorska Agencija [*Yugoslav Maritime Agency*] [*Belgrade*] (YU)
JUGOALAT ... Fabrika Alata [*Tool Factory*] [*Novi Sad*] (YU)
JUGOALKO ... Proizvodnja Alkoholnih Pijac [*Alcoholic Beverages Production*] [*Maribor*] (YU)
JUGOAUTO ... Yugoslav Automobile Import-Export [*Belgrade*] (YU)
JUGOAZBET ... Industrija Azbesta [*Asbestos Industry*] [*Mladenovac*] (YU)
JUGOBANKA ... Jugoslovenska Banka za Spoljnu Trgovinu [*Yugoslav Foreign Trade Bank*] (YU)
JUGODIJETETIKA ... Tvornica Farmaceutsko Dijetetskih Proizvoda [*Pharmaceutical and Dietetic Products Factory*] [*Zagreb*] (YU)
JUGODRVO ... Preduzece za Prodaju Drveta [*Establishment for the Sale of Lumber*] [*Beograd*] (YU)
JUGOELEKTRO ... Preduzece za Izvoz i Uvoz Elektricnog Materijala [*Electrical Equipment Export and Import Establishment*] (YU)
JUGOFOTO ... Yugoslovenska Foto Agencija [*Yugoslav Photograph Agency*] [*Beograd*] (YU)
JUGOFUND ... Jugoslovensko Preduzece za Fundiranje [*Yugoslav Establishment for Building Foundations*] [*Belgrade*] (YU)
JUGOINVEST ... Zajednica Preduzeca za Investicionu Izgradnju u Inostranstvu [*Union of Establishments for Foreign Investment Development*] [*Belgrade*] (YU)
JUGOKOZA ... Yugoslav Wool and Hide Trade (YU)
JUGOLEK .... Preduzece za Izvoz i Uvoz Lekova [*Yugoslav Pharmaceutical Export-Import Establishment*] (YU)
JUGOLINIJA ... Jugoslovenska Linijska Plovidba [*The Yugoslav Passenger Line*] [*Rijeka*] (YU)
JUGOMETAL ... Preduzece za Uvoz i Izvoz Ruda i Metala [*Yugoslav Ores and Metal Export-Import Establishment*] [*Belgrade*] (YU)
JUGOMINERAL ... Poduzece za Izvoz i Uvoz Ruda, Metala, Legura, i Nemetala [*Establishment for Export and Import of Ores, Metals, Alloys, and Nonmetals*] [*Zagreb*] (YU)
JUGOMONT ... Tvornica Montaznih Kuca [*Factory of Prefabricated Houses*] [*Zagreb*] (YU)
JUGONAFTA ... Preduzece za Uvoz i Izvoz Nafte i Naftinih Derivativa [*Export-Import Establishment for Petroleum and Its Derivatives*] [*Zagreb*] (YU)
JUGOPAPIR ... Preduzece za Spoljnu i Unutrasnju Trgovinu Papirom i Kancelarijskim Materijalom [*Establishment for Domestic and Foreign Trade in Paper and Office Equipment*] (YU)
JUGOPETROL ... Yugoslav Petrol and Petrol Derivatives Trade [*Zagreb*] (YU)
JUGOPLASTIKA ... Tvornica Plasticnih Masa [*Plastics Factory*] [*Kastel Sucurac*] (YU)
JUGOPRES ... Jugoslovenska Novinska Agencija [*Yugoslav News Agency*] [*Belgrade*] (YU)

JUGOPROEKT ... Proektantsko Pretprijatie [*Industrial Design Establishment*] [*Skopje*] (YU)
JUGOPROJEKT ... Preduzece za Izradu Gradevinskih i Elektromasinskih Projekata [*Enterprise for Drafting Construction and Electrical Engineering Designs*] (YU)
JUGORADIO ... Preduzece za Promet Radio Aparatima i Elektromaterijalom [*Radio Apparatus and Electric Materials Establishment*] (YU)
JUGOREGISTAR ... Jugoslovenski Registar Brodova [*Yugoslav Ships' Register*] (YU)
JUGOREKLAM ... Preduzece za Privrednu Reklamu [*Industrial Advertising Establishment*] (YU)
JUGORIBA ... Poduzece za Eksport-Import Ribljih Proizvoda [*Canned Fish Export-Import Establishment*] [*Zagreb*] (YU)
JUGOSANITARIJA ... Poduzece za Uvoz i Izvoz i Raspodelu Lekarskog i Sanitetskog Materijala [*Establishment for Import, Export, and Distribution of Medical Instruments and Apparatus*] (YU)
JUGOSEMEKOOP ... Proizvodnja Svih Vrsti Semena [*Yugoslav Seed Production Cooperative*] (YU)
jugosl .... Jugoslavenski [*Yugoslav*] (YU)
JUGOSPED ... Preduzece za Medunarodnu Spediciju i Javna Skladista [*Agency for International Forwarding and Public Warehouses*] (YU)
JUGOTEKSTIL ... Preduzece za Promet Tekstilom [*Yugoslav Textile Trade Establishment*] (YU)
JUGOTRANSPORT ... Yugoslav Agency for International Forwarding and Warehouses [*Zagreb*] (YU)
JUGOTURBINA ... Tvornica Parnih Turbina i Dizel Motora [*Yugoslav Steam Turbines and Diesel Engines Factory*] [*Karlovac*] (YU)
JUGOTURIST ... Preduzece za Turisticku Stamparsko-Izdavacku Delatnost [*Printing and Publishing Establishment for Tourism*] [*Belgrade*] (YU)
JUGOUGOSTITELJ ... Preduzece za Snabdevanje Ugostiteljstva Opremom [*Hotel and Catering Equipment Establishment*] (YU)
JUGOVINO ... Yugoslav Alcoholic Beverage Trade (YU)
JUGOVISKOZA ... Preduzece za Proizvodnju Viskoze [*Viscose Production Establishment*] [*Loznica*] (YU)
jugozap .... Jugozapadni [*Southwestern*] (YU)
Juil .... Juillet [*July*] [*French*]
jul .... Julho [*July*] [*Portuguese*] (GPO)
Jul .... Juli [*July*] [*German*] (GPO)
jul .... Julius [*July*] [*Hungarian*] (GPO)
julk .... Julkaisija [*Finnish*]
julk .... Julkaissut [*Finnish*]
JUMP.......... Jugoslovensko Udruzenje za Medunarodno Pravo [*Yugoslav International Law Association*] (YU)
jun .... Junho [*June*] [*Portuguese*] (GPO)
Jun .... Juni [*June*] [*German*] (GPO)
jun .... Junior [*German*]
jun .... Junior [*Finnish*]
jun .... Junior [*Junior*] [*Polish*]
jun .... Juniore [*Junior*] [*Italian*]
jun .... Junius [*June*] [*Hungarian*] (GPO)
JUN .... Junta Unificadora Nacional [*National Unifying Board*] [*Chilean*] (LA)
JUNA........... Juventude da Uniao Nacional Angolana [*Youth of the Angolan National Union*] (AF)
JUNAC .... Junta del Acuerdo de Cartagena [*Cartagena Agreement Board*] (LA1)
JUNAC .... Juventud Nacionalista Costarricense [*Costa Rican Nationalist Youth*] (LA)
JUNAEB ...... Junta Nacional de Auxilio Escolar y Becas [*National Board of School Aid and Scholarships*] [*Chilean*] (LA)
JUNAPLA.... Junta de Planificacion y Coordinacion Economica [*National Planning and Economic Coordination Board*] [*Ecuadorean*] (LA)
JUNAPRE.... Junta Nacional de Precios de Bienes Esenciales [*National Price Control Board for Essential Commodities*] [*Ecuadorean*] (LA)
JUNC.......... Jeunesse de l'Union Nationale Camerounaise [*Cameroonian National Union Youth*] (AF)
JUNC.......... Jeunesse d'Union Nationale Congolaise (MAR)
JUNCO .... Junta de la Comunidad de Cochabamba [*Cochabamba Community Board*] [*Bolivian*] (LA)
JUNRE........ Juventud Nacionalista Revolucionaria [*Revolutionary Nationalist Youth*] [*Ecuadorean*] (LA)
JUP............. Juventud Uruguaya de Pie [*Upstanding Uruguayan Youth*] (PD)
JUPA .... Junta da Uniao das Populacoes de Angola (MAR)
JUPA .... Juventude do Uniao de Populacoes Angolanas [*Youth of the Union of Angolan People*] (AF)
JUPA .... Juventudes Patrioticas [*Patriotic Youth*] [*Colombian*] (LA)
JUPCE......... Junta Permanente de Coordinacion Educativa [*Educational Permanent Coordination Board*] [*Peruvian*] (LA)
Jur .... Jurist [*German*]
JURDC .... Juventud Universitaria Revolucionaria Democrata Cristiana [*Christian Democratic Revolutionary Youth*] [*Costa Rican*] (LA)
JUS.............. Jugoslovenski Standard [*Yugoslav Standard*] (YU)
JUSAT......... Jugoslovensko-Sovjetski Aero-Transport [*Yugoslav-Soviet Air Transport*] (YU)
JUSPAD ...... Jugoslovensko-Sovjetsko Parabrodsko Akcionarsko Drustvo [*Yugoslav-Soviet Joint-Stock Shipping Company*] (YU)
JUSRDA ...... Jeunesse Union Soudanaise, Rassemblement Democratique Africain (MAR)
JUSTA......... Jugoslovensko-Sovjetska Mesovita Drustva [*Yugoslav-Soviet Mixed Companies*] (YU)
Justsl .... Justicni Sluzba [*Juridical Service*] (CZ)
JUSU .... Juba University Students Union [*Sudanese*] (MAR)
JUT.............. Jeunesse de l'Unite Togolaise (MAR)
JUT.............. Jugoslovenski Standard za Tekstil [*Yugoslav Standard for Textiles*] (YU)
JUTA .... Jamaica Union of Travelers Association (LA1)
JUTRA......... Jurutera [*Engineers*] (ML)
JUV............. Jednota Umelcu Vytvarnych [*Creative Artists' Association*] (CZ)
JUVENTO.... Justice-Union-Vigilance-Education-Nationalisme-Tenacite-Optimisme (MAR)
JUVENTO.... Juventus Togolensis (MAR)
JUVENTO.... Mouvement de la Jeunesse Togolaise (MAR)
JUWATA ..... Jumuia ya Wafanyakazi wa Tanzania [*Tanzanian Workers Association*] (AF)
juz .... Juzen [*Southern*] (YU)
jv .... Jihovychod [*Southeast*] (CZ)
j/v............... Jour de Vue [*French*]
JV .... Jugovzhod [*Southeast*] (YU)
JVC .... Juventud de Vanguardia Comunista [*Communist Vanguard Youth*] [*Venezuelan*] (LA)
JVC .... Juventud Vanguardista Costarricense [*Costa Rican Vanguardist Youth*] (LA)
JVP............. Janatha Vimukhti Peramuna [*People's Liberation Front*] [*Sri Lankan*] (PPW)
JVP............. Jongeren Vrijwilligers Programma [*Youth Volunteer Program*] [*Dutch*] (WEN)
JVS............. Jewish Vegetarian Society (EA)
JVU............. Jednota Vytvarnych Umelcu [*Creative Artists' Association*] (CZ)
JVUO.......... Jugoslovenska Vojska u Otadzbini [*Yugoslav Army in the Fatherland*] [*World War II*] (YU)
jw................ Jak Wyzej [*As Above*] (POL)
JW .... Jasnie Wielmozny [*The Honorable*] [*Polish*]
JW .... Justizwache [*German*]
JWAC .... Joint West Africa Committee (MAR)
JWAfrL........ Journal of West African Languages [*London*] [*A publication*] (MAR)
JWAL........... Journal of West African Languages [*London*] [*A publication*] (MAR)
JWP............ Jamaican Workers' Party (PPW)
JWP............ Jasnie Wielmozny Pan [*The Honorable Gentleman*] [*Polish*]
JWV............ Junge Welt Verlag [*"Junge Welt" (Young World) Publishing House*] (EG)
jz .... Jihozapad [*Southwest*] (CZ)
JZ .... Jodzahl [*Iodine Number*] [*German*]
JZ .... Jugoslovenske Zeleznice [*Yugoslav Railroads*] (YU)
JZ .... Jugozapad [*Southwest*] (YU)
JZD............. Jednotne Zemedelske Druzstvo [*Unified Agricultural Cooperative*] (CZ)
JZF .... Jeleniogorskie Zaklady Farmaceutyczne [*Jelenia Gora (Hirschberg) Pharmaceutical Plant*] (POL)
jzo .... Jegyzo [*Clerk, Notary*] (HU)
JZP............. Jeleniogorskie Zaklady Papiernicze [*Jelenia Gora (Hirschberg) Paper Mill*] (POL)
JZPT........... Jeleniogorskie Zaklady Porcelany Technicznej [*Jelenia Gora (Hirschberg) Industrial Porcelain Plant*] (POL)
JZT .... Jugoslovenski Zavod za Telekomunikaciju [*Yugoslav Telecommunication Institute*] (YU)

K

k .... Acid (RU)
k .... Acid, Sour (RU)
K .... Arbetarpartiet Kommunisterna [*Communist Workers' Party*] [*Swedish*] (WEN)
k .... Carat (RU)
K .... Cathode (BU)
K .... Cathode (RU)
k .... Cavalry (BU)
K .... Cobalt (RU)
K .... Coke (RU)
K .... Commandant (RU)
K .... Commandant's Post (RU)
k .... Coulomb (BU)
k .... Coulomb (RU)
K- .... Crane (RU)
k .... Curie (RU)
K .... Fortress, Citadel, Stronghold (RU)
K- .... Helicopter Designed by N. I. Kamov (RU)
K .... Kaap [*Cape*] [*Dutch*] (NAU)
k .... Kade [*Quay, Wharf*] [*Dutch*] (CED)
K .... Kadinlar [*Women*] (TU)
k .... Kaiserlich [*Imperial*] [*German*]
K .... Kallio [*Rock*] [*Finnish*] (NAU)
K .... Kalorie [*Calorie*] [*German*]
k .... Kalt [*Cold*] [*German*]
K .... Kammer [*German*]
K .... Kandidaat [*Academic degree*] [*Dutch*]
K .... Kandidaatti [*Finnish*]
K .... Kandidat [*Danish*]
K .... Kandidat [*Candidate*] [*Academic*] [*Russian*]
K .... Kandidat na Naukite [*Bulgarian*]
K .... Kandidat Ved [*Czechoslovak*]
K .... Kandidatsprof [*Academic examination*] [*Icelandic*]
K .... Kandidatus [*Hungarian*]
K .... Kap [*Cape*] [*Danish*] (NAU)
K .... Kap [*Cape*] [*German*] (NAU)
K .... Kap [*Cape*] [*Swedish*] (NAU)
K .... Kapitel [*Chapter*] [*German*]
K .... Kapp [*Cape*] [*Norwegian*] (NAU)
K .... Kari [*Rock, Reef*] [*Finnish*] (NAU)
K .... Kasse [*German*]
k .... Katu [*Street*] [*Finnish*]
K .... Kelet [*East*] [*Hungarian*] (GPO)
k .... Kelt [*Dated*] (HU)
°K .... Kelvin Degree (RU)
K .... Ker [*House*] [*Military map abbreviation*] [*World War I*] [*French*] (MTD)
k .... Kerulet [*District*] (HU)
K .... Khawr [*Inlet, Channel*] [*Arabic*] (NAU)
K .... Khowr [*Inlet, Channel*] [*Persian*] (NAU)
K .... Kilogramme [*Kilogram*] [*French*] (MTD)
k .... Kis [*Small*] (HU)
K .... Kivi [*Rock*] [*Finnish*] (NAU)
K .... Kleinlokomotive [*Standard Gauge Locomotive (Possessing any of the various types of motive power, with less than 150 HP, and a maximum speed of 30 KM/P/H. This term does not include small locomotives which are used solely in the service of repair yards and the like)*] (EG)
K .... Knight [*Chess*] (RU)
K .... Koder [*or Kodra*] [*Hill*] [*Albanian*] (NAU)
k .... Koeniglich [*Royal*] [*German*]
k .... Kolo [*Near*] [*Polish*]
k .... Konnyu [*Light (such as, light artillery)*] (HU)
k .... Konska Sila [*Horsepower*] (CZ)
K .... Konstante [*Constant*] [*German*]
k .... Kopeck (RU)
K .... Kotet [*Volume*] [*Hungarian*] (GPO)
K .... Koy [*Village*] (TU)
k .... Kozseg [*Village*] (HU)
K .... Kray (RU)
K .... Kuala [*Mouth of River (Name of towns, as Kuala Lumpur, Kuala Lupis)*] (ML)
K .... Kumanda [*or Kumandan*] [*Command or Commander*] (TU)
k .... Kuoli [*Finnish*]
k .... Kuollut [*Finnish*]
K .... Kuzey [*North*] (TU)
K .... Kwacha (MAR)
K .... Large-Caliber, Heavy-Caliber (RU)
K .... Map (BU)
K .... Master Gauge (RU)
K .... Red Banner (RU)
k .... Room (RU)
k .... Short-Distance [*City transit lines*] (RU)
K .... Silicon (RU)
K .... Stone [*Road-paving material*] [*Topography*] (RU)
K .... Stony [*Nature of bottom of a ford*] [*Topography*] (RU)
°K .... Stopien Kelvina [*Degree Kelvin*] [*Polish*]
K .... Well [*Topography*] (RU)
KA .... Activity Coefficient (RU)
KA .... Address Key (RU)
KA .... Army Commander (RU)
KA .... Catechol Amine (RU)
KA .... Cavalry Army (RU)
KA .... Communist Academy (RU)
KA .... Compass Azimuth (RU)
KA .... Corps Artillery (BU)
KA .... Corps Artillery (RU)
KA .... Helicopter Designed by N. I. Kamov (RU)
Ka .... Kaernten [*German*]
KA .... Kapitalistisches Ausland [*Capitalist Countries*] (EG)
Ka .... Karaatti(a) [*Finnish*]
Ka .... Kathode [*Cathode*] [*German*]
KA .... Katolicka Akce [*Catholic Action*] (CZ)
KA .... Katolicka Akcija [*Catholic Action*] (YU)
Ka .... Kawa [*River*] [*Japanese*] (NAU)
KA .... Kenya Airways (MAR)
K A .... Kepzomuveszeti Alap Kiadovallalata [*The Fine Arts Fund-Publishing House*] (HU)
ka .... Kiloampere (RU)
KA .... Koini Agora [*Common Market*] (GC)
KA .... Krajsky Aeroklub [*Regional Aero Club*] (CZ)
KA .... Ksiaznica Atlas [*"Atlas" Bookstore and Publishing House*] (POL)
KA .... Kulugyi Akademia [*Foreign Service Academy*] (HU)
KA .... Kypriakes Aerogrammes [*Cyprus Airlines*] (GC1)
KA .... Motion-Picture Projector (RU)
k-a .... Rear Admiral (RU)
KA .... Red Army [*1918-1946*] (RU)
KA .... Space Vehicle (RU)
KAA .... Cambodian Alumni Association (CL)
KAA .... Kendrikos Aerolimin Athinon [*Ellinikon (Athens) Airport*] (GC)
KAA .... Kentrikos Apokhetevtikos Agogos [*Central Sewage Pipe*] (GC1)
KAA .... Komma Adesmevtis Anexartisias [*Nonaligned Independence Party*] [*Greek*] (GC)
KAAA .... Kenya Amateur Athletics Association (MAR)
KAAPV .... Kendron Apokatastaseos Anapiron Paidon Voulas [*Voula Rehabilitation Center for Crippled Children*] [*Greek*] (GC)
kab .... Cable [*Topography*] (RU)
KAB .... Kabupaten [*Regency*] [*Replaced by DASWATI-II*] (IN)
KAB .... Katholieke Arbeidersbeweging [*Catholic Workers' Movement*] [*Defunct*] [*Dutch*] (WEN)
KAB .... Katholische Arbeitnehmerbewegung [*Catholic Employees' Movement*] [*Swiss*] (WEN)
KAB .... Kinevezesi es Alkalmazasi Bizottsag [*Personnel Committee*] (HU)
KAB .... Kontinuierliche Arbeitsplatzbelegung [*Personnel Continuously on Duty*] (EG)
KAB .... Kozgazdasagi Allando Bizottsag (Kolcsonos Gazdasagi Segitseg Tanacsa) [*Permanent Economic Commission (CEMA)*] (HU)

KAB............ Kozlekedesi Allando Bizottsag [*Standing Committee for Transportation (CEMA)*] (HU)
Kaba........... Kaba Konusma [*Coarse, Rough Speech*] (TU)
KABAG........ Kepala Bagian [*Division Chief, Section Chief*] (IN)
kab-balk..... Kabardino-Balkarian (RU)
Kabbalkgosizdat ... Kabardino-Balkarian State Publishing House (RU)
Kabbalkgosnatsizdat ... Kabardino-Balkarian State National Publishing House (RU)
Kabbalknatsizdat ... Kabardino-Balkarian National Publishing House (RU)
Kabgiz......... Kabardinian State Publishing House (RU)
KABI........... Kesatuan Aksi Buruh Indonesia [*Indonesian Workers Action Front*] (IN)
kabr............ Corps Artillery Brigade (BU)
KABr........... Corps Artillery Brigade (RU)
KAC............ Kenya Asbestos Cement Ltd. (MAR)
KAC............ Kenya Asbestos Company (MAR)
kach........... Qualitative, Quality, High-Grade (RU)
kachestv..... Qualitative, Quality, High-Grade (RU)
kach-vo....... Quality, Property, Grade (RU)
KAD............ Capacitive Induction Motor (RU)
KAD............ Commander of Division Artillery (RU)
KAD............ Division Artillery Commander (BU)
kad............. Kadet [*Cadet*] [*Polish*]
KAD............ Kendron Amesou Draseos [*Instant Response Center*] [*See also AD*] (GC1)
kad............. Rear Admiral (BU)
KADA.......... Kemubu Agriculture Development Association (ML)
KADAPOLMETRODJAYA ... Kepala Daerah Kepolisian Metropolitan Djakarta Raya [*Chief of the Metropolitan Djakarta Police Region*] (IN)
KADEP........ Kepala Departemen [*Department Head*] (IN)
kadet.......... Member of the Constitutional Democratic Party [*1905-1917*] (RU)
KADIN......... Kepala Dinas [*Service Chief*] (IN)
KADIR......... Kepala Direktorat [*Directorate Head*] (IN)
KADIS......... Kepala Dinas [*Service Chief*] (IN)
KADIT......... Kepala Direktorat [*Directorate Head*] (IN)
KADJATI..... Kepala Kedjaksaan Tinggi [*Chief of the District Attorney's Office*] (IN)
KADJAWA ... Kepala Djawatan [*Office Chief*] (IN)
KADKY........ Klados Asfaliseos Dimotikon kai Koinotikon Ypallilon [*Municipal and Communal Employees Insurance Branch*] [*Greek*] (GC)
kadm........... Kontradmiral [*Rear-Admiral*] [*Polish*]
k-adm......... Rear Admiral (RU)
KADU.......... Kenya African Democratic Union (PPW)
KADY.......... Kanonismos Allilografias Dimosion Ypiresion [*Public Services Correspondence Regulations*] [*Greek*] (GC)
KAE............ Aerological Observation Record Book (RU)
KAE............ Atomic Energy Commission (RU)
KAE............ Commission on Aerology (of the World Meteorological Organization) (RU)
KAE............ Complex Antarctic Expedition (RU)
KAE............ Kama Archaeological Expedition (RU)
KAE............ Komma Agroton kai Ergazomenon [*Agrarian and Workers Party*] [*Greek*] (GC)
KAEF.......... Katholisches Arbeitskreises Entwicklung und Frieden (MAR)
KAEV.......... Konnyuipari Alkatreszgyarto es Ellato Vallalat [*Spare Parts Manufacturing and Supply Enterprise of the Light Industry*] (HU)
KAF............ Kefalaion Apozimioseos Fortoekfortoton [*Stevedores Compensation Fund*] [*Greek*] (GC)
KAF............ Kenya Air Force (MAR)
KAF............ Kivalo Aruk Foruma [*Forum of Outstanding Goods*] (HU)
KAF............ Konrad Adenauer Foundation (MAR)
KAF............ "Red Banner" Amur Flotilla (RU)
KAFCO........ Kuwait Aviation Fueling Company (ME)
KAFM.......... Catholic Association of French Youth (RU)
KAFU.......... Kenya African Farmers' Union (MAR)
KAG............ Air Group Commander (RU)
KAG............ Corps Artillery Group (BU)
KAG............ Corps Artillery Group (RU)
KAG............ Korpusna Artiljeriska Grupa [*Corps Artillery Group*] (YU)
KAGGM....... Koy Arastirma ve Gelistirme Genel Mudurlugu [*Village Research and Development Directorate General*] (TU)
KAGI........... Kesatuan Aksi Guru Indonesia [*Indonesian Teachers Action Front*] (IN)
Kagit-Is....... Paper Workers Union (TU)
KAI............. Kazan' Aviation Institute (RU)
KAI............. Kuybyshev Aviation Institute (RU)
KAIS........... Kazakhstan Complex Scientific Research Institute of Structures and Building Materials (RU)
kaivost........ Kaivostyo [*Mining*] [*Finnish*]
KAJ............. Katholieke Arbeiders Jeugd [*Catholic Labor Youth*] [*Dutch*] (WEN)
KAJA........... Cambodian Alumni from Japan (CL)
KAK............ Corps Artillery Commander (BU)
KAK............ Kommunistisk Arbejdskreds [*Communist Labor Circle*] [*Danish*] (WEN)
kal.............. Calorie (BU)
kal.............. Calorie (RU)
kal.............. Kalastus [*Fishing*] [*Finnish*]
kal.............. Kalendarz [*Calendar*] [*Polish*]
kal.............. Kalori(a) [*Finnish*]
kal.............. Kaloria [*Calorie*] (HU)
Kal.............. Kalorifer [*or Kaloriferli*] [*Heater or Equipped with Heater*] (TU)
Kal.............. Kilogramm Kalorie [*Kilogram Calorie*] [*German*]
kalimag....... Potassium-Magnesium Sulfate Fertilizer (RU)
ka li sz........ Kotelezo Altalanos Ipari Szamlarendszer [*Compulsory Bookkeeping System (in industry)*] (HU)
Kalmgosizdat ... Kalmyk State Publishing House (RU)
Kalmizdat ... Kalmyk Publishing House (RU)
KALP.......... Kenya African Liberal Party (MAR)
KALSEL...... Kalimantan Selatan [*South Kalimantan*] (IN)
KALTARA ... Kalimantan Utara [*North Kalimantan (Sarawak, Sabah, Brunei)*] (IN)
KALTENG ... Kalimantan Tengah [*Central Kalimantan*] (IN)
KALTIM...... Kalimantan Timur [*East Kalimantan*] (IN)
kam............ Kamara [*Chamber*] (HU)
kam............ Kamat [*Interest*] (HU)
Kam............ Kamen [*Rock*] [*Russian*] (NAU)
Kam............ Kammer [*German*]
KAM........... Kenya African Movement (MAR)
KAM........... Konserwacja Architektury Monumentalnej [*Administration for the Conservation of Historical Buildings*] (POL)
KAM........... Panstwowe Przedsiebiorstwo Robot Konserwatorskich Architektury Monumentalnej [*State Enterprise for Conservation Work on Historical Buildings*] (POL)
kam............ Rock [*Topography*] (RU)
kam............ Stone Quarry [*Topography*] (RU)
kam............ Stone, Stony [*Topography*] (RU)
KAM........... Study Center for Aviation Medicine (RU)
KAMAMI..... Komtin'ny Artista Malagasy Mitolona [*National Committee of Artists and Musicians*] [*Malagasy*] (AF)
KAMBRUS ... Industrija Naravnih Brusnih Kamnov [*Natural Grindstones Industry*] [*Rogatec*] (YU)
Kamchatrybprom ... Kamchatka Oblast Fish Industry Administration (RU)
KAMDE....... Kanonismos Anatheseos Meleton Dimosion Ependyseon [*Regulation for the Assignment of Studies for Public Investments*] [*Greek*] (GC)
KamGES..... Kama Hydroelectric Power Plant (RU)
KAMI.......... Kesatuan Aksi Mahasiswa Indonesia [*Indonesian College Students Action Front*] (IN)
KAMK......... Krajsky Auto-Moto Klub [*Regional Motoring Club*] (CZ)
KAMPDE..... Kanonismos Anatheseos Meleton Programmatos Dimosion Ependyseon [*Regulation for the Assignment of Studies under the Public Investments Program*] [*Greek*] (GC)
KAMTIB...... Keamanan dan Ketertiban [*Security and Order*] (IN)
kam-ug....... Coal (RU)
KAMU-SEN ... Kibris Turk Kamu Gorevlileri Sendikasi [*Turkish Cypriot Civil Servant's Union*] [*Formerly, GOR-SEN*] (TU)
kamv.......... Worsted Mill [*Topography*] (RU)
kan............ Canal, Channel (RU)
Kan............ Kanal [*Canal, Channel*] [*Polish*] (NAU)
Kan............ Kanal [*Canal*] (TU)
kan............ Kanonier [*Gunner, Artilleryman*] [*Polish*]
kan............ Kanonik [*Cannon*] [*Polish*]
Kan............ Kanonikus [*German*]
KAN........... Klub Angazovanych Nestraniku [*Club of Committed Non-Party Persons (organized in 1968)*] (CZ)
Kanaz......... Kanaker Aluminum Plant (RU)
kanc........... Kancelaria [*or Kancelaryiny*] [*Office*] [*Polish*]
kanc........... Kanclerz [*Chancellor*] [*Polish*]
kand........... Candidate (RU)
kand........... Kandidaatti [*Finnish*]
kand........... Kandidatus [*Candidate*] (HU)
kand........... Kandydat [*Candidate*] [*Polish*]
kand n........ Kandydat Nauk [*Candidate of Science*] [*Polish*]
KANI.......... Kesatuan Aksi Nelajan Indonesia [*Indonesian Fishermen's Action Front*] (IN)
KANSAK..... Turk Kanser Arastirma ve Savas Kurumu [*Turkish Organization for Research and Combating Cancer*] (TU)
kansakop.... Kansakoulunopettaja [*Finnish*]
KANTAFU ... Kenya African National Traders and Farmers Union (MAR)
kants.......... Office Term (BU)
KANU......... Kenya African National Union (PPW)
KANZEKO... Kahama Nzega Co-Operative Union (MAR)
KAO........... Crimean Astrophysical Observatory (RU)
KAO........... Kalmyk Autonomous Oblast (RU)
KAO........... Kiev Astronomical Observatory (RU)
kaol.......... Kaolin Plant [*Topography*] (RU)
KAP........... Artillery Regiment Commander (RU)
kap........... Captain (RU)
KAP........... Combined Automatic Parachute (RU)
KAP........... Confederation of Arab Trade Unions [*CATU*] (RU)
KAP........... Corps Air Regiment (RU)
KAP........... Corps Artillery Regiment (RU)
KAP........... Horse Artillery Regiment (RU)
kap........... Kapelan [*Chaplain*] [*Polish*]
Kap........... Kapitel [*Chapter*] (EG)
kap........... Kapitel [*Chapter*] [*Danish*] (GPO)
kap........... Kapitel [*Chapter*] [*Norwegian*] (GPO)

kap .... Kapitel [*Chapter*] [*Swedish*] (GPO)
kap .... Kapitula [*Chapter*] [*Polish*]
Kap .... Kapitular [*German*]
Kap .... Kaplica [*Hot Spring*] (TU)
KAP .... Kapten [*Captain*] (IN)
KAP .... Kefalaion Asfaliseos Pistoseon [*Credit Insurance Fund*] [*Greek*] (GC)
kap .... Klauzula o Autorskom Pravu [*Copyright Clause*] (YU)
KAP .... Koini Agrotiki Politiki [*Joint Agricultural Policy*] (GC1)
KAP .... Komisija za Agitaciju i Propagandu [*Agitation and Propaganda Commission*] (YU)
KAP .... Kooperative Abteilung Pflanzenproduktion [*Cooperative Crop Production Department*] (EG)
KAP .... Large-Panel Reinforced Foam Concrete Slab (RU)
KAP .... "Red Banner" Air Regiment (RU)
KAP .... "Red Banner" Artillery Regiment (RU)
KAPAPs ...... Kendron Apokatastaseos Politikon Anapiron Psykhikou [*Psykhiko Rehabilitation Center for Handicapped Civilians*] [*Greek*] (GC)
KAPBI .... Kesatuan Aksi Pengemudi Betjak Indonesia [*Indonesian Pedicab Drivers Action Front*] (IN)
KAPFER ...... Turkiye Kapi ve Kalorifer Iscileri Sendikasi [*Turkish Building, Custodial, and Heating Plant Workers Union*] (TU)
KAPI .... Kesatuan Aksi Peladjar Indonesia [*Indonesian Students Action Front*] (IN)
kapit .... Capitalist (BU)
Kapl .... Kaplanei [*German*]
KAPNI .... Kesatuan Aksi Pengusaha Nasional Indonesia [*Indonesian National Businessmen's Action Front*] (IN)
KAPOLRI ..... Kepala Kepolisian Republik Indonesia [*Chief of the Republic of Indonesia Police Force*] (IN)
KAPP .... Karelian Association of Proletarian Writers [*1926-1932*] (RU)
KAPP .... Kenya African People's Party (MAR)
KAPP .... Korean Association of Proletarian Writers (RU)
KAPPI .... Kesatuan Aksi Pemuda Peladjar Indonesia [*Indonesian Youth and Students Action Front*] (IN)
KAPSh .... Engineer Shaposhnikov Arctic Frame Tent (RU)
kap str .... Capital Construction (BU)
kapt .... Kapteeni [*Finnish*]
kar .... Carat (RU)
KAR .... Corps Artillery Reserve (RU)
kar .... Horse Artillery (BU)
Kar .... Karakol [*Police Station, Outpost*] (TU)
KAR .... King's African Rifles (MAR)
kar .... Quarantine [*Topography*] (RU)
Karakalpakgiz ... Karakalpak State Publishing House (RU)
Karakalpakgosizdat ... Karakalpak State Publishing House (RU)
Karakalpakvodtrans ... Water Transportation Administration at the Council of Ministers, Karakalpak ASSR (RU)
karakul .... Karakul Sheep-Breeding [*Topography*] (RU)
karant .... Quarantine [*Topography*] (RU)
karap .... Machine-Gun Artillery Regiment (BU)
Karbat .... Guard Battalion (RU)
KARD .... Artillery Division Commander (RU)
kard .... Kardynal [*Cardinal*] [*Polish*]
Kargopol'lag ... Kargopol' Corrective Labor Camp (RU)
KARIS .... Karadeniz Nisasta-Glikoz-Misirozuyagi Sanayii ve Ticaret AS [*Black Sea Starch, Glucose, Corn Oil Industry and Marketing Corp.*] (TU)
Karlag .... Karaganda Corrective Labor Camp (RU)
KARM .... Corps Artillery Repair Shop (RU)
karn .... Karnagy [*Conductor (Music)*] (HU)
karnach .... Guard Commander (RU)
Karnt .... Kaernten [*German*]
KARO .... Kepala Biro [*Bureau Chief*] (IN)
kart .... Card (RU)
kart .... Kartars [*Colleague*] (HU)
kart .... Karton [*Cartoon*] [*Polish*]
kart .... Map [*Bibliography*] (RU)
kart .... Picture (BU)
kart .... Scene [*In theater*] (RU)
KARTGEOFOND ... Kartograficky a Geodeticky Fond [*Cartograhic and Geodetic Fund*] (CZ)
kartogr .... Cartogram (RU)
kartogr .... Kartografia [*or Kartograficzny*] [*Cartography or Cartographic*] [*Polish*]
Kartontol' .... Cardboard and Tar Paper Plant (RU)
KAS .... Medical Launch (RU)
KASAB .... Kepala Staf Angkatan Bersendjata [*Chief of Staff of the Armed Forces*] [*Also, KSAB*] (IN)
KASAD .... Kepala Staf Angkatan Darat [*Army Chief of Staff*] [*Also, KSAD*] (IN)
KASAL .... Kepala Staf Angkatan Laut [*Navy Chief of Staff*] [*Also, KSAL*] (IN)
KASAU .... Kepala Staf Angkatan Udara [*Air Force Chief of Staff*] [*Also, KSAU*] (IN)
KASI .... Kepala Seksi [*Section Chief*] (IN)
KASI .... Kesatuan Aksi Sardjana Indonesia [*Indonesian College Graduates Action Front*] (IN)
kasit .... Kasityo [*Needlework*] [*Finnish*]
KASK .... Kinisi Allagis Synetairistikou Kinimatos [*Movement for Change in the Cooperative Movement*] [*Greek*] (GC)
KASKhN ...... Kazakh Academy of Agricultural Sciences (RU)
KASP .... Commission for Complex Study of the Caspian Sea [*Of the Academy of Sciences, USSR*] (RU)
Kaspar .... Caspian Sea Steamship Line (RU)
Kaspflot ...... Caspian Dry-Cargo Steamship Line (RU)
Kaspmorput' ... Caspian Administration of Sea Routes (RU)
Kaspnefteflot ... Caspian Administration of Oil Tanker Fleet (RU)
KaspNIRO ... Caspian Scientific Research Institute of Sea Fisheries and Oceanography (RU)
Kasptanker ... Caspian Oil Tanker Steamship Line (RU)
KASS .... Kara-Bogas-Gol Salt Station (of the Academy of Sciences, USSR) (RU)
Kass .... Kassier [*German*]
KASS .... Kulturni a Spolecenska Strediska [*Cultural and Social Centers*] (CZ)
KASSR .... Kabardinian Autonomous Soviet Socialist Republic (RU)
KASSR .... Karelian Autonomous Soviet Socialist Republic [*1925-1936*] (RU)
KASSR .... Kazakh Autonomous Soviet Socialist Republic (RU)
KASU .... Kenya African Study Union (MAR)
kasv .... Kasvitiede [*Botany*] [*Finnish*]
kasvatustkand ... Kasvatustieteiden Kandidaatti [*Finnish*]
KASZ .... Kozalkalmazottak Szakszervezete [*Trade Union of Civil Service Workers*] (HU)
KAT .... Autotransformer for Motion-Picture Projector (RU)
kat .... Catalyst, Catalytic (RU)
Kat .... Catholic Cemetery [*Topography*] (RU)
KAT .... Control of Automotive Transport (BU)
kat .... Katalogus [*Catalog*] (HU)
kat .... Kataszteri [*Cadastral*] (HU)
kat .... Katedra [*Chair, Department*] [*Polish*]
kat .... Katedralny [*Cathedral*] [*Polish*]
Kat .... Kategorie [*German*]
kat .... Katolicki [*Catholic*] [*Polish*]
kat .... Katolikus [*Catholic*] (HU)
kat .... Katolinen [*Finnish*]
KAT .... Kendron Apokatastaseos Travmation [*Rehabilitation Center for the Injured*] [*Greek*] (GC)
KATAK .... Kibris Adasi Turk Azinlik Kurumu [*Turkish Minority Organization for the Island of Cyprus*] (GC)
katal .... Kateisalennus [*Finnish*]
katalitich ..... Catalytic (RU)
Katalogizdat ... State Publishing House of Catalogs (RU)
KATE .... Kendra Anoteras Tekhnikis Ekpaidevseos [*Higher Technical Education Centers*] [*Greek*] (GC)
KATEE .... Kendra Anoteras Tekhnikis kai Epangelmatikis Ekpaidevseos [*Higher Technical and Vocational Training Centers*] [*See also KATE*] (GC1)
KATEK .... Kuybyshev Automobile and Tractor Electrical Equipment and Carburetor Plant (RU)
kat h .... Kataszteri Hold [*Cadastral Yoke*] (HU)
kath .... Kathalisch [*Catholic*] [*German*] (GPO)
KATI .... Kesatuan Aksi Tani Indonesia [*Indonesian Farmers Action Front*] (IN)
katol .... Catholic (BU)
KATRIN .... Kilombero Agricultural Training and Research Institute (MAR).
KATS .... Ship Automatic Telephone Exchange (RU)
KATShch .... Mine-Sweeping Boat (RU)
KAU .... Kenya African Union (PPW)
kauch .... Rubber-Bearing (RU)
Kaucuk-Is ... Turkiye Kaucuk, Lastik ve Plastik Iscileri Sendikasi [*Turkish Rubber and Plastic Workers Union*] (TU)
KAUFE .... Oxyethylated Phenols from Coal Tar (RU)
kaup .... Kauppa [*Business, Trade*] [*Finnish*]
kaup .... Kaupunki [*Finnish*]
kaupp .... Kauppala [*Finnish*]
kaupp .... Kauppias [*Finnish*]
kauppatkand ... Kauppatieteiden Kandidaatti [*Finnish*]
kauppatlis ... Kauppatieteiden Lisensiaatti [*Finnish*]
kauppatmaist ... Kauppatieteiden Maisteri [*Finnish*]
kauppattri ... Kauppatieteiden Tohtori [*Finnish*]
kav .... Cavalry (RU)
kAV .... Continental Antarctic Air (RU)
kAV .... Continental Arctic Air (RU)
KAV .... Kavaleri [*Cavalry*] (IN)
KAV .... Kohaszati Alapanyagellato Vallalat [*Supply Enterprise of Basic Metallurgical Materials*] (HU)
KAV .... Krajsky Akcni Vybor [*Regional Action Committee*] (CZ)
kavk .... Caucasian (RU)
Kavkaznefterazvedka ... Caucasian Petroleum Exploration Trust (RU)
KAVNF .... Krajsky Akcni Vybor Narodni Fronty [*Regional Action Committee of the National Front*] (CZ)
KAVZ .... Automobile Made by the Kurgan Bus Plant (RU)
KAVZ .... Kurgan Bus Plant (RU)
KAWBBA ..... Kenya Amateur Weightlifting and Body-Building Association (MAR)
KAWC .... Kenya African Workers Congress (MAR)
KAWI .... Kesatuan Aksi Wanita Indonesia [*Indonesian Women's Action Front*] (IN)

KAWU .... Kenya African Workers Union (MAR)
Kay .... Kaynak [*Source, Spring*] (TU)
KAYA .... Young Cambodian Artists Association (CL)
Kaym .... Kaymakam [*District Governor*] [*Within a province*] (TU)
KAYO .... Kenya Anglican Youth Organization (MAR)
kayt .... Kaytetaan [*Is Used*] [*Finnish*]
KAZ .... Automobile Made by the Kurgan Bus Plant (RU)
KAZ .... Automobile Made by the Kutaisi Automobile Plant (RU)
kaz .... Barrack [*Topography*] (RU)
KAZ .... Kandalaksha Aluminum Plant (RU)
kaz .... Kazakh (RU)
KAZ .... Kazan' Railroad (RU)
KAZ .... Krasnoyarsk Aluminum Plant (RU)
KAZ .... Kurgan Bus Plant (RU)
KAZ .... Kutaisi Automobile Plant (RU)
Kazakhsel'mash ... Kazakh Agricultural Machinery Plant (RU)
Kazakhstanneft' ... Association of the Kazakhstan Petroleum Industry (RU)
KazFAN .... Kazakh Branch of the Academy of Sciences, USSR (RU)
Kazgeupr .... Kazakh Geodetic Administration (RU)
Kazgiprogorsel'stroy ... Kazakh State Planning Institute for the Planning of Urban and Rural Construction (RU)
KAZGIPRONIIKhIMMASH ... Kazakh State Planning and Scientific Research Institute of Chemical and Machinery Industries (RU)
Kazgiprotsvetmet ... Kazakh State Institute for the Planning of Establishments of Nonferrous Metallurgy (RU)
KAZGOSIZDAT ... Kazakh State Publishing House (RU)
KAZGOSLITIZDAT ... Kazakh State Publishing House of Belles Lettres (RU)
Kazgres .... Kazan' State Regional Electric Power Plant (RU)
KazGU .... Kazakh State University Imeni S. M. Kirov (RU)
KazIMS .... Kazakh Scientific Research Institute of Mineral Raw Materials (RU)
KazIOT .... All-Union Scientific Research Institute of Work Safety of the VTsSPS [*Kazan'*] (RU)
Kazkhlopkosoyuz ... Kazakh Kray Union of Cotton-Growing Cooperatives (RU)
Kazkhlopkotsentr ... Kazakh Center of Cotton-Growing Cooperatives (RU)
Kazmetallzavod ... Kazakh Metallurgical Plant (RU)
KazMI .... Kazakh Medical Institute (RU)
KazMZ .... Kazakh Metallurgical Plant (RU)
KazNIGMI ... Kazakh Scientific Research Hydrometeorological Institute (RU)
KazNIIAT ..... Kazakh Scientific Research Institute of Automobile Transportation (RU)
KazNIIE .... Kazakh Scientific Research Institute of Power Engineering (RU)
KazNIIVKh ... Kazakh Scientific Research Institute of Water Management (RU)
KazNIIZh ..... Kazakh Scientific Research Institute of Livestock Breeding (RU)
KazNIPIAT ... Kazakh Scientific Research and Planning Institute of Automobile Transportation (RU)
KazPI .... Kazakh Pedagogical Institute Imeni Abay (RU)
Ka Zrf .... Kapali Zarfi [*Sealed Envelope Bidding*] (TU)
Kazsel'khozgiz ... Kazakh State Publishing House of Agricultural Literature (RU)
Kazsel'mash ... Kazakh Agricultural Machinery Plant (RU)
KazSSR .... Kazakh Soviet Socialist Republic (RU)
KazTAG .... Kazakh News Agency (RU)
Kaztsentroarkhiv ... Central Archives Administration, Kazakh ASSR (RU)
KazTsIK ...... Central Executive Committee, Kazakh SSR (RU)
Kazuchpedgiz ... Kazakh State Publishing House of Textbooks and Pedagogical Literature (RU)
Kazvetinstitut ... Kazakh State Veterinary and Zootechnical Institute (RU)
KB .... Battery Commander (BU)
KB .... Cable Drum (RU)
kb .... Cable Length (RU)
Kb .... Cavalry Brigade (BU)
kb .... Cubic (RU)
KB .... Design Office (RU)
KB .... Kadry Bezpieczenstwa [*Security Cadres*] [*Military Battalions*] [*World War II*] (POL)
KB .... Kantor Berita [*News Agency*] (IN)
kb .... Karabin Bojowy [*Rifle*] [*Polish*]
KB .... Karadeniz Bakir [*Black Sea Copper Works*] [*See also KBI*] (TU)
KB .... Kazalisna Biblioteka [*Theater Library*] [*Zagreb*] (YU)
KB .... Kisa Boylu [*Short Length*] [*As of a timber*] (TU)
KB .... Komitet Blokowy [*City Block Committee*] (POL)
KB .... Kommunistischer Bund [*Communist Union (Radical Left)*] [*Austrian*] (WEN)
KB .... Komunalna Banka [*Communal Bank*] (YU)
KB .... Koninklijke Bibliotheek [*'s-Gravenhage*]
KB .... Korpusna Baza [*Corps Base*] (YU)
kb .... Korulbelul [*About, Approximately*] [*Hungarian*] (GPO)
K/B .... Kota Bahru [*Malaysian*] (ML)
K B .... Kozponti Bizottsag [*Central Committee*] (HU)
KB .... Kray Library (RU)
KB .... Kultur Bakanligi [*Ministry of Culture*] (TU)
KB .... Kulturbund [*Cultural League*] (EG)
KB .... Large Alidade (RU)
KB .... Monitor Unit (RU)
KB .... Paper Capacitor (RU)
KB .... Tower Crane (RU)
KBAO .... Kabardino-Balkarian Autonomous Oblast [*1922-1936*] (RU)
KBAP .... "Red Banner" Bomber Regiment (RU)
KBASSR ...... Kabardino-Balkarian Autonomous Soviet Socialist Republic (RU)
KBAT .... Design Office of Automation and Remote Control Equipment for the Petroleum and Gas Industry (RU)
KBAZ .... Base Commander (RU)
kbb .... Counterbattery Fire (RU)
KBB .... Kulak, Burun, ve Bogaz (Klinigi or Mutehassis) [*Ear, Nose, and Throat (Clinic or Specialist)*] (TU)
KBC .... Kenya Broadcasting Corporation (MAR)
KBDU .... Kom-Bum Development Union (MAR)
KBE .... Abridged Bulgarian Encyclopedia [*A publication*] (BU)
KBF .... "Red Banner" Baltic Fleet (RU)
KBG .... Hermetically Sealed Paper Capacitor (RU)
KBGS .... Design Office of Hydromechanical Structures (RU)
KBGS- .... Tower Crane for Hydraulic Engineering Construction (RU)
KBGU .... Kabardino-Balkarian State University (RU)
KBI .... Institute of Criticism and Bibliography (RU)
KBI .... Karadeniz Bakir Isletmeleri Anonim Sirketi [*Black Sea Copper Works Corporation*] [*See also KB*] (TU)
KBI .... Kontrollbericht der Industrie [*Industry Control Report*] (EG)
KBI .... Municipal and Personal Services Inspection (RU)
KBiGK .... Komisja Budownictwa i Gospodarki Komunalnej [*Commission for Construction and Communal Economy*] (POL)
KBKA .... Kesatuan Buruh Kereta Api [*Railway Workers Union*] (IN)
KBKI .... Kesatuan Buruh Kerakjatan Indonesia [*Indonesian Democratic Workers Federation*] (IN)
KBL .... Kilusan ng Bangong Lipunan [*New Society Movement*] [*Philippine*] (PD)
KbLg .... Kabellaenge [*Cable Length (Generally 600 feet)*] (EG)
KBM .... Kesatuan Buruh Marhaenis [*Marhaenist Workers Federation*] (IN)
kbn .... Candidate of Biological Sciences (RU)
KBNP .... Design Office for Oil Field Automation and Geophysical Instrument Making (RU)
KBO .... Kommunistischer Bund Oesterreichs [*Communist League of Austria*] (PPW)
KBO .... Kurs Borbene Obuke [*Combat Training Course*] (YU)
KBO .... Personal Services Kombinat (RU)
KBOt .... Klasicni Bojni Otrovi [*Classic Poison Gases*] [*Military*] (YU)
KBP .... Combat Training Course (RU)
KBP .... Flight Safety Control (RU)
KBP .... Komisaris Besar Polisi [*Chief Police Commissioner*] (IN)
KBP .... Paper Duct Capacitor (RU)
KBP .... Pulverulent Concentrate of Spent Sulfite Liquor (RU)
KBPL .... Communist League Proletarian Left [*Dutch*] (PPW)
KBPM .... Kesatuan Buroh Padang Minyak [*Oil Field Workers Union*] (ML)
KBRI .... Kedutaan Besar Republik Indonesia [*Embassy of the Republic of Indonesia*] (IN)
KBS .... Communal Public Services (BU)
KBS .... Kenya Bus Services Ltd. (MAR)
KBS .... Kiev Botanical Garden (RU)
KBS .... Kreisbuchungsstation [*Kreis Accounting Office*] (EG)
KBSh .... Kuybyshev Railroad (RU)
KBSK .... Carboxylated Butadiene-Styrene Rubber (RU)
kbt .... Cable Length (RU)
KBT .... Kongres Britanskih Tredjuniona [*Congress of British Trade-Unions*] (YU)
KBt .... Kontrabatiranje [*Counterbattery Fire*] (YU)
KBT .... Solid Concentrate of Spent Sulfite Liquor (RU)
KBTsMA ...... Design Office of Tsvetmetavtomatika (RU)
KBUiA .... Komitet Budownictwa, Urbanistyki, i Architektury [*Committee for Construction, Urban Development, and Architecture*] (POL)
KBV .... Traveling-Wave Ratio (RU)
KBW .... Kommunistischer Bund Westdeutschland [*Communist League of West Germany*] (PPW)
KBW .... Korpus Bezpieczenstwa Wewnetrznego [*Internal Security Corps*] (POL)
KBZ .... Komise pro Branne Zalezitosti [*Commission for Defense Matters*] (CZ)
KBZh .... Liquid Concentrate of Spent Sulfite Liquor (RU)
KC .... Kenya Coalition (MAR)
KC .... Klub Ctenaru [*Readers' Club*] (CZ)
KC .... Kodeks Cywilny [*Civil Code*] [*Polish*]
KC .... Komandir Cete [*Company Commander*] (YU)
KC .... Komitet Centralny [*Central Committee*] (POL)
Kc .... Koruna Ceskoslovenska [*Czechoslovak Koruna*] [*Currency*] (CZ)
Kc .... Kucuk [*Small, Minor*] (TU)
KCA .... Karting Club d'Abidjan (MAR)
KCA .... Kikuyu Central Association (MAR)
k-ca .... Knjizarnica [*Bookshop*] (YU)
kcal .... Kilo Kaloria [*Kilo Calorie*] (HU)
kcal .... Kilogramm Kalorie [*Kilogram Calorie*] [*German*]
kcal .... Kilokaloria [*Kilocalorie*] [*Polish*]
KCB .... Kernwaffen-, Chemische, und Biologische (Aufklaerung) [*Nuclear, Chemical, and Biological (Reconnaissance)*] (EG)
KCB-Anlage ... Kern, Chemische, Bakteriologische-Anlage [*ABC-Detector*] (EG)

KCC .... Kampala City Council (MAR)
KCC .... Kenya Co-Operative Creameries Ltd. (MAR)
KCCU .... Kilimanjaro Chagga Citizens' Union (MAR)
KCDB .... Kaduna Capital Development Board (MAR)
KCDC .... Kenya Citizens Democratic Congress (MAR)
KCFC .... Kenya Chemical and Food Corporation (MAR)
KCFC .... Kuwait Chemical Fertilizer Company (ME)
KC FPK .... Komitet Centralny Francuskiej Partii Komunistycznej [*Central Committee of the French Communist Party*] (POL)
KCh .... Black Silicon Carbide (RU)
KCh .... Commission for the Study of the Quaternary Period (of the Academy of Sciences, USSR) (RU)
KCh .... Frequency Corrector (RU)
kch .... Locksmith, Doorkeeper, Turnkey (BU)
KCh .... Malleable Iron (RU)
K-Chemie ... Kampfstoffchemie [*Chemical Warfare Chemistry*] (EG)
kch r .... Machine-Gun Company (BU)
KChSR .... Kuban'-Black Sea Soviet Republic [*1918*] (RU)
kch vd .... Machine-Gun Platoon (BU)
KChZhD ...... Chinese Ch'ang-Ch'un Railroad [*1945-1953*] (RU)
KCIA .... South Korean Central Intelligence Agency [*Later, Agency for National Security Planning*] (PD)
KCK .... Ketua Chawangan Khas [*Chief Special Branch*] (ML)
KC KPJ .... Komitet Centralny Komunistycznej Partii Japonii [*Central Committee of the Communist Party of Japan*] (POL)
KC KPP .... Komitet Centralny Komunistycznej Partii Polski [*Central Committee of the Communist Party of Poland*] (POL)
KC KPZR ..... Komitet Centralny Komunistycznej Partii Zwiazku Radzieckiego [*Central Committee of the Communist Party of the Soviet Union*] (POL)
KCLB .... Katholiek Centrum voor Lectuurinformatie en Bibliotheekvoorziening [*NBLC*] [*Dutch*]
KCMA .... Klub Cyklistu, Motocyklistu, a Automobilistu [*Bicycle, Motorcycle, and Automobile Club*] (CZ)
KCMC .... Kilimanjaro Christian Medical Centre (MAR)
KCMU .... Kumba Co-Operative Marketing Union (MAR)
KCNA .... Korean Central News Agency (CL)
KCOS .... Knihovna Ceskoslovenska Obce Sokolske [*Library of the Czechoslovak Sokol Organization*] (CZ)
KC PPR .... Komitet Centralny Polskiej Partii Robotniczej [*Central Committee of the Polish Workers Party*] (POL)
KC PZPR ..... Komitet Centralny Polskiej, Zjednoczonej Partii Robotniczej [*Central Committee of the Polish United Workers' Party*] (POL)
Kcs .... Csehszlovak Korona [*Czechoslovak Crown*] [*Currency*] (HU)
Kcs .... Koruna Ceskoslovenska [*Czechoslovak Koruna*] [*Currency*] (CZ)
KCSN .... Kralovska Ceska Spolecnost Nauk [*Royal Czech Society of Sciences*] (CZ)
KCSP .... Kontrola Cywilna Statkow Powietrznych [*Civil Aircraft Control*] (POL)
KCSR .... Kuwaiti Company for Shipbuilding and Repairs (ME)
KCST .... Klub Ceskoslovenskych Turistu [*Czechoslovak Tourist Club*] (CZ)
KCT .... Klub Ceskych Turistu [*Czech Tourist Club*] (CZ)
KCT .... Krajsky Cirkevni Tajemnik [*Regional Church Secretary*] (CZ)
KCTL .... Klub Ctenaru Technicke Literatury [*Club of Technical Literature Readers*] (CZ)
KCV .... Klub Ceskych Velocipedistu [*Czech Cycling Club*] (CZ)
KCVP .... Konservativ-Christlichsoziale Volkspartei [*Conservative Christian-Social Party*] [*Swiss*] (PPE)
KCWKP(b) ... Komitet Centralny Wszechzwiazkowej Komunistycznej Partii (Bolszewikow) [*Central Committee of the All-Union Communist Party (Bolsheviks)*] (POL)
KC ZMS ...... Komitet Centralny Zwiazku Mlodziezy Socjalistycznej [*Central Committee of the Socialist Youth Union*] [*Polish*]
KCZZ .... Komisja Centralna [*or Centralny*] Zwiazkow Zawodowych [*Central Commission of Trade Unions*] (POL)
KD .... Battalion Commander (BU)
KD .... Battalion Commander (RU)
KD .... Blood Pressure (RU)
Kd .... Cavalry Division (BU)
kd .... Conductor [*Railroad, Trolley, Bus*] (BU)
KD .... Constitutional Democrat (RU)
k-d .... Constitutional Democratic Party [*1905-1917*] (RU)
KD .... Detonating Cap (RU)
KD .... Division Commander (RU)
KD .... Kaini Diathiki [*New Testament*] (GC)
KD .... Kamenouhelne Doly [*Black Coal Mines*] (CZ)
kd .... Kansandemokraatti(nen) [*Finnish*]
KD .... Kartographischer Dienst der Nationalen Volksarmee [*National People's Army Cartographic Service*] (EG)
Kd .... Kidemli [*Senior, Seniority in Rank, Rating*] (TU)
KD .... Kisa Dalga [*Short Wave*] (TU)
KD .... Kladenske Doly [*Kladno Mines*] (CZ)
KD .... Klasyfikacja Dziesietna [*Decimal Classification*] [*Polish*]
KD .... Kolektivni Dum [*Communal (Social) Center*] (CZ)
Kd .... Komanda Divisiona [*Headquarters of Artillery Battalion*] (YU)
KD .... Komitet Dzielnicowy [*City Section Committee*] (POL)
KD .... Konvertible Devisen [*Convertible Foreign Exchange*] (EG)
KD .... Kreisdienststelle [*Kreis Agency*] (EG)
KD .... Kriegs Dekoration [*War Decoration*] [*German*]
KD .... Kuwaiti Dinar (ME)
kd .... Pack Horse Driver, Horseholder (BU)
KD .... Pressurizer (RU)
KDA .... Kenya Darts Association (MAR)
KDA .... Klub Demokratickych Akademikov [*Democratic University Students' Club*] (CZ)
k-da .... Komanda [*Command*] [*Military*] (YU)
KDA .... Kono Development Association (MAR)
K-daKoV ..... Komanda Kopnene Vojske [*Ground Forces Command*] (YU)
KDAS .... Koini Dievthynsis ton Aktoploikon Syngoinonion [*Coastal Communications Joint Directorate*] [*Greek*] (GC)
KDB .... Kenya Dairy Board (MAR)
KDB .... Kocaeli Devrimciler Birligi [*Kocaeli Revolutionaries' Union*] (TU)
KDC .... Klub Delnickych Cyklistu [*Workers' Cycling Club*] (CZ)
KDCI .... Kepala Daerah Chusus Ibukota [*Head of the Special Capital Region (Governor of Djakarta)*] (IN)
KDD .... Kasarni Dozorci Dustojnik [*Garrison Officer of the Day*] (CZ)
KDE .... Kendron Didaskalias Enilikon [*Adult Education Center*] [*Greek*] (GC)
Kde .... Klein-Durchgangseilgueterzug [*Small Express Through Freight Train*] (EG)
Kdg .... Kindergarten [*or Kindergaertnerin*] [*German*]
KDG .... Kinisi Dimokratikon Gynaikon [*Movement of Democratic Women*] [*Greek*] (GC)
Kdg .... Klein-Durchgangsgueterzug [*Small Through Freight Train*] (EG)
KDGTh .... Kinisis Dimokratikon Gynaikon Thessalonikis [*Movement of Salonica's Democratic Women*] (GC1)
KDH .... Kepala Daerah [*Chief of Region*] (IN)
KDK .... Ceramic Disc Capacitor (RU)
KDK .... Children Book Pool (RU)
KDK .... Commission for the Compilation of a Dialectological Map of the Russian Language (RU)
KDK .... Kozgazdasagtudomanyi Dokumentacios Kozpont [*Economics Documentation Center*] (HU)
KDK .... Kreis-Direktion fuer den Kraftverkehr [*Kreis Directorate for Motor Traffic*] (EG)
KDK .... State Control Commission (BU)
KDKE .... Kommounistiko Diethnistiko Kinima Elladas [*Communist Internationalist Movement of Greece*] (GC)
KDKhVD ...... Kray House of Children's Art Education (RU)
KDL .... Compagnie des Chemins de Fer Kinshasa-Dilolo-Lubumbashi [*Kinshasa-Dilolo-Lubumbashi Railway Company*] [*Zairian*] (AF)
KDL .... Kraje Demokracji Ludowej [*People's Democracies*] [*Polish*]
KDL .... Smoke and Volatility Coefficient (RU)
KDL .... Societe des Chemins de Fer Katanga-Dilolo-Leopoldville (MAR)
KDM .... Democratic Youth Committee (BU)
KD Malaya .. Kapal Di-Raja Malaya [*Royal Malayan Ship*] (ML)
KDMMA ...... Kadikoy Devlet Muhendislik ve Mimarlik Akademisi [*Kadikoy State Engineering and Architectural Academy*] [*Istanbul*] (TU)
KDMMA ...... Konya Devlet Muhendislik ve Mimarlik Akademisi [*Konya State Engineering and Architecture Academy*] (TU)
kdmos .... Kodarithmos [*Code Number*] (GC)
KDN .... Battalion Commander (RU)
KDNK .... Committee for State and People's Control (BU)
KDNK .... Keluaran Dalam Negeri Kasar [*Gross National Product*] (ML)
KDO .... Kendrika Dioikitika Organa [*Central Administrative Organs*] [*Greek*] (GC)
KDO .... Kendriki Dioikitiki Organosis [*Central Administrative Organization*] [*Greek*] (GC)
Kdo .... Kommando [*German*]
KDO .... Landing Detachment Commander (RU)
KDOSM .... Combine for the Extraction and Processing of Rock-Lining Materials (BU)
KDP .... Control Tower [*Aviation*] (RU)
KDP .... Differential Absorption Coefficient (RU)
KDP .... Dispatcher's Command Post (BU)
KDP .... Fire-Control Tower, Plotting Room [*Navy*] (RU)
KDP .... Horse-Drawn Decontamination Wagon (RU)
KDP .... Kanonovy Delostrelecky Pluk [*Gun Artillery Regiment*] (CZ)
KDP .... Krajske Divadlo Pracujicich [*Regional Workers' Theater*] (CZ)
KDP .... Kurdish Democratic Party (ME)
KDP .... Kurdistan Demokrat Partisi [*Kurdistan Democratic Party*] (TU)
KDP .... Peasants' Democratic Party [*German Democratic Republic*] (RU)
KDPG .... Peasant's Democratic Party of Germany [*German Democratic Republic*] (RU)
KDPI .... Kurdish Democratic Party of Iran (PPW)
KDR .... Code Relay (RU)
KDRMB .... Code Relay with Magnetic Blocking (RU)
KDRSh .... Code Relay with Plug Switching (RU)
KDRShMB ... Code Relay with Magnetic Blocking and Plug Switching (RU)
KDRSM .... Comite Democratique pour la Revolution Socialiste Malgache (MAR)

KDRSM .... Komity Demokratika Manohana ny Fototra Iorenan' ny Revolisiona Sosialista Malagasy [*Democratic Committee to Support the Malagasy Socialist Revolution*] (AF)
KDRT .... Code Relay for Jolting Conditions (RU)
KDS .... Kendrika Dioikitika Somata [*Central Administrative Bodies*] [*Greek*] (GC)
KDS .... Kendrikon Dioikitikon Symvoulion [*Central Administrative Council*] [*Greek*] (GC)
KDS .... Kendron Dierkhomenon Stratou [*Army Transients Center*] [*Greek*] (GC)
KDS .... Khusitan Development Service [*Iranian*] (MAR)
KDS .... Komma Demokratikou Sosialismou [*Party for Democratic Socialism*] [*Greek*] (PPE)
KDS .... Kristen Demokratisk Samling [*Christian Democratic Union*] [*Swedish*] (PPE)
KDS .... Oxygen-Producing Plant (RU)
KDSE .... Katholische Deutsche Studenten-Einigung [*German Catholic Student Union*] [*West German*] (EG)
Kdstg .... Klein-Dienstgutzug [*Intra-Enterprise Freight Train*] (EG)
KDSZ .... Kohaszati Dolgozok Szakszervezete [*Trade Union of Metallurgical Workers*] (HU)
KdT .... Kammer der Technik [*Chamber of Technology*] (EG)
kdt .... Komandant [*Commander*] (YU)
Kdt .... Kommandant [*German*]
KDTM .... Democratic Committee of Youth and Students for the Defense of the Malagasy Socialist Revolution (AF)
KDTTMB ..... Kibris Dahili Telekommunikasyon Turk Mustahdemler Birligi [*Union of Turkish Employees of Cyprus Inland Telecommunications*] (GC)
KDU .... Remote Control Device (RU)
KDV .... Kozlekedesi Dokumentacios Vallalat [*Transportation Documentation Enterprise*] (HU)
KDV .... Kvinnornas Demokratiska Varldsforbund [*Women's International Democratic Federation*] [*Use WIDF*] [*Swedish*] (WEN)
KDW .... Komitet Drobnej Wytworczosci [*Small-Scale Industries Committee*] (POL)
Kdz .... Karadeniz [*Black Sea*] (TU)
KDZ .... Kmetijska Delavna Zadruga [*Peasant Working Cooperative*] (YU)
kdzh .... Kilojoule (RU)
KDZTU .... Karadeniz Teknik Universitesi [*Black Sea Technical University*] (TU)
KE .... Acarid Encephalitis (RU)
ke .... Cavalry Squadron, Cavalry Troop (BU)
KE .... Cruiser Squadron (RU)
KE .... Electrolytic Capacitor (RU)
KE .... Kendriki Epitropi [*Central Committee*] (GC)
KE .... Kenya [*Two-letter standard code*] (CNC)
ke .... Keskiviikko(na) [*Finnish*]
KE .... Kinetic Energy (RU)
KE .... Komma Ellinosocialiston [*Greek Socialists Party*] (GC)
KE .... Kyvernitiki Epitropi [*or Kyvernitikos Epitropos*] [*Government Committee or Government Commissioner*] [*Greek*] (GC)
KE .... Oxygen Effect (RU)
ke .... Starch Equivalent (RU)
KEA .... Kendron Ekpaidevseos Anapiron [*Training Center for the Handicapped*] [*Greek*] (GC)
KEA .... Kendron Ethnikis Asfaleias [*National Security Center*] (GC)
KEA .... Kinima Eniaias Aristeras [*United Left Movement*] (GC1)
KEA .... Kinima Epanastatikis Aristeras [*Movement of the Revolutionary Left*] [*Greek*] (GC)
KEA .... Kinima Ethnikis Anagenniseos [*Movement of National Regeneration*] [*Greek*] (GC)
KEA .... Kinima Ethnikis Andistaseos [*National Resistance Movement*] [*Greek*] (GC)
KEA .... Kinisis Ethnikis Anadimiourgias [*National Regeneration Movement*] [*Grivas*] [*Greek*] (GC)
KEA .... Koini Evropaiki Agora [*European Common Market*] (GC)
KEA .... Komma Ethnikis Anagenniseos [*National Rebirth Party*] [*Greek*] (GC)
KEA .... Kratikon Ergostasion Aeroplanon [*State Aircraft Factory*] [*Greek*] (GC)
KEADEA ..... Kinima gia Ethniki Anexartisia Diethni Eirini kai Afoplismo [*Movement for National Independence, International Peace, and Disarmament*] (GC1)
KEAE .... Kendron Erevnon Atomikis Energeias (Andidrastir Kholargou) [*Atomic Energy Research Center (Kholargos Reactor)*] [*Greek*] (GC)
KEAK .... Kendriki Epitropi Apokatastaseos Kratoumenon [*Central Committee for the Rehabilitation of Prisoners*] [*Greek*] (GC)
KEAK .... Kinima Ethnikis Apokatastaseos Kyprou [*Movement for the National Restoration of Cyprus*] (GC)
KEAM .... Concentrate of Anthracene-Oil Emulsion (RU)
KEAP .... Kendron Ekpaidevseos Anorthodoxou Polemou [*Unconventional Warfare Training Center*] [*Greek*] (GC)
KeATA .... Kendriki Agora Trofimon Athinon [*Athens Central Food Market*] (GC)
KEB .... Konstruktions- und Entwicklungsbuero [*Design and Development Office*] (EG)
KEB .... Kozponti Ellenorzo Bizottsag [*Central Control Committee*] (HU)
KEBKOR ..... Kernbrandstofkorporasie [*Nuclear Fuel Corporation*] [*South African*] (AF)
KEBORA ..... Kebudajaan dan Olah Raga [*Culture and Sports*] (IN)
KEC .... Korean Engineering Company (MAR)
KECh .... Billeting Operation Unit (RU)
KED .... Customs Duty List [*EEC*] (GC1)
KED .... Erythema Dose (RU)
KED .... Kendriki Epitropi Daneion [*Central Loans Committee*] [*Greek*] (GC)
KED .... Kendriki Epitropi Diaitisias [*Central Arbitration Committee*] [*Greek*] (GC)
KED .... Kendron Ekpaidevseos Diavivaseon [*Communications Training Center*] [*Greek*] (GC)
KED .... Kinima Ethnikis Draseos [*Movement for National Action*] [*Greek*] (GC)
KED .... Komma Ethnikis Draseos [*National Action Party*] [*Greek*] (GC)
KED .... Kratiki Ekmetallevsis Dason [*State Exploitation of Forests*] [*Greek*] (GC)
KED .... Ktimatiki Etaireia Dimosiou [*Public Land Company*] (GC1)
KEDJAGUNG ... Kedjaksaan Agung [*Office of the Attorney General*] (IN)
KEDJARI ..... Kedjaksaan Negeri [*Office of the Public Prosecutor*] (IN)
KEDJATI ..... Kedjaksaan Tinggi [*Office of the District Attorney*] (IN)
KEDKE .... Kendriki Enosis ton Dimon kai Koinotiton tis Ellados [*Central Union of Municipalities and Communes of Greece*] (GC)
KEDUBES ... Kedutaan Besar [*Embassy*] (IN)
KEE .... Kendriki Elengtiki Epitropi [*Central Control Committee*] [*Cypriot*] (GC)
KEE .... Kendron Ekpaidevseos Efedron [*Reserves Training Center*] [*Greek*] (GC)
KEE .... Kendron Englimatologikon Erevnon [*Criminology Research Center*] [*Greek*] (GC)
KEE .... Koinoniki Enosis Epistimonon [*Social Union of Professionals*] [*Greek*] (GC)
KEE .... Komma Ergazomenon Ellados [*Greek Workers' Party*] (GC)
KEEA .... Kypriaki Enosis Epangelmation Avtokinitiston [*Cypriot Union of Professional Drivers*] (GC)
KEED .... Kinisis Ethnikis Enoseos Dexias [*National Unification Movement of the Right*] [*Cypriot*] (GC)
KEEE .... Kendriki Eklogiki Epitropi Ethnikofronon [*Central Electoral Committee of Nationalists*] [*Cypriot*] (GC)
KEEE .... Kiniton Epidimiologikon Ergastirion Erevnon [*Mobile Epidemiological Research Laboratory*] [*Greek*] (GC)
KEEF .... Kratikon Ergastirion Elengkhou Farmakon [*National Drug Control Laboratory*] [*Greek*] (GC)
KEEK .... Kentriki Epitropi Epilogis kai Kritirion [*Selection and Criteria Central Committee*] (GC1)
KEEM .... Kendron Ekpaidevseos Efodiasmou kai Metaforon [*Supply and Transportation Training Center*] [*Greek*] (GC)
KEEP .... Kendron Epikheirimatikis Epikoinonias kai Provolis [*Center for Entrepreneurial Communication and Projection*] (GC1)
KEEPTh ...... Kendriki Eforevtiki Epitropi Paidopoleon Thessalonikis [*Central Supervisory Committee for Salonica Children's Centers*] (GC)
KEES .... Komma Ethnikis ton Ellinon Sotirias [*Party for the National Salvation of Greeks*] (GC)
KEESING .... Keesing's Contemporary Archives [*A publication*] (MAR)
KEEThA ...... Kendron Erevnon Ethnikis Amynis [*National Defense Research Center*] [*Greek*] (GC)
KEF .... Kabinet pro Etnografii a Folkloristiku [*Ethnography and Folklore Department (of the Czechoslovak Academy of Sciences)*] (CZ)
kef .... Kefalaion [*Chapter (of Document)*] (GC)
KEFE .... Kendriki Enosis Froutoparagogon Ellados [*Central Fruitgrowers Union of Greece*] (GC)
KEFEM .... Kemenyfemipari Vallalat [*Hard Metal Industry Enterprise*] (HU)
kEFr .... Kilo Energetische Futtereinheit [*1,000 High Energy Fodder Units for Beef Cattle*] (EG)
KEG .... Examining and Evacuation Hospital (RU)
KEGE .... Kendron Erevnon kai Georgikis Ekpaidevseos [*Research and Agricultural Training Center*] (GC)
KEGE .... Kendron Georgikis Ekpaidevseos [*Agricultural Training Center*] [*Greek*] (GC)
KEGEPOA ... Kendriki Gnomodotiki Epitropi Programmatos Oikonomikis Politikis [*Central Advisory Committee for Economic Policy Programs*] [*Greek*] (GC)
KEI .... Commission for Expeditionary Research (of the Academy of Sciences, USSR) (RU)
KEI .... Kenoolaj Ellenorzo Intezet [*Quality Control Institute on Lubricating Oils*] (HU)
KEI .... Kozponti Eloadoi Iroda [*Central Office of Special Consultants*] (HU)
KEI .... Kozponti Elorejelzo Intezet [*Central Forecasting Institute*] (HU)
KEIB .... Chair of Epidemiology and Communicable Diseases (BU)
KEIS .... Kiev Experimental Research Plant [*Of the NIISMI*] (RU)
KEISZ .... Kepzomuveszek es Iparmuveszek Szovetsege [*Association of Artists and Designers*] (HU)
keitt .... Keittotaito [*Culinary Art, Cookery*] [*Finnish*]
KEK .... Kendron Epangelmatikis Katartiseos [*Vocational Training Center*] (GC1)

KEK............ Konferenz Evangelischer Kirchen Europas [*Conference of European Protestant Churches*] (EG)
KEK............ Kozepeuropa-Kupa [*Central Europe Cup (Sports)*] (HU)
KEK............ Kypriakon Ethnikon Komma [*Cypriot National Party (1944-1960)*] [*Greek Cypriot*] (PPE)
KEK............ Kyvernitiki Epitropi Kapnou [*Government Tobacco Committee*] [*Greek*] (GC)
KEK............ Marx Karoly Kozgazdasagi Egyetem Kozponti Konyvtara [*Central Library of the Karl Marx School of Economics*] (HU)
KEKATE...... Kendron Mathiteias kai Takhyrrythmou Epangelmatikis Katartiseos Enilikon [*Apprenticeship and Rapid Vocational Training Center for Adults*] (GC)
KeKE........... Kendriki Kallitekhniki Epitropi [*Central Artistic Committee*] [*Greek*] (GC)
KEKELE...... Jeunesse Ngufu-Madimba-Kinzambi-Kinfunda-Ladi (MAR)
KEKI............ Kozponti Elelmiszeripari Kutatointezet [*Central Research Institute of the Food Industry*] (HU)
KEKMA....... Kinisi gia Eniaio Komma Marxistikis Aristeras [*Movement for a United Party of the Marxist Left*] [*Greek*] (GC)
KEKN.......... Kendron Ergazomenon Koritsion kai Neotiton [*Center for Working Girls and Youths*] [*Greek*] (GC)
k ekv.......... Starch Equivalent (RU)
KEL............. Karntner Einheitsliste [*Carinthian Unity List*] [*Austrian*] (PPE)
KEL............. Koroska Enotna Lista [*Carinthian Unity List*] [*Austrian*] (PPE)
KELS........... Kendron Ekpaidevseos tou Limenikou Somatos [*Port Corps Training Center*] [*Greek*] (GC)
KELTEX...... Kelenfoldi Textilkombinat [*Kelenfold Textile Concern*] (HU)
KELV........... Kendriki Epitropi Logistikon Vivlion [*Central Accounts Board*] (GC)
KEM-........... Electromagnetic Classifier (RU)
kem............. Kemia [*Chemistry*] [*Finnish*]
KEM............ Kendron Ekpaidevseos Mikhanikou [*Engineers Training Center*] [*Greek*] (GC)
KEM............ Kendron Ekpaidevseos Mikhanokiniton [*Mechanized Forces Training Center*] [*Greek*] (GC)
KEM............ Kypriaki Etaireia Metaforon [*Cyprus Transport Company*] (GC)
KEMA.......... Keuringsinstituut Elektrotechnische Materialen Arnhem
KEMA.......... N. V. tot Keuring van Electrotechnische Materialen [*Office for the Inspection of Electrotechnical Material*] [*Dutch*] (WEN)
KEMAM....... Kesatuan Malaya Merdeka [*Free Malaya Front*] (ML)
KEMAS....... Kelantan Malay Syndicate (ML)
KEME.......... Kendron Ekpaidevtikon Meleton kai Epimorphosis [*Center for Educational Research and Training (Development)*] (GC1)
KEME.......... Kendron Epitheoriseos Mesis Ekpaidevseos [*Secondary Education Supervision Center*] (GC1)
KEMEDI...... Kendron Metafraston kai Diermineon [*Center for Translators and Interpreters*] (GC1)
KEMI........... Kereskedelmi Minosegellenorzo Intezet [*Commercial Quality Control Institute*] (HU)
KEMK.......... Kendron Ekpaidevseos Monadon Katadromon [*Raiding Forces Training Center*] [*Greek*] (GC)
KEML.......... Kinisi Ellinon Marxiston-Leniniston [*Movement of Greek Marxist-Leninists*] (GC)
KEMSA....... Kemik Urunleri Sanayi ve Ticaret AS [*Bone Products Industry and Trade Corp.*] (TU)
KEMZ.......... Kaluga Electromechanical Plant (RU)
KEMZ.......... Kemerovo Electromechanical Plant (RU)
KEMZ.......... Kiev Electromechanical Plant (RU)
KEMZ.......... Kurgan Electromechanical Plant (RU)
KEMZ.......... Moscow Motion-Picture Electromechanical Equipment Plant (RU)
KEMZ.......... Motion-Picture Electromechanical Equipment Plant (RU)
ken............. Candidate of Economic Sciences (RU)
KEN............ Kendron Ekpaidevseos Neosyllekton [*Recruit Training Center*] [*Greek*] (GC)
KEN............ Kenya [*Three-letter standard code*] (CNC)
KENDACOL... Industrias Kendall de Colombia Ltda. [*Bogota*] (COL)
KENE........... Kendriki Epitropi Nomothetikis Ergasias [*Central Legislative Processing Committee*] [*Greek*] (GC)
KENEXTEL... Kenya External Telecommunications Co. (MAR)
kenr............ Kenraali [*Finnish*]
kenrluutn.... Kenraaliluutnantti [*Finnish*]
kenrmaj...... Kenraalimajuri [*Finnish*]
KENSTA...... Kenya Stationers Ltd. (MAR)
KENTAS...... Kimya Endustrisi ve Ticaret Anonim Sirketi [*Chemical Industry and Trade Corporation*] (TU)
KEO............ Design and Experimental Department (RU)
KEO............ Housing Operation Department (RU)
KEO............ Kray Export Association (RU)
KEOK.......... Kulfoldieket Ellenorzo Orszagos Kozpont [*National Center of Alien Registration*] (HU)
KEOKH........ Kulfoldieket Ellenorzo Orszagos Kozponti Hatosag [*National Center of Alien Registration*] (HU)
KEOM.......... Kendron Ekpaidevseos Oreinon Metaforon [*Mountain Transport Training Center*] [*Greek*] (GC)
KEP............ Catelectrotonic Potential (RU)
KEP............ Electric Instruction Device (RU)
KEP............ Electropneumatic Instruction Device (RU)
KEP............ Examining and Evacuation Station (RU)
KEP............ Kendriki Epitropi Protathlimatos [*Central Championship Committee (of the Greek Soccer Federation)*] (GC)
KEP............ Kendron Ekpaidevseos Pyrovolikou [*Artillery Training Center*] [*Greek*] (GC)
KEP............ Kendron Epangelmatikou Prosanatolismou [*Occupational Orientation Center*] [*Greek*] (GC)
KEP............ Keputusan [*Directive*] (IN)
KEPA.......... Kendron Endatikon Programmaton Anaptyxeos [*Center of Intensive Development Planning*] (GC1)
KEPA.......... Kendron Paragogikotitos [*Productivity Center*] [*Greek*] (GC)
KEPE.......... Kendriki Epitropi Prosfygon Ellados [*Central Committee of Greek Refugees*] (GC)
KEPE.......... Kendron Programmatismou kai Oikonomikon Erevnon [*Center for Planning and Economic Research or Center for Planning and Research*] [*Greek*] (GC)
KEPEL........ Kynigetiki Enosis Poleos-Eparkhias Lemesou [*Limassol City and District Hunters Union*] [*Cypriot*] (GC)
KEPES........ Kendriki Epitropi Prostasias tis Engkhoriou Sitoparagogis [*Central Committee for the Protection of Domestic Wheat Production*] [*Greek*] (GC)
KEPOA........ Kendriki Epitropi Programmatos Oikonomikis Anaptyxeos [*Central Committee for the Economic Development Program*] [*Greek*] (GC)
KEPOS........ Koinofelis Epikheirisis Poleodomias, Oikismou, kai Stegaseos [*Town Planning and Housing Public Utility Enterprise*] (GC)
KEPOS........ Kratiki Epikheirisis Poleodomias, Oikismou, Stegaseos [*State Town Planning and Housing Enterprise*] [*Greek*] (GC)
KEPPE......... Kendriki Epitropi Politikon Prosfygon Ellados [*Central Committee of Greek Political Refugees*] (GC)
KEPPRES.... Keputusan Presiden [*Presidential Directive*] (IN)
KEPRO........ Office for Operation, Rental, and Servicing of Equipment (of the Metrostroy) (RU)
kepsomuv... Kepzomuveszetek [*or Kepzomuveszeti*] [*Fine Arts or Of Fine Arts*] (HU)
ker.............. Keraaminen Teollisuus [*Ceramics*] [*Finnish*]
ker.............. Kereszteny [*Christian*] [*Hungarian*] (GPO)
ker.............. Kerulet [*District*] [*Hungarian*] (GPO)
keram.......... Ceramics Plant [*Topography*] (RU)
Keramik-Is... Turkish Porcelain, Cement, Brick, and Soils Industries Workers Union (TU)
Keramostroj... Zavody na Vyrobu Keramickych Stroju [*Plants for the Manufacture of Ceramics Machinery*] (CZ)
KERAVILL... Kerekpar, Radio, es Villamossagi Kiskereskedelmi Vallalat [*Retail Trade Enterprise for Bicycles, Radios, and Electrical Appliances*] (HU)
KERAZ........ Keramicke Zavody [*Ceramics Works*] (CZ)
KERINFORG... Belkereskedelmi Ugyvitelszervezesi es Informaciofeldolgozasi Intezet [*Management Organization and Information Processing Institute of Domestic Trade*] (HU)
KERIPAR..... Kereskedelmi Asztalos es Lakatosipari Vallalat [*Carpenters and Locksmiths Trade Enterprise*] (HU)
Ker es Ip Kam... Kereskedelmi es Iparkamara [*Chamber of Commerce and Industry*] (HU)
KERM.......... Komitet Ekonomiczny Rady Ministrow [*Economic Committee of the Council of Ministers*] (POL)
KERMI......... Kereskedelmi Minosegellenorzo Intezet [*Commercial Quality Control Institute*] (HU)
kers............ Kersantti [*Finnish*]
KERTVALL... Kertgondozo Vallalat [*Park Maintenance Organization*] (HU)
KES............ Kendriki Epitropi Sporoparagogis [*Seed Production Central Committee*] [*Greek*] (GC)
KES............ Kendrikon Ekklisiastikon Symvoulion [*Central Ecclesiastical Council*] [*Greek*] (GC)
KES............ Kendrikon Epoptikon Symvoulion [*Central Supervisory Council*] [*Greek*] (GC)
KES............ Kinima Elevtherou Syndikalismou [*Free Labor Movement*] [*Greek*] (GC)
KES............ Konferencija Evropskih Statisticara [*Conference of European Statisticians*] (YU)
KES............ Kray Economic Conference (RU)
KES............ Motion-Picture Electric Power Unit (RU)
KES............ Space Power Plant (RU)
KESA.......... Kendron Ekpaidevseos Stratiotikis Astynomias [*Military Police Training Center*] [*Greek*] (GC)
Kesk........... Keskustapuolue [*Center Party*] [*Finnish*]
kesk........... Keskustapuoluelainen [*Finnish*]
KESMA....... Kenya Sugar Manufacturers' Association (MAR)
KESPEKRI... Kesatuan Pekerdja Keristen Indonesia [*Indonesian Christian Workers Association*] (IN)
KESSBANEG... Kesatuan Serikat-Serikat Sekerdja Bank-Bank Negara [*Federation of State Bank Trade Unions*] (IN)
kestom........ Kestomuodossa [*Progressive Form*] [*Finnish*]
kesz............ Keszitette [*Prepared By*] (HU)
KESZ.......... Kutatasi Ellatasi Szolgalat [*Research Supply Service*] (HU)
KET............ Kendron Ekpaidevseos Tethorakismenon [*Armored Forces Training Center*] [*Greek*] (GC)
KETA.......... Kenya External Trade Authority (MAR)
KETE.......... Kendra Epangelmatikis kai Tekhnikis Ekpaidevseos [*Vocational and Technical Education Centers*] [*See also KATE, KATEE*] (GC1)

KETI .... Kisipari Exportra Termelteto Iroda [*Office for Promoting Export Production by Artisans*] (HU)
KETJ .... Ketjamatan [*District*] (IN)
KETS .... Kendron Ekpaidevseos Tekhnikou Somatos [*Technical Corps Training Center*] [*Greek*] (GC)
KEU .... Housing Operation Administration (RU)
KEU .... Kommunalekonomiska Utredningen [*Swedish*]
kEV .... Continental Equatorial Air (RU)
KEV .... Enameled High-Voltage Composition [*Resistor*] (RU)
kev .... Kilo Electron Volt (RU)
KeV .... Kiloelektronenvolt [*Kilo Electron Volt*] (EG)
keV .... Kiloelektronovolt [*Kilo Electron Volt*] [*Polish*]
KEV .... Kozlekedesi Epito Vallalat [*Construction Enterprise for Transportation Facilities*] (HU)
KEVA .... Kendriki Epitropi Voreioipeirotikou Agonos [*Central Committee of the Northern Ipeiros Struggle*] [*See also KEVIA*] [*Greek*] (GC)
KEVA .... Kendron Ethnikis Viomikhanikis Anaptyxeos [*Center for National Industrial Development*] [*Greek*] (GC)
KEVA .... Kendron Viotekhnikis Anaptyxeos [*Center for Development of Crafts*] [*Greek*] (GC)
KEVE .... Kypriakon Emborikon kai Viomikhanikon Epimelitirion [*Cyprus Chamber of Commerce and Industry*] (GC)
KEVIA .... Kendriki Epitropi Voreioipeirotikou Agonos [*Central Committee of the Northern Ipeiros Struggle*] [*See also KEVA*] (GC)
KEVOP .... Kendron Ekpaidevseos Vareon Oplon Pezikou [*Infantry Heavy Weapons Training Center*] [*Greek*] (GC)
KEY .... Kendron Ekpaidevseos Ygeionomikou [*Medical Service Training Center*] [*Greek*] (GC)
KEYP .... Kendron Ekpaidevseos Ylikou Polemou [*Ordnance Training Center*] [*Greek*] (GC)
kez .... Kezelo [*Operator, Attendant*] (HU)
kezb .... Kezbesitve [*Delivered by Hand*] (HU)
kezirat gy .... Kezirat Gyanant [*In Manuscript Form*] (HU)
KF .... Caspian Flotilla (RU)
kf .... Cationite Filter (BU)
KF .... Creatine Phosphate (RU)
KF .... Fale Krotkie [*Short Waves*] [*Polish*]
KF .... Front Commander (RU)
KF .... Kabinet Filosofie [*Department of Philosophy (of the Czechoslovak Academy of Sciences)*] (CZ)
KF .... Kepzomuveszeti Foiskola [*Academy of Fine Arts*] (HU)
KF .... Keramidas Freres et Fils (MAR)
KF .... Komma Filelevtheron [*Liberal or Neo-Liberal Party*] [*Greek*] (GC)
KF .... Kommunistisk Forbund (M-L) [*Communist League (Marxist-Leninist)*] [*Danish*] (WEN)
KF .... Konservative Folkeparti [*Conservative People's Party (Commonly called the Conservative Party)*] [*Danish*] (PPE)
KF .... Kooperativa Forbundet [*Consumers' Cooperative Union*] [*Swedish*] (WEN)
KF .... Koroski Fuzinar [*Carinthian Ironsmith*] [*Gustanj*] [*A periodical*] (YU)
kf .... Kozepfoku [*Secondary (School)*] (HU)
KF .... Kratky Film Praha [*Film Shorts Prague*] (CZ)
KF .... Kultura Fizyczna [*Physical Culture*] (POL)
K + F .... Kutatas-Fejlesztes [*Research and Development*] (HU)
k/f .... Motion Picture (RU)
KfA .... Kammer fuer Aussenhandel [*Chamber for Foreign Trade*] (EG)
KFA .... Kenya Farmers Association Ltd. (MAR)
KFAED .... Kuwaiti Fund for Arab Economic Development (ME)
KFAN .... Kazan' Branch of the Academy of Sciences, USSR (RU)
KFAN .... Kola Branch of the Academy of Sciences, USSR (RU)
KFAP .... Krakowska Fabryka Aparatow Pomiarowych [*Krakow Measurement Apparatus Plant*] (POL)
KFB .... Kozsegi Foldigenylo Bizottsag [*Village Committee on Land Claims*] (HU)
KFC .... Kenya Film Corporation (MAR)
KFESRAS .... Kuveitskii Fond Ekonomicheskovo i Sotsial'novo Razvitiia Arabskikh Stran (MAR)
KFF .... Kenya Football Federation (MAR)
KFF .... Kvinnenes Frie Folkevalgte [*Women's Freely Elected Representatives*] [*Norwegian*] (PPE)
k fin n .... Candidate of Financial Sciences (BU)
KFK .... Kernforschungszentrum Karlsruhe [*West German*]
KFKI .... Kozponti Fizikai Kutato Intezet [*Central Research Institute of Physics*] (HU)
KFKis .... Committee for Physical Culture and Sports (RU)
KFKP .... Kodix Forologias Katharas Prosodou [*Net Income Tax Code*] [*Greek*] (GC)
KFL .... Kenya Federation of Labor (AF)
KfL .... Kreisbetrieb fuer Landtechnik [*Kreis Enterprise for Agricultural Equipment*] (EG)
kfm .... Kaufmaennisch [*Commercial*] (EG)
Kfm .... Kaufmann [*Merchant*] (EG)
KFML .... Kommunistiska Foerbundet Marxist-Leninisterna [*Communist League of Marxist-Leninists*] [*Swedish*] (PPE)
KFML(r) ...... Kommunistiska Foerbundet Marxist-Leninisterna (Revolutionar) [*Communist League of Marxists-Leninists (Revolutionary)*] [*Swedish*] (WEN)
k f-m n .... Candidate of Physical and Mathematical Sciences (RU)
kfn .... Candidate of Philological Sciences (RU)
kfn .... Candidate of Philosophical Sciences (RU)
k f n .... Candidate of Physical Sciences (BU)
KFN .... Komitet Frontu Narodowego [*Committee of the People's Front*] (POL)
KFP .... Komisja Funduszu Posmiertnego [*Commission on the Death Benefit Fund*] (POL)
KFP .... Konstitutionella Folkpartiet [*Constitutional People's Party*] [*Finnish*] (PPE)
KFP .... Kozponti Fejlesztesi Programok [*Central Development Programs*] (HU)
KFP .... Kristelig Folkeparti [*Christian People's Party*] [*Norwegian*] (WEN)
KFPC .... Kassala Fruit Processing Co. Ltd. [*Sudanese*] (MAR)
KFS .... Committee for Physical Culture and Sports (BU)
KFS .... Kallopistikos kai Filanthropikos Syllogos Aigaleo "I Proodos" [*"The Proodos" Beautification and Charitable Club of Aigaleo*] [*Greek*] (GC)
KFS .... Kodix Forologikon Stoikheion [*Tax Revenue Data Code*] (GC)
KFSKh .... Kinisi Foititon Skholis Khimikon [*Movement of Chemistry School Students*] [*Greek*] (GC)
KFSSR .... Karelo-Finnish Soviet Socialist Republic [*1940-1956*] (RU)
KFST .... Kuestenfunkstelle [*Coastal Radio Station*] (EG)
kft .... Korlatolt Felelossegu Tarsasag [*Limited Liability Company*] (HU)
KFTCIC .... Kuwait Foreign Trading, Contracting & Investment Company
KFTD .... Kibris Federe Turk Devleti [*Turkish Federated State of Cyprus*] (GC)
KFUT .... Klodzka Fabryka Urzadzen Technicznych [*Klodzko (Glatz) Technical Equipment Factory*] (POL)
KFV .... Koolajkutato es Feltaro Vallalat [*Enterprise for Oil Prospecting and Drilling*] (HU)
KF VNII .... Krasnodar Branch of the All-Union Scientific Research Institute of Petroleum and Gas (RU)
KFVNIIneft' ... Krasnodar Branch of the All-Union Scientific Research Institute of Petroleum and Gas (RU)
KfW .... Kreditanstalt fuer Wiederaufbau [*Reconstruction Credit Institution, Loan Bank*] [*West German*] (EG)
KFWM .... Krasnicka Fabryka Wyrobow Metalowych [*Krasnik Metal Products Plant*] (POL)
Kfz .... Kraftfahrzeug [*Motor Vehicle*] (EG)
KG .... Coke-Oven Gas (RU)
KG .... Corps Hospital (RU)
KG .... Kabinet pro Geomorfologii [*Department of Geomorphology (of the Czechoslovak Academy of Sciences)*] (CZ)
Kg .... Kampong [*or Kampung*] [*Village, Settlement*] [*Indonesian*] (NAU)
Kg .... Kampong [*or Kampung*] [*Village, Settlement*] [*Malay*] (NAU)
Kg .... Karang [*Coral Reef, Reef*] [*Malay*] (NAU)
KG .... Karta Gornicza [*Miner's Identity Card*] (POL)
KG .... Katastralgemeinde [*German*]
kg .... Kilo [*Finnish*]
kg .... Kilogram (BU)
kg .... Kilogram [*Kilogram*] (POL)
kg .... Kilogram (RU)
kG .... Kilogram Force (RU)
KG .... Kilogram Sily [*Kilogram-Force*] [*Polish*]
kg .... Kilogramm [*Kilogram*] (EG)
kg .... Kilogramm [*Kilogram*] (HU)
kg .... Kilogramma(a) [*Finnish*]
kg .... Kilogramme [*Kilogram*] [*French*]
Kg .... Kilogramo [*Kilogram*] [*Spanish*]
KG .... Kmetijsko Gospodarstvo [*Farm Economy*] (YU)
Kg .... Koenig [*German*]
KG .... Komenda Glowna [*Main Headquarters*] (POL)
KG .... Komitet Glowny [*Main Committee*] (POL)
KG .... Komitet Gminny [*Polish*]
KG .... Kommanditgesellschaft [*Limited Partnership*] [*German*] (WEN)
Kg .... Kompong [*Often part of a place name*] [*Cambodian*] (CL)
KG .... Konsumgenossenschaft [*Consumer Cooperative*] (EG)
KG .... Krajska Galeria [*Regional Gallery*] (CZ)
KG .... Main Contactor (RU)
KGA .... Mountain Horse Artillery (RU)
KGAP .... Kommunistische Gruppe Arbeiter-Politik [*Communist Group for Workers' Policies*] [*Swiss*] (WEN)
KGB .... Kampfgruppenbataillon [*Workers Militia Battalion*] (EG)
KGB .... Komitet Gossudarstvennoi Bezopasnosti [*Committee of State Security*] [*Russian*]
KGB .... State Security Committee [*At the Council of Ministers*] (RU)
KGC .... Kibris Gaziler Cemiyeti [*League of Cypriot Veterans*] [*Turkish Cypriot*] (GC)
kgcc .... Kilograme de Combustibil Conventional [*Kilograms of Conventional Fuel*] (RO)
KGDB .... Kozponti Gazdasagi Dontobizottsag [*Central Economic Arbitration Committee*] (HU)
KGE .... Concise Geographic Encyclopedia [*A publication*] (RU)
KGE .... Kendron Georgikis Ekpaidevseos [*Agricultural Training Center*] [*Greek*] (GC)
KGEN .... Kendriko Grafeio tis Ergatikis Neolaias [*Central Office for Working Youth*] [*Cypriot*] (GC)
k geogr k ..... Candidate of Geographic Sciences (BU)

KGH............ Kommunaler Grosshandel [*Communal Wholesale Enterprise*] (EG)
KGI............ Kompleksni Godisnji Izvestaj [*Consolidated Annual Report*] (YU)
KGK............ Hermetically Sealed Ceramic Capacitor (RU)
kgl............ Koeniglich [*Royal*] [*German*]
KGL............ Kombinatsgewerkschaftsleitung [*Combine Trade-Union Headquarters*] (EG)
kgl............ Kongelig [*Royal*] [*Danish*] (GPO)
KGM............ Karayollari Genel Mudurlugu [*Highways Directorate General*] (TU)
kGm............ Kilogram Meter (RU)
kgm............ Kilogrammametri(a) [*Finnish*]
KGM............ Koho- es Gepipari Miniszterium/Miniszter [*Ministry/Minister of Metallurgical and Machine Industries*] (HU)
KGM............ Kutuphaneler Genel Mudurlugu [*Libraries Directorate General*] [*Under Ministry of Culture*] (TU)
KGMI............ Kalinin State Medical Institute (RU)
KGMI............ Kazakh Mining and Metallurgical Institute (RU)
KGMI............ Kazan' State Medical Institute (RU)
KGMI............ Kemerovo State Medical Institute (RU)
KGMI............ Kishinev State Medical Institute (RU)
KGMI............ Kursk State Medical Institute (RU)
KGMI............ Kuybyshev State Medical Institute (RU)
k g-m n........ Candidate of Geological and Mineralogical Sciences (RU)
KGMP............ Data-Collecting Hydrometeorological Station (RU)
KGMTI........ Koho- es Gepipari Miniszterium Tervezo Irodai [*Planning Offices of the Ministry of Metallurgy and Machine Industry*] (HU)
KGMZ............ Kerch' State Metallurgical Plant Imeni P. L. Voykov (RU)
kgn............ Candidate of Geographical Sciences (RU)
KGO............ Kommunist Genclik Orgutu [*Communist Youth Organization (Network)*] (TU)
KGO............ Kozmikus Geodeziai Obszervatorium [*Cosmic Geodesic Observatory*] (HU)
KGP............ Commandant of Mountain Pass (RU)
KGP............ Kmetijsko Gozdarsko Posestvo [*Agricultural and Forest Property*] (YU)
KGP............ Komma Georgiou Papandreou [*Party of George Papandreou*] [*Greek*] (PPE)
KG PAN....... Komitet Geograficzny Polskiej Akademii Nauk [*Polish Academy of Sciences Committee on Geography*] (POL)
KGPI............ Kaluga State Pedagogical Institute (RU)
KGPI............ Kiev State Pedagogical Institute Imeni A. M. Gor'kiy (RU)
KGPI............ Kirgiz State Pedagogical Institute (RU)
KGPI............ Kishinev State Pedagogical Institute Imeni I. Kryange (RU)
KGPI............ Kuybyshev State Pedagogical Institute Imeni V. V. Kuybyshev (RU)
KGR............ Galvanic Skin Reflex (RU)
KGR............ Kierownictwo Grupy Robot [*Management of a Work Unit*] (POL)
kgr............ Kilogram (BU)
kgr............ Kizigranat [*Hand Grenade*] (HU)
Kgr............ Koenigreich [*Kingdom*] [*German*] [*Correspondence*]
KGRI............ Krivoy Rog Institute of Ore Mining (RU)
kgs............ Kilogram Force (RU)
KGS............ Kreisgeschaeftsstelle [*Kreis Business Office*] (EG)
KGSD............ Kibris Guzel Sanatlar Dernegi [*Cypriot Fine Arts Society*] [*Turkish Cypriot*] (GC)
KGST............ Kolcsonos Gazdasagi Segitseg Tanacsa [*Council for Mutual Economic Assistance (CEMA)*] (HU)
kgts............ Kilohertz, Kilocycles per Second (RU)
KGTY............ Kibris Gecici Turk Yonetimi [*Cyprus Provisional Turkish Administration*] (GC)
KGU............ Kampfgruppe Gegen Unmenschlichkeit [*Fighting Group Against Inhumanity*] (EG)
KGU............ Kazan' State University Imeni V. I. Ul'yanov (Lenin) (RU)
KGU............ Kenya Golf Union (MAR)
KGU............ Kiev State University Imeni T. G. Shevchenko (RU)
KGU............ Kirgiz State University (RU)
KGUP............ Kuwait Gas Utilization Project (ME)
KGV............ Konnyuipari Gepalkatresz es Anyagforgalmi Vallalat [*Machine Supply Enterprise for Light Industry*] (HU)
KGV............ Konsumgenossenschaftsverband [*Union of Consumer Cooperatives*] (EG)
KGVI............ Kazan' State Veterinary Institute Imeni N. E. Bauman (RU)
KGW............ Kolo Gospodyn Wiejskich [*Rural Housewives' Circle*] (POL)
KGW............ Komitet Gospodarki Wodnej [*Water Supply Committee*] (POL)
K Gy............ Kobanyai Gyogyszerarugyar [*Pharmaceutical Factory of Kobanya*] (HU)
KGZ............ Caucasian State Reservation (RU)
KGZ............ Committee for State Contracts (RU)
KGZS............ Koziarske a Gumarenske Zavody na Slovensku [*Leather and Rubber Plants in Slovakia*] (CZ)
Kgzv............ Kilogram Zive Vahy [*Kilogram of Live Weight*] (CZ)
KGZVI............ Kazan' State Zootechnical and Veterinary Institute (RU)
kh............ Administrative (Service of a Ship) (RU)
KH............ Cambodia [*Two-letter standard code*] (CNC)
kh............ Farmstead [*Topography*] (RU)
Kh............ Karargah [*Headquarters*] (TU)
Kh............ Khao [*Hill, Mountain*] [*Thai*] (NAU)
Kh............ Khatzi [*Cypriot*] (GC)
kh............ Kylpyhuone [*Finnish*]
kh............ Normal Running Fit (RU)
Kh............ Surgical Hospital (RU)
kh............ Thousand (BU)
Kha............ Hectare (BU)
KHA............ Kindergarten Headmistresses Association (MAR)
KhAAK........ Adipyl Chloride (RU)
KhAB............ Aerial Chemical Bomb (RU)
KhAB............ Chemical Air Bomb (BU)
KhabIIZhT... Khabarovsk Institute of Railroad Transportation Engineers (RU)
KhADI............ Khar'kov Highway Institute (RU)
KhAEE............ Khoresm Archaeological and Ethnographical Expedition (RU)
KhAF............ Chloroacetophenone (RU)
KhAI............ Khar'kov Aviation Institute (RU)
khakas........ Khakass (RU)
Khakasgiz... Khakass State Publishing House (RU)
Khakasoblnatsizdat ... Khakass Oblast National Publishing House (RU)
Khakgiz............ Khakass State Publishing House (RU)
Khakizdat... Khakass Book Publishing House (RU)
Khakknigizdat ... Khakass Book Publishing House (RU)
Khakoblgosizdat ... Khakass Oblast State Publishing House (RU)
khald............ Chaldean (RU)
KhAN............ Khristianiki Adelfotis Neon [*Young Men's Christian Association*] (GC)
KhAO............ Khar'kov Astronomical Observatory (RU)
Khargiprotrans ... Khar'kov State Planning and Surveying Institute (RU)
KhARZ............ Khar'kov Apparatus and Radiator Plant (RU)
Khas............ Hydroacoustic Station (BU)
KhATK............ Terephthalyl Chloride (RU)
KhAZOS...... Khar'kov Plant for Experimental Aircraft Construction (RU)
KhB............ Chemical Battalion (RU)
kh/b............ Cotton (RU)
KhBR............ Chemical, Bacteriological, and Radiological (RU)
kh br............ Thousand Issues (BU)
KhBS............ Cold White Light (Fluorescent Lamp) (RU)
khch............ Administrative and Supply Department (RU)
khch............ Chemically Pure (RU)
KHD............ Kloeckner-Humboldt-Deutz AG (MAR)
KhDP............ Chemical Decontamination Station (RU)
KhE............ Khristiano-Koinoniki Enosis [*Christian Socialist Union*] [*Greek*] (GC)
KhEG............ Chemical Generator of Electrical Energy (RU)
KhEG............ Hygiene-Epidemiological Group (BU)
KhEG............ Surgical Evacuation Hospital (RU)
KhEI............ Hygiene-Epidemiological Institute (BU)
KhELZ............ Khar'kov Electrotechnical Plant (RU)
KhEMZ............ Khar'kov Electromechanical Plant (RU)
KhEN............ Khristianiki Enosis Neanidon [*Young Women's Christian Association*] (GC)
KhEP............ Khrimatistirion Emborevmaton Peiraios [*Piraeus Commodity Exchange*] (GC)
KHES............ Krajska Hygienicko-Epidemiologicka Stanice [*Regional Public Health and Epidemiology Station*] (CZ)
KhETI............ Khar'kov Electrotechnical Institute (RU)
KhETZ............ Khar'kov Diesel Locomotive Electrical Equipment Plant (RU)
KhEU............ Hygiene-Epidemiological Administration (BU)
KhF............ Chemical Mine (RU)
KhF............ Chromium Phosphate Electrolyte (RU)
KhFDM............ Chlorophenyldimethylurea (RU)
KhFI............ Khar'kov Pharmaceutical Institute (RU)
KhFM............ Chlorophenyldimethylurea (RU)
KhFZ............ Chemical-Pharmaceutical Plant (BU)
KHG............ Kabinet pro Historickou Geografii [*Department of Historical Geography (of the Czechoslovak Academy of Sciences)*] (CZ)
KHG............ Kommunistische Hochschulgruppe [*Communist Student Organization*] [*West German*] (WEN)
KhG............ Surgical Hospital (RU)
KhGBI............ Khar'kov State Library Institute (RU)
KhGI............ Khar'kov Mining Institute (RU)
KhGIMIP..... Khar'kov State Institute of Measures and Measuring Instruments (RU)
KhGNMB..... Khar'kov State Scientific Medical Library (RU)
kh/gr............ Khiliogrammon [*Kilogram*] (GC)
KhGSEE...... Khristianiki Geniki Synomospondia Ergazomenon Ellados [*Christian General Confederation of Greek Workers*] (GC)
KhGU............ Khar'kov State University Imeni A. M. Gor'kiy (RU)
KhGU............ Surgical Reinforcement Group (RU)
KHGYP........ Kraliyet Hava Gucu Yardimci Polis ve Aylikci Mustahdemler Sendikasi [*Royal Air Force Auxiliary Police and Monthly Salaried Employees Union*] [*Turkish Cypriot*] (GC)
KhI............ Chlorinated Lime (RU)
KhI............ Khimiya i Industriya [*Chemistry and Industry*] [*A periodical*] (BU)
KHI............ Know-How International (MAR)
Khidrostroy ... Hydraulic Constructions Organization (BU)
KhIGS............ Khibiny Mountain Station (of the Academy of Sciences, USSR) (RU)

KhIIT .... Khar'kov Institute of Railroad Transportation Engineers Imeni S. M. Kirov (RU)
KhIK .... Chemical Institute Imeni L. Ya. Karpov (RU)
khil .... Thousand(s) (BU)
khim .... Chemical, Chemistry (BU)
khim .... Chemical, Chemistry (RU)
khim .... Chemical Plant [*Topography*] (RU)
KhIM .... Khar'kov Scientific Research Institute of Metals (RU)
khimbaklab ... Chemical and Bacteriological Laboratory (RU)
khimfak .... Division of Chemistry (RU)
khimfarm .... Chemical and Pharmaceutical (RU)
khim-farm ... Chemical and Pharmaceutical Plant [*Topography*] (RU)
Khimfarmprom ... Administration of the Chemical and Pharmaceutical Industry (RU)
Khimfarmproyekt ... Office for the Planning of Chemical and Pharmaceutical Plants (RU)
Khimfarmsbyt ... All-Union Trade Office for Chemical and Pharmaceutical Goods and Sanitary Articles (RU)
khimfugas ... Chemical Mine (RU)
Khimgaz ..... All-Union Scientific Research Institute of the Chemical Processing of Gases (RU)
Khimimport ... Enterprise for Import and Export of Chemicals and Drugs (BU)
Khimizdat ... State Publishing House of Scientific and Technical Chemical Literature (RU)
khimleskhoz ... Wood-Chemistry Establishment (RU)
Khimlesprom ... All-Union Trust for the Procurement and Processing of Lumber of the Glavkhimpromstroy (RU)
khimlespromkhoz ... Wood-Chemistry Industrial Establishment (RU)
Khimleszag ... State Trust for the Procurement of Industrial Raw Materials and Fuel of the Glavleskhim (RU)
khim mel ..... Chemical Soil Improvement (RU)
khimprom ... Chemical Industry (RU)
Khimr .... Chemical Company (RU)
khimrazvedka ... Chemical Reconnaissance (RU)
Khimsantekhmontazh ... All-Union Trust of the Glavkhimpromstroy (RU)
KHIMSNARYAD ... Chemical Shell (RU)
khim sost .... Chemical Composition (RU)
Khimtekhizdat ... State Publishing House of Chemical and Technical Literature (RU)
khimtrevoga ... Gas Alarm [*Military term*] (RU)
khimugolok ... Chemical Study Room (RU)
khim zn .... Chemical Symbol (RU)
KhIn .... Khimiya i Industriya [*Chemistry and Industry*] [*A periodical*] (BU)
KhINO .... Khar'kov Institute of Public Education (RU)
KhIOT .... Khar'kov Institute of Work Safety (RU)
KhIP .... Random Pulse Interference (RU)
khir .... Surgeon, Surgery (BU)
khir .... Surgery, Surgical (RU)
KhISI .... Khar'kov Construction Engineering Institute (RU)
khist .... Histology, Histologist (BU)
khizh .... Hut [*Topography*] (RU)
KhK .... Refrigeration Chamber (RU)
kh-ka .... Characteristic, Performance (RU)
khkh .... No-Load Condition (Electricity) (RU)
KhKhTI .... Khar'kov Institute of Chemical Technology Imeni S. M. Kirov (RU)
KHKO .... Kurt Halk Kurtulus Ordusu [*Kurdish Peoples' Liberation Army*] (TU)
KhKPV .... Chemical Combine for Polyester Fibers (BU)
KhKUKS ...... Chemical Courses for the Advanced Training of the Command Personnel of the RKKA (RU)
KhKZ .... Kherson Combine Plant (RU)
khl .... Belles Lettres (RU)
khl .... Chloroform (RU)
KhL .... Laboratory Chromathermograph (RU)
Khladpromstroy ... Construction and Installation Trust of the Rosmyasorybtorg of the Ministry of Trade, RSFSR (RU)
Khladstroy ... Refrigeration and Apparatus Plant (BU)
khlak .... Kihlakunta [*Finnish*]
khl-bum ...... Cotton (RU)
Khleboizdat ... Publishing House of Technical and Economic Literature on Problems of the Flour-Milling, Groats, and Combined-Fodder Industry and on Elevators and Storage Facilities (RU)
Khlebsbyt ... Moscow Office of the Administration of the Baking Industry of the Mosoblispolkom (RU)
khlf .... Chloroform (RU)
khlop .... Cotton (RU)
Khlor-IFK ..... Isopropyl Chlorophenylcarbamate (RU)
KhLS .... SONAR Station (BU)
kh lv .... Thousand Leva (BU)
KHM .... Cambodia [*Three-letter standard code*] (CNC)
khM .... Cold (Air) Mass (RU)
KhM .... Magnesium Chlorate (RU)
KhM .... Ship's Chemical Service (RU)
khm .... Thousand Meters (BU)
KhMA- .... Ammonia Refrigeration Unit (RU)
KhMB .... Chloromercuribenzoate (RU)
KhMDMB .... Chloromethyldimethylbenzene (RU)
KhMG .... Chemical Generator of Mechanical Energy (RU)
KhMI .... Khar'kov Medical Institute (RU)
KhMMI .... Khar'kov Institute of Mechanics and Mechanical Engineering (RU)
KhMO .... Khar'kov Mathematical Society (RU)
KhMS .... Hydrometeorological Service (BU)
KhMU .... Administrative and Materials Supply Management (RU)
KhN .... Chemical Attack [*Warning*] (RU)
KHN .... Komitet Historii Nauki [*Committee on the History of Science*] (POL)
KhNIKhFI .... Khar'kov Scientific Research Chemical and Pharmaceutical Institute (RU)
KhNOS .... Chemical Observation and Warning Service (RU)
KhNP .... Chemical Observation Post (BU)
KhNP .... Chemical Observation Post (RU)
KhNP .... Chemical Science and Industry (RU)
KhNSR .... Khoresm People's Soviet Republic [*1920-1923*] (RU)
KhNV .... Chemistry and Technology of Inorganic Substances (RU)
kho .... Chemical Defense (RU)
KhO .... Chemical Weapon (RU)
KhO .... Chemical Weapons (BU)
KHO .... Korkein Hallinto-Oikeus [*Supreme Administrative Court*] [*Finnish*] (WEN)
KhOGES ..... Khar'kov Oblast State Electric Power Plant (RU)
khol .... Cold (RU)
khol .... Dutch (BU)
kholod .... Cold Storage Plant [*Topography*] (RU)
khon prep ... Paid Instructor (BU)
KhOON .... United Nations Charter (BU)
khor .... Good (RU)
Khoremag ... State Enterprise for Hotels, Restaurants, and Stores (BU)
KhORGES ... Khar'kov Oblast State Electric Power Plant (RU)
khoz .... Economic, Economy, Establishment, Farm (RU)
Khozakarf ... Logistics Academy of the Red Army and Navy (RU)
khozmag ..... Household Goods Store (RU)
KhOZO .... Administrative and Supply Department (RU)
khoztorg ..... Specialized Organization for Trade in Household Goods (RU)
KhOZU .... Administrative and Supply Management (RU)
khozupr ...... Administrative and Supply Management (RU)
khoz-vo ...... Economy, Establishment, Farm (RU)
KhP .... Chemical Industry (RU)
KhP .... Chloroprene (RU)
KhP .... Cold Period [*Meteorology*] (RU)
KHP .... Keban Holding ve Ortaklari Plastik Sanayii AS [*Keban Holding and Partners Plastic Industry Corp.*] (TU)
KhP .... Khamili Piesis [*Low Pressure*] (GC)
KhPI .... Khar'kov Polytechnic Institute Imeni V. I. Lenin (RU)
KHPI .... Khimicheskii Poglotitel Izvestkovyi [*Chemical absorbent*] [*USSR*]
KhPI .... Lime Chemical Absorbent (RU)
KhPL .... Chemical Field Laboratory (RU)
KhPO .... Administrative and Production Department (RU)
KhPPB .... Mobile Field Surgical Hospital (BU)
KhPPG .... Mobile Field Surgical Hospital (BU)
KhPPG .... Mobile Field Surgical Hospital (RU)
KhPS .... Artistic and Political Council (RU)
KhPZ .... Khar'kov Locomotive Plant (RU)
KhR .... Chemical Company (RU)
KhR .... Chemical Reconnaissance (BU)
khr .... Christian (RU)
khr .... Chronometer (RU)
khr .... Farmstead [*Topography*] (RU)
khr .... Mountain Range [*Topography*] (RU)
kh-ra .... Farmsteads [*Topography*] (RU)
khra .... Kirkkoherra [*Finnish*]
Khramges ... Khrami Hydroelectric Power Plant (RU)
Khraneksport ... State Enterprise for the Export of Food Products (BU)
KhRD .... Chemical Reconnaissance Patrol (BU)
KhRD .... Chemical Reconnaissance Patrol (RU)
Khr e .... Christian Era [*In historic dates*] (RU)
khreb .... Mountain Range [*Topography*] (RU)
KhRIKE .... Khristiano-Dimokratikon Koinonikon Komma Ellados [*Greek Christian Democratic Party*] (GC)
KhRISKEL ... Khristiano-Dimokratikon Komma tis Ellados [*Christian Democratic Party of Greece*] (GC)
khrom .... Chromium Mines [*Topography*] (RU)
khromzavod ... Box Calf Plant (RU)
KhRR .... Chemical and Radiation Reconnaissance (RU)
KhRU .... Art Trade School (RU)
khrust .... Cut Glass Factory [*Topography*] (RU)
KhS .... Chemical Service (RU)
khs .... Connecting Trench (RU)
KhS .... Khamili Sykhnotis [*Low Frequency*] (GC)
KHS .... Kniznica Hudobneho Seminara [*Library of the Music Seminary (of the Slovak University)*] (CZ)
KHS .... Krosnienskie Huty Szkla [*Krosno Glass Works*] (POL)
KhS .... Sulfuryl Chloride (RU)
KhSh .... Household Refrigerator (RU)
KhSK .... Khristiano-Sosialistiki Kinisi [*Christian Socialist Movement*] [*Greek*] (GC)
KhSKhI .... Khar'kov Agricultural Institute Imeni V. V. Dokuchayev (RU)

KhSO .... Chemical Fragmentation Shell (BU)
KhSSR .... Khoresm Soviet Socialist Republic [*1923-1924*] (RU)
KhSSRZ ...... Kherson Shipyard Imeni Komintern (RU)
KhSZ .... Khar'kov Machine Tool Plant (RU)
KhSZ .... Use of Chemicals in Socialist Agriculture (RU)
KhT .... Chemical Alarm [*Military term*] (RU)
KhT .... Chromathermograph (RU)
kht .... Cold-Drawn (RU)
KhT .... Gas Alert (BU)
KHT .... Keskuskauppakamarin Hyvaksyma Tilintarkastaja [*Finnish*]
KhT .... Khamili Tasis [*Low Voltage*] (GC)
KhTG .... Chemical Generator of Heat (RU)
KhTG .... Chymotrypsinogen (RU)
KhTGZ .... Khar'kov Turbogenerator Plant Imeni S. M. Kirov (RU)
KhTI .... Chemical and Technical Institute (BU)
KhTM- .... Turbocompressor Refrigeration Unit (RU)
KHTMK .... Kibris Hukumeti Turk Memurin Kurumu [*Turkish Cypriot Civil Servants Association*] (GC)
KhTs .... Chordal Center (RU)
khts .... Hertz (BU)
KhTSZ .... Khar'kov Tractor Assembly Plant (RU)
KhTZ .... Khar'kov Tractor Plant Imeni Sergo Ordzhonikidze (RU)
KhTZ .... Khar'kov Turbine Plant Imeni S. M. Kirov (RU)
KhTZ .... Tractor Made by the Khar'kov Tractor Plant Imeni Sergo Ordzhonikidze (RU)
KHU .... Kenya Hockey Union (MAR)
khud .... Artist, Painter (RU)
KhudA .... Academy of Fine Arts (BU)
Khudozh ..... Artistic, Artist (BU)
khudozhpromsoyuz ... Art Crafts Producers' Association (RU)
khudruk ...... Art Adviser (RU)
Khut .... Farmstead [*Topography*] (RU)
Khutemast ... Art and Craft Shops (RU)
KhV .... Chromophil Substance (RU)
KHV .... Kozuti Hidfenntarto Vallalat [*Highway Bridge Maintenance Enterprise*] (HU)
KhVO .... Chemical Water Purification (BU)
kh-vo .... Economy, Establishment, Farm (RU)
KhVO .... Khar'kov Military District (RU)
KhVP .... Food Industry (BU)
KhVS .... Vertical Spindle Automotive Cotton Picker (RU)
KhVSh .... Vinyl-Perchloride Putty (RU)
KhVT .... Khar'kov Military Court (RU)
KhVZ .... Khar'kov Bicycle Plant (RU)
KHVZ .... Komise pro Hnuti Vynalezcu a Zlepsovatelu [*Commission for the Inventors' and Improvers' Movement*] (CZ)
KhVZD .... Chemical Delayed-Action Fuze (RU)
khyem .... Chemical Mass Unit (RU)
KhZ .... Chemical Defense (RU)
KhZ .... Chemical Plant (BU)
khz .... Chemical Plant (RU)
kHz .... Kiloherc [*Kilo-Cycle per Second*] [*Polish*]
KHz .... Kilohertz [*Kilohertz*] (EG)
KhZ .... Refrigeration Equipment Plant (BU)
KhZMI .... Khar'kov Plant of Mine Surveying Instruments (RU)
KhZTM .... Khar'kov Transportation Machinery Plant (RU)
KhZZM .... Khar'kov Dental Materials Plant (RU)
KI .... Communist International (RU)
Ki .... Corps Engineer (RU)
KI .... Fighter Airplane Compass (RU)
Ki .... Kali [*River*] [*Malaysian*] (NAU)
KI .... Keramicna Industrija [*Ceramic Industry*] (YU)
KI .... Kmetijski Inspektorat [*Inspectorate of Agriculture*] (YU)
KI .... Kommunista Internacionale [*Communist International (COMINTERN)*] (HU)
KI .... Komunisticka Internacionala [*Communist International (COMINTERN)*] (CZ)
KI .... Krajsky Inspektorat [*Regional Inspectorate*] (CZ)
KI .... Kulturni Informace [*Cultural Information Service (of the Ministry of Information)*] (CZ)
KI .... Oxygen Inhaler (RU)
KI .... Oxygen Utilization Factor (RU)
KIA .... Cambodian Information Agency [*Use AKI*] (CL)
KIA .... Kachin Independence Army [*Burmese*] (PD)
KIA .... Kenya Institute of Administration (MAR)
KIA .... Kilimanjaro International Airport (MAR)
K i A .... Monitoring and Automation [*Equipment*] (RU)
KIACS .... Kenya Independent Armoured Car Squadron (MAR)
KIAI .... Caucasian Historical and Archaeological Institute (RU)
KIAMC .... Kenya Institute of Administration Motor Club (MAR)
KIB .... Kikepzo Bazis [*Training Base*] (HU)
KIB .... Konstruktions- und Ingenieurbuero [*Design and Engineering Office*] (EG)
KIB .... Koy Isleri Bakanligi [*Village Affairs Ministry*] (TU)
KIB .... Kozigazgatasi Birosag [*Public Administration Court*] (HU)
KIB .... Kozigazgatasi Bizottsag [*Committee on Public Administration*] (HU)
KIB .... Kraftfahrzeuginstandsetzungsbetrieb [*Motor Vehicle Repair Enterprise*] (EG)
KIC .... Kuwait Investment Company (ME)
KICC .... Kenyatta International Conference Centre (MAR)
KIChP .... Commission for the Study of the Quaternary Period (RU)
KICOMI .... Kisamu Cotton Mills Ltd. (MAR)
KID .... Collegium of Foreign Affairs (RU)
KID .... Ion Diffusion Coefficient (RU)
KID .... Kranjska Industrijska Druzba [*Carniolan Industrial Society*] (YU)
KIDC .... Kenya Industrial Development Corporation (MAR)
KIDECO ...... Kilimanjaro Development Corporation (MAR)
KiDKP .... Ksztalcenie i Doskonalenie Kadr Pedagogicznych [*Education and Improvement of Pedagogical Personnel*] (POL)
KIDO .... Kish Island Development Organisation (MAR)
KIE .... Kenya Industrial Estates Ltd. (MAR)
KIE .... Kenya Institute of Education (MAR)
KIE .... Keresztyen Ifjusagi Egyesulet [*Young Men's Christian Association*] (HU)
kieg psag .... Kiegeszito Parancsnoksag [*Replacement Center*] (HU)
kiel .... Kielessa [*Finnish*]
kielit .... Kielitiede [*Finnish*]
Kier .... Kierownik [*Manager*] [*Polish*]
KIER .... Korea Institute of Energy and Resources
KIFCO .... Kuwait International Finance Company (ME)
KiG .... Kotar i Grad [*District and City*] (YU)
KIGM .... Kultur Isleri Genel Mudurlugu [*Cultural Affairs Directorate General*] (TU)
KIGVF .... Kiev Institute of the Civil Air Fleet (RU)
KIH .... Kaisar-I-Hind [*Indian medal*]
KIHUB .... Kompi Perhubungan [*Signal Company*] (IN)
KII .... Kiev Industrial Institute (RU)
KII .... Kuybyshev Industrial Institute Imeni V. V. Kuybyshev (RU)
KIIC .... Kuwait International Investment Company (ME)
kiir .... Kiireellinen [*Finnish*]
KIIVKh .... Kiev Institute of Hydraulic Engineers (RU)
kij .... Kijarat [*Exit*] (HU)
KIK .... Committee for Art and Culture (BU)
KIK .... Kamu Iktisadi Kuruluslari [*Public Economic Establishments*] (TU)
KIK .... Karma Isci Komitesi [*Mixed Workers' Committee*] [*Turkish Cypriot*] (GC)
KIK .... Keramicka Industrija Kumanovo [*Kumanovo Ceramic Industry*] (YU)
kik .... Kikepzes [*or Kikepzett*] [*Basic Training or Trained*] (HU)
KIK .... Kray Executive Committee (RU)
KIKhL .... Kazakh Institute of Belles Lettres (RU)
KIKhN .... Kiniton Kheirourgikon Nosokomeion [*Mobile (Army) Surgical Hospital*] (GC)
KIKI .... Kiev Institute of Motion Picture Engineers (RU)
KIL .... Caprylolactam (RU)
KIL .... Control and Measuring Laboratory (RU)
KIL .... Kapitalistisches Industrieland [*Capitalist Industrial Country*] (EG)
KIL .... Kontor fuer Import und Lagerung [*Import and Warehousing Agency*] (EG)
Kilo .... Kilogramme [*Kilogram*] [*French*] (MTD)
KILO-MOTO ... Office des Mines d'Or de Kilo-Moto (MAR)
KIM .... Communist Youth International (BU)
KIM .... Communist Youth International [*1919-1943*] (RU)
KIM .... Jacketed Small Composition [*Resistor*] (RU)
KIM .... Kenya Institute of Management (MAR)
kim .... Kimutatas [*Account, Financial Statement*] (HU)
Kim .... Kimya [*Chemistry, Chemical*] (TU)
KIM .... Kolej Islam Malaya [*Malayan Moslem College*] (ML)
KIM .... Kombinat Industrieller Mast [*Industrial Fattening Combine*] (EG)
KIM .... Komity Iobonan'ny Mpitolona [*Joint Struggle Committee*] [*Malagasy*] (AF)
KIM .... Komunisticka Internacionala Mladeze [*Communist Youth International*] (CZ)
KIM .... Konnyuipari Miniszterium/Miniszter [*Ministry/Minister of Light Industry*] (HU)
KIM .... Pulse-Code Modulation (RU)
KIMA .... Kompi Markas [*Headquarters Company*] (IN)
KIMC .... Kenya Institute of Mass Communication (MAR)
KIMESKh .... Kazakh Institute of Rural Mechanization and Electrification (RU)
Kimka .... Commission for Operation of Small Mines (RU)
KIMPA .... Hakim Perwira [*Military Judge*] (IN)
KIMS .... Caucasian Institute of Mineral Raw Materials (RU)
KIMS .... Checkout Magnetic Station (RU)
KIMSAT ...... Kimyevi Maddeler Ticaret ve Sanayi Ltd. Sti. [*Chemicals Trade and Industry, Inc.*] (TU)
KIMSZ .... Kommunista Ifjumunkasok Magyarorszagi Szovetsege [*Federation of Young Communist Workers in Hungary*] (HU)
KIMTES .... Kimya Tesisleri Sanayin Ticaret AS [*Chemical Equipment Industry and Corporation*] (TU)
KIMTUA ...... Hakim Ketua [*Chief Justice*] (IN)
kimut .... Kimutatas [*Account, Financial Statement*] (HU)
Kimya-Is ..... Turkiye Kimya Iscileri Sendikasi [*Turkish Chemical Workers Union*] [*See also Turkimya*] (TU)
k i n .... Candidate of Economic Sciences (BU)
kin .... Candidate of Historical Sciences (RU)

kin.............. Motion Picture Industry Plant [*Topography*] (RU)
KINAP......... Motion Picture Equipment Plant (RU)
KIND........... Kodix Idiotikou Navtikou Dikaiou [*Code of Private Maritime Law*] (GC)
Kinel'neft'... Kinel' Petroleum Industry Trust (RU)
kinetich....... Kinetic (RU)
Kinofotoizdat ... All-Union State Publishing House for Cinematography and Photography (RU)
Kinostroymontazh ... Construction and Installation Office of the Ministry of Cinematography, USSR (RU)
KINS........... Commission for the Study of the National Composition of the Population of the USSR (RU)
KIO............. Committee for Inventions and Discoveries (RU)
KIO............. Kenya Information Office (MAR)
KIO............. Kongres Industrijskih Organizacija [*Congress of Industrial Organizations*] (YU)
KiO............. Of Culture and Rest (RU)
KIOSZ......... Kisiparosok Orszagos Szervezete [*National Organization of Artisans*] (HU)
kip.............. Boiling (RU)
KIP............. Check-and-Test Apron (RU)
KIP............. Check-and-Test Point (RU)
KIP............. Control and Measuring Instrument (BU)
KIP............. Control and Measuring Instruments (RU)
KIP............. Control and Measuring Instruments Plant (RU)
KIP............. Insulating Oxygen Set (RU)
KIP............. Konfeksiyon Imalat Pazarlama Sanayi Ticaret AS [*Ready-Made Clothing Manufacture and Marketing Industry Corporation*] (TU)
KIP............. Measuring Instruments Set (RU)
KIP............. Red International of Trade Unions (RU)
KIPiA.......... Control and Measuring Instruments and Automation Equipment (RU)
KIPIG.......... Kibris Iktisadi Planlama Istisare Grubu [*Cyprus Economic Planning Consultative Group*] [*Turkish Cypriot*] (GC)
Kip M.......... Konnyuipari Miniszterium/Miniszter [*Ministry/Minister of Light Industry*] (HU)
KIPO........... Useful Volume Utilization Factor [*Of a blast furnace*] (RU)
KIPP........... Institute for Comprehensive Study and Design (BU)
KIPP........... Krasnodar Institute of the Food Industry (RU)
KIPS........... Mobile Check-and-Test Station (RU)
KIPS........... Permanent Commission for the Study of the Tribal Compositon of the Population of the USSR (at the Academy of Sciences, USSR) (RU)
KIPSZER..... Konnyuipari Szerelo es Epito Vallalat [*Light Industry Assembling and Construction Enterprise*] (HU)
KIR............. Khartoum Flight Information Region (MAR)
kir............... Kiralyi [*Royal*] (HU)
KIR............. Kirov Railroad (RU)
KIR............. Komisija za Izucavanje Rada i Radnih Uslova Sindikata Gradevinara [*Commission to Study Labor and Labor Conditions, Builders' Trade-Union*] (YU)
KiR............. Natural and Vulcanized Rubber (RU)
Kira-Kod..... Kisracilari Koruma Dernegi [*Associaton for the Protection of Tenants*] (TU)
KIRAPP....... Kirgiz Association of Proletarian Writers [*1930-1932*] (RU)
KIRDEP....... Kilimanjaro Regional Integrated Development Programme (MAR)
KIRDI.......... Kenya Industrial Research and Development Institute
kirend......... Kirendeltseg [*Local Office*] (HU)
kirg............. Kirgiz (RU)
KirgizFAN... Kirgiz Branch of the Academy of Sciences, USSR (RU)
Kirgizgosizdat ... Kirgiz State Publishing House (RU)
Kirgizneft'... Kirgiz Oil Field Administration (RU)
Kirgizuchpedgiz ... Kirgiz State Publishing House of Textbooks and Pedagogical Literature (RU)
KirgNIIZh.... Kirgiz Scientific Research Institute of Livestock Breeding (RU)
KirgNIIZhV ... Kirgiz Scientific Research Institute of Livestock Breeding and Veterinary Science (RU)
kirj.............. Kirjallisessa Tyylissa [*Literary*] [*Finnish*]
kirj.............. Kirjataan [*Finnish*]
kirj.............. Kirjoittanut [*Finnish*]
kirjall.......... Kirjallisuus [*Literature*] [*Finnish*]
kirjanp........ Kirjanpito [*Bookkeeping*] [*Finnish*]
kirjap.......... Kirjapaino [*Typography, Printing*] [*Finnish*]
kirj sid........ Kirjansidonta [*Bookbinding*] [*Finnish*]
kirk............. Kirkossa [*or Kirkollinen*] [*Ecclesiastic*] [*Finnish*]
kirp............. Brickyard [*Topography*] (RU)
KirSSR........ Kirgiz Soviet Socialist Republic (RU)
KirTAG........ Kirgiz News Agency (RU)
KIS............. Check-and-Test Station (RU)
KIS............. Kendrikon Israilitikon Symvoulion [*Central Jewish Council*] (GC)
KIS............. Keramicka Industrija Skopje [*Skopje Ceramic Industry*] (YU)
Kis.............. Kisi [*or Kisiler*] [*Individual or Individuals*] (TU)
KIS............. Klub Inzenyru a Stavitelu [*Engineers' and Builders' Club*] (CZ)
KIS............. Komisia pre Industrializaciu Slovenska [*Commission for the Industrialization of Slovakia*] (CZ)
KIS............. Kontrolna Isturena Stanica [*Advanced Control Station*] [*Military*] (YU)
KIS............. Krankenhaus Informations System
KIS............. Oxygen-Inhalation Station (RU)
KISA........... Kikuyu Independent Schools Association (MAR)
kiserl.......... Kiserleti [*Experimental*] (HU)
KISI............ Kiev Construction Engineering Institute (RU)
KISKER....... Kiskereskedelmi Vallalat [*Retail Enterprise*] (HU)
k isk n......... Candidate of Art Studies (RU)
k is n.......... Candidate of Historical Sciences (BU)
KISO........... Commission for Solar Research (of the Academy of Sciences, USSR) (RU)
KISOSZ....... Kiskereskedok Orszagos Szabadszervezete [*National Free Organization of Retailers*] (HU)
KISTEX....... Kispesti Textilgyar [*Kispest Textile Mill*] (HU)
KISZ........... Magyar Kommunista Ifjusagi Szovetseg [*Hungarian Communist Youth League*] (HU)
KISZOK....... Kommunista Ifjusagi Szovetseg Orszagos Kozpontja [*National Center of the Hungarian Communist Youth League*] (HU)
KISZOV....... Kisipari Szovetkezetek Szovetsege [*Association of Small Industrial Cooperatives*] (HU)
kit............... Chinese (BU)
kit............... Chinese (RU)
KIT............. Committee of Rural Union [*Malagasy*] (AF)
KIT............. Control and Measurement Engineering (RU)
KIT............. Kamu Iktisadi Tesebbusleri [*Public Economic Enterprises*] [*Turkish Cypriot*] (GC)
KIT............. Koninklijk Instituut voor de Tropen [*Amsterdam*]
KITA........... Kesatuan Insaf Tanah Air [*National Consciousness Party*] [*Malaysian*] (PPW)
KITE........... Kukorica es Iparinoveny Termelesi Egyuttmukodes [*Corn and Industrial Crop Growing Cooperation (Located at Nadudver)*] (HU)
KITI............ Kohoipari Tervezo Iroda [*Planning Office for Metallurgical Industry*] (HU)
KITSAB....... Kibris Turk Seyahat Acentalari Birligi [*Turksih Cypriot Travel Agents Association*] (TU)
KITSAK-SEN ... Kibris Turk Sanayi Kesimi Memurlar Sendikasi [*Turkish Cypriot Industrial Sector Employees Union*] (GC)
KITV........... Konnyuipari Tervezo Vallalat [*Light Industry Designing Enterprise*] (HU)
KIU............. Commission for the Study of the Ukraine (at the VUAN) (RU)
KIUA........... Kazakhstan Institute of Fertilizers and Soil Science (RU)
KIUTA......... Kiwanda cha Uchapaji cha Taifa (MAR)
KIUV........... Kiev Institute for the Advanced Training of Physicians (RU)
kiv.............. Kivitel [*Export*] (HU)
KIVB........... Kommunista Internacionale Vegrehajto Bizottsaga [*Executive Committee of the Communist International*] (HU)
KIvI............ Koninklijk Instituut van Ingenieurs [*'s-Gravenhage*]
KIVM........... Committee for Permafrost Study (of the Academy of Sciences, USSR) (RU)
KIVUMINES ... Compagnie Miniere de Kivu [*Mining Company of Kivu*] [*Zairian*] (AF)
KiW............ Ksiazka i Wiedza [*Book and Knowledge*] [*Publisher*] (POL)
KIWA.......... Keurings Instituut Waterleiding Artikelen [*Rijswijk*]
KIWZ.......... Kupiecki Instytut Wiedzy Zawodowej [*Institute of Business Administration*] (POL)
KIYa........... Foreign Language Courses (RU)
KIYaLI......... Kazan' Institute of Language, Literature, and History (of the Academy of Sciences, USSR) (RU)
Kiyevmetrostroy ... Construction Administration of the Kiev Subway (RU)
KiyevZNIIEP ... Kiev Zonal Scientific Research and Planning Institute for Standard and Experimental Planning of Residential and Public Buildings (RU)
KIYU........... Kibris-Yunanistan Dairesi General Mudurlugu [*Cyprus-Greece Office Directorate General*] [*of Foreign Affairs Ministry*] (TU)
KIZ............. Kazakh Scientific Research Institute of Agriculture (RU)
KIZ............. Kemijska Industrijska Zajednica [*Chemical Industrial Association*] [*Zagreb*] (YU)
KIZ............. Komisja dla Spraw Inwalidztwa i Zatrudnienia [*Commission on Problems of Disability and Employment*] (POL)
Kizelugol'.... Kizel Coal Basin (RU)
KIZh........... Communist Institute of Journalism (RU)
KIZILAY...... Turkiye Kizilay Dernegi [*Turkish Red Crescent Society*] [*Similar to Red Cross*] [*See also TKD*] (TU)
KiZPS......... Kopalnictwo i Zaklady Przetworcze Siarki [*Sulphur Mining and Processing Enterprise*] (POL)
KJ.............. Kilodzul [*Kilojoule*] [*Polish*]
KJ.............. Kostnicka Jednota [*Union of Constance*] (CZ)
KJ.............. Scierie Kakou Joseph (MAR)
KJB............ Katholieke Jeugdbeweging [*Catholic Youth Movement*] [*Dutch*] (WEN)
KJB............ Kommunistische Jugendbewegung [*Communist Youth Movement*] [*Austrian*] (WEN)
KJ K........... Kozlekedesi es Jogi Kiado [*Publishers of Economic and Legal Literature*] (HU)
KJOe.......... Kommunistische Jugend Oesterreichs [*Communist Youth of Austria*] (EG)
KJR............ Katholieke Jeugdraad voor Nederland [*Catholic Youth Council for the Netherlands*] (WEN)
KJSE.......... Kenya Junior Secondary Education (MAR)
KJV............ Kommunistischer Jugendverband [*Communist Youth Federation*] [*Swiss*] (WEN)

KJV............ Kraljevska Jugoslovenska Vojska [*Royal Yugoslav Army*] (YU)
KJVDM........ Kraljevska Jugoslovenska Vojska Draza Mihailovic [*Royal Yugoslav Army of Draza Mihailovic*] (YU)
k/k............ Candidate's Membership Card (RU)
kk............ Cavalry Corps (BU)
KK............ Cavalry Corps (RU)
KK............ Committee for Cinematography (BU)
KK............ Compass Course (RU)
KK............ Control Commission (RU)
KK............ End of Curve [*Railroads*] (RU)
KK............ Kabushiki Kaisha [*Public Limited Company*]
KK............ Kaiser Koenigliche
KK............ Kandang Kerbau (ML)
kk............ Kansakoulu [*Finnish*]
KK............ Kansallinen Kokoomus [*National Coalition (Conservative Party)*] [*Finnish*] (WEN)
KK............ Kara Komutani [*Ground (Forces) Commander*] (TU)
KK............ Kasvatustieteiden Kandidaatti [*Finnish*]
KK............ Kepala Keluarga [*Head of Family*] (IN)
KK............ Kepala Kepolisian [*Chief of Police*] (IN)
KK............ Khmer Krom [*Lower Cambodians*] [*Cambodians living in South Vietnam*] (CL)
kk............ Kiettokomero [*Finnish*]
kk............ Kihlakunta [*Finnish*]
kk............ Kirkonkyla [*Finnish*]
KK............ Kodeks Karny [*Penal Code*] [*Polish*]
KK............ Komisija za Katastar [*Cadastre Commission*] (YU)
KK............ Komitet Koordynacyjny [*Coordinating Committee*] (POL)
KK............ Komitet Kuracjuszy [*Health Resort Patients' Committee*] (POL)
KK............ Kommounistikon Komma [*Communist Party*] (GC)
KK............ Kommunista Kialtvany [*Communist Manifesto*] (HU)
kk............ Konekivaari [*Finnish*]
KK............ Konfliktkommission [*Conflict Commission*] (EG)
K k............ Konyvkiado [*Book Publishers*] (HU)
kk............ Korona [*Crown*] (HU)
K K............ Kossuth Kiado [*Kossuth Publishing House*] (HU)
KK............ Kozepeuropai Kupa [*Mid-European Cup*] (HU)
KK............ Krajska Konference [*Regional Conference*] (CZ)
KK............ Krasnodar Kray (RU)
KK............ Kuala Kangsar (ML)
KK............ Kulturni Komise [*Cultural Commission*] (CZ)
Kk............ Kunze-Knorr Bremse [*Kunze-Knorr Brake*] (EG)
kk............ Kuukaudet [*Finnish*]
kk............ Kuukausi [*or Kuukautta*] [*Finnish*]
KK............ Kuvvet Kontrollu [*Power Controlled*] [*As of a tractor for vehicles in tow*] (TU)
KK............ Quality Control (BU)
KK............ Red Cross (RU)
KK............ Spaceship (RU)
kk............ Trooper, Cavalryman (BU)
KKA............ Caucasian Red Army (RU)
KKA............ Kinima Kypriakis Andistaseos [*Cypriot Resistance Movement*] (GC)
KKA............ Kodix Koinonikis Asfaliseos [*Social Insurance Code*] [*Greek*] (GC)
KKA............ Kommounistikon Komma Alvanias [*Albanian Communist Party*] (GC)
kkal............ Kilocalorie (BU)
kkal............ Kilocalorie (RU)
KKASSR..... Karakalpak Autonomous Soviet Socialist Republic (RU)
KKAZ.......... Kuybyshev Carburetor and Fittings Plant (RU)
KKB............ Korespondencyjny Kurs Bibliotekarski [*Library Science Correspondence Course*] (POL)
KKB............ Kozlekedesi Konyvesbolt [*Transportation Publications Book Shop*] (HU)
KKBK.......... Kongres Kesatuan Buroh Kebangsaan [*National Trade Union Congress*] (ML)
KKDD.......... Katalog Kandidatskikh i Doktorskikh Dissertatsii [*A bibliographic publication*]
KKDDY........ Kodix Katastaseos Dimosion Dioikitikon Ypallilon [*Public Administrative Employees Schedule Code*] [*Greek*] (GC)
KKE............ Complex Kenimekh Expedition (RU)
KKE............ Kommunistiko Komma Ellados [*Communist Party of Greece*] (PPW)
KKEA.......... Kikuyu Karinga Educational Association (MAR)
KKEes......... Kommunistiko Komma Ellados - Esoterikou [*Communist Party of Greece - Interior*] (PPE)
KKEex......... Kommunistiko Komma Ellados - Exoterikou [*Communist Party of Greece - Exterior*] (PPE)
KKE/ML...... Kommunistiko Komma Elladas/Marxiston-Leniniston [*Communist Party of Greece/Marxist-Leninist*] (GC)
KKES.......... Kommunistiko Komma Ellados - Esoterikou [*Communist Party of Greece - Interior*] (PPW)
KKF............ Komitet Kultury Fizycznej [*Physical Culture Committee*] (POL)
KKF............ "Red Banner" Caspian Naval Flotilla (RU)
KKFiT.......... Komitet Kultury Fizycznej i Turystyki [*Physical Culture and Tourism Committee*] (POL)
KKG............ Kesatuan Kebangsaan Guru [*National Union of Teachers*] (ML)
KKG............ Kreiskonsumgenossenschaft [*Kreis Consumer Cooperative*] (EG)
Kkgbr.......... Kunze-Knorr-Bremse fuer Gueterzuege [*Kunze-Knorr Brake for Freight Trains*] (EG)
KKh............ Katastatikos Khartis [*Charter*] (GC)
KKh............ Koroi Khorikotitos [*Net Tons, Net Tonnage*] [*See also KKKh*] (GC)
Kkh............ Potassium Chloride (RU)
k kh n.......... Candidate of Chemical Sciences (BU)
kkhn............ Candidate of Chemical Sciences (RU)
KKhT.......... Ktimatologikon kai Khorometrikon Tmima [*Cadastral and Zoning Department*] [*See also TPPE*] (GC1)
KKhTI.......... Kazan' Institute of Chemical Technology Imeni S. M. Kirov (RU)
KKhTs.......... Kilohertz (BU)
KKhZ.......... By-Product Coke Plant (RU)
KKhZhD...... Kiev-Khar'kov Railroad (RU)
KKI............ Committee for Culture and Art (BU)
KKI............ Krajsky Kulturni Inspektorat [*Office of the Regional Inspector of Cultural Activities*] (CZ)
KKI............ Kulturkapcsolatok Intezete [*Institute for Cultural Relations*] (HU)
KKIK.......... Keramicno Kemicna Industrija Kamnik [*Kamnik Ceramic and Chemical Industry*] (YU)
KKiKP.......... Red Cross and Red Crescent [*Society*] (RU)
KKIV.......... Kiallitasokat Kivitelezo Ipari Vallalat [*Enterprise Affiliated with Industry for Arrangement of Exhibits*] (HU)
KKK............ End of Belt Line [*Railroads*] (RU)
KKK............ Kara Kuvvetler Komutani [*Ground Forces Commander*] (TU)
KKK............ Kesunyans Keltek Kernow [*Celtic League in Cornwall*]
KKK............ Khmer du Kampuchea Krom [*Association of Friends of the Khmer Krom*] [*Use AKKK*] [*Cambodian*] (CL)
KKK............ Kibris Koordinasyon Komitesi [*Cyprus Coordination Committee*] [*Turkish Cypriot*] (GC)
KKK............ Kommounistikon Komma Kyprou [*Communist Party of Cyprus*] [*See also AKEL*] (GC)
KKK............ Kosmofysikon kai Kosmotheikon Kinima [*Cosmophysic and Cosmotheist Movement*] [*Greek*] (GC)
KKK............ Krajsky Kynologicky Klub [*Regional Kennel Club*] (CZ)
KKK............ Kreiskontrollkommission [*Kreis Control Commission*] (EG)
KKK............ Switchboard for Checking Credit Rating (RU)
KKKA.......... Caucasian "Red Banner" Red Army (RU)
KKKh.......... Koroi Katharas Khorikotitos [*Net Register(ed) Tonnage*] [*See also KKh*] (GC)
KKKT.......... Canadian Catholic Confederation of Labor (RU)
KKL............ Card Hopper Contact (RU)
KKLK.......... Krajska Komise Lidove Kontroly [*Regional Commission of People's Control*] (CZ)
KKM............ Kereskedelem- es Kozlekedesugyi Miniszter [*Minister of Trade and Transportation*] (HU)
KkM............ Kulkereskedelmi Miniszterium/Miniszter [*Ministry/Minister of Foreign Trade*] (HU)
KKMP.......... Korespondencyjny Klub Mlodych Pisarzy [*Young Writers' Correspondence Club*] (POL)
KKN............ Krosnienskie Kopalnictwo Naftowe [*Krosno Oil Wells*] (POL)
KKO............ Cockpit Oxygen Equipment (RU)
KKO............ Kibris Kurtulus Ordusu [*Cyprus Liberation Army*] (TU)
kko............ Kirkko [*Finnish*]
KKO............ Komunalna Kasa Oszczednosci [*Communal Savings Bank*] (POL)
KKO............ Konflikt-Kommissionsordnung [*Conflict Commission Regulations*] (EG)
KKO............ Korps Komando [*Marine Corps*] (IN)
KKON.......... Koinonikon Kendron Oikogeneias kai Neotitos [*Family and Youth Social Center*] [*Greek*] (GC)
KKOV.......... Cossack Mutual Aid Committee (RU)
KKOV.......... Peasants' Public Mutual Aid Committee (RU)
KKP............ Canadian Communist Party (BU)
KKP............ Canadian Trade-Union Congress (RU)
KKP............ Chinese Communist Party (BU)
KKP............ Chinese Communist Party (RU)
KKP............ Cuban Communist Party (BU)
KKP............ Cypriot Communist Party (BU)
KKP............ Kendron Koinonikis Pronoias [*Social Welfare Center*] (GC)
KKP............ Kina Kommunista Partja [*Communist Party of China*] (HU)
KKP............ Konfederatsiia Kongolezskikh Profsoiuzov (MAR)
KKP............ Leather and Fur Industry (BU)
Kkpbr.......... Kunze-Knorr-Bremse fuer Personenzuege [*Kunze-Knorr Brake for Passenger Trains*] (EG)
KKPT.......... Kakitangan Khas Periksaan Tentera [*Special Military Intelligence Staff*] (ML)
KK-RKI........ Control Commission and Workers' and Peasants' Inspection [*1923-1934*] (RU)
KKS............ Aerial Surveying Compass Course (RU)
k ks............ Cavalry Corps (BU)
KKS............ Courses for Command Personnel (RU)
KKS............ Kolejowy Klub Sportowy [*Railway Workers' Sports and Athletics Club*] [*Polish*]
KKS............ Komisja Kontroli Stronnictwa [*Party Control Commission*] (POL)
KKS............ Kongres Kesatuan Sakerja [*Trade Union Congress (TUC)*] (ML)
Kksbr.......... Kunze-Knorr-Bremse fuer Schnellzuege [*Kunze-Knorr Brake for Express Trains*] (EG)

KKSFA........ Kypros - Koreatikos Syndesmos Filias kai Allilengyis [*Cyprus - Korea Friendship and Solidarity League*] (GC)
kkt.............. Kozos Kozsegi Tanacs [*Joint Village Council (of two of more villages)*] (HU)
KKT............. Kulturalis Kapcsolatok Tanacsa [*Council of Cultural Relations*] (HU)
KKTD.......... Kanunlar ve Kararlar Tetkik Dairesi [*Laws and Decisions' Investigation Office*] [*Under office of Premier*] (TU)
KKTSK........ Kucuk Kaymakli Turk Spor Kulubu [*Kucuk Kaimakli Turkish Sports Club*] [*Turkish Cypriot*] (GC)
KKU............. Kniznica Komenskeho Univerzity [*Comenius University Library*] [*Bratislava*] (CZ)
K Kuv.......... Kara Kuvvetleri [*Ground Forces*] (TU)
KKV............. Kiskereskedelmi Vallalat [*Retail Enterprise*] (HU)
KKv............. Komandir Komandnog Voda Baterije [*Commander of the Command Platoon of a Battery*] (YU)
KKV............. Kommounistikon Komma Voulgarias [*Bulgarian Communist Party*] (GC)
KKVI............ Komisija za Kulturne Veze sa Inostranstvom [*Commission for Cultural Relations with Foreign Countries*] (YU)
KKZ............. Kamyshin Crane Plant (RU)
KKZ............. Kinderbijslagwet voor Kleine Zelfstandigen [*Children's Allowance Act for Self-Employed of Small Means*] [*Dutch*] (WEN)
KKZA........... Heavy Caliber Antiaircraft Artillery (BU)
KKZVV......... Krajska Komise pro Zemedelskou Vyrobu a Vykup [*Regional Commission for Agricultural Production and Bulk Buying*] (CZ)
kl................. Caliber, Gauge (RU)
KL................ Caprolactam (RU)
kl................. Class [*or Category*] (BU)
kl................. Class, Sort, Grade (RU)
Kl................. Clinker [*Road-paving material*] [*Topography*] (RU)
kl................. Club (RU)
kl................. Cosmic Rays (RU)
kl................. Grade (BU)
KL................ Gunboat (RU)
Kl................. Kale [*Castle, Fortress*] (TU)
KL................ Kaufmaennische Leitung [*Business Management*] (EG)
kl................. Kevatlukukausi [*Finnish*]
kl................. Kiloliter (RU)
kl................. Kilolitre [*Kiloliter*] [*French*] (GPO)
Kl................. Kilolitro [*Kiloliter*] [*Spanish*]
kl................. Klapka [*Extension (Telephone)*] (CZ)
kl................. Klasa [*Class*] (YU)
kl................. Klasa [*Class*] (POL)
kl................. Klasifikacija [*Classification*] (YU)
kl................. Klasse [*Class*] [*Danish*] (GPO)
Kl................. Klasse [*Class*] [*German*] (GPO)
kl................. Klockan [*O'Clock*] [*Swedish*] (GPO)
kl................. Klokken [*O'Clock*] [*Danish*] (GPO)
KL................ Komisija za Lekove [*Pharmaceutical Commission*] (YU)
KL................ Komitet Lodzki
KL................ Kontrola Letenja [*Flight Control*] [*Military*] (YU)
KL................ Kozponti Laboratorium [*Central Laboratory*] (HU)
KL................ Kuala Lumpur (ML)
Kl................. Kuopion Laani(a) [*Finnish*]
KL................ Kurang Lebih [*More or Less, Approximately*] (IN)
KL................ Line Contactor (RU)
KL................ Pilot Lamp, Supervisory Lamp (RU)
k-l................ Some (RU)
kl................. Spring, Source [*Topography*] (RU)
KLA............. Kingdom of Libya Airways [*or Airlines*] (MAR)
Kla.............. Kuala [*River Mouth*] [*Indonesian*] (NAU)
Kla.............. Kuala [*River Mouth*] [*Malaysian*] (NAU)
KLA............. Kwazulu Legislative Assembly (MAR)
KLA............. Spacecraft (RU)
kladb........... Cemetery [*Topography*] (RU)
klasich........ Classic (BU)
klassich...... Classic (RU)
KLDR........... Korejska Lidove-Demokraticka Republika [*Korean People's Republic*] (CZ)
KLE............. Concise Literary Encyclopedia [*A publication*] (RU)
KLEG........... Kancelar Legii [*Office of Czechoslovak Legions (Attached to the Ministry of National Defense)*] (CZ)
Kleytuk....... Moscow Bone Glue and Fertilizer Plant (RU)
KLF............. Cambodian Liberation Front (CL)
KLFA........... Kenya Land Freedom Army (MAR)
KLFB........... Knihovna Lekarske Fakulty, Brno [*Library of the School of Medicine in Brno*] (CZ)
KLFI............ Kozponti Legkorfizikai Intezet [*Central Institute of Atmospheric Physics*] (HU)
KLFK........... Kniznica Lekarskej Fakulty, Kosice [*Library of the School of Medicine in Kosice*] (CZ)
KLFOL......... Knihovna Lekarske Fakulty v Olomouci [*Library of the School of Medicine in Olomouc*] (CZ)
KLFP........... Knihovna Lekarske Fakulty, Praha [*Library of the School of Medicine in Prague*] (CZ)
KLFPI.......... Knihovna Lekarske Fakulty, Plzen [*Library of the School of Medicine in Plzen*] (CZ)
KLGC........... Kuala Lumpur Garrison Command (ML)
KLI............... Kalinin Railroad (RU)
Kli................ Klinik [*Clinic*] (TU)
klim............. Climatic, Climatology (RU)
Klin.............. Klinik [*German*]
klinich......... Clinical (RU)
KLK............. Card-Tape-Card Machine (RU)
KLK............. Katolicky Literarni Klub [*Catholic Literary Club*] (CZ)
KLK............. Kelas Latehan Kerja [*Work (Job) Training Class*] (ML)
KLK............. Krajska Lidova Knihovna [*Regional People's Library*] (CZ)
klkh............. Kolkhoz [*Topography*] (RU)
klkh dv........ Kolkhoz Yard [*Topography*] (RU)
KLKhTI........ Leningrad "Red Banner" Institute of Chemical Technology Imeni Lensovet (RU)
KLKSNR...... Komise Lidove Kontroly Slovenske Narodni Rady [*Commission of People's Control of Slovakia's National Council*] (CZ)
klm.............. Kilolumen (RU)
KLM............. Koninklijke Luchtvaart Maatschappij [*Royal Dutch Airlines*] (WEN)
klm-ch........ Kilolumen-Hour (RU)
KLN............. Kypriaki Leskhi Neolaias [*Cypriot Youth Club*] [*London*] (GC)
k-lo............. Kello [*Hour, O'Clock*] [*Finnish*] (GPO)
KLO............. Krajevni Ljudski Odbor [*District People's Committee*] (YU)
KLP............. Flight Training Course (RU)
klp.............. Kai Loipa [*Et Cetera*] (GC)
KLP............. Kendrikon Limenarkheion Peiraios [*Piraeus Central Port Authority*] (GC)
KLP............. Krajowa Loteria Pieniezna [*National Lottery*] (POL)
KLR............. Kreislandwirtschaftsrat [*Kreis Agricultural Council*] (EG)
KLR............. Linear Expansion Coefficient (RU)
KLS............. Kommunisten und Linkssozialisten [*German*]
KLS............. Stationary Belt Conveyor (RU)
Klstr............ Kloster [*German*]
KLTE........... Kossuth Lajos Tudomanyegyetem [*Lajos Kossuth University of Sciences*] (HU)
Klurabis...... Club of Workers in the Arts (RU)
klv............... Kilowatt (BU)
KLW............ Karl-Liebknecht-Werke, Magdeburg [*Karl-Liebknecht Works, Magdeburg*] (EG)
KM.............. Acid Mucopolysaccharide (RU)
km............... Commandant (BU)
KM.............. Comoros [*Two-letter standard code*] (CNC)
KM.............. Contact Mechanism (RU)
KM.............. Crystal Modulator (RU)
KM.............. Cyril and Methodius (BU)
KM.............. Kabataang Makabayan [*Nationalist Youth*] [*Philippine*]
KM.............. Kablovska Mreza [*Cable Network*] [*Military*] (YU)
km............... Karabin Maszynowy [*Machine Gun*] [*Polish*]
km............... Kilometer (BU)
km............... Kilometer [*Kilometer*] (HU)
km............... Kilometer [*Kilometer*] [*German*]
km............... Kilometer (RU)
km............... Kilometr [*Kilometer*] (POL)
km............... Kilometre [*Kilometer*] [*French*]
km............... Kilometre [*Kilometer*] [*Turkish*] (GPO)
km............... Kilometri(a) [*Finnish*]
Km.............. Kilometro [*Kilometer*] [*Spanish*]
KM.............. Komanda Mesta [*Command of a City*] (YU)
KM.............. Komisija za Mehanizaciju [*Mechanization Commission*] (YU)
KM.............. Komitet Miejski [*City Committee*] (POL)
kM.............. Kommenden Monats [*Of Next Month*] [*German*]
KM.............. Kon Mechaniczny [*Horsepower*] [*Polish*]
KM.............. Koni Maszynowych [*Horsepower*] (POL)
KM.............. Kozellatasi Miniszterium/Miniszter [*Ministry/Minister of Supply*] (HU)
KM.............. Kozlekedesugyi Miniszterium/Miniszter [*Ministry/Minister of Transportation*] (HU)
km............... Kozmondas [*Proverb*] (HU)
KM.............. Kozoktatasugyi Miniszterium/Miniszter [*Ministry/Minister of Public Education (Since 1951)*] (HU)
KM.............. Krajske Muzeum [*Regional Museum*] (CZ)
KM.............. Kulugyminiszterium/Miniszter [*Ministry/Minister of Foreign Affairs*] (HU)
K M............. Kurucu Meclis [*Organizing Assembly*] (TU)
KM.............. Kutahya Manyezit Isletmeleri AS [*Kutahya Magnezite Operations Corp.*] (TU)
km............... Kyvika Metra [*Cubic Meters*] (GC)
KM.............. March Route Commandant (RU)
KM.............. March Route Commander (BU)
KM.............. Marrow (RU)
KM.............. Meteorological Observation Record Book (RU)
KM.............. Michaelis Constant (RU)
km............... My Italics (BU)
KM.............. Naval Fortress (RU)
KM.............. Oxygen Mask (RU)
Km.............. Potassium Magnesium Sulfate (RU)
KM.............. Stone Bridge (RU)
km^2............. Kilometr Kwadratowy [*Square Kilometer*] [*Polish*]
Km^2............ Kilometre Carre [*Square Kilometer*] [*French*] (MTD)
km^2............. Square Kilometer (BU)
km^3............. Kilometr Szescienny [*Cubic Kilometer*] [*Polish*]
KMA............ Kenya Medical Association (MAR)

KMA .... Kepzomuveszeti Alap [*Fine Arts Fund*] (HU)
KMA .... Koninklijke Militaire Academie [*Royal Military Academy*] [*Dutch*] (WEN)
KMA .... Kursk Magnetic Anomaly (RU)
KMAC .... Koztarsasagi Magyar Automobil Club [*Automobile Club of the Hungarian Republic*] [*Formerly Royal Hungarian Automobile Club*] (HU)
KMAS .... Kibris Madenler Anonim Sirketi [*Cyprus Mines Corporation*] [*Turkish Cypriot*] (GC)
KMAU .... Moscow "Red Banner" Aviation School (RU)
KMB .... Konstruktions-Montage-Buero [*Design and Assembly Office*] (EG)
KMB .... Public Libraries Pool (RU)
KMC .... Kenya Meat Commission (MAR)
KMC .... Klub Mladych Ctenaru [*Club of Young Readers*] (CZ)
km/ch .... Kilometers per Hour (BU)
KMD .... Kadikoy Musik Dernegi [*Kadikoy Music Association*] [*Istanbul*] (TU)
KM-DK .... Machine-Gun Mortar Decontamination Kit (BU)
kmdr .... Komandor [*Commodore*] [*Polish*]
kmdt .... Komendant [*Commander*] [*Polish*]
KME .... Kypriaki Metallevtiki Etaireia [*Cyprus Mines Corporation*] (GC)
KMEA .... Kinitai Monades Ethnofylakis Amynis [*National Guard Mobile Defense Units*] [*Greek*] (GC)
KMET .... Committee on Meteorites (of the Academy of Sciences, USSR) (RU)
KMF .... Kabinet Moderni Filologie [*Department of Modern Philology (of the Czechoslovak Academy of Sciences)*] (CZ)
kmf .... Kelt Mint Fent [*Date as Above*] (HU)
KMF .... Klub Modernich Filologu [*Modern Philology Club*] (CZ)
KMF .... Short Film (RU)
KMFD .... National Committee for Liberty and Decentralization [*Malagasy*] (AF)
KMFRV .... Committee in Support of the Demand for a New Republic [*Malagasy*] (AF)
KMG .... Cavalry Motorized and Mechanized Group (RU)
KMG .... Kendrikon Morfotikon Grafeion [*Central Educational Office*] (GC)
km/g .... Kilometry na Godzine [*Kilometers per Hour*] [*Polish*]
KMG .... Klynveld Main Goerdeler [*European accounting firm*]
KmG .... Kmecki Glas [*Peasant's Voice*] [*A periodical*] (YU)
KMG .... Kombinat za Montazne i Opste Gradevinske Radove [*Combine for General Construction Jobs*] (YU)
KMGV .... Pro-Military Government Committee in the Ambatondrazaka Subprefecture [*Malagasy*] (AF)
KMh .... Koniogodzina [*Horse-Power-Hour*] [*Polish*]
KMI .... Kaunas Medical Institute (RU)
KMI .... Kereskedelmi Minosegellenorzo Intezet [*Commercial Quality Control Institute*] (HU)
KMI .... Kiev Medical Institute Imeni Academician A. A. Bogomolets (RU)
KMI .... Kirgiz State Medical Institute (RU)
KMI .... Klub Mlodej Inteligencji [*Club of Young Intelligentsia*] (POL)
KMIAE .... Committee for the Peaceful Utilization of Atomic Energy (BU)
KMIP .... Committee on Measures and Measuring Instruments (RU)
KMiP .... Komitet Miejski i Powiatowy [*City and County (Party) Committee*] (POL)
KMIZ .... Correlation Methods in Earthquake Investigation (RU)
KMK .... Kibris Maden Kumpanyasi [*Cyprus Mining Company*] (TU)
KMK .... Krestanska Mirova Konference [*Christian Peace Conference*] (CZ)
KMK .... Kuznetsk Metallurgical Kombinat (RU)
KMK .... Medical Control Commission (BU)
kmk/kaemka ... Kozveszelyes Munkakerulo [*Work-Shirking That Endangers Public Order or Vagrancy*] (HU)
KMKS- .... Multipurpose Magnetic Logging Station (RU)
KML .... Kenya Muslim League (MAR)
KMM .... Etudiants des Provinces [*Provincial Students*] [*Malagasy*] (AF)
KMM .... Kesatuan Malaya Merdeka [*Free Malaya Front*] (ML)
KMM .... Mechanized Treadway Bridge (RU)
KMME .... Concentrate of Mineral-Oil Emulsion (RU)
KMME .... Kendron Marxistikon Meleton kai Erevnon [*Center for Marxist Studies and Research*] [*Greek*] (GC)
kmn .... Candidate of Medical Sciences (RU)
KMN .... Kasatria Mangku Negara [*Fourth Grade of Most Distinguished Order of Pangkuan Negara*] [*Malaysian*] (ML)
KMNI .... Komisija za Medicinsko-Naucna Istrazivanja [*Medical Research Commission*] (YU)
KMNO .... Kolegium Ministerstva Narodni Obrany [*Ministry of National Defense Advisory Board*] (CZ)
KMO .... After Engine Room (RU)
KMO .... Committee of Youth Organizations of the USSR (RU)
km/o .... Kilometer Ora [*Kilometers per Hour*] (HU)
KMO .... Kimya Muhendisleri Odasi [*Chamber of (Turkish) Chemical Engineers*] (TU)
KMO .... Music Education Courses (RU)
KMODD .... Kendron Metekpaidevseos Organon Dimosias Dioikiseos [*Advanced Training Center for Public Administration Officials*] [*Greek*] (GC)
KMOETs ...... Carboxymethyl Hydroxyethyl Cellulose (RU)
kmol' .... Kilogram Molecule, Kilomole (RU)
KMP .... Corps Medical Station (RU)
KMP .... International Law Commission (BU)
KMP .... Kabinet Mezinarodniho Prava [*Department of International Law (of the Czechoslovak Academy of Sciences)*] (CZ)
KMP .... Katipunang Manggagawang Pilipino [*Confederation of Trade Unions of the Philippines*]
KMP .... KERAMOPROJEKT - Statni Ustav pro Projektovani Zavodu Prumyslu Stavebnich Hmot a Keramiky [*State Planning Institute of Enterprises for Building Material and Ceramics Industry*] (CZ)
KMP .... Kommunistak Magyarorszagi Partja [*Communist Party of Hungary*] (PPE)
KMP .... Koyala Mazdoor Panchayat [*Indian*]
KMPI .... Kuwait Metal Pipes Industries (ME)
KMPiK .... Klub Miedzynarodowej Prasy i Ksiazki [*International Press and Book Club*] (POL)
KMPP .... Kisan Mazdoor Praja Party [*Indian*]
KMPV .... Correlation Method of Refracted Waves (RU)
KM PZPR ..... Komitet Miejski Polskiej Zjednoczonej Partii Robotniczej [*City Committee of the Polish United Workers Party*] (POL)
KMR .... Kulturno Masovni Rad [*Mass Culture Program*] [*Military*] (YU)
KMR .... Low-Speed Code Relay (RU)
KM RNP .... Correlation Modification of Controlled Directional Reception (RU)
KMS .... Komunalni Sluzba [*Public Service*] [*Civil defense*] (CZ)
KMSB .... Commander of Motorized Rifle Battalion (RU)
KMSB .... Komity Mpanazava ny Saim-Bahoaka [*National Public Information Committee*] [*Malagasy*] (AF)
KMSD .... Commander of Motorized Rifle Division (RU)
km/sek .... Kilometry na Sekunde [*Kilometers per Second*] [*Polish*]
KMSMRR .... Kapisanan ng mga Manggawa Sa MRR [*Manila Railroad Workers' Union*] [*Philippine*]
Kmsn .... Kommission [*German*]
KMSP .... Commander of Motorized Rifle Regiment (RU)
Kmsr .... Kommissaer [*German*]
KMST .... Courses of Masters of Socialist Labor (RU)
Kmst .... Karl-Marx-Stadt [*Karl-Marx-Stadt*] (EG)
KMSTIBF .... Kibris Maden Sirketi Turk Isciler Birligi Federasyonu [*Federation of Turkish Workers Unions of the Cyprus Mines Corporation*] (GC)
KMSU .... Komsomol Youth Construction Administration (RU)
KMT .... Cobalt-Manganese Thermistor (RU)
KMT .... Klub Milosnikow Teatru [*Theater Fans' Club*] [*Polish*]
KMT .... Kuomintang [*Nationalist Party of China*] (PD)
KMTB .... Kibris Milli Turk Birligi [*Cypriot National Turkish Union*] (PPE)
KMTP .... Committee for the Defense of the Revolution [*Malagasy*] (AF)
KMTs .... Carboxymethylcellulose (RU)
KMTS .... Office of Materials and Equipment Supply (RU)
KMTVE .... Komity Malagasy Momba ny Taonan'ny Vehivary Erantany (MAR)
KMU .... Karl-Marx-Universitat [*Karl Marx University*] (EG)
KMU .... Kurucu Meclis Uyesi [*Organizing Assembly Member*] (TU)
KMUJ .... Kolo Medykow Uniwerstetu Jagiellonskiego [*Medical Students' Circle of Jagiellonian University*] (POL)
KMUL .... Kolo Medykow Uniwersytetu Lodzkiego [*Medical Students' Circle of Lodz University*] (POL)
KMUMCS .... Kolo Medykow Uniwersytetu Marii Curie-Sklodowskiej [*Medical Students' Circle of Maria Curie-Sklodowska University*] (POL)
KMUR .... Komisja Miedzyministerialna Uplynnienia Remanentow [*Inter-Ministerial Commission on the Distribution of Surpluses*] (POL)
KMV .... Caucasian Spas [*Health resort area*] (RU)
KMV .... Kazan' Museum Herald [*A publication*] (RU)
KMV .... Kikuya Mission Volunteers (MAR)
KmV .... Kmetijski Vestnik [*Agricultural Review*] [*Koper*] [*A publication*] (YU)
KMW .... Kola Mlodziezy Wojskowej [*Military Youth Circle*] (POL)
KMZ .... Kazakh Metallurgical Plant (RU)
KmZ .... Kmecka Zena [*The Farm Woman*] [*A periodical*] (YU)
KMZ .... Kol'chugino Metal-Rolling Plant Imeni S. Ordzhonikidze (RU)
KMZ .... Komitim-Pirenena Miaro ny Zon' Olombelona [*Standing Committee of the National Congress*] [*Malagasy*] (AF)
KMZ .... Kraftfahrzeug- und Motorenwerk, Zwickau (VEB) [*Zwickau Motor Vehicle and Engine Plant (VEB)*] (EG)
KMZ .... Kuznetsk Metallurgical Plant (RU)
KmzlR .... Kommerzialrat [*German*]
kn .... Book [*or Volume*] (BU)
kn .... Book (RU)
k-n .... Captain (RU)
KN .... Horse Van (RU)
Kn .... Kainite (RU)
KN .... Katolicke Noviny [*Catholic News*] [*A newspaper*] (CZ)
Kn .... Kleiner Nahgueterzug [*Small Local Freight Train*] (EG)
Kn .... Knaben [*German*]
kn .... Kniga [*Book, Volume*] (YU)
Kn .... Knoten [*Knot*] [*German*]
KN .... Kopalnictwo Naftowe [*Oil Wells*] (POL)
KN .... Kuantan [*Malaysian*] (ML)
KN .... Low-Voltage Cable (RU)
kn .... Our Italics (BU)

KN .... Overall Adjustment (RU)
KN .... Petroleum Coke (RU)
kn .... Prince (BU)
KN .... St. Christopher-Nevis-Anguilla [*Two-letter standard code*] (CNC)
k-n .... Some (RU)
KNA .... Committee on New Alphabet (RU)
KNA .... Katholische Nachrichten-Agentur (MAR)
KNA .... Kenya National Archives [*Nairobi*] (MAR)
KNA .... Kenya News Agency (AF)
KNA .... Kommounistiki Neolaia Athinon [*Communist Youth of Athens*] (GC)
KNA .... Korean People's Army [*Korean People's Democratic Republic*] (RU)
KNA .... Kuki National Assembly [*Indian*] (PPW)
KNA .... St. Christopher-Nevis-Anguilla [*Three-letter standard code*] (CNC)
KNAAS .... Kenya National Academy for Advancement of Arts and Sciences (MAR)
KNAP .... Center for Agitation and Propaganda by Visual Means (RU)
KNAW .... Koninklijke Nederlandse Akademie van Wetenschappen [*Dutch*]
KNB .... Krajowa Narada Budownictwa [*All-Polish Conference on Construction*] (POL)
KNBC .... Kariba North Bank Company (MAR)
KNB PKN .... Komisja Normalizacyjna Budownictwa Polskiego Komitetu Normalizacyjnego [*Construction Standardization Commission of the Polish Committee on Standardization*] (POL)
KNBT .... Katholieke Nederlandse Boeren en Tuinbouwsbond [*Netherlands Catholic Farmers and Horticultural Workers Union*] (WEN)
KNC .... Kamerun National Congress [*Cameroonian*] (AF)
KNC .... Kamerun National Convention (MAR)
KNCJ .... Katalog Norm i Cen Jednostkowych [*Catalog of Norms and Unit Prices*] (POL)
KNCSS .... Kenya National Council of Social Services (MAR)
KNCU .... Kilimanjaro Native Co-Operation Union Ltd. (MAR)
KNCV .... Koninklijke Nederlandse Chemische Vereniging [*'s-Gravenhage*]
KND .... Directive Gain [*Antenna*] (RU)
KND .... Low-Pressure Chamber (RU)
KND .... Low-Pressure Compressor (RU)
KNDD .... Kendron Neotitos Dimou Athinaion [*Athens Municipality Youth Center*] (GC)
KNDK .... Kodix Nomon Dimon kai Koinotiton [*Law Code for Municipalities and Communes*] [*Greek*] (GC)
KNDK .... Koreai Nepi Demokratikus Koztarsasag [*Democratic People's Republic of Korea*] (HU)
KNDP .... Kamerun National Democratic Party [*Cameroonian*] (AF)
KNDR .... Korean People's Democratic Republic (RU)
KNDR .... People's Democratic Republic of Korea (BU)
KNDTP .... Kiev House of Scientific and Technical Propaganda (RU)
Kne .... Kleiner Naheilzug [*Small Local Express Train*] (EG)
KNE .... Komisija za Nuklearnu Energiju [*Nuclear Energy Commission*] (YU)
KNE .... Kommounistiki Neolaia Ellados [*Greek Communist Youth*] (GC)
KNEB .... Kozponti Nepi Ellenorzesi Bizottsag [*Central People's Control Committee*] (HU)
KNF .... Komma Neon Filelevtheron [*Young Liberals' Party*] [*Greek*] (GC)
KNFK .... Kodix Nomon Forologias Kapnou [*Code of Tobacco Tax Laws*] [*Greek*] (GC)
KNFU .... Kenya National Farmers Union (MAR)
kni .... Kumppani [*Finnish*]
knigoizd .... Knigoizdatelstvo [*Publishing House*] (YU)
knigotorg .... Book Trade Administration (RU)
knigotorg .... Book Trade Association (RU)
knigotorg .... Book Trade Office (RU)
knigouch .... Book Trade Apprenticeship School (RU)
KNII .... Complex Scientific Research Institute (RU)
KNIIKiF .... Kirgiz Scientific Research Institute of Health Resorts and Physiotherapy (RU)
KNIIOT .... Kazan' Scientific Research Institute of Work Safety (RU)
KNIIPP .... Krasnodar Scientific Research Institute of the Food Industry (RU)
KNIITIM .... Kuban' Scientific Research Institute for Testing Tractors and Agricultural Machinery (RU)
KNIK .... Committee for Science, Art, and Culture (BU)
KNIPI .... Complex Scientific Research and Design Institute (BU)
KNIPITIS .... Complex Scientific Research and Design Institute for Construction Standardization and Industrialization (BU)
KNIPI TUGA .... Complex Scientific Research and Design Institute of Territorial Structure, Urban Planning, and Architecture (BU)
KNiT .... Komitet Nauki i Techniki [*Committee for Science and Technology*] (POL)
KNIUI .... Karaganda Scientific Research Institute of Coal (RU)
KNIUI .... Kusnetsk Scientific Research Institute of Coal (RU)
KNIVI .... Kazan' Veterinary Scientific Research Institute (RU)
kn izd .... Book Publishing House (RU)
knizh .... Bookstore (BU)
knizh .... Literary (BU)
knj .... Knjiga [*Book, Volume*] (YU)
KNJJS .... Knjizevnost i Jezik u Skoli [*Literature and Language in the School*] [*Belgrade*] [*A periodical*] (YU)
KnjN .... Knjizevne Novine [*Literary News*] [*Belgrade*] [*A periodical*] (YU)
KNK .... Kinai Nepkoztarsasag [*Chinese People's Republic*] (HU)
KNK .... People's Youth Chamber (BU)
KNKP .... Committee for Scientific Consultation and Propaganda (of the Academy of Sciences, USSR) (RU)
KNLC .... Koninklijk Nederlands Landbouw Comite [*Royal Netherlands Agricultural Committee*] (WEN)
KNLF .... Karen National Liberation Front [*Burmese*] (PD)
KNM .... Kenya National Museum (MAR)
kn mag .... Bookstore (RU)
KNMI .... Koninklijk Nederlands Meteorologisch Instituut [*Royal Dutch Meteorological Institute*] (WEN)
KNN .... Khabouan (Kan) Neo Thang Noum [*Youth Front Movement*] [*Same as Parti des Jeunes*] [*Laotian*] (CL)
kn n .... Officer of the Guards (BU)
KNO .... Kotarski Narodni Odbor [*District People's Committee*] (YU)
kn o .... Truck Transport Squad (BU)
KNOA .... Chinese People's Liberation Army (BU)
KNOC .... Kuwait National Oil Company (ME)
KNOJ .... Korpus Narodnog Oslobodenja Jugoslavije [*National Liberation Corps of Yugoslavia*] (YU)
KNOPO .... Krajiski Narodnooslobodilacki Partizanski Odred [*Krajina National Liberation Partisan Detachment*] [*Croatia*] [*World War II*] (YU)
KNOPP .... Study Center for Scientific Organization of Industrial Establishments (of the Academy of Sciences, USSR) (RU)
KNOV .... Koninklijk Nederlands Ondernemersverbond [*Royal Dutch Employers' Association*] (WEN)
KNOV .... Korpus Narodnooslobodilacke Vojske [*National Liberation Army Corps*] (YU)
KNP .... Catholic People's Party [*Dutch*] (RU)
KNP .... Command Observation Point (BU)
KNP .... Command and Observation Post (RU)
KNP .... Commander's Observation Post (RU)
KNP .... Compagnie Kouilou Niari Pool (MAR)
KNP .... Katholieke Nationale Partij [*Catholic National Party*] [*Dutch*] (PPE)
KNP .... Kenya National Properties Ltd. (MAR)
KNP .... Komise Narodniho Pojisteni [*National Insurance Commission*] (CZ)
KNP .... Kongres Nauki Polskiej [*Congress of Polish Science*] (POL)
KNP .... Krajska Nemocenska Pojistovna [*Regional Health Insurance Agency*] (CZ)
KNPA .... Kilimanjaro Native Planters' Association (MAR)
KNPC .... Kuwait National Petroleum Company (ME)
KN PN .... Komisja Nadzorcza Panstw Neutralnych (w Korei) [*Neutral Nations Supervisory Commission (in Korea)*] (POL)
KNR .... Chinese People's Republic (RU)
KNR .... Komitet Nauk Rolniczych [*Committee on Agricultural Sciences*] (POL)
KNR .... People's Republic of China (BU)
KNRB .... Constitution of the Bulgarian People's Republic (BU)
KNRG .... Kwame Nkramah Revolutionary Guards (MAR)
KNRV .... Koninklijke Nederlandse Reder Vereniging [*Royal Netherlands Shipowners' Association*] (WEN)
KNS .... Kancelar Narodniho Shromazdeni [*The National Assembly Office*] (CZ)
KNS .... Kara-Bogaz-Gol Scientific Research Station (of the Academy of Sciences, USSR) (RU)
KNS .... Kenya News Service (AF)
KNS .... Kinisi Neon Sosialiston [*Movement of Young Socialists*] [*Greek*] (GC)
KNS .... Komise pro Narodni Spotrebu [*National Consumption Commission*] (CZ)
Kns .... Kumulativni Narodni Sprava [*Joint National Administration*] (CZ)
KNSC .... Kenya National Sports Council (MAR)
kn skl .... Book Warehouse (RU)
KnsR .... Konsistorialrat [*German*]
KNT .... Kereszteny Noi Tabor [*Assembly of Christian Women*] (HU)
KNTB .... Scientific and Technical Libraries Pool (RU)
KNTC .... Kenya National Trading Corporation (MAR)
KNThVE .... Kendron Nosimaton Thorakos Voreiou Ellados [*Northern Greece Center for Thoracic Diseases*] (GC)
Kntlr .... Kontrollor [*German*]
KNTM .... Knihovna Narodniho Technickeho Musea [*Library of the National Museum of Technology*] [*Prague*] (CZ)
KNTPVO .... Committee for Science, Technical Progress, and Higher Education (BU)
KNTT .... Committee on Scientific and Technical Terminology (of the Academy of Sciences, USSR) (RU)
KNU .... Karen National Union [*Burmese*] (PD)
KNU .... Kolarcev Naroden Univerzitet [*Kolarac People's University*] [*Belgrade*] (YU)
KNUB .... Koninklijke Nederlandse Uitgeversbond
KNUFNS .... Kampuchean National United Front for National Salvation (PD)

KNUST .... Kwame Nkrumah University of Science and Technology (MAR)
KNUT .... Kenya National Union of Teachers (MAR)
KNV .... Krajsky Narodni Vybor [*Regional National Committee*] (CZ)
KNVD .... Koninklijk Nederlands Verbond van Drukkerijen [*Royal Netherlands Printing Association*]
kn-vo .... Book Publishing House (RU)
KNW .... Kolektyw Norm Wewnetrznych [*Collective on Domestic Norms*] (POL)
kny .... Kozlony [*Bulletin*] (HU)
kny .... Kulonnyomat [*Reprint*] (HU)
knytb .... Kozsegi Nyilvanos Tavbeszelo Allomas [*Village Public Telephone*] (HU)
KO .... Acid Treatment (RU)
KO .... Check Point [*Aviation*] (RU)
KO .... Compensating Winding (RU)
KO .... Cooperative Organizations (BU)
KO .... Design Department (RU)
KO .... Detachment Commander (RU)
Ko .... Kaikyo [*Strait*] [*Japanese*] (NAU)
KO .... Kassenordnung [*Financial Decree (Usually relating to the state budget)*] (EG)
KO .... Kihlakunnanoikeus [*Finnish*]
KO .... Komandantska Osmatracnica [*Command Observation Post*] (YU)
KO .... Komisja Okregowa [*District Commission*] (POL)
Ko .... Komite [*Committee*] (TU)
KO .... Komitet Okregowy [*District Committee*] (POL)
KO .... Kommatiki Omas [*Party Group, Parliamentary Group*] (GC)
KO .... Kommatiki Organosis [*Party Organization*] [*Plus the initial letter of the district or sector of the organization*] [*Greek*] (GC)
KO .... Kongo Overzee (MAR)
KO .... Konkursordnung [*Legislation on Bankruptcy*] [*German*]
KO .... Koordinacioni Odbor (SIV) [*Coordinating Committee*] (YU)
KO .... Korkein Oikeus [*Supreme Court*] [*Finnish*] (WEN)
KO .... Krajevni Odbor [*Local Committee*] (YU)
KO .... Kulturalno-Oswiatowa (Prace) [*Cultural and Educational (Work)*] (POL)
ko .... Kyseessa Oleva [*Under Discussion, In Question*] [*Finnish*] (GPO)
ko .... Kysymyksessa Oleva [*Finnish*]
KO .... Organosilicon (RU)
KO .... Turnover Coefficient (RU)
KO .... Volume Compensator [*Nuclear energy*] (BU)
KoA .... Coenzyme A (RU)
KOA .... Kalinin Oblast State Archives (RU)
KOA .... Kommatiki Organosi Akhtidas [*Sector Party Organization*] (GC)
KOA .... Kommounistiki Organosis Aeroporias [*Communist Organization for the Air Force*] [*Greek*] (GC)
KOA .... Kommounistiki Organosis Athinon [*Communist Organization of Athens*] (GC)
KOA .... Kratiki Orkhistra Athinon [*Athens State Orchestra*] (GC)
KOA .... Kypriakos Organismos Anaptyxeos [*Cypriot Development Organization*] (GC)
KOA .... Kypriakos Organismos Athlitismou [*Cypriot Athletic Organization*] (GC)
KOAP .... Kommounistiki Organosis Astynomias Poleon [*Communist Organization for the Cities Police*] [*Greek*] (GC)
KoASSR ...... Komi Autonomous Soviet Socialist Republic (RU)
Koat .... Kommissariat [*German*]
KOB .... Public Safety Committee (RU)
KO Biuro ..... Kulturalno-Oswiatowe Biuro [*Office of Culture and Education*] (POL)
KOBP .... Komanda Odeljenja Borbenih Potreba [*Headquarters of Department of Combat Supplies*] (YU)
KOBue .... Konstruktionsbuero [*Designing Office*] (EG)
KOC .... Kuwait Oil Company (ME)
KOCGP .... Kuwait Oil Company Gas Project (ME)
koch .... Nomad Camp [*Topography*] (RU)
KOD .... Komisija za Opojne Droge [*Intoxicating Drugs Commission*] (YU)
KOD .... Krajske Oblastni Divadlo [*Regional Theater*] (CZ)
KOD .... Kurs pro Osvetove Dustojniky [*Instruction Course for Armed Forces Cultural and Education Officers*] (CZ)
KODAERAL ... Komando Daerah Angkatan Laut [*Naval Region Command*] (IN)
KODAM .... Komando Daerah Militer [*Military Region Command (Subordinate commands: KOREM, KODIM, KORAMIL)*] (IN)
KODAU .... Komando Daerah Udara [*Air Region Command*] (IN)
KODIM .... Komando Distrik Militer [*Military District Command*] [*See KODAM*] (IN)
KODISO ...... Komma Dimokratikou Sosialismou [*Democratic Socialism Party*] (GC1)
KODYA .... Kotamadya [*Municipality*] (IN)
KOE .... Kapnemboriki Omospondia tis Ellados [*Tobacco Merchants' Federation of Greece*] (GC)
KOE .... Kendron Oikonomikon Erevnon [*Center of Economic Research*] (GC1)
KOE .... Kendron Okeanologikon Erevnon [*Center for Oceanological Research*] (GC)
KOE .... Kommatiki Organosi Ellados [*Party Organization of Greece*] (GC)
KOE .... Kooperative Einrichtung [*Cooperative Facility*] (EG)
KOEE .... Kulfoldi Osztondijasok Egyetemi Elokeszitoje [*University Preparatory School for Foreign Scholarship Students*] (HU)
koef .... Coefficient (BU)
koef .... Coefficient (RU)
Koeff .... Koeffizient [*Coefficient*] [*German*]
Koeffiz .... Koeffizient [*Coefficient*] [*German*]
KOEK .... Kallitekhnikos Organismos Ellinikon Kinimatografon [*Artistic Organization of the Greek Cinema*] (GC)
KOEM .... Communist Organization of Aegean Macedonia (BU)
KOEP .... Kendron Oikonomikon Erevnon kai Programmatismou [*Economic Research and Programing Center*] [*Greek*] (GC)
KOF .... Fatherland Front Committee (BU)
KOFEM .... Szekesfehervar Konnyufemmu [*Szekesfehervar Light Metal Works*] (HU)
KOFIM .... Common Committee for the Struggle in Majunga [*Malagasy*] (AF)
KOG .... Kendrikon Organotikon Grafeion [*Central Organizational Office*] [*Cypriot*] (GC)
KOG .... Kendrikos Organotikos Grammatevs [*Central Organizational Secretary*] (GC)
KOGA .... Kalinin Oblast State Archives (RU)
KOGAB .... Komando Gabungan [*Joint Command*] (IN)
KOGE .... Magyar Kozhasznalatu Gepjarmuvallalatok Orszagos Egyesulete [*National Association of Public Motor Vehicle Enterprises in Hungary*] (HU)
KOGEC .... Kuwait Oil, Gas, and Energy Corporation (ME)
KOGEF .... Kibrislilar Ogrenim ve Genclik Federasyonu [*Cypriots' Education and Youth Federation*] (TU)
koger .... Coherent (RU)
KOGF .... Kibrislilar Ogrenim ve Genclik Federasyonu [*Cypriots' Education and Youth Federation*] [*Also, KOGEF*] [*Turkish Cypriot*] (GC)
KOGIZ .... Book Trade Association of State Publishing Houses (RU)
KOGV .... Kypriakos Organismos Galaktomikis Viomikhanias [*Cyprus Dairy Industry Organization*] (GC)
KOGYOGY ... Kobanyai Gyogyszerarugyar [*Pharmaceutical Factory of Kobanya*] (HU)
KOHANMARNAS ... Komando Pertahanan Maritim Nasional [*National Maritime Defense Command*] (IN)
KOHANUDNAS ... Komando Pertahanan Udara Nasional [*National Air Defense Command*] (IN)
KOHDOSZ ... Kohaszati Dolgozok Szakszervezete [*Trade Union of Metallurgical Workers*] (HU)
KOHERT ...... Kohoipari Ertekesito Kozpont [*Marketing Center of the Metallurgy Industry*] (HU)
KOHHIKI ..... Konzerv-, Hus- es Hutoipari Kutato Intezet [*Industrial Research Institute on Food Canning and Refrigeration*] (HU)
KOI .... Komorka Organizacji Inwestycji [*Investment Organization Unit*] (POL)
KOI .... Krajsky Osvetovy Inspektorat [*Office of the Regional Inspector of Cultural Affairs*] (CZ)
koill .... Koillinen [*Finnish*]
KOIP .... Komisija za Odobravanje Investicionih Programa [*Commission for Approval of Investment Programs*] (YU)
KOIZ .... All-Union Cooperative Joint Publishing House (RU)
KOJAL .... Kozegeszsegugyi es Jarvanyugyi Allomas [*Public Health and Medical Clinic for Contagious Diseases*] (HU)
kok .... Kai Outo Kathexis [*And So Forth*] (GC)
Kok .... Kansallinen Kokoomus [*National Coalition (Conservative Party)*] [*Finnish*]
KOK .... Kodix Odikis Kykloforias [*Traffic Code*] (GC)
kok .... Kokoomuslainen [*Finnish*]
KOK .... Krajsky Odbor Kultury [*Regional Department of Culture*] (CZ)
KOK .... Kynigetiki Omospondia Kyprou [*Cyprus Hunting Federation*] (GC)
KOKARMINDAGRI ... Korps Karyawan Pemerintahan Dalam Negeri [*Indonesian*]
KOKERT ...... Kozsegi Kenyergyarak Reszvenytarsasag [*Municipal Bakeries Limited (Prewar)*] (HU)
KOKEV .... Kohaszati Alapanyagokat Keszletezo Vallalat [*Stockpiling Enterprise for Metallurgical Primary Materials*] (HU)
KOKh .... Kommounistiki Organosis Khorofylakis [*Communist Organization for the Gendarmerie*] (GC)
kokh .... Koroi Olikis Khoritikotitos [*Gross Register Tons*] (GC)
KOKhIMI ..... Department of General Chemistry of the Irkutsk Medical Institute (RU)
KOKI .... Kiserleti Orvostudomanyi Kutato Intezet [*Research Institute in Experimental Medicine*] (HU)
koks .... By-Product Coke Plant [*Topography*] (RU)
KOKSI .... Kesatuan Organisasi Koperasi Seluruh Indonesia [*All-Indonesia Federation of Cooperatives*] (IN)
Koksokhimmontazh ... All-Union Trust for the Construction and Installation of By-Product Coke Plants (RU)
KOKSZ .... Kereskedok Orszagos Kozponti Szovetsege [*National Central Merchants Association*] (HU)

KO KV KSC ... Komise Obrany KV KSC (AV KSS) [*Defense Commission, Regional Committee of the Communist Party of Czechoslovakia (Regional Committee of the Communist Party of Slovakia)*] (CZ)
kol ... Collection (BU)
kol ... Colony [*Topography*] (RU)
kol ... Column (BU)
kol ... Kolega [*Colleague*] [*Polish*]
KOL ... Kolonel [*Colonel*] (IN)
kol ... Koloriert [*Colored*] [*German*]
Kol ... Kolumne [*Column*] [*German*]
kol ... Oscillation (RU)
kol'chugalyuminiy ... Aluminum Alloy Produced by the Kol'chugino Nonferrous Metals Plant [*1922*] (RU)
KOLEY SEN ... Kibris Turk Otel, Lokanta, ve Eglence Yerleri Iscileri Sendikasi [*Turkish Cypriot Hotel, Restaurant, and Amusement Place Workers' Union*] (TU)
kolich ... Quantitative, Quantity, Amount, Number (RU)
kolichestv ... Quantitative (RU)
Kolkhoztsentr ... All-Union Council of Collective Farms (RU)
koll ... Colloidal, Colloid (RU)
Koll ... Kollegium [*German*]
koll ... Ryhmasana, Kollektiivisesti [*Collective Noun*] [*Finnish*]
Koll Srt ... Kollektif Sirketi [*Corporation*] (TU)
Kolon ... Colony [*Topography*] (RU)
Kol Ort ... Kollektif Ortakligi [*Collective Partnership*] [*Turkish*] (CED)
kol red ... Kolegium Redakcyjne [*Editorial Staff*] [*Polish*]
Kol S ... Kollektif Sirketi [*Collective Company*] [*Turkish*] (CED)
KOLS ... Kommounistiki Organosis Limenikou Somatos [*Communist Organization for the Port Corps*] [*Greek*] (GC)
Kolstok ... State Commercial Grocery Enterprise (BU)
kolts ... Koltseg [*Cost, Expenses*] (HU)
KOLUC ... Kongolees Leuvens Universitair Centrum (MAR)
kol-vo ... Quantity, Amount, Number (RU)
KOM ... Commanding, Command, Command Element (BU)
kom ... Commissar (BU)
Kom ... Commissariat (RU)
kom ... Committee (BU)
kom ... Committee (RU)
kom ... Communist (RU)
KOM ... Compressor (RU)
kom ... Kilohm (RU)
KOM ... Kiniti Odondoiatriki Monas [*Mobile Dental Unit*] [*Greek*] (GC)
Ko M ... Kohaszati Miniszterium/Miniszter [*Ministry/Minister of Metallurgy*] (HU)
Kom ... Komando [*Commando*] (TU)
kom ... Komendant [*Commander*] [*Polish*]
Kom ... Komiser [*Commissioner*] [*As of a police department*] (TU)
KOM ... Komodor [*Commodore*] (IN)
KOM ... Kompeni [*Company*] (ML)
KOM ... Kraftomnibusse [*Motor Buses*] (EG)
KOMABAL ... Komando Markas Besar Angkatan Laut [*Navy Headquarters Command*] (IN)
KOMAFI ... Kooperative Malagasy Fitaterana [*Malagasy Transportation Cooperative*] (AF)
KOMAK ... Communist Academy (RU)
Komalyum ... Commission on Aluminum (RU)
KOMAMAFIMI ... Komity Maharitra Manohana ny Fitondra-Miaramila [*Permanent Committee to Support the Military Government*] [*Malagasy*] (AF)
KOMANDAK ... Komando Antar Daerah Kepolisian [*Police Interregional Command*] (IN)
komandarm ... Army Commander (RU)
KOMAO ... Caucasian Branch of the Moscow Archaeological Society (RU)
komartbat ... Artillery Battery Commander (RU)
komartform ... Commissar of Artillery Formations (RU)
kombat ... Battalion Commander (BU)
kombat ... Battalion Commander (RU)
kombat ... Battery Commander (RU)
kombed ... Committee of the Poor [*1918*] (RU)
KOMBESPOL ... Komisar Besar Polisi [*Chief Police Commissioner*] (IN)
kombik ... Combined-Fodder Plant [*Topography*] (RU)
kombizhir ... Mixed Fat (RU)
kombrig ... Brigade Commander (RU)
komchon ... Commander of Special-Purpose Units (RU)
KOMDAK ... Komando Daerah Kepolisian [*Police Region Command (Subordinate commands: KOMDIN, KOMRES, KOMDIS, KOMSEK)*] [*See KOMDAPOLMETRODJAYA*] (IN)
KOMDAPOLMETRODJAYA ... Komando Daerah Kepolisian Metropolitan Djakarta Raya [*Djakarta Metropolitan Police Region Command (Subordinate commands: KOMWIL, KOMSEKKO, KOMDET)*] (IN)
KOMDE ... Kratikos Organismos Mikhanimaton Dimosion Ergon [*State Organization for Public Works Machinery*] [*Greek*] (GC)
KOMDET ... Komando Detasemen [*Detachment Command*] [*See KOMDAPOLMETRODJAYA*] (IN)
KOMDIN ... Komando Daerah Inspeksi [*Inspection Region Command*] [*See KOMDAK*] (IN)
KOMDIS ... Komando Distrik [*District Command*] [*See KOMDAK*] (IN)
komdiv ... Battalion Commander (RU)
komdiv ... Division Commander (RU)
KOMDJEN ... Komisaris Djenderal [*Commissioner General*] (IN)
Komelprom ... Committee for Small Industry (RU)
koment ... Commentary (BU)
KOMENT ... Commentator, Commented (BU)
koment ... Komentarz [*Commentary*] [*Polish*]
KOMEP ... Kommounistiki Epitheorisi [*Communist Review*] [*Published abroad by the Greek Communist Party Central Committee during 1969-74*] [*A publication*] (GC)
komesk ... Squadron Commander [*Aviation*] (RU)
komeska ... Squadron Commander [*Aviation*] (RU)
KOMGF ... Commission for Soil Mechanics and Foundation Construction (RU)
KOMGRAP ... Komunalno Gradevinsko Preduzece [*Communal Building Establishment*] (YU)
komich ... Comical (RU)
Komigiz ... Komi State Publishing House (RU)
Komiles ... Kombinat of the Lumber Industry of the Komi ASSR (RU)
Kominform ... Communist Information Bureau (BU)
Kominformbyuro ... Communist Information Bureau (BU)
Komintern ... Communist International (BU)
Komintern ... Communist International [*1919-1943*] (RU)
komis ... Commission (RU)
Komisko ... Committee of the International Socialist Conference (BU)
komit ... Komitatiivi [*Finnish*]
komkhoz ... Department of Municipal Services (RU)
komkhoz ... Municipal Services (RU)
komkor ... Corps Commander (RU)
komm ... Commutator, Switchboard (RU)
komm ... Kommentiert [*Explained*] [*German*]
Komm ... Kommerzial [*German*]
Komm ... Kommunal [*German*]
komm ... Kommunisti(nen) [*Finnish*]
kommelprom ... Committee for Small Industry (RU)
komment ... Commentary (RU)
kommerch ... Commercial (RU)
Kommerpribor ... Committee of Measures and Measuring Instruments (at the Council of Ministers, USSR) (RU)
kommestprom ... Committee of Local Industry (RU)
Kommunenergoproyekt ... Office for the Planning of Municipal Electric Power Plants (RU)
Kommunenergostroy ... State Municipal Trust for the Installation and Construction of Power Engineering Installations (RU)
kommunkhoz ... Department of Municipal Services (RU)
kommunkhoz ... Municipal Services (RU)
komnachsostav ... Command Personnel (RU)
KOMNIS ... Komisija za Medicinsko-Naucna Istrazivanja [*Medical Research Commission*] (YU)
KOMOB ... Komando Mobil Brigade [*Mobile Brigade Command*] (IN)
Komones ... Commission for Cases Concerning Minors (RU)
komp ... Composed, Composer (BU)
Komp ... Kompanie [*Company*] (EG)
komp ... Komparatiivi [*Comparative*] [*Finnish*]
komp ... Kompenzacio [*Compensation*] (HU)
komp ... Komplett [*Complete*] [*German*]
kompar ... Komparatiivi(nen) [*Comparative*] [*Finnish*]
Kompartiya ... Communist Party (BU)
KOMPERINDRA ... Kompartimen Perindustrian Rakjat [*Indonesian*]
KOMPIPA ... National Synthesis Committee [*Malagasy*] (AF)
KOMPLEX ... KOMPLEX Nagyberendezesek Export-Import Vallalata [*KOMPLEX Export-Import Enterprise for Factory Equipment*] (HU)
Kompod ... Komunalni Podnik [*Communal Enterprise*] (CZ)
KOMPOL ... Komisaris Polisi [*Police Commissioner*] (IN)
Kompolk ... Regimental Commander (BU)
Kompomgol ... Famine Relief Committee (RU)
kompp ... Komppania [*Finnish*]
kompr ... Komprimiert [*Compressed*] [*German*]
kom red ... Komitet Redakcyjny [*Editorial Committee*] [*Polish*]
Komrem ... All-Russian Commission for Repair of Rolling Stock (RU)
KOMRES ... Komando Resort [*Area Command*] [*See KOMDAK*] (IN)
komroty ... Company Commander (RU)
KOMS ... Kaliningrad Oblast Experimental Reclamation Station (RU)
Kom S ... Komandit Sirketi [*Limited Partnership*] [*Turkish*] (CED)
KOMSEK ... Komando Seksi [*Section Command*] [*See KOMDAK*] (IN)
KOMSEKKO ... Komando Seksi Kota [*City Section Command*] [*See KOMDAPOLMETRODJAYA*] (IN)
komsod ... Commission for Assistance (RU)
Komsomol ... Communist Youth Union (BU)
Komspol ... Komanditni Spolecnost [*Limited Partnership Company*] (CZ)
Komstr ... Komunisticka Strana [*Communist Party*] (CZ)
KOMTA ... Commission on Heavy Aircraft (RU)
KOMThE ... Kommounistiki Theoritiki Epitheorisi [*Communist Theoretical Review*] (GC1)
Komtrud ... Committee for Universal Labor Service (RU)
Komtsvetfond ... Commission for the Establishment of a Special Fund for Financing Nonferrous Metallurgy (RU)
KOMUCh ... Committee of Members of the Constituent Assembly [*1918*] (RU)
komukr ... Commander of a Fortified Area (RU)
komun ... Communist (BU)
komus ... Commander of a Fortified Sector (RU)

KOMUS .... Komisija za Ucbenike in Skripta [*Textbooks Commission*] [*Ljubljana*] (YU)
komvuz .... Commanding Officer of a Military Educational Institution (RU)
Komvuz .... Communist Higher Educational Institution (RU)
komvzvod ... Platoon Commander (RU)
KOMWIL ...... Komando Wilajah [*Territory Command*] [*See KOMDAPOLMETRODJAYA*] (IN)
Komzag ...... Committee for Procurement of Agricultural Products (RU)
Komzet .... Land Settlement Committee for Jewish Workers (RU)
KON .... Convoy [*Navy*] (RU)
kon .... Horse-Breeding Sovkhoz [*Topography*] (RU)
KON .... Kendron Oikogeneias kai Neotitos [*Family and Youth Center*] [*Greek*] (GC)
Kon .... Konak [*Halting Place, Inn*] (TU)
Kon .... Koninklijke [*Royal*] [*Dutch*] (CED)
KONAKAT ... Confederation of Associations of Katanga (MAR)
konarm .... Cavalry Army (RU)
konart .... Horse Artillery (RU)
konartbat .... Horse Artillery Battery (RU)
konartvzvod ... Horse Artillery Platoon (RU)
KONB .... Office of Experimental Directed Drilling (RU)
kond .... Confectionery Factory [*Topography*] (RU)
kond .... Konditionaali(n) [*Conditional*] [*Finnish*]
kondit .... Konditionaali [*Conditional*] [*Finnish*]
konfigurats ... Configuration, Configurational (RU)
kongr .... Kongresszus [*Congress*] (HU)
kongreg ...... Kongregacio [*Congregation*] (HU)
KONI .... Komite Olahraga Nasional Indonesia
KONIIS .... Kiev Branch of the Central Scientific Research Institute of Communications (RU)
konj .... Konjunktiivi [*Subjunctive Mood*] [*Finnish*]
konj .... Konjunktio [*Conjunction*] [*Finnish*]
konkr .... Specifically (BU)
Konnyuip K ... Konnyuipari Kiado [*Light Industry Publishing House*] (HU)
konopl .... Hemp-Growing Sovkhoz [*Topography*] (RU)
Kon/polis .... Konstandinoupolis [*Constantinople*] [*Istanbul is preferred*] (GC)
kons .... Cannery [*Topography*] (RU)
kons .... Konsonantti [*Finnish*]
Kons .... Konsul [*or Konsulent*] [*German*]
Konservles ... All-Union Trust for Logging and Sawmilling of the Glavkonserv (RU)
Konservsteklotara ... All-Union Trust for the Manufacture of Glass Containers for the Canning Industry (RU)
Konst .... Constitutional (BU)
konst .... Konstant [*Constant*] [*German*]
KONSTAL ... Chorzowska Wytwornia Konstrukcji Stalowych [*Chorzow Steel Construction Plant*] (POL)
KONSUMEX ... KONSUMEX Kulkereskedelmi Vallalat [*KONSUMEX Foreign Trade Enterprise (Handles import of consumer goods and export of toys, musical instruments, objects of art, and commercial equipment)*] (HU)
Kontr .... Kontroll [*or Kontrollor*] [*German*]
Kontrol'pribor ... Moscow Experimental Plant of Control Instruments (RU)
konts .... Concentrated (RU)
konts .... Concentration (BU)
Kontsesskom ... Committee on Concessions (RU)
konts-iya ..... Concentration (RU)
konts-t .... Concentrate (RU)
KONV .... Komisia Okresneho Narodneho Vyboru [*Commission of the District National Committee*] (CZ)
konyvimpex ... Konyvimport-Export [*Book Export and Import Enterprise*] (HU)
konyvny ...... Konyvnyomda [*Book Printer*] (HU)
konyvvizsg ... Konyvvizsgalo [*Auditor, Accountant*] (HU)
KonZ .... Kontaminirano Zemljiste [*Contaminated Area*] [*Military*] (YU)
konz .... Konzentriert [*Concentrated*] [*German*]
Konz .... Konzipient [*German*]
KOOBIKh .... Cooperative of Bulgarian Engineers and Chemists (BU)
koop .... Cooperative (BU)
koop .... Cooperative (RU)
Koop .... Kooperatifleri [*Cooperative*] [*Turkish*] (CED)
Koop .... Kooperator [*German*]
koopinsoyuz ... Union of Disabled Persons' Cooperative Artels (RU)
Koop-Is .... Turkiye Tarim Kredi Kooperatifleri Personeli Sendikasi [*Turkish Agricultural Credit Cooperative Employees Union*] (TU)
Koopkredit ... Moscow Credit Association (RU)
Kooposyltorg ... Main Administration of Wholesale and Small-Scale Wholesale Mail-Order Trade (of the Tsentrosoyuz) (RU)
Koopstrakhsoyuz ... All-Russian Cooperative Insurance Union (RU)
Kooptorgreklama ... All-Union Office of Commercial Advertising (RU)
KOOSPOL ... Podnik Zahranicniho Obchodu pro Dovoz a Vyvoz Zemedelskych Vyrobku a Potreb [*Foreign Trade Enterprise for the Import and Export of Agricultural Products and Materials*] (CZ)
KO OV KSC ... Komise Obrany OV KSC (OV KSS) [*Defense Commission, District Committee of the Communist Party of Czechoslovakia (District Committee of the Communist Party of Slovakia)*] (CZ)
KOP .... Complex Experimental Station (BU)
KOP .... Corps Supply Relay Point (RU)
KOP .... Gunnery Training Course (RU)
KOP .... Klippfontain Organic Product Corp. (MAR)
KOP .... Komisia Ochrony Pracy [*Labor Protection Board*] [*Polish*]
KOP .... Komisja Oceny Projektow Inwestycyjnych [*Commission on the Evaluation of Investment Plans*] (POL)
KOP .... Komitet Obroncow Pokoju [*Committee of Partisans of Peace*] (POL)
KOP .... Kommatiki Organosi Perifereias [*Area Party Organization*] (GC)
KOP .... Kommatiki Organosi Poleos [*City Party Organization*] (GC)
KOP .... Kommatiki Organosis Periokhis [*Regional Party Organization*] [*Greek*] (GC)
KOP .... Kommounistiki Organosis Peiraios [*Communist Organization of Piraeus*] (GC)
KOP .... Koninski Okreg Przemyslowy [*Industrial Region of Konin*] [*Polish*]
kop .... Kopalnia [*or Kopalnictwo*] [*Mine or Mining*] (POL)
kop .... Kopeck (RU)
kop .... Kopeekka(a) [*Finnish*]
Kop .... Kopru [*Bridge*] (TU)
KOP .... Korpus Ochrony Pogranicza [*Polish*]
KOP .... Krakowski Okreg Przemyslowy [*Industrial Region of Cracow*] [*Polish*]
KOP .... Kypriaki Omospondia Podosfairou [*Cyprus Soccer Federation*] (GC)
KOP .... Leather and Footwear Industry (RU)
KOP .... Operation Code (RU)
KOPart .... Corps Artillery Supply Relay Point (RU)
KOPASGAT ... Komando Pasukan Gerak Tjepat [*Strike Troop Command (Air Force paratroops)*] (IN)
KOPELAPIP ... Komando Pelaksana Persiapan Industri Penerbangan [*Aviation Industry Development Command*] (IN)
KOPEP .... Kypriakos Organismos Protypon kai Elengkhou Poiotitos [*Cypriot Organization for Quality Control and Standards*] (GC)
KOPEX .... Przedsiebiorstwo Budowy Zakladow Gorniczych Zagranica [*Enterprise for the Construction of Mining Facilities Abroad*] (POL)
KOPI .... Komisja Oceny Projektow Inwestycyjnych [*Commission on the Evaluation of Investment Plans*] (POL)
KOPKAMTIB ... Komando Operasi Pemulihan Keamanan dan Ketertiban [*Command for the Restoration of Security and Order*] (IN)
KOPLAX ...... Compania Colombiana de Plasticos Koplax Ltda. [*Medellin*] (COL)
koprogen-aza ... Coproporphyrinogen Oxidase (RU)
KOPROSAN ... Komando Operasi Projek-Projek Sandang [*Indonesian*]
KOPS .... Komando Perjuangan Sarawak [*Sarawak Struggle Command (Chinese Communist)*] (ML)
KOPTAS ...... Kamyon, Otomobil, ve Yedek Parca Ticaret Anonim Sirketi [*Truck, Automobile, and Spare Parts Trade Corporation*] [*Istanbul*] (TU)
kor .... Correspondent (BU)
kor .... Correspondent (RU)
kor .... Cover (BU)
KOR .... Klub Oficerow Rezerwy [*Reserve Officers Club*] (POL)
kor .... Korean (RU)
kor .... Korona [*Crown*] (HU)
kor .... Korrigiert [*Corrected*] [*German*]
KOR .... Korzeti Orvosi Rendelo [*District Medical Center*] (HU)
KOR .... Krajska Odborova Rada [*Regional Trade Union Council*] (CZ)
kor .... Mounted Orderly (BU)
KOR .... Republic of Korea [*Three-letter standard code*] (CNC)
kor .... Short [*Film*] (RU)
KOR .... Social Self-Defense Committee [*Also, SSDC*] [*Polish*] (PD)
KOR .... Workers Defense Committee [*Polish*]
Kora .... Koramiral [*Vice Admiral*] (TU)
KORAG .... Koloniale Reichsarbeitsgemeinschaft (MAR)
Koralovag ... Ship, Locomotive, and Railroad Car Building Enterprise (BU)
KORAMIL .... Komando Rayon Militer [*Military Precinct Command*] [*See KODAM*] (IN)
KORAMO .... Kolinske Rafinerie Mineralnich Oleju [*Kolin Oil Refineries*] (CZ)
KORANDAK ... Koordinasi Antar Daerah Kepolisian [*Police Interregional Coordinating Command (May have replaced KOMANDAK)*] (IN)
KORBSO ..... Bulgarian-Soviet Shipbuilding Company (BU)
KORDSA ..... Kord Bezi Sanayi ve Ticaret AS [*Cord Cloth Industry and Trade Corp.*] (TU)
KOREM .... Komando Resort Militer [*Military Area Command*] [*See KODAM*] (IN)
koresp .... Korespondent [*or Korespondencyjny*] [*Correspondent or Correspondence*] [*Polish*]
koreysk .... Korean (RU)
Korg .... Korgeneral [*Lieutenant General*] (TU)
korl .... Korlevel [*Circular Letter*] (HU)
Korm .... Kormany [*Cabinet*] (HU)
korm yed ..... Feed Unit (RU)
kor opis ...... Imprint Description (BU)
korp .... Building [*In addresses*] (RU)
korpr .... Korpraali [*Finnish*]
korr .... Correspondent (RU)
korr .... Korrektura [*Proof Sheet*] (HU)

korr .... Korrespondierend [*German*]
korr .... Korrigiert [*Corrected*] [*German*]
Korsavas ..... Kore'de Savasanlar Dernegi [*Association of Korean Veterans*] (TU)
KORSEL ...... Korea Selatan [*South Korea*] (IN)
KORSTIC .... Korean Scientific and Technological Information Center
korttip .... Korttipeli [*Card Games*] [*Finnish*]
KORUT .... Korea Utara [*North Korea*] (IN)
kor zagl .... Cover Title (BU)
KOS .... Communications Section Commander (RU)
KOS .... Correction and Drainage System (BU)
KOS .... Counterintelligence Service (BU)
KOS .... Kendrikon Oikonomikon Symvoulion [*Central Economic Council*] [*Greek*] (GC)
KOS .... Kolkhoz Experimental Station (RU)
KOS .... Komise Organisace Stavebnictvi [*Organizational Commission for the Construction Industry*] (CZ)
KOS .... Kommounistiki Organosis Stratou [*Communist Organization for the Army*] [*Greek*] (GC)
KOS .... Komunisticka Omladina Srbije [*Communist Youth of Serbia*] (YU)
KOS .... Krajske Osvetove Stredisko [*Regional Cultural Center*] (CZ)
KOS .... Kuratorium Okregu Szkolnego [*School District Department*] (POL)
KOS .... Kyvernitikon Oikonomikon Symvoulion [*Government Economic Council*] (GC)
KOSARTOP ... Commission for Special Artillery Experiments (RU)
KOSATGAS ... Komando Satuan Tugas [*Task Force Command*] (IN)
kosc .... Kosciol [*Church*] [*Polish*]
KOSEK .... Coordinating Secretariat of National Unions of Students [*COSEC*] (RU)
KOSEK .... Coordination Secretariat of the National Students Unions (BU)
KOSGORO ... Kesatuan Organisasi Serba Guna Gotong Rojong [*Federation of Cooperating Multipurpose Organizations*] (IN)
kosm .... Cosmic, Space (RU)
kosm .... Cosmonautics [*or Astronautics*] (BU)
KOSMS .... Courses for Advanced Training of Officers of the Fleet Medical Service (RU)
KOSOS .... Design Department of the Experimental Land-Based Aircraft Construction (of the TsAGI) (RU)
KOSSA .... Kommatikos Organismos Stratou-Somaton Asfaleias [*or Kommounistiki Organosis Stratou kai Somaton Asfaleias*] [*Party Organization for the Army and Security Forces*] [*Greek*] (GC)
KOSSU .... Krajska Oddeleni Statniho Statistickeho Uradu [*Regional Departments of the State Office of Statistics*] (CZ)
KOSTRAD ... Komando Strategis Angkatan Darat [*Army Strategic Command*] (IN)
KOSTRANAS ... Komando Strategis Nasional [*National Strategic Command*] (IN)
Ko-T .... Co-Thiaminase (RU)
KOT .... Committee for Recreation and Tourism (BU)
KOT .... Kolarska Odznaka Turystyczna [*Tourist Bicycle Badge*] (POL)
KOT .... Konyvtarak Orszagos Tanacsa [*National Council of Libraries*] (HU)
KOT .... Kypriakos Organismos Tourismou [*Cyprus Tourism Organization*] (GC)
KOTA .... Korusok Orszagos Tanacsa [*National Council of Choruses*] (HU)
KOTC .... Kuwait Oil Tanker Company (ME)
KOTh .... Kommounistiki Organosis Thessalonikis [*Communist Organization of Salonica*] (GC)
KOTIB .... Commission for Healthier Working and Living Conditions (RU)
KOTINRO .... Kamchatka Branch of the Pacific Ocean Scientific Research Institute of Fisheries and Oceanography (RU)
KOTKA .... Konfekcija i Tkaonica [*Ready-Made Clothing and Textile Mill*] [*Krapina*] (YU)
kotl .... Hollow (RU)
KOTL .... Koolajbanyaszati Tudomanyos Laboratorium [*Scientific Laboratory of Petroleum Prospecting*] (HU)
Kotlostroy ... Boiler Plant (RU)
Kotlotermomontazh ... Trust for the Installation of Industrial Heating and Boiler Units (RU)
KOTRA .... Korea Trade Promotion Corporation (MAR)
KOTsM .... Nonferrous Metals Processing Combine (BU)
KOTUKI .... Kozuti Kozlekedesi Tudomanyos Kutato Intezet [*Scientific Research Institute for Highway Transport*] (HU)
kotv .... Kotveny [*Bond*] (HU)
KOTY .... Kiz Orta Talebeler Yurdu [*Women's Secondary Student Home*] [*Turkish Cypriot*] (GC)
koul .... Koulussa [*or Koululaiskielessa*] [*School*] [*Finnish*]
KOV .... Firing Platoon Commander (BU)
KOV .... Firing Platoon Commander (RU)
KOV .... Kabinet Odborarske Vychovy [*Department of Trade Union Education*] (CZ)
KOV .... Kommatiki Organosi Vaseos [*Base Party Organization*] (GC)
KOV .... Kommounistiki Organosis Vaseos [*Communist Organization of the Base*] (GC)
KOV .... Kooperationsverband [*Production Cooperation Association*] (EG)
KoV .... Kopnena Vojska [*Ground Forces*] (YU)
kov .... Kovetkezo [*Following*] [*Hungarian*] (GPO)
KOV .... Peasants' Mutual Aid Society (RU)
KOVAC .... Kobanya Vas es Acelontode [*Kobanya Iron and Steel Foundry*] (HU)
KOVAC .... Kovacsolt es Ontott Vas- es Acelmuvek [*Wrought Iron, Cast Iron, and Steel Factory*] (HU)
KOVAGO ..... Kiev Branch of the All-Union Astronomical and Geodetic Society (RU)
KOVM .... Committee for Permafrost Study (RU)
KOVN .... Kommounistiki Organosis Vasilikou Navtikou [*Communist Organization for the Royal Navy*] [*Greek*] (GC)
KOVO .... Podnik Zahranicniho Obchodu pro Dovoz z Vyvoz Vyrobku Presneho Strojirenstvi [*Foreign Trade Enterprise for the Import and Export of Products of the Precision Engineering Industry*] (CZ)
Kovona .... Tovarny na Kovovy Nabytek [*Metal Furniture Factories*] (CZ)
KOVOSMALT ... Narodni Podnik pro Prodej Kuchynskeho a Zelezneho Zbozi [*National Enterprise for the Retail Sale of Kitchen Ware and Hardware*] (CZ)
KOVR .... Harbor Defense Commander (RU)
KOWANI ...... Kongres Wanita Indonesia
KOWILMAN ... Komando Wilajah Pertahanan [*Defense Territorial Command*] (IN)
KOYHD .... Koy Ogretmenleri ile Haberlesme ve Yardimlasma Dernegi [*Society for the Promotion of Mutual Communication and Mutual Aid re Village Teachers*] (TU)
KOY-KOOP ... Koy Kalkinma ve Diger Tarimsal Amacli Kooperatifleri Birligi [*Union of Cooperatives for Village Development and Other Agricultural Goals*] (TU)
KOZ .... Kmetijske Obdelovalne Zadruge [*Peasant Working Cooperatives*] [*Collective farms*] (YU)
KOZDOK ..... Kozlekedesi Dokumentacios es Nyomtatvanyellato Vallalat [*Transportation Forms and Stationery Printing Enterprise*] (HU)
Kozdok .... Kozlekedesi Dokumentacios Vallalat [*Transportation Documentation Establishment*] (HU)
KOZEPTERV ... Kozlekedesuzemi Epulettervezo Vallalat [*Construction Designing Enterprise of the Transportation Establishments*] (HU)
KOZERT ...... Kozsegi Elelmiszerkereskedelmi Reszvenytarsasag [*Municipal Food Trade Company Limited (Prewar)*] (HU)
KOZGEP ..... Kozlekedesepitesi Gepjavito Vallalat [*Highway Construction Machine Repair Shop*] (HU)
kozh .... Tannery [*Topography*] (RU)
KOZhFURNITURA ... Trust of Auxiliary Establishments of the Leather and Footwear Industry (RU)
KOZHIR .... Kozponti Hirlapiroda [*Central Newspaper Office*] (HU)
Kozhsindikat ... All-Union Leather Syndicate (RU)
Kozhsyr'ye ... Moscow Plant for the Processing of Leather Raw Materials (RU)
Kozhtekhzamenitel' ... Moscow Plant for the Production of Industrial Leather Substitutes (RU)
Kozl K .... Kozlekedes- es Melyepitestudomanyi Kiado [*Transport and Civil Engineering Publishing House*] (HU)
Kozokt K ..... Kozoktatasugyi Kiado [*Public Education Publishing House*] (HU)
Kozp Stat Hiv ... Kozponti Statisztikai Hivatal [*Central Statistical Office*] (HU)
KO ZSP .... Komisja Okregowa Zrzeszenia Studentow Polskich [*District Commission of the Polish Student Association*] (POL)
kozv .... Kozvetlen [*Immediate, Close-Range*] (HU)
KP .... Blood-Penicillin Preparation (RU)
KP .... Bridge Crane (RU)
KP .... Cable Appliance (RU)
KP .... Cardan Suspension, Gimbal Suspension (RU)
KP .... Cathode Follower (RU)
kp .... Cavalry Regiment (BU)
KP .... Cavalry Regiment (RU)
KP .... Ceramic Coating [*For aircraft*] (RU)
KP .... Check Point (RU)
KP .... Checking Subroutine (RU)
KP .... Command Device (RU)
KP .... Command Post (BU)
KP .... Command Post (RU)
KP .... Communist Party (BU)
KP .... Communist Party (RU)
KP .... Compass Bearing (RU)
KP- .... Control Panel (RU)
KP .... Democratic Peoples Republic of Korea [*Two-letter standard code*] (CNC)
Kp .... Express Train (RU)
KP .... Gearbox, Gearshift (RU)
KP .... Kazneno-Popravni [*Penal-Reformatory*] (YU)
K/P .... Kedah/Perlis [*Malaysian*] (ML)
kp .... Kerekpar [*or Kerekparos*] [*Bicycle or Cyclist*] (HU)
KP .... Keskustapuolue [*Center Party of Finland*] (PPW)
kp .... Keszpenz [*Cash*] (HU)
KP .... Ketua Penguasa [*Chief Superintendent*] (ML)
Kp .... Kilopond [*1 kilogram of thrust*] (EG)
kp .... Kilopond [*1 kilogram of thrust*] [*Polish*]
Kp .... Kilopond [*Kilopond*] [*1 kilogram of thrust*] (HU)
kp .... Kleiner Personenzug [*Small Passenger Train*] (EG)

KP .... Kmetijsko Posestvo [*Agricultural Estate*] (YU)
Kp .... Kochpunkt, Siedepunkt [*Boiling Point*] [*German*]
KP .... Komisija za Plate [*Wage Commission*] (YU)
KP .... Komisija za Produktivnost i Norme [*Labor Productivity and Norms Commission*] (YU)
KP .... Komitet Powiatowy [*District Committee*] (POL)
KP .... Komma Panevropis [*Pan-European Party*] [*Greek*] (GC)
KP .... Komma Proodeftikon [*Progressive Party*] [*Greek*] (PPE)
KP .... Kommunista Part [*Communist Party*] (HU)
KP .... Kommunistesch Partei [*Communist Party of Luxembourg*] (PPE)
Kp .... Kompanie [*Company*] (EG)
kp .... Komunalni Podnik [*Communal Enterprise*] (CZ)
KP .... Komunalno Podjetje [*Communal Establishment*] (YU)
KP .... Komunisticka Partija [*Communist Party*] (YU)
KP .... Komunistyczna Partia [*Communist Party*] [*Polish*]
kp .... Konepistooli [*Finnish*]
kP .... Konstanter Preis [*Constant Price*] (EG)
KP .... Kooperativna Praktika [*Cooperative Practice*] [*A periodical*] (BU)
KP .... Kovinsko Podjetje [*Metallurgical Establishment*] (YU)
KP .... Kozos Piac [*Common Market*] (HU)
KP .... Krajska Poradna [*Regional Advisory Bureau (for folk arts activities)*] (CZ)
kp .... Kuollutta Painoa [*Finnish*]
KP .... Kutahya Porselen Sanayii AS [*Kutahya Porcelain Industry Corporation*] (TU)
KP- .... Loading Crane (RU)
KP .... Oxygen Apparatus (RU)
KP .... Oxygen Potential (RU)
KP .... Oxygen Tent (RU)
KP .... Red Crescent [*Society*] (RU)
KP .... Regimental Commander (RU)
KP .... River Crossing Commandant (RU)
KP .... Start Button (RU)
KP .... Transportation Committee (RU)
Kp 10 .... Kochpunkt bei 10mm Quecksilberdruck [*Boiling Point at 10 millimeters of Mercury Pressure*] [*German*]
KPA .... Communist Party of Albania (RU)
KPA .... Communist Party of Algeria (RU)
KPA .... Communist Party of Argentina (RU)
KPA .... Communist Party of Armenia (RU)
KPA .... Communist Party of Australia (RU)
KPA .... Communist Party of Austria (RU)
KPA .... Communist Party of Azerbaydzhan (RU)
KPA .... Cooperative Producers' Artel (RU)
KPA .... Domestic Fuel Laboratory [*Finnish*]
KPA .... Kikuyu Provincial Association (MAR)
KPA .... Kinisis Prosfygon Ammokhostou [*Famagusta Refugees Movements*] [*Cypriot*] (GC1)
KPA .... Kodeks Postepowania Administracyjnego [*Code of Administrative Proceedings*] [*Polish*]
KPA .... Komunisticka Partija Albanije [*Communist Party of Albania*] (YU)
KPA .... Komunistyczna Partia Algierii [*Algerian Communist Party*] [*Polish*]
KPA .... Komunistyczna Partia Australii [*Australian Communist Party*] [*Polish*]
KPA .... Komunistyczna Partia Austrii [*Austrian Communist Party*] [*Polish*]
KPA .... Kontrollpostamt [*Control Post Office*] (EG)
KPA .... Oblique Cross Reinforcement (RU)
KPAP .... Kendron Prostasias Anapirou Paidiou [*Center for the Protection of the Handicapped Child*] [*Greek*] (GC)
KPaS .... Krajska Poradna a Studovna [*Regional Advisory Bureau and Study Center*] (CZ)
KPB .... Battalion Command Post (RU)
KPB .... Communist Party of Belgium (RU)
KPB .... Communist Party of Belorussia (RU)
KPB .... Communist Party of Bolivia (RU)
KP(b) .... Communist Party (of Bolsheviks) [*1925-1952*] (RU)
KPB .... Communist Party of Brazil (RU)
KPB .... Communist Party of Burma (RU)
K-PB .... Kommandeur Panzerbataillon [*Tank Battalion Commander*] (EG)
KPB .... Kommunistische Partij van Belgie [*Communist Party of Belgium*] (PPE)
KPB .... Komunisticka Partija Bugarske [*Communist Party of Bulgaria*] (YU)
KPB .... Komunisticka Partija Burme [*Communist Party of Burma*] (YU)
KPB .... Komunistyczna Partia Belgii [*Belgian Communist Party*] [*Polish*]
KP(b) .... Komunistyczna Partia (Bolszewikow) [*Communist Party (Bolsheviks)*] (POL)
KPB .... Kuwait Planning Board (ME)
KPB .... Trade-Union Congress of Burma (RU)
KP(b)A .... Communist Party (of Bolsheviks) of Armenia [*1920-1952*] (RU)
KP(b)A .... Communist Party (of Bolsheviks) of Azerbaydzhan (RU)
KP(b)B .... Communist Party (of Bolsheviks) of Belorussia [*1919-1952*] (RU)
KP(b)E .... Communist Party (of Bolsheviks) of Estonia [*1940-1952*] (RU)
KP(b)G .... Communist Party (of Bolsheviks) of Georgia (RU)
KPBiH .... Komunisticka Partija Bosne i Hercegovine [*Communist Party of Bosnia and Hercegovina*] (YU)
KP(b)K .... Communist Party (of Bolsheviks) of Kazakhstan (RU)
KP(b)K .... Communist Party (of Bolsheviks) of Kirgizia (RU)
KP(b)L .... Communist Party (of Bolsheviks) of Latvia [*1919-1952*] (RU)
KP(b)L .... Communist Party (of Bolsheviks) of Lithuania [*1940-1952*] (RU)
KP(b)M .... Communist Party (of Bolsheviks) of Moldavia [*1940-1952*] (RU)
KP(b)T .... Communist Party (of Bolsheviks) of Tadzhikistan (RU)
KP(b)T .... Communist Party (of Bolsheviks) of Turkmenistan (RU)
KP(b)U .... Communist Party (of Bolsheviks) of the Ukraine [*1918-1952*] (RU)
KP(b)Uz .... Communist Party (of Bolsheviks) of Uzbekistan [*1924-1952*] (RU)
KPC .... Kenya Power Company (MAR)
KPC .... Kenya Press Club (MAR)
KPC .... Kodeks Postepowania Cywilnego [*Code of Civil Procedure*] (POL)
KPC .... Komunisticka Partija Cehoslovacke [*Communist Party of Czechoslovakia*] (YU)
KPCG .... Komunisticka Partija Crne Gore [*Communist Party of Montenegro*] (YU)
KPCh .... Communist Party of Chile (RU)
KPCh .... Communist Party of Czechoslovakia (RU)
KPCh .... Komunistyczna Partia Chin [*Chinese Communist Party*] [*Polish*]
KPCJ .... Kruh Pratel Ceskeho Jazyka [*Circle of Friends of the Czech Language*] (CZ)
KPCSR .... Komunisticka Partija Cehoslovacke Republike [*Communist Party of the Czechoslovak Republic*] (YU)
KPCz .... Komunistyczna Partia Czechoslowacji [*Communist Party of Czechoslovakia*] (POL)
KPD .... Battalion Command Post (RU)
KPD .... Carboxypeptidase (RU)
KPD .... Communist Party of Denmark (RU)
KPD .... Efficiency Factor (BU)
KPD .... Efficiency Factor (RU)
KPD .... Kazneno-Popravni Dom [*Penal-Reformatory Institution*] (YU)
KPD .... Kodix Poinikis Dikonomias [*Code of Criminal Procedure*] [*Greek*] (GC)
KPD .... Kodix Politikis Dikonomias [*Code of Civil Procedure*] [*Greek*] (GC)
KPD .... Kolejowe Przedsiebiorstwo Dowozowe [*Railroad Forwarding Enterprise*] (POL)
KPD .... Kommunistische Partei Deutschlands [*Communist Party of Germany*] [*West German*] (PPW)
KPD .... Kratiki Ploti Dexameni [*State Floating Dock*] [*Greek*] (GC)
KPD .... Kulturno-Prosvetno Drustvo [*Cultural and Educational Society*] (YU)
KPD .... Large-Panel Housing Construction (RU)
KPD .... Large-Panel Plant for Housing Construction (RU)
KPD-AO .... Kommunistische Partei Deutschlands - Aufbau-Organisation [*Communist Party of Germany - Party-Building Organization*] [*West German*] (EG)
KPD-ML .... Kommunistische Partei Deutschlands/Marxisten-Leninisten [*Communist Party of Germany/Marxists-Leninists*] [*West German*] (PPW)
KPdSU .... Kommunistische Partei der Sowjet Union [*Communist Party of the Soviet Union (CPSU)*] [*West German*] (WEN)
KPE .... Communist Party of Ecuador (RU)
KPE .... Communist Party of Estonia (RU)
KPE .... Kenya Preliminary Examination (MAR)
KPE .... Kenya Primary Education (MAR)
KPE .... Polyethylene for Cables (RU)
KPED .... Kendron Pyrinikon Erevnon Dimokritos [*Dimokritos Nuclear Research Center*] [*Greek*] (GC)
KPEE .... Kendro Politikis Erevnas kai Epimorfosis [*Center for Political Research and Training*] [*Greek*] (GC)
KPF .... Communist Party of Finland (RU)
KPF .... Communist Party of France (RU)
KPF .... Kolkhoz Poultry-Raising Farm (RU)
KPF .... Komisija za Pregled Filmova [*Film Control Commission*] (YU)
KPF .... Komitet Polonii Francuskiej [*Committee of the Poles in France*] (POL)
KPF .... Komunisticka Partija Francuske [*Communist Party of France*] (YU)
KPF .... Komunistyczna Partia Finlandii [*Finland Communist Party*] [*Polish*]
KPF .... Komunistyczna Partia Francji [*Communist Party of France*] (POL)
KPFN .... Kefalaion Prostasias Fymatikon Navtikon [*Insurance Fund for Tubercular Seamen*] [*Greek*] (GC)
KPFV .... Kancelar Predsednictva Federalni Vlady [*Office of the Presidium of the Federal Government*] (CZ)
KPG .... Communist Party of Georgia (RU)
KPG .... Communist Party of Germany (RU)
KPG .... Communist Party of Greece (RU)
KPG .... Communist Party of Holland (RU)
KPG .... Communist Party of Honduras (RU)
KPG .... Emergency Backwater Level (RU)
KPG .... Komisja Planowania Gospodarczego [*Economic Planning Committee*] (POL)
KPG .... Komunisticka Partija Grcke [*Communist Party of Greece*] (YU)

KPG............ Load Position Contact (RU)
KPGMPTM... Kesatuan Persekutuan Guru Melayu, Persekutuan Tanah Melayu [*Federation of Malay Teachers' Unions, Federation of Malaya*]
KPGY.......... Kobanyai Porcellangyar [*Porcelain Factory of Kobanya*] (HU)
KPH............ Kingston Public Hospital [*Jamaican*] (LA1)
KPH............ Kniznice "Podnikoveho Hospodarstvi" [*Publication Series "Podnikove Hospodarstvi" (Management)*] (CZ)
KPH............ Komunisticka Partija Hrvatske [*Communist Party of Croatia*] (YU)
KPH............ Komunistyczna Partia Hiszpanii [*Spanish Communist Party*] [*Polish*]
KPH............ Komunistyczna Partia Holandii [*Communist Party of Holland*] [*Polish*]
KPI............ Communist Party of India (RU)
KPI............ Communist Party of Indonesia (RU)
KPI............ Communist Party of Iraq (RU)
KPI............ Communist Party of Israel (RU)
KPI............ Communist Party of Italy (RU)
KPI............ Communist Party of Spain (RU)
KPI............ Information Transmission Channel (RU)
KPI............ Karelian Pedagogical Institute (RU)
KPI............ Kaunas Polytechnic Institute (RU)
KPI............ Kiev Polytechnic Institute (RU)
KPI............ Komunisticna Partija Italije [*Communist Party of Italy*] (YU)
KPI............ Komunistyczna Partia Indonezji [*Communist Party of Indonesia*] (POL)
KPIIIMK....... Committee for Field Research of the Institute of the History of Material Culture (of the Academy of Sciences, USSR) (RU)
KPJ............ Klub Pomoraca Jugoslavije [*Yugoslav Seamen's Club*] [*USA*] (YU)
KPJ............ Komunisticka Partija Jugoslavije [*Communist Party of Yugoslavia (1920-1952)*] (PPE)
KPJ............ Komunisticka Partija Jugoslavije [*Communist Party of Yugoslavia (1974-late 1970s)*] (PPE)
KPJ............ Komunistyczna Partia Japonji [*Communist Party of Japan*] (POL)
k pk............ Cavalry Regiment (BU)
KPK............ Commission of Party Control at the TsK VKP(b) [*1934-1952*] (RU)
KPK............ Commission of Personnel Training (of the Academy of Sciences, USSR) (RU)
KPK............ Committee of Party Control at the TsK KPSS [*1952-1962*] (RU)
KPK............ Communist Party of Canada (RU)
KPK............ Communist Party of Catalonia (RU)
KPK............ Communist Party of China (RU)
KPK............ Communist Party of Colombia (RU)
KPK............ Communist Party of Kazakhstan (RU)
KPK............ Communist Party of Kirgizia (RU)
KPK............ Communist Party of Korea [*1925-1946*] (RU)
KPK............ End of Transition Curve [*Railroads*] (RU)
KPK............ Ketua Pegawai Kechil [*Chief Petty Officer*] (ML)
KPK............ Kodeks Postepowania Karnego [*Code of Criminal Procedure*] (POL)
KPK............ Komunisticka Partija Kine [*Communist Party of China*] (YU)
KPK............ Komunistyczna Parti Kanady [*Communist Party of Canada*] [*Polish*]
KPK............ Krajska Planovacia Komisia [*Regional Planning Commission*] (CZ)
KPK............ Plans and Documents Control (BU)
KPK............ Short-Period Oscillation, Short-Period Vibration (RU)
KPK............ Trade-Union Congress of Canada (RU)
KPKA.......... Konstruktion und Projektierung Kerntechnischer Anlagen [*Enterprise for Design and Planning of Nuclear Installations*] (EG)
KPKhZ......... Collective Chemical Defense (RU)
KPKK.......... Kreisparteikontrollkommission [*Kreis Party Control Commission*] (EG)
KPKVCh...... Committee for Friendship and Cultural Relations with Foreign Countries (BU)
KPL............ Committee on Applied Linguistics (RU)
KPL............ Communist Party of Latvia (RU)
KPL............ Communist Party of Lithuania (RU)
KPL............ Communist Party of Luxembourg (RU)
kpl............ Drops (RU)
kpl............ Kappale(tta) [*Finnish*]
KPL............ Ketua Pegawai Laut [*Chief Naval Officer*] (ML)
KPL............ Kommunisticheskaia Partiia Lesoto (MAR)
KPLiB.......... Communist Party of Lithuania and Belorussia (RU)
KPLPH......... Komandan Pusat Latehan Polis Hutan [*Commander Central Training Police Field Force*] (ML)
KPM............ Combination Sprinkling and Washing Machine (RU)
KPM............ Communist Party of Mexico (RU)
KPM............ Communist Party of Moldavia (RU)
KPM............ Communist Party of Morocco (RU)
KPM............ Kancelar Prace a Mzdy [*Labor and Wage Office*] (CZ)
KPM............ Kesatuan Pelajar Melayu Melaka [*Malay Students' Union of Malacca*] (ML)
KPM............ Kombinovany Pontonovy Most [*Combined Pontoon Bridge*] (CZ)
KPM............ Komunisticka Partija Madarske [*Communist Party of Hungary*] (YU)
KPM............ Komunisticka Partija Makedonije [*Communist Party of Macedonia*] (YU)
KPM............ Kono Progressive Movement (MAR)
KPM............ Kontrolni Propousteci Misto [*Traffic Release Point*] (CZ)
KPM............ Kozlekedesi- es Postaugyi Miniszterium [*Ministry of Transportation and Postal Affairs*] (HU)
KPM............ Kumpulan Perubatan Medan [*Field Ambulance Corps*] (ML)
KPM............ Terminal Point [*Aviation*] (RU)
KPM............ Terminal Point of the March Route (BU)
KPMA.......... Komitim-Pirenena Miandraikitra ny Anaran-Tany [*National Committee on Geographic Names*] [*Malagasy*] (AF)
KP MO......... Komenda Powiatowa Milicji Obywatelskiej [*District Headquarters of the Civic Militia*] [*Polish*]
KPMS.......... Medical Service Command Post (RU)
kpn............ Candidate of Pedagogical Sciences (RU)
KPN............ Communist Party of Netherlands (RU)
KPN............ Communist Party of Norway (RU)
KPN............ Confederation for an Independent Poland (PD)
Kpn............ Kepulauan [*Archipelago*] [*Indonesian*] (NAU)
KPN............ Ketua Polis Negara [*Chief National Police*] (ML)
KPNLF......... Khmer People's National Liberation Front [*Kampuchean*] (PD)
KPNZ.......... Communist Party of New Zealand (RU)
KPO............ Control and Planning Department (RU)
KPO............ Cooperative Producers' Society (RU)
k po............ Junior Sergeant (BU)
KPO............ Kommunistische Partei Oesterreichs [*Communist Party of Austria*] (PPW)
KPO............ Kulturne-Propagacni Oddeleni [*Cultural and Propaganda Department*] (CZ)
KPO............ Kulturno-Prosvetnite Organizacii [*Cultural and Educational Organizations*] (YU)
KPO............ Kulturno-Prosvjetni Odbor [*Cultural and Educational Committee*] (YU)
KPOE.......... Kendron Programmatismou kai Oikonomikon Erevnon [*Center for Programing and Economic Research*] [*Greek*] (GC)
KPOe.......... Kommunistische Partei Oesterreichs [*Communist Party of Austria*] (EG)
KPOP.......... Komitet Porozumiewawczy Organizacji Podziemnych [*Underground Organizations' Consultative Committee*] [*World War II*] (POL)
KPOWU....... Kenya Petroleum and Oil Workers' Union (MAR)
KPP............ Check Point for Motor Transport (RU)
KPP............ Communist Party of Pakistan (RU)
KPP............ Communist Party of Poland [*1925-1938*] (RU)
KPP............ Communist Party of Portugal (RU)
KPP............ Congress of Industrial Organizations [*CIO*] (RU)
KPP............ Congress of Industrial Organizations (BU)
KPP............ Control and Check Point (RU)
KPP............ Control-Traffic Point/Post (BU)
KPP............ Kamerun People's Party (MAR)
KPP............ Kano People's Party [*Nigerian*] (AF)
KPP............ Ketua Egawai Polis [*Chief Police Officer*] (ML)
K-pp............ Komandir Pesadiskog Puka [*Infantry Regiment Commander*] (YU)
KPP............ Kombinat of Auxiliary Establishments (RU)
KPP............ Kombinat of Industrial Establishments (RU)
KPP............ Komisija za Plate u Privredi [*Industrial Wage Commission*] (YU)
KPP............ Komunisticka Partija Poljske [*Communist Party of Poland (1925-1938)*] (YU)
KPP............ Komunistyczna Partia Polski [*Communist Party of Poland (1925-1938)*] (PPE)
KPP............ Kontrollpassierpunkt [*Border Control Point*] (EG)
KPP............ Krajske Plachtarske Preteky [*Regional Glider Contest*] (CZ)
KPP............ Regimental Command Post (RU)
KPP i AFT.... Congress of Industrial Organizations and American Federation of Labor (BU)
KPPMS........ Kesatuan Pelajar-Pelajar Melayu Selangor [*Malayan Students' Association of Selangor*] (ML)
KPPR.......... Komunistyczna Partia Polska Robotnicza [*Communist Polish Workers' Party (1918)*] (POL)
KP PZPR..... Komitet Powiatowy Polskiej Zjednoczonej Partii Robotniczej [*District Committee of the Polish United Workers' Party*] [*Polish*]
k pr............ Cavalry Escort (BU)
KPR............ Communist Party of Romania [*1921-1948*] (RU)
KPR............ Company Command Post (RU)
KPR............ Control-Marshaling Post (BU)
KPR............ Demolition Set (RU)
KPR............ Kancelar Presidenta Republiky [*Office of the President*] (CZ)
kpr............ Kapral [*Corporal*] [*Polish*]
KPR............ Kenya Police Reserve (MAR)
KPR............ Kulturne-Propagacni Referat [*Cultural and Propaganda Section*] (CZ)
KPR............ River Crossing Commandant (RU)
KPRL.......... Kolejowe Przedsiebiorstwo Robot Ladunkowych [*Railroad Loading Enterprise*] (POL)
KPRM.......... Komitet Planowania przy Radzie Ministrow [*Council of Ministers Planning Committee*] (POL)
KPRP.......... Kampuchean People's Revolutionary Party (PD)

KPRP.......... Komunistyczna Partia Robotnicza Polski [*Communist Workers' Party of Poland (1918-1925)*] [*Polish*]
kps.......... Capsule (RU)
KPS.......... Communist Party of Slovakia (RU)
KPS.......... Ketua Penguasa Setor [*Chief Superintendent of Stores*] (ML)
kps.......... Kiloparsec (RU)
KPS.......... Kobanyai Polgari Serfozo Reszvenytarsasag [*Civic Brewery of Kobanya Limited*] (HU)
KPS.......... Komisija za Plati vo Stopanstvo [*Industrial Wage Commission*] (YU)
KPS.......... Kommunistische Partei der Schweiz [*Communist Party of Switzerland*] (PPE)
KPS.......... Kommunistische Partij Suriname [*Communist Party of Suriname*] (PPW)
KPS.......... Komunisticka Partija Srbije [*Communist Party of Serbia*] (YU)
KPS.......... Komunisticna Partija Slovenije [*Communist Party of Slovenia*] (YU)
KPS.......... Kotarska Poljoprivredna Stanica [*District Agricultural Station*] (YU)
KPS.......... Krajska Politicka Skola [*Regional Political School*] (CZ)
KPS.......... Krajsky Pedagogicky Sbor [*Regional Educational Board*] (CZ)
KPS.......... Kurs Politickeho Skoleni [*Political Training Course*] (CZ)
KPSAD.......... Komunisticka Partija Sjedinjenih Americkih Drzava [*Communist Party of the United States of America*] (YU)
KPSh.......... Communist Party of Sweden (RU)
KPSh.......... Communist Party of Switzerland (RU)
KPsO.......... Kendron Psykhagogias Opliton [*Enlisted Men's Recreation Center*] (GC)
KPSS.......... Communist Party of the Soviet Union (BU)
KPSS.......... Communist Party of the Soviet Union (RU)
KPSS.......... Kommunistcheska Partiia Sovetskogo Souizu [*Communist Party of the Soviet Union*] (PPE)
KPSS.......... Komunisticka Partija Sovjetskog Saveza [*Communist Party of the Soviet Union*] (YU)
KPSShA.......... Communist Party of the United States of America (RU)
KPSTO.......... Komunisticna Partija Svobodnega Trzaskega Ozemlja [*Communist Party of the Free Territory of Trieste*] (YU)
KPsY.......... Kendron Psykhikis Ygieinis [*Mental Health Center*] [*Greek*] (GC)
KPT.......... Communist Party of Thailand (RU)
KPT.......... Communist Party of Transjordan (RU)
KPT.......... Communist Party of Tunisia (RU)
KPT.......... Communist Party of Turkestan (RU)
KPT.......... Communist Party of Turkey (RU)
KPT.......... Communist Party of Turkmenia (RU)
kpt.......... Kapitan [*Captain*] [*Polish*]
Kpt.......... Kapitan [*Captain*] [*US equivalent: Captain*] (CZ)
kpt.......... Kaptajn [*Captain*] [*Danish*] (GPO)
KPT.......... Tank Regiment Commander (RU)
KPTF.......... Kolkhoz Poultry Farm (RU)
KPTI.......... Kozponti Pedagogus Tovabbkepzo Intezet [*Central Institute for Advanced Teacher Training*] (HU)
KPTP.......... Committee for Industry and Technological Progress (BU)
KPTs.......... Communist Party of Ceylon (RU)
KPU.......... Communist Party of the Ukraine (RU)
KPU.......... Communist Party of Uruguay (RU)
KPU.......... Kazneno-Popravne Ustanove [*Penal-Reformatory Institutions*] (YU)
K pu.......... Keleti-Palyaudvar [*Keleti (East) Railway Station (Budapest)*] (HU)
KPU.......... Kenya People's Union (AF)
KPU.......... Shipboard Intercommunication System (RU)
KPUG.......... Hunter-Killer Group [*Navy*] (RU)
KPUNIA.......... Fighter Aviation Ship's Control and Guidance Post (RU)
KPUV.......... Kanony Proti Utocne Vozbe [*Antitank Guns*] (CZ)
KPUz.......... Communist Party of Uzbekistan (RU)
KPV.......... Communist Party of Great Britain (RU)
KPV.......... Communist Party of Hungary [*1918-1948*] (RU)
KPV.......... Communist Party of Venezuela (RU)
kPV.......... Continental Modified Air (RU)
kPV.......... Continental Polar Air (RU)
KPV.......... [*The*] Culture and Literature of the East [*Bibliography*] (RU)
KPV.......... Kancelar Predsednictva Vlady [*Office of the Government Presidium*] (CZ)
KPV.......... Searchlight Platoon Commander (RU)
KPVDOSZ.......... Kereskedelmi, Penzugyi, es Vendeglatoipari Dolgozok Szakszervezete [*Trade Union of Workers in Commerce, Finance, and the Catering Industries*] (HU)
KPVO.......... Air Defense Ship, Antiaircraft Ship (RU)
kPVO.......... Antiaircraft Defense Corps (BU)
KPVRZ.......... Konotop Locomotive and Railroad Car Repair Plant (RU)
KPVS.......... Komise Pomoci Vychodnimu Slovensku [*Relief Commission for Eastern Slovakia*] (CZ)
KPWB.......... Komunistyczna Partia Wielkiej Brytanii [*Communist Party of Great Britain*] [*Polish*]
KPYa.......... Communist Party of Japan (RU)
KPYe.......... Variable Capacitor (RU)
KPYu.......... Communist Party of Yugoslavia [*1919-1952*] (RU)
KPZ.......... Kotarska Poljoprivredna Zadruga [*District Agricultural Cooperative*] (YU)
KPZ.......... Kulturno-Prosvetna Zajednica [*Cultural and Educational Association*] (YU)
KPZ.......... Pretrial Detention Cell (RU)
KPZB.......... Communist Party of Western Belorussia (RU)
KPZB.......... Kieleckie Przemyslowe Zjednoczenie Budowlane [*Kielce Industrial Construction Association*] (POL)
KPZB.......... Komunistyczna Partia Zachodniej Bialorusi [*Communist Party of Western Belorussia (Prewar)*] (POL)
KPZB.......... Krakowskie Przemyslowe Zjednoczenie Budowlane [*Krakow Industrial Construction Association*] (POL)
KPZDA.......... Komunisticna Partija Zdruzenih Drzav Amerike [*Communist Party of the United States of America*] (YU)
KPZF.......... Komisija za Poljoprivredni Zemljisni Fond [*Agricultural Land Fund Commission*] (YU)
KPZh.......... Liquid Cargo Container (RU)
KP ZMS.......... Komitet Powiatowy Zwiazku Mlodziezy Socjalistycznej [*District Committee of the Socialist Youth Union*] [*Polish*]
KPZR.......... Komunistyczna Partia Zwiazku Radzieckiego [*Communist Party of the Soviet Union*] (POL)
KPZRZ.......... Krakowskie Przedsiebiorstwo Zmechanizowanych Robot Ziemnych [*Krakow Mechanized Earthmoving Enterprise*] (POL)
KPZU.......... Communist Party of the Western Ukraine (RU)
KPZU.......... Komunistyczna Partia Zachodniej Ukrainy [*Communist Party of Western Ukraine (Prewar)*] (POL)
KPZZ.......... Krajsky Podnik Zemedelskeho Zasobevani [*Regional Agricultural Supply Enterprise*] (CZ)
KQMWU.......... Kenya Quarry and Mine Workers' Union (MAR)
KR.......... Area Commandant (BU)
KR.......... Area Commandant (RU)
KR.......... Box Car (RU)
KR.......... Code Register (RU)
kr.......... Commander [*or Officer in Charge*] (BU)
k-r.......... Commander, Commanding Officer, Leader (RU)
KR.......... Commander's Reconnaissance (RU)
KR.......... Company Commander (RU)
k-r.......... Condenser, Capacitor (RU)
KR.......... Cosmic Radiation (RU)
k-r.......... Counterrevolutionary (RU)
kr.......... Critical (RU)
KR.......... (Heavy) Cruiser (RU)
kr.......... Karat [*Carat*] [*Polish*]
KR.......... Kenya Regiment (MAR)
KR.......... Khmer Rouge [*or Khmers Rouges*] [*Red Cambodian*] (CL)
Kr.......... King [*Chess*] (RU)
KR.......... Kjeller Research Establishment [*Norwegian*]
KR.......... Kladensky Revir [*Kladno Basin (Coal)*] (CZ)
KR.......... Klasifikacija Robe [*Goods Classification*] (YU)
KR.......... Knihovni Rada [*Library Council (of the Local People's Committee)*] (CZ)
KR.......... Kolko Rolnicze [*Agricultural Cooperative*] [*Polish*]
KR.......... Koloniale Rundschau (MAR)
KR.......... Komandni Racunar [*Staff Computer*] [*Military*] (YU)
KR.......... Komisja Rewizyjna [*Board of Control*] [*Polish*]
KR.......... Komisja Rozjemcza [*Conciliation Commission*] (POL)
KR.......... Kontenrahmen [*Accounting System*] (EG)
Kr.......... Kran [*Crane*] [*German*]
Kr.......... Kranken [*German*]
kr.......... Kray (RU)
Kr.......... Kreis [*District*] [*German*]
KR.......... Kreutzer [*Monetary unit*] [*German*]
Kr.......... Kriminal [*German*]
kr.......... Krona [*Crown*] [*Swedish*] (GPO)
kr.......... Krone [*Crown*] [*Danish*] (GPO)
Kr.......... Krueng [*River*] [*Indonesian*] (NAU)
kr.......... Kruunu(a) [*Finnish*]
Kr.......... Krystallographie [*Crystallography*] [*German*]
KR.......... Kulon Rendelet [*Special Decree (Legal)*] (HU)
Kr.......... Kurus [*Kurus*] [*Piastre*] [*Monetary unit*] (TU)
kr.......... Machine Gun Company (BU)
KR.......... Major Repair, General Overhaul (RU)
KR.......... Mine-Clearing Set (RU)
KR.......... Oxygen Reducer (RU)
KR.......... Pilot Relay (RU)
Kr.......... Red [*Toponymy*] (RU)
KR.......... Republic of Korea [*Two-letter standard code*] (CNC)
kr.......... Shell Rock [*Topography*] (RU)
KRA.......... Kreis-Registrierabteilung [*Kreis Registration Department*] (EG)
k-ra.......... Office (RU)
KRA.......... Spotter Observation Aviation (BU)
KRA.......... Spotting and Reconnaissance Aviation (RU)
krae.......... Spotter Observation Aviation Squadron (BU)
krae.......... Spotting and Air Reconnaissance Squadron (RU)
KRAK.......... Kato Rossia, Ameriki, Kina [*Down with Russia, America, China (Movement)*] [*Greek*] (GC)
krakhm.......... Starch Plant [*Topography*] (RU)
krakhm.......... Starch and Syrup Plant [*Topography*] (RU)
KrAO.......... Crimean Astrophysical Observatory (RU)
KRAONA.......... Kraonita Malagasy (MAR)
krap.......... Spotter Observation Aviation Regiment (BU)
krap.......... Spotting and Air Reconnaissance Regiment (RU)

KRAS .... Check-and-Repair Aviation Station (RU)
KRAS .... Krasnoyarsk Railroad (RU)
Krasges....... Krasnoyarsk Hydro-Electric Power Plant (RU)
kraskom...... Red Commander (RU)
Kraslag .... Krasnoyarsk Corrective Labor Camp (RU)
Krasmash ... Krasnoyarsk Machinery Plant (RU)
krasnoarm ... Red Army (RU)
Krasnomash ... Krasnoyarsk Heavy Machinery Plant (RU)
Krasnoyargiz ... Krasnoyarsk State Publishing House (RU)
krat............. Kratica [*Abbreviation*] (YU)
krayekoso... Kray Economic Conference (RU)
krayeved..... Regional Studies (RU)
krayfo.......... Kray Finance Department (RU)
krayFU .... Kray Finance Administration (RU)
Kraygiz........ Kray State Publishing House (RU)
krayknigotorg ... Kray Book Trade Office (RU)
kraykomkhoz ... Kray Department of Municipal Services (RU)
kraykoopinsoyuz ... Kray Union of Disabled Persons' Cooperative Artels (RU)
kraykozhpromsoyuz ... Kray Leather Producers' Union (RU)
krayono....... Kray Department of Public Education (RU)
krayplan...... Kray Planning Commission (RU)
kraypoligrafizdat ... Department of Publishing Houses and Printing Industry of a Krayispolkom Cultural Administration (RU)
kraypotrebsoyuz ... Kray Union of Consumers' Societies (RU)
kraysobes... Kray Department of Social Security (RU)
kraysovprof ... Kray Council of Trade Unions (RU)
KrayTASS... Khabarovsk Kray Branch of the News Agency of the Soviet Union (RU)
krayVTEK ... Kray Medical Commission for Determination of Disability (RU)
krayzdrav.... Kray Department of Public Health (RU)
krayzo......... Kray Land Department (RU)
krayzu .... Kray Land Administration (RU)
KRAZ........... Automobile Made by the Kremenchug Automobile Plant (RU)
KRAZ........... Kremenchug Automobile Plant (RU)
kr b............. Brigade Commander (BU)
kr bt .... Battery Commander (BU)
KRCh........... Tuning-Fork Frequency Controller (RU)
KRD............. Collective Workers' Movement [*Philippines*] (RU)
KRD............. Krajska Rada Druzstev [*Regional Council of Cooperatives*] (CZ)
KRDA .... Kweneng Rural Development Association (MAR)
KRDC .... Kenya Rally Drivers' Club (MAR)
KRDP........... Karonga Rural Development Project (MAR)
kr dr .... Battalion Commander (BU)
Kr e .... Krisztus Elott [*Before Christ*] (HU)
KREIC .... Koweit Real Estate Investment Consortium (MAR)
kreik............ Kreikassa [*Finnish*]
kreik............ Kreikkaa [*or Kreikaksi*] [*Finnish*]
kreikk.......... Kreikkalainen [*Greek*] [*Finnish*]
kreikkal....... Kreikkalainen [*Greek*] [*Finnish*]
KREMENCO ... Kuwait Industrial Refinery, Maintenance, and Engineering Company (ME)
KremGES.... Kremenchug Hydroelectric Power Plant (RU)
KREMU .... Kenya Rangeland Ecological Monitoring Unit (MAR)
KREMZ........ Kalinin Electromechanical Plant (RU)
KREMZ........ Kiev Electromechanical Repair Plant (RU)
Krep .... Fortress, Citadel, Stronghold [*Topography*] (RU)
KRES........... Kiev Regional Electric Power Plant (RU)
KRES........... Krasnodar Regional Electric Power Plant (RU)
kr esk .... Troop Commander (BU)
Krestintern ... Peasants' International (RU)
krestkom .... Peasants' Mutual Aid Committee (RU)
Krestlit........ Lithuanian Red Cross (RU)
krestpom .... Peasants' Mutual Aid Committee (RU)
krest'yan..... Peasant (RU)
KRESZ .... A Kozuti Kozlekedes Rendjenek Szabalyzata [*Traffic Regulations for Public Thoroughfares*] (HU)
KREZ........... Konstantinovka Electrical Repair Plant (RU)
KrF .... Kristelig Folkpartiet [*Christian People's Party*] [*Norwegian*] (PPE)
KrF .... Kristeligt Folkeparti [*Christian People's Party*] [*Danish*] (PPE)
KRG............. Karaganda Railroad (RU)
KrG............. Kriegsgericht [*War Tribunal*] [*German*]
KRH............. Komisja Rozbudowy Hutnictwa [*Commission for Metallurgical Development*] (POL)
krik.............. Kriketti [*Cricket*] [*Finnish*]
Krim .... Kriminal [*German*]
KRINGRAMAT ... Krizevacka Industrija Gradevnog Materijala [*Krizevci Building Materials Industry*] (YU)
KRIPO .... Kriminalpolizei [*Ordinary Criminal Police*] [*German*]
KrISK .... Crimean Institute of Special Crops (RU)
krist............. Crystal, Crystalline (RU)
Krist .... Kristallisation [*Crystallization*] [*German*]
krist............. Kristallisiert [*or Kristallinisch*] [*Crystallized or Crystalline*] [*German*]
Kristal-Is..... Turkiye Sise, Cam, ve Kristal Sanayii Iscileri Sendikasi [*Turkish Bottle, Glass, and Crystal Industry Workers Union*] (TU)
kristallich.... Crystal, Crystalline (RU)
kristallokhim ... Crystal-Chemistry (RU)
krist sp........ Crystal Spectrometer (RU)
krit.............. Critical (RU)
krit.............. Kritisch [*Critical*] [*German*]
kritich .... Critical (RU)
Krivbass...... Krivoy Rog Iron Ore Basin (RU)
Krivorozhstal' ... Krivoy Rog Metallurgical Plant (RU)
KRIZTO .... Commission for Fisheries Research in the Western Pacific Ocean (RU)
krj................ Kirja(a) [*Finnish*]
krjm............. Krestni Jmeno [*Christian Name*] (CZ)
kr k............. Corps Commander (BU)
KRK............. Kreisrevisionskommission [*Kreis Audit Commission*] (EG)
krkat............ Kreikkalais-Katolinen [*Finnish*]
kr kdrt......... Blood Count Card (BU)
Krkh .... Krankenhaus [*German*]
KRKO .... Kibris Rum Kurtulus Ordusu [*Greek Cypriot Liberation Army*] [*EKAS is preferred*] [*Turkish Cypriot*] (GC)
KRKP........... Krajowa Rada Kobiet Polskich [*All-Polish Council of Women*] (POL)
Krkw .... Krankenkraftwagen [*Motor Ambulance*] (EG)
KRL .... Koreanska Republika Ludowa [*Korean People's Republic*] (POL)
KRL .... Light Cruiser (RU)
KRLD........... Koreanska Republika Ludowo-Demokratyczna [*Korean People's Democratic Republic*] [*Polish*]
KRLS........... Ship Radar (RU)
KRM .... Radio Range Beacon (RU)
KRN............. Krajowa Rada Narodowa [*National People's Council (1944-1947)*] [*Polish*]
krn............... Rhizome (RU)
KRNG.......... Kwame Nkrumah Revolutionary Guards (MAR)
krnpl .... Root Crop (RU)
KRNV .... Komise Rizeni Narodnich Vyboru [*Commission for the Direction of People's Committees*] (CZ)
KRO............. Counterintelligence Section of the OGPU (RU)
KRO............. Katholieke Radio Omroep [*Catholic Broadcasting Association*] [*Dutch*] (WEN)
KRO............. Krajska Rada Odboru [*Regional Trade Union Council*] (CZ)
KRO............. Reconnaissance Detachment Commander (RU)
KRO............. Workers' Education Center (RU)
KRO............. Workers' Training Courses (RU)
KROW .... Komitet Rozbudowy Otoczenia Wawelu [*Committee for Development of the Wawel Area*] (POL)
KRP .... Checking and Clearing Point [*At a decontamination station*] (RU)
KRP .... Compass Radio Bearing (RU)
KRP .... Kama River Steamship Line (RU)
KRP .... Keskusrikospoliisi [*Central Criminal Police*] [*Finnish*] (WEN)
KRP .... Knihovna Rudeho Prava [*Library of the "Rude Pravo" Newspaper*] (CZ)
KRP .... Komisija za Reviziju Projekata [*Design Revision Commission*] (YU)
KRP .... Kurdistan Revolutionary Party [*Iraqi*] (PPW)
KRPG .... Communist Workers' Party of Germany (RU)
kr pk............ Regimental Commander (BU)
KRPP .... Communist Workers' Party of Poland [*1918-1925*] (RU)
KRR............. Rat-Reticulocyte Reaction (RU)
KRRL........... Kabinet pro Studia Recka, Rimska, a Latinska [*Department of Greek, Roman, and Latin Studies (of the Czechoslovak Academy of Sciences)*] (CZ)
KRRS........... Kenya Rugby Referees Society (MAR)
KRS .... Cosmic Rocket System (RU)
krs............... Kerros [*Finnish*]
krs............... Krossi(a) [*Finnish*]
KrS.............. Kurirska Stanica [*Courier Station*] [*Military*] (YU)
Krs .... Kurus [*Piastre*] [*Monetary unit*] (TU)
KRSEDE...... Kendrikos Radiofonikos Stathmos Enoplon Dynameon Ellados [*Main Radio Station of the Armed Forces of Greece*] (GC)
KRSS........... Krajska Sprava Spoju [*Regional Administration Office for Communications*] (CZ)
KRT .... Code Relay Transformer (RU)
KRT .... Heavy Cruiser (RU)
KRT .... Khartoum International Airport (MAR)
krt............... Korut [*Avenue, Boulevard*] (HU)
kr-ts .... Red Army Soldier (RU)
KRU............. Category Distribution System [*Nuclear energy*] (BU)
KRU............. Control and Inspection Administration (RU)
KRU............. Directorate of Counterintelligence (RU)
Kr u .... Krisztus Utan [*Anno Domini*] (HU)
KRV .... Auxiliary Cruiser (RU)
KRV .... Komanda Ratnog Vazduhoplovstva [*Air Force Command*] (YU)
KRWRiOP.... Komisja Rzadowa Wyznan Religijnych i Oswiecenia Publicznego [*State Commission on Religious Denominations and Public Education*] [*Pre-World War II*] (POL)
kr-yets .... Red Army Soldier (RU)
Krymgosizdat ... Crimean State Publishing House (RU)
Krymizdat.... Crimean Oblast Book Publishing House (RU)
KrymTsIK.... Central Executive Committee of the Crimean ASSR (RU)
Kryst .... Krystall [*or Krystallisation or Krystallographie*] [*Crystal or Crystallization or Crystallography*] [*German*]
k-ryy........... Which, That, Who (RU)

KRZh.......... Railroads of the Korean People's Democratic Republic (RU)
KS.......... Apparent Resistance (RU)
KS.......... Boilermaking (RU)
KS.......... Cathode Glow (RU)
KS.......... Check Signal (RU)
KS.......... Combustion Chamber (RU)
KS.......... Command Personnel (RU)
KS.......... Communications Channel (RU)
KS.......... Compressor Station (RU)
ks.......... Control Station (RU)
ks.......... Corps (BU)
KS.......... Cybernetic Collection [*Bibliography*] (RU)
KS.......... Duty on Board [*Navy*] (RU)
KS.......... Gearbox (RU)
KS.......... Guard Duty (RU)
KS.......... Gunnery Training Course (RU)
ks.......... Horsepower (BU)
KS.......... Kamerunskii Soiuz (MAR)
KS.......... Kancelarske Stroje [*Office Machinery*] (CZ)
k-s.......... Kantasana [*Finnish*]
KS.......... Kapitalisticke Staty [*Capitalist States*] (CZ)
ks.......... Katso [*See, Compare*] [*Finnish*] (GPO)
KS.......... Keltic Society (EA)
KS.......... Kendrikon Symvoulion [*Central Council*] (GC)
KS.......... Kepala Staf [*Chief of Staff*] (IN)
KS.......... Kilosikl [*Kilocycle*] (TU)
Ks.......... Kisa [*Short*] (TU)
Ks.......... Kisim [*Section*] [*As of a publication*] (TU)
KS.......... Klanje Stoke [*Livestock Slaughter*] (YU)
KS.......... Klub Sportowy [*Sport Club*] (POL)
KS.......... Knjizevni Sever [*Literary North*] [*Subotica*] [*A periodical*] (YU)
KS.......... Kollisionsschutzanlage [*Anticollision Device*] (EG)
Ks.......... Kolpos [*Gulf*] [*Greek*] (NAU)
KS.......... Komisija za Standardizaciju [*Standardization Commission*] (YU)
KS.......... Komisija Strucnjaka [*Commission of Specialists*] (YU)
KS.......... Komitet Stoleczny [*Polish*]
KS.......... Komunisticka Strana [*Communist Party*] (CZ)
KS.......... Komunisticka Stranka [*Communist Party*] (YU)
KS.......... Konjska Sila [*Horsepower*] (YU)
KS.......... Konjska Snaga [*Horsepower*] (YU)
KS.......... Kontrolna Stanica [*Control Station*] [*Radio*] [*Military*] (YU)
KS.......... Krajska Sprava [*Regional Administration*] (CZ)
KS.......... Kritiki Syspirosi [*Critical Thinking Group*] [*Marxist-Leninist-Maoist*] [*Greek*] (GC)
KS.......... Krojastvo in Siviljstvo [*Tailoring and Dressmaking*] (YU)
ks.......... Ksiadz [*Priest, Reverend*] (POL)
ks.......... Ksiaze [*Duke*] [*Polish*]
KS.......... Kuestenschiff [*Coastal Ship*] (EG)
KS.......... Kuestenschutzboot [*Coastal Patrol Boat, Coastal Protection Boat*] (EG)
ks.......... Kus [*Each, Piece, Unit*] (CZ)
KS.......... Oscillating System (RU)
KS.......... Quartz Spectrograph (RU)
KS.......... Resistance Method in Logging (RU)
KS.......... Shim Rod [*Nuclear physics and engineering*] (RU)
KS.......... Spotter (RU)
KS.......... Stop Button (RU)
KS.......... Vitreous-Enamel Capacitor (RU)
KSA.......... Committee on Construction and Architecture (BU)
KSA.......... Krajska Sdruzeni Advokatu [*Regional Associations of Lawyers*] (CZ)
KSAC.......... Kingston-Saint Andrew Corporate Area [*Jamaican*] (LA1)
KSAVU.......... Kniznica Slovenskej Akademie Vied a Umeni [*Library of the Slovak Academy of Sciences and Arts*] (CZ)
KSB.......... Communal Economy and Public Works (BU)
KSB.......... Kozponti Statisztikai Bizottsag [*Central Statistical Committee*] (HU)
KSB.......... Ksiazka Sprzetu Budowlanego [*Record Book for Building Equipment*] (POL)
K Sb.......... Kumandan Subay [*Commanding Officer*] (TU)
KSB.......... Rifle Battalion Commander (RU)
KSC.......... Kenana Sugar Company [*Sudanese*] (MAR)
KSC.......... Komandir Streljacke Cete [*Commanding Officer of a Rifle Company*] (YU)
KSC.......... Komunisticka Strana Ceskoslovenska [*Communist Party of Czechoslovakia*] (PPW)
KSC.......... Krajsky Soud Civilni [*Regional Civil Court*] (CZ)
KSC.......... Krajsky Soud Obchodni [*Regional Court of Business Litigation*] (CZ)
KSCSN.......... Klub Svazu Ceskoslovenskych Novinaru [*Czechoslovak Journalists' Club*] (CZ)
KSCSS.......... Klub Svazu Ceskoslovenskych Soisovatelu [*Czechoslovak Writers' Club (Club of the Czechoslovak Writers' Union)*] (CZ)
KSD.......... Kodix Stratiotikis Dikaiosynis [*Code of Military Justice*] [*Greek*] (GC)
KSD.......... Krajove Slovenske Divadlo [*Slovak Regional Theater*] (CZ)
KSD.......... Medium-Pressure Compressor (RU)
KSD.......... Rifle Division Commander (RU)
KSES.......... Kendriki Synetairistiki Enosis Sykoparagogon (Sykiki) [*Central Fig Producers Cooperative Union*] [*Greek*] (GC)
KSG.......... Hermetically Sealed Mica Capacitor (RU)
KSGU.......... Knihovna Statniho Ustavu Geologickeho [*Library of the State Geological Institute*] (CZ)
KSGUCSR.......... Knihovna Statniho Ustavu Geologickeho Ceskoslovenske Republiky [*Library of the State Geological Institute of the Czechoslovak Republic*] (CZ)
KSh.......... Code Bus [*Computers*] (RU)
KSH.......... Kaplan Seiner Heiligkeit [*German*]
Ksh.......... Kenyan Shilling (MAR)
KSH.......... Kozponti Statisztikai Hivatal [*Central Statistical Office*] (HU)
KShA.......... Address Code Bus [*Computers*] (RU)
KShB.......... Children and School Libraries Pool (RU)
KShCh.......... Number Code Bus (RU)
KShR.......... Telephone Construction Company (RU)
ksht a.......... Army Commander (BU)
KShtM.......... Command Staff Car (BU)
ksht o a.......... Separate Army Commander (BU)
KShU.......... Command and Staff Exercise, Command Post Exercise (RU)
KShZ.......... Kirov Tire Plant (RU)
KSI.......... Kozponti Sportiskola [*Central Sports School*] (HU)
KSI.......... Red Sports International (RU)
KSIA.......... Brief Communications of the Institute of Archaeology (RU)
KSIE.......... Brief Communications of the Institute of Ethnography (RU)
ksieg.......... Ksiegarnia [*Bookshop*] (POL)
KSIIMK.......... Brief Communications on Reports and Field Research of the Institute of Material Culture (Academy of Sciences, USSR) (RU)
KSIV.......... Brief Communications of the Institute of Oriental Studies [*Academy of Sciences, USSR*] (RU)
KSK.......... Commission of Soviet Control (at the Council of People's Commissars, USSR) [*1934-1940*] (RU)
KSK.......... Committee for Economic Coordination (BU)
KSK.......... Kanser Savas Konseyi [*Council to Combat Cancer*] [*Under Ministry of Health and Social Welfare*] (TU)
KSK.......... Karsiyaka Spor Kulubu [*Karsiyaka Sports Club*] [*Izmir*] (TU)
KSK.......... Klub Socialisticke Kultury [*Socialist Culture Club*] (CZ)
KSK.......... Komise Stranicke Kontroly [*Party Control Commission*] (CZ)
KsK.......... Potassium Sulfate (RU)
KSKhI.......... Kishinev Agricultural Institute Imeni M. V. Frunze (RU)
KSKhI.......... Kuban' Agricultural Institute (RU)
k skh n.......... Candidate of Agricultural Sciences (BU)
k s-kh n.......... Candidate of Agricultural Sciences (RU)
KSKhOS.......... Complex Agricultural Experimental Station (RU)
KSKhSh.......... Communist Agricultural School (RU)
KSKO.......... Sovkhoz and Kolkhoz Education Center (RU)
KSKP.......... Kumpulan Sekuad Khas Polis [*Police Special Squad Group*] (ML)
Ksl.......... Kisla [*Barracks*] (TU)
KSL.......... Krajska Sprava Lesu [*Regional Forest Administration*] (CZ)
KSL.......... Kuala Selangor (ML)
KSL.......... Perforation Solenoid Contact (RU)
KSLS.......... Krajska Sprava Inseminacnich Stanic [*Regional Administration of Insemination Stations (Attached to the Regional National Committee)*] (CZ)
KSM.......... Building Materials Kombinat (RU)
KSM.......... Commission on Synoptic Meteorology (of the World Meteorological Organization) (RU)
ksm.......... Cubic Centimeter (BU)
KSM.......... Keyboard Calculating Machine (RU)
KSM.......... Young Communist League (RU)
KSMB.......... Young Communist League of Belorussia (RU)
KSME.......... Young Communist League of Estonia [*1921-1940*] (RU)
KSMIP.......... Committee of Standards, Measures, and Measuring Instruments (RU)
KSMK.......... Young Communist League of China (RU)
KSML.......... Young Communist League of Latvia [*1919-1936*] (RU)
KSML.......... Young Communist League of Lithuania [*1918-1940*] (RU)
KSMM.......... Katolickie Stowarzyszenie Mlodziezy Meskiej [*Catholic Association of Young Men*] (POL)
KSMU.......... Young Communist League of the Ukraine [*1919-1923*] (RU)
KSMW.......... Komitet Studiujacej Mlodziezy Wiejskiej [*Peasant Youth Student Committee*] (POL)
KSMZO.......... Komisija za Saradnju sa Medunarodnim Zdravstvenim Organizacijama [*Commission for Cooperation with International Health Organizations*] (YU)
KSN.......... Command Guidance System (RU)
KSN.......... Kabinet pro Spolecenske Nauky [*Department of Social Sciences*] (CZ)
KSN.......... Komunisticka Strana Nemecka [*Communist Party of Germany*] (CZ)
KSNDTC.......... Kiem Sat Nhan Dan Toi Cao [*People's Supreme Procurate*] (TVP)
KSNK.......... Katalog Scalonych Norm Kosztorysowych [*Catalog of Standard Norms for Cost Estimators*] (POL)
KSNKh.......... Caucasian Council of the National Economy (RU)
KSNKh.......... Kazakh Council of the National Economy (RU)
KSO.......... Karlovarsky Symfonicky Orchestr [*Karlsbad Symphony Orchestra*] (CZ)

KSO............ Kendron Symbarastaseos Oikogeneias [*Family Assistance Center*] [*Greek*] (GC)
KSO............ Pressed Mica Capacitor (RU)
KSOS.......... Koinopraxia Synetairistikon Organoseon Soultaninas [*Confederation of Sultana Cooperative Organizations*] [*Greek*] (GC)
KSP............ Braunkohlenkombinat "Schwarze Pumpe" (VEB) [*"Schwarze Pumpe" Brown Coal Combine (VEB)*] (EG)
KSP............ Instrument-Flight Control Room (RU)
KSP............ Kendrikos Stathmos Paragogis [*Central Productivity Station*] [*Greek*] (GC)
KSP............ Kenya Socialist Party (MAR)
KSP............ Komisija za Proucavnje Stanbene Problematike i Izgradnje [*Commission for the Study of Housing Problems and Construction*] (YU)
KSP............ Komma Sosialistikis Protovoulias [*Socialist Initiative Party*] [*Greek*] (GC)
KSP............ Kulturni Sluzba Pracujicim [*Cultural Service for the Working People*] (CZ)
KSP............ Rifle Regiment Commander (RU)
KSPC.......... Kuwait-Spanish Petroleum Company (ME)
KSPCA........ Kenya Society for the Prevention of Cruelty to Animals (MAR)
KSPS........... Kray Council of Trade Unions (RU)
KSPU........... Kniznica Statneho Pedagogickeho Ustavu [*Library of the State Pedagogical Institute*] [*Bratislava*] (CZ)
KSPY........... Kendron Syndonismou Pyron Ypostirixeos [*Fire Support Coordination Center*] [*Greek*] (GC)
KSPZ........... Kotarski Savez Poljoprivrednih Zadruga [*District Union of Agricultural Cooperatives*] (YU)
KSPZPR...... Komitet Stoleczny Polskiej Zjednoczonej Partii Robotniczej [*Warsaw Committee of the Polish United Workers Party*] (POL)
KSR............ Canonical Simplicial Partition (RU)
KSR............ Kenya-Somalia Relations (MAR)
KSR............ Kniznica Sovietskych Romanov [*Soviet Fiction Literary Series*] (CZ)
KSR............ Konferencja Samorzadu Robotniczego [*Workers' Self-Government Conference*] (POL)
KSR............ Krajsky Sbor Radioamateru [*Regional Board of Amateur Radio Operators*] (CZ)
KSR............ Rifle Company Commander (RU)
KSR............ Rifle Company Commander (BU)
KSR(b)........ Komunisticka Strana Ruska (Bolseviku) [*Communist Party of Russia (Bolshevik)*] (CZ)
KSRI........... Komandno-Stabne Ratne Igre [*Staff Officers' War Games*] (YU)
KSS............ Kenya Soil Survey (MAR)
KSS............ Kolo Srpskih Sestara [*Serbian Sisters Society*] [*Libertyville, IL*] (YU)
KSS............ Komunisticka Strane Slovenska [*Communist Party of Slovakia*] [*Czechoslovak*] (PPW)
KSS............ Krajevni Sindikalni Svet [*Local Council of Trade-Unions*] (YU)
KSS............ Kumpulan Simpan Senggara [*Ordnance Maintenance Group*] (ML)
KSSD.......... Krajsky Svaz Spotrebnich Druzstev [*Regional Union of Consumers' Cooperatives*] (CZ)
KSSR.......... Kazakh Soviet Socialist Republic (RU)
KSSR.......... Kirgiz Soviet Socialist Republic (RU)
KSSRZ........ Kiev Shipyard (RU)
KSSS.......... Komunisticka Strana Sovetskeho Svazu [*Communist Party of the Soviet Union*] (CZ)
KSSZF......... Komisija za Selsko-Stopanskiot Zemjisen Fond [*Agricultural Land Fund Commission*] (YU)
KST............ Compressor Station (RU)
KST............ Concentric Laminar Texture (RU)
KST............ Kendriki Synergatiki Trapeza [*Central Cooperative Bank*] [*Cypriot*] (GC)
Kst............ Kohlenstaub [*Powdered Coal*] (EG)
KST............ Kolcsonos Segito Takarekpenztarak [*Mutual Savings Banks*] (HU)
KST............ Komitet za Spoljnu Trgovinu (DSPRP) [*Foreign Trade Committee*] (YU)
KST............ Krajsky Trestni Soud [*Regional Criminal Court*] (CZ)
KSt............ Railroad Station Commandant (RU)
KSTC.......... Kenya Science Teachers College (MAR)
KSTL........... Klub Slovenskych Turistov Lyziarov [*Slovak Tourist and Skiing Club*] (CZ)
KSU............ Administration of Health Resorts and Sanatoriums (RU)
KSU............ Checking and Reading Device (RU)
KSU............ Commission for Assistance to Scientists (RU)
KSU............ Health Resort Administration (BU)
KSU............ Kniznica Slovenskej Univerzity [*Slovak University Library*] [*Bratislava*] (CZ)
KSU............ Switching-Connecting Device (RU)
KSUP.......... Kulturny Svaz Ukrajinskych Pracujucich [*Cultural Association of Ukrainian Workers*] [*Slovakia*] (CZ)
KSV............ Komandir Streljackog Voda [*Rifle Platoon Commander*] (YU)
KSV............ Kommunistische Studentenvereinigung [*Communist Students Union*] [*Austrian*] (WEN)
KSV............ Kommunistischer Studentenverband [*Communist Student Federation*] [*West German*] (WEN)
KSV............ Kotarsko Sindikalno Vece [*District Trade-Union Council*] (YU)
KSV............ Standing Wave Ratio (RU)
ksvb........... Corps Signal Battalion (BU)
KSVB........... Krajska Sprava Verejne Bezpecnosti [*Regional Administration of Public Security*] (CZ)
KSV-Kommission ... Knotenpunkt-Stueckgut-Verkehrs-Kommission [*Railroad Junction Commission for LCL Cargo or for General Cargo*] (EG)
KSVN........... Voltage Standing Wave Ratio (RU)
KSWC.......... Khartoum Spinning and Weaving Company (MAR)
KSWILWPG ... Kolo Studentow Wydzialu Inzynierii Ladowo-Wodnej Politechniki Gdanskiej [*Students' Circle of the Land and Water Engineering Department of the Gdansk (Danzig) Polytechnic Institute*] (POL)
KSZ............ Catalog of Weak Stars (RU)
KSZ............ Shipyard (BU)
KSZB.......... Kereskedelmi Szakoktatasi Bizottsag [*Committee on Specialized Commercial Training*] (HU)
KSZB.......... Kozponti Szabvanyositasi Bizottsag [*Central Standardization Committee*] (HU)
KSZDOSZ... Kozlekedesi es Szallitasi Dolgozok Szakszervezete [*Trade Union of Communication and Transportation Workers*] (HU)
KSZE.......... Konferenz fuer Sicherheit und Zusammenarbeit in Europa [*Conference on Security and Cooperation in Europe (CSCE)*] (EG)
KSZE.......... Kukoricatermelesi Szocialista Egyuttmukodes [*Socialist Cooperation in Corn Production (Located at Szekszard)*] (HU)
KSZh.......... Committee of Soviet Women (RU)
KSZh.......... Communist Union of Journalists (RU)
KSZI........... Kozonsegszervezo Iroda [*Office for Organizing People's Cultural Entertainment*] (HU)
KSZ K......... Kisipari Szovetkezetek Kiadovallalata [*Publishing House of the Producers' Cooperative Enterprises*] (HU)
KSZKBI....... Kisipari Szovetkezeti Kolcsonos Biztosito Intezet [*Mutual Insurance Institute for Cooperatives*] (HU)
KSZKV........ Kisipari Szovetkezeti Kiado Vallalat [*Cooperative Publishing Enterprise*] (HU)
K Sz M......... Kereskedelem- es Szovetkezetugyi Miniszter [*Minister of Commerce and Cooperatives*] (HU)
KSZS.......... Kovorobne a Strojarenske Zavody na Slovensku, Narodny Podnik [*Metallurgical and Machine Building Plants in Slovakia, National Enterprise*] (CZ)
KSZT.......... Kereskedelmi Szakoktatasi Tanacs [*Council on Specialized Commercial Training*] (HU)
KSzT.......... Kozponti Szallitasi Tanacs [*Central Transportation Council*] (HU)
KSZTB........ Kozalkalmazottak Szakszervezete Teruleti Bizottsag [*Trade Union of Government Employees, Territorial Committee*] (HU)
kt............... Captain [*Army*] (BU)
KT.............. Code Transformer (RU)
k-t.............. Committee (BU)
k-t.............. Committee (RU)
k-t.............. Concentrate (RU)
k-t.............. Credit (RU)
kt............... Critical Temperature (RU)
Kt............... Kereskedelmi Torveny [*Commercial Code*] (HU)
KT.............. Ketua Turus [*Chief of Staff*] [*Malaysian*] (ML)
kt............... Kiloton (RU)
k-t.............. Komandant [*Commander*] (YU)
KT.............. Komandni Toranj [*Control Tower*] [*Airport*] (YU)
k-t.............. Kombinat (RU)
kT.............. Konkrete Tatbestaende [*Concrete Facts*] [*German*]
KT.............. Kontrola Techniczna [*Technical Control Board*] (POL)
kt............... Korter [*Circle*] (HU)
kt............... Kozsegi Tanacs [*Village Council*] (HU)
KT.............. Kratki Talasi [*Short Waves*] (YU)
KT.............. Ktimatiki Trapeza [*Land Bank*] [*See also EKTE*] (GC1)
KT.............. Labor Code (BU)
k/t.............. Motion-Picture Theater (RU)
kt............... Room Temperature (RU)
KT.............. Television Camera (RU)
k-ta............ Acid (RU)
KTA............ Commercial News Agency (RU)
KTA............ Kendrikon Takhydromeion Athinon [*Athens Main Post Office*] (GC)
KTA............ Kibris Turk Alayi [*Turkish Cypriot Regiment*] (TU)
KTA............ Kozuletek Tamogatasi Alapja [*Relief Fund for Public Institutions*] (HU)
KTA............ Kraftfahrzeugtechnische Anstalt [*Motor Vehicle Technical Facility*] (EG)
KTA............ Kreistransportaktiv [*Kreis Transportation Aktiv*] (EG)
KTACYD..... Kibris Turk Autistik Cocuklara Yardim Dernegi [*Association for Aid to Turkish Cypriot Autistic Children*] (GC)
KTAD.......... Kibris Turk Anneler Dernegi [*Turkish Cypriot Mothers' Organization*] (TU)
KTAD.......... Kibris Turk Aydinlar Dernegi [*Turkish Cypriot Intellectuals Association*] (GC)

KTAF.......... Kibris Turk Atletizm Federasyonu [*Turkish Cypriot Athletic Federation*] (TU)
KTAMS....... Kibris Turk Amme Memurlari Sendikasi [*Turkish Cypriot Public Service Officials Union*] (GC)
KTAMS....... Kibris Turk Askeri Mustahdemler Sendikasi [*Turkish Cypriot Military Employees' Union*] [*See also As-Sen*] (TU)
KTAP.......... Corps Heavy Artillery Regiment (RU)
KTB............ Concert and Theatrical Office (RU)
ktb............. Corps Tank Battalion (BU)
KTB............ Design and Technological Office (RU)
KTB............ Kibris Tib Birligi [*Cypriot Medical Union*] [*Turkish Cypriot*] (GC)
KTB............ Kibris Turk Birligi [*Turkish Cypriot Unit*] [*Military*] (TU)
KTB............ Kooperacios Tarcakozi Bizottsag [*Interministerial Committee on Cooperation*] (HU)
KTB............ Tank Battalion Commander (RU)
KTBB.......... Kibris Turk Benzinciler Birligi [*Turkish Cypriot Gasoline Dealers' Union*] (TU)
KTBK.......... Kibris Turk Baris Kuvvetleri [*Turkish Cypriot Peace Forces*] (TU)
KTBK.......... Kibris Turk Birligi Kumandasi [*Turkish Cypriot (Military) Unit Command*] (TU)
KTBKK........ Kibris Turk Birligi Kara Kuvvetleri [*Turkish Cypriot Unit Ground Forces*] (TU)
KTBMC....... Kibris Turk Birlesmis Milletler Cemiyeti [*Turkish Cypriot United Nations' Society*] (GC)
KTBR.......... Tank Brigade Commander (RU)
ktbtk.......... Katonai Bunteto Torvenykonyv [*Military Penal Code, Articles of War*] (HU)
KTC............ Kawambwa Tea Company (MAR)
KTC............ Kibris Turk Cemiyeti [*Turkish Cypriot Society*] (TU)
KTCB.......... Kibris Turk Ciftciler Birligi [*Turkish Cypriot Farmers' Union*] (TU)
KTCEK........ Kibris Turk Cocuk Esirgeme Kurumu [*Turkish Cypriot Child Protection Association*] (GC)
KTCh.......... Confederation of Workers of Chile (RU)
KTCK.......... Kibris Turk Cografya Kurumu [*Turkish Cypriot Geographic Organization*] (TU)
KTCM.......... Kibris Turk Cemaat Meclisi [*Turkish Cypriot Communal Assembly*] (GC)
KTCMS....... Kibris Turk Cemaat Meclisi Sendikasi [*Turkish Cypriot Communal Assembly Union*] (GC)
KTD............ Collective Labor Contract (BU)
KTD............ Kemicna Tovarna Domzale [*Chemical Factory in Domzale*] (YU)
KTD............ Tank Division Commander (RU)
KTDA.......... Kenya Tea Development Authority (MAR)
KTDC.......... Kenya Tourist Development Corporation (MAR)
KTDD.......... Kibris Turk Demokrasi Dernegi [*Turkish Cypriot Democracy Society*] (TU)
k-t na demokr bulg zheni... Bulgarian Democratic Women's Committee (BU)
KTDI............ Kibris Turk Denizcilik Isletmesi [*Turkish Cypriot Maritime Operations Directorate General*] (TU)
KTDT.......... Kibris Turk Devlet Tiyatrolari [*Turkish Cypriot State Theatres*] (GC)
KTDU.......... Kabinet pro Theorii a Dejiny Umeni [*Department for the Study of the Theory and History of Art (of the Czechoslovak Academy of Sciences)*] (CZ)
KTE............ Kendron Tekhnologikon Efarmogon [*Applied-Technology Center*] [*Greek*] (GC)
KTE............ Koinonia ton Ethnon [*League of Nations*] (GC)
KTE............ Kozlekedestudomanyi Egyesulet [*Scientific Association of Transportation*] (HU)
KTEB.......... Kibris Turk Eczacilar Birligi [*Turkish Cypriot Pharmacists' Union*] (TU)
KTEE.......... Kendron Takhyrrythmou Ekpaidevseos Enilikon [*Accelerated Training Center for Adults*] [*Greek*] (GC)
KTEE.......... Kendron Takhyrrythmou Epangelmatikis Ekpaidevseos [*Accelerated Vocational Training Center*] [*Greek*] (GC)
KTEFA......... Koinon Tameion Eispraxeon Fortigon Avtokiniton [*Joint Freight Truck Collection Funds*] [*Greek*] (GC)
KTEK.......... Kibris Turk Elektrik Kurumu [*Turkish Cypriot Electric Power Enterprise*] (GC)
KTEK.......... Office for Container Shipments and Transportation and Forwarding Operations (RU)
KTEL.......... Koinon Tameion Eispraxeon Leoforeion [*Joint Bus Receipts Fund*] [*Greek*] (GC)
KTEMO....... Kibris Turk Elektrik Muhendisler Odasi [*Chamber of Turkish Cypriot Electrical Engineers*] (TU)
KTEP.......... Konstrukcne Technicke a Ekonomicke Pracoviste Investicni Vystavby Zeleznic [*Technical and Economic Development Center for Railroad Investment Construction*] (CZ)
KTEYL......... Koinon Tameion Eispraxeon Yperastikon Leoforeion [*Joint Urban Bus Receipts Fund*] [*Greek*] (GC)
KTF............ Kolkhoz Commodity Farm (RU)
KTF............ Koumiss Farm (RU)
KTFD.......... Kibris Turk Federe Devleti [*Turkish Cypriot Federated State*] (GC)
KTFDKM..... Kibris Turk Federe Devleti Kurucu Meclisi [*Constituent Assembly of the Turkish Cypriot Federated State*] (TU)
KTFF.......... Kibris Turk Futbol Federasyonu [*Turkish Cypriot Soccer Federation*] (GC)
KTFHB........ Kibris Turk Futbol Hakemler Birligi [*Turkish Cypriot Soccer Referees' Union*] (TU)
KTGA.......... Kenya Tea Growers Association (MAR)
KTGC.......... Kibris Turk Gazeteciler Cemiyeti [*Turkish Cypriot Journalists Association*] (GC)
KTGD.......... Kibris Turk Genclik Dernegi [*Turkish Cypriot Youth Association*] (TU)
KTGKD........ Kendrikon Tameion Georgias, Ktinotrofias, kai Dason [*Central Fund for Agriculture, Animal Raising, and Forests*] (GC)
KTH............ Krynickie Towarzystwo Hokejowe [*Krynica Hockey Society*] (POL)
KTHB.......... Kibris Turk Hakemler Birligi [*Turkish Cypriot Referees' Union*] (TU)
KTHB.......... Kibris Turk Hastabakicilar Birligi [*Turkish Cypriot Nurses' Union*] (GC)
KTHB.......... Kibris Turk Hekimler Birligi [*Turkish Cypriot Physicians' Union*] (TU)
KTHD.......... Kibris Turk Hematoloji Dernegi [*Turkish Cypriot Hematology Society*] (TU)
KTHD.......... Kibris Turk Hukukcular Dernegi [*Turkish Cypriot Jurists' Association*] (GC)
KTHHB........ Kibris Turk Hemsire ve Hastabakicilar Birligi [*Turkish Cypriot Union of Nurses and Nurses Aides*] (GC)
KTHKG........ Kibris Turk Hava Kuvvetlerini Guclendirme Vakfi [*Turkish Cypriot Air Force Strengthening Fund*] (TU)
KTHMK....... Kibris Turk Hukumeti Memurlari Kurumu [*Turkish Cypriot Government Employees' Association*] (GC)
KTHS.......... Kibris Turk Hekimler Sendikasi [*Turkish Cypriot Physicians' Union*] (TU)
KThVE......... Kratikon Theatron Voreiou Ellados [*State Theater of Northern Greece*] (GC)
KTHY.......... Kibris Turk Hava Yollari [*Turkish Cypriot Airlines*] (TU)
KTHYB........ Kibris Turk Hayvan Yetistiricileri ve Besleyicileri Birligi [*Turkish Cypriot Animal Raisers and Stock Feeders' Union*] (TU)
KTHYBB...... Kibris Turk Hayvan Yetistiricileri ve Besleyicileri Birligi [*Turkish Cypriot Animal Raisers and Stock Feeders' Union*] (GC)
KTI............. Kalinin Peat Institute (RU)
KTI............. Khartoum Technical Institute (MAR)
KTI............. Kostroma Textile Institute (RU)
KTI............. Krapinska Tekstilna Industrija [*Krapina Textile Industry*] (YU)
KTI............. Kriminaltechnisches Institut [*Criminological Institute*] (EG)
KTIBF.......... Kibris Turk Isci Birlikleri Federasyonu [*Federation of Turkish Cypriot Worker Unions*] (GC)
KTIBF.......... Kibris Turk Isciler Birlikleri Federasyonu [*Federation of Turkish Cypriot Worker Unions*] (TU)
KTIC........... Kibris Turk Islam Cemiyeti [*Turkish Cypriot Islamic Society*] (TU)
KTIC........... Kibris Turk Isverenler Cemiyeti [*Turkish Cypriot Employers' Association*] (TU)
KTICA......... Kibris Turk Ilmi Calismalar Akademisi [*Turkish Cypriot Academy of Science*] (GC)
KTID........... Kibris Turk Isverenler Dernegi [*Turkish Cypriot Employers' Association*] (TU)
kt III r.......... Lieutenant Commander [*Navy*] (BU)
kt II r........... Commander [*Navy*] (BU)
KTIKD......... Kibris Turk Islam Kultur Dernegi [*Turkish Cypriot Islamic Culture Association*] [*Turkish Cypriot*] (GC)
KTIL........... Koinon Tameion Idiotikon Leoforeion [*Joint Fund for Privately Owned Buses*] [*Greek*] (GC)
KTILP......... Kiev Technological Institute of Light Industry (RU)
KTIOS......... Kibris Turk Ilkokul Ogretmenler Sendikasi [*Turkish Cypriot Elementary School Teachers Union*] [*Later, KTOS*] (TU)
kt I r............ Captain [*Navy*] (BU)
KTiR........... Klub Techniki i Racjonalizacji [*Technology and Rationalization Club*] (POL)
KTIRP......... Kaliningrad Technical Institute of the Fish Industry and Fisheries (RU)
KTIS........... Kibris Turk Isverenler Sendikasi [*Turkish Cypriot Employers' Union*] (TU)
KTIS........... Standard Design and Technical Research Office (RU)
KTK............ Confederation of Workers of Colombia (RU)
KTK............ Confederation of Workers of Cuba (RU)
KTK............ Kauppatieteiden Kandidaatti [*Finnish*]
ktk.............. Kozos Tanacsu Kozseg [*Village Administrated by a Joint Village Council (of two or more villages)*] (HU)
KTK............ Kozponti Technologiai Konyvtar [*Central Technological Library*] (HU)
KTK............ Krakowskie Towarzystwo Kolarskie [*Krakow Cycling Society*] (POL)
KTK............ Quality Technical Control (BU)
KTK............ Tubular Ceramic Capacitor (RU)
KTKA.......... Kibris Turk Kuvvetleri Alayi [*Turkish Cypriot Forces Regiment*] (TU)
KTKB.......... Kibris Turk Kadinlar Birligi [*Turkish Cypriot Women's Association*] (TU)
KTKD.......... Kibris Turk Kizilay Dernegi [*Turkish Cypriot Red Crescent Organization*] (GC)
KTKD.......... Kibris Turk Kultur Dernegi [*Turkish Cypriot Culture Society*] (GC)
KTKK.......... Kibris Turk Kadinlar Komitesi [*Turkish Cypriot Women's Committee*] (TU)

KTKK .... Kibris Turk Kooperatifcilik Kurumu [*Turkish Cypriot Cooperatives' Association*] (GC)
KTKL .... Kozponti Technologiai Kutato Laboratorium [*Central Technological Research Laboratory of the Szekesfehervar Light Metal Works (Research on all aluminum semifinished goods)*] (HU)
KTKM .... Kibris Turk Kurucu Meclisi [*Turkish Cypriot Constituent Assembly*] (TU)
KTKMB .... Kibris Turk Kooperatif Merkez Bankasi [*Turkish Cypriot Cooperatives Central Bank*] (TU)
KTKMO .... Kibris Turk Kimye Muhendisleri Odasi [*Chamber of Turkish Cypriot Chemical Engineers*] (GC)
KTKOV .... Kommatikon Tmima Kommatikis Organosis Vaseos [*Base Party Organization Section*] (GC)
ktl .... Kai ta Loipa [*And the Rest, And So Forth*] (GC)
KTL .... Kauppatieteiden Lisensiaatti [*Finnish*]
KTLA .... Confederation of Workers of Latin America (RU)
KTLIS .... Kibris Turk Liman Iscileri Sirketi [*Turkish Cypriot Harbor Workers Corporation*] (TU)
KTM .... Code of Merchant Marine Navigation of the USSR (RU)
KTM .... Confederation of Workers of Mexico (RU)
KTM .... Kauppatieteiden Maisteri [*Finnish*]
KTM .... Kemicna Tovarna Moste [*Moste Chemical Factory*] (YU)
KTM .... Kenva Taitex Mills (MAR)
KTM .... Keretapi Tanah Melavu [*Malayan Railways*] (ML)
KTM .... Krajnja Tacka Marsrute [*Final Point of a March*] [*Army*] (YU)
KTM .... Merchant Navigation Code (BU)
KTMB .... Kibris Turk Milli Birligi Partisi [*Turkish Cypriot National Unity Party*] (GC)
KTMC .... Kibris Turk Musiki Cemiyeti [*Turkish Cypriot Music Society*] (GC)
KTMDES .... Kibris Turk Maarif Dairesi Egitimciler Sendikasi [*Turkish Cypriot Education Office Instructors' Union*] (GC)
KTMK .... Kaynak Teknigi Turk Milli Komitesi Yonetmeligi [*Turkish National Committee for Welding Techniques*] (TU)
KTMK .... Kereskedelmi Tovabbkepzo es Modszertani Kozpont [*Center of Refresher Courses and Methodology of Trade*] (HU)
KTMMOB .... Kibris Turk Muhendis ve Mimar Odalari Birligi [*Union of Turkish Cypriot Chambers of Engineers and Architects*] (TU)
KTMPB .... Kibris Turk Memurin ve Polis Birligi [*Union of Turkish Cypriot Workers and Police*] [*On British sovereign bases*] (GC)
KTMSUK .... Kibris Turk Meyva-Sebze Uretim Kooperatifi [*Turkish Cypriot Fruit and Vegetable Production Cooperative*] (GC)
ktn .... Candidate of Technical Sciences (BU)
ktn .... Candidate of Technical Sciences (RU)
Ktn .... Kaernten [*or Kaerntner*] [*German*]
KTN .... Kelantan [*Malaysian*] (ML)
KTNB .... Kibris Turk Narenciye Birligi [*Turkish Cypriot Orange Growers' Union*] (GC)
KTNUB .... Kibris Turk Narenciye Ureticiler Birligi [*Turkish Cypriot Citrus Fruit Producers' Union*] (TU)
KTO .... Coefficient of Heat Emission (RU)
KTO .... Kibris Turk Ocagi [*Turkish Cypriot Hearth*] [*Club*] (TU)
KTO .... Konto [*Account on Credit*] [*German*]
KTO .... Technical Inspection, Technical Control (RU)
KTOB .... Kibris Turk Ogretmenler Birligi [*Turkish Cypriot Teachers' Union*] (GC)
KTOEOB .... Kibris Turk Orta Egitim Ogretmenler Birligi [*Union of Turkish Cypriot Secondary Education Teachers*] (GC)
KTOEOS .... Kibris Turk Orta Egitim Ogretmenler Sendikasi [*Turkish Cypriot Secondary Education Teachers' Union*] (GC)
KTOK .... Kibris Turk Ogretmen Koleji [*Turkish Cypriot Teachers' College*] [*Kyrenia*] (TU)
KTOK .... Kibris Turk Otomobil Kurumu [*Turkish Cypriot Automobile Association*] (TU)
Kto-Nr .... Kontonummer [*Account Number*] (EG)
KTOS .... Kibris Turk Ogretmenler Sendikasi [*Turkish Cypriot Teachers' Union*] [*Formerly, KTIOS*] (TU)
KTOTSD .... Kibris Turk Oto Tamirciler ve Sanatkarlari Dernegi [*Turkish Cypriot Auto Mechanics' and Artisans' Organization*] (GC)
KTOYMO .... Kibris Turk Orman Yuksek Muhendisleri Odasi [*Turkish Cypriot Chamber of Senior Forestry Engineers*] (TU)
KTP .... Coefficient of Heat Transfer (RU)
Ktp .... Kitaplik [*Library, Book Shelves*] (TU)
KTP .... Komisija za Tehnicku Pomoc [*Technical Assistance Commission*] [*United Nations*] (YU)
KTP .... Korean Labor Party (BU)
KTP .... Korpus Techniczny Pozarnictwa [*Technical Fire Brigade*] (POL)
KTP .... Krajevno Trgovinsko Podjetje [*Local Commercial Establishment*] (YU)
KTP .... Tank Regiment Commander (RU)
KTP .... Technical Check Point [*Of tank workshops, etc.*] (BU)
KTP .... Technical Control Point (RU)
KTP .... Television Channel (RU)
KTPI .... Kaum-Tani Persatuan Indonesia [*Indonesian Farmers' Party*] [*Surinamese*] (PPW)
KTPR .... Thermal Conductivity Coefficient (RU)
KTPS .... Kibris Turk Petrolleri Sirketi [*Turkish Cypriot Petroleum Corporation*] (TU)
KTR .... Code Transmitter Relay (RU)
KTR .... Coefficient of Thermal Expansion (RU)
KTR .... Klub Techniki i Racjonalizacji [*Technology and Rationalization Club*] (POL)
K/TR .... Kuala Trengganu [*Capital of Trengganu State, Malaysia*] (ML)
ktr .... Tank Company Commander (RU)
KTRZ .... Committee for Labor and Wages (BU)
KTs .... Acid-Resistant Cement (RU)
KTS .... Commission on Labor Disputes (RU)
KTS .... Kriziacke Tazenie za Slobodu [*Crusade for Freedom*] (CZ)
KTS- .... Transportation Construction Crane (RU)
KTSA .... Commission for Technical Cooperation in Africa South of the Sahara (RU)
KTSAB .... Kibris Turk Seyahat Acentleri Birligi [*Turkish Cypriot Travel Agents' Union*] [*Turkish Cypriot*] (GC)
KTsADA .... Kiev Central Archives of Ancient Documents (RU)
KTSCD .... Kibris Turk Sosyal Calismacilar Dernegi [*Turkish Cypriot Social Workers' Organization*] (TU)
KTSD .... Kibris Turk Sanatcilar Dernegi [*Turkish Cypriot Artists' Organization*] (TU)
KTShCh .... Minesweeping Boat (RU)
KTSI .... Kibris Turk Sanayi Isletmeleri Holding Ltd. Sirketi [*Turkish Cypriot Industrial Operations Holding Corporation*] (GC)
k-tsiya .... Concentration (RU)
k-t s/ka .... Credit Account (BU)
KTsKhFD .... Cellulose, Paper, and Fodder Yeast Combine (BU)
KTsM .... Nonferrous Metals Combine (BU)
KTSO .... Kibris Turk Sanatcilar Ocagi [*Turkish Cypriot Artisans' Club*] (GC)
KTSOK .... Kibris Turk Devlet Senfoni Orkestra ve Korosu [*Turkish Cypriot State Symphony Orchestra and Chorus*] (TU)
KTsP .... Paper and Cellulose Industry (BU)
KTSPO .... Kibris Turk Sehir Plancilari Odasi [*Turkish Cypriot Chamber of City Planners*] (TU)
KTsU .... Central-Control Board [*Computers*] (RU)
KTsV .... Acid-Resistant and Waterproof Cement (RU)
ktsz .... Kisipari Termeloszovetkezet [*Artisan Cooperative*] (HU)
KTT .... Committee on Technical Terminology (of the Academy of Sciences, USSR) (RU)
KTT .... Kauppatieteiden Tohtori [*Finnish*]
KTTB .... Kibris Turk Tabibler Birligi [*Turkish Cypriot Physicians' Union*] (TU)
Kttbd .... Kattunband [*Cloth Binding*] [*German*]
KTTC .... Kenya Technical Teachers College (MAR)
KTTD .... Kibris Turk Telekomunikasyon Dairesi [*Turkish Cypriot Telecommunications Office*] (GC)
KTTD .... Kibris Turk Tuccarlar Dernegi [*Turkish Cypriot Merchants' Organization*] (TU)
KTTE .... Kibris Turk Tutun Endustrisi Limited Sirketi [*Turkish Cypriot Tobacco Industry Corporation*] (GC)
KTTI .... Kibris Turk Turizm Isletmeleri Ltd Sirketi [*Turkish Cypriot Tourism Operations Limited Liability Company*] (TU)
KTTILS .... Kibris Turk Turizm Isletmeleri Limited Sirketi [*Turkish Cypriot Tourism Operations Limited Liability Company*] (GC)
KTTK .... Kibris Turk Tarih Kurumu [*Turkish Cypriot Historical Society*] (TU)
KTTMS .... Kibris Telekomunikasyon Turk Mustahdemler Sendikasi [*Turkish Cypriot Telecommunications Employees Union*] (TU)
KTTO .... Kibris Turk Ticaret Odasi [*Turkish Cypriot Chamber of Commerce*] (TU)
KTTs .... Committee on Labor and Prices (BU)
KTTs .... Kiev Television Center (RU)
KTTTB .... Kibris Turk Turizm ve Tanitma Birligi [*Turkish Cypriot Tourism and Orientation Union*] (TU)
KTU .... Karadeniz Teknik Universitesi [*Black Sea Technical University*] (TU)
KTU .... Remote Control Key (RU)
KTU .... School of Office and Trade Apprenticeship (RU)
KTUC .... Kenya Trades Union Congress
kTV .... Continental Tropical Air (RU)
KTV .... Kunnallisten Tyontekijain ja Viranhaltijain Liitto [*Municipal Workers' Union*] [*Finnish*] (WEN)
KTVF .... Kibris Turk Voleybol Federasyonu [*Turkish Cypriot Volleyball Federation*] (TU)
KTVHB .... Kibris Turk Veteriner Hekimler Birligi [*Turkish Cypriot Veterinary Physicians' Union*] (GC)
KTVTL .... Katedra Telesne Vychovy a Telovychovneho Lekarstvi [*Chair of Physical Education and Medicine Related to Physical Education (at the Comenius University)*] (CZ)
KTVVSP .... Katedra Telesne Vychovy Vysoke Skoly Pedagogicke [*Chair of Physical Education at the College of Education*] (CZ)
KTY .... Kibris Turk Yonetimi [*Turkish Cypriot Administration*] (GC)
KTYe .... Final Thematic Unit [*Lexicography*] (RU)
KTYMC .... Kibris Turk Yapi Muteahhitleri Cemiyeti [*Turkish Cypriot Construction Contractors' Association*] (GC)
KTYOO .... Kiz Teknik Yusek Ogretmen Okulu [*Women's Advanced Technical Teachers' School*] (TU)
k tyt .... Karta Tytulowa [*Title Page*] (POL)
KTYYK .... Kibris Turk Yonetimi Yurutme Kurulu [*Turkish Cypriot Administration Executive Council*] (GC)
KTZ .... Kafue Textiles of Zambia (MAR)
KTZ .... Kaluga Turbine Plant (RU)

KTZ .... Klin Thermometer Plant (RU)
KTZ .... Krouzek Techniku-Zlepsovatelu [*Group of Technicians and Innovators*] (CZ)
KU .... Amplification Factor (RU)
KU .... Cable Section (RU)
KU .... Checking Device (RU)
KU .... Combined Attack (RU)
KU .... Commandant of a Sector (RU)
KU .... Conductometric Apparatus (RU)
KU .... Control Key (RU)
KU .... Correcting Device (RU)
KU .... Course Angle (RU)
KU .... Karlova Universita [*Charles University*] [*Prague*] (CZ)
KU .... Katastarska Uprava [*Cadastral Administration*] (YU)
KU .... Keuangan [*Finance*] (IN)
KU .... Komitet Uczelniany [*College (or University or Polytechnical School) Committee*] (POL)
KU .... Kriminalni Ustredna [*Criminal Investigation Bureau*] (CZ)
KU .... Kuasa Usaha [*Charge d'Affaires*] (IN)
Ku .... Kucuk [*Small, Little*] (TU)
Ku .... Kuyu [*Well, Pit*] (TU)
Ku .... Reduction Coefficient (RU)
KU .... Sector Commander (BU)
KU .... Stability Factor (RU)
KU .... Univerzita Komenskeho [*Comenius University*] [*Bratislava*] (CZ)
KuAI .... Kuybyshev Aviation Institute (RU)
KUAP .... Komisja Usprawnienia Administracji Publicznej [*Commission for Increasing the Efficiency of Public Administration*] (POL)
kub .... Cubic (BU)
kub .... Cubic (RU)
kub .... Kubisch [*Cubic*] [*German*]
Kub Gew ..... Kubik Gewicht [*Weight per Cubic Meters in Tons, Density*] [*German*]
kubm .... Cubic Meter (BU)
KUBP .... Combat Training Course (RU)
KUBS .... Commission for the Improvement of Students' Living Conditions (RU)
KUBU .... Commission for the Improvement of Scientists' Living Conditions (RU)
KUBUCH ..... Commission for the Improvement of Students' Living Conditions (RU)
KUC .... Kenyatta University College (MAR)
KUCP .... Kamerun United Commoners' Party (MAR)
KUD .... Komisija za Ustedu Drveta [*Commission for Wood Saving*] (YU)
kud .... Kudonta [*or Tekstiiliteollisuus*] [*Weaving, Textiles*] [*Finnish*]
KUD .... Kulturno-Umetnicko Drustvo [*Cultural and Artistic Society*] (YU)
KUF .... Kommunistisk Ungdoms Forbund [*Communist Youth League*] [*Danish*] (WEN)
KUG .... Ship Striking Force (RU)
KUH .... Kitab Undang-Undang Hukum [*Code of Laws*] (IN)
KUINS .... Committee for Registration and Study of Scientific Manpower (of the Academy of Sciences, USSR) (RU)
KUINZh .... Courses for Advanced Training of Engineers (RU)
KUJ .... Kenya Union of Journalists (MAR)
KUK .... Komitet Upowszechienia Ksiazki [*Committee on the Popularization of Books*] (POL)
KUK .... Koordinacni Ukrajinsky Komitet [*Ukrainian Coordination Committee*] (CZ)
KUK .... Krajska Ucitelska Knihovna [*Regional Teachers' Library*] (CZ)
Ku KM .... Kulkereskedelmi Miniszterium/Miniszter [*Ministry/Minister of Foreign Trade*] (HU)
KUKS .... Courses for Advanced Training of Command Personnel (RU)
KUKS .... Courses for Organizing Communist Personnel (BU)
kul .... Coulomb (RU)
KUL .... Katolicki Uniwersytet Lubelski [*Lublin Catholic University*] (POL)
Kulb .... Kulhanbey Agzi [*Coarse Speech, Vulgarity*] (TU)
kulf .... Kulfoldi [*Foreign*] (HU)
KULFORG ... Magyar Kulforgalmi Reszvenytarsasag [*Hungarian Foreign Trade Limited (Prewar)*] (HU)
Kulker Min ... Kulkereskedelmi Miniszterium/Miniszter [*Ministry/Minister of Foreign Trade*] (HU)
Kuloylag ...... Kuloy Corrective Labor Camp and Colonies (RU)
KULP .... Flight Training Course (RU)
kul't .... Cultural (RU)
kult .... Culture, Cultural (BU)
Kult .... Kultur Dairesi Genel Mudurlugu [*Cultural Office Directorate General*] [*Of Foreign Affairs Ministry*] (TU)
KULTEX ...... Kulonleges Textil- es Divatarukeszito Haziipari Szovetkezet [*Cooperative Enterprise for the Manufacture of Men's and Women's Fashion Wear*] (HU)
KULTINT ..... Kulturkapcsolatok Intezete [*Institute for Cultural Relations*] (HU)
kul'tmag ...... Store of Goods for Cultural Purposes (RU)
kul'tprop ..... Department of Culture and Propaganda (RU)
Kultprop ..... Kulturne-Propagacni Referat [*Culture and Propaganda Department (of the Communist Party of Czechoslovakia)*] (CZ)
Kultprop ..... Kulturni a Propagacni Oddeleni [*Culture and Propaganda Department (of the Communist Party of Czechoslovakia)*] (CZ)
kult-prosv ... Cultural and Educational (BU)
kul'ttorg ...... Organization for Trade in Goods for Cultural Purposes (RU)
KULTURA ... KULTURA Konyv es Hirlap Kulkereskedelmi Vallalat [*KULTURA Foreign Trade Enterprise for Books and Newspapers*] (HU)
Ku M .... Kulugyminiszterium/Miniszter [*Ministry/Minister of Foreign Affairs*] (HU)
kum .... Small Oriental Temple [*Topography*] (RU)
KUMAS .... Kutahya Manyezit Isletmeleri Anonim Sirketi [*Kutahya Magnesite Processing Corporation*] (TU)
KUML .... Kommunistisk Ungdom Marxister-Leninister [*Marxist-Leninist Communist Youth*] [*Danish*] (WEN)
KUMP .... Kray Administration of the Local Industry (RU)
kumpp .... Kumppani [*Finnish*]
KUMS .... Course for Advanced Training of Medical Personnel (RU)
KUMSAN ..... Kum Cakil Sanayii ve Ticaret AS [*Sand and Gravel Industry and Commercial Corporation*] (TU)
KUMZ .... Krasnoural'sk Copper-Smelting Plant (RU)
KUNC .... Kamerun United National Congress (MAR)
kungl .... Kunglig [*Royal*] [*Swedish*] (GPO)
KUNMV .... Communist University of National Minorities of the East (RU)
KUNMZ .... Komunisticki Univerzitet Nacionalnih Manjina Zapada [*Communist University of National Minorities of the West*] [*USSR*] (YU)
KUNS .... Courses for Advanced Training of Command Personnel (RU)
KUNZ .... Krajsky Ustav Narodniho Zdravi [*Regional Public Health Institute*] (CZ)
KUOMS .... Courses for Advanced Training of Medical Service Officers (RU)
KUOS .... Courses for Advanced Training of Officers (RU)
KUOS .... Krajske Ustredi Osvetovych Sboru [*Regional Center of Boards of Education*] (CZ)
KUP .... Khartoum University Press [*Sudanese*] (MAR)
KUPA .... Amplification Factor of Receiving Antenna (RU)
KUPON .... Communist University for Social Science Teachers (RU)
KUPROD ..... Kulturno-Prosvetno Drustvo [*Cultural and Educational Society*] (YU)
KUR .... Crimean Fortified Region (RU)
KUR .... Fortified Area Commandant (RU)
kur .... Health Resort [*Topography*] (RU)
Kur .... Kurat [*or Kurator*] [*German*]
kur .... Kurator [*School Superintendent*] [*Polish*]
Kur .... Kurmay [*Staff*] (TU)
Kur .... Kurum [*Organization, Society*] (TU)
KUR .... Relative Bearing of Radio Station (RU)
Kur Bak .... Kurmay Baskani [*Chief of Staff*] (TU)
kurg .... Hill, Tumulus [*Topography*] (RU)
Kurgansel'mash ... Kurgan Agricultural Machinery Plant (RU)
KurGPI .... Kursk State Pedagogical Institute (RU)
kur p .... Health Resort Settlement (RU)
kurs .... Kursiivi(a) [*Finnish*]
Kurupr .... Administration of Health Resorts (RU)
kur'yer .... Express [*Train*] (RU)
kurz .... Kurziv [*Italics*] (HU)
KUS .... Combined Speed Indicator (RU)
KUSCO .... Kenya United Steel Company Ltd. (MAR)
KUSES .... Kyoto University Scientific Expedition to the Sahara and the Surrounding Areas (MAR)
KuS-Fonds ... Kultur- und Sozialfonds [*Cultural and Social Fund*] (EG)
KUSH .... Kush; Journal of the Sudan Antiquities Service [*Khartum*] [*A publication*] (MAR)
KUSKS .... Courses for Advanced Training of Senior Command Personnel (RU)
kustprom .... Cottage Industry (RU)
KUSU .... Khartoum University Students' Union [*Sudanese*] (AF)
KUTESZ ...... Magyar Tudomanyos Akademia Kutatasi Eszkozoket Kivitelezo Vallalata [*Research Equipment Branch of the Hungarian Academy of Sciences*] (HU)
KUTSAN ..... Kutbi Ogullari Boya ve Vernik Sanayii AS [*Kutbi Sons Paint and Varnish Industry Corp.*] (TU)
Kutup .... Kutuphaneci [*Librarian*] (TU)
KUTV .... Communist University of Workers of the East (RU)
KUV .... Continental Air from Temperate Latitudes (RU)
KUV .... Course Wind Angle (RU)
kuv .... Kuvaannollisesti [*Figuratively*] [*Finnish*]
kuv .... Kuvittanut [*Finnish*]
KUVNAS ..... Advanced Training Courses for Higher Command Personnel (BU)
Kuvv .... Kuvvetler [*Force*] (TU)
Kuybyshevgaz ... Trust of the Kuybyshev Gas Industry (RU)
Kuybyshevgidrostroy ... Construction Administration of the Kuybyshev Hydroelectric Power Plant (RU)
Kuybyshevneft' ... Association of the Kuybyshev Petroleum Industry (RU)
Kuybyshevneftegeofizika ... Kuybyshev Administration of Geophysical Exploration (RU)
Kuybyshevugol' ... State Trust of Coal Establishments of the Kuybyshev Region (RU)
Kuzbass ...... Kuznetsk Coal Basin (RU)

Kuzbassgiproshakht ... State Institute for the Planning of Mines and Concentration Plants of the Kuznetsk Coal Basin (RU)
KUZhD .... Commission for the Improvement of Children's Living Conditions (RU)
KU ZMP....... Komitet Uczelniany Zwiazku Mlodziezy Polskiej [*College Committee of the Polish Youth Union*] (POL)
KU ZMS....... Komitet Uczelniany Zwiazku Mlodziezy Socjalistycznej [*College Committee of the Socialist Youth Union*] [*Polish*]
KUZNIUI...... Kuznetsk Scientific Research Institute of Coal (RU)
KU ZSP .... Komitet Uczelniany Zrzeszenia Studentow Polskich [*College Committee of the Polish Students' Association*] (POL)
Kuztekstil'mash ... Kuznetsk Textile Machinery Plant [*Penza oblast*] (RU)
kv .... Apartment (RU)
kv .... Billeting Detail, Quartering Party (BU)
KV .... Bottom Cup [*Ammunition*] (RU)
KV .... Breeding Ratio, Conversion Ratio [*Nuclear physics and engineering*], Reproduction Factor (RU)
KV .... Capillary Soil Moisture Capacity (RU)
kV............... Continental Air (RU)
KV .... Convalescent Party [*In a hospital*] (RU)
KV .... Cultural and Educational (RU)
kv .... District (BU)
KV .... End Switch (RU)
KV .... High-Voltage Cable (RU)
kv .... Kadervezeto [*Leader of Cadre*] (HU)
KV .... Karny Vybor [*Disciplinary Committee*] (CZ)
KV .... Kartellverband der Katholischen Oesterreichischen Studentenverbindungen [*Alliance of Austrian Catholic Student Associations*] (WEN)
K V.............. Kartografiai Kiadovallalat [*The Cartographic Institute Press*] (HU)
KV .... Kartografiai Vallalat [*Cartographic Enterprise*] (HU)
KV .... Kilovat [*Kilowatt*] (YU)
kV............... Kilovolt (EG)
kv .... Kilovolt (BU)
kv .... Kilovolt (RU)
kV............... Kilovoltti(a) [*Finnish*]
kv .... Kilowatt (BU)
kV............... Kilowolt [*Kilovolt*] [*Polish*]
KV .... Komisija za Vodoprivredu [*Commission for Water Management*] (YU)
KV .... Koncentraciona Vatra [*Concentration of Fire*] [*Military*] (YU)
KV .... Kongsberg Vaapenfabrikk [*Norwegian*]
kv .... Konyv [*Book*] (HU)
KV .... Koordinacni Vybor [*Coordinating Committee (of the Association of Czech and of Slovak Librarians)*] (CZ)
KV .... Kopnena Vojska [*Ground Forces*] (YU)
KV .... Kozponti Vezetoseg [*Central Committee*] (HU)
KV .... Kraftverkehr [*Motor Vehicle Traffic*] (EG)
KV .... Krajsky Vybor [*Regional Committee*] (CZ)
KV .... Kratka Vlna [*Shortwave*] (CZ)
kv .... Kriegsverwendungsfaehig [*Fit for Active Service*] (EG)
KV .... Platoon Commander (RU)
KV .... Potassium Tartrate (RU)
kv .... Quarter [*Of a year*] (RU)
KV .... Short Waves (BU)
KV .... Shortwave (RU)
kv .... Square (BU)
kv .... Square (RU)
KV-............. Water-Tube Boiler (RU)
kV............... Wilson Cloud Chamber (RU)
kva .... Kilovolt Ampere (BU)
kva .... Kilovolt Ampere (RU)
kVA .... Kilowoltoamper [*Kilovolt-Ampere*] [*Polish*]
KVA............. Kungliga Svenska Vetenskapsakademien [*Royal Swedish Academy of Sciences*] (WEN)
kVAr............ Kilowar [*Kilovar*] [*Polish*]
KVB............. Komintern Vegrehajto Bizottsaga [*Executive Committee of the COMINTERN*] (HU)
KVB............. Korpusna Veterinarska Bolnice [*Corps Veterinary Hospital*] (YU)
KVc .... Kilovat Cas [*Kilowatt-Hour*] (YU)
KVCh........... Cultural and Educational Section [*In a corrective labor camp*] (RU)
kvch .... Kilowatt Hour (BU)
KVCh........... Quartz-Crystal Clock (RU)
KVD............. High-Pressure Boiler (RU)
KVD............. High-Pressure Compressor (RU)
KVD............. Kurz-Vier-Dieselmotor [*Short-Stroke, Four-Cycle Diesel Engine*] (EG)
KVDP........... Catarrhal Inflammation of Upper Respiratory System (RU)
KVDR .... Koreanische Volksdemokratische Republik [*Democratic People's Republic of Korea (DPRK)*] (EG)
kve .... Kotve [*Bound*] (HU)
KVF .... Caspian Naval Flotilla (RU)
KVF .... Red Air Force (RU)
KVF .... Vacuum Canning Factory (BU)
KVG............. Kulonleges Villamos Gepgyar [*Special Electrical Machinery Factory*] (HU)
KVG............. Military Clinic (RU)
KVH............. Krajsky Vybor Hornicky [*Regional Mining Committee*] (CZ)
KVHV .... Katholiek Vlaams Hoogstudenten Verbond [*Flemish Catholic Secondary Students Union*] [*Belgian*] (WEN)
KVI .... Kazan' Veterinary Institute Imeni N. E. Bauman (RU)
KVI .... Scientific Research Institute of Dermatology and Venereal Diseases (RU)
KVK............. Internal Conversion Ratio (RU)
KvK .... Kamer van Koophandel
KVK............. Krajska Vodohospodarska Komise [*Regional Water Utilization Committee*] (CZ)
KVKSC......... Krajsky Vybor Komunisticke Strany Ceskoslovenska [*Regional Committee of the Communist Party of Czechoslovakia*] (CZ)
KVKSS......... Krajsky Vybor Komunisticke Strany Slovenska [*Regional Committee of the Communist Party of Slovakia*] (CZ)
KVL .... Corps Veterinary Hospital (RU)
KVL .... Designer's Waterline (RU)
KVM .... Driving Course (RU)
KVM .... Khmer Viet Minh [*Cambodian Viet Minh*] [*Term formerly used by Prince Sihanouk to refer to Cambodian leftists*] (CL)
kvm .... Square Meter (BU)
KVMK.......... Kronshtadt Naval Fortress (RU)
kvn .... Candidate of Military Sciences (RU)
kvn .... Candidate of Veterinary Sciences (RU)
KVNB .... Komise Vnitrni Narodni Bezpecnosti [*Internal National Security Commission*] (CZ)
KVNB .... Krajske Velitelstvi Narodni Bezpecnosti [*Regional National Security Corps Headquarters*] (CZ)
KVO............. Auxiliary Boiler Equipment (RU)
KVO............. Caucasian Military District (RU)
KVO............. Cultural and Educational Department [*In a corrective labor camp*] (RU)
KVO............. Kiev Military District (RU)
KVO............. Korpusna Vojna Oblast [*Corps Military Territory*] (YU)
k-vo............. Publishing House (BU)
KVOM.......... Krajsky Vybor Obrancu Miru [*Regional Committee of Peace Defenders*] (CZ)
KVOT .... Special Mutual Aid Fund (RU)
KVP............. Corps Military Prosecutor (RU)
KVP............. Kasernierte Volkspolizei [*Garrisoned People's Police*] (EG)
KVP............. Katholieke Volkspartij [*Catholic People's Party*] [*Dutch*] (PPE)
KVP............. Komisija za Verska Pitanja (SIV) [*Commission on the Religious Question*] (YU)
KVP............. Krajsky Vykupni Podnik [*Regional Purchasing Enterprise (for agricultural products)*] (CZ)
KVP............. Mutual Aid Fund (RU)
KVP............. Punched-Card Ejection Contact (RU)
KVPD-......... Constant-Pressure Capillary Viscometer (RU)
KVPD........... Kasernierte Volkspolizei-Dienststelle [*Garrisoned People's Police Office*] (EG)
KVPG .... Field Hospital for Dermatology and Venereal Diseases (RU)
KVPPG........ Mobile Field Hospital for Dermatology and Venereal Diseases (RU)
KVR............. Boiling-Water Reactor (RU)
KVR............. Capital Repair, Overhaul (BU)
KVRZ........... Kiev Railroad Car Repair Plant (RU)
KVS............. Auxiliary Ship Boiler (RU)
KVS............. Compressor Diving Station (RU)
KVS............. Kotarska Veterinarska Stanica [*District Veterinary Station*] (YU)
KVS............. Krajska Vodohospodarska Sluzba [*Regional Water Management Service*] (CZ)
KVS............. Krajska Vojenska Sprava [*Regional Military Directorate*] (CZ)
KVS............. Oxygen-Air Mixture (RU)
KVS............. Signal Platoon Commander (RU)
KVST........... Knihvony Vysokych Skol Technickych [*Libraries of the Institutes of Technology*] [*Prague*] (CZ)
KVST........... Kniznica Vysokej Skoly Technickej [*Library of the Institute of Technology*] [*Bratislava*] (CZ)
KVStB .... Krajske Velitelstvi Statni Bezpecnosti [*Regional State Security Headquarters*] (CZ)
KVSZMH...... Krajsky Vybor Svazu Zamestnancu Mistniho Hospodarstvi [*Regional Committee of the Union of Employees in the Local Economy*] (CZ)
KVT .... Committee for Internal Transportation (RU)
KVT .... Corps of Military Topographers (RU)
kvt .... Kilowatt (BU)
kvt .... Kilowatt (RU)
KVT .... Klub Vojskoveho Telesa [*Military Post Club*] (CZ)
kvt .... Konyvtar [*Library*] (HU)
kvtar............ Konyvtar [*Library*] (HU)
kvtch........... Kilowatt-Hour (BU)
kvt-ch.......... Kilowatt-Hour (RU)
KVTs........... Auxiliary-Shop Complex (RU)
KVTs........... Coordinating Computation Center (RU)
KVTVS .... Krajsky Vybor Telesnej Vychovy a Sportu [*Regional Committee for Physical Education and Sports*] (CZ)
KVU............. Headquarters Platoon Commander (BU)
KVU............. Headquarters Platoon Commander (RU)
KVU............. Klokneruv Vyzkumny Ustav [*Klokner Research Institute*] (CZ)
KVU............. Klub Vytvarnych Umelcu [*Creative Artists' Club*] (CZ)
KVU............. Krajsky Vyzkumny Ustav [*Regional Research Institute*] (CZ)

KVU............ Peripheral Equipment Switching Device (RU)
KVU-CO...... Krajske Vojenske Utvary, Civilni Obrany [*Regional Military Units, Civil Defense*] (CZ)
KVUZ........... Krajsky Vyzkumny Ustav Zemedelsky [*Regional Agricultural Research Institute*] (CZ)
KVV............ Koolajvezetek Vallalat [*Oil Pipeline Enterprise*] (HU)
KVV............ Krajske Vojenske Velitelstvi [*Regional Military Headquarters*] (CZ)
KVV............ Krajsky Volebni Vybor [*Regional Election Committee*] (CZ)
KVV............ Krajsky Vykorny Vybor [*Regional Executive Committee*] (CZ)
KVZ............ Committee for Military Contracts (RU)
KVZ............ Kalinin Railroad Car Plant (RU)
KVZ............ Kmetijska Vrtnarska Zadruga [*Horticultural Cooperative*] (YU)
KVZ............ Kryukovo Railroad Car Plant (RU)
KVZhD........ Chinese Eastern Railroad [*1903-1945*] (RU)
KVZP........... Antiaircraft Machine-Gun Platoon Commander (RU)
KW............. Kamera Werke, Niedersedlitz (VEB) [*Niedersedlitz Camera Works (VEB)*] (EG)
kW............. Kilowat [*Kilowatt*] [*Polish*]
kW............. Kilowatt [*Kilowatt*] (EG)
kW............. Kilowatt [*Kilowatt*] [*French*]
kW............. Kilowatti(a) [*Finnish*]
KW............. Komenda Wojewodzka [*Province Headquarters*] [*Polish*]
KW............. Komitet Warszawski [*Warsaw Committee*] [*Polish*]
KW............. Komitet Wojewodzki [*Province Committee*] [*Polish*]
KW............. Komitet Wykonawczy [*Executive Committee*] (POL)
KW............. Kreditanstalt fuer Wiederaufbau (MAR)
KW............. Kurzwelle [*Short Wave*] (EG)
KW............. Kuwait [*Two-letter standard code*] (CNC)
kw............. Kwadratowy [*Square*] (POL)
KW............. Kwanza (MAR)
kw............. Kwartal [*Three Months*] [*Polish*]
kwart.......... Kwartalnik [*or Kwartalny*] [*Quarterly*] [*Polish*]
KWE............ Knight of the White Eagle [*Polish*]
KWEBBOTU... Kweneng West Branch of the Botswana Teachers Union (MAR)
KwG............ Kesselwagen [*Tank Car*] (EG)
KWH............ Keramische Werke, Hermsdorf (VEB) [*Hermsdorf Ceramic Works (VEB)*] (EG)
kWh............ Kilowatogodzina [*Kilowatt-Hour*] [*Polish*]
kWh............ Kilowatt-Heure [*Kilowatt-Hour*] [*French*]
kWh............ Kilowattitunti [*Finnish*]
kWh............ Kilowattstunde [*Kilowatt-Hour*] (EG)
KWI............ Komorka Wykonawstwa Inwestycyjnego [*Unit for Investment Operations*] (POL)
KWK............ Kabelwerk Koepenick [*Koepenick Cable Works*] (EG)
KWK............ Kampfwagenkanone [*Tank Gun*] (EG)
KWK............ Kolonial-Wirtschaftliche Komitee (MAR)
KWK............ Kurs Wynikowy Kalkulacyjny [*Calculated Effective Rate*] [*Foreign trade*] (POL)
KWKZ.......... Komitet Wspolpracy Kulturalnej z Zagranica [*Committee on Cultural Cooperation with Foreign Countries*] (POL)
Kwl............. Kesselwagen Leitstelle [*Tank Car Operations Office*] (EG)
KWL............ Kinderbijslagwet voor Loontrekkenden [*Children's Allowance Act for Employees*] [*Dutch*] (WEN)
KW MO........ Komenda Wojewodzka Milicji Obywatelskiej [*Provincial Headquarters of the Civic Militia*] [*Polish*]
KW MZS...... Komitet Wykonawczy Miedzynarodowego Zwiazku Studentow [*Executive Committee of the International Union of Students*] (POL)
kwn............ Kwintal [*Quintal*] [*Polish*]
KWO............ Kabelwerk Oberspree (VEB) [*Oberspree Cable Works (VEB)*] (EG)
KWO............ Kenya Women's Organisation (MAR)
kWo............ Kilowatt Ora [*Kilowatt-Hour*] (HU)
KWP............ Kierownictwo Walki Podziemnej [*Command of the Underground Resistance Movement*] [*World War II*] (POL)
KWP............ Korean Workers' Party [*North Korean*] (PD)
KW PZPR.... Komitet Wojewodzki Polskiej Zjednoczonej Partii Robotniczej [*Provincial Committee of the Polish United Workers' Party*]
KWR............ Krosnienskie Warsztaty Remontowe [*Krosno Repair Shops*] (POL)
KWRN ZSP... Komitet Wykonawczy Rady Naczelnej Zrzeszenia Studentow Polskich [*Executive Committee of the Chief Council of the Polish Students' Association*] [*Polish*]
KWS............ Komisja do Walki ze Spekulacja [*Commission for the Struggle Against Speculation*] (POL)
KW SP......... Komenda Wojewodzka Sluzby Polsce [*Voivodship Headquarters of Service to Poland*] [*Semimilitary youth organization*] (POL)
Kwst............ Kilowattstunde [*Kilowatt-Hour*] [*German*]
KW-stoff...... Kohlenwasserstoff [*Hydrocarbon*] [*German*]
KWT............ Kuwait [*Three-letter standard code*] (CNC)
KW TUR...... Komitet Wykonawczy Towarzystwa Uniwersytetow Robotniczych [*Executive Committee of the Workers' Universities Society*] [*Polish*]
KWU............ Kommunales Wirtschaftsunternehmen [*Local Economic Enterprise*] (EG)
KWV............ Ko-Operative Wijnbouwers Vereniging van Zuid-Afrika (MAR)
KWV............ Kommunale Wohnungsverwaltung [*Municipal Housing Administration*] (EG)
KWW........... Kolo Wiedzy Wojskowej [*Military Science Circle*] (POL)
KWWL......... Kurs Wstepnych Wiadomosci Lotniczych [*Preliminary Aviation Course*] (POL)
KW ZMS...... Komitet Wojewodzki Zwiazku Mlodziezy Socjalistycznej [*Provincial Committee of the Socialist Youth Union*] [*Polish*]
KW ZSL....... Komitet Wykonawczy Zjednoczonego Stronnictwa Ludowego [*Executive Committee of the United Peasants' Party*] [*Polish*]
KY.............. Cayman Islands [*Two-letter standard code*] (CNC)
KY.............. Kabaka Yekka Party [*Ugandan*] (AF)
KY.............. Koy Yollari [*Village Roads*] (TU)
KY.............. Kratiki Ypiresia [*Government (Vehicle), For Government (Official) Use*] (GC)
KYa............ Aiming Box (RU)
KYCCA....... Kenya Youth Christian Choirs Association (MAR)
KYDEP........ Kendriki Ypiresia Diakhoriseos Enkhorion Proiondon [*Central Service for the Separation of Domestic Products*] [*Greek*] (GC)
KYDF.......... Istanbul Orta Ogretim Ogrencileri Koruma ve Yardim Dernekleri Federasyonu [*Federation of Organizations for the Protection and Aid to Secondary Students*] (TU)
KYeD.......... Cat Unit (RU)
k yed.......... Feed Unit (RU)
KYeD.......... Rat Unit (RU)
KYEP.......... Kendriki Ypiresia Erevnis Paraponon [*Central Service for the Investigation of Complaints*] [*In the Office of the Minister to the Premier*] [*Greek*] (GC)
KYEP.......... Koinoniki Ypiresia Ektakton Peristaseon [*Social Service for Special Cases*] [*Greek*] (GC)
KYePS........ Permanent Commission for the Study of Natural Productive Forces of the USSR (at the Academy of Sciences, USSR) (RU)
KYET.......... Kendron Ypodokhis Ekpaidevseos Tekhniton [*Technicians Training Reception Center*] [*Greek*] (GC)
Kyl............. Kymen Laani [*Finnish*]
KYP............ Kendriki Ypiresia Pliroforion [*Central Intelligence Service*] [*Greek*] (GC)
KYP............ Kypriaki Ypiresia Pliroforion [*Cyprus Information Service*] (GC)
KYPA.......... Kendriki Ypiresia Politikis Aeroporias [*State Civil Aviation Administration*] [*Greek*] (GC)
KYPE.......... Kendriki Ypiresia Paralavis Ekpombon [*Central Radio Monitoring Service*] [*Greek*] (GC)
KYPE.......... Kendriki Ypiresia Pliroforion kai Erevnon [*Central Service of Intelligence and Investigation*] (GC)
KYS............ Koinotikos Ygeionomikos Stathmos [*Community Medical Station*] (GC)
KYSE.......... Koy Yollar, Sular, ve Elektrik Isciler Sendikasi [*Village Roads, Water, and Electrification Workers Union*] (TU)
KYSEA........ Kyvernitikon Symvoulion Ethnikis Amynis [*Government Council for National Defense*] (GC1)
KYSME........ Kendrikon Ypiresiakon Symvoulion Mesis Ekpaidevseos [*Central Service Council for Secondary Education*] [*Greek*] (GC)
KYSOP........ Kyvernitiko Symvoulio Oikonomikis Politikis [*Government Council of Economic Policy*] (GC1)
KYSSE........ Kendrikon Ypiresiakon Symvoulion Stoikheiodous Ekpaidevseos [*Central Service Council for Elementary Education*] [*Greek*] (GC)
KYT............ Kendriki Ypiresia Takhydromeion [*Central Postal Service*] [*Greek*] (GC)
KYT............ Kendron Ypodokhis Tekhniton [*Technicians' Reception Center*] [*Greek*] (GC)
KYuA.......... Club of Young Automobilists (RU)
KYuBZ........ Group of Young Zoo Biologists (RU)
KYuGE........ Complex Southern Geological Expedition (RU)
KYuLF........ Club of Young Physics Amateurs (RU)
kyun........... Candidate of Laws (RU)
KYuTO........ South Pacific Commission [*SPC*] (RU)
KZ.............. Flight Commander (RU)
KZ.............. Kerosene Fueler, Kerosene Vehicle (BU)
KZ.............. Kerosene Refueling Truck (RU)
KZ.............. Kmetijska Zadruga [*Agricultural Cooperative*] (YU)
KZ.............. Kodeks Zobowiazan [*Law on Contracts*] (POL)
k-z............. Kolkhoz (RU)
KZ.............. Kolomna Locomotive Plant Imeni Kuybyshev (RU)
KZ.............. Komitet Zakladowy [*Plant Committee*] (POL)
KZ.............. konzentrationslager [*German*]
KZ.............. Konzervatorski Zavod [*Conservation Institute*] (YU)
KZ.............. Krajsky Zavod [*Regional Plant*] (CZ)
KZ.............. Krivicni Zakonik [*Criminal Code*] (YU)
KZ.............. Krojacka Zadruga [*Tailoring Cooperative*] (YU)
KZ.............. Kulturny Zivot [*Cultural Life*] [*A periodical*] (CZ)
kZ.............. Kurze Sicht [*Short Sight*] [*German*] [*Business and trade*]
KZ.............. Shipyard (BU)
KZ.............. Short Circuit, Short Circuited (RU)
KZ.............. Starch Grain (RU)
KZA............ Heavy Caliber Antiaircraft Artillery (BU)
KZA............ Knihovna Zemedelske Akademie [*Library of the Academy of Agriculture*] (CZ)

KZA............ Krajske Zdruzenie Advokatov [*Regional Association of Lawyers*] (CZ)
KZA............ Large-Caliber Antiaircraft Artillery (RU)
KZA............ Sound Control Unit (RU)
KZAG.......... Corps Antiaircraft Artillery Group (RU)
KZB............ Concert and Entertainment Office (RU)
KZBP.......... Krakowskie Zjednoczenie Budownictwa Przemyslowego [*Krakow Industrial Construction Association*] (POL)
KZD............ Kurz-Zwei-Dieselmotor [*Short-Stroke, Two-Cycle Diesel Engine*] (EG)
kz dr........... Bicycle Battalion (BU)
KZEMB........ Kibris Zahire Encumeni Mustahdemleri Birligi [*Union of Cypriot Cereals Committee Employees*] [*Turkish Cypriot*] (GC)
KZG............ Katowickie Zaklady Gastronomiczne [*Katowice Catering (or Restaurant) Establishments*] [*Polish*]
KZG............ Kieleckie Zaklady Gastronomiczne [*Kielce Catering (or Restaurant) Establishments*] [*Polish*]
KZG............ Kolejowe Zaklady Gastronomiczne [*Railroad Catering (or Restaurant) Establishments*] (POL)
KZG............ Krakowskie Zaklady Gastronomiczne [*Krakow Catering (or Restaurant) Establishments*] (POL)
kzh............. Treasurer, Cashier (BU)
KZhB........... Kustanay Iron Ore Basin (RU)
KZIP............ Katowickie Zjednoczenie Instalacji Przemyslowych [*Katowice Industrial Installation Association*] (POL)
KZIP............ Krakowskie Zjednoczenie Instalacji Przemyslowych [*Krakow Industrial Installation Association*] (POL)
KZK............ Kvalifikacni Zdokonalovaci Kurzy [*Specialty Improvement Courses*] (CZ)
KZKh........... Kazakh Railroad (RU)
Kzl.............. Kanzlei [*German*]
Kzlr............. Kanzler [*German*]
KZM............ Concentrate of Green-Oil Emulsion (RU)
KZM............ Komunistyczny Zwiazek Mlodziezy [*Communist Union of Youth*] (POL)
KZMA.......... Kiev Medical Equipment Plant (RU)
KZMH.......... Krajske Zakladny Mistniho Hospodarstvi [*Regional Centers of the Local Economy*] (CZ)
KZMP.......... Komunistyczny Zwiazek Mlodziezy Polskiej [*Communist Union of Polish Youth*] (POL)
KZMR.......... Komunistyczny Zwiazek Mlodziezy Robotniczej [*Communist Union of Working Youth*] (POL)
KZN............ Kabinet Zdenka Nejedleho [*Zdenek Nejedly Department (of the Czechoslovak Academy of Sciences)*] (CZ)
KZNS.......... Kujawskie Zaklady Naprawy Samochodow [*Kujawy Auto Repair Shop*] (POL)
KZO............ Foreign Organization Committee of the RSDRP [*1911-1917*] (RU)
KZO............ Komise pro Zahranicni Obchod [*Foreign Trade Commission*] (CZ)
KZoBSiO..... Marriage, Family, and Guardianship Code (RU)
KZoBSO...... Marriage, Family, and Guardianship Code (RU)
KZOMS....... Kursk Zonal Experimental Reclamation Station (RU)
KZOT.......... Labor Code (RU)
KZP............ Katowickie Zaklady Piekarnicze [*Katowice Bakeries*] (POL)
KZPG.......... Krakowskie Zaklady Przemyslu Gumowego [*Krakow Rubber Works*] (POL)
KZPS.......... Kotarski Zadruzni Poslovni Savez [*District Agricultural Cooperative Business Union*] (YU)
KZ PZPR..... Komitet Zakladowy Polskiej Zjednoczonej Partii Robotniczej [*Plant Committee of the Polish United Workers' Party*] (POL)
kz r............. Bicycle Company (BU)
KZS............ Antiaircraft Gunnery Courses (RU)
KZS............ Keramicke a Sklarske Zavody na Slovensku, Narodny Podnik [*Ceramics and Glass Factories in Slovakia, National Enterprise*] (CZ)
KZS............ Kontrolno Zastitna Sluzba [*Control Defense Service*] [*Army*] (YU)
KZS............ Krajowe Zawody Samolotowe [*Country-Wide Airplane Contests*] (POL)
KZSB.......... Krakowski Zwiazek Spoldzielni Branzowych [*Krakow Union of Business Cooperatives*] (POL)
KZSO.......... Kirov Sports Equipment Plant (RU)
KZSSLP...... Kmetijski Zemljiski Sklad Splosnega Ljudskega Premozenja [*Agricultural Land Fund of the National Property*] (YU)
KZST.......... Krajowy Zwiazek Spoldzielni Transportu [*National Union of Transport Cooperatives*] (POL)
KZTM.......... Kiev Commercial Machinery Plant (RU)
KZTS.......... Kiev Turning Lathe Plant (RU)
KZTS.......... Kolomna Heavy Machine Tool Plant (RU)
KZWI.......... Katowickie Zjednoczenie Wodno-Inzynierskie [*Katowice Hydraulic Engineering Association*] (POL)
KZWME....... Krakowskie Zaklady Wytworcze Materialow Elektrotechnicznych [*Krakow Electric Engineering Materials Plant*] (POL)
KZWME....... Krakowskie Zaklady Wytworcze Materialow Elektrycznych [*Krakow Electric Materials Plant*] (POL)
KZZhBK...... Kurakhovka Reinforced Concrete Structural Parts Plant (RU)
KZZM.......... Klasowy Zwiazek Zawodowy Metalowcow [*Class Trade Union of Metal Workers*] (POL)
KZ ZMS....... Komitet Zakladowy Zwiazku Mlodziezy Socjalistycznej [*Works Committee of the Socialist Youth Union*] [*Polish*]

L

l .... Eli [*Or*] [*Finnish*] (GPO)
L .... Free Fit, Easy-Running Fit (RU)
l .... Laan [*Lane*] [*Dutch*] (CED)
l .... Laani [*Finnish*]
L .... Lac [*or Lacul or Lacu*] [*Lake*] [*Romanian*] (NAU)
L .... Lac [*Lake*] [*French*] (NAU)
L .... Lago [*Lake*] [*Italian*] (NAU)
L .... Lago [*Lake*] [*Portuguese*] (NAU)
L .... Lago [*Lake*] [*Spanish*] (NAU)
L .... Lagoa [*Small Lake, Marsh*] [*Portuguese*] (NAU)
l .... Lakos [*Inhabitant*] (HU)
L .... Lamp, Tube (RU)
L .... Land [*German*]
l .... Lap [*Page*] (HU)
l .... Lasd! [*See*] [*Hungarian*] (GPO)
l .... Laudatur [*Latin*]
L .... Laurea [*Academic degree*] [*Italian*]
L .... Left, Left-Hand (RU)
L .... Lehrer [*German*]
L .... Leicanc [*License*] [*Afghan*]
L .... Lekarz [*Academic qualification*] [*Polish*]
L .... Leningrad (BU)
L .... Leningrad (RU)
l/ .... Leur [*Their, Your*] [*Business and trade*] [*French*]
l .... Lev, Leva (BU)
l .... Lever (BU)
l .... Lewy [*Left*] [*Polish*]
l .... Ley [*Law*] [*Spanish*]
L .... Liber [*Book*] [*Latin*] (GPO)
L$ .... Liberian Dollar (MAR)
l .... Libro [*Book*] [*Spanish*]
L .... Licence [*License*] [*French*]
L .... Licenciado [*One Who Is Licensed in a Profession*] [*Spanish*]
L .... Licenciado [*Licentiate*] [*Portuguese*]
L .... Licenciatura [*Master's degree*] [*Spanish*]
L .... Licenciatura [*Academic qualification*] [*Portuguese*]
L .... Licenciatus [*Academic degree*] [*Latin*]
L .... Licenta [*Academic qualification*] [*Romanian*]
L .... Licentiat [*Danish*]
l .... Liczba [*Number*] (POL)
l .... Lies [*Read*] [*German*]
L .... Light [*Class of river ship*] (RU)
l .... Line (RU)
L .... Line Contactor (RU)
l .... Links [*Left*] [*German*]
l .... Linksdrehend [*Counterclockwise*] [*German*]
L .... Lire [*Lira*] [*Italian*] (GPO)
L .... Lisans [*Turkish*]
L .... Lisensiaatti [*Finnish*]
l .... List [*Sheet*] (CZ)
l .... Liter (BU)
l .... Liter [*Liter*] (EG)
l .... Liter (RU)
l .... Litr [*Liter*] (POL)
l .... Litra(a) [*Finnish*]
l .... Litre [*Liter*] [*French*]
l .... Litro [*Liter*] [*Portuguese*] (GPO)
l .... Litro [*Liter*] [*Spanish*]
L .... Locus [*Place*] [*Latin*] (GPO)
l .... Loeslich [*Soluble*] [*German*]
l .... Loesung [*Solution*] [*German*]
L .... Long [*Of guns*] [*French*] (MTD)
L .... Luka [*Harbor, Port*] [*Yugoslav*] (NAU)
L .... Luksemburg [*Luxembourg*] [*Polish*]
l .... Person (BU)
l .... Person [*Grammar*] (RU)
l .... Physician (BU)
L .... Quinquaginta [*Fifty*] [*Latin*]
l .... Readily (Soluble) (RU)
L .... Rook, Castle [*Chess*] (RU)
L .... Selbstinduktionskoeffizient [*Inductivity*] [*German*]

l .... Sheet (BU)
l .... Sheet, Leaf (RU)
L .... Summer [*Automobile and tractor diesel fuel designation*] (RU)
L- .... Winch (RU)
LA .... Aircraft Designed by S. A. Lavochkin (RU)
La .... Laguna [*Lagoon*] [*Italian*] (NAU)
La .... Laguna [*Lagoon*] [*Norwegian*] (NAU)
La .... Laguna [*Lagoon*] [*Portuguese*] (NAU)
La .... Laguna [*Lagoon*] [*Spanish*] (NAU)
La .... Langsamfahrstellen [*Reduced Speed Track Sections*] (EG)
LA .... Lanska Akce [*"Lany Action" (Manpower recruitment drive)*] (CZ)
LA .... L'Anthropologie (MAR)
LA .... Laos [*Two-letter standard code*] (CNC)
la .... Lasd Alabb [*See Below*] (HU)
la .... Lauantai(na) [*Finnish*]
la .... Lege Artis [*According to the Rules of the Craft*] [*Latin*]
LA .... Lekka Atletyka [*Athletics, Track and Field Events*] [*Polish*]
LA .... Letecka Armada [*Air Army*] (CZ)
l/a .... Lettre d'Avis [*Letter of Advice*] [*French*]
LA .... Library Association [*British*]
La .... Licenza Accademia di Belli Arti [*Italian*]
LA .... Liga Africana (MAR)
LA .... Light Artillery (RU)
LA .... Lovacka Avijacija [*Fighter Aviation*] (YU)
LA .... Motorized Laboratory (RU)
LA .... Vehicle, Aircraft (RU)
LAA .... Libyan Arab Airlines (MAR)
laak .... Laaketiede [*Surgery*] [*Finnish*]
laaket .... Laaketiede [*Surgery*] [*Finnish*]
laaket(jakir)tri ... Laaketieteen (Ja Kirurgian) Tohtori [*Finnish*]
laaketkand ... Laaketieteen Kandidaatti [*Finnish*]
laaketlis ...... Laaketieteen Lisensiaatti [*Finnish*]
LAAS .... Laboratoire d'Automatique et d'Analyse des Systemes
LAAS .... Laboratoire d'Automatique et de ses Applications Spatiales
lab .... Labil [*Labile*] [*German*]
lab .... Laborant [*Laboratory Assistant*] [*Polish*]
lab .... Laboratorium [*Laboratory*] [*Polish*]
lab .... Laboratory (RU)
lab .... Laboratory Assistant (RU)
Lab .... Labuan [*or Labuhan*] [*Anchorage or Harbor*] [*Indonesian*] (NAU)
Lab .... Labuan [*or Labuhan*] [*Anchorage or Harbor*] [*Malaysian*] (NAU)
LAB .... Lloyd Aereo Boliviano [*Lloyd Bolivian Air Line*] (LA)
LABAN .... Lakas ng Bayan [*Peoples' Power Movement - Fight*] [*Philippine*] (PPW)
LABFROSST ... Laboratorio Frost de Colombia Ltda. [*Bogota*] (COL)
LAbg .... Landtagsabgeordneter [*German*]
LABIB .... Laboratory for the Study of Protein (of the Academy of Sciences, USSR) (RU)
LABIFR .... Laboratory of Biochemistry and Physiology of Plants (of the Academy of Sciences, USSR) (RU)
LABIOF .... Laboratory of Biophysics (of the Academy of Sciences, USSR) (RU)
LABIZh .... Laboratory of Biochemistry and Physiology of Animals (of the Academy of Sciences, USSR) (RU)
labj .... Labjegyzet [*Footnote*] (HU)
LABM .... Laboratoires d'Analyses Biologiques Medicales (MAR)
LABMEOZ ... Laboratorio Meoz Ltda. [*Bogota*] (COL)
Labn .... Labuan [*or Labuhan*] [*Anchorage or Harbor*] [*Indonesian*] (NAU)
Labn .... Labuan [*or Labuhan*] [*Anchorage or Harbor*] [*Malaysian*] (NAU)
labor .... Laboratory (RU)
labor .... Laboratory Assistant (RU)
LABr .... Light Artillery Brigade (RU)
lac .... Lacina [*or Lacinski*] [*Polish*]
LAC .... Liga Antituberculosa Colombiana [*Bogota*] (COL)
LACADEL ... La Casa de Electricidad Ltda. [*Medellin*] (COL)
LAChKh ...... Logarithmic Frequency Response Characteristic (RU)
LACOFA ...... La Cooperation Franco-Africaine (MAR)

LACOFACI ... Lacofa Cote-d'Ivoire (MAR)
LACSA .... Lineas Aereas Costarricenses, Sociedad Anonima [*Costa Rican airline*]
LACVW .... Landelijk Algemeen Christelik Verbond van Werkgevers [*Flemish General Association of Christian Rural Employers*] [*Belgian*] (WEN)
LADE .... Lineas Aereas del Estado [*State Airlines*] [*Argentine*] (LA)
LADH .... Liga Argentina por los Derechos del Hombre [*Argentine League for Human Rights*] (LA)
LADI .... Leningrad Highway Institute Imeni V. V. Kuybyshev (RU)
LADT .... Leningrad Highway Technicum (RU)
LAEEC .... Groupe International Laicat et Communaute Chretienne [*International Laity and Christian Community Group - ILCCG*] (EA)
LAER .... Laboratory of Aerial Methods (RU)
LAF .... Lebanese Armed Forces
LAFA .... Lao-Australian Friendship Association [*Use AALA*] (CL)
LAFB .... Libyan Arab Foreign Bank (MAR)
LAFE .... Laboratorio de Fisica Espacial [*Brazilian*]
LAFKhI .... Laboratory of Physiological Chemistry (RU)
LAFOKI .... Laboratory of Scientific Applied Photography and Cinematography (of the Academy of Sciences, USSR) (RU)
LAFR .... Laboratory for Plant Anatomy and Physiology (of the Academy of Sciences, USSR) (RU)
LAFRANCOL ... Laboratorio Franco Colombiano [*Cali*] (COL)
LAFTA .... Latin American Free Trade Association (LA)
LAG .... Arab League (RU)
lag .... Camp (RU)
LAG .... Laboratory of Genetics (of the Academy of Sciences, USSR) (RU)
lag .... Lagoon [*Topography*] (RU)
Lag .... Lagune [*Lagoon*] [*Military map abbreviation*] [*World War I*] [*French*] (MTD)
LAG .... Liga Arabskikh Gosudarstv (MAR)
LAG .... Liga Armada Gallega [*Armed Galician League*] [*Spanish*] (PD)
LAGE .... Lineas Aereas de Guinea Ecuatorial [*Airlines of Equatorial Guinea*] (AF)
LAGED .... Laboratory of Precambrian Geology (of the Academy of Sciences, USSR) (RU)
LAGG .... Aircraft Designed by S. A. Lavochkin, V. P. Gorbunov, and M. I. Gudkov (RU)
LAGO .... Laboratorio Argo [*Bucaramanga*] (COL)
LAGOVEN ... [*A*] Subsidiary of PETROVEN [*Venezuelan*] (LA)
LAGU .... Laboratory of Coal Geology (of the Academy of Sciences, USSR) (RU)
lah .... Lahemmin [*Finnish*]
lah .... Lahettaja [*Finnish*]
lah V .... Lahin Vastine [*Approximately*] [*Finnish*]
LAIC .... Les Argiles Industrielles du Cameroun (MAR)
LAICO .... Latinoamerican Investment Consultants [*Cali*] (COL)
LAICO .... Lineas Aereas Internacionales y Colombianas (COL)
LAJS .... Libyan American Joint Service for Agriculture and Natural Resources (MAR)
LAK .... Laboratory of Architectural Ceramics (RU)
lak .... Lakitermi [*Law, Juridical Term*] [*Finnish*]
lak .... Lakitiede [*Finnish*]
LAKh .... Logarithmic Frequency Response Characteristic (RU)
LAKhU .... Leningrad Administrative Office (of Institutions of the Academy of Sciences, USSR) (RU)
LAKI .... Lakkipari Kutato Intezet [*Research Institute for the Lacquer Industry*] (HU)
lakokr .... Varnish and Paint Plant [*Topography*] (RU)
LAKORED ... Laboratory for Document Preservation and Restoration (of the Academy of Sciences, USSR) (RU)
LAKOTERV ... Lako- es Kommunalis Epuleteket Tervezo Vallalat [*Planning Enterprise for Residential and Communal Buildings*] (HU)
LAKRIST ..... Laboratory of Crystallography (of the Academy of Sciences, USSR) (RU)
LAKSDA ...... Laksamana Muda [*Rear Admiral*] (IN)
LAKSDYA ... Laksmana Madya [*Vice Admiral*] (IN)
LAKSUS ...... Pelaksana Chusus [*Special Executive Officer*] (IN)
LAKSZER .... Lakatos es Szerszamkeszito Kisipari Termeloszovetkezet [*Small Industrial Producers' Cooperative of Locksmiths and Toolmakers*] (HU)
lakt .... Laktanya [*Barracks*] (HU)
LAKTERV .... Lakoepulettervezo Vallalat [*Designing Enterprise for Residential Dwellings*] (HU)
LAL .... Laboratoire de l'Accelerateur Lineaire [*French*]
LALP .... Leningrad Academy of Light Industry Imeni S. M. Kirov (RU)
LAM .... Laboratory of Aerial Methods (RU)
LAM .... Laboratory of Aviation Medicine (RU)
LAM .... Liberalium Artium Magister [*Master of the Liberal Arts*] [*French*] (GPO)
LAM .... Linhas Aereas de Mocambique (MAR)
LAM .... Litografia de Arte Moderno [*Cali*] (COL)
LAMCo .... Liberian-American-Swedish Minerals Company [*Liberian*] (AF)
LAMINACO ... Laminacion de Colombia Ltda. [*Medellin*] (COL)
LAN .... Chronicles of the Bulgarian Academy of Sciences (BU)
LAN .... Lembaga Administrasi Negara [*State Administration Institute*] (IN)
LAN .... Linea Aerea Nacional [*National Airline*] [*Chilean*] (LA)
LAN .... Pengadilan [*Court of Law*] (IN)
LANA .... Lignes Aeriennes Nord-Africaines (MAR)
LANAPHARM ... Laboratoire National Pharmaceutique (MAR)
LANC .... Liga Apararii Nationale Crestine [*League of National Christian Defense*] [*Romanian*] (PPE)
landw .... Landwirtschaftlich [*Agricultural*] (EG)
landwS .... Landwirtschaftliche Schule [*German*]
LANEFICO ... Lanera del Pacifico Ltda. [*Mengua-Cali*] (COL)
langj .... Langjaehrig [*For Many Years*] [*German*]
Langlei .... Langleitung [*Long Line (Telephones)*] (EG)
LANICA .... Linea Aerea de Nicaragua [*Nicaraguan Airline*] (LA)
LANMORA ... Landers Mora y Compania Ltda. [*Medellin*] (COL)
LANS .... Land Navigation System (MAR)
LANS .... Legion Argentina Nacional Sindicalista [*Argentine National Labor Union Legion*] (LA)
LANSA .... Lineas Aereas Nacionales Consolidadas, Sociedad Anonima
LANTAS ...... Lalu Lintas [*Traffic*] (IN)
LANTER ...... Laboratorios y Agencias Internacionales [*Cali*] (COL)
lantp .... Lantista Pituutta [*Finnish*]
LANU .... Pangkalan Udara [*Air Base*] (IN)
LANZACOL ... Lanzaceras Colombianas SA [*Medellin*] (COL)
LAO .... Laos [*Three-letter standard code*] (CNC)
LAO .... Ligue pour l'Avenir et l'Ordre [*Somali*] (MAR)
LAO .... L'vov Astronomical Observatory (RU)
LAOKh .... Laboratory of General Chemistry (of the Academy of Sciences, USSR) (RU)
LAOS .... Laikai Antistasiakai Omades Sambotaz [*Popular Resistance Sabotage Groups*] [*Greek*] (GC)
Lao-Viet ...... Pathet Lao-Viet Cong (CL)
LAP .... Liberation Action Party [*Trinidadian and Tobagan*] (PPW)
LAPAN .... Lembaga Penerbangan dan Antariksa Nasional [*National Aviation and Space Agency*] (IN)
LAPCO .... Laboratoires Pharmaceutiques du Congo (MAR)
LAPCO .... Lavan Petroleum Company [*Iranian*] (ME)
LAPI .... Leningrad Agricultural Pedagogical Institute (RU)
LAPIP .... Lembaga Persiapan Industri Penerbangan [*Aviation Industry Development Foundation*] (IN)
lapk .... Lapkiado [*Newspaper Publisher*] (HU)
lapp .... Lappalainen [*Finnish*]
LAPP .... Latvian Association of Proletarian Writers (RU)
LAPP .... Leningrad Association of Proletarian Writers (RU)
LAPRIZ .... Laboratory of Applied Zoology (of the Academy of Sciences, USSR) (RU)
LAR .... Libya Arap Cumhuriyeti [*Libyan Arab Republic*] (TU)
LAR .... Liniile Aeriene Romane [*Romanian Airlines*] (RO)
LAR .... Loita Armada Revolucionaria [*Armed Revolutionary Struggle*] [*Spanish*] (PD)
LARC .... Libyan-American Reconstruction Commission (MAR)
LARCO .... Laminados Metalicos y Aires Acondicionados [*Medellin*] (COL)
LARES .... Liniile Aeriene Romane Exploatate de Stat [*Bucharest*]
laring .... Laryngology, Laryngologist (BU)
LARMS .... Glacier Automatic Radiometeorological Station (RU)
LARZ .... Leningrad Automobile Repair Plant (RU)
LAS .... Air Rescue Dinghy (RU)
LAS .... Arab League (RU)
LAS .... Laboratory of Anisotropic Structures (of the Academy of Sciences, USSR) (RU)
LAS .... League of Arab States (MAR)
LASECNA ... L'Agence pour la Securite de la Navigation Aerienne en Afrique et Madagascar (MAR)
LASH .... Lighter Aboard Ship (MAR)
LASHIP .... Lighter Aboard Ship (MAR)
LASIN .... Laboratory for the Study and Synthesis of Vegetable and Animal Products (of the Academy of Sciences, USSR) (RU)
LASSA .... Lastik Sanayi ve Ticaret Anonim Sirketi [*Rubber Industry and Trade Corporation*] [*Istanbul*] (TU)
last .... Lastenkielta [*Baby Talk*] [*Finnish*]
LASZ .... Legfobb Allami Szamvevoszek [*Supreme State Auditing Office*] (HU)
lat .... Lateinisch [*German*]
lat .... Latin (BU)
lat .... Latin [*Latin*] (HU)
lat .... Latin (RU)
LAT .... Latin Alphabet (BU)
lat .... Latinaa [*or Latinaksi*] [*Latin*] [*Finnish*]
Lat .... Latince [*Latin*] (TU)
lat .... Latvian (RU)
LAT .... Latvian Railroad (RU)
LAT .... Lebanese Air Transport (Charter) Company SAL (ME)
l at .... Liczba Atomowa [*Atomic Number*] [*Polish*]
LATA .... Laboratoire Africain de Therapeutique Appliquee (MAR)
lat-amer ...... Latin American (RU)
Latgiprogorstroy ... Latvian State Institute for the Planning of Urban Construction (RU)
Latgiproprom ... Latvian State Institute for the Planning of Industrial Establishments (RU)
Latgiprosel'stroy ... Latvian State Institute for the Planning of Rural Construction (RU)
Latgiprovodkhoz ... Latvian State Institute for the Planning of Reclamation (RU)
Latgiz .... Latvian State Publishing House (RU)

Latgosizdat ... State Publishing House of the Latvian SSR (RU)
Latgosrybvod ... Latvian State Inspection for Fish Conservation and Reproduction and the Regulation of Fish Breeding (RU)
LatINTI .... Latvian Republic Institute of Scientific and Technical Information and Propaganda (RU)
l-atm .... Liter-Atmosphere (RU)
LatNIIGiM.... Latvian Scientific Research Institute of Hydraulic Engineering and Reclamation (RU)
LA TOGOLAISE ... Union pour le Commerce et l'Industrie au Togo (MAR)
Latpotrebsoyuz ... Latvian Republic Union of Consumers' Societies (RU)
Latpromsovet ... Council of Producers' Cooperatives of the Latvian SSR (RU)
LATR .... Laboratory Autotransformer (RU)
LATRAF ...... Laminoir Trefilerie d'Afrique (MAR)
LATU .... Laboratorio Tecnologico del Uruguay [*Technological Laboratory of Uruguay*] (LA)
latv .... Latvian (RU)
Latvenergo ... Administration of Power System Management of the Sovnarkhoz of the Latvian SSR (RU)
LatvSSR...... Latvian Soviet Socialist Republic (RU)
latysh .... Latvian (RU)
laus .... Lauseessa [*In a Sentence*] [*Finnish*]
lav .... Lava [*Field*] [*Topography*] (RU)
LAV .... Linea Aeropostal Venezolana
LAVD........... Laboratory of High Pressures and Temperatures (of the Academy of Sciences, USSR) (RU)
LA VOLTAIQUE ... Union pour le Commerce et l'Industrie en Haute-Volta (MAR)
LAW .... Leipziger Arzneimittelwerk (VEB) [*Leipzig Pharmaceutical Works (VEB)*] (EG)
LAWAN .... Labour Writers Association of Nigeria (MAR)
LAWASIA.... Law Association for Asia and the Western Pacific (EA)
LAY .... Leningrad Arctic School (RU)
LAYDER ...... Laminacion y Derivados Ltda. [*Medellin*] (COL)
LAZ .... Line Equipment Room (RU)
LAZ .... L'vov Bus Plant (RU)
LB................ Baccalaureus Literarum [*Bachelor of Letters*] [*Latin*] (GPO)
lb .... Lambert (RU)
LB................ Lebanon [*Two-letter standard code*] (CNC)
LB................ Lenin Library [*State Library of the USSR Imeni V. I. Lenin*] (RU)
lb .... Libra [*Pound*] [*Latin*] (GPO)
LB................ Line Battery (RU)
LB................ Lovci-Bombarderi [*Fighter Bombers*] (YU)
lb .... Port, Larboard (RU)
LB................ Ski Battalion (RU)
LBA .... Legiao Brasileira de Assistencia [*Brazilian Welfare Legion*] (LA)
LBA .... Lehrerbildungsanstalt [*German*]
LBA .... Licensed Buying Agent (MAR)
LBA .... Light Bombardment Aviation (RU)
LBA .... Lovacko-Bombarderska Avijacija [*Fighter-Bomber Aviation*] (YU)
lbak .... Light Bombardment Aviation Wing (BU)
LBAN........... L'vov Library of the Academy of Sciences, UkrSSR (RU)
LBAP............ Light Bomber Regiment (RU)
LBat............. Dummy Battery (RU)
LBB .... Light Bomber Brigade (RU)
LBC .... Landelijke Bibliotheek-Centrale [*Dutch*]
LBC .... Les Bois du Cameroun (MAR)
LBC .... Les Bois du Congo (MAR)
LBC .... Local Branch Committee [*Mauritian*] (AF)
LBD .... Les Bois Debites (MAR)
LBD .... Lidove Bytove Druzstvo [*People's Apartment Cooperative*] (CZ)
LBEPO .... Light Armored Train (RU)
LBH .... Land-, Bau-, und Holzbearbeitungsmaschinen [*Agricultural, Construction, and Woodworking Machines*] (EG)
LBIDI .... Liberian Bank for Industrial Development and Investment (AF)
LBK .... Landbaukombinat [*Rural Construction Combine*] (EG)
LBK .... Line Battery Switch (RU)
LBKD........... Chronicle of the Bulgarian Literary Society [*A publication*] (BU)
LBKM .... Lembaga Beasiswa Kenangan Maulud [*Mohammad's Birth Memorial Scholarship Foundation*] (ML)
LBN .... Lebanon [*Three-letter standard code*] (CNC)
LBP.............. Bomb Run (RU)
LBPJ............ Lembaga Bandaran Petaling Jaya [*Petaling Jaya Municipal Institute*] (ML)
LBR .... Liberia [*Three-letter standard code*] (CNC)
LBr .... Ski Brigade (RU)
LBS .... Les Bois de Sassandra (MAR)
lbs .... Libras [*Pounds*] [*Spanish*]
LBS .... Libyan Broadcasting Service (MAR)
lbs .... Lineman Battalion (RU)
LBSV........... Lineman Battalion (RU)
LBTP .... Laboratoire du Batiment et des Travaux Publics (MAR)
LBU .... Course-Line Deviation (RU)
LBV .... Traveling-Wave Tube [*Radio*] (BU)
LBV .... Traveling-Wave Tube (RU)
LBVM .... Traveling-Wave Magnetron-Type Tube (RU)
LBVP........... Le Bons Vins Pennone (MAR)
LBY .... Libya [*Three-letter standard code*] (CNC)
LBZ.............. Leitstelle fuer Baumaschinenersatzteile und -Zubehoer [*Control Office for Construction Machine Spare Parts and Accessories*] (EG)
LC................ Legislative Council (MAR)
LC................ Letter of Credit (MAR)
l/c................ Leur Compte [*French*]
LC................ Liberalt Centrum [*Liberal Center*] [*Danish*] (PPE)
LC................ Liga Comunista [*Communist League*] [*Spanish*] (WER)
lc .... Loco Citato [*In the Place Cited*] [*Latin*]
LC................ Lotta Continua [*Continuous Struggle*] [*Italian*] (PPE)
L de C.......... Lucha de Clases [*Class Struggle*] [*Spanish*] (WER)
LC................ Lumiere Centrale [*On cartridge bags*] [*Military*] [*French*] (MTD)
LC................ St. Lucia [*Two-letter standard code*] (CNC)
LCA .... Les Comptoirs Africains (MAR)
LCA .... Liga Comunista Armada [*Armed Communist League*] [*Mexican*] (LA)
LCA .... St. Lucia [*Three-letter standard code*] (CNC)
LCATC .... Livingstonia Central African Trading Company Ltd. (MAR)
LCC.............. Lagos City Council (MAR)
LCCLC .... Laboratorul Central de Cercetari Lacuri si Cerneluri [*Central Laboratory for Research on Varnishes and Inks*] (RO)
LCCS .... Laboratorul Central de Cercetari Stiintifice [*Central Laboratory for Scientific Research*] (RO)
LCDDH........ Ligue Congolaise pour la Defense des Droits de l'Homme (MAR)
Lcdo .... Licenciado [*Licensed*] [*Spanish*]
LCE .... Liga Comunista Espartaca [*Spartacus Communist League*] [*Mexican*] (LA)
LCh .... Poor Audibility (BU)
LCHF .... Laboratoire Centrale d'Hydraulique de France (MAR)
LCI............... Leerplancommissie Cursorisch Informatica-Onderwijs [*Dutch*]
LCI............... Liga Comunista Internacionalista [*International Communist League*] [*Portuguese*] (PPE)
LCIE .... Laboratoire Central des Industries Electriques [*French*]
LCL .... Labor Congress of Liberia (MAR)
LCMCFC..... Liaison Committee for Mediterranean Citrus Fruit Culture [*See also CLAM*] (EA)
LCom .... Lotta Comunista [*Communist Struggle*] [*Italian*] (WER)
LCOS .... London Conference on Overseas Students (MAR)
LCP .... League of Coloured Peoples (MAR)
LCP .... Lesotho Congress Party (AF)
LCPC........... Laboratoire Central des Ponts et Chaussees [*Main Highway Department Laboratory*] [*French*] (WER)
LCPE........... Leux & Cie. - Plomberie Electricite (MAR)
LCPR........... Liga Comunista Partidaria Reconstrutiva [*Communist League for the Reconstruction of the Communist Party*] [*Portuguese*] (WER)
LCPR........... Liga para a Construcao do Partido Revolucionario [*League for Construction of the Revolutionary Party*] [*Portuguese*] (WER)
LCR .... Laboratoire Central de Recherches [*French*]
l/cr .... Lettre de Credit [*Letter of Credit*] [*French*]
LCR .... Liga Comunista Revolucionaria [*Revolutionary Communist League*] [*Spanish*] (WER)
LCR .... Ligue Communiste Revolutionnaire [*Revolutionary Communist League*] [*French*] (PPW)
LCRI .... Lake Chad Research Institute [*Nigerian*] (AF)
LCsM........... Liga Ceskoslovenskych Motoristu [*Czechoslovak Motoring Club*] (CZ)
LCSS........... Laboratorio Central del Servicio de Sismologia
LCT .... Laboratoire Central de Telecommunications [*Central Telecommunications Laboratory*] [*French*] (WER)
LCT .... Laboratorio Central de Telecomunicaciones [*Central Telecommunications Laboratory*] [*Cuban*] (LA)
LCTC........... Lagos City Transport Corporation (MAR)
LCTES......... Lefke Cengiz Topel Erkek Sanat Enstitusu [*Lefke (Lefka) Cengiz Topel Men's Trade Institute*] [*Turkish Cypriot*] (GC)
LCTS........... Lagos City Transport Service (MAR)
LCTU........... Libyan Confederation of Trade Unions (MAR)
LCW .... Lesotho Council of Workers (MAR)
LCY .... League of Communists of Yugoslavia [*Savez Komunista Jugoslavije*] (PPW)
ld .... File Sheet, Dossier Sheet (RU)
LD................ Laiki Dimokratia [*or Laokratiki Dimokratia*] [*People's Republic*] (GC)
ld .... Lasd [*See, Refer To*] (HU)
LD................ Leader [*Navy*] (RU)
LD................ Lekarnicky Dum [*Pharmacists' Building*] (CZ)
LD................ Lethal Dose (RU)
LD................ Libyan Dinar (ME)
LD................ Licence de Docteur en Medecine [*French*]
L en D.......... Licencie en Droit [*Licentiate in Law*] [*French*]
LD................ Licni Dohodak [*Individual Income*] (YU)
LD................ Lidova Demokracie [*People's Democracy (Also name of a newspaper)*] (CZ)
LD................ Literarni Duvernik [*Book Agent*] (CZ)
LD................ Ljubljanski Dnevnik [*Ljubljana Daily*] [*A newspaper*] (YU)
LDA .... Lead Development Association (EA)
Lda .... Limitada [*Limited*] [*Spanish*]
lda .... Limitada [*Limited*] [*Portuguese*] (CED)
LDA .... Livestock Development Agency (MAR)

LDAN.......... Engine Laboratory of the Academy of Sciences, USSR (RU)
LDC............ Law Development Centre (MAR)
LDC............ Less Developed Country (AF)
LDC............ Liberian Development Corporation (MAR)
LDE............ Laiki Dimokratiki Enotita (Enotis) [*Popular Democratic Unity*] (GC1)
Lde............ Lande [*Heath, Moor*] [*Military map abbreviation*] [*World War I*] [*French*] (MTD)
LDE............ Locomotive Diesel si Electrice [*Diesel and Electric Locomotives*] (RO)
LDF............ Landesverband der Dolmetscher und Fremdsprachenlehrer [*National Association of Interpreters and Foreign Language Teachers*] [*West German*]
LDFK.......... Leningrad House of Physical Culture (RU)
LDFL.......... Lusaka and District Football League (MAR)
LDG............ Laiki Dimokratia Germanias [*German Democratic Republic*] (GC)
LDK............ Lodzki Dom Kultury [*Lodz Social and Recreation Club*] [*Polish*]
LDK............ Sawmilling and Woodworking Kombinat (RU)
LDKhVD...... Leningrad House of Children's Art Education (RU)
LDMPT....... Ligue Democratique-Mouvement pour le Parti du Travail (MAR)
LDNTP........ Leningrad House of Scientific and Technical Propaganda (RU)
LDO............ Leningrad House of Officers Imeni S. M. Kirov (RU)
LDO............ Lesni Druzstvo Obce [*Communal Forest Cooperative*] (CZ)
Ldo............ Licenciado [*One Who Is Licensed in a Profession*] [*Spanish*]
LDOK.......... Sawmilling and Woodworking Kombinat (RU)
LDP............ Leningrad Palace of Pioneers Imeni A. A. Zhdanov (RU)
LDP............ Letecky Dopravni Pluk [*Air Transport Regiment*] (CZ)
LDP............ Liberal-Democratic Party (SJT)
LDP............ Liberal-Democratic Party of Japan [*Jiyu-Minshuto*] (PPW)
LDP............ Liberal Demokratische Partei [*Liberal Democratic Party*] [*West German*] (PPE)
LDP............ Lietuviy Demokraty Partija [*Lithuanian Democratic Party*] (PPE)
LdP............ Ljudska Pravica [*The People's Rights*] [*A daily*] [*Ljubljana*] (YU)
LdP-B.......... Ljudska Pravica - Borba [*The People's Rights - Struggle*] [*A daily*] [*Ljubljana*] (YU)
LDPD.......... Liberal-Demokratische Partei Deutschlands [*Liberal Democratic Party of Germany*] [*East German*] (PPW)
LDPG.......... Liberal Democratic Party of Germany [*German People's Republic*] (RU)
LdProsv...... Ljudska Prosveta [*The People's Education*] [*A periodical*] [*Ljubljana*] (YU)
LDRN.......... Ligue de Defense de la Race Negre (MAR)
LDS............ Letecke Dispecerske Stanoviste [*Aviation (or Aircraft) Dispatch Center*] (CZ)
LDS............ Lidove Demokraticke Staty [*The People's Democratic Countries*] (CZ)
LDSA.......... Leningrad House of the Soviet Army (RU)
LDSK.......... Sawmilling and House Construction Kombinat (RU)
LDSOO........ Leningrad Voluntary Sports Society of Hunters (RU)
LdTd.......... Ljudski Tednik [*People's Weekly*] [*Trieste*] [*A publication*] (YU)
LDTM.......... Leningrad House of Machinery-Manufacturing Technology (RU)
LDTU.......... Leningrad House of Technical Training (RU)
LdU............ Landesring der Unabhaengigen [*Independent Party*] [*Swiss*] (PPE)
LDU............ Leningrad House of Scientists Imeni A. M. Gor'kiy (RU)
LDU............ Lenjingradsko Drustvo Univerziteta [*Leningrad Society of Universities*] [*Russian*] (YU)
Ldw............ Landwirt [*or Landwirtschaft*] [*German*]
l dz............ Liczba Dziennika [*Number on the Agenda*] [*Polish*]
LDZ............ Logarithmic Attenuation Ratio (RU)
LE.............. Egyptian Pound (ME)
LE.............. Laborator pro Elektrotechniku [*Electrical Engineering Laboratory (of the Czechoslovak Academy of Sciences)*] (CZ)
LE.............. Laiki Exousia [*Popular Power*] [*Communist organization*] [*Greek*] (GC)
Le.............. Laje [*Flat-Topped Rock*] [*Portuguese*] (NAU)
Le.............. Leone (MAR)
LE.............. Licence d'Enseignement [*Academic qualification*] [*French*]
LE.............. Lineal Element, Linear Element (RU)
LE.............. Literary Encyclopedia [*A publication*] (RU)
LE.............. Loero [*Horsepower*] (HU)
LE.............. Logarithmic Element (RU)
LEA............ Laiki Epanastatiki Andistasi [*Popular Revolutionary Resistance*] [*Greek*] (GC)
LEA............ Liga Ecuatoriana Anti-Tuberculosa [*Ecuadorean League Against Tuberculosis*] (LA)
LEA............ Lucha Espanola Antimarxista [*Spanish Anti-Marxist Struggle*] (WER)
LEAP.......... Loan and Educational Aid Programme (MAR)
LEAS.......... Laikos Ethnikos Apelevtherotikos Syndiasmos [*Popular National Liberation League*] [*Cypriot*] (GC)
LEBAMA..... Le Batiment Mauritanien (MAR)
Lebensl....... Lebenslauf [*Career*] [*German*]
LEC............ Lesotho Evangelical Church (MAR)
LEC............ Liberia Electricity Corporation (MAR)
lech............ Hospital, Clinic [*Topography*] (RU)
Lechsanupr... Medical and Sanitary Administration (RU)
LECO.......... Ferme Experimentale d'Elevage de la Songolo (MAR)
LECO.......... Librarie Evangelique au Congo (MAR)
LECUSA...... Lesotho Credit Union Scheme for Agriculture (MAR)
led............ Ice, Glacial (RU)
LED............ Icebreaker (RU)
LEDA.......... Ley de Desarrollo Agropecuario [*Agricultural-Livestock Development Law*] [*Mexican*] (LA1)
LEDB.......... Lagos Executive Development Board (MAR)
Ledflot........ Arctic Ocean Flotilla (RU)
ledn............ Glacier [*Topography*] (RU)
LEE............ L'Equatoriale Electronique (MAR)
LEEL.......... Leningrad Experimental Electrotechnical Laboratory (RU)
LEF............ Art's Left Front [*Literary group, 1923-1930*] (RU)
LEFI............ Leningrad Institute of Electrophysics (RU)
LEG............ General Lycee [*French*]
Leg............ Legation [*German*]
Leg............ Legation [*Legation*] [*French*] (MTD)
leg............ Legenyseg [*Enlisted Men, Privates*] (HU)
LEGCO........ Legislative Council (MAR)
legf............ Legfelso [*or Legfobb*] [*Highest or Supreme*] (HU)
Legf Bir....... Legfelso Birosag [*Supreme Court*] (HU)
Legf U.......... Legfobb Ugyeszseg [*Supreme Prosecutor's Office*] (HU)
Legg............ Legierungen [*Alloys*] [*German*]
legos............ Legoltalmi [*Officer in Civil Air Defense Work*] (HU)
LEGr-.......... Electric Cargo Winch (RU)
LEGTIS........ Lefkosa ve Kazasi Endustri ve Genel Turk Isciler Sendikasi [*Nicosia and District Industrial and Public Turkish Workers' Union*] [*Turkish Cypriot*] (GC)
Lehrb.......... Lehrbeauftragter [*German*]
leht............ Lehtori [*Finnish*]
leichtl.......... Leichtloeslich [*Easily Soluble*] [*German*]
Leig............ Leichter Gueterzug [*Light Freight Train*] (EG)
leik............ Leikillisesti [*Jocularly*] [*Finnish*]
LEIS............ Leningrad Electrotechnical Institute of Communications Imeni M. A. Bonch-Bruyevich (RU)
LEK............ Laiko Enotiko Komma [*Populist Union Party*] [*Greek*] (PPE)
LEK............ Laikon Enotikon Komma [*Populist Unionist Party*] [*Cypriot*] (GC)
lek............ Lecture (BU)
lek............ Lekarz [*Physician*] [*Polish*]
lekarstv....... Medicinal (RU)
Lekoop........ Physicians' Cooperative (BU)
Lekoopizdat... Physicians' Cooperative Publishers (BU)
LekPr.......... Lekarski Pregled [*Physicians' Review*] [*A periodical*] (BU)
Lekrastrest... State Trust for the Cultivation and Procurement of Medicinal Plant Raw Materials (RU)
LEKt............ Electric Whaling Winch (RU)
LELM.......... Leipzig Evangelical Lutheran Mission (MAR)
LEM............ Laboratory of Evolutionary Morphology (of the Academy of Sciences, USSR) (RU)
LEM............ Laboratory of Experimental Morphogenesis (RU)
LEM............ Laiki Etaireia Metaforon [*Popular Transport Company*] [*Cypriot*] (GC)
LEMB.......... Laborator pro Elektronovou Mikroskopii v Biologii [*Laboratory of Electron Microscopy in Biology (of the Czechoslovak Academy of Sciences)*] (CZ)
LEMHANNAS... Lembaga Pertahanan Nasional [*National Defense Institute*] (IN)
LEMI............ Leningrad Electromechanical Institute (RU)
LEMP.......... Lengyel Egyesult Munkaspart [*United Workers' Party of Poland*] (HU)
LEMT.......... Leningrad Electrotechnical Medical Technicum (RU)
LEMUK........ Leningrad Electromechanical Training Center for Railroad Transportation Engineers (RU)
LEMZ.......... Leningrad Electromechanical Plant (RU)
LEN............ [*Direction Generale de*] Liberation et d'Edification Nationale [*(Directorate General of) Liberation and National Construction*] [*Use LENA*] [*Cambodian*] (CL)
LENA.......... [*Direction Generale de*] Liberation et d'Edification Nationale [*(Directorate General of) Liberation and National Construction*] [*Cambodian*] (CL)
Lenbriketmash... Leningrad State Briquette Machinery Plant (RU)
Lendorstroy... Leningrad Road Construction Trust (RU)
LENDVI....... Leningrad Scientific Research Institute of Dermatology and Venereology (RU)
Lenenergo... Leningrad Regional Administration of Power System Management (RU)
LENFI.......... Leningrad Pharmaceutical Scientific Research Institute (RU)
Lenfil'm....... Leningrad Motion Picture Studio (RU)
Lengas.......... Gas Supply System Administration of Lengorispolkom (RU)
Lengeolnerud... Leningrad State All-Union Geological Exploration Trust for Nonmetallic Minerals (RU)
LenGES....... Leningrad State Electric Power Plant (RU)
LENGIDEP... Leningrad Branch of the All-Union State Planning Institute "Gidroenergoproyekt" (RU)
LenGIDUV... Leningrad State Institute for the Advanced Training of Physicians Imeni S. M. Kirov (RU)
Lengiprogaz... Leningrad State Institute for the Planning of Synthetic Liquid Fuel and Gas-Producing Establishments (RU)
Lengiprogor... Leningrad Branch of the State Institute for the Planning of Cities (RU)

Lengiprokhim ... Leningrad Branch of the State Institute for the Planning of Plants of the Basic Chemical Industry (RU)
Lengipromash ... Leningrad State Institute for the Planning of Machinery and Metalworking Plants (RU)
Lengiprorechtrans ... Leningrad State Institute for Planning in River Transportation (RU)
Lengiprotorf ... Leningrad Branch of the State Planning Institute for the Multipurpose Use of Peat in the National Economy (RU)
Lengiprotrans ... Leningrad State Planning and Surveying Institute of the State Industrial Committee for Transportation Construction, USSR (RU)
Lengiprovodkhoz ... Leningrad State Institute for the Planning of Water-Management and Reclamation Construction (RU)
Lengird .... Leningrad Group for the Study of Jet Propulsion [*1932-1934*] (RU)
Lengiz .... Leningrad Branch of the State Publishing House (RU)
Lengorispolkom ... Executive Committee of the Leningrad City Soviet of Workers' Deputies (RU)
Lengorono ... Leningrad City Department of Public Education (RU)
Lengorpromsovet ... Leningrad City Council of Producers' Cooperatives (RU)
Lengorsovet ... Leningrad City Soviet of Workers' Deputies (RU)
Lengorspravka ... Leningrad City Reference and Information Office (RU)
Lengortel'set' ... Leningrad City Telephone Network (RU)
Lengorvoyenkomat ... Leningrad City Military Commissariat (RU)
Lengoryos... Leningrad City Branch of the All-Russian Society for the Blind (RU)
Lengorzdravotdel ... Leningrad City Department of Public Health (RU)
Lengosfil..... Leningrad State Philharmonic (RU)
Lengosstroyizdat ... Leningrad Branch of the State Publishing House of Literature on Construction, Architecture, and Building Materials (RU)
Lengostoptekhizdat ... Leningrad Branch of the State Scientific and Technical Publishing House of the Petroleum and Mineral-Fuel Industry (RU)
leningr .... Leningrad (RU)
LenIUU........ Leningrad City Institute for the Advanced Training of Teachers (RU)
Lenizdat...... Newspaper, Periodical, and Book Publishing House of the Leningrad Oblast and City Committees of the KPSS (RU)
Lenkarz....... Leningrad Carburetor Plant (RU)
LENKER...... Len- Kender- es Muszaki Textilertekesito Vallalat [*Commercial Enterprise for Industrial Cordage and Textiles*] (HU)
Lenkhimles ... Leningrad State Trust of the Wood-Chemistry Industry (RU)
LenKhIMMASh ... Leningrad Branch of the All-Union Scientific Research and Design Institute of Chemical Machinery (RU)
Lenkhimsektor ... Leningrad Branch of the Chemical Department of the United Scientific and Technical Publishing House (RU)
Lenkhimtekhizdat ... Leningrad Branch of the State Chemical and Technical Publishing House (RU)
Lenkinap..... Leningrad Motion-Picture Equipment Plant (RU)
Lenkogiz..... Leningrad Oblast Branch of the Book Trade Association of State Publishing Houses (RU)
LENKOMBANK ... Leningrad City and Oblast Municipal Bank (RU)
Lenkubu...... Leningrad Commission for the Improvement of Scientists' Living Conditions (RU)
Lenlikvodzavod ... Leningrad Liqueur and Vodka Plant (RU)
Lenmashgiz ... Leningrad State Publishing House of Literature on Machinery Manufacture (RU)
Lenmetrostroy ... Leningrad Subway Construction Administration (RU)
lenn .... Lennatin [*Telegraph*] [*Finnish*]
Lennauchfil'm ... Leningrad Motion-Picture Studio of Popular Science Films (RU)
LENNIIKhIMMASH ... Leningrad Scientific Research and Design Institute of Chemical Machinery (RU)
LenNIILKh... Leningrad Scientific Research Institute of Forestry (RU)
LenNIKhFI... Leningrad Scientific Research Chemical and Pharmaceutical Institute (RU)
LENNILKhI ... Leningrad Scientific Research Institute of Wood Chemistry (RU)
LenNITO...... Leningrad Scientific, Engineering, and Technical Society (RU)
Lenoblispolkom ... Executive Committee of the Leningrad Oblast Soviet of Workers' Deputies (RU)
Lenoblono... Leningrad Oblast Department of Public Education (RU)
Lenoblpotrebsoyuz ... Leningrad Oblast Union of Consumers' Societies (RU)
Lenoblproyekt ... Institute for the Planning of Housing, Civil-Engineering, and Municipal Construction of the Lenoblispolkom (RU)
Lenoblsovet ... Leningrad Oblast Soviet of Workers' Deputies (RU)
Lenoblsovprof ... Leningrad Oblast Council of Trade Unions (RU)
Lenoblvetsnab ... Leningrad Oblast Veterinary Supply Office (RU)
Lenogiz....... Leningrad Association of State Publishing Houses (RU)
Lenokogiz... Leningrad Oblast Branch of the Book Trade Association of State Publishing Houses (RU)
Lenpartizdat ... Leningrad Branch of the Publishing House of the TsK VKP (b) (RU)
Lenpishchepromizdat ... Leningrad Branch of the State Scientific and Technical Publishing House of the Food Industry (RU)
Lenplan....... Planning Commission of the Lengorispolkom (RU)
Lenproyekt ... Institute for the Planning of Housing and Civil Engineering Construction of the Lengorispolkom (RU)
Lenshveymash ... Leningrad State Sewing-Machine Plant (RU)
Lensotsekgiz ... Leningrad Branch of the State Publishing House of Social and Economic Literature (RU)
Lensovet..... Leningrad Soviet of Workers' Deputies (RU)
Lensovnarkhoz ... Council of the National Economy of the Leningrad Economic Region (RU)
Lenstankolit ... Leningrad Machine Tool Castings Plant (RU)
LenTASS .... Leningrad Branch of the News Agency of the Soviet Union (RU)
Lentekstil'mash ... Leningrad Textile Machinery Plant (RU)
Lenteplopribor ... Leningrad State Plant of Electronic Heat-Control Instruments (RU)
Lentorfmash ... Leningrad Peat Machinery Plant (RU)
Lentrublit.... Leningrad Pipe-Casting Plant (RU)
lenugolok.... Lenin Corner (RU)
LENVAT...... Leningrad Oblast Office of the All-Union Gas-Welding Trust (RU)
LENVNIGI.... Leningrad Branch of the All-Union Scientific Research Institute of Gas and Synthetic Liquid Fuel (RU)
LENVNIIPT ... Leningrad Branch of the All-Union Scientific Research Institute of Industrial Transportation (RU)
Lenvodokanalstroy ... Leningrad Water Supply and Sewer System Construction Trust (RU)
Lenvodopribor ... Leningrad Water Supply Equipment Plant (RU)
Lenvodput' ... Administration of Leningrad Waterways (RU)
Lenvoyenport ... Leningrad Naval Port (RU)
Lenzagotmorsnab ... Leningrad Procurement Office of the Maritime Fleet (RU)
Lenzhet....... Leningrad Fats Trust (RU)
LEP............. Electric Power Transmission Line (RU)
LEP............. Laboratoires d'Electronique et de Physique Appliquee [*Electronics and Applied Physics Laboratory*] [*French*] (WER)
LEP............. Lycee d'Enseignement Professionnel [*Professional High School*] [*French*]
LEPRA......... Leprosy Relief Association [*Malawian*] (AF)
LEPSUK...... Leningrad Track Construction Training Center for Railroad Transportation Engineers (RU)
LER............. Liga de Economistas Revolucionarios [*League of Revolutionary Economists*] [*Mexican*] (LA)
LER............. Line Operation Company (RU)
LERM .... Line Maintenance and Repair Shop (RU)
LERSh......... Electrically and Manually Operated Boat Winch (RU)
LES .... Leipziger Eisen- und Stahlwerke [*Leipzig Iron and Steelworks*] (EG)
LES .... Locomobile Electric Power Station (RU)
LES .... Telecommunications Line (RU)
LESA........... Lecheria Higienica Sociedad Anonima [*Cartagena*] (COL)
Lesbumizdat ... State Publishing House of Literature of the Lumber and Paper Industries (RU)
LESC........... Licence es-Sciences Commerciales [*Master's Degree (License) in Commercial Sciences*] (CL)
Les fak .... School of Forestry (BU)
Lesmetprom ... State All-Union Lumber Industry Trust of the Ministry of Ferrous Metallurgy, USSR (RU)
Lesn .... Forester's House [*Topography*] (RU)
lesnich .... Forestry Section, Forest Range [*Topography*] (RU)
lesokhoz ..... Forest Management (RU)
LESOMA..... Socialist League of Malawi (AF)
Lesop .... Sawmill [*Topography*] (RU)
lesp .... Sawmill [*Topography*] (RU)
lesprom....... Lumber Industry (RU)
Lespromash ... All-Union Logging and Woodworking Trust of the Ministry of Machinery Manufacture and Instrument Making, USSR (RU)
Lespromtyazh ... All-Union Lumber Industry Trust of the Ministry of Heavy Machinery Manufacture, USSR (RU)
LET............. Leningrad Power Engineering Technicum (RU)
Let.............. Letectvo [*Air Force*] (CZ)
let............... Lettre [*Letter, Draft*] [*Business and trade*] [*French*]
Leta............ Latvian News Agency (RU)
LETAC .... Lexique Thematique de l'Afrique Centrale (MAR)
LETDA......... Letnan Dua [*Second Lieutenant*] (IN)
LETDJEN .... Letnan Djenderal [*Lieutenant General*] (IN)
LETEKS ...... Leskovacka Tekstilna Fabrika [*Textile Factory in Leskovac*] (YU)
LETI............ Leningrad Electrotechnical Institute Imeni V. I. Ul'yanov (Lenin) (RU)
LETIISS....... Leningrad Electrotechnical Institute of Signal and Communications Engineers [*1937-1951*] (RU)
LETIIZhT..... Leningrad Electrotechnical Institute of Railroad Transportation Engineers (RU)
LETKOL ...... Letnan Kolonel [*Lieutenant Colonel*] (IN)
letnab......... Aerial Observer (RU)
LETOV......... Letalska Tovarna [*Airplane Factory*] [*Ljubljana*] (YU)
Letpl............ Letecky Pluk [*Air Force Regiment*] (CZ)
LETs........... Airfield Center (BU)
LETTU......... Letnan Satu [*First Lieutenant*] (IN)
LETUL .... Lefkosa Turk Lisesi Musik Toplulugu [*Nicosia Turkish Lycee Musical Society*] (TU)
LETZ .... Leningrad Electrotechnical Plant (RU)
LETZ .... Lyskovo Electrotechnical Plant (RU)
LEU .... Medical and Evacuation Directorate (RU)

lev .... Left, Left-Hand (RU)
LEVAPAN.... Levaduras y Materias Primas para Panificacion y Biscocheria [*Bogota*] (COL)
LEW............ Lokomotivbau-Elektrotechnische Werke [*Locomotive Construction and Electrotechnical Plant*] (EG)
leyt .... Lieutenant (RU)
leyts .... Leucine (RU)
LEZ............ Electric Winch for the Gangway Ladder (RU)
LEZ............ Laboratory of Experimental Zoology (RU)
LEZM.......... Laboratory of Experimental Zoology and Animal Morphology (of the Academy of Sciences, USSR) (RU)
LF .... Front Line, Line of Battle (BU)
LF .... La Fraternidad [*Brotherhood of Locomotive Engineers and Firemen*] [*Argentine*] (LA)
LF .... Laborator pro Experimentalni a Theoretickou Fysiku [*Laboratory for Experimental and Theoretical Physics (of the Czechoslovak Academy of Sciences)*] (CZ)
lf .... Lasd Fent [*See Above*] (HU)
LF .... Leningrad Branch (RU)
LF .... Liberation Front [*Namibian*] (AF)
LF .... Listy Filologicke [*Journal of Philology*] [*A publication*] (CZ)
LFA............. Land Freedom Army (MAR)
LFA............. Local Football Association [*Sudanese*] (MAR)
LFC .... Libyan Finance Corporation (MAR)
LFCh .... Laborator Fysikalni Chemie [*Laboratory for Physical Chemistry (of the Czechoslovak Academy of Sciences)*] (CZ)
LFChKh....... Logarithmic Phase Frequency Characteristic (RU)
lfd............... Laufend [*Consecutive, Current, Running*] (EG)
Lfdm............ Laufender Meter [*Linear Meter*] (EG)
lfd Nr .... Laufende Nummer [*Serial Number, Running Number*] [*German*]
LFEI............ Leningrad Institute of Finance and Economics (RU)
LFEM........... Land Forces East Malaysia (ML)
LFF............. Liberian Frontier Force (MAR)
LFG .... Laboratory of Combustion Physics (RU)
Lfg .... Lieferung [*Installment, Issue, Part*] [*German*]
LFI.............. Leningrad Pharmaceutical Institute (RU)
LFJ .... Ljudska Fronta Jugoslavije [*People's Front of Yugoslavia*] (YU)
LFK............. Therapeutic Physical Culture (RU)
LFKh .... Logarithmic Phase Frequency Characteristic (RU)
LFKU........... Lekarska Fakulta Komenskeho [*Faculty of Medicine of Comenius University*] (CZ)
LFL............. La Forestiere de Lambarene (MAR)
LFLPU .... Libyan Federation of Labour and Professional Unions (MAR)
LFM............ La Forestiere de Moloundou (MAR)
Lfm............. Landforstmeister [*Regional Forester*] (EG)
lfm .... Laufender Meter [*Linear Meter*] (EG)
LFM............ Lieutenant Feld Marechal [*French*] (MTD)
LFM............ Lodzka Fabryka Mebli [*Lodz Furniture Factory*] (POL)
LFMI........... Laboratory of Physico-Mechanical Tests (RU)
LFMR.......... Lubelska Fabryka Maszyn Rolniczych [*Lublin Agricultural Machinery Plant*] (POL)
LFMT........... Leningrad Physico-Mechanical Technicum (RU)
LFMU .... Leningrad Machine Accounting and Computing Office (RU)
LFO .... Light Infantry Flamethrower (RU)
LFOC........... Lea-Francis Owners Club (EA)
LFP............. Liberala Folkpartiet [*Liberal People's Party*] [*Finnish*] (PPE)
LFP............. Track [*Aviation*] (RU)
LFPZ........... Lecebny Fond Postovnich Zamestnancu [*Postal Employees' Medical Fund*] (CZ)
Lfrg .... Lieferung [*Delivery, Installment, Part*] (EG)
LFS............. Lancucka Fabryka Srub [*Lancut Bolt and Nut Factory*] (POL)
LFSV .... Aircraft Telescopic Headlight (RU)
LFTI............ Leningrad Physico-Technical Institute (RU)
LFTL............ Leningrad Physico-Technical Laboratory (RU)
LFTsGVIA ... Leningrad Branch of the Central State Archives of Military History (RU)
LFTU .... Liberian Federation of Trade Unions (AF)
LfV.............. Landesamt fuer Verfassungsschutz [*State Office for the Protection of the Constitution*] [*West German*] (WEN)
LFVE .... Laboratory of High-Energy Physics (RU)
LFVZ .... Lecebny Fond Verejnych Zamestnancu [*Public Employees' Medical Fund*] (CZ)
LFW............ Lubelskie Fabryki Wag [*Lublin Scale Factories*] (POL)
LFZ............. Lubelska Fabryka Zgrzeblarek [*Lublin Flax Carding Factory*] (POL)
LFZ............. Lucobne a Farmaceuticke Zavody [*Chemical and Pharmaceutical Plants*] (CZ)
LG............... La Geographie [*A publication*] (MAR)
lg .... Lang [*Long, In Length*] [*German*]
lg .... Largo [*Broadway*] [*Italian*] (CED)
lg .... Largo [*Square*] [*Portuguese*] (CED)
Lg .... Lebendgewichtstatistik fuer Rinder und Schweine [*Live-Weight Statistics for Cattle and Hogs*] (EG)
LG............... Local Government (MAR)
lg .... Logarytm [*Logarithm*] [*Polish*]
LG............... Lokalno Gospodarstvo [*Local Economy*] (YU)
LG............... Luteinizing Hormone (RU)
LG-.............. Vacuum-Tube Generator, Vacuum-Tube Oscillator (RU)
LGA............ Local Government Area (MAR)
LGBI........... Leningrad State Library Institute Imeni N. K. Krupskaya (RU)
LGDJ........... Librairie Generale de Droit et de Jurisprudence [*North African*] (MAR)
LGES........... Leningrad State Electric Power Plant (RU)
LGG............ Gueterwagenleerzug aus Gedeckten Wagen [*Empty Freight Train Consisting of Covered Freight Cars*] (EG)
LGGP........... Laboratory of Hydrogeological Problems Imeni F. P. Savarenskiy (RU)
LGI .... Leningrad Mining Institute Imeni G. V. Plekhanov (RU)
LGIFK.......... Lithuanian State Institute of Physical Culture (RU)
LGILI .... Leningrad State Institute of Historical Linguistics (RU)
LGIUU .... Leningrad City Institute for the Advanced Training of Teachers (RU)
LGK............ Leningrad City Committee (RU)
LGK............ Leningrad State Conservatory Imeni N. A. Rimskiy-Korsakov (RU)
LGMI .... Leningrad Hydrometeorological Institute (RU)
LGMI .... Leningrad State Milk Inspection (RU)
LGMT .... Leningrad Hydrometeorological Technicum (RU)
LGO............ Gueterwagenleerzug aus Offenen Gueterwagen [*Empty Freight Train Consisting of Open Freight Cars*] (EG)
LGOLU .... Leningrad State "Order of Lenin" University Imeni A. A. Zhdanov (RU)
LGP .... Libyan Gas Producers (MAR)
LGPI .... Leningrad State Pedagogical Institute Imeni A. I. Gertsen (RU)
LGPIIYa....... Leningrad State Pedagogical Institute of Foreign Languages (RU)
LGPMI......... Leningrad State Institute of Pediatric Medicine (RU)
LGR............ Landesgerichtsrat [*German*]
LGRI........... Leningrad Institute of Geological Exploration (RU)
LGRI........... Leningrad State Quality Inspection of Fish (RU)
LGRS........... Leningrad City Radio Wire Broadcasting Network (RU)
LGRT........... Leningrad Trust for Geological Exploration (RU)
LGS .... Leningrad City Soviet (RU)
LGS .... Ligue pour la Grande Somalie (MAR)
LGSPS .... Leningrad City Council of Trade Unions (RU)
LGT .... Leningrad State Planning and Surveying Institute of the State Industrial Committee for Transportation Construction, USSR (RU)
LGTA........... Liga Geral dos Trabalhadores Angolanos [*Leopoldville*] (MAR)
LGTA........... Ligue Generale des Travailleurs de l'Angola [*General League of Angolan Workers*] (AF)
LGTS........... Leningrad City Telephone Network (RU)
LGU............ Latvian State University Imeni P. Stuchka (RU)
LGU............ Leningrad State University Imeni A. A. Zhdanov (RU)
LGU............ L'vov State University Imeni Ivan Franko (RU)
LGUMP......... Leningrad Branch of the State Administration of the Metallurgical Industry (RU)
LGV .... Legvedelem [*or Legvedelmi*] [*Air Defense or Antiaircraft (Gun)*] (HU)
LGWF .... Libyan General Workers' Federation (MAR)
LGWU.......... Libyan General Workers' Union (MAR)
LGZ .... Laboratorij Gradevinarstva - Zagreb [*Construction Laboratory in Zagreb*] (YU)
LGZhD......... Leningrad City Railways (RU)
LGZU........... Leningrad State Correspondence University (RU)
LH............... Laborator Hutnicka [*Metallurgical Laboratory (of the Czechoslovak Academy of Sciences)*] (CZ)
LH............... Landbouwhogeschool [*Wageningen*]
LH............... Lidova Hvezdarna [*People's Observatory*] (CZ)
LH............... Lorinci Hengermu [*Rolling Mills of Lorinc*] (HU)
LHD .... Literarum Humaniorum Doctor [*Doctor of the More Humane Letters*] [*Latin*] (GPO)
LHK .... Lebenshaltungskosten [*Cost of Living*] (EG)
LHM............ Landbau- und Holzbearbeitungsmaschinen [*Agricultural and Woodworking Machines*] (EG)
L'HOMME.... L'Homme; Cahier d'Ethnologie, de Geographie, et de Linguistique [*A publication*] (MAR)
LHptm .... Landeshauptmann [*German*]
LHS .... Laborator Heterocyklickych Sloucenin [*Laboratory for the Study of Heterocyclic Compounds (of the Czechoslovak Academy of Sciences)*] (CZ)
LI-............... Aircraft Designed by B. P. Lisunov (RU)
LI .... Final Selector (RU)
LI .... Lesna Industrija [*Lumber Industry*] (YU)
LI .... Liberal International (EA)
LI .... Liechtenstein [*Two-letter standard code*] (CNC)
Li .... Liman [*or Limani*] [*Harbor, Port*] [*Turkish*] (NAU)
li .... Links [*German*]
LI .... Literary Institute Imeni A. M. Gor'kiy (RU)
LI .... Lucka Intendatura [*Harbor Commissariat*] (YU)
LIA.............. Landtechnische Industrieanlagen (VEB LIA) [*Industrial Agricultural Technology Installations (VEB)*] (EG)
LIAC .... Liberian International American Corporation (MAR)
LIAM........... Liga Intensificadora da Accao Missionaria (MAR)
LIAP .... Leningrad Institute of Aviation Instruments (RU)
LIAT .... Leeward Island Air Transport (LA1)
LIAZ .... Automobile Made by the Likino Bus Plant (RU)
LIAZ .... Liberecke Automobilove Zavody [*Liberec Automobile Works*] (CZ)
LIAZ .... Likino Bus Plant (RU)
lib .... Liberaali(nen) [*Finnish*]

lib ... Libere [*Discharged, Liberated*] [*French*]
lib ... Libra [*Pound*] [*Spanish*]
lib ... Libro [*Book*] [*Spanish*]
LIBAS ... Libya Insaat ve Yatirim Anonim Sirketi [*Libyan Construction and Investment Corporation*] (TU)
LIBE ... Ligo Internacia de Blindaj Esperantistoj [*International League of Blind Esperantists - ILBE*] (EA)
LIBECO ... Societe Librevilloise de Constructions [*Libreville Construction Company*] [*Gabonese*] (AF)
LIBER ... Ligue des Bibliotheques Europeennes de Recherche
LIBERESE ... La Libertad-Compania de Seguros Generales SA [*Bogota*] (COL)
LIBIDI ... Liberian Bank for Industrial Development and Investment (MAR)
LIBIS ... Leuvens Integraal Bibliotheek en Informatie Systeem
LIBMISH ... United States Military Mission to Liberia (MAR)
LIBOR ... London Interbank Offered Rate (MAR)
LIBRA ... Linnas Brasileiras de Navegacao, SA [*Brazilian Steamship Lines*] (LA)
LIBRAPORT ... Entreprise Nationale d'Importation de Librairie (MAR)
LIBROCUBA ... Empresa de Comercio Exterior de Publicaciones [*Foreign Trade Enterprise for Periodicals*] [*Cuban*] (LA)
LIBSUCO ... Liberian Sugar Corporation (MAR)
lic ... Licenciado [*Spanish*]
lic ... Lizentiat [*German*]
LICCD ... Ligue Internationale Contre la Concurrence Deloyale [*International League Against Unfair Competition*] (EA)
LICENCIA ... LICENCIA Talalmanyokat Ertekesito Vallalat [*LICENCIA Marketing Enterprise for Inventions*] (HU)
LICh ... Linear Pulse Part (RU)
lich ... Personal [*Pronoun*] (BU)
lichn sost ... Personnel, Staff (RU)
LICI ... Limonaderie de la Cote-d'Ivoire (MAR)
LICOTRA ... L'Essor Ivoirien de Construction et de Travaux Publics (MAR)
LICOVALLE ... Industria de Licores del Valle [*Cali*] (COL)
LID ... Lectuur- en Informatie Dienst [*NBLC*] [*Dutch*]
LID ... Lehr Institut fuer Dokumentation
LIDA ... Laboratorio de Investigacion y Diagnostico de Avicultura [*Avian Research and Diagnosis Laboratory*] [*Cuban*] (LA)
LIDA ... Livestock Development Authority [*Tanzanian*] (AF)
LIDEE ... L'Investissement et la Distribution Economique Eburneenne (MAR)
LIDU ... Lega Internazionale dei Diritti dell' Uomo [*International League of Human Rights*] [*Italian*] (WER)
LIDUS ... Liberal-Demokratische Union der Schweiz [*Liberal Democratic Union of Switzerland*] (PPE)
LIE ... Liechtenstein [*Three-letter standard code*] (CNC)
Lief ... Lieferung [*Fascicle, Number*] [*German*]
LIEI ... Leningrad Institute of Economic Research (RU)
LIEI ... Leningrad Institute of Engineering Economics (RU)
LIEM ... Leningrad Institute of Experimental Meteorology (RU)
LIETIN ... Leningrad Scientific Research Institute for Determination of Disability and Organization of Work for Disabled Persons (RU)
LIETTIN ... Leningrad Scientific Research Institute for Determination of Disability and Employment of Disabled Persons (RU)
Lieut ... Lieutenant [*Lieutenant*] [*Military*] [*French*] (MTD)
Lieut Col ... Lieutenant-Colonel [*Lieutenant Colonel*] [*Military*] [*French*] (MTD)
LIFE ... Laboratorios Industriales Farmaceuticos Ecuatorianos [*Ecuadorean Pharmaceutical Industrial Laboratories*] (LA)
LIFEMO ... Liga Feminina de Mocambique [*Mozambique Women's League*] (AF)
LIFLI ... Leningrad Institute of History, Philosophy, and Literature (RU)
Liftoremont ... Moscow City Trust for the Repair of Elevators in Dwelling Houses (RU)
Liftstroy ... Administration of Elevator Construction (RU)
LIGEM ... Lomonosov Institute of Geochemistry, Crystallography, and Mineralogy (of the Academy of Sciences, USSR) (RU)
LIGENCO ... Liberian General Enterprises Company (MAR)
LIGI ... Leningrad Institute of Civil Engineers (RU)
LIGNA ... Podnik Zahranicniho Obchodu pro Dovoz a Vyvoz Dreva a Vyrobku Prumyslu Drevozpracujiciho a Papirenskeho [*Foreign Trade Enterprise for the Import and Export of Wood and Products of the Lumber and Paper Industries*] (CZ)
LIGNIMPEX ... LIGNIMPEX Fa, Papir, es Tuzeloanyag Kulkereskedelmi Vallalat [*LIGNIMPEX Foreign Trade Enterprise for Lumber, Paper, and Fuel*] (HU)
ligr ... Ligroin (RU)
LIGVF ... Leningrad Institute of the Civil Air Fleet (RU)
LII ... Flight Research Institute (RU)
LII ... Leningrad Industrial Institute (RU)
LIIGVF ... Leningrad Institute of Civil Air Fleet Engineers (RU)
liik ... Liike-Clama(ssa) [*Finnish*]
LIIKP ... Leningrad Institute of Motion-Picture Industry Engineers (RU)
LIIKS ... Leningrad Institute of Municipal Construction Engineers (RU)
LIIMP ... Leningrad Institute of Dairy Industry Engineers (RU)
LIIMSZ ... Leningrad Institute of Mechanical Engineers of Socialist Agriculture (RU)
LIIOP ... Leningrad State Institute of Engineers for Public Eating Facilities (RU)
LIIPS ... Leningrad Institute of Industrial Construction Engineers (RU)
LIIPT ... Leningrad Institute of Industrial Transportation Engineers (RU)
LIIVT ... Leningrad Institute of Water Transportation Engineers (RU)
LIIZhT ... Leningrad Institute of Railroad Transportation Engineers Imeni Academician V. N. Obraztsov (RU)
LIK ... Artificial Climate Laboratory (RU)
LIK ... Leman Industries Kaduna Ltd. (MAR)
LIK ... Lesno Industrijski Kombinat [*Industrial Combine in Wood Products*] [*Sostanj*] (YU)
LIK ... Switchboard Final Selector [*Telephony*] (RU)
LIK ... Zadruga Likovnih Umjetnika [*Representational Artists' Cooperative*] [*Sarajevo*] (YU)
LIKAT-IS ... Turkiye Liman ve Kara Tahmil-Tahliye Iscileri Sendikasi [*Turkish Longshoremen's Union*] (TU)
LIKb ... Large Exchange Final Selector [*Telephony*] (RU)
LIKh ... Leningrad Institute for Managerial Personnel (RU)
LIKhF ... Leningrad Institute of Chemical Physics (RU)
LIKhMP ... Leningrad Institute of the Refrigeration and Dairy Industries (RU)
LIKhT ... Leningrad Scientific Research Institute of Surgical Tuberculosis and Bone and Joint Diseases (RU)
LIKI ... Leningrad Institute of Motion-Picture Engineers (RU)
LIKP ... Leningrad Institute of the Confectionery Industry (RU)
likpunkt ... Center for the Elimination of Illiteracy (RU)
LIKUD ... Political Bloc [*Israeli*] (ME)
LIKUM ... Zadruga Likovnih Umjetnika Hrvatske [*Representational Artists' Cooperative of Croatia*] (YU)
Likvidkom ... Liquidation Commission (RU)
LILA ... Ligue Internationale de la Librairie Ancienne [*International League of Antiquarian Booksellers - ILAB*] (EA)
LILI ... Leningrad Institute of Historical Linguistics (RU)
lim ... Estuary, Firth [*Topography*] (RU)
LIM ... Final Trunk Selector (RU)
LIM ... Leningrad Institute of Metals (RU)
LIM ... Liberia Inland Mission (MAR)
lim ... Limes [*Limit*] [*Latin*]
LIM ... Livingstone Inland Mission (MAR)
LIM ... Livingstone Interior Mission (MAR)
LIM ... Materials-Testing Laboratory (RU)
LIMAN-SEN ... Kibris Turk Liman ve Tasit Iscileri Sendikasi [*Turkish Cypriot Harbor Workers and Stevedores' Union*] (GC)
LIMBRAVOD ... Limarsko-Bravarska i Vodoinstalaterska Radionica [*Tinsmiths, Locksmiths, and Plumbers Shop*] [*Titograd*] (YU)
LIMIG ... Ligue Luxembourgeoise des Mutiles et Invalides de Guerre (1940-1945) [*Luxembourg League of WWII Cripples and Invalids*] (WER)
LIMSKh ... Leningrad Institute of Agricultural Mechanization (RU)
LIMSZ ... Leningrad Institute for the Mechanization of Socialist Agriculture (RU)
LIN ... Institute for Forest Study (of the Academy of Sciences, USSR) (RU)
lin ... Linea [*Line*] [*Spanish*]
LINA ... Liberian National News Agency (AF)
LINACO ... Lignes Nationales Aeriennes Congolaises (MAR)
LINA-CONGO ... Lignes Nationales Aeriennes Congolaises (MAR)
LINBOV ... Leningrad Institute for Pest and Disease Control in Agriculture (RU)
lingv ... Linguistics (RU)
linksdr ... Linksdrehend [*Counterclockwise*] [*German*]
lin metur ... Linear Meter (BU)
LINOA ... Librairie Nouvelle de l'Ouest Africain (MAR)
LINOCO ... Societe Nationale des Petroles Libyens [*Libyan National Oil Corporation*] (MAR)
LINSU ... Liberian National Students Union (MAR)
LINW ... Lekarski Instytut Naukowo-Wydawniczy [*Medical Scientific Publishing Institute*] (POL)
LIO ... Laboratorio de Investigaciones Oncologicas [*Oncological Research Laboratory*] [*Cuban*] (LA)
LIO ... Laboratory for Artificial Insemination of Animals (RU)
LIO ... Lesno Industrijski Obrat [*Industrial Plant for Wood Products*] (YU)
LIOK ... Ludowy Instytut Oswiaty i Kultury [*People's Institute for Education and Culture*] (POL)
LIOOT ... Leningrad Scientific Research Institute of Work Organization and Safety (RU)
LIOT ... All-Union Scientific Research Institute of Work Safety of the VTsSPS [*Leningrad*] (RU)
LIP ... Liga Iberista Portuguesa [*Portuguese Iberian League*] (WER)
LIPA ... L'Industrie de Peche en Afrique [*African Fishing Industry*] [*Congolese*] (AF)
LIPAD ... Ligue Patriotique pour le Developpement [*Patriotic League for Development*] [*Upper Voltan*] (AF)
LIPETCO ... Compagnie Petroliere Libyenne (MAR)
LIPI ... Lembaga Ilmu Pengetahuan Indonesia [*Indonesian Council of the Sciences*] (IN)
LIPK ... Leningrad Scientific Research Institute of Blood Transfusion (RU)

LIPKKh........ Leningrad Institute for Improving the Qualifications of Managerial Personnel (RU)
LIPKRI......... Leningrad Institute for Improving the Qualifications of Workers in the Arts (RU)
LIPOS.......... Livnica i Tvornica Poljoprivrednih Sprava [*Foundry and Factory of Agricultural Tools*] [*Tuzla*] (YU)
LIPTOL........ Lignitorykheia Ptolemaidos [*Ptolemais Lignite Mines*] [*Greek*] (GC)
LIPZ............ Leningrad Scientific Research Institute of Occupational Diseases (RU)
liq............... Liquidation [*Liquidation, Settlement*] [*French*]
liq pr........... Liquidation Prochaine [*French*]
LIRCI........... Liga Internacional de Reconstruccion de la IV Internacional [*International Reconstruction League of the Fourth International*] [*Spanish*] (WER)
LIRG........... Leningrad Institute of Radiation Hygiene (RU)
LIRI............ Leather Industries Research Institute (MAR)
lirich........... Lyrical (RU)
LIS-............ Laboratory Salt-Content Indicator (RU)
LIS.............. Leningrad Scientific Research Institute of Structures and Building Materials (RU)
LIS.............. Liberian Information Service (AF)
lis............... Lisays [*Finnish*]
lis............... Lisensiaatti [*Finnish*]
LIS.............. Test Flight Station (RU)
LISCo.......... Liberian Iron and Steel Corporation (AF)
Lise-Der...... Lycee (High School) Students' Organization (TU)
LISI............. Leningrad Construction Engineering Institute (RU)
Lisp............ Special Final Selector [*Telephony*] (RU)
LISS........... Leningrad Institute of Soviet Construction Imeni M. I. Kalinin (RU)
LIST........... Leningrad Institute of Soviet Trade Imeni F. Engels (RU)
lit............... Foundry [*Topography*] (RU)
LIT............. Leningrad Industrial Technicum (RU)
lit............... Liter [*Liter*] (HU)
lit............... Literary, Literature (RU)
Lit.............. Literatur [*Literature*] (EG)
lit............... Literature, Literary (BU)
lit............... Lithographic, Lithography (RU)
lit............... Lithuanian (RU)
LIT............. Lithuanian Railroad (RU)
lit............... Olasz Lira [*Italian Lira*] (HU)
LITBANG..... Penelitian dan Pengembangan [*Research and Development*] (IN)
liter............ Literature, Literary (BU)
Litf............. Literaturen Front [*Literary Front*] [*A newspaper*] (BU)
litfak........... Division of Literature (Division of Russian Language and Literature) (RU)
Litfront........ Literaturen Front [*Literary Front*] [*A newspaper*] (BU)
LITIN.......... Leningrad Scientific Research Institute for the Study and Organization of Work for Disabled Persons (RU)
Litinstitut.... Moscow Literary Institute Imeni A. M. Gor'kiy (RU)
Litizdat........ State Publishing House of Belles Lettres (RU)
LITKhUDGIZ... State Publishing House of Belles Lettres (RU)
lit-khudozh... Belletristic (RU)
Litkoopinsoyuz... Republic Union of Disabled Persons' Cooperatives of the Lithuanian SSR (RU)
Litkruzhok... Literary Circle (BU)
LITM........... Leningrad Institute of Precision Mechanics (RU)
LITMiO........ Leningrad Institute of Precision Mechanics and Optics (RU)
LITMO........ Leningrad Institute of Precision Mechanics and Optics (RU)
LitNIIGiM.... Lithuanian Scientific Research Institute of Hydraulic Engineering and Reclamation (RU)
LITO........... Literary Publishing Division of Narkompros (RU)
litogr.......... Lithographed (RU)
litogr.......... Lithography, Lithographed, Lithographic (BU)
litogr.......... Litografia [*Lithography*] [*Polish*]
Litogr izd.... Lithographic Publication (BU)
LITOMETAL... Litografia en Metal SA [*Bogota*] (COL)
LITOPAN..... Litografia Panamericana Ltda. [*Bogota*] (COL)
LITOTAPAS... Fabrica Tapas Litografiadas Continental Ltda. [*Bogota*] (COL)
Litovenergo... Lithuanian Regional Administration of Power System Management (RU)
Litovtorsyr'ye... Lithuanian Republic Administration for the Procurement and Processing of Secondary Raw Materials (RU)
Litpotrebsoyuz... Lithuanian Republic Union of Consumers' Societies (RU)
Litpromsovet... Council of Producers' Cooperatives of the Lithuanian SSR (RU)
Lit-ra.......... Literature (BU)
Litrybvod.... Lithuanian Administration of Fish Conservation and Fish Culture (RU)
Litsel'energo... Lithuanian Republic Office for the Operation of Electric Power Plants (RU)
LitSSR......... Lithuanian Soviet Socialist Republic (RU)
LITT........... Leningrad Industrial Peat Technicum (RU)
LIU............. Combination Connector [*Telephony*] (RU)
LIU............. Light Wellpoint Apparatus (RU)
LIUU........... Leningrad City Institute for the Advanced Training of Teachers (RU)
liv.............. Livre [*Book (Usually a division of a volume)*] [*French*]
LIVD........... Leningrad Scientific Research Institute of High Pressures (RU)
LIVOCI........ L'Ivoirienne de Confection Industrielle (MAR)
LIVOTEX..... L'Ivoirienne de Textiles (MAR)
LIVOTI........ Leningrad Institute of Instrument Making of the All-Union Precision Industry Association (RU)
LIVT........... Leningrad Institute of Water Transportation (RU)
LIW............ Landtechnische Instandsetzungswerke [*Agricultural Equipment Maintenance Works*] (EG)
Liyepaysel'mash... Liepaja Agricultural Machinery Plant (RU)
LIZ............. Leningrad Tool Plant (RU)
liz.............. Lysine (RU)
LIZhT......... Leningrad Institute of Railroad Transportation (RU)
LIZhVYa...... Leningrad Institute of Living Oriental Languages (RU)
lJ.............. Laufenden Jahres [*Of the Current Year*] [*German*]
Lj.............. Ljubljana [*Ljubljana*] (YU)
LjD............ Ljubljanski Dnevnik [*Ljubljana Daily*] [*A newspaper*] (YU)
LjJA.......... Ljetopis Jugoslavenske Akademije Znanosti i Umjetnosti [*Annals of the Yugoslav Academy of Sciences and Arts*] [*Zagreb*] (YU)
LJM............ Liga da Juventude de Mocambique [*Mozambique Youth League*] (AF)
LjT............. Ljubljanska Tiskarna [*Ljubljana Printing House*] (YU)
LjV............. Ljevaonica Zeljeza Varazdin [*Varazdin Iron Foundry*] (YU)
LK.............. Battleship (RU)
LK.............. Commission for Liquidations (BU)
LK.............. False Combination (RU)
L/K............ Icebreaker (RU)
LK.............. Laaketieteen Kandidaatti [*Finnish*]
LK.............. Laiko Komma [*Populist Party*] [*Greek*] (PPE)
LK.............. Landeklappe [*Landing Flap (Airplane)*] (EG)
L/K............ Las/Koperal [*Lance Corporal*] (ML)
LK.............. Lebih Kurang [*More or Less, Approximately*] (IN)
lk............... Lehky Kulomet [*Light Machine Gun*] (CZ)
LK.............. Lekarska Komora [*Medical Association*] (CZ)
LK.............. Lekarske Knihkupectvi a Nakladatelstvi [*Sales and Publishing Firm for Medical Literature*] (CZ)
LK.............. Lidova Knihovna [*People's Library*] (CZ)
LK.............. Liga Kobiet [*League of Women*] (POL)
LK.............. Liman Kontrolu [*Harbor Control*] [*Turkish Cypriot*] (GC)
LK.............. Line Contactor (RU)
LK.............. Line-Switchboard (RU)
LK.............. Loziskovy Kov [*Bearing Metal*] (CZ)
lk............... Luokka [*Finnish*]
lk............... Lux [*Measures*] (RU)
LK.............. Lyzarsky Klub [*Ski Club*] (CZ)
LK.............. Medical Commission (BU)
LK.............. Pilot Lamp, Supervisory Lamp (RU)
LK.............. Red Light (RU)
LK.............. Sri Lanka [*Two-letter standard code*] (CNC)
LKA............ Landeskriminalamt [*State Criminal Police Office*] [*West German*] (WEN)
LKA............ Sri Lanka [*Three-letter standard code*] (CNC)
LKAB.......... Loussavaara-Kiirunavaara Aktiebolag [*The LKAB Mining Co.*] [*Swedish*] (WEN)
LKAO.......... Linear Combination of Atomic Orbitals (RU)
LKB............ Leistungs- und Kostenermittlungsbogen [*Form for Determination of Work Output and Costs*] (EG)
lk bk........... Scout Car (BU)
LKBN Antara... Lembaga Kantor Berita Nasional Antara [*Antara National News Agency*] (IN)
lkbs............ Cable-Laying Battalion (RU)
LKC............ Lekarska Komora pro Zemi Ceskou [*Medical Association of Bohemia*] (CZ)
LKD............ Light Cableway (RU)
LKDP.......... Lietuviu Krikscioniu Demokratu Partija [*Lithuanian Christian Democratic Party*] (PPE)
LKF............ Leningrad Cartographic Factory (RU)
LKFJN......... Lodzki Komitet Frontu Jednosci Narodu [*Lodz Committee of the National Unity Front*] [*Polish*]
LKG............ Leipziger Kommissions- und Grossbuchhandel [*Leipzig Commission and Wholesale Book Trade*] (EG)
lkh............. Logóu Kharin [*For Example*] (GC1)
LKhTI......... Leningrad Institute of Chemical Technology (RU)
LKhTIMP..... Leningrad Chemical Technology Institute of the Dairy Industry (RU)
LKI............. Leningrad Shipbuilding Institute (RU)
LKIP........... Laboratory of Control and Measuring Instruments (RU)
LKK............ Medical Consultation Commission (BU)
LKK............ Medical Control Commission (RU)
lk kch.......... Light Machine-Gun (BU)
LKKFiT....... Lodzki Komitet Kultury Fizycznej i Turystyki [*Lodz Committee for Physical Culture and Tourism*] [*Polish*]
LKM............ Lazna Komanda Mesta [*Fake Command Post*] (YU)
lkm............. Lekki Karabin Maszynowy [*Light Machine Gun*] [*Polish*]
LKM............ Lenin Kohaszati Muvek, Diosgyor [*Lenin Metallurgical Works of Diosgyor*] (HU)
lk mn.......... Light Mortar (BU)
LKO............ Cables-Lines Department (BU)
LKP............ Lembaga Kemajuan Perusahaan [*Industrial Promotion Board*] (ML)

LKP .... Liberaalinen Kansanpuolue [*Liberal People's Party*] [*Finnish*] (PPE)
LKP .... Lietuvos Komunisty Partija [*Communist Party of Lithuania*] (PPE)
LKP .... Light Cable Ferry, Light Rope Ferry (RU)
LKR .... Battle Cruiser (RU)
Lkr .... Landkreis [*Rural Kreis*] (EG)
LKR .... Lidove Kurzy Rustiny [*People's Russian Language Courses*] (CZ)
LKRD .... Laboratory of Document Preservation and Restoration (of the Academy of Sciences, USSR) (RU)
lkrs .... Cable-Laying Company (RU)
LKS .... Leningrad Cable Network (RU)
LKS .... Liberation Kanake Socialiste [*Socialist Kanak Liberation*] [*New Caledonian*] (PD)
LKS .... Lodzki Klub Sportowy [*Lodz Sports Club*] (POL)
LKS .... Ludowy Klub Sportowy [*Popular Sports and Athletics Club*] [*Polish*]
lk-sek .... Lux-Second (RU)
LKSM .... Lenin Young Communist League (RU)
LKSMA .... Lenin Young Communist League of Armenia (RU)
LKSMB .... Lenin Young Communist League of Belorussia (RU)
LKSMB .... Leninski Komunistychny Saiuz Moladzi Belarusi
LKSMD .... Lenin Young Communist League of Dagestan (RU)
LKSME .... Lenin Young Communist League of Estonia (RU)
LKSMG .... Lenin Young Communist League of Georgia (RU)
LKSMK .... Lenin Young Communist League of Kazakhstan (RU)
LKSML .... Lenin Young Communist League of Latvia (RU)
LKSML .... Lenin Young Communist League of Lithuania (RU)
LKSMM .... Lenin Young Communist League of Moldavia (RU)
LKSMT .... Lenin Young Communist League of Turkmenistan (RU)
LKSMU .... Lenin Young Communist League of the Ukraine (RU)
LKSMUz ...... Lenin Young Communist League of Uzbekistan (RU)
LKT .... Laaketieteen (Ja Kirurgian) Tohtori [*Finnish*]
LKT .... Leningrad Municipal Services Technicum (RU)
LKTP .... Lembaga Kemajuan Tanah Persekutuan [*Federal Land Development Authority - FLDA*] (ML)
l k-tsa .... Light Machine-Gun (BU)
LKU .... Lesnicke Kulturne Ustredie [*Forest Cultural Center*] (CZ)
LKVVA .... Leningrad "Red Banner" Air Force Academy (RU)
LKVVIA .... Leningrad "Red Banner" Air Force Engineering Academy (RU)
LKW .... Lastkraftwagen [*Truck*] (EG)
LKZ .... Leningrad Carburetor Plant (RU)
LKZ .... Leningrad Kirov Plant (RU)
ll .... Fluorescent Lamp (RU)
LL .... Laaketieteen Lisensiaatti [*Finnish*]
ll .... Laatsleden [*Last*] [*Dutch*] (GPO)
Ll .... Lapin Laani [*Finnish*]
ll .... Leicht Loeslich [*Easily Soluble*] [*German*]
L es L .... Licencie es Lettres [*Licentiate in Letters*] [*French*]
LL .... Liga para la Liberacion [*Liberation League*] [*Salvadoran*] (LA)
LL .... Liga Lotnicza [*Aeronautical League*] (POL)
LL .... Liiketyontekijain Liitto [*Retail Shop Clerks Union*] [*Finnish*] (WEN)
ll .... Loco Laudato [*In the Place Cited*] [*Latin*]
ll .... Sheets [*Manuscript*] (BU)
ll .... Sheets, Leaves (RU)
LLA .... Lesotho Liberation Army (PD)
LLAA .... Leurs Altesses [*Their Highnesses*] [*French*]
LLAARR ...... Leurs Altesses Royales [*Their Royal Highnesses*] (CL)
LLB .... Legum Baccalaureus [*Bachelor of Laws*] [*Latin*] (GPO)
LLC .... Lieutenant au Long Cours (MAR)
LLD .... Legum Doctor [*Doctor of Laws*] [*Latin*] (GPO)
LLDP .... Lilongwe Land Development Programme [*or Project*] (MAR)
LL EE .... Leurs Eminences [*Their Eminences*] [*French*] (MTD)
LLEE .... Leurs Excellences [*Their Excellencies*] [*French*] (CL)
LLI .... Leningrad Forest Institute (RU)
LLM .... Legum Magister [*Master of Laws*] [*Latin*] (GPO)
LLM .... Librairie de Madagascar "Quartier Latin" (MAR)
LLMM .... Leurs Majestes [*Their Majesties*] [*French*] (CL)
LLMM .... Loro Maesta [*Their Majesties*] [*Italian*] (GPO)
LLN .... Lembaga Letrik Negara [*National Electricity Board*] (ML)
LLO .... Laerlings Landsorganisation [*National Federation of Apprentices*] [*Danish*] (WEN)
LLOKh .... Leningrad Laboratory of General Chemistry (RU)
LLPP (Ministero dei) ... Ministero dei Lavori Pubblici [*Ministry of Public Works*] [*Italian*] (WER)
LLTD .... Leningrad Heat Engine Laboratory (RU)
LM .... Laboratory Agitator (RU)
Lm .... Laem [*Cape, Point*] [*Thai*] (NAU)
LM .... Leipziger Messeamt [*Leipzig Fair Office*] (EG)
LM .... Leitender Maschinist [*Chief Machinist*] [*Navy*] (EG)
LM .... Lesotho Maloti (MAR)
LM .... Letnan Muda [*Ensign*] (IN)
LM .... Leucocytes (RU)
LM .... Lidova Milice [*People's Militia*] (CZ)
LM .... Liga Morska [*Maritime League*] (POL)
lm .... Linear Meter (BU)
LM .... Ljudska Mladina [*People's Youth*] (YU)
lm .... Lumen [*Lumen*] [*Polish*]
lm .... Lumen (RU)
LM .... Slide Balance, Slide-Wire Bridge (RU)
LMA .... Livingstone Motors Assemblers (MAR)
LMB .... Landmaschinenbau (VEB) [*Farm Machine Construction Plant (VEB)*] (EG)
LMB .... Livestock and Meat Board (MAR)
LMC .... Laborator pro Mereni Casu [*Laboratory of Horology (of the Czechoslovak Academy of Sciences)*] (CZ)
LMC .... Lancia Motor Club (EA)
LMC .... Liberian Mining Company (AF)
lm-ch .... Lumen-Hour (RU)
LMD .... Liga Municipal Dominicana [*Dominican Municipal League*] [*Dominican Republic*] (LA1)
LME .... London Metal Exchange (MAR)
LMG .... Galitskiy Flying Bomb (RU)
LMGKhRM ... Laboratory of Mineralogy and Geochemistry of Rare Metals (of the Academy of Sciences, USSR) (RU)
lmh .... Lumenogodzina [*Lumen-Hour*] [*Polish*]
LMHI .... Liga Medicorum Homoeopathica Internationalis [*International Homoeopathic Medical League*] (EA)
LMI .... Lebensmittelindustrie [*Foodstuffs Industry*] (EG)
LMI .... Leningrad Institute of Mechanical Engineering (RU)
LMI .... Leningrad Mechanical Institute (RU)
LMI .... Leningrad Medical Institute (RU)
LMI .... Liga Monarquica Independente (MAR)
LMIM .... Labor Muszeripari Muvek [*Labor Instrument Industry Works*] (HU)
LMJ .... Ljudska Mladina Jugoslavije [*People's Youth of Yugoslavia*] (YU)
LMMC .... Livestock and Meat Marketing Corporation [*Sudanese*] (MAR)
LMMU .... Latin Mediterranean Medical Union [*See also UMML*] (EA)
lmn .... Liczba Mnoga [*Plural*] (POL)
LMN .... Small Pneumatic Boat (RU)
LMO .... Meadow Reclamation Detachment (RU)
LMP .... Lesotho Mounted Police (MAR)
LMP .... Light Bridge Train (RU)
LMR .... Ligne de Moindre Resistance [*Military*] [*French*] (MTD)
LMR .... Ligue Marxiste Revolutionnaire [*Revolutionary Marxist League*] [*Swiss*] (PPW)
LMR- .... River Boat Motor (RU)
LMS .... Laborator Matematickych Stroju [*Mathematical Instrument Laboratory (of the Czechoslovak Academy of Sciences)*] (CZ)
LMS .... Letopis Matice Slovenske [*Annals of Matica Slovenska (Slovenian Cultural Society)*] (YU)
LMS .... Letopis Matice Srpske [*Annals of Matica Srpska (Serbian Cultural Society)*] [*Novi Sad*] (YU)
LMS .... Ljudska Milicija Slovenije [*People's Police of Slovenia*] (YU)
LMS .... Ljudska Mladina Slovenije [*People's Youth of Slovenia*] (YU)
LMS .... London Missionary Society (MAR)
LMS .... Lumber Machinery Station (RU)
LMS .... Meadow Reclamation Station (RU)
lm-sek .... Lumen-Second (RU)
LMU .... Leningrad Nautical School (RU)
LMU .... Letecke Mimoradne Udalosti [*Air Accidents*] (CZ)
LMU .... Letnan Muda Udara [*Air Sublieutenant (Warrant officer)*] (IN)
LMY .... League of Malawi Youth (AF)
lmz .... Foundry and Machine Plant (RU)
LMZ .... Leningrad Metal Plant (RU)
LMZ .... Leningradskii Metallicheskii Zavod
LN .... Landwirtschaftliche Nutzflaeche [*Agricultural Area*] (EG)
LN .... Lembaran Negara [*State Gazette*] (IN)
Ln .... Limin [*Harbor*] [*Greek*] (NAU)
ln .... Line [*Measures*] (RU)
LN .... Lyon [*On cartridge bags*] [*Military*] [*French*] (MTD)
LN .... Neon Lamp (RU)
LN .... Nickel Brass (RU)
LN .... Sodium Laurate (RU)
LNA .... Laikon Nosokomeion Athinon [*Athens Public Hospital*] (GC)
LNA .... Liberation Press Agency [*of the NFLSV*] [*Use LPA*] [*South Vietnamese*] (CL)
LNA .... Liberian National Airlines (AF)
LNA .... Liberian News Agency (MAR)
LNA .... Libyan News Agency (AF)
LNA .... Liga Nacional Africana (MAR)
LNBS .... Lesotho National Broadcasting Service (MAR)
LNC .... Lega Nazionale delle Cooperative e Mutue [*National League of Cooperatives*] [*Italian*] (WER)
LNC .... Local Native Councils (MAR)
L-NCP .... Liberal-National Country Party [*Australian*] (PPW)
LND .... Loterie Nationale du Benin [*National Lottery of Benin*] (AF)
LNDC .... Lake Nasser Development Centre (MAR)
LNDC .... Lesotho National Development Corporation (MAR)
LNERV .... Laboratoire National de l'Elevage et de Recherches Veterinaires (MAR)
LNF .... Landwirtschaftliche Nutzflaeche [*Agricultural Area*] (EG)
LNF .... Latvian National Foundation (EA)
LNG .... Liberian National Guard (MAR)
LNGRI .... Leningrad Scientific Research Institute of Petroleum Geological Exploration (RU)
LNH .... Lisovny Novych Hmot [*Pressing Plants for New Materials*] (CZ)

LNII AKKh... Leningrad Scientific Research Institute of the Academy of Municipal Services Imeni K. D. Pamfilov (RU)
LNIIFK......... Leningrad Scientific Research Institute of Physical Culture (RU)
LNIIKKh...... Leningrad Scientific Research Institute of Municipal Services (RU)
LNIIP........... Leningrad Scientific Research Institute of Prosthetics (RU)
LNIKhO....... Leningrad Chemical Scientific Research Society (RU)
LNISI.......... Leningrad Shale Scientific Research Institute (RU)
LNIVI.......... Leningrad Veterinary Scientific Research Institute (RU)
LNIYa.......... Leningrad Scientific Research Institute of Linguistics (RU)
LNJP........... Ligue Nationale de la Jeunesse Patriotique [*National League of Patriotic Youth*] [*Beninese*] (AF)
LNK............ Lengyel Nepkoztarsasag [*Polish People's Republic*] (HU)
LNKhMGU... Laboratory of Inorganic Chemistry of the Moscow State University Imeni M. V. Lomonosov (RU)
LNOC.......... Libyan National Oil Corporation (MAR)
LNOJ........... League of Nations Official Journal [*A publication*] (MAR)
l'novod........ Flax-Growing Sovkhoz [*Topography*] (RU)
LNP............. Dummy Observation Point (RU)
Lnpl............ Letecky Nahradni Pluk [*Air Force Replacement Regiment*] (CZ)
LNR............. Lagos Notes and Records [*A publication*] (MAR)
LNR............. Lao National Radio (CL)
LNS............. Line of Least Resistance (RU)
LNT............. Loterie Nationale Togolaise (MAR)
LNTS........... League of Nations Treaty Series [*A publication*] (MAR)
LNUS........... Liberian National Union of Students (AF)
L'nyan......... Linen Goods Factory [*Topography*] (RU)
LNYO........... Liberian National Youth Organization (MAR)
LO................ Laborator Optiky [*Optical Laboratory (of the Czechoslovak Academy of Sciences)*] (CZ)
LO................ Landsorganisasjonen i Norge [*Norwegian Federation of Trade Unions*] (WEN)
LO................ Landsorganisation de Samvirkende Fagforbund [*Danish Federation of Trade Unions*] (WEN)
LO................ Landsorganisationen [*Swedish Federation of Trade Unions*] (WEN)
lo................. Lasd Ott [*See*] (HU)
LO................ Leningrad Branch (RU)
LO................ Leningrad Oblast (RU)
LO................ Letecky Okrah [*Air Force District*] (CZ)
l/o............... Leur Ordre [*French*]
LO................ Linija Otkrivanja [*Detection Line*] [*RADAR*] [*Air Force*] (YU)
LO................ Ljudski Odbor [*People's Committee*] (YU)
LO................ Lucha Obrera [*Workers' Struggle*] [*Spanish*] (WER)
LO................ Lutte Ouvriere [*Workers' Struggle*] [*French*] (PPW)
LOA............. Local Education Authority (MAR)
LOAC........... Ligne Ouvriere d'Action Catholique [*Workers' League for Catholic Action*] [*Mauritian*] (AF)
LOAOR........ Leningrad Oblast Archives of the October Revolution (RU)
LOAS........... Liga Oriental Antisemita [*Uruguayan Antisemitic League*] (LA)
LOAU........... Leningrad Oblast Archives Administration (RU)
LOB............. Leningrad Society of Bibliophiles (RU)
LOBK........... Leningrad Oblast Office of Regional Study (RU)
loc.............. Localita [*Italian*] (CED)
LOCAUTO... Societe Senegalaise de Location d'Automobiles (MAR)
loc cit......... Loco Citato [*In the Place Cited*] [*Latin*] (GPO)
LOCMAT..... Entreprise de Location de Materiel et de Terrassement (MAR)
Locre........... Locature [*Farmhouse*] [*Military map abbreviation*] [*World War I*] [*French*] (MTD)
LOEL........... Laiki Oinoviomikhaniki Etaireia Lemesou Ltd. [*Popular Distillers Company of Limassol*] [*Cypriot*] (GC)
LOFEUK...... Leningrad Oblast Finance and Economics Training Center (RU)
LOG............. Laboratory of Distant Hybridization (RU)
log.............. Logarytm [*Logarithm*] [*Polish*]
log.............. Logiikka [*Logic*] [*Finnish*]
LOG............. Logistik [*Logistics*] (IN)
LOGAIS....... Leningrad Branch of the State Academy for the Study of Art (RU)
LOGIDEP..... Leningrad Branch of the Gidroenergoproyekt (RU)
LOGIPROAVTOTRANS... Leningrad Branch of the Giproavtotrans (RU)
LOGTsKP.... Leningrad Branch of the State Central Book Chamber (RU)
LOI.............. Leningrad Institute of Optics (RU)
LOI.............. Leningrad Oblast Executive Committee (RU)
LOID............ Leningrad Branch of the Institute of Rainmaking (RU)
LOII............. Leningrad Branch of the Institute of History (of the Academy of Sciences, USSR) (RU)
LOIIMK........ Leningrad Branch of the Institute of the History of Material Culture (RU)
LOII RO....... Leningrad Branch of the Institute of History of the Academy of Sciences, USSR. Manuscript Division (RU)
LOIKFUN..... Leningrad Society of Researchers in the Culture of the Finno-Ugrian Peoples (RU)
LOINA......... Leningradsk Otdeleni Instituta Narodov Azii (MAR)
LOIP........... Leningrad Society of Naturalists (RU)
LOIPKKNO... Leningrad Branch of the Institute for Improving the Qualifications of Public Education Personnel (RU)
LOIZ............ Leningrad Oblast Publishing House (RU)
Loj.............. Lojman [*Housing, Quarters*] (TU)
LOK............. Leningrad Oblast Committee (RU)
LOK............. Leningrad Oblast Office (RU)
LOK............. Leningrad Society of Collectors (RU)
LOK............. Leveltarak Orszagos Kozpontja [*National Archives Center*] (HU)
LOK............. Liga Obrony Kraju [*National Defense League*] [*Formerly, LPZ*] (POL)
Lok.............. Locomotive (EG)
LOK............. Lokhos Oreinon Katadromon [*Mountain Raider Company*] [*Greek*] (GC)
lok............... Loxodromic (RU)
LOKA.......... Leningrad Branch of the Communist Academy (RU)
LOKB........... Leningrad City and Oblast Municipal Bank (RU)
LOKBI......... Leningrad Branch of the Scientific Research Institute of Criticism and Bibliography (RU)
Lokf............ Lokomotivfuehrer [*Locomotive Engineer*] (EG)
Lokh............ Lokomotivheizer [*Locomotive Fireman*] (EG)
LOKhO........ Leningrad Society of Orthopedic Surgeons (RU)
LOKK.......... League of Red Cross Societies (RU)
lokkm.......... Lokomotivni Kilometr [*Locomotive Kilometer*] (CZ)
Lokltkm...... Lokomotivleistungs-Tonnenkilometer [*Locomotive Performance Ton-Kilometers (Unit of measurement for locomotive performance)*] (EG)
Lokomotivproyekt... Locomotive Design Office (RU)
Lok P........... Loxodromic Bearing (RU)
LOKSPEDIT... Lokalno Transportno Speditersko Preduzece [*Local Transport and Shipping Establishment*] (YU)
LOKU........... Leningrad Oblast Communist University (RU)
Lokum......... Dinamit Lokumu [*Small Plastic Bomb or Explosive, Dynamite Bomb*] [*Turkish Cypriot*] (GC)
LOKUNMZ.. Leningrad Branch of the Communist University of National Minorities of the West (RU)
LOKZ........... Leningrad Oblast Collegium of Defense Lawyers (RU)
LOLGU........ Leningrad "Order of Lenin" State University Imeni A. A. Zhdanov (RU)
LOLLTA....... Leningrad "Order of Lenin" Forestry Engineering Academy Imeni S. M. Kirov (RU)
LOM............ Liga Obrera Marxista [*Marxist Labor League*] [*Mexican*] (LA1)
LOMI........... Leningrad Branch of the Institute of Mathematics Imeni V. A. Steklov (of the Academy of Sciences, USSR) (RU)
LOMO.......... Ljudski Odbor Mestne Obcine [*Municipal People's Committee*] (YU)
LOMZ.......... Leningrad Optical Instrument Plant (RU)
LON............ Special Assignment Camp [*Corrective labor camps*] (RU)
LONA.......... Local News Agency (MAR)
LONACI....... Loterie Nationale de Cote-d'Ivoire (MAR)
LONASE...... Loterie Nationale Senegalaise (MAR)
LONIIS........ Leningrad Branch of the Scientific Research Institute of Communications (RU)
LONIIV........ Leningrad Branch of the NIIV (RU)
LONITI......... Leningrad Branch of the Textile Scientific Research Institute (RU)
LONITO....... Leningrad Branch of the All-Union Scientific, Engineering, and Technical Society (RU)
LONITOE..... Leningrad Branch of the All-Union Scientific, Engineering, and Technical Society of Power Engineers (RU)
LONITOL..... Leningrad Branch of the All-Union Scientific, Engineering, and Technical Society of Foundry Workers (RU)
LONITOMASh... Leningrad Branch of the All-Union Scientific, Engineering, and Technical Society of Machine Builders (RU)
LONITOS..... Leningrad Branch of the All-Union Scientific, Engineering, and Technical Society of Welders (RU)
LONITOVT... Leningrad Branch of the All-Union Scientific, Engineering, and Technical Society of Water Transportation (RU)
LONPI.......... Leningrad Institute of Theoretical and Applied Ophthalmology (RU)
LONRHO..... London and Rhodesian Mining and Land Co. (MAR)
LONTO........ Leningrad Oblast Administration of the Scientific and Technical Society (RU)
LONTOVT... Leningrad Branch of the Scientific and Technical Society of Water Transportation (RU)
LOOGAPU... Leningrad Oblast Department of the Main Pharmaceutical Administration (RU)
LOOKKh...... Leningrad Oblast Department of Municipal Services (RU)
LOOMP....... Leningrad Association of Experimental Machine Establishments (RU)
LOONO........ Leningrad Oblast Department of Public Education (RU)
LOONTI....... Leningrad Branch of the United Scientific and Technical Publishing House (RU)
LOOSVOD... Leningrad Oblast Society for Assisting the Development of Water Transportation and Safeguarding Human Life on Waterways (RU)
LOOVOG..... Leningrad Oblast Branch of the All-Union Society of Deaf-Mutes (RU)
LOP............. Dummy Firing Position (RU)
LOP............. Liga Ochrony Przyrody [*League for the Preservation of Nature*] [*Polish*]
LOP............. Lodzki Okreg Przemyslowy [*Lodz Industrial Region*] [*Polish*]
LOPI........... Leningrad Oblast Pedagogical Institute (RU)
LOPOZRz.... Lodzkie Okregowe Przedsiebiorstwo Obrotu Zwierzetami Rzeznymi [*Lodz District Establishment for Marketing Animals for Slaughter*] (POL)
LOPP........... Liga Obrony Powietrznej Panstwa [*State Air Defense League*] (POL)

LOPP .... Liga Obrony Przeciwlotniczej i Przeciwgazowej [*Polish*]
LOPPE .... Ley Federal de Organizaciones Politicas y Procesos Electorales [*Federal Law on Political Organizations and Electoral Processes*] [*Mexican*] (LA1)
LOPU .... Leningrad District Assay Administration (RU)
loq .... Loquitur [*He (or She) Speaks*] [*Latin*] (GPO)
LOR .... Laboratory of Finishing Operations (RU)
LOR .... Otalaryngology, Otorhinolaryngology (RU)
LOR .... Otorhinolaryngology (CL)
LOS .... Forest Experimental Station (RU)
LOS .... Laboratory of Organic Synthesis (of the Academy of Sciences, USSR) (RU)
LOS .... Leningrad Oblast Soviet (RU)
LOS .... Letecke Obranne Stredisko [*Air Defense Center*] (CZ)
LOSA .... Leningrad Branch of the Union of Architects of the USSR (RU)
loshch .... Ravine, Hollow, Depression [*Topography*] (RU)
LOSKh .... Leningrad Branch of the Union of Artists of the RSFSR (RU)
losl .... Loeslich [*or Loeslichkeit*] [*Soluble or Solubility*] [*German*]
LOSNITO ..... Leningrad Oblast Council of Scientific, Engineering, and Technical Societies (RU)
LOSNTO ...... Leningrad Oblast Council of Scientific, Engineering, and Technical Societies (RU)
LOSO .... Leningrad Oblast Construction Association (RU)
LOSP .... Leningrad Branch of the Union of Writers of the USSR (RU)
LOSPO .... Leningrad Oblast Union of Consumers' Societies (RU)
LOSPS .... Leningrad Oblast Council of Trade Unions (RU)
LOSSKh ...... Leningrad Oblast Union of Soviet Artists (RU)
Losungsm ... Loesungsmittel [*Solvent*] [*German*]
losz .... Loszer [*Ammunition*] (HU)
LOT .... Dummy Emplacement (RU)
LOT .... Polish Airlines
LOTEYCA ... Lote y Casa Constructora [*Medellin*] (COL)
LOTI .... Leningrad Oblast Scientific Research Institute of Heat Engineering (RU)
lotn .... Lotnictwo [*Aircraft*] [*Polish*]
lotn .... Lotniczy [*Air*] [*Polish*]
LOTsES .... Leningrad Branch of the Central Electrotechnical Council (RU)
LOTsF .... Laboratory for the Processing of Color Films (RU)
LOTsGIA ..... Leningrad Branch of the Central State Historical Archives (RU)
LOTsIA .... Leningrad Branch of the Central Historical Archives (RU)
LOTsIYaP .... Leningrad Branch of the Central Scientific Research Institute of Language and Literature of Peoples of the USSR (RU)
LOTsNIIP .... Leningrad Branch of the Central Scientific Research Institute of Pedagogy (RU)
LOTsT .... Leningrad District Central Printing Office (RU)
LOTU .... Lefkosa Ozel Turk Universitesi [*Nicosia Special (Private) Turkish University*] (GC)
LOUChGIZ ... Leningrad Branch of the Publishing House of Textbooks and Pedagogical Literature (RU)
LOUMP .... Leningrad Oblast Administration of Local Industry (RU)
LOUMS .... Leningrad Oblast Administration of the Ministry of Communications, USSR (RU)
LOUYeGMS ... Leningrad Oblast Administration of United Hydrometeorological Service (RU)
LOV .... Backward-Wave Tube (RU)
lov .... Hunting (BU)
lov .... Lovas [*Mounted, Cavalry*] (HU)
LOVAGO ..... Leningrad Branch of the All-Union Astronomical and Geodetic Society (RU)
LOVEK .... Leningrad Branch of the All-Union Power Engineering Committee (RU)
LOVEO .... Leningrad Branch of the All-Union Electrotechnical Association (RU)
LOVET .... Leningrad Branch of the All-Union Electrotechnical Trust (RU)
LOVIShS ..... Leningrad Joint Military Engineering School of Communications (RU)
LOVIUAA .... Leningrad Branch of the All-Union Institute of Fertilizers, Soil Science, and Agricultural Engineering (RU)
LOVIZh .... Leningrad Branch of the All-Union Scientific Research Institute of Livestock Breeding (RU)
LOVM .... Magnetron-Type Backward-Wave Tube (RU)
LOVNITOE ... Leningrad Branch of the All-Union Scientific, Engineering, and Technical Society of Power Engineers (RU)
LOVNITOL ... Leningrad Branch of the All-Union Scientific, Engineering, and Technical Society of Foundry Workers (RU)
LOVODGEO ... Leningrad Branch of the All-Union Scientific Research Institute of Water Supply, Sewer Systems, Hydraulic Engineering Structures, and Engineering Hydrogeology (RU)
LOVSU .... Leningrad District Military Medical Directorate (RU)
LOVZITO ..... Leningrad Branch of the All-Union Correspondence Institute of Technical Education (RU)
LOWA .... Lokomotiv- und Waggonbau [*Locomotive and Railroad Car Construction Plant*] (EG)
LOYe .... Leningrad Society of Naturalists (RU)
LOYePA ...... Leningrad Branch of the United Party Archives (RU)
LOZKU .... Leningrad Oblast Communist Correspondence University (RU)
LP .... Airfield, Flying Field (RU)
LP- .... Collating and Gathering Machine (RU)
LP .... Forest Belt, Forest Zone (RU)
LP .... Foundry Production (RU)
LP .... Laboratorni Pristroje [*Laboratory Appliances*] (CZ)
LP .... Laboratory Penetrometer (RU)
LP .... Labour Party of South Africa (PPW)
LP .... Laburisticka Partija [*Labor Party*] (YU)
LP .... Laiki Paideia [*Popular Education (Group)*] [*Greek*] (GC)
LP .... Lasy Panstwowe [*State Forests*] (POL)
LP .... Leta Pane [*In the Year of Our Lord*] (CZ)
LP .... Letni Plan [*Year Plan*] [*Usually preceded by a number*] (CZ)
LP .... Liberaalinen Kansanpuolue [*Liberal Party*] [*Finnish*] (WEN)
LP .... Liberal Party [*Canadian*] (PPW)
LP .... Liberation Populaire [*People's Liberation*] [*French*] (WER)
LP .... Liberator Party [*Guyanese*] (PPW)
l p .... Liczba Pojedyncza [*Singular*] (POL)
lp .... Liczba Porzadkowa [*Ordinal number*] (POL)
LP .... Line of Sight (RU)
LP .... Linear Programing (RU)
LP .... Ljudski Pravnik [*People's Lawyer*] [*A periodical*] [*Ljubljana*] (YU)
lp .... Petal (RU)
LP .... Position Line (RU)
LP .... Steam Winch (RU)
LP .... Tree-Planting Machine, Tree Planter (RU)
LP .... Vacuum-Tube Potentiometer (RU)
LP-28 .... Ligas Populares de 28 de Febrero [*February 28 Popular Leagues*] [*Salvadoran*] (PD)
LPA .... Laboratoires Pharmaceutiques Africains (MAR)
LPA .... Liberation Press Agency [*of the NFLSV*] [*South Vietnamese*] (CL)
LPA .... Librairie-Editions du Peuple Africain (MAR)
LPA .... Liga Panstw Arabskich [*The Arab League*] [*Polish*]
LPA .... Local Planning Authority (MAR)
LPAA .... Laka Protivavionska Artiljerija [*Light Antiaircraft Artillery*] (YU)
LPAI .... Ligue Populaire Africaine pour l'Independance [*African People's League for Independence*] [*Djibouti*] (AF)
Lpaz .... Lokomotive mit Gepaeckwagen als Zug [*Locomotive with Baggage Car, Operated as a Train*] (EG)
LPD .... Line of Adjusted Ranges (RU)
LPD .... Line of Range Corrections (RU)
LPDSA .... Libyan Public Development and Stabilization Agency (MAR)
LPE .... Laboratorul de Proiectari Educationale [*Educational Design Laboratory*] (RO)
LPE .... Linear Energy Loss (RU)
LPER .... Lubelskie Przedsiebiorstwo Elektryfikacji Rolnictwa [*Lublin Enterprise for Electrification of Agriculture*] (POL)
LPF .... Lao Patriotic Front [*Use NLHS*] (CL)
LPFEI .... Leningrad Pedagogical Institute of Finance and Economics (RU)
LPG .... Landwirtschaftliche Produktionsgenossenschaft [*Agricultural Producer Cooperative*] (EG)
LPG .... Likid Petrol Gaz [*Liquefied Petroleum Gas, Butane Gas*] (TU)
LPG .... Liquefied Petroleum Gas (MAR)
LPH .... Letecke Pohonne Hmoty [*Aviation Fuels*] (CZ)
LPHM .... Letecke Pohonne Hmoty a Maziva [*Aviation Fuels and Lubricant*] (CZ)
LPI .... Leningrad Polytechnic Institute Imeni M. I. Kalinin (RU)
LPI .... Liberal Party of Italy (RU)
LPI .... L'vov Polytechnic Institute (RU)
LPI .... Societe Librairie Papeterie Ivoirienne (MAR)
LPK .... Laikon Proodevtikon Kinima [*People's Progressive Movement*] [*Greek*] (GC)
LPK .... Lao Pen Kang [*Lao Neutralist (Party)*] (CL)
LPK .... Lekarska Poradni Komise [*Medical Advisory Committee*] (CZ)
LPK .... Lumber Industry Complex (RU)
LPK .... Lumber Producers' Cooperatives (RU)
LPKh .... Lumber Industry Establishment (RU)
LPLA .... Lao People's Liberation Army (CL)
LPM .... Labor Party of Malaya (ML)
LPM .... Librairie Populaire du Mali (MAR)
LPM .... Tape Feed, Tape Mechanism, Tape-Drive Mechanism [*Computers*] (RU)
LPMC .... Liberian Produce Marketing Corporation (AF)
LPMI .... Leningrad Institute of Pediatric Medicine (RU)
LPN .... Lembaga Padi dan Beras Negara [*National Paddy and Rice Institute*] (ML)
LPN .... Ligue Progressiste des Interets Economiques et Sociaux des Populations du Nord Cameroun (MAR)
LPN .... Line of Adjusted Deflections (RU)
LPN .... Line of Deflection Corrections (RU)
LPO .... Letecky Poradni Organ [*Aviation Advisory Staff*] (CZ)
LPO .... Liberale Partei Oesterreichs [*Liberal Party of Austria*] (PPE)
l poj .... Liczba Pojedyncza [*Singular*] (POL)
LPP .... Lebowa People's Party [*South African*] (PPW)
LPP .... Liga dos Patriotas Presos [*League of Jailed Patriots*] [*Portuguese*] (WER)
LPP .... Light Bridge Train (RU)
lpp .... Light River-Crossing Fleet (BU)
LPPC .... Liberian Palm Products Corporation (MAR)
LPPP .... Lembaga Pemasaran Pertanian Persekutuan [*Federal Agricultural Marketing Association*] (ML)
l/pr .... Icing of Road and Slopes (Obstacle) [*Topography*] (RU)
l prom .... Light Industry Factory [*Topography*] (RU)

l prom.......... Light Industry Plant [*Topography*] (RU)
LPRP.......... Lao People's Revolutionary Party [*Phak Pasason Pativat Lao*] (PPW)
LPS.......... Aircraft Position Line (RU)
LPS.......... Flying Personnel (RU)
LPS.......... Les Planteurs du Sassandra (MAR)
LPS.......... Letecka Priprava a Sport [*Aviation Preparedness and Athletics*] (CZ)
LPS.......... Liberale Partei der Schweiz [*Liberal Party of Switzerland*] (PPE)
LPS.......... Limenikos Pyrosvestikos Stathmos [*Port Fire Station*] (GC)
LPT.......... Linear Rotary Transformer (RU)
LPTHE.......... Laboratoire de Physique Theorique et Hautes Energies
LPTP.......... Lubelska Przetwornia Tytoniu Przemyslowego [*Lublin Tobacco Factory*] (POL)
LPU.......... Establishment for Medical Preventive Treatment (RU)
LPU.......... Lembaga Pemilihan Umum [*General Election Board*] (IN)
LPU.......... Letecke Povetrnostni Ustredi [*Air Weather Center*] (CZ)
LPU.......... Line of Adjusted Deflections [*Artillery*] (RU)
LPU pri MNZST... Medical Prophylactic Administration of the Ministry of Public Health and Social Welfare (BU)
lpv.......... Light Antiaircraft Battery (BU)
LPV.......... Listos para Vencer [*Ready-to-Win*] [*Physical fitness program*] [*Cuban*] (LA)
LPVCS.......... Letectvo Protivzdusne Obrany Statu [*Aviation Component of National Air Defense*] (CZ)
LPW.......... Laboratorium Przemyslu Weglowego [*Laboratory of the Coal Industry*] (POL)
LPW.......... Laboratorium Przemyslu Welnianego [*Laboratory of the Wool Industry*] (POL)
LPW.......... Lotnicze Przysposobienie Wojskowe [*Pre-Military Air Training*] (POL)
Lpz.......... Leipzig (EG)
LPZ.......... Liga Przyjaciol Zolnierza [*League of Soldier's Friends*] (POL)
LPZ.......... Lugansk Locomotive Plant (RU)
LPZB.......... Lubelskie Przemyslowe Zjednoczenie Budowlane [*Lublin Industrial Construction Association*] (POL)
LR-.......... Hand Winch (RU)
lr.......... Lastno Rocno [*By One's Own Hand*] (YU)
lR.......... Laufend Rechnung [*Current Account*] [*German*] [*Business and trade*]
Lr.......... Lavoir [*Wash House*] [*Military map abbreviation*] [*World War I*] [*French*] (MTD)
LR.......... Left Hand (RU)
LR.......... Liberia [*Two-letter standard code*] (CNC)
LR.......... Line Distributor (RU)
LR.......... Line Relay (RU)
lr.......... Lira (RU)
LR.......... Ljudska Republika [*People's Republic*] (YU)
LR.......... Slightly Wounded (RU)
LRA.......... Light Rocket Artillery (BU)
LRA.......... Light Rocket Artillery (RU)
LRA.......... Line of Equal Azimuths (RU)
LRB.......... Lidova Republika Bulharska [*Bulgarian People's Republic*] (CZ)
LRBA.......... Laboratoire de Recherches Balistiques et Aerodynamiques [*Ballistic and Aerodynamic Research Laboratory*] [*French*] (WER)
LRBH.......... Ljudska Republika Bosna in Hercegovina [*People's Republic of Bosnia and Hercegovina*] (YU)
LRC.......... Liberia Refinery Company (MAR)
LRC.......... Local Referees Committee (MAR)
LRCG.......... Ljudska Republika Crna Gora [*People's Republic of Montenegro*] (YU)
LRD.......... Hunting and Fishing Association (BU)
LRD.......... Jet Propulsion Laboratory [*California*] (RU)
LRDG.......... Long Range Desert Group [*Arab*] (MAR)
LRE.......... Linear Power Consumption (RU)
LRG.......... Landscape Research Group (EA)
LRGRU.......... Leningrad Regional Geological Exploration Administration (RU)
LRH.......... Linija Radarskog Horizonta [*RADAR Horizon Line*] (YU)
LRH.......... Ljudska Republika Hrvatska [*People's Republic of Croatia*] (YU)
LRI.......... Legiforgalmi es Repuloter Igazgatosag [*Air Traffic and Airport Authority*] (HU)
LRK.......... Readily Soluble Component (RU)
LRM.......... Ljudska Republika Makedonija [*People's Republic of Macedonia*] (YU)
LRP.......... Lebanese Revolutionary Party (PD)
LRP.......... Lena River Steamship Line (RU)
LRP.......... Line of Equal Bearings (RU)
LRR.......... Land-Rover Register 1947-1951 (EA)
LRR.......... Letecky Rizena Raketa [*Air Guided Rocket*] (CZ)
LRR.......... Line of Equal Distance (RU)
LRRP.......... Line of Equal Radio Bearings (RU)
LRS.......... Hunting and Fishing Union (BU)
lrs.......... Line Signal Company (RU)
LRS.......... Ljudska Republika Slovenija [*People's Republic of Slovenia*] (YU)
LRS.......... Ljudska Republika Srbija [*People's Republic of Serbia*] (YU)
LRS.......... Ludovy Rybarsky Spolok [*People's Fishing Club*] (CZ)
LRSLP.......... Lietuvos Revoliuciniu Socialistu Liaudininkai Partija [*Revolutionary Socialist Populists Party of Lithuania*] (PPE)
LRT.......... Ligue Revolutionnaire des Travailleurs [*Revolutionary Workers' League*] [*Belgian*] (WER)
LRTA.......... Laboratoire Radio-Television Abidjan (MAR)
LRTA.......... Light Rail Transit Association (EA)
LRUK.......... Commander's Personal Radio Center (RU)
LRV.......... Line of Equal Altitudes (RU)
LS.......... Communication Line, Line, Circuit (RU)
ls.......... Horsepower (RU)
LS.......... Labologists Society (EA)
LS.......... Laborator Strojnicka [*Machine Building Laboratory (of the Czechoslovak Academy of Sciences)*] (CZ)
LS.......... Laboratory of Speleology (of the Academy of Sciences, USSR) (RU)
LS.......... Laererskoleeksamen [*Norwegian*]
LS.......... Laikos Synagermos [*People's Rally*] (GC)
LS.......... Lakheion Syndakton [*Editors Lottery*] (GC1)
lS.......... Lange Sicht [*Long Sight*] [*Business and trade*] [*German*]
L de S.......... Latinoamericana de Seguros SA [*Bogota*] (COL)
LS.......... Lekarz Stomatolog [*Dentist*] [*Polish*]
LS.......... Lesni Spolecenstva [*Forestry Corporations*] (CZ)
LS.......... Lesotho [*Two-letter standard code*] (CNC)
LS.......... Lexicographic Collection [*Bibliography*] (RU)
LS.......... Lidove Soudnictvi [*People's Judiciary*] [*A periodical*] (CZ)
LS.......... Lidovy Soudce [*People's Judge*] (CZ)
LS.......... Liga Socialista [*Socialist League*] [*Venezuelan*] (LA)
LS.......... Light Forces [*Navy*] (RU)
LS.......... Limenikon Soma [*Port Corps*] (GC)
LS.......... Linear Resistance (RU)
LS.......... Linksozialisten [*Left Socialists*] [*Austrian*] (PPE)
Ls.......... Lise [*High School, Lycee*] (TU)
LS.......... Livre Soudanaise (MAR)
LS.......... Ljudska Skupscina [*People's Assembly*] (YU)
LS.......... Locus Sigilli [*The Place of the Seal*] [*Latin*] (GPO)
LS.......... Loutkovy Soubor [*Puppet Theater Ensemble*] (CZ)
LS.......... Luftschutz [*Civil Defense, Passive Air Defense*] (EG)
LS.......... Lugar del Sello [*Place of the Seal*] [*Spanish*]
LS.......... Lute Society (EA)
LS.......... Medical Serum (RU)
LS.......... Personnel, Staff (RU)
LS.......... Signal Light (RU)
L/sa.......... Lefkosa [*Nicosia*] [*Turkish Federated State of Cyprus*] (GC)
LSAP.......... Letzeburger Sozialistesch Arbechter Partei [*Socialist Workers' Party of Luxembourg*] (PPE)
LSAP.......... Luxemburgische Sozialistische Arbeiterpartei [*Luxembourg Socialist Workers Party*] (WEN)
LSB.......... Belen'kiy's Therapeutic Serum (RU)
L es Sc.......... Licencie es Sciences [*Licentiate of Sciences*] [*French*]
lsc.......... Loco Supra Citato [*In the Place Cited Above*] [*Latin*] (GPO)
lsch.......... Horsepower per Hour (RU)
LSCR.......... Ligue des Societes de la Croix-Rouge
LSD.......... Lembaga Sosial Desa [*Village Social Agency*] (IN)
LSD.......... Lemnul Stratificat Densificat [*Stratified Densified Wood*] (RO)
LSD.......... Liberaler Studentenbund Deutschlands [*Liberal Student Federation of Germany*] [*West German*] (WEN)
LSD.......... Lidove Spotrebni Druzstvo [*People's Consumer Cooperative*] (CZ)
LSDP.......... Lietuvos Socialdemokratu Partija [*Social Democratic Party of Lithuania*] (PPE)
LSDP.......... Lithuanian Social Democratic Party (RU)
LSDPC.......... Lagos State Development and Property Corporation (MAR)
LSE.......... Lochkarten-Lese-Stanz-Einheit [*Punch Card Reader-Perforator*] (EG)
LSG.......... Lagos State Government (MAR)
LSG.......... Ligo Samseksamaj Geesperantistoj (EA)
Lsg.......... Loesung [*Solution*] [*German*]
Lsgg.......... Loesungen [*Solutions*] [*German*]
LSh.......... Light Attack Aircraft (RU)
LShchP.......... Line Switchboard (RU)
LSHD.......... Luftschutzhilfsdienst [*Civil Defense Auxiliary Service*] [*West German*] (WEN)
LSI.......... Landesschulinspektor [*German*]
LSK.......... Livsmedelsstadgekommitten [*Swedish*]
LSK.......... Luftschutz Kommando [*Civil Air Defense Command*] (EG)
LSK.......... Luftstreitkraefte [*Air Force*] (EG)
LSKhA.......... Latvian Agricultural Academy (RU)
LSKhI.......... Leningrad Agricultural Institute (RU)
LSK/LV.......... (Kommando der) Luftstreitkraefte und Luftverteidigung [*Air Forces and Air Defense (Command)*] (EG)
LSKT.......... Leningrad Glass and Ceramics Technicum (RU)
LSLDP.......... Lietuvos Socialistu Liaudininkai Demokratu Partija [*Socialist Populists Democratic Party of Lithuania*] (PPE)
LSLP.......... Lietuvos Socialistu Liaudininkai Partija [*Socialist Populists Party of Lithuania*] (PPE)
LSLRS.......... Ljudska Skupscina Ljudske Republike Slovenije [*People's Assembly of the People's Republic of Slovenia*] (YU)
LSM.......... Liberation Support Movement (MAR)
LSM.......... Lubelska Spoldzielnia Mieszkaniowa [*Lublin Housing Cooperative*] (POL)
LSMB.......... Lint and Seed Marketing Board (MAR)

LSMGI......... Leningrad Sanitation and Hygiene Medical Institute (RU)
l/smos......... Logariasmos [*Account*] (GC)
LSN............. Lei de Seguranca Nacional [*National Security Law*] [*Brazilian*] (LA)
LS/NE......... Laendersektion Nordeuropa [*North European Countries Section*] (EG)
LSNKh......... Leningrad Council of the National Economy (RU)
LSO............. Lesotho [*Three-letter standard code*] (CNC)
LSO............. Letecky Spojavaci Oddil [*Air Communications Battalion*] (CZ)
LSO............. Liberal Socialists Organization [*Egyptian*] (ME)
LSP............. Liberal Socialist Party [*Egyptian*] (PPW)
LSP............. Liberal Socialist Party [*Singapore*] (ML)
LSP............. Liberale Staatspartij [*Liberal State Party*] [*Netherlands*] (PPE)
lsp............... Sawmill [*Topography*] (RU)
LSPO........... Leningrad Union of Consumers' Societies (RU)
LSR............. Landesschulrat [*German*]
LSR............. Saw Frame, Log Frame (RU)
LSR............. Sectional Saw Frame (RU)
LSS............. Lubelska Spoldzielnia Spozywcow [*Lublin Consumers' Cooperative*] (POL)
LSSK........... Leningrad Union of Soviet Composers (RU)
LSSKh......... Leningrad Union of Soviet Artists (RU)
LSSR........... Latvian Soviet Socialist Republic (RU)
LSSR........... Lithuanian Soviet Socialist Republic (RU)
LST............. Leningrad Shipbuilding Technicum (RU)
LStR........... Lohnsteuer-Richtlinie [*Wages Tax Directives*] (EG)
LSU............. Liberalsoziale Union [*Liberal Social Union*] [*West German*] (PPW)
LSVS........... Lager-Speditionsversicherungsschein [*Warehouse Shipping Insurance Certificate*] (EG)
LSW............. Ludowa Spoldzielnia Wydawnicza [*People's Publishing House*] (POL)
lsz............... Leltari Szam [*Inventory Number*] (HU)
LSZ............. Leninogorsk Lead Plant (RU)
LSZ............. Lidova Skola Zemedelska [*People's Agricultural School*] (CZ)
LT............... Beam Tetrode (RU)
LT............... Conveyor Belt (RU)
lt................. Laatikko [*Finnish*]
lt................. Laut [*According To*] (EG)
Lt................ Leutnant [*Lieutenant*] [*German*]
Lt................ Lieutenant [*Lieutenant*] [*French*] (MTD)
l-t............... Lieutenant (RU)
LT............... Line Transformer (RU)
lt................. Litre [*Liter*] (TU)
LT............... Precision Casting (RU)
LT............... Technical Lycee [*French*]
LT............... Telegramme-Lettre [*Telegram-Letter*] (CL)
Lt................ Triebwagen-Leerzug [*Empty Rail Motor Car and Consist*] (EG)
LTA............. Land Tenure Act [*Rhodesian*] (AF)
LTA............. Lembaga Tenaga Atom [*Atomic Energy Institute*] (IN)
LTA............. Leningrad Forestry Engineering Academy Imeni S. M. Kirov (RU)
LTA............. Lettre de Transport Aerien [*French*]
LTA-........... Tape-Printing Apparatus (RU)
LTBB........... Lefkosa Turk Berberler Birligi [*Nicosia Turkish Barbers' Union*] (TU)
LTBMMS..... Lefkosa Turk Belediyesi Memur ve Mustahdemleri Sendikasi [*Nicosia Turkish Municipal Officials and Employees' Union*] [*Turkish Cypriot*] (GC)
LTBr........... Light Tank Brigade (RU)
LTC............. Land Tenure Center (MAR)
ltd............... Leitend [*Chief*] (EG)
LTD............. Letecka Technicka Divize [*Aviation (or Air) Technical Division*] (CZ)
Ltda............. Limitada [*Limited*] [*Spanish*]
Ltd S........... Limited Sirketi [*Limited Company, Corporation*] [*Turkish*] (CED)
Ltd Sti......... Limited Sirketi [*Limited Company, Corporation*] [*See also Sti, TAS*] (TU)
Lte.............. Lette [*Swamp*] [*Military map abbreviation*] [*World War I*] [*French*] (MTD)
LTEU........... Leningrad Tourist and Excursion Administration (RU)
LTF............. Laboratory of Theoretical Physics (RU)
LTF............. Telegramme-Lettre [*Telegram-Letter*] [*Use LT*] (CL)
Ltg.............. Leitung [*German*]
LTGH........... Lefkosa Turkiye Genel Hastane [*Nicosia Turkish General Hospital*] (TU)
LTI.............. Forestry Engineering Institute (RU)
LTI.............. Leningrad Technological Institute Imeni Lensovet (RU)
LTI.............. Leningrad Textile Institute Imeni S. M. Kirov (RU)
LTI.............. Lerotholi Freedom Party (MAR)
LTIPP.......... Leningrad Technological Institute of the Food Industry (RU)
ltk............... Laatikko [*Finnish*]
LTK............. Liiketyonantajain Keskusliitto [*Commercial Employers' Association*] [*Finnish*] (WEN)
LTK............. Luonnontieteiden Kandidaatti [*Finnish*]
LTKL........... Lefkosa Turk Kiz Lisesi [*Nicosia Turkish Women's Lycee*] (TU)
LTL............. Lefkosa Turk Lisesi [*Nicosia Turkish Lycee*] [*Cypriot*] (TU)
LTM............. Letecky Technicky Material [*Aviation Technical Equipment*] (CZ)
LTM-HB....... Sluzba Lesotechnickych Melioraci a Hrazeni Bystrin [*Forest Engineering and Flood Control Service*] (CZ)
LTN............. Laboratory for Technical Standarization (RU)
LTN............. Lodzkie Towarzystwo Naukowe [*Lodz Learned Society*] (POL)
ltn............... Luutnantti [*Finnish*]
LTO............. Lithuanian Theatrical Society (RU)
LTOP........... Lesnicko-Technicka Ochrana Pudy [*Technical Forest Soil Conservation*] (CZ)
LTP............. Laboratoire des Travaux Publics (MAR)
LTP............. Letecky Technicky Pluk [*Air Technical Regiment*] (CZ)
LTP............. Lucko Transportno Preduzece [*Port Transport Establishment*] (YU)
LTPA........... Lorraine de Travaux Publics Africains (MAR)
ltq............... Torok Font [*Turkish Pound*] (HU)
Ltr............... Leiter [*Leader, Manager*] (EG)
LTR............. Local Thermodynamic Equilibrium (RU)
LTs............. Flight Center (RU)
LTS............. Leichtes Torpedoschnellboot [*Light Motor Torpedo Boat*] (EG)
LTS............. Lesnicka Technicka Skola [*Technical School of Forestry*] (CZ)
LTS............. Loi Toa Soan [*Editorial Comment, Editorial Note*] (TVP)
LTSA........... Leningrad Theater of the Soviet Army (RU)
LTsIA.......... Leningrad Central Historical Archives (RU)
LTT............. Lignes Telegraphiques et Telephoniques [*Algerian*] (MAR)
Ltt D........... Literarum Doctor [*Doctor of Letters*] [*Latin*] (GPO)
LTTs........... Leningrad Television Center (RU)
LTU............. Lufttransport-Unternehmen GmbH [*Air Transportation Enterprise Company*] (EG)
LTU............. Tactical Flight Training (RU)
LTU............. Technical Flight Exercise (BU)
LTV............. Cable-Line Connection (BU)
LTV............. Letacko-Takticke Vezbe [*Tactical Flight Exercises*] (YU)
LTZ............. Lipetsk Tractor Plant (RU)
LTZhDT....... Leningrad Railroad Transportation Technicum Imeni F. E. Dzerzhinskiy (RU)
LU............... Amplifier Tube (RU)
LU............... Leningrad University (RU)
LU............... Lidova Universita [*People's University*] (CZ)
LU............... Liga Ultramarina (MAR)
LU............... Linear (Program) Part [*Automation*] (RU)
LU............... Ljudska Uprava [*People's Administration*] [*Ljubljana*] [*A periodical*] (YU)
LU............... Logarithmic Amplifier (RU)
Lu................ Luoto [*or Luodet*] [*Rock or Rocks*] [*Finnish*] (NAU)
LU............... Luxembourg [*Two-letter standard code*] (CNC)
LUAR........... Liga da Uniao e Accao Revolucionaria [*League for Unity and Revolutionary Action*] [*Portuguese*] (WER)
LUAR........... Liga Unida da Accao Revolucionaria (MAR)
LUAT........... Leningrad Administration of Automobile Transportation (RU)
lub.............. Bast Plant [*Topography*] (RU)
l ub............. Lata Ubiegle [*The Past Years*] [*Polish*]
LUBA........... Parti du Rassemblement des Peuples Luba (MAR)
LUBAKO...... Association Lumiere du Bas-Congo (MAR)
LUBREF...... Petromin Lubricating Refinery (MAR)
LUBTEX...... Societe Lubrifiants Texaco (MAR)
LUC............. Laborator Uzinal de Cercetari [*In-Plant Research Laboratory*] (RO)
LUCE........... L'Unione Cinematografica Educativa [*Italian*]
ludn............. Ludnosc [*The Population*] [*Polish*]
LUDRN........ Ligue Universelle pour la Defense de la Race Noire (MAR)
LUE............. Linear Electron Accelerator (RU)
Luep........... Laenge ueber Puffer [*Length over Buffers*] (EG)
LUF............. Labor Unity Front [*Nigerian*] (AF)
LUF............. Liberation and Unity Front [*Saharan*] (AF)
LUFO........... Legugyi Foosztaly [*Main Department of Aviation (Part of Kozlekedesi- es Postaugyi Miniszterium)*] (HU)
LUFPT......... Laktologicky Ustav Fakulty Potravinarske Technologie [*Milk Produce Research Institute of the Faculty of Food Technology*] [*Prague*] (CZ)
LUGMI......... Leningrad Administration of State Meat Inspection (RU)
LUGMS........ Leningrad Administration of the Hydrometeorological Service (RU)
LUI.............. Leningrad Teachers' Institute (RU)
LUI.............. Linear Ion Accelerator (RU)
LUINSA....... Laboratorios Unidos Interamericanos [*Bogota*] (COL)
LUK............. Lamellen und Kupplungsbau (MAR)
LuK............. Luonnontiet Kandidaatti [*Finnish*]
LUKS........... Leningrad Communications Training Center (RU)
luks............. Luksusowe (Wydanie) [*Deluxe (Edition)*] (POL)
lukus........... Lukusana [*Numeral*] [*Finnish*]
lun.............. Lunes [*Monday*] [*Spanish*]
LUNKhU...... Leningrad Administration of the Statistical Survey of the National Economy (RU)
Luonnondtiet Kand... Bachelor's Degree in Natural Science [*Finnish*]
luonnontkand... Luonnontieteiden Kandidaatti [*Finnish*]
LUPU........... Leningrad Junction Administration of Freight Loading and Unloading (RU)
LUR............. Linear Turn Lead (RU)
LUs............. Line Amplifier, Linear Amplifier (RU)
LUT............. Letecke Technicke Uciliste [*Aviation Technical Training Center*] (CZ)
LUT............. Lidova Umelecka Tvorivost [*Folk Arts Activities*] (CZ)

LUT .... Loge Unie des Theosophes
lut .... Luteranus [*Lutheran*] (HU)
LUTH .... Lagos University Teaching Hospital (MAR)
luth .... Lutherisch [*Lutheran*] (EG)
luutn .... Luutnantti [*Finnish*]
LUX .... Luxembourg [*Three-letter standard code*] (CNC)
LUXAIR .... Luxembourgeoise de Navigation Aerienne [*Luxembourg airline*]
LUZ .... La Universidad del Zulia [*The University of Zulia*] [*Venezuelan*] (LA)
LV .... Electron Tube Voltmeter, Tube Voltmeter (RU)
lv .... Influence Line (RU)
LV .... Landesverteidigung [*German*]
lv .... Leiviska [*Finnish*]
LV .... Lev [*Monetary unit in Bulgaria*]
lv .... Lev, Leva (BU)
LV .... Levazim [*Supplies, Provisions*] [*Military*] (TU)
LV .... Libreria Voluntad [*Bogota*] (COL)
LV .... Lid Volksraad [*Member of Parliament*] [*South African*] (AF)
LV .... Lieutenant de Vaisseau [*French*] (MTD)
LV .... Line Equalizer, Line Compensator (RU)
LV .... Linschoten Vereeniging, Werke (MAR)
LV .... Luftverteidigung [*Air Defense*] (EG)
L'V .... L'vov Railroad (RU)
LV .... Lytic Substance (RU)
LV .... Vacuum-Tube Rectifier (RU)
LVA .... Letecka Vojenska Akademie [*Air Force Academy*] (CZ)
LVD .... Luft-Verteidigungsdivision [*Air Defense Division*] (EG)
lv es .... Fighter Squadron (BU)
LVF .... Ladoga Naval Flotilla (RU)
LVF .... Legion des Volontaires Francais Contre le Bolchevisme
LVFS .... Lake Victoria Fisheries Service (MAR)
LVG .... Lehr- und Versuchsgut [*Training and Experimental Farm*] (EG)
L'vGU .... L'vov State University Imeni Ivan Franko (RU)
LVH .... Laborator pro Vodni Hospodarstvi [*Water Management Laboratory (of the Czechoslovak Academy of Sciences)*] (CZ)
LVI .... Leningrad Oriental Institute (RU)
LVI .... Leningrad Veterinary Institute (RU)
LVIMU .... Leningrad Higher Engineering Nautical School Imeni Admiral S. O. Makarov (RU)
LVIN .... Low Viscosity Index (MAR)
LVIPI .... Leningrad Higher Pedagogical Institute of Engineering (RU)
LVKSKhSh ... Leningrad Higher Communist School of Agriculture Imeni S. M. Kirov (RU)
LVM .... Light Suspension Bridge (RU)
LVMI .... Leningrad Military Mechanical Engineering Institute (RU)
LVMU .... Leningrad Higher Nautical School (RU)
LVNC .... Laborator Vyssi Nervove Cinnosti [*Laboratory of Higher Nervous Activity (of the Czechoslovak Academy of Sciences)*] (CZ)
LVO .... Leningrad Military District (RU)
LVO .... Lieferverordnung [*Delivery Regulations*] (EG)
L'vovsel'mash ... L'vov Agricultural Machinery Plant (RU)
LVRI .... Legiun Veteran Republik Indonesia [*Republic of Indonesia Veterans Legion*] (IN)
LVRZ .... Locomotive and Railroad Car Repair Plant (RU)
LVS .... Aqualung Diving Station (RU)
LVS .... Letecke Vycvikove Stredisko (Presov) [*Aviation Training Center (Presov)*] (CZ)
LVSCL .... Letecka Vysetrovaci Stanice Ceskoslovenskeho Letectva [*Czechoslovak Air Force Investigating Station*] (CZ)
LVShPD ...... Leningrad Higher School of Trade Unionism of the VTsSPS (RU)
LVT .... Linear Rotary Transformer (RU)
LVU .... Letecky Vyzkumny Ustav [*Aeronautic Research Institute*] [*Prague-Letnany*] (CZ)
lvv .... Liikevaihtovero [*Finnish*]
LVVA .... Leningrad Air Force Academy (RU)
lvveroineen ... Liikevaihtoveroineen [*Finnish*]
LVVIA .... Leningrad Air Force Engineering Academy Imeni A. F. Mozhayskiy (RU)
lvvineen ...... Liikevaihtoveroineen [*Finnish*]
LVVS .... Liquidatie Vermogens Verwaltung Sarphatistraat [*Amsterdam, The Netherlands*]
LVZ .... Locomotive and Railroad Cars Plant (BU)
LVZ .... L'vov Bicycle Plant (RU)
LVZh .... Inflammable Liquid (RU)
Lw .... Leinwand [*Linen, Cloth*] [*German*]
LW .... Leitungswaehler [*Final Selector, Line Selector*] (EG)
LW .... Lekarz Weterynarii [*Veterinarian*] [*Polish*]
lw .... Lichte Weite [*Inside Diameter*] [*German*]
LWB .... Lutherischer Weltbund [*Lutheran World Federation*] (EG)
LWCU .... Lebanese World Cultural Union (MAR)
Lwd .... Leinwand [*Linen, Cloth*] [*German*]
LWD .... Lotnicze Warsztaty Doswiadczalne [*Aeronautical Research Shops*] (POL)
LWD .... Louw Wepener Decoration (MAR)
LWF .... Labor Welfare Fund [*Iranian*] (ME)
LWF .... Lutheran World Federation [*See also FLM*] (EA)
LWF/WS ..... Lutheran World Federation/World Service (MAR)
LWM .... Louw Wepener Medal (MAR)
LWOST .... Low Water Ordinary Spring Tide (MAR)
LWP .... Ludowe Wojsko Polskie [*Polish People's Army*] (POL)
LWR .... Lagos Weekly Record [*A publication*] (MAR)
LWR .... Landwirtschaftsrat (beim Ministerrat) [*Agricultural Council (in the GDR Council of Ministers)*] (EG)
LWS .... Lutheran World Service (MAR)
LWSiS .... Lubelska Wytwornia Surowic i Szczepionek [*Lublin Serum and Vaccine Manufacturing Plant*] (POL)
LWTP .... Lubelska Wytwornia Tytoniu Przemyslowego [*Lublin Tobacco Factory*] (POL)
ly .... Lampoyksikko [*Finnish*]
LY .... Libya [*Two-letter standard code*] (CNC)
LY .... Lokhos Ygeionomikou [*Medical Company*] (GC)
LYaP .... Laboratory of Nuclear Problems (RU)
LYaPAS ...... Logical Language of Synthesis Algorithm Representation (RU)
LYaR .... Laboratory of Nuclear Reactions (RU)
LYeD .... Frog Unit [*Biology*] (RU)
lyh .... Lyhenne [*Finnish*]
lyh .... Lyhennetty [*Finnish*]
lyh .... Lyhennys [*or Lyhennettyna*] [*Abreviation*] [*Finnish*]
LYM .... Lagos Youth Movement (MAR)
LYuI .... Leningrad Law Institute Imeni M. I. Kalinin (RU)
lyut .... Lutheran (RU)
Lyut .... Lutheran Cemetery [*Topography*] (RU)
Lyut kir .... Lutheran Church [*Topography*] (RU)
LZ .... Delay Line (RU)
LZ .... Green Light (RU)
LZ .... Leksikografski Zavod [*Lexicographic Institute*] [*Zagreb*] (YU)
LZ .... Letecka Zakladna [*Air Force Base*] (CZ)
LZ .... Letecke Zavody, Narodni Podnik [*Aircraft Factories, National Enterprise*] (CZ)
LZ .... Ljubljanski Zvon [*Ljubljana Bell*] [*A periodical*] (YU)
Lz .... Lokleerfahrt [*Locomotive Run without Cars*] (EG)
l/z .... Sawmill [*Topography*] (RU)
LZAK .... Annals of the Work of the Archaeographical Commission (RU)
LZB .... Literaturen Zbornik Spisanije na Drustvoto za Makedonski Jazik i Literatura [*Literary Collection. Papers of the Society for Macedonian Language and Literature*] [*Skopje*] (YU)
LZB .... Lubelskie Zjednoczenie Budownictwa [*Lublin Construction Union*] (POL)
LZCh .... Lubelskie Zaklady Chmielarskie [*Lublin Hops Plant*] (POL)
LZETD .... Leninovy Zavody, Elektrotechnicka Tovarna v Plzni-Doudlevcich [*Lenin Works, Electric Machinery Plant in Plzen-Doudlevce*] [*Formerly, Skoda Works*] (CZ)
LZG .... Lodzkie Zaklady Gastronomiczne [*Lodz Restaurant Establishments*] (POL)
LZG .... Lubelskie Zaklady Gastronomiczne [*Lublin Restaurant Establishments*] (POL)
LZh .... Yellow Light (RU)
LZI .... Leningrad Zootechnical Institute (RU)
LZI .... Luminescent Symbol Indicator (RU)
LZII .... Leningrad Industrial Correspondence Institute (RU)
LZIP .... Lubelskie Zjednoczenie Instalacji Przemyslowych [*Lublin Association of Industrial Installations*] (POL)
LZITO .... Leningrad Correspondence Institute of Technical Education (RU)
LZK .... Lodzkie Zaklady Kinotechniczne [*Lodz Motion Picture Establishments*] (POL)
LZM .... Lodzki Zespol Miejski [*Lodz Metropolitan Area*] (POL)
LZM .... Lubelskie Zaklady Metalowe [*Lublin Metal Works*] (POL)
LZM .... Lubelskie Zaklady Miesne [*Lublin Meat Stores*] (POL)
LZMI .... Leningrad Correspondence Institute of Mechanical Engineering (RU)
LZO .... Lukowskie Zaklady Obuwia [*Lukow Footwear Factory*] (POL)
LZP .... Lubelskie Zaklady Piekarnicze [*Lublin Bakeries*] (POL)
LZP .... Planned Course Line, Desired Course Line (RU)
LZPHAPoPHSiPG ... Ludzkie Zjednoczenie Przedsiebiorstw Handlu Artykulami Przemyslowymi oraz Przedsiebiorstw Handlu Spozywczego i Przemyslu Gastronomicznego [*Lodz Union of Industrial Product Trade Enterprises and of Food Trade and Catering Industry Enterprises*] (POL)
LZPlzen .... Leninovy Zavody, Plzen [*Lenin Works, Plzen*] [*Formerly, Skoda Works*] (CZ)
LZPO .... Lodzki Zarzad Przemyslu Odziezowego [*Lodz Clothing Industry Administration*] (POL)
LZPOG .... Lodzkie Zaklady Przemyslu Obuwia Gumowego [*Lodz Rubber Footwear Plant*] (POL)
LZPP .... Lubelskie Zaklady Przemyslu Piekarniczego [*Lublin Bakeries*] (POL)
LZPS .... Lubelskie Zaklady Przemyslu Skorzanego [*Lublin Leather Industry Enterprise*] (POL)
LZPT .... Lodzkie Zaklady Przetworczo-Tluszczowe [*Lodz Fat Processing Plant*] (POL)
LZPT .... Lubelskie Zaklady Przemyslu Terenowego [*Lublin Local Industry Plants*] (POL)
LZS .... Forest Conservation Station (RU)
LZS .... Ludowe Zespoly Sportowe [*People's Sports Unions*] (POL)
LZS .... Ludowe Zrzeszenie Sportowe [*People's Sports Association*] (POL)
LZS .... Ludowy Zespol Sportowy [*People's Sports Union*] (POL)

LZSP .... Lodzki Zwiazek Spoldzielczosci Pracy [*Lodz Labor Cooperative Union*] (POL)

LZT i GT ...... Easily Inflammable Fluids and Combustible Fluids (BU)

LZTM........... Leningrad Commercial Machinery Plant (RU)

LZV............. Lovacka Zadruga Vojvodine [*Vojvodina Hunters' Cooperative*] (YU)

LZWS .... Lodzkie Zaklady Wyrobow Skorzanych [*Lodz Leather Goods Plant*] (POL)

M

M .... Boy [*In questionnaires*] (RU)
m .... Bridge (RU)
m .... Cape, Promontory [*Topography*] (RU)
M$ .... Dollar [*Monetary unit in Malaya*]
m .... International (RU)
M .... Little [*Toponymy*] (RU)
M .... Mach Number (RU)
m .... Madde [*Article, Paragraph*] (TU)
M .... Madre [*Mother*] [*Spanish*]
M .... Maedchen [*German*]
M .... Maestria [*Master's Degree*] [*Spanish*]
M .... Maestro [*Master*] [*Spanish*]
m .... Magan [*Private*] (HU)
M .... Magistar [*Academic qualification*] [*Yugoslav*]
M .... Magister [*Master*] [*Latin*] (GPO)
M .... Magistr [*Egyptian*]
m .... Magyar [*Hungarian*] (HU)
m .... Mahalle [*Ward, Quarter*] [*Turkish*] (CED)
M .... Maisteri [*Finnish*]
M .... Maitrise [*Master's Degree*] [*French*]
M .... Majestad [*Majesty*] [*Spanish*]
m .... Major [*Rank*] (BU)
m .... Major (RU)
M .... Man (MAR)
m .... Man [*Statistics*] (RU)
m .... Manana [*Tomorrow*] [*Spanish*]
M .... Manipulus [*Handful*] [*Latin*] (GPO)
M .... Marais [*Swamp*] [*Military map abbreviation*] [*World War I*] [*French*] (MTD)
M .... Mark [*Mark (Coin)*] [*German*] (GPO)
M .... Markt [*German*]
M .... Mas [*Farm*] [*Military map abbreviation*] [*World War I*] [*French*] (MTD)
m .... Masculine (Gender) (RU)
M .... Masse [*Mass*] [*German*]
M .... Mater [*German*]
M .... Mediano [*On an Examination: Fair*] [*Spanish*]
M .... Medicinae [*Of Medicine*] [*Latin*] (GPO)
m .... Mein [*My*] [*Business and trade*] [*German*]
M .... Meisteraprof [*Academic examination*] [*Icelandic*]
M .... Melantrich [*A publishing and printing firm*] (CZ)
M .... Mensuel [*Monthly*] [*French*]
M .... Merced [*Grace, Mercy*] [*Spanish*]
M .... Meridies [*Midnight, Noon*] [*Latin*] (GPO)
m .... Mes [*Month*] [*Business and trade*] [*Spanish*]
m .... Mester [*Master, Chief*] (HU)
M .... Mestre [*Master*] [*Portuguese*]
m .... Meta [*Meta*] [*German*]
m .... Meter (BU)
m .... Meter [*Meter*] (EG)
m .... Meter [*Meter*] (HU)
m .... Meter (RU)
m .... Metr [*Meter*] (POL)
M .... Metre [*Meter*] [*French*] (MTD)
m .... Metri(a) [*Finnish*]
m .... Metro [*Meter*] [*Portuguese*] (GPO)
m .... Metro [*Meter*] [*Spanish*]
m .... Mi [*My*] [*Business and trade*] [*Spanish*]
m .... Miasto [*City, Town*] (POL)
m .... Miesiac [*Month*] [*Polish*]
m .... Mieszkanie [*Apartment*] (POL)
M .... Miladi [*Anno Domini*] [*In the Year of Our Lord*] (TU)
M .... Mille [*One Thousand*] [*French*]
m .... Millions (BU)
m .... Mine (BU)
m .... Mint [*As*] (HU)
m .... Minute [*French*] (MTD)
m .... Minute (RU)
m .... Minute (BU)
m .... Minute [*Minute*] [*German*]
m .... Minuto [*Minute*] [*Spanish*]
m .... Minuutti [*Minute*] [*Finnish*] (GPO)
M .... MIR [*Peace*] [*A periodical*] (BU)
m .... Mit [*With*] [*German*]
M .... Mitrailleuse [*Machine Gun*] [*Military*] [*French*] (MTD)
M .... Mobilization Day (BU)
M .... Modele [*Model*] [*French*] (MTD)
M .... Moderata Samlingspartiet [*Moderate Coalition Party*] [*Swedish*] (WEN)
M .... Modernized (RU)
M .... Modifie [*Modified*] [*French*] (MTD)
M .... Modulator (RU)
m .... Mois [*Month*] [*French*]
M .... Molarity of Solution (RU)
M .... Molecular Weight (RU)
M .... Molekulargewicht [*Molecular Weight*] [*German*]
m/ .... Mon [*My*] [*French*] [*Business and trade*]
M .... Monat [*Month*] [*German*]
M .... Monsieur [*Mister*] [*French*]
M .... Montagne [*Of guns*] [*French*] (MTD)
m .... Month (BU)
m .... Month (RU)
M .... Mort [*or Morte*] [*Died*] [*French*]
M .... Morze [*Sea*] [*Polish*]
M .... Moscow [*Bibliography*] (RU)
M .... Moscow (BU)
M .... Mosyo [*Mister*] [*Turkish*] (GPO)
m .... Mozgositas [*Mobilization*] (HU)
M .... Muerto [*or Muerta*] [*Died*] [*Spanish*]
M .... Muff, Coupling, Clutch (RU)
m .... Myelocyte (RU)
m .... Myos [*Also*] [*Finnish*]
M .... Mys [*Cape*] [*Russian*] (NAU)
m .... Oil, Lubricant (RU)
M .... Scale (RU)
m .... Sea (RU)
M .... Shallow [*Ford or river crossing*] [*Topography*] (RU)
m .... Small Town [*Topography*] (RU)
m .... Subway [*Sign on stations*] (RU)
m .... Tomb, Grave [*Topography*] (RU)
M .... Torpedo Boat (RU)
m^2 .... Metr Kwadratowy [*Square Meter*] [*Polish*]
m^2 .... Metre Carre [*Square Meter*] [*French*] (GPO)
m^2 .... Negyzetmeter [*Square Meter*] (HU)
m^2 .... Neliometri(a) [*Finnish*]
m^2 .... Quadratmeter [*Square Meter*] (EG)
m^2 .... Square Meter (BU)
m^3 .... Cubic Meter (BU)
m^3 .... Kobmeter [*Cubic Meter*] (HU)
m^3 .... Kubikmeter [*Cubic Meter*] (EG)
m^3 .... Kuutiometri(a) [*Finnish*]
m^3 .... Metr Szescienny [*Cubic Meter*] [*Polish*]
MA .... Artillery Shop (RU)
MA .... Land-Surveying Archives (RU)
ma .... Maanantai(na) [*Finnish*]
MA .... Magister Artium [*Master of Arts*] [*Latin*] (GPO)
Ma .... Magistere [*French*]
MA- .... Magnetic Analyzer (RU)
MA .... Magnetic Azimuth (RU)
MA .... Makhitiki Aristera [*Militant Left*] [*Greek*] (GC)
MA .... Maleic Anhydride (RU)
MA .... Mangels Annahme [*For Non-Acceptance*] [*Business and trade*] [*German*]
MA .... Manufacture d'Armes [*French*] (MTD)
Ma .... Maria [*Spanish*]
MA .... Maroko [*Morocco*] [*Polish*]
Ma .... Matala [*Shoal*] [*Finnish*] (NAU)
MA .... Mechanized Army (BU)
MA .... Megas Alexandros [*Alexander the Great*] [*Greek*] (GC)
ma .... Mellekallomas [*Extension (Telephone)*] (HU)
MA .... Messageries Africaines (MAR)
MA .... Methyl Acetate (Solvent) (RU)

MA.............. Microammeter (RU)
MA.............. Milliammeter (RU)
ma.............. Milliampere (BU)
mA.............. Milliampere [*Milliampere*] (EG)
ma.............. Milliampere (RU)
MA.............. Mitarbeiter [*Staff Employee*] (EG)
MA.............. Mitotic Activity [*Biology*] (RU)
MA.............. Mittelalter [*German*]
ma.............. Mittelalterlich [*German*]
MA.............. Mohamed Egypt Aly (MAR)
MA.............. Monimos Andiprosopeia [*Permanent Delegation*] (GC)
MA.............. Morocco [*Two-letter standard code*] (CNC)
MA.............. Morphological Analysis (RU)
MA.............. Movimento Associativo de Estudantes [*Associative Movement of Students*] [*Portuguese*] (WER)
Ma.............. Muara [*River Mouth*] [*Malay*] (NAU)
ma.............. Mundartlich [*German*]
Ma.............. Mura [*Village*] [*Japanese*] (NAU)
MA.............. Muzeum Archeologiczne [*Archeological Museum*] (POL)
MA.............. Product Form Algorithm (RU)
MAA........... International Academy of Astronautics (RU)
MAA........... Maison de l'Agriculture Algerienne (MAR)
MAA........... Ministere des Affaires Africaines (MAR)
MAA........... Multichannel Pulse-Height Analyzer (RU)
MAAA.......... Malayan Amateur Athletic Association (ML)
MAACP....... Mediterranean African Airlift Command Post (MAR)
MAAE.......... International Atomic Energy Agency (BU)
MAAE.......... International Atomic Energy Agency [*IAEA*] (RU)
MAAE.......... Mezinarodni Agentura pro Atomovou Energii [*International Agency for Atomic Energy*] (CZ)
MAAF.......... Mediterranean Allied Air Forces (MAR)
MAAIF......... Mutuelle Assurance Automobile des Instituteurs de France [*French Teachers Mutual Automobile Insurance Association*] (WER)
maanmitt.... Maanmittaus [*Geodesy*] [*Finnish*]
maant.......... Maantiede [*Geography*] [*Finnish*]
MA'ARAKH ... Political Bloc [*Israeli*] (ME)
maar art...... Maaraava Artikkeli [*Definite Article*] [*Finnish*]
maas........... Maaseudunpuoluelainen [*Finnish*]
maat........... Maatalous [*Agriculture*] [*Finnish*]
MAATEC..... Mutuelle Algerienne d'Assurances des Travailleurs de l'Education et de la Culture [*Algerian Mutual Insurance Company for Educational and Cultural Workers*] (AF)
maatja metsatiettri ... Maatalous-Ja Metsatieteiden Tohtori [*Finnish*]
maatja metsatkand ... Maatalous-Ja Metsatieteiden Kandidaatti [*Finnish*]
maatja metsatlis ... Maatalous-Ja Metsatieteiden Lisensiaatti [*Finnish*]
MAB............ Aerial Antibridge Bomb (RU)
MAB............ Magyar Allami Biztosito [*Hungarian State Insurance Enterprise*] (HU)
MAB............ Man and Biosphere (MAR)
MAB............ Militaerische Abnahmebestimmungen [*Acceptance (Purchase) Terms for Military Commodities*] (EG)
mab............ Motorized Battalion of Submachine Gunners (BU)
MAB............ Naval Air Base (RU)
MABAD....... Markas Besar Angkatan Darat [*Army Headquarters*] [*Also, MBAD*] (IN)
MABAL........ Markas Besar Angkatan Laut [*Navy Headquarters*] [*Also, MBAL*] (IN)
MABAU....... Markas Besar Angkatan Udara [*Air Force Headquarters*] [*Also, MBAU*] (IN)
MABECY..... Manufacture Beninoise du Cycle (MAR)
MABEGOSZ ... Magyarorszagi Bercseplok es Gepkocsitulajdonosok Orszagos Szovetsege [*National Association of Threshing Machine and Automobile Owners*] (HU)
MABEOSZ... Magyar Belyeggyujtok Orszagos Szovetsege [*National Association of Hungarian Philatelists*] (HU)
MABI........... Meganalkalmazottak Biztosito Intezete [*Insurance Institute for Private Employees*] (HU)
MABLA........ Movimento Afro-Brasileiro para a Libertacao de Angola (MAR)
MABOSE..... Manufacture de Bonneterie Senegalaise (MAR)
MABR.......... Inter-American Development Bank [*IADB*] (RU)
MAC............ Macao [*Three-letter standard code*] (CNC)
Mac............ Macarca [*Hungarian*] (TU)
MAC............ Magyar Atletikai Club [*Hungarian Athletic Club*] (HU)
MAC............ Manufacture Africaine de Cycle (MAR)
MAC............ Manufacture d'Allumettes et Cigarettes [*Cigarette and Match Manufacturing Company*] [*Cambodian*] (CL)
MAC............ Ministerio de Agricultura y Cria [*Ministry of Agriculture and Livestock*] [*Venezuelan*] (LA)
MAC............ Misir Arap Cumhuriyeti [*Arab Republic of Egypt*] (TU)
MAC............ Mission Agricole Chinoise [*Chinese Agricultural Mission*] [*Zairian*] (AF)
MAC............ Moniteur Africain du Commerce et de l'Industrie (MAR)
MAC............ Moslem Action Committee [*Mauritian*] (AF)
MAC............ Mouvement d'Action Civique [*Civil Action Movement*] [*Belgian*] (WER)
MAC............ Mouvement Anti-Colonialiste [*Anti-Colonialist Movement*] (AF)
MAC............ Mouvement Autonomiste Canarien (MAR)
MAC............ Movimento Anti-Colonialista (MAR)
MAC............ Movimento Anticomunista [*Anticommunist Movement*] [*Brazilian*] (LA)
MAC............ Movimiento Amplio Colombiano [*Broad-Based Movement of Colombia*] (PPW)
MACAC....... Anti-Communist Commando Movement [*Portugal*] (WER)
MACACI...... Manufacture de Caoutchouc de la Cote-d'Ivoire (MAR)
MACC......... Manufacture d'Armes et de Cartouches Congolaises [*Congolese Weapons and Cartridges Manufacturing Company*] (AF)
MACEL........ Manufacturas de Cuero Ltda. [*Medellin*] (COL)
Macho......... Movimiento Anticomunista Hondureno [*Honduran Anti-Communist Movement*] (PD)
MACI........... Mutuelle Agricole de Cote-d'Ivoire (MAR)
MACIMEA... Materiel Automobiles, Carrieres, Industries, Mines, Entreprises Agricoles [*Moroccan*] (MAR)
MACIMO..... Compagnie Malgache des Ciments de Moramanga (MAR)
MACODEX ... Compagnie Malgache d'Elevage et d'Exportation (MAR)
MACODI...... Manufacture de Confection de Cote-d'Ivoire (MAR)
MACOMA.... Materiaux de Construction de Madagascar (MAR)
MACON....... Manufactura Colombiana de Carton [*Medellin*] (COL)
MACWUSA ... Motor Assemblies and Components Union of South Africa (MAR)
Mad............ Madame [*Madam*] [*French*] (MTD)
Mad............ Madde [*Article*] (TU)
MAD........... Mikta Apospasmata Dioxeos [*Joint Pursuit Detachments*] [*Greek*] (GC)
MAD........... Militaerischer Abschirmdienst [*Military Security Service*] [*West German*] (WEN)
MAD........... Military Action Dockers (MAR)
MAD........... Moscow Playwrights' Association (RU)
MADA.......... Malaysian Agriculture Development Association (ML)
MADAIR...... Societe Nationale Malgache de Transports Aeriens (MAR)
MADALI...... Manufacture Dakardse de Literie [*Senegalese*] (MAR)
MADAUTO ... Madagascar-Automobile (MAR)
MADCAP..... Societe Madecasse de Chapellerie et Autres Industries (MAR)
MADCONSERVES ... Madagascar-Conserves (MAR)
MADE.......... Movimento de Apoio aos Desempregados [*Movement for Assistance to the Unemployed*] [*Portuguese*] (WER)
MADECAUCHO ... Manufacturas de Caucho [*Medellin*] (COL)
MADECO .... Manufacturas de Cobre, SA [*Copper Manufactures, Inc.*] [*Chilean*] (LA)
MADECONCRETO ... Maderas Concreto [*Bogota*] (COL)
MADEINDECO ... Maderas Industriales de Colombia [*Bogota*] (COL)
MADEMA .... Manufacturas de Madera [*Bogota*] (COL)
MADEMSA ... Manufacturas de Metales, SA [*Metal Manufactures, Inc.*] [*Chilean*] (LA)
Maden Federasyonu ... Turkiye Maden Isci Sendikalari Federasyonu [*Turkish Mine Workers Federation*] (TU)
MADENGRAIS ... Madagascar-Engrais (MAR)
Maden-Is..... Turkish Mine, Metal, Metal Works, and Machine Industry Workers Union (TU)
MADETACO ... Manufacturas Corona Ltda. [*Barranquilla*] (COL)
MADGE........ Microwave Aircraft Digital Guidance Equipment (MAR)
MADI........... Moscow Highway Institute (RU)
MADIMPORT ... Comptoir Malgache d'Importation [*Malagasy Import Agency*] (AF)
MADISZ...... Magyar Demokratikus Ifjusagi Szovetseg [*Association of Hungarian Democratic Youth*] (HU)
MADK.......... Monoamino Dicarboxylic Acid (RU)
MADOC....... Magnetband Austauschformat fuer Dokumentationszweck
MADOME.... Magyar Dolgozok Muveszfenykepezo Egyesulete [*Art Photography Association of Hungarian Workers*] (HU)
MADU.......... Mombasa African Democratic Union (MAR)
MAE........... Magyar Agrartudomanyi Egyesulet [*Association of Hungarian Agricultural Sciences*] (HU)
MAE........... Magyar Agrartudomanyi Egyetem [*Hungarian Agricultural University*] (HU)
MAE........... Ministero degli Affari Esteri [*Ministry of Foreign Affairs*] [*Italian*] (WER)
MAE........... Ministerul Afacerilor Externe [*Ministry of Foreign Affairs*] (RO)
MAE........... Mision Andina del Ecuador [*Ecuadorean Andean Mission*] (LA)
MAE........... Mission Anti-Erosive (MAR)
MAE........... Movimiento de Accion Estudiantil [*Student Action Movement*] [*Argentine*] (LA)
MAE........... Museum of Anthropology and Ethnography (RU)
MAEA.......... Miedzynarodowa Agencja Energii Atomowej [*International Atomic Energy Agency*] (POL)
MAEDY....... Monas Aeroporikis Exypiretiseos Dimosion Ypiresion [*Public Services Air Service Unit*] [*Greek*] (GC)
MAEM......... Missao Antropologica e Etnologica de Mocambique (MAR)
MAER.......... Ministry of Agriculture, Eastern Region (MAR)
MAESON..... Marxist All-Ethiopian Socialist Movement (PD)
MAET.......... Mission Francaise d'Aide Economique et Technique [*French Mission for Economic and Technical Aid*] (CL)
MAF............ Front Militant Autonome [*Autonomous Militant Front*] [*French*] (PD)
MAF............ International Astronautical Federation [*IAF*] (RU)
MAF............ Malaysian Armed Forces (ML)
MAF............ Maroc, Algerie, France (MAR)
MAF............ Moscow Futurists' Association [*Publishing house*] (RU)
MAF............ Movimento de Arregimentacao Feminina [*Women's Regimentation Movement*] [*Brazilian*] (LA)
MAFA.......... Maison des Agriculteurs Francais d'Algerie (MAR)

Mafa .... Maschinenfabrik (Halle) [*Halle Machine Building Enterprise*] (EG)
MAFCO .... Mauritanian Fishery Company (MAR)
MAFDAL ..... National Religious Party [*Israeli*] (ME)
MAFI .... Magyar Allami Foldtani Intezet [*Hungarian State Geological Institute*] (HU)
MAFIA .... Morte Alla Francia Italia Anelo [*Death to the French is Italy's Cry*], or Movimento Anti Francesi Italiano Azione [*Italian Action Movement Against the French*] [*When used in reference to the secret society often associated with organized crime, "Mafia" is from the Sicilian word for boldness or lawlessness*]
MAFILM ...... Magyar Filmgyarto Vallalat [*Hungarian Film Producing Enterprise*] (HU)
MAFIRT .... Magyar Filmipari Reszvenytarsasag [*Hungarian Film Industry Limited (Prewar)*] (HU)
MAFISZ .... Magyar Forradalmi Ifjumunkas Szovetseg [*Hungarian Young Revolutionary Workers' Association*] (HU)
MAFKI .... Magyar Asvanyolaj es Foldgaz Kiserleti Intezet [*Hungarian Petroleum and Natural Gas Experimental Institute*] (HU)
MAFM-KTMA ... Union of Revolutionary Students [*Malagasy*] (AF)
MAFPADUM ... Mouvement Algerien des Forces Populaires et de l'Armee pour la Democratie et l'Union Maghrebine [*Algerian Movement of People's Forces and of the Army for Democracy and Maghreb Union*] (AF)
MAFRAM ..... Maison de l'Amitie Frano-Africaine et Malgache (MAR)
MAG .... High-Power Aerosol Generator (RU)
MAG .... International Association of Geodesy [*IAG*] (RU)
mag .... Magazine [*Military term*], Shop, Store (RU)
Mag .... Magistrat von Gross-Berlin [*Greater Berlin Magistrate*] (EG)
MAG .... Ministerio de Agricultura y Ganaderia [*Ministry of Agriculture and Cattle Breeding*] [*Nicaraguan*] (LA)
MAG .... Ministerio de Agricultura y Ganaderia [*Ministry of Agriculture and Cattle Breeding*] [*Salvadoran*]
mag .... Mohammedan Cemetery [*Topography*] (RU)
MAG .... Morska Agencja w Gdyni [*Maritime Agency in Gdynia*] (POL)
MAG .... Mutuello Agricole du Gabon (MAR)
MAGA .... International Association of Geomagnetism and Aeronomy [*IAGA*] (RU)
MAGA .... Magnetohydrodynamic Analogy (RU)
MAGAMOD ... Magasins Modernes Gabonais (MAR)
Mag arch ..... Magister Architecturae [*Latin*]
Mag arch ..... Magister der Architektur [*German*]
MAGATE ..... International Atomic Energy Agency [*IAEA*] (RU)
MAGD .... Mitteilungen der Afrikanischen Gesellschaft in Deutschland (MAR)
MAGERWA ... Magasins Generaux du Rwanda (MAR)
MAGETAT ... Magasin d'Etat d'Alimentation [*State Food Store*] [*Liquidated 1 July 1970*] [*Cambodian*] (CL)
MAGEV .... Muszaki Anyag- es Gepkereskedelmi Vallalat [*Technical Material and Machinery Trade Enterprise*] (HU)
magg .... Maggio [*May*] [*Italian*]
magg .... Maggiore [*Major*] [*Italian*]
MAGIC .... Mozambique, Angola, Guinea-Bissau Information Center (AF)
Magin .... Magasin [*Shop*] [*Military map abbreviation*] [*World War I*] [*French*] (MTD)
magn .... Magnetic (RU)
magn .... Magnetisch [*Magnetic*] [*German*]
magnet .... Magnetisch [*Magnetic*] [*German*]
magn rez ...... Magnetic Resonance (RU)
Mag pharm ... Magister Pharmaciae [*Latin*]
Mag pharm ... Magister der Pharmazie [*German*]
Mag phil ...... Magister Philosophiae [*Latin*]
Mag phil ...... Magister der Philosophie [*German*]
Mag phil fac theol ... Magister Philosophiae Facultatis Theologicae [*Latin*]
Mag phil fac theol ... Magister der Philosophie der Theologischen Fakultaet [*German*]
Mag rer nat ... Magister Rerum Naturalium [*Latin*]
Mag rer soc oec ... Magister Rerum Socialium Oeconomicarumque [*Latin*]
MAGRIN ...... Maquinaria Agricola e Industrial Ltda. [*Cali*] (COL)
Mag theol .... Magister Theologiae [*Latin*]
Mag theol .... Magister der Theologie [*German*]
MAGU .... Moscow City Trucking and Carting Administration (RU)
MAGW .... Mitteilungen der Anthropologischen Gesellschaft in Wien (MAR)
magy .... Magyar [*Hungarian*] (HU)
MAGZI .... Mission d'Amenagement et de Gestion des Zones Industrielles (MAR)
Mah .... Mahalle [*Quarter, Precinct*] [*of a city*] (TU)
MAH .... Mahkamah [*Court, Tribunal*] (IN)
Mah .... Mahkeme [*Court*] [*of law*] (TU)
MAH .... Milli Asayis Hizmeti [*Turkish National Security Service*] (TU)
MAHABI ...... Magyar Hajozasi Betegsegbiztosito Intezet [*Hungarian Health Insurance Institute for Seamen*] (HU)
MAHART ..... Magyar Hajozasi Reszvenytarsasag [*Hungarian Shipping Company Limited*] (HU)
MAHB .... Mobilna Armiska Hirurska Bolnica [*Mobile Army Surgical Hospital*] (YU)
mahd .... Mahdollinen [*Finnish*]
mahd .... Mahdollisesti [*Finnish*]
MAHIR .... Magyar Hirdeto Vallalat [*Hungarian Advertising Enterprise*] (HU)
MAHMILLUB ... Mahkamah Militer Luar Biasa [*Special Military Tribunal*] (IN)
Mahr .... Maehrchen [*Fairy Tale*] [*German*]
MAI .... International Institute of Agriculture (RU)
MAI .... Memoires de l'Academie des Inscriptions et Belles Lettres [*Paris*] [*A publication*] (MAR)
MAI .... Ministerio da Administracao Interna [*Ministry of Interior*] [*Portuguese*] (WER)
MAI .... Ministerium fuer Aussen- und Innerdeutschen Handel [*Ministry of Foreign and Inner-German Trade*] [*See also MfAI*] (EG)
MAI .... Ministre Attache a l'Interieur [*Minister Assigned to (Ministry of) Interior*] (CL)
MAI .... Moscow Aviation Institute Imeni Sergo Ordzhonikidze (RU)
MAI .... Moscow Institute of Architecture (RU)
MAI .... Movimento Antimilitarista Italiano [*Italian Anti-Militarist Movement*] (WER)
MAI .... Movimiento de Abogados Independientes [*Movement of Independent Lawyers*] [*Panamanian*] (LA)
MAIA .... Materiel Automobile Industriel Agricole [*Moroccan*] (MAR)
MAIA .... Ministerul Agriculturii si Industriei Alimentare [*Ministry of Agriculture and the Food Industry*] (RO)
MAIChP .... International Association on Quaternary Research [*INQUA*] (RU)
MAIM .... International Academy of the History of Medicine (RU)
MAIMA .... Manufacturas Maderas Industriales Ltda. [*Barranquilla*] (COL)
main .... Mainittu [*Finnish*]
MAINCOL .... Maquinaria Internacional de Colombia SA [*Cali*] (COL)
MAIPA .... Maranhao Industria de Pesca e Produtos Alimenticios [*Maranhao Fishing and Food Products Industry*] [*Brazilian*] (LA)
MAIPA .... Movimiento Anti-Imperialista Patriotico de Alicante [*Anti-Imperialist Patriotic Movement of Alicante*] [*Spanish*] (WER)
Maist .... Maisteri [*Master of Arts*] [*Finnish*] (GPO)
MAJ .... Majoor [*Major*] (IN)
maj .... Major [*Major*] [*US equivalent: Major*] (CZ)
Maj .... Major [*Major*] [*French*] (MTD)
maj .... Majuri [*Finnish*]
maj .... Majus [*May*] (HU)
MAJDJEN ..... Majoor Djenderal [*Major General*] (IN)
MAJE .... Movimento Angolano de Juventude Estudante (MAR)
mak .... Macedonian (RU)
MAK .... Magyar Altalanos Koszenbanya Reszvenytarsasag [*Hungarian General Coal Mines Limited (Prewar)*] (HU)
Mak .... Makina [*Machinery, Mechanical*] (TU)
MAK .... Maritime Arbitration Commission (RU)
MAK .... Materials on the Archaeology of the Caucasus (RU)
makb .... Camouflage Battalion (RU)
MAKh .... Museum of the Academy of Arts, USSR (RU)
MAKhD .... Moscow Association of Theatrical Scenery Painters (RU)
MAKI .... Israel Communist Party (ME)
MAKI .... Mathitiki Anexartiti Kinisi [*Student Independent Movement*] (GC)
Makiz .... Moscow Academic Publishing House (RU)
MakNII .... Makeyevka Scientific Research Institute for Work Safety in the Mining Industry (RU)
MAKODAM ... Markas Komando Daerah Militer [*Military Region Command Headquarters*] (IN)
MAKPROFIL ... Macedonian Mine Prospecting and Boring Establishment [*Skopje*] (YU)
MAKS .... Inter-African Committee on Statistics (RU)
MAKS .... International Seed Testing Association [*ISTA*] (RU)
MAKS .... Makina ve Klima Sanayii AS [*Machinery and Air Conditioning Industry Corp.*] (TU)
maks .... Maksanut [*Finnish*]
maks .... Maksettu [*Finnish*]
maks .... Maksimum [*or Maksymalny*] [*Maximum*] [*Polish*]
maks .... Maximum (RU)
MAKSA .... Mainzer Arbeitskreis Sudafrika (MAR)
maks davl ... Maximum Pressure (RU)
maksim .... Maximum (RU)
MAKTAS ..... Makarnacilik ve Ticaret Turk Anonim Sirketi [*Macaroni Manufacture and Trade Corporation*] (TU)
Mak Tec ...... Makina ve Techizat [*Machinery and Equipment*] (TU)
MAKTRANSPORT ... Macedonian Public Transportation Establishment [*Skopje*] (YU)
Mal .... Little, Small (RU)
MAL .... Malacca [*Malaysia*] (ML)
MAL .... Malaysian Air Lines (ML)
Mal .... Maliye [*Finance*] (TU)
mal .... Malowal [*Painted By*] (POL)
MAL .... Manufacturera Agricola [*Bogota*] (COL)
MALA .... Malawi Library Association (MAR)
MALACA ...... Manufacturas de Caucho [*Bogota*] (COL)
malaysk ...... Malay, Malayan (RU)
MALB .... Maliye Bakanligi [*Finance Ministry*] (TU)
MALEV .... Magyar Legikozlekedesi Vallalat [*Hungarian Air Transport Enterprise*] (HU)
Malgobekneft' ... Trust of the Malgobek Petroleum Industry (RU)
MALIAP .... Societe Malienne de Diffusion d'Appareils Electriques (MAR)

MALIGAZ .... Societe Malienne des Gaz Industriels (MAR)
MALIMAG ... Societe Malienne de Grands Magasins (MAR)
MALINET .... Master List of Medical Indexing Terms [*EM*] [*Amsterdam*]
Malre .... Maladrerie [*Hospital for Lepers*] [*Military map abbreviation*] [*World War I*] [*French*] (MTD)
MAM .... Madzi a Moyo (MAR)
MAM .... Memoires de l'Academie Malgache [*Tananarive*] [*A publication*] (MAR)
MAM .... Miroiterie Africaine Moderne (MAR)
mam .... Myriametre [*Myriameter*] [*French*] (GPO)
MAMBO ...... Mediterranean Association for Marine Biology and Oceanology (EA)
MAMG .... Magyar Allami Mezogazdasagi Gepuzem [*Hungarian State Agricultural Machine Factory*] (HU)
MAMI .... Moscow Aircraft Engine Institute (RU)
MAMI .... Moscow Institute of Automotive Engineering (RU)
MAMK .... Mistni Auto-Moto Klub [*Local Motoring Club*] (CZ)
MAMO .... International Association of Microbiological Societies [*IAMS*] (RU)
MAMR .... International Association of Marine Radio Interests (RU)
MAMT .... Moscow Technicum of Automative Engineering (RU)
MAMYu .... Former Moscow Archives of the Ministry of Justice, Kept at the TsGADA (RU)
man .... Manana [*Tomorrow*] [*Spanish*]
MAN .... Mandato de Accion y Unidad Nacional [*Mandate of Action and National Unity*] [*Bolivian*] (PPW)
MAN .... Manufacturers Association of Nigeria (AF)
MAN .... Marea Adunare Nationala [*Grand National Assembly*] (RO)
MAN .... Maschinenfabrik Augsburg-Nuernberg AG [*Augsburg-Nuernberg Machine Factory, Inc.*] (EG)
mAn .... Meiner Ansicht Nach [*In My Opinion*] (EG)
MAN .... Ministerul Apararii Nationale [*Ministry of National Defense*] (RO)
MAN .... Mouvement pour une Alternative Non-Violente [*Movement for a Nonviolent Alternative*] [*French*] (PPE)
MAN .... Movimiento de Accion Nacional [*National Action Movement*] [*Colombian*] (LA)
MAN .... Movimiento de Accion Nacional [*National Action Movement*] [*Venezuelan*] (LA)
MAN .... Movimiento Agricola Nacional [*National Agriculture Movement*] [*Colombian*] (LA)
MAN .... Movimiento Anti-Comunista Nacional [*National Anticommunist Movement*] [*Salvadoran*] (LA)
MAN .... Movimiento Antilliyana Nobo [*New Antillean Movement*] [*Netherlands Antillean*] (LA)
MANA .... Malawi News Agency (MAR)
MANAGRO ... Manufacturas Agroindustriales [*Bogota*] (COL)
MANAPO ..... Makedonski Narodni Pokret [*Macedonian National Movement*] (YU)
MANC .... Mocambique African National Congress (MAR)
MANC .... Mouvement d'Action Nationale Camerounaise (MAR)
MANCER ...... Manufacturas de Ceramica SA [*Medellin*] (COL)
MANCO .... Mocambique African National Congress (MAR)
MANE .... Magyar Allami Nepi Egyuttes [*Hungarian State Folk Ensemble*] (HU)
mangruppa ... Mobile Group, Maneuver Group (RU)
MANIPOL .... Manifesto Politik [*Political Manifesto*] (IN)
MANK .... International Scientific Film Association [*ISFA*] (RU)
mannl .... Maennlich [*German*]
MANO .... Movimiento Anti-Comunista Nacional Organizado [*Organized National Anticommunist Movement*] [*Bolivian*] (LA)
MANO .... Movimiento Anti-Comunista Nacional Organizado [*Organized National Anticommunist Movement*] [*Guatemalan*] (LA)
MANO .... Movimiento Argentino Nacional Organizado [*Argentine National Organized Movement*] (LA)
MANOPLAS ... Manufacturas Plasticas Ltda. [*Medellin*] (COL)
MANR .... Ministry of Agriculture and Natural Resources of Western Nigeria (MAR)
MANS .... Makedonsko-Avstraliski Naroden Sojuz [*Macedonian-Australian People's League*] [*Melbourne*] (YU)
Mant .... Mantik [*Logic*] (TU)
MANTEP ..... Management Training for Education Personnel (MAR)
MANU .... Makonde African National Union (MAR)
MANU .... Mozambique African National Union (AF)
MANUCACIG ... Manufacture Centrafricaine de Cigares (MAR)
MANUCAM ... Manufacture de Toiles et Baches du Cameroun (MAR)
MANUCONGO ... Societe Congolaise de Manutention (MAR)
Manufre ...... Manufacture [*Manufactory*] [*Military map abbreviation*] [*World War I*] [*French*] (MTD)
MANUGAB ... Manufacture Gabonaise (MAR)
MAO .... Mari Autonomous Oblast [*1920-1936*] (RU)
mao .... Med Andra Ord [*In Other Words*] [*Swedish*] (GPO)
mao .... Med Andre Ord [*In Other Words*] [*Norwegian*] (GPO)
MAO .... Monoamine Oxydase (BU)
MAO .... Mordvinian Autonomous Oblast [*1930-1934*] (RU)
MAO .... Moscow Archaeological Society (RU)
MAO .... Moscow Architectural Society [*1867-1930*] (RU)
MAO .... Movimiento Armado Obrero [*Workers' Armed Movement*] [*Guatemalan*] (LA)
MAO .... Movimiento de Asociaciones de Obreros [*Workers' Associations Movement*] [*Argentine*] (LA)
MAO .... Movimiento de Autodefensa de los Obreros [*Workers' Self-Defense Movement*] [*Colombian*] (LA)
MAORT .... Magyar-Amerikai Olajipari Reszvenytarsasag [*Hungarian-American Oil Company Limited*] (HU)
MAP .... International Association of Soil Science [*IASS*] (RU)
MAP .... Maghreb-Arabe Presse [*Maghreb-Arab Press Agency*] [*Moroccan*] (AF)
MAP .... Manufacture Abidjanaise de Plastiques (MAR)
MAP .... Masarykova Akademie Prace [*Masaryk Academy of Labor*] (CZ)
MAP .... Mikhanokinitos Astynomia Poleon [*Motorized Cities Police*] (GC1)
MAP .... Milicias de Accion Popular [*People's Action Militias*] [*Spanish*] (WER)
MAP .... Military Assistance Program (MAR)
MAP .... Ministerio de Agricultura e Pesca [*Ministry of Agriculture and Fisheries*] [*Portuguese*] (WER)
MAP .... Ministerstwo Administracji Publicznej [*Ministry of Public Administration*] (POL)
MAP .... Ministry of the Aircraft Industry, USSR (RU)
MAP .... Ministry of the Automobile Industry, USSR (RU)
MAP .... Moslem Association Party (MAR)
MAP .... Movimiento de Accion Patriotica [*Patriotic Action Movement*] [*Uruguayan*] (LA)
MAP .... Movimiento de Accion Popular [*Popular Action Movement*] [*Mexican*] (LA1)
MAP .... Movimiento Agrario Panameno [*Panamanian Agrarian Movement*] (LA)
MAP .... Mpitolona any Amin'ny Provansa [*Provincial Demonstrators*] [*Malagasy*] (AF)
MAP .... Muscle Adenylic Preparation (RU)
MAP .... Portuguese Action Movement (WER)
MAPA .... Malaysian Agricultural Producers Association (ML)
MAPA .... Movimento de Autodeterminacao para os Acores [*Movement for the Self-Determination of the Azores*] [*Portuguese*] (WER)
MAPAI .... Israel Workers Party (ME)
MAPAM .... United Workers Party (ME)
MAPAMA .... Manufacture Papetiere du Maroc (MAR)
MAPANTJAS ... Mahasiswa Pantjasila [*Pantjasila College Students Association*] (IN)
MAPAS .... Malatya Patron Sanayi ve Ticaret Anonim Sirketi [*Malatya Pattern Industry and Trade Corporation*] (TU)
MAPE .... Movimiento de Afirmacion y Progreso de la Educacion [*Educational Affirmation and Progress Movement*] [*Argentine*] (LA)
MAPHILINDO ... Malaysia, Philippines, and Indonesia (IN)
MAPI .... Mitsubishi Atomic Power Industries, Inc. (SJT)
MAPI .... Movimiento de Accion Popular Independiente [*Independent Popular Action Movement*] [*Colombian*] (LA)
MAPLAS ..... Plasticos y Maquinaria [*Bogota*] (COL)
MAPN .... International Political Science Association [*IPSA*] (RU)
MAPOLEX ... Muanyagfeldolgozo Kisipari Termeloszovetkezet [*Production Cooperative of Plastic Materials*] (HU)
MAPP .... International Association of Proletarian Writers (RU)
MAPP .... Moscow Association of Proletarian Writers (RU)
MAPPENAS ... Musjawarah Perentjanaan Pembangunan Indonesia [*Indonesia Development Planning Council*] (IN)
MAPRC .... Mediterranean Allied Photographic Reconnaissance Command (MAR)
MAPRE .... Maquinaria de Precision Ltda. [*Bogota*] (COL)
MAPRIAL .... Mezhdunarodnaja Assotsiatsija Professorov Russkogo Jazyka i Literatury [*International Association of Teachers of Russian Language and Literature*] (EA)
MAPRINTER ... Empresa Cubana Importadora de Materias Primas y Productos Intermedios [*Cuban Enterprise for Import of Raw Materials and Intermediate Products*] (LA)
MAPS .... International Superphosphate Manufacturers' Association [*ISMA*] (RU)
MAPU .... Matabeleland African Peoples Union [*Rhodesian*] (AF)
MAPU .... Movimiento de Accion Popular Unida [*Unified Popular Action Movement*] [*Chilean*] (PD)
MAPU .... Movimiento de Accion Popular Unitario [*Single Popular Action Movement*] [*Chilean*] (LA)
MAPU .... Movimiento de Avanzada Popular Universitario [*Advanced Popular University Movement*] [*Argentine*] (LA)
MAPU-OC ... Movimiento de Accion Popular Unitario - Obreros y Campesinos [*United Popular Action Movement - Workers and Peasants Faction*] [*Chilean*] (LA1)
MAQUIMPORT ... Empresa Cubana Importadora de Maquinaria y Equipos [*Cuban Enterprise for Import of Machinery and Equipment*] (LA)
MAQUINEGO ... Maquinaria y Negocios [*Medellin*] (COL)
MAQUIT ...... Comercial de Maquinas e Equipamentos [*Machinery and Equipment Marketing Company*] [*Brazilian*] (LA)
MAR- .... Automatic Recorder (RU)
MAR .... International Development Association [*IDA*] (RU)
MAR .... Magyar Allamrendorseg [*Hungarian State Police*] (HU)
mar .... Mari (RU)
mar .... Mark [*Currency*] (RU)
mar .... Marynarz [*Sailor, Mariner*] [*Polish*]

MAR .... Materials on Russian Archaeology (RU)
MAR .... Mezhdunarodnaia Assotsiats Razvitiia (MAR)
MAR .... Morocco [*Three-letter standard code*] (CNC)
MAR .... Movimento de Acao Revolucionaria [*Revolutionary Action Movement*] [*Brazilian*] (LA)
MAR .... Movimento di Azione Rivoluzionaria [*Revolutionary Action Movement*] [*Italian*] (PD)
MAR .... Movimiento de Accion Revolucionaria [*Revolutionary Action Movement*] [*Mexican*] (PD)
MAR .... Movimiento de Accion Revolucionaria [*Revolutionary Action Movement*] [*Guatemalan*] (LA)
MAR .... Movimiento de Accion Revolucionaria [*Revolutionary Action Movement*] [*Panamanian*] (LA)
MAR .... Movimiento de Accion Revolucionaria [*Revolutionary Action Movement*] [*Uruguayan*] (LA)
MAR .... Movimiento Armada Revolucionaria - Accion [*Armed Revolutionary Movement - Action*] [*Mexican*] (LA)
MARA .... Majlis Amanah Rakyat [*Council of Trust for the Indigenous People*] (ML)
MARA .... Ministere de l'Agriculture et de la Reforme Agraire [*Ministry of Agriculture and Agrarian Reform*] (AF)
MARA .... Movimiento Autentico de Recuperacion Argentino [*Argentine Authentic Renewal Movement*] (LA)
MARAGRA ... Marracuene Agricola Acucareira (MAR)
MARAIRMED ... Maritime Air Forces Mediterranean (MAR)
MarASSR .... Mari Autonomous Soviet Socialist Republic (RU)
MARAVEN .. [*A*] Subsidiary of PETROVEN [*Venezuelan*] (LA)
Marbas .... Maritsa Basin (BU)
marc .... Marcius [*March*] (HU)
MARC .... Mouvement d'Action pour la Resurrection du Congo [*Action Movement for the Resurrection of the Congo*] [*Zairian*] (PD)
MARC .... Movimiento Agrario Revolucionario del Campesinado Boliviano [*Revolutionary Movement of Bolivian Indian Peasants*] (PPW)
MARCOMAF ... Societe Commerciale au Service du Marche Commun et de l'Afrique (MAR)
MARDI .... Malaysian Agricultural Research and Development Institute (ML)
MARECS ..... Satellite de Communication Maritime [*Maritime Communications Satellite*] (LA1)
marg .... Margarine Plant [*Topography*] (RU)
margants .... Manganese Mines [*Topography*] (RU)
Marge .... Marecage [*Marsh*] [*Military map abbreviation*] [*World War I*] [*French*] (MTD)
Margosizdat ... Mari State Publishing House (RU)
margr .... Margrabia [*Margrave*] [*Polish*]
MARIMEX ... Maroc-Import-Export [*Moroccan Import-Export Co.*] (AF)
Marknigoizdat ... Mari Book Publishing House (RU)
marm .... Marmoriert [*Marbled*] [*Bookbinding*] [*German*]
MARN .... Movimento de Agricultores Rendeiros do Norte [*Northern Tenant Farmers Movement*] [*Portuguese*] (WER)
MARPE .... Movimiento de Afirmacion y Renovacion Peronista [*Peronist Renewal and Reaffirmation Movement*] [*Argentine*] (LA)
MARPESCA ... Empresa Cubana Importadora de Buques Mercantes y de Pesca [*Cuban Enterprise for the Import of Merchant and Fishing Ships*] (LA)
MARPORT ... Empresa Maritima Portuaria de Importacion [*Maritime and Ports Importation Enterprise*] [*Cuban*] (LA)
MARS .... Movimiento de Accion Revolucionaria Socialista [*Socialist Revolutionary Action Movement*] [*Costa Rican*] (LA)
MARSA .... Margarin Sanayi AS [*Margarine Industry Corp.*] (TU)
MARSAVCO ... Societe des Margarines et Savonneries Congolaises (MAR)
marsh .... Marshal (RU)
marsz .... Marszalek [*Marshal*] [*Polish*]
mart .... Martes [*Tuesday*] [*Spanish*]
MARTEKS ... Maras Tekstil Sanayii AS [*Maras Textile Industry Corp.*] (TU)
marts .... Martires [*Martyrs*] [*Spanish*]
MARU .... Instantaneous Automatic Gain Control (RU)
MARVIL .... Societe de Production Maraichere Vilmorin (MAR)
MARZ .... Moscow Automobile Repair Plant (RU)
MAS .... International Astronomical Union [*IAU*] (RU)
MAS .... Interplanetary Automatic Station (RU)
MAS .... Local Automatic System (RU)
MAS .... Malaysia Air System (ML)
MAS .... Maschinenausleihstation [*Machine Rental Station*] (EG)
MAS .... Ministerio dos Asountos Sociais [*Ministry of Social Affairs*] [*Portuguese*] (WER)
MAS .... Mission d'Amenagement du Fleuve Senegal (MAR)
MAS .... Monetary Authority of Singapore
MAS .... Moravske Akciove Strojirny, Narodni Podnik [*Moravian Machine Building Joint-Stock Company, National Enterprise*] (CZ)
MAS .... Mouvement d'Action Socialiste [*Socialist Action Movement*] [*Belgian*] (WER)
MAS .... Movimiento de Accion Social [*Social Action Movement*] [*Dominican Republic*] (LA)
MAS .... Movimiento de Afirmacion Social [*Social Affirmation Movement*] [*Argentine*] (LA)
MAS .... Movimiento al Socialismo [*Movement towards Socialism*] [*Venezuelan*] (PPW)
MAS .... Muerte a los Secuestradores [*Death to Kidnappers*] [*Colombian*] (PD)
mas .... Oil Mill [*Topography*] (RU)
MASA .... Medical Aid for Southern Africa (MAR)
MASA .... Medical Association of South Africa
MASA .... Mediterranean Allied Strategic Air Force (MAR)
MASA .... Mines-African Staff Association (MAR)
MASD .... Minimal Absolute Lethal Dose (RU)
MASD .... Movimiento al Socialismo Democratico [*Movement toward Democratic Socialism*] [*Bolivian*] (LA1)
mash .... Machine Shop [*Topography*] (RU)
mash .... Machinery Plant [*Topography*] (RU)
MAShGIZ .... State Scientific and Technical Publishing House of Literature on Machinery Manufacture (RU)
mashin .... Typewritten (BU)
mashinno-trakt ... Machine-and-Tractor (RU)
Mashinoimport ... All-Union Association for the Import of Machinery (RU)
Mashmetizdat ... State Publishing House of the Machinery, Metalworking, and Aircraft Industries (RU)
mash opyt st ... Machine Experimental Station [*Topography*] (RU)
Mashpriborstroy ... All-Union Construction and Installation Trust of the Ministry of Machinery Manufacture and Instrument Making, USSR (RU)
mashprom ... Machinery Industry (RU)
MASI .... Inter-American Statistical Institute [*IASI*] (RU)
mask .... Camouflage (RU)
MASK .... International Credit Insurance Association [*ICIA*] (RU)
mask .... Maskuliini [*Finnish*]
MASK .... Materials Warehouses and Stock Rooms (RU)
maskkov ..... Camouflage Drape (RU)
maskr .... Camouflage Company (RU)
maskv .... Camouflage Platoon (RU)
Masl .... Oil Mill [*Topography*] (RU)
masloprom ... Oil Industry (RU)
MASLOTsENTR ... Central Union of Dairy Cooperatives (RU)
MASMO ...... Medical Equipment Workshops (RU)
MASO .... International Social Security Association [*ISSA*] (RU)
MASPED ..... Magyar Altalanos Szallitmanyozasi Vallalat [*Hungarian General Shipping Enterprise*] (HU)
MASPLA ..... Movimiento por la Autodeterminacion y la Solidaridad de los Pueblos LatinoAmericanos [*Movement for the Self-Determination and Solidarity of Latin American Peoples*] [*Argentine*] (LA)
MASPS .... Moroccan Association for the Support of the Palestinian Struggle (AF)
masr .... Camouflage Company (RU)
MASSIFER ... F. Massiye and J. Ferras (MAR)
Masspartgiz ... State Publishing House of Mass Party Literature (RU)
MASSR .... Mari Autonomous Soviet Socialist Republic (RU)
MASSR .... Moldavian Autonomous Soviet Socialist Republic [*1924-1940*] (RU)
MASSR .... Mordvinian Autonomous Soviet Socialist Republic (RU)
mass yed .... Mass Unit (RU)
mast .... Ink (BU)
mast .... Workshop, Shop (RU)
MASTAS ..... Marmara Melamin Sanayi ve Ticaret Anonim Sirketi [*Marmara Melamine (Cyanuramide) Industry and Marketing Corporation*] (TU)
MASTER ..... Movimento de Agricultores sem Terras [*Landless Farmers Movement*] [*Brazilian*] (LA)
MASYDA ..... Materiaux de Synthese de Dakar (MAR)
MASZ .... Magyar Allami Szenbanyak [*Hungarian State Coal Mines*] (HU)
MASZ .... Magyar Atletikai Szovetseg [*Hungarian Athletic Association*] (HU)
maszek .... Magan Szektor [*Private Sector (of Economy) or Private Merchant or Craftsman, Moonlighter*] (HU)
MASZI .... Magyar Szabvanyugyi Intezet [*Hungarian Bureau of Standards*] (HU)
MASZOBAL ... Magyar-Szovjet Bauxit-Aluminium Reszvenytarsasag [*Hungarian-Soviet Bauxite Company Limited*] (HU)
MASZOLAJ RT ... Magyar-Szovjet Olajipari Reszvenytarsasag [*Hungarian-Soviet Industrial Oil Company Limited*] (HU)
MASZOVAL ... Magyar-Szovjet Bauxit-Aluminium Tarsasagok [*Hungarian-Soviet Bauxite Companies*] (HU)
MASZOVLET ... Magyar-Szovjet Polgari Legiforgalmi Tarsasag [*Hungarian-Soviet Civilian Airline*] (HU)
MASZOVOL ... Magyar-Szovjet Nyersolaj Reszvenytarsasag [*Hungarian-Soviet Crude Oil Company Limited*] (HU)
MAT .... International Automotive Transport (BU)
MAT .... Magyar Aluminiumipari Troszt [*Hungarian Aluminum Industry Trust*] (HU)
MAT .... Magyar Autonom Tartomany [*Hungarian Autonomous Territory (in Romania)*] (HU)
m at .... Masa Atomowa [*Atomic Mass*] [*Polish*]
mat .... Matematiikka [*Mathematics*] [*Finnish*]
Mat .... Matematik [*Mathematics*] (TU)
mat .... Matematyczny [*or Matematyka*] [*Mathematical or Mathematics*] (POL)
mat .... Mathematical (BU)
MAT .... Mathematical Association of Tanzania (MAR)
mat .... Mathematical, Mathematics (RU)

MAT .... Medical Association of Tanzania (MAR)
MAT .... Monades Andimetopiseos Tarakhon [*Riot Center Units*] [*See also MMAD, OAT*] (GC1)
MAT .... Monades Apokatastaseos Taxeos [*Order Restoration Units*] (GC1)
MAT .... Motorlu Araclar Ticaret AS [*Motorized Vehicles Trading Corporation*] (TU)
MATA .... Museums Association of Tropical Africa (AF)
MATAF .... Mediterranean Allied Tactical Air Force (MAR)
MATCO .... Materiales de Construccion Ltda. [*Santa Marta*] (COL)
MATE .... Merestechnikai es Automatizalasi Tudomanyos Egyesulet [*Scientific Association of Measures and Automation*] (HU)
MATE .... Modern Aids to Education (MAR)
MATEIP .... Magyar Textilipari Vallalat [*Hungarian Textile Mill*] (HU)
MATEL-AFRIC ... Materiel Electrique Africain (MAR)
MATELCA ... Societe Marocaine de Telecommunications par Cables Sousmarins [*Moroccan*] (MAR)
MATELCO ... Societe de Materiel Electrique du Congo (MAR)
MATELECS ... Materiales Electricos [*Bogota*] (COL)
MATELT ...... Ministere de l'Amenagement du Territoire, de l'Equipement, du Logement, et du Tourisme [*Ministry of Territorial Development, Equipment, Housing, and Tourism*] [*French*] (WER)
matem .... Mathematical (BU)
matemat ..... Mathematical, Mathematics (RU)
MATEOSZ ... Magyar Teherfuvarozok Orszagos Kozponti Szovetkezete [*National Central Cooperative of Hungarian Truckers*] (HU)
mater .... Materials (RU)
MATERAUTO ... Materiel Automobile et Industriel (MAR)
MATERMACO-Congo ... Materiel et Materiaux de Construction - Congo (MAR)
MATESZ ..... Magyar Tekezo Szovetseg [*Hungarian Bowling Association*] (HU)
MATESZ ..... Magyar Teruleti Szinhaz [*Hungarian Regional Theater*] (HU)
math .... Mathematisch [*German*]
MATI .... Magasepitesi Tervezo Intezet [*Designing Institute for Building Construction*] (HU)
MATI .... Ministry of Agriculture Training Institute (MAR)
MATI .... Moscow Aviation Technological Institute (RU)
MATICOSE ... Manufacture de Tissage et de Confection Senegalaise (MAR)
MATIN .... Ministry of Agriculture Training Institute at Nyegezi (MAR)
MATiShD .... Ministry of Automobile Transportation and Highways (RU)
MATMCGFF ... Ministerul Aprovizionarii Tehnico-Materiale si Controlul Gospodaririi Fondurilor Fixe [*Ministry of Technical-Material Supply and Control of the Management of Fixed Assets*] (RO)
MATOBA ..... Manufacture de Toiles et Baches (MAR)
MATP .... Ministry of the Automobile and Tractor Industry (RU)
Matrez .... Uprava Materijalnih Rezervi [*Administration of Material Reserves*] (YU)
MATS .... Long-Distance Automatic Telephone Communication (RU)
MATs .... Methylacetone (RU)
MATS .... Middle Africa Transportation Survey (MAR)
MATShD ..... Ministry of Automobile Transportation and Highways (RU)
MATShOSDOR ... Ministry of Automobile Transportation and Highways (RU)
MATTRA ..... Societe Mauritanienne de Transit, Transport, Representation, Assurances (MAR)
MATZPEN ... Political Party [*Israeli*] (ME)
MAU .... International Association of Universities [*IAU*] (RU)
MAUD .... Movimento Academico pela Uniao Democrata [*Academic Movement for Democratic Union*] [*Portuguese*] (PPE)
MAUK .... Moscow Automobile Training Center (RU)
MAUND .... Mouvement Algerien pour l'Unite Nationale et la Democratie [*Algerian Movement for National Unity and Democracy*] (AF)
MAUP .... International Association of Criminal Law (RU)
MAURELEC ... Societe Mauritanienne d'Electricite [*Mauritanian Electricity Company*] (AF)
MAUREX ..... Societe Mauritanienne d'Explosifs (MAR)
MAURINAP ... Societe Mauritanienne de Diffusion d'Appareils Electriques (MAR)
MAURIPEX ... Mauritania Import-Export (MAR)
MAUS .... Movimiento de Accion y Unidad Socialista [*Socialist Movement for Action and Unity*] [*Mexican*] (PPW)
MAV .... Magyar Allamvasutak [*Hungarian State Railways*] (HU)
mAV .... Maritime Antarctic Air (RU)
mAV .... Maritime Arctic Air (RU)
MAV .... Maximum Adsorptive Moisture Capacity (RU)
MAV .... Misti Akcni Vybor [*Local Action Committee*] (CZ)
MAV .... Small Amphibian (RU)
MAVAG .... Magyar Allami Vas, Acel-, es Gepgyarak [*Hungarian State Iron, Steel, and Machine Factories*] (HU)
MAVAS .... Monimos Andiprosopeia Voreio-Atlandikou Symfonou [*Permanent Delegation to NATO*] (GC)
MAVAUT ..... Magyar Allamvasutak Autobusz Uzeme [*Autobus Service of the Hungarian State Railways*] (HU)
MAVI .... Metopon Apelevtheroseos Voreiou Ipeirou [*Northern Ipeiros Liberation Front*] [*Greek*] (GC)
MAVIE .... Manufacture Voltaique d'Insecticides et d'Esthetique (MAR)
MAV Jegyny ... Magyar Allamvasutak Jegynyomdaja [*Ticket Printing Office of the Hungarian State Railroads*] (HU)
MAVOCI ...... Manufacture Voltaique de Cigarettes (MAR)
MAVOSZ ..... Magyar Vadaszok Orszagos Szovetsege [*National Association of Hungarian Hunters*] (HU)
MAVTI .... Magyar Allamvasutak Tervezo Intezet [*Planning Institute of Hungarian State Railways*] (HU)
MAVTRANS ... Magyar Allamvasutak Szallitmanyozasi Szolgalata [*Transfer Service of the Hungarian State Railroads*] (HU)
MAW .... Mauritius Alliance of Women (AF)
MAW .... Messegeraete- und Armaturenwerk, Magdeburg (VEB) [*Magdeburg Measuring Instrument and Fittings Plant (VEB)*] (EG)
MAW .... Militant Action Workers (MAR)
maW .... Mit Anderen Worten [*In Other Words*] [*German*]
MAWR .... Ministry of Agriculture, Western Region (MAR)
MAWU .... Mechanical and Allied Workers Union [*Liberian*] (AF)
max .... Maximum [*Maximum*] [*German*]
MAY .... Monades Asfaleias Ypaithrou [*Rural Security Units*] [*Greek*] (GC)
MAYC .... Malaysian Association of Youth Clubs (ML)
MAYe .... Maritime Astronomical Yearbook [*A publication*] (RU)
maymo .... Mayordomo [*Spanish*]
MAYSAN ..... Makine ve Yedekparca Sanayi ve Ticaret AS [*Machinery and Spare Parts Industry and Trade Corp.*] (TU)
MAYuD .... International Association of Democratic Lawyers (BU)
MAYuD .... International Association of Democratic Lawyers [*IADL*] (RU)
MAYuN .... International Association of Legal Science [*IALS*] (RU)
MAZ .... Automobile Made by the Minsk Automobile Plant (RU)
MAZ .... Magistrates Association of Zambia (MAR)
MAZ .... Minsk Automobile Plant (RU)
MAZh .... International Alliance of Women [*IAW*] (RU)
MAZhK .... International Railway Congress Association [*IRCA*] (RU)
MB .... Bridge Battalion (RU)
MB .... Local Battery (RU)
MB .... Local Office (RU)
MB .... Magnetic Drum (RU)
MB .... Magyar Bajnoksag [*Hungarian Championship*] (HU)
MB .... Majlis Bandar [*City or Town Council*] (ML)
MB .... Makedonska Bibliografija [*Macedonian Bibliography*] (YU)
MB .... Malaysia Barat [*West Malaysia*] (ML)
MB .... Markas Besar [*Main Headquarters*] (IN)
MB .... Medical Base (RU)
MB .... Medicinae Baccalaureus [*Bachelor of Medicine*] [*Latin*] (GPO)
mb .... Megyei Birosag [*County Court*] (HU)
MB .... Menteri Besar [*Chief Minister*] (ML)
mb .... Metr Biezacy [*Running Meter*] [*Polish*]
mb .... Millibar (BU)
mb .... Millibar (RU)
Mb .... Mineral Bath (BU)
MB .... Ministerstwo Bezpieczenstwa [*Ministry of Security*] (POL)
MB .... Ministerstwo Budownictwa [*Ministry of Construction*] (POL)
MB .... Minobacac [*Mine Thrower*] (YU)
MB .... Mobile Base, Tender [*Navy*] (RU)
mb .... Mortar Battalion (RU)
mb .... Mortar Battery (RU)
M/b .... Motorni Brod [*Motor Ship*] (YU)
MB .... Muslim Brothers (MAR)
mb .... Perhaps (RU)
m-b .... Scale (RU)
MBA .... Interlibrary Loan (RU)
MBA .... Military Basketball Association [*Sudanese*] (MAR)
MBAM .... Missao Botanica de Angola e Mocambique, Junta de Investigacoes do Ultramar (MAR)
mbar .... Milibar [*Millibar*] [*Polish*]
mbarn .... Millibarn (RU)
mbatr .... Meteorological Battery (BU)
MBB .... Magyar Beruhazasi Bank [*Hungarian Investment Bank*] (HU)
MBBB .... Marmara ve Bogazlari Belediyeleri Birligi [*Marmara and Straits (of Bosporus) Municipalities' Union*] (TU)
MBBS .... Boy Scouts International Bureau [*BSIB*] (RU)
MBBS .... Malaya Borneo Building Society Ltd. (ML)
MBC .... Malawi Broadcasting Corporation (AF)
MBC .... Mauritius Broadcasting Corporation (AF)
MBCEU .... Mauritius Broadcasting Corporation Employees Union (AF)
MBCS .... Manufacture de Bonneterie et de Confection Senegalaise (MAR)
MBD .... International Office of Railway Documentation (RU)
MBD .... Majlis Belia Daerah [*District Youth Council*] (ML)
MBD .... Millions of Barrels per Day (MAR)
MBDP .... Ministry of the Paper and Woodworking Industries (RU)
MBE .... Member of British Empire (ML)
MBER .... Inter-American Development Bank (RU)
mber .... Millirem (RU)
MBF .... Medunarodna Bibliotekarska Federacija [*International Federation of Library Associations*] (YU)
MBF .... Monobutyl Phosphate (RU)
MBG .... Milli Birligi Grupu [*National Unity Group*] [*See also MBK*] (TU)
MBG .... Mission Biologique du Gabon (MAR)
MBH .... Megyei Begyujtesi Hivatal [*County Crop Collection Office*] (HU)
mbH .... Mit Beschraenkter Haftung [*With Limited Liability*] (EG)
MBH .... Muzej Bosne i Hercegovine [*Museum of Bosnia and Hercegovina*] (YU)

MBHB.......... Malaysian Batik and Handicrafts Bureau (ML)
MBHS.......... Methodist Boys' High School (MAR)
MBI-.......... Biological Immersion Microscope (RU)
MBI.......... International Institute of Bibliography [*1895-1931*] (RU)
MBiDP.......... Ministry of the Paper and Woodworking Industries (RU)
MBIS.......... International Bank for Economic Cooperation (BU)
MBK.......... International Congress of Biochemistry (RU)
MBK.......... International Container Bureau [*ICB*] (RU)
MBK.......... Magyar Beke-Kongresszus [*Hungarian Peace Congress*] (HU)
MBK.......... Milli Birligi Kurulu [*National Unity Committee*] [*See also MBG*] (TU)
MBM.......... Majlis Belia Malaysia [*Malaysian Youth Council*] (ML)
MBM.......... Miedzykolkowe Bazy Maszynowe [*Inter-Circle Machine Bases*] [*Agriculture*] (POL)
MBM.......... Missao de Biologia Maritima, Junta de Investigacoes do Ultramar (MAR)
MBMiO.......... Ministerstwo Budownictwa Miast i Osiedli [*Ministry of City and Settlement Construction*] (POL)
MBO.......... Musterbetriebsordnung [*Model Factory Regulations, Model Shop Rules*] (EG)
MBOG.......... International Office of Public Hygiene [*1907-1946*] (RU)
MBOR.......... Miedzynarodowy Bank Odbudowy i Rozwoju [*International Bank for Reconstruction and Development*] [*Polish*]
mbp.......... Ammunition Supply Workshop (RU)
MBP.......... International Biological Program (RU)
MBP.......... Miedzynarodowe Biuro Pracy [*International Labor Office*] [*Polish*]
MBP.......... Miejska Biblioteka Publiczna [*Municipal Public Library*] [*Polish*]
MBP.......... Milli Birlik Partisi [*National Unity Party*] [*See also UBP*] [*Cypriot*] (TU)
MBP.......... Ministerstwo Bezpieczenstwa Publicznego [*Ministry of Public Security*] (POL)
MBP.......... Ministerstwo Budownictwa Przemyslowego [*Ministry of Industrial Construction*] (POL)
MBP.......... Moscow Trade-Union Office (RU)
MBPP.......... Middle Belt Peoples' Party (MAR)
MBPP.......... Movimento Brasileiro dos Partidarios da Paz [*Brazilian Movement of Peace Partisans*] (LA)
mbr.......... Bridge Brigade (RU)
MBR.......... Intercontinental Ballistic Missile (BU)
MBR.......... Intercontinental Ballistic Missile (RU)
MBR.......... International Labor Office [*ILO*] (RU)
MBR.......... Mineracoes Brasileiras Reunidas [*Brazilian Mines Association*] (LA)
Mbr.......... Mitropolija Broj [*Metropolis Number*] [*Orthodox Eastern Church*] [*Serbian*] (YU)
MBR.......... Naval Short-Range Reconnaissance Aircraft (RU)
MBRKh.......... International Office of Revolutionary Artists (RU)
MBRL.......... International Office of Revolutionary Literature (RU)
MBRR.......... International Bank for Reconstruction and Development [*IBRD*] (RU)
MBRR.......... Mezhdunarodni Bank Rekonstruktsii i Razvitiia (MAR)
MBS.......... Biological Stereomicroscope (RU)
MBS-.......... Boring and Polesetting Machine (RU)
MBS.......... Intercontinental Ballistic Missile (RU)
MBS.......... International Union of Biochemistry [*IUB*] (RU)
MBS.......... Mano Blanca Salvadorena [*Salvadoran White Hand*] (LA)
MBS.......... Medborgerlig Samling [*Citizens Rally*] [*Swedish*] (PPE)
MBS.......... Methodist Boys School (ML)
MBS.......... Ministerio de Bienestar Social [*Ministry of Social Welfare*] [*Nicaraguan*] (LA1)
MBT.......... International Labor Bureau (BU)
MBT.......... Local Remote-Control Unit (RU)
MBT.......... Magyar Beke-Tanacs [*Hungarian Peace Council*] (HU)
MbT.......... Mariborska Tiskarna [*Maribor Printers*] (YU)
MBT.......... Mercaptobenzothiazole (RU)
MBTK-.......... Mobile Tubular Tower Crane (RU)
MB-TKA.......... Motor Torpedo Boat Tender (RU)
MBU.......... Medical Reinforcement Brigade (RU)
MBU.......... Moscow Basin Administration (RU)
MBV.......... International Time Bureau (RU)
MBV.......... Mistni Bezpecnostni Vybor [*Local Security Committee*] (CZ)
MBVR.......... Local Clearinghouse (RU)
MBVV.......... International Wine and Vine Office [*IWO*] (RU)
MBW.......... Miedzynarodowe Biuro Wychowania [*International Education Bureau*] [*Polish*]
MC.......... Manganese Centre (EA)
Mc.......... Metre Cube [*Cubic Meter*] [*French*] (MTD)
mc.......... Metru Cub [*Cubic Meter*] (RO)
M/c.......... Mi Cuenta [*My Account, My Debit*] [*Business and trade*] [*Spanish*]
m-c.......... Miesiac [*Month*] [*Polish*]
MC.......... Milli Cephesi [*National Front (Government)*] (TU)
MC.......... Mining Corporation (MAR)
MC.......... Ministere des Colonies (MAR)
MC.......... Ministere du Congo Belge et du Ruanda-Urundi (MAR)
m/c.......... Mon Compte [*French*]
MC.......... Monaco [*Two-letter standard code*] (CNC)
MC.......... Monako [*Monaco*] [*Polish*]
M/c.......... Motorni Camac [*Motor Boat*] (YU)
M/c.......... Motorni Coln [*Motor Boat*] (YU)
MCA.......... Malaysian Chinese Association (PPW)
MCA.......... Member of Constituent Assembly (MAR)
mca.......... Miesiaca [*Month*] [*Polish*]
MCA.......... Mouvement Cooperatif Algerien [*Algerian Cooperative Movement*] (AF)
MCA.......... Muslim Committee of Action [*Mauritanian*] (MAR)
Mcal.......... Megakaloria, Termia [*Megacalorie, Ton Calorie, Therm*] [*Polish*]
MCBA.......... Malaysian Commercial Banks Association (ML)
MCC.......... Malawi Correspondence College (MAR)
MCC.......... Manufacture Camerounaise de Caoutchouc (MAR)
MCC.......... Manufacture de la Couture Camerounaise (MAR)
MCC.......... Member of Central Committee (MAR)
MCC.......... Mercado Comun Centroamericano [*Central American Common Market*] [*Use CACM*] (LA)
MCC.......... Military Co-Ordinating Committee (MAR)
MCC.......... Moslem Construction Company Ltd. (MAR)
MCC.......... Movimiento Civico Cristiano [*Civic Christian Movement*] [*Uruguayan*] (LA)
MCC.......... Movimiento Conciencia Catolica [*Catholic Awareness Movement*] [*Mexican*] (LA1)
MCCA.......... Malacca [*Malaysia*] (ML)
MCCI.......... Moto-Club de Cote-d'Ivoire (MAR)
MCCS.......... Ministry of Cooperation, Commerce, and Supply [*Sudanese*] (MAR)
MCD.......... Movimento Contra a Ditadura [*Movement Against Dictatorship*] [*Brazilian*] (LA)
MCE.......... Malayan Certificate of Education (ML)
MCE.......... Mercado Comun Europeo [*European Common Market*] (LA)
MCE.......... Ministerio de Comercio Exterior [*Ministry of Foreign Trade*] [*Portuguese*] (WER)
MCE.......... Movimiento Civil Ecuatoriano [*Ecuadorean Civil Movement*] (LA)
MCE.......... Movimiento Comunista de Espana [*Communist Movement of Spain*] (WER)
MCECEI.......... Ministerul Comertului Exterior si Cooperarii Economice Internationale [*Ministry of Foreign Trade and International Economic Cooperation*] (RO)
MCF.......... Missions Church Federation (MAR)
MCFI.......... Mauritius Chemical and Fertilizer Industry (AF)
MCG.......... Movimiento Comunista de Galicia [*Communist Movement of Galicia*] [*Spanish*] (WER)
MCG.......... Movimiento Cooperativista Guatemalteco [*Guatemalan Cooperationist Movement*] (LA)
MCh.......... Clockwork (RU)
MCh.......... Interval Frequency (BU)
m/ch.......... Machine/Hour (BU)
MCh.......... Magister Chirurgiae [*Master of Surgery*] [*Latin*] (GPO)
MCh.......... Materiel (RU)
MCH.......... Maternal Child Health (MAR)
MCh.......... Meridional Parts (RU)
MCH.......... Morska Centrala Handlowa [*Maritime Trade Center*] (POL)
m/chas.......... Machine/Hour (BU)
MChE.......... Magyar Chemikusok Egyesulete [*Association of Hungarian Chemists*] (HU)
Mche.......... Marche [*Market*] [*Military map abbreviation*] [*World War I*] [*French*] (MTD)
MCHFP.......... Maternity and Child Health and Family Planning Project [*Sudanese*] (MAR)
MChK.......... Moscow Extraordinary Commission for Combating Counterrevolution and Sabotage [*1917-1922*] (RU)
MChM.......... Ministry of Ferrous Metallurgy (RU)
MChP.......... Ministerstvo Chemickeho Prumyslu [*Ministry of the Chemical Industry*] (CZ)
MChZ.......... Method of Frequency Sounding (RU)
MChZ.......... Moravske Chemicke Zavody [*Moravian Chemical Plants*] (CZ)
MChZ.......... Moscow Watchmaking Plant (RU)
MCI.......... Ministerio de Comercio Interior [*Ministry of Domestic Commerce*] [*Portuguese*] (WER)
MCI.......... Ministerul Comertului Interior [*Ministry of Domestic Trade*] (RO)
MCI.......... Ministerul Constructiilor Industriale [*Ministry of Industrial Construction*] (RO)
MCI.......... Movimiento Campesino Independiente [*Independent Peasants Movement*] [*Guatemalan*] (LA)
Mcin.......... Medecin [*Doctor*] [*Military*] [*French*] (MTD)
MCInd.......... Ministerul Constructiilor Industriale [*Ministry of Industrial Construction*] (RO)
MCK.......... Mezinarodni Cerveny Kriz [*International Red Cross*] (CZ)
MCK.......... Miedzynarodowy Czerwony Krzyz [*International Red Cross*] [*Polish*]
MCKS.......... Makedonski Centralen Kooperativen Sojuz [*Macedonian Central Cooperative Union*] (YU)
MCL.......... Mauritius Confederation of Labor (AF)
MCL.......... Movimiento Comunista Liberatorio [*Liberatory Communist Movement*] [*Mexican*] (LA1)
MCLN.......... Mouvement Centrafricain de Liberation Nationale [*Central African Movement for National Liberation*] (PD)
MCM.......... Marche Commun Maghrebin (MAR)
MCM.......... Movimiento Catorce de Mayo [*14 May Movement*] [*Paraguayan*] (LA)

MCN .... Movimiento de Conciliacion Nacional [*National Conciliation Movement*] [*Dominican Republic*] (PPW)
MCn .... Triturated Gun Powder [*Symbol*] [*French*] (MTD)
MCNL .... Military Committee of National Liberation [*Malian*] (PPW)
mco .... Marco [*March*] [*Portuguese*] (GPO)
MCO .... Monaco [*Three-letter standard code*] (CNC)
MCP .... Malaria Control Plan (ML)
MCP .... Malawi Congress Party (PPW)
MCP .... Malayan Communist Party (ML)
MCP .... Mouvement Chretien pour la Paix [*Christian Peace Movement*] [*Belgian*] (WER)
MCP .... Movimento de Cultura Popular [*People's Culture Movement*] [*Brazilian*] (LA)
MCR .... Movimento Comunista Revolucionario [*Revolutionary Communist Movement*] [*Brazilian*] (LA)
MCR .... Movimiento Campesino Revolucionario [*Revolutionary Peasant Movement*] [*Chilean*] (LA)
MCR .... Movimiento Cristiano Revolucionario [*Revolutionary Christian Movement*] [*Nicaraguan*] (LA1)
MCRL .... Movimiento Costa Rica Libre [*Free Costa Rican Movement*] (LA)
MCS .... Malaysian Civil Service (ML)
MCS .... Ministerio da Comunicacao Social [*Ministry of Mass Communication*] [*Portuguese*] (WER)
MCS .... Movimento Convergencia Socialista [*Socialist Convergence Movement*] [*Brazilian*] (LA)
MCSA .... Malaysian Civil Service Association (ML)
MCSA .... Mountain Club of South Africa (MAR)
MCSP .... Mesic Ceskoslovensko-Sovetskeho Pratelstvi [*Czechoslovak-Soviet Friendship Month*] (CZ)
MCSZ .... Magyarorszagi Cionista Szovetseg [*Zionist Federation in Hungary*] (HU)
MCT .... Manufacture de Cigarettes du Tchad (MAR)
MCT .... Missao de Combate as Tripanosomiases (MAR)
MCT .... Mission de Controle du Transgabonais (MAR)
MCTA .... Mild Coffee Trade Association (MAR)
MCTC .... Movimiento Campesino Tupaj Catari [*Bolivian*] (PPW)
m/cte .... Mon Compte [*My Account*] [*Business and trade*] [*French*]
MCTU .... Mauritius Confederation of Trade Unions (AF)
MCU .... Meru Citizens Union (MAR)
MCU .... Mladez Ceskoslovenskych Unitaru [*Czechoslovak Unitarian Youth Group*] (CZ)
MCU .... Movimiento Civico Unitario [*United Civic Movement*] [*Chilean*] (LA)
MCV .... Movimiento Comunista Vascongado [*Basque Communist Movement*] [*Spanish*] (WER)
MCYL .... Malayan Communist Youth League [*South Thailand, supporting CTO*] (ML)
m cz .... Mala Czestotliwosc [*Low Frequency*] [*Polish*]
MD .... Air Madagascar (MAR)
MD- .... Differential Manometer, Differential Pressure Gauge (RU)
MD .... Dose Rate (RU)
MD .... Magnetic Disk (RU)
MD- .... Magnetographic Defectoscope (RU)
Md .... Marchand [*Merchant*] [*Business and trade*] [*French*]
MD .... Masarykovy Domovy v Krci [*Masaryk Homes for the Aged in Krc*] (CZ)
MD .... Masarykuv Dul [*Masaryk Mine*] [*Tynec*] (CZ)
MD .... Matica Dalmatinska [*A Dalmatian literary and publishing society*] [*Zadar*] (YU)
MD .... Mechanized Division (RU)
MD .... Medical Documentation (RU)
MD .... Medicinae Doctor [*Doctor of Medicine*] [*Latin*] (GPO)
MD .... Melayu Di-Raja [*Royal Malay*] (ML)
MD .... Mestske Divadlo [*Municipal Theater*] (CZ)
MD .... Meteorologischer Dienst [*Meteorological Service*] (EG)
MD .... Mevcut Degil [*Not Available*] (TU)
MD .... Mine Detonator (RU)
MD .... Mine Surveying (RU)
MD .... Ministerio de Defesa [*Ministry of Defense*] [*Portuguese*] (WER)
MD .... Ministerstvo Dopravy [*Ministry of Transportation*] (CZ)
MD .... Ministry of Supply [*Obsolete*] (BU)
MD .... Mitteldruck [*Intermediate Pressure*] [*German*]
md .... Mobilization Documents (RU)
MD .... Modulator (RU)
m/d .... Mois de Date [*French*]
MD .... Moroccan Dinar (MAR)
md .... Mortar Battalion (RU)
MD .... Movimiento Desarrollista [*Movement for Development*] [*Venezuelan*] (LA)
Md .... Mudur [*or Mudurlik*] [*Director or Directorate*] (TU)
Md .... Mudurlugu [*Management*] [*Turkish*] (CED)
Md .... Muhendis Diplomasi [*Engineering qualification*] [*Turkish*]
MD .... Mujeres Democraticas [*Democratic Women*] [*Spanish*] (WER)
md .... Placing of Troops (RU)
Md .... Range Scale [*Artillery*] (RU)
MD .... Road Mine (RU)
m^{3}d .... Cubic Meters per Day (BU)
MDA .... Metropolitan Development Agency (MAR)
Mdat .... Mandat [*Order*] [*Business and trade*] [*French*]
MDB .... Medical Disciplinary Board [*Iranian*] (ME)
MdB .... Mitglied des Bundestages [*Member of the Bundestag*] (EG)
MDB .... Movimento Democratico Brasileiro [*Brazilian Democratic Movement*] (PPW)
MDB .... Naval Long-Range Bomber (RU)
MDC .... Maison du Cycle (MAR)
MDC .... Malawi Development Corporation (MAR)
MDC .... Marine Diamond Corporation (MAR)
MDC .... Movimiento Democrata Cristiano [*Christian Democratic Movement*] (LA)
MDC .... Movimiento Democratico del Campesinado [*Democratic Movement of Rural Workers*] [*Spanish*] (WER)
MDC .... Mwananchi Development Corporation (MAR)
Mdch .... Maedchen [*German*]
MDCS .... Magyar Divatcsarnok [*Hungarian Fashion Store*] (HU)
MDD .... Digital Computer (RU)
MDD .... Mezinarodni Den Deti [*International Children's Day*] (CZ)
MDD .... Miedzynarodowy Dzien Dziecka [*International Children's Day*] (POL)
MDD .... Milli Demokratik Devrimciler [*National Democratic Revolutionaries*] (TU)
MDD .... Ministry of State Supply [*Obsolete*] (BU)
MDD .... Mouvement Democratique Dahomeen (MAR)
MDDSZ .... Magyarorszagi Delszlavok Demokratikus Szovetsege [*The Democratic Association of Southern Slavs in Hungary*] (HU)
MDE .... Magnetic Diode Element (RU)
Mde .... Marchande [*Merchant*] [*French*] (MTD)
MDF .... International Road Federation [*IRF*] (RU)
MDF .... Les Meubles de France [*Abidjan*] (MAR)
MDF .... Mednarodni Denarni Fond [*International Monetary Fund*] (YU)
MDF .... Mid-West Democratic Front (MAR)
MdF .... Ministerium der Finanzen [*Ministry of Finance*] (EG)
MDFKS .... Remote-Control Scale Photoelectric Copying System (RU)
MDFM .... Mezinarodni Demokraticka Federace Mladeze [*World Federation of Democratic Youth*] (CZ)
MDFV .... Magyar Diafilmgyarto Vallalat [*Hungarian Filmstrip Production Enterprise*] (HU)
MDFZ .... Mezinarodni Demokraticka Federace Zen [*Women's International Democratic Federatin*] (CZ)
MDFZh .... Women's International Democratic Federation [*WIDF*] (BU)
MDFZh .... Women's International Democratic Federation [*WIDF*] (RU)
MDG .... Madagascar [*Three-letter standard code*] (CNC)
MDG .... Movimento Democratico da Guine (MAR)
MdI .... Ministerium des Inneren [*Ministry of the Interior*] (EG)
MDI .... Mouvement pour la Democratie et l'Independance [*Movement for Democracy and Independence*] [*Central African*] (PD)
MDI .... Movimiento Democratico Independiente [*Independent Democratic Movement*] [*Venezuelan*] (LA)
MDIA .... Mouvement pour la Defense des Interets de l'Angola [*Movement for the Defense of Angolan Interests*] [*French*] (AF)
MDIA .... Movimento para a Defesa dos Intereses de Angola [*Movement for the Defense of Angolan Interests*] (MAR)
MDIN .... Mouvement de la Defense des Interets Nationaux (MAR)
MDIO .... Intergovernmental Economic Organizations (BU)
MdJ .... Ministerium der Justiz [*Ministry of Justice*] (EG)
MD-jedinica ... Moto-Desantna Jedinica [*Motorized Landing Unit*] (YU)
MDJO .... Mornaricko-Desantno-Jurisno Odeljenje [*Marine Landing Attack Department*] (YU)
MDK- .... Calcium Molybdate (RU)
MDK .... Copper Extraction Combine (BU)
MDK .... International Danube Commission (RU)
MDK .... Maximum Permissible Concentration (RU)
MD K .... Medicina Kiado [*Medicina Publishing House*] (HU)
MDK .... Medunarodna Decimalna Klasifikacija [*International Decimal Classification*] (YU)
MDK .... Miejski Dom Kultury [*Municipal Social and Recreation Club*] [*Polish*]
MDK .... Mistni Dopravni Komise [*Local Transportation Commission*] (CZ)
MDK .... Mlodziezowy Dom Kultury [*Youth House of Culture*] (POL)
MDK .... Moscow Dialectological Commission (RU)
MDK .... Muszaki Dokumentacios Kozpont [*Technical Documentation Center*] (HU)
MDKhP .... Ministry of Supply and Food Industry [*Obsolete*] (BU)
md l .... Doctor of Medicine (BU)
MDL .... Movimiento de Democratizacion Liberal [*Liberal Democratization Movement*] [*Colombian*] (LA)
MDLN .... Mouvement Democratique de Liberation Nationale (MAR)
MDLP .... Movimento Democratico para a Libertacao de Portugal [*Democratic Movement for the Liberation of Portugal*] (WER)
MDLPC .... Movimento Democratico de Libertacao de Portugal e Colonias (MAR)
MDM .... Magnetic Road Mine (RU)
MDM .... Marszalkowska Dzielnica Mieszkaniowa [*Marszalkowska Residential District*] (POL)
MDM .... Mestske Divadlo Mladych [*Municipal Young People's Theater*] [*Brno*] (CZ)
MDM .... Miedzynarodowy Dzien Mlodziezy [*International Youth Day*] [*Polish*]

M-DM .... Modulation-Demodulation (RU)
MDM .... Movimento Democratico de Mocambique [*Democratic Movement of Mozambique*] (AF)
MDM .... Movimento Democratico das Mulheres [*Women's Democratic Movement*] [*Portuguese*] (WER)
MDN .... International Children's Week (RU)
MDN .... Mark der Deutschen Notenbank [*Mark of the German Bank of Issue*] [*Later, M*] (EG)
MDN .... Movimiento Democratico Nacional [*National Democratic Movement*] [*Colombian*] (LA)
MDN .... Movimiento Democratico Nacionalista [*Nationalist Democratic Movement*] [*Guatemalan*] (LA)
MDN .... Movimiento Democratico Nicaraguense [*Nicaraguan Democratic Movement*] (PPW)
MDNF .... Minimal Disjunctive Normal Form (RU)
MDNS .... Ministrstvo za Drzavne Nabave Slovenije [*Ministry of State Supply of Slovenia*] (YU)
MDNT .... Moscow House of Folk Art (RU)
MDNTP .... Moscow House of Scientific and Technical Propaganda Imeni F. E. Dzerzhinskiy (RU)
MDO .... Mericsky Delostrelecky Oddil [*Survey Battalion*] (CZ)
MDO .... Mestsky Dum Osvety [*Municipal Cultural Center*] (CZ)
MDO .... Milli Devrim Ordusu [*National Revolutionary Army*] (TU)
MDO .... Mlodziezowy Dom Oswiaty [*Youth Education House*] [*Polish*]
MDO .... Road Machinery Detachment (RU)
MDOL .... Movimento pela Defesa do Ocidente Livre [*Movement for the Defense of the Free West*] [*Portuguese*] (WER)
MDP .... Madagascar-Presse (AF)
MDP .... Magyar Dolgozok Partja [*Hungarian Workers' Party*] (PPE)
MDP .... Maximum Dynamic Error (RU)
MDP .... Milli Duzenlik Partisi [*National Order Party*] (TU)
MDP .... Moslem Democratic Party [*Philippine*] (PPW)
MDP .... Mouvement Democrate Progressiste (MAR)
MDP .... Mouvement Democratique Populaire [*Moroccan*] (MAR)
MDP .... Movimento Democratico Portugues [*Portuguese Democratic Movement*] (PPE)
MDP .... Movimiento Democratico Peruano [*Peruvian Democratic Movement*] (LA)
MDP .... Movimiento Democratico Popular [*Democratic Popular Movement*] [*Ecuadorean*] (PPW)
MDPA .... Mines Domaniales des Potasses d'Alsace (MAR)
MDP/CDE ... Movimento Democratico Portugues/Commissao Democratica Eleitoral [*Portuguese Democratic Movement/Democratic Electoral Commission*] (WER)
MDPI .... Management Development and Productivity Institute (MAR)
MDPO .... Mission de Developpement du Perimetre d'Ombessa [*Mbam*] (MAR)
MDPPD .... Movimento Democratico Portugues de Ponta Delgada [*Portuguese Democratic Movement of Ponta Delgada*] (WER)
MDPT .... Ministerstvo Dopravy, Post, a Telekomunikacii [*Ministry of Transportation, Posts, and Telecommunications*] [*Slovakia*] (CZ)
MDR .... Naval Long-Range Reconnaissance Aircraft (RU)
MDRA .... Mouvement Democratique de Renouveau Algerien [*Democratic Movement for Algerian Renewal*] (AF)
MDRM .... Mouvement Democratique de Renovation Malgache [*Democratic Movement for Malagasy Renewal*] (AF)
MDRP .... Movimiento Democratico Reformista Peruano [*Peruvian Democratic Reformist Movement*] (PPW)
MDR PARMEHUTU ... Mouvement Democratique Republicain du Parti du Mouvement de l'Emancipation Hutu [*Republican Democratic Movement of the Hutu Emancipation Movement Party*] [*Rwandan*] (AF)
MDRRA .... Ministere du Developpement Rural et de la Reforme Agraire [*Ministry of Rural Development and Agrarian Reform*] [*Malagasy*] (AF)
MDRT .... Mouvement Democratique de Renovation Tchadienne [*Democratic Movement for Chadian Renewal*] (AF)
MDS .... International Falcon Movement [*IFM*] (RU)
MDS .... Magnetomotive Force (RU)
MDS .... Mezinarodni Druzstevni Svaz [*International Cooperative Alliance*] (CZ)
MDS .... Miedzynarodowy Dzien Spoldzielczosci [*International Co-Operative Day*] [*Polish*]
MDS .... Mitteilungen aus dem Deutschen Schutzgebieten (MAR)
MDS .... Mouvement Democrate Socialiste [*Democratic Socialist Movement*] [*French*] (PPW)
MDS .... Mouvement des Democrates Socialistes [*Movement of Socialist Democrats*] [*Tunisian*] (PPW)
MDS .... Mouvement Democratique et Social [*Democratic and Social Movement*] [*Reunionese*] (AF)
MDS .... Road Machinery Station (RU)
MDSA .... Malayan Democratic Students Alliance [*Selangor*] (ML)
MDSF .... Mouvement Democrate Socialiste de France [*Democratic Socialist Movement of France*] (PPE)
MDSh .... Naval Smoke Pot (RU)
MDSK .... International Movement of Catholic Students [*IMCS*] (RU)
MDSz .... Mezogazdasagi Dolgozok Szakszervezete [*Trade Union of Agricultural Workers*] (HU)
MDT .... Mezinarodni Desetinne Trideni [*International Decimal Classification System*] (CZ)
MDT .... Mezinarodni Dopravni Tarif [*International Transportation Tariff*] (CZ)
MDT .... Miejski Dom Towarowy [*Municipal Department Store*] [*Polish*]
MDU .... Moscow House of Scientists (RU)
MDU .... Remote-Control Device (RU)
MDV .... Maldives [*Three-letter standard code*] (CNC)
MDV .... Medizinischer Dienst des Verkehrswesens [*Medical Service for Transportation*] (EG)
MDV .... Miestny Dozorny Vybor [*Local Supervisory Committee*] (CZ)
MDV .... Mouvement Democratique Voltaique [*Voltan Democratic Movement*] (AF)
MDY .... Mutemerkiz Dingil Yuku [*Concentrated Axial Load*] (TU)
Mdyn .... Megadyna [*Megadyne*] [*Polish*]
MDZ .... Camouflaging Smoke Screen (RU)
MDZ .... Melitopol' Diesel Plant (RU)
MDZ .... Mezinarodni Den Zen [*International Women's Day*] (CZ)
ME .... International Units (BU)
ME .... Maailmanennatys [*Finnish*]
ME .... Mache-Einheit [*Mache Unit*] [*German*]
Me .... Madre [*Mother*] [*Spanish*]
ME .... Magnetoelectric Instrument (RU)
Me .... Maitre [*Master*] [*French*]
ME .... Majority Elements (RU)
ME .... Malaysian Engineers (ML)
ME .... Malomipari Egyesules [*Industrial Milling Cooperative*] (HU)
ME .... Masinstvo i Elektrotehnika [*Machinery and Electrical Engineering*] (YU)
ME .... Materials on Ethnography (RU)
mE .... Meines Erachtens [*In My Opinion*] (EG)
Me .... Memur [*Official, Employee*] [*Government*] (TU)
ME .... Mengeneinheit [*Unit of Quantity*] (EG)
ME .... Mercaptoethylamine (RU)
Me .... Metal (RU)
Me .... Metall [*Metal*] [*German*]
Me .... Methyl [*Methyl*] [*German*]
ME .... Mikton Epiteleion [*Joint Staff*] [*Greek*] (GC)
ME .... Milattan Evvel [*Before Christ*] (TU)
ME .... Ministerstvo Energetiky [*Ministry of Power Industry*] (CZ)
ME .... Ministerstwo Energetyki [*Ministry of Power*] (POL)
ME .... Ministry of Electrification [*Obsolete*] (BU)
Me .... Molhe [*Mole*] [*Portuguese*] (NAU)
Me .... Muelle [*Mole*] [*Spanish*] (NAU)
ME .... Muenze Einheit [*Coinage*] [*German*]
ME .... Muszaki Egyetem [*Technical University*] (HU)
ME .... Muszaki Eloirasok [*Technical Instructions*] (HU)
MEA .... International Economic Association [*IEA*] (RU)
MEA .... Metopon Ethnikis Adadimiourgias [*National Regeneration Front*] [*Greek*] (PPE)
MEA .... Metopon Ethnikis Anasyngrotiseos [*National Reconstruction Front*] [*Greek*] (GC)
MEA .... Monades Ethnikis Amynis [*National Defense Units*] [*Greek*] (GC)
MEAE .... Ministere d'Etat aux Affaires Etrangeres [*Ministry of State for Foreign Affairs*] [*Mauritanian*] (AF)
MEAF .... Mediterranean Expeditionary Allied Forces (MAR)
MEAF .... Middle East Air Force (MAR)
MEAFOPS ... Middle East Air Force Operations (MAR)
MEAFSA ..... Middle East, Southern Asia, and Africa South of the Sahara (MAR)
MEAN .... Mission d'Etude et d'Amenagement du Niger (MAR)
MEAP .... Mikroviologikon Ergastirion Afthodous Pyretou (Dimosion) [*Foot-and-Mouth Disease Microbiological Laboratory (Public)*] [*Greek*] (GC)
MEAU .... Missao de Estudos Apicolas do Ultramar Portugues, Junta de Investigacoes do Ultramar (MAR)
MEAUP .... Missao de Estudos Apicolas do Ultramar Portugues, Junta de Investigacoes do Ultramar (MAR)
meb .... Furniture Factory [*Topography*] (RU)
MEB .... International Office of Epizootics (RU)
MEB .... Milli Egitim Bakanligi [*National Education Ministry*] (TU)
MEB .... Movimiento de Educacao de Base [*Basic Education Movement*] [*Brazilian*] (LA)
MEBAN .... Menkul Degerler Bankerlik ve Finansman AS [*Securities Banking and Finance Corp.*] (TU)
MEBD .... Milchwirtschaftlicher Erzeugerberatungsdienst [*Dairy Producers Advisory Service*] (EG)
MEBECO ..... Menuiserie et Ebenisterie Congolaise (MAR)
MEBPA .... Missao de Estudos Broceanologicas e de Pesca de Angola (MAR)
MEC .... Masina Electronica de Calcul [*Electronic Calculator*] (RO)
mec .... Mecazi [*Figurative*] (TU)
Mec .... Meclisi [*Assembly*] (TU)
MEC .... Member of the Executive Council [*Namibian*] (AF)
MEC .... Mercato Europeo Comune [*European Common Market*] [*Use EEC*] [*Italian*] (WER)
MEC .... Ministerio da Educacao e Cultura [*Ministry of Education and Culture*] [*Brazilian*] (LA)
MEC .... Ministry of Education and Culture [*Mozambican*] (AF)

MEC .... Movimiento Estudiantil Cristiano [*Christian Student Movement*] [*Costa Rican*] (LA)
MECA......... Metal Metalica Colombiana de Accesorios Ltda. [*Cali*] (COL)
MECA......... Societe Congolaise de Mecanographie Congo (MAR)
MECANEMBAL ... Societe Africaine d'Emballages Metalliques (MAR)
MECAS .... Middle East Center for Arab Studies (MAR)
mech.......... Mechanika [*or Mechaniczny*] [*Mechanics or Mechanical*] (POL)
mechan....... Mechanisch [*Mechanical*] [*German*]
MECHIM...... Societe de Genie Metallurgique et Chimique [*Algerian*] (MAR)
Mechinstitut ... Institute of Infectious Diseases Imeni I. I. Mechnikov (RU)
MECIPA ...... Societe Malgache d'Etudes de Construction et d'Investissements Papetiers (MAR)
MECM .... Methodist Episcopal Congo Mission (MAR)
MECOL .... Metalurgica Colombiana Ltda. [*Bogota*] (COL)
med............ Medical (BU)
med............ Medical, Medicine (RU)
Med............ Medico [*Doctor*] [*Italian*]
Med............ Mediterranean (MAR)
Med............ Medizin [*or Medizinisch*] [*German*]
med............ Medycyna [*or Medyczny*] [*Medicine or Medical*] (POL)
MED .... Ministerio de Educacion [*Ministry of Education*] [*Nicaraguan*] (LA1)
MedA .... Medical Academy (BU)
MEDA.......... Mercaptoethyliminodiacetate (RU)
MEDA.......... Mouvement pour l'Evolution Democratique en Afrique (MAR)
MedAACSReg ... Mediterranean Airways and Communication Service Region (MAR)
MedA-Anl ... Medical Academy - Institute of Anatomy (BU)
MedA-Bioll ... Medical Academy - Institute of Biology (BU)
MEDAC .... Mouvement d'Evolution Democratique de l'Afrique Centrale (MAR)
MedA-DetKl ... Medical Academy - Pediatric Clinic (BU)
MedA-Fizioll ... Medical Academy - Institute of Physiology (BU)
MedA-GinKl ... Medical Academy - Gynecological Clinic (BU)
MedA-IBiolKhim ... Medical Academy - Institute of Biological Chemistry (BU)
MedA-IEpiz ... Medical Academy - Institute of Epizootiology (BU)
MedA-IFar... Medical Academy - Institute of Pharmacology (BU)
MedA-Ikhig ... Medical Academy - Institute of Hygiene (BU)
MedA-IKhistEmbr ... Medical Academy - Institute of Histology and Embryology (BU)
MedA-IMedfiz ... Medical Academy - Institute of Medical Physics (BU)
MedA-IMedKhim ... Medical Academy - Institute of Medical Chemistry (BU)
MedA-IPatAn ... Medical Academy - Institute of Pathological Anatomy (BU)
MedA-IPatfiziol ... Medical Academy - Institute of Pathological Physiology (BU)
MedA-IRadiolfiziot ... Medical Academy - Institute of Radiology and Physiotherapy (BU)
MedA-ISotsKhig ... Medical Academy - Institute of Social Hygiene (BU)
MedA-ISudMed ... Medical Academy - Institute of Forensic Medicine (BU)
MedA-ITrBol ... Medical Academy - Institute of Occupational Diseases (BU)
MedA-IVoennoMedPod ... Medical Academy - Institute for the Training of Military Physicians (BU)
MedA-IZuboprot ... Medical Academy - Institute of Dentistry (BU)
MedA-KhirPropKl ... Medical Academy - Clinic of Preliminary Medical Instruction (BU)
MedA-KlInfBol ... Medical Academy - Clinic for Communicable Diseases (BU)
MedA-KlOpZub ... Medical Academy - Clinic of Dental Surgery (BU)
MedA-KozhVenKl ... Medical Academy - Clinic for Skin and Venereal Diseases (BU)
MedA-MikrobiolSerl ... Medical Academy - Institute of Microbiology and Serology (BU)
MedA-NervPsikhKl ... Medical Academy - Neuropsychiatric Clinic (BU)
MedA-OchKl ... Medical Academy - Ophthalmological Clinic (BU)
MedA-OrtTravKl ... Medical Academy - Clinic of Orthopedics and Traumatology (BU)
MedA Pl ...... Medical Academy in Plovdiv (BU)
MEDAS .... Mobilya Ev Dekorasyonu Anonim Sirketi [*Furniture and Home Decoration Corporation*] (TU)
MedA-TerKl ... Medical Academy - Therapeutic Clinic (BU)
MedA-UshNGurKl ... Medical Academy - Clinic for Ear, Nose, and Throat Diseases (BU)
MedA-VutrKl ... Medical Academy - Internal Diseases Clinic (BU)
MedA-VutrPolikl ... Medical Academy - Internal Diseases Polyclinic (BU)
MedA-Yasli ... Medical Academy - Nursery (BU)
Med bibl...... Medical Library (BU)
MEDC.......... Menos Esquerra Democratica de Catalunya [*Catalonian Democratic Left*] [*Menos*] [*Spanish*] (WER)
MEDCENT... Central Mediterranean Area (MAR)
med ch........ Copper Number (RU)
MEDEAST... Eastern Mediterranean Area (MAR)
Medepl........ Copper-Smelting Plant [*Topography*] (RU)
MEDERCO ... Mouvement de l'Evolution et de Developpement Rural - Congo [*Movement for the Evolution and Rural Development - Congo*] [*Leopoldville*]
MEDESAN .. Melamin Desen Sanayi [*Melamin Ornamental Design and Metal Working Industry*] (TU)
Med fak....... School of Medicine (BU)
Medgiz........ State Publishing House of Medical Literature (RU)
MEDI .... Movimiento de Empresarios del Interior [*Movement of Managers from the Interior*] [*Argentine*] (LA1)
MEDICO...... Medical International Cooperation (CL)
MEDICOK ... Rontgen Kulkereskedelmi Vallalat [*Export-Import Enterprise for X-Ray Equipment*] (HU)
MEDICOR.... Orvosi Rontgenkeszulekek Vallalata [*Medical X-Ray Equipment Enterprise*] (HU)
MEDICUBA ... Empresa Cubana Importadora y Exportadora de Productos Medicos [*Cuban Enterprise for the Import and Export of Medical Products*] (LA)
MEDIMPEX ... MEDIMPEX Gyogyszer Kulkereskedelmi Vallalat [*MEDIMPEX Foreign Trade Enterprise for Pharmaceutical Products*] (HU)
Medit.......... Mediterranean (MAR)
MedL........... Meditsinski Letopis [*Medical Chronicle*] [*A periodical*] (BU)
MedLandEx ... Mediterranean Landing Exercise (MAR)
MEDLOC..... Mediterranean Lines of Communication (MAR)
MEDME....... Mediterranean and Middle East (MAR)
Medn.......... Copper Mines [*Topography*] (RU)
MEDNOREAST ... Northeast Mediterranean Area (MAR)
Medn-prov ... Copper Wire Plant [*Topography*] (RU)
MEDOC....... Mediterranean Occidental (MAR)
MEDOSZ..... Mezogazdasagi es Erdeszeti Dolgozok Szakszervezete [*Trade Union of Workers in Agriculture and Forestry*] (HU)
med p.......... Medical Station [*Topography*] (RU)
MEDRECO ... Mediterranean Refinery Company [*Lebanese*] (ME)
MedS........... Mediterranean Sea (MAR)
Medsanchast ... Medical Unit (BU)
Medsantrud ... Medical and Sanitary Workers' Trade Union (RU)
medsb......... Medical Battalion (RU)
medsb......... Medical Battalion, Medical Squadron (BU)
MEDSOUEAST ... Southeast Mediterranean Area (MAR)
MEDSUPPACT ... Mediterranean Support Activity (MAR)
medsv .... Medical Platoon (RU)
Meduchposobiye ... Republic Trust for Medical Educational Visual Aids (RU)
MEDUNSA ... Medical University of Southern Africa (MAR)
MEDY.......... Monas Exypiretiseos Dimosion Ypiresion [*Public Services Support Unit*] [*Greek*] (GC)
MEE............ Magyar Elektronikai Egyesulet [*Hungarian Electronics Association*] (HU)
MEE............ Magyar Elektrotechnikai Egyesulet [*Hungarian Electrotechnical Association*] (HU)
MEE............ Mikti Ergatiki Epitropi [*Mixed Labor Committee*] [*Greek*] (GC)
MEE............ Ministerul Energiei Electrice [*Ministry of Electric Power*] (RO)
MEEA.......... Mobil Exploration Equatorial Africa, Inc. [*Cameroonian*] (AF)
MEECI......... Mouvement des Etudiants et des Eleves de Cote-d'Ivoire [*Movement of Students and Pupils of the Ivory Coast*] (AF)
MEEI........... Magyar Elektrotechnikai Ellenorzo Intezet [*Hungarian Electrotechnical Control Institute*] (HU)
MEEN.......... Ministere d'Etat a l'Economie Nationale [*Ministry of State for National Economy*] [*Mauritanian*] (AF)
MEENEN ..... Monimos Ektimitiki Epitropi Navtikon Epitaxeon kai Navloseon [*Permanent Committee for Assessing Naval Requisitions and (Ship) Charters*] (GC)
MEES .... Middle East Economic Survey [*Lebanese*] (ME)
MEEU .... Missao de Estudos Economicos do Ultramar, Junta de Investigacoes do Ultramar (MAR)
MEF............ Mauritian Employers Federation (AF)
MEF............ Mediterranean Expeditionary Force (MAR)
MEF............ Methylphosphonic Acid (RU)
MEFEM .... Mechanikai es Femtomegcikk Kisipari Termeloszovetkezet [*Cooperative Enterprise for Manufacture of Metalware*] (HU)
MEFERT...... Magyar Ertekpapirforgalmi Reszvenytarsasag [*Hungarian Stock Brokerage Limited (Prewar)*] (HU)
MEFESZ...... Magyar Egyetemi es Foiskolai Egyesuletek Szovetsege [*Federation of Hungarian University and College Associations*] (HU)
MEFI........... Mezogepfejleszto Intezet [*Agricultural Machine Developing Institute*] (HU)
MEFMC .... Ministerul Economiei Forestiere si Materialelor de Constructii [*Ministry of the Forestry Economy and Construction Materials*] (RO)
MEFORI....... Mezogazdasagi Fordito Iroda [*Translation Office for Literature on Agriculture*] (HU)
MEFTER...... Magyar Folyam- es Tengerhajozasi Reszvenytarsasag [*Hungarian River and Sea Navigation Company Limited*] (HU)
Me-Ga .... Tvornica Metalne Galanterije i Pisacih Pera [*Factory of Metal Notions and Fountain Pens*] [*Zagreb*] (YU)
megb........... Megbeszeles [*Conference*] (HU)
megb........... Megbizott [*Trustee, Representative*] (HU)
MEGEV .... Mezogazdasagi Gepalkatresz Ellato Vallalat [*Agricultural Machinery Spare Parts Supply Enterprise*] (HU)
megh........... Meghalt [*Deceased*] (HU)
megh........... Meghatalmazott [*Proxy, Plenipotentiary*] (HU)
megh min.... Meghatalmazott Miniszter [*Minister Plenipotentiary*] (HU)
megj........... Megjegyzes [*Comment, Footnote*] (HU)
megsz .... Megszallas [*or Megszallo*] [*Occupation or Occupying*] (HU)
MEGVED..... Munkaegeszsegvedelmi es Gepiberendezeseket Keszito KTSZ [*Cooperative Manufacturing Enterprise for Industrial Safety Equipment*] (HU)

MEGYEVILL ... Megyei Villanyszerelo Vallalat [*County Electrical Engineering Enterprise*] (HU)
MEH .... Mellektermek es Hulladekgyujto Troszt [*Trash and Garbage Collection Trust*] (HU)
MEHNG .... Missao de Estudos do Habitat Nativo na Guine, Junta de Investigacoes do Ultramar (MAR)
MEHNT .... Missao de Estudos do Habitat Nativo em Timor (MAR)
MEHTAP ..... Merkezi Hukumet Teskilati Arastirma Projesi [*Central Government Organization Research Project*] (TU)
MEI .... Maatskappy vir Europese Immigrasie (MAR)
MEI .... Machine-Electrical Engineering Institute (BU)
MEI .... Madagascar Electro-Industrie (MAR)
MEI .... Ministerul Educatiei si Invatamintului [*Ministry of Education and Instruction*] (RO)
MEI .... Moscow Power Engineering Institute (RU)
MEI .... Moscow Power Institute (BU)
MEI .... Movimiento Estudiantil Independiente [*Independent Student Movement*] [*Argentine*] (LA)
MEI .... Societe Marocaine pour l'Entreprise et l'Industrie (MAR)
MEIC .... Ministerio de Economia, Industria, y Comercio [*Ministry of the Economy, Industry, and Commerce*] [*Costa Rican*] (LA1)
MEIC .... Ministerio de Educacao e Investigacao Cientifica [*Ministry of Education and Scientific Research*] [*Portuguese*] (WER)
MEICO .... Mecanica Industrial Colombiana [*Medellin*] (COL)
MEIDA .... Metals and Engineering Industries Development Association [*Tanzanian*] (AF)
MEIO .... Malaysian External Intelligence Organization (ML)
MEIS .... Moscow Electrotechnical Institute of Communications (RU)
MEISON ...... Me'ei Sone All Ethiopian Socialist Movement (MAR)
MEIZ .... Moscow Electrical Insulation Plant (RU)
Mej .... Mejuffrouw [*Miss*] [*Dutch*] (GPO)
MEK .... Budapesti Muszaki Egyetem Konyvtara [*Library of the Technical University of Budapest*] (HU)
MEK .... International Electrical Engineering Commission (BU)
MEK .... International Electrotechnical Commission [*IEC*] (RU)
MEK .... Mathitiko Ethnikistiko Kinima [*Student Nationalist Movement*] [*Greek*] (GC)
MEK .... Medical Education Kit (MAR)
MEK .... Megyei Mezogazdasagi Termekeket Ertekesito Kozpont [*County Agricultural Products Store and Distribution Center*] (HU)
mek .... Mekaniikka [*Mechanics*] [*Finnish*]
MEK .... Methyl Ethyl Ketone (RU)
MEK .... Mezogazdasagi Termekeket Ertekesito Szovetkezeti Kozpont [*Cooperative Center for Agricultural Marketing*] (HU)
MEK .... Mikhani Esoterikis Kavseos [*Internal Combustion Engine*] (GC)
mekh .... Mechanical, Mechanics, Mechanized (RU)
mekhanich ... Mechanical (RU)
MEKhANOBR ... All-Union Scientific Research and Planning Institute for the Mechanical Processing of Minerals (RU)
mekhfak ...... Division of Mechanics (RU)
mekhmat .... Division of Mechanics and Mathematics (RU)
mekh mat .... Mechanico-Mathematical (RU)
mekhom ...... Mechanical Ohm (RU)
Mekhtorg .... All-Union State Association for Trade in Fur Goods (RU)
MeKLK .... Mestska Komise Lidove Kontroly [*City Commission of People's Control*] (CZ)
MEKOROT ... National Water Company [*Israeli*] (ME)
meks .... Mexican (RU)
mekv .... Milliequivalent (RU)
mel .... Chalk Pit [*Topography*] (RU)
MEL .... Mantenimientos Electricos [*Medellin*] (COL)
mel .... Mill [*Topography*] (RU)
MEL .... Minimum Effective Level (MAR)
MEL .... Muzika Esperanto Ligo [*Esperantist Music League*] (EA)
mel .... Reclamation (RU)
MELA .... Middle East Librarians Association
MElektr .... Ministry of Electrification [*Obsolete*] (BU)
MELETEX .... Metall-, Lebensmittel, -Textil-GmbH Export und Import [*Metal, Foodstuffs, and Textile Export and Import Co.*] (EG)
MELI .... Marx-Engels-Lenin-Institut beim ZK der SED [*Marx-Engels-Lenin Institute of the SED Central Committee*] (EG)
meliorat ...... Reclamation (RU)
mell .... Muszaki Ellenor [*Technical Inspector, Supervisor*] (HU)
mell rass ..... Moller Scattering (RU)
Mel'n .... Mill [*Topography*] (RU)
MELS .... Marx-Engels-Lenin-Stalin-Institut beim ZK der SED [*Marx-Engels-Lenin-Stalin Institute of the SED Central Committee*] (EG)
MELT .... Mouseion Ellinikis Laikis Tekhnis [*Museum of Greek Folk Art*] (GC)
MELYEPTERV ... Melyepitesi Tervezo Vallalat [*Civil Engineering Designing Enterprise*] (HU)
MELYGEP ... Melyfurasi Szerszamgepgyarto es Gepjavito Vallalat [*Manufacturing and Repair Enterprise for Deep-Drilling Equipment*] (HU)
MELYTERV ... Melyepito Tervezo Iroda [*Civil Engineering Designing Office*] (HU)
MELZ .... Moscow Electric Bulb Plant (RU)
MEM .... Magyar Elet Mozgalma [*Movement of Hungarian Life*] (PPE)
MEM .... Mezogazdasagi es Elelmezesugyi Miniszterium [*Ministry of Agriculture and Food Industry*] (HU)
MEM .... Ministerio de Energia y Minas [*Ministry of Energy and Mines*] [*Venezuelan*] (LA)
MEM .... Ministry of Electrification and Land Reclamation [*Obsolete*] (BU)
MEM .... Mondpaca Esperantista Movado [*Esperantist Movement for World Peace - EMWP*] (EA)
MEM .... Moscow State Electrical Installation Trust (RU)
MEM .... Small Electron Microscope (RU)
MEMA .... Missao para o Estudo do Missionologia Africana, Junta de Investigacoes do Ultramar (MAR)
MEMAA .... Missao de Estudos dos Movimentos Associativos em Africa (MAR)
MEMACO .... Metal Marketing Corporation [*Zambian*] (MAR)
MEMATA .... Messageries Malgaches Tamataviennes (MAR)
MEM-DER ... Memurlar Dernegi [*Civil Servants Association*] (TU)
MEME .... Malaysian Electrical and Mechanical Engineers (ML)
MEME .... Missao de Estudos das Minorias Etnicas do Ultramar Portugues, Junta de Investigacoes do Ultramar (MAR)
MEMFHISZ ... Mellektermek es Maradek Feldolgozo Kisipari Termeloszovetkezet [*Domestic Industrial Production Cooperative for Processing Byproducts and Waste*] (HU)
MEMIIT .... Moscow Electromechanical Institute of Railroad Transportation Engineers Imeni F. E. Dzerzhinskiy (RU)
MEMOSZ .... Magyar Epitomunkasok Orszagos Szakszervezete [*National Union of Hungarian Construction Workers*] (HU)
MEMOSZ .... Magyar Epitomunkasok Orszagos Szovetsege [*National Union of Hungarian Construction Workers*] (HU)
MEM RSZ .... Mezogazdasagi es Elelmezesugyi Miniszterium Repulogepes Szolgalata [*Ministry of Agriculture and Food Industry's Aviation Service*] (HU)
MEMRZ .... Moscow Electromechanical Repair Plant (RU)
MEMSAN .... Mekanik ve Elektrik Muhendislik Sanayii Anonim Sirketi [*Mechanical and Electrical Engineering Industry Corporation*] (TU)
MEMSOCLING ... Memoire de la Societe de Linguistique [*A publication*] (MAR)
MEMT .... Moscow Electromechanical Technicum (RU)
MEMZ .... Moscow Electromechanical Plant (RU)
MEMZ .... Moscow Experimental Machine Plant (of the Glavgaz, USSR) (RU)
MEN .... Menteri [*Minister*] (IN)
MEN .... Ministerio de Educacion Nacional [*National Education Ministry*] [*Venezuelan*] (LA)
MEN .... Resimen [*Regiment*] (IN)
MENA .... Middle East News Agency (AF)
MENADA ..... Menuiserie de l'Adamaoua (MAR)
MENAG .... Menteri Agama [*Minister of Religious Affairs*] (IN)
MENDAGRI ... Menteri Dalam Negeri [*Minister of Internal Affairs*] (IN)
MENEVEN ... [A] Subsidiary of PETROVEN [*Venezuelan*] (LA)
meng .... Menguante [*Spanish*]
MENHANKAM ... Menteri Pertahanan dan Keamanan [*Minister of Defense and Security*] (IN)
MENI .... Movimiento Electoral Nacional Independiente [*Independent National Electoral Movement*] [*Venezuelan*] (LA)
MENKES ..... Menteri Kesehatan [*Minister of Health*] (IN)
MENKESRA ... Menteri Kesedjahteraan Rakjat [*Minister of People's Welfare*] (IN)
MENKO .... Muszaki Ertelmisegi Nok Kore [*Women's Technical-Intellectual Circle*] (HU)
MENKU .... Menteri Keuangan [*Minister of Finance*] (IN)
MENLU .... Menteri Luar Negeri [*Minister of Foreign Affairs*] (IN)
MENPEN ..... Menteri Penerangan [*Minister of Information*] (IN)
MENPERDA ... Menteri Perdagangan [*Minister of Commerce*] (IN)
MENPERHUB ... Menteri Perhubungan [*Minister of Communications*] (IN)
Mens .... Mensucat [*Textile*] (TU)
MENS .... Middle East Neurosurgical Society (MAR)
MENSA .... Mensucat Sanayi ve Ticaret AS [*Textile Industry and Trade Corporation*] [*Adana*] (TU)
MENSOS ..... Menteri Sosial [*Minister of Social Affairs*] (IN)
MENTAN ..... Menteri Pertanian [*Minister of Agriculture*] (IN)
MENTAS ..... Menkul Degerler Ticaret Anonim Sirketi [*Securities Trade Corporation*] (TU)
MENTEKER ... Menteri Tenaga Kerdja [*Minister of Manpower*] (IN)
MENTRANSKOP ... Menteri Transmigrasi dan Koperasi [*Minister of Resettlement and Cooperatives*] (IN)
MeNV .... Mestsky Narodni Vybor [*City National Committee*] (CZ)
MEO .... International Economic Organizations [*Reference book*] (RU)
MEO .... Mikti Ekpaidevtiki Omas [*Joint Training Unit*] [*Military*] [*Greek*] (GC)
MEO .... Mikti Epiteliki Omas [*Joint Staff Group*] (GC)
meo .... Minosegi Ellenorzo Osztaly [*Department of Quality Control*] (HU)
MEO .... Music Hall Association (RU)
MEO .... Muszaki Ellenorzo Osztaly [*Technical Inspection Department*] (HU)
MEOCAM .... Mouvement d'Etudiants de l'Organisation Commune Africaine, Malgache, et Mauricienne [*Student Movement of the Afro-Malagasy-Mauritian Common Organization*] (AF)

MEON......... Ministere d'Etat a l'Orientation Nationale [*Ministry of State for National Orientation*] [*Mauritanian*] (AF)
MEOP......... Mathitiki Epitropi Organotikis Protovoulias [*Student Committee for Organizational Initiative*] (GC)
MEOPTA..... Spojene Tovarny pro Jemnou Mechaniku a Optiku, Narodni Podnik [*United Factories for Precision and Optical Instruments, National Enterprise*] (CZ)
MEOS......... Mechanizace Oprav a Sluzeb [*Mechanization of Repairs and Services*] (CZ)
MEOSA....... Mikti Epiteliki Omas Somaton Asfaleias [*Security Corps Joint Staff Unit*] (GC)
MEP............ Electrode Potential Method (RU)
MEP............ Local Evacuation Station (RU)
MEP............ Magnetoelectric Converter (RU)
MEP............ Magyar Elet Partja [*Party of Hungarian Life*] (PPE)
MEP............ Mahajana Eksath Peramuna [*People's United Front*] [*Sri Lankan*] (PPW)
MEP............ Mestske Elektricke Podniky [*Municipal Electric Power Enterprises*] (CZ)
MEP............ Mikti Epitropi Prosopikou [*Mixed Committee of Personnel*] [*Cypriot*] (GC)
MEP............ Ministry of the Electrical Equipment Industry, USSR (RU)
MEP............ Ministry of the Electrotechnical Industry, USSR (RU)
MEP............ Mouvement d'Ecologie Politique [*Ecology Political Movement*] [*French*] (PPW)
MEP............ Movimiento Electoral del Pueblo [*People's Electoral Movement*] [*Netherlands Antillean*] (PPW)
MEP............ Movimiento Electoral del Pueblo [*People's Electoral Movement*] [*Venezuelan*] (PPW)
MEPA......... Mikti Epitropi Prosopikou Astynomias [*Police Mixed Personnel Committee*] [*Greek*] (GC)
MEPAI........ Mouvement Etudiant du Parti Africain de l'Independance [*Student Movement of the African Independence Party*] [*Senegalese*] (AF)
MEPEY........ Mikti Epitropi Prosopikou Ekpaidevtikis Ypiresias [*Mixed Committee of Educational Services Personnel*] [*Cypriot*] (GC)
MEPLACO... Fabrica Metales y Plasticos Colombiana Ltda. [*Medellin*] (COL)
MEPLASCO ... Mecanica y Plasticos Colombianos [*Medellin*] (COL)
MEPMPU..... Missao de Estudo dos Problemas Migratorios e do Povoamento no Ultramar, Junta de Investigacoes do Ultramar (MAR)
MEPOD....... (Ustav pre) Mechanizovanie Podohospodarskej Vyroby na Slovensku [*(Institute for) Mechanization of Agricultural Production in Slovakia*] (CZ)
MEPP.......... Societe Mauritanienne d'Entreposage de Produits Petroliers (MAR)
MEPR.......... Ministere d'Etat a la Promotion Rurale [*Ministry of State for Rural Development*] [*Mauritanian*] (AF)
MEPROBA... Mouvement des Etudiants Progressistes Burundi [*Movement of Burundi Progressive Students*] (AF)
MEPROBA... Mouvement Progressiste Bahutu [*Progressive Hutu Movement*] [*Burundi*] (AF)
Mepro-Valpro ... Rolled Metal Industry (BU)
MEPS.......... Ministere d'Etat a la Promotion Sociale [*Ministry of State for Social Development*] [*Mauritanian*] (AF)
MEPSA........ Metalurgica Peruana, Sociedad Anonima [*Peruvian Metalworks, Incorporated*] (LA)
MEPW......... Ministry of Economic Planning, Western Region (MAR)
MEPZA........ Mauritius Export Processing Zones Association [*Mauritanian*] (AF)
MER............ Maison d'Enfants de Rabat [*Moroccan*] (MAR)
mer.............. Merenkulku [*Seafaring, Nautical Term*] [*Finnish*]
Mer.............. Merkez [*Administrative Center, Capital*] (TU)
MERA.......... Manufacture Electronique et Mecanique du Rwanda (MAR)
MERA.......... Zjednoczenie Przemyslu Automatyki i Aparatury Pomiarowej [*Automation and Measuring Apparatus Industry Association*] (POL)
MERC.......... Materials and Energy Research Center [*Iranian*] (ME)
MERCAPAN ... Corporacion Antioquena de Mercados [*Medellin*] (COL)
MERCATOR ... MERCATOR KFT Export-Import Kereskedelmi Keviseletek [*MERCATOR Limited Liability Company/Export-Import Commercial Agencies*] (HU)
MERCOLA .. Mercantil Colombiana Ltda. [*Cali*] (COL)
MERCON..... Mercantil de Confecciones [*Bogota*] (COL)
MERHAI...... Ministere d'Etat aux Ressources Humaines et Affaires Islamiques [*Ministry of State for Human Resources and Islamic Affairs*] [*Mauritanian*] (AF)
merk............ Merkita [*Finnish*]
merk............ Merkitseva [*Finnish*]
merk............ Merkitty [*Finnish*]
merk............ Merkitys [*Finnish*]
MERN.......... Missao de Estudo do Rendimento Nacional do Ultramar (MAR)
MERRA........ Middle East Relief and Rehabilitation Administration (MAR)
MERS.......... Movimiento de Estudiantes Revolucionarios Salvadorenos [*Revolutionary Movement of Salvadoran Students*] (PD)
MERS.......... Movimiento de Estudiantes Revolucionarios de Secundaria [*Movement of Revolutionary High School Students*] [*Salvadoran*] (LA1)
MERSIFRICA ... Mercados, Silos, y Frigorificos del Distrito Federal [*Markets, Silos, and Packing Houses of the Federal District*] [*Venezuelan*] (LA)
mert............ Mertek [*Measure, Scale*] (HU)
MERT.......... Minosegi Ellenorzo Reszvenytarsasag [*Quality Control Company*] (HU)
MERU.......... Mechanical Engineering Research Unit (MAR)
MES............ Excavating Machine Station (RU)
MES............ International Telecommunications of the USSR (RU)
MES............ Machinery Manufacture. Encyclopedic Handbook [*A publication*] (RU)
MES............ Maharashtra Ekikaran Samithi [*Indian*] (PPW)
MES............ Ministerio de Educacion Superior [*Ministry of Higher Education*] [*Cuban*] (LA)
MES............ Ministry of Electric Power Plants, USSR (RU)
MES............ Mitropolitika Ekklisiastika Symvoulia [*Metropolitan Ecclesiastical Councils*] [*Greek*] (GC)
mes............. Month (RU)
mes............. Monthly (BU)
MES............ Movimento de Esquerda Socialista [*Movement of the Socialist Left*] [*Portuguese*] (PPE)
ME-SA......... Mesken Sanayii AS [*Housing Industry Corporation*] (TU)
MeSA.......... Mestske Sdruzeni Advokatu v Praze [*City Association of Lawyers, Prague*] (CZ)
MESA.......... Ministerio (Ministro) do Equipamento Social e do Ambiente [*Ministry (Minister) of Public Services and the Environment*] [*Portuguese*] (WER)
MESAN....... Mouvement de l'Evolution Sociale de l'Afrique Noire [*Movement for the Social Development of Black Africa*] [*Central African*] (AF)
MESC.......... Movimiento Estudiantil Social Cristiano [*Social Christian Student Movement*] [*Colombian*] (LA)
MESE.......... Morfotikos Ekpolitistikos Syllogos Elevsinos [*Elevsis Educational and Cultural Association*] [*Greek*] (GC)
MESEP........ Ministry of Electric Power Plants and the Electrical Equipment Industry, USSR (RU)
MESI.......... Ministere d'Etat a la Souverainete Interne [*Ministry of State for Internal Sovereignty*] [*Mauritanian*] (AF)
MESI.......... Moscow Institute of Economics and Statistics (RU)
MESiEP....... Ministry of Electric Power Plants and the Electrical Equipment Industry, USSR (RU)
Mesl........... Meslek [*Profession or Professional*] (TU)
MESM......... Small Electronic Computer (RU)
MESM-........ Small Electrostatic Microscope (RU)
MESRS........ Ministere de l'Enseignement Superieur et de la Recherche Scientifique [*Algerian*] (MAR)
MESS.......... Maden Esya Sanayicileri Sendikasi [*Metal Products Industrialists Union*] (TU)
MESSAGAL ... Messageries du Senegal (MAR)
Mest........... Mestsky [*Municipal, City, Urban*] (CZ)
mest........... Pronoun (BU)
mestoim...... Pronoun (RU)
Mestprom ... Local Industry (BU)
MESZ.......... Magyar Evezos Szovetseg [*Hungarian Rowing Association*] (HU)
MESZHART ... Magyar-Szovjet Hajozasi Reszvenytarsasag [*Hungarian-Soviet Shipping Company Limited*] (HU)
MESZOV..... Mezogazdasagi Termelo Szovetkezet [*Agricultural Production Cooperative*] (HU)
met............. Metal, Metallic (RU)
met............. Metallurgia [*Metallurgy*] [*Finnish*]
met............. Metallurgical, Metallurgy (RU)
met............. Metallurgical Plant [*Topography*] (RU)
met............. Metalware Plant [*Topography*] (RU)
met............. Metalworking Plant [*Topography*] (RU)
MET............ Modern Egitim Tesisleri AS [*Modern Training Facilities Corp.*] (TU)
metal.......... Metallurgy, Metallurgical (BU)
METALCAR ... Metalurgica el Carmen [*Bogota*] (COL)
METALCO... Productos Metalicos de Cartagena Ltda. (COL)
METALDOM ... Complejo Metalurgico Dominicano [*Dominican Metallurgical Complex*] [*Dominican Republic*] (LA1)
METALFA ... Industrias Metalicas Alfa [*Cali*] (COL)
METAL-GABON ... Societe Metallurgique du Gabon (MAR)
METALIMEX ... Podnik Zahranicniho Obchodu pro Dovoz a Vyvoz Rud, Kovu, a Tuhych Paliv [*Foreign Trade Enterprise for the Import and Export of Ores, Metals, and Solid Fuels*] (CZ)
METALIMPEX ... METALIMPEX Acel es Fem Kulkereskedelmi Vallalat [*METALIMPEX Foreign Trade Enterprise for Steel and Metal*] (HU)
Metal-Is....... Turkiye Metal, Celik, Muhimmat, Makine, Metalden Mamul Esya ve Oto Sanayii Isci Sendikalari Federasyonu [*Turkish Metal and Allied Workers Federation*] (TU)
METALKAT ... Societe Metallurgique du Katanga (MAR)
metall.......... Metallisch [*Metallic*] [*German*]
metallich..... Metal, Metallic (RU)
METALLO ... Societe de Constructions Metalliques (MAR)
METALLOGLOBUS ... Metalloglobus Femipari es Ertekesito Vallalat [*Trade Enterprise for Metal Products*] (HU)
metalloizol ... Waterproof Material Made from Metal Foil (RU)
metallopromsoyuz ... Producers' Union of the Metalworking Industry (RU)

metallopromsoyuz ... Union of Metal Producers' Cooperatives (RU)
Metallosbyt ... Administration for the Marketing of Ferrous Metals (RU)
Metallurgavtomatika ... Trust for the Automation of Metallurgical Establishments (RU)
METALLURGIZDAT ... State Scientific and Technical Publishing House of Literature on Ferrous and Nonferrous Metallurgy (RU)
Metallurgprokatmontazh ... Trust for the Installation of Rolling-Mill and Other Metallurgical Equipment (RU)
METAL SEN ... Metal Iscileri Sendikasi [*Metal Workers Union*] [*Cypriot*] (TU)
METAMAD ... Metale y Maderas, SA [*Cali*] (COL)
METAMIG ... Metais Minas Gerais [*Minas Gerais Metals*] [*Brazilian*] (LA)
METAS........ Izmir Metalurji Fabrikasi Turk Anonim Sirketi [*Izmir Metallurgy Factory Corporation*] (TU)
METAVAL... Metalurgica del Valle Ltda. [*Cali*] (COL)
METAZ........ Metalurgicke Zavody [*Metallurgical Works*] (CZ)
METE .... Magyar Elektrotechnikai Egyesulet [*Hungarian Electrotechnical Association*] (HU)
METE .... Magyar Elelmezesipari Tudomanyos Egyesulet [*Scientific Association of the Hungarian Food Industry*] (HU)
METE .... Mezoegazdasagi es Elelmiszeripari Tudomanyos Egyesulet
METECNA... Metalotecnica de Mocambique Lda. (MAR)
meteor .... Meteorologia [*Meteorology*] [*Finnish*]
meteor .... Meteorological, Meteorology (RU)
meteor .... Meteorology, Meteorological (BU)
meteorolog ... Meteorologiai [*Meteorological*] (HU)
METESZ....... Mernokok es Technikusok Szovetsege [*Federation of Engineers and Technicians*] (HU)
METESZ...... Muszaki es Termeszettudomanyi Egyesuletek Szovetsege [*Federation of Technological and Scientific Associations*] (HU)
Meth............ Methode [*Method*] [*German*]
met haz....... Metni Hazirlayan [*Prepared Text*] (TU)
METI............ Machine-Electrical Engineering Institute (BU)
METIISS...... Moscow Electrotechnical Institute of Signalization and Communications Engineers [*1932-1937*] (RU)
Metizsbyt.... All-Union State Office for the Marketing of Metalware (RU)
METKA........ Mehanicna Tkalnica [*Mechanized Textile Mill*] [*Celje*] (YU)
METO .... Middle East Treaty Organization (MAR)
metod.......... Systematic, Methodic, Methodological (RU)
METOPLASTICAS ... Industrias Metoplasticas Ltda. [*Bogota*] (COL)
metpromsoyuz ... Union of Metal Producers' Cooperatives (RU)
METRANS... Podnik pro Mezinarodni Zasilatelstvi [*International Freight Transportation Enterprise*] (CZ)
metrich .... Metric (RU)
Metrie.......... Metairie [*Small Farm*] [*Military map abbreviation*] [*World War I*] [*French*] (MTD)
METRIMPEX ... METRIMPEX Muszeripari Kulkereskedelmi Vallalat [*METRIMPEX Foreign Trade Enterprise of the Instrument Industry*] (HU)
Metrogiprotrans ... State Planning and Surveying Institute for the Construction of Subways and Transportation Facilities (RU)
METROP ..... Mesno Trgovinsko Podjetje [*Commercial Meat Establishment*] (YU)
Metroproyekt ... Technical Office for the Planning of the Moscow Subway (RU)
Metrostroy ... State Administration of Construction of the Moscow Subway (RU)
metr t .... Metric Ton (RU)
mets............ Metsastys [*Hunting*] [*Finnish*]
METs........... Motor Electric Power Plant (BU)
metsh.......... Metsanhoito [*Forestry*] [*Finnish*]
MEUPM....... Mouvement d'Entente et de l'Unite du Peuple Muluba (MAR)
MEUTU........ Movimiento Estudiantil de la Universidad del Trabajo del Uruguay [*Student Movement of the Labor University of Uruguay*] (LA)
MEV............. Macro-Economische Verkenning
MeV............. Megaelektronowolt [*Mega-Electron-Volt*] [*Polish*]
Mev .... Million Electronvolts (RU)
MEV............. Moravske Energeticke Vyrobny [*Moravian Electric Power Plants*] (CZ)
MEVEA........ Mesogeiakai Epikheiriseis Viomikhanias-Emboriou-Andiprosopeion [*Mediterranean Industrial, Commercial, and Distribution Enterprises*] [*Greek*] (GC)
MEVIEP....... Mezogazdasagi Vizi Epito Vallalat [*Agricultural Hydraulic Engineering Enterprise*] (HU)
Mevr........... Mevrouw [*Mrs.*] [*Dutch*] (GPO)
MEVRO .... Mezinarodni Vystava Rozhlasu [*International Radio Exposition*] (CZ)
MEVS .... Ministry of Electrification and Water Resources [*Obsolete*] (BU)
MEVT .... Moscow Technicum for Electric Vacuum Devices (RU)
MEWA .... Metallwaren-Industrie [*Hardware Industry*] (EG)
MEWAC .... Mediterranean Europe West Africa Conference (MAR)
MEWU .... Malayan Estate Workers' Union (ML)
MEX............. Meksyk [*Mexico*] [*Polish*]
MEX............. Mexico [*Three-letter standard code*] (CNC)
MEXCONCRETO ... Mezclas de Concreto Ltda. [*Cali*] (COL)
MEY............. Metallion Evdokimou Ypiresias [*Medal of Honorable Service*] [*Greek*] (GC)
Mey .... Meydan [*Public Square, Field*] (TU)
MEYAK .... Memur Yardimlasma Kurumu [*Government Employees Mutual Aid Society*] [*Under Prime Ministry*] (TU)
MEYBUZ ..... Meyve ve Buzlu Muhafaza ve Enternasyonal Nakliyat AS [*Fruit Refrigeration and International Transport Corp.*] (TU)
MEYEA........ Metales y Baterias SA [*Medellin*] (COL)
MEYSU........ Meyva Sulari Anonim Sirketi [*Fruit Juices Corporation*] (TU)
MEZ............ Mitteleuropaische Zeit [*Central European Time*] (EG)
MEZ............ Moravske Elektrotechnicke Zavody [*Moravian Electric Appliances Plants*] (CZ)
MEZ............ Moravskoslezske Elektrotechnicke Zavody, Narodni Podnik [*Moravian-Silesian Electric Appliances Plant, National Enterprise*] (CZ)
MEZ............ Oil Extraction Plant (RU)
mezhd......... Interjection [*Grammatical*] (BU)
mezhd......... Interjection (RU)
mezhdunar ... International (BU)
mezhdunar ... International (RU)
Mezhduved ... Interdepartmental (RU)
Mezhgorsvyaz'stroy ... All-Union State Trust for the Construction of Long-Distance Wire Communications Structures (RU)
Mezhkniga ... International Book [*All-Union Association for the International Book Trade*] (RU)
mezhkolkhozstroy ... Interkolkhoz Construction Organization (RU)
Mezhrabkom ... International Workers' Committee (RU)
Mezhrabpom ... International Workers' Relief (RU)
Mezhsovkhim ... Interdepartmental Conference on Chemical Defense (RU)
mezh st....... Landmark, Boundary Mark [*Topography*] (RU)
MEZOERT... Mezogazdasagi Termekeket Ertekesito Vallalat [*Agricultural Produce Market Enterprise*] (HU)
MEZOKER... Zoldseg- es Gyumolcs Ertekesito Szovetkezeti Kozpont [*Cooperative Center for the Sale of Vegetables and Fruit*] (HU)
MEZOMAG ... Mezogazdasagi Magkereskedelmi Vallalat [*Agricultural Seed-Trade Enterprise*] (HU)
MEZOSZOV ... Mezogazdasagi Eszkozoket Ertekesito Szovetkezet [*Sales Cooperative for Agricultural Epuipment*] (HU)
MEZOVILL ... Mezogazdasagi es Falusi Villanyszerelesi Vallalat [*Agricultural and Village Electrical Repair and Installation Enterprise*] (HU)
MF.............. Mali Franc (MAR)
MF.............. Mechanical Filter (BU)
MF.............. Medicine and Physical Culture Publishing House (BU)
MF.............. Mediterranean Fleet (MAR)
MF.............. Medufrekventni [*Intermediate Frequency*] (YU)
mf............... Merfold [*Mile*] (HU)
MF.............. Microphotometer (RU)
mf............... Millifarad (RU)
mf............... Milliphot (RU)
MF.............. Miniaturni Filips [*Miniature Phillips*] [*Radio*] (YU)
MF.............. Ministerio das Financas [*Ministry of Finance*] [*Portuguese*] (WER)
MF.............. Ministerstvo Financi [*Ministry of Finance*] (CZ)
MF.............. Ministerstwo Finansow [*Ministry of Finance*] (POL)
MF.............. Ministerul Finantelor [*Ministry of Finances*] (RO)
MF.............. Ministry of Finance (BU)
MF.............. Ministry of Finance (RU)
mf............... Mint Fent [*As Above*] (HU)
MF.............. Mlada Fronta [*The Youth Front (A newspaper and publishing house)*] (CZ)
Mf.............. Moeglichkeitsform [*German*]
MF.............. Monophosphate (RU)
MF.............. Moravska Filharmonie [*Moravian Philharmonic Orchestra*] (CZ)
MF.............. Moscow Branch (RU)
MF.............. Movimento Federalista [*Federalist Movement*] [*Portuguese*] (WER)
Mf.............. Mufettis [*Inspector*] (TU)
MF.............. Muszaki Foiskola [*Technical College*] (HU)
MF.............. Mzdovy Fond [*Wage Fund*] (CZ)
MFA............ International Astronautical Federation [*IAF*] (RU)
MFA............ International Phonetic Alphabet (RU)
MFA............ International Phonetic Association [*IPA*] (RU)
MFA............ Malawi Football Association (MAR)
MFA............ Manufacture Florence Actualite (MAR)
MFA............ Ministry of Foreign Affairs (ML)
MFA............ Movimento das Forcas Armadas [*Armed Forces Movement*] [*Portuguese*] (PPE)
MfAA.......... Ministerium fuer Auswaertige Angelegenheiten [*Ministry for Foreign Affairs*] (EG)
MfAI .... Ministerium fuer Aussen- und Innerdeutschen Handel [*Ministry for Foreign and Inner-German Trade*] [*See also MAI*] (EG)
MfaL........... Medaille fuer Ausgezeichnete Leistungen [*Medal for Distinguished Achievement*] (EG)
MFALP .... International Federation of Air Line Pilots Associations [*IFALPA*] (RU)
MFAM .... Missao de Fotogrametria Aerea de Mocambique (MAR)
MFAR .... Milicias del Frente Armado de Resistencia [*Militia of the Armed Fronts for Resistance*] [*Argentine*] (LA)
MFASM .... International Federation of Medical Students' Associations [*IFMSA*] (RU)
MFAts .... Methyl Fluoroacetate (RU)
MfB............ Ministerium fuer Bauwesen [*Ministry for Construction*] (EG)

MFBA .... International Federation of Library Associations [*IFLA*] (RU)
MFBRO .... Miedzynarodowa Federacja Bojownikow Ruchu Oporu [*International Federation of Fighters in the Resistance Movement*] [*Polish*]
MFC .... Messageries Fluviales de la Cuvette (MAR)
MfC .... Ministerium fuer Chemische Industrie [*Ministry for the Chemical Industry*] (EG)
MFD .... International Federation for Documentation [*IFD*] (RU)
MFD .... Mezinarodni Federace Dopravy [*International Transportation Federation*] (CZ)
MFDK .... Ministry of Finance and State Control [*Obsolete*] (BU)
MFDKhS ...... Dichloromethylphenylsilane (RU)
MFD-KLA .... Latin-American Committee of the International Federation for Documentation (RU)
MFDO .... International Federation of Children's Communities [*IFCC*] (RU)
MFDZ .... Mezinarodni Federace Demokratickych Zen [*International Federation of Democratic Women*] (CZ)
MFDZh .... International Federation of Democratic Women (BU)
MfE .... Ministerium fuer Eisenbahnwesen [*Ministry for Railroads*] (EG)
MfEE .... Ministerium fuer Elektrotechnik und Elektronik [*Ministry for Electrotechnology and Electronics*] (EG)
MFEI .... Moscow Institute of Finance and Economics (RU)
MfEMK .... Ministerium fuer Erzbergbau, Metallurgie, und Kali [*Ministry for Mining, Metalurgy, and Potash*] (EG)
MFF .... International Federation of Film Archives [*IFFA*] (RU)
MFF .... Mashonaland Field Force (MAR)
MFF .... Mezinarodni Filmovy Festival [*International Film Festival*] (CZ)
MFG .... Miners' International Federation [*MIF*] (RU)
MfG .... Ministerium fuer Gesundheitswesen [*Ministry for Health*] (EG)
MfG .... Ministerium fuer Grundstoffindustrie [*Ministry for the Raw Materials Industry*] (EG)
MFGS .... Mittheilungen von Forschungsreisenden und Gelehrten aus den Deutschen Schutzgebieten (MAR)
MFH .... Megyei Foldhivatal [*County Land Office*] (HU)
MfHV .... Ministerium fuer Handel und Versorgung [*Ministry for Trade and Supply*] (EG)
MFI .... Benakeion Fytopathologikon Institouton [*Benakeion Plant Pathology Institute*] [*Initial letters of Benakeion are "mp" in Greek*] (GC)
MFI .... Moscow Institute of Finance (RU)
MFI .... Moscow Pharmaceutical Institute (RU)
MFK .... International Finance Corporation [*IFC*] (RU)
MfK .... Ministerium fuer Kultur [*Ministry for Culture*] (EG)
MFKhP .... International Federation of Christian Trade Unions [*IFCTU*] (RU)
MFKM .... International Catholic Youth Federation [*ICYF*] (RU)
m fl .... Med Flera [*With Others*] [*Swedish*] (GPO)
mfl .... Med Flere [*With Others*] [*Danish*] (GPO)
m fl .... Med Flere [*And Others*] [*Norwegian*] (GPO)
MfL .... Ministerium fuer Leichtindustrie [*Ministry for Light Industry*] (EG)
MFLV .... Magyar Filmlaboratorium Vallalat [*Hungarian Film Laboratory*] (HU)
MFM .... International Metalworkers' Federation [*IMF*] (RU)
MfM .... Ministerium fuer Maschinenbau [*Ministry for Machine Building*] (EG)
MfM .... Ministerium fuer Materialwirtschaft [*Ministry for Material Management*] (EG)
MFM .... Mouvement pour le Pouvoir Proletarien [*or aux Petits*] [*Movement for Proletarian Power*] [*Malagasy*] (PPW)
MFM .... Mpitolona Hoan'ny Fanjakan'ny Madinika [*Militants for the Establishment of a Proletarian Regime*] [*Malagasy*] (AF)
MFMK .... International Federation of Young Cooperators [*IFYC*] (RU)
MFMM .... International Federation of Musical Youth (RU)
MFMPK .... Magyar Forradalmi Munkas- Paraszt Kormany [*Hungarian Revolutionary Workers' and Peasants' Government*] (HU)
MFMU .... Moscow Machine Accounting and Computing Office (RU)
MFN .... International Federation of Petroleum Workers [*IFPW*] (RU)
MFNF .... Magyar Fuggetlensegi Nepfront [*Hungarian Independence People's Front*] (HU)
MFNFOT ..... Magyar Fuggetlensegi Nepfront Orszagos Tanacsa [*National Council of the Hungarian Independence People's Front*] (HU)
MFNRM .... Ministarstvo na Financiite na Narodnata Republika Makedonija [*Ministry of Finance of Macedonia*] (YU)
MfNV .... Ministerium fuer Nationale Verteidigung [*Ministry for National Defense*] (EG)
MFO .... Interbranch Turnover [*Banking*] (RU)
MFO .... Moscow Finance Department (RU)
MFO .... Multinational Force and Observers (MAR)
MFP .... International Graphical Federation [*IGF*] (RU)
MFP .... Magyar Fuggetlensegi Part [*Hungarian Independence Party*] (HU)
MFP .... Marematlou Freedom Party [*Basotho*] (AF)
MFP .... Movimento Federalista Portugues [*Portuguese Federalist Movement*] (WER)
MFPA .... Mauritius Family Planning Association (AF)
MFPROO ..... International Federation of Unions of Employees in Public and Civil Services [*IFPCS*] (RU)
MFPRP .... International Federation of Professional Workers in Education (BU)
MFPRP .... World Federation of Teachers' Unions (RU)
MFR .... Member of the Order of the Federal Republic (MAR)
MFROK .... International Shoe and Leather Workers' Federation [*ISLWF*] (RU)
MFRP .... International Federation of Workers in Education (BU)
MFRPSKh ... International Federation of Plantation, Agriculture, and Allied Workers [*IFPAAW*] (RU)
MFS .... [*The*] International Shipping Federation Ltd. [*ISF*] (RU)
MFS .... Mezinarodni Fond Solidarity [*International Solidarity Fund*] (CZ)
MfS .... Ministerium fuer Staatssicherheit [*Ministry for State Security*] [*See also MISTAI, MSS*] (EG)
MFS .... Ministrstvo za Finance Slovenije [*Ministry of Finance of Slovenia*] (YU)
MFSA .... Maurel Freres Societe Anonyme (MAR)
MfSAB .... Ministerium fuer Schwermaschinen- und Anlagenbau [*Ministry for Heavy Machine Construction and Plant Construction*] (EG)
MFSD .... International Federation of Building and Woodworkers [*IFBWW*] (RU)
MFSF .... International Pharmaceutical Students' Federation [*IPSF*] (RU)
MFSM .... Miedzynarodowa Federacja Schronisko Mlodziezowych [*International Youth Hostel Federation*] [*Polish*]
MFSN .... Medzinarodna Federacia Slobodnych Novinarov [*International Federation of Free Journalists*] (CZ)
MFST .... International Federation of Commercial, Clerical, and Technical Employees [*IFCCTE*] (RU)
MFT .... International Transport Workers' Federation [*ITF*] (RU)
MFT .... Magyarhoni Foldtani Tarsulat [*Geological Society of the Hungarian Fatherland*] (HU)
MFT .... Megyei Foldbirtokrendezo Tanacs [*County Council on Redistribution of Land*] (HU)
MFT .... Methylphenyltriazene (RU)
MFT .... Militants pour la Concretisation de la Revolution [*Militants for the Realization of the Revolution*] [*Malagasy*] (AF)
MFTA .... Mouvement des Femmes Travailleuses de l'Angola [*Angolan Working Women's Movement*] (AF)
MFTI .... Moscow Physicotechnical Institute (RU)
MFTTShP .... International Textile and Garment Workers' Federation [*ITGWF*] (RU)
MFU .... Functional Micromodule Block (RU)
MFU .... Malayan Film Unit (ML)
MFU .... Mission Francaise d'Urbanisme (MAR)
MfV .... Ministerium fuer Verkehrswesen [*Ministry for Transport*] (EG)
MfVF .... Ministerium fuer Verarbeitungsmaschinen- und Fahrzeugbau [*Ministry for Processing-Machine and Vehicle Construction*] (EG)
MFVNIGRI ... Moscow Branch of the All-Union Scientific Research Institute of Geological Exploration (RU)
MFVNIIZh .... Moscow Branch of the All-Union Scientific Research Institute of Fats (RU)
MFW .... Miedzynarodowy Fundusz Walutowy [*International Monetary Fund*] [*Polish*]
MFZhUO ..... International Federation of University Women [*IFUW*] (RU)
mg .... Gecici Madde [*Temporary Article*] [*As of a bill*] (TU)
MG .... Gradient Method (RU)
mg .... Last Year (BU)
mg .... Last Year (RU)
MG .... Local Oscillator (RU)
MG .... Madagascar [*Two-letter standard code*] (CNC)
mg .... Magan [*Private, Privately Owned*] (HU)
Mg .... Magara [*Cavern, Grotto*] (TU)
MG .... Magnetic Head (RU)
MG .... Maharashtrawadi Gomantak [*Indian*] (PPW)
MG .... Maschinengewehr [*Machine Gun*] (EG)
MG .... Maximum Hygroscopicity (RU)
Mg .... Megagram (RU)
MG .... Methylene Blue (RU)
mg .... Miligram [*Milligram*] (POL)
mg .... Miligramo [*Milligram*] [*Spanish*]
mg .... Milligram (BU)
mg .... Milligram (RU)
mG .... Milligram Force (RU)
mg .... Milligramm [*Milligram*] (EG)
mg .... Milligramm [*Milligram*] (HU)
mg .... Milligramma(a) [*Finnish*]
mg .... Milligramme [*Milligram*] [*French*]
MG .... Mine-Surveying Gyrocompass (RU)
MG .... Ministarstvo Gradevina [*Ministry of Building*] (YU)
MG .... Ministerstwo Gornictwa [*Ministry of Mining*] (POL)
MG .... Ministry of Forests [*Obsolete*] (BU)
mG .... Mit Goldschnitt [*With Gilt Edges*] [*German*]
mg .... Mobile Group, Maneuver Group (RU)
MG .... Molekulargewicht [*Molecular Weight*] [*German*]
MG .... Mouvement Geographique (MAR)
MG .... Muvakkat Gol [*Temporary (Seasonal) Lake*] (TU)
M3G .... Marx, Mao, Marighella, e Guevara [*Marx, Mao, Marighella, and Guevara*] [*Brazilian*] (LA)
MGA .... International Association of Geodesy [*IAG*] (RU)

MGA........... Manufacture Generale Alimentaire (MAR)
MGA........... Ministry of Civil Aviation (RU)
MGA........... Missao Geografica de Angola [*Angola Geographical Mission*] (AF)
MGA........... Moscow Mining Academy (RU)
MGA........... Mushroom Growers Association (EA)
MGAL.......... Major General [*Major General*] (CL)
MGAMID..... Former Moscow Main Archives of the Ministry of Foreign Affairs, Kept at the TsGADA (RU)
MGAMID..... Moscow State Archives of the Ministry of Foreign Affairs (RU)
MGAMTs..... Moscow Main Air Weather Center (RU)
MGAP.......... Mouvement Gabonais d'Action Populaire [*Gabonese Popular Action Movement*] (AF)
mgb............ Megabar (RU)
MGB........... Ministry of State Security [*1946-1953*] (RU)
mgbatr........ Weather Battery [*Military term*] (RU)
MGBI........... Moscow State Library Institute (RU)
Mgbr........... Ministarstvo Gradevina Broj [*Ministry of Building Number*] (YU)
MGBT.......... Moscow City Library Technicum (RU)
MGC........... Maadi Golf Club [*Egyptian*] (MAR)
MGD........... Hydromagnetic (RU)
MGD........... Machine for Deep Drainage (RU)
MGD........... Magnetohydrodynamic (RU)
MGD........... Moscow City Administration (RU)
MGDG......... Magnetogas-Dynamic Generator (RU)
MGDG......... Magnetohydrodynamic Generator (RU)
MGDNT....... Moscow City House of Folk Art (RU)
MGDP.......... Moscow City House of Pioneers (RU)
MGDPO....... Moscow City Volunteer Fire Society (RU)
MGDSP....... Moscow City House of Hygiene Education (RU)
MGDU......... Moscow City Teacher's House (RU)
mgdzh......... Megajoule (RU)
MGE........... Magyar Geofizikusok Egyesulete [*Association of Hungarian Geophysicists*] (HU)
Mge............ Mouillage [*Anchorage*] [*French*] (NAU)
MGEI........... Moscow State Institute of Economics (RU)
mg-ekv........ Milligram-Equivalent (RU)
MGES.......... Moscow State Electric Power Plant (RU)
MGESA....... Manisa Genclik ve Spor Akademisi [*Manisa Youth and Sports Academy*] (TU)
mgev........... Million Electron-Volts (RU)
MGF........... Madagascar Franc (MAR)
MGF........... Moscow State Philharmonic (RU)
MGFHU....... Missao de Geografia Fisica e Humana do Ultramar, Junta de Investigacoes do Ultramar (MAR)
MGG-.......... Helical Depth Gage (RU)
MGG........... International Geophysical Year (BU)
MGG........... International Geophysical Year [*IGY*] (RU)
MGG........... Medunarodna Geofizicka Godina [*International Geophysical Year*] [*1957-1958*] (YU)
MGGE......... International Greenland Glaciological Expedition (RU)
MGGH......... Mitteilungen der Geographischen Gesellschaft in Hamburg [*A publication*] (MAR)
MGGS......... International Union of Geodesy and Geophysics [*IUGG*] (RU)
mggts.......... Megahertz, Megacycles per Second (RU)
MGI............ Imperial Ethiopian Mapping and Geographical Institute (MAR)
MGI............ Long-Distance Selector (RU)
MGI............ Marine Hydrophysical Institute (RU)
MGI............ Mining and Geological Institute (BU)
MGI............ Moscow Geodetic Institute (RU)
MGI............ Moscow Mining Institute (RU)
MGIAI......... Moscow State Institute of Historical Archives (RU)
MGiE.......... Ministerstwo Gornictwa i Energetyki [*Ministry of Mining and Power*] (POL)
MGIMIP....... Moscow State Institute of Measures and Measuring Instruments (RU)
MGIMO....... Moscow State Institute of International Relations (RU)
MGiON........ Ministry of Geology and Conservation of Mineral Resources (RU)
MGiSS......... Ministry of Urban and Rural Construction (RU)
MGIUU........ Moscow City Institute for the Advanced Training of Teachers (RU)
MGK........... Interdepartmental Geophysical Committee (RU)
MGK........... International Convention Concerning the Carriage of Goods by Rail (RU)
MGK........... International Geological Congress (RU)
MG K.......... Mezogazdasagi Konyv- es Folyoirat Kiado [*Publishers of Agricultural Books and Periodicals*] (HU)
MGK........... Milli Guvenlik Kurulu [*National Security Council*] (TU)
MGK........... Ministerstwo Gospodarki Komunalnej [*Ministry of Municipal Economy*] (POL)
MGK........... Ministry of State Control (RU)
MGK........... Moscow City Committee (RU)
MGK........... Moscow City Office (RU)
MGK........... Moscow State Conservatory Imeni P. I. Chaykovskiy (RU)
MGKA......... Moscow City Lawyers' Collegium (RU)
mgkal.......... Megacalorie (RU)
MGKhI......... Moscow State Art Institute Imeni V. I. Surikov (RU)
mgkhts........ Megahertz (BU)
MGKI.......... Magyar Gazdasagkutato Intezet [*Hungarian Institute of Economic Research*] (HU)
MGKI.......... Mezogazdasagi Gepkiserleti Intezet [*Experimental Institute for Agricultural Machinery*] (HU)
MGKT.......... Moscow State Chamber Theater (RU)
MGKU......... Mumbai Girni Kamgar Union [*Bombay Mill Workers' Union*] [*Indian*]
MGL............ Marine Hydrophysical Laboratory (RU)
MGL............ Miniere des Grands Lacs Africains [*African Great Lakes Mining Co.*] [*Zairian*] (AF)
MGLB.......... Moscow City Lecture Bureau (RU)
MGM........... Magasins Gabonais Modernes (MAR)
MGM........... Magyar Gordulocsapagy Muvek [*Hungarian Ballbearing Works*] (HU)
mgm........... Megameter (RU)
MGM........... Missao Geografica de Mocambique, Junta de Investigacoes do Ultramar (MAR)
MGM........... Muhasebat Genel Mudurlugu [*Directorate General of Accounting*] (TU)
MGMI.......... Magnitogorsk Mining and Metallurgical Institute Imeni G. I. Nosov (RU)
MGMI.......... Moscow Hydrometeorological Institute [*1930-1941*] (RU)
MGMI.......... Moscow Institute of Water Reclamation (RU)
MGMI.......... Second Moscow State Medical Institute Imeni N. I. Pirogov (RU)
MGMP......... Multispeed Hydromechanical Gear (RU)
MGN............ Majlis Gerakan Negara [*National Operations Council*] (ML)
mgn............ Millihenry (RU)
Mgne........... Montagne [*Mountain*] [*Military map abbreviation*] [*World War I*] [*French*] (MTD)
MGNITI........ Moscow City Scientific Research Institute of Tuberculosis (RU)
MGO............ Militaergerichtsordnung [*Rules of Procedure of a Military Court*] (EG)
MGO............ Moscow City Branch, Moscow City Department (RU)
mgom.......... Megohm (BU)
mgom.......... Megohm (RU)
MGON......... Ministry of Geology and Conservation of Mineral Resources, USSR (RU)
MGONI........ Moscow City Real Estate Department (RU)
MGOPS....... Ministry of Forests and Protection of Environment (BU)
MGOT.......... Moscow City Labor Department (RU)
MGOTS....... Long-Distance Oblast Telephone Exchange (RU)
MGOTZK..... Moscow City Association of Theater and Show Ticket Offices (RU)
MGP............ Magnetic Directional Gyro (RU)
MGP............ Marina de Guerra del Peru [*Peruvian Navy*] (LA)
MGP............ Metal-Film Hermetically Sealed Precision (Resistor) (RU)
MGP............ Milli Guven Partisi [*National Reliance Party*] (TU)
MGP............ Moscow City Administration (RU)
MGP-........... Piston Depth Gage (RU)
MGPDI......... Moscow State Pedagogical Institute of Defectology (RU)
MGPI........... Melekess State Pedagogical Institute (RU)
MGPI........... Moscow City Pedagogical Institute Imeni V. P. Potemkin (RU)
MGPI........... Moscow State Pedagogical Institute Imeni K. Liebknecht (RU)
MGPI........... Moscow State Pedagogical Institute Imeni V. I. Lenin (RU)
MGPIIYa...... First Moscow State Pedagogical Institute of Foreign Languages (RU)
MGP i MR.... Ministry of State Food and Material Reserves, USSR (RU)
MGPP.......... Mechanized Hospital Field Laundry (RU)
mgr............. Magister [*Master*] [*Latin*] (POL)
MGR............ Marina de Guerra Revolucionaria [*Revolutionary Navy*] [*Cuban*] (LA)
mgr............. Milligramm [*Milligram*] (HU)
Mgr............. Monseigneur [*My Lord*] [*French*] (GPO)
MGR............ Mouvement de la Gauche Reformatrice [*Movement of the Reformist Left*] [*French*] (PPW)
MGRI........... Moscow Institute of Geological Exploration Imeni Sergo Ordzhonikidze (RU)
MGRS.......... Moscow City Administration of the Radio Wire Broadcasting Network (RU)
MGRS.......... Moscow City Radio Wire Broadcasting Network (RU)
MGS............ International Freight Agreement (RU)
MGS............ International Gas Union [*IGU*] (RU)
MGS............ International Geographical Union (RU)
MGS............ International Geophysical Cooperation (RU)
MGS............ Methodist Girls School (ML)
MGS............ Mezhdunarodnoye Gruzovoye Soglasheniye [*Agreement Concerning International Railroad Freight Traffic (Between USSR and Satellites)*] (EG)
mgs............. Milligram Force (RU)
MGS............ Moscow City Soviet (RU)
MGS............ Museum of City Sculpture (RU)
MGSB.......... Local Geodetic Information Office (RU)
MGSC.......... Malaysian General Service Corps (ML)
MGSh.......... Naval General Staff (RU)
MGSNKh..... Moscow City Council of the National Economy (RU)
MGSovet..... Interdepartmental Geodetic Council (RU)
MGSPS....... Moscow City Council of Trade Unions (RU)
MGSS.......... International Year of the Quiet Sun [*IQSY*] (RU)
MGSS.......... Ministry of Urban and Rural Construction (RU)
Mgt............. Megaton (RU)
MGT............ Missao Geografica de Timor, Junta de Investigacoes do Ultramar (MAR)

MGTE.......... Moscow State Music Hall (RU)
MGTI........... Mezogeptervezo Iroda [*Office for the Design of Agricultural Machinery*] (HU)
MGTS.......... Long-Distance Telephone Exchange (RU)
Mgts........... Megahertz, Megacycles per Second (RU)
MGTS.......... Moscow City Telephone Network (RU)
MGU........... Mezogazdasagi Gepuzem [*Agricultural Machine Factory*] (HU)
MGU........... Moscow City Administration (RU)
MGU........... Moscow State University Imeni M. V. Lomonosov (RU)
MGU........... Powerful Loudspeaker (RU)
MGULP........ Moscow City Administration of Light Industry (RU)
MGUMP....... Moscow City Administration of Local Industry (RU)
mgvt........... Megawatt (RU)
mgvt-ch...... Megawatt-Hour (RU)
MGW........... Messgeraetewerk [*Measuring-Instrument Plant*] (EG)
MGYE.......... Magyar Gyogypedagogusok Egyesulete [*Association of Hungarian Teachers in Special Education*] (HU)
MGYT.......... Magyar Gyogyszertudomanyi Tarsasag [*Hungarian Pharmaceutical Association*] (HU)
MGZhD........ Moscow City Railways [*Trust*] (RU)
MGZPI......... Moscow State Pedagogical Correspondence Institute (RU)
MH.............. Almarhum [*Deceased*] (IN)
MH.............. Magyar Helikon [*Hungarian Helicon Publishing House*] (HU)
MH.............. Matica Hrvatska [*A Croatian literary and publishing society*] [*Zagreb*] (YU)
mh.............. Megallohely [*Stop*] (HU)
MH.............. Ministerstvo Hornictvi [*Ministry of Mining*] (CZ)
MH.............. Ministerstwo Hutnictwa [*Ministry of Metallurgy*] (POL)
MHA............ Madonna House Apostolate (EA)
MHaBZCH... Magnezitove Hute a Bane Zavodu Cervenej Hviezdy [*Red Star Magnetite Works and Mines*] (CZ)
MHAI........... Mott, Hay & Anderson International (MAR)
MHAP.......... Muzeum Historyczne Aptekarstwa Polskiego [*Historical Museum of Polish Pharmacy*] (POL)
3M(harom M)modszer ... Mozdulatelemzes, Munkatanulmanyozas es Munkakialakitas Modszer [*A Method Involving Time-Motion Study, Work Analysis and Formation of Work Procedures*] (HU)
MHAST........ Missao Hidrografica de Angola e Sao Tome (MAR)
MHAT.......... Moskovski Hudozestveni Akademski Teatr [*Moscow Academic Art Theater*] (YU)
MHC............ Mesovita Hemiska Ceta [*Mixed Chemical Company*] [*Military*] (YU)
MHCU.......... Ministere de l'Habitat, de la Construction, et de l'Urbanisme [*Algerian*] (MAR)
MHD............ Magyar Hajo es Darugyar [*Hungarian Ship and Crane Factory*] (HU)
MHD............ Meteorologischer-Hydrologischer Dienst [*Meteorological and Hydrological Service*] (EG)
MHD............ Miejski Handel Detaliczny [*Municipal Retail Trade*] (POL)
MHD............ Ministerstvo Hutniho Prumyslu a Rudnych Dolu [*Ministry of the Metallurgical Industry and Ore Mines*] (CZ)
MHD............ Ministerstwo Handlu Detalicznego [*Ministry of Retail Trade*] (POL)
mhd............ Mittelhochdeutsch [*German*]
MHDGS....... Ministarstvo Hrvatskog Domobranstva - Glavni Stozer [*Ministry of Croatian Home Defense - General Headquarters*] [*World War II*] (YU)
MHE............ Magyar Hajozasi Egyesulet [*Hungarian Shipping Association*] (HU)
MHF............ Mezinarodni Hudebni Festival [*International Music Festival*] (CZ)
MHG............ Mauritius Hotels Group (MAR)
MHJ............ Minosegi Hangszerkeszito es Javito Kisipari Termeloszovetkezet [*Cooperative Enterprise for the Production and Repair of Musical Instruments*] (HU)
MHK............ Medunarodna Hidrografska Konferencija [*International Hydrographic Conference*] (YU)
MHK............ Munkara Harcra Kesz [*Ready for Work and Defense*] (HU)
MHKD.......... Matica Hrvatskih Kazalisnih Dobrovoljaca [*Croatian Amateur Theatrical Society*] [*Zagreb*] (YU)
Mhl............. Mahalli [*Local, Quarter*] [*As of a city*] (TU)
Mhlbes........ Muehlenbesitzer [*German*]
MHM........... Miejski Handel Miesny [*Municipal Meat Trade*] (POL)
MHM........... Miejski Handel Mleczarski [*Polish*]
MHM........... Mill Hill Missionaries (MAR)
MHO............ Materiel Hospitalier Outre-Mer (MAR)
MHO............ Metallurgiques Hoboken Overpelt (MAR)
MHP............ Milli Hedef Partisi [*National Goal Party*] [*Turkish Cypriot*] (PPE)
MHP............ Milli Yetci Hareket Partisi [*Nationalist Action Party*] [*Formerly, CKMP*] (TU)
MHPRD....... Ministerstvo Hutniho Prumyslu a Rudnych Dolu [*Ministry of the Metallurgical Industry and Ore Mines*] (CZ)
MHR............ Members of the House of Representatives (MAR)
MHRD.......... Ministerstvo Hutniho Prumyslu a Rudnych Dolu [*Ministry of the Metallurgical Industry and Ore Mines*] (CZ)
MHRT.......... Magyar Hajozasi Reszvenytarsasag [*Hungarian Shipping Company Limited*] (HU)
MHS............ Matabele Home Society (MAR)
MHS............ Mladezne Hnuti za Svobodu [*Youth Freedom Movement*] (CZ)
MHSz.......... Magyar Helyesiras Szabalyai [*Hungarian Orthographic Rules*] (HU)
MHSZ.......... Magyar Honvedelmi Sportszovetseg [*Hungarian Sports Federation for National Defense*] (HU)
MHSZ.......... Magyar Honvedelmi Szovetseg [*Hungarian National Defense Association*] (HU)
MHT............ Magyar Hidrologiai Tarsasag [*Hungarian Hydrological Association*] (HU)
mht............. Med Hensyn Til [*With Regard To*] [*Danish*] (GPO)
mht............. Med Hensyn Til [*With Regard To*] [*Norwegian*] (GPO)
MHU............ Medunarodni Hidrografski Ured [*International Hydrographic Office*] (YU)
MHU............ Ministerio da Habitacao e Urbanismo [*Ministry of Housing and Urbanization*] [*Portuguese*] (WER)
MHV............ Magyar Hanglemezgyarto Vallalat [*Hungarian Sound Recording Enterprise*] (HU)
MHV............ Mellektermek- es Hulladekgyujto Vallalat [*Trash and Garbage Collection Enterprise*] (HU)
MHW........... Metallhuetten- und Halbzeugwerke, Berlin (VEB) [*Berlin Metallurgical and Semifinished Product Works (VEB)*] (EG)
MHW........... Ministerstwo Handlu Wewnetrznego [*Ministry of Domestic Trade*] (POL)
MHW........... Mittleres Hochwasser [*Mean High Water Mark*] (EG)
MHWU......... Mauritius Hotel Workers Union (AF)
MHz............ Megahertz [*Megahertz*] (EG)
MHZ............ Ministerstwo Handlu Zagranicznego [*Ministry of Foreign Trade*] (POL)
MI............... Groupe Musulman-Independent pour la Defense du Federalisme Algerien (MAR)
MI-.............. Helicopter Designed by M. L. Mil' (RU)
MI............... Induction Method (RU)
MI............... Institute of Mathematics (BU)
MI............... Institute of Mathematics Imeni V. A. Steklov (RU)
Mi............... Machi [*Town*] [*Japanese*] (NAU)
MI............... Magister Inzynier [*Master of Technical Sciences*] [*Polish*]
MI............... Marker Pulse (RU)
MI............... Masinski Institut [*Mechanical Engineering Institute*] (YU)
MI............... Mensa International (EA)
MI............... Meridional Index (RU)
MI............... Metalna Industrija [*Metal Industry*] (YU)
MI............... Midway Islands [*Two-letter standard code*] (CNC)
mi............... Miedzy Innymi [*Among Others*] (POL)
Mi............... Milchzug [*Milk Train*] (EG)
MI............... Ministerio da Industria [*Ministry of Industry*] [*Portuguese*] (WER)
MI............... Ministerstvo Informaci [*Ministry of Information*] (CZ)
MI............... Ministerul de Interne [*Ministry of the Interior*] (RO)
Mi............... Misaki [*Cape*] [*See also Mki*] [*Japanese*] (NAU)
MI............... Multiseater Fighter (RU)
MI............... Naval Fighter Airplane (RU)
mi............... Palace of Publication (RU)
MI............... Pulse Modulator (RU)
MI............... Testing Methods (RU)
MIA............. Marxista Ifjusagi Akademia [*Marxist Youth Academy*] (HU)
MIA............. Materials and Research on the Archaeology of the USSR (RU)
MIA............. Movimento para a Independencia de Angola (MAR)
MIA............. Movimiento Industrial Argentino [*Argentine Industrial Movement*] (LA)
MIA............. Murrumbidgee Irrigation Area [*Australian*] (MAR)
MIA............. Museum of the History of Architecture (RU)
MIAA........... Missao de Inqueritos Agricolas de Angola (MAR)
MIAM........... Manufacture Ivoirienne d'Articles de Menage (MAR)
MIAMSI....... Movimiento Internacional de Apostolado en los Medios Sociales Independientes [*International Movement of Apostolate in the Independent Social Milieux*] (EA)
MIAN........... Institute of Mathematics Imeni V. A. Steklov of the Academy of Sciences, USSR (RU)
Mian............ Kasa Imienia Mianowskiego [*Mianowski Fund*] [*For the Promotion of Science and Letters in Poland*] (POL)
MIAN........... Medunarodni Institut za Administrativne Nauke [*International Institute on Administration*] (YU)
MIAP........... Movimiento Independiente de Accion Popular [*Independent Movement for Popular Action*] [*Venezuelan*] (LA)
MIB............. Battelle Memorial Institute [*US*] (RU)
MIB............. Malaysian Infantry Brigade (ML)
MIB............. Mecanisation Industrielle des Bois (MAR)
mib............. Motorized Engineer Battalion (RU)
MIB............. Mouvement d'Insoumission Bretonne [*Breton Insubordination Movement*] [*French*] (PD)
MIBA........... Miniere de Bakwanga [*Bakwanga Mining Co.*] [*Zairian*] (AF)
MIBIEN........ Ministerio de Bienestar Social [*Ministry of Social Welfare*] [*Nicaraguan*] (LA1)
MIC............. Malaysian Indian Congress (PPW)
MIC............. Ministerio de Industria e Comercio [*Ministry of Industry and Commerce*] [*Brazilian*] (LA)
MIC............. Ministerul Industriei Chimice [*Ministry of the Chemical Industry*] (RO)
MIC............. Mouvement Chretien des Independents et des Cadres [*Christian Movement of Independents and Professionals*] [*Belgian*] (WER)

MIC.......... Movimiento de Integracion Cristiana [*Christian Integration Movement*] [*Colombian*] (LA)
MIC.......... Movimiento de Izquierda Cristiana [*Christian Left Movement*] [*Chilean*] (LA)
MICAI.......... Mines et Carrieres de l'Imerina (MAR)
MICE.......... Manufacture Ivoirienne de Confection Enfantine (MAR)
MICE.......... Ministerio de Comercio del Exterior [*Ministry of Foreign Trade*] [*Nicaraguan*] (LA1)
MICh.......... Ministerul Industriei Chimice [*Ministry of the Chemical Industry*] (RO)
MICI.......... Manufacture d'Imprimerie et de Cartonnage Ivoirienne (MAR)
MICK.......... Manufacture Industrielle de Cuirs de Kaedi [*Mauritanian*] (MAR)
MICM.......... Ministerul Industriei Constructiilor de Masini [*Ministry of the Machine Building Industry*] (RO)
MICMUE.......... Ministerul Industriei Constructiilor de Masini-Unelte si Electrotehnicii [*Ministry of the Machine Tool Building and Electrical Engineering Industry*] (RO)
MICOIN.......... Ministerio de Comercio Interior [*Ministry of Domestic Trade*] [*Nicaraguan*] (LA1)
MICOL.......... Manufacturas Industriales Colombianas Ltda. [*Bogota*] (COL)
MICONS.......... Ministerio de la Construccion [*Ministry of Construction*] [*Cuban*] (LA)
MICONS.......... Ministerio de la Construccion [*Ministry of Construction*] [*Nicaraguan*] (LA1)
MICTI.......... Ministerio de Industria, Comercio, Turismo, e Integracion [*Ministry of Industry, Commerce, Tourism, and Integration*] [*Peruvian*] (LA)
MICUMA.......... Societe des Mines de Cuivre de Mauritanie (MAR)
MID.......... International Institute for Documentation (RU)
MID.......... MacCarthy Island Division (MAR)
MID.......... Midway Islands [*Three-letter standard code*] (CNC)
MID.......... Military Intelligence Directorate [*Malaysian*] (ML)
MID.......... Ministry of Foreign Affairs (RU)
MID.......... Ministry of Interior and Defense [*Singapore*] (ML)
MID.......... Moscow Institute of Declamation (RU)
MID.......... Movimiento Independiente Democratico [*Independent Democratic Movement*] [*Panamanian*] (PPW)
MID.......... Movimiento de Integracion Democratica [*Democratic Integration Movement*] [*Dominican Republic*] (PPW)
MID.......... Movimiento de Integracion y Desarrollo [*Integration and Development Movement*] [*Argentine*] (LA)
MID.......... Movimiento de la Izquierda Democratica [*Movement of the Democratic Left*] [*Honduran*] (LA)
MID.......... Nederlandse Militaire Inlichtingendienst [*Dutch Military Intelligence Service*] (WEN)
MIDA.......... Movimiento de Integracion Democratica Anti-Reeleccionista [*Antireelection Democratic Integration Movement*] [*Dominican Republic*] (LA)
MIDAS.......... Managed Inputs Delivery Agricultural Services Project (MAR)
MIDEBOM.......... Mission de Developpement de l'Embouche Bovine de Mbandjock (MAR)
MIDEC.......... Middle East Industrial Development Projects Corporation (MAR)
MIDEM.......... Marche Internationale du Disque et de l'Edition Musical
MIDEMA.......... Minoteries de Matadi (MAR)
MIDERIM.......... Mission de Developpement de la Riziculture dans la Plaine des Mbo [*Cameroonian*] (MAR)
MIDEST.......... Marche International de la Sous-Traitance (MAR)
MIDEVIV.......... Mission de Developpement des Cultures Vivrieres Maraicheres et Fruitieres (MAR)
MIDF.......... Malaysia Industrial Development Finance Berhad [*Corporation*] (ML)
MIDINRA.......... Ministerio de Desarrollo Agropecuario y Reforma Agraria [*Ministry of Agricultural-Livestock Development and Agrarian Reform*] [*Nicaraguan*] (LA1)
MIDVIV.......... Mission de Developpement des Cultures Vivrieres, Maraicheres, et Fruitieres [*Cameroonian*] (MAR)
MIE.......... Magyar Iparjogvedelmi Egyesulet [*Association for the Protection of Hungarian Industrial Rights*] (HU)
MIE.......... Mauritius Institute of Education (AF)
MIEC.......... Pax Romana, Mouvement International des Etudiants Catholiques [*Pax Romana, International Movement of Catholic Students - IMCS*] (EA)
MIEC.......... Pax Romana, Movimiento Internacional de Estudiantes Catolicos [*Pax Romana, International Movement of Catholic Students - IMCS*] (LA)
MIEG.......... Mineraloel Import- und Export- GmbH [*Mineral-Oil Import and Export Co.*] (EG)
MIEI.......... Moscow Institute of Engineering Economics Imeni Sergo Ordzhonikidze (RU)
miejsc.......... Miejscowosc [*Place, Locality*] [*Polish*]
miekk.......... Miekkailu [*Fencing*] [*Finnish*]
MIEL.......... Malaysian Industrial Estates Limited (ML)
Miel.......... Mielizna [*Shoal*] [*Polish*] (NAU)
miel.......... Mieluummin [*Finnish*]
MIEM.......... Moscow Institute of Electronic Machinery (RU)
mierc.......... Miercoles [*Wednesday*] [*Spanish*]
mies.......... Miesiac [*or Miesiecznie or Miesiecznik*] [*Month or Monthly*] [*Polish*]
mieszk.......... Mieszkaniec [*Inhabitant*] [*Polish*]
MIF.......... MARC [*Machine Readable Cataloging*] International Format
MIF.......... Miners' International Federation [*See also FIM*] (EA)
mif.......... Mythology (RU)
MIFERGUI.......... Mines de Fer de Guinee [*Iron Mining Co. of Guinea*] (AF)
MIFERMA.......... Societe des Mines de Fer du Mauritanie [*Iron Mining Co. of Mauritania*] (AF)
MIFERSO.......... Societe des Mines de Fer du Senegal Oriental (MAR)
MIFI.......... Moscow Engineering Physics Institute (RU)
MIFLI.......... Moscow Institute of Philosophy, Literature, and History (RU)
MIFR.......... Materials and Research on the History of the Flora and Vegetation of the USSR (RU)
MIFRIFI.......... Mittelfristige Finanzplanung [*Medium-Term Financial Planning*] (EG)
MIG.......... Aircraft Designed by Artem Ivanovich Mikoyan and M. I. Gurevich (RU)
MIGERT.......... Muszer- es Irodagepertekesito Vallalat [*Instrument and Office Machine Marketing Enterprise*] (HU)
MIGSh.......... International Wool Study Group [*IWSG*] (RU)
MIH.......... Matica Iseljenika Hrvatske [*Society of Emigrants of Croatia*] (YU)
MIH.......... Miedzynarodowa Izba Handlowa [*International Chamber of Commerce*] (POL)
MII-.......... Interference Microscope (RU)
MII.......... Madjelis Industri Indonesia [*Indonesian Industrial Council*] (IN)
MII.......... State Fine Arts Museum Imeni A. S. Pushkin (RU)
MIIC.......... Pax Romana, Mouvement International des Intellectuels Catholiques [*Pax Romana, International Catholic Movement for Intellectual and Cultural Affairs - ICMICA*] (EA)
MIIC.......... Pax Romana, Movimiento Internacional de Intelectuales Catolicos [*Pax Romana, International Catholic Movement for Intellectual and Cultural Affairs - ICMICA*] (LA)
MIIGAIK.......... Moscow Institute of Engineers of Geodesy, Aerial Surveying, and Cartography (RU)
MIIGS.......... Moscow Institute of Urban Construction Engineers (RU)
MIIMSKh.......... Melitopol' Institute of Agricultural Mechanical Engineers (RU)
MIIOP.......... Moscow Institute of Engineers for Public Eating Facilities (RU)
MIIS.......... Manufacture Ivoirienne d'Isolants Synthetiques (MAR)
MIIS.......... Moscow Institute of Communications Engineers (RU)
MIIT.......... Milletlerarasi Iktisadi Isbirligi Teskilati Genel Sekreterligi [*International Economic Cooperation Organization General Secretariat*] [*of Finance Ministry*] (TU)
MIIT.......... Moscow Institute of Railroad Transportation Engineers (RU)
MIIVKh.......... Moscow Institute of Hydraulic Engineers (RU)
MIIZ.......... Moscow Institute of Land Use Measures Engineers (RU)
MIIZhT.......... Moscow Institute of Railroad Transportation Engineers (RU)
Mij.......... Maatschappij [*Society, Company*] [*Dutch*] (GPO)
MIJ.......... Movimiento Iglesia Joven [*Young Church Movement*] [*Chilean*] (LA)
MIJARC.......... Mouvement International de la Jeunesse Agricole et Rurale Catholique [*International Movement of Catholic Agricultural and Rural Youth - IMCARY*] (EA)
MIJARC.......... Movimiento Internacional de la Juventud Agraria y Rural Catolica [*International Movement of Catholic Agricultural and Rural Youth - IMCARY*] (LA)
MIJE.......... Magyar Iparjogvedelmi Egyesulet [*Association for the Protection of Hungarian Industrial Rights*] (HU)
MIJM.......... Mouvement International de Jeunesse Mazdaznan (MAR)
MIK.......... Maximale Immissionskonzentration [*Maximum Emission Concentration*] (EG)
MI K.......... Minerva Kiado [*Minerva Publishing House*] (HU)
MIKhM.......... Moscow Institute of Chemical Machinery (RU)
MIKI.......... Muszeripari Kutatointezet [*Research Institute of the Instrument Industry*] (HU)
MIKKh.......... Moscow Scientific Research Institute of Municipal Services (RU)
MIKP.......... Moscow Institute of the Leather Industry (RU)
mikr.......... Microbiology (RU)
mikr.......... Microscope (RU)
mikrobiol.......... Microbiological, Microbiology (RU)
MIKS.......... Multichannel Investigation of Vibrations of Structures and Soils (RU)
MI K YO.......... Mikhanografiko Kendron Ypourgeiou Oikonomikon [*Ministry of Finance Computer Center*] (GC1)
MIL.......... Manufacturas Industriales Ltda. [*Cali*] (COL)
mil.......... Militia (RU)
Mil.......... Millimetre [*Millimeter*] [*French*] (MTD)
MIL.......... Movimiento Iberico de Liberacion [*Iberian Liberation Movement*] [*Spanish*] (WER)
MIL.......... Movimiento Independiente Liberal [*Independent Liberal Movement*] [*Colombian*] (LA)
MIL.......... Movimiento de Integracion Liberal de la Guajira [*Movement for the Liberal Integration of Guajira*] [*Colombian*] (LA)
MILCO.......... Movimiento de Integracion Liberal de la Costa [*Movement for the Liberal Integration of the Coast*] [*Colombian*] (LA)
miless.......... Milesimas [*Spanish*]
milj.......... Miljoona(a) [*Finnish*]
mill.......... Milliliter (BU)
Mill.......... Million [*Million*] [*German*] (WEN)
MILLE.......... Movimento per l'Italia Libera nella Libera Europa [*Movement for a Free Italy in a Free Europe*] (WER)

MILPAS....... Milicias Populares Antisomocistas [*Anti-Somoza People's Militia*] [*Nicaraguan*] (LA)
MILTUR....... Milliyet Turizm Anonim Sirket [*Milliyet Tourism Corporation*] [*Turkish Cypriot*] (GC)
MILUBA....... Societe Miniere du Lualaba (MAR)
MIM............ Magnezitipari Muvek [*Magnesite Industry Works*] (HU)
MIM............ Marketing Internacional de Mocambique Lda. (MAR)
MIM............ Matica na Iselenicite od Makedonija [*Society of Emigrants of Macedonia*] (YU)
MIM............ Metal-Insulator-Metal [*Thin-film circuits*] (RU)
MIM............ Metallographic Microscope (RU)
Mim............ Mimarlik [*Architecture*] (TU)
MIM............ Ministerul Industriei Metalurgice [*Ministry of the Metallurgical Industry*] (RO)
MIM............ Mouvement Independantiste Martiniquais [*Martinique Independence Movement*] (PD)
MIM............ Movimiento Institucionalista Militar [*Military Institutionalist Movement*] [*Paraguayan*] (LA)
MIMESKh.... Moscow Institute of Rural Mechanization and Electrification (RU)
MIMO.......... Moscow State Institute of International Relations (RU)
mimorprof ... Mimoradny Professor [*Associate Professor*] (CZ)
min............ First Name Unknown (BU)
MIN............ Institute of Mineralogy (of the Academy of Sciences, USSR) (RU)
m in........... Miedzy Innymi [*Among Others*] [*Polish*]
min............ Mineral (RU)
Min............ Mineral Spring [*Topography*] (RU)
min............ Mineralogia [*Mineralogy*] [*Finnish*]
min............ Minimal [*or Minimum*] [*Minimum*] [*German*]
min............ Minimum, Minimal (RU)
min............ Mining (BU)
Min............ Minister [*Minister*] (POL)
Min............ Minister [*or Ministerial*] [*German*]
min............ Minister, Ministry (RU)
min............ Ministeri [*Finnish*]
Min............ Ministerstwo [*Ministry*] (POL)
Min............ Ministre [*or Ministere*] [*Minister or Ministry*] [*French*] (MTD)
min............ Miniszter [*Minister (In the cabinet)*] [*Hungarian*] (GPO)
min............ Minut [*Minute*] [*Polish*]
min............ Minute (BU)
Min............ Minute [*Minute*] (EG)
min............ Minute (RU)
min............ Minuuttia [*Finnish*]
Min............ Moulin [*Mill*] [*Military map abbreviation*] [*World War I*] [*French*] (MTD)
MIN............ Movimiento Industrial Nacional [*National Industrial Movement*] [*Argentine*] (LA1)
MIN............ Movimiento de Integracion Nacional [*National Integration Movement*] [*Dominican Republic*] (LA1)
MIN............ Movimiento de Integracion Nacional [*National Integration Movement*] [*Venezuelan*] (PPW)
MIN............ Movimiento de Integridad Nacional [*National Integrity Movement*] [*Venezuelan*] (LA)
MIN............ Movimiento de Intransigencia Nacional [*National Intransigency Movement*] [*Argentine*] (LA)
MIN............ Movimiento de Izquierda Nacional [*National Left-Wing Movement*] [*Bolivian*] (PPW)
MINA.......... Movimento para la Independencia Nacional de Angola (MAR)
Minaferes.... Ministre des Affaires Etrangeres [*or Ministere des Affaires Etrangeres*] [*Minister of Foreign Affairs or Ministry of Foreign Affairs*] [*Cambodian*] (CL)
MINAG........ Ministerio de Agricultura [*Ministry of Agriculture*] [*Cuban*] (LA)
Minagri........ Ministere de l'Agriculture [*or Ministre de l'Agriculture*] [*Ministry of Agriculture or Minister of Agriculture*] [*Cambodian*] (CL)
MINAGRI..... Ministerio de Agricultura [*Ministry of Agriculture*] [*Cuban*] (LA1)
MinAI.......... Ministero dell'Africa Italiana (MAR)
MINAL......... Ministerio de la Industria Alimenticia [*Ministry of the Food Industry*] [*Cuban*] (LA)
MINAT......... Ministere de l'Administration Territoriale (MAR)
Minaviaprom ... Ministry of the Aircraft Industry, USSR (RU)
Minavtoprom ... Ministry of the Automobile Industry, USSR (RU)
Minavtoshosdor ... Ministry of Automobile Transportation and Highways (RU)
MINAZ......... Ministerio de la Industria Azucarera [*Ministry of the Sugar Industry*] [*Cuban*] (LA)
minb........... Mortar Battalion (BU)
minb........... Mortar Battalion (RU)
MINBAS...... Ministerio de la Industria Basica [*Ministry of Basic Industry*] [*Cuban*] (LA)
minbatr....... Mortar Battery (BU)
minbatr....... Mortar Battery (RU)
MinBl.......... Ministerialblatt [*Ministerial Gazette*] (EG)
Minbumdrevprom ... Ministry of the Paper Industry (RU)
Minbumprom ... Ministry of the Paper Industry (RU)
minc........... Minometna Ceta [*Mortar Platoon*] (CZ)
MINCE......... Ministerio do Comercio Externo [*Ministry of Foreign Trade*] [*Angolan*] (AF)
MINCEX...... Ministerio de Comercio Exterior [*Ministry of Foreign Trade*] [*Cuban*] (LA)
Minchermet ... Ministry of Ferrous Metallurgy (RU)
MINCI.......... Ministerio do Comercio Interno [*Ministry of Internal Trade*] [*Angolan*] (AF)
MINCIN....... Ministerio de Comercio Interior [*Ministry of Domestic Trade*] [*Cuban*] (LA)
MINCOM..... Ministerio de Comunicaciones [*Ministry of Communications*] [*Cuban*] (LA)
Mincultes.... Ministere des Cultes [*or Ministre des Cultes*] [*Ministry of Religious Affairs or Minister of Religious Affairs*] [*Cambodian*] (CL)
MIND.......... Ministerio de Industria [*Ministry of Industry*] [*Nicaraguan*] (LA1)
mind........... Mortar Battalion (BU)
MINDECO ... Mining Development Corporation [*Zambian*] (AF)
MINDEF....... Ministry of Defense [*Singapore*] (ML)
Mindeveloppement ... Ministere de Developpement [*or Ministre de Developpement*] [*Ministry of Development or Minister of Development*] [*Cambodian*] (CL)
MINDIN....... Ministerio del Desarrollo Industrial [*Ministry of Industrial Development*] [*Cuban*] (LA)
mindn.......... Mortar Battalion (BU)
mindn.......... Mortar Battalion (RU)
mindr.......... Minometne Druzstvo [*Mortar Squad*] (CZ)
MINED......... Ministerio de Educacion [*Ministry of Education*] [*Cuban*] (LA)
Mineducanale ... Ministere de l'Education Nationale [*or Ministre de l'Education Nationale*] [*Ministry of National Education or Minister of National Education*] [*Cambodian*] (CL)
MINEL......... Ministarstvo Elektroprivrede [*Ministry of Electric Industries*] (YU)
MINEP......... Ministere de l'Economie et du Plan (MAR)
miner.......... Mineral (RU)
miner.......... Mineralogy, Mineralogical (BU)
MINERALIMPEX ... MINERALIMPEX Olaj- es Banyatermek Kulkereskedelmi Vallalat [*MINERALIMPEX Foreign Trade Enterprise for Oil and Mine Products*] (HU)
MINEROPERU ... Peruvian State Mining Enterprise (LA)
MINESEB.... Ministere de l'Enseignement Secondaire et de l'Education de Base (MAR)
MINFAR....... Ministerio de las Fuerzas Armadas Revolucionarias [*Ministry of the Revolutionary Armed Forces*] [*Cuban*] (LA)
Minfin.......... Ministry of Finance (RU)
Minfinances ... Ministre des Finances [*or Ministere des Finances*] [*Minister of Finance or Ministry of Finance*] [*Cambodian*] (CL)
MINFOC...... Ministere de l'Information et de la Culture (MAR)
MING.......... Movimento de Independencia Nacional da Guine Portuguesa (MAR)
Mingechaursel'mash ... Mingechaur Agricultural Machinery Plant (RU)
Mingorsel'stroy ... Ministry of Urban and Rural Construction (RU)
Mingoskontrol' ... Ministry of State Control (RU)
MINIE.......... Ministerio de la Industria Electrica [*Ministry of the Electric Power Industry*] [*Cuban*] (LA)
MINIL.......... Ministerio de la Industria Ligera [*Ministry of Light Industry*] [*Cuban*] (LA)
minim.......... Minimum, Minimal (RU)
Minindel...... Ministry of Foreign Affairs (RU)
MININT........ Ministerio del Interior [*Ministry of the Interior*] [*Cuban*] (LA)
MININT........ Ministerio del Interior [*Ministry of the Interior*] [*Nicaraguan*] (LA1)
Min ist......... Mineral Spring [*Topography*] (RU)
minist.......... Ministry (BU)
Minist suv ... Council of Ministers (BU)
MINITRFOP ... Ministere de l'Interieur et de la Fonction Publique (MAR)
MINJUS....... Ministerio de Justicia [*Ministry of Justice*] [*Cuban*] (LA)
Minjustice... Ministre de la Justice [*or Ministere de la Justice*] [*Minister of Justice or Ministry of Justice*] [*Cambodian*] (CL)
MINKh......... Moscow Institute of the National Economy Imeni G. V. Plekhanov (RU)
MINKhiGP... Moscow Institute of the Petrochemical and Gas Industry Imeni Academician I. M. Gubkin (RU)
Minkhimprom ... Ministry of the Chemical Industry, USSR (RU)
MINKhU...... Moscow Institute for the Statistical Survey of the National Economy (RU)
Minkomkhoz ... Ministry of the Municipal Economy (RU)
Minkomkhozizdat ... Publishing House of the Ministry of the Municipal Economy (RU)
Minlegprom ... Ministry of Light Industry (RU)
Minlesbumprom ... Ministry of the Lumber and Paper Industries (RU)
Minlesprom ... Ministry of the Lumber Industry (RU)
Minmash..... Ministry of Machinery Manufacture, USSR (RU)
Minmestprom ... Ministry of Local Industry (RU)
Minmetallurgkhimstroy ... Ministry of Construction of Establishments of the Metallurgical and Chemical Industries (RU)
Minmetallurgprom ... Ministry of the Metallurgical Industry, USSR (RU)
MINMG........ Ministerio de Mineria y Geologia [*Ministry of Mines and Geology*] [*Cuban*] (LA)
MINMINAS ... Ministro/Ministerio de Minas y Energia [*Minister/Ministry of Mines and Energy*] [*Colombian*] (LA)
Minmobigale ... Ministere de la Mobilisation Generale [*or Ministre de la Mobilisation Generale*] [*Ministry of General Mobilization or Minister of General Mobilization*] [*Cambodian*] (CL)
Minmorflot ... Ministry of the Maritime Fleet, USSR (RU)

Minmyasomolprom ... Ministry of the Meat and Dairy Industry (RU)
Minnefteprom ... Ministry of the Petroleum Industry (RU)
mino .... Ministro [*Minister*] [*Spanish*]
Minoboronprom ... Ministry of the Defense Industry, USSR (RU)
MINOKA .... Minoteries de Kakontwe (MAR)
MINORDIA ... Societe Africaine des Mines Or-Diamant (MAR)
MINOTLRS ... Ministrstvo Notranjih Poslov Ljudske Republike Slovenije [*Ministry of the Interior, People's Republic of Slovenia*] (YU)
minotryad ... Mine Detachment (RU)
minp .... Mortar Regiment (BU)
minp .... Mortar Regiment (RU)
MINPECO .... MINEROPERU Comercial [*Peruvian State Mineral Marketing Company*] (LA)
MINPES .... Ministerio de la Industria Pesquera [*Ministry of the Fishing Industry*] [*Cuban*] (LA)
Min PiT .... Ministerstwo Poczt i Telegrafow [*Ministry of Posts and Telegraphs*] (POL)
Minpred ...... Ministersky Predseda [*Prime Minister*] (CZ)
MINPROEKT ... Mine Designing Institute (BU)
Minpromprodtovarov ... Ministry of the Foodstuffs Industry (RU)
Minpros .... Ministry of Education (RU)
Min r .... Mine Company (BU)
minr .... Minometna Rota [*Mortar Company*] (CZ)
minr .... Mortar Company (BU)
minr .... Mortar Company (RU)
Minrechflot ... Ministry of the River Fleet (RU)
Minrefugies ... Ministre des Refugies [*or Ministere des Refugies*] [*Minister of Refugees or Ministry of Refugees*] [*Cambodian*] (CL)
MINREX .... Ministerio de Relaciones Exteriores [*Ministry of Foreign Relations*] [*Cuban*] (LA)
MinribNRH ... Ministarstvo Ribolova Narodna Republika Hrvatska [*Croatian Ministry of Fisheries*] (YU)
Minrybprom ... Ministry of the Fish Industry (RU)
MINSA .... Ministerio de Salud [*Ministry of Health*] [*Nicaraguan*] (LA1)
Minsante ..... Ministre de Sante [*or Ministere de Sante*] [*Minister of Health or Ministry of Health*] [*Cambodian*] (CL)
MINSAP ...... Ministerio de Salud Publica [*Ministry of Public Health*] [*Cuban*] (LA)
Minsecurinale ... Ministre de la Securite Nationale [*or Ministere de la Securite Nationale*] [*Minister of National Security or Ministry of National Security*] [*Cambodian*] (CL)
Minsel'khoz ... Ministry of Agriculture (RU)
MINSIME ..... Ministerio de la Industria Sidero-Mecanica [*Ministry of Steelworking Industry*] [*Cuban*] (LA)
Minsotsob ... Ministry of Social Security (RU)
Minsovkhoz ... Ministry of Sovkhozes (RU)
Minsredmash ... Ministry of Medium Machinery Manufacture, USSR (RU)
Minstroy ...... Mining Construction Administration (BU)
Minstroy ...... Ministry of Construction (RU)
Minstroydormash ... Ministry of Construction and Road Machinery Manufacture, USSR (RU)
Minsudprom ... Ministry of the Shipbuilding Industry, USSR (RU)
Minsvyazi .... Ministry of Communications (RU)
MINSZ .... Magyar Ifjusagi Nepi Szovetseg Uttoro Mozgalom [*Hungarian People's Youth Federation, Pioneer Movement*] (HU)
Mintekstil'prom ... Ministry of the Textile Industry (RU)
Mintorg .... Ministry of Trade (RU)
MINTRAB .... Ministerio del Trabajo [*Ministry of Labor*] [*Cuban*] (LA)
MINTRANS ... Ministerio del Transporte [*Ministry of Transportation*] [*Cuban*] (LA)
Mintransmash ... Ministry of Transportation Machinery Manufacture, USSR (RU)
Mintransstroy ... Ministry of Transportation Construction, USSR (RU)
Mintravo ..... Ministere des Travaux Publics [*or Ministre des Travaux Publics*] [*Ministry of Public Works or Minister of Public Works*] [*Cambodian*] (CL)
Mintsvetmet ... Ministry of Nonferrous Metallurgy (RU)
Mintsvetmetzoloto ... Moscow Institute of Nonferrous Metals and Gold Imeni M. I. Kalinin (RU)
Mintyazhmash ... Ministry of Heavy Machinery Manufacture, USSR (RU)
Mintyazhstroy ... Ministry of Construction of Heavy Industry Establishments, USSR (RU)
MINU .... Administrasi Umum [*General Administration*] (IN)
Minugleprom ... Ministry of the Coal Industry (RU)
Minuglestroy ... Ministry of Construction of Coal Industry Establishments (RU)
Minusinnefterazvedka ... Minusinsk Trust of Petroleum Exploration (RU)
minv .... Mortar Platoon (RU)
MINVAH ...... Ministerio de la Vivienda y Asentamientos Humanos [*Ministry of Housing and Human Settlements*] [*Nicaraguan*] (LA1)
Minville .... Ministere Charge de la Ville de Phnom Penh [*or Ministre Charge de la Ville de Phnom Penh*] [*Ministry for the City of Phnom Penh or Minister for the City of Phnom Penh*] [*Cambodian*] (CL)
Minvneshtorg ... Ministry of Foreign Trade, USSR (RU)
min-vo .... Ministry (RU)
Minvostokugol' ... Ministry of the Coal Industry of the Eastern Regions, USSR (RU)
min vr .... Past Tense (BU)
MINVU .... Ministerio de Vivienda y Urbanismo [*Ministry of Housing and Urban Affairs*] [*Chilean*] (LA)
minzag .... Minelayer (RU)
Minzag .... Ministry of Procurement (RU)
Minzapadugol' ... Ministry of the Coal Industry of the Western Regions, USSR (RU)
Minzdrav ..... Ministry of Public Health (RU)
MIO .... Ministerstvo Informaci a Osvety [*Ministry of Information and Culture*] (CZ)
MIO .... Montaz Instalacji Okretowej [*Assembly of Ship Equipment*] (POL)
MIOG .... Mitteilungen des Instituts fuer Oesterreichische Geschichtsforschung [*German*]
MIOI .... Magyar Izraelitak Orszagos Irodaja [*National Office of Hungarian Jews*] (HU)
MIOK .... Magyar Izraelitak Orszagos Kepviselete [*National Representation of the Hungarian Jews*] (HU)
MIOT .... Magyar Ifjusag Orszagos Tanacsa [*National Council of Hungarian Youth*] (HU)
MIOT .... Moscow Institute of Work Safety (RU)
MIP .... Between Foreign Ports (RU)
MIP .... Milicias de Izquierda Proletaria [*Militias of the Proletarian Left*] [*Spanish*] (WER)
MIP .... Ministarstvo Inostranih Poslova [*Ministry of Foreign Affairs*] (YU)
MIP .... Mouvement Independent Populaire [*Popular Independent Movement*] [*Luxembourg*] (PPE)
MIP .... Mouvement Islamique Progressiste [*Islamic Progressive Movement*] [*Tunisian*] (PD)
MIP .... Movimento Italiano della Pace [*Italian Peace Movement*] (WER)
MIPA .... Manufacture Ivoirienne des Plastiques Africains (MAR)
MIPC .... Manufacture Ivoirienne des Platres Chimiques (MAR)
MIPD .... Monoisopropyldiphenyl (RU)
MIPDI .... Moscow Institute of Applied and Decorative Art (RU)
MIPI .... Madjelis Ilmu Pengetahuan Indonesia [*Council for Sciences of Indonesia*]
MIPLAN .... Ministerio de Planificacion [*Ministry of Planning*] [*Argentine*] (LA)
MIPLAN .... Ministerio de Planificacion [*Ministry of Planning*] [*Nicaraguan*] (LA1)
MIPMR .... Muzeul Historic al Partidului Muncitoresc Roman [*Historical Museum of the Romanian Workers Party*] (RO)
MIPRA .... Mouvement Independant PRA [*Independent PRA Movement*] [*Upper Voltan*] (AF)
MIPTES .... Movimiento Independiente de Profesionales Salvadorenos [*Independent Movement of Salvadoran Professionals*] (LA1)
MIQ .... Ministerio de la Industria Quimica [*Ministry of the Chemical Industry*] [*Cuban*] (LA)
MIR .... Long-Distance Outgoing Register [*Telephony*] (RU)
MIR .... Malaysian Infantry Regiment (ML)
MIR .... Medicos Internos y Residentes [*Interns and Resident Doctors*] [*Spanish*] (WER)
MIR .... Monthly Intelligence Report (MAR)
MIR .... Morski Instytut Rybacki [*Maritime Fisheries Institute*] (POL)
MIR .... Mouvement pour l'Independance de la Reunion [*Movement for the Independence of Reunion*] (PD)
MIR .... Movimiento Independiente Revolucionario [*Independent Revolutionary Movement*] [*Ecuadorean*] (LA)
MIR .... Movimiento de Izquierda Revolucionaria [*Movement of the Revolutionary Left*] [*Bolivian*] (PPW)
MIR .... Movimiento de Izquierda Revolucionaria [*Movement of the Revolutionary Left*] [*Chilean*] (LA)
MIR .... Movimiento de Izquierda Revolucionaria [*Movement of the Revolutionary Left*] [*Peruvian*] (LA)
MIR .... Movimiento de Izquierda Revolucionaria [*Movement of the Revolutionary Left*] [*Venezuelan*] (LA)
MIR .... Museum of the History of Religion (RU)
MIR .... Muszer- es Irodagep Ertekesito Vallalat [*Trade Enterprise for Office Equipment*] (HU)
MIR .... Revolutionary Leftist Movement [*Spanish*] (WER)
MIRA .... Movimiento Independentista Armado [*Armed Pro-Independence Movement*] [*Puerto Rican*] (PD)
MIRA .... Movimiento de Izquierda Revolucionaria Argentina [*Argentine Movement of the Revolutionary Left*] (LA)
MIRA .... Museum of the History of Religion and Atheism (RU)
MIRAF .... Miroiteries Africaines a Pointe-Noire (MAR)
MIRCB .... Memoires de l'Institut Royal du Congo Belge [*Brussels*] [*A publication*] (MAR)
MIREK .... World Power Conference [*WPC*] (RU)
MIRGEM ...... Moscow Institute of Radio Electronics and Mining Electromechanics (RU)
MIRH .... Movimiento Independiente de Humanidades [*Independent Movement of Humanities*] [*Panamanian*] (LA)
MIRKOZ ...... Muszaki Irodai es Kozszuksegleti Cikkeket Gyarto es Javito Kisipari Szovetkezet [*Cooperative Enterprise for Manufacture and Repair of Office Equipment*] (HU)
MIR-ML .... Movimiento de Izquierda Revolucionaria - Marxista-Leninista [*Movement of the Revolutionary Left - Marxist-Leninist*] [*Peruvian*] (LA)

MIRN .... Movimento Independente da Reconstrucao Nacional [*Independent Movement of National Reconstruction*] [*Portuguese*] (PPE)
Mirongres ... Mironovskiy State Regional Electric Power Plant (RU)
Mir Vr .... Universal Time, Greenwich Time (RU)
MIS .... International Institute of Welding [*IIW*] (RU)
MIS .... Machine-Testing Station (RU)
MIS .... Manufacture d'Isolants Synthetiques (MAR)
MIS .... Matica Iseljenika Srbije [*Society of Emigrants of Serbia*] (YU)
MIS .... Moscow Institute of Steel (RU)
MIS .... Repeated-Use Circuit (RU)
MIS .... (Rotational) Speed Change Mechanism (RU)
MISC .... Malaysian International Shipping Corporation (ML)
mise .... Marchandise [*Merchandise*] [*French*]
MISh .... Pitch-Control Mechanism (RU)
MISI .... Moscow Construction Engineering Institute Imeni V. V. Kuybyshev (RU)
MISK .... Milliyetci Isci Sendikalar Konfederasyonu [*Confederation of Nationalist Labor Unions*] [*NAP-associated labor confederation*] (TU)
MISKT .... Moscow Institute of Soviet Cooperative Trade (RU)
MISO .... Mzumbe Institute Students Organisation (MAR)
MISR .... Malawi Institute of Social Research (MAR)
Misrair .... Egyptian Aviation Company (ME)
MISTASI ...... Ministerium fuer Staatssicherheit [*Ministry for State Security*] [*See also MfS, MSS*] (EG)
MISTRAL .... Memorisation d'Informations, Selection, Traitement, et Recherche Automatique [*CII*] [*French*]
MISURA ...... Miskito, Sumo, and Rama [*Nicaraguan Indian coalition*]
MISURASATA ... Miskito, Sumo, and Rama [*Nicaraguan Indian coalition*]
MISZ .... Magyar Ipari Szabvany [*Hungarian Industrial Standards*] (HU)
MISZ .... Magyar Irok Szovetsege [*Hungarian Writers' Association*] (HU)
MISZB .... Magyar Ipari Szabvanyosito Bizottsag [*Hungarian Committee of Industrial Standardization*] (HU)
MIT .... Milli Istihbarat Teskilati [*National Intelligence Organization*] (TU)
MIT .... Ministerio de Industria y Turismo [*Ministry of Industry and Tourism*] [*Peruvian*] (LA)
Mit .... Mitoloji [*Mythology*] (TU)
MIT .... Morski Instytut Techniczny [*Maritime Engineering Institute*] (POL)
MIT .... Mythological, Mythology (BU)
MITAS .... Maden Insaat Turk Anonim Sirketi [*Turkish Metal Construction Corporation*] (TU)
MITAS .... Modern Iplik Ticaret Anonim Sirketi [*Modern Thread Trade Corporation*] [*Urfa*] (TU)
MITE .... Mezogazdasagi Ipari Tudomanyos Egyesulet [*Scientific Association for Industries Related to Agriculture*] (HU)
MITEBI .... Manufacture Ivoirienne de Materiaux pour le Batiment et l'Industrie (MAR)
MITEP .... Moscow Institute of Standard and Experimental Planning (RU)
MITEX .... Societe Mitidja-Textiles (MAR)
MITF .... Milletlerarasi Islam Teskilatlari Federasyonu [*Federation of International Islamic Organizations*] (TU)
mitget .... Mitgeteilt [*Contributed*] [*German*]
Mitgl d BR ... Mitglied des Bundesrates [*German*]
MITI .... Ministerio de Industria, Turismo, e Integracion [*Peruvian*]
MITI .... Ministry of International Trade and Industry [*Japanese*] (SJT)
MITKA .... Movimiento Indio Tupaj Katari [*Tupaj Katari Indian Movement*] [*Bolivian*] (PPW)
MITKhT .... Moscow Institute of Fine Chemical Technology Imeni M. V. Lomonosov (RU)
MITOS .... Khar'kov Plant for Mechanical and Heat Treatment of Glass (RU)
MITRANS .... Ministerio de Transporte [*Ministry of Transportation*] [*Cuban*] (LA)
MITRANS .... Ministerio de Transporte [*Ministry of Transportation*] [*Nicaraguan*] (LA1)
Mitropa .... Mitteleuropaeische Schlaf- und Speisewagen-Aktiengesellschaft [*Central European Dining- and Sleeping-Car Corporation*] (EG)
MITsKE .... International Center of Research and Information on Collective Economy [*ICRICE*] (RU)
MITsMiZ ...... Moscow Institute of Nonferrous Metals and Gold Imeni M. I. Kalinin (RU)
MITsMZ ...... Moscow Institute of Nonferrous Metals and Gold Imeni M. I. Kalinin (RU)
MITT .... Materials on the History of Turkmenia and the Turkmenians (RU)
Mitt .... Mitteilung [*Report*] [*German*]
mitt .... Mittels [*By Means Of*] [*German*]
Mittlg .... Mitteilung [*Report*] [*German*]
MIU .... Ministerul Industriei Usoare [*Ministry of Light Industry*] (RO)
MIU .... Movimiento Izquierdista Universitario [*University Leftist Movement*] [*Ecuadorean*] (LA)
MIUK .... Monoiodoacetic Acid (RU)
MIULP .... Movimiento Indispensable Unido para Liberar al Pueblo [*United Vital Movement for the Liberation of the People*] [*Venezuelan*] (LA)
MIVI .... Manufacture Ivoirienne de Vitrages Isolants (MAR)
MIVOTI .... Moscow Institute of Instrument Making of the All-Union Precision Industry Association (RU)
MIZ .... Local Industry and Trades (BU)
MIZ .... Moscow Institute of Land Use Measures (RU)
MIZ .... Moscow Measuring Instruments Plant (RU)
MIZ .... Moscow Tool Plant (RU)
MIZ .... Workshop for Individual Orders (RU)
MIZh .... Moscow Institute of Journalism (RU)
MJ .... Makedonski Jazik [*Macedonian Language*] [*A periodical*] [*Skopje*] (YU)
mj .... Mezinarodni Jednotka [*International Unit (Pharmaceutical measure)*] (CZ)
MJ .... Ministerul Justitiei [*Ministry of Justice*] (RO)
MJ .... Mistni Jednota [*Local Unit*] (CZ)
mj .... Mjesec [*Month, Moon*] (YU)
mj .... Mjesto [*Place*] (YU)
MJC .... Mouvement de la Jeunesse Communiste [*Communist Youth Movement*] [*French*] (WER)
MJC .... Movimento da Juventude Comunista [*Communist Youth Movement*] [*Portuguese*] (WER)
MJC .... Movimiento Juvenil Cristiano [*Christian Youth Movement*] [*Costa Rican*] (LA)
MJL .... Mouvement de la Jeunesse Luxembourgeoise [*Luxembourg Youth Movement*] (WER)
MJOA .... Mouvement de la Jeunesse Ouvriere Angolaise [*Angolan Working Youth Movement*] (AF)
MJP .... Mouvement de la Jeunesse Panafricaine [*Panafrican Youth Movement*] (MAR)
MJP .... Movimiento de la Juventud Panamena [*Panamanian Youth Movement*] (LA)
MjPD .... Mjesecnik Pravnickog Drustva [*Lawyers' Society Monthly*] (YU)
Mjr .... Major [*German*]
mjr .... Major [*Major*] (CZ)
mjr .... Major [*Major*] [*Military rank*] (POL)
MJS .... Movimiento Juventud Sandinista [*Sandinist Youth Movement*] [*Nicaraguan*] (LA)
MJSz .... Magyar Jogasz Szovetseg [*Association of Hungarian Jurists*] (HU)
MJT .... Mouvement de la Jeunesse Tchadienne (MAR)
MJUPG .... Movimento da Juventude da Uniao Popular da Guine (MAR)
MJUPS .... Mouvement des Jeunes de l'Union Progressiste Senegalaise [*Youth Movement of the Senegalese Progressive Union*] (AF)
MK .... Bridge Logging Method (RU)
MK .... Camouflage Paint (RU)
MK- .... Erection Crane (RU)
MK .... Intergranular Corrosion (RU)
MK .... International Book [*All-Union Association for the International Book Trade*] (RU)
m/k .... Junior Commander (RU)
Mk .... Lighthouse, Beacon (RU)
MK .... Local Committee (RU)
MK .... Long-Distance Switchboard, Toll Switchboard (RU)
MK .... Magnetic Correction (RU)
MK .... Magnetic Course, Magnetic Heading (RU)
MK .... Magnetski Kurs [*Magnetic Course*] [*Aviation*] (YU)
MK .... Magveto Kiado [*Magveto Publishing House*] (HU)
MK .... Magyar Kozlony [*Hungarian Gazette*] (HU)
MK .... Magyar Koztarsasag [*Hungarian Republic*] (HU)
MK .... Magyar Kupa [*Hungarian Cup*] (HU)
MK .... Makedonski Komitet [*Macedonian Committee*] (YU)
MK .... Malawi Kwacha (MAR)
MK .... Marinekabel [*Marine Cable*] (EG)
Mk .... Mark [*Mark*] [*German*]
MK .... Markka [*Finnish currency*] (GPO)
MK .... Maschinen- und Kapazitaetserfassung [*Census of Machinery and Capacity*] (EG)
MK .... Meat Kombinat (RU)
MK .... Mechanized Corps (RU)
MK .... Medeni Kanun [*Civil Law*] (TU)
MK .... Mediteranska Komisija [*Mediterranean Commission*] (YU)
mk .... Megakykloi [*Megacycles*] (GC)
MK .... Member of Knesset (ME)
MK .... Mesni Komitet [*Local Committee*] (YU)
MK .... Mestska Knihovna [*Municipal Library*] (CZ)
MK .... Metallurgical Combine (BU)
MK .... Metarrithmistikon Komma [*Reformist Party*] [*Greek*] (PPE)
MK .... Methyl Red (Indicator) (RU)
mk .... Micron (RU)
MK .... Microphone Inset, Transmitter Inset [*Telephony*] (RU)
mk .... Mikroskopisch [*Microscopic*] [*German*]
mk .... Millicoulomb (RU)
MK .... Ministerstvo Kultury [*Ministry of Culture*] (CZ)
MK .... Ministerstwo Kolei [*Ministry of Railroads*] (POL)
MK .... Ministerstwo Komunikacji [*Ministry of Transportation*] (POL)
MK .... Ministry of Culture [*Obsolete*] (BU)
MK .... Ministry of Culture (RU)
MK .... Mitotic Index (RU)
M-K .... Monte Carlo Method (RU)
MK .... Moscow Committee (RU)
MK .... Motor Ship (BU)

MK............. Motorboat (RU)
Mk............. Muldenkipper [*Rail-Dump Car*] (EG)
MK-............. Multiple-Cut Trench Excavator (RU)
MK............. Pendulum Hammer, Impact Tester (RU)
mk............. Seaman [*or Sailor*] (BU)
m/k............. Small Caliber (BU)
mk............. Small-Caliber, Small-Bore (RU)
Mk............. Torque (RU)
MK............. Verband der Marianischen Studentenkongregationen Oesterreichs [*Federation of Sodalities of Our Lady for Students*] [*Austrian*] (WEN)
MK............. Youth Committee (BU)
MKA............. International Cooperative Alliance [*ICA*] (RU)
m-ka............. Marka [*Mark*] [*Polish*]
mka............. Microampere (BU)
mka............. Microampere (RU)
MKAD............. Moscow Belt Highway (RU)
Mkal............. Megacalorie (RU)
MKAP............. International Confederation of Arab Trade Unions [*ICATU*] (RU)
MKB............. International Cooperative Bank [*ICB*] (RU)
mkb............. Microbar (RU)
mkbar............. Microbar (RU)
mkber............. Microrem (RU)
MKBK............. Moscow Motion-Picture Equipment Design Office (RU)
MKBR............. Intercontinental Ballistic Missile (RU)
MKBS............. Intercontinental Ballistic Missile (RU)
MKCh............. International Tea Committee (RU)
MKChM............. Ferrous Metals Metallurgical Combine (BU)
MKCK............. Medunarodni Komitet Crvenog Krsta [*International Red Cross Committee*] (YU)
MKCK............. Miedzynarodowy Komitet Czerwonego Krzyza [*International Red Cross Committee*] [*Polish*]
MKD............. Magnetic Annular Arc (RU)
MKD............. Motorized Cavalry Division (RU)
MKDNRM............. Muzejsko-Konservatorsko Drustvo na Narodnata Republika Makedonija [*Museum and Preservation Society of Macedonia*] (YU)
MKDON............. Moscow-Kursk-Donbass Railroad (RU)
MKE............. A Magyar Koztarsasag Elnoke [*President of the Hungarian Republic*] (HU)
MKE............. Magyar Kemikusok Egyesulete [*Association of Hungarian Chemists*] (HU)
MKE............. Makina ve Kimya Endustri [*Machine and Chemical Industry*] [*See also MKEK*] (TU)
MKE............. Miejskie Koleje Elektryczne [*Municipal Electrical Railroads*] (POL)
MKE............. Militaerische Koerperertuechtigung [*Military Physical Training*] (EG)
MKEA............. International Conference of Agricultural Economists [*ICAE*] (RU)
MKEK............. Makina ve Kimya Endustri Kurumu [*The Machine and Chemical Industry Establishment*] [*See also MKE*] (TU)
MKF............. Magnetischer Kugelfernschalter [*Magnetic Ball Teleswitch*] (EG)
mkf............. Microfarad (BU)
mkf............. Microfarad (RU)
MKF............. Monocalcium Phosphate (RU)
MK FJN............. Miejski Komitet Frontu Jednosci Narodu [*National Unity Front City Committee*] (POL)
MKFN............. Miejski Komitet Frontu Narodowego [*Municipal Committee of the People's Front*] (POL)
MKG-............. Crawler Erection Crane (RU)
mkg............. Microgram (RU)
MKGM............. Milli Kutuphane Genel Mudurlugu [*National Library Directorate General*] (TU)
mkgn............. Microhenry (RU)
MKGR............. Musjawarah Kekeluargaan Gotong Rojong [*Consultative Council of Cooperative Groups*] (IN)
MKGSS............. Meter-Kilogram Force-Second [*System of units*] (RU)
MKGYa............. International Commission on Large Dams (BU)
MKH............. Magyar Kozponti Hirado [*Hungarian Central News Agency*] (HU)
MKh............. Meta Khristou [*In the Year of Our Lord*] (GC)
MKh............. Ministry of Grain Products, USSR (RU)
MKhAT............. Moscow Academic Art Theater of the USSR Imeni M. Gor'kiy (RU)
mkhg............. Mobile Surgical Group [*Navy*] (RU)
MKhI............. Moscow Art Institute Imeni V. I. Surikov (RU)
MKhIMP............. World Economy and World Politics (RU)
MKhORM............. International Young Christian Workers [*YCW*] (RU)
MKhP............. Mechanized Storage and Search (RU)
MKhP............. Ministry of Chemical Industry (BU)
MKhP............. Ministry of the Chemical Industry, USSR (RU)
MKhP............. Polarizing Microscope for Cotton (RU)
m/khs............. Camouflaged Communication Trench [*Topography*] (RU)
MKHS............. Medunarodna Konferencija Hriscanskih Sindikata [*International Federation of Christian Trade Unions (IFCTU)*] (YU)
MKhT............. Moscow Art Theater [*1898-1920*] (RU)
MKhT............. Moscow State Organization for the Baked Goods and Confectionery Retail Trade (RU)
MKhTI............. Moscow Institute of Chemical Technology Imeni D. I. Mendeleyev (RU)
MKhTIMP............. Moscow Institute of Chemical Technology of the Meat Industry (RU)
MKhTT............. Moscow Technicum of Chemical Technology (RU)
MKI............. Ministerstvo Kultury a Informaci [*Ministry of Culture and Information*] (CZ)
Mki............. Misaki [*Cape*] [*Japanese*] (NAU)
MKI............. Small Control Testing (RU)
MKINKK............. International Commission for the Study of Folk Culture in the Carpathians (RU)
MKIOlimp............. Miedzynarodowy Komitet Igrzysk Olimpijskich [*International Committee on the Olympic Games*] (POL)
MKiS............. Ministerstwo Kultury i Sztuki [*Ministry of Culture and Art*] (POL)
MKISZ............. Magyar Kommunista Ifjusagi Szovetseg [*Hungarian Communist Youth Association*] (HU)
M-Kiyev............. Moscow-Kiev Railroad (RU)
MKK............. International Advisory Committee on Bibliography, Documentation, and Terminology (RU)
MKK............. International Red Cross [*IRC*] (RU)
MKK............. International Whaling Commission (RU)
MKK............. Magyar Kepzomuveszeti Kiallitas [*Hungarian Fine Arts Exhibit*] (HU)
MKK............. Magyar Kereskedelmi Kamara [*Hungarian Chamber of Commerce*] (HU)
MKK............. Marine-Kunststoffkabel [*Plastic Marine Cable*] (EG)
mkk............. Microcoulomb (RU)
MKK............. Muszaki Konyvkiado [*Publishing House for Technical Books*] (HU)
MKK............. Muveszet Kis Konyvtara [*Small Library of Arts*] [*Name of publication series*] (HU)
MKKE............. Marx Karoly Kozgazdasagtudomanyi Egyetem [*Karl Marx University of Economic Sciences*] (HU)
MKKF............. International Telephone Consultative Committee (RU)
MKKF............. Miejski Komitet Kultury Fizycznej [*Municipal Committee on Physical Culture*] (POL)
MKKFiT............. Miejski Komitet Kultury Fizycznej i Turystyki [*City Committee for Physical Culture and Tourism*] (POL)
MKKH............. Magyar Kulkereskedelmi Hivatal [*Hungarian Foreign Trade Office*] (HU)
MKKh............. Ministry of the Municipal Economy (RU)
MKKh............. Moscow Department of Municipal Services (RU)
MKKhP............. International Federation of Christian Trade Unions [*IFCTU*] (RU)
MKKhU............. Ministry of the Municipal Economy, Ukrainian SSR (RU)
MKKI............. Magyar Kulkereskedelmi Igazgatosag [*Hungarian Foreign Trade Directorate*] (HU)
MKKK............. International Committee of the Red Cross [*ICRC*] (RU)
MKKL............. Merestechnikai Kozponti Kutato Laboratorium [*Central Research Laboratory for Measuring Technology*] (HU)
MKKM............. Mezinarodni Koaxialni Kabelova Magistrala [*International Coaxial Cable Line*] (CZ)
MKKP............. Miejska Komisja Kontroli Partyjnej [*City Party Control Commission*] (POL)
MKKPSS............. Moscow Committee of the KPSS (RU)
MKKR............. International Radio Consultative Committee (RU)
MKKT............. International Telegraph Consultative Committee (RU)
MKKT............. Muszaki Kutatasokat Koordinalo Tanacs [*Council for Coordinating Technical Research*] (HU)
MKKTT............. International Telegraph and Telephone Consultative Committee (RU)
mkkyuri............. Microcurie (RU)
mkl............. Microliter (RU)
MKL............. Miejska Komisja Lokalowa [*Municipal Housing Commission*] (POL)
MKL............. Muzeum Kultur Ludowych [*Folk Culture Museum*] (POL)
MKLK............. Mistni Komise Lidove Kontroly [*Local Commission of People's Control*] (CZ)
MKLMS............. Mladinski Komite Ljudske Mladine Slovenije [*Youth Committee of the People's Youth of Slovenia*] (YU)
MKM............. Magyar Kabel Muvek [*Hungarian Cable Works*] (HU)
mkm............. Micron (RU)
MKMH............. Mala Knjiznica "Matice Hrvatske" [*The "Mala Knjiznica" Publication Series, issued by the Matica Hrvatska Publishing House*] [*Zagreb*] (YU)
mkmk............. Micromicron (RU)
mkmkf............. Micromicrofarad (RU)
mkmkg............. Micromicrogram (RU)
mkmkv............. Micromicrovolt (RU)
mkmkvt............. Micromicrowatt (RU)
MKMMRT............. Magyar Kozlony, Minisztertanacsi es Miniszteri Rendeletek Tara [*Hungarian Gazette, Collection of Cabinet and Departmental Decrees*] (HU)
mkmol'............. Micromole (RU)
MKMR............. International Radio-Maritime Committee (RU)
MKMV............. International Committee on Weights and Measures (RU)
mkn............. Micron (RU)
MKN............. Minimal Controlled Level (BU)
MKN............. Muzeum Kultur Narodowych [*Polish*]
MKO............. Engine and Boiler Room (RU)

MKO........... International Commission on Illumination (BU)
MKO........... International Commission on Illumination [*CIE*] (RU)
m-ko........... Small Town (RU)
MKOI.......... Miedzynarodowy Komitet Olimpijski [*International Olympic Games Committee*] [*Polish*]
MKOM......... Intergovernmental Maritime Consultative Organization [*IMCO*] (RU)
mkom.......... Microhm (RU)
MKOS.......... Manych-Kuma Irrigation System (RU)
MKOSZ....... Magyar Kozalkalmazottak Orszagos Szovetsege [*National Federation of Hungarian Civil Servants*] (HU)
MKOW......... Miejski Komitet Odbudowy Warszawy [*Municipal Committee on the Reconstruction of Warsaw*] (POL)
M Kozlony... Magyar Kozlony Kiado [*"Magyar Kozlony" Publishing House*] (HU)
MKP........... International Propaganda Committee (RU)
MKP........... Magyar Kommunista Part [*Hungarian Communist Party*] (PPE)
MKP........... Maritime Coastal Navigation (BU)
MKP........... Marokanskaia Kommunisticheskaia Partiia [*Moroccan Communist Party*] (MAR)
MKP........... Masove-Kulturni Prace [*Mass Cultural Work*] (CZ)
MKP........... Mechanical Forging Press (RU)
MKP........... Medunarodna Konvencija o Prevozu Putnika [*International Convention Concerning the Carriage of Passengers and Luggage by Rail (CIV)*] (YU)
MKP........... Ministerstwo Kontroli Panstwowej [*Ministry of State Control*] (POL)
MKP........... Motorkerekpar [*Motorcycle*] (HU)
MKP........... Multiconfigurational Approximation (RU)
MKP-.......... Pneumatic Riveting Hammer (RU)
MKP-.......... Pneumatic-Tired Erection Crane (RU)
MK Pasa...... Mustafa Kemal Pasha [*Ataturk*] (TU)
mkpd........... Mechanical Efficiency (RU)
MKPG.......... Miejska Komisja Planowania Gospodarczego [*Municipal Commission on Economic Planning*] (POL)
MKPiK......... Miedzynarodowy Klub Prasy i Ksiazki [*International Press and Book Club*] (POL)
MKR........... International Rice Commission [*IRC*] (RU)
MKR........... Medunarodna Konvencija o Prevozu Robe na Zeleznicama [*International Convention Concerning the Carriage of Goods by Rail (CIM)*] (YU)
mkr............ Microroentgen (RU)
mkr............ Mikroskopisch [*Microscopic*] [*German*]
MKR........... Minus Control Relay [*Railroads*] (RU)
mkrad......... Microrad (RU)
MKRD.......... Blower Motor Jet Engines (BU)
MKRM......... Interkolkhoz Repair Shop (RU)
MKRYe........ International Commission on Radiological Units and Measurements [*ICRU*] (RU)
MKRZ.......... International Commission on Radiological Protection [*ICRP*] (RU)
MKS........... Crossbar Switch [*Telephony*] (RU)
MKS........... International Conference on Commodities (BU)
MKS........... Junior Command Personnel (RU)
MKS........... Makedonski Kooperativen Sojuz [*Macedonian Cooperative Union*] (YU)
MKS........... Maul- und Klauenseuche [*Foot-and-Mouth Disease*] (EG)
mks............ Maxwell (RU)
MKS........... Medunarodni Kongres Slavista [*International Congress of Specialists in Slavic Languages and Literature*] (YU)
MKS........... Meter-Kilogram-Second [*System of units*] (RU)
MKS........... Metr-Kilogram-Sekunda [*Meter-Kilogram-Second*] [*Polish*]
MKS........... Miedzyszkolny Klub Sportowy [*Inter-School Sports Club*] (POL)
MKS........... Miedzyuczelniany Klub Studencki [*Intercollegiate Students' Club*] [*Polish*]
MKS........... Milicyjny Klub Sportowy [*Militia Sports Club*] (POL)
MKS........... Mugla Kirec Sanayii AS [*Mugla Lime Industry Corporation*] (TU)
mks............ Potion [*Pharmacy*] (RU)
MKSA.......... Meter-Kilogram-Second-Ampere [*System of units*] (RU)
MKSAGS..... Meter-Kilogram-Second-Ampere-Degree Kelvin-Candle [*System of units*] (RU)
MKSB.......... Ministry of Communal Economy and Public Works [*Obsolete*] (BU)
MKSBI......... Ministry of Communal Economy and Public Works [*Obsolete*] (BU)
MKSBP........ Ministry of Communal Economy, Public Works, and Roads (BU)
MKSC.......... Motorna Konjska Snaga-Cas [*Motor Horsepower-Hour*] (YU)
mksek......... Microsecond (RU)
MKSG.......... Meter-Kilogram-Second-Degree Kelvin [*System of units*] (RU)
MKSK.......... Meter-Kilogram-Second-Coulomb [*System of units*] (RU)
MKSO.......... Interkolkhoz Construction Organization (RU)
MKSP.......... International Confederation of Free Trade Unions [*ICFTU*] (RU)
MKSP.......... International Conference of Free Trade Union (BU)
MKSS.......... Medunarodna Konferencija Slobodnih Sindikata [*International Conference of Free Trade Unions*] (YU)
MKSS.......... Meter-Kilogram-Second-Candle [*System of units*] (RU)
MKSZ.......... Magyar Kerekparos Szovetseg [*Hungarian Cyclists' Association*] (HU)
MKT........... Magyar Kozgazdasagi Tarsasag [*Hungarian Economic Society*] (HU)
MKT........... Manufacture Khmere de Tabacs [*Cambodian Tobacco Manufacturing Company*] (CL)
MKT........... Milletlerarasi Kalkinma Teskilati [*Agency for International Development - AID*] (TU)
MKT........... Moscow Chamber Theater (RU)
MKT-.......... Tractor-Mounted Erection Crane (RU)
Mk Tf.......... Makinali Tufek [*Machine Gun*] (TU)
MKTiR........ Miedzyzakladowy Klub Techniki i Racjonalizacji [*Inter-Plant Technique and Rationalization Club*] (POL)
MKTIS........ Magusa Genel Turk Isciler Sendikasi [*Famagusta Turkish Cypriot Workers Union*] (GC)
MKTs.......... Interchamber Pillar [*Mining*] (RU)
MKTS.......... Moscow Hard Alloys Kombinat (RU)
MKTU.......... Small Public Address System of a Ship (RU)
MKU-.......... Cinephotomicrography Unit (RU)
MKU........... Long-Distance Cable Center, Toll Cable Center (RU)
mkub.......... Cubic Meter (BU)
MKV........... Microswitch (RU)
mkv............ Microvolt (BU)
mkv............ Microvolt (RU)
MKV........... Mittelschueler-Kartellverband Katholischer Farbentraegender Korporationen Oesterreichs [*Union of the Austrian Catholic Student Associations*] (EG)
MKVLKSM... Moscow Committee of the VLKSM (RU)
MKVOKU.... Moscow "Red Banner" Higher Joint Command School Imeni Supreme Soviet of the RSFSR (RU)
mkvt........... Microwatt (BU)
mkvt........... Microwatt (RU)
m kw........... Metr Kwadratowy [*Square Meter*] [*Polish*]
MKWZZ....... Miedzynarodowa Konferencja Wolnych Zwiazkow Zawodowych [*International Conference of Free Trade Unions*] (POL)
Mkyuri......... Megacurie (RU)
mkyuri......... Millicurie (RU)
MKZ........... Manganorudni a Kyzove Zavody [*Manganese Ore and Pyrite Plants*] [*Chvaletice*] (CZ)
MKZ........... Mesarija Kmetijske Zadruge [*Agricultural Cooperative of Butchers*] (YU)
MKZ........... Moscow Carburetor Plant (RU)
MKZhG........ International Cooperative Women's Guild (RU)
MKZhM....... International Harvester Company (RU)
MKZhT........ International Rail Transport Committee (RU)
ml.............. Junior (RU)
ML............. Luminescence Microscope (RU)
ML............. Maalaisliitto [*Agrarian League*] [*Finnish*] (WEN)
ML............. Magnetic Tape (RU)
ML............. Mali [*Two-letter standard code*] (CNC)
Ml.............. Matmazel [*Miss*] [*Turkish*] (GPO)
ML............. Mechanikai Laboratorium [*Mechanical Laboratory*] (HU)
Ml.............. Mikkelin Laani(a) [*Finnish*]
ml.............. Mililitr [*Milliliter*] [*Polish*]
ml.............. Milliliter [*Milliliter*] (EG)
ml.............. Milliliter (RU)
ml.............. Millilitra(a) [*Finnish*]
ml.............. Millilitre [*Milliliter*] [*French*] (GPO)
ML............. Ministerstwo Lacznosci [*Ministry of Communications*] [*Polish*]
ML............. Ministerstwo Lesnictwa [*Ministry of Forestry*] (POL)
ML............. Mitgliedsland [*Member Country*] (EG)
ML............. Mlada Literatura [*New Literature*] [*A periodical*] [*Skopje*] (YU)
ML............. Mlade Leta (Vydavatelstvo Knih pro Mladez) [*Early Years (Publishing House for the Young)*] (CZ)
Ml.............. Mladsi [*Junior*] [*Attached to a name*] (CZ)
ML............. Mladsi Lekar [*Junior Physician*] [*Military*] (CZ)
ml.............. Mlodszy [*Junior*] [*Polish*]
Ml.............. Molality of Solution (RU)
ml.............. Moottorilaiva [*Finnish*]
M-L........... Moscow-Leningrad [*Bibliography*] (RU)
ml.............. Mukaan Luettuna [*Finnish*]
ml.............. Youth (BU)
MLA........... Interplanetary Vehicle (RU)
MLA........... Maramanga - Lac Alaotra (MAR)
MLA........... Member of the Legislative Assembly [*Namibian*] (AF)
MLA........... Movimento de Libertacao de Angola (MAR)
MLA........... Movimiento Liberal Autonomo [*Autonomous Liberal Movement*] [*Colombian*] (LA)
mladsh........ Junior (RU)
mlb............ Millilambert (RU)
MLBP.......... Ministry of the Lumber and Paper Industries (RU)
MLC........... Mauritius Labor Congress (AF)
MLC........... Member, Legislative Council (MAR)
MLC........... Movimiento Liberal Constitucionalista [*Liberal Constitutionalist Movement*] [*Nicaraguan*] (LA)
MLCN.......... Marxistisch-Leninistisch Centrum Nederland [*Marxist-Leninist Center, The Netherlands*] (WEN)
MLCV.......... Mouvement de Liberation des Iles du Cap Vert [*Movement for the Liberation of the Cape Verde Islands*] (AF)
mld............. Miliard [*Billion*] [*Polish*]
MLD........... Minimalni Licni Dohodak [*Minimum Individual Income*] (YU)
MLD........... Moldavian Railroad (RU)

MLD............ Monarquicos Liberal Democratas [*Liberal Democratic Monarchists*] [*Spanish*] (WER)
MLD............ Mouvement pour la Liberation de Djibouti [*Movement for the Liberation of Djibouti*] (PD)
MLD............ Movimento di Liberazione della Donna [*Women's Liberation Movement*] [*Italian*] (WER)
MLD............ Movimiento de Liberacion Dominicana [*Dominican Liberation Movement*] [*Dominican Republic*] (LA)
MLDP.......... Ministerstvo Lesu a Drevarskeho Prumyslu [*Ministry of Forests and the Lumber Industry*] (CZ)
MLE............ Magnetic Logical Element (RU)
Mle............ Modele [*Model*] [*French*] (MTD)
ML-12E........ Movimiento de Liberacion Doce de Enero [*12 January Liberation Movement*] [*Dominican Republic*] (LA)
MLEC.......... Mouvement pour la Liberation de l'Enclave de Cabinda [*Movement for the Liberation of the Cabinda Enclave*] [*Angolan*] (AF)
MLF............ Marxist-Leninistisk Fraktion [*Marxist-Leninist Fraction*] [*Swedish*] (WEN)
MLF............ Marxist-Leninistiske Front [*Marxist-Leninist Front*] [*Norwegian*] (WEN)
MLF............ Mauritius Labor Federation (AF)
MLF............ Mauritius Liberation Front (AF)
MLF............ Mouvement de Liberation des Femmes [*Women's Liberation Movement*] [*Luxembourg*] (WER)
MLFF.......... Manufacture de Laine et de Fibranne Filees [*Algerian*] (MAR)
MLG............ Local Lecturer Groups (BU)
MLG............ Marxist-Leninistiske Gruppene [*Marxist-Leninist Groups*] [*Norwegian*] (WEN)
MLG............ Movimento de Libertacao da Guine (MAR)
MLG............ Youth Lecturer Groups (BU)
MLGC.......... Mouvement de Liberation de la Guinee du Cap Vert (MAR)
MLGC.......... Movimento de Libertacao da Guine e Cabo Verde (MAR)
MLGCV........ Mouvement de Liberation de la Guinee du Cap Vert (MAR)
MLGCV........ Movimento de Libertacao da Guine e Cabo Verde (MAR)
MLGP.......... Movimento de Libertacao da Guine Portuguesa (MAR)
MLI............ Mali [*Three-letter standard code*] (CNC)
MLI............ Moscow Forest Institute (RU)
ML i BP........ Ministry of the Lumber and Paper Industries (RU)
MLICV.......... Mouvement de Liberation des Iles du Cap Vert [*Movement for the Liberation of the Cape Verde Islands*] [*French*] (MAR)
MLICV.......... Movimento de Libertacao das Ilhas de Cabo Verde [*Movement for the Liberation of the Cape Verde Islands*] [*Portuguese*] (WER)
Mli Mh Tsk ... Milli Muhafiz Teskilati [*National Guard Organization*] (TU)
MLiPD.......... Ministerstwo Lesnictwa i Przemyslu Drzewnego [*Ministry of Forestry and Timber Industry*] [*Polish*]
mlk............ Maalaiskunta [*Finnish*]
MLK............ Mistni Lidova Knihovna [*Local People's Library*] (CZ)
MLKE.......... Marxistiki Leninistiki Kinisi Ellados [*Marxist-Leninist Movement of Greece*] (GC)
ml k-r.......... Junior Commander (RU)
MLL............ Line Selector Electromagnet (RU)
MLL............ Masarykova Letecka Liga [*Masaryk Aviation League*] (CZ)
Mlle............ Mademoiselle [*Miss*] [*French*] (GPO)
Mlle............ Muelle [*Mole*] [*See also Me*] [*Spanish*] (NAU)
ml leyt........ Second Lieutenant (RU)
MLLH.......... Mezinarodni Liga Ledniho Hokeje [*International Ice Hockey League*] (CZ)
MLM............ Movimento de Libertacao das Mulheres [*Women's Liberation Movement*] [*Portuguese*] (WER)
MLN............ Melilla Airport (MAR)
mln............ Milion [*Million*] [*Polish*]
mln............ Million (BU)
mln............ Million (RU)
MLN............ Mouvement de Liberation Nationale [*National Liberation Movement*] [*Upper Voltan*] (AF)
MLN............ Movimiento de Liberacion Nacional [*National Liberation Movement*] [*Guatemalan*] (PPW)
MLN............ Movimiento de Liberacion Nacional [*National Liberation Movement*] [*Argentine*] (LA)
MLN............ Movimiento de Liberacion Nacional [*National Liberation Movement*] [*Mexican*] (LA)
MLN............ Movimiento de Liberacion Nacional - Tupamaros [*National Liberation Movement - Tupamaros*] [*Uruguayan*] (LA)
MLN-29........ Movimiento de Liberacion Nacional 29 de Noviembre [*29 November National Liberation Movement*] [*Panamanian*] (LA)
MLNA.......... Movimento de Libertacao Nacional de Angola (MAR)
ml nauchn sotr ... Junior Scientific Worker (RU)
MLNC.......... Mouvement de Liberation National des Comores [*National Liberation Movement of the Comoro Islands*] (AF)
ml n s.......... Junior Scientific Associate (BU)
MLO............ Marxisten-Leninisten Oesterreichs [*Marxists-Leninists of Austria*] (PPE)
MLO............ Mestni Ljudski Odbor [*Local People's Committee*] (YU)
MLP............ Malta Labor Party (PPW)
MLP............ Mauritius Labor Party (PPW)
MLP............ Ministerstvo Lehkeho Prumyslu [*Ministry of Light Industry*] (CZ)
MLP............ Ministry of Light Industry (RU)
MLP............ Ministry of the Lumber Industry (RU)
MLP............ Mouvement de Liberation du Peuple [*People's Liberation Movement*] [*Malagasy*] (AF)
MLP............ Movimento Libertario Portugues [*Portuguese Anarchist Movement*] (WER)
MLP............ Movimiento de Liberacion Proletaria [*Proletarian Liberation Movement*] [*Mexican*] (LA)
MLP............ Movimiento de Liberacion del Pueblo [*People's Liberation Movement*] [*Salvadoran*] (PD)
MLPB.......... Ministry of Light Industry, Belorussian SSR (RU)
MLPC.......... Mouvement de Liberation du Peuple Centrafricain [*Movement for the Liberation of the Central African People*] (PD)
MLPD.......... Marxistische-Leninistische Partei Deutschlands [*Marxist-Leninist Party of Germany*] (EG)
MLPN.......... Marxist-Leninist Party of the Netherlands (WEN)
MLPOe........ Marxistische-Leninistische Partei Oesterreichs [*Marxist-Leninist Party of Austria*] (WEN)
MLPS.......... Ministrstvo za Lokalni Promet Slovenije [*Ministry of Local Transportation of Slovenia*] (YU)
MLPU.......... Ministry of Light Industry, Ukrainian SSR (RU)
MLR............ Madarska Ludova Republika [*Hungarian People's Republic*] (CZ)
MLR............ Minimum Lending Rate (MAR)
MlR............ Mladinska Revija [*Youth Review*] (YU)
MLR............ Movimiento Laboral Revolucionario [*Revolutionary Labor Movement*] [*Peruvian*] (LA)
MLR............ Movimiento de Lucha Revolucionaria [*Revolutionary Struggle Movement*] [*Mexican*] (LA1)
mlrd............ Billion (BU)
mlrd............ Billion (RU)
mlrd/ME...... Billion International Units (BU)
MLS............ Lumber Machinery Station (RU)
MLS............ Malay Language Society (ML)
MLS............ Mouvement de Liberation du Sanwi [*Movement for the Liberation of the Sanwi*] [*Ghanaian*] (AF)
MLS............ Movimento per le Liberta Statuarie [*Movement for Statutory Liberty*] [*Sanmarinese*] (PPE)
MLS............ Movimiento de Liberacion Sebta [*Ceuta Liberation Movement*] [*Spanish*] (PD)
MLSA.......... Mines Local Staff Association (MAR)
MLSTP........ Mouvement pour la Liberation de Sao Tome et Principe [*Movement for the Liberation of Sao Tome and Principe*] (AF)
MLSTP........ Movimento de Libertacao de Sao Tome e Principe [*Movement for the Liberation of Sao Tome and Principe*] [*Portuguese*] (PPW)
Mlstrzm....... Mladsi Strazmistr [*Warrant Officer, Junior Grade*] (CZ)
MLSZ.......... Magyar Labdarugo Szovetseg [*Hungarian Soccer League*] (HU)
MLT............ Malta [*Three-letter standard code*] (CNC)
MLT............ Masarykova Liga Proti Tuberkulose [*Masaryk League for the Prevention of Tuberculosis*] (CZ)
MLT............ Varnished Metal-Film Heat-Resistant (Resistor) (RU)
MLTI............ Moscow Forestry Engineering Institute (RU)
MLTM.......... Maktab Latehan Tentera Malaysia [*Malaysian Military Training College*] (ML)
MLU............ Masarykuv Lidovychovny Ustav [*Masaryk Institute of Public Education*] (CZ)
MLUH.......... Martin-Luther-Universitaet Halle [*Martin Luther University, Halle*] (EG)
MLV............ Ministerstvo Lesniho a Vodniho Hospodarstvi [*Ministry of Forestry and Water Management*] (CZ)
MLZ............ Magnetostrictive Delay Line (RU)
Mlz............ Malzeme [*Materials, Equipment, Stock*] (TU)
MLZ............ Marxistische-Leninistische Zellen [*Marxist-Leninist Cells*] [*West German*] (WEN)
MLZhMS..... Women's International League for Peace and Freedom (RU)
MM............ Compagnie des Messageries Maritimes (MAR)
mm............ Last Month (BU)
MM............ Local Air Mass (RU)
MM............ Maailmanmestaruus [*Finnish*]
Mm............ Madam [*Mrs.*] [*Turkish*] (GPO)
MM............ Marker Beacon (RU)
MM............ Mars Matbaasi [*Mars Press*] [*Ankara*] (TU)
m/m............ Mas o Menos [*More or Less*] [*Spanish*]
MM............ Mathematical Model (RU)
mm............ Med Mera [*And So Forth*] [*Swedish*] (GPO)
mm............ Med Mere [*And So Forth*] [*Danish*] (GPO)
mm............ Med Mere [*And So Forth*] [*Norwegian*] (GPO)
Mm............ Megameter (RU)
Mm............ Megametre [*Metric System*] [*French*] (GPO)
MM............ Messieurs [*Plural of Mister*] [*French*]
mm............ Meta Mesimvrian [*Post Meridian*] (GC)
MM............ "Metalna", Tovarna Konstrukcij in Strojnih Naprav, Maribor [*"Metalna" Machinery Factory in Maribor*] (YU)
mm............ Metermazsa [*Quintal*] (HU)
MM............ Methodist Mission (MAR)
mm............ Milimetr [*Millimeter*] (POL)
mm............ Milimetro [*Millimeter*] [*Spanish*]
MM............ Millet Meclisi [*Grand National Assembly*] [*See also BMM*] (TU)
mm............ Millimeter (BU)

mm .... Millimeter [*Millimeter*] (EG)
mm .... Millimeter [*Millimeter*] (HU)
mm .... Millimeter (RU)
mm .... Millimetre [*Millimeter*] [*French*]
mm .... Millimetri(a) [*Finnish*]
mM .... Millimolarity (RU)
MM .... Mimar ve Muhendisler Ltd. [*Architects and Engineers Ltd.*] [*Manufacturers of aluminum kitchen ware*] (TU)
MM .... Ministerul Muncii [*Ministry of Labor*] (RO)
MM .... Ministry of Machinery Manufacture, USSR (RU)
Mm .... Miriametro [*Spanish*]
m/m .... Moi-Meme [*Myself*] [*French*]
MM .... Moravske Museum [*Moravian Museum*] [*Brno*] (CZ)
MM .... Moscow Subway (RU)
m a m .... Mot a Mot [*Word for Word*] [*French*]
MM .... Motor Method (RU)
mm .... Motorized and Mechanized (RU)
mm .... Muiden Muassa [*Finnish*]
MM .... muistomitali [*Finnish*]
mm .... Mutatis Mutandis [*With the Necessary Changes*] [*Latin*] (GPO)
mm .... Muun Muassa [*or Muuassa*] [*Among Other Things*] [*Finnish*]
MM .... Muvelodesugyi Miniszterium/Miniszter [*Ministry/Minister of Cultural Affairs*] (HU)
mm² .... Milimetr Kwadratowy [*Square Millimeter*] [*Polish*]
Mm² .... Millimetre Carre [*Square Millimeter*] [*French*] (MTD)
mm³ .... Milimetr Szescienny [*Cubic Millimeter*] [*Polish*]
Mm³ .... Millimetre Cube [*Cubic Millimeter*] [*French*] (MTD)
MMA .... Methyl Methacrylate (RU)
MMA .... Mine Management Associates (MAR)
MMA .... Revised Product Form Algorithm (RU)
MMA .... Small Medical Apparatus (RU)
MMAA .... Methylol Methacrylamide (RU)
MMA/ADA ... Mahaica-Mahaicony-Abary/Agricultural Development Authority [*Guyanese*] (LA)
MMAD .... Mikhanokinitos Monas Amesou Draseos [*Motorized Unit of Instant Action*] [*See also KAD*] (GC1)
MMAM .... Manufacture Marocaine d'Articles Metalliques (MAR)
MMB .... Meat Marketing Board (MAR)
MMB .... Motorized and Mechanized Brigade (RU)
MMB .... Muzeum Mesta Bratislavy [*Bratislava Municipal Museum*] (CZ)
MmC .... Millimetres Court [*French*] (MTD)
MMC .... Muhimbili Medical Centre (MAR)
MMCC .... Methodist Mission of Central Congo (MAR)
MMD .... Instantaneous Mine [*Navy*] (RU)
MMD .... Movimento Militar Democratico [*Democratic Military Movement*] [*British*] (LA)
Mme .... Madame [*Mrs.*] [*French*] (GPO)
MME .... Mikromesaies Epikheiriseis [*Small and Medium-Sized Enterprises*] (GC1)
MME .... Small Medical Encyclopedia (RU)
MMF .... Makine ve Muhendislik Fakultesi [*Faculty of Mechanics and Engineering*] [*Istanbul Technical University*] (TU)
MMF .... Meat and Dairy Farm (RU)
MMF .... Medunarodni Monetarni Fond [*International Monetary Fund*] (YU)
MMF .... Ministry of the Maritime Fleet, USSR (RU)
MMF .... Mission Militaire Francaise [*French Military Mission*] (CL)
MMFM .... Front des Journalistes [*Journalists Front*] [*Malagasy*] (AF)
MMFT .... Front des Enseignants [*Teachers Front*] [*Malagasy*] (AF)
MMG .... Mechanikai Meromuszerek Gyara [*Measuring Instruments Factory*] (HU)
MMG .... Milli Meclis Grupu [*National Assembly Group*] (TU)
MMG .... Mouvement Mixte Gabonais (MAR)
MMGS .... Local Interdepartmental Geodetic Council (RU)
MMGY .... Mechanikai Meromuszerek Gyara [*Measuring Instruments Factory*] (HU)
MMI .... Magyar Munkasmozgalmi Intezet [*Institute of the Hungarian Working Class Movement*] (HU)
MMI .... Materiel Mecanique et Industriel [*Moroccan*] (MAR)
MMI .... Medicus Mundi Internationalis [*International Organization for Cooperation in Health Care - IOCHC*] (EA)
MMI .... Moscow Mechanical Engineering Institute (RU)
MMI .... Moscow Medical Institute (RU)
MM I Arch ... Munkasmozgalmi Intezet Archivuma [*Archives of the Institute of the Hungarian Working Class Movement*] (HU)
MMiMP .... Ministry of the Meat and Dairy Industry (RU)
MMiP .... Ministry of Machinery Manufacture and Instrument Making, USSR (RU)
MMiSKhP .... Ministry of Local and Shale-Chemical Industries [*ESSR*] (RU)
MMiTP .... Ministry of Local and Fuel Industries (RU)
MMK .... International Maritime Committee [*IMC*] (RU)
MMK .... International Meteorological Committee (BU)
MMK .... International Meteorological Committee (RU)
MMK .... Magnitogorsk Metallurgical Kombinat (RU)
mmk .... Miljoona(a) Markkaa [*Finnish*]
mmk .... Millimicron (RU)
MMK .... Motorized and Mechanized Corps (RU)
mmkf .... Millimicrofarad (RU)
MMKO .... Intergovernmental Maritime Consultative Organization [*IMCO*] (RU)
MMKR .... Interrayon Shop for Major Repair (RU)
MmL .... Millimetres Long [*French*] (MTD)
m ml l .... Assistant Surgeon, Battalion Surgeon (BU)
MMLM .... Moroccan Marxist-Leninist Movement (AF)
Mml Me .... Muamelat Memuru [*Administrative Clerk*] (TU)
MMLS .... Muhendislik-Mimarlik ve Lisans Sonrasi [*Engineering and Architectural Postgraduate Degree*] (TU)
MMLV .... Movimiento Marxista-Leninista de Venezuela [*Marxist-Leninist Movement of Venezuela*] (LA)
MMM .... Mauritian Militant Movement (PD)
MMM .... Medical Missionaries of Mary (MAR)
MMM .... Messe der Meister von Morgen [*Fair of the Masters of Tomorrow*] (EG)
MMM .... Ministerio de Minas y Metalurgia [*Ministry of Mines and Metallurgy*] [*Cuban*] (LA)
MMM .... Mouvement Militant Mauricien [*Mauritian Militant Movement*] (PPW)
MMM .... Mouvement Mondial des Meres [*World Movement of Mothers - WMM*] (EA)
MMM .... Muebles Metalicos Manizales (COL)
MMMG .... Mosonmagyarovari Mezogazdasagi Gepgyar [*Agricultural Machine Factory of Mosonmagyarovar*] (HU)
MMMP .... Ministerio de la Marina Mercante y Puertos [*Ministry of Merchant Marine and Ports*] [*Cuban*] (LA)
MMMP .... Ministry of the Meat and Dairy Industry (RU)
MMMSP ...... Mouvement Militant Mauricien Socialiste Progressiste [*Mauritius Militant Socialist Progressive Movement*] (PPW)
MMMT .... Magyar Mezogazdasagi Muvelodesi Tarsasag [*Hungarian Society for Agricultural Education*] (HU)
MMMZ .... Magnitogorsk Metalware and Metallurgical Plant (RU)
MMN .... Metallurgic et Mechanique Nucleaires [*Belgian*]
MMND .... Analog Simulator (RU)
MMO .... International Meteorological Organization [*IMO*] (RU)
MMO .... Magnetic Meteorological Observatory (RU)
MMO .... Makina Muhendisleri Odasi [*Chamber of Mechanical Engineers*] (TU)
MMO .... Meteoroloji Muhendisleri Odasi [*Chamber of Meteorological Engineers*] (TU)
MMO .... Moscow Mathematical Society (RU)
MMO .... Reclamation Machine Detachment (RU)
MMO .... Small Magellanic Cloud (RU)
MMOB .... Mimar, Muhendis Odalari Birligi [*The Chambers of Architecture and Engineering Association*] (TU)
mmol' .... Millimole (RU)
MMP .... Magyar Megujulas Partja [*Party of Hungarian Renewal*] (PPE)
MMP .... Makedonski Medicinski Pregled [*Macedonian Medical Survey*] [*A periodical*] [*Skopje*] (YU)
MMP .... Ministry of Local Industry (RU)
MMP .... Ministry of the Metallurgical Industry, USSR (RU)
MMP .... Molecular Beam Method (RU)
MMPB .... Ministry of Local Industry, Belorussian SSR (RU)
MMPG .... Ministerul Minelor, Petrolului, si Geologiei [*Ministry of Mines, Petroleum, and Geology*] (RO)
MMPU .... Ministry of Local Industry, Ukrainian SSR (RU)
Mmq .... Millimetre Carre [*Square Millimeter*] [*French*] (MTD)
MMR .... Magazin von Merkwuerdigen Neuen Reisebeschreibungen (MAR)
MMR .... Ministry of Material Reserves, USSR (RU)
MMRF .... Ministry of the Maritime and River Fleets, USSR (RU)
MMS .... International Mathematical Union (RU)
MMS .... International Music Council [*IMC*] (RU)
MMS .... Malayan Medical Service (ML)
MMS .... Methodist Missionary Society (MAR)
MMS .... Militaermedizinische Sektion [*Military Medical Section*] (EG)
MMS .... Motorized and Mechanized Unit (RU)
MMS .... Reclamation Machine Station (RU)
MMSC .... Methodist Mission of South Congo (MAR)
MMSI .... Moscow Medical Stomatological Institute (RU)
MMSK .... Mednogorsk Copper and Sulfur Kombinat (RU)
MMSV .... Magyar Mezogazdak Szovetkezete [*Hungarian Farmers' Cooperative*] (HU)
MMT .... Copper-Manganese Thermistor (RU)
MMT .... Magyar Meteorologiai Tarsasag [*Hungarian Meteorological Society*] (HU)
MMT .... Magyar Muveszeti Tanacs [*Hungarian Council of Arts*] (HU)
MMTC .... Milton Margai Teachers College (MAR)
MMTC .... Mouvement Mondial des Travailleurs Chretiens [*World Movement of Christian Workers - WMCW*] (EA)
MMTF .... Meat and Dairy Farm (RU)
MMTS .... Malaysian Military Training School (ML)
MMTSzSz ... Magyar Mernokok es Technikusok Szabad Szakszervezete [*Free Trade Union of Hungarian Engineers and Technicians*] (HU)
mmv .... Maximum Molecular Moisture-Absorption Capacity (RU)
MMV .... Milli Mudafaa Vekaleti [*National Defense Ministry*] [*See also MSB*] (TU)
MMV .... Millimetric Waves (RU)
MMVZ .... Minsk Motorcycle and Bicycle Plant (RU)
MMZ .... Magadan Machine Plant (RU)
MMZ .... Moscow Machine Plant (RU)
MMZ .... Moscow Motorcycle Plant (RU)
MMZ .... Mytishchi Machinery Plant (RU)

MN.............. Bench Mark (RU)
MN.............. Interdepartmental Standard (RU)
MN.............. Machinery-Manufacturing Standard (RU)
MN.............. Mae Nam [*River*] [*Thai*] (NAU)
MN.............. Magnetic Saturation (RU)
MN.............. Magyar Nephadsereg [*Hungarian People's Army*] (HU)
Mn.............. Maison [*House*] [*French*]
mn.............. Many (RU)
Mn.............. Meganewton (RU)
mn.............. Mnoga [*Plural*] (POL)
mn.............. Mnozina [*Plural*] (YU)
M/n.............. Moneda Nacional [*Argentine Paper Money*] [*Business and trade*]
MN.............. Mongolia [*Two-letter standard code*] (CNC)
Mn.............. Moulin [*Mill*] [*French*] (NAU)
mn.............. Mutato Nomine [*The Name Being Changed*] [*Latin*] (GPO)
MN.............. Muzeum Narodowe [*National Museum*] (POL)
MN.............. Nonlinear Model (RU)
mn.............. Plural (RU)
m-n.............. Shop, Store (RU)
MN.............. Stationary Coupling (RU)
MNA.............. Malawi News Agency (AF)
Mna.............. Mladina [*Youth*] [*A periodical*] (YU)
MNA.............. Mouvement d'Action Politique et Sociale [*Political and Social Action Movement*] [*Swiss*] (PPW)
MNA.............. Mouvement National Algerien [*Algerian National Movement*] (AF)
MNA.............. Mouvement National Angolais [*Angolan National Movement*] (MAR)
MNA.............. Movimento Nacional de Angola [*Angolan National Movement*] (AF)
MNA.............. Movimiento Nacional Arosemenista [*National Arosemena Movement*] [*Ecuadorean*] (LA)
MNA.............. Movimiento Nueva Alternativa [*New Alternative Movement*] [*Venezuelan*] (LA1)
MNADREG... Movement of National Alliance for Democratic Restoration of Equatorial Guinea (AF)
M naznachenie... Mobilization Assignment (BU)
MNB.............. Magyar Nemzeti Bank [*Hungarian National Bank*] (HU)
MNB.............. Magyar Nemzeti Bizottmany, New York [*Hungarian National Council, New York*] (HU)
MNB.............. Metal Tanker-Barge (RU)
MNB.............. Ministerstvo Narodni Bezpecnosti [*Ministry of National Security*] (CZ)
MNB.............. Moroccan News Bulletin (MAR)
MNB.............. Movimento Nacionalista Brasileiro [*Brazilian Nationalist Movement*] (LA)
MNC.............. Mouvement National du Congo-Lumumba [*Congo National Movement-Lumumba*] [*Zairian*] (PD)
MNC.............. Mouvement Nationaliste du Congo (MAR)
MNC.............. Movimiento Nacionalista Cubano [*Cuban Nationalist Movement*] [*In exile*] (LA)
MNC.............. Multinational Corporation (MAR)
mn ch.............. Plural (BU)
mn ch.............. Plural (RU)
MNCK.............. Mouvement National Congolais Kalonji (MAR)
MNCL.............. Mouvement National Congolais Lumumba (MAR)
MNCP.............. Mbandzeni National Convention Party (MAR)
MNCR.............. Mouvement National Congolais de la Resistance (MAR)
MND.............. Ministry of National Development [*Guyanese*] (LA)
MND.............. Movimento Nacional Democratico [*National Democratic Movement*] [*Portuguese*] (PPE)
MNDP.............. Malawi National Democratic Party (MAR)
mn dr.............. Many Others (BU)
mn dr.............. Many Others (RU)
MNDSZ.............. Magyar Nok Demokratikus Szovetsege [*Hungarian Democratic Women's Union*] (HU)
MNDSZ.............. Magyarorszagi Nemetek Demokratikus Szovetsege [*Democratic Federation of Germans in Hungary*] (HU)
MNE.............. Ministerio de Negocios Estrangeiros [*Ministry of Foreign Affairs*] [*Portuguese*] (WER)
MNE.............. Superposed Epoch Method (RU)
MNEAP.............. Movimiento Nacional Estudiantil de Accion Popular [*National Student Movement of Popular Action*] [*Argentine*] (LA)
MNEF.............. Mutuelle Nationale des Etudiants de France (MAR)
MNET.............. Magyar Nepkoztarsasag Elnoki Tanacsa [*Presidential Council of the Hungarian People's Republic*] (HU)
MNF.............. Mizo National Front [*Indian*] (PD)
MNFF.............. Magyar Nemzeti Fueggetlensegi Front [*Hungarian National Independence Front*] (HU)
MNFP.............. Magyar Nemzeti Fueggetlensegi Part [*Hungarian National Independence Party*] (PPE)
MNG.............. Mongolia [*Three-letter standard code*] (CNC)
MNG.............. Movimiento Nueva Generacion [*New Generation Movement*] [*Panamanian*] (LA)
MNG.............. Movimiento Nueva Generacion [*New Generation Movement*] [*Venezuelan*] (LA1)
MNI.............. Malaysia National Insurance [*Subsidiary of PERNAS*] (ML)
MNI.............. Moscow Petroleum Institute Imeni Academician I. M. Gubkin (RU)
MNI.............. Movimento Nacional Independente (MAR)
MNI.............. Movimiento Nacionalista de Izquierda [*Bolivian*] (PPW)
MNII.............. Mari Scientific Research Institute (RU)
MNIIEM.............. Moscow Scientific Research Institute of Epidemiology and Microbiology (RU)
MNIIEMG.... Moscow Scientific Research Institute of Epidemiology, Microbiology, and Hygiene (RU)
MNIILKh...... Moscow Scientific Research Institute of Forestry [*1932-1938*] (RU)
MNIIP.............. Moscow Scientific Research Institute of Prosthetics (RU)
MNIIPTMash... Interbranch Scientific Research, Planning, and Technological Institute for Mechanization and Automation in Machinery Manufacture (RU)
MNIIVP.............. Moscow Scientific Research Institute of Virus Preparations (RU)
MNIIVS.............. Moscow Scientific Research Institute of Vaccines and Serums Imeni I. I. Mechnikov (RU)
MNIIYaLI..... Mordvinian Scientific Research Institute of Language, Literature, and History (RU)
MNIL.............. Malayan National Independence League (ML)
MNiR.............. Interdepartmental Norms and Wages, Interdepartmental Standards and Costs (RU)
MNiR.............. Local Norms and Wages, Local Standards and Costs (RU)
m-niye.............. Deposit, Layer (RU)
MNJ.............. Movimiento Nacional Justicialista [*National Justicialista Movement*] [*Argentine*] (LA)
MNJ.............. Movimiento Nacional de la Juventud [*National Youth Movement*] [*Dominican Republic*] (LA)
MNJA.............. Movimiento Nacional de Juventudes Anticomunistas [*National Movement of Anticommunist Youth*] [*Argentine*] (LA)
MNJD.............. Mouvement National de la Jeunesse Democratique [*National Movement of Democratic Youth*] [*Beninese*] (AF)
MNJR.............. Movimiento Nacional de la Juventud Revolucionaria [*National Movement of Revolutionary Youth*] [*Mexican*] (LA)
MNJTS.............. Mouvement National des Jeunes Travailleurs du Senegal [*National Movement of Young Senegalese Workers*] (AF)
MNK.............. Magyar Nemzetgyules Konyvtara [*Library of the Hungarian National Assembly*] (HU)
MNK.............. Magyar Nepkoztarsasag [*Hungarian People's Republic*] (HU)
MNK.............. Marine Nationale Khmere [*Cambodian National Navy*] [*Replaced MRK*] (CL)
MNK.............. Mesni Nacionalni Komitet [*Local National Committee*] (YU)
MNK.............. Multinationale Konzerne (MAR)
mn-k.............. Polygon (RU)
mnkem.............. Magyar Nepkoztarsasag Erdemes Muvesze [*Meritorious Artist of the Hungarian People's Republic*] (HU)
MNKK.............. Magyar Nephadsereg Kozponti Klubja [*The Central Club of the Hungarian People's Republic*] (HU)
mnkkm.............. Magyar Nepkoztarsasag Kivalo Muvesze [*Eminent Artist of the Hungarian People's Republic*] (HU)
MNL.............. Movimiento Nacional y Latinoamericano [*National and Latin American Movement*] [*Argentine*] (LA)
MNL.............. National Liberation Movement [*Guatemalan*] (PD)
MNL.............. Small Pneumatic Boat (RU)
MNLA.............. Malayan National Liberation Army [*Malayan Communist Party*] (IN)
MNLA.............. Movimento Nacional de Libertacao de Angola (MAR)
MNLF.............. Malayan National Liberation Front [*Singapore*] (PD)
MNLF.............. Moro National Liberation Front [*Philippine*] (PD)
MNLGE.............. Movimento Nacional da Libertacao de Guine Equatorial (MAR)
MNLL.............. Malayan National Liberation League (ML)
MNLT.............. Mouvement National de Liberation du Tchad (MAR)
MN-M.............. Small Nonlinear Electronic Simulator (RU)
MNME.............. Miskolci Nehezipari Muszaki Egyetem [*Heavy Industry Technical University of Miskolc*] (HU)
MNMT.............. Magyar Nepkoztarsasag Minisztertanacsa [*Council of Ministers of the Hungarian People's Republic*] (HU)
MNO.............. Mesni Narodni Odbor [*Local People's Committee*] (YU)
MNO.............. Ministarstvo Narodne Odbrane [*Ministry of National Defense*] (YU)
MNO.............. Ministerstvo Narodni Obrany [*Ministry of National Defense*] (CZ)
MNO.............. Ministry of National Defense (BU)
MNO.............. Moscow Numismatic Society (RU)
MNOFNRJ... Ministarstvo Narodne Odbrane Federativne Narodne Republike Yugoslavije [*Ministry of National Defense of the Federal People's Republic of Yugoslavia*] (YU)
mnogokr..... Iterative Aspect (RU)
mnogokr..... Multicolor (RU)
mnogopromsoyuz... Union of Multitrade Producers' Cooperatives (RU)
MNO/KS..... Ministerstvo Narodni Obrany/Kadrova Sprava [*Ministry of National Defense/Personnel Directorate*] (CZ)
MNOLO.............. Moscow Scientific Society of Otolaryngologists (RU)
MNOO.............. Mesni Narodnooslobodilacki Odbor [*Local National Liberation Committee*] (YU)
MNO/SVU... Ministerstvo Narodni Obrany/Stavebni Vyrobni Usek [*Ministry of National Defense/Building Production Sector*] (CZ)
MNOSZ.............. Magyar Nepkoztarsasagi Orszagos Szabvany [*Hungarian National Standards*] (HU)
MNOT.............. Magyar Nepkoztarsasagi Orszagos Tipusterv [*National Standards Plan of the Hungarian People's Republic*] (HU)

MNOT.......... Magyar Nok Orszagos Tanacsa [*National Council of Hungarian Women*] (HU)
MNO/TAS... Ministerstvo Narodni Obrany Tankova a Automobilova Sprava [*Ministry of National Defense/Tank and Automobile Directorate*] (CZ)
MNOTI......... Magyar Nepkoztarsasag Orszagos Tervezesi Iranyelv [*Hungarian People's Republic, National Planning Directive*] (HU)
MNO/VL...... Ministerstvo Narodni Obrany/Velitelstvi Letectva [*Ministry of National Defense/Air Force Headquarters*] (CZ)
mnozh......... Plural (RU)
MNP............ Malay Nationalist Party (ML)
MNP............ Milli Nizam Partisi [*National Order Party*] [*Ordered closed in May 1971*] (TU)
MNP............ Ministry of National Education (BU)
MNP............ Ministry of the Petroleum Industry (RU)
MNP............ Mouvement National des Pionniers [*National Pioneers Movement*] [*Congolese*] (AF)
MNP............ Movimiento Nacional Petrolero [*National Petroleum Movement*] [*PEMEX Union*] [*Mexican*] (LA)
MNP............ Movimiento Nacional Poncista [*National Poncista Movement*] [*Ecuadorean*] (LA)
MNP............ Movimiento Nacionalista Popular [*Popular Nationalist Movement*] [*Chilean*] (PD)
MNP............ Ungrounded Loop Method (RU)
MNPGD....... Mouvement National des Prisonniers de Guerre et des Deportes [*French*]
m npm......... Metrow Nad Poziomem Morza [*Meters above Sea Level*] [*Polish*]
MNPM......... Ministarstvo na Narodnata Prosveta na Makedonija [*Ministry of Education of Macedonia*] (YU)
MNPZ.......... Moscow Petroleum-Processing Plant (RU)
MNR............ Mediese Navorsingsraad [*Medical Research Council*] [*South African*] (AF)
MNR............ Milicias Nacionales Revolucionarias [*National Revolutionary Militias*] [*Cuban*] (LA)
MNR............ Mongolian People's Republic (BU)
MNR............ Mongolian People's Republic (RU)
MNR............ Mouvement National pour le Renouveau [*National Movement for Renewal*] [*Upper Voltan*] (AF)
MNR............ Mouvement National de la Revolution [*National Revolutionary Movement*] [*Congolese*] (AF)
MNR............ Mouvement Nationaliste Revolutionnaire [*Revolutionary Nationalist Movement*] [*French*] (PD)
MNR............ Movimiento Nacional Reformista [*National Reform Movement*] [*Argentine*] (LA)
MNR............ Movimiento Nacional Reformista [*National Reform Movement*] [*Guatemalan*] (LA)
MNR............ Movimiento Nacional Revolucionario [*National Revolutionary Movement*] [*Spanish*] (WER)
MNR............ Movimiento Nacional Revolucionario [*National Revolutionary Movement*] [*Salvadoran*] (PPW)
MNR............ Movimiento Nacionalista Revolucionario [*National Revolutionary Movement*] [*Bolivian*] (PPW)
MNR............ Movimiento Nacionalista Revolucionario Julio [*Revolutionary Nationalist Movement (Julio)*] [*Bolivian*] (PPW)
MNR............ Mozambique National Resistance (AF)
MNR............ Track-Setting Relay (RU)
MNRA.......... Mongolian People's Revolutionary Army (RU)
MNR-A........ Movimiento Nacionalista Revolucionario-Alianza [*Nationalist Revolutionary Movement-Alliance Faction*] [*Bolivian*] (LA1)
MNRA.......... Movimiento Nacionalista Revolucionario Autentico [*Authentic Nationalist Revolutionary Movement*] [*Bolivian*] (LA)
MNRCS....... Mouvement National pour la Revolution Culturelle et Sociale [*National Movement for the Cultural and Social Revolution*] [*Chadian*] (AF)
MNRD.......... Mouvement National de la Revolution Dahomeenne (MAR)
MNRG.......... Mouvement National de la Revolution Gabonaise [*Gabonese National Revolutionary Movement*] (AF)
MNRI........... Movimiento Nacionalista Revolucionario de Izquierda [*National Revolutionary Movement of the Left*] [*Bolivian*] (LA)
MNRP.......... Mongolian People's Revolutionary Party (BU)
MNRP.......... Mongolian People's Revolutionary Party (RU)
MNRP.......... Movimiento Nacionalista Revolucionario del Pueblo [*Nationalist Revolutionary People's Movement*] [*Bolivian*] (PPW)
MNRS.......... Machine for Continuous Pouring of Steel (RU)
MNR-U........ Movimiento Nacional Revolucionario-Unido [*National Revolutionary Movement-United Faction*] [*Bolivian*] (LA1)
MNS............ Junior Command Personnel (RU)
MNS............ Local People's Council (BU)
MNS............ Method of Steepest Descent (RU)
MNS............ Mladez Narodnich Socialistu [*National Socialist Party Youth*] (CZ)
MNS............ Mouvement National Somalien (MAR)
MNS............ Movimiento Nacional de Salvacion [*National Movement of Salvation*] [*Dominican Republic*] (PPW)
MNS............ Movimiento Nacional Suprapartidista [*National Supraparty Movement*] [*Salvadoran*] (LA)
MNS............ Movimiento Nacionalista Salvadoreno [*Salvadoran Nationalist Movement*] (LA1)
MNSDT....... Local People's Council of Deputies of the Working People (BU)
MNSZ.......... Zveno National Youth Union (BU)
MNT............ Makedonski Naroden Teatar [*Macedonian National Theater*] (YU)
MNTK.......... Movimiento Nacional Tupaj Katari [*Bolivian*] (PPW)
MNTV.......... Mistni Narodni Telovychovny Vybor [*Local Physical Education Board*] (CZ)
MNU............ Forced-Oil System (RU)
MNU............ Malayan Nurses Union (ML)
MNU............ Movement for National Unity [*St. Vincentian*] (LA1)
MNUC......... Mouvement National pour l'Unification du Congo (MAR)
MNUR.......... Mouvement National pour l'Union et la Reconciliation au Zaire [*National Movement for Union and Reconciliation in Zaire*] (PD)
MNUT.......... Muslim National Union of Tanganyika (MAR)
MNV............ Madarsky Narodny Vybor [*Hungarian National Committee*] (CZ)
MNV............ Mistni Narodni Vybor [*Local National Committee*] (CZ)
MNVN.......... Mien Nam Viet Nam [*South Vietnam*] (TVP)
MNW........... Mittleres Niedrigwasser [*Mean Low Water Mark*] (EG)
MNYC.......... Mauritius National Youth Council (AF)
MNZ............ Ministry of Public Health (BU)
MNZNRM.... Ministarstvo za Narodno Zdravje na Narodnata Republika Makedonija [*Ministry of Public Health of Macedonia*] (YU)
MNZS.......... Ministrstvo za Notranje Zadeve Slovenije [*Ministry of the Interior of Slovenia*] (YU)
MNZSG....... Ministry of Public Health and Social Welfare (BU)
MO.............. Deliberate Fire (RU)
MO.............. Local Defense (RU)
MO.............. Macao [*Two-letter standard code*] (CNC)
MO.............. Magnetic Observatory (RU)
MO.............. Massed Fire [*or Concentrated Fire*] (BU)
MO.............. Massed Fire [*Artillery*] (RU)
MO.............. Meteorological Observatory (RU)
MO.............. Methyl Orange (Indicator) (RU)
MO.............. Milattan Once [*Before Christ*] (TU)
MO.............. Milicja Obywatelska [*Citizens' Militia*] (POL)
MO.............. Miner's Pick, Pick Hammer (RU)
MO.............. Ministerstvo Obchodu [*Ministry of Trade*] (CZ)
MO.............. Ministerstwo Odbudowy [*Ministry of Reconstruction*] (POL)
MO.............. Ministerstwo Oswiaty [*Ministry of Education*] (POL)
MO.............. Ministry of Defense (RU)
MO.............. Mistni Organisace [*Local Organization*] (CZ)
MO.............. Mobilization Section (RU)
MO.............. Molecular Orbital (RU)
M/o............. Mon Ordre [*French*]
MO.............. Moravska Ostrava [*Moravian Ostrava*] (CZ)
Mo.............. Morro [*Headland, Hill*] [*Portuguese*] (NAU)
Mo.............. Morro [*Headland, Hill*] [*Spanish*] (NAU)
MO.............. Moscow Branch (RU)
MO.............. Moscow Oblast (RU)
MO.............. Motorized Detachment (RU)
mo.............. Oil Separator, Lubricant Separator (RU)
MO.............. Queueing Operation (RU)
MO.............. Release Magnet (RU)
MO.............. Small Submarine Chaser (RU)
MO.............. Submarine Chaser (RU)
MOA............ Mikti Orkhistra Athinon [*Athens Mixed Orchestra*] (GC)
MOA............ Milicias Obreras de la Alfabetizacion [*Literacy Workers Militias*] [*Nicaraguan*] (LA1)
MOA............ Ministry of Agriculture (MAR)
MOA............ Mokichi Okada Association [*Japanese*]
MOA............ Movimiento Obrero Autogestionario [*Self-Management Workers' Movement*] [*Spanish*] (WER)
MOAC......... Movimiento Obrero de Accion Catolica [*Catholic Action Workers Movement*] [*Argentine*] (LA)
MOAC......... Movimiento Obrero de Accion Catolica [*Catholic Action Workers Movement*] [*Uruguayan*] (LA)
MOAU......... Moscow Oblast Archives Administration (RU)
MOB............ International Refugee Organization (BU)
MOB............ International Refugee Organization [*IRO*] (RU)
MOB............ Magyar Olympiai Bizottsag [*Hungarian Olympic Committee*] (HU)
MOB............ Mistni Osvetova Beseda [*Local Cultural Group*] (CZ)
MOB............ Mobilisation Generale [*General Mobilization*] [*Cambodian*] (CL)
mob............ Mobilization (RU)
MOB............ Muemlekek Orszagos Bizottsaga [*National Committee on Historical Monuments*] (HU)
MOBBRIG.... Mobil Brigade [*Mobile Brigade*] (IN)
MOBEIRA.... Moagem de Beira Lda. (MAR)
MOBIGALE ... Mobilisation Generale [*General Mobilization*] [*Cambodian*] (CL)
MOBLRKI.... Moscow Oblast Workers' and Peasants' Inspection [*1920-1934*] (RU)
MOBO......... Mobilization Section (RU)
mobovsu..... Mobilization Section of the District Military Medical Directorate (RU)
MOBRAL..... Movimento Brasileiro de Alfabetizacao [*Brazilian Literacy Movement*] (LA)
MOBSA....... Moscow Society for Combating Alcoholism (RU)

MOBSTYA .. Malayan Outward-Bound School Trained Youth Association (ML)
MOBUP .... Moskva-Oka Basin Administration of Waterways (RU)
MOC .... Management Opleidings Centrum
MOC .... Metropolitan Owners' Club (EA)
MOC .... Mouvement des Ouvriers Chretiens [*Christian Workers Movement*] [*Belgian*] (WER)
MOC .... Movimiento Obrero Campesino [*Peasant Workers Union*] [*Argentine*] (LA)
MOC .... Movimiento Obrero Cristiano de Nicaragua [*Christian Labor Movement of Nicaragua*] (LA)
MOCAF .... Societe Motte Cordonnier Afrique (MAR)
MOCAMA.... Molinos Caracas Maracaibo, SA [*Venezuelan*]
MOCI.......... Moniteur Officiel du Commerce International (MAR)
MOCIL......... Mocambique Importadora (Beira) Lda. (MAR)
MOCK .... Medunarodni Odbor Crvenog Krsta [*International Committee of the Red Cross*] (YU)
MOD .... Mestske Oblastni Divadlo [*Municipal Regional Theater*] (CZ)
MOD .... Miedzynarodowa Organizacja Dziennikarska [*International Journalists' Organization*] (POL)
MOD .... Ministry of Defense [*Singapore*] (ML)
mod .... Model (RU)
Mod .... Modele [*Model*] [*French*] (MTD)
mod .... Modulator (RU)
MOD .... Respiratory Minute Volume (RU)
MODACAPI ... Movimiento de Accion Capitalina Independiente [*Movement for Capital Independent Action*] [*Dominican Republic*] (LA1)
MODECAR ... Montajes Industriales del Caribe Ltda. [*Barranquilla*] (COL)
MODEF .... Mouvement de Defense des Exploitations Familiales [*Movement for the Defense of Family Farms*] [*French*] (WER)
MODENI...... Movimiento Democratizador Nacionalista Independiente [*Nationalist Independent Democratizing Movement*] [*Honduran*] (LA1)
MODEPANA ... Movimiento en Defensa del Patrimonio Nacional [*Movement for the Protection of National Resources*] [*Argentine*] (LA)
MODEPAZ... Movimiento Peruano de Soberania Nacional, Solidaridad Internacional, y Paz Mundial [*Peruvian Movement of National Sovereignty, International Solidarity, and World Peace*] (LA)
MODEX .... Magyar Divataru Kulkereskedelmi Vallalat [*Hungarian Foreign Trade Enterprise for Fashionwear*] (HU)
MODNE .... Mathitiki Organosi Dimokratikis Neolaias Ellados [*Student Organization of Democratic Youth of Greece*] (GC)
MODNT .... Moscow Oblast House of Folk Art (RU)
MODPIK ...... Moscow Society of Playwrights and Composers (RU)
MODVF .... Moscow Society of Friends of the Air Force (RU)
MOEAK .... Mystiki Organosis Ethnikis Apelevtheroseos Kyprou [*Secret Organization for the National Liberation of Cyprus*] (GC)
moebl .... Moebliert [*Furnished*] (EG)
MOEC .... Movimiento Obrero, Estudiantil, y Campesino [*Worker-Student-Peasant Movement*] [*Colombian*] (LA)
MOEK .... Moscow Oblast Power Engineering Committee (RU)
MOEL .... Moscow Electric Bulb Plant (RU)
MOF .... Small Concentration Plant (RU)
MOF .... Youth Fatherland Front (BU)
MOFLOR ..... Mocambique Florestal (MAR)
MOG .... Milicias Obreras Guatemaltecas [*Guatemalan Workers' Militia*] (PD)
mog .... Tomb, Grave [*Topography*] (RU)
MOGA .... International Civil Aviation Organization [*ICAO*] (RU)
MOGAOR .... Moscow Oblast State Archives of the October Revolution (RU)
MOGAS .... Sociedade Mocambicana de Gases Comprimidos (MAR)
MOGES .... Moscow Association of State Electric Power Plants (RU)
MOGIA .... Moscow Oblast State Historical Archives (RU)
MOGIZ .... Moscow Branch of the Association of State Publishing Houses (RU)
mogl .... Moeglich [*Possible*] [*German*]
MOGPIIYa ... Moscow Oblast State Pedagogical Institute of Foreign Languages (RU)
MOGUR .... Movimiento Guerrillero Urbano [*Urban Guerrilla Movement*] [*Colombian*] (LA)
MOGURT ..... MOGURT Gepjarmu Kulkereskedelmi Vallalat [*MOGURT Foreign Trade Enterprise for Motor Vehicles*] (HU)
MOHOSZ ..... Magyar Honvedelmi Sportszovetseg [*Hungarian Sports Federation for National Defense*] (HU)
MOHOSZ ..... Magyar Onkentes Honvedelmi Szovetseg [*Hungarian Voluntary Home Defense Association*] (HU)
MOHOSZ ..... Magyar Orszagos Horgasz Szovetseg [*Hungarian National Anglers' Association*] (HU)
MOID .... Moroccan Office of Information and Documentation (MAR)
MOIDR .... Moscow Society of Russian History and Antiquities (RU)
MOIDS .... Moscow Experimental Research Station for Sprinkler Watering (RU)
MOIF .... Merkezi Odenekli Izin Fonu [*Central Compensation Fund*] [*Turkish Federated State of Cyprus*] (GC)
MOIK .... Moscow Oblast Executive Committee (RU)
MOIP .... Moscow Society of Naturalists (RU)
MOIR .... Movimiento Obrero Independiente Revolucionaria [*Independent Workers Revolutionary Movement*] [*Colombian*] (LA)
MOIR .... Movimiento Obrero Izquierdista Revolucionario [*Colombian*] (PPW)
MOiSW .... Ministerstwo Oswiaty i Szkolnictwa Wyzszego [*Ministry of Education and Higher Schools*] (POL)
MOIUU .... Moscow Oblast Institute for the Advanced Training of Teachers (RU)
MO IZMIRAN ... Murmansk Branch of the Institute of Terrestrial Magnetism, the Ionosphere, and Radio Wave Propagation (of the Academy of Sciences, USSR) (RU)
MOJA .... Movement for Justice in Africa [*Liberian*] (PPW)
MOK .... Copper Concentration Combine (BU)
MOK .... International Coffee Organization (RU)
MOK .... International Olympic Committee (BU)
MOK .... International Olympic Committee [*IOC*] (RU)
MOK .... Local Organizational Committee (BU)
MOK .... Mora Ferenc Kiado [*Ferenc Mora Publishing House*] (HU)
MOK .... Moscow Oblast Committee (RU)
MOK .... Moscow Oblast Office (RU)
MOK .... Mutuelle des Originaires de Krinjabo (MAR)
MOK .... Muzeumok Orszagos Kozpontja [*National Museum Center*] (HU)
MOKA .... Mystiki Organosi Kyprion Agoniston [*Underground Organization of Cypriot Fighters*] (GC)
mokham ...... Mohammedan (BU)
MOKI .... Magyar Orszagos Kozegeszsegugyi Intezet [*Hungarian National Institute of Public Health*] (HU)
MOKI .... Moscow Oblast Clinical Scientific Research Institute (RU)
MOKJ .... Mistni Odbor Kostnicke Jednoty [*Local Branch of the Union of Constance*] (CZ)
MOKO .... Moscow Oblast Department of Municipal Services (RU)
mokt .... Millioctave (RU)
mol .... Dairy [*Topography*] (RU)
mol' .... Gram Molecule, Mole (RU)
mol .... Molecular (RU)
Mol .... Molekuel [*or Molekul or Molekular*] [*Molecule or Molecular*] [*German*]
MOLA .... Moscow Society of Amateurs of Astronomy (RU)
MOLAJ .... Magyar-Szovjet Olaj Tarsasag [*Hungarian-Soviet Oil Enterprise*] (HU)
mol art .... Dairy Artel (RU)
MolASSR .... Moldavian Autonomous Soviet Socialist Republic [*1924-1940*] (RU)
MOLB .... Moscow Oblast Lecture Bureau (RU)
mold .... Moldavian (RU)
Moldavgiz ... Moldavian State Publishing House (RU)
MOLDEAGUA ... Molino Dagua Ltda. [*Cali*] (COL)
moleks .... Molecular Sieve (RU)
molektronika ... Molecular Electronics (RU)
Mol Gew ...... Molekulargewicht [*Molecular Weight*] [*German*]
MOLGK .... Moscow "Order of Lenin" Conservatory Imeni P. I. Chaykovskiy (RU)
MOLICA ...... Movimento de Libertacao da Cabinda [*Movement for the Liberation of Cabinda*] [*Angolan*] (AF)
MOLIFUGE ... Movimiento de Liberacion y Futuro de Guinea Ecuatorial (MAR)
MOLIMO ...... Movimento de Libertacao de Mocambique [*Mozambique Liberation Movement*] (AF)
MOLINACO ... Mouvement de Liberation Nationale des Comores [*National Liberation Movement of the Comoro Islands*] (AF)
MOLIPO ...... Movimento de Libertacao Popular [*People's Liberation Movement*] [*Brazilian*] (LA)
Molirena ...... Liberal Republican and Nationalist Movement [*Panamanian*] (PD)
MOLKh .... Moscow Society of Lovers of the Arts (RU)
molmash ..... Dairy Machinery Plant (RU)
MOLMI .... First Moscow "Order of Lenin" Medical Institute Imeni I. M. Sechenov (RU)
mol-myasn ... Dairy and Meat Sovkhoz [*Topography*] (RU)
Molotovneft' ... Molotov Petroleum Association (RU)
molprom ..... Dairy Industry (RU)
Molpromstroy ... All-Union Construction and Installation Trust of the Ministry of the Meat and Dairy Industry, USSR (RU)
Mol-Refr ...... Molekularrefraktion [*Molecular Refraction*] [*German*]
MolSSR .... Moldavian Soviet Socialist Republic (RU)
mol v .... Molecular Weight (RU)
Mol W .... Molekularwaerme [*Molecular Heat*] [*German*]
MOM .... Magyar Optikai Muvek [*Hungarian Optical Factory*] (HU)
Mom .... Megohm (RU)
mom .... Milliohm (RU)
MOM .... Ministry of General Machinery Manufacture, USSR (RU)
MOMA .... Miktai Omadai Mikhanimaton Anasyngrotiseos [*Joint Reconstruction Equipment Units*] [*See also SYKEA*] [*Greek*] (GC)
MOM-OB-DER ... Meslek Okullari Mezun ve Ogrencileri Birlesme ve Dayanisma Dernegi [*Professional School Graduates and Students' Unity and Mutual Solidarity Association*] (TU)
MOMS .... Mervardesskatt [*Value-Added Tax*] [*Swedish*] (WEN)

MOMS......... Miestny Odbor Matice Slovenskej [*Local Branch of the Matica Slovenska (A Slovak cultural organization)*] (CZ)
MOMU......... Missao Organizadora do Museu do Ultramar (MAR)
MOMZ......... Moscow Optical Instrument Plant (RU)
Mon............ Maison [*House, Firm, Family*] [*French*]
MON............ Makhitikai Omadai Neolaias [*Fighting Groups of Youth*] [*Greek*] (GC)
MON............ Member of the Order of the Niger (MAR)
MON............ Metal-Oxide Low-Resistance (Resistor) (RU)
MON............ Mezinarodni Organisace Novinaru [*International Organization of Journalists*] (CZ)
MON............ Ministerstwo Obrony Narodowej [*Ministry of National Defense*] (POL)
Mon............ Monastery, Cloister [*Topography*] (RU)
mon............ Monikko [*Finnish*]
mon............ Monikollisesti [*Finnish*]
mon............ Monikon [*Finnish*]
mon............ Monocytes (RU)
MON............ Movimiento de Opinion Nacional [*National Opinion Movement*] [*Argentine*] (LA)
MONALI...... Movement for National Liberation [*Barbadian*] (LA1)
MONALIGE ... Movimiento Nacional de Liberacion de la Guinea Ecuatorial (MAR)
MONAP....... Movimiento Nacional de Pobladores [*National Settlers Movement*] [*Guatemalan*] (LA)
MONAP....... Mozambique Nordic Agricultural Program (MAR)
MONARECO ... Movimiento Nacional Revolucionario de la Comunidad [*National Revolutionary Movement of the Community*] [*Argentine*] (LA)
MONAS....... Monumen Nasional [*National Monument*] (IN)
monasto...... Monasterio [*Monastery*] [*Spanish*]
Monatsh...... Monatshefte [*Monthly (As in a publication)*] [*German*]
mong.......... Mongolian, Mongol (RU)
MONIAG..... Moscow Oblast Scientific Research Institute of Obstetrics and Gynecology (RU)
MONIIAG..... Moscow Oblast Scientific Research Institute of Obstetrics and Gynecology (RU)
MONIIGS..... Moscow Branch of the State Scientific Research Institute of the Hydrolysis and Sulfite Liquor Industry (RU)
MONIKI....... Moscow Oblast Clinical Scientific Research Institute Imeni M. F. Vladimirskiy (RU)
MONIMA..... Mouvement National pour l'Independance de Madagascar [*National Movement for the Independence of Madagascar*] (PPW)
MONIMI....... Moscow Oblast Scientific Research Methods Institute (RU)
MONIMPEX ... MONIMPEX Kulkereskedelmi Vallalat [*MONIMPEX Foreign Trade Enterprise*] (HU)
MONITI........ Moscow Oblast Scientific Research Institute of Tuberculosis (RU)
MONITO...... Moscow Branch of the All-Union Scientific, Engineering, and Technical Society (RU)
MONITOE.... Moscow Branch of the All-Union Scientific, Engineering, and Technical Society of Power Engineers (RU)
MONITOL.... Moscow Branch of the All-Union Scientific, Engineering, and Technical Society of Foundry Workers (RU)
MONITOMASh ... Moscow Branch of the All-Union Scientific, Engineering, and Technical Society of Machine Builders (RU)
MONITOVT ... Moscow Branch of the All-Union Scientific, Engineering, and Technical Society of Water Transportation (RU)
MO NIZMIR ... Murmansk Branch of the Scientific Research Institute of Terrestrial Magnetism, the Ionosphere, and Radio Wave Propagation (RU)
MONK......... Commission on Mongolia (of the Academy of Sciences, USSR) (RU)
MONO......... Moscow Department of Public Education (RU)
MONOCLE ... Mise en Ordinateur d'une Notice Catalographique de Livre [*MARC-formaat van de Bibliotheque Universitaire de Grenoble*]
monokl........ Monoclinic (RU)
monokl s..... Monoclinic Syngony (RU)
Mons........... Monsenor [*Monsignor*] [*Spanish*]
mont............ Electrician, Assembler, Fitter (RU)
Montazhkhimzashchita ... Trust of the Glavteplomontazh of the Gosmontazhspetsstroy SSSR (RU)
Montazhlegmash ... Trust for the Installation of Technological Equipment of Establishments of Textile and Light Industries (RU)
Montazhsantekhsnab ... Supply Office for Sanitary Engineering Operations (RU)
Montazhstroymash ... Specialized Trust of the Glavstroy of the Ministry of the Machine Tool and Tool Industry, USSR (RU)
MONTEDISON ... Montecatini Edison (MAR)
MONTO....... Moscow Oblast Administration of the Scientific and Technical Society (RU)
MONTRAL... Montagargas y Tractores Ltda. [*Cali*] (COL)
MONTRAL... Movimiento Nacional de Trabajadores para la Liberacion [*National Movement of Workers for Liberation*] [*Venezuelan*] (LA)
MONTRI...... Movimiento Nacional de Trabajadores Independientes [*National Independent Workers Movement*] [*Venezuelan*] (LA)
Montt.......... Monument [*Monument*] [*Military map abbreviation*] [*World War I*] [*French*] (MTD)
MOO........... Macedonian-Odrin Volunteer Forces (BU)
MOO........... Moscow Oblast Branch, Moscow Oblast Department (RU)
MOO........... Moscow Society of Hunters (RU)
MOOM......... Monades Organoseos kai Methodon [*Organization and Methods Units*] [*Greek*] (GC)
MOOMP...... Moscow Oblast Department of Local Industry (RU)
MOONO...... Moscow Oblast Department of Public Education (RU)
MOOP......... Ministry for the Preservation of Public Order (RU)
MOOSO...... Moscow Oblast Department of Social Security (RU)
MOOT......... Moscow Oblast Labor Department (RU)
MOOZ......... Moscow Oblast Department of Public Health (RU)
MOP........... Interbranch Association of Trade Unions (RU)
MOP........... International Organization of Employers [*IOE*] (RU)
MOP........... International Society of Soil Scientists (RU)
MOP........... Junior Maintenance Personnel (BU)
MOP........... Junior Service Personnel (RU)
MOP........... Metal Processing Industry (BU)
MOP........... Mezinarodni Organizace Prace [*International Labor Organization*] (CZ)
MOP........... Miedzynarodowa Organizacja Pracy [*International Labor Organization*] (POL)
MOP........... Ministerio das Obras Publicas [*Ministry of Public Works*] [*Portuguese*] (WER)
MOP........... Ministerio de Obras Publicas [*Ministry of Public Works*] (COL)
MOP........... Ministerio de Obras Publicas [*Ministry of Public Works*] [*Salvadoran*]
MOP........... Ministerio de Obras Publicas [*Ministry of Public Works*] [*Venezuelan*] (LA)
MOP........... Ministry of the Defense Industry, USSR (RU)
MOP........... Moscow Department of the Press (RU)
MOP........... Moscow Oblast Administration (RU)
MOP........... Mouvement pour l'Ordre et la Paix [*Movement for Order and Peace*] [*New Caledonian*] (PD)
MOP........... Mouvement Ouvriers-Paysans [*Workers' and Peasants' Movement*] [*Haitian*] (PD)
MOP........... Small Experimental Underground Vault [*Permafrost investigation*] (RU)
MOP........... Trade Unions International (RU)
MOPA......... Moderno Pazarlama ve Dagitim AS [*Modern Marketing and Distributing Corporation*] (TU)
MOPAD....... Movement for Peace and Democracy (MAR)
MOPARE..... Movimiento Patriotico de Renovacion [*Patriotic Renewal Movement*] [*Chilean*] (LA)
MOPBF........ International Organization of Aid to Fighters Against Fascism (BU)
Moped......... Motor-Pedal [*Motorized Bicycle*] (EG)
moped......... Pedal Motorcycle (RU)
MOPEO....... Moscow Planning and Experimental Department (RU)
MOPEX........ Mozgokep Kiviteli Vallalat [*Motion Picture Export Enterprise*] (HU)
MOPG.......... Materials for General and Applied Geology (RU)
MOPG.......... Miners' Trade Unions International (RU)
MOPH.......... Ministerio das Obras Publicas e Habitacao [*Ministry of Public Works and Housing*] [*Mozambican*] (AF)
MOPI........... Moscow Oblast Pedagogical Institute Imeni N. K. Krupskaya (RU)
MOPI........... Moscow Oblast Polytechnic Institute (RU)
MOPI........... Movimiento Obrero Popular de Izquierda [*People's Labor Movement of the Left*] [*Colombian*] (LA)
MOPKhN..... Trade Unions International of Chemical, Oil, and Allied Workers (RU)
MOPLA........ Movimento Popular por la Libertacao de Angola (MAR)
MOPM......... Trade Unions International of Metal and Engineering Industries (RU)
MOPOCO.... Movimiento Popular Colorado [*Colorado Popular Movement*] [*Paraguayan*] (PD)
MOPP.......... Miedzyszkolny Osrodek Prac Pozalekcyjnych [*Inter-School Center for Extra-Curricular Work*] (POL)
MOPP.......... Miejski Osrodek Propagandy Partyjnej [*City Party Propaganda Center*] (POL)
MOPR.......... International Organization for Aid to Fighters for Revolution [*1922-1947*] (RU)
MOPR.......... International Organization for Aid to Revolutionary Fighters (BU)
MOPR.......... International Organization for Aid to Victims of the Revolution (BU)
MOPR.......... International Organization for Aid to Working People (BU)
MOPR.......... Miedzynarodowa Organizacja Pomocy Rewolucjonistom [*International Red Aid*] (POL)
MOPS.......... Multispectral Opium Poppy Sensor System [*Appears thus in Turkish newspapers*] (TU)
MOPSD....... Trade Unions International of Workers of the Building, Wood, and Building Materials Industries (RU)
MOPSh........ Moscow Party School (RU)
MOPShK..... Moscow Experimental Model Commune School (RU)
MOPSLKh... Trade Unions International of Agricultural and Forestry Workers [*TUIAFW*] (RU)
MOP(SP)..... Ministerstvo Ochrany Prace a Socialni Pece [*Ministry of Protection of Labor and of Social Welfare*] (CZ)

MOPT.......... Ministerio de Obras Publicas y Transportes [*Ministry of Public Works and Transportation*] [*Costa Rican*] (LA)
MOPTT........ Postal, Telegraph, and Telephone International [*PTTI*] (RU)
MOPU.......... Moscow Oblast Assay Administration (RU)
MOPUA....... Mouvement Populaire de l'Unite Angolaise [*Popular Movement of Angolan Unity*] (AF)
MOQED....... Political Party [*Israeli*] (ME)
MOR............ Medunarodna Organizacija Rada [*International Labor Organization (ILO)*] (YU)
MOR............ Mistni Odborova Rada [*Local Trade Union Council*] (CZ)
MOR............ Movimiento de Orientacion Reformista [*Reformist Orientation Movement*] [*Argentine*] (LA)
MOR............ Mundo Obrero Revolucionario [*Revolutionary Labor World*] [*Spanish*] (WER)
mor............. Nautical Term (BU)
mor............. Sea, Maritime, Naval (RU)
Morak.......... Naval Academy (RU)
Morarkh...... Main Naval Archives (RU)
MorASSR.... Mordvinian Autonomous Soviet Socialist Republic (RU)
MordASSR ... Mordvinian Autonomous Soviet Socialist Republic (RU)
Mordgiz....... Mordvinian State Publishing House (RU)
MORE.......... Movimiento Obrero Revolucionario [*Workers Revolutionary Movement*] [*Nicaraguan*] (LA1)
MORECO .... Mozambique Revolutionary Council (AF)
MOREHOB ... Mouvement de la Resistance des Hommes Bleus [*Blue Men Resistance Movement*] [*Moroccan*] (AF)
MORENA..... Mouvement de Renovation Nationale [*National Renewal Movement*] [*Malagasy*] (AF)
MORENA..... Movimiento Revolucionario Nacional [*National Revolutionary Movement*] [*Brazilian*] (LA)
MORENA..... Movimiento de Renovacion Nacional [*National Renewal Movement*] [*Venezuelan*] (PPW)
MORENA..... Movimiento Revolucionario Nacional [*National Revolutionary Movement*] [*Chilean*] (LA)
MORENURE ... Movimiento Revolucionario Nueva Republica [*New Republic Revolutionary Movement*] [*Dominican Republic*] (LA)
morf .... Morphological, Morphology (RU)
MORI .... Megyei Orvosi Rendelo Intezet [*County Medical Center*] (HU)
Moriskom ... Military History Commission for the Study and Utilization of the Experience of the 1914-1918 War at Sea (RU)
MORKI......... Moscow Branch of the Workers' and Peasants' Inspection (RU)
morlet .... Naval Aviator (RU)
Mormuz....... Naval Museum (RU)
Morozovsksel'mash ... Morozovsk Agricultural Machinery Plant (RU)
MORP.......... International Association of Revolutionary Writers (RU)
MORP.......... Metodyczny Osrodek Racjonalizacji Produkcji [*Production Rationalization Methods Center*] (POL)
Morput' .... Administration of Sea Routes (RU)
MORT.......... International Association of Revolutionary Theaters (RU)
Mortekhsnab ... State Procurement and Supply Office of the Ministry of the Maritime Fleet, USSR (RU)
MORU.......... Moscow Association of Accounting and Statistical Personnel (RU)
MOS .... International Organization for Standardization [*ISO*] (RU)
MOS .... International Organization for Standardization (BU)
MOS .... Mission Itinerante Ophtalmologique Saharienne (MAR)
MOS .... Mistni Osvetovy Sbor [*Local Cultural Council*] (CZ)
MOS .... Mobilni Operacni Sal [*Mobile Operations Van*] (CZ)
MOS .... Movimiento de Organizacion Socialista [*Socialist Organization Movement*] [*Mexican*] (LA)
MOSA.......... Moscow Branch of the Union of Architects, USSR (RU)
MOSA.......... Movimento de Solidariedade Africana (MAR)
MOSAL .... Mocambique Sobresselentes e Accesorios Limitada (MAR)
MOSAN....... Montaj ve Celik Imalat Ltd. Sti. [*Steel Manufacturing and Installation Corp.*] (TU)
MOSANII..... Moscow Branch of the Arctic Scientific Reseach Institute (RU)
Mosavtoremont ... Moscow City Trust of Automobile Repair Establishments (RU)
Mosavtotekhsnab ... Moscow City Trust of the Administration of Automobile Repair Plants and of Technical Supply of Automobile Transportation (RU)
Mosavtotrest ... Moscow Automobile Transportation Trust (RU)
Mosbass ..... Moscow Coal Basin (RU)
Mosdachtrest ... Moscow City Dacha Trust (RU)
Mosdolproyekt ... Moscow Oblast Planning Institute for Housing, Civil Engineering, and Municipal Construction (RU)
Moselektrik ... Moscow Electrotechnical Plant (RU)
Moselektromontazh ... Moscow State Electrical Installation Trust (RU)
Moselektrotrans ... Moscow Power Supply Trust of the City Electric Transportation System (RU)
Moselektrotransproyekt ... Moscow Planning Office of the Administration of Passenger Transportation (RU)
Mosenergo ... Moscow Regional Administration of Power System Management (RU)
Mosenergoproyekt ... Planning Office of the Mosenergo (RU)
Mosenergosnab ... Materials and Equipment Supply Office of the Mosenergo (RU)
Mosenergostroy ... Moscow Trust for the Construction and Installation of Thermal Electric Power Plants (RU)
Mosfil.......... Moscow State Philharmonic (RU)
Mosfilial...... Moscow Branch (RU)
MOSFIL'M... Moscow Motion-Picture Studio (RU)
Mosfinotdel ... Moscow Finance Department (RU)
Mosfundamentstroy ... Moscow State Trust for Foundation Construction (RU)
Mosgaz .... Trust of the Administration of the Gas Supply System of the Mosgorispolkom (RU)
Mosgazprovodstroy ... Moscow Trust for Gas Pipeline Construction (RU)
Mosgaztekhsnab ... Moscow City Trust of the Fuel and Power Supply System of the Mosgorispolkom (RU)
Mosgeo....... Moscow Geological Administration (RU)
Mosgeolnerud ... Moscow Geological Exploration Trust for Nonmetallic Minerals (RU)
Mosgiprobum ... Moscow Branch of the State Institute for the Planning of Establishments of the Pulp, Paper, and Hydrolysis Industry (RU)
Mosgipromash ... Moscow Branch of the State Institute for the Planning of Machinery Plants (RU)
Mosgiprotrans ... Moscow State Planning and Surveying Institute of the State Industrial Committee for Transportation Construction, USSR (RU)
Mosgoraptekoupravleniye ... Pharmaceutical Administration of the Mosgorispolkom (RU)
Mosgorarbitrazh ... Moscow City Arbitration Commission (RU)
Mosgorbank ... Moscow City Bank (RU)
Mosgorbytkommunsnab ... Moscow City Trust of the Administration of Personal and Municipal Services (RU)
Mosgorbytkommunstroy ... Construction and Installation Trust of the Administration of Personal and Municipal Services of the Mosgorispolkom (RU)
Mosgordets ... Moscow City Children's Excursion and Tourist Station (RU)
Mosgorekskursbyuro ... Moscow City Excursion Office (RU)
Mosgorelektroprom ... Moscow City Electrotechnical Industry Trust (RU)
Mosgorfinupravleniye ... Moscow City Finance Administration (RU)
Mosgorgeotrest ... Moscow City Trust for Geological, Geodetic, and Cartographic Work (RU)
Mosgorispolkom ... Executive Committee of the Moscow City Soviet of Workers' Deputies (RU)
Mosgorkinoprokat ... Moscow City Office for Motion-Picture Distribution (RU)
Mosgorkom ... Moscow City Committee (RU)
Mosgorkoopinsoyuz ... Moscow City Union of Disabled Persons' Cooperatives (RU)
Mosgorkozhobuv'prom ... Moscow City Trust of the Leather and Footwear Industry (RU)
Mosgorles... Moscow City Logging Trust (RU)
Mosgorleszag ... Moscow City Logging Trust (RU)
Mosgorlombard ... Administration of the Moscow City Pawnshop (RU)
Mosgormebel'prom ... Moscow City Trust of the Furniture Industry (RU)
Mosgormekhpogruz ... Mosgorispolkom Administration for the Mechanization of Loading and Unloading (RU)
Mosgormestprom ... Moscow City Local Industry Trust (RU)
Mosgormetalloprom ... Moscow City Trust of the Metals Industry (RU)
Mosgormetalloshirpotreb ... Moscow City Trust of the Consumers' Metalware Industry (RU)
Mosgormetrem ... Moscow City Trust for the Repair of Metalware, Watches, and Musical Instruments (RU)
Mosgorono ... Moscow City Department of Public Education (RU)
Mosgorotdelzags ... Department of the Civil Registry of the Mosgorispolkom (RU)
Mosgorplan ... Moscow City Planning Commission (RU)
Mosgorplastmass ... Moscow City Trust for the Manufacture of Plastic Consumers' Goods (RU)
Mosgorpogruz ... Moscow City Trust for Loading and Unloading (RU)
Mosgorpoligrafprom ... Moscow City Printing Trust (RU)
Mosgorpotrebsoyuz ... Moscow City Union of Consumers' Societies (RU)
Mosgorpromsnab ... Moscow City Trust for Industrial Supply (RU)
Mosgorpromsovet ... Council of Producers' Cooperatives of the City of Moscow (RU)
Mosgorshveyprom ... Moscow City Garment Industry Trust (RU)
Mosgorsobes ... Moscow City Department of Social Security (RU)
Mosgorsovet ... Moscow City Soviet of Workers' Deputies (RU)
Mosgorsovnarkhoz ... Council of the National Economy of the Moscow City Economic Region (RU)
Mosgorsovnarkhozstroy ... Construction and Installation Trust of the Mosgorsovnarkhoz (RU)
Mosgorspravka ... Moscow City Reference and Information Office (RU)
Mosgorstrakh ... Moscow City Administration of the Gosstrakh (RU)
Mosgorstromtrest ... Moscow City Building Materials Trust (RU)
Mosgorstroymontazh ... Moscow City Construction and Installation Trust (RU)
Mosgorsud ... Moscow City Court (RU)
Mosgorsvet ... Electric Power Supply Establishment for the Street Lighting of the City of Moscow (RU)
Mosgortekstil'prom ... Moscow City Textile Industry Trust (RU)
Mosgorteplo ... Moscow City Heat Engineering Office (RU)
Mosgortopsnab ... Moscow City Trust for Fuel Supply (RU)
Mosgortorgotdel ... Trade Department of the Ispolkom of the Mosgorsovet (RU)
Mosgortransproyekt ... Moscow Planning Office for Engineering, Industrial, and Electrotechnical Structures for City Transportation (RU)

Mosgortransstroy ... Construction Trust of the Administration of Passenger Transportation of the Mosgorispolkom (RU)
Mosgorvneshtek ... Moscow City Transportation and Forwarding Office for Out-of-Town Shipments (RU)
Mosgorvtek ... Moscow City Medical Commission for Determination of Disability (RU)
Mosgorzags ... Moscow City Department of the Civil Registry (RU)
Mosgorzdravotdel ... Moscow City Department of Public Health (RU)
Mosgosstrakh ... State Insurance Administration in the City of Moscow (RU)
MOSI .... Economic Data Machine Processing (BU)
MOSICP ...... Movimiento Sindical Cristiano del Peru [*Christian Labor Movement of Peru*] (LA)
Mosinodezhda ... Trust for Custom-Tailoring (RU)
Mosinzhproyekt ... Moscow Institute for the Planning of Engineering Installations (RU)
MOs i SW .... Ministerstwo Oswiaty i Szkolnictwa Wyzszego [*Ministry of Education and Schools of Academic Rank*] [*Polish*]
MOSK .... Moderna Socijalna Kronika [*Modern Social Chronicle*] [*Zagreb*] [*World War II*] [*A publication*] (YU)
Mosk .... Moscow (RU)
MOSK .... Moscow Railroad (RU)
Moskabel' ... Moscow Cable Plant (RU)
MOSKh .... Moscow Agricultural Society (RU)
MOSKh .... Moscow Branch of the Union of Artists of the RSFSR (RU)
Moskhimtrest ... Moscow State Chemical Trust (RU)
Moskhlebtorg ... Moscow State Organization for the Baked Goods and Confectionery Retail Trade (RU)
MOSKhOS ... Moscow Oblast Agricultural Experimental Station (RU)
Moskhoztorg ... Moscow City Trade Organization for Household Goods and Building Materials (RU)
Moskinap .... Moscow Motion-Picture Equipment Plant (RU)
Moskip .... Moscow Control and Measuring Instruments Plant (RU)
MOSKIYeV ... Moscow-Kiev Railroad (RU)
Moskniga .... Moscow City Book Trade Office (RU)
Mosknigotorg ... Moscow Oblast Book Trade Office (RU)
MOSKOMONES ... Moscow Commission for Cases Concerning Minors (RU)
Moskovstroy ... Moscow Trust for the Capital Construction of Water Supply and Sewer System Installations (RU)
Moskozh ..... Moscow Association of Leather Industry Establishments (RU)
Moskprofobr ... Moscow Subdivision of Vocational and Technical Education (RU)
Moskul'ttorg ... Moscow Organization for Trade in Goods for Cultural Purposes (RU)
Moskvugol' ... State Association of the Coal Industry of the Moscow Region Basin (RU)
Mosmashpriborstroy ... Moscow Construction Trust of the Glavstroy of the Ministry of Machinery Manufacture and Instrument Making, USSR (RU)
Mosmetroves ... Moscow Precision Scales and Measuring Instruments Plant (RU)
MosMGS ..... Moscow Interdepartmental Geodetic Council (RU)
Mosmoloko ... Moscow Milk and Dairy Products Trade Organization (RU)
Mosmolzhivtrest ... Moscow Trust of Dairy and Livestock Breeding Sovkhozes (RU)
Mosmoststroy ... Moscow Trust for Railroad Bridge Construction (RU)
Mosmuzradio ... Moscow Plant for Guaranteed Repairing of Radio Equipment and Renting and Repairing of Musical Keyboard Instruments (RU)
MOSNAV ..... Moscow Lifesaving Society (RU)
Mosneftekip ... Moscow Control and Measuring Instruments Plant for the Petroleum Industry (RU)
Mosnezhilotdel ... Department of Nonresidential Buildings of the Mosgorsovet (RU)
MOSNKh ..... Moscow Oblast Council of the National Economy (RU)
MOSO .... Moscow Department of Social Security (RU)
Mosoblarbitrazh ... State Arbitration Commission at the Moscow Oblast Executive Committee (RU)
Mosoblarkhivbyuro ... Moscow Oblast Archives Office (RU)
Mosoblavtotek ... Moscow Oblast Automobile Transportation and Forwarding Office (RU)
Mosobldorotdel ... Moscow Oblast Road Department (RU)
Mosobldorstroy ... Moscow Oblast Road and Bridge Construction Trust (RU)
Mosoblelektro ... Moscow Oblast Administration of Electric Power Plants and Networks (RU)
Mosoblelektro ... Moscow Oblast Administration of Power System Operation (RU)
Mosoblfinotdel ... Moscow Oblast Finance Department (RU)
Mosoblgorlit ... Administration of Literature and Publishing Houses of the City of Moscow and Moscow Oblast (RU)
Mosoblgosstrakh ... Administration of State Insurance in Moscow Oblast (RU)
Mosoblispolkom ... Executive Committee of the Moscow Oblast Soviet of Workers' Deputies (RU)
Mosoblkniga ... Moscow Oblast Book Trade Office (RU)
Mosoblmestpromsnab ... Moscow Oblast Trust for Materials and Equipment Supply of the Moscow Oblast Administration of Local Industry (RU)
Mosoblono ... Moscow Oblast Department of Public Education (RU)
Mosoblpishcheprom ... Administration of the Food Industry of the Mosoblispolkom (RU)
Mosoblplan ... Moscow Oblast Planning Commission (RU)
Mosoblpromsovet ... Council of Producers' Cooperatives of Moscow Oblast (RU)
Mosoblsovet ... Moscow Oblast Soviet of Workers' Deputies (RU)
Mosoblsovnarkhoz ... Council of the National Economy of the Moscow Oblast Economic Administrative Region (RU)
Mosoblsovprof ... Moscow Oblast Council of Trade Unions (RU)
Mosoblspetsstroy ... Specialized Trust of the Construction Administration of the Mosoblispolkom (RU)
Mosoblspravka ... Moscow Oblast Reference and Information Office (RU)
Mosoblspravkontora ... Moscow Oblast Reference and Information Office (RU)
Mosoblstatupravleniye ... Moscow Oblast Statistical Administration (RU)
Mosoblstroy ... Moscow Oblast Construction Trust (RU)
Mosoblstroymontazh ... Moscow Oblast Construction and Installation Trust (RU)
MosoblstroyTsNIL ... Central Scientific Research Laboratory for Construction of the Glavmosoblstroy (RU)
Mosobltekstil'prom ... Moscow Oblast Textile Trust (RU)
Mosobltop ... Administration of the Fuel Industry and Local Building Materials of the Mosoblispolkom (RU)
Mosoblvodokanal ... Moscow Oblast Water Supply and Sewer System Trust (RU)
Mosoblzags ... Moscow Oblast Department of the Civil Registry (RU)
Mosoblzdravotdel ... Moscow Oblast Department of Public Health (RU)
Mosoblzhilprom ... Moscow Oblast Trust for Materials and Equipment Supply of the Housing Administration of the Mosoblispolkom (RU)
Mosoblzhilupravleniye ... Moscow Oblast Housing Administration (RU)
Mosobshchepitstroy ... Trust of the Main Administration of Public Eating Facilities of the Mosgorispolkom (RU)
Mosochistvod ... Moscow Trust for Sewage Purification (RU)
MOSOKR .... Moscow Belt Railroad (RU)
Mosotdelstroy ... Moscow City Trust of the Administration of Finishing Work of the Glavmosstroy (RU)
MOSP .... Moscow Branch of the Union of Writers (RU)
MOSPB .... Ministry of Public Construction, Roads, and Public Works (BU)
Mosplastkozh ... Moscow Imitation Leather Plant (RU)
Mosplastmass ... Moscow Scientific Research Institute of Plastics (RU)
MOSPNI ...... Moscow State Institute of Neuropsychology (RU)
MOSPO .... Moscow Oblast Union of Consumers' Societies (RU)
Mospochtamt ... Moscow Post Office (RU)
Mospodzemproyekt ... Moscow Planning Institute of the Administration of the Mospodzemstroy (RU)
Mospodzemstroy ... Moscow State Trust for the Construction of Underground Structures (RU)
Mospodzemstroysnab ... Moscow City Trust for Materials and Equipment Supply of the Administration for the Construction of Underground Structures (RU)
Mospoligraf ... Moscow State Association of Printing Industry Establishments (RU)
Mospor .... Movement for the Struggle for Political Rights [*Ugandan*] (PD)
Mosprodsnab ... Moscow Office of Food Supply (RU)
Mosprodstroy ... Construction and Installation Trust of the Second Main Construction Administration of the Ministry of the Foodstuffs Industry, USSR (RU)
Mospromproyekt ... Moscow Institute of Industrial Planning (RU)
Mospromtrans ... Administration for the Servicing of Industrial Establishments of the Glavmosavtotrans (RU)
Mosproyekt ... Administration for the Planning of Housing, Civil Engineering, and Municipal Construction of the Mosgorispolkom (RU)
Mosproyekt ... Institute for the Planning of Housing and Civil Engineering Construction in the City of Moscow (RU)
MOSPS .... Moscow Oblast Council of Trade Unions (RU)
MOSPTTaR ... Mezinarodni Odborove Sdruzeni Zamestnancu Post, Telefonu, Telegrafu, a Rozhlasu [*International Federation of Trade Unions of Postal, Telephone, Telegraph, and Radio Employees*] (CZ)
Mosrechtek ... Moscow River Transportation and Forwarding Office (RU)
Mosremchas ... Moscow Watch Repair Plant (RU)
Mosremelektrobytpribor ... Moscow Plant for the Repair of Electrical Household Appliances (RU)
Mosremstanok ... Industrial and Technical Establishment for the Repair of Metal-Cutting Equipment of the Administration of Machinery Manufacture of the Mosgorsovnarkhoz (RU)
Mosrestorantrest ... Moscow Trust of Model Restaurants (RU)
MOSRYaZ ... Moscow-Ryazan' Railroad (RU)
Mosrybtrest ... Moscow Oblast Fish Industry Trust (RU)
MOSRYBVTUZ ... Moscow Technical Institute of the Fish Industry and Fisheries (RU)
Mossangaltrikotazh ... Moscow Factory for the Manufacture of Sanitary Notions and the Repair of Knit Goods (RU)
Mossannelektroprom ... Trust of the Administration of Installation, Electrical Installation, and Sanitary Engineering of the Glavmosstroy (RU)
Mossantekhstroy ... Moscow State Sanitary Engineering Trust of the Glavmosstroy (RU)
Mossel'elektro ... Moscow Oblast Trust of the Glavsel'elektro (RU)
Mossel'energo ... Moscow Oblast Office for the Operation of Rural Electric Power Installations (RU)
Mossel'khozaeros"yemka ... Moscow Office of Aerogeodetic Establishments of the Ministry of Agriculture, USSR (RU)

Mossel'khozpromstroy ... Moscow Construction and Installation Trust of the Moscow Oblast Administration of Agriculture (RU)
Mossel'mash ... Moscow Agricultural Machinery Plant (RU)
Mossel'prom ... Moscow Association of Establishments for Processing Products of the Agricultural Industry (RU)
Mossel'proyekt ... Design and Planning Office of the Administration of Planning Organizations of the Ministry of Urban and Rural Construction, RSFSR (RU)
Mossel'vodstroy ... Moscow Construction and Installation Office of Rural Water Management Projects (RU)
Mosshakhtostroy ... Trust for the Construction of Mine Installations in the Moscow Region Coal Basin (RU)
Mosshampanzavod ... Moscow Champagne Plant (RU)
MOSSKh..... Moscow Branch of the Union of Soviet Artists (RU)
Mosskuppromtorg ... Moscow City State Organization for Buying and Selling on Commission (RU)
Mossnabsbytkino ... Moscow Oblast Office for the Supply and Marketing of Motion-Picture Goods (RU)
Mossovet.... Moscow City Soviet of Workers' Deputies (RU)
MOSSP .... Moscow Branch of the Union of Soviet Writers (RU)
Mosspirtotrest ... Moscow Alcohol Trust (RU)
Mossredprom ... Moscow State Trust of Medium and Small Industries (RU)
Mosstankin ... Moscow Institute of Machine Tools and Tools (RU)
Mosstroy..... Moscow State Construction and Installation Trust (RU)
Mosstroykanalizatsiya ... Moscow Construction Trust for Sewer System Facilities (RU)
Mosstroymekhanizatsiya ... Moscow Trust for Mechanized Construction (RU)
Mosstroytop ... Construction Office of the Administration of the Fuel Industry of the Mosoblispolkom (RU)
Mosstroytrans ... Administration for Centralized Transportation of Construction Freight of the Glavmosavtotrans (RU)
Mossvetstroy ... Specialized Construction and Installation Administration for the Installation of Moscow City Street Lighting (RU)
most............ Bridge Crossing [*Topography*] (RU)
MOST.......... Militaeroberstaatsanwalt [*Military Senior Prosecutor*] (EG)
Mostara....... Moscow Trust for the Manufacture and Marketing of Packing Materials (RU)
mostb.......... Bridge Battalion (BU)
mostb.......... Bridge Battalion (RU)
mostbr........ Bridge Brigade (BU)
Mostekhfil'm ... Moscow Studio of Technical Films (RU)
Mostekhtorgsnab ... Materials and Equipment Supply Office of the Main Administration of Trade of the Ispolkom of the Moscow City Soviet of Workers' Deputies (RU)
Mostekstil' ... Moscow Oblast Textile Trust (RU)
Mostekstil'torg ... Moscow Specialized Trade Office for Textile Goods (RU)
Mostelefonstroy ... Moscow State Trust for the Construction of Telephone Structures (RU)
Mosteploset'stroy ... Construction and Installation Administration of the Mosenergostroy Trust (RU)
MOSTEU..... Moscow Tourist and Excursion Administration (RU)
MOSTiW...... Miejski Osrodek Sportu, Turystyki, i Wypoczynku [*City Sports, Touring, and Rest Center*] (POL)
Mostoremtonnel' ... All-Union Trust for the Reconstruction and Capital Repair of Bridges and Tunnels (RU)
Mostorg ...... Moscow City Department Store Trade Organization (RU)
Mostorg ...... Moscow Oblast Trust for Wholesale and Retail Trade (RU)
Mostorgin ... Moscow Disabled Persons' Trade and Producers' Cooperative Association (RU)
Mostorgsnab ... Materials and Equipment Supply Office of the Department of Trade of the Ispolkom of the Moscow City Soviet of Workers' Deputies (RU)
Mostorgstroy ... Construction and Installation Trust of the Main Administration of Trade of the Ispolkom of the Moscow City Soviet of Workers' Deputies (RU)
Mostorgtrans ... Administration of Commercial Transportation of the Main Administration of Trade of the Ispolkom of the Moscow City Soviet of Workers' Deputies (RU)
Mostostal.... Panstwowe Przedsiebiorstwo Budowy Mostow i Konstrukcji Stalowych [*State Enterprise for Bridge Building and Steel Constructions*] (POL)
Mostostroy ... Rayon Administration for Bridge Construction (RU)
Mostostroyprom ... All-Union Trust of Industrial and Construction Establishments of the Glavmostostroy (RU)
Mostotrest ... All-Union Trust for the Construction of Large and Supersize Bridges (RU)
Mostransstroy ... Moscow Construction and Installation Trust of Transportation Construction (RU)
mostsb........ Bridge-Building Battalion (BU)
mostsr......... Bridge-Building Company (BU)
Mostsvettorg ... Moscow Flower and Seedling Wholesale and Retail Trade Organization (RU)
Mosugol'..... Oblast Administration of the Moscow Region Coal Basin (RU)
MOSUKTEK ... Moscow Administration of Container Shipments and Transportation and Forwarding Operations (RU)
MOSV.......... Mednarodna Organizacija za Socialno Varstvo [*International Social Security Association*] (YU)
MOSVIPE.... Mikti Omas Stratiotikis Voitheias Inomenon Politeion en Elladi [*Joint US Military Assistance Unit in Greece*] (GC)
Mosvodokanalproyekt ... Institute for the Planning of Water Supply and Sewer System Installations of the Mosgorispolkom (RU)
Mosvodokanalsnab ... Moscow Water Supply Trust of the Water Supply and Sewer System Administration of the Mosgorispolkom (RU)
Mosvodoprovod ... Moscow Water Supply Trust of the Administration of Water Supply and Sewer Systems of the Mosgorispolkom (RU)
Mosvodstroy ... Moscow Water Management Construction Trust (RU)
Mosvuzstroy ... Moscow State All-Union Construction Trust of the Glavstroy of the Ministry of Higher Education, USSR (RU)
MOSYuN..... Moscow Oblast Station for Young Naturalists (RU)
MOSYuT ..... Moscow Oblast Station for Young Technicians (RU)
MOSZ.......... Magyar Orszagos Szabvany [*Hungarian National Standards*] (HU)
MOSZ.......... Magyar Orvos Szovetseg [*Hungarian Medical Association*] (HU)
Moszagotstroy ... Moscow Specialized Construction and Installation Trust of the Glavzagotstroy (RU)
Moszdravotdel ... Moscow Department of Public Health (RU)
Moszelenstroy ... Moscow State Landscaping Trust (RU)
Moszhilgoststroy ... Moscow Housing and Hotel Construction Trust (RU)
Moszhilotdel ... Moscow Housing Department (RU)
Moszhilproyekt ... Institute for the Planning of Major Housing Repair in the City of Moscow (RU)
Moszhilremsnab ... Office of the Administration of Major Housing Repair of the Mosgorispolkom (RU)
Moszhilspetsstroy ... Moscow Trust for Plastering and Other Special Finishing Operations (RU)
Moszhilstroy ... Moscow Housing Construction Trust (RU)
Moszhilupravleniye ... Moscow City Housing Administration (RU)
Moszhivotnovodles ... Republic Office of the Administration for the Procurement of Building Materials and Structural Parts of the Ministry of Sovkhozes, RSFSR (RU)
MOSZK .... Magyar Orszagos Szovetkezeti Kozpont [*National Center of Hungarian Cooperatives*] (HU)
MOSZSZ..... Magyar Orvosok Szabad Szakszervezete [*Free Trade Union of Hungarian Physicians*] (HU)
MOT .... International Labor Organization (BU)
MOT .... International Labor Organization [*ILO*] (RU)
MOT .... Magyar Orszagos Tudosito Reszvenytarsasag [*Hungarian National News Agency Limited (Prewar)*] (HU)
mot............. Motorized (RU)
Mot............. Motorlu [*Motorized*] (TU)
MOT .... Movimiento Obrero Tradicionalista [*Traditionalist Labor Movement*] [*Spanish*] (WER)
MOTAS .... Motorlu Araclar ve Aksamlari Subesi [*Motorized Vehicles and Parts Branch*] [*A subsidiary of ETI in the TFSC*] [*Turkish Cypriot*] (TU)
motd........... Mortar Section (RU)
MOTESZ..... Magyar Orszagos Torna Szovetseg [*Hungarian National Gymnastics Association*] (HU)
MOTESZ ..... Magyar Orvostudomanyi Tarsasagok es Egyesuletek Szovetsege [*Federation of Hungarian Medical Science Societies and Associations*] (HU)
MOTEZ........ Moscow Transformer and Electric Motor Plant (RU)
MOTF .... Milletlerarasi Ogrenci Teskilatlari Federasyonu [*Federation of International Student Organizations*] (TU)
MOTH.......... Memorable Order of Tin Hats [*South African*] (AF)
MOTI .... Magyar Orszagos Tervezesi Iranyelvek [*Hungarian National Planning Guidelines*] (HU)
MOTI .... Moscow Oblast Institute of Tuberculosis (RU)
MOTIM .... Magyarovar Timfold es Mukorundgyar [*Magyarovar Alumina and Alundum Factory*] (HU)
MOTO.......... Monatstonnen(metric) [*Metric Tons per Month*] [*German*]
MOTOCARSA ... Motores y Carrocerias de Colombia, Sociedad Anonima [*Bogota*] (COL)
MOTOCOLDA ... Motos de Colombia Ltda. [*Bogota*] (COL)
MOTOKOV ... Podnik Zahranicniho Obchodu pro Dovoz a Vyvoz Vozidel a Vyrobku Lehkeho Prumyslu [*Foreign Trade Enterprise for the Import and Export of Vehicles and Products of the Light Industry*] (CZ)
MOTOPAR ... Motor Parcalari Imalati, Ticaret, ve Sanayi AS [*Motor Parts Manufacture, Trade, and Industry Corp.*] (TU)
MOTORAGRI ... Societe pour le Developpement de la Motorisation de l'Agriculture [*Company for the Development and Mechanization of Agriculture*] [*Ivorian*] (AF)
MOTORCOL ... Distribuidora de Automotores Colombianos Ltda. [*Bogota*] (COL)
MOTOREP... Motores y Repuestos Ltda. [*Bogota*] (COL)
motorkm..... Motorovy Kilometr [*Motor-Kilometer*] [*Kilometer run by a motor-driven rail vehicle*] (CZ)
MOTORLET ... Tovarna na Motory a Letadla [*Automobile and Aircraft Factory*] [*Janonice*] (CZ)
MOTOTECHNA ... Narodni Podnik pro Prodej Jizdnich Kol a Motocyklu [*National Enterprise for the Retail Sale of Bicycles and Motorcycles*] (CZ)
MOTOVALLE ... Motores del Valle [*Cali*] (COL)
MOTsKTI..... Moscow Branch of the Central Scientific Research, Planning, and Design Boiler and Turbine Institute Imeni I. I. Polzunov (RU)

MOTsNIIRF ... Moscow Branch of the Central Scientific Research Institute of the River Fleet (RU)
mott rass .... Mott Scattering (RU)
MOTZK .... Moscow Association of Theater and Show Ticket Offices (RU)
MOU .... Metal-Oxide Ultrahigh-Frequency (Resistor) (RU)
MOU .... Movimiento Obrero Unido [*United Worker Movement*] [*Puerto Rican*] (LA)
MOULIAF .... Mouvement de Liberation Africaine [*African Liberation Movement*] (AF)
MOULP .... Moscow Oblast Administration of Light Industry (RU)
MOUMS ...... Moscow Oblast Administration of the Ministry of Communications, USSR (RU)
MOUR .... Moscow Department of Criminal Investigation (RU)
MOURP .... Moskva-Oka River Steamship Line Administration (RU)
MOUS .... Moscow Oblast Administration of Sovkhozes (RU)
MOUSKh ..... Moscow Oblast Administration of Agriculture (RU)
MOUVKh ..... Moscow Oblast Administration of Water Management (RU)
MOV .... Mezinarodni Olympijsky Vybor [*International Olympics Committee*] (CZ)
MOV .... Reflected Wave Method (RU)
MOVAGO .... Moscow Branch of the All-Union Astronomical and Geodetic Society (RU)
MOVANO .... Moscow Branch of the All-Union Scientific Architectural Society (RU)
MOVE .... Motosyklistikos Omilos Voreiou Ellados [*Motorcyclists Club of Northern Greece*] (GC)
MOVICAR ... Movilizadora de Cargamentos Ltda. [*Medellin*] (COL)
MOVIU .... Moscow District Military Engineering Directorate (RU)
MOVLEK ..... Moscow Oblast Visiting Medical and Epidemiological Consultation (RU)
MOVNIIGS ... Moscow Branch of the All-Union Scientific Research Institute of the Hydrolysis and Sulfite Liquor Industry (RU)
MOVOPC .... Mouvement de la Voix du Peuple Congolais (MAR)
MOVSU .... Moscow District Military Medical Directorate (RU)
Movzadt ...... Moscow Branch of the All-Union Correspondence Highway Technicum (RU)
mow .... Mehr oder Weniger [*More or Less*] [*Commodities*] [*German*]
MOW .... Ministry of Works (MAR)
MOZ .... Miedzyzakladowa Organizacja Zwiazkowa [*Inter-Factory Labor Union Organization*] (POL)
MOZ .... Miejscowa Organizacja Zwiazkowa [*Local Labor Union Organization*] (POL)
MOZ .... Mozambique [*Three-letter standard code*] (CNC)
MOZGOC .... Mozambique Gulf Oil Company (MAR)
MOZh .... International Organization of Journalists (BU)
MOZh .... International Organization of Journalists [*IOJ*] (RU)
Mozherez .... Moscow Railroad Repair Plant (RU)
MOZM .... International Organization for Legal Metrology (RU)
MOZO .... Moscow Land Department (RU)
MOZU .... Magnetic Internal Storage (RU)
MOZU .... Moscow Oblast Land Administration (RU)
MP .... Bridge Train (RU)
MP .... Council of Ministers Decree (BU)
MP .... Crossing Point [*Topography*] (RU)
MP .... Dead Space, Dead Ground [*Artillery*] (RU)
MP- .... Engine Drive (RU)
MP .... Feed Mechanism [*Automation*] (RU)
mp .... Local Production (BU)
MP .... Machine Translation, Mechanical Translation (RU)
MP .... Magnetic Bearing (RU)
MP .... Magnetic Belt [*Weld inspection device*] (RU)
MP .... Magnetic Field (RU)
MP .... Magnetic Starter (RU)
MP .... Magyar Posztogyar [*Hungarian Textile Factory*] (HU)
mp .... Mainittu Paikka [*Finnish*]
MP .... [*Remise en*] Mains Propres [*Personal*] (CL)
MP .... Malayan Party (ML)
mp .... Male Sex [*Statistics*] (RU)
MP .... Martens-Pensky Instrument [*For flash-point testing*] [*Pet.*] (RU)
mp .... Masodperc [*Second*] (HU)
MP .... Maximum Absorption (RU)
mp .... Mechanized Regiment (BU)
MP .... Medical Station (RU)
Mp .... Megapond [*Megapond*] [*1,000 kilograms of thrust*] (EG)
MP .... Megapond [*Megapond*] [*1,000 kilograms of thrust*] (HU)
MP .... Member of Parliament (MAR)
MP .... Mesi Piesis [*Intermediate Pressure, Mean Pressure*] (GC)
MP .... Mesto Pecata [*Place for Seal (Documents)*] (YU)
mp .... Metru Patrat [*Square Meter*] (RO)
MP .... Microswitch (RU)
mp .... Miespuolinen [*Finnish*]
MP .... Militaerpolizei [*Military Police*] (EG)
MP .... Millet Partisi [*Nation Party*] (TU)
MP .... Milli Partisi [*National Party*] [*Cypriot*] (TU)
MP .... Minefield (RU)
MP .... Ministarstvo Prosvete [*Ministry of Education*] (YU)
MP .... Ministerstvo Paliv [*Ministry of Fuels*] (CZ)
MP .... Ministerstvo Prumyslu [*Ministry of Industry*] (CZ)
MP .... Ministry of Education (RU)
MP .... Ministry of Industry [*Obsolete*] (BU)
MP .... Ministry of Justice (BU)
MP .... Mizarsko Podjetje [*Cabinetmakers' Establishment*] (YU)
MP .... Mlinsko Preduzece [*Military*] (YU)
MP .... Mobilization Plan (RU)
MP .... Monitor Polski [*Polish Monitor*] [*Law journal*] [*A publication*] (POL)
MP .... Mortar Regiment (RU)
mp .... Mortar Unit (RU)
M-P .... Moscow-Petrograd [*Bibliography*] (RU)
m/p .... Motor Sailer (RU)
MP .... Motorized Infantry (RU)
MP .... Motorized Regiment (RU)
MP .... Mouvement Populaire [*North African*] (MAR)
MP .... Movable Coupling (RU)
MP .... Place for Seal (RU)
MP .... Plastic Fuze for a Mine (RU)
MP .... Polarizing Microscope (RU)
MP .... Run Magnet (RU)
MP .... Small-Caliber Pistol, Small-Bore Pistol (RU)
MP .... Vertical Magnet (RU)
MP .... Weather Post, Meteorological Post (RU)
MPA .... Beef-Extract Agar (RU)
MPA .... Magasins Populaires d'Arrondissement [*District People's Warehouses*] [*Guinean*] (AF)
MPA .... Manevarska Protivavionska Artiljerija [*Maneuver Antiaircraft Artillery*] (YU)
MPA .... Manicaland Provincial Authority (MAR)
MPA .... Mercaptopropylamine (RU)
MPA .... Miejskie Przedsiebiorstwo Autobusowe [*Municipal Bus Service Enterprise*] (POL)
MPA .... Mission Presbyterienne Americaine (MAR)
MPA .... Mouvement Panafricain Anticommuniste [*Pan-African Anti-Communist Movement*] (AF)
MPA .... Mouvement Populaire Africain [*African People's Movement*] [*Upper Voltan*] (AF)
MPA .... Movimiento Popular Argentino [*Argentine People's Movement*] (LA)
MPAA .... Marasleios Paidagogiki Akadimia Athinon [*Marasleios Pedagogical Academy of Athens*] (GC)
MPAA .... Mornaricka Protivavionska Artiljerija [*Navy Antiaircraft Artillery*] (YU)
MPAA .... Movimento Popular Africano de Angola (MAR)
MPAC .... Movimento do Povo Anticolonista [*People's Anticolonial Movement*] [*Portuguese*] (WER)
MPAF .... Malaysian People's Action Front (ML)
MPAIAC ...... Movimiento para la Autodeterminacion y Independencia del Archipielago Canario [*Movement for the Self-Determination and Independence of the Canary Archipelago*] [*Canary Islands*] [*Spanish*] (PD)
MPAJ .... Mouvement Panafricaine de la Jeunesse (MAR)
MPAJA .... Malayan People's Anti-Japanese Army (ML)
MPAJU .... Malayan People's Anti-Japanese Union (ML)
MPAM .... Missao de Pedologia de Angola e Mocambique, Junta de Investigacoes do Ultramar (MAR)
MPAS .... Ministerio da Previdencia e Assistencia Social [*Ministry of Welfare and Social Security*] [*Brazilian*] (LA)
MPB .... Beef-Extract Broth (RU)
MPB .... Machine Rental Base (RU)
MPB .... Majlis Penimbangan Bersama [*Joint Consultative Council*] (ML)
mpb .... Motorized Infantry Battalion (BU)
MPB .... Mouvement Progressiste du Burundi (MAR)
MPB .... Turret Traversing Mechanism (RU)
mpbr .... Motorized Infantry Brigade (RU)
MPC .... Certificat de Mathematiques, Physique, et Chimie [*French*]
MPC .... Maharashtra Prajatantra Congress [*Indian*] (PPW)
MPC .... Maharashtra Progressive Congress [*Indian*] (PPW)
MPC .... Maison du Pneu et du Caoutchouc (MAR)
MPC .... Makedonska Pravoslavna Crkva [*Macedonian Orthodox Church*] (YU)
MPC .... Metales Preciosos Colombianos [*Bogota*] (COL)
MPC .... Ministerstwo Przemyslu Chemicznego [*Ministry of the Chemical Industry*] (POL)
MPC .... Ministerstwo Przemyslu Ciezkiego [*Ministry of Heavy Industry*] (POL)
MPC .... Mosul Petroleum Company (ME)
MPC .... Mouvement Progressive Congolais (MAR)
MPC .... Movimiento Popular Cristiano [*Popular Christian Movement*] [*Bolivian*] (LA)
MPCA .... Manpower Citizens Association [*Guyanese*] (LA)
MPCD .... Mouvement Populaire Constitutionnel Democratique [*Popular Democratic Constitutional Movement*] [*Moroccan*] (PPW)
MPCh .... Maximum Usable Frequency (RU)
MPCh .... Ministerstwo Przemyslu Chemicznego [*Ministry of the Chemical Industry*] (POL)
MPD .... Drill Feed Mechanism [*Pet.*] (RU)
MPD .... Magneto-Plasmadynamic (RU)
mpd .... Motorized Infantry Division (RU)
MPD .... Movimiento Popular Democratico [*Democratic People's Movement*] [*Salvadoran*] (LA1)

MPD .... Movimiento Popular Dominicano [*Dominican Popular Movement*] [*Dominican Republic*] (PPW)
MPD .... Portable Polarizing Microscope (RU)
MPDC........... Mouvement Populaire Democratique et Constitutionnel (MAR)
MPDiP.......... Ministerstwo Przemyslu Drzewnego i Papierniczego [*Ministry of the Lumber and Paper Industry*] (POL)
MPDiRz........ Ministerstwo Przemyslu Drobnego i Rzemiosla [*Ministry of Small Scale and Handicraft Industry*] (POL)
MPDL........... Malayan People's Democratic League (ML)
MPDU........... Malian People's Democratic Union (MAR)
MPE............. Ministerstvo Paliv a Energetiky [*Ministry of Fuel and Power*] (CZ)
MPEA........... Mouvement Populaire d'Evolution Africaine (MAR)
MPEC........... Miejskie Przedsiebiorstwo Energetyki Cieplnej [*Municipal Thermoelectric Power Enterprise*] (POL)
m pech'....... Open-Hearth Furnace (RU)
MPE-HSE.... Ministerstvo Paliv a Energetiky - Hlavni Sprava Elektraren [*Chief Administration of Electric Power Stations of the Ministry of Fuel and Power*] (CZ)
MPEI............ Moscow Institute of Industry and Economics (RU)
MPF............. International Industrial Federation (RU)
MPF............. Malayan Patriotic Front (ML)
MPF............. Marematlou Freedom Party [*Basotho*] (AF)
MPF............. Ministerio Publico Federal [*Federal Public Ministry*] [*Mexican*] (LA)
MPF............. Ministerium fuer Post und Fernmeldewesen [*Ministry for Postal Affairs and Telecommunications*] (EG)
MPF............. Moscow Printing Plant (of the Goznak) (RU)
MPFF........... Malay Police Field Force (ML)
MPFS........... Magnetic Periodic Focusing System (RU)
MPG............. International Polar Year (RU)
MPG............. Max Planck Gesellschaft zur Foerderung der Wissenschaft Eingetragener Verein [*Max Planck Society for the Promotion of Science*] [*West German*] (WEN)
MPG............. Maximum Backwater Level (RU)
MPG............. Milice Populaire Guineenne [*Guinean People's Militia*] (AF)
MPG............. Piston Depth Gauge (RU)
MPGA........... Beef-Extract Glucose Agar (RU)
MPGI........... Mouvement Populaire pour la Guadeloupe Independante [*Popular Movement for Independent Guadeloupe*] (PD)
MPGK........... Miejskie Przedsiebiorstwa Gospodarki Komunalnej [*Municipal Enterprises of Communal Economy*] (POL)
MPGP........... Mutuelle du Personnel de la Garde Provinciale [*Mutual Association of Provincial Guard Personnel*] [*Cambodian*] (CL)
MPGR........... Ministerstwo Panstwowych Gospodarstw Rolnych [*Ministry of State Farms*] (POL)
MPH............. Ministerstwo Przemyslu i Handlu [*Ministry of Industry and Trade*] (POL)
MPHV........... Manufacture des Plastiques de Haute-Volta (MAR)
MPI.............. International Patent Institute (RU)
MPI.............. Magyar Pamutipar [*Hungarian Cotton Enterprise*] (HU)
MPI.............. Matieres Premieres d'Importation [*Imported Raw Materials*] (CL)
MPI.............. Miejskie Przedsiebiorstwo Instalacji [*Municipal Installations Enterprise*] (POL)
MPI.............. Moscow Pedagogical Institute (RU)
MPI.............. Moscow Printing Institute (RU)
MPI.............. Movimiento Pro-Independencia de Puerto Rico [*Pro-Independence Movement of Puerto Rico*] (LA)
MPIA............ Miejskie Przedsiebiorstwo Imprez Artystycznych [*Municipal Show Business*] [*Polish*]
MPIA............ Movimento para a Independencia de Angola (MAR)
MPIEA.......... Malayan Planting Industry Employers Association (ML)
MPIGE.......... Movimiento Pro-Independencia de Guinea Ecuatorial (MAR)
MPIGM......... Milli Piyango Idaresi Genel Mudurlugu [*National Lottery Administration Directorate General*] (TU)
MPiH............ Ministerstwo Przemyslu i Handlu [*Ministry of Industry and Trade*] (POL)
MPII............. Magyar Parttorteneti Intezet Irattara [*Archives of the Hungarian Institute for Party History*] (HU)
MPIIYa......... Moscow Pedagogical Institute of Foreign Languages (RU)
MPiK............ Miedzynarodowa Prasa i Ksiazka [*International Press and Book Club*] (POL)
MPIKRIMA... Mpianatra Kristiana Malagasy [*Malagasy Christian Students*] (AF)
MPiOS......... Ministerstwo Pracy i Opieki Spolecznej [*Ministry of Labor and Social Welfare*] (POL)
MP i PL........ Machine Translation and Applied Linguistics [*Bibliography*] (RU)
MPiSA......... Ministry of Instrument Making and Means of Automation, USSR (RU)
MPiT............ Ministerstwo Poczt i Telegrafow [*Ministry of Posts and Telegraphs*] (POL)
MPJ............. Mouvement Panafricain de la Jeunesse [*Pan-African Youth Movement*] [*Use PAYM*] (AF)
MPJ............. Movimiento Popular Justicialista [*Popular Justicialist Movement*] [*Venezuelan*] (LA)
MPK............. International Classification of Patents (RU)
MPK............. International Convention Concerning the Carriage of Passengers and Luggage by Rail (RU)
MPK............. International Preparatory Committee (RU)
MPK............. Mechanized Movable Support [*Mining*] (RU)
mpk............. Meripeninkulma(a) [*Finnish*]
MPK............. Miejskie Przedsiebiorstwo Komunikacyjne [*Municipal Transportation Enterprise*] (POL)
MPK............. Mining and Processing Combine (BU)
MPK............. Ministry of Education and Culture [*Obsolete*] (BU)
MPK............. Modernized Flotation Suit [*Military term*] (RU)
MPK............. Small Antisubmarine Ship (RU)
MPKiO......... Moscow Park of Culture and Rest (RU)
MPL............. Blade-Operating Mechanism [*Nautical term*] (RU)
MPL............. Mashonaland Progressive League (MAR)
MPl.............. Ministerstvo Planovani [*Ministry of Planning*] (CZ)
MPL............. Ministerstwo Przemyslu Lekkiego [*Ministry of Light Industry*] (POL)
M pl............. Ministre Plenipotentiaire [*French*] (MTD)
MPL............. Mouvement Populaire de Liberation [*People's Liberation Movement*] [*Djibouti*] (AF)
MPL............. Movimento Politica dei Lavoratori [*Workers' Political Movement*] [*Italian*] (PPE)
MPL-............ Shunting Pneumatic Winch (RU)
MPLA........... Malaysian People's Liberation Army (ML)
MPLA........... Mouvement Populaire de Liberation de l'Angola (MAR)
MPLA........... Movimento Popular de Libertacao de Angola [*Popular Movement for the Liberation of Angola*] (AF)
MPLA-AN.... Movimento Popular de Libertacao de Angola-Agostinho Neto (MAR)
MPLAC........ Movimiento Popular Liberal del Archipielago Canario [*People's Liberal Movement of the Canary Islands*] [*Spanish*] (WER)
MPLA-PT.... Movimento Popular de Libertacao de Angola - Partido do Trabalho [*Popular Movement for the Liberation of Angola - Party of Labor*] (PPW)
MPLC........... Mouvement Populaire pour la Liberation du Congo (MAR)
MPLC........... Movimento Popular de Libertacao de Cabinda [*Popular Movement for the Liberation of Cabinda*] [*Angolan*] (PD)
MPLD........... Malorazni Protiletadlove Delostrelectvo [*Small Caliber Antiaircraft Artillery*] (CZ)
MPLD........... Mouvement Populaire pour la Liberation de Djibouti (MAR)
MPLF........... Malaysian People's Liberation Front (ML)
MPLN........... Movimento para a Libertacao Nacional [*National Liberation Movement*] [*Portuguese*] (WER)
MPLN........... Movimiento Popular de Liberacion Nacional [*People's National Liberation Movement*] [*Bolivian*] (LA1)
MPLO........... Malay Police Liaison Officer (ML)
MPLR........... Mongolska Partia Ludowo-Rewolucyjna [*Mongolian People's Revolutionary Party*] [*Polish*]
MPLR........... Mouvement pour la Liberation de la Reunion [*Movement for the Liberation of Reunion*] (AF)
MPLT........... Mouvement Populaire pour la Liberation du Tchad [*Popular Movement for the Liberation of Chad*] (AF)
MPLTT......... Mouvement Populaire pour la Liberation Totale du Tchad [*Popular Movement for the Total Liberation of Chad*] (AF)
MPM............ Junior Chamber International [*JCI*] (RU)
MPM............ Majlis Pelajaran Melayu [*Malayan Education Council*] (ML)
MPM............ Materiel de Protection Moderne (MAR)
MPM............ Mayotte People's Movement (MAR)
MPM............ Milli Produktivite Merkezi [*National Productivity Center*] (TU)
MPM............ Ministerstwo Przemyslu Maszynowego [*Ministry of the Machine Building Industry*] (POL)
MPM............ Ministerstwo Przemyslu Metalowego [*Ministry of the Metal Industry*] (POL)
MPM............ Mouvement Populaire Mahorais [*Mayotte People's Movement*] [*Comoran*] (PPW)
MPM............ Mouvement Populaire Marocain (MAR)
MPM............ Movimiento Peronista Montonero [*Peronist Montonero Movement*] [*Argentine*] (LA)
MPMB.......... Ministerstwo Przemyslu Materialow Budowlanych [*Ministry of the Building Materials Industry*] (POL)
MPMI........... Moscow Fur and Peltry Institute (RU)
MPMiM........ Ministerstwo Przemyslu Miesnego i Mleczarskiego [*Ministry of Meat and Dairy Industry*] (POL)
MPMiMP..... Ministry of the Meat and Dairy Products Industry (RU)
MPMM......... Movimiento por un Mundo Mejor [*Movement for a Better World*] [*Venezuelan*] (LA)
MPNC.......... Mouvement pour le Progres National Congolais (MAR)
MPO............ Coast Guard, Coast Guard Service (RU)
MPO............ Intergovernmental Organization (RU)
MPO............ Magnetic Bearing of the Checkpoint (RU)
MPO............ Makedoniki Politiki Organosis [*Macedonian Political Organization*] [*Bulgarian anti-Greek organization*] [*Greek*] (GC)
MPO............ Makedonska Politicka Organizacija [*Macedonian Political Organization*] (YU)
MPO............ Miejskie Przedsiebiorstwa Ogrodnicze [*Municipal Garden Enterprises*] (POL)
MPO............ Miejskie Przedsiebiorstwo Oczyszczania [*Municipal Sanitation Enterprise*] (POL)
MPO............ Ministerstvo Post [*Ministry of Postal Service*] (CZ)
MPO............ Moscow Consumers' Society (RU)
MPO............ Motorisovany Prezvedny Oddil [*Motorized Reconnaissance Battalion*] (CZ)

MPOM......... Miejskie Przedsiebiorstwo Oczyszczania Miasta [*Municipal Sanitation Enterprise*] (POL)
MPOZKZ..... Mesarsko Podjetje, Okrajna Zveza Kmetijskih Zadrug [*Butcher Establishment, District Union of Agricultural Cooperatives*] (YU)
MPP............ Madjelis Perusahaan dan Perniagaan [*Chamber of Commerce and Industry*] (IN)
MPP............ Manipur People's Party [*Indian*] (PPW)
MPP............ Mechanized Field Laundry (RU)
MPP............ Medical Aid Crossing Point (BU)
MPP............ Medical Station at a Water Crossing (RU)
MPP............ Mesarsko Preradivacko Preduzece [*Meat-Processing Establishment*] (YU)
MPP............ Mestske Plynarenske Podniky [*Municipal Gas Works*] (CZ)
MPP............ Mestske Prepravni Podniky [*Municipal Transportation Enterprises*] (CZ)
MPP............ Ministerstvo Potravinarskeho Prumyslu [*Ministry of the Food Industry*] (CZ)
MPP............ Ministry of the Food Industry (RU)
MPP............ Mouvement pour le Progres du Peuple (MAR)
MPP............ Movimento do Partido do Proletariado [*Proletariat Party Movement*] [*Portuguese*] (WER)
MPP............ Movimento Popular Portugues [*Popular Portuguese Movement*] (WER)
MPPA.......... Beef-Extract Liver Agar (RU)
MPPB.......... Beef-Extract Liver Broth (RU)
mppb.......... Bridge Train of a Pontoon Battalion (RU)
MPPP.......... Mauritius People's Progressive Party (MAR)
MPPP.......... Meteorological Receiving-Sending Station (RU)
MPPT.......... Ministry of the Foodstuffs Industry (RU)
m/pr............ Barely Noticeable Obstacles [*Topography*] (RU)
m pr............ By the Way (RU)
MPR............ Magnetic Bearing of a Radio Direction Finder (RU)
MPR............ Magnetic Bearing of a Radio Navigation Point (RU)
MPR............ Magnetic Bearing of a Radio Station (RU)
MPR............ Magnetic Bearing of a Rocket (RU)
MPr............ Makedonski Pregled [*Macedonian Review*] [*A periodical*] (BU)
mpr............ Mine Disposal Company (RU)
MPR............ Ministry of Food Reserves, USSR (RU)
MPR............ Mouvement Populaire de la Revolution [*Popular Revolutionary Movement*] [*Zairian*] (PD)
MPR............ Mouvement Populaire Revolutionnaire [*Popular Revolutionary Movement*] [*Tunisian*] (PD)
MPR............ Movimento Popolare Rivoluzionario [*Popular Revolutionary Movement*] [*Italian*] (PD)
MPR............ Movimiento Popular Revolucionario [*Popular Revolutionary Movement*] [*Ecuadorean*] (LA)
MPR............ Movimiento Popular Revolucionario [*Popular Revolutionary Movement*] [*Nicaraguan*] (LA1)
MPRB.......... Miejskie Przedsiebiorstwo Remontowo-Budowlane [*Municipal Repair and Construction Enterprise*] (POL)
MPRB.......... Miejskie Przedsiebiorstwo Robot Budowlanych [*Municipal Construction Enterprise*] (POL)
MPRD.......... Miejskie Przedsiebiorstwo Robot Drogowych [*Municipal Road Construction Enterprise*] (POL)
MPRDiM...... Miejskie Przedsiebiorstwo Robot Drogowych i Mostowych [*Municipal Road and Bridge Construction Enterprise*] (POL)
MPRI............ Miejskie Przedsiebiorstwo Robot Inzynieryjnych (Dawna "Metrobudowa") [*Municipal Engineering Enterprise (Formerly, "Metrobudowa")*] (POL)
MPRiS.......... Ministerstwo Przemyslu Rolnego i Spozywczego [*Ministry of the Agricultural and Food Industry*] (POL)
MPros.......... Ministry of Education (RU)
MPR-P.......... Miejskie Przedsiebiorstwo Rozbiorkowo-Porzadkowe [*Municipal Demolition and Disposal Enterprise*] (POL)
MPRP.......... Mongolian People's Revolutionary Party [*Mongol Ardyn Khuv'sgalt Nam*] (PPW)
MPRP.......... Moslem People's Republican Party [*Iranian*] (PPW)
MPRS.......... Madjelis Permusjawaratan Rakjat Sementara [*Provisional People's Consultative Congress*] (IN)
Mprv............ Mitprovisor [*German*]
MPRWiK...... Miejskie Przedsiebiorstwo Robot Wodociagowych i Kanalizacyjnych [*Municipal Water Supply and Sewer Construction Enterprise*] (POL)
MPS............ International Chamber of Shipping [*ICS*] (RU)
MPS............ International Industrial Secretariat (RU)
MPS............ Machine Rental Station (RU)
MPS............ Magasins-Pilotes Socialistes [*North African*] (MAR)
MPS............ Mashinoprokratnaia Stantsiia (MAR)
MPS............ Mathematical Programming Society (EA)
MPS............ Medical Station of a Unit [*Military term*] (RU)
MPS............ Medunarodni Poljoprivredni Sajam [*International Agricultural Fair*] [*Novi Sad*] (YU)
MPS............ Mestska Postovni Sprava [*City Postal Administration*] (CZ)
MPS............ Mezhdunarodnoye Passazhirskoye Soglasheniye [*Agreement Concerning International Railroad Passenger Traffic (Between USSR and satellites)*] (EG)
MPS............ Milicias Populares Sandinistas [*Sandinist People's Militias*] [*Nicaraguan*] (LA1)
MPS............ Ministerstvo Pracovnich Sil [*Ministry of Manpower*] (CZ)
MPS............ Ministry of Railroads, USSR (RU)
MPS............ Mobile Police Station (ML)
MPS............ Moscow State Trust for the Construction of Underground Structures (RU)
MPS............ Mouvement Populaire Senegalaise (MAR)
MPS............ Movimiento Popular Socialista [*Socialist Popular Movement*] [*Colombian*] (LA)
MPS............ Mucopolysaccharide (RU)
MPS............ Muy Poderoso Senor [*Spanish*]
MPS............ Scaling Circuit [*Computers*] (RU)
MPS............ Track Machine Station [*Railroads*] (RU)
MPSA.......... Ministry of Instrument Making and Means of Automation, USSR (RU)
MPSC.......... Movimiento Popular Socialcristiano [*Christian Social Popular Movement*] [*Salvadoran*] (PD)
MPSD.......... Moscow Proletarian Rifle Division (RU)
MPSF.......... Malayan People's Socialist Front (ML)
MPSM.......... Ministry of the Building Materials Industry (RU)
MPSP.......... Ministerstvo Prace a Socialni Pece [*Ministry of Labor and Social Welfare*] (CZ)
MPSP.......... Montazni Podnik Spoju [*Assembly Enterprise for Communications*] (CZ)
MPSP.......... Movimiento por la Paz y la Soberania de los Pueblos [*Movement for Peace and Sovereignty of Peoples*] [*Cuban*] (LA)
MPSS.......... Ministry of the Communications Equipment Industry, USSR (RU)
MPSV.......... Ministerstvo Prace a Socialnich Veci [*Ministry of Labor and Social Affairs*] (CZ)
MPSZ.......... Magyar Paraszt Szovetseg [*Hungarian Peasant Association*] (HU)
MPSZ.......... Magyar Penzugyi Szindikatus [*Hungarian Financial Syndicate*] (HU)
MPT............ Direct-Current Machine (RU)
MPT............ Madarska Partija Trudbenika [*Hungarian Workers' Party*] (YU)
MPT............ Miejskie Przedsiebiorstwo Taksowkowe [*or Taksowek*] [*Municipal Taxicab Enterprise*] (POL)
MPT............ Ministerstvo Post a Telekomunikaci [*Ministry for Postal Affairs and Telecommunications*] (CZ)
MPT............ Mouvement Populaire Tchadien (MAR)
MPT............ Mouvement Populaire Togolais [*Togolese Popular Movement*] (AF)
MPTShP...... Ministry of the Consumers' Goods Industry (RU)
MPTT.......... Ministry of Post, Telegraph, and Telephone [*Obsolete*] (BU)
MPTTR........ Ministry of Post, Telegraph, Telephone, and Radio [*Obsolete*] (BU)
MPTU.......... Technical Specifications of the Machinery Industry (RU)
MPTU.......... Technical Specifications of the Metallurgical Industry (RU)
MPU............ Local Control Post (RU)
MPU............ Magnetic Track Angle (RU)
MPU............ Moscow Political Administration (RU)
MPU............ Movimiento del Pueblo Unido [*United People's Movement*] [*Nicaraguan*] (LA)
mpuaz.......... Millipoise (RU)
MPUAZO..... Naval Antiaircraft Artillery Fire Control Device (RU)
MPUK.......... Local Industrial Training Center (RU)
mPV............ Maritime Polar Air (RU)
mpv............ Mine Disposal Platoon (RU)
MPV............ Moralno-Politicko Vaspitanje [*Moral and Political Education*] [*Military*] (YU)
MPV............ Refracted-Wave Method (RU)
MPV............ Small Time Constant (RU)
MPVKhO..... Local Antiaircraft and Chemical Defense (BU)
MPVKhO..... Local Antiaircraft and Chemical Defense (RU)
MPVO.......... Local Air Defense (RU)
MPVO.......... Local Antiaircraft Defense (BU)
MPVP.......... International Traveling Exhibition of Instruments and Measuring Devices (RU)
MPW............ Mouvement Populaire Wallon [*Walloon Popular Movement*] [*Belgian*] (WER)
MPYI............ Moble-Prefabrik Yapi Isletmesi [*Furniture-Prefabricated Structures Enterprise*] [*Turkish Cypriot*] (GC)
MPZ............ Mezinarodni Plachtarske Zavody [*International Glider Contests*] (CZ)
mpz............ Millipieze (RU)
mpz............ Millipoise (RU)
MPZ............ Mjesna Poljoprivredna Zadruga [*Local Agricultural Cooperative*] (YU)
MPZ............ Moravskoslezske Pletarske Zavody [*Moravian-Silesian Knitting Mills*] (CZ)
MPZh.......... Beef-Extract Gelatin (RU)
MPZU.......... Permanent Storage Matrix (RU)
MQ............ Martinique [*Two-letter standard code*] (CNC)
Mq............ Metre Carre [*Square Meter*] [*French*] (MTD)
Mqs............ Marquis [*Marquess*] [*French*] (MTD)
Mqse.......... Marquise [*Marchioness*] [*French*] (MTD)
MR............ Distance Scale (RU)
mr............ Gunner [*Artillery*] (BU)
MR............ High-Power Radio Station (RU)
MR............ Lever Micrometer (RU)
MR............ Magnetic Reverberator (RU)

m-r .... Major (RU)
MR .... Maldivian Rupee (MAR)
m r .... Male Gender (BU)
mr .... Martir [*Martyr*] [*Spanish*]
mr .... Masculine Gender (RU)
MR .... Mauritania [*Two-letter standard code*] (CNC)
MR .... Mauritius Rupee (MAR)
MR .... Maximum Relay, Over-Current Relay, Overload Relay (RU)
MR .... Mechanized Patrol (RU)
Mr .... Meester in de Rechten [*Academic qualification*] [*Dutch*]
MR .... Metallurgy and Ore Mining (BU)
MR .... Meteorological Rocket (RU)
MR .... Microroentgenometer (RU)
mr .... Milliroentgen (RU)
M-r .... Minister [*Government*] (BU)
m-r .... Minister (RU)
MR .... Ministerstwo Rolnictwa [*Ministry of Agriculture*] (POL)
MR .... Ministre Resident [*French*] (MTD)
MR .... Miniszteri Rendelet [*Ministerial Decree (Legal)*] (HU)
MR .... Mistni Rozhlas [*Local Radio Broadcasting*] (CZ)
MR .... Mladinska Revija [*Youth Review*] [*Ljubljana*] [*A publication*] (YU)
Mr .... Monsieur [*Mister*] [*French*] (MTD)
mr .... Mortar Company (RU)
mr .... Motorized Company (RU)
MR .... Museum of Revolution (RU)
MR .... Naval Reconnaissance (BU)
MR .... Naval Reconnaissance Aircraft (RU)
MR- .... Radioisotope Manometer (RU)
MR .... Repair Shop (RU)
MR .... Route Relay (RU)
m r .... Sea Level (BU)
mr .... Slightly Soluble (RU)
MR-8 .... Movimento Revolucionario 8 de Outubro [*8 October Revolutionary Movement*] [*Brazilian*] (LA1)
MR-13 .... Movimiento Revolucionario del 13 de Noviembre [*13 November Revolutionary Movement*] [*Guatemalan*] (LA)
MRA .... Market Research Africa (MAR)
MRA .... Ministerio da Republica para os Acores [*Ministry of the Republic for Azores*] [*Portuguese*] (WER)
MRA .... Mission pour la Reforme Administrative [*Administrative Reform Mission*] [*Chadian*] (AF)
MRA .... Moral Re-Armament (MAR)
MRA .... Movimiento Revolucionario Autentico [*Authentic Revolutionary Movement*] [*Costa Rican*] (LA)
MR-24A .... Movimiento Revolucionario Veinticuatro de Abril [*24 April Revolutionary Movement*] [*Dominican Republic*] (LA)
MRAC .... Musee Royal de l'Afrique Centrale (MAR)
mrad .... Millirad (RU)
mrae .... Naval Rocket-Launcher Air Squadron (RU)
mram .... Marble [*Quarry*] [*Topography*] (RU)
MRAP .... Mouvement Contre le Racisme, l'Anti-Semitisme, et pour la Paix [*Movement Against Racism, Antisemitism, and for Peace*] [*Later, Movement Against Racism and for Friendship between Peoples*] [*French*] (WER)
MRAP .... Movement Against Racism and for Friendship between Peoples [*Formerly, Movement Against Racism, Antisemitism, and for Peace*] (EA)
MRAP .... Movimiento de Resistencia Armada Puertorriquena [*Puerto Rican Armed Resistance Movement*] (PD)
MRAP .... Naval Reconnaissance Air Regiment (RU)
MRB .... Mouvement de Resistance Bakongo (MAR)
MRB .... Mouvement Rural du Burundi (MAR)
MRC .... Medical Research Council (MAR)
MRC .... Movimiento Rebelde Colombiano [*Colombian Rebel Movement*] (LA)
MRC .... Movimiento de Restauracion Conservadora [*Bogota*] (COL)
MRC .... Movimiento Revolucionario Campesino [*Peasant's Revolutionary Movement*] [*Salvadoran*] (LA1)
MRC .... South African Medical Research Council (MAR)
MRCA .... Multirole Combat Aircraft [*A joint English, German, and Italian project to develop a standard NATO fighter*] (WEN)
MRCB .... Musee Royal du Congo Belge (MAR)
MRD .... Malaysian Rubber Development Corporation (ML)
mrd .... Merced [*Grace, Mercy*] [*Spanish*]
mrd .... Miljardi(a) [*Finnish*]
Mrd .... Milliarde [*Billion*] [*German*] (WEN)
mrd .... Millirutherford (RU)
MRD .... Movement for the Restoration of Democracy [*Pakistani*] (PD)
MRD .... Movimento Revolucionario Democratico [*Democratic Revolutionary Movement*] [*Brazilian*] (LA)
MRD .... Movimiento de Reafirmacion Doctrinaria [*Movement of Doctrinaire Reaffirmation*] [*Argentine*] (LA1)
MRDB .... Museum of the Revolutionary Movement in Bulgaria (BU)
MRDN .... Mouvement Revolutionnaire pour la Democratie Nouvelle [*Revolutionary Movement for New Democracy*] (PD)
MRDP .... Mezinarodni Ruda Delnicka Pomoc [*International Workers' Red Aid*] (CZ)
MRDT .... Mouvement Democratique de la Renovation Tchadienne [*Democratic Movement for Chadian Restoration*] (AF)
MRE .... Movimiento Revolucionario Ecuatoriano [*Ecuadorean Revolutionary Movement*] (LA)
MRE .... Movimiento Revolucionario Espartaco [*Bolivian*] (PPW)
mrezerford ... Millirutherford (RU)
MRF .... Matabelaland Relief Force (MAR)
MRF .... Ministry of the River Fleet (RU)
MRG .... Miedzynarodowy Rok Geofizyczny [*International Geophysical Year*] [*Polish*]
MRG .... Mouvement des Radicaux de Gauche [*Movement of Left Radicals*] [*French*] (PPE)
MRG .... Mouvement de la Revolution Gabonaise (MAR)
mrg .... Myriagram (RU)
MRGT .... Caterpillar Tractor Repair Shop (RU)
MRI .... Megyei Rendelo Intezet [*County Ambulance Station*] (HU)
MRI .... Movimiento Republicano Independiente [*Independent Republican Movement*] [*Ecuadorean*] (LA)
MRI .... Radioactive Isotope Method (RU)
MRIC .... Revolutionary Movement of the Christian Left [*Ecuadorean*] (PPW)
MRiRR .... Ministerstwo Rolnictwa i Reform Rolnych [*Ministry of Agriculture and Agricultural Reforms*] [*Pre-World War II*] (POL)
MRIT .... Moscow Editing and Publishing Technicum (RU)
MR-14J .... Movimiento Revolucionario Catorce de Junio [*14 June Revolutionary Movement*] [*Dominican Republic*] (LA)
MRK .... Interrayon Office (of the Soyuzpechat') (RU)
MRK .... Local Wage Commission (RU)
MRK .... Marine Royale Khmere [*Royal Cambodian Navy*] [*Replaced by MNK*] (CL)
Mrk .... Merkez [*Central*] (TU)
MRKCh .... International Frequency Registration Board [*IFRB*] (RU)
MRKF .... Miedzyzwiazkowa Rada Kultury Fizycznej [*Inter-Union Council of Physical Culture*] (POL)
MRKI .... Moscow Workers' and Peasants' Inspection (RU)
MRL .... Minen-Raeum- und Legeboot [*Mine Sweeper and Layer*] (EG)
MRL .... Mongolska Republika Ludowa [*Mongolian People's Republic*] [*Polish*]
MRL .... Movimiento de Reintegracion Liberal [*Liberal Reintegration Movement*] [*Colombian*] (LA)
MRL .... Movimiento Revolucionario Liberal [*Liberal Revolutionary Movement*] [*Colombian*] (LA)
MRLA .... Malayan Races Liberation Army (ML)
MRLL .... Malay Races Liberation League (Communist) (ML)
MRM .... Engine Repair Shop (RU)
MRM .... Machine Repair Shop (RU)
MRM .... Marker Beacon (RU)
MRM .... Medical Microroentgenometer (RU)
MRM .... Metalurgija Raznobojnih Metala [*Nonferrous Metallurgy*] (YU)
MRM .... Ministerio da Republica para a Madeira [*Ministry of the Republic for Madeira*] [*Portuguese*] (WER)
MRM .... Mozambique Resistance Movement (MAR)
mrm .... Myriameter (RU)
MR/ML .... Movimento Revolucionario/Marxista-Leninista [*Revolutionary Movement/Marxist-Leninist*] [*Portuguese*] (WER)
MRN .... Miejska Rada Narodowa [*Municipal People's Council*] (POL)
MRN .... Mouvement de Renovation Nationale [*National Renovation Movement*] [*Haitian*] (LA)
MRN .... Movimiento de la Reforma Nacional [*National Reform Movement*] [*Argentine*] (LA)
MRN .... Movimiento de Renovacion Nacional [*Movement for National Renovation*] [*Colombian*] (PPW)
MRN .... Movimiento de Reorganizacion Nacional [*National Reorganization Movement*] [*Argentine*] (LA)
MRND .... Mouvement Revolutionnaire National pour le Developpement [*National Revolutionary Movement for Development*] [*Rwandan*] (PPW)
MRNP .... Controlled Directional Reception Method (RU)
MRO .... Interrayon Branch, Interrayon Department (RU)
Mro .... Maestro [*Master*] [*Spanish*]
MRO .... Mistni Rada Osvetova [*Local Cultural Board*] (CZ)
MRO .... Movimiento Revolucionario Oriental [*Uruguayan Revolutionary Movement*] (LA)
MROMIR ...... Mroue Miroiterie (MAR)
MROT .... Inter-American Regional Organization of Workers (RU)
MRP .... International Revolutionary Aid (RU)
MRP .... International Workers' Aid (RU)
MRP .... Magnetic Radio Bearing (RU)
MRP .... Magyar Radikalis Part [*Hungarian Radical Party*] (HU)
MRP .... Manufacture de Reconditionnement de Pneumatiques (MAR)
MRP .... Marker Beacon Receiver (RU)
MRP .... Medical Evacuation Distribution Station (RU)
MRP .... Mediterranean Regional Program (MAR)
MRP .... Ministry of the Fish Industry (RU)
MRP .... Ministry of the Radiotechnical Industry, USSR (RU)
MRP .... Moscow River Steamship Line (RU)
MRP .... Mouvement Republicain Populaire [*Popular Republican Movement*] [*French*] (PPE)
MRP .... Movimiento de Resistencia Popular [*Popular Resistance Movement*] [*Chilean*] (LA)
MRP .... Movimiento de la Revolucion Peruana [*Movement of the Peruvian Revolution*] (LA)

MRP .... Movimiento Revolucionario Pazestenssorista [*Paz Estenssoro Revolutionary Movement*] [*Bolivian*] (LA)
MRP .... Movimiento Revolucionario Popular [*Popular Revolutionary Movement*] [*Mexican*] (LA1)
MRP .... Movimiento Revolucionario del Pueblo [*People's Revolutionary Movement*] [*Costa Rican*] (LA)
MRP .... Movimiento Revolucionario del Pueblo - Ixim [*People's Revolutionary Movement - Ixim*] [*Guatemalan*] (PD)
MRPC .... Mouvement de Regroupement des Populations Congolaise (MAR)
Mr Ph .... Magister der Pharmazie [*German*]
MRPP .... Movimento Reorganizativo do Partido do Proletariado [*Movement for the Reorganization of the Proletariat Party*] [*Portuguese*] (WER)
mrprof .... Mimoradny Professor [*Associate Professor*] (CZ)
MRR .... Minimum Rediscount Rate (MAR)
MRR .... Movimento de Resistencia Republicana (MAR)
MRR .... Movimento de Resistencia Revolucionaria [*Revolutionary Resistance Movement*] [*Brazilian*] (LA)
MRRTA .... Long-Distance Radio-Relay Television Control Room (RU)
MRS .... Machine Repair Station (RU)
mrs .... Maravedises [*Old Spanish Coins*] [*Spanish*]
mrs .... Martires [*Martyrs*] [*Spanish*]
MRS .... Mechanized Fishing Station (RU)
MRS .... Mine-Detecting Service (RU)
Mrs .... Moerser [*Mortar*] (EG)
MRS .... Motorized Fishing Station (RU)
MRS .... Mouvement Republicain Senegalais [*Senegalese Republican Movement*] (PPW)
MRS .... Movimento Renovador Sindical [*Union Renewal Movement*] [*Brazilian*] (LA)
MRS .... Movimiento Reformista Salvadoreno [*Salvadoran Reformist Movement*] (LA1)
MRS .... Small Fishing Seiner (RU)
MRS .... Speed Control Mechanism (RU)
MRSh .... Meridional Difference of Latitute (RU)
Mrsl .... Maresal [*Marshal*] (TU)
MRSM .... Mongolian Revolutionary Youth League (RU)
MRSM .... Mouvement du Renouveau Social Malgache (MAR)
MR SSSR .... Maritime Register of the USSR (RU)
MRSZ .... Magyar Repulo Szovetseg [*Hungarian Aviation Association*] (HU)
mrt .... Maart [*March*] [*Dutch*] (GPO)
MRT .... Magyar Radio es Televizio Vallalat [*Hungarian Radio and Television Enterprise*] (HU)
MRT .... Makedonski Revolucionarni Teroristi [*Macedonian Revolutionary Terrorists*] (YU)
MRT .... Mauritania [*Three-letter standard code*] (CNC)
MRT .... Miedzynarodowy Rajd Tatrzanski [*International Tatra Mountains Rally*] [*Polish*]
MRT .... Moscow Revolutionary Tribunal (RU)
MRT .... Mouvement Revolutionnaire Tchadien (MAR)
MRT .... Movimento Revolucionario Tiradentes [*Revolutionary Tiradentes Movement*] [*Brazilian*] (PD)
MRT .... Small Fishing Trawler (RU)
MRTB .... Movimiento Revolucionario de los Trabajadores Bolivianos [*Revolutionary Movement of Bolivian Workers*] (LA1)
MRTK .... Movimiento Revolucionario Tupaj Katari [*Tupaj Katari Revolutionary Movement*] [*Bolivian*] (PPW)
MRTO .... International Workers' Theatrical Association (RU)
MRTO .... Small Fishing Trawler with Refrigerated Holds (RU)
MRTP .... Ministry of the Radiotechnical Industry, USSR (RU)
MRTs .... Route Control Interlocking System [*Railroads*] (RU)
MRTU .... Interrepublic Technical Specifications (RU)
MRTU .... Moscow Radio Wire Broadcasting Center (RU)
MRTU .... Moscow Radiotechnical Administration (RU)
MRU .... Interrayon Center [*Telephony*] (RU)
MRU .... Mano River Union (MAR)
MRV .... Diaphragm Control Valve (RU)
MRV .... Mercury-Water Gauge (RU)
MRV .... Mouvement du Regroupement Voltaique (MAR)
MRwCz .... Muzeum Regionalne w Czestochowie [*Czestochowa Regional Museum*] (POL)
MRZ .... Frost Resistance (RU)
MRZ .... Metal Lattice Lagging [*Mining*] (RU)
MRZ .... Motor Repair Plant (RU)
MRZh .... Medical Journal of Abstracts [*A publication*] (RU)
MRZhK .... Interrayon Livestock-Breeding Office (RU)
MS .... Aircraft Position [*In flight*] (RU)
MS .... Booby Trap (RU)
MS- .... Comparison Microscope (RU)
MS .... Council of Ministers (BU)
MS .... International Court of the United Nations (RU)
MS .... Interplanetary Station (RU)
MS .... Lubricating Oil (RU)
MS .... Manuscriptum [*Manuscript*] [*Latin*] (GPO)
MS .... Manuscrit [*Manuscript*] [*French*]
MS .... Manuscrito [*Manuscript*] [*Spanish*]
Ms .... Manuskript [*Manuscript*] (EG)
Ms .... Marais [*Swamp*] [*Military map abbreviation*] [*World War I*] [*French*] (MTD)
MS .... Marxistischer Studentenbund [*Marxist Student Federation*] [*West German*] (WEN)
MS .... Masinska Radionica [*Machine Shop*] (YU)
MS .... Mass Spectrometer (RU)
MS .... Matica Slovenska [*Slovak Foundation (A Slovak cultural organization)*] (CZ)
MS .... Matica Slovenska [*Slovenian Literary Society*] [*Ljubljana*] (YU)
MS .... Matica Srpska [*Serbian Literary and Publishing Society*] [*Novi Sad*] (YU)
MS .... Mechanization of Construction (RU)
MS .... Mechanized Unit [*Military term*] (RU)
MS .... Medical Department [*of naval ship*], Medical Service (RU)
m/s .... Medical Service (BU)
MS .... Mesi Sykhnotis [*Medium Frequency*] (GC)
MS .... Metal Sarajevo [*Wholesale Metallurgical Trade Establishment, Sarajevo*] (YU)
MS .... Metals Society (EA)
m/s .... Meter je Sekunde [*Meters per Second*] (EG)
MS .... Methylene Blue (RU)
MS .... Milattan Sonra [*In the Year of Our Lord*] (TU)
MS .... Ministarstvo Saobracaja [*Ministry of Transportation*] (YU)
MS .... Ministerstvo Skolstvi [*Ministry of Education*] (CZ)
MS .... Ministerstvo Spoju [*Ministry of Communications*] (CZ)
MS .... Ministerstvo Spravedlnosti [*Ministry of Justice*] (CZ)
MS .... Ministerstvo Stavebnictvi [*Ministry of Building*] (CZ)
MS .... Ministerstvo Strojirenstvi [*Ministry of the Machine Building Industry*] (CZ)
MS .... Ministerstwo Skupu [*Ministry of Procurement*] (POL)
MS .... Ministerstwo Sprawiedliwosci [*Ministry of Justice*] (POL)
MS .... Ministerul Sanatatii [*Ministry of Health*] (RO)
MS .... Ministry of Communications (RU)
MS .... Ministry of Construction [*Obsolete*] (BU)
MS .... Ministry of Construction (RU)
MS .... Ministry of Sovkhozes (RU)
MS .... Missionary Society (MAR)
MS .... Mistni Skupina [*Local Group*] (CZ)
MS .... Mittelschule [*German*]
ms .... Moins [*French*]
MS .... Molecular Sieve (RU)
MS .... Montserrat [*Two-letter standard code*] (CNC)
MS .... Moscow Soviet of Workers', Peasants', and Red Army Deputies (RU)
ms .... Motorized Unit [*Military term*] (RU)
MS .... Moulins Sentenac (MAR)
MS .... Musikschule [*German*]
MS .... Mutation Spectrum (RU)
MS .... Navy, Naval Forces (RU)
m/s .... Nurse (RU)
MS .... Parking Place [*Of aircraft*] (RU)
MS .... Screw Cap (RU)
MS .... Weather Service, Meteorological Service (RU)
MS .... Youth Union (BU)
MS .... Zeme Moravskoslezska [*Province (Land) of Moravia and Silesia*] (CZ)
MSA .... International Council on Archives [*ICA*] (RU)
MSA .... International Sociological Association [*ISA*] (RU)
MSA .... International Standard Atmosphere (RU)
MSA .... International Union of Architects (BU)
MSA .... International Union of Architects (RU)
MSA .... Malaysia-Singapore Airlines (ML)
MSA .... Mauritius Sports Association (MAR)
MSA .... Mercury Singapore Airlines (ML)
MSA .... Ministry of Construction and Architecture [*Obsolete*] (BU)
MSA .... Mouvement Socialiste Africain (MAR)
MSA .... Mouvement Souverainete Association [*Canadian*] (PPW)
MSA .... Movimento Separatista Angolano (MAR)
MSA .... Movimento dei Socialisti Autonomi [*Movement of Autonomous Socialists*] [*Italian*] (WER)
MSA .... Movimiento Socialista Andaluz [*Andalusian Socialist Movement*] [*Spanish*] (WER)
MSAN .... Morfotikoi Syllogoi Agrotikis Neolaias [*Agricultural Youth Educational Associations*] [*Greek*] (GC)
MSANO .... Ministerstvo Skolstvi a Narodni Osvety [*Ministry of Education and Culture*] (CZ)
MSAR .... Mouvement Solidarite Anti-Repression [*Solidarity and Anti-Repression Movement*] [*Mauritian*] (AF)
ms as .... Muchos Anos [*Spanish*]
MSAS .... Slow Anticoincidence and Coincidence Circuit (RU)
MSAT .... International Road Transport Union [*IRU*] (RU)
MSAT .... Mutuelles Senegalaises d'Assurances des Transporteurs (MAR)
MSAUD .... Muslim Students Association of the University of Dar Es Salaam (MAR)
MSAVP .... Moravsko-Slezska Akademie Ved Prirodnich [*Moravian and Silesian Academy of Natural Sciences*] (CZ)
MSB .... Battalion Medical Service (BU)
msb .... Bridge Construction Battalion (RU)
MSB .... International Socialist Bureau [*1900-1914*] (RU)
MSB .... Machine Computation Office, Machine Calculating Office (RU)
MSB .... Malaysian Special Branch (ML)

MSB .... Marxistischer Studentenbund [*Marxist Student Federation*] [*Austrian, West German*] (WEN)
MSB .... Medical Battalion (RU)
MSB .... Medicisko-Sanitetski Bataljoni [*Medical Hygiene Battalions*] (YU)
MSB .... Medium Naval Bomber (RU)
MSB .... Memoires de la Societe de Biogeographie [*A publication*] (MAR)
MSB .... Metal Dry-Cargo Barge (RU)
MSB .... Milli Savunma Bakanligi [*National Defense Ministry*] [*See also MMV*] (TU)
msb .... Millistilb (RU)
msb .... Motorized Rifle Battalion (BU)
MSB .... Motorized Rifle Battalion (RU)
MSB .... Motorized Rifle Brigade (RU)
MSB .... Movimiento Sindical de Base [*Rank and File Labor Union Movement*] [*Argentine*] (LA)
MSB .... Movimiento Socialista de Baleares [*Socialist Movement of the Balearic Islands*] [*Spanish*] (WER)
Msb .... Sbornik za Narodni Umotvoreniya, Nauka, i Knizhnina [*Collection of Folklore, Science, and Literature*] [*A periodical*] (BU)
MSBA .... Memoires de la Societe Royale Belge d'Anthropologie et de Prehistoire [*A publication*] (MAR)
MSBM .... Baltic Sea Naval Forces (RU)
MSC .... Maadi Sporting Club (MAR)
MSC .... Maharashtra Socialist Congress [*Indian*] (PPW)
MSC .... Malayan Service Corps (ML)
MSC .... Malaysian Solidarity Convention (ML)
MSC .... Material Systems Corporation (MAR)
MSC .... Mediterranean Shipping Company (MAR)
MSC .... Mediterranean Sub-Commission (MAR)
MSC .... Movimiento Socialista Catalan [*Catalan Socialist Movement*] [*Spanish*] (WER)
MSC .... Movimiento Socialista Colombiano [*Colombian Socialist Movement*] (LA)
MSC .... Muslim Supreme Council [*Ugandan*] (AF)
ms ch .... Bridge Unit (BU)
MSCh .... Medical Unit (RU)
MSCh .... Modified Gray Iron (RU)
MSChM .... Black Sea Naval Forces (RU)
MSChPF .... International Union of Pure and Applied Physics [*IUPAP*] (RU)
MSChV .... International Union of Private Railway Truck Owners' Associations (RU)
MSCP .... Mesic Sovetsko-Ceskoslovenskeho Pratelstvi [*Soviet-Czechoslovak Friendship Month*] (CZ)
MSD .... Doctor Medicinae Scientariae [*Doctor of Scientific Medicine*] (CZ)
MSD .... Masarykuv Studentsky Domov [*Masaryk Students' Home*] (CZ)
MSD .... Mechanical Services Department (MAR)
MSD .... Mechanical Services Director (MAR)
MSD .... Medical Battalion (RU)
MSD .... Minimal Lethal Dose (RU)
MSD .... Motorized Rifle Division (RU)
MSD .... Motostrelecka Divize [*Motorized Rifle Division*] (CZ)
MSD .... Movimento Social Democrata [*Social Democrat Movement*] [*Portuguese*] (PPE)
MSD .... Movimiento Social Democratico [*Social Democratic Movement*] [*Peruvian*] (LA)
MSDC .... Movimiento Social Democrata Cristiano [*Christian Social Democrat Movement*] [*Paraguayan*] (LA)
MSDF .... Maritime Self Defense Force (SJT)
MSDM .... Ministry of Construction and Road Machinery Manufacture, USSR (RU)
MSDP .... Mauritian Social Democratic Party (MAR)
MSDP .... Mezinarodni Sdruzeni Demokratickych Pravniku [*International Association of Democratic Lawyers*] (CZ)
ms dr .... Bridge Battalion (BU)
MSDR .... Ministry of Supply and State Reserves (BU)
MSDV .... Far Eastern Naval Forces (RU)
MSE .... International Telecommunication Union [*ITU*] (RU)
MSE .... Monimoi Synodikai Epitropai [*Permanent Synodical Committees*] [*Greek*] (GC)
MSE .... Movimiento Socialista Espanol [*Spanish Socialist Movement*] (WER)
MSE .... Mtibwa Sugar Estate Ltd. (MAR)
MSE .... Small Soviet Encyclopedia [*A publication*] (RU)
m/sek .... Meter pro Sekunde [*Meters per Second*] (EG)
msek .... Millisecond (RU)
MSES .... Ministry of Construction of Electric Power Plants, USSR (RU)
ms es .... Naval Squadron (BU)
Msf .... Mesafe [*Distance, Distant*] (TU)
MSF .... Multilateral Scientific Fund (MAR)
MSFK .... Moscow Union of Physical Culture (RU)
MSFNRJ .... Ministarstvo Saobracaja Federativne Narodne Republike Jugoslavije [*Ministry of Transportation of the Federal People's Republic of Yugoslavia*] (YU)
MSFNRJ .... Muzejski Savet Federativna Narodna Republika Jugoslavija [*Museum Council of Yugoslavia*] (YU)
MSG .... Makerere Students' Guild [*Ugandan*] (AF)
MSG .... Melanocyte-Stimulating Hormone (RU)
MSG .... Movimiento Socialista de Galicia [*Socialist Movement of Galicia*] [*Spanish*] (WER)
MSG .... Movimiento Socialista Guineano (MAR)
MSGB .... Muslim Society in Great Britain (MAR)
MSGG .... International Union of Geodesy and Geophysics [*IUGG*] (RU)
MSGNRM .... Ministarstvo za Socijalni Grizi na Narodnata Republika Makedonija [*Ministry of Social Assistance of Macedonia*] (YU)
Msgr .... Monsignore [*German*]
MSGV .... International (Railway) Wagon Union (RU)
MSH .... Ministerstvo Stavebnich Hmot [*Ministry of Building Materials*] (CZ)
MSh .... Nautical School (RU)
MSh .... Naval Staff (RU)
MSh .... Small Demolition Charge (RU)
MShchU .... Local Control Board (RU)
MShI .... Magnet of Step-by-Step Switch (RU)
MShT .... International Temperature Scale (RU)
MShU .... Low-Noise Amplifier (RU)
MShZ .... Moscow Tire Plant (RU)
MSI .... Medunarodni Statisticki Institut [*International Statistical Institute*] (YU)
MSI .... Moscow Institute of Sanitation (RU)
MSI .... Mouvement Sociologique International (MAR)
MSI .... Movimento Sociale Italiano [*Italian Social Movement*] (PPE)
MSI .... Second Independence Movement [*Ecuadorean*] (PPW)
MSiDM .... Ministry of Construction and Road Machinery Manufacture, USSR (RU)
MSI-DN .... Movimento Sociale Italiano - Destra Nazionale [*Italian Social Movement - National Right Wing*] (WER)
MSiIP .... Ministry of the Machine Tool and Tool Industry, USSR (RU)
MSIM .... International Council for the Exploration of the Sea [*ICES*] (RU)
MSIP .... Ministry of the Machine Tool and Tool Industry, USSR (RU)
MSIRI .... Mauritius Sugar Industry Research Institute (AF)
MSK .... Card-Sorting Magnet (RU)
MSK .... International Skating Union [*ISU*] (RU)
MSK .... International Students' Conference (BU)
MSK .... International Union of Crystallography [*IUCr*] (RU)
MSK .... Local Scholarship Commission (RU)
MSK .... Maritime Signal Book, Maritime Signal Code (RU)
MSK .... Masarykova Studentska Kolej [*Masaryk Students' Home*] (CZ)
MSK .... Medical Team (RU)
MSK .... Mistni Spravni Komise [*Local Administrative Commission*] (CZ)
MSK- .... Mobile Construction Crane (RU)
MSK- .... Mobile Folding Crane (RU)
MSK .... Moscow Time (RU)
MSKh .... Freewheeling Mechanism (RU)
MSKh .... Ministry of Agriculture (RU)
MSKhA .... Moscow Agricultural Academy Imeni K. A. Timiryazev (RU)
MSKhI .... Moscow Agricultural Institute (RU)
MSKhM .... Ministry of Agricultural Machinery Manufacture, USSR (RU)
MSKhZh .... International Agricultural Journal [*A publication*] (RU)
M-ski suv ..... Council of Ministers (BU)
MSKP .... Maritime Disease Control Point (RU)
Mskr .... Manuskript [*Manuscript*] (EG)
MSKRP .... International Special Committee on Radio Interference (RU)
msl .... Mesela [*For Example*] [*Turkish*] (GPO)
msl .... Mimo Sluzbu [*Retired, Inactive*] (CZ)
MSL .... Movimento Separatista Lusitano (MAR)
MSI .... Muzeum Slaskie [*Silesian Museum*] (POL)
MSL .... Small Collapsible Boat (RU)
MSM .... Mezinarodni Svaz Mladeze [*International Union of Youth*] (CZ)
MSM .... Midwest State Movement (MAR)
MSM .... Ministry of Medium Machinery Manufacture (RU)
MSM .... Mouvement Social du Maniema (MAR)
MSM .... Mouvement Social Muhutu [*Hutu Social Movement*] [*Rwandan*] (AF)
MSM .... Mouvement Socialiste Malgache [*Malagasy Socialist Movement*] (AF)
MSM .... Mouvement Socialiste Mauricien [*Mauritius Socialist Movement*] (AF)
MSM .... Mouvement Solidaire Moluba (MAR)
MSMO .... International Union of Railway Medical Services (RU)
MS MPVO .... Medical Service of the Local Antiaircraft Defense (RU)
MSMS .... International Union of Socialist Youth [*IUSY*] (RU)
MSN .... Movimiento de Salvacion Nacional [*National Salvation Movement*] [*Nicaraguan*] (LA)
MS-NK .... Matica Slovenska, Narodna Kniznica [*Matica Slovenska, National Library*] (CZ)
MSNK .... Small Council of People's Commissars [*1921-1930*] [*RSFSR*] (RU)
MSNKh .... Moscow Council of the National Economy (RU)
MSNRM .... Ministerstvo za Sumarstvo na Narodnata Republika Makedonija [*Ministry of Forestry of Macedonia*] (YU)
MSNS .... International Council of Scientific Unions [*ICSU*] (RU)
MSO .... Inter-American Defense Board [*IADB*] (RU)
MSO .... Interkolkhoz Construction Organization (RU)
MSO .... International Economic Organizations (BU)
MSO .... International Economic Trust (BU)
MSO .... International Tin Council [*ITC*] (RU)
MSO .... Local Construction Trust (BU)

MSO .... Medical Detachment (RU)
MSO .... Medical Section [*Military term*] (RU)
MSO .... Mezinarodni Svaz Odborovy [*International Trade Union Federation*] (CZ)
MSO .... Ministerstvo Skolstvi a Osvety [*Ministry of Education and Culture*] (CZ)
MSO .... Ministry of Social Security (RU)
MSO .... Misto Specielni Ocisty [*Special Decontamination Point*] (CZ)
MSO .... Moulin du Sud-Ouest (MAR)
MSO .... Mouvement Socialiste Occitan [*Occitanian Socialist Movement*] [*French*] (PPE)
MSOF .... Fleet Medical Department (RU)
MSOGVD .... Local Council for Social Welfare and Children's Education (BU)
Mson .... Maison [*House, Firm*] [*Business and trade*] [*French*]
MSOP .... International Union for the Protection of Nature [*IUPN*] (RU)
MSOS .... Meziministersky Sbor Obrany Statu [*Interdepartmental Committee for National Defense*] (CZ)
MSOT .... International Union of Public Transport (RU)
MSOT .... Magyar Sportorvosi Tanacs [*Hungarian Council of Sports Physicians*] (HU)
MSOTO .... International Union of Official Travel Organizations [*IUOTO*] (RU)
MSP .... International Trade-Union Secretariat (RU)
MSP .... Manufacture Senegalaise de Papiers Transformes (MAR)
m sp .... Methyl Alcohol (RU)
MSP .... Milli Selamet Partisi [*National Salvation Party*] (TU)
MSP .... Ministerio de Salud Publica [*Ministry of Public Health*] [*Uruguayan*] (LA)
MSP .... Ministerstvo Socialni Pece [*Ministry of Social Welfare*] (CZ)
MSP .... Ministerstvo Spotrebniho Prumyslu [*Ministry of Consumer Industry*] (CZ)
MSP .... Ministerstvo Stavebniho Prumyslu [*Ministry of the Building Industry*] (CZ)
MSP .... Ministry of Construction and Roads [*Obsolete*] (BU)
MSP .... Ministry of the Machine Tool Industry, USSR (RU)
MSP .... Ministry of the Shipbuilding Industry, USSR (RU)
MSP .... Moderata Samlingspartiet [*Moderate Unity Party*] [*Swedish*] (PPE)
msp .... Motorized Rifle Regiment (BU)
MSP .... Motorized Rifle Regiment (RU)
MSP .... Motostrelecky Pluk [*Motorized Rifle Regiment*] (CZ)
MSP .... Movimento Socialista Popular [*Popular Socialist Movement*] [*Portuguese*] (PPE)
MSP .... Movimiento Sindical Peronista [*Peronist Union Movement*] [*Argentine*] (LA)
MSPA .... Mauritius Sugar Producers Association (AF)
MSPADD ..... Mauritius Society for the Prevention of Alcohol and Drug Dependency (AF)
MSPCA .... Mauritius Society for the Prevention of Cruelty to Animals (MAR)
MSPD .... International Union for Child Welfare [*IUCW*] (RU)
MSPD .... Machine for Hoisting Operations [*Pet.*] (RU)
MSPM .... Ministry of Construction of Machinery-Manufacturing Establishments, USSR (RU)
MSPMKhP ... Ministry of Construction of Establishments of the Metallurgical and Chemical Industries, USSR (RU)
MSPNP .... Ministry of Construction of Petroleum Industry Establishments, USSR (RU)
MSPO .... Moscow Union of Consumers' Societies (RU)
MSpr .... Ministerstvo Spravedlnosti [*Ministry of Justice*] (CZ)
MSPr .... Motostrelecky Prapor [*Motorized Rifle Battalion*] (CZ)
MSPS .... International Student Aid Service (BU)
MSPT .... Movimientos Sindicales del Pueblo Trabajador [*Trade Union Movements of the Working People*] [*Nicaraguan*] (LA1)
MSPTI .... Ministry of Construction of Heavy Industry Establishments, USSR (RU)
MSPUP .... Ministry of Construction of Coal Industry Establishments (RU)
ms r .... Bridge Company (BU)
MSR .... Bridge Construction District (RU)
MSR .... Independent Tripping Mechanism (RU)
MSR .... Medical Company (RU)
MSR .... Montserrat [*Three-letter standard code*] (CNC)
msr .... Motorized Rifle Company (BU)
MSR .... Motorized Rifle Company (RU)
MSR .... Movimiento Socialista Revolucionario [*Revolutionary Socialist Movement*] [*Panamanian*] (PPW)
MSR .... Movimiento Socialista Revolucionario [*Revolutionary Socialist Movement*] [*Ecuadorean*] (LA1)
MSR .... Shunting Signal Relay (RU)
msrk .... Maaseurakunta [*Finnish*]
MSRK i KD ... Moscow Soviet of Workers', Peasants', and Red Army Deputies (RU)
MSRKKA ..... Naval Forces of the Workers' and Peasants' Red Army (RU)
MSS .... Hay-Cutting Machine Station (RU)
MSS .... Installation and Construction Station (RU)
MSS .... International Code [*Nautical term*] (RU)
MSS .... International Seismological Summary [*ISS*] (RU)
MSS .... International Union of Students (BU)
MSS .... International Union of Students [*IUS*] (RU)
MSS .... Machine Computation Station, Machine Calculating Station (RU)
MSS .... Manuscripta [*Manuscripts*] [*Latin*] (GPO)
MSS .... Manuscritos [*Manuscripts*] [*Spanish*]
MSS .... Medical Department [*of naval ship*], Medical Service (RU)
MSS .... Medical Station (RU)
MSS .... Medunarodni Studentski Savez [*International Students' Union*] (YU)
MSS .... Meter-Second-Candle [*System of units*] (RU)
MSS .... Mezinarodni Svaz Studentstva [*International Union of Students*] (CZ)
MSS .... Ministerium fuer Staatssicherheit [*Ministry for State Security*] [*See also MfS, MISTASI*] (EG)
MSS .... Ministerstvo Statnich Statku [*Ministry of State Farms*] (CZ)
MSS .... Ministry of Machine Tool Manufacture, USSR (RU)
MSS .... Muzealna Slovenska Spolocnost [*Slovak Museum Society*] (CZ)
MSS .... Ship's Engineering Department (RU)
MSSB .... Mistni Skupina Svazu Brannosti [*Local Group of the Union for Military Preparedness*] (CZ)
MSSh .... International Latitude Service [*ILS*] (RU)
MSSKh .... Moscow Union of Soviet Artists (RU)
MSSM .... Ministry of Construction and Construction Materials (BU)
MSSR .... Moldavian Soviet Socialist Republic (RU)
MSSRC .... Mediterranean Social Science Research Council (MAR)
MSSRZ .... Moscow Shipyard (RU)
MSSS .... International Satellite Communications System (BU)
MSSSh .... International Rapid Latitude Service (RU)
MSSU .... Malaysia Special Services Unit (ML)
MSSVD .... Medical Society for the Study of Venereal Diseases (EA)
MSSZ .... Magyar Si Szovetseg [*Hungarian Skiing Association*] (HU)
MSSZh .... International Sports Union of Railwaymen (RU)
MST .... Maitrise de Sciences et Techniques [*French*]
MST .... Maladies Sexuelles Transmissibles [*Transmittable Sexual Diseases*] [*French Guiana*] (LA1)
MST .... Mali Sorumluluk Tazminat [*Financial Responsibility Indemnification*] (TU)
MST .... Marokanskii Soiuz Truda (MAR)
mst .... Meteorological Station (BU)
m st .... Miasto Stoleczne [*Capital City*] (POL)
mst .... Millistoke (RU)
MST .... Ministarstvo Spoljne Trgovine [*Ministry of Foreign Trade*] (YU)
MST .... Ministerstvo Strojirenstvi [*Ministry of the Machine Building Industry*] (CZ)
MST .... Moravskoslezske Tiskarny [*Moravian-Silesian Printing Plant*] (CZ)
MST .... Moroccan Labor Union (RU)
MST .... Moscow Statistical Technicum (RU)
MST .... Movimiento Socialista de los Trabajadores [*Socialist Workers Movement*] [*Dominican Republic*] (LA1)
MST .... Museum of Science and Technology (MAR)
MST .... Weather Station, Meteorological Station (RU)
MstB .... Bridge Battalion (RU)
MSTC .... Mauritius Sugar Terminal Corporation (MAR)
Mstr .... Meister [*German*]
MSTS .... Moscow State Sanitary Engineering Trust of the Glavmosstroy (RU)
MSTSPACOM ... Mediterranean Military Sea Transportation Service Space Assignment Committee (MAR)
MSU .... Bridge Construction Installation (RU)
MSU .... Machine Computation Installation, Machine Calculating Installation (RU)
MSU .... Movimento Socialista Unificado [*Unified Socialist Movement*] [*Portuguese*] (WER)
MSUS .... Mouvement Socialiste d'Union Senegalaise (MAR)
MSV .... Medical Platoon (RU)
MSv .... Ministerstvo Stavebnictvi [*Ministry of Building*] (CZ)
MSV .... Missionary Sisters of Verona (MAR)
MSV .... Mistni Skolni Vybor [*Local School Committee*] (CZ)
MSV .... Moscow Shipyard (RU)
msv .... Motorized Rifle Platoon (RU)
MSVU .... Ministerstvo Skolstvi, Ved, a Umeni [*Ministry of Education, Sciences, and Arts*] (CZ)
MSVU .... Moravskoslezske Sdruzeni Vytvarnych Umelcu [*Moravian-Silesian Association of Creative Artists*] (CZ)
MSVVMP ..... Ministry of Construction of Military and Naval Establishments (RU)
MSW .... Miejski Sztab Wojskowy [*City Military Headquarters*] (POL)
MSW .... Ministerstwo Spraw Wewnetrznych [*Ministry of Internal Affairs*] (POL)
MSW .... Ministerstwo Szkolnictwa Wyzszego [*Ministry of Higher Education*] (POL)
MSWiN .... Ministerstwo Szkol Wyzszych i Nauki [*Ministry of Higher Schools and Science*] (POL)
m sz .... Maganszektor [*Private Sector*] (HU)
MSZ .... Magyar Szabvany [*Hungarian Standard*] (HU)
MSZ .... Mednarodna Studentska Zveza [*International Students' Union*] (YU)
MSZ .... Ministerstvo pro Sjednoceni Zakonu [*Ministry for the Unification of Law*] (CZ)
MSZ .... Ministerstwo Spraw Zagranicznych [*Ministry of Foreign Affairs*] (POL)
MSZ .... Minsk Machine Tool Plant (RU)

MSZ............ Moscow Grinding Machine Plant (RU)
M Szabadsagh Szov ... Magyar Szabadsagharcos Szovetseg [*Association of Hungarian Freedom Fighters*] (HU)
MSZB.......... Magyar Szavatossagi Bank [*Hungarian Insurance Bank*] (HU)
MSZBH........ Magyar-Szovjet Baratsag Honap [*Hungarian-Soviet Friendship Month*] (HU)
MSZBT........ Magyar-Szovjet Barati Tarsasag [*Hungarian-Soviet Friendship Society*] (HU)
MSZDP........ Magyar Szocial Demokrata Part [*Hungarian Social Democratic Party*] (PPE)
MSZDSZ..... Magyarorszagi Szlovakok Demokratikus Szovetsege [*Democratic Association of Slovaks in Hungary*] (HU)
MSZh.......... International Council of Women [*ICW*] (RU)
MSzH.......... Magyar Szabvanyugyi Hivatal [*Hungarian Bureau of Standards*] (HU)
MSZH.......... Magyar Szovjet Hirado [*Hungarian-Soviet New Agency*] (HU)
MSZHB........ Mezogazdasagi Szovetkezeti Hitelbank [*Agricultural Cooperative Credit Bank*] (HU)
MSZhD........ International Union of Railways (RU)
MSzhSD...... International Council of Social Democratic Women (RU)
MSZHSZ..... Magyar Szabadsagharcos Szovetseg [*Association of Hungarian Freedom Fighters*] (HU)
MSZI........... Magyar Szabvanyugyi Intezet [*Hungarian Bureau of Standards*] (HU)
MSZK.......... Mezogazdasagi Szovetkezeti Kozpont [*Agricultural Cooperative Center*] (HU)
MSzKSz...... Magyar Szovjet Kozgazdasagi Szemle [*Hungarian-Soviet Economic Review*] [*A publication*] (HU)
MSZMP....... Magyar Szocialista Munkaspart [*Hungarian Socialist Workers' Party*] (PPE)
MSZMT....... Magyar Szovjet Muvelodesi Tarsasag [*Hungarian-Soviet Cultural Society*] (HU)
MSZOSZ..... Mezogazdasagi Szakemberek Orszagos Szovetsege [*National Association of Agricultural Specialists*] (HU)
MSZSZ........ Magyar Szabadsagharcos Szovetseg [*Association of Hungarian Freedom Fighters*] (HU)
MSzSz......... Mozgo Szakorvosi Szolgalat [*Special Mobile Medical Service*] (HU)
MSZSZ........ Muveszeti Szakszervezetek Szovetsege [*Federation of Artists' Trade Unions*] (HU)
MSZSZOSZ ... Magyar Szabad Szakszervezetek Orszagos Szovetsege [*National Federation of Hungarian Free Trade Unions*] (HU)
MSZT.......... Magyar Szenbanyaszati Troszt [*Hungarian Coal Mining Trust*] (HU)
MSZT.......... Magyar-Szovjet Tarsasag [*Hungarian-Soviet Society*] (HU)
MT............... A Munka Torvenykonyve [*Labor Code*] (HU)
MT............... Dead Center (RU)
MT............... Internacia Asocio Monda Turismo [*International Association for World Tourism*] (EA)
mt................ Mainittu Teos [*Finnish*]
MT............... Makinali Tufek [*Machine Gun*] (TU)
MT............... Malta [*Two-letter standard code*] (CNC)
MT............... Manometric Thermometer (RU)
MT............... Mariborska Tiskarna [*Maribor Printing House*] (YU)
MT............... Matice Technicka [*Society for the Promotion of Technology*] (CZ)
Mt................ Megaton (RU)
MT............... Megyei Tanacs [*County Council*] (HU)
Mt................ Metre [*or Metreler*] [*Meter or Meters*] (TU)
MT............... Milliers de Tonnes (MAR)
MT............... Ministerio do Trabalho [*Ministry of Labor*] [*Portuguese*] (WER)
MT............... Ministerio do Trabalho [*Ministry of Labor*] [*Brazilian*] (LA)
MT............... Ministerstvo Techniky [*Ministry of Technology*] (CZ)
MT............... Ministerul Turismului [*Ministry of Tourism*] (RO)
MT............... Ministry of Trade (RU)
MT............... Ministry of Transportation (BU)
MT............... Minisztertanacs [*Council of Ministers*] (HU)
MT............... Modosito Tervezet [*Modified Draft*] (HU)
mt................ Molecular Weight (BU)
Mt................ Mont [*Mount, Mountain*] [*French*] (NAU)
Mt................ Montant [*Amount*] [*Business and trade*] [*French*]
M/t............... Motorni Tanker [*Motor Tanker*] (YU)
MT............... Navigation Tables (RU)
MT............... Telephone Handset, Hand Microtelephone (RU)
MTA............ Macedonian Telegraph Agency (BU)
MTA............ Maden Tetkik ve Arastirma Enstitusu [*The Mining Research Institute*] [*See also MTAE*] (TU)
MTA............ Magyar Tudomanyos Akademia [*Hungarian Academy of Sciences*] (HU)
MTA............ Malaysian Territorial Army (ML)
MTA............ Materiel Thermique Africain (MAR)
MTA............ Ministry of Tourism and Aviation [*Seychelles*] (AF)
MTAC.......... Management Training and Advisory Centre (MAR)
mtad........... Mine and Torpedo Aviation Division (BU)
MTAE.......... Maden Tetkik ve Arastirma Enstitusu [*The Mining Research Institute*] [*See also MTA*] (TU)
mtae........... Mine and Torpedo Aviation Squadron (BU)
MTAK.......... Magyar Tudomanyos Akademia Konyvtara [*Library of the Hungarian Academy of Sciences*] (HU)
MTAMEN-SEN ... Maden Tetkik ve Arastirma Enstitusu Genel Mudurlugu Isyeri Mensuplari Sendikasi [*Mining Technique and Research Institute Directorate General Site Employees Union*] [*Ankara*] (TU)
MTAMTO.... Magyar Tudomanyos Akademia Muszaki Tudomanyok Osztalya [*Hungarian Academy of Sciences, Division of Technical Sciences*] (HU)
MTAP.......... Mine and Torpedo Air Regiment (RU)
mtap........... Mine and Torpedo Aviation Regiment (BU)
MTAVA........ Mwananchi Tractor and Vehicles Assemblers Ltd. (MAR)
MTB............ Moscow Trolleybus (RU)
MTC............ Manufacture de Tabac de la Cote-d'Ivoire (MAR)
MTC............ Mauritius Turf Club (MAR)
MTC............ Medumurska Trikotaza (Cakovec) [*Medjumurje Knitted Goods Factory (Cakovec)*] (YU)
MTC............ Ministerio dos Transportes e Communicacoes [*Ministry of Transportation and Communication*] [*Portuguese*] (WER)
MTCF.......... Multilateral Technical Co-Operation Fund (MAR)
MTCI........... Manufacture des Tabacs de la Cote-d'Ivoire (MAR)
MTDiL......... Ministerstwo Transportu Drogowego i Lotniczego [*Ministry of Road and Air Transportation*] (POL)
MTE............ Magnetic Triode Element (RU)
MTE............ Maison Tunisienne de l'Edition (MAR)
MTE............ Makina - Takim Endustrisi AS [*Machinery and Equipment Industry Corporation*] (TU)
MTE............ Mezogazdasagi es Elelmiszeripari Tudomanyos Egyesulet [*Scientific Institute for Agriculture and the Food Industry*] (HU)
MTE............ Minisztertanacs Elnoke [*Prime Minister, Chairman of the Council of Ministers*] (HU)
Mte............. Monte [*Mount, Mountain*] [*Italian*] (NAU)
Mte............. Monte [*Mount, Mountain*] [*Portuguese*] (NAU)
Mte............. Monte [*Mount, Mountain*] [*Spanish*] (NAU)
MTE............ Munkas Torna Egylet [*Workers' Athletic Association*] (HU)
MTEI........... Manufacture Tunisienne d'Exploitation Industrielle (MAR)
MTEI........... Moscow Institute of Transportation Economics (RU)
MTEKSZ..... Magyar Tekezo Szovetseg [*Hungarian Bowling Association*] (HU)
M Term tud Tars ... Magyar Termeszettudomanyi Tarsasag [*Hungarian Natural Science Association*] (HU)
MTESZ........ Muszaki es Termeszettudomanyi Egyesuletek Szovetsege [*Federation of Technical and Scientific Associations*] (HU)
MTEU.......... Moscow Tourist and Excursion Administration (RU)
MTF............ Dairy Farm (RU)
MTF............ Meat Production Farm (RU)
mtf.............. Metaforikos [*Figuratively*] (GC)
MTF............ Trimethyltrithiophosphite (RU)
MTFL.......... Moscow Television Branch Laboratory (RU)
MTFP.......... Marema Tlou [*or Tloe*] Freedom Party (MAR)
MTG............ Magusa Turk Gucu [*Famagusta Turkish Strength*] [*Soccer team*] (TU)
Mtgl............ Mitglied [*German*]
MT H........... A Munkaerotartalekok Hivatala Elnokenek Vegrehajtasi Utasitasa [*Decree of the President of the Office of Labor Reserves*] (HU)
Mth............. Minisztertanacs Hatarozata [*Resolution of the Council of Ministers*] (HU)
Mth............. Minisztertanacsi Hatarozat [*Council of Ministers Resolution (Legal)*] (HU)
MT H........... Munkaerotartalekok Hivatala [*Office of Labor Reserves*] (HU)
MTI............. Hungarian Telegraph Information (BU)
MTI............. Magyar Tavirati Iroda [*Hungarian Telegraph Agency*] (HU)
MTI............. Massachusetts Institute of Technology [*MIT*] (RU)
MTI............. Moscow Peat Institute (RU)
MTI............. Moscow Textile Institute (RU)
MTI............. Mouvement de la Tendance Islamique [*Islamic Trend Movement*] [*Tunisian*] (PD)
MTILP.......... Moscow Technological Institute of Light Industry (RU)
MTIMMP..... Moscow Technological Institute of the Meat and Dairy Industry (RU)
MTIMP......... Moscow Technological Institute of Local Industry (RU)
MTIN........... Ministry of Trade and Industry, Northern Region (MAR)
MTiP........... Ministry of Trade and Industry (RU)
MTIPP......... Moscow Technological Institute of the Food Industry (RU)
MTiSKhM.... Ministry of Tractor and Agricultural Machinery Manufacture, USSR (RU)
MTiTM........ Ministry of Transportation and Heavy Machinery Manufacture, USSR (RU)
MTK............ Dairy Kolkhoz (RU)
MTK............ International Commission on Terminology (RU)
MTK-........... International Telegraph Code (RU)
MTK............ Maataloustuottajain Keskusliitto [*Agricultural Producers' Association*] [*Finnish*] (WEN)
MTK............ Magyar Tanacskoztarsasag [*Hungarian Soviet Republic*] (HU)
MTK............ Medunarodna Trgovinska Komora [*International Chamber of Commerce*] (YU)
MTK............ Metallurgie de Kolwezi (MAR)
MTK............ Miedzynarodowe Targi Ksiazki [*International Book Fair*] [*Polish*]
MTK............ Shallow Tubular Well (RU)
MTKhTU..... Moscow Theatrical Applied Art School (RU)

MTkI........... Mernoki Tovabbkepzo Intezet [*Institute for Extension Courses in Engineering*] (HU)
MTKI........... Munkavedelmi Tudomanyos Kutato Intezet [*Scientific Research Institute for Labor Safety*] (HU)
MTKJ........... Mezogazdasagi Termekek Kereskedelmi Jegyzeke [*Commercial Register of Agricultural Products*] (HU)
Mtkm........... Megatonnenkilometer [*Million Ton-Kilometers*] (EG)
MTL........... Maaseudun Tyonantajaliitto [*Agricultural Employers' Association*] [*Finnish*] (WEN)
mtl........... Monatlich [*Monthly*] (EG)
MTL........... Mouvement pour le Triomphe des Libertes Democratiques [*Movement for the Triumph of Democratic Liberties*] [*Algerian*] (MAR)
MTLD........... Mouvement pour le Triomphe des Libertes Democratiques [*Movement for the Triumph of Democratic Liberties*] [*Algerian*] (AF)
MTM........... Machine and Tractor Shop (RU)
MTM-........... Maksutov Meniscus-Lens Telescope (RU)
MTM........... Marches Tropicaux et Mediterraneens (MAR)
MTM........... Metodtidmatning [*Methods Time Measurement*] [*Swedish*] (WEN)
MTM........... Ministry of Heavy Machinery Manufacture, USSR (RU)
MTM........... Ministry of Transportation Machinery Manufacture, USSR (RU)
MTM........... Mouvement des Travailleurs Mauriciens [*Mauritian Workers Movement*] (AF)
MTN........... Multilateral Trade Negotiations (MAR)
MTO........... High-Powered Telephoto Lens (RU)
MTO........... International Trade Organization (RU)
MTO........... Maintenance Vehicle (RU)
MTO........... Masuri Tehnice-Organizative [*Technical-Organizational Measures*] (RO)
MTO........... Materials and Equipment Supply Department (RU)
MTO........... Materiel Support [*Military term*] (RU)
MTO........... Mediterranean Theater of Operations (MAR)
MTO........... Medunarodna Trgovinska Organizacija [*International Trade Organization*] (YU)
MTO........... Milletlerarasi Ticaret Odasi [*International Chamber of Commerce*] (TU)
MTO........... Milli Talebe Orgutu [*National Student Organization*] (TU)
MTO........... Mouvement Togolais pour la Democratie [*Togolese Movement for Democracy*] (PD)
MTO........... Thermomechanical Treatment (RU)
MTO........... Weather Situation (BU)
MTOA........... Manufacture des Tabacs de l'Ouest Africain (MAR)
MTOP........... Ministerio de Transporte y Obras Publicas [*Ministry of Transportation and Public Works*] [*Uruguayan*] (LA)
MTP........... International Chamber of Commerce [*ICC*] (RU)
MTP........... Junior Technical Personnel (RU)
MTP........... Magnetotelluric Profiling (RU)
MTP........... Maktab Tentera Persekutuan [*Federation Military College*] (ML)
MTP........... Manufacture Togolaise des Plastiques (MAR)
MTP........... Marema Tlou Party [*Basotho*] (AF)
MTP........... Miedzynarodowe Targi Poznanskie [*Poznan International Fair*] (POL)
MTP........... Ministerstvo Tezkeho Prumyslu [*Ministry of Heavy Industry*] (CZ)
MTP........... Ministry of the Fuel Industry (RU)
MTP........... Ministry of Heavy Industry [*Obsolete*] (BU)
MTP........... Ministry of the Textile Industry (RU)
MTPC........... Ministre des Travaux Publics [*Algerian*] (MAR)
MTPP........... Tactical Infantry Training Methods (RU)
MTPT........... Ministry of Commerce, Industry, and Labor [*Obsolete*] (BU)
MTPY........... Metokhikon Tameion Politikon Ypallilon [*Civil Servants Pension Fund*] [*Greek*] (GC)
MTQ........... Martinique [*Three-letter standard code*] (CNC)
MTR........... Magnetic Thermonuclear Reactor (RU)
MTR........... Magyar Telefonhirmondo es Radio Reszvenytarsasag [*Hungarian Closed-Circuit Transmission and Radio Company Limited*] (HU)
MTR........... Ministry of Labor Reserves (RU)
MTR........... Naval Transport Aircraft (RU)
mt r........... Turbid Solution (RU)
MTrans-TekhnB... Ministry of Transportation, Technical Library (BU)
MTRK........... Makedonskiot Taen Revolucioneren Komitet [*Macedonian Secret Revolutionary Committee*] (YU)
MTRZ........... Moscow Trolleybus Repair Plant (RU)
MTS........... Long-Distance Telephone Communications (RU)
MTS........... Long-Distance Telephone Exchange (RU)
MTS........... Long-Distance Telephone Network, Trunk Network (RU)
MTS........... Machine and Tractor Station (RU)
MTS........... Machine-Tractor Stations (BU)
MTS........... Magyar Testnevelesi es Sportmozgalom [*Hungarian Physical Education and Sports Movement*] (HU)
mts........... Mainittu Teos, Sivu [*Finnish*]
MTS........... Maschinen-Traktoren-Station [*Machine Tractor Station*] (EG)
MTS........... Masinsko-Traktorske Stanice [*Machine Tractor Stations*] (YU)
MTS........... Materials and Equipment Supply (RU)
MTs........... Mechanical Interlocking [*Railroads*] (RU)
MTS........... Mestska Telekomunikacni Sprava [*City Administration for Telecommunications*] (CZ)
MTS........... Meter-Ton-Second [*System of units*] (RU)
MTS........... Metokhikon Tameion Stratou [*Army Pension Fund*] [*Greek*] (GC)
MTS........... Miedzynarodowy Trybunal Sprawiedliwosci [*International Court of Justice*] [*Polish*]
MTS........... Miedzynarodowy Tydzien Studenta [*International Students' Week*] (POL)
MTS........... Ministerstvo Tezkeho Strojirenstvi [*Ministry of Heavy Machine Building Industry*] (CZ)
MTS........... Ministry of Transportation Construction (RU)
MTs........... Mitotic Cycle (RU)
m-ts........... Month (RU)
MTS........... Moscow Theater of Satire (RU)
MTsAOR........... Moscow Central Archives of the October Revolution (RU)
MTSB........... Megyei Testnevelesi es Sportbizottsag [*County Physical Education and Sports Committee*] (HU)
mtsb........... Motorcycle Battalion (BU)
MTsB........... Motorcycle Battalion (RU)
MTsD........... World Data Centers (RU)
MTSE........... Munkas Testedzo es Sport Egylet [*Workers' Physical Education and Sports Association*] (HU)
MTsEM........... Mathematical Digital Electronic Computer (RU)
MTSG........... Ministry of Labor and Social Welfare [*Obsolete*] (BU)
MTSH........... Magyar Testnevelesi es Sporthivatal [*Hungarian Office of Physical Education and Sports*] (HU)
MTsK........... Centralized-Check Machine (RU)
MTsM........... Ministry of Nonferrous Metallurgy (RU)
MTSNRM........... Ministerstvo na Trgovijata i Snabduenjeto na Narodnata Republika Makedonija [*Ministry of Commerce and Supply of Macedonia*] (YU)
mtsp........... Motorcycle Regiment (BU)
MTsR........... Interchain Reaction (RU)
mtsr........... Motorcycle Company (BU)
MTsRK........... Moscow Central Workers' Cooperative (RU)
MTSRTS........... Maschinen-Traktoren-Station Reparatur-Technische Station [*Machine Tractor Station Repair and Technical Station*] (EG)
MTsSB........... Central Bureau of the Association of Seismology and Physics of the Earth's Interior (RU)
MTST........... Magyar Testnevelesi es Sport Tanacs [*Hungarian Council for Physical Education and Sports*] (HU)
mtsv........... Motorcycle Platoon (RU)
MTsVIA........... Moscow Central Military History Archives (RU)
MTSZT........... Magyar Termeszetbarat Szovetseg Tanacsa [*Council of the Hungarian Nature Study Association*] (HU)
MTT........... Magyar Tarsadalomtudomanyi Tarsulat [*Hungarian Social Science Association*] (HU)
MTT........... Magyar Tudomanyos Tanacs [*Hungarian Scientific Council*] (HU)
MTT........... Mariborska Tekstilna Tovarna [*Maribor Textile Factory*] (YU)
MTT........... Milicias de Tropas Territoriales [*Territorial Troops Militia*] [*Cuban*] (LA1)
MTT........... Moscow Peat Technicum (RU)
mtt........... Multifrequency Voice-Frequency Telegraphy (RU)
MTT........... Technical Installation Trust (RU)
MTT........... Telluric Current Method (RU)
MTTB........... Mauritius Tourist and Travel Bureau (MAR)
MTTB........... Milli Turkiye Talebe Birligi [*Turkish National Student Union*] (TU)
MTTc........... Ministerul Transportului si Telecomunicatiilor [*Ministry of Transportation and Telecommunications*] (RO)
MTTE........... Malawian Traders Trust Extension (MAR)
MTTH........... Minisztertanacs Tanacsi Hivatala [*Bureau for Local Councils of the Council of Ministers*] (HU)
MTTI........... Moscow Institute of Trade and the Science of Commodities (RU)
MTTs........... Moscow Television Center (RU)
MTTT........... Magyar Termeszettudomanyi Tarsasag [*Hungarian Natural Science Association*] (HU)
mtty........... Maaratty [*Finnish*]
MTU........... Circuit Telecontrol [*Electricity*] (BU)
MTU........... Machine Technical School (BU)
MTU........... Methylthiouracil (RU)
MTU........... Mezimestska Telefonni Ustredna [*Long Distance Telephone Central*] (CZ)
MTU........... Mezinarodni Telekomunikacni Unie [*International Telecommunications Union*] (CZ)
MTU........... Motoren- und Turbinen Union [*West German*]
MTU........... Technical Installation Administration (RU)
MTU........... Weather Conditions (BU)
MTUC........... Malaysian Trade Union Congress (ML)
M Tud Akad... Magyar Tudomanyos Akademia [*Hungarian Academy of Sciences*] (HU)
mTV........... Maritime Tropical Air (RU)
MTV........... Materialtechnische Versorgung [*Procurement of Required Materials*] (EG)
mtv........... Megyei Tanacs ala Rendelt Varos [*Town Administered by a County Council*] (HU)
Mtv........... Mitverseher [*German*]
MTVA........... Metokhikon Tameion Vasilikis Aeroporias [*Royal Air Force Pension Fund*] [*Greek*] (GC)

MTVN .... Metokhikon Tameion Vasilikou Navtikou [*Royal Navy Pension Fund*] [*Greek*] (GC)
MTVO .... Regimental Shop for the Repair of Tank Armament and Optical Equipment (RU)
MTW .... Matthias-Thesen-Werft Wismar (VEB) [*Wismar Matthias-Thesen Shipyard (VEB)*] (EG)
MTWS .... Miedzynarodowe Towarzystwo Wagonow Sypialnych [*International Sleeping Car Association*] (POL)
MTY .... Millions of Tons per Year (MAR)
MTYuZ .... Moscow Young Spectator's Theater (RU)
MTZ .... Magnetotelluric Sounding (RU)
MTZ .... Materialne Technicke Zasobovani [*Technical and Material Procurement*] (CZ)
MTZ .... Minsk Tractor Plant (RU)
MTZ .... Moscow Brake Plant (RU)
MTZ .... Moscow Pipe Plant (RU)
MTZ .... Moscow Transformer Plant (RU)
MTZ .... "Tito" Metalski Zavod [*"Tito" Metal Institute*] [*Skopje*] (YU)
MTZ .... Tractor Made by the Minsk Tractor Plant (RU)
MU .... Installation [*Assembly*] Administration (RU)
MU .... Installation Administration (RU)
MU .... Local Control [*Computers*] (RU)
MU .... Magnetic Amplifier (RU)
MU .... Management Unit (MAR)
MU .... Masarykova Universita [*Masaryk University*] [*Brno*] (CZ)
MU .... Matematicky Ustav [*Mathematical Institute (of the Czechoslovak Academy of Sciences)*] (CZ)
MU .... Mauritius [*Two-letter standard code*] (CNC)
MU .... Metrologicky Ustav [*Metrological Institute*] (CZ)
MU .... Mezinarodni Telefonni Ustredna [*International Telephone Exchange*] [*Prague*] (CZ)
MU .... Microphone Amplifier (RU)
MU .... Montanni Unie [*European Coal and Steel Community*] (CZ)
MU .... Moviment Universitari [*University Movement*] [*Spanish*] (WER)
MU .... Multiplier [*Computers*] (RU)
mu .... Munkas [*Worker*] (HU)
mu .... Muszaki [*Technical, Engineering (Adjective)*] (HU)
MU .... Muzicka Akademija [*Music Academy*] (YU)
MU .... Mykologicky Ustav [*Institute of Mycology*] (CZ)
MU .... Naval Trainer, Naval Trainer Aircraft (RU)
MU .... Power Unit (RU)
MUA .... Mouvement Universitaire Algerien [*Algerian University Movement*] (AF)
Mua .... Muavini [*Assistant, Deputy*] (TU)
MU-AD .... Magnetic Amplifier-Induction Motor (RU)
MUAKI .... Muanyagipari Kutato Intezet [*Industrial Research Institute on Plastics*] (HU)
MUAN .... Musterek Guvenlik ve Anlasmalar Dairesi Genel Mudurlugu [*Joint Security and Agreements Office Directorate General*] [*of Foreign Affairs Ministry*] (TU)
MUART .... Muszaki Arut Ertekesito Vallalat [*Commercial Enterprise for Machines, Machine Tools, and Machine Products*] (HU)
MUB .... Miejski Urzad Bezpieczenstwa [*Municipal Security Office*] (POL)
MUB .... Mouvement de l'Unite Basonge (MAR)
MUBEF .... Mouvement Unifie Belge des Etudiants Francophones [*Belgian United Movement of French-Speaking Students*] (WER)
MUC .... Kandidat Mediciny [*Candidate for the Degree of Doctor of Medicine*] (CZ)
MUC .... Mezinarodni Umluva o Preprave Cestujicich po Zeleznici [*International Agreement on Railroad Passenger Transportation*] (CZ)
MUC .... Millions d'Unites de Compte [*Millions of Counting Units*] [*French Guiana*] (LA1)
MUC .... Mission Universitaire et Culturelle Francaise en Tunisie (MAR)
MUC .... Mouvement d'Union Camerounaise (MAR)
MUC .... Movimiento Universitario Catolico [*Catholic University Movement*] [*Venezuelan*] (LA)
MUC .... Movimiento Universitario del Centro [*Central University Movement*] [*Argentine*] (LA)
MUCEU .... Makarere University College Employees Union [*Ugandan*] (AF)
MUCF .... Mission Universitaire et Culturelle Francaise au Maroc (MAR)
MUCS .... Movimiento de Unificacion y Coordinacion Sindical [*Union Unification and Coordination Movement*] [*Argentine*] (LA)
MUD .... Ministarstvo Unutrasnjih Djela [*Ministry of Internal Affairs*] (YU)
MUD .... Mouvement Union Democratique [*Democratic Union Movement*] [*Monegasque*] (PPE)
MUD .... Movimento da Uniao Democratica [*Democratic Union Movement*] [*Portuguese*] (WER)
MUD .... Movimento Universitario de Desfavelamento [*University Antislum Movement*] [*Brazilian*] (LA)
Mud .... Muddet [*Period*] [*of time*] (TU)
MUDA .... Movimiento Universitario Democrata Argentino [*Argentine Democratic University Movement*] (LA)
MUDel .... Local Division Control [*Computers*] (RU)
MUDES .... Movimento Universitario de Desenvolvimento Economico e Social [*University Movement for Economic and Social Development*] [*Brazilian*] (LA)
MUDJ .... Movimento de Unidade Democratica - Juvenil [*Democratic Union Movement - Youth*] (MAR)
MUD-Juvenil ... Movimento Uniao Democratica - Juvenil [*Democratic Union Movement - Youth*] [*Portuguese*] (WER)
MUDOK .... Muszaki Dokumentacios Kozpont [*Technical Documentation Center*] (HU)
MUDr .... Doctor Medicinae Universae [*Doctor of Medicine*] (CZ)
MUE .... Movimiento de Unidad Estudiantil [*Movement of Student Unity*] [*Panamanian*] (LA)
Mue .... Muehle, Hammerwerk [*German*]
muegy .... Muegyetem [*Technical University*] (HU)
MUEL .... Mouvement pour l'Unite et l'Entente Lulua (MAR)
MUF .... Ultraviolet Microscope (RU)
MUFI .... Muszaki Fizikai Kutato Intezet [*Technical Physics Research Institute*] (HU)
MUFIS .... Manisa Unlu Maddeler ve Firin Iscileri Sendikasi [*Manisa Farinaceous Products and Bakery Workers' Union*] (TU)
MUFLNG .... Mouvement pour l'Unification des Forces de Liberation de la Guadeloupe [*Movement for the Unification of National Liberation Forces of Guadeloupe*] (PD)
MUFM .... Mouvement Universel pour une Federation Mondiale [*World Association of World Federalists*] [*Use WAWF*] (AF)
MUFONOA ... Mutuelle des Fonctionnaires de l'Ordre Administratif [*Administrative Government Employees Mutual Association*] [*Cambodian*] (CL)
MUG .... Muszaki Gumigyar [*Industrial Rubber Factory*] (HU)
MUGI .... Melyepitoipari Uzemgazdasagi Iroda [*Industrial Management Bureau in Civil Engineering*] (HU)
MUGI .... Musterek Guvenlik Isleri Dairesi Genel Mudurlugu [*Joint Security Affairs Office Directorate General*] [*of Foreign Affairs Ministry*] (TU)
Muh .... Muhabere [*Communications*] (TU)
Muh .... Muhasebe [*Accounting, Accountancy*] (TU)
muh .... Muhely [*Workshop*] (HU)
Muh .... Muhendis [*Engineer*] (TU)
Muh .... Muhtar [*Village Headman*] (TU)
MUHE .... Ministere de l'Urbanisme, de l'Habitat, et de l'Environnement (MAR)
Muh Mim Aka ... Muhendislik ve Mimarlik Akademisi [*Engineering and Architecture Academy*] (TU)
MUI .... Moscow University News [*A publication*] (RU)
MUI .... Movement for the Unity of the Left [*Ecuadorean*] (PPW)
MUIN .... Movimiento Universitario Integralista Nacional [*National University Integral Movement*] [*Argentine*] (LA)
Muist .... Muistutus [*Note*] [*Finnish*] (GPO)
MUJ .... Movimiento Universitario Juvenil [*University Youth Movement*] [*Costa Rican*] (LA)
muk .... Flour Mill [*Topography*] (RU)
MUK .... Local Control of Commands [*Computers*] (RU)
MUK .... Magnetic Chart Angle (RU)
MUK .... Marine Scientific Committee (RU)
Mu K .... Muszaki Kiado [*Publishing House of Technical Literature*] (HU)
Muka .... Mukavele [*Contract, Agreement*] (TU)
MUKhIN .... Moscow Institute of Coal Chemistry (RU)
mul .... Mit dem Urzeiger Laufend [*Clockwise*] [*German*]
MULPOC .... Centre Multinational de Programme et d'Execution de Projets de l'Afrique de l'Ouest [*Multinational Center for the Programming and Execution of West African Projects*] (AF)
Mulr .... Muletier (Sentier) [*Mule Path*] [*Military map abbreviation*] [*World War I*] [*French*] (MTD)
mult .... Mehrfach [*German*]
MULTIFERSELA ... Empresa Multinacional para la Comercializacion de Fertilizantes del Sistema Economico Latinoamericano [*Multinational Enterprise for the Marketing of Fertilizers of the Latin American Economic System*] (LA)
mu m .... A Munkaugyi Miniszter Rendelete, Utasitasa [*Decree of the Minister of Labor*] (HU)
MuM .... Muhasebe Mudurlugu [*Accounting Directorate*] [*of Foreign Affairs Ministry*] (TU)
Mu M .... Munkaugyi Miniszter [*Minister of Labor*] (HU)
MUN .... Metal-Film Ultrahigh-Frequency Unprotected (Resistor) (RU)
MUN .... Movimiento de Unidad Nacional [*National Unity Movement*] [*Chilean*] (LA)
MUN .... Movimiento de Unidad Nacional [*National Unity Movement*] [*Salvadoran*] (LA1)
MUN .... Movimiento Universitario Nacional [*National University Movement*] [*Argentine*] (LA)
Mun .... Munition [*Ammunition*] (EG)
MUNAF .... Movimento de Unidade Nacional Antifacista [*National United Antifascist Movement*] [*Portuguese*] (PPE)
Munas .... Munasebetler [*Relations*] (TU)
MUNAS .... Musjawarah Nasional [*National Conference*] (IN)
MUNC .... Mouvement d'Union Nationale Congolaise (MAR)
MUNGE .... Movimiento de Union Nacional de Guinea Ecuatorial (MAR)
MUNI .... Moscow Real Estate Administration (RU)
MUNICROF ... Movimiento Universitario y Profesional para la Organizacion de la Comunidad [*Bogota*] (COL)
MUNOSZER ... Mutragya- es Novenyvedoszer Ertekesito Szovetkezeti Vallalat [*Cooperative Enterprise for Selling Fertilizers and Products for Plant Protection*] (HU)
MUOp .... Local Control of Operations [*Computers*] (RU)
MUOp Sdv ... Local Shift Control (RU)

MUOSZ .... Magyar Ujsagirok Orszagos Szovetsege [*National Federation of Hungarian Journalists*] (HU)
MUP .... Mesno Usluzno Preduzece [*Local Services Establishment*] (YU)
MUP .... Mezinarodni Urad Prace [*International Labor Office*] (CZ)
MUP .... Ministarstvo Unutrasnjih Poslova [*Ministry of Internal Affairs*] (YU)
MUP .... Ministry of the Coal Industry (RU)
MUP .... Mouvement de l'Unite Populaire [*Popular Unity Movement*] [*Tunisian*] (PD)
MUP .... Movimento de Unidade Popular [*Popular Unity Movement*] [*Portuguese*] (WER)
MUPGE .... Movimiento de Union Popular de Liberacion de la Guinea Ecuatorial (MAR)
MUPV .... Ministry of the Coal Industry of the Eastern Regions, USSR (RU)
MUPZ .... Ministry of the Coal Industry of the Western Regions, USSR (RU)
MUR .... Morski Urzad Rybacki [*Deep Sea Fishing Administration*] (POL)
MUR .... Moscow Office of Criminal Investigation (RU)
MUR .... Mouvement Unifie de la Resistance (MAR)
MUR .... Movimiento de Unidad Reformista [*Reformist Unity Movement*] [*Dominican Republic*] (LA1)
MUR .... Movimiento Universitario Reformista [*University Reform Movement*] [*Argentine*] (LA)
MUR .... Movimiento Universitario Revolucionario [*Revolutionary University Movement*] [*Colombian*] (LA)
MUR .... Movimiento Universitario Revolucionario [*Revolutionary University Movement*] [*Ecuadorean*] (LA)
MUREBES... Mutuelle des Ressortissants de Bengassou-Esseyakro (MAR)
MURFAAMCE ... Mutual Reduction of Forces and Armaments and Associated Measures in Central Europe (WER)
murt .... Murteellinen [*Dialect*] [*Finnish*]
MUS .... Magnetic Amplifier with Self-Magnetization (RU)
MUS .... Mauritius [*Three-letter standard code*] (CNC)
Mus .... Musavir [*Adviser*] (TU)
Mus .... Museum [*German*]
mus .... Musiikki [*Music*] [*Finnish*]
Mus .... Musik [*German*]
mus .... Musor [*Schedule, Program*] (HU)
Mus B .... Musicae Baccalaureus [*Bachelor of Music*] [*Latin*] (GPO)
MUSC .... Movimiento Universitario Social Cristiano [*Social Christian University Movement*] [*Dominican Republic*] (LA1)
Mus D .... Musicae Doctor [*Doctor of Music*] [*Latin*] (GPO)
MUSERMA ... Association Mutuelle de Secours des Ressortissants Manianga du Territoire de Songololo (MAR)
M u-shte...... School of Music (BU)
MUSI .... Local Addition Control [*Computers*] (RU)
Mus M .... Musicae Magister [*Master of Music*] [*Latin*] (GPO)
Muspaed..... Musisch-Paedagogisch [*German*]
MUSPIDA.... Musjawarah Pimpinan Daerah [*Regional Executive Council*] (IN)
MUSS .... Medunarodno Udruzenje za Socijalnu Sigurnost [*International Social Security Association (ISSA)*] (YU)
Must .... Musterek [*Joint*] (TU)
MUSZ .... Magyar Uszo Szovetseg [*Hungarian Swimming Association*] (HU)
MUSZ .... Magyar Uttorok Szovetsege [*Hungarian Pioneers' Association*] (HU)
musz .... Muszak [*Work Shift*] (HU)
musz .... Muszaki [*Technical, Technological*] (HU)
musz .... Muszeresz [*Mechanic*] (HU)
MUSZ .... Muszertermelo Vallalat [*Synthetic Coal Production Enterprise*] (HU)
MUSZI .... Mezogazdasagi Ugyvitelszervezesi Iroda [*Office for the Organization of Agricultural Business Management*] (HU)
musz tud doktora ... Muszaki Tudomanyok Doktora [*Doctor of Technical Sciences*] (HU)
Mut .... Mutercim [*Translator*] (TU)
Mute .... Mutehassis [*Specialist*] (TU)
MUTI .... Movimento Unitario dos Trabalhadores Intelectuais para a Defesa da Revolucao [*United Movement of Intellectuals for the Defense of the Revolution*] [*Portuguese*] (WER)
MUTRACI.... Mutuelle des Transporteurs de Cote-d'Ivoire (MAR)
MUUmn .... Local Multiplication Control [*Computers*] (RU)
mUV .... Maritime Moderate Air (RU)
MUV .... Mlynarsky Ustav Vyzkumny [*Flour Milling Research Institute*] (CZ)
MUV .... Modernized Simplified Fuze (RU)
MUV .... Universal Mine Fuze (RU)
muvez .... Muvezeto [*Foreman, Chief of Factory Unit*] (HU)
MUZ .... Mezinarodni Umluva o Preprave Zbozi po Zeleznicich [*International Agreement on Railroad Freight Transportation*] (CZ)
MUZ .... Mineworkers Union of Zambia (AF)
muz .... Museum (RU)
muz .... Music, Musical (RU)
muz .... Music, Musical (BU)
Muz .... Muzik [*Music*] (TU)
muz .... Muzyka [*or Muzyczny*] [*Music or Musical*] (POL)
Muzfond...... Music Fund of the USSR (RU)
Muzgiz .... State Music Publishing House (RU)
muzhsk .... Masculine, Male (RU)
muz-nauch ... Musicological (BU)
MUZO .... Music Department (RU)
MUZO .... Musical Education (RU)
Muzpred ..... State Music Trust (State Association of Music Establishments) (RU)
MV .... Cutter (RU)
MV .... Driver-Mechanic (RU)
MV .... Height Scale (RU)
MV .... Low Water (RU)
mv .... Maanviljelija [*Finnish*]
MV .... Maldives [*Two-letter standard code*] (CNC)
mV .... Maritime Air (RU)
MV .... Masking Agent [*Chemistry*] (RU)
Mv .... Materialversorgung [*Material Supply, Procurement*] (EG)
mv .... Measures of Weight (RU)
MV .... Mechanical Rectifier (RU)
MV .... Mechanized Troops (RU)
MV .... Megali Vretannia [*Great Britain*] (GC)
MV .... Megawolt [*Megavolt*] [*Polish*]
MV .... Meter Waves, Metric Waves (RU)
MV .... Methylviologen (RU)
MV .... Microswitch (RU)
mV .... Miliwolt [*Millivolt*] [*Polish*]
MV .... Milletvekili [*Deputy*] (TU)
mv .... Millivolt (BU)
mv .... Millivolt (RU)
MV .... Mine Fuze (RU)
MV .... Ministerstvo Vnitra [*Ministry of Interior*] (CZ)
MV .... Ministry of Armaments, USSR (RU)
mv .... Mint Vendeg [*Visiting Artist*] (HU)
MV .... Mistni Velitelstvi [*Local Command Post*] (CZ)
Mv .... Mitvergangenheit [*German*]
m/v............. Mois de Vue [*French*]
MV .... Molecular Weight (RU)
mv .... Moottorivene [*Finnish*]
mv .... Mortar Platoon (RU)
mv .... Mrtva Vaha [*Dead Weight*] (CZ)
MV .... Mudafaa Vekaleti [*Defense Ministry*] (TU)
MV .... Multivibrator (RU)
Mv .... Naval Forces (BU)
MV .... Oil Circuit Breaker, Oil Switch (RU)
MV .... Rotary Magnet (RU)
MV .... Small-Bore Rifle (RU)
m-v............. Study of Materials (RU)
MV .... Vacuum Gauge, Vacuum Manometer (RU)
MVA .... Magyar Vasuti Arudijszabas [*Hungarian Railroad Freight Rates*] (HU)
mva .... Megavolt Ampere (BU)
MVA .... Megavoltamper [*Megavolt-Ampere*] (YU)
MVA .... Moscow Veterinary Academy (RU)
MVAA.......... Mitteilungen aus dem Verein zur Abwehr des Antisemitismus [*Berlin*] [*A publication*] (MAR)
MVD .... Air-Manganese Depolarization (RU)
MVD .... Ministry of Internal Affairs (RU)
MVDr.......... Doctor Medicinae Veterinariae [*Doctor of Veterinary Medicine*] (CZ)
MVDr.......... Veterinary Doctor [*Czechoslovak*]
MVE............ Matravideki Eromu [*Power Plant of the Matra Region*] (HU)
MVETs .... Microhydraulic Power Plant (BU)
MVEU .... Moscow Higher School of Power Engineering (RU)
MVF............ International Monetary Fund [*IMF*] (RU)
MVG .... Magyar Vagon- es Gepgyar, Gyor [*Railroad Car and Machine Factory, Gyor*] (HU)
MVGT .... Moscow Evening Mining Technicum (RU)
MVI............ Metallverarbeitende Industrie [*Metalworking Industry*] (EG)
MVI............ Moscow Veterinary Institute (RU)
MV i SSO.... Ministry of Higher and Secondary Special Education (RU)
MVK .... Magyar Voroskereszt [*Hungarian Red Cross*] (HU)
MVK .... Mevalonic Acid (RU)
Mvk .... Mevki [*Site, Locality*] (TU)
MVK .... Ministerstvo Vykupu [*Ministry for Bulk Purchases (of agricultural products)*] (CZ)
MVK .... Moscow-Volga Canal [*1937-1947*] (RU)
MVKh .... Ministry of Water Management (RU)
MVKhPU ..... Moscow Higher School of Industrial Art (RU)
MVKRCh..... Interdepartmental Commission on Radio Frequencies (RU)
MVL............ Maximal Pulmonary Ventilation (RU)
MVM........... Magyar Vegyimuvek [*Hungarian Chemical Factory*] (HU)
m³vm.......... Cubic Meter Capacity (BU)
MVMI.......... Moscow Evening Institute of Mechanical Engineering (RU)
MVMI.......... Moscow Evening Institute of Metallurgy (RU)
MVMU .... Murmansk Higher Nautical School (RU)
MVN .... Armed-Safe Mechanism (RU)
MVN .... Materialverbrauchsnorm [*Material Consumption Norm*] (EG)
MVNB.......... Mistni Velitelstvi Narodni Bezpecnosti [*Local Headquarters of the National Security Corps*] (CZ)
MVO .... Ministerstvo Vnitrniho Obchodu [*Ministry of Domestic Trade*] (CZ)
M-vo........... Ministry (BU)
m-vo........... Ministry (RU)

MVO .... Ministry of Higher Education (RU)
MVO .... Moscow Military District (RU)
M-vo elektr i melior ... Ministry of Electrification and Land Reclamation [*Obsolete*] (BU)
M-vo elektr vod prir bog ... Ministry of Electrification and Natural Resources [*Obsolete*] (BU)
M-vo fin....... Ministry of Finance (BU)
M-vo ind zan ... Ministry of Industry and Trades [*Obsolete*] (BU)
M-vo inf izk ... Ministry of Information and the Arts [*Obsolete*] (BU)
M-vo nar otbr ... Ministry of National Defense (BU)
M-vo nar prosv ... Ministry of National Education (BU)
M-vo nar zdr ... Ministry of Public Health (BU)
M-vo obsht sgr put blag ... Ministry of Public Buildings, Roads, and Public Works [*Obsolete*] (BU)
M-vo prav.... Ministry of Justice (BU)
M-vo sots polit ... Ministry of Social Policy [*Obsolete*] (BU)
M-vo na transp ... Ministry of Transportation (BU)
M-vo turg.... Ministry of Commerce [*Obsolete*] (BU)
M-vo v .... Ministry of War [*Obsolete*] (BU)
M-vo vunsh rab ... Ministry of Foreign Affairs (BU)
M-vo vunsh rab i izpv ... Ministry of Foreign Affairs and Religious Faiths [*Obsolete*] (BU)
M-vo vutr rab ... Ministry of Internal Affairs (BU)
M-vo zemed i durzh im ... Ministry of Agriculture and State Property [*Obsolete*] (BU)
M-vo zhel avtom vodni i vuzd suobsht ... Ministry of Railroads and Automobile, Water, and Air Communications [*Obsolete*] (BU)
M-vo zhel posht i telegr ... Ministry of Railroads, Posts, and Telegraphs [*Obsolete*] (BU)
MVP............ Correcting Mechanism (RU)
MVP............ Method of Induced Polarization (RU)
MVP............ Methylvinylpyridine (RU)
MVP............ Ministerstvo Verejnych Praci [*Ministry of Public Works*] (CZ)
MVP............ Refracted Wave Method, Refraction Method (RU)
MVPI........... Moscow Higher Pedagogical Institute (RU)
MVPP .... Metal Runway (RU)
MVR .... Ministry of Foreign Affairs (BU)
MVR .... Ministry of Internal Affairs (BU)
MVR .... Molecular-Weight Distribution (RU)
MVR .... Mongolische Volksrepublik [*Mongolian People's Republic*] (EG)
MVR-UPPZ ... Ministry of Internal Affairs, Fire Prevention Administration (BU)
mvs .... Maanviljelysseura [*Finnish*]
MVS .... Magnetic-Variation Station (RU)
MVS .... Masinska Visa Skola [*Advanced Machinery School*] (YU)
MVS .... Mezinarodni Vseodborovy Svaz [*International Federation of Trade Unions*] (CZ)
MVS .... Ministerstvo Vseobecneho Strojirenstvi [*Ministry of Machine Building*] (CZ)
MVS .... Ministerstvo Vysokych Skol [*Ministry of Institutions of Higher Education*] (CZ)
MVS .... Ministry of the Armed Forces (RU)
MVS .... Mistni Vojenska Sprava [*Local Military Administration*] (CZ)
MVS .... Valence Bond Theory (RU)
MVSN.......... Milizia Volontaria per la Sicurezza Nazionale [*Italian*]
MVSofSA .... Mine Ventilation Society of South Africa (MAR)
MVSSO .... Ministry of Higher and Secondary Special Education (RU)
MVSSz .... Magyar Vandorsport Szovetseg [*Hungarian Tourists Association*] (HU)
MVSZ .... Magyar Vivo Szovetseg [*Hungarian Fencing Association*] (HU)
MVSzPE...... Magyar Vasuti Szemely-, Poggyasz-, es Expresszarudijszabas [*Hungarian Railroad Passenger, Luggage, and Freight Rates*] (HU)
MVSZSZ ..... Magyar Vasutasok Szabad Szakszervezete [*Free Trade Union of the Hungarian Railroad Workers*] (HU)
MVT............ International Military Tribunal (RU)
Mvt .... Megawatt (RU)
mvt............ Milliwatt (BU)
mvt .... Milliwatt (RU)
MVT............ Ministerstvo Vystavby a Techniky [*Ministry of Development and Technology*] (CZ)
MVT............ Ministry of Foreign Trade (BU)
MVT............ Ministry of Foreign Trade, USSR (RU)
MVT............ Ministry of Internal Trade (BU)
MVT............ Scale Rotary Transformer (RU)
Mvt-ch......... Megawatt-Hour (RU)
MVTU .... Moscow Higher Technical School Imeni N. E. Bauman (RU)
MVTVS........ Mistni Vybor pro Telesnou Vychovu a Sport [*Local Committee for Physical Education and Sports*] (CZ)
MVU-........... General-Purpose Wheatstone Resistance Bridge (RU)
MVunshRab ... Ministry of Foreign Affairs (BU)
MVunshTurg ... Ministry of Foreign Trade (BU)
MVutrTurg ... Ministry of Internal Trade (BU)
MVV .... Propellant, Low-Order Explosive (RU)
MVVS .... Modelarske Vyzkumne a Vyvojove Stredisko [*Model Research and Development Center (of the Union for Cooperation with the Army)*] (CZ)
MVY .... Magyar Vitorlas Yachtszovetseg [*Hungarian Sailboat and Yachting Association*] (HU)
MVZ............ Ministerstvo Vyzivy [*Ministry of Food Supply*] (CZ)
MVZ............ Minsk Bicycle Plant (RU)
MVZ............ Moravskoklezske Vlnarske Zavody [*Moravian-Silesian Woolen Mills*] (CZ)
MVZI........... Moscow Higher Zootechnical Institute (RU)
MVZShPD ... Moscow Higher Correspondence School of Trade Unionism of the VTsSPS (RU)
MW .... Malawi [*Two-letter standard code*] (CNC)
MW .... Marynarka Wojenna [*Navy*] (POL)
MW .... Material Wybuchowy [*Explosive*] [*Polish*]
MW .... Megavat [*Megawatt*] (YU)
MW .... Megawat [*Megawatt*] [*Polish*]
mW .... Meines Wissens [*As Far As I Know*] (EG)
MW .... Messwert [*Constant Value*] (EG)
mW .... Miliwat [*Milliwatt*] [*Polish*]
MW .... Minenwerfer [*Military*] [*German*] (MTD)
MW .... Mittelwasser [*Medium Water Level*] (EG)
MW .... Muslim World [*Hartford*] [*A publication*] (MAR)
MWAFG....... Media Workers Association of Free Grenada (LA1)
MWASA ...... Media Workers' Association of South Africa (MAR)
MWc .... Megavat Cas [*Megawatt-Hour*] (YU)
MWEU .... Motor Workshop Employees' Union (ML)
MWG .... Magyar Waggon- es Gepgyar, Ltd. [*Hungarian Railroad Car and Machine Plant Limited*] (HU)
MWG .... Miedzynarodowa Wspolpraca Geofizyczna [*International Geophysical Cooperation*] [*Polish*]
MWI............ Malawi [*Three-letter standard code*] (CNC)
MWIA .... Medical Women's International Association [*See also AIFM*] (EA)
MWL........... Muslim World League (MAR)
m woj .... Miasto Wojewodzkie [*Capital of Province*] [*Polish*]
MWP........... Malta Workers Party (PPE)
MWP........... Muzeum Wojska Polskiego [*Polish Army Museum*] [*Polish*]
MWPLF .... Malayan Workers and Peasants Labor Front (ML)
MWSM .... Mid-West State Movement (MAR)
MWT........... Mazurska Wytwornia Tytoniu [*Mazury (Masuria) Tobacco Plant*] (POL)
Mw d V .... Mittelwort der Vergangenheit [*German*]
mx .... Au Mieux [*French*]
Mx .... Makswel [*Maxwel*] [*Polish*]
mx .... Maximum [*Maximum*] [*German*]
MX.............. Mexico [*Two-letter standard code*] (CNC)
MX .... Wytwornia Maszyn Numer X [*Number X Machine Building Plant*] (POL)
M-18-X .... Movimiento 18 de Octubre de Accion Revolucionaria Astra [*Astra 18th October Movement of Revolutionary Action*] [*Ecuadorean*] (PD)
MY.............. Malaysia [*Two-letter standard code*] (CNC)
MYA .... Monoiodoacetate (RU)
myasn .... Meat Industry Kombinat [*Topography*] (RU)
myasn .... Meat Industry Plant [*Topography*] (RU)
myasokomb ... Meat Kombinat [*Topography*] (RU)
myasomolprom ... Meat and Dairy Industry (RU)
Myasomoltara ... Administration of Packing Materials Manufacture for the Meat and Dairy Industry (RU)
MYC .... Maadi Yacht Club (MAR)
MYC .... Malayan Youth Council (ML)
MYCL........... Mauritius Young Communist League (AF)
MYe............. International Unit (RU)
MYe............. Mass Unit (RU)
MyeD........... International Unit of Activity [*Medicine*] (RU)
MYK .... Merkez Yonetim Kurulu [*Central Executive Committee*] [*of a political party*] (TU)
myl .... Soap Plant [*Topography*] (RU)
MYOD.......... Malatya Yuksek Ogrenim Dernegi [*Malatya Higher Education Association*] (TU)
MYP............. Malawi Youth Pioneers (AF)
MYS .... Malaysia [*Three-letter standard code*] (CNC)
myt .... Mytologia [*Mythology*] [*Finnish*]
MYu............. Ministry of Justice (RU)
MYuD .... International Youth Day [*1915-1945*] (RU)
MYuF........... Moscow Jewelry Factory (RU)
MYuI............ Moscow Law Institute (RU)
MYuS .... International Jurists' Union (BU)
MYuTAKE ... Materials of the South Turkmen Complex Archaeological Expedition (RU)
MYW........... Maendeleo ya Wanawake [*Women's Development Organization*] [*Kenyan*] (AF)
Mz .... Farmstead [*Topography*] (RU)
MZ.............. Front des Artistes [*Artists Front*] [*Malagasy*] (AF)
MZ.............. Machine Building Plant (BU)
MZ.............. Mangels Zahlung [*For Non-Payment*] [*Business and trade*] [*German*]
Mz .... Mehrzahl [*German*]
Mz .... Mesozoyik [*Mesozoic*] [*Geology*] (TU)
MZ.............. Metallurgical Plant (BU)
MZ.............. Metallurgical Plant (RU)
MZ-............. Microsonde (RU)
MZ .... Minelayer (RU)
MZ.............. Ministerstvo Zeleznic [*Ministry of Railroads*] (CZ)
MZ.............. Ministerstvo Zemedelstvi [*Ministry of Agriculture*] (CZ)

MZ .... Ministerstwo Zdrowia [*Ministry of Health*] (POL)
MZ .... Ministerstwo Zeglugi [*Ministry of Shipping*] (POL)
MZ .... Ministry of Agriculture [*Obsolete*] (BU)
MZ .... Ministry of Public Health (RU)
MZ .... Mizarska Zadruga [*Cabinetmakers' Cooperative*] (YU)
MZ .... Mlekarska Zadruga [*Milk Cooperative*] (YU)
MZ .... Mozambique [*Two-letter standard code*] (CNC)
MZ .... Muzeum Ziemi [*Geological Museum*] (POL)
MZ .... Oil Dispenser, Servicing Truck (BU)
MZ .... Oil-Servicing Truck (RU)
mz .... Ointment, Salve (RU)
MZ .... Winter Oil (RU)
MZA .... Light Antiaircraft Artillery (BU)
MZA .... Moravsky Zemsky Archiv [*Moravian Provincial Archives*] (CZ)
MZA .... Small-Caliber Antiaircraft Artillery (RU)
MZA .... Small Refueling Unit (RU)
MZAL .... Minsk Plant of Transfer Machines and Standard-Unit Machine Tools (RU)
MZ-B .... Cluster Minefield (RU)
MZB .... Light Antiaircraft Battery (BU)
MZ bat .... Light Antiaircraft Battery (BU)
MZBM .... Miejski Zarzad Budynkow Mieszkalnych [*Municipal Administration of Residential Buildings*] (POL)
MZD .... Delayed-Action Mine (RU)
MZd .... Ministerstvo Zdravotnictvi [*Ministry of Public Health*] (CZ)
MZDI .... Ministry of Agriculture and State Property [*Obsolete*] (BU)
MZDS .... Moscow Woodworking Machine Plant (RU)
MZ-E .... Electromagnetic Minefield (RU)
MZ-G .... Deep Minefield (RU)
MZG .... Mazowieckie Zaklady Gastronomiczne [*Mazovian Catering Establishments*] [*Polish*]
MZG .... Ministry of Agriculture and Forests [*Obsolete*] (BU)
MZG- .... Multiple Hardening Burner (RU)
MZGT .... Moscow Correspondence Mining Technicum (RU)
MZh .... Local Population (BU)
MZh .... Manufactured from Marine Animals (RU)
MZh .... Methyl Yellow (Indicator) (RU)
MZH .... Miejski Zarzad Handlu [*Municipal Administration of Trade*] [*Polish*]
MZhAVS .... Ministry of Railroads, Automobiles, and Water Communications [*Obsolete*] (BU)
MZhD .... Murmansk Railroad (RU)
mzhdb .... Railroad-Bridge Battalion (RU)
MZhDK .... International Railway Congress (RU)
mzhdp .... Railroad-Bridge Regiment (RU)
MZhGS .... Ministry of Housing and Civil Engineering Construction (RU)
MZhK .... International Railway Transport Committee (RU)
MZhK .... Oil and Fats Kombinat (RU)
MZhKG .... International Cooperative Women's Guild [*ICWG*] (RU)
MZhP .... Oil and Fats Industry (RU)
mzhpb .... Railroad Bridge Battalion (BU)
mzhpp .... Railroad Bridge Regiment (BU)
MZhS .... Livestock-Breeding Machine Station (RU)
MZhSO .... Women's International Zionist Organization [*WIZO*] (RU)
MZ-I .... Engineer Minefield (RU)
MZI .... Moscow Zootechnical Institute (RU)
MZIEI .... Moscow Correspondence Institute of Engineering Economics (RU)
MZIMP .... Moscow Correspondence Institute of the Metalworking Industry (RU)
MZiOS .... Ministerstwo Zdrowia i Opieki Spolecznej [*Ministry of Health and Social Welfare*] [*Polish*]
MZIShP .... Moscow Correspondence Institute of the Garment Industry (RU)
MZISSP .... Moscow Correspondence Institute of the Silicate and Construction Industries (RU)
MZK .... Interplant Cooperation, Interfactory Cooperation (RU)
MZK .... Miejskie Zaklady Komunikacyjne [*Municipal Transportation Establishments*] (POL)
mz k .... Military Band (BU)
MZKGG .... Miedzykomunalne Zaklady Komunikacyjne Gdansk-Gdynia [*Gdansk (Danzig)-Gdynia Inter-City Transportation Establishment*] (POL)
MZKhP .... Ministry of Agriculture and Food Industry (BU)
Mzl .... Mezarlik [*Cemetery*] (TU)
MZL .... Middle Zone League (MAR)
MZM .... Miejski Zaklad Mleczarski [*Municipal Dairy*] (POL)
MZ-M .... Sea Minefield (RU)
MZMA .... Moscow Small Automobile Plant (RU)
MZNRM .... Ministerstvo za Zemjodelie na Narodnata Republika Makedonija [*Ministry of Agriculture of Macedonia*] (YU)
MZO .... Miejskie Zaklady Oczyszczania [*Town Cleaning Department*] [*Polish*]
MZO .... Ministerstvo Zahranicniho Obchodu [*Ministry of Foreign Trade*] (CZ)
MZO .... Ministerstwo Ziem Odzyskanych [*Ministry of Recovered Territories*] (POL)
MZO .... Ministry of Public Health (RU)
MZO .... Moscow Correspondence Branch (RU)
MZO .... Moscow Defense Zone [*1941-1942*] (RU)
MZO/HTS .... Ministerstvo Zahranicniho Obchodu/Hlavni Technicka Sprava [*Ministry of Foreign Trade/Main Technical Directorate*] (CZ)
MZOTsM .... Moscow Plant for the Processing of Nonferrous Metals (RU)
MZP .... Barely Perceptible Obstacle [*Military term*] (RU)
MZP .... Rabbit Wire, Concealed Wire [*Military term*] (RU)
MZP .... Small-Caliber Antiaircraft Machine Gun (RU)
MZPA .... Moscow Correspondence Industrial Academy (RU)
MZPD .... Miedzynarodowe Zrzeszenie Prawnikow Demokratow [*International Association of Democratic Lawyers*] (POL)
MZPI .... Moscow Correspondence Pedagogical Institute (RU)
MZPI .... Moscow Correspondence Printing Institute (RU)
MZPT .... Moscow Correspondence Technicum for Instrument Making (RU)
MZPUK .... Miejski Zarzad Przedsiebiorstw i Urzadzen Komunalnych [*City Administration of Municipal Enterprises and Establishments*] (POL)
MZPW .... Mazowieckie Zaklady Przemyslu Welnianego [*Mazowsze (Masovia) Wool Plant*] (POL)
MZ-R .... River Minefield (RU)
MZS .... Interlibrary Loan Service (BU)
MZS .... Miedzynarodowe Zawody Szybowcowe [*International Glider Contest*] (POL)
MZS .... Miedzynarodowy Zwiazek Spoldzielczy [*International Cooperative Union*] (POL)
MZS .... Miedzynarodowy Zwiazek Studentow [*International Union of Students*] (POL)
MZS .... Ministerstvo na Zemjodelie i Sumarstvo [*Ministry of Agriculture and Forestry*] (YU)
MZS .... Motorized Station for Hunting Sea Animals (RU)
MZS .... Pile-Screwing Mechanism (RU)
MZS .... Winter Lubricating Oil (RU)
MZSh .... Moscow Grinding Accessories Plant (RU)
MZShV .... Moscow Champagne Plant (RU)
MZSM .... Miedzynarodowe Zawody Sportowe Mlodziezy [*International Youth Games*] (POL)
MZST .... Moscow Correspondence Statistical Technicum (RU)
MZSZ .... Magyar Zenemuveszek Szovetsege [*Association of Hungarian Musicians*] (HU)
MZTA .... Moscow Thermal Automation Plant (RU)
MZTI .... Moscow Correspondence Textile Institute (RU)
MZU .... Assembly Preparation Sector (RU)
MZU .... Magnetic Storage, Magnetic Memory (RU)
MZU .... Moravske Zemske Ustredi Obci, Mest, a Okresu [*Center of Communities, Towns, and Districts of the Province of Moravia*] (CZ)
MZU .... Small Floating Bucket Dredge (RU)
MZUB .... Magnetic Drum Storage (RU)
MZUL .... Magnetic Tape Storage (RU)
MZUMD .... Magnetic Disk Mini-Memory System (BU)
MZV .... Ministerstvo Zahranicnich Veci [*Ministry of Foreign Affairs*] (CZ)
MZVZ .... Ministerstvo Zemedelstvi a Vyzivy [*Ministry of Agriculture and Food*] (CZ)
MZZ .... Barely Perceptible Obstacle [*Military term*] (RU)
MZZ .... Masinsko Zemjodelska Zadruga [*Agricultural Machinery Cooperative*] (YU)
MZZ .... Mesna Zemljoradnicka Zadruga [*Local Agricultural Cooperative*] (YU)
MZZhKT .... Moscow Correspondence Communal Housing Technicum (RU)

N

n ... Chief, Superior Officer (BU)
N ... Electric Locomotive Made by the Novocherkassk Electric Locomotive Plant (RU)
N ... Gunner (RU)
N ... Leistung [*Output*] [*German*]
N ... Low Pressure [*Meteorology*] (RU)
N ... Lower [*Toponymy*] (RU)
N ... Nacelnik [*Chief*] (CZ)
n ... Nach [*After*] [*German*]
N ... Nachmittags [*Afternoon*] [*German*]
N ... Nachts [*At Night*] [*German*]
n ... Nacido [*or Nacida*] [*Born*] [*Spanish*]
n ... Nad [*On*] [*In geographical names*] [*Polish*]
N ... Nada (MAR)
n ... Nagy [*Great, Big*] (HU)
N ... Nahgueterzug [*Local Freight Train*] (EG)
n ... Narodni [*National*] (CZ)
N ... Nassdampf [*Wet (Saturated) Steam*] (EG)
n ... Nastepny [*Next, Following*] (POL)
N ... National [*German*]
N ... Natus [*Born*] [*Latin*] (GPO)
N ... Navire [*Ship*] [*French*] (MTD)
N ... Nehir [*River*] (TU)
n ... Nemzeti [*National*] (HU)
N ... Nepos [*Grandson*] [*Latin*] (GPO)
n ... Netto [*Net*] [*Business and trade*] [*German*]
n ... Neutral [*Neutral*] [*German*]
n ... Neutrophils (RU)
N ... New [*Toponymy*] (RU)
n ... Newton (RU)
N ... Newton [*Finnish*]
N ... Nigeria Naira (MAR)
N ... Nisos [*Island*] [*Greek*] (NAU)
N ... Nitroglycerin (RU)
N ... Niuton [*Newton*] [*Polish*]
n ... Noche [*Night*] [*Spanish*]
N ... Nocte [*At Night*] [*Latin*] (GPO)
n ... Noerdlich [*Northern*] [*German*]
n ... Noin [*About, Approximately*] [*Finnish*] (GPO)
N ... Nombre Ignorado [*Spanish*]
N ... Nomen [*or Nomina*] [*Name or Names*] [*Latin*] (GPO)
N ... Nominal [*Nominal*] [*French*]
N ... Nord [*or Nordre*] [*North or Northern*] [*Danish*] (NAU)
N ... Nord [*North*] [*French*] (MTD)
N ... Nord [*or Norden*] [*North*] [*German*]
N ... Nord [*or Nordre*] [*North or Northern*] [*Norwegian*] (NAU)
N ... Nord [*or Norr or Norra*] [*North or Northern*] [*Swedish*] (NAU)
N- ... Norm (RU)
n ... Normal [*Normal*] [*German*]
N ... Normal [*Bearing precision class*] (RU)
n ... Normal [*Chemistry*] (RU)
n ... Normal Solution [*Chemistry*] (RU)
N ... Norte [*North*] [*Spanish*]
N ... Norwegia [*Norway*] [*Polish*]
N ... Noster [*Our*] [*Latin*] (GPO)
N ... Nota [*Note*] [*Latin*]
N ... Notablemente Aprobado [*On an Examination: Credit*] [*Spanish*]
N ... Notar [*German*]
N ... Notos [*South*] (GC)
n/ ... Notre [*Our*] [*Business and trade*] [*French*]
N ... Nowy [*New*] [*Polish*]
N ... Numero [*Number*] [*Finnish*] (GPO)
n ... Nutzeffekt, Wirkungsgrad [*Efficiency*] [*German*]
N ... Observation (RU)
N ... Observation, Surveillance, Supervision (BU)
N ... Observer (RU)
N ... People (BU)
N ... Plant Standard (RU)
N ... Stationary, Fixed (RU)
N ... Tight Fit, Drive Fit (RU)
n ... Uninhabited, Uninhabitable [*Topography*] (RU)
NA ... Ground Artillery (RU)
NA ... Nacelnik Artiljerije [*Chief of Artillery*] (YU)
NA ... Namibia [*Two-letter standard code*] (CNC)
NA ... Napoleonic Association (EA)
NA ... National Assembly [*United Arab Republic*] (MAR)
NA ... Nationalaktion Gegen die Ueberfremdung von Volk und Heimat [*National Action Against Foreign Domination of People and Homeland*] [*Swiss*] (WEN)
NA ... Nationale Aktion fuer Volk und Heimat [*National Action for People and Homeland*] [*Swiss*] (PPE)
NA ... Native Authority (MAR)
NA ... New Alphabet (RU)
NA ... Nitramine (RU)
NA ... Normal Markov Algorithms (RU)
N del A ... Nota del Autor [*Author's Note*] [*Spanish*] (GPO)
na ... Nota del Autor [*Author's Note*] [*Spanish*]
NA ... Notes Africaines [*Dakar*] [*A publication*] (MAR)
NA ... Notioanatolikos [*Southeast*] (GC)
NA ... Ordinance on the Traffic With, Purchasing, and Storage of Containers in Commercial Circulation and Material and Technical Supply (BU)
na ... People's Artist (RU)
NA ... Rifled Artillery (RU)
NAA ... Army Artillery Commander (RU)
NAA ... Narody Azii i Afriki (MAR)
NAACAM ... National Association of Automotive Component and Allied Manufacturers (MAR)
NAACIE ... National Association of Agricultural, Commercial, and Industrial Employees [*Guyanese*] (LA)
NAAF ... North-African Air Force (MAR)
NAAM ... National Association for the Advancement of Muslims [*Ugandan*] (AF)
NAAMSA ... National Association of Automobile Manufacturers of South Africa (MAR)
NAAO ... North Africa Area Office (MAR)
NAASO ... Nigerian Afro-Asian People's Solidarity (AF)
nab ... Embankment, Quay (RU)
nab ... Nabozenstvi [*Religion*] (CZ)
NAB ... National Assembly Bill (MAR)
NAB ... National Security Agency [*NSA*] (RU)
NAB ... Nigeria-Arab Bank Ltd.
NAB ... Nigerian Agricultural Bank (MAR)
nab ... Observer (RU)
NAB ... Unexploded Aerial Bomb (RU)
nabl ... Observation Tower [*Topography*] (RU)
NABOCE ... National Bookkeeping Certificate (MAR)
NABSO ... Namibian Black Students Organization (AF)
NABT ... Nigerian Association of Building Technicians (MAR)
NAC ... National Action Committee (ML)
NAC ... National Advisory Council [*Sierra Leonean*] (AF)
NAC ... National Advisory Council [*Somali*] (AF)
NAC ... National African Company (MAR)
NAC ... National Air Charters Zambia Ltd. (MAR)
NAC ... Native Anglican Church (MAR)
NAC ... Nyasaland African Congress (MAR)
NACAF ... Northwest African Coastal Air Force (MAR)
NACAL ... North American Conference on Afroasiatic Linguistics (MAR)
NACAR ... National Advisory Committee on Aeronautical Research (MAR)
NACB ... Nigerian Agricultural and Co-Operative Bank (MAR)
NACDA ... National Cooperative Development Agency [*Grenadian*] (LA1)
nach ... Beginning (BU)
nach ... Beginning, Start, Source (RU)
nach ... Chief, Head, Commander (RU)
nach ... Initial, First, Elementary (RU)
nachart ... Artillery Commander (RU)
nachartdiv ... Division Artillery Commander (RU)
nachartkor ... Corps Artillery Commander (RU)
nachdiv ... Division Commander (RU)
Nachf ... Nachfolger [*Successor*] [*German*] (WEN)
nachfin ... Chief of Finance [*Military term*] (RU)
nachinsnab ... Chief of Engineer Supply [*Military term*] (RU)

nachinzh..... Chief of Engineer Service [*Military term*] (RU)
nachinzharm ... Chief of Engineer Service of an Army (RU)
nachkants... Office Chief (RU)
nachkar....... Guard Commander (RU)
nachkhim.... Chief of Chemical Service (RU)
nachkhoz.... Chief of Administrative and Supply Department (RU)
nachkhoz.... Chief of Administrative and Supply Management (RU)
nachkhozupr ... Chief of Administrative and Supply Management (RU)
nachm......... Nachmittags [*After Noon*] [*German*] (GPO)
nachmil....... Chief of Militia (RU)
NAChNII...... Scientific Archives of the Chuvash Scientific Research Institute of Language, Literature, History, and Economics (RU)
nachpo........ Chief of Political Section [*Military term*], Chief of Political Department (RU)
nachpoarm ... Chief of Political Section of an Army (RU)
nachpodiv... Chief of Political Section of a Division (RU)
nachprod.... Chief of Food Supply [*Military term*] (RU)
nachpu........ Chief of Political Directorate [*Military term*], Chief of Political Administration (RU)
NAChSANARM ... Chief Medical Administration of a Separate Army (BU)
nachsanarm ... Chief of Medical Service of an Army (RU)
nachsanbrig ... Chief of Medical Service of a Brigade (RU)
nachsandiv ... Chief of Medical Service of a Division (RU)
nachsankor ... Chief of Medical Service of a Corps (RU)
nachsanupr ... Chief of the Military Medical Directorate (RU)
nach sk....... Initial Velocity, Initial Speed (RU)
nachsnab.... Chief of Supply (RU)
nachsoch.... Chief of Secret Operations Unit (RU)
nachveshch ... Chief of Clothing and Equipment Supply [*Military term*] (RU)
nachvoyendor ... Chief of Military Roads (RU)
nachvto...... Chief of Military Topographic Section (RU)
Nachw......... Nachwort [*Epilogue*] [*German*]
NACLA........ North American Congress on Latin America (LA)
NACO.......... National Agricultural Company (MAR)
NACOA....... Nacional de Combustible de Aviacion, SA [*National Aviation Fuel Corporation, Inc.*] [*Mexican*] (LA)
NACP.......... National Association for Coloured People (MAR)
NACPHO..... Nigeria Association of Creative Photographers (MAR)
NACREL...... National Chemical Research Laboratory (MAR)
Nacst.......... Nacelnik Stabu [*Chief-of-Staff*] (CZ)
nacz............ Naczelny [*Chief, Main*] (POL)
NAD............. Air Division Commander (RU)
NAD............. Division Artillery Commander (RU)
NAD............. National Accountancy Diploma (MAR)
NAD............. New African Development (MAR)
NAD............. Nicotinamide-Adenine Dinucleotide (RU)
NAD............. Noradrenaline (RU)
NADA.......... Native Affairs Department Annual [*A publication*] (MAR)
NADECO..... National Development Corporation (MAR)
NADELCO... Nacional de Comercio [*Cali*] (COL)
NADF........... Nicotinamide-Adenine Dinucleotide Phosphate (RU)
NADI........... Nomenclatura Arancelaria y Derechos de Importacion [*Tariff List and Customs Duties*] [*Argentine*] (LA)
NADI........... Scientific Research Highway Institute (RU)
nadt zagl..... Text Heading (BU)
NAEB.......... North African Economic Board (MAR)
NAES.......... Pumped Storage Electric Power Plant (RU)
NAF............. Norsk Arbeidsgiverforening [*Norwegian Employers' Association*] (WEN)
NAF............. Nouvelle Action Francaise [*New French Action*] (PPE)
NAFA........... Night Aerial Camera (RU)
NAFA........... Night Aerial Photographic Equipment (BU)
NAFAC........ Societe Nord-Africaine d'Arbitrages et de Changes [*Moroccan*] (MAR)
NAFC.......... North African Forestry Commission (MAR)
NAFCO........ National Agricultural and Food Corporation (MAR)
NAFCO........ National Airways and Finance Corporation (MAR)
NAFCO........ National Feed Company [*Egyptian*] (MAR)
NAFCOC..... National African Federated Chamber of Commerce (MAR)
NAFEN........ Near and Far East News Ltd. (MAR)
NAFINSA..... Nacional Financiera, Sociedad Anonima [*National Finance Bank, Incorporated*] [*Mexican*] (LA1)
NAFK........... Naphthofurancarboxylic Acid (RU)
NAFOZ........ National Fishermen Organization of Zambia (MAR)
NAFPP......... National Accelerated Food Production Program (MAR)
NAFSLAC ... National Association of Federations of Syrian and Lebanese American Clubs (MAR)
NAFTA........ Polnocno-Atlantycki Obszar Wolnego Handlu [*North Atlantic Free Trade Area*] (POL)
NAFTI.......... National Film and Television Institute (MAR)
NAFU........... National African Federation of Unions [*Rhodesian*] (AF)
NAGEMA..... Nahrungsmittel-, Genussmittel-, und Verpackungsmaschinen (VVB) [*Foodstuffs, Fancy Foodstuffs, and Packing Machines (VVB)*] (EG)
NAGES........ Pumped Storage Hydro-Electric Power Plant (RU)
nagl............ Naglowek [*Heading*] (POL)
nagyker v.... Nagykereskedelmi Vallalat [*Wholesale Commercial Enterprise*] (HU)
NAH............. Ministry of Animal Health, Northern Region (MAR)
NAHAL........ Fighting Pioneer Youth [*Israeli*] (ME)
NAHCO....... Nigerian Aviation Handling Company (MAR)
Nahgef........ Nahgefecht [*Close Combat*] (EG)
Nahk........... Nahkampf [*Close Combat*] (EG)
nahk........... Nahkateollisuus [*Leather Industry*] [*Finnish*]
Nahz........... Vereinigte Nieder- und Hochdruck-Dampfheizung [*Combined Low and High Pressure Steam Heating System*] (EG)
NAI............. Nordiska Afrika Institutet (MAR)
naib............ Greatest, Largest, Maximum (RU)
NAIB........... Societe Nantaise d'Importation de Bois et de Quincaillerie [*Moroccan*] (MAR)
NAICO......... Nacional de Ingenieria y Construcciones Ltda. [*Cali*] (COL)
NAIET.......... Nord Africa Industria e Transporti (MAR)
NAIG........... Nippon Atomic Industry Group Co., Ltd. (SJT)
naim............ Smallest, Least, Minimum (RU)
NAIZ........... Scientific Association for the Study of the Peoples of the West (RU)
NAK............ Corps Artillery Commander (RU)
Nak............. Nakliyat [*or Nakliye*] [*Transport*] (TU)
NAK............ Nea Agrotiki Kinisis [*New Agrarian Movement*] [*Greek*] (GC)
NAK............ Nederlandsch Archief voor Kerkgeschiedenis (MAR)
NAK............ Neolaiistiko Andidiktatoriko Kinima [*Antidictatorial Movement of Youth*] [*Greek*] (GC)
NAK............ Neos Astikos Kodix [*New Code of Civil Procedure*] (GC)
NAKA.......... Valakinek A Partfogoltja [*or X. Y. ElvtarsNAK A KAdere*] [*Someone's Protege (slang)*] (HU)
NAKASA..... National Amateur Karate Association of South Africa (MAR)
NAKI........... Nagynyomasu Kiserleti Intezet [*High Pressure Testing Institute*] (HU)
nakl............ Bill of Lading, Waybill, Invoice (RU)
nakl............ Mood [*Grammar*] (RU)
nakl............ Naklad [*Issue*] (POL)
nakl............ Naklada [*Edition*] (YU)
nakl............ Nakladatelstvi [*Publisher*] (CZ)
nakl............ Nakladem [*Published By*] (POL)
nakm.......... Nakladni Kilometr [*Freight-Kilometer*] (CZ)
NaKo.......... Nahrungs- und Konsumgueter [*Foodstuffs and Consumer Goods*] (EG)
NAL............ National Agricultural Laboratories (MAR)
NAL............ National Alliance of Liberals [*Ghanaian*] (AF)
NAL............ Natsional'naia Afrikanskaia Liga (MAR)
NAL............ Notaufnahmelager [*Emergency Reception Camp*] [*West German*] (WEN)
NAL............ Scientific Automobile Laboratory [*1918-1920*] (RU)
NALCO........ Nacional de Ingenieria y Construcciones Ltda. [*Bogota*] (COL)
NALDDH..... Encuentro Nacional de los Argentinos por las Libertades Democraticas y los Derechos del Hombre [*National Assembly of Argentines for Democratic Liberties and Human Rights*] (LA)
NALLA........ Agencia Nacional de Linhas a Longa Distancia [*National Agency for Long Distance Lines*] [*Portuguese*] (WER)
NALMACO ... Nacional de Maquinas de Contabilidad Ltda. [*Cali*] (COL)
NALO.......... Nasional Lotere [*National Lottery*] (IN)
nam............ Namestek [*Deputy*] (CZ)
nam............ Namesti [*Square, Boulevard*] (CZ)
NAM........... Namibia [*Three-letter standard code*] (CNC)
NAM........... Nederlandse Aardolie Maatschappij [*Netherlands Natural Gas Company*] (WEN)
NAM........... Nonaligned Movement (AF)
NAM........... North Africa Mission (MAR)
NA-MA........ Narodni Magazin [*People's Department Store*] (YU)
NAMB.......... National Agricultural Marketing Board (MAR)
NAMBOARD ... National Agricultural Marketing Board (MAR)
Namfrel....... National Citizens Movement for Free Elections [*Philippine*]
NAMI-.......... Automobile Designed by the Scientific Research Institute of Automobiles and Automobile Engines (RU)
NAMI........... Central Scientific Research Institute of Automobiles and Automobile Engines (RU)
naml........... Naemlich [*Namely*] [*German*] (GPO)
naml........... Namligen [*Namely*] [*Swedish*] (GPO)
NAMOTI...... National Movement for True Independence [*Trinidadian and Tobagan*] (LA1)
NAMPI......... National Archeological Museum in Plovdiv (BU)
NAMS.......... National Archeological Museum in Sofia (BU)
NAMSO....... [*The*] Namibian Students Organization (AF)
NAMUCAR ... Naviera Multinacional del Caribe [*Caribbean Multinational Shipping Line*] (LA)
NAN............ News Agency of Nigeria (MAR)
NAN............ Ordinance on Amortization Norms (BU)
NANA.......... New Africa News Agency (MAR)
NANAW....... Naval Forces Northwest African Waters (MAR)
NANC.......... Nyasaland African National Congress (MAR)
NANICA...... Naviera Nicaraguense [*Nicaraguan Shipping Co.*] (LA1)
NANS.......... Air Navigation Service Manual (RU)
NANS.......... National Association of Nigerian Students (MAR)
NAOP.......... Artillery-Gunnery Manual (RU)
nap............. Napis [*or Napisal*] [*Inscription or Written By*] [*Polish*]
nap............. Naponkent [*Daily*] (HU)
NAP............ National Action Party [*Turkish*] (PD)
NAP............ National Alliance Party (MAR)
NAP............ National Association of Manufacturers [*US*] (RU)
NAP............ National Awami Party [*Pakistani*] (PD)

NAP............ Nationales Aufbauprogramm [*National Reconstruction Program*] (EG)
NAP............ Niger Agricultural Project (MAR)
NAP............ Nigeria Advance Party (MAR)
NAP............ Nosokomeion Anapiron Polemou [*Nursing Home for War Handicapped*] [*Greek*] (GC)
NAP............ Nouvelle Agence de Presse [*New Press Agency*] [*French*] (AF)
NAP............ Nuclei Armati Proletari [*Armed Proletarian Nuclei*] [*Italian*] (PD)
NAP............ Nucleos de Acao Partidaria [*Party Action Nuclei*] [*Brazilian*] (LA1)
NAP............ Nucleos de Accion Popular [*Nuclei of Popular Action*] [*Spanish*] (WER)
NAP............ Regimental Artillery Commander (RU)
NAP............ Regimental Artillery Officer (BU)
NAPA.......... Nyasaland African Progressive Association (MAR)
NAPAC........ Natal Performing Arts Council (MAR)
NAPAP........ Noyaux Armes pour l'Autonomie Populaire [*Armed Cells for Popular Autonomy*] [*French*] (PD)
NAPCh........ Nonlinear Active Frequency Transformer (RU)
NAPCO........ National Production Company (MAR)
NAPDO........ Namibian African People's Democratic Organisation (MAR)
napech........ Printed, Published (BU)
NAPHER...... Nigeria Association for Physical Health, Education, and Recreation (MAR)
napk............ Napkozi [*During the Day, Daytime, Day-Care Center*] (HU)
NAPK.......... National Agroindustrial Complex (BU)
NAPK.......... Nea Anexartitos Politiki Kinisis [*New Independent Political Movement*] [*Greek*] (GC)
NAPO.......... Chief of Political Section [*Military term*], Chief of Political Department (RU)
(na) podst... (Na) Podstawie [*Based (On)*] (POL)
NAPP.......... Nacelnik Artiljerije Pesadiskog Puka [*Artillery Chief of an Infantry Regiment*] (YU)
napr............ For Example (BU)
napr............ For Example, For Instance (RU)
napr............ Na Priklad [*For Example*] (CZ)
napr............ Naprimer [*For Example*] (YU)
NAPRA........ National Padi and Rice Authority (ML)
NAPROZA... Nabavna in Prodajna Zadruga [*Buying and Selling Cooperative*] (YU)
napulno prerab... Completely Revised (BU)
NAPV.......... Asynchronous Automatic Reclosing (RU)
nar.............. Adverb (BU)
NAR............ Beginning of Automatic Operation (RU)
nar.............. Narodni [*National*] (CZ)
nar.............. Narozen [*Born*] (CZ)
NAR............ National Archives of Rhodesia (MAR)
NAR............ Nuclei Armati Rivoluzionari [*Armed Revolutionary Nuclei*] [*Italian*] (PD)
nar.............. People's, National (BU)
nar.............. People's, Popular, National (RU)
NARCO....... National Ranching Company [*Tanzanian*] (AF)
NARD.......... National Alliance for the Restoration of Democracy (MAR)
nar-demokr rep... People's Democratic Republic (BU)
NARI........... Natal Agricultural Research Institute (MAR)
naris........... Painted, Drawn By (BU)
NAR-IS Koop... Kibris Turk Narenciye Pazarlama Kooperatif [*Turkish Cypriot Citrus Fruit Marketing Cooperative*] (TU)
Narizdat...... People's Publishing House (BU)
NARKO........ Narenciye ve Tarim Urunleri Uretim ve Pazarlama Kooperatifi [*Citrus Fruit and Agricultural Products Producing and Marketing Cooperative*] [*Mersin*] (TU)
narkom....... People's Commissar [*1917-1946*] (RU)
narkomat.... People's Commissariat [*1917-1946*] (RU)
Narkomchermet... People's Commissariat of Ferrous Metallurgy, USSR [*1939-1946*] (RU)
NARKOMELEKTRO... People's Commissariat of Electric Power Plants and the Electrical Equipment Industry, USSR (RU)
NARKOMFIN... People's Commissariat of Finance [*1924-1946*] (RU)
NARKOMGOSKON... People's Commissariat of State Control [*1940-1946*] (RU)
Narkomindel... People's Commissariat of Foreign Affairs [*1917-1946*] (RU)
narkomkhim... People's Commissariat of the Chemical Industry [*1939-1946*] (RU)
Narkomkhimprom... People's Commissariat of the Chemical Industry [*1939-1946*] (RU)
NARKOMKhOZ... People's Commissariat of the Municipal Economy (RU)
Narkomkomkhoz... People's Commissariat of the Municipal Economy (RU)
NARKOMLEGPROM... People's Commissariat of Light Industry (RU)
NARKOMLES... People's Commissariat of the Lumber Industry [*1932-1946*] (RU)
NARKOMMASh... People's Commissariat of Machinery Manufacture, USSR (RU)
NARKOMMESTPROM... People's Commissariat of Local Industry (RU)
Narkommyasomolprom... People's Commissariat of the Meat and Dairy Industry (RU)
NARKOMNATs... People's Commissariat for Nationalities, RSFSR (RU)
NARKOMNEFT'... People's Commissariat of the Petroleum Industry, USSR [*1939-1946*] (RU)
NARKOMPIShChEPROM... People's Commissariat of the Food Industry (RU)
NARKOMPOChTEL'... People's Commissariat of Postal and Telegraphic Service (RU)
NARKOMPROD... People's Commissariat of Food [*1917-1924*] (RU)
NARKOMPROS... People's Commissariat of Education [*1917-1946*] (RU)
NARKOMPUT'... People's Commissariat of Railroads, USSR [*1922-1946*] (RU)
NARKOMRABKRIN... People's Commissariat of Workers' and Peasants' Inspection [*1920-1934*] (RU)
NARKOMRECHFLOT... People's Commissariat of the River Fleet, USSR (RU)
Narkomrezinprom... People's Commissariat of the Rubber Industry, USSR (RU)
NarkomRKI... People's Commissariat of Workers' and Peasants' Inspection [*1920-1934*] (RU)
NARKOMRYBPROM... People's Commissariat of the Fish Industry [*1939-1946*] (RU)
NARKOMSNAB... People's Commissariat of Supply [*1930-1934*] (RU)
NARKOMSOBES... People's Commissariat of Social Security [*1918-1946*] (RU)
NARKOMSOVKhOZOV... People's Commissariat of Grain and Livestock-Breeding Sovkhozes (RU)
NARKOMSVYaZ'... People's Commissariat of Communications, USSR [*1932-1946*] (RU)
Narkomtekstil'... People's Commissariat of the Textile Industry (RU)
Narkomtop... People's Commissariat of the Fuel Industry (RU)
Narkomtorg... People's Commissariat of Foreign and Domestic Trade, USSR [*1924-1938*] (RU)
NARKOMTORG... People's Commissariat of Trade [*1938-1946*] (RU)
NARKOMTRUD... People's Commissariat of Labor [*1917-1933*] (RU)
Narkomtsvetmet... People's Commissariat of Nonferrous Metallurgy, USSR [*1939-1946*] (RU)
NARKOMTYaZh... People's Commissariat of Heavy Industry [*1932-1939*] (RU)
Narkomtyazhprom... People's Commissariat of Heavy Industry, USSR [*1932-1939*] (RU)
NARKOMUGOL'... People's Commissariat of the Coal Industry, USSR [*1939-1946*] (RU)
Narkomvneshtorg... People's Commissariat of Foreign Trade, USSR [*1923-1925, 1930-1946*] (RU)
NARKOMVNUDEL... Narodnyi Komissariat Vnutrennikh Del [*People's Commissariat of Internal Affairs (1917-1946)*] [*Also known as NKVD*] [*Soviet secret police organization*]
Narkomvnutorg... People's Commissariat of Domestic Trade [*1924-1938*] (RU)
NARKOMVOD... People's Commissariat of Water Transportation, USSR (RU)
Narkomvoyen... People's Commissariat for Military Affairs [*1918-1923*] (RU)
Narkomvoyenmor... People's Commissariat for Military and Naval Affairs, USSR [*1923-1934*] (RU)
Narkomvoyenmor... People's Commissariat of the Navy, USSR [*1937-1946*] (RU)
Narkomyust... People's Commissariat of Justice, USSR [*1936-1946*] (RU)
NARKOMZAG... People's Commissariat of Procurement, USSR [*1938-1946*] (RU)
NARKOMZDRAV... People's Commissariat of Public Health [*1936-1946*] (RU)
NARKOMZEM... People's Commissariat of Agriculture (RU)
Narkoop...... People's Cooperative (BU)
Narkoopizdat... People's Cooperative Publishing House (BU)
Nar kult....... Narodna Kultura [*People's Culture*] [*A periodical*] (BU)
Narmag....... People's Store (BU)
nar obr........ Public Education (RU)
Narobraz..... Department of Public Education (RU)
nar pech...... National Press (BU)
narpit.......... Public Eating Facilities (RU)
NARPIT....... Trade Union of Workers of Public Eating Facilities (RU)
Nar prosv.... Narodna Prosveta [*Public Education*] [*A periodical*] (BU)
NARS.......... National Agricultural Research Station (MAR)
NARS.......... Unguided Aircraft-Launched Missile (RU)
Narsoc........ Narodni Socialiste [*National Socialists*] (CZ)
Nar subr...... National Assembly (BU)
narsuvet...... People's Council (BU)
NarTeatur... National Theater (BU)
NARUBIN.... Nasr Company for Rubber Industries (MAR)
NARUS........ Narodohospodarsky Ustav Slovensky [*Slovak Institute of Economics*] (CZ)
NAS............ Nacelnik Automobilni Sluzby [*Chief, Motor Transport Service*] (CZ)
NAS............ Navtikos Athlitikos Syndesmos [*Naval Athletic League*] [*Greek*] (GC)
nas............. Population (BU)
nas............. Population (RU)
NASA.......... National Agricultural Settlement Authority [*Libyan*] (MAR)
NaSa.......... Nuestra Senora [*Our Lady*] [*Spanish*]
NASACO..... National Shipping Company Agencies Ltd. [*Tanzanian*] (AF)
NASAF........ North African Strategic Air Force (MAR)
NASAKOM... Nasionalis-Agama-Kimunis [*Nationalists, Religious Groups, Communists (Term symbolizing the apparent unity of principal political groups during the Sukarno era)*] (IN)

NASCO .... El Nasr Automotive Manufacturing Corporation [*Egyptian*] (MAR)
NASDA .... National Space Development Agency (SJT)
nasl .... Successors (RU)
NASS .... Nacelnik Aviosignalne Stanice [*Air Signal Station Chief*] (YU)
nast .... Nastepny [*Next*] (POL)
nast .... Present (Tense) (RU)
nasyshch .... Saturated, Impregnated (RU)
nasz .... Naszierend [*Nascent*] [*German*]
NAT .... Navtikon Apomakhikon Tameion [*Seamen's Retirement Fund*] [*Greek*] (GC)
NAT .... Normal Atmospheric Pressure (RU)
NATA .... Neighbors Aid to Asia (CL)
Nat-Bibl ...... Nationalbibliothek [*German*]
NATCO .... National Confectionary Company (MAR)
NATEX .... National Textile Industries Corp. Ltd. (MAR)
NATI .... State All-Union Scientific Research Institute of Tractors (RU)
NATIS .... National Information System [*UNESCO*]
NATIST .... National Translation Institute of Science and Technology of Japan
Natle .... Nationale [*National*] [*Military map abbreviation*] [*World War I*] [*French*] (MTD)
NATO .... North African Theater of Operations (MAR)
NATO .... North Atlantic Treaty Organization [*See also OTAN*]
NATO-Is ...... Federation of NATO Workers Union (TU)
NatR .... Nationalrat [*German*]
NATREF ...... National Petroleum Refiners of South Africa (MAR)
NATROMOLDES ... Compania Nacional de Troquelado y Moldeo SA [*Bogota*] (COL)
nats .... National (BU)
nats .... National (RU)
NATS .... National Association of Technological Students (MAR)
nats k-t .... National Committee (BU)
Naturv .... Naturvorkommen [*Natural Occurrence*] [*German*]
NAU .... Natal Agricultural Union [*South African*] (AF)
NAUCA .... Nomenclatura Arancelaria Uniforme Centroamericana [*Uniform Customs List of Central America*] (LA)
nauch .... Scientific (BU)
nauch .... Scientific (RU)
nauch-issled ... Scientific Research (RU)
nauch-izsl ... Scientific Research (BU)
nauch-popul ... Popular Science (RU)
nauch-tekhn ... Scientific and Technical (RU)
NAURP .... Lower Amur River Steamship Line Administration (RU)
NAUTS .... National Union of Tanganyika Students [*Tanzanian*] (AF)
NAUW .... Nigeria Association of University Women (MAR)
NAV .... Navassa Island [*Three-letter standard code*] (CNC)
NAV .... Scientific Association of Oriental Studies (RU)
NAVENAL ... Compania Nacional de Navegacion [*National Shipping Company*] [*Colombian*] (LA)
NAVF .... Norge Almenvitenskapelige Forskningsrad [*Norwegian Research Council for Science and the Humanities*] (WEN)
NAVICONGO ... Syndicat des Cies de Navigation et Consignataires de Navires du Congo (MAR)
NAVIDA .... Compania de Seguros la Nacional SA [*Bogota*] (COL)
Navig .... Navigable [*Navigable*] [*Military map abbreviation*] [*World War I*] [*French*] (MTD)
NAVIM .... Navigational Information for Mariners (RU)
NAVIP .... Narodno Vinarstvo i Podrumarstvo [*National Wine-Selling and Wine Cellars*] (YU)
NAVITOGO ... Syndicat des Compagnies de Navigation et des Consignataires de Navires du Togo (MAR)
NAVLOMAR ... Intreprinderea de Navlosire, Agenturare, si Aprovizonare Nave [*Ship Supply Enterprise and Chartering Agency*] (RO)
NAVOCFORMED ... Naval On-Call Force Mediterranean (MAR)
NAVROM ..... Directia Generala a Navigatiei Civile [*General Directorate for Civil Navigation*] (RO)
NAVROM ..... Navigatia Maritima si Fluviala Romana [*Romanian Maritime and River Navigation*] (RO)
NAW .... Nationales Aufbauwerk [*National Reconstruction Program (Voluntary, unpaid work)*] (EG)
NAWAL .... North American West African Line (MAR)
NAWOA .... National Automobile Workshop Owners' Association (MAR)
NAYLAMP ... Cooperativa de Trabajadores del Puerto de Pimental Ltda. [*Pimentel Port Workers Cooperative*] [*Peruvian*] (LA)
NAYO .... National Youth Organization (MAR)
NAZ .... Emergency Supplies, Emergency Reserve (RU)
NAZ .... Nadvoitsy Aluminum Plant (RU)
NAZ .... National Archives of Zambia (MAR)
NAZ .... Netball Association of Zambia (MAR)
Nazavs .... Science for All [*Monograph series*] (BU)
NAZhT .... Academy of Railroad Transportation (RU)
nazv .... Name, Title (BU)
nazv .... Name, Title (RU)
NaZw .... Nahrungsmittelzuweisung [*Foodstuffs Allotment*] (EG)
NB .... Magyar Nemzeti Bizottmany, New York [*Hungarian National Council, New York*] (HU)
n/B .... Nad Becvou [*On the Becva River*] (CZ)
NB .... Nagy-Britannia [*Great Britain*] (HU)
nb .... Nagybecsu [*Esteemed*] (HU)
NB .... Naoruzan Brod [*Armed Vessel*] (YU)
NB .... Narodna Banka [*National Bank*] (YU)
NB .... Narodna Biblioteka [*National Library*] (YU)
NB .... Narodni Bezpecnost [*National Security (Corps)*] (CZ)
NB .... Nemzeti Bajnoksag [*National Championship, National League (Soccer)*] (HU)
NB .... Nemzeti Bank [*National Bank*] (HU)
NB .... Nepbirosag [*People's Court*] (HU)
NB .... Nepbolt [*People's General Store*] (HU)
NB .... Nobel-Bozel (MAR)
NB .... Nonlinear Block (RU)
NB .... Normal Boy [*Normal (Average) Length*] (TU)
n/b .... Not Found [*On lists*] (RU)
NB .... Nota Bene [*Mark Well*] [*Latin*] (GPO)
NB .... Notez Bien [*Note Well*] [*French*] (WER)
NB .... Scientific Library (RU)
NB .... Tail Water (RU)
NB .... Wage Scale (BU)
Nba .... Neubauamt [*Office for New Construction*] (EG)
NBA .... Nigerian Bar Association (MAR)
NBA .... Night Bombardment Aviation (RU)
NBA .... Nuovo Banco Ambrosiano [*Italian*]
NBAC .... Nigerian Bank for Agriculture and Co-Operatives (MAR)
NBAD .... Night Bomber Division (RU)
NBAP .... Night Bomber Regiment (RU)
NBATT .... Nigerian Battalion (MAR)
NBB .... Nederlandse Boekverkopers Bond
NBC .... Narodni Banka Ceskoslovenska [*Czechoslovak National Bank*] (CZ)
NBC .... National Bank of Commerce (MAR)
NBC .... National Bibliographic Control (MAR)
NBC .... National Book Council [*United Kingdom*]
NBC .... Nederlands Bibliografisch Centrum
NBC .... Nigerian Broadcasting Corporation (MAR)
NBCC .... Nigerian-British Chamber of Commerce (MAR)
NBCI .... Nigerian Bank for Commerce and Industry (AF)
NBD .... Nederlandse Bibliotheekdienst [*'s-Gravenhage*]
NBE .... National Bank of Egypt (MAR)
NBE .... National Bank of Ethiopia (AF)
NBF .... Nationaal Bibliotheek Fonds [*Dutch*]
NBFNRJ ...... Narodna Banka Federativna Narodna Republika Jugoslavija [*National Bank of Yugoslavia*] (YU)
NBIMOD ...... Naukowo-Badawczy Instytut Mechanicznej Obrobki Drewna [*Research Institute of the Mechanical Finishing of Lumber*] (POL)
NBIW .... Naukowo-Badawczy Instytut Wlokienniczy [*Textile Scientific Research Institute*] (POL)
NBK .... Initial Point of Bomb Run (RU)
NBL .... Nigerian Breweries Limited (MAR)
NBLC .... Nederlands Bibliotheek- en Lectuur Centrum [*'s-Gravenhage*]
NBM .... Niet Boek Materialen [*Dutch*]
NBM .... Nouvelle Boulangerie de M'Balmayo (MAR)
NBNI .... Nasionale Bounavorsningsinstituut (MAR)
Nborba .... Narodna Borba [*National Struggle*] [*A journal*] (YU)
NBP .... Initial Point of Bomb Run (RU)
NBP .... Lower Sideband (RU)
NBP .... Narodowy Bank Polski [*Polish National Bank*] (POL)
nbp .... Zeroth Born Approximation (RU)
NBPDCh ...... Lower Sideband of Doppler Frequencies (RU)
NBPGR .... National Bureau of Plant Genetic Resources [*Indian*]
NBR .... Unguided Ballistic Missile (RU)
NBRI .... National Building Research Institute (MAR)
NBRS .... National Building Research Station (MAR)
NBS .... Chief of Ammunition Supply (RU)
NBS .... Nemzetkozi Barati Sportjatekok [*International Friendship Games*] (HU)
NBS .... Nigeria Building Society (MAR)
NBS .... Nigerian Broadcasting Service (MAR)
NBT .... Nederlandse Bond van Middelbare en Hogare Technici [*Netherlands Union of Professional Engineers*]
NBU .... Combat Sector Commander (RU)
NC .... Nastavni Centar [*Training Center*] [*Military*] (YU)
NC .... National Convention (MAR)
NC .... Native Commissioner (MAR)
NC .... New Caledonia [*Two-letter standard code*] (CNC)
NC .... Non Classe [*Of soldiers who have not qualified at target practice*] [*French*] (MTD)
nc .... Non Cote [*French*]
n/c .... Notre Compte [*French*]
NC .... Nouveau Cedi (MAR)
NCA .... Nigeria's Constituent Assembly (MAR)
NCA .... Norwegian Church Aid (MAR)
NC-AAPSO ... Nigerian Committee of the Afro-Asian People's Solidarity Organization (AF)
NCAJL .... National Council of Art in Jewish Life (MAR)
NCAL .... National Constituent Assembly of Libya (MAR)
NCAL .... National Council for Arts and Letters [*Sudanese*] (MAR)
NCB .... National Commercial Bank [*St. Lucian*] (LA1)
NCBWA .... National Congress of British West Africa (MAR)
NCC .... Namibia Council of Churches (AF)
NCC .... National Canefarming Committee [*Guyanese*] (LA)

NCC .... National Computing Centre [*United Kingdom*]
NCC .... National Construction Corporation Ltd. (MAR)
NCC .... National Consultative Council [*Ugandan*] (AF)
NCC .... Nederlandse Classificatie-Commissie [*'s-Gravenhage*]
NCC .... Nouvelle Cie. Commerciale (MAR)
NCC/AV ...... Nederlandse Classificatie-Commissie/Algemene Vergadering
NCC/BV ...... Nederlandse Classificatie-Commissie/Beleidsvoorbereiding
NCC/CGr .... Nederlandse Classificatie-Commissie/Studiecommissie voor Classificatie Grondslagen [*Waarinopgenomen Classificatie Research*]
NCCK .... National Christian Council of Kenya (MAR)
NCCL .... National Council for Civil Liberties (MAR)
NCCM .... Nchanga Consolidated Copper Mines [*Zambian*] (AF)
NCCO .... National Cold Chain Operations Ltd. (MAR)
NCC/Plen ... Nederlandse Classificatie-Commissie/Plenaire Vergadering
NCC/Thes ... Nederlandse Classificatie-Commissie/Thesaurusproblemen
NCC/UDC/Red ... Nederlandse Classificatie-Commissie/Redactiecommissie voor Herziening van de Nederlandse Teksten en voor de Tekst van een Register op de Nederlandse Verkorte UDC-Uitgave
NCD .... National Christian Democratic Party [*Namibian*] (AF)
NCDB .... National Co-Operative and Development Bank (MAR)
NCDP .... Namibia Christian Democratic Party (PPW)
NCDP .... National Christian Democratic Party [*Namibian*] (AF)
NCDTC .... National Cooperative Development and Training Centre [*Sudanese*] (MAR)
NCE .... National Certificate of Education (MAR)
nch .... Low Frequency (BU)
NCh .... Low Frequency (RU)
NCHE .... National Council for Higher Education [*Sudanese*] (MAR)
NChK .... Neutralized Black Contact Substance (RU)
NCHP .... Navale et Commerciale Havraise Peninsulaire [*Malagasy*] (MAR)
n Chr .... Nach Christus [*After Christ*] [*German*] (GPO)
NChS .... Low-Frequency Seismic Exploration (RU)
NChS .... Normal Human Serum (RU)
NChSS .... Low-Frequency Seismic Station (RU)
NChZ .... Novacke Chemicke Zavody [*Chemical Factories at Novaky*] (CZ)
NChZ .... Science Reading Room (RU)
NCI .... National Chemical Industries (MAR)
NCI .... No Currency Involved (MAR)
NCJCS .... National Conference of Jewish Communal Service (MAR)
NCL .... National Central Library [*United Kingdom*]
NCL .... New Caledonia [*Three-letter standard code*] (CNC)
NCLDO .... National Congress of Local Democratic Organs [*Guyanese*] (LA1)
NCLL .... National Council for the Liberation of Libya (MAR)
NCLP .... Nyasaland Congress Liberation Party (MAR)
NCMB .... Nigerian Cocoa Marketing Board (MAR)
NCMV .... National Christelijk Middenstands Verbond [*National Christian Middle Class Federation*] [*Belgian*] (WEN)
NCNA .... New China News Agency (CL)
NCNC .... National Convention of Nigerian Citizens (AF)
NCNC .... National Council of Nigeria and Cameroon (AF)
NCNL .... Nasionale Chemiese Navorsingslaboratorium (MAR)
NCNU .... National Commission of Nigeria for UNESCO (MAR)
NCOB .... Nederlandstalig Centrum voor Openbare Bibliotheken
NCOBPS ..... National Conference of Black Political Scientists (MAR)
NCP .... National Convention Party (ML)
NCP .... National Convention Party [*Gambian*] (PPW)
NCP .... Nepali Congress Party (PD)
NCPC .... National Committee for the Protection of the Consumer [*Iranian*] (ME)
NCPC .... National Cooperative Planning Committee [*Mauritian*] (AF)
NCPP .... National Colored Peoples Party [*South African*] (AF)
NCR .... National Council of Resistance for Liberty and Independence [*Iranian*] (PD)
NCR .... National Council of the Revolution [*Syrian*] (MAR)
NCR .... Nuclei Comunisti Rivoluzionari [*Communist Revolutionary Nuclei*] [*Italian*] (WER)
NCRC .... National Council of the Revolutionary Command [*Syrian*] (MAR)
NCRI .... National Cereals Research Institute (MAR)
NCRL .... National Chemical Research Laboratory (MAR)
NCRV .... Nederlandse Christelijke Radio Vereniging [*Netherlands Christian Broadcasting Association*] (WEN)
NCS .... National Catholic Secretariat (MAR)
NCS .... Nghien Cuu Sinh [*Research Student*] (TVP)
NCS .... Nigerian Chemical Services Ltd. (MAR)
NCSAV .... Nakladatelstvi Ceskoslovenske Akademie Ved [*Publishing House of the Czechoslovak Academy of Sciences*] (CZ)
NCSL .... National Council of Sierra Leone (MAR)
NCSPD .... National Civic Service for Participation in Development (MAR)
NCSR .... National Council for Scientific Research [*Zambian*]
NCSR .... National Council for Social Research (MAR)
NCSV .... Nederlandse Christen-Studenten Vereniging [*Dutch Christian Students' Union*] (WEN)
NCSVU .... Nakladatelstvi Ceskoslovenskych Vytvarnych Umelcu [*Publishing House of Czechoslovak Creative Artists*] (CZ)
NCSW .... National Council for Social Welfare [*Sudanese*] (MAR)
NCSY .... National Conference of Synagogue Youth (MAR)
NCT .... Nucleo Comunista de Trabajadores [*Communist Nucleus of Workers*] [*Dominican Republic*] (LA)
NCTS .... Nacelnik Centralne Telefonske Stanice [*Central Telephone Station Chief*] [*Military*] (YU)
NCTUN .... National Council of Trade Unions of Nigeria (MAR)
NCU .... National Conference for Unification [*South Korean*] (PPW)
NCU .... Northern Co-Operative Union (MAR)
NCV .... Nacelnik Centra Veze [*Chief of Communications Center*] [*Military*] (YU)
NCVD .... Nacelnik Centra Vatre Divisiona [*Chief of a Divisional Fire Center*] (YU)
NCVEVS ...... Dutch Committee for European Security and Cooperation [*Pro-Moscow*] (WEN)
NCW .... National Council of Women (MAR)
NCW .... Nederlands Christelijk Werkgeversbond [*Dutch Christian Employers' Union*] (WEN)
NCW .... Non-Communist World (MAR)
NCWA .... Nigerian Citizens Welfare Association (MAR)
NCWD .... National Council of Women in Development (MAR)
NCWK .... National Council of Women of Kenya (MAR)
NCWSA ...... National Council of Women of South Africa (MAR)
NCWTD .... Nationaal Centrum voor Wetenschappelijke en Technische Documentatie [*Belgian*]
ND .... Directive on Concluding Contracts between Socialist Organizations (BU)
ND .... Directive on Contracts (BU)
nd .... Division Commander (BU)
ND .... Low Pressure (RU)
ND .... Naczelna Dyrekcja [*Central Administration, Main Directorate*] (POL)
ND .... Narodni Divadlo [*National Theater*] (CZ)
ND .... Narodowa Demokracja [*National Democratic Party*] (POL)
ND .... Nea Demokratia [*New Democracy*] [*Greek*] (PPE)
Nd .... Niederdruck [*Low Pressure*] (EG)
Nd .... Niederschlag [*Precipitate*] [*German*]
ND .... Nomothetikon Diatagma [*Legislative Decree*] (GC)
ND .... Nontoxic Screening Smoke (RU)
ND .... Normal Pressure (RU)
ND .... Notiodytikos (Anemos) [*Southwesterly (Wind)*] (GC)
N-D .... Notre Dame [*Our Lady*] [*French*] (GPO)
ND .... Nov Den [*New Day*] [*A publishing establishment*] [*Skopje*] (YU)
ND .... Nova Doba [*New Time*] [*A periodical*] (CZ)
nd .... Observer (BU)
ND .... Oil Field Exploitation (RU)
n/D .... On the Dnepr [*Toponymy*] (RU)
n/D .... On the Don [*Toponymy*] (RU)
ND .... People's Militia (RU)
ND .... Slant Range (RU)
NDA .... Dicyclohexylamine Nitrite (RU)
NDA .... Naczelna Dyrekcja Administracyjna [*Chief Executive Administration*] (POL)
NDA .... National Drama Association (MAR)
NDA .... Nigerian Defence Academy (MAR)
NDANC .... Nairobi District African National Congress (MAR)
NDAP .... Naczelna Dyrekcja Archiwow Panstwowych [*Central Administration of State Archives*] (POL)
NDAP .... Nationale Deutsche Arbeiterpartei [*National German Labor Party*] [*West German*] (PPW)
NDAR .... Algerian People's Democratic Republic (RU)
NDAR .... Narodnaia Demokraticheskaia Alzhirskaia Respublika (MAR)
ndaw .... Nur Direkt ab Werk [*Only Directly from the Plant*] (EG)
NDAZ .... National Drivers Association of Zambia (MAR)
NDB .... Naczelna Dyrekcja Bibliotek [*Central Administration of Libraries*] (POL)
NDB .... Nomenclature Douaniere de Bruxelles (MAR)
NDC .... National Defense Council (ML)
NDC .... National Development Corporation (MAR)
NDC .... National Documentation Center [*Laotian*] (CL)
NDC .... Niger Delta Congress (MAR)
NDC .... Nippon Decimal Classification
NDCA .... National Development Credit Agency (MAR)
NDCC .... Ngie Development Consultative Committee (MAR)
NDCG .... Naucno Drustvo Crne Gore [*Learned Society of Montenegro*] [*Cetinje*] (YU)
NDD .... National Democratic Movement [*Portuguese*] (RU)
Ndd .... Niederschlaege [*Precipitates*] [*German*]
NDF .... National Democratic Front [*Iranian*] (PD)
NDF .... National Democratic Front [*Yemeni*] (PD)
NDF .... National Development Foundation (MAR)
NDFK .... Neon Dimokratikon Foititikon Kinima [*New Democracy Student Movement*] [*Greek*] (GC)
NDH .... Nezavisna Drzava Hrvatska [*Independent State of Croatia*] [*World War II*] (YU)
NDK .... Nemet Demokratikus Koztarsasag [*German Democratic Republic*] (HU)
NDKhSh ...... Nontoxic Screening Smoke Pot (RU)
Ndl .... Nederland [*Netherlands*] [*Dutch*] (GPO)
NDL .... Pneumatic Landing Boat (RU)
NDLR .... Note de la Redaction [*Editor's Note*] [*French*] (WER)
NDMC .... National Diamond Mining Company [*Sierra Leonean*] (AF)

NDMF .... National Development and Management Foundation (MAR)
NDMiOZ ...... Naczelna Dyrekcja Muzeow i Ochrony Zabytkow [*Central Administration of Museums and the Protection of Historical Relics*] (POL)
NDN .... Nemzetkozi Demokratikus Noszovetseg [*International Federation of Democratic Women*] (HU)
NDNA .... Navtiki Dioikisis Notiou Aigaiou [*Southern Aegean Naval Command*] [*Greek*] (GC)
NDNRBiH .... Naucno Drustvo Narodne Republike Bosne i Hercegovine [*Learned Society of Bosnia and Hercegovina*] (YU)
NDNSZ .... Nemzetkozi Demokratikus Noszovetseg [*International Federation of Democratic Women*] (HU)
NDO .... Naczelna Dyrekcja Ogolna [*Chief General Administration*] (POL)
NDOA .... Narodnoe Dvizhenie za Osvobozhdenie Angoly [*People's Movement for the Liberation of Angola*] [*Russian*] (MAR)
NDOZ .... Continuous Dipole Axial Sounding (RU)
NDP .... Narodno-Demokraticheskaia Partiia (MAR)
NDP .... National Democratic Party [*Egyptian*] (PPW)
NDP .... National Democratic Party [*German Democratic Republic*] (RU)
NDP .... National Democratic Party [*Indian*] (PPW)
NDP .... National Democratic Party [*Namibian*] (AF)
NDP .... National Democratic Party [*Pakistani*] (PD)
NDP .... National Democratic Party [*Solomon Islander*] (PPW)
NDP .... National Democratic Party [*St. Vincentian*] (LA1)
NDP .... National Development Plan (MAR)
NDP .... Nationaldemokratische Partei [*National Democratic Party*] [*Austrian*] (PPW)
NDP .... Natsional'no-Demokraticheskaia Partiia (MAR)
NDP .... Neo-Destour Party [*Tunisian*] (MAR)
NDP .... New Democratic Party [*Canadian*] (PPW)
NDP .... New Democratic Party [*Shinmin-Dang*] [*South Korean*] (PPW)
NDP .... New Democratic Party [*St. Vincentian*] (PPW)
NDP .... Noseci Dekontaminacioni Pribor [*Portable Decontamination Equipment*] [*Military*] (YU)
NDP .... Vereniging van de Nederlandsche Dagbladpers [*Association of the Netherlands Daily Press*] (WEN)
NDPC .... National Development Plan Council (ML)
NDPD .... National-Demokratische Partei Deutschlands [*National-Democratic Party of Germany*] (EG)
NDPG .... National Democratic Party of Germany [*German Democratic Republic*] (RU)
NDPO .... Novosibirsk Volunteer Fire Society (RU)
NDR .... Narodnaia Demokraticheskaia Respublika Iemen (MAR)
NDR .... National Democratic Revolution [*Ethiopian*] (AF)
NDR .... Natsional'noe Dvizhenie Revoliutsii (MAR)
NDR .... Nemacka Demokratska Republika [*German Democratic Republic (East Germany)*] (YU)
NDR .... Nemecka Demokraticka Republika [*German Democratic Republic (East Germany)*] (CZ)
NdR .... Nota della Redazione [*Editor's Note*] [*Italian*] (WER)
Ndrl .... Niederlassung [*Branch Establishment*] [*German*] (CED)
NDS .... Nakladatelstvi Dopravy a Spoju [*Publishing House for Literature on Transportation and Communications*] (CZ)
NDS .... Neo-Democrates Senegalais [*Senegalese Neo-Democrats*] (AF)
NDS .... Novinarsko Drustvo Slovenije [*Society of Journalists of Slovenia*] (YU)
NDSMK .... New Democratic Youth League of China (RU)
NDSO .... Novodemokratski Savez Omladine [*New Democratic Youth Federation*] [*Vietnam*] (YU)
NDSS .... Highest Permissible Degree of Compression (RU)
NDT .... Naczelna Dyrekcja Techniczna [*Chief Technical Administration*] (POL)
NDU .... National Democratic Union [*Zimbabwean*] (PPW)
NDUF .... National Democratic United Front [*Later, FNDF*] [*Burmese*] (PD)
NDUO .... National Democratic Unity Organisation (MAR)
NDV .... Nacelnik Delostreleckeho Vyzbrojovani [*Chief, Artillery Ordnance*] (CZ)
NDVSh .... Scientific Reports of Schools of Higher Education (RU)
NDYeF .... People's Democratic United Front of China (RU)
NDYL .... New Democratic Youth League (ML)
NDZ .... Nacelnik Delostreleckeho Zasobovani [*Chief of Artillery Supply Service*] (CZ)
NDZ .... Nontoxic Smoke Screen (RU)
NDZR .... Natsional'noe Dvizhenie v Zashchitu Revoliutsii (MAR)
ne .... Anno Domini [*In the Year of Our Lord*] (RU)
Ne .... Effektive Leistung [*Effective Horsepower*] [*German*]
NE .... Fixed Electrode (RU)
Ne .... Naheilgueterzug [*Local Express Freight Train*] (EG)
NE .... Narodna Enciklopedija Srpsko-Hrvatsko-Slovenacka (Stanojevic Stanoje) [*Stanoje Stanojevic's Serbo-Croatian-Slovenian National Encyclopedia*] (YU)
NE .... Nasa Era [*Our Era (In the Year of Our Lord)*] (YU)
ne .... Naszej Ery [*Our Era (In the Year of Our Lord)*] (POL)
ne .... Nemet [*German*] (HU)
NE .... Nepi Egyuttes [*Folk Ensemble*] (HU)
NE .... Nichtbundeseigene Eisenbahnen [*Non-Federal Railroads*] [*West German*] (WEN)
NE .... Nichteisen [*Nonferrous*] [*German*] (WEN)
NE .... Niger [*Two-letter standard code*] (CNC)
NE .... Nomarkhiaki Epitropi [*Nome Committee*] [*Greek*] (GC)
NE .... Nomismatiki Epitropi [*Currency Committee*] (GC)
NE .... Nonlinear Element (RU)
NE .... Nord Est [*Northeast*] [*French*] (MTD)
NE .... Nordeste [*Northeast*] [*Spanish*]
NE .... Nova Era [*Our Era (In the Year of Our Lord)*] (YU)
ne .... Our Era [*In the Year of Our Lord*] (BU)
NE .... Standard Cell (RU)
NEA .... Native Education Association (MAR)
NEA .... Nea Elliniki Aristera [*New Greek Left*] [*Greek*] (GC)
NEA .... Nebeneichamt [*German*]
NEA .... Nouvelles Editions Africaines [*New African Publishing Company*] (AF)
NEAFC .... North-East Atlantic Fisheries Commission (EA)
NEB .... National Electricity Board (ML)
NEB .... Nepi Ellenorzesi Bizottsag [*People's Control Committee*] (HU)
NEB .... Scientific Experimental Center (RU)
NEBVVS ...... Scientific Experimental Center of the Air Force (RU)
NEC .... National Economic Council [*Iranian*] (ME)
NEC .... National Executive Committee [*Malaysian*] (ML)
NEC .... National Executive Committee [*Mauritian*] (AF)
NEC .... National Executive Council [*Malaysian*] (ML)
NECA .... Nigerian Employers Consultative Association (MAR)
NECCO .... Nigerian Engineering and Construction Company (MAR)
nech .... Odd (RU)
NECLSA ...... North East Coalition for the Liberation of Southern Africa (MAR)
NECPP .... North Eastern Convention People's Party (MAR)
NECZAM ..... National Educational Company of Zambia (MAR)
Ned. .... Nederlands [*Netherlands*] [*Dutch*] (CED)
NED .... Neolaia Ethnikis Draseos [*Youth for National Action*] (GC)
NEDA .... Neolaia Eniaias Dimokratikis Arsteras [*Youth of the United Democratic Left*] [*See also EDA*] (GC1)
NEDC .... National Economic Development Council (MAR)
NEDCO .... National Estates and Designing Company Limited (MAR)
NEDE .... Nomos peri Eispraxeos Dimosion Esodon [*Law on Collection of Public Revenues*] [*Greek*] (GC)
NEDEPA ...... Nea Demokratiki Parataxi [*New Democratic Front*] [*Greek Cypriot*] (PPE)
NE DI K .... Neolaia Dimokratikou Kommatos [*Democratic Party Youth*] (GC)
NEDIPA .... Neolaia Dimokratikis Parataxis [*Youth of the Democratic Front*] (GC)
NEDKE .... Neon Ethnikon Dimokratikon Komma Ellinon [*New National Democratic Party of Greeks*] [*Greek*] (GC)
NEDO .... Nederlands Documentatiecentrum voor Ontwikkelingslanden (MAR)
NEE .... Navtikon Epimelitirion Ellados [*Merchant Marine Chamber of Greece*] (GC)
NEE .... Nukleer Enerji Enstitusu [*Nuclear Energy Institute*] [*Istanbul Technological University*] (TU)
NEED .... Near East Emergency Donations (MAR)
NEF .... Near East Foundation (MAR)
NEFO .... New Emerging Forces (IN)
neft .... Oil Well [*Topography*] (RU)
neft .... Oil-Well Derrick [*Topography*] (RU)
neft .... Petroleum, Oil (RU)
neft .... Petroleum Production [*Topography*] (RU)
Neft .... Petroleum Refinery [*Topography*] (RU)
neft .... Petroleum Reservoir [*Topography*] (RU)
Nefteburmashremont ... State Trust for the Repair of Drilling Equipment (RU)
Neftekhimavtomat ... Scientific Research and Planning Institute for Complex Automation of Production Processes in the Petroleum and Chemical Industries (RU)
NEFTEKIP ... Control and Measuring Instruments Plant for the Petroleum Industry (RU)
neftepereg ... Petroleum-Refining (RU)
Nefteprovodproyekt ... State All-Union Trust for Surveying and Planning of Petroleum Pipelines and Petroleum Storage Depots (RU)
Neftezavodproyekt ... All-Union Trust for the Planning of Petroleum Industry Plants (RU)
neg .... Negociable [*French*]
negt .... Negociant [*Merchant, Trader*] [*Business and trade*] [*French*]
neh .... Nehai [*Late*] (HU)
NEH .... Societe Nigerienne des Etablissements Herlicq (MAR)
NEHA .... Nederlands Economisch Historisch Archief
Nehezip K ... Nehezipari Kiado [*Publishing House on Heavy Industry*] (HU)
NEI .... Northern Engineering Industries (MAR)
NEIDA .... Network of Educational Innovation for Development in Africa (AF)
NEIS .... Novosibirsk Electrotechnical Institute of Communications (RU)
neizv .... Unknown (BU)
NEK .... Neo Elliniko Komma [*New Greek Party*] [*Greek*] (GC)
NEKA .... Nea Ergatiki Kinisis Athinon [*New Labor Movement of Athens*] (GC)
NEKA .... Nomarkhiaki Epitropi Katapolemiseos Analfavitismou [*Nome Anti-Illiteracy Committee*] [*Greek*] (GC)

NEKG .... Nova Hut Klementa Gottwalda [*New Metallurgical Works of Klement Gottwald*] [*Ostrava-Kuncice*] (CZ)
NEKIN .... Scientific Experimental Institute (RU)
NEKOLIM .... Neokolonialisme, Kolonialisme, dan Imperialisme [*Neocolonialism, Colonialism, and Imperialism*] (IN)
NEKOSZ ..... Nepi Kollegiumok Orszagos Szovetsege [*National Association of People's Colleges*] (HU)
nekr .... Obituary (BU)
NEL .... Scientific Experimental Laboratory (RU)
N(E)LE .... Nomarkhiaki (Eparkhiaki) Epitropi Laikis Epimorfosis [*Nomarchial (Provincial) Committee for Popular Advancement (Cultural, Vocational, Political, Recreational, etc.)*] (GC1)
nem .... German (BU)
nem .... German (RU)
nem .... Nemet [*German*] (HU)
NEM .... Northeastern Mediterranean (MAR)
NEMA .... Netzschkauer Maschinenfabrik (VEB) [*Netzschkau Machine Factory (VEB)*] (EG)
NEMAS .... Nouvelle Emaillerie Senegalaise (MAR)
NEMEDRI .... Northeast and Mediterranean Route Instruction (MAR)
NE-Metall .... Nichteisenmetall [*Nonferrous Metal*] (EG)
nem ez .... German Language (BU)
NEMPI .... National Ethnographic Museum in Plovdiv (BU)
nemzk .... Nemzetkozi [*International*] (HU)
NEN .... Nederlandse Norm
NENARACA ... Near East and North Africa Regional Agricultural Credit Association
nenasyshch ... Unsaturated (RU)
NEOCALI .... Compania Cali Neon Ltda. (COL)
neochishch ... Unpurified, Crude (RU)
neodobr ...... Disapproving (BU)
neopr .... Indefinite (Pronoun) (RU)
neopr .... Infinitive (Form of Verb) (RU)
NEP .... Nea Ergatoypalliliki Parataxis [*or Nea Ergatiki Parataxis*] [*New Labor Faction*] [*Greek*] (GC)
NEP .... Nemzeti Egyseg Partja [*Party of National Unity*] [*Hungarian*] (PPE)
nep .... Neper (RU)
NEP .... New Economic Policy [*Malaysian*] (ML)
NEP .... New Economic Policy [*1921-1936*] (RU)
NEP .... Novosadsko Elektricno Preduzece [*Novi Sad Electric Establishment*] (YU)
NEPA .... National Electric Power Authority [*Nigerian*] (MAR)
NEPA .... Nigerian Electric Power Authority (MAR)
NEPB .... Nigerian Enterprises Promotion Board (MAR)
NEPB .... Nigerian Enterprises Promotion Bureau (MAR)
NEPCO .... National Export Promotion Council (MAR)
neperekh .... Intransitive (Verb) (RU)
neperiodich ... Nonperiodic (RU)
NEPMUV MIN ... Nepmuvelesi Miniszterium/Miniszter [*Ministry/Minister of Public Education*] (HU)
neprekh ...... Intransitive (BU)
neprom .... Unchanged (BU)
nepsz .... Nepszeru [*Popular*] (HU)
NEPU .... Northern Elements Progressive Union [*Nigerian*] (AF)
nepul .... Incomplete (BU)
NER .... Niger [*Three-letter standard code*] (CNC)
NER .... North Eastern Region (MAR)
ner-vo .... Inequality [*Mathematics*] (RU)
NES .... Desk Encyclopedic Dictionary [*A publication*] (RU)
Nes .... Nisidhes [*Islet(s)*] [*Greek*] (NAU)
NES .... Nucleos Educativos Seleccionados [*Select Educational Centers*] [*Peruvian*] (LA)
NESAM .... Nucleo dos Estudantes Africanos Secundarios de Mocambique (MAR)
NESh .... Train Commander, Echelon Commander (RU)
NESHS .... Narodna Enciklopedija Srpsko-Hrvatsko-Slovenacka [*Serbian-Croatian-Slovenian National Encyclopedia*] [*Zagreb*] (YU)
nesk .... Several (RU)
neskl .... Indeclinable (Word) (RU)
nesov .... Imperfective (Aspect of Verb) (RU)
NESP .... National Economic Survival Programme (MAR)
NESPAK ...... National Engineering Services of Pakistan (MAR)
NESZ .... Nephadsereg Egeszsegugyi Szolgalata [*Health Service of the People's Army*] (HU)
NET .... Nepkoztarsasag Elnoki Tanacsa [*Presidium of the People's Republic*] (HU)
NET .... Nigerian External Telecommunications Ltd. (MAR)
NET .... Nouvelle Entreprise Togolaise (MAR)
NETAS .... Northern Electric Telekomunikasyon Anonim Sirketi [*Northern Electric Telecommunication Corporation*] (TU)
NETh .... Nepkoztarsasag Elnoki Tanacsanak Hatarozata [*Resolution of the Presidential Council of the People's Republic*] (HU)
NETI .... Nehezipari Epulettervezo Iroda [*Construction Designing Office for Heavy Industry*] (HU)
Nettokm ...... Nettotonnenkilometer [*Net Ton Kilometers (Product of the weight of the freight carried by a train multiplied by the kilometers traveled by that train)*] (EG)
neud .... Unsatisfactory (RU)
NEUM .... Non-European Unity Movement [*South African*] (PD)
neutr .... Neutralisiert [*Neutralize*] [*German*]
n ev .... Naptari Ev [*Calendar Year*] (HU)
NEVIKI .... Nehezvegyipari Kutato Intezet, Veszprem [*Research Institute for the Heavy Chemicals Industry, Veszprem*] (HU)
Nevkhimzavod ... Neva Chemical Plant (RU)
nevl .... Nevleges [*Nominal*] (HU)
Nevr .... Neurologist, Neurology (BU)
NEVZ .... Novocherkassk Electric Locomotive Plant (RU)
neytr .... Neutral, Inert (RU)
neytr-tsiya ... Neutralization (RU)
NEZA .... Nouvelles Entreprises Zairoises (MAR)
nezameshch ... Unsubstituted (RU)
NEZhK .... Nonesterified Fatty Acids (RU)
NF .... Impartible Fund (BU)
NF .... Inorganic Phosphate (RU)
NF .... Naphtoquinone (RU)
NF .... Narodna Fronta [*People's Front*] (YU)
NF .... Narodni Fronta [*National Front*] [*Czechoslovak*] (PPE)
NF .... National Front [*British*] (PPW)
NF .... National Front (RU)
NF .... Nationale Front [*National Front*] (EG)
NF .... Nemzeti Front [*National Front*] (HU)
nF .... Neue Folge [*New Series*] [*German*] (GPO)
NF .... Niederfrequenz [*Low Frequency*] (EG)
NF .... Nisko Frekventni [*Low Frequency*] (YU)
NF .... Norfolk Island [*Two-letter standard code*] (CNC)
NF .... Norsk Front [*Norwegian Front*] (PD)
NF .... Nouveau Franc [*New Franc (Monetary unit introduced in 1960)*] [*French*]
NF .... Nova Filatelija [*New Philately*] [*Ljubljana*] [*A periodical*] (YU)
NF .... Nueva Fuerza [*New Force*] [*Venezuelan*] (LA)
NF .... People's Front (BU)
NFA .... Nitrophenyl Acetate (RU)
NFC .... National Fisheries Company [*Grenadian*] (LA1)
NFCA .... National Federation of Credit Associations [*Japanese*]
NFD .... Northeast Frontier District [*Kenyan*] (AF)
NFD .... Northern Frontier Division (MAR)
NfD .... Nur fuer den Dienstgebrauch [*For Official Use Only*] (EG)
NFDR .... National Front for the Defense of the Revolution [*Malagasy*] (AF)
NFF .... Nemzeti Fueggetlensegi Front [*National Independence Front*] [*Hungarian*] (PPE)
NFFF .... National Federation of Fish Friers (MAR)
NFGD .... National Front of Democratic Germany (RU)
NFH .... Nacelnik Financniho Hospodarstvi [*Chief of Finance*] [*Military*] (CZ)
NFI .... Naturfreunde-Internationale [*International Friends of Nature - IFN*] (EA)
NFin .... Directive on Financing, Crediting, and Controlling Capital Investments (BU)
NFJ .... Narodna Fronta Jugoslavije [*National Front of Yugoslavia*] (YU)
NFK .... Norfolk Island [*Three-letter standard code*] (CNC)
NFK .... Novosadska Fabrika Kablova [*Novi Sad Cable Factory*] (YU)
NFKKK .... Directive on the Financial Crediting and Control of Capital Investments (BU)
NFLSV .... National Front for the Liberation of South Vietnam (CL)
NFLSVN ...... National Front for the Liberation of South Vietnam [*Use NFLSV*] (CL)
NFM .... Naroden Front na Makedonija [*People's Front of Macedonia*] (YU)
NFN .... Nouvelle Front NAZI [*New NAZI Front*] [*French*] (PD)
NFNCE .... Nucleus of Nonconventional Energy Sources of the Federal University of Ceara [*Brazilian*]
NFP .... National Federation Party [*Fijian*] (PPW)
NFP .... Physical Training Manual (RU)
NFP .... Science Fiction and Adventures (RU)
NFPP .... National Family Planning Program (MAR)
NFR .... Navigatia Fluviala Romana [*Romanian River Navigation Agency*] (RO)
NFS .... National Physical Culture Union (BU)
NFSL .... National Front for the Salvation of Libya
NFSS .... National Fund for Social Security [*Arabian*] (MAR)
NFT .... Nigeria Trust Fund (AF)
NF Vorstufe ... Niederfrequenz Vorstufe [*Low Frequency Input Stage*] (EG)
NFW .... Narodowy Front Wyzwolenia [*National Liberation Front*] [*South Vietnam*] (POL)
NFWIR .... National Federation of Women's Institutes of Rhodesia (MAR)
NFWP .... Nutritional Field Working Party (MAR)
NFWWP .... Narodowy Front Wyzwolenia Wietnamu Poludniowego [*South Vietnam National Liberation Front*] (POL)
NFZ .... Narodni Fronta Zen [*National Women's Front*] (CZ)
NFZ .... National Front of Zimbabwe (PPW)
NG .... Dumpy Level (RU)
NG .... Inert Gas (RU)
NG .... Naoruzanje s Nastavom Gadanja [*Armament with Target Practice (Subject in training)*] (YU)
NG .... Narodni Galerie [*National Gallery of Art*] (CZ)
NG .... Nase Gradevinarstvo [*Our Construction*] [*A periodical*] (YU)
NG .... Nastava Gadanja [*Target Practice*] (YU)
NG .... Natural Gutta-Percha (RU)
NG .... Neurological Hospital (RU)

NG............ Nigeria [*Two-letter standard code*] (CNC)
ng............ Post Commander (BU)
NGA............ Nigeria [*Three-letter standard code*] (CNC)
NGB............ German State Library (RU)
NGB............ Nemzeti Gondozo Bizottsag [*National Welfare Committee*] (HU)
NGB............ Nigerian Grains Board (MAR)
NGDR............ Nederlands Genootschap voor Document Reproductie
NGE............ Nigerian Guild of Editors (MAR)
NGEB............ Nemzetkozi Gazdasagi Egyuttmukodesi Bank [*International Bank for Economic Cooperation (CEMA)*] (HU)
ngez............ Nicht Gezaehlt [*By the Lot*] [*German*]
NGH............ Nepgondozo Hivatal [*People's Welfare Office*] (HU)
NGI............ Nederlands Genootschap voor Informatica
NGI............ Normal Histone (RU)
NGIMIP............ Novosibirsk State Institute of Measures and Measuring Instruments (RU)
NGJ............ Nigerian Geographical Journal [*A publication*] (MAR)
NGK............ Nederduitse Gereformeerde Kerk [*Dutch Reformed Church*] [*Namibian, South African*] (AF)
NGK............ Neutron-Gamma-Ray Logging (RU)
Ng-Kabel.... Netzgruppenkabel [*Regional Cable*] (EG)
NGKB............ Nemzetkozi Gazdasagi Kapcsolatok Bizottsaga [*Committee of International Economic Relations*] (HU)
NGKVTs...... Directive on Border Control of Foreign Currency Valuables (BU)
NGL............ Inhomogeneous Lorentz Group (RU)
NGL............ Nigerian Green Line (MAR)
NGL............ Nitroglycol (RU)
NGL............ Normal Gliadin (RU)
NGMB............ Nigerian Groundnuts Marketing Board (MAR)
NGMR............ Nederlands Genootschap voor Micrografie en Reprografie [*Formerly, NGDR*]
ngn............ Nanohenry (RU)
NGNB............ Lower Downstream Water Level (RU)
NGO............ Nur Gewerkschaftliche Opposition [*Trade-Union-Only Opposition*] (EG)
NGO............ Origin of Grouped Operation [*Computers*] (RU)
NGOMAT.... Ngomi-Matengo Cooperative Marketing Union (MAR)
NGP............ Neue Grosse Partei [*New Great Party*] [*West German*] (PPW)
NGPI............ Novosibirsk State Pedagogical Institute (RU)
NGPR............ Nederlands Genootschap voor Public Relations
NGR............ Nuevas Generaciones Revolucionarias [*New Revolutionary Generations*] [*Guatemalan*] (LA)
NGRI............ Petroleum Institute of Geological Exploration [*Moscow*] (RU)
NGRI............ State All-Union Scientific Research Institute of Geological Exploration [*Leningrad*] (RU)
NGS............ Directive on Chief Bookkeepers (BU)
NGS............ Nacelnik Generalniho Stabu [*Chief of the General Staff*] (CZ)
NGSEE............ Nea Geniki Synomospondia Ergatoypallilon Ellados [*New Greek General Confederation of Labor*] (GC)
NGSK............ Nederduitse Gereformeerde Sendingkerk (MAR)
NGSPA............ Nastava Gadanja Srednjokalibarska Protivavionska [*Target Practice for Medium Caliber Antiaircraft Guns*] (YU)
NGSZ............ Nemzetkozi Gazdalkodo Szervezet [*Internationally Operating Organization*] (HU)
Ngt............ Negociant [*Merchant*] [*French*] (MTD)
NGTs............ Nitroglycerine (RU)
NGU............ Nizhniy Novgorod State University (RU)
NGU............ Novosibirsk State University (RU)
NGV............ Nederlands Genootschap van Vertalers [*Netherlands Association of Translators*]
NGWIZAKO... Ngwizani a Kongo (MAR)
NH............ New Hebrides [*Two-letter standard code*] (CNC)
NH............ Nowa Huta (Przedsiebiorstwo Panstwowe) [*Nowa Huta (State Enterprise)*] (POL)
NHA............ National Housing Authority [*Jamaican*] (LA1)
NHB............ New Hebrides [*Three-letter standard code*] (CNC)
NHC............ National Housing Corporation (MAR)
NHC............ Shirika la Nyumba la Taifa [*National Housing Corporation*] [*Tanzanian*] (AF)
NHDC............ National Hotels Development Corporation Ltd. (MAR)
NHF............ Nemzeti Harci Front [*Militant National Front*] (HU)
NHFP............ New Hebrides Federal Party (PPW)
NHH............ Nagy Honvedo Haboru [*Great Patriotic War (of the Union of Soviet Socialist Republics)*] (HU)
NHI............ National Health Institute (MAR)
NHK............ Narodohospodarska Komise [*Economic Commission*] (CZ)
NHK............ Nederduits Hervormde Kerk van Afrika [*Dutch Reformed Church of Africa*] [*Namibian, South African*] (AF)
NHK............ Nihon/Nippon Hoso Kyokai [*Japan Broadcasting Corporation*] (SJT)
NHLMAC..... National High-Level Manpower Allocation Committee (MAR)
NHP............ National Hotels and Properties Ltd. [*Jamaican*] (LA1)
NHPM............ Narodni Hnuti Pracujici Mladeze [*National Movement of the Working Youth*] (CZ)
NHT............ National Housing Trust [*Jamaican*] (LA1)
Nhz............ Niederdruckdampfheizung [*Low Pressure Steam Heating System*] (EG)
NI............ Initial Pulse (RU)
NI............ Nacelnik Inzinjerije [*Engineering Corps Chief*] (YU)
NI............ Nautical Institute (EA)
NI............ Nepmuvelesi Intezet [*Institute of Public Education*] (HU)
NI............ Nicaragua [*Two-letter standard code*] (CNC)
NI............ Nonlinear Distortion (BU)
NI............ Nonmetallic Minerals (RU)
NI............ Nonmineral Deposits (BU)
Ni............ Numeri [*Numbers*] [*Italian*] (GPO)
ni............ Output Norm (BU)
NI............ Position and Homing Indicator (RU)
NI............ Science and Art Publishing House (BU)
NI............ Scientific Institute (RU)
NI............ Scientific Research (RU)
NIA............ Naczelna Izba Aptekarska [*Chief Pharmacy Chamber*] (POL)
NIA............ Nigerian Institute of International Affairs (MAR)
NIA............ Scientific Institute of Architecture (RU)
NIAB............ Air Research Bureau [*ARB*] (RU)
NIAFIZ......... Physics Scientific Research Association (RU)
NIAI............ Scientific Research Aviation Institute (RU)
NIAI............ Scientific Research Institute of Batteries (RU)
NIAKhIM..... Chemical Scientific Research Association (RU)
NIAKUP....... Scientific Research Association of the Coal and Shale Industry (RU)
NIAL............ Scientific Research Automobile Laboratory (RU)
NIAM............ Netherlands Institute for Audiovisual Media
NIAM............ Scientific Research Association of Marxists (RU)
NIAMASh.... Scientific Research Association of Machinery Manufacture and Metalworking (RU)
NIAMET....... Scientific Research Association of Ferrous Metallurgy (RU)
NIANKP....... Scientific Research Association for the Study of National and Colonial Problems (RU)
NIAP............ Artillery Scientific Test Range (RU)
NIAS............ Automatic Nonlinear Sampled-Data System (RU)
NIAS............ Engineer Aviation Service Manual (RU)
NIAT............ Scientific Institute of Automobile Transportation (RU)
NIAT............ Scientific Research Institute of Aviation Technology (RU)
NIATsVETMET... Scientific Research Association of Nonferrous Metallurgy (RU)
NIB............ National Insurance Board [*Jamaican*] (LA1)
NIB............ National Investment Bank (MAR)
NIB............ National Irrigation Board (MAR)
NIB............ Scientific Research Office (RU)
NIBMAR...... No Independence Before Majority African Rule (MAR)
NIBTN......... Scientific Research Office of Technical Standards (RU)
NIBV............ Scientific Research Office of Interchangeability (RU)
NIC............ Nastavna Intendantska Ceta [*Quartermaster Training Company*] (YU)
NIC............ Natal Indian Congress (MAR)
NIC............ National Industries Company [*Arabian*] (MAR)
NIC............ National Insurance Corporation [*Ugandan*] (AF)
NIC............ National Intelligence Committee [*Malaysian*] (ML)
NIC............ National Interim Council [*Sierra Leonean*] (AF)
NIC............ National Investment Commission (MAR)
NIC............ Nederlandse Informatie Combinatie [*'s-Gravenhage*]
NIC............ Newly Industrialized Country (MAR)
NIC............ Nicaragua [*Three-letter standard code*] (CNC)
NIC............ Nuclear Industry Consortium [*Also known as GPIN*] [*Belgian*]
NICI............ National Investment Company of Iran (ME)
NICON......... National Insurance Corporation of Nigeria (AF)
NICRO......... National Institute for Crime Prevention and Rehabilitation of Offenders (MAR)
nid............ Nidottu(na) [*Finnish*]
NiD............ Niepodleglosc i Demokracja [*Independence and Democracy*] [*Political movement*] (POL)
NID............ Nouvelle Imprimerie Dionysienne (MAR)
NIDA............ National Institute for Development Administration [*Bangkok, Thailand*]
NIDB............ Nigerian Industrial Development Bank (AF)
NIDCS......... National Industrial Development Corporation of Swaziland (MAR)
NIDER......... Nederlands Instituut voor Informatie, Documentatie, en Registratuur [*Later, NOBIN*]
NIDI............ Scientific Research Diesel Institute (RU)
NIDOC......... National Information and Documentation Centre [*Egyptian*] (MAR)
NIE............ Nonlinear Integrating Element [*Computers*] (RU)
NIEC............ National Import and Export Corporation Ltd. (MAR)
NIEE............ New Sources of Electric Power (RU)
NIEEI............ Scientific Research Institute of Electric Carbon Components (RU)
NIEFT......... Scientific Research Institute of Experimental Physiology and Therapy (RU)
NIEI............ Scientific Research Institute of Economics (RU)
NIEIRP......... Scientific Research and Experimental Institute of the Rubber Industry (RU)
NIEL............ Scientific Research Laboratory of Electric Automation (RU)
niem............ Niemiecki [*German*] (POL)
NIEM............ Scientific Research Institute of Epidemiology and Microbiology (BU)
NIEN............ Nosilevtikon Idryma Emborikou Navtikou [*Maritime Workers Nursing Home*] (GC)
NIEO............ New International Economic Order (WEN)

NIERA .... Scientific Research and Experimental Work on Containers (BU)
NIETh .... Nosilevtikon Idryma Ergaton Thalassis [*Maritime Workers Nursing Home*] [*Greek*] (GC)
NIF............... Scientific Research Branch (RU)
NIFI.............. Scientific Research Institute of Finance (RU)
NIFI.............. Scientific Research Institute of Physics (at the Leningrad State University Imeni A. A. Zhdanov) (RU)
NIFKhI......... Physicochemical Scientific Research Institute Imeni L. Ya. Karpov (RU)
NIFOR .... Nigerian Institute for Oil Palm Research (MAR)
NIFTA.......... Nouvelle Industrie de Filature et Tissage Algerienne (MAR)
NIG............. Scientific Research Group (RU)
NIGALEX..... Nigerian Aluminium Extrusions and Anodising (MAR)
NIGC .... National Iranian Gas Company (ME)
NIGELEC..... Societe Nigerienne d'Electricite [*Niger Electric Power Company*] (AF)
NIGERCEM ... Nigerian Cement Company (MAR)
NIG-GECIBA ... Societe Nigerienne de Genie Civil et Batiment (MAR)
NIGI............. Scientific Research Institute of Hydraulic Engineering (RU)
NIGIM.......... Central Scientific Research Institute of Geology and Mineralogy (RU)
NIGMI.......... Scientific Research Hydrometeorological Institute (RU)
NIGRI........... Scientific Research Institute of Geological Exploration (RU)
NIGRI........... Scientific Research Institute of Ore Mining (RU)
NIGRIS .... Scientific Research Ore-Mining Institute of the Lead and Zinc Industry (RU)
NIGRIZoloto ... Scientific Research Institute of Geological Exploration for Gold (RU)
niH............... Nicht im Handel [*Not for Sale*] [*German*]
NIHURST..... National Institute of Higher Education [*Trinidadian and Tobagan*] (LA1)
NII................ Negara Islam Indonesia [*Islamic State of Indonesia*] (IN)
NII................ Scientific Research Institute (BU)
NII................ Scientific Research Institute (RU)
NII................ Scientific Research Institute of Toys (RU)
NIIA .... Nigerian Institute of International Affairs (AF)
NIIA .... Scientific Research Institute of Aerial Surveying (RU)
NIIA .... Scientific Research Institute of Architecture (RU)
NIIAG .... Scientific Research Institute of Obstetrics and Gynecology (RU)
NIIAK........... Scientific Research Institute of Aeroclimatology (RU)
NIIAlmaz ..... State Scientific Research Institute of Diamond Tools and Diamond Machining Operations (RU)
NIIAntropologii ... Scientific Research Institute of Anthropology (RU)
NIIAP........... Scientific Testing Institute of Aviation Instruments (RU)
NIIAsbest.... Scientific Research Institute of the Asbestos-Processing Industry (RU)
NIIasbestotsement ... State Scientific Research Institute for Asbestos, Mica, Asbestos Cement Products, and for the Planning of Construction of Mica Industry Establishments (RU)
NIIASBESTTsEMENT ... Scientific Research Institute for Asbestos, Mica, Asbestos Cement Products, and for the Planning of Construction of Mica Industry Establishments (RU)
NIIasbotsement ... Scientific Research Institute for Asbestos, Mica, Asbestos Cement Products, and for the Planning of Construction of Mica Industry Establishments (RU)
NIIAT........... State Scientific Research Institute of Automobile Transportation (RU)
NIIAvtomatika ... Scientific Research Institute for the Automation of Production Processes in the Chemical Industry and Nonferrous Metallurgy (RU)
NIIAvtomatprom ... Scientific Research Institute for the Automation of Production Processes in Industry (RU)
NIIAvtopribor ... Scientific Research and Experimental Institute of Automobile and Tractor Electrical Equipment, Carburetors, and Instruments (RU)
NIIAvtopriborov ... Scientific Research and Experimental Institute of Automobile Electrical Equipment, Carburetors, and Instruments (RU)
NIIavtoprom ... Scientific Research Institute of the Automobile Industry (RU)
NIIB .... Scientific Research Botanical Institute (RU)
NIIBP........... Scientific Research Institute of the Ferment Industry (RU)
NIIBUMDREVMASh ... Scientific Research Institute for Paper and Woodworking Machinery (RU)
NIIBUMMASh ... Scientific Research Institute of Paper Machinery (RU)
NIIChASPROM ... Scientific Research Institute of the Watchmaking Industry (RU)
NIIChERMET ... Scientific Research Institute of Ferrous Metallurgy (RU)
NIID .... Scientific Research Institute of Defectology (of the Academy of Pedagogical Sciences, RSFSR) (RU)
NIIDI........... Scientific Research Institute of Children's Infections (RU)
NIIDREVMash ... Scientific Research Institute of Woodworking Machinery (RU)
NIIE .... Scientific Research Institute of Electrification (BU)
NIIEE........... Scientific Research Institute for Electrification and Electrical Industry (BU)
NIIEE........... Scientific Research Institute of Power Engineering and Electrification (RU)
NIIEG........... Scientific Research Institute of Epidemiology and Hygiene (RU)
NIIEG........... Scientific Research Institute of Experimental Hygiene (RU)
NIIEKhAil.... Scientific Research Institute of Experimental Surgical Equipment and Instruments (RU)
NIIEM .... Scientific Research Institute of Epidemiology and Microbiology (BU)
NIIEMG........ Scientific Research Institute of Epidemiology, Microbiology, and Hygiene (RU)
NIIES........... Scientific Research Institute of Economics of Construction (RU)
NIIF............. Scientific Research Institute of Pharmacology (BU)
NIIF............. Scientific Research Institute of Pharmacy (BU)
NIIF............. Scientific Research Institute of Physics (at the Moscow State University) (RU)
NIIF............. Scientific Research Institute of Physiology (RU)
NIIFK........... Scientific Research Institute of Finance and Credit (BU)
NIIFVUKh.... Scientific Research Institute for Physical Education and School Hygiene (BU)
NIIG............. Scientific Research Institute of Engineering Geology (RU)
NIIG............. Scientific Research Institute of Geography (RU)
NIIG............. Scientific Research Institute of Hydraulic Engineering (RU)
NIIGA .... Scientific Research Institute of Arctic Geology (RU)
NIIGAIK....... Novosibirsk Institute of Engineers of Geodesy, Aerial Surveying, and Cartography (RU)
NIIGGS........ Scientific Research Institute of Forests and Forestry Resources (BU)
NIIGiM......... Scientific Research Institute of Hydraulic Engineering and Reclamation (RU)
NII GKRE..... Scientific Research Institute of the State Committee of the Council of Ministers, USSR, for Radio Electronics (RU)
NIIGMP........ Scientific Research Institute of Hydrometeorological Instruments (RU)
NIIGorsel'stroy ... Scientific Research Institute of Urban and Rural Construction (RU)
NIIGP........... Scientific Research Institute of Forestry Industry (BU)
NIIGP........... Scientific Research Institute of Urban Construction and District Planning (RU)
NIIGR........... Scientific Research Institute of Geophysical Exploration Methods (RU)
NIIGrad .... Scientific Research Institute of Urban Construction (RU)
NIIGradostroitel'stva ... Scientific Research Institute of Urban Construction and District Planning (RU)
NIIGrazhdanstroy ... Scientific Research Institute of Civil Engineering Construction (RU)
NIIGS........... State Scientific Research Institute of the Hydrolysis and Sulfite Liquor Industry (RU)
NIIGVF .... Scientific Research Institute of the Civil Air Fleet of the USSR (RU)
NIIIAM......... Scientific Research and Testing Institute of Aviation Medicine (RU)
NIIInformstroydorkommunmash ... Scientific Research Institute of Information on Construction, Road, and Municipal Machinery Manufacture (RU)
NIIInfortyazhmash ... Scientific Research Institute of Information on Heavy, Power Engineering, and Transportation Machinery Manufacture (RU)
NIIIOM......... Scientific Research Institute of Industrial Economics and Organization in Machine Building (BU)
NIIK .... Scientific Research Institute of Culture (RU)
NIIKE........... Scientific Research Institute of Culture and Economics (RU)
NIIKF .... Scientific Research Institute for Health Resorts and Physiotherapy (BU)
NIIKh........... Scientific Research Institute of Chemistry (at the Khar'kov State University Imeni A. M. Gor'kiy) (RU)
NIIKhIM....... Scientific Research Institute of Hydraulic Engineering and Land Reclamation (BU)
NIIKhIMMASh ... All-Union Scientific Research and Design Institute of Chemical Machinery (RU)
NIIKhIMPolimer ... Scientific Research Institute of Chemicals for Polymer Materials (RU)
NIIKhK .... Scientific Research Institute of Haematology and Blood Transfusion (BU)
NIIKhM........ Scientific Research Institute of Hydrology and Meteorology (BU)
NIIKhP......... Scientific Research Institute of the Art Industry (RU)
NIIKhP......... Scientific Research Institute for Chemical Production (BU)
NIIKhV......... Scientific Research Institute of Art Education (RU)
NIIKKh .... Scientific Research Institute of Potato Growing (RU)
NIIKKOP...... Scientific Research Institute for the Leather, Rubber, and Shoe Industries (BU)
NIIKMA .... Scientific Research Institute for Problems of the Kursk Magnetic Anomaly (RU)
NIIKP........... Scientific Research Institute of the Cable Industry (RU)
NIIKP........... Scientific Research Institute of the Coal Industry (BU)
NIIKP........... Scientific Research Institute of the Starch and Syrup Industry (RU)
NIIKRP .... Scientific Research Institute of the Coal and Ore Mining Industries (BU)
NIIKS........... Novocherkassk Institute of Municipal Construction Engineers (RU)
NIIKS........... Scientific Research Institute of Motion-Picture Theater Construction (RU)

NIIKZ.......... Scientific Research Institute of Rabbit Breeding and Fur Farming (RU)
NIIL.............. Scientific Research Laboratory (RU)
NIILaborpribor ... Scientific Research Institute of Laboratory Instruments and Automation (RU)
NIILITMASH ... State Scientific Research Institute of Foundry Machinery and Technology (RU)
NIILK........... Scientific Research Institute of the Varnish and Paint Industry (RU)
NIILKh......... Scientific Research Institute of Forestry (RU)
NIILP........... Scientific Research Institute of Laboratory Instruments (RU)
NIILP........... Scientific Research Institute of the Lumber Industry (RU)
NIILTEKMASh ... Scientific Research Institute of Light and Textile Machinery (RU)
NIILV........... Scientific Research Institute of Bast Fibers (RU)
NIIM............. Scientific Research Institute of Mathematics (RU)
NIIM............. Scientific Research Institute of Metallurgy (RU)
NIIMASh..... Scientific Research Institute of Machinery Manufacture and Metalworking (RU)
NIIMash....... Scientific Research Institute of Technical Information on Machinery Manufacture (RU)
NIIMekhaniki ... Scientific Research Institute of Mechanics (RU)
NIIMESS..... Scientific Research Institute for the Mechanization and Electrification of Agriculture (BU)
NIIMESTTOPPROM ... Scientific Research Institute of Local and Fuel Industries (of the Gosplan UkrSSR) (RU)
NIIMetallurgkhimstroy ... Scientific Research Institute for Construction in the Metallurgical and Chemical Industries (RU)
NIIMETIZ..... Scientific Research Institute of Metalware Industry (RU)
NIIMF.......... Scientific Research Institute of Mechanics and Physics (RU)
NIIMKSBP... Scientific Research Institute of the Ministry of Communal Economy, Public Works, and Roads (BU)
NIIMM......... Scientific Research Institute of Mathematics and Mechanics (RU)
NIIMontazhspetsstroy ... Scientific Research Institute for Installation and Specialized Construction Work (RU)
NIIMosstroy ... Scientific Research Institute of the Glavmosstroy (RU)
NIIMostov ... Scientific Research Institute of Bridge Construction (RU)
NIIMP.......... Scientific Research Institute of the Fur Industry (RU)
NIIMP.......... Scientific Research Institute of the Meat Industry (RU)
NIIMRP........ Scientific Research Institute of Mechanization in the Fish Industry (RU)
NIIMRTP...... Scientific Research Institute of the Ministry of the Radiotechnical Industry (RU)
NIIMSK........ Scientific Research Institute of Monomers for Synthetic Rubber (RU)
NIINAvtsel'khozmash ... Scientific Research Institute of Information on Automobile, Tractor, and Agricultural Machinery Manufacture (RU)
NIINEFTEKhIM ... Scientific Research Institute of Petrochemical Industries (RU)
NIINP........... Scientific Research Institute of the Petroleum Industry (RU)
NIINSM........ Scientific Research Institute of New Building Materials, Structure Finishing, and Fitting (RU)
NIINStroymaterialov ... Scientific Research Institute of New Building Materials, Structure Finishing, and Fitting (RU)
NIIO............. Scientific Research Institute for Education (BU)
NIIO............. Scientific Research Institute of Reindeer Breeding (RU)
NIIOGAZ..... State Scientific Research Institute for Gas Purification in Industry and Sanitation (RU)
NIIOKh........ Scientific Research Institute of Vegetable Growing (RU)
NIIOMD....... Scientific Research Institute for the Protection of Motherhood and Childhood (BU)
NIIOMES..... Scientific Research Institute for the Organization, Mechanization, and Economics of Construction (RU)
NIIOMS....... Scientific Research Institute for the Economics, Organization, and Mechanization of Construction (BU)
NIIOMS....... Scientific Research Institute for the Organization and Mechanization of Construction (RU)
NIIOMSP..... Scientific Research Institute for the Organization and Mechanization of Construction Industry (RU)
NIIOMTP..... Scientific Research Institute for the Organization, Mechanization, and Technical Aids in Construction (RU)
NIIOPiK....... Scientific Research Institute of Organic Intermediates and Dyestuffs (RU)
NIIORKh...... Scientific Research Institute of Lake and River Fisheries (RU)
NIIOsnovaniy ... Scientific Research Institute of Foundations and Underground Structures (RU)
NIIOSP........ Scientific Research Institute of Foundations and Underground Structures (RU)
NIIOT........... Scientific Research Institute of Labor Safety (BU)
NIIOT........... Scientific Research Institute of Technology and Organization of Production (RU)
NIIOZ........... Scientific Research Institute of Public Buildings and Structures (RU)
NIIP............. Scientific Research Institute of Apiculture (RU)
NIIP............. Scientific Research Institute of Fruit Growing Imeni I. V. Michurin (RU)
NIIP............. Scientific Research Institute of Poultry Raising (RU)
NIIP............. Scientific Research Institute of Soil Science (RU)
NIIPG........... Scientific Research Institute of Applied Graphics (RU)
NIIPI........... Scientific Research Institute of Zoonotic Infections in Specific Geographic Areas (RU)
NIIPiN.......... Scientific Research Institute of Planning and Standards (RU)
NIIPIT.......... Scientific Research Institute of Printing and Publishing Technology (RU)
NIIPK........... Scientific Research Institute of Consumers' Cooperatives (RU)
NIIPKh......... Scientific Research Institute of Applied Chemistry (RU)
NIIPM.......... Scientific Research Institute of Plastics (RU)
NIIPM.......... Scientific Research Institute of Printing Machinery (RU)
NIIPOLIGRAFMASH ... Scientific Research Institute of Printing Machinery (RU)
NIIPP........... Scientific Research Institute of Polymerization Plastics (RU)
NIIPP........... Scientific Research Institute for the Prevention of Pneumoconiosis (RU)
NIIPPIES..... Scientific Research, Planning, and Design Institute for Power Projects Construction (BU)
NIIPRODMASh ... Scientific Research Institute of Food Machinery (RU)
NIIPS........... Scientific Research Institute of Industrial Buildings and Structures (RU)
NIIPT........... Scientific Research Institute of Direct Current (RU)
NIIPT........... Scientific Research Institute of Hoisting and Conveying Installations (RU)
NIIPT........... Scientific Research Institute of Industrial Transportation (RU)
NIIPTMASh ... Scientific Research, Planning, and Technological Institute of Machinery Manufacture (RU)
NIIPZiK........ Scientific Research Institute of Fur Farming and Rabbit Breeding (RU)
NIIPZK......... Scientific Research Institute of Fur Farming and Rabbit Breeding (RU)
NIIR............. National Institute of Industrial Research (MAR)
NIIR............. Scientific Research Institute of Rubber and Latex Products (RU)
NIIRKh......... Scientific Research Institute of Fisheries (RU)
NIIRP........... Scientific Research Institute of the Rubber Industry (RU)
NIIRT........... Scientific Research Institute of Radio Broadcasting and Television (RU)
NIIS............. Scientific Research Institute of Communications (RU)
NIIS............. Scientific Research Institute for Construction (BU)
NIIS............. Scientific Research Institute of Shipbuilding (RU)
NIIS............. Scientific Research Institute of Suggestology (BU)
NIISantekhniki ... Scientific Research Institute of Sanitary Engineering (RU)
NIISChETMASH ... Scientific Research Institute of Calculating Machines (RU)
NIISChETMAShMMiP ... Scientific Research Institute of Calculating Machines of the Ministry of Machinery and Instruments (RU)
NIISel'stroy ... Scientific Research Institute of Rural Construction (RU)
NIISEM........ Scientific Testing Institute of Communications and Electromechanics of the RKKA (RU)
NIISF........... Scientific Research Institute for Constructional Physics (RU)
NIISh........... Scientific Research Institute of the Wool Industry (RU)
NIIShP......... Scientific Research Institute of the Garment Industry (RU)
NIIShP......... Scientific Research Institute of the Tire Industry (RU)
NIIShP......... Scientific Research Institute of the Wool Industry (RU)
NIISI........... Scientific Research and Testing Sanitation Institute of the RKKA (RU)
NIISK........... Scientific Research Institute of Structural Parts (RU)
NIISKhOM... Scientific Research Institute of Agricultural Machinery (RU)
NIISM.......... Scientific Research Institute of Building Materials (RU)
NIISM.......... Scientific Research Institute of Forensic Medicine (RU)
NIISMI......... Scientific Research Institute of Building Materials and Products (RU)
NIISO........... Scientific Research Institute of Aircraft Equipment (RU)
NIISP........... Scientific Research Institute of the Construction Industry (RU)
NIISS........... Scientific Research Institute of Rural Buildings and Structures (RU)
NIISS........... Scientific Research Institute of Shipbuilding and Ship Standards (RU)
NIISS........... Scientific Research Institute of Synthetic Alcohols and Organic Products (RU)
NIIST........... Scientific Research Institute of Sanitary Engineering (RU)
NIIST........... Scientific Research Institute of Sorption Technology (RU)
NIIStrommash ... State Scientific Research Institute of Machinery for the Building Materials Industry (RU)
NIISTROY.... Scientific Research Institute for Construction (RU)
NIIStroykeramika ... State Scientific Research Institute of Building Ceramics (RU)
NIISV........... Scientific Research Institute of Glass Fibers (RU)
NIISZhIMS ... Scientific Research Institute of Synthetic Fat Substitutes and Detergents (RU)
NIIT............. Scientific Research Institute of Labor (RU)
NIIT............. Scientific Research Institute of Remote Control (RU)
NIIT............. Scientific Research Institute of Transportation (BU)
NIIT............. Scientific Research Institute of Transportation (RU)
NIIT............. Scientific Research Tobacco Institute (BU)
NIITA........... Scientific Research Institute of the History and Theory of Architecture (RU)
NIITAVTOPROM ... Scientific Research Institute of the Technology of the Automobile Industry (RU)

NIITEIR........ All-Union Scientific Research Institute of Technical and Economic Research and Information on Radio Electronics (RU)
NIITEKhIM ... Scientific Research Institute of Technical and Economic Research of the State Committee of the Council of Ministers, USSR, for Chemistry (RU)
NIITekhmash ... Scientific Research Institute of Machinery-Manufacturing Technology (RU)
NIItelevideniya ... Scientific Research Institute of Television (RU)
NIITEPLOPRIBOR ... Scientific Research Institute of Heat Power Engineering Equipment (RU)
NIITI .... Scientific Research Institute of the Theory and History of Architecture and Construction Engineering (RU)
NIITIG.......... Scientific Research Institute for Technological Research on Fuels (BU)
NIITII .... Scientific Research Institute of the Theory and History of the Fine Arts (RU)
NIITIM .... Kuban' Scientific Research Institute for Testing Tractors and Agricultural Machinery (RU)
NIITIP .... Scientific Research Institute of the Theory and History of Pedagogy (RU)
NIITKh......... Scientific Research Institute of Labor Hygiene (BU)
NIITM .... Scientific Research Institute of Automobile, Tractor, and Agricultural Machinery-Manufacturing Technology (RU)
NIITM .... Scientific Research Institute of Machinery-Manufacturing Technology (RU)
NIITMASh ... Scientific Research, Planning, and Design Institute of Machinery-Manufacturing Technology (RU)
NIITN.......... Scientific Research Institute of Technical Standardization (RU)
NIITO........... Scientific Research Institute of Traumatology and Orthopedics (RU)
NIITOP .... Scientific Research Institute of Trade and Public Eating Facilities (RU)
NIITP .... Scientific Research Institute of Knit Goods Industry (RU)
NIITP .... Scientific Research Institute for the Knitwear Industry (BU)
NIITraktorosel'khozmash ... Scientific Research Institute of Tractor and Agricultural Machinery-Manufacturing Technology (RU)
NIITraktorsel'khozmash ... Scientific Research Institute of Tractor and Agricultural Machinery-Manufacturing Technology (RU)
NIItransneft' ... Scientific Research Institute for Transportation and Storage of Petroleum and Petroleum Products (RU)
NIITruda...... Scientific Research Institute of Labor (RU)
NIITs........... Scientific Research Institute of the Cement Industry (RU)
NIITS .... Scientific Research Institute of Urban and Rural Telephone Communications (RU)
NIITsEMENT ... State All-Union Scientific Research Institute of the Cement Industry (RU)
NIITsemmash ... Scientific Research Institute of Cement Machinery (RU)
NIItsvetmet ... Scientific Research Institute of Nonferrous Metals (RU)
NIITU........... Scientific Research Institute of Packing Materials and Packaging (RU)
NIITVCh ...... Scientific Research Institute of High-Frequency Currents (RU)
NIITyaZhMASh ... Scientific Research, Design, and Technological Institute of Heavy Machinery Manufacture (RU)
NIIUgleobogashcheniye ... State Planning, Design, and Scientific Research Institute of Coal Enrichment and Briquetting (RU)
NIIUIF.......... Scientific Research Institute of Fertilizers, Insecticides, and Fungicides (RU)
NIIV .... Scientific Research Institute of Synthetic Fibers (RU)
NIIV .... Scientific Research Institute of Viscose (RU)
NIIVESPROM ... Scientific Research Institute of Scales and Instruments (RU)
NIIVKh......... Scientific Research Institute of Water Management (RU)
NIIVS........... Scientific Research Institute of Vaccines and Serums (RU)
NIIVT .... Novosibirsk Institute of Water Transportation Engineers (RU)
NIIVT .... Scientific Research Institute of Foreign Trade (BU)
NIIVT .... Scientific Research Institute of High Temperatures (RU)
NIIVVS .... Scientific Research Institute of the Air Force (RU)
NIIYaF .... Scientific Research Institute of Nuclear Physics (of the Moscow State University) (RU)
NIIYaLI .... Scientific Research Institute of Language, Literature, and History (RU)
NIIZ .... Scientific Research Institute of Grain and Grain Products (RU)
NIIZ .... Scientific Research Institute of Zoology (RU)
NIIZarubezhgeologiya ... Scientific Research Laboratory of Geology of Foreign Countries (RU)
NIIZh .... Scientific Research Institute of Animal Husbandry (BU)
NIIZh .... Scientific Research Institute of Housing (RU)
NIIZh .... Scientific Research Institute of Livestock Breeding (RU)
NIIZhB......... Scientific Research Institute of Concrete and Reinforced Concrete (RU)
NIIZhELEZOBETON ... Scientific Research Institute of Reinforced Concrete Products and Building and Nonmetallic Materials (RU)
NIIZhS......... Scientific Research Institute for the Industrialization of Housing Construction (RU)
NIIZhT......... Novosibirsk Institute of Railroad Transportation Engineers (RU)
NIIZhT......... Scientific Research Institute of Railroad Transportation (RU)
NIIZhV......... Scientific Research Institute of Livestock Breeding and Veterinary Science (RU)
NIIZK........... Scientific Research Institute of Fur Farming and Rabbit Breeding (RU)
NIIZK........... Scientific Research Institute of Truck Gardening (BU)
NIIZKh......... Scientific Research Institute of Grain Farming (RU)
NIIZM .... Scientific Research Institute of Terrestrial Magnetism (RU)
NIJ .... Nigerian Institute of Journalism (MAR)
NIK .... Naczelna Izba Kontroli [*Chief Board of Supervision*] [*Polish*]
NIK .... Najwyzsza Izba Kontroli [*Supreme Chamber of Control*] (POL)
NIK .... National Executive Committee (BU)
NIK .... Nehezipari Kozpont [*Heavy Industry Center*] (HU)
nik .... Nickel [*Mining location*] [*Topography*] (RU)
NIK .... Science, Art, and Culture (BU)
NIKE............ Nitrokemia Ipartelepek [*Nitrochemical Industrial Plants*] (HU)
NIKE............ Nosilevtikon Idryma Klirikon Ellados [*Nursing Home for Greek Clergy*] (GC)
NIKEX .... NIKEX Nehezipari Kulkereskedelmi Vallalat [*NIKEX Foreign Trade Enterprise for Heavy Industry Products*] (HU)
NIKFI .... All-Union Scientific Research Institute of Motion Pictures and Photography (RU)
NIKhB.......... Khristo Botev Scientific Institute (BU)
NIKhFI......... Scientific Research Chemical-Pharmaceutical Institute (BU)
NIKhFI......... Scientific Research Chemical and Pharmaceutical Institute (RU)
NIKhI .... National General Art Exhibit (BU)
NIKhI .... Scientific Research Chemical Institute (RU)
NIKhI .... Scientific Research Cotton Institute (RU)
NIKhIMP...... All-Russian Scientific Research Chemical Institute of Local Industry (RU)
NIKhPZ .... Scientific Research Institute for Hygiene and Occupational Diseases (BU)
NIKI .... Scientific Research Institute of Business Cycles (RU)
NIKIIMP....... Scientific Research and Design Institute for Testing Equipment, Instruments, and for Mass Measurement Devices (RU)
NIKIMP........ Scientific Research and Design Institute for Testing Equipment, Instruments, and for Mass Measurement Devices (RU)
NIKP............ Scientific Research Institute of the Leather Industry (RU)
NIKTI........... Scientific Research, Design, and Technological Institute (RU)
NIKVI........... Scientific Research Institute of Dermatology and Venereal Diseases (RU)
NIL.............. Niederlassung Import und Lagerung [*Import and Storage Branch*] (EG)
NIL.............. Scientific Research Laboratory (RU)
NILAT.......... Scientific Research Laboratory of Automobile Transportation (RU)
NILCO .... Nationaal Instituut voor de Landbouwstudie in Congo (MAR)
NILD .... Scientific Research Laboratory of Engines (RU)
NILET .... Scientific Research Laboratory of Experimental Therapy (RU)
NILK............ Scientific Research Institute of Varnishes and Paints (RU)
NILN............ Navorsingsinstituut vir die Leernywerheid (MAR)
NILNEFTEGAZ ... Scientific Research Laboratory of Geological Criteria for the Evaluation of Prospects of Oil and Gas Occurence (RU)
NILOS .... Scientific Research Forest Experimental Station (RU)
NILP .... Northern Ireland Labour Party (PPW)
NILSI .... Scientific Research Laboratory of Machine Tools and Tools (RU)
NILT .... Labor Standards Research Laboratory (RU)
NILTara....... Scientific Research Laboratory of Packing Materials (RU)
NILtekmash ... Scientific Research Institute of Light and Textile Machinery (RU)
NILUSDP..... Scientific Research Laboratory of Structural Parts (RU)
NILW .... Naukowy Instytut Lekarsko-Weterynaryjny [*Scientific Institute of Veterinary Medicine*] (POL)
NIM.............. National Institute of Metallurgy (MAR)
NIM.............. Nehezipari Miniszterium/Miniszter [*Ministry/Minister of Heavy Industry*] (HU)
NIM.............. New Ivanovo Textile Mill (RU)
nim .... Nimitetty [*Finnish*]
nim .... Nimittain [*Namely*] [*Finnish*] (GPO)
NIMD .... National Institute of Management Development [*Egyptian*] (MAR)
NIMDOK...... Nehezipari Miniszterium Muszaki Dokumentacios es Fordito Iroda [*Ministry of Heavy Industry Bureau of Technical Documentation and Translation*] (HU)
NIME .... Nehezipari Muszaki Egyetem [*Technical University for Heavy Industry*] (HU)
NIMGE......... Marine Geophysical Scientific Research Expedition (RU)
NIMI............. Novocherkassk Institute of Reclamation Engineering (RU)
NIMI............. Scientific Research Institute of the Dairy Trade and Industry (RU)
NIMIGUSZI ... Nehezipari Miniszterium Ipargazdsagi es Uzemszervezesi Intezet [*Ministry of Heavy Industry Institute of Industrial Economics and Systems Analysis*] (HU)
nimim.......... Nimimerkki [*Finnish*]
NIMIS .... Scientific Research Machine-Testing Station (RU)
NIM Kvt .... Nehezipari Miniszterium Muszaki Konyvtara [*Technical Library of the Ministry of Heavy Industry*] (HU)
NIMMI .... Naval Medical Scientific Research Institute (RU)
NIMR .... National Institute for Medical Research (MAR)
NIMS .... Permafrost Scientific Research Station (RU)
NIMSA......... Nigerian Medical Students Association (MAR)
NIMTS .... Nosilevtikon Idryma Metokhikou Tameiou Stratou [*Army Pension Fund Nursing Home*] [*Greek*] (GC)
NIN .... Nedeljne Informativne Novine [*Weekly News Bulletin*] (YU)

NIN .... Nueva Izquierda Nacional [*New National Left*] [*Spanish*] (WER)
NINGRI .... Petroleum Scientific Research Institute of Geological Exploration (RU)
NINKhI .... Scientific Research Institute of Neurosurgery (RU)
NIO .... Naucno Istrazivacke Organizacije [*Scientific Research Organizations*] (YU)
NIOC .... National Iranian Oil Company (ME)
NIOC .... National Iron Ore Company [*Liberian*] (AF)
NIOKh .... Scientific Research Institute of Vegetable Growing (RU)
NIOKhIM ..... Scientific Research Institute of Basic Chemistry (RU)
NIOKR .... Scientific Research and Experimental Design Work (RU)
NIOMTPS .... Scientific Research Institute for the Organization, Mechanization, and Technical Aids in Construction (RU)
NIOPIK .... Scientific Research Institute of Organic Intermediates and Dyestuffs (RU)
NIORKh .... State Scientific Research Institute of Lake and River Fisheries (RU)
NIOT .... Scientific Research Institute of Work Safety (RU)
NIOZ .... Nederlands Instituut voor Onderzoek der Zee [*Netherlands Institute for Maritime Research*] (WEN)
NIP .... National Independence Party [*Namibian*] (PPW)
NIP .... National Institute for Productivity (MAR)
NIP .... Novinarsko Izdavacko Poduzece [*Journalistic Publishing Establishment*] [*Zagreb*] (YU)
NIPC .... Nigerian Investment Property Company (MAR)
NIPCO .... Nile Petroleum Company [*Egyptian*] (ME)
NI-pd .... Nacelnik Inzinjerije Pesadiske Divizije [*Chief Engineer of an Infantry Division*] (YU)
NIPI .... Scientific Research Institute of Food Flavoring Industry (RU)
NIPIA .... Scientific Research Institute for Automation (BU)
NIPIGORMASh ... Scientific Research, Planning, and Design Institute of Mining and Concentrating Machinery (RU)
NIPINeftekhimavtomat ... Scientific Research and Planning Institute for Complex Automation of Production Processes in the Petroleum and Chemical Industries (RU)
NIPKEK .... Scientific Research Institute for Planning and Designing Electronic Calculators (BU)
NIPKIK .... Scientific Research Planning and Design Institute for Shipbuilding (BU)
NIPKIMMI .... Scientific Research Planning and Design Institute for Metal Cutting Machines and Instruments (BU)
NIPKIRE ...... Scientific Research Planning and Design Institute for Radio Electronics (BU)
Nip M .... Nehezipari Miniszter [*Minister of Heavy Industry*] (HU)
NIPO .... Netherlands Institute for Public Opinion (WEN)
NI-pp .... Nacelnik Inzinjerije Pesadiskog Puka [*Chief Engineer of an Infantry Regiment*] (YU)
NIPP .... Scientific Institute of Neuropsychiatry and Mental Hygiene (RU)
NIPPIES ...... Scientific Research Planning and Design Institute for Power Systems (BU)
NIPR .... National Institute for Personnel Research (MAR)
ni pri .... Nisi Prius [*Unless Before*] [*Latin*] (GPO)
NIPROC .... Nigeria Industrial and Produce Company (MAR)
NIPRORUDA ... Scientific Research Planning and Design Institute for Ore Mining and Concentration (BU)
NiR .... Norms and Wages, Standards and Costs (RU)
NIR .... Scientific Research and Development (BU)
NIR .... Scientific Research Work (RU)
NIRA .... Nucleare Italiana Reattori Avanzati [*Italian Nuclear Company for Advanced Reactors*] (WER)
NIRD .... Scientific and Development Work (BU)
NIRFI .... Scientific Research Institute of Radiophysics (at the Gor'kiy State University Imeni N. I. Lobachevskiy) (RU)
NIRIA .... Nederlandse Ingenieursvereniging "NIRIA"
NIRMMI .... All-Union Scientific Research Institute of Vegetable Oils and Margarine (RU)
NIRO .... Scientific Research Institute of Sea Fisheries and Oceanography (RU)
NIROWI .... Nigerian-Rumanian Wood Industries (MAR)
NIRP .... Scientific Research Institute of the Rubber Industry (RU)
NIRR .... National Institute for Road Research (MAR)
NIRT .... National Iranian Radio and Television (ME)
NIS .... Chief of Engineer Service (RU)
NiS .... Lookout and Communications [*Navy*] (RU)
NIS .... Nacelnik Intendancni Sluzby [*Chief of Quartermaster Service*] (CZ)
NIS .... National Insurance Scheme [*Guyanese*] (LA)
NIS .... National Insurance Scheme [*Jamaican*] (LA1)
Nis .... Nisis [*Islet(s)*] [*Greek*] (NAU)
NIS .... Scientific Research Council (BU)
NIS .... Scientific Research Department (RU)
NIS .... Scientific Research Sector (BU)
NIS .... Scientific Research Ship (RU)
NIS .... Scientific Research Station (RU)
NIS .... Standards Research Station (RU)
NISCO .... National Iranian Steel Company (ME)
NISER .... Nigerian Institute for Social and Economic Research (MAR)
NISI .... Scientific Research Institute for Construction (BU)
NISIC .... National Iranian Steel Industries Company (ME)
NISIR .... National Institute for Scientific and Industrial Research [*Malaysian*] (ML)
NISJOUR ..... Nigerian School of Journalism (MAR)
NISKhI .... Scientific Research Institute for Sanitation and Public Hygiene (BU)
NISKhOZ ..... Scientific Research Institute for Sanitation, Hygiene, and Organization of Public Health (BU)
NISO .... Lookout and Communications Service Section [*Navy*] (RU)
NISO .... Scientific Institute of Aircraft Equipment (RU)
NISP .... Lookout and Communications Service Station [*Navy*] (RU)
NISPP .... Lookout and Communications Service Mobile Station [*Navy*] (RU)
NISR .... Lookout and Communications Service Area [*Navy*] (RU)
NISS .... Scientific Research Institute of Shipbuilding (RU)
NISSP .... National Integral Sample Survey Programme (MAR)
NIST .... National Institute of Science and Technology [*Philippine*]
NIT .... Numero de Identificacion Tributaria [*Tax Identification Number*] [*Colombian*] (LA)
NITECO .... Nigerian Technical Company Ltd. (MAR)
NITEKhIM ... Scientific Research Institute of Technical and Economic Research of the State Committee of the Council of Ministers, USSR, for Chemistry (RU)
NITEX .... Societe Nigerienne des Textiles (MAR)
NITGEO .... Scientific Research Institute of Heat and Water Power Engineering Equipment (RU)
NITI .... Scientific Research Institute for Textiles (BU)
NITI .... Scientific Research Technological Institute (BU)
NITI .... Scientific Research Technological Institute (RU)
NITI .... Scientific Research Textile Institute (RU)
NITIVPP ...... Scientific Research Technological Institute for the Wine Making and Brewing Industry (BU)
NITKhI .... Scientific Research Institute of Chemical Technology (RU)
NITKhIB ...... Scientific Research Institute of Chemical Technology for Personal Services (RU)
NITO .... Scientific, Engineering, and Technical Society (RU)
NITOBUM .... Scientific, Engineering, and Technical Society of Paper Industry Workers (RU)
NITOLES ..... Scientific, Engineering, and Technical Society of the Lumber Industry (RU)
NITOLesprom ... Scientific Technical Society of the Lumber Industry (RU)
NITOLIT ...... Scientific, Engineering, and Technical Society of Foundry Workers (RU)
NITOM .... Scientific, Engineering, and Technical Society of General Metallurgy (RU)
NITON .... Scientific, Engineering, and Technical Society of Petroleum Workers (RU)
NITR .... National Institute for Telecommunications Research (MAR)
NITR .... Nigerian Institute of Trypanosomiasis Research (MAR)
NITRA .... Niger-Transit (MAR)
NITROVEN ... La Venezolana de Nitrogenos, SA [*Venezuelan Nitrogen Company, Inc.*] (LA)
NITRR .... National Institute for Transport and Road Research (MAR)
NITsMP .... Scientific Research Center for Machine Translation (RU)
NiTU .... Norms and Technical Specifications (RU)
NIU .... Niue [*Three-letter standard code*] (CNC)
NIU .... Scientific Institute for Fertilizers (RU)
NIUI .... Scientific Research Institute of Coal (RU)
NIUIF .... Scientific Research Institute of Fertilizers, Insecticides, and Fungicides Imeni Ya. V. Samoylov (RU)
NIV .... Commander of Engineer Troops (RU)
Nivages .... Niva Hydroelectric Power Plant (RU)
NIVB .... Navorsingsinstituut vir die Visserybedryf (MAR)
NIVE .... Nederlands Instituut voor Efficiency [*Later, Nederlandse Vereniging voor Management*] [*'s-Gravenhage*]
NIVI .... Scientific Research Vacuum Institute (RU)
NIVI .... Veterinary Scientific Research Institute (RU)
NIVK .... Scientific Research Institute of Naval Shipbuilding (RU)
NIVKhKI ...... Scientific Research Institute of Veterinary Hygiene and Control (BU)
NIVMI .... Army Medical Scientific Institute (BU)
NIVNO .... Nasionale Instituut vir Vuurpylnavorsingen-ontwikkeling [*South African*] (MAR)
NIVOS .... Veterinary Scientific Research Experimental Station (RU)
NIVR .... Nederlands Instituut voor Vliegtuigontwikkeling en Ruimtevaart [*Netherlands Institute for Aviation Research and Space Travel*] (WEN)
NIVRA .... Nederlands Instituut van Registeraccountants [*Amsterdam*]
NIVS .... Veterinary Scientific Research Station (RU)
NIVTE .... Scientific Research Institute for Medical Determination of Disability (RU)
NIVTEK .... Scientific Research Institute for Medical Determination of Disability (RU)
NIVV .... Institute for Studies on Peace and Security [*Dutch*] (WEN)
NIWIL .... Nigerian Wire Industries Limited (MAR)
NIWR .... National Institute for Water Research (MAR)
NIYaZ .... Scientific Research Institute of Linguistics (RU)
NIZ .... Nacelnik Intendancniho Zasobovani [*Chief of Quartermaster Service*] (CZ)
Niz .... Nizina [*Plain*] [*Polish*]
NIZENP .... Antiaircraft Artillery Scientific Test Range (RU)
Nizh .... Lower [*Toponymy*] (RU)
NiZh .... Science and Life (RU)

Nizhnevolgoneftegeofizika ... Administration of Geo-Physical Exploration of the Lower Volga Region (RU)
NIZI .... Scientific Research Institute of Zoology (BU)
NIZISNP ...... Zonal Scientific Research Institute of Horticulture of the Non-Black Earth Belt (RU)
nizm .... Lowland [*Topography*] (RU)
NIZMIR .... Scientific Research Institute of Terrestrial Magnetism, the Ionosphere, and Radio Wave Propagation (RU)
nJ .... Naechsten Jahres [*or Naechstes Jahr*] [*Of Next Year or Next Year*] (EG)
NJ .... Nas Jezik [*Our Language*] [*Belgrade*] [*A periodical*] (YU)
NJA .... Norrbottens Jarnverk AB [*Norrbottens Ironworks*] [*Swedish*] (WEN)
NJAC .... National Joint Action Committee [*Trinidadian and Tobagan*] (LA1)
NJCS .... National Jewish Committee on Scouting (MAR)
NJESS .... Nigerian Journal of Economic and Social Studies [*A publication*] (MAR)
NJM .... New JEWEL [*Joint Endeavor for Welfare, Education, and Liberation*] Movement [*Grenadian*] (MAR)
NJP .... Narodni Jednota Posumavska [*National Society for the Sumava Area*] (CZ)
NJS .... Narodni Jednota Severoceska [*National Society for Northern Bohemia*] (CZ)
NJSZT .... Neumann Janos Szamitastechnikai [*or Szamitogeptudomanyi*] Tarsasag [*Janos Neumann Society of Computer Technology*] (HU)
NJUASCO ... New Juabeng Secondary-Commercial School (MAR)
NJYC .... National Jewish Youth Council (MAR)
NK .... Air-Position Indicator (RU)
NK .... Beginning of Curve [*Railroads*] (RU)
Nk .... Chief (BU)
n-k .... Chief, Head, Commander (RU)
NK .... Constant Storage (RU)
NK .... Criminal Code (BU)
NK .... Design Norms, Design Standards (RU)
NK .... Naczelny Komitet [*Chief Committee*] [*Polish*]
NK .... Narodna Knjiznjica [*National Library*] [*Ljubljana*] (YU)
NK .... Narodni Knihovna [*The National Library (Also, a publication series)*] (CZ)
NK .... Narodopisny Kabinet [*Ethnological Section (of the Slovak Academy of Sciences)*] (CZ)
NK .... "Nasza Ksiegarnia" (Instytut Wydawniczy) [*"Our Book-Shop" (Publishing Institute)*] (POL)
NK .... National Committee (BU)
NK .... National Committee (RU)
NK .... Natural Rubber (RU)
NK .... Negative Culture (RU)
nk .... Nemzetkozi [*International*] (HU)
NK .... Neon Komma [*New Party*] [*Greek*] (PPE)
NK .... Neutral Red (Indicator) (RU)
NK .... Neutron Logging (RU)
NK .... New Books (RU)
NK .... Nickel-Cobalt (RU)
nk .... Niin Kuin [*Finnish*]
nk .... Niin Kutsuttu [*Finnish*]
NK .... Nogometni Klub [*Soccer Club*] (YU)
NK .... Normalkerze [*Candle Power*] [*German*]
NK .... Notarska Komora [*Notaries' Association*] (CZ)
NK .... Nucleic Acids (RU)
NK .... People's Commissariat [*1917-1946*] (RU)
NK .... Scientific Committee (RU)
NKAI .... Scientific Committee for Antarctic Research (RU)
NKAP .... People's Commissariat of the Aircraft Industry, USSR [*1939-1946*] (RU)
NKAT .... People's Commissariat of Automobile Transportation (RU)
NKAU .... National Committee of Automatic Control, USSR (RU)
NKB .... People's Commissariat of Ammunition, USSR (RU)
NKBK .... National Committee of Bulgarian Members of Cooperatives (BU)
NKChM .... People's Commissariat of Ferrous Metallurgy, USSR [*1939-1946*] (RU)
NKCP .... North Kalimantan Communist Party [*Malaysian*] (PD)
NKD .... Fixed Range Circle (RU)
NKD .... Najvyssi Kontrolny Dvor [*Supreme Accounting Office*] (CZ)
NKDA .... Nea Kinisi Dikigoron Athinon [*New Movement of Athens Attorneys*] (GC)
nke .... Normal Calomel Electrode (RU)
NKEP .... People's Commissariat of the Electrical Equipment Industry, USSR (RU)
NKES .... People's Commissariat of Electric Power Plants, USSR (RU)
NKES i EP ... People's Commissariat of Electric Power Plants and the Electrical Equipment Industry, USSR (RU)
NKF .... People's Commissariat of Finance [*1924-1946*] (RU)
NKFD .... Nationalkomitee Freies Deutschland [*National Free-Germany Committee*] [*West German*] (WEN)
NKFin .... People's Commissariat of Finance [*1924-1946*] (RU)
NKFV .... Nagyalfold Koolaj es Foldgastermelo Vallalat [*Great Plains Petroleum and Natural Gas Producing Enterprise*] (HU)
NKG .... Neutralized Acid Sludge (RU)
NKG .... Neutron-Gamma-Ray Logging Method (RU)
NKG .... New Kenya Group (MAR)
NKGB .... People's Commissariat of State Security (RU)
NKGG .... Nationalkomitee fuer Geodaesie und Geophysik [*National Committee for Geodesy and Geophysics*] (EG)
NKGK .... People's Commissariat of State Control [*1940-1946*] (RU)
NKGP .... People's Commissariat of the Mining Industry, USSR (RU)
NKh .... Petroleum Industry (RU)
NKhFI .... Scientific Chemical and Pharmaceutical Institute (RU)
NKhGS .... National Art Gallery in Sofia (BU)
NKhK .... Petrochemical Combine (BU)
NKhS .... Chief of Chemical Service (BU)
NKhS .... Chief of Chemical Service (RU)
NKhV .... Commander of Chemical Troops (RU)
n-ki .... Successors (RU)
NKID .... People's Commissariat of Foreign Affairs [*1917-1946*] (RU)
NKII .... Kwame N'Krumah Ideological Institute (MAR)
NKK .... Beginning of Belt Line [*Railroads*] (RU)
NKK .... Narodni Kulturni Komise [*National Cultural Commission*] (CZ)
NKK .... Nepkonyvtari Kozpont [*Administrative Center for People's Libraries*] (HU)
NKKhP .... People's Commissariat of the Chemical Industry, USSR [*1939-1946*] (RU)
NKKKh .... People's Commissariat of the Municipal Economy (RU)
NKKU .... Negara Kesatuan Kalimantan Utara [*Unified State of North Kalimantan*] (ML)
NKL .... Namik Kemal Lise [*Namik Kemal Lycee*] [*High school*] [*Cypriot*] (TU)
NKL .... People's Commissariat of the Lumber Industry [*1932-1946*] (RU)
NKLEGprom ... People's Commissariat of Light Industry (RU)
NKLes .... People's Commissariat of the Lumber Industry [*1932-1946*] (RU)
NKLP .... People's Commissariat of Light Industry (RU)
nkm .... Najciezszy Karabin Maszynowy [*Heaviest Machine Gun*] [*Polish*]
NKM .... Non-Relativistic Quantum Mechanics (RU)
NKM .... People's Commissariat of Machinery Manufacture, USSR (RU)
NKMash ...... People's Commissariat of Machinery Manufacture, USSR (RU)
NKMB .... Nederlandse Katholieke Middenstandsbond [*Netherlands Catholic Middle Class Association*] (WEN)
NKMestprom ... People's Commissariat of Local Industry (RU)
NKMF .... People's Commissariat of the Maritime Fleet, USSR (RU)
NKMGG .... Nacionalne Komisije za Medunarodnu Geofizicku Godinu [*National Commissions for the International Geophysical Year*] [*1957-1958*] (YU)
NKMMP .... People's Commissariat of the Meat and Dairy Industry (RU)
NKMP .... People's Commissariat of Local Industry (RU)
NKMTP .... People's Commissariat of the Local Fuel Industry (RU)
NKMV .... People's Commissariat of Mortar Weapons, USSR (RU)
NKMZ .... New Kramatorsk Machinery Plant (RU)
NKN .... Naczelny Komitet Narodowy [*Polish*]
NKN .... People's Commissariat for Nationalities, RSFSR (RU)
NKNLL .... North Kalimantan National Liberation League (ML)
NKNP .... People's Commissariat of the Petroleum Industry, USSR [*1939-1946*] (RU)
NKO .... People's Commissariat of Defense [*1934-1946*] (RU)
NKOF .... National Committee of the Fatherland Front (BU)
NK na OF ..... National Committee of the Fatherland Front (BU)
NKOJ .... Nacionalni Komitet Oslobodenja Yugoslavije [*National Committee for the Liberation of Yugoslavia*] (YU)
NKOL .... Nacelnik Kadroveho Oddilu Letectva [*Air Force Personnel Chief*] (CZ)
NKOM .... People's Commissariat of General Machinery Manufacture, USSR (RU)
NKOP .... People's Commissariat of the Defense Industry, USSR (RU)
N-k otd .... Section Chief (BU)
NKOYu .... National Committee for the Liberation of Yugoslavia (RU)
NKP .... Commander's Observation Post (RU)
NKP .... Nasionale Konserwatiewe Party [*National Conservative Party*] [*South African*] (PPW)
NKP .... Nemet Kommunista Part [*German Communist Party*] (HU)
NKP .... New Kenya Party (MAR)
NKP .... Norges Kommunistiske Parti [*Norwegian Communist Party*] (PPE)
NKP .... Observation and Spotting Post [*Artillery*] (RU)
NKP .... People's Commissariat of Education [*1917-1946*] (RU)
NKPishcheprom ... People's Commissariat of the Food Industry (RU)
NKPiT .... People's Commissariat of Postal and Telegraphic Service (RU)
NKPochtel' ... People's Commissariat of Postal and Telegraphic Service (RU)
NKPP .... People's Commissariat of the Food Industry (RU)
NKPROD ..... People's Commissariat of Food [*1917-1924*] (RU)
NKPros .... People's Commissariat of Education [*1917-1946*] (RU)
NKPS .... People's Commissariat of Railroads, USSR [*1922-1946*] (RU)
NKPSM .... People's Commissariat of the Building Materials Industry (RU)
NKPT .... People's Commissariat of Postal and Telegraphic Service (RU)
NKPZA .... Antiaircraft Artillery Observation and Spotting Post (RU)
Nkr .... Norjan Kruunu(a) [*Finnish*]
N Kr .... Norveg Korona [*Norwegian Krone*] (HU)
NKRF .... People's Commissariat of the River Fleet, USSR (RU)
NKRKI .... People's Commissariat of Workers' and Peasants' Inspection [*1920-1934*] (RU)

NKRP.......... People's Commissariat of the Fish Industry [*1939-1946*] (RU)
NKRP.......... People's Commissariat of the Rubber Industry, USSR (RU)
NKrS........... Nacelnik Kurirske Stanice [*Courier Station Chief*] [*Military*] (YU)
NKS............ People's Commissariat of Communications, USSR [*1932-1946*] (RU)
NKSG.......... National Committee of Soviet Geographers (RU)
NKSKh........ People's Commissariat of Grain and Live-Stock-Breeding Sovkhozes (RU)
NKSM.......... People's Commissariat of Medium Machinery Manufacture, USSR (RU)
NKSNAB..... People's Commissariat of Supply [*1930-1934*] (RU)
NKSO.......... People's Commissariat of Social Security [*1918-1946*] (RU)
NKSP.......... People's Commissariat of the Shipbuilding Industry, USSR (RU)
NKSS.......... People's Commissariat of Machine Tool Manufacture, USSR (RU)
NKSvyazi.... People's Commissariat of Communications, USSR [*1932-1946*] (RU)
nkt.............. Lower Critical Temperature (RU)
NKT............ People's Commissariat of Labor [*1917-1933*] (RU)
NKTG.......... National Confederation of Workers of Guinea (RU)
NKTiP.......... People's Commissariat of Trade and Industry (RU)
NKTL........... Ground Ejection-Seat Trainer (RU)
NKTM.......... People's Commissariat of Heavy Machinery Manufacture, USSR [*1939-1946*] (RU)
NKTM.......... People's Commissariat of Transportation Machinery Manufacture, USSR [*1945-1946*] (RU)
NKTOP........ People's Commissariat of the Fuel Industry (RU)
NKTorg....... People's Commissariat of Foreign and Domestic Trade, USSR [*1924-1938*] (RU)
NKTorg....... People's Commissariat of Trade [*1938-1946*] (RU)
NKTP.......... People's Commissariat of the Fuel Industry (RU)
NKTP.......... People's Commissariat of Heavy Industry, USSR [*1932-1939*] (RU)
NKTP.......... People's Commissariat of the Tank Industry, USSR (RU)
NKTP.......... People's Commissariat of the Textile Industry (RU)
NKTP.......... People's Commissariat of Trade and Industry (RU)
NKTrud....... People's Commissariat of Labor [*1917-1933*] (RU)
NKTsBP...... People's Commissariat of the Pulp and Paper Industry, USSR (RU)
NKTsM........ People's Commissariat of Nonferrous Metallurgy, USSR [*1939-1946*] (RU)
NKTyazhmash... People's Commissariat of Heavy Machinery Manufacture [*1939-1946*] (RU)
NKTYaZhprom... People's Commissariat of Heavy Industry, USSR [*1932-1939*] (RU)
NKU............ Nejvyssi Kontrolni Urad [*Supreme Accounting Office*] (CZ)
N-k u-nie..... Department Chief (BU)
NKUP.......... People's Commissariat of the Coal Industry USSR [*1939-1946*] (RU)
NKV............ Nederlands Katholiek Vakverbond [*Netherlands Catholic Workers Federation*] (WEN)
NKV............ People's Commissariat of Armaments, USSR (RU)
NKV............ People's Commissariat for Military Affairs [*1918-1923*] (RU)
NKVD.......... Narodnyi Komissariat Vnutrennikh Del [*People's Commissariat of Internal Affairs (1917-1946)*] [*Also known as NARKOMVNUDEL*] [*Soviet secret police organization*]
NKVD.......... Public Security Department [*Later, KGB*] [*Russian*] (PD)
NKVM.......... People's Commissariat for Military and Naval Affairs, USSR [*1923-1934*] (RU)
NKVMF........ People's Commissariat of the Navy, USSR [*1937-1946*] (RU)
NKVneshtorg... People's Commissariat of Foreign Trade, USSR [*1923-1925, 1940-1946*] (RU)
NKVnutorg... People's Commissariat of Domestic Trade [*1924-1938*] (RU)
NKVod......... People's Commissariat of Water Transportation, USSR (RU)
NKVoyen..... People's Commissariat for Military Affairs [*1918-1923*] (RU)
NKVoyenmor... People's Commissariat for Military and Naval Affairs, USSR [*1923-1934*] (RU)
NKVoyenmor... People's Commissariat of the Navy, USSR [*1937-1946*] (RU)
NKVP.......... People's Commissariat of Munitions, USSR (RU)
NKVR.......... Narodni Komitet pro Vedeckou Radiotechniku [*National Committee for Scientific Radio Engineering*] (CZ)
NKVT.......... People's Commissariat of Domestic Trade [*1924-1938*] (RU)
NKVT.......... People's Commissariat of Foreign Trade, USSR [*1923-1925, 1930-1946*] (RU)
NKVT.......... People's Commissariat of Water Transportation, USSR (RU)
NKW............ Naczelny Komitet Wykonawczy [*Chief Executive Committee*] (POL)
NKW............ Narodowy Komitet Wyzwolenia [*National Liberation Committee*] (POL)
NKW PSL.... Naczelny Komitet Wykonawczy Polskiego Stronnictwa Ludowego [*Chief Executive Committee of the Polish Peasant Party*] (POL)
NKW SD...... Naczelny Komitet Wykonawczy Stronnictwa Demokratycznego [*Chief Executive Committee of the Democratic Party*] (POL)
NKWV.......... Nederlands Katholiek Werkgevers Verbond [*Netherlands Catholic Employers Association*] (WEN)
NKW ZSL.... Naczelny Komitet Wykonawczy Zjednoczonego Stronnictwa Ludowego [*Chief Executive Committee of the United Peasant Party*] (POL)
NKYu.......... People's Commissariat of Justice, USSR [*1936-1946*] (RU)
NKYust........ People's Commissariat of Justice, USSR [*1936-1946*] (RU)
NKZ............ Narodno Kazaliste Zagreb [*Zagreb National Theater*] (YU)
NKZ............ People's Commissariat of Agriculture (RU)
NKZ............ People's Commissariat of Public Health [*1936-1946*] (RU)
NKZag......... People's Commissariat of Procurement, USSR [*1938-1946*] (RU)
NKzaUNICEF... Nacionalna Komisija za UNICEF [*Yugoslav National Commission for UNICEF*] (YU)
NKZdrav..... People's Commissariat of Public Health [*1936-1946*] (RU)
NKZem........ People's Commissariat of Agriculture (RU)
NKZM.......... National Committee for the Defense of Peace (BU)
NK ZSL........ Naczelny Komitet Zjednoczonego Stronnictwa Ludowego [*Chief Committee of the United Peasants' Party*] (POL)
NKZZhSKh... People's Commissariat of Grain and Live-Stock-Breeding Sovkhozes (RU)
NL............... Holandia [*Holland*] [*Polish*]
nL............... Nad Labem [*On the Elbe River*] (CZ)
nl................ Namelijk [*Namely*] [*Dutch*] (GPO)
NL............... Navigation Slide Rule (RU)
nl................ Nemlig [*Namely*] [*Norwegian*] (GPO)
NL............... Neo Lao [*Hak Sat*] [*Lao Patriotic Front*] [*Use NLHS*] (CL)
NL............... Netherlands [*Two-letter standard code*] (CNC)
nl................ Nicht Loeslich [*Not Soluble*] [*German*]
NL............... Niederlassung [*Branch Office, Field Office, Place of Business*] (EG)
n l............... Non Licet [*It Is Not Permitted*] [*Latin*] (GPO)
nl................ Non Liquet [*It Is Not Clear*] [*Latin*] (GPO)
nl................ Non Longe [*Not Far*] [*Latin*] (GPO)
NL............... Pneumatic Boat (RU)
NLA............ Nigerian Library Association (MAR)
NLAC.......... National Library Advisory Council (MAR)
NLAC.......... National Literacy Advisory Committee (MAR)
NLAF.......... National Language Action Front (ML)
NLB............ National Liquor Board (MAR)
NLB............ Nepkoztarsasag Legfelso Birosaga [*Supreme Court of the People's Republic*] (HU)
nlb.............. Nieliczbowane (Strony) [*Unpaged*] (POL)
NLBP.......... Night Light Bomber Regiment (RU)
NLC............ National Liberation Council [*Ghanaian*] (AF)
NLC............ New Liberal Club [*Shin Jiyu Club*] [*Japanese*] (PPW)
NLC............ Nigerian Labor Congress (AF)
NLCD.......... National Liberation Council Decree (MAR)
NLD............ Netherlands [*Three-letter standard code*] (CNC)
NLDP.......... National Liberal Democratic Party (MAR)
NLF............ National Front for the Liberation of South Vietnam [*Use NFLSV*] (CL)
NLF............ National Labour Federation (MAR)
NLF............ National Liberation Front [*Burmese*] (PD)
NLF............ National Liberation Front [*South African*] (PD)
NLFR.......... National Liberation Front of Reunion (MAR)
NLG............ National Lecturers Group (BU)
NLHS.......... Neo Lao Hak Sat [*Lao Patriotic Front*] (TVP)
NLHX.......... Neo Lao Hak Sat [*Lao Patriotic Front*] [*Use NLHS*] (CL)
NLJ............ Nigerian Law Journal [*A publication*] (MAR)
NLJU.......... New Liberal Jewish Union (MAR)
NLL............ National Lending Library for Science and Technology [*United Kingdom*]
NLM............ National Liberation Movement (MAR)
NLM............ Nile Liberation Movement [*Egyptian*] (MAR)
NLMA.......... Nigerian Livestock and Meat Authority (MAR)
NLMGB........ National Liberation Movement of Guinea-Bissau (MAR)
NLMWT....... Mouvement de Liberation Nationale du Togo Occidental [*National Liberation Movement of West Togo*] (AF)
NLMZ.......... New Lipetsk Metallurgical Plant (RU)
NLP............ Light Pneumatic Pontoon (RU)
NLP............ Narodnoliberalna Partiia [*National Liberal Party*] [*Bulgarian*] (PPE)
NLP............ National Liberal Party [*Lebanese*] (ME)
NLP............ National Liberation Party [*Gambian*] (PPW)
NLP............ Nigerian Labor Party (AF)
NLPC.......... National Livestock Production Company (MAR)
NLR............ Nationaal Lucht- en Ruimtevaartlaboratorium [*National Aeronautical and Astronautical Research Institute*] [*Dutch*] (WEN)
NLR............ Nemocnice Lehce Ranenych [*Hospital for Slightly Wounded*] (CZ)
NLRD.......... National Hunting and Fishing Society (BU)
NLRS.......... National Hunting and Fishing Union (BU)
NLSC.......... National Leather and Shoe Corporation (MAR)
NLVF.......... Norges Landbruksvitenskapelige Forskningsrad [*Norwegian Agricultural Research Council*] (WEN)
NM.............. Antidisturbance Mine, Antiremoval Mine (RU)
Nm.............. Mechanischer Wirkungsgrad [*Mechanical Efficiency*] [*German*]
Nm.............. Nachmittags [*Afternoon*] [*German*]
NM.............. Nacionalnite Malcinstva [*National Minorities*] (YU)
nM.............. Naechsten Monats [*Of Next Month*] (EG)
nm.............. Namiddag [*After Noon*] [*Dutch*] (GPO)

NM.............. Narodna Milicija [*People's Militia*] [*A periodical*] (YU)
NM.............. Narodna Milicija [*People's Militia*] [*Police*] (YU)
NM.............. Narodna Mladina [*People's Youth*] (YU)
NM.............. Narodni Museum [*National Museum*] (CZ)
NM.............. Nepjoleti Miniszterium/Miniszter [*Ministry/Minister of Public Welfare*] (HU)
NM.............. New World (RU)
NM.............. Newtonian Mechanics (RU)
Nm.............. Newtonmeter [*Newton Meter (Unit of mechanical efficiency)*] (EG)
NM.............. Nonmetallic Deposits (RU)
NM.............. Nord Magnetique [*French*] (MTD)
Nm.............. Normalmeter [*Standard Meter*] (EG)
NM.............. People's Militia (BU)
NM.............. People's Museum (BU)
NM-.............. Pressure Gauge (RU)
NMA............ Chief of Medical Service of an Army (RU)
NMA............ Nigerian Medical Association (MAR)
NMB............ Magnetic Drum Storage (RU)
NMB............ Nigeria Marketing and Regional Production Development Board (MAR)
NMB............ Scientific Medical Library (RU)
NMC............ Nairobi Motor Club (MAR)
NMC............ National Meteorological Center (SJT)
NMC............ National Military Council [*Surinamese*] (PD)
NMC............ National Milling Corporation [*Tanzanian*] (AF)
nmc............ Norme de Munca Conventionale [*Conventional Work Norms*] (RO)
NMCG.......... NATO Maritime Coordination Group (MAR)
NMCM.......... Nigerian Motor Components Manufacturers (MAR)
NMD............ Chief of Medical Service of a Division (RU)
NMDF.......... National Movement for the Defense of the Fatherland [*Replaced CDNI*] [*Lao*] (CL)
NMEP.......... Novyi Mezhduradnyi Ekonomicheskii Poriadok (MAR)
NMERI......... National Mechanical Engineering Research Institute (MAR)
NMJ............ Narodna Mladina na Jugoslavija [*People's Youth of Yugoslavia*] (YU)
NMK............ Chief of Medical Service of a Corps (RU)
NMK............ Low-Molecular-Weight Component (RU)
NMK............ Nonequilibrium Molecular Constellation (RU)
NMK............ Scientific Methodological Study Center (RU)
NMKh.......... People's Museum in Khisar (BU)
NML............ Magnetic Tape Storage (RU)
NMl............ Narodna Mladezh [*People's Youth*] [*A periodical*] (BU)
NMM............ Narodna Mladina na Makedonija [*People's Youth of Macedonia*] (YU)
NMM............ Nepjoleti es Munkaugyi Miniszterium/Miniszter [*Ministry/Minister of Public Welfare and Labor*] (HU)
NMM............ Nepmuvelesi Miniszterium/Miniszter [*Ministry/Minister of Public Education*] (HU)
NMN............ Nicotinamide Mononucleotide (RU)
NMO............ Forward Engine Room (RU)
NMO............ Scientific Methodological Department (RU)
NMP............ Chief of Medical Service of a Regiment (RU)
NMP............ National Maize Project (MAR)
NMP............ Nederlands Middenstands Partij [*Netherlands Middle Class Party*] (PPE)
NMPI........... People's Museum in Plovdiv (BU)
NMPP.......... Nouvelles Messageries de la Presse Parisienne [*New Distribution Service of the Parisian Press*] [*French*] (WER)
NMR............ National Movement for Renewal (MAR)
n mr s......... Commander of Naval Forces (BU)
NMS............ Chief of Medical Service (RU)
NMS............ Scientific Medical Council (RU)
NMS............ Scientific Methodological Council (RU)
NMS............ Scientific Methodological Department (RU)
NMT............ Bottom Dead Center (RU)
NMT............ Nigerian Machine Tool Company (MAR)
NMTC.......... National Marine Tanker Company (MAR)
NMU............ National Maritime Union [*Panamanian*] (LA)
NMU............ Nuba Mountains Union (MAR)
NMV............ Lower Low Water (RU)
NMWA......... National Mine Workers Association [*Liberian*] (AF)
NMWU......... National Mine Workers Union [*Liberian*] (AF)
NMWU......... National Mining Workers Union (ML)
NMWU......... Northern Mine Workers Union (MAR)
NMZhK........ Low-Molecular-Weight Fatty Acids (RU)
nN.............. Gesamtwirkungsgrad [*Total Efficiency*] [*German*]
NN.............. Ismeretlen Nevu [*Anonymous*] (HU)
NN.............. Low Voltage (RU)
nN.............. Nad Nisou [*On the Neisse River*] (CZ)
nn.............. Nastepne (Strony) [*Next (Pages)*] (POL)
nn.............. Nizke Napeti [*Low Voltage*] (CZ)
nn.............. Nomen Nescio [*Latin*] (GPO)
NN.............. Normalnull [*Datum Surface, Mean Sea Level*] [*German*] (WEN)
NN.............. Northern News (MAR)
NNA............ National News Agency [*Lebanese*] (ME)
NNA............ National People's Army (RU)
NNA............ Nigerian National Alliance (MAR)
NNA............ Notio-Notio-Anatolikos [*South-Southeast*] (GC)
NNC............ Naga National Council [*Indian*] (PD)
NNC............ Namibian National Convention (MAR)
NNC............ Native National Congress (MAR)
NNC............ Northern Nigerian Congress (MAR)
NNCAE........ Nigerian National Council for Adult Education (MAR)
NND............ Nigerian National Diploma (MAR)
NNDC.......... New Nigeria Development Company Ltd. (MAR)
NNDC.......... Northern Nigeria Development Corporation (MAR)
NNDP.......... Nigerian National Democratic Party (AF)
NNE............ Nord Nord Est [*North North-East*] [*French*] (MTD)
NNE............ Nornordeste [*North-Northeast*] [*Spanish*]
NNF............ Namibia National Front (PPW)
NNF............ National Science Foundation [*NSF*] (RU)
NNI............ Nederlands Normalisatie-Instituut [*Rijswijk*]
NNI 82......... Normcommissie Informatieverzorging [*Dutch*]
NNIL........... Northern Nigeria Investments Limited (MAR)
NNK............ Neutron-Neutron Logging (RU)
NNL............ Nigeria Newsletter [*A publication*] (MAR)
NNL............ Nigerian National Shipping Line (MAR)
NNLC.......... Ngwane National Liberation Congress [*Swazi*] (AF)
NNM............ Neutron-Neutron Method (RU)
NNMA.......... Nigerian National Merit Award (MAR)
NNMC.......... Nigerian Newsprint Manufacturing Company (MAR)
NNN............ Nemzetkozi Nonap [*International Women's Day*] (HU)
NNNA.......... North Nyasa Native Association (MAR)
NNO............ Nornoroeste [*North-Northwest*] [*Spanish*]
NNOC.......... Nigerian National Oil Corporation (AF)
NNP............ New National Party [*Grenadian*]
NNP............ Stationary Observation Post (RU)
NNP............ Vereniging van de Nederlandsche Nieuwsbladpers [*Association of the Netherlands Weekly Press*] (WEN)
NNPC.......... Nigerian National Petroleum Company (AF)
NNPC.......... Northern Nigerian Publishing Company (MAR)
NNRI........... National Nutrition Research Institute (MAR)
NNRLNT...... Decree on Job Placement of Persons with Diminished Working Capacity (BU)
NNS............ Nigeriiskii Natsional'nyi Soiuz (MAR)
NNSC.......... Nigerian National Supply Company (MAR)
NNSL.......... Nigerian National Shipping Lines (MAR)
NNTs.......... Low-Nitrated Cellulose (RU)
NNU............ Namibia National Union (AF)
NNUU.......... Naciones Unidas [*United Nations*] [*Use UN*] (LA)
NNW............ Niedrigstes Niedrigwasser [*Minimum Low Water Level*] (EG)
NNW............ Nord Nord Ouest [*North Northwest*] [*French*] (MTD)
NNZ............ Auxiliary Charge Carriers (RU)
NO.............. Chief of Operations Section (BU)
NO.............. Chief of Operations Section (RU)
no.............. Criminal Section (BU)
NO.............. Detachment Commander (RU)
NO.............. Directive on Workers' and Employees' Leaves and Rest Periods (BU)
NO.............. Nacelnik Oddeleni [*Chief of Department*] (CZ)
nO.............. Nad Odrou [*On the Oder River*] (CZ)
NO.............. Nadbiskupski Ordinarijat [*Chancery of the Catholic Archbishopric*] (YU)
no.............. Nain T Niin Ollen [*Finnish*]
NO.............. Naroden Odbor [*People's Committee*] (YU)
NO.............. Narodna Odbrana [*National Defense*] (YU)
NO.............. Narodna Omladina [*People's Youth*] (YU)
NO.............. Narodni Osvobozeni [*National Liberation*] [*A newspaper*] (CZ)
NO.............. Narodnooslobodilacki [*National Liberation*] (YU)
NO.............. National Okrug (RU)
NO.............. National Opera (BU)
NO.............. Navtikos Omilos [*Yacht Club*] (GC)
no.............. Netto [*Net*] [*German*] (GPO)
NO.............. Niederoesterreich [*or Niederoesterreichisch*] [*German*]
NO.............. Nordosten [*Northeast*] (EG)
NO.............. Noroeste [*Northwest*] [*Spanish*]
NO.............. Norway [*Two-letter standard code*] (CNC)
n/o............. Notre Ordre [*Our Order*] [*Business and trade*] [*French*]
NO.............. Nova Obzorja [*New Horizons*] [*Maribor*] [*A periodical*] (YU)
No.............. Novini [*News*] [*A newspaper*] (BU)
NO.............. Null-Balance Device [*Computers*] (RU)
No.............. Numer [*Number*] [*Polish*]
no.............. Numero [*Finnish*]
No.............. Numero [*Number, Issue*] [*French*]
No.............. Numero [*or Nummer*] [*Number*] [*German*] (GPO)
No.............. Numero [*Number*] [*Italian*] (GPO)
No.............. Numero [*Number*] [*Spanish*]
no.............. Numero [*Number*] [*Turkish*] (GPO)
n:o............. Numro [*Number*] [*Swedish*] (GPO)
n/o............. Over (RU)
NO.............. Public Education (RU)
NOA............ Nueva Organizacion Anticomunista [*New Anticommunist Organization*] [*Guatemalan*] (LA)
NOA............ Nueva Organizacion Antiterrorista [*New Anti-Terrorist Organization*] [*Guatemalan*] (PD)
NOA............ People's Army of Liberation [*Chinese People's Republic*] (RU)
NOA............ Scientific Testing Airfield (RU)
NOAA.......... National Oceanic and Atmospheric Administration (WER)
NOAK.......... People's Army of Liberation of China (RU)

NOAKMO .... Narodni Odbor Autonomne Kosovo-Metohijske Oblasti [*People's Committee of the Autonomous Region of Kosovo-Metohija*] (YU)
No Amr .... Nobetci Amiri [*Duty Officer*] (TU)
NoAptD .... Novo Aptechno Delo [*New Pharmacy Affairs*] [*A periodical*] (BU)
NOAS .... National Organization for Agricultural Settling (MAR)
NOB .... Narodnooslobodilacka Borba [*National Liberation Struggle*] (YU)
NOB .... Nemzetkozi Olimpiai Bizottsag [*International Olympic Committee*] (HU)
Nob .... Nobis [*For (or On) Our Part*] [*Latin*] (GPO)
NOBIN .... Nederlands Orgaan voor de Bevordering van de Informatieverzorging [*'s-Gravenhage*]
NO brigada ... People's Liberation Brigade (BU)
NOC .... National Oil Corporation [*Libyan, Nigerian*] (MAR)
NOC .... National Operations Committee [*Malaysian*] (ML)
NOCG .... Narodna Omladina Crne Gore [*People's Youth of Montenegro*] (YU)
NOCI .... Nederlandse Organisatie voor Chemische Informatie [*'s-Gravenhage*]
NOCI .... Nomenclature Cambodgienne des Industries [*Cambodian Nomenclature of Industries*] (CL)
NOCISEN .... Nouvelle Cimenterie du Senegal (MAR)
NOD .... Chief of Railroad Section (RU)
NOD .... Greatest Common Divisor (RU)
NODB .... Nacelnik Odboru [*Branch Chief*] (CZ)
NODO .... Narodnooslobodilacki Dobrovoljacki Odred [*National Liberation Volunteer Detachment*] [*World War II*] (YU)
NO-DO .... Noticiarios y Documentales Cinematograficos [*Documentary Films and Newsreel Co.*] [*Spanish*] (WER)
NOE .... Navtikos Omilos Ellados [*Yacht Club of Greece*] (GC)
NOE .... (Skholi) Nomikon kai Oikonomikon Epistimon [*(School of) Law and Economic Sciences*] [*See also SNOE*] (GC1)
N-Oefen ...... Niederschachtoefen [*Low-Shaft Furnaces (Installed at the West Metallurgical Combine in Calbe/Saale)*] (EG)
NOEI .... Nouvel Ordre Economique International [*New International Economic Order*] [*Use NIEO*] [*French*] (AF)
NOEI .... Nuevo Orden Economico Internacional [*New International Economic Order*] [*Spanish*] (LA)
noem .... November (BU)
NOeP .... Neue Oekonomische Politik [*New Economic Policy*] (EG)
NOeS .... Neues Oekonomisches System [*New Economic System*] (EG)
NOeSPL ...... Neues Oekonomisches System der Planung und Leitung [*New Economic Planning and Managing System*] (EG)
NOeSPL ...... Neues Oekonomisches System der Planung und Leitung der Volkswirtschaft [*New Economic System of Planning and Managing the Economy*] (EG)
NOF .... Narodnooslobodilacka Fronta [*National Liberation Front*] (YU)
NOF .... Narodnooslobodilacki Fond [*National Liberation Fund*] (YU)
NOF .... People's Liberation Front (BU)
NOFROA ..... Compagnie Norvegienne et Francaise de l'Ouest Africain (MAR)
NOG .... Narodni Odbor Grada [*City People's Committee*] (YU)
NOGEPA ..... Netherlands Oil and Gas Exploration and Production Association
NOGO .... Narodni Odbor Gradske Opstine [*Township People's Committee*] (YU)
NOGZ .... Narodni Odbor Grada Zagreba [*People's Committee of the City of Zagreb*] (YU)
Noi .... Nisoi [*Islands*] [*See also N*] [*Greek*] (NAU)
NOIP .... National Office of Industrial Property (MAR)
NOJ .... Narodno Oslobodenje Jugoslavije [*National Liberation of Yugoslavia*] (YU)
NOK .... Narodni Odbor Kotara [*District People's Committee*] (YU)
NOK .... National Olympic Committee (RU)
NOK .... Nationales Olympisches Komitee [*National Olympic Committee*] (EG)
NOKZ .... Narodni Odbor Kotara Zagreba [*People's Committee of the District of Zagreb*] (YU)
NOLIT .... Nova Literatura, Izdavacko Preduzece [*New Literature, Publishing Establishment*] [*Belgrade*] (YU)
NOLITAF ..... Nouvelle Literie Africaine (MAR)
nol pros ...... Nolle Prosequi [*Will Not Prosecute*] [*Latin*] (GPO)
nom .... Nominatif [*Nominative, Subject, Registered*] [*French*]
nom .... Nominatiivi [*Finnish*]
NOM .... Scientific Society of Marxists (RU)
NOMACO .... Nouvelle Mauritanie Commerciale (MAR)
NON .... Nuevo Orden Nacional [*New National Order*] [*Ecuadorean*] (LA)
NONAS .... Negroes Occidental National Agricultural School (MAR)
non cul .... Non Culpabilis [*Not Guilty*] [*Latin*] (GPO)
non obs .... Non Obstante [*Notwithstanding*] [*Latin*] (GPO)
non pros ...... Non Prosequitur [*He Does Not Prosecute*] [*Latin*] (GPO)
non seq .... Non Sequitur [*It Does Not Follow (Logically)*] [*Latin*] (GPO)
NOO .... Nacelnik Operacniho Oddeleni [*Chief of Operations Department*] (CZ)
NOO .... Narodni Odbor Opstine [*Municipal People's Committee*] (YU)
NOO .... Narodnooslobodilacki Odbor [*National Liberation Committee*] (YU)
NOP .... Narodnooslobodilacki Pokret [*National Liberation Movement*] [*World War II*] (YU)
NOP .... Netherlands Association of Trade Unions (RU)
NOP .... Novy Operativni Plan [*New Operational Plan*] (CZ)
NOPATO ..... Nouvelle Papeterie Togolaise (MAR)
NOPiDO ...... Narodnooslobodilacki Partizanski i Dobrovoljacki Odredi [*National Liberation Partisan and Volunteer Detachments*] [*World War II*] (YU)
NOPiDV ...... Narodnooslobodilacka Partizanska i Dobrovoljacka Vojska [*National Liberation Partisan and Volunteer Army*] [*World War II*] (YU)
NOPiDVJ ..... Narodnooslobodilacka Partizanska i Dobrovoljacka Vojska Jugoslavije [*National Liberation Partisan and Volunteer Army of Yugoslavia*] [*World War II*] (YU)
NOPiD(vojska) ... Narodnooslobodilacka Partizanska i Dobrovoljacka (Vojska) [*National Liberation Partisan and Volunteer (Army)*] [*World War II*] (YU)
NOPO .... Narodnooslobodilacki Partizanski Odredi [*National Liberation Partisan Detachments*] [*World War II*] (YU)
NOPOBiH .... Narodnooslobodilacki Partizanski Odredi Bosne i Hercegovine [*National Liberation Partisan Detachments of Bosnia and Hercegovina*] [*World War II*] (YU)
NOPOJ .... Narodnooslobodilacki Partizanski Odredi Jugoslavije [*National Liberation Partisan Detachments of Yugoslavia*] [*World War II*] (YU)
NOPPMB ..... Nigeria Oil Palm Produce Marketing Board (MAR)
NOPTU .... Scientific Organization of Production, Labor, and Management (BU)
NOPU .... Narodnooslobodilacki Partizanski Udarni [*National Liberation Partisan Shock Units*] (YU)
NOPV .... Narodnooslobodilacka Partizanska Vojska [*National Liberation Partisan Army*] [*World War II*] (YU)
NOR .... Narodnooslobodilacki Rat [*National Liberation War*] [*World War II*] (YU)
NOR .... Navtikos Omilos Rodou [*Rhodes Yacht Club*] (GC)
NOR .... Norway [*Three-letter standard code*] (CNC)
NORAD .... Norwegian Agency for Development (MAR)
NORCEM ...... Cement Company of Northern Nigeria (MAR)
NORCh .... Nonstandard Equipment and Spare Parts (BU)
NORDITA .... Nordisk Institut for Teoretisk Atomfysik [*Nordic Institute for Theoretical Nuclear Physics*] [*Danish*] (WEN)
NORG .... Nasserite Organisation Reform Group (MAR)
NORGABON ... Societe Miniere du Nord-Gabon (MAR)
Noril'lag ...... Noril'sk Corrective Labor Camp (RU)
NORINDOK ... Norwegian Committee for Information and Documentation
norj .... Norjaa [*or Norjaksi*] [*Finnish*]
norj .... Norjalainen [*Finnish*]
norl .... Norleucine (RU)
NORLA .... Northern Region Literature Agency (MAR)
NorLantMedArea ... North Atlantic and Mediterranean Area (MAR)
norm .... Normal (RU)
norm .... Normen [*Standards*] [*German*]
NORMETAL ... Empresa Metalmecanica del Norte [*Northern Metalworking Enterprise*] [*Peruvian*] (LA)
NORS .... Office of New Vegetable Raw Materials (RU)
NORSS .... Independent General Workers' Trade Union (BU)
NORTEC ..... Northern Technical College (MAR)
norv .... Norwegian (RU)
NorwP .... Norwegisches Patent [*Norwegian Patent*] [*German*]
NOS .... Chief of Axis of Communications (RU)
NOS .... Irrigation and Drainage System (BU)
NOS .... Nacelnik Operacni Skupiny [*Chief of Operational Detachment*] (CZ)
NOS .... Narodna Omladina Srbije [*People's Youth of Serbia*] (YU)
NOS .... Narodni Odbor Sela [*Village People's Committee*] (YU)
NOS .... Narodni Odbor Sreza [*District People's Committee*] (YU)
NOS .... Narodno Osvobojenje Slovenije [*National Liberation of Slovenia*] [*World War II*] (YU)
NOS .... Nederlandse Omroep Stichting [*Netherlands Broadcasting Foundation*] (WEN)
NOS .... Nouvel Ordre Social [*New Social Order*] [*Swiss*] (PD)
NOS .... Nulla Osta di Sicurezza [*Security Clearance*] [*Italian*] (WER)
NOSA .... National Occupational Safety Association (MAR)
NOSAB .... Night Signal Bomb (RU)
NOSCO .... Ndola Oil Storage Company (MAR)
NOSEC .... Nouvelle Societe Senegalaise de Commerce et d'Industrie (MAR)
NOSOCO ..... Nouvelle Societe Commerciale Africaine (MAR)
NOSONATRAM ... Nouvelle Societe Nationale des Transports Mauritaniens (MAR)
NOSWA .... National Organization of South-West Africa [*Namibian*] (AF)
NOSZF .... Nagy Oktoberi Szocialista Forradalom [*The Great October Socialist Revolution*] (HU)
NOT .... Magyar Nok Orszagos Tanacsa [*National Council of Hungarian Women*] (HU)
not .... Music [*Score of a composition*] (RU)
NOT .... Nacionalna Organizacija Tehnicara [*National Organization of Technicians*] (YU)
NOT .... Naczelna Organizacja Techniczna [*Chief Technical Organization*] (POL)

NOT............ Nepbirosagok Orszagos Tanacsa [*National Council of People's Courts*] (HU)
not.............. Numerot [*Finnish*]
NOT............ Scientific Organization of Labor (RU)
NOTEKh...... Chief of Technical Department (RU)
NOTh........... Navtikos Omilos Thessalonikis [*Salonica Yacht Club*] (GC)
noti............. Text with Music (BU)
Not il ed ...... Notlar Ilave Eden [*Notes Which Were Added*] (TU)
notl............. Notlen [*Unmarried*] (HU)
NOTT........... National Office of Technology Transfer (MAR)
NOTU .... National Organisation of Trade Unions (MAR)
NOTU .... Nederlandsche Organisatie van Tijdschriften-Uitgevers [*Netherlands Organization of Periodical Publishers*] (WEN)
NOU............ Narodnooslobodilacki Udarni [*National Liberation Shock Troops*] [*World War II*] (YU)
NOUB .... Narodnooslobodilacka Udarna Brigada [*National Liberation Shock Brigade*] [*World War II*] (YU)
NOU(Korpus) ... Narodnooslobodilacki Udarni Korpus [*National Liberation Shock Corps*] [*World War II*] (YU)
NOUP .... Narodnooslobodilacka Udarna Proleterska [*National Liberation Proletarian Shock (Unit)*] (YU)
NOUVELLE SIACA ... Societe Ivoirienne d'Ananas et de Conserves Alimentaires (MAR)
NOUZ .... Narodni Odborove Ustredi Zamestnancu [*National Trade Union Employees' Center*] (CZ)
NOV............ Narodna Omladina Vojvodine [*People's Youth of Vojvodina*] (YU)
NOV............ Narodnooslobodilacka Vojska [*National Liberation Army*] [*World War II*] (YU)
Nov............. New [*Toponymy*] (RU)
NOV............ Nonpersistent Gas (RU)
nov .... November [*November*] [*Danish*] (GPO)
nov .... November [*November*] [*Dutch*] (GPO)
Nov............. November [*November*] [*German*] (GPO)
nov .... November [*November*] [*Hungarian*] (GPO)
nov .... Novembre [*November*] [*French*]
nov .... Novembre [*November*] [*Italian*]
nov .... Novembro [*November*] [*Portuguese*] (GPO)
NOV............ People's Liberation Army (BU)
NOV............ Unstable Chemical Agents [*Military*] (BU)
NOVA .... Narodnooslobodilacka Vojska Albanije [*National Liberation Army of Albania*] [*World War II*] (YU)
Novbre .... Noviembre [*November*] [*Spanish*]
nove .... Noviembre [*November*] [*Spanish*]
NOVELTA ... Nouvelle Societe Commerciale de Tamatave (MAR)
NOVH .... Narodnooslobodilacka Vojska Hrvatske [*National Liberation Army of Croatia*] [*World War II*] (YU)
NOVI........... Nederlands Opleidingsinstituut voor Informatica [*Amsterdam*]
NOVIB .... Netherlands Organization for International Development Cooperation (WEN)
NOVJ........... Narodnooslobodilacka Vojska Jugoslavije [*National Liberation Army of Yugoslavia*] [*World War II*] (YU)
NOVM.......... Narodnooslobodilacka Vojska Makedonije [*National Liberation Army of Macedonia*] [*World War II*] (YU)
NovNIKhl .... Scientific Research Institute of Cotton Growing in the New Regions (RU)
novosib .... Novosibirsk (RU)
Novosibgiz ... Novosibirsk State Publishing House (RU)
Novosibirgiz ... Novosibirsk State Publishing House (RU)
Novosibproyekt ... Planning Institute of the Novosibirsk Gorispolkom (RU)
NOVOTEKS ... Tekstilna Tovarna, Novo Mesto [*Novo Mesto Textile Factory*] (YU)
NOVSlovenije ... Narodnoosvobodilna Vojska Slovenije [*National Liberation Army of Slovenia*] [*World War II*] (YU)
nov st .... New Style [*Gregorian calendar*] (RU)
NOW........... Narodowa Organizacja Wojskowa [*National Military Organization*] (POL)
NOZEMA..... Nederlandse Omroep Zender Maatschappij [*Netherlands Radio Broadcasting Company*] (WEN)
NOZh........... New Society of Painters [*1922-1924*] (RU)
NP .... Chief of Political Section [*Military term*], Chief of Political Department (RU)
NP .... Continuous Profiling (RU)
np............... Direction of Flight (RU)
NP .... Directive on Payments (BU)
NP .... Feed Pump (RU)
NP .... Forward Perpendicular [*Shipbuilding*] (RU)
NP .... Guide Plate (RU)
NP .... Irregular Semidiurnal Tides (RU)
NP .... Litter Post (RU)
np............... Na Przyklad [*For Example*] (POL)
np............... Naispuolinen [*Finnish*]
NP .... Narodnaia Partiia (MAR)
np............... Narodni Podnik [*National Enterprise*] (CZ)
NP .... Narodni Pojisteni [*National Insurance*] (CZ)
NP .... Nasionale Party van Suid-Afrika [*National Party of South Africa*] (PPW)
NP .... Nasionale Party van Suidwesafrika [*National Party of South West Africa*] [*Namibian*] (PPW)
NP .... Nation Party [*Millet Partisi*] [*Turkish*] (PPW)
NP .... National Party [*Nigerian*] (AF)
NP .... National Press (BU)
NP .... Nationalist Party [*Maltese*] (PPE)
NP .... Nauchen Pregled [*Scientific Review*] [*A periodical*] (BU)
NP .... Nebenprodukt [*Secondary Product, By-Product*] (EG)
NP .... Nepal [*Two-letter standard code*] (CNC)
np............... Neper [*Napier*] [*Polish*]
np............... Neper (RU)
NP .... Northern Province (MAR)
NP .... Nova Proizvodnja [*New Production*] [*Ljubljana*] (YU)
NP .... Nowe Prawo [*New Law*] [*A periodical*] (POL)
NP .... Nucleoprotein (RU)
NP .... Observation Instrument (RU)
NP .... Observation Point, Observation Station (BU)
NP .... Observation Post (RU)
NP .... Petroleum Industry (RU)
NP .... Piston Jump (RU)
NP .... Populated Place (RU)
NP .... Settlements (BU)
NP .... Undetermined Frequency of Publication (BU)
NP .... Ungrounded Loop (RU)
NP .... Unpolished (RU)
NPA............ Artillery Observation Post (RU)
NPA............ National Police Agency (SJT)
NPA............ New People's Army [*Philippine*] (PD)
NPA............ Nigerian Ports Authority (AF)
NPA............ Nine Pin Association (EA)
NPAN .... Newspaper Proprietors Association of Nigeria (MAR)
N PASOK .... Neolaia Panellinion Sosialistikon Kinima [*Panhellenic Socialist Movement Youth*] (GC)
NPB............ Coastal Lookout Station (RU)
NPB............ Nasionale Pers Beperk (MAR)
NPB............ Scientific Educational Library (RU)
NPC............ National People's Congress [*Chinese*] (PPW)
NPC............ National Petrochemical Company [*Iranian*] (ME)
NPC............ National Petroleum Corporation [*Barbadian*] (LA1)
NPC............ National Preparatory Committee [*Guyanese*] (LA)
NPC............ National Printing Company Ltd. (MAR)
NPC............ National Psychological Committee [*Malaysian*] (ML)
NPC............ Nauru Phosphate Corporation
NPC............ Northern People's Congress [*Nigerian*] (AF)
NPCh.......... Lowest Applicable Frequency (RU)
NPCh.......... Niezalezna Partia Chlopska [*Independent Peasant Party*] (POL)
NPCP.......... Nairobi People's Convention Party (MAR)
NPD............ National Democratic Party [*West German*] (PD)
NPD............ Nationaldemokratische Partei Deutschlands [*National Democratic Party of Germany*] [*West German*] (PPE)
NPD............ Nees Politikes Dynameis [*New Political Forces*] [*Greek*] (PPE)
NPDD .... Nomikon Prosopon Dimosiou Dikaiou [*Legal Entity of Public Law*] [*In reference to semi-government corporations*] [*Greek*] (GC)
NPDMC .... National Property Development and Management Company (MAR)
NPE .... Nomarkhiaki Peitharkhiki Epitropi [*Nome Disciplinary Committee*] [*Greek*] (GC)
NPF .... Napthene-Paraffin Fraction (RU)
NPF .... Narodni Pozemkovy Fond [*National Land Fund*] (CZ)
NPF .... National Patriotic Front [*Guyanese*] (LA)
NPF .... National Progressive Front [*Iraqi*] (PPW)
NPF .... National Progressive Front [*Syrian*] (PPW)
NPF .... National Provident Fund [*Zambian*] (AF)
NPF .... Nigeria Police Force (MAR)
NPF .... Northern Progressive Front (MAR)
NPFI .... Institute of Theoretical and Applied Pharmacy (RU)
NPG............ Narodowy Plan Gospodarczy [*National Economic Plan*] (POL)
NPG............ Negative Population Growth (MAR)
NPG............ Nile Provisional Government (MAR)
NPG............ Normal Backwater Level (RU)
NPH............ Napln Pohonych Hmot [*Gasoline Pump*] (CZ)
NPI .... National Productivity Institute (MAR)
NPI .... Novocherkassk Polytechnic Institute Imeni Sergo Ordzhonikidze (RU)
NPID........... Nomikon Prosopon Idiotikou Dikaiou [*Legal Entity of Private Law*] [*Greek*] (GC)
NPK............ Beginning of Transition Curve [*Railroads*] (RU)
NPK............ Criminal Procedure Code (BU)
NPK............ National Alliance [*Surinamese*] (PD)
NPK............ Nationale Partij Kombinatie [*National Party Alliance*] [*Surinamese*] (PPW)
NPK............ Nea Politiki Kinisis [*New Political Movement*] [*Greek*] (GC)
NPK............ Punched-Card Storage (RU)
NPK............ Scientific Production Combine (BU)
NPKP.......... Regimental Commander's Observation Post (RU)
NPKS .... People's Political Advisory Council [*Chinese People's Republic*] (RU)
NPKS .... People's Political Consultative Council (BU)
NPKSK........ People's Political Advisory Council of China (RU)
NPl .... Directive on Payments (BU)
NPl .... Directive on Planning (BU)
NPL .... Nauru Pacific Line
NPL .... Nepal [*Three-letter standard code*] (CNC)

NPL .... Nueva Prensa Latinoamericana [*Nueva Prensa Latinoamericana*] [*Press agency*] (LA)
NPL .... Punched-Tape Storage (RU)
NPLF .... Namibia People's Liberation Front (AF)
npm .... Nad Poziomem Morza [*Above Sea Level*] [*Polish*]
NpM .... Nepmuvelesi Miniszterium/Miniszter [*Ministry/Minister of Adult Education*] (HU)
NpMAJ .... Narodni Podnik Mistra Aloisa Jiraska [*Alois Jirasek National Enterprise*] [*Hronov*] (CZ)
NPMC .... National Petroleum Marketing Company [*Trinidadian-Tobagan*] (LA1)
NPMC .... Nigerian Produce Marketing Company Ltd. (MAR)
NPMO .... National Pasok Momogun Organization [*National Sons of the Soil Organization*] [*Sabah*] (ML)
NPN .... National Party of Nigeria (PPW)
NPNRD .... Directive on the Non-Normed Work Day (BU)
NPO .... Directive on Design Organizations (BU)
NPO .... Nacelnik Planovaciho Oddeleni [*Chief of the Planning Section*] [*Military*] (CZ)
NPO .... Nigerian Press Organisation (MAR)
NPO .... Nongovernmental Organizations (RU)
NPO .... Scientific Industrial Trust (BU)
npor .... Nadporucik [*Senior Lieutenant*] [*US equivalent: First Lieutenant*] (CZ)
NPP .... Close Infantry Support (BU)
NPP .... Direct Support of Infantry (RU)
NPP .... Flight Manual (RU)
NPP .... Narodnaia Progressivnaia Partiia (MAR)
NPP .... Nastavni Plan i Program [*Training Plan and Program*] [*Military*] (YU)
NPP .... Nemzeti Paraszt Part [*National Peasant Party*] [*Hungarian*] (PPE)
NPP .... Nepohybliva Palebna Prehrada [*Fixed Fire Barrage*] (CZ)
NPP .... Neprosredna Podrska Pesadije [*Close Support of Infantry*] (YU)
NPP .... Nigerian People's Party (PPW)
NPP .... Northern People's Party (MAR)
NPP .... People's Progressive Party [*British Guiana*] (RU)
NPPB .... Mobile Field Hospital for Neurological Diseases (BU)
NPPG .... Neurological Mobile Field Hospital (RU)
NPPPP .... Northern Province Progressive People's Party (MAR)
NPR .... Narodowa Partia Robotnicza [*National Workers Party*] [*Polish*] (PPE)
NPR .... Normal Protamine (RU)
NPRB .... Hand-to-Hand Combat Manual (RU)
NPRC .... Nigerian Petroleum Refinery Company (MAR)
NPRL .... National Physical Research Laboratory (MAR)
NPRN .... Directive on Planning, Assigning, and Job Placement of Young Specialists with Higher Education (BU)
NPRSP .... Narodowa Pozyczka Rozwoju Sil Polski [*National Loan for the Development of Poland's Resources*] (POL)
NPRT .... Nauru Phosphate Royalties Trust
NPS .... Nationale Partij Suriname [*Suriname National Party*] (PPW)
NPS .... Popular Science Series (RU)
NPS .... Scientific Pedagogical Section (RU)
NPSA .... Nouveau Programme Substantiel d'Action (MAR)
NPSC .... Nigeria Public Service Commission (MAR)
NPSD .... Chief of Message Center (RU)
NPSK"NEI" ... Scientific Production Combine "New Energy Sources" [*Bulgarian*]
NPSL .... Narodnaia Partiia Seppa-Leone (MAR)
NPSS .... Highest Useful Degree of Compression (RU)
NPSS .... Narodni Podnik Sberne Suroviny [*National Enterprise for the Collection of Raw Materials*] (CZ)
NPSS .... National Party of the Subjects of the Sultan of Zanzibar (MAR)
NPSSh .... Staff Field Manual (RU)
NPST .... National Party of South Thailand (ML)
NPSZ .... Nemocenska Pojistovna Soukromych Zamestnancu [*Private Employees' Health Insurance Agency*] (CZ)
NPT .... Nationalpreistraeger [*National Prize Winner*] (EG)
NPT .... Nuclear Nonproliferation Treaty (MAR)
NPTZh .... Directive on the Utilization of Women's Labor (BU)
NPU .... Ground Transmitter (RU)
NPU .... National People's Union [*Rhodesian*] (AF)
npu .... Nehezpuska [*Heavy Rifle*] (HU)
NPU .... Newspaper Press Union of South Africa (MAR)
NPU .... Normal Backwater Level (RU)
NPU .... Oil Field Administration (RU)
NPUA .... National Progressive Unionist Assembly [*Egyptian*] (MAR)
NPUG .... National Progressive Unionist Grouping (MAR)
NPUP .... National Progressive Unionist Party [*Egyptian*] (PPW)
NPV .... Lower High Water (RU)
NPV .... Naturpolitische Volkspartei [*People's Party for Nature Policy*] [*West German*] (PPW)
NPV .... Net Present Value (MAR)
NPVCh .... Lowest Applicable High Frequency (RU)
NPVO .... Air Defense Commander (RU)
NPWP .... Nigerian People's Welfare Party (MAR)
NPZ .... Nabavljacke Prodajna Zadruga [*Buying and Selling Cooperative*] (YU)
NPZ .... Nacelnik Proviantniho Zasobovani [*Chief of Food Supply*] [*Military*] (CZ)
NPz .... Nacelnik Pruzkumu [*Chief of Reconnaissance*] (CZ)
NPZ .... Petroleum-Processing Plant (RU)
NPZ .... Petroleum Refinery (BU)
NPZ .... Portable Contamination Apparatus [*Military term*] (RU)
NPZDZh ...... Directive on the Sale and Exchange of State Housing (BU)
NPZFK .... Directive on the Application of the Law on Financial Control (BU)
NPZP .... Narodnaia Partiia Zanzibara i Pemby (MAR)
NR .... Chief of Intelligence (BU)
NR .... Chief of Intelligence (RU)
nr .... Insoluble (RU)
NR .... Narodna Republika [*People's Republic*] (YU)
NR .... Narodni Rada [*National Council*] (CZ)
NR .... Nature Reserve (MAR)
NR .... Nauru [*Two-letter standard code*] (CNC)
NR .... Negro y Rojo [*Black and Red*] [*Spanish*] (WER)
NR .... Nigerian Railway (MAR)
NR .... Night Reconnaissance (RU)
N de la R ...... Nota de la Redaccion [*Editorial Note*] [*Spanish*] (GPO)
nr .... Numer [*Number*] (POL)
Nr .... Numero [*or Nummer*] [*Number*] [*German*] (GPO)
nr .... Nummer [*Number*] [*Danish*] (GPO)
nr .... Nummer [*Number*] [*Swedish*] (GPO)
NR .... People's Republic (BU)
NR .... People's Republic (RU)
NR .... Rodezja Polnocna [*North Rhodesia*] [*Polish*]
nr .... Service Company (BU)
NR .... Standard (RU)
NRA .... Albanian People's Republic (BU)
NRA .... Narodnaia Respublika Angola (MAR)
NRA .... National Resistance Army [*Ugandan*] (PD)
NRA .... Nemzeti Repulo Alap [*National Aviation Fund*] (HU)
nra .... Nuestra [*Our*] [*Spanish*]
NRA .... People's Republic of Albania (RU)
NRA .... People's Revolutionary Army of China [*1937-1945*] (RU)
NRAC .... Northern Rhodesia African Congress (MAR)
NRAMTU ..... Northern Rhodesia African Mineworkers' Trade Union (MAR)
NRAMU .... Northern Rhodesia African Mineworkers' Union (MAR)
NRANC .... Northern Rhodesia African National Congress (MAR)
NRAS .... Northern Rhodesia Administrative Service (MAR)
nras .... Nuestras [*Our*] [*Spanish*]
NRB .... Bulgarian People's Republic (BU)
NRB .... Narodnaia Respublika Benin (MAR)
NRB .... Narodni Rada Badatelska [*National Research Council*] (CZ)
NRB .... Natural Resources Board (MAR)
NRB .... People's Republic of Bulgaria (RU)
NRB .... Radiation Safety Norms (BU)
NRBiH .... Narodna Republika Bosna i Hercegovina [*People's Republic of Bosnia and Hercegovina*] (YU)
NRBPNS ...... Bulgarian People's Republic, National Assembly Presidium (BU)
NRBulg .... Bulgarian People's Republic (BU)
NRC .... Ferrocarriles Nacionales de Colombia [*National Railroads of Colombia*] (LA)
NRC .... Nacelnik Radio Centra [*Radio Center Chief*] [*Military*] (YU)
NRC .... Narodni Rada Ceskoslovenska [*Czechoslovak National Council*] (CZ)
NRC .... National Reconstruction Council (MAR)
NRC .... National Redemption Council [*Ghanaian*] (AF)
NRC .... National Reformation Council [*Sierra Leonean*] (AF)
NRC .... National Research Centre [*Egyptian*] (MAR)
NRC .... National Research Council of Ghana (MAR)
NRC .... National Resistance Council (MAR)
NRC .... Native Recruiting Corporation (MAR)
NRC .... Native Representative Council (MAR)
NRC .... Natural Resources College [*Malawian*] (AF)
NRC .... Niger River Commission (MAR)
NRC .... Nigerian Railway Corporation (MAR)
NRCC .... Ndoleleji Rural Community Centre (MAR)
NRCE .... National Research Council of Egypt (MAR)
NRCG .... Narodna Republika Crna Gora [*People's Republic of Montenegro*] (YU)
NRCP .... Northern Rhodesia Commonwealth Party (MAR)
NRD .... Natsional'noe Revoliutsionnoe Dvizhenie (MAR)
NRD .... Natural Resources Division (MAR)
NRD .... Niemiecka Republika Demokratyczna [*German Democratic Republic*] (POL)
NRD .... People's Revolutionary Movement [*Ecuadorean*] (RU)
NRDC .... National Research Development Corporation [*United Kingdom*]
NRDC .... Natural Resources Defence Council (MAR)
NRDC .... Northern Regional Development Corporation (MAR)
NRDP .... National Rural Development Progress (MAR)
NRF .... Neues Rotes Forum [*New Red Forum*] [*FRG student organization*] (EG)
NRF .... Niemiecka Republika Federalna [*German Federal Republic*] (POL)
NRF .... Nouvelle Revue Francaise [*Periodical title; initials also used on books published by Gallimard*]
NRF .... River Fleet Norms (RU)

NRG............ Northern Rhodesia Government (MAR)
NRG............ Scientific and Editorial Group (RU)
NRH............ Narodna Republika Hrvatska [*People's Republic of Croatia*] (YU)
NRIMS......... National Research Institute for Mathematical Sciences (MAR)
NRK............ Narodnaia Respublika Kongo (MAR)
NRK............ Norsk Rikskringkasting [*Norwegian Broadcasting Corporation*] (WEN)
Nrk............ Not Recommended (Term) (RU)
NRKCh........ Scientific Editing Map Compilation Department (RU)
NRKE.......... Latest Development in Quantum Electrodynamics (RU)
NRL............ Nizhniy Novgorod Radio Laboratory (RU)
NRLP.......... Northern Rhodesia Liberal [*or Liberty*] Party (MAR)
NRLTUC...... Native Races Liquor Traffic United Committee (MAR)
NRM............ Narodnaia Respublika Mozambik (MAR)
NRM............ National Resistance Movement [*Ugandan*] (PD)
NRM............ Negara Republik Malaya [*State of the Republic of Malaya*] (ML)
NRMG.......... Nederlands Rekenmachine Genootschap [*Amsterdam*]
NRMU.......... Northern Rhodesia Mineworkers' Union (MAR)
NRO............ Directive on Registering Insurers (BU)
NRO............ Narodni Rada Obchodnictva [*Merchants' National Council*] (CZ)
nro............ Nuestro [*Our*] [*Spanish*]
Nro............ Numero [*Number*] [*German*]
NROC.......... National Revolutionary Operations Command [*Ethiopian*] (AF)
NROS.......... Nejvyssi Rada Obrany Statu [*Supreme Counil for National Defense*] (CZ)
nros............ Nuestros [*Our*] [*Spanish*]
NROW.......... Naczelna Rada Odbudowy Warszawy [*Chief Council for the Reconstruction of Warsaw*] (POL)
NROW.......... Naczelna Rada Organizowania Wystaw [*Chief Council for the Organization of Exhibitions*] (POL)
NRP............ Narodni Ravnogorski Pokret [*Ravna Gora National Movement*] [*World War II*] (YU)
NRP............ National Religious Party [*Hamiflaga Hadatit Leumit*] [*Israeli*] (PPW)
NRP............ Nevis Reformation Party (LA1)
NRP............ New Republic Party [*South African*] (PPW)
NRP............ New Rhodesia Party (MAR)
NRP............ Observation and Reconnaissance Post (RU)
NRP............ People's Republican Party [*Turkish*] (RU)
NRPJ.......... Nezavisna Radnicka Partija Jugoslavije [*Independent Labor Party of Yugoslavia*] (YU)
NRPM.......... People's Revolutionary Government of Mongolia (RU)
NRPS.......... Independent Workers' Trade Union (BU)
NRR............ Net Reproduction Rate (MAR)
NRR............ Northern Rhodesia Regiment (MAR)
NRR............ Romanian People's Republic (BU)
NRRC.......... Natural Resources Research Council (MAR)
Nr rej.......... Numer Rejestracyjny [*Registration Number*] [*Polish*]
NRS............ Naczelna Rada Spoldzielcza [*Chief Council of Cooperatives*] (POL)
NRS............ Narodna Republika Slovenija [*People's Republic of Slovenia*] (YU)
NRS............ Narodna Republika Srbija [*People's Republic of Serbia*] (YU)
NRS............ National Refugee Service (MAR)
NRS............ People's Radio Sofia (BU)
NRS............ Unguided Missile (RU)
NRSC.......... National Road Safety Council (MAR)
NRSE.......... Narodna Radikalna Stranka u Egzilu [*National Radical Party in Exile*] (YU)
NRSI........... Narodna Republika Slovenija [*People's Republic of Slovenia*] (YU)
NRSLI.......... National Reference Library of Science and Invention [*United Kingdom*]
NRT............ Net Register Tonnage (RU)
NRT............ Net Register Tons (BU)
NRTSS........ Directive on Trying Labor Disputes by the Courts (BU)
NRU............ Hungarian People's Republic (BU)
NRU............ Nauru [*Three-letter standard code*] (CNC)
NRUTUC..... Northern Rhodesia United Trades Union Congress (MAR)
NRV............ Growth Stimulant from Petroleum (RU)
NRV............ Nacelnik Radio Veze [*Radio Communications Chief*] [*Military*] (YU)
NRV............ National Reserve of Volunteers (MAR)
NRV............ Net Register Tonnage (RU)
NRV............ Nigerian Revolutionary Vanguard (AF)
NRVS.......... People's Revolutionary Military Council [*Chinese People's Republic*] (RU)
n-ry............ Numery [*Numbers, Installments, Issues*] (POL)
NRY............ People's Republic of Yemen (BU)
NRZ............ Ground RADAR Interrogator (RU)
NRZ............ National Railways of Zimbabwe (MAR)
NRZK.......... Naczelna Rada Zrzeszen Kupieckich [*Chief Council of Merchant Associations*] (POL)
NRZPHiU..... Naczelna Rada Zrzeszen Prywatnego Handlu i Uslug [*Chief Council of Private Trade and Service Associations*] (POL)
NS.............. Chief Communications Officer, Chief Signal Officer (RU)
Ns.............. Chief of Service (BU)
NS.............. Chief of Signal Service (BU)
NS.............. Chief of Supply (RU)
NS.............. Command Personnel (RU)
NS.............. Direct Stabilization (RU)
NS.............. Initial Velocity, Initial Speed (RU)
NS.............. Irregular Diurnal Tides (RU)
NS.............. Irrigation System (BU)
ns.............. Limited Service (BU)
NS.............. Magnetizing Force (RU)
NS.............. Nacelnik Saniteta [*Chief of Medical Corps*] (YU)
NS.............. Nacelnik Staba [*Chief of Staff*] (YU)
NS.............. Nacelnik Stabu [*Chief of Staff*] (CZ)
NS.............. Nachschrift [*Postscript*] (EG)
nS.............. Nad Sazavou [*On the Sazava River*] (CZ)
nS.............. Naechste Seite [*Next Page*] [*German*]
NS.............. Narodna Skupstina [*National Assembly*] (YU)
NS.............. Narodna Suma, Zagreb [*National Forests*] [*Zagreb*] [*A periodical*] (YU)
NS.............. Narodne Starine [*National Antiquities*] [*Zagreb*] [*A periodical*] (YU)
NS.............. Narodni Shromazdeni [*National Assembly*] (CZ)
NS.............. Narodni Socialisticka Strana [*National Socialist Party*] (CZ)
NS.............. Narodni Sourucenstvi [*National Unity Party (Fascist, 1939)*] (CZ)
ns.............. Narodni Sprava [*or Spravce*] [*National Administration or Administrator*] (CZ)
NS.............. Narodno Stopanstvo [*National Economy*] (YU)
NS.............. Narodnye Sotsialisty [*Popular Socialists*] [*Russian*] (PPE)
NS.............. National Assembly (BU)
NS.............. National Council (BU)
NS.............. National Union (BU)
NS.............. Natjonal Samling [*National Union*] [*Norwegian*] (PD)
NS.............. Navadeci Stanoviste [*Fire Direction Center or Forward Observer Post*] (CZ)
NS.............. Nederlandsche Spoorwegen [*Netherlands Railroad Company*] (WEN)
NS.............. Negri Sembilan (ML)
NS.............. Nejvyssi Soud [*Supreme Court*] (CZ)
NS.............. Nemzeti Segely [*National Relief*] (HU)
NS.............. Neoi Sosialistai [*New Socialists*] [*Greek*] (GC)
ns.............. New Style [*Gregorian calendar*] (RU)
ns.............. Niin Sanottu [*So Called*] [*Finnish*] (GPO)
NS.............. Nisandzija [*First Gunner*] (YU)
NS.............. Noncombatant Duty (RU)
NS.............. Nonlinear Resistance (RU)
NS.............. Nord Sud [*North-South*] [*On maps*] [*French*] (MTD)
NS.............. Nostro Signore [*Our Lord*] [*Italian*]
NS.............. Novi Sad [*Novi Sad*] (YU)
NS.............. Novi Svet [*New World*] [*Ljubljana*] [*A periodical*] (YU)
NS.............. Nudel'man-Suranov Aircraft Wing Gun (RU)
NS.............. Nuestra Senora [*Our Lady*] [*Spanish*] (GPO)
NS.............. Nuestro Senor [*Our Lord*] [*Spanish*]
ns.............. Nuorisoseura [*Finnish*]
NS.............. People's Council (BU)
N-S............ Polnoc-Poludnie [*North-South*] [*Polish*]
NS.............. Scientific Council (BU)
ns.............. Train operates only on weekdays following Sundays and holidays [*See also S*] (EG)
n/s............ Unclassified (RU)
NSA............ Autoridade Nacional de Seguranca [*National Security Authority*] [*Portuguese*] (WER)
NSA............ Chief of Medical Administration (BU)
NSA............ Chief of Medical Service of an Army (RU)
NSA............ Natal Society of Artists (MAR)
NSA............ National Service Act [*Guyanese*] (LA)
NSA............ Nederlandse Studenten Akkoord [*Netherlands Students' Accord*] (WEN)
NSAC.......... Narodni Sdruzeni Americkych Cechu [*National Association of Czech Americans*] (CZ)
NSAC.......... National Space Activities Council (SJT)
NSAL.......... Nigerian South American Line (MAR)
NSAPV........ Narodna Skupstina Autonomne Provincije Vojvodine [*People's Assembly of the Autonomous Province of Vojvodina*] (YU)
NSB............ Narodni Svaz Brannosti [*National Association for Military Preparedness*] (CZ)
NSB............ Nationaal-Socialistische Beweging [*National Socialist Movement*] [*Netherlands*] (PPE)
NSB............ Natsional'n Sel'skokhoziaistvenn Bank [*Arab*] (MAR)
NSB............ Nemzeti Sport Bizottsag [*National Sports Committee*] (HU)
NSB............ Norges Statsbaner [*Norwegian State Railways*] (WEN)
NSB............ Nouvelle Societe du Bois (MAR)
NSC............ National Security Council [*Malaysian*] (ML)
NSC............ National Settlement Convention (MAR)
NSC............ National Sports Commission (MAR)
NSC............ National Sports Council (ML)
NSC............ National Standing Committee (MAR)
NSC............ Nigerian Sugar Company Ltd. (MAR)
NSC............ Noel-Schlosser & Compagnie (MAR)
NSCB.......... National Savings and Credit Bank (MAR)
NSCN.......... National Socialist Council of Nagaland [*Indian*] (PD)
NSCS.......... Narodopisna Spolecnost Ceskoslovenska [*Czechoslovak Ethnographical Society*] (CZ)

NSCSU........ Nabozenska Spolecnost Ceskoslovenskych Unitaru [*Religious Society of Czechoslovak Unitarians*] (CZ)
NSD............ Chief Signal Officer of a Division (RU)
NSd............ Nasa Sodobnost [*Our Time*] [*Ljubljana*] [*A periodical*] (YU)
NSD............ Small Arms Field Manual (RU)
NSDA.......... Nigeria Steel Development Authority (MAR)
NSDAP........ Nationalsozialistische Deutsche Arbeiterpartei [*National Socialist German Workers Party*] (EG)
NSDP.......... Independent Social Democratic Party of Germany (RU)
NSDPG........ Independent Social Democratic Party of Germany (RU)
NSDT.......... Directive on Tax and Fee Collection (BU)
NSDT.......... People's Council of Working People's Deputies (BU)
NSDV.......... Directive on the Collection of Debts to the State (BU)
NSE............ Nationalmuseets Skrifter, Etnografisk Raekke [*Copenhagen*] (MAR)
NSEM.......... Nouvelle Societe Equatoriale de Mecanographie (MAR)
n ser........... New Series (RU)
NSESA........ Nomarkhiakon Symvoulion Exoskholikis Somatikis Agogis [*Nomarchy Council of Extracurricular Physical Education*] [*Greek*] (GC)
NSFC.......... Nouvelle Societe France-Congo (MAR)
NSFNRJ...... Narodna Skupstina Federativne Narodne Republike Jugoslavije [*People's Assembly of the Federal People's Republic of Yugoslavia*] (YU)
NSFS.......... People's Union for Physical Culture and Sports (BU)
nsg............. Lower Horizontal Base Line (RU)
NSG............ Narodni Strelecka Garda [*National Association of Riflemen*] (CZ)
NSG............ Nouvelle Societe du Gabon (MAR)
NSGP.......... Navtikon Stratologikon Grafeion Peiraios [*Piraeus Naval Recruiting Office*] (GC)
NSGS.......... National Gymnastics and Sports Union (BU)
NSGT.......... Non-Self-Governing Territories (MAR)
NSh............ Chief of Staff (RU)
NSh-........... Gear Pump (RU)
NSH............ Nadmorska Spoldzielnia Hydrotechnikow [*Coastal Region Hydraulic Engineers' Cooperative*] (POL)
NSh............ Public School (RU)
NSh............ Pump Rod (RU)
NShS.......... Navigation Manual [*Aviation*] (RU)
NSht........... Chief of Staff (BU)
NShZO........ National Reserve Officers School (BU)
NSI............. National Sugar Institute [*Indian*]
NSI............. Nemzetkozi Statisztikai Intezet [*International Statistical Institute*] (HU)
NSIC........... National Small Industries Corporation (MAR)
NSIDK......... Nederlandse Stichting Informatie- en Documentatiecentrum voor de Kartografie [*Utrecht*]
NSIL........... Nouvelle Societe Immobiliere Librevilloise (MAR)
NSJ............ Narodna Skupstina na Jugoslavija [*National Assembly of Yugoslavia*] (YU)
NSJC.......... Notre Seigneur Jesus-Christ [*French*] (MTD)
NSJC.......... Nuestro Senor Jesucristo [*Our Lord Jesus Christ*] [*Spanish*]
NSK............ Chief Signal Officer of a Corps (RU)
NSK............ National Council of Cartographers, USSR (RU)
NSK............ Nizi Sanitetski Kurs [*Elementary Medical Course*] [*Military*] (YU)
NSK............ Nomikon Symvoulion tou Kratous [*State Legal Council*] [*Greek*] (GC)
NSK............ Scientific Council for Coordination (BU)
NSKE.......... Neolaia Sosialistikou Kommatos Ellados [*Youth of the Socialist Party of Greece*] (GC)
NSKhI......... Novosibirsk Agricultural Institute (RU)
NSKhI......... Scientific Research Institute of Sanitation and Public Hygiene (BU)
NSKRS........ Directive on Official Trips of Workers and Employees (BU)
N skv.......... Pressure Well (RU)
NSM........... German Peace Union [*Federal Republic of Germany*] (RU)
NSMB......... Northern States Marketing Board (MAR)
NSMS......... Natsional'nyi Soiuz Marokkanskikh Studentov (MAR)
NSN........... Officer in Charge of Communications (BU)
NSn........... Unguided Missile (RU)
NSNG......... National Council of Nigerian Citizens (RU)
NSNG......... Natsional'nyi Sovet Nigeriiskikh Grazhdan (MAR)
NSNK......... National Council of Nigeria and Cameroon (RU)
NSNK......... Natsional'nyi Sovet Nigerii i Kameruna (MAR)
NSNRBiH.... Narodna Skupstina Narodne Republike Bosne i Hercegovine [*People's Assembly of the People's Republic of Bosnia and Hercegovina*] (YU)
NSNRCG..... Narodna Skupstina Narodne Republike Crne Gore [*People's Assembly of the People's Republic of Montenegro*] (YU)
NSNRM....... Narodno Sobranie na Narodnata Republika Makedonija [*People's Assembly of the People's Republic of Macedonia*] (YU)
NSNRS........ Narodna Skupstina Narodne Republike Slovenije [*People's Assembly of the People's Republic of Slovenia*] (YU)
NSNRS........ Narodna Skupstina Narodne Republike Srbije [*People's Assembly of the People's Republic of Serbia*] (YU)
NSNS.......... National Union of People's Forces [*Moroccan*] (RU)
NSNS.......... Natsional'nyi Soiuz Narodnykh Sil (MAR)
NSNTI........ National Scientific and Technical Information System (BU)
NSO............ Chief of Communications of a Military District (RU)
NSO............ Directive on Bookkeeping Accountability (BU)
NSO............ National Security Organization [*Nigerian*] (AF)
NSO............ National Statistical Office (MAR)
NSO............ Standard Cost of Processing (RU)
NSO............ Student Scientific Society (RU)
NSOA.......... Nouvelles Savonneries de l'Ouest Africain (MAR)
NSOF.......... National Council of the Fatherland Front (BU)
nsolo.......... Sa Neogranicenom Solidarnom Odgovornoscu [*With Unlimited Joint Liability*] [*Yugoslav*] (CED)
NSP............ National Salvation Party [*Milli Selamet Partisi*] [*Turkish*] (PPW)
NSP............ National Seoposengwe Party [*Bophuthatswana*] (PPW)
NSP............ National Socialist Party [*New Zealander*] (PD)
NSP............ Nationalist Social Party [*Lebanese*] (MAR)
NSP............ Nederlandsch Scheepsbouwkundig Proefstation [*Netherlands Naval Testing Station*] (WEN)
NSP............ People's Socialist Party [*Republic of India*] (RU)
NSP............ Routine Storage (RU)
NSP............ Sanitary Planning Norms (RU)
NSPK.......... People's Socialist Party of Cuba (RU)
NSPK.......... Routine and Constant Storage (RU)
NSPOGF..... Directive on Haymowing, Pastures, and Forest Resources (BU)
NSPRI......... Nigerian Stored Products Research Institute (MAR)
NSR............ Natsional'nyi Soiuz Ruandy (MAR)
NSR............ Nederlands Studenten Raad [*National Student Council*] [*Dutch*] (WEN)
NSR............ Nemecka Spolkova Republika [*German Federal Republic*] (CZ)
Nsr............. Nesriyat [*Publication*] (TU)
NSR............ Nueva Sociedad Rural [*New Rural Society*] [*Spanish*] (WER)
NSR............ Soviet People's Republic [*1920-1924*] (RU)
NSRA.......... National Shoe Retailers Association (MAR)
NSRA.......... Nigeria Squash Racket Association (MAR)
NSRASA..... National Smallbore Rifle Association of South Africa (MAR)
NSRC.......... Narodni Shromazdeni Republiky Ceskoslovenske [*National Assembly of the Czechoslovak Republic*] (CZ)
NSRC.......... National Science Research Council [*Guyanese*]
NSRI........... Nelspruit Subtropical Research Institute (MAR)
NSRKP........ Nigeriiskaia Sotsialisticheskaia Raboche-Krest'ianskaia Partiia (MAR)
NSRZ.......... Neva Ship Repair Yard (RU)
NSS............ National Security Service [*Djibouti*] (AF)
NSS............ National Security Service [*Somali*] (MAR)
NSS............ National Student Union (RU)
NSS............ Nederlandse Stichting voor Statistiek [*'s-Gravenhage*]
NSS............ Nejvyssi Spravni Soud [*Supreme Administrative Court*] (CZ)
NSSh.......... Incomplete Secondary School, Seven-Year School (RU)
NSSM......... National Security Study Memorandum (MAR)
NSST.......... National Sports and Technology Union (BU)
n st............. Gregorian Calendar Dates (BU)
n st............. New Style [*Gregorian calendar*] (RU)
NstA........... Archives of the National Economy [*A publication*] (BU)
NSTA.......... National Science and Technology Agency (MAR)
NSTA.......... National Science and Technology Authority [*Philippine*]
NSTC.......... Nyegezi Social Training Centre (MAR)
NSTDA........ National Science and Technology Development Agency (MAR)
N-stvo........ Authorities, Chiefs, Superiors, Board of Trustees (BU)
NSU............ Novinarsky Studijni Ustav [*Research Institute of Journalism*] (CZ)
NSU............ Nuova Sinistra Unita [*New United Left*] [*Italian*] (PPE)
NSU............ Unidentified Vessel (RU)
NSV............ Chief of Communications Center (BU)
n/sv........... No Information (RU)
NSVN......... Nosokomeion Stelekhon Vasilikou Navtikou [*Royal Navy Cadre Hospital*] (GC)
NSW........... Nichtsozialistisches Waehrungsgebiet [*Non-Socialist Monetary Area*] (EG)
NSYA.......... Nomarkhiakon Symvoulion Ygeias kai Asfaliseos [*Nomarchy Health and Insurance Council*] (GC)
NSYO.......... Nukleer Silahlarin Yayilmasinin Onlenmesi Antlasma [*Nuclear Arms Anti-Proliferation Agreement*] (TU)
NSZ............ Narodowe Sily Zbrojne [*National Armed Forces*] (POL)
NSZE.......... Nemet Szocialista Egysegpart [*Socialist Unity Party of Germany*] (HU)
NSZEP........ Nemet Szocialista Egysegpart [*Socialist Unity Party of Germany*] (HU)
nszhdv........ Chief Signal Officer of Railroad Troops (RU)
NSZK.......... Nemet Szovetseges Koztarsasag [*Federal Republic of Germany*] (HU)
NSZP.......... Nemzeti Szabadelvu Part [*National Liberal Party*] [*Hungarian*] (PPE)
NT.............. Chief of Rear Services (BU)
NT.............. Initial Point (RU)
NT.............. Iraq-Saudi Arabia Neutral Zone [*Two-letter standard code*] (CNC)
NT.............. Low-Temperature (RU)
NT.............. Nahradni Teleso [*Replacements Unit (Depot)*] (CZ)
NT.............. Naphthotocopherol (RU)
NT.............. Narodna Tehnika [*People's Technology*] [*A society*] (YU)
NT.............. National Taranesc [*National Peasant Party*] [*Romanian*] (PPE)
NT.............. Nea Taxis [*New Order*] (GC)
Nt.............. Negociant [*Merchant*] [*French*] (MTD)

nt .... Nem Tenyleges [*Nonprofessional, Irregular*] [*Military*] (HU)
NT .... Nepgazdasagi Tanacs [*People's Economic Council*] (HU)
NT .... Nikola Tesla [*Nikola Tesla*] (YU)
NT .... Nisanska Tacka [*Target Point*] (YU)
nt .... Nit (RU)
NT .... Nomarkhiakon Tameion [*Nomarchy Fund*] (GC)
NT .... Nontransforme [*Military*] [*French*] (MTD)
NT .... Normal Temperature, Reference Temperature (RU)
N del T .... Nota del Traductor [*Translator's Note*] [*Spanish*] (GPO)
NT .... Nula Tacka [*Zero Point*] (YU)
NT .... Oil Tanker (RU)
NT .... Superacoustic Telegraphy (RU)
Nt .... Thermischer Wirkungsgrad [*Thermal Efficiency*] [*German*]
NTA .... National Teachers Association (MAR)
NTA .... New Turkish Alphabet (RU)
NTA .... Nigerian Television Authority (MAR)
NTB .... Nachrichtentechnisches Buero [*Communications Office*] (EG)
NTB .... Nigerian Tourist Board (MAR)
NTB .... Norwegian News Bureau (RU)
NTB .... Nusatenggara Barat [*West Lesser Sundas*] (IN)
NTB .... Scientific and Technical Library (RU)
NTB .... Scientific and Technical Office (RU)
NTC .... National Trading Company [*or Corporation*] (MAR)
NTC .... National Transport Commission [*or Corporation*] (MAR)
NTC .... Nigerian Tobacco Company (MAR)
NTCh .... Scientific and Technical Department (RU)
NTD .... Scientific and Technical Society (BU)
Ntf .... Naturforscher [*Scientific Investigator*] [*German*]
NTF .... Nucleotide Triphosphate (RU)
NTGO .... Scientific and Technical Mining Society (RU)
NTGU .... Novosibirsk Territorial Geological Administration (RU)
NTI .... Naucno Tekhniceskaja Informcija [*Science and Technical Information*] [*USSR*]
Nti .... Neiti [*Miss*] [*Finnish*] (GPO)
NTI .... Scientific and Technical Information (RU)
NTI .... Scientific and Technical Information (BU)
NTI .... Scientific and Technical Publication (RU)
NTJ .... Nigeria Trade Journal [*A publication*] (MAR)
NTK .... Directive on Workers' Record Books (BU)
NTK .... Lower Large Intestine (RU)
NTK .... Scientific and Technical Club (RU)
NTK .... Scientific and Technical Committee (RU)
NTL .... News of Technical Literature (RU)
NTM .... Narodni Technicke Museum [*National Museum of Technology*] (CZ)
NTMK .... Nizhniy Tagil Metallurgical Kombinat (RU)
NTMZ .... Novotul'skiy Metallurgical Plant (RU)
NTN .... Najwyzszy Trybunal Narodowy [*Supreme National Tribunal*] (POL)
NTNF .... Norges Teknisk-Natuvitenskapelige Forskningsrad [*Norwegian Council for Scientific and Industrial Research*] (WEN)
NTO .... National Theatre Organisation (MAR)
n-to .... Net (RU)
nto .... Netto [*Net*] (HU)
NTO .... Scientific and Technical Department (RU)
NTO .... Scientific and Technical Society (RU)
NTO Belmashprom ... Belorussian Republic Branch of the All-Union Scientific and Technical Society of the Machinery Industry (RU)
NTOChM .... Scientific and Technical Society of Ferrous Metallurgy (RU)
NTOEP .... Scientific and Technical Society of the Power Industry (RU)
NTO GKh i AT ... Scientific and Technical Society of Urban Economy and Automobile Transportation (RU)
NTOLes .... Scientific and Technical Society of the Lumber Industry (RU)
NTOLesprom ... Scientific and Technical Society of the Lumber Industry (RU)
NTOLP .... Scientific and Technical Society of the Lumber Industry (RU)
NTOMASh ... Scientific and Technical Society of Machine Builders (RU)
NTOMashprom ... Scientific and Technical Society of the Machinery Industry (RU)
NTOMashpromlit ... Scientific and Technical Society of the Machinery Industry, Foundry Section (RU)
NTO NGP .... Scientific and Technical Society of the Petroleum and Gas Industry (RU)
NTONP .... Scientific and Technical Society of the Petroleum Industry (RU)
NTORiE .... Scientific and Technical Society of Radio Engineering and Telecommunications Imeni A. S. Popov (RU)
NTOS .... Chief of Topographic Service (RU)
NTO SKh ..... Scientific and Technical Society of Agriculture (RU)
NTOSP .... Scientific and Technical Society of the Shipbuilding Industry (RU)
NTOSS .... All-Union Scientific and Technical Society of Shipbuilding and Navigation (RU)
NTOSTIGKh ... Scientific and Technical Society of Sanitary Engineering and Urban Economy (RU)
NTOVT .... Scientific and Technical Society of Water Transportation (RU)
NTP .... Naukowe Towarzystwo Pedagogiczne [*Pedagogical Learned Society*] (POL)
NTP .... Normatywy Techniczne Projektowania [*Norms for Technical Planning*] (POL)
NTP .... Scientific and Technical Propaganda (RU)
NTP .... Technological Planning Norms (RU)
NTPS .... Local Telegraphic Communications Post (RU)
ntra .... Nuestra [*Our*] [*Spanish*]
ntras .... Nuestras [*Our*] [*Spanish*]
NTRL .... National Telecommunications Research Laboratory (MAR)
ntro .... Nuestro [*Our*] [*Spanish*]
ntros .... Nuestros [*Our*] [*Spanish*]
NTRU .... Northern Transvaal Rugby Union (MAR)
NTS .... Chief of Technical Service (RU)
NTs .... Directive on Prices (BU)
NTS .... Nacelnik Telegrafske Stanice [*Telegraph Station Chief*] [*Military*] (YU)
NTS .... Narodno Trudovoi Soyuz [*People's Labor Union*] [*Russian*] (PD)
NTs .... National Center (RU)
NTS .... National Labor Union (RU)
NTS .... National Tourist Union (BU)
NTs .... Nitrocellulose (RU)
NTS .... Scientific and Technical Council (RU)
NTS .... Scientific and Technical Union (BU)
NTsAP .... National Weather Analysis Center [*NAWAC*] (RU)
NTS GUGP ... Scientific and Technical Council of the Main Administration of the Mining Industry (RU)
NTS MSP .... Scientific and Technical Council of the Ministry of the Shipbuilding Industry (RU)
NTSS .... Directive on Trying Labor Disputes by the Courts (BU)
NTsUVS ...... Chief of the Central Directorate of Military Communications (RU)
NTT .... Newton's Theory of Gravitation (RU)
NTT .... [*The*] Nippon Telegraph & Telephone Public Corp. (SJT)
NTT .... Nusatenggara Timur [*East Lesser Sundas*] (IN)
NTTA .... Nigeria Table Tennis Association (MAR)
NTTM .... Scientific and Technical Creativity among the Youth (BU)
ntto .... Netto [*Net*] [*German*] (GPO)
NTU .... Namibia Transnational Unit (MAR)
NTU .... Scientific and Technical Administration (RU)
NTU .... Standard Technical Specifications (RU)
NTUC .... National Trade Union Congress (ML)
NTUC .... Nigerian Trade Union Congress (AF)
NTUF .... Nigerian Trade-Union Federation (AF)
NTV .... National Television Authority (MAR)
NTWL .... Nederlandse Technische en Natuur Wetenschappelijke Literatuur
NTZ .... Iraq-Saudi Arabia Neutral Zone [*Three-letter standard code*] (CNC)
NTZ .... New Pipe Plant (RU)
NU .... Chief of Administration (RU)
NU .... Lower Level (RU)
NU .... Nahdlatul Ulama [*Moslem Scholars Party*] (IN)
NU .... Nakhimov School [*Navy*] (RU)
NU .... Naphthylacetic Acid (RU)
NU .... Narodopisny Ustav [*Ethnological Institute (of the Slovak Academy of Sciences)*] (CZ)
NU .... National Union (MAR)
NU .... Nations Unies (MAR)
NU .... Nepugyeszseg [*Office of the People's Attorney*] (HU)
NU .... Niue [*Two-letter standard code*] (CNC)
Nu .... Numara [*Number*] (TU)
NU .... Scientific Establishment (RU)
NUAK .... National Aeronautics and Space Administration [*NASA*] (RU)
NUASA .... Nairobi University Agriculture Students Association (MAR)
NUB .... Nacizmus Uldozotteinek Bizottsaga [*Committee of the Victims of Nazism*] (HU)
NUB .... Novacke Uholni Bane [*Novaky Coal Mines*] (CZ)
NUBE .... National Union of Bank Employees (ML)
NUBEGW .... National Union of Building, Engineering, and General Workers (MAR)
NUC .... Natal University College (MAR)
NUC .... National Unity Council (ML)
NUC .... National Universities Commission (MAR)
NUC .... Nationale UNESCO Commissie
NUC .... Nejvyssi Urad Cenovy [*Supreme Price Office*] (CZ)
NUCC .... Nairobi University Chemical Club (MAR)
NUCLAM ..... NUCLEBRAS Auxiliar de Mineracao, SA [*NUCLEBRAS Mining Assistance, Inc.*] [*Brazilian*] (LA)
NUCLEBRAS ... Empresas Nucleares Brasileiras, SA [*Brazilian Nuclear Corporations*] (LA)
NUCLEI .... NUCLEBRAS Enriquecimento Isotopico, SA [*NUCLEBRAS Isotope Enrichment, Inc.*] [*Brazilian*] (LA)
NUCLEMON ... NUCLEBRAS de Monazita e Associados Ltda. [*NUCLEBRAS Monazite and Associated Elements Ltd.*] [*Brazilian*] (LA)
NUCLEN ...... NUCLEBRAS Engenharia, SA [*NUCLEBRAS Engineering, Inc.*] [*Brazilian*] (LA)
NUCLEP ...... NUCLEBRAS de Equipamentos Pesados, SA [*NUCLEBRAS Heavy Equipment, Inc.*] [*Brazilian*] (LA)
NUCON .... NUCLEBRAS Construtora de Centrais Nucleares, SA [*NUCLEBRAS Nuclear Plant Construction, Inc.*] [*Brazilian*] (LA1)
NUCS .... National Union of Cameroon Students (MAR)
NUCW .... National Union of Cameroon Workers (AF)
NUCW .... National Union of Cinema Workers (ML)

NUCW .... National Union of Commercial Workers (ML)
NUDA .... Nigerian Unions of Dispensing Assistants (AF)
NUDO .... National United Democratic Organization [*Namibian*] (PPW)
NUEPI .... National Union of Employees in the Printing Industry (ML)
NUES .... National Union of Ethiopian Students (AF)
NUEUS .... National Union of Ethiopian University Students (AF)
NUF .... National Unifying Force [*Zimbabwean*] (PPW)
NUF .... National United Front (MAR)
NUF .... National Unity Front [*Polish*] (PPW)
NUFC .... National United Front of Cambodia [*Use FUNK*] (CL)
NUFCOR ..... Nuclear Fuels Corporation [*South African*] (AF)
NUFFIC .... Netherlands Universities Foundation For International Cooperation
NUFK .... National United Front of Cambodia [*Use FUNK*] (CL)
NUGS .... National Union of Ghanaian Students (AF)
NUHA .... National Union of Hospital Assistants (ML)
NUJ .... National Union of Journalists [*Malaysian*] (ML)
NUJ .... Nigerian Union of Journalists (AF)
NUJS .... Novosadsko Udruzenje Jugoslovenskih Studenata [*Yugoslav Students Association in Novi Sad*] (YU)
NUK .... Naphthylacetic Acid (RU)
NUK .... Narodna in Univerzitetna Knjiznica [*National and University Library*] [*Ljubljana*] (YU)
NUK .... Narodni a Universitni Knihovna [*National and University Library*] (CZ)
NUKS .... National Union of Kenya Students (AF)
NUKU .... Nejvyssi Ucetni Kontrolni Urad [*Supreme Accounting Office*] (CZ)
NUL .... National Union for Liberation [*Philippine*] (PPW)
NUL .... National University of Lesotho (MAR)
NULGE .... Nigerian Union of Local Government Employees (AF)
num .... Above Sea Level (RU)
NUM .... National Union of Mineworkers [*South African*]
num .... Numero [*Number*] [*Spanish*]
NUMCO .... Nigerian Uranium Mining Company (MAR)
numer .... Numbered (RU)
NUMM .... Chief of the Directorate for Mechanization and Motorization (RU)
NUMMS .... National Union of Malaysian Muslim Students (ML)
numo .... Numero [*Number*] [*Spanish*]
NUMS .... National Union of Malaysian Students (ML)
nums .... Numeros [*Numbers*] [*Spanish*]
NUNBE .... National Union of Nigerian Bank Employees (AF)
NUNS .... National Union of Nigerian Students (AF)
NUNW .... National Union of Namibia Workers (MAR)
NUNW .... National Union of Newspaper Workers [*Malaysian*] (ML)
nuor .... Nuorempi [*Finnish*]
NUP .... Nacionalno Udruzenje za Planiranje [*National Planning Association*] [*USA*] (YU)
NUP .... National Union [*or Unionist*] Party [*Sudanese*] (MAR)
NUP .... Uncontrolled Repeater Station (RU)
NUPAW .... National Union of Plantation and Agricultural Workers [*Ugandan*] (AF)
NUPF .... National Union of Popular Forces [*Moroccan*] (MAR)
NUPOD .... Nakupna Ustredny Potravnych Druzstev [*Central Purchase Office of Food Cooperatives*] (CZ)
NUPOSA ..... National Undergraduate Program for Overseas Study of Arabic (MAR)
NUPP .... National Unionist Progressive Party [*Egyptian*] (MAR)
NUPSE .... National Union of Public Service Employees [*Guyanese*] (LA)
NUPW .... National Union of Plantation Workers (ML)
NUR .... Unguided Missile (RU)
NUR .... Unguided Rocket (BU)
NURD .... Nueva Union Republicana-Democratica [*New Democratic Republican Union*] [*Venezuelan*] (LA)
NURDSR ..... Directive on Extending the Working Day for Seasonal Work (BU)
NURS .... National Union of Rhodesia Students (AF)
NURS .... Unguided Missile (RU)
NURS .... Unguided Rocket Projectile (BU)
NURTW .... National Union of Road Transport Workers [*Nigerian*] (AF)
NUrV .... Lower Water Level (RU)
NUS .... Chief of Communications Center (RU)
NUS .... National Union of Students (MAR)
NUS .... Nonpartisan Teachers' Union (BU)
NUSAS .... Nasionale Unie van Suid-Afrikaanse Studente [*National Union of South African Students*] (AF)
NUSDE .... National Union of Shop and Distributive Employees [*Nigerian*] (AF)
NUSG .... National Union of Students of Ghana (MAR)
NUSS .... National Union of Students of Sierra Leone (MAR)
NUSS .... National Union of Syrian Students (ME)
NUSU .... Nanyang University Student Union (ML)
NUSU .... Nanyang University Students Union [*Singapore*] (ML)
NUSWAS ..... National Union of South-West African Students [*Namibian*] (AF)
NUT .... National Union of Teachers [*Kenyan*] (AF)
NUT .... National Union of Teachers (ML)
NUT .... Nigerian Union of Teachers (MAR)
NUTA .... National Union of Tanganyika Workers [*Tanzanian*] (AF)
NUTAE .... Nuffield Unit of Tropical Animal Ecology (MAR)
NUTV .... Narodni Ustredni Telovychovny Vybor [*National Committee for Physical Education*] (CZ)
NUTW .... National Union of Tanganyika Workers (MAR)
NUTW .... National Union of Textile Workers (MAR)
NUUS .... National Union of Uganda Students (AF)
NUWA .... National Urban Water Supply Authority (MAR)
NUWM .... National Union of Workers in Mali (MAR)
NUYO .... National Union of Youth Organizations [*Ugandan*] (AF)
NUZS .... National Union of Zambia Students (AF)
n/v .... Low-Voltage (RU)
NV .... Magnetizing Fork [*Weld inspection device*] (RU)
NV .... Minimum Moisture Capacity (of Soil) (RU)
NV .... Naamloze Vennootschap [*Limited Liability Company*] [*Dutch*] (GPO)
NV .... Nacelnik Veze [*Communications Chief*] [*Military*] (YU)
nV .... Nad Vahom [*On the Vah River*] (CZ)
nV .... Nad Vltavou [*On the Vltava River*] (CZ)
NV .... Narodni Vybor [*National Committee*] (CZ)
NV .... Nas Vrt [*Our Garden*] [*Zagreb*] [*A periodical*] (YU)
NV .... Nase Vojsko [*Our Army*] [*A publishing house*] (CZ)
NV .... Navassa Island [*Two-letter standard code*] (CNC)
NV .... Nederlandse Staatsmiinen [*Dutch State Mines*] (WEN)
NV .... Nemzetkozi Vasar [*International Fair*] (HU)
NV .... Neposredna Vatra [*Direct Fire*] [*Military*] (YU)
NV .... Nichtverbreitung [*Nonproliferation*] [*German*] (WEN)
NV .... Niski Vodostaj [*Low Tide*] (YU)
NV .... North Vietnam [*or North Vietnamese*] (CL)
n/v .... Notre Ville [*Our City*] [*French*] [*Business and trade*]
n/V .... On the Volga [*Toponymy*] (RU)
NV .... People's Army (BU)
NV .... Rotor, Main Rotor (RU)
nv .... Time Norm (BU)
NVA .... Nationale Volksarmee [*National People's Army*] (EG)
NVA .... Nederlandsche Vereeniging van Antiquaren
NVA .... Nemzetkozi Vasuti Arudijszabas [*International Railroad Freight Tariff*] (HU)
NVA .... Vietnam People's Army [*Use VPA*] [*North Vietnamese*] (CL)
NVas .... Nasa Vas [*Our Village*] [*Ljubljana*] [*A periodical*] (YU)
NVB .... Narodni Vybor Bezpecnosti [*National Security Board*] (CZ)
NVB .... National Party Netherlands (WEN)
NVB .... National Security Brigade [*Dutch*] (WEN)
NVB .... National Volunteer Brigade (MAR)
NVB .... Nationale Vrouwenraad van Belgie [*National Council of Belgian Women*] (WEN)
NVB .... Nederlandse Vereniging van Bibliothecarissen
NVB .... Nederlandse Volksbeweging [*Dutch People's Movement*] (PPE)
NVB .... Nederlandse Vrouwenbeweging [*Netherlands Women's Movement*] (WEN)
NVBA .... Nederlandse Vereniging van Bedrijfsarchivarissen [*'s-Gravenhage*]
NVB/CLO .... Sectie Centrum Literatuuronderzoekers van de Nederlandse Vereniging van Bibliothecarissen
NVB/SSB .... Sectie Speciale Bibliotheken van de Nederlandse Vereniging van Bibliothecarissen
NVB/SWB ... Sectie Wetenschappelijke Bibliotheken van de Nederlandse Vereniging van Bibliothecarissen
NVD .... Chief of Military Roads (RU)
NVD .... Commander of Airborne Force (RU)
NVD .... Normal-Hub, Vier-Takt Dieselmotor [*Standard Stroke, Four-Cycle Diesel Engine*] (EG)
nvd .... Service Platoon (BU)
nve .... Normal Hydrogen Equivalent (RU)
NVE .... Standard Hydrogen Electrode (RU)
NVF .... Lower-Volga Branch (RU)
NVF .... Nederlandse Vereniging van Fotojournalisten [*Netherlands Association of Photo Journalists*] (WEN)
NVII .... Noril'sk Evening Industrial Institute (RU)
NVj .... Nastavni Vjesnik [*Teaching Review*] [*Zagreb*] (YU)
NVK .... Low-Voltage Contact (RU)
NVK .... Nacelnik Vojenskeho Klubu [*Military Club Officer*] (CZ)
nvkf .... Nemzeti Vallalat Korlatolt Felelosseggel [*National Enterprise with Limited Liability*] (HU)
NVL .... Person Called Is Not Here [*Telephone*] (BU)
NVMB .... Naval Base Commander (RU)
NVN .... North Vietnam [*or North Vietnamese*] (CL)
NVNIIGG ..... Lower Volga Scientific Research Institute of Geology and Geophysics (RU)
NVN/VC ...... North Vietnamese/Viet Cong [*or North Vietnam/Viet Cong*] (CL)
NVO .... Low-Voltage Equipment (RU)
NVO .... Neuererverordnung [*Innovator Decree*] (EG)
NVo .... People's Army (BU)
NVOPNZh ... Directive Temporarily Restricting the Admission of New Residents in Large Cities and Other Settlements (BU)
NVP .... Nahverkehrspreisverordnung [*Price Regulation Governing Local Transportation*] (EG)
NVP .... Nederlandse Vereniging van Persbureaux [*Netherlands Association of Press Bureaus*] (WEN)
NVPOSL ...... Nacelnik Protivzdusne Obrany Statu a Letectva [*Chief of National Air Defense and Aviation*] (CZ)

NVP-U .... Nationale Volkspartij - Unie [*National United People's Party*] [*Netherlands Antillean*] (PPW)
NVR .... Nederlandse Vredesraad [*Netherlands Peace Council*] (WEN)
NVRI .... Vom National Veterinary Research Institute (MAR)
NVRP .... Lower Volga River Steamship Line (RU)
NVRZ .... Novorossiysk Railroad Car Repair Plant (RU)
NVS .... Chief of Military Communications (RU)
NVS .... Nacelnik Vycvikove Skupiny [*Chief of Training Detachment*] (CZ)
NVS .... Nacelnik Vysadkove Sluzby [*Chief of Airborne Service*] (CZ)
NVS .... Narodna Vlada Slovenije [*National Government of Slovenia*] (YU)
NVS .... Nejvyssi Vojensky Soud [*Supreme Military Court*] (CZ)
NVT .... Nepokretne Vatrene Tacke [*Fixed Targets*] [*Military*] (YU)
NVTI .... National Vocational Training Institute (MAR)
NVU .... Nederlandse Volksunie [*Dutch People's Union*] (WEN)
NVU .... People's Military Academy (BU)
NVV .... Nederlands Verbond van Vakverenigingen [*Netherlands Federation of Trade Unions*] (WEN)
NVV .... Nederlandse Bond van Vervoerspersoneel [*Netherlands Association of Transportation Personnel*] (WEN)
NVVR .... Nasionale Verkeersveiligheidsraad [*National Traffic Safety Council*] [*South African*] (AF)
NVVS .... Chief of the Air Force (RU)
NVW .... Nederland in de Vijf Werelddeelen, Leyden 1947 (MAR)
n vz .... Chief of Aerostation (BU)
NVZ .... Noninterchangeability (RU)
n vz f .... Commander, Army Air Force (BU)
nvzu .... Chief of Military School (BU)
NW .... Nord Ouest [*Northwest*] [*French*] (MTD)
NW .... Nordwesten [*Northwest*] (EG)
Nw .... Wirtschaftlicher Nutzeffekt Wirkungsgrad [*Economical Efficiency*] [*German*]
NWC .... National Working Committee (MAR)
NWC .... Nigerian Workers Council (AF)
NWDR .... Nordwestdeutscher Rundfunk [*Northwest German Radio Network*] [*West German*] (WEN)
NWFP .... North-West Frontier Province [*Pakistani*] (PD)
NWGA .... National Wool Growers' Association (MAR)
NWKV .... Nasionale Wolkwekersvereniging van Suid-Afrika (MAR)
NWM .... National Workers Movement [*St. Vincentian*] (LA1)
NWO .... National Women's Organization [*Grenadian*] (LA1)
NWP .... Najwiekszy Wspolny Podzielnik [*Highest Common Divisor*] [*Polish*]
NWRC .... New World Resource Center (MAR)
NWU .... National Workers Union [*Seychelles*] (AF)
NWU .... National Workers Union [*St. Lucian*] (LA1)
NWU .... National Workers Union [*Jamaican*] (LA1)
NWU .... National Workers Union [*Dominican Republic*] (LA1)
NWW .... Najmniejsza Wspolna Wielokrotnosc [*Smallest Common Multiple*] [*Polish*]
ny .... Nyilvanos [*Public*] (HU)
ny .... Nyilvantartas [*Record, Register*] (HU)
ny .... Nyugalmazott [*Retired*] (HU)
Ny .... Nyugat [*West*] [*Hungarian*] (GPO)
NYC .... Nigerian Youth Congress (MAR)
NYC .... Nigerian Youth Council (AF)
NYCN .... National Youth Council of Nigeria (MAR)
NYE .... Nomiki Ypiresia tis Ekklisias [*Church Legal Service*] [*Greek*] (GC)
NYeZh .... Rudder, Propeller Designed by N. Ye. Zhukovskiy (RU)
nyilv .... Nyilvanos [*Public*] (HU)
nyilv rend .... Nyilvanos Rendes [*Full (Professor)*] (HU)
nyk .... Nykyinen [*or Nykyisin*] [*Modern, In Our Days*] [*Finnish*] (GPO)
ny kotv .... Nyeremenykotveny [*Premium Bond*] (HU)
NYKV .... Nyersborgyujto es Keszletezo Vallalat [*Raw Hide Collection and Storage Enterprise*] (HU)
NYM .... National Youth Movement [*Sierra Leonean*] (AF)
NYM .... Nigerian Youth Movement (MAR)
NYMG .... National Youth Movement of Ghana (MAR)
NYO .... National Youth Organisation (MAR)
NYO .... National Youth Organization [*Grenadian*] (LA1)
nyomt .... Nyomtatta [*Printed By*] (HU)
nyomtatv ..... Nyomtatvany [*Printed Matter*] (HU)
Nyomtell ..... Nyomtatvanyellato Vallalat [*Office Stationery Supply Enterprise*] (HU)
nyomtv .... Nyomtatvany [*Printed Matter*] (HU)
NYPC .... National Youth Pioneer Corps (ML)
NYPDOSZ ... Nyomda- es Papiripari Dolgozok Szakszervezete [*Trade Union of Workers and Employees of the Printing and Paper Industries*] (HU)
ny r .... Nyilvanos Rendes [*Full (Professor)*] (HU)
ny rk .... Nyilvanos Rendkivuli [*Associate (Professor)*] (HU)
nyrkk .... Nyrkkeily [*Boxing*] [*Finnish*]
NYS .... National Youth Service (MAR)
NYSC .... National Youth Service Corps [*Nigerian*] (AF)
NYTC .... Nigerian Youth Thinkers Club (AF)
NYTIL .... Nyanza Textile Industries Limited (MAR)
NYU .... National Youth Union (MAR)
Nyug pu ...... Nyugati Palyaudvar [*West Railway Station*] [*Budapest*] (HU)
NZ .... Criminal Law (BU)
NZ .... Na Znanje [*Take Note*] (YU)
Nz .... Nachzug [*Second Section of a Train (Operated separately)*] (EG)
NZ .... Nadnormativni Zasoby [*Supplies Exceeding the Standards*] (CZ)
nz .... Nagradni Zaloha [*Replacement Reserves*] (CZ)
NZ .... Narodna Zascita [*National Defense*] [*Slovenia*] (YU)
NZ .... Narodne Zhromazdenie [*National Assembly*] (CZ)
NZ .... Narody Zjednoczone [*United Nations*] (POL)
NZ .... Nasa Zena [*Our Woman*] [*Ljubljana*] [*A periodical*] (YU)
NZ .... Nedotknutelna Zasoba [*War Reserve Supplies*] (CZ)
NZ .... Neutral Zone, No-Man's-Land (RU)
NZ .... New Zealand [*Two-letter standard code*] (CNC)
NZ .... Nieuwezijds [*New Side*] [*Dutch*] (CED)
NZ .... Nova Zalozba [*New Publishing House*] (YU)
NZ .... Nova Zeta [*New Zeta*] [*Cetinje*] [*A periodical*] (YU)
NZ .... Plant Standard (RU)
NZ .... Reserve Supplies, Individual Reserves (RU)
NZBr .... Law on Marriage (BU)
nzch .... Low Audio Frequency (RU)
NZD .... Normal-Hub, Zwei-Takt Dieselmotor [*Standard-Stroke, Two-Cycle Diesel Engine*] (EG)
NZd .... Nova Zadruga [*New Cooperative*] [*A periodical*] (YU)
NZFS .... New Zealand Forest Service
NZH .... Nakladni Zavod Hrvatske [*Publishing Institute of Croatia*] (YU)
NZH .... Narodna Zastita Hrvatske [*National Defense of Croatia*] (YU)
NZhDO .... Chief of Railroad Guard (RU)
NZI .... Nationaal Ziekenhuis-Instituut [*Utrecht*]
nzk .... Sustained Oscillations (RU)
NZKTD .... Directive on Collective Labor Contracts (BU)
NZL .... Neva Machinery Plant Imeni V. I. Lenin (RU)
NZL .... New Zealand [*Three-letter standard code*] (CNC)
NZO .... Standing Barrage (BU)
NZO .... Standing Barrage (RU)
NZPB .... Directive on Payment for Work Stoppage and Waste in Industry, Transportation, and Construction (BU)
NZPL .... Nadodrzanskie Zaklady Przemyslu Lniarskiego [*Odra River Linen Mills*] (POL)
NZPP .... Najnoviji Nacrt Zakona o Parnicnom Postupku [*Most Recent Draft Law on Civil Procedure*] (YU)
NZR .... Nationale Ziekenhuisraad [*Utrecht*]
NZS .... Nacelnik Zdravotnicke Sluzby [*Chief of Medical Service*] (CZ)
NZS .... Neobsluhovana Zesilovaci Stanice [*Unattended Booster Stations (Amplifier stations on coaxial cable line) (Underground metal tanks)*] (CZ)
NZS .... Netitalni Zarizeni Staveniste [*Unspecified Building Equipment (for current use)*] (CZ)
NZSG .... Public Health and Social Welfare (BU)
NZSR .... Directive on the Substitution of Employees and Holding Several Jobs (BU)
NZSTs .... Law on Supply and Prices (BU)
NZTD .... Law on Labor Contracts (BU)
NZUVT .... Law on the Regulation of Internal Trade (BU)
NZV .... Nepokretna Zaprecna Vatra [*Fixed Barrage Fire*] [*Military*] (YU)
NZZn .... Narodno Zemedelsko Zname [*People's Agrarian Banner*] [*A newspaper*] (BU)

O

o/ ... A l'Ordre De [*French*]
o ... Father [*Ecclesiastic*] (RU)
O ... Flash Ranging (RU)
O ... Gun (RU)
o ... Island (BU)
o ... Island (RU)
O ... Lake [*Vessel class according to the river register*] (RU)
o ... Oben [*Above*] (EG)
O ... Ober [*German*]
o ... Oblast (RU)
O ... Ocean [*Ocean*] [*Polish*]
O ... Octarius [*Pint*] [*Latin*] (GPO)
O ... Odde [*or Odden*] [*Point*] [*Norwegian*] (NAU)
o ... Oder [*Or*] (EG)
O ... Oeste [*West*] [*Spanish*]
O ... Oesterreich [*or Oesterreichisch*] [*Austria or Austrian*] [*German*] (GPO)
O ... Officier [*of the Legion of Honor*] [*French*] (MTD)
o ... Ohne [*Without*] (EG)
o ... Ojciec [*Polish*]
O ... Oklevel [*Hungarian*]
O ... Okres [*District*] (CZ)
o ... Oldal [*Page*] (HU)
o ... Ora [*Hour, Time*] (HU)
o ... Orden [*Order*] [*Business and trade*] [*Spanish*]
o ... Ordentlich [*German*]
O/ ... Order [*Business and trade*] [*German*]
o ... Ordinaer [*Ordinary Grade*] [*German*]
O ... Ordinary [*Level of General Certificate of Education*] [*Ghanaian*]
o/ ... Ordre [*Order*] [*Business and trade*] [*French*]
o ... Ore [*Half Farthing*] [*Norwegian*] (GPO)
O ... Ormos [*Bay*] [*Greek*] (NAU)
O ... Orszagos [*National (Adjective)*] (HU)
o ... Ortho [*Ortho*] [*German*]
o ... Orvos [*Physician*] (HU)
O ... Oscilloscope (RU)
O ... Ost [*or Osten*] [*East*] [*German*] (EG)
O ... Ostrov [*or Ostrova*] [*Island or Islands*] [*Russian*] (NAU)
O ... Ostrov [*or Ostrovul or Ostrovu*] [*River Island*] [*Romanian*] (NAU)
o ... Osztaly [*Class, Department, Division*] (HU)
O ... Otocic [*or Otocici*] [*Islet or Islets*] [*Yugoslav*] (NAU)
O ... Otok [*or Otoci*] [*Island or Islands*] [*Yugoslav*] (NAU)
O ... Oxygonon [*Oxygen*] (GC)
O ... Oy [*or Oya or Toy*] [*Island*] [*Norwegian*] (NAU)
O ... Splinter, Fragmentation (RU)
O ... Tin (RU)
OA ... Amplitude Limiter (RU)
OA ... Antenna Mounting (RU)
OA ... Axial Reinforcement (RU)
OA ... Contaminated Atmosphere (RU)
OA ... Obalska Artilerija [*Coastal Artillery*] (YU)
oa ... Oder Aehnlich [*Or Something Similar*] [*German*]
oa ... Og Annet [*And Others*] [*Norwegian*] (GPO)
OA ... Oklopni Automobil [*Armored Car*] (YU)
OA ... Olymbiaki Aeroporia [*Olympic Airlines*] (GC1)
oa ... Onder Andere [*Among Others*] [*Dutch*] (GPO)
OA ... Operational Airfield (RU)
oa ... Orszagos Allatvasar [*National Livestock Fair*] (HU)
OAA ... Omilos Andisfairiseos Athinon [*Athens Lawn Tennis Club*] (GC)
OAAA ... Organismos Apaskholiseos kai Asfaliseos Anergias [*or Organismos Apaskholiseos kai Asfaliseos Kata tis Anergias*] [*Organization for Unemployment Insurance and Employment*] [*Greek*] (GC)
OAACE ... Organisation Afro-Asiatique de Cooperation Economique [*Afro-Asian Organization for Economic Cooperation*] [*Use AFRASEC*] (AF)
OAAEE ... Organosis Aoraton Agoniston Ellinikou Ethnous [*Organization of Invisible Fighters of the Greek Nation*] [*Also, SNNYS*] (GC)
OAAH ... Organisation Afro-Asiatique pour l'Habitation [*Afro-Asian Housing Organization*] [*Use AAHO*] (AF)
OAAH ... Orszagos Anyag es Arhivatal [*National Material and Price Office*] (HU)
OAAPS ... Organisation for Afro-Asian Peoples Solidarity (MAR)
OAARR ... Organisation Afro-Asiatique pour la Reconstruction Rurale [*Afro-Asian Rural Reconstruction Organization*] [*Use AARRO*] (AF)
OAB ... Aerial Fragmentation Bomb (RU)
OAB ... Ordem dos Advogados do Brasil [*Brazilian Bar Association*] (LA)
OAB ... Organisation Africaine du Bois [*African Wood Organization*] (AF)
OAB ... Orszagos Atomenergia Bizottsag [*National Atomic Energy Committee*] (HU)
OAB ... Separate Air Brigade (RU)
oabr ... Gun Artillery Brigade (BU)
OAC ... Obus en Acier a Amorcage de Culot [*Military*] [*French*] (MTD)
OAC ... Oost Afrikaansche Compagnie (MAR)
OACI ... Organisation de l'Aviation Civile Internationale [*International Civil Aviation Organization*] [*Use ICAO*] (AF)
OACI ... Organizacion de Aviacion Civil Internacional [*International Civil Aviation Organization*] [*Use ICAO*] (LA)
OACIE ... Oost Afrikaansche Compagnie (MAR)
OACV ... Office Algerien des Colonies de Vacances (MAR)
OACV ... Operation Arachides et Cultures Vivrieres (MAR)
OAD ... Bidirectional Amplitude Limiter (RU)
oad ... Gun Artillery Division (BU)
OAD ... Oficiul de Aprovizionare si Desfacere [*Office of Supply and Sales*] (RO)
OAD ... Organization of American States (BU)
OAD ... Orszagos Autobuszmenetrend es Dijszabas [*National Bus Timetable and Rate List*] (HU)
OAD ... Separate Artillery Battalion (RU)
OADA ... Organisation Arabe pour le Developpement Agricole [*Arab Agricultural Development Organization*] (AF)
OADMA ... Organismos Anegerseos Dikastikou Megarou Athinon [*Organization for Constructing the Athens Court House*] (GC)
oadn ... Separate Artillery Battalion (RU)
OADS ... Organisation Arabe de Defense Sociale (Contre le Crime) (MAR)
OAE ... Office d'Approvisionnement de l'Etat [*State Supply Office*] [*Beninese*] (AF)
OAE ... Omospondia Andistasiakon Ellados [*Greek Federation of Resisters*] (GC)
OAE ... Organisasie van Afrika-Eenheid [*Organization of African Unity*] [*Use OAU*] (AF)
OAE ... Organisation der Afrikatischen Einheit (MAR)
OAE ... Organismos tis Afrikanikis Enotitos [*Organization of African Unity*] (GC)
OAE ... Organizatiia Afrikanskovo Edinstva (MAR)
OAED ... Organismos Apaskholiseos Ergatikou Dynamikou [*Labor Force Employment Organization*] [*Greek*] (GC)
OAER ... Base Airfield (RU)
OAES ... Separate Air Communications Squadron (RU)
OAFT ... Orszagos Allattenyesztesi es Takarmanyozasi Felugyeloseg [*National Animal Breeding and Fodder Inspectorate*] (HU)
OAG ... Organization of American States [*OAS*] (RU)
OAI ... Public Automobile Inspector (RU)
OAIC ... Office Algerien Interprofessionnel des Cereales [*Interoccupational Algerian Grains Office*] (AF)
OAIM ... Organisme Arabe pour l'Industrialisation Militaire (MAR)
OAK ... Organismos Amerikanikon Kraton [*Organization of American States*] (GC)
oak ... Orszagos Allat- es Kirako [*or Kirakodo*] Vasar [*National Livestock and Merchandise Fair*] (HU)
OAK ... Ostravsky Aeroklub [*Ostrava Aero Club*] (CZ)
OAK ... Reports of the Archaeological Commission [*A publication*] (RU)
OAKh ... Society of Architect Artists [*1903-1932*] (RU)

OAL............ Organisation pour l'Afrique Libre [*Organization for Free Africa*] (AF)
OAL............ Special Automobile Laboratory (RU)
OAL i MP..... Department of Mathematical Linguistics and Machine Translation (RU)
o all............ Osszeallitotta [*Compiled By*] (HU)
OALS........... Organizacion Avanzada para la Liberacion del Sahara [*Forward Organization for the Liberation of the Sahara*] (AF)
OAM............ Automatic Optimizer (RU)
OAM............ Organisation Africaine et Malgache (MAR)
OAM............ Relative Amplitude Modulation (RU)
OAMCAF..... Organisation Africaine et Malgache du Cafe [*African and Malagasy Coffee Organization*] (AF)
OAMCE....... Organisation Africaine et Malgache de Cooperation Economique (MAR)
OAMJTB..... Organisation pour l'Afrique des Mouvements de Jeunesse et du Travail Benevole (MAR)
OAMK......... Okresni Auto-Motoklub [*District Motoring Club*] (CZ)
OAMNII....... Joint Scientific Research Institutes for Aviation Medicine (BU)
OAMO......... Obshchaia Afro-Malagasiiskaia Organizatsiia (MAR)
OAMPI......... Office Africain et Malgache de la Propriete Industrielle (MAR)
OAN............ Organismos Anelkyseos Navagion [*Ship Salvage Organization*] [*Greek*] (GC)
OAO............ General Administrative Department (RU)
OAO............ Separate Air Detachment (RU)
OAOLPP...... Oficina de Atencion a los Organos Locales del Poder Popular del Consejo de Ministros [*Local People's Government Department of the Council of Ministers*] [*Cuban*] (LA)
OAP............ Austrian Trade-Union Association (RU)
oap............ Gun Artillery Regiment (BU)
OAP............ Office Algerien de Peches [*Algerian Fishing Office*] (AF)
OAP............ Organismos Apokhetevseos Protevousis [*Capital Area Drainage Organization*] [*Greek*] (GC)
OAP............ Separate Air Regiment (RU)
OAPCKKPM... Odelenie za Agitacija i Propaganda pri Centralni Komitet na Komunistickata Partija na Makedonija [*Department of Agitation and Propaganda in the Central Committee of the Communist Party of Macedonia*] (YU)
OAPEC........ Oficina Administrativa para Programas Educativos Conjuntos [*Later, ICCE*] [*Bogota*] (COL)
OAPEC........ Organization of Arab Petroleum Exporting Countries (ME)
OAPF........... Main Motor Highway to the Front (BU)
OAPI........... Organisation Africaine pour la Propriete Intellectuelle [*African Organization for Intellectual Rights*] (AF)
OAPV........... Single-Phase Automatic Reclosing (RU)
OAPVO........ Separate Antiaircraft Defense Army (BU)
OAR............ Basic Repair Service (BU)
OAR............ Detached Motor Transport Company (BU)
OAR............ Obedinennaia Arabskaia Respublika (MAR)
OAR............ United Arab Republic (BU)
OAR............ United Arab Republic [*UAR*] (RU)
OARB.......... Separate Motor Vehicle Repair Battalion (RU)
oaremb....... Separate Motor Vehicle Repair Battalion (RU)
OARI........... Organizacion de Accion Revolucionaria Independiente [*Independent Revolutionary Action Organization*] [*Venezuelan*] (LA)
OARM.......... District Motor Vehicle Repair Shop (RU)
OARM.......... Organisation Arabe des Ressources Minieres [*Moroccan*] (MAR)
oarp............ Separate Motor Transport Company (RU)
OARTU........ District Artillery Directorate (RU)
OAS............ Airfield Construction Section (RU)
OAS............ Airfield Service Section (RU)
OAS............ Aviation Supply Section (RU)
O-as............ Nullas [*Finest Quality*] (HU)
OAS............ Organisacni Akciova Spolecnost [*Organizational Joint-Stock Company*] (CZ)
OAS............ Organisation de l'Armee Secrete [*Secret Army Organization*] [*French*] (PD)
OAS............ Organismos Astikon Syngoinonion [*Urban Communications Organization*] [*Greek*] (GC)
OAS............ Organization of American States (LA)
oashr.......... Separate Army Disciplinary Company (RU)
OASR.......... Separate Motorized Medical Company (RU)
OASTh........ Organismos Astikon Syngoinonion Thessalonikis [*Organization of Salonica City Communications*] (GC)
OAT............ Obus en Acier a Amorcage de Tete [*Military*] [*French*] (MTD)
OAT............ Omades Andimetopiseos Tarachon [*Riot Control Groups*] [*See also MAT*] (GC1)
OAT............ Organisation Arabe du Travail [*North African*] (MAR)
OAT............ Ouvrages d'Art et Travaux (MAR)
OATB.......... Separate Motor Transport Battalion (RU)
oatbo.......... Separate Technical Support Battalion for an Airfield (BU)
OATh........... Organismos Apokhetevseos Thessalonikis [*Salonica Drainage Organization*] (GC1)
oatro........... Separate Technical Support Company for an Airfield (BU)
OATS.......... Terminal Automatic Telephone Exchange (RU)
OATUU........ Organization of African Trade Union Unity (AF)
OAU............ Okrug Pharmaceutical Administration (BU)
OAU............ Organization of African Unity (PD)
OAULC........ Organisation for African Unity Liberation Committee (MAR)
OAV............ Oesterreichischer Alpen Verein [*Austrian Alpine Club*]
OAV............ Okresni Akcni Vybor [*District Action Committee*] (CZ)
OAV............ Organization Autonome de la Vallee [*Autonomous Organization of the Valley*] [*Senegalese*] (AF)
oavtb.......... Separate Motor Transport Battalion (RU)
oaz............. Oasis (RU)
OAZ............ Odessa Automobile Assembly Plant (RU)
OB.............. Common Base (RU)
OB.............. Concentration (RU)
ob.............. Obacz [*See*] (POL)
Ob.............. Ober [*German*]
ob.............. Obiit [*He (or She) Died*] [*Latin*] (GPO)
ob.............. Obispo [*Bishop*] [*Spanish*]
ob.............. Obiter [*Incidentally*] [*Latin*] (GPO)
OB.............. Oblast Library (RU)
ob.............. Obligation [*Obligation*] [*Business and trade*] [*French*]
ob.............. Obywatel [*Citizen*] (POL)
oB.............. Ohne Befund [*Without Findings*] (EG)
OB.............. Oktanski Broj [*Octane Number*] [*Navy*] (YU)
OB.............. Olympiai Bajnoksag [*Olympic Championship*] (HU)
OB.............. Openbare Bibliotheek [*Dutch*]
OB.............. Operational Base [*Navy*] (RU)
OB.............. Organizacao de Base [*Primary Organization*] [*Brazilian*] (LA)
OB.............. Organosi Bolsevikon [*Organization of Bolsheviks*] [*Greek*] (GC)
OB.............. Orszagos Bekebizottsag [*National Peace Committee*] (HU)
OB.............. Ossewabrandwag (MAR)
OB.............. Osvetova Beseda [*Cultural Center*] (CZ)
ob.............. Revolution (RU)
OB.............. Uniovular Twins (RU)
ob.............. United, Joint (BU)
OBA............ Old Boys' Association (ML)
OBAD.......... Report of the Bulgarian Archeological Society (BU)
OBAE.......... Office des Bois d'Afrique Equatoriale [*Equatorial Africa Forestry Office*] (AF)
OBAE.......... Separate Bomber Squadron (RU)
OBAI........... Report of the Bulgarian Archeological Institute (BU)
OBAS.......... Obchodni Akciova Spolecnost [*Joint-Stock Trading Company*] (CZ)
OBATO........ Separate Airfield Technical Support Battalion (RU)
obats.......... Separate Tank Truck Battalion (RU)
OBB............ Burgas Okrug Library (BU)
Obb............ Oberbayern [*Upper Bavaria*] [*West German*] (WEN)
OBB............ Oesterreichische Bundesbahnen [*Austrian Federal Railways*] (WEN)
OBB............ Orszagos Bali Bizottsag [*National Social Dancing Committee*] (HU)
OBBF........... Front Hospital Base Section (BU)
OB-Centar... Obavestajni Centar [*Information Center*] [*Military*] (YU)
ob ch.......... Part by Volume (RU)
Obczak........ Obcansky Zakon [*Civil Law Code*] (CZ)
OBD............ Obecne Prospesne Bytove Druzstvo [*General Apartment Cooperative*] (CZ)
obdm.......... Separate Area Decontamination Battalion (BU)
obdm.......... Separate Ground Decontamination Battalion (RU)
OBE............ Oberste Bauleitung fuer Elektrifizierung [*Construction Headquarters for Electrification*] (EG)
OBE............ Order of the British Empire (ML)
OBE............ Relative Biological Effectiveness (RU)
OBEA.......... Office of Economic Analysis Based on Public Participation (RU)
OBECI......... Office Beninois de Cinema [*Benin Cinema Office*] (AF)
Obekoso..... Oblast Economic Conference (RU)
OBEMAP..... Office Beninois des Manutentions Portuaires [*Beninese Office of Port Management*] (AF)
Obes........... Oblast Economic Conference (RU)
obevak........ Oblast Evacuation Station (RU)
obg............. Detour [*Railroads*] (RU)
OBI............. Office du Baccalaureat International [*International Baccalaureate Office - IBO*] (EA)
OBI............. Outillage pour la Batiment et l'Industrie [*Moroccan*] (MAR)
OBiDN......... Osrodek Bibliografii i Dokumentacji Naukowej [*Center for Bibliography and Scientific Documentation*] (POL)
obikn........... Ordinary, Ordinarily (BU)
obit............ Separate Antitank Battalion (RU)
OBIV........... Separate Engineer Troops Battalion (RU)
obj.............. Objekti [*Object*] [*Finnish*]
obj.............. Objetosc [*Size, Volume*] (POL)
obk............. Combat Ship Squadron (RU)
OBK............ Office des Bauxites de Kindia (MAR)
OBK............ Organisation pour l'Amenagement et la Mise en Valeur du Bassin de la Kagera (MAR)
OBKE.......... Orszagos Banyaszati es Kohaszati Egyesulet [*National Association for Mining and Metallurgy*] (HU)
ob/khs........ Approach Trench Adapted for Defense [*Topography*] (RU)
OBKhS........ Department for Combating the Embezzlement of Socialist Property and Speculation (RU)
OBKhSS...... Department for Combating the Embezzlement of Socialist Property and Speculation (RU)
obkhz......... Separate Chemical Attack Protection Battalion (BU)
obkhz......... Separate Chemical Defense Battalion (RU)
OBKI........... Orszagos Balneologiai Kutato Intezet [*National Research Institute of Balneology*] (HU)

obl .... Cover (RU)
obl .... Oblast (BU)
obl .... Oblast (RU)
Oblarkhiv .... Oblast Archives Administration (RU)
Oblastop ..... Oblast Fuel Administration (RU)
Oblbytpromsoyuz ... Oblast Producers' Union for Personal Services to the Population (RU)
obldortrans ... Oblast Administration of Highways, Dirt Roads, Trucking, and Carting (RU)
obldrevmebel'prom ... Oblast Administration of the Furniture and Woodworking Industry (RU)
oblekoso ..... Oblast Economic Conference (RU)
Oblfizkul't ... Oblast Committee for Physical Culture and Sport (RU)
Oblfo .... Oblast Finance Department (RU)
oblFU .... Oblast Finance Administration (RU)
oblgalkhimpromsoyuz ... Oblast Producers' Union of the Notions and Chemical Industries (RU)
Oblgalpromsoyuz ... Oblast Notions Producers' Union (RU)
Oblgiz .... Oblast State Publishing House (RU)
Oblgosstrakh ... Oblast Administration of State Insurance (RU)
oblig .... Obligation [*French*]
oblIUU .... Oblast Institute for the Advanced Training of Teachers (RU)
oblkhimpromsoyuz ... Oblast Producers' Union of the Chemical Industry (RU)
oblknigotorg ... Oblast Book Trade Office (RU)
Oblkomkhoz ... Oblast Department of Municipal Services (RU)
oblkonupr ... Oblast Administration of Horse Breeding (RU)
Oblkoopinsoyuz ... Oblast Disabled Persons' Cooperative Union (RU)
Oblkozhpromsoyuz ... Oblast Leather Producers' Union (RU)
Obl k-t .... Oblast Committee (BU)
Obllegprom ... Oblast Administration of Light Industry (RU)
obllit .... Oblast Administration for the Protection of Military and State Secrets in the Press (RU)
Oblmel'trest ... Oblast Rural Flour-Milling Trust (RU)
oblmestprom ... Oblast Administration of Local Industry (RU)
oblmesttopprom ... Oblast Administration of Local and Fuel Industries (RU)
Oblmostorg ... Moscow Oblast Wholesale and Retail Trade Establishment (RU)
Oblnitoles ... Oblast Scientific, Engineering, and Technical Society of the Sawmilling Industry (RU)
ObLO .... Obcinski Ljudski Odbor [*Municipal People's Committee*] (YU)
OBLO .... Oblastni Ljudski Odbor [*Regional People's Committee*] (YU)
oblo .... Separate Light Flame-Thrower Battalion (RU)
oblONO .... Oblast Department of Public Education (RU)
oblorgnabor ... Oblast Department for Resettlement and Organized Recruitment of Workers (RU)
oblosvod ..... Oblast Branch of the Society for Furthering the Development of Water Transportation and for the Safeguarding of Human Lives on Waterways (RU)
oblpishcheprom ... Oblast Department of the Food Industry (RU)
Oblplan .... Oblast Planning Commission (RU)
oblpoligrafizdat ... Department of Publishing Houses and the Printing Industry of the Administration of Culture of an Oblispolkom (RU)
oblpotrebsoyuz ... Oblast Union of Consumers' Societies (RU)
oblprofsovet ... Oblast Council of Trade Unions (RU)
oblpromstrom ... Oblast Administration of the Building Materials Industry (RU)
oblpromtekhsnab ... Oblast Office of Materials and Equipment Supply of an Oblpromsovet (RU)
oblproyekt ... Oblast Planning Office (RU)
oblproyekt ... Planning Institute of an Oblispolkom (RU)
oblRATAU ... Oblast Branch of the Ukrainian News Agency (RU)
Oblrechtrans ... Oblast Administration for Transportation Development of Small Rivers (RU)
Oblrybolovpotrebsoyuz ... Oblast Union of Fishermen's Cooperatives (RU)
Oblsel'stroy ... Oblast Administration for Rural and Kolkhoz Construction (RU)
oblSES .... Oblast Sanitary and Epidemiological Station (RU)
Oblshveypromsoyuz ... Oblast Garment Producers' Union (RU)
OblSNKh ..... Oblast Council of the National Economy (RU)
Oblsobes .... Oblast Department of Social Security (RU)
oblsortsemovoshch ... Oblast Office for the Procurement and Marketing of High-Quality Vegetable Seeds (RU)
oblsovprof ... Oblast Council of Trade Unions (RU)
oblsportsoyuz ... Oblast Council of the Union of Sports Societies and Organizations (RU)
Oblstrompromsoyuz ... Oblast Producers' Cooperative Union for the Manufacture of Building Materials (RU)
Oblstromtrest ... Oblast Trust of the Building Materials Industry (RU)
Oblt .... Oberleutnant [*German*]
oblTEK .... Oblast Transportation and Forwarding Office (RU)
Obltekstil'promsoyuz ... Oblast Textile Producers' Cooperative Union (RU)
obltekstil'shveypromsoyuz ... Oblast Producers' Union of the Textile and Garment Industries (RU)
oblTEU .... Oblast Tourist and Excursions Administration (RU)
obltop .... Oblast Administration of the Fuel Industry (RU)
Obltrikotazhpromsoyuz ... Oblast Knit Goods Producers' Union (RU)
obl ts .... Oblast Center (RU)
OBLUNKhU ... Oblast Administration of the Statistical Survey of the National Economy (RU)
oblurs .... Oblast Administration of Workers' Supply (RU)
oblUSKh ..... Oblast Administration of Agriculture (RU)
OblV .... Oblastni Velitelstvi [*Regional Headquarters (of the National Security Corps)*] (CZ)
oblvodkhoz ... Oblast Administration of Water Management (RU)
oblvoyenkomat ... Oblast Military Commissariat (RU)
OblVTEK ..... Oblast Medical Commission for Determination of Disability (RU)
oblzags .... Oblast Department of the Civil Registry (RU)
Oblzdrav ..... Oblast Department of Public Health (RU)
oblzo .... Oblast Land Department (RU)
Oblzoovetsnab ... Oblast Veterinary Technical Supply Office (RU)
oblzu .... Oblast Land Administration (RU)
Obm .... Obmann [*German*]
OBM .... Office Bugesera-Mayaga (MAR)
ob/min .... Revolutions per Minute (BU)
OBMP .... Separate Marine Battalion (RU)
OBN .... Department of Biological Sciences (of the Academy of Sciences, USSR) (RU)
OBN .... Osrodek Badan Naukowych [*Scientific Research Center*] (POL)
obn .... Published, Made Public (BU)
OBNI .... Orszagos Bor- es Nemikortani Intezet [*National Institute for Dermatology and Venereal Diseases*] (HU)
OBNYH .... Orszagos Bunugyi Nyilvantarto Hivatal [*National Office of Criminal Records*] (HU)
OB-O .... Obavestajno Odeljenje [*Information Department*] [*Military*] (YU)
OBO .... Oddzial Budowy Osiedli [*Branch of Settlement Construction*] (POL)
OBO .... Oklopni Borbeni Odredi [*Armored Combat Detachments*] (YU)
obo .... Separate Maintenance Battalion (BU)
obo .... Separate Service Battalion (RU)
Oborongiz ... State Scientific and Technical Publishing House of Literature on Defense (RU)
obp .... Ammunition Supply Section (RU)
OBP .... Combat Training Section (RU)
OBP .... Ochrana Bezpecnosti Praca [*Labor Safety*] (CZ)
OBP .... Reciprocal Bearing (RU)
OBP .... Single Sideband (RU)
OBP .... Total Lateral Displacement [*Navy*] (RU)
obpo .... Obispo [*Bishop*] [*Spanish*]
obr .... Image, Face, Portrait (BU)
obr .... Model [*Accompanied by year*] (RU)
Obr .... Obavestenje Broj [*Information Number*] (YU)
obr .... Obrot [*Revolution*] [*Polish*]
OBr .... Oklopna Brigada [*Armored Brigade*] (YU)
OBR .... Overseas Business Reports (MAR)
OBR .... Ruse Okrug Library (BU)
obrab .... Revised (BU)
obrabot .... Processed, Worked, Machined (RU)
obr/min .... Obrotow na Minute [*Revolutions per Minute*] [*Polish*]
obro .... Outubro [*October*] [*Portuguese*] (GPO)
obrs .... Separate Signal Brigade (RU)
obs .... Observer [*Observe*] [*Danish*] (GPO)
obs .... Observera [*Observe*] [*Swedish*] (GPO)
OBS .... Outward-Bound Schools (ML)
OBS .... Separate Signal Battalion (RU)
OBSA .... Joint Standardization Office of the Aircraft Industry (TsAGI) (RU)
observ .... Observatory (RU)
obshch .... General, Common, Aggregate (RU)
obshchedostup ... Moderately Priced, Open to All, Generally Accessible (RU)
obshchepit ... Public Eating Establishment (RU)
obshch tit l ... General Title Page, Main Title Page (RU)
obshtestv ... Social (BU)
Obsht podem ... Obshtestven Podem [*Social Uplift*] [*A periodical*] (BU)
ob sp .... Obiit sine Prole [*Died without Issue*] [*Latin*] (GPO)
Obsre .... Observatoire [*Observatory*] [*Military map abbreviation*] [*World War I*] [*French*] (MTD)
OBSS .... Office Beninois de Securite Sociale [*Benin Office of Social Security*] (AF)
Obst .... Oberst [*German*]
Obstal' .... Obukhov Steel Foundry (RU)
Obstlt .... Oberstleutnant [*German*]
OBTI .... Association of Technical Publishing Houses (RU)
OBTI .... Oblast Office of Technical Information (RU)
OBTI .... Office of Technical Information Based on Public Participation (RU)
OBTI .... Specialized Office of Technical Information (RU)
OBTO .... Separate Armored Detachment (RU)
obtrr .... Separate Loading-Unloading Operations Battalion (BU)
OBU .... Oblastni Telefonni Ustredna [*Regional Telephone Exchange*] (CZ)
OBU .... Obvodny Bansky Urad [*District Mining Office*] (CZ)
obuch .... Teaching, Instruction, Training (RU)
OBV .... Department for Agricultural Pest Control (RU)
Obv .... Oberbauvorschriften [*Track Superstructure Regulations*] (EG)
OBV .... Okresni Branny Vybor [*District Defense Committee*] (CZ)
obv .... Separate Convalescent Battalion (RU)
OBV .... Varna Okrug Library (BU)

ob v .... Volumetric Weight (RU)
OBVNO........ Separate Battalion of People's Militia (RU)
ob-vo.......... Society, Company (RU)
ObVS........... Obvodni Vybor Svazu [*Area Trade Union Committee*] (CZ)
obw .... Obwieszczenie [*Proclamation*] (POL)
obw .... Obwoluta [*Book Jacket*] (POL)
obwol .... Obwoluta [*Book Jacket*] [*Polish*]
obyasn .... Explained, Explanatory (BU)
ob"yasn ...... Explanation (RU)
ob"yavl .... Announcement, Declaration (RU)
ob"yemn..... Volume, Volumetric (RU)
ob"yemn ch ... Part by Volume (RU)
ob"yemnotsentrir ... Body-Centered (RU)
ObZ .... Obranne Zpravodajstvi [*Counterintelligence*] (CZ)
obz .... Separate Smokescreen Battalion (BU)
OBZAMINI... Ministerstvo Zahranicniho Obchodu [*Ministry of Foreign Trade (Cable address)*] (CZ)
Oc................ Ocean [*Ocean*] [*Polish*]
OC............... Office Central pour la Cooperation Industrielle Internationale (MAR)
oc .... Oktanove Cislo [*Octane Number*] (CZ)
oc .... Opere Citato [*In the Work Cited*] [*Latin*] (GPO)
OC............... Ordnance Corps (ML)
OCA .... Office de Commercialisation Agricole [*Agricultural Marketing Bureau*] [*Guinean*] (AF)
OCA .... Operation Crossroads Africa (MAR)
OCA .... Organisation Combat Anarchiste [*Anarchist Combat Organization*] [*French*] (PPW)
OCA .... Organizacao dos Comunistas de Angola (MAR)
OCA .... Organizacao Cultural dos Angolanos (MAR)
OCA .... Organizacion de Cooperativas Americanas [*Organization of American Cooperatives*] (LA)
OCABE........ Office de Coordination Atomique de Belgique [*Belgian Office of Atomic Coordination*] (WER)
OCAD.......... Office de Commercialisation Agricole du Dahomey (MAR)
OCAD.......... Office de Commercialisation des Produits Agricoles du Dahomey (MAR)
OCAD.......... Oficiul Central de Aprovizionare si Desfacere [*Central Office for Supply and Sales*] (RO)
OCAL .... Organization of Communist Action in Lebanon (PD)
OCAM .... Organisation Commune Africaine et Mauricienne [*African-Mauritian Common Organization*] (AF)
OCAMM ...... Organisation Commune Africaine, Malgache, et Mauricienne (MAR)
OCAPAM .... Office Central Africain de Productions Agronomiques et Medicinales (MAR)
OCAS.......... Office de Commercialisation Agricole du Senegal [*Agricultural Marketing Office of Senegal*] (AF)
OCAU.......... Office de Cooperation et d'Accueil Universitaire (MAR)
OCB............ Organisation Camerounaise de la Banane (MAR)
OCBC.......... Overseas Chinese Banking Corporation [*Singapore*]
OCBN.......... Organisation Commune Benin-Niger des Chemins de Fer et des Transports [*Joint Benin-Niger Railroad and Transport Organization*] (AF)
OCBV.......... Office Communautaire du Betail et de la Viande [*Community Livestock and Meat Office*] (AF)
OCC .... Octagon Car Club (EA)
OCC .... Office Commercial Camerounais (MAR)
OCC .... Oficina de Circulacion Certificada [*Bogota*] (COL)
OCC .... Organisation Clandestine du Continent [*Algerian*] (MAR)
OCC .... Organisation Combat Communiste [*Communist Combat Organization*] [*French*] (PPW)
OCCE.......... Office Congolais du Commerce Exterieur (MAR)
OCCGE .... Organisation de Coordination et de Cooperation pour la Lutte Contre les Grandes Endemies en Afrique de l'Ouest [*Organization for Coordination and Cooperation in the Control of Major Endemic Diseases in West Africa*] (AF)
OCCGEAC ... Organisation de Coordination et de Cooperation Contre les Grandes Endemies en Afrique Centrale (MAR)
OCCI .... Officer in Charge - Criminal Investigation (ML)
OCD .... Office de Cooperation au Developpement [*Office of Cooperation in Developmental Activity*] [*Belgian*] (AF)
OCDE.......... Organisation de Cooperation et de Developpement Economique [*Organization for Economic Cooperation and Development*] [*Use OECD*] [*French*] (WER)
OCDE.......... Organizacao de Cooperacao e Desenvolvimento Economico [*Organization for Economic Cooperation and Development*] [*Use OECD*] [*Portuguese*] (WER)
OCDN.......... Organisation Commune Dahomey-Niger des Chemins de Fer et des Transports (MAR)
OCE............ Office de Commercialisation et d'Exportation [*Marketing and Export Office*] [*Moroccan*] (AF)
OCE............ Office de Controle et d'Exportation [*Control and Export Office*] [*Moroccan*] (AF)
OCEAC .... Organisation de Coordination pour la Lutte Contre les Endemies en Afrique Centrale [*Organization for Coordination in Control of Endemic Diseases in Central Africa*] (AF)
OCE-BR ...... Organizacion Comunista de Espana - Bandera Roja [*Communist Organization of Spain - Red Flag*] (WER)
OCF............ Oficiul Central Farmaceutic [*Central Pharmaceutical Office*] (RO)
OCFL.......... Office Congolaise des Chemins de Fer des Grands Lacs (MAR)
OCFLN........ Organisation Civile du Front de Liberation Nationale [*Algerian*] (MAR)
OCF-ML ...... Organisation Communiste de France - Marxiste-Leniniste [*Communist Organization of France - Marxist-Leninist*] (PPW)
OCFT.......... Office du Chemin de Fer Transcamerounais (MAR)
OCG .... Ostry Casovy Granat [*Time Fuse Grenade*] (CZ)
OCh............ Ink Oscillograph (RU)
OCh............ Octane Number (RU)
OCH .... Office Congolais de l'Habitat [*Congolese Housing Office*] (AF)
och .... Very, Very Much, Greatly (RU)
ochishch..... Purified, Cleaned, Refined (RU)
OChK .... Detachable Wing Sections (RU)
OChM......... Relative Frequency Modulation (RU)
OChS .... General Libraries Association (BU)
OChS .... Okoliya Library Council (BU)
OChS .... Okrug Library Council (BU)
OChT.......... Octane Number of Fuel (RU)
OChT.......... Relative Frequency Telegraphy (RU)
OChZ.......... Orel Watchmaking Plant (RU)
OChZ.......... Ostravske Chemicke Zavody [*Ostrava Chemical Plants*] (CZ)
OChZ.......... Public Reading Room (RU)
OCI............ Integrated Revolutionary Organizations [*Cuban*] (PPW)
OCI............ Office of Criminal Investigation (ML)
OCI............ Oficina Central de Informacion [*Central Information Office*] [*Peruvian*] (LA)
OCI............ Oficina Central de Informacion [*Central Information Office*] [*Venezuelan*] (LA)
OCI............ Organisation Communiste Internationaliste [*Internationalist Communist Organization*] [*French*] (PPW)
OCI............ Organisation de la Conference Islamique [*Organization of the Islamic Conference - OIC*] (EA)
OCI............ Organisation pour la Cooperation Industrielle [*Industrial Cooperation Organization*] [*Algerian*] (AF)
OCI............ Organisme de Cooperation Industrielle (MAR)
OCIBEC ...... Office de Commerce et de l'Industrie de la Belgique et du Congo (MAR)
OCIBU......... Office des Cultures Industrielles du Burundi [*Burundi Industrial Crops Office*] (AF)
OCIC .... Office Cherifien Interprofessionnel des Cereales [*Moroccan*] (MAR)
OCIC .... Organisation Catholique Internationale du Cinema [*International Catholic Organization for Cinema and Audiovisuals*] (EA)
OCIMF......... Oil Companies International Marine Forum (EA)
OCINAM...... Office Cinematographique National du Mali (MAR)
OCIP........... Oficina Central de Informacion de Personas [*Missing Persons Information Center*] [*Uruguayan*] (LA)
OCIP........... Organisme Commun des Institutions de Prevoyance [*Algerian*] (MAR)
OCIR........... Office des Cultures Industrielles du Rwanda [*Rwandan Industrial Crops Office*] (AF)
OCIRU .... Office des Cafes Indigenes du Ruanda et Burundi (MAR)
OCIRU .... Office des Cultures Industrielles du Ruanda-Urundi (MAR)
OCL............ Organizatia Comerciala Locala [*Local Trade Organization*] (RO)
OCL............ Overseas Containers Ltd. (MAR)
OCLAE .... Organizacion Continental Latinoamericana de Estudiantes [*Continental Organization of Latin American Students*] (LA)
OCLALAV ... Organisation Commune de Lutte Antiacridienne et de Lutte Antiaviaire [*Joint Anti-Locust and Anti-Aviarian Organization*] (AF)
OCLC .... Organizacion Comunista "Lucha de Clases" [*"Class Struggle" Communist Organization*] [*Spanish*] (WER)
OCLEAC ..... Organisation de Coordination pour la Lutte Contre les Endemies en Afrique Centrale [*Organization for Coordination in Control of Endemic Diseases in Central Africa*] [*Use OCEAC*] (AF)
OCLPP .... Oficiul pentru Construirea de Locuinte Proprietate Personala [*Office for the Construction of Privately Owned Housing*] (RO)
OCM........... Office des Changes Marocaines (MAR)
OCM........... Oficiul de Control al Marfurilor [*Office for the Control of Goods*] (RO)
OCMAD....... Organizatia Cooperativei Mestesugaresti de Aprovizionare si Desfacere [*Artisan Cooperative Organization for Supply and Sales*] (RO)
OCMB .... Officer in Charge - Marine Branch (ML)
OCMI.......... Organizacion Consultiva Maritima Intergubernamental [*Intergovernmental Maritime Consultative Organization*] [*Use IMCO*] (LA)
OCM-LP ...... Organizacao Comunista Marxista-Leninista Portuguesa [*Portuguese Communist Organization, Marxist-Leninist*] (PPE)
OCMLR .... Organisation Communiste Marxiste-Leniniste de la Reunion [*Reunionese Communist Organization, Marxist-Leninist*] (PPW)

OCN .... Organizacion Contrasubversiva Nacional [*National Counter-Subversive Organization*] [*Spanish*] (WER)
OCO .... Office Congolais de l'Okoume (MAR)
OCOA .... Organismo Coordinador de Operaciones Antisubversivas [*Counter-Subversive Operations Coordinating Agency*] [*Uruguayan*] (LA)
OCOD .... Officer Commanding Ordnance Directorate (ML)
OCORA .... Office de Cooperation Radiophonique [*Office of Radio Cooperation*] [*French*] (AF)
OCOT .... Oficiul de Cadastru si Organizarea Teritoriului [*Office for Cadaster and Territorial Organization*] (RO)
OCP .... Office Cherifien des Phosphates [*Moroccan Phosphates Office*] (AF)
OCP .... Oncocarciasis Control Programme (MAR)
OCP .... Organisation Commerciale de la Production Bananiere de la Cote-d'Ivoire (MAR)
OCP .... Organisation de Controle des Pollutions (MAR)
OCP .... Organizacion Comunista Proletaria [*Proletarian Communist Organization*] [*Mexican*] (LA1)
OCPC .... Officer in Charge of Police Circle (ML)
OCPE .... Office Communautaire de Promotion des Echanges [*Community Trade Promotion Office*] (AF)
OCPHV .... Office de Commercialisation des Produits de Haute Volta [*Marketing Office for Products of Upper Volta*] (AF)
OCPI .... Office Central de la Presse Illustree [*Illustrated Press Central Office*] [*French*] (AF)
OCPT .... Office Congolais des Postes et Telecommunications (MAR)
OCR .... Organisation des Chantiers de la Revolution [*Organization of Work Camps of the Revolution*] [*Guinean*] (AF)
OCR .... Organisation for the Collaboration of Railways [*See also OSShD*] (EA)
OCRA .... Organisation Clandestine de la Revolution Algerienne [*Clandestine Organization of the Algerian Revolution*] (AF)
OCRS .... Organisation Commune des Regions Sahariennes [*Common Organization of the Saharan Regions*] (AF)
OCS .... Office de la Canne et du Sucre [*Cane and Sugar Office*] [*Malagasy*] (AF)
OCS .... Officer in Charge - Station (ML)
OCS .... Organisme de Cooperation Scientifique [*Organization for Scientific Cooperation*] [*Algerian, French*] (AF)
OCSB .... Officer in Charge - Special Branch (ML)
OCSE .... Organizzazione di Cooperazione e di Sviluppo Economico [*Organization for Economic Cooperation and Development*] [*Use OECD*] [*Italian*] (WER)
OCSMA .... Organisme Central du Service Militaire Adapte (MAR)
OCSS .... Officer in Charge - Secret Societies (ML)
oct .... October [*October*] [*Dutch*] (GPO)
oct .... Octobre [*October*] [*French*]
OCT .... Office du Commerce de Tunisie [*Tunisian Trade Office*] (AF)
OCT .... Office de Cooperation du Travail [*Office of Labor Cooperation*] [*Zairian*] (AF)
OCT .... Okresni Cirkevni Tajemnik [*District Church Secretary*] (CZ)
OCT .... Organisation Communiste des Travailleurs [*Communist Organization of Workers*] [*French*] (PPW)
Octbre .... Octubre [*October*] [*Spanish*]
octe .... Octubre [*October*] [*Spanish*]
OCTI .... Office Central des Transports Internationaux par Chemins de Fer [*Central Office for International Railway Transport*] (EA)
OCTK .... Office Central du Travail au Katanga (MAR)
OCTNU .... Oficina de Cooperacion Tecnica de las Naciones Unidas [*United Nations Technical Cooperation Office*] (LA)
OCTRA .... Office du Chemin de Fer Transgabonais [*Trans-Gabonese Railroad Office*] (AF)
OCU .... Organizacion de Consumidores y Usuarios [*Organization of Consumers and Users*] [*Spanish*] (WER)
OCV .... Office des Cultures Vivrieres (MAR)
OCV .... Orszagos Cirkusz Vallalat [*National Circus Enterprise*] (HU)
OD .... Cutoff Throttle Valve (RU)
od .... Detachment (BU)
od .... Och Dylikt [*And the Like*] [*Swedish*] (GPO)
od .... Oder [*Or*] (EG)
OD .... Odessa Railroad (RU)
OD .... Oditur [*Judge Advocate*] (IN)
OD .... Oklopna Divizija [*Armored Division*] (YU)
OD .... Okonomisk Demokrati [*Economic Democracy*] [*Danish*] (WEN)
OD .... Operacni Dustojnik [*Operations Officer*] (CZ)
OD .... Operations Duty Officer (BU)
OD .... Operations Duty Officer, Duty Officer (RU)
OD .... Optimal Distribution [*Linguistics*] (RU)
OD .... Optisches Drehungsvermoegen [*Optical Rotation*] [*German*]
OD .... Opus Dei [*Catholic Lay Organization*] [*Spanish*] (WER)
OD .... Ordnance Directorate (ML)
OD .... Orta Dalga [*Medium Wave*] (TU)
OD .... Osmotic Pressure (RU)
ODA .... Oblastni Dum Armady [*Regional Armed Forces Building*] (CZ)
ODA .... Official Development Assistance (MAR)
ODA .... Okrug State Archive (BU)
ODA-IPER ... Ankara Ticaret Odalari Personnel Sendikasi [*Ankara Chamber of Commerce Personnel Union*] (TU)
ODAMAP ..... Office Dahomeen des Manutentions Portuaires (MAR)
ODAS .... Osrednji Drzavni Arhiv Slovenije [*Central State Archives of Slovenia*] (YU)
OdAZ .... Odessa Automobile Assembly Plant (RU)
odb .... Odbitka [*Copy*] [*Polish*]
ODB .... Separate Decontamination Battalion (RU)
ODB .... Separate Landing Battalion (RU)
odb .... Separate Smoke Battalion (BU)
odc .... Odcinek [*Section, Sector*] [*Polish*]
ODC .... Office Douanier Congolais (MAR)
ODC .... Oficiul de Desfacere a Carnii [*Office for Meat Sales*] (RO)
ODCA .... Organizacion Democrata Cristiana de America [*Christian Democratic Organization of the Americas*] (LA)
ODCD .... Oficiul pentru Deservirea Corpului Diplomatic [*Office for Service to the Diplomatic Corps*] (RO)
ODD .... "Friends of Children" Society [*1924-1935*] (RU)
odd .... Oddeleni [*Department*] (CZ)
odd .... Oddil [*Battalion*] [*Military*] (CZ)
ODD .... Organisation "Dienst fuer Deutschland" [*"Service for Germany" Organization*] (EG)
ODDEP .... Organismos Dioikiseos kai Diakheiriseos Ekklisiastikis Periousias [*Organization for the Administration and Management of Church Property*] [*Greek*] (GC)
od dgl .... Oder Dergleichen [*Or the Like*] (EG)
ODDJEN .... Oditur Djenderal [*Judge Advocate General*] (IN)
ODDS .... Organizzazione delle Donne Democratiche Somale (MAR)
oddz .... Oddzial [*Branch, Department, Section*] (POL)
ODE .... Oficiul de Documentare Energetica [*Office for Power Documentation*] (RO)
ODEACEC ... Organizacion de Asociaciones Contra el Comunismo [*Organization of Associations Against Communism*] [*Guatemalan*] (LA)
ODEB .... Separate Road Maintenance Battalion (RU)
ODECA .... Organizacion de Estados Centroamericanos [*Organization of Central American States*] [*Use OCAS*] (LA)
ODECABE ... Organizacion Deportiva Centroamericana y del Caribe [*Central American and Caribbean Sports Organization*] [*Guatemalan*] (LA)
ODECOB ..... Organismo de Desarrollo del Complejo Bayovar [*Agency for Development of the Bayovar Complex*] [*Peruvian*] (LA)
ODEF .... Office National de Developpement et d'Exploitation des Ressources Forestieres [*National Agency for the Development and Exploitation of Forest Resources*] [*Togolese*] (AF)
ODEKA .... Organisation pour l'Amenagement et le Developpement du Bassin de la Riviere Kagera (MAR)
ODEM .... Office des Engins Mecaniques [*Office of Mechanical Equipment*] [*Cambodian*] (CL)
ODEM .... Orta Dogu Etitim Merkezi [*Middle East Training Center*] [*Preparatory school*] (TU)
ODEMO .... Organisation de Developpement du Moyen Ouest [*Middlewest Development Organization*] [*Malagasy*] (AF)
ODEP .... Organismos Dioikiseos Ekklisiastikis Periousias [*Organization for the Administration of Church Property*] [*Greek*] (GC)
ODEPA .... Oficina de Planificacion Agricola [*Agriculture Planning Office*] [*Chilean*] (LA)
ODEPA .... Organizacion Deportiva Panamericana [*Pan American Sports Organization - PASO*] (EA)
ODEPES .... Organismos Diakheiriseos Eidikon Poron Ergasiakon Somateion [*Organization for the Management of Labor Union Special Funds*] (GC)
ODEPLAN ... Oficina de Planificacion Nacional [*National Planning Office*] [*Chilean*] (LA)
ODETA .... Organisation pour le Developpement du Tourisme Africain [*Organization for the Development of African Tourism*] (AF)
ODF .... Department of Prerevolutionary Holdings [*In archives*] (RU)
ODF .... Finishing Decorative Plywood (RU)
OdF .... Opfer des Faschismus [*Victim of Fascism*] (EG)
ODG .... Optical Index Head (RU)
ODG .... Ordine del Giorno [*Order of the Day, Agenda*] [*Italian*] (WER)
ODG .... Organosis Dimokratikon Gynaikon [*Organization of Democratic Women*] [*Cypriot*] (GC)
ODG .... Reversible Generator (BU)
o dgl .... Oder Dergleichen [*Or the Like, Or Similar*] [*German*]
ODI .... Office pour le Developpement Industrial du Royaume du Maroc [*Moroccan*] (MAR)
ODI .... Okresni Dopravni Inspektorat [*District Traffic Inspection Bureau*] (CZ)
ODI .... Open Door International (EA)
ODI .... Orszagos Dietetikai Intezet [*National Dietetic Institute*] (HU)
ODISY .... Organismos Diakheiriseos (Pleonazondos) Symmakhikou Ylikou [*Allied (Surplus) Materiel Management Organization*] [*Greek*] (GC)
odj .... Odjezd [*Departure*] (CZ)
ODJ .... Opinion des Jeunes (MAR)
ODJR .... Organisation Democratique de la Jeunesse Reunionnaise [*Reunionese Democratic Youth Organization*] (AF)
ODK .... Long-Term Credit Department (RU)
ODK .... Okregowa Dyrekcja Kolejowa [*District Railroad Administration*] (POL)

ODK .... Orszagos Dokumentacios Kozpont [*National Documentation Center*] (HU)
ODKD .... Organismos Dimosion Ktimaton Dodekanisou [*Organization of Public Properties of the Dodecanese*] [*Greek*] (GC)
ODKO .... Osrodek Doskonalenia Kadr Oswiatowych [*Center for the Improvement of Teaching Personnel*] (POL)
OdI .... Oberdispatcherleitung [*Head Dispatching Office*] (EG)
ODLT .... Oblastni Dum Lidove Tvorivosti [*Regional Folk Arts Center*] (CZ)
ODM .... Overseas Development Ministry (MAR)
ODMO .... All-Union House of Clothing Models (RU)
ODMP .... Organismos Diakheiriseos Monastiriakis Periousias [*Organization for Administration of Monastery Property*] [*Greek*] (GC)
ODMTS .... Okoliya Depot of the Machine-Tractor Station (BU)
ODN .... "Down with Illiteracy" Society (RU)
odnokr .... Momentary (Aspect of Verb) (RU)
ODNT .... Oblast House of Folk Art (RU)
ODO .... Bath and Disinfection Unit (RU)
ODO .... Decontamination Unit (RU)
ODO .... District House of Officers (RU)
odobr .... Approved (BU)
odobr .... Approved (RU)
ODOKSAN ... Osmaneli Dokum Sanayi ve Ticaret AS [*Osmaneli Foundry Industry and Trade Corp.*] (TU)
ODOOS .... Osrodek Dokumentacji Obrabiarek i Obrobki Skrawaniem [*Machine Tool and Machining Documentation Center*] (POL)
ODOT .... Orszagjaro Diakok Orszagos Talalkozoja [*National Meeting of Touring Students*] (HU)
ODP .... Bath and Decontamination Station (RU)
ODP .... Bird Pox-Diphtheria (RU)
odp .... Foundations of the State and Law (BU)
odp .... Odpoledne [*Afternoon*] (CZ)
ODP .... Okrug State Enterprise (BU)
OdP .... Ordnung der Planung [*Order on Planning*] (EG)
ODP .... Organisation de Defense Populaire (MAR)
ODP .... Organizacao da Defensa Popular [*People's Defense Organization*] [*Angolan*] (AF)
ODP .... Supply and Maintenance Section (BU)
ODPG .... Organisation du Developpement de la Plaine de Gonaives [*Organization for the Development of the Gonaives Plain*] [*Haitian*] (LA)
ODPK .... Department of Long-Term Industrial Credit (RU)
ODPP .... Department of Long-Range Weather Forecasts (RU)
ODPT .... Oficiul de Documentare si Publicatii Tehnice [*Office for Documentation and Technical Publications*] (RO)
odpto .... Separate Antitank Battalion (RU)
odpvo .... Separate Air Defense Battalion (RU)
ODR .... Bath and Disinfection Company (RU)
ODR .... Organismo de Desarrollo Regional [*Regional Development Body*] [*Peruvian*] (LA)
ODR .... Society of Friends of Radio (RU)
ODRA .... Department of Ancient Manuscripts and Documents of the Institute of History of the Academy of Sciences, USSR (RU)
o drgl .... Oder Dergleichen [*Or the Like, Or Similar*] [*German*]
ODRL .... Department of Old Russian Literature (RU)
ODRP .... Oblast House of Education Workers (RU)
ODSB .... Separate Road-Building Battalion (RU)
ODSK .... Society of Friends of Soviet Cinematography (RU)
ODSNF .... Joint Far Eastern Fleet Observation Service (RU)
ODSP .... Consolidated State Economic Enterprises (BU)
ODSS .... Society of Friends of the Soviet Union (RU)
odst .... Odstavec [*Paragraph*] (CZ)
ODSZ .... Obchod Drobnym Spotrebnim Zbozim [*Retail Store of Small Consumer Goods*] (CZ)
ODT .... Organisation des Democrates Tunisiens [*Organization of Tunisian Democrats*] (AF)
ODTA .... Organisation pour le Developpement du Tourisme Africain [*Organization for the Development of African Tourism*] (AF)
ODTKA .... Separate Motor Torpedo Boat Division (RU)
ODTM .... Saponified Distilled Tall Oil (RU)
ODTO .... Special Road Transportation Department (RU)
ODTP .... Okrug State Commercial Enterprise (BU)
ODTS .... Department of Scenery and Technical Equipment [*Motion-picture studio*] (RU)
ODTU .... Orta Dogu Teknik Universitesi [*Middle East Technical University*] [*Ankara*] (TU)
ODTU-DER ... Orta Dogu Teknik Universitesi Talebe Dernegi [*Middle East Technical University Student Association*] (TU)
ODTUKMB ... Orta Dogu Teknik Universitesi Kibrisli Mezunlar Birligi [*Middle East Technical University Cypriot Graduates Union*] (TU)
ODU .... Bath and Disinfection Installation (RU)
ODU .... Integrated Dispatching Control (RU)
ODV .... Okresni Doplnovaci Velitelstvi [*District Headquarters of Military Records and Reserves*] (CZ)
ODVA .... Organisation du Developpement de la Vallee d'Artibonite [*Organization for the Development of the Artibonite Valley*] [*Haitian*] (LA)
ODVA .... Special Far Eastern Army (RU)
ODVF .... Society of Friends of the Air Fleet [*1923-1925*] (RU)
ODVO .... Odessa Military District (RU)
ODYE .... Omospondia Dikastikon Ypallilon Ellados [*Federation of Judiciary Employees of Greece*] (GC)
ODZ .... Blinding Smoke Screen (RU)
ODZS .... State Farms Trust (BU)
OE .... Common Emitter (RU)
Oe .... Ersted [*Oersted*] [*Unit of magnetizing intensity*] [*Polish*]
OE .... Oikonomiki Epitropi [*Finance Committee*] [*Greek*] (GC)
OE .... Omada "Epanastasi" [*"Revolution" Group*] [*Greek*] (GC)
oe .... Omorrythmos Etaireia [*Unlimited General Partnership*] (GC)
OE .... Otu Edo (MAR)
OEA .... Automobile Operation Department (RU)
OEA .... Organismos Epikourikis Asfaliseos [*Auxiliary Insurance Organization*] [*Greek*] (GC)
OEA .... Organizacion de Estados Americanos [*Organization of American States*] [*Use OAS*] (LA)
OEA .... Orszagos Energiagazdalkodasi Alap [*National Fund for Power Economy*] (HU)
OEA .... Orszagos Epuletjavitasi Alap [*National Fund for Building Repairs*] (HU)
OeAAB .... Oesterreichischer Arbeiter- und Angestelltenbund [*Austrian Workers' and Employees' League*] [*OeVP affiliate*] (WEN)
OeAMC .... Oesterreichische Alpine Montangesellschaft [*Austrian Alpine Mining Company*] (WEN)
OEAS .... Organismos Elengkhou ton di Aftokiniton Syngoinonion [*Organization for the Control of Automotive Communications*] [*Greek*] (GC)
OEB .... Separate Evacuation Battalion (RU)
OeBB .... Oesterreichische Bauernbund [*Austrian Farmers' League*] [*OeVP affiliate*] (WEN)
OeBB .... Oesterreichische Bundesbahnen [*Austrian State Railways*] (WEN)
OEBK .... Organisation pour l'Equipement Banana-Kinshasa (MAR)
OEBU .... Organizacion de Exiliados Brasilenos en Uruguay [*Organization of Brazilian Exiles in Uruguay*] (LA)
OEC .... Office d'Etudes sur le Caoutchouc [*Rubber Studies Office*] (CL)
OEC .... Office des Etudiants Cambodgiens [*Office of Cambodian Students*] (CL)
OEC .... Organisation Europeenne du Charbon [*European Coal Organization*] [*French*] (WER)
OEC .... Oxford Editions of Cuneiform Texts (MAR)
OECD .... Organization for Economic Cooperation and Development [*Formerly, Organization for European Economic Cooperation*]
OECDC .... Organization for Economic Cooperation among Developing Countries (AF)
OECD-NEA ... Organization for Economic Cooperation and Development, Nuclear Energy Agency (SJT)
OECE .... Organisation Europeenne de Cooperation Economique [*Organization for European Economic Cooperation*] [*Use OEEC*] [*Replaced by OECD*] [*See also OCDE*] [*French*] (WER)
OECE .... Organizacion Europea de Cooperacion Economica [*Organization for European Economic Cooperation*] [*Use OEEC*] (LA)
OECF .... Japanese Overseas Economic Cooperation Fund (MAR)
OECGD .... Overseas Export Credit Guarantee Department (MAR)
OECS .... Organization of Eastern Caribbean States (LA)
oed .... Oper Edei Deixei [*Which Was To Be Demonstrated*] (GC)
OEDE .... Omospondia Ergaton Dermatos Ellados [*Federation of Greek Leather Workers*] (GC)
OEDOSZ ..... Orvos-Egeszsegugyi Dolgozok Szakszervezete [*Trade Union of Workers and Employees in the Medical Services*] (HU)
OEDV .... Organismos Ekdoseos Didaktikon Vivlion [*Organization for the Publication of Textbooks*] [*Formerly, OESV*] [*Greek*] (GC)
OEE .... Omospondia Efimeridopolon Ellados [*Federation of Greek Newspaper Vendors*] (GC1)
OEE .... Orszagos Erdeszeti Egyesulet [*National Forestry Association*] (HU)
OEEC .... Organization for European Economic Cooperation (SJT)
OEESIO .... Omospondia Elevtheron Ergatikon Somateion Imikratikon Organismon [*Federation of Free Labor Unions of Semi-Governmental Organizations*] (GC)
OEEYDKE ... Omospondia Ergatotekhniton kai Ektakton Ypallilon Dimon kai Koinotiton Ellados [*Federation of Workers, Technicians, and Temporary Employees of the Municipalities and Communes of Greece*] (GC)
OEF .... Orszagos Erdeszeti Foigazgatosag [*National Directorate of Forestry*] (HU)
OEFEK .... Omospondia Ethnikon Foititikon Enoseon Kyprou [*Federation of National Student Unions of Cyprus*] (GC)
OEFJ .... Orszagosan Egyseges Foglalkozasi Jegyzek [*Nationally Uniform Employment Register*] (HU)
OEFK .... Oikonomiki Eforia Forologias Klironomion [*Directorate of Inheritance Taxation*] [*Greek*] (GC)
OEFPN .... Department of Economic, Philosophical, and Legal Sciences (of the Academy of Sciences, USSR) (RU)
OeGB .... Oesterreichischer Gewerkschaftsbund [*Austrian Trade Union Federation*] (WEN)

OEGH .... Orszagos Energiagazdalkodasi Hatosag [*National Energy Management Authority*] (HU)
OEH .... Orszagos Energiagazdalkodasi Hatosag [*National Energy Management Authority*] (HU)
OEH .... Orszagos Epitesugyi Hivatal [*National Construction Office*] (HU)
OEI .... Oficina de Educacion Iberoamericana [*Ibero-American Bureau of Education - IABE*] (EA)
OEI .... Orszagos Epitoipari Igazgatosag [*National Directorate of the Building Industry*] (HU)
OEIFAE .... Omospondia Epangelmation Idioktiton Fortigon Avtokiniton Ellados [*Federation of Professional Truck Owners of Greece*] (GC)
OeIG .... Oesterreichische Industrieverwaltungs-Gesellschaft [*Austrian Industries Management Company*] (WEN)
OEIS .... Odessa Electrotechnical Institute of Communications (RU)
Oek .... Oekonomie [*German*]
OEK .... Omospondia Ergodoton Kyprou [*Federation of Cypriot Employers*] (GC1)
OEK .... Organisation d'Etudiants Khmers [*Organization of Cambodian Students*] (CL)
OEK .... Organismos Ellinikis Katoikias [*Greek Housing Organization*] (GC)
OEK .... Organismos Ergatikis Katoikias [*Workers' Housing Organization*] [*Greek*] (GC)
OEK .... Orszagos Epitesugyi Kormanybiztos [*National Commissioner of Construction*] (HU)
OEK .... Orszagos Epuletjavitasi Kozpont [*National Center of Building Repairs*] (HU)
OEKAE .... Omospondia Ergaton, Keramopoion, kai Angeioplaston Ellados [*Federation of Tile, Brick, and Ceramic Workers of Greece*] (GC)
OEKhVE ...... Omospondia Ergatoypallilon Khimikis Viomikhanias Ellados [*Federation of Chemical Industry Workers of Greece*] (GC)
OEKULEI ..... Oekonomisch-Kultureller Leistungsvergleich [*Economic-Cultural Comparison, Economic-Cultural Competition*] (EG)
OEKVE .... Omospondia Ergatoypallilon Kapnoviomikhanias Ellados [*Federation of Greek Tobacco Industry Workers and Employees*] (GC)
OEL .... Oil Exploration License (MAR)
OeLB .... Oertlicher Landwirtschaftlicher Betrieb [*Local Agricultural Enterprise*] (EG)
OELMEK ..... Omospondia Ellinon Leitourgon Mesis Ekpaidevseos Kyprou [*Federation of Greek Secondary School Teachers of Cyprus*] (GC)
OELTEK ...... Omospondia Ellinon Leitourgon Tekhnikis Ekpaidevseos Kyprou [*Federation of Greek Technical School Teachers of Cyprus*] (GC)
OEM .... Omospondia Ergaton Metallou [*Metal Workers' Federation*] [*Greek*] (GC)
OEM .... Organizacion Editorial Mexicana [*Mexican Publishing Organization*] (LA)
OEME .... Organotiki Epitropi Mathitikon Ekdiloseon [*Organizational Committee for Student Demonstrations*] [*Cypriot*] (GC)
OEMEE .... Omospondia Ergatotekhniton Metallevtikon Epikheiriseon Ellados [*Federation of Workers and Technicians of Mining Enterprises of Greece*] (GC)
OEMG .... Omospondia Ergaton Metaforon kai Georgias [*Federation of Transport and Farm Workers*] [*Cypriot*] (GC)
OEMI .... Oficina de Emergencia del Ministerio del Interior [*Interior Ministry Emergency Office*] [*Chilean*] (LA)
OEML .... Organosi Ellinon Marxiston-Leniniston [*Organization of Greek Marxist-Leninists*] (GC)
OeMV .... Oesterreichische Mineraloelverwaltung AG [*Austrian Oil Administration*] (WEN)
OEN .... Organosis Ethnikis Neolaias [*Organization of Nationalist Youth*] [*Cypriot*] (GC)
OENO .... Omospondia Ellinikon Navtergatikon Organoseon [*Federation of Greek Maritime Worker Organizations*] (GC)
OEOS .... Organismos Evropaikis Oikonomikis Synergasias [*Organization for European Economic Cooperation*] (GC)
OEP .... Consolidated Electric Power Enterprises (BU)
OeP .... Oekonomische Planinformation [*Economic Plan Information*] (EG)
OEP .... Omospondia Epangelmation Peiraios [*Piraeus Tradesmen's Federation*] (GC)
OEP .... Organosi "Ergatiki Pali" [*"Worker Struggle" Organization*] [*Greek*] (GC)
OEPD .... Organismos Ellinikou Papoutsiou kai Dermatos [*Greek Shoe and Leather Organization*] (GC)
OEPL .... Organisation de l'Enseignement Prive Laic [*Private Lay Education Organization*] [*Cameroonian*] (AF)
OEPT .... Office Equatorial des Postes et Telecommunications (MAR)
OER .... Organizatsiia Ekonomicheskovo Razvitiia (MAR)
OER .... Separate Evacuation Company (RU)
OeRF .... Oesterreichischer Rundfunk-Fernsehen [*Austrian Radio and Television System*] (WEN)
OeRG .... Oesterreichischer Rundfunk GmbH [*Austrian Broadcasting Co.*] (WEN)
OERM .... Organisation Economique Regionale du Maghreb (MAR)
OERS .... Organisation des Etats Riverains du Fleuve Senegal [*Organization of Senegal River States*] (AF)
OES .... All-Union Institute for the Planning of Electric Power Projects (RU)
OES .... Base-Load Electric Power Plant (RU)
OES .... Integrated Power System, Grid System (RU)
OES .... Oblast Economic Conference (RU)
OES .... Organisation des Etats Sahariens (MAR)
OES .... Organotiki Epitropi Syndiaskepsis [*Conference Organization Committee*] (GC1)
oes .... Osztrak Schilling [*Austrian Schilling*] (HU)
OESE .... Omospondia Ekdromikon Somateion Ellados [*Federation of Hiking Clubs of Greece*] (GC)
OESO .... Organisatie voor Economische Samenwerking en Ontwikkeling [*Organization for Economic Cooperation and Development*] [*Use OECD*] [*Dutch*] (WEN)
OESR .... Organization for Economic Cooperation and Development [*OECD*] (RU)
OeSS .... Oekonomisches System des Sozialismus [*Economic System of Socialism*] (EG)
OESU .... Integrated Power System of the Ukrainian SSR (RU)
OeSU .... Oesterreichische Studenten Union [*Austrian Students' Union*] [*OeVP affiliate*] (WEN)
OESV .... Organismos Ekdoseos Skholikon Vivlion [*Later, OEDV*] [*Greek*] (GC)
OESVE .... Omospondia Ergoliptikon Syndesmon Voreiou Ellados [*Federation of Contractors Associations of Northern Greece*] (GC)
OESz .... Orvos-Egeszsegugyi Szakszervezet [*Medical Sanitation Trade Union*] (HU)
OET .... Orszagos Epitesugyi Tanacs [*National Council on Construction*] (HU)
OETE .... Omospondia Ergaton Typou Ellados [*Federation of Greek Press Workers*] (GC)
OETI .... Orszagos Elelmezes- es Taplalkozastudomanyi Intezet [*National Institute of Food and Nutrition*] (HU)
OETs .... United Evangelical Churches (BU)
OETTI .... Orszagos Elelmezes- es Taplalkozastudomanyi Intezet [*National Institute of Food and Nutrition*] (HU)
OeTV .... Oeffentlicher Dienst, Transport, und Verkehr [*Public Service, Transportation, and Communications (Labor Union)*] [*West German*] (EG)
OETY .... Omospondiaki Epitropi Trapezikon Ypallilon [*Federative Committee of Bank Employees*] (GC)
OEVA .... Office de l'Experimentation et de la Vulgarisation Agricoles [*Tunisian*] (MAR)
OEVA .... Omospondia Epangelmation kai Viotekhnon Athinon [*Federation of Tradesmen and Craftsmen of Athens*] [*The last initial varies according to location*] (GC)
OeVB .... Oertlicher Volkseigener Betrieb [*Locally Administered State Enterprise*] (EG)
OeVP .... Oesterreichische Volkspartei [*Austrian People's Party*] (WEN)
OeVW .... Oertliche Versorgungswirtschaft [*Local Public Utilities*] (EG)
OeWB .... Oesterreichischer Wirtschaftsbund [*Austrian Business League*] [*OeVP affiliate*] (WEN)
OEY .... Omospondia Eforiakon Ypallilon [*Federation of Tax Assessors*] (GC1)
OEY .... Omospondia Emborikon Ypallilon [*Federation of Commercial Employees*] [*Cypriot*] (GC)
OEYSK .... Omospondia Ergatotekhniton kai Ypallilon Stratiotikon Katastimaton [*Federation of Military Establishment Personnel*] [*Cypriot*] (GC)
OEYTE .... Omospondia Ergatotekhniton-Ypallilon Tsimenton Ellados [*Federation of Greek Cement Industry Workers and Employees*] (GC)
OEZ .... Osteuropaeische Zeit [*East European Time*] [*German*] (WEN)
of .... Commissioned Officer (BU)
OF .... Concentration Plant (RU)
OF .... Fatherland Front (BU)
OF .... Fatherland Front [*People's Republic of Bulgaria*] (RU)
OF .... High Explosive Fragmentation (BU)
OF .... High-Explosive Fragmentation [*Shell, bomb*] (RU)
OF .... Offensif Fusant [*Military*] [*French*] (MTD)
of .... Oficina [*Office*] [*Spanish*]
oF .... Ohne Fortsetzung [*No More*] [*German*]
OF .... Organisation Fraternelle [*Fraternal Organization*] [*Mauritian*] (AF)
OF .... Orta Frekans [*Medium Frequency*] (TU)
OF .... Oslobodilacka Fronta [*Liberation Front*] [*World War II*] (YU)
OF .... Otechestven Front [*Fatherland Front*] [*A periodical*] (BU)
OFA .... Omnium Forestier Africain (MAR)
OFA .... Organizacion Farmaceutica Americana [*Bogota*] (COL)
OFAA .... Omilos Filon Astynomikon Athinon [*Association of Friends of Athens Police Officers*] (GC)
OFAB .... Aerial High-Explosive Fragmentation Bomb (RU)
OFAB .... Office d'Amenagement de Boke [*Boke Development Office*] [*Guinean*] (AF)
OFALAC ...... Office Algerien d'Action Commerciale [*Algerian Office of Business Activity*] (AF)
OFASA .... Organizacion Farmaceutica Americana Sociedad Anonima [*See also OFA*] [*Bogota*] (COL)

OFB .... Orszagos Foldbirtokrendezo Birosag [*Central Court for Land Redistribution*] (HU)
OFBO .... Hydroxyphenylbenzoxazole (RU)
OFBT .... Orszagos Foldbirtokrendezo Tanacs [*National Council for Land Redistribution*] (HU)
OFCA .... Office d'Exploitation des Carrieres [*Office for the Exploitation of Quarries*] [*Chadian*] (AF)
OFDE .... Organisation de Fraternite et de Developpement Economique [*Organization for the Promotion of Fraternity and Economic Development*] [*Mauritian*] (AF)
OFDI .... Office of Foreign Direct Investment (MAR)
OFE .... Omospondia Fortoekfortoton Ellados [*Federation of Greek Longshoremen*] (GC)
OFEDES ...... Office des Eaux du Sous-Sol [*Office of Subsoil Water*] [*Niger*] (AF)
OFENET ...... Office des Entreprises de l'Etat [*Office of State Enterprises*] [*Cambodian*] (CL)
OFERMAT ... Office Francais de Cooperation pour les Chemins de Fer et les Materiels d'Equipement (MAR)
OFEROM ..... Office Central des Chemins de Fer d'Outre-Mer [*French Overseas Railroad Office*] (MAR)
OFF- .... Freon Drier and Filter (RU)
off .... Oeffentlich [*German*]
off .... Offert [*French*]
Off .... Officier [*or Officiel*] [*Officer or Official*] [*French*] (MTD)
OFFI .... Orszagos Fordito es Forditashitelesito Iroda [*National Office for Official Translations and Affidavits*] (HU)
OFFINACO ... Office National de Cooperation [*National Cooperatives Office*] [*Replaced OROC*] [*Cambodian*] (CL)
off red .... Offres Reduites [*French*]
Offz .... Offizier [*German*]
Offzl .... Offizial [*German*]
OFH .... Orszagos Foldhivatal [*National Land Office*] (HU)
OFI .... Orientation a la Fonction Internationale (MAR)
OFI .... Orszagos Foldhitelintezet [*National Agricultural Credit Bank*] (HU)
OFICODA .... Oficinas de Control de Distribucion de Abastecimientos [*Supply Distribution Control Offices*] [*Cuban*] (LA)
OFIDA .... Office des Douanes et Accises [*Customs and Excise Office*] [*Zairian*] (AF)
OFIL .... Oficiul Filatelic [*Philatelic Office*] (RO)
OFIMAD ...... Omnium Financier de Madagascar (MAR)
OFIPA .... Societe Omnium Financier de Produits Alimentaires (MAR)
OFIPLAN ..... Oficina de Planificacion Nacional [*National Planning Office*] [*Costa Rican*] (LA)
OFITEC .... Office Tunisien de l'Expansion Commerciale et du Tourisme (MAR)
ofits .... Official (RU)
ofits .... Official, Formal (BU)
OFK .... Orthophosphoric Acid (RU)
OFKO .... Omospondia Filathlon Kynigetikou Oplou [*Hunting Weapon Sportsmen's Federation*] [*Greek*] (GC)
o fl .... Og Flere [*And So On*] [*Norwegian*] (GPO)
OFL .... (Ortskomitee der) Organisation Freiwilliger Luftschutzhelfer [*(Local Committee of the) Organization of Volunteer Civil Defense Assistants*] (EG)
OFLA .... Office des Fruits et Legumes d'Algerie [*Fruit and Vegetable Office of Algeria*] (AF)
Ofm .... Oberforstmeister [*Chief Forest Supervisor*] (EG)
OFM .... Relative Phase Modulation (RU)
OFMAVINS ... Office Malgache de Vins (MAR)
OFMI .... Orszagos Foldmerestani Intezet [*National Institute of Land Surveying*] (HU)
OFMN .... Department of Physical and Mathematical Sciences (of the Academy of Sciences, USSR) (RU)
OFN .... Operation Feed the Nation (MAR)
OFNACER ... Office National des Cereales (MAR)
OFNACOM ... Office National de Commerce [*National Marketing Office*] [*Congolese*] (AF)
OFO .... Oficir z Oruda [*Officer in Charge of Arms*] (YU)
OFOM .... Office de la France d'Outre-Mer (MAR)
OFOMENTO ... Oficina de Fomento [*Development Office*] [*Colombian*] (LA)
OFON .... Officer of the Order of the Niger (MAR)
OFOR .... October Revolution Holdings Department [*Archives*] (RU)
OFOTERT .... Optikai, Finommechanikai, es Fotocikkeket Ertekesito Vallalat [*Marketing Enterprise for Optical, Fine Mechanical, and Photograhic Items*] (HU)
OFP .... Obchodni-Financni Plan [*Business and Financial Plan*] (CZ)
OFPE .... Office de la Formation Professionnelle et de l'Emploi [*Vocational Training and Employment Bureau*] [*Tunisian*] (AF)
OFR .... Officer of the Federal Republic (MAR)
OFR .... Oficiul Farmaceutic Regional [*Regional Pharmaceutic Office*] (RO)
OFR .... Opsonocytophagic Test (RU)
OFR .... Order of the Federal Republic (MAR)
OFRATEME ... Office Francais des Techniques Modernes d'Education
ofs .... Offset (RU)
OFS .... Orange Free State (MAR)
OFS .... Osvobodilna Fronta Slovenije [*Liberation Front of Slovenia*] (YU)
OFSIT .... Orange Free State Investment Trust Ltd. (MAR)
OFSZSZK .... Orosz Federativ Sozcialista Szovjet Koztarsasag [*Russian Socialist Federative Soviet Republic*] (HU)
OFT .... Obus en Fonte a Amorcage de Tete [*Military*] [*French*] (MTD)
OFT .... Orszagos Foldbirtokrendezo Tanacs [*National Council for Land Redistribution*] (HU)
OFT .... Orszagos Foldmuvelesugyi Tanacs [*National Agricultural Council*] (HU)
OFT .... Relative Phase Telegraphy (RU)
oftalm .... Ophthalmology, Ophthalmologist (BU)
OFTH .... Orszagos Foldugyi es Terkepeszeti Hivatal [*National Bureau of Geodesy and Cartography*] (HU)
OFU .... Organization for Free Ugandans (AF)
OFUNC .... Organisation des Femmes de l'Union Nationale Camerounaise [*Women's Organization of the Cameroonian National Union*] (AF)
OFV .... Obuka Oficira za Vatru [*Training of Fire Control Officer*] [*Military*] (YU)
OFY .... Operation Feed Yourself (MAR)
og .... Oben Genannt [*Above Named*] [*German*]
OG .... Oberstes Gericht [*Supreme Court*] [*German*] (WEN)
OG .... Obudai Gazgyar [*Gas Works of Obuda*] (HU)
OG .... Oddzial Glowny [*Main Branch*] (POL)
OG .... Official Gazette (MAR)
Og .... Ogretmen [*Teacher*] (TU)
OG .... Operation Chart (RU)
OG .... Operativna Grupa [*Operational Group*] [*Military*] (YU)
OG .... Organization Gestosis, Society for the Study of Pathophysiology of Pregnancy (EA)
OG .... Organotikos Grammatevs [*Organizational Secretary*] (GC)
og .... Osztag [*Detachment, Squad*] (HU)
og .... Ova Godina [*This Year*] (YU)
OG .... Reference Generator (RU)
OG .... Task Force, Task Group (RU)
OGA .... Office General de l'Air (MAR)
OGA .... Oficiul de Gospodarire a Apelor [*Water Management Office*] (RO)
OGA .... Organizzazione Giovanile Africana (MAR)
OGA .... Organosis Georgikon Asfaliseon [*Farm Insurance Organization*] [*Greek*] (GC)
OGA .... Orszagos Geodeziai Adattar [*National Documentation Center for Geodesy*] (HU)
OGABI .... Omnium Gabonais Immobilier (MAR)
OGAPROV ... Office Gabonais d'Amelioration et de Production de Viande (MAR)
OGB .... Oesterreichischer Gewerkschaftsbund [*Austrian*]
OGB .... Urban Improvement Department (RU)
OGC .... Office de Gestion, Compatibilite (MAR)
OGChPP ...... Joint Numerical Weather Prediction Unit [*US*] (RU)
OGD .... Operativna Grupa Divizija [*Operational Group of the Divisions*] [*Military*] (YU)
OGE .... Chief Power Engineer Department (BU)
OGE .... Chief Power Engineer's Department (RU)
OGE .... Omospondia Gynaikon Ellados [*Federation of Greek Women*] (GC)
OGE .... Relative Genetic Effectiveness (RU)
OGEDEP ..... Office de Gestion de la Dette Publique [*Office for the Management of the Public Debt*] [*Zairian*] (AF)
og esh .... Assault Echelon (BU)
OGG .... Oxyhemogram (RU)
OGGN .... Department of Geological and Geographical Sciences (of the Academy of Sciences, USSR) (RU)
OGH .... Oberster Gerichtshof [*German*]
OGI .... Chief Engineer's Department (RU)
OGI .... Geodetic Surveying Organization (BU)
OGIL .... Koolaj es Foldgazbanyaszati Ipari Kutato Laboratorium [*Oil and Natural Gas Exploring Industrial Research Laboratory*] (HU)
ogiptd .... Separate Guards Antitank Battalion (RU)
OGIS .... Department of Geophysics and Seismology (of the Academy of Sciences, Turkmen SSR) (RU)
OGIZ .... Association of State Publishing Houses [*1930-1949*] (RU)
OGK .... Chief Designer's Department (RU)
OGK .... Odessa State Conservatory Imeni A. V. Nezhdanova (RU)
OGK .... Terminal Gas Logging (RU)
OGK-STO .... Chief Designers' Department for the Planning of Machine Tools and Technological Equipment (RU)
Ogl .... Ogloszony [*Published*] (POL)
ogl .... Table of Contents (RU)
OGM .... Chief Mechanic Department (BU)
OGM .... Chief Mechanic's Department (RU)
OGMD .... Separate Guards Mortar Battalion (RU)
OGMET .... Chief Metallurgist Department (BU)
OGMet .... Chief Metallurgist's Department (RU)
OGMI .... Odessa Hydrometeorological Institute (RU)
OGMkh .... Chief Mechanic's Department (RU)
OGN .... Department of Humanities (of the Academy of Sciences, USSR) (RU)
ogn .... Firearm (BU)
OGNB .... Odessa State Scientific Library Imeni A. M. Gor'kiy (RU)
ogneup .... Refractory Products Plant [*Topography*] (RU)

OGO .... End of Grouped Operation [*Computers*] (RU)
OgOGM .... Ogretmen Okullari Genel Mudurlugu [*Teachers Schools Directorate General*] (TU)
ogp .... Flame Thrower (BU)
OGPEC .... Officially Guaranteed Private Export Credits (MAR)
OGPI .... Odessa State Pedagogical Institute Imeni K. D. Ushinskiy (RU)
OGPI .... Orel State Pedagogical Institute (RU)
OGPU .... United State Political Administration at the Council of People's Commissars, USSR [*1922-1934*] (RU)
Ogr .... Ogrenci [*Student*] (TU)
OGRAPS ..... Opste Gradevinsko Preduzece Srbije [*General Construction Establishment of Serbia*] (YU)
Ogret-Bir ..... Ogretmenler Yardim ve Dayanisma Birligi [*Teachers' Aid and Solidarity Union*] [*Cypriot*] (TU)
Ogret-Bir ..... Ogretmenler Yardimlasma ve Dayanisma Dernegi [*Teachers' Mutual Aid and Solidarity Association*] [*Ankara*] (TU)
OGREVOPROMET ... Preduzece za Promet Ogrevnim Materijalom [*Fuel Trading Establishment*] (YU)
Ogrt .... Ogretmen [*Teacher*] (TU)
OGS .... Omospondia Georgikon Synetairismon [*Federation of Agricultural Cooperatives*] [*Greek*] (GC)
OGSA .... Organisation de Gestion et de Securite Aeronautique [*Aeronautical Management and Safety Organization*] [*Algerian*] (AF)
ogsb .... Separate Guards Rifle Battalion (RU)
ogsbr .... Separate Guards Rifle Brigade (RU)
OGSD .... German-Soviet Friendship Organization (RU)
OGSE .... Omospondia Georgikon Synetairismon Ellados [*Federation of Greek Agricultural Cooperatives*] (GC)
OGSM .... Fuel and Lubricants Section (RU)
OGSS .... Organizzazione Generale degli Studenti Somali [*Organization of Somali Students*] [*Italian*]
OGSt .... Oberstes Gericht Strafsachen [*Supreme Court for Criminal Cases*] [*West German*] (WEN)
OGT .... Chief Technologist's Department (BU)
OGT .... Chief Technologist's Department (RU)
OGT .... Orszagos Gazdasagi Tanacs [*National Economic Council*] (HU)
OGT .... Ortak Gumruk Tarife No. [*Joint Customs Tariff Number*] [*As in EEC transactions*] (TU)
OGTsA .... Organization of Central American States (RU)
Ogt Svy .... Ogretim Seviyesi [*Level of Education*] (TU)
OGU .... Odessa State University Imeni I. I. Mechnikov (RU)
OGVD .... Social Welfare and Education of Children (BU)
OGVF .... Civil Air Fleet Association (RU)
ogvl .... Rolling Barrage, Creeping Barrage (BU)
ogvsbr .... Separate Guards Rifle Brigade (RU)
OGvTPP ...... Separate Guards Break-Through Tank Regiment (RU)
Ogy .... Orszaggyules [*National Assembly*] (HU)
OGYE .... Orszagos Gyogyszeresz Egyesulet [*National Association of Pharmacists*] (HU)
OGYIT .... Orszagos Gyermek- es Ifjusagvedelmi Tanacs [*National Council for the Protection of Children and Youth*] (HU)
OGySSzK .... Orszagos Gyogynoveny- es Selyemguboforgalmi Szovetkezeti Kozpont [*National Cooperative for Medicinal Plants and Silk Cocoons*] (HU)
OGZ .... Obst- und Gemuese-Zentrale [*Fruit and Vegetable Center*] (EG)
OGZ .... Opci Gradanski Zakonik [*General Civil Code*] (YU)
OH .... Olympijske Hry [*Olympic Games*] (CZ)
OHAD .... Oral History and Antiquities Department (MAR)
OHB .... Orszagos Honvedelmi Bizottmany [*National Defense Council*] (HU)
OHC .... Order of the Holy Cross, Liberian Mission (MAR)
OHE .... Orszagos Hitelvedo Egylet [*National Credit Protection Association*] (HU)
OHES .... Okresni Hygienicko-Epidemiologicka Stanice [*District Public Health and Epidemiology Station*] (CZ)
OHF .... Orszagos Halaszati Felugyeloseg [*National Fishing Inspectorate*] (HU)
OHG .... Offene Handelsgesellschaft [*Partnership*] (EG)
OHH .... Orszagos Hadigondozo Hivatal [*National War Relief Office*] (HU)
OHJ .... Oborova Hospodarska Jednorka [*Sectoral Economic Unit*] (CZ)
OHKI .... Orszagos Husipari Kutatointezet [*National Meat Industry Research Institute*] (HU)
OHLM .... Office des Habitations a Loyer Moderes [*Office of Moderate Rent Housing*] [*Senegalese*] (AF)
OHP .... Ochotnicze Hufce Pracy [*Volunteer Labor Brigades*] (POL)
OHT .... Orszagos Halgazdasagi Tanacs [*National Council of Fisheries*] (HU)
OHT .... Orszagos Hitelugyi Tanacs [*National Council on Credit*] (HU)
OHU .... Odborne Hornicke Uciliste [*Training Center for Mining Specialists*] (CZ)
OHV .... Osszetett Honvedelmi Verseny [*Combined National Defense Competition*] (HU)
OHZ .... Hydroxylzahl [*Hydroxyl Number*] [*German*]
Ohz .... Ofenheizung [*Stove Heating*] (EG)
OI .... Actuating Element (RU)
OI .... Final Sum (RU)
OI .... Information Department (RU)
OI .... Information Processing (RU)
OI .... Oberingenieur [*Chief Engineer*] (EG)
Oi .... Oberirdisch [*Above Ground*] (EG)
OI .... Orijentalni Institut [*Oriental Institute*] (YU)
OI .... Orvostovabbkepzo Intezet [*Institute for Postgraduate Medical Training*] (HU)
OI .... Oscillometric Index (RU)
OI .... Single Flash (RU)
OIA .... Omnium Industriel Africain (MAR)
OIA .... Organizacion Internacional del Azucar [*International Sugar Organization - ISO*] (EA)
oiab .... Separate Engineer Airdrome Battalion (BU)
oiab .... Separate Engineer Aviation Battalion (RU)
OIAC .... Oboade Institute of African Culture (MAR)
OIAC .... Organisation Interafricaine du Cafe [*Inter-African Coffee Organization*] [*Use IACO*] (AF)
OIAM .... Department for Testing Aviation Materials (RU)
OIAM .... Organisation Interafricaine et Malgache (MAR)
OIAONI .... Department for the Study, Analysis, and Generalization of Scientific Information (of the All-Union Electrotechnical Institute Imeni V. I. Lenin) (RU)
OIC .... Office Ivoirien des Chargeurs (MAR)
OIC .... Oficina de Investigacion Criminal [*Office of Criminal Investigation*] [*Ecuadorean*] (LA)
OIC .... Organisation Internationale du Cafe [*International Coffee Organization*] [*French*] (AF)
OIC .... Organisation Internationale du Commerce [*French*]
OIC .... Organizacion Internacional de Cafe [*International Coffee Organization*] [*Spanish*] (LA)
OIC .... Organizacion Izquierda Cristiana [*Christian Left Organization*] [*Chilean*] (LA)
OIC .... Organization of the Islamic Conference [*See also OCI*] (EA)
OICE .... Organizacion de Izquierda Comunista de Espana [*Organization of the Communist Left of Spain*] (WER)
OICI .... Omnium Immobilier de Cote-d'Ivoire (MAR)
OICMA .... Organisation Internationale pour le Controle du Criquet Migrateur Africain [*International African Migratory Locust Organization*] (AF)
OICS .... Organe International de Controle des Stupefiants [*International Narcotics Control Board*] [*Use INCB*] (CL)
OID .... Ofensiva de Izquierda Democratica [*Offensive of the Democratic Left*] [*Bolivian*] (PPW)
OIDR .... Society of History and Russian Antiquities (at the Moscow University) (RU)
OIE .... Office International des Epizooties [*International Office of Epizootics*] (CL)
OIE .... Omospondia Ilektrotekhniton Ellados [*Federation of Greek Electricians*] (GC)
OIE .... Organosis Inomenon Ethnon [*United Nations Organization*] (GC)
OIE .... Separate Fighter Squadron (RU)
OIEA .... Organizacion Internacional de Energia Atomica [*International Atomic Energy Agency*] [*Use IAEA*] (LA)
OIEC .... Office International de l'Enseignement Catholique [*Catholic International Education Office - CIEO*] (EA)
OIEE .... Omospondia Idiotikon Ekpaidevtikon Ellados [*Federation of Private Teachers of Greece*] (GC)
OIEKO .... Omospondia Ilektrismou kai Epikheiriseon Koinis Ofeleias [*Electric Power and Public Utilities Federation*] [*Greek*] (GC)
OIELE .... Omospondia Idiotikon Ekpaidevtikon Leitourgon Ellados [*Federation of Greek Private School Teachers*] (GC)
OIEN .... Organosis Ithikou Exoplismou Neotitos [*Youth Moral Rearmament Organization*] [*Greek*] (GC)
OIETA .... Office Inter-Etats du Tourisme Africain [*Inter-State Office for African Tourism*] (AF)
OIF .... Department of Historical Sciences and Philology (of the Academy of Sciences, USSR) (RU)
OIF .... Oficiul de Imbunatatiri Funciare [*Land Improvement Office*] (RO)
OIF .... Opsti Investicioni Fond [*General Investment Fund*] (YU)
OIFPCA .... Oficiul de Imbunatatiri Funciare si Proiectare Constructii in Agricultura [*Office for Land Improvements and Construction Design in Agriculture*] (RO)
OIG .... Oklopna Izvidacka Grupa [*Armored Reconnaissance Group*] (YU)
OIG .... Organizzazione Internazionale dei Giornalisti [*International Organization of Journalists*] [*Use IOJ*] [*Italian*] (WER)
OIGPE .... Okregowy Inspektorat Gospodarki Paliwowo-Energetycznej [*District Fuel and Power Management Inspectorate*] (POL)
OIH .... Orszagos Idegenforgalmi Hivatal [*National Tourist Office*] (HU)
OII .... Department of Fine Arts (RU)
OIIMF .... Odessa Institute of Engineers of the Maritime Fleet (RU)
OIIVKh .... Experimental Research Institute of Water Management (RU)
OIJ .... Organisation Internationale des Journalistes [*International Organization of Journalists - IOJ*] [*French*] (EA)
OIJ .... Organismo de Investigacion Judicial [*Judicial Investigation Agency*] [*Costa Rican*] (LA1)
OIK .... Accountability and Election Conferences (BU)
OIK .... Negative Impedance Converter (RU)
oik .... Oikealla [*Finnish*]

oik .... Oikeastaan [*Really, Properly*] [*Finnish*] (GPO)
oikeustkand ... Oikeustieteen Kandidaatti [*Finnish*]
oikeustlis .... Oikeustieteen Lisensiaatti [*Finnish*]
oikeusttri .... Oikeustieteen Tohtori [*Finnish*]
OIKh .... Tool Supply Department (RU)
OIL .... Organizzazione Internazionale del Lavoro [*International Labor Organization*] [*Use ILO*] [*Italian*] (WER)
OILB .... Organisation Internationale de Lutte Biologique Contre les Animaux et les Plants Nuisibles [*International Organization for Biological Control of Noxious Animals and Pests - IOBC*] (EA)
OILP .... Odigoi Idiotikon Leoforeion Peiraios [*Drivers of Piraeus Privately Owned Buses*] (GC)
OIM .... Organizatia Internationala a Muncii [*International Labor Organization*] (RO)
OIM .... Society of Marxist Historians (RU)
OIML .... Organisation Internationale de Metrologie Legale [*International Organization of Legal Metrology*] (EA)
OIMS .... Society for the Study of Interplanetary Communications (RU)
OIN .... Department of Historical Sciences (of the Academy of Sciences, USSR) (RU)
OIN .... Oficinas de Impuestos Nacionales [*National Tax Offices*] [*Colombian*] (LA)
OInAB .... Separate Engineer Aviation Brigade (RU)
OIO .... Omospondia Imikratikon Organoseon [*Federation of Semi-Governmental Organizations*] [*Cypriot*] (GC)
OIOT .... Orszagos Ifjusagpolitikai es Oktatasi Tanacs [*National Youth Policy and Education Council*] (HU)
O i OV .... Errors and Misspellings Are Possible (RU)
OIP .... General True Bearing (RU)
OIP .... Oficina de Ingenieria del Proyecto [*Project Engineering Office*] [*Spanish*] (WER)
OIP .... Oklopna Izvidacka Patrola [*Armored Reconnaissance Patrol*] (YU)
OIP .... Organisation Internationale de Psychophysiologie [*International Organization of Psychophysiology - IOP*] (EA)
OIP .... Organizacion Iberoamericana de Pilots [*Ibero-American Organization of Pilots - IOP*] (EA)
OIP .... Organizacion Internacional de Periodistas [*International Organization of Journalists*] [*Use IOJ*] (LA)
OIP .... Reciprocal True Bearing (RU)
OIP .... True Bearing Reading (RU)
OIPC .... Organisation Internationale de la Police Criminelle [*International Criminal Police Organization*] [*Use INTERPOL*] [*French*] (CL)
OIPC .... Organizacion Internacional de Policia Criminal [*International Criminal Police Organization*] [*Use INTERPOL*] [*Spanish*] (LA)
OIPC .... Organizatia Internationala de Politie Criminala [*International Criminal Police Organization*] (RO)
OIPCh .... Single-Phase Gas Tube Frequency Converter (RU)
OIPI .... Omsk Institute of Zoonotic Infections in Specific Geographic Areas (RU)
oiptap .... Separate Antitank Artillery Regiment (RU)
OIPTD .... Separate Antitank Battalion (RU)
oiptd .... Separate Tank Destroyer Battalion (BU)
OIR .... Institute of Workers Engaged in Joint Research (RU)
OIR .... Oficina de Informaciones y Radiodiffusion de la Presidencia de la Republica [*Presidential Press and Radio Office*] [*Chilean*] (LA)
OIR .... Organisation Internationale pour les Refugies (MAR)
OIRD .... Separate Engineer Reconnaissance Patrol (RU)
OIRP .... Reciprocal True Radio Bearing (RU)
OIRSA .... Organismo Internacional Regional de Sanidad Agropecuaria [*Regional International Organization for Plant Protection and Animal Health*] (LA)
OIRT .... Organisation Internationale de Radiodiffusion et Television [*International Radio and Television Organization*] (EA)
OIS .... Okoliya Statistics Inspector (BU)
OISA .... Organization of Information Agencies of the Countries of Asia (RU)
OISB .... Orszagos Ifjusagi Sport Bizottsag [*National Committee for Physical Education of the Youth*] (HU)
OISCA .... Organization for Industrial, Spiritual, and Cultural Advancement International (EA)
OISS .... Organizacion Iberoamericana de Seguridad Social [*Ibero-American Social Security Organization*] (LA)
OIT .... Organisation Internationale du Travail [*International Labor Organization*] [*Use ILO*] [*French*] (AF)
OIT .... Organizacao Internacional do Trabalho [*International Labor Organization*] [*Use ILO*] [*Portuguese*] (WER)
OIT .... Organizacion Internacional del Trabajo [*International Labor Organization*] [*Use ILO*] [*Spanish*] (LA)
OIT .... Orszagos Idegenforgalmi Tanacs [*National Council on Tourism*] (HU)
OIT .... Orszagos Iparoktatasi Tanacs [*National Council on Industrial Training*] (HU)
OIT .... Osrodek Informacji Turystycznej [*Tourist Information Center*] [*Polish*]
OITI .... Orszagos Idegsebeszeti Tudomanyos Intezet [*National Scientific Institute on Neurosurgery*] (HU)
OITIS .... Overseas Industrial and Trade Investment Services (MAR)
OITK .... Special Corrective Labor Colony (RU)
OITR .... Corrective Labor Department (RU)
OITS .... Organizacion Internacional de Telecomunicaciones [*International Organization of Telecommunications*] [*Use IOTS*] (LA)
OITZ .... Oddeleni Inzenyrsko-Technickeho Zasobovani [*Engineer-Technical Supply Department*] (CZ)
OIU .... Omdurman Islamic University [*Sudanese*] (MAR)
OIUK .... Hydroxyindoleacetic Acid (RU)
OIYaI .... Joint Institute of Nuclear Research (RU)
OIYE .... Omospondia Idiotikon Ypallilon Ellados [*Greek Federation of Private Employees*] (GC)
OIZ .... Joint Publishing House (RU)
OIZ .... Opsti Imovinski Zakonik [*General Civil Code*] (YU)
OIZ .... Organizatia Internationala a Ziaristilor [*International Organization of Journalists*] (RO)
OIZ .... Publications Department (of the People's Commissariat of Defense) (RU)
OIZ .... Society of Inventors (RU)
oJ .... Ohne Jahr [*or Jahre*] [*No Date (of publication)*] [*German*] (EG)
OJ .... Oklopna Jedinica [*Armored Unit*] (YU)
OJ .... Osvetova Jizba [*Cultural Room*] (CZ)
OJA .... Organizacja Jednosci Afrykanskiej [*Organization of African Unity*] [*Polish*]
OJE .... Organizacion Juvenil Espanola [*Spanish Youth Organization*] (WER)
OJK .... Organisation de la Jeunesse Khmere [*Cambodian Youth Organization*] (CL)
OJM .... Organizacao da Juventude Mocambicana [*Mozambique Youth Organization*] (AF)
OJO .... Organizacion Juvenil de Octubre [*October Youth Organization*] [*Spanish*] (WER)
OJT .... Orang Jahat Tempatan [*Local Bad Character*] (ML)
OK .... Check Valve (RU)
ok .... Circa (BU)
OK .... Common Collector (RU)
OK .... Compensating Winding (RU)
OK .... Deflecting Coil (RU)
OK .... Joint Command (RU)
ok .... Near, About, Approximately (RU)
OK .... Obchodni Komora [*Chamber of Commerce*] (CZ)
OK .... Oblasni Komitet [*Regional Committee*] (YU)
OK .... Oblast Committee (RU)
ok .... Ocean (RU)
OK .... Oceanographic Commission (RU)
OK .... Odvodni Komise [*Draft Board*] (CZ)
oK .... Ohne Kosten [*Without Cost*] [*Business and trade*] [*German*]
ok .... Oka [*or Okades*] [*Unit of weight equal to 2.8 pounds*] (GC)
ok .... Okoliya (BU)
OK .... Okoliya Committee (BU)
ok .... Okolnik [*Administrative Instruction*] (POL)
ok .... Okolo [*Approximately*] (POL)
OK .... Okresna Komisia [*District Commission*] (CZ)
OK .... Okrug Committee (BU)
OK .... Okruzni Komitet [*County Committee*] (YU)
Ok .... Okulu [*School*] (TU)
Ok .... Okunur [*Readable, Worthy of Being Read*] (TU)
OK .... Olympic Committee (RU)
OK .... Olympic Committee (BU)
OK .... Optical Quadrant (RU)
OK .... Organizational Committee of the RSDRP (RU)
OK .... Orszaggyules Konyvtara [*Library of the National Assembly*] (HU)
ok .... Orszagos Kirako Vasar [*National Merchandise Fair*] (HU)
OK .... Orszagos Kozpont [*National Center*] (HU)
ok .... Osszekoto [*Liaison, Contact*] (HU)
OK .... Personnel Department (RU)
ok .... Reflux Condensate (RU)
OK .... Release Key (RU)
OK .... Reverse Course (RU)
OKA .... Organismoi Koinonikis Asfaliseos [*Social Insurance Organizations*] [*Greek*] (GC)
OKA .... Pulmotor, Resuscitating Oxygen Apparatus (RU)
OKA .... Separate Caucasian Army (RU)
OKA .... Separate "Red Banner" Army (RU)
OKAD .... Single-Phase Capacitive Induction Motor (RU)
OKAE .... Separate Spotting Air Squadron (RU)
OKAL-KOOP ... Omorfo Kalkinma Kooperatif Sirketi [*Omorfo Development Cooperative*] (TU)
OKAP .... Okrajna Avtoprevozniska Podjetja [*District Motor Transport Establishments*] (YU)
okap .... Surface Gunnery Support Force (RU)
okarab .... Separate Machine Gun Artillery Battalion (BU)
OKB .... Design Office Based on Public Participation (RU)
OKB .... Experimental Design Office (RU)
OKB .... Odeljak Korpusne Baze [*Detachment of Corps Depot*] (YU)
OKB .... Oesterreichische Kontrollbank [*Austrian*]
OKB .... Special Design Office (RU)
OKBA .... Experimental Design Office for Automation (RU)

OKBK.......... Orszagos Konyvforgalmi es Bibliografiai Kozpont [*National Book Circulation and Bibliography Center*] (HU)
OK(b)P........ Oroszorszagi Kommunista (Bolsevik) Part [*Russian Communist Party (Bolsheviks)*] (HU)
OKBT.......... Orszagos Kozlekedesbiztonsagi Tanacs [*National Traffic Safety Council*] (HU)
OKChPH..... Okresni Klub Chovatelu Postovnich Holubu [*District Club of Carrier Pigeon Breeders*] (CZ)
ok csop....... Osszekoto Csoport [*Liaison Group*] (HU)
OKCT.......... Odbor Klubu Ceskych Turistu [*Branch of the Czech Tourist Club*] (CZ)
OKD............ Ostravsko-Karvinske Doly [*Ostrava-Karvina Mines*] (CZ)
OKD............ Ostravsko-Karvinske Kamenouhelne Doly [*Ostrava-Karvina Coal Mines*] (CZ)
OKDE.......... Organosi Kommouniston Diethniston Elladas [*Organization of Communist Internationalists of Greece*] (GC)
OKDVA........ Special "Red Banner" Far Eastern Army (RU)
OKE............ Omas Koinovoulevtikou Ergou [*Group of Parliamentary Work*] (GC1)
OKE............ Omospondia Kafepolon Ellados [*Greek Coffee Merchants Federation*] (GC)
OKE............ Omospondia Klostoyfandourgon Ellados [*Federation of Greek Textile Workers*] (GC)
OKET.......... Orszagos Kozegeszsegugyi Tanacs [*National Council of Public Health*] (HU)
OKF-........... Photometric Ocular (RU)
OK FJN........ Ogolnopolski Komitet Frontu Jednosci Narodu [*All-Poland National Unity Front Committee*] (POL)
OKFN.......... Obwodowy Komitet Frontu Narodowego [*District Committee of the People's Front*] (POL)
OKFN.......... Ogolnopolski Komitet Frontu Narodowego [*All-Poland Committee of the People's Front*] (POL)
OKFP.......... Oddzialowa Komisja Funduszu Posmiertnego [*Departmental Commission of the Death Benefit Fund*] (POL)
OKFS.......... Okoliya Committee for Physical Culture and Sports (BU)
OKFS.......... Okrug Committee for Physical Culture and Sports (BU)
OKG............ Laser (RU)
OKG............ Obuv - Kuze - Guma [*Shoes - Leather - Rubber (A national enterprise)*] (CZ)
OKGT.......... Orszagos Koolaj es Gazipari Troszt [*National Oil and Gas Industry Trust*] (HU)
OKGV.......... Organismos Kypriakis Galakto-Viomikhanias [*Cypriot Dairy Industry Organization*] (GC)
OKh............ Fragmentation Chemical [*Shell*] (RU)
OKH............ Orszagos Kozellatasi Hivatal [*National Office of Public Supply*] (HU)
OKH............ Orszagos Kozponti Hitelszovetkezet [*National Central Credit Society*] (HU)
OKhAB........ Fragmentation Chemical Aerial Bomb (RU)
okhb............ Separate Chemical Battalion (RU)
OKhEN........ Orthodoxos Khristianiki Enosis Neon [*Union of Orthodox Christian Youth*] [*Cypriot*] (GC)
OKhI............ General Art Exhibit (BU)
OKhK........... Okhta Chemical Kombinat (RU)
OkhK........... Society of Book Artists (RU)
okhlazhd..... Cooled, Chilled, Refrigerated (RU)
okhmatdet... Institute of Mother and Child Care (RU)
OKhMK........ Orsko-Khalilovskiy Metallurgical Kombinat (RU)
OKhN.......... Department of Chemical Sciences (of the Academy of Sciences, USSR) (RU)
OKhOA........ Organismos Khrimatodotiseos Oikonomikis Anaptyxeos [*Economic Development Funding Organization*] [*Greek*] (GC)
OKhOBR..... Department of Art Education (RU)
okhot........... Hunting (RU)
okhotn......... Hunter's Cabin [*Topography*] (RU)
OKhR........... Association of Realist Artists (RU)
OKhR........... Roadstead Defense (RU)
okhr............ Separate Chemical Company (RU)
okhr sl......... Security Service (BU)
okh rz.......... Security Patrol [*Cavalry*] (BU)
OKhTs......... Department of Art Treasures (RU)
OKhVY........ Omospondia (Ergaton, Tekhniton, kai Ypallilon) Khimikis Viomikhanias kai Ygieinis [*Federation (of Workers, Technicians, and Employees) of the Chemical Industry and Sanitation*] [*Greek*] (GC)
OKhZ........... Administration of United State Chemical Plants (RU)
OKI............. Okresni Kulturni Inspektorat [*Office of the District Inspector of Cultural Activities*] (CZ)
OKI............. Orszagos Kardiologiai Intezet [*National Institute of Cardiology*] (HU)
OKI............. Orszagos Kozegeszsegugyi Intezet [*National Institute of Public Health*] (HU)
OKIP............ Department of Control and Measuring Instruments (RU)
OKiP............ Oswiata, Ksiazka, i Prasa [*Education, Book, and Press (Club)*] (POL)
OKISAR....... Special Committee for the Study of Union and Autonomous Republics (of the Academy of Sciences, USSR) (RU)
okisl pl........ Oxidizing Flame (RU)
OKISZ......... Kisipari Szovetkezetek Orszagos Szovetsege [*National Federation of Artisan Cooperatives*] (HU)
okk.............. Joint Force Command Code (RU)
OKK............ Oblast Control Commission (RU)
OKK............ Okregowa Komisja Ksiezy [*District Commission of Clergy*] (POL)
OKK............ Orszagos Kereskedelmi Kamara [*National Chamber of Commerce*] (HU)
OKK............ Orszagos Konyvtari Kozpont [*National Library Center*] (HU)
OKK............ Red Cross Society (RU)
OKKGM....... Orman Koylerini Kalkindirma Genel Mudurlugu [*Forest Villages Development Directorate General*] (TU)
OKKMA....... Special Commission for the Kursk Magnetic Anomaly (RU)
OKKPJ........ Okruzni Komitet Komunisticke Partije Jugoslavije [*County Committee of the Communist Party of Yugoslavia*] (YU)
OKKSC....... Okresni Komise Komunisticke Strany Ceskoslovenska [*District Commission of the Czechoslovak Communist Party*] (CZ)
okl.............. Okladka [*Book Cover*] (POL)
okl.............. Okleveles [*Certified, Possessing a Diploma (for example, Okl. Gepesz Mernok, Certified Mechanical Engineer)*] (HU)
OKL............. Optikai es Finommechanikai Kozponti Kutato Laboratorium [*Central Research Laboratory for Optics and Precision Mechanics*] (HU)
OKLA.......... Organismos Kendrikis Lakhanagoras Athinon [*Athens Central Vegetable-Market Organization*] (GC)
OKLE........... "Organosi Kommouniston Laiki Exousia" [*"Popular Power Organization of Communists"*] [*Greek*] (GC)
OKLK.......... Okresni Komise Lidove Kontroly [*District Commission of People's Control*] (CZ)
OKM............ Department of Clinical Medicine (RU)
OKML.......... District Courses for Junior Lieutenants (RU)
OKMP.......... Oddeleni Kulturni-Masove Prace [*Cultural and Propaganda Department*] (CZ)
OKMZ.......... Osvetova Komise Ministerstva Zemedelstvi [*Cultural Commission of the Ministry of Agriculture*] (CZ)
OKN............ Okregowa Komisja Narciarska [*District Ski Commission*] (POL)
okn.............. Reflux Condensate Pump (RU)
OKNE.......... Omospondia Kommounistikis Neolaias Ellados [*Federation of Greek Communist Youth*] (GC)
OKNO.......... Okruzni Komitet Narodne Omladine [*County Committee of the People's Youth*] (YU)
OKO............ All-Russian Association of Cinematographic Societies (RU)
OKO............ Oficer Kulturalno-Oswiatowy [*Culture and Education Officer*] (POL)
OKO............ Plan Position Indicator (RU)
OKOK-DER... Ogretmen, Kolejliler, Ogretim, ve Kultur Dernegi [*Teachers', College Students', Teaching and Cultural Organization*] [*Cypriot*] (TU)
okol............. Okoliya (BU)
Okol k-t....... Okoliya Committee (BU)
Okol nar suvet... Okoliya People's Council (BU)
Okorg.......... Okoliya Organizer (BU)
OKOS.......... Officer Personnel Section (RU)
OKP............. Compass Bearing Reading (RU)
OKP............. Laser (RU)
OKP............. Ogolnopolski Komitet Pokoju [*All-Poland Peace Committee*] [*Polish*]
OKP............. Okresni Komunalni Podnik [*District Communal Enterprise*] (CZ)
OKP............. Okrug Committee on Transportation (RU)
OKP............. Olasz Kommunista Part [*Italian Communist Party*] (HU)
OKP............. One Kameroon Party (MAR)
OKP............. Organismoi Koinonikis Politikis [*Social Policy Organizations*] [*Greek*] (GC)
OKP............. Reciprocal Compass Bearing (RU)
OKP............. Surface Support Force (RU)
OKP............. United Peasants' Party [*Polish People's Republic*] (RU)
OKPG.......... United Communist Party of Germany (RU)
okpp........... Separate Border Control Post (RU)
OKPS.......... General Leather Workers Trade Union (BU)
OKPS.......... Okoliya Trade Unions Committee (BU)
OKPUV........ Oddil Kanonu Proti Utocne Vozbe [*Antitank Battalion*] (CZ)
OKR............. Counterintelligence Section (RU)
OKR............. Experimental Design Work (RU)
OKR............. Major Repair Department, General Overhaul Department (RU)
okr.............. Okreg [*District, Region*] (POL)
OKR............. Okregowy Klub Racjonalizacji [*Regional Rationalization Club*] (POL)
okr.............. Okres [*District*] (CZ)
okr.............. Okrug (BU)
okr.............. Okrug, District (RU)
OKR............. Ostravsko-Karvinsky Revir [*Ostrava-Karvina Coal Basin*] (CZ)
OKR............. Ostravsky Kamenouhelny Revir [*Ostrava Coal Basin*] (CZ)
okr.............. Outskirts [*Topography*] (RU)
okrae........... Separate Spotting and Air Reconnaissance Squadron (RU)
okrae........... Separate Spotting and Reconnaissance Aviation Squadron (BU)
OKRAM....... Society of Marxist Students of Local Lore (RU)
OKRAP........ Separate Spotting and Air Reconnaissance Regiment (RU)
okrap........... Separate Spotting and Reconnaissance Aviation Regiment (BU)
Okres.......... Okrug Economic Conference (RU)
okrfo........... Okrug Finance Department (RU)

Okr KFS ...... Okrug Committee for Physical Culture and Sports (BU)
okrkom .... Okrug Committee (RU)
Okr ns .... Okrug People's Council (BU)
okrono .... Okrug Department of Public Education (RU)
okrprofsovet ... Okrug Council of Trade Unions (RU)
okrsobes..... Okrug Department of Social Security (RU)
OKRSPS...... Okrug Council of Trade Unions (RU)
okr ts.......... Okrug Center (RU)
okrvetupr.... District Military Veterinary Directorate (RU)
okrzagot ..... Okrug Procurement Point (RU)
okrzdrav ..... Okrug Department of Public Health (RU)
okrZU .... Okrug Land Administration (RU)
oks .... Armed, Fuzed [*Ammunition*] (RU)
OKS............ Capital Construction Department (RU)
OKS............ Hydroxycorticosteroid (RU)
OKS............ Okresna Konzumna Sluzba [*District Consumers' Service*] (CZ)
OKS............ Okrug Cooperative Union (BU)
OKS............ Omospondia Katanalotikon Synetairismon [*Federation of Consumer Cooperatives*] [*Greek*] (GC)
OKS............ Orbital Space Station (RU)
OKS............ Organismos tou Kendrikou Symfonou [*Central Treaty Organization*] (GC)
OKS............ Single-Cable Logging Station (RU)
OKSD .... Sino-Soviet Friendship Society (RU)
OKSE .... Omospondia Kyvernitikon kai Stratiotikon Ergaton [*Federation of Government and Military Workers*] [*Cypriot*] (GC)
OKShR........ Separate Telephone Construction Company (RU)
OKSKhOS... Oblast Complex Agricultural Experimental Station (RU)
OKSKOJ ..... Okruzni Komitet Saveza Komunisticke Omladine Jugoslavije [*County Committee of the League of Communist Youth of Yugoslavia*] (YU)
OKSMW ...... Okregowy Komitet Stowarzyszenia Mlodziezy Wiejskiej [*District Committee of the Association of Peasant Youth*] (POL)
OK na SNM ... Okoliya Committee of the People's Youth Union (BU)
oksr............ Separate Telephone Construction Company (BU)
OKSS .... Okresni Sprava Spoju [*District Administration Office for Communications*] (CZ)
okt.............. Octave (RU)
okt.............. October (BU)
okt.............. October (RU)
OKT............ October Railroad (RU)
okt.............. Oktober [*October*] (HU)
okt.............. Oktober [*October*] [*Danish*] (GPO)
Okt.............. Oktober [*October*] [*German*] (GPO)
Okt.............. Oktyabr'skiy [*Toponymy*] (RU)
OKT............ Orszagos Konyvtarugyi Tanacs [*National Council on Libraries*] (HU)
OKT............ Orszagos Kozmuvelodesi Tanacs [*National Public Culture Council*] (HU)
OKT............ Orszagos Koznevelesi Tanacs [*National Council on Public Education*] (HU)
oktaedr .... Octahedral (RU)
OKTB .... Design and Technological Office Based on Public Participation (RU)
oktc............ Oktanove Cislo [*Octane Number*] (CZ)
OKThE .... Organismos Kratikon Theatron Ellados [*Greek State Theater Organization*] (GC)
OKTI........... Orszagos Koranyi Tbc Intezet [*National Koranyi Tuberculosis Institute*] (HU)
oktr .... Separate Telephone Exchange Company (RU)
OKU............ Laser Amplifier (RU)
OKU............ Oblastni Kriminalni Ustredna [*Regional Criminal Investigation Bureau*] (CZ)
OKU............ Okrug Cooperative Administration (BU)
OKU............ Ozdi Kohaszati Uzemek [*Ozd Metallurgical Works*] (HU)
OKUD .... Omladinsko Kulturno Umjetnicko Drustvo [*Youth Cultural and Artistic Society*] (YU)
OKUOMS .... District Courses for Advanced Training of Medical Service Officers (RU)
OKV............ Odvolaci Karny Vybor [*Disciplinary Board of Appeal*] (CZ)
OKV............ Peasants' Mutual Aid Association [*German Democratic Republic*] (RU)
OKVB .... Osszoroszorszagi Kozponti Vegrehajto Bizottsag [*All-Union Central Executive Committee (USSR)*] (HU)
OKVDP........ Acute Catarrhal Inflammation of Upper Respiratory System (RU)
OKVK .... Special Supreme Control Collegium for Land Disputes [*1922-1930*] (RU)
OKVT .... Orszagos Kornyezetvedelmi Tanacs [*National Council of Environmental Protection*] (HU)
OKWFN....... Okregowy Komitet Wyborczy Frontu Narodowego [*District Electoral Committee of the People's Front*] (POL)
OKWOM...... Ogolnopolski Komitet Wspolpracy Organizacji Mlodziezowych [*All-Poland Committee for the Cooperation of Youth Organizations*] (POL)
OKZ............ Opsti Krivicni Zakonik [*General Criminal Code*] (YU)
OKZ............ Short-Circuit Ratio (RU)
OKZVV........ Okresni Komise Zemedelskych Vykrmen Vepru [*District Agricultural Commission for Hog Fattening Stations*] (CZ)
OKZZ........... Okregowa Komisja Zwiazkow Zawodowych [*District Commission of Trade Unions*] (POL)
OKZZ........... Okregowy Komitet Zwiazkow Zawodowych [*District Committee of Trade Unions*] (POL)
OL............... Base Line [*Of a ship*] (RU)
OL............... Clearing Lamp (RU)
OL............... Oberbaustofflager [*Superstructure Material Depot*] (EG)
OL............... Obrana Lidu [*People's Defense*] [*A newspaper*] (CZ)
OL............... October League (MAR)
oL .... Ohne Lieferplan [*Without Delivery Schedule*] (EG)
ol .... Olasz [*Italian*] (HU)
OL............... Order of Lenin (RU)
OL............... Orszagos Leveltar [*National Archives*] (HU)
OL............... Otravne Latky [*Chemical Agents, Toxicants*] (CZ)
Ol................ Oulun Laani [*Finnish*]
OLA............. All-Slavic Linguistic Atlas (RU)
OLA .... Ogaden Liberation Army [*Ethiopian*] (AF)
OLA .... Orbital Space Vehicle, Orbital Spacecraft (RU)
OLA .... Organosis Laikis Amynis [*People's Defense Organization*] [*Greek*] (GC)
OLADE .... Organizacion Latinoamericana de Energia [*Latin American Energy Organization*] (LA)
OLAFRIC..... Compagnie Huilerie Africaine (MAR)
Olajert Kirend ... Olajertekesito Vallalat Kirendeltsege [*Branch Office of the Oil Distribution Enterprise*] (HU)
OLAJTERV ... Koolaj es Gazipari Tervezo Vallalat [*Petroleum and Gas Industry Planning Enterprise*] (HU)
OLANI .... Office du Lait du Niger (MAR)
OLAS........... Organisation Locale des Affaires Sociales (MAR)
OLAS........... Organizacion Latinoamericana de Solidaridad [*Latin American Solidarity Organization*] [*Use LASO*] (LA)
OLB............. Orszagos Letszambizottsag [*National Census Committee*] (HU)
OLBS........... Separate Line Signal Battalion (RU)
OLC............. Organizacion para Liberacion del Comunismo [*Organization for Liberation from Communism*] [*Salvadoran*] (LA1)
OLC............. Overseas Liaison Committee (MAR)
OLCP-EA .... Organisation de Lutte Contre le Criquet Pelerin dans l'Est Africain [*Desert Locust Control Organization for Eastern Africa*] [*Use DCLO-EA*] (AF)
old .... Oldal [*Page*] (HU)
OLDEPESCA ... Organismo Latinoamericano para el Desarrollo de la Pesca [*Latin American Organization for Developing Fishing*] (LA1)
OLDP........... Society of Amateurs of Ancient Literature (RU)
OLDPI.......... Society of Amateurs of Literature and Art (RU)
OLDS........... Oddeleni Letecke Dopravni Spravy [*Department of Air Transport Directorate*] (CZ)
OLE .... Organosi Laikis Exousias [*Organization of Popular Sovereignty*] (GC)
OLEAHV...... Organisation Libre des Enseignants Africains de Haute Volta [*Free Organization of African Teachers of Upper Volta*] (AF)
OLEOCOL... Oleaginosas Colombiana Ltda. [*Barranquilla*] (COL)
OLEOPAC... Oleoducto del Pacifico, SA [*Cali*] (COL)
OLEYIS .... Turkiye Otel, Lokanta, ve Eglence Yerleri Iscileri Sendikasi [*Hotel, Restaurant, and Amusement Places Employees Union of Turkey*] [*See also TOLEYIS*] (TU)
OLF .... Oromo Liberation Front [*Ethiopian*] (PD)
Olfm .... Oberlandforstmeister [*Chief Regional Forester*] (EG)
OLG............. Okoliya Lecture Group (BU)
OLG............. Okrug Lecture Group (BU)
OLGR .... Oberlandesgerichtsrat [*German*]
OLH .... Oblastni Lidova Hvezdarna [*Regional Public Observatory*] (CZ)
OLHSZ .... Orszagos Lakasepitesi Hitelszovetkezet [*National Credit Cooperative for Housing Construction*] (HU)
OLICAR....... Oliveira et Cardoso (MAR)
OLIE .... Omospondia Leitourgon Idiotikis Ekpaidevseos [*Federation of Private School Teachers*] [*Greek*] (GC)
OLIZ .... Specialized Laboratory of Electric Measurements (RU)
OLK............. Okresni Lidova Knihovna [*District People's Library*] (CZ)
OLK............. Organismos Limenon Kyprou [*Cyprus Port Authority*] (GC)
OLKO .... Omorfo, Lefke, ve Bolgesi Kooperatifleri Birligi [*Morfou, Lefka, and Regional Cooperatives Union*] (TU)
OlKP............ Olasz Kommunista Part [*Italian Communist Party*] (HU)
OLLA........... Organizacion de Lluita Armada [*Armed Struggle Organization*] [*Spanish*] (WER)
OLM .... Office des Logements Militaires [*North African*] (MAR)
Olm .... Olum Yili [*Year of Death*] (TU)
Olm .... Olumu [*Death*] (TU)
OLM .... Organisation Locale Membre [*Local Member Organization*] (AF)
OLME.......... Omospondia Leitourgon Mesis Ekpaidevseos [*Federation of Secondary School Teachers*] [*Greek*] (GC)
OLMUK .... Mukavva Sanayii ve Ticaret AS [*Cardboard Industry and Trade Corporation*] (TU)
OLND .... Office de la Loterie Nationale pour le Developpement [*National Lottery Development Office*] [*Lao*] (CL)
OLNE........... Organosis Leninistikis Neolaias Ellados [*Organization of Leninist Youth of Greece*] (GC)
OLO............. All-Army Hunting Organization (BU)
OLO............. Okrajni Ljudski Odbor [*District People's Committee*] (YU)
OLP .... Organisation de Liberation de Palestine [*Palestine Liberation Organization*] [*Use PLO*] [*French*] (AF)

OLP .... Organismos Limenos Peiraios [*Piraeus Port Authority*] (GC)
OLP .... Organizacao de Libertacao da Palestina [*Palestine Liberation Organization*] [*Use PLO*] [*Portuguese*] (WER)
OLP .... Orszagos Legvedelmi Parancsnoksag [*National Air Defense Command*] (HU)
OLP .... Separate Camp Station (RU)
OLP .... Single-Wire Transmission Line (RU)
OLPN .... Association of Persons Persecuted During the Nazism [*Federal Republic of Germany*] (RU)
OLR .... Organisation pour la Liberation du Rwanda (MAR)
OLRS .... General Hunting and Fishing Union (BU)
olrs .... Separate Line Signal Company (RU)
OLS .... Light Forces Detachment [*Navy*] (RU)
OLS .... Odred Lekara Specijalista [*Medical Specialists Detachment*] (YU)
OLS .... Okresny Ludovy Sud [*District People's Court*] (CZ)
olsb .... Separate Telephone Construction Battalion (BU)
OLSHOD ..... Organization for the Liberation of Saguia El-Hamra and Oued El-Dheb (MAR)
olszv .... Orszagos Lo- es Szamarvasar [*National Horse and Donkey Fair*] (HU)
OLT .... Osjecka Ljevaonica i Tvornica Strojeva [*Osijek Foundry and Machinery Factory*] (YU)
OLTBr .... Separate Light Tank Brigade (RU)
OLTEK .... Organosis Leitourgon Tekhnikis Ekpaidevsis Kyprou [*Organization of Technical Education Teachers of Cyprus*] (GC)
OLTG .... Ordnung ueber den Lufttransport Gefaehrlicher Gueter [*Regulation on Air Transport of Hazardous Goods*] (EG)
OLTh .... Organismos Limenos Thessalonikis [*Salonica Port Authority*] (GC)
OLTL Im AM ... Oddzial Lodzki Towarzystwa Literackiego Imienia Adama Mickiewicza [*Lodz Branch of Adam Mickiewicz Literary Society*] (POL)
OLTP .... Separate Light Tank Regiment (RU)
olv .... Olvasd [*Read*] (HU)
olv .... Orszagos Lovasar [*National Horse Fair*] (HU)
OLYa .... Department of Literature and Language (of the Academy of Sciences, USSR) (RU)
OLYeAiE ..... Society of Amateurs of the Natural Sciences, Anthropology, and Ethnography (RU)
OM- .... Metal Settling Tank (RU)
OM .... Militia Station (RU)
OM .... Obranci Miru [*Peace Defenders*] (CZ)
OM .... Odmorovaci Misto [*Decontamination Point*] (CZ)
OM .... Oduma Magazine, Rivers State Council for Arts and Culture [*Nigerian*] [*A publication*] (MAR)
OM .... Officier Mecanicien (MAR)
OM .... Officine Mecchaniche [*Algerian*] (MAR)
OM .... Okresni Milice [*District Militia*] (CZ)
OM .... Okrug Museum (BU)
OM .... Oktatasugyi Miniszterium/Miniszter [*Ministry/Minister of Education*] (HU)
OM .... Oman [*Two-letter standard code*] (CNC)
om .... Omistaja [*Finnish*]
OM .... Omospondia Metallorykhon [*Federation of Miners*] [*Cypriot*] (GC)
O ve M .... Organizasyon ve Metot Grubu [*Organization and Methods Group*] [*In various ministries*] (TU)
OM .... Organosi "Makhitis" [*"Fighter" Organization*] [*Greek*] (GC)
OM .... Osadni Milice [*Hamlet Militia*] (CZ)
OM .... Osrodek Maszynowy [*Machine Station*] (POL)
OM .... Ovce Mleko [*Sheep Milk*] (YU)
om .... Ovog Meseca [*Of This Month*] (YU)
OM .... Power Governor (RU)
OM .... Single-Band Modulation (RU)
OM .... Small Offset (RU)
OM .... Teaching Machine (RU)
OMA .... Department of Mechanization and Automation (RU)
OMA .... Inverse Matrix Algorithm (RU)
OMA .... Ocean Mining Associates (MAR)
oma .... Om Akustyczny [*Acoustical Ohm*] [*Polish*]
OMA .... Organizacao das Mulheres Angolanas [*Organization of Angolan Women*] (AF)
OMAAEEC ... Organisation Mondiale des Anciens et Anciennes Eleves de l'Enseignement Catholique [*World Organization of Former Pupils of Catholic Schools*] (EA)
OMADEX ..... Office Malgache d'Exportation (MAR)
OMAG .... Armed Forces Supply and Repair Depot [*Portuguese*] (WER)
OMAG .... Separate Naval Air Group (RU)
OMAIR .... Department of Mechanization and Automation of Information Work (RU)
OMAKhR ..... Youth Society of the Association of Revolutionary Artists (RU)
OMAPAG .... Omnium Maghrebien de Participations et de Gestion (MAR)
OMB .... Oblast Medical Library (RU)
OMB .... Obshtina Mineral Baths (BU)
OMB .... Openbare Muziek Bibliotheek [*Dutch*]
OMB .... Organisation Moderne du Bureau (MAR)
OMB .... Orszagos Munkabermegallapito Bizottsag [*or Orszagos Munkaber Bizottsag*] [*National Wage Board*] (HU)
OMBEVI ...... Office Malien du Betail et de la Viande (MAR)
OMBIT .... Okrug Interunion Office of Engineers and Technicians (RU)
OMBKE .... Orszagos Magyar Banyaszati es Kohaszati Egyesulet [*National Hungarian Association of Mining and Metallurgy*] (HU)
OMBN .... Department of Medical and Biological Sciences (of the Academy of Medical Sciences, USSR) (RU)
OMBSN .... Separate Special-Purpose Medical Battalion (RU)
OMBVI .... Office Malien du Betail et de la Viande (MAR)
OMC .... Ocean Minerals Company (MAR)
OMC .... Office Mauritanien de Cereales [*Mauritanian Grain Office*] (AF)
OMCE .... Orszagos Magyar Cecilia Egyesulet [*National Hungarian Cecilia Association (Music)*] (HU)
OMCh .... Materiel Inspection (RU)
OMCI .... Omnium Marocain Commercial et Industriel [*Moroccan Commercial and Industrial Trading Company*] (AF)
OMCI .... Organisation Maritime Consultative Intergouvernementale [*Intergovernmental Maritime Consultative Organization*] [*Use IMCO*] (AF)
OMCO .... Ocean Minerals Company (MAR)
OMCOM ...... Oficina de Mejoramiento Comunal [*Community Improvement Office*] [*Salvadoran*] (LA1)
OMD .... Institute of Mother and Child Care (RU)
OMD .... Mother and Child Care (RU)
OMD .... Oblastni Madarske Divadlo [*Hungarian Regional Theater*] (CZ)
OMD .... Ochrana Matek a Deti [*Mother and Child Care*] (CZ)
OMDKRB ..... Organization for the Management and Development of the Kagera River Basin (MAR)
OME .... Omospondia Metallevton Ellados [*Federation of Greek Miners*] (GC)
OME .... Organisation Mondiale de l'Emballage [*World Packaging Organization - WPO*] (EA)
OMECA .... Office de Mecanographie (MAR)
OMECOMS ... Organisation pour la Mecanographie, la Comptabilite, et le Secretariat (MAR)
OMEH .... Orszagos Munkaerogazdalkodasi Hivatal [*National Labor Institute*] (HU)
OMEK .... Orszagos Mezogazdasagi es Elelmezesipari Kiallitas es Vasar [*National Agricultural and Food Industry Exhibition and Fair*] (HU)
OMELF .... Office Marocain de l'Exportation de Legumes et Fruits (MAR)
OMEP .... Organisation Mondiale pour l'Education Prescolaire [*World Organization for Early Childhood Education*] (EA)
OMETI .... Orszagos Munkaegeszsegugyi Intezet [*National Institute for Workers' Health Protection*] (HU)
OMF .... Obzornik za Matematiko in Fiziko [*Journal of Mathematics and Physics*] [*Ljubljana*] [*A publication*] (YU)
OMFB .... Orszagos Muszaki Fejlesztesi Bizottsag [*National Technical Development Committee*] (HU)
OMFI/OMFKI ... Orszagos Mezogazdasagi Fajtakiserleti Intezet [*National Agricultural Type-Experimentation Institute*] (HU)
OMFT/OMFMT ... Orszagos Mezogazdasagi Fajtaminosito Tanacs [*National Agricultural Type-Classifying Council*] (HU)
OMGE .... Organisation Mondiale de Gastroenterologie [*World Organization of Gastroenterology - WOG*] (EA)
OMGE .... Organizacion de la Mujer de Guinea Ecuatorial (MAR)
OMGH .... Orszagos Munkaero Gazdalkodasi Hivatal [*National Manpower Office*] (HU)
Omgiz .... Omsk State Publishing House (RU)
OMgK .... Orszagos Mezogazdasagi Konyvtar [*National Agricultural Library*] (HU)
OMGR .... Department of Marine Geophysical Work [*of the VNIIGeofizika*] (RU)
OMH .... Odbor Mistniho Hospodarstvi [*Local Economy Department*] (CZ)
OMH .... Orszagos Meresugyi Hivatal [*National Scaling Office*] (HU)
OMI .... Oblate Fathers of Mary Immaculate (MAR)
OMI .... Ocean Management, Incorporated (MAR)
OMI .... Odessa State Medical Institute Imeni N. I. Pirogov (RU)
OMI .... Omnium Marocain d'Investissement [*Moroccan Investment Trading Company*] (AF)
OMI .... Organisation Maritime Internationale [*International Maritime Organization - IMO*] (EA)
OMI .... Orszagos Munkaegeszsegugyi Intezet [*National Institute for Workers' Health Protection*] (HU)
OMIC .... Omnium Marocain Industriel et Chimique [*Moroccan Industrial and Chemical Trading Company*] (AF)
OMIH .... Orszagos Magyar Idegenforgalmi Hivatal [*Hungarian National Office of Tourism*] (HU)
OmIIT .... Omsk Institute of Railroad Transportation Engineers (RU)
OMIKE .... Orszagos Magyar Izraelita Kozmuvelodesi Egyesulet [*Hungarian National Jewish Educational Association*] (HU)
OMIKI .... Orszagos Mezogazdasagi Ipari Kiserleti Intezet [*National Agricultural Experimental Station*] (HU)
OMINC .... Ocean Management, Incorporated (MAR)
OMIR .... Department of Mechanization of Engineering and Technical Calculations (RU)
OMK .... General Mine Committee (BU)
OMK .... Orszagos Muszaki Konyvtar [*National Technical Library*] (HU)
OMKDK .... Orszagos Muszaki Konyvtar es Dokumentacios Kozpont [*National Technical Library and Documentation Center*] (HU)

OMKER .... Orvosi Muszer es Fogaszati Cikk Kereskedelmi Vallalat [*Commercial Enterprise for Medical and Dental Instruments and Appliances*] (HU)
OMKh .... Society of Moscow Artists (RU)
OMKMR ...... Department of Mechanization of Copying and Duplicating (RU)
OML .... Fundamentals of Marxism-Leninism (RU)
OML .... Oil Mining License (MAR)
OMLE .... Organization of Spanish Marxist-Leninists (PD)
OMLE .... Organosis Marxiston-Leniniston Elladas [*Organization of Marxist-Leninists of Greece*] (GC)
o/m/m .... A l'Ordre de Moi-Meme [*French*]
OMM .... Mother and Child Care (RU)
OMM .... Operation Mils in Mali (MAR)
OMM .... Organisation Meteorologique Mondiale [*World Meteorological Organization - WMO*] [*French*] (EA)
OMM .... Organizacao das Mulheres Mocambicanas [*Organization of Mozambique Women*] (AF)
OMM .... Organizacion Meteorologica Mundial [*UN World Meteorology Organization*] [*Use WMO*] [*Spanish*] (LA)
OMM .... Orszagos Magyar Munkasbizottsag [*National Committee of Hungarian Workers*] (HU)
OMM .... Scientific Research Institute of Mother and Child Care (RU)
OMMI .... Orszagos Mezogazdasagi Minosegvizsgalo Intezet [*National Research Institute on Quality Standards in Agriculture*] (HU)
OMMSA ...... Organisation of Monuments, Museums, and Sites of Africa (MAR)
OMMSS .... Oeuvres Mama Mobutu Sese Seko [*Mama Mobutu Sese Seko Projects*] [*Zairian*] (AF)
OMN .... Department of Medical Sciences (RU)
OMN .... Oman [*Three-letter standard code*] (CNC)
OMNIREX .... Omnium de Recherches et Exploitations Petrolieres [*Petroleum Exploration and Exploitation Company*] [*Algerian*] (AF)
OMNIS .... Office Militaire National pour les Industries Strategiques [*National Military Office for Strategic Industries*] [*Malagasy*] (AF)
OMNIVI .... Omsk Veterinary Scientific Research Institute (RU)
omo .... Medical Support Detachment (BU)
OMO .... Music Education Department (RU)
OMO .... Orman Muhendisleri Odasi [*Chamber of Forestry Engineers*] [*Turkish Cypriot*] (GC)
OMO .... Separate Medical Detachment (RU)
OMOCI .... Office de la Main-d'Oeuvre de Cote-d'Ivoire (MAR)
OMOS .... Experimental Naval Aircraft Construction Section (RU)
OMP .... Department of Local Industry (RU)
OMP .... Magnetic Bearing Reading (RU)
OMP .... Mass-Destruction Weapon (RU)
omp .... Ominaispaino [*Finnish*]
OMP .... Ordnance Maintenance Park (ML)
OMP .... Reciprocal Magnetic Bearing (RU)
omp .... Separate Mortar Regiment (RU)
ompb .... Separate Motorized Pontoon Battalion (RU)
OMPI .... Organizacion Mundial de la Propiedad Intelectual [*World Intellectual Property Organization*] [*Use WIPO*] (LA)
OMPKA .... Organismos Mathitikis Pronoias kai Andillipseos [*Students' Training and Welfare Organization*] [*Greek*] (GC)
OMPP .... Ochrana Majetku Proti Pozaru [*Protection of Property Against Fire*] (CZ)
OMPSA .... Organisation Mondiale pour le Promotion Sociale des Aveugles [*World Council for the Welfare of the Blind - WCWB*] (EA)
OMPTOB ..... Separate Motorized Antitank Flamethrower Battalion (RU)
OMPU .... Great Circle Magnetic Track Angle (RU)
OMPU .... Oficina Municipal de Planeamiento Urbano [*Municipal Office of Urban Planning*] [*Venezuelan*] (LA)
OMR .... Obermedizinalrat [*Chief Public Health Officer (In the GDR, title awarded for special merit)*] (EG)
OMR .... Office Mauritanien de la Radiodiffusion [*Mauritanian Broadcasting Office*] (AF)
OMR .... Organizacion Magisterial Revolucionaria [*Revolutionary Teachers Organization*] [*Salvadoran*] (LA1)
omr .... Separate Camouflage Company (RU)
OMRE .... Orszagos Magyar Repulo Egyesulet [*Hungarian National Aviation Association*] (HU)
OMRP .... Reciprocal Magnetic Radio Bearing (RU)
OMS .... Experimental Reclamation Station (RU)
OMS .... Okresni Mericske Stredisko [*District Geodetic Center*] (CZ)
OMS .... Okresni Myslivecky Svaz [*District Foresters' Union*] (CZ)
OMS .... Omsk Railroad (RU)
OMS .... Organisation Mondiale de la Sante [*World Health Organization*] [*Use WHO*] [*French*] (WER)
OMS .... Organizacao Mundial de Saude [*World Health Organization*] [*Portuguese*] (MAR)
OMS .... Organizacion Mundial de la Salud [*World Health Organization*] [*Use WHO*] [*Spanish*] (LA)
OMS .... Organizacni a Mobilizacni Sprava [*Organization and Mobilization Directorate*] (CZ)
OMS .... Organization and Mechanization of Construction (BU)
OMS .... Organizzazione Mondiale della Sanita [*World Health Organization*] [*Italian*] (MAR)
OMS .... Organosi Mathitikou Syndikalismou [*Organization of Student Unionism*] [*Greek*] (GC)
OMS .... Telephone Call Canceled at Moment of Connection (BU)
OMSB .... Separate Bridge Construction Battalion (RU)
omsb .... Separate Medical Battalion (RU)
omsb .... Separate Motorized Rifle Battalion (RU)
omsdON ...... Separate Special-Purpose Motorized Rifle Division (RU)
OM sektsiya ... General Mobilization Section (BU)
OMSEN .... Omnium Senegal (MAR)
OMSKhI ...... Omsk Agricultural Institute Imeni S. M. Kirov (RU)
OMSR .... Separate Medical Company (RU)
omsr .... Separate Motorized Rifle Company (RU)
OMSZ .... Orszagos Mento Szolgalat [*National Ambulance Service*] (HU)
OMSZ .... Orszagos Meteorologiai Szolgalat [*National Meteorological Service*] (HU)
OMSzK .... Orszagos Meheszeti Szovetkezeti Kozpont [*National Center of Beekeepers' Cooperatives*] (HU)
OMT .... Organisation Mondiale du Tourisme [*World Tourism Organization*] (CL)
OMTAS .... Otomotiv Transmisyon Aksami Sanayi ve Ticaret Anonim Sirketi [*Automotive Transmission Parts Industry and Commerce Corporation*] (TU)
OMTK .... Orszagos Magyar Tejertekesito Kozpont [*National Hungarian Center for Milk Distribution*] (HU)
OMTO .... Materiel Support Section [*Miltary term*], Materials and Equipment Supply Department (RU)
OMTS .... Materials and Equipment Supply Department (RU)
OMTUR .... Organizacja Mlodziezy Towarzystwa Uniwersytetow Robotniczych [*Youth Organization of the Society of Workers' Universities (Extension courses)*] (POL)
OMTVGE ..... Omospondia Mikhanikon kai Thermaston Viomikhanias kai Georgias Ellados [*Federation of Greek Industrial and Agricultural Mechanics and Stokers*] (GC)
OMTVK .... Omospondia Misthoton Typou kai Viomikhanias Khartou [*Federation of Salaried Press and Paper Industry Employees*] [*Greek*] (GC)
OMU .... Department for Stocktaking of Materials (RU)
OMU .... Operational Magnetic Amplifier (RU)
OMU .... Simultaneous Multiplier (RU)
OM Uzmani ... Organizasyon ve Method Uzmani [*Organization and Methods Specialist*] (TU)
OMV .... Office de Mise en Valeur [*Development Office*] [*Cambodian*] (CL)
OMVA .... Office de Mise en Valeur Agricole [*Moroccan*] (MAR)
OMVG .... Organisation de Mise en Valeur du Fleuve Gambie [*Gambia River Development Organization*] (AF)
OMVK .... Okresni Mimoradna Vyzivovaci Komise [*District Special Food Commission*] (CZ)
OMVR .... Department of Mechanization of Computation (RU)
OMVS .... Organisation pour la Mise en Valeur du Fleuve Senegal [*Senegal River Development Organization*] (AF)
OMVSD .... Office de Mise en Valeur de Sategui-Deressia (MAR)
OMVVM .... Office de Mise en Valeur de la Vallee de la Medjerda [*Office for Developing the Medjerda Valley*] [*Tunisian*] (AF)
OMYeN .... Department of Mathematical and Natural Sciences (of the Academy of Sciences, USSR) (RU)
OMZ .... Experimental Magnesium Plant (RU)
OMZ .... Optical Instrument Plant (RU)
OMZB .... Separate Small-Caliber Antiaircraft Battery (RU)
OMZD .... Delayed-Action Fragmentation Mine (RU)
omzhdb .... Separate Motorized Railroad Battalion (RU)
On .... Canon [*Cannon*] [*Short form used in commands only*] [*French*] (MTD)
on .... Concentrated Artillery Fire (RU)
ON .... League of Nations (BU)
ON .... Main Direction, Base Line (RU)
On .... Onorevole [*Honorable*] [*Italian*] (GPO)
ON .... Operativni Normy [*Operational Standards*] (CZ)
ON .... Orden Nuevo [*New Order*] [*Spanish*] (WER)
ON .... Ordine Nuovo [*New Order*] [*Italian*] (WER)
ON .... Ortsnetz [*Local Telephone Network*] (EG)
ON .... Primary Direction [*Military*] (BU)
ON .... Reference Voltage (RU)
on .... Special-Purpose (RU)
ON .... Specialized Standards (RU)
ON .... Stress-Control Winding (RU)
ON .... Supercharger (RU)
ON .... United Nations (BU)
ONA .... Office des Nouvelles Algeriennes [*Algerian News Office*] (AF)
ONA .... Omnium Nord-Africain [*North African Trading Company*] (AF)
ONAA .... Office National de l'Artisanat d'Art (MAR)
ONAA .... Oficina Nacional de Apoyo Alimentario [*National Office for Food Support*] [*Peruvian*] (LA)
ONAAC .... Office National d'Alphabetisation et d'Action Communautaire [*National Office for Literacy and Community Action*] [*Haitian*] (LA)
ONAB .... Office National des Aliments du Betail [*Algerian*] (MAR)
ONACER ..... Office National des Cereales [*National Grain Office*] [*Zairian*] (AF)
ONACIBE .... Office National du Cinema du Benin (MAR)
ONACO .... Office National Algerien de Commercialisation [*Algerian National Marketing Office*] (AF)

ONACT........ Organizacion Nicaraguense Americana de Cooperacion Tecnica [*Nicaraguan American Organization of Technical Cooperation*] (LA)
ONADEC..... Organisation Nationale des Entreprises Congolaises [*National Organization of Congolese Enterprises*] (AF)
ONAF.......... Office National d'Affretements (MAR)
ONAF.......... Office National des Forets [*National Forests Office*] [*Congolese*] (AF)
ONAFEX...... Office National Algerien des Foires et des Expositions Commerciales (AF)
ONAFITEX... Office National des Fibres Textiles [*National Textile Fiber Office*] [*Zairian*] (AF)
ONAGI......... Office National de Gestion des Biens Immobiliers de l'Etat [*National Office for Management of State Real Estate*] [*Zairian*] (AF)
ONAH.......... Office National d'Hydrocarbures [*National Hydrocarbons Office*] [*Guinean*] (AF)
ONAHA....... Office National des Amenagements Hydro-Agricoles (MAR)
ONAI........... Organisation of Nigerian Agricultural Industries (MAR)
ONAJ........... Oficina Nacional de Asuntos Juridicos [*National Legal Affairs Office*] [*Peruvian*] (LA)
ONAKO....... Office National du Kouilou (MAR)
ONAL.......... Organisation Nouvelle pour l'Afrique Libre [*New Organization for Free Africa*] (AF)
ONALAI....... Office National du Lait et des Produits Laitiers [*Algerian*] (MAR)
ONALFA...... Office National de l'Alfa [*North African*] (MAR)
ONAMA....... Office National du Materiel Agricole [*National Agricultural Equipment Office*] [*Algerian*] (AF)
ONAMHYD... Office National du Materiel Hydraulique (MAR)
ONAMO....... Office National Algerien de la Main-d'Oeuvre [*National Algerian Manpower Bureau*] (AF)
ONAMS....... Oficina Nacional de Apoyo a la Mobilizacion Social [*National Office for Support of Social Mobilization*] [*Peruvian*] (LA)
ONAP.......... Oficina Nacional de Administracion Publica y Personal [*National Bureau for Personnel and Public Administration*] [*Dominican Republic*] (LA)
ONAPED..... Organizacion Nacional de Periodistas Democraticos [*National Organization of Democratic Journalists*] [*Venezuelan*] (LA)
ONAPO........ Office National des Produits Oleicoles [*National Olive Products Office*] [*Algerian*] (AF)
ONAREM..... Office National des Ressources Minieres [*National Office of Mineral Resources*] [*Niger*] (AF)
ONAREST... Office National de la Recherche Scientifique et Technique [*National Office of Scientific and Technical Research*] [*Cameroonian*] (AF)
ONAREXH... Office National de Recherches et d'Exploitation des Hydrocarbures [*Moroccan*] (MAR)
ONAT.......... Office National Algerien du Tourisme [*Algerian National Tourist Office*] (AF)
ONATA........ Office National de l'Artisanat Traditionnel Algerien [*National Office of Algerian Traditional Handicrafts*] (AF)
ONATHO..... Office National du Tourisme et de l'Hotellerie [*National Tourism and Hotel Office*] [*Beninese*] (AF)
ONATRA..... Office National des Transports [*National Transportation Office*] [*Zairian*] (AF)
ONATRATE... Oficina Nacional de Transporte Terrestre [*National Office for Land Transportation*] [*Dominican Republic*] (LA1)
ONB............. Office National du Bois [*National Lumber Office*] [*Zairian*] (AF)
Onb............. Onbasi [*Corporal*] (TU)
ONBG.......... Office National des Bois du Gabon (MAR)
ONBI............ Office National des Barrages et de l'Irrigation (MAR)
ONC............ Office National du Cafe [*National Coffee Office*] [*Zairian*] (AF)
ONC............ Office National des Changes [*National Exchange Office*] [*Cambodian*] (CL)
ONC............ Office National de Commerce [*National Trade Office*] [*Burundi*] (AF)
ONCA.......... Office National de Commercialisation Agricole [*National Office for Agricultural Marketing*] [*Gabonese*] (AF)
ONCAD....... Office National de Cooperation et d'Assistance pour le Developpement [*National Office of Cooperation and Assistance for Development*] [*Senegalese*] (AF)
ONCE.......... Oficina Nacional del Censo [*National Census Office*] [*Cuban*] (LA)
ONCF.......... Office National de Chemins de Fer [*National Railroad Office*] [*Moroccan*] (AF)
ONCFM....... Office National des Chemins de Fer du Maroc (MAR)
ONCIC......... Office National pour la Commercialisation des Industries Cinematographiques [*National Marketing Bureau for the Cinematographic Industries*] [*Algerian*] (AF)
ONCL.......... Office National Cinematographique du Laos [*National Motion Picture Office of Laos*] (CL)
ONCPA........ Office National de Commercialisation des Produits Agricoles [*National Office for the Marketing of Agricultural Products*] [*Congolese*] (AF)
ONCPB........ Office National de Commercialisation des Produits de Base [*National Basic Necessities Marketing Office*] [*Cameroonian*] (AF)
ONCS.......... Office National Catholique des Moyens de Communications Sociales (MAR)
ONCSA....... Orszagos Nep- es Csaladvedelmi Alap [*National Welfare Fund*] (HU)
ONCT.......... Office National Congolais du Tourisme (MAR)
ONCV.......... Office National de Commercialisation des Produits Viti-Vinicoles [*National Office for Marketing Wine and Wine Products*] [*Algerian*] (AF)
OND............ Greatest Common Divisor (RU)
OND............ Ordinary National Diploma (MAR)
OND............ Pressure Increase Limiter (RU)
ONDC.......... Office National de Developpement de Cacao (MAR)
ONDE.......... Office National de Developpement de l'Elevage [*National Livestock Development Office*] [*Zairian*] (AF)
ONDEC....... Oficina Nacional de Educacion Catolica [*National Catholic Education Office*] [*Peruvian*] (LA)
ONDECOOP... Oficina Nacional de Fomento Cooperativo [*National Cooperative Development Office*] [*Peruvian*] (LA)
ONDEPA..... Organizacion Nacional de Profesionales Agropecuarios [*National Agricultural and Livestock Professionals Association*] [*Colombian*] (LA)
ONDEPJOV... Oficina Nacional de Desarrollo de Pueblos Jovenes [*National Office for the Development of New Settlements*] [*Peruvian*] (LA)
ONDR.......... Office National Tchadien de Developpement Rural [*Chadian National Office for Rural Development*] (AF)
ONDS.......... Office National du Sucre [*National Sugar Office*] [*Zairian*] (AF)
ONE............ Oeuvre Nationale d'Entraide [*National Welfare Fund*] [*Cambodian*] (CL)
ONE............ Office National de l'Electricite [*National Electricity Office*] [*Moroccan*] (AF)
One............ Oyane [*or Oyene*] [*Islands*] [*Danish*] (NAU)
One............ Oyane [*or Oyene*] [*Islands*] [*Norwegian*] (NAU)
ONEC.......... Oficina Nacional de Estadisticas y Censo [*National Office for Statistics and Census*] [*Peruvian*] (LA)
ONED.......... Organismos Neolaias Enoseos Kendrou [*Center Union (Party) Youth Organization*] (GC1)
Oneglag...... Onega Corrective Labor Camp (RU)
ONEP.......... Office National d'Eau Potable [*National Drinking Water Office*] [*Algerian*] (AF)
ONERA........ Office National d'Etudes et de Recherches Aerospatiales [*National Office for Aerospace Studies and Research*] [*French*] (WER)
ONEREP...... Omnium Cherifien de Negoce et de Representations Internationales (MAR)
ONERN........ Oficina Nacional de Evaluacion de Recursos Nacionales [*National Bureau for Evaluating National Resources*] [*Peruvian*] (LA)
ONERSOL... Office Nigerien de l'Energie Solaire [*Nigerien Solar Energy Office*] [*Niger*] (AF)
ONF............ Fatherland People's Front [*Hungarian People's Republic*] (RU)
ONF............ Ob'edinennyi Natsional'nyi Front (MAR)
ONF............ Okresny Narodny Front [*District National Front Organization*] (CZ)
ONFP.......... Office National de Formation Professionnelle (MAR)
ong............. Ongeveer [*About, Approximately*] [*Dutch*] (GPO)
ONG............ Organisations Non-Gouvernementales [*Nongovernmental Organizations*] (AF)
ONGT.......... Office National Gabonais du Tourisme [*Gabonese National Tourist Office*] (AF)
ONH............ Office National de l'Huile [*National Olive Oil Office*] [*Tunisian*] (AF)
ONHA.......... Office National de l'Huilerie d'Abeche (MAR)
ONI............. Office National d'Irrigation [*National Irrigation Office*] [*Moroccan*] (AF)
ONI............. Office National de l'Ivoire (MAR)
ONI............. Office des Nouvelles Internationales [*International News Office*] [*French*] (AF)
ONI............. Oficina Nacional de Informacion [*National Information Office*] [*Peruvian*] (LA)
ONI............. Oficina Nacional de Integracion [*National Integration Office*] [*Peruvian*] (LA)
ONI............. Organizacion Nacional Independiente [*National Independent Organization*] [*Venezuelan*] (LA)
ONI............. Orszagos Nevelestudomanyi Intezet [*National Pedagogical Institute*] [*Kecskemet*] (HU)
ONIA.......... Office National Industriel de l'Azote (MAR)
ONII............ Institute of Scientific Research Based on Public Participation (RU)
ONIITEM..... Oficina Nacional de Invenciones, Informacion Tecnica, y Marcas [*National Office for Inventions, Technical Information, and Trademarks*] (LA)
ONIL........... Office National d'Industrialisation Libyen (MAR)
ONIS........... Oficina Nacional de Informacion Social [*National Social Information Office*] [*Peruvian*] (LA)
ONISEP....... Office National d'Information sur les Enseignements et les Professions [*French*]
ONIT........... Oficina Nacional de Integracion [*National Integration Office*] [*Peruvian*] (LA)
ONJ............ Organizacao Nacional de Jornalistas [*National Organization of Journalists*] [*Mozambican*] (AF)
ONK............ Optimum Irregular Code (RU)
ONK............ Oristikos Navtikos Katalogos [*Definitive Naval List*] [*Greek*] (GC)

ONL............ Office National de Logement [*National Housing Office*] [*Zairian*] (AF)
ONM............ Least Common Multiplier (RU)
ONM............ Office National Meteorologique [*French*]
ONM............ Office National des Mines [*National Mines Office*] [*Tunisian*] (AF)
ONM............ Office National de Modernisation [*National Modernization Office*] [*Central African*] (AF)
ONM............ Office du Niger au Mali (MAR)
ONM............ Organisation National des Moudjahidine [*National Veterans' Organization*] [*Algerian*] (AF)
ONMB.......... Oblast Scientific Medical Library (RU)
ONMI........... Opera Nazionale Maternita e Infanzia [*National Institute for Mother and Child Welfare*] [*Italian*] (WER)
ONMI........... Opera Nazionale per il Mezzogiorno d'Italia [*National Institute for the Improvement of Southern Italy*] (WER)
ONMR.......... Office National de la Modernisation Rurale [*National Office for Rural Modernization*] [*Moroccan*] (AF)
ONMT.......... Office National Marocain de Tourisme [*Moroccan National Tourist Office*] (AF)
ONMT.......... Office National Mauritanien du Tourisme [*Mauritanian National Tourism Office*] (AF)
ONNED........ Organosis Neon tis Neas Dimokratias [*Youth Organization of the New Democracy (Party)*] [*Greek*] (GC)
ONO............ Department of Public Education (RU)
ONO............ Oblasten Naroden Odbor [*Regional People's Committee*] (YU)
ONO............ Oesnoroeste [*West-Northwest*] [*Spanish*]
ONO............ Office National de l'Okoume (MAR)
ONO............ Okruzni Narodni Odbor [*County People's Committee*] (YU)
ONO............ Opstinski Narodni Odbor [*Municipal People's Committee*] (YU)
ONOAKMO ... Okruzni Narodni Odbor Autonomne Kosovo-Metohiske Oblasti [*County People's Committee of the Autonomous Kosovo-Metohija Region*] (YU)
ONOO.......... Okruzni Narodnooslobodilacki Odbor [*County National Liberation Committee*] (YU)
ONP............ Association of German Trade Unions [*West German*] (RU)
ONP............ Office National de Peche [*National Fishing Office*] [*Algerian*] (AF)
ONP............ Office National de Peche [*National Fishing Office*] [*Tunisian*] (AF)
ONP............ Office National de Peche [*National Fishing Office*] [*Zairian*] (AF)
ONP............ Office National Pharmaceutique (MAR)
ONP............ Office National des Ports [*National Ports Office*] [*Algerian*] (AF)
ONP............ Okresni Narodni Pojistovna [*District National Insurance Agency*] (CZ)
ONP............ Okresni Nemocenska Pojistovna [*District Health Insurance Agency*] (CZ)
ONP............ Scientific Propaganda Department (RU)
ONP............ Separate Observation Post (RU)
ONPC.......... Office National des Ports du Cameroun (MAR)
ONPDD........ Omospondia Nomikon Prospopon Dimosiou Dikaiou [*Federation of Legal Entities of Public Law*] [*Greek*] (GC)
ONPFEP...... Office National du Planning Familial et de la Population (MAR)
ONPFP........ Office National du Planning Familial et de la Population (MAR)
ONPI........... Office National de la Propriete Industrielle [*National Office for Industrial Properties*] [*Algerian*] (AF)
ONPM.......... Office National des Peches Maritimes [*Moroccan*] (MAR)
ONPPC........ Office National des Produits Pharmaceutiques et Chimiques [*National Office of Pharmaceutical and Chemical Products*] [*Niger*] (AF)
ONPT........... Office National des Postes et Telecommunications [*National Postal and Telecommunications Office*] [*Congolese*] (AF)
ONPTZ........ Office National des Postes et Telecommunications du Zaire [*Zairian National Posts and Telecommunications Office*] (AF)
ONPTZa...... Office National des Postes et Telecommunications du Zaire [*Zairian National Posts and Telecommunications Office*] (AF)
ONPU.......... Oficina Nacional de Planeamiento y Urbanismo [*National Planning and Urban Renewal Bureau*] [*Peruvian*] (LA)
ONPZ.......... Obrtno Nabavna Prodajna Zadruga [*Handicraft Buying and Selling Cooperative*] (YU)
ONR............ Oboz Narodowo-Radykalny [*Radical Nationalist Camp*] [*Polish*] (PPE)
ONR............ Organization for National Reconstruction [*Trinidadian and Tobagan*] (LA1)
ONRA.......... Office National de la Reforme Agraire [*National Office for Agrarian Reform*] [*Algerian*] (AF)
ONRA.......... Oficina Nacional de la Reforma Agraria [*National Office for Agrarian Reform*] [*Peruvian*] (LA)
ONRD.......... Office National de Recherches et de Developpement [*National Research and Development Office*] [*Zairian*] (AF)
ONRI........... Orde van Nederlandse Raadgevende Ingenieurs [*'s-Gravenhage*]
ONRS.......... Office National de la Recherche Scientifique [*National Office for Scientific Research*] [*Algerian*] (AF)
ONRSD........ Office National de la Recherche Scientifique et du Developpement [*National Office for Scientific Research and Development*] [*Zairian*] (AF)
ONS............ Office National des Sports (MAR)
ONS............ Okoliya People's Council (BU)
ONS............ Okrug People's Council (BU)
ONS............ Ordinary National Assembly (BU)
ONS............ Oriental Numismatic Society (EA)
ONSC.......... Oficina Nacional del Servicio Civil [*National Civil Service Office*] [*Uruguayan*] (LA)
ONSDT........ Okoliya People's Council of Deputies of the Working People (BU)
ONSDT........ Okrug People's Council of Deputies of the Working People (BU)
ONSiW........ Osrodek Nauk Spolecznych i Wojskowych [*Social and Military Science Center*] (POL)
ONSS.......... Office National de la Securite Sociale [*National Office of Social Security*] [*Belgian*] (WER)
ONSSU........ Office National des Sports Scolaires et Universitaires [*National Office of Scholastic and University Sports*] [*Congolese*] (AF)
ONT............ Department of Labor Standardization (RU)
ONT............ Office National de Textiles [*National Textiles Office*] [*Tunisian*] (AF)
ONT............ Office National du Tourisme (MAR)
ONT............ Office National des Transports [*National Transportation Office*] [*Moroccan*] (AF)
ONT............ Oficiul National de Turism [*National Office for Tourism*] (RO)
ONT............ Orszagos Nepmuvelesi Tanacs [*National Council of Adult Education*] (HU)
ONTB.......... Basic Scientific and Technical Library (RU)
ONTB.......... Specialized Scientific and Technical Library (RU)
ONTEJ......... Organizacion Nacional de Turismo Estudiantil y Juvenil [*National Organization of Student and Youth Tourism*] [*Peruvian*] (LA)
ONTF........... Office National des Travaux Forestiers (MAR)
ONTI............ Association of Scientific and Technical Publishing Houses (RU)
ONTI............ Department of Scientific and Technical Information (RU)
ONTI............ Joint Scientific and Technical Publishing House (RU)
ONTIZ.......... Association of Scientific and Technical Publishing Houses (RU)
ONTM.......... Office National de Tourisme Marocaine (MAR)
ONTP........... Office National des Transports Publics (MAR)
ONTPiO....... Department of Scientific and Technical Information and Propaganda (RU)
ONTS.......... Oblast Scientific and Technical Council (RU)
ONTS.......... Office National du The et du Sucre [*National Tea and Sugar Office*] [*Moroccan*] (AF)
ONTT........... Office National Togolais du Tourisme (MAR)
ONTT........... Office National du Tourisme et du Thermalisme [*National Office of Tourism and Thermal Springs*] [*Tunisian*] (AF)
ONTV.......... Okresni Narodni Telovychovny Vybor [*District Physical Education Committee*] (CZ)
ONU............ Organisation des Nations Unies [*United Nations Organization*] [*Use UN*] [*French*] (AF)
ONU............ Organizacao das Nacoes Unidas [*United Nations*] [*Use UN*] [*Portuguese*] (WER)
ONU............ Organizacion de las Naciones Unidas [*United Nations*] [*Use UN*] [*Spanish*] (LA)
ONU............ Organizatia Natiunilor Unite [*United Nations*] [*Use UN*] (RO)
ONUC.......... Organisation des Nations Unies au Congo (MAR)
ONUDI......... Organisation des Nations Unies pour le Developpement Industriel [*United Nations Industrial Development Organization*] [*Use UNIDO*] [*French*] (WER)
ONUDI......... Organizacion de las Naciones Unidas para el Desarrollo Industrial [*United Nations Industrial Development Organization*] [*See UNIDO*] [*Spanish*] (LA)
ONUDI......... Organizatia Natiunilor Unite pentru Dezvoltare Industriala [*United Nations Industrial Development Organization*] [*Use UNIDO*] (RO)
ONV............ Obvodni Narodni Vybor [*District National Committee*] (CZ)
ONV............ Okresni Narodni Vybor [*District National Committee*] (CZ)
ONW............ Okreg Naukowy Warszawski [*Warsaw Academic District*] (POL)
ONZ............ Least Common Denominator (RU)
ONZ............ Main Charge Carriers (RU)
ONZ............ Odbor za Narodno Zdravlje (SIV) [*Public Health Committee*] (YU)
onz.............. Onza [*Ounce*] [*Spanish*]
ONZ............ Organizacja Narodow Zjednoczonych [*United Nations*] [*Use UN*] (POL)
OO.............. Deviation Detection (RU)
OO.............. Oberoesterreich [*or Oberoesterreichisch*] [*German*]
oO.............. Ohne Ort [*No Place (of Publication)*] [*German*]
oo............... Ojcowie [*Polish*]
OO.............. Okresni Odbor [*District Branch*] (CZ)
OO.............. Okresni Organisace [*District Organization*] (CZ)
OO.............. Okruzni Odbor [*County Committee*] (YU)
OO.............. Operations Section (RU)
OO.............. Opstinski Odbor [*Municipal Committee*] (YU)
OO.............. Organizational Department (RU)
OO.............. Osnovna Organizacija [*Basic Organization*] (YU)
OO.............. Social Insurance (BU)
OO.............. Special Section, Special Department (RU)
OOA............ Ochranna Organizace Autorska [*Authors' Protective Organization (Copyright)*] (CZ)
OOB............ Okresni Osvetova Beseda [*District Cultural Group*] (CZ)

oob .... Separate Flame-Throwing Battalion (BU)
OOB .... Separate Flamethrower Battalion (RU)
OOCL .... Overseas Ocean Carrier Limited [*Hong Kong*]
OOD .... Company with Limited Liability (BU)
OOD .... Movement Support Detachment (RU)
OOD .... Traffic Control Detachment (BU)
oO Dr u J .... Ohne Ort, Druckernamen, und Jahr [*German*]
OODS .... Okresna Organizacia Demokratickej Strany [*District Organization of the Democratic Party*] (CZ)
OOD-vo .... Company with Limited Liability (BU)
OOE .... Odiki Omospondia Ellados [*Greek Roads Federation*] (GC)
OOGE .... Omospondia Oikodomon kai Genikon Ergaton [*Federation of Construction and General Workers*] [*Cypriot*] (GC)
OOGM .... Orta Ogretim Genel Mudurlugu [*Secondary Education Directorate General*] (TU)
OOI .... Okresni Osvetovy Inspektorat [*Office of the District Inspector of Cultural Activities*] (CZ)
OOI .... Orszagos Onkologiai Intezet [*National Oncological Institute*] (HU)
OOK .... Odred Obezbedenja Kretanja [*Movement Protecting Detachment*] [*Military*] (YU)
OOK .... Odred za Opravku Komunikacija [*Detachment for Communications Repair*] [*Military*] (YU)
OOK .... Okresni Odbor Kultury [*District Cultural Department*] (CZ)
OOK .... Orszagos Orvostorteneti Konyvtar [*National Library of Medical History*] (HU)
OOK .... Ovambo Ontwikkelingskorporasie [*Ovambo Development Corporation*] [*Namibian*] (AF)
OOKiDKN .... Okregowe Osrodki Ksztalcenia i Dokształcania Kadr Nauczycielskich [*District Centers for the Education and Improvement of Teaching Personnel*] (POL)
OOMP .... Oblast Department of Local Industry (RU)
OON .... Department of Social Sciences (of the Academy of Sciences, USSR) (RU)
OON .... Order of the Niger (MAR)
OON .... Organizacija na Obedinenite Narodi [*United Nations Organization*] (YU)
OON .... Organizatsiia Ob'edinennykh Natsii (MAR)
OON .... Special-Purpose Detachment (RU)
OON .... United Nations Organization (BU)
OON .... United Nations Organization [*UNO*] (RU)
OONAZ .... Special-Purpose Detachment (RU)
OOOF .... Okrozni Odbor Osvobodilne Fronte [*County Committee of the Liberation Front*] (YU)
OOOID .... Report of the Odessa Society of History and Antiquities (RU)
OOP .... Oddzialowa Organizacja Partyjna [*Branch Party Organization*] (POL)
OOP .... Okregowa Organizacja Partyjna [*District Party Organization*] (POL)
OOP .... Primary Defense Zone (RU)
OOR .... Obvodna Osvetova Rada [*District Cultural Council*] (CZ)
OOR .... Okresni Odborova Rada [*District Trade-Union Council*] (CZ)
OOR .... Separate Flamethrower Company (RU)
OOS .... Negative Feedback (RU)
OOS .... Okresni Osvetovy Sbor [*District Cultural Board*] (CZ)
OOSA .... Organismos Oikonomikis Synergasias kai Anaptyxeos [*Organization for Economic Cooperation and Development*] (GC)
OOSA .... Separate Detachment of Ambulance Motor Sleds (RU)
OOSB .... Okresni Odbor Svazu Brannosti [*District Branch of the Union for Military Preparedness*] (CZ)
OOSK .... Osnovna Organizacija Saveza Komunista [*Basic Organization of the League of Communists*] (YU)
OOSMP .... Separate Specialized Medical Aid Detachment (RU)
OOSSNU .... Separate Dog-Team Sled-Litter Detachment (RU)
OOSSRN .... Osnovna Organizacija Socijalisticki Savez Radnog Naroda [*Basic Organization of the Socialist Alliance of Working People*] (YU)
OOT .... Work Safety Department (RU)
OOUP .... Odbor za Organizaciono-Upravna Pitanja (SIV) [*Committee on Organizational and Administrative Problems*] (YU)
OOUR .... Osnova Organizacija Udruzenog Rada [*Basic Organization of Workers*] [*Yugoslav*] (CED)
OOVB .... Okresni Oddeleni Verejne Bezpecnosti [*District Department for Public Security*] (CZ)
OOZB .... Okrozni Odbor Zveze Borcev [*County Committee of the Union of Veterans*] (YU)
OP .... Bath Station (RU)
op .... Experimental (RU)
OP .... Experimental Field [*Agriculture*] (RU)
OP .... Firing Position (RU)
OP .... Firing Position [*Artillery*] (BU)
OP .... Flight Control Section (RU)
OP- .... Foam Fire Extinguisher (RU)
op .... Inventory, List (RU)
op .... List, Inventory of Goods, Schedule (BU)
OP .... N-Type Conductivity, Negative Conductivity (RU)
OP .... Obalna Plovidba [*Coastal Navigation*] (YU)
OP .... Obcansky Prukaz [*Citizen's Identification Card*] (CZ)
OP .... Oborovy Podnik [*Sectoral Enterprise*] (CZ)
OP .... Obrtno Poduzece [*Handicraft Establishment*] (YU)
OP .... Observation Post (RU)
op .... Obvodni Podnik [*District Enterprise*] [*Czechoslovak*] (CED)
OP .... Odbor za Privredu (SIV) [*Committee on Economics*] (YU)
OP .... Oddzial Powiatowy [*County Branch*] (POL)
OP .... Odevni Prodejny [*Clothing Stores*] (CZ)
OP .... Odevni Prumysl [*Garment Industry*] (CZ)
OP .... Okoliya Management (BU)
OP .... Okresni Pojistovna [*District Insurance Agency*] (CZ)
OP .... Okresni Poradna [*District Advisory Office*] (CZ)
OP .... Okrug Enterprise (BU)
OP .... Okrug Management (BU)
op .... Olvadaspont [*Melting Point*] (HU)
OP .... Omospondia Pratirioukhon [*Federation of Gas Station Owners*] [*See also SP*] (GC1)
op .... Opera [*Works*] [*Latin*] (GPO)
OP .... Operation Order (RU)
OP .... Operationnel [*Operational*] [*French*] (CL)
OP .... Operativni Planovani [*Operational Planning*] (CZ)
op .... Opettaja [*Finnish*]
op .... Opus [*Work*] [*Latin*] (GPO)
OP .... Opus Pacis [*Opus Pacis (Hungarian Catholic peace movement)*] (HU)
OP .... Ordre des Precheurs [*Dominicans*] [*French*]
OP .... Osnovni Pravac [*Main Direction*] [*Military*] (YU)
OP .... Osobni Prukaz [*Personal Identity Card*] (CZ)
OP .... Osvecova Prace [*Cultural Work*] [*A periodical*] (CZ)
OP .... Otets Paisiy [*Father Paisiy*] [*A periodical*] (BU)
OP .... Otkupno Preduzece [*Purchasing Establishment*] (YU)
OP- .... Pneumatic Irrigator (RU)
OP .... Process Time (RU)
OP .... Propaganda Department (RU)
OP .... Reciprocal Bearing (RU)
OP .... Reflected and Refracted [*Wave*] (RU)
OP .... Rotary Converter (RU)
OP .... Stopping Point (RU)
OP .... Strongpoint (RU)
OP .... Supply Relay Point [*Military term*] (RU)
op- .... Telescopic Sight (RU)
OP .... Terminal Point (RU)
OPA .... Austrian Liberation Party (RU)
OPA .... Offre Publique d'Achat [*Public Offer to Purchase*] [*French*] (WER)
OPA .... Omada gia mia Proletariaki Aristera [*Group for a Proletarian Left*] [*Greek*] (GC)
OPA .... Onafhankelijke Partij [*Independent Party*] [*Dutch*] (PPW)
OPA .... Organisation des Pionniers Angolais [*Organization of Angolan Pioneers*] [*French*] (MAR)
OPA .... Organismos Prolipseos Atykhimaton [*Accident Prevention Organization*] [*Greek*] (GC)
OPA .... Organizacao de Pioneiros Angolanos [*Organization of Angolan Pioneers*] [*Portuguese*] (AF)
OPA .... Organizacja Panstw Amerykanskich [*Organization of American States*] [*Polish*]
OPA .... Propaganda and Agitation Section (BU)
opab .... Separate Machine-Gun and Artillery Battalion (RU)
OPAC .... Office des Produits Agricoles de Costermansville (MAR)
OPAD .... Separate Gun Artillery Battalion (RU)
OPAEP .... Organisations des Pays Arabes Exportateurs de Petrole (MAR)
OPAIE .... Organismos Perithalpseos kai Apokatastaseos Israiliton Ellados [*Organization for Aid and Resettlement of Jews of Greece*] (GC)
OPAK .... Office des Produits Agricoles de Kivu [*Zairian*] (MAR)
OPAKFI .... Optikai, Akusztikai, es Filmtechnikai Egyesulet [*Optics, Acoustics, and Film Technology Association*] (HU)
OPAM .... Office des Produits Agricoles du Mali [*Malian Agricultural Products Office*] (AF)
OPANAL .... Organizacion para la Proscripcion de Armas Nucleares en la America Latina [*Organization for the Proscription of Nuclear Arms in Latin America*] (LA)
OPANDAD .... Ortak Pazar Nezdinde Daimi Delegelik [*Turkish Permanent Delegation to the Common Market*] (TU)
OPAP .... Organismos Prognostikon Agonon Podosfairou [*Organization of Soccer Game Forecasters*] [*Greek*] (GC)
OPAS .... Office des Produits Agricoles de Stanleyville (MAR)
OPaS .... Okresni Poradna a Studovna [*District Advisory Bureau and Study Center*] (CZ)
OPAS .... Organisation de Propagande et d'Action Speciale [*Algerian*] (MAR)
OPAT .... Office des Ports Aeriens de Tunisie [*Tunisian Airport Office*] (AF)
OPAT .... Office des Produits Agricoles du Togo [*Togo Agricultural Products Office*] (AF)
OPB .... Optical Bombsight (RU)
OPB .... Security Service [*Civil defense*] (RU)
OPB .... Separate Machine-Gun Battalion (RU)
OPBM .... Okregowe Przedsiebiorstwa Barow Mlecznych [*District Milk Bar Enterprises*] (POL)
OPC .... Oblast Union of Consumers' Societies (RU)
OPC .... Oddil Polniho Cetnictva [*Military Police Battalion*] (CZ)
OPC .... Oil Palm Company (MAR)
OPC .... Ovamboland People's Congress (MAR)

OPC............ Own Produce Consumed (MAR)
OPCA.......... Oficiul de Proiectari pentru Constructii in Agricultura [*Office for Design for Agricultural Constructions*] (RO)
OPCC.......... Organisation of Petroleum Consuming Countries (MAR)
OPCC.......... Organisme Provincial de Cooperation et de Coordination [*Provincial Cooperation and Coordination Organization*] [*Cambodian*] (CL)
OPCh.......... Optimum Working Frequency (RU)
op cit.......... Opere Citato [*In the Work Cited*] [*Latin*] (GPO)
OPD............ Oberpostdirektion [*Main Postal Directorate*] (EG)
OpD............ Operativer Diensthabender [*Officer of the Day*] (EG)
opdesb........ Separate River Crossing Assault Battalion (RU)
OPDP.......... Odbor za Perspektivni Drustveni Plan (SIV) [*Committee for the Prospective Economic Plan*] (YU)
OPDSNP..... General Regulations on the Procurement of Consumer Goods (BU)
OPE............ Organismos Prolipseos Englimatos [*Organization for Crime Prevention*] [*Greek*] (GC)
OPE............ Organismos Proothiseos Exagogon [*Organization for Exports Promotion*] (GC1)
OPE............ Organosis Pankypriakis Enotitas [*Organization for Pan-Cyprian Unity*] (GC)
OPE............ Oulamos Prolipseos Englimatos [*Crime Prevention Squad*] [*Cypriot*] (GC)
OPEAGRO... Organizacion de Paises Exportadores de Productos Agropecuarios [*Organization of Exporting Countries of Agricultural and Livestock Products*] (LA)
OPEB.......... Experimental Model Excursion Center (RU)
OPEB.......... Organizacao de Pesquisas Espaciais do Brasil [*Brazilian Space Research Organization*] (LA)
OPEC.......... Organization of Petroleum Exporting Countries (ME)
OPECD........ Organismos Populares de la Educacion, Cultura, y Deportes [*People's Educational, Cultural, and Sports Organizations*] [*Cuban*] (LA)
OPECNA..... OPEC [*Organization of Petroleum Exporting Countries*] News Agency (MAR)
OPEI............ Office National de Promotion d'Entreprise Ivoirienne [*National Office for the Promotion of Ivorian Enterprises*] (AF)
OPEK.......... Organosis Prostasias Ellinon Kyprion [*Organization for the Protection of Greek Cypriots*] (GC)
OPEMA....... Office des Peches Maritimes [*Maritime Fishing Office*] [*Guinean*] (AF)
OPEN.......... Office de Promotion de l'Entreprise Nigerienne [*Office for the Promotion of Nigerien Enterprises*] [*Niger*] (AF)
OPEOE........ Omospondia Pandopolon, Edodimopolon, kai Oinopandopolon Ellados [*Federation of Grocers, Food Dealers, and Wine Merchants of Greece*] (GC)
OPEP.......... Omospondia Prosopikou Etaireion Petrelaioeidon [*Federation of Personnel of Petroleum Products Companies*] [*Greek*] (GC)
OPEP.......... Organisation des Pays Exportateurs de Petrole [*Organization of Petroleum Exporting Countries*] [*Use OPEC*] [*French*] (AF)
OPEP.......... Organismos Protypon kai Elenkhou Poiotitos [*Standards and Quality Control Organization*] (GC1)
OPEP.......... Organizacao dos Paises Exportadores de Petroleo [*Organization of Petroleum-Exporting Countries*] [*Use OPEC*] [*Portuguese*] (WER)
OPEP.......... Organizacion de Paises Exportadores de Petroleo [*Organization of Petroleum Exporting Countries*] [*Use OPEC*] [*Spanish*] (LA)
OPEP.......... Unit of a Field Evacuation Station (RU)
OPERCOL... Operaciones Comerciales Industriales Ltda. [*Barranquilla*] (COL)
OPERU........ Transactions Office [*Gosbank*] (RU)
OPEV.......... Office de Promotion de l'Entreprise Voltaique (MAR)
OPEX.......... Organization and Operations Executive (MAR)
OPEZ.......... Office pour la Promotion des Entreprises Zairoises [*Office for the Promotion of Zairian Enterprises*] (AF)
OPF............ Organisation Panafricaine des Femmes [*Pan-African Women's Organization*] (AF)
OPF............ Orszagos Penzugyi Felugyeloseg [*National Inspectorate of Revenue*] (HU)
OPFB.......... Forward Front Logistical Installation Subsection (BU)
OPFB.......... Unit of Advanced Front-Line Base (RU)
OPFPS........ Supply Relay Point Railhead for Courier Postal Communications (BU)
OPG............ Ground Surface Mark (RU)
OPG............ Ostry Prubojny Granat [*Armor-Piercing Grenade*] (CZ)
OPHAM....... Office Pharmaceutique Malgache (MAR)
OPHO.......... Okregowe Przedsiebiorstwo Handlu Opalem [*District Fuel Trade Enterprise*] (POL)
OPI.............. Odessa Pedagogical Institute Imeni K. D. Ushinskiy (RU)
OPI.............. Odessa Polytechnic Institute (RU)
OPI.............. Office de Promotion de l'Entreprise Ivoirienne (MAR)
OPI.............. Oposicion de Izquierda [*Leftist Opposition*] [*Spanish*] (WER)
OPIC.......... Oficina Permanente Internacional de la Carne [*Permanent International Meat Office*] (EA)
OPIC.......... Overseas Private Investment Corporation (LA)
OPIF.......... Orient Press International Federation (MAR)
OPIGIM....... Manuscript Department of the State Historical Museum (RU)
OPII............ Institute of Planning and Research Based on Public Participation (RU)
OPINA......... Opinion Nacional (Partido) [*National Opinion (Party)*] [*Venezuelan*] (LA)
OPIR............ Organizacion Popular Independiente Revolucionaria [*Popular Independent Revolutionary Organization*] [*Venezuelan*] (LA)
OPJ............. Office [*or Officier*] de la Police Judiciaire (MAR)
OPJA.......... Opasni Prostori u Jadranskom i Jonskom Moru [*Dangerous Areas in the Adriatic and Ionian Seas*] (YU)
OPJM.......... Organizacion de Pioneros Jose Marti [*Organization of Jose Marti Pioneers*] [*Cuban*] (LA)
OPK............ Department of Blood Transfusion (RU)
OPK............ Obrona Powietrzna Kraju [*Home Air Defense*] (POL)
OPK............ Odbor za Prosvetu i Kulturu (SIV) [*Committee on Education and Culture*] (YU)
OPK............ Oddeleni Pohranicni Kontroly [*Frontier Control Department*] (CZ)
OPK............ Okoliya Industrial Combine (BU)
OPK............ Orszagos Pedagogiai Konyvtar [*National Education Library*] (HU)
OPK............ Personnel-Training Department (RU)
OPK............ Separate Outguard (RU)
OPKh.......... Experimental Model Farm (RU)
OPKhV........ Omospondia Prosopikou Khimikis Viomikhanias [*Federation of Chemical Industry Personnel*] [*Greek*] (GC)
OPKI.......... Onkopatologiai Kutato Intezet [*Research Institute in Tumor Pathology*] (HU)
OPL............ Adjustable-Blade Reversible Runner (of a Hydraulic Turbine) (RU)
OPL............ Obrana Proti Letadlum [*Antiaircraft Defense*] (CZ)
OPL............ Obrona Przeciw Lotnicza [*Antiaircraft Defense*] (POL)
OPL............ Oil Prospecting License (MAR)
OPLA.......... Oficina de Planificacion Agricola [*Agricultural Planning Office*] [*Chilean*] (LA)
OPLA.......... Omades Prostasias Laikou Agonos [*Units for the Protection of the People's Struggle*] [*Greek*] (GC)
OPLC.......... Organizacion para la Liberacion de Cuba [*Organization for the Liberation of Cuba*] (PD)
OPLO.......... Oromo People's Liberation Organization [*Ethiopian*] (AF)
OPLOH........ Organisation de Production et de Logistique OTAN [*Organisation du Traite de l'Atlantique Nord*] du HAWK (MAR)
OPLot.......... Obrona Przeciwlotnicza [*Antiaircraft Defense*] [*Polish*]
OPM............ First Aid Detachment (RU)
OPM............ Oberster Patent- und Markensenat [*German*]
OPM............ Oddeleni Prace a Mezd [*Labor and Wage Department*] (CZ)
OPM............ Oddzial Przedsiebiorstwa Mierniczego [*Branch of the Surveying Enterprise*] (POL)
OPM............ Okregowe Przedsiebiorstwo Miernicze [*District Surveying Enterprise*] (POL)
OPM............ Okresni Pece o Mladez [*District Youth Welfare Organization*] (CZ)
Opm............ Opmerking [*Remark*] [*Dutch*] (GPO)
OPM............ Organisasi Papua Merdeka [*Papua Independent Organization*] [*Indonesian*] (PD)
OPM............ Organizacion Politico-Militar [*Politico-Military Organization*] [*Paraguayan*] (PD)
OPM............ Single-Sideband Modulation (RU)
OPM............ Society of Marxist Teachers (RU)
OPN............ Association of Trade Unions of Norway (RU)
OPNT.......... Office des Ports Nationaux Tunisiens (MAR)
OPO............ Basic Plan of Operations [*Military term*] (RU)
OPO............ Department for the Exchange of Production Experience (RU)
OPO............ Fire Prevention Department (RU)
OPO............ Operations and Production Department (RU)
OP-O.......... Operativni Otsek [*Operation Section*] [*Military*] (YU)
OPO............ Organization and Planning Department (RU)
OPO............ Ortsparteiorganisation [*Local Party Organization*] (EG)
OPO............ Oslobodilacki Partizanski Odred [*Partisan Liberation Detachment*] (YU)
OPO............ Osnovnata Partiska Organizacija [*Basic Party Organization*] (YU)
OPO............ Ovamboland People's Organisation (MAR)
OPO............ Separate Border Guard Detachment (RU)
OPOC.......... Omnium Photo Optique Cinema (MAR)
OPODD....... Omospondia Prosopikou Organismon Dimosiou Dikaiou [*Federation of Personnel of Public Law Organizations*] [*Greek*] (GC)
OPOEKh...... Organosis Politikis kai Oikonomikis Epistratevseos tis Khoras [*Organization for the Political and Economic Mobilization of the Nation*] [*Greek*] (GC)
OPOY.......... Omospondia Perifereiakon Oikonomikon Ypallilon [*Federation of Regional Finance Employees*] [*Greek*] (GC)
OPOYaZ...... Society for the Study of the Theory of Poetic Language [*1914-1923*] (RU)
OPOZRz...... Okregowe Przedsiebiorstwa Obrotu Zwierzetami Rzeznymi [*District Slaughter Animal Trade Enterprise*] (POL)
OPP............ Department of Industrial Establishments (RU)
OPP............ Experimental Industrial Establishment (RU)
OPP............ Mail Transportation Department (RU)

OPP .... Main Direction-Finding Station (RU)
OPP .... Okrug Industrial Enterprise (BU)
OPP .... Okrug Printing Enterprise (BU)
OPP .... Omades Politikis Protovoulias [*Political Initiative Groups*] [*Greek*] (GC)
opp .... Oppilas [*Finnish*]
OPP .... Organos de Poder Popular [*Organs of People's Government*] [*Cuban*] (LA)
OPP .... Organoseis Prostasias Perivallondos [*Environmental Protection Organizations*] (GC)
OPP .... Political Propaganda Department (RU)
OPP .... Propaganda and Press Department (RU)
OPPA .... Party Propaganda and Agitation Department (RU)
OPPE .... Omospondia Palaion Polemiston Ellados [*Federation of Greek Veterans*] (GC)
OPPE .... Organismos Palaion Polemiston Ellados [*Organization of Greek Veterans*] (GC)
OPPIR .... Portable Optical Pyrometer (RU)
OPPME .... Office de Promotion des Petites et Moyennes Entreprises (MAR)
OPPP .... Organisation des Pays Producteurs de Petrole [*North African*] (MAR)
OPPS .... Okoliya Fire-Fighting Service (BU)
OPPS .... Optique Photo et Precision du Senegal (MAR)
OPPU .... Association of Proletarian Writers of the Ukraine (RU)
OPPV .... Experimental Model Ground of the Vsevobuch (RU)
OPPZ .... Department for Resettlement and Preparation of an Area for Flooding [*Hydroelectric developments*] (RU)
OPQCB .... Office Professionel de Qualification et de Classification des Entreprises du Batiment (MAR)
OPR .... Basic Planned Repair (BU)
OPR .... Covering Detachment, Covering Force (RU)
OPR .... Field Repair Section (RU)
OPR .... Odred za Pranje Rublja [*Laundry Detachment*] [*Military*] (YU)
Opr .... Operator [*Surgeon*] (TU)
opr .... Oprawa [*or Oprawiony*] [*Binding or Bound*] (POL)
OPR .... Organisasi Perlawanan Rakjat [*People's Resistance Organization*] (IN)
OPR .... Organisation du Peuple Rodriguais [*Organization of the Rodrigues People*] [*Mauritian*] (AF)
Opr .... Supreme Court Decision (BU)
OPR-33 .... Organizacion Popular Revolucionaria-33 [*Popular Revolutionary Organization-33*] [*Uruguayan*] (LA)
oprac .... Opracowal [*or Opracowane*] [*Prepared By or Prepared*] (POL)
OPRAG .... Office des Ports et Rades du Gabon [*Gabon Ports and Roadsteads Office*] (AF)
oProf .... Ordentlicher Professor [*Full Professor*] [*German*] (WEN)
OPROL .... Oddeleni Protiradiolokace [*Radar Countermeasures Department*] (CZ)
oprol .... Oxyproline (RU)
OPRON .... Organization of Progressive Nationals (LA1)
OPRP .... Organizacion Politica de la Revolucion Peruana [*Political Organization of the Peruvian Revolution*] (LA)
OPRS .... Oddeleni Protiradiotechnicke Sluzby [*Counter Radiotechnical Service Department*] (CZ)
OPRS .... Oil Palm Research Station (MAR)
OPS .... Field Communications Section (RU)
OPS .... General Rules of Signalization (RU)
OPS .... Hydroxypropyl Alcohol (RU)
OPS .... Oblasni Privredni Sud [*Regional Economic Court*] (YU)
OPS .... Ogledna Poljoprivredna Stanica [*Agricultural Experiment Station*] (YU)
OPS .... Okresni Pedagogicky Sbor [*District Board of Education*] (CZ)
OPS .... Okresni Pracovni Stredisko [*District Labor Center*] (CZ)
OPS .... Okruhova Politicka Sprava [*Zonal Political Directorate*] (CZ)
OPS .... Okruzni Privredni Sud [*County Economic Court*] (YU)
OPS .... Operations [*Operations*] [*French*] (CL)
OPS .... Oral Protez Sanayii AS [*Oral Prosthetics Industry Corp.*] (TU)
OPS .... Organisasi Perusahaan-Perusahaan Sedjenis [*Organization of Similar Enterprises*] (IN)
OPS .... Organizacion Panamericana de la Salud [*Pan American Health Organization*] [*Use PAHO*] (LA)
OPS .... Own Produce Sold (MAR)
OPS .... Separate Signal Regiment (RU)
OPS .... Single Flip-Flop (RU)
OPS .... Underground Structures Department (RU)
OPSA .... Oficina de Planeamiento del Sector Agropecuario [*Agricultural-Livestock Sector Planning Office*] [*Colombian*] (LA)
OPSA .... Operavereniging van Suid-Afrika (MAR)
OPSCO .... Operations Sub-Committee (ML)
OPSD .... Society of Polish-Soviet Friendship (RU)
OPSh .... Shpagin Flare Pistol (RU)
OPSJ .... Organisatie van Progressieve Studerende Jeugd [*Organization of Progressive Student Youth*] [*Dutch*] (WEN)
OPSSZZ ...... Otkupno Preduzece Sreskog Saveza Zemljoradnickih Zadruga [*Purchasing Establishment of the District Agricultural Cooperatives Union*] (YU)
OPSUS .... Operasi Chusus [*Special Operations*] (IN)
OPSZS .... Otkupno Preduzece Sreskog Zadruznog Saveza [*Purchasing Establishment of the District Cooperative Union*] (YU)
OPT .... Joint Force Message Code Table (RU)
OPT .... Office des Postes et des Telecommunications [*Postal and Telecommunications Office*] [*Gabonese*] (AF)
opt .... Optical, Optics (RU)
opt .... Optics, Optical (BU)
opt .... Optiikka [*Optics*] [*Finnish*]
opt .... Optisch [*Optical*] [*German*]
OPT .... Osrodek Postepu Technicznego [*Technical Progress Center*] (POL)
OPT .... Society of Proletarian Tourism (RU)
optabr .... Separate Antitank Artillery Brigade (RU)
OPTD .... Separate Antitank Battalion (RU)
OPTE .... All-Union Voluntary Society of Proletarian Tourism and Excursions [*1928-1936*] (RU)
OPTI .... Department of Industrial and Technical Information (RU)
OPTI .... Orszagos Palyavalasztasi Tanacsado Intezet [*National Career Selection Advisory Institute*] (HU)
optich .... Optical (RU)
OPTICOM .... Optimum Community (MAR)
OPTiE .... All-Union Voluntary Society of Proletarian Tourism and Excursions [*1928-1936*] (RU)
OPTIMA ...... Organization for the Phyto-Taxonomic Investigation of the Mediterranean Area (EA)
optorg .... Wholesale (RU)
OPTRA .... Office Professionnel des Transports [*Professional Transportation Bureau*] [*French*] (WER)
OPTS .... Office des Postes et des Telecommunications du Senegal [*Senegal Postal and Telecommunications Office*] (AF)
OPTT .... Ob'edinenie Profsoiuzov Trudiashchikhsia Tunisa (MAR)
OPU .... Experimental Model Institution (RU)
OPU .... Great Circle Track Angle (RU)
opubl .... Published (RU)
opulab .... Separate Machine-Gun and Artillery Battalion (RU)
opulap .... Separate Machine-Gun and Artillery Regiment (RU)
OPV .... Office Pharmaceutique Veterinaire (MAR)
OPVDC .... Organizacao Provincial de Voluntarios e Defesa Civil (MAR)
OPVDCA ..... Organizacao Provincial de Voluntarios e Defesa Civil de Angola (MAR)
OPVK .... Department of Industrial Veterinary Control (RU)
OPVN .... Office des Produits Vivriers du Niger [*Nigerien Foodstuffs Office*] [*Niger*] (AF)
OPVTR .... General Rules for Internal Work Order (BU)
OPW .... Joint Freight Car Pool (Bloc) [*Russian*] (EG)
OPW .... Ogolny Park Wagonow [*General Freight Car Pool*] [*Polish*] (CZ)
OPXAE .... Omospondia Prosopikou Xenon Aeroporikon Etaireion [*Federation of Foreign Airline Company Personnel*] [*Greek*] (GC)
OPYK .... Omospondia Politon Ygron Kavsimon [*Federation of Liquid Fuel Dealers*] [*Greek*] (GC)
opyt .... Experimental (RU)
OPZ .... Obstacle-Forcing Detachment (RU)
OPZ .... Obucarsko Preradivacka Zadruga [*Shoe Finishing Cooperative*] (YU)
OPZ .... Opca Poljoprivredna Zadruga [*General Agricultural Cooperative*] (YU)
OPZ .... Opca Privredna Zadruga [*General Economic Cooperative*] (YU)
OPZB .... Olsztynskie Powiatowe Zjednoczenie Budowlane [*Olsztyn (Allenstein) County Construction Association*] (POL)
OPZB .... Olsztynskie Przemyslowe Zjednoczenie Budowlane [*Olsztyn (Allenstein) Industrial Construction Association*] (POL)
OPZG .... Trade-Union Association of West Germany (RU)
OPZHN .... Operacni Plan Zbrane Hromadneho Niceni [*Operations Plan for Weapons of Mass Destruction*] (CZ)
OPZPHiU ..... Ogolnopolskie Zrzeszenie Prywatnego Handlu i Uslug [*All-Poland Private Trade and Services Association*] (POL)
OPZZ .... Department for Preparation of an Area for Flooding [*Hydroelectric developments*] (RU)
OQ .... Ouvrier Qualitie [*French*]
OR .... Controlled Member (RU)
OR .... Danger Area (RU)
OR- .... Experimental Rocket [*Engine*] (RU)
or .... Flamethrower Company (RU)
or .... Greenhouse [*Topography*] (RU)
or .... Gun (RU)
or .... Gun, Piece (BU)
or .... Landmark, Reference Point, Checkpoint (BU)
OR .... Main Register (RU)
OR .... Oborove Reditelstvi [*Sectoral Directorate*] (CZ)
OR .... Obvodni Rada [*District Council*] (CZ)
OR .... Octrooiraad [*Rijswijk*]
OR .... Odborova [*or Odborovy*] Rada [*Trade-Union Council or Trade-Union Counselor (Title of government official)*] (CZ)
OR .... Odborove Riaditelstvo [*Sectoral Directorate*] (CZ)
OR .... Odluka o Renti [*Land Rent Decision*] [*Law*] (YU)
O-R .... Oesterreich-Reihe (Taschenbuecher) [*German*]
OR .... Oklopne Rezerve [*Armored Reserves*] (YU)
OR .... Okresni Referent [*District Official*] (CZ)
OR .... Olah Raga [*Sports, Athletics*] (IN)
OR .... Onderwijsraad
OR .... Order of the Rokel (MAR)
or .... Orderly, Messenger (BU)
OR .... Ordonnance Royale [*Royal Ordinance*] [*Cambodian*] (CL)

OR .... Organizacija Rada [*Organization of Work*] (YU)
OR .... Organizacion de Revolucionarios [*Organization of Revolutionaries*] [*Venezuelan*] (LA)
or .... Orosz [*Russian*] (HU)
Or .... Orta [*Secondary*] (TU)
or .... Orvosi Rendelo [*Medical Consultation Room*] (HU)
Or .... Reference Point, Marker (RU)
OR .... Regulating Winding (RU)
OR .... Roadstead Defense (RU)
OR .... Separate Mounted Patrol (RU)
OR .... Single Operating Mode [*Computers*] (RU)
OR .... Telephone Call Canceled (BU)
OR .... Working Winding (RU)
ORA .... All-Russian Association of Workers' Artels (RU)
ORA .... Oramiral [*Vice Admiral*] (TU)
ORA .... Organisation Revolutionnaire Anarchiste [*Revolutionary Anarchist Organization*] [*French*] (PPE)
ORA .... Organizacion de Reparaciones Automotoras [*Bogota*] (COL)
ORA .... Organizacion de Resistencia Armada [*Organization of Armed Resistance*] [*Chilean*] (LA)
ORAC .... Omnium de Refrigeration et Amenagements Coloniaux (MAR)
ORAD .... Oficiul Regional de Aprovizionare si Desfacere [*Regional Office for Supply and Sales*] (RO)
ORAD .... Separate Artillery Reconnaissance Battalion (RU)
orad .... Separate Reconnaissance Artillery Battalion (BU)
ORAE .... Separate Air Reconnaissance Squadron (RU)
ORAF .... Organisation Regionale Africaine (MAR)
ORAF .... Organisation de la Resistance de l'Algerie Francaise (MAR)
ORAF .... Ortadogu ve Afrika Dairesi Genel Mudurlugu [*Middle East and Africa Office Directorate General*] [*of Foreign Affairs Ministry*] (TU)
ORAMEI .... Oeuvre Reine Astrid de la Mere et de l'Enfant Indigenes (MAR)
ORAMS .... Oficina Regional de Apoyo a la Mobilizacion Social [*Regional Office of Support to Social Mobilization*] [*Peruvian*] (LA)
OR-AN .... Orta Anadolu Insaat AS [*Central Anatolian Construction Corp.*] (TU)
ORANA .... Organisme de Recherches sur l'Alimentation et la Nutrition Africaine [*African Food and Nutrition Research Organization*] (MAR)
ORAP .... Separate Air Reconnaissance Regiment (RU)
Orat .... Oratoire [*Oratory*] [*Military map abbreviation*] [*World War I*] [*French*] (MTD)
orato .... Separate Airfield Technical Support Company (RU)
orats .... Separate Tank Truck Company (RU)
ORAYCON .... Organizacion Administrativa y Contable Draycon Ltda. [*Bogota*] (COL)
ORB .... Operaciske Recne Baze [*Operational River Bases*] [*Navy*] (YU)
ORB .... Orman Bakanligi [*Ministry of Forestry*] (TU)
orb .... Separate Ammunition Supply Company (RU)
ORB .... Separate Radio Battalion (RU)
ORB .... Separate Reconnaissance Battalion (RU)
ORBA .... Orde Baru [*The New Order*] (IN)
ORC .... Oficina de Registro de Consumidores [*Consumers Registration Office*] [*Cuban*] (LA)
ORCD .... Organisation for Regional Cooperation and Development [*Iranian*] (MAR)
ORCG .... Organe de Recherche des Criminels de Guerre (MAR)
ORCh .... Optimum Working Frequency (RU)
ORCOREL .... Organizacao Comercial de Representacoes Limitada (MAR)
ORD .... Oddil Rizeni Dopravy Verejne Bezpecnosti [*Highway Traffic Control Battalion of Public Security*] (CZ)
ORD .... Office du Ranch de la Dihesse (MAR)
ORD .... Offices Regionaux de Developpement [*Regional Development Offices*] [*Central African*] (AF)
ORD .... Okresni Rada Druzstev [*District Council of Cooperatives*] (CZ)
ord .... Ordinaire [*Ordinary*] [*Type of rice*] [*Cambodian*] (CL)
ord .... Ordinaire [*French*]
Ord .... Ordnung [*Order*] [*German*]
ORD .... Organisation Rurale de Developpement [*Rural Development Organization*] [*Upper Voltan*] (AF)
ORD .... Organisme Regional de Developpement (MAR)
ORD .... Separate Reconnaissance Battalion (RU)
ORD .... Separate Reconnaissance Patrol (BU)
ORD .... Separate Reconnaissance Patrol (RU)
ORDEN .... Organizacion Democratica Nacionalista [*Nationalist Democratic Organization*] [*Salvadoran*] (LA)
ORDEZA .... Organismo Regional para de Desarrollo de la Zona Afectada [*Regional Organization for the Development of the Earthquake Disaster Area*] [*Peruvian*] (LA)
ORDOK .... Orvostudomanyi Dokumentacios Kozpont [*Medical Documentation Center*] (HU)
Ord Prof .... Ordinaryus Profesor [*Full Professor*] (TU)
ORDZh .... Ordzhonikidze Railroad (RU)
ORE .... Organizacion Revolucionario de Estudiantes [*Revolutionary Organization of Students*] [*Spanish*] (WER)
ORE .... Ornitologia Rondo Esperantlingva [*Esperantist Ornithologists' Association*] (EA)
OREL .... Organizacion de Relaciones Estudiantiles Latinoamericanas [*Organization for Latin American Student Relations*] (LA)
OREP .... Department for the Distribution and Dispatch of Publications (RU)
ORF .... General Recursive Function (RU)
ORF .... Orszagos Rendorfokapitanysag [*National Police Headquarters*] (HU)
ORFA/CSV .... Organizacao das Forcas Armadas Comites de Soldados Vermelhos [*Armed Forces Organization/Committee of Red Soldiers*] [*Portuguese*] (WER)
ORFI .... Orszagos Reuma- es Furdougyi Intezet [*National Institute on Rheumatism and Curative Spas*] (HU)
ORFIDEM .... Organizacion y Financiacion de Empresas [*Bogota*] (COL)
ORFM .... Oficiul de Rezerve Forte de Munca [*Office for Labor Reserves*] (RO)
ORFS .... Organizacion de Rehabilitacion Fisico-Social [*Bogota*] (COL)
ORG .... Officer of the National Order of the Republic of the Gambia (MAR)
ORG .... Order of the Republic of Gambia (MAR)
org .... Organic (RU)
org .... Organisch [*Organic*] [*German*]
org .... Organization, Organizational (BU)
org .... Organizational (RU)
Org .... Orgeneral [*Full General*] (TU)
ORG .... Separate Reconnaissance Group (RU)
ORGA .... Organizacion Regional Gallega Autonoma [*Regional Galician Autonomy Organization*] [*Spanish*] (PPE)
ORGABON .... Compagnie des Mines d'Or du Gabon (MAR)
Orgametall .... Trust for the Rationalization of Production in the Machinery and Metalworking Industry (RU)
Organa .... Organisch-Chemische Industrie (VVB) [*Organic Chemical Industry (VVB)*] (EG)
ORGANDA .... Organisasi Gabungan Angkutan Darat [*Federation of Transport Firms*] (IN)
organich .... Organic (RU)
ORGATEC .... Societe Africaine d'Etudes Techniques (MAR)
Orgavtoprom .... State All-Union Institute of Automobile Technology (RU)
Orgbyuro .... Organizational Bureau (BU)
Orgchermet .... Scientific Research Institute for the Organization of Ferrous Metallurgy (RU)
ORGECO .... Organisation Generale des Consommateurs [*French*]
Orgelektrotrans .... Republic Trust of the City Electric Transportation System Administration [*RSFSR*] (RU)
Orgenergostroy .... All-Union Institute for the Planning of Electric Power Projects (RU)
Orggaz .... Republic Trust for the Adjustment and Control of Gas Equipment of the Urban Gas Supply System [*RSFSR*] (RU)
orgger .... Organizovani Gerilci [*Organized Guerrillas*] [*World War II*] (YU)
Orgkhim .... State All-Union Trust of the State Committee of the Chemical Industry, USSR (RU)
Orgmashpribor .... All-Union Planning and Technological Experimental Institute of the Ministry of the Machinery and Tool Industry (RU)
Orgmashuchet .... Special Office for the Organization of Machine Accounting and Computing in Heavy Industry (RU)
orgnabor .... Department of Resettlement and Organized Recruitment of Workers (RU)
orgnabor .... Organized Recruitment (RU)
Or Gn Kh .... Ordu Genel Karargah [*Army General Staff*] (TU)
Orgotdel .... Organizational Department (BU)
Orgproyekttsement .... All-Union State Special Office for Starting, Adjustment, Planning, and Design Work in the Cement Industry (RU)
orgraspred .... Organization and Distribution Department of the TsK VKP(b) (RU)
ORGREB .... Organisation fuer Abnahme, Betriebsfuehrung, und Rationalisierung von Energieanlagen [*Organization for Acceptance, Operation, and Rationalization of Energy Facilities*] (EG)
ORGRES .... State Trust for the Organization and Rationalization of Regional Electric Power Plants and Networks (RU)
ORGREZ .... Organizace pro Racionalizaci Energetickych Zavodu [*Organization for Rationalization of Electric Power Plants*] (CZ)
Orgsekretar .... Organizational Secretary (BU)
Orgstankinprom .... State Planning, Technological, and Experimental Institute (for the Organization of the Machine-Tool and Tool Industry) (RU)
Orgstroy .... State Institute for the Introduction of Advanced Operational and Labor Methods in Construction (RU)
OrgVCMD .... Organizacijski Vestnik Cirilmetodijskega Drustva Katoliskih Duhovnikov LRS [*Organizational Review of the Cyril-Methodius Society of Catholic Priests of Slovenia*] [*Ljubljana*] (YU)
Orgvodokanal .... State Republic Adjustment and Repair Trust of the Water Supply and Sewer System Administration [*RSFSR*] (RU)
OrgVOFS .... Organizacijski Vestnik Osvobodilne Fronte Slovenije [*Organizational Review of the Liberation Front of Slovenia*] [*Ljubljana*] (YU)
Orgvosstroy .... Office for Organization and Standardization of Construction and Restoration Work (RU)
OrgVSZDL .... Organizacijski Vestnik Socijalisticne Zveze Delovnega Ljudstva Slovenije [*Organizational Review of the Socialist Union of Working People of Slovenia*] [*Ljubljana*] (YU)
orgy .... Ornagy [*Major*] [*Military*] (HU)

ORI .... Association of Workers in the Fine Arts (RU)
ORI .... Ocean Research Institute [*Japanese*]
ORIF .... Oficiul Regional de Imbunatatire Funciara [*Regional Office for Land Improvement*] (RO)
orig .... Original (BU)
orig b podp ... Unsigned Original (BU)
orig s avtogr ... Autographed Original (BU)
orig s avtogr i pech ... Autographed and Sealed Original (BU)
orig s pech ... Sealed Original (BU)
ORIK .... Organisation de la Region Industrielle du Koullou (MAR)
ORINFOR .... Office Rwandaise d'Information [*Rwandan Information Office*] (AF)
ORINTAS .... Organize Insaat Sanayi ve Ticaret Ltd. Sti. [*Organized Construction Industry and Trade Corp.*] (TU)
Or-Is .... Turkiye Orman Iscileri Sendikasi [*Turkish Forestry Workers' Union*] [*Izmir*] (TU)
ORIT .... Organizacion Regional Interamericana de Trabajadores [*Inter-American Regional Organization of Workers*] (LA)
ORJUNA ...... Organizacija Jugoslovenskih Nacionalista [*Organization of Yugoslav Nationalists*] (YU)
ORK .... Ob'edinennaia Respublika Kamerun (MAR)
ORK .... Oekumenische Rate der Kirchen (MAR)
ORK .... Okresni Rolnicka Komise [*District Agricultural Commission*] (CZ)
ORK .... Okresni Rozhodci Komise [*District Arbitration Commission*] (CZ)
ork .... Orkiestra [*Orchestra*] [*Polish*]
ORK .... Orszagos Rendorkapitanysag [*National Police Headquarters*] (HU)
ORK .... Radio Compass Reading (RU)
ORKFiSp ..... Okregowa Rada Kultury Fizycznej i Sportu [*District Council of Physical Culture and Sport*] (POL)
orkhrr .... Separate Chemical and Radiation Reconnaissance Company (BU)
orkhrr .... Separate Chemical and Radiation Reconnaissance Company (RU)
ORKhZ .... Separate Chemical Defense Company (RU)
orkhz .... Separate Company for Protection Against Chemical Attacks (BU)
ORKI .... Ontozesi es Rizstermelesi Kutato Intezet [*Irrigation and Rice Cultivation Research Institute*] (HU)
ORKIMD ...... Association of Revolutionary Composers and Personages Active in Music [*1924-1929*] (RU)
ORKLB .... Rare Book Division of the Lenin Library (RU)
ORKOY .... Orman Koy Iliskileri Genel Mudurlugu [*Forest Village Affairs Directorate General*] (TU)
ORKOY .... Orman Koyleri Projesi [*Forest Villages Project*] (TU)
ORL .... Office de Radiodiffusion Lao [*Lao Radiobroadcasting Office*] (CL)
ORL .... Surveillance Radar (RU)
ORLA .... Orde Lama [*The Old Order*] (IN)
ORLAK .... Orszagos Lakasepitesi Vallalat [*National Enterprise for Apartment Construction*] (HU)
ORLB .... Manuscript Division of the Lenin Library (RU)
orlpo .... Separate Light Infantry Flame-Thrower Company (BU)
OR-LS .... Organizacion de Revolucionarios-Liga Socialista [*Organization of Revolutionaries-Socialist League*] [*Venezuelan*] (LA1)
orlsb .... Separate Radio-Relay Communications Battalion (BU)
ORM- .... Experimental Jet Engine (RU)
ORM- .... Experimental Rocket Engine (RU)
ORM .... Operation Riz Mopti [*Malian*] (MAR)
Orm .... Orman [*or Ormancilik*] [*Forest or Forestry*] (TU)
orm .... Ormester [*Sergeant*] (HU)
ORMAS .... Organisasi Massa [*Mass Organization*] (IN)
ORMO .... Ochotnicza Rezerwa Milicji Obywatelskiej [*Volunteer Reserve of Citizens' Militia*] (POL)
ORMU .... Detached Company for Medical Reinforcement of the Army (BU)
ORMU .... Separate Medical Reinforcement Company (RU)
ORMVA .... Offices Regionaux de Mise en Valeur Agricole (MAR)
ORMVAD ..... Office Regional de Mise en Valeur Agricole des Doukkala [*Tunisian*] (MAR)
ORMVAL ..... Office Regional de Mise en Valeur Agricole de Loukkos (MAR)
ORN .... Order of the River Niger (MAR)
ORN .... Organization of Revolutionaries of the North [*Lebanese*] (PD)
orn .... Ornamentirt [*German*]
ORN .... Osiedlowa Rada Narodowa [*People's Settlement Council*] [*Polish*]
ORNB .... Orenburg Railroad (RU)
ORNIIMSK .. Orenburg Scientific Research Institute for the Breeding of Beef and Dairy Cattle (RU)
ORNITS .... Society of Workers of Science and Technology for Assistance to the Building of Socialism in the USSR (RU)
ORNOGE ..... Organizacion Nacional de la Oposicion de Guinea Ecuatorial en el Exilio [*National Organization of Opposition of Equatorial Guinea in Exile*] (AF)
ORO .... Okresni Rada Odboru [*District Trade-Union Council*] (CZ)
ORO .... Okresni Rada Osvetova [*District Cultural Council*] (CZ)
ORO .... Organisation-Renseignement-Operation [*Algerian*] (MAR)
oro .... Separate Maintenance Company (BU)
oro .... Separate Service Company (RU)
ORO .... Special Reconnaissance Detachment (RU)
ORO .... United Revolutionary Organizations of Cuba (RU)
OROC .... Office Royal de Cooperation [*Royal Cooperatives Office*] [*Replaced by OFFINACO*] [*Cambodian*] (CL)
OROTEKS ... Oroslavska Tekstilna Industrija [*Oroslavlje Textile Industry*] (YU)
OROUBANGUI ... Societe d'Exploitation Auriferes de l'Oubangui (MAR)
ORP .... Oddeleni Radu a Predpisu [*Department for Military Manuals and Regulations*] (CZ)
ORP .... Oficina de Regulacion de Precios [*Price Control Office*] [*Panamanian*] (LA)
ORP .... Okret Rzeczypospolitej Polskiej [*Polish Navy Ship*]
ORP .... Orange River Project (MAR)
ORP .... Organisation de la Resistance Populaire [*Popular Resistance Organization*] [*Algerian*] (AF)
ORP .... Publications Distribution Department (RU)
ORP .... Reciprocal Radio Bearing (RU)
ORP .... Society of Revolutionary Poster Designers (RU)
ORPA .... Organizacion Revolucionaria del Pueblo en Armas [*Revolutionary Organization of the People in Arms*] [*Guatemalan*] (PD)
ORPADE ...... Organisation Panafricaine des Juristes et Economistes pour l'Assistance et le Developpement [*Pan-African Organization of Jurists and Economists for Assistance and Development*] (AF)
ORPC .... Organizacion Revolucionaria Punto Critico [*Critical Point Revolutionary Organization*] [*Mexican*] (LA1)
ORPC-ML .... Organizacao para a Reconstrucao do Partido Comunista-Marxista-Leninista [*Organization for the Reconstruction of the Communist Party/Marxist-Leninist*] [*Portuguese*] (WER)
ORPO .... Department of Leading Party Bodies (RU)
ORPO .... Organization and Planning Department (RU)
ORPOL .... Organisasi Politik [*Political Organization*] (IN)
ORPS .... General Workers Trade Union (BU)
ORPS .... General Workers' Trade Union [*People's Republic of Bulgaria*] (RU)
ORPV .... Office Regional de Produits Vivriers [*Regional Foodstuffs Office*] [*Togolese*] (AF)
orpv .... Separate Field Water Supply Company (RU)
ORR .... Separate Reconnaissance Company (RU)
orrb .... Separate Radio Relay Battalion (RU)
ORRD .... River Traffic Control Department (RU)
orrd .... Separate Radio Relay Battalion (RU)
orreg .... Separate Traffic Control Company (RU)
ORRO .... Separate Portable Flamethrower Company (RU)
orro .... Separate Portable Flamethrowers Company (BU)
ORRS .... Manpower Distribution Department (RU)
ORS .... Department of Workers' Supply (RU)
ORS .... General Workers Supply (BU)
ORS .... Irrigation System (RU)
ORS .... Obsluga Ratalnej Sprzedazy [*Installment Sales Service*] (POL)
ORS .... Oficiul de Rezerve de Stat [*Office for State Reserves*] (RO)
ORS .... Opci Radnicki Savez [*General Workers Union*] (YU)
ORS .... Operation Riz Segou [*Malian*] (MAR)
ORS .... Operation Riz Sikasso [*Malian*] (MAR)
ORS .... Operativna Ratna Sluzba [*Operational Military Service*] (YU)
ORS .... Orange River Sovereignty (MAR)
ORS .... Separate Signal Company (RU)
ORS .... Separate Supply Company (RU)
ORS .... Society of Russian Sculptors [*1925-1932*] (RU)
ORSA .... Officiers de Reserve en Situation d'Activite sous Contrat [*Reserve Officers on Active Duty under Contract*] [*French*] (WER)
ORSC .... Office de la Recherche Scientifique Coloniale (MAR)
ORSEC .... Organisation des Secours [*Disaster Relief Organization*] [*French*] (WER)
ORSI-CONGO ... Societe Commerciale et Industrielle Orsi (MAR)
ORSL .... Order of the Republic of Sierra Leone (MAR)
ORSS .... General Workers Trade Union (BU)
ORSTOM ..... Office de la Recherche Scientifique et Technique d'Outre-Mer [*Overseas Scientific and Technical Research Office*] [*French*] (AF)
orszgy hat ... Orszaggyulesi Hatarozat [*Resolution of the National Assembly*] (HU)
orsz ut .... Orszagut [*State Highway*] (HU)
ORT .... Obsluga Ruchu Turystycznego [*Tourist Traffic Service*] [*Polish*]
ORT .... Organisation, Reconstruction, Travail (MAR)
ORT .... Organizacion Revolucionaria de Trabajadores [*Workers Revolutionary Organization*] [*Spanish*] (WER)
ORT .... Organizacion Revolucionaria de los Trabajadores [*Workers Revolutionary Organization*] [*Salvadoran*] (LA)
Ort .... Ortakligi [*Partnership*] [*Turkish*] (CED)
Ort .... Ortaklik [*Partnership*] (TU)
ort .... Orthodox [*Orthodox*] (HU)
ort .... Orthodromic (RU)
ort .... Orthopedics, Orthopedist (BU)
ort .... Ortograficzny [*Orthographic*] (POL)
ORTB .... Office de Radiodiffusion et Television du Benin [*Radio and Television Broadcasting Office of Benin*] (AF)
ORTB .... Separate Radio Battalion (RU)

ortcheka ..... Special Extraordinary River Transportation Commission for Combating Counterrevolution and Sabotage (RU)
ORTChK ...... Rayon Branch of the Extraordinary Transportation Commission (RU)
ORTF .... Office de Radiodiffusion et de Television Francaise [*Office of French Broadcasting and Television*] (WER)
ORTN .... Obrigacoes Reajustaveis do Tesouro Nacional [*National Treasury Readjustable Bonds*] [*Brazilian*] (LA1)
ORTN .... Office de Radiodiffusion-Television du Niger [*Niger Radio and Television Broadcasting Office*] (AF)
ORTP .... Orthodromic Bearing (RU)
ORTPN .... Office Rwandais du Tourisme et des Parcs Nationaux (MAR)
ortr .... Electronic Reconnaissance Detachment (BU)
ortr .... Separate Radio Company (RU)
ORTRAG ..... Orbital Transport und Raketen Gesellschaft (MAR)
ortrr .... Separate Loading-Unloading Works Company (BU)
ORTZ .... Society for the Dissemination of Technical Knowledge (RU)
ORU .... Association of Accounting and Statistical Personnel (RU)
ORU .... Odborova Rada Ucitelska [*Teachers' Trade-Union Council*] (CZ)
ORU .... Organizacion Revolucionaria Universitaria [*Revolutionary University Organization*] [*Dominican Republic*] (LA1)
ORU .... Outdoor Distribution System (BU)
ORU .... Outdoor Distribution System [*Electricity*] (RU)
ORUD .... Department of Rayon Administration of Roads (RU)
ORUD .... Traffic Control Department (RU)
ORUM .... Open-Pit Mining of Coal Deposits (RU)
ORUS .... Orman Urunleri Sanayii Genel Mudurlugu [*Forest Products' Industry Directorate General*] (TU)
orv .... Orvos [*Physician*] (HU)
orvb .... Separate Maintenance and Recovery Battalion (RU)
orvb .... Separate Repair and Reconstruction (Engineer) Battalion (BU)
ORVP .... Casualty Search and Evacuation Detachment (RU)
orvr .... Separate Maintenance and Recovery Company (RU)
ORW .... Organizacja Rodzin Wojskowych [*Military Dependents Organization*] (POL)
ORWN .... Osrodek Rozpowszechniania Wydawnictw Naukowych [*Center for the Dissemination of Scientific Publications*] (POL)
ORWNPAN ... Osrodek Rozpowszechniania Wydawnictw Naukowych Polskiej Akademii Nauk [*Polish Academy of Scientific Publications Dissemination Center*] (POL)
ORYa .... Gun Junction Box (RU)
ORYaS .... Department of Russian Language and Literature (of the Academy of Sciences, USSR) (RU)
oryg .... Oryginal [*or Oryginalny*] [*Original or Genuine*] (POL)
ORZ .... Organisations- und Rechenzentrum [*Organization and Computer Center*] (EG)
ORZATU ...... Department of Relay Protection, Automation, Remote Control, and Stability (RU)
ORZZ .... Okregowa Rada Zwiazkow Zawodowych [*District Council of Trade Unions*] (POL)
ORZZN .... Zemedelske Zasobovani a Nakup, Oborove Reditelstvi [*Agricultural Supply and Purchasing, Sectoral Directorate*] (CZ)
o/s .... Argentine Gold Currency
OS .... Axis of Communications (RU)
OS .... Experimental Station [*Agriculture*] (RU)
OS .... Experimental Vessel (RU)
os .... Expert Rifleman (RU)
OS .... Feedback (RU)
OS .... General Assembly, General Meeting (BU)
OS .... General Session (of the Academy of Sciences, USSR) (RU)
OS .... General Supply Depot (RU)
OS .... Insurance Department (RU)
OS .... Lean Caking [*Coal*] (RU)
OS .... Negative Resistance (RU)
OS .... Obchodni Skola [*Commercial School*] (CZ)
OS .... Oblasni Stab [*Regional Headquarters*] [*World War II*] (YU)
OS .... Oblast Soviet (RU)
OS .... Oblastni Sberna [*Regional Depot*] (CZ)
OS .... Odborna Skola [*Vocational School*] (CZ)
OS .... Odborna Skupina [*Group of Specialists*] (CZ)
OS .... Odborovy Svaz [*Trade Union*] (CZ)
OS .... Odvodni Soupis [*Conscription Inventory*] (CZ)
os .... Ogleden Sonra [*Afternoon*] (TU)
OS .... Ogledna Stanica [*Experiment Station*] (YU)
OS .... Okoliya Council (BU)
OS .... Okresni Sekretariat [*District Secretariat*] (CZ)
OS .... Okresni Soud [*District Court*] (CZ)
OS .... Okrug Council (BU)
os .... Omaa Sukua [*Finnish*]
OS .... Omada "Gia ton Sosialismo" [*Group "For Socialism"*] [*Greek*] (GC)
OS .... Operacni Sprava [*Operations Directorate*] (CZ)
OS .... Operativna Sala [*Operations Room*] [*Military*] (YU)
OS .... Optical Sensitizer (RU)
OS .... Optimal System (RU)
OS .... Orange Glass (RU)
OS- .... Orange Light Filter (RU)
OS .... Orasul Stalin [*Stalin City*] (RO)
OS .... Order of Suvorov (RU)
OS .... Organisation Secrete (MAR)
OS .... Organisation Speciale [*Algerian*] (MAR)
OS .... Organisme Saharienne (MAR)
OS .... Organisme Stockeurs (MAR)
OS .... Organizacni Sluzba [*Organization Service*] (CZ)
os .... Osasto [*Finnish*]
Os .... Osiedle [*Settlement*] [*Polish*]
OS .... Osjecki Sajam [*Osijek Fair*] (YU)
OS .... Osmatracka Stanica [*Observation Station*] [*Military*] (YU)
OS .... Osnovna Sredstva [*Fixed Assets*] (YU)
os .... Osoba [*Person*] [*Polish*]
OS .... Osobni Spis [*Personal Record*] (CZ)
os .... Osoite [*Finnish*]
OS .... Otkupna Stanica [*Purchasing Station*] (YU)
OS .... Ouvrier Specialise [*Specialized or Skilled Worker*] [*French*] (WER)
OS .... Self-Excitation Winding (RU)
OS .... Single-Digit Adder (RU)
OS .... Special Conference (RU)
OS .... Special Worker (RU)
OS .... Supply Section, Supply Department (RU)
OS .... Support Force, Convoy Detachment [*Navy*] (RU)
OS .... Very Old (RU)
OSA .... Ochranny Svaz Autorsky [*Copyright Association*] (CZ)
OSA .... Office Senegalais de l'Artisanat (MAR)
OSA .... Oficerska Szkola Artylerii [*Artillery Officers' School*] (POL)
osa .... Om Svar Anhalles [*An Answer Is Requested*] [*Swedish*] (GPO)
OSA .... Omnibus Services Authority (MAR)
OSA .... Operativna Sala Aerodroma [*Operations Room of an Airport*] [*Military*] (YU)
OSA .... Organic Soil Association of Southern Africa (MAR)
OSA .... Society of Modern Architects (RU)
osad .... Separate Self-Propelled Artillery Battalion (RU)
OSADC .... Ogun State Agricultural Development Corporation (MAR)
OSAE .... Separate Medical Air Squadron (RU)
OSAKVU ..... Joint Central Asian "Red Banner" Military School (RU)
OSAM .... Separate Fixed Air Maintenance Depot (RU)
OSAN .... General Session of the Academy of Sciences, USSR (RU)
OSAP .... Oficerska Szkola Artylerii Przeciwlotniczej [*Polish*]
OSAP .... Oficerska Szkola Artylerii Przeciwpancernej [*Anti-Tank Artillery Officers' School*] (POL)
OSAP .... Separate Medical Air Regiment (RU)
OSAPlot ...... Oficerska Szkola Artylerii Przeciwlotniczej [*Antiaircraft Artillery Officers' School*] (POL)
OSAS .... Overseas Service Aid Scheme (MAR)
OSAZ .... Okresni Sporitelna a Zalozna [*District Savings and Deposit Bank*] (CZ)
OSB .... Order of St. Benedict (MAR)
OSB .... Separate Combat Engineer Battalion (RU)
OSB .... Separate Rifle Battalion (RU)
osb .... Separate Signal Battalion (BU)
OSBC .... Ondo State Broadcasting Corporation [*Nigerian*] (MAR)
OSBI .... General Union of Bulgarian Industrialists (BU)
osbr .... Separate Rifle Brigade (BU)
osbr .... Separate Rifle Brigade (RU)
OSBT .... General Union of Bulgarian Merchants (BU)
OSBZK .... General Union of Bulgarian Agricultural Cooperatives (BU)
OSC .... Organizacija Srpskih Cetnika [*Organization of Serbian Chetniks*] [*Chicago*] (YU)
OSC .... Overseas School Certificate (ML)
os ch .... Of Extreme Purity (RU)
o/sch .... Open Account (RU)
OSCI .... Organizacion Simpatizante de la IV Internacional [*Organization Sympathizing with the Fourth International*] [*Spanish*] (WER)
OSCO .... Oil Service Company of Iran (MAR)
OSCOPROGASDE ... Oficina de Supervigilancia y Control de las Propiedades del General Anastasio Somoza y Debayle [*Office for the Supervision and Control of the Properties of General Anastasio Somoza Debayle*] [*Nicaraguan*] (LA)
OSCP .... Ocean Sedimentary Coring Programme (MAR)
OSD .... Okresni Spotrebni Druzstvo [*District Consumer Cooperative*] (CZ)
OSD .... Osrodek Szkolenia Dziennikarskiego [*Journalism Educational Center*] (POL)
OSDEC .... Orientacion Social de Dirigentes de Empresa Colombiana [*Bogota*] (COL)
OSDEM .... Society for Furthering Demilitarization and Disarmament (RU)
OSE .... Administracion de Obras Sanitarias del Estado [*State Board of Sanitation*] [*Uruguayan*] (LA)
OSE .... Oeuvre Sociale pour Enfants [*Moroccan*] (MAR)
OSE .... Omospondia Syndaxioukhon Ellados [*Federation of Greek Pensioners*] (GC)
OSE .... Organismos Sidirodromon Ellados [*Railways Organization of Greece*] [*Formerly, Sidirodromoi Ellinikou Kratous (SEK)*] (GC)
OSE .... Organosi Sosialistikis Epanastaseos [*Socialist Revolutionary Organization*] [*Greek*] (GC)
Ose .... Oseraie [*Osier-Bed*] [*Military map abbreviation*] [*World War I*] [*French*] (MTD)

OSEDT........ Oficiul Special pentru Editarea si Distrubuirea Timbrelor [*Special Office for the Publication and Distribution of Stamps*] (RO)
OSELMA..... Organismos Synetairistikis Ekmetallevseos Limnothalassis Mesolongiou kai Aitolikou [*Organization for the Cooperative Exploitation of the Mesolongion and Aitolikon Marshlands*] (GC)
OSEN.......... Organization of Petroleum Exporting Countries [*OPEC*] (RU)
OSEO.......... Sanitary and Epidemiological Detachment of a District (RU)
OSER.......... Office de Securite Routiere (MAR)
oset............. Ossetian, Ossetic (RU)
OSF............. Odznaka Sprawnosci Fizycznej [*Physical Fitness Badge*] (POL)
OSF............. OPEC [*Organization of Petroleum Exporting Countries*] Special Fund (MAR)
OSF............. Osrodek Sprawnosci Fizycznej [*Physical Fitness Center*] (POL)
OSFPS........ Railhead Section for Courier Postal Communications (BU)
OSFS.......... Oblates of Saint Francis De Sales [*Roman Catholic religious order*] (MAR)
OSG............ Fuel Supply Section, Fuel Supply Department (RU)
OSGA.......... Department for Construction of Hydrogliders and Motor Sleds (RU)
OSGK.......... General Assembly of the Civil Collegium (BU)
OSh............. Consumer Goods Department (RU)
OSh............. Feathering Hinge (RU)
OSh............. Fuze (RU)
OSH............. Orszagos Sporthivatal [*National Sports Office*] (HU)
OShA........... Asphalt-Coated Fuze (RU)
oshb............ Separate Disciplinary Battalion (RU)
OShDA........ Double Asphalt-Coated Fuze (RU)
OSHE.......... Office de Soutien de l'Habitat Economique [*Low-Cost Housing Support Office*] [*Ivorian*] (AF)
OShOSDOR... Department of Highways (RU)
OShP........... Association of Swiss Trade Unions (RU)
oshr............. Separate Disciplinary Company (RU)
osht ar......... GHQ Reserve (BU)
osht ar rz..... GHQ Artillery (BU)
OShYu......... Oblast School of Young Correspondents (RU)
OShZ........... Omsk Tire Plant (RU)
OSI............... Deflecting System of Indicator (RU)
OSI............... Office Special d'Imposition (MAR)
OSI............... Office of Special Investigations (MAR)
OSI............... Opitna Stanica za Impregnaciju [*Animal Impregnation Experiment Station*] [*Slavonski Brod*] (YU)
OSI............... Orszagos Sportorvosi Intezet [*National Institute of Sports Medicine*] (HU)
OSIM........... Oficiul de Stat pentru Inventii si Marci [*State Office for Inventions and Trademarks*] (RO)
OSK............. Okresna Spravna Komisia [*District Administrative Commission*] (CZ)
OSK............. Omospondia Syndaxioukhon Kapnergaton [*Federation of Pensioned Tobacco Workers*] [*Greek*] (GC)
OSK............. Organismos Skholikon Ktirion [*School Buildings Organization*] [*Greek*] (GC)
osk.............. Orszagos Sertes es Kirako Vasar [*National Hog and Merchandise Fair*] (HU)
osk.............. Oskarzony [*The Accused*] [*Polish*]
OSK............. Osrodek Szkolenia Kadr [*Training Center of Personnel In*] (POL)
OSKhI......... Odessa Agricultural Institute (RU)
oskm........... Osobovy Kilometr [*Passenger-Kilometer*] (CZ)
OSKOM....... Special Committee of the Council of Defense (RU)
Oskow......... Ogolnopolski Szkolny Komitet Odbudowy Warszawy [*All-Poland School Committee for the Reconstruction of Warsaw*] (POL)
OSKS.......... General Students' Cooperative Association (BU)
OSL............. Oficerska Szkola Lacznosci [*Signal Officers' School*] (POL)
OSL............. Oficerska Szkola Lotnicza [*Air Force Officers' School*] (POL)
OSL............. Single Pilot Lamp (RU)
OSM............ Oberschaltmechaniker [*Chief Control Mechanic (At missile installation)*] (EG)
OSM............ Oficiul de Stat pentru Metrologie [*State Office for Metrology*] (RO)
OSM............ Okregowa Spoldzielnia Mleczarska [*District Dairy Cooperative*] (POL)
OSM............ Okresni Starostlivost o Mladez [*District Youth Welfare Organization*] (CZ)
Osm............. Osmanlica [*Ottoman*] [*Historical*] (TU)
OSMP.......... Specialized Medical Aid Detachment (RU)
OSMR.......... Basic Single-Stage Decision Model (RU)
OSMU.......... Separate Construction and Installation Administration (RU)
OSMU.......... Special Construction and Installation Site (RU)
OSMW......... Oficerska Szkola Marynarki Wojennej [*School for Naval Officers*] (POL)
OSN............. Experimental Statistical Norms (RU)
osn.............. Founded, Created (RU)
osn.............. Fundamental, Basic, Principal (RU)
OSN............. Oficina de Seguridad Nacional [*Office of National Security*] [*Nicaraguan*] (LA)
OSN............. Organisace Spojenych Narodu [*United Nations*] (CZ)
OSN............. Orzecznictwo Sadu Najwyzszego [*Decisions of the Supreme Court*] (POL)
OSN............. Ottuv Slovnik Naucny [*Otto's Encyclopedia*] (CZ)
OSN............. Standardization Department (RU)
OSNA.......... Osmatranje Dejstva Neprijateljski Artiljerije [*Observation of Enemy Artillery Action*] (YU)
OSNAA........ Organization for Afro-Asian Peoples Solidarity (RU)
Osnav.......... Society for Lifesaving on Waterways of the USSR [*1928-1931*] (RU)
OSNAZ........ Special-Purpose Detachment (RU)
OSNIE......... Omospondia Syllogon Nosilevtikon Idrymaton Ellados [*Federation of Greek Nursing Home Societies*] (GC)
OSNK.......... General Assembly of the Criminal Law Collegium (BU)
osnov.......... Founded, Created (RU)
OSNP.......... All-China National People's Congress (BU)
OSNP.......... Association of Free German Trade Unions [*East German*] (RU)
osn prerab... Completely Revised (BU)
OSNS.......... General Students' National Union (BU)
OSNU.......... Dog-Team Sled - Litter Unit (RU)
OSO............ Decontamination Section (RU)
OSO............ Department of Social Security (RU)
OSO............ Oessudoeste [*West-Southwest*] [*Spanish*]
OSO............ Oposicion Sindical Obrera [*Workers Trade Union Opposition*] [*Spanish*] (WER)
OSO............ Public Sanitation Officers (BU)
OSO............ Ship Equipment Department (RU)
OSO............ Society for Assistance to the Defense of the USSR [*1926-1927*] (RU)
Osoaviakhim... Society for Assistance to the Defense, Aviation, and Chemical Construction of the USSR [*1927-1948*] (RU)
osobkm....... Osobni Kilometr [*Passenger-Kilometer (A unit of measure on railroads)*] (CZ)
Osobproyektmontazh... State All-Union Special Planning and Installation Trust (RU)
Osodmil...... Society for Assistance to the Militia (RU)
OSOMPP..... Okresni Sekce Organisacne-Masove Prace a Propagandy [*District Section for Mass Organizational Work and Propaganda*] (CZ)
OSOS.......... Organizacion Secreta de Oficiales [*Secret Organization of Officers*] [*Guatemalan*] (LA1)
Osotop........ Special Conference on Fuel (RU)
OSOV.......... Obalska Sluzba Obavestavanja i Veze [*Coastal Information and Communications Service*] [*Military*] (YU)
OsP............. Basic Regulations (BU)
OSP............. Consolidated Economic Enterprise (BU)
OSP............. Instrument-Landing Equipment (RU)
OSP............. Liaison Section with Infantry [*Artillery*] (RU)
OSP............. Limited Scope of Application [*Computer programing*] (RU)
osp.............. Obciansky Sudny Poriadok [*Code of Civil Procedure*] (CZ)
OSP............. Obshtina Economic Enterprise (BU)
OSP............. Ochotnicza Straz Pozarna [*Volunteer Fire Brigade*] (POL)
OSP............. Oficerska Szkola Piechoty [*School for Infantry Officers*] (POL)
OSP............. Oficina de Seguridad Politica [*Office for Political Security*] [*Ecuadorean*] (LA)
OSP............. Okresna Socialna Poistovna [*District Social Insurance Agency*] (CZ)
OSP............. Okresny Stavebny Podnik [*District Construction Enterprise*] (CZ)
OSP............. Okrug Economic Enterprise (BU)
OSP............. Orientarea Scolara/Profesionala [*Educational/Vocational Orientation*] (RO)
OSP............. Osrodek Szkolenia Partyjnego [*Party Training Center*] (POL)
osp.............. Separate Signal Regiment (BU)
OSP............. United Socialist Party [*French*] (RU)
OSPA.......... Oficina Sectorial de Planificacion Agropecuaria [*Area Office for Agricultural-Livestock Planning*] [*Salvadoran*] (LA1)
OSPAA........ Organisation de la Solidarite des Peuples Afro-Asiatiques [*Afro-Asian Peoples' Solidarity Organization*] [*Use AAPSO*] [*French*] (AF)
OSPAA........ Organizzazione di Solidarieta dei Popoli Afroasiatici [*Afro-Asian Peoples' Solidarity Organization*] [*Use AAPSO*] [*Italian*] (WER)
OSPAAAL... Organisation de Solidarite des Peuples Afro-Asiatiques et d'Amerique Latine [*Afro-Asian Latin-American Peoples' Solidarity Organization*] [*Use AALAPSO*] [*French*] (AF)
OSPAAAL... Organizacion de Solidaridad con los Pueblos de Africa, Asia, y America Latina [*Afro-Asian-Latin American Peoples' Solidarity Organization*] [*Use AALAPSO*] [*Spanish*] (LA)
OSPAP........ Odbytove Sdruzeni Papirenskeho Prumyslu [*Market Associations of the Paper Industry*] (CZ)
OSPB.......... General Popular Banks' Union (BU)
OSPC.......... Officer Superintending Police Circle (ML)
OSPF........... Oblasni Sekretarijat za Poslove Finansija [*Regional Secretariat of Finance*] [*Pristina*] (YU)
OSPK.......... United Socialist Party of Catalonia (RU)
OSPN.......... Oborove Stredisko pro Projektove Normy Spoju [*Sectoral Center for Planning Standards of Communications*] (CZ)
OSPO.......... Oblast Union of Consumers' Societies (RU)
OSPO.......... Okoliya Council of Trade Organizations (BU)
OSPS.......... General Council of Trade Unions (BU)
OSPS.......... Oblast Council of Trade Unions (RU)
OSPS.......... Okrug Council of Trade Unions (BU)
OSPS.......... Okrug Council of Trade Unions (RU)

OSPT.......... Osrodek Szkolnictwa Pocztowo-Telekomunikacyjnego [*Postal and Telecommunications Training Center*] (POL)
OSPVL........ Organizace pro Spolupraci v Prumyslu Valivych Lozisek [*Organization for Cooperation in Ball Bearing Industry*] (CZ)
OSPZK........ Okoliya Council of Consumers' Agricultural Cooperatives (BU)
OSR............ Comparison Element, Comparator (RU)
OSR............ Oficerska Szkola Radiotechniczna (Jelenia Gora) [*Radio Engineering Officers' School (Jelenia Gora)*] (POL)
OSR............ Oktobarska Socijalisticka Revolucija [*October Socialist Revolution*] [*Russian Revolution, 1917*] (YU)
OSR............ Ortsschulrat [*German*]
Osr............. Osrodek [*Center*] [*Polish*]
OSR............ Separate Combat Engineer Company (RU)
OSR............ Special Construction Area (RU)
OSRB.......... Overseas Services Resettlement Bureau (MAR)
osrb............ Separate Signal Brigade (BU)
OSRG.......... Okregowe Stacje Ratownictwa Gorniczego [*District Mine Rescue Stations*] (POL)
OSRO.......... Office of Sahel Relief Organisations (MAR)
OSRO.......... Office for Special Relief Operations (MAR)
OSRV.......... Rayon Terminal Broadcasting Station (RU)
OSS............ Experimental Selection Station (RU)
OSS............ General Union of Syndicates (BU)
OSS............ Land-Based Aircraft Section (of the TsKB of the Aviatrest) (RU)
OSS............ Obilna Spolocnost na Slovensku [*Grain Company in Slovakia*] (CZ)
OSS............ Oddzial Sprzetu Sanitarnego [*Sanitary Equipment Branch*] (POL)
OSS............ Oficerska Szkola Samochodowa [*Motor Transport Officers' School*] (POL)
OSS............ Oficiul de Stat pentru Standarde [*State Office for Standards*] (RO)
OSS............ Okoliya Syndicate Council (BU)
OSS............ Organizace Spoluprace Socialistickych Zemi v Oboru Elektrickych a Postovnich Spoju [*Organization of Cooperation of Socialist Countries in the Field of Electrical and Postal Communications*] (CZ)
Oss............. Wydawnictwo Zakladu Narodowego Imienia Ossolinskich [*Publishing House of the Ossolinski National Institution*] (POL)
OSSC.......... Oyo State Sports Council (MAR)
OSSD.......... Okresni Svaz Spotrebnich Druzstev [*District Union of Consumer Cooperatives*] (CZ)
OSSh.......... Single-Phase Dry-Type Mine Transformer (RU)
OSShD........ Organisation fuer die Zusammenarbeit der Eisenbahnen [*Organisation for the Collaboration of Railways - OCR*] (EA)
OSSO.......... Experimental Horticultural and Vegetable-Growing Station (RU)
OSSO.......... Special Conference (RU)
OSSU.......... Organisation du Sport Scolaire et Universitaire Togolais (MAR)
OSSUC........ Organisation des Sports Scolaires et Universitaires du Cameroun (MAR)
OST............ All-Union Standard [*1925-1940*] (RU)
ost............. Obsolete (BU)
OST............ Oddzial Sprzetowo-Transportowy [*Equipment and Transportation Department*] (POL)
OST............ Office for Science and Technology (MAR)
OST............ Organizacion Socialista de los Trabajadores [*Socialist Workers' Organization*] [*Bolivian*] (PPW)
OST............ Organizacion Socialista de los Trabajadores [*Socialist Workers' Organization*] [*Costa Rican*] (PPW)
OST............ Osrodek Szkolenia Teatralnego [*Center for Dramatic Training*] (POL)
OST............ Society of Easel Painters [*1925-1932*] (RU)
ostar........... Obsolete Term (BU)
ostekhbyuro ... Special Technical Office (RU)
Osterr.......... Oesterreichisch [*Austrian*] [*German*] (GPO)
OSTI........... Office for Scientific and Technical Information [*United Kingdom*]
OSTiW......... Osrodek Sportu, Turystyki, i Wypoczynku [*Sports, Tourism, and Recreation Center*] [*Polish*]
O St J.......... Officer of the Order of St. John (ML)
ostl............. Oestlich [*German*]
ost p........... Railroad Stop [*Topography*] (RU)
OSTP.......... Separate Sentry Post (RU)
OSTPZK...... General Union of Labor Productive Artisans' Cooperatives (BU)
OS na TPZK ... General Union of Labor Productive Cooperatives (BU)
OSTRAMEC ... Organizacion Sindical de Trabajadores de Medios de Comunicacion [*Trade Union Organization of Communication Media Workers*] [*Nicaraguan*] (LA1)
OSTT.......... General Agreement on Tariffs and Trade [*GATT*] (RU)
OSTT.......... Orszagos Sport- es Testnevelesi Tanacs [*National Council on Sports and Physical Education*] (HU)
OSTZ.......... Separate Outpost Support (RU)
OSU............ Oficerska Szkola Uzbrojenia [*Ordnance Officers' School*] (POL)
OSU............ Okregowy Sad Ubezpieczen Spolecznych [*District Court of Social Security*] (POL)
OSU............ Okrug Statistical Administration (BU)
OSU............ Separate Construction Site (RU)
OSU............ Special Construction Administration (RU)
OSUS.......... Okregowy Sad Ubezpieczen Spolecznych [*District Court of Social Insurance*] [*Polish*]
OSUZ.......... Organization of Students of Secondary Educational Institutions (RU)
osv............. Och Sa Vidare [*And So Forth*] [*Swedish*] (GPO)
OSV............ Oddeleni Sluzby Vojsk [*Troop Services Department*] (CZ)
osv............. Og Sa Videre [*And So Forth*] [*Danish*] (GPO)
osv............. Og Sal Videre [*And So Forth*] [*Norwegian*] (GPO)
OSV............ Okresni Skolni Vybor [*District Board of Education*] (CZ)
OSV............ Opcinsko Sindikalno Vijece [*Municipal Trade-Union Council*] (YU)
OSV............ Organisation Sociale des Volontaires [*Social Organization of Volunteers*] [*Upper Voltan*] (AF)
OSV............ Organismos tou Symfonou tis Varsovias [*Warsaw Pact*] (GC)
OSVA.......... Organismos tou Synthikis tou Voreiou Atlandikou [*North Atlantic Treaty Organization*] (GC)
Osvag.......... Information Agency (RU)
OSVIM......... Experimental Station of the All-Union Scientific Research Institute of Agricultural Mechanization (RU)
OSVO.......... Oblastni Sprava Vychovy a Osvety [*Regional Educational and Cultural Administration*] (CZ)
OSVOD........ Society for Furthering the Development of Water Transportation and for the Safeguarding of Human Lives on Waterways of the USSR [*1931-1956*] (RU)
OSVOK........ Special Conference on the Restoration of Basic Industrial Capital (RU)
OSVS.......... General Union of Water-Power Syndicates (BU)
OSVV.......... Organization of the Soviet War Veterans (RU)
OSWChem ... Oficerska Szkola Wojsk Chemicznych [*Chemical Warfare Officers' School*] (POL)
OSWP.......... Oficerska Szkola Wojsk Pancernych [*Armored Troop Officers' School*] (POL)
OSWZ.......... Oficerska Szkola Wojsk Zmechanizowanych [*Mechanized Troop Officers' School*] (POL)
OSYGO....... Omospondia Synetairistikon Ypallilon Georgikon Organoseon [*Federation of Employees of Agricultural Cooperative Organizations*] [*Greek*] (GC)
OSZ............ Experimental Welding Plant (RU)
OSZ............ Okregowa Skladnica Zaopatrzenia [*District Supply Depot*] (POL)
OSZ............ Okresni Sporitelna a Zalozna [*District Savings and Deposit Bank*] (CZ)
OSZB.......... Orszagos Szakmai Bertablazat [*National Occupational Wage Table*] (HU)
OSZB.......... Orszagos Szamviteli Bizottsag [*National Committee on Accounting*] (HU)
OSZD(b)P ... Oroszorszagi Szocialdemokrata (Bolsevik) Part [*Russian Social Democratic Party (Bolsheviks)*] (HU)
OSZDMP..... Oroszorszagi Szocialdemokrata Munkaspart [*Russian Social Democratic Workers' Party*] (HU)
OSZFSZK.... Oroszorszagi Szovjet Foderativ Szocialista Koztarsasag [*Russian Socialist Federative Soviet Republic*] (HU)
OSZH.......... Orszagos Szovetkezeti Hitelintezet [*National Cooperatives Credit Institute*] (HU)
OSZhD........ Organization for Railroad Cooperation among Socialist Countries (BU)
OSZhD........ Railroad Cooperation Organization (RU)
OSZI........... Orszagos Szamitastechnika Alkalmazasi Iroda [*National Computer Technology Application Office (A component of Kozponti Statisztikai Hivatal)*] (HU)
OSZJ........... Orszagos Szakmunkas Jegyzek [*National Skilled Worker Register*] (HU)
OSZK.......... Oroszorszagi Szovjet Koztarsasag [*Russian Soviet Republic*] (HU)
OSZK.......... Orszagos Szechenyi Konyvtar [*Szechenyi National Library*] (HU)
OSZK(b)P ... Osszszovetsegi Kommunista (Bolsevik) Part [*All-Union Communist Party (Bolsheviks)*] (HU)
Osz KP........ Osztrak Kommunista Part [*Austrian Communist Party*] (HU)
oszl........... Oszlop [*Column*] [*Military*] (HU)
OSZM.......... Basic Single-Stage Maximum Problem (RU)
OSZP.......... Olasz Szocialista Part [*Italian Socialist Party*] (HU)
OSZSZ........ Orszagos Szabadsagharcos Szovetseg [*National Association of Freedom Fighters*] (HU)
OSZSZT...... Orszagos Szenbanyaszati Szaktanacs [*National Coal Mining Council*] (HU)
OSZT.......... Orszagos Szakszervezeti Tanacs [*National Trade Union Council*] (HU)
O SZ T........ Orszagos Szovetkezeti Tanacs [*National Council of Cooperatives*] (HU)
oszt........... Osztaly [*Class, Department, Battalion*] (HU)
OSZT.......... Ozdi Szenbanyaszati Troszt [*Coal Mining Trust of Ozd*] (HU)
osztr.......... Osztrak [*Austrian*] (HU)
Osztr KP..... Osztrak Kommunista Part [*Austrian Communist Party*] (HU)
OSZV.......... Orszagos Szamitogeptechnikai Vallalat [*National Computer Technology Enterprise*] (HU)
OSZVB........ Orszagos Szamviteli Bizottsag [*National Committee on Accounting*] (HU)

OSZZ.......... Osnovni Savez Zemljoradnickih Zadruga [*Basic Union of Agricultural Cooperatives*] (YU)
OSZZSD...... Organizatsiya Sotrudnichestva Zheleznykh Dorog [*Organization for Cooperation among Railroads (of CEMA)*] (HU)
OT.............. All Clear Signal (RU)
OT.............. Current Limiter (RU)
OT.............. Current Winding (RU)
OT.............. Departure [*Railroads*] (RU)
OT.............. Emplacement (RU)
OT.............. Flamethrower Tank (RU)
ot................ Heating Load (RU)
OT.............. Labor Department (RU)
OT.............. Landmark, Reference Point (BU)
OT.............. Obojzivelne Tanky [*Amphibious Tanks*] (CZ)
OT.............. Obrneny Transporter [*Armored Personnel Carrier*] (CZ)
OT.............. Oddzial Terenowy [*Local Department*] (POL)
OT.............. Oikeustieteen Kandidaatti [*Finnish*]
OT.............. Optical Theodolite (RU)
OT.............. Organisation Trotskiste [*Trotskyite Organization*] [*French*] (WER)
OT.............. Organizacion Trotskista [*Trotskyite Organization*] [*Spanish*] (WER)
ot................ Orszagos Tanacs [*National Council*] (HU)
OT.............. Orszagos Tervhivatal [*National Planning Office*] (HU)
Ot................ Ortsteil [*Section (of town)*] (EG)
OT.............. Osnovna Tarifa [*Basic Tariff*] [*Railroads*] (YU)
ot................ Section, Division, Department (BU)
OT.............. Sectorial Standard (BU)
OT.............. Unidirectional Texture (RU)
OTA............ Office Technique d'Assurances (MAR)
OTA............ Omnium Tchadien d'Alimentation (MAR)
OTA............ Organisation Mondiale du Tourisme et de l'Automobile [*World Tourism and Auto Organization*] [*Luxembourg*] (WER)
OTA............ Organismoi Topikis Avtodioikiseos [*Organizations of Local Self-Government*] [*Greek*] (GC)
OTA............ Orszagos Testnevelesi Alap [*National Fund for Physical Education*] (HU)
OTAH.......... Orszagos Tervhivatal, Arhivatal [*National Planning Office, Office of Price Control*] (HU)
OTAL.......... OT Africa Line (MAR)
OTAN.......... Organisation du Traite de l'Atlantique Nord [*North Atlantic Treaty Organization*] [*Use NATO*] [*French*] (WER)
OTAN.......... Organizacion del Tratado del Atlantico Norte [*North Atlantic Treaty Organization*] [*Use NATO*] (LA)
OTAS.......... Organizacion del Tratado del Atlantico Sur [*South Atlantic Treaty Organization*] [*Use SATO*] (LA)
OTASE........ Organisation du Traite de l'Asie Sud-Est [*Southeast Asia Treaty Organization*] [*Use SEATO*] (CL)
OTASE........ Organisation du Traite de Defense Collective pour l'Asie du Sud-Est [*Southeast Asia Treaty Organization*] [*Use SEATO*] [*French*] (WER)
OTB............ Office du The du Burundi [*Burundi Tea Office*] (AF)
OTB............ Separate Tank Battalion (RU)
OTB............ Separate Transport Battalion (RU)
OTB............ Special Technical Office (RU)
OTB............ Technological Office Based on Public Participation (RU)
OTBP.......... Department of Trade and Personal Service Facilities (RU)
otbr............ Separate Tank Brigade (RU)
OTCA.......... Overseas Technical Cooperation Agency [*Japanese*] (CL)
OTCZ.......... Office des Transports en Commun du Zaire (AF)
otd.............. Department, Branch, Section (RU)
otd.............. Department, Section, Separate, From Below (BU)
OTD............ Office des Terres Domaniales [*National Land Office*] [*Tunisian*] (AF)
otd.............. Separate, Independent, Detached (RU)
otdavt........ Submachine-Gun Unit (RU)
Otdelstroy... Trust for Special Finishing Work (RU)
OTDJEN...... Oditurat Djenderal [*Office of the Judge Advocate General*] (IN)
otd l............ Separate Sheet (RU)
Otd mat tekh snab ... Material and Technical Supply Department [*or Section*] (BU)
otd-niye...... Department, Branch, Section (RU)
otd otpech ... Separate Imprint (BU)
otd ott......... Offprint, Reprint, Separate Copy (RU)
otd prop i agit ... Propaganda and Agitation Section (BU)
otd svkh...... Sovkhoz Branch [*Topography*] (RU)
OTE............ Omospondia Thiroron Ellados [*Federation of Concierges of Greece*] (GC)
OTE............ Operativne-Technicka Evidence [*Operational and Technical Reporting*] (CZ)
OTE............ Organismos Tilepikoinonion Ellados [*Greek Telecommunications Organization*] (GC)
OTE............ Wage Rate and Economics Department (RU)
OTEC.......... Ocean Thermal Exchange Conversion (LA1)
OTEF.......... Office Tchadien d'Etudes Ferroviaires (MAR)
OTEF.......... Organisation Tunisienne de l'Education et de la Famille [*Tunisian Education and Family Organization*] (AF)
OTEINA....... Omnium Technique Electro-Industriel NA [*North African*] (MAR)
OTEK.......... Association of Transportation and Forwarding Offices (RU)
OTEK.......... Consolidated Transportation and Shipping Offices (BU)
OTEM.......... Otelcilik ve Turizm Egitim Merkezleri [*Hotel Operation and Tourism Training Centers*] [*Kyrenia*] (TU)
OTEN.......... Department of Technical Sciences (of the Academy of Sciences, USSR) (RU)
oter............ Separate Telegraph Operating Company (BU)
OTER.......... Separate Telephone-Operating Company (RU)
OTERI......... Office Technique de Realisation Industrielle [*Lebanese*] (MAR)
OTF............ Sheep-Breeding Farm (RU)
OTFB.......... Service Section of Front Logistical Installation (BU)
OTFB.......... Unit of a Rear Base of a Front (RU)
OTFZ.......... Oddeleni Tylove Frontove Zakladny [*Rear Service Department of the Frontline Base*] (CZ)
otg.............. From Above (BU)
OTG............ Ogolnopolski Tygodnik Gospodarczy [*All-Poland Economic Weekly*] (POL)
OTG............ Oklopna Takticka Grupa [*Armored Tactical Group*] (YU)
OTG............ Organismos Trofimon kai Georgias [*Food and Agriculture Organization (of the United Nations)*] (GC)
otg.............. Responsible, In Charge (BU)
otglag.......... Verbal (RU)
OTGS.......... Department of City Telephone Networks (RU)
OTH............ Orszagos Talalmanyi Hivatal [*National Patent Office*] (HU)
OTH............ Orszagos Tervhivatal [*National Planning Office*] (HU)
OThAK........ Organismos Theatrikis Anaptyxeos Kyprou [*Organization for the Theatrical Development of Cyprus*] (GC)
OTI............. Department of Technical Information (RU)
OTI............. Department of Technical Information and Inventions (RU)
OTI............. Organizacion de Television Iberoamericana
OTI............. Orszagos Tarsadalombiztosito Intezet [*National Institute for Social Security*] (HU)
OTI............. Otonom Turk Idaresi [*Autonomous Turkish Administration*] [*Cypriot*] (TU)
OTII............ Department of Technical Information and Inventions (RU)
OTIPKhP..... Odessa Technological Institute of the Food and Refrigeration Industry (RU)
OTIR........... Department of Technical Information and Rationalization (RU)
OTiR........... Osrodek Techniki i Racjonalizacji [*Technology and Rationalization Center*] (POL)
OTIZ........... Department of Technical Information and Inventions (RU)
OTiZ........... Labor and Wages Department (RU)
OTIZ........... Specialized State Publishing House (RU)
OTK............ Department of Technical Control (RU)
OTK............ Main Transportation Commission (RU)
OTK............ Obrona Terytorialna Kraju [*National Territorial Defense*] (POL)
OTK............ Oddeleni Technicke Kontroly [*Technical Control Department*] (CZ)
OTK............ Okresni Technicka Kontrola [*District Technical Control*] (CZ)
OTK............ Omospondia Tourko-Kypriakou Kratous [*Turkish-Cypriot Federated State*] (GC1)
otk.............. Onallo Tanacsu Kozseg [*Village with Independent Council*] (HU)
OTK............ Opatreni k Upevneni Technologicke Kazne [*Measures for the Strengthening of Technological Discipline*] (CZ)
OTK............ Organisace Technicke Kontroly [*Technical Control Organization*] (CZ)
OTK............ Organization of Technical Control (BU)
OTK............ Otdel Tekhnicheskogo Kontrolya [*Department of Technical Control*] [*Russian*] (TVP)
OTK............ Public Control by Members of the Communist Party (RU)
OTK............ Separate Tank Corps (RU)
OTK............ Special Transportation Commission (RU)
OTK............ Technical Control Section (BU)
Otkomkhoz ... Department of Municipal Services (RU)
otl.............. Excellent [*Mark in school*] (RU)
OTL............ Oberstleutnant [*Lieutenant Colonel*] (EG)
OTL............ Oikeustieteen Lisensiaatti [*Finnish*]
otm............. Mark, Notation, Reading [*Instrument*], Blip [*RADAR*] (BU)
otm............. Mark, Sign, Index (RU)
otm............. Revoked [*or Anulled or Abolished*] (BU)
OTM............ Small Optical Theodolite (RU)
OTMS.......... Organization and Tactics of Medical Service (RU)
OTN............ Department of Technical Sciences (of the Academy of Sciences, USSR) (RU)
otn.............. Relative (RU)
otnos.......... Relative [*Pronoun*] (BU)
otnosit........ Relative (RU)
otnt............ Specific Gravity/Weight (BU)
otn vlazhn... Relative Humidity (RU)
otn yed....... Relative Unit (RU)
OTO............ General Theory of Relativity (RU)
oto.............. Oman Toimensa Ohella [*Finnish*]
Oto............. Otomobil [*Automobile*] (TU)
OTO............ Technical Training Department (RU)
OTOE.......... Omospondia Trapezo-Ypallilikon Organoseon Ellados [*Federation of Greek Bank Employee Organizations*] (GC)
otol............ Otology, Otologist (BU)
otor............ Separate Flamethrower Tank Company (RU)
otorg.......... Chief Organizer (RU)
OTP............ Consolidated Commercial Enterprise (BU)
OTP............ Department of Commercial Ports (RU)

OTP .... Obalsko Transportno Preduzece [*Shore Transport Establishment*] [*Novi Sad*] (YU)
OTP .... Oddeleni Technicke Pomoci [*Technical Assistance Department*] (CZ)
OTP .... Office Togolais des Phosphates [*Togolese Phosphates Office*] (AF)
OTP .... Okrug Commercial Enterprise (BU)
OTP .... Omnium Technique de Pipelines [*Sudanese*] (MAR)
OTP .... Opce Trgovinsko Poduzece [*General Commercial Establishment*] (YU)
OTP .... Optimum Temperature Sequence (RU)
OTP .... Organismos Touristikis Pisteos [*Tourist Credit Organization*] [*Greek*] (GC)
OTP .... Orszagos Takarekpenztar [*National Savings Bank*] (HU)
otp .... Separate Tank Regiment (RU)
otpech .... Printed, Print [*Offprint*] (BU)
OTPP .... Department of Technical Preparation of Production (RU)
otpp .... Separate Breakthrough Tank Regiment (RU)
Otpr .... Departure [*Railroads*] (RU)
OTPS .... General Labor Trade Union (BU)
OTR .... Close Support Missile (RU)
otr .... Detachment (RU)
OTR .... Group of Supply Ships, Convoy [*Navy*] (RU)
otr .... Negative [*Grammar*] (BU)
OTR .... Oddeleni Technickych Rozboru [*Technical Analysis Department*] (CZ)
otr .... Separate Transport Company (RU)
otrab .... Separate Transport Aviation Base (BU)
OTRACO ..... Office d'Exploitation des Transports Coloniaux (MAR)
OTRACO ..... Office de Transit de la Cote d'Afrique (MAR)
OTRACO ..... Office des Transports Congolaises (MAR)
OTRADI .... Office de Transit de la Cote-d'Ivoire (MAR)
OTRAG .... Orbital Transport- und Raketen- Aktiengesellschaf [*Orbital Transport and Rocket, Inc.*] [*West German*] (AF)
OTRAZ .... Office d'Exploitation des Transports au Zaire (MAR)
otrazh spos ... Reflectivity, Reflectance, Reflection Factor (RU)
otrazh sv ..... Reflected Light (RU)
otremb .... Separate Tank Repair Battalion (RU)
OTrI .... Orszagos Traumatologiai Intezet [*National Institute of Traumatology*] (HU)
otritsat .... Negative (RU)
OTs .... Heating Plant (BU)
OTS .... Medium Optical Theodolite (RU)
OTS .... Negative Glow (RU)
OTs .... Operational Center (BU)
OTS .... Tank Task Force (RU)
OTS .... Technical Supply Section, Technical Supply Department (RU)
OTS .... Terminal Telephone Exchange (RU)
OTsAG .... Organization of Central American States [*OCAS*] (RU)
OTSB .... Orszagos Testnevelesi es Sportbizottsag [*National Committee for Sports and Physical Culture*] (HU)
OTsDP .... Operator of the Central Dispatcher's Station, Operator of the Central Control Post (RU)
otsekr .... Executive Secretary (RU)
Otsenkom ... Valuation Commission (RU)
OTSh .... Departure [*Nautical term*] (RU)
OTSH .... Orszagos Testnevelesi es Sport Hivatal [*National Office for Sports and Physical Education*] (HU)
OTShL .... Experimental Technical Sewing Laboratory (RU)
OTSI .... Orszagos Testneveles- es Sportegeszsegugyi Intezet [*National Institute of Physical Education and Sports Hygiene*] (HU)
OTSI .... Orszagos Testnevelesi es Sportorvosi Intezet [*National Physical Education and Sports Physician Institute*] (HU)
OTsK .... Body-Centered Cubic (RU)
OTsK .... United Central Committee (RU)
OTsR .... Basic Cysteine Reaction (RU)
otsr .... Separate Telegraph Construction Company (BU)
OTSSE .... Omospondia Topikon Spoudastikon Syllogon Ellados [*Federation of Local Student Clubs of Greece*] (GC)
OT st .... Emplacement for Heavy Machine Gun (RU)
otsv .... Signal Section, Communications Section (RU)
OTsZ .... Lead and Zinc Plant (BU)
OTT .... Basic Technical Requirements (RU)
ott .... Copy, Print, Impression (RU)
OTT .... Ocean Transport and Trading (MAR)
OTT .... Oikeustieteen Tohtori [*Finnish*]
ott .... Ottobre [*October*] [*Italian*]
OTT .... Single-Channel Carrier Telegraphy (RU)
OTT .... Society for Technical Creativity (BU)
OTTKT .... Orszagos Tavlati Tudomanyos Kutatasi Terv [*National Long-Range Scientific Research Plan*] (HU)
OTTP .... Omnium Technique des Transports par Pipelines (MAR)
ottp .... Separate Heavy Tank Regiment (RU)
OTTU .... Odessa Streetcar and Trolleybus Administration (RU)
OTU .... Terminal Repeater (RU)
OTUS .... Office Tunisien de Standardisation (MAR)
otv .... Hardening, Solidification (RU)
OTV .... Oeffentlicher Dienst, Transport, und Verkehr [*Public Service, Transportation, and Traffic (Trade union)*] [*West German*] (WEN)
otv .... Responsible (RU)
OTVA .... Allied Tactical Air Force [*NATO*] (RU)
otvet .... Responsible (RU)
OTVH .... Orszagos Termeszetvedelmi Hivatal [*National Bureau of Conservation*] (HU)
otv red .... Editor in Chief (RU)
otvruk .... Official in Charge (RU)
OTVT .... Orszagos Termeszetvedelmi Tanacs [*National Council for Plant and Wildlife Protection*] (HU)
OTY .... Omospondia Takhydromikon Ypallilon [*Federation of Post Office Employees*] [*Greek*] (GC)
OTYE .... Omospondia Trapezikon Ypallilon Ellados [*Federation of Bank Employees of Greece*] (GC)
OTZ .... Labor and Wages Department (RU)
OTZ .... Onega Tractor Plant (RU)
otzdrav .... Department of Public Health (RU)
OU .... Administrative Department (RU)
OU- .... Carbon Dioxide Fire Extinguisher (RU)
OU .... Control Device (RU)
OU .... Control Winding (RU)
OU .... Feedback Control (RU)
OU .... Lighting Device (RU)
OU .... Obalovy Ustav [*Packaging Institute*] (CZ)
OU .... Obecni Urad [*Community Office*] (CZ)
OU .... Oblast Center [*Communications*] (RU)
OU .... Obvodny Urad [*District Office*] (CZ)
OU .... Odborne Uciliste [*Vocational School*] (CZ)
OU .... Oductovaci Ustredna [*Accounting Center*] (CZ)
OU .... Okresni Telefonni Ustredna [*District Telephone Exchange*] (CZ)
OU .... Opisy Udoskonalen [*Descriptions of Improvements*] (POL)
OU .... Oposicion Unida [*United Opposition*] [*Dominican Republic*] (LA1)
OU .... Optical Goniometer (RU)
OU .... Optimal Control (RU)
OU .... Orientalni Ustav [*Institute of Oriental Studies (of the Czechoslovak Academy of Sciences)*] (CZ)
OU .... Osidlovaci Urad [*Resettlement Office*] (CZ)
OU .... Osvetove Ustredie [*Cultural Center*] (CZ)
OU .... Replacement Section [*Military term*] (RU)
OU .... Terminal [*Computers*] (RU)
OUA .... Orchestre de l'Universite d'Abidjan (MAR)
OUA .... Organisation de l'Unite Africaine [*Organization of African Unity*] [*Use OAU*] [*French*] (WER)
OUA .... Organizacao da Unidade Africana [*Organization of African Unity*] [*Use OAU*] [*Portuguese*] (WER)
OUA .... Relative Specific Activity (RU)
OUB .... Overseas Union Bank [*Singapore*]
OUCFA .... Office Universitaire et Culturelle Francaise en Algerie [*French Cultural and University Office in Algeria*] (AF)
OUD .... General Delivery Conditions [*Council for Economic Mutual Assistance*] (BU)
OUD .... Separate Training Battalion [*Artillery*] (RU)
OUDSI .... General Conditions for the Procurement of Goods for Export (BU)
OUED .... Organizacion Unitaria de Estudiantes de Deusto [*Unitary Organization of Deusto Students*] [*Spanish*] (WER)
OUF .... Orszagos Ugyvitelgepesitesi Felugyelet [*National Business Operations Mechanizing Supervision*] (HU)
OUF .... Overseas Union Finance [*Singapore*]
OUG .... Okrajna Uprava za Gozdarstvo [*District Forestry Administration*] (YU)
OUG .... Okregowe Urzedy Gornicze [*District Mining Administration*] (POL)
OUG .... Organisation de l'Unite Guineenne [*Organization of Guinean Unity*] (PD)
OUGK .... Oblastni Ustav Geodesie a Kartografie [*Regional Geodetic and Cartographic Institute*] (CZ)
OUGS .... Okrug Forestry Resources Administration (BU)
OUK .... Oblastna Uradovna Presidlovacej Komisie [*Regional Office of the Resettlement Commission*] (CZ)
OUK .... Okresni Ucitelska Knihovna [*District Teachers' Library*] (CZ)
OUK .... Okresni Uverova Komise [*District Loan Commission*] (CZ)
OUK .... Training Ship Detachment (RU)
OULG .... Organisation Unifiee pour la Liberation de la Guinee [*Unified Organization for the Liberation of Guinea*] (AF)
OuLiPo .... Ouvroir de Litterature Potentielle [*Workshop of Potential Literature*]
OUM .... Okregowy Urzad Miar [*District Office of Measures*] [*Polish*]
OUMEREP ... Outre-Mer Representation (MAR)
OUMP .... Oblast Administration of Local Industry (RU)
OUMVR .... Okrug Administration of the Ministry of Internal Affairs (BU)
OUN .... Association of Ukrainian Nationalists (RU)
OUN .... Organisace Ukrajinskych Nacionalistu [*Organization of Ukrainian Nationalists*] (CZ)
OUN .... Organizacija Ujedinjenih Nacija [*United Nations Organization*] (YU)
OUN .... Organizacja Ukrainskich Nacjonalistow [*Organization of Ukrainian Nationalists*] (POL)
OUN .... Organizatsiia Ukrains'kykh Natsionalistiv [*Organization of Ukrainian Nationalists*]

OUNZ .... Obvodni Ustav Narodniho Zdravi [*District Public Health Institute*] (CZ)
OUNZ .... Okresni Ustav Narodniho Zdravi [*District Public Health Institute*] (CZ)
OUO .... Obalsko Utvrdenje Otseka [*Coastal Fortification Section*] (YU)
OUOP .... Okresny Urad Ochrany Prace [*District Labor Protection Office*] (CZ)
OUP .... Attended Repeater Station (RU)
OUP .... Odbor za Unutrasnju Politiku (SIV) [*Committee on Internal Policy*] (YU)
OUP .... Official Unionist Party [*Northern Ireland*] (PPW)
OUPP .... Separate Training Glider Regiment (RU)
OUPT .... Okregowy Urzad Pocztowo-Telegraficzny [*District Post and Telecommunications Office*] (POL)
OUPT .... Okregowy Urzad Pocztowy i Telekomunikacyjny [*District Post and Telecommunications Office*] (POL)
OUPZ .... Odborne Uciliste Pracovnich Zaloh [*Training School for Labor Reserves*] (CZ)
OUR .... Department of Criminal Investigation (RU)
OUR .... Organizacion de Unidad Revolucionaria [*Organization of Revolutionary Unity*] [*Bolivian*] (PPW)
our .... Relative Specific Radioactivity (RU)
OURD .... Overseas Uranium Resources Development Company Ltd. (MAR)
OUS .... Odborne Uciliste Spoju [*Center for Professional Instruction in Communications*] (CZ)
OUS .... Okregowe Urzedy Samochodowe [*District Automotive Vehicle Administration*] (POL)
OUS .... Reference Repeater Station (RU)
OUSA .... Organisation de l'Unite Syndicale Africaine [*Organization of African Trade Union Unity*] [*Use OATUU*] (AF)
OUSA .... Organizacion de Unidad Sindical Africana [*Organization of African Trade Union Unity*] (LA)
OUSIV .... CEMA [*Council for Economic Mutual Assistance*] General Conditions (BU)
OUSKh .... Oblast Administration of Agriculture (RU)
OUSPZ .... Odborne Uciliste Statnich Pracovnich Zaloh [*Training School for State Labor Reserves*] (CZ)
OUT .... Organizacao Unida de Trabalhadores [*United Organization of Workers*] [*Portuguese*] (PPE)
OUT .... Orszagos Ugyvedi Tanacs [*National Council of Lawyers*] (HU)
OUTB .... Separate Training Tank Battalion (RU)
ouv .... Ouverture [*French*]
Ouvr .... Ouvrages Exterieurs [*Outworks*] [*Military map abbreviation*] [*World War I*] [*French*] (MTD)
OUVS .... District Directorate of Military Supply (RU)
OUZ .... Department of Educational Institutions (RU)
OUZD .... Okrozni Urad za Zavarovanje Delavcev [*District Office of Workers' Insurance*] (YU)
OV .... Chemical Warfare Agent (BU)
OV .... Dangerous Goods [*Railroads*] (RU)
OV .... Errors Are Possible (RU)
OV .... Field Winding (RU)
OV .... Firing Platoon (RU)
OV .... Flammable Substance (RU)
o-v .... Island (BU)
o-v .... Island (RU)
OV .... Obrnena Vozba [*Armored Corps*] (CZ)
OV .... Obvodni Vybor [*District Committee, Borough Committee*] (CZ)
OV .... Okresni Velitelstvi [*District Headquarters*] (CZ)
OV .... Okresni Vybor [*District Committee*] (CZ)
OV .... Organic Matter (RU)
OV .... Orszagos Vezetoseg [*National Directorate*] (HU)
OV .... Ortsvereinigungen [*Local Associations*] (EG)
ov .... Osztalyvezeto [*Department Head/Chief*] (HU)
Ov .... Ova [*Plain, Field*] (TU)
OV .... Process Time (RU)
ov .... Purified Water (RU)
OV .... Single-Shot Multivibrator (RU)
OV .... Toxic Agent (RU)
o-va .... Islands (RU)
OVA .... Organismos Viomikhanikis Anaptyxeos [*Organization for Industrial Development*] [*Greek*] (GC)
OVAPAM .... Office de Valorisation Pastorale et Agricole du Mutara (MAR)
OVB .... Oddeleni Verejne Bezpecnosti [*Public Security Department*] (CZ)
OVB .... Onafhankelijk Verbond van Bedrijfsorganisaties [*Independent Federation of Industrial Organizations*] [*Dutch*] (WEN)
ovb .... Separate Reconstruction Battalion (RU)
OVBD .... Okresni Vystavbove Bytove Druzstvo [*District Association for Apartment Construction*] (CZ)
OVD .... Motor Field Winding (RU)
OVD .... Offizier vom Dienst [*Duty Officer*] (EG)
OVDNKh .... Oblast Exhibition of Achievements of the National Economy (RU)
OVEF .... Orszagos Vetomagfelugyeloseg [*National Seed Inspectorate*] (HU)
OVET .... Orszagos Villamosenergiagazdalkodasi Tanacs [*National Council on the Utilization of Electric Power*] (HU)
OVF .... Orszagos Villamosenergia Felugyelet [*National Electric Power Inspectorate*] (HU)
OVF .... Orszagos Vizugyi Foigazgato [*National Director General for Water Power and Hydraulic Engineering*] (HU)
OVG .... District Military Hospital (RU)
OVG .... Generator Field Winding (RU)
OVGE .... Omospondia Viomikhanikon kai Genikon Ergaton [*Federation of Industrial and General Workers*] [*Cypriot*] (GC)
OVH .... Orszagos Vizgazdalkodasi Hivatal [*National Water Bureau*] (HU)
OVH .... Orszagos Vizugyi Hivatal [*National Bureau of Water Conservation*] (HU)
OVH .... Osztalyvezetohelyettes [*Deputy Department Head*] (HU)
OVI .... Clothing and Equipment Supplies (RU)
OVI .... Interior Installations Trust (BU)
OVI .... Okrug Water Installation (BU)
OVIE .... Or Vert Ivoirien Societe d'Expansion (MAR)
OVIKSh .... Joint "Red Banner" Military Engineering School (RU)
OVILLEF .... Orszagos Villamosenergia Felugyelet [*National Electric Power Authority*] (HU)
OVIMU .... Odessa Higher Engineering Nautical School (RU)
OVIR .... Visa and Registration Department (RU)
OVIS .... Military Engineering Supply Section (RU)
OVIT .... Orszagos Villamostavvezetek Vallalat [*National Enterprise for Power Line*] (HU)
OVIU .... District Military Engineering Directorate (RU)
OVK .... Oblast Military Commissariat (RU)
OVK .... Orszagos Vezetokepzo Kozpont [*National Management Training Center*] (HU)
OVKT .... Orszagos Vizgazdalkodasi Keretterv [*National General Plan on Water Economy*] (HU)
OVM .... Motor Field Winding (RU)
OVM .... Society of Militant Materialists (RU)
OVMD .... Society of Militant Dialectical Materialists (RU)
Ov mot art polk ... Combined Arms Motorized Artillery Regiment (BU)
ovnasl .... Ovojni Naslov [*Jacket Title*] (YU)
OVNI .... Objet Volant Non-Identifie [*Unidentified Flying Object*] [*Use UFO*] (AF)
OVNI .... Objeto Volador No Identificado [*Unidentified Flying Object*] [*Use UFO*] (LA)
OVO .... Oddeleni Vychovy a Osvety [*Department of (Political) Education and Culture*] [*Armed forces*] (CZ)
OVO .... Outside Service Department [*of a library*] (RU)
O-vo .... Society, Company (BU)
o-vo .... Society, Company (RU)
OVO .... Special Military District (RU)
OVOMA .... Omby Voafantina Malagasy (MAR)
OVOS .... Okresny Vybor Odbojovych Sloziek [*District Committee of Resistance Units*] (CZ)
ovoshch .... Vegetable Storage [*Topography*] (RU)
ovoshchn .... Vegetable Sovkhoz [*Topography*] (RU)
OVP .... Joint Force Training (RU)
OVP .... Joint Rolling Stock [*Railroads*] (BU)
OVP .... Oesterreichische Volkspartei [*Austrian People's Party*] (PPW)
OVP .... Okresni Vykupni Podnik [*District Bulk Purchasing Enterprise (for agricultural products)*] (CZ)
OVP .... Oxidation-Reduction Potential (RU)
OVPP .... Military Field Post Section (RU)
OVPS .... Ob'edinennyi Velikii Progressivnyi Soiuz (MAR)
OVR .... Calling-Answering Relay (RU)
OVR .... Harbor Defense (RU)
ovr .... Ravine [*Topography*] (RU)
OVRK .... Okrug Military Revolutionary Committee (BU)
OVRP .... Organizacion de Voluntarios para la Revolucion Puertorriquena [*Organization of Volunteers for the Puerto Rican Revolution*] (PD)
OVS .... Clothing and Equipment Depot (RU)
OVS .... Clothing and Equipment Supply (RU)
OVS .... Clothing and Equipment Supply Section (RU)
OVS .... Foreign Relations Section [*Military term*] (RU)
OVS .... Joint Armed Forces (RU)
OVS .... Joint Force Communications (RU)
OVS .... Okresni Vojenska Sprava [*District Military Directorate*] (CZ)
OVS .... Oxidation-Reduction Medium (RU)
OVS .... Separate Signal Platoon (RU)
OVSA .... Omospondia Viotekhnikon Somateion Athinon [*Federation of Athens Handicrafts Associations*] (GC)
OVSL .... Organisation Voltaique des Syndicats Libres [*Voltan Organization of Free Trade Unions*] (AF)
OVSR .... Separate Medical Company (RU)
OVSS .... Military Medical Service Section (RU)
OVSTM .... Operation Vallee du Senegal Tesekele-Magui (MAR)
OVSU .... District Military Medical Directorate (RU)
OVSZ .... Orszagos Vertranszfuzios Szolgalat [*National Blood Transfusion Service*] (HU)
OVSZKTI .... Orszagos Vertranszfuzios Szolgalat Kozponti Tudomanyos Kutato Intezete [*Central Scientific Research Institute of the National Blood Transfusion Service*] (HU)
OVT .... All Clear [*Air-raid warning*] (RU)
OVT .... All-Clear Antiaircraft Defense Signal (BU)
OVT .... Orszagos Villamos Tavvezetek Vallalat [*National Enterprise for Power Lines*] (HU)
OVTs .... Computation Service Center (RU)

ovts .... Sheep-Breeding Sovkhoz [*Topography*] (RU)
ovtsy .... Military Censorship Section (RU)
OVTT .... Orszagos Vezetotovabbkepzesi Tudomanyos Tanacs [*National Science Council for Advanced Management Training*] (HU)
OVTVS .... Okresni Vybor pro Telesnou Vychovu a Sport [*District Committee for Physical Education and Sports*] (CZ)
OVU .... Ocelarsky Vyzkumny Ustav [*Steel Research Institute*] (CZ)
OVU .... Optical Calculator (RU)
OVUZ .... Department of Higher Educational Institutions (RU)
OVV .... Exciter Field Winding (RU)
OVV .... Okresni Vojenske Velitelstvi [*District Military Headquarters*] (CZ)
OVV .... Okresni Volebni Vybor [*District Election Committee*] (CZ)
OVVK .... District Military Medical Commission (RU)
OVZ .... Expectation of External Start [*Computers*] (RU)
OVZ .... Orekhovo-Zuyevo Scales Plant (RU)
oW .... Oesterreichische Waehrung [*Austrian Currency*] [*German*]
oW .... Ohne Wert [*Without Value*] [*Business and trade*] [*German*]
OW .... Okreg Wojskowy [*Military District*] (POL)
Owa .... Ostrov [*Islands*] [*See also O*] [*Russian*] (NAU)
OWAEC .... Organization for West African Economic Co-Operation (MAR)
OWAL .... Oficina de Washington para America Latina [*Washington Office on Latin America*] [*Use WOLA*] (LA1)
OWB .... Opleiding tot Wetenschappelijk Bibliothecaris
OWD .... Ogolne Warunki Dostaw [*General Conditions of Delivery*] (POL)
OWG .... Ordnungswidrigkeiten-Gesetz [*Misdemeanors Law*] (EG)
OWI .... Oddzial Wykonawstwa Inwestycyjnego [*Investment Operations Branch*] (POL)
OWKS .... Okregowy Wojskowy Klub Sportowy [*District Military Sport Club*] (POL)
OWP .... Oboz Wielkiej Polski [*Camp of Great Poland*] (PPE)
OWP .... Odrodzone Wojsko Polskie [*Restored Polish Army*] [*Polish*]
OWP .... Ogolnopolska Wystawa Plastyki [*All-Poland Exhibition of Plastic Arts*] (POL)
OWP .... Organization of Working People [*Guyanese*] (LA)
OWRM .... Okregowe Warsztaty Remontowo-Montazowe [*District Repair and Assembly Shops*] (POL)
OWTU .... Oil Workers Trade Union (LA)
Oxd .... Oxydation [*or Oxydieren*] [*Oxidation*] [*German*]
oxdd .... Oxydierend [*Oxidizing*] [*German*]
OXFAM .... Oxford Committee for Famine Relief (CL)
OXICOL .... Fabrica Colombiana de Oxigeno [*Bogota*] (COL)
OXIQUIM .... Establecimientos Industriales Quimicos Ltda. [*Chemical Industrial Establishments Ltd.*] [*Chilean*] (LA)
OXNE .... Organosis Xenonon Neotitos Ellados [*Youth Hostel Organization of Greece*] (GC)
Oxyka .... Sauerstoffindustrie (VVB) [*Oxygen Industry (VVB)*] (EG)
Oy .... Osakeyhtioe [*Limited Company*] [*Finnish*]
OYAK .... Ordu Yardimlasma Kurumu [*Army Mutual Aid Association*] [*See also OYKGM*] (TU)
OYaP .... Generalized Programing Language (RU)
OYeES .... Organization for European Economic Cooperation [*OEEC*] (RU)
OYEKO .... Omospondia Ypallilon Epikheiriseon Koinis Ofeleias [*Federation of Public Utility Employees*] [*Greek*] (GC)
OYI .... Organismos Ydrevseos kai Ilektrofotismou [*Water Supply and Electric Lighting Organization*] [*Followed by initial letter of location*] [*Greek*] (GC)
OYK .... Omas Ypovrikhion Katastrofon [*Underwater Demolition Squad*] (GC)
OYKGM .... Ordu Yardimlasma Kurumu Genel Mudurlugu [*Army Mutual Aid Association Directorate General*] [*See also OYAK*] (TU)
OYPAE .... Omospondia Ypallilikou Prosopikou Avtokiniton Ellados [*Federation of Transport Personnel of Greece*] (GC)
OYTh .... Organismos Ydrevseos Thessalonikis [*Salonica Water Supply Organization*] (GC)
OZ .... Barrage [*Artillery*] (RU)
OZ .... Center of Contamination (RU)
OZ .... Consolidated Plants (BU)
OZ .... Department of Public Health (RU)
oz .... Lake (RU)
OZ .... Obrtna Zbornica [*Chamber of Craftsmen*] (YU)
OZ .... Obstacle Detachment (RU)
OZ .... Obucarska Zadruga [*Shoemakers Cooperative*] (YU)
OZ .... Oddeleni Zbrani [*Weapons Department (Part of general staff)*] (CZ)
OZ .... Odevne Zavody [*Clothing Enterprises*] (CZ)
OZ .... Okregowy Zwiazek [*District Union*] [*Polish*]
OZ .... Operativna Zona [*Zone of Operation*] [*Military*] (YU)
OZ .... Opravarenske Zavody [*Repair Shops*] (CZ)
OZ .... Osvetove Zarizeni [*Equipment of Cultural Establishments*] (CZ)
OZ .... Oudezijds [*Old Side*] [*Dutch*] (CED)
Oz .... Ozero [*Lake*] [*Russian*] (NAU)
oz .... Reserve [*Military*] (BU)
ozab .... Separate Antiaircraft Artillery Battery (RU)
OZAC .... Office Zairois de Controle [*Zairian Control Office*] (AF)
OZACAF .... Office Zairois du Cafe [*Zairian Coffee Office*] (AF)
ozad .... Separate Antiaircraft Artillery Battalion (BU)
OZAD .... Separate Antiaircraft Artillery Battalion (RU)
OZAKOM .... Special Transcaucasian Committee [*1917-1920*] (RU)
OZAMS .... Oficina Zonal de Apoyo a la Mobilizacion Social [*Zonal Office of Support to Social Mobilization*] [*Peruvian*] (LA)
OZAP .... Obchodni Zarizeni [*Business Equipment*] (CZ)
OZAP .... Separate Antiaircraft Artillery Regiment (RU)
OZATE .... Ordzhonikidze Automobile and Tractor Electrical Equipment Plant (RU)
OZB .... Osnovni Zakon o Braku [*Basic Law on Marriage*] (YU)
OZBCO .... Osobni Zdravotnicky Balicek Civilni Obrany [*Civil Defense First-Aid Kit*] (CZ)
OZBS .... Osnovni Zakon o Zastiti Bilja od Bolesti i Stetocina [*Basic Law on the Protection of Plants Against Diseases and Injurious Insects*] (YU)
OZBW .... Okregowy Zarzad Budownictwa Weglowego [*District Administration of Coal Industry Construction*] (POL)
OZC .... Okregowy Zwiazek Cechow [*District Union of Guilds*] (POL)
OZCh .... Green Tea Infusion (RU)
OZD .... Object Zvlastni Dulezitosti [*Specially Important Target*] (CZ)
OZDiP .... Child and Youth Health Care (RU)
OZE .... Osnovni Zakon o Eksproprijaciji [*Basic Law on Expropriation*] (YU)
OZEBiH .... Zavod za Ekonomsku Propagandu i Publicitet Bosne i Hercegovine [*Institute of Economic Propaganda and Publicity of Bosnia and Hercegovina*] [*Sarajevo*] (YU)
OZenAD .... Separate Antiaircraft Artillery Battalion (RU)
OZenAP .... Separate Antiaircraft Artillery Regiment (RU)
OZET .... All-Union Society for Land Settlement of Jewish Workers in the USSR (RU)
ozetl .... Ozetleyen [*Summarized, Abridged*] (TU)
OZG .... Okregowe Zaklady Gastronomiczne [*District Catering Establishments*] [*Polish*]
Ozgur Haber-Is ... Turkish Postal, Telegraph, Telephone, Radio, and Television Workers Union (TU)
ozh .... Liquid Trap (RU)
OZH .... Oglasni Zavod Hrvatske [*Advertising Institute of Croatia*] [*Zagreb*] (YU)
OZH .... Ogrodnicze Zaklady Handlowe [*Garden Produce Sales Establishments*] (POL)
OZH .... Ogrodnicze Zaklady Hodowlane [*Horticultural Establishments*] (POL)
ozhad .... Separate Railroad Artillery Battalion (RU)
ozhdrb .... Separate Railroad Repair Battalion (RU)
OZHS .... Odbytova Zakladna Hlavni Spravy [*Main Administration, Distribution Unit*] (CZ)
oz i .... Ozel Isim [*Proper Noun*] (TU)
OZIPS .... General Artisan and Trade Union (BU)
Oz-Is .... Ozgur Is Sendikalar Konfederasyonu [*Confederation of Free Trade Unions*] (TU)
Oz Is .... Turkiye Ozgur Isci Sendikalari Konfederasyonu [*Confederation of Free Trade Unions*] (TU)
OZK .... Obchodni a Zivnostenska Komora [*Chamber of Commerce*] (CZ)
OZK .... Odborna Zavodna Kniznica [*Factory Technical Library*] (CZ)
OZK .... Odborna Zavodni Knihovna [*Factory Technical Library*] (CZ)
OZK .... Odborova Zavodni Knihovna [*Trade Union Factory Library*] (CZ)
OZK .... Oddzialy Zaopatrzenia Kolejowego [*Railroad Supply Branches*] (POL)
OZK .... Okregowy Zarzad Kin [*District Movie Theatre Administration*] (POL)
OZK .... Okresni Zivnostenska Komise [*District Trade Commission*] (CZ)
OZKZ .... Okrajna Zveza Kmetijskih Zadrug [*District Union of Agricultural Cooperatives*] (YU)
OZL .... Plant Laboratory (RU)
OZLP .... Okregowy Zarzad Lasow Panstwowych [*District Administration of State Forests*] (POL)
OZM .... Fragmentation Barrier Mine (RU)
OZMO .... Opoczynskie Zaklady Materialow Ogniotrwalych [*Opoczno Fireproof Material Plant*] (POL)
OZMR .... Opci Zakon o Morskom Ribolovu [*General Law on Sea Fishing*] (YU)
OZN .... Oboz Zjednoczenia Narodowego [*National Unity Camp*] [*Pre-World War II*] (POL)
OZN .... Organizacija Zdruzenih Narodov [*United Nations Organization*] (YU)
OZNNS .... Organization for the Protection of the Population and the National Economy (BU)
OZNO .... Opsti Zakon o Narodnim Odborima [*General Law on People's Committees*] (YU)
OZO .... Correspondence Training Department (RU)
OZO .... Odbor Zasobovaci a Odbytovy [*Supply and Marketing Department*] (CZ)
OZOE .... Osnovni Zakon o Eksproprijaciji [*Basic Law on Expropriation*] (YU)
ozog .... Harassing Fire (BU)
OZON .... Oboz Zjednoczenia Ogolno-Narodowego [*National Unity Camp*] [*Pre-World War II*] (POL)
OZORD .... Opsti Zakon o Odnosima Roditelja i Dece [*General Law on Parent and Child Relations*] (YU)
OZOS .... Olsztynskie Zaklady Opon Samochodowych [*Olsztyn Tire Plant*] (POL)

OZP .... Oddeleni Zahranicni Pomoci [*Foreign Aid Department*] (CZ)
OZP .... Odraz Zabezpeceni Pohybu [*March Security Detachment*] (CZ)
OZP .... Oglas za Pomorce [*Notice to Mariners*] [*A periodical*] (YU)
OZP .... Osnovni Zakon o Prekrsajima [*Basic Law on Misdemeanors*] (YU)
OZPGR .... Okregowy Zarzad Panstwowych Gospodarstw Rolnych [*District Administration of State Farms*] (POL)
OZPO .... Ostrowieckie Zaklady Przemyslu Odziezowego [*Ostrowiec Clothing Factory*] (POL)
OZPP .... Ogolnopolskie Zrzeszenie Prywatnego Przemyslu [*All-Polish Association of Private Industry*] (POL)
OZPP .... Osnovni Zakon o Drzavnim Privrednim Preduzecima [*Basic Law on State Economic Establishments*] (YU)
OZPPChSiR ... Ogolnopolskie Zrzeszenie Prywatnego Przemyslu Chemicznego, Spozywczego, i Roznych [*All-Polish Association of Private Chemical, Food, and Miscellaneous Industries*] (POL)
OZPS .... General Agrarian Trade Union (BU)
OZR .... Oddzial Zaopatrzenia Robotniczego [*Workers' Supply Branch*] (POL)
OZR .... Osrodek Zaopatrzenia Robotniczego [*Workers' Supply Center*] (POL)
OZRA .... Plant Protection Department (RU)
OZS .... Flame and Incendiary Agent (RU)
OZS .... Oddeleni Zahranicnich Styku [*Foreign Affairs Department*] (CZ)
OZS .... Okresni Zdravotni Sprava [*District Health Administration*] (CZ)
OZS .... Osnovni Zakon o Stărateljstvu [*Basic Law on Guardianship*] (YU)
OZT .... Fragmentation Incendiary Tracer (RU)
OZT .... Office Zairois du Tourisme (MAR)
OZTs .... Waiting on Cement (RU)
OZU .... Internal Storage, Internal Memory (RU)
OZU .... Internal Storage System [*Data processing*] (BU)
OZU .... Land Improvement Department (RU)
OZU .... Opci Zakon o Univerzitetima [*General Law on Universities*] (YU)
OZV .... Determination of Air Contamination (RU)
OZV .... Flame and Incendiary Agent (RU)
OZVD .... Otrokovicko-Zlinsko-Vizovicka Draha [*Otrokovice-Zlin-Vizovice Railroad*] (CZ)
OZZ .... Okregowe Zaklady Zbozowe [*District Grain Elevators*] (POL)
OZZ .... Opsta Zemjodelska Zadruga [*General Agricultural Cooperative*] (YU)
OZZZ .... Osnovni Zakon o Zemljoradnickim Zadrugama [*Basic Law on Agricultural Cooperatives*] (YU)

P

P ..... Advanced, Forward, Leading (RU)
P ..... Apiary [*Topography*] (RU)
P ..... Bound [*Bibliography*] (RU)
p ..... Bystreet, Lane, Alley (RU)
p ..... Case [*Grammar*] (RU)
P ..... De Position [*Said of a battery*] [*Military*] [*French*] (MTD)
P ..... Diamond Pyramid [*Vickers hardness test*] (RU)
p ..... First Lieutenant (BU)
P ..... Fixed Light [*Nautical term*] (RU)
p ..... Folder, File, Dossier (BU)
p ..... Food (RU)
P ..... For Desert Backgrounds [*Designation of camouflage materials*] (RU)
P ..... Fruit (RU)
P ..... Infantry (RU)
P ..... Instrument, Device, Apparatus (RU)
p ..... Interference, Noise (RU)
P ..... Padre [*Father, Priest*] [*Spanish*]
p ..... Page [*Page*] [*French*]
p ..... Pagina [*Page*] [*Portuguese*] (GPO)
p ..... Painos [*Finnish*]
p ..... Pair [*French*]
p ..... Pair, Couple (RU)
p ..... Paiva(a) [*Day, Date*] [*Finnish*] (GPO)
p ..... Palsta [*Finnish*]
P ..... Pan [*or Pani*] [*Mr., Mrs., Miss*] [*Polish*]
P ..... Papa [*Pope*] [*Spanish*]
P ..... Papa [*Pope*] [*Latin*] (GPO)
p ..... Par [*By, Per, Through, From*] [*French*]
p ..... Para [*Para*] [*German*]
p ..... Paragraph, Clause (RU)
P ..... Parameter (RU)
P ..... Parc (a Bestiaux) [*Peak, Cattle Pen*] [*Military map abbreviation*] [*World War I*] [*French*] (MTD)
P ..... Parkirozo (Hely) [*Parking Place*] (HU)
p ..... Partim [*In Part*] [*Latin*] (GPO)
P ..... Pasir [*Part of place name, i.e. Pasir Puteh*] (ML)
P ..... Patent (RU)
P ..... Pater [*Father*] [*Latin*] (GPO)
p ..... Patrz [*See*] (POL)
P ..... Pawn [*Chess*] (RU)
p ..... Paye [*Paid*] [*French*]
P ..... Pengo [*Pengo*] (HU)
p ..... Penni(a) [*Penny or Pence*] [*Finnish*] (GPO)
p ..... Per [*By*] [*Latin*] (GPO)
p ..... Per [*For*] [*Italian*]
p ..... Perc [*Minute*] (HU)
P ..... Personenzuglokomotive [*Passenger Train Locomotive, Local Passenger Train Locomotive*] (EG)
p ..... Persoona [*Person*] [*Finnish*]
P ..... Peso [*Spanish*]
P ..... Petrograd (RU)
P ..... Pharmacien [*Apothecary*] [*French*]
p ..... Piazza [*Place*] [*Italian*] (CED)
P ..... Pic [*Peak*] [*Military map abbreviation*] [*World War I*] [*French*] (MTD)
p ..... Pietro [*Floor, Story*] (POL)
p ..... Pieze (RU)
p ..... Pius [*Holy*] [*Latin*] (GPO)
P ..... Piyade [*Infantry*] (TU)
P ..... Plowland, Plowed Field [*Topography*] (RU)
p ..... Point, Post (RU)
p ..... Poise (RU)
p ..... Pole (RU)
P ..... Pond [*Gram of Thrust*] [*See also Kp (Kilopond) and Mp (Megapond)*] (EG)
P ..... Pond [*Gram of Thrust*] [*See also Kp (Kilopond) and Mp (Megapond)*] (HU)
p ..... Pond [*Gram of Thrust*] (CZ)
p ..... Pondere [*By Weight*] [*Latin*] (GPO)
P ..... Pont [*Bridge*] [*Military map abbreviation*] [*World War I*] [*French*] (MTD)
P ..... Pontifex [*Bishop*] [*Latin*] (GPO)
P ..... Populus [*People*] [*Latin*] (GPO)
p ..... Porownaj [*Compare*] [*Polish*]
P ..... Port [*Port*] [*French*] (NAU)
P ..... Port [*Malaysian*] (ML)
P ..... Portugalia [*Portugal*] [*Polish*]
p ..... Post [*After*] [*Latin*] (GPO)
P ..... Post (RU)
p ..... Pour [*For*] [*French*]
P ..... Pour [*For*] [*In the context of signatures at the end of memos or documents*] (CL)
P ..... Powder [*Pharmacy*] (RU)
P ..... Pozorovatelna [*Observation Post*] (CZ)
P ..... Pregunta [*Question*] [*Spanish*]
P ..... Prepositional [*Case*] (RU)
p ..... Prime [*First, Prime*] [*French*]
p ..... Primus [*First*] [*Latin*] (GPO)
p ..... Pro [*For*] [*Latin*] (GPO)
P ..... Produktion [*Production*] (EG)
P ..... Professional Qualification [*Finnish*]
P ..... Professional Qualification [*Indonesian*]
P ..... Program Module [*Computers*] (RU)
P ..... Proteste [*French*]
P ..... Ptychion [*Greek*]
P ..... Puaz [*Poise*] [*Polish*]
p ..... Puhelin [*Finnish*]
P ..... Pulau [*Part of place name, i.e. Pulau Penang/Pinang Malaysia*] (ML)
p ..... Punkt [*Point*] [*Polish*]
p ..... Pyha [*Finnish*]
P ..... Receiver (RU)
P ..... Regiment (RU)
p ..... Right, Right-Hand (RU)
P ..... Route, Track [*Topography*] (RU)
P ..... Sand [*Topography*] (RU)
P ..... Sandy [*Topography*] (RU)
P ..... Settlement [*Topography*] (RU)
P ..... Splinterproof Structures [*Topography*] (RU)
P ..... Square [*Topography*] (RU)
p ..... Stabnuclear (RU)
P ..... Starter Button (RU)
P ..... Steam Locomotive (RU)
P ..... Subcaliber (RU)
P ..... Suburb [*Topography*] (RU)
P ..... Switch (RU)
P ..... Trailer (RU)
p ..... Train (RU)
P1 ..... Teknikum Ingenior [*Professional qualification*] [*Danish*]
P2 ..... Akademingenior [*Professional qualification*] [*Danish*]
P3 ..... Civilingenior [*Professional qualification*] [*Danish*]
P4 ..... Nurse, Midwife [*Professional qualification*] [*Danish*]
P4 ..... Pegawai Pengangkutan Pasokan Polis [*Police Force Transport Officer*] (ML)
PA ..... Address Delivery Pulse [*Computers*] (RU)
PA ..... Anatomical Forceps (RU)
PA ..... Antenna Strip (RU)
PA ..... Black Prismatic Powder [*Symbol*] [*French*] (MTD)
PA ..... Field Airdrome (RU)
PA ..... Field Army (BU)
PA ..... Field Army (RU)
PA ..... Field Artillery (RU)
PA ..... Field Balloon (RU)
PA ..... Intermediate Equipment [*Computers*] (RU)
pA ..... Micromicro Ampere [*Micromicro Ampere ($1/10^{12}$ Amperes)*] (EG)
PA ..... Mobile Directional Antenna (RU)
PA ..... Pacte de Solidarite Sociale [*Pact of Social Solidarity*] [*Belgian*] (WER)
PA ..... Pacto Andino [*Andean Pact*] [*Use Andean Group*] (LA)

pa............... Paino Arkki [*Printed Sheet*] [*Finnish*] (GPO)
PA............... Panama [*Panama*] [*Polish*]
PA............... Panama [*Two-letter standard code*] (CNC)
pa............... Para [*For, Toward*] [*Spanish*]
PA............... Parc d'Artillerie [*Military*] [*French*] (MTD)
PA............... Parizsky Archiv [*Paris Archives (of the Ministry of Foreign Affairs)*] (CZ)
PA............... Parti de l'Action [*Party of Action*] [*Moroccan*] (PPW)
PA............... Partido Autentico [*Authentic Party*] [*Argentine*] (LA)
PA............... Patentanmeldung [*Patent Application*] (EG)
PA............... People's Alliance [*Althydubandalag*] [*Icelandic*] (PPW)
PA............... People's Assembly [*Egyptian*] (MAR)
pa............... Per Adres [*Care Of*] [*Dutch*] (GPO)
pA............... Per Adresse [*Care Of*] [*German*] (GPO)
pa............... Per Annum [*Yearly*] [*Latin*] (GPO)
PA............... Perwira [*Officer*] (IN)
PA............... Petroleumaether [*Petroleum Ether*] [*German*]
PA............... Pistolet Automatique [*Automatic Pistol*] (CL)
PA............... Plataformas Anti-Capitalistas [*Anti-Capitalist Platforms*] [*Spanish*] (WER)
Pa............... Playa [*Beach*] [*Spanish*] (NAU)
PA............... Politische Abteilung [*Political Department*] (EG)
PA............... Polyamide (RU)
PA............... Por Ausencia [*Because of Absence*] [*Spanish*]
PA............... Por Autoridad [*By Authority*] [*Spanish*]
PA............... Por Autorizacion [*For Authorization*] [*Spanish*]
pa............... Postal Address (RU)
PA............... Postamt [*Post Office*] (EG)
PA............... Poste Administratif (MAR)
PA............... Pour Ampliation [*French*]
Pa............... Praia [*Beach*] [*Portuguese*] (NAU)
PA............... Presence Africaine (MAR)
Pa............... Prima [*First Class*] [*Business and trade*] [*German*]
PA............... Prirocnik za Agitacija [*Handbook for Agitators*] [*A periodical*] (YU)
pa............... Pro Anno [*For the Year*] [*Latin*] (GPO)
PA............... Proletariaki Aristera [*See also Omada gia mia Proletariaki Aristera (OPA)*] (GC)
PA............... Propaganda and Agitation (BU)
PA............... Propyl Acetate (RU)
PA............... Protivavionski [*Antiaircraft*] (YU)
Pa............... Pruefungsamt [*Inspection Office*] (EG)
PA............... Regimental Artillery (BU)
PA............... Regimental Artillery (RU)
PA............... Sand-Oil Blender Unit [*Pet.*] (RU)
PA............... Straightforward Algorithm (RU)
PA............... Transverse Reinforcement (RU)
PAA............. Pan African Airlines (MAR)
PAA............. Problems of the Arctic and Antarctic [*A publication*] (RU)
PAA............. Protivavionska Artiljerija [*Antiaircraft Artillery*] (YU)
PAA............. Prueba de Aptitud Academica [*Spanish*]
PAAB........... Field Army Air Base (RU)
PAAECI....... Pan American Association of Educational Credit Institutions [*See also APICE*] (EA)
PAAFL......... Pan-African Air Freight Lines (MAR)
PAAG.......... Protivavionska Artiljeriska Grupa [*Antiaircraft Artillery Group*] (YU)
PAAORLBE ... Pan-American Association of Oto-Rhino-Laryngology and Broncho-Esophagology (EA)
paar............ Antiaircraft Artillery (BU)
paarr........... Army Mobile Ordnance Repair Depot (BU)
PAAS........... Army Field Ammunition Depot (RU)
PAAS........... Field Army Artillery Depot (BU)
PAASOK...... Pankyprion Agrotikon Koinoniko-Dimokratikon Komma [*Pan-Cyprian Agrarian Social-Democratic Party*] (GC1)
paav............ Paaverbi [*Principal Verb*] [*Finnish*]
PAB............. Advanced Army Base (RU)
PAB............. Aerial Practice Bomb (RU)
PAB............. Gun Artillery Battery (RU)
PAB............. Mobile Army Base (BU)
PAB............. Mobile Army Base (RU)
PAB............. Parti des Paysans, Artisans, et Bourgeois [*Farmers', Artisans', and Burghers' Party*] [*Swiss*] (PPE)
PAB............. Periscopic Aiming Circle [*Artillery*] (BU)
PAB............. Periscopic Aiming Circle [*Artillery*] (RU)
PAB............. Periskopska Artiljeriska Busola [*Periscopic Artillery Compass*] (YU)
PAB............. Semiautomatic Block System [*Railroads*] (RU)
PABAN........ Perwira Bantuan [*Officer Support Group*] (ML)
PABEKO...... Parti de l'Alliance des Bena-Koshi (MAR)
PABISA....... Party Bisamah' Sarawak (ML)
PABK........... Pan-American Coffee Bureau [*PACB*] (RU)
PABK........... Para-Aminobenzoic Acid (RU)
Pable........... Payable [*French*]
PABR........... Gun Artillery Brigade (RU)
PABX........... Private Automatic Branch Exchange (MAR)
PAC............. Pan-Africanist Congress [*South African*] (AF)
PAC............. Partido de Accion y Cambio [*Action and Change Party*] [*Costa Rican*] (LA)
PAC............. Partido Accion Constitucional [*Constitutional Action Party*] [*Dominican Republic*] (LA1)
PAC............. Patrulla Aerea Civil [*Bogota*] (COL)
PAC............. Planning Advisory Council (MAR)
PAC............. Politique Agricole Commune (MAR)
PAC............. Pomocna Armadni Cesta [*Secondary Army Route*] (CZ)
PAC............. Positive Action Campaign (MAR)
PAC............. Productivity Advisory Council (MAR)
PAC............. Programa de Acao Concentrada [*Concentrated Action Program*] [*Brazilian*] (LA)
PAC............. Programme d'Action Commerciale (MAR)
PAC............. Public Accounts Committee [*Mauritian*] (AF)
PAC............. Pulk Artylerii Ciezkiej
PACA........... Pan-Africanist Congress of Azania [*South African*] (MAR)
PACB........... Portuguese Administrative Council of the Cahora Basa (MAR)
PACLA......... Pan African Christian Leadership Assembly (MAR)
PACOFS...... Performing Arts Council of the Orange Free State (MAR)
PACOREDO ... Partido Comunista de la Republica Dominicana [*Also, PCRD*] [*Communist Party of the Dominican Republic*] (LA)
PAC-SA...... Pan-Africanist Congress of South Africa (AF)
PACT........... Performing Arts Council of the Transvaal (MAR)
PACT........... Private Agencies Collaborating Together, Inc. (MAR)
pad............. Case [*Grammar*] (BU)
pad............. Case [*Grammar*] (RU)
PAD............. Gun Artillery Division (RU)
PAD............. Partido Autentico Democratico [*Authentic Democratic Party*] [*Guatemalan*] (LA)
pad............. Ravine [*Topography*] (RU)
PAD............. Solid-Propellant Generator, Solid-Reactant Gas Generator (RU)
PADA........... Partico de Accion Democratica Anticomunista [*Anticommunist Democratic Action Party*] (LA)
PADAK........ Papeterie Dakaroise SA (MAR)
PADASA...... Pazarlama Dagitim ve Satis Ltd. Sti. [*Marketing, Distribution, and Sales Limited Corp.*] (TU)
PADELPA.... Papeles del Pacifico Ltda. [*Cali*] (COL)
PADENA...... Parti Democrate National (MAR)
PADENA...... Partido Democratico Nacional [*National Democratic Party*] [*Chilean*] (LA)
PADEPA...... Papelera del Pacifico, SA [*Pacific Paper, Inc.*] [*Chilean*] (LA)
PADES........ Programa de Accion del Desarrollo Economico y Social [*Socioeconomic Development Action Program*] [*Bolivian*] (LA)
PADESM..... Parti des Desherites de Madagascar [*Party of the Deprived of Madagascar*] (AF)
PADIK......... Pankyprion Dimokratikon Kinima [*Pan-Cyprian Democratic Movement*] (GC)
PADIS......... Pan-African Documentation and Information System [*Addis Ababa, Ethiopia*]
padn............ Gun Artillery Battalion (RU)
PADO.......... Antiairborne Defense (RU)
PADOG........ Plan d'Amenagement et d'Organisation (MAR)
PADP........... Partido Accion Democratico Popular [*Popular Democratic Action Party*] [*Costa Rican*] (LA)
PADPM........ Pan-African Democratic Party of Malawi (AF)
PAdr............ Per Adresse [*Care Of*] (EG)
PAE............. Panellinios Aktoploiki Enosis [*Panhellenic Coastal Shipping Union*] (GC)
PAE............. Parataxis Agroton kai Ergazomenon [*Agrarian and Labor Faction*] [*Greek*] (GC)
pae............. Partes Aequales [*Equal Parts*] [*Latin*] (GPO)
PAE............. Preduzece za Automatizaciju i Elektroniku [*Establishment for Automation and Electronics*] (YU)
PAEEK........ Podosfairiki Athlitiki Enosi Eparkhias Kyrineias [*Kyrenia District Athletic Soccer Union*] (GC)
PAEGAE...... Pronomioukhos Anonymos Etaireia Genikon Apothikon Ellados [*Chartered General Warehouses Joint Stock Company of Greece*] (GC)
paepstl........ Paepstlich [*German*]
PAF............. Mobile Photographic Laboratory (RU)
PAF............. Pan-African Federation (MAR)
PAF............. Pan-African Festival (MAR)
PAF............. Police de l'Air et des Frontieres [*Air and Frontier Police*] [*French*] (WER)
PAF............. Polyazophenylene (RU)
PAF............. Semiautomatic Apparatus for Packaging Lozenges (RU)
PAFAMS..... Pan American Federation of Associations of Medical Schools [*See also FEPAFEM*] (EA)
Pafawag...... Panstwowa Fabryka Wagonow [*State Railroad Car Factory*] (POL)
PAFMECA... Pan-African Freedom Movement for East and Central Africa (MAR)
PAFMECSA ... Pan African Freedom Movement for East, Central, and Southern Africa [*Superseded in 1963 by the liberation committee of the Organization of African Unity*] (PD)
PAFNA........ Pan-African News Agency (AF)
PAFT........... Pan-American Federation of Labor (RU)
pag............. Diving Gyro Horizon (RU)
PAG-........... Gyro Horizon Converter (RU)
pag............. Pagina [*Page*] [*Spanish*]
pag............. Pagina [*Page*] [*Italian*]
pag............. Pagination (BU)
pag............. Pagination (RU)

pag .... Paginiran [*Paginated*] (YU)
PAG .... Panstwowy Arbitraz Gospodarczy [*State Office for Economic Arbitration*] (POL)
PAG .... Para-Aminohippuric Acid (RU)
PAG .... Party for the Autonomy of Gibraltar (PPW)
PAG .... Prince Alfred's Guard (MAR)
PAG .... Protivavionska Grupa [*Antiaircraft Group*] (YU)
PAG .... Pukovska Artiljeriska Grupa [*Regimental Artillery Group*] (YU)
PAG .... Regimental Artillery Group (BU)
PAG .... Regimental Artillery Group (RU)
PAGART ...... Polska Agencja Artystyczna [*Polish Art Agency*] (POL)
pagdo .... Pagadero [*Payable*] [*Business and trade*] [*Spanish*]
Paged .... Polska Agencja Drzewna [*Polish Lumber Agency*] (POL)
PAGED .... Polska Agencja Eksportu Drewna [*Polish Agency for the Export of Timber*] [*Polish*]
PAGENA ..... Papeterie Generale de l'Afrique Occidentale (MAR)
PAGENA ..... Participation Generale Africaine (MAR)
PAGENACI ... Participation Generale Africaine de la Cote-d'Ivoire (MAR)
PAGOR .... [*R.*] Pailhoux et G. Goret (MAR)
PAGRAL ...... Proveedora Agroindustrial [*Cali*] (COL)
PAGS .... Parti de l'Avant-Garde Socialiste [*Socialist Vanguard Party*] [*Algerian*] (PD)
PAHO .... Pan American Health Organization
PAHUB .... Perwira Perhubungan [*Communications Officer*] (IN)
PAI .... Paideuma (MAR)
PAI .... Parti Africain de l'Independance [*African Independence Party*] [*Senegalese*] (PPW)
PAI .... Parti Africain de l'Independance [*African Independance Party*] [*Upper Voltan*] (AF)
PAI .... Partido Africano da Independencia da Guine Dita Portuguesa (MAR)
PAI .... Plan de Accion Inmediata [*Plan for Immediate Action*] [*Peruvian*] (LA)
PAI .... Portable Aerosol Inhalator (RU)
PAICV .... Parti Africain de l'Independance du Cap-Vert [*African Party for the Independence of Cape Verde*] (MAR)
PAID .... Pan-African Institute for Development (MAR)
PAIGC .... Partido Africano da Independencia da Guine e do Cabo Verde [*African Party for the Independence of Guinea and Cape Verde*] (PPW)
PA IIL TsK KPU ... Party Archives of the Institute of the History of the Party of the Central Committee of the Communist Party of the Ukraine (RU)
paik .... Paikasta [*About a Place*] [*Finnish*]
Pain .... Prochain [*Next, Nearest*] [*French*]
paini .... Painissa [*Wrestling*] [*Finnish*]
painoll .... Painollisena [*Stressed, Accented*] [*Finnish*]
painott .... Painottomana [*Unaccented*] [*Finnish*]
PAIS .... Public Affairs Information Service (MAR)
PAJ .... Protivavionska Odbrana Jedinice [*Antiaircraft Defense Units*] (YU)
PAJAR .... Parti Rakyat Jati Sarawak [*Sarawak Native People's Party*] [*Malaysian*] (PPW)
PAJU .... Pan-African Journalists Union (AF)
PAK .... Industrial-Agrarian Complex (BU)
PAK .... Paidagogiki Akadimia Kyprou [*Pedagogic Academy of Cyprus*] (GC)
pak .... Paketti [*Finnish*]
PAK .... Pakistan [*Pakistan*] [*Polish*]
PAK .... Pakistan [*Three-letter standard code*] (CNC)
PAK .... Panafrikanskii Kongress (MAR)
PAK .... Panellinion Apelevtherotikon Kinima [*Panhellenic Liberation Movement*] (GC)
PAK .... Pankyprio Andistasiako Kinima [*Pan-Cyprian Resistance Movement*] (GC)
PAK .... Panzerabwehrkanone [*Antitank Gun*] (EG)
PAK .... Pomiary - Automatyka -Kontrola [*Measurements - Automation - Control*] [*A monthly periodical*] (POL)
PAK .... Projet Agricole de Kibuye (MAR)
PAK .... Transfer of Instruction Address [*Computers*] (RU)
PAKh .... Motorized Field Bakery (BU)
PAKh .... Motorized Field Bakery (RU)
PAKh .... Passenger Automobile Transportation Establishment (RU)
PAKOE .... Panellinion Kendron Oikologikon Erevnon [*Panhellenic Center of Ecological Research*] (GC1)
PAKOMATIC ... Empacomatic de Colombia Ltda. [*Barranquilla*] (COL)
PA KPE .... Party Archives of the Central Committee of the Communist Party of Estonia (RU)
PAKTAS ...... Pamuk Ticaret ve Sanayi Anonim Sirketi [*Cotton Trade and Industry Corporation*] (TU)
PAKuyb obl ... Party Archives of the Kuybyshev Oblast (RU)
Pal .... Chamber (RU)
PAL .... Laboratory of Pathological Anatomy (RU)
pal .... Palazzo [*Palace*] [*Italian*] (CED)
PAL .... Parc d'Artillerie Lourde [*Military*] [*French*] (MTD)
PAL .... Placi Aglomerate din Lemn [*Chipboard*] (RO)
PAL .... Polska Akademia Literatury [*Polish Academy of Literature*] [*Pre-World War II*] (POL)
PAL .... Polska Armia Ludowa [*Polish People's Army (1943-1944)*] [*Polish*]
PAL .... Pomocny Prumysl Automobilni a Letecky [*Instrument and Accessory Industry for Aircraft and Automobiles*] (CZ)
PAL .... Povrchove Aktivni Latky [*Surface Active Agents (Oils)*] (CZ)
PAL .... Progressive Alliance of Liberia (PPW)
PAL .... Transfer Machine Line (RU)
PALAD .... Peralatan Angkatan Darat [*Army Ordnance*] (IN)
paleol .... Paleolithic (RU)
paleon .... Paleontology (RU)
paleont .... Paleontology, Paleontological (BU)
PALF .... Pyridoxal Phosphate (RU)
PALGA .... Pathologisch-Anatomisch Landelijk Geautomatiseerd Archief [*Dutch*]
PALM .... People's Action Labor Movement [*Grenadian*] (LA)
PALMEVEAS ... Palmiers et Heveas du Gabon (MAR)
PALMITEX ... Industrias Textiles de Palmira (COL)
PALMO .... Panellinios Organosis Laikis Symbarastaseos [*Panhellenic Organization of Popular Support*] (GC)
PALP .... Palebne Postaveni [*Firing Position*] (CZ)
PALR .... Panzerabwehrlenkrakete [*Antitank Guided Rocket*] (EG)
Pals .... Palais [*Palace*] [*Military map abbreviation*] [*World War I*] [*French*] (MTD)
Pals .... Palheiros [*Fishing Village*] [*Portuguese*] (NAU)
PALSS .... Physical and Life Sciences Society (MAR)
PALU .... Parti Lumumbiste de l'Unite (MAR)
PALU .... Progressive Arbeiders- en Landbouwersunie [*Progressive Workers' and Farm Laborers' Union*] [*Surinamese*] (PPW)
Pam .... Field Air Maintenance Shop (RU)
PAM .... Mobile Air Maintenance Shop (RU)
PAM .... Mobile Artillery Shop (RU)
Pam .... Monument [*Topography*] (RU)
PAM .... Panafricaine des Metaux (MAR)
PAM .... Patriotikon Antidiktatorikon Metopon [*Patriotic Antidictatorial Front*] [*Greek*] (GC)
PAM .... Patriotikon Apelevtherotikon Metopon [*Patriotic Liberation Front*] [*Greek*] (GC)
PAM .... People's Action Movement [*St. Kitts-Nevis*] (PPW)
PAM .... Periodistas Asociados de Manizales (COL)
PAM .... Pokrajinski Arhiv v Mariboru [*Provincial Archives in Maribor*] (YU)
PAM .... Pomorska Akademia Medyczna [*Pomeranian Medical Academy*] (POL)
PaM .... Prace a Mzdy [*Work and Wages*] (CZ)
PAM .... Programme Alimentaire Mondial [*World Food Program*] [*Use WFP*] (AF)
PAM .... Protivatomska Maska [*Antiatomic Mask*] (YU)
PAM .... Protivavionski Mitraljez [*Antiaircraft Machine Gun*] (YU)
PAM .... Regimental Artillery Shop (RU)
PAMA .... Perwira Pertama [*Junior Officer (Lieutenant to captain)*] (IN)
PAME .... Pan-Democratic Agrarian Front of Greece (PPW)
PAME .... Pandemokratiki Agrotikon Metapon Ellados [*Pan-Democratic Agrarian Front of Greece*] (PPE)
PAME .... Pankyprio Anorthotiko [*Pancyprian Renewal Front*] [*Greek Cypriot*] (PPE)
PAME .... Pankyprion Ananeotikon Metopon [*Pan-Cyprian Renewal Front*] (GC1)
PAMEN .... Perwira Menengah [*Field Grade Officer (Major to colonel)*] (IN)
PAMF .... Pyridoxamine Phosphate (RU)
PAMI .... Plan de Asistencia Medica Integral [*Comprehensive Medical Assistance Plan*] [*Argentine*] (LA)
PAMID .... Centrul de Calcul si Lucrari Auxiliare si Rare [*Center for Computation and Auxiliary and Rare Projects*] (RO)
PAMIL .... Imo State Palm Industrial (MAR)
PAMK .... Panellinia Agonistiki Mathitiki Kinisi [*Panhellenic Militant Student Movement*] (GC)
PAMMD .... Public Administration, Manpower, and Management Division (MAR)
PAMOL .... Plantations Pamol du Cameroun Ltd. (MAR)
PAMS .... Army Field Medical Depot (RU)
PAMS .... Mobile Artillery Weather Station (RU)
PAMSS .... Army Field Medical Depot (RU)
PAMTEKS ... Pamukkale Tekstil Sanayi ve Ticaret AS [*Pamukkale Textile Industry and Trade Corp.*] (TU)
PAMTS .... Semiautomatic Long-Distance Telephone Communication (RU)
PAN .... Automatic Aiming Device [*Artillery*] (RU)
PAN .... Industrial-Agrarian Trust (BU)
PAN .... National Action Party [*Mexican*] (PD)
PAN .... Panama [*Three-letter standard code*] (CNC)
PAN .... Panitia [*Committee*] (IN)
PAN .... Partido de Accion Nacional [*National Action Party*] [*Spanish*] (WER)
PAN .... Partido de Accion Nacional [*National Action Party*] [*Mexican*] (LA)
PAN .... Partido Agrario Nacional [*National Agrarian Party*] [*Bolivian*] (LA)
PAN .... Partiia Alzhirskovo Naroda (MAR)
PAN .... Polish Academy of Sciences (RU)
PAN .... Polska Akademia Nauk [*Polish Academy of Sciences*] (POL)
PAN .... Programa Alimentario Nacional [*National Food Program*] [*Nicaraguan*] (LA1)
PAN .... Project voor Automatische Namenverwerking [*Dutch*]
PAN .... Pyridylazonaphthol (RU)

PAN .... Semiautomatic Aiming [*Artillery*] (RU)
PANA .... Pan-African Information Agency (MAR)
PANA .... Pan-African News Agency [*Use PAFNA*] (AF)
PANA .... Pan Asia News Agency (SJT)
PANA .... Pan Asia News Alliance (CL)
PANA .... Parti Nationaliste (MAR)
PANAC .... Parti National Chretien (MAR)
PANAC .... Plantations Association of Nigeria and the Cameroons (MAR)
PANACH ..... Pan-African Chemical Industries (MAR)
PANACO ..... Parti Nationaliste Congolais (MAR)
PANACOL ... Panamericana de Comercio Ltda. [*Bogota*] (COL)
PANAF .... Pan-Africaine d'Affichage (MAR)
PAN-AF .... Pan-African News Agency (MAR)
PANAF .... Parti National Africain (MAR)
PANAFTEL ... Pan-African Telecommunications Network (AF)
PANAI .... Patronato Nacional de Ancianos e Invalidos [*Venezuelan*]
PANAJECO ... Parti National de la Jeunesse Congolaise (MAR)
PANALI .... Parti National de la Liberte (MAR)
PANALU ...... Parti National Lumumba (MAR)
PANANKO ... Parti Nationaliste Nkonga (MAR)
PANARE ...... Parti National de Reconstruction (MAR)
PANAS .... Parti Negara Sarawak [*Sarawak State Party*] (ML)
PANATRA ... Parti National du Travail (MAR)
PANBE .... Pansements du Benin (MAR)
Pancar-Is .... Turkiye Seker ve Seker Pancari Sanayii Iscileri [*Turkish Sugar and Sugar Beet Industry Workers' Union*] [*Ankara*] (TU)
PANDECA ... Partido Nacional para Democracia, Desarrollo, y Educacion Civica (MAR)
PANG .... Panglima [*Commander*] (IN)
PANIDA .... Societe de Panification de Doala (MAR)
PANJU .... Pan-African Union of Journalists (MAR)
Pankobirlik ... Pancar Kooperatifler Birligi [*Turkish Beet Producers' Union*] (TU)
PANP .... Prazska Akumulatorka [*Prague Battery Plant*] (CZ)
Pans .... Pansiyon [*Pension, Boarding House*] (TU)
PANS .... Protivavionske Nisanske Sprave [*Antiaircraft Aiming Mechanism*] (YU)
panstw .... Panstwowy [*National, State*] (POL)
PANTEKS ... Pancevacka Tekstilna Industrija [*Pancevo Textile Industry*] (YU)
PANTEX ...... Textiles Panamericanos SA [*Medellin*] (COL)
PANTUR ...... Panamericana de Viajes y Turismo [*Bogota*] (COL)
PAO .... Panathinaikos Athlitikos Omilos [*Pan-Athenian Athletic Club*] (GC)
PAO .... Panellinios Apelevtherotiki Organosis [*Panhellenic Liberation Organization*] (GC)
PAO .... Panellinios Athlitiki Organosis [*Panhellenic Athletic Organization*] (GC)
PAO .... Preisanordnung [*Price Order*] (EG)
PAO .... Protiatomova Ochrana [*Antinuclear Defense*] (CZ)
PAO .... Protivavionska Odbrana [*Antiaircraft Defense*] (YU)
PAO .... Societe de Plantations de l'Afrique Occidentale (MAR)
PAODYE ...... Pankyprios Anexartitos Omospondia Dimotikon Ypallilon kai Ergaton [*Pan-Cyprian Independent Federation of Civil Service Employees and Workers*] (GC)
PAOK .... Panthessalonikeios Athlitikos Omilos Konstandinoupoleos [*Pan-Salonica Athletic Club of Istanbul*] (GC)
PAOR .... Permanente Accion Organizada Revolucionaria [*Permanent Organized Revolutionary Action*] [*Peruvian*] (LA)
pa otb .... Antiaircraft Defense (BU)
PAOWU .... Port Authority and Other Workers Union [*Mauritian*] (AF)
PAP .... Agentia Polona de Presa [*Polish Press Agency*] (RO)
PAP .... Atypical Primary Pneumonia (RU)
PAP .... Gun Artillery Regiment (RU)
pap .... Paperiteollisuus [*Paper Industry*] [*Finnish*]
PAP .... Paris-Afrique Presse [*Paris-Africa Press Agency*] [*French*] (AF)
PAP .... Parole au Peuple [*Voice to the People*] [*Belgian*] (WER)
PAP .... Parti d'Action Paysanne (MAR)
PAP .... Partido Aprista Peruano [*Aprista Party of Peru*] (LA)
PAP .... People's Action Party [*Singaporean*] (PPW)
PAP .... People's Action Party [*Ghanaian*] (AF)
PAP .... Plano de Accao Politico [*Political Action Plan*] [*Portuguese*] (WER)
PAP .... Politiki Aneksartitos Parataksis [*Independent Political Front*] [*Greek*] (PPE)
PAP .... Polska Agencja Prasowa [*Polish Press Agency*] (POL)
PAP .... Poultry and Animal Products Ltd. (MAR)
PAP .... Powiatowe Archiwum Panstwowe [*County State Archives*] (POL)
PAP .... Pulk Artylerii Polowej [*Polish*]
PAPAS .... Partai Pesaka Anak Sarawak [*Sarawak Sons Pesaka Party*] (ML)
PAPC .... Public Agricultural Production Corporation [*Sudanese*] (MAR)
PAPEC .... Societe Africaine de Production d'Articles en Papier et d'Emballages en Carton (MAR)
PAPERI .... Parti Persaudaraan Islam [*Islamic Brotherhood Party*] (ML)
Papie .... Papeterie [*Paper Manufactory*] [*Military map abbreviation*] [*World War I*] [*French*] (MTD)
PAPIR .... Programme d'Action Prioritaire d'Initiative Regionale (MAR)
PAPIRPROMET ... Preduzece za Promet Papirom [*Paper Trade Establishment*] (YU)
PAPMAD ..... Papeteries de Madagascar (MAR)
Papo .... Popular Action Party [*Panamanian*] (PD)
PAPOMO ..... Partido Popular de Mocambique [*Mozambique Popular Party*] (AF)
PAPP .... Partido de Accion Patriotica Progresista [*Progressive Patriotic Action Party*] [*Ecuadorean*] (LA1)
PAPS .... Army Field Food Depot (RU)
PAPS .... Partido Alianza Popular Socialista [*Socialist Popular Alliance Party*] [*Costa Rican*] (LA)
PAPU .... Pan-African Postal Union (MAR)
PAR .... Airfield Homing Radio Station (RU)
Par .... Ferry [*Topography*] (RU)
par .... Field Artillery (BU)
PAR .... Panstwowa Administracja Rolna [*State Administration of Agriculture*] (POL)
PAR .... Panzerabwehrreserve [*Antitank Reserve*] (EG)
PAR .... Paracel Islands [*Three-letter standard code*] (CNC)
par .... Paragraf [*Paragraph*] [*Polish*]
par .... Paragraf [*Paragraph, Section*] (CZ)
par .... Paragrafos [*Paragraph*] (GC)
par .... Parrafo [*Paragraph*] [*Spanish*]
PAR .... Partido Accion Renovadora [*Renovation Action Party*] [*Salvadoran*] (LA)
PAR .... Partido Accion Revolucionaria [*Revolutionary Action Party*] [*Dominican Republic*] (LA1)
PAR .... Partido Accion Revolucionaria [*Revolutionary Action Party*] [*Nicaraguan*] (LA)
PAR .... Partido Aragonese Regional [*Aragonese Regional Party*] [*Spanish*] (PPW)
PAR .... Partito Anti-Reformista [*Anti-Reform Party*] [*Maltese*] (PPE)
par .... Perfume Factory [*Topography*] (RU)
PAR .... Polska Agencja Reklamy [*Polish Advertising Agency*] (POL)
PAR .... Powszechna Agencja Reklamy [*General Advertising Agency*] [*Polish*]
PAR .... Protivavionski Reflektori [*Antiaircraft Searchlights*] (YU)
PAR .... Pyridylazoresorcinol (RU)
PAR .... Regimental Artillery Repair Shop (BU)
Par .... Steamship Line (RU)
PAR .... Track Emergency Relay (RU)
para .... Paragrafos [*Paragraph*] (GC)
PARA .... Parti d'Action Revolutionnaire Angolaise (MAR)
PARAC .... Parlementair Automatiserings Centrum
PARAKOAD ... Para Komando Angkatan Darat [*Army Paracommando Troops*] (IN)
PARAKU ..... Pasukan Rakjat Kalimantan Utara [*North Kalimantan People's Forces*] (ML)
paral .... Parallel (BU)
paral .... Parallel (RU)
parall .... Parallel (RU)
PARAM .... Mobile Army Artillery Repair Shop (RU)
PARAMOSA ... Pastas Ramos y Semolas SA [*Cali*] (COL)
parash v ...... Parachute Tower [*Topography*] (RU)
parashyut ... Paratroop Field [*Topography*] (RU)
PARB .... Mobile Aircraft Repair Base (RU)
parb .... Mobile Automotive Repairs Battalion (BU)
PARB .... Mobile Motor Vehicle Repair Base (BU)
PARB .... Mobile Motor Vehicle Repair Base (RU)
PARD .... People Against Racial Discrimination (MAR)
PARDA .... Parca Dagitim Ticaret ve Sanayi AS [*Parts Distribution, Trade, and Industry Corporation*] (TU)
PARECO ..... Parti de Regroupement Congolais (MAR)
PARGA .... Paris-Gabon (MAR)
PARIBAS ..... Compagnie Financiere de Paris et des Pays-Bas (MAR)
PARK- .... Portable Radioactive Logging Equipment (RU)
PARKE .... Parataxis Kendrou [*Array of the Center*] (GC1)
PARKINDO ... Partai Keristen Indonesia [*Indonesian Christian Party*] (IN)
par krakhm ... Steam-Driven Starch Factory [*Topography*] (RU)
parl .... Parlamentti [*Parliamentary*] [*Finnish*]
parl .... Parliamentary Expression (BU)
parl .... Parliamentary Expression (RU)
par lesp .... Steam-Driven Sawmill [*Topography*] (RU)
PARM .... Field Aircraft Repair Shop (RU)
PARM .... Mobile Motor Vehicle Repair Shop (RU)
PARM .... Partido Autentico de la Revolucion Mexicana [*Authentic Party of the Mexican Revolution*] (PPW)
PARM .... Regimental Aircraft Repair Shop (RU)
PARM .... Regimental Artillery Repair Shop (RU)
PARM .... Regimental Motor Vehicle Repair Shop (RU)
PARMD .... Division Mobile Motor Vehicle Repair Shop (RU)
PARMEHUTU ... Parti du Mouvement de l'Emancipation Hutu [*Hutu Emancipation Movement Party*] [*Rwandan*] (AF)
Par mel'n .... Steam-Driven Mill [*Topography*] (RU)
PARMP .... Regimental Mobile Motor Vehicle Repair Shop (RU)
Par muk ...... Steam-Driven Flour Mill [*Topography*] (RU)
PARMUSI .... Partai Muslimin Indonesia [*Indonesian Moslem Party*] (IN)
PARN .... Partido de Accion y Reconstruccion Nacional [*National Action and Reconstruction Party*] [*Guatemalan*] (LA)
Parovozo-remont ... Locomotive Repair Shop [*Topography*] (RU)
PARR .... Regimental Artillery Repair Shop (BU)
parsag .... Parancsnoksag [*Headquarters*] [*Military*] (HU)

PARSAN...... Makina Parcalari Sanayii AS [*Machinery Spare Parts Industry Corp.*] [*Ankara*] (TU)
parsek......... Parallax-Second, Parsec (RU)
PARSOCILIBRE ... Parti Socialiste Libre du Burundi (MAR)
P art............ Parc d'Artillerie [*Artillery Park*] [*French*] (MTD)
part............ Partizan [*Partisan*] (HU)
part............ Party (BU)
part............ Party, Party Member (RU)
partalk........ Partalkalmazott [*Party Employee*] (HU)
partep......... Partepites [*Party Development*] (HU)
Partgruporg ... Party Group Organizer (RU)
PARTINDO ... Partai Indonesia [*Indonesian Party*] (IN)
partis.......... Partisiippi [*Participle*] [*Finnish*]
partit........... Partitiivi [*Finnish*]
Partizdat..... Communist Party Publishing House (BU)
Partizdat..... Party Publishing House (RU)
Partkom...... Party Committee (BU)
part k-t...... Party Committee (BU)
Partorg........ Party Organizer (BU)
Partorga...... Party Organization (BU)
parts........... Partial (RU)
partsz.......... Partszervezet [*Party Organization*] (HU)
partszerv .... Partszervezet [*Party Organization*] (HU)
partszolg..... Partszolgalat [*or Partszolgalatos*] [*Communist Party Activity or Participant in the Party Activity*] (HU)
PartT........... Partizanska Tiskarna [*Partisan Printers*] (YU)
PARU.......... Semiautomatic Gain Control (RU)
Paryadro..... Party Nucleus (BU)
PARZ.......... Mobile Motor Vehicle Repair Plant (RU)
PARZ.......... Mobile Motor Vehicle Repair Plant (BU)
PAS............ Acid Para-Aminosalicilic [*Para-Aminosalicylic Acid*] (RO)
PAS............ Advanced Ammunition Depot (RU)
PAS............ Advanced Army Depot (RU)
Pas............ Apiary [*Topography*] (RU)
PAS............ Army Field Depot (RU)
PAS............ Artillery Firing Regulations (RU)
PAS............ Field Ammunition Depot (RU)
PAS............ Panellinios Andialkooliki Stavroforia [*Panhellenic Anti-Alcohol Crusade*] (GC)
PAS............ Parti Islanse Malaysia [*Islamic Party of Malaysia*] (PPW)
PAS............ Partido de Accion Socialista [*Socialist Action Party*] [*Costa Rican*] (PPW)
PAS............ Partito de Azione de Sardegna [*Sardinian Action Party*] [*Italian*] (PPW)
pas............ Pasture [*Topography*] (RU)
PAS............ Persatuan Agama Se-Melayu [*Pan-Malayan Religious Union*] (ML)
PAS............ Plano de Amparo Social [*Social Assistance Program*] [*Brazilian*] (LA)
PAS............ Regimental Ammunition Depot (RU)
PAS............ Regimental Artillery Depot (BU)
PAS............ Soil and Agricultural Station (RU)
PASA.......... Poligono do Acustica Submarina dos Acores [*Azores Submarine Acoustic Range*] [*Portuguese*] (WER)
PASC.......... Palestine Armed Struggle Command (PD)
PASC.......... Pan-African Student Conference (AF)
PASC.......... Pan American Standards Commission [*See also COPANT*] (EA)
PASC.......... Partido Socialista Autonomista de Canarias [*Autonomous Socialist Party of the Canary Islands*] [*Spanish*] (WER)
PASCAL...... Programme Applique a la Selection et a la Compilation Automatique de la Litterature [*French*]
PASCT........ Pan American Society for Chemotherapy of Tuberculosis [*See also SAQT*] (EA)
PASD.......... Public Administration Studies Division (MAR)
PASEGES ... Panellinios Anotati Synomospondia Enoseon Georgikon Synetairismon [*Panhellenic Supreme Confederation of Unions of Agricultural Cooperatives*] (GC)
PASEP........ Plano de Assistencia ao Servidor Publico [*Civil Servants Welfare Fund*] [*Brazilian*] (LA)
PASEV........ Panellinios Syndesmos Ekdoton Vivliou [*Panhellenic Association of Book Publishers*] (GC1)
PASINKO.... Pasukan Induk Komando [*Main Marine Force*] (IN)
PASK.......... Para-Aminosalicylic Acid (RU)
PASKE........ Panellinia Agonistiki Syndikalistiki Kinisi Ergazomenon [*Panhellenic Militant Workers Trade Union Movement*] (GC)
PASKOARMA ... Pasukan Komando Armada [*Fleet Marine Force*] (IN)
PASM.......... Pan-African Student Movement (AF)
PASO.......... Pan American Sports Organization [*See also ODEPA*] (EA)
PASO.......... Partido Accion Socialista [*Socialist Action Party*] [*Costa Rican*] (LA)
PASO.......... Partido Socialista [*Socialist Party*] [*Honduran*] (LA1)
PASOA........ Pan-African Students Organization in the Americas (AF)
PASOCO..... Parti Socialiste des Comores [*Comoros Socialist Party*] (AF)
PASOK........ Panellinion Sosialistikon Kinema [*Pan-Hellenic Socialist Movement*] [*Greek*] (PPE)
PASP.......... Panellinia Agonistiki Spoudastiki Parataxi [*Panhellenic Militant Student Faction*] (GC)
PASPE........ Pandeios Anotati Skholi Politikon Epistimon [*Pandeios Supreme School of Political Sciences*] [*Greek*] (GC)
PASPE........ Ptykhioukhoi tis Anotatis Skholis Politikon Epistimon [*Graduates of the Supreme School of Political Sciences*] [*Greek*] (GC)
PASS.......... Army Field Medical Depot (RU)
pass.......... Passage [*Lane*] [*French*] (CED)
pass.......... Passenger (Train) (RU)
pass.......... Passiivi(n) [*Passive Voice*] [*Finnish*]
pass.......... Passim [*Everywhere*] [*Latin*] (GPO)
PASSAT...... Programm zur Automatischen Selektion von Stichwoertern aus Teksten [*German*]
PASS-B....... Army Ammunition Dump (BU)
pass -tov..... Passenger and Freight (Train) (RU)
PAST.......... Ambulance Station (RU)
past............ Pastori [*Finnish*]
PASTAGALLO ... Fabrica de Pastas el Gallo Ltda. [*Bogota*] (COL)
PASU.......... Pan-African Socialist Union [*Rhodesian*] (AF)
PASUS........ Pasukan Chusus [*Special Forces*] (IN)
PASV.......... Partiia Arabskovo Sotsialisticheskovo Vozrozhdeniia (MAR)
PASYDY...... Pankyprios Syndekhnia Dimosion Ypallilon [*Pan-Cyprian Union of Civil Servants*] (GC)
PAT............ Automation and Telemechanics Enterprise (BU)
pat............ Patent (RU)
pat............ Pathologic, Pathological, Pathology (RU)
pat............ Patriarca [*Spanish*]
PAT............ Polska Agencja Telegraficzna [*Polish Telegraph Agency*] (POL)
PAT............ Prazska Akciova Tiskarna [*Prague Printing Joint-Stock Company*] (CZ)
PATA.......... P A Tiele Akademie [*'s-Gravenhage*]
PATA.......... Pacific Area Travel Association (CL)
PatA.......... Patentamt [*German*]
pat -anat..... Pathologicoanatomical (RU)
PAT-ELS..... Steam-Turbine Electric Power Plant (RU)
path............ Pathologisch [*German*]
PATI............ Perwira Tinggi [*General Officer*] (IN)
PATKh........ Passenger Automobile Transportation Establishment (RU)
patl............ Pataljoona [*Finnish*]
pato............ Patologia [*Pathology*] [*Finnish*]
patol........... Pathology, Pathologist (BU)
patologich ... Pathologic, Pathological (RU)
PATU.......... Panafrican Telecommunications Union (MAR)
PATYOLAT ... Vegytisztito Vallalat [*Dry Cleaning Enterprise*] (HU)
PAtZ.......... Protivatomska Zastita [*Antiatomic Defense*] (YU)
PAU............ Complete Author Index (RU)
PAU-.......... Field Automatic Welding Unit (RU)
PAU............ Mobile Nitrogen Unit (RU)
PAU............ Pangkalan Angkatan Udara [*Air Force Base*] (IN)
PAU............ Personnel Autonome de l'Universite [*Autonomous University Staff Personnel*] [*Malagasy*] (AF)
PAU............ Polska Akademia Umiejetnosci [*Polish Academy of Sciences and Letters*] (POL)
Pau............ Poteau [*Fingerpost, Guidepost*] [*Military map abbreviation*] [*World War I*] [*French*] (MTD)
PAUJ.......... Pan-African Union of Journalists (MAR)
PAUP.......... Automatic Program Setup Device (RU)
PAV............ Army Field Veterinary Depot (RU)
pav............ Pavilion (RU)
PAV............ Pomoc Americke Vlade [*US Government Economic Aid*] [*Tripartite Aid Program*] (YU)
PAV............ Programme d'Assistance Volontaire [*Voluntary Assistance Program*] [*Telecommunications*] [*Laotian*] (CL)
PAV............ Surface-Active Agents (BU)
PAV............ Surface-Active Substance (RU)
PAV............ Variable Attenuation Equalizer (RU)
PAVCO........ Pisos de Asfalto y Vinilo SA [*Bogota*] (COL)
PAVETs....... Pumping-Storage Hydroelectric Plant (BU)
PAVINAL..... Pavimentadora Nacional [*Medellin*] (COL)
PAVI............ Pomoc Americke Vlade u Hrani [*US Government Aid in Food*] (YU)
PAVMP........ Fully Automatic High-Quality Machine Translation (RU)
PAVN.......... Vietnam People's Army [*Use VPA*] [*North Vietnamese*] (CL)
PAVS.......... Army Field Veterinary Depot (RU)
PAW............ Polska Agencja Wydawnicza [*Polish Publishing Agency*] (POL)
PAWC.......... Pan-African Women's Conference (AF)
PAWC.......... Pan-African Workers Congress (AF)
PAX............ Instytut Wydawniczy "Pax" [*"Pax" Publishing Institute*] (POL)
PAYDS........ Panellinios Agon Yperaspiseos tis Dimokratias kai tou Syndagmatos [*Panhellenic Struggle for the Defense of Democracy and the Constitution*] (GC)
PAYM.......... Pan-African Youth Movement (AF)
PAYO.......... Pan-African Youth Organization (AF)
PAYP.......... Prokekhorimeni Apothiki Ylikou Polemou [*Advanced Ordnance Depot*] [*Greek*] (GC)
PAZ............ Atomic Defense, Antiatomic Defense (RU)
PAZ............ Automobile Made by the Pavlovo Bus Plant Imeni A. A. Zhdanov (RU)
paz............ Barrage Balloons Regiment (RU)
paz............ Barrage Balloons Regiment (BU)
PAZ............ Nuclear Defense (BU)
PAZ............ Pavlovo Bus Plant Imeni A. A. Zhdanov (RU)
PAZ............ Plan d'Amenagement des Zones [*French*]
PAZ............ Podol'sk Battery Plant (RU)

PAZ .... Pohybliva Armadni Zakladna [*Mobile Army Base*] (CZ)
PAZ .... Protivavionska Zastita [*Antiaircraft Defense*] (YU)
PAZhK .... Pan-American Railway Congress Association [*PARCA*] (RU)
PB .... Benzoyl Peroxide (RU)
PB .... Dive Bomber (RU)
PB .... Etablissements Pierre Balet (MAR)
PB .... Floating Base, Depot Ship, Tender (RU)
pb .... Infantry Battalion (BU)
pb .... Infantry Battalion (RU)
PB .... Leading Battalion (BU)
pb .... Machine-Gun Battalion (RU)
PB .... Panzerbataillon [*Tank Battalion*] (EG)
P/b .... Parabrod [*Steamer*] (YU)
pb .... Partbizottsag [*Party Committee*] (HU)
pb .... Party Membership Card (RU)
PB .... Pejabat Besar [*Head Office*] (ML)
PB .... Penzugyi Bizottsag [*Finance Committee*] (HU)
PB .... Pesadiski Bataljon [*Infantry Battalion*] (YU)
pb .... Plus Bas [*French*]
PB .... Polis Besar [*Police District*] (ML)
PB .... Politburo (BU)
PB .... Politburo (RU)
PB .... Politikai Bizottsag [*Political Committee*] (HU)
PB .... Poljska Bolnica [*Field Hospital*]
pb .... Pontoon Battalion (RU)
PB .... Privatbetrieb [*Private Enterprise*] (EG)
PB .... Propan-Butan [*Propane-Butane*] (HU)
PB .... Proportional Unit [*Computers*] (RU)
PB .... Proprietes Baties (MAR)
PB .... Prukaz Brance [*Conscription Certificate*] (CZ)
PB .... Prvni Brnenska Strojirna [*First Machine Factories in Brno*] (CZ)
pb .... Regimental Battery (RU)
PB .... Safety Regulations (RU)
Pb .... St. Petersburg (RU)
PB .... Standing Bureau (BU)
pb .... Starboard (RU)
PBA .... Floating Battery [*Artillery*] (RU)
PBA .... Mobile Drill Unit (RU)
PBA .... Partido Barrientista Autentico [*Bolivian*] (PPW)
PBA .... Polska Bibliografia Analityczna [*Polish Analytical Bibliography*] (POL)
pbatr .... Maintenance Battery (BU)
PBB .... Forward Hospital Base (BU)
PBB .... Perserikatan Bangsa-Bangsa [*United Nations*] (IN)
PBC .... Poljski Bolnicki Centar [*Field Hospital Center*] (YU)
PBC .... Provinciale Bibliotheek Centrale
PBD .... Pomorsko-Brodarsko Drustvo [*Maritime Shipping Society*] (YU)
PBDCT .... Plano Basico de Desenvolvimento Cientifico e Tecnologico [*Basic Plan for Scientific and Technological Development*] [*Brazilian*] (LA1)
PBE .... Panstwowe Budownictwo Elektryczne [*State Power Engineering*] (POL)
PBE .... Pasar Biasa Eropa [*European Common Market*] (IN)
PBE .... Regulation for the Safety and Operation of Hoisting Machinery (BU)
PBF .... Pravoslavni Bogoslovski Fakultet [*Orthodox Theological Faculty*] (YU)
PBFL .... Planning for Better Family Living [*FAO*] (MAR)
PBG .... Porphobilinogen (RU)
PBI .... Producto Bruto Interno [*Gross Domestic Product*] [*Use GDP*] (LA)
PBICSGH ..... Permanent Bureau of International Congresses for the Sciences of Genealogy and Heraldry (EA)
PB institut ... Eastern Orthodox Theological Institute (BU)
PBK .... Mobile Pressure Chamber (RU)
PBK- .... Pneumatic-Tired Tower Crane (RU)
PBK .... Przedsiebiorstwo Budowy Kopaln [*Mine Construction Enterprise*] (POL)
p bl .... Field Hospital (BU)
pble .... Payable [*Payable*] [*Business and trade*] [*French*]
pble .... Posible [*Possible*] [*Business and trade*] [*Spanish*]
PBLK .... Przedsiebiorstwo Budowy Linii Kablowych [*Cable Line Construction Enterprise*] (POL)
PBM .... Antitransmit-Receive Tube (RU)
PBM .... Przedsiebiorstwo Budownictwa Miejskiego [*Town Building Enterprise*] [*Polish*]
PBM .... Ranging Combat Vehicle (RU)
PBMF .... Bulgarian Maritime Navigation Administration (BU)
PBMUM .... Persatuan Bahasa Melayu Universiti Malaysia [*Malayan Language Association of the University of Malaysia*] (ML)
PBN .... Non-Self-Propelled Floating Base (RU)
PBn .... Poudres Brunes [*Symbol*] [*Military*] [*French*] (MTD)
PBN .... Przeglad Bibliograficzny "Nafty" [*Bibliographical Review of the Journal "Nafta" (Petroleum)*] (POL)
PBNII .... Perm' Biological Scientific Research Institute (RU)
PBNP .... Observation Post Tank (RU)
PBn S .... Poudre Brune de Siege [*Military*] [*French*] (MTD)
PBO .... Field Bath Detachment (RU)
PBO .... Plan and Budget Organization [*Iranian*] (ME)
PBO .... Protibiologicka Ochrana [*Antibiological Defense*] (CZ)
PBO .... Right Flank Protection (RU)
PBO .... Single-Cotton Covered Wire (RU)
PBP .... Ammunition Supply Point (RU)
PBP .... Panstwowe Budownictwo Przemyslowe [*State Industrial Construction Enterprise*] (POL)
PBP .... Pesadiska Borbena Pravila [*Infantry Combat Rules*] (YU)
PBP .... Polskie Biuro Podrozy "Orbis" [*"Orbis" Polish Travel Bureau*]
PBP .... Powiatowe Biblioteki Pedagogiczne [*County School Libraries*] (POL)
PBP .... Przedsiebiorstwo Budownictwa Przemyslowego [*Industrial Construction Enterprise*] (POL)
PBP Orbis ... Polskie Biuro Podrozy "Orbis" [*"Orbis" Polish Travel Bureau*] (POL)
PBR .... Combat Deployment Point [*Aviation*] (RU)
pbr .... Infantry Brigade (RU)
PBR .... Panstwowy Bank Rolny [*State Agricultural Bank*] (POL)
PBR .... Programm zur Bekaempfung des Rassismus (MAR)
PBR .... Prostor Bojoveho Rozmisteni [*Combat Deployment Sector*] (CZ)
pbrgr .... Infantry Brigade Group (RU)
pbro .... Presbitero [*Spanish*]
PBRP .... Bulgarian River Navigation Administration (BU)
PBrV .... Pomoc Britanske Vlade [*Economic Aid of British Government*] [*Tripartite Aid Program*] (YU)
PBS .... Field Ballistic Station (BU)
PBS .... Field Ballistic Station [*Artillery*] (RU)
PBS .... Persatuan Bawean Singapura [*Bawean Association of Singapore*] (ML)
PBS .... Popularna Biblioteka Sportowa [*Popular Sports Series*] (POL)
PBS .... Poradkova a Bezpecnostni Sluzba [*Discipline and Security Service*] [*Civil defense*] (CZ)
PBS .... Self-Propelled Floating Base (RU)
PBSE .... Przedsiebiorstwo Budowy Sieci Elektrycznych [*Electrical Network Construction Enterprise*] (POL)
PBTO .... Polsko-Brytyjskie Towarzystwo Okretowe
PBU .... High-Powered Magnifying Instrument (RU)
PBU .... Teacher's Pedagogical Library (RU)
PBV .... Pomoc Belgiske Vlade [*Economic Aid of Belgian Government*] (YU)
PBVI .... Pomoc Belgijske Vlade u Hrani [*Aid of Belgian Government in Food*] (YU)
PBW .... Pedagogiczna Biblioteka Wojewodzka [*Voivodship Pedagogical Library*] (POL)
PBZ .... Antibacteriological Defense (BU)
PBZ .... Antibacteriological Protection, Bacteriological Protection (RU)
PBZ .... Field Concrete Plant (RU)
PBZ .... Pojizerske Bavlnarske Zavody, Narodni Podnik [*Jizera River Area Cotton Mills, National Enterprise*] (CZ)
PBZPC .... Przedsiebiorstwo Budowy Zakladow Przemyslu Ciezkiego [*Enterprise for the Construction of Heavy Industry Establishments*] (POL)
PC .... Communist Party [*Peruvian*] (PD)
pc .... Pancelos [*Armored*] (HU)
PC .... Paramount Chief (MAR)
PC .... Parti Communiste [*Communist Party*] [*French*]
PC .... Parti Communiste [*Communist Party*] [*Luxembourg*] (PPW)
PC .... Parti de Conservation (MAR)
PC .... Partido Carlista [*Carlist Party*] [*Spanish*] (WER)
PC .... Partido Colorado [*Colorado Party*] [*Uruguayan*] (PPW)
PC .... Partido Comunista [*Communist Party*] (LA)
PC .... Partido Conservador [*Conservative Party*] [*Ecuadorean*] (PPW)
PC .... Partido Conservador [*Conservative Party*] [*Colombian*] (LA)
pc .... Pas Cote [*French*]
PC .... Patrolni Camac [*Patrol Boat*] (YU)
pc .... Paye au Comptant [*Paid in Cash*] [*Business and trade*] [*French*]
PC .... Peace Corps (MAR)
PC .... People's Committee (MAR)
PC .... People's Conference [*Indian*] (PPW)
PC .... Pesadiska Ceta [*Infantry Company*] (YU)
PC .... Points de Contact [*Military*] [*French*] (MTD)
PC .... Policia de Control [*Bogota*] (COL)
PC .... Pomocna Ceta [*Auxiliary Company*] (YU)
PC .... Portion Centrale [*French*] (MTD)
PC .... Poste de Commandement [*Command Post*] [*Use CP*] [*French*] (WER)
PC .... Poudre Composition [*Military*] [*French*] (MTD)
pc .... Pour Cent [*French*]
p/c .... Pour Compte [*French*]
pc .... Praca [*Square*] [*Portuguese*] (CED)
PC .... Prazske Cihelny [*Prague Brick Works*] (CZ)
PC .... Preparatory Committee (MAR)
pc .... Pro Centum [*Percent*] [*Latin*]
pc .... Procento [*Percent*] (CZ)
PC .... Producciones Colombia - Inravision [*Bogota*] (COL)
PC .... Productora de Controles Ltda. [*Medellin*] (COL)
PC .... Provincial Commissioner [*Kenyan*] (AF)
PC .... Trust Territory of the Pacific Islands [*Two-letter standard code*] (CNC)
PCA .... Parc de Corps d'Armee [*Military*] [*French*] (MTD)
PCA .... Parti Communiste Algerien [*Algerian Communist Party*] (AF)

PCA .... Partido Comunista de Angola [*Communist Party of Angola*] (AF)
PCA .... Partido Comunista Angolano (MAR)
PCA .... Partido Comunista de Argentina [*Communist Party of Argentina*] (PD)
p-ca .... Pecatnica [*Printing House*] (YU)
PCA .... Poste de Controle Administratif [*Administrative Control Post*] [*Congolese*] (AF)
PCA-CNRR ... Partido Comunista de Argentina - Comite Nacional para la Reivindicacion Revolucionaria [*Communist Party of Argentina - National Committee for Revolutionary Demands*] (LA)
PCAD .... Post de Commandement d'Artillerie Divisionnaire [*Military*] [*French*] (MTD)
PCB .... Parti Communiste de Belgique [*Communist Party of Belgium*] (PPE)
PCB .... Partido Comunista de Bolivia [*Communist Party of Bolivia*] (PPW)
PCB .... Partido Comunista do Brasil [*Brazilian Communist Party*] (PPW)
PCB .... People's Cooperative Bank [*Jamaican*] (LA1)
PCB .... Physique, Chimie, Biologie [*Physics, Chemistry, and Biology (Certificate)*] [*French*] (WER)
PCB-ML ...... Partido Comunista Marxista-Leninista de Bolivia [*Marxist-Leninist Communist Party of Bolivia*] (PPW)
PCBR .... Partido Comunista Brasileiro Revolucionario [*Brazilian Revolutionary Communist Party*] (LA)
PCC .... Partido Carlista de Cataluna [*Carlist Party of Catalonia*] [*Spanish*] (WER)
PCC .... Partido Comunista Canario [*Communist Party of the Canary Islands*] [*Spanish*] (WER)
PCC .... Partido Comunista Chileno [*Communist Party of Chile*] (PD)
PCC .... Partido Comunista de Colombia [*Communist Party of Colombia*] (LA)
PCC .... Partido Comunista Cubano [*Communist Party of Cuba*] (PPW)
PCC .... Partido Conservador Colombiano [*Conservative Party of Colombia*] (PPW)
PCC .... Partie Communiste Chinois (MAR)
PCC .... People's Caretaker Council [*Rhodesian*] (AF)
PCC .... Pour Copie Conforme [*French*]
PCC .... Price Control Center [*Iranian*] (ME)
PCC .... Public Complaints Commission (MAR)
PCCA .... Poste de Commandement de Corps d'Armee [*Military*] [*French*] (MTD)
PCCh .... Partido Comunista de Chile [*Chilean Communist Party*] (LA)
PCC-ML ...... Partido Comunista Colombiano - Marxista-Leninista [*Colombian Communist Party - Marxist-Leninist*] (LA)
PCCN .... Parti Congolais de Conscience Nationale (MAR)
PCCNRR ..... Partido Comunista - Comite Nacional de Recuperacion Revolucionaria [*Communist Party - National Committee for Revolutionary Recovery*] [*Argentine*] (LA)
PCCS .... Parti Conservateur Chretien-Social [*Conservative Christian-Social Party*] [*Swiss*] (PPE)
PCD .... Democratic Conservative Party [*Nicaraguan*] (PD)
PCD .... Panstwowa Centrala Drzewna [*State Lumber Center*] (POL)
PCD .... Partido Comunista Dominicano [*Dominican Communist Party*] [*Dominican Republic*] (PPW)
PCD .... Partido Conservador Democrata [*Democratic Conservative Party*] [*Nicaraguan*] (LA1)
PCD .... Plataforma de Convergencia Democratica [*Platform of Democratic Convergence*] [*Spanish*] (WER)
PCD .... Programme Communal de Developpement [*Communal Development Program*] [*Algerian*] (AF)
PCD .... Pueblo, Cambio, y Democracia [*People, Change, and Democracy*] [*Ecuadorean*] (LA1)
PCDA .... Partido Cristao Democratico de Angola [*Christian Democratic Party of Angola*] (AF)
PCDI .... Poste de Commandement de Division d'Infanterie [*Military*] [*French*] (MTD)
PCd'I (M-L) ... Partito Comunista d'Italia (Marxista-Leninista) [*Communist Party of Italy (Marxist-Leninist)*] (WER)
PCDO .... Provincial Community Development Officer (MAR)
PCdoB .... Partido Comunista do Brasil [*Communist Party of Brazil*] (PPW)
PCE .... Parti Communiste Egyptien (MAR)
PCE .... Partido Comunista Ecuatoriano [*Communist Party of Ecuador*] (PPW)
PCE .... Partido Comunista de Espana [*Communist Party of Spain*] (PPE)
PCEA .... Parti Congolais de l'Entente Africaine (MAR)
PCEA .... Presbyterian Church of East Africa (MAR)
Pceau .... Ponceau [*Culvert*] [*Military map abbreviation*] [*World War I*] [*French*] (MTD)
PCEHS .... Publications du Comite des Etudes Historiques et Scientifiques de l'AOF (MAR)
PCEI .... Partido Comunista de Espana (Internacional) [*Spanish Communist Party (International)*] (WER)
PCEM .... Premier Cycle d'Etudes Medicales [*French*]
PCE-ML ...... Partido Comunista del Ecuador-Marxista Leninista [*Communist Party of Ecuador-Marxist Leninist Faction*] [*Ecuadorean*] (LA1)
PCE/ML ...... Partido Comunista de Espana Marxista-Leninista [*Marxist-Leninist Spanish Communist Party*] (WER)
PCE-R .... Reconstituted Spanish Communist Party (PD)
PCES .... Partido Comunista de El Salvador [*Communist Party of El Salvador*] (LA)
PCF .... Parti Communiste Francais [*French Communist Party*] (PPW)
PCG .... Parti Communiste de Guadeloupe [*Communist Party of Guadeloupe*] (PPW)
PCG .... Partido Carlista de Galicia [*Carlist Party of Galicia*] [*Spanish*] (WER)
pch .... Ammunition Bearer [*or Carrier*] (BU)
pch .... Because (RU)
PCh .... Digital Plethysmograph with Ink Registration (RU)
p ch .... Furnace/Hour (BU)
PCh .... Intermediate Frequency (RU)
PCH .... Panstwowa Centrala Handlowa [*State Trade Center*] (POL)
PCH .... Partido Comunista de Honduras [*Communist Party of Honduras*] (PD)
p/ch .... Political Unit [*Military term*] (RU)
PCh .... Program Clock (RU)
PCh .... Pseudorandom Number (RU)
PChM .... Frequency Manipulation Attachment [*Computers*] (RU)
PChM .... Program Clock Mechanism (RU)
PChO .... Protichemicka Ochrana [*Antichemical Defense*] (CZ)
pchor .... Podchorazy [*Ensign*] [*Polish*]
PChP .... Absorption Limiting Frequency (RU)
PChP .... Progressistskaia Chadskaia Partiia (MAR)
p Chr n .... Post Christum Natum [*After the Birth of Christ*] [*Latin*]
PchU .... Printer [*Computers*] (RU)
PChZ .... Povazske Chemicke Zavody [*Chemical Plants of the Vah River*] (CZ)
PChZ .... Prazske Chemicke Zavody [*Prague Chemical Works*] (CZ)
PCI .... Parti Communiste Internationaliste [*Internationalist Communist Party*] [*French*] (PPE)
PCI .... Parti Communiste Italien (MAR)
PCI .... Partidul Comunist Italian [*Italian Communist Party*] (RO)
PCI .... Partito Comunista Italiano [*Italian Communist Party*] (WER)
PCI .... Pax Christi International (EA)
PCI .... Paza Contra Incendiilor [*Fire Prevention*] (RO)
PCI .... Pecheries de Cote-d'Ivoire (MAR)
PCI .... Trust Territory of the Pacific Islands [*Three-letter standard code*] (CNC)
PCIAOH .... Permanent Commission and International Association on Occupational Health (EA)
PCICS .... Permanent Council of the International Convention of Stresa on Cheeses (EA)
PCIEC .... Permanent Committee for International Eucharistic Congresses (EA)
PCIJ .... Permanent Court of International Justice (MAR)
PCIM .... Parti du Congres de l'Independance (MAR)
PCI/ML .... Partito Comunista d'Italia/Marxista-Leninista [*Italian Communist Party/Marxist-Leninist*] (WER)
PCJ .... Partido Catorce de Junio [*14 June Party*] [*Dominican Republic*] (LA1)
PCK .... Pengarah Chawangan Khas [*Director Special Branch (Police)*] (ML)
PCK .... Pilotni Cvicna Kabina [*Pilot Training Cabin*] (CZ)
PCK .... Polski Czerwony Krzyz [*Polish Red Cross*] (POL)
PCK .... Portatif Celik Konstruksiyon Sanayi ve Ticaret AS [*Portable Steel Construction Industry and Trade Corp.*] (TU)
PCK .... Puna Cena Kostanja [*Full Cost*] (YU)
PCKD .... Pegawai Chawangan Khas Daerah [*District Special Branch Officer*] (ML)
PCKD .... Polski Centralny Komitet Doradczy [*Central Polish Advisory Committee*] (POL)
PCL .... Parti Communiste Libanais [*Lebanese Communist Party*] (PPW)
PCL .... Parti Communiste de Luxembourg [*Communist Party of Luxembourg*] (PPE)
PCLPN Las ... Panstwowa Centrala Lesnych Produktow Niedrzewnych "Las" [*"Las" (Forest) State Agency of Non-Timber Forest Products*] (POL)
PCM .... Papeterie Cartonniere Moderne [*Algerian*] (MAR)
PCM .... Parti des Classes Moyennes [*Middle Class Party*] [*Luxembourg*] (PPE)
PCM .... Parti Communiste Malgache [*Malagasy Communist Party*] (AF)
PCM .... Parti Communiste Marocain [*Moroccan Communist Party*] (AF)
PCM .... Parti Communiste Martiniquais [*Communist Party of Martinique*] (PPW)
PCM .... Partido Comunista Mexicano [*Mexican Communist Party*] (PPW)
PCM .... Pineapple Canning of Malaysia (ML)
PCM .... Pravoslavna Crkva vo Makedonija [*Orthodox Church in Macedonia*] (YU)
PCM .... Produits en Ciment Moule (MAR)
PC-ML .... Marxist-Leninist Communist Party [*Bolivian*] (PPW)
PCML .... Parti Communiste Marxiste-Leniniste [*Marxist-Leninist Communist Party*] [*French*] (PPW)
PCML .... Partido Comunista Marxista-Leninista [*Marxist-Leninist Communist Party*] [*Argentine*] (LA)

PCML .... Partito Comunista Marxista-Leninista [*Marxist-Leninist Communist Party*] [*Sanmarinese*] (PPE)
PCMLB .... Parti Communiste Marxiste-Leniniste de Belgique [*Marxist-Leninist Communist Party of Belgium*] (WER)
PCMLF .... Parti Communiste Marxiste-Leniniste Francais [*Marxist-Leninist Communist Party*] [*French*] (PPW)
PC(ML)I ...... Partito Comunista (Marxista-Leninista) de Italia [*Communist Party of Italy (Marxist-Leninist)*] (PPE)
PCMU .... Plan Communal de Modernisation Urbaine (MAR)
PCN .... Certificat de Physique, Chimie, Sciences Naturelles [*French*]
PCN .... National Reconciliation Party [*Salvadoran*] (PD)
PCN .... Partido Comunista de Nicaragua [*Communist Party of Nicaragua*] (PD)
PC de N .... Partido Comunista de Nicaragua [*Communist Party of Nicaragua*] (LA1)
PCN .... Partido de Conciliacion Nacional [*National Reconciliation Party*] [*Salvadoran*] (PPW)
PCN .... Partido Conservador Nicaraguense [*Nicaraguan Conservative Party*] (PPW)
PCN .... Pitcairn [*Three-letter standard code*] (CNC)
PCO .... Partido Comunista Ortodoxo [*Orthodox Communist Party*] [*Dominican Republic*] (LA1)
Pco .... Picco [*Peak*] [*Italian*] (NAU)
Pco .... Pico [*Peak*] [*See also Po*] [*Portuguese*] (NAU)
Pco .... Pico [*Peak*] [*See also Po*] [*Spanish*] (NAU)
PCO .... Poste de Commandement Operationnel [*Operational Command Post*] [*Cambodian*] (CL)
PCO .... Pripraven k Civilni Obrane [*Prepared for Civil Defense (Badge)*] (CZ)
PCO .... Programme Complementaire Optionnel (MAR)
PCO .... Protiletecka Civilni Obrana [*Civil Air Defense*] (CZ)
PCOD .... Permanente Commissie voor Overheids-Documentatie [*'s-Gravenhage*]
PCOE .... Partido Comunista Obrero Espanol [*Spanish Workers Communist Party*] (WER)
PCP .... Palestinian Communist Party (PD)
PCP .... Panafrican Congress of Prehistory (MAR)
PCP .... Partido Communista Portugues [*Portuguese Communist Party*] (WER)
PCP .... Partido Comunista Paraguayano [*Paraguayan Communist Party*] (PD)
PCP .... Partido Comunista Peruano [*Peruvian Communist Party*] (PPW)
PCP .... Partido Comunista Portugues [*Portuguese Communist Party*] (PPE)
PCP .... Partido Comunista Puertorriqueno [*Puerto Rican Communist Party*] (PPW)
p cp .... Petites Coupures [*French*]
PCP .... Progressive Conservative Party [*Canadian*] (PPW)
PCP .... Progressive Constitutionalist Party [*Maltese*] (PPE)
PCP .... Puerto Rican Communist Party (PD)
PCPAZ .... Permanente Commissie voor Post- en Archiefzaken [*'s-Gravenhage*]
PCP-M .... Partido Comunista Peruano - Mayoria [*Peruvian Communist Party - Majority Faction*] (LA)
PCP M-L ...... Partido Comunista de Portugal, Marxista-Leninista [*Marxist-Leninist Communist Party of Portugal*] (PPE)
PCP(R) .... Partido Comunista Portugues Reconstruido [*Portuguese Communist Party - Reformed*] (WER)
PCP-U .... Partido Comunista Peruano - Unidad [*Peruvian Communist Party - Unidad Faction*] (LA)
PCPV .... Partit Carli del Pais Valencia [*Carlist Party of the Valencian Country*] [*Spanish*] (WER)
PCR .... Parti du Centre [*Center Party*] [*Mauritian*] (AF)
PCR .... Parti Communiste Reunionnais [*Communist Party of Reunion*] (PPW)
PCR .... Partido Comunista Revolucionario [*Revolutionary Communist Party*] [*Argentine*] (LA)
PCR .... Partido Comunista Revolucionario [*Revolutionary Communist Party*] [*Chilean*] (LA)
PCR .... Partido Comunista Revolucionario [*Revolutionary Communist Party*] [*Spanish*] (WER)
PCR .... Partidul Comunist Roman [*Romanian Communist Party*] (PPE)
PCR .... Partito Comunista Rivoluzionario [*Revolutionary Communist Party*] [*Italian*] (WER)
PCR .... Program to Combat Racism (MAR)
PCRD .... Partido Comunista de la Republica Dominicana [*Also, PACOREDO*] [*Communist Party of the Dominican Republic*] (LA)
PCRML .... Parti Communiste Revolutionnaire - Marxiste-Leniniste [*Revolutionary Marxist-Leninist Communist Party*] [*French*] (PPW)
PCRV .... Parti Communiste Revolutionnaire Voltaique [*Voltan Revolutionary Communist Party*] (AF)
pcs .... Parancs [*Order, Command*] (HU)
PCS .... Parti Chretien-Social [*Christian Social Party*] [*Luxembourg*] (PPW)
PCS .... Parti Communiste Senegalais [*Senegalese Communist Party*] (AF)
PCS .... Parti Communiste Suisse [*Communist Party of Switzerland*] (PPE)
PCS .... Partido Comunista Salvadoreno [*Salvadoran Communist Party*] (PPW)
PCS .... Partito Comunista Sammarinese [*Communist Party of San Marino*] (PPE)
PCS .... Postupak Crkvenih Sudova [*Ecclesiastic Courts Procedure*] (YU)
PCSD .... Partido Cristao Social Democratico [*Christian Social Democratic Party*] [*Portuguese*] (PPE)
PCS/ML ...... Parti Communiste Suisse/Marxiste-Leniniste [*Swiss Communist Party/Marxist-Leninist*] (WER)
PCST .... Public Corporation for Sugar Trade [*Sudanese*] (MAR)
PCSU .... Plan Communal Semi-Urbain [*Algerian*] (MAR)
pct .... Panceltoro [*Armor-Piercing, Antitank (Shell, Gun)*] (HU)
PCT .... Parti Communiste Tunisien [*Tunisian Communist Party*] (PD)
PCT .... Parti Congolais du Travail [*Congolese Labor Party*] (PPW)
PCT .... Partido Comunista de los Trabajadores [*Communist Party of the Workers*] [*Formerly, OPI*] [*Spanish*] (WER)
PCT .... Poste de Commandement Tir (MAR)
p ct .... Prosent [*Percent*] [*Norwegian*] (GPO)
p/cta .... Por Cuenta [*On Account*] [*Spanish*]
PCTP .... Partido Comunista dos Trabalhadores Portugueses [*Portuguese Workers' Communist Party*] (PPW)
PCU .... Partido Comunista del Uruguay [*Communist Party of Uruguay*] (LA)
PCUd'I .... Partito Comunista Unificato d'Italia [*United Communist Party of Italy*] [*Pro-Chinese*] (WER)
PCUI .... Partito Comunista Unificado de Italia [*Unified Communist Party of Italy*] (PPE)
PCUS .... Parti Communiste de l'Union Sovietique (MAR)
PCUS .... Partidul Comunist al URSS [*Communist Party of the USSR*] (RO)
PCV .... Groupement Petits Commercants Voltaique (MAR)
P et CV .... Parcs et Convois [*Military*] [*French*] (MTD)
PCV .... Partido Comunista Venezolana [*Venezuelan Communist Party*] (PPW)
PCW .... Parti Communiste Wallon [*Walloon Communist Party*] [*Belgian*] (WER)
PCW .... Polichlorek Winylu [*Polyvinyl Chloride*] [*Polish*]
PCWF .... Panstwowa Centrala Wychowania Fizycznego [*State Center of Physical Education*] (POL)
PCWM .... Panstwowe Centrum Wyszkolenia Morskiego [*State Center for Nautical Education*] (POL)
PCWU .... Public Cleansing Workers' Union [*Singapore*] (ML)
PCZ .... Canal Zone [*Three-letter standard code*] (CNC)
p cz .... Posrednia Czestotliwosc [*Intermediate Frequency*] [*Polish*]
PCZ .... Priroda, Clovek, Zdravje [*Nature, Man, Health*] [*A periodical*] [*Ljubljana*] (YU)
PD .... Democratic Party [*Ecuadorean*] (PD)
PD- .... Dispatcher's Console (RU)
PD .... Increased Pressure (RU)
pd .... Infantry Division (BU)
PD .... Infantry Division (RU)
PD .... Palaia Diathiki [*Old Testament*] (GC)
PD .... Parti Democratique [*Democratic Party*] [*Luxembourg*] (PPE)
pd .... Partial Pressure (RU)
PD .... Partido Democrata [*Democratic Party*] [*Costa Rican*] (PPW)
PD .... Partido Democratico [*Democratic Party*] [*Brazilian*] (LA1)
PD .... Partido Democratico [*Democratic Party*] [*Spanish*] (WER)
PD .... Peak Detector (RU)
pd .... Peldany [*Copy*] (HU)
PD .... Pemangku Djabatan [*Acting (Manager, Chairman)*] (IN)
PD .... Perifereia Dimou [*Municipal District*] (GC)
PD .... Pesadiska Divizija [*Infantry Division*] (YU)
PD .... Petrol Dairesi [*Petroleum Office*] (TU)
PD .... Piece Droite [*In a turret*] [*Military*] [*French*] (MTD)
pd .... Pied [*Foot*] [*Business and trade*] [*French*]
PD .... Piezobirefringence (RU)
PD .... Piston Engine (RU)
PD .... Planinsko Drustvo [*Alpine Society*] (YU)
PD .... Poljoprivredno Dobro [*State Farm*] (YU)
Pd .... Poludnie [*or Poludniowy*] [*South or Southern*] [*Polish*]
P/D .... Port Dickson (ML)
pd .... Port Du [*French*]
PD .... Posdata [*or Post Data*] [*Postscript*] [*Spanish*] (GPO)
PD .... Potentiometric Transducer (RU)
PD .... Poverenictvo Dopravy [*Office of the Commissioner of Transportation*] (CZ)
PD .... Poverenictvo Dopravy a Verejnych Prac [*Office of the Commissioner of Transportation and Public Works*] (CZ)
PD .... Presernova Druzba [*Preseren Society*] (YU)
PD .... Pressedienst [*Press Service*] (EG)
pd .... Pressurized, Under Pressure (RU)
PD .... Prime Mover (RU)
PD .... Proedrikon Diatagma [*Presidential Decree*] [*Greek*] (GC)
PD .... Program Transmitter [*Computers*] (RU)
PD .... Programa Democratico [*Democratic Program*] [*Spanish*] (PPE)
PD .... Proportional Differentiator (RU)
PD .... Prosvetni Delavec [*Educational Worker*] [*A periodical*] [*Ljubljana*] (YU)
PD .... Protivdesantni [*Antilanding*] [*Military*] (YU)
PD .... Pulse Pressure (RU)

PD .... Pushkin House (RU)
PD .... Semiconductor Diode (RU)
PD .... Starting Motor (RU)
PD .... Suspended Decontaminator (RU)
PD .... Switching Diode (RU)
pd .... Useful Effect (RU)
PDA .... Emergency-Signal Transmitter (RU)
PdA .... Partei der Arbeit [*Labor Party*] [*Swiss*] (PPE)
PDA .... Partido Democratico de Angola [*Democratic Party of Angola*] (AF)
PDA .... Partit Democrata d'Andorra [*Andorran Democratic Party*] (PPW)
Pd'A .... Partito d'Azione [*Action Party*] [*Italian*] (PPE)
Pda .... Pedra [*Rock*] [*Portuguese*] (NAU)
PDA .... Perifereia Dimou Athinon [*Athens Municipal Area*] (GC)
Pda .... Piedra [*Rock*] [*Spanish*] (NAU)
PDA .... Posadkovy Dum Armady [*Army Post Recreation Building*] (CZ)
pda .... Pour Dire Adieu [*To Say Goodbye*] [*French*]
PDA .... Preventive Detention Act (MAR)
PDA .... Produktions- und Dienstleistungsabgabe [*Production and Services Tax (A type of turnover tax)*] (EG)
PDA .... Proleter Devrimci Aydinlik Grubu [*Proletarian Revolutionary Enlightenment Group*] [*See also PDAG*] (TU)
PDA .... Regulation on the Application of the Law on State Arbitration (BU)
PDAG .... Proleter Devrimci Aydinlik Grubu [*Proletarian Revolutionary Enlightenment Group*] [*See also PDA*] (TU)
PDAP .... Programa Autonomo de Desenvolvimento Agro-Pecuario [*Autonomous Agricultural-Livestock Development Program*] [*Portuguese*] (WER)
PDAVO .... Verordnung ueber die Produktionsabgabe und Dienstleistungsabgabe der VEW [*Ordinance Concerning the Production Tax and Services Tax of the State Economy*] (EG)
pdb .... Airborne Battalion (BU)
PDB .... Paradichlorobenzene (RU)
PDB .... Paratroop Battalion (RU)
PDB .... Partei der Deutschsprachigen Belgier [*Party of German-Speaking Belgians*] (PPW)
PDB .... Parti Democrate du Burundi (MAR)
PDB .... Partido Democrata Boliviano [*Bolivian Democratic Party*] (LA)
PDB .... Partido Democratico Brasileiro [*Brazilian Democratic Party*] (LA)
PDB .... Petrol Dairesi Baskanligi [*Petroleum Office Chairmanship*] (TU)
PDB .... Production Dispatch Office (RU)
PDBB .... Airdrop Fuel and Lubricant Tank (RU)
pdbr .... Paratroop Brigade (RU)
PDC .... Christian Democratic Party [*Panamanian*] (PD)
PDC .... Pacte Democratica per Catalunya [*Democratic Pact for Catalonia*] [*Spanish*] (PPE)
PDC .... Parti Democrate Chretien [*Christian Democratic Party*] [*Malagasy*] (AF)
PDC .... Parti Democrate Chretien du Burundi [*Christian Democratic Party of Burundi*] (AF)
PDC .... Parti Democrate-Chretien Suisse [*Christian Democratic Party of Switzerland*] (PPE)
PDC .... Parti Democratique Congolais (MAR)
PDC .... Parti Democratique Constitutionel [*Constitutional Democratic Party*] [*Moroccan*] (AF)
PDC .... Parti Democratique de la Cote-d'Ivoire (MAR)
PDC .... Partido da Democracia Cristao [*Christian Democratic Party*] [*Portuguese*] (PPW)
PDC .... Partido Democracia Cristiana [*Christian Democratic Party*] [*Guatemalan*] (PPW)
PDC .... Partido Democrata Cristiano [*Christian Democratic Party*] [*Bolivian*] (PPW)
PDC .... Partido Democrata Cristiano [*Christian Democratic Party*] [*Costa Rican*] (PPW)
PDC .... Partido Democrata Cristiano [*Christian Democratic Party*] [*Honduran*] (PPW)
PDC .... Partido Democrata Cristiano [*Christian Democratic Party*] [*Mexican*] (LA)
PDC .... Partido Democrata Cristiano [*Christian Democratic Party*] [*Paraguayan*] (PPW)
PDC .... Partido Democrata Cristiano [*Christian Democratic Party*] [*Peruvian*] (PPW)
PDC .... Partido Democrata Cristiano [*Christian Democratic Party*] [*Salvadoran*] (LA)
PDC .... Partido Democrata Cristiano [*Christian Democratic Party*] [*Spanish*] (WER)
PDC .... Partido Democrata Cristiano [*Christian Democratic Party*] [*Uruguayan*] (LA)
PDC .... Partido Democratico Cristao [*Christian Democratic Party*] [*Brazilian*] (LA)
PDC .... People's Defence Committee [*Ghanaian*] (PD)
PDC .... Societe du Palace de Cocody (MAR)
PDCh .... Doppler Frequency Converter (RU)
PDCH .... Partido Democrata Cristiano de Honduras [*Honduran Christian Democratic Party*] (LA)
PDCI .... Parti Democratique de la Cote-d'Ivoire [*Democratic Party of the Ivory Coast*] (PPW)
PDCL .... Partido Democrata de Castilla y Leon [*Democratic Party of Castille and Leon*] [*Spanish*] (WER)
PDCM .... Parti Democrate Chretien de Madagascar [*Christian Democratic Party of Madagascar*] (AF)
PDCR .... Partido Democrata Cristiano Revolucionario [*Revolutionary Christian Democratic Party*] [*Bolivian*] (LA)
PDCS .... Partito Democratico Cristiano Sammarinese [*Christian Democratic Party of San Marino*] (PPE)
PDD .... Maximum Permissible Dose (RU)
PDD .... Panstwowy Dom Dziecka [*State Children's Home*] (POL)
PDD .... Parti Democratique Dahomeen (MAR)
PDD .... Pertubohan Pemuda Daerah [*Rural Youth Organization*] (ML)
PDD .... Posadkovy Dozorci Dustojnik [*Garrison Officer of the Day*] (CZ)
PDD .... Proportional Pressure Transducer (RU)
PDD .... Tree-Type Decoder [*Computers*] (RU)
PDDD .... Protovathmion Dioikitikon kai Diaititikon Dikastirion [*First Instance Administrative and Arbitration Court*] [*Greek*] (GC)
PDE .... Programma Dimosion Ependyseon [*Public Investments Program*] (GC1)
PDEB .... Partiia Dvizheniia za Emansipatsiiu Bakhutu (MAR)
PDEG .... Panelliniki Dimokratiki Enosis Gynaikon [*Panhellenic Women's Democratic Union*] (GC)
PDELAR ...... Presidencia de la Republica [*Presidency of the Republic*] [*Mexican*] (LA)
PDelo .... Prosvetno Delo [*Cultural Journal*] [*A periodical*] [*Skopje*] (YU)
pdesb .... River Crossing Assault Battalion (RU)
pdesr .... River Crossing Assault Company (RU)
pdesv .... River Crossing Assault Platoon (RU)
PDF .... People's Defense Force [*Singapore*] (ML)
PDF .... Periscopic Long-Focus Camera (RU)
PDF .... Pionniers de France [*French Pioneers*] (WER)
PDFLP .... Popular Democratic Front for the Liberation of Palestine (ME)
PDG .... Parti Democratique Gabonais [*Gabonese Democratic Party*] (PPW)
PDG .... Parti Democratique de Guinee [*Democratic Party of Guinea*] (PPW)
PDG .... Partido Democrata Galego [*Galician Democratic Party*] [*Spanish*] (WER)
P-DG .... President-Directeur General [*President-Director General*] [*French*] (WER)
PDH .... Pedagosko Drustvo Hrvatske [*Pedagogic Society of Croatia*] (YU)
PDH .... Povjesno Drustvo Hrvatske [*Croatian Historical Society*] (YU)
PDH .... Prirodoslovno Drustvo Hrvatske [*Croatian Natural Sciences Society*] (YU)
PDHA .... Produktions-, Dienstleistungs-, und Handelsabgabe [*Production, Services, and Trade Tax*] (EG)
PDHV-RDA ... Parti Democratique de la Haute Volta--Rassemblement Democratique Africain [*Democratic Party of Upper Volta--African Democratic Rally*] (AF)
PDI .... Partai Demokrasi Indonesia [*Indonesian Democratic Party*] (PPW)
PDI .... Parti Dahomeen de l'Independance (MAR)
PDI .... Parti Democratique de l'Independance [*Moroccan*] (MAR)
PDI .... Partito Democratica Italiana [*Italian Democratic Party*] (PPE)
PDI .... Prise Ombilicale Derniers Instants
PDI .... Regulation on State Property (BU)
PDiBM .... Przedsiebiorstwo Detalu i Barow Mlecznych [*Milk Retail and Milk Bar Enterprise*] (POL)
PDIC .... Public Demands Implementation Convention [*Indian*] (PPW)
PDID .... Parti pour la Defense des Institutions Democratiques (MAR)
PDiRz .... Ministerstwo Przemyslu Drobnego i Rzemiosla [*Ministry of Small Scale and Handicraft Industry*] (POL)
PDIUM .... Partito Democratico Italiano di Unita Monarchica [*Italian Democratic Party of Monarchical Unity*] (PPE)
PDJTB .... Parti Democratique des Jeunes Travailleurs du Burundi (MAR)
PDK .... Maximum Permissible Concentration (BU)
PDK .... Maximum Permissible Concentration (RU)
PDK .... Panstwowy Dom Kultury [*State House of Culture*] (POL)
PDK .... Phileleftheron Demokratikon Kendron [*Liberal Democratic Union*] [*Greek*] (PPE)
PDK .... Phileleftheron Demokratikon Komma [*Liberal Democratic Party*] [*Greek*] (PPE)
PDK .... Planove-Dispecerska Kancelar [*Management and Plan Control Bureau*] (CZ)
PDK .... Potentiometric Remote-Indicating Compass (RU)
PDK .... Powiatowe Domy Kultury [*County Houses of Culture*] (POL)
PDK .... Pres, Dokum, ve Kromaj Fabrikalari [*Stamping, Foundry, and Chrome Plating Factories*] (TU)
PDk .... Primorski Dnevnik [*Maritime Region Daily*] [*Trieste*] (YU)
PDKN .... Maximum Permissible Concentration of Unidentified Radioactive Isotopes (RU)
PDL .... Poverty Datum Level [*or Line*] (MAR)
PDL .... Proposta di Legge [*Parliamentary Bill*] [*Italian*] (WER)
PDLM .... Direction des Peches Legunaires et Maritimes [*Lagoon and Marine Fishery Administration*] [*Ivorian*] (AF)
PDLP .... Front Democratique pour la Liberation de Djibouti [*Democratic Front for the Liberation of Djibouti*] (PD)
PDM .... Ground Decontamination Device (RU)
PDM .... Parti Democratique Malgache (MAR)

PDM .... Partido Democratico Mexicano [*Mexican Democratic Party*] (LA)
PDM .... People's Democratic Movement [*Turks and Caicos Islands*] (PPW)
PDM .... People's Democratic Movement [*St. Vincentian*] (LA1)
PDM .... Progres et Democratie Moderne [*Progress and Modern Democracy*] [*French*] (PPE)
PDM .... Railroad Track Maintenance Shops (RU)
PDMA .... Propyldimethacrylamide (RU)
PDMD .... Panstwowy Dom Malego Dziecka [*State Infants' Home*] [*Polish*]
PDMM .... Airdrop Flexible Bag (RU)
PDMP .... Field Divisional Aid Station (BU)
PDMS .... Railroad Track Machinery Station (RU)
PDN .... Negative-Deciphering Apparatus (RU)
PDN .... Partito Democratico Nazionalista [*Democratic Nationalist Party (1921-1926)*] [*Maltese*] (PPE)
PDN .... Perusahaan Dagang Negara [*State Trading Company*] (IN)
PDO .... Advance Landing Detachment (RU)
PDO .... Antiamphibious Defense, Antilanding Defense (RU)
PDO .... Laundry and Disinfection Detachment (RU)
PDO .... Pankyprios Didaskaliki Organosis [*Pan-Cyprian Teachers Organization*] (GC)
pdo .... Pasado [*Past*] [*Spanish*]
PDO .... Perifereiaka Dioikitika Organa [*Regional Administrative Organs*] [*Greek*] (GC)
PDO .... Petroleum Development Oman (ME)
PDO .... Production Dispatch Department (RU)
PDO .... Production Dispatching Department (BU)
PDO .... Prostor za Degazaciju Oruzja [*Arms Decontamination Area*] (YU)
PDO .... Protivdesantna Odbrana [*Antilanding Defense*] (YU)
PDO .... Weapon Decontamination Site (RU)
pd ob .... Supply Train [*Regimental*] (BU)
PDOC .... Partido Democrata Obrero Campesino [*Democratic Worker-Peasant Party*] [*Dominican Republic*] (LA1)
PDOG .... Pankypriaki Dimokratiki Organosis Gynaikon [*Pan-Cyprian Democratic Women's Organization*] (GC)
PDOSOM .... Enterprise for the Extraction and Processing of Quarry-Lining Materials (BU)
PDOV .... Prostor za Degazaciju Oruzja i Vozila [*Arms and Vehicles Decontamination Area*] (YU)
pdp .... Airborne Regiment (BU)
PDP .... Laundry and Disinfection Station (RU)
PDP .... Mobile Control Tower [*Aviation*] (RU)
PDP .... Pakistan Democratic Party (PD)
PDP .... Paratroop Regiment (RU)
PDP .... Parti Democrate Populaire [*Popular Democratic Party*] [*French*] (PPE)
PDP .... Partido Democrata Popular [*People's Democratic Party*] [*Argentine*] (LA)
PDP .... Partido Democrata Popular [*People's Democratic Party*] [*Dominican Republic*] (PPW)
PDP .... Partido Democrata Popular [*People's Democratic Party*] [*Spanish*] (WER)
PDP .... Partido Democrata Progresista [*Progressive Democratic Party*] [*Argentine*] (LA)
PDP .... Partido da Direita Portuguesa [*Party of the Portuguese Right*] (PPE)
PDP .... Partido de los Pobres [*Poor People's Party*] [*Mexican*] (LA)
PdP .... Partido del Pueblo [*People's Party*] [*Panamanian*] (LA)
PDP .... Partito Democratico Populare [*Popular Democratic Party*] [*Sanmarinese*] (PPE)
PDP .... People's Democratic Party [*Bahamian*] (LA1)
PDP .... Peoples' Democratic Party [*Sudanese*] (MAR)
PDP .... Progressive Democratic Party [*Montserrat*] (PPW)
PDP .... Suspended Decontamination Apparatus (RU)
PDPA .... People's Democratic Party of Afghanistan (PPW)
PDPC .... Parti Democratique du Peuple Cabindais [*Democratic Party of the Cabindan People*] [*Angolan*] (AF)
PDPL .... Programme pour le Developpement de la Production Laitiere [*Dairy Herd Development Program*] [*Mauritian*] (AF)
PDPS .... Standing Production Conference (RU)
PDPT .... Parti Democratique des Populations Togolaises (MAR)
pdr .... Airborne Company (BU)
pdr .... Infantry Battalion (BU)
PDR .... Paratroop Company (RU)
PDR .... Parti Democrate Rural (MAR)
PDR .... Parti Democratique de la Reconstruction (MAR)
PDR .... Partido de la Democracia Radical [*Radical Democratic Party*] [*Chilean*] (LA)
PDR .... Partido Democratico Republicano [*Republican Democratic Party*] [*Brazilian*] (LA)
PDR .... Personnes Deplacees et Refugiees (MAR)
PdR .... Praesident der Republic [*President of the Republic*] (EG)
PDR .... Programme de Developpement Rural [*Tunisian*] (MAR)
PDREUF .... Public Daily-Rated Employees' Union Federation (ML)
PDRP .... Partido Democrata Reformista Peruano [*Peruvian Reformist Democratic Party*] (LA)
PDRTs .... Radio Transmission Center (RU)
PDRY .... People's Democratic Republic of Yemen (ME)
pds .... Paratroop Gunner (RU)
PDS .... Paratroop Service (RU)
PDS .... Parti Democratique Senegalais [*Senegalese Democratic Party*] (PPW)
PDS .... Partido Democrata Socialista [*Socialist Democratic Party*] [*Panamanian*] (PPW)
PDS .... Partido Democratico Social [*Social Democratic Party*] [*Brazilian*] (LA)
PDS .... Partito di Democrazia Socialista [*Socialist Democracy Party*] [*Sanmarinese*] (PPW)
PDS .... Pedagosko Drustvo Srbije [*Pedagogic Society of Serbia*] (YU)
PDS .... Plantations de la Savane de Dabou (MAR)
PDS .... Plukovni Delostrelecka Skupina [*Regiment Artillery Group*] (CZ)
PDS .... Poddustojnicka Skola [*School for Noncommissioned Officers*] (CZ)
PDS .... Senior Roadmaster [*Railroads*] (RU)
PDS .... Synchronization Transmitter (RU)
PDSI .... Co-Phasing Pulse Transmitter (RU)
PDSN .... Pnevmatikos Desmos Spoudaston tis Neolaias [*Cultural Bond of Student Youth*] (GC)
PDSO .... Regulation on State Economic Organizations (BU)
PDSO .... Voluntary Trade Union Sports Organization (BU)
PDSU- .... Mobile Crushing and Grading Unit (RU)
PDT .... Panstwowa Dyrekcja Tramwajowa [*State Administration of Streetcars*] (POL)
PDT .... Panstwowy Dom Towarowy [*State Department Store*] (POL)
PdT .... Parti du Travail [*Labor Party*] [*Swiss*] (PPE)
PDT .... Partido Democratico Trabalhista [*Democratic Worker's Party*] [*Brazilian*] (LA1)
PDT .... Powszechny Dom Towarowy [*General Department Store*] (POL)
PDT .... Pretprijatie za Dalekovodi i Trasfostanici [*Establishment for Long-Distance Transmission Lines and Transformer Stations*] [*Skopje*] (YU)
PDT .... Transportation Decontamination Site (RU)
PDTZh .... Container for Air-Dropping of Liquids (RU)
PDU .... Control Transmitter (RU)
PDU .... Maximum Permissible Level (RU)
PDU .... Mobile Stone Crusher (RU)
PDU .... Parti Dahomeen de l'Unite (MAR)
PDU .... Parti Democratique Unifie [*Unified Democratic Party*] [*Upper Voltan*] (AF)
PDU .... Remote Control Panel (RU)
PDU .... Transmitting Installation (RU)
PDUP .... Partito dell'Unita Proletaria [*Proletarian Unity Party*] [*Italian*] (WER)
PdUP .... Partito di Unita Proletaria per il Comunismo [*Democratic Party of Proletarian Unity for Communism*] [*Italian*] (PPE)
PDUR .... Airdrop Packing Straps (RU)
PDV .... Call Sender (RU)
pdv .... Paratroop Platoon (RU)
PDV .... Parti Democratique Voltaique [*Voltan Democratic Party*] (AF)
PdVP .... Praesidium der Volkspolizei [*People's Police Presidium*] (EG)
PDVSA .... Petroleos de Venezuela, SA [*Venezuelan Petroleum, Inc.*] (LA)
PDW .... Progress Dritte Welt (MAR)
pd-wsch .... Poludniowo-Wschodni [*South-East*] [*Polish*]
PDZ .... Penza Diesel Plant (RU)
PDZ .... Pervoural'sk Dinas Brick Plant (RU)
pd-zach .... Poludniowo-Zachodni [*South-West*] [*Polish*]
pdz/khs .... Underground Connecting Trench [*Topography*] (RU)
Pe- .... Aircraft Designed by V. M. Petlyakov (RU)
PE .... Electronic Psychrometer (RU)
PE- .... Electropneumatic Transducer (RU)
PE .... Enameled Wire (Resistor) (RU)
PE .... Field Clearing Station (RU)
Pe .... Padre [*Father, Priest*] [*Spanish*]
pe .... Par Exemple [*For Example*] [*French*]
pe .... Parelthondos Etous [*Of the Past Year, Last Year's*] (GC)
PE .... Parni Elektrarna [*Steam Power Plant*] (CZ)
PE .... Passeinheit [*Unit of Fit*] [*German*]
PE .... Pedagogical Encyclopedia (RU)
PE .... Perifereiaki Epitropi [*Regional Committee*] (GC1)
pe .... Perjantai(na) [*Finnish*]
PE .... Peru [*Peru*] [*Polish*]
PE .... Peru [*Two-letter standard code*] (CNC)
PE .... Piyade Er [*Private, Infantry*] (TU)
PE .... Police d'Etat [*State Police*] [*Algerian*] (AF)
PE .... Polietilen [*Polyethylene*] (TU)
PE .... Politischer Erzieher, Politische Erziehung [*Political Educator, Political Education*] (EG)
PE .... Poljoprivredna Ekonomija [*Agricultural Economy*] (YU)
PE .... Polyethylene (RU)
PE .... Polytechnische Bildung und Erziehung [*Polytechnical Training and Education*] (EG)
PE .... Pomorska Enciklopedija [*Marine Encyclopedia*] (YU)
pe .... Ponte [*Bridge*] [*Portuguese*] (CED)
pe .... Por Ejemplo [*For Example*] [*Correspondence*] [*Spanish*]
PE .... Port Elizabeth (MAR)
PE .... Poste d'Ecoute [*Listening Station*] [*Military*] [*French*] (MTD)
PE .... Potencijalna Evaporacija [*Potential Evaporation*] [*Geography*] (YU)

PE............... Semiconductor Element (RU)
PE............... Threshold Element [*Computers*] (RU)
PE............... Utricular Elements (RU)
PEA............ Pankypriaki Enosis Apomakhon [*Pan-Cyprian Veterans Union*] (GC)
PEA............ People's Education Association (MAR)
PEA............ Polyethylene Azelate (RU)
PEA............ Portuguese East Africa (MAR)
PEA............ Press Employees Association [*Mauritian*] (AF)
PEA............ Programma Evropaikis Anorthoseos [*European Recovery Program*] (GC)
PEA............ Proodevtiki Enosis Agoniston [*Progressive Fighters Union*] [*Cypriot*] (GC)
PEAEA........ Panellinios Enosis Agoniston Ethnikis Andistaseos [*Panhellenic Union of National Resistance Fighters*] (GC)
PEAK.......... Panavstraliaki Epitropi Avtodiatheseos Kyprou [*Pan-Australian Committee for the Self-Determination of Cyprus*] [*Cypriot*] (GC)
PEAK.......... Panellinios Epitropi Avtodiatheseos Kyprou [*Panhellenic Committee for the Self-Determination of Cyprus*] (GC)
PEAKEL...... Panellinia Enosis Allilengyis ston Kypriako Lao [*Panhellenic Union of Solidarity with the Cypriot People*] (GC1)
PEAM.......... Pankypriako Ethniko Apelevtherotiko Metopo [*Pan-Cyprian National Liberation Front*] (GC)
PEAN.......... Panellinios Enosis Agonizomenon Neon [*Panhellenic Union of Fighting Youth*] (GC)
PEAN.......... Patriotiki Enosis Agonizomenis Neolaias [*Patriotic Union of Fighting Youth*] [*Greek*] (GC)
PEAP.......... Panellinios Enosis Apomakhon Polemou [*Panhellenic Union of War Veterans*] (GC)
PEAP.......... Pankyprios Enosis Anakoufiseos Pathondon [*or Pankyprios Epitropi Apokatastaseos Pathondon*] [*Pan-Cyprian Union for Relief of the Distressed*] (GC)
PEAT.......... Protypa Ergastiria Andikeimenon Tekhnis [*Model Art Craft Workshops*] [*Greek*] (GC)
PEATEA...... Panellinios Enosis Anapiron kai Travmation Ethnikis Andistaseos Periodou 1941-1944 [*Penhellenic Union of Wounded and Disabled of the National Resistance Period, 1941-1944*] (GC)
PEAThP....... Panellinios Enosis Anapiron kai Thymaton Polemou [*Panhellenic Union of Disabled and Victims of War*] (GC)
PEAYEA...... Panellinios Enosis Axiomatikon-Ypaxiomatikon Ethnikis Andistaseos [*Panhellenic Union of Officers and Noncommissioned Officers of the National Resistance*] (GC)
PEB............ Economic Planning Office (RU)
PEB............ Preduzece za Eksploataciju Boksita [*Bauxite Exploitation Establishment*] [*Cetinje*] (YU)
PEB............ Putno-Eksploatacioni Bataljon [*Road Maintenance Battalion*] [*Military*] (YU)
PeB............ Statni Pedagogicka Knihovna v Brne [*State Pedagogical Library in Brno*] (CZ)
PEBCO........ Port Elizabeth Black Civic Organization [*South African*] (PD)
PEC............ Parti pour l'Evolution des Comores [*Party for the Evolution of the Comoros*] (AF)
PEC............ Partido Estat Catala [*Catalan State Party*] [*Spanish*] (WER)
PEC............ Protocolo de Expansion Comercial [*Protocol Office for Trade Expansion*] [*Uruguayan*] (LA)
PEC............ Prova Elementi Combustibili [*An Italian fast reactor*]
PEC............ Proyecto Electrico Campeche [*Campeche Electrification Project*] [*Mexican*] (LA)
PECAM....... Pecheries Camerounaises (MAR)
Pech........... Pechota [*Infantry*] (CZ)
pech........... Press (BU)
pech........... Printed (RU)
pech........... Printing Plant, Printed (BU)
Pechie......... Pecherie [*Fishery*] [*Military map abbreviation*] [*World War I*] [*French*] (MTD)
pech l......... Printer's Sheet (RU)
PECHOR..... Pechora Railroad (RU)
Pechorlag... Pechora Railroad Corrective Labor Camp (RU)
PechorNIUI... Pechora Scientific Research Institute of Coal (RU)
PECI........... Plastiques et Elastomeres de la Cote-d'Ivoire (MAR)
PECIG......... Pecheries Industrielles Gabonaises [*Gabonese Fishing Industries*] (AF)
PECIG......... Societe de Pecheries Industrielles du Gabon (MAR)
PECO.......... Centrala de Desfacere a Produselor Petroliere [*Central for the Sale of Petroleum Products*] (RO)
PECSAR...... Permanent Committee for Search and Rescue (MAR)
PED............ Pays en Developpement (MAR)
ped............ Pedagogical (BU)
ped............ Pedagogical (RU)
Ped............ Pedagoji [*Pedagogy*] (TU)
ped............ Pediatrics (BU)
PEDAEP...... Projet d'Experimentation et de Demonstration en Arboriculture, Elevage, et Paturage [*Tunisian*] (MAR)
pedag......... Pedagogical, Pedagogy (RU)
Pedag......... Professional Education Specialization (BU)
pedag u-shta... Normal Schools (BU)
PEDE.......... Programa Estrategico de Desenvolvimento [*Strategic Development Program*] [*Brazilian*] (LA)
PEDEVESA... Petroleos de Venezuela, SA [*Venezuelan Petroleum, Inc.*] [*Use Spanish*] (LA)
pedin.......... Pedagogical Institute (RU)
PEDMEDE... Panellinios Enosis Diplomatoukhon Mikhanikon Ergolipton Dimosion Ergon [*Panhellenic Union of Licensed Engineer Public Works Contractors*] (GC)
PEDMIEDE... Panellinios Enosis Diplomatoukhon Mikhanikon kai Ilektrologon Ergolipton Dimosion Ergon [*Panhellenic Union of Licensed Mechanical and Electrical Engineer Public Works Contractors*] (GC)
PEDPA........ Perifereiaki Dievthynsis Politikis Amynis [*Regional Civil Defense Directorate*] [*Cypriot*] (GC)
PEE............ Panellinia Enosis Ethnikofronon [*Panhellenic Union of Nationalists*] (GC)
PEE............ Pankypriaki Epitropi Eirinis [*Pan-Cyprian Peace Committee*] (GC)
PEE............ Pankypriaki Epitropi Englovismenon [*Pan-Cyprian Committee of Enclaved Persons*] (GC)
PEEA.......... Panellinios Enosis Efedron Axiomatikon [*Panhellenic Union of Reserve Officers*] (GC)
PEEA.......... Pankyprios Enosis Epangelmation Avtokinitiston [*Pan-Cyprian Union of Professional Drivers*] (GC)
PEEA.......... Pequenas Empresas de Extraccion de Anchoveta [*Small Enterprises for Anchovy Fishing*] [*Peruvian*] (LA)
PEEA.......... Politiki Epitropi Ethnikis Apelevtheroseos [*Political Committee for National Liberation*] [*Greek*] (GC)
PEEEPP....... Panellinia Enosis Epanapatristhendon Ellinon Politikon Prosfygon [*Panhellenic Union of Repatriated Greek Political Refugees*] (GC1)
PEEG.......... Panellinios Enosis Ergazomenon Gynaikon [*Panhellenic Union of Working Women*] (GC)
PEEK.......... Panellinios Epitropi Enoseos Kyprou [*Panhellenic Committee for the Union of Cyprus*] (GC)
PEEL........... Panellinios Enosis Epangelmation Logiston [*Panhellenic Union of Professional Accountants*] (GC)
PEETh......... Panellinios Enosis Elevtherou Theatrou [*Panhellenic Union of the Free Theater*] (GC)
PEF............ Recurrent Figure Elements [*Cybernetics*] (RU)
PEFCO........ Private Export Funding Corporation (MAR)
PEFND........ Panellinios Enosis Filon Neas Dimokratias [*Panhellenic Union of Friends of New Democracy*] (GC)
PEFP.......... Panellinios Enosis Filon ton Polyteknon [*Panhellenic Union of Friends of Parents of Large Families*] (GC)
PEG............ Panelladiki Enosis Gynaikon [*Panhellenic Women's Union*] (GC)
PEG............ Pegawai [*Officer, Official*] [*Malaysian*] (ML)
Peg............ Pegunungan [*Mountain Range*] [*Indonesian*] (NAU)
PEG............ Polyethylene Glycol (RU)
PEGA.......... Petrol ve Gas Endustrisi AS [*Petroleum and Gas Industry Corporation*] (TU)
PEGA.......... Proodevtiki Enosis Gynaikon Ammokhostou [*Progressive Union of Famagusta Women*] (GC)
PEGAB........ Pecheries Gabonaises [*Fisheries of Gabon*] (AF)
PEGO.......... Pankypriaki Ethniki Gynaikeia Organosis [*Pan-Cyprian National Women's Organization*] (GC)
PEGSAAA... Pankypria Epitropi Goneon kai Syngenon Adiloton Aikhmaloton kai Agnooumenon [*Pan-Cyprian Committee of Parents and Relatives of Undeclared Prisoners and Missing Persons*] (GC)
PEGSAAAKT... Panellinios Epitropi Goneon kai Syngenon Adiloton Aikhmaloton kai Agnooumenon tis Kypriakis Tragodias [*Panhellenic Committee of Parents and Relatives of Undeclared Prisoners and Missing Persons of the Cyprus Tragedy*] (GC)
PEGSM....... Mobile Electric and Gas Welding Shop (RU)
PEGUPCO... Persian Gulf Petroleum Company [*Iranian*] (ME)
PEI............ Polyethyleneimine (RU)
PEI............ Pravno-Ekonomski Institut [*Law and Economic Institute*] (YU)
PEIAIKh...... Panellinios Enosis Idioktiton Avtokiniton Idiotikis Khriseos [*Panhellenic Union of Owners of Private Use Vehicles*] (GC)
PEiZh.......... Power and Damage Control Station [*Navy*] (RU)
PEJ............ Pejabat [*Office*] (ML)
pej............ Por Ejemplo [*For Example*] [*Spanish*]
PEK............ Cohesive Energy Density (RU)
PEK............ Mailing Office (RU)
PEK............ Panagrotiki Enosis Kyprou [*Pan Agrarian Union of Cyprus*] (GC)
PEK............ Panellinios Enosis Kinimatografiston [*Panhellenic Cinematographers Union*] (GC)
PEK............ Pecsi Tudomanyegyetem Konyvtara [*Library of the University of Pecs*] (HU)
PEK............ Perifereiakai Epitropai Katanomon [*Regional Apportionment Committee*] [*Greek*] (GC)
PEK............ Politicka Ekonomie Kapitalismu [*Political Economics of Capitalism*] (CZ)
PEK............ Problems of Economics [*A publication*] (RU)
PEK............ Proodevtiki Enotiki Kinisi [*Progressive Union Movement*] (GC)
PEKA.......... Pankyprios Enosis Kyprion Agoniston [*Pan-Cyprian Union of Cypriot Fighters*] (GC)

PEKA.......... Panspoudastiki Epitropi Kypriakou Agonos [*All-Students Committee of the Cyprus Struggle*] [*Cypriot*] (GC)
PEKA.......... Politiki Epitropi Kypriakou Agonos [*Political Committee of the Cyprus Struggle*] [*Cypriot*] (GC)
Pekachem... Przedsiebiorstwo Konstrukcji Aparatury Chemicznej [*Chemical Equipment Designing Enterprise*] (POL)
PEKAM........ Parti Keadilan Masharakat [*Social Justice Party*] (ML)
PEKEMAS... Pertubohan Kebangsaan Melayu Singapore [*Malayan National Organization in Singapore*] (ML)
pekh........... Infantry (RU)
PEKh........... Pankyprios Enosis Khimikon [*Pan-Cyprian Chemists Union*] (GC)
Pel.............. Parcel [*Shoal*] [*Portuguese*] (NAU)
PEL.............. Pelajaran [*Education*] (ML)
Pel.............. Peloton [*Half of a Company, Quarter of a Squadron*] [*Military*] [*French*] (MTD)
PEL.............. Philatelic Esperanto League [*See also ELF*] (EA)
PEL.............. Programmes d'Equipements Locaux [*Algerian*] (MAR)
peld............. Peldany [*Copy*] (HU)
PELDA......... Pembantu Letnan Dua [*Second Sublieutenant*] (IN)
pelit............. Pelitermi [*Games*] [*Finnish*]
PELITA........ Pembangunan Lima Tahun [*5-Year Development (Plan)*] (IN)
PELMASI..... Pelopor Mahasiswa Sosialis Indonesia [*Indonesian Socialist College Student Pioneers*] (IN)
PELNI.......... Pelajaran Nasional Indonesia [*Indonesian National Maritime Company*] (IN)
PELTU......... Pembantu Letnan Satu [*First Sublieutenant*] (IN)
PEM............. Pankypriaki Enosis Mikrokatastimatarkhon [*Pan-Cyprian Union of Small Shopkeepers*] (GC)
PEM............. Pankypriakon Enotikon Metopon [*Pan-Cyprian Unifying Front*] (GC)
PEM............. Pankyprion Ergatoagrotikon Metopon [*Pan-Cyprian Labor Agrarian Front*] (GC)
PEM............. Plast- und Elastverarbeitungsmaschinen [*Machines for Processing Plastic and Elastic Materials*] (EG)
PEMA.......... Pankyprion Eniaion Metopon Agoniston [*Pan-Cyprian United Fighters' Front*] (GC)
PEMAECO... Societe de Peche Maritime du Congo (MAR)
PEMARZA... Societe des Peches Maritimes du Zaire [*Zaire Maritime Fishing Company*] (AF)
PEME.......... Programa de Expansao e Melhoria do Ensino [*Program for Expansion and Improvement of Education*] [*Brazilian*] (LA)
PEME.......... Proodevtiki Enosi Miteron Ellados [*Progressive Union of Greek Mothers*] (GC)
PEMEK........ Panellinios Enosis Mikhanikon Esoterikis Kavseos [*Panhellenic Union of Internal Combustion Engineers*] (GC)
PEMEN........ Panellinios Enosis Mikhanikon Emborikou Navtikou [*Panhellenic Union of Merchant Marine Engineers*] (GC)
PEMEX......... Petroleos Mexicanos [*Mexican Petroleum*] (LA)
PEMILU........ Pemilihan Umum [*General Election*] (IN)
PEMKO........ Profilo Elektrik Motorlari ve Kompresor Sanayii AS [*Profilo Electric Motors and Compressor Industry Corp.*] (TU)
PEMOEA..... Panellinios Enosis Makhiton Omadon Ethnikis Andistaseos [*Panhellenic Union of Fighter Groups of the National Resistance*] (GC)
PEMS.......... Paris Evangelical Missions Society (MAR)
PEN............. International PEN [*Poets, Playwrights, Essayists, Editors, and Novelists*] (EA)
PEN............. Panellinios Enosis Navton [*Panhellenic Seamen's Union*] (GC)
PEN............. Pankypriaki Ethniki Neolaia [*Pan-Cyprian Nationalist Youth*] (GC)
PEN............. Parti de l'Entente Nationale (MAR)
PEN............. Penang City [*Malaysia*] (ML)
Pen............. Peninsula [*Peninsula*] [*Spanish*] (NAU)
PEN............. Penolong [*Assistant*] (ML)
PEN............. Pnevmatiki Estia Nikaias [*Nikaia Cultural Home*] [*Greek*] (GC)
PEN............. Poder Ejecutivo National [*National Executive Body*] [*Argentine*] (LA)
PENAD........ Penerangan Angkatan Darat [*Army Information Office*] (IN)
PEND........... Low-Pressure Polyethylene (RU)
PENE........... Panellinios Ethniki Navtergatiki Enosis [*Panhellenic National Maritime Workers Union*] (GC)
PENEN........ Panellinios Enosis Navtomageiron Emborikis Navtilias "O Agios Spyridon" [*Panhellenic Union of Merchant Marine Cooks*] (GC)
PENEN........ Panellinios Enosis Navton Emborikis Navtilias [*Panhellenic Union of Merchant Marine Seamen*] (GC)
pen'k trep... Hemp Mill [*Topography*] (RU)
PENP........... Partiia Edinstva i Natsional'novo Progressa (MAR)
PENPRES.... Penetapan Presiden [*Presidential Decision*] (IN)
PENS........... Partido Espanol Nacional Socialista [*Spanish National Socialist Party*] (WER)
pent............ Pentek [*Friday*] (HU)
Penz............ Penza Railroad (RU)
Penzig......... Penzforgalmi Igazgatosag [*Directorate of Money Circulation*] (HU)
Penzkhimmash... Penza Chemical Machinery Plant (RU)
Penzmash... Penza Machinery Plant (RU)
PEO............. Economic Planning Department (RU)
PEO............. Pankyprios Ergatiki Omospondia [*or Pankypriaki Ergatiki Omospondia*] [*Pan-Cyprian Labor Federation*] (GC)
PEOIATA..... Panellinios Ethniki Omospondia Idioktiton Avtokiniton Taxi kai Agoraion [*Panhellenic National Federation of Owners of Taxis and Vehicles for Hire*] (GC)
PEOM......... Pankypria Ethniki Organosis Mathiton [*Pan-Cyprian National Students Organization*] (GC)
PEON.......... Pankyprios Ethniki Organosis Neolaias [*or Pankyprios Ethniki Organosis Neon*] [*Pan-Cyprian National Youth Organization*] (GC)
PEOPEF...... Panellinios Enosis Oikogeneion Politikon Exoriston kai Fylakismenon [*Panhellenic Union of Families of Political Exiles and Prisoners*] (GC)
PEP............ Converter of Electrical Quantities [*Computers*] (RU)
PEP............ Field Evacuation Station (RU)
PEP............ Pankyprios Epitropi Prosfygon [*Pan-Cyprian Refugee Committee*] (GC)
PEP............ Parti d'Emancipation Populaire (MAR)
PEP............ Parti Evangelique Populaire [*Popular Protestant Party*] [*Swiss*] (PPE)
PEP............ Preduzece za Eksploataciju Pristanista [*Harbor Exploitation Establishment*] (YU)
PEP............ Recurrent Representation Elements [*Cybernetics*] (RU)
PEP............ State All-Union Planning Institute for the Planning of Construction of Industrial Heat and Electric Power Plants for Supplying Power to Industrial Establishments in All Branches of the National Economy (RU)
PeP............ Statni Pedagogicka Knihovna v Praze [*State Pedagogical Library in Prague*] (CZ)
PEPEN........ Panellinios Enosis Ploiarkhon Emborikis Navtilias [*Panhellenic Union of Merchant Marine Masters*] (GC)
PEPEN (PT)... Panellinios Enosis Ploiarkhon Emborikis Navtilias (Pasis Taxeos) [*Panhellenic Union of Merchant Marine Masters (of All Classes)*] (GC1)
PEPESCA... Empresa Pesquera Mixta del Peru [*Peruvian Mixed Fisheries Enterprise*] (LA)
PEPG.......... Pankyprios Enosis Proodevtikon Gynaikon [*Pan-Cyprian Union of Progressive Women*] (GC)
Pepre.......... Pepiniere [*Nursery Garden*] [*Military map abbreviation*] [*World War I*] [*French*] (MTD)
PEPU.......... Protectorate Education Progress Union (MAR)
PEQUIVEN... Petroquimica de Venezuela, CA [*Petrochemical Company of Venezuela*] (LA)
Per............. Alternating Light [*Nautical term*] (RU)
per............. Binding (RU)
per............. Bystreet, Lane, Alley [*Topography*] (RU)
Per............. Ferry, Water-Crossing Point [*Topography*] (RU)
Per............. Mountain Pass [*Topography*] (RU)
PER............ Perikatan [*Alliance*] (ML)
per............. Period (RU)
PER............ Peru [*Three-letter standard code*] (CNC)
PER............ Przedsiebiorstwa Elektryfikacji Rolnictwa [*Agriculture Electrification Enterprises*] (POL)
per............. Transitive [*Grammar*] (RU)
per............. Translation, Translator (RU)
PER............ Transmitter (RU)
PERAKU...... Pergerakan Rakyat Kalimantan Utara [*North Kalimantan People's Movement*] (ML)
Perap.......... Perapohjola [*Finnish*]
PERBARA... Perhimpunan Bangsa-Bangsa Asia Tenggara [*Association of South East Asian Nations (ASEAN)*] (IN)
PERBUM..... Persatuan Buruh Minjak [*Oil Workers Union*] (IN)
percent....... Per Centum [*By the Hundred*] [*Latin*] (GPO)
pereizd........ Reprint, Reprinted (RU)
perek........... Shoal [*Topography*] (RU)
perekh........ Transitive (Verb) (RU)
perem......... Alternating (Current) (RU)
peren.......... Figurative (Sense) (RU)
perepech.... Reprinted (RU)
perepl......... Binding (RU)
perer........... Revised [*Bibliography*] (RU)
peresm........ Reviewed, Revised (RU)
perev.......... Translation, Translator (RU)
perf............ Perfekti [*Perfect Tense*] [*Finnish*]
Per Gr Pr..... Alternating Group-Flashing Light [*Nautical term*] (RU)
Per Gr Zatm... Alternating Group-Occulting Light [*Nautical term*] (RU)
PERHIMI...... Perhimpunan Mahasiswa Indonesia [*Indonesia College Students Association*] (IN)
period........ Periodic, Periodical, Recurring (RU)
period........ Periodical (BU)
period dr..... Repeating Decimal, Recurring Decimal (RU)
periodich.... Periodic, Intermittent (RU)
PERKAPPEN... Persatuan Karyawan Perusahaan Perkebunan Negara [*Association of Employees of State Plantations*] (IN)
PERKATEXI... Persatuan Karyawan Textil Indonesia [*Indonesian Textile Workers Union*] (IN)
PERKIM....... Pertubohan Kebajikan Islam Malaysia [*Malaysian Muslim Welfare Organization*] (ML)
PERMINA.... Pertambangan Minjak Nasional [*National Oil Company*] (IN)
PermNIUI.... Perm' Scientific Research Institute of Coal (RU)
PERNAS...... Perbadanan National [*National Corporation*] (ML)
PERNIDA..... Perniagaan dan Perdagangan (Sharikat) [*Trade and Commerce Company*] (ML)

PERP .... Load Transfer Point (RU)
PERP .... Programma Elenkhou Rypanseos Perivallondos [*Pollution and Environment Control Program*] (GC1)
Per P Gr Pr ... Alternating Fixed Light with a Group of Flashes [*Nautical term*] (RU)
Per P Pr .... Alternating Fixed Light with Flashes [*Nautical term*] (RU)
Per Pr .... Alternating Flashing Light [*Nautical term*] (RU)
PERPRES .... Peraturan Presiden [*Presidential Ordinance*] (IN)
Pers .... Persembe [*Thursday*] (TU)
pers .... Persiaa [*or Persiaksi*] [*Finnish*]
pers .... Persialainen [*Finnish*]
pers .... Persian (BU)
pers .... Persian (RU)
PERS .... Personnel Dairesi Genel Mudurlugu [*Personnel Office Directorate General*] [*of Foreign Affairs Ministry*] (TU)
pers .... Persoona [*Finnish*]
PERSAGI ..... Persatuan Ahli Gizi Indonesia
Persa-Is .... Perde ve Sahne Sanatcilari Sendikasi [*Screen and Stage Artists Union*] (TU)
PERSIT .... Persatuan Isteri Tentara [*Army Wives Association*] (IN)
pers pron .... Persoonapronomini [*Personal Pronoun*] [*Finnish*]
PERTAMA ... Perkumpulan Tenaga Utama [*Association of Eminent Persons*] [*Malaysian*] (ML)
PERTAMIN ... Pertambangan Minjak Indonesia [*Indonesian Oil Company*] (IN)
PERTAMINA ... Pertambangan Minjak dan Gas Bumi Nasional [*National Oil and Natural Gas Company*] (IN)
PERTAS ...... Perakende Giyim ve Tuketim Maddeleri Ticaret ve Sanayii [*Retail Wearing Apparel and Consumer Articles Industry and Trade Corp.*] (TU)
PERTI .... Persatuan Tarbijah Islamijah [*Islamic Education Union (Political party)*] (IN)
perv .... Originally (RU)
perv .... Primary, Initial (RU)
pervonach .. Originally (RU)
PERZA .... Sistema de Control Periodo de Zafra [*Sugar Harvest Period Control System*] [*Cuban*] (LA)
Per Ztm .... Alternating Occulting Light [*Nautical term*] (RU)
per zv .... Variable Star (RU)
PES .... Economic Planning Sector (RU)
PES .... Mobile Electric Power Plant (RU)
PES .... Peak-Load Electric Power Plant (RU)
pes .... Per Esempio [*For Example*] [*Italian*]
PES .... Plastiques et Elastomeres du Senegal (MAR)
PES .... Politicka Ekonomie Socialismu [*Political Economics of Socialism*] (CZ)
Pes .... Sand [*Topography*] (RU)
pes .... Sandy [*Topography*] (RU)
PES .... Tidal Electric Power Plant (RU)
PESCAPERU ... Empresa Publica de Produccion de Harina y Aceite de Pescado [*State Fishmeal and Fish Oil Production Agency*] [*Peruvian*] (LA)
PESCOCEAN ... Pesca Oceanica Ecuatoriana [*Ecuadorean Fishing Enterprise*] (LA)
PESCONSA ... Pesquerias Espanoles Sovieticos Conjuntos [*Soviet-Spanish Joint Fisheries, Inc.*] [*Spanish*] (WER)
PESD .... Moderate-Pressure Polyethylene (RU)
PESEA .... Panellinios Enosis Syndesmon Ethnikis Andistaseos [*Panhellenic Union of National Resistance Associations*] (GC)
PESEDE .... Panellinios Enosis Syndesmon Ergolipton Dimosion Ergon [*Panhellenic Union of Public Works Contractors Associations*] (GC)
PESEN .... Panellinios Enosis Syndaxioukhon Emborikou Navtikou [*Panhellenic Union of Merchant Marine Pensioners*] (GC)
PESESY ...... Syndekhnia Ypallilon Symvoulion Ydatopromitheias [*Union of Water Supply Boards Employees*] [*Cypriot*] (GC)
Peshch .... Cave, Cavern [*Topography*] (RU)
PESI .... Panellinia Enosi Sofronistikon Idrymaton [*Panhellenic Union of Correctional Institutions*] (GC1)
PESINE .... Aluminum of Greece Corporation (GC1)
PESK .... Panellinios Epitropi Symbarastaseos Kyprou [*Panhellenic Committee for Aid to Cyprus*] (GC)
PESLA .... Pekarsko Slasticarska Nabavna Zadruga [*Bakery and Cake Supply Cooperative*] (YU)
PESN .... Panellinios Ergazomeni kai Spoudazousa Neolaia [*Panhellenic Working and Studying Youth*] (GC)
PESP .... Pankypriaki Elliniki Sosialistiki Profylaki [*Pan-Cyprian Greek Socialist Vanguard*] (GC)
PESP .... Proodevtiki Ergatiki Syndikalistiki Parataxi [*Workers Progressive Trade Union Faction*] [*Greek*] (GC)
PESPEF .... Panellinios Enosis Syngenon Politikon Exoriston kai Fylakismenon [*Panhellenic Union of Relatives of Political Exiles and Prisoners*] (GC)
PESU- .... Electropneumatic Signal Device (RU)
PET .... People's Experimental Theatre (MAR)
pet .... Petiitti(a) [*Finnish*]
PET .... Politiets Efterretningstjeneste [*Police Intelligence Service*] [*Danish*] (WEN)
PET .... Przepisy Eksploatacji Technicznej [*Rules for Technical Operation*] (POL)
PETA .... Pemuda Tanah Ayer [*National Youth Association*] [*Malayan*] (ML)
PETANI .... Persatuan Tani Nasional Indonesia [*Indonesian National Farmers Union*] (IN)
PETAS .... Plastik Endustri ve Ticaret Anonim Sirketi [*Plastic Industry and Trade Corporation*] (TU)
PETF .... Polyethylene Terephthalate (RU)
PETGAZ ...... Turkiye Petrol ve Urunleri Sanayii Nakil ve Satis Iscileri Sendikasi [*Turkish Petroleum and Products Industry Transport and Sales Workers Union*] (TU)
PETh .... Panellinios Enosis Thalamipolon [*Panhellenic Union of Stewards*] (GC)
PETh .... Pronoia Ergaton Thalassis [*Maritime Workers Welfare*] [*Greek*] (GC)
PEThGK ...... Panellinios Enosis Thimaton Germanikis Katokhis "O Foinix" [*"Phoenix" Panhellenic Union of Victims of the German Occupation*] (GC)
PEThTh .... O Stefenson Panellinios Enosis Thermaston Thalassis [*Panhellenic Union of Sea Stokers*] (GC)
PETKIM .... Petrokimya Anonim Sirketi [*Petrochemical Corporation*] (TU)
PETKIM-IS ... Petroleum and Chemical Workers Union (TU)
PETO .... Petrol Ofisi [*Turkish Petroleum Office*] (TU)
petr .... Petrographic (RU)
PETRANGOL ... Companhia de Petroleos de Angola [*Angola Petroleum Company*] (AF)
petr ef .... Petroleum Ether (RU)
PETRIN .... Petrographic Institute (of the Academy of Sciences, USSR) (RU)
PETROBRAS ... Petroleo Brasileiro SA [*Brazilian Petroleum Corporation*] (LA)
PETROCHIM ... Intreprinderea Petrochimica [*Petrochemical Enterprise*] (RO)
PETROCI ..... Societe Nationale d'Operations Petrolieres de la Cote-d'Ivoire [*Ivorian Petroleum Company*] (AF)
PETROCID ... Petromin Sulphuric Acid Plant (MAR)
PETROGAB ... Societe Nationale des Petroles Gabonais (MAR)
PETROLBER ... Petrolkemiai Beruhazasi Vallalat [*Petrochemical Investment Enterprise*] (HU)
PETROLGAS ... Petroleum and Gas Equipment Establishment [*Belgrade*] (YU)
Petrol-Is ...... Turkiye Petrol, Kimya, Azot, ve Atom Iscileri Sendikasi [*Turkish Petroleum, Chemical, Nitrogen, and Atomic Workers Union*] (TU)
PETROMAD ... Compagnie Malgache de Transports Petroliers (MAR)
PETROPAR ... Societe de Participations Petrolieres [*North African*] (MAR)
PETROPERU ... Petroleras de Peru [*State Petroleum Agency*] [*Peruvian*] (LA)
PETROQUISA ... PETROBRAS Quimica, Sociedade Anonima [*PETROBRAS Chemical Corporation*] [*Brazilian*] (LA)
PETROVEN ... Petroleos de Venezuela, SA [*Venezuelan Petroleum, Inc.*] (LA)
PETT .... Professeurs d'Enseignement Technique Theorique [*Theoretical Technical Education Teachers*] [*Senegalese*] (AF)
PETV .... Program for Educational Television (MAR)
pet vit .... Petit Vitesse [*Slow Speed*] [*Correspondence*] [*French*]
PEU .... Economic Planning Administration (RU)
PEU .... Epidemic Control Administration (RU)
PEU .... Steam Power Plant [*Nautical term*] (RU)
PEV .... Enameled, Moisture-Resistant, Wire-Wound (Resistor) (RU)
PEV .... Panellinios Enosis Vasilofronon [*Panhellenic Union of Royalists*] (GC)
PEV .... Programme Elargi de Vaccination [*Expanded Vaccination Program*] [*Zairian*] (AF)
PEVA .... Piyasa Etud ve Arastirma Burosu [*Market Study and Research Bureau*] (TU)
PEVD .... High-Pressure Polyethylene (RU)
PEVD .... Panellinion Kinima Vasilevomenis Dimokratias [*Panhellenic Movement for a Royalist Republic*] (GC)
PEVEV .... Panellinios Ethniki Vasiliki Enosi Voreioelladiton [*Panhellenic National Royalist Union of Northern Greeks*] (GC)
PEVR .... Enameled, Moisture-Resistant, Adjustable Wire-Wound (Resistor) (RU)
PEVT .... Direct, Enameled, Heat-Resistant Wire-Wound (Resistor) (RU)
PEWC .... Public Electricity and Water Corporation [*Sudanese*] (MAR)
pex .... Par Exemple [*For Example*] [*French*] (GPO)
PEYAK .... Personel Yardimlasma Kooperatifi Ltd. [*Personnel Mutual Aid Cooperatives Corp.*] [*Cypriot*] (TU)
PEYKE .... Panellinios Enosis Ypallilon Kinimatografikon Epikheiriseon [*Panhellenic Union of Employees of Motion Picture Enterprises*] (GC)
Pez .... Pezikon [*Infantry*] (GC)
PEZ .... Recurrent Sign Elements [*Cybernetics*] (RU)
Pezetcha ..... Przemyslowo-Handlowa Zaklady Chemiczne [*Industrial and Commercial Chemical Establishments*] (POL)
Pezetgees ... Powiatowy Zwiazek Gminnych Spoldzielni [*County Union of Rural Communal Cooperatives*] (POL)
PEZh .... Power and Damage Control Station [*Navy*] (RU)
PEZZ .... Poljoprivredna Ekonomija Zemljoradnicke Zadruge [*Farm Economy of Agricultural Cooperatives*] (YU)
PF .... Band Filter, Band-Pass Filter (RU)
PF .... Field Fortifications (Manual) (RU)
PF .... French Polynesia [*Two-letter standard code*] (CNC)

PF............... High-Explosive Cartridge (RU)
pf............... Pafta [*Section (of a map)*] (TU)
pf............... Pancelos Fegyvernem [*Armored Forces*] (HU)
PF............... Patriotic Front [*Zimbabwean*] (PPW)
pf............... Penzugyi Felugyelo [*Financial Inspector, Treasury Inspector*] (HU)
pf............... Perfelvetel [*Appearance (In the court)*] (HU)
Pf............... Pfarre [*German*]
Pf............... Pfarrexpositur [*German*]
Pf............... Pfennig [*Penny*] [*German*] (GPO)
pf............... Pfennigi(a) [*Finnish*]
Pf............... Pferd [*Horsepower*] [*German*]
Pf............... Pfund [*Pound*] [*German*]
PF............... Phase-Reversing Switch (RU)
pf............... Picofarad (BU)
pf............... Picofarad (RU)
pF............... Pikofarad [*Picofarad*] [*Polish*]
PF............... Plasticizer, Softener (RU)
PF............... Polar Front (RU)
PF............... Polisario Front [*Popular Front for the Liberation of Saguia El Hamra and Rio De Oro*] [*Moroccan*] (PD)
PF............... Poljoprivredni Fakultet [*Faculty of Agriculture*] (YU)
PF............... Polyphenylene (RU)
Pf............... Postfach [*Post Office Box*] [*German*] (CED)
pf............... Pour Feliciter [*To Congratulate*] [*French*]
PF............... Poverenictvo pre Financie [*Office of the Commissioner of Finance*] (CZ)
PF............... Pravni Fakultet [*Faculty of Law*] (YU)
PF............... Prefecture [*Prefecture*] [*Military map abbreviation*] [*World War I*] [*French*] (MTD)
PF............... Prefilter (RU)
PF............... Puncher (RU)
PF............... Pyrophosphate (RU)
PF............... Underwater Lamp (RU)
pf............... Vertical Photography [*Aviation*] (RU)
PFA............... Parti Federaliste Africain (MAR)
PFA............... Parti de la Federation Africaine (MAR)
PFA............... Penang Football Association (ML)
PFA............... Perak Football Association (ML)
PFA............... Polyformaldehyde (RU)
PFA............... Produktionsfondsabgabe [*Production Fund Tax*] (EG)
PFAC............... Parti Federal de l'Afrique Centrale (MAR)
Pfadm............... Pfarradministrator [*German*]
PFAE............... Panstwowa Fabryka Aparatow Elektrycznych [*State Electrical Equipment Factory*] (POL)
PFB............... Advance Front Logistical Installation (BU)
PFB............... Advanced Frontline Base (RU)
PFB............... Panstwowa Filharmonia Baltycka [*State Baltic Philharmonic Orchestras*] (POL)
PFB............... Partei Freier Buerger [*Free Citizens' Party*] [*West German*] (PPW)
PFCI............... Peche et Froid de Cote-d'Ivoire (MAR)
PFD............... Demodulator Band Filter (RU)
Pfd............... Pfund [*Pound*] [*Money, weight*] [*German*]
PFD............... Protovathmion Forologikon Dikastirion [*First Instance Tax Court*] [*Greek*] (GC)
p fel............... Penzugyi Felugyelo [*Financial Inspector, Treasury Inspector*] (HU)
PfExPrv............... Pfarrexcurrendoprovisor [*German*]
PFF............... Police Field Force (ML)
PFFSLD............... Peoples Force Front to Slay Leftist Disestablishmentarianism (MAR)
Pfg............... Pfennig [*Penny*] (EG)
PFI............... Presse Francaise et Internationale [*French and International Press*] (AF)
PFI............... Pyatigorsk Pharmaceutical Institute (RU)
PFK............... Field Physical Therapy Office (RU)
PFK............... Pan-Foititikon Kinima [*Pan-Student Movement*] (GC1)
PFK............... Permanent Finance Commission (BU)
PFKSZ............... Preliminary General Catalog of Fundamental Faint Stars (RU)
PFL............... Laotian Patriotic Front (RU)
Pfl............... Pflanze [*Plant*] [*German*]
PFL............... Placi Fibrolemnoase [*Fiberboard*] (RO)
PFLE............... Popular Front for the Liberation of Eritrea [*Ethiopian*] (AF)
PFLKh............... Polyphenol from Wood Chemicals (RU)
PFLM............... People's Forces for the Liberation of Mozambique (MAR)
PFLO............... Popular Front for the Liberation of Oman (PD)
PFLOAG............... Popular Front for the Liberation of Oman and the Arabian Gulf (PD)
PFLP............... Popular Front for the Liberation of Palestine (PD)
PFLP-GC............... Popular Front for the Liberation of Palestine - General Command (PD)
PFM............... Modulator Band Filter (RU)
PFN............... Parti des Forces Nouvelles [*New Forces Party*] [*French*] (PPW)
PFO............... Financial Planning Department (RU)
PFO............... Ration and Forage Section [*Military term*] (RU)
PFP............... Pakistan Trade-Union Federation (RU)
PFP............... Popular Front Party [*Ghanaian*] (PPW)
PFP............... Porcelain and Faience Industry (BU)
PFP............... Progressiewe Federale Party [*Progressive Federal Party*] [*South African*] (PPW)
Pfprv............... Pfarrprovisor [*German*]
Pfr............... Pfarrer [*German*]
Pfrexprv............... Pfarrexcurrendoprovisor [*German*]
Pfrmprv............... Pfarrmitprovisor [*German*]
Pfrmvk............... Pfarrmitvikar [*German*]
PFS............... Farm Crop Rotation (RU)
PFS............... Pakistan Foreign Service (CL)
PFS............... Panellinios Farmakevtikos Syllogos [*Panhellenic Pharmaceutical Society*] (GC)
PFS............... Pankyprios Farmakevtikos Syndesmos [*Pan-Cyprian Pharmaceutical Society*] (GC)
PFS............... Projector for Facade Illumination, Floodlight (RU)
PFS............... Ration and Forage Supply (RU)
PFS............... Ration and Forage Supply Depot (RU)
pfsa............... Pour Faire Ses Adieux [*To Say Goodbye*] [*French*] (GPO)
PFSh............... Partia Fashismit e Shqiperise [*Fascist Party of Albania*] (PPE)
PFSJ............... Panstwowa Fabryka Sztucznego Jedwabiu [*State Artificial Silk Factory*] (POL)
PFU............... Functional Block Using Film Circuits (RU)
PFU............... Parti Feministe Unifie [*Unified Women's Party*] [*Belgian*] (WER)
PFUM............... Pabianicka Fabryka Urzadzen Mechanicznych [*Pabianice Machine Tool Factory*] (POL)
PFV............... Pomoc Francuske Vlade [*French Government Economic Aid*] [*Tripartite Aid Program*] (YU)
pfv............... Pour Faire Visite [*To Make a Call*] [*French*]
PfVk............... Pfarrvikar [*German*]
PFVI............... Pomoc Francuske Vlade u Hrani [*Aid of French Government in Food*] (YU)
Pfvw............... Pfarrverweser [*German*]
PfVwes............... Pfarrverweser [*German*]
pfvzo............... Palyafelvigyazo [*Track Watchman*] (HU)
PFZ............... Panstwowy Fundusz Ziemi [*State Land Fund*] (POL)
PFZ............... Patrioticheskii Front Zimbabve (MAR)
PFZ............... Polni Frontove Zabezpeceni [*Frontline Field Support*] (CZ)
PFZ............... Post- und Fernmeldetechniches Zentralamt [*Central Office for Postal and Telecommunications Operations*] (EG)
PFZA............... Panstwowa Fabryka Zwiazkow Azotowych (w Chorzowie) [*State Nitrogen Compound Factory (in Chorzow)*] (POL)
PF-ZAPU............... Patriotic Front - Zimbabwe African People's Union (PD)
PG............... Antitank Grenade (RU)
PG............... Carrier Pigeon, Homing Pigeon (RU)
PG-............... Clamshell Loader, Grab Loader [*Mining*] (RU)
PG............... Field Hospital (RU)
PG............... Flash Absorber, Flash Eliminator, Flash Suppressor [*Artillery*] (RU)
PG............... Foam Generator (RU)
PG............... Hydraulic Press (RU)
pg............... Last Year (RU)
PG............... Machine-Gun Nest (RU)
PG............... Papua New Guinea [*Two-letter standard code*] (CNC)
PG............... Partido Galleguista [*Galician Party*] [*Spanish*] (WER)
PG............... Partido Garriques [*Garriques Party*] [*Spanish*] (WER)
PG............... Penang (ML)
Pg............... Peso Guineen (MAR)
Pg............... Petrograd (RU)
PG............... Piece Gauche [*In a turret*] [*Military*] [*French*] (MTD)
PG............... Pigment Granule (RU)
PG............... Pneumogram (RU)
PG............... Pokretna Grupa [*Mobile Group*] [*Military*] (YU)
PG............... Politechnika Gdanska [*Gdansk Polytechnical School*] (POL)
PG............... Politikon Grafeion [*Politburo*] (GC)
PG............... Post-Grado [*Spanish*]
PG............... Prisonnier de Guerre [*Prisoner of War*] [*French*]
PG............... Procuratore Generale [*Attorney General*] [*Italian*] (WER)
PG............... Produktionsgenossenschaft [*Producer Cooperative*] (EG)
PG............... Propyl Gallate (RU)
pg............... Przez Grzecznosc [*Polish*]
PG............... Pyrolytic Graphite (RU)
PG............... Steam Generator (BU)
PG............... Steam Generator [*Nuclear physics and engineering*] (RU)
PG............... Trigger Generator (RU)
PGA............... Mobile Army Group (RU)
PGA............... Press Gallery Association (MAR)
PGAP............... Pneudraulic Autopilot (RU)
PGAP............... Poleodomikon Grafeion Athinon kai Perikhoron [*City Planning Office of Athens and Suburbs*] (GC)
PGB............... Panglima Gagah Berani [*Federation Gallantry Decoration*] [*Malaysian*] (ML)
PGB............... Pusat Gerakan Bersama [*Joint Operations Center*] (ML)
pgd og............... Normal Barrage (BU)
Pge............... Passage [*Passage*] [*Military map abbreviation*] [*World War I*] [*French*] (MTD)
P Gen............... Parc du Genie [*Military*] [*French*] (MTD)
P Gen A............... Parc du Genie d'Armee [*Military*] [*French*] (MTD)
PGG............... Piston Gas Generator (RU)
PGG............... Przemysl Guzikarsko-Galanteryjny [*Haberdashery Goods Industry*] (POL)
PGG............... Steam and Gas Generator (RU)
PGH............... Pengarah [*Director*] (ML)
PGH............... Produktionsgenossenschaft des Handwerks [*Artisan Producer Cooperative*] (EG)

PGI .... Partido Gallego Independiente [*Independent Galician Party*] [*Spanish*] (WER)
PGI .... Partido Galleguista de Izquierdas [*Galician Leftist Party*] [*Spanish*] (WER)
PGI .... Polar Geophysical Institute (of the Kola Branch of the Academy of Sciences, USSR) (RU)
Pgio .... Poggio [*Mound, Small Hill*] [*Italian*] (NAU)
PGJDF .... Procuraduria General de Justicia del Distrito Federal [*Federal District Attorney General's Office*] [*Mexican*] (LA)
PGK .... Pflanzungsgesellschaft Kpeme (MAR)
PGK .... Proodevtiki Gynaikeia Kinisi [*Progressive Women's Movement*] [*Cypriot*] (GC)
PGKU .... Pasukan Gerilja Kalimantan Utara [*North Kalimantan Guerrilla Force*] (IN)
PGL .... Panstwowe Gospodarstwa Lesne [*State Forest Properties*] (POL)
PGI .... Politechnika Gliwicka [*Engineering College of Gliwice*] [*Polish*]
PGL .... Proodevtikai Gynaikai Larnakos [*Progressive Women of Larnaca*] (GC)
PGI .... Prosvetni Glasnik [*Educational Bulletin*] [*Belgrade*] [*A publication*] (YU)
PGM .... Plovdiv City Museum (BU)
Pg(M) .... Posgraduacao (Mestrado) [*Academic degree*] [*Portuguese*]
PGMO .... Poltava Gravimetric Observatory (RU)
PGN .... Procurador General de la Nacion [*National Attorney General*] [*Colombian*] (LA)
PGN .... Procuraduria General de la Nacion [*Office of the National Attorney General*] [*Colombian*] (LA)
PGNP .... Pedal-Operated Parametric Generator (RU)
PGO .... Polar Geophysical Observatory (RU)
PGO .... Poltava Gravimetric Observatory (RU)
PGP .... Maximal Annual Penetration [*Radioactivity*] (BU)
PGP .... Pomorsko Gradevno Preduzece [*Maritime Construction Establishment*] (YU)
PGPN .... Przedsiebiorstwo Geofizyki Przemyslu Naftowego [*Geophysical Enterprise of the Petroleum Industry*] (POL)
PGPP .... State Contract and Delivery Regulations (RU)
PGR .... Field Radiometer for Gamma-Beta Radiation (RU)
PGR .... Panstwowe Gospodarstwa Rolne [*State Farms*] (POL)
PGR .... Procurador General Regional [*Regional Attorney General*] [*Colombian*] (LA)
PGR .... Procuradoria General Regional [*Office of the Regional Attorney General*] [*Colombian*] (LA)
PGRI .... Persatuan Guru Republik Indonesia [*Republic of Indonesia Teachers Union*] (IN)
PGRK- .... Field Logging Radiometer for Gamma-Beta Radiation (RU)
PGRKU .... Pasokan Gerilya Kalimantan Utara [*North Kalimantan Guerrilla Forces*] [*Formerly, PGRS, changed June 1970 to conform with new CPNK, Communist Party of North Kalimantan*] (ML)
PGRM .... Parti Gerakan Rakyat Malaysia [*Malaysian People's Movement Party*] (PPW)
P Gr Pr .... Fixed Light with a Group of Flashes [*Nautical term*] (RU)
PGRS .... Oil-Field Gas-Control Station (RU)
PGRS .... Pasokan Gerilya Rakyat Sarawak [*Sarawak People's Guerrilla Forces*] [*Replaced by PGRKU*] (ML)
PG Ryb .... Panstwowe Gospodarstwa Rybackie [*State Fishing Farms*] [*Polish*]
PGS .... Battle Position, Battle Zone (RU)
pg s .... Frontier Sector (BU)
PGS .... Industrial Loudspeaker Communications (RU)
PGS .... Panellinios Gymnastikos Syllogos [*Panhellenic Gymnastic Club*] (GC)
PGS .... Panionios Gymnastikos Syllogos [*Pan-Ionian Gymnastic Club*] [*Greek*] (GC)
PGS .... Pravila Garnizonske Sluzbe [*Garrison Service Rules*] (YU)
PGSD .... Partido Galego Social-Democrata [*Galician Social Democratic Party*] [*Spanish*] (WER)
PGSDN .... Partido Galego Social-Democrata Nacionalista [*Nationalist Social Democratic Galician Party*] [*Spanish*] (WER)
PGT .... Micarta-Textolite Plastic (RU)
PGT .... Partido Guatemalteco del Trabajo [*Guatemalan Labor Party*] (PD)
PGT .... Pasukan Gerak Tjepat [*Strike Troops (Air Force paratroops)*] (IN)
PGT .... Plus Gravement Touches (MAR)
PGT .... Urban-Type Settlement (RU)
PGTV .... Pecsi Geodeziai es Terkepeszeti Vallalat [*Geodesic and Cartographic Enterprise of Pecs*] (HU)
PGU .... Intercommunication Loudspeaker System (RU)
PGU .... Mobile Hydraulic Excavator [*Min.*] (RU)
PGU .... Perm' State University Imeni A. M. Gor'kiy (RU)
PGU .... Underground Gasification of Coal (RU)
PGU .... Universal Hydraulic Blowout Preventer [*Pet.*] (RU)
PGV .... Checking Vertical-Flight Gyroscope (RU)
PGV .... Privatgueterwagen-Vorschriften [*Regulations for Private Freight Cars*] (EG)
PGZA .... Pravila Gadanja Zemaljske Artiljerije [*Ground Artillery Fire Rules*] (YU)
PH .... Paedagogische Hochschule [*Advanced School for Teacher Training*] (EG)
ph .... Pecset Helye [*Seal*] (HU)
Ph .... Phare [*Lighthouse*] [*Military map abbreviation*] [*World War I*] [*French*] (MTD)
PH .... Philippines [*Two-letter standard code*] (CNC)
ph .... Plus Haut [*French*]
ph .... Postahivatal [*Post Office*] (HU)
PH .... Pre Hrista [*Before Christ*] (YU)
PH .... Produktionsmittelhandel [*Trade in Production Equipment*] (EG)
PH .... Pruzkumna Hlidka [*Reconnaissance Patrol*] (CZ)
pH .... Wasserstoffexponent [*Hydrogen Exponent*] [*German*]
Pharm .... Pharmazie [*German*]
Pharma .... Pharmazeutische Industrie (VVB) [*Pharmaceutical Industry (VVB)*] (EG)
PHARMARIN ... Office National de Pharmacie [*Mauritanian*] (MAR)
PHARMEX ... Pharmaceutical Import Company [*Syrian*] (ME)
PHARMEX ... Public Organization for the Import of Specialized Pharmaceuticals (MAR)
PHB .... Perhubungan [*Communications*] (IN)
PhB .... Philosophiae Baccalaureus [*Bachelor of Philosophy*] [*Latin*] (GPO)
PHCI .... Plantations et Huileries de Cote-d'Ivoire [*Ivory Coast Plantations and Oil Works*] (AF)
PHCP .... Primary Health Care Programme (MAR)
PhDr .... Doctor Philosofiae [*Doctor of Philosophy (PhD)*] (CZ)
PhDr .... Doctor of Philosophy [*Czechoslovak*]
PhDr .... Doktor der Philosophie [*German*]
PHG .... Pahang (ML)
phil .... Philosophisch [*German*]
philol .... Philologisch [*German*]
philos .... Philosophisch [*German*]
PHL .... Philippines [*Three-letter standard code*] (CNC)
PHM .... Pohonne Hmoty a Mazadla [*Petroleum Products and Lubricants*] (CZ)
PhMr .... Magister Farmaciae [*Pharmacist (Academic degree)*] (CZ)
PHP .... Plantations du Haut-Penja (MAR)
PHR .... Peloton hors Range [*Military*] [*French*] (MTD)
PHSch .... Parteihochschule "Karl Marx" der SED [*"Karl Marx" Party Advanced School of the SED*] (EG)
PHSR .... Przedsiebiorstwo Handlu Sprzetem Rolniczym [*Farm Equipment Trade Enterprise*] (POL)
PHU .... Postovni Hospodarska Ustredna [*Central Postal Management Office*] (CZ)
phys .... Physikal [*or Physikalisch*] [*Physical*] [*German*]
Phys .... Physikat [*or Physikus*] [*German*]
physik .... Physikal [*or Physikalisch*] [*Physical*] [*German*]
PHZ .... Plan Hmotneho Zasobovani [*Materiel Procurement Plan*] (CZ)
Phz .... Presskohlenheizung [*Briquette Heating*] (EG)
PHZ .... Protivhemiska Zastita [*Antichemical Defense*] [*Military*] (YU)
PHZ .... Przedsiebiorstwo Handlu Zagranicznego [*Foreign Trade Enterprise*] (POL)
PI .... Design Institute (BU)
PI .... Filipiny [*Philippines*] [*Polish*]
PI .... Information Transmission Device (RU)
PI .... Institute of Paleontology (RU)
PI .... Intermediate Total (RU)
PI .... Paedagogisches Institut [*Pedagogical Institute*] (EG)
pi .... Palaion Imerologion [*Old Calendar*] (GC)
PI .... Paracel Islands [*Two-letter standard code*] (CNC)
PI .... Parti Islam [*Islamic Party*] (ML)
PI .... Partido Intransigente [*Intransigent Party*] [*Argentine*] (PD)
PI .... Partido Intransigente [*Intransigent Party*] [*Uruguayan*] (LA)
PI .... Paysans Independants (MAR)
PI .... Pazarisen Inspektorat [*Market Inspectorate*] (YU)
PI .... Pedagogiai Intezet [*Pedagogical Institute*] (HU)
PI .... Pedagogical Institute (RU)
PI .... Planning Institute (RU)
PI .... Point Initial [*Military*] [*French*] (MTD)
PI .... Polytechnic Institute (RU)
pi .... Posebno Izdanje [*Special or Separate Edition*] (YU)
PI .... Poverenictvo pre Informacie [*Office of the Commissioner of Information*] (CZ)
PI .... Prehranbena Industrija [*Food Industry*] (YU)
PI .... Preselection, Preselector [*Telephony*] (RU)
PI .... Primary Meter (RU)
PI .... Proportional-Integral (Law) (RU)
PI .... Proportional Integrator (RU)
PI .... Regimental Engineer (RU)
PIA .... Pakistan International Airlines Corp.
PIA .... Polski Instytut Archeologiczny [*Polish Archeological Institute*] (POL)
PIACT .... Program for the Introduction and Adaptation of Contraceptive Technology (MAR)
PIALLO .... Programa Alto Llano Occidental [*Upper Western Plains Program*] [*Venezuelan*] (LA)
PIAN .... Institute of Paleontology of the Academy of Sciences, USSR (RU)
PIANC .... Permanent International Association of Navigation Congresses (EA)
PIAR .... Piyasa Arastirma Merkezi [*Market Research Center*] (TU)

PIAR .... Proyectos Integrales de Asentamiento Rural [*Integral Projects for Rural Settlement*] [*Peruvian*] (LA)
PIARC .... Permanent International Association of Road Congresses [*See also AIPCR*] (EA)
PIAWU .... Printing Industry and Allied Workers Union [*Guyanese*] (LA)
PIB .... Planning and Research Office (RU)
PIB .... Prices and Incomes Board (MAR)
PIB .... Producto Interno Bruto [*Gross Domestic Product*] (LA)
PIB .... Produit Interieur Brut [*North African*] (MAR)
PIB .... Produits Interieurs Bruts [*Gross National Product*] [*Use GNP*] (CL)
PIB .... Pukovska Intendantska Baza [*Regimental Quartermaster Base*] (YU)
PIBAS .... Plastik Ip ve Bant Sanayi ve Tic Anonim Sirketi [*Plastic Cord and Tape Industry and Trade Corporation*] (TU)
PIBD .... Panstwowy Instytut Biologii Doswiadczalnej [*State Institute of Experimental Biology*] (POL)
PIBR .... Pig Industry Board of Rhodesia (MAR)
PIBSL .... Panstwowy Instytut Badania Sztuki Ludowej [*State Institute of Folk Art Research*] (POL)
PIBU .... Parti pour l'Independance du Burundi (MAR)
PIC .... Pecheries Industrielles du Congo [*Congo Industrial Fisheries*] (AF)
PIC .... Petrochemical Industries Company [*Kuwaiti*] (ME)
PIC .... Piping Industrial Contractors Ltda. [*Bogota*] (COL)
PIC .... Planification Industrielle Christian R. Champroux & Cie. (MAR)
PIC .... Plantations Industrielles de Cocotiers (MAR)
PIC .... Police Information Center [*Jamaican*] (LA1)
PIC .... Policia de Investigacao Criminal [*Criminal Investigation Police*] [*Mozambican*] (AF)
PICG .... Programme International de Correlation Geologique [*International Geological Correlation Programme - IGCP*] (EA)
PICO .... Pacific International Company Ltd. (MAR)
PID .... Partido Institucional Democratico [*Democratic Institutional Party*] [*Guatemalan*] (LA)
PID .... Planlama ve Insaat Dairesi [*Planning and Construction Office*] [*Turkish Cypriot*] (GC)
PID .... Planlama ve Insaat Dairesi Karayollari [*Planning and Construction Office of Highways Directorate*] [*Turkish Cypriot*] (GC)
PID .... Proletari in Divisa [*Proletarians in Uniform*] [*Italian*] (WER)
PID .... Provision pour Investissements Diversifies (MAR)
PIDC .... Programme International de Developpement de la Communication (MAR)
PIDE .... Pakistan Institute of Development Economics [*Islamabad*]
PIDE .... Policia Internacional e de Defesa do Estado [*International and State Defense Police*] [*No longer in existence*] [*Portuguese*] (WER)
PIDER .... Programa de Inversiones para el Desarrollo Rural [*Rural Development Investment Program*] [*Mexican*] (LA)
pidgineng ... Pidginenglantia [*Pidgin English*] [*Finnish*]
PIDO .... Problems of History of Precapitalistic Societies [*A publication*] (RU)
PIDO .... Problemy Istorii Dokapitalisticheskikh Obshchestv (MAR)
PID-regulyator ... Proportional-Integral-Differential Controller (RU)
PIDSA .... Population Information and Documentation System for Africa [*Accra, Ghana*]
PIE .... Przedsiebiorstwo Instalacji Elektrycznych [*Electrical Installations Enterprise*] (POL)
PIERT .... Budapesti Papir es Irodaszer Ertekesito Vallalat [*Budapest Trade Enterprise for Stationery and Office Supplies*] (HU)
PIEU .... Pioneer Industries Employees Union (ML)
PIF .... Engineer Field Photographic Laboratory (RU)
PIG .... Floating Integrating Gyroscope (RU)
PIG .... Panstwowy Instytut Geologiczny [*State Geological Institute*] (POL)
PIGM .... Panstwowa Inspekcja Gospodarki Materialowej [*State Inspectorate for the Management of Materials*] (POL)
PIGR .... Prefets Inspecteurs Generaux Regionaux [*Algerian*] (MAR)
PIH .... Panstwowa Inspekcja Handlowa [*State Trade Inspectorate*] (POL)
PIH .... Panstwowy Instytut Higieny [*State Institute of Hygiene*] (POL)
PIHiSIJA ...... Prirodoslovna Istrazivanja Hrvatske i Slavonije, Jugoslavenske Akademije [*National Science Studies of Croatia and Slavonia, Issued by the Yugoslav Academy of Sciences and Arts*] [*Zagreb*] (YU)
PIHM .... Panstwowy Instytut Hydrologiczno-Meteorologiczny [*State Institute of Hydrology and Meteorology*] (POL)
PIHPs .... Panstwowy Instytut Higieny Psychicznej [*State Institute of Mental Hygiene*] (POL)
PIHS .... Panstwowy Instytut Historii Sztuki [*State Institute of the History of Art*] (POL)
PIHZ .... Polska Izba Handlu Zagranicznego [*Polish Chamber of Foreign Trade*] (POL)
PII .... Pemuda Islam Indonesia [*Indonesian Moslem Youth Organization*] (IN)
PIIMM i SKhP ... Planning and Research Institute of the Ministry of Local and Shale-Chemical Industries, ESSR (RU)
PIK .... Panstwowy Instytut Ksiazki [*State Book Institute*] (POL)
PIK .... Planning and Surveying Office (RU)
PIK .... Runway [*Airfield*] (BU)
PIKON .... Film Corrosion Inhibitor for Petroleum-Extracting Equipment (RU)
pikor .... Pioneer Correspondent (RU)
PIKPA .... Patriotikon Idryma Koinonikis Prononias kai Andilipseos [*Patriotic Institute of Social Aid and Welfare*] (GC)
pil .... Pilot [*Pilot*] [*Polish*]
pil .... Pilula [*Pill*] [*Latin*] (GPO)
PIL .... Soil Adhesiveness Meter (RU)
PILCAM .... Societe Camerounaise de Fabrication de Piles Electriques (MAR)
PILOTUR ..... Agencia de Viajes y Turismo [*Bogota*] (COL)
Pilr .... Pilier [*Pillar*] [*Military map abbreviation*] [*World War I*] [*French*] (MTD)
PILSA .... Plastik Sanayi AS [*Plastic Industry Corporation*] (TU)
PIM .... Pahalilik ve Issizlikle Mucadele Dernegi [*Association for the Struggle Against High Prices and Unemployment*] (TU)
PIM .... Panstwowa Inspekcja Materialowa [*State Inspectorate of Materials*] (POL)
PIM .... Panstwowy Instytut Meteorologiczny [*Polish*]
PIM .... Pasokan Infanteri Malaysia [*Malaysian Infantry Regiment*] (ML)
PIM .... Pneumatic Actuator (RU)
PIM .... Principal Infirmier-Major (MAR)
PIM .... Providence Industrial Mission (MAR)
PIM .... Safety Actuator (RU)
PIMAS .... Plastik Insaat Malzemeleri Anonim Sirketi [*Plastic Construction Materials Corporation*] (TU)
PIMat .... Panstwowy Instytut Matematyczny [*State Mathematical Institute*] (POL)
PIME .... Pontificum Institutum Mediolanese pro Missionibus Exteris [*Pontifical Institute for Foreign Missions*] (MAR)
PIN .... Institute of Paleontology (of the Academy of Sciences, USSR) (RU)
PIN .... Partido do Integracao Nacional [*National Integration Party*] [*Brazilian*] (LA1)
PIN .... Programa de Integracao Nacional [*National Integration Program*] [*Brazilian*] (LA)
PIN .... Regulations and Standards for the Construction of Cities (RU)
PINA .... Programa Integrado de Nutricion Aplicada [*Neiva*] (COL)
PINDAD .... Perindustrian Angkatan Darat [*Army Industrial Plant*] (IN)
PING .... Panstwowy Instytut Naukowo-Gospodarczy [*State Economic Research Institute*] (POL)
PINGW .... Panstwowy Instytut Naukowy Gospodarstwa Wiejskiego [*State Research Institute of Rural Economy*] (POL)
PINM .... Planned Building of Settlements (BU)
PINRO .... Polar Scientific Research Institute of Sea Fisheries and Oceanography Imeni N. M. Knipovich (RU)
PINSAL .... Pinturas Salvadorenas, SA [*Salvadoran Paints Corp.*]
PINSER .... Petites Industries Senegalaises Reunies (MAR)
PINSTECH ... Pakistan Institute of Nuclear Science and Technology
PINTUCO .... Pinturas Colombianas [*Bogota*] (COL)
PINU .... Partido de Innovacion y Unidad [*Innovation and Unity Party*] [*Honduran*] (LA)
PIO .... Information Reception from Operator [*Computers*] (RU)
PIO .... Poets International Organisation (EA)
PIO .... Poverenictvo Informacii a Osvety [*Office of the Commissioner of Information and Culture*] (CZ)
pion .... Pioneer (RU)
PIP .... Pan-Iranist Party (PPW)
PiP .... Panstwo i Prawo [*State and Law*] [*A periodical*] (POL)
PIP .... Partido Independentista Puertorriqueno [*Puerto Rican Independence Party*] (PPW)
PIP .... Plantations Industrielles de Palmiers (MAR)
PIP .... Policia de Investigaciones de Peru [*Peruvian Investigative Police*] (LA)
PIP .... Polski Instytut Prasoznawczy [*Polish Press Institute*] (POL)
PIP .... Primary Measuring Instrument (RU)
PIP .... Programa de Inversiones Publicas [*Public Investments Program*] [*Nicaraguan*] (LA1)
PIP .... Puerto Rican Independence Party (PD)
PIP .... Semiconductor Measuring Instrument (RU)
PIPMES .... Design Institute for Industrial, Mining, and Power Industry Construction (BU)
PIPSA .... Productora e Importadora de Papel, Sociedad Anonima [*Paper Importer and Producer, Incorporated*] [*Mexican*] (LA1)
PIR .... Engineer Reconnaissance Periscope, Trench Periscope (RU)
PIR .... Partido de Izquierda Radical [*Leftist Radical Party*] [*Chilean*] (LA)
PIR .... Partido de la Izquierda Revolucionaria [*Party of the Revolutionary Left*] [*Bolivian*] (PPW)
PIR .... Prakticna Izobrazba Rukovodioca [*Manager Training in Industry*] (YU)
PIR .... Prewarning Relay [*Railroads*] (RU)
PIR .... Pukovska Intendantska Radionica [*Regimental Quartermaster Workshop*] (YU)
PIR .... Sound-Flash Survey Post [*Artillery*] (RU)
Piram .... Pyramidal (RU)
PIRI .... Paint Industries Research Institute (MAR)
PIS .... Panellinios Iatrikos Syllogos [*Panhellenic Medical Association*] (GC)

PIS.............. Pankyprios Iatrikos Syllogos [*Pan-Cyprian Medical Association*] (GC)
PIS.............. Panstwowa Inspekcja Sanitarna [*State Sanitary Inspectorate*] (POL)
PIS.............. Panstwowy Instytut Sztuki [*State Institute of Art*] (POL)
PIS.............. Prazska Informacni Sluzba [*Prague Information Service*] (CZ)
PIS.............. Programa de Integracao Social [*Social Integration Program*] [*Brazilian*] (LA)
PIS.............. Przedsiebiorstwo Imprez Sportowych [*Sport Event Enterprise*] (POL)
PIS.............. Pukovsko Intendantsko Slagaliste [*Regimental Quartermaster Depot*] (YU)
pisat.......... Writer (RU)
Pisch bum... Paper Factory [*Topography*] (RU)
PISE........... Partido por la Independencia Socialista de Euzkadi [*Party for the Socialist Independence of the Basque Country*] [*Spanish*] (WER)
PISh........... History Teaching in the School (RU)
pishch......... Food, Alimentary (RU)
pishch......... Food Industry Plant [*Topography*] (RU)
pishchemash ... Food Machinery Plant (RU)
pishcheprom ... Food Industry (RU)
Pishchepromizdat ... State Scientific and Technical Publishing House of the Food Industry (RU)
Pishchevkus ... Trade Union of Workers of the Food and Flavoring Industry of the USSR (RU)
pishch konts ... Food Concentrates (RU)
pish mash... Typewriter (RU)
PISM........... Panstwowy Instytut Spraw Miedzynarodowych [*State Institute of International Affairs*] (POL)
PISM........... Polski Instytut Spraw Miedzynarodowych [*Polish Institute of International Affairs*] (POL)
PISPESCA ... Asociacion Colombiana de Piscicultura y Pesca [*Bogota*] (COL)
PISS........... Polskie Instalacje Sily i Swiatla [*Polish Power and Light Installations*] (POL)
PISS........... Rules of the Economic and Social Council (BU)
PISwL.......... Polski Instytut Socjologiczny w Lodzi [*Polish Sociological Institute in Lodz*] (POL)
pit.............. Drinking Water (RU)
pit.............. Feeding, Nutrition (RU)
pit.............. Nursery [*for plants or animals*] [*Topography*] (RU)
PIT.............. Panstwowy Instytut Telekomunikacyjny [*State Institute of Communication*] (POL)
pit.............. Pitaja [*Finnish*]
PIT.............. Przemyslowy Instytut Telekomunikacji [*Industrial Institute of Communication*] (POL)
PIT.............. Punkt Informacji Turystycznej [*Tourist Information Center*] [*Polish*]
pit frukt....... Fruit-Tree Nursery [*Topography*] (RU)
PIU-............ Breakdown Tester (RU)
PIU.............. Pioneer Industries Union [*Singapore*] (ML)
PIU.............. Pneumatic Level Indicator (RU)
PIUC........... Parti pour l'Independance et l'Unite des Comores (MAR)
Piv.............. Brewery [*Topography*] (RU)
PIV.............. Pamutszovo Ipari Vallalat [*Cotton Mill*] (HU)
PIVE........... Regulations for the Manufacture of Explosion-Proof Electrical Equipment (RU)
Piv zav........ Brewery [*Topography*] (RU)
PIW.............. Panstwowy Instytut Wydawniczy [*State Publishing Institute*] (POL)
PIW.............. Petroleum Intelligence Weekly [*A publication*] (MAR)
PIWR........... Panstwowy Instytut Wydawnictw Rolniczych [*State Institute of Agricultural Publications*] (POL)
PIWU........... Pineaple Industry Workers Union (ML)
P i Zh.......... Law and Life [*A publication*] (RU)
PIZOLUB..... Societe Pizo de Formulation de Lubrifiants (MAR)
Pj................ Parteijargon [*Party Jargon*] (EG)
PJ................ Partido Justicialista [*Justicialista Party*] [*Argentine*] (LA)
PJ................ Petaling Jaya [*Near Kuala Lumpur*] (ML)
PJ................ Police Judiciaire [*Criminal Investigation Police*] [*French*] (WER)
PJ................ Poste de Jonction [*Military*] [*French*] (MTD)
pj................ Puheenjohtaja [*Finnish*]
PJA.............. Pretprijatie za Javen Avtotransport [*Public Motor Transport Establishment*] (YU)
PJF.............. Policia Judicial Federal [*Federal Judicial Police*] [*Mexican*] (LA)
PJG.............. Pingat Jasa Gemilang [*Meritorious Medal*] [*Singapore*] (ML)
PJK.............. Pingat Jasa Kebaktian [*Loyal Service Medal*] (ML)
PJP.............. Police Judiciaire des Parquets [*Investigatory Police of the Public Prosecutor*] [*Belgian*]
PJP.............. Pusat Jabatan Polis [*Police Department Headquarters*] (ML)
PK.............. Border Guard Commandant's Office (RU)
PK.............. Border Guard Cutter (RU)
PK.............. Bypass Valve, Bypass (RU)
PK.............. Cavalry Support (RU)
PK.............. Check Button [*Telephony*] (RU)
p-k.............. Colonel (RU)
PK.............. Conciliation Commission (BU)
PK-............. Continuously Operating Coil Boiler, Single-Pass Boiler (RU)
PK.............. Cooking Kettle (RU)
PK.............. Coordinate Converter (RU)
pk.............. Correspondence Censorship (RU)
PK.............. Course Correction (RU)
PK.............. Entry-Driving Machine, Sinking Machine [*Mining*] (RU)
PK.............. Field Switchboard (RU)
PK.............. Fire Brigade (RU)
PK.............. Fire Cock (RU)
PK.............. Fire Hydrant (RU)
PK.............. Flotation Suit, Non-Sinkable Suit (RU)
PK.............. Forward Edge, Main Line of Resistance [*Military term*] (RU)
PK.............. Industrial Combine (BU)
PK.............. Intermediate Cascade (RU)
PK.............. Intermediate Switching (RU)
PK.............. Outguard (RU)
PK.............. Paddle Steamer (RU)
PK.............. Pakistan [*Two-letter standard code*] (CNC)
pk.............. Pakka(a) [*Finnish*]
PK.............. Panzerkompanie [*Tank Company*] (EG)
pk.............. Parancsnok [*Commander*] (HU)
PK.............. Park Kultury [*Park of Culture*] (CZ)
pk.............. Partonkivuli [*Non-Party*] (HU)
PK.............. Party Commission (RU)
PK.............. Party Committee (RU)
PK.............. Patriotiko Kinima [*Patriotic Movement*] [*Greek*] (GC)
PK.............. Pensions Commission (BU)
PK.............. Penyata Keadaan [*Situation Report*] (ML)
PK.............. Perak (ML)
PK.............. Permanent Commission (BU)
Pk.............. Petrolatum, Acid (RU)
PK.............. Pferdekraft [*Horsepower*] [*German*]
PK.............. Phileleftheron Komma [*Liberal Party*] [*Greek*] (PPE)
pk.............. Pikakivaari [*Finnish*]
PK.............. Piston Compressor (RU)
PK.............. Pneumatic Contactor (RU)
PK.............. Poinikos Kodix [*Penal Code*] (GC)
PK.............. Pokrajinski Komitet [*Provincial Committee*] (YU)
PK.............. Polar Commission (of the Academy of Sciences, USSR) (RU)
PK.............. Politechnika Krakowska [*Technical University of Cracow*] [*Polish*]
PK.............. Politicka Knihovna [*Political Library*] (CZ)
PK.............. Politicki Komitet [*Political Committee*] (YU)
PK.............. Poljoprivredna Komora [*Chamber of Agriculture*] (YU)
PK.............. Polycarbonates (RU)
PK.............. Pomocne Kursy [*Auxiliary Courses*] (CZ)
PK.............. Posta Kutusu [*Post Office Box*] (TU)
PK.............. Potassium Persulfate (RU)
PK.............. Poteau Kilometre [*Kilometer Post*] (CL)
PK.............. Powiatowy Komitet [*County Committee*] (POL)
PK.............. Prehranbeni Kombinat [*Food Combine*] (YU)
PK.............. Presernova Knjiznica [*Preseren Library*] [*Ljubljana*] (YU)
PK.............. Preventive Debugging [*Computers*] (RU)
PK.............. Primary Loop, Primary Circuit [*Nuclear physics and engineering*] (RU)
PK.............. Problems of Cybernetics [*Bibliography*] (RU)
PK.............. Proedros Kyverniseos [*President*] [*Automobile license plate designation*] (GC)
PK.............. Projektierung Kernkraftwerke [*Project Planning of Nuclear Power Plants*] (EG)
PK.............. Proodevtikon Komma [*Progressive Party*] (GC)
PK.............. Prothypourgos Kyverniseos [*Premier*] [*Automobile license plate designation*] (GC)
PK.............. Provozni Komise [*Production Commission*] (CZ)
PK.............. Punched Card (RU)
pk.............. Putnicka Kola [*Passenger Car*] [*Railroads*] (YU)
PK.............. Pyrocatechol (RU)
pk.............. Regiment (BU)
PK-............. Relief Valve, Emergency Valve, Safety Valve (RU)
PK.............. Semiconductor Key (RU)
PK.............. Start Button (RU)
PK.............. Steam Boiler (RU)
PK-............. Steam Crane (RU)
p/k............. Steamship (BU)
PK-............. Straight-Through Combine (RU)
p/k............. Subcutaneously, Hypodermically [*Pharmacy*] (RU)
PK.............. Television Camera (RU)
PK.............. Transit Cascade (RU)
PK.............. Transit Curve, Transition Curve [*Railroads*] (RU)
PK.............. Transmitting Complex (RU)
PKA............ Paket-Kontrollpostamt [*Parcel Post Inspection Office*] (EG)
PKA............ Panstwowa Komisja Arbitrazowa [*State Arbitration Commission*] (POL)
P-ka........... Polyclinic (BU)
PKA............ Pyrocatechol Monoacetate (RU)
PKAE.......... Politikon Komma Agroton Ellados [*Farmers' Political Party of Greece*] (GC)
pkb............ Area Road Traffic Control Battalion (BU)
PKB............ Parti Kemajuan Brunei [*Brunei Progressive Party*] (ML)
PKB............ Planning and Design Office (RU)
PKB............ Projektierungs- und Konstruktionsbuero [*Project-Planning and Designing Office*] (EG)
PKBAsboshifer ... Planning and Design Office of the Asbestos Shingle, Mica, and Asphalt Roofing Industry (RU)

pkbr .... Area Traffic Control Brigade (BU)
PKC .... Panstwowa Komisja Cen [*State Price Commission*] (POL)
PKCh .... Pilot-Frequency Receiver (RU)
PkCV .... Pokretni Centar Veze [*Mobile Communications Center*] [*Military*] (YU)
PKD .... Planlama ve Koordinasyon Dairesi [*Plans and Coordination Office*] [*of Turkish Electric Power Directorate General*] (TU)
PKD .... Press for Annular Parts (RU)
PKD .... Simple Cableway, Simple Ropeway (RU)
PKDZ .... Posudkova Komise Duchodoveho Zabezpeceni [*Pension Review Commission*] (CZ)
PKE .... Panstwowa Komisja Etatow [*State Personnel Commission*] (POL)
PKEN .... Pnevmatiki Kinisis Ellinikis Neolaias [*Intellectual Union of Young Greek Professionals*] (GC)
PKENNE ...... Pnevmatiki Kinisis Ellinikis Neolaias Neon Epistimonon [*Intellectual Movement of Greek Youth and Young Professionals*] (GC)
pkesk .... Puhelinkeskustelu [*Finnish*]
PKF .... Persatuan Karyawan Fadjarbhakti [*Fadjar Bhakti State Trading Enterprise Workers' Union*] [*Indonesian*]
PKF .... Polska Kronika Filmowa [*Polish Film Chronicle*] (POL)
PK FJN .... Powiatowy Komitet Frontu Jednosci Narodu [*National Unity Front County Committee*] (POL)
PKG .... Cardiopneumography (RU)
PKh .... Ahead Running, Forward Running (RU)
pkh .... Infantry (BU)
PKh .... Interstage Cooler [*Refrigeration*] (RU)
p kh .... Paradeigmatos Kharin [*For Example*] (GC)
PKh .... Planned Economy (RU)
PKh .... Pro Khristou [*Before Christ*] (GC)
p/kh .... Steamship (RU)
PKh .... Transfer Characteristic (RU)
PKhB .... Polychlorobenzene (RU)
PKhD .... Food, Clothing, and Equipment Supply Point (RU)
PKhL .... Chemical Field Laboratory (RU)
PKhL .... Field Chemical Laboratory (BU)
PKhM .... Perchloromethyl Mercaptan (RU)
PKhN .... Chemical Observation Post (RU)
PKhO .... Chemical Defense (RU)
PKhOR .... Chemical Defense Company (RU)
PKhP .... Chemical Defense Kit (RU)
PKhP .... Chemical Defense Training (RU)
PKhP .... Field Bakery (RU)
PKhR .... Chemical Agent Detection Kit (BU)
PKhR .... Chemical Defense Company (RU)
PKhR .... Gas Detection Device, Chemical Monitoring Device, Chemical Reconnaissance Instrument (RU)
PKhS .... Chemical Defense Kit (RU)
PKhS .... Chemical Defense Service (RU)
PKhV .... Perchlorovinyl (RU)
PKhV .... Polyvinyl Chloride (RU)
PKhZ .... Antichemical Defense (BU)
PKhZ .... Chemical Defense (RU)
PKhZ .... Field Bakery (RU)
PKhZR .... Chemical Defense Company (RU)
PKI .... Information Command Converter [*Computers*] (RU)
PKI .... Partai Komunis Indonesia [*Indonesian Communist Party*] (IN)
PKI .... Piackutato Iroda [*Marketing Research Office*] (HU)
PKI .... Posta Kiserleti Intezet [*Postal Service Experimental Institute*] (HU)
PKI .... Primary Cosmic Radiation (RU)
PKiEUWM ... Przedsiebiorstwo Konserwacji i Eksploatacji Urzadzen Wodno-Melioracyjnych [*Enterprise for the Conservation and Operation of Land Reclamation and Improvement Installations*] (POL)
PKiN .... Palac Kultury i Nauki [*Palace of Culture and Science*] (POL)
PKiO .... Park of Culture and Rest (RU)
PKIPishcheprom ... Planning and Design Institute for Complex Automation of Production Processes in the Food Industry (RU)
PKJ .... Pitanje Knjizevnosti i Jezika [*Literary and Linguistic Problems*] [*A periodical*] [*Sarajevo*] (YU)
PKJIF .... Prilozi za Knjizevnost, Jezik, Istoriju, i Folklor [*Contributions to Literature, Language, History, and Folklore*] [*A periodical*] (YU)
PKJU .... Posta Kozponti Javito Uzem [*Central Post Office Repair Shops*] (HU)
PKK .... Kurdish Workers' Party [*Turkish*] (PD)
PKK .... Panstwowa Komisja Klasyfikacyjna [*State Qualification Commission*] (POL)
PKK .... Parteikontrollkommission [*Party Control Commission*] (EG)
PKK .... Pasokan Keselamatan Kawasan [*Area Security Unit*] (ML)
PKK .... Pilot Channel Receiver (RU)
PKK .... Planning and Design Office (RU)
PKK .... Political Consultative Committee [*of member countries of the Warsaw Treaty*] (RU)
PKKB .... Panstwowy Korespondencyjny Kurs Bibliotekarski [*State Correspondence Course for Librarians*] (POL)
PKKF .... Powiatowy Komitet Kultury Fizycznej [*County Committee on Physical Culture*] (POL)
PKKFiT .... Powiatowy Komitet Kultury Fizycznej i Turystyki [*County Committee for Physical Culture and Tourism*] (POL)
PKKh .... Fireproof Chemical Composition (RU)
PKKP .... Powiatowa Komisja Kontroli Partyjnej [*County Party Control Commission*] (POL)
PKKPJ .... Pokrajinski Komitet Komunisticke Partije Jugoslavije [*Provincial Committee of the Communist Party of Yugoslavia*] (YU)
PKKPJ .... Politicki Komitet Komunisticke Partije Jugoslavije [*Political Committee of the Communist Party of Yugoslavia*] (YU)
PKKPJM ...... Pokrainski Komitet na Komunistickata Partija na Jugoslavija za Makedonija [*Regional Committee of the Communist Party of Yugoslavia for Macedonia*] (YU)
PKKR .... School for Improving Qualifications of Kolkhoz Managers [*1936-1941*] (RU)
PKL .... Panstwowa Komisja Lokalowa [*State Housing Commission*] (POL)
PKL .... Polskie Koleje Linowe [*Polish Funicular (or Cable) Railways*] (POL)
PKL- .... Switch (RU)
pk lch .... Regimental Dispensary (BU)
PKM .... Parti des Kadihines de Mauritanie [*Party of Mauritanian Toilers*] (AF)
PKM .... Parti Komunis Malaya [*Malayan Communist Party*] (ML)
PKM .... Pasokan Kelengkapan Malaysia [*Malaysian Ordnance Corps*] (ML)
PKM .... Pneumatic Forging Hammer (RU)
PKM .... Pokrajinski Komitet Makedonije [*Provincial Committee of Macedonia*] [*Communist Party*] (YU)
PKM .... Pomocna Komanda Mesta [*City Auxiliary Military Command*] (YU)
PKM .... Projektierungs-, Konstruktions-, und Montagebuero [*Planning, Design, and Assembly Office*] (EG)
pkm .... Putnicki Kilometar [*Passenger-Kilometer*] (YU)
PKMB .... Pertubohan Kebangsaan Melayu Bersatu [*United Malayan National Organization*] (ML)
PKN .... Number-to-Voltage Converter (RU)
PKN .... Pekan [*Malaysia*] (ML)
PKN .... Polish Standardization Committee (RU)
PKN .... Polski Komitet Normalizacyjny [*Polish Committee on Standardization*] (POL)
PKNM .... Partiia Kongressa Nezavisimosti Madagaskara (MAR)
PKNPN .... Regulation on Crediting Population Consumer Needs (BU)
PKNS .... Perbadanan Kemajuan Negeri Selangor [*Selangor State Development Organization*] (ML)
PKO .... Antisatellite Defense, Spacecraft Defense (RU)
PKO .... Defense Against Motor Torpedo Boats (RU)
PKO .... Differential Compound Winding (RU)
PKO .... Panellinios Kapnergatiki Omospondia [*or Pandelladiki Kapnergatiki Omospondia*] [*Panhellenic Tobacco Workers Federation*] (GC)
PKO .... Park Kultury a Oddechu [*Park of Culture and Recreation*] (CZ)
PKO .... Polska Kasa Opieki [*Polish Security Bank*] (POL)
PKO .... Powszechna Kasa Oszczednosci [*General Savings Bank*] (POL)
PKO .... Regulation on Cooperative Organizations (BU)
pk ob .... Regimental Train (BU)
PKOE .... Panellinion Kendron Oikologikon Erevnon [*Panhellenic Center of Ecological Research*] [*See also PAKOE*] (GC1)
PKOJF .... Park Kultury a Oddechu Julia Fucika [*Julius Fucik Park of Culture and Recreation*] (CZ)
PKOI .... Polski Komitet Olimpijski [*Polish Olympic Games Committee*] (POL)
pkom .... Politicki Komesar [*Political Commissar*] [*Communist Party*] (YU)
PKONS .... Pensions Commission of the Okrug People's Council (BU)
PKOP .... Polski Komitet Obroncow Pokoju [*Polish Committee of Partisans of Peace*] (POL)
PKO SA .... Polska Kasa Opieki Spolka Akcyjna [*Polish Guardian Bank Ltd.*] [*Polish*]
PKP .... Advanced Command Post (RU)
PKP .... Edge-Punched Card (RU)
PKP .... Infantry Heavy-Caliber Machine Gun (RU)
PKP .... Partido Komunista ng Pilipinas [*Communist Party of the Philippines*] (PPW)
PKP .... Pegawai Kechil Polis [*Subordinate Police Officer*] (ML)
PKP .... Perustuslaillinen Kansanpuolue [*Constitutional People's Party*] [*Finnish*] (PPE)
PKP .... Polityczny Komitet Porozumiewawczy [*Polish*]
PKP .... Poljoprivredno Komunalno Preduzece [*Communal Agricultural Establishment*] (YU)
PKP .... Polskie Koleje Panstwowe [*Polish State Railroads*] (POL)
PKP .... Portuguese Communist Party (BU)
PKP .... Portuguese Communist Party (RU)
PKP .... Simple Cableway, Simple Rope Crossing (RU)
PKPG .... Panstwowa Komisja Planowania Gospodarczego [*State Economic Planning Commission*] (POL)
PKPG .... Powiatowa Komisja Planowania Gospodarczego [*County Economic Planning Commission*] (POL)
PKPiW .... Przedsiebiorstwo Kolportazu Prasy i Wydawnictw [*Press and Publication Circulation Enterprise*] (POL)
PKPI .... Panstwowa Komisja Plac [*State Wages Commission*] (POL)

PKPM .... Perserikatan Kebangsaan Pelajar Malaysia [*Malaysian Students National Association*] (ML)
PKPO .... Proletarian Cultural and Educational Organization (RU)
PKPP .... Epicyclic Gearbox [*Tanks*] (RU)
PKPP .... Pejabat Ketua Pegawai Polis [*Office of the Chief Police Officer*] (ML)
PKPR .... Panstwowa Komisja Planowania Rolniczego [*State Commission on Agricultural Planning*] (POL)
PKPR .... Polski Komitet Pomocy Repatriantom [*Polish Committee for Assisting Repatriates*] (POL)
PKPR .... Polski Korpus Przysposobienia i Rozmieszczenia [*Polish Training and Resettlement Corps (in exile)*] (POL)
PKPS .... Polski Komitet Pomocy Spolecznej [*Polish Social Assistance Committee*] (POL)
pkr .... Area Road Traffic Control Company (BU)
PKr .... Politechnika Krakowska [*Technical University of Cracow*] [*Polish*]
PKR .... Powiatowa Komenda Rejonowa [*District Army Command*] [*Polish*]
PKR .... Privremeni Komandni Racunar [*Temporary Staff Computer*] [*Military*] (YU)
PKR .... Switch Relay (RU)
pkr .... Winged Missiles Regiment (BU)
PKS .... Panstwowa Komisja Samochodowa [*Polish*]
PKS .... Panstwowa Komunikacja Samochodowa [*State Motor Transport*] (POL)
PKS .... Panstwowa Komunikacja Samolotowa [*State Airlines*] (POL)
PKS .... Parti Komunis Sarawak [*Sarawak Communist Party*] (ML)
PKS .... Periphery Communications Channel (RU)
PKS .... Political Consultative Council [*Chinese People's Republic*] (RU)
PKS .... Regulation on Capital Construction (BU)
PKS- .... Semiautomatic Logging Station (RU)
PKSh .... Partia Komuniste e Shqiperise [*Communist Party of Albania*] [*Later, PPSh*] (PPE)
PKSKOJ .... Politicki Komitet Saveza Komunisticke Omladine Jugoslavije [*Political Committee of the League of Communist Youth of Yugoslavia*] (YU)
PKSvJ .... Pucka Knjiznica Izdavana Drustvom Svetog Jeronima [*Popular Library Published by the Saint Jerome Society*] (YU)
PKT .... Partai Komunis Tjina [*Chinese Communist Party*] (IN)
PKT .... Passagers-Kilometres Transportes (MAR)
PKT .... Penangkis Kapal Terbang [*Fighter Plane*] (ML)
pkt .... Punkt [*Center, Point*] (POL)
Pkt .... Punkt [*Point*] (EG)
PKTCh .... Assistant Commander for Technical Matters (RU)
PKTI .... Planning and Design Technological Institute (RU)
PKTP .... Regulation on Categorization of Labor for Pensioning (BU)
PKU .... Powiatowa Komenda Uzupelnien [*County Military Reserve Headquarters*] (POL)
PKV .... Postupna Koncentracija Vatre [*Progressive Concentration of Fire*] [*Military*] (YU)
PKV .... Short-Wave Direction Finder (RU)
PKVD .... Panellinios Kinisis Vasilevomenis Dimokratias [*Panhellenic Movement for a Crowned Republic*] (GC)
PKVP .... Projekcne Konstrukcni Vyvojove Pracoviste [*Project Design and Development Center*] (CZ)
PKW .... Personenkraftwagen [*(Motor) Car*] (EG)
PKW .... Powiatowy Komitet Wykonawczy [*County Executive Committee*] (POL)
PKWN .... Polski Komitet Wyzwolenia Narodowego [*Polish Committee of National Liberation*] (POL)
PKWZ .... Przedsiebiorstwo Kolportazu Wydawnictw Zagranicznych [*Enterprise for the Circulation of Foreign Publications*] (POL)
PKWZSL .... Powiatowy Komitet Wykonawczy Zjednoczonego Stronnictwa Ludowego [*County Executive Committee of the United Peasant Party*] (POL)
PKZ .... Pavlodar Combine Plant (RU)
PKZ .... Pedagosko-Knjizevni Zbor [*Pedagogic-Literary Society*] [*Zagreb*] (YU)
PKZ .... Penza Compressor Plant (RU)
PkZC .... Pokretni Zicni Centar [*Mobile Wire Center*] [*Military*] (YU)
PKZD .... Antiaircraft Battalion Commander's Post (RU)
PKZh .... Iron Pentacarbonyl (RU)
PKZh .... Large Reinforced Concrete Slab (RU)
PKZh .... Reinforced Concrete Roof Slab (RU)
PKZhS .... Regulations on Housing Construction Crediting (BU)
PKZP .... Pracownicza Kasa Zapomogowo-Pozyczkowa [*Workers' Slate Club*] [*Polish*]
PKZSL .... Powiatowy Komitet Zjednoczonego Stronnictwa Ludowego [*District Committee of the United Peasants' Party*] [*Polish*]
PL .... Adjustable-Blade [*Nautical term*] (RU)
pl .... Colonel (BU)
Pl .... Flake (Powder), Plate (Powder) (RU)
Pl .... Light-Press Fit (RU)
pl .... Melting (RU)
PL .... Mobile Laboratory (RU)
pl .... Mountain (BU)
pl .... Paaluokka [*Finnish*]
PL .... Parti Liberal [*Liberal Party (1974-1979)*] [*Belgian*] (PPE)
PL .... Partido Laborista [*Labor Party*] [*Argentine*] (LA)
PL .... Partido Liberal [*Liberal Party*] [*Bolivian*] (LA)
PL .... Partido Liberal [*Liberal Party*] [*Chilean*] (LA)
PL .... Partido Liberal [*Liberal Party*] [*Colombian*] (LA)
PL .... Partido Liberal [*Liberal Party*] [*Ecuadorean*] (LA)
PL .... Partido Liberal [*Liberal Party*] [*Panamanian*] (PPW)
PL .... Partido Liberal [*Liberal Party*] [*Paraguayan*] (PPW)
PL .... Partido Liberal [*Liberal Party*] [*Portuguese*] (PPE)
PL .... Partido Liberal [*Liberal Party*] [*Spanish*] (PPE)
PL .... Pathet Lao [*Originally an underground organization set up in Laos to overthrow the French, now popularly used to refer to the leftists or communists in Laos or the military arm of the NLHS*] (CL)
PL .... Pelatun [*Platoon*] (ML)
pl .... Peldaul [*For Example*] (HU)
Pl .... Piazzale [*Place, Square*] [*Italian*] (CED)
pl .... Pills [*Pharmacy*] (RU)
PL .... Pilot's Parachute (RU)
Pl .... Plac [*Square*] [*Polish*]
pl .... Place [*French*] (CED)
pl .... Plan (BU)
pl .... Plan [*or Planek or Planovani*] [*Plan or Planning*] (CZ)
pl .... Planche [*Full-Page Illustration, Plate*] [*French*]
pl .... Plane (RU)
PL .... Planimeter (RU)
pl .... Plass [*Place*] [*Norwegian*] (CED)
pl .... Platinum (RU)
pl .... Plats [*Square*] [*Swedish*] (CED)
Pl .... Platz [*German*]
Pl .... Plaza [*Spanish*]
pl .... Plein [*Square*] [*Dutch*] (CED)
Pl .... Plicina [*Shoal*] [*Yugoslav*] (NAU)
Pl .... Ploshchad' [*Russian*]
Pl .... Ploshtad [*Bulgarian*]
pl .... Plotno [*Cloth Binding*] [*Polish*]
pl .... Plural [*Plural*] [*German*]
PL .... Poland [*Two-letter standard code*] (CNC)
PL .... Politechnika Lodzka [*Engineering College of Lodz*] [*Polish*]
PL .... Polska [*Poland*] [*Polish*]
PL .... Postilokero [*Post Office Box*] [*Finnish*]
PL .... Pravo Lidu [*The People's Right*] [*A newspaper*] (CZ)
pl .... Printer's Sheet (RU)
PL .... Produktionsleitung [*Production Management*] (EG)
Pl .... Projection Lamp (RU)
PL .... Protiletecky [*Antiaircraft*] (CZ)
PL .... Punched Tape (RU)
pl .... Puolilihava [*Finnish*]
Pl .... Raft [*Topography*] (RU)
pl .... Railroad Platform [*Topography*] (RU)
pl .... Square (BU)
Pl .... Square [*Topography*], Area (RU)
PL .... Submarine (RU)
PlA .... Amphibian (RU)
PLA .... Pakistan Liberation Army (PD)
PLA .... Palestine Liberation Army (ME)
PLA .... Patriotic Liberation Army [*Burmese*] (PD)
PLA .... Pedro Leon Abroleda Brigade [*Colombian*] (PD)
PLA .... People's Liberation Army [*Indian*] (PD)
Pla .... Plateau [*Tableland, Sunken Flat*] [*French*] (NAU)
PLAB .... Aerial Depth Charge, Airborne Depth Charge (RU)
plae .... Antisubmarine Air Squadron (RU)
plae .... Antisubmarine Aviation Squadron (BU)
PLAF .... People's Liberation Armed Forces [*South Vietnamese*] (CL)
PLAN .... People's Liberation Army of Namibia (PPW)
plan .... Planned, Planning, Plan (RU)
PLAN .... Polska Ludowa Akcja Niepodleglosciowa [*Polish People's Independence Movement*] (POL)
PLANAME .... Plano Nacional de Mecanizacao [*National Mechanization Program*] [*Brazilian*] (LA)
PLANARCO .... Planeacion Arquitectura Construccion [*Medellin*] (COL)
PLANDES .... Sociedad Chilena de Planificacion y Desarrollo [*Chilean Association for Planning and Development*] (LA)
PLANHAP .... Plano Nacional de Habitacao Popular [*National Low-Cost Housing Plan*] [*Brazilian*] (LA)
PLANICOL .... Planificadora Industrial de Colombia [*Bogota*] (COL)
PLANITEC .... Planeacion Tecnica [*Bogota*] (COL)
Plankhozgiz .... State Publishing House of Literature on Planned Economy (RU)
Plankomtel' .... Telegraph Communications Planning Commission (RU)
PLANZO .... All-Union Correspondence Institute of Planning (RU)
pl ar .... Pack Artillery (BU)
PLASAN .... Planlama Sanayi ve Ticaret Yatirim AS [*Planned Industrial and Commercial Investment Corp.*] (TU)
PLASCO .... Plasticos Colombianos Ltda. [*Manizales*] (COL)
plast .... Plastic (RU)
Plasta .... Betriebe zur Herstellung von Kunststoffen und Plastischen Massen (VVB) [*Plants for Production of Synthetic and Plastic Materials (VVB)*] (EG)
PLASTICAM .... Plastique Camerounaise (MAR)
PLASTICOL .... Plasticos Colombia Ltda. [*Palmira*] (COL)
plastm .... Plastics Plant [*Topography*] (RU)

Plastmasstroy ... State Trust for the Organization and Development of the Production of Plastics and Plastic Articles (RU)
plat .... Platinum [*Place of mining*] [*Topography*] (RU)
Platf .... Platform [*Railroads, topography*] (RU)
PLATIN .... Institute for the Study of Platinum and Other Precious Metals [*1918-1934*] (RU)
Platre .... Platriere [*Plaster Quarry*] [*Military map abbreviation*] [*World War I*] [*French*] (MTD)
Plau .... Plateau [*Table-Land*] [*Military map abbreviation*] [*World War I*] [*French*] (MTD)
plav .... Smelting Works, Foundry [*Topography*] (RU)
plavk .... Fusibility (RU)
plavl .... Melting (RU)
Plavmornin ... Floating Marine Scientific Research Institute (RU)
PLAYDECA ... Plasticos y Derivados, Compania Anonima [*Venezuelan*]
PLB .... Short-Range Submarine (RU)
plCO .... Pluk Civilni Obrany [*Civil Defense Regiment*] (CZ)
PLD .... Long-Range Submarine (RU)
pld .... Mountain Infantry Division (BU)
PLD .... Partido de la Liberacion Dominicana [*Dominican Liberation Party*] [*Dominican Republic*] (PPW)
PLD .... Partido Liberal Democratico [*Democratic Liberal Party*] [*Nicaraguan*] (LA)
pld .... Peldany [*Copy, Sample*] (HU)
pld .... Poludnie [*or Poludniowy*] [*South or Southern*] (POL)
PLD .... Protiletadlova Divize [*Antiaircraft Division*] (CZ)
PLD .... Protiletadlove Delostrelectvo [*Antiaircraft Artillery*] (CZ)
PLDO .... Antisubmarine Defense (RU)
PLDO .... Protiletadlovy Delostrelecky Oddil [*Antiaircraft Artillery Battalion*] (CZ)
PLDP .... Parti Liberal Democrate et Pluraliste [*Belgian*] (PPW)
PLDP .... Political Leadership Development Program, AIPAC (MAR)
PLDP .... Poverenictvo Lesneho a Drevarskeho Priemyslu [*Office of the Commissioner of the Forest and Lumber Industry*] (CZ)
PLDS .... Polnohospodarske a Lesnicke Dokumentacne Stredisko [*Documentation Center for Agriculture and Forestry*] [*Kosice*] (CZ)
plem .... Pedigreed (RU)
plem .... Pedigreed Livestock Breeding Sovkhoz [*Topography*] (RU)
Plemzagotkontora ... Office for Pedigreed Cattle Procurement (RU)
Plenbezh ..... Committee for Prisoner and Refugee Affairs (RU)
PLF .... Palestine Liberation Front (PD)
PLF .... People's Liberation Forces [*Ethiopian*] (AF)
PLF/GC .... People's Liberation Forces/General Command [*Ethiopian*] (AF)
PLG .... Center Lecturers Groups (BU)
PLG .... Partido Liberal Galego [*Galician Liberal Party*] [*Spanish*] (WER)
PLG .... Provisional Libyan Government (MAR)
PLH .... Partido Liberal de Honduras [*Liberal Party of Honduras*] (PPW)
PLHDWU ..... Port Louis Harbor and Dock Workers Union [*Mauritian*] (AF)
PLI .... Line-Pulse Receiver (RU)
PLI .... Partido Liberal Independiente [*Independent Liberal Party*] [*Nicaraguan*] (PPW)
PLI .... Partito Liberale Italiano [*Italian Liberal Party*] (PPW)
PLI .... Payp-Layn Endustrisi [*Pipeline Industry*] (TU)
PLIS .... Planungs Informations Systeme
PLISA .... Plasticos Internacionales Ltda. [*Bogota*] (COL)
plk .... Palkkausluokka [*Finnish*]
plk .... Plukovnik [*Colonel*] [*US equivalent: Colonel*] (CZ)
PLK .... Prague Linguistic Circle (RU)
PLK .... Prazsky Linguisticky Krouzek [*Prague Linguistic Circle*] (CZ)
PLK .... Protiletadlovy Kanon [*Antiaircraft Cannon*] (CZ)
PLK .... Protiletecky Kryt [*Antiaircraft Shelter*] (CZ)
plk .... Pulkownik [*Colonel*] (POL)
pl/khos .... Ploiarkhos [*Captain (Navy), Master (Merchant Marine)*] (GC)
PLKI .... Enterprise for Cast Stoneware (BU)
PLL .... Polskie Linie Lotnicze [*Polish Air Lines*] (POL)
Plle .... Passerelle [*Footbridge*] [*Military map abbreviation*] [*World War I*] [*French*] (MTD)
PLM .... Pakistan Liberation Movement (PD)
PLM .... Paris-Lyon-Mediterranee [*Railway*] [*French*] (MTD)
PLM .... Partido Leninista-Marxista [*Leninist-Marxist Party*] [*Colombian*] (LA)
PLM .... Partido de Libertacao de Mocambique (MAR)
PLM .... People's Liberation Movement [*Montserrat*] (PPW)
plm .... Plnometr [*Cubic Meter*] (CZ)
PLM .... Progressive Labor Movement [*Antiguan*] (LA)
plm .... Prostorovy Metr [*Cubic Meter*] (CZ)
plm .... Small Submarine (RU)
PLMA .... Pomoc Lekarska Mlodziezy Akademickiej [*Medical Aid for University Youth*] (POL)
pl m-k .... Lightship (RU)
PLMP .... Progressive Labor Movement Party (LA1)
PLN .... Partido Liberacion Nacional [*National Liberation Party*] [*Costa Rican*] (PPW)
PLN .... Partido Liberal Nacionalista [*Nationalist Liberal Party*] [*Nicaraguan*] (LA)
Pln .... Pelabohan [*Roadstead, Anchorage*] [*Indonesian*] (NAU)
Pln .... Pelabohan [*Roadstead, Anchorage*] [*Malaysian*] (NAU)
pln .... Polnoc [*or Polnocny*] [*North or Northern*] (POL)
PLO .... Antisubmarine Defense (RU)
PLO .... Palestine Liberation Organization (PD)
PLO .... Panstwowe Liceum Okretowe [*State Merchant Marine School*] (POL)
PLO .... Polskie Linie Oceaniczne [*Polish Ocean Lines*] (POL)
PLO .... Polskie Linie Okretowe [*Polish Shipping Lines*] (POL)
PLO .... Pravila Letacke Obuke [*Flight Training Rules*] [*Air Force*] (YU)
PLO .... Protiletadlovy Oddil [*Antiaircraft Battalion*] (CZ)
Plodkoop .... Fruit Cooperative (BU)
plodoovoshch ... Fruit and Vegetable Sovkhoz [*Topography*] (RU)
Plon .... Plantation [*Plantation*] [*Military map abbreviation*] [*World War I*] [*French*] (MTD)
pl opt os ...... Optic Axial Plane (RU)
pl or .... Mountain Gun (BU)
Pl OS .... Pleven Oblast Court (BU)
ploshch .... Square [*Topography*], Area (RU)
PLOSU .... Protiletadlova Obrana Statniho Uzemi [*Air Defense of National Territory*] (CZ)
plot .... Dam, Dike, Weir (RU)
plotn .... Carpentry (RU)
plotn .... Density (RU)
Plovmornin ... Floating Marine Scientific Research Institute (RU)
PLP .... Panstwowe Liceum Pedagogiczne [*State Pedagogical School*] (POL)
PLP .... Parti Liberal Progressiste [*Liberal Progressive Party*] [*Moroccan*] (PPW)
PLP .... Parti de la Liberte et du Progres [*Party of Liberty and Progress*] [*Belgian*] (PPE)
PLP .... Partido de Liberacion Popular [*Popular Liberation Party*] [*Ecuadorean*] (LA)
PLP .... Partido de Liberacion del Pueblo [*People's Liberation Party*] [*Mexican*] (LA)
PLP .... Partido Liberal Progresista [*Progressive Liberal Party*] [*Guatemalan*] (LA)
PLP .... Partido de los Pobres [*Poor People's Party*] [*Mexican*] (PD)
PLP .... People's Liberation Party [*Liberian*] (AF)
PLP .... Podniky Lesneho Priemyslu [*Enterprise of the Forest Industry*] (CZ)
PLP .... Poverenictvo Lahkeho Priemyslu [*Office of the Commissioner of Light Industry*] (CZ)
PLP .... Progressive Labor Party [*Bermudian*] (LA1)
PLP .... Progressive Labor Party [*St. Lucian*] (LA1)
PLP .... Progressive Liberal Party [*Bahamian*] (PPW)
PLP .... Protiletadlovy Pluk [*Antiaircraft Regiment*] (CZ)
PLP .... Pusat Latehan Polis [*Police Training Center*] (ML)
PLP .... Soil Vacuum-Tube Potentiometer (RU)
PLPAR .... Regulations on Internal Passports and Address Registration (BU)
PL/PI .... Proletarische Linke/Partei Initiative [*Proletarian Left/Party Initiative*] [*West German*] (WEN)
plplt .... Polplotno [*Half-Cloth Binding*] [*Polish*]
PLPP .... Pegawai Laut Pasokan Polis [*Police Force Marine Officer*] (ML)
PLPPH .... Pusat Latehan Polis Pasokan Hutan [*Police Field Force Training Center*] (ML)
PLR .... Constructions Metalliques Panz et Laon Reunis (MAR)
PLR .... Partido Liberal Radical [*Radical Liberal Party*] [*Ecuadorean*] (PPW)
PLR .... Partido Liberal Radical [*Radical Liberal Party*] [*Paraguayan*] (PPW)
PLR .... Pusat Latehan Rikerut [*Recruit Training Center*] (ML)
PLRA .... Partido Liberal Radical Autentico [*Authentic Liberal Radical Party*] [*Paraguayan*] (PD)
PLRO .... Protiletecky Raketovy Oddil [*Antiaircraft Rocket Battalion*] (CZ)
PLRS .... Protiletecke Ridici Strely [*Air Defense Guided Missiles*] (CZ)
PLRT .... Protiletadlova Raketova Technika [*Air Defense Rocket Technology*] (CZ)
PLRV .... Protiletadlove Raketove Vojsko [*Antiaircraft Rocket Troops*] (CZ)
PLRZ .... Protiletadlove Raketove Zbrane [*Antiaircraft Rocket Weapons*] (CZ)
pls .... Medium Submarine (RU)
PLS .... Parti Liberal Suisse [*Liberal Party of Switzerland*] (PPE)
PLS .... Parti de la Liberation et du Socialisme [*Party of Liberation and Socialism*] [*Moroccan*] (AF)
PLS .... Plynarenska Sluzba [*Gas Supply Service*] [*Civil defense*] (CZ)
PLS .... Position Laterale de Securite (MAR)
plsbr .... Mountain Rifle Brigade (BU)
plsd .... Mountain Rifle Division (BU)
plskg .... Plateau (RU)
plsp .... Mountain Rifle Regiment (BU)
PLST .... Small Railroad Station [*Topography*] (RU)
PLT .... Pembantu Letnan [*Sublieutenant*] (IN)
PLT .... Permanent Labour Tribunal (MAR)
plt .... Plotno [*Cloth Binding*] [*Polish*]
PLT .... Portable Tank Lamp [*Military term*] (RU)
PLT .... Trenching Plow, Plow-Type Trench Excavator (RU)
PLTI .... Volga Region Forestry Engineering Institute Imeni M. Gor'kiy (RU)
PLU- .... Lecturer's Projector Unit (RU)
PLU .... Partido Liberal Unido [*United Liberal Party*] [*Paraguayan*] (LA)

PLU .... Partido Liberal Unificado [*Unified Liberal Party*] [*Paraguayan*] (PPW)
PLUA .... Partido da Luta dos Africanos de Angola [*Party for the Struggle of the Africans of Angola*] (AF)
PLUNA .... Primeras Lineas Uruguayas de Navegacion Aerea [*Uruguayan National Airlines*] (LA)
PLURO .... Antisubmarine Guided Weapon (RU)
PLURS .... Antisubmarine Guided Missile (RU)
PLUS .... Prima Leben und Sparen [*Quality Living and Saving*] [*Brand name and discount store chain in West Germany and US*]
pluskv .... Pluskvamperfekti [*Pluperfect*] [*Finnish*]
plut .... Plutonowy [*Sergeant*] [*Polish*]
plv .... Postilahetysvekseli [*Finnish*]
PLW .... Panstwowe Lecznice Weterynaryjne [*State Veterinary Hospitals*] (POL)
Plw .... Polwysep [*Peninsula*] [*Polish*]
PLYF .... Port Louis Youth Federation [*Reunionese*] (AF)
PLZ .... Minelaying Submarine (RU)
PLZ .... Plantations Lever au Zaire (MAR)
PLZ .... Polni Letistni Zabezpeceni [*Field Airfield Support*] (CZ)
PLZ .... Postleitzahl [*German*]
PLZ .... Protiletalska Zascita [*Antiaircraft Protection*] [*Civil defense*] (YU)
PLZpriMINOT ... Protiletalska Zascita pri MINOT [*Antiaircraft Defense in the Ministry of the Interior*] (YU)
PM .... Antipersonnel Mine (RU)
PM .... Blasting Unit, Blasting Machine (RU)
PM .... Feeder, Feed Mechanism (RU)
PM .... Field Shop [*Military term*] (RU)
PM .... Field Weather Post (RU)
PM .... Film (RU)
PM .... Groupe Pierre Mariotte [*French*]
pm .... Last Month (RU)
PM .... Magnetic Starter (RU)
PM .... Makarov Pistol (RU)
PM .... Mechanical Packer [*Pet.*] (RU)
PM .... Medical Aid Station (RU)
PM .... Mobile Shop (RU)
PM .... Padre Maestro [*Spanish*]
PM .... Partito Monarchico [*Monarchist Party*] [*Italian*] (PPE)
pm .... Pasado Meridiano [*Spanish*] (GPO)
PM .... Patriotikon Metopon [*Patriotic Front*] [*Greek Cypriot*] (PPE)
PM .... Penzugyminiszterium [*Ministry of Finance*] (HU)
pM .... Per Monat [*Per Month*] [*Business and trade*] [*German*]
pm .... Pistolet Maszynowy [*Machine-Gun*] [*Polish*]
PM .... Pistolet Mitrailleur [*Machine Pistol*] (CL)
PM .... Plan-Methodik (Unterabteilung der Abteilung Plankoordinierung) [*Planning Methodology (A Subdivision of the Department of Plan Coordination)*] (EG)
PM .... Pneumatic Hammer (RU)
PM .... Policia Militar [*Military Police*] [*Portuguese*] (WER)
pm .... Pomeridiane [*After Noon*] [*Italian*] (GPO)
pm .... Post Meridiem [*Afternoon*] [*Latin*] (GPO)
PM .... Post Mortem [*After Death*] [*Latin*] (GPO)
PM .... Pravna Misul [*Legal Thought*] [*A periodical*] (BU)
PM .... Precizna Mehanika [*Precision Instruments*] (YU)
PM .... Prehrada Mladeze [*"Youth" Dam*] (CZ)
PM .... Preparation Militaire [*French*]
PM .... Preteky Mieru [*Peace Race*] (CZ)
PM .... Prevote Militaire [*Military Police*] [*Cambodian*] (CL)
pm .... Pro Minute [*Per Minute*] [*German*]
PM .... Programing Mechanism (RU)
PM .... Proletarian Thought [*Publishing house*] (RU)
PM .... Promemoria [*Finnish*]
PM .... Przemysl Meblarski [*Furniture Industry*] (POL)
PM .... Pseudomonoclinic (RU)
pm .... Puscani Metak [*Rifle Bullet*] (YU)
PM .... Ranging Mortar (RU)
PM .... Repair Ship, Floating Shop (RU)
PM .... St. Pierre and Miquelon [*Two-letter standard code*] (CNC)
PM .... Semisoft (RU)
PM .... Steam Engine (RU)
PM .... Vertical Magnet, Lifting Magnet (RU)
PM- .... Watering Truck, Sprinkler Truck (RU)
4PM .... Persatuan Persuratan Pemuda Pemudi Melayu [*Malayan Youth Literary Association*] [*Singapore*] (ML)
PMA .... Panstwowe Muzeum Archeologiczne [*State Archaeological Museum*] (POL)
PMA .... Pays les Moins Avances (MAR)
PMA .... Polymethyl Acrylate (RU)
PMA .... Programa Mundial de Alimentos [*UN World Food Program*] [*Use WFP*] (LA)
PMA .... Propylmethacrylamide (RU)
PMAC .... Provisional Military Administrative Council [*Ethiopian*] (PD)
PMAC .... Provisional Military Advisory Council (MAR)
PMADK .... Permanent International Association of Road Congresses [*PIARC*] (RU)
PMAEA .... Port Management Association of Eastern Africa (MAR)
PMAKS .... Permanent International Association of Navigation Congresses [*PIANC*] (RU)
PMAN .... Prezidiul Marii Adunari Nationale [*Presidium of the Grand National Assembly*] (RO)
PMAV .... Prazsky Mestsky Akcni Vybor [*Prague City Action Committee (of the National Front)*] (CZ)
PMAWCA .... Port Management Association of West and Central Africa (MAR)
pmb .... Pontoon Bridge Battalion (RU)
PMB .... Private Mail Bag (MAR)
PMB .... Protivminobacacka Borba [*Antimortar Defense*] (YU)
PMB .... Punkt des Maneuverbeginns [*Start of Maneuver (In intercepting enemy planes)*] (EG)
pmb .... Road and Bridge Battalion (BU)
PMB .... Turret Traversing Mechanism (RU)
PMBr .... Pontoon Bridge Brigade (RU)
PMC .... Palabora Mining Company (MAR)
PMC .... Parquets et Moulures du Cameroun (MAR)
PMC .... Pekarsko-Mesarska Ceta [*Bakers and Butchers Company*] (YU)
PMC .... Permanent Mandates Commission (MAR)
PMC .... Planning and Management Consultancy [*Sudanese*] (MAR)
PMC .... Political Military Committee (MAR)
PMCh .... Paramagnetic Particle (RU)
PMC (S) ...... Pan Malaysia Cement Works (Singapore) (ML)
PmCV .... Pomocni Centar Veze [*Auxiliary Communications Center*] [*Military*] (YU)
PMCW .... Pan Malaysia Cement Works (ML)
PMD .... Pembangunan Masjarakat Desa [*Village Community Development*] (IN)
PMD .... Pro Merito Decoration (MAR)
PMD .... Protivpesadiska Mina-Drvena [*Wooden Anti-Infantry Mine*] (YU)
PMD .... Wooden Antipersonnel Mine (RU)
PMDB .... Partido do Movimento Democratico Brasileiro [*Brazilian Democratic Movement Party*] (LA1)
PMDK .... Machine-Gun and Mortar Decontamination Kit (RU)
PME .... Petites et Moyennes Entreprises [*Small and Medium-Size Businesses*] [*French*] (WER)
PME .... Plan de Modernisation et d'Equipement (MAR)
PME .... Popular Medical Encyclopedia [*A publication*] (RU)
PME .... Pteryx Miktis Ekpaidevseos [*Mixed Training Wing*] [*Air Force*] [*Greek*] (GC)
pmet .... Puscani Metak [*Rifle Bullet*] (YU)
PMEZ .... Pyshma Copper Electrolytic Plant (RU)
PMF .... Full-Length Film, Feature Film (RU)
PMFAT .... Personnel Militaire Feminin de l'Armee de Terre [*Army Female Military Personnel*] [*French*] (WER)
PMG .... Pemangku [*Acting*] (ML)
PMG .... Przeladunki Morskie Gdansk [*Gdansk Cargo Handling Enterprise*] (POL)
PMH .... Polska Marynarka Handlowa [*Polish Merchant Marine*] (POL)
Pm-Handel ... Produktionsmittelhandel [*Trade in the Means of Production*] (EG)
PMI .... Partai Muslimin Indonesia [*Indonesian Moslem Party (Same as PARMUSI)*] (IN)
PMI .... Petites et Moyennes Industries [*Small and Medium-Size Industries*] (AF)
PMI .... [*Service Nationale de*] Protection Maternelle Infantile [*(National) Infant and Maternal Protection (Department)*] [*Laotian*] (CL)
PMiM .... Applied Mathematics and Mechanics (RU)
Pmin .... Angle of Safety [*Artillery*] (RU)
PMIP .... Pan-Malayan Islamic Party (ML)
PMK .... Mobile Mechanized Column (RU)
PMK .... Pecsi Moso- es Kokszmu [*Coal Processing and Coke Plant of Pecs*] (HU)
PMK .... Polymethacrylic Acid (RU)
PMK .... Popularni Motoristicka Knihovna [*Popular Publications Series on Motors*] (CZ)
PMKh .... Mechanized Field Bakery (RU)
PMLI .... Partito Marxista-Leninista Italiano [*Italian Marxist-Leninist Party*] (WER)
PMLM .... Parti Marxiste-Leniniste Malgache (MAR)
PMLM .... Parti Marxiste Leniniste Mauricien [*Mauritian Marxist-Leninist Party*] (AF)
PMM .... Applied Mathematics and Mechanics (RU)
PMM .... Mobile Machine Shop (RU)
PMM .... Pro Merito Medal (MAR)
PMMA .... Polymethylmethacrylate (RU)
PMMS .... Primitive Methodist Missionary Society (MAR)
PMN .... Mine Observation [*Navy*] (RU)
PMN .... Panglima Mangku Negara [*Knight of the Most Distinguished Order of the Defender of the Realm*] (ML)
PMN .... Partido de Movilizacion Nacional [*National Mobilization Party*] [*Nicaraguan*] (LA)
PMN .... Progettazioni Meccanico Nucleare [*Nuclear Machinery Planning*] [*Italian*] (WER)
PMO .... Mine Defense, Antimine Defense (RU)
PMO .... Pangosmios Meteorologikos Organismos [*World Meteorological Organization (of the United Nations)*] (GC)
PMO .... Portable Target Equipment (RU)
PMP .... Bridge Train (RU)

PMP............ Field Weather Post (RU)
pmp............ Marine Regiment (BU)
pmp............ Marine Regiment (RU)
PMP............ Mechanized Field Laundry (RU)
PMP............ Medical Aid Station (RU)
PMP............ Parti du Mouvement Populaire de la Cote Francaise des Somalis (MAR)
PMP............ Partito Monarchico Popolare [*Popular Monarchist Party*] [*Italian*] (PPE)
PMP............ Planetary Traversing Mechanism [*of a tank turret*] (RU)
PMP............ Preliminary Master Plan (MAR)
PMP............ Regimental Aid Station (BU)
PMP............ Regimental Medical Station (RU)
PMP............ Semiconductor-Metal-Semiconductor [*Thin-film circuits*] (RU)
PMPO.......... Mechanized Field Laundry Detachment (RU)
PMR............ Partidul Muncitoresc Roman [*Romanian Workers' Party*] (RO)
PMR............ Portable Microroentgenometer (RU)
pmr............ Road and Bridge Company (BU)
PMR............ Trailer Minelayer (RU)
PMR-1.......... Protivpesadiska Mina-Rasprskava Juca [*Anti-Infantry Fragmentation Mine*] (YU)
PMRC.......... Programa de Modernizacao e Reorganizacao da Comercializacao [*Marketing Reorganization and Modernization Program*] [*Brazilian*] (LA)
PMRGT........ Mobile Repair Shop for Artillery Caterpillar Tractors (RU)
PMRN.......... Prezydium Miejskiej Rady Narodowej [*Presidium of the People's Town Council*] [*Polish*]
PMRO.......... Protivpesadiska Mina-Rasprskavajuca Otskocna [*Anti-Infantry Fragmentation Rebounding Mine*] (YU)
PMRS.......... Protivpesadiska Mina-Rasprskavajuca, Svetleca [*Anti-Infantry Fragmentation Flare Mine*] (YU)
PMRV.......... Plan Mobilizacniho Rozvinuti Vojsk [*Mobilization Plan for Troop Deployment*] (CZ)
PMRW.......... Panstwowa Muzyczna Rada Wydawnicza [*State Musical Publication Council*] (POL)
PMS............ Council of Ministers Decree (BU)
PMS............ Council of Ministers Letter (BU)
PMS............ Device for Determination of Mechanical Properties of Plants (RU)
PMS............ Field Weather Station (RU)
PMS............ Mine Service Regulations [*Military term*] (RU)
PMS............ Panstwowy Monopol Spirytusowy [*State Alcohol Monopoly*] (POL)
PMS............ Paris Missionary Society (MAR)
PMS............ Permanent-Magnet System Instrument [*Metrology*] (RU)
PMS............ Poljoprivredno-Masinska Stanica [*Agricultural Machinery Station*] (YU)
PMS............ Polski Monopol Solny [*Polish Salt Monopoly*] (POL)
PMS............ Polymethyl Siloxane (RU)
PMS............ Pontonova Mostova Souprava [*Pontoon Bridging Section*] (CZ)
PMS............ Preparation Militaire Superieure [*Advanced Military Preparatory Training*] [*French*] (WER)
PMS............ Problems of Peace and Socialism [*A publication*] (RU)
PMS............ Track Machinery Station [*Railroads*] (RU)
PMSD.......... Parti Mauricien Social-Democrate [*Mauritian Social Democratic Party*] (PPW)
PMSMZ....... Ministry of Agriculture Pasture Reclamation Service (BU)
PMSP.......... Proodevtiki Mathitiki Spoudastiki Parataxi [*Progressive Student Faction*] [*Greek*] (GC)
PMSP.......... Proodevtiki Mathitiki Syndikalistiki Parataxi [*Progressive Student Trade Union Faction*] [*Greek*] (GC)
PMSU.......... Partidul Muncitoresc Socialist Ungur [*Hungarian Socialist Workers' Party*] (RO)
PMT............ Instrument for Determination of Microhardness (RU)
PMT............ Panstwowy Monopol Tytoniowy [*State Tobacco Monopoly*] (POL)
PMT............ Partido Mexicano de los Trabajadores [*Mexican Workers' Party*] (PPW)
PMT............ Partija Madarskih Trudbenika [*Hungarian Workers' Party*] (YU)
PMT............ Polski Monopol Tytoniowy [*Polish Tobacco Monopoly*] (POL)
PMT............ Prumyslova Tiskarna [*Industrial Printing Plant*] (CZ)
PMTF.......... Applied Mechanics and Technical Physics (RU)
PMTs-.......... Copper-Zinc Solder (RU)
PMTZ.......... Plan Materielne-Technickeho Zasobovani [*Plan for the Procurement of Materiel and Equipment*] (CZ)
PMU............ Fertilizer Containing Several Trace Elements (RU)
PMU............ Pari Mutuel Urbain [*Legal Parimutuel System*] [*French*] (WER)
PMU............ Peninsula Malay Union (ML)
PMU............ Police Mobile Unit [*Zambian*] (AF)
PMU............ Production-Installation Administration (BU)
PMU............ Programme de Modernisation Urbaine [*Urban Modernization Program*] [*Algerian*] (AF)
PMU............ Simple Meteorological Condition (BU)
PMUM.......... Persatuan Mahasiswa Universiti Malaya [*Students' Union, University of Malaya*] (ML)
PMUM.......... Societe d'Exploitation pour le Pari Mutuel Urbain au Maroc (MAR)
PMUP.......... Partidul Muncitoresc Unit Polonez [*Polish United Workers' Party*] (RO)
PMV............ Pro Mundi Vita (EA)
pm vl.......... Prearranged Barrage (BU)
PMW............ Polska Marynarka Wojenna [*Polish Navy*] [*Polish*]
PMZ............ Discontinuous Magnetic Recording, Intermediate Magnetic Recording (RU)
PMZ............ Industrial Installations Plant (BU)
PMZ............ Panstwowe Muzeum Zoologiczne [*State Zoological Museum*] (POL)
PMZ............ Panstwowy Monopol Zapalczany [*State Match Monopoly*] (POL)
PMZ............ Penza Machinery Plant (RU)
PMZ............ Pneumatic Stoker (RU)
PMZ............ Podol'sk Machine Plant (RU)
PMZD.......... Delayed Action Railroad Mine (RU)
pmzhpb...... Pontoon-Bridge Railroad Battalion (BU)
PN............ Actuating Pump, Starting Pump (RU)
PN............ Booster Pump [*Aviation*] (RU)
pn............ Cartridge (BU)
PN............ Direction Post (RU)
PN............ Guidance Point, Aiming Point (BU)
pn............ Monday (RU)
PN............ Observer's Parachute (RU)
pn............ Ordinal Number, Number in a Series, Atomic Number (RU)
PN............ Partido Nacional [*National Party*] [*Honduran*] (PPW)
PN............ Partido Nacional [*Blanco Party*] [*Uruguayan*] (PPW)
PN............ Partido Nacional [*National Party*] [*Chilean*] (LA)
PN............ Party Negara [*National Party*] (ML)
pn............ Patrz Nizej [*See Below*] [*Polish*]
PN............ Perusahaan Negara [*State Company*] (IN)
PN............ Peti Nitrogenmuvek [*Nitrogen Factory of Pet*] (HU)
Pn............ Pinar [*Spring, Fountain*] (TU)
PN............ Pitcairn [*Two-letter standard code*] (CNC)
Pn............ Piton [*Peak*] [*French*] (NAU)
pn............ Pod Nazwa [*Called*] [*Polish*]
PN............ Pohlavni Nemoci [*Venereal Diseases*] (CZ)
PN............ Polemikon Navtikon [*Navy*] (GC)
PN............ Police Nationale [*National Police*] (CL)
PN............ Policia Nacional [*National Police*] [*Salvadoran*] (LA1)
PN............ Politicka Nastava [*Political Training*] [*Military*] (YU)
pn............ Polnoc [*North*] [*Polish*]
PN............ Polskie Normy [*or Polska Norma*] [*Polish Standards*] (POL)
PN............ Polynucleotide (RU)
PN............ Preventive Adjustment, Preventive Maintenance (RU)
PN............ Projet de Norme
PN............ Proviantni Nacelnik [*Food Service Chief*] (CZ)
PN............ Puolustusneuvosto [*Defense Council*] [*Finnish*] (WEN)
PN............ Pyridine Nucleotide (RU)
PN............ Saturated Steam (RU)
PN............ Voltage Switch (RU)
pna............ Paivana [*Finnish*]
PNA............ Pakistan National Alliance (PD)
PNA............ Parti National Africain [*African National Party*] [*Angolan*] (AF)
PNA............ Programa Nacional do Alcool [*National Alcohol Program*] [*Brazilian*] (LA)
PNA............ Temporary Directional Antenna (RU)
PNAS.......... Proceedings of the National Academy of Sciences [*A publication*] (MAR)
PNB............ Product National Brut [*Gross National Product*] (RO)
PNB............ Produit National Brut [*Gross National Product*] [*French*]
PNB............ Proprietes Non Baties (MAR)
PNBFT........ Programa Nacional de Banano y Frutas Tropicales [*National Banana and Tropical Fruit Program*] [*Ecuadorean*] (LA)
PNC............ Palestine National Council (PD)
PNC............ Partidual Nationale Crestine [*National Christian Party*] [*Romanian*] (PPE)
PNC............ People's National Congress [*Guyanese*] (PD)
PNC............ Personnel Navigant Commercial (MAR)
PNCP.......... Parti National de la Convention du Peuple (MAR)
pn d............ Engineer Combat Battalion (BU)
PND............ Low-Pressure Heater (RU)
PND............ Low-Pressure Polyethylene (RU)
PND............ Parti Nationaliste du Dahomey (MAR)
PND............ Partidul National-Democratic [*National Democratic Party*] [*Romanian*] (PPE)
PND............ Plano Nacional de Desenvolvimento [*National Development Plan*] [*Brazilian*] (LA)
PND............ Slant-Range Correction (RU)
PNDC.......... Provisional National Defence Council [*Ghanaian*] (PD)
PNDU.......... Programa Nacional do Desenvolvimento Urbano [*National Urban Development Program*] [*Brazilian*] (LA)
PNE............ PASOK Nomarkhiaki Epitropi [*PASOK Nome Committee*] (GC1)
PNE............ Polskie Normy Elektryczne [*Polish Electrical Standards*] (POL)
pne............ Przed Nasza Era [*Before Our Era (Before Christ)*] (POL)
PNEMEM..... Programa Nacional de Exportacao de Material de Emprego Militar [*National Policy for Export of Material for Military Use*] [*Brazilian*] (LA1)
pnev............ Pneumatic, Compressed-Air (RU)
PNF............ Palestine National Front (PD)
PNF............ Partito Nazionale Fascista [*National Fascist Party*] [*Italian*] (PPE)
PNF............ Polynucleotide Phosphorylase (RU)

PNF .... Progressive National Front [*Syrian*] (MAR)
PNG .... Papua New Guinea [*Three-letter standard code*] (CNC)
PNG .... Partido Nacional Guevarista [*Ecuadorean*] (PPW)
PNH .... Partido Nacional de Honduras [*National Party of Honduras*] (LA)
PNI .... Partai Nasional Indonesia [*Indonesian National Party*] (IN)
PNI .... Partido Nacional Independiente [*National Independent Party*] [*Costa Rican*] (PPW)
PNI .... Partido Nacional Integracionista [*National Integration Party*] [*Venezuelan*] (LA)
PNIC .... Pleasure Navigation International Joint Committee [*See also CINP*] (EA)
PNII .... Pediatric Scientific Research Institute (RU)
PNIIIS .... Industrial and Scientific Research Institute for Engineering Surveys in Construction (RU)
PNIP .... Device for Beam Observation and Measurement [*Nuclear physics and engineering*] (RU)
PNIRO .... Polar Scientific Research Institute of Sea Fisheries and Oceanography (RU)
PNIUI .... Moscow Region Scientific Research, Planning, and Design Institute of Coal (RU)
PNIUI .... Perm' Scientific Research Institute of Coal (RU)
p niz .... Patrz Nizej [*See Below*] [*Polish*]
pnk .... Peninkulma [*Finnish*]
PNKA .... Perusahaan Negara Kereta Api [*State Railway Company*] (IN)
PNKD .... Polski Narodowy Komitet Demokratyczny [*Polish National Democratic Committee*] [*In exile*] (POL)
PNL .... Parti National Liberal [*National Liberal Party*] [*Lebanese*] (PPW)
PNL .... Partidul National Liberal [*National Liberal Party*] [*Romanian*] (PPE)
PNL .... Prodotto Nazionale Lordo [*Gross National Product*] [*Use GNP*] [*Italian*] (WER)
PNM .... Partito Nazionale Monarchico [*National Monarchist Party*] [*Italian*] (PPE)
PNM .... People's National Movement [*Trinidadian and Tobagan*] (PD)
PNN .... Ground Observation Post (RU)
PNN .... Low-Pressure Superheater (BU)
PNN .... Prefectura Nacional Naval [*National Navy Prefecture*] [*Uruguayan*] (LA)
PNN .... Profesores Non Numerarios [*Extraordinary Professors*] [*Spanish*] (WER)
PNNV .... Net Positive Suction Head (RU)
PNO .... Assistant Chief of the Operations Section (RU)
PNO .... Deputy Chief of Staff for Operations (BU)
PNO .... Panellinios Navtiki Omospondia [*Panhellenic Seamen's Federation*] (GC)
PNO .... Parti Nationaliste Occitan [*Occitanian Nationalist Party*] [*French*] (PPE)
PNOC .... Philippine National Oil Company
PNOH .... Pozorista Narodnog Oslobodenja Hercegovine [*National Liberation Theaters of Hercegovina*] (YU)
PNOU .... Proleterska Narodnooslobodilacka Udarna [*Proletarian National Liberation Shock Troops*] (YU)
PNOUB .... Proleterska Narodnooslobodilacka Udarna Brigada [*Proletarian National Liberation Shock Brigade*] [*World War II*] (YU)
PNP .... Converter of Nonelectrical Parameters [*Computers*] (RU)
PNP .... Forward Observation Post (BU)
PNP .... Forward Observation Post (RU)
PNP .... Mobile Observation Post (RU)
PNP .... Pakistan National Party (PD)
PNP .... Parti National Populaire [*National Popular Party*] [*Canadian*] (PPW)
PNP .... Parti National du Progres (MAR)
PNP .... Partido Nacional Portugues [*Portuguese Nationalist Party*] (WER)
PNP .... Partido Nacionalista del Pueblo [*Bolivian*] (PPW)
PNP .... Partido Nuevo Progresista [*New Progressive Party*] [*Puerto Rican*] (PPW)
PNP .... Partidul National Poporului [*National People's Party*] [*Romanian*] (PPE)
PNP .... People's National Party [*Ghanaian*] (PPW)
PNP .... People's National Party [*Jamaican*] (PPW)
PNP .... Polish People's Republic (BU)
PNP .... Popular Nationalist Party [*Panamanian*] (PD)
PNP .... Progressive National Party (LA1)
PNP .... Progressivnaia Nigerskaia Partiia (MAR)
PNP- .... Steam Reciprocating Pump, Steam Piston Pump (RU)
PNPDD .... Praxeis Nomikon Prosopon Dimosiou Dikaiou [*Acts of Legal Entities of Public Law*] [*Greek*] (GC)
pn pk .... Engineer Combat Regiment (BU)
PNPNOKDK ... Regulations on Imposing Fines by Organs of the State Control Commission (BU)
PNPYO .... People's National Party Youth Organization [*Jamaican*] (LA1)
PNR .... Partido Nacional Reformista [*Reformist National Party*] [*Guatemalan*] (LA)
PNR .... Partido Nacional Republicano [*National Republican Party*] [*Portuguese*] (PPE)
PNR .... Partido Nacionalista Revolucionario [*Revolutionary Nationalist Party*] [*Ecuadorean*] (PPW)
PNR .... Partij Nationalistische Republiek [*Nationalist Republic Party*] [*Surinamese*] (PPW)
PNR .... Policia Nacional Revolucionaria [*National Revolutionary Police*] [*Cuban*] (LA)
PNR .... Polish People's Republic (RU)
PNR .... Starting and Adjusting Operations (BU)
PNR-44 .... Partido Nacional Revolucionario de 44 [*National Revolutionary Party of 44*] [*Colombian*] (LA)
PNRD .... Partido Nacionalista Revolucionario Democratico [*Democratic Revolutionary National Party*] [*Dominican Republic*] (LA1)
PNRSM .... Production Standards of Building Material Expenditure (RU)
pn rt .... Engineer Combat Company (BU)
PNS .... National Assembly Presidium (BU)
PNS .... Observation and Signal Post (RU)
PNS .... Plovdiv People's Council (BU)
PNS .... Pomocnik Nacelnika Stabu [*Assistant Chief-of-Staff*] (CZ)
PNS .... Postovni Novinova Sluzba [*Postal Newspaper Subscription Service*] (CZ)
PNS .... Prozatimni Narodni Shromazdeni [*Provisional National Assembly*] (CZ)
PNSFO .... Pomocnik Nacelnika Staba za Fizicku Obuku [*Assistant to Chief of Staff for Physical Training*] [*Military*] (YU)
PNSh .... Assistant Chief of Staff (RU)
PNShR .... Assistant Chief of Staff for Intelligence (RU)
PNSht .... Deputy Chief of Staff (BU)
PNSO .... Plovdiv People's Sports Organization (BU)
PNT .... Device for the Adjustment of Television Sets (RU)
PNT .... It Is Clear [*Telegraphy*] (RU)
PNT .... Partidul National Taranesc [*National Peasant Party*] (RO)
PNT .... Party of New Turkey (RU)
PNT .... Personnel Navigant Technique (MAR)
Pnt .... Point [*Point*] [*Military map abbreviation*] [*World War I*] [*French*] (MTD)
PNT .... Ponitrianske Tehelne [*Nitra Brick Works*] (CZ)
PNTC .... Parti National Travailliste Camerounais [*Cameroonian National Labor Party*] (AF)
PNTL .... Polskie Naukowe Towarzystwo Lesne [*Polish Scientific Society for Forestry*] (POL)
PNTs .... Guidance and Target Identification Point (RU)
PNU .... Mobile Magnetizer [*Weld inspection device*] (BU)
PNU .... Mobile Magnetizer [*Weld inspection device*] (RU)
PNU .... Postovni Novinovy Urad [*Postal Newspaper Subscription Office*] (CZ)
PNU .... Regulations on Teachers' Appointments (BU)
PNUD .... Programa de las Naciones Unidas para el Desarrollo [*United Nations Development Program*] [*Use UNDP*] (LA)
PNUD .... Programme des Nations Unies pour le Developpement [*United Nations Development Program*] [*Use UNDP*] (CL)
PNUD .... Programul Natiunilor Unite pentru Dezvoltare [*United Nations Development Program*] (RO)
PNUDE .... Programa das Nacoes Unidas para o Desenvolvimento [*United Nations Development Program*] [*Portuguese*] (WER)
PNUE .... Programme des Nations Unies pour l'Environnement [*United Nations Environment Program*] [*Use UNEP*] (AF)
PNUI .... Parti National Uni de l'Independance (MAR)
PNULAD .... United Nations Program for Drug Abuse Control [*Use UNPDAC*] (AF)
PNUO .... Progressive National Unionist Organization [*Egyptian*] (ME)
PNV .... Basque Nationalist Party [*Spanish*] (PD)
PNV .... High Pressure Superheater (BU)
PNV .... National Velasquista Party [*Ecuadorean*] (PPW)
PNV .... Night Vision Device (RU)
PNV .... Parti National Voltaique (MAR)
PNV .... Partido Nacionalista Vasco [*Basque Nationalist Party*] [*Spanish*] (PPE)
PNV .... "Voltage-Time" Converter (RU)
PNVC .... Partido Nacional de Veteranos Civiles [*Civilian Veterans National Party*] [*Dominican Republic*] (LA1)
pn-wsch .... Polnocno-Wschodni [*North-East*] [*Polish*]
PNYME .... Papir- es Nyomdaipari Muszaki Egyesulet [*Technical Association of the Paper and Printing Industry*] (HU)
PNZ .... Panstwowe Nieruchomosci Ziemskie [*Polish*]
PNZ .... Poljoprivredni Nakladni Zavod [*Agricultural Publishing Institute*] [*Zagreb*] (YU)
pn-zach .... Polnocno-Zachodni [*North-West*] [*Polish*]
PNZP .... Polnohospodarsky Nakupny a Zasobovaci Podnik [*Agricultural Supply and Purchase Enterprise*] (CZ)
PO .... Advance Detachment (BU)
PO .... Advance Detachment (RU)
PO .... Aircraft Designed by N. N. Polikarpov (RU)
PO .... Auxiliary Organization (BU)
PO .... Border Guard (RU)
PO .... Border Guard Detachment (RU)
PO .... Bypass Switch (RU)
PO .... Check Point Bearing (RU)
PO .... Consumers' Society (RU)
PO .... Cross Pollination (RU)
PO .... Departure Yard, Advance Yard [*Railroads*] (RU)
PO .... Exhaust Steam (RU)
PO .... Foaming Agent, Frothing Agent (RU)
PO .... Mobile Defense (RU)

PO .... Pamiatnik Oslobodenia [*Liberation Memorial*] (CZ)
PO .... Par Ordre [*Military*] [*French*] (MTD)
PO .... Par Ordre De [*By Order Of*] [*In the context of signatures at the end of memos or documents*] (CL)
po .... Partisan Detachment (RU)
PO .... Partizanski Odredi [*Partisan Detachments*] [*World War II*] (YU)
po .... Pelniacy Obowiazki [*Acting Chief*] (POL)
PO .... Petrol Ofisi [*Petroleum Office*] [*of Turkish government*] [*See also TPO*] (TU)
Po .... Pico [*Peak*] [*See also Pco*] [*Portuguese*] (NAU)
Po .... Pico [*Peak*] [*See also Pco*] [*Spanish*] (NAU)
PO .... Pionyrska Organisace [*Pioneer Organization*] (CZ)
po .... Pitaa Olla [*Finnish*]
PO .... Planning Department, Planning Section (RU)
PO .... Poder Obrero [*Worker Power*] [*Argentine*] (LA)
PO .... Podnikova Organisace [*Enterprise Organization*] [*A periodical*] (CZ)
PO .... Podvodno Oruzje [*Underwater Weapons*] [*Military*] (YU)
PO .... Political Department, Political Section (RU)
PO .... Politicke Oddeleni [*Political Department*] (CZ)
PO .... Politicky Oddil [*Political Department*] (CZ)
PO .... Por Orden [*By Order*] [*Spanish*]
po .... Posebni Odtis [*Special Reprint*] (YU)
PO .... Post Office (RU)
PO .... Poste d'Observation [*Military*] [*French*] (MTD)
Po .... Postzug [*Mail Train*] (EG)
PO .... Potere Operaio [*Workers' Power*] [*Italian*] (WER)
Po .... Pouce [*Inch*] [*French*] (MTD)
Po .... Pour Ordre [*French*] (MTD)
PO .... Prednji Odred [*Advanced Detachment*] [*Military*] (YU)
PO .... Privremeno Otsutan [*Temporarily Absent*] [*Census*] (YU)
PO .... Processing Station (RU)
PO .... Projektne Organizacije [*Industrial Designing Organizations*] (YU)
PO .... Protiletecka Obrana [*Antiaircraft Defense*] (CZ)
PO .... Pruzkumny Oddil [*Reconnaissance Battalion*] (CZ)
po .... Puheena Oleva [*Finnish*]
Po .... Pulo [*Island*] [*Indonesian*] (NAU)
Po .... Pulo [*Island*] [*Malaysian*] (NAU)
PO .... Receiving-Departure Yard [*Railroads*] (RU)
PO .... Refracted and Reflected (Wave) (RU)
PO .... Security on the March, March Security (RU)
PO .... Starting Unit (RU)
p/o .... Subdivision (RU)
PO .... Turnover Period (RU)
PO .... Verification Paid [*Telegraphy*] (RU)
POA .... Panellinios Omospondia Aliergaton [*Panhellenic Federation of Fishing Industry Workers*] (GC)
POA .... Panellinios Omospondia Artergaton [*Panhellenic Federation of Bakery Workers*] (GC)
POA .... Pankyprios Organosis Anapiron [*Pan-Cyprian Organization of the Disabled*] (GC)
POA .... Pezoporikos Omilos Athinon [*Athens Walking Club*] (GC)
POA .... Pontifica Opera di Assistenza [*Pontifical Relief Organization*]
POA .... Public Order Act [*Mauritian*] (AF)
POAA .... Pankyprios Organosis Apokatastaseos Anapiron [*Pan-Cyprian Rehabilitation Organization for the Handicapped*] (GC)
POAAP .... Panellinios Omospondia Astegon Aston Prosfygon [*Panhellenic Federation of Homeless Urban Refugees*] (GC)
POAAPS ...... Permanent Organization for Afro-Asian Peoples Solidarity (MAR)
POAEA .... Panellinios Organosis Agoniston Ethnikis Andistaseos [*Panhellenic Organization of National Resistance Fighters*] (GC)
POAP .... Pangosmios Omospondia Adelfopoiimenon Poleon [*World Federation of Sister Cities*] (GC1)
poarm .... Army Political Section (RU)
POAS .... Pankyprios Omospondia Anexartiton Syndekhnion [*Pan-Cyprian Federation of Independent Trade Unions*] (GC)
POAYA .... Panellinios Omospondia Artergaton kai Ypallilon Artou [*Panhellenic Federation of Bakery Workers*] (GC)
POAYL .... Panellinios Omospondia Avtokinitiston Yperastikon Leoforeion [*Panhellenic Federation of Interurban Bus Drivers*] (GC)
POAYS .... Panellinios Omospondia Avtokinitiston Yperastikon Syngoinonion [*Panhellenic Federation of Drivers in Interurban Transportation*] (GC)
POB .... Parti Ouvrier Belge [*Belgian Workers' Party*] [*Later, Belgian Socialist Party*] (PPE)
POB .... Partizansko Obavestajni Biro [*Partisan Information Bureau*] [*World War II*] (YU)
pober .... Shore, Coast (RU)
POBNS .... Regulation on Relations with Banks in the National Economy (BU)
POC .... Parti des Ouvriers Chretiens [*Christian Workers Party*] [*Belgian*] (WER)
POC .... Pevecka Obec Ceskoslovenska [*Czechoslovak Choral Society*] (CZ)
POC .... Public Order Company (ML)
POCH .... Progressiven Organisationen der Schweiz [*Progressive Organizations of Switzerland*] (PPE)
poch .... Spadix [*Botany*], Cop [*Textiles*] (RU)
po Chr .... Po Chrystusie [*Polish*]
pocht .... Post Office (RU)
pocht .... Post, Postal, Mail (RU)
pocht -tel .... Postal and Telegraphic, Post and Telegraph (RU)
pochv .... Soil, Ground (RU)
pochv gidr ... Soil Hydrology (RU)
pochv kompl ... Soil Complex (RU)
pochv Min ... Soil Mineralogy (RU)
pochvoobr ... Soil-Cultivating (RU)
pochvoobr ... Soil-Forming (RU)
POCSM .... Pionierska Organizacia Ceskoslovenskeho Svazu Mladeze [*Pioneer Organization of the Czechoslovak Union of Youth*] (CZ)
pod .... Approach Road, Porch, Entrance (RU)
POD .... Division Dressing Detachment (RU)
POD .... Pracownicze Ogrody Dzialkowe [*Employees' Garden Plots*] (POL)
POD .... Preduzece za Obradu Duvana [*Tobacco Processing Establishment*] (YU)
pod .... Signature (BU)
pod .... Similar (BU)
pod .... Similar, Like, Such (RU)
PODERI .... Programa de Desarrollo Rural Integral [*Integral Rural Development Program*] [*Nicaraguan*] (LA1)
PODG .... Pangosmios Organismos Dimokratikon Gynaikon [*World Federation of Democratic Women*] (GC)
podgot .... Preparation, Prepared (RU)
podgr .... Subgroup [*Artillery*] (BU)
podigr .... Ironical (BU)
podiv .... Political Section of a Division (RU)
PODKO .... Powiatowy Osrodek Doskonalenia Kadr Oswiatowych [*County Center for Improvement of Educational Personnel*] (POL)
Podlodkomin ... Minelaying Submarine (RU)
PODN .... Pangosmios Organosis Dimokratikis Neolaias [*World Federation of Democratic Youth*] (GC)
podn .... Podnaslov [*Subtitle*] (YU)
podobr .... Improved (BU)
Podolskhar ... Podol'sk Branch of the Sugar Trust (RU)
podp .... Signature, Signed (RU)
podp k pech ... Approved for Printing (RU)
podplav .... Underwater Navigation (RU)
podpolk ...... Lieutenant Colonel (RU)
podr .... Podrecznik [*Textbook*] (POL)
pod red .... Edited By (BU)
pod red .... Edited By (RU)
PODREM ..... Rolling Stock Repair Train (RU)
pod rukovod ... Under the Leadership Of (RU)
podsem .... Subfamily (RU)
podst el .... Electric Substation (RU)
podstroch ... Interlinear (RU)
podstroch primech ... Footnote (RU)
podv .... Bound [*Book*] (BU)
podv .... Underwater [*Topography*] (RU)
podvizh .... Mobile, Movable (RU)
PODY .... Pankyprios Organosis Dimokratikon Gynaikon [*Pan-Cyprian Organization of Democratic Women*] (GC)
Pod"yemtranskomplekt ... Trust for Making Up Complete Sets of Hoisting and Conveying Equipment (RU)
podzagl .... Subtitle (BU)
podzagol ..... Subtitle, Subhead (RU)
Podzemgaz ... All-Union Experimental Office for the Surveying, Planning, and Construction of Experimental Mines for Underground Coal Gasification (RU)
POE .... Patriarkhiki Oikonomiki Epitropi [*Patriarchal Finance Committee*] (GC)
POE .... Plan of Organization of Operations (RU)
POE .... Polyoxyethylene Glycol (RU)
POEA .... Pankypria Omospondia Efedron Axiomatikon [*Pan-Cyprian Federation of Reserve Officers*] (GC)
POED .... Pankyprios Organosis Ellinon Didaskalon [*Pan-Cyprian Greek Teachers Organization*] (GC)
POEEYTE .... Panellinios Omospondia Ergaton Episitismou kai Ypallilon Touristikon Epangelmaton [*Panhellenic Federation of Food Supply and Tourist Trades Workers*] (GC)
POEI .... Panellinios Omospondia Ergatoypallilon Imatismou [*Panhellenic Federation of Garment Workers and Employees*] (GC)
POEK .... Panellinios Omospondia Ergatoypallilon Kreatos [*Panhellenic Federation of Meat Industry Workers and Employees*] (GC)
POEKO .... Panellinia Omospondia Emborikon Kladikon Organoseon [*Panhellenic Federation of Commercial Branch Organizations*] (GC1)
POELIME .... Pankyprios Organosis Ellinon Leitourgon Idiotikis Mesis Ekpaidevseos [*Pan-Cyprian Organization of Greek Private Secondary School Teachers*] (GC)
POEM .... Palm Oil Estates Managers (MAR)
POEM .... Panellinios Omospondia Ergaton Metallou [*Panhellenic Federation of Metal Workers*] (GC)
POEO .... Panellinios Omospondia Ergatotekhniton Oikodomon [*Panhellenic Federation of Building Trades Workers*] (GC)

POEOX........ Panellinios Omospondia Ergatoypallilon Oikodomon kai Xylou [*Panhellenic Federation of Construction and Lumber Workers*] (GC)
POES........... Pangosmios Omospondia ton Ergatikon Syndikaton [*World Federation of Trade Unions*] (GC)
poet............ Poetic (RU)
poet............ Poetic Word (BU)
POEYGTP ... Panellinios Omospondia Ergatotekhniton-Ypallilon Galaktos, Trofimon, kai Poton [*Panhellenic Federation of Milk, Food, and Beverage Personnel*] (GC)
POEYPEPG ... Panellinios Omospondia Ergatotekhniton kai Ypallilon Paragogis, Epexergasias, kai Poliseos Galaktos [*Panhellenic Federation of Milk Production, Processing, and Sales Personnel*] (GC)
POF .... Complete Evaluative Functions (RU)
POF .... Fixed Capital Increment (RU)
POFE........... Panellinios Organosis Filelevtheron Ellinidon [*Panhellenic Organization of Liberal Women*] (GC)
POFI .... Panellinios Omospondia Fotos kai Ikhou [*Panhellenic Federation of Light and Sound*] (GC1)
POFIS.......... Postovni Filatelisticka Sluzba [*Postal Stamp Collector Service*] (CZ)
POFNE .... Pankypria Omospondia Foititon kai Neon Epistimonon [*Pan-Cyprian Federation of Students and Young Professionals*] (GC)
POG............. Panelladiki Omospondia Gynaikon [*Panhelladic Federation of Women*] (GC)
pogl............ Absorption (RU)
pog m.......... Linear Meter, Running Meter (RU)
POGO.......... Pankyprios Omospondia Gynaikeion Organoseon [*Pan-Cyprian Federation of Women's Organizations*] (GC)
pogov.......... Proverb (RU)
POGR .... President's Own Guard Regiment (MAR)
pogresk....... Border Guard Troop [*Cav.*] (RU)
pogr kom .... Border Guard Commandant's Office [*Topography*] (RU)
pogr st .... Frontier Post [*Marker*] [*Topography*] (RU)
pogruz......... Loading and Unloading Platform [*Topography*] (RU)
pogr zast..... Frontier Post (RU)
POGSJAM... Propagandno Odelenje pri Glavniot Stab na Jugoslovenskata Armija za Makedonija [*Propaganda Department in the General Headquarters of the Yugoslav Army of Macedonia*] [*World War II*] (YU)
POH............. Partizanski Odredi Hrvatske [*Croatian Partisan Detachments*] [*World War II*] (YU)
pohj............ Pohjois [*Northern*] [*Finnish*]
poHr........... Po Hrista [*In the Year of Our Lord*] (YU)
POIA........... Panstwowa Organizacja Imprez Artystycznych [*Polish*]
POIA Artos ... Panstwowa Organizacja Imprez Artystycznych "Artos" [*"Artos" State Organization for Artistic Performances*] (POL)
POIAL.......... Panellinios Omospondia Idioktiton Astikon Leoforeion [*Panhellenic Federation of Urban Bus Owners*] (GC)
POIDON ...... Regulation on Expropriation of Property for State and Public Needs (BU)
POiE........... Pomorska Odlewnia i Emaliernia [*Pomerania Metal-Working and Enameling Plant*] (POL)
POIEKO....... Panellinios Omospondia Ilektrismou kai Epikheiriseon Koinis Ofeleias [*Panhellenic Federation of Electric Power and Public Utility Enterprises*] (GC)
POIT........... Powiatowy Osrodek Informacji Turystycznej [*District Tourist Information Center*] [*Polish*]
POJ .... Partizanski Odredi Jugoslavije [*Partisan Detachments of Yugoslavia*] [*World War II*] (YU)
POJ .... Pionyrske Oddily Junaka [*Pioneer Units of the Junak Organization*] (CZ)
poj.............. Pojedynczy [*Single*] (POL)
POK............ Panellinion Oikologikon Kinima [*Panhellenic Ecological Movement*] (GC1)
pok............. Pokoj [*Room*] (POL)
POK............ Postai Oktatasi Kozpont [*Postal Training Center*] (HU)
POKB .... Panstwowy Osrodek Ksztalcenia Bibliotekarzy [*State Center for the Education of Librarians*] (POL)
POKE .... Panellinios Organosis Kinimatografikon Epikheiriseon [*Panhellenic Organization of Motion Picture Enterprises*] (GC)
POKh.......... [*The*] Organic Chemistry Industry (RU)
POKhl.......... Plovdiv Okrug Art Exhibit (BU)
POKLJDZ.... Preduzece za Opravku Kola i Lokomotiva Jugoslovanske Drzavne Zeleznice [*Car and Locomotive Repair Establishment of the Yugoslav Railroads*] (YU)
Pokobank ... Bank of Consumers' Cooperatives (RU)
pok prel ...... Index of Refraction, Refractive Index (RU)
POKY .... Panellinios Omospondia Koinotikon Ypallilon [*Panhellenic Federation of Communal Employees*] (GC)
pol.............. Glade, Clearing [*Topography*] (RU)
pol.............. Half (RU)
POL .... Panellinios Omospondia Logiston [*Panhellenic Accountants Federation*] (GC)
POL .... Petroleum, Oil, and Lubricants (CL)
POL .... Poland [*Three-letter standard code*] (CNC)
pol.............. Polarization (RU)
pol.............. Polish (BU)
pol.............. Politiikka [*Politics*] [*Finnish*]
pol.............. Politika [*or Politikai*] [*Politics or Political*] (HU)
pol.............. Politisch [*German*]
Pol.............. Polizei [*German*]
pol.............. Polowa [*Half*] (POL)
pol.............. Polski [*Polish*] (POL)
Pol.............. Poluostrov [*Peninsula*] [*Russian*] (NAU)
POLAG........ Panellinios Omospondia Leoforeioukhon Agonon Grammon [*Panhellenic Federation of Unprofitable Bus Line Operators*] (GC)
POL-DER..... Polis Dernegi [*Police Association*] [*of a particular city*] (TU)
POLDOK ..... Politische Dokumentation
polem.......... Polemika [*Polemic*] (POL)
polg............ Polgari [*Civilian*] (HU)
polg m......... Polgarmester [*Mayor*] (HU)
Polgos......... Polskie Wydawnictwa Gospodarcze [*Polish Publishing House for Economics*] (POL)
Pol grad ...... Polymerizationsgrad [*Degree of Polymerization*] [*German*]
POLICOLDA ... Poliolefinas Colombiana Ltda. [*Girardota-Antioquia*] (COL)
poligr .... Polygraphic (BU)
poligr .... Printing (RU)
poligr .... Printing Industry Factory [*Topography*] (RU)
poligr .... Printing Industry Kombinat [*Topography*] (RU)
Poligrafizdat ... Department of Publishing Houses and the Printing Industry (RU)
Poligrafkniga ... Book and Magazine Printing Trust (RU)
poligrafprom ... Printing Industry (RU)
Poligrafsoyuz ... Union of Printing Trade Workers (RU)
pol ikonom ... Political Economy (BU)
POLINAL..... Policia Nacional [*Bogota*] (COL)
Polinale....... Police Nationale [*National Police*] [*Cambodian*] (CL)
polir............ Polished (RU)
polir shl....... Polished Section (RU)
POLIS.......... Politische Informations Systeme
POLISARIO ... Frente Popular para la Liberacion de Saguia El Hamra y Rio De Oro [*Popular Front for the Liberation of Saguia El Hamra and Rio De Oro*] [*Saharan*] (AF)
polit............ Political (BU)
polit............ Political (RU)
polit............ Politisch [*German*]
Politbyuro... Political Bureau (BU)
Politbyuro na TsK na BKP ... Politburo of the BCP [*Bulgarian Communist Party*] Central Committee (BU)
politekhn .... Polytechnic, Polytechnical (RU)
Politemigrant ... Political Exile (BU)
Politizdat .... Publishing House of Political Literature (RU)
politkom ..... Political Commissar (RU)
politkom ..... Politicki Komesar [*Political Commissar*] [*Communist Party*] (YU)
Politotdel .... Political Department (BU)
politprosvet ... Political Education Administration, Political Education Directorate (RU)
politprosvet ... Political Education Committee (RU)
Politsekretar ... Political Secretary (BU)
politupr .... Political Administration, Political Directorate (RU)
Politupravlenie ... Political Administration (BU)
Politvod....... Political Administration of Water Transportation (RU)
Politzatvornik ... Political Prisoner (BU)
POLJCOPSKBA ... Poduzece za Opskrbu Poljoprivrede [*Agricultural Supply Establishment*] (YU)
POLJOOTKUP ... Poljoprivredno Otkupno Preduzece [*Agricultural Purchasing Establishment*] (YU)
POLJOPRODUKT ... Preduzece za Promet Poljoprivrednih Proizvoda [*Agricultural Products Trade Establishment*] (YU)
POLJOPROIZVOD ... Preduzece za Promet Poljoprivrednih Proizvoda [*Agricultural Products Trade Establishment*] (YU)
POLJOPROMET ... Preduzece za Promet Poljoprivrednih Proizvoda [*Agricultural Products Trade Establishment*] (YU)
POLJOTRGOVINA ... Preduzece za Promet Poljoprivrednih Proizvoda [*Agricultural Products Trade Establishment*] (YU)
polk............ Colonel (BU)
polk............ Colonel (RU)
polkinzh...... Regimental Engineer (RU)
polkom........ Political Commissar (RU)
polkom........ Politicki Komesar [*Political Commissar*] [*Communist Party*] (YU)
Polnar .... Polska Wytwornia Narzedzi [*Polish Tool Plant*] (POL)
Poln sobr soch ... Complete Collection of Works, Complete Works (RU)
Polocean..... Polskie Linie Oceaniczne [*Polish Ocean Lines*] (POL)
POLOCENTRO ... Programa de Desenvolvimento dos Cerrados [*Scrublands Development Program*] [*Brazilian*] (LA1)
Polokr .... Politicky Okres [*Political District*] (CZ)
POLONORDESTE ... Programa de Desenvolvimento de Areas Integradas do Nordeste [*Program for the Development of Integrated Areas of the Northeast*] [*Brazilian*] (LA)
Polotn .... Linen Factory [*Topography*] (RU)
polozh......... Positive (BU)
polozhit....... Positive (RU)
pol post svkh ... Sovkhoz Field Structures [*Topography*] (RU)
Polpred .... Political Representative (BU)

polr............ Polrocznie [*Semiannual*] (POL)
POLRI.......... Kepolisian Negara Republik Indonesia [*Republic of Indonesia State Police*] (IN)
pol'sk.......... Polish (RU)
polsk........... Polskorek [*Half-Binding*] [*Polish*]
pol st........... Field Camp [*Topography*] (RU)
pol st........... Polar Station (RU)
polud........... Poludnie [*South*] [*Polish*]
polupl.......... Poluplatno [*Half-Linen*] [*Binding*] (YU)
poluprovodn ... Semiconductor (RU)
Polw............ Polwysep [*Peninsula*] [*Polish*]
POLYAG...... Panellinios Omospondia Leoforeioukhon Yperastikon Agonon Grammon [*Panhellenic Federation of Unprofitable Interurban Bus Line Operators*] (GC)
polyarograf ... Polarographic (RU)
Polyg........... Polygone [*Proving Ground, Artillery Range*] [*Military map abbreviation*] [*World War I*] [*French*] (MTD)
POLZAR...... Polis Pazari [*Police Market*] (TU)
pom............. Assistant (BU)
pom............. Assistant, Deputy (RU)
pom............. Building [*In addresses*] (RU)
POM............ Panstwowe Osrodki Maszynowe [*State (Agricultural) Machine Stations*] (POL)
POM............ Polisi Militer [*Military Police*] (IN)
pom............. Pomeridiane [*After Noon*] [*Italian*] (GPO)
POM............ Postaugyi Miniszterium/Miniszter [*Ministry/Minister of the Post*] (HU)
POMAG....... Societe de Grands Magasins de Pointe-Noire (MAR)
pomb........... Pontoon-Bridge Battalion (BU)
pomb........... Pontoon Bridge Battalion (RU)
pombr......... Pontoon-Bridge Brigade (BU)
pombr......... Pontoon Bridge Brigade (RU)
pombrig...... Assistant Brigade Leader (RU)
POME.......... Panellinios Omospondia Mousikon Ellados [*Panhellenic Federation of Greek Musicians*] (GC)
pomgol........ Committee for Famine Relief [*1921-1922*] (RU)
pomkombat ... Assistant Battalion Commander (RU)
pomkombrig ... Assistant Brigade Commander (RU)
pomkomdiv ... Assistant Division Commander (RU)
pomkomroty ... Assistant Company Commander (RU)
pomkomvzod ... Assistant Platoon Commander (RU)
pomkomvzvoda ... Assistant Platoon Commander (RU)
POMM......... Panellinios Omospondia Milergato-Ypallilon kai Makaronotekhniton [*Panhellenic Federation of Mill and Macaroni Workers and Employees*] (GC)
pomnach..... Assistant Chief (RU)
POMOA....... Provisional Office for Mass Organizational Affairs [*Ethiopian*] (AF)
pomocn....... Pomocniczy [*Auxiliary*] (POL)
POMONA.... Compagnie pour le Commerce International de Fruits et Primeurs (MAR)
pomp........... Pontoon-Bridge Regiment (BU)
pomp........... Pontoon Bridge Regiment (RU)
POMR.......... Partido Obrero Marxista Revolucionario [*Marxist Revolutionary Workers Party*] [*Peruvian*] (LA)
pomrezh..... Assistant Producer (RU)
Pomvetsl..... Pomocna Veterinarska Sluzba [*Auxiliary Veterinary Service*] (CZ)
pomzav....... Assistant Manager, Assistant Chief (RU)
Pomzdrasl ... Pomocna Zdravotnicka Sluzba [*Auxiliary Medical Service*] (CZ)
PON............ Panellinios Omospondia Navtikon [*Panhellenic Seamen's Federation*] (GC)
PON............ Panellinios Organosis Neolaias [*Panhellenic Youth Organization*] (GC)
Pon............. Pavillon [*Pavilion*] [*Military map abbreviation*] [*World War I*] [*French*] (MTD)
PON............ Popularna Odznaka Narciarska [*Popular Ski Badge*] [*Polish*]
ponb........... Pontoon-Bridge Battalion (BU)
ponbr......... Pontoon-Bridge Brigade (BU)
ponmostb ... Pontoon Bridge Battalion (RU)
ponmostbr ... Pontoon Bridge Brigade (RU)
ponmostp ... Pontoon Bridge Regiment (RU)
ponp........... Pontoon Bridge Regiment (RU)
PONTECO... Societe Commerciale Pontenegrine-Oubangui (MAR)
ponv........... Pontoon Platoon (RU)
POO............ Protivoklopna Odbrana [*Antiarmor Defense*] (YU)
POONSDT... Design Organizations of Okrug People's Councils of Deputies of the Working People (BU)
POP............ Panstwowy Osrodek Pedagogiczny [*State Pedagogical Center*] (POL)
POP............ Parti Ouvrier et Populaire (Parti Suisse du Travail) [*Labor Party*] [*Swiss*] (WER)
POP............ Partido de Orientacion Popular [*Popular Orientation Party*] [*Ecuadorean*] (LA)
POP............ Patrullas de Orden Publico [*Public Order Patrols*] [*Cuban*] (LA)
POP............ Podstawowa Organizacja Partyjna [*Primary Party Organization (of the Polish United People's Party)*] (POL)
POP............ Poduzece za Odrzavanje Pruge JZ [*Yugoslav Railroads Track Maintenance Establishment*] (YU)
POP............ Preduzece za Odrzavanje Puteva [*Road Maintenance Establishment*] (YU)
POP............ Property Owners' Protection (MAR)
POP............ Prumysl-Obchod-Politika [*Industry-Commerce-Politics (The secretariats of the Communist Party)*] (CZ)
POP............ Regimental Supply Relay Point (RU)
POP............ Regulations on Social Assistance (BU)
POPD.......... Panellinia Omospondia Prosopikou Diylistirion [*Panhellenic Confederation of Refinery Employees*] (GC)
POP-DEI...... Panellinios Omospondia Prosopikou Dimosia Epikheirisis Ilektrismou [*Panhellenic Federation of Public Power Corporation Personnel*] (GC)
POPEO........ Panellinios Omospondia Paragogis kai Emborias Oporokipevtikon [*Panhellenic Federation of Fruit and Vegetable Producers and Marketers*] (GC)
POPN.......... Przedsiebiorstwo Obrotu Produktami Naftowymi [*Petroleum Products Marketing Enterprise*] (POL)
POPO.......... People's Organizing Provisional Office (MAR)
POPODD..... Panellinios Omospondia Prosopikou Organismon Dimosiou Dikaiou [*Panhellenic Federation of Personnel of Public Law Organizations*] (GC)
POPP.......... Pangosmios Omospondia Palaion Polemiston [*World Veterans Federation*] (GC)
POPP.......... Preduzece za Odrzavanje Plovnog Puta [*River Navigation Maintenance Establishment*] (YU)
POPPG........ Party of the People's Progress Groups [*Trinidadian and Tobagan*] (LA)
popr........... Corrected (BU)
popr........... Poprawione [*Corrected*] (POL)
POPS.......... Panellinios Omospondia Politikon Syndaxioukhon [*Panhellenic Federation of Civil Pensioners*] (GC)
POPsY......... Pangosmios Organismos Psykhikis Ygeias [*World Federation for Mental Health*] (GC)
popul.......... Popular (BU)
popul.......... Popular (RU)
populn........ Enlarged (BU)
POPVC........ Puestos de Observacion y Vigilancia Costera [*Observation and Coastal Vigilance Posts*] [*Cuban*] (LA)
p or............ Field Gun (BU)
Por............. Gunpowder Plant [*Topography*] (RU)
POR............ Parti Ouvrier Revolutionnaire [*Revolutionary Workers Party*] [*Belgian*] (WER)
POR............ Partido Obrero Revolucionario [*Revolutionary Workers' Party*] [*Bolivian*] (PPW)
POR............ Partido Obrero Revolucionario [*Revolutionary Workers Party*] [*Peruvian*] (LA)
POR............ Partido Operario Revolucionario [*Revolutionary Workers Party*] [*Brazilian*] (LA)
por.............. Porownaj [*Compare*] (POL)
por.............. Porucik [*Lieutenant*] [*US equivalent: Second Lieutenant*] (CZ)
por.............. Porucznik [*Lieutenant*] (POL)
POR............ Ranging Gun (RU)
Por............. Rapids [*Topography*] (RU)
POR............ Work Organization Plan (RU)
PORA.......... Parti Ouvrier Revolutionnaire Arabe (MAR)
PORBISI...... Persatuan Organisasi Buruh Islam Seluruh Indonesia [*All-Indonesian Federation of Moslem Workers Organizations*] (IN)
PORC.......... Partido Obrero Revolucionario-Combate [*Revolutionary Struggle Workers' Party*] [*Bolivian*] (PPW)
porc............ Poradove Cislo [*Consecutive Number*] (CZ)
PORE.......... Partido Obrero Revolucionario de Espana [*Revolutionary Labor Party of Spain*] (WER)
POREM........ Railroad Rolling-Stock Repair Train (RU)
por no.......... Ordinal Number (BU)
por nom...... Ordinal Number (BU)
Poroshkogr ... Powder Pattern (RU)
PORP.......... Polish United Workers' Party (BU)
PORP.......... Polish United Workers' Party (RU)
PORPISI...... Persatuan Organisasi Pemuda Islam Seluruh Indonesia [*All-Indonesia Federation of Moslem Youth Organizations*] (IN)
porpor......... Second Lieutenant (RU)
Por skl......... Powder Magazine [*Topography*] (RU)
porssi.......... Porssitermi [*Stock Exchange*] [*Finnish*]
PORT.......... Partido Obrero Revolucionario Trotskista [*Trotskyite Revolutionary Labor Party*] [*Peruvian*] (LA)
POR-T......... Partido Operario Revolucionario-Trotskista [*Trotskyite Revolutionary Labor Party*] [*Brazilian*] (LA)
port............ Portaikko [*Finnish*]
port............ Portugalia [*or Portugaliksi*] [*Finnish*]
port............ Portugalilainen [*Finnish*]
port............ Portuguese (RU)
Portio.......... Porticciolo [*Small Port*] [*Italian*] (NAU)
PORTOBRAS ... Empresa de Portos do Brasil [*Brazilian Ports Enterprise*] (LA)
PORTP........ Partido Obrero Revolucionaria Trotskista Posadista [*Bolivian*] (PPW)
portr........... Portrait (BU)
portr........... Portrait (RU)
portug......... Portuguese (RU)
poryadk....... Ordinal (Number) (RU)
PORZ Orbis ... Przedsiebiorstwo Obslugi Ruchu Zagranicznego Orbis [*Orbis Foreign Travel Agency*] (POL)

pos .... Adequate [*Mark in school*] (RU)
POS .... Feedback Potentiometer (RU)
POS .... Hunters' Trading Station (RU)
POS .... Mirror-Image Firing Device (RU)
p-os .... Paikallisosasto [*Finnish*]
POS .... Panellinios Odondiatrikos Syllogos [*Panhellenic Dental Society*] (GC)
POS .... Panellinios Omospondia Sidirodromikon [*Panhellenic Railwaymen's Federation*] (GC)
POS .... Parti de l'Objectif Socialiste (MAR)
POS .... Partido Obrero Socialista [*Socialist Labor Party*] [*Mexican*] (LA1)
POS .... Partiia Osvobozhdeniia i Sotsializma (MAR)
POS .... Plovdiv Oblast Court (BU)
POS .... Polskie Organizacje Studenckie [*Polish Student Organizations*] (POL)
POS .... Polytechnische Oberschule [*German*]
POS .... Pomorski Obalski Sektor [*Naval Coastal Sector*] (YU)
pos .... Posel [*Deputy*] [*Polish*]
Pos .... Position [*Position*] (EG)
POS .... Pskov Provincial Dictionary (RU)
pos .... Settlement (RU)
POS .... Successive Concentration of Fire [*Artillery*] (BU)
POS- .... Tin-Lead Solder (RU)
POSD .... Panellinios Omospondia Syndesmon Dasoponon [*Panhellenic Federation of Forestry Workers' Associations*] (GC)
Posekr .... Political Secretariat (RU)
POSF .... Panstwowa Odznaka Sprawnosci Fizycznej [*State Badge for Physical Fitness*] [*Polish*]
POSG .... Panellinios Omospondia Syndesmon Geoponon [*Panhellenic Federation of Agriculturists' Associations*] (GC)
POSK .... Panellinios Omospondia Syndaxioukhon Kapnergaton [*Panhellenic Federation of Pensioned Tobacco Workers*] (GC)
POSL .... Parti Ouvrier Socialiste Luxembourgeois [*Luxembourg Socialist Workers Party*] (WER)
Posl .... Poslanec [*Member of the National Assembly*] (CZ)
posl .... Proverb (RU)
poslbydl ...... Posledni Bydliste [*Last Address*] (CZ)
posled .... [*The*] Last One (BU)
Posledgol .... Central Commission for Combating the After-Effects of Famine (RU)
Posledgol .... Commission for Combating the After-Effects of Famine (RU)
poslesl .... Epilogue (RU)
poslesl .... Postword (BU)
posm .... Posthumous (BU)
POSM .... Quarry Materials Processing Enterprise (BU)
posmert ...... Posthumous (RU)
POSNAA ..... Permanent Organization for Afro-Asian Peoples Solidarity (RU)
Pos pl .... Landing Site [*Helicopters*], Landing Area (RU)
pospo .... Settlement Consumers' Society (RU)
posr .... Adequate [*Mark in school*] (RU)
POSS .... Panellinios Omospondia Syndaxioukhon Sidirodromikon [*Panhellenic Federation of Railroad Pensioners*] (GC)
poss pron .... Possessivipronomini [*Possessive Pronoun*] [*Finnish*]
posssuff ...... Possessiivisuffiksi [*Finnish*]
pos such ..... Opere Citato [*In the Work Cited*] (BU)
post .... Decision, Resolution, Decree (RU)
post .... Decree (BU)
post .... Direct [*Current*], Permanent, Constant (RU)
POSTI .... Przedsiebiorstwo Obrotu Spozywczymi Towarami Importowanymi [*Sales Enterprise for Imported Food Goods*] (POL)
postitoim .... Postitoimisto [*Finnish*]
POSTiW ...... Powiatowy Osrodek Sportu, Turystyki, i Wypoczynku [*County Sports, Touring, and Rest Center*] (POL)
Postkutiya ... Post Office Box (BU)
Post na Min suvet ... Council of Ministers Decree (BU)
postroykom ... Construction Committee (RU)
Posyltorg .... Republic Mail Order Trade Office (RU)
POT .... Motor Vehicle Decontamination Site (RU)
POT .... Parish Organizing Teams [*Grenadian*] (LA1)
POT .... Permis d'Occupation Temporaire [*Temporary Occupation Permit*] (CL)
POT .... Petit Observateur Togolais (MAR)
Pot .... Potamos [*River*] [*Greek*] (NAU)
pot .... Potentiaali(n) [*Finnish*]
POT .... Pretprijatie za Obrabotka na Tutun [*Tobacco Processing Establishment*] (YU)
POT .... Punkt Obslugi Turystycznej [*Tourist Service*] [*Polish*]
POTA .... Prosopikon Organismon Topikis Avtodioikiseos [*Personnel of Local Self-Government Organizations*] [*Greek*] (GC)
POTAB .... Postal es Tavkozlesi Allando Bizottsag [*Standing Committee for Posts and Communications (CEMA)*] (HU)
potash .... Potash Plant [*Topography*] (RU)
potd .... Machine-Gun Section (RU)
p/otd .... Subdivision (RU)
POTE .... Pecsi Orvostudomanyi Egyetem [*Medical University of Pecs*] (HU)
potents .... Potential (RU)
POTI .... Postai Tervezo Iroda [*Postal Planning Office*] (HU)
POTKSPZ .... Poduzece za Otkup i Trgovinu KSPZ [*Purchase and Trade Establishment, District Union of Agricultural Cooperatives*] (YU)
POTOR .... Panstwowy Osrodek Technicznej Obslugi Rolnictwa [*State Center for Technical Services to Agriculture*] (POL)
potreb .... Consumers' (RU)
potrebsoyuz ... Union of Consumers' Societies (RU)
POU .... Mobile Desalting Unit (RU)
Poudie .... Poudrerie [*Powder Works*] [*Military map abbreviation*] [*World War I*] [*French*] (MTD)
Poudre .... Poudriere [*Powdermill, Powder Magazine*] [*Military map abbreviation*] [*World War I*] [*French*] (MTD)
POUM .... Partido Obrero de Unificacion Marxista [*Marxist Unification Labor Party*] [*Spanish*] (WER)
POUS .... Partido Operario Unificado Socialista [*Unified Socialist Workers Party*] [*Portuguese*] (PPE)
pov .... Attorney (RU)
pov .... Confidential (BU)
POV .... Fuel and Lubricant Research Laboratory [*Finnish*]
pov .... Imperative Mood (RU)
POV .... Pocatecni Obdobi Valky [*Initial Period of War*] (CZ)
POV .... Podminky Omezene Valky [*Limited Warfare Conditions*] (CZ)
Pov .... Poluostrov [*Peninsula*] [*See also Pol*] [*Russian*] (NAU)
pov .... Povolani [*Occupation*] (CZ)
POV .... Projekty Organisace Vystavby [*Organizational Plans for Construction*] (CZ)
pov .... Raised, Increased, Stepped-Up (RU)
POV .... Semipersistent Toxic Agent, Semipersistent War Gas (RU)
POVA .... Promithevtikos Organismos Vasilikis Aeroporias [*Royal Air Force Procurement Organization*] [*Greek*] (GC)
POVB .... Pohranicni Oddeleni Verejne Bezpecnosti [*Frontier Department of Public Security*] (CZ)
POVDOP ..... Poverenictvo Dopravy [*Office of the Commissioner of Transportation*] (CZ)
POVEK .... Pankyprios Organosis Viotekhnon, Epangelmation, kai Katastimatarkhon [*Pan-Cyprian Organization of Artisans, Tradesmen, and Shopkeepers*] (GC)
povel .... Imperative Mood (RU)
poverkhn .... Surface, Superficial (RU)
POVIR .... Polar Branch of the All-Union Scientific Research Institute of Plant Growing (RU)
povor .... Turning, Rotary (RU)
POVP .... Statute of Military Crimes (RU)
povr .... Damaged (BU)
povstankom ... Insurrectionary Committee (RU)
POW .... Polska Organizacja Wojskowa [*Polish Military Organization*] (POL)
POW .... Pomorski Okreg Wojskowy [*Pomeranian Military District*] (POL)
pow .... Powiat [*County*] (POL)
pow .... Powierzchnia [*Surface*] [*Polish*]
powiel .... Powielany [*Mimeographed*] (POL)
POWO .... Przedsiebiorstwo Obrotu Warzywami i Owocami [*Enterprise for Fruit and Vegetable Marketing*] (POL)
POY .... Pangosmios Organosis Ygeias [*World Health Organization*] (GC)
POYA .... Panellinios Omospondia Yperastikon Avtokinitiston [*Panhellenic Federation of Interurban Drivers*] (GC)
POYA .... Popular Youth Association (MAR)
poyasn .... Explanation (RU)
poyasnit ...... Explanatory (RU)
POYPA .... Panellinios Omospondia Ypallilikou Prosopikou Avtokiniton [*Panhellenic Federation of Automotive Personnel*] (GC)
POZ .... Mobile Obstacle Detachment (RU)
POZ .... Mobile Obstacle Unit (BU)
POZ .... Podol'sk Tin Plant (RU)
POZ .... Pohyblivy Odrad Zatarasovaci [*Mobile Detachment for Roadblocks*] (CZ)
POZ .... Pokretni Odrdi za Zaprecavanje [*Mobile Barrage Detachments*] (YU)
poz .... Positive (RU)
poz .... Pozycja [*Item*] (POL)
pozh .... Fire Station [*Topography*] (RU)
pozh .... Fire Tower [*Topography*] (RU)
pozh .... Firehouse [*Topography*] (RU)
pozhch .... Fire Station, Firehouse (RU)
pozh kal ...... Fire Tower [*Topography*] (RU)
PozHL .... Pozorovaci Hlidka [*Observation Patrol*] (CZ)
POZP .... Pretprijatie za Odrzavnje na Zeleznicki Prugi [*Railroad Track Maintenance Establishment*] [*Skopje*] (YU)
pozv .... Fortification Platoon (RU)
PP .... Antipersonnel (BU)
PP .... Antipersonnel (RU)
PP .... Approach Area, Approach Zone [*Aviation*] (RU)
PP .... Border Post (RU)
PP .... Bridge Train (RU)
PP .... Cartridge Carrier (RU)
PP .... Compiler [*Computers*] (RU)
PP .... Converting Substation (RU)
PP .... Covered Space, Covered Surface (RU)
PP .... Direct-Current Potentiometer (RU)

PP .... Direct Wire (RU)
PP .... Dressing Station (RU)
PP .... Field Gun (RU)
PP .... Field Mess [*Military term*] (RU)
PP .... Field Plotter [*Artillery*] (RU)
pp .... Field Post, Field Station (RU)
PP .... Field Postal Service (RU)
PP .... Fire Fighting (BU)
PP .... Floating (Observation and Communications) Post (RU)
PP .... Food Industry (RU)
PP .... Fuse (RU)
PP .... Hydrant Base (RU)
pp .... In Order, In Sequence, In Succession (RU)
PP .... Industrial Enterprise (BU)
PP .... Industrial Vacuum Cleaner (RU)
PP .... Infantry Regiment (RU)
PP .... Infantry Regiment (BU)
PP .... Infantry Support (RU)
PP .... Intermediate Product (RU)
pp .... Intermediate Superheat, Intermediate Superheater (RU)
PP .... Landing Site [*Helicopters*], Landing Area (RU)
pp .... Lieutenant Colonel (BU)
p/p .... Lieutenant Colonel (RU)
pp .... Loss on Calcination (RU)
p/p .... Money Order, Postal Order (RU)
p/p .... On the Instructions Of, On a Commission From, On Behalf Of (RU)
p/p .... Original Signed (RU)
pp .... Paginas [*Pages*] [*Portuguese*] (GPO)
PP .... Palebny Prumer [*Fire Diameter; Basic Load of Ammunition*] (CZ)
PP .... Panels Manufacturing Enterprise (BU)
PP .... Pangu Pati [*Papua New Guinean*] (PPW)
PP .... Panowie [*or Panie or Panstwo*] [*Messrs., Mesdames, Mr. and Mrs.*] [*Polish*]
pp .... Par Procuration [*By Procuration*] [*French*]
pp .... Paragraphs (RU)
PP .... Parna Pekara [*Steam Bakery*] (YU)
PP .... Parna Pivara [*Steam Brewery*] (YU)
PP .... Parnicni Postupak [*Civil Procedure*] (YU)
PP .... Parti du Peuple (MAR)
PP .... Partia Popullore [*Popular Party*] [*Albanian*] (PPE)
PP .... Partido Panamenista [*Panamanian Party*] (PPW)
PP .... Partido Popular [*Popular Party*] [*Brazilian*] (LA1)
PP .... Partido Popular [*Popular Party*] [*Spanish*] (PPE)
PP .... Partido do Progresso [*Progress Party*] [*Portuguese*] (WER)
pp .... Partisiipin Perfekti [*Past Participle*] [*Finnish*]
PP .... Pasokan Peninjau [*Reconnaissance Corps*] (ML)
PP .... Patrol Pengintip [*Reconnaissance Patrol*] (ML)
pp .... Pawns [*Chess*] (RU)
PP .... Pedal Switch (RU)
PP .... Pegawai Penyiasat [*Investigation Officer*] (ML)
PP .... Pekarsko Poduzece [*Baking Establishment*] (YU)
PP .... Pengurus Pusat [*Central Executive Council*] (IN)
Pp .... Per Procura [*or Procuram*] [*By Proxy (Signature of authorized official)*] [*Latin*] (EG)
PP .... Peraturan Pemerintah [*Government Ordinance*] (IN)
PP- .... Perforating Gun, Gun Perforator [*Pet.*] (RU)
P & P .... Pertes et Profits [*French*]
PP .... Pesadiski Puk [*Infantry Regiment*] (YU)
PP .... Pesurohjaya Polis [*Commissioner of Police*] (ML)
PP .... Petgodisni Plan [*Five-Year Plan*] (YU)
PP .... Pjesacka Pukovnija [*Infantry Regiment*] (YU)
PP .... Plachtarske Preteky [*Glider Contests*] (CZ)
PP .... Plan Prace Podniku [*Factory Work Plan*] (CZ)
PP .... Podnikovy Plan [*Factory Work Plan*] (CZ)
pp .... Points, Paragraphs, Clauses (RU)
pp .... Polgari Perrendtartas [*Civil Procedure, Code of Civil Procedure*] (HU)
PP .... Policia de Proteccao [*Protective Police*] [*Mozambican*] (AF)
PP .... Politechnika Poznanska [*Engineering College of Poznan*] [*Polish*]
PP .... Political Education Staff (RU)
PP .... Poljoprivredno Preduzece [*Agricultural Establishment*] (YU)
PP .... Polypropylene (RU)
PP .... Pomazi Posztogyar [*Textile Mill of Pomaz*] (HU)
PP .... Por Poder [*Power of Attorney*] [*Law*] [*Spanish*]
pp .... Port Paye [*French*]
PP .... Portable Potentiometer (RU)
PP .... Porte Pagado [*Spanish*]
PP .... Portion Principale [*French*] (MTD)
pp .... Posle Podne [*Afternoon*] (YU)
p-p .... Post Scriptum (BU)
PP- .... Powder Cartridge (RU)
P-P .... Powietrze-Powietrze [*Air-to-Air (Missile)*] [*Polish*]
PP .... Praemissis Praemittendis [*Omitting Titles, To Whom It May Concern*] [*Latin*] (WEN)
PP .... Predionica Pamuka [*Cotton Mill*] (YU)
PP .... Prehranbeno Preduzece [*Food Supply Establishment*] (YU)
PP .... Prilepska Pivara [*Prilep Brewery*] (YU)
PP .... Printer Switch [*Computers*] (RU)
PP .... Privredna Preduzeca [*Economic Establishments*] (YU)
PP .... Privredni Pregled [*Economic Survey*] [*Belgrade*] [*A periodical*] (YU)
PP .... Privremena Pravila [*Provisional Rules*] [*Military*] (YU)
PP .... Privremeno Prisutni [*Temporarily Present*] [*Census*] (YU)
PP .... Productora de Papeles [*Yumbo-Valle*] (COL)
PP .... Productos Philips [*Medellin*] (COL)
PP- .... Program Switch (RU)
PP .... Progress [*or Progressive*] Party (MAR)
PP .... Projektno Preduzece [*Industrial Design Establishment*] (YU)
pp .... Prokuuraoikeuden Najalla [*Finnish*]
PP .... Proodeftiki Parataxis [*Progressive Front*] [*Greek Cypriot*] (PPE)
Pp .... Protipechotni [*Anti-Infantry*] (CZ)
PP .... Protivpesadiski [*Anti-Infantry*] (YU)
PP .... Prumysl Pradla [*The Undergarment Industry*] (CZ)
PP .... Przedsiebiorstwo Panstwowe [*State Enterprise*] (POL)
pp .... Publie Par [*Published By*] [*French*]
PP .... Pulau-Pulau [*Group of Islands*] [*Indonesian*] (NAU)
PP .... Pulau-Pulau [*Group of Islands*] [*Malaysian*] (NAU)
PP .... Receiving Device, Receiver (RU)
PP .... Reception Sidings [*Railroads*] (RU)
PP .... Recharging Station (RU)
pp .... Second Lieutenant (BU)
PP .... Semiconductor (RU)
p/p .... Semifinished Material, Intermediate (RU)
PP .... Semitrailer (RU)
PP .... Small-Arms Ammunition Supply Point (RU)
PP .... Standing Committee (BU)
pp .... Steam Transformer (RU)
PP .... Submachine Gun (RU)
PP .... Superheated Steam (RU)
PP .... Switching Station (RU)
pp .... Teacher, Instructor (RU)
PP .... Track Arrival [*Railroads*] (RU)
PP .... Track Bearing (RU)
PP .... Transfer Index (RU)
PP .... Underwater Sound Detector (RU)
PP .... Warning Post (RU)
pp a .... Adjektiivina Kaytetty Partisiipin Perfekti [*Past Participle Used as an Adjective*] [*Finnish*]
PPA .... Longitudinal Transverse Reinforcement (RU)
PPA .... Parti Populaire Africain (MAR)
PPA .... Parti Progressiste Africain [*African Progressive Party*] [*Senegalese*] (AF)
PPA .... Parti Progressiste Angolais [*Angolan Progressive Party*] (AF)
PPA .... Partido Autentico Peronista [*Authentic Peronist Party*] [*Argentine*] (PD)
PPA .... Partido Patriotico Arubano [*Aruban Patriotic Party*] [*Netherlands Antillean*] (PPW)
PPA .... People's Progressive Alliance [*Gambian*] (AF)
ppa .... Per Procura [*By Proxy (Signature of authorized official)*] [*Latin*] (EG)
PPA .... Programa para el Pequeno Agricultor [*Small Farmer Program*] [*Dominican Republic*] (LA1)
PPA .... Programa de Protecao Ambiental [*Environmental Protection Program*] [*Brazilian*] (LA)
PPAA .... Parti Populaire Algerien (MAR)
PPAB .... Mobile Army Field Hospital (BU)
PPAC .... Personnalites Publiques de l'Afrique Centrale (MAR)
PPAG .... Planned Parenthood Association of Ghana (MAR)
PPAM .... Pasokan Perkhidmatan Am Malaysia [*Malaysian General Service Corps*] (ML)
PPAO .... Personnalites Publiques de l'Afrique de l'Ouest (MAR)
PPAP .... People's Party of Arunachal Pradesh [*Indian*] (PPW)
PPB .... Battalion Dressing Station (RU)
PPB .... Field Ammunition Supply Point (RU)
PPB .... Panstwowe Przedsiebiorstwo Budowlane [*State Ccnstruction Enterprise*] (POL)
PPB .... Partido Popular Barrientista [*Barrientist People's Party*] [*Bolivian*] (LA)
PPB .... Pertubohan Pembangunan Bandar [*City Development Organization*] (ML)
PPB .... Police Paramilitary Battalion [*Zambian*] (AF)
PPB .... Regimental Ammunition Dump (BU)
PPB .... Regimental Ammunition Supply Point (RU)
PPBB .... Partai Pesaka Bumiputra Bersatu [*United Traditional Bumiputra Party*] [*Malaysian*] (PPW)
PPB HiL .... Przedsiebiorstwo Przemyslowe Budowy Huty Imienia Lenina [*Industrial Enterprise for the Construction of Lenin Metallurgical Plant*] (POL)
PPBM .... Panstwowe Przedsiebiorstwa Budowlano-Montazowe [*State Construction and Installation Enterprises*] (POL)
PPBP .... Pegawai Penjaga Balai Polis [*Officer in Charge - Police Station*] (ML)
PPBP .... Privremena Pesadiska Borbena Pravila [*Temporary Infantry Combat Rules*] (YU)
PPBT .... Panstwowe Przedsiebiorstwo Budownictwa Terenowego [*State Local Construction Enterprise*] (POL)
PPC .... Parti Populaire Congolais (MAR)
PPC .... Parti Progressiste Congolais (MAR)

PPC .... Partido Popular Catala [*Catalan People's Party*] [*Spanish*] (WER)
PPC .... Partido Popular Cristiano [*Christian Popular Party*] [*Peruvian*] (PPW)
PPC .... Partido Popular Cristiano [*Popular Christian Party*] [*Argentine*] (LA)
PPC .... Partido Progresista Cristiano [*Progressive Christian Party*] [*Dominican Republic*] (LA1)
PPC .... Partitu Populare Corsu [*Corsican*] (PD)
PPC .... Petroleum Planning Committee (MAR)
PPC .... Pour Prendre Conge [*To Take Leave*] [*French*]
PPCDRP...... Partido Pueblo, Cambio, y Democracia Roldosista del Pueblo [*People, Change, and Democracy Roldosist People's Party*] [*Ecuadorean*] (LA1)
PPCEA .... Parti Populaire Congolais de l'Entente Africaine (MAR)
PPCK........... Pegawai Penjaga Chawangan Khas [*Officer in Charge - Special Branch*] (ML)
PPCO .... Parti Progressiste Congolais (MAR)
PPCPL......... Pegawai Penjaga Chawangan Polis Laut [*Officer in Charge - Marine Police Branch*] (ML)
PPD .... Degtyarev Submachine Gun (RU)
PPD .... Maintenance of Reservoir Pressure, Repressuring (RU)
PPD .... Message Center (RU)
PPD .... Parti Populaire du Dahomey (MAR)
PPD .... Parti Populaire Djiboutien [*Djibouti*] (PD)
PPD .... Parti Progressiste Dahomeen (MAR)
PPD .... Partido Popular Democratico [*Popular Democratic Party*] [*Portuguese*] (WER)
PPD .... Partido Popular Democratico [*Popular Democratic Party*] [*Puerto Rican*] (PPW)
PPD .... Planning and Programming Department (MAR)
PPD .... Variable-Length Field (RU)
PPDA........... Partido Popular Democratico Acoriano [*Azorean Popular Democratic Party*] [*Portuguese*] (WER)
PPDC........... Paraguayan People's Documentation Center (EA)
PPDC........... Partido Popular Democratica Cristiana [*Popular Christian Democratic Party*] [*Spanish*] (PPE)
PPDC........... Partido Progresista Democrata Cristiano [*Christian Democratic Progressive Party*] [*Dominican Republic*] (LA1)
PPD Dalmor ... Panstwowe Przedsiebiorstwo Dalekomorskie [*"Dalmor" State Maritime Enterprise*] (POL)
Ppd III KD.... Regulations on the Application of Title III of the Labor Code (BU)
ppdo............ Proximo Pasado [*Last Month*] [*Spanish*]
PPDP........... Pegawai Penjaga Daerah Polis [*Officer in Charge - Police District*] (ML)
PPE .... Electropneumatic Transducer (RU)
PPE .... Partido Popular Extremeno [*Extremaduran People's Party*] [*Spanish*] (WER)
PPE .... Supply and Evacuation Route (RU)
PPEG........... Mobile Epidemic Control Group (RU)
PPEO........... Mobile Epidemic Control Detachment (RU)
PPER........... Electrical Installation Plan (RU)
PPF............. Ferrite-Testing Device (RU)
PPF............. Parti Populaire Francais [*French Popular Party*] (PPE)
PPF............. Privatefoeretagarnas Partioganisation i Finland [*Finnish Private Entrepreneurs' Party*] (PPE)
PPF............. Projet Pilote Forestier (MAR)
PPFG........... People's Progressive Front of Ghana (MAR)
PPF prepyatstviya ... Antipersonnel Fortification Obstacles (BU)
PPG............. Mobile Field Hospital (RU)
PPG............. Physical Planning Group (MAR)
PPG............. Rectangular Hysteresis Loop (RU)
PPGK .... Panstwowe Przedsiebiorstwa Geodezji i Kartografii [*State Geodetic and Cartographic Enterprises*] (POL)
PPH .... Pasokan Polis Hutan [*Police Field Force*] (ML)
PPI.............. Panitia Pemilihan Indonesia [*Indonesian Election Committee*] (IN)
PPI.............. Partito Popolare Italiano [*Italian Popular Party*] (WER)
PPI.............. Persatuan Peladjar Indonesia [*Indonesian Students Association*] (IN)
PPI.............. Persatuan Pelaut Indonesia [*Indonesian Seamen's Association*] (IN)
PPIB .... Productivity, Prices, and Incomes Board (MAR)
PPIE .... Panstwowe Przedsiebiorstwo Imprez Estradowych [*State Show Business*] [*Polish*]
PPINM .... Regulations on the Planned Construction of Settlements (BU)
PPiPT(mine) ... Protivpesadiske i Protivtenkovske (Mine) [*Anti-Infantry and Antitank Mines*] (YU)
PPIS .... Panstwowe Przedsiebiorstwo Imprez Sportowych [*State Enterprise for Sporting Events*] [*Polish*]
PPiUR.......... Przedsiebiorstwo Polowow i Urzadzen Rybackich [*Fisheries and Fishing Facilities Enterprise*] (POL)
PPK .... G-Suit (RU)
PPK .... Industrial and Political Courses (RU)
PPK .... Panstwowe Przedsiebiorstwo Kolportazu [*State Enterprise for Circulation of Publications*] (POL)
PPK .... Pasokan Propaganda Khas [*Special Propaganda Force*] (ML)
PPK .... Pegawai Pentadbir Kontijen [*Contingent Administrative Officer*] (ML)
PPK .... Protiv Petokolonaski [*Anti-Fifth Column*] (YU)
PPK .... Regulations on Arbitration Commissions (BU)
PPK .... Soil Absorbing Complex (RU)
PPK .... Steam Superheater Channel (RU)
PPKAM........ Panstwowe Przedsiebiorstwo Konserwacji Architektury Monumentalnej [*State Enterprise for the Conservation of Monumental Architecture*] (POL)
PPKB........... Pertubohan Pasokmomogan Kadazan Bersatu [*United Kadazan Sons of the Soil Organization*] [*Sabah*] (ML)
PPKEN .... Poinikos kai Peitharkhikos Kodix Emborikou Navtikou [*Merchant Marine Penal and Disciplinary Code*] [*Greek*] (GC)
PPKh........... Mobile Field Bakery (RU)
PPKIM......... Persatuan Pelajar Kolej Islam Malaya [*Students Union of the Malayan Muslim College*] (ML)
PPKK........... Panstwowe Przedsiebiorstwa Krawiecko-Kusnierskie [*State Enterprises for Tailoring and Furriery*] (POL)
PPKLJDZ .... Pretprijatie za Popravka na Koli i Lokomotivi Jugoslovanske Drzavne Zeleznice [*Car and Locomotive Repair Establishment, Yugoslav State Railroads*] (YU)
PPKO .... Pusat Pendidikan Komando [*Marine Training Center*] (IN)
PPKRM........ Pusat Perjuangan Kebangsaan Rakyat Malaya [*Malayan People's National Struggle Center*] (ML)
PPK Ruch.... Panstwowe Przedsiebiorstwo Kolportazu "Ruch" [*"Ruch" State Enterprise for the Circulation of Periodicals and Newspapers*] (POL)
PPL.............. Aid Station for the Slightly Wounded (RU)
PPL.............. Landing Area, Landing Field (RU)
PPL.............. Parti Populaire Liberal (MAR)
PPL.............. Partido Popular de Liberacion [*Popular Liberation Party*] [*Argentine*] (LA)
Ppl.............. Pesi Pluk [*Infantry Regiment*] (CZ)
PPL.............. Phak Pasason Lao [*Lao Communist Party*] (CL)
PPL.............. Poder Popular Local [*Local People's Government*] [*Cuban*] (LA)
ppl.............. Polplotno [*Half-Linen*] [*Book cover*] (POL)
PPL.............. Submarine Position (RU)
pplk............. Podplukovnik [*Lieutenant Colonel*] [*US equivalent: Lieutenant Colonel*] (CZ)
pplk............. Podpulkownik [*Lieutenant Colonel*] (POL)
PPLP .... Pegawai Penjaga Latehan Polis [*Officer in Charge of Police Training*] (ML)
PPM............. Antipersonnel Mine (RU)
PPM............. First Aid Stations (BU)
PPM............. Medical First Aid Station (RU)
PPM............. Moving Permanent Magnet (RU)
PPM............. Panstwowe Przedsiebiorstwo Melioracyjne [*State Land Reclamation Enterprise*] (POL)
PPM............. Panstwowe Przedsiebiorstwo Miernicze [*State Surveying Enterprise*] (POL)
PPM............. Parti Pekerja-Pekerja Malaysia [*Workers' Party of Malaysia*] (PPW)
PPM............. Parti du Peuple Mauritanien [*Mauritanian People's Party*] (AF)
PPM............. Parti Progressiste Martiniquais [*Progressive Party of Martinique*] (PPW)
PPM............. Partido Popular Monarquico [*Popular Monarchist Party*] [*Portuguese*] (WER)
PPM............. Partido del Pueblo Mexicano [*Mexican People's Party*] (PPW)
PPM............. Pasokan Perkhidmatan Malaysia [*Malaysian Service Corps*] (ML)
PPM............. Pemerentah Pasokan Meriam [*Battery Commander*] (ML)
PPM............. People's Popular Movement [*Trinidadian and Tobagan*] (LA1)
PPM............. People's Pressure Movement [*Barbadian*] (LA1)
PPM............. Pingat Peringatan Malaysia [*Commemoration Medal - Malaysia*] (ML)
PPM- .... Pneumatic Polishing Machine (RU)
PPM............. Poder Popular Municipal [*Municipal People's Government*] [*Cuban*] (LA)
PPM............. Policia Popular de Mocambique [*Mozambican People's Police*] (AF)
PPM............. Programme Prioritaire Minimal (MAR)
PPM............. Protivpesadiske Mine [*Anti-Infantry Mines*] (YU)
PPM............. Pulkowe Pogotowie Medyczne [*Regimental Ambulance Services*] (POL)
PPM............. Regimental Dressing Station (BU)
PPM............. Regimental Medical Aid Station (RU)
PPM............. Rock Loader, Dirt Loader [*Mining*] (RU)
PPM............. Turning Point [*Aviation*] (RU)
PPMI............ Perserikatan Perhimpunan-Perhimpunan Mahasiswa Indonesia [*Federation of Indonesian College-Student Organizations*] (IN)
PP mini........ Antipersonnel Mines (BU)
PPMO.......... Primary Party Mass Organization (BU)
PPMP .... Antipersonnel Mine Field (BU)
PPMP .... Antipersonnel Mine Field (RU)
PPMP .... Protipechotni Minove Pole [*Anti-Infantry Mine Field*] (CZ)
PPMP .... Prvni Prazsky Mestansky Pivovar [*First Municipal Breweries in Prague*] (CZ)
PPN .... Direct Legal Norms (BU)
PPN .... Flight Instruments, Flight Instrumentation (RU)
PPN .... Night Machine-Gun Sight (RU)

PPN .... Parti Progressiste Nigerien [*Nigerien Progressive Party*] [*Niger*] (AF)
PPN .... Perusahaan Perkebunan Negara [*State Plantation*] (IN)
PPN .... Pingat Pangkuan Negara [*Medal to the Orders of Chivalry - Malaysia*] (ML)
PPN .... Poder Popular Nacional [*National People's Government*] [*See ANP*] [*Cuban*] (LA)
PPN .... Proizvodnja i Prerada Nafte [*Naphtha Production and Refining*] (YU)
PPNUNPO ... Regulations on the Application of the Ukase on Naming and Renaming Sites of National and Local Significance (BU)
PPO .... Field Laundry Detachment (RU)
PPO .... Field Postal Section [*Military term*] (RU)
PPO .... Fire-Fighting Equipment (RU)
PPO .... Periodicke Preventivni Opravy [*Periodical Preventive Repairs*] (CZ)
PPO .... Planovani a Provadeni Preventivnich Oprav [*Planning and Preventive Repair Work*] (CZ)
PPO .... Poverenictvo Priemyslu a Obchodu [*Office of the Commissioner of Industry and Commerce*] (CZ)
PPO .... Primary Party Organization (BU)
PPO .... Production Planning Department (RU)
PPO .... Protivpodmornicka Odbrana [*Antisubmarine Defense*] (YU)
PPO .... Scheduled Preventive Maintenance Inspection (RU)
PPOC .... Papeterie Principale de l'Oubangui-Chari (MAR)
PPOK .... Premiowa Pozyczka Odbudowy Kraju [*Loan for the Reconstruction of the Country*] (POL)
p/polk .... Lieutenant Colonel (RU)
p pon .... Par Procuration [*By Procuration*] [*French*]
PPOO .... Provisional People's Organizing Office [*Ethiopian*] (AF)
ppor .... Podporucik [*Junior Lieutenant*] [*US equivalent: Lieutenant, Junior Grade*] (CZ)
ppor .... Podporucznik [*Second Lieutenant*] [*Polish*]
PPOV .... Pripraven k Praci a Obrane Vlasti [*Prepared for Work and National Defense (Badge)*] (CZ)
PPP .... Advanced Dressing Station (RU)
PPP .... Antipersonnel Obstacle (RU)
PPP .... Dressing Station and Field Mess (RU)
PPP .... First Aid Station (RU)
PPP .... Industrial Production Personnel (BU)
ppp .... Loss on Calcination (RU)
PPP .... Pakistan People's Party (PD)
PPP .... Partai Persatuan Pembangunan [*Development Unity Party*] [*Indonesian*] (PPW)
PPP .... Parti du Progres du Peuple (MAR)
PPP .... Partido Patriotico Popular [*Popular Patriotic Party*] [*Ecuadorean*] (LA)
PPP .... Partido Popular Progresista [*Popular Progressive Party*] [*Honduran*] (LA)
PPP .... Partido del Pueblo de Panama [*Panamanian People's Party*] (PPW)
PPP .... People's Patriotic Party [*Burmese*] (PD)
PPP .... People's Political Party [*St. Vincentian*] (PPW)
PPP .... People's Popular Party (MAR)
PPP .... People's Progress Party [*Papua New Guinean*] (PPW)
PPP .... People's Progressive Party [*Gambian*] (PPW)
PPP .... People's Progressive Party [*Guyanese*] (PD)
PPP .... People's Progressive Party [*Solomon Islander*] (PPW)
PPP .... People's Progressive Party [*Anguilla*] (PPW)
PPP .... People's Progressive Party [*Mauritian*] (AF)
PPP .... People's Progressive Party [*Malaysian*] (ML)
PPP .... People's Progressive Party of Perak [*Malaysian*] (PPW)
PPP .... Poder Popular Provincial [*Provincial People's Government*] [*Cuban*] (LA)
PPP .... Progressive People's Party [*Liberian*] (PPW)
PPP .... Proodevtiki Panspoudastiki Parataxi [*Progressive Pan-Student Faction*] [*Greek*] (GC)
PPP .... Protivprojektilski Projektil [*Antimissile Missile*] (YU)
PPP .... Prumysl Polevkovych Pripravku [*Dehydrated Soup Industry*] (CZ)
PpP .... Przyjaciel przy Pracy [*Friend at Work*] [*A periodical*] (POL)
PPP .... Ration Supply Point (RU)
PPP .... Receiving-Sending Post (RU)
PPP .... Regimental Small-Arms Ammunition Supply Point (RU)
PPP .... Send-Receive Switch (RU)
PPPB .... Pegawai Penjaga Polis Bahagian [*Officer Superintending Police Sector*] (ML)
PPPC .... Parti des Paysans et de Proletaires Congolais (MAR)
PPPD .... Pegawai Penjaga Polis Daerah [*Officer in Charge - District Police*] (ML)
PPPP .... Pegawai Pengangkutan Pasokan Polis [*Police Force Transport Officer*] (ML)
PPPPC .... Petroleum Products Pipeline Public Corporation [*Sudanese*] (MAR)
PPPPM .... Persatuan Persuratan Pemuda Pemudi Melayu [*Malayan Youth Literary Association*] [*Singapore*] (ML)
PPPR .... Poverenictvo Podohospodarstva a Pozemkovej Reformy [*Office of the Commissioner for Agriculture and Land Reform*] (CZ)
PPR .... Antirepeat Relay (RU)
PPR .... Clearing Station for the Wounded (BU)
P Pr .... Fixed Light with Flashes [*Nautical term*] (RU)
p/pr .... On Presentation, At Sight (RU)
PPR .... Parti Progresif Rakyat [*People's Progressive Party*] (ML)
PPR .... Pasokan Penchegah Rusohan [*Riot Prevention Unit*] (ML)
PPR .... Planned Preventive Repairs (BU)
PPR .... Poder Popular Regional [*Regional People's Government*] [*Cuban*] (LA)
ppr .... Podporucznik [*Polish*]
PPR .... Political Education Work (RU)
PPR .... Politieke Partij Radikalen [*Radical Political Party*] [*Dutch*] (PPE)
PPR .... Polska Partia Robotnicza [*Polish Workers' Party (1942-1948)*] (POL)
PPR .... Preliminary Work Preparation (RU)
PPR .... Price List by Rayon Rates (RU)
PPR .... River Crossing Point for the Wounded (RU)
PPR .... Scheduled Preventive Maintenance, Scheduled Overhaul, Regular Overhaul (RU)
p/pr .... Simple Portable Obstacles [*Military term, topography*] (RU)
PPR .... Work Plan (RU)
Pprap .... Pesi Prapor [*Infantry Battalion*] (CZ)
PPRC .... Panstwowe Przedsiebiorstwo Robot Czerpalnych [*State Enterprise for Dredging*] (POL)
PPRD .... Panstwowe Przedsiebiorstwo Robot Drogowych [*Polish*]
PPRK .... Panstwowe Przedsiebiorstwo Robot Komunikacyjnych [*State Enterprise for Transportation Projects*] (POL)
PPRN .... Prezydium Powiatowej Rady Narodowej [*Presidium of the People's District Council*] (POL)
PPRPiC .... Panstwowe Przedsiebiorstwo Robot Podwodnych i Czerplanych [*State Enterprise for Underwater Work and Dredging*] (POL)
PPRV .... Recall Receiver (RU)
PPRV- .... Regulations on Transporting Radioactive Substances (RU)
PPS .... Auroral Radio Wave Absorption (RU)
PPS .... Field Postal Station (RU)
PPS .... Fire Fighting Service (BU)
PPS .... Forward Message Center (RU)
PPS .... Mobile Post Offices (BU)
PPS .... Parti du Progres et du Socialisme [*Party of Progress and Socialism*] [*Moroccan*] (PPW)
PPS .... Partido Popular Salvadoreno [*Salvadoran Popular Party*] (PPW)
PPS .... Partido Popular Socialista [*Popular Socialist Party*] [*Mexican*] (LA)
PPS .... Partie Populaire Syrienne [*See also SNP, SSNP*] [*Lebanese*] (ME)
PPS .... Pasokan Polis Sukarela [*Police Volunteer Reserve*] (ML)
PPS .... Pingat Perkhidmatan Setia [*Federation Long Service and Good Conduct Medal - Malaysian*] (ML)
PPS .... Plovdiv Court of Reconciliation (BU)
PPS .... Polska Partia Socjalistyczna [*Polish Socialist Party (1892-1948)*] (POL)
PPS .... Pozarna Preventivna Sluzba [*Fire Prevention Service*] (YU)
PPS .... Prazska Paroplavebni Spolecnost [*Prague Steamship Lines*] (CZ)
PPS .... Primary Collecting Point (RU)
PPS .... Primo-Predajna Sekcija [*Receiving and Transmitting Section*] [*Radio*] (YU)
PPS .... Progressivnaia Partiia Svazilenda (MAR)
PPS .... Project Planning Section (MAR)
PPS .... Projet "Production Primaire au Sahel" (MAR)
PPS .... Proyecto Partido Socialista [*Socialist Party Project*] [*Dominican Republic*] (LA1)
PPS .... Regimental Food Supply Depot (RU)
PPS .... Rules for Sailing Competitions (RU)
PPS .... Sudayev Submachine Gun (RU)
PPSC .... Partido Popular Social Cristiano [*Popular Social Christian Party*] [*Nicaraguan*] (LA1)
PPSEAWA ... Pan-Pacific and South-East Asia Women's Association (EA)
PPS-FR .... Polska Partia Socjalistyczna-Frakcja Rewolucyjna [*Polish Socialist Party-Revolutionary Faction*] (PPE)
PPSh .... Partia e Punes e Shqiperise [*Labor Party of Albania*] [*Formerly, PKSh*] (PPE)
PPSh .... Polar Cap Absorption (RU)
PPSh .... Shpagin Submachine Gun (RU)
PPSJ .... Pegawai Penjaga Siasatan Jenayat [*Criminal Investigation Officer*] (ML)
PPsluzhba ... Fire Fighting Service (BU)
PPSP .... Proodevtiki Panspoudastiki Syndikalistiki Parataxi [*Progressive Pan-Student Trade Union Faction*] [*Greek*] (GC)
PPSS .... Regulations for Preventing Collisions at Sea (RU)
PP stantsiya ... Mobile Post Office (BU)
PPS-WRN .... Polska Partia Socjalistyczna-Wolnosc, Rownosc, Niepodleglosc [*Polish Socialist Party-Freedom, Equality, Independence*] (PPE)
PPT .... Parti Progressiste du Tchad [*Progressive Party of Chad*] (AF)
PPT .... Pegawai Perisekan Tentera [*Military Intelligence Officer*] (ML)
PPT .... Poverenictvo pre Posty a Telegraf [*Office of the Commissioner of Postal and Telegraph Service*] (CZ)
PPT .... Przedsiebiorstwo Przemyslu Terenowego [*Local Industry Enterprise*] (POL)

PPT............ Semiconductor Triode (RU)
PPTit............ Poczta Polska, Telegraf, i Telefon [*Polish Administration of Posts, Telegraphs, and Telephones*] (POL)
PPTM............ Partido Popular Trabajador Mexicano [*Mexican Working People's Party*] (LA)
PPTM............ Persatuan Perkhidmatan Tadbir Malaya [*Malayan Civil Service Association*] (ML)
PPT Orbis... Przedsiebiorstwo Podrozy i Turystyki Orbis [*Orbis Travel and Tourist Enterprise*] (POL)
PPTR............ Pukovske Protivtenkovske Rezerve [*Regimental Antitank Reserves*] (YU)
PPTS............ Panstwowe Przedsiebiorstwo "Totalizator Sportowy" [*State Enterprise "Sporting Pool"*] [*Polish*]
PPTT............ Poczta Polska, Telegraf, i Telefon [*Polish Administration of Posts, Telegraphs, and Telephones*]
PPTV............ High-Resistance Direct-Current Potentiometer (RU)
PPU............ Anti-G Device (RU)
PPU............ Foam Polyurethan (RU)
PPU............ Noise-Suppressing Device (RU)
PPU............ Planning and Production Administration (RU)
PPU............ Planovita Preventivni Udrzba [*Planned Preventive Maintenance*] (CZ)
PPU............ Starting and Switching Device (RU)
PPU............ Steam Generating Unit, Steam Generating System (RU)
Ppuk............ Potpukovnik [*Lieutenant Colonel*] (YU)
PPUZhS...... Regulations on the Application of the Ukase on Encouraging and Assisting Cooperative and Individual Housing Construction (BU)
PPV............ Advanced Veterinary Station (RU)
PPV............ Maximal Field Moisture [*Agriculture*] (BU)
PPV............ Maximum Field Moisture Capacity of Soil (RU)
PPV............ Mobile Shot Point (RU)
PPV............ Rules for the Use of Railroad Cars in International Passenger and Railroad Freight Traffic (RU)
PPW............ Panstwowe Przedsiebiorstwo Wydzielone [*State Exempted Enterprise Of*] (POL)
PPWK............ Panstwowe Przedsiebiorstwo Wydawnictw Kartograficznych [*State Map Publication Enterprise*] (POL)
PPWNH....... Przedsiebiorstwo Panstwowe Wyodrebnione "Nowa Huta" [*"Nowa Huta" State Exempted Enterprise*] (POL)
PPWP............ Panstwowe Przedsiebiorstwo "Wiercenia Poszukiwawcze" [*State "Exploratory Drilling" Enterprise*] (POL)
PPYa............ Armature-Testing Device (RU)
PPYa............ Bee Venom Preparation (RU)
PPYU............ Party of Popular Yemenite Unity (PD)
PPZ............ Fire Fighting (BU)
PPZ............ Ignition Tester (RU)
PPZ............ Papudziska Preradivacka Zadruga [*Slipper Production Cooperative*] (YU)
PPZ............ Pneumatic Grain Elevator (RU)
PPZB............ Poznanskie Przemyslowe Zjednoczenie Budowlane [*Poznan Industrial Construction Association*] (POL)
PPZDA........ Regulations on the Application of the Law on State Arbitration (BU)
PPZDvP....... Regulations on the Application of the Law on Road Traffic (BU)
PPZG............ Regulations on the Application of the Law on Forests (BU)
PPZIR............ Regulations on the Application of the Law on Inventions and Rationalizations (BU)
PPZM............ Polskie Przedsiebiorstwo Zeglugi Morskiej [*Polish Maritime Shipping Enterprise*] (POL)
PPZNO........ Regulations on the Application of the Law on Rentals (BU)
PPZNSNZ.... Regulations on the Application of the Law on Scientific Degrees and Titles (BU)
PPZNZ......... Regulations on the Application of the Law on Public Health (BU)
PPZP............ Regulations on the Application of the Law on Pensions (BU)
PPZPZSK.... Regulations on the Application of the Law on the Pensioning of Cooperative Farmers (BU)
PPZSG........ Regulations on the Application of the Law on Citizens' Property (BU)
PPZSt............ Regulations on the Application of the Law on Standardization (BU)
PPZTSU...... Regulations on the Application of the Law on Territorial and Settlement Organization (BU)
PPZVO........ Regulations on the Application of the Law on Higher Education (BU)
PPZVT......... Regulations on the Application of the Law on Foreign Trade (BU)
PPZZ............ Poljoprivredno Preduzece Zemljoradnicke Zadruge [*Farm Establishment of an Agricultural Cooperative*] (YU)
PQD............ Partido Quisqueyano Democrata [*Quisqueyan Democratic Party*] [*Dominican Republic*] (PPW)
PR............ Aircraft Deployment Point (RU)
pr............ Avenue (RU)
pr............ Before (BU)
pr............ Canal, Channel [*Topography*] (RU)
PR............ Flashing Light [*Nautical term*] (RU)
PR............ Foaming Agent (RU)
PR............ Homing Radio Station (RU)
pr............ Infantry Company (BU)
PR............ Infantry Company (RU)
PR............ Infantry Reconnaissance (RU)
pr............ Intermediate [*Nuclear physics and engineering*] (RU)
PR-............ Intermediate Relay (RU)
PR............ Log Trailer (RU)
PR............ Machine-Gun Company (RU)
PR............ Maximum Load, Peak Level (RU)
PR............ Mobile Radio Station (RU)
pr............ Other (RU)
PR............ Output Punch [*Computers*] (RU)
pr............ Overloaded Operating Condition (RU)
PR............ Paedagogischer Rat [*Pedagogical Council*] (EG)
P/r............ Parni Remorker [*Steam Tugboat*] (YU)
PR............ Parti Rakyat (Malaysia) [*People's Party of Malaysia*] (ML)
PR............ Parti de la Reconciliation (MAR)
PR............ Parti Republicain [*Republican Party*] [*French*] (PPW)
PR............ Partido Radical [*Radical Party*] [*Spanish*] (PPE)
PR............ Partido Radical [*Radical Party*] [*Chilean*] (LA)
PR............ Partido Reformista [*Reformist Party*] [*Dominican Republic*] (PPW)
PR............ Partido Reformista [*Reformist Party*] [*Costa Rican*] (LA)
PR............ Partido Republicano [*Republican Party*] [*Brazilian*] (LA)
PR............ Partido Republicano [*Republican Party*] [*Costa Rican*] (LA)
PR............ Partido Revolucionario [*Revolutionary Party*] [*Guatemalan*] (PPW)
PR............ Partito Radicale [*Radical Party*] [*Founded, 1955*] [*Italian*] (PPE)
pr............ Passage, Thoroughfare (RU)
pr............ Past, Last (RU)
PR............ Patria Roja [*Red Fatherland*] [*Peruvian*] (PD)
PR............ Pekarska Radnja [*Bakery*] (YU)
PR............ Peking Review [*A publication*] (MAR)
PR............ Perang Rakjat [*People's War*] (IN)
PR............ Periodic Recording (RU)
PR............ Periscope, Trench Periscope (RU)
PR............ Piano Regolatore [*Zoning Regulations*] [*Italian*] (WER)
PR............ Planned Repairs (BU)
PR-............ Pneumatic Relay (RU)
PR............ Podkarpatska Rus [*Subcarpathian Ukraine*] (CZ)
PR............ Podnikova Rada [*Factory Committee*] (CZ)
PR............ Podnikove Reditelstvi [*Enterprise Management*] (CZ)
PR............ Pojistovaci Rada [*Insurance Council*] (CZ)
PR............ Polarized Relay (RU)
PR............ Policejni Reditelstvi [*Police Headquarters*] (CZ)
PR............ Polskie Radio [*Polish Radio*] (POL)
Pr............ Pond [*Topography*] (RU)
pr............ Por [*By, Through*] [*Spanish*]
PR............ Position Area [*Artillery*] (RU)
PR............ Positioning Relay (RU)
PR............ Poste Restante [*French*]
PR............ Povolavaci Rozkaz [*Draft Order*] (CZ)
pr............ Powder [*Medicine*] (RU)
Pr............ Praesident [*German*]
Pr............ Prairie [*Meadow*] [*Military map abbreviation*] [*World War I*] [*French*] (MTD)
pr............ Praktisch [*Practical, Applied*] [*German*]
pr............ Praktoreion [*Agency, Agent's Office*] (GC)
PR............ Pravila (Nastava) [*Training Rules*] [*Military*] (YU)
Pr............ Pravosudie [*Justice*] [*A periodical*] (BU)
pr............ Prawy [*Right*] [*Polish*]
PR............ President de la Republique [*President of the Republic*] (CL)
PR............ Presidente da Republica [*President of the Republic*] [*Portuguese*] (WER)
Pr............ Press Fit (RU)
PR............ Pretsednik Republike [*President of the Republic*] (YU)
PR............ Prezydium Rzadu [*Presidium of the Government*] (POL)
pr............ Prime [*First, Prime*] [*French*]
Pr............ Prince [*Prince*] [*French*] (MTD)
pr............ Prochain [*Next, Nearest*] [*French*]
Pr............ Professeur [*Professor or Teacher*] (CL)
PR............ Profile, Section, Cross Section (RU)
Pr............ Prolaz [*Passage*] [*Yugoslav*] (NAU)
PR............ Proportional Controller, Proportional Governor (RU)
PR............ Propylene (RU)
PR............ Puerto Rico [*Spanish*]
PR............ Puerto Rico [*Two-letter standard code*] [*Postal code*] (CNC)
PR............ Radioactive Densimeter (RU)
PR............ Receiver (RU)
PR............ Reproducing Puncher [*Computers*] (RU)
pr............ Right Hand (RU)
pr............ Right, Right-Hand (RU)
pr............ Right Tributary [*Topography*] (RU)
PR............ Rubber-Covered Wire (RU)
PR............ Solubility Product (RU)
pr............ Spatial (BU)
PR............ Starting Relay, Initiating Relay (RU)
PR............ Starting Rheostat (RU)
PR............ Station Bearing (RU)
pr............ Strait, Sound (RU)
PR............ Taxi Strip, Taxiway [*Aviation*] (RU)
PR............ Test Relay (RU)
pr............ Therefore, Hence, Then, And So Forth (BU)
Pr............ Titulo de Profesor [*Spanish*]

PR............ Track Relay [*Railroads*] (RU)
PR............ Trigger Register (RU)
p/r............ Under the Leadership Of (RU)
PR............ Zone of Destruction (RU)
PRA............ Emergency-Pulse Receiver (RU)
PRA............ Parti du Regroupement Africain [*African Regroupment Party*] [*Niger*] (PD)
PRA............ Parti de Regroupement Africain [*African Regroupment Party*] [*Upper Voltan*] (AF)
PRA............ Parti de Regroupement Africain [*African Regroupment Party*] [*Zairian*] (AF)
PRA............ Partido Revolucionario Autentico [*Authentic Revolutionary Party*] [*Bolivian*] (PPW)
PRA............ People's Regional Assembly [*Sudanese*] (MAR)
PRA............ People's Republic of Angola (MAR)
PRA............ People's Revolutionary Army [*Grenadian*] (LA1)
PRA............ Postrechnungsamt [*Postal Accounting Office*] (EG)
PRA............ Start-Regulating Equipment (RU)
prac............ Pracownik [*Worker, Employee*] [*Polish*]
PRAC............ Pyrethrum Research Advisory Committee (MAR)
P Racc............ Points de Raccordement [*Military*] [*French*] (MTD)
Prachtex..... Prachtexemplar [*Splendid Copy*] [*German*]
PRADA........ Societe de Produits Agricoles du Dahomey (MAR)
PRADHOTEL ... Compania Hotel del Prado SA [*Barranquilla*] (COL)
pr Adr.......... Per Adresse [*Care Of*] [*Correspondence*] [*German*]
PRAF............ People's Revolutionary Armed Forces [*Grenadian*] (LA1)
PRAG............ Public Relations Association of Ghana (MAR)
PRAI............ Proyecto de Reconstruccion y Accion Inmediata [*Reconstruction and Immediate Action Program*] [*Nicaraguan*] (LA1)
prakt............ Praktisch [*Practical, Applied*] [*German*]
pral............ Principal [*Spanish*]
PRAM............ Partido Revolucionario Abril y Mayo [*April-May Revolutionary Party*] [*Salvadoran*] (LA)
PRAM............ Partido Revolucionario Abril y Mayo [*April-May Revolutionary Party*] [*Guatemalan*] (LA)
PRAMEN..... Narodni Podnik pro Prodej Lahudkarskeho Zbozi [*National Enterprise for the Retail Sale of Delicatessen Merchandise*] (CZ)
PRAMOB..... Pravila Mobilizacije [*Mobilization Regulations*] (YU)
PRAMUKA ... Pradja Muda Karana [*The Youth Are the Hope of the State (State scouting organization)*] (IN)
prap............ Prapor [*Battalion*] (CZ)
PRAR............ Partido Republicano Argentino [*Argentine Republican Party*] (LA)
PRAR............ Partido Revolucionario Autentico Rios [*Bolivian*] (PPW)
PRAS............ Parti du Regroupement Africain-Senegalais (MAR)
Pras............ Praeses [*German*]
Pras............ Praesident [*German*]
prav............ Correct, Accurate, True (RU)
prav............ Right, Right-Hand (RU)
Prav............ Russian Orthodox Cemetery [*Topography*] (RU)
pravl............ Administration, Management (RU)
pravosl........ Russian Orthodox (RU)
Prav ZZZI.... Regulations on the Application of the Law on Mandatory Property Insurance (BU)
PRB............ Ammunition-Unloading Point (RU)
PRB............ Distribution Planning Office (RU)
PRB............ Field Repair Base (RU)
PRB............ Mobile Repair Base (RU)
PRB............ Partai Rakyat Brunei [*Brunei People's Party*] (ML)
PRB............ Parti Rakyat Bersatu [*United People's Party*] [*Singapore*] (ML)
PRB............ Partido Revolucionario Barrientista [*Barrientist Revolutionary Party*] [*Bolivian*] (LA)
PRB............ Poudreries Reunies de Belgique [*Belgian United Powder Factories*] (WER)
PRB............ Radio Direction-Finding Unit (Radiosonde) (RU)
PRB............ Societe des Plantations Rhoniers-Bora (MAR)
PRBC............ People's Revolutionary Broadcasting Corporation [*Libyan*] (MAR)
PRBiRS....... Przedsiebiorstwo Remontowo-Budowlane i Robot Specjalnych [*Enterprise for Repair and Construction and for Special Projects*] (POL)
pr br............ Antiarmored (BU)
PRC............ Parti Republicain Congolais (MAR)
PRC............ Parti des Ressortissants Congolais (MAR)
PRC............ Partido Republicano Calderonista [*Calderonista Republican Party*] [*Costa Rican*] (PPW)
PRC............ Partido Revolucionario Cristiano [*Christian Revolutionary Party*] [*Argentine*] (LA)
PRC............ Partido Revolucionario Cristiano [*Christian Revolutionary Party*] [*Dominican Republic*] (LA1)
PRC............ People's Redemption Council [*Liberian*] (PD)
PRC............ People's Republic of China (MAR)
PRC............ Revolutionary Socialist Party [*Peruvian*] (PD)
PrCHO......... Prapor Chemicke Orchrany [*Chemical Defense Battalion*] (CZ)
PRCI............ Parti Republicain de Cote-d'Ivoire (MAR)
PRCiP.......... Przedsiebiorstwo Robot Czerpalnych i Podwodnych [*Enterprise for Dredging and Underwater Work*] (POL)
pr compt..... Pour Compte [*By Cash*] [*Business and trade*] [*French*]
PRCP.......... Partido Revolucionario del Proletariado Chileno [*Revolutionary Party of the Chilean Proletariat*] (LA)
PRCS.......... Palestinian Red Crescent Society (MAR)
PRD............ Parti Radical-Democratique Suisse [*Radical Democratic Party of Switzerland*] (PPE)
PRD............ Parti Republicain du Dahomey (MAR)
PRD............ Partido Radical Democrata [*Radical Democratic Party*] [*Ecuadorean*] (LA)
PRD............ Partido de Renovacion Democratica [*Democratic Renewal Party*] [*Costa Rican*] (PPW)
PRD............ Partido Revolucionario Democratico [*Democratic Revolutionary Party*] [*Panamanian*] (PPW)
PRD............ Partido Revolucionario Dominicano [*Dominican Revolutionary Party*] [*Dominican Republic*] (PPW)
PRD............ Powder Rocket Engine (RU)
PRD............ Pribramske Rudne Doly, Narodni Podnik [*Pribram Ore Mines, National Enterprise*] (CZ)
PRD............ Property Registration Department [*Iranian*] (ME)
PRD............ Proportional Pressure Regulator (RU)
PRD............ Przedsiebiorstwo Robot Drogowych [*Road Construction Enterprise*] (POL)
PRD............ Ramjet Engine (RU)
PRD............ Transmitter (RU)
PRDC.......... Partido Revolucionario Democrata Cristiano [*Revolutionary Christian Democratic Party*] [*Venezuelan*] (LA)
PRDD.......... Partiia Respublikanskovo Demokraticheskovo Dvizheniia (MAR)
PrDI............ Regulation on State Property (BU)
PRD-NR....... Partido Radical Democrata por una Nueva Republica [*Radical Democratic Party for a New Republic*] [*Ecuadorean*] (LA)
prd tr.......... Supply Train [*Division and corps*] (BU)
PRE-............ Electromechanical Converter (RU)
PRE............ Partido Republicano Evolucionista [*Republican Evolutionist Party*] [*Portuguese*] (PPE)
PRE............ Spanish Catalonian Battalion (PD)
pred............ Chairman (RU)
pred............ Preceding, Previous, Foregoing (RU)
pred............ Predikatiivinen [*Predicative*] [*Finnish*]
pred............ Predseda [*Chairman*] (CZ)
pred............ Preface, Foreword (RU)
predg.......... Introduction [*or Preface*] (BU)
predik......... Predicative (BU)
predisl......... Preface (BU)
predisl......... Preface, Foreword (RU)
predl............ Prepositional (Case) (RU)
predlg.......... Preposition (BU)
predm.......... Subject (RU)
predsed rep ... Presidency of the Republic (BU)
Predsprosbyuro ... Goods Supply and Demand Office (RU)
predst.......... Prefix (BU)
PreduzecePTTSaobracaja ... Preduzece Postanskog, Telegrafskog, i Telefonskog Saobracaja [*Postal, Telegraph, and Telephone Establishment*] (YU)
PreduzeceZOP ... Preduzece za Odrzavanje Pruge [*Railroad Track Maintenance Establishment*] (YU)
predzavkom ... Chairman of a Plant Committee (RU)
PREE............ Partido Revolucionario de Educadores Ecuatorianos [*Revolutionary Party of Ecuadorean Educators*] (LA)
prees............ Preesens [*Present Tense*] [*Finnish*]
PREF............ Plande Redressement Economique et Financier [*Senegalese*]
pref............ Prefecture (RU)
pref............ Preference [*Preference*] [*French*]
pref............ Prefiksi, Etuliite [*Prefix*] [*Finnish*]
PREFAB-CAMEROUN ... Societe de Prefabrication Camerounaise de Maisons Populaires (MAR)
PREFANTIOQUIA ... Prefabricaciones Antioquia Ltda. [*Medellin*] (COL)
pregl............ Reviewed (BU)
preim............ Mainly, Chiefly, Principally (RU)
prejm............ Prejmenovan [*Renamed*] (CZ)
prekh............ Transitive [*Verb*] (BU)
PREMAR..... Prefet Maritime [*Maritime Prefect*] [*French*] (WER)
PREMOTO... Promotion de Representation Automobile (MAR)
pren............ Figuratively (BU)
prenebr....... Slighting (BU)
prenebr....... Slighting, Scornful (RU)
prep............ Copy, Transcript (BU)
prep............ Prepositio [*Preposition*] [*Finnish*]
prep............ Teacher [*or Instructor*] (BU)
prep............ Teacher (RU)
Prepak........ People's Revolutionary Party of Kungleipak [*Indian*] (PD)
PREPAL...... Societe Africaine de Preparations Alimentaires (MAR)
prep i chern ... Copy and Carbon Copy (BU)
PREPE......... Plano de Reequipamento Especial para o Exercito [*Special Reequipment Plan for the Army*] [*Brazilian*] (LA1)
prepech...... Reprinted (BU)
prep mashina ... Typewritten Copy (BU)
prepod........ Teacher (RU)
prerab......... Revised, Revised By (BU)
prerab izd... Revised Edition (BU)
prerazk....... Retold By (BU)

PREREPUBLIQUE ... President de la Republique [*President of the Republic*] [*Cambodian*] (CL)
pres .... President [*President*] (CZ)
presb .... Presbitero [*Spanish*]
pressl .... Presencni Sluzba [*Actual Military Service*] (CZ)
PREST .... Comite pour la Politique de la Recherche Scientifique et Technique [*EG*] [*Luxembourg*]
PREUSSAG ... Preussische Bergwerks- und Huetten-AG [*PREUSSAG Mining and Metallurgical Corp.*] (EG)
prev .... Prevedel [*Translated By*] (YU)
prev .... Translator, Translated By, Translation (BU)
PREVAC ...... Promotora Nacional de Prevencion de Accidentes [*Bogota*] (COL)
prevoskh st ... Superlative Degree (RU)
prev ot .... Translated From (BU)
prev st .... Superlative (BU)
PREXMIN .... Prospections et Exploitations Minieres [*Malagasy*] (MAR)
prez .... President (RU)
prez .... Prezes [*Chairman*] [*Polish*]
prez .... Prezydent [*President*] [*Polish*]
Prez .... Prezydium [*Presidium*] [*Polish*]
prezr .... Contemptuous, Scornful, Disdainful (RU)
prezr .... Contemptuously (BU)
PRF .... Partido Revolucionario Febrerista [*Febrerista Revolutionary Party*] [*Paraguayan*] (PPW)
PRF .... Podjetje za Razdeljevanje Filmov [*Motion Picture Distributing Establishment*] (YU)
PRF .... Primitive Recursive Function (RU)
PRFLP .... Popular Revolutionary Front for the Liberation of Palestine (ME)
pr/g .... Last Year (RU)
PRG .... Parachute Reconnaissance Group (BU)
Prg .... Paragraf [*Paragraph*] [*of a program or bill*] (TU)
PRG .... People's Revolutionary Government [*Grenadian*] (PD)
PRG .... Police des Renseignements Generaux [*General Investigation Police*] (AF)
PRG .... Provisional Revolutionary Government [*of the Republic of South Vietnam*] [*Use PRGRSV*] (CL)
PRGMTs ...... Subregional Hydrometeorological Center (RU)
PRGRSV ...... Provisional Revolutionary Government of the Republic of South Vietnam (CL)
PRH .... Partido Revolucionario Hondureno [*Honduras Revolutionary Party*] (PPW)
PRI .... Institutional Revolutionary Party [*Mexican*] (PD)
PRI .... Parti de la Republique Islamique [*Iranian*] (MAR)
PRI .... Partido Revolucionario Independiente [*Independent Revolutionary Party*] [*Guatemalan*] (LA)
PRI .... Partido Revolucionario Institucional [*Institutional Revolutionary Party*] [*Mexican*] (LA)
PRI .... Partito Repubblicano Italiano [*Italian Republican Party*] (PPW)
PRI .... Plastics and Rubber Institute (EA)
PRI .... Prevention Routiere Internationale [*International Prevention of Road Accidents*] (EA)
Pri .... Priroda [*Nature*] [*A periodical*] (BU)
PRI .... Puerto Rico [*Three-letter standard code*] (CNC)
prib .... Additional, Surplus (RU)
prib .... Arrival (RU)
pribalt .... Baltic Region (RU)
pribav .... Added, Addition (BU)
pribavl .... Addition, Supplement (RU)
pribl .... Approximately (RU)
PribVO .... Baltic Military District (RU)
prich .... Participle (BU)
prich .... Participle (RU)
PRIDA .... Programa Integral de Desarrollo Agricola [*Integral Agricultural Development Program*] [*Venezuelan*] (LA)
PRIDECO .... Programa Integral de Desarrollo Comunal [*Integral Program of Community Development*] [*Salvadoran*] (LA1)
Prig .... Suburb [*Topography*] (RU)
prij .... Prijezd [*Arrival*] (CZ)
prikl .... Applied (RU)
PrikVO .... Carpathian Military District (RU)
pril .... Adjective (BU)
pril .... Adjective (RU)
pril .... Appendix (BU)
pril .... Supplement (BU)
pril .... Supplement, Appendix, Enclosure (RU)
prim .... Annotation, Footnote, Remark (RU)
prim .... Primaer [*Primary*] [*German*]
Prim .... Primarius [*German*]
PRIMARCO ... Confecciones Primavera SA [*Medellin*] (COL)
PRIMAS .... Program fuer Rectorchieren und Indexieren mit Maschinenhilfe
primech ...... Annotation, Footnote, Remark (RU)
Primizdat .... Primorskiy Kray Publishing House (RU)
prim perev ... Translator's Note (RU)
primred .... Primedba Redakcije [*Editorial Comment*] (YU)
prim ref .... Abstractor's Note (RU)
PrimTASS ... Primorskiy Kray Branch of the News Agency of the Soviet Union (RU)
PRIN .... Partido Revolucionario de Integracion Nacional [*Revolutionary Party of National Integration*] [*Venezuelan*] (LA)
PRIN .... Partido Revolucionario de la Izquierda Nacionalista [*National Leftist Revolutionary Party*] [*Bolivian*] (PPW)
PRING .... Partido Revolucionario de Izquierda Nacional Gueiler [*Bolivian*] (PPW)
PRINM .... Partido Revolucionario de la Izquierda Nacional Moller [*Bolivian*] (PPW)
PRIO .... International Peace Research Institute of Oslo (MAR)
Priorodo-mat fak ... Department of Natural History and Mathematics (BU)
pr i ot .... Arrival and Departure (RU)
prir .... Priredil [*Prepared By*] (YU)
PRiS .... Przemysl Rolny i Spozywczy [*Agricultural and Food Industry*] (POL)
PRISA .... Public Relations Institute of South Africa (MAR)
Prist .... Landing Stage, Wharf, Pier [*Topography*] (RU)
prit .... Addition, Supplement (BU)
prit mest ..... Possessive Pronoun (BU)
PRiTV .... Polskie Radio i Telewizja [*Polish Radio and Television*] [*Polish*]
priv .... Privat [*Private*] (EG)
priv .... Privilegie [*Privileged, Licensed*] [*French*]
priv .... Privilegio [*Spanish*]
priv-dots ..... Privatdocent (RU)
PriVO .... Volga Military District (RU)
prizm .... Prismatic (RU)
PRK .... Democratic Peoples Republic of Korea [*Three-letter standard code*] (CNC)
prk .... Enemy (RU)
PRK .... Mobile X-Ray Unit (RU)
PRK .... People's Republic of Kampuchea [*Formerly, Cambodia*] (PD)
PRK .... Pneumatic Control Valve, Pneumatic Governor (RU)
PRK .... Przedsiebiorstwo Robot Kolejowych [*Railroad Construction Enterprise*] (POL)
PRK .... Radiation Monitoring Post (RU)
PRK .... Radio Control Point (BU)
PRK .... Semiautomatic Distributing Conveyor (RU)
PRK .... Straight Mercury-Quartz Discharge Lamp (RU)
PRKhM .... Mobile Repair Shop for Chemical Equipment (RU)
pr Khr .... Before Christ (BU)
PRKhU .... Field Collapsible Refrigeration Unit (RU)
PrKoop .... Regulation on Cooperative Organizations (BU)
PRKP .... Parachute Oxygen Apparatus (RU)
pr kub .... Simple Cubic Lattice (RU)
PRL .... Homing Radar (RU)
PRL .... Landing Radar (RU)
PRL .... Mobile Radiological Laboratory (RU)
PRL .... Parti Reformateur Liberal [*Liberal Reform Party*] [*Belgian*] (PPW)
PRL .... Parti Republicain de la Liberte [*Republican Party of Liberty*] [*French*] (PPE)
PRL .... Passive Radar (RU)
PRL .... Polska Rzeczpospolita Ludowa [*Polish People's Republic*] (POL)
PRL .... Pouvoir Revolutionnaire Local [*Local Revolutionary Authorities*] [*Guinean*] (AF)
PRLU .... Portable Radiological Field Laboratory (RU)
PRLW .... Parti des Reformes et de la Liberte de Wallonie [*Belgian*] (PPW)
PRM .... Field Oil-Reclaiming Plant (RU)
PRM .... Homing Beacon (RU)
pr m .... Last Month (RU)
PRM .... Mobile Repair Shop (RU)
PRM .... Partai Rakyat Malaya [*Malayan People's Party*] (ML)
PRM .... Parti de Regroupement Mauritanien [*Mauritanian Regroupment Party*] (AF)
PRM .... Portable Microroentgenometer (RU)
PrM .... Pravna Misul [*Legal Thought*] [*A periodical*] (BU)
PRM .... Prezes Rady Ministrow [*President of the Council of Ministers*] (POL)
PRM .... Prezydium Rady Ministrow [*Presidium of the Cabinet*] [*Polish*]
PRM .... Radio Beacon Signal Receiver (RU)
Prm .... Receiver (RU)
pr/min .... Idle Strokes per Minute (RU)
Prmj .... Proslog Mjeseca [*Preceding Month*] (YU)
PRN .... Parti de Regroupement National [*National Regroupment Party*] [*Upper Voltan*] (AF)
PRN .... Partido Republicano Nacionalista [*National Republican Party*] [*Costa Rican*] (LA)
PRN .... Partido de la Revolucion Nacional [*Party of the National Revolution*] [*Bolivian*] (PPW)
PRN .... Partido Revolucionario Nacionalista [*Nationalist Revolutionary Party*] [*Venezuelan*] (LA)
PRN .... Powiatowa Rada Narodowa [*County People's Council*] (POL)
PRNC .... Parti de Reconstruction Nationale du Congo (MAR)
PRNCA .... Parti de Reconstruction Nationale du Congo et de l'Afrique (MAR)
pr ne .... Before Christ (BU)
prne .... Pre Nase Ere [*Before Our Era (Before Christ)*] (YU)
PRNM .... Parti de la Renaissance Nationale Mauritanienne (MAR)
PRNM .... Pergerakan Revolusioner Nasional Malaya [*Malayan National Revolutionary Movement*] (ML)
PrNo .... Prazdnichni Novini [*Holiday News*] [*A newspaper*] (BU)
PRNR .... Public Resort Nature Reserve (MAR)

PRO .... Antimissile Defense (BU)
PRO .... Antimissile Defense, Missile Defense, Antirocket Defense (RU)
PRO .... Partido Revolucionario Ortodoxo [*Orthodox Revolutionary Party*] [*Guatemalan*] (LA)
PRO .... Partido Revolucionario Ortodoxo [*Orthodox Revolutionary Party*] [*Honduran*] (LA)
PRO .... Passport Registration Department (RU)
PRO .... Polskie Ratownictwo Okretowe [*Polish Ship Salvage Enterprise*] (POL)
Pro .... Prostori [*Scope*] [*A periodical*] (BU)
PRO .... Protiraketova Obrana [*Antimissile Defense*] (CZ)
PRO .... Public Relations Officer (MAR)
PROA .... Plantations Reunies de l'Ouest Africain (MAR)
PROAGRO... Programa de Apoio a Atividade Agropecuaria [*Agriculture and Livestock Activity Support Program*] [*Brazilian*] (LA)
PROAIBN .... Programa de Apoio as Industrias Basicas do Nordeste [*Northeast Basic Industry Support Program*] [*Brazilian*] (LA)
PROAIUN .... Programa de Apoio a Infraestrutura Urbana do Nordeste (of Northeast Bank of Brazil) [*Northeast Urban Infrastructure Support Program*] [*Brazilian*] (LA)
PROALCOOL ... Programa Nacional do Alcool [*Alcohol Production Program*] [*Brazilian*] (LA1)
PROAVES ... Procesadora del Valle SA [*Cali*] (COL)
PROAZU...... Asociacion de Productores de Azufre [*Sulfur Producers Association*] [*Chilean*] (LA)
prob .... Proboszcz [*Parish-Priest*] [*Polish*]
PROBI-SA ... Application Industrielle des Progres en Biologie (MAR)
probl .... Problems (RU)
proc............ Procent [*Per Cent*] [*Polish*]
proc............ Procesion [*Spanish*]
PROCA........ Programa de Cooperacion con las Islas del Caribe [*Program of Cooperation with the Caribbean Islands*] [*Venezuelan*] (LA)
PROCACI.... Societe des Produits de Cacao de la Cote-d'Ivoire (MAR)
PROCAER... Progetti Costruzioni Aeronauticae [*Italian*]
PROCAMA ... Union des Producteurs de Cacao et de Cafe d'Akposo, Canton Ouma (MAR)
PROCAMOU ... Union des Producteurs d'Amou (MAR)
PROCAMPO ... Asesoramiento Tecnico al Campo [*Technical Counseling for Rural Areas*] [*Nicaraguan*] (LA1)
PROCANA... Asociacion de Productores de Cana de Azucar [*Association of Sugarcane Producers*] [*Salvadoran*] (LA1)
PROCAR ..... Productora de Carton Ltda. [*Medellin*] (COL)
PROCARFAL ... Productora de Cartones Asfalticos Ltda. [*Cali*] (COL)
PROCAUCHO ... Productos de Caucho SA [*Medellin*] (COL)
Proc Conf Cult Ecol ... Proceedings of the Conference of Cultural Ecology [*A publication*] (MAR)
PROCEBADA ... Asociacion para el Fomento del Cultivo de la Cebada [*Bogota*] (COL)
PROCEMASA ... Procesadora del Mar, Sociedad Anonima [*Seafoods Processing Enterprise, Incorporated*] [*Ecuadorean*] (LA)
PROCHILE ... Instituto de Promocion de Exportaciones [*Institute for Export Promotion*] [*Chilean*] (LA)
PROCHIMAD ... Societe des Produits Chimiques de Madagascar (MAR)
PROCHIMAT ... Compagnie de Produits Chimiques et Materiaux (MAR)
prochit .... Read [*Bibliography*] (RU)
PROCI .... Societe de Conditionnement de Produits Cote-d'Ivoire (MAR)
PROCIDA .... Societe des Produits Chimiques, Industriels, et Agricoles (MAR)
PROCOHARINAS ... Productora Colombiana de Harinas [*Bogota*] (COL)
PROCOLDER ... Proveedora Colombiana de Repuestos [*Medellin*] (COL)
PROCOLMA ... Productos Colombianos de Madera [*Medellin*] (COL)
PROCOLSA ... Productos Colombianos para Automotores [*Bogota*] (COL)
PROCOLSA ... Promotora Colombiana Sociedad Anonima [*Bogota*] (COL)
PROCON..... Proyectos y Construcciones [*Cali*] (COL)
PROCONTROLES ... Productora de Controles Ltda. [*Cali*] (COL)
PROCOS..... Produits Congeles au Senegal (MAR)
PROCOVEX ... Promotora de Ventas y Comercio Exterior Ltda. [*Bogota*] (COL)
prod .... Food (RU)
PROD .... Personal Relations and Organizational Development Programme (MAR)
Prod .... Produkt [*Product*] [*German*]
PRODALUM ... Productos de Aluminio Arquitectionico Ltda. [*Cali*] (COL)
PRODAPAM ... Programa Setorial de Desenvolvimento Agropecuario do Amazonas [*Amazonas Agricultural and Stockraising Development Program*] [*Brazilian*] (LA)
PRODASEN ... Centro de Processamento de Dados do Senado Federal [*Federal Senate Data Processing Center*] [*Brazilian*] (LA)
PRODB........ Supply Base (BU)
PRODECO... Programa de Promocion Educativa Comunal [*Program for the Promotion of Community Education*] [*Nicaraguan*] (LA1)
PRODEL...... Societe Frigorifique des Produits des Eleveurs Tchadiens (MAR)
PRODELCO ... Promociones del Comercio [*Cali*] (COL)
PRODEMA ... Productores de Madera de El Salvador [*Wood Producers of El Salvador*] (LA1)
PRODEMA ... Productos de Madera Ltda. [*Bogota*] (COL)
PRODEPAL ... Productos de Papel Ltda. [*Cali*] (COL)
PRODESARROLLO ... Centro para la Promocion de la Ciencia y el Desarrollo Socioeconomico [*Center for Promotion of Socioeconomic Development and Science*] [*Costa Rican*] (LA1)
PRODESTE ... Programa de Desenvolvimento de Centro-Oeste [*Central-West Development Program*] [*Brazilian*] (LA)
PRODIAL..... Promotion des Usages Industriels de l'Alcool (MAR)
Prodintorg ... All-Union Export-Import Association of the Ministry of Foreign Trade, USSR (RU)
prodkom ..... Food Committee (RU)
prodmash ... Food Machinery Manufacture (RU)
prodmash ... Food Machinery Plant (RU)
Prodmontazh ... State Planning and Installation Trust of the Glavtekhmontazh of the Ministry of Construction, RSFSR (RU)
prodolzh ..... Continuation, Sequel (RU)
Prodrasmet ... Central Committee of the VSNKh for the Stocktaking, Distribution, and Sale of Heavy Ores and Metals (RU)
Prodsnab .... Office of Food Supply for Workers and Employees (RU)
produlzh ..... Continuation (BU)
PRODUNAL ... Productos Nacionales [*Cali*] (COL)
Proektneftespetsmontazh ... Planning Office of the Glavneftemontazh of the Ministry of Construction, RSFSR (RU)
PROEMPAQUES ... Productora Nacional de Empaques Ltda. [*Bogota*] (COL)
PROEXPO ... Fondo de Promocion de Exportaciones [*Export Promotion Fund*] [*Colombian*] (LA)
prof .... Profesor [*Professor*] (POL)
prof .... Profesor [*Professor*] (CZ)
Prof .... Profesor [*Professor*] (TU)
prof .... Professional, Vocational, Occupational, Trade (BU)
Prof .... Professor [*German*]
prof .... Professor [*Professor*] (HU)
prof .... Professor (BU)
prof .... Professor (RU)
prof .... Professori [*Finnish*]
prof .... Profeta [*Spanish*]
prof .... Trade-Union (RU)
prof .... Vocational, Occupational, Professional (RU)
PROFAMILIA ... Centro de Planificacion Familiar [*Cali*] (COL)
Profgrupa.... Trade Union Group (BU)
Profgruporg ... Trade Union Group Organizer (BU)
PROFICOL ... Productos Fitosanitarios de Colombia [*Bogota*] (COL)
profil punkt ... Prophylactic Station [*Topography*] (RU)
Profintern ... Red International of Trade Unions (RU)
Profizdat..... Trade-Union Publishing House (RU)
Profkomitet ... Trade Union Committee (BU)
profkor........ Trade-Union Correspondent (RU)
profobr........ Administration for Vocational Education of the Population (RU)
PROFOG ..... Promotion du Foyer Guadeloupeen [*Promotion of the Guadeloupean Home*] (LA1)
Proforganizatsiya ... Trade Union Organization (BU)
Profpredsedatel ... Trade Union Chairman (BU)
Profsekretariat ... Trade Union Secretariat (BU)
Profsovet .... Council of Trade Unions (RU)
Profsozh ..... Railroad Workers' Trade Union (RU)
Profsuyuz.... Trade Union (BU)
Prof-t.......... Trade Union Committee (BU)
Proftekhizdat ... All-Union Publishing House of Textbooks and Pedagogical Literature of the State Committee of the Council of Ministers, USSR, for Vocational and Technical Education (RU)
PROGAN ..... Productos Ganaderos Chile Ltda. [*Chilean Livestock Products Ltd.*] (LA)
PROGAS ..... Proveedora de Gas Ltda. [*Bogota*] (COL)
Progimn...... Junior High School (BU)
PROGRE...... City Planning and Zoning Organization (BU)
PROHUZA ... Centre d'Etudes et Informations des Problemes Humains dans les Zones Arides (MAR)
PROINCO.... Proyectos Ingenieria Construccion [*Bogota*] (COL)
PROINPA..... Promotora Industrial Panamericana [*Bogota*] (COL)
PROINSA .... Promociones de Credito e Inversiones Sociedad Anonima [*Cali*] (COL)
proizn.......... Pronounced (RU)
proizv.......... Production (BU)
Proizv.......... Scientific-Production Specialization (BU)
proizv-vo..... Production, Manufacture (RU)
proj............. Projekt [*Project*] [*Polish*]
proj............. Projektowal [*Designed By*] (POL)
Prok .... Prokuratur [*or Prokurist*] [*German*]
prol............. Prologo [*Spanish*]
prol............. Strait, Sound (RU)
PROLECHE ... Procesadora de Leches SA [*Medellin*] (COL)
prolet .... Proletarian (RU)
Proletkul't... "Proletarian Culture" [*1917-1932*] (RU)
proletstud... Proletarian Students (RU)
prom .... Industrial (BU)
prom .... Industrial, Industry (RU)
Prom .... Promontorio [*Promontory*] [*Spanish*] (NAU)
prom .... Promotor [*Professor conferring a degree*] [*Polish*]
PROMECAR ... Productos Metalicos de Cartagena Ltda. [*Cartagena*] (COL)

Promenergo ... Industrial and Technical Establishment for the Adjustment, Planning, and Repair of Power-Engineering Equipment (RU)
Promenergomontazh ... Industrial Power Installation (BU)
Promenergoproyekt ... State All-Union Planning Institute for the Planning of Construction of Industrial Heat and Electric Power Plants for Supplying Power to Industrial Establishments of All Branches of the National Economy (RU)
PROMETAL ... Productos de Metal [*Medellin*] (COL)
PROMETALICOS ... Productos Metalicos de Colombia Ltda. [*Manizales*] (COL)
PROMEXCOL ... Promotora de Explotaciones y Cultivos Ltda. [*Medellin*] (COL)
promezh ..... Intermediate, Interstitial (RU)
Promfinplan ... Industrial Finance Plan (BU)
Promgrazhdanstroy ... State Trust for Industrial and Civil Engineering Construction (RU)
PROMIV ...... Promotion Ivoirienne (MAR)
Promizdat ... Industrial Publishing House (RU)
Promkombinat ... Industrial Combine (BU)
promkoop ... Producers' Cooperatives (RU)
prommetsoyuz ... Union of Metal Producers' Cooperatives (RU)
Prommontazh ... Industrial Assemblies (BU)
PROMOCAM ... Societe Camerounaise de Promotion (MAR)
PROMOCI ... Promotion des Cultures Industrielles (MAR)
PROMOGABON ... Agence Gabonaise de Promotion Industrielle et Artisanale [*Gabonese Agency for Industrial and Handicrafts Promotion*] (AF)
PROMOPLAST ... Societe de Promotion des Matieres Plastiques (MAR)
PROMOTEC ... Producciones y Montajes Tecnicos Ltda. [*Cali*] (COL)
PROMOVIL ... Propaganda Movil Ltda. (COL)
Promplan .... Industrial Planning Commission (RU)
prom prod ... Intermediate Product (RU)
Promproekt ... Industrial Designs (BU)
prom sch ... Industrial Accounting (BU)
promsovet ... Council of Producers' Cooperatives (RU)
promsoyuz ... Union of Producers' Cooperatives (RU)
prom-st' ...... Industry (RU)
Promstal'konstruktsiya ... Planning Office of the Glavstal'konstruktsiya of the Ministry of Construction of Establishments of the Metallurgical and Chemical Industries, USSR (RU)
promstrakhkassa ... Mutual Insurance and Mutual Aid Fund of Producers' Cooperatives (RU)
promstrakhsovet ... Insurance Council of Artels of Producers' Cooperatives (RU)
Promstromenergomontazh ... All-Union Trust for the Installation of Power Engineering Equipment of the Glavstroymash of the Ministry of the Building Materials Industry, USSR (RU)
Promstroyizdat ... State Publishing House of Literature on Building Materials (RU)
Promstroyproyekt ... All-Union Trust of Construction Planning of Industrial Establishments and Structures of Ferrous and Nonferrous Metallurgy and Machinery Manufacture (RU)
Promstroyproyekt ... State Institute for Sanitary-Engineering and General-Construction Planning of Industrial Establishments [*Leningrad*] (RU)
Promstroyproyekt ... State Planning Institute for General-Construction and Sanitary-Engineering Planning of Industrial Establishments [*Moscow*] (RU)
Promsvyaz'montazh ... Trust for the Installation of Communications for Industrial Establishments (RU)
Promsyr'yeimport ... All-Union Import-Export Association for Industrial Raw Materials (RU)
Promtara ..... Industrial Packing Materials Trust (RU)
promtekhsnab ... Department of Technical Supply at the Council of Producers' Cooperatives (RU)
promtorg .... Manufactured Goods Trade Organization (RU)
Promtransproyekt ... State Planning Institute for the Development of Plans of Structures and for the Organization of Industrial Transportation (RU)
Promvoyensovet ... Council of War Industry (RU)
Promzernoproyekt ... State Institute for the Planning of Flour-Milling and Groats Industry Establishments, Elevators and Storage Facilities (RU)
promzhilstroy ... Industrial Housing Construction (RU)
pron .... Pronomini [*Pronoun*] [*Finnish*]
PRONAN ..... Programa Nacional de Alimentacao e Nutricao [*National Food and Nutrition Program*] [*Brazilian*] (LA)
PRONASE ... Productura Nacional de Semillas [*National Seed Producers Organization*] [*Mexican*] (LA)
PRONTEL .... Programa Nacional de Teleducacao [*National Television Education Program*] [*Brazilian*] (LA)
PROP .... Panstwowa Rada Ochrony Przyrody [*State Council for the Protection of Nature*] (POL)
prop .... Propagandistic, Propaganda (RU)
PrOP .... Regulation on Social Assistance (BU)
PROPAL ...... Productora de Papeles [*Yumbo-Valle*] (COL)
PROPAN ...... Productora de Pan [*Medellin*] (COL)
Pr za op na kn ... Rules for Descriptive Cataloging in Public Libraries (BU)
PRO-PO .... Prognostika Podosfairou [*Soccer Forecasts*] (GC)
PROQUICOL ... Productos Quimicos Colombianos SA [*Medellin*] (COL)
PROQUINAL ... Fabrica de Productos Quimicos Nacionales Ltda. [*Bogota*] (COL)
pror .... Procurador [*Spanish*]
PROROCHE ... Productos Roche SA [*Bogota*] (COL)
pros .... Prosody (RU)
PROSAB ...... Antiaircraft Bomb (RU)
prosh .... Past (Tense) (RU)
PROSI .... Public Relations Office of the Sugar Industry (MAR)
PROSID .... Transformation de Produits Siderurgiques (MAR)
prosm .... Reviewed, Revised (RU)
prosmotr ..... Reviewed (RU)
prosp .... Avenue (RU)
prosp .... Prospekt [*Leaflet*] [*Polish*]
prost .... Colloquial Expression (RU)
prost .... Colloquial Word (RU)
prosv .... Education (BU)
prosvet .... Enlightening, Educational (RU)
prot .... Canal, Channel [*Topography*] (RU)
prot .... Minutes, Proceedings (RU)
prot .... Protestans [*Protestant*] (HU)
Prot .... Protestant [*Protestant*] (CZ)
PROT .... Protocol Dairesi Genel Mudurlugu [*Protocol Office Directorate General*] [*of Foreign Affairs Ministry*] (TU)
PROTABACO ... Productora Tabacalera de Colombia SA [*Bogota*] (COL)
Pro Tan .... Proje Tanzimi [*Organizing of Project*] (TU)
PROTECO ... Productos Tecnicos Colombianos [*Buenaventura*] (COL)
Prot ekz s .... Minutes of the Exarchy Council (BU)
PROTELA .... Fabrica de Productos Textiles Protela Boger & Compania [*Bogota*] (COL)
pro tem .... Pro Tempore [*For the Time Being*] [*Latin*] (GPO)
PROTENAL ... Productos Tecnicos Nacionales [*Cali*] (COL)
PROTERRA ... Programa de Redistribuicao de Terras e de Estimulo as Atividades Agro-Pecuarias do Nordeste e do Norte [*Land Redistribution and Agricultural and Livestock Incentive Program for the Northeast and North*] [*Brazilian*] (LA)
PROTEXSY ... Office de Promotion du Textile Synthetique en Cote-d'Ivoire (MAR)
prots .... Percent (RU)
PROTZ .... Regulation on Recording and Reporting Labor Accidents (BU)
Prov .... Province [*Province*] [*French*] (MTD)
prov .... Province (RU)
Prov .... Provincia [*Province*] [*Spanish*] (GPO)
Prov .... Provinz [*Province*] (EG)
Prov .... Provision [*Commission*] [*Business and trade*] [*German*]
prova .... Provincia [*Province*] [*Spanish*]
PROVALLE ... Promotora del Valle Ltda. [*Cali*] (COL)
provbr .... Provozni Brigada [*Traffic Brigade*] [*Motor pool for ministries*] (CZ)
provd .... Provdana [*Married (Female)*] (CZ)
PROVICALI ... Promotora de Vivienda de Cali (COL)
PROVICCOP ... Promotora de Vivienda Cooperativa [*Cali*] (COL)
PROVICO .... Promotora de Vivienda Popular [*Bogota*] (COL)
PROVINC .... PROVINC Kereskedelmi Egyesules [*PROVINC Trade Association*] (HU)
Provol .... Wire Plant [*Topography*] (RU)
provor .... Provisor [*Spanish*]
provzheldor ... Cable Railway (RU)
Prox .... Proximo [*In (or Of) the Next*] [*Latin*] (GPO)
Proyektgidromekhanizatsiya ... State Planning Institute for the Complex Planning of Hydraulic Mining Establishments of Nonmetallic Building Materials and for the Rendering of Technical Assistance in Putting Such Establishments in Operation and Servicing Them (RU)
Proyektstal'konstruktsiya ... State Institute for the Planning, Research, and Testing of Steel Structures and Bridges (RU)
Proz .... Prozent [*or Prozentig*] [*Percent or Percentage*] [*German*]
proz .... Versification (BU)
Prozamet .... Biuro Projektowania Zakladow Przemyslu Metalowego i Elektrotechnicznego [*Bureau of Plans for Metal and Electrical Industry Plants*] (POL)
prozodezhda ... Work Clothes (RU)
PRP- .... Manual Pneumatic Riveting Press (RU)
PRP .... Parti Republicain du Progres [*Republican Progress Party*] [*Central African*] (PD)
PRP .... Parti de la Revolution Populaire [*People's Revolutionary Party*] [*Zairian*] (PD)
PRP .... Partido Republicano Portugues [*Portuguese Republican Party*] (PPE)
PRP .... Partido Revolucionario Popular [*Popular Revolutionary Party*] [*Portuguese*] (PPE)
PRP .... Partido Revolucionario do Proletariado [*Revolutionary Party of the Proletariat*] [*Portuguese*] (WER)
PRP .... Partido Revolucionario do Proletariado [*Revolutionary Party of the Proletariat*] [*Brazilian*] (LA)
PRP .... Partido Revolucionario Proletario [*Proletarian Revolutionary Party*] [*Chilean*] (LA)
PRP .... People's Redemption Party [*Nigerian*] (PPW)
PRP .... People's Revolution Party [*Singapore*] (ML)
PRP .... Progressive Reform Party (MAR)
PRP .... Track Relay Repeater (RU)

PRPA........... Partido de Reunificacao do Povo Angolano [*Party for the Reunification of the Angolan People*] (AF)
PRPB........... Parti de la Revolution Populaire du Benin [*Benin People's Revolutionary Party*] (PD)
PRP-BR....... Partido Revolucionario do Proletariado-Brigadas Revolucionarias [*Revolutionary Party of the Proletariat-Revolutionary Brigades*] [*Portuguese*] (WER)
PrPK............ Regulation on Conciliation Commissions (BU)
pr pl............. Before Noon (BU)
PRPL............ Light Sectional Floating Pier (RU)
PrPS............ Prapor Pohranicni Straze [*Border Guard Battalion*] (CZ)
PRPS............ Relay and Broadcasting Equipment Enterprise (BU)
PRPT............ Parti Revolutionnaire du Peuple Tunisien [*Revolutionary Party of the Tunisian People*] (PD)
PRPUP......... Przedsiebiorstwo Robot Przemyslowych Urzadzen Podziemnych [*Industrial Underground Construction Enterprise*] (POL)
PRR.............. Mode Selector Switch (RU)
PRR.............. Poljoprivredna Remontna Radionica [*Agricultural Repair Shop*] (YU)
PRRI-PERMESTA... Pemerintah Revolusioner Republik Indonesia - Perdjuangan Semesta [*Revolutionary Government of the Republic of Indonesia - Total Struggle Movement*] (IN)
PRRWM....... Przedsiebiorstwo Rejonowych Robot Wodno-Melioracyjnych [*Regional Irrigation and Land Reclamation Enterprise*] (POL)
PRS.............. Antimissile Missile (RU)
PRS.............. Homing Radio Station (RU)
PRS.............. Mobile Regulating Station (RU)
PRS.............. Partai Rakyat Singapura [*Singapore People's Party*] (ML)
PRS.............. Partei fuer Renten-, Steuer-, und Soziale Gerechtigkeit [*Party for Equitable Pensions, Taxation, and Social Services*] [*West German*] (PPW)
PRS.............. Parti du Regroupement Soudanais (MAR)
PRS.............. Parti Republicain Senegalais [*Senegalese Republican Party*] (AF)
PRS.............. Parti de la Revolution Socialiste [*Party of the Socialist Revolution*] [*Algerian*] (AF)
PRS.............. Partido de la Revolucion Salvadorena [*Salvadoran Revolutionary Party*] (LA)
PRS.............. Partido Revolucionario Socialista [*Socialist Revolutionary Party*] [*Colombian*] (LA)
Prs................ Personel [*Personnel*] (TU)
PRS.............. Polski Rejestr Statkow [*Polish Register of Ships*] (POL)
PRS.............. Projet Rural de Sedhiou (MAR)
PRS.............. Radio Range Station (BU)
PRS.............. Sailing Vessel (RU)
PRS.............. Train Radio Station (RU)
PRSB............ Parti de la Revolution Socialiste du Benin (MAR)
PRSC............ Partido Revolucionario Social Cristiano [*Christian Social Revolutionary Party*] [*Dominican Republic*] (LA)
pr sch.......... Proportional Counter (RU)
Prsdt............ Praesident [*German*]
PRSI............. Co-Phasing Pulse Receiver (RU)
pr/smos....... Proypologismos [*Budget*] (GC)
PRSNT......... Parti Republicain pour le Salut National Tchadien [*Republican Party for Chadian National Salvation*] (AF)
PRSS............ Parti Republicain Social du Senegal (MAR)
PRSS............ Powszechna Robotnicza Spoldzielnia Spozywcza [*General Worker's Consumer Cooperative*] (POL)
PrSt.............. Predigtstation [*German*]
PRT-............. Device for Programed Temperature Control (RU)
Prt................ Parit [*Stream, Canal, Ditch*] [*Malay*] (NAU)
PRT.............. Partido Republicano Trabalhista [*Republican Workers Party*] [*Brazilian*] (LA)
PRT.............. Partido Revolucionario Trabajador [*Revolutionary Workers' Party*] [*Argentine*] (LA)
PRT.............. Partido Revolucionario de los Trabajadores [*Workers' Revolutionary Party*] [*Argentine*] (PD)
PRT.............. Partido Revolucionario de los Trabajadores [*Workers' Revolutionary Party*] [*Mexican*] (LA1)
PRT.............. Partido Revolucionario de los Trabajadores [*Revolutionary Workers' Party*] [*Uruguayan*] (PD)
PRT.............. Partido Revolucionario dos Trabalhadores [*Workers' Revolutionary Party*] [*Portuguese*] (WER)
PRT.............. Partido Rural Trabalhista [*Rural Labor Patry*] [*Brazilian*] (LA)
PRT.............. Plovni Recni Trenovi [*River Convoys*] [*Navy*] (YU)
PRT.............. Portugal [*Three-letter standard code*] (CNC)
PRT.............. Proportional Temperature Control (RU)
PRT.............. Przedsiebiorstwo Robot Telekomunikacyjnych [*Communication Construction Enterprise*] (POL)
PRT.............. Workers' Revolutionary Party [*Peruvian*] (PD)
prtb.............. Mobile Missile Maintenance Depot (BU)
PRTB... .... Mobile Repair and Technical Base (RU)
PRTB............ Partido Revolucionario de Trabajadores Bolivianos [*Bolivian Workers' Revolutionary Party*] (PD)
PRTBR......... Partido Revolucionario de los Trabajadores de Bolivia Romero [*Bolivian*] (PPW)
PRTC............ Partido Revolucionario de Trabajadores Centroamericanos [*Revolutionary Party of Central American Workers*] [*Salvadoran*] (PD)
PRTI............. Telemetering Receiver (RU)
PRTS............ Portable Radiotelegraph Station (RU)
PRTs............ Receiving Radio Center (RU)
PrTS............ Regulation on Hearing Labor Disputes (BU)
PRTs............ Transmitting Radio Center (RU)
PRTZ............ Partisans, Guerrillas (BU)
PRU.............. Control Pulse Receiver (RU)
PRU.............. Manual Control Panel (RU)
PRU.............. Mobile X-Ray Unit (RU)
PrU.............. Model Statutes (BU)
PRUD............ Partido Revolucionario de Unificacion Democratica [*Revolutionary Party of Democratic Unification*] [*Salvadoran*] (LA1)
PrUDP......... Regulation on the Application of the Ukase on State Pensions (BU)
Pruflsgg...... Pruefloesungen [*Testing Solutions*] [*German*]
PRUM........... Underground Working of Coal Deposits (RU)
PRUMO....... Progresso Unido de Mocambique [*United Progress of Mozambique*] (AF)
PRUN............ Partido Republicano de Unidad Nacional [*National Unity Republican Party*] [*Guyanese*] (LA)
PrUNRM...... Regulation on the Application of the Ukase on Encouraging a Higher Birth Rate and Large Families (BU)
PRUPC......... Parti Revolutionnaire de l'Union des Populations du Cameroun (MAR)
PrUTKZS..... TKZS [*Labor Cooperative Farm*] Model Statutes (BU)
PrUZUP....... Regulation on the Structure and Tasks of the Pensions Administration and Its Local Organs (BU)
PRV.............. Call Receiver (RU)
PRV.............. Float-Type Regulating Valve (RU)
PRV.............. Partido de la Revolucion Venezolana [*Party of the Venezuelan Revolution*] (LA)
prv............... Pour Rendre Visite [*To Return a Call*] [*French*]
Prv............... Proliv [*Channel, Strait*] [*Russian*] (NAU)
Prv............... Provisor [*or Provisorisch*] [*German*]
pr-vo........... Government (RU)
pr-vo........... Representation, Delegation (RU)
PrVOBL....... Preisverordnungsblatt [*Price Regulations Gazette*] (EG)
PrVT............ Prosecutor of a Military Tribunal (RU)
PrVTAK....... Regulation on Proceedings before the Foreign Trade Arbitration Commission (BU)
PRW............. Przysposobienie Rolnicze i Wojskowe [*Agricultural and Military Training*] (POL)
PRY.............. Paraguay [*Three-letter standard code*] (CNC)
pryam.......... In the Direct Sense (RU)
PRZ.............. Locomotive Repair Plant (RU)
PRZ.............. Przedsiebiorstwo Robot Zmechanizowanych [*Mechanized Construction Enterprise*] (POL)
PrZDA......... Regulation on the Implementation of the Law on State Arbitration (BU)
P Rz d/s...... Pelnomocnik Rzadu do Spraw [*Government Plenipotentiary for*] [*Polish*]
przed Chr.... Przed Chrystusem [*Polish*]
przedr......... Przedruk [*Reprint*] (POL)
przedst....... Przedstawienie [*Performance*] [*Polish*]
przejrz......... Przejrzane [*Examined*] (POL)
przekl.......... Przeklad [*Translation*] (POL)
przel............ Przelozyl [*Translated By*] [*Polish*]
przerob....... Przerobione [*Revised*] (POL)
przetl........... Przetlumaczyl [*Translated By*] [*Polish*]
przew.......... Przewodniczacy [*President*] [*Polish*]
przew.......... Przewodnik [*Guide*] [*Polish*]
PRZh............ Radioisotopic Liquid Density Meter (RU)
PrZhG.......... Regulation for Accepting, Examining, and Settling Civil Grievances (BU)
PRZS............ Mobile Repair and Charging Station (RU)
przyg........... Przygotowal [*Prepared By*] [*Polish*]
przyp........... Przypisek [*Footnote, Postscript*] (POL)
PRZZ............ Powiatowa Rada Zwiazkow Zawodowych [*County Council of Trade Unions*] (POL)
PS................ Absorber (RU)
PS................ Adjustment Fire [*Artillery*] (RU)
PS................ Aiming Rest, Aiming Stand (RU)
PS................ Aircraft Bearing (RU)
PS................ Anti-Icing System (RU)
PS................ Bias Bleeder (RU)
PS................ Boom Position [*Nautical term*] (RU)
PS................ Card-Reader Punch [*Computers*] (RU)
PS................ Ceskoslovenska Lekarska Spolecnost J. E. Purkyne [*J. E. Purkyne Czechoslovak Medical Society*] (CZ)
ps................. Coast Guard Vessel (RU)
PS................ Communications Post (RU)
PS................ Corpo delle Guardie di Pubblica Sicurezza [*Corps of Public Security Guards*] [*Italian*] (WER)
PS................ Correction for Displacement [*Artillery*] (RU)
PS................ Direct Coupling (RU)
PS................ Dispatch Vessel (RU)
PS................ Field Crop Station (RU)
PS................ Field Service (RU)
PS................ Firing Regulations (RU)
ps................. Handwritten Pages (BU)

PS.............. Intermediate Station (RU)
PS.............. Interstage Cooler [*Refrigeration*] (RU)
PS.............. Lines of Communication [*Military term*], Routes of Communication (RU)
PS.............. Marshalling Yard, Classification Yard [*Railroads*] (RU)
PS.............. Message Center (RU)
ps.............. Opere Citato (BU)
PS.............. Pandeios Skholi [*School*] [*See also PASPE*] (GC1)
ps.............. Parallax-Second, Parsec (RU)
PS.............. Partecipazioni Statali [*State Participations*] [*Italian*] (WER)
PS.............. Parteischule [*Party School*] (EG)
PS.............. Parti Socialiste [*Socialist Party*] [*French*] (WER)
PS.............. Partido Socialista [*Socialist Party*] [*Chilean*] (LA)
PS.............. Partido Socialista [*Socialist Party*] [*Portuguese*] (WER)
PS.............. Partido Socialista Portuguesa [*Portuguese Socialist Party*] (PPE)
PS.............. Partido Socialista Uno [*Socialist Party*] [*Bolivian*] (PPW)
Ps.............. Pasa [*Pasha*] [*Turkish*] (GPO)
PS.............. Pasca Sarjana [*Academic degree*] [*Indonesian*]
PS.............. Pasne Skupnosti [*Pastures Held in Common*] (YU)
PS-.............. Passenger Aircraft (RU)
PS-.............. Patrol Vessel (RU)
PS.............. Pedagogicky Sbor [*Board of Education*] (CZ)
PS.............. Perifereiakon Symvoulion [*Regional Council*] (GC)
PS.............. Personenschutz [*Protection of Persons (MfS Department, supplies guards for officials, etc.)*] (EG)
ps.............. Pesos [*Spanish*]
PS.............. Pferdestaerke [*Horsepower*] [*German*] (GPO)
PS.............. Pisnovy Soubor [*Choral Ensemble*] (CZ)
PS.............. Plastic Scintillator (RU)
PS.............. Pocetnicka Sluzba [*Accounting Service*] (CZ)
PS.............. Podaci Stanice [*Distribution Stations*] (CZ)
PS.............. Poddustojnicka Skola [*Non-Commissioned Officers' School*] (CZ)
PS.............. Podnikova Sprava [*Plant Management*] (CZ)
PS.............. Pohranicni Straz [*Border Guard*] (CZ)
PS.............. Pojistovaci Soud [*Insurance Court*] (CZ)
PS.............. Policia Sandinista [*Sandinist Police*] [*Nicaraguan*] (LA1)
PS.............. Politechnika Szczecinska [*Engineering College of Szczecin*] [*Polish*]
PS.............. Politicka Sprava [*Political Directorate*] (CZ)
PS.............. Poljoprivredna Stanica [*Agricultural Station*] (YU)
PS.............. Polni Soud [*Military Court*] (CZ)
PS.............. Polni Straz [*Reconnaissance Unit*] (CZ)
PS.............. Polyester Resin (RU)
PS.............. Polystyrene (RU)
PS.............. Polystyrene for Foaming (RU)
PS.............. Popis Stanovnistva [*Population Census*] (YU)
PS.............. Posadkova Sprava [*Garrison Directorate*] (CZ)
PS.............. Position Speciale [*Special Appointment*] [*Cambodian*] (CL)
PS.............. Positive Column [*Electricity*] (RU)
PS.............. Post Office Station (RU)
PS.............. Poste de Secours [*Dressing Station*] [*Military*] [*French*] (MTD)
PS.............. Postenska Stedilnica [*Postal Savings Bank*] (YU)
PS.............. Postovni Sporitelna [*Postal Savings Agency*] (CZ)
PS.............. Postscriptum [*Postscript*] [*Latin*] (GPO)
ps.............. Postskriptum [*Postscript*] [*Danish*] (GPO)
PS.............. Postskriptum [*Postscript*] [*German*]
ps.............. Postskriptum [*Postscript*] [*Swedish*] (GPO)
PS.............. Povazske Strojarne [*Machine Building Factories of the Vah River Area*] (CZ)
PS.............. Poverenictvo Spojov [*Office of the Commissioner of Communications*] (CZ)
PS.............. Poverenictvo Spravodlivosti [*Office of the Commissioner of Justice*] (CZ)
PS.............. Powszechna Samoobrona [*General Civil Defense*] (POL)
PS.............. Pozemni Stavby [*Surface Construction*] [*A periodical*] (CZ)
PS.............. Pravni Savet (SIV) [*Legal Council*] (YU)
P/S.............. Pretovarne Stanice [*Transshipment Stations*] (YU)
P/S.............. Pripusna Stanica [*Admission Station*] (YU)
PS.............. Privredni Savet [*Economic Council*] (YU)
PS.............. Privredni Savetnik [*Economic Counselor*] [*A periodical*] (YU)
PS.............. Privredni Sud [*Economic Court*] (YU)
PS.............. Prumyslova Skola [*Industrial School*] (CZ)
PS.............. Przedsiebiorstwo Samorzadowe [*Municipal Enterprise*] (POL)
ps.............. Pseudonim [*Pseudonym*] [*Polish*]
PS.............. Pur Sang [*Thoroughbred*] [*Of a horse*] [*French*] (MTD)
PS.............. Purple Glass (RU)
PS.............. Pyrosvestikon Soma [*Fire Corps*] (GC)
PS-.............. Recording Potentiometer (RU)
p/s.............. Sailing Ship (RU)
PS-.............. Scaler (RU)
PS.............. Settlement Soviet of Workers' Deputies (RU)
PS.............. Signal Device (RU)
PS.............. Signal Regiment (RU)
PS.............. Solenoid Drive (RU)
PS.............. Spontaneous Polarization (Method) (RU)
PS-.............. Starter Panel (RU)
PS.............. Substation (RU)
ps.............. Supply Wharf, Supply Pier (RU)
PS.............. Total Correction [*Topography*] (RU)
PS.............. Trade Union (RU)
PS.............. Union of Consumers' Societies (RU)
PS.............. Well Potential [*Pet.*] (RU)
PS,.............. Indizierte Pferdestaerke [*Indicated Horsepower*] [*German*]
PS-1.............. Socialist Party - One [*Bolivian*] (PD)
PSA.............. Pangosmion Synedrion Apodimon [*World Congress of Repatriates*] (GC1)
PSA.............. Pankyprios Syndesmos Agoniston [*Pan-Cyprian League of Fighters*] (GC)
PSA.............. Parti Socialiste Africain (MAR)
PSA.............. Parti Socialiste Autonome [*Autonomous Socialist Party*] [*French*] (PPE)
PSA.............. Parti Solidaire Africain (MAR)
PSA.............. Parti Sportif Algerien (MAR)
PSA.............. Partido Socialista de Andalucia [*Socialist Party of Andalusia*] [*Spanish*] (WER)
PSA.............. Partido Socialista Aponte [*Bolivian*] (PPW)
PSA.............. Partido Socialista de Aragon [*Socialist Party of Aragon*] [*Spanish*] (WER)
PSA.............. Partido Socialista Argentino [*Argentine Socialist Party*] (LA)
PSA.............. Partido Solitario Africano (MAR)
PSA.............. Partito Socialista Autonomo [*Autonomous Socialist Party*] [*Swiss*] (PPW)
PSA.............. People's Supreme Assembly [*Yemeni*] (PPW)
PSA.............. Port of Singapore Authority (ML)
PSA.............. Postsparkassenamt [*Postal Savings Office*] (EG)
PSA.............. Public Service Association [*Guyana*]
PSAA.............. Panellinios Synomospondia Agoniston Andistaseos [*Panhellenic Federation of Resistance Fighters*] (GC)
PSAAThAX... Panellinios Syndesmos Axiomatikon Asyrmatou Thalassis, Aeros kai Xiras [*Panhellenic Association of Marine, Air, and Land Radio Officers*] (GC)
psag.............. Parancsnoksag [*Headquarters*] [*Military*] (HU)
PSAN.............. Partit Socialista d'Alliberament Nacional dels Paisos Catalans [*National Liberation Socialist Party of the Catalan Regions*] [*Spanish*] (WER)
PSAPY........ Panellinios Syndesmos Atmoploikon kai Praktoreiakon Ypallilon [*Panhellenic Association of Shipping and Travel Agency Employees*] (GC)
P S ar.............. Pur Sang Arabe [*French*] (MTD)
PSAS.............. Parti Senegalais d'Action Socialiste (MAR)
PSAThP...... Panellinios Syndesmos Anapiron kai Thymaton Polemou 1912-1941 [*Panhellenic Association of Disabled and Victims of Wars 1912 and 1941*] (GC)
PSB.............. Parti Socialiste Belge [*Belgian Socialist Party*] (WER)
PSB.............. Partido Socialista de Bolivia [*Bolivian Socialist Party*] (LA)
PSB.............. Partido Socialista Brasileiro [*Brazilian Socialist Party*] (LA)
psb.............. Road Construction Battalion (BU)
PSBK.............. Poradni Sbor pro Bytovou Kulturu [*Homemaking Advisory Council*] (CZ)
PSC.............. Congolese Socialist Party [*Zairian*] (PD)
PSC.............. Nicaraguan Social Christian Party (PD)
PSC.............. P. Soucail & Cie. (MAR)
PSC.............. Parti Social Chretien [*Christian Social Party*] [*Belgian*] (WER)
PSC.............. Parti Socialiste Camerounais [*Cameroonian Socialist Party*] (AF)
PSC.............. Parti Socialiste Centrafricain [*Central African Socialist Party*] (PD)
PSC.............. Parti Socialiste des Comores [*Comoro Socialist Party*] (AF)
PSC.............. Parti Socialiste Congolais (MAR)
PSC.............. Partido Social Cristiano [*Christian Social Party*] [*Spanish*] (WER)
PSC.............. Partido Social Cristiano [*Social Christian Party*] [*Ecuadorean*] (PPW)
PSC.............. Partido Social Cristiano [*Social Christian Party*] [*Bolivian*] (LA)
PSC.............. Partido Socialcristiano Nicaraguense [*Nicaraguan Social Christian Party*] (PPW)
PSC.............. Partido Socialista de Catalunya [*Catalan Socialist Party*] [*Spanish*] (PPE)
PSC.............. Police Service Commission [*Jamaican*] (LA1)
PSC.............. Project Support Communication (MAR)
PSC.............. Public Service Commission [*Trinidadian and Tobagan*] (LA1)
PSCC.............. Private Sector Co-Ordinating Committee (MAR)
PSD.............. Destour Socialist Party [*Tunisian*] (PD)
PSD.............. Medium-Pressure Heater (RU)
PSD.............. Message Center (BU)
PSD.............. Message Center (RU)
PSD.............. Panglima Setia Di-Raja [*First Grade of the Most Honorable Order of Setia Di-Raja*] (ML)
PSD.............. Parti Social-Democrate [*Social Democratic Party*] [*Luxembourg*] (WER)
PSD.............. Parti Social-Democrate [*Social Democratic Party*] [*Malagasy*] (AF)
PSD.............. Parti Social Democrate de Madagascar et des Comores (MAR)
PSD.............. Parti Socialiste Democrate [*Democratic Socialist Party*] [*French*] (PPW)
PSD.............. Parti Socialiste Democratique [*Moroccan*] (MAR)
PSD.............. Parti Socialiste Destourien [*Destourian Socialist Party*] [*Tunisian*] (AF)
PSD.............. Partido Social Democrata [*Social Democrat Party*] [*Portuguese*] (PPE)

PSD .... Partido Social-Democrata [*Social-Democrat Party*] [*Spanish*] (PPE)
PSD .... Partido Social Democrata [*Social Democratic Party*] [*Bolivian*] (PPW)
PSD .... Partido Social Democrata [*Social Democratic Party*] [*Chilean*] (LA)
PSD .... Partido Social Democratico [*Social Democratic Party*] [*Portuguese*] (WER)
PSD .... Partido Social Democratico [*Social Democratic Party*] [*Nicaraguan*] (PPW)
PSD .... Partido Social Democratico [*Social Democratic Party*] [*Argentine*] (LA)
PSD .... Partido Social Democratico [*Social Democratic Party*] [*Brazilian*] (LA)
PSD .... Partido Social Democratico [*Social Democratic Party*] [*Salvadoran*] (LA)
PSD .... Partido Socialista Democratico [*Democratic Socialist Party*] [*Guatemalan*] (PD)
PSD .... Partido Socialista Democratico [*Democratic Socialist Party*] [*Ecuadorean*] (LA)
PSD .... Partido Socialista Democratico [*Democratic Socialist Party*] [*Venezuelan*] (LA)
PSD .... Polish Social Democracy (RU)
PSD .... Public Services Department [*Malaysian*] (ML)
PSD .... Punkt Sprzedazy Detalicznej [*Retail Sales Center*] (POL)
PSD .... Social Democratic Party [*Mexican*] (PD)
PSD .... Social Democratic Party [*Nicaraguan*] (PD)
PSDC .... Partido Social Democrata Cristiano [*Bogota*] (COL)
PSDC .... Partido Social Democratico Cristiano [*Christian Democratic Socialist Party*] [*Colombian*] (LA)
PSDCL .... Partido Social Democrate de Castilla y Leon [*Social Democratic Party of Castille and Leon*] [*Spanish*] (WER)
PSDE........... Partido Social Democratico Espanol [*Spanish Social Democratic Party*] (WER)
PSDG .... Partido Social Democratico Gallego [*Galician Social Democratic Party*] [*Spanish*] (WER)
PSDI............ Partido Social Democratico Independente [*Independent Social Democratic Party*] [*Portuguese*] (PPE)
PSDI .... Partito Socialista Democratico Italiano [*Italian Social Democratic Party*] (WER)
PSDIS.......... Partito Socialista Democratico Indipendente Sammarinese [*Independent Social Democratic Party of San Marino*] (PPE)
PSDMI......... Panellinios Syllogos Diplomatoukhon Mikhanologon-Ilektrologon [*Panhellenic Association of Licensed Mechanics and Electricians*] (GC)
PSDMR........ Partidul Social-Democrat al Muncitorilor din Romania [*Social-Democratic Workers' Party of Romania*] (RO)
PSDP........... Regimental Message Center (RU)
PSDP........... Regimental Sanitary and Decontamination Station (RU)
PSDS........... Partito Socialista Democratico Sammarinese [*Social Democratic Party of San Marino*] (PPE)
PSe.............. Effective Pferdestaerke [*Effective Horsepower*] [*German*]
PSE .... Panellinios Syndesmos Exagogeon [*Panhellenic Exporters Association*] (GC)
PSE .... Pangosmion Symvoulion Ekklision [*World Council of Churches*] (GC)
PSE .... Pangosmios Synomospondia Ergaton [*World Confederation of Labor*] (GC)
PSE .... Pankyprion Symvoulion Eirinis [*Pan-Cyprian Peace Council*] (GC)
PSE .... Pankyprion Symvoulion Evimerias [*Pan-Cyprian Welfare Council*] (GC)
PSE .... Partido Socialista de Ecuador [*Socialist Party of Ecuador*] (LA)
PSEA........... Panellinios Synomospondia Efedron Axiomatikon [*Panhellenic Confederation of Reserve Officers*] (GC)
PSEA........... Politiki Skhediaseos Ektaktou Anangis [*Emergency Planning Policy*] (GC)
PSEDN .... Pankyprion Soma Ethelondikis Douleias Neolaias [*Pan-Cyprian Youth Corps for Volunteer Work*] (GC)
PSEEPP ...... Pankyprios Syndesmos Ellinon Ethelondon Palaion Polemiston [*Pan-Cyprian League of Greek Volunteer Veterans*] (GC)
PSEGS .... Panellinios Synomospondia Enoseon Georgikon Synetairismon [*Panhellenic Confederation of Unions of Agricultural Cooperatives*] (GC)
PSEGSE...... Panellinios Synomospondia Enoseon Georgikon Synetairismon Ellados [*Panhellenic Confederation of Agricultural Cooperative Unions of Greece*] (GC)
PSEMA........ Parti Social d'Education des Masses Africaines [*Social Party for Education of the African Masses*] [*Upper Voltan*] (AF)
PSEMA........ Parti Social d'Evolution des Masses Africaines (MAR)
PSEODM..... Panellinios Syndesmos Epikheiriseon Odikon Diethnon Metaforon [*Panhellenic Association of International Road Transport Enterprises*] (GC)
PSEPE......... Proodevtiki Syndikalistiki Ergatoypalliliki Parataxis Ellados [*Progressive Labor Employee Faction of Greece*] (GC)
PSEPP......... Proodevtiki Syndikalistiki Ergatoypalliliki Parataxis Peiraios [*Progressive Labor Employee Faction of Piraeus*] (GC)
pseud .... Pseudonim [*Pseudonym*] [*Polish*]
Pseud .... Pseudonym [*German*]
Psevd .... Pseudonym (BU)
psevd .... Pseudonym (RU)
PSF .... Parti Social Francais [*French Social Party*] (PPE)
PSF .... Popular Struggle Front [*Palestinian*] (PD)
PSF .... Problems of Modern Physics (RU)
PSF .... Progres Social Francais [*French Social Progress*] (PPE)
PSG............ Parti Socialiste Guyanais [*Guiana Socialist Party*] (PPW)
PSG............ Partido Social Guatemalteco [*Guatemalan Social Party*] (LA)
PSG............ Partido Socialista Galego [*Galician Socialist Party*] [*Spanish*] (WER)
PSG............ Peoples' Sacrifice Guerrillas [*Iranian*] (ME)
PSG............ Planning and Estimate Group (RU)
PSG............ Problems of Soviet Geology [*A publication*] (RU)
PSG............ Regimental Fuel Depot (RU)
PSG............ Search and Sorting Party [*Military term*] (RU)
PSGII........... PSG Industrial Institute [*Indian*]
PSGTECH ... PSG College of Technology [*Indian*]
PSGU .... Prace Statniho Ustavu Geologickeho [*Transactions of the State Geological Institute*] (CZ)
PSh .... Hose Mask (RU)
PSH .... Partido Socialista de Honduras [*Socialist Party of Honduras*] (LA)
Psh .... Pferdestaerkestunde [*Horsepower-Hour*] [*German*]
PSh .... Plug Switch (RU)
PSh .... Regimental School (RU)
psh .... Rifle (BU)
PSh .... Wire-Stitching Machine (RU)
P S'ham ...... Port Swettenham (ML)
PShch .... Intermediate Distributing Frame [*Telephony*] (RU)
PShOK .... Party Schools of Okrug Committees (BU)
PShP .... Ball-Bearing Suspension (RU)
PShS .... Navigation Service Regulations (RU)
PSI.............. Collecting Point for Equipment (RU)
PSI.............. Partai Sosialis Indonesia [*Indonesian Socialist Party*] (IN)
PSI.............. Partido Socialista Interior [*Interior Socialist Party*] [*Spanish*] (WER)
PSI.............. Partido Socialista de Izquierda [*Workers Leftist Socialist Party*] [*Mexican*] (LA)
PSI.............. Partido Socialista de Izquierda [*Workers Leftist Socialist Party*] [*Peruvian*] (LA)
PSI.............. Partito Socialista Italiano [*Italian Socialist Party*] (PPE)
Psi .... Psikoloji [*Psychology*] (TU)
PSI.............. Public Service International [*See also ISP*] (EA)
PSI.............. Static Test Device [*Artillery*] (RU)
PSIA .... Public Security Investigation Agency (SJT)
PSII............. Partai Serikat Islam Indonesia [*Indonesian Islamic Union Party*] (IN)
psikh .... Psychiatry, Psychiatrist (BU)
PSIKH.......... Psychology (BU)
psikh bol'n ... Psychiatric Hospital [*Topography*] (RU)
psikhol........ Psychological (RU)
PSIOE.......... Pankyprios Syndesmos Idioktiton Okhimaton Enoikiaseos [*Pan-Cyprian Association of Car Rental Owners*] (GC)
PSISC .... Port-Said International Sporting Club [*Egyptian*] (MAR)
PSIT .... Parti Socialiste Independant du Tchad (MAR)
PSIUP.......... Partito Socialista Italiano di Unita Proletaria [*Italian Socialist Party of Proletarian Unity (1945-1947)*] (PPE)
PSIUP.......... Partito Socialista Italiano di Unita Proletaria [*Italian Socialist Party of Proletarian Unity (1964-1972)*] (PPE)
PSIYM .... Panellinios Syllogos Idiotikon Ypallilon Mikhanografiseos [*Panhellenic Association of Private Machine Accounting Employees*] [*Greek*] (GC)
PSJ............. Parti Socialista Jurassien [*Jura Socialist Party*] [*Swiss*] (WER)
Psj .... Pasaj [*Passage, Arcade*] (TU)
PSJ............. Pegawai Siasatan Jenayat [*Criminal Investigation Officer*] (ML)
PSJM........... Popis Svjetionika Jadranskog i Jonskog Mora [*List of Lighthouses of the Adriatic and Ionian Seas*] (YU)
PSJU .... Privremeni Savet Juznoslovenskog Ujedinjenja [*Provisional Council of South Slavic Unification*] [*World War I*] (YU)
PSK .... Coast Guard Vessel (RU)
PSK .... Panellinion Sosialistikon Kinima [*Panhellenic Socialist Movement*] [*PASOK is preferred*] (GC)
PSK .... Panspoudastiki Syndikalistiki Kinisi [*Pan-Student Trade Union Movement*] [*Greek*] (GC)
PSK .... Parti Socialiste Koulamalliste (MAR)
PSK .... Pasokan Simpanan Persekutuan [*Federal Reserve Unit (Police)*] (ML)
PSK .... Pharmaceutical Society of Kenya (MAR)
PSK .... Postal Savings Office (BU)
PSK .... Proodevtiko Syndikalistiko Kinima [*Progressive Trade Union Movement*] [*Greek*] (GC)
PSK .... Przedsiebiorstwo Spedycji Krajowej [*Domestic Dispatching Enterprises*] (POL)
PSKh-.......... Precision Synchronoscope (RU)
PSKh........... Synchro Generator of a Transmitting Station (RU)
PSKhM........ Panellinios Syllogos Khimikon Mikhanikon [*Panhellenic Association of Chemical Engineers*] (GC)
PSKhO .... Food and Agriculture Organization of the United Nations [*FAO*] (RU)
PSKJ .... Pitanja Savremenog Knjizevnog Jezika [*Problems of the Modern Literary Language*] [*Sarajevo*] [*A periodical*] (YU)
PSKN .... Shipboard Regulations (RU)

PSL............ Collecting Point for Slightly Wounded (RU)
PSL............ Panellinios Synomospondia Logiston [*Panhellenic Confederation of Accountants*] (GC)
PSI............ Politechnika Slaska [*Engineering College of Silesia*] [*Polish*]
PSL............ Polska Sztuka Ludowa [*Polish Folk Art*] (POL)
PSL............ Polskie Stronnictwo Ludowe [*Polish Peasant Party (1945-1947)*] (PPE)
PSL............ Polskie Stronnictwo Ludowe [*Polish Peasant Party (1913-1931, 1945-1949)*] (POL)
PSL............ Polskie Stronnictwo Ludowe [*Polish Peasant Party (1903-1913)*] (PPE)
PSLI........... Partito Socialista dei Lavoratori Italiani [*Socialist Party of Italian Workers*] (PPE)
PSL-Lewica... Polskie Stronnictwo Ludowe-Lewica [*Polish Peasant Party-Left (1913-1920)*] (PPE)
PSL-Lewica... Polskie Stronnictwo Ludowe-Lewica [*Polish Peasant Party-Left (1947-1949)*] (PPE)
PSL-NW...... Polskie Stronnictwo Ludowe-Nowe Wyzwolenie [*Polish Peasant Party-New Liberation*] (PPE)
PSL-Piast.... Polskie Stronnictwo Ludowe-Piast [*Polish Peasant Party-Piast*] (PPE)
PSL-Wyzwolenie... Polskie Stronnictwo Ludowe-Wyzwolenie [*Polish Peasant Party-Liberation*] (PPE)
PSM............ Mauritian Socialist Party (PD)
PSM............ Panglima Setia Mahkota [*Second Grade of Darjah Yang Mulia Setia Mahkota Malaysia*] (ML)
PSM............ Panstwowa Szkola Morska [*State Maritime School*] (POL)
PSM............ Parti Socialiste Malgache [*Malagasy Socialist Party*] (AF)
PSM............ Parti Socialiste Monegasque [*Monaco Socialist Party*] (PPW)
PSM............ Pflanzenschutz- und Schaedlingsbekaempfungsmittel [*Plant Protection Products and Pesticides*] (EG)
PSM............ Politicke Skoleni Madaru [*Political Education of Hungarian Nationals*] (CZ)
PSM............ Politicke Skoleni Muzstva [*Political Training of Enlisted Personnel*] (CZ)
PSM............ Por Su Mandato [*By His Orders*] [*Spanish*]
PSM............ Poznanska Spoldzielnia Mieszkaniowa [*Poznan Housing Cooperative*] (POL)
PSM............ Simple Means of Mechanization (RU)
PSMS.......... Construction Materials and Construction Industry (BU)
PSMS.......... Poradni Sbor pro Mechanisaci Stavebnictvi [*Advisory Board for the Mechanization of the Construction Industry*] (CZ)
PSMSL........ Permanent Service for Mean Sea Level (EA)
PSMU.......... Pevecke Sdruzeni Moravskych Ucitelu [*Moravian Teachers' Choral Society*] (CZ)
PSMZH........ Progressivnyi Soiuz Marokkanskikh Zhenshchin (MAR)
PSN............ Base-End Station (BU)
PSN............ Inflatable Life Raft (RU)
PSN............ Nicaraguan Socialist Party (PD)
PSN............ Parti de la Solidarite Nationale [*Party of National Solidarity*] [*Luxembourg*] (PPE)
PSN............ Partido Socialista Nicaraguense [*Nicaraguan Socialist Party*] (PPW)
PSNL.......... Poradny a Studovny Marxismu-Leninismu [*Advisory and Study Centers of Marxism and Leninism*] (CZ)
PSNS.......... Poslovnik Savezne Narodne Skupstine [*Rules of Procedure of the Federal People's Assembly*] (YU)
PSO............ Antisatellite Defense (RU)
PSO............ Decontamination Station (RU)
PSO............ Fire Watch Service (RU)
PSO............ Pankyprios Synergatiki Omospondia [*Pan-Cyprian Cooperative Federation*] (GC)
PSO............ Polymerizable Oligomer (RU)
PSO............ Port and Shipping Organization [*Iranian*] (ME)
PSO............ Portable Firing-Ground Equipment (RU)
PSO............ Poverenictvo Skolstva a Osvety [*Office of the Commissioner of Education and Culture*] (CZ)
PSO............ Pratik Sanat Okulu [*Practical Trade School*] (TU)
PSO............ Progressieve Studenten Organisatie [*Progressive Student Organization*] [*Dutch*] (WEN)
PSO............ Proletarian Sports Society (RU)
PSO............ Successive Concentration of Fire (BU)
PSO............ Successive Fire Concentration (RU)
PSOA.......... Platre Sies de l'Ouest Africain (MAR)
PSOE.......... Partido Socialista Obrero Espanol [*Spanish Socialist Workers' Party*] (PPE)
PSOJ.......... Private Sector Organization of Jamaica (LA1)
PSOKhS...... Panellinios Synomospondia Orthodoxon Khristianikon Syndikaton [*Panhellenic Confederation of Orthodox Christian Trade Unions*] (GC)
Pson........... Prison [*Prison*] [*Military map abbreviation*] [*World War I*] [*French*] (MTD)
PSOW.......... Punkt Skupu Owocow i Warzyw [*Fruit and Vegetable Purchase Center*] (POL)
PSP............ Economic Marketing Enterprise (BU)
PSP............ Field Hospital Train (RU)
PSP............ Instrument Landing System Indicator (RU)
PSP............ Intermediate Patching Bay [*Telephony*] (RU)
PSP............ Intermediate Rendezvous Point [*Aviation*] (RU)
PSP............ Pacifist Socialist Party [*Netherlands*] (RU)
PSP............ Pacifistisch Socialistische Partij [*Pacifist Socialist Party*] [*Dutch*] (WEN)
PSP............ Parti Socialiste Progressiste [*Socialist Progressive Party*] [*Mauritian*] (AF)
PSP............ Partido Social Progressista [*Social Progressive Party*] [*Brazilian*] (LA)
PSP............ Partido Socialista del Peru [*Peruvian Socialist Party*] (LA)
PSP............ Partido Socialista Popular [*Popular Socialist Party*] [*Argentine*] (LA)
PSP............ Partido Socialista Popular [*Popular Socialist Party*] [*Chilean*] (LA)
PSP............ Partido Socialista Popular [*Popular Socialist Party*] [*Pre-1965*] [*Cuban*] (LA)
PSP............ Partido Socialista Popular [*Popular Socialist Party*] [*Dominican Republic*] (LA)
PSP............ Partido Socialista Popular [*Popular Socialist Party*] [*Peruvian*] (PPW)
PSP............ Partido Socialista Popular [*Popular Socialist Party*] [*Spanish*] (PPE)
PSP............ Partido Socialista Portuguesa [*Portuguese Socialist Party*] (PPW)
PSP............ Partido Socialista Puertorriqueno [*Puerto Rican Socialist Party*] (LA)
PSP............ Pasokan Simpanan Persekutuan [*Federal Reserve Unit (Police)*] (ML)
PSp............ Periodichesko Spisanie na Bulgarskoto Knizhovno Druzhestvo [*Periodical of the Bulgarian Learned Society*] (BU)
PSP............ Ploigikos Stathmos Peiraios [*Piraeus Shipping Pilots Station*] (GC)
PSP............ Policia de Seguranca Publica [*Public Security Police*] [*Portuguese*] (WER)
PSP............ Popular Socialist Party [*Cuban*] (PPW)
PSP............ Portuguese Socialist Party (RU)
PSP............ Postupne Soustredeni Palby [*Rolling Fire Barrage*] (CZ)
PSP............ Pracownia Sztuk Plastycznych [*Plastic Arts Studio*] (POL)
PSP............ Praja Socialist Party [*Indian*] (PPW)
PSP............ Pravnicka Skola Pracujicich [*Workers' Law School*] (CZ)
PSP............ Prazske Pevecke Sdruzeni [*Prague Choral Society*] (CZ)
PSP............ Predsednictvo Sboru Poverenikov [*Presidium of the Board of Commissioners*] (CZ)
PSP............ Progressive Socialist Party [*Lebanese*] (ME)
PSP............ Proodevtiki Syndikalistiki Parataxis [*Progressive Labor Faction*] [*Greek*] (GC)
PSP............ Puerto Rican Socialist Party (PD)
PSP............ Regular Hospital Train (RU)
PSP............ Rules of Formation Cruising (RU)
ps pd og...... Successive Concentration of Fire (BU)
PSPF.......... Pokrajinski Sekretarijat za Poslove Finansija [*Provincial Secretariat of Finance*] [*Vojvodina*] (YU)
PSPG.......... Partido Socialista do Povo Galego [*Socialist Party of the Galician People*] [*Spanish*] (WER)
PSPP.......... Pegawai Senjata Pasokan Polis [*Police Force Armament Officer*] (ML)
PSPPD........ Partido Socialista Portugues de Ponta Delgada [*Portuguese Socialist Party of Ponta Delgada*] (WER)
PSPS.......... Panellinios Syndesmos Politikon Syndaxioukhon [*Panhellenic League of Civil Pensioners*] (GC)
PSPU.......... Pokrajinski Sekretarijat za Pravosudnu Upravu [*Provincial Secretariat of Justice*] [*Vojvodina*] (YU)
PSPV.......... Partit Socialista del Pais Valencia [*Socialist Party of the Valencian Country*] [*Spanish*] (WER)
PSPV.......... Regimental Collecting Point for Prisoners of War (RU)
PSR............ Parti Socialiste Republicain [*Socio-Republican Party*] [*Cambodian*] (CL)
PSR............ Parti Socialiste Reunionnais [*Reunionese Socialist Party*] (AF)
PSR............ Partido Socialista Revolucionario [*Revolutionary Socialist Party*] [*Mexican*] (PPW)
PSR............ Partido Socialista Revolucionario [*Revolutionary Socialist Party*] [*Peruvian*] (PPW)
PSR............ Partido Socialista Revolucionario [*Revolutionary Socialist Party*] [*Portuguese*] (PPE)
PSR............ Party Socialiste Revolutionnaire [*Socialist Revolutionary Party*] [*Lebanese*] (PPW)
PSR............ Point Operating Relay [*Railroads*] (RU)
psr............. Road Construction Company (BU)
PSR............ Socialist Revolutionary Party (RU)
PSRD.......... Woodworkers' Trade Union (RU)
PSRE.......... Partido Socialista Revolucionario Ecuatoriano [*Socialist Revolutionary Party of Ecuador*] (PPW)
PSRL.......... Complete Collection of the Russian Chronicles (RU)
PSRM.......... Panstwowa Szkola Rybolowstwa Morskiego [*State School of Deep-Sea Fishing*] [*Polish*]
PSRM.......... Parti Sosialis Rakyat Malaya [*People's Socialist Party of Malaya*] (ML)
PSRM.......... Parti Sosialis Rakyat Malaysia [*Malaysian People's Socialist Party*] (PPW)
PSR-ML....... Partido Socialista Revolucionario - Marxista-Leninista [*Socialist Revolutionary Party - Marxist-Leninist*] [*Peruvian*] (LA)
PSRS.......... Parti Socialiste Revolutionnaire Somalien [*Somali Revolutionary Socialist Party*] [*Use SRSP*] (AF)

PSRS .... Partito Socialista Rivoluzionario Somalo [*Somali Revolutionary Socialist Party*] [*Use SRSP*] (AF)
PSRSSKhP ... Agricultural and Food Industry Workers Trade Union (BU)
PSS .... Mountain Rescue Service (BU)
PSS .... Parti Socialiste Suisse [*Social Democratic Party of Switzerland*] (PPE)
PSS .... Parti de la Solidarite Senegalaise (MAR)
PSS .... Partito Socialista Sammarinese [*Socialist Party of San Marino*] (PPE)
PSS .... Poletno-Sletna Staza [*Take-off and Landing Runway*] [*Military*] (YU)
PSS .... Postscripta [*Postscripts*] [*Latin*] (GPO)
PSS .... Poverenictvo pre Socialnu Starostlivost [*Office of the Commissioner of Social Welfare*] (CZ)
PSS .... Powszechna Spoldzielnia Spozywcow [*Universal Consumers' Cooperative*] [*Polish*]
PSS .... Prevention of Ship Collision at Sea (RU)
PSS .... Privredni Savet Srbije [*Economic Council of Serbia*] (YU)
PSS .... Station Operator's Link (RU)
PSSA .... Pharmaceutical Society of South Africa (MAR)
PSSA .... Photogrammetric [*or Photographic*] Society of South Africa (MAR)
PSSA .... Private Secondary Schools Authority [*Mauritian*] (AF)
Psse .... Princesse [*Princess*] [*French*] (MTD)
PSSh .... Staff Field Service [*Regulations*] (RU)
PSSIIS .... Partito Socialista: Sezione Italiana del Internazionale Socialista [*Socialist Party: Italian Section of International Socialism*] (PPE)
PSSM .... Panstwowa Srednia Szkola Muzyczna [*State Secondary Music School*] (POL)
PSSNB .... Pohranicni Straz Sboru Narodni Bezpecnosti [*National Security Corps Border Guard Troops*] (CZ)
PST .... Ambulance Loading Post, Ambulance Relay Post (RU)
P/St .... Border Station (RU)
PST .... Field Collecting Point (RU)
PST .... Pankyprios Syndesmos Tourkoplikton [*Pan-Cyprian Association of Victims of Turks*] (GC)
PST .... Panstwowa Szkola Techniczna [*State Technical School*] [*Polish*]
PST .... Parti Suisse du Travail [*Swiss Labor Party*] [*Communist*] (WER)
PST .... Partido Social Trabalhista [*Social Workers Party*] [*Brazilian*] (LA)
PST .... Partido Socialista de los Trabajadores [*Socialist Workers' Party*] [*Argentine*] (LA)
PST .... Partido Socialista de los Trabajadores [*Socialist Workers' Party*] [*Colombian*] (PPW)
PST .... Partido Socialista de los Trabajadores [*Socialist Workers' Party*] [*Mexican*] (PPW)
PST .... Partido Socialista de los Trabajadores [*Socialist Workers' Party*] [*Peruvian*] (LA)
PST .... Partido Socialista de los Trabajadores [*Socialist Workers' Party*] [*Venezuelan*] (LA)
PST .... Peseta [*Monetary unit in Spain and Latin America*]
pst .... Pistil, Pistillate [*Botany*] (RU)
pst .... Pond Sterling [*Pound Sterling*] [*Dutch*] (GPO)
P st .... Post Office Station [*Topography*] (RU)
P/St .... Small Railroad Station, Flag Station, Whistle Stop [*Topography*] (RU)
P/St .... Substation (RU)
PSTA .... Partido Socialista Tito Atahuichi [*Bolivian*] (PPW)
psta .... Puolesta [*Finnish*]
PSTR .... Transportation Workers' Trade Union (RU)
PSTs .... Steam Power Shop (RU)
PSTU .... Private Secondary Teachers Union [*Mauritian*] (AF)
PSTUC .... Pan-Sarawak Trade Union Congress (ML)
PSU .... Control Signal Receiver (RU)
PSU .... Parti Socialiste Unifie [*Unified Socialist Party*] [*French*] (PPW)
PSU .... Partido Socialista Uruguayo [*Uruguayan Socialist Party*] (PD)
PSU .... Partidul Socialist Unitar [*Unitary Socialist Party*] [*Romanian*] (PPE)
PSU .... Partito Socialista [*Socialist Unity Party*] [*Sanmarinese*] (PPE)
PSU .... Partito Socialista Unificato [*Unified Socialist Party*] [*Italian*] (PPE)
PSU .... Partito Socialista Unitario [*Unitary Socialist Party (1949-1951)*] [*Italian*] (PPE)
PSU .... Partito Socialista Unitario [*Unitary Socialist Party (1922-1926)*] [*Italian*] (PPE)
PSU .... Partito Socialista Unitario [*Socialist Unity Party*] [*Sanmarinese*] (PPW)
PSU .... Public Service Union [*Guyanese*] (LA)
PSU .... Steam Power Plant [*Nautical term*] (RU)
PSU- .... Universal Welding Transformer (RU)
PSUA .... Partido Socialista Unificado da Alemanha [*Socialist Unity Party of East Germany*] [*Use SED*] (AF)
PSUC .... Partit Socialista Unificat de Catalunya [*Unified Socialist Party of Catalonia*] [*Spanish*] (PPE)
PSULI .... Partito Socialista Unitario de Lavoratori Italiani [*Unitary Socialist Party of Italian Workers*] (PPE)
PSUM .... Partido Socialista Unificado de Mexico [*Unified Socialist Party of Mexico*] (LA1)
PSUP .... Partido Socialista de Unidad Popular [*Socialist Party of Popular Unity*] [*Colombian*] (LA)
PSUP .... Pokrajinski Sekretarijat za Unutrasnje Poslove (APV) [*Provincial Secretariat of Internal Affairs*] [*Vojvodina*] (YU)
PSUZ .... Regulation on School Scholarships (BU)
PSV .... Parti Socialiste Voltaique [*Voltan Socialist Party*] (AF)
PSV .... Partido Socialista de Venezuela [*Socialist Party of Venezuela*] (LA)
PSV .... Polni Sled Veleni [*Field Command Echelon*] (CZ)
PSV .... Poslovnik Saveznog Veca [*Rules of Procedure of the Federal Council*] (YU)
PSV .... Pridruzena Stavebni Vyroba [*Subsidiary Construction Activity*] (CZ)
PSV .... Progressieve Surinaamse Volkspartij [*Progressive Suriname People's Party*] (PPW)
PSVB .... Pomocna Straz Verejne Bezpecnosti [*Auxiliary Public Security Corps*] (CZ)
PSvHS .... Poverenictvo Stavebnictva, Hlavna Sprava [*Office of the Commissioner of Construction, Main Administration*] (CZ)
PSVK .... High-Frequency Intermediate Patching Bay [*Telephony*] (RU)
PSVPO .... Preduzece za Spasavanje i Vadenje Potopljenih Objekata [*Establishment for Rescue and Salvage of Submerged Objects*] [*Shipping*] (YU)
PSVTI .... Regimental Materiel Depot (RU)
PSVU .... Poverenictvo Skolstva, Vied, a Umeni [*Office of the Commissioner of Education, Sciences, and Arts*] (CZ)
psyk .... Psykologia [*Psychology*] [*Finnish*]
PSZ .... Pedagogiai Szeminarium [*Pedagogical Seminar*] (HU)
PSZ .... Pedagogus Szakszervezet [*Teachers Trade Union*] (HU)
PSz .... Politechnika Szczecinska [*Engineering College of Szczecin*] [*Polish*]
PSZ .... Polskie Sily Zbrojne [*Polish Armed Forces*] (POL)
psz .... Probaszolgalatos [*On Probation*] (HU)
PSz .... Przemysl Szklarski [*Glass Industry*] (POL)
PSZdrRab ... Public Health Workers Trade Union (BU)
PSzH .... Pancelozott Szalito Harcjarmu [*Armored Transport Vehicle*] [*Military*] (HU)
PSZR .... Health Workers Trade Union (BU)
PSZT .... Pecsi Szenbanyaszati Troszt [*Coal Mining Trust of Pecs*] (HU)
PSzW .... Powiatowy Sztab Wojskowy [*County Military Headquarters*] (POL)
PT .... Amphibious Personnel Carrier (RU)
PT .... Amphibious Tank (RU)
PT .... Antitank (BU)
PT .... Antitank (RU)
PT .... Brake Test [*Railroads*] (RU)
PT- .... Cable Trailer [*Oceanography*] (RU)
P & T .... Direccion General de Correos y Telecommunicacion [*General Directorate of Posts and Telecommunications*] [*Spanish*] (WER)
PT .... Fire Alarm (RU)
pt .... Friday (RU)
PT- .... Heavy-Duty Trailer, Giant Trailer (RU)
PT .... Industrial Television (RU)
PT .... Message Code Table (RU)
PT .... Parti Travailliste [*Labor Party*] [*Mauritian*] (AF)
PT .... Partido Trabajador [*Workers Party*] [*Argentine*] (LA)
PT .... Partido de los Trabajadores [*Workers Party*] [*Dominican Republic*] (LA1)
PT .... Partido del Trabajo [*Labor Party*] [*Spanish*] (WER)
PT .... Partido dos Trabalhadores [*Workers Party*] [*Brazilian*] (LA1)
PT .... Pegawai Turus [*Staff Officer*] (ML)
PT .... Pelnym Tytulem [*Full-Titled*] [*Polish*]
PT .... Perseroan Terbatas [*Limited Company*] (IN)
Pt .... Personenzugtenderlokomotive [*Local Passenger Train Tender Locomotive*] (EG)
Pt .... Petit [*Small*] [*Military map abbreviation*] [*World War I*] [*French*] (MTD)
PT .... Pleno Titulo [*Polish*]
pt .... Pod Tytulem [*Entitled, Under the Title*] (POL)
PT .... Pogon na Plinsku Turbinu [*Gas Turbine Power*] (YU)
PT .... Policia de Transito [*Traffic Police*] [*Mozambican*] (AF)
PT .... Polis Tentera [*Military Police*] (ML)
PT .... Polskie Towarzystwo [*Polish Society*] (POL)
Pt .... Pont [*Bridge*] [*Military map abbreviation*] [*World War I*] [*French*] (MTD)
Pt .... Port [*Harbor*] [*Military map abbreviation*] [*World War I*] [*French*] (MTD)
PT .... Portugal [*Two-letter standard code*] (CNC)
PT .... Poste e Telecomunicazioni [*Post and Telecommunications*] [*Italian*] (WER)
P et T .... Postes et Telecommunications [*Postal and Telecommunications Administration*] [*French*] (WER)
PT .... Potential Trigger (RU)
PT .... Poverenictvo pre Techniku [*Office of the Commissioner of Technology*] (CZ)
PT .... Precise Wire-Wound (Resistor) (RU)
PT .... Predilnica i Tkalnica [*Spinning and Weaving Mills*] [*Maribor*] (YU)
Pt .... President [*President*] (AF)
PT .... Protitankovy [*Antitank*] (CZ)

PT............ Protivtenkovski [*Antitank*] (YU)
PT............ Publicidad Tecnica [*Bogota*] (COL)
Pt............ Punt [*Point*] [*Dutch*] (NAU)
PT............ Putnicka Tarifa [*Passenger Rate*] (YU)
Pt............ Pynt [*or Pynten*] [*Point*] [*Norwegian*] (NAU)
Pt............ Pynt [*Point*] [*Danish*] (NAU)
PT............ Semiconductor Triode (RU)
PT............ Steam Turbine (RU)
p/t............ Steamship (RU)
PT............ Textolite for Machine Parts (RU)
PT............ Tokarev Pistol (RU)
PT............ Training Parachute (RU)
pT............ With Full Title [*Correspondence*] [*German*]
PTA............ Antitank Artillery (RU)
PTA............ Parti du Travail Albanais [*Albanian Workers' Party (AWP)*] [*French*] (WER)
PTA............ Perifereiakon Tameion Agrofylakis [*Rural Police Regional Fund*] [*Greek*] (GC)
pta............ Peseta [*A Spanish coin*]
PTA............ Petrograd News Agency [*1915-1918*] (RU)
PTA............ Plataformas de Trabajadores Anti-Capitalistas [*Platforms of Anti-Capitalist Workers*] [*Spanish*] (WER)
PTA............ Platinum-Titanium Anode (RU)
P-ta............ Poczta [*Post Office*] [*Polish*]
PTA............ Polish Telegraph Agency (BU)
PTA............ Polskie Towarzystwo Akustyczne [*Polish Acoustical Society*] [*Polish*]
PTA............ Polskie Towarzystwo Archeologiczne [*Polish Archeological Society*] (POL)
Pta............ Ponta [*Point*] [*Portuguese*] (NAU)
pta............ Porta [*Gate*] [*Italian*] (CED)
PTA............ Poste Telephonique Artillerie [*Military*] [*French*] (MTD)
PTA............ Pracovni Tabory [*Labor Camps*] (CZ)
PTA............ Preferential Trade Agreements (MAR)
PTA............ Preferential Trade Area (MAR)
PTA............ Primary Tungsten Association (EA)
PTA............ Protivtenkovska Artiljerija [*Antitank Artillery*] (YU)
Pta............ Punta [*Point*] [*Italian*] (NAU)
Pta............ Punta [*Point*] [*Spanish*] (NAU)
PTAB............ Aerial Antitank Bomb (RU)
PTAB............ Protivtenkovske Aviobombe [*Antitank Air Bombs*] (YU)
PTAD............ Protivtenkovski Artiljeriski Divizion [*Antitank Artillery Division*] [*Military*] (YU)
PTAL............ Professeur Technique d'Atelier de Lycee (MAR)
PTAr............ Polskie Towarzystwo Archeologiczne [*Polish Archeological Society*] [*Polish*]
PTARZ............ Mobile Tank-Component Repair Plant (RU)
ptas............ Pesetas [*Spanish*]
PTB............ Antitank Battery (RU)
PTB............ Industrial Safety Regulations (BU)
PTB............ Parti des Travailleurs Burundi (MAR)
PTB............ Partido Trabalhista Brasileiro [*Brazilian Labor Party*] (PPW)
PTB............ Polskie Towarzystwo Biochemiczne [*Polish Biochemical Society*] (POL)
PTB............ Polskie Towarzystwo Botaniczne [*Polish Botanical Society*] (POL)
PTB............ Pradelny a Tkalcovny Bavlny [*Cotton Spinning and Weaving Mills*] (CZ)
PTB............ Producto Territorial Bruto [*Gross National Product*] [*Use GNP*] (LA)
PTB............ Safety Engineering Regulations (RU)
PTBat............ Protitankova Baterie [*Antitank Battery*] (CZ)
PTBW............ Przedsiebiorstwo Transportu Budownictwa Weglowego [*Mine Equipment Transportation Enterprise*] (POL)
PTC............ Panstwowe Teatry Czestochowskie [*Czestochowa State Theatres*] (POL)
PTC............ Partido de Trabajadores Colombianos [*Colombian Labor Party*] (LA)
PTC............ Penang Turf Club (ML)
PTC............ Perak Turf Club (ML)
PTC............ Pioneer Tobacco Company (MAR)
PTC............ Polskie Towarzystwo Cybernetyczne [*Polish Cybernetic Society*] [*Polish*]
PTCA............ Plains Tribal Council of Assam [*Indian*] (PPW)
PTCh............ Polskie Towarzystwo Chemiczne [*Polish Chemical Society*] (POL)
ptd............ Antitank Battalion (BU)
PTD............ Antitank Battalion (RU)
PTD............ Panstwowe Teatry Dramatyczne [*State Drama Theatres*] (POL)
PTD............ Polskie Towarzystwo Dermatologiczne [*Polish Dermatological Society*] (POL)
PTD............ Turboram Jet Engine (RU)
PTDD............ Support by Long-Range Tanks (RU)
PTDP............ Partido Trabalhista Democratico Portugues [*Portuguese Democratic Workers Party*] (WER)
PTDP............ Perifereia Teos Dioikiseos Protevousis [*Former Athens Administrative Area*] (GC)
PTDWP............ Panstwowy Teatr Domu Wojska Polskiego [*State Theatre of the House of the Polish Army*] (POL)
PTE............ Experimental Instruments and Techniques (RU)
PTE............ Pangosmios Takhydromiki Enosis [*Universal Postal Union*] (GC)
pte............ Parte [*Part*] [*Spanish*]
PTE............ Partido de Trabajadores Espanoles [*Spanish Workers' Party*] (PPE)
PTE............ Partido del Trabajo de Espana [*Spanish Labor Party*] (WER)
PTE............ Partiia Togolezskovo Edinstva (MAR)
PTE............ Permis Temporaires d'Exploitation (MAR)
Pte............ Petite [*Small*] [*Military map abbreviation*] [*World War I*] [*French*] (MTD)
Pte............ Pointe [*Point*] [*French*] (NAU)
PTE............ Politicno Teritorijalna Enota [*Political and Territorial Unit*] (YU)
PTE............ Polskie Towarzystwo Ekonomiczne [*Polish Economic Society*] (POL)
PTE............ Polskie Towarzystwo Elektryczne [*Polish Electrical Society*] (POL)
Pte............ Ponte [*Bridge*] [*Italian*] (NAU)
Pte............ Porte [*Gate*] [*Military map abbreviation*] [*World War I*] [*French*] (MTD)
Pte............ Poste [*Post*] [*Military map abbreviation*] [*World War I*] [*French*] (MTD)
PTE............ Technical Operation Rules (RU)
PTE............ Technical Operations Regulations (BU)
Pte de D...... Poste de Douane [*Military map abbreviation*] [*World War I*] [*French*] (MTD)
PTEk............ Polskie Towarzystwo Ekonomiczne [*Polish Economic Society*] (POL)
PTEMPS...... Rules for Technical Operation of the Ministry of Railroads, USSR (RU)
Ptesi............ Pazartesi [*Sunday*] (TU)
PTF............ Polskie Towarzystwo Farmaceutyczne [*Polish Pharmaceutical Society*] (POL)
PTF............ Polskie Towarzystwo Filologiczne [*Polish Philological Society*] (POL)
PTF............ Polskie Towarzystwo Fizyczne [*Polish Physics Society*] (POL)
PTF............ Polskie Towarzystwo Fotograficzne [*Polish Photographic Society*] (POL)
PTF............ Poultry-Raising Farm (RU)
PTF............ Spinning and Weaving Factory (RU)
PTFE............ Polytetrafluoroethylene (RU)
PTFilozof.... Polskie Towarzystwo Filozoficzne [*Polish Philosophical Society*] (POL)
PTFiz............ Polskie Towarzystwo Fizyczne [*Polish Physics Society*] (POL)
PTG............ Amphibious Tracked Personnel Carrier (RU)
PTG............ Pneumotachography (RU)
PTG............ Polskie Towarzystwo Geograficzne [*Polish Geographical Society*] (POL)
PTG............ Polskie Towarzystwo Geologiczne [*Polish Geological Society*] (POL)
PTG............ Polskie Towarzystwo Gleboznawcze [*Polish Soil Science Society*] (POL)
PTGU............ Steam-Turbine Generator Unit (RU)
PTH............ Polskie Towarzystwo Historyczne [*Polish Historical Society*] (POL)
pth............ Posta- es Tavirohivatal [*Post and Telegraph Office*] (HU)
PTHZ............ Polskie Towarzystwo Handlu Zagranicznego [*Polish Society for Foreign Trade*] [*Polish*]
PTI............ Pedagogiai Tudomanyos Intezet [*Scientific Institute of Pedagogy*] (HU)
PTI............ Planning and Technological Institute (RU)
PTI............ Polytechnic Institute (RU)
PTI............ Poste Telephonique Infanterie [*Military*] [*French*] (MTD)
PTI............ Press Trust of India (MAR)
PTIMASh..... Khar'kov Planning and Design Technological Institute of Machinery Manufacture (RU)
Ptits............ Poultry-Raising Sovkhoz [*Topography*] (RU)
PTJ............ Policia Tecnica Judicial [*Judicial Technical Police*] [*Venezuelan*] (LA)
PTJ............ Polskie Towarzystwo Jezykoznawcze [*Polish Philological Society*] [*Polish*]
PTK............ Channel Selector (RU)
PTK............ Field Telephone Cable (RU)
PTK............ Industrial and Technical Courses (RU)
PTK............ Panstwowe Technikum Korespondencyjne [*State Correspondence Technical School*] (POL)
PTK............ Polgari Torvenykonyv [*Civil Code*] (HU)
PTK............ Polskie Towarzystwo Krajoznawcze [*Polish Local Studies Society*] (POL)
ptk............ Poytakirja [*Finnish*]
PTK............ Protitankove Kanony [*Antitank Guns*] (CZ)
PTK............ Provozne-Technicke Knihovny [*Technical and Management Reference Libraries*] (CZ)
PTK............ Steam Turbocompressor (RU)
ptk............ Tank Commander's Panoramic Telescope (RU)
PTK............ Vocational and Technical Courses (RU)
PTKh............ Constant Table of Characteristics (RU)
PTKMPS..... Regulations on Technical Control of Motor Vehicles (BU)
Ptkp............ Postatakarekpenztar [*Postal Savings Bank*] (HU)
PTKS............ Polskie Towarzystwo Kulturalno-Spoleczne [*Polish Cultural and Social Society*] (POL)

PTL............ Polskie Towarzystwo Lekarskie [*Polish Medical Society*] [*Polish*]
PTL............ Polskie Towarzystwo Ludoznawcze [*Polish Folklore Society*] (POL)
PTL............ Propeller-Turbinenluftstrahlmotor [*Turboprop Aircraft Engine*] (EG)
PTL............ Protivtenkovska Linija [*Antitank Line*] (YU)
PTM............ Antitank Mine (RU)
PTM............ Cloth Dust Mask (RU)
PTM............ Panstwowe Technikum Mechaniczne [*State Mechanical Technical School*] (POL)
PTM............ Panstwowe Technikum Morskie [*State Maritime Technical School*] (POL)
PTM............ Parti Travailliste Mauricien (MAR)
PTM............ Persekutuan Tanah Melayu [*Federation of Malaya*] (ML)
PTM............ Pocetna Tacka Marsrute [*Starting Point of a March*] [*Army*] (YU)
PTM............ Polis Tentera Malaysia [*Malaysian Military Police*] (ML)
PTM............ Polskie Towarzystwo Matematyczne [*Polish Mathematical Society*] (POL)
PTM............ Predilnica i Tkalnica [*Spinning and Weaving Mills*] [*Maribor*] (YU)
PTM............ Protivtenkovske Mine [*Antitank Mines*] (YU)
PTMA.......... Polskie Towarzystwo Milosnikow Astronomii [*Polish Society of Friends of Astronomy*] (POL)
PTMA.......... Poznanskie Towarzystwo Milosnikow Astronomii [*Poznan Society of Friends of Astronomy*] (POL)
PTMB.......... Przemysl Terenowy Materialow Budowlanych [*Local Industry of Building Materials*] (POL)
PTMI........... Protitankova Mina [*Antitank Mine*] (CZ)
PT mini........ Antitank Mines (BU)
PTMOW....... Polskie Towarzystwo Matematyczne, Oddzial Wroclawski [*Wroclaw (Breslau) Branch of the Polish Mathematical Society*] (POL)
PTMP.......... Antitank Mine Field (BU)
PTMP.......... Antitank Minefield (RU)
PTMP.......... Protitankove Minove Pole [*Antitank Mine Field*] (CZ)
PTN............ Labor Party of the Netherlands (RU)
PTN............ Partido Trabalhista Nacional [*National Labor Party*] [*Brazilian*] (LA)
PTN............ Polskie Towarzystwo Neurologiczne [*Polish Neurological Society*] (POL)
PTN............ Regulations on Labor Norms (BU)
PTN............ Technical Observation Point (BU)
PTN............ Technical Observation Post (RU)
PTN............ Turbine-Driven Feed Pump (RU)
PTN............ Voice-Frequency Dialing Set [*Telephony*] (RU)
PTNII.......... Planning, Technological, and Scientific Research Institute (RU)
PTNV.......... Voice-Frequency Dialing and Ringing Set (RU)
PTO............ Antitank Cannon, Antitank Gun (RU)
PTO............ Antitank Defense (BU)
PTO............ Antitank Defense (RU)
PTO............ Antitorpedo Defense (RU)
PTO............ Hoisting and Conveying Equipment (RU)
PTO............ Industrial Transportation Department (RU)
PTO............ Part- es Tomegszervezeti Osztaly [*Party and Mass Organization Department*] (HU)
Pt O........... Partszervezesi Osztaly [*Department of Party Organization*] (HU)
pto............. Patio [*Court*] [*Portuguese*] (CED)
PTO............ Polskie Towarzystwo Orientalistyczne [*Polish Society for Oriental Studies*] (POL)
Pto............. Porto [*Port*] [*Italian*] (NAU)
Pto............. Porto [*Port*] [*Portuguese*] (NAU)
PTO............ Post and Telegraph Office (RU)
PTO............ Principal Training Officer (MAR)
PTO............ Production and Technical Department (RU)
PTO............ Protitankova Obrana [*Antitank Defense*] (CZ)
PTO............ Protitankovy Oddil [*Antitank Battalion*] (CZ)
PTO............ Protivtenkovska Odbrana [*Antitank Defense*] (YU)
PTO............ Protivtorpedna Odbrana [*Antitorpedo Defense*] (YU)
Pto............. Puerto [*Port*] [*Spanish*] (NAU)
PTO............ Technical Inspection Point (RU)
PTO............ Technical Production Department (BU)
PTO............ Technical Service Point (RU)
PTOM.......... Pays et Territoires d'Outre-Mer (MAR)
Pton............ Ponton [*Pontoon*] [*Military map abbreviation*] [*World War I*] [*French*] (MTD)
PTOP.......... Antitank Strongpoint (RU)
PTOR.......... Antitank Cannon (BU)
PTOR.......... Antitank Cannon, Antitank Gun (RU)
PTOR.......... Antitank Defense Area (RU)
PTOZ.......... Antitank Barrage Fire, Antitank Barrage (RU)
PTP............ Antitank Cannon, Antitank Gun (RU)
PTP............ Antitank Obstacle, Antitank Barrier (RU)
PTP............ Direct Heat Flow (RU)
PTP............ Panstwowy Teatr Polski [*Polish State Theater*] (POL)
PTP............ Parti Togolais du Progres [*Togolese Progress Party*] (AF)
PTP............ Plan de Trabajos Publicos [*Public Works Plan*] [*Argentine*] (LA)
PTP............ Polskie Towarzystwo Pediatryczne [*Polish Pediatric Society*] [*Polish*]
PTP............ Polskie Towarzystwo Prehistoryczne [*Polish Prehistorical Society*] (POL)
PTP............ Polskie Towarzystwo Przyrodnikow [*Polish Naturalists' Society*] (POL)
PTP............ Pomocny Technicky Prapor [*Technical Support Battalion*] (CZ)
PTP............ Privremeni Tehnicki Propisi [*Provisional Technical Regulations*] (YU)
PTP............ Protitankova Puska [*Antitank Rifle*] (CZ)
PTP............ Protitankovy Pluk [*Antitank Regiment*] (CZ)
PTP............ Spot-Landing Parachute (RU)
PTP............ Step-Down Transformer Substation (RU)
PTP............ Technical Aid Point (RU)
PTP............ Television Program Selector (RU)
PtPb........... Putnicki Parabrod [*Passenger Steamer*] (YU)
PTPN.......... Poznanskie Towarzystwo Przyjaciol Nauk [*Poznan Society of Friends of Science*] (POL)
PTPreh........ Polskie Towarzystwo Prehistoryczne [*Polish Prehistorical Society*] (POL)
PTR............ Antitank Defense Area (RU)
PTR............ Antitank Ditch (RU)
PTR............ Antitank Fortified Area (BU)
PTR............ Antitank Rifle (RU)
PTR............ Parti Tindakan Ra'yat [*People's Action Party*] [*Singapore*] (ML)
PTR............ Parti Travailliste [*Labor Party*] [*Mauritian*] [*Use PT*] (AF)
ptr............. Pietro [*Floor, Story*] (POL)
PTR............ Plan Technickeho Rozvoje [*Technical Development Plan*] (CZ)
PTR............ Pneumatic Friction Handsaw (RU)
PTR............ Polskie Towarzystwo Radiologiczne [*Polish Radiological Society*] [*Polish*]
PTR............ Polskie Towarzystwo Reumatologiczne [*Polish Rheumatological Society*] [*Polish*]
PTR............ Protivtenkovska Rezerva [*Antitank Reserve*] (YU)
PTR............ Pukovske Tenkovske Rezerve [*Regimental Tank Reserves*] (YU)
PTRB.......... Field Tractor Repair Base (RU)
ptrb............ Mobile Tank Maintenance Battalion (BU)
PTRB.......... Mobile Tank Maintenance Depot (BU)
PTRB.......... Mobile Tank Repair Base (RU)
PTRD.......... Degtyarev Antitank Rifle (RU)
PTrez.......... Antitank Reserve (BU)
PTRez......... Antitank Reserve (RU)
PTRK.......... Technical Radio Control Post (RU)
Ptrl............ Patrouillenfuehrer [*German*]
PTRM.......... Panstwowe Technikum Rybolowstwa Morskiego [*State Technical School for Deep-Water Fishing*] (POL)
PTRS.......... Philosophical Transactions of the Royal Society of London [*A publication*] (MAR)
PTRS.......... Simonov Antitank Rifle (RU)
PTRU.......... Antitank Line (RU)
PTRZ.......... Mobile Tank Maintenance Plant (BU)
PTRZ.......... Mobile Tank Repair Plant (RU)
PTRZ.......... Planowo-Terminowe Remonty Zapobiegawcze [*Planned and Undeferrable Preventive Repairs*] (POL)
PTS............ Composite Video Signal (RU)
PTS............ Conveyor System (RU)
PTS............ Fish Receiving and Transport Vessel (RU)
PTS............ Heater Thermistor (RU)
PTS............ Mobile Television Unit (RU)
pts............. Pesetas [*Spanish*]
PTS............ Podohospodarska-Technicka Skola [*Agricultural School*] (CZ)
PTS............ Polskie Towarzystwo Statystyczne [*Polish Statistical Society*] (POL)
Pts............. Puits [*Well*] [*Military map abbreviation*] [*World War I*] [*French*] (MTD)
PTS............ Pyrotechnic Agents (RU)
PTs-........... Tank Trailer (RU)
PTS............ Telephone Relay Exchange (RU)
PTS............ Thermistor (RU)
PTS............ Tractor Trailer Snowplow (RU)
PTS............ Wire-Wound Resistance Tensometer (RU)
p-tsa.......... Printing Press (BU)
PTSEEU...... Private Tea and Sugar Estates Employees Union [*Mauritian*] (AF)
Ptsi............ Pazartesi [*Sunday*] (TU)
PTS-K......... Thermistor with Indirect Heating (RU)
PTsKO........ Permanent Central Opium Board [*PCOB*] (RU)
pt sl........... Patrol Service (BU)
PTSL.......... Przedsiebiorstwo Transportu Samochodowego Lacznosci [*Automotive Postal Service Enterprise*] (POL)
PTsN.......... Gear-Driven Centrifugal Supercharger (RU)
pts et pts..... Profits et Pertes [*Profit and Loss*] [*French*]
PTsR.......... Gear-Driven Centrifugal Governor, Gear-Driven Centrifugal Regulator (RU)
pts sl.......... Military Police Service (BU)
PTsU.......... Control Circuit Switch, Pilot Circuit Switch (RU)
PTsUK........ Mobile Flight Control Center (RU)
PTsUK........ Transfer to Central Command Control [*Computers*] (RU)
pts vd......... Military Police Platoon (BU)
PTT............ Intermediate Current Transformer (RU)

PTT............. Pasokan Pertahanan Tempatan [*Local Defense Corps*] (ML)
PTT............. Politikai Tanacskozo Testulet [*Political Consultative Commission (of the Warsaw Pact)*] (HU)
PTT............. Polskie Towarzystwo Tatrzanskie [*Polish Tatra Mountains Society*] (POL)
PTT............. Post, Telegraph, and Telephone [*Saudi Arabian*] (ME)
PTT............. Posta, Telefon, Telgraf [*Post, Telephone, and Telegraph Administration*] (TU)
PTT............. Posta, Telegraf, si Telefon [*Posts, Telegraphs, and Telephones*] (RO)
PTT............. Posta, Telegraf, Telefon [*Post, Telegraph, Telephone*] (YU)
Ptt............. Postansko-Telegrafsko-Telefonski [*Postal, Telegraph, and Telephone*] (YU)
PTT............. Postes et Telecommunications [*Posts and Telecommunications*] (AF)
PTT............. Postes, Telegraphes, et Telephones [*Post, Telegraph, and Telephone*] [*General Post Office*] [*French*]
PTT............. Posts, Telegraphs, and Telephones (BU)
PtT............. Ptujski Tednik [*Ptuj Weekly*] [*A periodical*] (YU)
PTT............. Public Telephone and Telegraph
PTT............. Television Picture Tube (RU)
PTT............. Tokarev Pistol (RU)
PTTI............. Postal, Telegraph, and Telephone International [*See also IPTT*] (EA)
PTTK............. Polskie Towarzystwo Turystyczno-Krajoznawcze [*Polish Tourist and Local Studies Society*] (POL)
PTTR............. Posta, Telegraf, Telefon, si Radio [*Posts, Telegraphs, Telephones, and Radio*] (RO)
PTTR............. Posts, Telegraphs, Telephones, and Radio (BU)
PTTS............. Postal, Telegraph, and Telephone Stations (BU)
PTU............. Fire-Fighting Technical School (RU)
PTU............. Industrial Television Unit (RU)
PTU............. Intermediate Repeater (RU)
PTU............. Professional-Technical School [*Russian*]
PTU............. Remote-Control Board (RU)
PTU............. Steam Turbine Unit (RU)
PTU............. Technical Vocational School (BU)
PTU............. Television Receiver, Television Set (RU)
PTU............. Underwater Television Unit (RU)
PTU............. Vocational and Technical School (RU)
PTUMP............. Antitank Controlled Mine Field (BU)
PTUMP............. Antitank Controlled Mine Field (RU)
PTUR............. Antitank Guided Missile (BU)
PTUR............. Antitank Guided Missile (RU)
PTURS............. Antitank Guided Missile (RU)
PTURS............. Antitank Guided Self-Propelled Missile (BU)
PTV............. Parti Travailliste Voltaique [*Voltan Labor Party*] (AF)
PTV............. Programma Tekhnikis Voitheias [*Technical Assistance Program*] (GC)
PTV............. Voice-Frequency Ringing Receiver [*Telephony*] (RU)
PTV............. Workers' Party of Vietnam (RU)
PTVU............. Voice-Frequency Ringing and Control Receiver (RU)
PTWK............. Polskie Towarzystwo Wydawcow Ksiazek [*Polish Publishers' Association*] [*Polish*]
PTWU............. Post and Telecommunications Workers Union [*Guyanese*] (LA)
PTZ............. Polskie Towarzystwo Zootechniczne [*Polish Animal Husbandry Society*] (POL)
PTZ............. Protitankova Zaloha [*Antitank Reserve*] (CZ)
PTZO............. Antitank Barrage Fire (RU)
PU............. Adapter (RU)
PU............. Auxiliary Steering Equipment [*River vessels*] (RU)
PU............. Control Panel, Console (RU)
PU............. Control Post (RU)
PU............. Control Switch (RU)
PU............. Converter Unit [*Computers*] (RU)
PU............. Direct Control (RU)
PU............. Dust Extractor, Dust Allayer, Dust Trap [*Mining*] (RU)
PU............. Field Command (RU)
PU............. Field Service Regulations (RU)
PU............. Launcher [*Rocketry*] (RU)
PU............. Normal School (BU)
PU............. Palackeho Universita [*Palacky University*] [*Olomouc*] (CZ)
pu............. Palyaudvar [*Railroad Station*] (HU)
PU............. Pangkalan Udara [*Air Base*] (IN)
PU............. Parametric Amplifier (RU)
PU............. Patentni Urad [*Patent Office*] (CZ)
PU............. Pechotni Uciliste [*Infantry School*] (CZ)
PU............. Pedagogicky Ustav [*Pedagogical Institute*] (CZ)
PU............. Pijacna Uprava [*Market Administration*] (YU)
PU............. Plynarensky Ustav [*Gas Works*] [*Bechovice*] (CZ)
PU............. Polarograficky Ustav [*Polarographic Institute*] [*Czechoslovak Academy of Sciences*] (CZ)
PU............. Political Administration (BU)
PU............. Political Administration, Political Directorate (RU)
PU............. Polyurethane (RU)
PU............. Polyurethane Foam (RU)
PU-............. Portable Photographic Enlarger (RU)
PU............. Pravnicky Ustav Ministerstva Spravedlnosti [*Law Institute of the Ministry of Justice*] (CZ)
PU............. Preamplifier (RU)
PU............. Prehistoricky Ustav [*Prehistoric Institute*] [*Charles University*] [*Prague*] (CZ)
PU............. Printer [*Computers*] (RU)
PU............. Privredna Udruzenja [*Economic Associations*] (YU)
PU............. Privredne Ustanove [*Economic Institutions*] (YU)
PU............. Profesores Universitarios [*University Professors*] [*Spanish*] (WER)
PU............. Programer, Program Device (RU)
PU............. Proleterski Udarni [*Proletarian Shock Troops*] (YU)
Pu............. Pulau [*or Pulu*] [*Island*] [*Malay*] (NAU)
Pu............. Pulau [*or Pulu*] [*Island*] [*Indonesian*] (NAU)
pu............. Puska [*Rifle*] (HU)
PU............. Receiver (RU)
PU............. Switching Device (RU)
PU............. Testing Device (RU)
PU............. Track Angle (RU)
PU............. United States Miscellaneous Pacific Islands [*Two-letter standard code*] (CNC)
PU-............. Universal Track-Shifting Machine [*Railroads*] (RU)
PUA............. Accelerometer Tester (RU)
PUA............. Parti de l'Unite Africaine (MAR)
PUAO............. Fire Director [*Artillery*] (RU)
Puarm............. Army Political Directorate (RU)
PUAS............. Postal Union of the Americas and Spain [*See also UPAE*] (EA)
PUAZO............. Antiaircraft Fire Control Instrument (BU)
PUAZO............. Antiaircraft Fire Director (RU)
PUB............. Parti de l'Unite Basonge (MAR)
PUB............. Partido Union Boliviana [*Bolivian Unity Party*] (PPW)
PuB............. Penzugyi Bizottsag [*Financial Committee*] (HU)
PUB............. Prazska Uverni Banka [*Prague Credit Bank*] (CZ)
PUB............. Public Utilities Board [*Singapore*] (ML)
p/ub............. Shelter for Small-Arms Ammunition Supply Point [*Topography*] (RU)
publ............. Public (RU)
publ............. Publication (RU)
publ............. Publication, Published (BU)
Publ............. Publikation [*German*]
publ bibl...... Public Library (BU)
PUBLICOM... Agentia de Publicitate pentru Comertul Exterior [*Romanian Publicity Agency for Foreign Trade*] (RO)
PUBLICONTA... Contaduria Publica Ltda. [*Cali*] (COL)
PUBLIDELTA... Delta Publicidad [*Medellin*] (COL)
PUBLI-PERU... Empresa de Publicidad del Peru [*Peruvian Advertising Enterprise*] (LA)
publits............. Journalism (RU)
PUBP............. Powiatowy Urzad Bezpieczenstwa Publicznego [*County Administration of Public Security*] (POL)
PUBPS............. Privredno Udruzenje Bioskopskih Preduzeca Srbije [*Economic Association of Motion Picture Theaters of Serbia*] (YU)
PUC............. Parti de l'Unite Congolaise (MAR)
PUC............. Partido Union Civica [*Civic Union Party*] [*Dominican Republic*] (LA1)
PUC............. Pontificia Universidade Catolica [*Pontifical Catholic University*] [*Brazilian*] (LA)
PUC............. Proteine Unicellulaire (MAR)
PUC............. Public Utilities Commission [*Trinidadian and Tobagan*] (LA1)
PUCA............. Partido Unionista Centro Americano [*Central American Unionist Party*] (LA)
PUCH............. Parti Uni des Communistes Haitiens [*United Party of Haitian Communists*] (LA)
PUCHE............. Potchefstroom University for Christian Higher Education (MAR)
PUCO............. Partido Unificacion de Campesinos y Obreros [*Workers and Peasants Unification Party*] [*Guatemalan*] (LA)
PUD............. Partido Unificacion Democratica [*Democratic Unification Party*] [*Guatemalan*] (LA)
PUD............. Plans d'Urbanisme Directeur [*Algerian*] (MAR)
PUDH............. Parti d'Union des Democrates Haitiens [*Union Party of Haitian Democrats*] (LA)
PUDN............. Partido Union Democratica Nacionalista [*National Democratic Union Party*] [*Salvadoran*] (LA)
PUDNOVJ... Partizanska Udarna Divizija Narodnooslobodilacke Vojske Jugoslavije [*Partisan Shock Division of the National Liberation Army of Yugoslavia*] (YU)
PUDOC............. Centrum voor Landbouwpublikaties en Landbouwdocumentatie [*Wageningen*]
PUE............. Rules for Setting Up Electrical Installations (RU)
PUF............. People's United Front [*Papua New Guinean*] (PPW)
PUF............. Presses Universitaires de France [*French University Press*] (WER)
PUG............. Hunter-Killer Group [*Navy*] (RU)
PUG............. Przeglad Ustawodawstwa Gospodarczego [*Review of Economic Legislation*] (POL)
PUGN............. Full Deflection [*Artillery*] (RU)
puh............. Puhelin [*Telephone*] [*Finnish*]
puhek............. Puhekieli [*Finnish*]
puhkesk...... Puhelinkeskustelu [*Finnish*]
puhutt............. Puhutteluna [*Address*] [*Finnish*]
PUI............. Engineer's Control Post (RU)
PUI............. Model Statutes of the Labor Production Cooperatives of Disabled Persons (BU)

PUI .... Partido Universitario Independiente [*Independent University Party*] [*Spanish*] (WER)
PUK .... Patriotic Union of Kurdistan [*Iraqi*] (PD)
PUK .... Pechiney-Ugine-Kuhlmann Company [*France*] (WER)
PUKO .... Propagacni Ustredi Kraje Olomouckeho [*Propaganda Headquarters for the Olomouc Region*] (CZ)
PUL .... Linear Control Point [*Automation*] (RU)
pulab .... Machine-Gun and Artillery Battalion (RU)
PULADA ...... Pusat Latehan Darat [*Army Training Center*] (ML)
pulap .... Machine-Gun and Artillery Regiment (RU)
PULO .... Pattani United Liberation Organization [*Thai*] (PD)
pul otd .... Machine-Gun Section (RU)
PULPAPEL ... Celulosa y Papel de Colombia SA [*Bogota*] (COL)
PUM .... Parti de l'Unite Marocaine (MAR)
PUMO .... Mortar Fire Director (RU)
PUMS .... Pokrajinska Uprava Poljoprivrednih Masinskih Stanica [*Provincial Administration of Agricultural Machinery Stations*] [*Vojvodina*] (YU)
PUMS .... Pravnicky Ustav Ministerstva Spravedlnosti [*Law Institute of the Ministry of Justice*] (CZ)
PUMV .... Publikacni Ustav Ministerstva Vnitra [*Publishing Institute of the Ministry of the Interior*] (CZ)
PUMZ .... Pervoural'sk Metalware Plant (RU)
PUN .... Control and Guidance Post (RU)
PUN .... Partido Unico Nacional [*National Single Party*] [*Equatorial Guinean*] (AF)
PUN .... Partido de Unificacion Nacional [*National Unification Party*] [*Costa Rican*] (LA)
PUN .... Partido Union Nacional [*National Union Party*] [*Peruvian*] (LA)
PUNA .... Parti de l'Unite Nationale (MAR)
PUNG .... Parti de l'Unite Nationale de Guinee (MAR)
PUNGA .... Parti de l'Unite Nationale Gabonaise (MAR)
PUNGE .... Partido Unido Nacional de Guinea Ecuatorial (MAR)
PUNIA .... Fighter Aviation Control and Guidance Post (RU)
PUNR .... Regulation on the Application of the Ukase on Encouraging the Birth Rate (BU)
PUNS .... Parti de l'Unite Nationale Sahraouie (MAR)
PUNT .... Partido Unico Nacional de los Trabajadores [*Workers National Single Party*] [*Equatorial Guinean*] (AF)
PUO .... Fire Direction Instrument (BU)
PUO .... Fire Director [*Artillery*] (RU)
PUOKR .... Political Directorate of a Military District (RU)
puol .... Puolaa [*or Puolaksi*] [*Finnish*]
puol .... Puolalainen [*Finnish*]
PUOZA .... Antiaircraft Fire Director (RU)
PUP .... Parti de l'Union Populaire [*People's Union Party*] [*Haitian*] (LA)
PUP .... Parti de l'Unite du Peuple (MAR)
PUP .... Partido da Unidade Popular [*Popular Unity Party*] [*Portuguese*] (WER)
PUP .... People's United Party [*Belizean*] (PPW)
PUP .... Popular Unity Party [*Bangladesh*] (PPW)
PUP .... Pracovni Utvar Potrestanych [*Convict Labor Unit*] (CZ)
PUPch .... Intermediate-Frequency Preamplifier (RU)
PUPG .... Partido Union do Povo Galego [*United Party of the Galician People*] [*Spanish*] (WER)
PUPiK .... Przedsiebiorstwo Upowszechniania Prasy i Ksiazki [*Enterprise for Book and Press Distribution - "Ruch"*] [*Polish*]
PUPiK Ruch ... Panstwowy Urzad Publikacji i Kolportazu "Ruch" [*"Ruch" State Bureau for Publishing and for Circulation of Publications*] (POL)
PUR .... Panstwowy Urzad Repatriacyjny [*State Repatriation Administration*] (POL)
PUR .... Political Directorate of the Revvoyensovet (RU)
PUR .... Polyurethan [*Polyurethane*] (EG)
PUR .... Przedsiebiorstwo Uplynnienia Remanentow [*Enterprise for Distribution of Surpluses*] (POL)
PURA .... Partido de Union Republicana Autentica [*Authentic Republican Union Party*] [*Costa Rican*] (LA)
PuRD .... Pulse Jet Engines (BU)
PURKKA ..... Political Directorate of the Workers' and Peasants' Red Army (RU)
PURNES ...... Regulation on the Management, Order, and Supervision of Floor Ownership (BU)
PURP .... Poljska Ujedinjena Radnicka Partija [*Polish United Workers Party*] (YU)
PURS .... Antitank Guided Missile (RU)
PURS .... Guided Missile Fire Director (RU)
PURS .... Partido Unido de la Revolucion Sandinista [*United Party of the Sandinist Revolution*] [*Nicaraguan*] (LA)
PURS .... Partido de la Union Republicana Socialista [*Socialist Republican Union Party*] [*Bolivian*] (LA)
Purvon .... First, Elementary (BU)
PUS .... Fire Director [*Artillery*] (RU)
PUS .... Panstwowy Urzad Samochodowy [*State Automobile Administration*] (POL)
PUS .... Pile-Setting Device (RU)
PUS .... Plans d'Utilisation des Sols [*North African*] (MAR)
PUS .... Postovni Urad Sekovy [*Postal Check Office*] (CZ)
PUS .... Przeglad Ubezpieczen Spolecznych [*Social Security Review*] [*A magazine*] (POL)
PUS .... United States Miscellaneous Pacific Islands [*Three-letter standard code*] (CNC)
PUSF .... Rapid Film Drier (RU)
PUSKOPAD ... Pusat Koperasi Angkatan Darat [*Army Cooperative*] (IN)
PUSM .... Pravnicky Ustav Ministerstva Spravedlnosti [*Law Institute of the Ministry of Justice*] (CZ)
PUSO .... Decontamination Station (RU)
PUSO .... Sanitary Processing and Decontamination Centers (BU)
PUSPAMARA ... Pusat Perdagangan MARA [*MARA Sales Center*] (ML)
PUSPENAL ... Pusat Penerangan Angkatan Laut [*Navy Information Center*] (IN)
Pust .... Desert [*Topography*] (RU)
PUT .... Parti de l'Unite Togolaise [*Togolese Unity Party*] (AF)
PUT .... Pekerdjaan Umum dan Tenaga [*Public Works and Power*] (IN)
PUTCO .... Public Utility Transport Company (MAR)
PUTERA ...... Pusat Tenaga Ra'ayat [*Manpower Center*] (ML)
PU-TKZS ...... Model Statutes of the Labor Cooperative Farms (BU)
put p .... Control Point [*Railroads*] (RU)
PUTPK .... Model Statutes of Labor Productive Cooperatives (BU)
Put'rem .... Administration of Railroad Track-Repair Plants (RU)
put'rem .... Track-Repair Train (RU)
PUTS .... Torpedo Director (RU)
PUTs .... Vocational Training Center (BU)
puus .... Puusepantyot [*Carpentry*] [*Finnish*]
puut .... Puutarhanhoito [*Horticulture*] [*Finnish*]
PUV .... Pluk Utocne Vozby [*Combat Tank Regiment*] (CZ)
PUV .... Prazsky Ustredni Vybor [*Prague Central Committee*] (CZ)
PUV .... Predsednictvo Ustredniho Vyboru [*Presidium of the Central Committee*] (CZ)
PUVN .... Full Elevation [*Artillery*] (RU)
PuVRD .... Pulsejet Engine (RU)
PUW .... Panstwowy Urzad Wydawniczy [*State Publishing Office*] (POL)
PUWF .... Panstwowy Urzad Wychowania Fizycznego [*State Office of Physical Education*] (POL)
PUWP .... Polish United Workers' Party (PD)
PUZ .... Portowy Urzad Zdrowia [*Port Health Administration*] (POL)
PUZUP .... Regulation on the Organization and Tasks of the Pensions and Welfare Administration and Its Local Organs (BU)
PV .... Aircraft Sound Detector (RU)
PV .... Antiaircraft (BU)
PV .... Antiaircraft (RU)
pv .... Assistant Driver (RU)
PV .... Border Troops (RU)
PV .... Debarkation Point (RU)
PV .... Driving Engine (RU)
PV .... Drop Point [*Aviation*] (RU)
pv .... Feedwater (RU)
PV .... Field Railroad Car [*Military term*] (RU)
PV .... Final Bracket, Last Bracket [*Artillery*] (RU)
PV .... Full Moisture Capacity [*of soil*] (RU)
PV .... Fuse Link (RU)
PV .... General Delivery [*For telegrams*] (RU)
PV .... High Water, High Tide (RU)
PV .... Instituto de Promocion de la Vivienda Ltda. [*Bogota*] (COL)
PV .... Interference Field (RU)
PV .... Intermediate Waves (RU)
PV .... Machine-Gun Platoon (RU)
PV .... Military Port, Naval Port (RU)
PV .... Parachute Troops, Paratroops (RU)
PV .... Patraci Vozidlo [*Reconnaissance Vehicle*] (CZ)
p-v .... Peninsula (BU)
p-v .... Peninsula (RU)
PV .... Petite Vitesse [*On handwheel of turrets separated by steam*] [*French*] (MTD)
PV .... Phong Vien [*Signature on Newspaper Articles*] (TVP)
pv .... Pienviljelija [*Finnish*]
PV .... Planinski Vestnik [*Alpine Review*] [*Ljubljana*] [*A periodical*] (YU)
PV .... Planmaessig Vorbeugende Instandsetzung (System) [*Planned Preventive Maintenance*] (EG)
PV .... Plantations Villageoises (MAR)
PV .... Polar Air (RU)
PV .... Posadkove Velitelstvi [*Garrison Headquarters*] (CZ)
PV .... Posadkovy Velitel [*Garrison Commander*] (CZ)
PV .... Poverenictvo Vyzivy [*Office of the Food Commissioner*] (CZ)
PV .... Pradelny Vlny [*Woolen Mills*] (CZ)
PV .... Preignition (RU)
PV .... Problems of Oriental Studies [*A publication*] (RU)
PV .... Proces-Verbal [*French*]
PV .... Proedros Voulis [*President of Chamber of Deputies*] [*Automobile license plate designation*] [*Greek*] (GC)
PV .... Protected Village (MAR)
PV .... Prumyslove Vydavatelstvi [*Industrial Publishing House*] (CZ)
P/V .... Pyrovolikon [*Artillery*] (GC)
PV .... Receiving Puncher [*Computers*] (RU)
PV .... Reclosure, Reclosing (RU)
PV .... Regulation on Entries (BU)
PV .... Relative Switching-In Duration (RU)
PV .... Rotary Switch (RU)
PV .... Semiconductor Rectifier (RU)
PV .... Shot Point [*Geophysics*] (RU)

PV........ Surface-Active Substance (RU)
PV........ Switching Time (RU)
PV........ Vertical Plotter (RU)
PVA........ Longitudinal Helical Reinforcement (RU)
PVA........ Polyvinyl Acetate (RU)
PVA........ Pukovska Veterinarska Ambulanta [*Regimental Veterinary Station*] (YU)
PVAE........ Polyvinyl Acetate Emulsion (RU)
PVAWG........ Pruefungsverband der Arbeiterwohnungsbaugenossenschaft [*Control Association of the Workers Housing Construction Cooperative*] (EG)
PVB........ Polyvinyl Bromide (RU)
PVBA........ Persoonlijke Vennootschap met Beperkte Aansprakelijkheid [*Limited Company*] [*Dutch*] (CED)
PVC........ Partido Vanguardia Comunista [*Communist Vanguard Party*] [*Argentine*] (LA)
PVC........ Plantations Villageoises de Cocotiers (MAR)
PVC........ Policlorura de Vinil [*Polyvinyl Chloride*] (RO)
PVC........ Polivinilklorur [*Polyvinylchloride*] [*By-product of Petro-Chemical Industry*] (TU)
PVC........ Polyvinylchlorid [*Polyvinyl Chloride*] (CZ)
PVC........ Polyvinylchlorid [*Polyvinyl Chloride*] (EG)
PVD........ High-Pressure Heater (RU)
PVD........ High-Pressure Superheater (RU)
PVD........ Pays en Voie de Developpement [*Developing Countries*] [*French*] (WER)
PVD........ Pressure Head, Pitot-Static Head (RU)
PVD........ Produits Fabriques par les Pays en Voie de Developpement (MAR)
PVD........ Ramjet, Ramjet Engine (RU)
PvdA........ Partij van de Arbeid [*Labor Party*] [*Dutch*] (PPE)
PvdA/PTA... Partij van de Arbeid van Belgiee/Parti du Travail de Belgique [*Belgian Labor Party*] (PPW)
pvdd........ Airborne Infantry Division (RU)
PVDE........ Policia de Vigilancia e Defesa do Estado [*Vigilance and State Defense Police*] [*Portuguese*] (WER)
PVDO........ Antiairborne Defense (RU)
PVDS........ Pravilnik o Vojno-Disciplinskim Sudovima [*Guide for Military Disciplinary Tribunals*] (YU)
PVDSK........ Regulation for Deposits at the State Savings Bank (BU)
PvdV........ Partij van de Vrijheid [*Party of Freedom*] [*Dutch*] (PPE)
PVE........ Pteryga Vasikis Ekpaidevseos [*Basic Training Wing*] [*Greek*] (GC)
PVEE........ Pronoia Voreion Eparkhion Ellados [*Greek Northern Provinces Welfare*] (GC)
PVFSE........ Plano de Valorizacao Economica da Regiao da Fronteira Sudoeste do Pais [*Plan for Economic Promotion of the Southwest Border Region*] [*Brazilian*] (LA)
PVFZ........ Planetary High-Altitude Frontal Zone (RU)
PVK........ Pedion Volis Kritis [*Crete Firing Range*] (GC1)
PVK........ Pyruvic Acid (RU)
PVK........ Vibrating Roller Trailer (RU)
PVK........ Water-Resistant Pressboard (RU)
PVKh........ Polyvinyl Chloride (BU)
PVKh........ Polyvinyl Chloride (RU)
PVKhO........ Air and Chemical Defense (RU)
PVKhO........ Antiaircraft and Chemical Warfare Defense (BU)
PVKM........ Steam-Air Forging Hammer (RU)
PVL........ Epidemic Pneumonia (RU)
PVL........ Regimental Veterinary Hospital (RU)
PVL........ Veterinary Field Hospital (RU)
pvm........ Paivamaara [*Finnish*]
pvm........ Posta Vonalmester [*Postal Inspector*] (HU)
PVM........ Program-Timing Mechanism (RU)
PVM........ Protein, Vitamin, and Mineral Concentrate (MAR)
PVM........ Punched-Card Computer, Punched-Tape Computer (RU)
PVM........ Suspension Footbridge (RU)
PVN........ Air Observation Post (RU)
PVNOS........ Aircraft-Warning Service Post (RU)
PVO........ Air Defense (RU)
PVO........ Antiaircraft Defense (BU)
PVO........ Antiaircraft Gun (RU)
PVO........ Preisverordnung [*Price Regulation*] (EG)
PVO........ Private Voluntary Organization (MAR)
p-vo........ Production, Manufacture (RU)
PVO........ Protivvazdusna Odbrana [*Antiaircraft Defense*] (YU)
PVO........ Protivzdusna Obrana [*Air Defense*] (CZ)
PVOP........ Polgari Vedelem Orszagos Parancsnoksag [*National Civil Defense Command*] (HU)
PVOPP........ Air Defense of Loading Points (RU)
PVOS........ Protivzdusna Obrana Statu [*Territorial Air Defense Command*] (CZ)
PVOV........ Protivzdusna Obrana Vojsk [*Troop Air Defense*] (CZ)
PVOZN........ Air Defense of Population (RU)
PVP........ Approach Way, Approach Zone [*Aviation*] (RU)
PVP........ High-Density Polyethylene (RU)
PVP........ Padakovy Vysadkovy Pluk [*Airborne Parachute Regiment*] (CZ)
PVP........ Partido Vanguardia Popular [*Popular Vanguard Party*] [*Costa Rican Communist Party*] (LA)
PVP........ Partido de la Victoria del Pueblo [*People's Victory Party*] [*Uruguayan*] (LA)
PVP........ Plantations Villageoises Palmiers (MAR)
PVP........ Podjetje za Vzdrzavanje Prog [*Railroad Track Maintenance Establishment*] (YU)
PVP........ Polyvinylpyridine (RU)
PVP........ Polyvinylpyrrolidone (RU)
PVP........ Poslovnik Veca Proizvodaca [*Rules of Procedure of the Council of Producers*] (YU)
PVP........ Veterinary Aid Station (RU)
pvp........ Water-Soluble Powder [*Pharmacy*] (RU)
PVPJDZ........ Podjetje za Vzdrzevanje Proge Jugoslovanske Drzavne Zeleznice [*Rail Maintenance Establishment of the Yugoslav Railroads*] (YU)
pv pn........ Aid Station (BU)
PVPN........ Partido Vanguardia Popular Nacionalista [*Nationalist Popular Vanguard Party*] [*Venezuelan*] (LA)
PVPr........ Padakovy Vysadkovy Prapor [*Airborne Parachute Battalion*] (CZ)
PVR........ Antiaircraft Reconnaissance [*Civil defense*] (RU)
PVR........ Posredna Vatra Rusenja [*Indirect Demolition Fire*] [*Military*] (YU)
PVRD........ Ramjet Engine (BU)
PVRD........ Ramjet, Ramjet Engine (RU)
PVRDT........ Solid-Fuel Ramjet Engine (RU)
PVRDZh........ Liquid-Fuel Ramjet Engine (RU)
PVRGS........ Regulation on Keeping State Civil Status Records (BU)
PVRZ........ Locomotive and Railroad Car Repair Plant (RU)
PVS........ Dust Vacuuming Service [*Industrial*] (BU)
PVS........ Ground-Air Liaison Post (RU)
pvs........ Ground-Air Panel (RU)
PVS........ Partido Vanguardia Socialista [*Socialist Vanguard Party*] [*Argentine*] (LA)
PVS........ Polyvinyl Alcohol (RU)
PVS........ Predsunute Velitelske Stanoviste [*Advance Command Post*] (CZ)
PVS........ Presidium of the Supreme Soviet (RU)
PVS........ Regimental Clothing and Equipment Depot (RU)
PVSK........ Industrial Veterinary and Sanitary Control (BU)
PVSNRB........ Plenum of the Supreme Court of the Bulgarian People's Republic (BU)
PVSP........ Regular Military Hospital Train (RU)
PVSV........ Permanent All-Union Construction Exhibition (RU)
pvt........ Par Voie Telegraphique [*By Telegraph*] [*French*]
PVT........ Planning and Reconstruction Trust (RU)
PVT........ Policia de Viacao e Transito [*Traffic and Highway Police*] [*Portuguese*] (WER)
Pvt........ Privat [*German*]
PVTAK........ Regulations of the Foreign Trade Arbitration Commission (BU)
Pvtdz........ Privatdozent [*German*]
pv tpk........ Polgari Vedelmi Torzsparancsnok [*Civil Defense Staff Commander*] (HU)
PVTS........ Pravila Vazduhoplovne Tehnicke Sluzbe [*Air Technical Service Rules*] (YU)
PVU........ Calling and Ringing Device [*Telephony*] (RU)
PVU-........ High-Resistance Indicating Converter (RU)
pvuch........ Air Defense Training Point (RU)
PVUZ........ Higher Pedagogical Educational Institution (BU)
PVV........ Partij voor Vrijheid en Vooruitgang [*Freedom and Progress Party*] [*Belgian*] (PPW)
PVV........ Prazsky Vzorkovy Veletrh [*Prague Sample Fair*] (CZ)
PVV........ Predsednictvo Vysokoskolskeho Vyboru [*Presidium of the University Committee*] (CZ)
PVV........ Prirodovedecke Vydavatelstvi [*Natural Sciences Publishing House*] (CZ)
PVVP........ Posadkove Velitelstvi Velke Prahy [*Garrison Headquarters for Greater Prague*] (CZ)
PVVPOVO... Posadkove Velitelstvi Velke Prahy, Oddeleni Vychovy a Osvety [*Garrison Headquarters for Greater Prague, Department of Education and Culture*] (CZ)
PVZ........ High-Voltage Protection Station (RU)
PVZ........ Pancevacka Vodna Zajednica [*Pancevo Water Community*] (YU)
PVZ........ Perm' Bicycle Plant (RU)
PVZ........ Potiska Vodna Zajednica [*Potisje Water Community*] [*Zrenjanin*] (YU)
PVZ........ Poverenictvo pre Vyzivu a Zasobovanie [*Office of the Commissioner of Food Supply*] (CZ)
PVZ........ Protivvazdusna Zastita [*Antiaircraft Defense*] [*Army*] (YU)
Pvzl........ Provinzial [*German*]
PW........ Parti Wallon [*Walloon Party*] [*Belgian*] (WER)
PW........ Politechnika Warszawska [*Warsaw Polytechnical School*] (POL)
PW........ Prasa Wojskowa [*Military Press*] [*Publishing house*] (POL)
PW........ Przemysl Weglowy [*Coal Industry*] (POL)
PW........ Przysposobienie Wojskowe [*Military Training*] (POL)
PWBBC........ Professional Wrestling and Boxing Board of Control (MAR)
PwF........ Produktionsgenossenschaften Werktaetiger Fischer [*Production Cooperatives of Working Fishermen*] (EG)
PWG........ Polskie Wydawnictwa Gospodarcze [*Polish Publishing House for Economics*] (POL)

PWI............ Permanent Way Institution (EA)
PWI............ Persatuan Wartawan Indonesia [*Indonesian Journalists Association*] (IN)
PWiT........... Przedsiebiorstwo Wystaw i Targow [*Exhibitions and Fairs Bureau*] [*Polish*]
PWKS.......... Panstwowe Wydawnictwo Ksiazek Szkolnych [*State Publishing House for School Books*] (POL)
PWM........... Polskie Wydawnictwa Muzyczne [*Polish Music Publishing House*] (POL)
PWN............ Panstwowe Wydawnictwo Naukowe [*State Publishing House for Scholarly Works*] (POL)
PWP............ Peasants' and Workers' Party [*Indian*] (PPW)
PWPN.......... Panstwowe Wydawnictwo Popularno-Naukowe [*Popular Science State Publishing House*] (POL)
PWPW.......... Panstwowa Wytwornia Papierow Wartosciowych [*State Office for the Printing of Bonds and Paper Money*] (POL)
PWr............. Politechnika Wroclawska [*Engineering College of Wroclaw*] [*Polish*]
PWR............ Powiatowa Wystawa Rolnicza [*County Agricultural Exhibition*] (POL)
PWRiL.......... Panstwowe Wydawnictwo Rolnicze i Lesne [*State Agriculture and Forestry Publishing House*] (POL)
PWRM.......... Polaroid Workers Revolutionary Movement (MAR)
PWRN.......... Prezydium Wojewodzkiej Rady Narodowej [*Presidium of the People's Province Council*] [*Polish*]
PWS............ Panstwowe Wydawnictwa Szkolne [*State School Publishing House*] (POL)
PWSA.......... Panstwowa Wyzsza Szkola Aktorska [*State Higher School for Actors*] (POL)
PWSAG........ Panstwowa Wyzsza Szkola Administracji Gospodarczej [*State Higher School for Economic Administration*] (POL)
PWSF.......... Panstwowa Wytwornia Sprzetu Filmowego [*State Film Equipment Plant*] (POL)
PWSF.......... Panstwowa Wyzsza Szkola Filmowa [*State Higher School of Motion Pictures*] (POL)
PWSM.......... Panstwowa Wyzsza Szkola Muzyczna [*State Higher School of Music*] (POL)
PWSP.......... Panstwowa Wyzsza Szkola Pedagogiczna [*State Higher Pedagogical School*] (POL)
PWSSP........ Panstwowa Wyzsza Szkola Sztuk Plastycznych [*State Higher School of Plastic Arts*] (POL)
PWST.......... Panstwowa Wyzsza Szkola Teatralna [*State Higher School of Dramatics*] (POL)
PWSTiF....... Panstwowa Wyzsza Szkola Teatru i Filmu [*State Higher School of Stage and Screen*] (POL)
PWSZ.......... Panstwowe Wydawnictwa Szkolnictwa Zawodowego [*State Publishing House for Vocational Training*] (POL)
PWT............ Panstwowe Wydawnictwo Techniczne [*State Technical Publishing House*] (POL)
PWT............ Parti Wallon des Travailleurs [*Walloon Workers Party*] [*Belgian*] (WER)
PWT............ Pasokan Wanita Tambahan [*Women's Auxiliary Corps*] (ML)
PWU............ Plantation Workers Union [*Mauritian*] (AF)
PWU............ Public Workers Union [*Grenadian*] (LA1)
PWV............ Pretoria, Witwatersrand, Vereeniging Industrial Area [*South African*] (AF)
p wyz.......... Patrz Wyzej [*See Above*] [*Polish*]
PWZ............ Powiatowy Wydzial Zdrowia [*County Health Department*] (POL)
PX.............. Prumyslova Komise [*Industrial Commission*] (CZ)
PY.............. Paraguay [*Two-letter standard code*] (CNC)
PY.............. Paragwaj [*Paraguay*] [*Polish*]
pya............. Post-Office Box (RU)
PYaZ........... Antinuclear Defense, Nuclear Defense (RU)
PYC............ People's Youth Corps (ML)
PYC............ Presbyterian Youth Centre (MAR)
PYE............ Protovathmios Ygeionomiki Epitropi [*First Degree Medical Board*] [*Greek*] (GC)
PYF............ French Polynesia [*Three-letter standard code*] (CNC)
PYMECO..... Asociacion de Pequenos y Medianos Comerciantes Autonomos [*Association of Small and Medium Independent Businessmen*] [*Spanish*] (WER)
PYO............ Progressive Youth Organization [*Guyanese*] (LA)
PYP-........... Pyrosvestiki Ypiresia Poleos [*Fire Department of the City Of*] [*Followed by initial letter of city name*] (GC)
PYRESA...... Prensa y Radio Espanola Sociedad Anonima [*Spanish Press and Radio, Incorporated*] (AF)
PYS............ Praxis Ypourgikou Symvouliou [*Act of the Ministerial Council*] (GC)
PYS............ Protovathmion Ypiresiakon Symvoulion [*First Degree Service Council*] [*Greek*] (GC)
pys............. Pysakki [*Finnish*]
PYSDE........ Perifereiakon Ypiresiakon Symvoulion Dimotikis Ekpaidevseos [*Regional Service Council for Elementary Education*] [*Greek*] (GC)
PYSME........ Perifereiakon Ypiresiakon Symvoulion Mesis Ekpaidevseos [*District Service Council for Secondary Education*] [*Greek*] (GC)
PYSSE......... Perifereiakon Ypiresiakon Symvoulion Stoikheiodous Ekpaidevseos [*District Service Council for Elementary Education*] [*Greek*] (GC)
PZ.............. Auxiliary Parachute (RU)
PZ.............. Canal Zone [*Two-letter standard code*] (CNC)
pz.............. Contamination Zone (RU)
PZ.............. Floating Point (RU)
PZ.............. Incendiary Bullet (RU)
PZ.............. Incendiary-Ranging (RU)
PZ.............. Loading Device (RU)
Pz.............. Paleozoyik [*Paleozoic*] [*Geology*] (TU)
PZ.............. Passenger Building (RU)
PZ.............. Pekarska Zadruga [*Baking Cooperative*] (YU)
pz.............. Pieze (RU)
pz.............. Poise (RU)
PZ.............. Poljoprivredna Zadruga [*Agricultural Cooperative*] (YU)
PZ.............. Poljoprivredni Zavod [*Agricultural Institute*] (YU)
PZ.............. Postolarska Zadruga [*Shoemakers' Cooperative*] (YU)
pz.............. Praca Zbiorowa [*Symposium*] (POL)
PZ.............. Pracovni Zalohy [*State Labor Reserves*] (CZ)
PZ.............. Prazska Zelezarska Spolecnost, Narodni Podnik [*Prague Iron Company, National Enterprise*] (CZ)
PZ.............. Proizvodacka Zadruga [*Producers' Cooperative*] (YU)
PZ.............. Projektantski Zavod [*Industrial Design Institute*] (YU)
PZ.............. Pulk Zmechanizowany [*Mechanized Regiment*] (POL)
PZ.............. Setup and Dismantling Time (RU)
PZ.............. Societe Paterson Zochonis and Co. Ltd. (MAR)
PZ.............. Statni Pracovni Zalohy [*State Labor Reserves*] (CZ)
PZ.............. Total Blackout Condition (RU)
PZ.............. Underwater Protection [*of a ship*] (RU)
PZA............ Polski Zwiazek Atletyczny [*Polish Athletic Union*] (POL)
PZA............ Postzollamt [*Postal Customs Office*] (EG)
PZANN........ Pomorskie Zaklady Aparatury Niskiego Napiecia [*Pomerania Enterprise for Low Tension Equipment*] (POL)
PZB............ Polski Zwiazek Bokserski [*Polish Boxing Union*]
PZB............ Przemyslowe Zjednoczenie Budowlane [*Industrial Construction Association*] (POL)
PZBM.......... Pomorskie Zaklady Budowy Maszyn [*Pomerania Machine Construction Plant*] (POL)
PZBWP........ Polski Zwiazek Bylych Wiezniow Politycznych [*Polish Union of Former Political Prisoners*] (POL)
PzC............. Pruzkumna Ceta [*Reconnaissance Platoon*] (CZ)
PZChK......... Panstwowe Zaklady Chowu Koni [*State Horse-Breeding Stations*] (POL)
PZD............ Politische Zeitschriftendokumentation
PZD............ Poverenictvo Zdravotnictva [*Office of the Commissioner of Health*] (CZ)
PZD............ Powiatowy Zarzad Drogowy [*County Road Administration*] (POL)
PZDA.......... Regulation on the Application of the Law on State Arbitration (BU)
PzDB........... Pruzkumna Delostrelecka Baterie [*Artillery Reconnaissance Battery*] (CZ)
pzdk........... Field Wood Structures Plant (BU)
PzDO........... Pruzkumne Zpravodajske Delostrelecke Oddeleni [*Artillery Intelligence Reconnaissance Detachment*] (CZ)
PZE............ Panstwowy Zaklad Emerytalny [*State Retirement Bureau*] (POL)
PZE............ Polski Zwiazek Esperantystow [*Polish Association of Esperantists*] [*Polish*]
PZF............ Poljoprivredni Zemljisni Fond [*Agricultural Land Fund*] (YU)
PZF............ Polski Zwiazek Filatelistow [*Polish Association of Philatelists*] [*Polish*]
PZFA.......... Polski Zwiazek Fabryk Azotowych [*Polish Union of Nitrogen Factories*] (POL)
PZG............ Panstwowe Zaklady Graficzne [*State Printing Plants*] (POL)
PZG............ Polski Zwiazek Gimnastyczny [*Polish Gymnastic Union*] [*Polish*]
PZG............ Polski Zwiazek Gluchych [*Polish Association of the Deaf*] [*Polish*]
PZG............ Poznanskie Zaklady Gastronomiczne [*Poznan Restaurant Enterprises*] (POL)
PZG............ Poznanskie Zaklady Graficzne [*Poznan Printing Plant*] (POL)
PZGS.......... Powiatowy Zarzad Gminnych Spoldzielni [*County Administration of Rural Commune Cooperatives*] (POL)
PZGS.......... Powiatowy Zwiazek Gminnych Spoldzielni [*County Union of Rural Commune Cooperatives*] (POL)
PZGS.......... Powiatowy Zwiazek Gminnych Spoldzielni "Samopomoc Chlopska" [*District Association of the Village Cooperatives "Peasants' Self-Help"*] [*Polish*]
PZGWiTS.... Polskie Zrzeszenie Gazownikow, Wodociagowcow, i Technikow Sanitarnych [*Polish Association of Gas, Water Supply, and Sanitation Workers*] (POL)
PZh............ Journal of Paleontology [*A publication*] (RU)
PZH............ Panstwowy Zaklad Higieny [*State Institute of Hygiene*] (POL)
PzH............ Pruzkumna Hlidka [*Reconnaissance Patrol*] (CZ)
PZh-........... Steam-Driven Locomotive Crane (RU)
PZhD.......... Perm' Railroad (RU)
pzhdb......... Railroad Track-Laying Battalion (RU)
PZhG.......... Horizontal Searchlight (RU)
PZhI........... Semi-Higher Railway Institute (BU)
PZHK.......... Polski Zwiazek Hodowcow Koni [*Polish Union of Horse Breeders*] [*Polish*]
PZHL.......... Polski Zwiazek Hokeja na Lodzie [*Polish Ice Hockey Union*] (POL)
pzhpb......... Railway Transportation Battalion (BU)

PZHR.......... Panstwowe Zaklady Hodowli Roslin [*State Plant Breeding Station*] (POL)
PZhR.......... Radioactive Liquid Density Meter (RU)
PZhR-.......... Radioisotopic Liquid Density Meter (RU)
PZhS.......... Searchlight Station (RU)
PZHT.......... Polski Zwiazek Hokeja na Trawie [*Polish Hockey Union*] [*Polish*]
PZhV.......... Vertical Searchlight (RU)
PZInz.......... Panstwowe Zaklady Inzynierii [*State Engineering Plant*] (POL)
PZITB.......... Polski Zwiazek Inzynierow i Technikow Budowlanych [*Polish Union of Construction Engineers and Technicians*] (POL)
PZJ.......... Polski Zwiazek Jezdziecki [*Polish Riding Union*] [*Polish*]
PzJgd Trupp ... Panzerjagd Trupp [*Tank Pursuit Squad*] (EG)
PZK.......... Polski Zwiazek Kajakowy [*Polish Kayak Union*] (POL)
PZK.......... Polski Zwiazek Krotkofalowcow [*Polish Short-Wave Radio Operators Union*] (POL)
PZK.......... Powder Chamber Measuring Device (RU)
PZK.......... Underwater Protection of a Ship (RU)
PZKB.......... Panstwowy Zaoczny Kurs Bibliotekarski [*State Correspondence Course for Librarians*] (POL)
PZKiOR....... Polish Union of Agricultural Circles and Organizations (PD)
PZKKR........ Panstwowy Zaklad Korespondencyjnego Ksztalcenia Rolniczego [*State Institute for Correspondence Courses on Agriculture*] (POL)
PZKKS........ Polski Zwiazek Koszykowki, Siatkowki, i Szczypiorniaka [*Polish Basketball, Volleyball, and Handball Union*] (POL)
PZKO.......... Polski Zwiazek Kulturalno-Oswiatowy [*Polish Culture and Education Union*] (POL)
PZKO.......... Polski Zwiazek Kulturalno-Oswiatowy w Czechoslowacji [*Polish Union of Culture and Enlightenment in Czechoslovakia*] (CZ)
PZKol.......... Polski Zwiazek Kolarski [*Polish Cycling Union*] (POL)
PZKosz....... Polski Zwiazek Koszykowki [*Polish Basketball Union*] [*Polish*]
PZKR.......... Powiatowy Zwiazek Kolek Rolniczych [*District Union of Agricultural Co-Operatives*] [*Polish*]
PZL.......... Polski Zwiazek Lowiecki [*Polish Hunting Union*] (POL)
PZL.......... Polski Zwiazek Luczniczy [*Polish Archery Union*] [*Polish*]
PZL.......... Polski Zwiazek Lyzwiarski [*Polish Skaters' Union*] (POL)
PZL.......... Polskie Zaklady Lotnicze [*Polish Aviation Plant*] (POL)
PZL.......... Powiatowy Zarzad Lacznosci [*County Communications Administration*] (POL)
PzL.......... Pruzkumne Letectvo [*Reconnaissance Aviation (or Aircraft)*] (CZ)
PZLA.......... Polski Zwiazek Lekkiej Atletyki [*Polish Light Athletic Union*] (POL)
PZLPO........ Panstwowe Zenskie Liceum Przemyslu Odziezowego [*State Clothing Industry School for Women*] (POL)
PZLZ.......... Panstwowy Zaklad Leczniczy dla Zwierzat [*State Animal Hospital*] (POL)
PZM.......... Paleozoological Museum (of the Academy of Sciences, USSR) (RU)
PZM.......... Panstwowy Zaklad Mleczarski [*Polish*]
PZM.......... Polska Zegluga Morska [*Polish Steamship Company*] (POL)
PZM.......... Polski Zwiazek Motocyklowy [*Polish Motorcyclists' Union*] (POL)
PZM.......... Polski Zwiazek Motorowy [*Polish Motorists' Union*] (POL)
PZM.......... Powiatowe Zaklady Mleczarskie [*County Dairies*] (POL)
PZMB.......... Pruszkowskie Zaklady Materialow Biurowych [*Pruszkow Office Supplies Plant*] (POL)
PZMot.......... Polski Zwiazek Motorowy [*Polish Motorists' Union*] (POL)
PZN.......... Polski Zwiazek Narciarski [*Polish Ski Union*] (POL)
PZN.......... Polski Zwiazek Niewidomych [*Polish Union of the Blind*] (POL)
PZNF.......... Poznanskie Zaklady Nawozow Fosforowych [*Poznan Phosphorous Fertilizer Establishments*] (POL)
Pzo.......... Pizzo [*Peak*] [*Italian*] (NAU)
PZO.......... Podnik Zahranicniho Obchodu [*Foreign Trade Enterprise*] (CZ)
PZO.......... Polskie Zaklady Optyczne [*Polish Optical Plants*] (POL)
PZO.......... Pripraven k Zdravotni Obrane [*Prepared for Health Defense (Badge)*] (CZ)
PZO.......... Protiletecka Zavodni Obrana [*Factory Antiaircraft Defense*] (CZ)
PzO.......... Pruzkumny Odrad [*Reconnaissance Detachment*] (CZ)
PZO.......... Rolling Barrage, Creeping Barrage (BU)
PZO.......... Rolling Barrage, Creeping Barrage (RU)
PZOO.......... Polski Zwiazek Obroncow Ojczyzny [*Polish Union for National Defense (Prewar)*] (POL)
PZP.......... Poznanskie Zaklady Piekarnicze [*Poznan Bakeries*] (POL)
PZP.......... Przedsiebiorstwa pod Zarzadem Panstwowym [*Enterprises under State Administration*] (POL)
PZPB.......... Panstwowe Zaklady Przemyslu Bawelnianego [*State Cotton Plants*] (POL)
PZPB.......... Panstwowe Zaklady Przemyslu Budowlanego [*State Construction Industry Plants*] (POL)
PZPB.......... Prudnickie Zaklady Przemyslu Bawelnianego [*Prudnik (Neustadt) Cotton Plant*] (POL)
PZPI.......... Pokrajinski Zavod za Poljoprivredna Istrazivanja [*Provincial Institute for Agricultural Research*] [*Novi Sad*] (YU)
PZPiT.......... Panstwowy Zespol Piesni i Tanca [*State Song and Dance Ensemble*] [*Polish*]
PZPJG......... Panstwowe Zaklady Przemyslu Jedwabniczego i Galanterii [*State Silk and Haberdashery Plant*] (POL)
PZPN.......... Polski Zwiazek Pilki Noznej [*Polish Soccer Union*] (POL)
PZPO.......... Poznanskie Zaklady Przemyslu Odziezowego [*Poznan Clothing Plant*] (POL)
PZPR.......... Polska Zjednoczona Partia Robotnicza [*Polish United Workers' Party - PUWP*] (PPW)
PZPR.......... Polski Zwiazek Pilki Recznej [*Polish Handball Union*] (POL)
PzPr.......... Pruzkumny Prapor [*Reconnaissance Battalion*] (CZ)
PZPS.......... Panstwowe Zaklady Pomocy Szkolnej [*State School Supply Establishment*] (POL)
PZPS.......... Poznanskie Zaklady Przemyslu Spirytusowego [*Poznan Alcohol Plant*] (POL)
PZPW.......... Panstwowe Zaklady Przemyslu Welnianego [*State Wool Plants*] (POL)
PZR.......... Powiatowy Zarzad Rolnictwa [*County Agricultural Administration*] (POL)
PzR.......... Pruzkumna Rota [*Reconnaissance Company*] (CZ)
PZRK.......... Perenosnyi Zenitnyi Raketnyi Kompleks [*Portable Air Defense Missile Complex*] [*Russian*]
PZS.......... Field Battery Charging Station (RU)
PZS.......... Mobile Battery Charging Station (RU)
PZS.......... Panstwowa Zegluga Srodladows [*State Administration of Inland Navigation*] (POL)
PZS.......... Panstwowe Zaklady Samochodowe [*State Automobile Plants*] (POL)
PZS.......... Planinska Zveza Slovenije [*Alpine Union of Slovenia*] (YU)
PZS.......... Poljodjelska Znanstvena Smotra [*Agricultural Scientific Survey*] [*Zagreb*] [*A periodical*] (YU)
PZS.......... Polski Zwiazek Szermierczy [*Polish Fencing Union*] (POL)
PZS.......... Prazska Zelezarska Spolecnost, Narodni Podnik [*Prague Iron Company, National Enterprise*] (CZ)
PzS.......... Pruzkumna Skupina [*Reconnaissance Detachment*] (CZ)
PZSO.......... Poznanskie Zaklady Srodkow Odzywczych [*Poznan Health Food Enterprise*] (POL)
PZSP.......... Powiatowy Zwiazek Spoldzielni Produkcyjnych [*County Union of Producer Cooperatives (Collective farms)*] (POL)
PZSR.......... Poznanskie Zaklady Surowcow Roslinnych [*Poznan Agricultural Raw Material Establishment*] (POL)
PZSz.......... Polski Zwiazek Szermierczy [*Polish Fencing Union*] [*Polish*]
P Z Sz I........ Panstwowy Zaklad Szkolenia Inwalidow [*State Disabled Persons' Rehabilitation Institute*] (POL)
PZT.......... Polski Zwiazek Tenisowy [*Polish Tennis Union*] (POL)
PZT.......... Polski Zwiazek Turystyczny [*Polish Tourist Union*] (POL)
pzt.......... Poza Tekstem [*Outside of the Text*] (POL)
PZTS.......... Polski Zwiazek Tenisa Stolowego [*Polish Table Tennis Union*] (POL)
PZTW.......... Polski Zwiazek Towarzystw Wioslarskich [*Polish Union of Rowing Associations*]
PZU.......... Intermediate Storage (RU)
PZU.......... Mobile Suction Dredge (RU)
PZU.......... Panstwowy Zaklad Ubezpieczen [*State Insurance Bureau*] (POL)
PZU.......... Permanent Storage [*Data processing*] (RU)
PZU.......... Permanent Storage System [*Data processing*] (BU)
PZU.......... Stability Margin Indicator (RU)
PZUW.......... Powszechny Zadlad Ubezpieczen Wzajemnych [*General Mutual Insurance Company*] (POL)
PZV.......... Ignition Delay Period (RU)
PZV.......... Pokretna Zaprecna Vatra [*Mobile Barrage Fire*] [*Military*] (YU)
PZVA.......... Postzeitungsvertriebsamt [*Postal Newspapers and Periodicals Distribution Office*] (EG)
PZVO.......... Postzeitungsvertriebsordnung [*Postal Newspaper and Periodical Distribution Regulations*] (EG)
PZW.......... Polski Zwiazek Wedkarski [*Polish Angling Union*] [*Polish*]
PZW.......... Powiatowy Zarzad Weterynarii [*County Veterinary Administration*] (POL)
PZw.......... Przeglad Zwiazkowy [*Union Review*] [*A periodical*] (POL)
PZWANN..... Pomorskie Zaklady Wytworcze Aparatury Niskiego Napiecia [*Pomerania Low Tension Apparatus Plant*] (POL)
PZWet.......... Powiatowy Zarzad Weterynarii [*County Veterinary Administration*] (POL)
PZWL.......... Panstwowy Zaklad Wydawnictw Lekarskich [*State Medical Publishing House*] (POL)
PZWM.......... Poznanskie Zaklady Wyrobow Metalowych [*Poznan Metal Products Plant*] (POL)
PZWME....... Pomorskie Zaklady Wytworcze Materialow Elektrotechnicznych [*Pomerania Electric Engineering Plant*] (POL)
PZWS.......... Panstwowe Zaklady Wydawnictw Szkolnych [*State Textbook Publishing House*] (POL)
PZZ.......... Panstwowe Zaklady Zbozowe [*State Grain Elevators*] (POL)
PZZ.......... Polski Zwiazek Zachodni [*Polish Union of the Western Territories*] (POL)
PZZ.......... Polski Zwiazek Zapasniczy [*Polish Wrestling Union*] [*Polish*]
PZZ.......... Polski Zwiazek Zeglarski [*Polish Sailing Union*] (POL)
PZZ.......... Polski Zwiazek Zielarski [*Polish Union of Herbalists*] (POL)
PZZ.......... Powiatowe Zaklady Zbozowe [*County Grain Elevators*] (POL)
PZZ.......... Prodavnica Zemljoradnicke Zadruge [*Sales Department of Agricultural Cooperative*] (YU)

Q

Q.................. Carre [*French*] (MTD)
Q.................. Elektrizitaetsmenge [*Electrical Quantity*] [*German*]
q.................. Kwintal [*Quintal*] [*Polish*]
q.................. Metermazsa [*Quintal*] (HU)
q.................. Metricky Cent [*Quintal*] (CZ)
Q.................. Quadrat [*Square*] [*German*]
q.................. Quai [*Quay, Wharf*] [*French*] (CED)
q.................. Quintal [*Quintal*] [*French*] (GPO)
q.................. Quintal (Kvintal) [*Quintal*] (CZ)
Q.................. Waermemenge [*Heat Quantity*] [*German*]
QA............... Qatar [*Two-letter standard code*] (CNC)
QAFCO........ Qatar Fertilizer Company (ME)
Qal............... Quintal [*Measurements*] [*French*]
QANTAS..... Queensland & Northern Territory Aerial Service [*Later, QANTAS Airways Ltd.*] [*Australian airline*]
QAT............. Qatar [*Three-letter standard code*] (CNC)
QBSM.......... Que Besa Su Mano [*Who Kisses Your Hand*] [*Formal correspondence*] [*Spanish*]
QBSP.......... Que Besa Sus Pies [*Who Kisses Your Feet*] [*Formal correspondence*] [*Spanish*]
QC............... Queen's Counsel (MAR)
qcm............. Quadratcentimeter [*Square Centimeter*] [*German*]
qd................ Quasi Dicat [*As If One Should Say*] [*Latin*] (GPO)
qd................ Quasi Dictum [*As If Said*] [*Latin*] (GPO)
qd................ Quasi Dixisset [*As If He Had Said*] [*Latin*] (GPO)
QDA............. Qattara Depression Authority [*Egyptian*] (MAR)
QDG............. Que Dios Guarde [*Spanish*]
qdm............. Quadratdecimeter [*Square Decimeter*] [*German*]
qe................ Que [*Who, Whom, Which, That*] [*Spanish*]
qe................ Quod Est [*Which Is*] [*Latin*] (GPO)
QED............. Quod Erat Demonstrandum [*Which Was to Be Demonstrated*] [*Latin*] (GPO)
QEF............. Quod Erat Faciendum [*Which Was to Be Done*] [*Latin*] (GPO)
QEGE.......... Que en Gloria Este [*Deceased*] [*Spanish*]
QEI.............. Quod Erat Inveniendum [*Which Was to Be Found Out*] [*Latin*] (GPO)
qepd............ Que en Paz Descanse [*Rest in Peace*] [*Spanish*]
QESC.......... Queen Elizabeth Sports Center [*Bahamian*] (LA1)
QG............... Quartier General [*Headquarters*] [*French*] (WER)
QGA............ Quartier General d'Armee [*Military*] [*French*] (MTD)
QGAA.......... Quartier General d'Administration et d'Accompagnement [*Administration and Support Headquarters*] [*Cambodian*] (CL)
QG/AA........ Quartier General de l'Armee Active [*Regular Army General Headquarters*] [*Cambodian*] (CL)
QG/DN........ Quartier General de la Defense Nationale [*National Defense General Headquarters*] [*Cambodian*] (CL)
QG/EMG..... Quartier General de l'Etat Major General [*General Staff General Headquarters*] [*Cambodian*] (CL)
QGPO.......... Qatari General Petroleum Organization (ME)
q/ha............ Quintal per Hectare [*100 Kilograms per Hectare*] (HU)
qkm............. Quadratkilometer [*Square Kilometer*] (EG)
ql................. Quantum Libet [*As Much as You Please*] [*Latin*] (GPO)
qm............... Quadratmeter [*Square Meter*] (EG)
QML............ Qayyum Moslem League [*Pakistani*] (PD)
qmm............ Quadratmillimeter [*Square Millimeter*] [*German*]
qn................ Quien [*Who, Whom*] [*Spanish*]
QNA............. Qatar News Agency (ME)
QOCH.......... Queen's Own Cameroon Highlanders (MAR)
QPC............. Qatar Petroleum Company (ME)
qpl............... Quantum Placet [*As Much as Seems Good*] [*Latin*] (GPO)
qq................ Quelqu'un [*Anyone, Someone*] [*Correspondence*] [*French*]
Qqe............. Quelque [*Any, Some*] [*Correspondence*] [*French*]
qqv.............. Quae Vide [*Which See*] [*Plural*] [*Latin*] (GPO)
Qr................ Quartier [*Quarter*] [*Military map abbreviation*] [*World War I*] [*French*] (MTD)
QRMN.......... Qualified Registered Mental Nurses (MAR)
qs................ Quantum Sufficit [*Sufficient Quantity*] [*Latin*] (GPO)
QS............... Quecksilber-Saeule [*Mercury Column*] [*German*]
QS............... Quecksilber-Stand [*Mercury Level*] [*German*]
qsgh............ Que Santa Gloria Haya [*Spanish*]
qta............... Quinta [*Farm, Estate*] [*Portuguese*] (CED)
qual............. Qualitativ [*Qualitative*] [*German*]
quant........... Quantitativ [*Quantitative*] [*German*]
Queb........... Quebrada [*Cut, Ravine*] [*Portuguese*] (NAU)
Queb........... Quebrada [*Cut, Ravine*] [*Spanish*] (NAU)
QUIMIDENT... Industria Quimica Dental Ltda. [*Barranquilla*] (COL)
QUIMIMPORT... Empresa Cubana Importadora de Productos Quimicos [*Cuban Enterprise for Import of Chemical Products*] (LA)
QUINACAM... Quinquina du Cameroun (MAR)
qv................ Quantum Vis [*As Much as You Will*] [*Latin*] (GPO)
qv................ Quod Vide [*Which See*] [*Latin*] (GPO)

R

R.................. Angle-Off (RU)
R.................. Basin, Bowl [*Topography*] (RU)
R.................. Burst (RU)
r.................. Company (BU)
r.................. Company (RU)
R.................. Control, Regulator, Governor (RU)
R.................. Distributor (RU)
R.................. Elektrischer Widerstand [*Electrical Resistance*] [*German*]
r.................. Gender [*Grammar*], Species, Kind (RU)
R.................. Genitive (Case) (RU)
R.................. Jet, Reactive (RU)
R.................. Knife Switch (RU)
r.................. Line, Order (BU)
r.................. Private (BU)
r.................. Rada [*Series*] (CZ)
r.................. Radikal [*Radical*] [*A newspaper*] (BU)
r.................. Radius [*Radius*] [*German*]
R.................. Rail (RU)
R.................. Rat [*German*]
R.................. Rayon, City District (RU)
r.................. Real [*Coin*] [*Spanish*]
R.................. Reaumur [*Reaumur (Thermometric scale)*] (EG)
°R.................. Reaumur Degree (RU)
R.................. Reaumuria [*Finnish*]
R.................. Recessive (RU)
R.................. Rechnung [*German*]
R.................. Recht [*German*]
r.................. Rechtsdrehend [*Clockwise*] [*German*]
r.................. Recommande [*French*]
R.................. Reconnaissance [*Aircraft*] (RU)
R.................. Recto [*Right-Hand Page*] [*Latin*] (GPO)
r.................. Recu [*French*]
R.................. Reducer (RU)
r.................. Referalo [*Reviewing*] (HU)
r.................. Reggel [*Morning*] (HU)
R.................. Regina [*Queen*] [*Latin*] (GPO)
r.................. Registriert [*German*]
R.................. Regulating [*or Controlling*] (BU)
R.................. Reisezugverkehr [*Passenger Train Transportation*] (EG)
R.................. Reka [*River*] [*Russian*] (NAU)
R.................. Relay (RU)
R.................. Rendelet [*Decree (Legal)*] (HU)
r.................. Rendor [*Policeman*] (HU)
r.................. Rentgen [*Roentgen Unit*] [*Polish*]
R.................. Report [*French*]
R.................. Reprobado [*On an Examination: Failed*] [*Spanish*]
R.................. Responde [*Spanish*]
R.................. Respublica [*Commonwealth*] [*Latin*] (GPO)
R.................. Respuesta [*Answer*] [*Spanish*]
R.................. Reverencia [*Reverence*] [*Spanish*]
R.................. Reverendo [*Reverend*] [*Spanish*]
R$.................. Rhodesian Dollar (MAR)
R.................. Ridder [*Knight*] [*Danish*] (GPO)
r.................. Riisi(a) [*Finnish*]
R.................. Rio [*River*] [*Portuguese*] (NAU)
R.................. Rio [*River*] [*Spanish*] (NAU)
R.................. River [*Topography*] (RU)
R.................. River [*Type of boat*] (RU)
r.................. River (BU)
R.................. Rivier [*River*] [*Dutch*] (NAU)
R.................. Riviere [*River*] [*French*] (NAU)
r.................. Rodzaj [*Kind*] [*Polish*]
r.................. Roentgen (RU)
R.................. Rok [*Year*] (POL)
r.................. Rok [*Year*] (CZ)
R.................. Rotte (Mehrere Haeuser in Lockerer Siedlung) [*German*]
R.................. Route [*Route, Road, Highway*] (CL)
r.................. Rua [*Street*] [*Portuguese*] (CED)
R.................. Rubin [*Name of inventor*] [*Found on fuses*] [*French*] (MTD)
R.................. Ruble (RU)
R.................. Rud [*River*] [*Persian*] (NAU)
R.................. Rudnichar [*Miner*] [*A periodical*] (BU)
r.................. Rue [*Street*] [*French*] (CED)
r.................. Ruins [*Topography*] (RU)
R.................. Rumunia [*Romania*] [*Polish*]
R.................. Russian (RU)
R.................. Rzeka [*River*] [*Polish*] (NAU)
R.................. Siding Track [*Topography*] (RU)
°R.................. Stopien Reaumura [*Degree Reaumur*] [*Polish*]
r.................. Was Born (RU)
RA.............. Address Register [*Computers*] (RU)
RA.............. Agglutination Reaction (RU)
RA.............. Emergency Relay (RU)
Ra.............. Radical [*Chemistry*] (BU)
RA.............. Radio Alger (MAR)
RA.............. Radio Plate Battery (RU)
r/a.............. Radioactivity (RU)
RA.............. Rdeca Armada [*Red Army*] (YU)
RA.............. Recherches Africaines. Etudes Guineennes [*Conakry*] [*A publication*] (MAR)
RA.............. Rechtsanwalt [*German*]
RA.............. Reconnaissance Aviation (BU)
RA.............. Reconnaissance Aviation (RU)
RA.............. Redacteur Adjoint (MAR)
RA.............. Rentgen Aparat [*X-Ray Apparatus*] (YU)
RA.............. Republica Argentina [*Argentine Republic*]
ra.............. Repuloallomas [*Airport, Airbase*] (HU)
RA.............. Resguardo Aduanero [*Customs Police*] [*Peruvian*] (LA)
RA.............. Revue Africaine, Bulletin de la Societe Historique Algerienne [*Alger*] [*A publication*] (MAR)
RA.............. Robotnicka Akademia [*Workers' Academy*] (CZ)
Ra.............. Roca [*Rock*] [*Spanish*] (NAU)
Ra.............. Rocha [*Rock*] [*Portuguese*] (NAU)
RA.............. Rocket Artillery (RU)
RA.............. Royal Artillery (ML)
RA.............. Ruda Armada [*Red Army*] (CZ)
RA.............. Rudnik Antimona [*Antimony Mine*] (YU)
RA.............. Russian Archives (RU)
RA.............. Subscriber's Meter (RU)
RAA.............. Recueil des Actes Administratifs de l'Algerie (MAR)
RAA.............. Royal Australian Artillery (ML)
raam............ Raamatussa [*or Raamatun Kielessa*] [*In the Bible or Biblical Phrase*] [*Finnish*]
raap............ Reconnaissance Artillery Regiment (BU)
raav............ Army Aviation Company (BU)
RAB............ Raad van Advies voor Bedrijfsinformatie [*Rotterdam*]
Rab............ Rabatt [*Discount*] [*German*]
RAB............ Rasprskavajuce Aviobombe [*Fragmentation Air Bombs*] (YU)
RAB............ Rentjana Anggaran Belandja [*Draft Budget*] (IN)
RAB............ Republic Address Bureau (RU)
RAB............ Republik Arab Bersatu [*United Arab Republic*] (ML)
rab............ Worker (RU)
rab............ Worker (BU)
rabatr.......... Artillery Reconnaissance Battery (RU)
rabbat.......... Labor Battalion (RU)
rabbrig........ Work Brigade, Operating Crew (RU)
Rabfak........ Workers' School Department (BU)
rab gor........ Workers' Settlement [*Topography*] (RU)
RABIS.......... Trade Union of Workers in the Arts (RU)
Rabiz.......... Art Workers' Trade Union (BU)
Rabkhim...... Trade Union of Chemical Industry Workers (RU)
Rabkop........ Digger [*Mining*] (BU)
Rabkor........ Workers' Newspaper Correspondent (BU)
Rabkrin........ Workers' and Peasants' Inspection [*1920-1934*] (RU)
rab pos........ Workers' Settlement [*Topography*] (RU)
Rabpros...... Trade Union of Education Workers (RU)
Rabsel.......... Worker-Peasant Solidarity (BU)
Rabselkor... Workers' and Peasants' Correspondent (BU)
Rabshveyprom... Trade Union of Garment Industry Workers (RU)
Rabsnab...... State Workers' Supply Enterprise (BU)
rac.............. Racemisch [*Racemic*] [*German*]
RAC.............. Recueil de Pieces sur l'Administration et le Commerce (MAR)

RAC............ Regies d'Approvisionnement et de Commercialisation (MAR)
RAC............ Representantes de Ambientes Cristianos [*Representatives of Christian Surroundings*] [*Spanish*] (WER)
RAC............ Research Analysis Corporation (MAR)
RAC............ Rijks Advies Commissie voor de Openbare Bibliotheken
RAC............ Routiere Automobile Casablancaise (MAR)
RAC............ Royal African Company (MAR)
RAC............ Royal Air Cambodge [*Royal Air Cambodia*] (CL)
RAC............ Royal Automobile Club (MAR)
RACAM....... Rassemblement Camerounais (MAR)
RACC.......... Rhodesian African Chamber of Commerce (AF)
RAD............ Artillery Reconnaissance Battalion (RU)
rad.............. Radian (RU)
rad.............. Radio [*Radio*] [*Finnish*]
rad.............. Radio Plant [*Topography*] (RU)
rad.............. Radioallomas [*Radio Station*] (HU)
rad.............. Radioengineering (BU)
Rad.............. Radyo [*Radio*] (TU)
RAD............ Royal Academy of Dancing (MAR)
RADAM....... RADAR da Amazonia [*Amazon RADAR*] [*Brazilian*] (LA)
radb............ Radio Battalion (BU)
radd............ Radio Battalion (RU)
RADECO..... Rassemblement des Democrats du Congo (MAR)
RADELKISZ... Radioaktiv es Elektronikus Merokeszulekeket Kivitelezo Kisipari Termeloszovetkezet [*Artisan Cooperative of Measuring Instruments for Radioactivity and Electronics*] (HU)
RADEM....... Regie Autonome de Distribution d'Eau et d'Electricite Meknes (MAR)
RADEO........ Rassemblement Democratique Congolais (MAR)
RADER........ Rassemblement Democratique Ruandaise (MAR)
rad gen........ Radiation Genetics (RU)
Radierg....... Radierung [*Etching*] [*German*]
RADIOBRAS... Empresa Brasileira de Radiodifusao [*Brazilian Radiobroadcasting Company*] (LA)
Radiometeotsentr... Radio-Meteorological Center (RU)
Radioprom... Radio Industry (BU)
radiost......... Radio Station (RU)
Radiostroy... Construction of Radio Stations (BU)
Radiostroy... Trust of the Ministry of Communications, USSR (RU)
radn............ Reconnaissance Artillery Battalion (BU)
RADO.......... Regional Agriculture Development Officer (MAR)
radp............ Radio Regiment (BU)
RADP.......... Republique Algerienne Democratique et Populaire [*Democratic and People's Republic of Algeria*] (AF)
radr............ Radio Company (BU)
radr............ Radio Company (RU)
rad st.......... Radio Station [*Topography*] (RU)
RAD-UDRT... Respect voor Arbeid en Democratie/Union Democratique pour le Respect du Travail [*Respect for Labor and Democracy/ Democratic Union for the Respect of Labor*] [*Belgian*] (PPE)
radz............ Radziecki [*Soviet*] [*Polish*]
RAE............ Air Reconnaissance Squadron (RU)
RAe............ Rechtsanwalte [*Attorneys at Law*] [*German*]
RAE............ Republique Arabe d'Egypte (MAR)
RAE............ Royal Australian Engineers (ML)
RaEl............ Radium Element [*Radium Element*] [*German*]
RAF............ Radiofelderites [*Radio Reconnaissance*] (HU)
Raf.............. Rafineri [*Refinery*] (TU)
raf............... Reconnaissance Aviation Squadron (BU)
RAF............ Rhodesian Air Force (AF)
RAF............ Rote Armee Fraktion [*Red Army Faction (Baader-Meinhof Group)*] (EG)
RAFAMET... Raciborska Fabryka Obrabiarek [*Raciborz Machine Tool Plant*] (POL)
RAFECO...... Rassemblement Federal Congolais (MAR)
raff.............. Raffiniert [*Refined*] [*German*]
RAFI............ Political Party [*Israeli*] (ME)
Rafie............ Raffinerie [*Refinery*] [*Military map abbreviation*] [*World War I*] [*French*] (MTD)
RAFILM....... Radio- es Filmmechanikai Szolgalat [*Radio and Motion Picture Repair Service*] (HU)
RAG-........... Deep-Water Radiometer (RU)
Rag.............. Ragione [*Business Establishment*] [*Italian*] (CED)
RAG............ Reconnaissance Air Group [*British*] (RU)
RAG............ Referees Association of Ghana (MAR)
Ragaz.......... Mixed Russian-American Compressed Gas Joint-Stock Company (RU)
RAGK.......... High Command Artillery Reserve (RU)
rahv............ Rahvaanomaista Kielta [*Vulgar*] [*Finnish*]
RAI............. Baterai [*Battery (Artillery)*] (IN)
RAI............. Radioactive Isotope (RU)
RAI............. Rijwiel- en Automobiel-Industrie [*Bicycle and Automobile Manufacturers' Organization*] [*Dutch*] (WEN)
RAID........... Regie Autonome Intercommunale de Distribution d'Eau et d'Electricite [*Autonomous Intercommunal Administration for the Distribution of Water and Electricity*] [*Moroccan*] (AF)
RAI (MDLP in Portugal)... Rede de Accao Interna [*Internal Action Net*] [*Portuguese*] (WER)
RAIMK......... Russian Academy of the History of Material Culture (RU)
RAI-TV........ Radio Audizioni Italiane-Televisione [*Italian Radio Broadcasting and Television Company*] (WER)
RAIZ........... Russian-American Tool Plant (RU)
rajz............. Rajzolta [*Drawn By*] (HU)
rak.............. Observation Air Wing (BU)
rak.............. Rakentaminen [*or Rakennustyot*] [*Building*] [*Finnish*]
RAK............ Rayon Administrative Commission (RU)
RAK............ Regeln fuer die Alphabetische Katalogisierung
RAKAH........ New Communist List [*Israeli*] (ME)
RAKhN........ Russian Academy of Art Sciences (RU)
rakp............ Rakpart [*Dock, Embankment*] (HU)
RAL............ Republique Arabe Libyenne (MAR)
RAL............ Rotary Transfer Machine (RU)
RALE.......... Railway Association of Locomotive Enginemen (MAR)
RALIS.......... Regimento de Artilharia de Lisboa [*Artillery Regiment of Lisbon*] [*Portuguese*] (WER)
RALSC......... Rhodesian African Labor Supply Commission (MAR)
RAM............ Royal Air Maroc (MAR)
RAM............ "Russian Aircraft Engine" - Aircraft Engine Designed by A. D. Shvetsov [*1923*] (RU)
RAM............ Societe de Representation Automobile et Materiaux (MAR)
RAMO.......... Rafinerie Mineralnich Oleju [*Mineral Oil Refinery*] (CZ)
RAMS.......... Rural Assessment/Manpower Study (MAR)
RAMSA........ Radioaeronautica Mexicana, Sociedad Anonima [*Mexican Aeronautical Radio, Incorporated*] (LA)
RAN............ Power System Active Load Distributor (RU)
RAN............ Regie des Chemins de Fer Abidjan-Niger [*Abidjan-Niger Railway Administration*] (AF)
RAN............ Reseau Abidjan-Niger (MAR)
RAN............ Resistencia Armada Nacionalista [*Nationalist Armed Resistance*] [*Brazilian*] (LA)
RAN............ Russian Academy of Sciences [*1724-1925*] (RU)
RANA.......... Rassemblement National Congolais (MAR)
RANA.......... Rhodesia and Nyasaland Airways Ltd. (MAR)
RANFAN...... Rassemblement National des Francais Rapatries d'Afrique du Nord et d'Outre-Mer
RANIION..... Russian Association of Scientific Research Institutes of Social Sciences [*1923-1930*] (RU)
RANION....... Russian Association of Scientific Research Institutes of Social Sciences [*1923-1930*] (RU)
ranis............ Science and Art Workers (RU)
ransk........... Ranskaa [*or Ranskaksi*] [*Finnish*]
ransk........... Ranskan Kielta [*or Ranskalainen*] [*French*] [*Finnish*]
rao.............. Airfield Maintenance Company (RU)
RAO............ Russian Archaeological Society (RU)
RAP............ Air Reconnaissance Regiment (RU)
rap.............. Artillery Reconnaissance Regiment (RU)
RAP............ Automatic Start Relay (RU)
RAP............ Regie des Agglomeres du Pays [*Saharan*] (MAR)
RAP............ Regie Autonome des Petroles (MAR)
RAP............ Regiment d'Artillerie Parachutiste [*Algerian*] (MAR)
RAP............ Reglement d'Administration Publique [*North African*] (MAR)
RAP............ Republik Arab Persatuan [*United Arab Republic*] (IN)
RAP............ Rezervni Delovi, Alata, i Pribora [*Spare Parts, Equipment, and Tools*] [*Military*] (YU)
RAP............ Rhodesian Action Party (AF)
RAP............ Robotnicza Agencja Prasowa [*Worker's Press Agency*] (POL)
RAPA.......... Ramassage du Paddy [*Paddy Harvesting*] [*Cambodian*] (CL)
RAPC.......... Regie d'Acconage du Port de Casablanca (MAR)
RAPELU...... Rassemblement des Peuples Luba (MAR)
RAPIR.......... Radiation Pyrometer (RU)
RAPKh........ Russian Association of Proletarian Artists [*1931-1932*] (RU)
RAPM.......... Russian Association of Proletarian Musicians [*1923-1930*] (RU)
RAPO.......... Russian Pharmaceutical Association (RU)
RAPP.......... Russian Association of Proletarian Writers [*1923-1932*] (RU)
RAPRA........ Rubber and Plastics Research Association (EA)
RAR............ Rhodesian African Rifles (MAR)
RARK.......... Automatic Radiometer for Radioactive Logging (RU)
RARK.......... Sectional Equipment for Radioactive Logging (RU)
RARU.......... Rural Access Road Unit (MAR)
RARZ.......... Rayon Automobile Repair Plant (RU)
RARZ.......... Riga Automobile Repair Plant (RU)
RAS............ Purified Alkyl Aryl Sulfonate (RU)
RAS............ Relay-Controlled Automatic System (RU)
RAS............ Rijks Archief School
RAS............ Royal Academy of Science [*London*]
RASC.......... Royal Agricultural Society of the Commonwealth (MAR)
RASD.......... Republique Arabe Sahraoui Democratique [*Saharan Democratic Arab Republic*] [*Use SDAR*] (AF)
RASIT.......... RADAR de Surveillance au Sol (MAR)
RASK.......... Royal Agricultural Society of Kenya (MAR)
RASO.......... Russian-British Raw Materials Company (RU)
rasp............ Disintegration, Decay [*Nuclear physics and engineering*] (RU)
rasp/min..... Disintegrations per Minute (RU)
raspredpunkt... Distribution Center (RU)
rasp/sek..... Disintegrations per Second (RU)
rassh........... Expanded (RU)
RAST.......... Analytical Computer Station (BU)
rast............. Plant [*Botany*] (BU)
rast............. Vegetation (RU)

rastsenkom ... Wage Commission (RU)
rastv .... Solubility (RU)
RAT .... Rad Anafalbetskih Tecajeva [*Program of Courses for Illiterates*] [*Military*] (YU)
RAT .... Radio Autotransformer (RU)
RAT .... Red Andina de Telecomunicaciones [*Andean Telecommunications Network*] (LA)
RAT .... Relay Autotransformer (RU)
RAT .... Reseau des Amis de la Terre [*Network of Friends of the Earth*] [*French*] (PPE)
RAT .... Resistance Armee Tunisienne [*Tunisian Armed Resistance*] (PD)
RATAA .... Regione Autonoma Trentino Alto Adige [*Autonomous Region of Trentino South Tyrol*] [*Italian*] (WER)
RATAC .... RADAR de Tir de l'Artillerie de Campagne (MAR)
RATAO .... Russian-Austrian Joint-Stock Trade Company (RU)
RATAU .... Ukrainian News Agency (RU)
RATC .... Regie Autonome des Transports de la Ville de Casablanca [*North African*] (MAR)
RATECO ..... Radio Tecnica Colombiana [*Bogota*] (COL)
rato............ Airfield Technical Support Company (RU)
RATO .... Russian-Austrian Joint-Stock Trade Company (RU)
RATP........... Regie Autonome des Transports Parisiens [*Independent Parisian Transport System*] [*French*] (WER)
rats............. Rationalization, Efficiency-Expert (RU)
rats............. Rationalizer, Rationalization (BU)
Rats............ Ratsionalizatsiya [*Rationalization*] [*A periodical*] (BU)
RATS........... Rayon Automatic Telephone Exchange (RU)
Ratsbyuro ... Rationalizations Bureau (BU)
ratsemich ... Racemic (RU)
ratsiya......... Radio Station [*Topography*] (RU)
Rats predlozh ... Rationalization Suggestion (RU)
RATU........... Rated Atmospheric Temperature Conditions (RU)
RATZ........... Rustavi Nitrogen Fertilizer Plant (RU)
Rau............. Radeau [*Raft*] [*Military map abbreviation*] [*World War I*] [*French*] (MTD)
RAU............ Railway African Union [*Ugandan*] (AF)
RAU............ Rand Afrikaans University (MAR)
RAU............ Republique Arabe Unie [*French*]
Rau............. Ruisseau [*Stream*] [*French*] (NAU)
RAUK .... Reservialiupseerikoulu [*Finnish*]
raut............. Rautatiet [*Railways*] [*Finnish*]
RAV............ Rahmen-Absatzvertrag [*Basic Sales Contract*] (EG)
Rav .... Ravin [*Ravine*] [*Military map abbreviation*] [*World War I*] [*French*] (MTD)
RAVE.......... Registro de Aspirantes a Viviendas de Emergencia [*Registry of Emergency Housing Candidates*] [*Uruguayan*] (LA)
RAVEL......... Posta Radioveteltechnikai es Elektroakusztikai Uzeme [*Post Office Branch for Radio Reception and Acoustics*] (HU)
RAVISZ .... Radio es Villamossagi Szolgalat Kisipari Termeloszovetkezet [*Artisan Cooperative for Radio and Electric Service Enterprise*] (HU)
ravp............ Air Reconnaissance Regiment (RU)
Ravt............ Ravitaillement [*Revictualing*] [*Military*] [*French*] (MTD)
rav-vo.......... Equality, Equation (RU)
RAW........... Rationalisatie en Automatisering Wegenbouw [*Ede*]
RAW........... Reichsbahnausbesserungswerk [*GDR Railroad Repair Yard*] (EG)
RAWB.......... Raad van Advies voor het Wetenschapsbeleid [*'s-Gravenhage*]
RAWU.......... Railway Associated Workers Union [*Rhodesian*] (AF)
Ray .... Rayon [*German*]
ray .... Rayon, City District (RU)
raydorkhoz ... Rayon Highway Department (RU)
rayfo........... Rayon Finance Department (RU)
raygosstrakh ... Rayon State Insurance Inspection (RU)
rayGUMTO ... Rayon Office of the Main Administration of Materials and Equipment Supply (RU)
Raykom....... Rayon Committee (BU)
Raykoman... Rayon Commandant's Office (BU)
Raykomisiya ... Rayon Commission (BU)
Raykomitet ... Rayon Committee (BU)
raykomkhoz ... City District Department of Municipal Services (RU)
raykommunkhoz ... City District Department of Municipal Services (RU)
raykomol..... Rayon Committee of the Young Communist League (RU)
raykompart ... Rayon Party Committee (RU)
RAYKOMVOD ... Rayon Committee of the Water Transportation Workers' Trade Union (RU)
Raykoop...... Rayon Cooperative Union (BU)
raykprofsozh ... Rayon Committee of the Railroad Workers' Trade Union (RU)
raykul'tvod ... Rayon Committee for the Cultural Education of Water Transportation Workers (RU)
raykurupr.... Rayon Administration of Health Resorts (RU)
rayles .... Rayon Forest Commission (RU)
rayleskhoz ... Rayon Lumber Industry Establishment (RU)
rayleskom... Rayon Forest Commission (RU)
raymag........ Rayon Store, City District Store (RU)
raynarobraz ... Rayon Department of Public Education (RU)
raynezhilotdel ... Rayon Department of Nonresidential Buildings (RU)
rayONO....... Rayon Department of Public Education (RU)
rayplan........ Rayon Planning Commission (RU)
raypo........... Rayon Consumers' Society (RU)
raypotrebsoyuz ... Rayon Union of Consumers' Societies (RU)
rayprofsovet ... Rayon Trade Union Council (RU)
rayprofsozh ... Rayon Committee of the Railroad Transportation Workers' Trade Union (RU)
raypromtrest ... Rayon Industry Trust (RU)
raypur .... Rayon Administration (RU)
raySES........ Rayon Sanitary and Epidemiological Station (RU)
raysobes..... Rayon Department of Social Security (RU)
raysovkhoz ... Rayon Sovkhoz Department (RU)
Raysuvet..... Rayon Council (BU)
raytekhsnab ... Rayon Office of Materials and Equipment Supply (RU)
raytop.......... Rayon Department of the Local Fuel Industry (RU)
raytorgotdel ... Rayon Trade Department (RU)
rayupolminzag ... Rayon Representative of the Ministry of Procurement (RU)
Rayvetlechebnitsa ... Rayon Veterinary Hospital (RU)
rayvodkhoz ... Rayon Water Management Department (RU)
rayVTEK...... Rayon Medical Commission for Determination of Disability (RU)
rayzag .... Rayon Procurement Office (RU)
rayzags .... Rayon Civil Registry Office (RU)
Rayzankoop ... Rayon Artisans' Cooperative (BU)
rayzdrav...... Rayon Department of Public Health (RU)
rayzhilkommunotdel ... Rayon Communal Housing Department (RU)
rayzhilupr ... Rayon Housing Administration (RU)
Rayzo .... Rayon Land Department (RU)
rayzu .... Rayon Land Administration (RU)
raz.............. Different [*or Various*] (BU)
RAZ .... Referees Association of Zambia (MAR)
RAZ .... Revolutionaere Aufbauorganisation Zurich [*Zurich Revolutionary Organizing Committee*] [*Swiss*] (WEN)
raz .... Ruins [*Topography*] (RU)
raz .... Siding Track [*Topography*] (RU)
razb............ Diluted, Thinned (RU)
RAZB.......... Reconnaissance Battery (RU)
razbat......... Reconnaissance Battalion (BU)
Razch s/ka pri BNB ... Checking Account at the Bulgarian National Bank (BU)
razd............ Section, Chapter (RU)
raz der........ Destroyed Village (RU)
razd pag...... Broken Pagination (BU)
razd pag...... Separate Pagination (RU)
razg............ Colloquial (BU)
razg............ Colloquial Word (RU)
RAZh-.......... Radioactive Liquid Analyzer (RU)
RAZhA .... Regional'naia Assotsiatsia Zhitelei Angoly (MAR)
razm........... Dimensions, Proportions, Measures (BU)
Raznoeksport ... All-Union Association for the Export of Miscellaneous Goods (RU)
Raznoimport ... All-Union Association for the Import of Miscellaneous Goods (RU)
Raznoiznos ... State Commercial Enterprise for Export and Import (BU)
razr............. Class, Category (RU)
razr............. Destroyed, Demolished [*Topography*] (RU)
razrabot ...... Development, Elaboration [*Bibliography*] (RU)
razresh....... Authorized, Permitted (RU)
razsh .... Expanded [*Edition*] (BU)
RAZU.......... Razprave Akademije Znanosti in Umetnosti [*Transactions of the Slovenian Academy of Sciences*] [*Ljubljana*] [*A publication*] (YU)
razv .... Ruins [*Topography*] (RU)
razv d .... Village Ruins [*Topography*] (RU)
razv kh .... Farmstead Ruins [*Topography*] (RU)
razv pos ...... Settlement Ruins [*Topography*] (RU)
razv ukr...... Fortification Ruins [*Topography*] (RU)
raz zam .... Castle Ruins [*Topography*] (RU)
Rb............... Battalion Radio Station (RU)
RB............... Biovular Twins (RU)
Rb............... Blocking Relay (RU)
RB............... Bombing Manual (RU)
rb............... Diluted, Thinned (RU)
Rb............... Fishing Boat (RU)
RB............... Hand Ram (RU)
RB............... Labor Battalion (RU)
rb............... Missile Base (BU)
RB............... Racunovodstveni Biro [*Accounting Bureau*] (YU)
RB............... Rada Bezpecnosti [*Security Council*] [*United Nations*] (CZ)
RB............... Radio Beograd [*Radio Belgrade*] (YU)
RB............... Radio Unit [*of a radiosonde*] (RU)
RB............... Razvod Braka [*Divorce*] (YU)
rb............... Reconnaissance Battalion (BU)
RB............... Reconnaissance Battalion (RU)
RB............... Regulating Unit (RU)
Rb............... Reichsbahn [*GDR Railroad*] (EG)
Rb............... Repair Base, Maintenance Base (RU)
RB............... Republic Library (RU)
R/b.............. Ribarski Brod [*Fishing Boat*] (YU)
rb............... Riz Blanc [*Polished Rice*] (CL)
rb............... Rok Biezacy [*or Roku Biezacego*] [*This Year*] [*Polish*]
rb............... Rubel [*Ruble*] (POL)
rb............... Ruble (RU)

RB............... Rucna Bomba [*Hand Grenade*] (YU)
RB............... Rucni Bacac [*Hand Thrower*] (YU)
RB............... Rudne Bane [*Mines for Non-Ferrous Metal Ores*] (CZ)
RB............... Rudnik Bakra [*Copper Mine*] [*Majdanpek*] (YU)
RB............... Rudnik Barita [*Barite Mine*] (YU)
RB............... Rudnik Boksita [*Bauxite Mine*] (YU)
RB............... Ruhazati Bolt [*Clothing Store*] (HU)
RBA............ Rabat Airport (MAR)
RBA............ Rehoboth Baster Association [*Namibian*] (PPW)
RBA............ Reichsbahnamt [*GDR Railroad Division*] (EG)
RBB............ Sondervorschrift fuer die Regelung des Betriebes auf der Elektrischen Berliner S-Bahn [*Special Traffic Regulations for the Berlin Electric S-Bahn*] (EG)
RbbD.......... Reichsbahnbaudirektion [*GDR Railroad Construction Directorate*] (EG)
Rbbu.......... Reichsbahnbauunion [*GDR Railroad Construction Enterprise*] (EG)
RBC............ Regional Border Committee [*Thai-Malay border*] (ML)
RBC............ Rhodesia Broadcasting Company (AF)
RBCO......... Regional Border Committee Office [*Thai-Malay border*] (ML)
RBD............ Powder-Propelled Rocket Engine (BU)
RBD............ Reichsbahndirektion [*GDR Railroad Directorate*] (EG)
RBD............ Short-Range Missile (RU)
RBDF.......... Royal Bahamian Defense Force (LA1)
RBEI........... Revenu Brut des Entrepreneurs Individuels (MAR)
rbetr........... Concrete Construction Company (RU)
rbetr........... Concrete Works Company (BU)
Rbf.............. Rangierbahnhof [*Classification Yard*] (EG)
RBF............ Recurrent Boolean Function (RU)
Rbi.............. Recibi [*Spanish*]
RB II........... Radio Beograd II [*Radio Belgrade, Station 2*] (YU)
RBL............ Research Bureau Limited (MAR)
rbl.............. Szovjet Rubel [*Soviet Ruble*] (HU)
RBM............ Richards Bay Minerals (MAR)
RBMU......... Regions Beyond Missionary Union (MAR)
RBN-.......... Radioisotope Blocking Attachment (RU)
RBO............ Russian Botanical Society (RU)
RBOMU...... Russian Bibliographic Society at the Moscow State University (RU)
RBP............ Radar Bomb Sight (RU)
RBPC.......... Roads and Bridges Public Corporation [*Sudanese*] (MAR)
rbr.............. Missile Brigade (BU)
rbrtr............ Armored Carrier Company (RU)
RBS............ Radiolosko Borbena Sredstva [*Radiological Combat Equipment*] (YU)
RBS............ Russian Biographical Dictionary [*A publication*] (RU)
RBT............ Roadstead Diesel Tugboat (RU)
rbtr............. Armored Carrier Company (RU)
RBU............ Concrete Mortar Unit (RU)
RBU............ Depth-Charge Rocket Launcher (RU)
RBU-.......... Radioisotope Blocking Device (RU)
RBU............ Revirni Bansky Urad [*Coal Basin Mining Office*] (CZ)
RBV............ Radiologiai, Biologiai, es Vegyi Vedelem [*Radiological, Biological, and Chemical Defense*] (HU)
RBVA.......... Rhodesian Bantu Voters' Association (MAR)
RBVZ.......... Russian-Baltic Railroad-Car Plant (RU)
RC............... Chiny [*China*] [*Polish*]
RC............... Radio Centar [*Radio Center*] [*Military*] (YU)
RC............... Radio-Cevi [*Radio Tubes*] (YU)
RC............... Raymond Candau (MAR)
RC............... Registrar of Companies (MAR)
RC............... Registre du Commerce [*French*]
RC............... Rest Camp (MAR)
RC............... Retenues Collinaires (MAR)
RC............... Ribolovni Centar [*Fishing Center*] (YU)
RC............... Ridici Cviceni [*Exercise Umpires*] (CZ)
RC............... Riz Cargo [*Brown Rice*] [*Cambodian*] (CL)
RC............... Roman Catholic Church (MAR)
RC............... Route Coloniale [*Colonial Highway*] (CL)
RCA............ Regional Committee for Africa (MAR)
RCA............ Republique Centrafricaine [*Central African Republic*] [*Use CAR*] (AF)
RCA............ Rozpravy Ceske Akademie Ved a Umeni [*Transactions of the Czech Academy of Sciences and Arts*] [*A publication*] (CZ)
RCA............ Rozpravy Ceskoslovenske Akademie Ved [*Transactions of the Czechoslovak Academy of Sciences*] [*A publication*] (CZ)
RCB............ Rationalisation des Choix Budgetaires [*Rationalization of Budgetary Choices*] [*French*] (WER)
RCC............ Residual Oil Catalytic Conversion Process [*Libyan*] (MAR)
RCC............ Revolution Command Council [*Libyan*] (ME)
RCC............ Revolution Command Council [*Liberian*] (AF)
RCC............ Revolutionary Command Council [*Iraqi*] (PD)
RCC............ Rijks Computer Centrum
RCCC.......... Regiment Colonial de Chasseurs de Chars (MAR)
RCCKP....... Rassemblement des Chefs Coutumiers du Kongo Portugais (MAR)
RCD............ Regional Co-Operation for Development (MAR)
RCDS.......... Ring Christlich-Demokratischer Studenten [*Christian-Democratic Student Ring*] [*West German*] (WEN)
RCDTC....... Regional Cooperative Development and Training Centre [*Sudanese*] (MAR)
RCFM.......... Regie du Chemin de Fer du Mali (MAR)
RCFS........... Regie des Chemins de Fer du Senegal (MAR)
RCG............ Rhodesia Christian Group (MAR)
RCH............ Chile [*Chile*] [*Polish*]
RCh............. Number Register (RU)
RCh............. Working Drawing (RU)
RCh............. Worm Reducer (RU)
RChG.......... Partial Group Relay (RU)
RChK.......... Rayon Extraordinary Commission for Combating Counterrevolution and Sabotage (RU)
Rchn........... Rechnung [*German*]
RChO.......... Rota Chemicke Ochrany [*Chemical Defense Company*] (CZ)
RChPz......... Rota Chemickeho Pruzkumu [*Chemical Reconnaissance Company*] (CZ)
RChPzH...... Radiacni a Chemicka Pruzkumna Hlidka [*Radiation and Chemical Reconnaissance Patrol*] (CZ)
RChRPz....... Rota Chemickeho a Radiacniho Pruzkumu [*Chemical and Radiation Reconnaissance Company*] (CZ)
RChS........... Solution for Cleaning Firearm Barrels (RU)
RChV........... Sensitivity Time Control (RU)
RCiK........... Rada Czytelnictwa i Ksiazki [*Council on Reading and Books*] [*Polish*]
RCK............ Rada Czytelnictwa i Ksiazki [*Council on Reading and Books*] (POL)
RCK............ Rasinski Cetnicki Korpus [*Rasina Chetnik Corps*] [*World War II*] (YU)
RCLB.......... Revolutionary Communist League of Britain (PPW)
RCM............ Rassemblement Chretien de Madagascar [*Christian Rally of Madagascar*] (AF)
RCM............ Roan Consolidated Mines (MAR)
RCM............ Roman Catholic Missions (MAR)
RCN............ Radio Cadena Nacional [*Medellin*] (COL)
RCN............ Reactor Centrum Nederland [*Netherlands Reactor Center*] [*Later, ECN*] (WEN)
RCO............ Rota Civilni Obrany [*Civil Defense Company*] (CZ)
RCP............ Regiment de Chasseurs Parachutistes [*Algerian*] (MAR)
RCP............ Republican Colored Party [*South African*] (AF)
RCP............ Revolutionary Communist Party of India (PPW)
RCR............ Riaditelstvo pre Cestovny Ruch [*Central Bureau for the Promotion of Tourist Trade*] (CZ)
RCRF.......... Rei Cretariae Romanae Favtores [*Society of Roman Ceramic Archaeologists*] (EA)
RCS............ Regiment de Commandement et de Soutien [*Headquarters and Support Regiment*] [*Upper Voltan*] (AF)
RCS............ Republika Ceskoslovenska [*Czechoslovak Republic (until 1960)*] (CZ)
RCTL.......... Regio Corpo Truppe Libiche (MAR)
RCU............ Rungwe Central Union (MAR)
RCU............ Rural Cooperative Union [*Iranian*] (MAR)
RCV............ Rezervni Centar Veze [*Reserve Communications Center*] [*Military*] (YU)
RCVV.......... Rhodesiese Christelike Vrouevereniging (MAR)
RCWT......... Reseau des Chemins de Fer et du Wharf du Togo [*Togo Railroad and Wharf Network*] (AF)
RD............... Difference of Longitudes (RU)
RD............... "Distance Record" [*Aircraft designed by A. N. Tupolev, also called ANT-25*] (RU)
RD............... Distributing Board (RU)
RD............... Jet Engine (RU)
RD............... Long-Range Reconnaissance Aircraft (RU)
RD............... Maternity Home (RU)
rd................ Missile Battalion (BU)
RD............... Observation Battalion [*Artillery*] (RU)
RD............... Pressure-Regulator (RU)
RD............... Pressure Relay (RU)
RD............... Rabotnichesko Delo [*Workers' Affairs*] [*A periodical*] (BU)
rd................ Radian [*Radian (Unit of arc measure)*] [*Polish*]
RD............... Radio Battalion (RU)
RD............... Radio-Frequency Two-Frequency [*Cable*] (RU)
RD............... Radioisotopic Pickup (RU)
Rd............... Rand (MAR)
RD............... Reconnaissance Patrol (BU)
RD............... Reconnaissance Patrol (RU)
RD............... Reditelstvi Drah [*Railroad Directorate*] (CZ)
Rd............... Reduktion [*Reduction*] [*German*]
RD............... Reforma Democratica [*Democratic Reform*] [*Spanish*] (WER)
RD............... Republica Democratica [*Democratic Republic*] (RO)
RD............... Reversible Diesel Engine, Reversible Engine (RU)
RD............... Rivista Dalmatica [*Dalmatian Review (in Italian)*] [*Zadar*] [*A publication*] (YU)
RD............... Rizeni Dopravy [*Transport Direction Center*] (CZ)
RD............... Rocket Engine (BU)
RD............... Rocket Engine, Rocket Motor (RU)
RD............... Rolnicke Druzstvo [*Agricultural Cooperative*] (CZ)
rd................ Rund [*About, Approximately*] [*German*]
rd................ Rutherford (RU)
RD............... Rychla Divise [*Assault Division*] (CZ)
RD............... Taxiway (RU)
RDA............ Automatic Pressure Regulator (RU)
RDA............ Manual Respirator (RU)
RDA............ Rassemblement Democratique Afar (MAR)

RDA............ Rassemblement Democratique Africain [*Niger*] (PD)
RDA............ Rassemblement Democratique Africain [*Ivorian*] (PPW)
RDA............ Rassemblement Democratique Algerien (MAR)
RDA............ Republica Democratica Alema [*German Democratic Republic*] [*Use GDR*] [*Portuguese*] (WER)
RDA............ Republique Democratique Allemande [*German Democratic Republic - GDR*] (CL)
RDA............ Ruvuma Development Association (MAR)
RDAG.......... Rassemblement Democratique Africain de la Guinee (MAR)
Rda M.......... Reverenda Madre [*Reverend Mother*] [*Spanish*]
RdB............ Rat des Bezirkes [*Bezirk Council*] (EG)
RDB............ Reddingsdaadbond [*Aid Society*] [*South African*] (AF)
RDB............ Reisebeschreibungen von Deutschen Beamten und Kriegsleuten im Dienst der Niederlaendischen West- und Ost-Indischen Kompagnien [*The Hague*] (MAR)
RDC............ Radiodiffusion du Cameroun (MAR)
RDC............ Rassemblement Democratique Caledonien [*Caledonian Democratic Rally*] (PPW)
RDC............ Republique Democratique du Congo (MAR)
RDC............ Rural Development Centre [*Sudanese*] (MAR)
RDC............ Saudi Company for Research and Development (ME)
RDD............ Long-Range Missile (RU)
RDD............ Rassemblement Democratique Dahomeen (MAR)
RDD............ Regional Development Director (MAR)
RDD............ Republik Demokratik Djerman [*German Democratic Republic*] (IN)
RDD............ Rolnicke Dobytkarske Druzstvo [*Farmers' Livestock Cooperative*] (CZ)
RDE............ Regie Autonome Intercommunale de Distribution d'Eau et d'Electricite (MAR)
RDETS........ Republic Children's Excursion and Tourist Station (RU)
RDF............ Reddingsdaafonds (MAR)
RDG............ Republica Democratica Germana [*German Democratic Republic*] (RO)
RDG............ Smoke Hand Grenade (BU)
RDG............ Smoke Hand Grenade (RU)
RDJ............ Rudne Doly Jesenik [*Jesenik Mines for Non-Ferrous Metal Ores*] (CZ)
RD-1J.......... Rucni Dvogled Prvi Jugoslovenski [*Hand Binocular, 1st Yugoslav Model*] (YU)
RDJA.......... Rassemblement Democratique de la Jeunesse Angolaise (MAR)
RDK............ Rayon House of Culture (RU)
RDLGE........ Democratic Movement for the Liberation of Equatorial Guinea (PD)
RDLK.......... Rassemblement Democratique du Lac du Kwango et Kwilu (MAR)
rdm............ Company Decontamination Area (BU)
rdm............ Ground Decontamination Company (RU)
RDM............ Incremental-Code Modulation (RU)
RDM............ Rand Daily Mail (MAR)
RDM............ Republique Democratique de Madagascar [*Democratic Republic of Madagascar*] (AF)
RDN............ Low-Pressure Relay (RU)
rdn............ Missile Battalion (BU)
rdn............ Missile Battalion (RU)
Rdnot.......... Randnoten [*Marginal Notes*] [*German*]
RDNP.......... Rassemblement Democratique Nationaliste et Progressiste [*Progressive Nationalist and Democratic Assembly*] [*Haitian*] (PD)
RDNT.......... Workers' House of Folk Art (RU)
RDO............ Reaction to Moving Object (RU)
Rdo P.......... Reverendo Padre [*Reverend Father*] [*Spanish*]
RDP............ Area Traffic Control Point (RU)
RDP............ Direct Action Pressure Regulator (RU)
RDP............ Knapsack Decontamination Apparatus (RU)
RDP............ Manual Decontamination Apparatus (RU)
RDP-............ Pilot Pressure Regulator [*Oil equipment*] (RU)
RDP............ Portable Decontamination Apparatus (BU)
RDP............ Rassemblement Democratique Paysan (MAR)
RDP............ Regiment de Dragons Parachutistes [*Algerian*] (MAR)
RDP............ Rehoboth Democratic Party [*Namibian*] (AF)
RDP............ Rural Development Program (MAR)
RDP............ Snorkel (RU)
RDPA.......... Rayon House of Party Activists (RU)
RDPC.......... Rassemblement Democratique des Peuples Comoriens [*Democratic Rally of Comoro Peoples*] (AF)
RDPTT........ Radionica Direkcije PTT [*Workshop of the Postal, Telegraph, and Telephone Administration*] (YU)
RDR............ Rada Delegatow Robotniczych [*Council of Workers' Delegates*] (POL)
RDR............ Radiation Reconnaissance (BU)
RDRK.......... Republik Demokratik Rakjat Korea [*Korean People's Democratic Republic*] (IN)
RDS............ Area Traffic Control Service (RU)
RDS............ Has Worked with Radio Stations of the Democratic Countries [*Diploma for amateur radio operators*] (BU)
RDS............ Long-Range Radio Station (RU)
RDS............ Pressure Signal Relay (RU)
RDS............ Repubblica Democratica Somala (MAR)
RDS............ Traffic Control Area (RU)
RDS............ Two-Chamber Oxygen Pressure Reducer (RU)
RDS............ "Worked with All Countries of People's Democracy" [*Amateur radio operator's diploma*] (RU)
RDT............ Repubblica Democratica Tedesca [*German Democratic Republic*] [*Use GDR*] [*Italian*] (WER)
RDT............ Rolniczy Dom Towarowy [*Agricultural Department Store*] (POL)
RDT............ Solid-Propellant Rocket Engine (RU)
RDTT.......... Solid-Propellant Rocket Engine (RU)
RDV-............ Air Reducer (RU)
RDV............ High-Pressure Relay (RU)
RDV............ Republica Democratica Vietnam [*Democratic Republic of Vietnam*] (RO)
RDV............ Republik Demokratik Vietnam [*Democratic Republic of Vietnam*] (IN)
RDV............ Republique Democratique du Viet-Nam [*Democratic Republic of Vietnam*] [*Use DRV or North Vietnam*] (CL)
RDVN.......... Republique Democratique du Viet-Nam [*Democratic Republic of Vietnam*] [*Use DRV or North Vietnam*] (CL)
Rdy Nsr....... Radyo Nesriyati [*Radio Broadcast*] (TU)
RE............... Capacitance Regulator (RU)
RE............... Electromagnetic Relay (RU)
RE............... Fuel-Flow Regulator (RU)
RE............... Rada Europejska [*Council of Europe*] [*Polish*]
RE............... Radio Engineering and Electronics (RU)
re................ Rechts [*German*]
Re............... Recipe [*Spanish*]
RE............... Reconnaissance Squadron [*Aviation*] (RU)
Re............... Regelleistung [*Standard Capacity*] (EG)
RE............... Regimento de Engenharia [*Engineering Regiment*] [*Portuguese*] (WER)
RE............... Regulating Element, Control (RU)
RE............... Renovacion Espanola [*Spanish Renovation*] (PPE)
RE............... Retirado [*Retired*] [*Argentine*] (LA)
RE............... Reunion [*Two-letter standard code*] (CNC)
RE............... Revue d'Egyptologie [*Paris*] [*A publication*] (MAR)
Re............... Reynolds Number (RU)
Re............... Roche [*Rock*] [*French*] (NAU)
RE............... Roupie Mauricienne [*Mauritian*] (MAR)
RE............... Royal Engineers (ML)
REA............ Radio and Electronic Equipment (RU)
REA............ Radioelectronic Apparatus (BU)
REA............ Regie des Eaux Agricoles [*Agricultural Water Administration*] [*Tunisian*] (AF)
REAB.......... Radiotechnikai es Elektronikai Ipari Allando Bizottsaga (Kolcsonos Gazdasagi Segitseg Tanacsa) [*Council for Mutual Economic Assistance Permanent Committee for the Radio Technology and Electronics Industry*] (HU)
reabr.......... Rocket Artillery Brigade (RU)
reabr.......... Rocket-Launching Artillery Brigade (BU)
read............ Rocket-Launching Artillery Battalion (BU)
REAF.......... Royal Egyptian Air Force (MAR)
REAL.......... Recherches et Expansion d'Alimentation [*Nutrition Research and Expansion*] [*Ivorian*] (AF)
REAMERICA... Representaciones America Ltda. [*Medellin*] (COL)
reap............ Rocket Artillery Regiment (RU)
reap............ Rocket-Launching Artillery Regiment (BU)
REB............ Maintenance and Operation Base (RU)
reb.............. Roentgen Equivalent Man (RU)
REB............ Rural Electricity Board (MAR)
REBAR........ Regie des Batiments du Rwanda (MAR)
rebatr.......... Rocket Battery (RU)
rebatr.......... Rocket-Launching Battery (BU)
REBIA.......... Regional Building Institute for Africa (MAR)
REBIA.......... Regional Educational Building Institute for Africa (MAR)
rec.............. Recenzja [*or Recenzent*] [*Critic, Review or Reviewer*] [*Polish*]
RECE.......... Representacion Cubana en el Exilio [*Cuban Representation in Exile*] (LA)
rech............ Fluvial, River (RU)
Rechizdat... "River Transportation" Publishing House (RU)
rechn.......... River, Fluvial (RU)
Rechsudotrest... All-Union River Shipbuilding Trust (RU)
Rechtek...... River Transportation and Forwarding Office (RU)
RECOCIDI... Representation Commerciale de Cote-d'Ivoire (MAR)
RECOFLOR... Reforma Colombiana de la Flor [*Bogota*] (COL)
RECOL........ Representacoes Comerciais Lda. (MAR)
RECOPE...... Refinadora Costarricense de Petroleo [*Costa Rican Oil Refinery*] (LA)
RECSAM..... Regional Center for Education in Science and Mathematics [*Subsidiary of SEAMEC*] (CL)
RECSAM..... Regional Centre for Science and Mathematics (ML)
red.............. Editor, Editorial Board, Editorial Office (RU)
red.............. Editorial Office, Editor, Edited (BU)
red.............. Redagowal [*Edited By*] (POL)
red.............. Redakce [*Editorial Staff*] (CZ)
red.............. Redakcja [*Editorial Board, Editorial Office*] (POL)
RED............ Redaksi/Redaktur [*Editorial Staff/Editor*] (IN)
Red............ Redakteur [*or Redaktion*] [*German*]
red.............. Redaktor [*Editor*] (CZ)
red.............. Redaktor [*Editor*] [*Danish*] (GPO)
red.............. Redaktor [*Editor*] [*Swedish*] (GPO)
red.............. Redaktor [*Editor*] (POL)

Red............ Redan [*Redan*] [*Military map abbreviation*] [*World War I*] [*French*] (MTD)
red............ Reditel [*Director, Manager*] (CZ)
Red............ Reduktion [*Reduction*] [*German*]
RED............ Regional Economic Development [*Center*] (CL)
red............ Regular (BU)
red............ Rocket Battalion (RU)
RED............ Thread Tolerance Unit (RU)
REDAN........ Redes e Artefactos Nacionais Lda. (MAR)
redbr.......... Redni Broj [*Ordinal Number*] (YU)
redd........... Reduzierend [*Reducing*] [*German*]
Rede........... Redoute [*Redoubt*] [*Military map abbreviation*] [*World War I*] [*French*] (MTD)
REDF.......... Real Estate Development Fund (MAR)
red gimn u-tel ... Regular High School Teacher (BU)
redizdat...... Editorial and Publishing Section (RU)
redkol......... Editorial Board (RU)
Redkolegiya ... Editorial Board (BU)
red k-t........ Editorial Committee (BU)
redn........... Rocket-Launching Battalion (BU)
red nach u-ka ... Regular Woman Elementary School Teacher (BU)
red nach u-l ... Regular Male Elementary School Teacher (BU)
red nacz...... Redaktor Naczelny [*Chief Editor*] [*Polish*]
red nauk...... Redaktor Naukowy [*Scientific Supervisor*] [*Polish*]
REDP.......... Rada Ekonomiczna Drog Publicznych [*Economic Council on Public Roads*] (POL)
REDP.......... Rejony Eksploatacji Drog Publicznych [*Public Road Exploitation Districts*] (POL)
red prit........ Regular Supplement (BU)
redprof........ Redni Profesor [*Full Professor*] (YU)
red progimn u-l ... Regular Junior High School Teacher (BU)
REDSO........ Regional Economic Development Services Office (MAR)
red sost....... Editor-Compiler (RU)
red-stop...... Editor and Owner (BU)
ref............. Abstract, Paper (RU)
ref............. Referat [*or Referent*] [*Section or Section Head*] [*Polish*]
Ref............. Referate [*Reports, Abstracts*] [*German*]
ref............. Reference [*Reference, Allusion*] [*French*]
Ref............. Referent [*German*]
ref............. Referowal [*Report Made By*] (POL)
ref............. Reformatus [*Reformed (Church)*] (HU)
ref............. Roentgen Equivalent Physical (RU)
REFAMOL ... Representacoes Farmaceuticas de Mocambique Lda. (MAR)
refl............. Refleksiivi(nen) [*Finnish*]
refl............. Refleksiiviverbi [*Reflexive Verb*] [*Finnish*]
refr............ Refractometry (RU)
REG............ Electrohydraulic Regulator (RU)
REG............ Hydroelectric Steering Apparatus (RU)
REG............ Maintenance and Recovery Group (RU)
reg............. Regenerator (RU)
Reg............. Regens [*German*]
reg............. Regeny [*Novel*] (HU)
reg............. Regierte [*German*]
Reg............. Regiment [*Regiment*] [*French*] (MTD)
reg............. Regione [*Italian*] (CED)
reg............. Register (RU)
reg............. Registriert [*German*]
REG............ Remontno Evakuaciona Grupa [*Repair and Evacuation Group*] [*Military*] (YU)
reg............. Repair and Evacuation Group (BU)
REGALCO... Etablissements Regal & Cie. (MAR)
reg dv......... Traffic Control (RU)
REGIC......... Regie Generale d'Industries du Cameroun (MAR)
REGIDESO ... Regie de Distribution d'Eau et d'Electricite [*Water and Power Distribution Administration*] [*French*] (AF)
REGIFERCAM ... Regie des Chemins de Fer du Cameroun [*Cameroonian Railway Administration*] (AF)
REGLES...... Repartition du Surproduit Petrolier Particuliere a la Saoura et aux Oasis (MAR)
reglt........... Reglement [*Settlement, Adjustment, Regulation*] [*French*]
Regotmas ... All-Union Office for Regeneration of Used Petroleum Lubricants (RU)
reg t........... Register Ton (RU)
REH............ Radioelektronikai Hadviseles [*Radio Electronic Warfare*] (HU)
REHOTELES ... Reservacion de Hoteles [*Bogota*] (COL)
REI............. Radio Espana Independiente [*Radio Independent Spain*] (WER)
REI............. Regie Exploitations Industrielles [*Moroccan*] (MAR)
REI............. Revue des Etudes Islamiques [*Paris*] [*A publication*] (MAR)
REJ............. Rejimen [*Regiment*] (ML)
REJECO...... Regroupement de la Jeunesse Congolaise (MAR)
rek.............. Being Recommended, Recommended (RU)
REK............ Rekening [*Account (Financial, Bank)*] (IN)
Rek............. Reklamcilik [*Advertising, Publicity*] (TU)
REK MEK.... Russian Electrotechnical Committee of the International Electrotechnical Commission (RU)
Rekput'....... All-Union Trust for the Reconstruction of Railroads (RU)
rekt............ Rector (RU)
rekt............ Rekisteritonni(a) [*Finnish*]
rektn.......... Rekisteritonni(a) [*Finnish*]
REL............. Rassemblement Europeen de la Liberte [*European Liberty Rally*] [*French*] (PPE)
rel.............. Relie [*Bound*] [*French*]
Rel............. Religion [*Religion*] (EG)
rel.............. Religion (BU)
RELAP........ Replaciones Publicas y Tecnicas Publicitarias Ltda. [*Bogota*] (COL)
RELC.......... Regional English Language Center [*Subsidiary of SEAMEC*] (CL)
relig............ Religious (RU)
relyativ........ Relativistic (RU)
rem............. Masseinheit fuer Strahlungsdosis [*Unit of Measure for Radiation Dosage*] (EG)
Rem............ Remise [*Remittance*] [*Business and trade*] [*French*]
rem............. Repair (RU)
REM............ Resort Militer [*Military Area (KOREM)*] (IN)
REMA.......... Societe de Reception et de Magasin (MAR)
remabatr..... Rocket-Launching Mortar Battalion [*Artillery*] (BU)
remadn....... Rocket-Launching Mortar Battalion [*Artillery*] (BU)
remap......... Rocket-Launching Mortar Regiment (BU)
REMAR........ Representaciones Maritimas [*Bogota*] (COL)
remb........... Maintenance Battalion (RU)
remb........... Remboursable [*Repayable, Redeemable*] [*French*]
Rembt......... Remboursement [*Reimbursement*] [*Business and trade*] [*French*]
REME.......... Royal Electrical and Mechanical Engineers [*Jordanian*] (ME)
remesl......... Trade, Artisan (RU)
remletuchka ... Mobile Repair Shop (RU)
Remmashtrest ... Trust for the Repair of Metal-Cutting Machine Tools and Forging and Pressing Equipment (RU)
rem mast.... Repair Shop [*Topography*] (RU)
Remmekh ... Machine Repair Plant (RU)
REMO.......... Societe Ouest Africaine de Distribution Ets. Rene Montenay & Cie. (MAR)
REMOL........ Representacoes de Mocambique Limitada (MAR)
remont........ Repair Shop [*Topography*] (RU)
REMPOD..... Radio-Elektromehanisko Podjetje [*Radio and Electrical Engineering Establishment*] (YU)
remzavod.... Repair Plant (RU)
RENA.......... Rede Nacional de Abastecimento [*National Supply Network*] [*Brazilian*] (LA)
RENAB........ Empresa Estatal de Reparacoes Navais de Beira (MAR)
RENAC........ Retele Nationale de Calculatoare [*National Computer Networks*] (RO)
RENAIBAKO ... Renaissance du Bas-Kongo (MAR)
RENAICAM ... Renaissance Camerounaise (MAR)
Renaiss....... Renaissance [*German*]
RENAPE...... Rede Nacional de Pesca [*National Fishing Network*] [*Brazilian*] (LA)
RENAVE...... Empresa de Reparos Navais [*Ship Repair Company*] [*Brazilian*] (LA)
rend............ Rendelet [*Decree (Legal)*] (HU)
rendk.......... Rendkivuli [*Extraordinary*] (HU)
rend pu....... Rendezo Palyaudvar [*Marshalling Yards (Railway)*] (HU)
RENEC........ Registraduria Nacional del Estado Civil [*National Civil Registry Office*] [*Colombian*] (LA)
RENFE......... Red Nacional de los Ferrocarriles Espanoles [*Spanish National Railroads*] (WER)
rentg........... X-Ray, Roentgen (RU)
REO............ Regional Education Officer (MAR)
REO............ Russian Economic Society (RU)
REP............ Distribution Clearing Station [*Military*] (BU)
REP............ Distribution and Shipping of Printed Matter (BU)
REP............ Evacuation Distribution Station (RU)
REP............ Exploration and Extraction Establishment (RU)
REP............ Regiment Etranger de Parachutistes [*Foreign Paratroop Regiment*] (AF)
rep.............. Repartition [*French*]
rep.............. Report [*French*]
Rep............. Report [*Report*] [*German*]
rep.............. Reportaz [*or Reporter*] [*Report or Reporter*] [*Polish*]
rep.............. Repulo [*Flying, Flyer, Aircraft*] (HU)
REP............ Subscription System for the Distribution of the Daily Press (BU)
REPAHA...... Regional Educational Program for Animal Health Assistants [*Guyanese*] (LA)
REPELITA ... Rentjana Pembangunan Lima Tahun [*5-Year Development Plan (1969-1973)*] (IN)
Repertkom ... Main Committee for the Control of Repertoire and Spectacles (RU)
repertkom... Repertoire Committee (RU)
REPLEK...... Republicko Pretprijatie za Promet so Lekovi [*Republican (i.e., Macedonian) Pharmaceutical Trade Establishment*] [*Skopje*] (YU)
REPRECOL ... Representacoes e Construcoes Lda. (MAR)
reprod......... Reproduction (BU)
REPSA........ Refineria Paraguaya, Sociedad Anonima [*Paraguay Refineries, Incorporated*] (LA)
repter.......... Repuloter [*Airfield*] (HU)
RER............ Reseau Express Regional [*Paris subway*]
Rer............. Rocher [*Rock*] [*French*] (NAU)
RER............ Rural Economy Research (MAR)
RERU.......... Rural Economy Research Unit (MAR)

RES .... Electric Contact-Roller Welding (RU)
RES .... Rayon Electric Power Plant (RU)
RES .... Reformed Ecumenical Synod [*South African*] (AF)
Res .... Reserve [*German*]
Res .... Resmi [*Official*] (TU)
RES .... Reticuloendothelial System (RU)
RES .... Revue d'Ethnographie et de Sociologie [*A publication*] (MAR)
RESADOC ... Reseau Sahelien d'Information et de Documentation Scientifiques et Techniques [*Bamako, Mali*]
RESELCO ... Fabrica de Resistencias Electricas Colombianas [*Medellin*] (COL)
RESHD .... Electric Reaction Step Motor (RU)
Resid .... Residence [*or Resident*] [*Residence or Resident*] [*French*] (MTD)
RESIDA .... Reporteros Sindicalizados de Antioquia [*Medellin*] (COL)
RESKRIM .... Reserse Kriminil [*Criminal Investigations*] (IN)
RESMAC ..... Red Sismica Mexicana de Apertura Continental [*Continental Mexican Seismic Network*] (LA)
RESOLCOL ... Resortes de Colombia Ltda. [*Palmira*] (COL)
RESOS .... Radio-Electrical Equipment and Communications Station (RU)
resp .... Republic (RU)
resp .... Respectively (BU)
resp .... Respektive [*Respectively*] [*German*]
RESPOL ...... Resguardo y Policia Aduanera [*Customs Security and Police*] [*Chilean*] (LA)
Respta .... Respuesta [*Answer*] [*Business and trade*] [*Spanish*]
rest .... Restauriert [*Repaired*] [*German*]
reszl .... Reszleg [*Section, Detachment*] (HU)
RET .... Radiation-Effective Temperatures (RU)
RET .... Radioellentevekenyseg [*Radio Countermeasures*] (HU)
ret .... Retoriikka [*Rhetoric*] [*Finnish*]
RETE .... Radioellentevekenyseg Elharitasa [*Defense Against Radio Countermeasures*] (HU)
RETECSA ... Representaciones Tecnicas, Sociedad Anonima [*Venezuelan*]
RETP .... Revue d'Ethnographie et des Traditions Populaires [*A publication*] (MAR)
Retrnt .... Retranchement [*Intrenchment*] [*Military map abbreviation*] [*World War I*] [*French*] (MTD)
rets .... Recessive (RU)
rets .... Review, Reviewer (RU)
RETU .... River Technical Operations Administration (RU)
REU .... Reunion [*Three-letter standard code*] (CNC)
REU .... Rhodesia Electoral Union (MAR)
REUS .... Importadora de Repuestos Usados Ltda. [*Cali*] (COL)
REUV .... Universal Electronic Explosionproof Relay (RU)
REV .... Rechnungseinzugsverfahren [*Invoice Collection System (Cashless system of paying bills)*] (EG)
Rev .... Revident [*or Revier*] [*German*]
Rev .... Revisyon [*Revision*] (TU)
rev .... Revolver (RU)
REVALCO ... Remaches y Valvulas Colombianas Ltda. [*Bogota*] (COL)
Revis .... Revisor [*German*]
reviz .... Inspector, Auditor (RU)
rev kom .... Revolutionary Committee (RU)
revol .... Revolutionary (BU)
rev var .... Revenu Variable [*Variable Income*] [*French*]
Revvoyensovet ... Revolutionary Military Council [*1918-1934*] (RU)
revvoyentribunal ... Revolutionary Military Tribunal (RU)
REW .... Reichsbahnentwicklungswerk [*GDR Railroad Development Works*] (EG)
REYA .... Revolutionary Ethiopian Youth Association (MAR)
REYDIN .... Representaciones y Distribuciones Industriales Ltda. [*Cali*] (COL)
rez .... Electrified Wire Entanglement Company (RU)
rez .... Reserve (RU)
rez .... Reservoir, Tank, Cistern (RU)
rez .... Resume, Summary (BU)
rez .... Rezyser [*Director*] [*Polish*]
REZ .... Riga Electrical Machinery Plant (RU)
rez .... Rubber (RU)
rez .... Rubber Products Plant [*Topography*] (RU)
rez .... Rutherford (RU)
Rezinoproyekt ... State Institute for the Planning of Establishments of the Rubber Industry (RU)
Rezinotekhnika ... Industrial Rubber Products Plant (RU)
Rezinotrest ... State Trust of the Rubber Industry (RU)
Rezinproyekt ... State Institute for the Planning of Establishments of the Rubber Industry (RU)
rez ras .... Resonance Scattering (RU)
rf .... Abstract, Paper (RU)
RF .... Distribution Feeder (RU)
RF .... Excitation-Forcing Relay (RU)
RF .... Forcing Relay (RU)
rf .... Radphot (RU)
rf .... Refractometry (RU)
RF .... Republique Francaise [*French Republic*] [*French*] (GPO)
rf .... Revenu Fixe [*Fixed Income*] [*French*]
RF .... Rhodesian Front (AF)
Rf .... Rif [*Reef*] [*Dutch*] (NAU)
Rf .... Riff [*Reef*] [*German*] (NAU)
RF .... Rwanda Franc (MAR)
RFA .... Republica Federal Alema [*Federal Republic of Germany*] [*Use FRG*] [*Portuguese*] (WER)
RFA .... Republique Federale d'Allemagne [*Federal Republic of Germany*] [*Use FRG*] (AF)
RFA .... Retard a la Fermeture de l'Admission [*French*] (MTD)
RFB .... Roter Frontkaempferbund [*League of Red Front Fighters*] [*West German*] (WEN)
RFC .... Raljska Fabrika Cementa [*Ralja Cement Factory*] (YU)
RFCWA .... Regional Fisheries Commission for Western Africa (MAR)
RFD .... Republik Federal Djerman [*Federal Republic of Germany*] (IN)
RFDK .... Republic Long-Term Credit Fund (RU)
RFE .... Retard a la Fermeture de l'Echappement [*French*] (MTD)
RFEI .... Rostov-Na-Donu Institute of Finance and Economics (RU)
RFF .... Rede Ferroviaria Federal [*Federal Railway Network*] [*Brazilian*] (LA)
RFG .... Follicle-Stimulating Hormone Reaction (RU)
RFG .... Rayon Physical Culture Group (BU)
RFG .... Republica Federala Germana [*Federal Republic of Germany*] (RO)
RFG .... Rhodesian Financial Gazette [*A publication*] (MAR)
RFI .... Radio France Internationale (MAR)
RFI .... Republicki Finansiski Inspektorat [*Republic Financial Inspectorate*] (YU)
RFIC .... Republique Federale Islamique des Comores [*Islamic Federal Republic of the Comoros*] (AF)
RFJ .... Ring Freiheitlicher Jugend [*Liberal Students Organization*] [*FPOe affiliate*] [*Austrian*] (WEN)
RFK .... Radio Free Kabul (EA)
RFK .... Ribosephosphoric Acid (RU)
RFKhO .... Russian Physicochemical Society [*1878-1930*] (RU)
RFMA .... Rassemblement Franco-Musulman Algerien (MAR)
RFN .... Rybnicka Fabryka Maszyn [*Rybnik Machine Factory*] (POL)
RFO .... Rayon Finance Department (RU)
RFO .... Russian Photographic Society (RU)
RFO .... Russian Physical Society (RU)
RFPOS .... Rada Federalna Polskich Organizacji Studenckich [*Federal Council of Polish Student Organizations*] (POL)
RFQ .... Request for Quotation (MAR)
Rfr .... Ranskan Frangi(a) [*Finnish*]
RFRN .... Redeemable Floating Rate Note (MAR)
RFS .... Radio Broadcasting Station (RU)
RFS .... Ring Freiheitlicher Studenten [*Liberal Party Students Circle*] [*Austrian*] (WEN)
RFSRR .... Rosyjska Federacyjna Socjalistyczna Republika Radziecka [*Russian Soviet Federated Socialist Republic*] (POL)
RFT .... Reactor for Physics and Engineering Research (RU)
RFT .... Repubblica Federale Tedesca [*Federal Republic of Germany*] [*Use FRG*] [*Italian*] (WER)
RFT .... Rundfunk- und Fernmeldetechnik [*Radio and Telecommunications Technology*] (EG)
RFTO .... Russian Physicotechnical Society (RU)
RFV .... Excitation Fixation Relay (RU)
RFV .... Russian Philological Herald [*1879-1917*] [*A publication*] (RU)
RFZ .... Rundfunk- und Fernsehtechnisches Zentralamt [*Radio and Television Central Office*] (EG)
RG .... Hand Grenade (RU)
RG .... Rada Glowna [*Central Council*] (POL)
RG .... Rada Gospodarcza [*Economic Council*] (POL)
RG .... Rdultovskiy Point Detonation Fuze (RU)
RG .... Realgymnasium [*German*]
RG .... Reconnaissance Group (RU)
Rg .... Regierung [*German*]
RG .... Renseignements Generaux [*General Information (Intelligence)*] (CL)
RG .... Resmi Gazete [*Official Journal (for the Turkish Federated State of Cyprus)*] [*A publication*] (GC)
RG .... Revue de Geographie [*A publication*] (MAR)
RG .... Rhombic Horizontal [*Antenna*] (RU)
RG .... Volume Control (RU)
RGA .... Hemagglutination Reaction (RU)
Rga .... Rangieraufseher [*Classification Yard Supervisor*] (EG)
RGA .... Responsible Government Association (MAR)
RGA .... Rubber Growers' Association (EA)
rgb .... Deep Drilling Company (RU)
RGB .... Republic of Guinea-Bissau (MAR)
RGCFTP ..... Regie Generale de Chemins de Fer et de Travaux Publics [*General Railroad and Public Works Agency*] [*Cameroonian*] (AF)
RGCL .... Reunion General Confederation of Labor (MAR)
RGD .... Degtyarev Hand Grenade (RU)
RGD .... Depth Remote Flow Meter (RU)
RGD .... Double Rhombic Horizontal [*Antenna*] (RU)
RGD .... Revue de Geomorphologie Dynamique [*A publication*] (MAR)
RGDIP .... Revue Generale de Droit International Public [*North African*] [*A publication*] (MAR)
RGE- .... Gamma-Electron Relay (RU)
Rge .... Refuge [*Shelter*] [*Military map abbreviation*] [*World War I*] [*French*] (MTD)
RGE .... Regroupement des Guineens a l'Exterieur [*Rally of Guineans Abroad*] (PD)
RGGA .... State Riga City Archives of the Latvian SSR (RU)

RGHE .... Revue de Geographie Humaine et d'Ethnologie [*A publication*] (MAR)
RGI .... Rivista Geografica Italiana [*Florence*] [*A publication*] (MAR)
RGI .... Russian Hydrological Institute (RU)
RGK .... City District Committee (RU)
RGK .... General Headquarters Reserve (BU)
RGK .... Reserve of the High Command (RU)
rglm .... Regelmaessig [*Regular*] [*German*] (GPO)
RGM .... Rdultovskiy Membrane-Type Point Detonating Fuze (RU)
RGMI .... Rostov State Medical Institute (RU)
RGMTs .... Regional Hydrometeorological Center (RU)
RGN .... Rada Gospodarki Narodowej [*Council on the National Economy*] (POL)
RG NOT .... Rada Glowna Naczelnej Organizacji Technicznej [*High Council of the Chief Technical Organization*] [*Polish*]
RGNU .... Royal Government of National Union of Cambodia [*Use GRUNK*] (CL)
RGNUC .... Royal Government of National Union of Cambodia [*Use GRUNK*] (CL)
RGO .... Rada Glowna Opiekuncza [*Main Charity Council*] [*World War II*] (POL)
RGO .... Realisation de Grands Ouvrages [*Algerian*] (MAR)
RGO .... Regelungstechnik, Geraetebau und Optik [*Regulating Technology, Appliance and Optical Tools Industry*] (EG)
RGO .... Revolutionaere Gewerkschafts-Opposition [*Revolutionary Trade-Union Opposition*] (EG)
RGO .... Russian Geographic Society [*1845-1924*] (RU)
RGP .... Responsible Government Party (MAR)
RGP .... Rhodesian Government Party (MAR)
RGP .... Rijksgeschied-Kundige Publicaties (MAR)
RGPGD .... Revue de Geographie Physique et de Geologie Dynamique [*A publication*] (MAR)
RGPH .... Rada Glowna Przyjaciol Harcerstwa [*Chief Council of Friends of Scouting*] (POL)
RGR .... Rassemblement des Gauches Republicaines [*Assembly of the Republican Left*] [*French*]
RGR .... Rassemblement des Gaullistes Reunionnais (MAR)
RGS .... Horizontal Welded Petroleum Tank (RU)
RGS .... Reforma General de Salarios [*General Wage Reform*] [*Cuban*] (LA1)
RGSKhOS ... Republic State Agricultural Experimental Station (RU)
Rgt .... Regiment [*Regiment*] [*Military*] [*French*] (MTD)
RGT .... Reuniao Geral de Trabalhadores [*General Meeting of Workers*] [*Portuguese*] (WER)
RGU .... Rostov State University (RU)
RGV .... Estimated Water Level, Rated Water Level (RU)
RGV .... Rauhfuttergrossvieheinheit [*500 Kilograms of Live Weight of Domestic Animals Feeding on Coarse Fodder*] (EG)
RGVV .... Estimated High-Water Level, Rated High-Water Level (RU)
RGW .... Rat fuer Gegenseitige Wirtschaftshilfe [*Council for Economic Mutual Assistance (CEMA)*] [*German*] (WEN)
RGZKP .... Rada Glowna Zwiazku Kompozytorow Polskich [*Main Council of the Union of Polish Composers*] (POL)
RG ZLZS ..... Rada Glowna Zrzeszenia Ludowych Zespolow Sportowych [*Chief Council of Peasant Sports and Athletics Clubs Association*] [*Polish*]
RH .... Haiti [*Haiti*] [*Polish*]
RH .... Revisionist History [*An association*] (EA)
RH .... Revue Hispanique [*A publication*] (MAR)
RH .... Rhodesia Herald [*A publication*] (MAR)
rh .... Rovid Hullamu [*Shortwave*] (HU)
RH .... Southern Rhodesia [*Two-letter standard code*] (CNC)
RHA .... Resmi Hizmet Arac [*Official Service Vehicle*] (TU)
Rhj .... Rechnungshalbjahr [*Half of Fiscal Year*] (EG)
RHO .... Southern Rhodesia [*Three-letter standard code*] (CNC)
RHOKAT ...... Rhodesia-Katanga Company Limited (MAR)
RHONICK .... Rhodesian Nickel Corporation Ltd. (MAR)
RHP .... Regiment de Hussards Parachutistes [*Algerian*] (MAR)
Rhuzi .... Rhodesian Uzi (MAR)
RHV .... Rada Hospodarska Vsestatni [*National Economic Council*] (CZ)
rhW .... Rheinische Waehrung [*Rhenish Currency*] [*German*]
RI .... Computing Engineer (RU)
RI .... Indonezja [*Indonesia*] [*Polish*]
RI .... Insulation Rubber (RU)
RI .... Pulse Distributor (RU)
RI .... Pulse Relay (RU)
RI .... Pulse Storing Device (RU)
RI .... Radioactive Isotope (RU)
RI .... Recommended Inventions (RU)
RI .... Regiment d'Infanterie [*Infantry Regiment*] [*French*] (WER)
RI .... Register Selector (RU)
RI .... Rendelo Intezet [*Clinic for Ambulatory Patients*] (HU)
RI .... Republicains Independants [*Independent Republicans*] [*French*] (WER)
RI .... Republik Indonesia [*Republic of Indonesia*] (IN)
RI .... Rockwell International
RI .... Selector Relay (RU)
RI .... Servo Relay (RU)
RIA .... Regiment d'Infanterie Autonome [*Autonomous Infantry Regiment*] [*Cambodian*] (CL)
RIA .... Regiment Interarmes d'Appui [*Inter-Service Support Regiment*] [*Upper Voltan*] (AF)
RIAM .... Regiment Interarmes Malgache [*Malagasy Inter-Service Regiment*] (AF)
RIAN .... Radium Institute Imeni V. G. Khlopin of the Academy of Sciences, USSR (RU)
RIAOM .... Regiment Interarmes d'Outre-Mer [*Overseas Inter-Service Regiment*] [*French*] (AF)
RIAS .... Research Institute for Animal Science (MAR)
RIAS .... Rundfunk im Amerikanischen Sektor [*Radio in the American Sector (of Berlin)*] [*German*] (WEN)
RIAT .... Ramogi Institute of Advanced Technology (MAR)
RIB .... "Russian Historical Library" [*1872-1927*] (RU)
RIBIB .... Revista Interamericana de Bibliotecologia [*Medellin*] [*A publication*] (COL)
RIC .... Regiment d'Infanterie Commando [*Infantry Commando Regiment*] [*Upper Voltan*] (AF)
RIC .... Reuniao Inter-Camaras [*Inter-Chamber Meeting*] [*Portuguese*] (WER)
RICM .... Regiment d'Infanterie Coloniale de Maroc (MAR)
RICOCI .... Representations Industrielles et Commerciales de l'Ouest de la Cote-d'Ivoire (MAR)
RICOM .... Comptoir du Rip (MAR)
RICU .... Reformed Industrial and Commercial Workers' Union (MAR)
RID .... Radioisotopic Engine (RU)
RID .... Reactor Instituut te Delft [*Delft Reactor Institute*] [*Dutch*] (WEN)
RID .... Regiment d'Infanterie Derive [*Derived Infantry Regiment*] [*French*] (WER)
RID .... Reglement International Concernant le Transport des Merchandises Dangereuses par Chemins de Fer
RID .... Repatriement Integral des Devises [*Full Repatriation of Foreign Exchange*] (CL)
RIDA .... Rural and Industrial Development Authority [*Malaysian*] (ML)
RIDEP .... Regional Integrated Development Project (MAR)
RIEG .... Radioisotopic Electrogenerator (RU)
RIEM .... Republic Institute of Experimental Medicine (BU)
RIEM .... Rostov Institute of Epidemiology and Microbiology (RU)
RIEx .... Reglement International Concernant le Transport des Colis Express [*International Regulation for the Transportation of Express Freight*] (EG)
RIFR .... Radio Pulse Phase Discriminator (RU)
RIFT .... Regiment d'Infanterie des Forces du Territoire [*Territorial Forces Infantry Regiment*] [*French*] (WER)
RIG .... Editing and Publishing Group (RU)
Rig .... Rigole [*Gully*] [*Military map abbreviation*] [*World War I*] [*French*] (MTD)
RIG .... Route d'Interet General [*General Use Highway*] (CL)
Rigasel'mash ... Riga Agricultural Machinery Plant (RU)
RIGOPS .... Rayon Forest and Environmental Protection Inspectorate (BU)
RIGPN .... Rayon State Fire Inspection (RU)
RIH .... Roboty Inzynierskie i Hydrotechniczne [*Engineering and Hydraulic (Enterprise)*] (POL)
RIHED .... Regional Institute for Higher Education and Development (CL)
RIIA .... Royal Institute of International Affairs, London (MAR)
RIIC .... Rural Industries Innovation Centre [*Botswana*]
RIIGVF .... Riga Institute of Civil Air Fleet Engineers (RU)
RIITKhPZ .... Republic Scientific Research Institute for Labor Hygiene and Occupational Diseases (BU)
RIIZh .... Rayon Animal Husbandry Research Institute (BU)
RIIZh .... Republic Animal Husbandry Research Institute (BU)
RIIZhT .... Rostov Institute of Railroad Transportation Engineers (RU)
RIJ .... Romano Internacionalno Jekhethanibe [*Romani Union*] (EA)
RIK .... Radiofonikon Idryma Kyprou [*Cyprus Broadcasting Corporation*] (GC)
RIK .... Rayon Executive Committee (RU)
RIL .... Regulating Artificial Line (RU)
RILEM .... Reunion Internationale des Laboratoires d'Essais et de Recherches sur les Materiaux et les Constructions [*International Union of Testing and Research Laboratories for Materials and Structures*] (EA)
RILKO .... Research into Lost Knowledge Organisation Trust (EA)
RIM .... Quantized Pulse Modulation (RU)
RIM .... Regimiento de Infanteria Motorizada [*Motorized Infantry Regiment*] [*Cuban*] (LA)
RIM .... Republique Islamique de Mauritanie [*Islamic Republic of Mauritania*] (AF)
RIM .... Rhodesian Institute of Management (MAR)
Rim .... Rimesse [*Remittance*] [*Business and trade*] [*German*]
RIMA .... Regiment d'Infanterie de la Marine [*Marine Corps Regiment*] [*French*] (WER)
rim-kat .... Roman Catholic (RU)
RIN .... Non-Unified Characteristics Selector Relay (RU)
RIN .... Resimen Induk [*Training Regiment*] (IN)
Rin .... Rhinology, Rhinologist (BU)
RInS .... Ratna Intendantska Sluzba [*War Quartermaster Service*] (YU)
RINTI i P ...... Republic Institute of Scientific and Technical Information and Propaganda (RU)
RIO .... Editorial and Publishing Section (RU)
RIO .... Inspection Department (RU)
RIO .... Rijecka Industrija Odjece [*Rijeka Clothing Industry*] (YU)

RIO .... Routine Information Processing (RU)
RIO .... Russian Historical Society [*1866-1917*] (RU)
RIO .... Unified Characteristics Selector Relay (RU)
RionGES ..... Rion Hydroelectric Power Plant (RU)
RIP .... Requiescat [*or Requiescant*] [*May He (She or They) Rest in Peace*] [*Latin*] (GPO)
RIP .... Route Intraprovinciale [*Intraprovincial Highway*] (CL)
RIP .... Rural Industries Promotions [*Botswana*]
RIPC .... Regiment d'Infanterie Parachutiste de Choc [*Algerian*] (MAR)
RIPN .... Controlled Direct-Current Power Supply (RU)
RIPS .... Regional Institute for Population Studies [*Accra, Ghana*]
RIPSA .... Rutas Internacionales Peruanas, Sociedad Anonima [*Peruvian International Routes, Incorporated*] (LA)
ris .... Drawing (BU)
ris .... Drawing, Illustration, Diagram (RU)
RIS .... Editing and Publishing Council (BU)
RIS .... Impulse Signal Relay (RU)
RIS .... Ratna Intendantska Sluzba [*War Quartermaster Service*] (YU)
ris .... Rice [*Topography*] (RU)
RIS .... Synchronization Pulse Separator (RU)
RISCO .... Rhodesian Iron and Steel Company (MAR)
RISCOM ...... Rhodesian Iron and Steel Commission (MAR)
Rise .... Remise [*Military map abbreviation*] [*World War I*] [*French*] (MTD)
RISI .... Rostov-Na-Donu Construction Engineering Institute (RU)
RISKh .... Rostov Institute of Agricultural Machinery (RU)
RISKhI .... Republic Scientific Research Institute of Sanitation and Hygiene (BU)
RISO .... Editorial and Publishing Council (RU)
RISONPALM ... Rivers State Nigerian Palm Ltd. (MAR)
RIT- .... Radioactive Thickness Gauge (RU)
RIT .... Rassemblement Interprofessionnel du Togo (MAR)
RIT .... Regiment Interarmes Togolais [*Togolese Inter-Service Regiment*] (AF)
RITA .... Reseau Integre de Transmissions de l'Armee de Terre [*Integrated Communications Network of the Army*] [*French*] (WER)
RITENA .... Reunion Internacional de Tecnicos de la Nutricion Animal [*International Meeting of Animal Nutrition Experts*] (EA)
RITES .... Rail India Technical and Economic Services (MAR)
RITLA .... Red Tecnologica Latinoamericana [*Latin American Technological Network*] (LA)
ritor .... Rhetorical (RU)
RIU .... Radioactive Level Indicator (RU)
RIV .... Republicko Izvrsno Vece [*Republic Executive Council*] (YU)
Riv .... Riviere [*River*] [*French*] (NAU)
RIV .... Time Pulse Relay (RU)
RIVO .... Rijksinstituut voor Visserijonderzoek [*Government Institute for Fishery Research*] [*Dutch*] (WEN)
RIW .... Radiowy Instytut Wydawniczy [*Radio Publishing Institute*] (POL)
RIzslIZhiv St Z ... Rayon Animal Husbandry Research Institute in Stara Zagora (BU)
RJA .... Rad Jugoslavenski Akademije [*Papers of the Yugoslav Academy of Sciences and Arts*] [*Zagreb*] [*A publication*] (YU)
RJA .... Rhodesian Judo Association (MAR)
RJAF .... Royal Jordanian Air Force (MAR)
RJCT .... Radio Jugoslovanske Cone Trsta [*Radio of Yugoslav Zone of Trieste*] (YU)
RJN .... Rada Jednosci Narodowej [*Council of National Unity*] (POL)
RJPIC .... Revue Juridique et Politique. Independance et Cooperation [*North African*] [*A publication*] (MAR)
RJPUF .... Revue Juridique et Politique de l'Union Francaise [*North African*] [*A publication*] (MAR)
RK .... Capital Repair (RU)
RK .... Channel Distributor (RU)
RK .... Command Register (RU)
RK .... Compounding Regulator (RU)
RK .... Compressor Relay (RU)
RK .... Discharge Cascade (RU)
RK .... Distributing Head (RU)
RK .... Final Relay, Operating Relay (RU)
RK .... Logging Radiometer (RU)
r-k .... Mine (RU)
RK .... Natural Rubber (RU)
RK- .... Oxygen Reducer (RU)
RK- .... Pocket Radiometer (RU)
RK .... Rade Koncar, Tvornica Elektricnih Strojeva [*Rade Koncar Electric Machinery Works*] [*Zagreb*] (YU)
RK .... Radiation Circuit (RU)
RK .... Radiation Monitor (RU)
RK .... Radio Compass (RU)
RK .... Radio Klub [*Radio Club*] (YU)
RK .... Radioactive Logging (RU)
RK .... Rayon Committee (BU)
RK .... Rayon Committee (RU)
RK .... Rdeci Kriz [*Red Cross*] (YU)
Rk .... Reaktion [*Reaction*] [*German*]
RK .... Regulator Box (RU)
rk .... Rendkivuli [*Extraordinary*] (HU)
RK .... Repair Office (RU)
RK .... Republic Committee (RU)
RK .... Republic Office (RU)
RK .... Rimsko-Katolicky [*Roman Catholic*] (CZ)
RK .... Ristic-Kangrga (Recnik) [*Serbian-German Dictionary*] [*A publication*] (YU)
RK .... Robna Kuca, Trgovinsko Poduzece [*Store*] [*Commercial*] (YU)
rk .... Romai Katolikus [*Roman Catholic*] (HU)
RK .... Roman Catholic (RU)
RK .... Runner (RU)
RK .... Separation Capacitor (RU)
RK .... Supervisory Relay, Control Relay (RU)
RK .... Workers' and Peasants' (RU)
RKA .... Fish Gelatin Agar (RU)
RKChF .... Workers' and Peasants' Black Sea Fleet (RU)
RKD .... Pressure Control Relay (RU)
RkD .... Rocket Engine, Rocket Motor (RU)
RKD .... X-Ray Diffraction Chamber (RU)
RKED .... Revoliutsionnyi Komitet Edinstva i Deistviia (MAR)
RKF- .... Focusing X-Ray Camera (RU)
RKF .... Oxygen-Flux Cutter (RU)
RKF .... Workers' Congress of Philippines (RU)
RKFS .... Rayon Committee for Physical Culture and Sports (BU)
RKGTO .... Republic Program "Ready for Work and Defense" (BU)
RKh .... Birth of Christ [*BC in dates*] (RU)
RKh .... Forward Stroke, Driving Stroke (RU)
RKhA .... Russian Art Archives (RU)
rkhch .... Radiochemically Pure (RU)
RKhK .... Rubezhnoye Chemical Kombinat (RU)
RKhO .... Russian Chemical Society (RU)
RKhP .... Receiver Performance (RU)
RKhR .... Radiation and Chemical Reconnaissance (RU)
rkhrr .... Chemical and Radiation Reconnaissance Company (RU)
rkhrr .... Chemical and Radio Reconnaissance Company (BU)
rkh s .... Supply Dump, Distributing Point (BU)
RKhT .... Republic Office for Wholesale Trade in Household Goods [*RSFSR*] (RU)
RKhZ .... Chemical Barrage Area (RU)
rkhz .... Chemical Defense Company (RU)
RKI .... Workers' and Peasants' Inspection [*1920-1934*] (RU)
RKIE .... Reformatus Kereszteny Ifjusagi Egyesulet [*Reformed Church Christian Youth Association*] (HU)
RK i KD .... Of Workers', Peasants', and Red Army Deputies (RU)
RKK- .... Air-Regenerating Gas Mask Designed by Kovshov and Kuz'menko (RU)
RKK .... Mediation Commission for Price Adjustment (BU)
RKK .... Radiation-Induced Catalytic Cracking (RU)
Rkk .... Reaktionen [*Reactions*] [*German*]
RKK .... Requisitioning Commission (BU)
RKK .... Wage Rate and Dispute Commission (RU)
RKK .... Workers' and Peasants' Control (RU)
RKKA .... Workers' and Peasants' Red Army [*1918-1946*] (RU)
RKKAF .... Workers' and Peasants' Red Army and Navy (RU)
RKKF .... Workers' and Peasants' Red Navy (RU)
RKKh .... Rayon Department of Municipal Services (RU)
RKKM .... Workers' and Peasants' Red Militia (RU)
rk kov .... Rendkivuli Kovet [*Ambassador Extraordinary*] (HU)
RKKS .... Workers' and Peasants' Red Armed Forces (RU)
RKKVF .... Workers' and Peasants' Red Air Force (RU)
RKL .... Line Control Relay (RU)
rkl .... Ruokalusikallinen [*Finnish*]
RK-LS- .... Radioactive Logging with Luminescent Counters (RU)
RKM .... Cable Trunk Region (RU)
rkm .... Mounted Militia Reserve (RU)
RKM- .... Radiographic Camera-Monochromator (RU)
rkm .... Rakennusmestari [*Finnish*]
RKM .... Reczny Karabin Maszynowy [*Light Machine Gun*] (POL)
RKM .... Relativistic Quantum Mechanics (RU)
RKM .... Rendorsegi Korzeti Megbizott [*District Policeman*] (HU)
RKM .... Rezervno Komandno Mesto [*Reserve Command Post*] (YU)
RKM .... Workers' and Peasants' Militia (RU)
RKN .... Standard Round Relay (RU)
RKN .... Voltage Control Relay (RU)
RKNP .... Republican Peasants' National Party [*Turkish*] (RU)
RKO .... Disconnection Circuit Control Relay (RU)
RKO .... Operation Code Register (RU)
RKO .... Rayon Municipal Department (RU)
rkp .... Manuscript (RU)
rkp .... Rakpart [*Embankment*] (HU)
RKP .... Rejonowe Komitety Porozumiewawcze [*Regional Consultative Committees*] (POL)
rkp .... Rekopis [*Manuscript*] (POL)
RKP .... Roman Kommunista Part [*Romanian Communist Party*] (HU)
RKP .... Romanian Communist Party (BU)
RKP .... Romanian Communist Party (RU)
RKP .... Ruotsalainen Kansanpuolue [*Finnish*]
RKP .... Russian Communist Party (RU)
RKP(b) .... Ruska Komunisticka Partija (Boljsevici) [*Russian Communist Party (Bolsheviks)*] (YU)
RKP(b) .... Russian Communist Party (of Bolsheviks) [*1918-1925*] (RU)
RKPB .... Workers' and Peasants' Party of Burma (RU)

rkpINU .... Rukopis Instituta za Narodnu Umjetnost u Zagrebu [*Manuscript of the Folk Art Institute in Zagreb*] [*A publication*] (YU)
rkpMH .... Rukopis Matice Hrvatske [*Manuscript of Matica Hrvatska, a Croatian cultural society*] [*Zagreb*] [*A publication*] (YU)
RKPN .... Rooms Katholieke Partij Nederland [*Roman Catholic Party of the Netherlands*] (PPE)
RKPS .... Rayon Committees for Production Consultation (BU)
RKPS .... Working Committees of the Trade Union (BU)
RKPZ .... Rabotnicki Kulturno-Prosvetni Zavod [*Workers Cultural and Educational Institute*] (YU)
RKR .... Reversible Annular Register (RU)
Rkr .... Ruotsin Kruunu(a) [*Finnish*]
RKRT .... Rejonowe Kierownictwo Robot Telekomunikacyjnych [*District Management of Telecommunications Construction Work*] (POL)
RKRWM .... Rejonowe Kierownictwo Robot Wodno-Melioracyjnych [*District Administration for Irrigation and Land Reclamation Work*] (POL)
RKS .... Control Radio Station (RU)
RKS .... End-of-Count Relay (RU)
RKS .... Lubrication Control Relay (RU)
RKS .... Radiometric Control Station (RU)
RKS .... Raeum- und Kuestensicherungsdivision [*Mine-Sweeping and Coastal Security Division*] (EG)
RKS .... Rayon Communications Office (RU)
RKS .... Rayon Cooperative Union (BU)
RKS .... Record Keeping System (LA1)
RKS .... Robotniczy Klub Sportowy [*Workers' Sports Club*] (POL)
RKS .... Synchronism Control Relay (RU)
RKS .... Velocity Control Relay, Speed Control Relay (RU)
RKSh .... Rayon Kolkhoz School (RU)
RKSM .... Russian Young Communist League [*1918-1924*] (RU)
RKSP .... Rooms Katholieke Staatspartij [*Roman Catholic State Party*] [*Dutch*] (PPE)
rkt .... Jet Propulsion Technology (RU)
RKT .... Workers' and Peasants' Theater (RU)
RKTOF .... Workers' and Peasants' Pacific Fleet (RU)
RKTs .... Relay-Code Central Control (RU)
RKU .... Radiokomunikacni Kontrolni Urad [*Radio Communications Control Office*] (CZ)
RKU .... Rejonowa Komenda Uzupelnien [*District Headquarters of Military Reserves*] (POL)
RKU .... Relative Bearing (RU)
RKU .... Reonska Katastarska Uprava [*Regional Cadaster Administration*] (YU)
RKU .... Rudnik Kamenog Uglja [*Coal Mine*] (YU)
RKUD .... Radnicko Kulturno Umetnicko Drustvo [*Workers' Cultural and Artistic Society*] (YU)
RKV .... Oxygen-Air Mixture Regulator (RU)
RKV .... Rahmenkollektivvertrag [*Skeleton Collective Labor Agreement*] (EG)
RKVMF .... Workers' and Peasants' Navy (RU)
RKVP .... Rooms Katholieke Volkspartij [*Roman Catholic People's Party*] [*Dutch*] (PPE)
RKVT .... Rada Klubu Vojenskeho Telesa [*Committee of the Military Post Club*] (CZ)
RKZ .... Charging Control Relay (RU)
RKZM .... Rosyjski Komunistyczny Zwiazek Mlodziezy [*Russian Communist Youth Union*] (POL)
rl .... Demarcation Line (RU)
r-l .... Leader, Manager (BU)
RL .... Liban [*Lebanon*] [*Polish*]
RL .... Line Relay (RU)
RL .... Manual Laboratory (RU)
RL .... Radar (RU)
RL .... Radio Link, Wire Broadcasting Line (RU)
RL .... Radioactivni Latky [*Radioactive Agents*] (CZ)
RL .... Radiolokator [*RADAR*] (CZ)
rl .... Rajoitettu Lisamaksuvelvollisuus [*Finnish*]
RL .... Reactance Tube (RU)
Rl .... Real [*Real, Royal*] [*Spanish*]
RL .... Rikoslaki [*Finnish*]
RL .... Route Laterale [*Secondary Road*] (CL)
RL .... Rudnik Lignita [*Lignite Mine*] (YU)
rl .... Rulla(a) [*Finnish*]
RL .... X-Rays, Roentgen Rays (RU)
RLA .... Radar Devices (RU)
RLA .... Rocket Vehicle (RU)
rlb .... Radar Battalion (BU)
rlb .... Radar Battalion (RU)
RLB .... Radar Battery (RU)
RLB .... Radar Complex (BU)
RLD .... Republika Ludowo-Demokratyczna [*People's Democratic Republic*] (POL)
RLF .... Rabotnicheski Literaturen Front [*Workers' Literary Front*] [*A periodical*] (BU)
RLF .... Riksforbundet Landsbygdens Folk [*National Farmers Union*] [*Swedish*] (WEN)
RLG .... Luteinizing Hormone Reaction (RU)
RLG .... Royal Lao Government (CL)
RLI .... Rhodesia Light Infantry (MAR)
RLj .... Radio Ljubljana (YU)
RLK .... Rada Lidovych Komisaru [*Council of People's Commissars*] (CZ)
rlk .... Radar (RU)
rlk .... Radlux (RU)
RLKSM .... Russian Lenin Young Communist League [*1924-1926*] (RU)
RLN .... External Line Disconnecting Switch (RU)
RLN .... Raete fuer Landwirtschaftliche Produktion und Nahrungsgueterwirtschaft [*Councils for Agricultural Production and the Foodstuffs Industry*] (EG)
RLO .... Rajonski ljudski Odbor [*Precinct People's Committee*] (YU)
RLP .... Radar Post (BU)
RLP .... Radar Post (RU)
RLP .... Rally of the Lao People (CL)
RLP .... Rassemblement Liegeois pour la Paix [*Liege Assemblage for Peace*] [*French*] (WER)
RLP .... Rejon Lasow Panstwowych [*State Forest District*] (POL)
RLP .... Rhodesian Labor Party (MAR)
RLPS .... Russian Lumber Industry Council (RU)
RLR .... Radar Company (BU)
rlr .... Radar Company (RU)
RLR .... Rumunska Lidova Republika [*Romanian People's Republic*] (CZ)
RLS .... Estimated Resistance Line (RU)
RLS .... Radar Station (BU)
RLS .... Radar Station (RU)
RLS .... Radar System (BU)
RLS .... Radio Relay Communications Line (RU)
RLS .... Raketenleitstation [*Missile Control Center*] (EG)
RLSS .... Red Lion and Sun Society [*Red Cross*] [*Iranian*] (ME)
RLSVD- .... Superhigh-Pressure Mercury-Vapor Lamp (RU)
Rltb .... Realitaetenbesitzer [*German*]
rlto .... Airdrome Maintenance Support Company (BU)
rlts .... Stigma (RU)
RLU .... Rozhlasova Ludova Univerzita [*People's Radio University (Extension courses)*] (CZ)
RLU .... Workers' Literature University (RU)
RLZ .... Reditelstvi Lesnich Zavodu [*Directorate of Forest Enterprises*] (CZ)
RM .... Company Mortar (RU)
RM .... Design Model (RU)
RM .... Fix [*Aviation*] (RU)
RM .... Magnetic Relay (RU)
RM .... Main-Line Reserve (RU)
RM .... Maximum Relay (RU)
rm .... Militia Reserve (RU)
RM .... Overload Relay, Over-Current Relay (RU)
RM .... Power Disconnecting Switch (RU)
RM .... Rada Miejska [*Town Council*] [*Polish*]
RM .... Rada Ministrow [*Council of Ministers*] (POL)
RM .... Radio Beacon (RU)
RM .... Rare Metals (BU)
RM .... Ratna Mornarica [*Navy*] (YU)
rm .... Raummeter [*Cubic Meter*] [*German*]
RM .... Region Militaire [*Military Region*] (CL)
RM .... Reichsmark [*Mark*] [*German*]
RM .... Repair Shop (RU)
RM .... Reverenda Madre [*Reverend Mother*] [*Spanish*]
RM .... River Mine (RU)
RM .... Robni Magazin [*Store*] [*Commercial*] (YU)
RM .... Roentgenometer (RU)
RM .... Roupie Mauricienne (MAR)
RM .... Royal Marines (ML)
RM .... Rudarstvo i Metalurgija [*Mining and Metallurgy*] (YU)
RM .... Steering Engine (RU)
RMAF .... Royal Malayan Air Force (ML)
RMB .... Machine-Repair Base (BU)
RMCRS .... Royal Motonautique Club de Rabat Sale [*Moroccan*] (MAR)
RMF .... Rhodesian Mining Federation (MAR)
RMI .... Rostov Institute of Mechanical Engineering (RU)
RMI .... Rudarsko-Metalurski Inspektorat [*Mining and Metallurgic Inspectorate*] (YU)
rmint .... Mine Sweeper Company (RU)
RMIP .... Region Militar de Isla de Pinos [*Isle of Pines Military Region*] [*Cuban*] (LA)
rmisk .... Mine Detector Company (RU)
RMK .... Dismountable Metal Pile Driver (RU)
RML .... Revolutionaere Marxistische Liga [*Marxist Revolutionary League*] [*Swiss*] (WEN)
RMM .... Dismountable Metal Bridge (RU)
RMM .... Mechanical Repair Shop (RU)
RMM .... Rakosi Matyas Muvek, Csepel [*Matyas Rakosi Works, Csepel*] (HU)
RMM .... Revue du Monde Musulman [*Paris*] [*A publication*] (MAR)
RMM .... Rum Milli Muhafiz [*Greek National Guard (on Cyprus)*] (GC)
RMMO .... Rum Milli Muhafiz Ordusu [*Greek Cypriot National Guard Army*] (GC)
RMMZ .... Revda Metalware and Metallurgical Plant (RU)
r mn .... Genitive Plural (RU)
RMN .... Maximum Voltage Relay (RU)

RMN .... Regiao Militar do Norte [*Northern Military Region*] [*Portuguese*] (WER)
RMN .... Royal Malayan Navy (ML)
RMNO.......... Rozkaz Ministra Narodni Obrany [*Order by the Minister of National Defense*] (CZ)
RMNV- .... Multianode Mercury-Arc Rectifier (RU)
RMO .... Rafinerie Mineralnich Oleju [*Mineral Oil Refinery*] (CZ)
RMO .... Rezerwa Milicji Obywatelskiej [*Citizens' Militia Reserve*] (POL)
RMO .... Russian Musical Society (RU)
RMP............ Company Medical Station (RU)
rmp .... Marine Company (BU)
rmp .... Marine Company (RU)
rmp .... Motorized Infantry Company (RU)
RMP............ Roman Munkaspart [*Romanian Workers' Party*] (HU)
RMP............ Royal Malaysian Police (ML)
RMPI........... Mining of Subsurface Mineral Deposits (RU)
RM PRL .... Rada Ministrow Polskiej Rzeczpospolitej Ludowej [*Council of Ministers of the Polish People's Republic*] (POL)
RMr .... Radio Mreza [*Radio Network*] (YU)
RMR .... Royal Malay Regiment (ML)
RMS .... Council of Ministers Decision (BU)
RMS .... Mechanical Repair Station (RU)
RMS .... Motorized Fishing Station (RU)
RMS .... Radical Mass Spectrometer (RU)
RMS-........... Radio-Frequency Mass Spectrometer (RU)
RMS .... Region Militaire Speciale [*Special Military Region*] [*Cambodian*] (CL)
RMS .... Republik Maluku Selatan [*Republic of South Moluccas*] (IN)
RMS .... Workers' Youth League [*Bulgarian*] (RU)
RMS .... Workers' Youth Union (BU)
RMT............ Maximum Current Tripping Device (RU)
RmT .... Minimum Current Tripping Device (RU)
RMT............ Regiment de Marche du Tchad (MAR)
RMTs........... Distance between Centers (RU)
RMTs........... Mechanical Repair Shop (RU)
RMTs........... Radio-Meteorological Center (RU)
RMTs........... Workers' Youth Center (BU)
rmu............. Bridge Launcher Company (RU)
RMU .... Rudnik Mrkog Uglja [*Brown Coal Mine*] (YU)
RMU .... Small-Angle X-Ray Scattering (RU)
RM WP .... Rada Mlodziezowa Wojska Polskiego [*Youth Council, Polish Army*] (POL)
RMZ............ Machine-Repair Plant (BU)
RMZ............ Mechanical Repair Plant (RU)
RMZ............ Repair and Assembly Plant (RU)
RMZ............ Riga Machine Plant (RU)
RMZ............ Rostov Machine Plant (RU)
RMZ............ Workers' Youth Detachment (BU)
RN .... Carrier Rocket (RU)
RN .... Load Regulator (RU)
RN .... Load Resolution (RU)
RN .... Neutralization Reaction (RU)
RN .... Neutron Radiation Meter, Neutron Detector (RU)
RN .... Noncombatant Private (RU)
RN .... Rada Naczelna [*Chief Council*] (POL)
RN .... Rada Narodowa [*National Council (in London); People's Council (in Poland)*] (POL)
RN .... Radio Filament Battery (RU)
RN .... Rafinerija Nafte [*Naphtha Refinery*] (YU)
RN .... Rassemblement National [*Canadian*] (PPW)
r-n .... Rayon, City District, Area (RU)
RN .... Regular Miner's Lamp (RU)
RN .... Resistencia Nacional [*National Resistance*] [*Salvadoran*] (LA)
RN .... Revenu National [*North African*] (MAR)
RN .... Route Nationale [*National Highway*] [*French*] (WER)
RN .... Stress Relaxation (RU)
RN .... Voltage Regulator (RU)
RN .... Voltage Relay (RU)
RN .... Work Norm (RU)
RN .... Zero Relay (RU)
RNA............ Rassemblement National Arabe [*Arab National Rally*] [*Tunisian*] (PD)
RNA............ Repulogepes Novenyvedo Allomas [*Agricultural Air Station*] (HU)
RNA............ Rhodesian Native Association (MAR)
RNB............ Reditelstvi Narodni Bezpecnosti [*National Security Directorate*] (CZ)
RNB............ River Tank Barge (RU)
RNB............ Worker of the New Bulgaria (BU)
RNbA........... Reichsbahn-Neubauamt [*GDR Railroad Office for New Construction*] (EG)
RNBN .... Non-Self-Propelled River Tank Barge (RU)
RNBS........... Self-Propelled River Tank Barge (RU)
RNC............ Royal Natal Carbineers (MAR)
RNCFM .... Reseau National de Chemins de Fer Malgache [*Malagasy National Railroad System*] (AF)
RND............ Arc Voltage Regulator (RU)
RND............ Low-Pressure Rotor (RU)
RND............ Rassemblement National Democratique [*National Democratic Rally*] [*Senegalese*] (PPW)
RND............ Rijks Nijverheids Dienst [*Dutch*]
RNDr .... Doktor Prirodnich Ved [*Doctor of Natural Sciences*] (CZ)
RNE............ Radio Nacional de Espana [*Spanish National Radio*] (WER)
Rne............. Ruine [*Ruins*] [*Military map abbreviation*] [*World War I*] [*French*] (MTD)
RNET.......... Regie Nationale des Eaux du Togo (MAR)
RNFL........... Rhodesia National Football League (MAR)
RNFU.......... Rhodesian National Farmers Union (AF)
rng.............. Roentgen (RU)
RNGC .... Royal Nairobi Golf Club (MAR)
RNI .... Rassemblement National des Independants [*National Rally of Independents*] [*Moroccan*] (AF)
RNIFI .... Republic Pharmaceutical Scientific Research Institute (BU)
RNII .... Scientific Research Institute of Jet Propulsion (RU)
RNII AKKh... Rostov Scientific Research Institute of the Academy of Municipal Services Imeni K. D. Pamfilov (RU)
RNIIEM........ Republic Scientific Research Institute of Epidemiology and Microbiology (BU)
RNIIKF......... Republic Scientific Research Institute of Health Resorts and Physiotherapy (BU)
RNIIKhK ...... Republic Scientific Research Institute of Bone Surgery (BU)
RNIKF.......... Republic Scientific Research Institute for Clinical Physiology (BU)
RNIKVI .... Republic Scientific Research Institute of Skin and Venereal Diseases (BU)
RNITI .... Republic Scientific Research Institute on Tuberculosis (BU)
r-niye........... Plant (RU)
RNK............ Radiodiffusion Nationale Khmere [*Cambodian National Radio*] (CL)
RNK............ Ribonucleic Acid (RU)
RNK............ Roman Nepkoztarsasag [*Romanian People's Republic*] (HU)
RNK-aza...... Ribonuclease (RU)
RNL .... Radiodiffusion Nationale Lao [*Lao National Radio*] (CL)
RNL .... Rijecki Novi List [*Rijeka New Journal*] [*Rijeka-Fiume, 1907-1915*] [*A publication*] (YU)
RNM .... Minimum Voltage Relay (RU)
RNM .... Radio Diffusion Nationale Marocaine (MAR)
RNM .... Rassemblement National Malgache [*Malagasy National Rally*] (AF)
RNM .... Resistencia Nacional Mocambicana [*Mozambican National Resistance*] (PD)
RNMB.......... Republic Scientific Medical Library (RU)
RNN............ Zero Voltage Relay (RU)
RNO............ Single-Phase Voltage Regulator (RU)
RNP .... Controlled Directional Reception (RU)
RNP .... Radio Navigation Point (RU)
RNP .... Regie Nationale des Palmeraies (MAR)
RNP .... Rhodesia National Party (AF)
RNP .... Ribonucleoprotein (RU)
RNPC .... Regie Nationale des Palmeraies du Congo (MAR)
RNPE........... Regie Nationale des Plantations de l'Equateur (MAR)
RNPISMP .... Republic Scientific and Practical Institute for Emergency Medical Aid (BU)
RNPS........... Regie Nationale des Plantations de la Sangha (MAR)
RNR............ Romanian People's Republic (BU)
RNR............ Romanian People's Republic (RU)
RNS............ Nonlogical Combinations Relay (RU)
RNS............ Radio Navigation Station (RU)
RNS............ Radio Navigation System (RU)
RNS............ Radio Navigation System (BU)
RNS............ Rated-Speed Relay (RU)
RNS............ Rayon People's Councils (BU)
RNS............ Start-of-Count Relay (RU)
RNS............ Starter Voltage Relay (RU)
RNT .... Radio Navigation Point (RU)
RNT .... Radiodiffusion Nationale Tchadienne [*Chadian National Broadcasting*] (AF)
RNT .... Three-Phase Voltage Regulator (RU)
RNT .... Zero Current Relay (RU)
RNTA........... Rassemblement National des Travailleurs Algeriens [*National Rally of Algerian Workers*] (AF)
RNTA........... Regie Nationale des Tabacs et Allumettes (MAR)
RNTB........... Regie Nationale des Transports Brazzavillois (MAR)
RNTB........... Republic Scientific and Technical Library (RU)
RNTP........... Regie Nationale des Transports et des Travaux Publics [*Congolese*] (MAR)
RNU............ Lower Level Relay (RU)
RNUR .... Regie Nationale des Usines Renault (MAR)
RNVR........... Royal Naval Volunteer Reserve (ML)
RNW .... Radio Nederland Wereldomroep [*Radio Netherlands World Broadcasting Foundation*] (WEN)
r-nyy............ Rayon, City District, Area (RU)
RN ZBOWiD ... Rada Naczelna Zwiazku Bojownikow o Wolnosc i Demokracje [*Chief Council of the Association of Combatants for Liberty and Democracy*] [*Polish*]
RNZSP .... Rada Naczelna Zrzeszenia Studentow Polskich [*Chief Council of the Polish Student Association*] (POL)
RO .... Biro [*Bureau*] (IN)
RO .... Cutting-Off Relay, Disconnecting Relay (RU)
RO .... Electronic Equipment, Electronic and Radio Equipment [*Aircraft maintenance*] (RU)
RO .... Fallout Radiometer (RU)

RO .... Flamethrower Company (RU)
RO .... Intelligence Agency (RU)
RO .... Intelligence Department (RU)
RO .... Intelligence Service Department (BU)
RO .... Limiting Relay (RU)
RO- .... Manual Sprinkler (RU)
RO .... Portable Flamethrower (RU)
RO .... Raastuvanoikeus [*Finnish*]
RO .... Rada Okregowa [*District Council*] [*Polish*]
RO .... Radial-Axial (RU)
RO .... Radio Marker Beacon (RU)
RO .... Radna Organizacija [*Organization of Workers*] [*Yugoslav*] (CED)
RO .... Raketometny Oddil [*Rocket Launcher Battalion*] (CZ)
RO .... Rayon Department, City District Department (RU)
RO .... Real Orden [*Spanish*]
RO .... Reconnaissance Detachment (BU)
RO .... Reconnaissance Detachment (RU)
RO .... Regulator, Adjusting Device (RU)
RO .... Republiski Odbor [*Republic Committee*] (YU)
RO .... Rocket Launcher (RU)
RO .... Rocket Weapon (RU)
RO .... Romania [*Two-letter standard code*] (CNC)
RO .... Stopping Relay (RU)
ROA .... Retard a l'Ouverture de l'Admission [*French*] (MTD)
ROA .... Ruska Oslobodilacka Armija [*Russian Liberation Army*] [*Organized by the Germans from Soviet prisoners*] [*World War II*] (YU)
ROAK .... Ruch Oporu Armii Krajowej [*Resistance Movement of the Home Army*] (POL)
ROBAN .... Manuscript Division of the Library of the Academy of Sciences, USSR (RU)
RO BIS .... Manuscript Division of the State Public Library Imeni Saltykov-Shchedrin (RU)
ROC .... Republic of China (MAR)
ROC .... Rhodesia Omnibus Company (MAR)
ROCCON .... Road Construction Company of Nigeria Ltd. (MAR)
ROCH .... Ruch Oporu Chlopskiego [*Movement of Peasant Resistance*] [*Polish*] (PPE)
roczn .... Rocznie [*Yearly*] (POL)
roczn .... Rocznik [*Yearbook*] (POL)
rod .... Born (BU)
rod .... Born (RU)
rod .... Genitive [*Case*] (RU)
rod .... Spring, Source [*Topography*] (RU)
roddom .... Maternity Home (RU)
RODK .... Russian Book Friends' Society (RU)
rodn .... Spring, Source [*Topography*] (RU)
ROE .... Resistencia de Obreros y Estudiantes [*Worker and Student Resistance Group*] [*Uruguayan*] (LA)
ROE .... Sedimentation Rate [*Medicine*] (RU)
ROF .... Rayon Physical Culture Organization (BU)
ROG .... General-Group Relay (RU)
ROGBL .... Manuscript Division of the State Library Imeni Lenin (RU)
RO GIM .... State Historical Museum. Manuscript and Old Book Division (RU)
ROGN .... Flamethrower Company (RU)
RO GPB .... Manuscript Division of the State Public Library Imeni Saltykov-Shchedrin (RU)
ROH .... Revolucne Odborove Hnutie [*Revolutionary Trade-Union Movement*] (CZ)
RO IRLI .... Manuscript Division of the Institute of Russian Literature (RU)
ROIT .... Regionalny Osrodek Informacji Turystycznej [*Regional Tourist Information Center*] [*Polish*]
ROKK .... Red Cross Society of the RSFSR (RU)
ROLTEX .... Rovidaru es Lakastextil Kiskereskedelmi Vallalat [*State Dry Goods Stores*] (HU)
ROM .... City District Militia Department (RU)
ROM .... City District Militia Station (RU)
ROM .... Magnetic Revolution Regulator (RU)
ROM .... Open-Sea Reconnaissance Aircraft (RU)
rom .... Roemisch [*German*]
rom .... Roman [*Romanian*] (HU)
ROM .... Romania [*Three-letter standard code*] (CNC)
rom .... Romaniaa [*or Romaniaksi*] [*Finnish*]
rom .... Romanialainen [*Finnish*]
Rom .... Romorker [*Trailer*] (TU)
roman .... Romanisch [*German*]
romboedr .... Rhombohedral (RU)
romb s .... Rhombic Syngony (RU)
ROMCONSULT ... Institutul Roman de Consulting [*Romanian Consulting Institute*] (RO)
rom kat .... Romai Katolikus [*Roman Catholic*] (HU)
rom-kath .... Roemisch-Katholisch [*German*]
ROMM .... Revue de l'Occident Musulman et de la Mediterranee [*A publication*] (MAR)
ROMO .... Republic General Machinery Manufacture Association [*RSFSR*] (RU)
ROMTRANS ... Intreprinderea de Stat pentru Transporturi si Expeditii Internationale [*State Enterprise for International Transportation and Shipments*] (RO)
RO/MVD .... Investigating Section of the Ministry of Internal Affairs (RU)
ROMVD .... Rayon Branch of the Ministry of Internal Affairs (RU)
RON .... Eskadron [*Squadron*] (IN)
RONFIN .... Republic of Nauru Finance Corp.
RONO .... Rayon Department of Public Education (RU)
rontg .... Rontgen [*X-Ray*] (HU)
roomal .... Roomalainen [*Finnish*]
roomkat .... Roomalais-Katolinen [*Finnish*]
ROOP- .... Portable Pneumatic Fire Extinguisher-Sprinkler (RU)
rop .... Company Strong Point (RU)
ROP .... Field Failure Relay (RU)
ROP .... Referat Ochrony Przemyslowej [*Industrial Security Office*] (POL)
ROP .... Russian Society of Pathologists (RU)
ROPIK .... Russian Society for the Study of the Crimea (RU)
ROPIT .... Russian Steamship Line and Trade Society (RU)
ROPWiM .... Rada Ochrony Pomnikow Walki i Meczenstwa [*Council for Conservation of Monuments of Struggle and Martyrdom*] (POL)
RORI .... Russian Society of Radio Engineers [*1918-1929*] (RU)
ros .... Area Communications Section (RU)
ROS .... General-Signal Relay (RU)
ROS .... Operating Exchange Capacity [*Nuclear energy*] (BU)
ROS .... Radarska Osmatracka Stanica [*RADAR Observation Station*] (YU)
ROS .... Radiova Odposlouchavaci Sluzba [*Radio Monitoring Service*] (CZ)
ROS .... Remontowa Obsluga Statkow [*Ship Repair Service*] (POL)
ros .... Rosyjski [*Russian*] (POL)
ROS .... Speed-Limiting Relay (RU)
Rosavtoobsluzhivaniye ... Republic Trust of Filling Stations and Automobile Service Stations (RU)
Rosavtoremont ... Republic Trust of Automobile Repair Plants and Shops (RU)
Rosbakaleya ... Republic Office of the Wholesale Trade in Sugar, Confectionery, Canned Goods, Tobacco, Salt, and Other Groceries [*RSFSR*] (RU)
Rosbriket ... Republic Briquette Trust [*RSFSR*] (RU)
Rosdrozhzhi ... Republic Trust of Yeast Industry [*RSFSR*] (RU)
Rosformomaterialy ... State Republic Trust for the Extraction of Casting Sand and Clay (RU)
Rosgalantereya ... Republic Office of the Wholesale Trade in Notions, Perfume, Cosmetics, and Soap [*RSFSR*] (RU)
Rosgazstroy ... Republic Trust for the Construction of Gas Networks [*RSFSR*] (RU)
Rosgiprogorsel'stroy ... Republic State Planning Institute for the Planning of Urban and Rural Construction of the RSFSR (RU)
Rosgiprosel'khozstroy ... Republic State Planning Institute for the Planning of Agricultural Construction [*RSFSR*] (RU)
Rosgiprosovkhozstroy ... Republic State Institute for the Planning of Sovkhoz Construction [*RSFSR*] (RU)
Rosgiprovodkhoz ... Republic State Institute for the Planning of Water-Management and Reclamation Construction of the Gosvodkhoz RSFSR (RU)
Rosgiprozem ... Republic State Planning Institute for Land Use Measures [*RSFSR*] (RU)
Rosgizmestprom ... State Publishing House of Local Industry of the RSFSR (RU)
Rosglavavtotraktorosnabsbyt ... Main Administration for the Supply and Marketing of Automobiles, Tractors, Motors, Agricultural Machinery, and Spare Parts [*RSFSR*] (RU)
Rosglavbumprom ... Main Administration of the Paper Industry [*RSFSR*] (RU)
Rosglavbumsnabsbyt ... Main Administration for the Supply and Marketing of Products of the Pulp and Paper, Wood Chemistry, and Furniture Industries (RU)
Rosglavchermetsnabsbyt ... Main Administration of Supply and Marketing of Ferrous Metals, Metalware, Ores, Fluxes, By-Product Coke, and Refractory Products [*RSFSR*] (RU)
Rosglavelektrosnabsbyt ... Main Administration of Supply and Marketing of Electrotechnical Equipment, Cable Products, and Electrotechnical Consumer Goods (RU)
Rosglavfil'm ... Main Administration of Motion-Picture Production [*RSFSR*] (RU)
Rosglavgosrybvod ... Main State Inspection for Fish Conservation and Reproduction and for Control of Fishing [*RSFSR*] (RU)
Rosglavkhimkomplekt ... Main Administration for Supplying Complete Sets of Equipment, Devices, Cables, and Other Products and Basic Materials to Chemical Industry Establishments Being Constructed or Repaired [*RSFSR*] (RU)
Rosglavkhimsnabsbyt ... Main Administration of Supply and Marketing of Chemical, Rubber, and Asbestos Products [*RSFSR*] (RU)
Rosglavkniga ... Main Administration of the Book Trade [*RSFSR*] (RU)
Rosglavkonserv ... Main Administration of the Canning and Vegetable Drying Industry [*RSFSR*] (RU)
Rosglavkoopkhoztorg ... Main Administration for Trade in Building Materials, Hardware, and Goods Used in Industry (RU)
Rosglavkoopkul'ttorg ... Main Administration for Trade in Goods for Cultural Purposes [*RSFSR*] (RU)

Rosglavkoopmyasoptitsa ... Main Administration for the Procurement, Processing, and Marketing of Meat, Eggs, and Dairy Products [*of the Rospotrebsoyuz*] (RU)
Rosglavkooppromtorg ... Main Administration for Trade in Industrial Goods [*of the Rospotrebsoyuz*] (RU)
Rosglavkoopsnab ... Main Administration of Materials and Equipment Supply [*of the Rospotrebsoyuz*] (RU)
Rosglavkoopzhivsyr'ye ... Main Administration for the Procurement, Processing, and Marketing of Livestock Raw Materials, Secondary Raw Materials, Livestock Products, and Fur (RU)
Rosglavkozh ... Main Administration of the Leather Industry [*RSFSR*] (RU)
Rosglavkul'tsnabsbyt ... Main Supply and Marketing Administration of the Ministry of Culture, RSFSR (RU)
Rosglavlegsnab ... Main Administration of Materials and Equipment Supply of the Ministry of Light Industry, RSFSR (RU)
Rosglavlegsnabsbytsyr'ye ... Main Administration for Supplying and Marketing Raw Materials of Light Industry (RU)
Rosglavlen ... Main Administration of the Flax and Hemp Industry [*RSFSR*] (RU)
Rosglavles ... Main Administration of the Lumber Industry [*RSFSR*] (RU)
Rosglavlesosbyt ... Main Administration for the Marketing of Lumber [*RSFSR*] (RU)
Rosglavlesosnab ... Main Administration of Materials and Equipment Supply of the Ministry of the Lumber Industry, RSFSR (RU)
Rosglavlessnabsbyt ... Main Administration for Supply and Marketing of Products of the Logging and Woodworking Industry [*RSFSR*] (RU)
Rosglavmashdetal' ... Main Administration of Machine Part Manufacture [*RSFSR*] (RU)
Rosglavmashsnabsbyt ... Main Administration for the Supply and Marketing of Machinery [*RSFSR*] (RU)
Rosglavmaslosyrprom ... Main Administration of the Butter and Cheese Industry [*RSFSR*] (RU)
Rosglavmedsnab ... Main Medical Supply Administration [*RSFSR*] (RU)
Rosglavmekh ... Main Administration of the Fur and Sheepskin-Coat Industry [*RSFSR*] (RU)
Rosglavmyasomolsnab ... Main Administration of Materials and Equipment Supply of the Ministry of the Meat and Dairy Products Industry, RSFSR (RU)
Rosglavmyasomolstroy ... Main Construction Administration of the Ministry of the Meat and Dairy Products Industry, RSFSR (RU)
Rosglavmyasoptitseprom ... Main Administration of the Meat and Poultry Processing Industry [*RSFSR*] (RU)
Rosglavneftesnabsbyt ... Main Administration of Supply and Marketing of Petroleum and Petroleum Products (RU)
Rosglavoboronsnabsbyt ... Main Supply and Marketing Administration of the Defense Industry [*RSFSR*] (RU)
Rosglavobuv' ... Main Administration of the Footwear Industry [*RSFSR*] (RU)
Rosglavparfyumer ... Main Administration of the Perfume, Cosmetics, and Essential-Oil Industry (RU)
Rosglavpishchesnabsbytsyr'ye ... Main Administration of Supply and Marketing of Food Raw Materials (RU)
Rosglavpivo ... Main Administration of the Brewing and Soft Drink Industry [*RSFSR*] (RU)
Rosglavpriborsnabsbyt ... Main Administration of Supply and Marketing of Instruments and Automation Equipment [*RSFSR*] (RU)
Rosglavprodsnab ... Main Administration of Materials and Equipment Supply of the Ministry of the Foodstuffs Industry, RSFSR (RU)
Rosglavradiosnabsbyt ... Main Administration of Supply and Marketing of Communications Equipment and Radiotechnical Products [*RSFSR*] (RU)
Rosglavraszhirmaslo ... Main Administration of the Oil and Fats Industry [*RSFSR*] (RU)
Rosglavrybsnab ... Main Administration of Materials and Equipment Supply of Fish Industry Establishments [*RSFSR*] (RU)
Rosglavrybsnabsbyt ... Main Administration of Supply and Production Marketing of the Fish Industry [*RSFSR*] (RU)
Rosglavrybstroy ... Main Construction Administration of the Ministry of the Fish Industry, RSFSR (RU)
Rosglavrybtara ... Main Administration of Logging and Manufacture of Packing Materials of the Ministry of the Fish Industry, RSFSR (RU)
Rosglavsadpitomnik ... Main Administration of Horticulture, Nurseries, Sericulture, and Apiculture [*RSFSR*] (RU)
Rosglavsakhar ... Main Administration of the Sugar Industry [*RSFSR*] (RU)
Rosglavsel'snab ... Main Administration of Materials and Equipment Supply of the Ministry of Agriculture, RSFSR (RU)
Rosglavsetesnast' ... Main Administration of the Netting and Rigging Industry [*RSFSR*] (RU)
Rosglavsherst' ... Main Administration of the Wool Industry [*RSFSR*] (RU)
Rosglavshveyprom ... Main Administration of the Garment Industry [*RSFSR*] (RU)
Rosglavsol' ... Main Administration of the Salt Industry [*RSFSR*] (RU)
Rosglavspirt ... Main Administration of the Alcohol, Liqueur, and Vodka Industry (RU)
Rosglavstankoinstrumentsnabsbyt ... Main Administration of Supply and Marketing of Machine Tools, Forging-and-Pressing Equipment, Tools, and Abrasives [*RSFSR*] (RU)
Rosglavsteklo ... Main Administration of the Glass Industry [*RSFSR*] (RU)
Rosglavstromsnab ... Main Supply Administration of the Building Materials Industry [*RSFSR*] (RU)
Rosglavstroy ... Main Construction Administration [*RSFSR*] (RU)
Rosglavstroysnabsbyt ... Main Administration of Supply and Marketing of Building Materials and Sanitary Engineering Equipment [*RSFSR*] (RU)
Rosglavtabak ... Main Administration of the Tobacco and Tea Industries (RU)
Rosglavtekstil'galantereya ... Main Administration of the Textile and Notions Industries [*RSFSR*] (RU)
Rosglavtekstil'snabsbytsyr'ye ... Main Administration of Supply and Marketing of Textile Industry Raw Materials [*RSFSR*] (RU)
Rosglavtopmash ... Main Administration of Fuel Machinery [*RSFSR*] (RU)
Rosglavtorfbriket ... Main Administration of the Peat and Peat-Briquette Industry [*RSFSR*] (RU)
Rosglavtrikotazh ... Main Administration of the Knit Goods Industry [*RSFSR*] (RU)
Rosglavtselinstroy ... Main Administration of Sovkhoz Construction on Virgin and Fallow Lands [*RSFSR*] (RU)
Rosglavtsvetmetsnabsbyt ... Main Administration of Supply and Marketing of Nonferrous and Rare Metals, Nonferrous Rolled Products, and Metalware [*RSFSR*] (RU)
Rosglavtyazhmashsnabsbyt ... Main Administration of Supply and Marketing of Products of Heavy Transportation, Construction, and Road Machinery [*RSFSR*] (RU)
Rosglavugleneft' ... Main Administration of the Coal and Petroleum Industries [*RSFSR*] (RU)
Rosglavuglesnabsbyt ... Main Administration of Supply and Marketing of Coal Fuel, Shale, and Peat [*RSFSR*] (RU)
Rosglavvalprom ... Main Administration of the Felt Industry [*RSFSR*] (RU)
Rosglavvino ... Main Administration of the Wine-Making Industry [*RSFSR*] (RU)
Rosglavvitaminprom ... Main Administration of the Vitamin Industry [*RSFSR*] (RU)
Rosglavvodsnab ... Main Administration of Materials and Equipment Supply of the Ministry of Water Management, RSFSR (RU)
Rosgorstroy ... Republic Trust of Civil Engineering and Housing Construction [*RSFSR*] (RU)
Rosgosstrakh ... Administration of State Insurance for the RSFSR (RU)
Roskhlebtorg ... Main Administration of the Grain Trade [*RSFSR*] (RU)
Roskhmel'... Russian Republic Office for Hop Growing (RU)
Roskhoztorg ... Republic Office for Wholesale Trade in Household Goods [*RSFSR*] (RU)
Roskhoztrans ... Main Administration of Automobile Transportation of the Ministry of Sovkhozes, RSFSR (RU)
Roskombank ... Russian Commercial Bank (RU)
Roskonservlestara ... Trust for the Procurement and Processing of Lumber and for the Manufacture of Packing Materials of the Rosglavkonserv [*RSFSR*] (RU)
Roskooplestara ... Republic Trust for the Procurement of Lumber and for the Manufacture of Packing Materials of the Rosglavkoopsnab (RU)
Roskoopprodkontora ... Republic Office for Food Trade (RU)
Roskooppromproyekt ... Republic Planning Office of the Rospromsovet (RU)
Roskul'ttorg ... Republic Office for Wholesale Trade in Goods for Cultural Purposes and Sporting Goods [*RSFSR*] (RU)
Roslegpromstroy ... State Republic Construction and Installation Trust of the Ministry of Light Industry, RSFSR (RU)
Roslesotopsbyt ... Administration of Fuel Marketing and Lumber Supply [*RSFSR*] (RU)
Roslesstroytorg ... Republic Office for the Trade in Lumber and Building Materials [*RSFSR*] (RU)
Rosleszag ... Republic Logging Trust [*RSFSR*] (RU)
Rosmashdortrest ... Republic Trust for the Management of Road Machine Stations [*RSFSR*] (RU)
Rosmaslosindikat ... All-Russian Syndicate of the Vegetable Oil Industry (RU)
Rosmedsnabtorg ... Office for Purchasing, Procurement, and Supply of Chemicopharmaceutical Goods, Reagents, Sanitation and Hygiene Articles, and Other Pharmaceutical Products [*RSFSR*] (RU)
Rosmetalloproyekt ... Office for the Planning of Machinery and Metalworking Plants [*RSFSR*] (RU)
Rosmyasomolproyekt ... Republic Planning and Surveying Office of the Ministry of the Meat and Dairy Products Industry, RSFSR (RU)
Rosmyasorybtorg ... Republic Office for the Wholesale Trade in Meat, Butter, and Fish (RU)
ROSNIIMS... Republic Scientific Research Institute of Local Building Materials [*RSFSR*] (RU)
Rosobuv'torg ... Republic Office of the Wholesale Trade in Footwear [*RSFSR*] (RU)
Rosokhotsoyuz ... Union of Hunters' Societies of the RSFSR (RU)
Rosoptpromtorg ... Republic Office of the Wholesale Trade in Industrial Goods [*RSFSR*] (RU)
Rospotrebsoyuz ... Union of the Consumers' Societies of the RSFSR (RU)
Rosprodproyekt ... Republic Planning Office of the Ministry of the Foodstuffs Industry, RSFSR (RU)
Rospromsovet ... Council of Producers' Cooperatives of the RSFSR (RU)
Rospromtorg ... Main Administration for Trade in Industrial Goods [*RSFSR*] (RU)

Rosproyekt ... Institute for Publication and Distribution of Standard Designs for Rural Construction [*RSFSR*] (RU)
ROSS .... Roudnicke Strojirny a Slevarny [*Roudnice Engineering Works and Foundries*] (CZ)
Rossel'khoztekhnika ... All-Russian Association of the Council of Ministers of the RSFSR for the Sale of Agricultural Machinery, Spare Parts, Mineral Fertilizers, and Other Materials and Equipment, Repair Organization, and Machine Utilization in Kolkhozes and Sovkhozes (RU)
Rossel'stroy ... Republic Construction Trust of the Ministry of Agriculture, RSFSR (RU)
Rosshelk..... Russian Republic Office for Sericulture (RU)
Rosskotsyr'ye ... Republic Office for Supply of Animal Raw Materials and for Fattening of Cattle [*RSFSR*] (RU)
Rossnabso ... Administration of Materials and Equipment Supply of the Ministry of Social Security, RSFSR (RU)
Rossortsemovoshch ... Republic Office for the Procurement and Marketing of High-Quality Vegetable Seeds [*RSFSR*] (RU)
Rossovkhozstroy ... Republic Construction Trust of the Ministry of Sovkhozes, RSFSR (RU)
Rossovkhoztrans ... Main Administration of Automobile Transportation of the Ministry of Sovkhozes, RSFSR (RU)
Rosspetsstroy ... Republic Specialized Trust of the Glavspetsstroy [*RSFSR*] (RU)
Rosstromproyekt ... State Planning Institute for the Planning of Building Materials Plants [*RSFSR*] (RU)
Rosstroymontazh ... Republic Construction and Installation Trust [*RSFSR*] (RU)
Rosta........... Russian News Agency [*1918-1935*] (RU)
Rostekhizdat ... Publishing House of Scientific and Technical Literature of the RSFSR (RU)
Rostekstil'torg ... Republic Office for Wholesale Trade in Textiles [*RSFSR*] (RU)
Rostizdat .... Rostov Publishing House (RU)
Rostorgmestprom ... Rostov City Administration of Local Industry (RU)
Rostorgmontazh ... Republic Specialized Trust for the Installation of the Refrigeration and Trade Equipment [*RSFSR*] (RU)
Rostorgodezhda ... Republic Office of Wholesale Clothing Trade [*RSFSR*] (RU)
Rostorgreklama ... Republic Office of Trade Advertising [*RSFSR*] (RU)
Rostorgsnab ... Main Administration of Materials and Equipment Supply of the Ministry of Trade, RSFSR (RU)
Rostorgstroy ... Construction and Installation Trust of the Ministry of Trade, RSFSR (RU)
Rostovenergo ... Rostov Power System (RU)
Rostsel'mash ... Rostov Agricultural Machinery Plant (RU)
Rosvalmashproyekt ... Design, Planning, and Installation Office of the State Committee on Light Industry of the Gosplan SSSR (RU)
Rosvattrest ... Republic Cotton and Wadding Trust [*RSFSR*] (RU)
Rosvodstroy ... Republic Reclamation Construction Trust [*RSFSR*] (RU)
Rosvuzizdat ... Publishing House of the Ministry of Higher and Secondary Special Education, RSFSR (RU)
Rosyuvelirtorg ... Republic Office for Jewelry Manufacture and Trade [*RSFSR*] (RU)
Roszoovetsnab ... Republic Office for the Supply of Veterinary and Zootechnical Equipment, Instruments, and Drugs [*RSFSR*] (RU)
ROT............. Reverse-Current Relay (RU)
ROT............. Reverse-Current Tripping Device (RU)
ROT............. Temperature Regulator (RU)
ROTs........... Cycle Termination Relay (RU)
ROTZ........... Reactor with a Heat-Transfer Agent and Organic Moderator (RU)
ROU............. Manual Carbon Dioxide Fire Extinguisher (RU)
ROU............. Pressure-Reducing and Cooling Unit (RU)
Roubne .... Roubine [*Military map abbreviation*] [*World War I*] [*French*] (MTD)
ROUE .... Revolutionary Organization of Uganda (AF)
rov............... Rovat [*Newspaper Column*] (HU)
ROW............ Rybnicki Okreg Weglowy [*Rybnik Coal Basin*] [*Polish*]
roz............... Rozena [*Nee (Maiden name)*] (CZ)
rozdz........... Rozdzial [*Chapter*] (POL)
rozp............. Rozporzadzenie [*Instruction*] (POL)
rozsz .... Rozszerzone [*Enlarged*] (POL)
Rp................ Bench Mark (RU)
RP................ Casualty Sorting Station (RU)
RP................ Company Machine Gun (RU)
RP................ Distinctive Attributes (RU)
RP................ Distribution Field (RU)
RP................ Distribution Point [*Electricity*] (RU)
RP................ Excavations and Studies (BU)
RP................ Field Radiometer (RU)
rp................ Genitive Case (RU)
RP................ Initiating Relay (RU)
RP................ Intermediate Relay (RU)
RP................ Light Machine Gun (RU)
RP................ Loading Point, Entrucking Point (RU)
RP................ Miner's Lamp with Increased Reliability (RU)
rp................ Observation Post, Reconnaissance Post (RU)
RP................ Operating Field [*Computers*] (RU)
RP................ Polarized Relay (RU)
RP................ Precipitation Test (RU)
RP-.............. Precision Roentgen Meter (RU)
RP................ Rada Panstwa [*State Council*] [*Polish*]
RP................ Radiation Pyrometer (RU)
RP................ Radio Direction Finder (BU)
RP................ Radio Director Finder, Radiogoniometer (RU)
RP................ Radio Prijemnik [*Radio Receiver*] (YU)
rp................ Rakpart [*Embankment*] (HU)
Rp................ Rampe [*Ramp, Loading Platform*] (EG)
RP................ Rayon Substation (RU)
RP................ Reconnaissance by Radio Direction Finding (RU)
RP................ Recorder (RU)
RP................ Reditelstvi Post [*Postal Directorate*] (CZ)
RP................ Reform Party (MAR)
RP................ Regulating Post, Commanding Post (RU)
RP................ Reichs Patent [*State Patent*] [*German*]
rp................ Rekopis [*Manuscript*] (POL)
RP................ Reponse Payee [*Prepaid Reply*] [*French*] (CL)
RP................ Republikeinse Party van Suidwesafrika [*Republican Party of South West Africa*] [*Namibian*] (PPW)
RP................ Resolver (RU)
RP................ Reverend Pere [*Reverend Father*] [*French*]
RP................ Reverendo Padre [*Reverend Father*] [*Spanish*]
RP................ Rhodesian Party (MAR)
RP................ Ribarsko Poduzece [*Fishing Establishment*] (YU)
RP................ Rocni Plan [*Year Plan*] (CZ)
RP................ Route Provinciale [*Provincial Highway*] (CL)
RP................ Rude Pravo [*The Red Right*] [*A newspaper*] (CZ)
RP................ Rudny Projekt [*Mining Investments Planning Office*] (CZ)
RP................ Rzeczpospolita Polska [*Polish Republic*] (POL)
RP................ Searchlight Radar (RU)
RP................ Unloading Platform, Detrucking Platform (RU)
RP................ Workers' Party (BU)
rp................ Workers' Settlement (RU)
RPA-............ Lure-Distributing Truck (RU)
RPA .... Parabolic Horn Antenna (RU)
RPA .... Radio Reception Equipment Room (RU)
RPA .... Rassemblement Populaire Africain (MAR)
RPA .... Rationalist Press Association (EA)
RPA .... Rechapage Pneus Afrique (MAR)
RPA .... Republica Popular de Angola (MAR)
RPA .... Republica Populara Albania [*Albanian People's Republic*] (RO)
RPA .... Republik Persatuan Arab [*United Arab Republic*] (IN)
RPA .... Republika Poludniowej Afryki [*Republic of South Africa*] [*Polish*]
RPA .... Republique Populaire d'Angola (MAR)
RPA .... Rice Producers Association [*Guyanese*] (LA)
RPAC .... Resistencia do Povo Anti-Colonista [*Peoples Anti-Colonialist Resistance*] [*Portuguese*] (WER)
RPAJ .... Radnicke Protivavionske Jedinice [*Workers' Antiaircraft Units*] [*Army*] (YU)
RPAL .... Rubber Planters Association of Liberia (MAR)
RPB .... Company Ammunition Supply Point (RU)
RPB .... Nonceramic Polarized Relay (RU)
RPB .... Radar Bombsight (RU)
rpb .... Radio Direction-Finding Battalion (BU)
RPB .... Rassemblement Populaire du Burundi (MAR)
RPB .... Repair and Rental Base (RU)
RPB .... Republica Populara Bulgara [*Bulgarian People's Republic*] (RO)
RPB .... Republique Populaire du Benin (MAR)
RPB .... Workers' Party of Burma (RU)
RPC .... Regiment Parachutiste Commando [*Paratrooper Commando Regiment*] [*Upper Voltan*] (AF)
RPC .... Regiment de Parachutistes Coloniaux [*Algerian*] (MAR)
RPC .... Regional Police Commander (MAR)
RPC .... Republica Populara Chineza [*People's Republic of China*] (RO)
RPC .... Republique Populaire de Chine (MAR)
RPC .... Reunionese Peace Committee (MAR)
RPC .... Rivers People's Congress (MAR)
RPCh........... Frequency Starting Relay (RU)
RPCh........... Manual Heterodyne Frequency Trim (RU)
RPCh........... Radio Pulse Frequency Converter (RU)
RPCM.......... Rassemblement Populaire Caledonien et Metropolitain [*Caledonian and Metropolitan Popular Rally*] (PPW)
RPCR........... Rassemblement pour la Caledonie dans la Republique [*Popular Caledonian Rally for the Republic*] (PPW)
RPD .... Degtyarev Light Machine Gun (RU)
RPD .... Direct-Action Controller (RU)
RPD .... Electronic Radio Countermeasures (BU)
RPD .... Pressure Regulator (RU)
RPD .... Radio Countermeasures (RU)
RPD .... Ramjet Engine (RU)
RPD .... Rerum Politicarum Doctor [*Doctor of Political Science*] [*Latin*] (GPO)
RPD .... Rotary Piston Engine (RU)
RPDC .... Republique Populaire Democratique de Coree [*Democratic People's Republic of Korea*] [*Use DPRK or North Korea*] (CL)
RPDK........... Republica Populara Democrata Coreeana [*Korean Democratic People's Republic*] (RO)

rpdn .... Missile Maintenance Battalion (BU)
RPF .... Front Distribution Port (RU)
RPF .... Rassemblement du Peuple Francais [*Rally of the French People*] (WER)
RPF .... Reformatorische Politieke Federatie [*Reformist Political Federation*] [*Netherlands*] (PPE)
RPG .... Antitank Hand Grenade (RU)
RPG .... Antitank Rocket Launcher (RU)
RPG .... Fire Chief (BU)
rpg .... Radio Direction-Finding Group (BU)
RPHM .... Referent Zasobovani Pohonne Hmoty a Mazadla [*Officer-in-Charge of Petroleum Products and Lubricants*] (CZ)
RPI .... Rassemblement du Peuple Issa [*Somali*] (MAR)
RPI .... Rassemblement Populaire pour l'Independance [*People's Rally for Independence*] [*Djibouti*] (PPW)
RPI .... Rayon Fire Inspector (RU)
RPI .... Relay Selector Panel (RU)
RPI .... Republican Party of India (PPW)
RPI .... Republican Party of Italy (RU)
RPI .... Riga Polytechnic Institute (RU)
RPI .... Rostov Pedagogical Institute (RU)
RPIMA .... Regiment Parachutiste d'Infanterie de Marine [*Naval Infantry Paratrooper Regiment*] [*French*] (AF)
RPK .... Automatic Direction Finder (RU)
RPK .... Command Radio Transmitter (RU)
RPK .... Rayon Industrial Kombinat (RU)
RPK .... Rayon Party Committee (RU)
RPK .... Rayon Studbook (RU)
RPK .... Rumunska Partia Komunistyczna [*Communist Party of Romania*] [*Polish*]
RPKAD .... Resimen Para Komando Angkatan Darat [*Army Para Commando Regiment*] (IN)
rpkhz .... Chemical Defense Company (RU)
RPKO .... Automatic Direction Finder-Recorder (RU)
RP-Kredite ... Richtsatz-Plankredite [*Standard Planned Credits*] (EG)
RPL .... Rassemblement du Peuple Lao [*Rally of the Lao People*] [*Use RLP*] (CL)
RPL .... Rejon Przemyslu Lesnego [*Forest Industry District*] (POL)
RPl .... Richtlinie des Plenums des Obersten Gerichts [*Guidelines of the Plenum of the Supreme Court*] (EG)
rpl .... Rupla(a) [*Finnish*]
RPM .... Company Aid Station (BU)
RPM .... Mantissa Transfer Register [*Computers*] (RU)
RPM .... Neutral Flat Magnetic Relay (RU)
RPM .... Oil-Pumping Relay (RU)
RPM .... Republica Popular de Mocambique (MAR)
RPM .... Republica Populara Mongola [*Mongolian People's Republic*] (RO)
RPM .... Reverendo Padre Maestro [*Spanish*]
RPM .... Rivers People's Movement (MAR)
RPM- .... Rotary Loader (RU)
RPM .... Sorting and Selecting Machine (RU)
RPN .... Load-Supply Relay (RU)
RPN .... Manual Fire Pump (RU)
RPN .... Regulation Under Load (RU)
RPN .... Standard Flat Relay (RU)
RPO .... Constant-Speed Governor (RU)
RPO .... Intermediate Disconnection Relay (RU)
rpo .... Radio Direction-Finding Detachment (BU)
RPO .... Russian Palestine Society (RU)
RPO .... Starting Revolution Relay (RU)
RPP .... Company Small-Arms Ammunition Supply Point (RU)
RPP .... Mercury-Arc Rectifier Substation (RU)
RPP .... Mobile Radio Direction-Finding Station (RU)
RPP .... Number Sequence Transfer Register [*Computers*] (RU)
RPP .... Polarity Reversal Relay (RU)
RPP .... Rassemblement Populaire pour le Progres [*Popular Rally for Progress*] [*Djibouti*] (PPW)
RPP .... Rayon Public Telephone (RU)
RPP .... Republica Populara Polona [*Polish People's Republic*] (RO)
RPP .... Republican People's Party [*Cumhuriyet Halk Partisi - CHP*] [*Turkish*] (PPW)
RPP .... Workers Progressive Party [*Canada*] (BU)
RPPI .... Resurgence Party of the People of Iran [*Rastakhiz Party*] [*Iranian*] (ME)
RPPS .... Robotnicza Partia Polskich Socjalistow [*Workers Party of Polish Socialists*] (PPE)
RPPS-Lewica ... Robotnicza Partia Polskich Socjalistow-Lewica [*RPPS-Left*] (PPE)
RPPT .... Regroupement des Partis Politiques du Tchad (MAR)
RPR .... Company Antitank Defense Area (RU)
rpr .... Radio Direction-Finding Company (BU)
RPR .... Rassemblement pour la Republique [*Rally for the Republic*] [*French*] (WER)
RPR .... Rassemblement pour la Republique [*Rally for the Republic*] [*French Guiana*] (PPW)
RPR .... Rassemblement pour la Republique [*Rally for the Republic*] [*French Polynesian*] (PPW)
RPR .... Rassemblement pour la Republique [*Rally for the Republic*] [*Wallis and Futuna Islander*] (PD)
RPr .... Rodopski Pregled [*Rhodope Mountains Review*] [*A periodical*] (BU)
RPRG .... Republique Populaire Revolutionnaire de Guinee (MAR)
RPS .... Intermediate Lock-On Relay (RU)
RPS .... Intermediate Signal Relay (RU)
RPS .... Portable Reconnaissance Station (RU)
RPS .... Radio Direction-Finding Station (RU)
RPS .... Rayon Union of Consumers' Societies (RU)
RPS .... Referat Pracovnich Sil [*Manpower Department (attached to the National Committees)*] (CZ)
RPS .... Reunion Presse Service [*Reunion Press Service*] (AF)
RPS .... Reversible Scaling Circuit (RU)
RPS .... Steady-Speed Regulator [*Computers*] (RU)
RPS .... Warning Signaling Relay (RU)
RPSh .... Manually Controlled Saw Frame (RU)
rpsh .... Shpagin Light Machine Gun (RU)
RPSN- .... Radiometric Device for Automatic Determination of Sulfur in a Stream of Petroleum Products (RU)
RPSNT .... Republican Party for Chadian National Salvation [*Use PRSNT*] (AF)
rpsv .... Psychological Warfare Company (BU)
RPT .... Alternating-Current Intermediate Relay (RU)
RPT .... Fuel-Pumping Relay (RU)
RPT .... Limit Current Regulator (RU)
RPT .... Radioisotopic Portable Thickness Gauge (RU)
RPT .... Rassemblement du Peuple Togolais [*Rally of the Togolese People*] (PPW)
RPT .... Rayon Food Trade Organization (RU)
RPTI .... Ryazan' Planning and Technological Institute (RU)
RPTOP .... Company Antitank Strong Point (BU)
RPTOP .... Company Antitank Strong Point (RU)
RPTT .... Post, Telegraph, and Telephone Workers (BU)
RPU .... Republica Populara Ungara [*Hungarian People's Republic*] (RO)
RPU .... Wire Broadcasting Adapter (RU)
rpv .... Field Water-Supply Company (RU)
RPV .... Intermediate Switching on Relay (RU)
RPV .... Reclosure Relay (RU)
RPV .... Water-Pumping Relay (RU)
RPVC .... Racionalni Provozne-Vycvikovy Cykl [*Rational Temporary Training Cycle*] (CZ)
RPYa .... Gas Mask Repair Box (RU)
RPYS .... Republique Populaire du Yemen du Sud (MAR)
RPZ .... Rada Pomocy Zydom (MAR)
RPz .... Radiovy Pruzkum [*Radio Reconnaissance*] (CZ)
RPZB .... Rzeszowskie Przemyslowe Zjednoczenie Budowlane [*Rzeszow Industrial Construction Association*] (POL)
RPzP .... Radiovy Pruzkumny Pluk [*Radio Reconnaissance Regiment*] (CZ)
RQ .... Ravitaillement Quotidien [*Daily Revictualing*] [*Military*] [*French*] (MTD)
RR .... Cutoff Relay (RU)
RR .... Deployment Area [*Military term*] (RU)
r-r .... Dimensions, Size (RU)
RR .... Discharge Relay (RU)
RR .... Labor Company (RU)
rr .... Manual Control (RU)
RR .... Manual Control Rheostat (RU)
RR .... Rad Republiky [*Order of the Republic (a decoration)*] (CZ)
RR .... Rada Robotnicza [*Workers' Council*] [*Polish*]
RR .... Radial Rada Ltda. [*Medellin*] (COL)
RR .... Radio Renascenca [*Radio Station*] [*Portuguese*] (WER)
RR .... Radioteleviziunea Romana [*Romanian Radiotelevision*] (RO)
rr .... Rarissime [*Very Rarely*] [*Latin*] (GPO)
RR .... Reconcentracion Revolucionaria [*Revolutionary Reconcentration*] [*Peruvian*] (LA)
rr .... Reconnaissance Company (BU)
rr .... Reconnaissance Company (RU)
RR .... Regulating Relay (RU)
RR .... Remontna Radionica [*Repair Shop*] (YU)
RR .... Repair Shop (BU)
RR .... Reversing Relay (RU)
RR .... Revirni Reditelstvi [*Coal Basin Directorate*] (CZ)
RR .... Rhodesia Regiment (MAR)
RR .... Rhodesian Railways (MAR)
RR .... Rijecka Revija [*Rijeka Review*] [*A periodical*] (YU)
rr .... Rivers (RU)
RR .... Rodna Rech [*Native Language*] [*A periodical*] (BU)
r-r .... Solution (RU)
rr .... Species, Kinds (RU)
R/r .... Traffic Control Company (RU)
RR .... Turcja [*Turkey*] [*Polish*]
RRA .... Automobile Regulating Relay (RU)
RRAB .... Rotary-Scattering Aerial Bomb (RU)
RRAF .... Royal Rhodesian Air Force (MAR)
rrazm .... Mine Clearance Company (RU)
rrb .... Radio-Relay Battalion (BU)
rrb .... Radio-Relay Battalion (RU)
RRC .... Ethiopian Relief and Rehabilitation Commission (MAR)
RRC .... Rhodesian Reformed Church (MAR)
RRCh .... Manual Frequency Control (RU)

RRD .... Dilution, Scattering, and Decontamination (RU)
rrd .... Radio Relay Battalion (RU)
RRD .... Rocket Jet Engine (RU)
RRD .... Rocket Jet Engines (BU)
rrd .... Traffic Control Company (RU)
RRF .... Recna Ratna Flotila [*Naval River Flotilla*] (YU)
RRG .... Manual Volume Control (RU)
RRI .... Radio Republik Indonesia (IN)
RRI .... Rubber Research Institute [*Malaysian*] (ML)
RRI .... Ryazan' Radiotechnical Institute (RU)
r-rimost' ...... Solubility (RU)
RRIN .... Rubber Research Institute of Nigeria (MAR)
r-ritel' .... Solvent (RU)
RRK .... Radiodiffusion de la Republique Khmere [*Radio of the Cambodian Republic*] (CL)
RRK .... Regulator-Distributor Box (RU)
RRL .... Radio Relay Line (RU)
RRL .... Rumunska Republika Ludowa [*Romanian People's Republic (1952-1965)*] [*Polish*]
RRP .... Republican Reliance Party [*Cumhuriyetci Guven Partisi - CGP*] (PPW)
RRP .... Romanian Workers' Party (BU)
RRP .... Romanian Workers' Party (RU)
RRP .... Rudnik Rjavega Premoga [*Brown Coal Mine*] (YU)
RRP .... Rumunska Radnicka Partija [*Rumanian Labor Party*] (YU)
rrr .... Radio-Relay Company (BU)
RRRC .... Resettlement, Relief, and Rehabilitation Commission [*Sudanese*] (MAR)
RRS .... Radio Relay Station (RU)
RRSA .... Radio Republic of South Africa (MAR)
RRSS .... Ruska Ratna Sluzba Stabova [*Russian War Staff Service*] (YU)
RR SSSR ..... River Register of the USSR (RU)
RRT .... Braking Reverse Relay (RU)
RRT .... Republik Rakjat Tiongkok [*People's Republic of China*] (IN)
RRT .... Tank Regulating Relay (RU)
RRT .... Tractor Regulating Relay (RU)
RRTI .... Ryazan' Radiotechnical Institute (RU)
RRU .... Company Ultrashort-Wave Radio (RU)
RRU .... Manual Amplification Control (RU)
RRWU .... Rhodesia Railways Workers Union (AF)
RRZ .... Mining Equipment Repair Plant (RU)
RRZD .... Rolniczy Rejonowy Zaklad Doswiadczalny [*Regional Agricultural Experimental Station*] (POL)
RS .... Bent Rhombic [*Antenna*] (RU)
RS .... Counting Relay (RU)
r/s .... Design Computation (RU)
RS .... Discharge Resistance (RU)
RS .... Flow Relay (RU)
RS .... Intelligent Service Section (BU)
RS .... Medium Repair (RU)
RS .... Mixture Controller (RU)
RS .... Privates, Rank and File (RU)
RS .... Radial Drill (RU)
RS .... Radio Communications (RU)
R/s .... Radio Net (RU)
RS .... Radio Sarajevo (YU)
RS .... Radio Slovenija [*Radio Slovenia*] (YU)
r/s .... Radio Stanica [*Radio Station*] (YU)
RS .... Radio Station (RU)
RS .... Radna Snaga [*Manpower*] [*Army*] (YU)
RS .... Radnicki Sindikat [*Trade-Union*] (YU)
RS .... Radnicko-Sluzbenicki [*Workers and Employees*] (YU)
rs .... Radnih Sati [*Working Hours*] (YU)
RS .... Ratio Controller (RU)
RS .... Ratio Relay (RU)
RS .... Ratna Sluzba [*Military Service*] (YU)
RS .... Rayon Council (BU)
RS .... Rayon Soviet of Workers' Deputies (RU)
Rs .... Reales [*Spanish*]
RS .... Realschule [*German*]
RS .... Recette Subordonnee [*Subordinate Revenue (Office)*] [*Cambodian*] (CL)
RS .... Reconstruccion Socialista [*Socialist Reconstruction*] [*Spanish*] (WER)
RS .... Register of the USSR (RU)
RS .... Regular Session (BU)
RS .... Regulating Station (RU)
Rs .... Reis [*Money*] [*Portuguese*]
RS .... Relaxation Strength (RU)
RS .... Repair Ship, Floating Repair Base (RU)
RS .... Republic Council (RU)
RS .... Republicains Sociaux [*Social Republicans*] [*French*] (PPE)
RS .... Reversive Counter (RU)
RS .... Revolutionary Council (RU)
RS .... Rocket, Missile (RU)
RS .... Rocket Shell (BU)
RS .... Rumah Sakit [*Hospital*] (IN)
RS .... Seiner [*Boat*] (RU)
RS .... Signal Company (RU)
RS .... Signal Relay (RU)
rs .... Silver Ruble (RU)
RS .... Sliding Relay (RU)
RS .... Speed Regulator (RU)
RS .... Speed Relay (RU)
RS .... Starter Relay (RU)
RS .... Turret Lathe (RU)
RS .... Wire Broadcasting Network (RU)
RS .... Workers' Supply (RU)
RSA .... Army Regulating Station (RU)
RSA .... Artillery Reconnaissance Service (RU)
RSA .... Radio South Africa (MAR)
RSA .... Regional Studies Association (EA)
RSA .... Report from South Africa [*A publication*] (MAR)
RSA .... Republic of South Africa [*Use SA*] (AF)
RSAAF .... Royal South African Air Force (MAR)
RSAF .... Royal Saudi Air Force (ME)
RSAP .... Revolutionaire Socialistische Arbeiders Partij [*Revolutionary Socialist Workers' Party*] [*Dutch*] (PPE)
rsau .... Self-Propelled Gun Company (RU)
rsb .... Battalion Radio (RU)
RS-B .... Bomber Radio (RU)
RSB .... Regionale Steun Bibliotheek [*Bibliotheek met een regionale steunfunctie*]
RSBCA .... Regional School Building Centre for Africa (MAR)
RSBKE .... Dictionary of the Contemporary Bulgarian Literary Language (BU)
RSC .... Rada Svobodneho Ceskoslovenska [*Council of Free Czechoslovakia*] (CZ)
RSC .... Republica Socialista Cehoslovaca [*Czechoslovak Socialist Republic*] (RO)
RSC & G ...... Roux Seguela Cayzac & Goudard [*French advertising agency*]
RSCsl .... Rodopisna Spolecnost Ceskoslovenska [*Czechoslovak Genealogy Society*] (CZ)
RSD .... Medium-Range Missile (RU)
RSD .... Reditelstvi Statnich Drah [*State Railroad Directorate*] (CZ)
RSD .... Rolnicke Skladistni Druzstvo [*Agricultural Warehouse Cooperative*] (CZ)
RSDP .... Russian Social Democratic Party (BU)
RSDP(o) ...... Workers' Social Democratic Party (United) (BU)
RSDr .... Doctor Rerum Socialium [*Doctor of Social Sciences*] [*Latin*] (CZ)
RSDRF .... Russian Social Democratic Workers' Faction (RU)
RSDRP .... Rossiiskaia Sotsial-Demokraticheskaia Rabochaya Partiia [*Russian Social Democratic Workers' Party*] (PPE)
RSDRP .... Ruska Socijal-Demokratska Radnicka Partija [*Russian Social-Democratic Workers Party*] (YU)
RSDRP .... Russian Social Democratic Workers' Party [*1898-1912*] (RU)
RSDRP(b) ... Russian Social Democratic Workers' Party (of Bolsheviks) [*1912-1918*] (RU)
RSE .... Radio Slobodna Europa [*Radio Free Europe*] (CZ)
RSE .... Reforma Social Espanola [*Spanish Social Reform*] (WER)
rse .... Remise [*French*]
RSER .... Optimalizing-Control Relay Systems, Extremum Relay Systems (RU)
RSF .... Front Regulating Station (RU)
RSF .... Rhodesia Settlement Forum (MAR)
RSFI .... Republica Socialista Federativa Iugoslavia [*Socialist Federal Republic of Yugoslavia*] (RO)
RSFSR .... Ruska Sovjetska Federativna Socijalisticka Republika [*Russian Soviet Federative Socialist Republic*] (YU)
RSFSR .... Russian Soviet Federative Socialist Republic (BU)
RSFSR .... Russian Soviet Federative Socialist Republic (RU)
RSh .... Block Terminal, Control Box (RU)
rsh .... Deciphering (RU)
RSh .... Difference of Latitudes (RU)
RSh .... Loudspeaker Cord (RU)
RSh .... Miner's Measuring Tape (RU)
RShch .... Control Board (RU)
RShch .... Distributing Board (RU)
RShN .... Manual Bull Pump (RU)
rsh og .... Destruction Fire (BU)
RS-I .... Fighter Radio (RU)
RSI .... Mixing Relay Selector (RU)
RSI- .... Pulse-Counting Relay (RU)
RSI .... Pulse Pickup Relay (RU)
RSK .... Complement-Fixation Reaction (RU)
RSK .... Rayon Savings Bank (RU)
RSK .... Repair and Construction Office (RU)
RSKh .... Rayon Seed Production Farm (RU)
RSL .... Reditelstvi Statnich Lesu [*Directorate of State Forests*] (CZ)
RSL .... Reditelstvi Statnich Loterii [*State Lottery Directorate*] (CZ)
RSL .... Trunk Line Relay (RU)
RSL .... Workers' Union of Lithuania (RU)
RSL-DS .... Trunk Line and Four-Wire Termination Relay (RU)
RSLK- .... Rubber-Glass-Lacquer Tissue (RU)
RSLMF .... Republic of Sierra Leone Military Forces (MAR)
RSLO .... Terminal Trunk Line Relay (RU)
RSLT .... Tandem Trunk Line Relay (RU)
RSLU .... Multiplex Trunk Line Relay (RU)
RSLUI .... Outgoing Multiplex Trunk Line Relay (RU)
RSLUIM .... Outgoing Long-Distance Multiplex Trunk Line Relay (RU)
RSLUV .... Incoming Multiplex Trunk Line Relay (RU)

RSLUVM ..... Incoming Long-Distance Multiplex Trunk Line Relay (RU)
RSM .... Clarity, Audibility, Quality of Modulation (RU)
RSM .... Mantissa Sum Register [*Computers*] (RU)
RSM .... Revolution Socialiste Malgache [*Malagasy Socialist Revolution*] (AF)
RSM .... Robotnicza Spoldzielnia Mieszkaniowa [*Workers' Housing Cooperative*] (POL)
RSM .... Rostov Agricultural Machinery Plant (RU)
RSM .... Ruf- und Signalmaschine [*Telephone and Signal Equipment*] (EG)
RSMK .... Repair, Construction, and Installation Office (RU)
RSN .... Rassemblement pour le Salut National [*Rally for National Salvation*] [*Senegalese*] (PD)
RSNDT .... Rayon People's Councils of Deputies of the Working People (BU)
RSNKh .... Rayon Council of National Economy (RU)
RSNT .... Revised Single Negotiating Text (MAR)
RSO .... Building and Repair Organization (BU)
RSO .... Radio Identification System (RU)
RSO .... Revolutionaere Sozialisten (Oesterreichs) [*Revolutionary Socialists (Austria)*] (PPE)
RSON .... Detection and Guidance Radar Station (RU)
RSOP .... Rzeszowska Spoldzielnia Ogrodniczo-Pszczelarska [*Rzeszow Gardening and Beekeeping Cooperative*] (POL)
RSP .... Communications Company with Infantry (RU)
RSP .... Number Sequence Sum Register [*Computers*] (RU)
RSP- .... Radioisotopic Object Counter (RU)
RSP .... Rayon Construction Enterprise (BU)
RSP .... Recessive, Sex-Linked [*Biology*] (RU)
RSp .... Resolution of Coincidence (RU)
RSP .... Reversible Counter-Converter (RU)
RSP .... Revolutionaire Socialistische Partij [*Revolutionary Socialist Party*] [*Dutch*] (PPE)
RSP .... Revolutionary Socialist Party [*Indian*] (PPW)
RSpB .... Resolution of Coincidence on a Magnetic Drum (RU)
RSPI .... Rzemieslnicza Spoldzielnia Pracy Introligatorow [*Labor Cooperative of Book-Binders*] (POL)
RSpL .... Resolution of Coincidence on Magnetic Tapes (RU)
RSPS .... Republic Trade-Union Council (RU)
RSPV .... Reconstruccio Socialista del Pais Valencia [*Socialist Reconstruction of the Valencian Country*] [*Spanish*] (WER)
RSR .... Republica Socialista Romana [*Socialist Republic of Romania*] (RO)
rsrto .... Radio Technical Support Signal Company (BU)
RSS .... Regiae Societatis Sodalis [*Fellow of the Royal Society*] [*Latin*] (GPO)
RSS .... Remote Sensing Society (EA)
RSS .... Resolving Coincidence Circuit (RU)
RSS .... Ribbed Smoked Sheets [*of Rubber*] (CL)
RSS .... Rok Stranickeho Skoleni [*Party Indoctrination Year*] (CZ)
RSS .... Signal Pickup Relay (RU)
RSS .... Stop-Signal Relay (RU)
RSS .... Tracking Radio Station (RU)
RSSM .... Republica Sovietica Socialista Moldova [*Soviet Socialist Republic of Moldavia*] (RO)
RSSS .... Rashtriya Swayam Sewak Sangh [*National Union of Selfless Servers*] [*Indian*] (PD)
r st .... Mercury Column (RU)
RST .... Radio Sistema Tricolar (COL)
RSt .... Radio Station (RU)
RST .... Repair and Construction Trust (RU)
RST .... Revolutia Stiintifico-Tehnica [*Scientific-Technical Revolution*] (RO)
RST .... Rhodesian Selection Trust (MAR)
RST .... Roan Selection Trust (MAR)
Rst .... Rostock (EG)
RSTMH .... Royal School of Tropical Medicine and Hygiene (MAR)
RSTO .... Radiotechnical and Illuminating Engineering Support [*Aviation*] (RU)
RSTPK .... Rayon Union of Labor Productive Cooperatives (BU)
rstv .... Solubility (RU)
RSU .... Amplified Power Ratio Regulator (RU)
RSU- .... Radioisotopic Follow Level Gauge (RU)
RSU .... Repair and Construction Administration (RU)
RSv .... Company Communications (RU)
RSV .... Restaurants and Sleeping Cars [*Railroads*] (BU)
RSV .... Rimamurany- Salgotarjani Vasmu Reszvenytarsasag [*Rimamurany- Salgotarjan Iron Works Limited*] (HU)
RSV .... Troop Assembly Area (RU)
RSVP .... Repondez, S'il Vous Plait [*The Favor of an Answer Is Requested*] [*French*]
RSVP .... Royal St. Vincent Police (LA1)
RSW .... Rada Szkol Wyzszych [*Council on Higher Schools*] (POL)
RSW .... Robotnicza Spoldzielnia Wydawnicza [*Polish*]
RSW .... Rolnicza Spoldzielnia Wytworcza [*Agricultural Production Cooperative*] (POL)
RSW Prasa ... Robotnicza Spoldzielnia Wydawnicza "Prasa" [*"Prasa" (Press) Worker's Cooperative Publishing House*] (POL)
RSYe .... Radio Station "Free Europe" (RU)
RSZ .... Equisignal Zone (RU)
RSZ .... Rada Slovenskych Zien v Exile [*Council of Slovak Women in Exile*] (CZ)
RSZ .... Ratarsko Sjemenska Zadruga [*Agricultural Seed Cooperative*] (YU)
RSZ .... Rektorat Sveucilista u Zagrebu [*Rectorate of the University of Zagreb*] (YU)
RSZ .... Repulo Szovetseg [*Aviation Association*] (HU)
RSZ .... Repulogepes Szolgalat [*Aviation Service (of Ministry of Agriculture and Food Industry)*] (HU)
RSZ .... Revolutionaere Studentenschaft Zuerich [*Revolutionary Student Organization of Zurich*] [*Swiss*] (WEN)
RSZ .... Riaditelstvo Statnych Zeleznic [*State Railroads Directorate*] (CZ)
RSZ .... Ryazan' Machine Tool Plant (RU)
RSZB .... Reonska Stanica za Zastitu Bilja [*Regional Plant Protection Station*] (YU)
r szk .... Rok Szkolny [*School Year*] [*Polish*]
RT .... Electric Current Recording (RU)
RT .... Electric Current Relay (RU)
RT .... Exploration Theodolite (RU)
RT .... Expulsion-Type Arrester (RU)
RT .... Fishing Trawler (RU)
RT .... Fuel Regulator (RU)
RT .... Magyarorszagi Rendeletek Tara [*Collection of Decrees of Hungary*] (HU)
RT .... Radio Engineering (RU)
RT .... Radio Tank, Tank Radio (RU)
RT- .... Radioisotopic Thermoregulator (RU)
RT .... Raumteil [*Part by Volume*] [*German*]
RT .... Reference Point (RU)
RT .... Relay Transformer (RU)
rt .... Reszvenytarsasag [*Corporation*] (HU)
RT .... Robna Tarifa [*Commodity Freight Rates*] [*Railroads*] (YU)
RT .... Rocket Engineering (RU)
RT .... Rukun Tetangga [*Neighborhood Association*] (IN)
RT .... Sound Corrector (RU)
RT .... Temperature Regulator (RU)
RT .... Temperature Relay, Thermal Relay (RU)
RT .... X-Ray Tube (RU)
RTA- .... Page-Printing Apparatus (RU)
RTA .... Radio-Television Algerienne [*Algerian Radio and Television*] (AF)
RTA .... Rhodesian Tobacco Association (AF)
rtb .... Radio Battalion (RU)
RTB .... Radiodiffusion Television Belge [*Belgian Radio Broadcasting and Television System*] (WER)
rtb .... Radioengineering Battalion (BU)
RTB .... Rassemblement des Travailleurs Burundi (MAR)
RTB .... Rudarsko-Topionicki Basen [*Mining and Foundry Basin*] [*Bor*] (YU)
RTBISC .... Radiodiffusion-Television Belge - Institut des Services Comuns [*Belgian Radio Broadcasting and Television - Common Services Institute*] (WER)
rtbr .... Radioengineering Brigade (BU)
RTC .... Radio Tecnica Colombiana [*Bogota*] (COL)
RTC .... Radiodiffusion Television Congolaise [*Congolese Radio and Television*] (AF)
RTC .... Regional Trading Company (MAR)
RTC .... River Transport Corporation [*Sudanese*] (MAR)
RTC .... Rural Training Center (MAR)
RTChK .... Rayon Transportation Extraordinary Commission for Combating Counterrevolution and Sabotage (RU)
RTD .... Radio Tanzania Dar Es Salaam (MAR)
RTD .... Radiodiffusion Television de Djibouti (MAR)
RTD .... Turbojet Engine (RU)
rte .... Remite [*or Remitente*] [*Sender, From*] [*Spanish*]
Rte .... Route Nationale [*National Road*] [*Military map abbreviation*] [*World War I*] [*French*] (MTD)
RTF .... Radiodiffusion-Television Francaise [*French Radio Broadcasting and Television System*] (WER)
RTF .... Radiotelephone (RU)
RTg .... Radiotelegrafija [*Radiotelegraphy*] (YU)
RTG .... Reaktor Tevsii Proje Grubu [*Reactor Distribution Project Group*] (TU)
rtg .... Rentgen [*Roentgen (Unit of radiation)*] (CZ)
RTG .... Rentgen [*Roentgen (Unit of radiation)*] (YU)
rtg .... Rontgen [*Roentgen (Unit of radiation)*] (HU)
RTGA .... Hemagglutination-Inhibition Test (RU)
RTgC .... Radiotelegrafska Centrala [*Radiotelegraphic Center*] (YU)
RTGR .... Radiotelegraph (RU)
RTGW .... Rettungsgeraetewagen [*Rescue Equipment Truck (Used by fire department)*] (EG)
Rthr .... Reichsthaler [*German*]
RTI .... Industrial Rubber Products (RU)
RTI .... Industrial Rubber Products Plant (RU)
RTI .... Radiodiffusion Television Ivoirienne [*Ivory Coast Radio and Television*] (AF)
RTI .... Radiotechnical Equipment (RU)
RTI .... Ruska Tekstilna Industrija [*Ruse Textile Industry*] (YU)
RTJ .... Rad Tovarysstva Jezisova [*Society of Jesus*] (CZ)

RTJ............ Robotnicka Telocvicna Jednota [*Workers' Gymnastic Association*] (CZ)
RTK............ City District Theater Box Office (RU)
RTK............ Radiation-Induced Thermal Cracking (RU)
RTK............ Repulestudomanyi es Tajekoztato Kozpont [*Center for Aviation Science and Information*] (HU)
RTK............ Wheel Trench Digger (RU)
RTM............ Guiding Technical Materials (RU)
RTM............ Maximum Thermal Relay (RU)
RTM............ Radio-Television Malgache [*Malagasy Radio and Television*] (AF)
RTM............ Radio-Television Marocaine [*Moroccan Radio and Television*] (AF)
RTM............ Regie des Transports du Mali [*Mali Transportation Administration*] (AF)
RTM............ Regimen de Tirailleurs Marocains (MAR)
rtm............ Rotmistrz [*Captain (of Horse)*] [*Polish*]
RTN............ Forcing Temperature Regulator (RU)
RTNC.......... Radio-Television Nationale Congolaise (MAR)
RTO............ Radio Equipment (RU)
RTO............ Radio Telegraph Installation (BU)
RTO............ Radio Telegraph Section (RU)
RTO............ Russian Technical Society [*1866-1929*] (RU)
RTO............ Technical Service Company (RU)
RTO............ Technical Support Company (RU)
RTP............ Fire-Fighting Instructor (RU)
RTP............ Radio Post (RU)
rtp............ Radio Regiment (RU)
RTP............ Radio Televisao Portuguesa [*Portuguese Radio-Television System*] (WER)
RTP............ Radioengineering Post (BU)
rtp............ Radioengineering Regiment (BU)
RTP............ Radiotechnical Industry (RU)
RTP............ Recno Transportno Preduzece [*River Transport Establishment*] (YU)
RTPA.......... Regie des Transports de la Province de l'Atlantique (MAR)
RTPD.......... Direct Action Temperature Regulator (RU)
RTPD.......... Radio Countermeasures (RU)
RTPD.......... Robotnicze Towarzystwo Przyjaciol Dzieci [*Workers Society of Friends of Children*] (POL)
RTPR.......... Radiotechnicky Prapor [*Radiotechnical Battalion*] (CZ)
RTPz.......... Radiotechnicky Pruzkum [*Radiotechnical Reconnaissance*] (CZ)
RTPzP........ Radiotechnicky Pruzkumny Pluk [*Radiotechnical Reconnaissance Regiment*] (CZ)
rtr............ Radio Company (RU)
rtr............ Radioengineering Company (BU)
RTR............ Royal Tank Regiment (ML)
RTs............ Centrifugal Relay (RU)
RTs............ Expanding Cement (RU)
RTS............ Manual Exchange (RU)
RTS............ Radio-Television Scolaire [*French*]
RTS............ Radio Wire Broadcasting Network (RU)
RTS............ Radioengineering Station (BU)
RTS............ Radiotechnical Equipment (RU)
RTS............ Radiotechnical Personnel (RU)
RTS............ Radiotechnical Service (RU)
RTS............ Radiotelegraph Station (BU)
RTS............ Radiotelegraph Station (RU)
RTS............ Radiotelemetering Station (RU)
RTS............ Radiotelemetering System (RU)
RTs............ Rayon Center (RU)
RTS............ Rayon Telephone Exchange (RU)
RTS............ Rayon Telephone Network (RU)
RTs............ Reactor Shop (BU)
RTS............ Regie des Transports du Senegal [*Senegal Transportation Administration*] (AF)
RTS............ Regiment des Transmissions et Services [*Signals and Services Regiment*] [*Malagasy*] (AF)
RTS............ Remontno-Tehnicke Stanice [*Technical Repair Stations*] (YU)
RTS............ Repair and Technical Station (RU)
RTS............ Reparaturtechnische Station [*Equipment Repair Station*] (EG)
rts............ Review, Critique (RU)
RTS............ Television Relay Station (RU)
RTs............ Track Circuit (RU)
r-tsa.......... Workshop (BU)
RTSh.......... Workers' Technical School (RU)
RTShch....... Roadstead Mine Sweeper (RU)
r-tsiya........ Reaction (RU)
RTSK.......... Rayon Transportation and Warehouse Kombinat (RU)
RTSM.......... Republic Trust for the Manufacture of Building Materials (RU)
RTsO.......... Centralized Disconnecting Relay (RU)
RTSS.......... Revue Tunisienne de Sciences Sociales [*Tunis*] [*A publication*] (MAR)
rt st............ Mercury Column (RU)
RTsT.......... Radial-Flow Centripetal Turbine (RU)
RTsU.......... Recording Digital Unit (RU)
RTT............ Radio Television Tunisien [*Tunisian Radio and Television*] (AF)
RTT............ Regie des Telegraphes et des Telephones [*Telegraph and Telephone Administration*] [*Belgian*] (WER)
RTT............ Regiment de Tirailleurs Tunisiens (MAR)
RTT............ Temperature Regulator of Heat-Transfer Agent (RU)
Rttm............ Rittmeister [*German*]
RTTs.......... Radio Relay Center (BU)
RTTs.......... Riga Television Center (RU)
RTTsS........ Radio Relay Station (BU)
RTU............ Development and Technical Improvements Fund (BU)
RTU............ Radio Wire Broadcasting Center (RU)
RTU............ Radiotechnical Installations (RU)
RTU............ Rayon Radio Wire Broadcasting Installation (RU)
RTU............ Relay Center (RU)
RTU............ Remote Control Relay (RU)
RTU............ Repair and Technical Administration (RU)
RTU............ Republic Technical Specifications (RU)
RTUC.......... Reformed Trade Union Congress (MAR)
RTV............ Direccion General de Radiodifusion y Television [*Directorate General of Radio Broadcasting and Television*] [*Spanish*] (WER)
RTV............ Radio Relay Point (BU)
RTV............ Radio Television (MAR)
RTV............ Radio Troops (RU)
RTV............ Radiotechnicke Vojsko [*Radiotechnical Troops*] (CZ)
RTV............ Rhodesian Television (AF)
RTV............ Rikstrygdeverket [*National Social Insurance System*] [*Norwegian*] (WEN)
RTV............ Ruhaipari Tervezo Vallalat [*Designing Enterprise of the Clothing Industry*] (HU)
RTV............ Thermal Time Relay (RU)
RTV............ Valve-Type Lightning Arrester (RU)
RTVD.......... Radiotelevision Dominicana [*Dominican Radio and Television*] [*Dominican Republic*] (LA1)
RTZ............ Radio Tanzania Zanzibar (MAR)
RTZ............ Radiotechnicke Zabepeceni [*Radiotechnical Support (Security)*] (CZ)
RTZ............ Rakovnicke Tukove Zavody, Narodni Podnik [*Rakovnik Fat Rendering Factories, National Enterprise*] (CZ)
RTZ............ Rio Tinto Zinc [*British, Namibian*] (AF)
RTZ............ Rota Tezkych Zbrani [*Heavy Weapons Company*] (CZ)
RTZ............ Ruzomberske Textilne Zavody [*Ruzomberok Textile Mills*] (CZ)
RTZ............ Tank Repair Plant (RU)
RU............ Accelerating Relay (RU)
RU............ Control Relay (RU)
RU............ Decision Amplifier (RU)
RU............ Demagnetizing Device (RU)
RU............ Directorate of Intelligence (RU)
RU............ Distribution System [*Electricity*] (RU)
RU............ Estimated Angle (RU)
RU............ Gain Control (RU)
RU............ Guiding Regulations (RU)
RU............ Indicator Relay (RU)
Ru............ Knife Switch (RU)
RU-............ Level Regulator (RU)
RU............ Manual Control (RU)
RU............ Ore Mining Administration (BU)
RU............ Radio Center (RU)
RU............ Radio Control (RU)
RU............ Rasinjski Ugljenokop [*Rasinja Coal Pit*] (YU)
RU............ Rayon Center [*Communications*] (RU)
RU............ Recno Uporiste [*River Stronghold*] [*Navy*] (YU)
RU............ Recognition Device (RU)
RU............ Reconnaissance Device (RU)
RU............ Recorder (RU)
RU............ Reduction-Cooling Unit (RU)
RU-............ Regulator, Controller (RU)
RU............ Revolutionary Union (MAR)
RU............ Rhodes University (MAR)
RU............ River Navigation School (RU)
Ru............ Rubha [*Point*] [*Gaelic*] (NAU)
RU............ Rudnik Uglja [*Coal Mine*] (YU)
Ru............ Ruine [*German*]
RU............ Scanner (RU)
RU............ Separate Balancing (RU)
RU............ Separation Node (RU)
RU............ Steering Gear (RU)
RU............ Trade School (RU)
RU-............ Unit Rheostat (RU)
RU............ X-Ray Unit (RU)
RUA............ Photo Reproducing and Enlargement Apparatus (RU)
RUA............ Resistencia Unida Angolesa (MAR)
RUAM.......... Radio-Controlled Model Airplane (BU)
RuB............ Ring um Berlin [*Ring around Berlin (Railroad)*] (EG)
r ub............ Rok Ubiegly [*or Roku Ubieglego*] [*Last Year*] [*Polish*]
RUB............ Ruble [*Monetary unit in the USSR*]
rubr............ Heading, Column (RU)
rubr............ Rubryka [*Column*] [*Polish*]
RUC............ Republique Unie du Cameroun (MAR)
RUCA.......... Rijks Universitair Centrum Antwerpen
ruch............ Brook, Stream [*Topography*] (RU)
Rucks.......... Rueckseite [*Verso*] [*German*]
RUD............ Diagnostic X-Ray Unit (RU)
RUD............ Engine Control Lever (RU)
rud............ Mine [*Topography*] (RU)

RUD............ Republicka Uprava za Dohotke [*Republic Revenue Administration*] (YU)
RUD............ Rosicke Uhelne Doly [*Rosice Coal Mines*] (CZ)
RUD............ Rosicko-Oslavanske Uhelne Doly [*Rosice-Oslavany Coal Mines*] (CZ)
RUD............ Street Traffic Control (BU)
RUD............ Street Traffic Control (RU)
Rudmetal.... State Commercial Enterprise for Import and Export of Metal Ores (BU)
rudn........... Mine (RU)
RUDNAP..... Rudarsko Nabavno Prodajno Preduzece Eksport-Import [*Export-Import Mining Establishment*] [*Belgrade*] (YU)
Rueckst....... Rueckstoss [*Recoil, Repulse*] (EG)
RUFAST...... Recueil a l'Usage des Fonctionnaires de l'Administration en Service Territorial [*A publication*] (MAR)
RUG............ Rijks Universiteit Gent
RUG............ Rijks Universiteit Groningen
RUGSh........ Intelligence Directorate of the General Staff (RU)
RUH............ Statni Vyzkumny Ustav Rybarsky a Hydrologicky [*State Research Institute of Fishing and Hydrology*] (CZ)
RUK............ Commander's Radio Center (RU)
ruk.............. Leader, Manager, Instructor (RU)
ruk.............. Manager (BU)
ruk.............. Manuscript (RU)
RUK............ Reserviupseerikoulu [*Finnish*]
ruk.............. River Branch [*Topography*] (RU)
rukop.......... Manuscript (BU)
rukop.......... Manuscript (RU)
rukov.......... Manual, Textbook (RU)
rukovod....... Manager, Management (BU)
RUL............ Rejonowy Urzad Likwidzcyjny [*District Liquidation Office*] (POL)
rum............. Controlled-Mine-Laying Company (RU)
RUM........... Medical X-Ray Unit (RU)
RUM........... Radio-Controlled Mechanism (RU)
RUM........... Radio-Controlled Model (RU)
RUM........... Rayon Militia Administration (RU)
rum............. Romanian (BU)
rum............. Romanian (RU)
RUMA.......... Rayon Mechanization and Motor Vehicle Transport Administration (BU)
rum ez......... Romanian Language (BU)
RUN............ Carbon Voltage Regulator (RU)
RUN............ Normal Level Relay (RU)
RUN............ Rol Unico Nacional [*Centralized National Registry*] [*Chilean*] (LA)
RUNI........... Rayon Real Estate Administration (RU)
RUNV.......... Rada Ustredniho Narodniho Vyboru [*Council of the Central National Committee*] (CZ)
RUO............ Manual Carbon-Dioxide Fire Extinguisher (RU)
ruots........... Ruotsalainen [*Finnish*]
ruots........... Ruotsalaiset [*Finnish*]
ruots........... Ruotsia [*or Ruotsiksi*] [*Finnish*]
RUP............ Field Acceleration Relay (RU)
RUP............ Industrial X-Ray Unit (RU)
RUP............ Position Indicator Rheostat (RU)
RUP............ Ukrainian Revolutionary Party (RU)
RUP-........... Universal Field Radiometer (RU)
RUPD.......... Republiska Uprava za Posredovanje Dela [*Republic Employment Agency*] (YU)
RUPR.......... Republicka Uprava za Posredovanje Rada [*Republic Employment Agency*] (YU)
RUPSh......... Sleeve Float Level Regulator (RU)
RUR............ Reduction Cooling System [*Nuclear energy*] (BU)
RURALMINAS... Fundacao Rural Mineira [*Minas Gerais Rural Foundation*] [*Brazilian*] (LA)
RURT.......... Rayon Administration of River Transportation (RU)
RUS............ Air-Search Radar (RU)
RUS............ Regional Communications Center (RU)
Rus............. Rusca [*Russian*] (TU)
rus.............. Russian (RU)
rus.............. Russian (BU)
RUS-........... Universal Scintillation Radiometer (RU)
Rusavstrotorg... Mixed Russian-Austrian Trading and Industrial Company (RU)
Rusavsttorg... Mixed Russian-Austrian Trading and Industrial Company (RU)
rus ez.......... Russian Language (BU)
Rusgertorg... Russian-German Trading and Industrial Company (RU)
RUSN.......... Switching and Busing Arrangement Supplying the Station Auxiliaries (RU)
rus per........ Russian Translation (RU)
russ............ Russian (RU)
russk........... Russian (RU)
RUT............ Carbon Current Regulator (RU)
RUT............ Rejonowy Urzad Telekomunikacyjny [*District Office of Telecommunication*] [*Polish*]
RUT............ Remote Control Device Distributor (RU)
RUT............ Therapeutic X-Ray Unit (RU)
rutkod......... Russian Universal Telegraph Code (RU)
RUTT.......... Rejonowy Urzad Telefoniczno-Telegraficzny [*District Telephone and Telegraph Office*] [*Polish*]
RUU............ Rentjana Undang-Undang [*Draft Law*] (IN)
RUV............ Manual Fuze Setter (RU)
RUV............ Time-Dependent Gain Control (RU)
RUV-........... Water Level Regulator (RU)
RUVAT........ Ruhaipari Anyagellato Vallalat [*Clothing Industry Supply Enterprise*] (HU)
ruz.............. Ruzny [*Various*] (CZ)
ruzh............ Rifle (RU)
Ruzh............ Rifle Plant [*Topography*] (RU)
RU ZSP........ Rada Uczelniana Zrzeszenia Studentow Polskich [*College Council of the Polish Students' Association*] [*Polish*]
RV.............. Air Controller (RU)
RV.............. Call Distributor, Traffic Distributor [*Telephony*] (RU)
RV.............. Control Screw (RU)
rv............... Convalescent Company (RU)
rv............... Corporal of the Guards (BU)
RV.............. Excitation Regulator (RU)
RV.............. Explosion-Proof Miner's Lamp (RU)
RV.............. Humidity Regulator (RU)
RV.............. Mercury-Arc Rectifier (RU)
RV.............. Radical Left [*Danish*] (WEN)
RV.............. Radikale Venstre [*Radical Liberals*] [*Danish*] (PPE)
RV.............. Radio Altimeter (BU)
RV.............. Radio Altimeter (RU)
RV.............. Radio Altitude (RU)
RV.............. Radio Veze [*Radio Communications*] (YU)
RV.............. Radio Wave (RU)
RV.............. Radioactive Contamination, Radioactive Substance (RU)
RV.............. Radioactive Substance (BU)
RV.............. Railroad Car Repair (RU)
RV.............. Ratno Vazduhoplovstvo [*Air Force*] (YU)
RV.............. Reactor Venezolano [*Venezuelan*]
rv............... Reconnaissance Platoon (BU)
rv............... Reconnaissance Platoon (RU)
RV.............. Reducing Substance (RU)
RV.............. Richtverband [*Radio Relay*] (EG)
RV.............. Rod Valgallianse [*Red Electoral Alliance*] [*Norwegian*] (PPE)
RV-............. Rotary Viscosimeter (RU)
RV.............. Rotary Voltmeter (RU)
RV.............. Timing Relay (RU)
RV.............. Waiting Area [*Military term*] (RU)
RV.............. Wassermann Reaction (RU)
RVA............ Missile Troops and Artillery (BU)
RVA............ Recueil de Divers Voyages Faits en Afrique et en Amerique [*Paris, 1674*] [*A publication*] (MAR)
RVA............ Regie des Voies Aeriennes [*Airlines Administration*] [*Zairian*] (AF)
RVA............ Regroupements des Villages Animes (MAR)
Rva............. Rouva [*Madam*] [*Finnish*] (GPO)
RVB............ Maintenance and Recovery Battalion (RU)
RVB............ Maintenance and Recovery Brigade (RU)
rvb............. Repair and Reconstruction Battalion (BU)
RVC............ Rapport Valeur-Cout (MAR)
RVC............ Reditelstvi Vodnich Cest [*Waterways Directorate*] (CZ)
RVC............ Republicki Vazduhoplovni Centar [*Republic Aviation Center*] (YU)
RVD............ Air Traffic Control (BU)
RVD-........... Auxiliary Two-Coil Relay (RU)
RVD............ High-Pressure Relay (RU)
RVD............ High-Pressure Rotor (RU)
RVE............ Electronic Timing Relay (RU)
RVF............ Regie des Voies Fluviales [*River Lines Administration*] [*Zairian*] (AF)
RVG............ Richtverbindungsgeraete [*Microwave Relay Set*] (EG)
RVGK.......... Reserve of the Supreme Command (RU)
RVHP.......... Rada Vzajemne Hospodarske Pomoci [*Council of Economic Mutual Aid*] (CZ)
RVI............. Interval Switch-On Relay (RU)
RVI............. Ratni Vojni Invalidi [*Disabled Veterans*] (YU)
RVK............ Has Worked with All Continents [*Diploma for amateur radio operators*] (BU)
RVK............ Rayon Military Commissariat (RU)
RVK............ Vertical Riveted Petroleum Tank (RU)
RVKV.......... Rada Vytvarne Kultury Vyroby [*Council for Creative Designing of Products*] [*See CID*] (CZ)
RVL............ Reditelstvi Vojenskych Lesu [*Directorate of Military Forests*] (CZ)
RVM............ Excitation Regulator with a Motor Drive (RU)
RVM............ Pendular Timing Relay (RU)
RVM............ Regie des Voies Maritimes [*Shiplines Administration*] [*Zairian*] (AF)
RVM............ Rohrenvoltmeter [*Vacuum Tube Voltmeter*] (EG)
RVO............ Rijksverdedigingsorganisatie [*National Defense Research Organization*] [*Dutch*] (WEN)
RVOG.......... Radio Voice of the Gospel (MAR)
Rvoir........... Reservoir [*Tank*] [*Military map abbreviation*] [*World War I*] [*French*] (MTD)
rvp............. Military Police Company (BU)
RVP............ Pneumatic Timing Relay (RU)

RVP .... Rolnicka Vzajomna Pokladnica [*Agricultural Mutual Savings Bank*] (CZ)
RVR .... Maintenance and Recovery Company (RU)
RVS .... Audio Signal Cut-In Relay (RU)
RVS .... Diving Station with Manual Equipment (RU)
RVS .... Radio Broadcasting Station (RU)
RVS .... Radiove Vysilaci Stredisko [*Radio Broadcast Center*] (CZ)
RVS .... Revolutionary Military Council (of the Union of SSR) [*1922-1934*] (RU)
RVS .... Rollfuhrversicherungsschein [*Freight Insurance Policy*] (EG)
RVS .... Vertical Welded Petroleum Tank (RU)
RVSN .... Strategic Missile Troops (BU)
RVSR .... Republic Revolutionary Military Council [*1918-1922*] (RU)
RVSU .... Distributing Shaft of the Servomechanism (RU)
RVSU .... Rakety Vojensko-Strategickeho Urceni [*Strategic Missiles*] (CZ)
RVT .... High-Voltage Traction Disconnector (RU)
RVT .... Reditelstvi Vodnich Toku [*Watercourse Directorate*] (CZ)
RVT .... Revolutionary Military Tribunal (RU)
RVT .... Rozvoj Vedy a Techniky [*Development of Science and Technology*] (CZ)
RVTD .... Decimeter-Range Radio Altimeter (RU)
RVTU .... Republic Provisional Technical Specifications (RU)
RVU .... Mercury-Arc Rectifier Unit (RU)
RVU .... Radio Broadcasting Center (RU)
RVU .... Upper-Level Relay (RU)
RVV .... Excitation Switch-On Relay (RU)
RVV .... Rectifier Switch-On Relay (RU)
RVV .... Respublika Verkhnaia Vol'ta (MAR)
RVZ .... Radiosonde Observation (RU)
RVZ .... Riga Railroad Car Plant (RU)
RW .... Rassemblement Wallon [*Walloon Rally*] [*Belgian*] (WER)
RW .... Reichswaehrung [*German Currency*] [*German*]
RW .... Rukun Warga [*Precinct Association (Composed of Rukun Tetanggas - RT)*] (IN)
RW .... Rwanda [*Two-letter standard code*] (CNC)
RWA .... Rwanda [*Three-letter standard code*] (CNC)
RWE .... Rheinisch-Westfaelisches Elektrizitaetswerk AG [*Rhine-Westphalian Electricity Works, Inc.*] (EG)
RWG .... Regional Work Group (MAR)
RWPG .... Rada Wzajemnej Pomocy Gospodarczej [*Council for Economic Mutual Assistance*] (POL)
RWS .... Rhodesian Women's Service (MAR)
RWU .... Railway Workers Union [*Ugandan*] (AF)
RWUZ .... Railway Workers Union of Zambia (MAR)
ry .... Rahayksikko [*Finnish*]
RY .... Rakas Ystava (Kirjeissa) [*Finnish*]
ry .... Rehuyksikko(a) [*Finnish*]
ry .... Rekisteroity Yhdistys [*Registered Association*] [*Finnish*]
r-y .... Size, Dimensions (RU)
r-y .... Solutions (RU)
ryad .... Rare (BU)
RYaNSh .... Russian Language in the National School [*Bibliography*] (RU)
RYaS .... Russian Language and Literature [*Bibliography*] (RU)
RYaSh .... Russian Language in the School [*Bibliography*] (RU)
Ryazmekhzavod ... Ryazan' Machine Plant (RU)
Ryazsel'mash ... Ryazan' Agricultural Machinery Plant (RU)
Ryaztsvetmet ... Ryazan' Plant for the Production and Processing of Nonferrous Metals (RU)
ryb .... Fish Culture (RU)
ryb .... Fish Industry Plant, Fishery [*Topography*] (RU)
ryb dv .... Fisherman's Yard [*Topography*] (RU)
rybkop .... Fish Smokehouse [*Topography*] (RU)
rybol .... Fishing (RU)
Rybosudoproyekt ... Central Design Office for Shipbuilding of the Ministry of the Fish Industry, USSR (RU)
Rybosudostroy ... Administration of Fishing-Boat Building (RU)
rybov .... Fish Culture (RU)
ryb pos .... Fishermen's Settlement [*Topography*] (RU)
ryb pr .... Fisheries [*Topography*] (RU)
rybtrest .... State Fish Trust (RU)
rybzavod .... Fish Product Plant (RU)
ryb zim .... Fishermen's Winter Camp [*Topography*] (RU)
ryc .... Rycina [*Illustration*] (POL)
Rygawar .... Warszawsko-Ryska Fabryka Wyrobow Gumowych [*Warsaw-Riga Rubber Products Plant*] (POL)
rykm .... Rykmentti [*Finnish*]
rys .... Rysowal [*Drawn By*] (POL)
rys .... Rysunek [*Drawing*] (POL)
RZ .... Company Reserve (RU)
RZ .... Contaminated Area (RU)
RZ .... Delay Regulator (RU)
RZ .... Grounding Relay, Protective Relay (RU)
RZ .... Land Surveyor's Tape (RU)
RZ .... Rada Zakladowa [*Works Committee*] [*Polish*]
RZ .... Radio Zagreb (YU)
RZ .... Radioactive Contamination (RU)
RZ .... Radiosonde (RU)
RZ .... Raketna Zrna [*Rocket Shells*] (YU)
RZ .... Rare Earths (RU)
RZ .... Ratni Zlocini [*War Crimes*] (YU)
RZ .... Rdeca Zastava [*Red Flag*] (YU)
RZ .... Rdeca Zvezda [*Red Star*] (YU)
RZ .... Rechenzentrum [*Computer Center*] (EG)
RZ .... Referativity Zhurnal-Informaties
RZ .... Regiment de Zouaves (MAR)
RZ .... Repair Plant (RU)
rz .... Reserve (BU)
RZ .... Revolutionary Legality (RU)
RZ .... Ribarska Zadruga [*Fishing Cooperative*] (YU)
RZ .... Rozvodovy Zavod Elektricke Energie [*Electric Power Distributing Plant*] (CZ)
rz .... Rzeka [*River*] [*Polish*]
RZAP .... Reserve Air Regiment (RU)
RZD .... Razprave Znanstvenega Drustva za Humanisticne Vede v Ljubljani [*Transactions of the Learned Society for Humanistic Studies in Ljubljana*] [*A publication*] (YU)
rzd .... Siding Track [*Topography*] (RU)
RZDR .... Rechenzentrum der Deutschen Reichsbahn [*GDR Railroad Computer Center*] (EG)
RZE .... Rare-Earth Elements (RU)
r-zh .... Boundary, Line (RU)
RZh .... Journal of Abstracts [*A publication*] (RU)
RZhAstr .... Journal of Abstracts: Astronomy [*A publication*] (RU)
RZhBiol .... Journal of Abstracts: Biology [*A publication*] (RU)
RZhE .... Journal of Abstracts: Electrical Engineering [*A publication*] (RU)
RZhFiz .... Journal of Abstracts: Physics [*A publication*] (RU)
RZhGeo .... Journal of Abstracts: Geology [*A publication*] (RU)
RZhGeogr ... Journal of Abstracts: Geography [*A publication*] (RU)
RZhGfiz .... Journal of Abstracts: Geophysics [*A publication*] (RU)
RZhKhim .... Journal of Abstracts: Chemistry [*A publication*] (RU)
RZhMash .... Journal of Abstracts: Machinery Manufacture [*A publication*] (RU)
RZhMekh .... Journal of Abstracts: Mechanics [*A publication*] (RU)
RZhMet .... Journal of Abstracts: Metallurgy [*A publication*] (RU)
RZhO .... Rayon Housing Department (RU)
RZhU .... Railroad Trade School (RU)
RZhU .... Rayon Housing Administration (RU)
RZJD .... Rejonowe Zjednoczenie Jajczarsko-Drobiarskie [*District Egg and Poultry Cooperative*] (POL)
RZK .... Ruski Zastitni Korpus [*Russian Defense Corps*] [*World War II*] (YU)
RZKT .... Republic Correspondence Cooperative Technicum of the Rospotrebsoyuz (RU)
RZM .... Loader-Unloader (RU)
RZM .... Radomskie Zaklady Miesne [*Radom Meat Establishment*] (POL)
RZM .... Rare-Earth Metals (RU)
RZM .... Rewolucyjny Zwiazek Mlodziezy [*Revolutionary Union of Youth*] (POL)
RZMO .... Rogoznickie Zaklady Materialow Ogniotrwalych [*Rogoznik (Rosenig) Fireproof Materials Plant*] (POL)
RZMP .... Rozdelovna Zemedelskych Mechanisacnich Potreb [*Distribution Agency of Agricultural Mechanization Equipment*] [*Prague*] (CZ)
RZNO .... Rada Zidovskych Nabozenskych Obci [*Council of Jewish Religious Congregations*] (CZ)
RZO .... Radomskie Zaklady Obuwia [*Radom Shoe Plant*] (POL)
RZO .... Rayon Land Department (RU)
Rz P .... Rzeczpospolita Polska [*Polish Republic*] (POL)
RZPD .... Radomszczanskie Zaklady Przemyslu Drzewnego [*Radomsko Lumber Plant*] (POL)
Rzpl .... Rzeczpospolita [*Republic*] [*Polish*]
Rzplita .... Rzeczpospolita [*Republic*] [*Polish*]
RZPT .... Radomskie Zaklady Przemyslu Terenowego [*Radom Local Industry Plant*] (POL)
RZPW .... Rudzkie Zaklady Przemyslu Weglowego [*Ruda Coal Plant*] (POL)
RZPW .... Rybnickie Zjednoczenie Przemyslu Weglowego [*Rybnik Coal Industry Association*] (POL)
RZR .... Rhodesia Zimbabwe, Registrar of Pension and Provident Fund (MAR)
RZR .... Rudnik Zeljezne Rude [*Iron Ore Mine*] (YU)
RZS .... Audio Signal Relay (RU)
RZS .... Mercury-Arc Rectifier Charging Station (RU)
RZS .... Republicki Zavod za Statistiku [*Republic Statistical Institute*] (YU)
RZS .... Robotnicze Zespoly Spoldzielcze [*Polish*]
RZS .... Rolnicze Zrzeszenie Spoldzielcze [*Agricultural Cooperative Association*] (POL)
RZS .... Rolniczy Zespol Spoldzielczy [*Agricultural Cooperative Union*] (POL)
RZS .... Rudnik Zivega Srebra [*Mercury Mine*] [*Idrija*] (YU)
RZSSh .... Republic Correspondence Secondary School (RU)
RZSZL .... Republiski Zavod za Socialno Zavarovanje v Ljubljani [*Republic Institute of Social Insurance in Ljubljana*] (YU)
RZU .... Radio Zpravodajsky Utvar [*Radio Intelligence Regimental Unit*] (CZ)
RZV .... Antiaircraft Reconnaissance Platoon (RU)
RZV .... Rudnici Zlata i Volframa [*Gold and Tungsten Mines*] [*Kucevo*] (YU)

RZZ .... Rejonowa Zbiornica Zlomu [*District Scrap Metal Collection Point*] (POL)

Rz Z G .... Rzeszowskie Zaklady Gastronomiczne [*Rzeszow Restaurant Establishments*] (POL)

S

S .... Adder [*Computers*] (RU)
S- .... Ambulance Aircraft (RU)
S .... Balance (RU)
S .... Bishop [*Chess*] (RU)
S- .... Coupling (RU)
S .... Displacement [*Artillery*] (RU)
S .... For Snow Background [*Camouflage*] (RU)
s .... Kind, Quality, Grade (RU)
S .... Medical (Department of a Ship) (RU)
S .... Nakladatelstvi Svoboda [*Svoboda Publishing House*] (CZ)
s .... Neuter [*Gender*] (RU)
s .... North (BU)
S .... North, Northern (RU)
s .... Page (BU)
s .... Page (RU)
s/ .... Sa [*Their, Your*] [*Business and trade*] [*French*]
S .... Saeure [*Acid*] [*German*]
s .... Sahife [*Page*] [*Turkish*] (GPO)
S .... Saint [*Saint*] [*French*] (MTD)
S .... San [*or Santo*] [*Saint*] [*Spanish*]
s .... Sana [*Word*] [*Finnish*]
S .... Sao [*Saint*] [*Portuguese*] (GPO)
S .... Sarjana [*Academic degree*] [*Indonesian*]
S .... Scandia (MAR)
S .... Schloss [*German*]
S .... Schnellzuglokomotive [*Fast Express Train Locomotive*] (EG)
S .... Schule [*German*]
s .... Second (RU)
s .... Second [*French*]
S .... Seconde [*French*] (MTD)
s .... Seged [*Assistant*] (HU)
S .... Sehen [*See*] [*Business and trade*] [*German*]
S .... Sehid [*Martyr*] (TU)
S .... Seite [*Page*] [*German*] (GPO)
s .... Sekunda [*or Sekundy*] [*Second or Seconds*] [*Polish*]
S .... Sekunde [*Second*] [*German*]
s .... Sekunti(a) [*Finnish*]
S .... Self-Propelled (RU)
s .... Semi [*Half*] [*Latin*] (GPO)
S .... Sepultus [*Buried*] [*Latin*] (GPO)
s/ .... Ses [*Their, Your*] [*Business and trade*] [*French*]
S .... Sever [*North*] (YU)
s .... Sever [*North*] (CZ)
S .... Shipboard [*Nuclear physics and engineering*] (RU)
S .... Shushi [*Japanese*]
s .... Sida [*Page*] [*Swedish*] (GPO)
s .... Side [*Page*] [*Danish*] (GPO)
s .... Side [*Page*] [*Norwegian*] (GPO)
s .... Sider [*Pages*] [*Danish*] (GPO)
S .... Siege [*Siege*] [*French*] (MTD)
s .... Siehe [*See*] (EG)
s .... Signe [*Signed*] [*French*]
s .... Sillinki [*Finnish*]
S .... Sily (MAR)
S .... Sinif [*Class*] (TU)
S .... Situs [*Lies*] [*Latin*] (GPO)
s .... Sivu [*Page*] [*Finnish*] (GPO)
s .... Sivuilla [*Finnish*]
s .... Sivu(lla) [*Finnish*]
s .... Sivut [*Finnish*]
s/ .... Sobre [*On*] [*Business and trade*] [*Spanish*]
S .... Sobresaliente [*On an Examination: Distinction*] [*Spanish*]
S .... Socialdemokratiet [*Social Democratic Party*] [*Danish*] (WEN)
S .... Societas [*Society*] [*Latin*] (GPO)
S .... Socius [*or Sodalis*] [*Fellow*] [*Latin*] (GPO)
S .... Sofia (BU)
s .... Sokak [*Street*] [*Turkish*]
s .... Solidus [*Shilling*] [*Latin*] (GPO)
s .... Son (RU)
s/ .... Son [*Their, Your*] [*Business and trade*] [*French*]
s .... Sondre [*South*] [*Norwegian*] (GPO)
S .... Soudruh [*or Soudruzka*] [*Comrade*] (CZ)
S/ .... Sous [*Sub or Under*] [*Prefix*] [*French*] (CL)
S .... Spartacus [*Sports society*] (RU)
S .... Staz Szpitalny [*Hospital Practice*] [*Polish*]
s .... Ster [*Stere*] [*Polish*]
s .... Stron [*Pages*] (POL)
S .... Su [*Water, Stream*] (TU)
s/ .... Su [*Your*] [*Business and trade*] [*Spanish*]
S .... Sud [*South*] [*French*] (MTD)
S .... Sudska Uprava [*Judicial Administration*] (YU)
S .... Sued [*or Sueden*] [*South*] (EG)
S .... Superhigh [*Bearing precision grade*] (RU)
s/ .... Sur [*Geographic*] [*French*]
S .... Sur [*South*] [*Spanish*]
S .... Sveriges Socialdemokratiska Arbetareparti [*Social Democratic Party*] [*Swedish*] (WEN)
s .... Swiety [*Saint*] [*Polish*]
s .... Symmetrisch [*Symmetric*] [*German*]
s .... Syn [*Son*] [*Polish*]
s .... Syntyaan [*Finnish*]
s .... Syntynyt [*Finnish*]
S .... Szwecja [*Sweden*] [*Polish*]
S .... Trains Run Only on Sundays and the Following Holidays: New Year, Good Friday, Easter Monday, 1 May, 8 May (Day of Liberation), 7 October (Day of the Republic), 1st and 2nd day of Christmas, Ascension Day, Day of Penitence, Whit-Monday (EG)
s .... Village (BU)
s .... Village, Settlement (RU)
S .... Whistle [*Railroads*] (RU)
SA .... Agricultural Academy (BU)
SA .... Ammunition Depot (RU)
SA .... Djaksa [*Government Prosecuting Attorney*] (IN)
SA .... Power Unit (RU)
Sa .... Saari [*or Saaret*] [*Island or Islands*] [*Finnish*] (NAU)
Sa .... Saat [*Hour*] (TU)
Sa .... Saege [*German*]
sa .... Sajto Alatt [*In Press*] (HU)
sa .... Saka [*Jocular*] (TU)
SA .... Salgotarjani Acelarugyar [*Salgotarjan Steel Factory*] (HU)
sa .... Sama [*Finnish*]
SA .... Samohodna Artiljerija [*Self-Propelled Artillery*] (YU)
SA .... Saudi Arabia [*Two-letter standard code*] (CNC)
sa .... Secundum Artem [*According to Art*] [*Latin*] (GPO)
SA .... Self-Propelled Artillery (RU)
Sa .... Senora [*Madam, Lady*] [*Spanish*]
Sa .... Serra [*Mountain Range*] [*Portuguese*] (NAU)
SA .... Service Automobile [*Military*] [*French*] (MTD)
SA .... Service Auxiliaire [*Military*] [*French*] (MTD)
Sa .... Shima [*Island*] [*Japanese*] (NAU)
sa .... Siehe Auch [*See Also*] (EG)
Sa .... Sierra [*Mountain Range*] [*Spanish*] (NAU)
SA .... Signaling Device (RU)
sa .... Sine Anno [*Without Date*] [*Latin*] (GPO)
SA .... Slovenska Akademija Znanosti in Umetnosti [*Slovenian Academy of Sciences and Arts*] [*Ljubljana*] (YU)
SA .... Sociedad Anonima [*Stock Company*] [*Spanish*]
SA .... Sociedade Anonima [*Public Limited Company*] [*Portuguese*]
SA .... Societe Anonyme [*Joint Stock Company*] [*French*]
SA .... Sols Africains [*A publication*] (MAR)
SA .... Son Altesse [*His (or Her) Highness*] (CL)
SA .... Sonder-Abdruck [*Reprint*] [*German*]
SA .... Sosyete Anonim [*Joint Stock Company*] (TU)
SA .... South Africa (AF)
SA .... Soviet Archaeology (RU)
SA .... Soviet Arctic (RU)
SA .... Soviet Army (RU)
SA- .... Soviet Automatic Coupling (RU)
SA .... Spolka Akcyjna [*Company Limited*] [*Polish*]
SA .... Srpska Akademija [*Serbian Academy*] (YU)
SA .... Standard Atmosphere (RU)

SA .... Statni Arbitraz [*State Arbitration Office*] (CZ)
SA .... Sturmabteilung [*German*] (PPE)
SA .... Su Alteza [*His (or Her) Highness*] [*Spanish*]
SA .... Sua Altezza [*His (or Her) Highness*] [*Italian*]
SA .... Sudamerica [*South America*] [*Spanish*]
SA .... Sudanese Army (MAR)
Sa .... Summa [*or Summe*] [*Sum or Total*] (EG)
SA .... Syntactic Analysis (RU)
Sa .... Train Operates Only on Saturday (EG)
SAA .... Saudi Arabian Army (ME)
SAA .... Service des Activites Aeriennes [*Aerial Activities Service*] [*French*] (WER)
SAA .... Societe Aefienne d'Assurances (MAR)
SAA .... Societe Africaine d'Ambulances (MAR)
SAA .... Societe Agricole de l'Agneby (MAR)
SAA .... Societe Algerienne d'Assurance (MAR)
SAA .... Societe Auxiliaire Africaine (MAR)
SAA .... Societe Auxiliaire Africaine pour le Developpement du Commerce, de l'Industrie, et de l'Agriculture en Afrique Occidentale (MAR)
SAA .... South African Airways (AF)
SAA .... South African Alliance (PPW)
SAA .... South African Army (MAR)
SAA .... South African Artillery (MAR)
SAA .... South African Aviation Corps (MAR)
SAA .... Syndesmos Apostraton Axiomatikon [*Alliance of Retired Officers*] [*Followed by initial letter of service branch name*] [*Greek*] (GC)
SAA .... Syndicat Agricole Africain (MAR)
SAA .... Syrian Arab Airlines (MAR)
SAAA .... Sarawak Amateur Athletes Association (ML)
SAAA .... South African Association of Arts (MAR)
SAAA .... Sudanese Amateur Athletic Association (MAR)
SAAAS .... South African Association for the Advancement of Science (MAR)
SAAAU .... South African Amateur Athletic Union (MAR)
SAAB .... South African Archaeological Bulletin [*A publication*] (MAR)
SAAB .... Svenska Aeroplan Aktiebolaget [*Swedish automobile manufacturer; acronym used as name of its cars*]
SAAB .... Syndicat des Agents de l'Administration du Burundi [*Burundi Union of Administrative Employees*] (AF)
SAABED .... Societe Africaine d'Application des Bitumes et Derives (MAR)
SAABU .... South African Amateur Body-Building Union (MAR)
SAAC .... Societe Africaine d'Automobile et de Courtage (MAR)
SAAC .... South African Army Corps (MAR)
SAACE .... South African Association of Consulting Engineers (MAR)
SAACI .... Syndicat Agricole Africain de la Cote-d'Ivoire (MAR)
SAAE .... Societe Algerienne d'Accumulateurs Electriques (MAR)
SAAEB .... South African Atomic Energy Board (AF)
SAAF .... South African Air Force (AF)
SAAFA .... South African Air Force Association (MAR)
SAAFA .... South African Amateur Fencing Association (MAR)
SAAFA .... Special Arab Aid Fund for Africa (MAR)
SAAGU .... South African Amateur Gymnastics Union (MAR)
SAAJA .... South African Amateur Judo Association (MAR)
SAAK .... Synetairismoi Apokatastaseos Aktimonon Kalliergiton [*Cooperatives for the Rehabilitation of Landless Farm Workers*] [*Greek*] (GC)
SAAL .... Syrian Arab Airlines Limited (ME)
SAAMBR .... South African Association for Marine Biological Research (MAR)
saann .... Saannollinen [*Regular*] [*Finnish*]
SAAO .... Societe Auxiliaire d'Afrique Occidentale (MAR)
SAAO .... South African Astronomical Observatory (MAR)
SAAP .... Sociedad Argentina de Artes Plasticas [*Argentine Society of Plastic Arts*] (LA)
SAAPC .... Sudanese Animal & Agricultural Production Company (MAR)
SAAR .... Societe Africaine des Artisans Reunis (MAR)
SAARBS .... South African Angora Ram Breeders' Society (MAR)
SAARU .... South African Amateur Rowing Union (MAR)
SAASigs .... South African Army Signals (MAR)
SAATC .... Southern African Air Transport Council (MAR)
SAATU .... South African Amateur Trampoline Union (MAR)
SAAU .... South African Agricultural Union (MAR)
SAAU .... South African Athletic Union (MAR)
SAAWF .... South African Amateur Wrestling Federation (MAR)
SAAWU .... South African Allied Workers Union (AF)
SAAWU .... South African Amateur Weight-Lifting Union (MAR)
SAB .... Air-Dropped Parachute Flare (BU)
SAB .... Illuminating Aerial Bomb (RU)
sab .... Sabado [*Saturday*] [*Spanish*]
SAB .... Self-Propelled Artillery Brigade (RU)
SAB .... Singapore Armoured Brigade (ML)
SAB .... Societe Africaine des Bois (MAR)
SAB .... Societe Africaine de Bonneterie (MAR)
SAB .... Societe des Allumettes du Benin (MAR)
SAB .... Societe Anonyme Belge pour le Commerce du Haut-Congo (MAR)
SAB .... Society for Applied Bacteriology (EA)
SAB .... South African Bond (MAR)
SAB .... South African Breweries (MAR)
SAB .... Staf Angkatan Bersendjata [*Armed Forces Staff*] (IN)
SAB .... Svetleca Aviobomba [*Flare Aerial Bomb*] (YU)
SABA .... Societe Abidjanaise de Batiment (MAR)
SABA .... Societe Agricole Bananiere de l'Agneby (MAR)
SABA .... Societe Anonyme des Barytes Algeriennes (MAR)
SABA .... South African Black Alliance (PPW)
SABAIC .... Societe Anonyme de Batiments Ivoiro-Celtique (MAR)
SABC .... Societe Anonyme des Brasseries du Cameroun [*Cameroon Brewery Company*] (AF)
SABC .... South Africa Broadcasting Corporation (AF)
SABCI .... Societe d'Application des Bois a la Construction et a l'Industrie en Cote-d'Ivoire (MAR)
SABDN .... Societe Agricole et Bananiere de Divo Nord (MAR)
SABE .... Societe Africaine de Beton Equatoriaux (MAR)
SABE .... Societe Africaine des Bois Equatoriaux (MAR)
SABE .... Societe Africaine des Bois de l'Est (MAR)
SABE .... Societe Africaine d'Exploitation des Brevets "Eries" (MAR)
SABENA .... Societe Anonyme Belge d'Exploitation de la Navigation Aerienne [*SABENA Belgian World Airlines*]
SABEX .... Societe Abidjanaise d'Expertises (MAR)
SABI .... Societe Africaine de Biscuiterie (MAR)
SABI .... Societe Africaine de Bordelaise Industrielle [*Moroccan*] (MAR)
SABIC .... Societe Africaine des Bois Industrielle et Commerciale (MAR)
SABIMA .... Societe Abidjanaise d'Importation de Materiel Industriel (MAR)
SABLI .... Societe Agro-Animale Benino-Arabe-Libyenne (MAR)
Sablre .... Sabliere [*Sand Pit*] [*Military map abbreviation*] [*World War I*] [*French*] (MTD)
SABM .... Societe Africaine de Beton Manufacture (MAR)
SABM .... Societe Africaine des Bois du M'bam (MAR)
SABO .... Societe Agricole d'Abobo (MAR)
SABOGAB .... Societe Anonyme des Bois du Gabon (MAR)
sabr .... Self-Propelled Artillery Brigade (RU)
SABRA .... South African Bureau of Racial Affairs (AF)
SABRA .... Suid-Afrikaanse Bureau vir Rasse Aangeleenthede (MAR)
SABS .... South African Bureau of Standards (MAR)
SABSA .... South African Billiards and Snooker Association (MAR)
SABSWA .... South African Black Social Workers Association (AF)
SABTP .... Societe Africaine de Batiments et de Travaux Publics (MAR)
SABTS .... South African Blood Transfusion Service (MAR)
SABV .... Suid-Afrikaanse Bybelvereniging (MAR)
SABV-CP .... Societe Africaine de Betail et Viande, Cuirs, et Peaux (MAR)
SAC .... Schweizer Alpen Club [*Swiss Alpine Club*]
SAC .... Scientific Advisory Council to the Prime Minister (MAR)
SAC .... Service d'Action Civique [*Civic Action Service*] [*French*] (WER)
SAC .... Servicio de Asesoramiento Ciudadano [*Civic Advisory Service*] [*Spanish*] (WER)
SAC .... Sociedad de Agricultores de Colombia [*Farmers Association of Colombia*] (LA)
SAC .... Societe d'Achat et de Commission (MAR)
SAC .... Societe d'Action Coloniale (MAR)
SAC .... Societe d'Action Cooperative avec les Territoires d'Outre-Mer (MAR)
SAC .... Societe Africaine de Chaussures (MAR)
SAC .... Societe Africaine de Confection (MAR)
SAC .... Societe Africaine de Constructions (MAR)
SAC .... Societe Africaine de Culture (MAR)
SAC .... Societe Agricole Constant et Compagnie (MAR)
SAC .... Societe d'Assistance Comptable (MAR)
SAC .... Society of African Culture (AF)
SAC .... South African College (MAR)
SAC .... Southern Africa Committee (MAR)
SAC .... Space Activities Commission (SJT)
SAC .... Sudan Air Cargo (MAR)
SAC .... Sugar Association of the Caribbean (EA)
SAC .... Supreme Agricultural Council (MAR)
SAC .... Sveriges Arbetares Central-Organisation [*Central Organization of Swedish Workers*] (WEN)
SACA .... Societe Agricole de Cote-d'Afrique (MAR)
SACA .... Societe Anonyme Commerciale Agricole [*Paris Representantes Bogota*] (COL)
SACA .... Societe des Automobiles de la Cote-d'Afrique (MAR)
SACA .... Societe Auxiliaire de Commerce Africain (MAR)
SACA .... South African Cricket Association (MAR)
SACAB .... Societe Anonyme Camerounaise de Bonneterie (MAR)
SACAF .... Societe Anonyme de Constructions en Afrique (MAR)
SACAF .... Societe Centrafricaine du Sac (MAR)
SACAM .... Societe Africaine de Carreaux Agglomeres de Marbre (MAR)
SACAM .... Societe Agricole du Cameroun (MAR)
SACANGO .... Southern Africa Committee on Air Navigation and Ground Operation (MAR)
SACAPH .... Societe Agricole des Caoutchoucs d'Anphu-Ha (MAR)
SACAR .... Societe Abidjanaise de Carrelage (MAR)
SACB .... South African Cricket Board (MAR)
SACB .... South African Criminal Bureau (MAR)
SACBC .... Southern Africa Catholic Bishops' Conference (MAR)
SACBTP .... Societe Africaine de Construction de Batiments et Travaux Publics (MAR)
SACC .... Societe Anonyme Camerounaise de Chaussures et Valises (MAR)
SACC .... Societe Artisanale Camerounaise de Chaussures (MAR)
SACC .... South African Council of Churches (AF)

SACCAM .... Societe Artisanale des Coutures Camerounaises (MAR)
SACCB .... Societe Anonyme des Cultures au Congo Belge (MAR)
SACCIE .... Societe Algerienne de Commission, Consignation, Courtage d'Import-Export (MAR)
SACDA .... South African Copper Development Association (MAR)
SACDC .... South African Coastal Defence Corps (MAR)
SACE .... Sociedad de Amistad Cubana-Espanola [*Spanish-Cuban Friendship Society*] (LA)
SACEC .... Societe Africaine de Cooperation Economique [*Senegalese*] (MAR)
SACEG .... Societe Africaine de Constructions et d'Entreprises Generales (MAR)
SACEL .... Societe Anonyme Camerounaise d'Electronique (MAR)
SACEM .... Societe Anonyme Cherifienne d'Etudes Minieres [*Moroccan Mining Studies Corporation*] (AF)
SACEM .... Societe des Auteurs, Compositeurs, et Editeurs de Musique [*Society of Authors, Composers, and Music Publishers*] [*French*] (WER)
SACER .... Societe Africaine de Commerce et de Representation (MAR)
SACER .... Societe Africaine de Constructions Economiques et Rapides (MAR)
SACF .... South African Canoe Federation (MAR)
SACFER ...... Societe Africaine de Construction et de Fabrication d'Engins Roulants (MAR)
SACG .... Societe d'Alimentation et de Commerce Generale (MAR)
sachl .... Saechlich [*German*]
Sachv .... Sachverstaendiger [*German*]
Sachw .... Sachwalter [*German*]
SACI .... Andre Pagliano et Cie., Societe Africaine de Commission et d'Importation (MAR)
SACI .... Societe Africaine de Commerce et d'Industrie [*African Trade and Industry Company*] [*Ivorian*] (AF)
SACI .... Societe Auxiliaire de Constructions Immobilieres (MAR)
SACIA .... Societe Africaine pour le Commerce, l'Industrie, et l'Agriculture (MAR)
SACIA .... Societe Agricole, Commerciale, et Industrielle de l'Agneby (MAR)
SACIA .... Societe Auxiliaire du Commerce et de l'Industrie en Afrique (MAR)
SACIACI ..... Societe Africaine Commerciale, Industrielle, et Agricole de Cote-d'Ivoire (MAR)
SACIET .... Societe Africaine de Commerce, Import, Export, Transport (MAR)
SACIL .... Sociedade Agricola & Comercial (Imala) Lda. (MAR)
SACJK .... Societe Africaine des Comptoirs J. A. Klein (MAR)
SACL .... South African Confederation of Labor (AF)
SACLANT ... Supreme Allied Atlantic Command (WER)
SACM .... Societe Abidjanaise de Constructions Mecaniques (MAR)
SACM .... Societe Africaine de Constructions Metalliques (MAR)
SACM .... Societe Alsacienne de Constructions Mecaniques (MAR)
SACM .... Societe Anonyme de Confection Malgache (MAR)
SACM .... South Arabian Common Market (MAR)
SACNA .... South African Club of North America (MAR)
SACO .... Service Administratif Canadien Outre-Mer (MAR)
SACO .... Societe Abidjanaise de Construction (MAR)
SACO .... Societe Africaine de Cacao (MAR)
SACO .... Societe Africaine de Commerce (MAR)
SACO .... Societe Anonyme de la Carrosserie d'Oloumi (MAR)
SACO .... Sveriges Akademikers Central-Organisation [*Swedish Confederation of Professional Associations*] (WEN)
SACOCI ...... Societe Africaine de Commerce et d'Industrie en Cote-d'Ivoire (MAR)
SACOD .... Societe Anonyme de Commercialisation d'Or et de Diamants (MAR)
SACOD .... South African Congress of Democrats (MAR)
SACOM .... Societe Agricole et Commerciale de la Mananjeba (MAR)
SACOM .... Societe Anonyme Cherifienne d'Organisation Moderne [*Moroccan*] (MAR)
SACOMAIT ... Societe Algerienne de Construction, de Materiel Agricole Industriel, et de Travaux Publics [*Algerian Construction, Agricultural and Industrial Equipment, and Public Works Company*] (AF)
SACOMAT ... Societe Africaine de Construction et Materiaux (MAR)
SACOME ..... Societe Africaine de Constructions Metalliques et d'Entreprise (MAR)
SACOMI ...... Societe Africaine de Commerce et d'Industrie (MAR)
SACOMINE ... Societe Agricole, Commerciale, et Miniere (MAR)
SACOOP ..... Sociedad Auxiliadora de Cooperativas [*Cooperatives Assistance Agency*] [*Chilean*] (LA)
SACOPS ..... Societa Anonima Case Operaie Petrolibia Silca (MAR)
SACOS .... South African Council for Sport (AF)
SACOTRA ... Societe Africaine de Consignation et de Transit (MAR)
SACOTRAPDA ... Societe Arabe pour le Commerce, le Transport Public, et le Developpement Agricole (MAR)
SACP .... South Africa Communist Party (AF)
SACP .... Systeme d'Armes Courte Portee [*Short-Range Weapons System*] [*French*] (WER)
SACPAC ..... South African Co-Ordinating Performing Arts Council (MAR)
SACPO .... South African Coloured People's Organization (MAR)
SACRA .... Societe Africaine de Courtage et de Representation d'Assurances (MAR)
SACRA .... Societe Nord Africaine de Construction et de Representation Agricole et Mecanique (MAR)
SACS .... Societe Agricole et Commerciale de la Sangha (MAR)
SACS .... South African College School (MAR)
SACS .... South African Corps of Signals (MAR)
SACSA .... South African Conservative Students Association (AF)
SACSIR .... South African Council for Scientific and Industrial Research (MAR)
SACSJ .... Student and Academic Campaign for Soviet Jewry (MAR)
SACSSR ..... Svaz Architektu Ceskoslovenske Socialisticke Republiky [*Union of Architects of the Czechoslovak Socialist Republic*] (CZ)
SACT .... Societe Africaine de Commerce et de Transports (MAR)
SACT .... Societe Algerienne de Construction Telephonique (MAR)
SACTA .... Societe Agricole de Collecte de Tabac (MAR)
SACTU .... South African Congress of Trade Unions (AF)
SACTW .... South African Council of Transport Workers (AF)
SACU .... South African Cricket Union (MAR)
SACU .... South African Customs Union
SACUA .... Southern African Customs Union Agreement (MAR)
SACY .... Societe Anonyme des Anciens Ets. Cauvin-Yvose (MAR)
SAD .... Composite Air Division (RU)
sad .... Composite Aviation Division (BU)
SAD .... Schweizerischer Aufklaerungsdienst [*Swiss Intelligence Service*] (WEN)
SAD .... Self-Propelled Artillery Battalion (RU)
SAD .... Servicos de Accao Directa [*Services for Direct Action*] [*Portuguese*] (WER)
SAD .... Sistema Automatizado de Direccion [*Automated Data Addressing System*] [*Cuban*] (LA)
SAD .... Sjedinjene Americke Drzave [*United States of America*] (YU)
SAD .... Societe Africaine de Detergents (MAR)
SAD .... Societe Africaine de Domiciliation (MAR)
SAD .... Societe Agricole de Diby (MAR)
SAD .... Sowjetische Administration Deutschlands [*Soviet Administration of Germany*] (EG)
SAD .... Spolecnost Antonina Dvoraka [*Antonin Dvorak Society*] (CZ)
SADA .... Sendikalararasi Dayanisma Konseyini [*Inter-Union Solidarity Council*] (TU)
SADA .... Servico de Apoio e Desenvolvimento Agrario [*Service for Agrarian Support and Development*] [*Portuguese*] (WER)
SADA .... Sinai Arastirma Danisma Ajansi [*Industrial Research Advisory Agency*] [*Ankara*] (TU)
SADA .... Societe Agricole d'Ampombilawa (MAR)
SADAB .... Societe Africaine des Automobiles M. Berliet (MAR)
SADACEB ... Societe Anonyme des Anciens Chantiers d'Entreprise Borsetti (MAR)
SADAEA ..... Societe Anonyme des Anciens Ets. Amouroux (MAR)
SADAIC .... Sociedad Argentina de Autores, Interpretes, y Compositores de Musica [*Argentine Society of Songwriters, Singers, and Composers*] (LA)
SADAMI ...... Service Auxiliaire de l'Assistance Medicale aux Indigenes (MAR)
SADAPE ...... Sociedad Anonima de Aplicaciones Electronicas [*Bogota*] (COL)
SADARET ... Societe Anglaise d'Etudes et de Realisations d'Energie et de Telecommunications (MAR)
SADC .... Singapore Air Defence Command (ML)
SADCA .... Societe Anonyme des Conserves Alimentaires [*Tunisian*] (MAR)
SADCC .... Southern African Development Co-Ordination Conference
SADCOP ..... Petroleum Products Distribution Organization [*Syrian*] (ME)
SADE .... Services, Agriculture, Developpement, Elevage (MAR)
SADE .... Sociedad Argentina de Escritores [*Argentine Writers Association*] (LA)
SADE .... Suramericana de Electrificacion [*Bogota*] (COL)
SADEC .... Societe Africaine d'Etudes et Constructions (MAR)
SADEC .... Societe Auxiliaire d'Entreprises de Constructions en Afrique (MAR)
SADEC-CI ... Societe Auxiliaire d'Entreprises de Constructions en Cote-d'Ivoire (MAR)
SADEC Haute-Volta ... Societe Auxiliaire d'Entreprises de Constructions en Haute-Volta (MAR)
SADECO ..... Societe Africaine pour le Developpement du Commerce (MAR)
SADEM .... Societe Africaine des Eaux Minerales (MAR)
SADEMI ...... Sociedad Abastecedora de la Mineria [*Mining Supply Company*] [*Chilean*] (LA)
SADEO .... Synergazomenoi Agonistikoi Dimokratikoi Organismoi Ergazomenon [*Cooperating Democratic Militant Workers and Employee Organizations*] (GC1)
SADER .... Societe Africaine de Deroulage des Ets. Rougier & Fils (MAR)
SADER .... Societe d'Amenagement et du Developpement Regional du Gharb (MAR)
SADEVO ..... Societe Nationale d'Amenagement et de Developpement de la Vallee de l'Oueme (MAR)
SADF .... South African Defense Forces (AF)
SADI .... Saratov Highway Institute (RU)
SADI .... Service d'Approvisionnement et de Distribution des Produits Importes [*Imports Distribution and Supply Department*] [*Subsidiary of OROC--replaced by EPS*] [*Cambodian*] (CL)
SADI .... Societe Africaine de Developpement Industriel (MAR)
SADIA .... Societe Africaine de Diffusion Industrielle et Automobile (MAR)

SADIAMIL ... Societe Africaine du Developpement de l'Industrie Alimentaire du Millet et du Sorgho [*African Society for the Development of the Millet- and Sorghum-Based Food Industry*] (AF)
SADIC .... Societe Anonyme pour le Developpement Interieur Commercial et Industriel (MAR)
SADICO ...... Societe Africaine de Diffusion de Cosmetiques (MAR)
SADICOM ... Distribuidora Comercial SA [*Bogota*] (COL)
SADIF.......... Societe Africaine de Diffusion (MAR)
SADIH .... Societe Algerienne pour le Developpement de l'Industrie Hoteliere et Touristique (MAR)
SADIKS....... Soviet Association of Friendship and Cultural Cooperation with the Countries of Latin America (RU)
SADIN .... Societe Africaine de Distillation Industrielle [*Moroccan*] (MAR)
SADITA .... Societe Africaine d'Importation et de Distribution de Tabacs et Articles Divers (MAR)
SADITEX..... Societe d'Approvisionnement et de Distribution Textiles (MAR)
SADITEX-Mauritanie ... Societe Mauritanienne d'Approvisionnement et de Distribution Textiles (MAR)
SADIVOIRE ... Societe Africaine de Diffusion Ivoire (MAR)
SADM.......... Sociedad Argentina de Derechos de las Mujeres [*Women's Rights Association*] [*Argentine*] (LA)
SADO .... Societe Agricole d'Offa (MAR)
SADOI .... Sociedad Argentina de Organizacion Industrial [*Argentine Association of Industrial Organization*] (LA)
SADP........... Double-Side Photostat Machine (RU)
SADR .... Saharan Arab Democratic Republic [*Moroccan*] (PD)
SADRAC ..... South African Defence Research Advisory Committee (MAR)
SADTA .... South African Dancing Teachers' Association (MAR)
sae............. Composite Air Squadron (RU)
sae............. Composite Aviation Squadron (BU)
SAE .... Medical Air Ambulance Squadron (RU)
SAE .... Societe Africaine d'Edition (MAR)
SAE .... Societe Anonyme Egyptienne (MAR)
SAE .... Societe Auxiliaire d'Entreprises (MAR)
SAE .... Soviet Antarctic Expedition (RU)
SAEB........... Societe Africaine d'Entreprises et de Batiment [*Dakar*] (MAR)
SAEB........... Societe Africaine d'Exploitation des Bois (MAR)
SAEC .... Societe Abidjanaise d'Expansion Chimique (MAR)
SAEC .... Societe Africaine d'Expansion Chimique (MAR)
SAEC .... South African Engineers' Corps (MAR)
SAEC-CAMEROUN ... Societe Africaine d'Expansion Chimique - Cameroun (MAR)
SAECO........ Societe Abidjanaise d'Exploitations Commerciales (MAR)
SAECP .... Societe Africain d'Exportation de Cuirs et Peaux (MAR)
SAED .... Societe Africaine d'Etudes et de Developpement (MAR)
SAED .... Societe d'Agriculture et d'Elevage du D'jiminy (MAR)
SAED .... Societe d'Amenagement et d'Exploitation des Terres du Delta du Fleuve Senegal (MAR)
SAEE........... Syndesmos Anaptyxeos Ellinikon Exoplismon [*Association for the Development of Greek Armaments*] (GC)
SAEEI.......... Societe Africaine d'Equipement Electrique et Industriel des Ets. Verger et Delporte (MAR)
SAEF .... Societe Anonyme des Entreprises J. Fornero (MAR)
SAEG .... Societe Africaine des Entreprises Girardin [*Moroccan*] (MAR)
SAEGHT...... Societe Africaine d'Exploitation et de Gestion Hoteliere et Touristique (MAR)
SAEI............ Service des Affaires Economiques et Internationales [*Economic and International Affairs Service*] [*French*] (WER)
SAEI............ Sumitomo Atomic Energy Industries Ltd. (SJT)
SAEM.......... Synergazomenon Andidictatorikon Ergatiko Kinima [*Cooperating Antidictatorial Labor Movement*] [*See also AEM*] (GC1)
SAEN .... Societe des Anciens Etablissements Nicolas & Cie. (MAR)
SAEP........... Societe l'ACTION d'Edition et de Presse [*Tunisian*] (MAR)
SAEP........... Societe Africaine d'Editions et de Publicite (MAR)
SAEP........... Societe d'Agriculture et d'Elevage du Pool (MAR)
SAER........... Srpsko-Austriski i Evropski Rat [*Serbo-Austrian and European War*] [*World War I*] (YU)
SAERO .... Societe des Anciens Ets. A. Reymond de Ouagadougou (MAR)
SAET........... Societe Africaine d'Etudes Topographiques (MAR)
SAETO .... Sociedad Aereo del Tolina [*Colombia*]
SAEWA .... South African Electrical Workers' Association (MAR)
SAF .... Savonnerie Africaine des Ets. Fakhry (MAR)
SAF .... Service Administratif et Financier [*Administrative and Financial Service*] [*French*] (WER)
SAF .... Singapore Armed Forces (ML)
SAF .... Sistema de Asesoramiento y Fiscalizacion [*Advisory and Inspection System*] [*Peruvian*] (LA)
SAF .... Societe Africaine des Etablissements Fakhry (MAR)
SAF .... Societe Africaine Forestiere [*Libreville*] (MAR)
SAF .... Societe Agricole et Forestiere (MAR)
SAF .... Societe Agricole de Foumbo (MAR)
SAF .... Societe Alimentaire Fine (MAR)
SAF .... Societe Automobile Fassie [*Moroccan*] (MAR)
SAF .... South African Foundation (MAR)
SAF .... Sultan's Armed Forces [*Omani*] (ME)
SAF .... Svenska Arbetsgivareforeningen [*Swedish Employers' Confederation*] (WEN)
SAFA........... Societe d'Achats France-Afrique (MAR)
SAFA........... Societe Africaine Forestiere et Agricole (MAR)
SAFA........... South African Freedom Association (MAR)
SAFA........... Southern Amateur Football Association (MAR)
SAFACAM .... Societe Africaine Forestiere et Agricole Cameroun (MAR)
SAFAF......... South Arabian Federal Air Force (MAR)
SAFAL......... Societe Africaine de Fonderie d'Aluminium (MAR)
SAFAMI....... Societe Africaine de Fabrications Metalliques Industrielles (MAR)
SAFAR .... Societe Africaine de Fabrication des Automobiles Renault (MAR)
SAFARRIV .. Societe Africaine d'Assurances et de Reassurances en Republique de Cote-d'Ivoire (MAR)
SAFAS .... Saf Plastik Sanayi ve Ticaret Anonim Sirketi [*Clear Plastic Industry and Trade Corporation*] (TU)
SAFBAIL ..... Societe Africaine de Credit Bail (MAR)
SAFC........... Societe Africaine Financiere de Commission et de Courtage (MAR)
SAFCA .... Societe Africaine de Courtage d'Assurances (MAR)
SAFCA .... Societe Africaine de Credit Automobile (MAR)
SAFCA .... Societe Africaine de Fabrication de Cahiers (MAR)
SAFCA .... Societe Africaine de Fabrication de Cycles et Accessoires (MAR)
SAFCA .... South African Society of Composers, Authors, and Music Publishers (MAR)
SAF-CAP .... Sistema de Asesoramiento y Fiscalizacion para las Cooperativas Agrarias de Produccion [*Advisory and Supervisory System for Agrarian Production Cooperatives*] [*Peruvian*] (LA)
SAFCI.......... Societe Administrative et Financiere de Cote-d'Ivoire (MAR)
SAFCI.......... Societe Africaine Financiere, Commerciale, et Immobiliere (MAR)
SAFCO........ Saudi Arabian Fertilizers Company (ME)
SAFCO........ Societe Africaine Colombani & Cie. (MAR)
SAFCO........ Societe Africaine de Conserverie (MAR)
SAFCO........ Societe Africaine de Construction (MAR)
SAFCO........ Societe Afrique Commerce (MAR)
SAFCOM..... Societe Africaine de Constructions Metalliques (MAR)
SAFCOP...... Societe Africaine de Commercialisation des Produits de la Mer (MAR)
SAFD........... Societe des Ateliers et Fonderies Denis-Huet (MAR)
SAFE........... Servicio Auxiliar Femenino del Ejercito [*Army Women's Auxiliary Service*] [*Chilean*] (LA)
SAFE........... Societe Africaine d'Entreposage (MAR)
SAFE........... South African Friends of England (MAR)
SAFECOL ... Safe Colombiana, SA [*Bogota*] (COL)
SAFEFCON ... South Africa Far East Freight Conference (MAR)
SAFEGE...... Societe Anonyme Francaise d'Etudes, de Gestion, et d'Entreprise (MAR)
SAFEL......... Societe Africaine d'Elevage (MAR)
SAFEL......... Societe Africaine de Fruits et Legumes (MAR)
SAFELEC.... Societe Africaine d'Electricite (MAR)
SAFEM........ Societe Africaine de Froid Electro-Menager (MAR)
SAFER......... Societe d'Amenagement Foncier et d'Etablissement Rural [*Real Estate and Rural Development Company*] [*French*] (WER)
SAFF........... South African Field Force (MAR)
SAFFUC...... Sudan African Freedom Fighters Union of Conservatives (MAR)
SAFGRAD... Semi-Arid Food Grain Research and Development (MAR)
SAFI............ Saudi Arabian Financial Institution Company (ME)
SAFI............ Societe Africaine de Fabrication Industrielle (MAR)
SAFI............ Societe Africaine d'Investissements (MAR)
SAFIC.......... Societe Africaine Forestiere Industrielle et Commerciale (MAR)
SAFICA .... Societe Africaine de Fabrication et d'Impression de Cahiers (MAR)
SAFICO....... Sistema Andino de Financiamiento de Comercio [*Andean Commercial Financing System*] (LA)
SAFICOCI... Societe Abidjanaise de Fournitures pour l'Industrie et les Constructions en Cote-d'Ivoire (MAR)
SAFICOM.... Societe Africaine pour l'Industrie et le Commerce (MAR)
SAFIE.......... Societe Africaine d'Installations Electriques (MAR)
SAFIEX........ Societe Africaine d'Importation et d'Exportation (MAR)
SAFIL.......... Societa Agricola Fondiaria Italo-Libica (MAR)
SAFIL.......... Societe Africaine de Filterie (MAR)
SAFINA .... Societe Africaine Industrielle et Agricole de Sebikotane (MAR)
SAFINELEC ... Societe Africaine d'Injection et d'Electricite (MAR)
SAFIR.......... Societe Africaine de Fabrications Industrielles et de Representation (MAR)
SAFM .... Societe Africaine de Fabrication Metallique (MAR)
SAFMARINE ... South African Marine Corp. Ltd. (MAR)
SAFMSA ..... Sudanese Armed Forces Military Sports Association (MAR)
SAFO........... Societe Anonyme des Safaris Jean d'Orgeix (MAR)
SAFONKS... Societe Anonyme des Anciens Ets. Maurice Fonks (MAR)
SAFOP .... Societe Africaine de Formation Professionnelle (MAR)
SAFOR .... Societe Sanaga Forestiere (MAR)
SAFRA .... Societe Africaine d'Assurances (MAR)
SAfrD .... South African Dutch (MAR)
SAFRED...... Societe Africaine d'Emballage et de Demenagement (MAR)
SAFREP ...... Societe Anonyme Francaise de Recherches et d'Exploitation de Petrole [*French Petroleum Exploration and Exploitation Corporation*] [*Algerian*] (AF)
SAFREX ...... Societe Africaine d'Exploration Petroliere (MAR)
SAFRIC .... Societe Africaine de Confection (MAR)

SAFRIC .... Societe Africaine de Cooperation Commerciale [*Moroccan*] (MAR)
SAFRICA..... Societe Africaine de Representations Industrielles, Commerciales, et d'Assurances (MAR)
SAFRICO .... Societe Africaine de Construction (MAR)
SAFRIM....... Societe Africaine de Mecanographie (MAR)
SAFRIMEX ... Sociedade Africana de Importacao e Exportacao Lda. (MAR)
SAFRINEX... Societe Africaine d'Exploitation Vinicole (MAR)
SAFRIPA ..... Societe Africaine de Parfumerie (MAR)
SAFRITEX... Societe Africaine de Textile (MAR)
SAFRITIS .... Societe Africaine "Les Tissandiers" (MAR)
SAFT .... Societe Africaine de Filature et de Tissage [*Moroccan*] (MAR)
SAFTEL....... Societe Africaine d'Electronique et de Telecommunications (MAR)
SAFTI .... Singapore Armed Forces Training Institute (ML)
SAFTO .... South African Foreign Trade Organization (AF)
SAFTU .... South African Federation of Trade Unions (MAR)
SAFUES...... South African Federation of University Engineering Students (MAR)
Sag.............. Saglik [*Health*] (TU)
SAG............. Scierie, Atelier, et Garage (MAR)
SAG............. Secretaria de Agricultura y Ganaderia [*Secretariat of Agriculture and Livestock*] [*Mexican*] (LA)
SAG............. Servicio Agricola y Ganadero [*Agriculture and Livestock Service*] [*Chilean*] (LA)
SAG............. Sociedad de Agricultores y Ganaderos [*Bogota*] (COL)
SAG............. Societe Africaine de Groupage (MAR)
SAG............. Societe Agricole du Gabon (MAR)
SAG............. Societe Agricole de Guinee [*Agricultural Company of Guinea*] (AF)
SAG............. Societe Algerienne de Geophysique [*Algerian Geophysics Company*] (AF)
SAG............. Sowjetische Aktiengesellschaft [*Soviet Corporation*] [*SAGs were plants confiscated by the USSR after WWII and operated under Soviet auspices until the mid-50's*] (EG)
SAG............. Sozialistische Arbeitsgemeinschaft [*Socialist Work Group*] (EG)
SAGA .... Savonnerie du Gabon (MAR)
SAGA .... Societe Africaine de Groupement d'Achats (MAR)
SAGA .... Societe Anonyme de Gerance et d'Armement (MAR)
SAGA .... South African Gymkhana Association (MAR)
SAGAL .... Sociedade Agricola Algodoeira (MAR)
SAGAPE...... Societe d'Approvisionnement de Gaz Algerien pour l'Europe [*Company for Supplying Algerian Gas to Europe*] (AF)
SAGC .... Societe Africaine de Genie Civil (MAR)
SAGCA .... Societe Auxiliaire de Garantie et de Courtage d'Assurances (MAR)
SAGCI .... Societe d'Affretement et de Groupage de Cote-d'Ivoire (MAR)
SAGD .... Suid-Afrikaanse Geneeskundige Dienst (MAR)
SAGE .... Societe Africaine de Gestions d'Entreprises (MAR)
SAGE .... Symvoulion Arkhigon Genikon Epiteleion [*General Staff Officers Council*] [*Greek*] (GC)
SAGEC........ Societe Africaine de Genie Civil (MAR)
SAGECCOM ... Societe Africaine de Genie Civil et de Constructions Metalliques (MAR)
SAGECI....... Societe d'Agriculture et d'Elevage de la Cote-d'Ivoire (MAR)
SAGECO ..... Societe Abidjanaise de Gerance et d'Exploitation Commerciale (MAR)
SAGEM .... Societe Africaine des Articles Galvanises et Emailles (MAR)
SAGEMAR ... Societe d'Agence de Marques (MAR)
SAGI............ South African Garrisons Institutes (MAR)
SAGICAM ... Societe Agro-Industrielle du Cameroun (MAR)
SAGICOE.... Societe Agricole et Industrielle de la Cote Est (MAR)
SAGIS .... Societe Agricole et Industrielle de Sassandra (MAR)
SAGJ........... South African Geographical Journal [*Johannesburg*] [*A publication*] (MAR)
Saglik-Is ..... Turkiye Saglik Iscileri Sendikasi [*Turkish Health Workers Union*] (TU)
SAGM.......... South African General Mission (MAR)
SAGRICOL ... Societe Agricole et d'Elevage Khmero-Chinoise [*Cambodian-Chinese Agricultural and Livestock Company*] (CL)
SAGRINA .... Societe Agricole de la Nanoua (MAR)
SAGROCOL ... Sociedad Agrologica Colombiana Ltda. [*Bogota*] (COL)
SAGU .... Central Asian State University Imeni V. I. Lenin (RU)
SAGU .... South African Golf Union (MAR)
SAGUF .... Schweizerische Arbeitsgemeinschaft fuer Umweltforschung [*Swiss Association for Environmental Studies*] (WEN)
Sah .... Sahachivin [*Mr. or Ms.*] [*Literally Comrade; formerly used as a term of address for a member of the Sangkum Reastr Niyum (Prince Sihanouk's party)*] [*Cambodian*] (CL)
SAH .... Secteur d'Administration et d'Habitation (MAR)
SAHA .... South African Heavy Artillery (MAR)
sahk .... Sahkotekniikka [*Electricity*] [*Finnish*]
SAHM.......... Societe Africaine des Halles Modernes (MAR)
SAHM.......... Societe Algerienne des Huiles Minerales (MAR)
SAHOP........ Secretaria de Asentamientos Humanos y Obras Publicas [*Secretariat for Human Settlements and Public Works*] [*Mexican*] (LA)
SAHP........... Societe Anonyme de l'Hotel du Plateau (MAR)
SAI .... Service des Affaires Indigenes [*Bureau of Native Affairs*] (MAR)
SAI .... Sindicato de Auxiliares de Ingenieria [*Union of Engineering Assistants*] [*Salvadoran*] (LA)
SAI .... Societe Africaine d'Importation (MAR)
SAI .... Societe Arabe d'Investissements (MAR)
SAI .... South African Infantry (MAR)
SAI .... Su Alteza Imperial [*Spanish*]
SAIA............ Societe Agricole et Industrielle de l'Ankara [*Malagasy*] (MAR)
SAIA............ Solidariedade Africana para a Independencia de Angola (MAR)
SAIAO .... Societe Auxiliaire Immobiliere d'Afrique Occidentale (MAR)
SAIB............ Societa Agricola Industriale Bengasi (MAR)
SAIB............ Societe Africaine des Industries du Batiment (MAR)
SAIB............ Societe Algerienne pour l'Industrie du Batiment (MAR)
SAIBE.......... Societe Automobile et Industrielle du Benin (MAR)
SAIC............ South African Indian Congress (PD)
SAIC............ South African Indian Council (AF)
SAICA .... Societa Anonima Industriale Commerciale Automobilistica (MAR)
SAICA .... Societe Africaine Industrielle, Commerciale, et Agricole (MAR)
SAICA .... Societe Agricole et Industrielle de la Cote d'Afrique (MAR)
SAICCOR.... South African Industrial Cellulose Corporation (Pty) Ltd. (MAR)
SAICE .... South African Institute of Civil Engineers (MAR)
SAIChemE ... South African Institution of Chemical Engineers (MAR)
SAICI........... Societe Agricole et Industrielle de la Cote-d'Ivoire (MAR)
SAICOS....... Societe Agricole, Industrielle, et Commerciale du Senegal (MAR)
SAIDA .... Societa Anonima Italiana Distilleria Agraria (MAR)
SAIDC .... South African Inventions Development Corporation (MAR)
SAIDE .... Services Aeriens Internationaux d'Egypte (MAR)
SAIE .... South Africa Institute of Engineers (MAR)
SAIEA .... Societe Auxiliaire Immobiliere des Etats d'Afrique (MAR)
SAIEA .... South Africa Institute Employers' Association (MAR)
SAIEE.......... South Africa Institute of Electrical Engineers (MAR)
SAIET.......... Societa Anonima Impianti Elettrici Tripoli (MAR)
SAIET.......... Societe Africaine d'Importation et d'Exportation Tchadienne (MAR)
SAIF .... South African Industrial Federation (MAR)
SAIF .... South African Institute of Foundrymen (MAR)
SAIGIMS ..... Central Asian Scientific Research Institute of Geology and Mineral Raw Materials (RU)
SAIH............ Societe Africaine Immobiliere et Hoteliere (MAR)
SAII .... Central Asian Industrial Institute (RU)
SAII .... Societe Africaine d'Impressions Industrielles (MAR)
SAIIA........... South African Institute of International Affairs (AF)
SAIMCI........ Societe Anonyme Immobiliere des Magasins de Cote-d'Ivoire (MAR)
SAIME......... Central Asian Scientific Research Institute for the Mechanization and Electrification of Irrigation Farming (RU)
SAIMechE... South African Institute of Mechanical Engineers (MAR)
SAIM-KEBE ... Societe Anonyme Immobiliere - Kebe (MAR)
SAIMM .... South African Institute of Mining and Metallurgy (MAR)
SAIMR......... South African Institute for Medical Research (MAR)
SAINA .... Societe Anonyme Industrielle Nord-Africaine [*North African Industrial Company*] [*Tunisian*] (AF)
SAIPA.......... South African Institute for Public Administration (MAR)
SAIR .... Societe Agricole et Industrielle de la Ruzizi (MAR)
SAIR .... Son Altesse Imperiale Royale [*French*] (MTD)
SAIRAC....... South African Institute of Refrigeration and Air-Conditioning (MAR)
SAIRR......... South African Institute of Race Relations (AF)
SAIS .... Sociedad Agricola de Interes Social [*Social Interest Agricultural Organization*] [*Peruvian*] (LA)
SAIS .... Societa Agricola Italo-Somala (MAR)
SAIS .... Societe Agricole et Industrielle du Soja [*Moroccan*] (MAR)
SAIS .... South African Information Service (AF)
SAIS .... South African Interplanetary Society (MAR)
SAISA .... South African Ice-Skating Association (MAR)
SAISC .... South African Institute of Steel Construction (MAR)
SAIT .... Societa per l'Africa Italiana Tripoli (MAR)
SAIT .... Societe Africaine d'Importation de Textiles (MAR)
SAIT .... South African Institute of Translators (MAR)
SAIV .... South African Institute of Valuers (MAR)
SAIVA .... Societe Anonyme d'Importation et de Vente d'Alimentation (MAR)
SAIW .... South African Institute of Welding (MAR)
SAiW .... Stowarzyszenie Ateistow i Wolnomyslicieli [*Association of Atheists and Freethinkers*] (POL)
SAIZR.......... Central Asian Institute for the Protection of Plants (RU)
saj .... Sajat [*Personal, Private*] (HU)
SAJ.............. Society for the Advancement of Judaism (MAR)
SAJ.............. Sozialistische Arbeiterjugend [*Socialist Workers Youth*] [*West German*] (WEN)
SAJA........... Sociedad de Agricultores Japoneses [*Palmira*] (COL)
SAJA........... South African Jewellers Association (MAR)
SAJAA .... South African Journal of African Affairs [*Pretoria*] [*A publication*] (MAR)
SAJB........... South African Jukskei Board (MAR)
SAJE .... South African Journal of Economics [*Johannesburg*] [*A publication*] (MAR)
SAJS .... South African Journal of Science [*Johannesburg*] [*A publication*] (MAR)

SAK .... Composite Air Corps (RU)
sak .... Composite Aviation Corps (BU)
SAK .... Coupled Subscriber's Line Equipment (RU)
SaK .... Medical Launch (RU)
SAK .... Slovensky Autoklub [*Slovak Automobile Club*] (CZ)
SAK .... Socialisticka Akademie [*Socialist Academy*] (CZ)
SAK .... Societe Agricole de la Kaedi (MAR)
SAK .... Spolecnost Aplikovane Kybernetiky [*Society for Applied Cybernetics*] (CZ)
SAK .... Spoudastiki Andi-Imperialistiki Kinisi [*Student Anti-Imperialist Movement*] [*Greek*] (GC)
SAK .... Strategic Air Command (BU)
SAK .... Strategic Air Command [*SAC*] (RU)
SAK .... Suomen Ammattiyhdistysten Keskusliitto [*Central Federation of Finnish Trade Unions*] (WEN)
SAK .... Sveriges Arbetarepartiet Kommunisterna [*Swedish Workers' Communist Party*] (PPW)
SAKB .... Special Architectural Design Office (RU)
SAKELA ...... Societe Agricole de l'Ekela (MAR)
SAKh .... Mean Aerodynamic Chord (RU)
sakh .... Sugar Plant [*Topography*] (RU)
Sakharles ... All-Union Office for Wooden Packing Materials of the Glavsakhar (RU)
SAKhKNII ... Sakhalin Complex Scientific Research Institute (of the Siberian Department of the Academy of Sciences, USSR) (RU)
Sakhremsnab ... Trust for the Supply of Sugar Industry Establishments of the Rosglavsakhar with Materials and Equipment (RU)
sakh trost .... Sugarcane [*Topography*] (RU)
sakki .... Sakkipeli [*Chess*] [*Finnish*]
saks .... Saksaa [*or Saksaksi*] [*Finnish*]
saks .... Saksalainen [*or Saksan Kielta*] [*German*] [*Finnish*]
SAKU .... Central Asian Communist University Imeni V. I. Lenin (RU)
SAKVA .... Suid-Afrikaanse Konfederasie van Arbeid [*South African Labor Confederation*] (AF)
SAL .... Laboratory Drier (RU)
Sal .... Saline [*Salt Pit*] [*Military map abbreviation*] [*World War I*] [*French*] (MTD)
Sal .... Signal [*Signal*] [*Military map abbreviation*] [*World War I*] [*French*] (MTD)
SAL .... Societe Africaine de Lubrifiants (MAR)
SAL .... Societe Anonyme Libanaise (MAR)
SAL .... Societe d'Anthropologie de Lyon (MAR)
SAŁ .... South African Pound (MAR)
SAL .... South Arabian League (MAR)
SAL .... Subsecretaria de Asuntos Legislativos [*Undersecretariat of Legislative Affairs*] [*Argentine*] (LA)
SAL .... Suid-Afrikaanse Lugdiens [*South African Airways*] (AF)
SAL .... Winch Power Unit (RU)
SALA .... South African Library Association (MAR)
SALAM .... Societe Africaine de Lampes et d'Appareils Menagers (MAR)
SALCI .... Societe Alsacienne de la Cote-d'Ivoire (MAR)
SALCI .... Societe des Ananas de la Cote-d'Ivoire (MAR)
SALDRU ...... Southern Africa Labour and Development Research Unit (MAR)
SALE .... Syndesmos Anaptyxeos Larnakos kai Eparkhias [*Larnaca City and District Development Association*] (GC)
SALF .... Somali Abo Liberation Front [*Ethiopian*] (PD)
SALF .... Sudan African Liberation Front (MAR)
SALH .... Svetove Akademicke Letni Hry [*World Student Summer Sports Games*] (CZ)
SALINTO ..... Societe des Salines du Togo (MAR)
SALJ .... South African Law Journal [*A publication*] (MAR)
SALM .... Suid-Afrikaanse Lugmag [*South African Air Force*] [*Use SAAF*] (AF)
SALMAR ..... Societe Algerienne des Travaux Publics et Maritimes [*Algerian Public and Maritime Works Company*] (AF)
SALP .... Societe Africaine de Librairie et de Papeterie (MAR)
SALP .... South African Labour Party (MAR)
Salpie .... Salpetrerie [*Saltpeter Works*] [*Military map abbreviation*] [*World War I*] [*French*] (MTD)
SALS .... South African Logopedic Society (MAR)
SALT .... Societe Agricole Logone Tchad (MAR)
SALTU .... South African Lawn Tennis Union (MAR)
SAM .... Fixed Air Maintenance Depot (RU)
SAM .... Punched-Card Machine (RU)
SAM .... Punched-Card Machine Plant (RU)
SAM .... Senegal Agricole Materiel (MAR)
SAM .... Servico Aereo de Mocambique (MAR)
SAM .... Sindicato Argentino de Musicos [*Argentine Musicians Union*] (LA)
SAM .... Sistema Alimentario Mexicano [*Mexican Food Supply System*] [*Mexican*] (LA1)
SAM .... Slaska Akademia Medyczna [*Silesian Academy of Medicine*] [*Polish*]
SAM .... Slavomakedonikon Apelevtherotikon Metopon [*Slav-Macedonian People's Liberation Front*] [*Greek*] (GC)
SAM .... Sociedad Aeronautica de Medellin (COL)
SAM .... Societa Anonima Meccanidraulica (MAR)
SAM .... Societe Abidjanaise Metallurgique (MAR)
SAM .... Societe Africaine de Menuiserie (MAR)
SAM .... Societe Africaine de Mines [*African Mines Company*] [*French*] (AF)
SAM .... Societe Agricole de la Mambere (MAR)
SAM .... Societe Agricole de M'banga (MAR)
SAM .... Societe Automobile et Mecanique (MAR)
SAM .... Specialites Automobiles de Meknes (MAR)
SAM .... Squadre di Azione Mussolini [*Mussolini Action Squads*] [*Italian*] (WER)
SAMA .... Saudi Arabian Monetary Agency (ME)
SAMA .... Societe d'Approvisionnement Maritime (Adams & Cie.) (MAR)
SAMA .... Societe d'Assurances Millot Andre pour les Pays d'Outre-Mer (MAR)
SAMA .... Societe d'Avitaillement Maritime d'Abidjan (MAR)
SAMA .... South African Museums Association (MAR)
SAMA .... Stati Africani e Malgascio Associati (MAR)
SAMAB .... South African Museums Association. Bulletin [*A publication*] (MAR)
SAMAC .... Societe Africaine de Manufacture et de Commerce (MAR)
SAMAC .... Societe Africaine de Materiaux Ceramiques (MAR)
SAMAF .... Societe Auxiliaire du Manganese de Franceville (MAR)
SAMAFORTAL ... Societe Auxiliaire de Materiel Africain Ortal (MAR)
SAMAG .... Societe Algerienne des Magasins Generaux (MAR)
SAMANGOKY ... Societe Malgache d'Amenagement et la Mise en Valeur de la Vallee du Bas Mangoky [*Malagasy Company for the Development and Utilization of the Lower Mangoky Valley*] (AF)
SAMAO .... Societe Auxiliaire de Materiel pour l'Afrique Occidentale (MAR)
SAMAPA ..... Servicio Municipal de Agua Potable y Alcantarillado [*Municipal Waterworks and Sewerage Service*] [*Bolivian*] (LA)
SAMAR .... Societe Agricole de Marambitsy (MAR)
Samarco ..... Saudi Maritime Company Ltd. (ME)
SAMARTO ... Societe Anonyme Martini Pinto et Cie. (MAR)
SAMAT .... Societe Africaine de Representation de Materiel Automobile et Technique (MAR)
SAMATAGOR ... Societe Auxiliaire de Materiel Agricole [*Senegalese*] (MAR)
SAMATAGOR ... Societe Auxiliaire de Materiel Agricole Ortal [*Senegalese*] (MAR)
sambo .... Self-Defense without Weapons (RU)
SAMC .... South African Medical Corps (MAR)
SAMCO .... Societe Anonyme de Manufacture de Confection (MAR)
SAMCOA .... Syndicat des Agents Maritimes de la Cote Occidentale d'Afrique (MAR)
SAMDU .... Servico de Assistencia Medica Domiciliar e de Urgencia [*Home and Emergency Medical Assistance Service*] [*Brazilian*] (LA)
SAMEC .... Societe Africaine de Materiel d'Entreprise et de Construction (MAR)
SAMEGE ..... Societe Anonyme Marocaine d'Etudes, de Gestion, et d'Entreprise (MAR)
SAMELA ..... Societe des Ateliers Metalliques et d'Entreprises de Laon-Afrique (MAR)
SAMER .... Societe d'Armament et de Manutention de la Mer Rouge [*Red Sea Shipping Company*] [*Djibouti*] (AF)
SAMES .... Societe Anonyme des Machines Electrostatiques [*Electrostatic Machines Corporation*] [*French*] (WER)
SAMET .... Societe Africaine de Menuiserie Ebenisterie et Tapisserie (MAR)
SAMF .... Societe Africaine de Mobilier et Ferronnerie (MAR)
SAMGGM .... Sehit Aileleri Malul Gaziler ve Gorev Malulleri Dernegi [*Society for the Families of Those Killed and Wounded in Action*] [*Turkish Cypriot*] (GC)
SamGU .... Samarkand State University Imeni Alisher Navoi (RU)
SAMI .... Central Asian Medical Institute (RU)
SAMI .... Service de l'Assistance Medicale aux Indigenes (MAR)
SAMI .... Sistema Aereo Militar Interamericano [*Inter-American Military Air System*] (LA)
SAMI .... Societe Africaine de Materiel Industriel (MAR)
SAMIA .... Societe Arabe des Industries Metallurgiques Mauritano-Koweitienne [*Mauritanian-Kuwaiti Arab Metallurgical Industries Company*] (AF)
SAMINE ...... Societe Anonyme d'Entreprises Minieres [*Moroccan*] (MAR)
SAMI-PRADEC ... Societe Anonyme de Miroiterie, Peinture, Ravalement, Decoration (MAR)
SAMIR .... Societe Anonyme Marocaine Italienne de Raffinage [*Moroccan-Italian Refining Corporation*] (AF)
SAMI-TCHAD ... Societe Africaine de Materiel Industriel du Tchad (MAR)
SAML .... Nationella Samlingspartiet [*National Coalition Party*] [*Finnish*] (PPE)
sam lpb .... Independent Light Antiaircraft Battery (BU)
SAMM .... Servicos de Assistencia Medica Militar [*Military Medical Assistance Services*] [*Angolan*] (AF)
SAMMA .... Societe Anonyme d'Acconage et de Manutention en Mauritanie (MAR)
SAMOA .... Societe Agence Maritime de l'Ouest Africain [*Senegalese*] (MAR)
SAMOA .... Societe Agence Maritime de l'Ouest Africain Cameroun (MAR)
SAMOA .... Societe Agence Maritime de l'Ouest Africain Cote-d'Ivoire (MAR)
SAMOA .... Societe Anonyme des Metaux Oeuvres en Afrique [*Moroccan*] (MAR)
SAMOR .... Societe d'Approvisionnement du Monde Rural (MAR)
SAMOREM ... Societe Africaine de Montage et de Reparation Mecanique (MAR)

SAMP......... Sociedad Suramericana de Metales Preciosos SA [*Bogota*] (COL)
SAMPA....... South African Modern Pentathlon Association (MAR)
SAMPI........ Suid-Afrikaanse Mielieprodusente-Instituut [*South African Corn Producing Institute*] (AF)
SAMR......... South African Mounted Riflemen (MAR)
SAMRAF..... South African Military Refugee Aid Fund (MAR)
SAMRO....... South African Music Rights Organisation (MAR)
SAMS......... Saudi Arabian Mining Syndicate (MAR)
SAMSO....... Suid-Afrikaanse Mieliespesialiteite Organisasie [*South African Corn Specialty Organization*] (AF)
SAM-SOFRATOP ... Societe Auxiliaire de Materiel de la Societe Francaise de Travaux Topographiques et Photogrammetriques (MAR)
samt........... Saemtliche [*Complete*] [*German*]
SAMWU...... South African Mineworkers Union (AF)
SAN............ Pump Power Unit (RU)
San............ Sanaat [*Art, Craft*] (TU)
san............ Sanatorium [*Topography*] (RU)
San............ Sanayi [*Industry*] (TU)
San............ Sanitaets [*Medical*] (EG)
san............ Sanitation, Sanitary, Medical (RU)
san............ Sanomalehdet [*Journalism*] [*Finnish*]
San............ Santiye [*Construction Site*] (TU)
SAN............ Science Association of Nigeria (MAR)
SAN............ Slovak Academy of Sciences (RU)
SAN............ Srpska Akademija Nauka [*Serbian Academy of Sciences*] (YU)
SANA.......... Southern Afrikan News Agency (MAR)
SANA.......... Syrian Arab News Agency (ME)
SANAB........ South African Narcotics Bureau (MAR)
SANAE........ South African National Antarctic Expedition (MAR)
sanap.......... Medical Aviation Regiment (RU)
SANAR........ Sanitaere Einrichtungen und Armaturen [*Sanitary Plumbing Equipment and Fittings*] (EG)
SANAS........ Service d'Alimentation et Nutrition Appliquee du Senegal (MAR)
Sanat........... Sanatorium [*Sanatorium*] [*Military map abbreviation*] [*World War I*] [*French*] (MTD)
SANAUTOS ... Compania Santandereana de Automoviles Ltda. [*Bucaramanga*] (COL)
SANB.......... Sanayi ve Teknoloji Bakanligi [*Ministry of Industry and Technology*] (TU)
SANB.......... Societe Agricole du Nasso et de la Bia (MAR)
SANB.......... South African National Bibliography (MAR)
SANBIM...... Santral Bilgi Islem Merkezi, AS [*Central Data Processing Headquarters, Inc.*] (TU)
SANBRA..... Sociedade Algodoeira do Nordeste Brasileiro, SA [*Northeast Brazil Cotton Association, Inc.*] (LA)
SANCA........ South African National Council on Alcoholism and Drug Dependence (MAR)
SANCAR..... South African National Committee for Antarctic Research (MAR)
sancha........ Medical Unit [*Military term*] (RU)
SANCI......... South African National Committee on Illumination (MAR)
SANCOR..... South African National Committee for Oceanographic Research (MAR)
SANDRAMINE ... Compagnie Miniere Haut Sassandra [*Haut Sassandra Mining Company*] [*Ivorian*] (AF)
Sandruzhina ... Medical Battalion (BU)
SANEGRAM ... Plano de Saneamento de Grande Sao Paulo [*Greater Sao Paulo Sanitation Plan*] [*Brazilian*] (LA)
SANEPID..... Centrul Sanitaro-Anti-Epidemic [*Health and Anti-Epidemic Center*] (RO)
Sanepidstantsiya ... Medical Epidemiological Station (BU)
SANF........... South African Naval Forces (MAR)
SANF........... Sudan African National Front (MAR)
SAN GruzSSR ... Communications of the Academy of Sciences, Georgian SSR [*A publication*] (RU)
SANIGMI..... Central Asian Scientific Research Hydrometeorological Institute (RU)
SANIIRI....... Central Asian Scientific Research Institute of Irrigation (RU)
SANIISh...... Central Asian Scientific Research Institute of Sericulture (RU)
SANIKIS...... Central Asian Scientific Research Complex Institute of Structures (RU)
SaNIS.......... Observation and Communication Aircraft (RU)
SANKO........ Santral Konfeksiyon Sanayii ve Ticaret AS [*Central Ready-Made Clothing Industry and Trade Corp.*] (TU)
sankom....... Sanitary Commission (RU)
SANLAM..... Suid-Afrikaanse Nasionale Lewensassuransie-Maatskappy [*South African National Life Assurance Co. Ltd.*] (MAR)
SANLC........ South African Native Labor Corps (MAR)
SANNC........ South African Native National Congress (MAR)
SANO.......... Medical Section, Sanitary Department (RU)
SANOVNO ... Medical Section of a Military Scientific Society (RU)
SANPA........ Turk Sanayi Arastirma, Nesriyat, ve Pazarlama Merkezi [*Turkish Industrial Research, Publicity, and Marketing Center*] (TU)
Sanpost...... Medical Center (BU)
sanprosvet ... Sanitary Education (RU)
SANRA........ South African National Rifle Association (MAR)
SANROC..... South African Non-Racial Open Committee for Olympic Sports (AF)
SANS.......... Slovensko-Ameriski Narodni Svet [*Slovenian-American National Council*] (YU)
SANS.......... South African Naval Service (MAR)
SANS.......... Sudano-Afrikanskii Natsional'nyi Soiuz (MAR)
Sans Et....... Sansur Edilmistir [*Censored*] (TU)
SANTA........ South African National Tuberculosis Association (MAR)
SANTAM..... Suid-Afrikaanse Trust- en Assuransie-Maatskappy (MAR)
Santekhproyekt ... State Planning Institute for Industrial Sanitary Engineering Planning of the Gosstroy SSSR (RU)
Santekhstroy ... State Trust of Sanitary Engineering Construction (RU)
SANTUR...... Compania Santandereana de Turismo [*Bucaramanga*] (COL)
SANU.......... Slovenacka Akademija na Naukite i Umetnosta [*Slovenian Academy of Sciences and Arts*] [*Ljubljana*] (YU)
SANU.......... Somali African National Union (AF)
SANU.......... Sudan African National Union (MAR)
sanupr........ Sanitary Administration (RU)
SANY.......... Societe Auxiliaire de N'Gor Yoff (MAR)
SAO............ Automatic Optimization System (RU)
SAO............ Smithsonian Astrophysical Observatory (MAR)
SAO............ Societe Agricole de l'Ouest (MAR)
SAO............ Strafor Afrique Occidentale [*Dakar*] (MAR)
SAOB.......... Stuurgroep Automatisering Openbare Bibliotheken
SAOBTA..... Societe Anonyme Oddos Bois Tozan Agneby (MAR)
SAOC.......... South African Olympic Committee (MAR)
SAOC.......... South African Ordnance Corps (MAR)
SAOGIDEP ... Central Asian Branch of the Gidroenergoproyekt (RU)
SAOI........... Sindicato Autonomo del Omnibus Interdepartmental [*Autonomous Union of Interdepartmental Bus Drivers*] [*Uruguayan*] (LA)
SAON.......... Sindicato Argentino de Obreros Navales [*Argentine Union of Shipyard Workers*] (LA)
SAON.......... Socialist Academy of Social Sciences (RU)
SAONGA..... South African Olympic and National Games Association (MAR)
SAOU.......... Suid-Afrikaanse Onderwysersunie (MAR)
SAOV.......... Symvoulion Amoivaias Oikonomikis Voitheias [*Council for Mutual Economic Assistance*] (GC)
SAP............ Automatic Search System (RU)
sap............ Composite Air Regiment (BU)
sap............ Composite Air Regiment (RU)
SAP............ Nouvelle Societe Africaine de Plastiques (MAR)
SAP............ Sabah Alliance Party (ML)
sap............ Saper [*Combat Engineer*] [*Polish*]
SAP............ Seccao de Agitacao e Propaganda [*Agitation and Propaganda Section*] [*Of PCB*] [*Brazilian*] (LA)
sap............ Self-Propelled Artillery Regiment (RU)
SAP............ Servicio de Aprovisionamientos [*Supply Department*] [*Spanish*] (WER)
SAP............ Sidirodromoi Athinon-Peiraios [*Athens-Piraeus Railways*] (GC)
SAP............ Sintered Aluminum Powder (RU)
SAP............ Slovenija Avtopromet [*Slovenian Motor Transport*] [*Ljubljana*] (YU)
SAP............ Societe Africaine des Peaux (MAR)
SAP............ Societe Africaine de Peinture (MAR)
SAP............ Societe Africaine des Petroles [*African Petroleum Company*] [*Senegalese*] (AF)
SAP............ Societe Africaine Pigeon et Compagnie (MAR)
SAP............ Societe Africaine de Pneumatique (MAR)
SAP............ Societe Agricole de Prevoyance [*Algerian*] (MAR)
SAP............ Societe Algerienne des Polymeres (MAR)
SAP............ Societes Africaines de Prevoyance (MAR)
SAP............ Soma Amesou Paramvaseos [*Instant Intervention Corps*] (GC1)
SAP............ Soma Astynomias Poleon [*Cities Police (Corps)*] [*Greek*] (GC)
SAP............ South African Party (PPW)
SAP............ South African Police (MAR)
SAP............ Soysal Adelet Partisi [*Social Justice Party*] [*Turkish Cypriot*] (PPE)
SAP............ Sozialistische Arbeiterpartei [*Socialist Workers' Party*] [*West German*] (WEN)
SAP............ Special Action Programme (MAR)
SAP............ Stowarzyszenie Architektow Polskich [*Association of Polish Architects*] (POL)
SAP............ Suid-Afrikaanse Partij (MAR)
SAP............ Suramericana de Promociones Ltda. [*Bogota*] (COL)
SAP............ Sveriges Socialdemokratiska Arbetareparti [*Swedish Social Democratic Labor Party*] (PPW)
SAP............ Symvoulion Ambelourgikon Proiondon [*Vine Products Council*] [*Cypriot*] (GC)
SAP............ Syndesmos Anapiron Polemou [*League of War Disabled*] [*Greek*] (GC)
SAPA.......... Societe Africaine des Peches de l'Atlantique (MAR)
SAPA.......... Societe Africaine de Produits Alimentaires (MAR)
SAPA.......... South African Polo Association (MAR)
SAPA.......... South African Poultry Association (MAR)
SAPA.......... South African Powerboat Association (MAR)
SAPA.......... South African Publishers' Association (MAR)
SAPA.......... Suid-Afrikaanse Press Agentskaap [*South African Press Agency*] (AF)
SAPAC........ Societe Anonyme de Peche, d'Armement et de Conservation (MAR)

SAPA-CAMEROUN ... Societe d'Application de Peintures en Afrique - Cameroun (MAR)
SAPACI .... Societe des Papeteries de Cote-d'Ivoire (MAR)
SAPAL .... Societe Africaine de Produits Alimentaires (MAR)
SAPAL .... Societe Agro-Pastorale et de Legumes (MAR)
SAPAT .... South African Picture Analysis Test (MAR)
sapb .... Combat-Engineer Battalion (BU)
sapb .... Combat-Engineer Battalion (RU)
SAPB .... Societe Anonyme Plantations Guy de Brecey & Cie. (MAR)
SAPC .... Societe Africaine de Plomberie et de Couverture (MAR)
SAPCA .... Societe Anonyme de Pecheries et Conserves Alimentaires [*Moroccan*] (MAR)
SAPCAM ..... Societe Africaine de Produits Chimiques Agricoles et Menagers (MAR)
SAPCE .... Societe Algerienne de Produits Chimiques et d'Engrais [*Algerian Chemical and Fertilizer Products Company*] (AF)
SAPCO .... Societe d'Amenagement de la Petite Cote (MAR)
SAPCS .... Societe Africaine des Produits Chimiques Shell [*Ivorian*] (MAR)
sape .... Combat Engineer Troop (RU)
SAPEA .... Syndesmos Agoniston Poleos kai Eparkhias Ammokhostou [*Famagusta Town and District Fighters League*] (GC)
SAPEBA ...... Societe Agricole pour l'Exploitation de la Banane (MAR)
SAPEC .... Societe de Peche et Conserves [*Fishing and Canning Company*] [*Tunisian*] (AF)
SAPECO ..... Societe Africaine de Promotion Economique (MAR)
SAPEF .... Societe Africaine de Publicite et d'Editions Fusionnees (MAR)
SAPEGA ...... Societe d'Approvisionnement et de Peche du Gabon (MAR)
SAPEL .... Syndesmos Agoniston Poleos kai Eparkhias Lemesou [*Limassol Town and District Fighters League*] (GC)
SAPELEC .... Societe Africaine des Piles Electriques (MAR)
SAPERI .... Societe d'Application et de Perfectionnement Industriel (MAR)
SAPEVA ...... Syndicat des Producteurs de Vanille [*Vanilla Growers Trade Union*] [*Malagasy*] (AF)
SAPF .... Auxiliary Front Motor Road (BU)
SAPF .... South African Permanent Force (AF)
SAPF .... South African Pioneer Force (MAR)
SAPH .... Societe Africaine de Plantations d'Heveas [*African Rubber Plantation Company*] [*Ivorian*] (AF)
SAPI .... Societe Africaine de Peche Industrielle (MAR)
SAPI .... Societe Africaine des Produits pour l'Industrie (MAR)
SAPIC .... Societe Anonyme des Plantations d'Industries et de Commerce (MAR)
SAPIG .... Sociedad Anonima Pesquera Industrial Gallega [*Galician Industrial Fishing Corporation*] [*Spanish*] (WER)
SAPK .... Societe Anonyme des Plantations de Komono (MAR)
SAPLE .... Societe Anonyme de Peintures, Liants, et Enduits (MAR)
SAPLOCAM ... Sanitaires et Plomberie au Cameroun (MAR)
SAPM .... Societe Africaine de Produits Manufactures [*Senegalese*] (MAR)
SAPN .... Societe Agricole et Pastorale du Niari (MAR)
SAPO .... Samocinny Pocitac [*Computer*] (CZ)
SAPO .... Sarawak People's Organization [*Malaysian*] (PPW)
SAPOA .... South Africa Property Owners' Association (MAR)
SAPONET ... South African Post Office Network (MAR)
sap otd .... Combat Engineer Squad (RU)
SAPP .... Skholi Anapiron Paidon "Parnassou" [*Parnassos Crippled Children's School*] [*Greek*] (GC)
SAPPI .... South African Pulp and Paper Industries Ltd. (MAR)
sapr .... Combat-Engineer Company (BU)
sapr .... Combat-Engineer Company (RU)
SAPRAF ...... Societe d'Achats de Produits de l'Afrique Francaise (MAR)
SAPRAK ...... Samakum Pravatavitu Khmer [*Cambodian Historians Association*] (CL)
Sapre .... Sapiniere [*Firwood*] [*Military map abbreviation*] [*World War I*] [*French*] (MTD)
SAPRIM .... Societe Abidjanaise de Promotions Industrielles et Immobilieres (MAR)
SAPROC ..... Societe d'Achats de Produits du Cameroun (MAR)
SAPROCHIM ... Societe Africaine de Produits Chimiques (MAR)
SAPROCSY ... Societe Africaine de Produits Chimiques et de Synthese (MAR)
SAPROLAIT ... Societe Africaine de Produits Laitiers (MAR)
SAPROMA ... Societe Africaine de Produits Manufactures (MAR)
SAPROV ...... Societe pour l'Exploitation des Procedes Velut (MAR)
SAPROZI ..... Societe d'Amenagement et de Promotion de la Zone Franche Industrielle (MAR)
SAPS .... Servico de Alimentacao da Previdencia Social [*Social Welfare Food Service*] [*Brazilian*] (LA)
SAPS .... South African Price Schedule (MAR)
SAPSI .... Algorithm Designing for Textual Information Processing (RU)
SAPT .... Societe Africaine de Photogrammetrie et de Topographie (MAR)
SAPT .... Societe Anonyme Pierre Treche & Cie. (MAR)
SAPTCO ..... Saudi Public Transport Company (MAR)
sapv .... Combat Engineer Platoon (RU)
SAPV .... Suid-Afrikaanse Pluimvee Vereniging (MAR)
SAQT .... Sociedad Americana de Quimioterapia de la Tuberculosis [*Pan American Society for Chemotherapy of Tuberculosis - PASCT*] (EA)
SAR .... Automated Control System (BU)
SAR .... Automatic Control Station (RU)
SAR .... Automatic Control System (RU)
Sar .... Sarnic [*Cistern, Reservoir, Tank*] (TU)
SAR .... Schemas d'Armature Rurale [*North African*] (MAR)
SAR .... Secteur d'Amelioration Rurale [*Rural Development Sector*] [*Algerian*] (AF)
SAR .... Section Artisanale Rurale (MAR)
sar .... Shed, Barn [*Topography*] (RU)
SAR .... Siriiskaia Arabskaia Respublika (MAR)
SAR .... Sjednocena Arabska Republika [*United Arab Republic (UAR)*] (CZ)
SAR .... Societe Africaine Radioelectrique (MAR)
SAR .... Societe Africaine de Raffinage [*African Refining Company*] [*Senegalese*] (AF)
SAR .... Societe Africaine de Ravitaillement (MAR)
SAR .... Societe Africaine de Representation (MAR)
SAR .... Societe Algeroise du Radiateur (MAR)
SAR .... Son Altesse Royale [*His (or Her) Royal Highness*] [*French*] (GPO)
SAR .... South Africa Rand (MAR)
SAR .... South African Railways (MAR)
SAR .... Su Alteza Real [*His (or Her) Royal Highness*] [*Spanish*]
SAR .... Suedlicher Aussenring [*(Berlin) Southern Outer Freight Ring*] (EG)
SAR .... Syrian Arab Republic (ME)
SARA .... Servico de Assistencia aos Refugiados de Angola (MAR)
SARA .... Societe Abidjanaise de Ravitaillement et d'Alimentation (MAR)
SARA .... South African-Rhodesian Association (MAR)
SARA .... Stichting Academisch Rekencentrum Amsterdam
Saratovgaz ... Saratov Gas Industry Trust (RU)
SARB .... South African Reserve Bank (MAR)
SARB .... South African Rugby Board (MAR)
SARBUMUSI ... Sarekat Buruh Muslimin Indonesia [*Indonesian Moslem Workers Union*] (IN)
SARBUPRI ... Sarekat Buruh Perkebunan Republik Indonesia [*Republic of Indonesia Plantation Workers Union*] (IN)
SARCAS ..... Societe Arachides Casamance (MAR)
SARCCUS ... Southern African Regional Committee for the Conservation and Utilisation of the Soil (MAR)
SARCI .... Societe Abidjanaise de Representation Commerciale Industrielle (MAR)
SARCO .... Saudi Arabian Refining Company (ME)
SARCO .... Societe d'Exploitation des Ets. Raoul de Comarmond (MAR)
SARCU .... Sociedad Argentina por las Relaciones Culturales con la Union Sovietica [*Argentine Society for Cultural Relations with the USSR*] (LA)
sard .... Sardoba [*Water reservoir in Central Asia*] [*Topography*] (RU)
SARDA .... Sociedad de Amigos de la Republica Democratica Alemana [*Society of Friends of the German Democratic Republic*] [*Ecuadorean*] (LA)
SAREC .... Societe Africaine de Revetements, d'Etancheite, de Carrelages (MAR)
SARECCI .... Societe Africaine de Revetements, d'Etancheite, de Carrelages de Cote-d'Ivoire (MAR)
SARECO ..... Societe Africaine de Restauration Collective (MAR)
SARED .... Societe Anonyme de Representations et de Diffusions (MAR)
SAREDIS ..... Societe Anonyme de Representation et de Distribution (MAR)
SAREM .... Societe Africaine Radio Electro-Menager (MAR)
SAREMCA ... Societe Anonyme de Recherches et d'Explorations Minieres en RCA (MAR)
SAREMCI .... Societe Anonyme de Recherches et d'Exploitation Minieres en Cote-d'Ivoire [*Ivory Coast Mining Exploration and Exploitation Corporation*] (AF)
SAREP .... Societe Africaine de Representation (MAR)
SAREP .... Southern African Refugee Education Project (MAR)
SAREPA ...... Societe Africaine de Recherches et d'Etudes pour Aluminium (MAR)
SARET .... Societe Africaine de Recuperation et de Transformation (MAR)
SARG .... Societe Africaine de Representations Generales (MAR)
SARGRE ...... Service des Assurances sur Risques de Guerre et Risques Exceptionnels [*War and Special Risks Insurance Department*] [*Cambodian*] (CL)
SarGRES ..... Saratov State Regional Electric Power Plant (RU)
SARH .... Secretaria de Agricultura y Recursos Hidraulicos [*Secretariat of Agriculture and Water Resources*] [*Mexican*] (LA)
SAR and H ... South African Railways and Harbors (AF)
SAR & H ...... South African Railways and Harbors (MAR)
SARI .... Societe Africaine de Representations Industrielles (MAR)
SARI .... Societe pour la Riz et l'Industrie (MAR)
SARIA .... Societe Anonyme de Realisations Industrielles en Afrique (MAR)
SARIACI ...... Societe Anonyme de Realisations Industrielles en Afrique-Cote-d'Ivoire (MAR)
SARIA-Haute-Volta ... Societe Anonyme de Realisations Industrielles en Afrique-Haute-Volta (MAR)
SARIA-Niger ... Societe Anonyme de Realisations Industrielles en Afrique-Niger (MAR)
SARIC .... L'Auxiliaire de Realisations Immobilieres et Commerciales (MAR)
SARICECO ... Sanaga Rice Corporation (MAR)
Sarkombayn ... Saratov Combine Plant (RU)

SARL.......... Sociedade Anonima de Responsabilidade Limitada [*Joint Stock Company*] [*Portuguese*] (CED)
SARL.......... Societe a Responsabilite Limitee [*Limited Liability Company*] [*French*] (WER)
SARL.......... South African Radio League (MAR)
SARLA........ South African Rock Lobster Association (MAR)
SARM.......... Fixed Aircraft Repair Shop (RU)
SARM.......... Societe Anonyme de Ravitaillement Maritime [*Moroccan*] (MAR)
SARMAG..... Societe Africaine de Ravitaillement Maritime et d'Approvisionnements Generaux (MAR)
SARN.......... Automatic Voltage Regulator Frame (RU)
SARP.......... Stowarzyszenie Architektow Rzeczypospolitej Polskiej [*Association of Architects of the Polish Republic*] (POL)
SARPI.......... Societe Algerienne de Realisation et de Promotion Industrielle [*Algerian Industrial Development Company*] (AF)
SARSA........ Societa Anonima Raccolta Sparta Alfa (MAR)
SARST........ Societe Auxiliaire de la Recherche Scientifique et Technique (MAR)
SART.......... Societe Africaine de Realisations Touristiques (MAR)
SART.......... Societe Algerienne de Radio-Television (MAR)
SART.......... South African Railway Troops (MAR)
SARTOC..... South Africa Regional Tourism Council (MAR)
SARU.......... South African Rugby Union (MAR)
SARZ.......... Spornoye Automobile Repair Plant (RU)
SAS............ Ammonium Nitrate-Superphosphate (RU)
SAS............ Composite Air Unit (RU)
SAS............ Medical Aviation Station (RU)
SAS............ Sahne Artistleri Sendikasi [*Theatre Artists Union*] [*Izmir*] (TU)
SAS............ Sanidad y Asistencia Social [*Health and Social Welfare*] [*Venezuelan*] (LA)
SAS............ Scandinavian Airlines System (WEN)
SAS............ Section Administrative Specialisee (MAR)
SAS............ Servicio Nacional de Asistencia Social [*Formerly, SENDAS*] [*Bogota*] (COL)
SAS............ Servizio Attivita Spaziale [*Space Activity Service*] [*Italian*] (WER)
saS............ Siehe Auch Seite [*See Also Page*] [*German*]
SAS............ Slovensky Abstinentny Svaz [*Slovak Temperance Union*] (CZ)
SAS............ Societa in Accomandita Semplice [*Limited Partnership*] [*Italian*]
SAS............ Societatis Antiquariorum Socius [*Fellow of the Society of Antiquaries*] [*Latin*] (GPO)
SAS............ Societe Africaine des Silicates (MAR)
SAS............ Societe Alimentaire Sucriere (MAR)
SAS............ Societe Automobile Senegalaise (MAR)
SAS............ South African Ship (MAR)
SAS............ Special Air Services (ML)
SAS............ State Auxiliary Services (MAR)
SAS............ Su Alteza Serenisima [*His (or Her) Most Serene Highness*] [*Spanish*]
SAS............ Suid-Afrikaanse Spoorwee (MAR)
SAS............ Sveti Arhijerejski Sinod [*Holy Synod of Bishops*] [*Serbian Orthodox Church*] (YU)
SAS............ Ukrainian Soviet Socialist Republic Author's Certificate [*Patent*] (RU)
SASA.......... South African Skating Association (MAR)
SASA.......... South African Softball Association (MAR)
SASA.......... South African Sugar Association (AF)
SASA.......... Suni ve Sentetik Elyaf Sanayi Anonim Sirketi [*Artificial and Synthetic Fibers Industry Corporation*] (TU)
SASAC........ South African Council for Automation and Computation (MAR)
SASAP........ South African Society of Animal Production (MAR)
SASBANK... Suid-Afrikaanse Spaar- en Voorskotbank (MAR)
SASC.......... South African Service Corps (MAR)
SASC.......... Statutory Authorities Service Commission [*Trinidadian and Tobagan*] (LA1)
SASCA........ Sassandra-Cavally (MAR)
SASCAM..... South African Society for the Care of Mentally Handicapped (MAR)
SASCON..... Southern Africa Solidarity Conference (AF)
SASCON..... Southern African Solidarity Congress [*Zimbabwean*] (PPW)
SASEDIN.... South Asia Socio-Economic Development Information Network [*Proposed*]
SASEM........ Societe Africaine de Stockage et d'Embarquement (MAR)
SASEP........ Societe Africaine de Serigraphie et de Publicite [*Moroccan*] (MAR)
SASET........ Societe Auxiliaire Senegalaise des Exploitations de Thies (MAR)
SASG.......... Sosialistiske Arbeids og Studie Grupper [*Socialist Labor and Study Groups*] [*Norwegian*] (WEN)
SAS en H..... Suid Afrikaanse Spoorwee en Hawens [*South African Railways and Harbors*] [*Use SAR and H*] (AF)
SAShLP...... Stalingrad Aviation School for Pilots (RU)
SASht.......... United States of America (BU)
SASI............ South African Standards Institution (MAR)
SASIF.......... Societe Africaine de Sondages, Injections, Forages (MAR)
SASIF-CI..... Societe Africaine de Sondages, Injections, Forages de Cote-d'Ivoire (MAR)
SASIO......... South African Society of Insurance Officials (MAR)
SASJ........... South African Society of Journalists (MAR)
SASK.......... Suid-Afrikaanse Seinkorp (MAR)
SASLO........ South African Scientific Liaison Office (MAR)
SASM.......... Southern African Students Movement (AF)
SASM.......... Suid-Afrikaanse Staande Mag [*South African Permanent Force*] [*Use SAPF*] (AF)
SASMAL..... South African Sugar Millers Association Limited (MAR)
SASNA........ Syllogikon Amyndikon Symfonon Notioanatolikis Asias [*Southeast Asia Treaty Organization*] (GC)
SASO.......... South African Students' Organization (PD)
SASOL........ Suid-Afrikaanse Steenkool- Olie- en Gaskorporasie [*South African Coal, Oil, and Gas Corporation*] (AF)
SASP........... South African Society of Physiotherapy (MAR)
SASP........... Southern African Student Program (MAR)
SASPY........ Syndesmos Allilovoitheias Syndaxioukhon Politikon Ypallilon [*Mutual Aid Society for Pensioned Civil Employees*] [*Greek*] (GC)
SASRA........ South African Surf Riders' Association (MAR)
SASSAR...... South African Spoorwee, South African Railways (MAR)
SASSE........ Servico de Assistencia e Seguro Social dos Economiarios [*Assistance and Social Security Service for Domestic Servants*] [*Brazilian*] (LA)
SASSh........ United States of America [*USA*] (RU)
SASTA........ South African Sugarcane Technologists Association (MAR)
SASTROUF... Senegalaise de Transports Routieres et Fluviaux (MAR)
SASVIA....... Suid-Afrikaanse Studente Vereeniging in Amsterdam (MAR)
SAT............ Acoustic Homing Torpedo (RU)
SAT............ Kesatuan/Saruan [*Unit, Organization (Military)*] (IN)
sat............. S A Tobbi [*Et Cetera*] (HU)
sat............. Satynowy (Papier) [*Satin (Paper)*] (POL)
SAT............ Sennacieca Asocio Tutmonda [*Nationless Worldwide Association*] (EA)
SAT............ Societe Abidjanaise des Tabacs (MAR)
SAT............ Societe Abidjanaise de Torrefaction (MAR)
SAT............ Societe Abidjanaise de Transports (MAR)
SAT............ Societe Africaine de Transit (MAR)
SAT............ Societe Africaine de Transports Routiers (MAR)
SAT............ Societe Africaine de Travaux (MAR)
SAT............ Societe Amar Taleb (MAR)
SAT............ Syndicat Autonome du Tchad (MAR)
SATA.......... Sociedade Acoriana de Transportes Aereos Ltda. [*Portuguese*]
SATA.......... Societe Africaine de Transit et d'Affretement (MAR)
SATA.......... Societe Africaine de Transports Automobiles (MAR)
SATA.......... Societe Algero-Tunisienne Alfatiere (MAR)
SATA.......... South African Teachers' Association (MAR)
SATAC........ Societe d'Applications Techniques Agricoles et Caoutchoutieres (MAR)
SATACI....... Societe Africaine de Transit et d'Affretement Cote-d'Ivoire (MAR)
SATA-CONGO... Societe Africaine de Transit et d'Affretement Congo (MAR)
SATAER...... Societe Algerienne de Transports Aeriens (MAR)
SATA-GABON... Societe Africaine de Transit et d'Affretement au Gabon (MAR)
SATAK........ Societe Anonyme de Transports et d'Acconage de Kribi (MAR)
SATAM........ Societe Anonyme pour Tous Appareillages Mecaniques (MAR)
SATAR........ Societe Africaine de Transport et d'Affretement Routier (MAR)
SATAS........ Societe Anonyme des Transports Automobiles du Souss (MAR)
SATA-SENEGAL... Societe Africaine de Transit et d'Affretement Senegal (MAR)
SATC.......... Societe Abidjanaise de Tissus et Confections (MAR)
SATC.......... Societe d'Applications Techniques au Cameroun (MAR)
SATC.......... South African Tank Corps (MAR)
SATCC........ Southern African Transport and Communications Commission (MAR)
SATCO........ Societe Africaine de Terrassements et Constructions [*Moroccan*] (MAR)
SATEBA...... Societe Anonyme de Traverse en Beton Arme [*Moroccan*] (MAR)
SATEBA...... Societe des Tuileries et Briqueteries Africaines (MAR)
SATEC........ Sociedade Angolana de Tecidos Estampados [*Printed Fabric Company of Angola*] (AF)
SATEC........ Societe Africaine de Traitements Electrochimiques (MAR)
SATEC........ Societe d'Aide Technique et de Cooperation [*Technical Aid and Cooperation Company*] [*French*] (AF)
SATEC........ Societe d'Assistance Technique et de Credit Social d'Outre-Mer (MAR)
SATEG........ Societe Anonyme de Transports et d'Exploitations Generales (MAR)
SATEL......... Societe Africaine des Techniques Electroniques (MAR)
SATELIT..... Societe des Telecommunications Internationales du Togo [*International Telecommunications Company of Togo*] (AF)
SATELM...... Societe Africaine de Transport et de Location de Materiel (MAR)
SATEM........ Societe Anonyme de Terrassements Mecaniques (MAR)
SATENA...... Servicio de Aeronavegacion en Territorios Nacionales [*National Territorial Aerial Service*] [*Colombian*] (LA)
SATEP......... Service d'Achat, de Traitement, et d'Ecoulement des Poissons de Mer [*Salt Water Fish Purchasing, Processing, and Distribution Department*] [*Cambodian*] (CL)
SATEPO...... Southern African Team for Employment Promotion (MAR)

SATET......... Societe Africaine de Travaux et d'Etudes Topographiques [*African Topographic Projects and Studies Company*] [*Congolese*] (AF)
SATET-CENTRAFRIQUE ... Societe Centrafricaine de Travaux et d'Etudes Topographiques (MAR)
SATET-GABON ... Societe Gabonaise de Travaux et d'Etudes Topographiques (MAR)
SATET-TCHAD ... Societe Tchadienne de Travaux et d'Etudes Topographiques (MAR)
SATEX .... Societe Africaine de Textiles (MAR)
SATEX-CI ... Societe Africaine de Textiles de Cote-d'Ivoire (MAR)
SATEXCO ... Compania Textil Colombiana SA [*Medellin*] (COL)
SATFL......... Societe d'Affretements et des Transports Fluviaux Lao [*Lao River Transport and Charter Company*] (CL)
SATI .... Servicio de Asistencia Tecnica a la Industria [*Service for Technical Assistance to Industry*] [*Argentine*] (LA)
SATI .... Societe Africaine de Torrefaction Industrielle (MAR)
SATI .... Sudan American Textile Industry (MAR)
SATIM......... Societe Africaine de Tissage et d'Impressions, Morocco (MAR)
SAT-IS .... Turkiye Satis Iscileri Sendikasi [*Turkish Sales Workers Union*] [*Erzurum*] (TU)
SATK........... Suid-Afrikaanse Toeristekorporasie (MAR)
SATM.......... Societe Auxiliaire de Transport et de Materiel (MAR)
SATMACI.... Societe d'Assistance Technique pour la Modernisation Agricole de la Cote-d'Ivoire [*Technical Assistance Company for the Agricultural Modernization of the Ivory Coast*] (AF)
SATMAR..... South African Torbanite Mining and Refining Co. (MAR)
SATO .... Societe Anonyme de Torrefaction de l'Oubangui (MAR)
SATOC........ Societe Anonyme Travaux Oubangui Chari (MAR)
SATOM .... Societe Anonyme de Travaux d'Outre-Mer [*Overseas Construction Corporation*] [*Algerian*] (AF)
SATOUR ..... South African Tourist Corporation (MAR)
SATP........... Societe Africaine de Travaux Publics (MAR)
SATP........... Southern African Training Program (MAR)
SATPEC...... Societe Anonyme Tunisienne de Production et d'Expression Cinematographique [*North African*] (MAR)
SATRA .... Shoe and Allied Trades Research Association [*Later, Footwear Technology Centre*] (EA)
SATRA .... Societe Africaine de Travaux (MAR)
SATRACOM ... Societe Africaine pour le Transport et le Commerce (MAR)
SATRAM..... Societe Africaine de Travaux Maritimes et Fluviaux (MAR)
SATRAM..... Societe Auxiliaire de Transports et de Materiel (MAR)
SATRAP...... Societe Africaine de Travaux Publics et Prives (MAR)
SATRAR...... Service d'Achat, de Transformation, et de Reconditionnement du Riz [*Rice Purchasing and Processing Department*] [*Cambodian*] (CL)
SATRECO... Societe Africaine de Terrassements et Routes Economiques (MAR)
SATS........... Societe Africaine de Tolerie et Soudure (MAR)
SATS........... South African Training Ship (MAR)
SATS........... Union of Actors and Theater Employees (BU)
SATSA......... South African Tour and Safari Association (MAR)
SATT........... Societe Africaine de Transports et de Terrassements (MAR)
SATT........... Societe Africaine des Transports Tropicaux [*Algerian*] (MAR)
SATT........... Societe Africaine de Travaux et de Transports [*Ivorian*] (MAR)
SATTA .... Societe Africaine de Transactions, Transports, et Automobiles (MAR)
SATTs......... Sofia Direct Dialing Telephone Exchange (BU)
SATU........... Singapore Association of Trade Unions (ML)
SATU........... South African Tennis Union (MAR)
SATU........... South African Theatre Union (MAR)
SATU........... South African Typographical Union (MAR)
SATUC........ South African Trade Union Council (AF)
SATUDAS.... Sakarya Tarim Urunleri Uretme ve Degerlendirme Anonim Sirketi [*Sakarya Agricultural Products Cultivation and Enhancement (Improvement) Corporation*] (TU)
SATURO ..... Societe Africaine de Tubes et Robinetterie [*Moroccan*] (MAR)
SAU............. Abbreviated Author Index (RU)
SAU............. Aircraft Power Plant (RU)
SAU............. Automatic Control System (RU)
SAU............. Saudi Arabia [*Three-letter standard code*] (CNC)
SAU............. Sections Administratives Urbains [*Algerian*] (MAR)
SAU............. Self-Propelled Artillery (BU)
SAU............. Self-Propelled Gun (RU)
SAU............. Societe d'Architecture et d'Urbanisme (MAR)
SAU............. Surface Agricole Utile [*Algerian*] (MAR)
SAUCAF ...... Societe d'Achats et d'Usinage de Cafe (MAR)
SAUCM....... Societe Anonyme des Usines a Cafe du Mungo (MAR)
SAUCO .... Servicios de Automacion Contable, SA [*Automatic Data Processing Services, Inc.*] [*Spanish*] (WER)
SAUDIA....... Saudi Arabian Airlines (ME)
SAUDICORP ... Saudi Capital Corporation (MAR)
SAUJS......... South African Union of Jewish Students (MAR)
SAUK .... Suid-Afrikaanse Uitsaaikorporasie [*South Africa Broadcasting Corporation*] [*Use SABC*] (AF)
SAUM.......... South African Unity Movement (MAR)
SAUP........... Automated Management System (RU)
SAUPCI....... Societe d'Achats et d'Usinage des Produits de la Cote-d'Ivoire (MAR)
SAUR .... Societe d'Amenagement Urbain et Rural (MAR)
SAUR-AFRIQUE ... Societe d'Amenagement Urbain et Rural pour l'Afrique (MAR)
SAUU .... South African Underwater Union (MAR)
SAUXAF...... Societe Auxiliaire de Afrique Francaise (MAR)
SAV............. Savanna [*Zaria*] (MAR)
sav.............. Savart (RU)
SAV............. Slovenska Akademia Vied [*Slovak Academy of Sciences*] (CZ)
SA'V............ Stathmos Proton Voitheion [*First Aid Station*] (GC)
SAV............. Strollad ar Vro [*French*] (PPW)
SAVA .... Savonneries Associees [*Kinkala*] (MAR)
SAVA .... Societe Africaine de Vehicules Automobiles (MAR)
SAVAG........ Sociedade Anonima Viacao Aerea Gavzha [*Brazilian*]
SAVAK......... Sazman-e Ettela'at va Amniyat-e Keshvar [*National Intelligence and Security Organization*] [*Iranian*] (ME)
SAVAP .... Societe Anonyme de Vente et d'Application de Peinture (MAR)
SAVAS-IS ... Askeri Savas Tesisleri Iscileri Sendikasi [*Military Encounter Installations Workers' Union*] [*Sinop*] (TU)
SAVC .... South African Veterinary Corps (MAR)
SAVCA......... Savonneries S. Calafatas & Cie. [*Cameroonian*] (MAR)
SAVCONGO ... Savonnerie du Congo (MAR)
SAVEC .... Societe Africaine de Vente et de Consignation (MAR)
SAVECAO... Societe d'Achats et de Ventes de Cacao et de Cafe (MAR)
SAVF........... Suid-Afrikaanse Vrouefederasie (MAR)
SAVI............ Suid-Afrikaanse Vertalers-Instituut (MAR)
SAVIEM....... Societe de Vehicules Industriels et d'Equipements Mecaniques [*Industrial Vehicles and Mechanical Equipment Company*] [*French*] (WER)
SAVIL.......... Societe Abidjanaise de Vente pour les Importations de Luxe (MAR)
SAVIMO ...... Societe Agricole et Vinicole Maghrebine (MAR)
SAVN .... Societe d'Amenagement de la Vallee du Niari (MAR)
SAVRA......... South African Vehicle Renting Association (MAR)
SAVU .... Slovenska Akademia Vied a Umeni [*Slovak Academy of Sciences and Arts*] (CZ)
SAVU .... System Automatizace ve Veleni [*Automated System of Troop Command*] (CZ)
SAW............ Suid-Afrikaanse Weermag [*South African Defense Force*] [*Use SADF*] (AF)
SAWA.......... South African Water-Ski Association (MAR)
SAWAS .... South African Women's Auxiliary Services (MAR)
SAWAU .... South African Women's Agricultural Union (MAR)
SAWBA .... South African Womens' Bowling Association (MAR)
SAWEDO .... Samenwerkende Werkplaats-Technische Documentatiediensten
SAWFA .... South African Wine Farmers Association (MAR)
SAWGU....... South African Wattle Growers Union (MAR)
SAWHA....... South African Women's Hockey Association (MAR)
SAWNA....... South African Women's Netball Association (MAR)
SAWS.......... Seventh Day Adventist Welfare Service (CL)
SAWSO....... Salvation Army World Service Office (MAR)
SAWTRI ...... South African Wool Textile Research Institute (MAR)
SAY............ Suomi-Amerikka Yhdistys [*Finnish-American Society*] (WEN)
SAYA .... Sarawak Advanced Youth Association (Communist) (ML)
SAYA .... South African Yachting Association (MAR)
SAYC .... Southern Association of Youth Clubs [*Mauritian*] (AF)
SAYCO........ Sociedad de Autores y Compositores de Colombia [*Medellin*] (COL)
SAYeZhD .... Union of European Railways Road Services (RU)
SAYRH........ Secretaria de Agricultura y Recursos Hidraulicos [*Secretariat of Agriculture and Water Resources*] [*Mexican*] (LA)
SAZ............ Sporitelna a Zalozna [*Savings and Deposit Bank*] (CZ)
SAZ............ Sumgait Aluminum Plant (RU)
SAZh........... Flyer's Life Jacket (RU)
sazh............ Sagene (RU)
SAZH.......... Svetove Akademicke Zimni Hry [*World Student Winter Sports Games*] (CZ)
SAZhU .... Automatic Rigid Control System (RU)
SAZPI......... Central Asian Polytechnic Institute (RU)
SAZU........... Slovenska Akademija Znanosti in Umetnosti [*Slovenian Academy of Sciences and Arts*] [*Ljubljana*] (YU)
sb .... Collection (BU)
sb .... Collection [*Bibliography*] (RU)
sb .... Construction Battalion (RU)
SB .... Convergence of Meridians, Grid Declination (RU)
SB .... Distress Signal (RU)
SB .... High-Speed Bomber (RU)
SB .... Medium Bomber (RU)
SB .... Rendezvous Point [*Aviation*] (RU)
SB .... Rifle Battalion (BU)
SB .... Rifle Battalion (RU)
sb .... Saturday (RU)
sb .... Sbirka [*Collection*] (CZ)
Sb............... Sbirka Zakonu Ceskoslovenske Socialisticke Republiky [*Laws of the Czechoslovak Socialist Republic*] (CZ)
Sb............... Signalbuch [*Signal Book*] (EG)
SB .... Sitzungsberichte (MAR)
SB .... Slovenska Bibliografija [*Slovenian Bibliography*] (YU)
SB .... Sluzba Bezpieczenstwa [*Security Service*] (POL)
SB .... Solomon Islands [*Two-letter standard code*] (CNC)
SB .... Sotsialisticheska Borba [*Socialist Struggle*] [*A periodical*] (BU)
SB .... Soviet Botany (RU)

SB .... Sowjetische Botschaft [*Soviet Embassy*] (EG)
SB .... Spravce Budov [*Superintendent of Buildings*] (CZ)
SB .... Statisticki Bilten [*Statistical Bulletin*] [*A publication*] (YU)
SB .... Statni Banka Ceskoslovenska [*Czechoslavak State Bank*] (CZ)
SB .... Statni Studijni Knihovna Dra. Zdenka Nejedleho, Ceske Budejovice [*Dr. Zdenek Nejedly State Research Library in Ceske Budejovice*] (CZ)
sb .... Stilb (RU)
Sb .... Subay [*Officer*] (TU)
Sb .... Sube [*Branch*] (TU)
Sb .... Subesi [*Branch*] [*Turkish*] (CED)
sb .... Substantiivi [*Noun*] [*Finnish*]
SB .... Sumerbank [*Sumer Bank*] (TU)
SB .... Svaz Banictva [*Slovak Mining Association*] (CZ)
SB .... Svaz Brannosti [*Association for Military Preparedness*] (CZ)
SBA .... Bulgarian Automobile Association (BU)
SBA .... Singapore Base Area (ML)
SBA .... Small Business Association [*St. Lucian*] (LA1)
SBA .... Small Business Association [*Barbadian*] (LA1)
SBA .... Societe des Bois d'Assinie (MAR)
SBA .... Societe Bordelaise Africaine (MAR)
SBA .... Sudan Basketball Association (MAR)
SBAC .... Societe des Tabacs, Cigars, et Cigarettes J. Bastos de l'Afrique Centrale (MAR)
sbap .... High-Speed Bomber Regiment (RU)
SBAT .... Service Botanique et Agronomique de Tunisie (MAR)
sbatr .... Launching [*Rocket-Firing*] Battery (BU)
sbatr .... Launching Battery (RU)
SBAW .... Statistisches Bundesamt, Wiesbaden [*A publication*] (MAR)
SBB .... Societe des Brasseries de Bouake (MAR)
SbBAN .... Sbornik na Bulgarskata Akademiya na Naukite [*Collection of the Bulgarian Academy of Sciences*] [*A periodical*] (BU)
SBBSI .... Serikat Buruh Bank Seluruh Indonesia [*All-Indonesia Bank Employees Union*] (IN)
SBC .... Societe de Batiments et de Constructions (MAR)
SBC .... Stichting Bouwcentrum Ratiobouw
SBCBC .... Societe de Bitumes et Cut-Backs du Cameroun (MAR)
SBCI .... Societe Bamakoise du Commerce et de l'Industrie (MAR)
SBCS .... Statna [*or Statni*] Banka Ceskoslovenska [*Czechoslovak State Bank*] (CZ)
SBD .... Samenwerking Bedrijfseconomische Documentatie
SBD .... Societe de Bauxite de Dabola [*Dabola Bauxite Company*] [*Guinean*] (AF)
SBD .... Srpsko Biolosko Drustvo [*Serbian Biological Society*] (YU)
SBD .... Srpsko Brodarsko Drustvo [*Serbian Shipping Establishment*] (YU)
SBD .... Stavebni Bytove Druzstvo [*Association for Apartment Construction*] (CZ)
SBDA .... Stichting Bibliotheek- en Documentatie-Academies [*'s-Gravenhage*]
SBDK .... Solombala Paper and Woodworking Kombinat (RU)
SBDS .... Stichting Bibliotheek- en Documentatie-Scholen [*Later, SBDA*]
SBEE .... Societe Beninoise d'Electricite et d'Eau [*Benin Water and Electricity Company*] (AF)
sbf .... Sauf Bonne Fin [*French*]
SBF .... Siyasi Bilgileri Fakultesi [*Political Science Faculty of Ankara University*] (TU)
SBF .... Sociedade Brasileira de Fisica [*Brazilian Physics Association*] (LA)
SBFKB .... Siyasal Bilgiler Fakultesi Kibrislilar Birligi [*Cypriot Union of Ankara University School of Political Sciences*] [*Turkish Cypriot*] (GC)
Sbg .... Salzburg [*or Salzburger or Salzburgisch*] [*German*]
SBG .... Societe des Bois du Gabon (MAR)
SBG .... Societe Boucherie Generale (MAR)
SBGG .... Societe de Boissons Gazeuses du Gabon (MAR)
SBHO .... Societe des Brasseries du Haut-Ogooue [*Gabonese*] (MAR)
SBI .... Science-Based Industries (MAR)
SBI .... Societe Belge d'Investissement International (MAR)
SBI .... Societe des Bois Ivoiriens (MAR)
SBI .... Societe des Bois de Sassandra-Issia (MAR)
SBK .... Bibliographic Information File (RU)
SBK- .... Construction Tower Crane (RU)
SBK .... Societe des Brasseries de Kinshasa (MAR)
SBK .... Spezialbaukombinat [*Special Constructions Combine*] (EG)
SBK .... Stationary Pressure Chamber (RU)
SBK .... Union of Bulgarian Composers (BU)
SBKA .... Serikat Buruh Kereta Api [*Railway Workers Union*] (IN)
SBKB .... Serikat Buruh Kendaraan Bermotor [*Motor Vehicle Workers Union*] (IN)
SBKhSS ...... Office for Combating the Embezzlement of Socialist Property and Speculation (RU)
SBKI .... Reinforced Concrete Structures and Goods (BU)
SBKM .... Reinforced Concrete Structures and Installations (BU)
SBKM .... Spezialbaukombinat Magdeburg [*Magdeburg Special Construction Combine*] (EG)
SbKNV .... Sbirka Obezniku pro Krajske Narodni Vybory [*Collection of Directives for Regional National Committees*] (CZ)
SBL .... Slovenski Biografski Leksikon [*Slovenian Biographical Dictionary*] (YU)
SBLGI .... Serikat Buruh Listrik dan Gas Indonesia [*Indonesian Gas and Electrical Workers Union*] (IN)
SBM .... Societe Bananiere du Mambe (MAR)
SBM .... Societe Bois et Metal [*Tunisian*] (MAR)
SBMC .... State Building Materials Company (MAR)
SBMD .... Soviet-Bulgarian Mining Company (BU)
SBMS .... Sbornik Matice Slovenskej [*Journal of the Matica Slovenska*] [*A publication*] (CZ)
SBNL .... Bulgarian National Legions Union (BU)
SBNOR .... Savez Boraca Narodnooslobodilackog Rata [*Union of Combatants of the National Liberation War*] (YU)
SBNOV .... Sojuz na Borcite od Narodnoosloboditelnata Vojna [*Union of Combatants of the National Liberation War*] (YU)
SbNU .... Sbornik za Narodni Umotvoreniya, Nauka, i Knizhnina [*Collection of Folklore, Science, and Literature*] [*A periodical*] (BU)
SBO .... Jet Flame Blasthole Drill (RU)
SBO .... Societe Auxiliaire pour la Brasserie d'Outre-Mer (MAR)
SBO .... Stoleczne Biuro Odbudowy [*Warsaw Reconstruction Office*] (POL)
SBOA .... Stop Banking on Apartheid (MAR)
Sbob .... Sbirka Obezniku [*Collection of Directives (for Regional People's Committees)*] (CZ)
SBOL .... Stihaci Bombardovaci Letectvo [*Fighter-Bomber Airforce (or Aircraft)*] (CZ)
SBOLD .... Stihaci Bombardovaci Letecka Divize [*Fighter-Bomber Airforce Division*] (CZ)
SBOM .... Societe des Brasseries de l'Ogooue Maritime [*Gabonese*] (MAR)
SBOT .... Stoleczne Biuro Obslugi Turysty [*Warsaw Tourist Service Office*] (POL)
SBP .... Pile-Driver Ferry (RU)
SBP .... Soziale Buergerpartei [*Social Citizen's Party*] [*West German*] (PPW)
SBP .... Sprava Bojove Pripravy [*Combat Training Directorate*] (CZ)
SBP .... Srpska Bratska Pomoc [*Serbian Fraternal Aid*] [*USA*] (YU)
SBP .... Stowarzyszenie Bibliotekarzy Polskich [*Polish Librarians' Association*] (POL)
SBP .... Union of Bulgarian Writers (BU)
SBPC .... Sociedade Brasileira para o Progresso da Ciencia [*Brazilian Society for the Advancement of Science*] (LA)
SBPF .... Union of Fighters Against Fascism (BU)
SBPN .... Societe des Boulangeries et Patisseries Nouvelles (MAR)
SBPPI .... Serikat Buruh Pelajaran dan Pelabuhan Indonesia [*Indonesian Harbor and Maritime Workers Union*] (IN)
SBPT .... Serikat Buruh Perhubungan dan Transpor [*Transport and Communications Workers Union*] (IN)
SBPUT .... Serikat Buruh Pekerdjaan Umum dan Tenaga [*Public Works and Power Workers Union*] (IN)
SBR .... Bomb Release (RU)
SBR .... Deliver Only to the Addressee [*Telegraphy*] (RU)
SBRU .... Sectional Switching Structure (RU)
SBS .... Sevastopol' Biological Station Imeni A. O. Kovalevskiy (RU)
SBS .... Societe de Banques Suisse (MAR)
SBS .... Societe des Bois de la Sanaga (MAR)
SBS .... Spojene Strojirny a Slevarny Bohumira Smerala, Narodni Podnik [*Bohumir Smeral Consolidated Machine Building Plants and Foundries, National Enterprise*] (CZ)
SBS .... Svaz Bojovniku za Svobodu [*Union of Fighters for Freedom*] (CZ)
SBSA .... Standard Bank of South Africa (MAR)
SBSD .... Union of Bulgarian-Soviet Societies (BU)
SBSK .... Samakhom Bokkholik Seksa Khmer [*Association of Cambodian Education Personnel*] (CL)
SBStJ .... Serving Brother of the Order of St. John (ML)
SBT .... Societe de Batelage de Tulear (MAR)
SBT .... Societe de Bois Tropicaux (MAR)
SBTI .... Armored Equipment Depot (RU)
sb tr .... Collection of Transactions (RU)
SBTS .... Sistema Brasileiro de Comunicacao por Satelites [*Brazilian System for Satellite Communication*] (LA1)
SBU .... Sociedade Brasileira de Urbanismo, SA [*Brazilian Urban Development Company, Inc.*] (LA)
SBU .... Sociedades Biblicas Unidas (MAR)
SbV .... Sammlung Betrieblicher Vorschriften [*Collection of Operational Regulations*] (EG)
SBV .... Stredisko Branne Vychovy [*Military Education Center*] (CZ)
SBV .... Svaz Branne Vychovy [*Union for Military Education*] (CZ)
Sb VS .... Collection of Supreme Court Practice (BU)
SBWA .... Standard Bank of West Africa Ltd. (MAR)
SBWP .... Stowarzyszenie Bylych Wiezniow Politycznych [*Association of Former Political Prisoners*] (POL)
Sbytminvod ... All-Union Mineral Water Marketing Office (RU)
SBZ .... Sdruzene Bavlnarske Zavody [*United Cotton Mills*] (CZ)
SBZ .... Slezske Bavlnarske Zavody [*Silesian Cotton Mills*] (CZ)
SBZ .... Slovenske Bavlnarske Zavody [*Slovak Cotton Mills*] (CZ)
SBZ .... Sowjetische Besatzungszone [*Soviet Zone of Occupation*] (EG)
Sbzaknar .... Sbirka Zakonu a Narizeni Republiky Ceskoslovenske [*Collection of Laws and Degrees of the Czechoslovak Republic*] (CZ)
SBZh .... Union of Bulgarian Journalists (BU)

sc .... Scene [*Scene*] [*French*]
sc .... Scilicet [*Namely*] [*Latin*] (GPO)
Sc .... Scogliera [*Ridge of Rocks*] [*Italian*] (NAU)
sc .... Sculpsit [*He (or She) Carved or Engraved It*] [*Latin*] (GPO)
SC .... Secretaria de Comercio [*Secretariat of Commerce*] [*Mexican*] (LA)
SC .... Sekretarijat Centra za Unapredenje Gradevinarstva [*Secretariat of the Center for Advancement of Building*] (YU)
SC .... Senior Counsel (MAR)
SC .... Service en Campagne [*Military*] [*French*] (MTD)
sc .... Seul Cours [*French*]
SC .... Seychelles [*Two-letter standard code*] (CNC)
S en C .... Sociedad en Comandita [*Special Partnership, Limited Partnership*] [*Business and trade*] [*Spanish*]
s/c .... Son Compte [*French*]
SC .... State Constituency (MAR)
SC .... State Counsel (MAR)
SC .... Steering Committee [*NATO*] (MAR)
SC .... Strazarski Camac [*Patrol Boat*] (YU)
SC .... Stronnictwo Chlopskie [*Peasants' Party*] [*Polish*] (PPE)
SC .... Su Cargo [*Your Debit*] [*Business and trade*] [*Spanish*]
SC .... Su Casa [*His (or Her) House*] [*Spanish*]
SC .... Suez Canal (MAR)
SCA .... Sabah Chinese Association (ML)
SCA .... Sarawak Chinese Association (ML)
SCA .... Save the Children Alliance (EA)
SCA .... Sociedad Colombiana de Arquitectos [*Bogota*] (COL)
SCA .... Sociedad en Comandita por Acciones [*Limited Company*]
SCA .... Sociedade Cultural de Angola (MAR)
SCA .... Societa Anonima Strade Costruzioni Asfalti (MAR)
SCA .... Societe Camerounaise pour l'Automobile (MAR)
SCA .... Societe des Ciments d'Abidjan [*Ivorian*] (MAR)
SCA .... Societe Commerciale Africaine (MAR)
SCA .... Societe Commerciale d'Assurances (MAR)
SCA .... Soil Conservation Authority [*Australian*] (MAR)
SCA .... Statiune de Cercetare Agricola [*Agricultural Research Station*] (RO)
SCA .... Suez Canal Authority (MAR)
SCAAP .... Special Commonwealth African Assistance Plan (MAR)
SCAAS .... Sindicato de Carpinteros, Armadores, Albaniles, y Similares [*Trade Union of Carpenters, Fitters, Masons, and Related Trades Workers*] [*Nicaraguan*] (LA1)
SCAB .... Societe des Chantiers et Ateliers du Bassin de Diego-Suarez (MAR)
SCAC .... Societe de Carrieres Africaines et de Constructions (MAR)
SCAC .... Societe Commerciale d'Affretements et de Combustibles (MAR)
SCAC .... Societe Commerciale et Agricole du Cameroun (MAR)
SCAD .... Societe Centrafricaine de Deroulage (MAR)
SCADA .... Salisbury Council of Alcoholism and Drug Addiction [*Zimbabwean*] (MAR)
SCADOA .... Service Commun d'Armements Desservant l'Ouest Africain (MAR)
SCAEPC .... Societe Centrafricaine d'Engrais et de Produits Chimiques (MAR)
SCAER .... Societe de Credit Agricole et d'Equipement Rurale du Mali (MAR)
SCAF .... Compagnie des Scieries Africaines [*Ivorian*] (MAR)
SCAF .... Societe des Conserves Africaines Alimentaires (MAR)
SCAF .... Supreme Council of the Armed Forces [*Sudanese*] (MAR)
SCAFA .... Societe Centrafricaine d'Affretements et d'Acconage (MAR)
SCAFO .... Societe Commerciale d'Afrique Occidentale (MAR)
SCAG .... Societe Commerciale et Agricole de Guinee (MAR)
SCAG .... Societe Cooperative des Artisans de la Guyane [*Cooperative Association of Artisans of French Guiana*] (LA1)
SCAH .... Secteur de Commerce, Artisanat, et Habitation (MAR)
SCAHUR .... Societe Congolaise d'Amenagement de l'Habitat Urbain et Rural (MAR)
SCAI .... Societe Commerciale Abidjanaise d'Importation (MAR)
SCAL .... Societe Commerciale Andre Le Tellier (MAR)
SCALA .... Societa Coloniale Anonima Lavori Africa (MAR)
SCALOM .... Societe Camerounaise de Location de Materiel et de Travaux Publics (MAR)
SCAM .... Societe de Colonisation Agricole au Mayumbe (MAR)
SCAM .... Societe Commerciale Afrique-Maroc (MAR)
SCAM .... Societe Cooperative Agricole Marocaine (MAR)
SCAM .... Standing Committee on Agricultural Machinery (MAR)
SCAMAT .... Societa Commercio Attrezzi Macchinari Affini Tripoli (MAR)
SCAMIC .... Societe Camerounaise pour l'Expansion Industrielle et Commerciale (MAR)
SCAMTRA .... Societe Camerounaise de Manutention, de Transport, et de Transit (MAR)
SCANDOC .... Scandinavian Documentation Centre
SCAO .... Standing Conference of Atlantic Organisations (EA)
SCAPA .... Sociedade de Comercializacao e Apoio a Pesca Artesanal [*Company for Marketing and Support for Industrial Fishing*] [*Cape Verdean*] (AF)
SCAR .... Scientific Committee on Antarctic Research (EA)
SCAROMINES .... Societe Centrafricano-Roumaine des Mines (MAR)
SCAS .... State College of Arts and Science (MAR)
SCAS .... Statiunea Centrala de Apicultura si Sericultura [*Central Station for Apiculture and Sericulture*] (RO)
SCAT .... Societe Commerciale Andre Testas (MAR)
SCATRA .... Societe Centrafricaine de Travaux (MAR)
SCAUL .... Standing Conference of African University Libraries (MAR)
SCAULEA .... Standing Conference of African University Libraries, Eastern Area (MAR)
SCAULWA .... Standing Conference of African University Libraries, Western Area (MAR)
SCAV .... Societe Cherifienne d'Articles de Voyages (MAR)
SCB .... Savings and Credit Bank [*Cambodian*] (CL)
Sc B .... Scientiae Baccalaureus [*Bachelor of Science*] [*Latin*] (GPO)
SCB .... Societe Camerounaise de Banque [*Cameroonian Banking Company*] (AF)
SCB .... Societe Camerounaise des Bois (MAR)
SCB .... Societe des Ciments du Benin [*Benin Cement Company*] (AF)
SCB .... Societe Commerciale de Bouake (MAR)
SCB .... Societe de Constructions des Batignolles (MAR)
SCB .... Societe d'Etude et de Developpement de la Culture Bananiere (MAR)
SCB .... Spolek Ceskych Bibliofilu [*Society of Czech Bibliophiles*] (CZ)
SCB .... Statni Vedecka Knihovna, Ceske Budejovice [*State Research Library in Ceske Budejovice*] (CZ)
SCB .... Syndicat Chretien du Burundi [*Christian Labor Union of Burundi*] (AF)
SCBE .... Societe Camerounaise de Bois Equatoriaux (MAR)
SCBI .... Societe de Banque en Cote-d'Ivoire (MAR)
SCBI .... Societe Commerciale des Bois Ivoirienne (MAR)
SCBK .... Societe Congolaise des Brasseries Kronenbourg (MAR)
SCBM .... Societe Camerounaise de Beton Manufacture (MAR)
SCBT .... Shirika la Chakula Bora Tanzania (MAR)
SCC .... Severoceske Cihelny [*North Bohemian Brick Works*] (CZ)
SCC .... Seychelles Construction Company (MAR)
SCC .... Societe Camerounaise de Construction (MAR)
SCC .... Societe Commerciale Camerounaise (MAR)
SCC .... Soweto Community Council [*South African*] (AF)
SCC .... State Cinema Corporation [*Sudanese*] (MAR)
SCC .... Sudan Council of Churches (MAR)
SCCAS .... Statiunea Centrala de Cercetari pentru Apicultura si Sericultura [*Central Research Station for Apiculture and Sericulture*] (RO)
SCCB .... Sociedad Cubana de Ciencias Biologicas [*Cuban Biological Sciences Society*] (LA)
SCCC .... Societe Cinematographique et Commerciale de Casamance (MAR)
SCCC .... Societe de Coulee Continue de Cuivre (MAR)
SCCCE .... Statie Centrala de Cercetari pentru Combaterea Eroziunii [*Central Research Station for Combatting Soil Erosion*] (RO)
SCCE .... Societe Camerounaise de Conditionnement et d'Entreposage (MAR)
SCCG .... Societe Camerounaise pour le Commerce General (MAR)
SCCGA .... Societe Camerounaise de Controle et de Gestion Administrative (MAR)
SCCI .... Societe pour le Compoundage en Cote-d'Ivoire (MAR)
SCCI .... Societe de Construction de Cote-d'Ivoire (MAR)
SCCM .... Societe de Courtage et de Consignation Maritime (MAR)
SCCOM .... Societe de Courtage et de Consignation Maritime (MAR)
SCCP .... Statiunea de Cercetari pentru Cresterea Porcinelor [*Research Station for Hog Breeding*] (RO)
SCCRM .... Sacra, Cesarea, Catolica, Real Majestad [*Spanish*]
SCCT .... Societe Cambodgienne de Cultures Tropicales [*Cambodian Tropical Crop Company*] (CL)
SCCT .... Societe Camerounaise de Commerce et de Transports (MAR)
SCCTP .... Societe Congolaise de Construction et de Travaux Publics (MAR)
Sc D .... Scientiae Doctor [*Doctor of Science*] [*Latin*] (GPO)
SCD .... Servicio Central de Documentacion [*Central Documentation Service*] [*Venezuelan*] (LA)
SCD .... Societe des Ciments du Dahomey (MAR)
SCD .... Societe Commerciale de Dolisie (MAR)
SCD .... Sporting Club Dakarois (MAR)
SCD .... Studie Centrum voor Documentatie [*NIDER*]
SCDC .... Societe Camerounaise de Diffusion Commerciale (MAR)
SCDE .... Societe Camerounaise d'Expansion Economique (MAR)
SCDF .... Sdruzeni Ceskych Demokratickych Federalistu [*Association of Czech Democratic Federalists*] (CZ)
SCDP .... Societe Camerounaise des Depots Petroliers (MAR)
SCDU .... Svaz Ceskoslovenskych Divadelnich Umelcu [*Union of Czechoslovak Theater Artists*] (CZ)
SCE .... Severoceske Energeticke Zavody [*North Bohemian Electric Power Plants*] (CZ)
SCE .... Societe Camerounaise d'Equipement (MAR)
SCE .... Societe Cherifienne d'Engrais et de Produits Chimiques [*Moroccan*] (MAR)
Sce .... Source [*Spring*] [*Military map abbreviation*] [*World War I*] [*French*] (MTD)
SCE .... Stredoceske Elektrarny, Narodni Podnik [*Central Bohemian Electric Power Works, National Enterprise*] (CZ)
SCEA .... Societe Cooperative d'Entreprise Africaine (MAR)
SCEA .... Supreme Committee for Energy Affairs [*Iraqi*] (ME)

SCEC .... Societe Commerciale d'Exploitation de Carrieres (MAR)
SCEC .... Societe de Compatibilite et d'Expertises Comptables (MAR)
SCECA .... Servicio Cooperativo de Educacion Colombo Americana [*Bogota*] (COL)
SCECSAL ... Standing Conference of Eastern, Central, and Southern African Librarians (MAR)
SCED .... Sociedade Comercial de Exportacas e Distribuicas, SARL (MAR)
SCED .... Societe Centrafricaine d'Exploitation Diamantifere [*Central African Company for Diamond Mining*] (AF)
SCED .... Svaz Ceskobratrskeho Evangelickeho Duchovenstva [*Association of the Clergy of the Church of the Bohemian Brethren*] (CZ)
SCEF .... Societe Camerounaise d'Exploitation Forestiere (MAR)
SCEF .... Southern Conference Educational Fund (MAR)
SCEFL .... Societe Camerounaise Equatoriale de Fabrication de Lubrifiants (MAR)
scel .... Scellino [*Shilling*] [*Italian*]
SCEL .... Standing Committee on Education in Librarianship [*United Kingdom*]
SCE Mory & Cie ... Societe Camerounaise des Ets. Mory & Cie. (MAR)
SCEP .... Societe Commerciale des Ets. J. V. Piraube (MAR)
SCEPAG ..... Societe pour le Conditionnement et l'Exportation des Produits Agricoles (MAR)
SCEPOM ..... Societe de Construction et d'Exploitation du Pont de Moossou (MAR)
SCESO .... Societe de Cabotage et d'Entreposage du Sud-Ouest (MAR)
SCET .... Societa Cooperativa Eolilizia Tripoli (MAR)
SCET .... Societe Centrafricaine d'Equipement Touristique (MAR)
SCET .... Societe Centrale d'Equipement du Territoire [*Central Company for Territorial Equipment*] [*French*] (AF)
SCET-INTERNATIONAL ... Societe Centrale pour l'Equipement du Territoire International (MAR)
SCET-Ivoire ... Societe Centrale pour l'Equipement du Territoire en Cote-d'Ivoire (MAR)
SCETO .... Societe Centrale pour l'Equipement Touristique (MAR)
SCF .... Save the Children Fund (MAR)
SCFFC .... Societe Commerciale et Forestiere Fouet & Compagnie (MAR)
SCFG .... Societe Commerciale et Forestiere Gabonaise (MAR)
SCFM .... Societe de Conserves Franco-Mauritaniennes (MAR)
SCFT .... Societe Commerciale France-Tropiques (MAR)
SCG .... Societe Colas de Guinee (MAR)
SCGB .... Societe des Caoutchoucs de Grand Bereby (MAR)
SCGI .... Societe Congolaise de Gaz Industriels [*Congolese Industrial Gas Company*] (AF)
SCGNC .... Societe de Commerce General N'Dingue & Cie. (MAR)
SCGWTUF ... Sudan Central Government Workers' Trade-Union Federation (MAR)
sch .... Bill, Account (RU)
s/ch .... Combat Unit (RU)
SCH .... Friend or Foe [*Identification*] (RU)
SCh .... Gray Pig Iron (RU)
SCh .... Medical Unit (RU)
SCh .... Medium Frequency (RU)
SCh .... Natural Frequency (RU)
SCh .... Random Number (RU)
Sch .... Reading, Readout [*Computers*] (RU)
SCh .... Samopomoc Chlopska [*Peasants' Mutual Aid*] (POL)
Sch .... Schwerin [*One of the GDR Railroad Directorate units*] (EG)
s/ch .... Secret Unit (RU)
SCH .... Societe Commerciale et Hoteliere (MAR)
sch .... Strain Purity, Varietal Purity (RU)
SCH .... Svaz Ceskeho Herectva [*Union of Czech Actors*] (CZ)
sch .... Today, This Day (RU)
SChA .... "Man-Machine" System (RU)
Schad .... Schadwagenzug [*Damaged-Car Train*] (EG)
Schh .... Schutzhaus [*German*]
SchK .... Control Counter, Instruction Counter (RU)
SChK .... Four-Wire Patching Rack (RU)
SchK .... Schiedskommission [*Arbitration Commission*] (EG)
SChK i ChP ... Soviet Red Cross and Red Crescent (BU)
SChKh .... Drafting Facilities (RU)
SchKK .... Checking-Code Counter (RU)
SchKO .... Schiedskommissionsordnung [*Arbitration Commission Regulations*] (EG)
Schl .... Schloss [*Castle*] [*German*] (NAU)
Schliessf ..... Schliessfach [*Post Office Box*] [*German*] (CED)
Schlussbl .... Schlussblatt [*Last Leaf*] [*German*]
SChM .... "Man-Machine" System (RU)
SChM .... Modified Gray Pig Iron (RU)
schm .... Schmelzend [*Melting*] [*German*]
schm .... Schmilzt [*Melts*] [*German*]
Schmp .... Schmelzpunkt [*Melting Point*] [*German*]
Schmpt .... Schmelzpunkt [*Melting Point*] [*German*]
SCHO .... Societe Commerciale et Hoteliere de l'Ouest (MAR)
SChP .... Four-Wire Switching Bay (RU)
SchP .... Schmelzpunkt [*Melting Point*] [*German*]
schr .... Schreiben [*To Write*] [*German*]
schr .... Schriftlich [*In Writing*] [*German*]
Schrp .... Schrankenposten [*Crossing Guard, Guarded Crossing*] (EG)
SChS .... Black Sea Medium Seiner (RU)
SChS .... Medium-Frequency Seismic Exploration (RU)
SChSD .... Union of Czechoslovak-Soviet Friendship (RU)
sch sr .... Flank Guard (BU)
SchV .... Time Counter (RU)
Schw .... Schwedisch [*Swedish*] [*German*]
Schw .... Schweizerisch [*Swiss*] [*German*]
Schw .... Schwerin (EG)
Schw .... Schwester [*Sister, Nun*] (EG)
schwerl .... Schwerloeslich [*Only Slightly Soluble*] [*German*]
Schwnsl .... Schweinsleder [*Pig Skin*] [*German*]
Schww .... Schwellenwerk [*Tie Factory (or Shop), Tie Concentration Yard, Tie Storage Depot*] (EG)
Sci .... Scogli [*Rock(s), Reef(s)*] [*Italian*] (NAU)
SCI .... Silicate de Cote-d'Ivoire (MAR)
SCI .... Sociedad Colombiana de Ingenieros [*Colombian Engineers Association*] (LA)
SCI .... Societe Camerounaise d'Impregnation (MAR)
SCI .... Societe Camerounaise Industrielle (MAR)
SCI .... Societe Commerciale Interoceanique (MAR)
SCIA .... Societe Civile Immobiliere Africaine (MAR)
SCIA .... Societe Commerciale et Immobiliere de l'Atlantique (MAR)
SCIA .... Societe Commerciale Industrielle et Agricole (MAR)
SCIAC .... Societe Commerciale Industrielle et Agricole Centrafricaine (MAR)
SCIAS .... Societa Commerciale Italiana Africa Settentrionale (MAR)
SCIBE .... Societe de Construction Ivoirienne de Batiment et Entretien (MAR)
SCIC .... Sudanese Chemical Industries Company (MAR)
SCICA .... Societe Chimique et Industrielle Camerounaise (MAR)
SCICD .... Societe Centrale Immobiliere de la Caisse des Depots (MAR)
SCID .... Societe Commerciale et Industrielle Dahomeenne (MAR)
SCIDIECI ..... Societe Commerciale et Industrielle Doka-Importation Exportation Cote-d'Ivoire (MAR)
Scie .... Scierie [*Sawmill*] [*Military map abbreviation*] [*World War I*] [*French*] (MTD)
SCIE .... Societe Camerounaise d'Importation et d'Exportation (MAR)
SCIE .... Societe Camerounaise d'Installations Electriques (MAR)
SCIE .... Societe Commerciale et Industrielle d'Expansion [*Hotel de France*] (MAR)
SCIEC .... Societe Civile et Immobiliere des Entrepots de Coton (MAR)
SCIEC .... Syndicat des Commercants Importateurs et Exportateurs du Cameroun (MAR)
SCIF .... Societe Cherifienne de Materiel Industriel et Ferroviaire (MAR)
SCIG .... Societe Commerciale et Industrielle du Gabon (MAR)
SCII .... Societe Commerciale Ivoirienne d'Importation (MAR)
SCIK .... Savezni Centar za Izobrazbu Kadrova [*Federal Center for Instruction of Cadres*] (YU)
SCIL .... Societe Commerciale et Industrielle de Lambarene (MAR)
SCIME .... Societe Cherifienne d'Import, de Materiel d'Entreprises (MAR)
SCIMO .... Societe Commerciale et Industrielle pour la Metropole et Outre-Mer (MAR)
SCIMPEX .... Syndicat des Commercants, Importateurs, et Exportateurs [*Importers and Exporters Union*] (MAR)
SCIMPEX-COTE-D'IVOIRE ... Syndicat des Commercants, Importateurs, et Exportateurs de la Cote-d'Ivoire (MAR)
SCIMPEXDA ... Syndicat des Commercants, Importateurs, et Exportateurs du Dahomey (MAR)
SCIMPEX-HAUTE VOLTA ... Syndicat des Commercants, Importateurs, et Exportateurs de Haute-Volta (MAR)
SCIMPEX-MALI ... Syndicat des Commercants, Importateurs, et Exportateurs du Mali (MAR)
SCIMPEXNI ... Syndicat des Commercants, Importateurs, et Exportateurs du Niger (MAR)
SCIMPEXRIM ... Syndicat des Commercants, Importateurs, et Exportateurs de la Republique Islamique de Mauritanie (MAR)
SCIMPEXTO ... Syndicat des Commercants Importateurs et Exportateurs du Togo [*Trade Union of Togolese Importers and Exporters*] (AF)
SCIMPOS .... Societe Camerounaise d'Injection et de Modelage de Produits Organiques et Synthetiques (MAR)
SCIO .... Sarawak Communist International Organization [*Also known as SCO*] (ML)
SCIP .... Societe Civile Immobiliere du Plateau (MAR)
SCIP .... South Chad Irrigation Project (MAR)
SCIPLAC .... Societe Sciages et Placages Centrafricains (MAR)
SCIPP .... South Chad Irrigation Pilot Project (MAR)
SCIRIKA .... Societe Commerciale et Industrielle "Rika" (MAR)
SCISP .... Servicio Cooperativo Interamericano de Salud Publica [*Bogota*] (COL)
SCJ .... Service Civique de la Jeunese (MAR)
SCK .... Svaz Ceskych Knihovniku [*Union of Czech Librarians*] (CZ)
SCKN .... Societe Commerciale du Kouilou Niari (MAR)
SCKN .... Svaz Ceskych Knihkupcu a Nakladatelu [*Union of Czech Booksellers and Publishers*] (CZ)
SCKN-CENTRAFRIQUE ... Societe Commerciale du Kouilou Niari - Centrafrique (MAR)
SCKN-CONGO ... Societe Commerciale du Kouilou Niari - Congo (MAR)
SCL .... Society for Caribbean Linguistics (EA)
SCL .... Somali Confederation of Labour (MAR)
SCL .... Spolek Ceskych Lekaru [*Society of Czech Physicians*] (CZ)
SCM .... Sacra Catolica Majestad [*Spanish*]

SCM .... Societe Camerounaise de Machines (MAR)
SCM .... Societe Camerounaise Michelin (MAR)
SCM .... Societe Camerounaise de Minoterie (MAR)
SCM .... Societe de Caution Mutuelle (MAR)
SCM .... Societe de Construction de Madagascar (MAR)
SCM .... Sous-Commission de Co-Ordination des Questions Forestieres Mediterraneennes (MAR)
SCM .... State Committee Member of Communist Terrorist Organization (CTO) [*Malaysian*] (ML)
SCM .... Student Christian Movement (MAR)
SCM .... Svaz Ceskoslovenske [*or Ceske*] Mladeze [*Union of Czechoslovak (or Czech) Youth*] (CZ)
SCMA .... Servicio Colombiano de Metereologia e Hidrologia [*Cali*] (COL)
SCMB .... Societe de Construction Metallique de Bouake (MAR)
SCMBZ .... Spojene Ceske a Moravske Bavlnarske Zavody [*United Czech and Moravian Cotton Mills*] (CZ)
SCMCI .... Societe Commerciale de la Moyenne Cote-d'Ivoire (MAR)
SCMIC .... State Constructional Materials Import Company [*Iraqi*] (ME)
SCMM .... Selections from China Mainland Magazines (MAR)
SCMP .... Survey of China Mainland Press (MAR)
SCN .... Sindicato de Carreteras Nacionales [*National Highways Union*] [*Colombian*] (LA)
SCN .... Slovenske Cirkevne Nakladatelstvo [*Slovak Church Publishing House*] (CZ)
SCN .... Svaz Ceskych Novinaru [*Union of Czech Journalists*] (CZ)
SCNO .... Srpski Centralni Narodni Odbor [*Serbian Central National Committee*] [*Chicago*] (YU)
SCNOCB ..... Societe Cooperative Nationale Ouvriere de Construction et de Batiment [*Tunisian*] (MAR)
SCNT .... Suez Canal Net Ton (MAR)
SCO .... Sarawak Communist Organization [*Also known as SCIO*] (ML)
Sco .... Scoglio [*Rock(s), Reef(s)*] [*Italian*] (NAU)
SCO .... Societe des Ciments d'Onigbolo (MAR)
SCO .... Societe des Ciments d'Owendo (MAR)
SCO .... Societe Commerciale de l'Ogooue (MAR)
SCOA .... Societe Commerciale de l'Ouest Africain [*West African Trading Company*] [*French*] (AF)
SCOC .... Societe Commerciale de l'Ouest Cameroun (MAR)
SCODAP ..... Sous-Comite de Defense et d'Action Psychologique [*Defense Psychological Action Subcommittee*] [*In the Ministry of Agriculture*] [*Cambodian*] (CL)
SCODI .... Societe de Conserves de la Cote-d'Ivoire (MAR)
SCOFA .... Societe Commerciale France-Afrique (MAR)
SCOFIDEX ... Societe Commerciale Federale Camerounaise d'Importation et d'Exportation (MAR)
SCOG .... Service Central d'Organization et de Gestions [*Central Organization and Management Department*] [*Burundi*] (AF)
SCOGO .... Special Commission on Government Operations (MAR)
SCOI .... Societe Charbonniere de l'Ocean Indien (MAR)
SCOLMA ..... Standing Conference on Library Materials on Africa (MAR)
SCOM .... Service Central d'Organisation et de Methodes du Ministere de la Fonction Publique (MAR)
SCOM .... Societe Commerciale de l'Ouest Mauritanien (MAR)
SCOMAD .... Service de Controle du Conditionnement de Madagascar (MAR)
SCOMB .... Societe Cooperative de Meubles et de Batiments (MAR)
SCONUL ..... Standing Conference of National and University Libraries [*United Kingdom*]
SCOPE .... Scientific Committee on Problems of the Environment (MAR)
SCOPEC ..... Societe Industrielle et Commerciale de la Petite Cote (MAR)
SCOPED ..... Societe Commerciale du Petit Diboum (MAR)
SCOPO .... Standing Committee on Parastatal Organisations (MAR)
SCOPSS ..... Societe Cooperative-Ouvriere de Production de Sidi-Salem [*Algerian*] (MAR)
SCOR .... Scientific Committee on Oceanic Research (EA)
SCOR .... Security Council Official Records (MAR)
SCOR .... Societe Commerciale des Reassurance (MAR)
SCORESA ... Societe Commerciale de la Region des Savanes (MAR)
SCOT .... Soweto Committee of Ten [*South African*] (AF)
SCOT .... State College of Technology (MAR)
SCOT .... Syrian Company for Oil Transport (ME)
SCOTT .... Shipping Corporation of Trinidad and Tobago (LA1)
SCOV .... Svaz Ceskoslovenskych Oslepenych Vojinu [*Union of Czechoslovak Blind Veterans*] (CZ)
SCP .... Saudi Civil Police (ME)
SCP .... Sdruzeni Ceskych Partyzanu [*Association of Czech Partisans*] (CZ)
SCP .... Social Credit Party of Canada [*Parti Credit Social du Canada*] (PPW)
SCP .... Sociedad Colombiana de Planificacion [*Colombian Planning Society*] (LA)
SCP .... Societe Camerounaise de Publications (MAR)
SCP .... Societe Cherifienne de Petrole [*Moroccan Petroleum Company*] (AF)
SCP .... Societe de Commercialisation des Peaux (MAR)
SCP .... Sudanese Communist Party (PD)
SCP .... Syrian Communist Party (PPW)
SCPA .... Singapore Country People's Association [*Pro-Communist Barisan Sosialis Front organization*] (ML)
SCPA .... Societe Commerciale des Potasses et de l'Azote (MAR)
SCPC .... Societe Camerounaise de Collecte des Peaux et Cuirs (MAR)
SCPF .... Societe Commerciale Panayotis Freres (MAR)
SCPI .... Societe Civile de Participation Immobiliere [*North African*] (MAR)
SCPL .... Societe Camerounaise Pierre Lemonnier (MAR)
SCPM .... Societe Cherifienne des Produits Manufactures (MAR)
SCPS .... Sociaal Cultureel Planbureau
SCPS .... Supreme Council for Popular Sports [*Sudanese*] (MAR)
SCPUvN ...... Sdruzeni Ceskoslovenskych Politickych Uprchliku v Nemecku [*Association of Czechoslovak Political Refugees in Germany*] (CZ)
SCR .... Societe Centrale de Representation (MAR)
SCR .... Svetova Rada Cirkvi [*World Council of Churches*] (CZ)
Scra .... Scogliera [*Ridge of Rocks*] [*Italian*] (NAU)
SCRCSA ..... Statiunea Centrala de Reproductie si Combatere Sterilitatii la Animale [*Central Station for Reproductions and Combating Sterility in Animals*] (RO)
SCREG .... Societe Chimique Routiere et d'Entreprise Generale [*French*]
SCREW .... Student Committee for the Reevaluation of Escalated Warfare (MAR)
SCRG .... Societe Chimique et Routiere de la Gironde (MAR)
SCRP .... Severocesky Rudny Pruzkum [*North Bohemian Ore Prospecting*] (CZ)
SCS .... Slovensky Cyklisticky Svaz [*Slovak Cycling Association*] (CZ)
SCS .... Societe Camerounaise de Sacherie (MAR)
SCS .... Societe Commerciale Senegalaise (MAR)
SCS .... Societe de Construction du Senegal (MAR)
SCS .... Soil Conservation Service of New South Wales (MAR)
SCS .... Svaz Ceskoslovenskych Skladatelu [*Czechoslovak Composers' Union*] (CZ)
SCS .... Syndikat Ceskych Spisovatelu [*Czech Writers' Syndicate*] (CZ)
SCSA .... Ski Club of South Africa (MAR)
SCSA .... Supreme Council for Sports in Africa (MAR)
SCSF .... Svaz Ceskoslovenskych Filatelistu [*Union of Czechoslovak Philatelists*] (CZ)
SCSFUT ...... Syndikat Ceskoslovenskych Filmovych Umelcu a Techniku [*Czechoslovak Film Artists and Technicians Trade Union*] (CZ)
SCSH .... Svaz Ceskoslovenskeho Hasicstva [*Union of Czechoslovak Firemen*] (CZ)
SCSH .... Svaz Ceskoslovenskych Horolezcu [*Czechoslovak Mountain Climbers' Association*] (CZ)
SCSI .... Svaz Ceskoslovenskych Invalidu [*Union of Czechoslovak Disabled Persons*] (CZ)
SCSN .... Svaz Ceskoslovenskych Novinaru [*Czechoslovak Journalists' Union*] (CZ)
SCSP .... Svaz Ceskoslovensko-Sovietskeho Priatelstva [*Czechoslovak-Soviet Friendship League*] (CZ)
SCSS .... Svaz Ceskoslovenskych Spisovatelu [*Czechoslovak Writers' Union*] (CZ)
SCSV .... Svaz Ceskoslovenskych Vytvarniku [*Union of Czechoslovak Creative Artists*] (CZ)
SCSVU .... Svaz Ceskoslovenskych Vytvarnych Umelcu [*Union of Czechoslovak Creative Artists*] (CZ)
SCT .... Secretaria de Comunicaciones y Transportes [*Secretariat of Communications and Transport*] [*Mexican*] (LA)
Sct .... Section [*Section, Division*] [*Military*] [*French*] (MTD)
SCT .... Servicio de Cooperacion Tecnica [*Technical Cooperation Service*] [*Chilean*] (LA)
SCT .... Severoceske Tiskarny [*North Bohemian Printing Plants*] (CZ)
SCT .... Societe Camerounaise du Tabac (MAR)
SCT .... Societe Cotonniere Transoceanique (MAR)
SCTA .... Societe Camerounaise de Transport et d'Affretement (MAR)
SCTA .... Societe Commerciale de Transport des Amis (MAR)
SCTC .... Societe de Commerce et de Transports du Cameroun (MAR)
SCTG .... Societe Cotiere de Transport de Grumes (MAR)
SCTH .... Security Council Truce Commission [*Palestinian*] (MAR)
SCTIP .... Service de Cooperation Technique Internationale de Police [*International Police Technical Cooperation Service*] (CL)
SCTM .... Societe Commerciale et de Travaux Mecaniques [*Cameroonian*] (MAR)
SCTN .... Societe Cherifienne de Transports et de Navigation (MAR)
SCTNB .... Societe Commerciale des Techniques Nouvelles du Batiment (MAR)
SCTO .... Societe Cotonniere Transoceanique (MAR)
SCTRH .... Societe Camerounaise de Transports Routiers d'Hydrocarbures (MAR)
SCTS .... Societe Centrafricaine des Transports de la Haute-Sangha (MAR)
SCTS .... Societe des Cooperatives de Transportateurs du Senegal (MAR)
SCTT .... Societe Commerciale de Transports Transatlantiques (MAR)
SCTTAO ..... Societe Commerciale de Transports Transatlantiques Afrique Occidentale (MAR)
SCTT-CI ...... Societe Commerciale de Transports Transatlantiques Cote-d'Ivoire (MAR)
SCTTM .... Societe Commerciale de Transports Transatlantiques de Madagascar (MAR)
SCTT-MAURITANIENNE ... Societe Commerciale de Transports Transatlantiques Mauritanienne (MAR)

SCTTOI....... Societe Commerciale de Transports Transatlantiques Ocean Indien (MAR)
SCTT-TAMATAVE ... Societe Commerciale de Transports Transatlantiques de Tamatave (MAR)
SCU............ Supreme Council of Universities [*Saudi*] (ME)
SCUA.......... Suez Canal Users Association (MAR)
SCUB.......... Societe pour le Commerce et l'Usinage des Bois (MAR)
SCUG.......... Svaz Ceskych Umelcu a Grafiku [*Union of Czech Artists*] (CZ)
SCUGH....... Sdruzeni Ceskych Umelcu Grafiku "Hollar" [*Hollar Association of Czech Graphic Artists*] (CZ)
SCV............ Service de la Carte de la Vegetation [*Vegetation Map Service*] [*French*] (WER)
SCV............ Sindicatos Cap Verde (MAR)
SCV............ Societe Commerciale Voltaique "La Moderne" (MAR)
SCV............ Societe Credit et Vente (MAR)
SCVHU........ Svaz Ceskych Vykonnych Hudebnich Umelcu [*Czech Musicians' Union*] (CZ)
SCVPB........ Slovenska Centralna Vojno-Partizanska Bolnisnica [*Slovenian Central Partisan Military Hospital*] (YU)
SCVZO........ Svaz Ceskoslovenskych Vojaku Zahranicniho Odboje [*Union of Czechoslovak Veteran Partisans Abroad*] (CZ)
SCYCOMIMPEX ... Syndicat des Commercants Importateurs et Exportateurs de l'Afrique Equatoriale (MAR)
SCZ............ Svaz Ceskoslovenskeho Zivnostnictva [*Czechoslovak Small Business Association*] (CZ)
SCZ............ Svaz Ceskych Zen [*Union of Czech Women*] (CZ)
SCZV.......... Svaz Ceskoslovenskych Zahranicnich Vojaku [*Union of Czechoslovak Veterans of Foreign Wars*] (CZ)
SD.............. Aircraft and Engine [*Aircraft maintenance*] (RU)
s/d.............. Children's Show (RU)
s/d.............. Daily Ration (RU)
SD.............. Degtyarev Heavy Machine Gun (RU)
SD.............. Flank Patrol (BU)
SD.............. Lethal Dose (RU)
SD.............. Mean Pressure, Medium Pressure (RU)
SD.............. Medical Unit (RU)
SD.............. Rifle Division (RU)
SD.............. Salutem Dicit [*Sends Greetings*] [*Latin*] (GPO)
sd.............. Samma Dag [*The Same Day*] [*Swedish*] (GPO)
sd.............. Samme Dato [*Same Date*] [*Danish*] (GPO)
sd.............. Sans Date [*No Date (of publication)*] [*French*]
SD.............. Schemas Directeurs [*Moroccan*] (MAR)
SD.............. Sciere de Duckoue (MAR)
SD.............. Se Despide [*Spanish*]
SD.............. Sekolah Dasar [*Elementary School*] (IN)
SD.............. Senatorial District (MAR)
SD.............. Servomotor (RU)
sd.............. Siedend [*Boiling*] [*German*]
Sd.............. Siedepunkt [*Boiling Point*] [*German*]
sd.............. Siehe Dies [*See This, Which See*] [*German*]
sd.............. Siehe Dort [*See There*] [*German*]
sd.............. Sine Die [*Indefinitely*] [*Latin*] (GPO)
SD.............. Slovensky Dennik [*The Slovak Daily*] [*A newspaper*] (CZ)
sd.............. Social Democrat (BU)
s-d.............. Social Democrat (RU)
SD.............. Socialdemokratiet i Danmark [*Social Democratic Party of Denmark*] (PPE)
SD.............. Socialne Demokraticka Strana Delnicka [*Social Democratic Workers' Party*] (CZ)
SD.............. Solar Engine (RU)
SD.............. Solar Pickup (RU)
sd.............. Sosiaalidemokraatti(nen) [*Finnish*]
SD.............. Sous-Directeur (MAR)
SD.............. Southern Cross Decoration (MAR)
SD.............. Spontaneous Fission (RU)
SD.............. Sportsko Drustvo [*Sport Society*] (YU)
SD.............. Spotrebni Druzstvo [*Consumers Cooperative*] (CZ)
SD.............. Srpski Dom [*Serbian Home*] [*A periodical*] (YU)
SD.............. Stathmos Dioikiseos [*Command Post*] (GC)
SD.............. Stokta Degil [*Not in Stock*] (TU)
SD.............. Stronnictwo Demokratyczne [*Democratic Party*] [*Polish*] (PPE)
SD.............. Stycny Dustojnik [*Courier Officer*] (CZ)
SD.............. Sudan [*Two-letter standard code*] (CNC)
Sd.............. Sund [*Sundet*] [*Sound*] [*Danish*] (NAU)
Sd.............. Sund [*Sundet*] [*Sound*] [*Norwegian*] (NAU)
SD.............. Superheterodyne Demodulator (RU)
SD.............. Synchronous Motor (RU)
SD.............. Synchronous Transducer (RU)
sd.............. Today (RU)
SD.............. Transmitting Selsyn (RU)
SDA............ Self-Propelled Sprinkler (RU)
SDA............ Seventh Day Adventist Church (MAR)
SDA............ Sjedinjene Drzave Amerike [*United States of America*] (YU)
SDA............ Sozialistische Demokratische Aktion [*Socialist Democratic Action*] [*Swiss*] (WEN)
SDA............ Stratiotiki Dievthynsis Athinon [*Athens Military Directorate*] (GC)
SDAC.......... Societe d'Application Cinematographique (MAR)
SDAG.......... Sowjetisch-Deutsche Aktiengesellschaft [*Soviet-German Corporation (Wismut)*] (EG)
SDAI........... Societe de Developpement Agricole et Industriel [*Agricultural and Industrial Development Company*] [*Senegalese*] (AF)
SDAJ........... Savez Drustava Arhitekta Jugoslavije [*Federation of Architects' Societies of Yugoslavia*] (YU)
SDAJ........... Sozialistische Deutsche Arbeiterjugend [*Socialist German Workers Youth*] [*West German*] (WEN)
SDAM.......... Seventh Day Adventist Mission (MAR)
SDAM.......... Stratiotiki Dioikisis Anatolikis Mesogeiou [*Military Directorate for the Eastern Mediterranean*] [*Greek*] (GC)
SDAN........... Skholi Diakonisson Adelfon kai Nosokomon [*School for Deaconesses and Nurses*] [*Greek*] (GC)
SDAP........... Sociaal-Democratische Arbeiders Partij [*Social Democratic Workers' Party*] [*Dutch*] (PPE)
SDAR........... Saharan Democratic Arab Republic (AF)
SDARFNRJ ... Savez Drustava Arhivskih Radnika Federativna Narodna Republika Jugoslavija [*Federation of Archivists' Societies of Yugoslavia*] (YU)
SDAT........... Societe pour le Developpement Agricole du Togo (MAR)
sdat op........ Inventory, Transfer List (RU)
SDB............ Les Scieries du Baoule Anciens Ets. Jean Nivet (MAR)
SDB............ Salesians of Don Bosco (MAR)
SDB............ Sociaal-Democratische Bond [*Social Democratic League*] [*Dutch*] (PPE)
SDB............ Societe Dahomeenne de Banque (MAR)
SDC............ Social Development Commission [*Jamaican*] (LA1)
SDC............ Societe de Developpement et de Confection [*Moroccan*] (MAR)
SDC............ Sudan Development Corporation (MAR)
SDC............ Sugar Development Corporation (MAR)
SDCA.......... Societe de Conserves Africaines [*Senegalese*] (MAR)
SDCI........... Servico Director e Coordinador de Informacoes [*Director and Coordinator of Information Service*] [*Portuguese*] (WER)
SDCM.......... Societe Dahomeenne de Ciments et Materiaux (MAR)
SDCP........... Service de Diffusion Cinematographique Populaire [*People's Movie Dissemination Service*] [*Algerian*] (AF)
SDD............ Collection of Effective Treaties, Agreements, and Conventions Concluded with Foreign States (RU)
SDD............ Skola Dustojnickeho Dorostu [*Officers' Candidate School*] (CZ)
SDD............ Social Development Division (MAR)
SDD............ Srpsko Dobrotvorno Drustvo [*Serbian Welfare Society*] [*Chicago*] (YU)
SDD............ Two-Cycle Light Range Finder (RU)
SDDE.......... Societe Dahomeenne pour le Developpement Economique (MAR)
SDDF.......... Sosyal Demokrasi Dernekleri Federasyonu [*Federation of Social Democracy Organizations*] (TU)
SDDOM....... Societe pour le Developpement des Departements d'Outre-Mer (MAR)
SDE............ Service de Documentation Economique (MAR)
SDE............ Societe Dakaroise d'Entreposage (MAR)
SDE............ Sosialistiki Dimokratiki Enosis [*Socialist Democratic Union*] [*Greek*] (GC)
SDE............ Statiunea Didactica si Experimentala [*Teaching and Experimental Station*] (RO)
SDE............ Symvoulion Dimosion Ergon [*Public Works Council*] [*Greek*] (GC)
SDEC.......... Sudan Desert Encroachment Control and Rehabilitation Programme (MAR)
SDECE........ Service de Documentation Exterieure et de Contre-Espionnage [*Foreign Intelligence and Counterintelligence Service*] [*French*] (WER)
SDEE........... Sindicato Democratico de Estudiantes de Espana [*Democratic Union of Students of Spain*] (WER)
SDEJ........... Savez Drustava Ekonomista Jugoslavije [*Federation of Societies of Economists of Yugoslavia*] (YU)
SDEK........... Stratiotikon Deltion Epilogis kai Katastaseos [*Military Selection and Status Bulletin*] [*A publication*] (GC)
SDEM.......... Societe d'Entreprise de Montages (MAR)
SDEPM........ Syndicat des Directeurs des Etablissements d'Enseignement Prive de Madagascar [*Malagasy Union of Principals of Private Education Institutions*] (AF)
SDEPP......... Societe Dahomeenne d'Entreposage de Produits Petroliers (MAR)
SDF............ Saudi Development Fund (ME)
SDF............ Social Democratic Federation [*Shaminren*] [*Japanese*] (PPW)
SDF............ Social Democratic Front [*Ghanaian*] (PPW)
SDF............ Sofia State Philharmonic (BU)
SDF............ Sudan Defence Forces (MAR)
SDFD.......... Societe Africaine de Distribution de Fournitures Dentaires (MAR)
SDFK.......... Swiatowa Demokratyczna Federacja Kobiet [*Women's International Democratic Federation*] (POL)
SDFM.......... World Federation of Democratic Youth (BU)
SDG............ Societe de Droguerie du Gabon (MAR)
SDG............ Soli Deo Gloria Szovetseg [*Soli Deo Gloria Association*] (HU)
SDG............ Syllogos Dimokratikon Gynaikon [*Association of Democratic Women*] [*Greek*] (GC)
SDGK.......... Supreme Command Signal Battalion (BU)
SDGS.......... Srpska Drzavna Granicna Straza [*Serbian Frontier Guard*] [*World War II*] (YU)

SDH............ Spoldzielczy Dom Handlowy [*Cooperative Department Store*] [*Polish*]
SDI.............. Sivitanideion Dimosion Idryma [*Sivitanideios Public Foundation*] [*Greek*] (GC)
SDI.............. Societe d'Etudes pour le Developpement des Industries Agricoles au Senegal (MAR)
SDI.............. Statni Drevarska Inspekce [*State Inspection Office for Wood and Wood Products*] (CZ)
SDIAS......... Societe pour le Developpement des Industries Agricoles au Senegal (MAR)
SDIBC......... Syndicat de Defense des Interets Bananiers au Cameroun (MAR)
SDIC............ Societe de Developpement Industriel du Cameroun (MAR)
SDIEGEE..... Somateion Daktylografon Idiotikon Epikheiriseon-Grafeion kai Elevtheron Epangelmaton [*Union of Typists of Private Enterprises, Offices, and Liberal Professions*] [*Greek*] (GC)
SDIH............ Societe Dakaroise Immobiliere d'Habitations (MAR)
SDIM........... Systeme de Documentation et d'Information Metallurgique [*EG*] [*Luxembourg*]
S Dist.......... Section de Distribution [*Military*] [*French*] (MTD)
SDJAP......... Sportsko Drustvo Jugoslovenske Armije Partizan [*The Partisan Sport Club of the Yugoslav Army*] (YU)
SDJO........... Service de Distribution de Jus d'Orange [*Orange Juice Distribution Department*] [*In SKD*] [*Cambodian*] (CL)
SDK............. Seljacko-Demokratska Koalicija [*Peasant-Democratic Coalition*] [*Yugoslav*] (PPE)
SDK............. Sprava Dalkovych Kabelu [*Administration Office for Long-Distance Cables*] (CZ)
SDK............. Srpski Dobrovoljacki Korpus [*Serbian Volunteer Corps*] [*World War II*] (YU)
SDKhA........ Sofia State Art Academy (BU)
SDKP.......... Socjaldemokracja Krolestwa Polskiego [*Social-Democratic Party of the Kingdom of Poland (1893-1900)*] [*Polish*]
SDKPiL....... Socjal-Demokracja Krolestwa Polskiego i Litwy [*Social-Democratic Party of the Kingdom of Poland and of Lithuania (Before World War I)*] (POL)
SDKU.......... Decoding Device (RU)
SDL............. Collapsible Landing Boat (RU)
SDL............. Social Democratic Party of Latvia (RU)
SDL............. Sprava Dopravnich Letist [*Administration Office for Transport Plane Airports*] (CZ)
SDL............. Sprava Dopravniho Letectva [*Transport Airforce Directorate*] (CZ)
SDL............. Wooden Engineer Boat (RU)
Sdlg............ Siedlung [*German*]
SDLP........... Social Democratic and Labour Party [*Northern Ireland*] (PPW)
SDLZ........... Skola Dustojniku Letectva v Zaloze [*School for Reserve Air Force Officers*] (CZ)
SDLZ........... Slovenske Divadelne a Literarne Zastupitelstvo [*Slovak Theatrical and Publishing Agency*] (CZ)
SDM............ Diesel Pile Hammer (RU)
SDM............ Sienkiewiczowska Dzielnica Mieszkaniowa [*Sienkiewicz Residential District*] (POL)
SDM............ Societe Diallo Moctar & Cie. [*Senegalese*] (MAR)
SDM............ Srpsko-Dalmatinski Magazin [*Serbian-Dalmatian Magazine*] [*Zadar*] [*A publication*] (YU)
SDM............ Su Divina Majestad [*Spanish*]
SDM............ Synetairismoi Dytikis Makedonias [*Cooperatives of Western Macedonia*] (GC)
SDM............ Szczecinska Dzielnica Mieszkaniowa [*Szczecin (Stettin) Residential District*] (POL)
SDM-........... Ten-Key Adder (RU)
SDME.......... Sous-Direction des Moyens d'Essais [*Sub-Directorate of Means of Testing*] [*French*] (WER)
SDMMA....... Sakarya Devlet Muhendislik ve Mimarlik Akademesi [*Sakarya State Engineering and Architecture Academy*] (TU)
SDN............ Secretaria de la Defensa Nacional [*Secretariat of National Defense*] [*Mexican*] (LA)
SDN............ Sendirian [*Private Business Company*] (ML)
SDN............ Societe des Nations [*League of Nations*] [*French*]
SDN............ Sudan [*Three-letter standard code*] (CNC)
Sdn Bhd...... Sendirian Berhad [*Private Limited Company*]
SDNL.......... Suomen Demokraattinen Nuorisoliitto [*Finnish Democratic Youth League*] (WEN)
SDO............ Clothing Decontamination Station (BU)
SDO............ Clothing Decontamination Station (RU)
SDO............ Early-Warning System (RU)
Sdo............. Suido [*Channel*] [*Japanese*] (NAU)
sdo............. Supply Section (BU)
SDOE.......... Syndesmos Diplomatoukhon Oikonomikon kai Emborikon Epistimon [*League of Economic and Commercial Sciences Graduates*] (GC)
S-Don.......... Northern Donets Railroad (RU)
SDOP.......... Spolecnost Dunajsko-Oderskeho Pruplavu [*Danube-Oder Canal Company*] (CZ)
SDP............ Double-Track Snowplow (RU)
SDP............ Mean Square Dynamic Error (RU)
SDP............ Remote Feeder Transmission Bay (RU)
SDP............ Sanitary and Decontamination Station (RU)
SDP............ Savannah Development Project [*Sudanese*] (MAR)
SDP............ Savezni Drustveni Plan [*Federal Economic Plan*] (YU)
SDP............ Seychelles Democratic Party (AF)
Sdp............. Siedepunkt [*Boiling Point*] [*German*]
SDP............ Social Democratic Party [*Althyduflokkurinn*] [*Icelandic*] (PPW)
SDP............ Social Democratic Party [*Thai*] (PPW)
SDP............ Social Democratic Party [*Trinidadian and Tobagan*] (PPW)
SDP............ Social Democratic Party (RU)
SDP............ Socialdemokratska Partija [*Social Democratic Party*] (YU)
SDP............ Sosyalist Devrimci Partisi [*Revolutionary Socialist Party*] (TU)
SDP............ Sozial Demokratesch Partei [*Social Democratic Party*] [*Luxembourg*] (PPE)
SDP............ Stowarzyszenie Dziennikarzy Polskich [*Polish Journalist Association*] [*Polish*]
SdP............. Sudetendeutsche Partei [*Sudeten German Party*] [*Czechoslovak*] (PPE)
SDP............ Suomen Sosialidemokraattinen Puolue [*Finnish Social Democratic Party*] (WEN)
SDP............ Swaziland Democratic Party (AF)
SDPE.......... Sistema de Direccion y Planificacion de la Economia [*Economic Management and Planning System*] [*Cuban*] (LA)
SDPF.......... Social Democratic Party of Finland (RU)
SDPG.......... Social Democratic Party of Germany (RU)
SDPITFNRJ... Savez Drustava Poljoprivrednih Inzenjera i Tehnicara Federativna Narodna Republika Jugoslavija [*Federation of Societies of Agricultural Engineers and Technicians of Yugoslavia*] (YU)
SDPL.......... Social Democratic Party of Lithuania [*1896-1935*] (RU)
SDPL.......... Suomen Demokratian Pioneerien Liitto [*Finnish League of Democratic Pioneers*] (WEN)
SDPLS........ Service de Distribution de Parfumerie, Liqueur, et Spiritueux [*Perfumes, Liqueurs, and Alcoholic Beverages Distribution Department*] [*Cambodian*] (CL)
SDPM.......... Societe Dakaroise des Petroles Mory (MAR)
SDPNS........ Stenographic Records of the First National Assembly (BU)
SDPRR(b)... Socjaldemokratyczna Partia Robotnicza Rosji (Bolszewikow) [*Social-Democratic Workers' Party of Russia (Bolsheviks)*] [*Polish*]
SDPSh........ Social Democratic Party of Sweden (RU)
SDPV.......... Social Democratic Party of Hungary (RU)
SDR............ Societe de Developpement Regional [*Regional Development Company*] [*Belgian*] (WER)
SDR............ Somali Democratic Republic (AF)
SDR............ Special Drawing Right (MAR)
SDR............ Strelecke Druzstvo [*Rifle Squad*] (CZ)
SDRA.......... Service de Documentation, Renseignement, et Action [*Documentation, Intelligence, and Action Service (Security and Counterintelligence Branch)*] [*Belgian*] (WER)
SDRA.......... Societe pour le Developpement de la Riviera Africaine [*Company for the Development of the African Riviera*] [*Ivorian*] (AF)
SDRC.......... Service de Documentation, Renseignement, et Chiffre [*Documentation, Intelligence, and Cipher Service (Ciphers Branch)*] [*Belgian*] (WER)
SDRDP........ South Darfur Rural Development Programme [*Sudanese*] (MAR)
SDRI........... Service de Documentation, Renseignement, et Information [*Documentation, Intelligence, and Information Service (Intelligence Branch)*] [*Belgian*] (WER)
SDRM.......... Societe de Developpement Rural de Medouneu (MAR)
SDrog.......... Staatliches Erfassungs- und Absatzkontor fuer Arznei- und Gewuerzpflanzen [*State Procurement and Sales Office for Medicinal Plants and Herbs*] (EG)
SDRP.......... Social Democratic Workers' Party (RU)
SDRP.......... Societe Dahomeenne de Rechapage de Pneumatiques (MAR)
SDRPL......... Social Democratic Workers' Party of Latvia [*1917-1934*] (RU)
SDRPR........ Socijal-Demokratska Radnicka Partija Rusije [*Social-Democratic Workers Party of Russia*] (YU)
SDRS.......... Societe pour le Developpement des Regions Sahariennes [*Saharan Regional Development Company*] [*Algerian*] (AF)
SDRS.......... Societe de Developpement Rizicole du Senegal (MAR)
SDRT.......... Sous-Direction des Recherches Techniques [*Sub-Directorate of Technological Research*] [*French*] (WER)
SDS............ Listened to Democratic Radio Stations [*Amateur radio operator's diploma*] (BU)
SDS............ Long-Distance Service Office (RU)
SDS............ Samostalna Demokratska Stranka [*Independent Democratic Party*] [*Yugoslav*] (PPE)
SdS............ Servizio di Sicurezza [*Internal Security Service*] [*Anti-Terrorism*] [*Italian*] (WER)
SDS............ Ship Remote-Indicating Station (RU)
SDS............ Slovenska Demokraticka Strana [*Slovak Democratic Party*] (CZ)
SDS............ Slovenska Demokratska Stranka [*Slovenian Democratic Party*] (YU)
SDS............ Socijal Demokratska Stranka [*Social-Democratic Party*] (YU)
SDS............ Sosyal Demokrat Sendikalari [*Social Democrat Unions*] (TU)
SDS............ Sozialistischer Deutscher Studentenbund [*German Socialist Students Association*] (EG)
SDS............ Srpska Drzavna Straza [*Serbian State Guard*] [*World War II*] (YU)
SDS............ Statni Divadelni Studio [*State Theater Studio*] (CZ)

SDS .... Stratiotiki Dioikisis Sidirodromon [*Military Administration of Railroads*] [*Greek*] (GC)
SDSA .... Selangor Democratic Students Association (Communist) (ML)
SDSI .... Scientific Data Systems Israel (MAR)
SDSK .... Sosyal Demokrat Sendikacilar Konseyi [*Council of Social Democrat Unionists*] (TU)
SDSO .... Students' Voluntary Sports Society (RU)
SDSPF .... Savezni Drzavni Sekretarijat za Poslove Finansija [*Federal State Secretariat for Financial Affairs*] (YU)
SDT .... (Program) Compiling Diagnostic Tables (RU)
SDT .... Societe Dahomeenne de Transports (MAR)
SDT .... Spoldzielczy Dom Towarowy [*Cooperative Store*] [*Polish*]
SDT .... Stations for Decontamination and Deactivation of Transport (BU)
SDT .... Transport Decontamination Station (RU)
SDTA .... Scottish Dance Teacher's Alliance (EA)
SDTC .... South Darfur Transport Company [*Sudanese*] (MAR)
SDTI .... Societe pour le Developpement Touristique Interafricain (MAR)
SDTJ .... Svaz Delnickych Telocvicnych Jednot Ceskoslovenskych [*Federation of Czechoslovak Workers' Gymnastic Associations*] (CZ)
SDTJC .... Svaz Delnickych Telocvicnych Jednot Ceskoslovenskych [*Federation of Czechoslovak Workers' Gymnastic Associations*] (CZ)
SDTs .... Moving-Target Selector [*or Selection*] (RU)
SDU .... Savezna Drzavna Uprava [*Federal State Administration*] (YU)
SDU .... Secondary Girls School (BU)
SDU .... Sofia State University (BU)
SDU .... Soziale Demokratische Union [*Social Democratic Union*] [*West German*] (PPW)
SDU .... Standardized Pressure Indicator (RU)
SDV .... Kombinat of Synthetic Fragrant Substances (RU)
SDV .... Scule, Dispositive, si Verificatoare [*Tools, Devices, and Controls*] (RO)
SDV .... Sprava Delostreleckeho Vyzbrojovani [*Artillery Ordnance Directorate*] (CZ)
SDV .... Sprava Doplnovani Vojsk [*Directorate for Troop Replacements*] (CZ)
SDV .... Synthetic Fragrant Substances (RU)
SDVNS .... Stenographic Records of the Grand National Assembly (BU)
SDVU .... Statny Drevarsky Vyskumny Ustav [*State Research Institute for Wood*] (CZ)
SDYA .... Selangor Democratic Youth Association (Communist) (ML)
SDYaV .... Extremely Toxic Poisons (RU)
SDZ .... Skola Dustojniku v Zaloze [*School for Reserve Officers*] (CZ)
SDZ .... Slovenska Demokratska Zveza [*Slovenian Democratic Union*] [*Trieste*] (YU)
SDZ .... Slovenska Dijaska Zveza [*Slovenian Student Union*] (YU)
SDZ .... Srpski Dijalektoloski Zbornik [*Collection of Serbian Papers on Dialectology*] [*A publication*] (YU)
SDZ .... Svaz Dopravnich Zamestnancu [*Transport Employees' Union*] (CZ)
SDZb .... Srpski Dijalektoloski Zbornik, Srpske Akademije Nauka [*Serbian Dialect Journal, Serbian Academy of Sciences*] [*Belgrade*] [*A publication*] (YU)
SDZS .... Svaz Dopravnych Zamestnancov Slovenska [*Slovak Transport Employees' Union*] (CZ)
SE .... Electric Meter (RU)
SE .... Electromagnetic Separator (RU)
SE .... Ferroelectric (RU)
SE .... Free-Electron [*Method*] (RU)
se .... Launcher [*Rocket-Firing*] Squadron (BU)
SE .... Opaque Screen (RU)
Se .... Sable [*Sand*] [*Military map abbreviation*] [*World War I*] [*French*] (MTD)
SE .... Sanat Enstitusu [*Trade Institute*] (TU)
SE .... Scieries de l'Equateur (MAR)
Se .... Secca [*or Secche*] [*Shoal or Shoals*] [*Italian*] (NAU)
SE .... Secretaria de Estado [*Secretariat of State*] [*Portuguese*] (WER)
SE .... Secretariat [*or Secretaire*] d'Etat (MAR)
Se .... Sema [*or Schema*] [*Sketch, Drawing*] (TU)
SE .... Siberian Ethnography (RU)
SE .... Skholi Evelpidon [*Army Cadets Academy*] (GC1)
SE .... Slovenske Elektrarne [*Slovak Electric Power Plants*] (CZ)
SE .... Slovenski Etnograf [*The Slovenian Ethnographer*] [*Ljubljana*] [*A periodical*] (YU)
SE .... Smallpox Eradication Programme (MAR)
SE .... Solar Cell (RU)
SE .... Soma Edonopoulon [*United Democratic Youth Organization Corps*] [*Cypriot*] (GC)
SE .... Son Eminence [*His Eminence*] [*French*] (MTD)
SE .... Son Excellence [*His (or Her) Excellency*] [*French*] (CL)
SE .... Sovetskaia Etnografiia (MAR)
SE .... Soviet Ethnography (RU)
SE .... Spanish Solidarity (PD)
SE .... Sport Egylet [*Athletic Club*] (HU)
SE .... Statisticko-Ekonomicke Oddeleni [*Statistical and Economic Department*] (CZ)
SE .... Su Excelencia [*His (or Her) Excellency*] [*Spanish*]
SE .... Sua Eccellenza [*His (or Her) Excellency*] [*Italian*]
SE .... Sud Est [*Southeast*] [*French*] (MTD)
SE .... Sudeste [*Southeast*] [*Spanish*]
SE .... Suomen Ennatys [*Finnish*]
SE .... Sweden [*Two-letter standard code*] (CNC)
SE .... Symvoulevtiki Epitropi [*Consultative Committee*] (GC)
SE .... Symvoulion Epikrateias [*Council of State*] [*Greek*] (GC)
SE .... Synchronous Electric Motor (RU)
SE .... Syndikalistiki Enotita [*Syndicalist Unity*] (GC)
SEA .... Service Economique Africain [*African Economic Service*] [*Tunisian*] (AF)
SEA .... Servicios Especiales Aereos Ltda. [*Cucuta*] (COL)
SEA .... Sindicato de Educadores Argentinos [*Argentine Teachers Union*] (LA)
SEA .... Skholai Efedron Axiomatikon [*Reserve Officers Schools*] [*Greek*] (GC)
SEA .... Skholi Ethnikis Amynis [*National Defense School*] [*Greek*] (GC)
SEA .... Sociedad de Economistas Agrarios [*Association of Agrarian Economists*] [*Chilean*] (LA)
SEA .... Sociedad de Estudios y Accion Ciudadana [*Civic Action and Studies Group*] [*Argentine*] (LA)
SEA .... Societe d'Entreprises Africaines [*Cameroonian*] (MAR)
SEA .... Societe Equatoriale d'Assurances (MAR)
SEA .... Societe d'Equipement pour l'Afrique (MAR)
SEA .... Soma Ellinon Alkimon [*Corps of Valiant Greeks*] (GC)
SEA .... Syllogos Emboroypallilon Athinon [*Association of Athens Commercial Employees*] (GC)
SEA .... Syndesmos Efedron Axiomatikon [*Reserve Officers Association*] [*Cypriot*] (GC)
SEA .... Syndesmos Ellinikis Anexartisias [*Greek Independence League*] (GC)
SEAKh ...... Skholi Epimorfoseos Anoteron Axiomatikon Khorofylakis [*Gendarmerie Senior Officer Training School*] [*Greek*] (GC)
SEAAPP ...... Syndesmos Eispraktoron Avtokiniton Athinon-Peiraios-Perikhoron [*Union of Bus Collectors for Athens, Piraeus, and Suburbs*] (GC)
SEAAS .... Syllogos Ellinon Apofoiton Anotaton Skholon [*Society of Greek Graduates of Advanced Schools*] [*Cypriot*] (GC)
SEABC .... Southeast Asia Business Council (ML)
SEABM .... Societe d'Exploitation Agricole du Bas-Mangoro (MAR)
SEAC .... Societe Economique Africaine du Congo (MAR)
SEAC .... Societe d'Equipement pour l'Afrique-Cameroun (MAR)
SEAC .... South and East African Conference (MAR)
SEAC .... Southeast Asia Command (ML)
SEACI .... Societe d'Equipement pour l'Afrique, Cote-d'Ivoire (MAR)
SEACI .... Societe Eurafricain pour le Commerce et l'Industrie (MAR)
SEACO .... Societe d'Equipement pour l'Afrique-Congo (MAR)
SEADAG ..... Southeast Asia Development Advisory Group (CL)
SEAE .... Service des Etudes et de l'Analyse Economique (MAR)
SEAF .... Servicio de Empleo y Accion Formativa [*Employment and Training Action Service*] [*Venezuelan*] (LA)
SEAG .... Societe d'Equipement pour l'Afrique-Gabon (MAR)
SEA-HV .... Societe d'Equipement pour l'Afrique-Haute-Volta (MAR)
SEAK .... Spoudastiki Enotiki Andi-Imperialistiki Kinisi [*Student Unifying Anti-Imperialist Movement*] [*Greek*] (GC)
SEAK .... Syndonistiki Epitropi Agoniston Kyprou [*Coordinating Committee of Cypriot Fighters*] (GC)
SEAKEE ...... Syndonistiki Epitropi Andidiktatorikis Kinisis Ekpatrismenon Ellinidon [*Coordinating Committee for the Antidictatorial Movement of Expatriated Greek Women*] (GC)
SEAL .... Scandinavian East Africa Line [*Reunionese*] (AF)
SEAM .... Servicios Agricolas Mecanizados [*Mechanized Agricultural Services*] [*Chilean*] (LA)
SEAM .... Societe d'Equipement pour l'Afrique-Mauritanie (MAR)
SEAMEC ...... Southeast Asia Ministers of Education Council (CL)
SEAMEO ...... Southeast Asia Ministers of Education Organization (CL)
SEAMES ..... Southeast Asia Ministers of Education Secretariat (CL)
SEAMP .... Southeast Asia Microform Project (ML)
SEAN .... Skholi Episkeptrion Adelfon Nosokomon [*Visiting Nurses School*] (GC)
SEAN .... Societe d'Equipement pour l'Afrique-Niger (MAR)
SEANA .... Societe d'Etudes pour l'Amelioration de la Nutrition en Afrique (MAR)
SEANZA ...... Southeast Asia, New Zealand, and Australia Council (ML)
SEAP .... Secretaria Especial de Abastecimento e Precos [*Special Secretariat for Supply and Prices*] [*Brazilian*] (LA1)
SEAP .... Sociedad Economica de Amigos del Pais [*Economic Society of Friends of the Country*] [*Colombian*] (LA)
SEAP .... Southeast Asian Peninsula (CL)
SEAP .... Syndikalistiki Ergatiki Agonistiki Parataxi [*Labor Union Struggle Faction*] [*Greek*] (GC)
SEAPCTIT ... Southeast Asia Promotion Center for Trade, Investment, and Tourism (CL)
SEAPK .... Syllogos Exoriston kai Apofylakisthendon Politikon Kratoumenon [*Association of Exiled and Released Political Prisoners*] [*Greek*] (GC)
SEAPTIT ..... Southeast Asia Promotion Center for Trade, Investment, and Tourism [*Use SEAPCTIT*] (CL)
SEARCA ..... Southeast Asia Regional Center for Agriculture [*Subsidiary of SEAMEC*] (ML)
SEARO .... Southeast Asian Regional Office (ML)

SEAS.......... Secretaria de Estado dos Assuntos Sociais [*State Secretariat for Social Affairs*] [*Angolan*] (AF)
SEAS.......... Societe d'Equipement pour l'Afrique-Senegal (MAR)
SEASOE...... Syndonistiki Epitropi Andidiktatorikon Organoseon Ellados [*Coordinating Committee of Antidictatorial Organizations of Greece*] (GC)
SEAT.......... Sociedad Espanola de Automoviles de Turismo, SA [*Spanish Passenger Car Company, Inc.*] (WER)
SEAT.......... Syndekhnia Ergatoypallilon tis Arkhis Tilepikoinonion [*Union of Telecommunications Authority Employees*] [*Cypriot*] (GC)
SEATAC...... Southeast Asia Transportation and Communications (CL)
SEATLAS.... Compania de Seguros Atlas SA [*Manizales*] (COL)
SEATO........ Southeast Asia Treaty Organization (CL)
SEAUSO..... Southeast Asian University Students Organization (ML)
SEB............ Clearing and Evacuation Base (RU)
SEB............ Marshaling Evacuation Hospital (BU)
SEB............ Medical Evacuation Base (RU)
SEB............ Sabah Electricity Board (ML)
SEB............ Societe d'Exploitation du Parc a Bois de Belabo (MAR)
SEBA.......... Severoceske Bavlnarske Zavody [*North Bohemian Cotton Mills*] (CZ)
SEBACAM... Societe des Bauxites du Cameroun [*Cameroon Bauxite Company*] (AF)
SEBAM........ Societe Eburneenne d'Armement (MAR)
SEBAT........ Societe Eburneenne de Batiment (MAR)
SEBC.......... Societe d'Exploitation des Bois du Cameroun (MAR)
SEBC.......... Societe d'Exploitation des Bois du Congo (MAR)
SEBCA........ Societe d'Exploitation des Bois et Contreplaques en Algerie (MAR)
SEBCI......... Societe d'Exploitation Forestiere de Cote-d'Ivoire (MAR)
SEBCO........ Societe d'Exploration des Bois du Sud-Ouest (MAR)
SEBF.......... Slovenska Evanjelicka Bohoslovecka Fakulta [*Slovak Protestant Theological School*] [*Modra*] (CZ)
SEBICOB.... Societe Industrielle de Biscuiterie et Confiserie du Benin (MAR)
SEBIMA...... Societe d'Exploitation des Bitumes du Maroc (MAR)
SEBLIMA.... Societe d'Exploitation des Bitumes et Lubrifiants Irano-Morocaine (MAR)
SEBM.......... Societe d'Exploitation des Briqueteries du Mali (MAR)
SEBOGA..... Societe pour l'Expansion des Boissons Hygieniques au Gabon (MAR)
SEBPTM...... Syndicat des Entrepreneurs, Batiment, Travaux Publics, et Mines du Togo (MAR)
SEBRIMA.... Societe d'Exploitation des Briqueteries du Mali (MAR)
SEBROKO... Societe Hotelliere et Touristique de la Baie du Banco (MAR)
SEBSO........ Societe d'Exploitation des Bois du Sud-Ouest (MAR)
SEBT.......... Societe d'Exportation des Bois Tropicaux (MAR)
SEBUMI...... Serikat Buruh Minjak Indonesia [*Indonesian Oil Workers Union*] (IN)
sec............. Secundum [*According To*] [*Latin*] (GPO)
sec............. Sekunde [*or Sekundaer*] [*Second or Secondary*] [*German*]
SEC............ Sindicato de Educadores Costarricenses [*Costa Rican Educators Union*] (LA)
SEC............ Societe d'Echanges Commerciaux (MAR)
SEC............ Societe d'Expertise Compatable (MAR)
SEC............ State Enterprise for Food Canning [*Iraqi*] (MAR)
SEC............ Syndicat des Employes du Commerce (MAR)
SEC............ Systeme Europeen de Comptes Economiques Integres [*European Integrated Economic Accounting System*] (WER)
SECA.......... Societe pour l'Expansion Commerciale Africaine (MAR)
SECA.......... Societe d'Exploitation des Carrieres d'Azaguie (MAR)
SECA.......... Societe d'Exploitation Commerciale et Agricole (MAR)
SECA.......... Societe pour l'Exportation des Cafes du Sud (MAR)
SECAB........ Secretaria Permanente del Convenio Andres Bello [*Bogota*] (COL)
SECAM....... Sequentiel Couleurs a Memoire [*Sequential Memory Color*] [*Television system*] [*French*] (WER)
SECAM....... Symposium of Episcopal Conferences of Africa and Madagascar (MAR)
SECAN........ Societe d'Expertises Comptables en Afrique Noire (MAR)
SECAP........ Servicio Ecuatoriano de Capacitacion Profesional [*Ecuadorean Professional Training Service*] (LA)
SECAT........ Societe d'Exploitation Cinematographique du Tchad (MAR)
SECBA........ Societe des Exportateurs et Commissionnaires en Bois Africains (MAR)
SECCA........ Sociedad Ecuatoriana del Carbon [*Ecuadorean Coal Company*] (LA)
SECCO........ Societe d'Etudes Contre la Corrosion (MAR)
SECED........ Servicio Central de Documentacion de la Presidencia del Gobierno [*Central Service Organization for the Prime Minister's Office (Intelligence Unit)*] [*Spanish*] (WER)
SECF.......... Serviciul de Exploatare Cai Ferate [*Railway Utilization Service*] (RO)
SECFFASEN... Societe d'Expertises Comptables Fiduciaires France-Afrique-Senegal (MAR)
SECGPS..... Syndicat des Employes de la CGPS (MAR)
sech............ Section (RU)
SECh.......... Sociedad de Escritores de Chile [*Writers Association of Chile*] (LA)
SECI........... Societa Elettrica Coloniale Italiana (MAR)
SECI........... Societe Equatoriale de Commerce et l'Industrie (MAR)
SECI........... Societe d'Equipement de la Cote-d'Ivoire (MAR)
SECI........... Societe d'Exploitation des Carrieres Ivoiriennes (MAR)
SECIG......... Service d'Etudes et de Coordination de l'Information Gouvernementale [*Service for Research and Coordination of Government Information*] [*Congolese*] (AF)
sec leg........ Secundum Legem [*According to Law*] [*Latin*] (GPO)
SECMA....... Societe d'Exploitation Cinematographique Africaine (MAR)
SECMI......... Societe d'Entreprise de Constructions et Montage Ivoirienne (MAR)
sec nat........ Secundum Naturam [*According to Nature*] [*Latin*] (GPO)
SECO.......... Societe d'Elevage et de Commerce (MAR)
SECO.......... Societe d'Entreprises Congolaises (MAR)
SECOAMA... Syndicat des Comptables Agrees de Madagascar [*Malagasy Union of Certified Public Accountants*] (AF)
SECOFIN.... Secretaria de Comercio y Fomento Industrial [*Secretariat of Commerce and Industrial Development*] [*Mexican*] (LA1)
SECOINSA... Sociedad Espanola de Comunicaciones e Informatica, SA [*Spanish Company of Communications and Data Processing, Inc.*] (WER)
SECOLAS... Societe d'Expansion Commerciale de l'Atlas (MAR)
SECOM....... Secretaria de Comercio [*Secretariat of Commerce*] [*Mexican*] (LA1)
SECOM....... Secretaria de Comunicacao Social [*Mass Media Secretariat*] [*Brazilian*] (LA)
SECONOM... Service de Coordination de la Normalisation Maghrebine (MAR)
SECONS..... Sector de Construccion [*Construction Sector*] [*Cuban*] (LA)
SECOR........ Societe Equatoriale de Commerce et de Representation [*Pointe Noire*] (MAR)
SECOREB... Secretariat de la Conference des Ordinaires du Rwanda et du Burundi (MAR)
SECP.......... Societe Eburneenne de Cuirs et Peaux (MAR)
SECRAC..... Societe d'Entreprises Chimiques et Routieres au Cameroun (MAR)
SECRAE...... Societe d'Entreprises Chimiques et Routieres de l'Afrique Equatoriale (MAR)
sec reg........ Secundum Regulam [*According to Rule*] [*Latin*] (GPO)
SECREN...... Societe d'Exploitation pour la Construction et la Reparation Navale [*Naval Construction and Repair Company*] [*Malagasy*] (AF)
secreta........ Secretaria [*Spanish*]
SECT........... Societe d'Exploitation des Cultures Tropicales (MAR)
SECT........... Syndicat des Enseignants Catholiques du Togo [*Catholic Teachers Union of Togo*] (AF)
SECTA........ Societe d'Entreprise de Construction et de Travaux en Afrique (MAR)
SECTA........ Syndicat Belge des Employes Techniques et Cadres d l'Aeronautique [*Belgian Union of Aeronautical Technical Employees and Managerial Personnel*] (WER)
SECTCI....... Societe d'Exploitations de Carrieres et de Transports de la Cote-d'Ivoire (MAR)
SECTO........ Syndicat des Employes du Commerce du Togo [*Commercial Employees Union of Togo*] (AF)
SECTUR...... Secretaria de Cultura y Turismo [*Secretariat of Culture and Tourism*] [*Honduran*] (LA1)
SECYNEI..... Secretaria de Comercio y Negociaciones Economicas Internacionales [*Secretariat of Commerce and International Economic Negotiations*] [*Argentine*] (LA)
SED............ Secretaria de Educacao e Cultura [*Brazilian*]
SED............ Socialist Unity Party [*East German*] (PD)
SED............ Societe d'Equipement du Dahomey (MAR)
SED............ Sozialistische Einheitspartei Deutschlands [*Socialist Unity Party of Germany*] [*East German*] (PPW)
SED............ Stathmoi Elengkhou Diavatirion [*Passport Control Stations*] (GC)
SED............ Syndesmos Ellinon Diaitiiton [*League of Greek Arbitrators*] (GC)
SED............ Syndikalistiki Ergatiki Dimokratia [*Labor Union Democracy*] [*Greek*] (GC)
SEDA.......... Societe des Etablissements Donzel Andre & Cie. (MAR)
SEDA.......... Societe d'Etudes pour le Developpement de l'Afrique (MAR)
SEDAC........ Societe des Etablissements Donzel Andre & Cie. (MAR)
SEDAGRI.... Societe d'Etudes et de Developpement Agricole (MAR)
SEDAM....... Societe d'Etudes et de Developpement des Aeroglisseurs Marins, Terrestres, et Amphibies (MAR)
SEDAS........ Sociedad Elaboradora de Articulos de Seda [*Bogota*] (COL)
SEDB.......... SEAMEO [*Southeast Asia Ministers of Education Organization*] Education Development Bonds (CL)
SEDC.......... Societe d'Exploitation Dorland et Cedolin (MAR)
SEDC.......... State Economic Development Corporations (ML)
SEDCI......... Societe d'Etudes pour le Developpement de la Cote-d'Ivoire (MAR)
SEDCO........ Small Enterprises Development Company (MAR)
sedd........... Sans Engagement de Dates [*French*]
SEDEC........ Secretaria de Estado de Educacao e Cultura [*Brazilian*]
SEDECA...... Societe Senegalaise d'Exploitation de Carrieres (MAR)
SEDECO..... Sindicato de Empleados de Desarrollo Comunal [*Trade Union of Community Development Employees*] [*Costa Rican*] (LA1)

SEDEFITA... Societe d'Etude et de Developpement des Perimetres du Fiherenana et de la Taheza [*Fiherenana and Taheza Area Planning and Development Company*] [*Malagasy*] (AF)
SEDEIS....... Societe d'Etudes et de Documentation Economiques Industrielles en Sociales [*French*]
SEDES........ Sociedade de Estudos para Desenvolvimento Economico e Social [*Society of Studies for Economic and Social Development*] [*Portuguese*] (WER)
SEDES........ Societe d'Etudes pour le Developpement Economique et Social [*Economic and Social Development Studies Company*] [*French*] (AF)
SEDES........ Synomospondia Elevtheron Dimokratikon Ergatikon Syndikaton [*Confederation of Free Democratic Labor Unions*] [*Greek*] (GC)
SEDESAF.... Societe Seydou Demba Samake Fils & Compagnie (MAR)
SEDF........... SEAMEO [*Southeast Asia Ministers of Education Organization*] Education Development Fund (CL)
SEDI............ Secretaria de Desarrollo Industrial [*Secretariat of Industrial Development*] [*Argentine*] (LA)
SEDI............ Societe d'Etudes de Developpement Industriel [*Company for Studies of Industrial Development*] [*Ivorian*] (AF)
SEDIA......... Sociedad Ecuatoriana de Ingenieros y Arquitectos [*Ecuadorean Society for Engineers and Architects*] (LA)
SEDIA......... Societe d'Etude du Developpement Industriel et Agricole [*Algerian*] (MAR)
SEDIA......... Societe d'Etudes et de Distribution Interafricaine (MAR)
SEDIAC....... Societe pour l'Etude et le Developpement de l'Industrie, l'Agriculture, et le Commerce [*Company for the Study and the Development of Industry, Agriculture, and Commerce*] [*French*] (AF)
SEDIC......... Sociedade de Distribuicao Industrial e Commercial Lda. (MAR)
SEDICAL..... Societe d'Exploitation et de Distribution de Carburants et Lubrifiants (MAR)
SEDICO....... Societe d'Industrie et de Commerce (MAR)
SEDICSS.... Societe Senegalaise pour le Developpement Industriel et Commercial du Sine Saloum (MAR)
SEDIEK....... Syndekhnia Ergatoypallilon Dimon kai Imidimosion Epikheiriseon Kyprou [*Union of Employees of Municipal and Semi-Public Enterprises of Cyprus*] (GC)
SEDIEX....... Societe Senegalaise de Distribution Import-Export (MAR)
SEDIGEP..... Synergatiki Enosis Diatheseos Georgikon Proiondon [*Agricultural Products Cooperative Marketing Union*] [*Cypriot*] (GC)
SEDIP.......... Societe Senegalaise de Distribution de Primagaz (MAR)
SEDITEX..... Societe d'Etudes pour le Developpement de l'Industrie Textile (MAR)
SEDITRO..... Societe Senegalaise d'Importation et de Distribution des Fruits Tropicaux (MAR)
sedm........... Weekly (BU)
SEDMEK..... Syndesmos Ellinon Dievthyndon Mesis Ekpaidevseos Kyprou [*League of Greek Secondary School Principals of Cyprus*] (GC)
SEDN.......... Syndesmos Ellinon Dimokratikon Nomikon [*League of Greek Democratic Lawyers*] (GC)
SEDO.......... Societe d'Entreprise et de Debardage de l'Ogooue (MAR)
SEDO.......... Syndonistiki Epitropi Dimosio-Ypallilikon Organoseon [*Coordinating Committee of Public Employee Organizations*] [*Greek*] (GC)
SEDOC........ Service de Documentation [*Documentation Service*] [*Cameroonian*] (AF)
SEDOC........ Service d'Etudes et de Documentation [*Studies and Documentation Department*] [*Cambodian*] (CL)
SEDOCAR... Service de Documentation Scientifique et l'Armement [*French*]
SEDRE........ Societe d'Equipement du Departement de la Reunion (MAR)
SEDUM....... Sindicato Democratico de Estudiantes de la Universidad de Madrid [*Democratic Student Union of the University of Madrid*] [*Spanish*] (WER)
SEDYK........ Syndekhnia Epistimonon Ypallilon Kyprou [*Union of Professional Civil Servants of Cyprus*] (GC)
SEE............. Sanford Exploring Expedition (MAR)
SEE............. Societe d'Etudes et d'Expansion [*Studies and Expansion Society - SES*] (EA)
SEE............. Sosialistiki Epanastatiki Enosi [*Socialist Revolutionary Union*] [*Greek*] (GC)
SEE............. Symvoulion Evropaikis Enoseos [*European Union Council*] [*Greek*] (GC)
SEE............. Symvoulion Exoterikou Emboriou [*Foreign Trade Council*] [*Greek*] (GC)
SEE............. Syndesmos Ellinidon Epistimonon [*League of Greek Professional Women*] (GC)
SEEB........... Societe d'Exploitation et d'Exportation de Bois (MAR)
SEED........... Soldiers Employed in Economic Development (MAR)
SEEE........... Societe Equatoriale d'Energie Electrique (MAR)
SEEF........... Societe Eburneenne d'Exploitation Forestiere (MAR)
SEEFA......... Syndonistiki Epitropi Ellinon Foititon Anglias [*Coordinating Committee of Greek Students in England*] (GC)
SEEG........... Societe d'Energie et d'Eau du Gabon [*Gabon Power and Water Company*] (AF)
SEEG........... Syndonistiki Epitropi Ergazomenon Gynaikon [*Coordinating Committee of Working Women*] [*Greek*] (GC)
SEEGE........ Syndonistiki Epitropi Ergazomenon Gynaikon Ellados [*Coordinating Committee of Working Women of Greece*] (GC)
SEEI............ Savet za Energetiku i Ekstraktivnu Industriju [*Council on Power and the Extractive Industry*] (YU)
seem........... Seemaennisch [*German*]
SEEM.......... Societe d'Exploitation des Ets. Moubarack (MAR)
SEEN........... Syndicat d'Etudes d'Energie Nucleaire [*Nuclear Energy Research Union*] [*Belgian*] (WER)
SEENE........ Syndonistiki Epitropi Ergazomenon Neon Ellados [*Coordinating Committee of Working Youth of Greece*] (GC)
SEENGP...... Syndesmos Ellinon Exagogeon Nopon Georgikon Proiondon [*League of Greek Exporters of Fresh Agricultural Products*] (GC)
SEEPE......... Section des Rencontres des Etudiants Portugais a l'Etranger (MAR)
SEES........... Societe d'Entreprises Electriques et Sanitaires (MAR)
SEES........... Synomospondia Elevtheron Ergatikon Syndikaton [*Confederation of Free Labor Unions*] [*Cypriot*] (GC)
Seesa.......... Societe d'Expansion Economique du Satikana (MAR)
SEEY........... (Pankypria) Syndekhnia Ergaton Ependysis kai Ypodisis [*(Pan Cyprian) Union of Garment and Shoe Workers*] (GC)
SEF............. Serviciul de Exploatare Feroviar [*Railway Utilization Service*] (RO)
SEF............. Societe d'Exploitation Forestiere (MAR)
SEF............. Syndesmos Ellinoaigyptiakis Filias [*Greek-Egyptian Friendship Association*] (GC)
SEFA........... Secretaria de Estado do Fomento Agrario [*Secretariat of State for Agricultural Development*] [*Portuguese*] (WER)
SEFA........... Societe d'Exploitations Forestieres Africaines (MAR)
SEFA........... Syllogos Ergaton Fotaeriou Athinon [*Athens Gas Workers Union*] [*Also, SFA*] (GC1)
SEFAC........ Societe d'Etudes Franco-Africaine des Constructions (MAR)
SEFAC........ Societe d'Exploitation Forestiere et Agricole du Cameroun (MAR)
SEFAN........ Societe des Entreprises Frigorifiques de l'Afrique du Nord [*Moroccan*] (MAR)
SEFBT......... Societe d'Exploitation Forestiere de Bois du Togo (MAR)
SEFCA......... Societe des Entrepots Frigorifiques de la Casamance (MAR)
SEFCAM..... Societe d'Exploitation Forestiere du Cameroun (MAR)
SEFERIF...... Societe d'Exploitation du Fer du Rif [*Moroccan*] (MAR)
SEFG........... Syllogos Ellinon Foititon Gallias [*Club of Greek Students in France*] (GC)
SEFI............ Societe d'Exploitation Forestiere d'Issia (MAR)
SEFI............ Societe d'Exploitations Forestieres et Industrielles (MAR)
SEFI............ Syndicat des Entreprises Francaises de Travaux Publics a Vocation Internationale (MAR)
SEFIC.......... Societe d'Exploitations Forestieres et Industrielles du Cameroun (MAR)
SEFITA........ Societe d'Effilochage, Filature, Tissage, et Apprets [*Moroccan*] (MAR)
SEFLI.......... Societe d'Equipement et de Fabrication pour la Luminescence et l'Incandescence [*Moroccan*] (MAR)
SEFOC........ Societe d'Exploitations Forestieres du Comoe (MAR)
SEFS........... Societe d'Exploitation des Frigorifiques Survif [*Mauritanian*] (MAR)
SEFS........... Syllogos Ergazomenon Foititon Spoudaston [*Association of Working Students*] [*A fifth letter is added for name of city in which located*] (GC)
SEFTRA...... Societe d'Exploitations Forestiere et de Transports Routiers Africains (MAR)
SEG............. Clearing and Evacuation Hospital (RU)
seg............. Present [*Tense*] (BU)
SEG............. Societe d'Exploitations Gabonaises (MAR)
SEG............. Syllogos Ellinon Geologon [*Greek Geologists Association*] (GC1)
SEG............. Syndesmos Ellinon Germanias [*Association of Greeks in Germany*] (GC)
SEGA.......... Societe d'Entreprises Generales Africaines (MAR)
SEGA.......... Societe d'Etudes Gabonaises (MAR)
SEGA.......... Societe d'Exploitation des Gravieres en Afrique (MAR)
SEGAB........ Societe Generale Arts et Batiments (MAR)
Segal.......... Secretaire General [*Secretary General*] (CL)
SEGANS..... Societe d'Etude du Transport et de la Valorisation des Gaz Naturels du Sahara (MAR)
SEGAS........ Syndesmos Ellinikon Gymnastikon kai Athlitikon Somateion [*Association of Greek Gymnastic and Athletic Clubs*] (GC)
SEGAZCAM... Societe d'Etudes pour la Mise en Valeur du Gaz Naturel Camerounais (MAR)
SEGBA........ Servicios Electricos del Gran Buenos Aires [*Greater Buenos Aires Electrical Services*] [*Argentine*] (LA)
SEGD.......... (Pankypria) Syndekhnia Ergaton Georgias kai Dason [*(Pan-Cyprian) Union of Farm and Forest Workers*] (GC)
SEGECI....... Societe d'Entreprises Generales et de Constructions Industrielles (MAR)
SEGECO..... Societe d'Entreprise Generale Equatoriale de Constructions (MAR)
SEGECOT... Societe d'Etudes Generales et de Cooperation Technique (MAR)
SEGEDAN... Societe d'Etudes et de Gestion de l'Afrique Noire (MAR)

SEGENI....... Societe Generale Senegalaise pour le Negoce et l'Industrie (MAR)
SEGESA...... Societe d'Etudes Geographiques, Economiques, et Sociologiques Appliquees (MAR)
SEGGTH..... Service des Etudes Generales des Grands Travaux de l'Hydraulique [*Major Construction and Water Works General Studies Service*] [*Algerian*] (AF)
SEGI............ Societe d'Exploitation du Granit Ivoirien (MAR)
SEGIC......... Societe d'Etudes Generales de Constructions Industrielles et Civiles (MAR)
SEGMA....... Societe d'Etudes du Gaz Marin [*Tunisian*] (MAR)
SEGO.......... Societe d'Exploitation des Grumes de l'Ouest (MAR)
SEGOA........ Societe Senegalaise d'Oxygene et d'Acetylene (MAR)
SEGOR........ Societe d'Etudes de Gestion et d'Organisation (MAR)
SEGP........... Socialist Unity Party of Germany (BU)
SEGR........... Societe d'Exploitation de la Gare Routiere (MAR)
SEGRA........ System of Elements of the Hydraulic Control Automation (RU)
SEGRAM..... Societe Equatoriale des Grands Magasins (MAR)
SEH............. Secretariat d'Etat a l'Hydraulique [*Secretariat of State for Hydraulic Engineering*] [*Algerian*] (AF)
Seh.............. Sehir [*City, Town*] (TU)
SEHA........... Societe d'Exploitation Hoteliere en Afrique [*Congolese*] (MAR)
SEHCI......... Societe pour l'Equipement Hydraulique en Cote-d'Ivoire (MAR)
SEHOBAREST... Sindicato de Empleados de Hoteles, Bares, y Restaurantes [*Trade Union of Hotel, Bar, and Restaurant Employees*] [*Dominican Republic*] (LA1)
SEHOMA..... Societe de Conseil et d'Expansion Commerciale Hollando-Malienne (MAR)
SEHPG........ Societe d'Exploitation Hoteliere de Port-Gentil (MAR)
SEHR........... Societe d'Exploitation des Hydrocarbures de Hassi R'Mel [*Algerian*] (MAR)
SEI.............. Electric-Pulse Counter (RU)
SEI.............. Secretaria Especial de Informatica [*Special Secretariat of Informatics*] [*Brazilian*] (LA1)
SEI.............. Societas Ergophthalmologica Internationalis [*International Ergophthalmological Society*] (EA)
SEI.............. Societe de Constructions et d'Embranchements Industriels (MAR)
SEI.............. Societe d'Etudes Speciales et d'Installations Industrielles (MAR)
SEI.............. Societe Senegalaise d'Entreprises Industrielles (MAR)
SEI.............. Somateion Ellinon Ithopoion [*Greek Actors Association*] (GC)
SEI.............. Statni Energeticka Inspekce [*State Power Inspectorate*] (CZ)
SEIB............ Societe d'Electricite Industrielle et Batiments (MAR)
SEIB............ Societe Electrique et Industrielle de Baol [*Senegalese*] (MAR)
SEIB............ Statistical and Economic Information Bulletin for Africa [*A publication*] (MAR)
SEIC............ Societe Electrique et Industrielle de la Casamance (MAR)
SEIC............ Societe d'Exploitation Industrielle et Commerciale (MAR)
SEICI.......... Societe d'Exportation et d'Importation de la Cote-d'Ivoire (MAR)
SEIDE.......... Sociedad de Estudios Internacionales de la Democracia Espanola [*Society of International Studies of Spanish Democracy*] (WER)
SEIFSA....... Steel and Engineering Industries Federation of South Africa (AF)
SEIM........... Secretaria de Intereses Maritimos [*Secretariat of Maritime Interests*] [*Argentine*] (LA)
SEIM........... Syndicat des Entreprises et Industries du Mali (MAR)
SEIMAD...... Societe d'Equipement Immobilier de Madagascar [*Realty Equipment Company of Madagascar*] (AF)
SEIMAF....... Societe d'Exportation et d'Importation de Materiel en Afrique (MAR)
SEIR............ Societe Senegalaise d'Energie et d'Irrigation (MAR)
SEIS............ Sociedad de Estudiantes de Ingenieria y Arquitectura Salvadorenos [*Society of Salvadoran Engineering and Architecture Students*] (LA)
SEIT............ Societe Electrique et Industrielle de Tambacounda (MAR)
SEITA.......... Service d'Exploitation Industrielle des Tabacs et des Allumettes [*Commercial Tobacco and Match Manufacturing Agency*] [*French*] (WER)
SEITC.......... Section d'Etudes et d'Information des Troupes Coloniales (MAR)
SEITRA....... Societe d'Etudes Industrielles et de Travaux (MAR)
SEIVA.......... Sindicato de Empleados de la Industria del Vidrio y Afines [*Union of Employees of the Glass and Related Industries*] [*Argentine*] (LA)
SEJ.............. Slovenska Evanjelicka Jednota [*Slovak Evangelical Union*] (CZ)
SEJS........... Secretariat d'Etat a la Jeunesse et aux Sports (MAR)
SEK............. Economic Power Combine (BU)
SEK............. International Electric Power Conference (BU)
sek.............. Second (BU)
sek.............. Second (RU)
SEK............. Sekretariat [*or Sekretaris*] [*Secretariat or Secretary*] (IN)
sek.............. Sekunda [*or Sekundy*] [*Second or Seconds*] [*Polish*]
Sek............. Sekundar [*German*]
sek.............. Sekunnissa [*Finnish*]
sek.............. Sekunti(a) [*Finnish*]
SEK............. Sidirodromoi Ellinikou Kratous [*Greek State Railways*] [*See also OSE*] (GC)
SEK............. Sut Endustrisi Kurumu [*Dairy Industry Association*] (TU)
SEK............. Symvoulion Ethnikon Klirodotimaton [*National Bequests Council*] [*Greek*] (GC)
SEK............. Syndesmos Ergodoton Kyprou [*Cyprus Employers Association*] (GC)
SEK............. Synomospondia Ergaton Kyprou [*Confederation of Cypriot Workers*] (GC)
SEKA.......... Syndonistiki Epitropi Kypriakou Agonos [*Coordinating Committee of the Cyprus Struggle*] (GC)
SEKA.......... Turkiye Seluloz ve Kagit Fabrikalari Isletmesi [*Turkish Cellulose and Paper Factories Administration*] (TU)
SEKA-IS...... Turkiye Seluloz, Kagit, ve Mamulleri Iscileri Sendikasi [*Turkish Cellulose, Paper, and Paper Products Workers' Union*] (TU)
SEKAM....... Syndonistiki Epitropi Kanonismou Anatheseos Meleton [*Coordinating Committee for Regulation of Research Assignments*] [*Greek*] (GC)
SEKBER GOLKAR... Sekretariat Bersama Golongan Karya [*Joint Secretariat of Functional Groups*] (IN)
SEKDJEN.... Sekretaris Djenderal [*Secretary General*] (IN)
SEKE........... Sosialistikon Ergatikon Komma tis Elladas [*Socialist Labor Party of Greece*] [*Forerunner of Greek Communist Party (KKE)*] (GC)
SEKE........... Sosialistikon Ergatikon Komma Ellados [*Socialist Workers' Party of Greece*] (PPE)
SEKE........... Synetairistiki Enosis Kapnoparagogon Ellados [*Cooperative Union of Greek Tobacco Growers*] (GC)
SEKEP........ Symvoulio Emborias Kypriakon Elaiokomikon Proiondon [*Cypriot Olive Products Marketing Council*] (GC)
Seker-Is...... Turkiye Seker Sanayii Iscileri Sendikasi [*Sugar Industry Workers Union of Turkey*] (TU)
SEKF........... Syndonistiki Epitropi Kyprion Foititon [*Cypriot Students Coordinating Committee*] [*Greek*] (GC)
SEKI........... Somateion Ellinon Kyprion Ithopion [*Greek-Cypriot Actors Association*] (GC)
SEKO.......... Syndonistiki Epitropi Kommaton kai Organoseon [*Coordinating Committee of Parties and Organizations*] [*Cypriot*] (GC)
SEKOVE...... Synetairistika Ergostasia Konservopoiias Voreiou Ellados [*Northern Greece Cooperative Canning Factories*] (GC)
SEKP........... Symvoulion Emborias Kypriakon Pataton [*Cyprus Potato Marketing Council*] [*See also SEP*] (GC1)
sekr............ Confidential, Confidentially (RU)
sekr............ Secretary (RU)
Sekr............ Sekretaer [*or Sekretariat*] [*German*]
sekr............ Sekretarz [*Secretary*] [*Polish*]
SEKRIMA..... Fivondrononam Ben'ny Sendika Kristianina Malagasy [*Christian Confederation of Malagasy Trade Unions*] (AF)
seksot......... Secret Agent (RU)
Sekt............ Sektion [*German*]
SEKXA........ Syndikaton Ergatotekhniton Katergasias Xylou Athinon [*Athens Union of Technicians and Workers in Wood Processing*] (GC)
SEL............. Sanitary and Epidemiological Laboratory (RU)
SEL............. Scouts' Esperanto League (EA)
SEL............. Selangor (ML)
sel.............. Selective, Selection (RU)
sel.............. Selig [*Deceased*] [*German*] (GPO)
sel.............. Selis [*or Selides*] [*Page or Pages*] (GC)
SEL............. Sindicato de Ensenanza Libre [*Trade Union of Free Education*] [*Spanish*] (WER)
SEL............. Socialist Electoral League [*Norwegian*] (PPW)
SEL............. Societe d'Exploitation Limonadiere (MAR)
SEL............. Standard Elektrik Lorenz (MAR)
SEL............. Syndesmos Efedron Lemesou [*League of Limassol Reserves*] (GC)
SEL............. Syndesmos Ellinon Logotekhnon [*League of Greek Writers*] (GC)
sel.............. Village (RU)
SELA.......... Sistema Economico Latinoamericano [*Latin American Economic System*] (LA)
SELAF........ Societe pour l'Etudes des Langues Africaines [*Paris*] (MAR)
SELCA........ Societe d'Exploitation la Cascade [*Cameroonian*] (MAR)
SELEK........ Synergatiki Enosi Lemonoparagogon Kyrineias [*Kyrenia Lemon Growers Marketing Union*] (GC)
Sel'elektro... Main Administration of Rural Electrification (RU)
Sel'elektrostroy... Moscow Construction and Installation Trust of the Glavsel'elektrostroy (RU)
SELENCO... Sound Electronic Compagnie (MAR)
SELETE....... Skholi Ekpaidevtikon Leitourgon Epangelmatikis kai Tekhnikis Ekpaidevseos [*School for Teachers in Trades and Technical Education*] [*Greek*] (GC)
SELFCI........ Societe des Etablissements Louis Feltrin de Cote-d'Ivoire (MAR)
sel'ges........ Rural Hydroelectric Power Plant (RU)
SELIS.......... Societe d'Equipement pour l'Infrastructure Saharienne [*Saharan Infrastructure Equipment Company*] [*Algerian*] (AF)
Selitr.......... Saltpeter Plant [*Topography*] (RU)
Sel'khozaerofotos"yemka... Administration of Agricultural Aerial Surveying (RU)

Sel'khozgiz ... State Publishing House of Agricultural Literature, Journals, and Posters (RU)
Sel'khozizdat ... Publishing House of Agricultural Literature, Journals, and Posters [*Moscow*] (RU)
Sel'khozizdat ... Publishing House of Agricultural Literature (in the Republics) (RU)
sel'khozuch ... Agricultural Training School (RU)
Sel'khozVNITO ... All-Union Scientific, Engineering, and Technical Society of Agriculture (RU)
SELKIM .... Seluloz Kimya Sanayi ve Ticaret AS [*Cellulose Chemical Industry and Trade Corporation*] (TU)
Sel'kolkhozgiz ... State Agricultural, Cooperative, and Kolkhoz Publishing House (RU)
Selkoop ...... Village Cooperative (BU)
Selkor .... Village Correspondent (BU)
s ell .... Segedellenor [*Assistant Supervisor*] (HU)
Sel'leszag ... Logging Administration of the Ministry of Agriculture, USSR (RU)
Sel'mash ..... All-Russian Syndicate of Agricultural Machines and Implements (RU)
Sel'mashsnabsbyt ... All-Union Office for Supply of Agricultural Machinery Plants and for Marketing of Their Production (RU)
SELPE .... Syndesmos Epikheiriseon Lianikis Poliseos Ellados [*Association of Retail Enterprises of Greece*] (GC)
SELSA .... Servicio de Lucha Sanitaria [*Health Promotion Service*] [*Argentine*] (LA)
SELSA .... Sindicato de Empresa La Laguna, SA [*Union of the La Laguna Enterprise, Inc.*] [*Salvadoran*] (LA)
Sel'skosovet ... Council of Agricultural Cooperative Centers (RU)
Sel'skosoyuz ... All-Russian Union of Agricultural Cooperatives (RU)
sel st .... Plant Breeding Station [*Topography*] (RU)
sel stop .... Agricultural (BU)
Selsuvet ...... Village People's Council (BU)
SELT .... Syndicat d'Enseignants Laics du Togo [*Lay Teachers Union of Togo*] (AF)
SELTA .... Societe Electro-Technique Africaine (MAR)
SELTI .... Sudan English Language Teaching Institute (MAR)
Seluloz-Is .... Turkiye Seluloz ve Mamulleri Iscileri Sendikasi [*Turkish Cellulose and Cellulose Products Workers Union*] (TU)
SEM .... Aircraft Electric Meteorograph (RU)
sem .... Family (BU)
sem .... Family [*Biology*] (RU)
sem .... Seed (RU)
Sem .... Semaphore [*Semaphore*] [*Military map abbreviation*] [*World War I*] [*French*] (MTD)
SEM .... Semboyan [*Signals (Army)*] (ML)
SEM .... Servicio de Equipos Mecanicos [*Mechanical Equipment Service*] [*Peruvian*] (LA)
SEM .... Servicio Nacional de Erradicacion de la Malaria [*National Service for Malaria Eradication*] [*Colombian*] (LA1)
SEM .... Servicios Electromecanicos Ltda. [*Cali*] (COL)
SEM .... Sila Elektromotoryczna [*Electromotive Force*] [*Polish*]
SEM .... Sociedade de Estudos de Mocambique (MAR)
SEM .... Societe d'Emaillage et de Galvanisation du Mali (MAR)
SEM .... Societe d'Energie de Madagascar (MAR)
SEM .... Societe d'Equipement de la Mauritanie (MAR)
SEM .... Societe Senegalaise d'Etudes Maritimes (MAR)
SEM .... Soma Efodiasmou kai Metaforon [*Supply and Transportation Corps*] [*Army*] [*Greek*] (GC)
S Em .... Son Eminence [*French*]
SEM .... Son Excellence Monsieur _____ [*His Excellency Mr. _____*] (AF)
SEM .... Statie de Evidenta Mecanizata [*Station for Mechanized Records*] (RO)
SEMA .... Secretaria Especial do Meio-Ambiente [*Special Secretariat for the Environment*] [*Brazilian*] (LA)
SEMA .... Secteurs Experimentaux de Modernisation Agricole (MAR)
SEMA .... Societe d'Economie et de Mathematiques Appliquees (MAR)
SEMA .... Societe d'Equipement du Mali (MAR)
SEMA .... Societe d'Equipement de Materiel Aeronautique (MAR)
SEMA .... Societe d'Etudes Minieres Africaines (MAR)
SEMA .... Societe d'Exploitation Miniere de l'Androy (MAR)
SEMA .... Societe de Materiaux de Construction (MAR)
SEMAB .... Secteur Experimental de Modernisation Agricole de Bongor (MAR)
SEMABLE ... Secteur Experimental de Modernisation Agricole du Ble (MAR)
SEMAC .... Societe d'Exploitation des Magasins et Ateliers Casino (MAR)
SEMACO ..... Societe d'Exploitation de Materiaux de Construction (MAR)
SEMAG .... Societe Senegalaise des Grands Magasins (MAR)
SEMALK ..... Secteur Experimental de Modernisation Agricole de Lai et Kelo (MAR)
SEMARP ..... Societe d'Etude du Marche du Plateau (MAR)
SEMAS .... Standart Elektrik Malzemesi Ticaret ve Sanayii Anonim Sirketi [*Standard Electrical Equipment Trade and Industry Corporation*] (TU)
SEMCA .... Secteur Experimental de Modernisation des Cultures d'Altitude (MAR)
SEMCENTRE ... Secteur Experimental de Modernisation Agricole du Centre (MAR)
SEMCI .... Societe Ebenisterie, Menuiserie de Cote-d'Ivoire (MAR)
SEME .... Societe d'Entreprise et de Materiel Electrique (MAR)
SEMECA ..... Sociedad de Estudiantes de Medicina Emilio Alvarez [*Emilio Alvarez Association of Medical Students*] [*Salvadoran*] (LA)
SEMEDE ..... Servicio Medico Departamental [*Cali*] (COL)
SEMEDE ..... Servicio Medico para Empleados Departamentales [*Colombian*]
SEMEFO ..... Servicio Medico Forense [*Forensic Medicine Service*] [*Mexican*] (LA)
Semenovodsoyuz ... All-Russian Seed-Growing Union of Agricultural Cooperatives (RU)
SEMEO .... Southeast Asia Ministers of Education Organization [*Use SEAMEO*] (CL)
SEMEST ..... Secteur Experimental de Modernisation Agricole de l'Est (MAR)
SEMEYK ..... Syndekhnia Epistimonon Mikhanikon Ekpaidevtikis Ypiresias Kyprou [*Union of Professional Engineers of the Cyprus Educational Service*] (GC)
SEMI .... Societe des Eaux Minerales Ivoiriennes (MAR)
SEMI .... Societe d'Expertises Maritimes et Industrielles (MAR)
SEMI .... State Enterprise for Mechanical Industries in Iskandariyah [*Iraqi*] (MAR)
Semin .... Seminaire [*Seminary*] [*Military map abbreviation*] [*World War I*] [*French*] (MTD)
SEMIPI .... Preparatory School for Student Officers [*Malagasy*] (AF)
SEMKUR ..... Sebze ve Meyva Kurutma Sanayii AS [*Fruit and Vegetable Drying Industry Corp.*] (TU)
seml .... Semleges [*Neutral*] (HU)
SEM MARITIME ... Secteur Experimental de Modernisation Maritime (MAR)
SEMME .... Syllogos Ergazomenon Mathiton Mesis Ekpaidevseos Athinon [*Association of Working Students in Secondary Education*] [*Greek*] (GC)
SEMNORD ... Secteur Experimental de Modernisation et d'Action Rurale du Nord [*North Modernization and Rural Action Experimental Sector*] [*Cameroonian*] (AF)
SEMO .... Syndonistiki Epitropi ton Metallourgikon Organoseon [*Coordinating Committee of Metallurgical Organizations*] [*Greek*] (GC)
SEMP .... Statens Etnografiska Museum. Publications (MAR)
SEMPA .... Syndicat des Entrepreneurs de Manutention du Port d'Abidjan (MAR)
SEMPAO ..... Syndicat des Entreprises de Manutention de Ports d'Afrique Occidentale [*West African Port Handling Enterprises Union*] [*Senegalese*] (AF)
SEMPIMA .... Sendikan'ny Mpivarotra Malagasy [*Malagasy Businessmen's Association*] (AF)
SEMPOK ..... Syndicat des Entreprises de Manutention du Port de Kaolack (MAR)
SEMRY .... Societe d'Expansion et de Modernisation de la Riziculture de Yagoua (MAR)
SEMT .... Skholi Ekpaidevseos Mikhanikon Tilepikoinonias [*Training School for Telecommunications Engineers*] [*Greek*] (GC)
SEMU .... Servicio Electrico Municipal (MAR)
SEMULTRA ... Servicio Multimodal Transismico [*Transisthmian Multimodal Service*] [*Mexican*] (LA1)
SEMUP .... Self-Excited Magnetized Dynamoelectric Amplifier (RU)
Sen .... Senat [*German*]
SEN .... Senegal [*Three-letter standard code*] (CNC)
sen .... Senior [*Latin*]
Sen .... Senior [*Senior*] [*Dutch*] (GPO)
sen .... Senior [*or Der Aeltere*] [*Senior or The Elder*] (EG)
sen .... Senior [*Polish*]
SEN .... Sistema Energetico Nacional [*National Power System*] [*Cuban*] (LA)
SEN .... Sistemul Energetic National [*National Power System*] (RO)
SEN .... Skholi Emborikou Navtikou [*Merchant Marine Academy*] (GC1)
SEN .... Societe Equatoriale de Navigation (MAR)
SEN .... Soma Ellinon Navtoproskopon [*Greek Sea Scouts*] (GC)
SEN .... Soma Elpidoforon Neon [*Corps of Hopeful Youth*] [*Cypriot*] (GC)
SEN .... Somateion Ellinidon Nomikon [*Association of Greek Women Attorneys*] [*Greek*] (GC)
SEN .... State Enrolled Nurses (MAR)
SEN .... Symvoulion Emborikou Navtikou [*Merchant Marine Council*] [*Greek*] (GC)
SENA .... Servicio Nacional de Aprendizaje [*National Apprenticeship Service*] [*Colombian*] (LA)
SENA .... Symvoulion Elengkhou Navtikon Atykhimaton [*Council for the Control of Marine Accidents*] [*Greek*] (GC)
SENAA .... Syndonistiki Epitropi Neolaion Andimonarkhikou Agona [*Coordinating Committee of Youth of the Antimonarchical Struggle*] [*Greek*] (GC)
SENAC .... Servico Nacional de Aprendizagem Comercial [*Brazilian*]
SENAC .... Servico Nacional do Comercio [*National Trade Service*] [*Brazilian*] (LA)
SENAC .... Societe Senegalaise de l'Amiante Ciment (MAR)
SENACA ..... Servicio Nacional del Control Animal [*National Animal Control Service*] [*Uruguayan*] (LA)
SENADEM .. Secretaria Nacional de Educacion Media [*National Secretariat of Intermediate Education*] [*Venezuelan*] (LA)
SENAFER .... Servicio Nacional de Fertilizantes [*National Fertilizer Service*] [*Peruvian*] (LA)

SENAI .... Servico Nacional da Aprendizagem Industrial [*National Industrial Apprenticeship Service*] [*Brazilian*] (LA)
SENAM .... Servico Nacional de Assistencia aos Municipios [*National Municipal Aid Service*] [*Brazilian*] (LA)
SENAM .... Societe Senegalaise de Navigation Maritime (MAR)
SENAMEHI ... Servicio Nacional de Meteorologia e Hidrologia [*National Meteorological and Hydrographic Service*] [*Peruvian*] (LA)
SENAPET.... Servicio Nacional de Programacion y Evaluacion Tecnica [*National Technical Programing and Evaluation Service*] [*Argentine*] (LA)
SENARA...... Servicio Nacional de Radiodifusion [*National Broadcasting Service*] [*Argentine*] (LA)
SENASA...... Servicio Nacional de Sanidad Animal [*National Animal Health Service*] [*Argentine*] (LA)
Senat arkh ... Senate Archives (RU)
SENATI .... Servicio Nacional de Adiestramiento en Trabajo Industrial [*National Service for Industrial Work Training*] [*Peruvian*] (LA)
SENCIE....... Societe Senegalaise de Scierie (MAR)
SENDAS ..... Servicio Nacional de Asistencia Social [*Later, SAS*] [*Bogota*] (COL)
SENDET...... Secretaria Ejecutiva Nacional de Detenidos [*National Executive Secretariat of Prisoners*] [*Chilean*] (LA)
SENDIP .... Secretaria Nacional de Informacion Publica [*National Public Information Secretariat*] [*Ecuadorean*] (LA)
SENDOC ..... Small Enterprises National Documentation Centre [*Indian*] (MAR)
SENDU .... Servicio Nacional de Desarrollo Urbano [*National Urban Development Service*] [*Bolivian*] (LA)
SENE........... Syndonistiki Epitropi Neon Ergazomenon [*Coordinating Committee of Working Youth*] [*Greek*] (GC)
SENEGALAP ... Societe Senegalaise de Diffusion d'Appareils Electriques (MAR)
SENELEC.... Societe Senegalaise de Distribution d'Energie Electrique (MAR)
SENEPESCA ... Societe Senegalaise pour l'Expansion de la Peche Cotiere, Surgelation, et Conditionnement des Aliments (MAR)
SENEPHARMA ... Societe Pharmaceutique Senegalaise (MAR)
SENEPNEU ... Societe Senegalaise de Pneumatiques (MAR)
SENETEX.... Societe Senegalaise des Textiles (MAR)
SENETRANSCARS ... Senegalaise de Transports par Cars (MAR)
SENETRANSFIL ... Societe Senegalaise de Transformation du Fil de Metal (MAR)
SENG .... Secretaria de Estado dos Negocios do Governo [*Brazilian*]
SENGA......... Societe d'Entreposage du Gabon (MAR)
SENGAZ...... Societe Senegalaise des Gaz (MAR)
SENICOM ... La Senegalaise Industrielle Commerciale (MAR)
SENIMCO ... Senegalaise Immobiliere et Commerciale (MAR)
SENIMEX.... Senegal Import-Export (MAR)
SENINFOR ... Societe Senegalaise de Travaux Informatiques (MAR)
SENLAIT..... Societe Industrielle de Produits Laitiers (MAR)
SENN .... Societa Elettronucleare Nazionale [*Italian*]
SENO .... Syndonistiki Epitropi Neon Oikodomon [*Coordinating Committee of Young Construction Workers*] [*Greek*] (GC)
SENOTEL.... Societe Anonyme de Construction et de Gestion Immobiliere et Hoteliere (MAR)
SENPA .... Servicio Nacional de Productos Agrarios [*National Service for Agricultural Products*] [*Spanish*] (WER)
SENPRUC ... Secretaria Nacional de Preuniversitarios Cristianos [*Bogota*] (COL)
sent............ September (RU)
s-ent........... Sous-Entendu [*Understood*] [*French*]
SEO............. Department of Sanitation and Epidemiology (RU)
SE & O......... Salvo Errore et Omission [*Latin*]
SEO............. Sanitary and Epidemiological Detachment (RU)
SEO............. Sauf Erreur ou Omission [*Error or Omission Excepted*] [*French*] (GPO)
SEO............. Soma Ellinidon Odigon [*Greek Women Drivers Corps*] (GC)
SEO............. Symvoulevtiki Oikonomiki Epitropi [*Advisory Economic Committee*] (GC1)
SEO............. Symvoulion Epilogis Opliton [*Soldier Selection Council*] [*Greek*] (GC)
SEO............. Syndesmos Ellinon Oreivaton [*Greek Mountain Climbers League*] (GC)
SEOED........ Skholi Eidikon Oplon Enoplon Dynameon [*Armed Forces Special Weapons School*] [*Greek*] (GC)
SEOI........... Secretaria de Estado da Ordem Interna [*State Secretariat for Internal Security*] [*Angolan*] (AF)
SEOIL.......... Syndesmos Ergazomenon kai Odigon Idioktiton Leoforeion [*Association of Employees and Drivers of Privately Owned Buses*] [*Greek*] (GC)
SEOPAN ..... Grupo de Empresas de Obras Publicas de Ambito Nacional [*Group of Public Works Enterprises of National Scope*] [*Spanish*] (WER)
SEOPP .... Syndonistiki Epitropi Organoseon Prostasias tou Perivalondos [*Coordinating Committee of Organizations for the Protection of the Environment*] [*Greek*] (GC)
SEP .... Medical Evacuation Point (RU)
SEP .... Secretaria de Educacion Publica [*Secretariat of Public Education*] [*Mexican*] (LA)
SEP .... Secretariat d'Etat au Plan [*Algerian*] (MAR)
SEP .... Skholi Epangelmatikou Prosanatolismou [*Trade Orientation School*] [*Greek*] (GC)
SEP .... Smallpox Eradication Programme (MAR)
SEP .... Societe Equatoriale Pharmaceutique (MAR)
SEP .... Societe Europeenne de Propulsion [*European Propellant Co.*] [*French*] (WER)
SEP .... Societe pour l'Expansion des Exportations (MAR)
SEP .... Soma Ellinon Proskopon [*Greek Boy Scouts*] (GC)
SEP .... Sosialistiki Epanastatiki Pali [*Socialist Revolutionary Struggle*] [*Greek*] (GC)
SEP .... Special Electrotechnical Regulations (RU)
SEP .... Stichting Economische Publikaties
SEP .... Stowarzyszenie Elektrykow Polskich [*Association of Polish Electrical Engineers*] (POL)
SEP .... Suboticko Elektricno Preduzece [*Subotica Electrical Establishment*] (YU)
SEP .... Sumadisko Elektricno Preduzece [*Sumadija Electrical Establishment*] [*Vreoci*] (YU)
SEP .... Surrendered Enemy Personnel (ML)
SEP .... Symfonia Emboriou kai Pliromon [*Commerce and Payments Agreement*] [*Greek*] (GC)
SEP .... Symvoulion Elaiokomikon Proiondon [*Olive Oil Products Council*] [*Greek*] (GC)
SEP .... Symvoulion Emborias Pataton [*Potato Marketing Council*] [*Cypriot*] (GC)
SEP .... Symvoulion Exagogikis Politikis [*Export Policy Council or Board*] (GC1)
SEP .... Systima Enorganis Prosgeioseos [*Instrument Landing System*] (GC1)
SEPA........... Science Education Program for Africa (AF)
SEPA........... Servicios Periodisticos Asociados [*Associated Journalistic Services*] [*Chilean*] (LA)
SEPA........... Societe d'Edition et de Presse Africaine (MAR)
SEPA........... Societe des Engrais Phosphates Azotes [*Phosphate and Nitrate Fertilizer Company*] [*Tunisian*] (AF)
SEPAC .... Secretaria de Promocion y Asistencia de la Comunidad [*Volunteer Service of the Secretariat of Community Assistance and Development*] [*Argentine*] (LA)
SEPAC .... Societe Egyptienne pour la Fabrication des Articles en Caoutchouc (MAR)
SEPACAM ... Societe d'Exploitation pour l'Assainissement du Cameroun (MAR)
SEPAM........ Societe d'Exportation des Produits Animaux du Mali (MAR)
SEPAMA ..... Societe d'Exploitation des Produits d'Arachides du Mali (MAR)
SEPAN .... Servicio Publicitario de Alimentos y Nutricion [*Bogota*] (COL)
SEPANAL.... Secretaria del Patrimonio Nacional [*Secretariat of National Patrimony*] [*Mexican*] (LA)
SEPANI .... Societe d'Exploitation des Produits d'Arachides du Niger (MAR)
SEPAP .... Severoceske Papirny [*North Bohemian Paper Works*] (CZ)
SEPBA .... Societe d'Exploitation du Parc a Bois d'Abidjan [*Ivorian*] (MAR)
SEPBC .... Societe d'Exploitation des Parcs a Bois du Cameroun (MAR)
SEPC........... Societe d'Exploitation des Produits de Cote-d'Ivoire (MAR)
SEPCAE...... Societe des Engrais et des Produits Chimiques d'Afrique Equatoriale (MAR)
SEPCEM ..... Societe d'Etude pour la Promotion de la Culture et l'Exploitation du Mais au Cameroun (MAR)
SEPCM........ Societe d'Engrais et de Produits Chimiques de Madagascar (MAR)
SEPCON ..... Saudi Economic and Petroleum Consulting Group (MAR)
SEPDTh ...... Syndikalistiki Epitropi dia tin Prostasian ton Dimokratikon Thesmon [*Trade Union Committee for the Defense of Democratic Institutions*] [*Greek*] (GC)
SEPEM........ Societe d'Exploitation de Peche en Mer (MAR)
SEPEN .... Secretariat d'Etat au Plan et a l'Economie Nationale [*Tunisian*] (MAR)
SEPEO .... Syndonistiki Epitropi Provolis Ellinikis Oikonomias [*Coordinating Committee for the Promotion of the Greek Economy*] (GC)
SEPFI .... Societe d'Etudes et de Participation Financieres et Immobilieres [*North African*] (MAR)
SEPG........... Societe d'Energie de Port-Gentil (MAR)
SEPHOS...... Societe d'Etudes et de Participations Phosphatieres [*Phosphate Studies and Participations Company*] [*French*] (WER)
SEPIA.......... Societe d'Etudes de Production Industrielle en Afrique (MAR)
SEPIC.......... Societe d'Etude et de Promotion des Industries de la Cellulose (MAR)
SEPICA .... Societe d'Etudes et de Promotion Industrielle des Camerounais (MAR)
SEPIPSA ..... Servicio Peruano de Ingenieros de Petroleo del Oriente, Sociedad Anonima [*Peruvian Service of Petroleum Engineers for Eastern Peru, Incorporated*] (LA)
SEPLACODI ... Secretaria de Planamiento, Coordinacion, y Difusion [*Information, Coordination, and Planning Secretariat*] [*Uruguayan*] (LA)
SEPLAN ...... Secretaria de Planejamento [*Planning Secretariat*] [*Brazilian*] (LA)
SEPM .... Statiunea Experimentala de Preparate Microbiologice [*Experimental Station for Microbiological Preparations*] (RO)

SEPMI .... Sociedad para la Educacion Patriotico-Militar [*Society for Patriotic-Military Education*] [*Cuban*] (LA)
SEPO .... Societe d'Exploitation des Produits Oleagineaux [*Moroccan*] (MAR)
SEPOGA ..... Societe d'Exploitation des Produits Oleagineux du Gabon [*Gabonese Oleaginous Products Exploitation Company*] (AF)
SEPOM .... Societe d'Exploitation des Produits Oleagineux du Mali (MAR)
SEPP .... Societe d'Entreposage des Produits Petroliers (MAR)
SEPPIC .... Section de Peche et de Pisciculture du Cameroun (MAR)
SEPRA .... Sociedad Explotadora de Productos Agricolas Ltda. [*Agricultural Products Promotional Company Ltd.*] [*Chilean*] (LA)
SEPREP ...... Secretaria de Prensa de la Presidencia de la Republica [*Press Secretariat of the Presidency*] [*Peruvian*] (LA)
SEPRIC .... Societe d'Etudes pour la Promotion de l'Industrie Cafeiere (MAR)
SEPRONAL ... Sociedad Explotadora de Productos Nacionales Ltda. [*Bogota*] (COL)
sept .... September (BU)
sept .... September [*September*] [*Danish*] (GPO)
sept .... September [*September*] [*Dutch*] (GPO)
Sept .... September [*September*] [*German*] (GPO)
sept .... Septembre [*September*] [*French*]
SEPT .... Syndicat des Enseignants Protestants Togolais [*Togolese Protestant Teachers Union*] (AF)
septe .... Septiembre [*September*] [*Spanish*]
SEPVPS ...... Somateion Ergatikou Prosopikou Viomikhanion Plastikon Ylon kai Synafon Athinon-Peiraios-Perikhoron [*Union of Working Personnel of the Plastics and Related Industries of Athens, Piraeus, and Suburbs*] (GC)
seq .... Sequens [*The Following*] [*Latin*] (GPO)
ser .... Middle (RU)
ser .... Seria [*Series*] (POL)
ser .... Serial (RU)
Ser .... Serie [*Series*] [*German*]
ser .... Series (BU)
ser .... Series (RU)
ser .... Serine (RU)
SER .... Servicio Estatal de Radiodifusion [*State Radiobroadcasting Service*] [*Panamanian*] (LA)
SER .... Servico de Radiodifusao Educativa [*Educational Radiobroadcasting Service*] [*Brazilian*] (LA)
ser .... Silver (RU)
SER .... Sociaal Economische Raad [*Social Economic Council*] [*Dutch*] (WEN)
SER .... Societe Equatoriale de Raffinage [*Equatorial Refining Company*] [*Gabonese*] (AF)
SER .... System of Optimalizing Control (RU)
SERA .... Social and Economic Revolutionary Army (MAR)
SERA .... Societe d'Etudes et de Realisations Agricoles (MAR)
SERA .... Societe d'Etudes et de Representation en Afrique (MAR)
SERADIS ..... Societe Senegalaise de Representation, d'Approvisionnements et de Distribution (MAR)
SERAM .... Service d'Etudes et de Recherches Antimalariennes (MAR)
SERAO .... Societe d'Engineering et de Realisations en Afrique de l'Ouest (MAR)
SERAS .... Societe d'Exploitation des Ressources Animales du Senegal (MAR)
serb .... Serbiaa [*or Serbiaksi*] [*Finnish*]
serb .... Serbialainen [*Finnish*]
SERBAUD ... Serikat Buruh Angkatan Udara [*Air Transport Workers Union*] (IN)
SERBIUM .... Serikat Buruh Industri dan Umum [*General and Industrial Workers Union*] (IN)
serbskokhorv ... Serbo-Croatian (RU)
SERC .... Saudi-Egyptian Reconstruction Company (ME)
SERC .... Societe d'Equipement de la Republique du Congo (MAR)
SERCA .... Secteur Experimental de Rationalisation du Circuit de l'Arachide [*Senegalese*] (MAR)
SERCA .... Societe d'Exploitation de la Republique Centrafricain (MAR)
SERCO .... Service et Commerce (MAR)
SERCOGIM ... Societe de Services Communs et de Gestion Immobiliere (MAR)
SERCOTEC ... Servicio de Cooperacion Tecnica [*Technical Cooperation Service*] [*Chilean*] (LA)
SEREC .... Societe d'Etudes de Representation et de Controle (MAR)
SEREC-CI ... Societe d'Etudes, de Recherches, et d'Exploitations de Carrieres en Cote-d'Ivoire (MAR)
SEREG .... Societe d'Etudes, de Realisations, et de Gestion (MAR)
SEREM .... Societe d'Etudes, de Recherches, et l'Exploitation Minieres (MAR)
SEREPCA ... Societe de Recherches et d'Exploitation des Petroles du Cameroun [*Petroleum Prospecting and Exploitation Company of Cameroon*] (AF)
SEREPT ...... Societe Francaise d'Exploitation et de Recherches Petroliers en Tunisie [*French Company for Petroleum Exploitation and Prospecting in Tunisia*] (AF)
SERESA ...... Societe d'Etudes de la Realisation Economique et Sociale en l'Agriculture (MAR)
SEREX .... Secretaria Ejecutiva de Relaciones Economicas Externas [*Executive Secretariat for Foreign Economic Relations*] [*Chilean*] (LA)
SERFHAU ... Servico Federal de Habitacao e Urbanismo [*Federal Housing and Urban Planning Service*] [*Brazilian*] (LA)
SERGAL ...... Sociedade de Exportacoes, Representacoes Gerais, e Agencias Limitada (MAR)
SERGTHI ..... Societe d'Etudes et de Realisation des Grands Travaux Hydrauliques et Industriels [*Algerian*] (MAR)
serh ed .... Serh Eden [*Annotated*] [*As of a literary work*] (TU)
SERI .... Societe d'Etudes et de Realisations Industrielles [*Moroccan*] (MAR)
SERIA .... Societe d'Etudes et de Realisations Industrielles d'Abidjan (MAR)
SERIAO .... Societe d'Equipement Rural et Industriel d'Afrique Occidentale (MAR)
SERIC .... Societe d'Etudes et de Realisation pour l'Industrie Cafeiere et Cacaoyere (MAR)
SERIC .... Societe pour l'Exploitation de Representations Industrielles et Commerciales (MAR)
SERICC .... Societe d'Etudes et de Recherches pour l'Industrie et le Commerce Camerounais (MAR)
SERICODI ... Societe d'Etudes et de Realisations Industrielles de Cote-d'Ivoire (MAR)
SERIM .... Societe d'Etudes et de Realisations Industrielles Modernes (MAR)
SERI-RENAULT ENGINEERING ... Societe d'Etudes et de Realisations Industrielles Renault-Engineering (MAR)
SERM .... Societe d'Etudes et de Recherches Minieres de Madagascar [*Mining Studies and Prospecting Company of Madagascar*] (AF)
Serma .... Serenisima [*Spanish*]
SERMAN ..... Societe d'Exploitation et de Recherches Minieres dans l'Afrique du Nord (MAR)
SERMENA ... Servicio Medico Nacional de Empleados [*National Employees Medical Service*] [*Chilean*] (LA)
SERMI .... Societe d'Etudes et de Realisations Minieres et Industrielles (MAR)
SERMIS .... Societe d'Etudes et de Recherches Minieres du Senegal (MAR)
Sermo .... Serenisimo [*Spanish*]
SERP .... Sindicato de Educadores de la Revolucion Peruana [*Union of Educators of the Peruvian Revolution*] (LA)
SERPAL ...... Servicio Radiofonico para America Latina [*Radio Service for Latin America*] [*Costa Rican*] (LA1)
SERPAR ...... Servicio de Parques [*Park Service*] [*Peruvian*] (LA)
SERPE .... Superintendencia dos Servicos de Estatistica [*Brazilian*]
SERPED ...... Service d'Etudes et de Recherches Pedagogiques pour les Pays en Voie de Developpement (MAR)
SERPRO ...... Servico Federal de Processamento de Dados [*Federal Data Processing Service*] [*Brazilian*] (LA)
SERST .... Secretariat d'Etat a la Recherche Scientifique (MAR)
SERTAF ...... Services Techniques Africains Cote-d'Ivoire (MAR)
SERTEC ...... Societe d'Etudes et de Realisations Techniques (MAR)
SERTECI ..... Syndicat des Entreprises de Remorquage et de Transport par Eau de la Cote-d'Ivoire (MAR)
SERTI .... Studio-Ecole de la Radiodiffusion Television Ivoirienne (MAR)
SERTID .... Societe d'Etudes et de Realisation pour le Textile et les Industries Diverses (MAR)
SERVIGAS ... Servicio de Gas a Domicilio [*Bogota*] (COL)
SERVIPOL ... Servicio Tecnico de Pozos [*Cali*] (COL)
SERVITEC ... Empresa de Servicios Tecnicos de Computacion [*Enterprise for Technical Computation Services*] [*Cuban*] (LA)
SERVITECO ... Servicio Tecnico y Comercial Ltda. [*Pereira*] (COL)
servo .... Servicio [*Service*] [*Spanish*]
servor .... Servidor [*Spanish*]
serzh .... Sergeant (RU)
SES .... Butt Resistance Electric Welding (RU)
SES .... Medical Epidemiological Station (BU)
SES .... Sanitarno Epidemioloske Stanice [*Sanitary Epidemic Stations*] (YU)
SES .... Sanitary and Epidemiological Station (RU)
SES .... Sekretaris [*Secretary*] (IN)
SES .... Soviet Encyclopedic Dictionary [*A publication*] (RU)
SES .... Standardliste Eisen und Stahl [*Standard List for Iron and Steel Products*] (EG)
SES .... Station Operating Department [*Railroads*] (RU)
SES .... Studies and Expansion Society [*See also SEE*] (EA)
SES .... Sumska Eksperimentalna Stanica [*Forestry Experiment Station*] [*Erdelija*] (YU)
SES .... Syndesmos Ethnikofronon Somateion [*or Synomospondia Ethnikon Somaton*] [*League of Nationalist Associations or League of Nationalist Groups*] [*Cypriot*] (GC)
SES .... Syndicat des Enseignants du Senegal [*Teachers Union of Senegal*] (AF)
SESAF .... Societe Anonyme pour les Echanges entre la Suisse et l'Afrique (MAR)
SESAM .... Systeme Electronique de Selection Automatique de Microfilms
SESAME ..... Systeme d'Etudes pour un Schema d'Amenagement [*French*]
SESC .... Servico Social do Comercio [*Commercial Social Service*] [*Brazilian*] (LA)
SESCO .... Sarawak Electricity Supply Corporation (ML)

SESCYP...... Societe d'Exploitation des Salons de Coiffure Yetty et Patricia (MAR)
SESDA........ Secretariat de Sante Dentaire de l'Afrique (MAR)
SESI............ Servico Social da Industria [*Industrial Social Service*] [*Brazilian*] (LA)
SESIM......... Secours Social aux Invalides Militaires [*Social Aid for Disabled Military Personnel*] [*Cambodian*] (CL)
SESIN.......... Service Central de Surete des Installations Nucleaires [*Nuclear Installation Central Safety Service*] [*French*] (WER)
SESKOABRI ... Sekolah Staf dan Komando Angkatan Bersendjata Republik Indonesia [*Republic of Indonesia Armed Forces Staff and Command School*] (IN)
SESM.......... Special-Purpose Electronic Computer (RU)
SESMD .... Sudan Stock Exchange and Securities Market Developments (MAR)
SESP........... Servico Especial de Saude Publica [*Special Public Health Service*] [*Brazilian*] (LA)
SESR........... Esperantists' Union of Soviet Republics (RU)
SESUAM..... Societe d'Etudes Sucrieres en Afrique et a Madagascar (MAR)
SESUCHARI ... Societe d'Etudes Sucrieres du Chari (MAR)
SESUCHARI ... Societe d'Etudes Sucrieres du Tchad (MAR)
SESUHV...... Societe d'Etudes Sucrieres de Haute-Volta (MAR)
SET .... Aircraft Electric Tachometer (RU)
SET .... Sekretariat [*Secretariat*] (IN)
set .... Setembro [*September*] [*Portuguese*] (GPO)
SET .... Skholai Ekpaidevseos Tekhniton [*Technicians Training Schools*] [*Greek*] (GC)
SET .... Societe d'Etudes et de Travaux Topographiques (MAR)
SET .... Suboticki Elektricni Tramvaj [*Subotica Electric Streetcar*] (YU)
SETA........... Sociedad Tecnica Agropecuaria Ltda. [*Bucaramanga*] (COL)
SETA........... Societe Electronique Africaine (MAR)
SETA........... Societe d'Equipements Techniques et Automobiles (MAR)
SETA........... Societe des Ets. Tanoh (MAR)
SETA........... Societe d'Etudes Topographiques Africaines (MAR)
SETAC .... Syndicat des Entrepreneurs de Batiments, Travaux Publics, et Activites Connexes de la Republique du Congo (MAR)
SETACI....... Societe Ivoirienne d'Equipements Techniques et Automobiles (MAR)
SETAM........ Societe d'Etudes et de Travaux d'Art du Maroc (MAR)
SETAO .... Societe d'Etudes et de Travaux pour l'Afrique Occidentale (MAR)
SETAO .... Societe d'Etudes et de Travaux pour l'Afrique de l'Ouest (MAR)
SETAP......... Societe pour l'Etude Technique d'Amenagement Planifie (MAR)
SETBOG ..... Syndicat des Exploitants et Transformateurs du Bois de Guyane [*Trade Union of Growers and Processors of the French Guianese Forest*] (LA1)
SETCA .... Societe d'Etudes pour le Tourisme en Casamance (MAR)
SETCA .... Syndicat des Employes Techniciens et Cadres [*Technical Employees and Cadres Trade Union*] [*Belgian*] (WER)
SETCI.......... Societe d'Extrusion et de Tissage de Cote-d'Ivoire (MAR)
SETCO .... Societe d'Editions Techniques Coloniales (MAR)
sete .... Setiembre [*September*] [*Spanish*]
SETEC .... Societe d'Etudes Techniques et de Coordination du Batiment (MAR)
SETEC .... Societe d'Etudes Techniques et Economiques [*Technical and Economic Studies Company*] [*French*] (AF)
SETEF......... Societe d'Etudes Economiques et Financieres (MAR)
SETEGA...... Servicios Tecnicos y Ganaderos [*Bogota*] (COL)
SETELEC.... Societe d'Etudes et Travaux d'Electricite (MAR)
SETEM........ Societe d'Etudes et de Travaux Electromecaniques (MAR)
SETEM........ Syndesmos Ergolipton Tekhnikon Ergon Makedonias [*Association of Macedonia Technical Projects Contractors*] (GC)
SETEN .... Secretariat d'Etat Tunisien a l'Education Nationale (MAR)
SETER......... Societe d'Etudes et de Travaux pour l'Electronique et la Radio (MAR)
SETETh....... Syndesmos Ergolipton Tekhnikon Ergon Thessalonikis [*Association of Salonica Technical Projects Contractors*] (GC)
SETH........... Societe d'Etudes et de Travaux Hydrauliques (MAR)
SETH........... Societe d'Exploitation de l'Hotel Tiama (MAR)
SETHEM ..... Societe d'Etudes Hydrauliques, Electriques, et Mecaniques (MAR)
SETI .... Service d'Etudes et Travaux d'Infrastructure [*Infrastructure Studies and Construction Service*] [*Algerian*] (AF)
SETI .... Societe d'Exploitation des Techniques Industrielles [*Industrial Techniques Exploitation Company*] [*Tunisian*] (AF)
SETIA.......... Sindicato de Empleados Textiles de la Industria y Afines de la Republica Argentina [*Union of Employees of the Textile and Related Industries of the Argentine Republic*] (LA)
SETIC.......... Societe d'Etudes des Industries du Ciment [*Senegalese*] (MAR)
SETIF .... Societe d'Etudes Techniques Industrielles et Frigorifiques (MAR)
SETIM .... Societe d'Etudes et de Coordination Industrielle Marocaine [*Moroccan Industrial Studies and Coordination Company*] (AF)
SETIMEG .... Societe Anonyme d'Etudes, de Travail Immobilier, et de Gestion (MAR)
Set'mash .... Khar'kov Electrical Network and Installation Machinery Plant (RU)
SETMC........ Societe d'Etudes Topographiques Maffone & Cie. (MAR)
SETOM........ Societe d'Etudes de Travaux d'Outre-Mer [*Overseas Projects Studies Company*] [*French*] (AF)
SETOP .... Secretaria de Transporte y Obras Publicas [*Secretariat of Transportation and Public Works*] [*Argentine*] (LA)
SETP .... Societe Soudanaise d'Entreprise et de TP (MAR)
SETR .... Societe d'Expansion et de Transformation des Resines (MAR)
SETRA .... Societe d'Etudes et de Travaux (MAR)
SETRA-Congo ... Societe d'Etudes et de Travaux au Congo (MAR)
SETRAPEM ... Societe Equatoriale de Travaux Petroliers Maritimes (MAR)
sett .... Settembre [*September*] [*Italian*]
SETT .... Societe d'Exploitation de Transports et de Taxis (MAR)
SETTAO...... Syndicat des Entrepreneurs de Transports et Transitaires de l'Afrique Occidentale (MAR)
SETTD......... Syndicat des Entrepreneurs de Transport et Transitaires de Dakar (MAR)
SETTE......... Societe d'Entreprise de Travaux Topographiques et d'Edition (MAR)
SETU........... Societe d'Equipement des Terrains Urbains (MAR)
SETUBA...... Societe d'Etudes et de Travaux pour l'Utilisation du Beton Arme (MAR)
SETUBA-Bangui ... Societe d'Etudes et de Travaux pour l'Utilisation du Beton Arme en Oubangui (MAR)
SETUBA-Cameroun ... Societe d'Etudes et de Travaux pour l'Utilisation du Beton Arme en Cameroun (MAR)
SETUBA-TCHAD ... Societe d'Etudes et de Travaux pour l'Utilisation du Beton Arme au Tchad (MAR)
SETUG .... Societe d'Etudes et de Gestion [*North African*] (MAR)
setzag .... Netlayer [*Navy*] (RU)
SEU .... Sindicato Espanol Universitario [*Spanish University Union*] (WER)
SEU .... Sociedad Editorial Uruguaya [*Uruguayan Publishing Society*] (LA)
SEU .... Studia Ethnographica Upsaliensia (MAR)
seuo .... Sulvo Error u Omision [*Spanish*]
seur .... Seuraava [*Following, Next*] [*Finnish*] (GPO)
SEURECA ... Societe d'Etudes pour l'Urbanisme, l'Equipement, et les Canalisations (MAR)
SEURMAD ... Societe d'Equipement Urbain et Rural de Madagascar (MAR)
seurr........... Seuraavat [*Finnish*]
SEUSS .... Sociedad de Estudiantes Universitarios San Salvador [*Association of San Salvador University Students*] [*Salvadoran*] (LA)
SEV .... Council for Mutual Economic Assistance [*CMEA*] (RU)
Sev .... North, Northern (RU)
sev.............. North, Northern (BU)
SEV .... Northern Railroad (RU)
SEV .... Sekundaer-Elektronvervielfacher [*Secondary Electron Emission Multiplier*] (EG)
sev.............. Severen [*Northern*] (YU)
SEV .... Slovenske Energeticke Vyrobne [*Slovak Electric Power Producing Plants*] (CZ)
SEV .... Societe d'Ethologie Veterinaire [*Society for Veterinary Ethology - SVE*] (EA)
SEV .... Societe d'Exploitation de Viandes (MAR)
SEV .... Srednje Evropsko Vreme [*Middle European Time*] (YU)
SEV .... Syndesmos Ellinon Viomikhanon [*Association of Greek Industrialists*] (GC)
SEVAM's..... Societe d'Exploitation de Verreir du Marocs (MAR)
SEVAP .... Syndesmos Ergaton Vyrsodepson Athinon-Peiraios [*Union of Athens-Piraeus Tannery Workers*] (GC)
Sev Dobr..... North Dobrudzha (BU)
Sevdvinlag ... Northern Dvina Corrective Labor Camp (RU)
SEVE........... (Pankypria) Syndekhnia Emborikon kai Viomikhanikon Ergatoypallilon [*(Pan-Cyprian) Union of Commercial and Industrial Workers*] [*Cypriot*] (GC)
SEVE........... Syndesmos Ergatotekhniton Viomikhanias Elastikou [*Union of Rubber Industry Workers and Technicians*] [*Greek*] (GC)
SEVEGEP.... Synergatiki Etaireia Viomikhanikis Epexergasias Agrotikis Paragogis [*Cooperative Company for Industrial Processing of Agricultural Produce*] [*Cypriot*] (GC)
Severenergo ... Northern Power Administration (BU)
SEVIMA....... Societe d'Exploitation de la Viande a Madagascar (MAR)
Sev-Kav ...... North Caucasian (RU)
Sevl O S...... Sevlievo Oblast Court (BU)
SEVMACAM ... Societe d'Exploitation et de Colorisation des Marbres, Cipolins, et Aragonites a Madagascar (MAR)
Sevmorbaza ... Sevastopol' Naval Base (RU)
Sevmorput' ... Northern Sea Route (RU)
Sevmorzavod ... Sevastopol' Shipyard (RU)
SevNIIGiM... Northern Scientific Research Institute of Hydraulic Engineering and Reclamation (RU)
SevNIIGM.... Northern Scientific Research Institute of Hydraulic Engineering and Reclamation (RU)
SevNIIP .... Northern Scientific Research Industrial Institute (RU)
SEVOL .... Societe d'Equipement de la Haute-Volta (MAR)
SEVOP .... Syndesmos Ellinon Viomikhanon Oinon kai Poton [*Association of Greek Industrialists of Wines and Beverages*] (GC)
SEVT........... Statisticke a Evidencni Vydavatelstvi Tiskopisu [*Publishing House for Statistical and Record Forms*] (CZ)
Sevurallag ... Northern Ural Corrective Labor Camps (RU)

sev-vost ...... Northeast, Northeastern (RU)
Sevvostlag ... Northeastern Corrective Labor Camps (RU)
sev-zap .... Northwest, Northwestern (RU)
Sevzapgiprogorsel'stroy ... Northwestern State Planning Institute for the Planning of Urban and Rural Construction (RU)
SEVZAPPROYeKTPORTIZ ... Administration for the Study and Planning of the Northern and Western Ports (RU)
Sevzaptransles ... Northwestern Lumber Transportation Trust (RU)
Sevzheldorlag ... Northern Railroad Corrective Labor Camp (RU)
SEW .... Societe des Etablissements Wanner (MAR)
SEW .... Sozialistische Einheitspartei Westberlins [*Socialist Unity Party of West Berlin*] [*West German*] (PPW)
SEWMRPG ... Southern European-Western Mediterranean Regional Planning Group (MAR)
S Exc .... Son Excellence [*His (or Her) Excellency*] [*French*] (CL)
S Excia .... Sua Excel(l)encia [*His Excellency*] [*Portuguese*] (GPO)
SEYD .... Subay Esleri Yardimlasma Dernegi [*Officers Wives Mutual Aid Society*] (TU)
SEYET .... Syndikalistiki Enotita Ypallilon Ethnikis Trapezis [*Syndicalist Unity of National Bank Employees*] [*Greek*] (GC)
sez .... Sezione [*Section*] [*Italian*]
SEZ .... Slovenske Elektrotechnicke Zavody [*Slovak Electrical Equipment Plants*] (CZ)
SEZb .... Srpski Etnografski Zbornik [*Serbian Ethnographic Papers*] [*Issued by the Serbian Academy*] (YU)
SEZID .... Societe d'Equipement des Zones d'Industrialisation Decentralisee [*Decentralized Industrialization Area Equipment Company*] [*French*] (WER)
SF .... Finlandia [*Finland*] [*Polish*]
SF .... Northern Fleet (RU)
SF .... Photon Counter (RU)
SF .... Sameignarfelag [*Partnership*] [*Icelandic*] (CED)
SF .... Sans Frais [*French*]
SF .... Security Forces [*Malaysian*] (ML)
SF .... Sicherungs- und Fernmeldewesen [*Protective Devices and Telecommunications*] [*See also SFW, SuF*] (EG)
sf .... Sin Fecha [*No Date*] [*Spanish*]
SF .... Slovenska Filharmonia [*Slovak Philharmonic Orchestra*] (CZ)
SF .... Socialist Front [*Malaysian*] (ML)
SF .... Socialistisk Folkeparti [*Socialist People's Party*] [*Danish*] (WEN)
SF .... Soma Frondiston [*Quartermaster Corps*] (GC)
SF .... Sosialistisk Folkepartiet [*Socialist People's Party*] [*Norwegian*] (PPE)
SF .... Soviet Fleet (RU)
SF- .... Spectrophotometer (RU)
SF .... Sport Fotanacs [*Main Sports Council*] (HU)
SF .... Statni Filharmonie [*State Philharmonic*] (CZ)
SFA .... Sarawak Farmers Association (Communist) (ML)
SFA .... Societe Forestiere d'Azingo (MAR)
SFA .... Soviet Philatelic Association (RU)
SFA .... Sudan Football Association (MAR)
SFAB .... Societe Franco-Africaine des Bois (MAR)
SFAB .... Svenska Flygmotor AB [*Swedish Airplane Motor Corp.*] [*Swedish*] (WEN)
SFAC .... Societe Fermiere Agricole et Commerciale de Mananjary (MAR)
SFAC .... Societe des Forges et Ateliers du Creusot [*French*]
SFACOM-Dahomey ... Societe Francaise pour le Developpement du Commerce au Dahomey (MAR)
SFACS .... Societe Forestiere Agricole et Commerciale do Sombadjeck (MAR)
SFAD .... Societe Forestiere Andre Desbrosses (MAR)
SFADECO ... Societe Franco-Africaine d'Expansion Commerciale (MAR)
SFADO .... Societe Francaise d'Approvisionnement et Distribution (MAR)
SFAE .... Societe Franco Africaine d'Exploitation (MAR)
SFAG .... Societe Financiere et Auxiliaire de Gestion (MAR)
SFAG .... Societe Forestiere et Agricole du Gabon (MAR)
SFAL .... Societe Forestiere Africaine de la Louali (MAR)
SFAT .... Societe Franco-Africaine de Transports (MAR)
SFB .... Sender Freies Berlin [*Radio Free Berlin*] [*West German*] (WEN)
SFBL .... Societe Forestiere Bertrand-Lupo (MAR)
SFBO .... Societe Forestiere du Bas-Ogooue (MAR)
SFBP .... Societe Francaise des Petroles BP (MAR)
SFBS .... Spoleczny Fundusz Budowy Stolicy [*People's Fund for the Construction of Warsaw*] (POL)
SFBS .... Spoleczny Fundusz Budowy Szkol [*Social School Construction Fund*] (POL)
SFBSil .... Spoleczny Fundusz Budowy Szkol i Internatow [*Social Fund for the Construction of Schools and Boarding Schools*] (POL)
SFBW .... Spoleczny Fundusz Budowy Warszawy [*People's Fund for the Construction of Warsaw*] (POL)
SFC .... Societe Forestiere du Cameroun (MAR)
SFC .... State Farms Corporation (MAR)
SFC .... State Fishing Corporation (MAR)
SFCE .... Societe Francaise du Commerce Europeen (MAR)
SFCM .... Societe Francaise de Commerce a Madagascar (MAR)
SFCT .... Societe Franco-Camerounaise des Tabacs (MAR)
SFD- .... Diffraction Spectrophotometer (RU)
SFD .... Societe Forestiere de Dolisie (MAR)
SFDA .... Societe Forestiere Delbeil et Antoine (MAR)
SFDC .... Societe Financiere pour le Developpement du Cameroun (MAR)
SF/DE/SKKE ... Sosialismos Filelevtheron/Dimokratiki Enosis/Sosialistiko Komma Kinima Ellados [*Liberals' Socialism/Democratic Union/Socialist Party Movement of Greece*] [*Greek*] (GC)
SFDIC .... Societe Francaise des Distilleries d'Indochine [*French Distillery Company of Indochina*] (CL)
SFDL .... Societe Forestiere du Dja et Lobo (MAR)
SFDM .... Svetova Federace Demokraticke Mladeze [*World Federation of Democratic Youth*] (CZ)
SFDO .... Svetska Federacija Demokratske Omladine [*World Federation of Democratic Youth*] (YU)
SFDP .... Special Fisheries Development Project (MAR)
SFDTUC ...... Sarawak First Division Trade Union Congress (ML)
SFDZ .... Svetova Federace Demokratickych Zen [*World Federation of Democratic Women*] (CZ)
SFE .... Societe Financiere Europeenne (MAR)
SFE .... Societe Forestiere d'Ezanga (MAR)
SFE .... Societe Francaise des Electriciens [*French*]
SFEB .... Societe Francaise d'Etudes du Batiment (MAR)
SFEDTP ...... Societe Francaise d'Entreprises de Dragages et de Travaux Publics (MAR)
SFEM .... Societe Forestiere et d'Entretien Mecanique (MAR)
sfenoid .... Sphenoidal (RU)
SFERMA ..... Societe Francaise d'Entretien et de Reparation de Materiel Aeronautique [*French*]
SFES .... Sindicato de Fotografos de El Salvador [*Union of Photographers of El Salvador*] (LA)
SFF .... Skopski Filozofski Fakultet [*Faculty of Philosophy in Skopje*] (YU)
SFF .... Staatlicher Futtermittelfonds [*State Fodder Fund*] (EG)
SFFA .... System der Fehlerfreien Arbeit [*System of Error-Free Work*] (EG)
SFFAI .... Societe Francaise de Fournitures pour l'Automobile et l'Industrie (MAR)
SFG .... Societe Forestiere de la Goree (MAR)
SFGT .... Societe Forestiere Georges Thomas (MAR)
SFHL .... Societe Forestiere de la Haute-Lobaye (MAR)
SFHM .... Sondages Forages Hydrogeologiques et Miniers (MAR)
SFI .... Savezni Finansiski Inspektorat (DSPF) [*Federal Financial Inspectorate*] (YU)
SFI .... Sindacato Ferrovieri Italiani [*Union of Italian Railroad Workers*] (WER)
SFI .... Societe Financiere Internationale [*International Finance Corporation*] [*Use IFC*] (CL)
SFI .... Societe Forestiere d'Iguela (MAR)
SFI .... Societe Forestiere d'Issia (MAR)
SFI .... Societe de Froid et d'Importation (MAR)
SFIA .... Societe Forestiere et Industrielle de l'Azobe (MAR)
SFIC .... Societe Financiere et Immobiliere Couret (MAR)
SFID .... Societe Forestiere et Industrielle de la Doume (MAR)
SFIL .... Societe Forestiere Industrielle de la Lokoundje (MAR)
SFIM .... Societe Forestiere et Industrielle de la Makobe (MAR)
SFIM .... Societe Forestiere et Industrielle de Man (MAR)
SFIO .... Section Francaise de l'Internationale Ouvriere [*French Section of the Workers International (French Socialist Party)*] (WER)
SFIS .... Societe Forestiere et Industrielle de la Sangha (MAR)
SFIT .... Societe Franco-Ivoirienne de Transports (MAR)
SFJ .... Savez Filatelista Jugoslavije [*Federation of Yugoslav Philatelists*] (YU)
SFJA .... Service de la Formation des Jeunes en Algerie (MAR)
SFK .... Council of Physical Culture (RU)
SFK .... Northern Fergana Canal (RU)
SFK .... Rural Physical Culture Collective (BU)
SFK .... Savet za Fizicku Kulturu (SIV) [*Council on Physical Culture*] (YU)
SFK .... Selbstfahrkanone [*Self-Propelled Gun*] (EG)
SFK .... Sosyalist Fikir Klubu [*Socialist Idea Club*] (TU)
SFKD .... Swiatowa Federacja Kobiet Demokratycznych [*Polish*]
SFKh .... Collection of Regulations, Orders, and Instructions on Financial and Economic Problems (RU)
SFKhV .... Collection of Regulations, Orders, and Instructions on Financial and Economic Problems (RU)
SFKp .... Selbstfahrerlafettenkompanie [*Assault Gun Company*] (EG)
SFL .... Selbstfahrlafette [*Self-Propelled Carriage (Self-propelled gun)*] (EG)
SFL .... Syndicat des Fonctionnaires du Laos [*Lao Government Employees Union*] (CL)
SFLG .... Societe Forestiere du Lac Gome (MAR)
SFLG .... Societe Forestiere du Littoral Gabonais (MAR)
SFM .... Signal- und Fernmeldemeisterei [*Signal and Telecommunications Group*] (EG)
SFM .... Societe Forestiere du Maine (MAR)
SFM .... Societe Francaise des Mecaniciens
SFM .... Swiatowa Federacja Mlodziezy [*Polish*]
SFMB .... Swiatowa Federacja Miast Blizniaczych [*World Federation of Twin Cities*] [*Polish*]
SFMD .... Swiatowa Federacja Mlodziezy Demokratycznej [*World Federation of Democratic Youth*] (POL)

SFMD .... Swiatowy Festiwal Mlodziezy Demokratycznej [*World Festival of Democratic Youth*] (POL)
SFMex .... Sociedad Forestal de Mexico
SFMK .... Societe Forestiere de Mouyondzi Kintouka (MAR)
SFMO .... Societe Forestiere du Moyen Ogooue (MAR)
SFMS .... Societe Forestiere du Maine-Senegal (MAR)
SFN .... Sistema Financiero Nacional [*National Financial System*] [*Nicaraguan*] (LA1)
SFN .... Societe Forestiere du Niari (MAR)
SFND .... Societatea Franceza de Navigatie Danubiana [*French Society for Navigation of the Danube*] (RO)
SFNG .... Societe Forestiere de la N'gounie (MAR)
SFNI .... Suikerfabrieknavorsingsinstituut (MAR)
SFNL .... Societe Forestiere du Nyong et Lobo (MAR)
SFNO .... Sklad Fondu Narodni Obnovy [*Depot of the National Reconstruction Fund*] (CZ)
SFO .... Seefrachtordnung [*Ocean Freight Regulation*] (EG)
SFO .... Spoleczny Fundusz Oszczedzania [*People's Savings Fund*] (POL)
SFO .... Svetova Federace Odboru [*World Federation of Trade-Unions*] (CZ)
SFOA .... Societe Financiere de l'Ouest Africain [*Senegalese*] (MAR)
SFOA .... Spoudazousa Foititiki Organosis Athinon [*Athens Organization of Enrolled Students*] (GC)
SFOI .... Saint-Freres Ocean Indien (MAR)
SFOKiS .... Spoleczny Fundusz Odbudowy Kraju i Stolicy [*Social Fund for Rebuilding the Counry and the Capital (1948-1956)*] [*Polish*]
SFOM .... Societe Financiere pour les Pays d'Outre-Mer [*Overseas Finance Company*] [*French*] (AF)
SFOPP .... Spoleczny Fabryczny Osrodek Propagandy Partyjnej [*Plant Social Party Propaganda Center*] (POL)
SFOR .... Spoleczny Fundusz Oszczednosciowy Rolnictwa [*Farmers' Community Savings Fund*] (POL)
SFOS .... Spoleczny Fundusz Odbudowy Stolicy [*People's Fund for the Reconstruction of Warsaw*] (POL)
SFP .... Sociedade Financeira Portuguesa [*Portuguese Financial Society*] (WER)
SFP .... Svaz Filmovych Pracovniku [*Union of Film Workers*] (CZ)
SFP .... Svenska Folkpartiet [*Swedish People's Party*] [*Finnish*] (PPE)
SFP .... Syllogos Foititon Peiraios [*Piraeus Students Club*] (GC)
SFP .... World Federation of Trade-Unions (BU)
SFPN .... Swiatowa Federacja Pracownikow Nauki [*World Federation of Scientific Workers*] (POL)
SFPP .... Sanidad de las Fuerzas Policiales del Peru [*Health Service of the Peruvian Police Forces*] (LA)
SFPR .... Servico Federal de Prevencao e Repressao (aos Crimes Contra e Fazenda Nacional) [*Federal Service for Prevention and Suppression (of Crimes Against the National Treasury)*] [*Brazilian*] (LA)
SFPS .... Postal Courier Communications Station (BU)
SFPS .... World Federation of Trade-Unions (BU)
SFR .... Calculation of Financial Estimate (RU)
SFR .... Streak Camera (RU)
SFRA .... Societe Francaise de Representation pour l'Afrique (MAR)
SFRJ .... Socjalistyczna Federacyjna Republika Jugoslawii [*Socialist Federative Republic of Yugoslavia*] [*Polish*]
SFRJ .... Sozialistische Foederative Republik Jugoslawien [*Socialist Federative Republic of Yugoslavia*] [*West German*] (WEN)
SFRM .... Societe de Fabrications Radioelectriques Marocaines (MAR)
SFRV .... Schweizerische Fernseh- und Radio-Vereinigung [*Swiss Television and Radio Broadcasting Association*] (WEN)
SFRYu .... Socialist Federated Republic of Yugoslavia (BU)
SFRYu .... Socialist Federated Republic of Yugoslavia (RU)
SFS .... Societe Forestiere de Sangha (MAR)
SFS .... Srpska Fabrika Stakla [*Serbian Glass Factory*] [*Paracin*] (YU)
SFS .... Sveriges Forenade Studentkarer [*Swedish United Student Union*] (WEN)
SFSF .... Svenska Freds ochs Skiljedomsforeningen [*Swedish Society for Peace Arbitration*] (WEN)
SFSM .... Societe Fonciere du Sud de Madagascar (MAR)
SF-SN .... Smrt Fasizmu - Sloboda Narodu [*Death to Fascism - Freedom to the People*] [*Standard phrase in official documents*] (YU)
SFT .... Scierie, Foret, Transport (MAR)
SFT .... Societe Forestiere Tropicale (MAR)
SFT .... Societe Francaise des Traducteurs [*French Society of Translators*]
SFT .... Sport Fotanacs [*Main Sports Council*] (HU)
SFT .... Standard Fuel Tonnes [*Arab*] (MAR)
SFTB .... Societe Forestiere Tailleur & Baizet (MAR)
SFTI .... Siberian Physicotechnical Institute (RU)
SFTU .... Swaziland Federation of Trade Unions (MAR)
SFU .... Statni Fotomericky Ustav [*State Institute of Photogrammetry*] (CZ)
SFUFNRJ .... Savez Farmaceutskih Udruzenja FNRJ [*Federation of Pharmaceutical Associations of Yugoslavia*] (YU)
SFUP .... Swidnicka Fabryka Urzadzen Przemyslowych [*Swidnica (Schweidnitz) Industrial Equipment Factory*] (POL)
SFVP .... Svetova Federacia Vedeckych Pracovnikov [*World Federation of Scientific Workers*] (CZ)
SFVU .... Slovensky Fond Vytvarnych Umeni [*Slovak Creative Arts Foundation*] (CZ)
SFW .... Sicherungs- und Fernmeldewesen [*Blocking and Telecommunications (Railroad) System*] (EG)
SFW .... Signal- und Fernmeldewesen [*Signal and Telecommunications System*] (EG)
SFW .... Stellenbosch Farmers' Winery (MAR)
SFWTU .... Sudan Federation of Workers' Trades Unions (MAR)
SFZZ .... Swiatowa Federacja Zwiazkow Zawodowych [*World Federation of Trade Unions*] [*Polish*]
sg .... Centigram (RU)
SG .... Cophasal Horizontal [*Antenna*] (RU)
SG- .... Depth Recorder (RU)
SG .... Goryunov Heavy (Machine Gun) (RU)
SG .... Sa Grandeur [*His Grace*] [*French*] (MTD)
sg .... Same Year (BU)
Sg .... Schnellgueterzug [*Fast Freight Train*] (EG)
SG .... Secretaire General [*Secretary General*] (CL)
SG .... Secretaria de Gobernacion [*Secretariat of Government*] [*Mexican*] (LA)
SG .... Secretariat General [*Secretariat General*] (CL)
SG .... Secretary General (MAR)
SG .... Service Geographique (MAR)
Sg .... Sgeir [*Rock*] [*Gaelic*] (NAU)
SG .... Sicherheitsgruppe [*Security Group*] [*West German*] (EG)
SG .... Signal Generator (RU)
sg .... Signalman (BU)
SG .... Singapore [*Two-letter standard code*] (CNC)
sg .... Singulaari, Yksikko [*Singular*] [*Finnish*]
SG .... Skolsko Gadanje [*Target Practice*] (YU)
SG .... Social Hygiene (RU)
SG .... Societe Generale de Credit (MAR)
sg .... Sogenannt [*So-Called*] [*German*]
sG .... Spezifisches Gewicht [*Specific Gravity*] [*German*]
SG .... Spoldzielnia Gminna [*Rural Commune Cooperative*] (POL)
SG .... Sudan Government (MAR)
SG .... Sumsko Gazdinstvo [*Forestry Management*] (YU)
SG .... Synchronous Generator (RU)
sg .... This Year, Current Year (RU)
SG .... Welding Torch (RU)
SGA .... Main Air Depot (RU)
SGA .... Sekolah Guru Atas [*Senior Teachers School*] (IN)
SGA .... Societe Gabonaise d'Assainissement (MAR)
SGA .... Societe de Geologie Appliquee aux Gites Mineraux [*Society of Geology Applied to Mineral Deposits*] (EA)
SGAC .... Secretariat General d'Aviation Civile [*Secretariat General for Civil Aviation*] [*French*] (CL)
SGAC .... Societe Gabonaise d'Assurances et Courtage (MAR)
SGAEI .... Societe Gabonaise d'Amenagement et d'Equipement Immobiliers (MAR)
SGAIMK .... Communications of the State Academy of the History of Material Culture [*A publication*] (RU)
SGAMS .... Services Generaux Autonome de la Maladie du Sommeil (MAR)
SGAU .... Sofia City Pharmacy Administration (BU)
SGAV .... Statisztikai Gepi Adatfeldolgozo Vallalat [*Enterprise for Mechanical Processing of Statistical Data*] (HU)
SGB .... Schweizerischer Gewerkschaftsbund [*Swiss Trade Union Federation*] (WEN)
SGB .... Societe Gabonaise des Bois (MAR)
SGB .... Societe Generale de Banque au Cameroun (MAR)
SGB .... Societe Generale de Belgique (MAR)
SGB .... Societe Nationale des Grands Barrages [*National Large Dam Company*] [*Use SNGB*] [*Cambodian*] (CL)
SGB .... Sozialistischer Grosshandelsbetrieb [*Socialist Wholesale Enterprise*] (EG)
SGB .... Sudan Gezira Board (MAR)
SGBC .... Societe Generale de Banques au Cameroun [*General Banking Company of Cameroon*] (AF)
SGBC .... Societe Generale de Banques au Congo (MAR)
SGBCI .... Societe Generale de Banques en Cote-d'Ivoire [*General Banking Company of the Ivory Coast*] (AF)
SGBM .... Societe Guineenne de Beton Manufacture (MAR)
SGBS .... Societe General de Banque du Senegal [*General Banking Company of Senegal*] (AF)
SGC .... Societe Generale de Construction [*General Construction Company*] [*Zairian*] (AF)
SGCFG .... Societe de Gestion de la Compagnie Francaise du Gabon (MAR)
SGCI .... Societe Generale de la Cote-d'Ivoire (MAR)
SGCTP .... Societe Gabonaise de Constructions de TP (MAR)
SGD .... Srpsko Geografsko Drustvo [*Serbian Geographical Society*] (YU)
SGD .... Storehouse for Finished Parts (RU)
SGDG .... Sans Garantie du Gouvernement [*Without Government Guarantee*] [*French*] (WER)
SGDR .... Societe Gabonaise de Developpement Rural (MAR)
SGDT .... Societe de Gestion du Depot de Tamatave (MAR)
SGE .... All-Union Helminthological Expedition (RU)
SGE .... Service de Lutte Contre les Grandes Endemies (MAR)
SGE .... Societe Gabonaise d'Entreposage (MAR)
SGE .... Societe Gabonaise d'Entreprises (MAR)

SGE .... Societe Generale d'Electricite (MAR)
SGE .... Societe Generale d'Entreprise [*French*]
SGE .... Societe Guineenne d'Equipement [*Guinean Equipment Company*] (AF)
SGEA .... Societe Generale d'Entreprise d'Algerie (MAR)
SGEEM .... Societe Generale d'Entreprises Electromecaniques (MAR)
SGEFE .... Syndonistikon Grafeion Ellinon Foititon Exoterikou [*Coordinating Bureau of Greek Students Abroad*] (GC)
SGEFI .... Syndonistikon Grafeion Ellinon Foititon Italias [*Coordinating Office for Greek Students in Italy*] (GC)
SGEG .... Syndicat General de l'Education en Guadeloupe (PD)
SGEH .... Societe Gabonaise d'Etude Hoteliere (MAR)
SGEI .... Societe Gabonaise d'Etudes et Interventions (MAR)
SGEK .... Stathmoi Georgikis Erevnis kai Ktinotrofias [*Agricultural Research and Animal Breeding Stations*] [*Greek*] (GC)
SGEN .... Syndicat General de l'Education Nationale [*French*]
SGEP .... Sindicatura General de Empresas Publicas [*General Trusteeship of Public Enterprises*] [*Argentine*] (LA)
SGEPC .... Societe Guineenne d'Engrais et de Produits Chimiques (MAR)
SGEPP .... Societe Gabonaise d'Entreposage de Produits Petroliers (MAR)
SGES .... Centimeter/Gram/Erg/Second (RU)
SGET .... Sofia City Electric Transport (BU)
SGETP .... Societe Gabonaise d'Entreprises de Travaux Publics (MAR)
SGETPI .... Societe Generale d'Entreprises pour les Travaux Publics & Industriels (MAR)
SGF .... Societe Ganamet Freres (MAR)
SGF .... Societe Generale Fonciere (MAR)
SGGG .... Societe Generale du Golfe de Guinee (MAR)
SGGG-Togo ... Societe Generale du Golfe de Guinee-Togo (MAR)
SGGiD .... Collection of State Deeds and Treaties (RU)
SGGW .... Szkola Glowna Gospodarstwa Wiejskiego [*Central School of Agriculture*] (POL)
SGH .... Szkola Glowna Handlowa [*Main School of Commerce*] (POL)
SGHC .... Societe des Grands Hotels du Cameroun (MAR)
SGHMP .... Service Generale d'Hygiene Mobile et de Prophylaxie (MAR)
SGI .... Societe de Gestion d'Interets (MAR)
SGI .... Sverdlovsk Mining Institute Imeni V. V. Vakhrushev (RU)
SGIA .... Societe de Gerances Industrielles et Agricoles (MAR)
SGIFK .... Smolensk State Institute of Physical Culture (RU)
SGiP .... Soviet State and Law (RU)
SGJ .... Statisticki Godisnjak Federativna Narodna Republika Jugoslavija [*Statistical Yearbook of Yugoslavia*] [*A publication*] (YU)
SGK .... Horizontal Seismograph Designed by Kirnos (RU)
SGK .... Savezna Gradevinska Komora [*Federal Chamber of Construction*] (YU)
SGK .... Staatliche Geologische Kommission [*State Geological Commission*] (EG)
SGL .... Schulgemeinschaftsleitung [*School Community Leadership*] (EG)
S/Gl .... Secretaire General [*Secretary General*] [*Cambodian*] (CL)
sgl .... Sklad Glowny [*Main Warehouse*] (POL)
SGl .... Sumarski Glasnik [*Forestry Bulletin*] [*Belgrade*] [*A publication*] (YU)
SGM .... Goryunov Modernized Heavy (Machine Gun) (RU)
SGM .... Scottish Geographical Magazine [*Edinburgh*] [*A publication*] (MAR)
SGM .... Scripture Gift Mission (MAR)
SGM .... Societe Gabonaise de Mecanique (MAR)
SGM .... Societe Generale de Minerais [*General Ores Company*] [*Zairian*] (AF)
SGM .... Syndicat des Gens de Mer (MAR)
SGMB .... Societe Generale Marocaine de Banques (MAR)
SGMC .... State Gold Mining Corporation (MAR)
SGMI .... Saratov State Medical Institute (RU)
SGMI .... Sverdlovsk State Medical Institute (RU)
SGMT .... Societe Generale des Moulins du Togo (MAR)
SGMT .... Sverdlovsk Mining and Metallurgical Technicum Imeni I. I. Polzunov (RU)
SGMTP .... Service de Gestion du Materiel des Travaux Publics [*Public Works Equipment Management Department*] [*Zairian*] (AF)
SGN .... Group Carrier Bay (RU)
SGN- .... Nephelometer (RU)
SGN .... Societe Gabonaise de Negoce (MAR)
SGNCh- .... Low-Frequency Seismic Generator (RU)
SGNS .... Sofia City People's Council (BU)
SGNSDT ..... Sofia City People's Council of Working People's Deputies (BU)
SGO .... Group Equipment Bay (RU)
SGO .... Societe Gabonaise de l'Okoume (MAR)
SGODA .... Sofia City and Okrug State Archives (BU)
SGOM .... Societe de Gestion pour l'Outre-Mer (MAR)
SGOPC .... Sindicato Gremial de Obreros de Productos de Cemento [*Union of Cement Products Workers*] [*Salvadoran*] (LA)
SGP- .... Gas-Pressure Welding Machine (RU)
SGP .... Group Conversion Bay (RU)
SGP .... Sindicato Gremial de Peleteros [*Union of Leather Workers*] [*Salvadoran*] (LA)
SGP .... Singapore [*Three-letter standard code*] (CNC)
SGP .... Sistema General de Preferencias [*General Preference System*] (LA)
SGP .... Staatkundig Gereformeerde Partij [*Political Reformed Party*] [*Dutch*] (PPE)
SGP .... Storehouse for Finished Products (RU)
SGP .... Stowarzyszenie Geodetow Polskich [*Association of Polish Geodesists*] (POL)
SGP .... Sumsko Gradevinsko Preduzece [*Forestry Construction Establishment*] (YU)
SGPA .... Sovjetska Glavna Pomorska Agencija [*Soviet Central Maritime Agency*] [*Belgrade*] (YU)
SGPI .... Saratov State Pedagogical Institute (RU)
SGPI .... Smolensk State Pedagogical Institute Imeni Karl Marx (RU)
SGPI .... Stalinabad State Pedagogical Institute Imeni T. G. Shevchenko (RU)
SGPI .... Sverdlovsk State Pedagogical Institute (RU)
SGPIS .... Szkola Glowna Planowania i Statystyki [*Main School of Planning and Statistics*] (POL)
SGPK .... All-Union Geological Exploration Office (RU)
SGPT .... Societe Generale de Photo-Topographie (MAR)
SGPU .... Northern Mining Industry Administration (RU)
S Gr .... Sa Grandeur [*French*]
SGR .... Saudi Government Railroad (MAR)
SGR .... Service General du Renseignement [*General Intelligence Service*] [*Belgian*] (WER)
Sgr .... Sgeir [*Rock*] [*Gaelic*] (NAU)
Sgr .... Silbergroschen [*Old Prussian coin worth about 2 1/2 cents*] [*German*]
SGR .... Slovenska Glasbena Revija [*Slovenian Musical Journal*] [*Ljubljana*] [*A publication*] (YU)
SGR .... Societe Guineenne de Revetements (MAR)
SGR .... Spanski Gradanski Rat [*Spanish Civil War*] (YU)
SGRA .... Special Horizontal Photographic Reproduction Apparatus (RU)
SGRRO .... Saudi Government Railroad Organization (MAR)
SGRT .... Societe Gabonaise de Radio et Television (MAR)
SGS .... Centimeter-Gram-Second [*System of units*] (RU)
SGS .... Hydrographic Service Vessel (RU)
SGS .... Societe Gabonaise de Sciace (MAR)
SGS .... Societe Generale de Surveillance (MAR)
SGS .... Sudan Gezira Scheme (MAR)
SGSB .... Staatliches Guss- und Schmiedebuero, Berlin [*Berlin State Casting and Forging Office*] (EG)
SGSE .... Cgs Electrostatic System (RU)
SGSM .... Cgs Electromagnetic System (RU)
SGSM .... Fuel and Lubricants Depot (RU)
SGSR .... Generator and Compressor-Expander Frame (RU)
SGSZ .... Szkola Glowna Sluzby Zagranicznej [*Main School for the Foreign Service*] (POL)
sgt .... Segedtiszt [*Adjutant, Aide-de-Camp*] (HU)
Sgt .... Sergent [*Sergeant*] [*Military*] [*French*] (MTD)
SGT .... Societe Generale de Transports [*Moroccan*] (MAR)
SGT .... Societe Guineenne de Transport (MAR)
SGTC .... Service General des Troupes Coloniales (MAR)
SGTC .... Societe Gabonaise de Transports et de Carrieres (MAR)
SGTE .... Societe Generale de Techniques et d'Etudes (MAR)
SGTE .... Societe Generale de Traction et d'Exploitations (MAR)
SGTICES .... Sindicato General de Trabajadores de la Industria de la Construccion de El Salvador [*General Union of Workers of the Construction Industry of El Salvador*] (LA)
SGTM .... Societe Generale des Transports Maritimes [*French*]
SGTMA .... Societe Gabonaise de Transports Maritimes et d'Affretement (MAR)
SGTS .... Societe Generale Textiles et Soieries (MAR)
SGU .... Northern Geodetic Administration (RU)
SGU .... Saratov State University Imeni N. G. Chernyshevskiy (RU)
SGU .... Savezna Geodetska Uprava [*Federal Geodetic Administration*] (YU)
SGU .... Schweizerische Gesellschaft fuer Umweltschutz [*Swiss Association for Environmental Protection*] (WEN)
SGU .... Slovensky Geologicky Urad [*Slovak Geological Office*] (CZ)
SGU .... Smolensk State University (RU)
SGU .... Statni Geologicky Ustav CSR [*State Geological Institute of the Czechoslovak Republic*] (CZ)
SGU .... Statny Geologicky Ustav [*State Geological Institute*] (CZ)
SGV .... Northern Group of Armed Forces (RU)
SGWTU .... Sudan Government Workers' Trade Union (MAR)
SGWTUF ..... Sudan Government Workers' Trade-Union Federation (MAR)
SGZ .... Srpski Gradanski Zakonik [*Serbian Civil Code*] (YU)
Sh- .... Aircraft Designed by V. B. Shavrov (RU)
Sh .... Glider Designed by Sheremet'yev (RU)
sh .... Highway (RU)
sh .... Latitude (RU)
Sh .... Loose Fit (RU)
Sh .... Powdered Coal (RU)
Sh .... Sahife [*Page*] (TU)
Sh .... Sahra [*Field*] (TU)
SH .... St. Helena [*Two-letter standard code*] (CNC)
SH .... Sanayi Holding [*Industrial Holding Corporation*] [*Turkish Cypriot*] (GC)
SH .... Sardjana Hukum [*Bachelor of Laws*] (IN)
Sh .... Schutzhaltesignal [*Protective Stop Signal*] (EG)

sh .... Shillinki(a) [*Finnish*]
Sh .... Shturmovik [*Attack aircraft*] (RU)
Sh .... Staff, Headquarters (RU)
SH .... Svaz Zamestnancu v Hornictvi [*Mineworkers Union*] (CZ)
ShA .... Attack Aviation (RU)
SHA .... Sosyal Hizmetler Akademisi [*Social Services Academy*] (TU)
ShAAZ .... Shadrinsk Automobile Subassembly Plant (RU)
SHAC .... Societe Havraise Africaine de Commerce (MAR)
SHAC .... Societe Hoteliere d'Afrique Centrale (MAR)
SHAC .... Societe Hussein Ayad & Cie. (MAR)
ShAD .... Attack Air Division (RU)
ShAE .... Attack Air Squadron (RU)
ShAGES .... Shatura State Electric Power Plant (RU)
shakh .... Checkerboard Arrangement (RU)
shakh .... Mine, Shaft [*Topography*] (RU)
shakhm .... Chess (RU)
ShakhtNIUI ... Shakhty Scientific Research, Planning and Design Institute of Coal (RU)
Shakhtospetsstroy ... State Trust for Construction and Sinking of Shafts of the Glavspetspromstroy [*RSFSR*] (RU)
Shaks .... Shakespearella [*Shakespeare*] [*Finnish*]
ShAL .... [*An*] Extensive Air Shower, Auger Shower (RU)
ShAP .... Attack Air Regiment (RU)
SHAS .... Sephardi Torah Guardians [*Israeli political party*]
ShAU .... Wide-Band Antenna Amplifier (RU)
ShB .... Disciplinary Battalion (RU)
SHB .... Samenwerkende Havenbedrijven [*Co-operating Harbor Concerns*] [*Dutch*] (WEN)
SHB .... Societe Hoteliere du Barachois (MAR)
SHB .... Societe Hotelleries de Bamako (MAR)
SHB .... Societe Hydroelectrique de Boali (MAR)
SHB .... Sozialdemokratischer Hochschulbund [*Social Democratic University Student Association*] [*West German*] (EG)
ShBM .... Drum-Type Ball Mill (RU)
SHC .... Societe Hoteliere du Cambodge [*Hotel Company of Cambodia*] (CL)
SHC .... State Housing Corporation (MAR)
Shch .... Crushed Stone [*Road-paving material*] [*Topography*] (RU)
ShchDU .... Remote-Control Panel (RU)
ShchE .... Aircraft Designed by S. O. Shcherbakov (RU)
shchel .... Alkaline (RU)
shchel-zem ... Alkaline-Earth (RU)
shchet .... Brush (RU)
ShchKD .... Jaw Crusher (RU)
ShchMPB .... Alkaline Meat-Peptone Bouillon (RU)
shch oks .... Alkali Metal Oxalate (RU)
ShchOM .... Crushed Stone Cleaning Machine (RU)
ShchSP .... Fuse Panel of the Switch Control Relay [*Railroads*] (RU)
ShchU- .... Control Panel (RU)
shch/ub .... Slit Shelter [*Topography*] (RU)
ShchUK .... Oxalacetic Acid (RU)
ShchVP .... Auxiliary Instrument Panel (RU)
SHCJ .... Society of the Holy Child Jesus (MAR)
SHCP .... Secretaria de Hacienda y Credito Publico [*Secretariat of Finance and Public Credit*] [*Mexican*] (LA)
SHD .... Seehydrographischer Dienst [*Maritime Hydrographic Service*] (EG)
SHD .... Severoceske Hnedouhelne Doly [*North Bohemian Lignite (Brown Coal) Mines*] (CZ)
SHD .... Srpsko Hemisko Drustvo [*Serbian Chemical Society*] (YU)
ShD .... Step Motor [*Automation*], Step-by-Step Motor [*Electric machines*] (RU)
ShDM .... School of Peasant Youth [*Uzbekistan and Tadzikistan*] (RU)
SHDM .... Sportovni Hry Delnicke Mladeze [*Young Workers' Athletic Games*] (CZ)
ShDMRTs .... Centralized Interlocking Relay Mine Traffic Control (RU)
ShDRTs .... Centralized Relay Mine Traffic Control (RU)
SHDS .... [*Centre for*] Strengthening Health Delivery Systems (MAR)
ShE .... Bypass Element (RU)
ShE .... Scotch Encephalitis (RU)
sheg .... Jocular (BU)
SHEHFA .... Societe Hoteliere et d'Exploitation Hoteliere Franco-Africaine (MAR)
SHEHGYD ... Sakarya Halk Egitimi Hizmetlerini Gelistirme Yayma Dernegi [*Sakarya Organization for the Development and Spread of Popular Educational Services*] [*Turkish Cypriot*] (GC)
shelk .... Sericultural Sovkhoz [*Topography*] (RU)
shelk .... Silk-Reeling Factory [*Topography*] (RU)
ShELKOPRAVLENIYe ... Administration of Associated Silk Factories (RU)
SHELL BENINREX ... Societe Shell Beninoise de Recherches et d'Exploitation (MAR)
SHELL-CAMREX ... Societe Shell Camerounaise de Recherches et d'Exploitation (MAR)
SHELL-DAHOREX ... Societe Shell Dahomeenne de Recherches et d'Exploitation (MAR)
SHELL-IVOREX ... Societe Shell Ivoirienne de Recherches et d'Exploitation (MAR)
SHELL-MAUREX ... Societe Shell Mauritanienne de Recherches et d'Exploitation (MAR)
SHELL-NIGEREX ... Societe Shell Nigerienne de Recherche et d'Exploitation (MAR)
SHELL-SENREX ... Shell Senegalaise de Recherches et d'Exploitation (MAR)
SHELL-TOGOREX ... Societe Shell Togolaise de Recherches et d'Exploitation (MAR)
Shf .... Sahife [*Page*] (TU)
ShFZO .... Industrial Training School (BU)
ShG .... Noise Generator (RU)
Shh .... Sihhiye [*Hygiene*] (TU)
SHHA .... Self Help Housing Agency (MAR)
ShI .... Boarding School (RU)
SHI .... Societe Hoteliere Ivoirienne (MAR)
ShI .... Step-by-Step Switch (RU)
SHIAL .... Societe pour l'Histoire des Israelites d'Alsace-Lorraine (MAR)
SHIC .... Societe Hoteliere et Immobiliere du Congo (MAR)
SHICA .... Societe Hoteliere et Immobiliere de la Chaine des Alizes (MAR)
shif .... Slate Plant [*Topography*] (RU)
SHIHATA .... Shirika la Habari la Tanzania [*Tanzania News Agency*] (AF)
shil .... Shilling (RU)
ShIM .... Impulse Duration Modulation (RU)
SHINUI .... Political Party [*Israeli*] (ME)
ShIR .... Cord Register Finder (RU)
shir .... Width (RU)
ShIRAS .... Artillery Shell Burst Simulator (RU)
shiv .... Rapids [*Topography*] (RU)
Shizo .... Penal Isolation Cell (RU)
ShK .... Broad Gauge (RU)
ShK .... Cord Set Assembly (RU)
ShK- .... Pilot Balloon Set (RU)
shk .... School (RU)
SHK .... Societe Hoteliere du Kouilou (MAR)
SHK .... Societe Hydroelectrique du Kouilou (MAR)
SHK .... Statni Vedecka Knihovna, Hradec-Kralove [*State Scientific Library in Hradec-Kralove*] (CZ)
SHK .... Sun Hung Kai Securities [*Hong Kong*]
ShK .... Track Gauge (RU)
ShKAS .... Shpital'nyy, Komarnitskiy Rapid-Fire Aircraft (Machine Gun) (RU)
shkh .... Mine, Shaft (RU)
ShKM .... Kolkhoz Youth School (RU)
ShKM .... Peasant Youth School (RU)
ShKN .... Primary School (RU)
Shkolfil'm ... Central Motion Picture Laboratory of the Ministry of Education, RSFSR (RU)
shkrab .... Teacher, School Worker (RU)
ShKU .... Plug-In Switchboard (RU)
ShKU .... School of Cook Apprenticeship and Course Organization (RU)
ShL- .... Headset (RU)
shl .... Lock, Sluice [*Topography*] (RU)
Shl .... Slag [*Road-paving material*] [*Topography*] (RU)
shl-bet .... Slag Concrete (RU)
ShM- .... Ball Mill (RU)
ShM .... Helmet-Mask (Gas Mask) (RU)
ShM .... Mine Mill (RU)
ShM .... Plastering Machine (RU)
SHM .... Societe de la Haute-Mondah (MAR)
SHM .... Societe Hoteliere de Mauritanie (MAR)
SHM .... Societe des Hotelleries du Mali (MAR)
SHM .... Spoldzielcze Hurtownie Miedzypowiatowe [*Intercounty Cooperative Wholesale Warehouses*] (POL)
SHM .... Sportovne [*or Sportovni*] Hry Mladeze [*Young People's Athletic Games*] (CZ)
ShMA .... Axial Shaft Mill (RU)
ShMAS .... School for Junior Aviation Specialists (RU)
ShMO .... Nautical Training School (RU)
ShMO .... Odessa Nautical School (RU)
SHMP .... Service d'Hygiene Mobile et de Prophylaxie du Cameroun (MAR)
ShMT .... Shaft-Mill Furnace (RU)
ShMT .... Tangential Shaft Mill (RU)
ShMU .... Nautical Apprenticeship School (RU)
SHMU .... Statny Hydrologicky a Meteorologicky Ustav [*State Hydrological and Meteorological Institute*] [*Bratislava*] (CZ)
shmutstit .... Half Title (RU)
ShMVU .... School of Masters of Abundant Harvests (RU)
SHMZ .... Savezni Hidrometeoroloski Zavod [*Federal Hydrometeorological Institute*] [*Belgrade*] (YU)
SHN .... St. Helena [*Three-letter standard code*] (CNC)
SHN .... Societe des Huileries du Niger (MAR)
SHNC .... Societe Hoteliere Nord-Cameroun (MAR)
ShO .... Assault Force (RU)
ShO .... Bifilar Oscillograph, Soft-Iron Oscillograph (RU)
ShO .... Cryptographic Section (RU)
SHO .... Societe Commerciale Industrielle et Agricole du Haut-Ogooue (MAR)
SHOA .... Societe Hoteliere de l'Ouest Africain (MAR)
SHOC .... Societe Horlogerie du Congo (MAR)
ShOK .... Siauliai Footwear Kombinat (RU)
SHORTIE .... Short Range Thermal Imaging Equipment (MAR)
S Hos .... Section d'Hospitalisation [*Military*] [*French*] (MTD)
shoss .... Highway (RU)
shotl .... Scottish (RU)

ShOV.......... Shunt Field Winding (RU)
ShP............ Cord Switch (RU)
ShP............ Hachure Device (RU)
ShP............ Listening Sonar (RU)
ShP............ Pilot Balloon (RU)
SHPB.......... Specijalizovana Hirurska Poljska Bolnica [*Field Hospital for Specialized Surgery*] (YU)
ShPI............ Siauliai Pedagogical Institute (RU)
ShPM.......... Tie Tamper [*Railroads*] (RU)
SHPN.......... Savez Hrvatskih Privatnih Namjestenika [*Federation of Croatian Private Employees*] (YU)
ShPO.......... Full Hole Joint (RU)
ShPP.......... Detection Band Width (RU)
ShPP.......... Mine Surface Substation (RU)
ShPR.......... Hand-Operated Ship Steam Windlass (RU)
ShPS.......... Listening Sonar Station (RU)
ShPSS........ Wide-Band Seismic Station (RU)
ShPT.......... Swiss Labor Party (RU)
SHPz.......... Skupina Hloubkoveho Pruzkumu [*Deep Reconnaissance Detachment*] (CZ)
SHQ............ Supreme Headquarters (MAR)
ShR............ Bypass Relay (RU)
ShR............ Bypass Rheostat (RU)
ShR............ Circuit Resonator (RU)
ShR............ Connecting Cord Relay (RU)
ShR............ Plug-and-Jack (RU)
SHR............ Severcesky Hnedouhelny Revir [*North Bohemian Lignite (Brown Coal) Basin*] (CZ)
SHR............ Shire Highlands Railway Co. (MAR)
shr............. Shrapnel (BU)
ShR............ Shunt Regulator (RU)
SHR............ Statni Hospodarska Rada [*State Economic Council*] (CZ)
ShR............ Step Monitor [*Computers*] (RU)
ShR............ Step-by-Step Distributor (RU)
shr............. Type [*Printing*] (BU)
ShR............ Wall Socket (RU)
ShRB.......... Tire-Repair Base (RU)
SHRCS........ Svaz Horolezcu Republiky Ceskoslovenske [*Mountain Climbing Association of the Czechoslovak Republic*] (CZ)
SHRD.......... Svaz Zamestnancu Hutniho Prumyslu a Rudnych Dolu [*Union of Employees in the Metallurgical Industry and Ore Mines*] (CZ)
ShRD.......... Total Band Width (RU)
SHRM.......... Sportovne Hry Robotnickej Mladeze [*Athletic Games for Young Workers*] (CZ)
ShRM.......... Workers' Youth School (RU)
ShRS.......... School of Helmsmen and Signalmen (RU)
ShRV.......... Bypass Rheostat of an Exciter (RU)
ShRV.......... Radio Broadcasting Station (RU)
ShRYu........ Young Workers' School (RU)
SHS............ Kraljevina Srba, Hrvata, i Slovenaca [*Kingdom of Serbs, Croats, and Slovenes*] (YU)
ShS............ Mine Construction (RU)
SHS............ Scieries du Haut-Sassandra (MAR)
SHS............ Slovenska Historicka Spolocnost [*Slovak Historical Society*] (CZ)
SHS............ Slovensky Hokejovy Svaz [*Slovak Ice Hockey Association*] (CZ)
SHS............ Societatis Historiae Socius [*Fellow of the Historical Society*] [*Latin*] (GPO)
SHS............ Srbi, Hrvati, i Slovenci [*Serbs, Croats, and Slovenes*] (YU)
SHS............ Sudan Horticultural Society (MAR)
SHS............ Svaz Hokejistov Slovenska [*Slovak Ice Hockey Association*] (CZ)
ShShS........ Headquarters Cryptographic Service (RU)
SHSHV........ Societe des Huiles et Savohs de Haute-Volta (MAR)
SHSiKA....... Sekcja Historii Sztuki i Krytyki Artystycznej [*Section on the History of Art and Art Criticism*] (POL)
SHSKM....... Stowarzyszenie Historykow Sztuki i Kultury Materialnej [*Association of Historians of Art and Material Culture*] (POL)
ShSM.......... Rural Youth School (RU)
SHSM.......... Sportovni Hry Skolni Mladeze [*Student Athletic Games*] (CZ)
sht.............. Adit, Gallery [*Topography*] (RU)
sh t............. Hardness Scale (RU)
sht.............. Piece (RU)
SHT............ Salvo Honoris Titulo [*Latin*]
SHT............ Societe Hoteliere du Tchad (MAR)
SHT............ Societe Hoteliere de Treichville (MAR)
sht.............. Staff, Headquarters (BU)
sht.............. Staff, Headquarters (RU)
sht.............. State, Staff (RU)
ShT............ Tanzanian Shilling (MAR)
shta............ Army Headquarters (BU)
ShtA........... Ground Attack Aviation (BU)
shtabokr..... District Headquarters (RU)
shtabrig...... Brigade Headquarters (RU)
shtadiv....... Division Headquarters (RU)
shtaesk....... Squadron Headquarters (RU)
shtakor....... Corps Headquarters (RU)
Shtalvo........ Leningrad Military District Headquarters (RU)
Shtamorsichern... Black Sea Naval Headquarters (RU)
SHTAMPOZHEST'... Stamped Sheet Metalware Plant (RU)
Shtamvo..... Moscow Military District Headquarters (RU)
ShtAO........ Instrument Section Control Panel [*Nuclear energy*] (BU)
shtarm........ Army Headquarters (RU)
Shtbobm..... Baltic Sea Coast Defense Headquarters (RU)
shtd............ Division Headquarters (BU)
shtda.......... General Headquarters (BU)
Shtergres.... Shterovka State Regional Electric Power Plant (RU)
SHTFNRJ.... Savez Hemicara-Tehnologa Federativna Narodna Republika Jugoslavija [*Union of Chemical Technologists of Yugoslavia*] (YU)
shtks.......... Corps Headquarters (BU)
Shtl............ Sehitlik [*Cemetery*] [*Military*] [*See also Mzl*] (TU)
SHTM......... Societe des Hotelleries et du Tourisme du Mali (MAR)
shtoa.......... Separate Army Headquarters (BU)
ShTP.......... Braided Telephone Cord (RU)
shtpk.......... Regimental Headquarters (BU)
ShTS.......... Connection Contact (RU)
ShTsV......... Water Chromaticity Scale (RU)
SHTT.......... Societe Hoteliere et Touristique de Tunisie (MAR)
ShTT.......... Tank Technicians' School (RU)
ShTU.......... Trade Apprenticeship School (RU)
ShTV.......... Twisted Telephone Cord (RU)
ShU............ Shilling Ugandan (MAR)
SHU............ Statni Historicky Ustav [*State Historical Institute*] (CZ)
ShUMP........ Apprenticeship School in Mass-Employment Skills (RU)
ShUNS........ School for Advanced Training of the Command Staff (RU)
SHV............ Statni Hudebni Vydavatelstvi [*State Music Publishing House*] (CZ)
shv............. Sub Hac Voce [*or Sub Hoc Verbo*] [*Under This Word*] [*Latin*] (GPO)
shv............. Swedish (RU)
ShVAK........ Shpital'nyy-Volkov Aircraft Wing Cannon (RU)
SHVD.......... Sportovni Hry Vojenskeho Dorostu [*Junior Military Athletic Games*] (CZ)
SHVEYPROM... Garment Industry (RU)
SHVEYPROMSOYUZ... Producers' Union of the Garment Industry (RU)
shveyts....... Swiss (RU)
ShVLP......... School of Advanced Flight Training (RU)
SHVM.......... Sportovni Hry Vysokoskolske Mladeze [*University Youth Sports Games*] (CZ)
SHVP.......... Societe Hoteliere Victory Palace (MAR)
ShVZ.......... Siauliai Bicycle Plant (RU)
SHZ............ Savezni Hidrometeoroloski Zavod [*Federal Hydrometeorological Institute*] (YU)
Shz............. Sounding Balloon (RU)
SHZ............ Sportovni Hry Zactva [*Student Athletic Games*] (CZ)
SHZ............ Sulfat-Huettenzement [*Sulfate Blast Furnace Cement*] (EG)
SHZ............ Svaz Zamestnancu v Hornictvi [*Union of Employees in the Mining Industry*] (CZ)
ShZh.......... Silk Gland (RU)
ShZO.......... Reserve Officers School (BU)
SI............... Hunting Switch (RU)
si............... Inertia (RU)
SI............... Infrared Spectroscopy (RU)
SI............... International System [*of units*] (RU)
SI............... Northeast (BU)
SI............... Pulse Counter (RU)
Si............... Saki [*Cape, Point*] [*Japanese*] (NAU)
SI............... Sanitarni Inspektorat [*Sanitary Inspectorate*] (YU)
SI............... Sekretarijat za Industriju (SIV) [*Secretariat of Industry*] (YU)
SI............... Sekretarijat za Informacije (SIV) [*Secretariat of Information*] (YU)
SI............... Seksi [*Section*] (IN)
SI............... Servicio de Informaciones [*Information Service*] [*Peruvian*] (LA)
SI............... Severo-Istok [*Northeast*] (YU)
Si............... Sidi [*Tomb*] [*Arabic*] (NAU)
SI............... Skholi Ippikou [*Cavalry School*] [*Greek*] (GC)
SI............... Sociedad de Industrias [*Industrial Association*] [*Peruvian*] (LA)
SI............... Societe d'Intervention (MAR)
SI............... Soroptimist International (EA)
SI............... Spratly Islands [*Two-letter standard code*] (CNC)
SI............... Staroslovenski Institut [*Institute for Church Slavonic Studies*] (YU)
SI............... Statni Inspekce [*State Inspection*] (CZ)
SI............... Statutory Instrument (MAR)
SI............... Sub-Inginer [*Romanian*]
Si............... Sungai [*or Sungei*] [*River*] [*Indonesian*] (NAU)
Si............... Sungai [*or Sungei*] [*River*] [*Malay*] (NAU)
SI............... Survival International (EA)
SI............... Synchronizing Pulse, Timing Pulse (RU)
SI............... Systeme International (MAR)
SI............... Szkola Inzynierska [*Engineering School*] (POL)
Si............... True North (RU)
SI............... Union of Industrialists (BU)
SIA............. Service Intercontinental d'Assurances [*Moroccan*] (MAR)
SIA............. Skholi Iptamenon Aeroporon [*Air Force Flying School*] [*Greek*] (GC)
SIA............. Societe Immobiliere Africaine (MAR)
SIA............. Societe Interafricaine d'Assurances (MAR)

SIA .... Societe d'Investissements Africains (MAR)
SIA .... Societe Ivoirienne d'Assurances (MAR)
SIA .... Solkanska Industrija Apna [*Solkan Lime Industry*] [*Nova Gorica*] (YU)
SIA .... Spolek Ceskoslovenskych Inzenyru a Architektu [*Society of Czechoslovak Engineers and Architects*] (CZ)
SIA .... Statiunea de Intretinere Auto [*Automotive Maintenance Station*] (RO)
SIAA .... Societe Ivoirienne d'Appareils Automatiques (MAR)
SIAAC .... Syndicat des Intermediaires d'Assurances Agrees au Cameroun (MAR)
SIAB .... Societe Industrielle et Automobile Bennouna [*Moroccan*] (MAR)
SIAC .... Societe Immobiliere Africaine et de Commerce (MAR)
SIAC .... Societe Internationale des Artistes Chretiens [*International Society for Christian Artists*] (EA)
SIAC .... Societe Nationale des Industries Algeriennes de la Chaussure (MAR)
SIAC's .... Specialized Information Analysis Centres
SIACA .... Societe Immobiliere Africaine de Courtage et d'Assurances (MAR)
SIACA .... Societe Ivoiro-Allemande de Conserves d'Ananas (MAR)
SIACAF .... Societe Industrielle et Agricole Centrafricaine (MAR)
SIACI .... Societe des Industries Alimentaires en Cote-d'Ivoire (MAR)
SIA-Congo ... Societe Industrielle et Agricole du Congo (MAR)
SIADA .... Societe Industrielle et Agricole pour le Developpement de l'Alaotra (MAR)
SIADES .... Sociedad de Ingenieros Agronomos de El Salvador [*Association of Salvadoran Agricultural Engineers*] (LA1)
SIAE .... Societa Italiana degli Autori ed Editori [*Italian*]
SIAE .... Societe Abidjanaise Import-Export (MAR)
SIAEK .... Syndesmos Ilektonikon Asfaleias Enaerias Kykloforias [*Association of Air Traffic Controllers*] (GC1)
SIAEX .... Societe Ivoirienne d'Achat et d'Exportation (MAR)
SIAF .... Societe Internationale Africaine [*Moroccan*] (MAR)
SIAG .... Societe Industrielle et Automobile de Guinee (MAR)
SIAGRUZ .... Inversiones Agropecuarias SA [*Cali*] (COL)
SIAIEX .... Societe Inter-Africaine d'Import-Export (MAR)
SIAL .... Sociedade Imobiliaria e de Administracoes Limitada (MAR)
SIAL .... Societe Industrielle et Agricole de la Lobaye (MAR)
SIAM .... Sociedad Industrial de Articulos Metalicos Ltda. [*Bogota*] (COL)
SIAM .... Societe Industrielle Alimentaire de Magaria (MAR)
SIAM .... Societe d'Investissements Agricoles a Madagascar (MAR)
SIAM .... Societe Ivoirienne d'Acconage et de Manutention (MAR)
SIAMA .... Society for Interests of Active Missionaries in Asia, Africa, and America (EA)
SIAMAR .... Societe d'Investissements Agricoles au Maroc (MAR)
SIAMO .... Syndicat Interprofessionnel pour l'Acheminement de la Main-d'Oeuvre (MAR)
SIAN .... Institute of Seismology of the Academy of Sciences, USSR (RU)
SIAN .... Societe Industrielle d'Adjame Nord (MAR)
SIAN .... Societe Industrielle et Agricole du Niari [*Niari Industrial and Agricultural Company*] [*Congolese*] (AF)
SIANI .... Societe Industrielle et Automobile du Haut-Niger (MAR)
SIAO .... Societe Immobiliere de l'Afrique Occidentale (MAR)
SIAO .... Societe d'Investissement d'Affaires Occidentales [*Paris*] (MAR)
SIAOC .... Societe d'Investissement d'Affaires Occidentales (MAR)
SIAP .... Societe Industrielle Africaine de Plastiques (MAR)
SIAP-CONGO ... Societe Industrielle d'Articles en Papier du Congo (MAR)
SIAPE .... Societa Industriale Automatismo Prodotti Electronici [*Industrial Firm for Automatic Electronic Equipment*] [*Italian*] (WER)
SIAPE .... Societe Industrielle d'Acide Phosphorique et d'Engrais [*Phosphoric Acid and Fertilizer Manufacturing Company*] [*Tunisian*] (AF)
SIARA .... Societe Interafricaine de Representations Automobile (MAR)
SIARM .... Societe Ivoirienne d'Approvisionnement et de Restauration Maritime (MAR)
SIAS .... Scandinavian Institute of African Studies (AF)
SIAS .... Small Industries Advisory Service (MAR)
SIAS .... Societe Ivoirienne Azar et Salame (MAR)
SIAT .... Seccion Investigacion de Accidentes del Transito [*Traffic Accidents Investigation Section*] [*Chilean*] (LA)
SIAT .... Societe Immobiliere d'Afrique Tropicale (MAR)
SIAT .... Societe Industrielle et Agricole du Tabac Tropical (MAR)
SIAT .... Societe d'Investissement Arabe de Tunisie [*Arab Investment Company of Tunisia*] (AF)
SIAT .... Societe Ivoirienne Agricole de Tiassale (MAR)
SIB .... Saudi International Bank (MAR)
SIB .... Servico de Informacoes Bibliograficas [*Brazilian*]
sib .... Siberia, Siberian (RU)
SIB .... Sociedade Interplanetaria Brasileira [*Brazilian*]
SIB .... Societe Industrielle Bobolaise (MAR)
SIB .... Societe Industrielle du Boina (MAR)
SIB .... Societe Industrielle des Bois (MAR)
SIB .... Societe Ivoirienne de Banque [*Ivorian Banking Company*] (AF)
SIB .... Sovjetski Informativni Biro [*Soviet Information Bureau*] (YU)
SIB .... Special Investigations Bureau (ML)
SIBA .... Societe d'Importation de Beaux Ameublements (MAR)
SIBA .... Societe Industrielle des Blanchisseries Africaines (MAR)
SIBA .... Societe Industrielle de Bois Africains (MAR)
SIBA .... Societe Industrielle de Briqueteries Africaines (MAR)
SIBA .... Societe Intercontinentale de Banque Societe Anonyme (MAR)
SIBACI .... Societe Industrielle des Beaux-Arts de l'Ameublement de Cote-d'Ivoire (MAR)
SIBACO .... Societe Immobiliere de la Baie de Cocody (MAR)
SibADI .... Siberian Highway Institute Imeni V. V. Kuybyshev (RU)
SIBAF .... Societe Industrielle de Bois Africains (MAR)
SIBAG .... Societe d'Industries de Bois au Gabon (MAR)
SIBAGEC .... Societe Ivoirienne de Batiment et de Genie Civil (MAR)
SIBAT .... Societe Industrielle du Batiment (MAR)
SIBAT .... Societe Ivoirienne Burguiere & Ambrosino des Transports (MAR)
SIBC .... Societe Immobiliere du Boulevard Carde [*Ivorian*] (MAR)
Sibe .... Sicherheitsbeauftragter [*Security Officer*] (EG)
SIBE .... Societe d'Importation des Bois Exotiques (MAR)
SIBEKA .... Societe d'Entreprise et d'Investissement du Beceka (MAR)
Sibgiprobum ... State Institute for the Planning of Pulp and Paper Industry Establishments in Siberia and the Far East (RU)
Sibgiprogormash ... Siberian State Planning, Design, and Experimental Institute of Mining Machinery (RU)
Sibgiprotorg ... Siberian State Planning Institute of Trade (RU)
Sibgiprotrans ... Siberian State Planning and Surveying Institute of the State Industrial Committee for Transportation Construction of the USSR (RU)
SIBIA .... Societe Ivoirienne des Boulangeries et des Industries Alimentaires (MAR)
SIBICOB .... Societe Industrielle de Biscuiterie et Confiserie du Benin (MAR)
Sib IZMIR .... Siberian Institute of Terrestrial Magnetism, Ionosphere and Radio Wave Propagation (of the Siberian Department of the Academy of Sciences, USSR) (RU)
SibIZRA .... Siberian Institute for the Protection of Plants (RU)
SIBKIS .... Siberian Complex Institute of Structures and Building Materials (RU)
SIBMAS .... Societe Internationale des Bibliotheques et Musees des Arts du Spectacle [*International Association of Libraries and Museums of the Performing Arts*] (EA)
SibNIA .... Siberian Scientific Research Aviation Institute (RU)
SibNIILKhE ... Siberian Scientific Research Institute of Forestry and Forest Utilization (RU)
SIBNIISKhOZ ... Siberian Scientific Research Institute of Agriculture (RU)
SibNIIZh .... Siberian Scientific Research Institute of Livestock Breeding (RU)
SIBNIIZKhOZ ... Siberian Scientific Research Grain Institute (RU)
SibNIVI .... Siberian Scientific Research Veterinary Institute (RU)
SIBO .... Societe Industrielle de Bonneterie (MAR)
SIBO .... Societe Ivoirienne des Bois de l'Est (MAR)
SIBOIS .... Societe Industrielle Ivoirienne des Bois (MAR)
SIBP .... Societe Ivoirienne des Petroles BP (MAR)
SIBRAS .... Societe Industrielle de Brasseries du Senegal (MAR)
Sibrybvod ... Administration of Fish Conservation and Fisheries in Siberia (RU)
SIB-SA .... Societe Immobiliere du Benin (MAR)
Sibsantekhmontazh ... Siberian Sanitary Engineering Installation Trust (RU)
Sibsel'mash ... Novosibirsk Agricultural Machinery Plant (RU)
SIBT .... Societe Ivoirienne des Bois de Tiassale (MAR)
Sibtyazhmash ... Siberian Heavy Machinery Plant (RU)
SIBVO .... Siberian Military District (RU)
SIC .... La Specialisation Industrielle et Chimique (MAR)
SIC .... Sabah Indian Congress (ML)
SIC .... Science de l'Intelligence Creatrice (MAR)
SIC .... Secretaria de Industria y Comercio [*Secretariat of Industry and Commerce*] (LA)
SIC .... Servei d'Informacio Catala [*Catalan Information Service*] [*Spanish*] (WER)
SIC .... Servicio de Inteligencia Colombiano [*Colombian Intelligence Service*] (LA)
SIC .... Servicio de Inteligencia Criminal [*Criminal Intelligence Service*] [*Ecuadorean*] (LA)
SIC .... Small Industries Corporation [*Guyanese*] (LA)
SIC .... Sociedade Intercontinental de Comercio Lda. (MAR)
SIC .... Societe Immobiliere du Cameroon [*Cameroon Real Estate Company*] (AF)
SIC .... Societe d'Import et de Commission (MAR)
SIC .... Societe Industrielle des Cacaos [*Cameroonian*] (MAR)
SIC .... Societe Industrielle et Commerciale [*Industrial and Commercial Company*] [*Senegalese*] (AF)
SIC .... Societe Industrielle pour le Traitement des Caroubes [*North African*] (MAR)
SIC .... Societe Ivoirienne de Cinema (MAR)
SIC .... Srp i Cekic [*Hammer and Sickle*] (YU)
SIC .... State Insurance Corporation (MAR)
SICA .... Sociedade Industrial e Comercial Africana Lda. [*Nampula*] (MAR)
SICA .... Societe Immobiliere Centrafricaine (MAR)
SICA .... Societe Immobiliere de la Cote-d'Afrique (MAR)
SICA .... Societe Industrielle et Commerciale Africaine (MAR)
SICA .... Societe Industrielle et Commerciale d'Approvisionnements (MAR)
SICA .... Societe Industrielle de l'Est Camerounais (MAR)
SICAB .... Societe Immobiliere Cocody Abidjan (MAR)

SICAB .... Societe Industrielle Camerounaise des Bois (MAR)
SICABLE..... Societe Ivoirienne de Cables (MAR)
SICABO....... Societe Cooperative Agricole de Bonoua (MAR)
SICABO....... Societe Ivoirienne de Carrosserie Bois (MAR)
SICAC .... Societe Industrielle Commerciale Agricole de la Casamance (MAR)
SICAF.......... Societe Industrielle Chimique Africaine (MAR)
SICAF.......... Societe Industrielle de Couvertures Africaines (MAR)
SICAF.......... Societe Ivoirienne de Culture d'Ananas Frais (MAR)
SICAFE .... Sindicato de la Industria del Cafe [*Union of the Coffee Industry*] [*Salvadoran*] (LA)
SICAG......... Societe Industrielle Commerciale et Agricole de Guinee (MAR)
SICAG......... Societe Ivoirienne de Cautionnement de Garantie (MAR)
SICA-HR ..... Societe d'Interet Collectif Agricole-Habitat Rural [*Rural Agriculture-Habitat Collective Interest Society*] [*Guadeloupe*] (LA1)
SICAI........... Societa d'Ingegneria e Consulenza Attivita Industriali (MAR)
SICAI........... Societa Italo-Congolese Attivita Industriali (MAR)
SICAI........... Societe Italo-Congolaise d'Aide a l'Industrie (MAR)
SICAL.......... Societe Industrielle, Commerciale, et Agricole de la Likouala (MAR)
SICAN .... Societe Industrielle et Commerciale de l'Afrique du Nord d'Engrais et Produits Agricoles [*Algerian*] (MAR)
SICAO .... Societe Industrielle et Commerciale de l'Afrique de l'Ouest (MAR)
SICAP .... Societe Immobiliere du Cap-Vert (MAR)
SICAPE .... Societe Italo-Congolaise d'Armement et de Peche (MAR)
SICAR .... Societe Ivoirienne de Courtage, d'Assurances, et de Reassurances (MAR)
SICAT .... Societe Immobiliere et Commerciale de l'Afrique Tropicale (MAR)
SICAV .... Societe d'Investissement a Capital Variable [*Variable-Capital Investment Co.*] [*French*] (WER)
SICCA .... Societe Industrielle des Cuirs et Caoutchouc (MAR)
SICCI .... Societe Industrielle et Commerciale de Cote-d'Ivoire (MAR)
SICCT .... Secretaria da Industria, Comercio, Ciencia, e Tecnologia do Estado de Sao Paulo [*Brazilian*]
SICE .... Societe Industrielle et Commerciale de l'Emyrne (MAR)
SICELP .... Societa Italiana Costruzioni e Lavori Pubblici (MAR)
SICES .... Sindicato de la Industria del Cemento de El Salvador [*Union of the Cement Industry of El Salvador*] (LA)
SICFA.......... Societa Italiana Commercio Ferramenta e Affini nelle Colonie (MAR)
SICFA.......... Societe Industrielle et Commerciale Franco-Africaine (MAR)
SICFOM ...... Societe Immobiliere et Commerciale pour la France et l'Outre-Mer (MAR)
SICI .... Societe Immobiliere et Commerciale Ivoirienne (MAR)
SICK............ Societe Immobiliere et Commerciale du Kouilou (MAR)
SICM .... Societe Internationale de Construction et de Menuiserie (MAR)
SICM .... Societe Ivoirienne de Ciments et Materiaux (MAR)
SICMA......... Societe Industrielle et Commerciale des Materiaux [*Senegalese*] (MAR)
SICMEOS.... Societe Industrielle et Commerciale de Materiel d'Equipement d'Organisation et de Securite [*Senegalese*] (MAR)
SICN............ Societe Industrielle de Combustibles Nucleaires [*French*]
SICN............ Societe Industrielle et Commerciale Nigerienne (MAR)
SICN............ Systeme Ivoirien de Compatibilite Nationale (MAR)
SICNA .... Societe Industrielle et Commerciale Nord-Africaine d'Engrais et Produits Agricoles [*Moroccan*] (MAR)
SICND .... Societe Immobiliere du Comptoir National du Diamant (MAR)
SICO .... Sociedad Importadora Comercial [*Cali*] (COL)
SICO .... Societe Industrielle et Commerciale en Oubangui (MAR)
SICO .... Societe Ivoirienne pour le Commerce avec l'Om (MAR)
SICOA......... Societe Immobiliere et Commerciale de l'Ouest Africain Cote-d'Ivoire (MAR)
SICOB .... Salon des Industries du Commerce et de l'Organisation du Bureau [*Exposition of Office and Business Supply Industries and Office Organization*] [*French*] (WER)
SICOBOIS... Societe Industrielle et Commerciale des Bois Tropicaux (MAR)
SICOC......... Societe Industrielle et Commerciale des Oleagineux Centrafricains (MAR)
SICOCAM ... Societe Industrielle et Commerciale du Cameroun (MAR)
SICOD .... Societe Industrielle de Cosmetiques et Derives (MAR)
SICODEM-CI ... Societe Industrielle et Commerciale pour le Developpement du Mais en Cote-d'Ivoire (MAR)
SICOE .... Societe Industrielle et Commerciale de la Cote Est (MAR)
SICOF .... Societe de l'Industrie de la Confection de Fes [*Moroccan*] (MAR)
SICOF .... Societe Industrielle, Commerciale, et Financiere (MAR)
SICOFAA .... Sistema de Cooperacion entre las Fuerzas Aereas Americanas [*System of Cooperation among American Air Forces*] (LA)
SICOFEM.... Societe Ivoirienne de Confections Feminines et Masculines (MAR)
SICOFREL... Societe Ivoirienne pour la Commercialisation des Fruits et Legumes (MAR)
SICOGERE ... Societe Ivoirienne de Copropriete et de Gerance (MAR)
SICOGI........ Societe Ivoirienne de Construction et de Gestion Immobiliere (MAR)
SICOL .... Sociedade Importadora Commercial Limitada (MAR)
SICOM .... Societe Industrielle et Commerciale (MAR)
SICOM .... Societe Industrielle et Commerciale de Marrakech (MAR)
SICOM .... Societe Industrielle et Commerciale de M'Balmayo (MAR)
SICOM .... Societe Industrielle de Constructions Metalliques (MAR)
SICOMA...... Societe Immobiliere et Commerciale Africaine (MAR)
SICOMA...... Societe Industrielle et Commerciale de Mauritanie (MAR)
SICOMA...... Societe Ivoirienne de Construction et de Materiaux (MAR)
SICOMAD ... Societe Industrielle de la Cote Ouest de Madagascar (MAR)
SICOMAR ... Societe Ivoirienne de Consignation, de Manutention, et d'Armement (MAR)
SICOME ...... Societe Industrielle de Confection a Meknes [*Moroccan*] (MAR)
SICOMED ... Societe Ivoirienne de Construction Medicale (MAR)
SICOMO...... Societe Industrielle de Confection Moderne (MAR)
SICON......... Societe Industrielle et Commerciale du Niger (MAR)
SICONEXIM ... Societe Intercontinentale de Constructions et d'Exploitations Immobiliers, Madagascar (MAR)
SICONGO ... Societe Immobiliere du Congo (MAR)
SICONIEX ... Societe Industrielle Commerciale Nigerienne d'Import-Export (MAR)
SICONIGER ... Societe Industrielle et Commerciale du Niger (MAR)
SICOP .... Sistemul Integrat de Conducere a Productiei de Constructii-Montaj [*Integrated Management System for the Production of Constructions and Assemblies*] (RO)
SICOPECHE ... Societe Ivoirienne de Cooperation Internationale pour la Peche (MAR)
SICOPEG .... Societe Internationale de Conditionnement, de Participation, et d'Entreprise Generale (MAR)
SICOPHAR ... Societe Industrielle du Coton Pharmaceutique (MAR)
SICOR .... Societe Ivoirienne de Coco Rape (MAR)
SICOT .... Societe Internationale de Chirurgie Orthopedique et de Traumatologie [*International Society of Orthopaedic Surgery and Traumatology*] (EA)
SICOTOUR ... Societe Casamance Investissement Touristique (MAR)
SICOTP .... Societe Ivoirienne Commerciale Ouvriere de Travaux Publics et de Batiments (MAR)
SICOVO ...... Societe Industrielle et Commerciale Voltaique (MAR)
SICPAD....... Societe Industrielle Centrafricaine des Produits Alimentaires et Derives (MAR)
SICRUS....... Societe Ivoirienne de Crustaces (MAR)
SICS........... Societe Immobiliere de la Cote Sauvage (MAR)
SICSC.......... State Intelligence Counter-Subversive Committee (ML)
SICT............ Societe Industrielle Chimique de Tiko (MAR)
SICT............ Societe Industrielle et Commerciale du Tchad (MAR)
SICTA .... Societe Ivoirienne de Controle Technique Automobile et Industriel (MAR)
SICY............ Societe Industrielle et Commerciale du Yatenga (MAR)
SID .... Secretaria de Imprensa e Divulgacao [*Secretariat of Press and Publishing*] [*Brazilian*] (LA1)
SID .... Service d'Information et de Documentation [*Information and Documentation Service*] [*Haitian*] (LA)
SID .... Servicio de Informacion de la Defensa [*Defense Intelligence Service*] [*Uruguayan*] (LA)
SID .... Servizio Informazioni della Difesa [*Defense Intelligence Service*] [*Italian*] (WER)
sid .... Sidor [*Pages*] [*Swedish*] (GPO)
sid .... Sidottu(na) [*Finnish*]
SID .... Sociedad Industrial Dominicana [*Dominican Industrial Association*] [*Dominican Republic*] (LA)
SID .... Societe Industrielle Dakaroise (MAR)
SID .... Societe Internationale pour le Developpement (MAR)
SID .... Societe Ivoirienne de Distribution (MAR)
SID .... Standard Industrial Development Co. Ltd. (MAR)
SIDA........... Societe d'Information et de Diffusion Abidjanaise (MAR)
SIDA........... Swedish International Development Authority (AF)
SIDADT .... Societe Industrielle pour le Developpement Automobile au Dahomey et au Togo (MAR)
SIDAL.......... Societe Ivoirienne d'Ascenseurs et d'Appareils de Levage (MAR)
SIDAM......... Societe Ivoirienne d'Assurances Mutuelles (MAR)
SIDAM......... Somali Institute of Development Administration and Management (MAR)
SIDAT.......... Societe Industrielle pour le Developpement Automobile au Dahomey et au Togo (MAR)
SIDB........... Societe Industrielle des Bois [*Congolese*] (MAR)
SIDB........... Societe Industrielle Dakaroise du Bois (MAR)
SIDC........... Societe Industrielle Dahomeenne de Confection (MAR)
SIDCA .... Societe Industrielle Dakaroise de Conserves Alimentaires (MAR)
SIDE........... Secretaria de Informacion de Estado [*State Intelligence Secretariat*] [*Argentine*] (LA)
SIDE........... Servicio de Inteligencia del Ejercito [*Army Intelligence Service*] [*Uruguayan*] (LA)
SIDE........... Servicio de Investigaciones de Crimenes Economicos [*Investigating Service for Economic Crimes*] [*Chilean*] (LA)
SIDE........... Sistemul Informational Demografic [*Demographic Information System*] (RO)
SIDE........... Sociedad de Ingenieria del Ecuador [*Ecuadorean Engineering Society*] (LA)
SIDE........... Societe Ivoirienne d'Entreprises (MAR)
SIDEAC....... Societe Industrielle d'Engrais de l'Afrique Centrale (MAR)
SIDEB.......... Societe Ivoirienne de Distribution et d'Equipement de Bureaux (MAR)

SIDEC .... Societe Senegalaise d'Importation, de Distribution, et d'Exploitation Cinematographique (MAR)
SIDEC .... Stanford International Development Education Center (MAR)
SIDECI .... Societe Ivoirienne pour le Developpement de la Construction Industrialisee (MAR)
SIDECO....... Sindicato Profesional de Duenos de Establecimientos Comerciales de Chile [*Professional Union for Proprietors of Chilean Commercial Establishments*] (LA)
SIDEFCOOP ... Sociedad Interamericana de Desarrollo de Financiamiento Cooperativo [*Inter-American Society for the Development of Cooperative Financing*] (EA)
SIDEL.......... Sociedad Industrial de Ladrillo Ltda. [*Bogota*] (COL)
SIDELAF ..... Societe Ivoirienne d'Electrification (MAR)
SIDELPA..... Siderurgica del Pacifico SA [*Cali*] (COL)
SIDEM......... International Desalinization Company [*French*] (WER)
SIDEM......... Societe Ivoirienne d'Entreprises Maritimes (MAR)
SIDEMA ...... Societe Industrielle pour le Developpement du Machinisme Agricole [*Industrial Company for the Development of Agricultural Mechanization*] [*Malagasy*] (AF)
SIDEMA ...... Societe Ivoirienne d'Electro-Menager et d'Ameublement (MAR)
SIDEMAS.... Sivas Demiryol Makina Sanayii ve Muessessi [*Sivas Railway Machinery Industry Establishment*] [*Under Turkish State Railways*] (TU)
SIDEMPA.... Servicio Internacional de Marcas y Patentes [*Bogota*] (COL)
SIDENA....... Siderurgia Nacional [*National Iron and Steel Company*] [*Mexican*] (LA)
SIDERAFRIC ... Centre d'Information et de Promotion des Produits Siderurgiques et des Tubes d'Acier Francais en Afrique (MAR)
SIDERAMA ... Companhia Siderurgica da Amazonia [*Amazon Iron and Steel Company*] [*Brazilian*] (LA)
SIDERBRAS ... Siderurgica Brasileira, SA [*Brazilian Iron and Steel Corp.*] (LA)
SIDERFIL .... Siderurgica de Filadelphia Ltda. [*Bucaramanga*] (COL)
SIDERNA .... La Siderurgie Nationale [*Zairian*] (MAR)
SIDERPERU ... Empresa Siderurgica del Peru [*Peruvian State Iron and Steel Enterprise*] (LA)
SIDERRIO ... Acerias Paz Del Rio SA Siderurgica Paz Del Rio [*Bogota*] (COL)
SIDERSA..... Empresa Siderurgica Boliviana [*Bolivian Iron and Steel Enterprise*] (LA)
SIDES.......... Societe Industrielle pour le Developpement de la Securite en Algerie [*Industrial Company for the Development of Security in Algeria*] (AF)
SIDESA .... Siderurgica de la Sabana [*Bogota*] (COL)
SIDEST .... Societe Independante de Documentation et d'Editions Scientifiques et Techniques [*French*]
SIDETRA..... Societe Industrielle de Deroulage et de Tranchage (MAR)
SIDEX.......... Societe d'Importation de Distribution et d'Exportation (MAR)
SIDEXCA .... Societe Ivoirienne d'Exportation et de Transformation de Cafe, de Cacao, et de Produits Agricoles et Industriels (MAR)
SIDF .... Saudi Industrial Development Fund (ME)
SIDF .... Societe Ivoirienne de Developpement et de Financement (MAR)
SIDI .... Societe Ivoirienne de Developpement Industriel (MAR)
SIDIA.......... Sistema Integrado de Direccion de la Industria Azucarera [*Sugar Industry Integrated Management System*] [*Cuban*] (LA)
SIDIAMIL .... International Company for the Development of Food Industries Using Sorghum and Millet [*African*] (MAR)
SIDICAS...... Societe Immobiliere de Distribution de Carburants au Sahara (MAR)
SIDICO........ Societe Ivoirienne d'Exportation et de Diffusion des Colas (MAR)
SIDIMAG..... Societe Ivoirienne de Distribution de Marchandises Generales (MAR)
SIDINSA...... Siderurgica Integrada, Sociedad Anonima [*Integrated Iron and Steel Company, Incorporated*] [*Argentine*] (LA)
SIDITEX ...... Societe Internationale pour le Developpement de l'Industrie Textile (MAR)
S i DM.......... Construction and Road Machinery Manufacture (RU)
SIDO............ Small Industries Development Organization [*Tanzanian*] (AF)
SIDOR .... Siderurgica del Orinoco [*Orinoco Iron and Steelworks*] [*Venezuelan*] (LA)
SIDP .... Societe Ivoirienne de Distribution Petroliere (MAR)
SIDS............ Societe Internationale de Defense Sociale [*International Society for Social Defence - ISSD*] (EA)
SIDT .... Societe Industrielle de Transformation (MAR)
S(id)TPR..... Transistorized Scintillation Counter (with an Integrating Discriminator) (RU)
SIDUCAM ... Sindicato de Duenos de Camiones [*Truckowners Union*] [*Chilean*] (LA)
SIDUCO ...... Societe Industrielle d'Usinage et de Conditionnement (MAR)
SIE............... Service Import Export [*Import-Export Department*] [*In SKD*] [*Cambodian*] (CL)
SIE............... Servicio de Informaciones del Ejercito [*Army Intelligence Service*] [*Argentine*] (LA)
SIE............... Servicio de Informaciones del Ejercito [*Army Intelligence Service*] [*Peruvian*] (LA)
SIE............... Societe Immobiliere ELAEIS (MAR)
SIE............... Societe Ivoirienne des Etiquettes (MAR)
SIE............... Soviet Encyclopedia of History [*A publication*] (RU)
SIEB............ Societe Ivoirienne d'Exploitation Bananiere (MAR)
SIEBA.......... Societe Industrielle d'Exploitation des Bois Africains [*Douala*] (MAR)
SIEBEG .... Societe Ivoirienne d'Exploitation des Bois en Grumes (MAR)
SIEC............ Societe Internationale pour l'Enseignement Commercial [*International Society for Business Education*] (EA)
SIEC............ Societe Ivoirienne d'Expansion Commerciale (MAR)
SIECA .... Secretaria de Integracion Economica Centroamericana [*Secretariat of Central American Economic Integration*] (LA)
SIECA .... Societe Ivoirienne d'Exploitation de Carrieres (MAR)
SIEC-Benin ... Societe Immobiliere pour l'Equipement et la Construction au Benin (MAR)
SIECD .... Societe Internationale d'Education Continue en Dentisterie [*International Society of Continuing Education in Dentistry - ISCED*] (EA)
SIEC-Dahomey ... Societe Immobiliere pour l'Equipement et la Construction au Dahomey (MAR)
sied .... Siedend [*Boiling*] [*German*]
SIED............ Societe pour l'Importation et l'Exportation de Metaux Precieux au Dahomey (MAR)
SIED............ Societe Ivoirienne d'Ebenisterie et Decoration (MAR)
SIEDS.......... Societe Internationale d'Etude du Dix-Huitieme Siecle [*International Society for Eighteenth-Century Studies - ISECS*] (EA)
SIEFA.......... Syndesmos Idioktiton Elafron Fortigon Aftokiniton [*League of Light Weight Truck Owners*] [*Greek*] (GC)
SIEF-CONGO ... Societe Immobiliere et Fonciere Congo (MAR)
SIEFP .... Societe Industrielle d'Exploitation Forestiere du Plateau (MAR)
SIEF-RCA ... Societe Immobiliere et Fonciere RCA (MAR)
SIEF-Tchad ... Societe Immobiliere et Fonciere Tchad (MAR)
SIEG............ Societe Industrielle d'Emaillage et de Galvanisation (MAR)
SIEHT.......... Societe Ivoirienne d'Equipement Hotelier et Touristique (MAR)
SIEID........... Syndicat Interprofessionnel des Entreprises Industrielles du Dahomey (MAR)
SIEIT .... Syndicat Interprofessionnel des Entreprises Industrielles du Togo (MAR)
SIEL .... Sociedad Industrial Electronica Ltda. [*Bogota*] (COL)
SIEL .... Syllogos Idiotikon Ekpaidevtikon Leitourgon [*Association of Private School Teachers*] (GC)
SIELOR .... Societe Ivoirienne d'Electronique, Optique, et Radio (MAR)
SIELTE........ Societa Impianti Elettrici e Telefonici Sistema "Ericsson" (MAR)
SIEM .... Societe Industrielle Electro-Mecanique (MAR)
SIEM .... Societe Ivoirienne d'Emballages Metalliques (MAR)
SIEMENS .... Siemens Aktien-Gesellschaft (Berlin-Muenchen) [*Siemens Corporation (Berlin-Munich)*] (EG)
SIEMI .... Societe d'Importation et d'Exportation de Materiel Industriel (MAR)
SIEMI-RCA ... Societe d'Importation et d'Exportation de Materiel Industriel en RCA (MAR)
SIEN............ Sistema de Informacion Estadistica Nacional [*National Statistical Information System*] [*Cuban*] (LA)
SIERA.......... Scierie et Ebenisterie de l'Ira (MAR)
SIERI .... Societe Internationale d'Etude et de Recherche Industrielle [*Moroccan*] (MAR)
SIERI .... Societe Ivoirienne d'Etudes et de Realisations Industrielles (MAR)
SIEROMCO ... Sierra Leone Ore and Metal Company (MAR)
SIEROMOCO ... Sierra Leone Ore and Metal Company (MAR)
SIERTA .... Societe Ivoirienne d'Etudes et de Realisation de Travaux Agricoles (MAR)
sierz .... Sierzant [*Sergeant*] [*Polish*]
SIES .... Secretariat for International Ecology, Sweden (MAR)
SIES .... Sindicato de la Industria Electrica de El Salvador [*Union of the Electrical Industry Workers of El Salvador*] (LA)
SIES .... Societe Industrielle d'Engrais au Senegal (MAR)
SIESC .... Secretariat International des Enseignants Secondaries Catholiques [*International Secretariat of Catholic Secondary School Teachers*] [*Acronym used in association name, SIESC Pax Romana*] (EA)
SIESCA....... Societe Ivoirienne d'Elevage, de Salasion, et de Commerce Alimentaire (MAR)
SIETA.......... Societe Internationale d'Etudes et de Travaux en Afrique (MAR)
SIETHO .... Societe Ivoirienne d'Expansion Touristique et Hoteliere (MAR)
SIETI .... Small Industry Extension Training Institute [*Indian*] (MAR)
SIETRANS ... Ivorian Maritime Transport and International Logistics Engineering (MAR)
SIEXI .... Societe Ivoirienne d'Exportation et d'Importation (MAR)
SIF.............. Societe Ivoirienne de Financement (MAR)
SIF.............. Societe Sondages-Injections-Forages (MAR)
SIF.............. Sveriges Industriforbund [*Federation of Swedish Industries*] (WEN)
SIFA .... Servicio de Inteligencia de la Fuerza Aerea [*Air Force Intelligence Service*] [*Argentine*] (LA)
SIFA .... Servicio de Inteligencia de la Fuerza Aerea [*Air Force Intelligence Service*] [*Chilean*] (LA)
SIFA .... Servicio de Inteligencia de las Fuerzas Armadas [*Armed Forces Intelligence Service*] [*Dominican Republic*] (LA)

SIFA .... Servicio de Inteligencia de las Fuerzas Armadas [*Armed Forces Intelligence Service*] [*Venezuelan*] (LA)
SIFA .... Societe Industrielle Forestiere et des Allumettes (MAR)
SIFA .... Syndesmos Idioktiton Fortigon Avtokiniton [*League of Truck Owners*] [*Greek*] (GC)
SIFAC .... Societe Industrielle Forestiere en Afrique Centrale (MAR)
SIFAC .... Societe Industrielle Forestiere et Agricole de la Casamance (MAR)
SIFACE .... Societe Ivoirienne de Fabrication et de Commercialisation d'Appareillages Electriques et Electroniques (MAR)
SIFACOL ..... Societe Ivoirienne de Fabrication de Colles et Liants (MAR)
SIFAL .... Societe Ivoirienne de Fabrication de Lubrifiants (MAR)
SIFAR .... Servizio Informazioni delle Forze Armate [*Armed Forces Intelligence Service*] [*Italian*] (WER)
SIFAS .... Sentetik Iplik Fabrikalari Anonim Sirketi [*Synthetic Silk Factories Corporation*] [*Bursa*] (TU)
SIFAS .... Societe Industrielle de Fabrication d'Articles Scolaires [*School Supplies Manufacturing Company*] [*Cambodian*] (CL)
SIFAV .... Societe Industrielle de Fabrication d'Articles de Voyage (MAR)
SIFCAM ...... Societe Industrielle et Forestiere du Cameroun (MAR)
SIFCCA .... Societe Immobiliere Financiere et Commerciale de la Cote-d'Afrique (MAR)
SIFCCA .... Societe Industrielle Forestiere et Commerciale Camerounaise (MAR)
SIFCI .... Societe Industrielle et Forestiere de Cote-d'Ivoire [*Ivory Coast Industrial and Forestry Company*] (AF)
SIFCODER ... Societe Ivoirienne d'Importation et d'Exportation, de Fabrication, Construction, Confection, Distribution, d'Echanges, et de Representations (MAR)
SIFCODI ...... Societe Ivoirienne de Fabrication, Conditionnement, et Distribution (MAR)
SIFCP .... Societe Industrielle de Fabrication de Chaussures Plastuques (MAR)
SIFEC .... Societe d'Isolation Frigorifique et d'Entreprise de Construction (MAR)
SIFEDIB ...... Societe Ivoirienne Forestiere et de Developpement des Industries du Bois (MAR)
SIFEL .... Societe Ivoirienne de Fabrication d'Elastiques (MAR)
SIFELEC ..... Societe Ivoirienne de Fabrication de Materiel Electrique et de Compteurs a Eau (MAR)
SIFEP .... Societe d'Importation Fruits et Primeurs (MAR)
SIFERCOM ... Societe Ivoirienne d'Entreprise et de Construction (MAR)
SIFF .... Societe Ivoirienne Farhat Freres (MAR)
SIFI .... Societe Immobiliere Financiere et Industrielle (MAR)
SIFIDA .... Societe Financiere pour les Investissements et le Developpement en Afrique [*Financial Company for Investments and Development in Africa*] [*Tunisian*] (AF)
SIFIDA .... Societe Internationale Financiere pour les Investissements et le Developpement en Afrique [*North African*] (MAR)
SIFLI .... Societe Ivoirienne de Fabrication de Lubrifiants et d'Insecticides (MAR)
SIFMA .... Societe Ivoirienne de Fabrication et de Montage Automobile (MAR)
SIFMAP .... Somateion Idioktiton Fortigon kai Motosykletton Athinon-Peiraios [*Association of Athens-Piraeus Truck and Motorcycle Owners*] (GC)
SIFMCOL .... Siemmens Colombiana Ltda. [*Bogota*] (COL)
SIFO .... Sociedad Industrial de Fundicion de Occidente (COL)
SIFO .... Svenska Institutet for Opinions-Undersokningar [*Swedish Institute for Public Opinion Polls*] (WEN)
SIFOMAT .... Societe Ivoirienne de Fournitures et de Materiaux (MAR)
SIFOR .... Societe Industrielle de Fort-Dauphin (MAR)
SIFRA .... Societe Industrielle des Fruits Africains (MAR)
SIFRIA .... Societe Immobiliere de Fria (MAR)
SIFROID ...... Societe Industrielle du Froid du Benin (MAR)
SIFT .... Societe Industrielle et Forestiere de Tchanga (MAR)
SIFTAM .... Societa Immobiliare Fondiaria Tripolina Ahmed Muntasser (MAR)
Sig .... Signore [*Sir or Mister*] [*Correspondence*] [*Italian*]
Sig .... Sigorta [*Insurance*] (TU)
SIG .... Societe Industrielle Generale [*General Industrial Company*] [*Tunisian*] (AF)
SIG .... Societe Ivoirienne de Gaufretterie (MAR)
SIG .... Societe Ivoirienne de Gerances (MAR)
SIG .... Societe Ivoirienne de Groupage (MAR)
SIGA .... Societe Ivoirienne de Gestion Agricole (MAR)
SIGAC .... Sindicato de la Industria Gastronomica y Actividades Conexas [*Union of Workers in the Restaurant Industry and Related Activities*] [*Salvadoran*] (LA)
SIGAL .... Societe Ivoirienne de Galvanisation (MAR)
SIGAMA ...... Societe Italo-Gabonaise des Marbres (MAR)
SIGAS .... Societe d'Ingenierie, de Gestion, et de Service en Afrique (MAR)
SIGC .... Servicio de Investigacion de la Guardia Civil [*Investigation Service of the Civil Guard*] [*Spanish*] (WER)
SIGEBAN .... Sindicato de la Industria General de Empresas Bancarias y Asociaciones de Ahorro y Prestamo [*Trade Union of the General Industry of Banking and Savings and Loan*] [*Salvadoran*] (LA1)
SIGEFOR ..... Societe Ivoirienne de Gestion et d'Exploitation Forestiere (MAR)
SIGEM .... Salon International du Genie et de l'Equipement Municipal (MAR)
SIGES .... Societe Ivoirienne de Gestion, d'Etudes, et des Services (MAR)
SIGEXA .... Societe Ivoirienne de Gestion et d'Exploitation Automobiles (MAR)
Sigg .... Signori [*Sirs*] [*Italian*]
SIGI .... Societe Ivoirienne de Gestion Immobiliere (MAR)
Sigl .... Signal [*Signal*] [*Military map abbreviation*] [*World War I*] [*French*] (MTD)
SIGLOI .... Societe d'Importation et de Distribution de Gaz Liquefies pour l'Ocean Indien (MAR)
SIGMA .... Fabrika Signalnih Uredaja i Masina [*Signal Equipment and Machinery Factory*] [*Subotica*] (YU)
SIGMATP .... Societe Industrielle Gabonaise de Materiaux de Travaux Publics (MAR)
Sign .... Call Number [*Book*] (BU)
SIGNETEL ... Societe de Signalisation Electronique et de Telecommunications (MAR)
SIGP .... Societe Industrielle de la Grande Peche (MAR)
SIGRA .... Sociedad Industrial de Grasas SA [*Bogota*] (COL)
SIGRAG .... Societe Industrielle d'Exploitation des Granits Guineens (MAR)
sigte .... Siguiente [*Following, Next*] [*Spanish*]
SIGUE .... Society for Developments in Guinea (MAR)
SIH .... Societe Ivoirienne d'Habillement (MAR)
SIH .... Societe Ivoirienne d'Hotellerie (MAR)
SIHAM .... Societe Industrielle des Huiles au Maroc (MAR)
SIHTCO .... Societe Ivoirienne Hoteliere et Touristique de la Comoe (MAR)
SII .... Societe d'Imprimerie Ivoirienne (MAR)
SIIAEC .... Secretariat International des Ingenieurs, des Agronomes, et des Cadres Economiques Catholiques [*International Secretariat of Catholic Technologists, Agriculturists, and Economists*] (EA)
SIII .... Communications of the Institute of the History of the Arts (of the Academy of Sciences, USSR) [*A publication*] (RU)
SIII .... Societe Industrielle et Immobiliere Ivoirienne (MAR)
SIJVPP .... Statni Inspekce Jakosti Vyrobku Potravinarskeho Prumyslu [*State Inspection Office for Quality of Food Industry Products*] (CZ)
SIJZV .... Statni Inspekce Jakosti Zemedelskych Vyrobku [*State Inspection Office for Quality of Agricultural Products*] (CZ)
SIK .... Savezna Industriska Komora [*Federal Chamber of Industry*] (YU)
SIK .... Societe Immobiliere de Koutou (MAR)
SIK .... Sostanjska Industrija Konfekcije [*Sostanj Ready-Made Clothing Industry*] (YU)
SIKD "Njegos" ... Srpsko Istorisko-Kulturno Drustvo "Njegos" [*"Njegos" Serbian Historical and Cultural Society*] [*Chicago*] (YU)
SIKN .... Societe Immobiliere du Kouilou-Niari (MAR)
SIKO .... Societe Industrielle du Kouilou (MAR)
SIL .... Societe Internationale de la Lepre (MAR)
sil .... Tower Silo [*Topography*] (RU)
SILA .... Sistema Informativo Latinoamericano [*Latin American Information System*] (LA)
SILCA .... Societa Italo-Libica Commercio Automobili (MAR)
SILCO .... Societe Ivoiro-Libanaise de Commerce (MAR)
SILDA .... Sociedad Industrial Litografica Ltda. [*Bogota*] (COL)
SILE .... Service d'Information de la Legion Etrangere (MAR)
SILETI .... Sierra Leone Timber Industry and Plantation Company (MAR)
SILF .... Societe Internationale de Linguistique Fonctionelle [*International Society of Functional Linguistics*] (EA)
silik .... Silicate Industry Plant [*Topography*] (RU)
SILIORIOS ... Silicatos y Viorios Ltda. [*Cartagena*] (COL)
SILMT .... Syndesmos Idioktiton Leoforeion Meizonos Typou [*League of Owners of Large Buses*] [*Greek*] (GC)
SILOM .... Societe d'Investissements Laitiers Outre-Mer (MAR)
SILP .... Societe Ivoirienne de Librairie et de Papeterie (MAR)
SILPA .... Societa Industria Lavorazione Pietra Azizia (MAR)
SILS .... Societe d'Investissements Libano-Senegalaise (MAR)
SILU .... Sugar Industry Laborers Union [*Mauritian*] (AF)
SILWF .... Sugar Industry Labor Welfare Fund [*Mauritian*] (AF)
SILWFC .... Sugar Industry Labour Welfare Fund Committee [*Guyanese*]
SiM .... "Hammer and Sickle" Plant (RU)
SIM .... Servicio de Inteligencia Militar [*Military Intelligence Service*] [*Chilean*] (LA)
SIM .... Servicio de Inteligencia Militar [*Military Intelligence Service*] [*Dominican Republic*] (LA)
SIM .... Servizio Informazioni Militare [*Military Intelligence Service*] [*Italian*] (WER)
SIM .... Siberian Scientific Research Institute of Metals (RU)
sim .... Siemens (RU)
SIM .... Slovenska Izseljenska Matica [*Slovenian Emigration Society*] (YU)
SIM .... Sociedad Industrial de Materiales [*Bogota*] (COL)
SIM .... Sociedad Industrial Metalica Ltda. [*Manizales*] (COL)
SIM .... Societe Immobiliere de Madagascar (MAR)
SIM .... Societe d'Importation et d'Achat du Mali (MAR)
SIM .... Societe Industrielle de Menuiserie (MAR)
SIM .... Societe Senegalaise d'Investissements Maritimes (MAR)
SIM .... Spolka Inzynierow Mechanikow [*Mechanical Engineers Company*] (POL)
SIM .... Standards Institution of Malaysia (ML)

SIM .... Sudan Interior Mission (MAR)
sim .... Symmetrical (RU)
SIMA .... Servicio Industrial de Marina [*Maritime Industrial Service*] [*Peruvian*] (LA)
SIMA .... Sociedad de Intercambio Mercantil Ltda. [*Medellin*] (COL)
SIMA .... Societe d'Importation et d'Exportation Centrafricaine (MAR)
SIMA .... Societe Industrielle de Metaux pour l'Afrique (MAR)
SIMA .... Societe Ivoirienne de Menuiserie et d'Ameublement (MAR)
SIMAA .... Societe d'Importation de Materiel Automobile et Agricole (MAR)
SIMAC .... Societe Immobiliere d'Afrique Centrale (MAR)
SIMACO .... Societe Ivoirienne de Materiaux de Construction (MAR)
SIMAF .... Societe Industrielle Moderne d'Ameublement et de Ferronnerie (MAR)
SIMAFCI .... Societe Immobiliere Africaine de la Cote-d'Ivoire (MAR)
SIMAFRUIT ... Societe Interprofessionnelle Maritime et Fruitiere (MAR)
SIMAI .... Servicio Industrial de la Marina de Iquitos [*Iquitos Industrial Marine Service*] [*Peruvian*] (LA)
SIMAP .... Servicio de Informacion de Mercadeo Agropecuario [*Peruvian*]
SIMAR .... Societe Ivoirienne de Maroquinerie (MAR)
SIMAS .... Sindicato de la Industria de Muebles, Accesorios, y Similares [*Union of the Furniture and Related Industries*] [*Salvadoran*] (LA)
SIMAVIN .... Societe d'Importation Africaine Vinicole (MAR)
SIMC .... Societe Immobiliere Congolaise (MAR)
SIMC .... Societe Immobiliere du Moyen-Congo (MAR)
SIMC .... Societe Internationale de Medecine de Catastrophe [*International Society for Disaster Medicine*] (EA)
SIMC .... Societe Ivoirienne de Montages et de Constructions (MAR)
SIMCA .... Societe Industrielle de Mecanique et de Carrosserie Automobile [*French automobile manufacturer; acronym used as name of its cars*]
SIMCI .... Societe Industrielle de Matelas de Cote-d'Ivoire (MAR)
SIMCO .... Societe Immobiliere et de Constructions du Tchad (MAR)
SIMDA .... Sociedad de Importaciones Ltda. [*Bucaramanga*] (COL)
SIME .... Industria Sideromecanica [*Steelworking Industry*] [*Cuban*] (LA)
SIME .... Servicio Integral de Medicina Escolar. Universidad del Valle [*Cali*] (COL)
SIME .... Societe d'Importation de Materiel Electrique (MAR)
SIME .... Societe Industrielle de Materiaux et d'Etancheite (MAR)
SIMEA .... Societa Italiana Meriadionale per l'Energia Atomica [*Italian*]
SIMEA .... Societe Ivoirienne de Montage et d'Exploitation Automobile (MAR)
SIMECA .... Sociedade Importadora de Maquinas, Equipamentos, Carros, e Acessorios Lda. (MAR)
SIMECO .... Societe Ivoirienne de Menuiserie, d'Ebenisterie, et de Constructions Immobilieres (MAR)
SIMEF .... Societe des Industries Mecaniques et Electriques de Fes (MAR)
SIMEI .... Societe Ivoirienne de Materiaux Etanches et Isolants (MAR)
SIMENT .... Societe Imerinienne d'Entreprises (MAR)
SIMESA .... Siderurgica de Medellin Sociedad Anonima (COL)
SIMEUBLES ... Societe Ivoirienne de Meubles (MAR)
SIMEX .... Societe d'Importation et d'Exportation (MAR)
SIMEX .... Syrian Import and Export Company (ME)
SIMEXCO .... Societe Ivoirienne d'Importation, d'Exportation et de Commission (MAR)
SIMG .... Societas Internationalis Medicinae Generalis [*International Society of General Practice*] (EA)
SIMGAL .... Societe d'Importation du Senegal (MAR)
SIMI .... Societe Ivoirienne de Machettes Industrielles (MAR)
SIMITAS .... Sosyal Isletmeler ve Mesken Insaati Turk Anonim Sirketi [*Social Administration and Housing Construction Corporation*] (TU)
SIMKh .... Saratov Institute of Agricultural Mechanization Imeni M. I. Kalinin (RU)
SIMO .... Societe Ivoirienne des Materiels d'Organisation (MAR)
SIMO .... Somateion Ithopion Melodramatos kai Operas [*Association of Musical Stage and Opera Performers*] [*Greek*] (GC)
SIMOCA .... Societe Industrielle du Moyen-Orient au Cameroun [*Arab*] (MAR)
SIMOPA .... Societe Industrielle Moderne de Parfumerie (MAR)
SIMOTUR .... Sindicato de Motoristas del Transporte Urbano [*Trade Union of Urban Transportation Drivers*] [*Nicaraguan*] (LA1)
SIMP .... Stowarzyszenie Inzynierow i Technikow Mechanikow Polskich [*Association of Polish Mechanical Engineers and Technicians*] (POL)
SIMPA .... Societe Industrielle Moderne de Plastiques Africains (MAR)
SIMPAFRIC ... Societe d'Impressions Africaines (MAR)
SIMPEX .... Syndicat des Importateurs et Exportateurs du Gabon (MAR)
SIMPOL .... Societe Ivoirienne de Mousse Polyester (MAR)
sim/ros .... Simaioforos [*Ensign*] [*Navy rank*] (GC)
SIMS .... Societa Italiana di Medicina Sociale [*Italian*]
SIMSKh .... Saratov Institute of Agricultural Mechanization Imeni M. I. Kalinin (RU)
SIMSOC .... Societe Immobiliere Socomotra & Cie. (MAR)
SIMU .... Local Control Synchronizing Pulse [*Computers*] (RU)
SIMUN .... Empresa Siderurgica del Muna SA [*Bogota*] (COL)
SIN .... Servicio de Informaciones Navales [*Naval Intelligence Service*] [*Argentine*] (LA)
SIN .... Servicio de Inteligencia Nacional [*National Intelligence Service*] [*Peruvian*] (LA)
SIN .... Sistemul Informatic National [*National Data Processing System*] (RO)
SIN .... Societe Industrielle de Nouveautes [*North African*] (MAR)
sin .... Synonym (RU)
SINA .... Sindicato de la Industria Nacional del Azucar [*Union of the National Sugar Industry*] [*Salvadoran*] (LA)
SINA .... Societe Ivoirienne de Navigation (MAR)
SINABAN .... Sindicato Nacional de Empleados Bancarios de Panama [*National Union of Bank Employees of Panama*] (LA)
SINACAM ... Sistema Nacional de Controle Ambiental [*National Environmental Control System*] [*Brazilian*] (LA)
SINACHOD ... Sindicato Nacional de Choferes Dominicanos [*National Trade Union of Dominican Drivers*] [*Dominican Republic*] (LA1)
SINADEPS ... Sistema Nacional de Desarrollo de Propiedad Social [*National System for Social Property Development*] [*Peruvian*] (LA1)
SINADI .... Sistema Nacional de Informacion [*National Information System*] [*Peruvian*] (LA)
SINAES .... Societe Industrielle des Applications de l'Energie Solaire [*Senegalese*] (MAR)
SINAFCO .... Societe Inter-Africaine pour la Cooperation Commerciale [*Senegalese*] (MAR)
SINAFORP ... Sistema Nacional de Formacion Profesional [*National System for Professional Training*] [*Nicaraguan*] (LA1)
SINAMOS .... Sistema Nacional de Apoyo a la Mobilizacion Social [*National System for Support to Social Mobilization*] [*Peruvian*] (LA)
SINAP .... Sistema Nacional de Ahorros y Prestamos [*National Savings and Loan System*] [*Chilean*] (LA)
SINARA .... Sistema Nacional de Radiodifusion [*National Broadcasting System*] [*Argentine*] (LA)
SINAREX .... Societe Nationale de Recherche et d'Exploitation Minieres (MAR)
SINART .... Sistema Nacional de Radio y Television Cultural [*National System for Cultural Radio and Television*] [*Costa Rican*] (LA1)
SINATRA .... Sindicato Nacional de Trabajadores de la Radio [*National Radio Workers Union*] [*Colombian*] (LA)
SINATRASTEDO ... Sindicato Autonomo de Trabajadores de Sacos y Tejidos Dominicanos [*Autonomous Trade Union of Dominican Sacking and Textile Workers*] [*Dominican Republic*] (LA1)
SINBI .... Societe Nouvelle de Broderies et d'Impressions [*North African*] (MAR)
SINC .... Nicaraguan International Rescue from Communism (PD)
SINC .... Servei d'Informacio Nacional Catala [*Catalan National Information Service*] [*Spanish*] (WER)
SINCAP .... Societe Industrielle du Cap-Vert [*Senegalese*] (MAR)
SINCATEX ... Societe Industrielle Camerounaise des Textiles (MAR)
SINCO .... Societa Incremento e Commerciale (MAR)
SINCO .... Societe Internationale de Commerce (MAR)
SINCOLIT .... Societe Industrielle et Commerciale de Literie (MAR)
SINCONI .... Societe Industrielle Commerciale Nigerienne (MAR)
SINCRO .... Societe Informatique, de Conseils, et de Recherches Operationnels (MAR)
sind .... Syndicate (RU)
SINDACO .... Sindicato Angolano dos Camponeses et Operarios (MAR)
SINDEIT .... Sindicato de Empleados del Instituto Tecnologico [*Trade Union of Technological Institute Employees*] [*Costa Rican*] (LA1)
SINDELEN ... Sociedad de Industrias Electricas Nacionales [*Society of National Electrical Industries*] [*Chilean*] (LA)
SINDEMU .... Sociedad Industrial de Muebles Ltda. [*Medellin*] (COL)
SINDEP .... Sindicato Nacional de la Empresa Privada [*National Private Enterprise Union*] [*Costa Rican*] (LA)
SINDEU .... Sindicato de Trabajadores de la Universidad de Costa Rica [*Trade Union of Costa Rica University Workers*] (LA1)
SINDICOL ... Sindicato Unico de Trabajadores de Coltejer [*Medellin*] (COL)
SINDICONS ... Sindicato Obrero de la Construccion de Antioquia [*Medellin*] (COL)
SINDU .... Servicio Interamericano sobre el Desarrollo Urbano [*Inter-American Urban Development Information Service*] (LA)
SINECELH ... Sindicato Nacional de Empleados de Comunicaciones Electricas de Honduras [*National Union of Electrical Communication Employees of Honduras*] (LA)
SINEG .... Societe Ivoirienne de Negoce (MAR)
SINE-IS .... Turkiye Sinema Iscileri Sendikasi [*Turkish Cinema Workers Union*] [*Istanbul*] (TU)
SINEPUDERH ... Sindicato de Empleados Publicos de Educacion Rural en Honduras [*Trade Union of Honduran Rural Education Public Employees*] (LA1)
SINFDOK .... Swedish Council for Scientific Information and Documentation
SINFELTA ... Sindicato Ferroviario del Pacifico [*Cali*] (COL)
SINK .... Individual Carrier-Channels and Pilot-Frequency Bay (RU)
SINMUH .... Sindicato Musical de Honduras [*Honduran Musical Trade Union*] [*Honduran*] (LA1)
SINN .... Societe de l'Imprimerie Nationale du Niger (MAR)
Sinod k-vo ... Synodic Publishing House (BU)
SINOMAPE ... Sindicato Nacional de Operadores de Maquinas Pesadas [*National Union of Heavy Machinery Operators*] [*Dominican Republic*] (LA)
SINOPTAL ... Societe Industrielle d'Optique Algerie (MAR)
SINOTASHIP ... Sino-Tanzanian Joint Shipping Company (MAR)
SINPA .... Societe d'Interet National des Produits Agricoles [*National Agricultural Products Company*] [*Malagasy*] (AF)

SINPAR .... Servicio Investigativo Particular [*Bogota*] (COL)
SINPEP .... Sindicato Nacional de Profesores de Educacion Primaria [*National Union of Elementary Education Teachers*] [*Peruvian*] (LA)
SINPES .... Sindicato Nacional de Profesores de Educacion Secundaria [*National Union of Secondary School Teachers*] [*Peruvian*] (LA)
SINPET .... Sindicato Nacional de Profesores de Educacion Tecnica [*National Union of Technical Education Teachers*] [*Peruvian*] (LA)
sint .... Synthetic (RU)
SINTAE .... Sindicato Nacional de Trabajadores de Artes y Espectaculos [*National Union of Entertainment Workers*] [*Cuban*] (LA)
SINTAS .... Sosyal Sehircilik Insaat ve Ticaret Anonim Sirketi [*Social City Planning Construction and Trade Corporation*] (TU)
SINTECO .... Sociedad Industrial Tecnica Ltda. [*Cali*] (COL)
SINTEF .... Foundation of Scientific and Industrial Research [*Norwegian*]
SINTEL .... Sindicato de Telecomunicacoes [*Telecommunications Workers Union*] [*Portuguese*] (WER)
sintetich ...... Synthetic (RU)
SINTP .... Societe d'Interet National des Travaux Publics [*National Public Works Company*] [*Malagasy*] (AF)
SINTRABANCOL ... Sindicato Nacional de Trabajadores del Banco de Colombia [*Bogota*] (COL)
SINTRABE ... Sindicato de Trabajadores de Editorial y Tipografia Bedout [*Medellin*] (COL)
SINTRAFEC ... Sindicato de Trabajadores de la Federacion Nacional de Cafeteros de Colombia [*Chinchina-Caldas*] (COL)
SINTRAFERRAT ... Sindicato de Trabajadores Ferrocarriles del Atlantico [*Atlantico Railroad Workers Union*] [*Colombian*] (LA)
SINTRAIMEC ... Sindicato de Trabajadores de las Industrias Metalicas de Colombia [*Colombian Metal Workers Union*] (LA)
SINTRAQUIN ... Sindicato Nacional de Trabajadores de la Industria Quimica [*Cali*] (COL)
SINTRASALUD ... Sindicato de Trabajadores de Salud [*Trade Union of Health Workers*] [*Dominican Republic*] (LA1)
SINTRAVA ... Sindicato Nacional de Trabajadores de Avianca [*Bogota*] (COL)
SIO .... Aircraft Icing Gauge (RU)
SIO .... Individual Equipment Bay (RU)
SIO .... Random Information Processing (RU)
SIO .... Rural Election District (RU)
SIO .... Sekretarijat za Industrijo in Obrt [*Secretariat of Industry and Trade*] (YU)
SIO .... Social Insurance Organization [*Saudi*] (ME)
SIO .... Societe Industrielle d'Owendo (MAR)
SIO .... Studio za Industrijsko Oblikovanje [*Studio for Industrial Design*] [*Zagreb*] (YU)
SIODC .... Swaziland Iron Ore Development Company Limited (MAR)
SIOI .... Societa Italiana per l'Organizzazione Internazionale [*Italian*]
SIOM .... Societe Industrielle Oleicole Marocaine (MAR)
SIOMA .... Societe Impressions Ofset Maroc (MAR)
SIOP .... Societe Internationale d'Oncologie Pediatrique [*International Society of Pediatric Oncology*] (EA)
SIORBA .... Societe Immobiliere Ornano-Jean-Bart [*Moroccan*] (MAR)
SIOS .... Servizio Informasioni Operativa e Situazione [*Operational Intelligence and Situation Services*] [*Italian*] (WER)
SIOT .... All-Union Scientific Research Institute of Work Safety of the VTsSPS [*All-Union Central Trade-Union Council*] (Sverdlovsk) (RU)
SIP .... Individual Frequency-Converter Bay (RU)
SIP .... Secretaria de Informacion Publica [*Secretariat of Public Information*] [*Argentine*] (LA)
SIP .... Sindicato de la Industria del Pescado [*Fishing Industry Union*] [*Argentine*] (LA)
SIP .... Sindicato de la Industria Pesquera [*Fishing Industry Union*] [*Salvadoran*] (LA)
SIP .... Sindicato de Industriales Panamenos [*Panamanian Industrialists Union*] (LA)
SIP .... Sociedad Interamericana de Prensa [*Inter-American Press Association*] [*Use IAPA*] (LA)
SIP .... Societa Italiana per l'Esercizio Telefonico [*Italian Telephone Company*] (WER)
SIP .... Societe Indigene de Prevoyance (MAR)
SIP .... Societe Industrielle Pharmaceutique (MAR)
SIP .... Societe Ivoirienne de Peche (MAR)
SIP .... Societe Ivoirienne de Peinture (MAR)
SIP .... Societes Indigenes de Prevoyance [*North African*] (MAR)
SIP .... Spoleczne Inspekcje Pracy [*People's Labor Inspectorate*] (POL)
SIP .... Spoleczny Inspektor Pracy [*People's Labor Inspector*] (POL)
SIP- .... Step Pulse Interrupter (RU)
SIP .... Sumsko Industrisko Poduzece [*Forestry Industrial Establishment*] (YU)
SIPA .... Servicio de Investigacion y Promocion Agrarias [*Agrarian Research and Development Service*] [*Peruvian*] (LA)
SIPA .... Societe d'Importation des Pieces Automobiles (MAR)
SIPA .... Societe Industrielle des Plastiques Abidjanais (MAR)
SIPA .... Societe Industrielle de Produits Africains (MAR)
SIPA .... Somali Institute of Public Administration (MAR)
SIPAC .... Societe Ivoirienne de Plomberie, Assainissement, et Canalisation (MAR)
SIPAD .... Preduzece za Izvoz Drveta, Sarajevo (Sumsko Industrisko Preduzece Akcionarsko Drustvo) [*Wood Export Establishment*] [*Sarajevo*] (YU)
SIPAG .... Societe Industrielle de Panification de Guinee (MAR)
SIPAG .... Syndicat des Instituteurs, Professeurs, et Agents de la Guadeloupe (PD)
SIPAL .... Societe Industrielle de Preparations Alimentaires [*Togolese*] (MAR)
SIPALAC ..... Sindicato de la Industria de Productos Alimenticios, Lacteos, y Actividades Conexas [*Union of the Food, Dairy, and Related Industries*] [*Salvadoran*] (LA)
SIPAM .... Societe Industrielle de Peche a Madagascar (MAR)
SIPAM .... Societe Industrielle des Produits Alimentaires du Nord-Marocain (MAR)
SIPAR .... Societe Ivoirienne de Peche et d'Armement [*Ivorian Fishing and Shipping Company*] (AF)
SIPARCO .... Societe Industrielle de Parfumerie et de Cosmetique (MAR)
SIPAROCI ... Societe Industrielle de Parfumerie et de Cosmetique (MAR)
SIPCA .... Societe Industrielle de Produits Chimiques et Aromatiques (MAR)
SIPCI .... Societe Ivoirienne de Promotion Commerciale et Industrielle (MAR)
SIPCO .... Societe Ivoirienne de Produits Congeles (MAR)
SIPE .... Savezni Institut za Poljoprivrednu Ekonomiku [*Federal Institute of Agricultural Economics*] (YU)
SIPE .... Sociedade Industrial de Produtos Electricos [*Industrial Company for Electrical Products*] [*Portuguese*] (WER)
SIPEC .... Societe Industrielle des Peches au Cameroun (MAR)
SIPEC .... Societe Ivoirienne de Peintures et Colorants (MAR)
SIPECO .... Societe Industrielle des Peintures de Conakry (MAR)
SIPEGA .... Societe Industrielle des Peches du Gabon (MAR)
SIPER .... Societe Ivoirienne de Peinture et Revetement (MAR)
SIPES .... Sindicato de la Industria Portuaria de El Salvador [*Union of Port Workers of El Salvador*] (LA)
SIPG .... Societe Internationale de Participation et de Gestion (MAR)
SIPG .... Societe Internationale de Pathologie Geographique [*International Society of Geographical Pathology*] (EA)
SIPH .... Societe Indochinoise de Plantations d'Heveas [*Indochinese Rubber Plantation Industry*] (MAR)
SIPHAC .... Societe Industrielle Pharmaceutique du Cameroun (MAR)
SIPHO .... Societe Immobiliere de Promotion d'Etudes et de Realisations Hotelieres (MAR)
SIPI .... Societe Ivoirienne de Promotion Industrielle [*Ivorian Company for Industrial Promotion*] (AF)
SIPIHO .... Societe Ivoirienne pour l'Industrie Hoteliere (MAR)
SIPJB .... Societe Industrielle de Parfumerie Jazzar Bitar (MAR)
SIPL .... Societe Industrielle de Produits Laitiers (MAR)
SIPLA .... Societe Immobiliere et de Placement (MAR)
SIPMAD ...... Societe Industrielle de Peche de Madagascar (MAR)
SIPMAG ...... Societe Ivoirienne de Papiers et Materiels d'Arts Graphiques (MAR)
SIPOA .... Societe Industrielle Pharmaceutique de l'Ouest Africain (MAR)
SIPOL .... Seccion de Investigacion Policiaca [*Police Investigation Section*] [*Mexican*] (LA)
SIPPO .... Societe Ivoirienne des Pieces et Pneumatiques d'Occasion (MAR)
SIPPTAL ..... Sindicato de Productores Propietarios de Tierras Agropecuarias del Litoral [*Union of Coastal Agricultural and Livestock Landowners and Producers*] [*Ecuadorean*] (LA)
SIPR .... Societe Ivoirienne de Plomberie et Revetements (MAR)
SIPRA .... Societe Ivoirienne de Productions Animals (MAR)
SIPRAG .... Societe Ivoirienne de Promotion Agricole (MAR)
SIPREDI ...... Societe Internationale de Presse, d'Edition, et de Diffusion (MAR)
SIPRI .... Stockholm International Peace Research Institute (EA)
SIPRIM .... Societe Ivoirienne de Promotion et de Realisations Immobilieres (MAR)
SIPROA .... Societe Ivoirienne de Produits Agricoles (MAR)
SIPROM ...... Societe Industrielle des Produits Metallurgiques [*Moroccan*] (MAR)
SIPRON .... Sistema de Protecao ao Programa Nuclear Brasileiro [*Protective System for the Brazilian Nuclear Program*] (LA1)
SIPROSEM ... Societe Ivoirienne de Production de Sel Marin (MAR)
SIPRO-TOURIST ... Societe Ivoirienne de Promotion Touristique (MAR)
SIPS .... Societe Industrielle de Papeterie au Senegal (MAR)
SIPS .... Societe Ivoirienne de Plomberie Sanitaire (MAR)
SIPTP .... Societe Industrielle de Plomberie, Travaux Publics, et Particuliers [*Senegalese*] (MAR)
sir .... Namely (BU)
SIR .... Singapore Infantry Regiment (ML)
SIR .... Societe Ivoirienne de Raffinage [*Ivorian Refining Company*] (AF)
SIRAMA ...... Societe Siramamy Malagasy [*Malagasy Sugar Company*] (AF)
SIRAPS .... Sistema Intersectorial Regional de Apoyo a la Propiedad Social [*Intersectoral Regional System for Support of Social Property*] [*Peruvian*] (LA)

SIRAT.......... Societe Ivoirienne de Realisations Artisanales et Touristiques (MAR)
SIRCA......... Societe des Importateurs Reunis du Cameroun (MAR)
SIRCA......... Societe Industrielle de la Republique Centrafrique (MAR)
SIRCOM...... Societe Ivoirienne de Representation et de Commission (MAR)
SIRCOMA... Societe Industrielle de Representations et Commerciale en Mauritanie (MAR)
SIRDI.......... Societe Immobiliere de Representation et de Distribution (MAR)
SIREGCI...... Societe Immobiliere et de Representations Generales de Cote-d'Ivoire (MAR)
SIREG-Dakar... Societe Immobiliere et de Representations Generales de Dakar (MAR)
SIREL.......... Societe Industrielle et Routiere des Entreprises Lair (MAR)
SIRELE........ Societe Ivoirienne de Realisation Electrique (MAR)
SIREP.......... Societe Internationale pour la Recherche et l'Exploitation du Petrole (MAR)
SIRI............. Societe Ivoirienne de Representation Industrielle (MAR)
SIRI............. Sugar Industry Research Institute (MAR)
SIRIEM........ Societa Italiana Ricerche Idriche e Minerarie (MAR)
SIRIP........... Societe Irano-Italienne des Petroles [*Irano-Italian Petroleum Company*] (ME)
SIRMCE...... Societe Internationale pour la Recherche sur les Maladies de Civilisation et l'Environment [*International Society for Research on Civilization Diseases and Environment*] (EA)
SIRWA......... Societe Industrielle du Rwanda (MAR)
SIS.............. Reference and Information Service (RU)
SIS.............. Secteur Industriel Socialiste [*Socialist Industrial Sector*] [*Algerian*] (AF)
SIS.............. Societa Internazionale Scotista [*International Scotist Society - ISS*] (EA)
SIS.............. Societe Immobiliere du Senegal (MAR)
SIS.............. Societe Industrielle de Sacherie (MAR)
SIS.............. Societe Ivoirienne de Spectacles (MAR)
SIS.............. Sovetska Informacni Sluzba [*Soviet Information Service*] (CZ)
SIS.............. Special Investigation Section (ML)
SIS.............. Stratiotiki Iatriki Skholi [*Army Medical School*] [*Greek*] (GC)
SIS.............. Symvoulion Iatrikon Syllogon [*Medical Associations Council*] (GC)
SIS.............. Well Induction Seismic Detector (RU)
SISA............ Seguros e Inversiones, Sociedad Anonima [*Insurance and Investments Corporation*] [*Salvadoran*]
SISA............ SITRAM [*Societe Ivoirienne de Transport Maritime*] International Shipping Agencies [*Ivorian*] (AF)
SISA............ Societa Italiana Strade Africa (MAR)
SISAP.......... Societe d'Installations Sanitaires, d'Assainissement, et de Plomberies (MAR)
SISC............ Societe Industrielle Senegalaise de Confections (MAR)
SISCOMA... Societe Industrielle Senegalaise de Constructions Mecaniques et de Materiels Agricoles (MAR)
SISEA.......... Sugar Industry Staff Employees Association [*Mauritian*] (AF)
SISEF.......... Societe Industrielle de Sciage et d'Exploitation Forestiere (MAR)
SISEP.......... Societe Ivoirienne de Soufflage et d'Emballage Plastique (MAR)
SISFER........ Societe Ivoirienne de Serrurerie et Ferronerie (MAR)
SISH............ Societe Internationale de la Science Horticole [*International Society for Horticultural Science - ISHS*] (EA)
SISIR........... Singapore Institute of Standards and Industrial Research (ML)
SISK............ Sosyalist Isci Sendikalari Konfederasyonu [*Confederation of Socialist Worker Unions*] (TU)
SISO............ Schema voor de Indeling van de Systematische Catalogus in Openbare Bibliotheken [*Dutch*]
SISS............ Societe Industrielle des Silicones [*French*]
sist.............. Make, System, Systematic (RU)
SISUGA....... Societe d'Investissements Sucriers au Gabon (MAR)
SISWO........ Stichting Interuniversitair Instituut voor Sociaal-Wetenschappelijk Onderzoek [*Amsterdam*]
SIT............... Coeducational Technical School of Economics (BU)
sit................ Es Igy Tovabb [*Et Cetera*] (HU)
SIT............... Sindicato Industria Textil [*Union of the Textile Industry*] [*Salvadoran*] (LA)
SIT............... Singapore Improvement Trust (ML)
SIT............... Sistemul Informatic Teritorial [*Territorial Data Processing System*] (RO)
SIT............... Societe Indochinoise de Transports [*Indochinese Transport Company*] (CL)
SIT............... Societe Industrielle Thanry (MAR)
SIT............... Societe Industrielle de Transports (MAR)
SIT............... Societe Interafricaine de Transports (MAR)
SIT............... Societe Ivoirienne de Topographie (MAR)
SIT............... Societe Ivoirienne de Transit (MAR)
SIT............... Societe Ivoirienne de Transports (MAR)
SIT............... Soma Ippikou kai Tethorakismenon [*Cavalry and Armored Corps*] (GC)
SIT............... Statiile de Intretinere Tehnica [*Technical Maintenance Stations*] (RO)
SIT............... Stowarzyszenie Inzynierow i Technikow [*Association of Engineers and Technicians*] (POL)
SiT............... Wydawnictwo "Sport i Turystyka" [*"Sport and Turystyka" (Sport and Tourism) Publishing House*] (POL)
SITA............ Sociedade Internacional de Trilogia Analitica [*International Society of Analytical Trilogy - ISAT*] (EA)
SITA............ Societe Industrielle de Transports Automobiles (MAR)
SITA............ Societe Internationale de Telecommunications Aeronautiques [*International Aeronautical Telecommunications Company*] (CL)
SITA............ Societe de Transports Automobile de l'Imerina (MAR)
SITAB.......... Societe Ivoirienne des Tabacs (MAR)
SITAC.......... Societe Internationale des Tabacs au Cameroun (MAR)
SITAF.......... Societe Industrielle des Transports Automobiles Africains (MAR)
SITAM......... Societe Industrielle des Tabacs Malgaches (MAR)
SITAO......... Societe Immobiliere et Touristique de l'Afrique de l'Ouest (MAR)
SITAOF....... Syndicat d'Initiative et de Tourisme de l'AOF (MAR)
SITAP.......... Syndesmos Idioktiton Taxi Athinon kai Proasteion [*Athens and Suburbs Taxi Owners Association*] (GC)
SITB............ Societe Ivoirienne de Transformation du Bois (MAR)
SITC............ Standard International Trade Classification [*of Commodities*] (MAR)
SITC............ Sultan Idris Training College (ML)
SITCHAD.... Societe Immobiliere du Tchad (MAR)
SITCIB........ Societe Ivoirienne de Transport, de Commerce, et d'Industrie du Bois (MAR)
SITCOG....... Societe Ivoirienne de Transformation de Corps Gras (MAR)
SITE............ Sindicato Independiente de Trabajadores de la Ensenanza [*Independent Trade Union of Educational Workers*] [*Spanish*] (WER)
SITEB.......... Societe Industrielle de Travaux en Batiments [*Chadian*] (MAR)
SITECO....... Sociedad de Investigaciones Tecnicas Colombianas [*Society of Colombian Technical Research*] (LA)
SITECOHDEFOR... Sindicato de Trabajadores de la Corporacion de Desarrollo Forestal [*Trade Union of the Forestry Development Corporation Workers*] [*Honduran*] (LA1)
SITEF.......... Societe Ivoirienne de Tacheronnage et d'Exploitation Forestiere (MAR)
SITEL.......... Societe Ivoirienne de Telecommunications (MAR)
SITEP.......... Societe Italo-Tunisienne d'Exploitation Petroliere [*Italian-Tunisian Petroleum Exploitation Company*] (AF)
SITER.......... Societe Ivoirienne de Technique Electronique et de Radio (MAR)
SITET.......... Sindicato Industrial de Trabajadores Electricos y de Telecomunicaciones [*Industrial Union of Electrical and Telecommunications Workers*] [*Costa Rican*] (LA)
SITEX.......... Societe Ivoirienne des Textiles (MAR)
SITG............ Stowarzyszenie Inzynierow i Technikow Gornictwa [*Association of Mining Engineers and Technicians*] (POL)
SITH............ Societe Internationale de Technique Hydrothermale (MAR)
SITHA.......... Salon International du Textile et de l'Habillement (MAR)
SITIAMAH... Sindicato de Trabajadores de la Industria del Acero, Metales, y Similares [*Trade Union of Steel, Metal, and Related Industries Workers*] [*Honduran*] (LA1)
SITIAMAH... Sindicato de Trabajadores de la Industria Azucarera, Mieles, Alcoholes, y Similares de Honduras [*Trade Union of Honduran Sugar, Molasses, Alcohol, and Related Industries Workers*] [*Honduran*] (LA1)
SITIEF......... Societe Ivoirienne de Travaux Topographiques et Fonciers (MAR)
SITIM.......... Societe Internationale des Techniques d'Imagerie Mentals [*International Society for Mental Imagery Techniques in Psychotherapy and Psychology*] (EA)
SITIYO........ Sisli Iktisadi Ticari Ilimler Yuksek Okulu [*Sisli College of Economic and Commercial Science*] [*Istanbul*] (TU)
SITJ............ Savez Inzenjera i Tehnicara Jugoslavije [*Union of Engineers and Technicians of Yugoslavia*] (YU)
SITK............ Stowarzyszenie Inzynierow i Technikow Komunikacji [*Association of Transportation Engineers and Technicians*] (POL)
SITLD.......... Stowarzyszenie Inzynierow i Technikow Lesnictwa i Drzewnictwa [*Association of Forestry and Lumber Engineers and Technicians*] (POL)
SITLiD......... Stowarzyszenie Inzynierow i Technikow Lesnictwa i Drzewnictwa [*Association of Forestry and Lumber Engineers and Technicians*] (POL)
SITMA......... Societe Ivoirienne de Transports de Materiaux (MAR)
SITO............ Societe Industrielle de Traitement des Oleagineux (MAR)
SITO............ Societe Ivoirienne des Transports de l'Ouest (MAR)
SITOM......... Societe Industrielle de Traitement des Ordures Menageres (MAR)
SITP............ Aircraft Temperature Pulsation Gauge (RU)
SITP............ Societe Ivoirienne de Transports Publics (MAR)
SITPCh........ Stowarzyszenie Inzynierow i Technikow Przemyslu Chemicznego [*Association of Engineers and Technicians of the Chemical Industry*] (POL)
SITPChem... Stowarzyszenie Inzynierow i Technikow Przemyslu Chemicznego [*Association of Engineers and Technicians of the Chemical Industry*] (POL)
SITPH.......... Stowarzyszenie Inzynierow i Technikow Przemyslu Hutniczego [*Association of Engineers and Technicians of the Metallurgical Industry*] (POL)

SITPN.......... Stowarzyszenie Inzynierow i Technikow Przemyslu Naftowego [*Association of Engineers and Technicians of the Petroleum Industry*] (POL)
SITPP.......... Stowarzyszenie Inzynierow i Technikow Przemyslu Papierniczego [*Association of Engineers and Technicians of the Paper Industry*] (POL)
SITPP.......... Stowarzyszenie Naukowo-Techniczne Inzynierow i Technikow Przemyslu Papierniczego [*Scientific and Technical Association of Engineers and Technicians of the Paper Industry*] (POL)
SITPPW....... Stowarzyszenie Inzynierow i Technikow Polskiego Przemyslu Weglowego [*Association of Engineers and Technicians of the Polish Coal Industry*] (POL)
SITPSpoz.... Stowarzyszenie Inzynierow i Technikow Przemyslu Spozywczego [*Association of Food Industry Engineers and Technicians*] (POL)
SITPWI........ Stowarzyszenie Inzynierow i Technikow Przemyslu Wlokienniczego [*Association of Engineers and Technicians of the Textile Industry*] (POL)
SITR........... Stowarzyszenie Inzynierow i Technikow Rolnictwa [*Association of Engineers and Technicians in Agriculture*] (POL)
SITRA.......... Societe Ivoirienne de Transit (MAR)
SITRA.......... Societe Ivoirienne de Travaux (MAR)
SITRABA..... Societe Ivoirienne des Travaux Publics et Travaux Publics et Batiments (MAR)
SITRAC....... Sindicato da Trabajadores Concord [*Concord Workers Union*] [*Argentine*] (LA)
SITRAC....... Sindicato de Trabajadores Cordoba [*Trade Union of Cordoba Workers*] [*Argentine*] (LA1)
SITRAC....... Societe Industrielle de Transformation Centrafricaine (MAR)
SITRACA.... Sindicato de Trabajadores del Calzado [*Trade Union of Footwear Workers*] [*Costa Rican*] (LA1)
SITRACO.... Societe Interprofessionnelle de Transit et de Commissariat en Douane (MAR)
SITRACOCS... Sindicato de Trabajadores de la Construccion y Conexas Salvadorenas [*Trade Union of Salvadoran Workers in Construction and Related Activities*] (LA1)
SITRADIQUE... Sindicato de Trabajadores de la Division de Quepos [*Union of Workers of the Quepos Division*] [*Costa Rican*] (LA)
SITRAFENAT... Sindicato de Trabajadores Ferrocarrileros y Portuarios [*Trade Union of Railroad and Port Workers*] [*Costa Rican*] (LA1)
SITRAHCONAV... Sindicato de Trabajadores Hondurenos de Companias Navieras [*Trade Union of Honduran Shipping Companies Workers*] (LA1)
SITRAICE.... Sindicato de Trabajadores de la Industria Ceramica [*Trade Union of Ceramic Industry Workers*] [*Nicaraguan*] (LA1)
SITRAIM...... Sindicato de Trabajadores de la Industria de Muebles [*Trade Union of Furniture Industry Workers*] [*Nicaraguan*] (LA1)
SITRAINA.... Sindicato de Trabajadores del Instituto Nacional Agrario [*Workers Union of the National Agrarian Institute*] [*Honduran*] (LA)
SITRAM....... Sindicato de Trabajadores Materfer [*Materfer Workers Union*] [*Argentine*] (LA)
SITRAM....... Societe Industrielle de Transformation des Metaux (MAR)
SITRAM....... Societe Ivoirienne de Transport Maritime [*Ivorian Marine Transport Company*] (AF)
SITRANE..... Societe Ivoirienne de Transport et de Nettoiement (MAR)
SITRANS-BOIS... Societe Ivoirienne de Transformation des Bois (MAR)
SITRAPOSTH... Sindicato de Trabajadores Postales de Honduras [*Trade Union of Honduran Postal Workers*] (LA1)
SITRAPROVEC... Sindicato Nacional de Trabajadores de Empresas de Produccion, Extraccion, Venta, y Mercadeo de Materiales de la Construccion [*National Union of Workers of Companies Producing, Selling, and Marketing Contruction Materials*] [*Panamanian*] (LA)
SITRASFCO... Sindicato Industrial de la Standard Fruit Company [*Industrial Union of the Standard Fruit Company*] [*Costa Rican*] (LA)
SITRATERCO... Sindicato de Trabajadores de la Tela Railroad Company [*Union of Tela Railroad Company Workers*] [*Honduran*] (LA)
SITRATEX... Sindicato de Trabajadores de la Industria Textil [*Trade Union of Textile Industry Workers*] [*Nicaraguan*] (LA1)
SITRECO..... Sindicato de Trabajadores de Empresas Comerciales [*Trade Union of Commercial Enterprise Workers*] [*Nicaraguan*] (LA1)
SITS............ Engineering and Technical Personnel Section (RU)
SITS............ Syndicat des Ingenieurs et Techniciens du Senegal [*Engineers and Technicians Union of Senegal*] (AF)
SITSDIJ....... Savez Inzenjera i Tehnicara Sumarstva i Drvne Industrije Jugoslavije [*Union of Engineers and Technicians of the Forestry and Wood-Working Industries of Yugoslavia*] (YU)
SITsU.......... Central Control Synchronizing Pulse [*Computers*] (RU)
SITT............ Societe d'Industrie Textile Togolaise (MAR)
SITTELCOM... Sindicato Nacional de Trabajadores de la Empresa Nacional de Telecomunicaciones [*National Union of Workers of the National Telecommunications Enterprise*] [*Colombian*] (LA)
SITUAM...... Sindicato Independiente de Trabajadores de la Universidad Autonoma Metropolitana [*Independent Trade Union of Workers of the Metropolitan Autonomous University*] [*Mexican*] (LA1)
SITUN.......... Sindicato de Trabajadores de la Universidad Nacional [*Trade Union of National University Workers*] [*Costa Rican*] (LA1)
SITUS.......... Sindicato de Trabajadores Universitarios Salvadorenos [*Trade Union of Salvadoran University Workers*] (LA1)
SIU............. Societe Internationale d'Urologie [*International Society of Urology - ISU*] (EA)
SIUB............ Societe Ivoirienne d'Usinage des Bois (MAR)
SIUCHODISNA... Sindicato Unido de Choferes del Distrito Nacional [*United Trade Union of National District Drivers*] [*Dominican Republic*] (LA1)
SIUP............ Seychelles Islands United Party (AF)
SIV............. Council for Economic Mutual Assistance (BU)
SIV............. Savezno Izvrsno Vece [*Federal Executive Council*] (YU)
SIV............. Sistema de Inspeccion de Vuelo [*Flight Inspection System*] [*Venezuelan*] (LA)
Siv............. Sivil [*Civil*] (TU)
siv............. Sivulla [*Pages*] [*Finnish*] (GPO)
SIV............. Societe Immobiliere de la Volta (MAR)
SIV............. Societe Immobiliere de Vridi (MAR)
SIV............. Societe Senegalaise pour l'Industrie du Vetement (MAR)
SIVA........... Sociedad Importadora de Vehiculos (COL)
SIVA........... Societe Industrielle de Vetements en Afrique (MAR)
SIVA........... Societe Ivoirienne d'Agriculture (MAR)
SIVA........... Societe Ivoirienne du Village d'Azuretti (MAR)
SIVAE.......... Societe Ivoirienne d'Amenagement et d'Entretien (MAR)
SIVAK.......... Societe Ivoirienne Agricole et Industrielle du Kenaf (MAR)
SIVAM......... Statia de Incercari si Verificari de Aparatura Medicala [*Station for Testing and Checking Medical Apparatus*] (RO)
SIVE........... Societe Ivoirienne d'Importation de Vehicules et d'Equipement (MAR)
SIVEL.......... Societe Ivoirienne d'Electricite (MAR)
SIVELEC..... Societe Ivoirienne d'Electricite (MAR)
SIVEM......... Societe Ivoirienne d'Emballage (MAR)
SIVENG....... Societe Ivoirienne d'Engrais (MAR)
SIVENSA..... Siderurgica Venezolana Steel, Sociedad Anonima
SIVETI........ Societe Ivoirienne de Vetements sur Mesures Industrielles (MAR)
SIVIE.......... Societe Ivoirienne d'Installations Electriques (MAR)
SIVIMEX...... Societe Ivoirienne d'Importation et d'Exportation (MAR)
SIVIT.......... Societe des Industries de la Viande du Tchad (MAR)
SIVITOUR.... Societe Senegalo-Suedoise de Villages Touristiques (MAR)
SIVOA......... Societe Ivoirienne d'Oxygene et d'Acetylene (MAR)
SIVOITEX.... Societe Industrielle Ivoirienne de Textiles (MAR)
SIW............. Spoldzielczy Instytut Wydawniczy [*Cooperative Publishing Institute*] (POL)
SIWU........... Shoe Industry Workers' Union (ML)
SIXPOOL..... Sdruzeni Sesti Leteckych Spolecnosti Socialistickych Zemi [*Association of Six Airline Companies of Socialist Countries*] (CZ)
SIZ.............. Sestroretsk Tool Plant Imeni Voskov (RU)
SIZ.............. Sportske Igre Ucenika i Ucenica Srednjih i Strucnih Skola Zagreba [*School Games of Secondary and Technical Schools in Zagreb*] (YU)
SIZAI........... Societe Italo-Zairese Attivita Industriali (MAR)
SIZB............ Savezni Institut za Zastitu Bilja [*Federal Institute for Plant Protection*] (YU)
SIZK............ Samara Institute of Grain Crops (RU)
SIZSK.......... Savezni Institut za Zastitu Spomenika Kulture [*Federal Institute for the Preservation of Cultural Monuments*] (YU)
SJ............... Society of Jesus (MAR)
SJ............... Sozialistische Jugend [*Socialist Youth*] [*Austrian*] (WEN)
SJ............... Svalbard and Jan Mayen [*Two-letter standard code*] (CNC)
SJ............... Sveriges Statens Jarnvagar [*Swedish State Railways*] (WEN)
SJAA........... St. John's Ambulance Association (ML)
SJAB........... St. John's Ambulance Brigade (ML)
SJCC........... Suburban Jewish Community Center (MAR)
SJE............. Savez Jugoslovenske Elektroprivrede [*Yugoslav Electric Industries Union*] [*Belgrade*] (YU)
sjev............ Sjeverni [*Northern*] (YU)
SJF............. Suburban Jewish Folkshul (MAR)
SJI.............. Statni Jakostni Inspekce [*State Quality Inspection*] (CZ)
SJL............. Savez Jugoslovenskih Laboratorija [*Union of Yugoslav Laboratories*] (YU)
SJM............ Svalbard and Jan Mayen [*Three-letter standard code*] (CNC)
SJP............. Savezno Javno Pravobraniostvo [*Federal Body of Government Attorneys*] (YU)
SJP............. Social Justice Party [*Malaysian*] (ML)
SJT............. Savezno Javno Tuziostvo (SIV) [*Federal Public Prosecutors*] (YU)
SK.............. Classified Catalog (RU)
SK.............. Column Counter (RU)
Sk.............. Compass North (RU)
SK.............. Composers' Union (RU)
SK.............. Compounding System (RU)
SK-............ Conic Separator (RU)
sk.............. Declension (RU)
sk.............. Economic Combine (BU)

SK .... End of Communication (RU)
SK .... Express Train (RU)
SK .... Family Code (BU)
SK .... Feeble-Prisoner Crew [*Corrective labor camps*] (RU)
SK- .... Jib Crane (RU)
SK .... Patrol Cutter (RU)
sk .... Rifle Corps (BU)
SK .... Rifle Corps (RU)
sk .... Rock, Cliff [*Topography*] (RU)
sk .... Sa Kallad [*So Called*] [*Swedish*] (GPO)
sk .... Sajat Kezevel [*Signed*] [*Hungarian*] (GPO)
sk .... Sajatkezuleg [*In One's Own Handwriting*] (HU)
sk .... Sakki(a) [*Finnish*]
SK .... Salicylic Acid (RU)
SK .... Saobracajna Kontrola [*Transportation Control*] (YU)
SK .... Sarajevski Kiseljak, Preduzece za Eksploataciju Lekovitog Vrela "Kiseljak" [*"Kiseljak" Mineral Spring Enterprise*] [*Sarajevo*] (YU)
SK .... Savet za Kulturu [*Cultural Council*] (YU)
SK .... Savez Komunista [*League of Communists*] (YU)
SK .... Scierie de Koumassi (MAR)
sk .... Sector (BU)
Sk .... Sekil [*Figure, Sketch*] (TU)
sk .... Sekunde [*Second*] [*German*]
Sk .... Skar [*or Skaret*] [*Rock above Water*] [*Swedish*] (NAU)
sk .... Sketch (BU)
SK .... Skladnica Ksiegarska [*Book Store*] [*Polish*]
sk .... Skola, Skolni, Skolsky, Skolstvi [*School (noun and adjective), Education*] (CZ)
Sk .... Skolj [*Skoljic*] [*Island, Reef*] [*Yugoslav*] (NAU)
SK .... Skolni Knihovna [*School Library*] (CZ)
SK .... Skolska Knjiga [*A textbook publishing establishment*] [*Zagreb*] (YU)
Sk .... Skopelos [*Skopeloi*] [*Reef(s)*] [*Greek*] (NAU)
sk .... Skora (Oprawa) [*Leather (Binding)*] [*Polish*]
SK .... Slavic Committee (BU)
SK .... Slovanska Knihovna [*Slavic Library*] (CZ)
SK .... Slovenska Kniha [*The Slovak Book (part of the Czechoslovak National Bibliography)*] (CZ)
SK .... Slovenska Koroska [*Slovenian Carinthia*] [*A periodical*] (YU)
Sk .... Sokak [*Street*] [*See also Sok*] (TU)
SK .... Solana Kreka [*Kreka Salt Mine*] [*Tuzla*] (YU)
SK .... Soldatenkommitte [*Soldiers' Committee*] [*Swiss*] (WEN)
SK .... Solenoid Valve (RU)
SK .... Soviet Books (RU)
SK .... Special Committee (RU)
sk .... Speed, Velocity (RU)
SK .... Sport Kor [*Sport Club*] (HU)
S K .... Sport Lap- es Konyvkiado [*Publishers of Sports Periodicals and Books*] (HU)
SK .... Sportovni Klub [*Sports Club*] (CZ)
SK .... Sports Club (RU)
SK .... Stabilizing Circuit (RU)
SK .... Station Commandant (RU)
SK .... Surat Kabar [*Newspaper*] (IN)
SK .... Survey of Kenya (MAR)
SK .... Synchronous Compensator (RU)
SK .... Synthetic Rubber (RU)
SKA .... "Academy" Sports Club (RU)
s-ka .... Account (BU)
SKA .... Army Sports Club (RU)
SKA .... Patrol Cutter (RU)
SKA .... Slovenska Kulturna Akcija [*Slovenian Cultural Action*] [*Buenos Aires*] (YU)
SKA .... Somateion Ktiston Athinon [*Union of Athens Builders*] (GC)
s-ka .... Spolka [*Partnership, Company*] (POL)
SKA .... Srednjokalibarska Artiljerija [*Medium Caliber Artillery*] (YU)
SKA .... Srpska Kraljevska Akademija [*Serbian Royal Academy*] (YU)
SKA .... Studienkommission for Atomenergie [*Swiss*]
SKA .... Symvoulion Koininikis Asfaliseos [*Social Insurance Council*] [*Greek*] (GC)
SKA .... Syndesmos Koniaston Athinon [*Union of Athens Plasterers*] (GC)
SKA .... Syndonistikon Klimakion Arogis [*Detachment for Coordination of Assistance*] [*Greek*] (GC)
s-ka akc .... Spolka Akcyjna [*Joint Stock Company*] (POL)
SKAAL .... Solidaritaets-Komitee fuer Afrika Asien und Lateinamerika (MAR)
SKAF .... Swedish Paperboard Research Group
SKAF .... Syndikalistiki Kinisis Aristeron Filelevtheron [*Labor Movement of Leftist Liberals*] [*Greek*] (GC)
SKAI .... International Special Committee on Antarctic Research (RU)
skalenoedr ... Scalenohedral (RU)
SKAN .... Srpska Kraljevska Akademija Nauka [*Serbian Royal Academy of Sciences*] (YU)
skand .... Scandinavian (RU)
skand .... Skandinaavinen [*Finnish*]
SKAPP .... North Caucasian Union of Associations of Proletarian Writers (RU)
skaz .... Predicate (RU)
SKAZ .... Samara Carburetor and Fittings Plant (RU)
SKB .... Independent Design Office (RU)
SKB .... Machine Tool Design Office (RU)
SKB .... Special Design Office (RU)
SKB .... Synthetic Butadiene Rubber (RU)
SKBANN ..... Special Design Office for the Automation of Petroleum Processing and Petrochemistry (RU)
SKBAP .... Special Design Office of Analytical Instrument Making (RU)
SKBiH .... Savez Komunista Bosne i Hercegovine [*League of Communists of Bosnia and Hercegovina*] (YU)
SKB KOM .... Special Design Office for the Planning of Leather and Footwear Machines (RU)
SKBM .... Serikat Kaum Buruh Minjak [*Oil Workers Union*] (IN)
SKBM .... Synthetic Butadiene-Sodium Rubber with High Frost Resistance (RU)
SKBNM .... Special Design Office of Petroleum Machinery (RU)
SKBProdmash ... Special Design Office of Food Machinery (RU)
SKBPSA ...... Independent Design Office of Automation Instruments and Devices (RU)
SKBSil .... Spoleczny Komitet Budowy Szkol i Internatow [*Social Committee for the Building of Day and Boarding Schools*] [*Polish*]
SKBSN .... Special Design Office for the Standardization of Instrument Making (RU)
SKBTM .... Special Design Office of Textile Machinery (RU)
SKBTO .... Special Design Office of Weaving Equipment (RU)
SKCG .... Savez Komunista Crne Gore [*League of Communists of Montenegro*] (YU)
SKChF .... Black Sea Fleet Sports Club (RU)
SKD .... Reference Documentation Files (RU)
SKD .... Self-Adjusting Two-Cantilever Crane (RU)
SKD .... Severoceske Konsumni Druzstvo [*North Bohemian Consumer Cooperative*] (CZ)
SKD .... Slovenske Komorne Divadlo [*Slovak Chamber Theater*] (CZ)
SKD .... Slovensko Kemijsko Drustvo [*Slovenian Chemical Society*] (YU)
SKD .... Societe Khmere des Distilleries [*Cambodian Distilleries Company*] (CL)
SKDA .... Sportkomitee der Befreundeten Armeen [*Sports Committee of the Allied Armies*] (EG)
SKDA .... Sports Committee of Friendly Armies (RU)
SKDL .... Suomen Kansan Demokraattinen Liitto [*Finnish People's Democratic League*] (PPW)
sk dv .... Cattle Yard [*Topography*] (RU)
SKE .... Scandinavian Cooperative Exports (RU)
SKE .... Sosialistikon Komma Ellados [*Socialist Party of Greece*] (GC)
SKE .... Steinkohleneinheit [*Hard Coal Unit*] (EG)
SKE .... Svetska Konferencija za Energiju [*World Power Conference*] (YU)
SKE .... World Energy Conference (BU)
SKEA .... Staatliches Komitee fuer Erfassung und Aufkauf [*State Committee for Procurement and Purchase*] (EG)
SKEF .... Societe Khmere d'Exploitation Forestiere [*Cambodian Forest Exploitation Company*] (CL)
SK-ELD .... Sosialistikon Komma - Enosis Laikis Dimokratias [*Socialist Party - Union of Popular Democracy*] [*Greek*] (GC)
SKEPA .... Syndonistiki Kinisis tou Ethnikou Pandimokratikou [*Coordinating Movement for the National Democratic Struggle*] [*Greek*] (GC)
SKF .... AB Svenska Kullagerfabrik [*Swedish Ballbearing Works*] (WEN)
SKF .... Navy Sports Club (RU)
SKF .... Sosialistiko Kinima Foititon [*Student Socialist Movement*] [*Greek*] (GC)
SKF .... Staatliches Komitee fuer Forstwirtschaft [*State Forestry Committee*] (EG)
SKFCM .... Statni Komise pro Finance, Ceny, a Mzdy [*State Commission for Finance, Prices, and Wages*] (CZ)
SKFP .... Soviet Motion-Picture and Photo Industry (RU)
SKG- .... Caterpillar Jib Crane (RU)
SKG .... Sekretarijat za Kmetijstvo in Gozdarstvo (ISLRS) [*Secretariat of Agriculture and Forestry*] (YU)
SKG .... Srpski Knjizevni Glasnik [*Serbian Literary Bulletin*] [*A periodical*] (YU)
SKGJ .... Stalna Konferencija Gradova Jugoslavije [*Permanent Conference of Yugoslav Towns*] (YU)
SKGSM .... Fuels and Lubricants Depot (RU)
SKGU .... North Caucasian Geological Administration (RU)
SKGU .... North Caucasian State University (RU)
s/kh .... Agricultural (RU)
SKh .... Agricultural Aircraft (RU)
skh .... Agriculture (RU)
SKh .... Artists' Union (RU)
skh .... Diagram, Circuit (RU)
SKh .... Painters' Union (BU)
SKH .... Savez Komunista Hrvatske [*League of Communists of Croatia*] (YU)
skh .... Scheme, Plan, Project (BU)
SKh .... Socialist Economy (RU)
SKh .... Stathmos Khorofylakis [*Gendarmerie Station*] (GC)
SKh .... Steady-State Characteristic (RU)
SKhA .... Agricultural Academy (RU)

SkhB .... Block Diagram (RU)
SKhB .... Union of Bulgarian Painters (BU)
SKhE .... Agricultural Encyclopedia (RU)
SkhE .... Elementary Diagram (RU)
SKhEM .... Syndikaton Khersaion Emborevmatikon Metaforon [*Land Commercial Transports Trade Union*] [*Greek*] (GC)
SkhF .... Functional Circuit (RU)
SKhG .... State Publishing House of Agricultural Literature, Journals, and Posters (RU)
SKhI .... Agricultural Institute (RU)
s-kh inv .... Agricultural Implements (RU)
SKhIU .... Sofia School of Industrial Art (BU)
SKhKB .... Special Artistic Design Office (RU)
SKhL .... Cast Chromium Steel (RU)
SKhL .... Medical Chemistry Laboratory (BU)
SKhL .... Medico-Chemical Laboratory (RU)
SKhLR .... Agricultural Workers' and Lumbermen's Trade Union (RU)
SKhM .... Syllogos Khimikon Mikhanikon [*Association of Chemical Engineers*] [*Greek*] (GC)
SkhM .... Wiring Diagram (RU)
s-kh mekh ... Agricultural Mechanics (RU)
s-kh mekh ... Agricultural Mechanization (RU)
s-kh mel ...... Agricultural Reclamation (RU)
s-kh met ..... Agricultural Meteorology (RU)
s-kh min ...... Agricultural Mineralogy (RU)
SKhOS .... Agricultural Experimental Station (RU)
SKhPK .... Agricultural Producers' Cooperative (RU)
SKhPPG ...... Specialized Surgical Mobile Field Hospital (RU)
SKhR .... Chemical Scout Kit (RU)
SKhR .... Special Chemical Reconnaissance (RU)
SKhRU .... Sofia School of Fine Arts (BU)
SKhS .... Agricultural Station (RU)
SkhSp .... Coincidence Circuit (RU)
SKhU .... Agricultural Apprenticeship School (RU)
s kh-vo .... Agriculture (RU)
SKhZ .... Medico-Chemical Defense (RU)
SKI .... Channel Test Bay (RU)
SKI- .... Selective System Equipment Endframe (RU)
Ski .... Seriki [*Partner*] [*Turkish*] (CED)
SKI .... Soma Ktiniatrikou kai Ipponeion [*Veterinary and Remount Corps*] (GC)
SKI .... Spolek Komercnich Inzenyru [*Society of Graduates of Schools of Business Administration*] (CZ)
SKI .... Syndikalistiki Kinisi Iatrikis [*Medical Trade Union Movement*] [*Greek*] (GC)
SKI .... Synthesis of Isoprene Rubber (RU)
SKIKhA .... Syllogos Katokhon Idiotikis Khriseos Avtokiniton [*Society of Private Automobile Owners*] [*Greek*] (GC)
SKIP .... Strojno-Kovinsko Industrijsko Podjetje [*Machinery and Metallurgical Works*] [*Ljubljana*] (YU)
Skip .... Turpentine Plant [*Topography*] (RU)
SKJ .... Savez Kompozitora Jugoslavije [*Union of Composers of Yugoslavia*] (YU)
SKJ .... Savez Komunista Jugoslavije [*League of Communists of Yugoslavia*] (YU)
SKJ .... Sojuzot na Komunistite na Jugoslavija [*League of Communists of Yugoslavia*] (YU)
SKJ .... Statystyczna Kontrola Jakosci [*Statistical Quality Control*] [*Polish*]
SKK .... Allied Control Commission (BU)
SKK .... Soviet Control Commission (RU)
SKK .... Sowjetische Kontrollkommission [*Soviet Control Commission*] (EG)
SKK .... Spoleczna Komisja Kontroli [*People's Control Commission*] (POL)
SKK .... Staatliche Kontrollkommission [*State Control Commission*] (EG)
SKK .... Staatliches Kohle-Kontor [*State Coal Office*] (EG)
SKK .... Swiatowy Kongres Kobiet [*World Congress of Women*] (POL)
SKK .... Szkola Kadr Kierowniczych [*School for (Party) Leaders in ______*] (POL)
SKKF .... Stoleczny Komitet Kultury Fizycznej [*Warsaw Committee on Physical Culture*] (POL)
SKKF .... Syndesmos Kypro-Koreatikis Filias [*League of Cypriot-Korean Friendship*] (GC)
SKKZ .... Spoleczna Komisja Kontroli Zaopatrzenia [*People's Control Commission on Supplies*] (POL)
skl .... Declension (RU)
SKL .... Schwermaschinenbau "Karl Liebknecht," Magdeburg (VEB) [*"Karl Liebknecht" Heavy Machine Construction Plant, Magdeburg (VEB)*] (EG)
SKL .... Seismic Logging Laboratory (RU)
skl .... Storehouse, Depot [*Topography*] (RU)
SKL .... Suomen Kristillinen Litto [*Finnish Christian League*] (PPE)
Skl gor .... Fuel Depot [*Topography*] (RU)
SKLOEXPORT ... Podnik Zahranicniho Obchodu pro Vyvoz Skla [*Foreign Trade Enterprise for the Export of Glass*] (CZ)
sklon .... Declension (RU)
SKLP .... St. Kitts Labor Party (LA1)
SKM .... Savez Komunista Makedonije [*League of Communists of Macedonia*] (YU)
SKM .... Sojuz na Komunistite na Makedonija [*League of Communists of Macedonia*] (YU)
SKM .... Statny Kulturny Majetok [*State Cultural Properties*] (CZ)
SKM .... Szybka Kolej Miejska [*Metropolitan Railway*] [*Polish*]
SKM .... Szybkobiezna Kolej Miejska [*Municipal Express Railroad*] (POL)
SKM .... Young Communist League (RU)
SKMA .... Societe Khmere de Montage Automobile [*Cambodian Automobile Assembly Company*] (CL)
SKMGG .... Special Committee for the International Geophysical Year (RU)
SKMJ .... Sojuz na Komunistickata Mladina na Jugoslavija [*Union of Communist Youth of Yugoslavia*] (YU)
SKMR .... Szkolenie Kadr Mechanizacji Rolnictwa [*Training of Personnel for the Mechanization of Agriculture*] (POL)
SKMS .... Svaz Komunistickych Mladorobotnikov Slovenska [*Union of Young Communist Workers of Slovakia*] (CZ)
SKMZ .... Old Kramatorsk Machinery Plant Imeni S. Ordzhonikidze (RU)
SKN .... Sanockie Kopalnictwo Naftowe [*Sanok Oil Wells*] (POL)
SKN .... Sekuaderan [*Squadron*] (ML)
SKN .... Studencka Konferencja Naukowa [*Students' Scientific Conference*] (POL)
SKN .... Symvoulion Kriseos Nomarkhon [*Council for Judging Nomarchs*] [*Greek*] (GC)
SKN .... Syndekhnia Kyvernitikon Nosokomon [*Union of Government Nurses*] [*Cypriot*] (GC)
SKN .... Synthetic Butadienenitrile Rubber (RU)
SKNE .... Savezna Komisija za Nuklearnu Energiju [*Federal Commission for Nuclear Energy*] (YU)
Skne .... Skjerane [*or Skjaerane*] [*Rocks above Water*] [*Norwegian*] (NAU)
SKNII .... Sakhalin Complex Scientific Research Institute (of the Academy of Sciences, USSR) (RU)
SKNIVI .... North Caucasian Scientific Research Veterinary Institute (RU)
SKNO .... Sreski Komitet Narodne Omladine [*District Committee of the People's Youth*] (YU)
SKO .... Association of Sanatoriums and Health Resorts (RU)
SKO .... Compander-Equipment Bay (RU)
SKO .... Construction and Billeting Section (RU)
SKO .... Saobracajno-Komercijalno Odeljenje [*Transportation Commercial Department*] [*Railroads*] (YU)
SKO .... Serial Production Design Department (RU)
SKO .... Sieges-Kilometres Offerts (MAR)
SKO .... Surveillance Radar (RU)
SKO .... Szkolna Kasa Oszczednosci [*School Savings Bank*] [*Polish*]
SKO .... Szkolne Kola Oszczednosciowe [*School Savings Circles*] (POL)
SKO .... Szkolny Komitet Opiekunczy [*School Assistance Committee*] (POL)
SKODAM .... Staf Komando Daerah Militer [*Staff of Military Region Command*] (IN)
SkOE .... Skopevtiki Omospondia Ellados [*Marksmen's Federation of Greece*] (GC)
SKOGA .... Soviet-Chinese Civil Aviation Society (RU)
SKOJ .... Savez Komunisticke Omladine Jugoslavije [*Union of Communist Youth of Yugoslavia*] (YU)
SKOJ .... Soupravy pro Kontrolu Ozareni Jednotlivce [*Detectors of Radiation in Personnel*] (CZ)
SKOK .... Commission for Admittance to Sanatoriums and Health Resorts (RU)
SKOM .... Stratiotiki Kommounistiki Organosis Makronisou [*Makronisos Communist Army Organization*] [*Greek*] (GC)
SKOO .... Scandinavian Cooperative Wholesale Society (RU)
SKOP .... Slasko-Krakowski Okreg Przemyslowy [*Industrial Region of Cracow and Silesia*] [*Polish*]
SKOP .... Swiatowy Komitet Obroncow Pokoju [*World Committee of Partisans of Peace*] (POL)
SKOP .... Symvoulion Koinonikis kai Oikonomikis Politikis [*Social and Economic Policy Council*] (GC1)
skor .... Express [*Railroads*] (RU)
skot .... Cattle-Breeding [*Topography*] (RU)
SKOT .... Stredni Kolovy Obrneny Transporter [*Medium APC (Armored Personnel Carrier)*] (CZ)
skotl .... Skotlantilainen [*Scotch*] [*Finnish*]
Skotob .... Slaughterhouse [*Topography*] (RU)
Skotoimport ... Office for the Import of Cattle (RU)
skot ov .... Cattle Barn, Stable [*Topography*] (RU)
skotov .... Cattle Breeding (RU)
SKOW .... Szkolny Komitet Odbudowy Warszawy [*School Committee on the Reconstruction of Warsaw*] (POL)
SKP .... Accounting and Clerical Personnel (RU)
SKP .... Disease Control Station (RU)
SKP .... Flank Control Post (BU)
SKP .... Flight Command Post (RU)
SKP .... Launcher [*Rocket-Firing*] Command Post (BU)
SKP .... Medical Control Point (BU)
SKP .... Savet za Komunalne Poslove [*Communal Affairs Council*] (YU)
SKP .... Savezna Komisija za Plate [*Federal Wage Commission*] (YU)
SKP .... Sine-Cosine Potentiometer (RU)
SKP .... Societe Khmere de Pneumatiques [*Cambodian Tire Company*] (CL)
SKP .... Soma Kyprion Proskopon [*Boy Scouts of Cyprus*] (GC)
SKP .... Spanyol Kommunista Part [*Spanish Communist Party*] (HU)

SKP .... Startkontrollpunkt [*Take-Off Control Center*] (EG)
SKP .... Statni Katalog Prace [*State Labor Catalog*] (CZ)
SKP .... Stowarzyszenie Ksiegarzy Polskich [*Association of Polish Booksellers*] [*Polish*]
SKP .... Stowarzyszenie Ksiegowych Polskich [*Association of Polish Accountants*] (POL)
SKP .... Suomen Kommunistinen Puolue [*Communist Party of Finland*] (PPW)
SKP .... Sveriges Kommunistiska Partiet [*Communist Party of Sweden*] (PPE)
SKP .... Svesavezna Komunisticka Partija [*All-Union Communist Party*] (YU)
SKP(b) .... Sovjetska Komunisticka Partija (Boljsevika) [*Soviet Communist Party (Bolsheviks)*] (YU)
SKP(b) .... Svesavezna Komunisticka Partija (Boljsevika) [*All-Union Communist Party (Bolsheviks)*] (YU)
SKPD .... Savez Kulturno-Prosvetnih Drustava [*Federation of Cultural and Educational Societies*] (YU)
SKPDS .... Savez Kulturno-Prosvetnih Drustava Srbije [*Federation of Cultural and Educational Societies of Serbia*] (YU)
SKPF .... Savezna Komisija za Pregled Filmova [*Federal Commission for Film Censorship*] (YU)
SKPH .... Societe Khmere de Plantations d'Heveas [*Cambodian Rubber Plantation Company*] (CL)
SKPP .... Savezna Komisija za Plate u Privredi [*Federal Commission on Industrial Wages*] (YU)
SKPPE .... Union for Coordinating Production and Distribution of Electricity (RU)
skpt .... Stabni Kapitan [*Senior Captain*] [*Military rank*] (CZ)
SKPU .... Savet za Komunalne Poslove i Urbanizam (SIV) [*Council on Communal Affairs and City Planning*] (YU)
SKP ZSSR ... Szkolne Kolo Przyjaciol ZSSR [*School Circle of Friends of the USSR*] (POL)
skr .... Abbreviated, Abbreviation (BU)
SKR .... Corona Stabilitron Tube (RU)
SKR .... Cruise Missiles (BU)
SKR .... Escort Ship (RU)
SKR .... Raman Spectrum (RU)
Skr .... Sekretariat [*German*]
Skr .... Skaer [*or Skjaer*] [*Rock above Water*] [*Danish*] (NAU)
Skr .... Skjaer [*or Skjer or Skjeret*] [*Rock above Water*] [*Norwegian*] (NAU)
SKR .... Slovenska Kniznicna Rada [*Slovak Library Council*] (CZ)
SKR .... Societe Khmere de Raffinage de Petrole [*Cambodian Petroleum Refining Company*] [*Use SKRP*] (CL)
SKR .... Staatliches Komitee fuer Nichtmetallische Rohstoffreserven [*State Committee for Non-Metallic Raw Material Reserves*] (EG)
skr .... Sved Korona [*Swedish Krona*] (HU)
SKRB .... Stoleczny Klub Racjonalizatorow Budownictwa [*Warsaw Club of Construction Rationalizers*] (POL)
SKRK .... Spoleczny Komitet Radiofonizacji Kraju [*People's Committee on Country-Wide Radio Installation*] (POL)
SKRO .... Statni Komise pro Rizeni a Organizaci [*State Commission for Management and Organization*] (CZ)
SKRP .... Societe Khmere de Raffinage de Petrole [*Cambodian Petroleum Refining Company*] (CL)
SKRU .... Combined Motion-Picture and Radio Installation (RU)
SKS .... Savez Komunista Slovenije [*League of Communists of Slovenia*] (YU)
SKS .... Savez Komunista Srbije [*League of Communists of Serbia*] (YU)
SKS .... Savezna Komisija za Standardizaciju [*Federal Commission on Standardization*] (YU)
SKS .... Self-Propelled Compressor Station (RU)
SKS- .... Self-Propelled Logging Station (RU)
SKS .... Services Kataeb de Securite (MAR)
SKS .... Simonov Self-Loading Carbine (RU)
SKS .... Slovenska Katoliska Skupnost [*Slovenian Catholic Unity*] [*USA*] (YU)
SKS .... Soviet Committee of Slavicists (RU)
SKS .... Sovieto-Kypriakos Syndesmos [*Soviet-Cypriot Association*] (GC1)
SKS .... Spoldzielczy Klub Sportowy [*Cooperative Sport Club*] (POL)
SKS .... Staendige Kommission des RGW fuer Standardisierung [*CEMA Permanent Commission for Standardization*] (EG)
SKS .... Suomalaisen Kirjallisuuden Seura [*Finnish Literary Society*] (WEN)
SKS .... Suomi-Kiina Seura [*Finland-China Society*] (WEN)
SKS .... Synthetic Butadiene Styrene Rubber (RU)
SKS .... Szkolne Kolo Sportowe [*School Sports and Athletics Circle*] [*Polish*]
SKS .... Szkolny Klub Sportowy [*School Sports and Athletics Club*] [*Polish*]
SKSE .... (Pankypria) Syndekhnia Kyvernitikon kai Stratiotikon Ergaton [*(Pan-Cyprian) Union of Government and Military Workers*] [*Cypriot*] (GC)
SKSO .... Samarkand Oblast Reference Book [*A publication*] (RU)
SKSO .... Union of Communes of the Northern Oblast [*1936-1937*] (RU)
SKSP .... Skupina Svepomoci [*Self-Help Group*] (CZ)
SKSV .... Statni Knihovna Spolecenskych Ved [*State Social Science Library*] [*Prague*] (CZ)
Skt .... Sankt [*Saint*] [*German*] (GPO)
SKT .... Spoldzielnia Komunikacyjno-Transportowa [*Transportation Cooperative*] (POL)
SKT .... Statni Komise pro Techniku [*State Commission for Technology*] (CZ)
SKT .... Synergatiki Kendriki Trapeza [*Cooperative Central Bank*] [*Cypriot*] (GC)
SKTB .... Special Design and Technological Office (RU)
SKTBSP ...... Independent Design and Technological Office for the Planning of Glass Devices and Apparatus (RU)
SKTP .... Preassembled Transformer Substation Set (RU)
SKU .... Coding Device (RU)
SKU .... Housing Construction Administration (RU)
SKU .... Medical Health Resort Administration (BU)
SKU- .... Standardized Jib Crane (RU)
SKUD .... Sindikalno Kulturno-Umetnisko Drustvo [*Trade-Union Cultural and Artistic Society*] (YU)
SKUGMS ..... North Caucasian Administration of the Hydrometeorological Service (RU)
SKUPDBiH ... Savez Kulturno-Umjetnickih i Prosvjetnih Drustava Bosni i Hercegovine [*Federation of Cultural, Artistic, and Educational Societies of Bosnia and Hercegovina*] (YU)
skv .... Drill Hole, Oil Well (RU)
SKV .... Savezna Komisija za Vodoprivredu [*Federal Commission for Water Power*] (YU)
SKV .... Union of Shortwave Amateur Radio Operators (RU)
SKVH .... Svatni Komise pro Vedecke Hodnosti [*State Commission for Scientific Awards*] (CZ)
SKVO .... Military District Sports Club (RU)
SKVO .... North Caucasian Military District (RU)
SKVP .... Short Takeoff and Landing Aircraft (RU)
SKVT .... Sine-Cosine Rotating Transformer (RU)
SKVT .... Statni Komise pro Rozvoj a Koordinaci Vedy a Techniky [*State Commission for Development and Coordination of Science and Technology*] (CZ)
SKVUZ .... Council of Commissars of Higher Educational Institutions (RU)
SKVV .... Soviet Committee of War Veterans (RU)
SKVVI .... Stathmos Koinonikon Voitheion Vasilikou Idrymatos [*Social Assistance Station of the Royal Foundation*] [*Greek*] (GC)
SKW .... Schlauchkraftwagen [*Hose-Equipped Truck (Fire Department equipment)*] (EG)
SKW .... Szkolne Komisje Wspolzawodnictwa [*School Competition Commissions*] (POL)
SKYaD .... Holding Release of Toxic Smoke (RU)
SKYP .... Skholi Klostikis Yfandikis kai Plektikis [*Spinning, Weaving, and Knitting School*] [*Greek*] (GC)
SKYP .... Suomen Kansan Yhtenaeisyyden Puolue [*People's Unity Party*] [*Finnish*] (PPW)
SKYu .... Union of Communists of Yugoslavia (RU)
SKZ .... Slovenski Knjizni Zavod [*Slovenian Book Institute*] [*Ljubljana*] (YU)
SKZ .... Srpska Knjizevna Zadruga [*Serbian Literary Society*] [*Society and publishing house*] (YU)
SKZ .... Sveucilisna Knjiznica, Zagreb [*University Library, Zagreb*] (YU)
SKZ .... Syzran' Combine Plant (RU)
SKZA .... Medium-Caliber Antiaircraft Artillery (BU)
SKZM .... Soviet Committee for the Protection of Peace (RU)
SKZP .... Staatliches Kontor fuer Zellstoff und Papier [*State Office for Pulp and Paper*] (EG)
sl .... Centiliter (RU)
SL .... Collapsible Boat (RU)
SL .... Decoy Ship, Q-Ship (RU)
sl .... Follow, Following (BU)
sl .... Following, Next (RU)
Sl .... Large Village, Settlement [*Toponymy*] (RU)
sl .... Sans Lieu [*No Place (of publication)*] [*French*]
sl .... Sauf Livraison [*French*]
sl .... Schwer Loeslich [*Only Slightly Soluble*] [*German*]
SL .... Sendero Luminoso [*Shining Path*] [*Peruvian*] (PD)
sl .... Service [*Telephony*] (RU)
SL .... Sierra Leone [*Two-letter standard code*] (CNC)
SL .... Signal Lamp (RU)
sl .... Sin Lugar [*No Place (of publication)*] [*Spanish*]
sl .... Slangia [*Slang*] [*Finnish*]
Sl .... Slecna [*Miss*] (CZ)
SL .... Slesvigske Parti [*Schleswig Party*] [*Danish*] (PPE)
Sl .... Slovensko [*Slovakia*] (CZ)
sl .... Slovensky [*Slovak*] (CZ)
SL .... Sluzbeni List [*Official Gazette*] (YU)
SL .... Sociedad de Responsabilidad Limitada [*Private Limited Company*] [*Spanish*]
SL .... Starsi Lekar [*Senior Physician*] [*Army*] (CZ)
SL .... Statni Studijni Knihovna [*State Research Library in Liberec*] (CZ)
SL .... Statni Vedecka Knihovna, Liberec [*State Research Library in Liberec*] (CZ)
SL .... Steeloscope (RU)
SL .... Stihaci Letectvo [*Fighter Airforce (or Aircraft)*] (CZ)

SL .... Stronnictwo Ludowe [*Peasant Party (1944-1949)*] [*Polish*] (PPE)
SL .... Stronnictwo Ludowe [*Peasant Party (1931-1945)*] [*Polish*] (PPE)
SL .... Sumarski List [*Forestry Journal*] [*Zagreb*] [*1877-1946*] [*A publication*] (YU)
SL .... Svaz Lyzaru [*Skiing Association*] (CZ)
SL .... Sveriges Lantbruksforbund [*Federation of Swedish Farmers' Associations*] (WEN)
SL .... Swaziland Lilangeni (MAR)
SL .... Syrian Lira (MAR)
sl .... Syyslukukausi [*Finnish*]
SL .... Trunk [*Telephony*] (RU)
sl .... Weakly, Slightly, Lightly (RU)
sl .... Word (RU)
SLA .... Sabi-Limpopo Authority (MAR)
SLA .... Sekolah Landjutan Atas [*Senior Secondary School*] (IN)
SLA .... Sudanese Liquid Air Co. (MAR)
SLA .... Svenska Lantarbetsgivareforeningen [*Swedish Agricultural Employers' Association*] (WEN)
slaav .... Slaavilainen [*Finnish*]
SLAC .... Structures Lamellees d'Afrique Centrale (MAR)
Sladkoop .... Confectioners' Cooperative (BU)
SLAEAA ...... (Pankypria) Syndekhnia Limenergaton, Akhthoforon, kai Ergaton Apothikon kai Alieias [*(Pan-Cyprian) Union of Port Workers, Porters, and Warehouse and Fishing Workers*] (GC)
SLAIC .... Soweto Local Authority Interim Committee (MAR)
SLAJ .... Sierra Leone Association of Journalists (MAR)
SLAM .... St. Lucia Labor Action Movement (LA1)
SLAM .... Sierra Leone Alliance Movement (PD)
SLAMI .... Societe Lyonnaise Agricole, Miniere, et Industrielle (MAR)
slan .... Sine Loco, Anno, vel Nomine [*Without Place, Date, or Name*] [*Latin*] (GPO)
slants .... Shale Field [*Topography*] (RU)
SLAPCO ...... Sierra Leone Production Company (MAR)
slav .... Slavic (BU)
slav .... Slavic (RU)
Slavizdat ..... Slavic Publishing House (BU)
slaw .... Slawisch [*German*]
SLB .... Solomon Islands [*Three-letter standard code*] (CNC)
SLB .... Studia ad Tabulas Cuneiformes Collectas a FMTh de Liagre Boehl Pertinentia [*Leiden*] (MAR)
Slbr .... Sluzbeno Broj [*Official Number*] (YU)
SLBS .... Sierra Leone Broadcasting Service (MAR)
SLCL .... Sierra Leone Council of Labour (MAR)
SLD .... Savezno Lovacko Drustvo [*Federal Hunting Society*] (YU)
SLD .... Skholi Limenikon Dokimon [*Port Cadets School*] [*Greek*] (GC)
SLD .... Sofia Hunting Association (BU)
SLD .... Stihaci Letecka Divize [*Fighter Airforce Division*] (CZ)
SLD .... Union of Hunting Societies (BU)
SLDC .... Sierra Leone State Development Corporation (MAR)
SLDJ .... Savez Lekarskih Drustava Jugoslavije [*Federation of Medical Societies of Yugoslavia*] (YU)
SLE .... Sierra Leone [*Three-letter standard code*] (CNC)
SIE .... Slovenski Etnograf [*The Slovenian Ethnographer*] [*Ljubljana*] [*A periodical*] (YU)
sle .... Succursale [*Branch Agency, Sub-Office*] [*French*]
SLEB .... Societe Laiterie d'Elevage de Brazzaville (MAR)
sled .... Follows, Next, Consequently (BU)
sled .... Therefore, Consequently, Following, Next (RU)
sled obr ...... In the Following Way, As Follows (RU)
SLENCA ...... Sierra Leone Nature Conservation Association (MAR)
SLF .... Simplicial Linear Function (RU)
SIF .... Slovenska Filharmonie [*Slovak Philharmonic*] (CZ)
SLF .... Slovensky Literarny Fond [*Slovak Literary Foundation*] (CZ)
SLF .... Somali Liberation Front (AF)
SLF .... Svetova Luteranska Federacia [*Lutheran World Federation*] (CZ)
SLFA .... Sierra Leone Football Association (MAR)
SLFL .... Sierra Leone Federation of Labour (MAR)
SLFP .... Sri Lanka Freedom Party (PPW)
SLGJ .... Sierra Leone Geographical Journal [*Freetown, Sierra Leone*] [*A publication*] (MAR)
Slgl .... Sluzbeni Glasnik [*Official Gazette*] [*Serbia*] [*A publication*] (YU)
SLGMS .... Snow Avalanche Hydrometeorological Station (RU)
SLH .... Secteur de Loisir et d'Habitation (MAR)
SLH .... Sprava Lesniho Hospodarstvi [*Forest Management Administration*] (CZ)
SLI .... Statni Letecka Inspekce [*State Air Inspection Office*] (CZ)
SLIC .... Saudi Light Industry Company (MAR)
SLIK .... Slovansky Literarni Klub [*Slavic Literary Club*] (CZ)
SLIM .... Sierra Leone Independence Movement (MAR)
SLIM .... Societe Librairie Imprimerie Messagerie [*Tunisian*] (MAR)
SLIRE .... Societa Libica Incremento Razze Equine (MAR)
SLITA .... Societe Lilloise d'Imprimerie de Tananarive (MAR)
SLK .... Line Distribution Bay (RU)
SLK .... Red Signal Lamp (RU)
SLK .... Slovenska Lekarska Kniznica [*Slovak Medical Library*] (CZ)
SLK .... Statni Lekarska Knihovna [*State Medical Library*] [*Prague*] (CZ)
Sl-Kh .... Chemical Service (RU)
sl Khr .... After Christ (BU)
Sl Kuv .... Silahli Kuvvetler [*Armed Forces*] (TU)
SLKV .... Sport Lap- es Konyvkiadovallalat [*Publishing House for Sport Periodicals and Books*] (HU)
SLL .... Sarawak Liberation League [*Communist - Same leadership as NKCP*] (ML)
sll .... Sehr Leicht Loeslich [*Very Easily Soluble*] [*German*]
SILAKMO .... Sluzbeni List Autonomna Kosovo-Metohiska Oblast [*Official Gazette, Autonomous Kosovo-Metohija Region*] [*A publication*] (YU)
SLLC .... Sierra Leone Labour Congress (MAR)
SILFNRJ ...... Sluzbeni List Federativna Narodna Republika Jugoslavija [*Official Gazette of Yugoslavia*] [*A publication*] (YU)
SILNRBiH .... Sluzbeni List Narodna Republika Bosna i Hercegovina [*Official Gazette of Bosnia and Hercegovina*] [*A publication*] (YU)
SLM .... Dry Leucocytes (RU)
SLM .... Magnetic Recording Logometer (RU)
SLM .... Simplicial Linear Methods (RU)
SLNA .... Sierra Leone News Agency (MAR)
slnd .... Sans Lieu ni Date [*French*]
SLO .... Sarawak Labor Organization (ML)
SLO .... Socialist Liberals' Organization [*Egyptian*] (MAR)
sl ob .... Afternoon (BU)
sl obr .... In the Following Way, As Follows (RU)
SLOCA .... Service to Livestock Owners in Communal Areas (MAR)
SLO-FITES ... Svaz Slovenskych Filmovych a Televiznych Umelcov [*Union of Slovak Film and Television Artists*] (CZ)
Slon .... Solovetskiy Special Camp (RU)
SLOTFOM ... Service de Liaison des Originaires des Territoires de la France d'Outre-Mer (MAR)
slov .... Dictionary, Glossary (RU)
slov .... Slovene, Slovenian (BU)
SLOVUC ..... Slovensky Urad pre Veci Cirkevne [*Slovak Office for Church Affairs*] (CZ)
SLOVZAKU ... Slovensky Zememericsky a Kartograficky Ustav [*Slovak Geodetic and Cartographic Institute*] (CZ)
slow .... Slowenisch [*German*]
slowen .... Slowenisch [*German*]
SIOZA .... Slaski Okregowy Zwiazek Atletyczny [*Silesian Regional Athletic Association*] [*Polish*]
SIOZB .... Slaski Okregowy Zwiazek Bokserski [*Silesian Regional Boxing Association*] [*Polish*]
SLP .... St. Lucia Labor Party (LA)
SLP .... Scottish Labour Party (PPW)
SLP .... Simanovskiy, Lebedev, and Prokof'yev Gun Camera (RU)
slp .... Sine Legitima Prole [*Without Lawful Issue*] [*Latin*] (GPO)
SLP .... Socialist Labor Party [*Egyptian*] (PPW)
SLPA .... Sierra Leone Ports Authority (MAR)
SLPIM .... Sierra Leone Progressive Independence Movement (MAR)
SLPK .... Slovenska Planovacia Komisia [*Slovak Planning Commission*] (CZ)
sl pl .... Afternoon (BU)
SLPMB .... Sierra Leone Produce Marketing Board (MAR)
SLPP .... Sierra Leone People's Party (PD)
Sl PS .... Sliven Court of Reconciliation (BU)
SLPT .... Socialist Labor Party of Turkey [*Turkiye Sosyalist Isci Partisi*] (PPW)
SLPZ .... Village Medical Prophylactic Center (BU)
Sl-R .... Radiotechnical Service (RU)
SLR .... Sierra Leone Regiment (MAR)
SIR .... Slavisticna Revija [*Slavistics Review*] [*Ljubljana*] [*A publication*] (YU)
SLRP .... Society for Strategic and Long Range Planning (EA)
SLS .... Sierra Leone Studies [*Freetown, Sierra Leone*] [*A publication*] (MAR)
SLS .... Slovenska Ljudska Stranka [*Slovene People's Party*] [*Yugoslav*] (PPE)
SL'S .... Slovenska l'Udova Strana [*Slovak People's Party*] [*Also, HSL'S*] (PPE)
SLS .... Statne [*or Statni*] Lesy a Statky [*State Forests and Farms*] (CZ)
SLS .... Stowarzyszenie Lekarzy Sportowych [*Association of Sports Physicians*] (POL)
SLST .... Sierra Leone Selection Trust (AF)
Slt .... Selat [*Strait*] [*Malay*] (NAU)
S Lt .... Sous-Lieutenant [*Second Lieutenant*] [*French*] (MTD)
SLTA .... Sudan Lawn Tennis Association (MAR)
SLTB .... Syndicat Libre des Travailleurs du Burundi [*Free Union of Workers of Burundi*] (AF)
SLTs .... Aircraft Colored Lamp (RU)
SLU .... Svenska Landsbygdens Ungdomsforbund [*Swedish Rural Youth Association*] (WEN)
SLUB .... Svaz Ludovych Protifasistickych Bojovnikov [*People's Union of Fighters of Fascism*] (CZ)
sluch .... Sluchacz [*Student*] [*Polish*]
sluch .... Sluchowisko [*Radio Play*] [*Polish*]
SLUFAE ...... Surface-Launched Fuel Air Explosive (MAR)
SLUJ .... Savez Likovnih Umetnika Jugoslavije [*Yugoslav Association of Representational Artists*] (YU)
SLUK .... Slovensky Ludovy Umelecky Kolektiv [*Slovak People's Artistic Ensemble*] (CZ)

SLUKO .... Studijni a Lidovychovny Ustav Olomouckeho Kraje [*Research Institute for Adult Education in Olomouc Region*] (CZ)
SLUSZ .... Slovensky Urad Socialneho Zabezpecenia [*Slovak Social Security Office*] (CZ)
SLUT .... Soutez Lidove Umelecke Tvorivosti [*Folk Arts Contest*] (CZ)
sluzh .... Employee (RU)
sluzh .... Office, Business (RU)
SLV .... El Salvador [*Three-letter standard code*] (CNC)
SlV .... Slovenski Vestnik [*Slovenian Review*] [*A publication*] (YU)
SLvA .... Slovenska Liga v Amerike [*Slovak League in America*] (CZ)
SLVOM .... Slovensky Vybor Obrancov Mieru [*Slovak Committee of the Defenders of Peace*] (CZ)
SlVTS .... Slovenska Viedeckotechnicka Spolocnost [*Slovak Scientific-Technical Society*] (CZ)
SlVTVS .... Slovensky Vybor pre Telesnu Vychovu a Sport [*Slovak Physical Education and Athletic Committee*] (CZ)
SL-Wola Ludu ... Stronnictwo Ludowe-Wola Ludu [*Peasant Party-People's Will*] [*Polish*] (PPE)
SLZ .... Green Signal Lamp (RU)
SM .... Aircraft Meteorograph (RU)
SM .... Blue Camouflage Lamp (RU)
SM .... Calculator, Calculating Machine (RU)
sm .... Centimeter (BU)
sm .... Centimeter (RU)
SM .... Council of Ministers (RU)
SM .... Drilling Machine (RU)
SM .... Drone Aircraft (RU)
SM .... Economic Militia (BU)
SM .... Machine Builder's Handbook (RU)
SM- .... Machine for the Manufacture of Building Materials (RU)
Sm .... Magnetic North (RU)
SM- .... Membrane Signaler (RU)
SM .... Middle Marker Beacon (RU)
sm .... Mixed (BU)
sm .... Mixed, Mixer (RU)
SM .... (Pankypria) Syndekhnia Metallorykhon [*(Pan-Cyprian) Miners Union*] (GC)
SM .... Sa Majeste [*His (or Her) Majesty*] [*French*] (CL)
SM .... Samarkand Museum (RU)
sm .... Same Month (BU)
SM .... San Marino [*Two-letter standard code*] (CNC)
SM .... Santimetre [*Centimeter*] (TU)
SM .... Sarjana Muda [*Academic degree*] [*Indonesian*]
Sm .... Schmelzpunkt [*Melting Point*] [*German*]
Sm .... Schmilzt [*Melts*] [*German*]
sm .... See (RU)
sm .... Seemeile [*Nautical Mile*] (EG)
SM .... Seine Majestaet [*His Majesty*] [*German*]
SM .... Servomotor (RU)
SM .... Siege et Montague [*Military*] [*French*] (MTD)
SM .... Signal Mine (RU)
SM .... Skholi Mathiteias [*Apprenticeship School*] [*Greek*] (GC)
SM .... Slovenske Muzeum [*Slovak Museum*] [*Bratislava*] (CZ)
SM .... Snowplow (RU)
SM .... Socialist Youth (BU)
SM .... Southern Cross Medal (MAR)
SM .... Soviet Mission (RU)
SM .... Soviet Music (RU)
SM .... Splosno Mizarstvo [*General Cabinetmaking*] (YU)
SM .... Station Magasin [*Military*] [*French*] (MTD)
SM .... Statne Majetky [*State Farms*] (CZ)
SM .... Stopwatch (RU)
SM .... Student Youth (BU)
SM .... Su Majestad [*His (or Her) Majesty*] [*Spanish*]
SM .... Sumska Manipulacija [*Forestry Management*] (YU)
sm .... Suomalainen [*Finnish*]
sm .... Suomea [*or Suomeksi*] [*Finnish*]
SM .... Suomen Mestaruus [*Finnish*]
SM .... Surete Militaire [*Military Security*] (AF)
SM .... Synchronous Machine (RU)
SM .... Sztandar Mlodych [*Banner of the Young*] [*Polish*]
sm .... This Month (RU)
SM .... Twelve-Sports Event (BU)
SM .... Washing Machine (RU)
SmA .... Address Adder [*Computers*] (RU)
SMA .... Automatic Washing Machine (RU)
SMA .... European Convention on International Highways (BU)
SMA .... Scouts Musulmans Algeriens [*Algerian Moslem Scouts*] (AF)
SMA .... Secteurs de Modernisation Agricole (MAR)
SMA .... Section de Munitions d'Artillerie [*Military*] [*French*] (MTD)
SMA .... Sekolah Menengah Atas [*Senior Middle School*] (IN)
SMA .... Servicio Militar Activo [*Active Military Service*] [*Cuban*] (LA1)
SMA .... Servico Meteorologico de Angola (MAR)
SMA .... Singapore Monetary Authority (ML)
SMA .... Skholi Mikhanikon Aeroporias [*Air Force Engineer School*] (GC)
SMA .... Sowjetische Militaerische Administration [*Soviet Military Administration*] (EG)
SMA .... Statiuni pentru Mecanizarea Agriculturii [*Stations for the Mechanization of Agriculture*] (RO)
SMA .... Stredisko Automatizace a Mechanizace [*Automation and Mechanization Center*] (CZ)
SMA .... Union of International Associations [*UIA*] (RU)
SMAC .... Societe Maghrebine de Courtage et d'Assurances (MAR)
SMAC .... Societe Miniere Ajax & Cie. (MAR)
SMACA .... Societe Marocaine d'Approvisionnement Carrosserie Automobile (MAR)
SMACI .... Societe Miniere et Agricole de la Cote-d'Ivoire (MAR)
SMACP .... Sociedad Mexicana de Amistad con China Popular [*Mexican Society of Friendship with People's China*] (LA)
SMACT .... Societe Marocaine d'Affretement de Consignation et de Tourisme (MAR)
SMAD .... Sowjetische Militaradministration in Deutschland [*Soviet Military Administration in Germany*] (EG)
SMAE .... Collection of the Museum of Anthropology and Ethnography (RU)
SMAE .... Servicos Municipalizados de Agua et Electricidade (MAR)
SMAEI .... Societe Malgache d'Entreprises Industrielles (MAR)
SMAG .... Salaire Minimum Agricole Garanti [*Agricultural Guaranteed Minimum Wage*] [*French*] (AF)
SMAG .... Societe Meuniere et Avicole du Gabon (MAR)
SMAGF .... Societe Medicale des Antilles-Guyane Francaises [*Medical Society of Antilles-French Guiana*] (LA1)
SMAP .... Societe Malgache de Peinture (MAR)
SMAR .... Societe Malgache d'Assurances et de Representations (MAR)
SMAR .... Societe Mauritanienne d'Assurances et de Reassurances (MAR)
SMAT .... Societe Maritime du Togo (MAR)
SMATA .... Sindicato de Mecanicos y Afines del Transporte Automotor [*Union of Mechanics and Related Automotive Transport Workers*] [*Argentine*] (LA)
SMATAGOR ... Societe Auxiliaire de Materiel Agricole Ortal (MAR)
SMATEC .... Societe Marocaine d'Agglomeres et de Tuyaux en Ciment (MAR)
SMb .... (Abteilung) Schwermaschinenbau (der Staatlichen Plankomission) [*Heavy Machine-Building Department (of the State Planning Commission)*] (EG)
SMB .... Lightproof and Weatherproof Camouflage Paper (RU)
SMB .... Societe Mauritanienne de Banque (MAR)
SMB .... Societe Miniere des Bandamas [*Bandamas Mining Company*] [*Ivorian*] (AF)
SMB .... Societe Multinationale de Bitumes [*Ivorian*] (MAR)
SMB .... Union of Bulgarian Musicians (BU)
SMBA .... Societe Anonyme des Mines de Bou Arfa (MAR)
SMBPA .... Societe Malienne de Biscuiterie et Pates Alimentaires (MAR)
SMBS .... Societe des Mines de Bou-Skour [*Moroccan*] (MAR)
SMC .... Savings and Mortgage Corporation [*Ethiopian*] (AF)
SMC .... Severomoravske Cihelny [*North Moravian Brick Works*] (CZ)
SMC .... Singapore Maritime Command (ML)
SMC .... Societe Malgache de Cultures (MAR)
SMC .... State Motor Corporation (MAR)
SMC .... Statni Maloobchodni Ceny [*State Retail Prices*] (CZ)
SMC .... Su Majestad Catolica [*Spanish*]
SMC .... Sudan Military College (MAR)
SMC .... Supreme Military Council [*Nigerian*] (AF)
SMC .... Surveyor Menninger Chenevet [*North African*] (MAR)
SMCA .... Societe Malgache de Conteneurs et d'Affretement (MAR)
SMCADY .... Societe de Manutention de Carburants Aviation de Dakar-Yoff (MAR)
SMCh .... Modified Gray Pig Iron (RU)
SMCM .... Societe Marocaine Charbonniere et Maritime (MAR)
SMCV .... Scierie, Menuiserie Charpente de Haute-Volta Georges Jacob (MAR)
SMD .... Societe Marocaine de Distribution d'Eau, de Gaz, et d'Electricite (MAR)
SMD .... Societe des Mines du Djado (MAR)
SMDN .... Societe Miniere du Dahomey Niger (MAR)
SMDP .... Societe Maghrebine de Distribution de Papiers (MAR)
SMDR .... Societe Mutuelle de Developpement Rural (MAR)
SME .... Severomoravske Energeticke Zavody [*North Moravian Electric Power Plants*] (CZ)
SME .... Sindicato Mexicano de Electricistas [*Mexican Electricians Union*] (LA)
SME .... Skholi Metekpaidevseos Enilikon [*Advanced Training School for Adults*] [*Greek*] (GC)
SME .... Societe Malgache d'Edition (MAR)
SME .... Societe Malgache Electronique (MAR)
SME .... Societe des Mission Evangeliques de Paris (MAR)
SME .... Stato Maggiore dell' Esercito [*Army General Staff*] [*Italian*] (WER)
SME .... Systeme Monetaire Europeen [*European Monetary System*] [*Use EMS*] (AF)
SMEA .... Stratiotikai Monades Ethnofylakis Amynis [*National Guard Military Defense Units*] [*Greek*] (GC)
SMEC .... Societe de Menuiserie, Ebenisterie, et Charpente (MAR)
SMECA .... Societe Malgache d'Exploitation des Calcaires de l'Ankaratra (MAR)
SMECMA .... Societe Malienne d'Etude et de Construction de Materiel Agricole (MAR)
SMEF .... Societe Generale Malgache d'Exploitations Forestieres (MAR)

SMEITJ .... Savez Masinskih i Elektrotehnickih Inzenjera i Tehnicara Jugoslavije [*Union of Mechanical and Electrical Engineers and Technicians of Yugoslavia*] (YU)
SMEK .... Economic Mining and Power Complex (BU)
SM elj .... Siemens Martin Eljaras [*Siemens-Martin Process*] (HU)
SMEM .... Societe Marocaine d'Engrainages et de Mecanique (MAR)
SMEO .... Menuiserie et Ebenisterie d'Ouloumi (MAR)
SMEO .... Societe Miniere de l'Est Oubangui [*Paris*] (MAR)
SMEP .... Societe Marocaine des Engrais Pulverises (MAR)
SMEP .... Societe de Menuiserie et d'Ebenisterie du Port (MAR)
SMEP .... Societe des Missions Evangeliques de Paris (MAR)
SMER .... Societe Maghrebine de Construction et d'Entretien des Routes [*Moroccan*] (MAR)
SMERSH ..... Smert' Shpionam [*Russian phrase meaning "Death to the Spies," and name of a special division of USSR state security organizations charged with elimination of internal opposition to the regime from 1942 into postwar years*] [*Best known outside of USSR for role of its agents in the popular James Bond series of espionage stories*]
SMERT .... Societe Malienne d'Exploitation des Ressources Touristiques (MAR)
SMEX .... Societe Malgache d'Expertises (MAR)
SMF .... Special Mobile Force [*Mauritian*] (AF)
SMF .... Su Majestad Fidelisima [*Spanish*]
SMF .... Svenska Missionsforbundet [*Swedish Missionary Society*] (WEN)
SMF .... Syllogos Megareon Foititon [*Association of Megara Students*] [*Greek*] (GC)
SMFELE ...... Service du Moral et Foyer d'Entraide de la Legion Etrangere (MAR)
SMG .... Servicio Militar General [*General Military Service*] [*Cuban*] (LA)
SMG .... Sistemik Mayi Gubre [*Systemic Liquid Fertilizer*] (TU)
SMG .... Societe Mecanique Gabonaise (MAR)
SMG .... Societe Mesnil et Gajewski (MAR)
SMGC .... Societe Miniere Gabon-Congo (MAR)
SMGE .... (Pankypria) Syndekhnia Metaforon kai Genikon Ergaton [*(Pan-Cyprian) Union of Transport and General Workers*] (GC)
SMGI .... Societe Mauritanienne des Gaz Industriels (MAR)
SMGI .... Societe des Minerais de la Grande-Ile (MAR)
SMGL .... Scieries Modernes de Grand-Lahou [*Grand-Lahou Modern Sawmills*] [*Ivorian*] (AF)
SMGS .... Abkommen ueber den Internationalen Eisenbahngueterverkehr (Abk d Russ Bez) [*Agreement on International Railroad Freight Traffic (Russian abbreviation)*] (EG)
SMGS .... Agreement on International Railroad Freight Traffic (RU)
SMH .... Schroeder, Muenchmeyer, Hengst [*Bank*] [*West German*]
SMI .... (Pankypria) Syndekhnia Mikhanotekhniton kai Ilektrotekhniton [*(Pan-Cyprian) Union of Machinists and Electricians*] (GC)
SMI .... Sa Majeste Imperiale [*His (Her) Imperial Majesty*] [*French*]
SMI .... Sanidad del Ministerio del Interior [*Interior Ministry Health Service*] [*Peruvian*] (LA)
SMI .... Saratov State Medical Institute (RU)
SMI .... Section de Munitions d'Infanterie [*Military*] [*French*] (MTD)
SMI .... Siberian Institute of Metallurgy (RU)
SMI .... Smolensk State Medical Institute (RU)
SMI .... Societe Miniere Intercoloniale (MAR)
SMI .... Societe Miniere Intertropicale (MAR)
SMI .... Su Majestad Imperial [*His (or Her) Imperial Majesty*] [*Spanish*]
SmI .... Summing Integrator (RU)
SMIA .... Societe Marocaine pour l'Industrie Agricole (MAR)
SMIC .... Salaire Minimum de Croissance [*Minimum Growth Wage*] [*French*] (LA1)
SMIC .... Salaire Minimum Interprofessionnel de Croissance [*Interoccupational Minimum Growth Wage*] [*French*] (WER)
SMIC .... Societe Malgache d'Investissement et de Credit (MAR)
SMID .... Council of Ministers of Foreign Affairs [*1945-1955*] (RU)
SMIE .... Societe Mauritanienne d'Importation et d'Exportation (MAR)
SMIG .... Salaire Minimum Interprofessionnel Garanti [*Interoccupational Guaranteed Minimum Wage*] [*French*] (CL)
SMII .... Societe Malgache d'Impressions Industrielles (MAR)
SMIP .... Mass Information and Propaganda Media (BU)
SMIS .... Special Military Intelligence Staff (ML)
SMISB .... Societe Mauritanienne des Industries Secondaires du Batiment (MAR)
SMITH .... Societe Mauritanienne du Tourisme et d'Hotellerie (MAR)
S Mitr .... Section de Mitrailleuses [*Military*] [*French*] (MTD)
SMIVE .... Syllogos Mikhanologon-Ilektrologon Voreiou Ellados [*Association of Engineers-Electricians of Northern Greece*] (GC)
SMJ .... Society of Malawi. Journal [*Blantyre, Malawi*] [*A publication*] (MAR)
SMJ .... Spoldzielnie Mleczarsko-Jajczarskie [*Milk and Egg Cooperatives*] (POL)
SMJCM .... Societe de Caution Mutuelle des Jeunes Commercants du Mungo [*Cameroonian*] (MAR)
SMK .... Construction and Installation Combine (BU)
SMK- .... Construction and Installation Crane (RU)
SMK .... Construction and Installation Office (RU)
SMK .... Societe Miniere de Kisenge (MAR)
SMK .... Statni Mzdova Komise [*State Wage Board*] (CZ)
Smk .... Suomen Markka(a) [*Finnish*]
SML .... Forensic Medicine Laboratory (RU)
sml .... Sammenlign [*Compare*] [*Danish*] (GPO)
Smlg .... Sammlung [*German*]
SmM .... Mantissa Adder [*Computers*] (RU)
SMM .... Servicio Meteorologico de Mocambique (MAR)
SMM .... Societe Miniere de M'Passa (MAR)
SMM .... Sucreries Marseillaises de Madagascar (MAR)
SMMI .... Siberian Institute of Mechanics and Machinery Manufacture (RU)
SMMM .... Sindicato de Mecanicos y Metalurgicos de Managua [*Trade Union of Managua Mechanics and Metalworkers*] [*Nicaraguan*] (LA1)
SMN .... Senior Naval Commander (RU)
SMN .... Seri Maharajah Mangku Negara [*Grand Knight of the Most Distinguished Order of the Defender of the Realm*] (ML)
SMN .... Societe des Melasses du Niari (MAR)
SMN .... Societe des Mines du Niger [*Niger Mining Company*] (AF)
SMNL .... Sudan Movement for National Liberation (MAR)
SMNO .... Singapore Malays National Organization [*Pertubohan Kebangsaan Melayu Singapore*] (PPW)
SMNS .... Senior Medical Officer of a Sector (RU)
SMNZ .... Societe des Mines du N'Zako (MAR)
SMO .... Service Militaire Obligatoire [*Obligatory Military Service*] [*Cambodian*] (CL)
SMO .... Servicio Militar Obligatorio [*Obligatory Military Service*] [*Peruvian*] (LA)
SMO .... Sevastopol' Naval Observatory (RU)
SMO .... Sportnomedicinske Objave [*Sport Medicine News*] [*Ljubljana*] [*A periodical*] (YU)
SMO .... Svetova Meteorologicka Organizace [*World Meteorological Organization*] (CZ)
SMO .... Svetska Meteoroloska Organizacija [*World Meteorological Organization*] (YU)
SMOA .... Societe Marocaine d'Oxygene et d'Acetylene (MAR)
SMOA .... Societe des Mines d'Or de l'Andavkoera [*Malagasy*] (MAR)
SMOA .... Specialized Automation Installations Organization (BU)
SMOF .... Slavomakedonski Osloboditelniot Front [*Slavo-Macedonian National Liberation War*] (YU)
SMOG .... Smelost', Mysl', Obraz, Glubina [*Boldness, Thought, Image, Depth*] or Samoye Molodoye Obyedinenie Geniev [*Youngest Federation of Geniuses*] [*Clandestine group of writers in Moscow, USSR*]
SMOL .... Societe Miniere de l'Ogooue-Lobaye (MAR)
smol .... Tar Works [*Topography*] (RU)
Smolgiz .... Smolensk State Publishing House (RU)
SMOMPK .... Collection of Materials Describing Localities and Tribes of the Caucasus (RU)
SMOS .... Samorzad Mieszkancow Osiedla Studenckiego [*Residents' Autonomous Administration of the Students' Settlement*] (POL)
SMOT .... Free Interprofessional Association of Soviet Workers (PD)
SMOTIG ...... Service de la Main-D'Oeuvre des Travaux d'Interet General (MAR)
SMP .... Code of Marine Regulations (RU)
SMP .... Construction and Installation Train (RU)
SMP .... First Aid (RU)
SMP .... Northern Sea Route (RU)
SmP .... Number Sequence Adder [*Computers*] (RU)
SMP .... Rivet Gun (RU)
SMP .... Second Malaysia Plan (ML)
SMP .... Secteur Experimental de Modernisation des Palmeraies (MAR)
SMP .... Secteurs de Modernisation du Paysannat [*North African*] (MAR)
SMP .... Sekolah Menengah Pertama [*Junior Middle School*] (IN)
SMP .... Semiautomatic Washing Machine (RU)
smp .... Sine Mascula Prole [*Without Male Issue*] [*Latin*] (GPO)
SMP .... Societe des Magasins Prisunic (MAR)
SMP .... Societe Malgache de Publicite (MAR)
SMP .... Societe des Mines de Poura (MAR)
SMP .... Societe Moderne de Peche (MAR)
SMP .... Sosialistiki Mathitiki Parataxi [*Socialist Student Faction*] [*Greek*] (GC)
SMP .... Sprava Materialniho Planovani [*Materiel Planning Directorate*] (CZ)
SMP .... Suomen Maaseudun Puolue [*Finnish Rural Party*] (PPW)
Sm p .... Tar Furnace [*Topography*] (RU)
SMpec .... Siemens-Martinova Pec [*Open-Hearth Furnace*] (CZ)
SMPL .... Smiseny Letecky Pluk [*Mixed Aircraft Regiment*] (CZ)
SMPL .... Societe Malgache de Produits Laitiers (MAR)
SMPMG .... Societe Mauritanienne de Papeterie et Mobilier General (MAR)
SMPP .... Societe Marocaine des Produits du Petrole (MAR)
SMPP .... Societe de Mecanique du Port de Peche (MAR)
SMPR .... Secteur de Modernisation et de Production Rurale (MAR)
SMPR .... Societes Mutuelles de Production Rurale (MAR)
SMPS .... Abkommen ueber den Internationalen Eisenbahnpassagier-Verkehr [*Agreement on International Railroad Passenger Traffic (Russian abbreviation)*] (EG)
SMPS .... Convention for International Road Communications (BU)
SMR .... Construction and Installation Work (BU)
SMR .... Mechanically Recording Seismograph (RU)

SMR .... San Marino [*Three-letter standard code*] (CNC)
SMR .... Serviciul Maritim Roman [*Romanian Maritime Service*] (RO)
SMR .... Societe Malgache de Raffinerie [*Malagasy Refining Company*] (AF)
SMR .... Standard Malaysia Rubber (ML)
SMR .... Su Majestad Britanica [*Spanish*]
SMR .... Washing Machine with Manual Wringer (RU)
SMRI .... Sugar Milling Research Institute (MAR)
SMRSSZZ ... Servisna Masinska Radionica (SSZZ) [*Machine Servicing Shop*] (YU)
SMRT .... Societes Mutuelles Rurales Togolaises (MAR)
SMS .... Serviciul Medical si Sanatate [*Medical and Health Service*] (RO)
SMS .... Sindicatul Muncitorilor din Sanatate [*Union of Health Workers*] (RO)
SMS .... Stredni Mostova Souprava [*Medium Bridging Section*] (CZ)
sms .... Synthesis of Systems That Are Optimal in the Minimax Sense (RU)
SMS .... Syro-Mesopotamian Studies (MAR)
sm sled kart ... See the Following Card (RU)
SMSM .... Missionary Sisters of the Society of Mary (MAR)
SMSM .... Societe Miniere du Sud de Madagascar (MAR)
SMSR .... Servicio Medico Social Rural [*Rural Medical-Social Service*] [*Cuban*] (LA)
SMST .... System of Modular Jet-Type Elements (RU)
SMT .... Intercity Television Service (RU)
SMT .... Multiple Telephony System (RU)
SMT .... Sistema Multimodal Transistmico [*Transisthmian Multimodal System*] [*Mexican*] (LA1)
SMT .... Spoljna Mrtva Tacka [*Outer Dead Center*] (YU)
SMT .... Statiuni de Masini si Tractoare [*Machine and Tractor Stations*] (RO)
SMTF .... Societe Miniere de Tenke-Fungurume [*Tenke-Fungurume Mining Company*] [*Zairian*] (AF)
SMTH .... Societe Mauritanienne du Tourisme et d'Hotellerie (MAR)
SMTK .... Standardna Medunarodna Trgovinska Klasifikacija [*Standard International Trade Classification*] (YU)
SMTM .... Societe Malgache de Transports Maritimes [*Malagasy Marine Transport Company*] (AF)
SMTs .... Sofia Interurban Telephone Exchange (BU)
SMTT .... Societe Marocaine de Transports Touristiques (MAR)
SMTTs .... Capital Interurban Telephone Exchange (BU)
SMTWL .... Stichting voor Moeilijk Toegankelijke Wetenschappelijke Literatuur [*Dutch*]
SMU .... Adverse Meteorological Conditions (RU)
SMU .... Blackout Device (RU)
SMU .... Complex Meteorological Conditions (BU)
SMU .... Construction and Installation Administration (RU)
SMU .... Sindicato Medico del Uruguay [*Medical Labor Union of Uruguay*] (LA)
SMU .... Statni Meteorologicky Ustav [*State Meteorological Institute*] (CZ)
smugr .... Suomalais-Ugrilainen [*Finnish*]
SMUH .... Savez Muzickih Udruzenja Hrvatske [*Federation of Musical Associations of Croatia*] (YU)
SMUH .... Secretariat des Missions d'Urbanisme et d'Habitat (MAR)
SMUR .... Construction and Installation Administration for the Development of Radio Facilities (RU)
SMUW .... Seminarium Matematyczne Uniwersytetu Warszawskiego [*Mathematics Seminar of Warsaw University*] (POL)
SMV .... Centimeter Waves (RU)
SMV .... Centimeter Waves (BU)
S-MV .... Sprava Ministerstva Vnitra [*Directorate of the Ministry of Interior (Directorates are designated by numbers)*] (CZ)
SMW .... Stowarzyszenie Mlodziezy Wiejskiej [*Association of Peasant Youth*] (POL)
SMY .... Skholi Monimon Ypaxiomatikon [*Regular Noncommissioned Officers School*] [*Greek*] (GC)
SMYa .... Union of International Fairs (RU)
SMZ .... Serikali ya Mapinduzi ya Zanzibar (MAR)
SMZ .... Serpukhov Motorcycle Plant (RU)
SMZ .... Slovenska Misionska Zveza [*Slovenian Missionary Union*] [*Buenos Aires*] (YU)
SMZ .... Slovenske Magnezitove Zavody [*Slovak Magnesite Plants*] (CZ)
SMZ .... Societe Miniere du Zamza (MAR)
SMZ .... Solikamsk Magnesium Plant (RU)
SMZ .... Stocarska Mlekarska Zadruga [*Cattle and Dairy Cooperative*] (YU)
SMZhS .... Convention on International Railroad Communications (BU)
SN .... Bench Adjustment (RU)
SN .... Combined Observation, Bilateral Observation (RU)
SN .... Combined Observation, Bilateral Spotting (BU)
SN .... Construction Norms (RU)
sn .... From the Bottom (RU)
SN .... Homing (RU)
SN .... House Supplies [*Electric power plant*] (BU)
sn .... Medic, Stretcher Bearer (BU)
SN .... Medium Voltage (RU)
SN .... Observation Service (RU)
SN .... Sad Najwyzszy [*Supreme Court*] (POL)
sn .... Samoin [*Finnish*]
Sn .... San [*Mountain*] [*Japanese*] (NAU)
Sn .... San [*Saint*] [*Spanish*]
Sn .... Saniye [*Second*] [*of time*] (TU)
Sn .... Santo [*Saint*] [*Spanish*]
Sn .... Sayin [*Esteemed*] (TU)
SN .... Securite Nucleaire [*Nuclear Security Service*] [*Belgian*] (WER)
Sn .... Sene [*Year*] (TU)
SN .... Senegal [*Two-letter standard code*] (CNC)
SN .... Servicio Nacional [*Spanish*]
SN .... Severoceske Nakladatelstvi [*North Bohemian Publishing House*] (CZ)
s/n .... Sin Numero [*Without Number*] [*Spanish*] (CED)
sn .... Sine Nomine [*Without Name*] [*Latin*] (GPO)
SN .... Skarb Narodowy [*Polish*]
SN .... Slovanske Nakladatelstvi [*Slavic Publishing House*] (CZ)
S/n .... Sobre Nosotros [*On Us*] [*Business and trade*] [*Spanish*]
SN .... Soviet of Nationalities (RU)
SN .... Spojene Narody [*United Nations*] (CZ)
SN .... Spojovaci Nacelnik [*Communications Chief*] (CZ)
SN .... Spolecnost Narodu [*League of Nations*] (CZ)
SN .... Statni Nakladatelstvi [*State Publishing House*] (CZ)
sn .... Sthene (RU)
SN .... Stratiotikos Nomos [*Military Law*] [*Greek*] (GC)
SN .... Stronnictwo Narodowe [*Nationalist Party*] [*Polish*] (PPE)
SN .... Studium Nauczycielskie [*Teachers' College*] [*Polish*]
SN .... Sunday Nation [*Nairobi*] [*A publication*] (MAR)
SN- .... Voltage Stabilizer (RU)
SNA .... Saudi News Agency (ME)
SNA .... Secretary of Native Affairs (MAR)
SNA .... Servico Nacional de Ambulancia [*National Ambulance Service*] [*Portuguese*] (WER)
SNA .... Sindicato Nacional Agricola [*National Agricultural Union*] [*Cuban*] (LA)
SNA .... Sociedad Nacional Agraria [*National Agrarian Society*] [*Peruvian*] (LA)
SNA .... Sociedad Nacional de Agricultura [*National Agricultural Society*] [*Chilean*] (LA)
SNA .... Societe Nationale d'Allumettes [*National Match Company*] [*Malagasy*] (AF)
SNA .... Societe Nationale d'Assurances [*National Insurance Company*] [*Cambodian*] (CL)
SNA .... Societe Nationale d'Assurances et de Reassurances de la Republique de Guinee (MAR)
SNA .... Somali National Army (AF)
SNA .... Sudan News Agency (MAR)
SNA .... Syndesmos Neon Axiomatikon [*League of Young Officers*] [*Greek*] (GC)
SNA .... System of National Accounts (MAR)
SNA .... Union of the Peoples of Angola [*Party*] (RU)
snabd .... Supplied (BU)
Snabprommontazh ... Office of Materials and Equipment Supply of the Soyuzprommontazh Trust (RU)
snabsbyt ..... Supply and Marketing Administration (RU)
snabsbyt ..... Supply and Marketing Department (RU)
Snabstroymost ... Supply Office of the Mostotrest (RU)
Snabstroyvuz ... All-Union Office of the Main Administration of Capital Construction of the Ministry of Higher Education, USSR (RU)
SNABT .... Societe Nationale d'Amenagement de la Baie de Tanger (MAR)
Snabtoprom ... Office for the Supply of Fuel Industry Establishments (RU)
SNAC .... Societe Nationale de Confection [*North African*] (MAR)
SNAC .... Societe Nord-Africaine de Construction [*Moroccan*] (MAR)
SNAC .... Societe Nouvelle d'Assurance du Cameroun (MAR)
SNACI .... Societe Nouvelle d'Assurances de Cote-d'Ivoire (MAR)
SNAE .... Societe Nord Africaine des Eaux (MAR)
SNAF .... Societe Nord Africaine de Constructions Mecaniques et Ferroviaires [*Algerian*] (MAR)
SNAF .... Student National Action Front (ML)
SNAFOR ...... Societe Nationale pour le Developpement Forestier [*National Company for Forestry Development*] [*Beninese*] (AF)
SNAHDA ..... Societe Nationale des Huileries du Dahomey (MAR)
SNAI .... Societa Nazionale per l'Agricoltura e l'Industria (MAR)
SNAM .... Societa Nazionale Metanodotti [*National Gas Pipeline Company*] [*Italian*] (WER)
SNAM .... Societe Nigerienne d'Application Mecanique (MAR)
SNAP .... Sarawak National Party [*Malaysian*] (PPW)
SNAP .... Societe Nigerienne d'Application de Peinture (MAR)
SNAR .... Artillery Ground Reconnaissance Station (RU)
SNAR .... Servicio Nacional de Acueductos Rurales [*National Service for Rural Aqueducts*] [*Dominican Republic*] (LA1)
SNARI .... Societe Nouvelle Algerienne de Representation Internationale [*New Algerian International Representation Company*] (AF)
SNAS .... Societe Nord Africaine du Sac [*Algerian*] (MAR)
SNASP .... Servico Nacional de Seguranca Popular [*National People's Security Service*] [*Mozambican*] (AF)
SNAT .... Societe Nationale d'Acconage et de Transit (MAR)
SNAT .... Societe Nationale de l'Artisanat Traditionnel [*North African*] (MAR)

SNATCH ..... Societe Nationale Algerienne de Transport et de Commercialisation des Hydrocarbures [*Algerian National Hydrocarbons Transportation and Marketing Company*] (AF)
SNATRAC... Syndicat National des Travailleurs du Commerce (MAR)
SNAV .... Union of Lifesaving Societies (RU)
SNAVR........ Rescue and Emergency Damage Repair Work (BU)
SNB............. Battery Combined Observation (RU)
snb.............. Battery Observation Service (RU)
SNB............. Lateral Observation Post (BU)
SNB............. Savezna Narodna Banka [*Federal National Bank*] (YU)
SNB............. Sbor Narodni Bezpecnosti [*National Security Corps*] (CZ)
SNB............. Sekcja Naukowo-Badawcza [*Scientific Research Section*] (POL)
SNB............. Sinif Numara Birinci [*Number One Quality*] (TU)
SNB............. Straz Narodni Bezpecnosti [*National Security Guard*] (CZ)
SNB............. Superintendencia Nacional de Bancos [*National Superintendency of Banks*] [*Colombian*] (LA)
SNBATI....... Syndicat National du Beton Arme et des Techniques Industrialisees (MAR)
SNBC .... Sucreries de Nossi-Be et de la Cote Est SA (MAR)
SNBG .... Societe Nationale des Bois du Gabon (MAR)
SNBG .... Societe Nouvelle des Bois en Grumes (MAR)
SNBO .... Senior Commander of Coastal Defense (RU)
SNBr .... Brigade Combined Observation (RU)
SNC............. Servicio Nacional de Caminos [*Bolivian*]
SNC............. Societa in Nome Collettivo [*Partnership*] [*Italian*]
SNC............. Societe Nationale du Cameroun (MAR)
SNC............. Societe Nationale de Cimenterie (MAR)
SNC............. Societe Nationale de Cinema (MAR)
SNC............. Societe Nationale de Comptabilite (MAR)
SNC............. Societe Nationale de Construction [*National Construction Company*] [*French*] (AF)
SNC............. Societe Navale Caennaise [*Caen Shipbuilding Company*] [*French*] (WER)
SNC............. Societe Nigerienne des Ciments [*Nigerien Cement Company*] (AF)
SNC............. Swazi National Council (AF)
SNC............. Swiss Nonvaleurs Club (EA)
SNCA .... Societe Navale de l'Ouest Africain (MAR)
SNCASE ..... Societe Nationale de Construction Aeronautique du Sud-Est [*French*]
SNCASO..... Societe Nationale de Construction Aeronautique du Sud-Ouest [*French*]
SNCB .... Societe Nationale des Chemins de Fer Belges [*Belgian National Railroads*] (WER)
SNCC.......... Societe Nantaise de Cultures Cafeieres (MAR)
SNCDR........ Societe Nationale Congolaise de Developpement Rural [*Congolese National Enterprise for Rural Development*] (AF)
SNCDV........ Societe Navale Chargeurs Delmas-Vieljeux (MAR)
SNCE .... Societe Nationale du Commerce Exterieur (MAR)
SNCF........... Societe Nationale des Chemins de Fer Francais [*French National Railroad Company*] (AF)
SNCFA........ Societe Nationale des Chemins de Fer Algeriens [*Algerian National Railroad Company*] (AF)
SNCFT .... Societe Nationale des Chemins de Fer Tunisiens [*Tunisian National Railroad Company*] (AF)
SNCG.......... Societe Nationale de Corps Gras [*Algerian*] (MAR)
SNCh........... Carrier-Frequency Mixing (RU)
SNCh........... Union of People's Libraries (BU)
SNCIP .... Societe Nationale de Construction et de Travaux Publics [*National Construction and Public Works Company*] [*Algerian*] (AF)
SNCM.......... Societe Nationale des Constructions Mecaniques [*Algerian*] (MAR)
SNCMEC.... Societe Nationale des Constructions Mecaniques [*Algerian*] (MAR)
SNCMETAL ... Societe Nationale de Construction Metalliques [*Algerian*] (MAR)
SNCOTEC... Societe Nationale de Commercialisation des Textiles et des Cuirs [*North African*] (MAR)
SNCT .... Societe Nationale Centrafricaine de Travaux (MAR)
SNCTP .... Societe Nationale de Construction et de Travaux Publics [*National Construction and Public Work Company*] [*Beninese*] (AF)
SNCV .... Societe Nationale des Chemins de Fer Vicinaux [*National Local Railroads*] [*Belgian*] (WER)
SNCV .... Societe Nouvelle de Confiserie de Vridi (MAR)
SNCZ .... Societe Nationale des Chemins de Fer du Zaire [*Zairian National Railroad Company*] (AF)
SND............. Battalion Combined Observation [*Artillery*] (RU)
snd.............. Battalion Observation Service [*Artillery*] (RU)
SND............. Severoceske Narodni Divadlo [*North Bohemian National Theater*] (CZ)
SND............. Skholi Navtikon Dokimon [*Naval Academy*] [*Greek*] (GC)
SND............. Slezske Narodni Divadlo [*Silesian National Theater*] [*Opava*] (CZ)
SND............. Slovenske Narodne Divadlo [*Slovak National Theater*] (CZ)
SND............. Srpsko Naucno Drustvo [*Serbian Learned Society*] (YU)
SND............. Stronnictwo Narodowo-Demokratyczne [*Polish*]
SND............. Student Scientific Society (BU)
SNDA .... Secretaria Nacional de Defesa Agropecuaria [*National Secretariat for Agricultural Protection*] [*Brazilian*] (LA1)
SNDE .... Societe Nationale de Distribution d'Eau (MAR)
SNDF........... Second National Development Plan (MAR)
SNDK .... Slovenske Nakladatelstvo Detskej Knihy [*Slovak Publishing House of Juvenile Literature*] (CZ)
SNDK .... Statni Nakladatelstvi Detske Knihy [*State Publishing House of Juvenile Literature*] (CZ)
SNDL........... Suomen Naisten Demokraattinen Liitto [*Finnish Women's Democratic League*] (WEN)
SNDV .... Societe Navale Delmas-Vieljeux (MAR)
SNE............. All-Union Association for the Export and Import of Petroleum and Petroleum Products (RU)
SNE............. Servico Nacional de Emprego [*National Employment Service*] [*Portuguese*] (WER)
SNE............. Sistema Nacional de Estadisticas [*National Statistics Service*] [*Peruvian*] (LA)
SNE............. Societe National d'Electricite [*National Electric Company*] [*Guinean*] (AF)
SNE............. Societe Nationale des Eaux (MAR)
SNE............. Societe Nationale d'Energie (MAR)
SNEA .... Societe Nationale ELF [*Essences et Lubrifiants de France*] Aquitaine [*National ELF (Essences et Lubrifiants de France) Aquitaine Company*] (AF)
SNEA .... Societe Nationale d'Exploitation Agricole (MAR)
SNEA .... Syndicat National des Enseignants Angolais (MAR)
SNEAHV...... Syndicat National des Enseignants Africains de Haute Volta [*National Union of African Teachers of Upper Volta*] (AF)
SNEC .... Nouvelle Societe Commerciale des Ets. Charbonneau (MAR)
SNEC .... Syndicat National de l'Education et de la Culture [*National Educational and Cultural Association*] [*Malian*] (AF)
SNECC........ Syndicat National des Employes et Cadres du Commerce (MAR)
SNECI .... Sindicato Nacional dos Empregados do Comercio e da Industria de Provincia de Mocambique (MAR)
SNECIPA .... Sindicato Nacional dos Empregados do Comercio e da Industria da Provincia de Angola (MAR)
SNED .... Societe Nationale d'Edition et de Diffusion [*Algerian*] (MAR)
SNEELD...... Syndicat National des Enseignants des Ecoles Libres du Dahomey (MAR)
SNEF........... Societe Nouvelle des Ets. Farner & Cie. (MAR)
SNEFAC...... Societe Nouvelle d'Entreprises Franco-Africaines de Constructions (MAR)
SNEG .... Syndicat National des Enseignants de Guinee [*National Teachers Union of Guinea*] (AF)
SNEHM .... Societe Nationale d'Exploitation des Huileries du Mali (MAR)
SNEI............ Societe Nouvelle d'Editions Industrielles (MAR)
SNEL........... Societe Nationale d'Electricite (MAR)
SNEM.......... Servicio Nacional de Erradicacion de la Malaria [*National Malaria Eradication Service*] [*Ecuadorean*] (LA)
SNEM.......... Servicio Nacional de Erradicacion de la Malaria [*National Malaria Eradication Service*] [*Nicaraguan*] (LA1)
SNEMA .... Societe Nationale Eaux Minerales Algeriennes (MAR)
SNEN .... Syndicat National des Enseignants du Niger [*National Teachers Union of Niger*] (AF)
SNEP........... Servicio Nacional de Erradicacion del Paludismo [*National Service for Eradication of Malaria*] [*Cuban*] (LA)
SNEP........... Societe Nationale d'Edition et de Publicite [*Algerian*] (MAR)
SNEP........... Societe Nationale d'Electrolyse et de Petrochimie [*Moroccan*] (MAR)
SNEP........... Societe Nationale des Entreprises de Presse (MAR)
SNEP........... Stredisko pro Normovani a Ekonomiku Prace [*Center for Standardization and Economics of Labor*] (CZ)
SNEPPCI..... Syndicat National de l'Enseignement Primaire Public de Cote-d'Ivoire [*Ivory Coast National Public Primary Education Union*] (AF)
SNERI.......... Societe Nationale d'Etudes, de Gestion, de Realisations, et d'Exploitation Industrielles [*National Company for Industrial Studies, Management, Achievement, and Exploitation*] [*Algerian*] (AF)
SNES........... Symmetric Nonlinear Electrical Resistance (RU)
SNES........... Syndicat National de l'Enseignement Secondaire [*National Union of Secondary School Teachers*] [*French*]
SNES........... Syndicat National de l'Enseignement Superieur [*National Union of Advanced Education Teachers*] [*Moroccan*] (AF)
SNESup ...... Syndicat National de l'Enseignement Superieur [*National Union of Advanced Education Teachers*] [*French*] (WER)
SNET........... Syndicat National de l'Enseignement Technique [*National Union of Technical School Teachers*] [*French*]
SNETA .... Societe Nationale pour l'Etudes des Transports Aeriens (MAR)
SNETHA...... Societe Nationale d'Etudes et de Travaux Hydrauliques et Agricoles du Niger (MAR)
Snf............... Sinif [*Class*] (TU)
SNF .... Slovensky Narodny Front [*Slovak National Front*] (CZ)
SNF .... Sudanese National Front (PD)
SNFK........... Compensation-Type Ferromagnetic Voltage Stabilizer with Magnetized Actuating Mechanisms (RU)
SNFP .... Parametric-Type Ferromagnetic Voltage Stabilizer (RU)
Sng.............. Sans Notre Garantie [*Without Our Guarantee*] [*Business and trade*] [*French*]

SNG............ Santierul Naval Galati [*Galati Naval Shipyard*] (RO)
SNG............ Slovenska Narodna Galeria [*Slovak National Art Gallery*] (CZ)
SNG............ Slovensko Narodno Gledalisce [*Slovenian National Theater*] (YU)
SNGB.......... Societe Nationale des Grands Barrages [*National Large Dam Company*] [*Cambodian*] (CL)
SNGE.......... Societe Nationale Gabonaise d'Etudes (MAR)
SNGOD....... Special NGO [*Nongovernmental Organization*] Committee on Disarmament (EA)
SNGTN........ Societe Nationale de Grands Travaux du Niger (MAR)
SNH............ Societe Nationale de l'Habitat [*National Housing Company*] [*Central African*] (AF)
SNH............ Societe Nationale des Hydrocarbures (MAR)
SNI............. National Intelligence Service [*Zairian*] (PD)
SNI............. Secretaria Nacional Internacional [*National-International Secretariat*] [*Argentine*] (LA)
SNI............. Secretariado Nacional da Informacao [*National Secretariat of Information*] [*Portuguese*] (WER)
SNI............. Servico Nacional de Informacoes [*National Intelligence Service*] [*Brazilian*] (LA)
SNI............. Sistema Nacional de Informacion [*National Information System*] [*Bogota*] (COL)
SNI............. Sistema Nacional de Informacion [*National Information System*] [*Peruvian*] (LA)
SNI............. Sociedad Nacional de Industrias [*National Association of Industries*] [*Peruvian*] (LA)
SNI............. Societa Nazionale Italiana [*Italian*]
SNI............. Societe Nationale d'Investissements [*National Investment Company*] [*Cameroonian, Malagasy, Moroccan*] (AF)
SNI............. Syndicat National des Instituteurs [*National Union of Teachers*] [*French*]
SNIAS......... Societe Nationale Industrielle Aerospatiale [*French*]
SNIB........... Societe Nationale des Industries du Bois [*North African*] (MAR)
SNIC........... Sindicato Nacional de la Industria de la Carne [*National Union of the Meat Industry*] [*Salvadoran*] (LA)
SNIC........... Sistem National Informational pentru Conducere [*Natonal Data Processing System for Management*] (RO)
SNIC........... Societe Nationale des Industries de la Cellulose (MAR)
SNIC........... Societe Nationale des Industries Chimiques [*Algerian*] (MAR)
SNIC........... Societe Nouvelle de l'Imprimerie Centrale (MAR)
SNICS......... Societe Nationale pour l'Industrie et le Commerce au Senegal (MAR)
SNIE........... Servicio Nacional de Identificacion y Extranjeria [*National Identification and Alien Service*] [*Venezuelan*] (LA)
SNIE........... Societe Navale d'Importation et d'Exportation (MAR)
SNIEM......... Societe Nationale d'Importation et Exportation Mauritanienne (MAR)
SNII............ Council of Scientific Research Institutes (BU)
SNIIGGIMS... Siberian Scientific Research Institute of Geology, Geophysics, and Mineral Raw Materials (RU)
SNIIGiM...... Northern Scientific Research Institute of Hydraulic Engineering and Reclamation (RU)
SNIIGM....... Northern Scientific Research Institute of Hydraulic Engineering and Reclamation (RU)
SNIILP......... Sverdlovsk Scientific Research Institute of the Lumber Industry (RU)
SNIING........ Stalingrad Scientific Research Institute of Petroleum and Gas (RU)
SNIIP.......... All-Union Scientific Research Institute of Instrument Making (RU)
SNIISPP...... All-Union Scientific Research Institute of the Synthetics and Perfume Industry (RU)
SNIITMASh... Stalingrad Scientific Research Institute of Machinery-Manufacturing Technology (RU)
SNIL........... Selangor National Independence League (ML)
SNIM.......... Societe Nationale Industrielle et Miniere [*National Industrial and Mining Company*] [*Mauritanian*] (AF)
SNIMA........ Service de Normalisation Industrielle Marocaine (MAR)
SNIP........... Construction Norms and Regulations (RU)
SNIP........... Societe Nationale de Financement des Recherches de Petrole [*National Petroleum Prospecting Financing Company*] [*Algerian*] (AF)
SNIS........... Guidance and Liaison Aircraft (RU)
SNIS........... Lookout and Communications Service [*Navy*] (RU)
SNIT........... Societe Nationale Immobiliere de Tunisie [*Tunisian National Real Estate Company*] (AF)
SNIV........... Societe Nationale des Industries Verrieres [*National Glass Industries Company*] [*Algerian*] (AF)
SNJ............ Savez Novinara Jugoslavije [*Federation of Journalists of Yugoslavia*] (YU)
SNK............ Carrier and Control Frequencies Bay (RU)
SNK............ Council of People's Commissars [*1917-1946*] (RU)
SNK............ Soiuz Narodov Kameruna (MAR)
SNKh.......... Council of the National Economy (RU)
SNKhB........ Bulgarian National Choral Union (BU)
SNKL.......... Statni Nakladatelstvi Krasne Literatury [*State Publishing House of Belles-Lettres*] (CZ)
SNKLHU...... Statni Nakladatelstvi Krasne Literatury, Hudby, a Umeni [*State Publishing House of Belles-Lettres, Music, and Art*] (CZ)
SNKom........ Council of People's Commissars [*1917-1946*] (RU)
SNL............ Societe Nationale des Lieges [*North African*] (MAR)
SNL............ Somali National League (MAR)
SNL............ Syndicat National des Lyceens [*Moroccan*] (MAR)
SNLB.......... Societe Nationale des Industries des Lieges et du Bois [*National Cork and Wood Industries Company*] [*Algerian*] (AF)
SNLE.......... Sous-Marin Nucleaire Lanceur d'Engins [*Missile-Launching Nuclear Submarine*] [*French*] (WER)
SNLP.......... Societe Nationale Libyenne des Petroles (MAR)
SNM........... German Free Youth League (RU)
SNM........... People's Youth League [*Bulgarian*] (RU)
SNM........... People's Youth Union (BU)
SNM........... Slovenske Narodne Muzeum [*Slovak National Museum*] [*Turciansky Sv. Martin*] (CZ)
SNM........... Slovenske Narodopisne Muzeum [*Slovak Ethnographic Museum*] [*Turciansky Sv. Martin*] (CZ)
SNM........... Sociedad Nacional de Mineria [*National Mining Association*] [*Chilean*] (LA)
SNM........... Societe Nantaise de Madagascar (MAR)
SNM........... Somali National Movement (PD)
SNM........... Spolecnost Narodniho Muzea [*National Museum Society*] (CZ)
snm............ Sthene-Meter (RU)
SNMAREP... Societe Nationale de Materiel pour la Recherche et l'Exploitation du Petrole (MAR)
SNMC......... Societe Nationale des Materiaux de Construction [*National Building Materials Company*] [*Algerian*] (AF)
SNMD......... Union of Scientific Medical Societies (BU)
SNMES....... Syndicat National Marocain de l'Enseignement Superieur (MAR)
SN METAL... Societe Nationale des Constructions Metalliques [*National Metal Construction Company*] [*Algerian*] (AF)
SNMFM....... Sindicato Nacional dos Motoristas, Ferroviarios, e Metallurgicos (MAR)
SNMTs........ List of Settlements in the Bulgarian Kingdom (BU)
SNMVT........ Societe Nationale de Mise en Valeur du Sud Tunisien (MAR)
SNNA.......... Somali National News Agency (MAR)
SNNGA........ Societe Nationale des Materiaux de Construction [*National Construction Materials Company*] [*Algerian*] (AF)
SNNIS......... Observation, Guidance, and Liaison Aircraft (RU)
SNNMCC.... Sistema Nacional de Normalizacion, Metrologia, y Control de Calidad [*National System of Standardization, Weights and Measures, and Quality Control*] [*Cuban*] (LA)
SNO............ Ground Support Equipment (RU)
sn o........... Medical Section (BU)
SNO............ Societe Nantaise d'Outre-Mer (MAR)
SNO............ Sreski Narodni Odbor [*District People's Committee*] (YU)
SNO............ Srpska Narodna Odbrana [*Serbian National Defense*] [*A society*] [*Chicago*] (YU)
SNO............ Students' Scientific Society (RU)
SNO............ Svaz Narodniho Osvobozeni [*National Liberation League*] (CZ)
SNOA.......... Srpska Narodna Odbrana u Americi [*Serbian National Defense Council in America*] [*Chicago*] (YU)
SNOA.......... Syndicat des Negociants de l'Ouest Africain (MAR)
SNOAT........ Societe Nouvelle d'Ouvrages d'Art et Travaux (MAR)
SNOB.......... Slovenska Narodnoosvobodilna Borba [*Slovenian National Liberation Struggle*] (YU)
SNO Brigada... Sofia People's Liberation Brigade (BU)
SNOE.......... Skholi Nomikon kai Politikon Epistimon [*School of Law and Political Sciences*] [*See also MOE*] (GC1)
SNOF.......... Societe Nouvelle d'Organisation Forestiere (MAR)
SNOI........... Sumarski Naucno Opiten Institut [*Forestry Scientific Research Institute*] (YU)
SNOO.......... Slovenski Narodnoosvobodilni Odbor [*Slovenian National Liberation Committee*] (YU)
SNOO.......... Sreski Narodnooslobodilacki Odbor [*District National Liberation Committee*] (YU)
SNOS.......... Slovenski Narodnoosvobodilni Svet [*Slovenian National Liberation Council*] (YU)
SNOUB........ Slovenska Narodnoosvobodilna Udarna Brigada [*Slovenian National Liberation Shock Brigade*] [*World War II*] (YU)
SNOW......... Operation Peace for the Galilee [*Acronym from the Hebrew title for the invasion of Lebanon, 1982*]
SNP............ Concealed Observation Post (RU)
SNP............ Free People's Party [*Federal Republic of Germany*] (RU)
SNP............ Regimental Combined Observation (RU)
SNP............ Scottish National Party (PPW)
SNP............ Sistema Nacional de Pensiones [*National Pensions System*] [*Peruvian*] (LA)
SNP............ Slovenske Narodne Povstanie [*Slovak National Uprising*] (CZ)
SNP............ Social Nationalist Party [*Lebanese*] (ME)
SNP............ Socialist People's Party [*Denmark, Norway*] (RU)
SNP............ Sociedad Nacional de Pesca [*National Fishing Society*] [*Chilean*] (LA)
SNP............ Somali National Police (AF)
SNPA.......... Societe Nationale des Petroles d'Aquitaine [*Aquitaine National Petroleum Company*] [*French*] (AF)
SNPA.......... Substantial New Programme of Action (MAR)
SNPAE........ Syndesmos Neon dia ton Pyrinikon Afoplismon kai tin Eirinin "Bertrand Russell" [*Youth League for Nuclear Disarmament and Peace*] [*Frequently referred to as the "Bertrand Russell League"*] [*Greek*] (GC)
SNPE........... Societe Nationale des Poudres et Explosifs [*National Powder and Explosives Company*] [*French*] (WER)

SNPE .... Societe Nationale de Presse et d'Edition [*National Press and Publishing Company*] [*Mauritanian*] (AF)
SNPEP .... Secretaria Nacional de Propaganda y Educacion Politica [*National Secretariat for Political Propaganda and Education*] [*Nicaraguan*] (LA1)
SNPG .... Societe Nouvelle des Pecheries Gabonaises (MAR)
SNPJ .... Slovenska Narodna Podporna Jednota [*Slovenian National Welfare Society*] (YU)
SNPK .... Syndesmos Navtikon Praktoron Kyprou [*Association of Cypriot Shipping Agents*] (GC)
SNPL .... Statni Nakladatelstvi Politicke Literatury [*State Publishing House of Political Literature*] (CZ)
SNPL .... Syndicat National des Pilotes de Lignes [*French*]
SNPM .... Societe Nationale de Presse Marocaine [*Moroccan National Press Company*] (AF)
SnPn .... Powder for Siege and Fortress Guns [*Symbol*] [*French*] (MTD)
SNPP .... Sindicato Nacional de Periodistas Profesionales [*National Union of Professional Journalists*] [*Dominican Republic*] (LA)
SNPP .... Societe Nationale des Produits Petroliers [*National Petroleum Products Company*] [*Moroccan*] (AF)
SNPSB .... Servico Nacional de Producao de Sementes Basicas [*National Service for Producing Basic Seeds*] [*Brazilian*] (LA1)
SNPT .... Societe Nationale de Promotion Touristique (MAR)
SN PTT .... Sekcja Narciarska Polskiego Towarzystwa Tatrzanskiego [*Ski Section of the Polish Tatra Mountains Society*] (POL)
SNR .... Missile Guidance Station (RU)
SNR .... Section of Scientific Workers (RU)
Snr .... Senhor [*Mister or Lord*] [*Portuguese*] (GPO)
SNR .... Slovenska Narodna Rada [*Slovak National Council*] (CZ)
SNR .... Societe Nationale de Raffinage [*National Refining Company*] [*Algerian*] (AF)
SNR .... Sudan Notes and Records [*A publication*] (MAR)
SNR .... Svaz Narodni Revoluce [*National Revolution League*] (CZ)
SNR .... Union of Scientific Workers (BU)
Snra .... Senhora [*Mrs.*] [*Portuguese*] (GPO)
SNRB .... Union of Bulgarian Scientific Workers (BU)
SN REPAL ... Societe Nationale de Recherches et d'Exploitation des Petroles en Algeria [*National Company for Petroleum Prospecting and Exploitation in Algeria*] (AF)
SNRH .... Sabor Narodne Republike Hrvatske [*Assembly of Croatia*] (YU)
Snrta .... Senhorita [*Miss*] [*Portuguese*] (GPO)
SNRvZ .... Slovenska Narodna Rada v Zahranici [*Slovak National Council in Exile*] (CZ)
SNS .... Ground Stereophotogrammetry (RU)
SNS .... Savezna Narodna Skupstine [*Federal People's Assembly*] (YU)
SNS .... Self-Adjusting System (RU)
SNS .... Servicio Nacional de Salud [*National Health Service*] [*Chilean*] (LA)
SNS .... Societe Nationale de Siderurgie [*National Steel Company*] [*Algerian*] (AF)
SNS .... Societe Niger-Soudan (MAR)
SNS .... Societe Nouvelle Safric (MAR)
SNS .... Sofia People's Council (BU)
SNS .... Srpski Narodni Savez [*Serbian National Federation*] [*Chicago*] (YU)
SNS .... Studieforbundet Naringsliv och Samhalle [*Research Association for Industry and Society*] (WEN)
SNS .... Suomi-Neuvostoliitto-Seura [*Finland-Soviet Union Society*] (WEN)
SNS .... Village People's Council (BU)
SNSEMPAC ... Societe Nationale de Semouleries, Meuneries, Fabrique de Pates Alimentaires Couscous [*Algerian*] (MAR)
SNSO .... Union of People's Sports Organizations (BU)
SNSOGATRA ... Societe Nouvelle Societe Gabonaise de Travaux (MAR)
SNT .... Collection of Scientific Transactions [*A publication*] (RU)
SNT .... Navigation Light (RU)
SNT .... Societe Nationale de Transports [*National Transportation Company*] [*Tunisian*] (AF)
SNT .... Societe Nigerienne de Television (MAR)
SNT .... Stowarzyszenie Naukowo-Techniczne [*Scientific and Technical Association*] [*Polish*]
SNTA .... Sindicato Nacional de Trabajadores Azucareros [*National Trade Union of Sugar Industry Workers*] [*Cuban*] (LA1)
SNTA .... Sindicato Nacional de Trabajadores de Salud [*National Health Workers Union*] [*Cuban*] (LA)
SNTA .... Societe Nationale des Tabacs et Allumettes [*Algerian*] (MAR)
SNTA .... Societe Nigerienne de Transports Automobiles (MAR)
SNTAF .... Sindicato Nacional de Trabajadores Agricolas y Forestales [*National Union of Agricultural and Forestry Workers*] [*Cuban*] (LA)
SNTAG .... Sindicato Nacional de Trabajadores de Artes Graficas [*National Union of Workers in the Graphic Arts Industry*] [*Cuban*] (LA)
SNTAP .... Sindicato Nacional de Trabajadores de Administracion Publica [*National Union of Public Administration Workers*] [*Cuban*] (LA)
SNTC .... Sindicato Nacional de Trabajadores del Calzado [*National Footwear Workers Union*] [*Costa Rican*] (LA)
SNTC .... Sindicato Nacional de Trabajadores de Comercio [*National Commercial Workers Union*] [*Cuban*] (LA)
SNTC .... Sindicato Nacional de Trabajadores de la Construccion [*National Union of Construction Workers*] [*Cuban*] (LA)
SNTC .... Societe Nationale Tunisienne de Cellulose (MAR)
SNTCA .... Sindicato Nacional de Trabajadores del Comercio y la Administracion [*National Union of Workers in Commerce and Administration*] [*Cuban*] (LA)
SNTCFAR ... Sindicato Nacional de Trabajadores Civiles de las Fuerzas Armadas Revolucionarias [*National Union of FAR Civilian Workers*] [*Cuban*] (LA)
SNTCG .... Sindicato Nacional de Trabajadores del Comercio y Gastronomia [*National Commercial and Restaurant Workers Union*] [*Cuban*] (LA)
SNTD .... Union of Scientific and Technical Societies (BU)
SNTE .... Sindicato Nacional de Trabajadores de la Educacion [*National Trade Union of Education Workers*] [*Mexican*] (LA1)
SNTEC .... Sindicato Nacional de Trabajadores de la Educacion y Cultura [*National Union of Education and Cultural Workers*] [*Cuban*] (LA)
SNTF .... Societe Nationale des Transports Ferroviaires [*Algerian*] (MAR)
SNTF .... Societe Nigerienne de Transports Fluviaux et Maritimes (MAR)
SNTFM .... Societe Nationale des Transports Ferroviaires Mauritaniens [*Mauritanian National Railroad Transportation Company*] (AF)
SNTGP .... Stowarzyszenie Naukowo-Techniczne Geodetow Polskich [*Scientific and Technical Association of Polish Geodesists*] (POL)
SNTH .... Societe Nationale des Travaux d'Hydraulique (MAR)
SNTI .... Societe Nationale de Tomates Industrielles (MAR)
SNTI .... Stowarzyszenie Naukowo-Techniczne Inzynierow [*Scientific and Technical Association of Engineers*] (POL)
SNTIA .... Sindicato Nacional de Trabajadores de la Industria Azucarera [*National Union of Sugar Industry Workers*] [*Cuban*] (LA)
SNTIAL .... Sindicato Nacional de Trabajadores de la Industria Alimenticia [*National Food Industry Workers Union*] [*Cuban*] (LA)
SNTIiTG ...... Stowarzyszenie Naukowo-Techniczne Inzynierow i Technikow Gornictwa [*Scientific and Technical Association of Mining Engineers and Technicians*] (POL)
SNTIiTP ...... Stowarzyszenie Naukowo-Techniczne Inzynierow i Technikow Przemyslu [*Scientific and Technical Association of Engineers and Technicians of the Industry*] (POL)
SNTIL .... Sindicato Nacional de Trabajadores de la Industria Ligera [*National Union of Light Industry Workers*] [*Cuban*] (LA)
SNTIQE .... Sindicato Nacional de Trabajadores de las Industrias Quimica y Energetica [*National Chemical and Energy Industry Workers Union*] [*Cuban*] (LA)
SNTIT .... Sindicato Nacional de Trabajadores de la Industria Tabacalera [*National Union of Tobacco Industry Workers*] [*Cuban*] (LA)
SNTIT .... Sindicato Nacional de Trabajadores de la Industria de Transporte [*National Transportation Industry Workers Union*] [*Salvadoran*] (LA)
SNTITK .... Stowarzyszenie Naukowo-Techniczne Inzynierow i Technikow Komunikacji [*Scientific and Technical Association of Transportation Engineers and Technicians*] (POL)
SNTITP .... Stowarzyszenie Naukowo-Techniczne Inzynierow i Technikow Przemyslu [*Scientific and Technical Association of Engineers and Technicians of the Industry*] (POL)
SNTITPP ..... Stowarzyszenie Naukowo-Techniczne Inzynierow i Technikow Przemyslu Papierniczego [*Scientific and Technical Association of Paper Industry Engineers and Technicians*] (POL)
SNTITWM ... Stowarzyszenie Naukowo-Techniczne Inzynierow i Technikow Wodno-Melioracyjnych [*Scientific and Technical Association of Irrigation and Land Reclamation Engineers and Technicians*] (POL)
SNTL .... Statne Nakladatelstvo Technickej Literatury [*State Publishing House of Technical Literature*] (CZ)
SNTL .... Statni Nakladatelstvi Technicke Literatury [*State Publishing House of Technical Literature*] (CZ)
SNTM .... Sindicato Nacional de Trabajadores de la Medicina [*National Medical Workers Union*] [*Cuban*] (LA)
SNTMM .... Sindicato Nacional de Trabajadores Mineros y Metalurgicos [*National Union of Miners and Metalworkers*] [*Cuban*] (LA)
SNTMMP ..... Sindicato Nacional de Trabajadores de la Marina Mercante y Puertos [*National Union of Merchant Marine and Port Workers*] [*Cuban*] (LA)
SNTMVCI .... Syndicat National des Transports de Marchandises et Voyageurs de la Cote-d'Ivoire (MAR)
SNTN .... Societe Nationale des Transports Nigeriens (MAR)
SNTO .... Students' Scientific and Technical Society (RU)
SNTP .... Low-Frequency Transit and Channel Transfer Bay (RU)
SNTP .... Sindicato Nacional Textil y de las Pieles [*National Union of Textile and Leather Workers*] [*Cuban*] (LA)
SNTP .... Sindicato Nacional de Trabajadores de Petroleo [*National Union of Oil Workers*] [*Cuban*] (LA)
SNTP .... Sindicato Nacional de Trabajadores de la Prensa [*National Press Workers Union*] [*Venezuelan*] (LA)
SNTP .... Societe Nationale de Travaux Publics (MAR)
SNTPL .... Sindicato Nacional de Trabajadores de la Prensa y el Libro [*National Press and Book Workers Union*] [*Cuban*] (LA)

SNTPVO...... Council for Science, Technical Progress, and Higher Education (BU)
SNTQE........ Sindicato Nacional de Trabajadores de la Quimica y la Energetica [*National Union of Chemical and Power Industries Workers*] [*Cuban*] (LA)
SNTR........... Societe Nationale des Transports Routiers [*Algerian*] (MAR)
SNTRM........ Sindicato Nacional de Trabajadores Petroleros de la Republica Mexicana [*Mexican National Oil Workers Union*] (LA)
SNTS........... Sindicato Nacional de Trabajadores de la Salud [*National Trade Union of Health Workers*] [*Cuban*] (LA1)
SNTS........... Sindicato Nacional de Trabajadores Sastres [*National Union of Tailors*] [*Ecuadorean*] (LA)
SNTS........... Store Nordiske-Telegraf-Selskap Fabriken A/S [*Great Northern Telegraph Co. Factory, Ltd.*] [*Danish*] (WEN)
SNTS........... Studiorum Novi Testamenti Societas (MAR)
SNTSS........ Sindicato Nacional de Trabajadores del Seguro Social [*National Trade Union of Social Security Workers*] [*Mexican*] (LA1)
SNTTC........ Sindicato Nacional de Trabajadores de Transportes y Comunicaciones [*National Union of Transportation and Communications Workers*] [*Cuban*] (LA)
SNTU........... Societe Nationale de Transports Urbains (MAR)
SNTU........... Societe Nigerienne de Transport Urbain (MAR)
SNTUC........ Singapore National Trade Unions Congress (ML)
SNTV........... Societe Nationale des Transports de Voyageurs [*Algerian*] (MAR)
SNTZ........... Syndicat National des Travailleurs Zairois (MAR)
SNU............. Skopski Naroden Univerzitet [*Skopje People's University*] (YU)
SNU............. Somali National Union (MAR)
SNUJ........... Singapore National Union of Journalists (ML)
SNUP........... Sahara National Union Party (MAR)
SNUS........... Sistema Nacional Unico de Salud [*Sole National Health Program*] [*Nicaraguan*] (LA1)
SNV............. Sabiraliste Neispravnih Vozila [*Assemblage of Defective Vehicles*] [*Military*] (YU)
SNV............. Sbor Napravne Vychovy [*Correctional Training Corps*] (CZ)
SNYS........... Seychelles National Youth Service (MAR)
SNZ............. Savet za Narodno Zdravlje [*Public Health Council*] (YU)
SNZ............. Sekretarijat za Narodno Zdravlje (SIV) [*Secretariat of Public Health*] (YU)
SNZ............. Sprava Napravneho Zarizeni [*Correctional Facilities Directorate*] (CZ)
SNZSP........ Savet za Narodno Zdravlje i Socijalnu Politiku [*Council on Public Health and Social Policy*] (YU)
SO............... Concentrated Fire (RU)
SO............... Convergent Fire [*or Concentrated Fire*] (BU)
SO............... Deviation Signaling (RU)
SO............... Economic Trust (BU)
SO............... Flank Guard, Flank Detachment (BU)
so............... Launching [*Rocket-Firing*] Detachment (BU)
so............... Launching Detachment (RU)
SO............... Medical Aid Section (RU)
SO............... Saobracajno Odeljenje [*Transportation Department*] (YU)
so............... Sauf Omission [*French*]
SO............... Savezni Odbor [*Federal Committee*] (YU)
SO............... Savezni Organi [*Federal Organs*] (YU)
SO............... Schienenoberkante [*Top of Rail*] (EG)
so............... Se On [*That Is*] [*Finnish*] (GPO)
SO............... Seasonal Servicing [*of automobiles*] (RU)
SO............... Secret Department, Secret Section (RU)
SO............... Secteur Operationnel [*Operational Sector*] (CL)
SO............... Security at the Halt or in Bivouac (RU)
s/o.............. Self-Propelled Cannon (BU)
SO............... Self-Propelled Gun (RU)
SO............... Sergo Ordzhonikidze [*Locomotive series*] (RU)
So............... Seto [*Strait*] [*Japanese*] (NAU)
SO............... Siberian Department (of the Academy of Sciences, USSR) (RU)
so............... Siehe Oben [*See Above*] [*German*] (GPO)
SO............... Social Security (RU)
SO............... Somali [*Two-letter standard code*] (CNC)
s/o.............. Son Ordre [*French*]
SO............... Spojene Ocelarny [*United Steel Works*] [*Kladno*] (CZ)
SO............... Sports Society (RU)
SO............... Srpski Odbor [*Serbian Committee*] (YU)
SO............... Standard Model, Standard Sample (RU)
so............... Standard Purification [*of gases*] (RU)
SO............... Statni Studijni Knihovna v Ostrave [*State Research Library in Ostrava*] (CZ)
SO............... Statni Vedecka Knihovna v Ostrave [*State Research Library in Ostrava*] (CZ)
SO............... Studijni Oddeleni [*Study Section*] (CZ)
SO............... Sudoeste [*Southwest*] [*Spanish*]
SO............... Suedosten [*Southeast*] (EG)
SOA............. Societe Occidentale Africaine (MAR)
SOA............. Societe Omnisports de l'Armee (MAR)
SOA............. Soldats de l'Opposition Algerienne [*Soldiers of the Algerian Opposition*] (AF)
SOACAM.... Societe Avicole de l'Ouest Cameroun (MAR)
SOACIA...... Societe Auxiliaire pour le Commerce et l'Industrie en Afrique (MAR)
SOACO....... Societe Anonyme de Constructions (MAR)
SOACO....... Societe Ouest-Africaine de Commission (MAR)
SOADIP....... Societe Africaine de Diffusion et de Promotion (MAR)
SOAE.......... State Organization for Administration and Employment [*Iranian*] (ME)
SOAEM....... Societe Ouest-Africaine d'Entreprises Maritimes (MAR)
SOAF.......... Sultan of Oman Air Force (MAR)
SOAFCO..... Societe Africaine de Commerce et de Courtage (MAR)
SOAG.......... Stichting Ontwikkeling van de Automatisering bij de Gemeenten [*'s-Gravenhage*]
SOAGA....... Sindicato Obrero de Artes Graficas Autonomo [*Autonomous Trade Union of Graphic Arts Workers*] [*Dominican Republic*] (LA1)
SOAGCI...... Societe d'Affretement et de Groupage de Cote-d'Ivoire (MAR)
SOAGE........ Sindicatos de Obreros y Administrativos de General Electric [*Union of General Electric Workers*] [*Uruguayan*] (LA)
SOALCO..... Societe Nationale des Conserveries Algeriennes (MAR)
SOAM.......... Societe d'Oxygene et d'Acetylene de Madagascar (MAR)
SOAM.......... Stratiotikos Oikos tis Avtou Megaleiotitos [*His Majesty's Military Aides*] [*Greek*] (GC)
SOAN.......... Siberian Department of the Academy of Sciences, USSR (RU)
SOAO.......... North Ossetian Autonomous Oblast [*1924-1936*] (RU)
SOAP.......... Societe Ouest-Africaine de Presse (MAR)
SOAS.......... School of Oriental and African Studies [*University of London*] (MAR)
SOASSR..... North Ossetian Autonomous Soviet Socialist Republic (RU)
SOAT.......... Public Automotive Transportation Association (BU)
SOATO........ Societe Africaine de Torrefaction (MAR)
soavt.......... Coauthor (RU)
SOB............ Lead-Covered Armored Signal Cable (RU)
SOB............ Sanayi Odalari Birligi [*Union of Chambers of Commerce*] (TU)
SOB............ Senior Battery Officer [*Artillery*] (BU)
SOB............ Sluzbena Obvestila [*Official Announcements*] (YU)
SOBAB........ Societe de Bois d'Abengourou (MAR)
SOBAKA...... Societe Bananiere de la Kavi (MAR)
SOBAKI....... Societe Belgo-Africaine du Kivu (MAR)
SOBAMAD... Societe Bananiere de Madagascar (MAR)
SOBANO..... Societe du Batelage de Nossi-Be (MAR)
SOBANOA... Societe Bananiere de la Nonoa (MAR)
SOBEFI....... Societe Bertrand Fils (MAR)
SOBEGI....... Societe Beninoise des Gaz Industries (MAR)
SOBEK........ Societe Beninoise du Kenaf (MAR)
SOBEMAC... Societe Beninoise des Materiaux de Construction [*Beninese Construction Material Company*] (AF)
SOBENA..... Sociedade Brasileira de Engenharia Naval [*Brazilian Naval Engineering Society*] (LA)
SOBEPALH... Societe Beninoise de Palmier a Huile [*Beninese Oil Palm Company*] (AF)
sobes.......... Department of Social Security (RU)
sobes.......... Social Security (RU)
SOBETEX.... Societe Beninoise des Textiles [*Beninese Textile Company*] (AF)
SOBIASCO... Societe Bitume et de l'Asphalt du Congo (MAR)
SOBIL.......... Sociedade de Administracoes de Bens e Mobiliarios Lda. (MAR)
sobir........... Collective Noun (RU)
SOBOA........ Societe des Brasseries de l'Ouest Africain (MAR)
SOBOCA...... Societe des Bois du Sud Ouest Cameroun (MAR)
SOBOCAM... Societe de Conditionnement, de Fabrication, et de Transformation de Boissons du Cameroun (MAR)
SOBOCI...... Societe des Boissons Hygieniques de la Cote-d'Ivoire (MAR)
SOBOCO..... Societe de Bonnetterie et Confection Dakaroise (MAR)
SOBOFRI.... Societe Bobolaise de Friperie (MAR)
SOBOGAZ... Societe des Boissons Gazeuses du Benin (MAR)
SOBOHA..... Societe des Bois de la Hana (MAR)
SOBOMA.... Societe des Bois de la Manzan (MAR)
SOBOMA.... Societe des Boissons de Mauritanie (MAR)
SOBOMA.... Societe Bonnetiere Malagasy (MAR)
sobr............ Collection (RU)
SOBRADO... Societe des Brasseries du Dahomey (MAR)
SOBRAGA... Societe des Brasseries du Gabon (MAR)
SOBRAGUI... Societe des Brasseries de Guinee (MAR)
SOBRAT...... Societe des Brasseries du Tchad (MAR)
SOBRI......... Sentral Organisasi Buruh Republik Indonesia [*Republic of Indonesia Federation of Workers Organizations*] (IN)
SOBRICI...... Societe de Briqueteries de Cote-d'Ivoire (MAR)
SOBRIMA.... Societe des Briqueteries du Mali (MAR)
sobr soch.... Collected Works (RU)
Sobr Uzak... Collection of Laws and Decrees of the Workers' and Peasants' Government of the RSFSR (RU)
sobst izd..... Private Publication (BU)
sobstv......... Proper, Properly, Strictly (RU)
SOBUMINES... Societe Burundaise des Mines (MAR)
SOBV.......... Svaz Obcanu Bez Vyznani [*Union of Citizens without Religious Affiliation*] (CZ)
SOC............ Secundaria Obrera-Campesina [*Workers and Peasants Secondary School*] [*Cuban*] (LA)
SOC............ Social Overhead Costs (MAR)
SOC............ Solidaritat Obrera da Catalunya [*Workers Solidarity of Catalonia*] [*Spanish*] (WER)
SOC............ Superacion Obrera-Campesina [*Workers and Peasants Educational Improvement*] [*Cuban*] (LA)
SOCA.......... Societe de Carrosserie Abidjanaise (MAR)

SOCA.......... Societe Commerciale Africaine (MAR)
SOCA.......... Societe des Compteurs Africains (MAR)
SOCA.......... Societe Olympic Centrafricaine pour le Diamant et Metaux Precieux (MAR)
SOCA.......... State Organisation for Civil Aviation [*Iraqi*] (MAR)
SOCAB........ Societe Agricole du Bandama (MAR)
SOCAB........ Societe Camerounaise de Bonneterie (MAR)
SOCAB........ Societe de Construction Automobile du Benin (MAR)
SOCABAIL ... Societe Camerounaise de Credit Bail (MAR)
SOCABEX... Societe d'Application des Bois Exotiques (MAR)
SOCABO..... Societe Camerounaise des Boulangers (MAR)
SOCABU..... Societe d'Assurances du Burundi (MAR)
SOCACAO ... Societe Camerounaise de Cacaos (MAR)
SOCACI...... Societe Commerciale et Agricole de la Cote-d'Ivoire (MAR)
SOCACIG.... Societe Centrafricaine de Cigarettes (MAR)
SOCACOLIE ... Societe Camerounaise de Commerce Local d'Importation et d'Exportation (MAR)
SOCACOTRA ... Societe Camerounaise de Commerce et de Transport (MAR)
SOCAD .... Societe Camerounaise de Dietetique et d'Alimentation (MAR)
SOCAD .... Societe de Commercialisation et de Credit Agricole du Dahomey (MAR)
SOCADE..... Societe Camerounaise de Developpement (MAR)
SOCADEM ... Societe Camerounaise d'Emballages Metalliques (MAR)
SOCADI ...... Societe Centrafricaine de Diamant Industriel (MAR)
SOCADIESEL ... Societe Camerounaise du Diesel (MAR)
SOCADIMP ... Societe Abidjanaise d'Importation (MAR)
SOCADIS.... Societe Camerounaise de Distribution (MAR)
SOCAF........ Societe Cinematographique de l'Ouest Africain (MAR)
SOCAF........ Societe Commerciale Africaine [*Ivorian*] (MAR)
SOCAF........ Societe Commerciale Centrafricaine (MAR)
SOCAFER... Societe Camerounaise de Plomberie et de Ferronerie (MAR)
SOCAFIC.... Societe Camerounaise de Fournitures pour l'Industrie et les Constructions (MAR)
SOCAFIEX ... Societe Commerciale Africaine d'Importation et d'Exportation (MAR)
SOCAFLI..... Societe Africaine de Librairie "Les Heures Claires" (MAR)
SOCAFRIC ... Societe Camerounaise de Representation Industrielle et Commerciale (MAR)
SOCAFRICA ... Societe Africaine d'Achats (MAR)
SOCAFROID-Ivoire ... Societe Africaine du Froid Cote-d'Ivoire (MAR)
SOCAGEL... Societe Gabonaise de Cellulose (MAR)
SOCAGI...... Societe Centrafricaine des Gaz Industriels (MAR)
SOCAHIT.... Societe Camerounaise Hoteliere, Immobiliere, et Touristique (MAR)
SOCAHO..... Societe Camerounaise Hoteliere (MAR)
SOCAJU...... Sociedade Comercial e Industrial de Caju (MAR)
SOCAL........ Sociedad de Cultivos Agricolas Limitada (COL)
SOCAL........ Societe des Conserves Alimentaires (MAR)
SOCALDET ... Societe Algerienne de Developpement Touristique (MAR)
SOCALDEX ... Societe Algerienne de Developpement et d'Expansion (MAR)
SOCALIMINES ... Societe Mixte Centrafricano-Arab-Libyenne des Mines [*Joint Central African-Arab-Libyan Mining Company*] (AF)
SOCAM....... Societe Camerounaise de Menuiserie (MAR)
SOCAM....... Societe Commerciale Africaine d'Importation (MAR)
SOCAM....... Societe des Conserves Alimentaires du Mali (MAR)
SOCAMBOIS ... Societe Camerounaise des Bois (MAR)
SOCAMCAP ... Societe Camerounaise d'Elevage et de Capture d'Animaux Sauvages (MAR)
SOCAMCO ... Societe Camerounaise de Conserveries (MAR)
SOCAME..... Societe Camerounaise des Engrais (MAR)
SOCAMEC ... Societe Camerounaise d'Expansion de la Culture (MAR)
SOCAMETA ... Societe Camerounaise de Construction Metallique (MAR)
SOCAMEX ... Societe Camerounaise d'Exportation (MAR)
SOCANA..... Societe Camerounaise de Navigation (MAR)
SOCANA..... Societe des Plantations de Cafe Nana de Carnot (MAR)
Soc Ane ...... Societe Anonyme [*Stock Company*] [*French*] (GPO)
SOCANIGER ... Societe des Allumettes du Niger (MAR)
SOCAPA ..... Societe Camerounaise des Anciens Ets. Joseph Paris (MAR)
SOCAPA ..... Societe Camerounaise pour le Developpement de l'Automobile (MAR)
SOCAPA ..... Societe Camerounaise de Produits Africains (MAR)
SOCAPALM ... Societe Camerounaise de Palmeraies (MAR)
SOCAPAR... Societe Camerounaise des Anciens Ets. Joseph Paris (MAR)
SOCAPE ..... Societe Camerounaise de Presse et d'Edition (MAR)
SOCAPET... Societe Camerounaise des Petroles (MAR)
SOCAPROD ... Societe Camerounaise de Production et de Distribution de Boissons Hygieniques (MAR)
SOCAPS ..... Societe Camerounaise des Produits Shell (MAR)
SOCAR........ Societe Camerounaise d'Assurances et de Reassurances (MAR)
SOCAR........ Societe Camerounaise de Carrosserie (MAR)
SOCAREC... Societe Africaine de Rectification (MAR)
SOCARET... Societe Camerounaise de Reparations et Transports (MAR)
SOCARMAR ... Sociedade de Cargas e Descargas Maritimas, SARC [*Maritime Loading and Unloading Society*] [*Portuguese*] (WER)
SOCARP ..... Societe Commerciale Agricole du Rip [*Senegalese*] (MAR)
SOCARSEL ... Societe Camerounaise de Raffinage de Sel (MAR)
SOCAS........ Sociedades de Cooperacion Agricola [*Agricultural Cooperation Associations*] [*Chilean*] (LA)
SOCAS........ Societe de Conserves Alimentaires du Senegal (MAR)
SOCASE ..... Societe Commerciale Agricole Senegalaise (MAR)
SOCASEP... Societe Camerounaise de Sepultures et Transports Speciaux (MAR)
SOCAT........ Societe Cherifienne d'Articles Transformes (MAR)
SOCATCI.... Societe des Caoutchoucs de Cote-d'Ivoire (MAR)
SOCATEM ... Societe Camerounaise de Tresses d'Eponges Menageres (MAR)
SOCATEX... Societe Camerounaise de Confection et de Bonneterie (MAR)
SOCATI....... Societe Centrafricaine de Telecommunications Internationales (MAR)
SOCATRAL ... Societe Camerounaise de Transformation de l'Aluminium (MAR)
SOCATUC... Societe Camerounaise de Tuyauteries et de Cordes en Plastique (MAR)
SOCAVER... Societe Camerounaise de Verrerie (MAR)
SOCC.......... Solidaridad Obrera Cristiana de Cataluna [*Christian Workers Solidarity of Catalonia*] [*Spanish*] (WER)
SOCCA....... Societe Camerounaise de Credit Automobile (MAR)
SOCCDE..... Societe Commerciale Camerounaise pour le Developpement et l'Economie (MAR)
SOCCONAT ... Societe Cambodgienne de Consignation de Navires et de Transit [*Cambodian Ship Consignment and Transit Company*] (CL)
SOCCP........ Societe de l'Ouest Cameroun pour le Commerce et la Photographie (MAR)
Socd........... Sociedad [*Company*] [*Business and trade*] [*Spanish*]
Socdem ...... Socialni Demokrat [*Social Democrat*] (CZ)
SOCDYL ..... Sarawak Overseas Chinese Democratic Youth League (ML)
SOCEA........ Societe Eau et Assainissement (MAR)
SOCECO..... Societe Camerounaise d'Etudes et de Constructions (MAR)
SOCECO..... Societe Senegalaise de Commerce (MAR)
SOCECOD ... Societe Senegalaise pour le Commerce et le Developpement (MAR)
SOCECOM ... Societe Commerciale de Keur Soce (MAR)
SOCEF .... Societe de Construction et d'Exploitation des Installations Frigorifiques [*Refrigeration Plant Construction and Operation Company*] (AF)
SOCEFI....... Societe Centrafricaine d'Exploitations Forestieres et Industrielles (MAR)
SOCEI .... Societe Commerciale Camerounaise d'Exportation et d'Importation (MAR)
SOCEL .... Sociedade Industrial de Celuloses [*Industrial Society of Cellulose*] [*Portuguese*] (WER)
SOCEPA ..... Societe Anonyme d'Etudes et de Participations Immobilieres (MAR)
SOCEPAR... Sociedad de Celadores Particulares [*Bogota*] (COL)
SOCEPAR... Societe Anonyme d'Etudes et de Participations Immobilieres (MAR)
SOCERAM ... Societe Malgache de Ceramique (MAR)
SOCETEC... Societe d'Etudes Techniques (MAR)
SOCETODAK ... Societe d'Etudes du Thon Dakarois (MAR)
SOCEXPLAN ... Societe d'Exploitation de Plantations Societe Socfinol (MAR)
SOCFEIC .... Societe Khmero-Francaise d'Entreprises Industrielles et Commerciales [*Cambodian-French Industrial and Commercial Enterprises Company*] (CL)
SOCh .... Secret Operations Unit (RU)
soch .... Works [*Bibliography*] (RU)
SOCHAMAD ... Societe Anonyme de Confection Malgache (MAR)
SOCHEGIC ... Societe Cherifienne de Gestion Industrielle et Commerciale (MAR)
SOCHETI .... Societe Cherifienne d'Etudes et d'Entreprises (MAR)
SOCHOT ..... Societe Hoteliere du Cambodge [*Hotel Company of Cambodia*] (CL)
SOCI .... Societe de l'Ouest de la Cote-d'Ivoire (MAR)
SOCI .... State Organisation for Construction Industries [*Iraqi*] (MAR)
SOCIA......... Societe Commerciale Industrielle et Agricole (MAR)
SOCIABE.... Societe Agricole de M'Be (MAR)
SOCIACI..... Societe Commerciale et Industrielle Africaine de la Cote-d'Ivoire (MAR)
SOCIAGRI... Societe Ivoirienne d'Expansion Agricole (MAR)
SOCIAL....... Sociedade Comercial, Industrial, e de Agencias Limitada (MAR)
SOCIBEMA ... Societe des Ciments et Betons Manufactures (MAR)
SOCICA ...... Societe Cinematographique Africaine (MAR)
SOCICO ...... Societe Immobiliere et Commerciale du Congo (MAR)
SOCICO ...... Societe Immobiliere de la Communaute (MAR)
SOCIDA ...... Societe Commerciale et Industrielle Dakaroise (MAR)
SOCIDIS ..... Societe Ivoirienne d'Importation et de Distribution (MAR)
SOCIE .... Societe Commerciale d'Import Export [*Dakar*] (MAR)
SOCIEM...... Societe de Commerce General d'Importation et d'Exportation de Mauritanie (MAR)
SOCIEP....... Societe d'Importation et d'Exportation des Produits (MAR)
SOCIFRANCE ... Societe Immobiliere Francaise (MAR)
SOCIGA ...... Societe de Cigarettes du Gabon (MAR)
SOCIGAB.... Societe Commerciale et Industrielle au Gabon (MAR)
SOCIGLACE ... Societe des Glacieres d'Abidjan (MAR)
SOCIM .... Societe Centrafricaine d'Investissements Immobiliers (MAR)
SOCIM .... Societe Commerciale et Industrielle de Mauritanie [*Mauritanian Commercial and Industrial Company*] (AF)

SOCIMA...... Societe des Ciments du Mali (MAR)
SOCIMAD ... Societe Cinema de Madagascar (MAR)
SOCIMAF.... Societe Commerciale et Mobiliere de l'Afamba (MAR)
SOCIMAT.... Societe des Ciments et Materiaux (MAR)
SOCIMEX.... Societe d'Importation et d'Exportation de l'Ocean Indien (MAR)
SOCIP......... Societe Cristal Pailin SA [*Pailin Crystal Company, Inc.*] [*Cambodian*] (CL)
SOCIPAR.... Societe Ivoirienne de Participation (MAR)
SOCIPEC.... Societe Ivoirienne de Participations Economiques (MAR)
SOCIPECHE ... Societe Cote Ivoirienne de Peche (MAR)
SOCIPRA.... Societe Industrielle de Peinture et Ravalement (MAR)
SOCIR......... Societe Congolaise Italienne de Raffinage (MAR)
SOCITAS.... Societe Ivoirienne de Textiles Artificiels et Synthetiques (MAR)
SOCITEL..... Societe Ivoirienne des Telephones (MAR)
SOCITO....... Societe Industrielle Togolaise (MAR)
SOCITOUR ... Societe Casamancaise d'Investissement Touristique (MAR)
SOCITRABAR ... Societe Commerciale et Industrielle des Transports de Banjoun Reunis (MAR)
SOCITRACAM ... Societe Camerounaise Interprofessionnelle pour la Fourniture des Traverses et de Bois Debites au Transcamerounais (MAR)
SOCIVEL..... Societe Ivoirienne de Vetements du Luxe (MAR)
SOCIVER.... Societe Ivoirienne de Verrerie (MAR)
SOCIVIM..... Societe Ivoirienne d'Importation (MAR)
SocK........... Socialisticno Kmetijstvo [*Socialist Agriculture*] [*Ljubljana*] [*A periodical*] (YU)
SocM........... Socialisticna Misel [*Socialist Thought*] [*Ljubljana*] [*A periodical*] (YU)
SOCMA....... Societe Commerciale de Materiel Automobile [*Automobile Equipment Company*] [*Cambodian*] (CL)
SOCMEQ.... Societe Cambodgienne de Materiels Electriques et de Quincaillerie [*Cambodian Electrical Equipment and Hardware Company*] (CL)
SOCO.......... Societe Commerciale et Hoteliere du Gabon (MAR)
SOCOAF..... Societe Cinematographique de l'Ouest Africain (MAR)
SOCOAF..... Societe Commerciale Africaine du Sine Saloum (MAR)
SOCOAGRO ... Sociedad de Construcciones y Operaciones Agropecuarias, SA [*Agriculture and Livestock Construction and Operations Association, Inc.*] [*Chilean*] (LA)
SOCOB....... Societe Commerciale des Woulad Boussaba (MAR)
SOCOB....... Societe Cooperative Ouvriere de Batiments de Bamako (MAR)
SOCOBA..... Societe Commerciale du Baol (MAR)
SOCOBA..... Societe Commerciale Voltaique Raymond et Abid Bachour (MAR)
SOCOBA..... Societe Congolaise du Batiment (MAR)
SOCOBA..... Societe de Construction de Batiments [*Gabonese*] (MAR)
SOCOBACAM ... Societe Commerciale du Baleng du Cameroun (MAR)
SOCOBAM ... Societe Commerciale du Mbam (MAR)
SOCOBANQUE ... Societe Congolaise de Banque (MAR)
SOCOBAO ... Societe Commerciale de Balumbi-Ouest (MAR)
SOCOBE..... Societe Commerciale du Benin (MAR)
SOCOBIS.... Societe Confiserie et Biscuitiere (MAR)
SOCOBLE.... Societe Cooperative de Ble de Tunisie (MAR)
SOCOBO.... Societe Cooperative de Bonoua (MAR)
SOCOBOD ... Societe Commerciale Bock-Dieuf (MAR)
SOCOBOIS ... Societe Congolaise des Bois (MAR)
SOCOBOM ... Societe Commerciale Mauritanienne Boussahab et Mouloud (MAR)
SOCOC....... Societe Commerciale de l'Ouest Cameroun (MAR)
SOCOCI...... Societe Commerciale de la Cote-d'Ivoire (MAR)
SOCOCIM... Societe Ouest-Africaine des Ciments [*West African Cement Company*] [*Senegalese*] (AF)
SOCOCO.... Sociedad Colombiana de Construcciones Ltda. [*Bogota*] (COL)
SOCOCOM ... Compania Nacional de Combustibles SA [*Bogota*] (COL)
SOCODA..... Sociedad Constructora Ltda. [*Medellin*] (COL)
SOCODAK ... Societe Commerciale Dakaroise (MAR)
SOCODESE ... Societe Commerciale et de Decorticage du Senegal (MAR)
SOCODEXCO ... Sociedad Colombiana de Expansion Comercial [*Bogota*] (COL)
SOCODI...... Societe Commerciale de Distribution (MAR)
SOCODI...... Societe Congolaise de Disques (MAR)
SOCODIA.... Societe Commerciale pour le Developpement Industriel en Afrique (MAR)
SOCODIM... Societe Commerciale d'Importation (MAR)
SOCODIMA ... Societe de Construction et Distribution de Materiaux (MAR)
SOCODROG ... Societe de Courtage pour la Droguerie (MAR)
SOCOFADIS ... Societe Commerciale Famille Dimelente du Senegal (MAR)
SOCOFAM ... Sociedad Colombiana de Fabricantes Mecanicos [*Duitama-Boyaca*] (COL)
SOCOFAOCAM ... Societe Commerciale Familiale de l'Ouest-Cameroun (MAR)
SOCOFEL ... Sociedade Comercial de Ferragens Limitada (MAR)
SOCOFER... Societe Coloniale du Fer (MAR)
SOCOFFA... Societe Commerciale et Financiere Franco-Africaine [*Franco-African Trading and Finance Company*] (AF)
SOCOFI....... Societe Commerciale Financiere et Industrielle (MAR)
SOCOFI....... Societe Commerciale Franco-Ivoirienne (MAR)
SOCOFI....... Societe J. Corsetti et Fils (MAR)
SOCOFIAM ... Societe Cooperative Forestiere Industrielle et Agricole de la Marahoue (MAR)
SOCOFIDE ... Societe Congolaise de Financement du Developpement [*Congolese*] (MAR)
SOCOFOA ... Societe Commerciale Francaise de l'Ouest Africain (MAR)
SOCOFOR... Societe Commerciale et Forestiere du Saloum (MAR)
SOCOFRA... Societe Commerciale Francaise (MAR)
SOCOFRACIM ... Societe Commerciale Franco-Africaine des Ciments (MAR)
SOCOFRALE ... Societe de Courtage de la France Australe (MAR)
SOCOFRAN ... Societe du Congo Francais (MAR)
SOCOFROID ... Societe Congolaise de Conservation et de Congelation (MAR)
SOCOGABON ... Societe Commerciale et Hoteliere du Gabon (MAR)
SOCOGECI ... Societe de Constructions du Genie Civil (MAR)
SOCOGEDA ... Societe de Construction Generale de Danane (MAR)
SOCOGEL... Societe de Commerce General (MAR)
SOCOGIF.... Societe de Constructions Giraudel Freres (MAR)
SOCOGIM... Societe de Construction et de Gestion Immobiliere de Mauritanie (MAR)
SOCOGRASAS ... Sociedad Colombiana de Grasas Vegetales Ltda. [*Barranquilla*] (COL)
SOCOGUI.... Sociedad Colonial de Guinea (MAR)
SOCOIMA... Societe Commerciale et Industrielle du Mali (MAR)
SOCOIMPORT ... Societe Commerciale d'Importation du Sine Saloum (MAR)
SOCOINAF ... Societe des Commercants Industriels et Agriculteurs Africains (MAR)
SOCOINCO ... Ingenieros Constructores Contratistas [*Bogota*] (COL)
SOCOLA..... Societe Commerciale de Lamina (MAR)
SOCOLAG ... Societe Commerciale du Laghem (MAR)
SOCOLDA... Sociedad Colombiana de Administradores de Empresas [*Colombian Managers Society*] (LA)
SOCOLETRA ... Societe Coloniale d'Etudes et de Travaux (MAR)
SOCOLEX... Societe Coloniale d'Expansion Economique (MAR)
SOCOM....... Societe Commerciale du Mungo (MAR)
SOCOMA.... Societe Commerciale de Keur-Madiabel (MAR)
SOCOMA.... Societe Commerciale Marocaine (MAR)
SOCOMA.... Societe Commerciale de la Mauritanie (MAR)
SOCOMA.... Societe Commerciale du Mayumba (MAR)
SOCOMA.... Societe des Conserves du Mali (MAR)
SOCOMAB ... Societe Congolaise de Manutention des Bois [*Congolese Company for the Administration of Forests*] (AF)
SOCOMAB ... Societe Congolaise de Manutention des Bois au Port Pointe-Noire (MAR)
SOCOMAF ... Societe Commerciale Africaine (MAR)
SOCOMAF ... Societe Commerciale du Mali - M. Fourzoli & Cie. (MAR)
SOCOMAGAZ ... Societe Commerciale et Agricole d'Azaguie (MAR)
SOCOMAL ... Societe Commerciale d'Alimentation (MAR)
SOCOMAN ... Societe Commerciale et Miniere pour l'Afrique du Nord [*Moroccan*] (MAR)
SOCOMAR ... Societe Commerciale et Maritime (MAR)
SOCOMASS ... Societe de Construction, Montage, et Appareillage de Station Services (MAR)
SOCOMATHA ... Societe Commerciale Mauritanienne Thaofique (MAR)
SOCOMAUM ... Societe Commerciale Mauritanienne Mohamed Moloud et Cie. (MAR)
SOCOME.... Societe de Constructions Metalliques, Chad (MAR)
SOCOMEC ... Societe Cooperative Mecanographique (MAR)
SOCOMELA ... Societe de Constructions Metalliques (MAR)
SOCOMELEC-Ivoire ... Societe Commerciale de Materiel Electrique [*Ivorian*] (MAR)
SOCOMENA ... Societe du Complexe Industriel et Maritime de Menzel Bourguiba [*Moroccan*] (MAR)
SOCOMENA ... Societe Tunisienne Commerciale, Mecanique, et Maritime [*Tunisian Commercial, Mechanical, and Maritime Company*] (AF)
SOCOMETAL ... Sociedad de Construcciones Metalicas, SA [*Metal Construction Company, Inc.*] [*Chilean*] (LA)
SOCOMETAL ... Societe de Constructions Metalliques (MAR)
SOCOMETRA ... Societe Commerciale d'Etudes et de Travaux (MAR)
SOCOMI...... Societe Commerciale de Materiel Industriel (MAR)
SOCOMIA ... Societe Commerciale pour l'Equipement Industriel et Agricole, Madagascar (MAR)
SOCOMO.... Societe Commerciale Moderne (MAR)
SOCOMO.... Societe Commerciale de Morondava (MAR)
SOCOMO.... Societe Commerciale de l'Oubangui (MAR)
SOCOMOL ... Sociedade Comercial de Mocambique Lda. (MAR)
SOCOMOR ... Societe Commerciale Moramangaise [*Malagasy*] (MAR)
SOCONA..... Societe de Constructions Navales (MAR)
SOCONAF.... Societe Commerciale Nord-Africaine [*Moroccan*] (MAR)
SOCONDOF ... Societe Commerciale de N'Doffane [*Senegalese*] (MAR)
SOCONOCA ... Societe de Constructions du Nord Cameroun (MAR)
SOCONOMAR ... Societe Commerciale d'Affretements Maritimes (MAR)
SOCONORD ... Societe Commerciale du Nord (MAR)
SOCONOVILLE ... Societe Commerciale Nouvelle de Treichville (MAR)
SOCONTI.... Sociedad Colombiana de Contadores Publicos Titulados [*Bogota*] (COL)
SOCONY..... Societe Commerciale du Nyong (MAR)
SOCOODER ... Societe Cooperative de Developpement Rural (MAR)
SOCOODJALO ... Societe Commerciale Ondona du Dja et Lobo (MAR)
SOCOOPED ... Societes Cooperatives d'Epargne et de Developpement (MAR)
SOCOPAF... Societe Commerciale de Produits Africains (MAR)
SOCOPAL... Societe des Conserves des Poissons a l'Huile [*Tunisian*] (MAR)

SOCOPAN ... Sociedad Constructora de Pavimentos America [*Bogota*] (COL)
SOCOPAP ... Societe Commerciale de Papeterie [*Commercial Paper Company*] [*French*] (WER)
SOCOPASS ... Societe Commerciale de Passy [*Senegalese*] (MAR)
SOCOPECRO ... Societe Commerciale de Peche au Crocodile (MAR)
SOCOPEIN ... Societe Commerciale de Peintures (MAR)
SOCOPEINT ... Societe Congolaise de Peinture (MAR)
SOCOPETROL ... Societe Congolaise d'Entreposage de Produits Petroliers (MAR)
SOCOPIM ... Societe Commerciale pour l'Industrie au Maroc (MAR)
SOCOPRE ... Societe Senegalaise de Commercialisation des Produits de l'Elevage (MAR)
SOCOPRISE ... Societe Africaine d'Entreprises Industrielles et Immobilieres (MAR)
SOCOPRO ... Societe de Commerce et de Produits (MAR)
SOCOPSA ... Societe Cooperative des Planteurs de Saa (MAR)
SOCORA ..... Sociedad de Comercializacion de la Reforma Agraria [*Agrarian Reform Marketing Association*] [*Chilean*] (LA)
SOCORAM ... Societe de Constructions Radio-Electriques du Mali (MAR)
SOCORAP ... Societe de Cocos Rapes (MAR)
SOCOREP ... Societe Congolaise de Recherche de Petrole (MAR)
SOCORINA ... Societe de Constructions et de Reparations Industrielles et Navales (MAR)
SOCORP ..... Sociedad Colombiana de Ralaciones Publicas [*Barranquilla*] (COL)
SOCORWA ... Societe de Confection du Rwanda (MAR)
SOCOSA ..... Societe du Commerce Sarakole (MAR)
SOCOSAC ... Societe Commerciale et Industrielle du Sac [*Senegalese*] (MAR)
SOCOSAL ... Societe Commerciale du Saloum [*Senegalese*] (MAR)
SOCOSE ..... Societe de Constructions Senegalaises (MAR)
SOCOTA ..... Societe Commerciale de Tananarive (MAR)
SOCOTA ..... Societe Commerciale de Transactions (MAR)
SOCOTCHAD ... Societe Commerciale du Tchad (MAR)
SOCOTEC ... Societe de Controle Technique et d'Expertise de la Construction (MAR)
SOCOTEIN ... Sociedad Colombiana de Tecnicos Industriales [*Bogota*] (COL)
SOCOTEX ... Societe de Commercialisation des Textiles [*Tunisian*] (MAR)
SOCOTIC .... Societe Commerciale de Transports et d'Importation au Cameroun (MAR)
SOCOTO ..... Societe Commerciale du Togo (MAR)
SOCOTOB ... Societe Commerciale Tournebize (MAR)
SOCOTOU ... Societe Commerciale de Toumodi (MAR)
SOCOTRAM ... Sociedade de Comercializacao e Transformacao de Madeira [*Lumber Processing and Marketing Company*] (AF)
SOCOTRAN ... Societe de Compatibilite Transit Gestion Divers [*Senegalese*] (MAR)
SOCOTRAV ... Societe Cooperative des Transporteurs Voltaiques (MAR)
SOCOVACK ... Societe Commerciale de Vack Ngouna [*Senegalese*] (MAR)
SOCOVI ...... Societe Commerciale Vivriere du Mungo (MAR)
SOCOVIAS ... Sociedad Constructora de Vias [*Bogota*] (COL)
SOCOWAG ... Societe Commerciale Wague Freres & Cie. (MAR)
SOCPA .... Societe Congolaise de Produits Alimentaires (MAR)
SOCRAA ..... Societe de Commerce et de Representation Automobile et Assurances (MAR)
SOCRARROZ ... Sociedad de Cultivos y Recoleccion de Arroz Ltda. [*Neiva*] (COL)
SOCRATAL ... Societe Camerounaise pour la Transformation de l'Aluminium (MAR)
SOCREC ..... Societe de Constructions, Representations, et Etudes du Cambodge [*Cambodian Construction, Sales, and Studies Company*] (CL)
SOCTROPIC ... Societe Khmere des Cultures Tropicales [*Cambodian Tropical Crop Company*] (CL)
SOCUMA .... Societe des Mines de Cuivre de Mauritanie (MAR)
SOCUTCHAD ... Societe Sucriere du Tchad (MAR)
SOD .... Skholi Opliton Diavivaseon [*Enlisted Men's Signal Corps School*] [*Greek*] (GC)
SOD .... Studencki Osrodek Dyskusyjny [*Students' Discussion Center*] (POL)
SOD .... Studiekring voor Documentatie en Administratieve Organisatie der Overheid [*'s-Gravenhage*]
SOD .... Synchronous Single-Phase Motor (RU)
SODACA ..... Societe Dahomeenne de Credit Automobile (MAR)
SODACA-LITIME ... Societe de Developpement et d'Approvisionnement du Canton d'Akposso-Litime (MAR)
SODACAP ... Societe de Distribution d'Articles en Caoutchouc et Plastiques (MAR)
SODACI ...... Societe Dahomeenne Cinematographique (MAR)
SODACO ..... Societe Dahomeenne de Comptabilite (MAR)
SODACOM ... Societe Dahomeenne de Commerce (MAR)
SODACOM ... Societe Dakaroise de Constructions Metalliques (MAR)
SODACOT ... Societe Dahomeenne de Consignation et de Transit (MAR)
SODACRUS ... Societe Dahomeenne de Crustaces (MAR)
SODAF .... Societe Dahomeenne d'Ananas et Fruits (MAR)
SODAF .... Somali Democratic Action Front (AF)
SODAFE ...... Societe pour le Developpement de l'Afrique Equatoriale (MAR)
SODAGA ..... Societe Dakaroise des Boissons Gazeuses (MAR)
SODAGA ..... Societe Generale d'Approvisionnement du Dahomey (MAR)
SODAGRI .... Societe de Developpement Agricole et Industriel du Senegal (MAR)
SODAI .... Societe Dahomeenne pour le Developpement Industriel et Commercial (MAR)
SODAIC ...... Societe Dahomeenne pour le Developpement de l'Industrie et du Commerce (MAR)
SODAICA .... Societe de Developpement Agricole et Industriel de la Casamanca (MAR)
SODAK .... Societe Dahomeenne Agricole et Industrielle du Kenaf (MAR)
SODAK .... Societe Dakaroise de Negoce (MAR)
SODAL .... Societe de Diffusion d'Articles de Luxe (MAR)
SODAMETRO ... Societe Dahomeenne de Messageries et de Transports Routiers (MAR)
SODAMI ...... Societe Dahomeenne de Minoterie (MAR)
SODAP .... Synergatikos Organismos Diatheseos Ambelourgikon Proiondon [*Vine Products Cooperative Marketing Union Ltd.*] (GC)
SODAPEC ... Societe Dahomeenne de Peintures et Colorants (MAR)
SODA-PECHE ... Societe Dahomeenne de Peche (MAR)
SODA-PECHE ... Societe Dakaroise de Peche (MAR)
SODA-PLASTICA ... Societe Dahomeenne de Plastique (MAR)
SODAS .... Sodyum Sanayii Anonim Sirketi [*Sodium Industry Corporation*] [*Ankara*] (TU)
SODASEL ... Societe Dahomeenne de Sel (MAR)
SODATEX ... Societe Dahomeenne de Textiles (MAR)
SODATOURISME ... Societe d'Equipement et d'Exploitation Hoteliere et Touristique du Dahomey (MAR)
SODATRA ... Societe Dakaroise de Transit (MAR)
SODB .... Sdruzeni pro Odbyt Dehtovych Barviv [*Association for Marketing of Aniline Dyes*] (CZ)
SODEA .... Societe de Developpement Agricole [*Agricultural Development Company*] [*Moroccan*] (AF)
SODE(A) ..... Synergatikos Organismos Diatheseos Esperidoeidon (Ammokhostos) [*Famagusta Citrus Fruit Cooperative Marketing Union*] (GC)
SODEAM ..... Societe pour le Developpement de l'Electricite en Afrique et a Madagascar (MAR)
SODEBATEL ... Societe de Developpement pour le Batiment et l'Electricite (MAR)
SODEBLE ... Societe de Developpement pour la Culture et la Transformations du Ble [*Cameroonian*] (MAR)
SODEC .... Societe de Decorticage [*Senegalese*] (MAR)
SODECA ..... Societe pour le Developpement de l'Elevage et des Cultures de l'Alaotra [*Malagasy*] (MAR)
SODECAO ... Societe de Developpement du Cacao (MAR)
SODECI .... Societe de Distribution d'Eau de la Cote-d'Ivoire (MAR)
SODECO ..... Societe Dakaroise d'Entreprises et de Constructions (MAR)
SODECO ..... Societe pour le Developpement du Commerce (MAR)
SODECOTON ... Societe de Developpement du Coton [*Cameroonian*] (MAR)
SODEFEL .... Societe pour le Developpement de la Production des Fruits et Legumes [*Company for the Development of Fruit and Vegetable Production*] [*Ivorian*] (AF)
SODEFITEX ... Societe de Developpement des Fibres Textiles (MAR)
SODEFOR ... Societe pour le Developpement des Plantations Forestieres [*Forest Cultivation Development Company*] [*Ivorian*] (AF)
SODEFRAMA ... Societe des Echanges Franco-Marocaines (MAR)
SODEGBESS ... Societe de Developpement et de Gestion des Sites de Sali (MAR)
SODEGIC .... Societe d'Entreprises Generales Industrielles et Commerciales (MAR)
SODEINCO ... Societe de Developpement Industriel et Commercial (MAR)
SODELAC ... Societe de Developpement du Lac Chad (MAR)
SODELAC ... Societe d'Exploitation du Lac Tchad (MAR)
SODELEC ... Societe d'Electrification et de Canalisation (MAR)
SODE(M) .... Synergatikos Organismos Diatheseos Esperidoeidon (Morfou) [*Morfou Citrus Fruit Cooperative Marketing Union*] (GC)
SODEMA ..... Societe d'Etudes pour le Developpement de l'Industrie Mechanique en Algerie (MAR)
SODEMHE ... Societe de Mise Hors d'Eau (MAR)
SODEMI ...... Societe pour le Developpement Minier de la Cote-d'Ivoire [*Ivory Coast Mining Development Company*] (AF)
SODEMO .... Societe pour le Developpement de la Region de Morondava [*Company for the Development of Morondava Region*] [*Malagasy*] (AF)
SODENI .... Societe d'Embouteillage du Niger (MAR)
SODENIA .... Societe de Developpement des Niayes (Thies) [*Senegal*] (MAR)
SODENICOB ... Societe de Developpement Regional de la Vallee du Niari et de Jacob (MAR)
SODENKAM ... Societe de Developpement du Nkam [*Nkam Development Company*] [*Cameroonian*] (AF)
SODEP .... Societe d'Extrusion des Plastiques (MAR)
SODEPA ..... Committee on Society, Development, and Peace, Kenya (MAR)
SODEPA ..... Societe de Developpement et d'Exploitation des Produits Animaux [*Cameroonian*] (MAR)
SODEPALM ... Societe pour le Developpement et l'Exploitation du Palmier a Huile [*Company for the Development and Exploitation of Oil Palm*] [*Ivorian*] (AF)
SODEPAX ... Exploratory Committee on Society, Development, and Peace of the Roman Catholic Church and the World Council of Churches (MAR)

SODEPRA ... Societe pour le Developpement des Productions Animales [*Company for the Development of Animal Production*] [*Ivorian*] (AF)
SODERA ..... Societe de Developpement des Ressources Animales (MAR)
SODERDA ... Societe de Developpement de la Republique du Dahomey (MAR)
SODERIM .... Societe de Developpement de la Riziculture dans la Plaine des Mbo [*Cameroonian*] (MAR)
SODERIZ ..... Societe pour le Developpement de la Riziculture (MAR)
SODERMAN ... Sociedad de Desarrollo Regional de La Mancha [*Company for Regional Development of La Mancha*] [*Spanish*] (WER)
soderzh .... Content, Contents (RU)
SODESUCRE ... Societe pour le Developpement des Plantations de Canne a Sucre, l'Industrialisation et Commercialisation du Sucre [*Company for the Development of Sugar Cane Plantations, and the Industrialization and Marketing of Sugar*] [*Ivorian*] (AF)
SODETCHAD ... Societe de Developpement du Tchad (MAR)
SODETEG ... Societe d'Etudes Techniques et d'Entreprises Generales [*Technical Studies and General Enterprises Company*] [*French*] (WER)
SODETEGAO ... Societe d'Etudes Techniques d'Entreprises Generales Afrique de l'Ouest (MAR)
SODETEL .... Sociedad de Tejidos Limitada [*Medellin*] (COL)
SODETI .... Sociedad de Desarrollo de Tecnico Industrial [*Spanish*]
SODETO ..... Societe des Detergents du Togo (MAR)
SODETODAK ... Societe d'Etudes du Thon Dakarois (MAR)
SODETRAF ... Societe pour le Developpement des Transports Aeriens en Afrique (MAR)
SODETRAM ... Societe d'Etudes pour Realisations en Outre-Mer (MAR)
SODEVA ..... Societe de Developpement et de Vulgarisation Agricole (MAR)
SODEVEA ... Societe pour le Developpement et l'Exploitation de l'Hevea (MAR)
SODEXA ..... Societe d'Exploitation Agricole (MAR)
SODEXAFRIC ... Societe d'Exploitation de Magasins en Centrafrique (MAR)
SODEXHO ... Societe d'Exploitations Hotelieres, Maritimes, Aeriennes, et Terrestres (MAR)
SODEZONN ... Societe de Developpement de la Zone Njock-Nkoue (MAR)
SODF .... Synergatikos Organismos Diatheseos Ftharton [*Cooperative Organization for the Marketing of Perishables*] [*Cypriot*] (GC)
SODIACAM ... Societe de Distribution Alimentaire de Cameroun (MAR)
SODIACE .... Societe pour le Developpement de l'Industrie et l'Agriculture de la Cote Est (MAR)
SODIAL .... Societe de Diffusion d'Articles de Luxe (MAR)
SODIAM ...... Societe Diamantifere Centrafricaine de Diamants (MAR)
SODIAMA ... Societe de Diffusion Automobile de Madagascar (MAR)
SODIAMCI ... Societe Diamantifere de la Cote-d'Ivoire (MAR)
SODIAN ...... Sociedad para el Desarrollo Industrial de Andalucia [*Company for the Industrial Development of Andalusia*] [*Spanish*] (WER)
SODIAR .... Sociedad Industrial de Armenia (COL)
SODIC .... Societe de Developpement Ivoirien de la Construction (MAR)
SODIC .... Societe de Distribution Industrielle et Commerciale [*Moroccan*] (MAR)
SODICAM ... Societe Generale de Distribution au Cameroun (MAR)
SODICAN .... Sociedad para el Desarrollo Industrial Canario [*Company for Industrial Development of the Canary Islands*] [*Spanish*] (WER)
SODICONGO ... Societe Diamantaire du Congo (MAR)
SODIEX .... Sociedad para el Desarrollo Industrial de Extremadura [*Company for Industrial Development of Extremadura*] [*Spanish*] (WER)
SODIMA ...... Societe de Distribution de Materiel Automobile et Technique (MAR)
SODIMAF .... Societe de Distribution des Grandes Marques pour l'Africa (MAR)
SODIMICO ... Societe de Developpement Industriel et Miniere du Congo (MAR)
SODIMIZA ... Societe de Developpement Industriel et Miniere du Zaire [*Industrial Development and Mining Company of Zaire*] (AF)
SODIMPEX ... Societe Commercial d'Import-Export (MAR)
SODIM-TP ... Societe de Distribution de Materiel de Travaux Publics (MAR)
SODIPA .... Societe de Diffusion et Importation de Produits Alimentaires [*Senegalese*] (MAR)
SODIPHAC ... Societe de Diffusion Pharmaceutique en Afrique Centrale (MAR)
SODIREP ..... Societe de Diffusion et de Representation (MAR)
SODIS .... Societe de Diffusion Industrielle et Scientifique (MAR)
SODISHUIL ... Societe de Distribution de l'Huile (MAR)
SODISSER ... Societe de Distribution et de Services (MAR)
SODISTAR ... Societe de Diffusion des Produits de la Star (MAR)
SODITAS .... Solvent Distributorlugu Anonim Sirketi [*Solvent Distributorship Corporation*] (TU)
SODITEX ..... Sociedad Distribuidora de Textiles [*Bogota*] (COL)
SODIZI .... Societe du Domaine Industriel de Ziguinchor (MAR)
SODMC .... Sdruzeni Organizaci Deti a Mladeze CSR [*Association of Organizations of Children and Youth of the Czech Socialist Republic*] (CZ)
SODOJEL .... Societe du Domaine des Ouled Jellal (MAR)
SodP .... Sodobna Pedagogika [*Contemporary Pedagogy*] [*Ljubljana*] [*A periodical*] (YU)
SODRANOR ... Societe de Dragage du Nord (MAR)
SODRE .... Servicio Oficial de Difusion Radioelectrica [*Official Radio Broadcasting Service*] [*Uruguayan*] (LA)
SODSC .... Secretariado de Orientacion de la Democracia Social Cataluna [*Orientation Secretariat for the Social Democracy of Catalonia*] [*Spanish*] (WER)
SODUCAF ... Societe d'Usinage de Cafe du Cameroun (MAR)
SODUCO ..... Societe Durand et Compagnie (MAR)
SODY .... Stegastikos Organismos Dimosion Ypallilon [*Civil Servants' Housing Organization*] [*Greek*] (GC)
SOE .... Erythrocyte Sedimentation Rate (RU)
soe .... Socially Dangerous Element (RU)
SOEI .... Syndicat des Ouvriers et Employes des Industries (MAR)
SOEKOR ..... State-Owned Oil Exploration Company (MAR)
SOEKOR ..... Suidelike Olie-Eksplorasie-Korporasie [*Southern Oil Exploration Company*] [*South African*] (AF)
SOELACI ..... Societe Agriculture de Cote-d'Ivoire (MAR)
SOEME .... Sindicato de Obreros y Empleados del Ministerio de Educacion [*Union of Workers and Employees of the Ministry of Education*] [*Argentine*] (LA)
SOEMO .... Services d'Observation et d'Education en Milieu Ouvert [*Algerian*] (MAR)
SOEMPEDRO ... Sociedad Empacadora de Drogas [*Cali*] (COL)
SOERNI .... Societe d'Etudes et de Representations Navales Industrielles RCA (MAR)
SOEXAL ...... Societe d'Exploitation des Anciens Ets. Luiz (MAR)
SOEXCO ..... Sociedad Exportadora de Confecciones Ltda. [*Cali*] (COL)
sof .... Sofia (BU)
sof .... Sofort [*or Sofortigen*] [*Immediate*] [*German*]
SOF .... Soldier of Fortune (MAR)
SOF .... Svetova Odborova Federace [*World Federation of Trade Unions*] (CZ)
SOFAC .... Societe de Financement d'Achats a Credit (MAR)
SOFACAM ... Societe Familiale Africaine du Cameroun (MAR)
SOFACAMA ... Societe de Fabrication de Canalisations de Madagascar (MAR)
SOFACO ..... Societe Africaine de Fabrication, de Formulation, et de Conditionnement (MAR)
SOFALCA ... Societe de Fabrication d'Alcaloides (MAR)
SOFAM .... Societe Franco-Africaine de Metallurgie (MAR)
SOFAMAR .. Sociedade de Fainas de Mar e Rio, SARC [*Sea and River Labor Society, Inc.*] [*Portuguese*] (WER)
SOFAMI ...... Societe de Fabrication Metallique Ivoirienne (MAR)
SOFAN .... Societe et Fournisseurs d'Afrique Noire et de Madagascar (MAR)
SOFAR .... Sociedade de Farinhos [*Flour Company*] [*Angolan*] (AF)
SOFARIN ..... Sociedad Farmaceutica Internacional [*Bogota*] (COL)
SOFASA ...... Sociedad de Fabricantes de Automotores [*Envigado-Antioquia*] (COL)
SOFBA .... Societe Francaise des Bois Africains (MAR)
Sofbas .... Sofia Basin (BU)
SOFCAR ..... Societe de Fabrication de Carbones (MAR)
SOFEM .... Societe Forestiere et d'Elevage de Mouyondzi Soffer & Cie. (MAR)
SOFEMOL ... Sociedade de Ferragens e Motores Lda. (MAR)
Sofenergo ... Sofia Electric Power Administration (BU)
SOFFIN .... Societe Financiere France-Ingelheim (MAR)
SOFFO .... Societe Financiere pour la France et les Pays d'Outre-Mer (MAR)
SOFGM .... Societe Algerienne de Fabrication Electro-Mecanique (MAR)
SOFI .... Systeme d'Ordinateurs pour le Fret International (MAR)
SOFIBEL ..... Societe Forestiere et Industrielle de Belabo (MAR)
SOFIBOI ...... Societe Forestiere et Industrielle des Bois Ivoiriens (MAR)
SOFIBOIS ... Societe Financiere des Bois Tropicaux (MAR)
SOFICA .... Societe Forestiere Industrielle et Commerciale [*Cameroonian*] (MAR)
SOFICA .... Societe de Fournitures pour l'Industrie et les Constructions Africaines [*Senegalese*] (MAR)
SOFICAL ..... Societe de Financement Industriel Commercial et Agricole (MAR)
SOFICO .... Societe des Fibres Coloniales (Matsende) (MAR)
SOFICO .... Societe Industrielle de Fournitures et de Chaussures "L'Ours" [*Tunisian*] (MAR)
SOFICOMAF ... Societe Financiere et Commerciale Africaine (MAR)
SOFICRIN ... Societe Francaise des Crins Vegetaux [*Moroccan*] (MAR)
SOFIDAK .... Societe de la Foire Internationale de Dakar (MAR)
SOFIDE .... Societe Financiere de Developpement [*Finance Company for Development*] [*Zairian*] (AF)
SOFIDEG .... Societe Financiere de Developpement Economique en Guyane [*Financial Society for the Economic Development of French Guiana*] (LA1)
SOFIFA .... Societe Financiere et Immobiliere Franco-Africaine (MAR)
SOFIKE .... Societe Forestiere et Industrielle de la Nkebe (MAR)
SOFIMEC .... Societe de Fibres et Mecanique (MAR)
SOFIMEC .... Societe Francaise pour l'Industrie Miniere au Cameroun [*French Mining Industry Company in Cameroon*] (AF)
SOFIMO ...... Societe Financiere pour le Moyen-Orient (MAR)
SOFIOM ...... Societe Francaise des Ingenieurs d'Outre-Mer (MAR)
SOFIPA .... Societe Financiere Internationale de Participation (MAR)

SOFIRAN..... Societe Francaise des Petroles d'Iran [*French Petroleum Company of Iran*] (ME)
SOFIREP..... Societe Franco-Ivorienne de Representation (MAR)
SOFISEDIT ... Societe Financiere Senegalaise pour le Developpement de l'Industrie et du Tourisme [*Senegalese Financial Company for the Development of Industry and Tourism*] (AF)
SOFITEX..... Societe des Fibres Textiles [*Textile Fiber Company*] [*Beninese*] (AF)
SOFITIS ...... Societe de Filature et Tissage (MAR)
SOFITRANS ... Societe Financiere pour le Developpement des Transports et du Tourisme (MAR)
SOFOCI....... Societe Forestiere de la Cote-d'Ivoire (MAR)
SOFODECI ... Societe Forestiere de la Cote-d'Ivoire (MAR)
SOFOFA...... Sociedad de Fomento Fabril [*Industrial Development Association*] [*Chilean*] (LA)
SOFOHI....... Societe pour le Forestiere du Hein (MAR)
SOFONAL ... Societe de Fonderie des Alliages Legers (MAR)
SOFOPLAST ... Societe de Fabrication d'Objets en Plastique (MAR)
SOFOR........ Societe Forestiere (MAR)
SOFOR-IS ... Turkiye Soforler ve Otomobilciler Federasyonu [*Turkish Chauffeurs and Automobile Drivers Federation*] (TU)
SOFORMA ... Societe Forestiere du Mayumbe (MAR)
SOFOTE...... Societe Forestiere de la Tene (MAR)
SOFRACIMA ... Societe Franco-Africaine de Cinema (MAR)
SOFRACO... Societe Francaise de Constructions (MAR)
SOFRACOL ... Sociedad Franco Colombiana de Especialidades Farmaceuticas Ltda. [*Bogota*] (COL)
SOFRADI..... Societe Francaise de Distribution [*Senegalese*] (MAR)
SOFRAFIMEX ... Societe Franco-Africaine d'Importation et d'Exportation (MAR)
SOFRAMER ... Societe Francaise d'Achats pour l'Outre-Mer (MAR)
SOFRATEP ... Societe Franco-Tunisienne d'Exploitation Petroliere (MAR)
SOFRATI..... Societe Franco-Africaine de Tissus (MAR)
SOFRATOP ... Societe Francaise de Travaux Topographiques et Photogrammetriques [*French Topographic and Photogrammetric Projects Company*] (AF)
SOFRA-TP ... Societe Francaise de Travaux Publics [*French Public Works Company*] (AF)
SOFRAVIN ... Societe Francaise des Vins (MAR)
SOFRECOM ... Societe Francaise d'Etudes des Telecommunications [*French Telecommunications Studies Company*] (CL)
SOFRED...... Societe Francaise d'Etudes et de Developpement [*French Research and Development Company*] (AF)
SOFREDOC ... Societe Francaise d'Etudes et d'Editions Documentaires (MAR)
SOFREGAZ ... Societe Francaise d'Etudes et de Realisations d'Equipements Gaziers (MAR)
SOFREL ...... Societe des Fruits et Legumes (MAR)
SOFRELEC ... Societe Francaise d'Etudes et de Realisations d'Equipements Electriques (MAR)
SOFREMINES ... Societe Francaise d'Etudes Minieres (MAR)
SOFREPAL ... Societe Francaise de Recherches et d'Exploitation des Petroles en Algerie (MAR)
SOFRERAIL ... Societe Francaise d'Etudes et de Realisations Ferroviaires [*French Railroad Design and Construction Company*] (AF)
SOFRES...... Societe Francaise d'Enquetes par Sondage [*French Opinion Polling Company*] (WER)
SOFRES...... Societe Francaise d'Etudes Statistiques
SOFRESID ... Societe Francaise d'Etude d'Installations Siderurgiques (MAR)
SOFRETES ... Societe Francaise d'Etudes Thermique et d'Energie Solaire (MAR)
SOFRETRANSPORTS-URBAINS ... Societe Francaise d'Etudes et des Realisations de Transports Urbains [*French*] (MAR)
SOFRETU.... Societe Francaise d'Etudes et des Realisations de Transports Urbains [*French*]
SOFRIGAL ... Societe des Frigorifiques du Senegal (MAR)
SOFRIMA.... Societe des Frigorifiques de Mauritanie (MAR)
SOFRINA..... Societe Francaise pour l'Industrie en Afrique [*French Company for Industry in Africa*] (AF)
SOFRINOR ... Societe des Entrepots Frigorifiques du Nord (MAR)
SOFRITAO ... Societa Franco-Italiana per l'Africa Occidentale [*Senegalese*] (MAR)
SOFRO........ Societe Francaise de Recherche Operationnelle
SOFRUIPRIM ... Societe Primeurs Frais Nouveaux Selectionnes (MAR)
Sofstroy...... Sofia Construction Administration (BU)
SOFUMAD ... Societe des Futs Metalliques de Madagascar (MAR)
Sof u-t......... Sofia University (BU)
SOFV........... Societe Okoume du Fernan-Vaz (MAR)
Sofzhilfond ... Sofia Housing Facilities (BU)
SOG .... Sindicato de Obreros Gallegos [*Trade Union of Galician Workers*] [*Spanish*] (WER)
SOG .... Sindicato de Obreros del Gas [*Gas Workers Union*] [*Uruguayan*] (LA)
SOG .... Societe Ouvriere Gabonaise (MAR)
sog .... Sogenannt [*So-Called*] [*German*] (GPO)
SOGA.......... Society of General Affairs, SA [*Cambodian*] (CL)
SOGABAIL ... Societe Gabonaise de Credit Bail (MAR)
SOGABOL... Societe Gabonaise des Oleagineux (MAR)
SOGACA..... Societe Gabonaise de Credit Automobile (MAR)
SOGACAM ... Societe Gabonaise de Cabotage Maritime et Fluvial (MAR)
SOGACAR ... Societe Gabonaise de Carrieres (MAR)
SOGACCO ... Societe Gabono-Coreenne de Commerce (MAR)
SOGACEL... Societe Gabonaise de Cellulose [*Gabonese Cellulose Company*] (AF)
SOGACHIM ... Societe Gabonaise de Chimie (MAR)
SOGACI ...... Societe Gabonaise Commerciale et Industrielle (MAR)
SOGACI ...... Societe de Gestion et d'Assurances de la Cote-d'Ivoire (MAR)
SOGACO..... Societe Gabonaise de Commerce (MAR)
SOGAD .... Societe Gabonaise d'Amenagements et de Decoration (MAR)
SOGADEHO ... Societe Gabonaise d'Exploitation Hoteliere (MAR)
SOGADI ...... Societe Gabonaise de Distribution (MAR)
SOGAFER... Societe Gabonaise Ferroviaire (MAR)
SOGAFERRO ... Societe Gabonaise des Ferro-Alliages (MAR)
SOGAFINEX ... Societe Gabonaise de Financement et d'Expansion [*Gabonese Company for Financing and Expansion*] (AF)
SOGAFRIC ... Societe Gabonaise Froid et Representations Industrielles et Commerciales (MAR)
SOGAID ...... Societe Gabonaise d'Agence Immobiliere et de Demenagement (MAR)
SOGAIMEX ... Societe Gabesienne d'Importation et d'Exportation [*North African*] (MAR)
SOGAKOR ... Societe des Boissons Gazeuses du Kasai Oriental (MAR)
SOGALIVRE ... Societe Gabonaise du Livre (MAR)
SOGALU ..... Societe Gabonaise de l'Aluminium (MAR)
SOGAMA .... Societe de Gestion d'Assurances de Madagascar (MAR)
SOGAMAR ... Societe Gabonaise de Marbre et de Materiaux (MAR)
SOGAME..... Societe Gabonaise de Materiel et d'Equipement (MAR)
SOGAMIRE ... Societe Gabonaise de Miroiterie et Ebenisterie (MAR)
SOGANI ...... Societe des Gaz Industriels du Niger (MAR)
SOGAPAR... Societe Gabonaise de Participation et de Developpement (MAR)
SOGAPECHE ... Societe Gabonaise de Peche [*Gabonese Fishing Company*] (AF)
SOGAPLAST ... Societe Gabonaise de Plastique (MAR)
SOGAPRAL ... Societe Gabonaise de Produits Alimentaires (MAR)
SOGAPRESSE ... Societe Gabonaise de Presse (MAR)
SOGAPROM ... Societe Gabonaise de Promotion (MAR)
SOGARA ..... Societe Gabonaise de Raffinage [*Gabonese Refining Company*] (AF)
SOGAREC... Societe Gabonaise de Rectification et de Mecanique Generale (MAR)
SOGAREM ... Societe Gabonaise de Recherche et d'Exploitation Minieres [*Gabonese Mine Prospecting and Exploitation Company*] (AF)
SOGARES... Societe Gabonaise de Realisation de Structures (MAR)
SOGARET... Societe Gabonaise de Revetements et Travaux (MAR)
SOGARI....... Societe Gabonaise de Realisations Industrielles (MAR)
SOGATOL... Societe Gabonaise de Toles et Produits Siderurgiques (MAR)
SOGATRA... Societe Gabonaise de Travaux (MAR)
SOGATRAM ... Societe Gabonaise de Transport Maritime (MAR)
SOGATRANSCO ... Societe Gabonaise de Transit et de Consignation (MAR)
SOGB .... Societe des Caoutchoucs de Grand-Bereby (MAR)
SOGCHIM ... Societe Generale Industrielle et Chimique de Jadotville (MAR)
SOGDJZ...... Saobracajno Odeljenje Generalne Direkcije Jugoslovenskih Zeljeznica [*Transportation Department, Yugoslav General Railroad Administration*] (YU)
SOGEA........ Societe Generale pour l'Agriculture (MAR)
SOGEBA ..... Societe Generale de Batiments (MAR)
SOGEBAC... Societe Generale de Banque en Cote-d'Ivoire [*General Bank Company of the Ivory Coast*] (AF)
SOGEBE ..... Societe Generale du Benin (MAR)
SOGEC .... Societe Gabonaise d'Electrification et de Canalisation (MAR)
SOGECA..... Societe Gabonaise d'Exploitation de Carrieres (MAR)
SOGECA..... Societe Generale pour le Commerce en Afrique (MAR)
SOGECA..... Societe Generale de Credit Automobile (MAR)
SOGECALTEX ... Societe de Gestion des Depots "Caltex" (MAR)
SOGECHIM ... Societe Generale Industrielle et Chimique du Katanga (MAR)
SOGECI ...... Societe Generale de Commerce et d'Importation [*Moroccan*] (MAR)
SOGECO..... Sociedad General de Comercio [*Bogota*] (COL)
SOGECO..... Societe Generale de Comptabilite (MAR)
SOGECO..... Societe Generale de Consignation et d'Entreprises Maritimes [*Mauritanian*] (MAR)
SOGECOA ... Societe Generale de Collecte et d'Approvisionnement (MAR)
SOGECOM ... Societe Generale de Compensation (MAR)
SOGECOM ... Societe de Gerance et de Commerce (MAR)
SOGECOR ... Societe Generale de Conseil et de Representation Internationale (MAR)
SOGEDEM ... Societe Gabonaise d'Etude et de Developpement Maritimes (MAR)
SOGEDESCA ... Societe de Gestion Descours et Cabaud (MAR)
SOGEDI....... Societe Generale d'Edition et d'Imprimerie (MAR)
SOGEDI....... Societe Guineenne des Ets. Duffour et Igon (MAR)
SOGEDIA.... Societe de Gestion et de Developpement des Industries Alimentaires [*Food Industries Management and Development Company*] [*Algerian*] (AF)
SOGEDIS.... Societe Generale de Distribution (MAR)
SOGEDIS.... Societe de Gestion et de Developpement des Industries de Sucre (MAR)
SOGEF........ Societe de Gestion d'Entrepots Frigorifiques en Cote-d'Ivoire (MAR)

SOGEFIHA ... Societe de Gestion Financiere de l'Habitat [*Company for the Financial Management of Housing*] [*Ivorian*] (AF)
SOGEFINANCE ... Societe Generale de Financement et de Participation en Cote-d'Ivoire (MAR)
SOGEFOR ... Societe Generale des Forces Hydroelectriques du Katanga (MAR)
SOGEI .... Societe Generale d'Exploitations Industrielles (MAR)
SOGEK .... Societe Generale Khmere de Commerce et de Representation [*Cambodian General Trade Agency*] (CL)
SOGEK .... Synergatikos Organismos Genikou Emboriou Kyprou [*General Trade Cooperative Organization of Cyprus*] (GC)
SOGEL .... Sociedade Geral de Empreitadas Lda. (MAR)
SOGEL .... Societe Gabonaise d'Elevage (MAR)
SOGELEC ... Societe Generale Africaine d'Electricite (MAR)
SOGELEM ... Societe Generale d'Electricite de Mauritanie (MAR)
SOGEMA ..... Societe Generale Maritime Congolaise (MAR)
SOGEMAR ... Societe Guineenne de Gerance Maritime (MAR)
sogen .... Sogenannt [*So-Called*] [*German*]
SOGENA ..... Societe Generale Africaine (MAR)
SOGEP .... Societe Generale d'Etudes et de Planification (MAR)
SOGEP .... Societe Generale de Produits Chimiques (MAR)
SOGEPAC ... Societe Generale de Materiaux de Construction (MAR)
SOGEPAL ... Societe de Gestion et de Participations d'Industries Alimentaires (MAR)
SOGEPAR ... Societe Generale d'Etudes et de Participations en Cote-d'Ivoire (MAR)
SOGEPO ..... Societe d'Exploitation de Garages et d'Entrepots [*Senegalese*] (MAR)
SOGERA ..... Societe de Gestion des Participants de la Regie Autonome de Petroles (MAR)
SOGER-AO ... Societe Generale de Representations Industrielles et de Travaux Publics (MAR)
SOGERAP ... Societe de Gestion des Participations de la Regie Autonome des Petroles [*Saharan*] (MAR)
SOGERCA ... Societe Generale d'Entreprise de Centrales Atomiques [*General Atomic Power Plants Contracting Company*] [*French*] (WER)
SOGERCO ... Societe de Gerance de Representation et de Courtage (MAR)
SOGEREM ... Societe Generale de Recherches et d'Exploitation Minieres [*Upper Voltan*] (MAR)
SOGERES ... Societe de Gestion de Restaurants et de Spectacles (MAR)
SOGESETRA ... Societe Generale Senegalaise de Batiments et Travaux Publics (MAR)
SOGESUCRE ... Compagnie Sucriere Congolaise (MAR)
SOGET .... Societe de Gestion d'Entreprise et de Transport (MAR)
SOGETA ..... Societe de Gestion des Terres Agricoles [*Agricultural Land Management Company*] [*Moroccan*] (AF)
SOGETEC ... Societe Generale de Topographie, Photogrammetrie, et d'Etudes de Genie Civil (MAR)
SOGETEG ... Societe d'Etudes Techniques et d'Entreprises Generales (MAR)
SOGETEL ... Societe Generale de Travaux et Constructions Electriques (MAR)
SOGETHA ... Societe Generale des Techniques Hydroagricoles [*General Hydroagricultural Techniques Company*] [*Niger*] (AF)
SOGETHEL ... Societe Generale d'Exploitation Touristique et Hoteliere du Laos [*General Hotel and Tourism Company of Laos*] (CL)
SOGETISS ... Societe Generale de Tissage [*Tunisian*] (MAR)
SOGETOCAM ... Societe de Gestion pour le Tourisme au Cameroun (MAR)
SOGETRA ... Societe Generale de Travaux Routiers (MAR)
SOGETRAF ... Societe Generale de Travaux et de Representations en Afrique (MAR)
SOGETRAM ... Societe Generale de Travaux Maritimes et Fluviaux (MAR)
SOGETRANS ... Societe de Gestion et de Transport (MAR)
SOGEX .... Societe de Gestion pour l'Exploitation du Parc a Bois du Port de Douala (MAR)
SOGEXI .... Societe Generale d'Exportation et Importation (MAR)
SOGFERRO ... Societe Gabonaise des Ferro-Alliages (MAR)
SOGIA .... Societe Generale des Industries Alimentaires (MAR)
SOGIC .... Societe Gabonaise d'Importation et de Commerce (MAR)
SOGIC .... Societe Generale de l'Industrie de Confection [*Tunisian*] (MAR)
SOGICO ...... Societe Generale des Industries Cotonnieres (MAR)
SOGICOT .... Societe Generale des Industries Cotonnieres en Tunisie (MAR)
SOGIEXI ...... Societe Generale d'Importation et d'Exportation de Cote-d'Ivoire (MAR)
SOGIL .... Societe Generale des Industries Lainieres [*Tunisian*] (MAR)
SOGIMEX .... Societe Generale d'Importation et d'Exportation [*Senegalese*] (MAR)
SOGIP .... Societe Generale pour l'Industrialisation de la Peche [*General Company for the Industrialization of Fishing*] [*Ivorian*] (AF)
SOGISMA ... Societe des Gaz Industriels de Madagascar (MAR)
SOGIT .... Societe Generale des Industries Textiles [*Tunisian*] (MAR)
SOGITEX ..... Societe Generale des Industries Textiles [*Tunisian*] (MAR)
SOGODAN ... Societe Goudrons et Derives de l'Afrique du Nord [*Moroccan*] (MAR)
SOGOV .... Societe des Gestions et d'Outillages Publics de la Province de Vientiane [*Land and Water Transportation Company*] [*Literally, Vientiane Province Public Management and Equipment Company; same as Borisat Khon Song Thang Nam Lae Thang Bok*] [*Laotian*] (CL)
SOGPI .... North Ossetian State Pedagogical Institute Imeni K. L. Khetagurov (RU)
SOGRA .... Sociedade Grafica Lda. (MAR)
SOGRAD ..... Splosno Gradbeno Podjetje [*General Construction Establishment*] (YU)
SOGREAH ... Societe Grenobloise d'Etudes et d'Applications Hydrauliques [*French*]
SOGS .... Sanitetski Odred Glavnog Staba [*Medical Detachment of the General Staff*] (YU)
SOGUET ..... Societe Guineenne d'Engineering et d'Equipement Technique (MAR)
SOGUIP .... Societe Guineenne des Petroles (MAR)
SOGUIREP ... Societe Guineenne de Rechapage de Pneus (MAR)
SOHA .... Societe Hoteliere de l'Atlantique (MAR)
SOHICO ...... Societe Hoteliere et Immobiliere de Cocody (MAR)
SOHIMA ...... Societe Hoteliere et Immobiliere de Madagascar (MAR)
SOHLI .... Societe Hoteliere du Littoral (MAR)
SOHMA .... Servicio de Oceanografia, Hidrografia, y Meteorologia de la Armada [*Naval Oceanographic, Hydrographic, and Weather Service*] [*Uruguayan*] (LA)
SOHORA ..... Societe des Hotels de la Riviera Africaine (MAR)
SOHOTCI .... Societe Hoteliere et Touristique de Cote-d'Ivoire (MAR)
SOI .... Standards Organization of Iran (MAR)
SOI .... Statni Obchodni Inspekce [*State Commerce Inspection*] (CZ)
SOIAP .... Secretaria de Organizacion e Inspeccion de la Presidencia de la Republica [*Bogota*] (COL)
SOICO .... Sociedad Impermeabilizadora Colombiana [*Cali*] (COL)
SOID .... State Organisation for Industrial Development [*Iraqi*] (MAR)
SOIDI .... Societe Ivoirienne de Distribution (MAR)
SOIM .... Northern Branch of the Institute of Permafrost Study Imeni V. A. Obruchev (of the Academy of Sciences, USSR) (RU)
SOIMA .... Sindicato de Obreros de la Industria de Madera y Anexos [*Union of Workers of the Lumber and Related Industries*] [*Uruguayan*] (LA)
SOIMPEX .... Sociedade Importadora de Pecas (MAR)
SOIP .... Societe Ivoirienne de Pecheries (MAR)
SOIS .... Sosyal Isler Dairesi Genel Mudurlugu [*Social Affairs Office Directorate General*] [*of Foreign Affairs Ministry*] (TU)
SOIVA .... Sindicato Obrero de la Industria del Vestido y Afines [*Union of Workers of the Garment and Related Industries*] [*Argentine*] (LA)
SOJ .... Savez Obucara Jugoslavije [*Yugoslav Shoemakers Union*] (YU)
SOJECOCAM ... Societe des Jeunes Commercants de l'Ouest du Cameroun (MAR)
SOJUFA ...... Societe des Jus de Fruits d'Antsirabe (MAR)
SOJUFRUIT ... Societe des Jus de Fruits de la Mitidja [*Algerian*] (MAR)
SOK .... Sluzba Ochrony Kolei [*Railroad Security Service*] (POL)
Sok .... Sokagi [*Street, Lane*] [*See also Sk*] (TU)
SOK .... Straz Ochrony Kolejowej [*Railroad Security Guard*] (POL)
SOK .... Synergatikos Organismos Kapnoparagogon [*Tobacco Growers Cooperative*] [*Cypriot*] (GC)
SOK .... System of Remainder Classes [*Computers*] (RU)
SOKAO .... Soviet-Korean Aviation Society (RU)
SOKAVET ... Societe Khmere des Agences de Voyages et de Tourisme, SA [*Cambodian Tourism and Travel Agency Company, Inc.*] (CL)
SOKCIA ...... Societe Khmere pour la Commerce, l'Industrie, et l'Agriculture, SA [*Cambodian Commerce, Industry, and Agriculture Company, Inc.*] (CL)
SOKCT .... Societe Khmere des Cultures Tropicales [*Cambodian Tropical Crop Company*] (CL)
SOKEC .... Societe Khmere d'Entreprises de Constructions [*Cambodian Construction Enterprises Company*] (CL)
SOKECHI .... Societe Khmere d'Usine d'Engrais Chimique [*Cambodian Chemical Fertilizer Manufacturing Company*] (CL)
SOKECIA .... Societe Khmere d'Entreprises Commerciales, Industrielles, et Agricoles [*Cambodian Commercial, Industrial, and Agricultural Enterprise Company*] (CL)
SOKEPH ...... Societe Khmere d'Exploitation Pharmaceutique [*Cambodian Pharmaceutical Company*] (CL)
SOKFEM ..... Societe Khmere de Fabrication d'Emballages Metalliques [*Cambodian Metal Container Manufacturing Company*] (CL)
SOKHA .... Societe Khmere des Auberges [*Cambodian Hotel Company*] [*Replaced SOKHAR*] (CL)
SOKHAR ..... Societe Khmere d'Auberges Royales [*Royal Cambodian Hotel Company*] [*Replaced by SOKHA*] (CL)
SOKILAIT .... Societe Khmere pour l'Industrie Laitiere [*Cambodian Dairy Industry Company*] (CL)
SOKIMET .... Societe Kaedienne d'Importation, d'Exportation, et de Transport (MAR)
SOKIMEX .... Societe Khmere Import et Export [*Cambodian Import and Export Company*] (CL)
SOKINAC .... Societe Khmere Industrielle d'Applications Chimiques [*Cambodian Industrial Chemical Company*] (CL)
SOKJUTE .... Societe Khmere de Jute [*Cambodian Jute Company*] (CL)
SOKK .... Sovetsk Obshchestvo Krasnovo Kresta i Krasnovo Polumesiatsa (MAR)
SOKK i KP .. Union of Red Cross and Red Crescent Societies of the USSR (RU)
SOKME .... Societe Khmere de Materiels Electriques [*Cambodian Electrical Equipment Company*] (CL)

SOKNII .... Smolensk Oblast Scientific Research Institute of Regional Studies (RU)
SOKOA .... Societe Khmere d'Oxygene et d'Acetylene [*Cambodian Oxygen and Acetylene Company*] (CL)
SOKOFA ..... Solidaritat-Komitee Freies Afrika (MAR)
SOKOTAN... Sokoto Tannery (MAR)
SOKPHOS... Societe Khmere de Phosphates [*Cambodian Phosphate Company*] (CL)
SOKPROMA ... Societe Khmere de Productions Metallurgiques et Artisanales [*Cambodian Metallurgical and Handicrafts Production Company*] (CL)
sokr .... Abbreviated, Abbreviation (RU)
SOKRENA... Societe Khmere de Representation et Navigation [*Cambodian Representation and Navigation Company*] (CL)
SOKRI .... Societe Khmere pour le Riz et l'Industrie [*Cambodian Rice and Industry Company*] (CL)
Sokr SZ....... Abridged Collection of Laws of the USSR and RSFSR [*A publication*] (RU)
SOKSA........ Sinop Orme ve Konfeksiyon ve Ticaret AS [*Sinop Knitted Goods and Ready-Made Clothing Corp.*] (TU)
SOKSI .... Swadiri Organisasi Karya Sosialis Indonesia [*Federation of Indonesian Socialist Workers Organizations*] (IN)
SOKTRANSCO ... Societe Khmere de Transports de Commerce et d'Equipements Industriels [*Cambodian Commercial and Industrial Equipment Transport Company*] (CL)
SOKU .... Saratov Oblast Communist University Imeni V. I. Lenin (RU)
sol .... Salt Mine, Salt Water, Salt-Water Lake [*Topography*] (RU)
Sol............... Saltern, Saltworks [*Topography*] (RU)
SOL .... Sindicato de Obreros Libres [*Trade Union of Free Workers*] [*Mexican*] (LA1)
SOL .... Societe l'Okoume de Libreville (MAR)
SOL .... Soma Orkoton Logiston [*Certified Accountants Corps*] [*Greek*] (GC)
SOL .... Sosialistinen Opiskelijain Liitto [*Socialist Students' League (Communist-SKDL)*] [*Finnish*] (WEN)
SOLADO ..... Societe de Laminage de Douala (MAR)
SOLANI....... Societe Laitiere du Niger (MAR)
SOLARCO... Societe Libano-Arabe pour le Commerce (MAR)
SOLEMA ..... Societe de Lavages et Montages Metalliques Africains [*Senegalese*] (MAR)
SOLEMOA ... Societe de Lavages et Montages Metalliques Africains [*Senegalese*] (MAR)
SOLIBRA..... Societe de Limonaderies et Brasseries d'Afrique (MAR)
SOLICAM.... Societe du Linge de Maison au Cameroun (MAR)
SOLICO....... Societe Limonadiere de la Cote du Benin (MAR)
SOLICO....... Societe de Littoral Congolais (MAR)
SOLIMA ...... Solitany Malagasy [*Malagasy Petroleum Company*] (AF)
SOLIMAC.... Societe Libano-Ivoirienne de Materiaux de Construction (MAR)
SOLINCI...... Societe de Lingerie de Cote-d'Ivoire (MAR)
SOLINGRAL ... Suelos Integral Ltda. [*Medellin*] (COL)
SOLISE .... Comptoir de Literie du Senegal (MAR)
sol ist .... Salt Spring [*Topography*] (RU)
Sollbest ...... Sollbestand [*Authorized Strength*] (EG)
Sol mag....... Salt Storehouse [*Topography*] (RU)
SOLOMA..... Societe de Location de Materiel d'Entreprises (MAR)
sol prom...... Salt Mines [*Topography*] (RU)
SOLT........... Societe des Oleagineux du Logone-Tchad (MAR)
SOLUCO ..... Societe Luzienne de Conserves (MAR)
SOLVECO... Industrial de Disolventes y Productos Quimicos Ltda. [*Bogota*] (COL)
SOM .... Construction-Finishing Machine (RU)
SOM .... Radio Mast Signal Light (RU)
SOM .... Somali [*Three-letter standard code*] (CNC)
Som............. Sommet [*Summit*] [*French*] (NAU)
SOM .... Spoldzielcy Osrodek Maszynowy [*Cooperative Machine Station*] (POL)
SOM .... Stichting Onderzoek Massacommunicatie [*Amsterdam*]
SOM .... Swiatowa Organizacja Meteorologiczna [*World Meteorological Organization*] [*Polish*]
SOM .... World Meteorological Organization (BU)
SOMA.......... Sociedad Medica Antioquena [*Medellin*] (COL)
SOMA.......... Societe Malienne d'Assurances (MAR)
SOMA.......... Societe Maritime de Madagascar (MAR)
SOMABIPAL ... Societe Malienne de Biscuiterie et Pates Alimentaires (MAR)
SOMABRI.... Societe Malgache de Briqueterie (MAR)
SOMAC....... Societe Malienne de la Casamance (MAR)
SOMACA .... Societe Marocaine de Construction Automobile (MAR)
SOMACAT-SA ... Societe Mauritanienne d'Affretement, de Consignation, de Transit, et d'Acconage (MAR)
SOMACI...... Societe Malienne de Commerce et d'Industrie (MAR)
SOMACI...... Societe Marseillaise de la Cote-d'Ivoire (MAR)
SOMACIB ... Societe Marocaine pour le Commerce et l'Artisanat de la Bijouterie [*North African*] (MAR)
SOMACO .... Societe des Ets. Massiera & Cie. (MAR)
SOMACO .... Societe Majungaise de Commerce (MAR)
SOMACOA ... Societe Malgache de Construction Automobile (MAR)
SOMACOB ... Societe Malienne de Commercialisation du Betail (MAR)
SOMACODIS ... Societe Malgache de Collecte et de Distribution [*Malagasy Collection and Distribution Company*] (AF)
SOMACOM ... Societe Malgache de Commerce (MAR)
SOMACOM ... Societe Manoise de Commerce (MAR)
SOMACOM ... Societe Maritime et Commerciale (MAR)
SOMACOM ... Societe Mauritanienne de Construction Metallique (MAR)
SOMACOTP ... Societe Mauritanienne de Construction et de Travaux Publics (MAR)
SOMACOTRET ... Societe Mauritanienne de Commerce, de Transport, de Representation et de Transit (MAR)
SOMACOU ... Societe Malgache de Couvertures (MAR)
SOMADEC ... Societe Malgache d'Electricite [*Malagasy Electric Power Company*] (AF)
SOMADEC ... Societe Mauritanienne de Developpement et de Commerce (MAR)
SOMADEL... Societe Marocaine d'Electricite (MAR)
SOMADEP ... Societe Mauritanienne de Diffusion d'Energie Portable (MAR)
SOMADET ... Societe Marocaine pour le Developpement Touristique (MAR)
SOMADEX ... Societe Malgache d'Exploitation des Mines et Carrieres (MAR)
SOMADIR.... Societe Marocaine de Distribution et de Rectification (MAR)
SOMAF .... Societe Malienne de l'Automobile et du Froid (MAR)
SOMAF .... Societe Marbriere Africaine (MAR)
SOMAF .... Societe Marocaine du Froid [*Moroccan*] (MAR)
SOMAFAM ... Societe Malienne de Fabrication d'Articles Metalliques (MAR)
SOMAFCO ... Societe Marocaine Fonciere et Commerciale (MAR)
SOMAFOME ... Societe Marocaine de Fonderie et de Mecanique (MAR)
SOMAG....... Societe Soudanaise de Grands Magasins (MAR)
SOMAGA .... Societe Marseillaise du Gabon (MAR)
SOMAGEC ... Societe Maghrebienne de Genie Civil [*Moroccan*] (MAR)
SOMAGEL ... Societe Malgache des Gelatine (MAR)
SOMAIR...... Societe des Mines de l'Air [*Air Region Mining Company*] [*Niger*] (AF)
SOMALAC ... Societe Malgache d'Amenagement du Lac Alaotra [*Lake Alaotra Development Company*] [*Malagasy*] (AF)
SOMALAVAL ... Societe Malgache des Laques Valentine (MAR)
SOMALCO ... Societe Malgache de Cosmetiques et de Parfumerie (MAR)
SOMALGAZ ... Societe Mixte Franco-Algerienne de Gaz (MAR)
SOMALIBO ... Societe Malienne de Boissons Gazeuses (MAR)
SOMALIVRE ... Societe Mauritanienne du Livre (MAR)
SOMALTEX ... Somali Textile Factory (MAR)
SOMAP .... Societe Marocaine de Prevoyance (MAR)
SOMAP .... Societe Mauritanienne d'Armement et de Peche (MAR)
SOMAPA..... Societe Malienne de Parfumerie (MAR)
SOMAPA..... Societe Mauritanienne de Produits Alimentaires (MAR)
SOMAPALM ... Societe Malagasy pour le Palmier a Huile [*Malagasy Oil Palm Company*] (AF)
SOMAPECHE ... Societe Malgache de Pecherie (MAR)
SOMAPEX... Societe d'Exportation et de Peche (MAR)
SOMAPIL .... Societe Malienne de Piles Electriques (MAR)
SOMAPRIM ... Societe Mauritanienne de Promotion Industrielle et Immobiliere (MAR)
SOMAR .... Societe Marocaine d'Importation et d'Exportation (MAR)
SOMARCO ... Societe Maritime et Commerciale du Senegal (MAR)
SOMARD..... Societe Marocaine d'Etude (MAR)
SOMAREDE ... Societe Marocaine de Recherches, d'Etudes, et de Developpement (MAR)
SOMARGA ... Societe Maritime Gabonaise (MAR)
SOMARPE... Societe Oubangai Marques Pereira (MAR)
SOMASA..... Societe Malienne de Sacherie (MAR)
SOMASAC ... Societe Malienne de Sacherie (MAR)
SOMASAK ... Societe Malgache d'Amenagement de la Sakay [*Malagasy Company for the Development of Sakay*] (MAR)
SOMASAKA ... Societe Malagasy d'Amenagement de la Sakay [*Malagasy Company for the Development of Sakay*] (AF)
SOMASET... Societe Mauritano-Senegalaise de Transit, de Manutention, et de Transport (MAR)
SOMASON ... Societe Malgache du Son (MAR)
SOMAT .... Societe Maritime Atlantique du Togo (MAR)
SOMAT .... Societe du Materiel Agricole du Tchad (MAR)
SOMATAM ... Societe Marocaine de Tannerie et Megisserie (MAR)
SOMATEC ... Societe Mauritanienne de Techniques, d'Etudes, et Applications Comptables (MAR)
SOMATEL... Societe Malgache de Telephonie et d'Application Electriques (MAR)
SOMATELSAT ... Societe Marocaine de Telecommunications par Satellites [*Moroccan Satellite Telecommunications Company*] (AF)
SOMATEM ... Societe de Fabrication Industrielle de Matelas et Emballages Plastiques (MAR)
SOMATEX... Societe Marocaine de Textiles (MAR)
SOMATIB.... Societe Marocaine de Tissage et de Bonneterie (MAR)
SOMATRA ... Societe Malienne de Transports (MAR)
SOMATRAC ... Societe Mauritanienne de Distribution de Materiel de Travaux Publics (MAR)
SOMAUPECO ... Societe Mauritanienne de Peche et de Conserves Audeux Chatelet (MAR)
SOMAURAL ... Societe Mauritanienne des Allumettes (MAR)
SOMB.......... Societe Mauritanienne Boussade & Cie. (MAR)
SOMBEPEC ... Societe Malienne du Betail, des Peaux, et de Cuir (MAR)
SOMBRISA ... Sombrereria Industrial Ltda. [*Medellin*] (COL)
SOMDIAA ... Societe Multinationale de Developpement pour les Industries Alimentaires et Agricoles (MAR)
SOMEA .... Societe Nationale de Constructions Mecaniques et Aeronautiques d'Algerie (MAR)
SOMEAF ..... Societe Metallurgique Africaine (MAR)

SOMEC .... Sindicato de Operadores y Mecanicos de Equipos Camineros [*Union of Road-Building Equipment Operators and Mechanics*] [*Ecuadorean*] (LA)
SOMEC .... Societe de Materiel d'Entreprise et de Construction (MAR)
SOMEC .... Societe Mutuelle d'Etudes et de Cooperation Industrielle (MAR)
SOMECA..... Societe de Mecanique Appliquee (MAR)
SOMECA..... Societe de Mecanique Automobile et de Representation Industrielle (MAR)
SOMECA..... Societe Mecanographique Africaine (MAR)
SOMECAF ... Societe d'Ateliers Mecaniques Africains (MAR)
SOMECAFRIQUE ... Societe pour la Mecanisation des Entreprises en Afrique (MAR)
SOMECAFRIQUE-CENTRAFRIQUE ... Societe pour la Mecanisation des Entreprises de Centrafrique (MAR)
SOMECUP ... Societe Malienne d'Exploitation des Cuirs et Peaux (MAR)
SOMEDO .... Sociedad Medica Domiciliaria Ltda. [*Bogota*] (COL)
SOMEL........ Sociedade Importadora de Movies e Electrodomesticos Lda. (MAR)
SOMEL........ Societe Malgache d'Elevage (MAR)
SOMENGO ... Menuiserie Ebenisterie du Mungo (MAR)
SOMEP .... Societe Malgache d'Elements Prefabriques (MAR)
SOMEPAG ... Societe Mediterraneenne de Produits Agricoles [*Algerian*] (MAR)
SOMEPI ...... Societe Mauritanienne d'Etudes et de Promotion Industrielles (MAR)
SOMEPIA.... Societe Meroueh des Papiers Industriels Africains (MAR)
SOMERECI ... Societe de Mecanique et de Rectification de Cote-d'Ivoire (MAR)
SOMETER... Societe Mauritanienne d'Etudes Techniques et de Representation (MAR)
SOMETINA ... Societe Metallurgique et Industrielle Africaine (MAR)
SOMETRA... Societe Mediterraneenne de Transports (MAR)
SOMEX .... Sociedad Mexicana de Credito Industrial [*Mexican Society for Industrial Credit*] (LA)
SOMEXPA... Societe Malgache d'Exploitation et de Participation (MAR)
SOMIA......... Societe Mauritanienne pour l'Industrie de l'Automobile (MAR)
SOMIAN...... Societe Mobiliere et Immobiliere de l'Afrique Noire (MAR)
SOMIBA...... Societe Miniere de Moba [*Moba Mining Company*] [*Zairian*] (AF)
SOMICA...... Societe Miniere de Carnot (MAR)
SOMICOA... Societe Maritime et Industrielle de la Cote Occidentale d'Afrique (MAR)
SOMICOA-Gabon ... Societe Maritime et Industrielle de la Cote Occidentale d'Afrique - Gabon (MAR)
SOMICOA-Senegal ... Societe Maritime et Industrielle de la Cote Occidentale d'Afrique - Senegal (MAR)
SOMIDA...... Societe des Mines d'Ampandrandava (MAR)
SOMIDA...... Societe des Mines du Djebel Azared (MAR)
SOMIDANI ... Societe Miniere du Dahomey Niger (MAR)
SOMIEX ...... Societe Malienne d'Importation et d'Exportation (MAR)
SOMIFER .... Societe des Mines de Fer de Mekambo [*Mekambo Iron Mines Company*] [*Gabonese*] (AF)
SOMIFIMA ... Societe Miniere et Financiere de Madagascar (MAR)
SOMIGA...... Societe Miniere Gaziello & Cie. [*Dakar*] (MAR)
SOMIKA...... Societe Miniere de Karongo [*Karongo Mining Company*] [*Burundi*] (AF)
SOMIMA ..... Societe Miniere de Mauritanie [*Mining Company of Mauritania*] (AF)
SOMINI .... Societe Minoterie Nigerienne (MAR)
SOMINKI..... Societe Miniere et Industrielle du Kivu [*Mining and Industrial Company of Kivu*] [*Zairian*] (AF)
SOMINOR ... Societe des Mines du Congo Septentrional (MAR)
SOMIP......... Societe Anonyme Marocaine Italienne des Petroles (MAR)
SOMIP......... Societe Mauritanienne des Industries de la Peche (MAR)
SOMIPEX.... Societe Mauritanienne d'Importation, d'Exportation, et de Representation (MAR)
SOMIQUE ... Sociedade de Comercio e Metais de Mozambique (MAR)
SOMIRAMAD ... Societe des Minerais Rares de Madagascar (MAR)
SOMIREMA ... Societe d'Exploitation Miniere et de Recherches de Mauritanie [*Mining Exploitation and Prospecting Company of Mauritania*] (AF)
SOMIREN.... Societa Minerali Radiaettini Energia Nucleare [*Italian*]
SOMIRWA... Societe des Mines du Rwanda [*Rwandan Mining Company*] (AF)
SOMISA ...... Sociedad Mixta Siderurgica Argentina [*Argentine Joint Iron and Steel Association*] (LA)
SOMITAM... Societe Miniere de Tambao (MAR)
SOMITRAM ... Societe Malienne d'Ingenierie en Transports Maritimes (MAR)
SOMMIA ..... Societe Marocaine de Mecanique Industrielle (MAR)
SOMO .... Nonfat Milk Solids (RU)
SOMO .... Societe de l'Okoume du Moyen-Congo (MAR)
SOMOBAF ... Societe d'Assistance Technique pour la Modernisation de la Culture Bananiere et Fruitiere (MAR)
SOMOCAT-SA ... Societe Mauritanienne d'Affretement de Consignation de Transit et d'Acconage (MAR)
SOMOL .... Sociedade Mocambicana Lda. (MAR)
SOMONI...... Societe du Moyen Niger (MAR)
SOMOP....... Slovenske Oddelenie Ministerstva Obchodu a Priemyslu [*Slovak Department of the Ministry of Commerce and Industry*] (CZ)
SOMOPAL ... Sociedade de Produtos Alimentares Lda. (MAR)
SOMOREL... Sociedade Mocambicana de Representacoes Ltd. (MAR)
SOMOVA .... Societe de Montage et de Distribution de Vehicules Automobiles (MAR)
SOMPELO... Fabrica de Sombreros de Pelo [*Bogota*] (COL)
SOMSS .... Slovenske Oddelenie Ministerstva Socialnej Starostlivosti [*Slovak Department of the Ministry of Social Welfare*] (CZ)
Somt .... Sommet [*Summit*] [*Military map abbreviation*] [*World War I*] [*French*] (MTD)
SOMTIS ...... Societe Maribane de Tissage [*Morroccan*] (MAR)
SOMU.......... Sindicato de Obreros Maritimos Unidos [*United Maritime Workers Union*] [*Argentine*] (LA)
SOMUDER ... Societes Mutuelles du Developpement Rural (MAR)
SOMUKI...... Societe Miniere de Muhinga et de Kigali (MAR)
SOMZ.......... Suksun Optical Instrument Plant (RU)
SON............. Fire Control RADAR, Gun Locator (BU)
SON............. Gun Laying Radar (RU)
SON............. Sbornik Operativnich Norem [*Collection of Operational Standards*] (CZ)
SON............. Slovenske Odborne Nazvoslovie [*Slovak Specialized Terminology*] [*A publication*] (CZ)
SON............. Stacja Oceny Nasion [*Seed Testing Station*] (POL)
SON............. Stichting Scheikundig Onderzoek in Nederland [*Foundation for Chemical Research in the Netherlands*] (WEN)
SONA .... Somali National News Agency (MAR)
SONABA..... Societe Nationale d'Amenagement de la Baie d'Agadir (MAR)
SONABA..... Societe Nationale du Batiment (MAR)
SONABA..... Societe Nationale de la Ceramique Artisanale et Industrielle du Benin (MAR)
SONAC .... Societe Nationale Camerounaise pour le Commerce, l'Industrie, et le Developpement (MAR)
SONAC .... Societe Nationale de la Ceramique Artisanale et Industrielle du Dahomey (MAR)
SONAC .... Societe Nationale de Confection [*Tunisian*] (MAR)
SONAC .... Societe Nationale de Construction [*National Construction Company*] [*Liquidated 15 June 1970*] [*Cambodian*] (CL)
SONACAT... Societe Nationale de Commercialisation et d'Applications Techniques de Materiel Electro-Domestique, Electrique, Radio-Television, de Conditionnement d'Air, et de Refrigeration [*Algerian*] (MAR)
SONACEB... Societe Nationale de Commercialisation et d'Exportation du Benin [*National Marketing and Export Company of Benin*] (AF)
SONACHAR ... Societe Nigerienne du Charbon (MAR)
SONACI ...... Societe Nationale Commerciale et Industrielle [*National Commercial and Industrial Company*] [*Senegalese*] (AF)
SONACIMENT ... Societe Nationale de Ciment [*National Cement Company*] [*Cambodian*] (CL)
SONACLUB ... Sociedad Nacional de Clubes Ltda. [*Manizales*] (COL)
SONACO..... Societe Nationale Agricole pour le Coton [*National Agricultural Company for Cotton*] [*Beninese*] (AF)
SONACO..... Societe Nationale de Commerce [*National Trading Company*] [*Malagasy*] (AF)
SONACO..... Societe Nationale de Conditionnement [*National Packaging Company*] [*Ivorian*] (AF)
SONACO..... Societe Nationale de Confection [*Tunisian*] (MAR)
SONACO..... Societe Nationale de Constructions (MAR)
SONACO..... Societe Nationale de Contreplaques [*National Plywood Company*] [*Cambodian*] (CL)
SONACOB ... Societe Nationale de Commercialisation des Bois et Derives (MAR)
SONACOB ... Societe Nationale de Construction de Batiments (MAR)
SONACOM ... Societe Nationale de Commerce [*National Trading Company*] [*Togolese*] (AF)
SONACOM ... Societe Nationale de Commercialisation des Plantes Medicinales (MAR)
SONACOMA ... Societe Nationale des Commercants de Mauritanie (MAR)
SONACOME ... Societe Nationale de Constructions Mecaniques [*National Mechanical Engineering Company*] [*Algerian*] (AF)
SONACOP ... Societe Nationale de Commercialisation des Produits Petroliers [*National Petroleum Products Marketing Company*] [*Beninese*] (AF)
SONACOP ... Societe Nationale de Conserverie de Poisson [*National Fish Canning Company*] [*Cambodian*] (CL)
SONACOS ... Societe Nationale de Commercialisation des Oleagineux du Senegal (MAR)
SONACOS ... Societe Nationale de Commercialisation des Semences [*National Company for the Marketing of Seeds*] [*Moroccan*] (AF)
SONACOT ... Societe Nationale de Commercialisation du Tchad (MAR)
SONACOTRAP ... Societe Nationale de Construction et de Travaux Publics [*National Construction and Public Works Company*] [*Beninese*] (AF)
SONADE ..... Societe Nationale de Distribution d'Eau Potable et Industrielle [*National Company for the Distribution of Drinking Water and Water for Industrial Use*] [*Algerian*] (AF)
SONADER... Societe Nationale de Developpement Rural [*National Rural Development Company*] [*Mauritanian*] (AF)
SONADER... Societe Nationale pour le Developpement Rural du Dahomey (MAR)

SONADIG.... Societe National d'Investissement du Gabon [*National Investment Company of Gabon*] (AF)
SONADIS.... Societe Nationale d'Investissement du Senegal [*National Investment Company of Senegal*] (AF)
SONAE........ Societe Nationale d'Equipement [*National Equipment Company*] [*Beninese*] (AF)
SONAF........ Societe Nationale de Financement (MAR)
SONAFEL.... Societe Nationale pour le Developpement des Fruits et Legumes [*National Company for Development of Fruits and Vegetables*] [*Beninese*] (AF)
SONAFI....... Societe Nationale de Financement [*National Financing Company*] [*Ivorian*] (AF)
SONAFOR... Societe Nationale des Forages (MAR)
SONAFRIG ... Societe Nationale des Frigorifiques (MAR)
SONAGA..... Societe Nationale de Garantie et d'Assistance au Commerce (MAR)
SONAGAR ... Societe Nationale Gabonaise d'Assurances et de Reassurances (MAR)
SONAGECI ... Societe Nationale de Genie Civil [*National Civil Engineering Company*] [*Ivorian*] (AF)
SONAGIM ... Societe Nationale pour la Gestion Immobiliere [*National Company for Real Estate Management*] [*Beninese*] (AF)
SONAGRI.... Societe Nationale pour la Production Agricole [*National Company for Agricultural Production*] [*Beninese*] (AF)
SONAGTHER ... Societe Nationale des Grands Travaux Hydrauliques et d'Equipement Rural [*Algerian*] (MAR)
SONAKOP... Societe Nationale de Conserverie de Poisson [*National Fish Canning Company*] [*Use SONACOP*] [*Cambodian*] (CL)
SONALCO... Sociedad Nacional de Confecciones Ltda. [*Bogota*] (COL)
SONALCO... Societe Nationale des Conserveries Algeriennes (MAR)
SONALDI .... Sociedad Nacional de Inversiones Ltda. [*Manizales*] (COL)
SONAM....... Societe Nationale d'Assurances Mutuelles du Senegal (MAR)
SONAMA .... Societe National de Manutention [*National Freight Handling Company*] [*Algerian*] (AF)
SONAMEL... Societe Nationale de Materiel Electrique et Electromenager [*National Electrical Material and Appliances Company*] [*Beninese*] (AF)
SONAMI...... Sociedad Nacional de Mineria [*National Mining Association*] [*Chilean*] (LA)
SONAMIS.... Societe Nationale Miniere de Sounda-Kaka-Moeka (MAR)
SONAM-VIE ... Societe Nationale d'Assurance Mutuelle Vie (MAR)
SONAP........ Sociedad Anonima de Navegacion Petrolera [*Oil Tanker Corporation*] [*Chilean*] (LA)
SONAP........ Sociedad Nacional de Profesores [*National Teachers Association*] [*Chilean*] (LA)
SONAP........ Sociedade Nacional de Petroleos de Mocambique (MAR)
SONAP........ Societe Nationale des Articles de Papeterie (MAR)
SONAP........ Societe Nouvelle d'Alimentation et de Panification (MAR)
SONAPA ..... Societe Nationale de la Production Animale [*National Animal Production Company*] [*Beninese*] (AF)
SONAPAL ... Societe Nationale de Papeterie et de Librairie [*National Book Store and Stationery Company*] [*Beninese*] (AF)
SONAPAP ... Societe Nationale de Papier [*National Paper Company*] [*Liquidated 19 February 1971*] [*Cambodian*] (CL)
SONAPECHE ... Societe Nationale d'Armement et de Peche [*National Shipping and Fishing Company*] [*Beninese*] (AF)
SONAPEX ... Societe Nationale pour le Developpement du Commerce Exterieur [*Moroccan*] (MAR)
SONAPH ..... Societe Nationale pour le Developpement des Palmeraies et des Huileries [*National Society for the Development of Palm Tree Plantations and Palm Oil Resources*] [*Togolese*] (AF)
SONAPNEU ... Societe Nationale de Pneumatiques [*National Tire Company*] [*Cambodian*] (CL)
SONAPRESS ... Societe Nationale de Presse, d'Edition, et de Publicite (MAR)
SONAPRIM ... Societe Nationale de Distribution des Produits Importes [*National Imports Distribution Company*] [*Liquidated 8 May 1970*] [*Cambodian*] (CL)
SONAR........ Societe Nationale d'Approvisionnement du Monde Rural (MAR)
SONAR........ Societe Nationale d'Assurance et de Reassurance [*National Insurance and Reinsurance Company*] [*Beninese*] (AF)
SONARA ..... Societe Nationale de Raffinage (MAR)
SONARA ..... Societe Nigerienne de Commercialisation de l'Arachide [*Niger Peanut Marketing Company*] (AF)
SONARAF ... Societe Nationale de Raffinage [*National Refining Company*] [*Beninese*] (AF)
SONAREM ... Societe Nationale de Recherches et d'Exploitation Miniere [*National Mine Prospecting and Exploitation Company*] [*Algerian*] (AF)
SONAREM ... Societe Nationale de Recherches et d'Exploitation des Ressources Minieres du Mali [*National Company for Prospecting and Exploitation of Malian Mining Resources*] (AF)
SONAREP ... Sociedade Nacional de Refinacao de Petroleos (MAR)
SONAREX ... Societe Nationale de Recherches et d'Exploitations Minieres [*National Mine Prospecting and Exploitation Company*] [*Central African*] (AF)
SONAS........ Societe Nationale d'Assurances [*National Insurance Company*] [*Zairian*] (AF)
SONASCIE ... Societe Nationale de Scierie [*National Sawmill Company*] [*Liquidated 15 June 1970*] [*Cambodian*] (CL)
SONASUCRE ... Societe Nationale de Sucre [*National Sugar Company*] [*Cambodian*] (CL)
SONASUT... Societe Nationale Sucriere du Tchad (MAR)
SONATAM ... Societe Nationale des Tabacs et Allumettes du Mali (MAR)
SONATEM ... Societe Nationale des Travaux d'Eaux et Barrages [*Algerian*] (MAR)
SONATEX... Societe Nationale d'Importations Textiles (MAR)
SONATEX... Societe Nationale de Textiles [*National Textile Company*] [*Cambodian*] (CL)
SONATEXTILE ... Societe Nationale de Textiles [*National Textile Company*] [*Use SONATEX*] [*Cambodian*] (CL)
SONATHERM ... Societe Nationale Algerienne de Thermalisme (MAR)
SONATHYD ... Societe Nationale des Travaux Hydrauliques [*Algerian*] (MAR)
SONATIBA ... Societe Nationale de Travaux d'Infrastructure et de Batiments [*National Infrastructure and Building Construction Company*] [*Algerian*] (AF)
SONATITE ... Societe Nationale des Travaux d'Infrastructure des Telecommunications [*National Telecommunications Infrastructure Construction Company*] [*Algerian*] (AF)
SONATMAG ... Societe Nationale de Transit et de Magasins Generaux [*North African*] (MAR)
SONATO ..... Societe Nouvelle pour l'Expansion Commerciale Togolaise (MAR)
SONATOUR ... Societe Nationale Algerienne de Tourisme et d'Hotellerie (MAR)
SONATRA... Societe Nationale des Transports Aeriens [*National Air Transport Company*] [*Senegalese*] (AF)
SONATRAB ... Societe Nationale de Transformation du Bois (MAR)
SONATRAC ... Societe Nationale de Tracteurs [*National Tractor Company*] [*Cambodian*] (CL)
SONATRAC ... Societe Nationale de Transit et de Consignation [*National Transit and Consignment Company*] [*Beninese*] (AF)
SONATRACH ... Societe National du Transport et de Commercialisation des Hydrocarbons [*National Company for the Transport and Marketing of Hydrocarbons*] [*Algerian*] (AF)
SONATRAM ... Societe Nationale des Transports Maritimes [*National Maritime Transport Company*] [*Gabonese*] (AF)
SONATRAM ... Societe Nationale des Travaux Maritimes [*Algerian*] (MAR)
SONATRANS ... Sociedad Nacional Transportadora Ltda. [*Bogota*] (COL)
SONATRO... Societe Nationale des Travaux Routiers [*National Highway Construction Company*] [*Algerian*] (AF)
SONAVING ... Sociedad Nacional de Vigilantes [*Bogota*] (COL)
SONAVOCI ... Societe Nationale Voltaique de Cinema (MAR)
SONEA........ Societe Nationale pour l'Exploitation des Abattoirs (MAR)
SONEAB ..... Societe Nationale d'Exploitation des Arachides de Bouche (MAR)
SONECOR... Societe Nationale d'Equipement et de Constructions Routieres (MAR)
SONED........ Societe Nationale des Etudes de Developpement (MAR)
SONEDE ..... Societe Nationale d'Exploitation et de Distribution des Eaux [*National Water Exploitation and Distribution Company*] [*Algerian*] (AF)
SONEDIC .... Societe Nationale d'Equipement et de Developpement Industriel du Cameroun (MAR)
SONEES...... Societe Nationale des Eaux et Electricite du Senegal [*Senegalese National Water and Electricity Company*] (AF)
SONEF .... Societe Nationale d'Exploitation Forestiere [*National Forest Exploitation Company*] [*Cambodian*] (CL)
SONEG........ Societe Nationale d'Entreprise Generale (MAR)
SONEL .... Societe Nationale de l'Electricite [*National Electricity Company*] [*Cameroonian*] (AF)
SONEL .... Societe Nationale d'Elevage (MAR)
SONELEC ... Societe Nationale Algerienne de Fabrication et de Montage du Materiel Electrique et Electronique [*Algerian National Company for the Manufacture and Installation of Electrical and Electronic Equipment*] (AF)
SONELEC ... Societe Nationale d'Eau et d'Electricite (MAR)
SONELGAZ ... Societe Nationale d'Electricite et du Gaz [*National Electricity and Gas Company*] [*Algerian*] (AF)
SONEMS..... SONATRACH Ente Minerario Siciliano [*North African*] (MAR)
SONEOH ..... Societe Nationale d'Entretien et d'Exploitation d'Ouvrages Hydrauliques (MAR)
SONEP .... Societe Nationale d'Etudes et de Promotion Industrielle (MAR)
SONEPI .... Societe Nationale d'Etudes et de Promotion Industrielle (MAR)
SONEPRESS ... Societe Nationale d'Edition et de Presse (MAR)
SONERAN... Societe Nigerienne d'Exploitation des Ressources Animales (MAR)
SONETRA ... Societe Nationale d'Entreprise et de Travaux Publics (MAR)
SONETRA ... Societe Senegalaise de Transit (MAR)
SONEXI....... Societe Nigerienne d'Exploitation Cinematographique (MAR)
SONEXIM..... Societe Nationale d'Exportation et d'Importation [*National Export-Import Company*] [*Cambodian*] (CL)
SONEXPEXT ... Societe Nationale pour les Exportations Extremes [*National Special Exports Company*] [*Cambodian*] (CL)
SONEXPIERRE ... Societe Nationale pour l'Exploitation de Gisements des Pierres et Metaux Precieux et Semi-Precieux [*National Company for the Exploitation of Deposits of Precious and Semi-Precious Stones and Metals*] [*Cambodian*] (CL)

SONEXPIERROR ... Societe Nationale pour l'Exploitation de Gisements des Pierres et Metaux Precieux et Semi-Precieux [*National Company for the Exploitation of Deposits of Precious and Semi-Precious Stones and Metals*] [*Use SONEXPIERRE*] [*Cambodian*] (CL)
SONG .... Societe d'Okoume de la N'Gounie (MAR)
SONI-Afrique ... Societe Nouvelle d'Importation Afrique (MAR)
SONIAH .... Societe Nationale d'Irrigation et d'Amenagement Hydro-Agricole [*National Irrigation and Hydro-Agricultural Development Company*] [*Beninese*] (AF)
SONIB .... Societe Nationale d'Importation du Benin [*National Import Company of Benin*] (AF)
SONIC .... Societe Nationale d'Industrie et de Commerce (MAR)
SONIC .... Societe Nationale des Industries de la Cellulose [*National Cellulose Industries Company*] [*Algerian*] (AF)
SONIC .... Societe Nationale et Internationale Compagnie (MAR)
SONI-CA ..... Societe Nigerienne de Carrelage (MAR)
SONICA ...... Societe Nigerienne de Credit Automobile (MAR)
SONICAR .... Societe Nigerienne de Carrelage (MAR)
SONICERAM ... Societe Nigerienne de Produits Ceramique (MAR)
SONICHAR ... Societe Nigerienne de Charbon (MAR)
SONICO ...... Societe Nationale pour l'Industrie et le Commerce (MAR)
SONICOB .... Societe Nationale d'Industrialisation et de Commercialisation du Betail (MAR)
SONICOCIT ... Societe Nigerienne de Commerce International (MAR)
SONICOG ... Societe Nationale pour l'Industrie des Corps Gras [*National Company for the Fatty Substance Industry*] [*Beninese*] (AF)
SONIDA ...... Societe Nigerienne pour le Developpement de l'Autoroute (MAR)
SONIDEP .... Societe Nigerienne de Produits Petroliers [*Nigerien Petroleum Products Company*] [*Niger*] (AF)
SONIFAME ... Societe Nigerienne de Fabrications Metalliques (MAR)
SONII .... North Ossetian Scientific Research Institute (RU)
SONIMACI ... Societe Nippo-Malgache Commerciale et Industrielle [*Japanese-Malagasy Commercial and Industrial Company*] (AF)
SONIMCO .... Societe Nationale d'Impression en Continu (MAR)
SONIMEX .... Societe Nationale d'Importation et d'Exportation (MAR)
SONIPEC .... Societe Nationale des Industries des Peaux et Cuirs [*National Leather and Hides Industries Company*] [*Algerian*] (AF)
SONIPLA ..... Societe Nigerienne de Plastique (MAR)
SONITAB .... Societe Nigerienne de Batiment et de Travaux Publics (MAR)
SONITAN .... Societe Nigerienne de Tannerie (MAR)
SONITEX ..... Societe Nationale de l'Industrie Textile [*National Textile Industry Company*] [*Algerian*] (AF)
SONITEXTIL ... Societe Nouvelle Nigerienne des Textiles (MAR)
SONITRA .... Societe Nationale Ivoirienne de Travaux [*Ivorian National Construction Company*] (AF)
SONIVEX ..... Societe Nigerienne de Viandes d'Exportation (MAR)
SONIVIEX .... Societe Nigerienne de Viandes d'Exportation (MAR)
SONMIVA .... Societe Nationale de Mise en Valeur du Sud [*National Company for Development of the South*] [*Tunisian*] (AF)
SONMIVAS ... Societe Nationale de Mise en Valeur du Sud [*National Company for Development of the South*] [*Tunisian*] (MAR)
SONNA .... Somali National News Agency (AF)
SONOBAT ... Societe Nouvelle de Batiments (MAR)
SONOKIT .... Societe Nouvelle Khmere d'Importation et de Transit [*New Cambodian Import and Transit Company*] (CL)
SONOMUSICA ... Sociedad Nacional de Musica [*Medellin*] (COL)
SONP .... Spojene Ocelarny, Narodni Podnik [*United Steel Works, National Enterprise*] [*Kladno*] (CZ)
SONUCI ...... Societe Nigerienne d'Urbanisme et de Construction Immobiliere (MAR)
SONY .... South Nyanza (MAR)
SOO .... Clothing Disinfection Station (RU)
SOO .... Secret Operations Section (RU)
SOO .... Smotra Oruzja i Opreme [*Inspection of Arms and Equipment*] (YU)
SOO .... Synetairistikos Oinopoiitikos Organismos [*Cooperative Wine-Making Organization*] [*Greek*] (GC)
soobshch .... Communication [*Bibliography*], Information, Report (RU)
SOOP .... Senior Firing Position Officer (BU)
SOP .... Fixed Bath Station (RU)
sop .... Hill, Small Volcano [*Topography*] (RU)
SOP .... Permanent Decontamination Stations (BU)
SOP .... Sekcija za Odrzavanje Pruge [*Railroad Track Maintenance Section*] (YU)
SOP .... Sekcija za Odrzavanje Puteva [*Road Maintenance Section*] (YU)
SOP .... Spoldzielnie Oszczednosciowo-Pozyczkowe [*Savings and Loan Cooperatives*] (POL)
SOP .... Standard of Limited Application (RU)
SOP .... Staropolski Okreg Przemyslowy [*Old Polish Industrial Region*] [*Polish*]
SOP .... Straz Ochrony Przyrody [*Nature Preserving Guard*] [*Polish*]
SOP .... Szkola Oficerow Pozarnictwa [*Fire-Fighting Officers' School*] [*Polish*]
SOPA .... Societe Oranaise d'Entreprise Prefabrication [*Algerian*] (MAR)
SOPA .... Societe Pharmaceutique Africaine (MAR)
SOPA .... Societe des Produits Alimentaires (MAR)
SOPA .... Societe de Publicite Abidjanaise (MAR)
SOPAB .... Societe des Pansements du Benin (MAR)
SOPACOR ... Societe des Palmeraies du Cameroun Oriental (MAR)
SOPAD .... Societe de Produits Alimentaires et Dietetiques (MAR)
SOPAGEF ... Societe de Participation, de Gestion, et de Financement (MAR)
SOPAME ..... Societe des Palmeraies de Mbongo et d'Eseka (MAR)
SOPANI .... Societe de Parfumerie Nigerienne (MAR)
SOPAO .... Societe de Peche de l'Afrique Occidentale (MAR)
SOPAR .... Societe Parisienne d'Articles de Luxe (MAR)
SOPARCA ... Societe de Fabrication de Parfumerie au Cameroun (MAR)
SOPARCO ... Societe Africaine de Parfumerie et de Cosmetique (MAR)
SOPARMOD ... Societe de Parfums Modernes (MAR)
SOPAZ .... Synergatikos Organismos Paragogis Zootrofon [*Animal Feeds Production Cooperative*] [*Cypriot*] (GC)
SOPC .... Sub-Oficiales Profesionales de Carrera [*Professional Career Noncommissioned Officers*] [*Venezuelan*] (LA)
SOPCAM ..... Sopecoba Cameroun (MAR)
SOPD .... Dangerous Pressure Drop Indicator (RU)
SOPE .... Etaireia Prostasias Syngrafikon Dikaiomaton [*Society for the Protection of Authors' Rights*] [*Cypriot*] (GC)
SOPEC .... Sociedade de Produtos para o Fomento Pecuario Lda. (MAR)
SOPECA ..... Societe de Pecherie de Casamance [*Senegalese*] (MAR)
SOPECAM ... Societe de Presse et d'Editions du Cameroun [*Cameroon News and Publishing Corporation*] (AF)
SOPECAS ... Sociedade de Pecas e Automoveis (MAR)
SOPECI .... Societe de Peinture en Cote-d'Ivoire (MAR)
SOPECOBA ... Societe des Pecheries Cotieres a la Baleine (MAR)
SOPEFAL .... Societe Petroliere Francaise en Algerie [*French Petroleum Company in Algeria*] (AF)
SOPEG .... Societe Petroliere de Gerance [*Petroleum Management Company*] [*Algerian*] (AF)
SOPESEA ... Societe des Pecheries Senegalaises de l'Atlantique (MAR)
SOPESUR ... Sociedad Periodistica del Sur [*Southern Newspaper Company*] [*Chilean*] (LA)
SOPHRUC ... Societe de Planteurs d'Heveas pour le Ramassage et l'Usinage du Caoutchouc [*Rubber Planters Company for the Collection and Processing of Latex*] [*Cambodian*] (CL)
SOPI .... Societe de Participations et d'Etudes Industrielles [*Moroccan*] (MAR)
SOPICAD .... Societe Pituach Centrafricaine de Diamants (MAR)
SOPICOMA ... Societe pour la Promotion Industrielle et Commerciale de Madagascar [*Industrial and Commercial Promotion Company of Madagascar*] (AF)
SOPILEC ..... Societe des Piles Electriques du Gabon (MAR)
SOPIMA ...... Societe des Piles de Madagascar (MAR)
SOPIMER .... Societe Civile d'Etude du Pipeline Mediterranee (MAR)
SOPIVOLTA ... Societe des Piles de Haute-Volta (MAR)
SOPLAREF ... Sociedad de Plasticos Reforzados Ltda. [*Cali*] (COL)
Sopo .... Poets' Union (RU)
SOPO-AUTOS ... Societe Senegalaise des Poids Lourds Automobiles (MAR)
SOPOFI .... Societe Pontenegrine Financiere Immobiliere (MAR)
SOPONICRO ... Societe de Polissage, Nickelage, et Chromage (MAR)
SOPOTEC ... Societe Pompes et Techniques (MAR)
SOPP .... Sekcija za Odrzavanje Plovnih Puteva [*River Navigation Maintenance Section*] (YU)
SOPP .... Sekretarijat za Opste Privredne Poslove (SIV) [*Secretariat of General Economic Affairs*] (YU)
sopr .... Resistance, Strength (RU)
SOPRA .... Societe de Peinture et Ravalement (MAR)
SOPRAL .... Societe de Produits Alimentaires (MAR)
SOPRAVIT ... Sopravit de Peinture, Ravalement, et Vitrerie (MAR)
SOPREMER ... Societe d'Exploitation des Produits de la Mer [*Sea Products Exploitation Company*] [*Cambodian*] (CL)
SOPRIVO .... Societe de Produits Ivoiriens (MAR)
SOPROA ..... Sociedad Productora de Alimentos [*Food Processing Company*] [*Chilean*] (LA)
SOPRODA ... Societe d'Exploitation de Produits Agricoles et Forestiers [*Agricultural and Forest Products Exploitation Company*] [*Cambodian*] (CL)
SOPRODAV ... Societe d'Etude pour le Developpement de la Culture de l'Avocatier (MAR)
SOPRODAV-CI ... Societe d'Etude pour la Production de l'Avocat en Cote-d'Ivoire (MAR)
SOPROGI .... Societe pour la Promotion et la Gestion Industrielle (MAR)
SOPROHOT ... Societe de Promotion Hoteliere et Touristique de Tunisie (MAR)
SOPROIN .... Sociedad Profesional de Inversiones [*Bogota*] (COL)
SOPROLE ... Sociedad de Productores de Leche [*Society of Milk Producers*] [*Chilean*] (LA)
sopromat .... Strength of Materials (RU)
SOPROMET ... Sociedad Promotora de Exportaciones Metalurgicas [*Association for the Promotion of Metallurgical Exports*] [*Chilean*] (LA)
SOPROSEN ... Societe de la Promotion Senegalaise (MAR)
SOPS .... Council for the Study of Productive Resources (RU)
SOPV .... Sdruzeni Osvetimskych Politickych Veznu [*Association of Former Political Prisoners in the Oswieczym Concentration Camp*] (CZ)
SOPV .... Svaz Osvobozenych Politickych Veznu [*Union of Liberated Political Prisoners*] (CZ)

SOPVP .... Svaz Osvobozenych Politickych Veznu a Pozustalych po Obetech Nacismu [*Association of Liberated Political Prisoners and Relatives of the Victims of Nazism*] (CZ)

SOQUIMICH ... Sociedad Quimica y Minera Chilena [*Chilean Chemical and Mining Association*] (LA)

SOR .... Rudder Deflection Recorder (RU)

SOR .... Servicio Oficial de Radiodifusion [*Official Broadcasting Service*] [*Argentine*] (LA1)

SOR .... Slovenska Odborova Rada [*Slovak Trade Union Council*] (CZ)

SOR .... Stacja Obslugi Radiotechnicznej [*Radio-Engineering Service Station*] [*Polish*]

SOR .... Stacje Obslugi Radiofonicznej [*Broadcasting Service Stations*] (POL)

SORABA ..... Societe de Ravitaillement du Baol (MAR)

Sorabis .... Union of Workers in the Arts (RU)

Sorabpros... Union of Education Workers (RU)

SORAD........ Societe Regionale d'Amenagement et de Developpement (MAR)

SORADEC... Societe Raad & Cie. (MAR)

SORAF .... Societe de Representations Africaines (MAR)

SORAFOM ... Societe de la Radiodiffusion d'Outre-Mer [*Overseas Broadcasting Company*] [*French*] (AF)

SORAL .... Societe de Ravitaillement Alimentaire (MAR)

SORANI....... Societe des Transitaires Reunis SARL [*United Forwarding Agents Company, Inc.*] (CL)

SORAPA ..... Societe de Ramassage du Paddy [*Paddy Harvesting Company*] [*Cambodian*] (CL)

SORARAF ... Societe de Representation d'Assurances et de Reassurances Africaines (MAR)

SORECAL ... Societe Regionale de Construction d'Alger (MAR)

SORECAM ... Societe de Rechapage du Cameroun (MAR)

SORECO ..... Societe Regionale de Construction de Constantine [*Algerian*] (MAR)

SORECOR... Societe Regionale de Construction d'Oran (MAR)

SOREDIA .... Societe de Recherches et d'Exploitations Diamantiferes (MAR)

SOREFA...... Societe de Reparations et Fournitures Auto (MAR)

SOREKAT ... Societe de Recherches au Katanga (MAR)

SOREL .... Synergatikos Organismos Elaioparagogon [*Olive Producers' Cooperative Organization*] [*Cypriot*] (GC)

SORELEC ... Societe de Rebobinage et Electricite (MAR)

SOREMAC ... Societe de Recherches et d'Exploitations Miniere pour l'Afrique Centrale (MAR)

SORENA ..... Sociedad Refinadora Nacional [*National Refining Company*] [*Chilean*] (LA)

SOREPCA... Societe de Recherches et d'Exploitation des Petroles du Cameroun (MAR)

SOREPEL.... Societe de Reparation Electromecanique F. Riviere & Cie. (MAR)

SOREPZA ... Societe de Recherche et d'Exploitation des Petroles au Zaire (MAR)

SORES .... Societe de Realisations d'Equipements Scolaires (MAR)

SORES .... Societe de Restauration Senegalaise (MAR)

SORETRAP ... Societe Regionale des Travaux Publics [*Tunisian*] (MAR)

SORETRAS ... Societe Regionale de Transports du Gouvernorat de Sfax [*Tunisian*] (MAR)

SOREX .... Societe de Recherches et d'Exploitation de Kairouan [*Tunisian*] (MAR)

SORFACE ... Societe Franco-Arabe d'Assurance et de Reassurance SAL (MAR)

SORGO .... Central Asian Branch of the Russian Geographical Society (RU)

SORI .... Societe Regionale d'Investissements du Centre Sud (MAR)

SORICA....... Societe de Representation, d'Industrie, et de Commerce pour l'Adamaoua (MAR)

SORIFEMA ... Societe Rizicole et Feculiere Malagasy [*Malagasy Rice and Potato Production Company*] (AF)

SORIMEX.... Societe Regionale d'Importation et d'Exportation [*Tunisian*] (MAR)

SORiT.......... Stacja Obslugi Radiowej i Telewizyjnej [*Radio and Television Service Station*] [*Polish*]

SORIV .... Societe Route Ivoire (MAR)

SORMAS..... Sogut Refrakter Malzemeleri Anonim Sirketi [*Sogut Refractory Materials Corporation*] (TU)

SORO .... Special Operations Research Office (MAR)

SOROTEL ... Societe Royale d'Hotellerie [*Royal Hotel Trade Company*] [*Cambodian*] (CL)

SORS .... Unipolar Communication Operations Bay (RU)

sorsz .... Sorszam [*Serial Number*] (HU)

sort............... Marshaling Yard [*Topography*] (RU)

SORT............ Stacja Obslugi Radiowej i Telewizyjnej [*Radio and Television Service Station*] [*Polish*]

SORTEX...... Soroksari Textilipar Reszvenytarsasag [*Textile Industry of Soroksar Limited*] (HU)

Sortsemovoshch ... Republic Office for the Production, Procurement, and Sale of High-Quality Seeds of Vegetables, Melons, and of Fodder Root Crops (RU)

sort st.......... Marshaling Yard [*Topography*] (RU)

SORZ.......... Optical Character Recognition System [*Computers*] (RU)

SOS............ Feedback Sylphon (RU)

SOS............ Sierra Leone Organisation Society (MAR)

SOS............ Societe l'Okoume de Sindara (MAR)

SOS............ Societe d'Organisations et de Services (MAR)

SOS............ Sofia Okrug Court (BU)

SoS .... Sonderschule [*German*]

SOS............ SOS Detske Vesnice [*SOS Childrens' Villages (SOS is Morse code for "Help!")*] (CZ)

sos.............. Sosea [*Road*] [*Romanian*]

Sos .... Sosyoloji [*Sociology*] (TU)

SOS............ Straz Obrany Statu [*State Defense Guard*] (CZ)

SOS............ Sumska Ogledna Stanica [*Forestry Experiment Station*] (YU)

SOSA .... Snaps Old Students Association (MAR)

SOSAC........ Societe Senegalaise d'Armement a la Crevette (MAR)

SOSAP........ Societe Senegalaise d'Armement a la Peche (MAR)

SOSAP........ Sofia Obshtina Pharmaceutical Economic Enterprise (BU)

sosdem....... Sosiaalidemokraatti(nen) [*Finnish*]

SOSEBA ..... Societe Senegalaise d'Entreprise de Batiment (MAR)

SOSECHAL ... Societe Senegalaise de Chalutage (MAR)

SOSECI....... Societe Senegalaise pour le Commerce et l'Industrie (MAR)

SOSECOD .. Societe Senegalaise pour le Commerce et le Developpement (MAR)

SOSECODA ... Societe Senegalaise de Courtages et d'Assurances (MAR)

SOSECOMI ... Societe Senegalaise de Commerce et d'Importation [*Senegalese*] (MAR)

SOSECOREP ... Societe Senegalaise de Courtage et de Representation (MAR)

SOSEDA ..... Societe Senegalaise de Developpement Agricole (MAR)

SOSEDA ..... Societe Senegalaise pour le Developpement de l'Automobile (MAR)

SOSEFIL ..... Societe Senegalaise de Fileterie (MAR)

SOSEG........ Societe Senegalaise d'Emaillage et de Galvanisation (MAR)

SOSEGA ..... Societe Senegalaise de Courtage et de Gestion d'Assurances (MAR)

SOSEGBA... Societe Senegalaise d'Entreprise de Batiment (MAR)

SOSELF...... Societe Senegalaise des Etablissements Louis Feltrin (MAR)

SOSEPA...... Societe Senegalaise de Produits Alimentaires (MAR)

SOSEPE...... Societe Senegalaise de Peches (MAR)

SOSEPROCI ... Societe Senegalaise de Promotion Commerciale et Industrielle (MAR)

SOSEREM... Societe Senegalaise de Renflouement et d'Exploitation du Montana (MAR)

SOSETA...... Societe Senegalaise de Transports Automobiles (MAR)

SOSETAM... Societe Senegalaise de Tannerie-Megisserie (MAR)

SOSETER ... Societe Senegalaise de Terrassements (MAR)

SOSETRAM ... Societe Senegalaise de Transports et de Mecanique (MAR)

SOSETRAUR ... Societe Senegalaise de Travaux Urbains et Ruraux (MAR)

SOSEXCATRA ... Societe Senegalaise d'Exploitation de Carrieres et de Transports (MAR)

SoSh .... Somali Shilling (MAR)

SOSI........... Service d'Ornement de Sepulture Ivoirien (MAR)

SOSIDE....... Societe E. Simeonides et E. Devanakis (MAR)

SOSILOS .... Societe des Silos du Senegal (MAR)

SOSIMABI... Societe Sino-Malgache de Bouteilles Isolantes (MAR)

SOSIPO....... Societe des Silos Portuaires [*Moroccan*] (MAR)

SOSKhI....... North Ossetian Agricultural Institute (RU)

SOSOBA ..... Societe d'Entreprise Soudanaise de Batiment (MAR)

SOSR .... Sekretarijat za Opsti Stopanski Raboti (IVNRM) [*Secretariat of General Economic Affairs*] (YU)

SOSR .... Stacja Oceny Sprzetu Rolniczego [*Farm Equipment Evaluation Station*] (POL)

SOSS .... Sofia Okoliya Trade Union Council (BU)

SOSSRNJ.... Savezni Odbor Socialisticki Sojuz na Rabotniot Narod na Jugoslavija [*Federal Committee, Socialist Alliance of Working People of Yugoslavia*] (YU)

sost .... Compiled, Compiler (RU)

SOSTEM ..... Societe de Stations Thermales et des Eaux Minerales [*Tunisian*] (MAR)

SOSU .... Societe Sucriere Voltaique (MAR)

SOSUCAM ... Societe Sucriere du Cameroun [*Cameroon Sugar Company*] (MAR)

SOSUHO ..... Societe Sucriere du Haut-Ogooue [*Upper Ogooue Sugar Company*] (MAR)

SOSU-HV.... Societe Sucriere Voltaique [*Voltan Sugar Company*] (AF)

SOSUMAV ... Societe Sucriere de la Mahavavy [*Mahavavy Sugar Company*] (MAR)

SOSUNI....... Societe Sucriere Nigerienne [*Niger Sugar Company*] (MAR)

SOSUNIARI ... Societe Sucriere du Niari [*Niari Sugar Company*] [*Congolese*] (AF)

SOSUTCHAD ... Societe Sucriere du Tchad [*Chad Sugar Company*] (MAR)

SOSYAL-IS ... Social Workers Union (TU)

SOT............ Concealed Emplacement (RU)

SOT............ Sabiraliste Ostecene Tehnike [*Assemblage of Damaged Technical Equipment*] (YU)

sot .... Sotet [*Dark*] (HU)

sot .... Sotilassana [*Military Term*] [*Finnish*]

SOT............ Stacja Obslugi Telewizyjnej [*Television Service Station*] [*Polish*]

SOT............ Systeemontwerptechnieken

SOT............ Weapon on Disappearing Mount in Position (BU)

SOTA .... Societe des Transports Africains (MAR)

SOTAC........ Societe des Transports Automobiles de la Corniche [*Algerian*] (MAR)

SOTACh...... Sociedad de Tecnicos Agricolas de Chile [*Association of Agricultural Experts of Chile*] (LA)

SOTAD........ Societe Tuniso-Americaine de Developpement (MAR)

SOTAF .... Societe Textile de l'Afrique Occidentale (MAR)
SOTAGRO... Servicios Tecnicos Agropecuarios [*Tulua-Valle*] (COL)
SOTAL .... Societe Tunisienne d'Aluminium (MAR)
SOTALMA... Societe Touristique Algero-Marocaine (MAR)
SOTAPO ..... Societe des Tanneries Poyet (MAR)
SOTATRIC ... Societe Tuniso-Allemande de Confection et de Broderie (MAR)
SOTE........... Semmelweis Orvostudomanyi Egyetem [*Semmelweis Medical University*] (HU)
SOTEC .... Sociedad Tecnica [*Medellin*] (COL)
SOTEC .... Sociedade Tecnica e Comercial Lda. (MAR)
SOTECAS... Societe des Techniciens Associes (MAR)
SOTECNICA ... Sociedade Tecnica e Comercial Lda. (MAR)
SOTEF .... Societe Oranaise de Tissage et Filature [*North African*] (MAR)
SOTEGA ..... Societe Industrielle Textile du Gabon (MAR)
SOTEHPA ... Societe Togolaise d'Extraction d'Huile de Palme (MAR)
SOTEIC....... Societe Tropicale d'Entreprises Industrielles et Commerciales (MAR)
SOTEKCI .... Societe des Techniciens Khmers pour le Commerce et l'Industrie [*Cambodian Commercial and Industrial Technicians Company*] (CL)
SOTEL......... Sociedade Tecnica e Comercial Lda. (MAR)
SOTEM........ Societe Commerciale du N'Tem (MAR)
SOTEMA..... Societe Textile de Majunga [*Majunga Textile Company*] [*Malagasy*] (AF)
SOTEMI ...... Societe Tunisienne d'Expansion Miniere (MAR)
SOTEMU..... Societe Tunisienne d'Explosifs et de Munitions (MAR)
SOTEREL.... Sociedade Tecnica de Representacoes Lda. (MAR)
SOTESA...... Societa Tecnica pe lo Siviluppo Agricols (MAR)
SOTEXCO... Societe des Textiles du Congo (MAR)
SOTEXCOCAM ... Societe des Textiles et de Commerce du Cameroun (MAR)
SOTEXI .... Societe Industrielle Textile de Cote-d'Ivoire (MAR)
SOTEXIM.... Societe Togolaise d'Exportation et d'Importation [*Togolese Export-Import Company*] (AF)
SOTEXKA ... Societe Textile de Kaolack (MAR)
SOTHA........ Societe de Travaux Hydrauliques et Agricoles (MAR)
SOTHRA...... Societe de Transport de Gaz Naturel d'Hassi R'Mel a Arzew [*Algerian*] (MAR)
SOTIBA....... Societe de Teinture, Blanchissement, et Apprets (MAR)
SOTIBA-SIMPAFRIC ... Societe de Teinture, Blanchissement, Apprets, et d'Impressions Africaines [*Senegalese*] (MAR)
SOTIC .... Societe Tamatavienne d'Industries et de Cultures (MAR)
SOTICI .... Societe de Transformation Industrielle de Cote-d'Ivoire (MAR)
SOTIL.......... Sindicato de Obreros del Transporte Interdepartamental de Leche [*Milk Transport Workers Union*] [*Uruguayan*] (LA)
SOTIL.......... Sociedade Luso Tipografica Lda. (MAR)
SOTIMA ...... Societe de Tissages Maghrebins [*Algerian*] (MAR)
SOTIMPEX ... Societe Togolaise d'Importation et d'Exportation (MAR)
SOTIPA .... Societe de Transformation Industrielle du Papier (MAR)
SOTIZEM .... Societe Tiriss Zemmour (MAR)
SOTMES..... Sindicato Obrero Textil de Mejoramiento Social [*Trade Union for Social Improvement of Textile Workers*] [*Salvadoran*] (LA1)
SOTO .... Socialist Exchange of Technical Experience (BU)
SOTO .... Societe Dakaroise de Tolerie (MAR)
SOTOCA..... Societe Industrielle et Commerciale Togolaise du Cafe (MAR)
SOTOCAM ... Societe de Topographie au Cameroun (MAR)
SOTOCO..... Societe Togolaise du Coton [*Togolese Cotton Company*] (AF)
SOTODECO ... Societe Togolaise de Distribution Economique (MAR)
SOTOGIC.... Societe Togolaise de Gestion Immobiliere et de Constructions (MAR)
SOTOHOMA ... Societe Touristique et Hoteliere de Madagascar (MAR)
SOTOM .... Societe de Topographie de Madagascar (MAR)
SOTOMA..... Societe des Tabacs et Oleagineux de Madagascar (MAR)
SOTOMA..... Societe Togolaise de Marbrerie et Materiaux (MAR)
SOTOMAREY ... Societe Togolaise des Mareyeurs (MAR)
SOTOMARIAUX ... Societe Togolaise de Materiaux (MAR)
SOTOMECIA ... Societe Togolaise de Mecanisation Industrielle et Agricole (MAR)
SOTOPEMA ... Societe Togolaise des Pecheries Maritimes (MAR)
SOTOPLANT ... Societe Togolaise de Plantation (MAR)
SOTOPOLEF ... Societe Togolaise de Poissons et Legumes Frais (MAR)
SOTOPROCO ... Societe Togolaise d'Exportation de Produits Tropicaux (MAR)
SOTORAM ... Societe Touristique Royal Air Maroc (MAR)
SOTOREP ... Societe Togolaise de Rechapage de Pneus (MAR)
SOTOTRAC ... Societe Togolaise de Transit et de Consignation (MAR)
SOTP........... Societe Tunisienne de Petrole (MAR)
sotr............. Collaborator, Member of the Staff, Contributor (RU)
SOTRA .... Societe des Transports Abidjanais (MAR)
SOTRAB...... Societe de Transit du Benin (MAR)
SOTRAB-CI ... Societe de Travaux Publics et de Batiments Cote-d'Ivoire (MAR)
SOTRABO... Societe de Transformation du Bois (MAR)
SOTRABOI ... Societe de Transformation des Bois Ivoiriens (MAR)
SOTRAC ..... Societe de Transports en Commun du Cap-Vert (MAR)
SOTRACCA ... Societe de Transformation et de Commercialisation du Caoutchouc SA [*Rubber Processing and Marketing Company, Inc.*] [*Cambodian*] (CL)
SOTRACM ... Societe de Transports Routiers et de Commerce du Mungo (MAR)
SOTRACOB ... Societe de Transit et de Consignation du Benin [*Benin Transit and Storage Company*] (AF)
SOTRACOL ... Sociedad Transportadora Colombiana Ltda. [*Medellin*] (COL)
SOTRACOSS ... Societe de Transports en Common du Sine-Saloum (MAR)
SOTRAF...... Societe de Transit en Afrique Equatoriale (MAR)
SOTRAFOM ... Societe de Travaux Publics et de Terrassements de France et d'Outre Mer (MAR)
SOTRAFRIC ... Societe de Transports Africains (MAR)
SOTRAGAU ... Societe de Tranchage de la Gaume (MAR)
SOTRAHO... Societe de Travaux du Haut Ogooue (MAR)
SOTRAL...... Societe des Transports en Commun Librevillois (MAR)
SOTRALEC ... Societe de Travaux, d'Entretien, de Plomberie, et d'Electricite (MAR)
SOTRALLANO ... Sociedad Transportadora del Llano Ltda. [*Cali*] (COL)
SOTRAM..... Societe de Transports Mauritaniens (MAR)
SOTRAM..... Societe de Transports et de Reparations Automobiles de M'Balmayo (MAR)
SOTRAMEG ... Transformation de la Melasse [*Moroccan*] (MAR)
SOTRAMET ... Societe de Travaux Metalliques (MAR)
SOTRAMIL ... Societe de Transformation du Mil (MAR)
SOTRAMO ... Societe des Transports Modernes [*Tunisian*] (MAR)
SOTRANCO ... Societe de Transit de Consignation (MAR)
SOTRANEX ... Societe Auxiliaire de Transports et d'Exploitation de Bois Kouilou Niari (MAR)
SOTRANORD ... Societe Camerounaise de Transport du Nord-Cameroun (MAR)
SOTRANSO ... Societe des Transports de l'Ouest (MAR)
SOTRAPAR ... Societe de Travaux et de Participations (MAR)
SOTRASAN ... Sociedad Santandereana de Transportes [*Bucaramanga*] (COL)
SOTRASSUM ... Societe de Traitement des Sables du Sud de Madagascar (MAR)
SOTRASUM ... Societe des Terres Rares du Sud de Madagascar (MAR)
SOTRAT...... Societe de Transitaires Tchadiens (MAR)
SOTRATRANSCAM ... Societe Auxiliaire de Travaux Publics pour la Construction du Transcamerounais (MAR)
SOTRAUSQUE ... Sociedad de Transportes Unidos el Bosque Ltda. [*Barranquilla*] (COL)
SOTRAVIL .. Societe des Transports de Libreville (MAR)
SOTREC...... Societe des Trefileries et Clouteries en Cote-d'Ivoire (MAR)
SOTRECA... Societe des Transports en Centrafrique (MAR)
SOTREF ...... Societe Tropicale d'Exploitations Forestieres (MAR)
SOTREP...... Societe Tchadienne de Realisation et d'Entreprise de Pneumatiques (MAR)
SOTRI.......... Societe d'Exploitation des Ets. Tricon (MAR)
SOTRI.......... Societe de Transports Ivoiriens (MAR)
SOTRICO .... Societe Togolaise de Relance de l'Industrie et du Commerce (MAR)
SOTRIPA..... Societe de Transformation Industrielle des Produits Agricoles (MAR)
SOTROPAL ... Societe Tropicale des Allumettes (MAR)
SOTROPCO ... Societe Tropicale de Commerce (MAR)
sots .... Social, Socialist (RU)
sots .... Socialist (BU)
SOTS........... Society for Old Testament Study (MAR)
sots-dem .... Social Democrat, Social Democratic (RU)
Sotsekgiz.... State Publishing House of Literature on Social Sciences and Economics (RU)
Sotsintern... Socialist International (RU)
sotsiol .... Sociology (RU)
SOTSIRIZ.... Societe Tsimihety du Riz (MAR)
sotsobr........ Social Education (RU)
Sots pravo ... Sotsialistichesko Pravo [*Socialist Law*] [*A periodical*] (BU)
sotsvos .... Social Education (RU)
sotsvos .... Social Education Subdivision of the Department of Public Education (RU)
SOTUBAL ... Societe des Tubes d'Algerie (MAR)
SOTUC........ Societe des Transports Urbains du Cameroun (MAR)
SOTUCIB .... Societe Tunisienne de Ciment Blanc (MAR)
SOTUMACO ... Societe Tunisienne de Materiaux de Construction [*Tunisian Building Materials Company*] (AF)
SOTUMEX... Societe Tunisienne de Matieres Premieres Textiles (MAR)
SOTUPRI...... Societe Tunisienne de Production Industrielle [*Tunisian*] (MAR)
SOU............. Optical Light Device (RU)
SOU............. Sekretarijat za Opstu Upravu (SIV) [*Secretariat of General Administration*] (YU)
SOUH .... Statni Odborne Uciliste Hornicke [*State Training Center for Mining Specialists*] (CZ)
SOUR .... Slozena Organizacija Udruzenog Rada [*Collective Organization of Workers*] [*Yugoslav*]
sov.............. Perfective [*Aspect*] (RU)
SOV............. Persistent Chemical Agent (BU)
SOV............. Persistent Gas (RU)
SOV............. Series Field Winding (RU)
SOV............. Slovensky Oslobodzovaci Vybor [*Slovak Liberation Committee*] (CZ)
sov.............. Soviet (RU)
SOVANORD ... Societe de Valorisation de l'Anacardier du Nord (MAR)
SOVAPIA .... Societe de Vaporisation Industrielle Abidjanaise (MAR)
Sovbolstroy ... Soviet-Bulgarian Construction Company (BU)

sovdep........ Soviet of Workers', Peasants', and Red Army Deputies [*1917-1936*] (RU)
SOVE .... Symfoniki Orkhistra Voreiou Ellados [*Northern Greece Symphony Orchestra*] (GC)
SOVEA........ Societe Voltaique d'Exploitation Automobile (MAR)
SOVEC........ Societe Voltaique d'Etancheite et de Carrelage (MAR)
SOVECA ..... Societe de Vente de Cycles d'Alimentation (MAR)
SOVEDAE... Sociedad Venezolana de Derecho Aeronautico y Espacial [*Venezuelan Society of Aeronautical and Space Law*] (LA)
SOVEG........ Societe Voltaique d'Engineering et de Gestion (MAR)
Soveksportfil'm ... All-Union Association for the Export and Import of Motion Pictures (RU)
SOVEL .... Societe Voltaique d'Electronique, Radio, Electricite, Optique Electro-Acoustique (MAR)
SOVEM .... Societe pour la Vente d'Equipements et de Materiels (MAR)
SOVEMA..... Societe de Vente de Metaux et Alliages (MAR)
SOVEMA..... Societe Verrerie Malagasy (MAR)
SOVEMAN ... Societe de Vetements Manufactures (MAR)
SOVERPAL ... Societe de Vente de Produits Alimentaires (MAR)
sovers pererabot ... Completely Revised (RU)
soveshch .... Conference, Meeting (RU)
SOVETCO... Societe pour la Vente de Thons Congeles [*Frozen Tuna Marketing Company*] [*Ivorian*] (AF)
SOVETIV..... Societe des Vetements Ivoiriens (MAR)
Sovfrakht.... All-Union Association for the Chartering of Foreign Tonnage (RU)
SOVHOTEL ... Societe Voltaique d'Hotellerie et de Tourisme (MAR)
SOVI............ Societe Voltaique d'Infrastructures (MAR)
SOVIAMAD ... Societe des Viandes de Madagascar (MAR)
SOVIBO....... Societe des Vins et Boissons (MAR)
SOVIBOR .... Societe Vinicole Bordelaise (MAR)
SOVIC .... Societe Voltaique de l'Industrie du Cuir (MAR)
SOVICA....... Societe Voltaique d'Interet Collectif Agricole (MAR)
SOVICA....... Societe Voltaique d'Intervention et de Cooperation avec l'Agriculture (MAR)
SOVIEX .... Societe d'Exportation de Viandes (MAR)
SOVIMAS.... Societe Voltaique d'Importation Azar et Salem (MAR)
SOVINCI ..... Societe des Vins de la Cote-d'Ivoire (MAR)
SOVINCO.... Societe des Vins du Congo (MAR)
SOVINDAH ... Societe des Vins du Dahomey (MAR)
Sovinformbyuro ... Soviet Information Bureau [*Press agency*] (RU)
SOVINGAB ... Societe des Vins du Gabon (MAR)
SOVINGUI... Societe des Vins de la Guinee (MAR)
SOVINTO .... Sodas et Vins du Togo (MAR)
SOVITOUR ... Senegals Suedoise de Villages Touristiques (MAR)
sovkhozuch ... Sovkhoz Apprenticeship School (RU)
sovmin .... Council of Ministers (RU)
SOVOBRA... Societe Voltaique de Brasserie (MAR)
SOVOCA..... Societe Voltaique de Credit Automobile (MAR)
SOVODA..... Societe Voltaique pour le Developpement de l'Automobile (MAR)
SOVODIA.... Societe Voltaique de Diffusion Automobile et Aeronautique [*Ougadougou*] (MAR)
SOVOFA ..... Societe Voltaique des Ets. Faddoui (MAR)
SOVOFER ... Societe Voltaique de Ferronnerie et de Charpentes Metalliques (MAR)
SOVOG .... Societe Voltaique de Groupage (MAR)
SOVOG .... Sozialistiche Volksorganisation [*Socialist National Community*] [*Lithuanian*] (PPE)
SOVOIC ...... Societe Voltaique Industrielle et Commerciale (MAR)
SOVOLCI .... Societe Voltaique de Commerce et d'Industrie (MAR)
SOVOLCOM ... Societe Voltaique de Commercialisation (MAR)
SOVOLDIA ... Societe Voltaique de Diffusion Industrielle et Automobile (MAR)
SOVOLPLAS ... Societe Voltaique de Plastique (MAR)
SOVOLTA ... Societe Voltaique de Tanneries et des Industries du Cuir (MAR)
SOVOMEA ... Societe Voltaique de Montage et d'Exploitation Automobile (MAR)
SOVORES... Societe Voltaique de Revetement et Sanitaire (MAR)
SOVOTRA... Societe Voltaique d'Entreprise Hadiffe & Cie. (MAR)
sovp .... Coincidence (RU)
Sov p.......... Soviet Patent (RU)
sovprof........ Trade-Union Council (RU)
sovr .... Modern, Contemporary, Up-to-Date (RU)
SOVROM..... Intreprinderea Sovietica-Romana [*Soviet-Romanian Enterprise*] (RO)
SOVS .... Sanitetsko Odeljenje Vrhovnog Staba [*Medical Department of the General Staff*] (YU)
sov sekr ...... Top Secret (RU)
sovsod .... Assistance Council (RU)
SOVT........... Socialist Exchange of Experience in Water Transportation (RU)
Sovtorgflot ... Soviet Merchant Marine (RU)
SOW............ Slaski Okreg Wojskowy [*Silesian Military District*] (POL)
SOWI........... Samodzielny Oddzial Wykonawstwa Inwestycyjnego [*Autonomous Investment Operations Branch*] (POL)
SOXGE........ (Pankypria) Syndekhnia Oikodomon, Xylourgon, kai Genikon Ergaton [*(Pan-Cyprian) Union of Construction Workers, Carpenters, and General Workers*] (GC)
SOY............. Soma Oikonomikon Ypiresion [*Finance Corps*] [*Army*] (GC)
SOYe........... Static Exchange Capacitance (RU)
soyed .... Compound (RU)
SOYP........... Servicio Oceanografico y de Pesca [*State Oceanographic and Fisheries Service*] [*Uruguayan*] (LA)
SOYTAS...... Sosyal Yatirmlar Organizasyon ve Ticaret Anonim Sirketi [*Social Investments Organization and Trade Corporation*] (TU)
Soyuzalyuminiy ... All-Union Administration of the Aluminum Industry (RU)
Soyuzantiseptik ... State Trust for Antiseptic Treating and Preservation of Wood in Construction of the Glavspetspromstroy (RU)
Soyuzavtosel'mash ... Main Administration for Interrepublic Deliveries of Automobiles, Tractors, Agricultural Machines, and Their Spare Parts (RU)
Soyuzbummash ... All-Union Trust for Machinery and Spare Parts Manufacture of the Ministry of the Paper and Woodworking Industries, USSR (RU)
SOYuZDORNII ... State All-Union Scientific Research Institute of Roads and Highways (RU)
Soyuzdorproyekt ... State Institute for the Planning and Surveying of Highways of the State Industrial Committee for Transportation Construction, USSR (RU)
Soyuzdvigatel'remmontazh ... All-Union Trust for the Repair of Internal-Combustion Engines and Locomobiles of the Glavdizel' (RU)
Soyuzenergoremtrest ... State All-Union Trust for the Repair of Power Engineering Equipment of the Glavenergoremont of the State Industrial Committee for Power Engineering and Electrification, USSR (RU)
Soyuzgaz .... State Trust for the Extraction and Processing of Natural Gas and Helium (RU)
Soyuzgeomash ... All-Union Trust for the Manufacture of Geological Exploration Equipment and Geophysical Instruments (RU)
Soyuzgeoneftepribor ... State All-Union Trust for Geophysical and Petroleum Instrument Making (RU)
Soyuzgidromekhanizatsiya ... State All-Union Trust for Planning and Performing Hydraulic Mechanized Operations (RU)
Soyuzgiprotorg ... All-Union State Institute for the Planning of Trade Establishments and Public Eating Facilities (RU)
Soyuzglavenergo ... Main Power Engineering Administration (RU)
Soyuzglavkhim ... Main Administration for Interrepublic Deliveries of Chemical and Industrial Rubber Products (RU)
Soyuzglavkhimkomplekt ... Main Administration for Ensuring the Supply of Complete Sets of Equipment, Instruments, Cables, and Other Products for High-Priority Construction Projects of the Chemical and Pulp and Paper Industries (RU)
Soyuzglavkomplekt ... Main Administration for Ensuring the Supply of Complete Sets of Equipment, Instruments, Cables, and Other Manufactures for High-Priority Construction Projects in the Coal, Petroleum, and Other Branches of Industry (RU)
Soyuzglavlegpromsyr'ye ... Main Administration for Interrepublic Deliveries of Raw Materials for Light Industry (RU)
Soyuzglavmash ... Main Administration for Interrepublic Deliveries of Machinery (RU)
Soyuzglavmetall ... Main Administration for Interrepublic Deliveries of Metal Products (RU)
Soyuzglavmetallurgkomplekt ... Main Administration for Ensuring the Supply of Complete Sets of Equipment, Instruments, Cables, and Other Products for High-Priority Construction Projects of Ferrous and Nonferrous Metallurgy (RU)
Soyuzglavneft' ... Main Administration for Interrepublic Deliveries of Petroleum Products (RU)
Soyuzglavpishchepromsyr'ye ... Main Administration for Interrepublic Deliveries of Raw Materials for the Food Industry (RU)
Soyuzglavradiokomplekt ... Main Administration for Ensuring the Supply of Complete Sets of Equipment, Instruments, Cables, and Other Products for High-Priority Construction Projects of the Radio Electronics Industry (RU)
Soyuzglavstroykomplekt ... Main Administration for Ensuring the Supply of Complete Sets of Equipment, Instruments, Cables, and Other Products for High-Priority Construction Projects of the Building Materials and Construction Industries (RU)
Soyuzglavstroymaterialy ... Main Administration for Interrepublic Deliveries of Lumber and Building Materials (RU)
Soyuzglavtorg ... Main Administration for Interrepublic Deliveries of Consumer Goods (RU)
Soyuzglavtyazhmash ... Main Administration for Interrepublic Deliveries of Heavy Machinery (RU)
Soyuzglavugol' ... Main Administration for Interrepublic Deliveries of Coal (RU)
Soyuzgostsirk ... All-Union Association of State Circuses (RU)
Soyuzkhimeksport ... All-Union Association for the Export and Import of Chemicals (RU)
Soyuzkhimfarmtorg ... All-Union Office for Trade in Chemicals, Pharmaceuticals, and Hygienic Goods (RU)
Soyuzkislorodmontazh ... All-Union State Trust for the Installation of Oxygen Plants and Units (RU)
Soyuzkniga ... All-Union Book Trade Association (RU)
Soyuzkoopvneshtorg ... All-Union Cooperative Foreign Trade Association (RU)
Soyuzleksyr'ye ... All-Union Office for the Procurement of Medicinal Plants (RU)

Soyuzlessempitomnik ... All-Union Association of Tree Nurseries and Seed Procurement (RU)
Soyuzlift...... State Trust of the Glavtekhmontazh of the Gosmontazhspetsstroy SSSR (RU)
Soyuzliftomontazh ... All-Union Office for the Supply and Installation of Elevators (RU)
Soyuzmarkshtrest ... All-Union Mine-Surveying Trust (RU)
Soyuzmedinstrumenttorg ... All-Union Office for the Procurement, Marketing, and Sale of Medical Instruments and Equipment (RU)
Soyuzmedoborudovaniye ... All-Union Office for the Supply and Sale of Medical Equipment (RU)
Soyuzmorniiproyekt ... State Planning, Design, and Scientific Research Institute of Marine Transportation of the Ministry of the Maritime Fleet, USSR (RU)
Soyuzmorproyekt ... State Institute for the Planning of Seaports and Ship-Repair Establishments (RU)
Soyuzmul'tifil'm ... All-Union Animated Cartoon Studio (RU)
Soyuznefteburmashremont ... State All-Union Trust for the Repair of Drilling Equipment of the Ministry of the Petroleum Industry, USSR (RU)
Soyuznefteeksport ... All-Union Association for the Export and Import of Petroleum and Petroleum Products (RU)
Soyuznefteپribor ... All-Union Technical Office for the Supply of Complete Sets of Control and Measuring Instruments and Automation Equipment of the Ministry of the Petroleum Industry, USSR (RU)
Soyuzneftestroymekhanizatsiya ... All-Union Trust of the Glavneftestroymekhanizatsiya (RU)
Soyuzneftetara ... State All-Union Trust for the Manufacture of Petroleum Containers (RU)
Soyuznerudstroy ... State All-Union Trust for the Construction of Nonmetallic Building Materials Establishments (RU)
SoyuzNIKhI ... All-Union Scientific Research Institute of Cotton Growing (RU)
SoyuzOSVOD ... Union of Societies for Furthering the Development of Water Transportation and for the Safeguarding of Human Lives on Waterways of the USSR [*1931-1956*] (RU)
Soyuzpechat' ... Main Administration for the Distribution of Publications (RU)
Soyuzplodotara ... All-Union Packing Materials Office of the Glavkoopplodoovoshch (RU)
Soyuzposyltorg ... All-Union Mail-Order Office (RU)
Soyuzprokatmontazh ... State All-Union Trust for the Installation of Mechanical Equipment in Rolling Mills of Metallurgical Plants (RU)
Soyuzpromeksport ... All-Union Association of the Ministry of Foreign Trade, USSR (RU)
Soyuzprommekhanizatsiya ... Planning and Installation Trust of the Glavtekhmontazh of the Ministry of Construction, RSFSR (RU)
Soyuzprommontazh ... State All-Union Construction and Installation Trust of the Ministry of Construction of Establishments of the Metallurgical and Chemical Industries, USSR (RU)
Soyuzpushnina ... All-Union Association for the Export and Import of Fur Goods (RU)
Soyuzreaktivsbyt ... All-Union Office for the Marketing of Chemically Pure Reagents (RU)
Soyuzrybpromkadry ... All-Union Office for the Organized Hiring of Workers for the Fish Industry (RU)
Soyuzsel'elektro ... All-Union Association for Rural Electrification (RU)
Soyuzshlak ... All-Union Trust for the Processing of Industrial Slags (RU)
Soyuzsnav ... Union of Societies for Lifesaving on Waterways of the USSR [*1928-1931*] (RU)
Soyuzsortsemovoshch ... All-Union Office for the Production, Procurement, and Sale of High-Quality Seeds of Vegetables, Melons, and Food Roots (RU)
Soyuzsovkhozremmash ... Administration of Repair and Machine Plants of the Ministry of Sovkhozes, USSR (RU)
Soyuzspetsstroy ... All-Union Trust for Special Operations of the Glavspetsstroy (RU)
Soyuzsportproyekt ... All-Union Institute for the Planning of Sports Installations (RU)
Soyuzsteklosbyt ... All-Union Office for the Marketing of Glassware (RU)
Soyuzsteklostroy ... State All-Union Construction and Installation Trust of the Ministry of the Building Materials Industry of the USSR (RU)
Soyuztelefonstroy ... All-Union Trust of the Ministry of Communications, USSR (RU)
Soyuzteplostroy ... State Trust of the Glavteplomontazh of the Gosmontazhspetsstroy SSSR (RU)
Soyuztorgtrans ... All-Union Transportation Trust of the Ministry of Trade, USSR (RU)
Soyuztsemremont ... All-Union Trust for the Repair of Cement Plant Equipment (RU)
Soyuztverdosplav ... All-Union Trust of the Hard Alloys Industry (RU)
Soyuzvzryvprom ... Trust for Drilling and Blasting Operations of the Glavspetspromstroy (RU)
Soyuzzagottrans ... Main Administration of Automobile Transportation of the Ministry of Procurement, USSR (RU)
Soyuzzcovetsnab ... All-Union Trust for the Supply of Agriculture with Veterinary and Zootechnical Equipment, Instruments, and Drugs (RU)
Soyuzzdravpromstroy ... All-Union Construction Trust of the Administration of Capital Construction of the Ministry of Public Health, USSR (RU)
Soyuzzhivkontora ... All-Union Office for the Procurement and Marketing of Pedigree Cattle (RU)
SOZ............ Association for Common Land Cultivation (RU)
SOZ............ Samodzielne Oddzialy Zaopatrzenia [*Independent Supply Branches*] (POL)
SOZ............ Soviet Zone of Occupation (BU)
SOZ............ Swiatowa Organizacja Zdrowia [*World Health Organization*] [*Polish*]
SOZ............ World Health Organization (BU)
SOZACOM ... Societe Zairoise de Commercialisation des Minerais [*Zairian Company for the Marketing of Ores*] (AF)
SOZATEF.... Societe Zairoise de Tenke Fungurumi (MAR)
SOZh.......... Railroad Workers' Union (RU)
SOZIR.......... Societe Zairo-Italienne de Raffinage [*Zairian-Italian Refining Company*] (AF)
sp .... Alcohol, Ethel Alcohol (RU)
SP................ Blasting Cable, Firing Wire (RU)
SP................ Blinker, Blinking Device (RU)
SP................ Call Sign Selector (RU)
sp .... Centipoise (RU)
SP................ Clearing Station [*Military medicine*] (RU)
sp .... Cleavage (RU)
SP................ Collection of Government Regulations and Decrees (RU)
sp .... Combat Engineer (RU)
SP................ Connecting Point (RU)
SP................ Construction Industry (RU)
SP................ Deadmelt (RU)
SP................ Economic Enterprise (BU)
SP................ Erste Staatspruefung [*German*]
SP................ Feeder Bay (RU)
SP................ Freight Car with Perishable Goods (RU)
SP................ Instrument Landing (RU)
SP................ Joint Enterprises (BU)
SP- .... Landing System (RU)
SP................ Le Saint Pere [*French*] (MTD)
sp .... Magazine, Periodical, Journal (BU)
SP................ Medical Station (RU)
SP................ Monitoring Station (RU)
SP- .... North Pole [*Drifting station*] (RU)
SP................ Receiving Selsyn (RU)
sp .... Rifle Regiment (BU)
SP................ Rifle Regiment (RU)
SP................ Routine [*Computers*] (RU)
SP................ Sanford Papers (MAR)
SP................ Saobracajno Preduzece [*Transportation Establishment*] (YU)
SP................ Sapeurs-Pompiers [*French*]
SP................ Savezno Pravobraniostvo (SIV) [*Federal Body of Government Attorneys*] (YU)
SP................ Sbor Poverenikov [*Board of Commissioners*] (CZ)
SP................ Secteur Postal [*French*]
SP................ Section de Parc de Campagne [*Military*] [*French*] (MTD)
SP................ Seismic Detector (RU)
SP................ Sekcija za Puteve [*Roads Section*] (YU)
SP................ Sekretarijat za Promet (ISLRS) [*Secretariat of Trade*] (YU)
SP................ Self-Discharging Flatcar (RU)
SP................ Self-Polarization (RU)
SP................ Semensko Preduzece [*Seeds Establishment*] (YU)
SP................ Senggara Perhubongan [*Line of Communication*] (ML)
SP................ Senoi Praaq [*Fighting People*] (ML)
Sp................ Senterpartiet [*Center Party*] [*Norwegian*] (PPE)
SP................ Seri Pahlawan Gagah Perkasa [*Supreme Gallantry (Decoration)*] [*Malaysian*] (ML)
SP................ Service de Presse [*French*]
SP................ Servodrive (RU)
SP................ Shipbuilding Industry (RU)
SP................ Siege et Place [*Guns*] [*French*] (MTD)
SP................ Sikkim Parishad [*Indian*] (PPW)
SP................ Sindicato de la Prensa [*Journalists Union*] [*Venezuelan*] (LA)
sp .... Sine Prole [*Without Issue*] [*Latin*] (GPO)
SP................ Skupni Pasnik [*Collective Pasture*] (YU)
SP................ Slovenske Pohlady [*The Slovak View*] [*A periodical*] (CZ)
SP................ Slovenski Porocevalec [*Slovenian Reporter*] [*Ljubljana*] [*A periodical*] (YU)
SP................ Slovenski Pravopis [*Slovenian Orthography*] [*A periodical*] (YU)
SP................ Sluzba Polsce [*Service to Poland*] [*Semimilitary youth organization (1948-1955)*] (POL)
SP................ Socialistiska Partiet [*Socialist Party*] [*Swedish*] (WEN)
SP................ Sodobna Pedagogika [*Contemporary Pedagogy*] [*A periodical*] (YU)
SP................ Sofia Enterprise (BU)
SP- .... Solar Furnace (RU)
SP................ Sosialistiki Poreia [*Socialist Path*] [*Greek*] (GC)
SP................ Sosyalist Partisi [*Socialist Party*] [*Organized May 30, 1975*] (TU)

SP .... Sotsialisticheskо Pravo [*Socialist Law*] [*A periodical*] (BU)
SP .... Souhrny Plan [*Master Plan*] (CZ)
Sp .... Sous-Prefecture [*Sub-Prefecture*] [*Military map abbreviation*] [*World War I*] [*French*] (MTD)
SP .... Soviet Law (RU)
SP .... Sozialistische Partei [*Socialist Party*] (EG)
Sp .... Spalte [*Column*] [*German*] (GPO)
sp .... Spanyol [*Spanish*] (HU)
SP .... Sparkasse [*Savings Bank*] (EG)
sp .... Special (BU)
SP .... Speditersko Poduzece [*Forwarding Establishment*] (YU)
sp .... Spisanie [*Periodical*] (YU)
SP .... Spoldzielnia Pracy [*Polish*]
SP .... Spoldzielnia Produkcyjna [*Producer Cooperative*] [*Collective farm*] (POL)
sp .... Sport (BU)
sp .... Sport [*Sport*] (HU)
SP .... Staff Paper (MAR)
SP .... Stamparsko Preduzece [*Printing Establishment*] (YU)
SP .... Start Position (RU)
SP .... Statni Pojistovna [*State Insurance Agency*] (CZ)
SP .... Statni Studijni Knihovna, Plzen [*State Research Library in Plzen*] (CZ)
SP .... Statni Vedecka Knihovna, Plzen [*State Research Library in Plzen*] (CZ)
SP .... Steady-State Parameter (RU)
SP .... Steam Separator (RU)
SP .... Stolarsko Preduzece [*Carpentry Establishment*] (YU)
SP .... Strojevo Pravilo [*Regulation on Military Formations*] (YU)
SP .... Stronnictwo Pracy [*Labor Party*] (POL)
SP .... Sudan Programme (MAR)
SP .... Sudanese Pound (MAR)
SP .... Sudija za Prekrsaje [*Magistrate for Misdemeanors*] (YU)
SP .... Sumarsko Preduzece [*Forestry Establishment*] (YU)
sp .... Swietej Pamieci [*The Late*] (POL)
SP .... Syllogos (Synomospondia) Pratirioukhon [*Association of (Confederation of) Gas Station Owners*] (GC1)
SP .... Syndaktiki Praxis [*Constituent Act*] (GC)
SP .... Sztandar Pracy [*Banner of Labor*] [*Award*] (POL)
SP .... Trunks [*Telephony*] (RU)
SP .... Trusteeship Council (BU)
SP .... Union of Writers (RU)
Sp1 .... Spesialis I [*Academic degree*] [*Indonesian*]
Sp2 .... Spesialis II [*Academic degree*] [*Indonesian*]
SPA .... Singapore People's Alliance (ML)
SPA .... Sistema de Produccion Agropecuaria [*Agriculture and Livestock Production System*] [*Peruvian*] (LA)
SPA .... Slovenska Polnohospodarska Akademia [*Slovak Agricultural Academy*] (CZ)
SPA .... Socialist Party of Austria (RU)
SPA .... Sociedade Portuguesa de Autores [*Portuguese Authors' Society*] (WER)
SpA .... Societa per Azioni [*Public Limited Company*] [*Italian*]
SPA .... Societe Protectrice des Animaux [*Society for the Prevention of Cruelty to Animals*] [*French*] (WER)
SPA .... Somali Ports Authority (MAR)
SPA .... Spolek Posluchacu Architektury [*Society of University Students of Architecture*] (CZ)
SPA .... Stoleczne Przedsiebiorstwo Aptek [*Warsaw Pharmaceutical Enterprise*] (POL)
SPA .... Sudanese Press Agency (MAR)
SPA .... Sugar Producers Association [*Barbadian*] (LA1)
SPA .... Surohanjaya Pelajaran Awam [*Commissioner of Public Education*] (ML)
SPA .... Symvoulion Pliroforion kai Asfaleias [*Intelligence and Security Council*] [*Greek*] (GC)
SPAA .... Srednjokalibarska Protivavionska Artiljerija [*Medium Caliber Antiaircraft Artillery*] (YU)
SPABA .... Societe des Plantations de l'Ake Befia et Anonkoua (MAR)
SPAC .... Societe Senegalaise de Produits Alimentaires Congeles (MAR)
SPAC .... Society for the Promotion of African Culture (MAR)
SPACI .... Societe de Pecheries Africaines de Cote-d'Ivoire (MAR)
SPAD .... Sistem de Prelucrare Automatica a Datelor [*Automatic Data Processing System*] (RO)
SPAD .... Societe des Produits Agnis-Diabes (MAR)
SPADI .... Societe des Plantations d'Ananas de Divo (MAR)
SPAFE .... Societe des Petroles d'Afrique Equatoriale [*Petroleum Company of Equatorial Africa*] [*French*] (AF)
SPAFI .... Societe Pan-Africaine d'Investissement (MAR)
SPAFIF .... Southern Province African Farming Improvement Fund (MAR)
SPAGA .... Syndicat Professionnel des Agents Generaux d'Assurances (MAR)
SPAH .... Champs Elysees. Societe Parisienne et Africaine d'Habillement (MAR)
SPAK .... Synepis Politikon Aristeron Kinima [*Consistent Political Movement of the Left*] [*Greek*] (GC)
SPAM .... Damaged-Vehicle Collecting Point (RU)
SPAM .... Stowarzyszenie Polskich Artystow Muzykow [*Polish Musicians' Association*]
SPAM .... Wrecked Motor Vehicles Collecting Point (BU)
SPAMF .... Seychelles Popular Anti-Marxist Front (PD)
SPAN .... Societe des Plantations d'Ananas de Nianda (MAR)
SPANA .... Society for the Protection of Animals in North Africa (MAR)
SPAP .... Sidirodromoi Peiraios-Athinon-Peloponnisou [*Piraeus-Athens-Peloponnisos Railways*] (GC)
SPAR .... Federation des Societes Publiques d'Action Rurale [*Togolese*] (MAR)
SPARS .... Skypower Automated Reservation System (MAR)
SPAS .... Societatis Philosophiae Americanae Socius [*Fellow of the American Philosophical Society*] [*Latin*] (GPO)
SPAS .... Societe Professionnelle et Agricole de la Sakay (MAR)
SPAS .... Syndicat des Professeurs Africains du Senegal [*Union of African Professors of Senegal*] (AF)
SPASK .... Service Provincial de l'Agriculture de Sud Kivu (MAR)
spas st .... Lifesaving Station [*Topography*] (RU)
SPAT .... Societe des Produits Agricoles Tropicaux (MAR)
SPATiF .... Stowarzyszenie Polskich Artystow Teatru i Filmu [*Association of Polish Film and Theatre Actors*] (POL)
SPB .... Bombsight Interference Station (RU)
spb .... Epidemic-Control Battalion (RU)
SPB .... High-Speed Dive Bomber (RU)
SPB .... Information and Bibliographic Office (RU)
SPb .... Saint Petersburg (BU)
SPB .... Saint Petersburg (RU)
SPB .... Sbor Pohranicni Bezpecnosti [*Border Region Security Corps*] (CZ)
SPB .... Societe des Plantations Boudou (MAR)
SPB .... Special Planning Office (RU)
SPB .... Spoleczne Przedsiebiorstwo Budowlane [*People's Construction Enterprise*] (POL)
SPB .... Stoleczne Przedsiebiorstwo Budowlane [*Warsaw Construction Enterprise*] (POL)
SPB .... Svaz Protifasistickych Bojovniku [*Union of Anti-Fascist Fighters*] (CZ)
SpBAkN .... Spisanie na Bulgarskata Akademiya na Naukite [*Journal of the Bulgarian Academy of Sciences*] [*A publication*] (BU)
SpBAN .... Spisanie na Bulgarskata Akademiya na Naukite [*Journal of the Bulgarian Academy of Sciences*] [*A publication*] (BU)
SpBAN kl ist fil ... Journal of the Bulgarian Academy of Sciences, History and Philology Section [*A publication*] (BU)
SPBIAD .... Spisanie na Bulgarskoto Inzhenerno-Arkhitektno Druzhestvo [*Journal of the Bulgarian Engineers and Architects Association*] [*A publication*] (BU)
SpBID .... Spisanie na Bulgarskoto Ikonomichesko Druzhestvo [*Journal of the Bulgarian Society of Economists*] [*A publication*] (BU)
SpBIkD .... Spisanie na Bulgarskoto Ikonomichesko Druzhestvo [*Journal of the Bulgarian Society of Economists*] [*A publication*] (BU)
Sp na Bulg akad na naukite ... Spisanie na Bulgarskata Akademiya na Naukite [*Journal of the Bulgarian Academy of Sciences*] [*A publication*] (BU)
Sp na Bulg geol d-vo ... Spisanie na Bulgarskoto Geologichesko Druzhestvo [*Journal of the Bulgarian Geological Society*] [*A publication*] (BU)
Sp Bulg geol d-vo ... Spisanie na Bulgarskoto Geologichesko Druzhestvo [*Journal of the Bulgarian Geological Society*] [*A publication*] (BU)
SPBZ .... Sokolovsky Pretek Brannej Zdatnosti [*Sokolov Defense Preparedness Contest*] (CZ)
SPC .... Sea Ports Corporation [*Sudanese*] (MAR)
SPC .... Societe des Potasses du Congo [*Congolese Potash Company*] (AF)
SPC .... Societe de Promotion Commerciale (MAR)
SPC .... Srpska Pravoslavna Crkva [*Serbian Orthodox Church*] (YU)
SPC .... Sudan Petrol Corporation (MAR)
SPC .... Supreme People's Council (MAR)
SPC .... Syrian Petroleum Company (ME)
SPCA-THUBET ... Societe Parisienne de Comptoirs Africains A. Thubet (MAR)
SPCDRO .... Secretariat Permanent du Comite Directeur de la Recherche Operationnelle [*Permanent Secretariat of the Managing Committee on Operations Research*] [*French*] (WER)
sp ch .... Spectroscopically Pure (RU)
SPCI .... Societe de Promotion Commerciale Ivoirienne (MAR)
SPCK .... Society for Promoting Christian Knowledge (MAR)
SPCN .... Sciences Physiques, Chimiques, Naturelles (Certificat) [*Certificate in Physical, Chemical, and Natural Sciences*] (CL)
SPCN .... Societe des Plantations de Cafe de la Nome (MAR)
SPCN .... Societe des Produits Chimiques du Niger (MAR)
SPD .... Free-Piston Engine (RU)
SPD .... Message Center (RU)
SPD .... Secretaria de Prensa y Difusion [*Press and Propaganda Secretariat*] [*Argentine*] (LA)
SPD .... Slovensko Planinsko Drustvo [*Slovenian Alpine Society*] (YU)
SPD .... Sosyal Planlama Dairesi [*Social Planning Office*] [*Under State Planning Organization*] (TU)
SPD .... Sozialdemokratische Partei Deutschlands [*Social Democratic Party of Germany*] [*West German*] (WEN)
SPD .... Srpsko Pevacko Drustvo [*Serbian Singing Society*] (YU)
SPD .... Stredíska Pracujiciho Dorostu [*Young Workers' Centers*] (CZ)
SPD- .... Train Dispatcher Communications (RU)
SPDA .... Societe Peinture Decoration Africaine (MAR)

SPDB.......... Production Dispatch Office Communications System (RU)
SPDC.......... Societe du Palace de Cocody (MAR)
SPDK.......... Free-Piston Diesel Compressor (RU)
SPDO.......... Production Dispatch Department Communications System (RU)
SPDP.......... Caplan & Cie., Societe des Plantations Djongo-Penja (MAR)
SPDV.......... Societe pour le Developpement du Petrole Vert [*French*]
SPE.......... All-Union Association for the Export of Industrial Equipment (RU)
SPE.......... Senegalaise de Plomberie et d'Equipement (MAR)
SPE.......... Service Presidentiel Zairois des Etudes (MAR)
SPE.......... Sociedad Peruana de Escritores [*Association of Peruvian Writers*] (LA)
SPE.......... Societe des Plantations d'Elima (MAR)
SPE.......... Sosialistiki Panspoudastiki Enosi [*Socialist All-Student Union*] [*Greek*] (GC)
SPE.......... Symvoulion Proothiseos Exagogon [*Exports Promotion Council*] (GC)
SPEA.......... Servico de Pesquisas Economicas Aplicadas [*Applied Economic Research Bureau*] [*Brazilian*] (LA)
SPEA.......... Synergatiki Promithevtiki Enosis Ammokhostou-Larnakos [*Famagusta-Larnaca Cooperative Supply Union*] (GC)
speb.......... Epidemic Control Battalion (RU)
SPEC.......... Service Provisoire des Eaux du Cameroun (MAR)
spec.......... Specialis [*Special*] (HU)
spec.......... Specifisch [*Specific*] [*German*]
S pech.......... With Seal (BU)
SPECI.......... Societe de Publication de l'Edition de Cote-d'Ivoire (MAR)
SPECIA.......... Societe Parisienne d'Expansion Chimique (MAR)
SPECOMME ... Specified Command, Middle East (MAR)
SPED.......... Epidemic Control Team (RU)
SPED.......... Syndicat du Personnel de l'Enseignement Libre du Dahomey (MAR)
SPEIA.......... Syndicat Patronal des Entreprises et Industries Agricoles (MAR)
SPEIN.......... Syndicat Patronal des Entreprises et Industries du Niger (MAR)
SPEKA.......... Synetairistiki Promithevtiki kai Emboriki Enosi [*Cooperative Supply and Commercial Union*] [*Greek*] (GC)
SPEKO.......... Special Counterintelligence Section (RU)
spektr an..... Spectral Analysis (RU)
SPEL.......... Synergatiki Promithevtiki Enosis Ltd., Lefkosias [*Nicosia Cooperative Supply Union Ltd.*] (GC)
SPEM.......... Societe de Presse et d'Edition de Madagascar (MAR)
speo.......... Antiepidemiological Medical Detachment (BU)
SPEO.......... Epidemic Control Detachment (RU)
SPEPREV.... Societe de Peinture Entretien Plomberie Revetement Etancheite Vitrerie (MAR)
SPER.......... Syndicat des Industries de Materiel Professionnel Electronique et Radio Electrique (MAR)
spets.......... Special, Special Term (RU)
spets.......... Special, Specialist (BU)
spetskurs.... Special Course (BU)
Spetslag..... Special [*Corrective Labor*] Camp (RU)
Spetslagpunkt ... Special [*Corrective Labor*] Camp Section (RU)
Spetsrybmontazh ... State All-Union Specialized Trust of the Glavrybstroy (RU)
Spetsset'stroy ... Trust for the Construction of Power Transmission Lines and Substations of the Glavvostokelektroset'stroy (RU)
spetsstroy... Special Construction Projects Enterprise (BU)
Spetsstroy ... State All-Union Trust of Specialized Operations of the Glavstroy (RU)
Spetsstroymontazh ... Specialized Construction and Installation Trust (RU)
spetsVTEK ... Special Medical Commission for Determination of Disability (RU)
Spetszhelezobetonstroy ... State Specialized Trust for Reinforced Concrete Structures (RU)
SPEU.......... Singapore Printing Employees Union (ML)
spez.......... Specifisch [*Specific*] [*German*]
spez.......... Speziell [*Especially*] [*German*]
Spez Gew ... Spezifisches Gewicht [*Specific Gravity*] [*German*]
spezif.......... Spezifisch [*Specific*] [*German*]
SPF.......... Secours Populaire Francais [*French Popular Relief*] (WER)
SPF.......... Societe des Plantations de Foumban (MAR)
SPF.......... Societe de Prospections Forestieres (MAR)
SPF.......... Socijalisticka Partija Francuske [*Socialist Party of France*] (YU)
SPF.......... Storehouse for Semifinished Products (RU)
SPF.......... Trade-Union Council of the Philippines (RU)
SPFI.......... Secretaria de Patrimonio y Fomento Industrial [*Secretariat of Patrimony and Industrial Development*] [*Mexican*] (LA)
SPFS.......... Societe des Palmeraies de la Ferme Suisse [*Cameroonian*] (MAR)
SPG.......... Goryunov Heavy Machine Gun (RU)
SPG.......... Section de Parc du Genie [*Military*] [*French*] (MTD)
SPG.......... Sekolah Pendidikan Guru [*Teacher-Training Institutions*] [*Indonesian*]
SPG.......... Sistema de Preferencias Generalizadas [*Most-Favored-Nations System*] [*Spanish*] (WER)
SPG.......... Societe Pharmaceutique Guyanaise [*Pharmaceutical Society of French Guiana*] (LA1)
SPG.......... Society for the Propagation of the Gospel in Foreign Parts (MAR)
Sp G.......... Spezifisches Gewicht [*Specific Gravity*] [*German*]
SPG.......... Systeme des Preferences Generalisees [*System of Generalized Preferences*] [*French*] (AF)
SPGB.......... Socialist Party of Great Britain (PPW)
SPGC.......... Societe de Participation et de Gestion au Congo (MAR)
SPGG.......... Free-Piston Gas Generator, Free-Piston Gasifier (RU)
SPH.......... Savjet za Prosvjetu Hrvatske [*Educational Council of Croatia*] (YU)
SPH.......... Socialisticke Podnikove Hospodarstvi [*Socialist Enterprise Management*] (CZ)
SPHB.......... Societe des Plantations et Huileries de Bingerville (MAR)
SPHC.......... Societe de Plantations d'Heveas et de Cafeiers (MAR)
SPHM.......... Sprava Pohonne Hmoty a Mazadla [*Petroleum Products and Lubricants Directorate*] (CZ)
SPHU.......... Societe Proprietaire de l'Hotel de l'Union (MAR)
SPI.......... Saratov Polytechnic Institute (RU)
SPI.......... Savet za Preradivacku Industriju [*Council for the Manufacturing Industry*] (YU)
SPI.......... Service Pedologique Interafricain (MAR)
SPI.......... Servico de Protecao aos Indios [*Indian Protection Service*] [*Brazilian*] (LA)
SPI.......... Soviet and Party Publishing Houses (RU)
SPIA.......... Service Pedologique Interafricain (MAR)
SPIC.......... Societe de Participations Industrielles et Commerciales (MAR)
SPIC.......... Societe de Promotion Immobiliere du Cameroun (MAR)
spich.......... Match Factory [*Topography*] (RU)
SPICh.......... Spolek Posluchacu Chemickotechnologickeho Inzenyrstvi [*Association of University Students of Chemical Engineering*] (CZ)
SPIDS.......... Syndicat Patronal des Industries de Dakar et du Senegal [*Industry Employers Association of Dakar and Senegal*] (AF)
SPIE.......... Secretariat Professionnel International de l'Enseignement [*International Federation of Free Teachers' Unions - IFFTU*] (EA)
SPIE.......... Societe Parisienne pour l'Industrie Electrique (MAR)
SPIEA.......... Syndicat Professionnel de l'Industrie des Engrais Azotes (MAR)
SPIF.......... Societe de Participations Industrielles and Financieres (MAR)
Sp IGDS...... Spisanie i Izvestiya na Glavnata Direktsiya na Statistikata [*Journal and Bulletin of the Main Statistical Office*] [*A publication*] (BU)
SPIK.......... Spolek Posluchacu Inzenyrstvi Komercniho [*Association of School of Business Administration Students*] (CZ)
SPIM.......... Syndikalistiki Parataxi Ilektrologon-Mikhanologon [*Trade Union Faction of Electricians and Mechanics*] [*Greek*] (GC)
SPIN.......... Societa per Imprese Nucleari [*Nuclear Contracting Company*] [*Italian*] (WER)
SPIPAP....... Service de Presse, d'Information, de Propagande, et d'Action Psychologique [*Press, Information, Propaganda, and Psychological Action Department*] [*Cambodian*] (CL)
SPiR.......... Collection of Regulations and Decrees of the Council of People's Commissars of the USSR (RU)
SPIR.......... Society for the Protection of Individual Rights (MAR)
spirit.......... Spiritismi [*Spiritism*] [*Finnish*]
Spirt.......... Alcohol and Vodka Distillery [*Topography*] (RU)
SPIS.......... Spolek Posluchacu Inzenyrskeho Stavitelstvi [*Association of Architectural Engineering Students*] (CZ)
SPIVHLB..... Societe Proprietaire du Village Hotel de la Langue de Barbarie (MAR)
SPJ.......... Socijalisticka Partija Jugoslavije [*Socialist Party of Yugoslavia*] (PPE)
SPK.......... Arctic Circle (RU)
SPK.......... Blood Transfusion Station (RU)
SPK.......... Hydrofoil Vessel (RU)
SPK.......... Interrupter Contact (RU)
SPK-.......... Parabolic Cylinder Solar Range (RU)
SPK.......... Savet za Prosvetu i Kulturu [*Educational and Cultural Council*] (YU)
SPK.......... Savez Poljoprivrednih Komora [*Union of Chambers of Agriculture*] (YU)
SPK.......... Savezna Planska Komisija [*Federal Planning Commission*] (YU)
SPK.......... Sekretarijat za Prosvetu i Kulturu (SIV) [*Secretariat of Education and Culture*] (YU)
SPK.......... Severocesky Prumysl Kamene [*North Bohemian Stone Cutting Industry*] [*Liberec*] (CZ)
SPK.......... Sijil Persekolahan Kejuruan [*Vocational School Certificate*] (ML)
SPK.......... Siyasi Partiler Kanunu [*Political Parties Law*] (TU)
SPK.......... Skola Pesadiskih Komandira [*School for Infantry Commanders*] (YU)
SPK.......... Sozialistisches Patientenkollektiv [*Socialist Patients' Collective*] (EG)
Sp K.......... Special Satellite Capsule (RU)
SPK.......... Sreska Poljoprivredna Komora [*District Chamber of Agriculture*] (YU)
SPK.......... Staatliche Plankommission [*State Planning Commission*] (EG)
SPK.......... Statni Pedagogicka Knihovna [*State Pedagogical Library*] (CZ)
SPK.......... Statni Planovaci Komise [*State Planning Commission*] (CZ)
SPK.......... Stowarzyszenie Polskich Kombatantow [*Association of Polish Veterans*] (POL)

SPK .... Stratiotikos Poinikos Kodix [*Military Penal Code*] (GC)
SPK .... Svet za Prosveto in Kulturo Ljudska Republika Slovenija [*Cultural and Educational Council of Slovenia*] (YU)
SPKB .... Special Planning and Design Office (RU)
SPKI .... Spolek Posluchacu Komercniho Inzenyrstvi [*Association of School of Business Administration Students*] (CZ)
SPKK .... Statni Pedagogicka Knihovna Komenskeho [*Comenius State Pedagogical Library*] [*Prague*] (CZ)
SPKP .... Suomen Perustuslaillinen Kansanpuolue [*Finnish Constitutional People's Party*] (PPW)
SPKT .... Symvoulion Paragogikon kai Koinonikon Taxeon [*Council of Social and Productive Classes*] (GC)
sp l .... Spectral Line (RU)
SPL .... Spolecnost Pracovniho Lekarstvi [*Industrial Medicine Association*] (CZ)
Spl .... Supplement [*Supplement*] [*German*]
SPLA .... Saharan People's Liberation Army [*Arab*] (MAR)
SPLA .... Seychel Popular Liberation Army (MAR)
SPLAJ .... Socialist People's Libyan Arab Jamahirya (MAR)
SPLAM .... Societe d'Acconage et de Manutention [*Moroccan*] (MAR)
SPM .... Fixed Medical Aid Station (RU)
SPM .... Modern Problems of Mathematics [*Book series*] (RU)
SPM .... Permanent Medical Aid Stations (BU)
SPM .... Punched-Card Computer, Punched-Tape Computer (RU)
SPM .... St. Pierre and Miquelon [*Three-letter standard code*] (CNC)
SPM .... Servicos Prisionais Militares [*Military Prisons Service*] [*Portuguese*] (WER)
SPM .... Sijil Pelajaran Malaysia [*Malaysian Language Education Certificate*] (ML)
SPM .... Societe des Petroles de Madagascar (MAR)
SPM .... Sovet na Prosveta na Makedonija [*Council of Education of Macedonia*] (YU)
SPMA .... Syllogos Politikon Mikhanikon Athinon [*Athens Civil Engineers Association*] (GC)
SPMA .... Syndesmos Politikon Mikhanikon kai Arkhitektonon [*League of Civil Engineers and Architects*] [*Cypriot*] (GC)
SPN .... Auxiliary Laying Point [*Artillery*] (BU)
SPN .... Combat Engineer Observation Post (RU)
SPN .... Sekcja Piki Noznej [*Soccer Section*] (POL)
SPN .... Slovenske Pedagogicke Nakladatelstvo [*Slovak Pedagogical Publishing House*] (CZ)
SPN .... Stabilized Director [*Navy*] (RU)
SPN .... Statne Podohospodarski Nakladatelstvo [*State Agricultural Publishing House*] (CZ)
SPN .... Statni Pedagogicke Nakladatelstvi [*State Pedagogical Publishing House*] (CZ)
SPNC .... Sindicato Profesional Nacional de Choferes [*National Professional Drivers Union*] [*Chilean*] (LA)
SPND .... Societe des Plantations de N'Dafia (MAR)
Sp NII .... Spisanie na Nauchnoizsledovatelskite Instituti [*Journal of the Scientific Research Institutes*] [*A publication*] (BU)
SPNK .... Savet za Prosvetu, Nauku, i Kulturu [*Educational, Scientific, and Cultural Council*] (YU)
SPNP .... Societe des Plantation des Nyombe-Penja (MAR)
SPO .... Consumers' Societies Union (RU)
SPO .... Gun Ammunition Supply Point (RU)
SPO .... Sociaal Pedagogisch Onderwijs
SPO .... Sozialistische Partei Oesterreichs [*Socialist Party of Austria*] (PPW)
SPO .... Sport Popular Orasenesc [*Urban People's Sport*] (RO)
SPO .... Sprawny do Pracy i Obrony [*Fit for Work and Defense*] [*Badge*] (POL)
SPO .... Stomatologic Polyclinic (RU)
SPO .... Warning and Identification System (RU)
SPOA .... Souprava Prepravniku pro Osobni Automobily [*Passenger Automobile Transporter*] (CZ)
SPOA .... Syndesmos Palaion Odigon Avtokinitiston [*Association of Veteran Drivers*] [*Greek*] (GC)
SPOe .... Sozialistische Partei Oesterreichs [*Socialist Party of Austria*] (EG)
Spofa .... Spojene Farmaceuticke Zivody [*United Pharmaceutical Factories*] (CZ)
SPOJC .... Spojovaci Ceta (Dopnit Zkratkou prislus Velitelstvi) [*Communications Platoon (Abbreviation is augmented by adding initials of pertinent headquarters)*] (CZ)
SPOJP .... Spojovaci Pluk [*Communications Regiment*] (CZ)
Spoj r .... Spojovaci Rota [*Communications*] (CZ)
Spoj voj .... Spojovaci Vojsko [*Communications Troops (Signal Corps)*] (CZ)
SPOK .... Statni Populacni Komise [*State Population Commission*] (CZ)
spoldz .... Spoldzielcza [*or Spoldzielnia*] [*Cooperative*] (POL)
SPOLP .... Synergatiki Promithevtiki Organosis Lemesou-Pafou [*Limassol-Paphos Cooperative Supply Organization*] (GC)
SPOM .... Stanica Poljoprivrednih Oruda i Masina [*Agricultural Tools and Machines Station*] (YU)
SPOM .... Syndicat des Producteurs d'Oleagineux d'Outre-Mer (MAR)
SPON .... Social and Legal Protection of Minors (RU)
sp z oo .... Spolka z Ograniczena Odpowiedzialnoscia [*Limited Company*] [*Polish*]
sp z op .... Spolka z Ograniczona Poreka [*Company with Limited Liability*] [*Polish*]
sport .... Sporting, Sports, Sport (RU)
Sportintern ... Red Sports International (RU)
sportl .... Sportlich [*German*]
Sportsnab ... Sports Equipment Supplies (BU)
sport-toto ... Pari-Mutuel Betting (BU)
SPOSA .... St. Paul's Old Students Association (MAR)
Spowa .... Sport- und Wanderbedarf [*Sports and Hiking Needs*] (EG)
SPP .... Medical Control Point (BU)
SPP .... Medical Transfer Station [*Military term*] (RU)
SPP- .... Plastic Life Raft (RU)
SPP .... Program Interruption System (RU)
SPP .... Reinforced Concrete Panels Enterprise (BU)
SPP .... Searchlight Beam Field (RU)
SPP .... Secretaria de Programacion y Presupuesto [*Secretariat of Programing and Budget*] [*Mexican*] (LA)
SPP .... Sekretarijat za Pravosudne Poslove (SIV) [*Secretariat of Judicial Affairs*] (YU)
SPP .... Separator-Steam Superheater [*Nuclear energy*] (BU)
SPP .... Sindicato de Periodistas de Panama [*Journalists Union of Panama*] (LA)
SPP .... Societe de Peche Pontenegrine (MAR)
SPP .... Sofia Industrial Enterprise (BU)
SPP .... Southern Pacific Properties (MAR)
SPP .... Stable Intermediate Products (RU)
SPP .... Stanice Polni Posty [*Field Post Office*] (CZ)
SPP .... Statna Pamiatkova Peclivost [*State Institute for the Preservation of Monuments and Historical Relics*] (CZ)
SPP .... Statni Plynarenske Podniky [*State Gasworks*] (CZ)
SPP .... Stoleczna Przetwornia Papiernicza [*Warsaw Paper Factory*] (POL)
SPP .... Strojirny Potravinarskeho Prumyslu [*Food Industry Engineering Works*] (CZ)
SPP .... Swaziland Progressive Party (AF)
SPP .... Syndikalistiki Proodevtiki Parataxis [*Progressive Labor Faction*] [*Greek*] (GC)
SPP .... Szkola Przysposobienia Przemyslowego [*Industrial Training School*] (POL)
SPPB .... Sorting Mobile Field Hospital (BU)
SPPF .... Seychelles People's Progressive Front (PPW)
SPPFKAS .... Syndikalistiki Parataxis Proodevtikon Filelevtheron kai Anexartiton Syndikaliston [*Labor Faction of Progressive Liberals and Independent Syndicalists*] [*Greek*] (GC)
SPPG .... Societe Prehistorique et Protohistorique Gabonaise (MAR)
SPPG .... Specialized Mobile Field Hospital (RU)
SPPM .... Damaged Vehicle Collecting Point (RU)
SPPM .... Societe des Plantes a Parfums de Madagascar (MAR)
SPPM .... Wrecked Motor Vehicles Collecting Point (BU)
SPPP .... Service de Presse, Propagande, et Publicite [*Press, Propaganda, and Publicity Department*] [*Cambodian*] (CL)
SPPS .... Spolek Posluchacu Prumyslovych Skol [*Society of Students of Industrial Schools*] (CZ)
SPPW .... Szkoly Przysposobienia do Przemyslu Weglowego [*Coal Industry Training Schools*] (POL)
spr .... Conjugation (RU)
SPR .... Food Supply Depot (RU)
spr .... Information, Inquiry (BU)
SPR .... Socialne-Politicky Referat [*Section for Social and Political Affairs*] (CZ)
SPR .... Spratly Islands [*Three-letter standard code*] (CNC)
SPR .... Standarta Presidenta Republiky [*Standard of the President of the Republic*] (CZ)
SPR .... Strategic Petroleum Reserve [*Arab*] (MAR)
SPR .... Strelecky Prapor [*Rifle Battalion*] (CZ)
SPR .... Suomen Punainen Risti [*Finnish*]
SPR .... Szkoly Przysposobienia Rolniczego [*Agricultural Training Schools*] (POL)
S-Praaq .... Senoi Praaq [*Fighting People*] (ML)
SPRCO .... Samostatny Prapor Civilni Obrany [*Separate Civil Defense Battalion*] (CZ)
spre .... Siempre [*Always*] [*Spanish*]
SPRI .... Staf Pribadi [*Personal Staff*] (IN)
s pril .... With Supplement (BU)
SPRINTERS ... Screen Printers de Colombia [*Cali*] (COL)
SPRL .... Societe de Personnes a Responsabilite Limitee [*Private Limited Company*] [*French*]
Sprl .... Sprachlehre [*German*]
SPRM .... Societe des Plantations Reunies de Mimot [*United Plantation Company of Mimot*] [*Cambodian*] (CL)
SPROA .... Societe des Plantations Reunies de l'Ouest Africain (MAR)
SPROCAS ... Study Project on Christianity in Apartheid Society (MAR)
SPROLS ...... Societe de Promotion des Logements Sociaux (MAR)
SPRP .... Track Switch Relay Repeater (RU)
SPRS .... Aircraft Full-Sweep Radar (RU)
SPS .... Meter Receiving Selsyn (RU)
SPS .... St. Patrick's Missionary Society (MAR)
SPS .... Salvage Vessel, Rescue Ship (RU)
SPS .... Sekretarijat za Poljoprivredu i Sumarstvo (SIV) [*Secretariat of Agriculture and Forestry*] (YU)
sps .... Sine Prole Superstite [*Without Surviving Issue*] [*Latin*] (GPO)
SPS .... Socialistische Partij Suriname [*Suriname Socialist Party*] (PPW)

SPS .... Societe des Petroles du Senegal (MAR)
SPS .... Societe de Savon et Produits Similaires (MAR)
SPS .... Sofia Court of Arbitration (BU)
SPS .... Sozialdemokratische Partei der Schweiz [*Social Democratic Party of Switzerland*] (PPE)
SPS .... Sozialdemokratische Partei Suedtirols [*Social Democratic Party of South Tirol*] [*Italian*] (PPE)
SPS .... Spolecnost Pratel Starozitnosti [*Society for the Appreciation of Antiques*] (CZ)
SPS .... Srednja Poljoprivredna Skola [*Secondary Agricultural School*] (YU)
SPS .... Sreska Poljoprivredna Stanica [*District Agricultural Station*] (YU)
SPS .... Srpski Potporni Savez [*Serbian Welfare Union*] (YU)
SPS .... Statni Plavebni Sprava [*State Administration Office for Navigation*] (CZ)
SPS .... Statni Prumyslova Skola [*State Industrial School*] (CZ)
SPS .... Sudan Plantations Syndicate (MAR)
SPS .... Supersonic Airliner (RU)
SPS .... Svaz Partizanov Slovenska [*Union of Slovak Partisans*] (CZ)
SPS .... Trade-Union Council (RU)
SPS .... Universal Postal Union (BU)
SpSAN .... Spomenik Srpske Akademije Nauka [*Papers of the Serbian Academy of Sciences*] [*Belgrade*] [*A publication*] (YU)
SPSC .... Societatea de Propagatie Stiinta si Cultura [*Society for the Propagation of Science and Culture*] (RO)
SPSh .... Soviet and Party School (RU)
SPSK .... Savez Poljoprivredno-Sumarskih Komora [*Union of Chambers of Agriculture and Forestry*] (YU)
sp sovp ...... Magnetic Spectrometer Used to Study Coincidences (RU)
SPSP .... Societe des Plantations Saint-Georges (MAR)
sp S pr .... Spisanie Sotsialistichesko Pravo [*Socialist Law*] [*A periodical*] (BU)
SPSSSR ...... Svaz Pratel SSSR [*Union of Friends of the USSR*] (CZ)
SPSSSR ...... Svaz Priatelov SSSR [*Union of Friends of the USSR*] (CZ)
sp st .... Lifesaving Station [*Topography*] (RU)
SpStopR ..... Spisanie na Instituta za Stopanska Ratsionalizatsiya [*Journal of the Institute for Economic Rationalization*] [*A publication*] (BU)
SPSTU .... Secondary and Preparatory School Teachers' Union [*Mauritian*] (AF)
SPSU .... Statni Planovaci a Statisticky Urad [*State Planning and Statistical Office*] (CZ)
SPSz .... Soproni Poszto- es Szonyeggyar [*Textile and Carpet Factory of Sopron*] (HU)
SPT- .... Semimounted Tractor Snowplow (RU)
SPT .... Shromazdiste Poskozene Techniky [*Assembly Point for Damaged Equipment*] (CZ)
SPT .... Sijil Persekolahan Tinggi [*Higher Education Certificate*] (ML)
SPT .... Slovenski Pomorski Tehnikum [*Slovenian Merchant Marine School*] [*Piran*] (YU)
SPT .... Spolek Posluchacu Techniky [*Technical Institute Students' Association*] (CZ)
SPT .... Surmoulage de Pneu du Togo (MAR)
SPTA .... Slovenska Pomorsko-Trgovska Akademija [*Slovenian Merchant Marine Academy*] [*Piran*] (YU)
SPTF .... Societe pour Transports Forestiers (MAR)
SPTI .... Saglik Propagandasi ve Tibbi Istatistik Genel Mudurlugu [*Health Propaganda and Medical Statistics Directorate General*] (TU)
SPTM .... Societe des Plantations de Tabac de Malaimbandy, Madagascar (MAR)
SPTs .... Moving-Target Selection (RU)
SPTU .... Secondary Technical-Vocational School (BU)
SPU .... Aircraft Intercom (RU)
SPU .... Auxiliary Command Post (BU)
SPU .... Diagrammatic Method of Planning and Control [*Aircraft maintenance*] (RU)
SPU- .... Intermediate-Repeater Bay (RU)
SPU .... Medical Antiepidemiological Administration (BU)
SPU .... Power Supply and Control Bay (RU)
SPU .... Programed Control Systems [*Nuclear energy*] (BU)
SPU .... Savezne Privredne Ustanove [*Federal Economic Institutions*] (YU)
SPU .... Selective Perforation Unit (RU)
SPU .... Selective Switching Device (RU)
SPU .... Slovensky Planovaci Urad [*Slovak Planning Office*] (CZ)
SPU .... Statni Pamatkovy Ustav [*State Institute for the Preservation of Historical Monuments*] (CZ)
SPU .... Statni Pozemkovy Urad [*State Land Reform Office*] (CZ)
SPU .... Svetova Postovni Unie [*World Postal Union*] (CZ)
SPU .... Synchronizer with a Steady Lead Angle (RU)
SPUO .... Statni Projektovy Ustav Obchodu [*State Project Planning Institute for Trade*] (CZ)
SPUP .... Seychelles People's United Party (PPW)
SPUR .... Singapore Planning and Urban Research Group (ML)
SPURT- .... Three-Position Radioisotope Level Indicator (RU)
SPUSPG ...... Syndicat Professionnel des Usines de Sciage et Placages du Gabon (MAR)
SPV .... Average Inclusion Potential (RU)
SPV .... Gun Armament [*Aviation*] (RU)
SPV .... Servico de Protecao ao Voo [*Flight Protection Service*] [*Brazilian*] (LA)
SPV .... Societe des Petroles de Valence (MAR)
sp V .... Spezifisches Volumen [*Specific Volume*] [*German*]
SPV .... Standard Field Viscosimeter (RU)
SPVEA .... Superintendencia do Plano de Valorizacao Economica da Amazonia [*Superintendency for the Amazon Area Economic Promotion Program*] [*Brazilian*] (LA)
SPVFS .... Superintendencia do Plano Valorizacao da Fronteira Sudoeste [*Superintendency for the Southwest Border Promotion Program*] [*Brazilian*] (LA)
SPVP .... Fixed Veterinary Aid Station (RU)
SPVRD .... Supersonic Ramjet Engine (RU)
SPW .... Schuetzenppanzerwagen [*Armored Personnel Carrier*] (EG)
sp W .... Spezifische Waerme [*Specific Heat*] [*German*]
SPWFY .... Socialist Party of Workers, Farmers, and Youths (MAR)
SPY .... Siyasal Partiler Yasasi [*Political Parties' Code of Laws*] (TU)
SPYa .... Socialist Party of Japan (RU)
SPYu .... Trade-Union Council of Yugoslavia (RU)
SpYuD .... Spisanie na Yuridicheskoto Druzhestvo [*Journal of the Juridical Association*] [*A publication*] (BU)
spz .... Centipoise (RU)
SPZ .... Flank Guard (BU)
SPZ .... Savez Poljoprivrednih Zadruga [*Union of Agricultural Cooperatives*] (YU)
SPZ .... Sdruzeni Parlamentnich Zpravodaju [*Association of Parliament Reporters*] (CZ)
SPZ .... Slavonsko-Podravska Vicinalna Zeleznica [*Slovenian Drava Valley Local Railroad*] (YU)
SPZ .... Slovenska Prosvetna Zveza [*Slovenian Educational Federation*] [*Trieste*] (YU)
SPZ .... Statni Pracovni Zalohy [*State Labor Reserves*] (CZ)
SPZ .... Svaz Pracovniku v Zemedelstvi [*Agricultural Workers' Union*] (CZ)
SPZ .... Szkola Przysposobienia Zawodowego [*Vocational Training School*] (POL)
SPZB .... Sosnowieckie Przemyslowe Zjednoczenie Budowlane [*Sosnowiec Industrial Construction Association*] (POL)
SPzCKV ...... Samostatna Pruzkumna Ceta Krajskeho Velitele [*Separate Reconnaissance Platoon of the Regional Commander*] (CZ)
SPzH .... Samostatna Pruzkumna Hlidka [*Separate Reconnaissance Patrol*] (CZ)
SPZM .... Strediska Pracujici Zemedelske Mladeze [*Centers for Young Agricultural Workers*] (CZ)
SpZOIB .... Spisanie na Zemedelskite Opitni Instituti v Bulgariya [*Journal of the Agricultural Experimental Institutes in Bulgaria*] [*A publication*] (BU)
SQ .... Secondo Quantita [*According to Quantity*] [*Italian*]
sq .... Square [*Park, Square*] [*In addresses*] [*French*] (CED)
sr .... Alcohol-Soluble (RU)
sr .... Compare (RU)
SR- .... Counter-Collator (RU)
sr .... Easily Soluble (RU)
sr .... For a Term, For a Period (RU)
sr .... Guard (BU)
sr .... Mean, Medium (RU)
SR .... Medium Bomber (RU)
SR .... Medium Repair (RU)
Sr .... Middle [*Toponymy*] (RU)
sr .... Neuter [*Gender*] (RU)
SR .... Partiia Sotsialistov Revolyutsionerov [*Socialist Revolutionary Party*] [*Russian*] (PPE)
SR .... Reactive Power Meter (RU)
SR .... Rhodesia Meridionale [*Southern Rhodesia*] [*Italian*]
SR .... Rifle Company (BU)
SR .... Rifle Company (RU)
SR .... Sacra Rota [*Sacred Roman*] [*Italian*]
Sr .... Sanitetski Referent [*Sanitary Inspector*] [*Military*] (YU)
SR .... Sans Retard [*Military*] [*French*] (MTD)
SR .... Saudi Riyal (ME)
SR .... Schapper-Riegler Wert [*Schopper-Riegler Value*] [*German*]
Sr .... Schwester [*German*]
Sr .... See, Compare (BU)
SR .... Sekretarijat za Rad (SIV) [*Secretariat of Labor*] (YU)
SR .... Selection Register [*Computers*] (RU)
Sr .... Senhor [*Mister, Lord*] [*Portuguese*] (GPO)
sr .... Senior [*Latin*]
Sr .... Senior [*Senior*] [*Dutch*] (GPO)
SR .... Senor [*Sir, Mister*] [*Spanish*]
SR .... Service de Renseignements [*French*]
SR .... Seychelles Rupee (MAR)
Sr .... Sieur [*In legal papers*] [*French*] (MTD)
SR .... Signal Relay (RU)
SR .... Siri [*Series*] (ML)
SR .... Skala Reaumur [*Reaumur Scale*] [*German*]
SR .... Slavisticna Revija [*Slavistics Review*] [*A publication*] (YU)
SR .... Slovensky Rozhlas [*Slovak Radio*] (CZ)
s-r .... Socialist-Revolutionary (RU)
SR .... Sokolovsky Revir [*Sokolov Coal Basin*] (CZ)
SR .... Southern Rhodesia (MAR)

SR............... Sprava Radiokomunikaci [*Administration Office for Radio-Communications*] (CZ)
sr................ Sredni [*or Srednio*] [*Average*] [*Polish*]
sr................ Srednica [*Diameter*] [*Polish*]
SR............... Sredstva za Rad [*Working Tools*] [*Army*] (YU)
sr................ Srez [*District*] (YU)
SR............... Stabilization and Unloading (BU)
SR............... Statsjanstemannens Riksforbund [*National Federation of Government Employees*] [*Swedish*] (WEN)
sr................ Steradian (RU)
SR............... Strategic Missile (RU)
Sr................ Stronzio [*Strontium*] [*Italian*]
sr................ Successeur [*Successor, Heir*] [*French*]
SR............... Sucre Raffine [*Refined Sugar*] [*Reunionese*] (AF)
SR............... Sudan's Railways (MAR)
SR............... Surinam [*Two-letter standard code*] (CNC)
SR............... Synekhes Revma [*Direct Current*] (GC)
sr................ Urgent, Pressing (RU)
SR............... Urgent Telegram (RU)
sr................ Wednesday (RU)
SRA............. Secretaria de la Reforma Agraria [*Secretariat of Agrarian Reform*] [*Mexican*] (LA)
Sra.............. Senhora [*Mrs.*] [*Portuguese*] (GPO)
Sra.............. Senora [*Mrs.*] [*Spanish*]
SRA............. Service de Renseignements de l'Artillerie [*Military*] [*French*] (MTD)
SRA............. Societe de la Raffinerie d'Alger (MAR)
SRA............. Societe de Representation et d'Agreage (MAR)
SRA............. Summer Rainfall Agriculture Program (MAR)
SRA............. Sveriges Radio Aktiebolaget [*Swedish Broadcasting Corporation*] (WEN)
SRAIN......... Societe de Representations Automobiles et Industrielles au Niger (MAR)
SRANC........ Southern Rhodesian African National Congress (MAR)
SRAS........... Southern Rhodesian Air Services (MAR)
sravn........... Comparative (BU)
sravnit st..... Comparative Degree (RU)
sravn st....... Comparative Degree (RU)
S Ravt......... Section de Ravitaillement [*Military*] [*French*] (MTD)
SRB............. Flash Ranging Battery (RU)
SRB............. "Russian Botanists" Dictionary [*A publication*] (RU)
SRB............. Schweizerische Republikanische Bewegung [*Swiss Republican Action Movement*] (WEN)
SRB............. Sociedade Rural Brasileira [*Brazilian Rural Association*] (LA)
SRB............. Societe Rapide des Bois (MAR)
SRBB........... Sdruzeni Revolucnich Bojovnich a Barikadniku [*Association of Fighters in the (1945) Uprising*] (CZ)
SRBG........... Societe de Reception des Bois du Gabon (MAR)
SRBiH.......... Savez Radioamatera Bosne i Hercegovine [*Union of Radio Amateurs of Bosnia and Hercegovina*] (YU)
SRBOAGENCIJA ... Agencija za Posredovanje u Prometu Robom [*Serbian General Business Agency*] [*Belgrade*] (YU)
SRC............. Santa Romana Chiesa [*Holy Roman Church*] [*Italian*]
SRC............. Scientific Research Council [*Jamaican*]
SRC............. Security State (MAR)
SRC............. Servico de Radiocomunicacoes [*Radio Communications Service*] [*Brazilian*] (LA)
SRC............. Sociedad Regular Colectiva [*General Partnership*] [*Spanish*] (CED)
SRC............. Societe Regionale de Commerce [*Tunisian*] (MAR)
SRC............. Students Representative Council [*South African*] (AF)
SRC............. Subject-Fields Reference Code [*FID*] [*'s-Gravenhage*]
SRC............. Supreme Revolutionary Council [*Somali*] (AF)
SRC............. Svetova Rada Cirkvi [*World Council of Churches*] (CZ)
SRCC........... Societe Nationale pour la Renovation et le Developpement de la Cacaoyere et de la Cafeiere Togolaises [*National Society for the Renewal and Development of Togolese Cocoa and Coffee Resources*] (AF)
SRCD........... Societe Routiere Colas du Dahomey (MAR)
SRCI............ Societe Routiere Colas de la Cote-d'Ivoire (MAR)
SRCOA......... Societe Routiere Colas de l'Ouest Africain (MAR)
SRD............. Radio Range Station (RU)
SRD............. Slovenska Rada Druzstiev [*Slovak Council of Cooperatives*] (CZ)
SRD............. Societatea Romana Danubiana [*Romanian Danube Society*] (RO)
SRD............. Societe Regionale de Developpement [*Regional Development Company*] [*Tunisian*] (AF)
srd.............. Steradian [*Steradian*] [*Polish*]
SRD............. Stredoceske Rudne Doly [*Central Bohemian Ore Mines*] [*Pribram*] (CZ)
SRD............. Traffic Regulation Service (RU)
SRDI............ Societe Regionale de Developpement de l'Imbo (MAR)
SRDP........... Special Rural Development Programme (MAR)
SRDR........... Secteurs Regionaux de Developpement Rural (MAR)
SRE............. Secretaria de Relaciones Exteriores [*Secretariat of Foreign Relations*] [*Mexican*] (LA)
sred............. Mean, Medium, Middle (RU)
Sredazgintsvetmet ... Central Asian Branch of the State Scientific Research Institute of Nonferrous Metals (RU)
Sredazgiprovodkhlopok ... Central Asian State Institute for the Planning of Irrigation Structures and Rural Electric Power Plants (RU)
Sredazkhimmash ... Central Asian Chemical Machinery Plant (RU)
Sredazkomstaris ... Central Asian Committee for Museums and the Protection of Relics of the Past, Art, and Nature (RU)
Sredazmet ... Central Asian Meteorological Service (RU)
Sredazneft' ... Central Asian Petroleum Association (RU)
Sredaznefterazvedka ... Central Asian Petroleum Exploration Trust (RU)
SredazNIKhI ... Central Asian Scientific Research Institute for Cotton Growing (RU)
SredazNILKh ... Central Asian Scientific Research Institute of Forestry (RU)
Sredazvodkhoz ... Water Management Administration of Central Asia (RU)
sredneaz..... Central Asian (RU)
SREDNEVOLGOLES ... State Association of the Middle Volga Region Lumber Industry (RU)
Sredvolgeomin ... Middle Volga Branch of the Scientific Research Institute of Geology and Mineralogy (RU)
s a rend....... Sajto ala Rendezte [*Prepared for Publication By*] (HU)
S Res.......... Section de Reserve [*Military*] [*French*] (MTD)
Sres............ Senores [*Sirs*] [*Spanish*]
sr ez........... Serbian Language (BU)
SRF............. Sveriges Redareforening [*Shipowners' Association of Sweden*] (WEN)
SRFCAM..... Section de Recherches Forestieres au Cameroun (MAR)
SRGE.......... Societe Royale de Geographie d'Egypte (MAR)
SRGS.......... South Rhodesia Geological Survey (MAR)
SRH............ Secretaria de Recursos Hidraulicos [*Secretariat of Water Resources*] [*Mexican*] (LA)
SRHB.......... Society for Research into Hydrocephalus and Spina Bifida (EA)
SRI............. Sacro Romano Impero [*Holy Roman Empire*] [*Italian*]
SRI............. Samodzielny Referat Informacyjny [*Autonomous Information Office*] (POL)
SRI............. Santa Romana Iglesia [*Spanish*]
SRI............. Stabna Ratna Igra [*Staff War Game*] [*Military*] (YU)
sria............. Secretaria [*Secretary*] [*Spanish*]
SRiKO......... Workers' and Peasants' Defense Council [*1918-1920*] (RU)
SRIO........... Collection of the Russian Historical Society [*A publication*] (RU)
srio............. Secretario [*Secretary*] [*Spanish*]
SRIO........... Skola za Rezervne Intendantske Oficire [*Reserve Quartermaster Officers School*] (YU)
SR i SD........ Soviet of Workers' and Soldiers' Deputies [*1917-1918*] (RU)
SRJ............. Savez Radioamatera Jugoslavije [*The Yugoslav Union of Radio Amateurs*] (YU)
srk.............. Seurakunta [*Finnish*]
SRK............ Sovet Revoliutsionnovo Komandovaniia (MAR)
SRK............ Swiatowa Rada Kosciolow [*World Council of Churches*] [*Polish*]
SRK............ Union of Cinematography Workers of the USSR (RU)
SRKh.......... Dictionary of Russian Artists [*A publication*] (RU)
SRKiKD....... Soviet of Workers', Peasants', and Red Army Deputies [*1917-1936*] (RU)
SRKKh........ Union of Workers of Municipal Services (RU)
SRL............ Section de Reperage par les Lueurs [*Military*] [*French*] (MTD)
SRL............ Sociedad de Responsabilidad Limitada [*Private Limited Company*] [*Spanish*]
S de RL....... Sociedad de Responsabilidad Limitada [*Private Limited Company*] [*Spanish*]
SRL............ Societa a Responsabilita Limitata [*Private Limited Company*] [*Italian*]
SRL............ Societe a Responsabilite Limitee [*Private Limited Company*] [*French*] (MAR)
SRL............ Society of Romance Linguistics (EA)
SRLP.......... Socialist and Revolutionary Labour Party [*Gambian*] (PD)
SRLR.......... Societatea Romana de Lingvistica Romanica [*Romanian Society for Romance Linguistics*] (RO)
SRM............ Computer Mechanism (RU)
SRM............ Ship Repair Shops (RU)
SRM............ Sindicato de Redactores de Mexico [*Union of Mexican Journalists*] (LA)
SRM............ Su Real Majestad [*Spanish*]
SRM............ Suara Revolusi Malaya [*Voice of the Malayan Revolution (Communist)*] (ML)
SRM............ Sue Riverite Mani [*Personal for Addressee*] [*Italian*]
SRM............ Svetova Rada Mieru [*World Peace Council*] (CZ)
SRM............ Szkola Rybolowstwa Morskiego [*School of Deep-Sea Fishing*] [*Polish*]
SRMC.......... Southern Rhodesian Missionary Conference (MAR)
sr mkh........ Medium Mortar (BU)
SRMO.......... Slovenske Rafinerie Mineralnych Olejov, Narodny Podnik [*Slovak Petroleum Refineries, National Enterprise*] (CZ)
SRMRJ........ Sindikati Rudarskih i Metalurgiskih Radnika Jugoslavije [*Trade-Unions of Miners and Metallurgic Workers of Yugoslavia*] (YU)
SRMZ.......... Stavropol' Ship Repair and Machine Plant (RU)
SRN............ Sangkum Reastr Niyum [*Prince Sihanouk's party, dissolved in 1970*] [*Cambodian*] (CL)
SRN............ Stoleczna Rada Narodowa [*Warsaw People's Council*] (POL)
SRNK.......... Instruction-Number Counter Register [*Computers*] (RU)
SRO............ Aircraft Radar Responder (RU)
SRO............ Spolecnost s Rucenim Omezenym [*Company with Limited Liability*] (CZ)

SRO............ State Railways Organization [*Iranian*] (ME)
SR & O......... Statutory Rules and Orders (MAR)
SROT........... Service des Renseignements de l'Observation du Terrain [*Military*] [*French*] (MTD)
SROT........... Situations Resumes des Operations du Tresor (MAR)
SROZ........... Slovenska Rada Odborovych Zvazov [*Slovak Council of Trade Unions*] (CZ)
SRP............ Aircraft Radar Sight (RU)
SRP............ Assembling-Disassembling Device (RU)
SRP............ Computer Device (RU)
SRP............ Construction and Repair Train (RU)
SRP............ Education Workers' Union (BU)
SRP............ Regimental Medical Company (BU)
SRP-........... Scintillation Survey Radiometer (RU)
SRP............ Sekretarijat za Robni Promet [*Secretariat of Goods Trade*] (YU)
SRP............ Serengeti Research Project (MAR)
SRP............ Shipborne Radio Direction Finder (RU)
SRP............ Socialist Revolution Party [*Sosyalist Devrim Partisi*] [*Turkish*] (PPW)
SRP............ Socialisticka Radnicka Partija Jugoslavije [*Socialist Workers' Party of Yugoslavia*] (PPE)
SRP............ Societatea Romana Petroliera [*Romanian Petroleum Society*] (RO)
SRP............ Sozialistische Reichspartei [*Socialist Reich Party*] [*West German*] (PPE)
SRP............ Swiatowa Rada Pokoju [*World Council of Peace*] [*Polish*]
SRPJ(k)....... Socijalisticka Radnicka Partija Jugoslavije (Komunista) [*Socialist Workers Party of Yugoslavia (Communists)*] (YU)
SRP(k)........ Socijalisticka Radnicka Partija (Komunista) [*Socialist Workers Party (Communists)*] (YU)
SRPP........... Printing Industry Workers' Union (RU)
SRPS........... Sdruzeni Rodicu a Pratel Skoly [*Parent-Teacher Association*] (CZ)
SRPV........... Pulse Wave Propagation Velocity (RU)
sr r............ Neuter Gender [*Grammar*] (BU)
sr r............ Neuter Gender (RU)
SRR............ Romanian Socialist Republic (BU)
SRR............ Socjalistyczna Republika Radziecka [*Soviet Socialist Republic*] (POL)
SRR............ Sozialistische Republik Rumaenien [*Socialist Republic of Romania*] [*West German*] (WEN)
SRRA........... Singapore Rural Residents' Association (ML)
SRS............ Aircraft Radio Communication Set (RU)
SRS............ Aircraft Reconnaissance Station (RU)
SRS............ Fixed Radio Station (RU)
SRS............ Piece Rate System (BU)
SRS............ Police Dog (RU)
SRS............ Savez Radioamatera Srbije [*Serbian Union of Radio Amateurs*] (YU)
SRS............ Section de Reperage par le Son [*Military*] [*French*] (MTD)
SRS............ Slovenska Republikanska Stranka [*Slovenian Republican Party*] (YU)
SRS............ Societatis Regiae Socius [*or Sodalis*] [*Fellow of the Royal Society*] [*Latin*] (GPO)
SRS............ Srpska Radikalna Stranka [*Serbian Radical Party*] [*Yugoslav*] (PPE)
SRSC........... Societatea pentru Raspindirea Stiintei si Culturii [*Society for the Dissemination of Science and Culture*] (RO)
SRSD........... Stredisko pro Rozvoj Silnic a Dalnic [*Center for Construction Development of Roads and Highways*] (CZ)
SRSDM......... Union of Social Democratic Workers' Youth (BU)
sr sk........... Mean Velocity, Average Speed (RU)
SRSP........... Somali Revolutionary Socialist Party (AF)
sr st........... Comparative Degree (RU)
SRT............ Medium Fishing Trawler (RU)
SRT............ Section de Reperage par la Terre [*Military*] [*French*] (MTD)
Srta............ Senorita [*Miss, Young Woman*] [*Spanish*] (GPO)
SRTK........... Societe Regionale de Transports de Kasserine [*Tunisian*] (MAR)
SRTM........... Medium Fishing Trawler-Freezer (RU)
SRTR........... Medium Fishing Trawler-Refrigerator (RU)
SRTs........... Computer and Control Center [*Space vehicle guidance*] (RU)
SRTs........... Filter Center [*Military*] (BU)
SRTs........... Reconnaissance and Target Designation Station [*Artillery*] (RU)
SRTUC......... Southern Rhodesian Trades Union Congress (AF)
SRU-........... Computing Device (RU)
sr uch......... Secondary School (BU)
SrV............ Medium-Frequency Waves (RU)
srv............ See, Compare (BU)
Srv............ Servis [*Service*] (TU)
SRV............ Ship Repair Yard (RU)
SRV............ Spolecnost pro Racionalni Vyzivu [*Society for Rational Nutrition*] (CZ)
SRVD........... Sprava Raketoveho a Delostreleckeho Vyzbrojovani [*Rocket and Artillery Ordnance Directorate*] (CZ)
SRVD........... Sprava Raketovych Vojsk a Delostrelectva [*Rocket Troops and Artillery Directorate*] (CZ)
sr vek......... Medieval (BU)
sr-vek......... Medieval (RU)
sr vr........... Mean Time (RU)
SRVU........... Radio Broadcasting Center Studio (RU)
sr vv........... Middle Ages (RU)
SRW............ Schiffbau- und Reparatur Werft [*Ship Building and Repair Yard*] (EG)
SRWA........... Swiss Review of World Affairs [*Zurich*] [*A publication*] (MAR)
SRWU........... Sudan Railway Workers' Union (MAR)
SRZ............ Seismograph for Registering Destructive Earthquakes (RU)
SRZ............ Selanska Rabotna Zadruga [*Peasant Work Cooperative*] [*Collective Farm*] (YU)
SRZ............ Ship Repair Yard (RU)
SRZ............ Susuman Repair Plant (RU)
SS.............. Aircraft Construction (RU)
SS.............. Ambulance Aircraft (RU)
SS.............. Blue Glass (RU)
SS.............. Coincidence Circuit (RU)
SS.............. Comparison Circuit (RU)
SS.............. Counter, Counting Circuit (RU)
SS.............. Existence Doubtful [*Nautical term*] (RU)
SS.............. Line Counter (RU)
SS.............. Milizia di Protezione Nazista [*SS Troops*] [*Italian*]
SS.............. Miscellaneous Bay (RU)
SS.............. Sa Saintete [*His Holiness*] [*French*] (GPO)
SS.............. Sa Seigneurie [*His Lordship*] [*French*]
SS.............. Saeuren [*Acids*] [*German*]
SS.............. Saints [*Saints*] [*French*] (MTD)
SS.............. Saison Seche (MAR)
SS.............. Sanitetska Sluzba [*Medical Service*] [*Military*] (YU)
SS.............. Santa Sede [*Holy See*] [*Italian*]
SS.............. Santi [*Saints*] [*Italian*]
SS.............. Santissimo [*Most Holy*] [*Italian*]
SS.............. Savet za Skolstvo [*Council for Schools*] (YU)
SS.............. Savez Sindikata [*Council of Trade-Unions*] (YU)
ss.............. Sayfalar [*Pages*] (TU)
SS.............. Sberne Suroviny [*Raw Materials Collection (Enterprise)*] (CZ)
SS.............. Schutzstaffel [*NAZI Elite Troops*] (EG)
ss.............. Scilicet [*Namely*] [*Latin*] (GPO)
SS.............. Securite Sociale [*Social Security*] [*French*] (WER)
SS.............. Security Council (BU)
SS.............. Sedma Sila, Novinsko Izdavacko Preduzece Udruzenja Novinara Srbije [*Sedma Sila, a newspaper publishing enterprise of the Serbian Association of Journalists*] (YU)
SS.............. Seguridad Social [*Social Security*] [*Spanish*] (WER)
SS.............. Seismic Station (RU)
SS.............. Sekretarijat za Saobrakaj [*Secretariat of Transportation*] (YU)
SS.............. Sekretarijat za Sumarstvo [*Secretariat of Forestry*] (YU)
SS.............. Selenium Column (RU)
SS.............. Self-Propelled Missile (BU)
SS.............. Sempervivium Society (EA)
SS.............. Servicio Seccional Radial Ltda. [*Medellin*] (COL)
ss.............. Severna Sirina [*Northern Latitude*] (YU)
SS.............. Sidirodromikos Stathmos [*Railroad Station*] (GC)
sS.............. Siehe Seite [*See Page*] [*German*]
SS.............. Simeiosis Syndaxeos [*Editorial Note*] (GC)
SS.............. Sindikati Srbije [*Trade-Unions of Serbia*] (YU)
SS.............. Sluzbena Saopstenja [*Official Communications*] (YU)
SS.............. Somalia Shilling (MAR)
SS.............. Sommersemester [*Summer Term*] (EG)
SS.............. Sovetski Sojuz [*Soviet Union*] (YU)
SS.............. Soviet North (RU)
SS.............. Soviet Union (RU)
SS.............. Strada Statale [*Main Road*] [*Italian*]
SS.............. Strana Slobody [*Freedom Party*] (CZ)
ss.............. Strony [*Pages*] [*Polish*]
SS.............. Su Santidad [*Spanish*]
SS.............. Su Senoria [*Spanish*]
SS.............. Sua Santita [*His Holiness*] [*Italian*]
SS.............. Sumsko Stopanstvo [*Forestry Management*] (YU)
s/s............. Supply Depot (BU)
SS.............. Supply Service (RU)
SS.............. Supply Station (RU)
Ss.............. Svet Sovetu [*The Soviet World*] [*A periodical*] (CZ)
ss.............. Swieci [*Saints*] [*Polish*]
SS.............. Synchronization Pulse Selector (RU)
SS.............. Top Secret (RU)
SS.............. Village Soviet of Workers' Deputies (RU)
ss.............. Villages (RU)
SSA............ Agricultural Academy (BU)
SSA............ Agricultural Aviation (BU)
SSA............ Sanitetska Sluzba Armije [*Army Medical Service*] (YU)
SSA............ Secretaria de Salubridad y Asistencia [*Secretariat of Health and Assistance*] [*Mexican*] (LA)
SSA............ Shan State Army [*Burmese*] (PD)
SSA............ Soviet Architects' Union (RU)
SSA............ Star of South Africa (MAR)
SSA............ Svaz Slovenskych Architektov [*Union of Slovak Architects*] (CZ)
SSAA........... Societe Senegalaise des Artisans Associes (MAR)
SSAA........... Stichting Studiecentrum voor Administratieve Automatisering [*Later, SSI*]
SSAA........... Sus Altezas [*Spanish*]

SSA-AgrF ... Agricultural Academy - School of Agronomy (BU)
SSA-AgrF-KAgrKhim ... Agricultural Academy - School of Agronomy. Soil Chemistry Department (BU)
SSA-AgrF-KDarvGenSel ... Agricultural Academy - School of Agronomy. Department of Darwinism, Genetics, and Selection (BU)
SSA-AgrF-KGr ... Agricultural Academy - School of Agronomy. Horticulture Department (BU)
SSA-AgrF-KlozVin ... Agricultural Academy - School of Agronomy. Department of Viticulture and Oenology (BU)
SSA-AgrF-KMarksL ... Agricultural Academy - School of Agronomy. Department on Foundations of Marxism-Leninism (BU)
SSA-AgrF-KMekh ... Agricultural Academy - School of Agronomy. Department of Mechanization (BU)
SSA-AgrF-KOrgSPredpr ... Agricultural Academy - School of Agronomy. Department of Farm Management (BU)
SSA-AgrF-KPochv ... Agricultural Academy - School of Agronomy. Department of Soil Science (BU)
SSA-AgrF-KPolitIkon ... Agricultural Academy - School of Agronomy. Department of Political Economy (BU)
SSA-AgrF-KRast ... Agricultural Academy - School of Agronomy. Department of Plant Breeding (BU)
SSA-AgrF-KRastZasht ... Agricultural Academy - School of Agronomy. Department of Plant Protection (BU)
SSA-AgrF-KZBot ... Agricultural Academy - School of Agronomy. Department of Agricultural Botany (BU)
SSA-AgrF-KZIkon ... Agricultural Academy - School of Agronomy. Department of Agricultural Economics (BU)
SSAE........... Societe Shell de l'Afrique Equatoriale [*Equatorial Africa Shell Company*] [*Congolese*] (AF)
SSA-LesotekhnF ... Agricultural Academy - School of Forestry Engineering (BU)
SSA-LesotekhnF-KDendr ... Agricultural Academy - School of Forestry Engineering. Department of Dendrology (BU)
SSA-LesotekhnF-KDurvoprerab ... Agricultural Academy - School of Forestry Engineering. Department of Lumbering (BU)
SSA-LesotekhnF-KGeod GStr ... Agricultural Academy - School of Forestry Engineering. Department of Geodesy Forestry Construction (BU)
SSA-LesotekhnF-KGKult ... Agricultural Academy - School of Forestry Engineering. Department of Forest Crops (BU)
SSA-LesotekhnF-KIkonPIGs ... Agricultural Academy - School of Forestry Engineering. Department of Forest Resources Economics and Planning (BU)
SSA-LesotekhnF-KLesoop ... Agricultural Academy - School of Forestry Engineering. Department of Forest Conservation (BU)
SSA-LesotekhnF-KLesopol ... Agricultural Academy - School of Forestry Engineering. Department of Forest Exploitation (BU)
SSA-LesotekhnF-KLesoustr ... Agricultural Academy - School of Forestry Engineering. Department of Forest Management (BU)
SSA-LesotekhnF-KLesov ... Agricultural Academy - School of Forestry Engineering. Department of Silviculture (BU)
SSA-LesotekhnF-KLovS ... Agricultural Academy - School of Forestry Engineering. Department of Game Resources (BU)
SSA-LesotekhnF-KMash ... Agricultural Academy - School of Forestry Engineering. Department of Machine Engineering (BU)
SSA-LesotekhnF-KOPor ... Agricultural Academy - School of Forestry Engineering. Department of Fortification of Floodbeds (BU)
SSAO .... Societe Shell de l'Afrique Occidentale (MAR)
SSAS........... Star of South Africa Silver (MAR)
SSAS........... Stratiotiki Skholi Axiomatikon Somaton [*Corps Officers Military School*] (GC)
SSA-VetF.... Agricultural Academy - School of Veterinary Medicine (BU)
SSA-VetF-AkKl ... Agricultural Academy - School of Veterinary Medicine. Veterinary Obstetrics Clinic (BU)
SSA-VetF-IAn ... Agricultural Academy - School of Veterinary Medicine. Institute of Anatomy (BU)
SSA-VetF-IFar ... Agricultural Academy - School of Veterinary Medicine. Institute of Pharmacology (BU)
SSA-VetF-IFiziol ... Agricultural Academy - School of Veterinary Medicine. Institute of Physiology (BU)
SSA-VetF-IKhim ... Agricultural Academy - School of Veterinary Medicine. Institute of Chemistry (BU)
SSA-VetF-IKhirTekhnol ... Agricultural Academy - School of Veterinary Medicine. Institute of Hygiene and Technology (BU)
SSA-VetF-IkhranProd ... Agricultural Academy - School of Veterinary Medicine. Institute of Food Products (BU)
SSA-VetF-IMikrbiol ... Agricultural Academy - School of Veterinary Medicine. Institute of Microbiology (BU)
SSA-VetF-IParazitol ... Agricultural Academy - School of Veterinary Medicine. Institute of Parasitology (BU)
SSA-VetF-IPat ... Agricultural Academy - School of Veterinary Medicine. Institute of Pathology (BU)
SSA-VetF-IPatAn ... Agricultural Academy - School of Veterinary Medicine. Institute of Pathological Anatomy (BU)
SSA-VetF-IPatofiziol ... Agricultural Academy - School of Veterinary Medicine. Institute of Pathophysiology (BU)
SSA-VetF-ISudMed ... Agricultural Academy - School of Veterinary Medicine. Institute of Forensic Medicine (BU)
SSA-VetF-KhirKl ... Agricultural Academy - School of Veterinary Medicine. Surgical Clinic (BU)
SSA-VetF-VutrKl ... Agricultural Academy - School of Veterinary Medicine. Clinic for Internal Diseases (BU)
SSA-ZootekhnF ... Agricultural Academy - School of Animal Husbandry (BU)
SSA-ZootekhnF-KDomZhiv ... Agricultural Academy - School of Animal Husbandry. Department of Domestic Animals (BU)
SSA-ZootekhnF-KFur Proizv ... Agricultural Academy - School of Animal Husbandry. Department of Fodder Production (BU)
SSA-ZootekhnF-KGov ... Agricultural Academy - School of Animal Husbandry. Department of Cattle Breeding (BU)
SSA-ZootekhnF-KKhrDomZhiv ... Agricultural Academy - School of Animal Husbandry. Department of Domestic Animal Nutrition (BU)
SSA-ZootekhnF-KKon ... Agricultural Academy - School of Animal Husbandry. Department of Horse Breeding (BU)
SSA-ZootekhnF-KMI ... Agricultural Academy - School of Animal Husbandry. Dairy Department (BU)
SSA-ZootekhnF-KPrilZool ... Agricultural Academy - School of Animal Husbandry. Department of Applied Zoology (BU)
SSA-ZootekhnF-KRazvGen ... Agricultural Academy - School of Animal Husbandry. Department of Breeding Genetics (BU)
SSA-ZootekhnF-KSvin ... Agricultural Academy - School of Animal Husbandry. Department of Hog Breeding (BU)
SSB .... Bomb Sight Jamming Station (BU)
SSB .... Sarawak Special Branch (ML)
SSB .... Sectie Speciale Bibliotheken [*NVB*] [*'s-Gravenhage*]
SSB .... Societatea de Stiinte Biologice [*Society for Biological Sciences*] (RO)
SSB .... Special Service Battalion (MAR)
SSB .... Sulfite-Liquor Waste (RU)
SSB MEN.... Seccion de Servicios Bibliotecarios del Ministerio de Educacion Nacional [*Bogota*] (COL)
SSBR........... Samakum Sangkruos Bokkalik Rotthabal [*Administrative Government Employees Mutual Association*] [*Use MUFONOA*] [*Cambodian*] (CL)
SSBU........... Savez Studenta Beogradskog Univerziteta [*Union of Students of Belgrade University*] (YU)
SSC .... Sarawak Struggle Command (Communist) (ML)
SSC .... SILEC Semi-Conducteurs (MAR)
SSC .... Societas Sanctae Crucis [*Society of the Holy Cross*] [*Latin*] (GPO)
SSC .... State Security Committee (ML)
SSC .... State Security Council (MAR)
SSCB .... Sovyet Sosyalist Cumhuriyetleri Birligi [*Union of Soviet Socialist Republics*] (TU)
SSCM.......... Societe Nationale des Sciences Naturelles et Mathematiques de Cherbourg, Memoires [*A publication*] (MAR)
SSCP........... Severoslovenske Celulozky a Papierne [*North Slovakian Cellulose and Paper Works*] (CZ)
SSD .... Sindikalno Sportno Drustvo [*Trade-Union Sport Club*] (YU)
SSD .... Soma Stratiotikis Dikaiosynis [*(Army) Legal Corps*] (GC)
SSD .... Soviet of Soldiers' Deputies (RU)
SSD .... Staatssicherheitsdienst [*State Security Service*] (EG)
SSD .... Svaz Spotrebnich Druzstev [*Union of Consumer Cooperatives*] (CZ)
SSD .... Transmitting Selsyn (RU)
SSDC .... Social Self-Defense Committee [*Polish*] (PD)
SSDE........... Syndonistikon Symvoulion Dimosion Ependyseon [*Public Investments Coordinating Council*] [*Greek*] (GC)
SSDP........... Suomen Sosialidemokraattinen Puolue [*Finnish Social Democratic Party*] (PPW)
SSDU .... Svaz Slovenskych Divadelnych Umelcov [*Union of Slovak Theater Artists*] (CZ)
SSDUJ......... Sindikat Sluzbenika Drzavnih Ustanova Jugoslavije [*Trade-Union of Employees in Government Institutions of Yugoslavia*] (YU)
SSE .... Servico Secreto do Exercito [*Army Secret Service*] [*Brazilian*] (LA)
SSE .... Siberian Soviet Encyclopedia [*A publication*] (RU)
SSE .... Stratiotiki Skholi Evelpidon [*Military Cadet Academy*] [*Greek*] (GC)
SSE .... Stredoslovenske Energeticke Zavody [*Electric Power Plants, Central Slovakia*] (CZ)
SSE .... Sud Sud Est [*South Southeast*] [*French*] (MTD)
SSE .... Sudsudeste [*South Southeast*] [*Spanish*]
SSE .... Syllogiki Symvasis Ergasias [*Collective Labor Agreement*] (GC)
SSE .... Synelevsis Symvouliou Evropis [*Meeting of the Council of Europe*] (GC)
SSEC .... State Security Executive Committee (Sabah) (ML)
SSEMP........ Syndesmos Spoudaston Ellinikou Metsoviou Polytekhneiou [*Students Association of the Greek Metsovion Polytechnic School*] (GC)
SSEPC .... Societe Senegalaise d'Engrais et de Produits Chimiques (MAR)
SSES........... Syndonistikon Symvoulion ton Emborikon Syllagon [*Coordinating Council of Trade Boards*] (GC)
SSF .... Somali Salvation Front (PD)
SSF .... Spolok Slovenskych Filozofov [*Slovak Philosophical Society*] (CZ)
SSF .... Svetska Sindikalna Federacija [*World Federation of Trade-Unions*] (YU)
SSFC........... Shooting Stars Football Club (MAR)
SSFV........... Sondervorschrift fuer Selbsttaetige Signalanlagen [*Special Regulations for Automatic Signal Installations*] (EG)

SSG............ Savezno Sumarsko Gazdinstvo [*Federal Forest Economy*] (YU)
SSG............ Self-Excited Synchronous Generator (RU)
SSG............ Self-Powered Welding Head (RU)
SSGK.......... Slovenska Sprava Geodezie a Kartografie [*Slovak Geodetic and Cartographic Administration*] (CZ)
SSGKBI....... Serikat Sekerdja Gabungan Koperasi Batik Indonesia [*Association of Indonesian Batik Cooperatives Trade Union*] (IN)
SSGM.......... Union of Free German Youth (BU)
SSGZ.......... Sekretarijat za Splosne Gospodarske Zadeve (ISLRS) [*Secretariat of General Economic Affairs*] (YU)
SSh............ Ambulance Boat (RU)
SSh............ High-Speed Attack Aircraft (RU)
ssh............ North Latitude (RU)
SSH............ Savez Sindikata Hrvatske [*Council of Trade-Unions of Croatia*] (YU)
SSh............ Secondary School (RU)
SSh-........... Self-Propelled Chassis (RU)
SSH............ Socialisticke Statkove Hospodareni [*Socialist Farm Management*] (CZ)
SSH............ Svetove Studentske Hry [*World Student Sports Festival*] (CZ)
SShA.......... United States of America (RU)
SShch......... Power-Distributing Board (RU)
s-shche....... Temporary Settlement (RU)
SShG-......... Self-Propelled Mountain Chassis (RU)
SShI........... United States of Indonesia [*1949-1950*] (RU)
SShK.......... Valve-Grinding Machine (RU)
SSHM.......... Society for the Social History of Medicine (EA)
SShM.......... Sports School for Young People (RU)
SShO.......... Secret Cryptographic Section (RU)
SSHR.......... Sprava Statnich Hmotnych Rezerv [*Administration of State Material Reserves*] (CZ)
SShtA......... United States of America (BU)
s-shtu......... Versus (BU)
SShZ.......... Sverdlovsk Tire Plant (RU)
SSI............ Savezni Sanitarni Inspektorat [*Federal Sanitary Inspectorate*] (YU)
SSI............ Service Social International [*International Social Service - ISS*] (EA)
SSI............ Sever Severo-Istok [*North North-East*] (YU)
SSI............ Spolok Slovenskych Inzinierov [*Society of Slovak Engineers*] (CZ)
SSI............ Stichting Studiecentrum Informatica [*Amsterdam*]
Ssi............ Surekasi [*Company*] [*Turkish*] (GPO)
SSIE........... Smithsonian Science Information Exchange, Inc. (MAR)
SSIELF........ Societe du Sud d'Import-Export en Legumes et Fruits [*Tunisian*] (MAR)
SSIEM......... Society for the Study of Inborn Errors of Metabolism (EA)
SSIH........... Societe Suisse pour l'Industrie Horlogere [*Swiss watch manufacturer*]
ss il........... Illustrated Pages (BU)
SSJ............ Savez Sindikata Jugoslavije [*Council of Trade-Unions of Yugoslavia*] (YU)
SSJ............ Savez Slepih Jugoslavije [*Yugoslav Union of the Blind*] (YU)
SSJ............ Savez Sportova Jugoslavije [*Yugoslav Sports Federation*] (YU)
SSJ............ Savez Strelaca Jugoslavije [*Association of Yugoslav Riflemen*] (YU)
SSK............ Coupling-Cable Bay (RU)
SSK............ Sanitetska Sluzba Korpusa [*Corps Medical Service*] (YU)
SSK............ Savezna Saobracajna Komora [*Federal Chamber of Transportation*] (YU)
SSK............ Savezna Spoljno-Trgovinska Komora [*Federal Chamber of Foreign Trade*] (YU)
SSK............ Shooting Sport Club (RU)
SSK............ Sosialistiki Syndikalistiki Kinisi [*Socialist Trade Union Movement*] [*Greek*] (GC)
SSK............ Sosyal Sigortalari Kurumu Genel Mudurlugu [*Social Security Organization Directorate General*] (TU)
SSK............ Soviet Composers' Union (RU)
SSK............ Sportovy Strelecky Klub [*Sports Gun Club*] (CZ)
SSK............ Statna Studijna Kniznica Kosiciach [*Kosice State Research Library*] (CZ)
SSKG.......... Collection of Information on Caucasian Mountaineers [*A publication*] (RU)
SSKh.......... Soviet Artists' Union (RU)
SSKNRM...... Selsko-Stopanska Komora Narodne Republike Makedonije [*Chamber of Agriculture of Macedonia*] (YU)
SSI............ Sanitetska Sluzba [*Medical Service*] [*Military*] (YU)
SSL............ Soweto Students League [*South African*] (AF)
SSL............ Sprava Statnych Lesov [*State Forest Administration*] (CZ)
SSL............ Stredni Slovensko [*Central Slovakia*] (CZ)
SSL............ Sudan Shipping Line (MAR)
SSLC.......... Secondary-School-Leaving Certificate [*Brazilian*]
SSLM.......... South Sudan Liberation Movement (MAR)
SSM............ Seri Setia Mahkota [*First Grade of Darjah Yang Mulia Setia Mahkota Malaysia*] (ML)
SSM............ Socialist Youth League [*Bulgaria, Poland*] (RU)
SSM............ Socialist Youth Union (BU)
SSM............ Societatea de Stiinte Medicale [*Society for Medical Sciences*] (RO)
SSM............ Sojuz na Sindikatite za Makedonija [*Council of Trade-Unions of Macedonia*] (YU)
SSM............ Sprava Studentskeho Majetku [*Administration of Student Property*] (CZ)
SSM............ Svaz Slovenskej Mladeze [*Union of Slovak Youth*] (CZ)
SSM............ Svaz Socialisticke Mladeze [*Union of Socialist Youth*] (CZ)
SSMM.......... Sus Majestades [*Spanish*]
SSmo.......... Santisimo [*Most Holy*] [*Spanish*]
SSmoP........ Santisimo Padre [*Most Holy Father*] [*Spanish*]
SSMR.......... Societe Shell de Madagascar et de la Reunion (MAR)
SSMY.......... Su Sayaclari Muayene ve Ayar Yonetmeligi [*Water Meter Examination and Calibration Administration*] [*Under Ministry of Commerce*] (TU)
SSN............ Airspeed Pressure Indicator (RU)
ssn............ Centisthene (RU)
SSN............ Sdruzeni pro Spojene Narody [*Association for the United Nations*] (CZ)
SSN............ Svaz Slovenskych Novinarov [*Union of Slovak Journalists*] (CZ)
SSn............ Winged Missile (RU)
SSNAA........ Council of Solidarity of the Nations of Asia and Africa (RU)
SSNG.......... Societatea de Stiinte Naturale si Geografice [*Society for Natural and Geographhic Sciences*] (RO)
SSNIT.......... Social Security and National Insurance Trust (MAR)
SSNLO........ Shan State Nationalities Liberation Organization [*Burmese*] (PD)
SSNM.......... German Free Youth League [*German Democratic Republic*] (RU)
SSno........... Escribano [*Notary*] [*Spanish*]
SSNP........... Syrian Social Nationalist Party (ME)
SSNPG........ Southern Sudan Negro Provisional Government (MAR)
SSO............ Schema de Structure et d'Orientation [*Moroccan*] (MAR)
SSO............ State Security Office (ML)
SSO............ Strana Slovenskej Obrody [*Slovak Rebirth Party*] (CZ)
SSO............ Student Socialist Organization (BU)
SSO............ Sudsudoeste [*South Southwest*] [*Spanish*]
SSO............ Svaz Slovenskych Obchodnikov [*Union of Slovak Businessmen*] (CZ)
SSOJ.......... Savez Socialisticke Omladine Jugoslavije [*League of Socialist Youth of Yugoslavia*] (PPE)
SSOM.......... Shell des Services d'Outre-Mer (MAR)
SSP............ First Aid Station (RU)
SSP............ Receiving Selsyn (RU)
SSP............ Savet za Stanbene Poslove [*Housing Council*] (YU)
SSP............ Secretaria de Seguranca Publica [*Secretariat of Public Security*] [*Brazilian*] (LA)
SSP............ Seguro Social del Peru [*Peruvian Social Security*] (LA)
SSP............ Sekretarijat za Saobracaj i Puteve [*Secretariat of Transportation and Roads*] (YU)
SSP............ Slovenska Strana Prace [*Slovak Workers' Party*] (CZ)
SSP............ Sofia Agricultural Enterprise (BU)
SSP............ Sofia Economic Enterprise (BU)
SSP............ Sosialistiki Spoudastiki Pali [*Socialist Student Struggle*] [*Greek*] (GC)
SSP............ Sous Seing Prive [*French*]
SSP............ Standard Subroutines System [*Computers*] (RU)
SSP............ Svaz Slovenskych Partizanov [*Union of Slovak Partisans*] (CZ)
SSP............ Synchronous Tracking Transmission (RU)
SSP............ Synomospondia dia tin Sotirian tou Paidiou [*Save the Children Federation*] (GC)
SSP............ Union of Soviet Writers (RU)
SSPG.......... Southern Sudan Provisional Government (MAR)
SSPP.......... Societe Senegalaise de Presse et de Publication (MAR)
SSPS.......... Savezni Sekretarijat za Personalnu Sluzbu [*Federal Secretariat for Civil Service*] (YU)
SSPT.......... Societe Senegalaise des Phosphates de Taiba (MAR)
SSPT.......... Societe Senegalaise des Phosphates de Thies (MAR)
SSPT.......... Societe Senegalaise de Publicite et de Tourisme [*Senegalese Advertising and Tourism Company*] (AF)
SSPU.......... Self-Adjusting Program Control System [*Automation*] (RU)
SSR............ Sir Seewoosagur Ramgoolam [*Mauritian*] (AF)
SSR............ Slovenska Socialisticka Republic [*Slovak Socialist Republic (since 1960)*] (CZ)
SSR............ Sous-Sections Regionales (MAR)
SSR............ Soviet Socialist Republic (RU)
SSR............ Sovjetska Socijalisticka Republika [*Soviet Socialist Republic*] (YU)
SSRA.......... Socialist Soviet Republic of Armenia (RU)
SSRB.......... Socialist Soviet Republic of Belorussia (RU)
SSRC.......... Soweto Students Representative Council (MAR)
SSRG.......... Socialist Soviet Republic of Georgia (RU)
SSRM.......... Socialist Workers' Youth League (RU)
SSRN.......... Socijalisticki Savez Radnog Naroda [*Socialist Alliance of Working People*] (YU)
SSRNBiH..... Socijalisticki Savez Radnog Naroda Bosne i Hercegovine [*Socialist Alliance of Working People of Bosnia and Hercegovina*] (YU)
SSRNJ......... Socijalisticki Sojuz na Rabotniot Narod na Jugoslavija [*Socialist Alliance of Working People of Yugoslavia*] (YU)
SSRNJ......... Socijalisticka Savez Radnog Naroda Jugoslavije [*Socialist Alliance of Working People of Yugoslavia - SAWPY*] (PPE)

SSRNJzaVojvodinu ... Socijalisticki Savez Radnog Naroda Jugoslavije za Vojvodinu [*Socialist Alliance of Working People of Yugoslavia in Vojvodina*] (YU)
SSRNM .... Socijalisticki Sojuz na Rabotniot Narod na Makedonija [*Socialist Alliance of Working People of Macedonia*] (YU)
SSRNV .... Socijalisticki Savez Radnog Naroda Vojvodine [*Socialist Alliance of Working People of Vojvodina*] (YU)
Ssro .... Spolecnost s Rucenim Omezenym [*Company with Limited Liability (Ltd.)*] (CZ)
SSRP .... Official Communications of Industrial Managers (RU)
SSRP .... Societe Saharienne de Recherches Petroliers (MAR)
SSRP .... Somali Socialist Revolutionary Party (MAR)
SSRP .... Specialized Assembling-Disassembling Device (RU)
SSRSC .... Saudi-Sudanese Red Sea Commission (MAR)
SSRT .... Societe Senegalaise de Realisation Touristique (MAR)
SSRT .... Societe Senegalaise de Realisations Touristiques, Club Aldiana (MAR)
SSRZ .... Shipyard (RU)
SSS .... Centimeter-Second-Candle (RU)
SSS .... Has Listened to the Countries of the World [*Radio operator's diploma*] (BU)
SSS .... Selkciona Stocarska Stanica [*Selective Livestock Station*] (YU)
SSS .... Servicio de Seguro Social [*Social Security Service*] [*Chilean*] (LA)
SSS .... Sklarske Strojirny a Slevarny [*Glass Engineering Works and Foundries*] (CZ)
SSS .... Slovenska Strana Svobody [*Slovak Freedom Party*] (CZ)
SSS .... Sogut Seramik Sanayii AS [*Sogut Ceramics Industry Corporation*] (TU)
SSS .... Sprava Statnich Silnic [*State Highway Administration*] (CZ)
SSS .... State Security Service [*Mauritian*] (AF)
SSS .... Statne Strojove Stanice [*State Machine Tractor Stations*] (CZ)
SSS .... Statni Strojni Stanice [*State Machine Station*] (CZ)
SSS .... Su Seguro Servidor [*Your Faithful Servant*] [*Correspondence*] [*Spanish*]
SSS .... Svaz Slovenskeho Studentstva [*Slovak Student Union*] (CZ)
SSS .... Svaz Slovenskych Skladatelov [*Union of Slovak Composers*] (CZ)
SSS .... Svaz Slovenskych Spisovatelov [*Union of Slovak Writers*] (CZ)
SSSaS .... Sdruzeni Socialistickych Skautu a Skautek [*Association of Socialist Boy Scouts and Girl Scouts*] (CZ)
SSSD .... Slovensky Svaz Spotrebnych Druzstiev [*Slovak Union of Consumer Cooperatives*] (CZ)
SSSL .... Samostatny Stihaci Letecky Sbor [*Separate Fighter Air Corps*] (CZ)
SSSP .... Sindicato de Sastres y Similares de Panama [*Union of Tailors and Related Workers of Panama*] (LA)
SSSR .... Soyuz Sovetskikh Sotsialisticheskikh Respublik [*Union of Soviet Socialist Republics*]
SSSR .... Svaz Sovetskych Socialistickych Republik [*Union of Soviet Socialist Republics (USSR)*] (CZ)
SSSR .... Union of Soviet Socialist Republics (BU)
SSSS .... Samakum Sang Sangkum Serei Reath [*Serei Reath Social Work Association*] [*Cambodian*] (CL)
SSSS .... Samo Sloga Srbina Spasave [*Only Unity Will Save the Serbs*] [*Serbian motto*] (YU)
SSSS .... Svaz Slovenskych Spevackych Sborov [*Union of Slovak Choral Societies*] (CZ)
SSSU .... Sojuz na Studentite od Skopskiot Univerzitet [*Union of Students of Skopje University*] (YU)
SSSU .... Spevacky Sbor Slovenskych Ucitelov [*Slovak Teachers' Choral Society*] (CZ)
sst .... Centistoke (RU)
SST .... Severoslovenske Tehelne [*North Slovak Brick Works*] (CZ)
SST .... Sivil Savunma Teskilati [*Civil Defense Organization*] [*Turkish Federated State of Cyprus*] (GC)
SST .... Societe Senegalaise des Tabacs (MAR)
SST .... Spiral Laminar Texture (RU)
SST .... Stanica Sanitetskog Transporta [*Medical Transport Station*] [*Military*] (YU)
SST .... Tank Support Aircraft (RU)
SSTA .... Schiffstammabteilung [*Naval Cadre Section*] (EG)
SSTK .... Savezna Spoljno-Trgovinska Komora [*Federal Chamber of Foreign Trade*] (YU)
SSTK .... Sud Casti Spoljnotrgovinske Komore [*Court of Honor of the Chamber of Foreign Trade*] (YU)
SSTNYu .... Socialist Union of Working People of Yugoslavia (RU)
SSTP .... Suomen Sosialistinen Tyovaenpuolue [*Finnish Socialist Workers' Party*] (WEN)
SSTs- .... Spiral Centrifugal Cleaner (RU)
SSTU .... Statny Stavebny Urad [*State Construction Office*] (CZ)
SSTV .... Sistema Sandinista de Television [*Sandinist Television Service*] [*Nicaraguan*] (LA1)
SSU .... Grid-Control System (RU)
SSU .... Selangor Students Union (Communist) (ML)
SSU .... Ship Power Plant (RU)
SSU .... Slezsky Studijni Ustav [*Silesian Research Institute*] (CZ)
SSU .... Slovensky Statisticky Urad [*Slovak Statistical Office*] (CZ)
SSU .... Statni Statisticky Urad [*State Office of Statistics*] (CZ)
SSU .... Sudanese Socialist Union (AF)
SSU .... Sveriges Socialdemokratiska Ungdomsforbund [*Swedish Social Democratic Youth Association*] (WEN)
SSU .... Swaziland Students Union (AF)
SSUB .... Staatlicher Strassenbau- und Unterhaltungsbetrieb [*State Road Building and Road Repair Enterprise*] (EG)
SSUJ .... Studium Slowianskie Uniwerstytetu Jagiellonskiego [*Slavic Department of Jagiellonian University*] (POL)
SSV .... Council for Mutual Economic Aid (BU)
s sv .... Luminous Intensity, Candlepower (RU)
SSV .... North-Northeast (RU)
SSV .... Sekretarijat za Saobracaj i Veze (SIV) [*Secretariat of Transportation and Communications*] (YU)
SSV .... Sevastopol' Shipyard (RU)
SSV .... Severo-Severovychod [*North-Northeast*] (CZ)
SSV .... Spolok Svateho Vojtecha [*St. Adalbert Society*] (CZ)
SSV .... Sresko Sindikalno Vece [*District Council of Trade Unions*] (YU)
SSV .... Standard Selling Value (MAR)
SSV .... Suedschleswigscher Waehlerverband - Sydslesvigsk Vaelgerforening [*South Schleswig Voters' Association*] [*West German*] (PPW)
SSVP .... Society of St. Vincent De Paul (EA)
SSVT .... Societe Senegalaise de Voyages et de Tourisme (MAR)
SSVZ .... Svaz Statnych a Verejnych Zamestnancov [*Union of Government and Public Employees*] (CZ)
SSW .... Suedschleswiger Waehlerverband [*South Schleswig Voter's League*] [*West German*] (PPE)
SSW .... Szkola Sanitariuszy Weterynaryjnych [*School for Veterinary Assistants*] (POL)
SSYB .... Saglik ve Sosyal Yardim Bakanligi [*Ministry of Health and Social Welfare*] (TU)
SSYM .... Saglik ve Sosyal Yardim Mudurlugu [*Directorate of Health and Social Welfare*] [*Under Health Ministry*] (TU)
SSZ .... Machine Tool Plant (RU)
SSZ .... North-Northwest (RU)
SSZ .... Samouprava Socialnega Zavarovanja [*Autonomous Administration of Social Insurance*] [*Ljubljana*] [*A periodical*] (YU)
SSZ .... Savet za Socijalnu Zastitu [*Social Insurance Council*] (YU)
SSZ .... Sekretarijat za Socijalnu Zastitu (SIV) [*Secretariat of Social Insurance*] (YU)
SSZ .... Sever Severo-Zapad [*North Northwest*] (YU)
SSZ .... Severo-Severozapad [*North-Northwest*] (CZ)
SSZ .... Shipyard (RU)
SSZ .... Stol Sedmorice u Zagrebu [*Supreme Court in Zagreb*] (YU)
SSZ .... Svaz Slovenskych Zien [*Union of Slovak Women*] (CZ)
SSZS .... Savez Studenata Zagrebackog Sveucilista [*Union of Students of Zagreb University*] (YU)
SSZZ .... Sreski Savez Zemljoradnickih Zadruga [*District Union of Agricultural Cooperatives*] (YU)
ST .... Adding Transformer (RU)
ST .... Aircraft Engine High-Temperature Grease (RU)
st .... Article (BU)
st .... Article (RU)
ST .... Center of Impact, Mean Point of Impact (RU)
st .... Century (RU)
st .... Column (RU)
ST .... Construction Technical School (BU)
st .... Degree (RU)
ST .... Degree, Rank, Grade (BU)
ST .... Dry-Cargo Motor Ship (RU)
st .... Economic (BU)
ST- .... End-Window Counter (RU)
ST .... Jet, Jet Stream [*Meteorology*] (RU)
ST .... Laminar Texture (RU)
ST .... Launching Carriage (RU)
st .... Master Sergeant, First Sergeant, Chief Petty Officer (RU)
ST .... Medium-Hard (RU)
st .... Old (RU)
ST .... Old Equipment (BU)
st .... Old Style [*Julian calendar*] (RU)
ST .... Patrol Boat (RU)
ST .... Rear Area Service, Supply Service (RU)
St .... Saint [*Saint*] [*French*] (MTD)
St .... San [*or Santo*] [*Saint*] [*Italian*]
St .... Sankt [*Saint*] [*German*] (GPO)
ST .... Sao Tome and Principe [*Two-letter standard code*] (CNC)
St .... Schnellzugtenderlokomotive [*Fast Express Train Tank Locomotive*] (EG)
ST .... Secretaria de Turismo [*Secretariat of Tourism*] [*Mexican*] (LA)
st .... Segedtiszt [*Assistant, Aide*] (HU)
ST .... Sekolah Teknik [*Technical School*] (IN)
ST .... Sekretarijat za Trud (IVNRM) [*Secretariat of Labor*] (YU)
ST .... Selsyn-Transformer (RU)
st .... Senior, Chief (RU)
ST- .... Ship Thermograph (RU)
ST .... Signal Transformer (RU)
ST .... Soviet Teletype (RU)
ST .... Srednji Talasi [*Medium Waves*] [*Aviation*] (YU)
St .... Staat [*German*]
st .... Stabilizer (RU)
ST .... Stabilizing Transformer (RU)

St........ Stacja [*Station*] [*Polish*]
St........ Stadt [*German*]
st........ Stage, Grade, Step (RU)
St........ Stahl [*Steel*] [*German*]
ST........ Standard (RU)
ST........ Standards der Deutschen Demokratischen Republik [*German Democratic Republic Standards*] (EG)
St........ Starsi [*Senior*] (CZ)
st........ Starszy [*Older, Senior*] [*Polish*]
ST........ Starter (RU)
St........ Station [*Station*] [*Military map abbreviation*] [*World War I*] [*French*] (MTD)
st........ Station (RU)
st........ Statistical (RU)
st........ Statni [*State (adjective)*] (CZ)
st........ Statt [*Instead Of*] [*German*]
st........ Stav [*Paragraph, Chapter, Section*] (YU)
st........ Stavka [*Paragraph, Chapter, Section*] (YU)
St........ Stelle [*German*]
st........ Stere [*Stere*] [*French*] (GPO)
st........ Stoke (RU)
st........ Stoletje [*Century*] (YU)
st........ Stopien [*or Stopnie*] [*Degree or Degrees*] [*Polish*]
st........ Stotinka (BU)
St........ Stueck [*Each*] [*German*]
St........ Stunde [*Hour*] [*German*]
st........ Style (BU)
ST........ Superheavy (RU)
st........ Sutun [*Column*] [*As of a newspaper*] (TU)
ST-........ Temperature Recorder (RU)
ST........ Temperature Signaler (RU)
Sta........ Santa [*Saint*] [*Portuguese*] (GPO)
Sta........ Santa [*Saint*] [*Spanish*]
StA........ Schlauchtransportanhaenger [*Hose Reel Trailer (Fire department vehicle)*] (EG)
STA........ Science and Technology Agency (SJT)
Sta........ Senorita [*Miss, Young Woman*] [*Spanish*]
STA........ Service Technique de l'Aeronautique [*Military*] [*French*] (MTD)
STA........ Skholi Tekhnikon Aeroporias [*Air Force Technical School*] [*Greek*] (GC)
STA........ Societe des Tabacs Algeriens (MAR)
STA........ Societe des Tabacs et Allumettes [*North African*] (MAR)
STA........ Societe de Transport de l'Administration (MAR)
STA........ Societe de Transport Algerien (MAR)
STA........ Societe de Transports Africains (MAR)
STA........ Societe des Transports des Amis (MAR)
STA........ Societe de Travail Aerien [*Algerian*] (MAR)
STA........ Somateion Typografon Athinon [*Union of Athens Printers*] (GC)
StA........ Staatsanwalt [*or Staatsanwaltschaft*] [*German*]
STA........ Start-Stop Apparatus, Teletype (RU)
StA........ Starter Battery (RU)
STA........ Stredoevropska Tiskova Agentura [*Central European Press Agency*] (CZ)
STA........ Sustredovacie Tabory [*Detention Camps*] (CZ)
STA........ Sveriges Televerket [*Swedish Telecommunications Administration*] (WEN)
STAAIM........ Syndicat des Travailleurs Agricoles et Artisans de l'Ile Maurice [*Agricultural Workers and Artisans Union of Mauritius Island*] (AF)
Staatl........ Staatlich [*State or Federal*] [*German*] (GPO)
STAB........ Service des Transports Aeriens du Burundi [*Burundi Air Transportation Service*] (AF)
STAB........ Sociedad de Tecnicos Azucareros y Alcoholeros del Brasil
STAB........ Societe de Travaux Auxiliaires de Batiment (MAR)
stab........ Stabilizer, Regulator [*Electricity*] (BU)
STAB........ Svenska Tandsticks AB [*The Swedish Match Co. Ltd.*] (WEN)
STABACO... Sociedad Tabacalera Antioquena [*Medellin*] (COL)
STABEX........ Stabilization of Export Earnings from Commodities (MAR)
STACA........ Servicio Tecnico Agricola Colombiano-Americano [*Colombian-American Agricultural Technical Service*] (LA)
STACC........ Staccato [*Detached, Distinct*] [*Italian*]
stad........ Stadium [*Topography*] (RU)
STAE........ Sogdian-Tadzhik Archaelogical Expedition (RU)
STAEI........ Societe de Transit et d'Affretement Export-Import (MAR)
StAeVO........ Steueraenderungsverordnung [*Tax Amendment Decree*] (EG)
STAFARM... State Farms Corporation (MAR)
STAFO........ Statsjenestemanns Forbundet [*Federation of Civil Servants*] [*Norwegian*] (WEN)
STAG........ Servicio Tecnico Agricola [*Palmira*] (COL)
STAG........ Sindicato de Trabajadores de Artes Graficas [*Union of Graphic Arts Workers*] [*Salvadoran*] (LA)
STAG........ Sociedade Tecnica de Artes Graficas Mocambique Lda. (MAR)
StAG........ Staatsanwaltschaftsgesetz [*Public Prosecutors Law*] (EG)
STAGE........ Societe Africaine des Grands Travaux de l'Est (MAR)
STAGEK MEM... Statisztikai es Gazdasagelemzo Kozpont, Mezogazdasagi es Elelmezesugyi Miniszterium [*Statistical and Economic Analysis Center, Ministry of Agriculture and Food Industry*] (HU)
STAI........ Sindicato de Trabajadores Agroindustriales [*Trade Union of Agroindustrial Workers*] [*Nicaraguan*] (LA1)
STAKO........ Committee for the Study of Scientific Principles of Standardization (RU)
STAL........ Sociedade Tecnica de Acessorios Lda. (MAR)
stal........ Steel Foundry [*Topography*] (RU)
STALAG........ Stammlager [*Prisoner-of-War Camp*] [*German*]
Stalhurt........ Warszawska Hurtownia Zelaza, Stali, i Wyrobow Zelaznych [*Warsaw Wholesale House of Iron, Steel, and Ferrous Products*] (POL)
Stal'konstruktsiya... Trust of the Glavstal'konstruktsiya of the Gosmontazhspetsstroy SSSR (RU)
Stal'montazh... State Trust of the Glavstal'konstruktsiya of the Gosmontazhspetsstroy SSSR (RU)
Stal'most........ All-Union Trust for the Manufacture and Assembly of Metal Structures of the Glavmostostroy (RU)
Stal'proyekt... State All-Union Institute for the Planning of Units for Steel Foundry and Rolling Mill Production in Ferrous Metallurgy (RU)
STAM........ Societe de Travaux Agricoles Marocains (MAR)
STAM........ Societe Tunisienne d'Acconage et de Manutention (MAR)
STAMICO.... State Mining Corporation [*Tanzanian*] (AF)
STAMVIE.... Societe Tropicale d'Assurances Mutuelles et Vie [*Ivorian*] (MAR)
stan........ Stanitsa, Cossack Village (RU)
stan........ Temporary Settlement [*Topography*] (RU)
STANAVFORLANT... Standing Naval Force, Atlantic [*NATO*]
stand........ Standard (RU)
Standartdomsbyt... Central Office of the Rosglavlessnabsbyt (RU)
Standartgiz... State Publishing House of Standards (RU)
STANKIN.... Moscow Institute of Machine Tools and Tools (RU)
Stankoimport... All-Union Association of the Ministry of Foreign Trade, USSR (RU)
Stankolit..... Moscow Iron Foundry for the Production of Castings for Machine Tool Manufacture (RU)
Stankonormal'... Moscow Plant of Standard Parts for Machine Tools (RU)
STAP........ Secretariado Tecnico dos Assuntos Politicos [*Technical Secretariat for Political Affairs*] [*Portuguese*] (WER)
STAPE........ Secretariado Tecnico dos Assuntos Politicos e Eleitorais [*Technical Secretariat for Political and Election Matters*] [*Portuguese*] (WER)
STAPO........ Staatspolizei [*State Police*] [*Austrian*] (WEN)
Star........ Old [*Toponymy*] (RU)
STAR........ Service Technique Africain de Radio-Television (MAR)
STAR........ Societe Senegalaise de Transports et Affretements Routiers (MAR)
STAR........ Societe Tananarivienne de Refrigeration et de Boissons Gazeuses [*Malagasy*] (MAR)
STAR........ Societe de Transport Aerien du Rwanda (MAR)
STAR........ Societe Tunisienne d'Assurance et de Reassurance (MAR)
STARC........ Societe de Transports et d'Affretements Routiers au Cameroun (MAR)
starin........ Ancient (RU)
starkom........ Senior Commissar (RU)
starleyt........ Senior Lieutenant (RU)
starmekh.... Senior Mechanic [*Navy*] (RU)
starmornach... Senior Naval Officer (RU)
star neft kol... Abandoned Oil Well [*Topography*] (RU)
starogr........ Ancient Greek (BU)
starpom........ Senior Assistant [*Navy*] (RU)
starsh........ Senior, Chief (RU)
START........ Science Association of the Republic of Tanzania (MAR)
star zhel rud... Abandoned Iron Mine [*Topography*] (RU)
STAS........ Standarde de Stat [*State Standards*] (RO)
STASI........ Staatssicherheitsdienst [*State Security Service*] (EG)
st asist........ Senior Assistant (BU)
STAT........ Societe Tchadienne d'Affretement et de Transit (MAR)
stat........ Statim [*Immediately*] [*Latin*] (GPO)
stat........ Statistical, Statistics (RU)
statist........ Statistical (BU)
Stat K........ Statisztikai Kiado [*Statistical Publishing House*] (HU)
statupr........ Statistical Administration (RU)
Stavostroj... Zavody na Vyrobu Stavebnich Stroju [*Construction Machinery Plants*] (CZ)
STAZ........ Stalinsk Aluminum Plant (RU)
STAZA........ Stalinovy Zavody [*Stalin Plants*] (CZ)
STAZRA........ Plant Protection Station (RU)
stb........ Old Bulgarian Language (BU)
stb........ S A Tobbi [*Et Cetera*] (HU)
STB........ Sacrae Theologiae Baccalaureus [*Bachelor of Sacred Theology*] [*Latin*] (GPO)
STB........ Sanayi ve Teknoloji Bakanligi [*Ministry of Industry and Technology*] (TU)
STB........ Societe Togolaise de Boissons (MAR)
STB........ Societe des Transports Brazzavillois (MAR)
STB........ Societe Tropicale des Bois (MAR)
STB........ Societe Tunisienne de Banque [*Tunisian Banking Company*] (AF)
StB........ Statni Bezpecnost [*State Security (Police)*] (CZ)
STB........ Technical Estimate Office (RU)
STBC........ Swaziland Television Broadcasting Corporation (MAR)
StbEvSt........ Staatsbuergerschaftsevidenzstelle [*German*]
STBG........ Societe de Transports de Bois en Grumes (MAR)

STBL .... Spojene Tovarny na Barvy a Laky [*United Paint and Lacquer Factories*] (CZ)
STBO .... Societe de Transformation du Bois de l'Ouest (MAR)
St BOT .... Stoleczne Biuro Obslugi Turystycznej [*Warsaw Tourist Service Office*] (POL)
Stbr .... Steinbruch [*German*]
StbsRttm .... Stabsrittmeister [*German*]
STBTP .... Syndicat des Travailleurs du Batiment et Travaux Publics (MAR)
Stbv .... Staatsbuergerschaftsverband [*German*]
STC .... Customs Cooperation Council [*CCC*] (RU)
STC .... Singapore Traction Company [*Bus company*] (ML)
STC .... Societe Tchadienne de Confection (MAR)
STC .... Societe Tchadienne de Credit (MAR)
STC .... Societe de Transports et Construction (MAR)
STC .... State Trading Corporation [*Jamaican*] (LA1)
STC .... Statistical Training Centre (MAR)
STCA .... Section Topographique de Corps d'Armee [*Military*] [*French*] (MTD)
STCA .... Service Telegraphique de Corps d'Armee [*Military*] [*French*] (MTD)
STCAN .... Service Technique des Constructions et Armes Navales [*Technical Service for Naval Construction and Ordnance*] [*French*] (WER)
STCAU .... Service Technique Central d'Amenagement et Urbanisme (MAR)
STCHS .... Stavebne Technicka Sluzba [*Construction and Technical Service*] [*Civil defense*] (CZ)
STCI .... Societe de Transports de la Cote-d'Ivoire (MAR)
STCSP .... Sindicato de Trabajadores de la Construccion y Similares de Panama [*Union of Construction Workers and Workers in Related Trades of Panama*] (LA)
STCT .... Sindicato de Trabajadores de la Colombiana de Tabaco [*Colombian Tobacco Company Workers Union*] (LA)
STCT .... Sindicato dos Trabalhadores dos Correios e Telecomunicacoes [*Union of Postal and Telecommunications Workers*] [*Portuguese*] (WER)
STCTP .... Societe Togolaise de Commerce et de Travaux Publics (MAR)
STD .... Sacrae Theologiae Doctor [*Doctor of Sacred Theology*] [*Latin*] (GPO)
STD .... Sao Tome and Principe Dobra (MAR)
STD .... Societe Textile Dahomeenne (MAR)
STD .... Societe Tunisienne de Diffusion (MAR)
std .... Standartti(a) [*Finnish*]
Std .... Studien [*German*]
std .... Stuendig [*For Hour*] [*German*]
Std .... Stunde [*Hour*] [*German*]
Stde .... Stunde [*Hour*] [*German*]
stdg .... Stuendig [*For Hour*] [*German*]
STDI .... Section Topographique de Division d'Infanterie [*Military*] [*French*] (MTD)
Stdn .... Stunden [*Hours*] [*German*]
StdsA .... Standesamt [*German*]
STE .... Entreprise Socialiste des Travaux de l'Est (MAR)
Ste .... Sainte [*Saint*] [*French*] (MTD)
STE .... Skholi Touristikon Epangelmation [*Tourist Trades School*] [*Greek*] (GC)
Ste .... Societe [*Company*] [*French*]
STE .... Societe Togolaise d'Entreposage (MAR)
STE .... Societe Travaux Electriques (MAR)
STE .... Stredoceske Energeticke Zavody [*Electric Power Plants, Central Bohemia*] (CZ)
STE .... Studii Tehnico-Economice [*Technical-Economic Studies*] (RO)
STE .... Symvoulion tou Ethnous [*Council of State*] [*See also SE*] (GC1)
STEA .... Societe des Travaux d'Electrification et d'Adduction [*Electrification and Water Supply Construction Company*] [*Beninese*] (AF)
STEA .... Stammeichamt [*German*]
STEAG .... Steinkolen-Elektrizitaet Aktiengesellschaft (MAR)
STEAM .... Skholi Tekhnikis Ekpaidevseos Axiomatikon Mikhanikou [*Technical Training School for Engineer Corps Officers*] [*Greek*] (GC)
STEB .... Societe des Travaux d'Entretien de Batiments (MAR)
STEBT .... Societe de Transformation et d'Exploitation des Bois Tropicaux (MAR)
STEC .... Societe de Transport, d'Elevage, et de Commerce (MAR)
STECDIP ..... Societe Tunisienne d'Etudes, de Cooperation, et de Defense de l'Industrie Phosphatiere (MAR)
STECI .... Societe de Travaux d'Equipement de la Cote-d'Ivoire (MAR)
STECTA ...... Societe Technique et Commerciale des Canalisations Souterraines en Tubes d'Acier (MAR)
STEE .... Societe Tchadienne d'Energie Electrique (MAR)
STEEP .... Societe Tchadienne d'Entreposage de Produits Petroliers (MAR)
STEES .... Sindicato de Trabajadores de la Educacion de El Salvador [*Union of Educational Workers of El Salvador*] (LA)
STEF .... Societe de Transport et d'Entrepots Frigorifiques (MAR)
STEG .... Societe Tchadienne d'Entreprises Generales (MAR)
STEG .... Societe de Techniques, d'Entreprises, et de Gestion (MAR)
STEG .... Societe Tunisienne d'Electricite et du Gaz [*Tunisian Gas and Electric Company*] (AF)
StEG .... Strafrechtsergaenzungsgesetz [*Penal Code Amendment*] (EG)
STEI .... Societe Transafricaine d'Etudes et d'Investissements (MAR)
STEIA .... Sociedade Tecnica de Equipamentos Industriais e Agricolas Lda. (MAR)
steir .... Steirisch [*German*]
stekhiometrich ... Stoichiometric (RU)
stekl .... Glass Plant [*Topography*] (RU)
steklogr ...... Hyalography (RU)
Stellv .... Stellvertreter [*German*]
STEM .... Societe Tropicale d'Entrepots et de Magasinage (MAR)
STEM .... Southern Technical and Economic Movement [*South African*] (AF)
STEMI .... Societe de Transports et Manutentions Industriels (MAR)
STEN .... Societe Togolaise des Engrais (MAR)
sten .... Stenographic (RU)
stenkor .... Wall Newspaper Correspondent (RU)
stenogr .... Shorthand Record, Verbatim Report (RU)
stenogr .... Verbatim Report (BU)
Stenpechat ... Wall News Sheets (BU)
stenvestnik ... Wall Newspaper (BU)
STEP .... Societe Togolaise d'Electronique Parby (MAR)
STEP .... Societe de Travaux d'Electricite et Plomberie (MAR)
STEP .... Societe Tunisienne d'Exportation du Petrole (MAR)
STEPC .... Societe Tropicale d'Engrais et de Produits Chimiques (MAR)
STEPHOS ... Societe Tunisienne d'Exploitation Phosphatiere (MAR)
STEPO .... Spojene Tovarny na Technicky Porculan, Narodni Podnik [*United Industrial Ceramic Factories, National Enterprise*] (CZ)
ster .... Steradian (RU)
STER .... Stichting Etherreclame [*Airways Advertising Foundation*] [*Dutch*] (WEN)
stereot .... Stereotype (RU)
stereot izd .. Stereotype Publication (BU)
STET .... Societa Finanziaria Telefonica [*Telephone Finance Corporation*] [*Italian*] (WER)
STEUNAM ... Sindicato de Trabajadores y Estudiantes de la Universidad Nacional Autonoma de Mexico [*Workers and Students Union of the National Autonomous University of Mexico*] (LA)
STF .... Societe des Transports Ferre (MAR)
STF .... Supremo Tribunal Federal [*Federal Supreme Court*] [*Brazilian*] (LA)
STFAG .... Syndicat des Travailleurs de la Foret et de Agriculture (MAR)
StFB .... Staatlicher Forstwirtschaftsbetrieb [*State Forestry Enterprise*] (EG)
STFC .... Service du Transport Fluvial Centrafricain [*Central African River Transportation Service*] (AF)
STFO .... Societe Technique de la Foret d'Okoume [*Okoume Forest Technical Company*] [*Gabonese*] (AF)
Stft .... Stift [*German*]
STG .... Pipe Bender (RU)
STG .... Somatotropic Hormone (RU)
StGB .... Strafgesetzbuch [*Penal Code*] (EG)
STH .... Societe Togolaise d'Hotellerie (MAR)
STH .... Societe Togolaise des Hydrocarbures [*Togolese Hydrocarbons Company*] (AF)
STHRA .... Societe de Transport d'Hassi R'Mel-Arzew [*North African*] (MAR)
STI .... Information Telecommunication System (RU)
STI .... Institute of Sanitary Engineering (RU)
STI .... Savezni Trzisni Inspektorat (DSPRP) [*Federal Market Inspectorate*] (YU)
STI .... Secretaria de Tecnologia Industrial [*Secretariat for Industrial Technology*] [*Brazilian*] (LA1)
STI .... Siberian Technological Institute (RU)
Sti .... Sirketi [*Company*] [*See also Ltd Sti*] (TU)
STI .... Societe Tchadienne d'Investissement (MAR)
STI .... Somborska Tekstilna Industrija [*Sombor Textile Industry*] (YU)
STI .... Sudan Textile Industry (MAR)
S-Ti .... Suedtirol [*German*]
STI .... Technical Information Service (RU)
STIA .... Societe Tunisienne d'Industrie Automobile (MAR)
STIADES ..... Sindicato de Trabajadores de la Industria Electrica [*Trade Union of Electric Industry Workers*] [*Salvadoran*] (LA1)
STIB .... Societe de Transformation Industrielle des Bois (MAR)
STIC .... Societe des Traducteurs et Interpretes du Canada [*Society of Translators and Interpreters of Canada*]
STIC .... Sudan Textile Industry Company (MAR)
STICA .... Servicio Tecnico Interamericano de Cooperacion Agricola [*Inter-American Technical Service of Agricultural Cooperation*] (LA)
STICEC .... Australian National Scientific and Technical Information Authority
STICPA .... Societe Tchadienne Industrielle et Commerciale des Produits Animaux (MAR)
STICS .... Syndicat des Travailleurs Indigenes Congolais Specialises (MAR)
STIES .... Sindicato de Trabajadores de la Industria Electromecanica y Similares [*Trade Union of Electricians and Related Trades Workers*] [*Nicaraguan*] (LA1)

STIGCES .... Sindicato de Trabajadores de las Industrias Graficas y Conexas de El Salvador [*Union of Workers in the Graphics and Related Industries of El Salvador*] (LA)
STIL .... Societe des Transitaires Internationaux du Laos [*International Forwarding Agents Company of Laos*] (CL)
STIL .... Societe Tunisienne de l'Industrie Laitiere (MAR)
STIMA .... Societe de Techniques Industrielles et Maritimes (MAR)
STIMAD ...... Societe des Telecommunications Internationales de la Republique Democratique Malgache [*International Telecommunications Company of the Democratic Republic of Madagascar*] (AF)
STIMBS .... Sindicato de Trabajadores de Industrias Metalicas Basicas y Similares [*Union of Workers of the Basic Metals and Allied Industries*] [*Salvadoran*] (LA)
STIMCES .... Sindicato de Trabajadores de la Industria Minera y Conexas de El Salvador [*Trade Union of Salvadoran Mining and Related Industries Workers*] (LA1)
STIMEAFRIQUE ... Societe Technique d'Importation de Materiel d'Entreprise pour l'Afrique, Senegal (MAR)
STIMMB ...... Sindicato de Trabajadores de la Industria Mecanica y Metalicas Basicas [*Union of Workers of the Mechanical and Basic Metals Industries*] [*Salvadoran*] (LA)
STIP .... Sindicato de Trabajadores de la Industria Plastica [*Trade Union of Plastic Industry Workers*] [*Nicaraguan*] (LA1)
STIP .... Societe Tunisienne des Industries de Pneumatiques (MAR)
STIR .... Societe de Transports Internationaux du Rwanda (MAR)
STIR .... Societe Tunisio-Italienne de Raffinage [*Tunisian-Italian Refining Company*] (AF)
STIRTTES ... Sindicato de Trabajadores de la Industria de Radio, Teatro, y Television de El Salvador [*Union of Workers in the Radio, Theater, and Television Industry of El Salvador*] (LA)
STISSS .... Sindicato de Trabajadores del Instituto Salvadoreno del Seguro Social [*Union of the Salvadoran Social Security Institute Workers*] (LA)
STITASSC ... Sindicato de Trabajadores Industrias Textil, Algodon, Sinteticas, Similares, y Conexas [*Union of Workers in Textile, Cotton, Synthetic, Similar, and Related Industries*] [*Salvadoran*] (LA)
STIUSA .... Sindicato Textil Industrias Unidas, Sociedad Anonima [*Union of United Textile Industries, Inc.*] [*Salvadoran*] (LA)
STJ .... Slovenska Telocvicna Jednota [*Slovak Gymnastic Association*] (CZ)
STK .... Savez Trgovinskih Komora [*Union of Chambers of Commerce*] (YU)
STK .... Societe des Transports de Kinshasa [*Kinshasa Transport Company*] [*Zairian*] (AF)
STK .... Sreska Trgovinska Komora [*Distict Chamber of Commerce*] (YU)
STK .... Stacni Technicka Knihovna [*State Technical Library*] [*Brno*] (CZ)
STK .... Stadart Topografik Karta [*Standard Topographic Map*] (TU)
STK .... Stanje Teretnih Kola [*Condition of Freight Cars*] [*Railroads*] (YU)
STK .... Suomen Tyonantajain Keskusliitto [*Finnish Employers' Association*] (WEN)
STK .... Technical Supervisory Service (RU)
STK .... Telemetric Monitoring System (RU)
STK .... Voice-Frequency Patching Rack (RU)
STK .... Worker's Union of Colombia (RU)
StKK .... Staatliches Komitee fuer Kultur (und Sport) [*State Committee for Culture (and Sport)*] (EG)
StKKF .... Stoleczny Komitet Kultury Fizycznej [*Warsaw Committee on Physical Culture*] (POL)
Stkr .... Stadtkreis [*Urban Kreis (Administrative unit)*] (EG)
StKTA .... Stellvertreter Kommandeur der Technischen Ausruestung [*Deputy Commander for Technical Equipment*] (EG)
STKV .... Mean Temperature Coefficient of Viscosity (RU)
STL .... Pilot's Aerial Gunnery Trainer (RU)
StL .... Studentski List [*Students Journal*] [*A publication*] (YU)
STL .... Suomen Tukkukauppiaiden Liitto [*Finnish Federation of Wholesalers*] (WEN)
stlb .... Column (RU)
STLBW .... Stedelijke Technische Leergangen voor Bibliotheek Wezen
st lt .... Senior Lieutenant (RU)
STM .... Construction Technicum of the Mosgorispolkom (RU)
STM .... International Group of Scientific, Technical, and Medical Publishers (EA)
STM .... Sindicato del Transporte Maritimo [*Maritime Transport Workers Union*] [*Uruguayan*] (LA)
STM .... Societe de Transport de Merchandises [*Tunisian*] (MAR)
stm .... Sotamies [*Finnish*]
STM .... Soutez Tvorivosti Mladeze [*Young People's Creative Activities Competition*] (CZ)
Stm .... Starkstrommeisterei [*High-Voltage Section Shop*] (EG)
STM .... Stavby a Trati Mladeze [*Structures and Railroad Tracks (Built by Youth Brigade)*] (CZ)
Stm .... Steiermark [*or Steiermaerkisch*] [*German*]
STM .... Superior Tribunal Militar [*Superior Military Court*] [*Brazilian*] (LA)
STM .... Szybkie Tramwaje Miejskie [*Express Trolleys*] (POL)
STMA .... Syndicat des Transports Maritimes et Acconiers (MAR)
st mar .... Starszy Marynarz [*Able-Bodied Seaman*] [*Polish*]
Stmk .... Steiermark [*or Steiermaerkisch*] [*German*]
STML .... Sindicato de Trabajadores Municipales de Limon [*Trade Union of Limon Municipal Workers*] [*Costa Rican*] (LA1)
STML .... Working Youth League of Latvia (RU)
st m lk .... Surgeon, Regimental Surgeon (BU)
STMNC .... Sindicato de Trabajadores de Marmoles y Cementos Nare [*Nare Union of Marble and Cement Workers*] [*Colombian*] (LA)
STMV .... Working Youth League of Vietnam [*North Vietnamese*] (RU)
STN .... Societe des Terres Neuves (MAR)
STN .... Societe de Transports du Nord Cameroun (MAR)
STN .... Sportovni a Turisticke Nakladatelstvi [*Publishing House for Literature on Sport and Tourism*] (CZ)
Stn .... Station [*Station*] [*Military map abbreviation*] [*World War I*] [*French*] (MTD)
Stn .... Straten [*Straits*] [*See also Str*] [*Dutch*] (NAU)
STN .... Studenckie Towarzystwo Naukowe [*Students' Scientific Society*] (POL)
st No .... Old Number (BU)
STNP .... Strojarne Nakupnych Podnikov Bratislava [*Maintenance Shops of Purchasing Enterprises, Bratislava*] (CZ)
st n s .... Senior Scientific Associate (BU)
STO .... Council of Labor and Defense [*1920-1937*] (RU)
STO .... Labor and Defense Council (BU)
Sto .... Santo [*Saint*] [*Spanish*]
STO .... Savez za Tehnicki Odgoj [*Union for Technical Training*] (YU)
STO .... Special Theory of Relativity (RU)
STO .... Svobodno Trzasko Ozemlje [*Free Territory of Trieste*] (YU)
STO .... Technical Servicing Station (RU)
STOBAVO ... Stores Baches Haute-Volta (MAR)
STOC .... Societe de Transports Oubangui-Cameroun (MAR)
STOC .... Societe de Transports Ouest-Centrafricaines [*Bangui*] (MAR)
STOCA .... Societe Togolaise de Credit Automobile (MAR)
Stockpkt ..... Stockpunkt [*Solidifying Point*] (EG)
st ogn .... Starszy Ogniomistrz [*Battery Sergeant Major*] [*Polish*]
STOK .... Syndicat de Tajalt Oum Kadiar (MAR)
stol .... Stoleczny [*Of the Capitol*] [*Warsaw*] (POL)
STOL .... Stoleti [*Century*] (CZ)
STOM .... Societe de Transports de l'Ogooue Maritime (MAR)
Ston .... Station [*Station*] [*Military map abbreviation*] [*French*] (MTD)
stop .... Economic (BU)
STOP .... Public Freight Transport Association (BU)
STOP .... Public Transport Enterprise (BU)
STOP .... Sociedade Tecnica de Obras e Projectos Lda. (MAR)
STOP .... Standard of Limited Application (RU)
STOP .... Stowarzyszenie Techniczne Odlewnikow Polskich [*Polish Foundry Workers' Technical Association*] (POL)
STORES ...... Syntactic Tracer Organized Retrospective Enquiry System [*IWIS/TNO*] [*'s-Gravenhage*]
storozh b ..... Watch Box [*Topography*] (RU)
storozh v ..... Watchtower [*Topography*] (RU)
stow .... Stowarzyszenie [*Association*] (POL)
STP .... Center of Impact, Mean Point of Impact (RU)
STP .... Launching Platform (RU)
STP .... Sacrae Theologiae Professor [*Professor of Sacred Theology*] [*Latin*] (GPO)
STP .... Sao Tome and Principe [*Three-letter standard code*] (CNC)
STP .... Sentry Post (RU)
STP .... Sijil Tinggi Pelajaran [*Higher Education Certificate*] (ML)
STP .... Societe Togolaise des Plastiques (MAR)
STP .... Societes Tunisiennes de Prevoyance (MAR)
STP .... Splosno Trgovinsko Podjetje [*General Commercial Establishment*] (YU)
STP .... Suomen Tyovaenpuolue [*Finnish Workers' Party*] (WEN)
STPA .... Service de Transports Publics Aeriens (MAR)
STPA .... Seychelles Taxpayers and Producers Association (MAR)
STPC .... Societe des Tanneries et Peausseries du Cameroun (MAR)
STPI .... Technical Aid and Information Department (RU)
STPL .... Sosialistinen Tyovaen ja Pienviljelijain Liitto [*Socialist Workers and Small Holders League*] [*Finnish*] (WEN)
St planina ... Balkan Mountains (BU)
STPN .... Societe des Transports Publics de Nouakchott (MAR)
StPO .... Strafprozessordnung [*Code of Criminal Procedure*] [*West German*] (EG)
s t/pr .... Antitorpedo Net (RU)
st prep .... Senior Instructor (BU)
STPRM .... Sindicato de Trabajadores Petroleros de la Republica Mexicana [*Mexican Petroleum Workers Union*] (LA)
STPS .... Secretaria del Trabajo y Prevision Social [*Labor and Social Security Secretariat*] [*Mexican*] (LA)
STPZK .... Union of Labor Productive Craftsmen's Cooperatives (BU)
STQ .... Society of Translators of Quebec [*Canada*]
str .... Construction (BU)
STR .... Glow-Discharge Stabilitron Tube (RU)
str .... Line (RU)
STR .... Medical Transport Vessel (RU)
str .... Page (BU)
str .... Page (RU)
str .... Steradian (RU)
Str .... Steuer [*German*]

Str .... Straat [*or Straten*] [*Strait or Street*] [*Dutch*] (NAU)
Str .... Strada [*Street*] [*Italian*]
Str .... Strada [*Street*] [*Romanian*]
Str .... Straede [*Street*] [*Danish*]
Str .... Straeti [*Street*] [*Icelandic*]
Str .... Strasse [*Street*] [*German*] (GPO)
STR .... Stredni [*Secondary*] (CZ)
str .... Stronica [*Page*] (POL)
str .... Under Construction [*Topography*] (RU)
strad .... Passive Voice (RU)
strakh .... Insurance (RU)
STRC .... Scientific, Technical, and Research Commission [*of the OAU*] (AF)
STRE .... Telemetering System of Electric Power Consumption (RU)
StRG .... Strafregistergesetz [*Criminal Records Law*] (EG)
STRHA .... Sindicato de Trabajadores del Ingenio Rio Haina [*Trade Union of Rio Haina Sugar Mill Workers*] [*Dominican Republic*] (LA1)
StRK .... Staatliches Rundfunkkomitee [*State Radio Committee*] (EG)
str m .... Building Materials Plant [*Topography*] (RU)
STRM .... Sindicato de Telefonistas de la Republica Mexicana [*Trade Union of Telephone Operators of the Mexican Republic*] (LA1)
STRN .... Societe des Transports Routiers du Niger (MAR)
StRN .... Stoleczna Rada Narodowa [*Warsaw People's Council*] (POL)
stroit .... Construction Term (RU)
STROJEXPORT ... Podnik Zahranicniho Obchodu pro Vyvoz Stroju a Strojnich Zarizeni [*Foreign Trade Enterprise for the Export of Machines and Mechanical Equipment*] (CZ)
STROJIMPORT ... Podnik Zahranicniho Obchodu pro Dovoz Stroju a Prumyslovych Zarizeni [*Foreign Trade Enterprise for the Import of Machines and Industrial Installations*] (CZ)
STROMBYuRO ... All-Union Office of the Building Materials Industry (RU)
strommashina ... Machine for the Manufacture of Building Materials (RU)
Stromotdel ... Department of the Building Materials Industry (RU)
Strompromsoyuz ... Building Materials Producers' Union (RU)
Stroybank ... All-Union Bank for the Financing of Capital Investments (RU)
stroybat ...... Construction Battalion (RU)
Stroydetal' ... All-Union Trust for the Manufacture of Structural Parts (RU)
Stroydormash ... Construction and Road Machinery Plant (RU)
Stroygrupa ... Construction Group (BU)
Stroyizdat ... State Publishing House of Construction Literature (RU)
Stroymash ... Construction Machinery Plant (RU)
Stroymashsbyt ... Marketing Administration of the Ministry of Construction and Road Machinery Manufacture, USSR (RU)
Stroymat ..... Construction Materials (BU)
Stroymatmetiz ... State Commercial Enterprise for Construction Materials and Metal Products (BU)
Stroymekhanizatsiya ... Trust of the Administration for the Mechanization of Specialized and Installation Operations of the Ministry of Construction, RSFSR (RU)
Stroymekhzapchast' ... All-Union Office of the Glavstroymekhanizatsiya of the State Industrial Committee for Transportation Construction, USSR (RU)
Stroymontazh ... Trust of the Glavmetallurgmontazh of the Gosmontazhspetsstroy SSSR (RU)
Stroynefteurs ... Administration of Workers' Supply of the Ministry of Construction of Petroleum Industry Establishments, USSR (RU)
Stroyobedinenie ... Construction Trust (BU)
Stroytermoizolyatsiya ... Trust of the Glavteplomontazh of the Gosmontazhspetsstroy SSSR (RU)
stroytrest .... Building Materials Trust (RU)
stroyuch ...... Construction Apprenticeship School (RU)
Stroyvoyenmorizdat ... Publishing House of the Ministry of Construction of Military and Naval Establishments, USSR (RU)
Strpovbr ..... Strogo Poverljivo Broj [*Strictly Confidential Number*] (YU)
Strpovopbr ... Strogo Poverljivo Operativni Broj [*Strictly Confidential Operational Number*] [*Military*] (YU)
STRS .... Starsina [*Master Sergeant*] (CZ)
str-vo .... Construction, Construction Site (RU)
strz .... Strzelec [*Rifleman, Gunner*] [*Polish*]
sts .... Coupling, Clutch (RU)
STS .... Hyperfine Structure (RU)
STS .... Medical Transport Vessel (RU)
st s .... Old Style [*Julian calendar*] (RU)
STs .... Random Number (RU)
STS .... Rural Telephone Network (RU)
STs .... Silver-Zinc Battery (RU)
STS .... Slezska Tiskova Sluzba [*Silesian Press Service*] (CZ)
STS .... Slovensky Tenisovy Svaz [*Slovak Tennis Association*] (CZ)
STS .... Societe Textile du Senegal (MAR)
STS .... Societe des Transports Sauvage Pere & Fils (MAR)
STS .... Solar Heat Power Plant (RU)
STs .... Somite Center (RU)
STS .... Spojene Tovarny na Stuhy [*United Ribbon Factories*] (CZ)
STS .... Srednja Tehnicka Skola [*Secondary Technical School*] (YU)
STS .... State All-Union Construction and Installation Trust of Flame Heat Engineering (RU)
STS .... State Travel Service (MAR)
STS .... Statni Traktorova Stanice [*State Tractor Station*] (CZ)
STS .... Strojni Traktorove Stanice [*Machine Tractor Stations*] (CZ)
STS .... Studencki Teatr Satyryczny [*Students' Satirical Theater*] (POL)
STsB .... Signalization, Centralization, and Block System (RU)
STsGT .... All-Union Central Geophysical Trust (RU)
st sierz .... Starszy Sierzant [*Company Sergeant Major*] [*Polish*]
st sl .... Active Duty, Field Duty (BU)
stsl .... Old Slavonic (BU)
STsLN .... Aspiring Centrifugal Vane Pump (RU)
STsM .... Center-of-Mass System (RU)
STsM .... Special-Purpose Digital Computer (RU)
STSO .... Societe des Transporteurs du Senegal Oriental (MAR)
STSO .... Societe des Transports du Sud-Ouest (MAR)
STSPS .... Statni Spojova Sluzba [*State Communication Service*] [*Civil defense*] (CZ)
STsS .... Addition Cycle Counter (RU)
sts sp .... Scintillation Spectrometer (RU)
sts sp sovp ... Scintillation Coincidence Spectrometer (RU)
st st .... Old Style [*Julian calendar*] (BU)
stst .... Stari Stil [*Old Style*] [*Julian calendar*] (YU)
STsT .... Stereoscopic Color Television (RU)
st strz .... Starszy Strzelec [*Lance-Corporal*] [*Polish*]
STsV .... Antimony-Cesium Vacuum Phototube (RU)
st szer .... Starszy Szeregowy [*Leading Aircraftman*] [*Polish*]
STT .... Slobodna Teritorija Trsta [*Free Territory of Trieste*] (YU)
STT .... Societe des Textiles du Tchad (MAR)
STT .... Societe Tous Transports (MAR)
STT .... Suomen Tietotoimisto [*Finnish News Bureau*] (WEN)
STT .... Syndicat de Travailleurs du Tchad (MAR)
St-TB .... Stiasny-Taschenbuecher [*German*]
STTK .... Suomen Teknillisten Toimihenkilojarjestojen Keskusliitto [*Finnish Central Federation of Technical Functionaries*] (WEN)
StTO .... Stueckgut-Transport-Ordnung [*Less than Carload (Freight) Transportation Regulations*] (EG)
st tov .... Freight Station [*Topography*] (RU)
STTP .... Societe Tchadienne de Travaux Publics (MAR)
STTs .... Sofia Telephone Exchange (BU)
st-tsa .... Stanitsa, Cossack Village [*Topography*] (RU)
STT-VUJNA ... Slobodna Teritorija Trsta - Vojna Uprava Jugoslovenske Narodne Armije [*Free Territory of Trieste - Military Government of the Yugoslav People's Army*] (YU)
STU .... St. Lucia Teachers Union (LA1)
STU .... Sanitary Engineering Facility (RU)
STU- .... Sovnarkhoz Technical Specifications (RU)
STU .... Statni Typisacni Ustav [*Research Institute for Standardization*] (CZ)
STU .... Studijni a Typisacni Ustav [*Research Institute for Standardization*] (CZ)
STUC .... Seychelles Trade Union Congress (MAR)
stud .... Studentisch [*German*]
studbat .... Student Battalion (RU)
studkom ..... Student Committee (RU)
Stue .... Statue [*Statue*] [*Military map abbreviation*] [*World War I*] [*French*] (MTD)
STUF .... Sudan Trade Unions Federation (MAR)
STUFIT .... Societe Tunisienne Filature Tissage (MAR)
Stug .... Studiengesellschaft fuer Kohlenstaubfeuerung auf Lokomotiven [*Research Association for Powdered Coal Firing of Locomotives*] (EG)
STUNAM ..... Sindicato de Trabajadores de la Universidad Autonoma de Mexico [*Trade Union of the National Autonomous University of Mexico*] (LA1)
Sturshelkor ... Newspaper Correspondent (BU)
StUst .... Starkstromunterhaltungsstelle [*High Voltage Maintenance Shop*] (EG)
STV .... Savez za Telesno Vaspitanje [*Federation for Physical Education*] (YU)
STV .... Societe de Transports Vergnaud (MAR)
STV .... Solidaridad de Trabajadores Vascos [*Solidarity of Basque Workers*] [*Spanish*] (WER)
StV .... Staatsverlag der DDR [*GDR State Publishing House*] (EG)
StV .... Stellvertretender Vorsitzender [*Deputy Chairman*] (EG)
STV .... Voice-Frequency Ringing Bay (RU)
StVA .... Strafvollzugsanstalt [*Penal Institution*] [*West German*] (WEN)
StVO .... Strassenverkehrsordnung [*Street Traffic Regulations*] (EG)
StVZO .... Strassenverkehrszulassungsordnung [*Street Traffic Licensing Regulations*] (EG)
stw .... Steenweg [*Dutch*] (CED)
Stw .... Stellwerk [*Signal and Switch Control Tower*] (EG)
stwg .... Steenweg [*Dutch*] (CED)
STY .... Soma Tekhnikon Ypiresion [*(Army) Technical Corps*] (GC)
STZ .... High-Voltage Equipment Plant (BU)
STZ .... Low-Voltage Equipment Plant (BU)
STZ .... Outpost Support, Picket (RU)
STZ .... Severoceske Tukove Zavody [*North Bohemian Fat Rendering Factories (Usti Nad Labem)*] (CZ)
STZ .... Sinarskaya Pipe Plant (RU)
STZ .... Slobodna Trgovinska Zona [*Free Trade Zone*] (YU)
STZ .... Stalingrad Tractor Plant (RU)
St Zj .... Stany Zjednoczone [*United States*] (POL)
St Zjedn ...... Stany Zjednoczone [*United States*] [*Polish*]

St z OS .... Stara Zagora Oblast Court (BU)
Su .... Aircraft Designed by P. O. Sukhoy (RU)
SU .... Coal Depot (RU)
SU .... Collection of Laws (RU)
SU .... Concentrated Attack, Concentrated Thrust (RU)
SU .... Construction Administration (BU)
SU .... Construction Administration (RU)
SU .... Construction School (RU)
SU .... Drill Regulations, Drill Manual (RU)
SU .... Point Indicator (RU)
SU- .... Reader (RU)
SU .... Savet za Urbanizam [*City Planning Council*] (YU)
SU .... Secretariat Unifie [*Unified Secretariat*] [*Of 4th International*] [*French*] (WER)
SU .... Sejm Ustawodawczy [*Sejm (Parliament)*] (POL)
SU .... Selcuk Universitesi [*Selcuk University*] (TU)
SU- .... Self-Propelled Gun (RU)
SU .... Senggara Udara [*Air Maintenance*] (ML)
su .... Siehe Unten [*See Below*] [*German*] (GPO)
SU .... Signaler (RU)
SU .... Slovansky Ustav [*Slavic Institute (of the Czechoslovak Academy of Sciences)*] (CZ)
SU .... Slovenska Univerzita [*Slovak University*] [*Bratislava*] (CZ)
S-U .... Socjalno-Ubezpieczeniowa Komisja [*Social Insurance Commission*] (POL)
SU .... Sofia University (BU)
Su .... Sormovo Higher-Powered [*Locomotive*] (RU)
SU .... Sowjetunion [*Soviet Union*] (EG)
SU .... Special Administration (RU)
SU .... Spojovaci Uzel [*Communications Center*] (CZ)
SU- .... Stationary Installation (RU)
SU .... Statistical Administration (RU)
SU .... Stopper (RU)
SU .... Stubicki Ugljenokopi [*Stubica Coal Pits*] [*Tugonica*] (YU)
su .... Sunnuntai(na) [*Finnish*]
SU .... Suvorov School [*Military term*] (RU)
su .... Svar Udbedes [*An Answer Is Requested*] [*Danish*] (GPO)
SU .... Synchronizer (RU)
SU .... Union of Soviet Socialist Republics [*Two-letter standard code*] (CNC)
SU- .... Universal Saccharimeter (RU)
s-u .... Versus (BU)
SUA .... Slovensky Ustredny Archiv [*Slovak Central Archives*] (CZ)
SUA .... Sport Universitaire Algerien (MAR)
SUA .... Statele Unite ale Americii [*United States of America*] (RO)
SUAD .... Service d'Utilite Agricole de Developpement (MAR)
SUAD .... Staf Umum Angkatan Darat [*Army General Staff*] (IN)
SUAE .... Level Shift of Atomic Electrons (RU)
SUAITELAR ... Fabrica San Jose de Suaita SA [*Bogota*] (COL)
SUANP .... Sindicato Unico de la Administracion Nacional de Puertos [*Single Union of the National Ports Administration*] [*Uruguayan*] (LA)
suavt .... Coauthor (BU)
SUB .... Slovenske Uholne Bane [*Slovak Coal Mines*] (CZ)
sub .... Subaudi [*Understand*] [*Latin*] (GPO)
Sub .... Subdivision [*Subdivision*] (CL)
subcut .... Subkutan [*Subcutaneous*] [*German*]
SUBE .... Societe d'Utilization des Bois Exotiques (MAR)
SUBI .... Statni Ustredni Banska Inspekce [*Central State Mining Inspection Bureau*] (CZ)
subir .... Collective Noun (BU)
subj .... Subjekti [*Subject*] [*Finnish*]
subl .... Sublimiert [*Sublimes*] [*German*]
SUBOL .... Sociedade Ultramarina de Borracha Limitada [*Acessorios em Borracha*] (MAR)
SU-BP .... Statni Ustav pro Projektovani Uhelnych Dolu a Zavodu Naftoveho Prumyslu, Banske Projekty [*State Institute for the Planning of Coal Mines and Petroleum Industry Establishments, Mining Projects*] (CZ)
SUBP .... Statny Ustav Banskych Projektov [*State Institute of Mining Projects*] (CZ)
SUBR .... Severoural'sk Bauxite Mines (RU)
subst .... Substantiivi [*Finnish*]
Subst .... Substanz [*Substance*] [*German*]
SUC .... Savezni Ured za Cene [*Federal Office of Prices*] (YU)
SUC .... Societe d'Usinage de Cafe (MAR)
SUC .... Statni Urad pro Veci Cirkevni [*State Bureau for Church Affairs*] (CZ)
Suc .... Sucursal [*Branch*] [*Business and trade*] [*Spanish*]
SUC .... Syndicats Unifies du Congo (MAR)
SUCAM .... Superintendencia de Campanhas de Saude Publica [*Superintendency for Public Health Campaigns*] [*Brazilian*] (LA)
SUCAPITAL ... Suramericana de Capitalizacion SA [*Medellin*] (COL)
SUCCI .... Societe d'Urbanisme et de Constructions de la Cote-d'Ivoire (MAR)
SUCEE .... Socialist Union of Central and Eastern Europe (PD)
such .... Work, Composition (BU)
suchet .... Combination (BU)
SUCI .... Socialist Unity Center of India (PPW)
Sucie .... Sucrerie [*Sugar Mill*] [*Military map abbreviation*] [*World War I*] [*French*] (MTD)
SUCIN .... Societe d'Urbanisme et de Construction Immobiliere de Nouakchott (MAR)
SUCO .... Service Universitaire Canadien d'Outre-Mer (MAR)
SUCO .... Sucrerie du Congo (MAR)
SUCOMA .... Sugar Corporation of Malawi (AF)
SUCOMAD ... Societe Sucriere de la Cote Est de Madagascar (MAR)
SUCOMET ... Sociedad Uruguaya de Coque Metalurgico [*Uruguayan Society for Metallurgical Coke*] (LA)
SUCRAF ...... Sucrerie et Raffinerie de l'Afrique Centrale (MAR)
SUCSEL ...... Syndicat Unique des Cadres de la Sante et de l'Elevage (MAR)
SUCT .... Statia de Utilaje Constructii si Transporturi [*Station for Construction and Transportation Equipment*] (RO)
SUCVUT ...... Stavebni Ustav Ceskeho Vysokehe Uceni Technickeho [*Construction Center of the Czech Institute of Technology*] (CZ)
sud .... Ship Repair Yard [*Topography*] (RU)
sud .... Shipyard [*Topography*] (RU)
SUD .... Srpsko Uceno Drustvo [*Serbian Learned Society*] (YU)
SUD .... Stredoceske Uhelne Doly [*Central Bohemian Coal Mines*] (CZ)
SUDAM .... Superintendencia do Desenvolvimento da Amazonia [*Superintendency for the Development of the Amazon Region*] [*Brazilian*] (LA)
SUDAP .... Superintendencia da Agricultura e Producao [*Superintendency of Agriculture and Production*] [*Brazilian*] (LA)
SUDECO ..... Sugar Development Corporation [*Tanzanian*] (AF)
SUDECO ..... Superintendencia do Desenvolvimento da Regiao Centro Oeste [*Center-West Development Superintendency*] [*Brazilian*] (LA)
SUDELPA .... Superintendencia de Desenvolvimento Economico do Litoral Paulista [*Superintendency for Economic Development of Sao Paulo Coast*] [*Brazilian*] (LA)
SUDENE ...... Superintendencia do Desenvolvimento do Nordeste [*Superintendency for Development of the Northeast*] [*Brazilian*] (LA)
SUDEPE ...... Superintendencia do Desenvolvimento da Pesca [*Superintendency for Development of the Fishing Industry*] [*Brazilian*] (LA)
SUDES .... Syndicat Unique et Democratique des Enseignants du Senegal [*Sole Democratic Trade Union of Senegalese Teachers*] (AF)
SUDESUL ... Superintendencia da Regiao Sul [*Superintendency of the Southern Region*] [*Brazilian*] (LA)
SUDHEVEA ... Superintendencia da Borracha [*Superintendency of the Rubber Industry*] [*Brazilian*] (LA)
sud-khim .... Forensic Chemistry (RU)
sudkom ...... Ship Committee (RU)
sudl .... Suedlich [*German*]
sud med ...... Sudebna Meditsina [*Forensic Medicine*] [*A periodical*] (BU)
sudmedlab ... Forensic Medicine Laboratory (RU)
Sudoimport ... All-Union Association for the Import of Ships (RU)
SUDOP .... Statni Ustav Dopravniho Projektovani [*State Institute for Transport Design and Planning*] (CZ)
SUDP .... Sistema Unico de Documentacion de Proyectos [*Central System for Plan Documentation*] [*Cuban*] (LA)
SUDP .... Statny Ustav Dopravneho Projektovania [*State Institute for Transportation Projects*] [*Bratislava*] (CZ)
Sud pr .... Judicial Practice of the Supreme Court of the USSR (RU)
sudprom ..... Shipbuilding Industry (RU)
Sudpromgiz ... State All-Union Publishing House of the Shipbuilding Industry (RU)
Sudpromizdat ... State Publishing House of Literature for the Shipbuilding Industry (RU)
sudurzh .... Content (BU)
SUDZ .... Statni Urad Duchodoveho Zabezpeceni [*State Pension Office*] (CZ)
SUE .... Carbon Disulfide Emulsion (RU)
SUEL .... Syndicat Unifie des Enseignants Laics [*Unified Union of Lay Teachers*] [*Senegalese*] (AF)
SUEP .... Savet za Uzajamnu Ekonomsku Pomoc [*Council for Mutual Economic Aid*] [*Moscow*] [*East European Economic Integration*] (YU)
SuF .... Sicherungs- und Fermeldewesen [*Protective Devices and Telecommunications*] (EG)
SUF .... Socialist Unity Front [*Romanian*] (PPW)
SUF .... Sosialistisk Ungdomsforbund [*Socialist Youth Federation*] [*Norwegian*] (WEN)
SUF .... Swaziland United Front (MAR)
suff .... Suffiksi, Loppuliite [*Suffix*] [*Finnish*]
SUFRAMA ... Superintendencia da Zona Franca de Manaus [*Superintendency of the Manaus Free Trade Zone*] [*Brazilian*] (LA)
SUG .... Universal Welding Generator (RU)
SUGI .... Savezna Uprava za Geoloska Istrazivanja [*Federal Administration of Geological Research*] (YU)
SUGMS .... Northern Administration of the Hydrometeorological Service (RU)
SUGRES ...... Sredneural'sk State Regional Electric Power Plant (RU)
SUGU .... Sindicato Unico de Gastronomicos Uruguayos [*Single Union of Food and Restaurant Workers*] [*Uruguayan*] (LA)

SUGVF........ Northern Territorial Administration of the Civil Air Fleet (RU)
SuH............ Siemens und Halske (EG)
SUH............ Statni Ustav Hydrologicky T. G. Masaryka [*T. G. Masaryk State Hydrological Institute*] (CZ)
SUHS.......... Savezna Uprava Hidrometeoroloske Sluzbe [*Federal Administration of the Hydrometeorological Service*] (YU)
SUIN............ Union of Teachers-Internationalists (RU)
SU-IS........... Su Isciler Sendikasi [*Water Workers' Union (Guzelyurt)*] [*Turkish Cypriot*] (GC)
Su-Is........... Turkiye Baraj, Enerji, Su, ve Sulama Iscileri Sendikasi [*Turkish Dam, Energy, Water, and Irrigation Workers' Union*] (TU)
suiv............ Suivant [*Following*] [*French*]
SUJNA........ Sanitetska Uprave Jugoslovenske Narodne Armije [*Medical Administration of the Yugoslav People's Army*] (YU)
SUK............ Savez Ugostiteljskih Komora Federativna Narodna Republika Jugoslavija [*Yugoslav Federation of Chambers of the Hotel and Catering Trade*] (YU)
SUK............ Sreska Ugostiteljska Komora [*District Chamber of the Hotel and Catering Trade*] (YU)
SUK............ Srpski Udarni Korpus [*Serbian Shock Corps*] [*World War II*] (YU)
SUK............ Sun Compass (RU)
suk............ Woolen Mill [*Topography*] (RU)
sukh........... Dry [*Topography*] (RU)
Sukhumges... Sukhumi Regional Hydroelectric Power Plant (RU)
SUKK.......... Slovenske Ustredie Kniznej Kultury [*Slovak Center for Book Culture*] (CZ)
SUKL........... Statni Ustav pro Kontrolu Leciv [*State Control Institute for Pharmaceutical Products*] (CZ)
SUKP........... Sekretarijat za Urbanizam i Komunalne Poslove [*Secretariat of City Planning and Communal Affairs*] (YU)
sukr............ Abridged, Abbreviated (BU)
SUL............ Special Unnumbered License (MAR)
Sul............. Sulanmasi [*Irrigation*] (TU)
SULRA......... Sulawesi Tenggara [*Southeast Sulawesi*] (IN)
SULSEL....... Sulawesi Selatan [*South Sulawesi*] (IN)
SULTENG... Sulawesi Tengah [*Central Sulawesi*] (IN)
SULUT......... Slovenske Ustredie Ludovej Umeleckej Tvorivosti [*Slovak Folk Arts Center*] (CZ)
SULUT......... Sulawesi Utara [*North Sulawesi*] (IN)
SUM............ Save Uganda Movement (AF)
SUM............ Sea Level Recorder (RU)
SUM............ Socialist Unionist Movement [*Al Haraka at Tawhidiyya al Ishtirakiyya*] [*Syrian*] (PPW)
SUM............ Statni Ustav Meteorologicky [*State Meteorological Institute*] (CZ)
SUM............ Sudan United Mission (MAR)
SUM............ Sulfonated Vegetable Oil (RU)
SUM............ Szczecinski Urzad Morski [*Szczecin (Stettin) Maritime Office*] (POL)
SUMAS........ Su Makinalari Sanayii Kollektif Sirketi [*Water Pump Industry Corporation*] [*Mersin*] (TU)
SUMATEC.. Sociedad Colombo Sueca de Maquinaria y Tecnica Ltda. [*Bogota*] (COL)
SUMATEX... Sud-Madagascar Textile (MAR)
SUMBAR.... Sumatera Barat [*West Sumatra*] (IN)
SUMCE........ Sistema Unificado de Maquinas Computadoras Electronicas [*Unified Electronic Computer System*] [*Cuban*] (LA)
SUMED........ Suez-Mediterranean [*Pipeline*] [*Egyptian*] (ME)
SUMMA....... Sociedad Umana Moreno [*Bogota*] (COL)
SUMOC........ Superintendencia da Moeda e do Credito [*Superintendency of Money and Credit*] [*Brazilian*] (LA)
SUMUT........ Sumatera Utara [*North Sumatra*] (IN)
SUMZ.......... Sredneural'sk Copper Smelting Plant (RU)
SUN............ Service des Urgences de Nuit (MAR)
SUN............ Sofia School Board (BU)
SUN............ Union of Soviet Socialist Republics [*Three-letter standard code*] (CNC)
SUNA.......... Sudan [*or Sudanese*] News Agency (AF)
SUNAB........ Sucrerie Nationale du Beth [*Moroccan*] (MAR)
SUNAB........ Superintendencia Nacional de Abastecimento [*National Superintendency of Supplies*] [*Brazilian*] (LA)
SUNACAS... Sucrerie Nationale de Cannes du Sebou [*Moroccan*] (MAR)
SUNAG......... Sucreries Nationales du Gharb [*Moroccan*] (MAR)
SUNAMAM... Superintendencia Nacional de Marinha Mercante [*National Merchant Marine Superintendency*] [*Brazilian*] (LA)
SUNCA......... Sindicato Unico Nacional de la Construccion y Anexos (Afines) [*National Single Union of Construction and Related Workers*] [*Uruguayan*] (LA)
SUNFED...... Special United Nations Fund for Economic Development (MAR)
SUNTM........ Sindicato Unico Nacional del Transporte Maritimo [*Single Union of Marine Transport Workers*] [*Uruguayan*] (LA)
suom........... Suomalainen [*Finnish*]
suom........... Suomentanut [*Finnish*]
SUOPO........ Suojelupoliisi [*Security Police*] [*Finnish*] (WEN)
SUP............ Control Station for Periodically Working Oil Wells (RU)
SUP............ Savez Udruzenja Pravnika [*Union of Lawyers' Associations*] (YU)
SUP............ Savezna Uprava za Patente [*Federal Patents Administration*] (YU)
SUP............ Savezna Uprava Prihoda (DSPF) [*Federal Revenue Administration*] (YU)
SUP............ Savezna Uprava za Puteve [*Federal Roads Administration*] (YU)
SUP............ Savjet za Unutrasnje Poslove [*Internal Affairs Council*] (YU)
SUP............ Sekretarijat za Unutrasnje Poslove [*Secretariat of Internal Affairs*] (YU)
SUP............ Somali United Party (MAR)
SUP............ Statni Urad Planovaci [*State Planning Office*] (CZ)
SUP-........... Stereo Deflection and Parallax Meter (RU)
SUP............ Student Unification Party [*Liberian*] (AF)
Sup............. Superior [*German*]
sup............. Suplica [*Spanish*]
sup............. Supra [*Above*] [*Latin*] (GPO)
SUPA........... Sindicato Unido de Portuarios Argentinos [*United Argentine Port Workers Union*] (LA)
SUPE........... Sindicato Unido de Petroleros del Estado [*Union of State Petroleum Workers*] [*Argentine*] (LA)
SUPELSA.... Suramericana de Peliculas Sociedad Anonima [*Bogota*] (COL)
superl.......... Superlatiivi [*Superlative*] [*Finnish*]
SUPERSER... Suramericana de Servicios y Perforaciones SA [*Bogota*] (COL)
supertte...... Superintendente [*Spanish*]
SUPEX........ Superintendencia dos Contratos de Exploracao [*Superintendency of Exploration Contracts*] [*Of PETROBRAS*] [*Brazilian*] (LA)
SUPJ........... Savez Udruzenja Pravnika Jugoslavije [*Federation of Lawyers' Associations of Yugoslavia*] (YU)
suplte......... Suplente [*Spanish*]
SUPOBU..... Usines de Poissons du Burundi (MAR)
SUPOM....... Stavebni Urad pro Obnovu Mesta [*City Reconstruction Office*] (CZ)
SUPP........... Sarawak United People's Party [*Malaysian*] (PPW)
SUPPOP...... Statni Ustav Pamatkove Pece a Ochrany Prirody [*State Institute for Care of Historical Monuments and Nature Conservation*] (CZ)
SUPR........... Handbook of Consolidated Indexes of Expenditure of Labor and Materials [*A publication*] (RU)
SUPR........... Special Unit on Palestinian Rights [*United Nations*] (MAR)
SUPR........... Switch Starting Control Relay (RU)
SUPRA........ Superintendencia de Planejamento da Reforma Agraria [*Superintendency of Agrarian Reform Planning*] [*Brazilian*] (LA)
SUPRA........ Superintendencia para la Reforma Agraria [*Superintendency for Agrarian Reform*] [*Cuban*] (LA)
SUPS........... Handbook of Consolidated Indexes of Planning Operations Cost of the Gosstroy [*A publication*] (RU)
SUPSAN...... Motor Supaplari Sanayii ve Ticareti AS [*Motor Valves Industry and Trade Corp.*] (TU)
SUPSFNRJ... Savez Udruzenja Pravoslavnog Svestenstva Federativna Narodna Republika Jugoslavija [*Federation of Orthodox Clergy Associations of Yugoslavia*] (YU)
supte........... Suplicante [*Spanish*]
SUPV........... Savezna Uprava za Poslove Veterinarstva [*Federal Veterinary Service Administration*] (YU)
SUR............ Collection of Laws and Decrees of the Workers' and Peasants' Government (RU)
SUR............ Surinam [*Three-letter standard code*] (CNC)
SURA.......... Shan United Revolutionary Army [*Burmese*] (PD)
Sured.......... Coeditor (BU)
SURGELENMER... Societe Ivoirienne de Peche et de Congelation en Mer (MAR)
SURGEL-IVOIRE... Societe Ivoirienne de Commerce des Produits Alimentaires Surgele's (MAR)
Surgo.......... Surgidero [*Anchorage, Roadstead*] [*Spanish*] (NAU)
SURP........... Siberian Administration of Riverways (RU)
SURP........... Statni Ustav pro Rajonove Planovani [*State Institute for Regional Planning*] (CZ)
SUS............ (Motor) sa Unutrasnjim Sagorevanjem [*Internal Combustion Engine*] (YU)
SUS............ Severocesky Uhelny Syndikat [*North Bohemian Coal Syndicate*] (CZ)
SUS............ Statni Urad Statistacky [*State Statistical Office*] (CZ)
SUSAM........ Superintendencia do Servico Medico ao Amazonia [*Superintendency for Medical Service to the Amazon Region*] [*Brazilian*] (LA)
SUSEME..... Superintendencia de Servicos Medicos [*Superintendency of Medical Services*] [*Brazilian*] (LA)
SUSEP........ Superintendencia de Seguros Privados [*Superintendency of Private Insurance*] [*Brazilian*] (LA)
sush............ Dryer, Grain Dryer [*Topography*] (RU)
sushch........ Noun (RU)
susht........... Noun [*Grammar*] (BU)
SUSIPE....... Superintendencia do Sistema Penitenciario [*Superintendency of the Penitentiary System*] [*Brazilian*] (LA)
SUSN.......... Handbook of Consolidated Estimate Norms [*A publication*] (RU)
Susp........... Pont Suspendu [*Suspension Bridge*] [*Military map abbreviation*] [*World War I*] [*French*] (MTD)
SUSR........... Slovenska Ustredna Sportova Rada [*Slovak Central Sports Council*] (CZ)

sust .... Compiled By (BU)
SUSZ .... Statni Urad Socialnihe Zabezpeceni [*State Social Security Office*] (CZ)
sut .... Day, Twenty-Four Hours (RU)
SUT .... Societe d'Urbanisation du Tchad (MAR)
SUT .... Statia de Utilaje Transport [*Transportation Equipment Station*] (RO)
SUT .... Statni Ustav Tesnopisny [*State Stenographic Institute*] (CZ)
SUTA .... La Sucrerie du Tadla [*Moroccan*] (MAR)
SUTC .... Sindicato Unico de Trabajadores de Coltejer [*Coltejer Workers Union*] [*Colombian*] (LA)
SUTC .... Sindicato Unico de Trabajadores de la Compania Colombiana de Tejidos [*Sole Trade Union of Colombian Textile Company Workers*] (LA1)
SUTC .... Sindicato Union de Trabajadores de la Construccion [*United Trade Union of Construction Workers*] [*Salvadoran*] (LA1)
SUTEIN .... Slovensky Ustav pre Technicke a Ekonomicke Informacie [*Slovak Institute for Technical and Economic Information*] (CZ)
SUTEP .... Sindicato Unico de Trabajadores de la Ensenanza [*Single Union of Education Workers*] [*Peruvian*] (LA)
SUTEP .... Sindicato Unico de Trabajadores de Espectaculos Publicos [*National Public Entertainment Workers Union*] [*Argentine*] (LA)
SUTERM ..... Sindicato Unico de Trabajadores Electricistas de la Republica Mexicana [*Mexican Electrical Workers Union*] (LA)
SUTHD .... Slovensky Ustav pre Technicku a Hospodarsku Dokumentaciu [*Slovak Institute for Technical and Economic Documentation*] (CZ)
SUTIN .... Sindicato Unico de Trabajadores de la Industria Nuclear [*Sole Trade Union of Nuclear Industry Workers*] [*Mexican*] (LA1)
SUTINEN ..... Sindicato Unico de Trabajadores del Instituto Nacional de Energia Nuclear [*National Nuclear Energy Institute Workers Union*] [*Mexican*] (LA)
SUTM .... Sindicato Unico del Transporte Maritimo [*Single Union of Maritime Transport*] [*Uruguayan*] (LA)
sutr .... Collaborator, Collaboration, Collaborated (BU)
SUTRA .... Sindicato Unico de Trabajadores [*Sole Trade Union of Workers*] [*Nicaraguan*] (LA1)
SUTRADO ... Sindicato Unico de Trabajadores Docentes [*Single Union of Educational Workers*] [*Venezuelan*] (LA)
SUTRAFADO ... Sindicato Unido de Trabajadores de Falconbridge [*United Trade Union of Falconbridge Workers*] [*Dominican Republic*] (LA1)
SUTRASFCO ... Sindicato Unificado de Trabajadores de la Standard Fruit Co. [*Unified Union of Standard Fruit Company Workers*] [*Honduran*] (LA)
SUTU .... Universal Telephone Repeater Bay (RU)
SUTV .... Statni Urad pro Telesnou Vychovu [*State Office for Physical Education*] (CZ)
SUTVS .... Statni Urad pro Telesnou Vychovu a Sport [*State Office for Physical Education and Sports*] (CZ)
SUUG .... Sbornik Ustredniho Ustavu Geologickeho [*Journal of the Central Geological Institute*] [*A publication*] (CZ)
SUUP .... Savezna Uprava za Unapredenje Proizvodnje [*Federal Administration of Production Development*] (YU)
SUV .... Code Command System (RU)
SUV .... Slovensky Ustredny Vybor [*Slovak Central Committee*] (CZ)
SUV .... Soldados Unidos Vencerao [*Soldiers United Will Win*] [*Portuguese*] (WER)
Suv .... Suvremennik [*Contemporary*] [*A periodical*] (BU)
SUV .... Troop Control System (RU)
SUV .... Water Level Recorder (RU)
SUVESS ...... Syndicat Unique Voltaique des Enseignants du Secondaire et du Superieur [*Sole Voltan Union of Teachers of Secondary and Higher Education*] (AF)
SUVP .... Statni Urad pro Valecne Poskozence [*State Office for Victims of War*] (CZ)
Suvrem .... Suvremennik [*Contemporary*] [*A periodical*] (BU)
suvursh prerab ... Completely Revised (BU)
SUW .... Spoldzielnia Uslugowo-Wytworcza [*Production-and-Service Cooperative*] (POL)
SUZ .... Control and Safety Rods (RU)
SUZ .... Control and Shielding System [*Nuclear energy*] (BU)
SUZ .... Savezni Ustavni Zakon [*Federal Constitutional Law*] (YU)
SUZB .... Savezna Uprava za Zastitu Bilja [*Federal Administration for Plant Protection*] (YU)
SUZOR .... Savezni Ured za Osiguranje Radnika [*Federal Workers Insurance Office*] (YU)
SUZOR .... Sredisni Ured za Osiguranje Radnika [*Central Office for Workers Insurance*] (YU)
SV .... Altitude Indicator (RU)
sv .... Bundle (RU)
sv .... Candle (RU)
SV .... El Salvador [*Two-letter standard code*] (CNC)
SV .... Flash Ranging [*Artillery*] (RU)
sv .... Installment, Fascicule (BU)
SV .... Liaison Aircraft (RU)
sv .... Mean Time (RU)
SV .... Medical Platoon (RU)
SV .... Medium-Frequency-Wave (RU)
SV .... Medium Waves (BU)
SV .... Northeast, Northeastern (RU)
sv .... Over, Beyond (RU)
sv .... Rifle Platoon (BU)
sv .... Rifle Platoon (RU)
sv .... Saint (BU)
sv .... Saint (RU)
sv .... Samana Vuonna [*Same Year*] [*Finnish*] (GPO)
sv .... Sans Valeur [*French*]
SV .... Savezno Vece [*Federal Council*] (YU)
SV .... Sciences et Voyages (MAR)
SV .... Sdruzeni Vytvarniku [*Creative Artists' Association*] (CZ)
SV .... Selbst-Verlag [*German*]
SV .... Selenium Rectifier (RU)
SV .... Self-Excitation (RU)
SV .... Semiautomatic Rifle (RU)
sv .... Severo-Vzhod [*Northwest*] (YU)
sv .... Severovychod [*Northeast*] (CZ)
SV .... Sleeping Car (RU)
SV .... Slovenska Vlastiveda [*Slovak Encyclopedia*] [*A publication*] (CZ)
SV .... Slovensky Vybor [*Slovak Committee*] (CZ)
SV .... Sluzben Vesnik [*Official Gazette*] [*Skopje*] [*A publication*] (YU)
SV .... Solenoid Valve (RU)
SV .... Sosialistisk Valgforbund [*Socialist Electoral Alliance*] [*Norwegian*] (PPE)
SV .... Sosialistisk Venstreparti [*Socialist Left Party*] [*Norwegian*] (PPE)
SV .... Sovetskoe Vostokovedenie (MAR)
SV .... Soviet Oriental Studies (RU)
SV .... Sozialversicherung [*Social Insurance*] (EG)
SV .... Spolek Vytvarniku [*Creative Artists' Association*] (CZ)
SV .... Sredstva Veze [*Communications Equipment*] [*Army*] (YU)
SV .... Stanoviste Velitelstvi [*Command Post*] (CZ)
SV .... Stopanski Vesnik [*Economic Review*] [*Skopje*] [*A publication*] (YU)
SV .... Stravovaci Vybor [*Food Supply Committee*] (CZ)
SV .... Stredoslovenske Vydavatelstvo [*Central Slovakia Publishing House*] (CZ)
sv .... Sub Verbo [*or Voce*] [*Under the Word or Heading*] [*Latin*]
Sv .... Suceava [*Suceava*] (RO)
SV .... Sudiyski Vestnik [*Judges' Newspaper*] [*A publication*] (BU)
sv .... Svajci [*Swiss*] (HU)
sv .... Svazek [*Volume*] (CZ)
sv .... Sved [*Swedish*] (HU)
SV .... Svoboda [*Liberty*] [*A periodical*] (BU)
Sv .... Vertical Displacement [*Artillery*] (RU)
sv .... Wind Speed (RU)
SVA .... Communicate to All Addresses [*Telegraphy*] (RU)
Sva .... Liaison with the Attaches (BU)
SVA .... Ringing Signal Set (RU)
SVA .... Schiffbau-Versuchsanstalt [*Shipbuilding Research Institute*] (EG)
SVA .... Service de Vente des Alcools [*Alcohol Sales Department*] [*Cambodian*] (CL)
SVA .... Sovjetska Vojna Administracija [*Soviet Military Administration*] (YU)
SVA .... Sozialversicherungsanstalt [*Social Insurance Agency*] (EG)
SVA .... Statni Vyrobny Autodilu [*State Plants for Automobile Parts*] (CZ)
SVA .... Strafvollzugsanstalt [*Penal Institution*] [*West German*] (WEN)
SVA .... Strategic Air Command [*USA*] (RU)
SVA .... Surface Utile Agricole [*Algerian*] (MAR)
SVADP .... Shire Valley Agricultural Development (MAR)
SVAG .... Soviet Military Administration in Germany (RU)
SVAI .... Service de Vente des Alcools Importes [*Imported Alcohol Sales Department*] [*Cambodian*] (CL)
SVAM .... Anisotropic Glass-Fiber Material (RU)
SVAM .... Societe de Ventes d'Armes et de Munitions au Tchad (MAR)
SVARM .... Fixed Military Aircraft Repair Shop (RU)
SVARZ .... Sokol'niki Railroad Car Building and Repair Plant (RU)
Svazarm ...... Svaz pro Spolupraci s Armadou [*Union for Cooperation with the Army*] (CZ)
svb .... Signal Battalion (RU)
svb .... Signal Battalion (BU)
SVB .... Sprava Verejne Bezpecnosti [*Public Safety Directorate*] (CZ)
SVB .... Studenten Bakbeweging [*Student Trade Union Movement*] [*Belgian, Dutch*] (WEN)
SVB .... Union of Militant Atheists [*1922-1947*] (RU)
svbk .... Corps Signal Battalion (RU)
SVBP .... Service de Vente des Boissons et des Parfums [*Beverage and Perfume Sales Department*] [*Cambodian*] (CL)
SVBP .... Societe Voltaique des Petroles BP (MAR)
svb-ssv .... Signal Battalion Auxiliary Communications Center (BU)
SVC .... Shadow Village Council [*Mauritian*] (AF)
SVC .... Slovansky Vybor Ceskoslovenska [*Slavic Committee of Czechoslovakia*] (CZ)
SVCh .... High Frequency Signal (RU)
SVCh .... Superhigh Frequency (RU)
SVCh .... Ultra-High Frequency (BU)
SVCP .... Societe Voltaique des Cuirs et Peaux (MAR)

SVD .... Societas Verbi Divini [*Society of the Divine Word*] [*Roman Catholic men's religious order*] (MAR)
SVD .... Spolok Vytvarneho Dorostu [*Association of Young Creative Artists*] (CZ)
SVD .... Sprava Vojenske Dopravy [*Military Transport Directorate*] (CZ)
SVD .... Superhigh Pressure (RU)
SVD .... Svaz Vyrobnich Druzstev [*Association of Manufacturing Cooperatives*] (CZ)
SVD .... Warsaw Pact Countries (RU)
SVDE .... Sidirodromoi Voreiodytikis Ellados [*Railways of Northwestern Greece*] (GC)
SVDP .... Free Democratic Party [*German Federal Republic*] (RU)
SVDP .... Mobile Decontamination Spreader (RU)
SVE .... Society for Veterinary Ethology [*See also SEV*] (EA)
SVE .... Soviet Military Encyclopedia [*A publication*] (RU)
SVE .... Soviet Naval Squadron (RU)
SVE .... Svaz Zamestnancu v Energetice [*Union of Employees in the Power Industry*] (CZ)
SVE .... Syndesmos Viomikhanon Endyseos [*Clothing Industries Association*] [*Cypriot*] (GC)
SVEA .... Schweizerischer Verband Evangelischer Arbeitnehmer [*Swiss Union of Protestant Workers*] (WEN)
SVED .... Severoceske Vyrobni Elektrotechnicke Druzstvo [*North Bohemian Manufacturing Cooperative for Electrical Products*] (CZ)
SVEE .... Societe Voltaique d'Expansion Economique (MAR)
Svegintsvetmet ... Sverdlovsk State Institute of Nonferrous Metals (RU)
svekl .... Beet-Growing Sovkhoz [*Topography*] (RU)
Sverdlgiz .... Sverdlovsk State Publishing House (RU)
Sverdlovgiz ... Sverdlovsk State Publishing House (RU)
SverdNIPTIMASh ... Sverdlovsk Scientific Research, Planning, and Technological Institute of Machinery Manufacture (RU)
Svesht .... Priest (BU)
svfr .... Svajci Frank [*Swiss Franc*] (HU)
SVG .... Highest Level (RU)
sv g .... Light Year (RU)
SVG .... Staatliches Vertragsgericht [*State Contract Court*] (EG)
SVGVB .... Highest Level of the Head Water (RU)
SVI .... Mean Probable Wear (RU)
SVI .... Servicio de Vigilancia Interior [*Interior Guard Service*] [*Cuban*] (LA)
SVI .... Socialistas Valencians Independents [*Valencian Independent Socialists*] [*Spanish*] (WER)
SVI .... Statni Vodohospodarske Inspekce [*State Inspection Centers for Water Management*] (CZ)
SVIAM .... Statia de Verificare si Intretinere a Aparaturii Medicale [*Station for the Testing and Maintenance of Medical Instruments*] (RO)
SVIAT .... Societa Valorizzazioni Industriali Agrarie Tripolitane (MAR)
SVICA .... Societe Voltaique d'Intervention et de Co-Operation avec l'Agriculture (MAR)
SVIE .... Skholi Voithon Iatrikon Epangelmaton [*Medical Assistants School*] [*Greek*] (GC)
SVIMEZ .... Associazione per lo Sviluppo dell' Industria nel Mezzogiorno [*Association for the Industrial Development of the South*] [*Italian*] (WER)
svin .... Hog-Breeding Sovkhoz [*Topography*] (RU)
svints .... Lead Mine [*Topography*] (RU)
SVIP .... Sociedad Venezolana de Ingenieros de Petroleo [*Venezuelan Association of Petroleum Engineers*] (LA)
Svit .... Scroll, Roll (BU)
SVJC .... Savezni Vazduhoplovni Jedrilicki Centar [*Federal Aeronautic Glider Center*] [*Vrsac*] (YU)
SVK .... Channel Separation Bay (RU)
SVK .... Sozialversicherungskasse [*Social Insurance Finance Office*] (EG)
SVK .... Statna Vedecka Kniznica [*State Research Library*] [*Kosice*] (CZ)
SVK .... Statni Vedecka Knihovna [*State Science Library*] (CZ)
SVK .... Vertical Seismograph Designed by Kirnos (RU)
svkh .... Sovkhoz [*Topography*] (RU)
SVKL .... Slovenske Vydavatelstvo Krasnej Literatury [*Slovak Belles-Lettres Publishing House*] (CZ)
SVKR .... Sprava Vojenske Kontrarozvedky [*Military Counterintelligence Directorate*] (CZ)
svkr .... Sved Korona [*Swedish Krona*] (HU)
SVKT .... Sdruzenie Byvalych Vaznov Koncentracnvch Taborov [*Association of Former Prisoners in Concentration Camps*] (CZ)
SVL .... Medium Wave Line (RU)
svlb .... Line Signal Battalion (BU)
Svl Hv Mey ... Sivil Hava Meydani [*Civil Airfield*] (TU)
svlkb .... Line and Cable Signal Battalion (BU)
svlkr .... Line and Cable Signal Company (BU)
SVLP .... St. Vincent Labor Party (LA1)
svlr .... Line Signal Company (BU)
svlsb .... Line Construction Signal Battalion (BU)
svlsr .... Line Construction Signal Company (BU)
Svl Svn .... Sivil Savunma [*Civil Defense*] (TU)
SVM .... Saint, Victor, Modeste & Cie. (MAR)
SVM .... Societe de Vente de Materiel (MAR)
SVM .... Soviet Military Mission (RU)
SVM .... Stanje Voznog Materijala [*Condition of Rolling Stock*] (YU)
SVM .... Svaz Vojenske Mladeze [*Military Youth Union*] (CZ)
SVM .... Synthetic High-Polymer Materials (RU)
SVN .... Aspiring Centrifugal Pump (RU)
Svn .... Savunma [*Defense*] (TU)
SvN .... Svoboden Narod [*Free People*] [*A newspaper*] (BU)
SVNRM .... Sluzben Vesnik na Narodna Republika Makedonija [*Official Gazette of Macedonia*] [*A publication*] (YU)
SVO .... Mean Probable Deviation (RU)
SVO .... Siberian Military District (RU)
SVo .... Sovetskoe Vostokovedenie [*Moscow*] (MAR)
SVO .... Sozialversicherung der Arbeiter und Angestellten [*Social Insurance of Workers and Employees*] (EG)
SVO .... Special Water Purification [*Nuclear energy*] (BU)
SVO .... Stredni Vojensky Okruh [*Central Military District*] (CZ)
SVO .... Water Purification System [*Nuclear energy*] (BU)
SVOC .... Societe Verite de l'Ouest Cameroun (MAR)
SVOJ .... Sluzba Veze, Osmatranja, i Javljanja [*Military Communications, Reconnaissance, and Information Service*] (YU)
Sv Ok .... Suvari Okulu [*Cavalry School*] (TU)
SVOK .... Svaz Verejnych Obecnich Knihovniku [*Union of Librarians of Public Libraries*] (CZ)
SVOM .... Slovensky Vybor Obrancov Mieru [*Slovak Committee of Peace Defenders*] (CZ)
SVP- .... Blast Point Station (RU)
SVP .... Military Service Code (RU)
SVP .... Schweizerische Volkspartei [*Swiss People's Party*] (WEN)
svp .... Signal Regiment (BU)
svp .... Signal Regiment (RU)
svp .... S'il Vous Plait [*Please*] [*French*] (GPO)
SVP .... Societe Voltaique de Plastique (MAR)
SVP .... Societe de Vulgarisation de Procedes (MAR)
SVP .... Stabilized Sight [*Navy*] (RU)
SVP .... Statni Vodohospodarsky Plan [*State Plan for Water Utilization*] (CZ)
SVP .... Stredoceske Vyrobny Plynu, Narodny Podnik [*Central Bohemian Gas Works, National Enterprise*] (CZ)
SVP .... Suedtiroler Volkspartei [*South Tirol People's Party*] [*Italian*] (WEN)
SVP .... Superhigh Steam Parameters (RU)
SVP .... Syndagmatiki Vasiliki Parataxis [*Constitutional Royalist Faction*] [*Greek*] (GC)
SVP .... Welding (RU)
SVPC .... Societe Voltaique de Peintures et Colorants (MAR)
SVPCh .... Independent Militarized Fire Brigade (RU)
SVPI .... Societe de Ventes de Produits Industriels (MAR)
SVPL .... Slovenske Vydavatelstvo Podohospodarskej Literatury [*Slovak Agricultural Literature Publishing House*] (CZ)
SVPL .... Slovenske Vydavatelstvo Politickej Literatury [*Slovak Publishing House of Political Literature*] (CZ)
SVPS .... Through Sleeping Car (RU)
svr .... Signal Company (BU)
SVR .... Statni Vyzkumna Rada [*State Research Council*] (CZ)
SVRP .... Central Volga River Steamship Line (RU)
svrrkb .... Radio-Relay Cable Signal Battalion (BU)
svr-ssb .... Signal Company Auxiliary Communications Center (BU)
SVS .... Savezni Vrhovni Sud [*Federal Supreme Court*] (YU)
SVS .... Sbor Vezenske Straze [*Prison Guard Corps*] (CZ)
SVS- .... Simonov Semiautomatic Rifle (RU)
SVS .... Sofia Military Court (BU)
SVS .... Speditionsversicherungsschein [*Shipping Insurance Policy*] (EG)
SVS .... Sprava Vojenskych Skol [*Military Schools Directorate*] (CZ)
SVS .... Sreska Veterinarska Stanica [*District Veterinary Station*] (YU)
SVS .... Stocarsko-Veterinarska Stanica [*Livestock Veterinary Station*] (YU)
SVS .... Svaz Vysokoskolskeho Studentstva [*Union of University Students*] (CZ)
SVS .... Svaz Vysokoskolskych Studentov [*Union of University Students*] (CZ)
svseb .... Construction and Operational Signal Battalion (BU)
sv'sek .... Candle-Second (RU)
svser .... Construction and Operational Signal Company (BU)
SVSJ .... Suomen Vaestonsuojelujarjesto [*Finnish Population Protection Organization*] (WEN)
SVSO .... Slovenska Vysoka Skola Obchodna [*Slovak School of Business Administration*] (CZ)
SVST .... Slovenska Vysoka Skola Technicka [*Slovak Institute of Technology*] (CZ)
SVT .... Air-Raid Warning (RU)
SVT .... Severoceske Vystavni Trhy [*North Bohemian Sample Fairs*] [*Liberec*] (CZ)
SVT .... Tokarev Semiautomatic Rifle (RU)
SVTI .... Military Technical Equipment Depot (RU)
SVTL .... Slovenske Vydavatelstvo Technickej Literatury [*Slovak Technical Literature Publishing House*] (CZ)
SVTM .... Sprava Vodnich Toku a Meliorace [*Administration of Water Ways and Melioration Projects*] (CZ)
SVTVS .... Statni Vybor pro Telesnou Vychovu a Sport [*State Physical Education and Athletic Committee*] (CZ)

SVTVS .... Statny Vybor pre Telesnu Vychovu a Sport [*State Committee of Physical Education and Sports*] (CZ)
SVU .... Computer (RU)
SVU .... Saveznicka Vojna Uprava [*Allied Military Government*] (YU)
SVU .... Signaling-Calling Device (RU)
SVU .... Spolek Vytvarnych Umelcu [*Creative Artists' Association*] (CZ)
SVU .... Sprava Vojenskych Ucilist [*Military Training Centers Directorate*] (CZ)
SVU .... Statni Vybor pro Veci Umeni [*State Fine Arts Committee*] (CZ)
SVU .... Stavebni Vyrobni Usek [*Construction Materials Production Sector*] (CZ)
SVU .... Suvorov Military School (RU)
SVUESP ...... Statni Vyzkumny Ustav Ekonomiky ve Spotrebnim Prumyslu [*State Research Institute of Economy in Consumer Industry*] (CZ)
SVUK .... Statni Vyzkumny Ustav Kozedelny [*State Research Institute for Leather Tanning*] (CZ)
SVUL .... Suomen Voimistelu- ja Urheiluliitto [*Finnish Gymnastics and Sports League*] (WEN)
SVUM .... Sdruzeni Vytvarnych Umelcu Moravskych [*Association of Moravian Creative Artists*] (CZ)
SVUM .... Statni Vyzkumny Ustav Materialu [*State Research Institute for Engineering Materials*] (CZ)
SVUManes ... Spolek Vytvarnych Umelcu Manes [*Manes Association of Creative Artists*] (CZ)
SVUOM .... Statni Vyzkumny Ustav Ochrany Materialu G. V. Akimova [*G. V. Akimov State Research Institute for Protection of Metals*] (CZ)
SVUP .... Statny Vyskumny Ustav Polnohospodarsky [*State Agricultural Research Institute*] (CZ)
SVURH .... Statni Vyzkumny Ustav Rybarsky a Hydrobiologicky [*State Research Institute of Fish Culture and Hydrobiology*] (CZ)
SVUS .... Statni Vyzkumny Ustav Sklarsky [*State Glass Research Institute*] (CZ)
SVUSS .... Statni Vyzkumny Ustav pro Stavbu Stroju [*State Research Institute for Machinery Construction*] (CZ)
SVUST .... Statni Vyzkumny Ustav Sklarske Techniky [*State Research Institute for Glass Technology*] (CZ)
SVUT .... Statni Vyzkumny Ustav Textilni [*State Research Institute for Textiles*] (CZ)
SVUV .... Spolek Vytvarnych Umelcu Vychodoceskych [*Society of East Bohemian Creative Artists*] (CZ)
SVUZ .... Statni Vyzkumne Ustavy Zemedelske [*State Agricultural Research Institutes*] (CZ)
SVUZ .... Svaz Vyzkumnych Ustavu Zemedelskych [*Union of Agricultural Research Institutes*] (CZ)
SVV .... Sadjarstvo, Vinarstvo, in Vrtnarstvo [*Fruit Culture, Viticulture, and Horticulture*] [*Ljubljana*] [*A periodical*] (YU)
svv .... Signal Platoon (RU)
SVV .... Superlong Draft [*Spinning*] (RU)
SVVE .... Syndesmos Viomikhanon Voreiou Ellados [*Federation of Industrialists of Northern Greece*] (GC)
sv-vo .... Property (RU)
Sv V P .... Military Service Code (RU)
SVVP .... Vertical Takeoff and Landing Aircraft (RU)
SVVS .... Stredni Vseobecne Vzdelavaci Skola [*Secondary General Education School*] (CZ)
SVWG .... Strafvollzugs- und Wiedereingliederungsgesetz [*Law on Punishment and Reintegration*] (EG)
Svyaz'izdat ... State Publishing House of Literature on Communications and Radio (RU)
Svyaz'kabel'stroy ... All-Union Trust for the Construction of Intercity Cable Communication Trunk Lines (RU)
Svyaz'radioizdat ... State Publishing House of Literature on Communications and Radio (RU)
Svyaz'rem ... Railway Communications Repair Train (RU)
Svyaz'tekhizdat ... State Publishing House of Literature on Communications Engineering (RU)
SVZ .... Slovenske Vinarske Zavody [*Slovak Wine Enterprises*] (CZ)
SVZ .... Slovenske Vlnarske Zavody, Narodny Podnik [*Slovak Woolen Mills, National Enterprise*] (CZ)
SVZ .... Smederevska Vinogradska Zadruga [*Smederevo Viticulture Cooperative*] (YU)
SVZ .... Sverdlovsk Bicycle Plant (RU)
SVZN .... Stredisko pro Vynalezy a Zlepsovaci Navrhy [*Center for Inventions and Improvement Proposals*] (CZ)
SW .... Sicherheitswache [*German*]
SW .... Signalwerkstatt [*Signal Shop*] (EG)
SW .... Spezifische Waerme [*Specific Heat*] [*German*]
SW .... Sud Ouest [*Southwest*] [*French*] (MTD)
SW .... Sueddeutsche Waehrung [*South German Currency*] [*German*]
SW .... Suedwesten [*Southwest*] (EG)
sw .... Swiadek [*Witness*] [*Polish*]
sw .... Swiety [*Saint*] (POL)
SWA .... South-West Africa (AF)
SWA .... Sudanese Women's Association (MAR)
SWABC .... South-West African Broadcasting Corporation [*Namibian*] (AF)
SWACO .... South West Africa Coloureds' Organization (MAR)
SWACO .... South West Africa Company [*Namibian*] (MAR)
SWAFP .... Socialist Workers and Farmers Party [*Nigerian*] (AF)
SWAGH .... Stowarzyszenie Wychowankow Akademii Gorniczo-Hutniczej [*Alumni Association of the Academy of Mining and Metallurgy*] (POL)
SWAKARA ... South West Africa Karakul Auction (MAR)
SWAKOR .... South West Africa Oil Exploration Corporation (MAR)
SWAL .... Scandinavian West Africa Line (MAR)
SWALU .... Suedwest-Afrikanische Landwirtschafts-Union [*South-West African Agriculture Union*] [*Swazi*] (AF)
SWAM .... Stop-the-War-Against-Angola-and Mozambique (MAR)
SWAMA ...... South-West Africa Municipal Association [*Swazi*] (AF)
SWAMSA .... South-West African Municipal Staff Association [*Swazi*] (AF)
SWAN .... Sports Writers Association of Nigeria (MAR)
SWANIO ...... South West Africa United National Independence Organization (MAR)
SWANLA ..... South-West Africa Native Labor Association [*Namibian*] (AF)
SWANLIF .... South-West Africa National Liberation Front (MAR)
SWANOV .... South-West African Black Teachers Union [*Namibian*] (AF)
SWANTITER ... South-West Africa Anti-Terrorism Fund [*Swazi*] (AF)
SWANU .... South West Africa National Union [*Namibian*] (PPW)
SWANUF ..... South-West African National United Front [*Namibian*] (AF)
SWAOU .... South-West African Teachers Union [*Namibian*] (AF)
SWAOU .... Suidwes-Afrikaanse Onderwysersunie (MAR)
SWAPA .... South West Progressive Africa Association (MAR)
SWAPDUF ... South-West Africa People's Democratic United Front [*Namibian*] (AF)
SWAPO .... South West Africa People's Organization [*Namibian*] (PD)
SWAPO-D ... South-West African People's Organization Democrats [*Namibian*] [*Political party*] (AF)
SWAPOU ..... South-West African Professional Teachers Union [*Namibian*] (AF)
SWAUNIO ... South-West African United National Independence Organization [*Namibian*] (AF)
SWAWEK .... South-West Africa Water and Electricity Supply Commission [*Namibian*] (AF)
SWAZ .... Swaziland (MAR)
SWAZIMAR ... Royal Swaziland Maritime Company (MAR)
SWB .... Sectie Wetenschappelijke Bibliotheken [*NVB*] [*'s-Gravenhage*]
SWB .... Summary of World Broadcasts [*British Broadcasting Corporation*] (MAR)
SWC .... Somali Workers' Council (MAR)
SWDO .... Somali Women's Democratic Organization (AF)
SWE .... Sweden [*Three-letter standard code*] (CNC)
SWEC .... State War Executive Committee (ML)
SWF .... Studium Wychowania Fizycznego [*College of Physical Training*] [*Polish*]
SWF-Dienst ... Selbstwaehlferndienst [*Long-Distance Telephone Dialing Service*] (EG)
SWFP .... Socialist Workers and Farmers Party [*Nigerian*] (AF)
SWIFT .... Society for Worldwide Interland Financial Telecommunication
SWISSAIR ... Swiss Air Transport Co. Ltd.
SWK .... Scott Wilson Kirkpatrick and Partners (MAR)
swl .... Sehr Wenig Loeslich [*Very Slightly Soluble*] [*German*]
SWO .... Seewasserstrassenordnung [*High Seas International Rules of the Road*] (EG)
SWP .... Socialist Workers' Party [*British*] (PPW)
SWP .... Stowarzyszenie Wynalazcow Polskich [*Association of Polish Inventors*] (POL)
SWR .... Samodzielne Warsztaty Remontowe [*Independent Repair Shops*] (POL)
SWSA .... Social Welfare Services in Africa (MAR)
SWTUF .... Sudanese Workers' Trade Unions Federation (MAR)
SWU .... St. Lucia Workers Union (LA1)
swu .... Siehe Weiter Unten [*See Below*] [*German*]
SWU .... Sudan Women's Union (MAR)
SWWTU .... Seamen and Waterfront Workers Trade Union [*Trinidadian and Tobagan*] (LA1)
SWZ .... Swaziland [*Three-letter standard code*] (CNC)
SXEKA .... (Pankypria) Syndekhnia Ergaton Xenodokheion, Estiatorion kai Kendron Anapsykhis [*(Pan-Cyprian) Union of Hotel, Restaurant, and Recreation Center Workers*] (GC)
Sy .... Seyyar [*Mobile*] (TU)
SY .... Syria [*Two-letter standard code*] (CNC)
SYA .... Somateion Ypodimatergaton Athinon [*Union of Athens Shoeworkers*] (GC)
SYa .... Standard Language (RU)
SYAF .... Syrian Air Force (MAR)
SYAPCO ..... South Yemeni-Algerian Petroleum Company (ME)
SYBAZ .... Syndicat du Batiment du Zaire (MAR)
SYBETRA .... Syndicat Belge d'Entreprise a l'Etranger [*Belgian Foreign Contracting Syndicate*] (WER)
SYBOCOA ... Syndicat Bordelais du Commerce Ouest Africain (MAR)
SYC .... Seychelles [*Three-letter standard code*] (CNC)
SYC .... Somali Youth Club (MAR)
SYCOMIMPEX ... Syndicat des Commercants Importateurs-Exportateurs [*Import-Export Businessmen's Union*] [*Central African*] (AF)
SyD .... Synodiki Dioikisis [*Synodical Administration*] [*Greek*] (GC)
SYDATRABA ... Syndicat Dahomeen des Entreprises de Travaux Publics et de Batiment (MAR)
SYDICAM .... Syndicat des Commercants Importateurs Camerounais (MAR)

SYDNE........ Syndesmos Dimokratikon Neon Ellados [*League of Greek Democratic Youth*] (GC1)
sye............... Strontium Unit (RU)
SYeP........... Socialist Unity Party (RU)
SYePG......... Socialist Unity Party of Germany (RU)
SYePI.......... Socialist Unity Party of Iceland (RU)
SYET........... Syllogos Ypallilon Emborikis Trapezis [*Association of Employees of the Commercial Bank*] [*Greek*] (GC)
SYETh......... Somateion Ypovoleon Ellinikou Theatrou [*Greek Theater Prompters Union*] (GC)
sygn............ Sygnatura [*Signature*] [*In a book*] (POL)
SYKA........... Syndekhnia Kypriakon Aerogrammon [*Cyprus Airways Trade Union*] (GC)
SYKB........... Sinai Yatirim ve Kredi Bankasi [*Industrial Investment and Credit Bank*] (TU)
SYKEA......... Stratiotiki Ypiresia Kataskevis Ergon Anasyngrotiseos [*See also MOMA*] [*Military Service for the Construction of Reconstruction Projects*] [*Greek*] (GC)
SYKFA......... Syllogos Kyprion Foititon Anglias [*League of Cypriot Students in England*]
SYMETAIN... Syndicat Miniere de l'Etain [*Tin Mining Workers Union*] [*Zairian*] (AF)
SYMETRA... Syndicat des Entrepreneurs Metropolitains de Travaux Publics Travaillant Outre-Mer (MAR)
syn.............. Syndrofos [*Comrade*] (GC)
SYN............. Syntheses Revue Mensuelle Internationale [*Brussels*] [*A publication*] (MAR)
SYNABOIS... Syndicat National des Forestiers Producteurs des Bois (MAR)
SYNAC......... Syndicat National des Agriculteurs et Cultivateurs de Haute-Volta [*National Union of Farmers and Cultivators of Upper Volta*] (AF)
SYNACAAB... Syndicat des Agents de la Caisse Autonome d'Amortissement du Benin [*Union of Agents of the Independent Amortization Fund of Benin*] (AF)
SYNACADA... Syndicat National des Commercants Africains du Dahomey (MAR)
SYNACIB.... Syndicat National des Commercants et Industriels Africains du Benin [*National Union of African Merchants and Industrialists of Benin*] (AF)
SYNACID.... Syndicat National des Commercants et Industriels Africains du Dahomey (MAR)
SYNACODA... Syndicat des Cies de Navigation et des Consignataires de Navires du Dahomey (MAR)
SYNAD......... Syndicat des Administrateurs Civils [*Civil Administrators Union*] [*Malagasy*] (AF)
SYNAEM...... Syndicat National de l'Enseignement Moyen General Publique [*National Union of General Public Middle Education*] [*Beninese*] (AF)
SYNAESS... Syndicat National des Professeurs des Enseignements Secondaire et Superieur [*National Trade Union of Teachers of Secondary and Higher Education*] [*Beninese*] (AF)
SYNAGELSCAM... Syndicat des Gerants Libres de Station Service au Cameroun (MAR)
SYNAGRI.... Syndicat National des Agents d'Agriculture [*National Union of Agricultural Agents*] [*Upper Voltan*] (AF)
SYNAICAN... Systeme National d'Information Camerounais
SYNARES... Syndicat Africain de la Recherche et de l'Enseignement Superieur [*African Union for Research and Higher Education*] [*Ivorian*] (AF)
SYNCAB...... Syndicat National du Commerce, des Banques, du Credit, et des Assurances (MAR)
SYNCOBENI... Syndicat des Cheminots de l'OCBN [*OCBN Railroad Workers Trade Union*] (AF)
SYNDAGRI... Syndicat des Employeurs Agricoles (MAR)
SYNDIBOIS... Syndicat du Bois du Congo (MAR)
SYNDIMINES... Syndicat des Entreprises Minieres au Gabon (MAR)
SYNDINAVI... Syndicat des Compagnies de Navigation et Consignataires de Navires en Cote-d'Ivoire (MAR)
SYNDUSTREF... Syndicat des Industries de l'Afrique Equatoriale (MAR)
SYNDUSTRICAM... Syndicat des Industriels du Cameroun (MAR)
Syne............ Synagogue [*Synagogue*] [*Military map abbreviation*] [*World War I*] [*French*] (MTD)
SYNEBACI... Syndicat National Unique des Entrepreneurs en Batiment de Cote-d'Ivoire [*Sole National Union of Building Contractors of the Ivory Coast*] (AF)
SYNECECI... Syndicat National des Educateurs, Conseillers d'Education de Cote-d'Ivoire (MAR)
SYNECI....... Syndicat National des Enseignants du Second Degre de Cote-d'Ivoire [*National Union of Secondary Teachers of the Ivory Coast*] (AF)
SYNECTO... Syndicat des Employes de Commerce du Togo [*Togolese Business Employees Trade Union*] (AF)
SYNEIS....... Syndicat National de l'Enseignement Laic du Senegal (MAR)
SYN Eksport... Sinai Mamulleri Yatirim Nakliyat, Ihracat, ve Ithalat AS [*Industrial Products Investment, Transport, Export, and Import Corp.*] (TU)
SYNELS....... Syndicat National de l'Enseignement Laic du Senegal [*National Union of Lay Teachers of Senegal*] (AF)
SYNEPPCI... Syndicat National de l'Enseignement Primaire Public de Cote-d'Ivoire [*Ivory Coast National Public Primary Education Union*] (AF)
SYNERGAZ... Synergatikos Organismos Emfyaloseos Ygraeriou [*Gas Bottling Cooperative Organization*] [*Cypriot*] (GC)
SYNESCI.... Syndicat National des Enseignants du Second Degre [*National Secondary School Teachers Union*] [*Ivorian*] (AF)
SYNMAD..... Syndicat des Manutentionnaires du Dahomey (MAR)
synt............. Syntynyt [*Finnish*]
SYNTADE... Syndicat National des Travailleurs des Administrations d'Etat (MAR)
SYNTECAM... Societe Camerounaise pour la Fabrication de Tissus Synthetiques (MAR)
SYNTEP...... Syndicat des Travailleurs des Entreprises Petroliers (MAR)
SYP............. Soma Ylikou Polemou [*(Army) Ordnance Corps*] (GC)
SYP............. Sosialistinen Yhtenaisyyspuolue [*Socialist Unity Party*] [*Finnish*] (WEN)
SYP............. Suomen Yksityisyrittaejaein Puolúejaerjesto [*Finnish Private Entrepreneurs' Party*] (PPE)
SYPACOA... Syndicat Parisien du Commerce Ouest Africain (MAR)
SYPAOA..... Syndicat Patronal et Artisanal de l'Ouest Africain [*West African Employers and Artisans Union*] (AF)
SYPE........... Symvoulion Prostasias Perivallondos [*Environment Protection Council*] (GC1)
SYPO........... Sarawak Young People's Organization (Communist) (ML)
syr............... Cheese Dairy [*Topography*] (RU)
SYR............. Syria [*Three-letter standard code*] (CNC)
Syst No....... System Nummer [*System Number*] [*German*]
SYT............. Sayistay [*Court of Accounts*] (TU)
SYTANE...... Synergatikon Tamievtirion Spoudazousis Neolaias [*Cooperative Savings Bank for Students*] [*Cypriot*] (GC)
SYTYRIK..... Syndekhnia Tekhnikon Ypallilon Radiofonikon Idryma Kyprou [*Union of Cyprus Broadcasting Corporation Technical Personnel*] [*Cypriot*] (GC)
SYu............. Soviet Justice (RU)
SYU............. Sudanese Youth Union (MAR)
SYuI............ Sverdlovsk Law Institute (RU)
SYuK........... League of Communists of Yugoslavia (BU)
SYuN........... Young Naturalists' Station (RU)
SYuT........... Young Technicians' Station (RU)
SZ................ Antisubmarine Net (RU)
SZ................ Collection of Laws of the USSR (RU)
SZ................ Concentrated Charge (RU)
sz................ Conjunction (BU)
SZ................ Glassware Plant (BU)
SZ................ Northwest (BU)
SZ................ Northwest, Northwestern (RU)
SZ................ Saeurezahl [*Acid Number*] [*German*]
Sz................ Samozalozba [*Privately Printed*] (YU)
sZ................ Seinerzeit [*At That Time*] (EG)
SZ................ Sekretarijat za Zemjodelstvo (IVNRM) [*Secretariat of Agriculture*] (YU)
SZ................ Severo-Zapad [*Northwest*] (YU)
sz................ Severozapad [*Northwest*] (CZ)
SZ................ Skodovy Zavody [*Skoda Works*] (CZ)
SZ................ Smeralovy Zavody [*Smeral Plants*] (CZ)
SZ................ Socialisticke Zeme [*Socialist Countries*] (CZ)
SZ................ Socijalisticka Zora [*Socialist Dawn*] [*Skopje*] [*A periodical*] (YU)
SZ................ Socijalisticko Zemjodelie [*Socialist Agriculture*] [*Skopje*] [*A periodical*] (YU)
SZ................ Sound Signal (RU)
SZ................ Sovjetska Zveza [*Soviet Union*] (YU)
SZ................ Sowjetische Zone [*Soviet Zone*] (EG)
SZ................ Stalinovy Zavody [*Stalin Works*] [*Most*] (CZ)
SZ................ Statni Zastupitelstvi [*State Prosecutor's Office*] (CZ)
SZ................ Stocarska Zadruga [*Livestock Cooperative*] (YU)
SZ................ Stolarska Zadruga [*Carpentry Cooperative*] (YU)
SZ................ Svaz Zamestnancu [*Employees' Union*] (CZ)
SZ................ Svermovy Zavody [*Sverma Works*] (CZ)
SZ................ Svet za Zdravstvo [*Health Council*] (YU)
SZ................ Swaziland [*Two-letter standard code*] (CNC)
sz................ Szabad [*Free*] (HU)
sz................ Szakasz [*Platoon*] (HU)
sz................ Szanowny [*Honorable*] [*Polish*] (GPO)
sz................ Szazad [*Century, One One-Hundredth, Military Company*] (HU)
sz................ Szent [*Saint*] (HU)
sz................ Szovetkezet [*Cooperative*] (HU)
sz................ Szuletett [*Born*] (HU)
SZA............. Medium Antiaircraft Artillery (RU)
SZA............. Medium-Caliber Antiaircraft Artillery (BU)
sz a............. Szam Alatt [*Number*] (HU)
szab............ Szabalyozo [*Regulating, Controlling or Regulator, Controller*] (HU)
SZAB........... Szabvanugyi Allando Bizottsag (Kolcsonos Gazdasagi Segitseg Tanacsa) [*Permanent Committee on Standards (CEMA)*] (HU)
SZAB........... Szamitastechnikai Alkalmazasi Bizottsagok [*Committees for the Application of Computer Technology*] (HU)
sz adag....... Szabvany Adag [*Ration*] (HU)
SZAK........... Szakasz [*Platoon (Military, Section, Detachment)*] (HU)

szakip .... Szakiparos [*Skilled Craftsman*] (HU)
szaku .... Szakuzlet [*Special Shop*] (HU)
szall............ Szallito [*Carrier, Transporting*] (HU)
szam .... Szamozott [*Numbered*] (HU)
SZAMGEP... Szamitastechnikai es Ugyvitelgepesitesi Vallalat [*Computer Technology and Management Mechanization Enterprise*] (HU)
SZAMKI ...... Szamitastechnikai Kutato Intezet [*Computer Technology Research Institute*] (HU)
SZAMOK..... Szamitastechnikai Oktato Kozpont [*Computer Technology Training Center*] (HU)
SZB .... Slovenske Zeleznorudne Bane [*Slovak Iron Ore Mines*] (CZ)
SZB .... Szabadalmi Birosag [*Patent Court*] (HU)
szb .... Szabvany [*Standard, Norm*] (HU)
SZB .... Szakszervezeti Bizottsag [*Trade Union Committee*] (HU)
szb .... Szerb [*Serbian*] (HU)
SZBM .... Stoleczny Zarzad Budynkow Mieszkalnych [*Warsaw Residential Building Administration*] (POL)
Szb M .... Szenbanyaszati Miniszterium/Miniszter [*Ministry/Minister of Coal Mining*] (HU)
SZBT........... Szakszervezetek Budapesti Tanacsa [*Budapest Council of Trade Unions*] (HU)
SZBZ........... Sokolovsky Zavod Branne Zdatnosti [*Sokolov Military Fitness Contest*] (CZ)
SZCB........... Strzelinskie Zaklady Ceramiki Budowlanej [*Strzelin (Strehlen) Building Tile Plant*] (POL)
szczeg......... Szczegolowy [*Detailed*] (POL)
SZD .... Svaz Zemedelskych Druzstev [*Union of Agricultural Cooperatives*] (CZ)
szd .... Szazad [*Company (Infantry), Battery (Artillery), Squadron*] (HU)
SZD .... Szybowcowy Zaklad Doswiadczalny [*Glider Proving Grounds*] (POL)
SZDBiH .... Savez Zenskih Drustava Bosne i Hercegovine [*Federation of Women's Clubs of Bosnia and Hercegovina*] (YU)
SZDCG........ Savez Zenskih Drustava Crne Gore [*Federation of Women's Clubs of Montenegro*] (YU)
SZDH........... Savez Zenskih Drustava Hrvatske [*Federation of Women's Clubs of Croatia*] (YU)
SZDJ .... Savez Zenskih Drustava Jugoslavije [*Federation of Women's Clubs of Yugoslavia*] (YU)
SZDK........... Statni Zkusebna pro Drahe Kovy [*State Testing Center for Precious Metals*] (CZ)
SZDLLRS .... Socialisticna Zveza Delavnega Ljudstva Slovenije [*Socialist Union of Working People of Slovenia*] (YU)
SZDN........... Statni Zdravotnicke Nakladatelstvi [*State Publishing House for Public Health Literature*] (CZ)
SZDP........... Szocialdemokrata Part [*Social Democratic Party*] (HU)
SZDS........... Savez Zenskih Drustava Srbije [*Federation of Women's Clubs of Serbia*] (YU)
szds............ Szazados [*Captain*] (HU)
SZE .... Integrated Power System of the Northwest (RU)
SZE .... Szabad Europa (Radio) [*Radio Free Europe*] (HU)
sze.............. Szerda [*Wednesday*] (HU)
SZEB........... Szovetseges Ellenorzo Bizottsag [*Allied Control Commission*] (HU)
SZEBMGH... Szovetseges Ellenorzo Bizottsag Magyar Gazdasagi Hivatala [*Hungarian Economic Office of the Allied Control Commission*] (HU)
SZEFU......... Szekerfuvarozasi Vallalat [*Carting Enterprise*] (HU)
SzEK .... Szegedi Tudomanyegyetem Konyvtara [*Library of the University of Szeged*] (HU)
szem o .... Szemelyzeti Osztaly [*Personnel Department*] (HU)
szenb .... Szenbanya [*Coal Mine*] (HU)
Szepirod K ... Szepirodalmi Kiado [*Publishing House for Belles Lettres*] (HU)
szept .... Szeptember [*September*] (HU)
SZER........... Szabad Europa Radio [*Radio Free Europe*] (HU)
szer .... Szerokosc [*or Szeroki*] [*Breadth or Broad*] [*Polish*]
szer geogr... Szerokosc Geograficzna [*Latitude*] [*Polish*]
szerk .... Szerkesztette [*Edited By*] [*Hungarian*] (GPO)
szero .... Szeroszlop [*Army Supply Column*] (HU)
szesc........... Szescienny [*Cubic*] [*Polish*]
SZESZ......... Szocialista Egyuttmukodesi Szerzodes [*Socialist Cooperation Contract*] (HU)
SZET mozgalom ... Szakmunkasok Egyetemi Tanulasa Mozgalom [*"Skilled Workers to Attend University" Movement*] (HU)
sz ev........... Szoko Ev [*Leap Year*] (HU)
SZF............. Blocking-Filter Bay (RU)
SZF I........... Szinhaz- es Filmtudomanyi Intezet [*Theater and Film Research Institute*] (HU)
SZFK .... Savezni Zavod za Fizicku Kulturu [*Federal Institute of Physical Culture*] (YU)
SZg............. Signale an Zuegen [*Signals on Trains*] (EG)
SZG .... Szczecinskie Zaklady Gastronomiczne [*Szczecin Catering Establishments*] [*Polish*]
SZGA .... Saratov Gas Equipment Plant (RU)
SZGRP .... Northwestern State River Steamship Line (RU)
SZGRT .... Northwestern Geological Exploration Trust (RU)
SZGT........... Supersonic Gas Turbine (RU)
Sz Gy........... Szabvanygyujtemeny [*Collection of Standards, List of Standards*] (HU)
SZh............. Inflatable Life Jacket (RU)
SZh............. Lead Fluid [*Additive for gasoline*] (RU)
SZh............. Saccharose, Gelatin (RU)
SZH .... Svaz Zamestnancu v Hornictvi [*Mining Employees' Union*] (CZ)
szh .... Szekhely [*County Seat*] (HU)
SZhA .... Saccharose, Gelatin, Agar (RU)
SZhB .... Union of Bulgarian Journalists (BU)
Sz Hi........... Szabvanyugyi Hivatal [*Office of Standardization*] (HU)
SZhK .... Serum of Mares in Foal (RU)
SZhK .... Synthetic Fatty Acid (RU)
SZhS .... Synthetic Aliphatic Alcohol (RU)
SZhZ .... Synthetic Fat Substitutes (RU)
szi............... Szemelyiranyito [*Personnel Director (Office, Officer)*] (HU)
szig .... Szigorlo [*Candidate for Doctoral Degree*] (HU)
SZIKKTI/SZIKTI ... Szilikatipari Kozponti Kutato es Tervezo Intezet [*Central Research and Planning Institute of the Silicate Industry*] (HU)
SZIM........... Szerszamgepipari Muvek [*Machine Tool Industry Works*] (HU)
SZIM........... Szocialista Ifjumunkas Szovetseg [*Socialist Young Workers' Association*] (HU)
SZIMCS ...... Szamitastechnikai Ideglenes Munkacsoport [*Temporary Work Group for Computer Technology*] (HU)
SZINV.......... Savjet za Zakonodavstvo i Izgradnju Narodne Vlasti [*Council for Legislation and Development of People's Government*] (YU)
SZISLSLRS ... Sekretarijat za Zakonodajo Izvrsnega Sveta Ljudske Skupscine Ljudske Republike Slovenije [*Secretariat for Legislation of the Executive Council of the People's Assembly of Slovenia*] (YU)
SZIT .... Szakszervezeti Ifjumunkas es Tanoncmozgalom [*Movement of Socialist Young Workers and Apprentices*] (HU)
SZK .... Savez Zanatskih Komora [*Union of Chambers of Artisans*] (YU)
SZ K .... Szepirodalmi Kiado [*Fiction and Poetry Publishing House*] (HU)
SzK(b)P ...... Szovjetunio Kommunista (Bolsevik) Partja [*Communist Party of the Soviet Union (Bolshevik)*] (HU)
SZKFP......... Szamitastechnikai Kozponti Fejlesztesi Program [*Central Development Program for Computer Technology*] (HU)
SzKP .... Szovjetunio Kommunista Partja [*Communist Party of the Soviet Union*] (HU)
SZKPKB...... Szovjetunio Kommunista Partjanak Kozponti Bizottsaga [*Central Committee of the Communist Party of the Soviet Union*] (HU)
SZKSH .... Szovjetunio Kozponti Statisztikai Hivatala [*Central Statistical Office of the Soviet Union*] (HU)
SZKU........... Statni Zememericsky a Kartograficky Ustav [*State Geodetic and Cartographic Institute*] (CZ)
SZKU........... Statni Zemepisny a Kartograficky Ustav [*State Geographic and Cartographic Institute*] (CZ)
szkv............ Szakaszvezeto [*Junior Sergeant*] (HU)
szkv............ Szolgalatonkivuli [*Retired*] (HU)
szla............. Szamla [*Invoice*] (HU)
szle............. Szemle [*Review*] (HU)
SzlKP .... Szlovakia Kommunista Partja [*Communist Party of Slovakia*] (HU)
SZLTE .... Szovjet-Unio Legfelsobb Tanacsanak Elnoksege [*Presidium of the Supreme Soviet of the Soviet Union*] (HU)
SZM............ Skawinskie Zaklady Metalurgiczne [*Skawina Metallurgical Plant*] (POL)
SZMGSZ ..... Szovjet Magyar Gazdasagi Szerzodes [*Soviet-Hungarian Economic Pact*] (HU)
SZMT .... Szakszervezetek Megyei Tanacsa [*Megye (County) Trade Union Council*] (HU)
SZN .... Statni Zemedelske Nakladatelstvi [*State Agricultural Publishing House*] (CZ)
SZ N .... Szabad Nep [*Free People (Daily Newspaper of the Hungarian Communist Party)*] (HU)
SZNIIGM ..... Northwestern Scientific Research Institute of Hydraulic Engineering and Reclamation (RU)
SZNIISKh.... Northwestern Scientific Research Institute of Agriculture (RU)
SZN Kvt ...... Szocialista Neveles Konyvtara [*Library of Socialist Education*] (HU)
SZNZ........... Savezni Zavod za Narodno Zdravlje [*Federal Institute of Public Health*] (YU)
SZO .... Correspondence Training Section (RU)
SZO .... Northwestern Branch, Northwestern Department (RU)
SZO .... Samostatny Zdravotnicky Oddil [*Separate Medical Battalion*] (CZ)
SZO .... Sekretarijat za Zakonodavstvo i Organizaciju (SIV) [*Secretariat of Legislation and Organization*] (YU)
SZO .... Svetova Zdravotnicka Organizace [*World Health Organization*] (CZ)
SZO .... Svetska Zdravstvena Organizacija [*World Health Organization*] (YU)
szocdem ..... Szocial Demokrata [*Social Democrat*] (HU)
SZOE.......... Szegedi Orvostudomanyi Egyetem [*Medical University of Szeged*] (HU)
SZO K.......... SZOVOSZ Kiadovallalat (Szovetkezetek Orszagos Szovetsege Kiadovallalata) [*SZOVOSZ Publishing House (Publishing House of the National Association of Cooperatives)*] (HU)
SZOMATEX ... Szombathelyi Pamutipar [*Cotton Mill of Szombathely*] (HU)
szomb .... Szombat [*Saturday*] (HU)

SZOSZ .... Szakszervezetek Orszagos Szovetsege [*National Federation of Trade Unions*] (HU)
SzOT .... Szakszervezetek Orszagos Tanacsa [*National Council of Trade Unions*] (HU)
SZOTE .... Szeged Orvostudomanyi Egyetem [*Szeged Medical University*] (HU)
SZOVARU ... Szovetkezetek Orszagos Arubeszerzo es Ertekesito Kozos Vallalata [*Cooperatives National Joint Enterprise for Procuring Goods and Sales*] (HU)
SZOVAUT ... Kozepmagyarorszagi Foldmuvesszovetkezetek Szallitasi Vallalat [*Transportation Enterprise of the Agricultural Cooperatives in Central Hungary*] (HU)
SZOVERT.... Szovetkezetek Orszagos Felvasarlo es Ertekesito Kozpontja [*National Purchasing and Marketing Center of Cooperatives*] (HU)
SZOVOSZ ... Szovetkezetek Orszagos Szovetsege [*National Federation of Cooperatives*] (HU)
szp .... Gravitation Force (RU)
SZP .... Slaskie Zaklady Przemyslowe [*Silesia Industrial Plants*] (POL)
SZP .... Szczecinskie Zaklady Pralnicze [*Szczecin (Stettin) Laundries*] (POL)
szp .... Szpalta [*Column*] (POL)
SZPI .... Northwestern Correspondence Polytechnic Institute (RU)
SZPO........... Szczecinskie Zaklady Przemyslu Odziezowego [*Szczecin (Stettin) Clothing Plant*] (POL)
SZPP .... Savezni Zavod za Privredno Planiranje (DSPRP) [*Federal Institute of Economic Planning*] (YU)
SZPP .... Svaz Zamestnancu v Peneznictvi a Pojistovnictvi [*Union of Employees in the Field of Finance and Insurance*] (CZ)
SZPR........... Savezni Zavod za Produktivnost Rada [*Federal Institute for Labor Productivity*] (YU)
SZPSPP ...... Savezni Zavod za Proucavanje Skolskih i Prosvetnih Pitanje [*Federal Institute for the Study of School and Cultural Problems*] (YU)
SZPT .... Stoleczny Zarzad Przemyslu Terenowego [*Warsaw Local Industry Administration*] (POL)
SZPU........... Statni Zastavni a Pujcovni Urad [*State Loan Office and Pawnshop*] (CZ)
SZPW .... Slaskie Zaklady Przemyslu Welnianego [*Silesia Wool Plants*] (POL)
SZR .... Green-Light Signal Relay (RU)
SZR .... Public Health Employees Union (BU)
SZR .... Statni Zdravotni Rada [*State Public Health Council*] (CZ)
sz r .... Szabalyrendelet [*Bylaw, Statute, Ordinance*] (HU)
sz r .... Szamu Rendelet [*Decree Numbered*] (HU)
SzRI............. Szakorvosi Rendelo Intezet [*Center of Medical Specialists*] (HU)
SZRP........... Northwestern River Steamship Line (RU)
SZRSJ......... Sindikat Zeljeznickih Radnika i Sluzbenika Jugoslavije [*Trade-Union of Railroad Workmen and Employees of Yugoslavia*] (YU)
SZS .... Blue-Green Glass (RU)
SZS .... Savezni Zavod za Statistiku (DSPRP) [*Federal Statistical Office*] (YU)
SZS .... Slovenska Zemepisna Spolocnost [*Slovak Geographic Society*] (CZ)
SZS .... Sreski Zadruzni Savez [*District Cooperative Union*] (YU)
SZS .... Srpska Zemljoradnicka Stranka [*Serbian Agrarian Party*] [*Yugoslav*] (PPE)
SZS .... Staatliche Zentralverwaltung fuer Statistik [*State Central Administration for Statistics*] (EG)
SZS .... Svaz Zamestnancov Skolstva [*Union of Employees in Educational Institutions*] (CZ)
SZS .... Szkolny Zwiazek Sportowy [*School Athletics and Sports Association*] [*Polish*]
SZSO........... Savezni Zavod za Socijalno Osiguranje [*Federal Institute of Social Insurance*] (YU)
SZSO........... Svaz Zamestnancu Skolstvi a Osvety [*Union of Educational and Cultural Employees*] (CZ)
SZSU........... Statny Zdravotne-Socialny Ustav [*State Public Health and Social Institute*] (CZ)
sz szakszerv ... Szabad Szakszervezet [*Free Trade Union*] (HU)
SZSZK .... Szovjet Szocialista Koztarsasag [*Soviet Socialist Republic*] (HU)
SZSZKSZ.... Szovjet Szocialista Koztarsasagok Szovetsege [*Union of Soviet Socialist Republics*] (HU)
SZSZNSZ.... Szabad Szakszervezetek Nemzetkozi Szovetsege [*International Federation of Free Trade Unions*] (HU)
s Zt .... Seiner Zeit [*Then*] [*German*]
SZT .... Standard Fuze (RU)
SZT .... Szakszervezeti Tanacs [*Trade Union Council*] (HU)
SZT .... Szechenyi Tarsasag [*Szechenyi Association*] (HU)
SzT.............. Szegedi Textilmuvek [*Textile Factory of Szeged*] (HU)
Szt .... Szent [*Saint*] (HU)
SZTA........... Szovjet-Unio Tudomanyos Akademiaja [*Academy of Sciences of the Soviet Union*] (HU)
SZTAKI .... MTA Szamitastechnikai es Automatizlasi Kutato Intezet [*Computer Technology and Automation Research Institute of the Hungarian Academy of Sciences*] (HU)
SZTE .... Szilikatipari Tudomanyos Egyesulet [*Scientific Association of the Silicate Industry*] (HU)
Szt Gl .... Sztab Glowny [*General Staff*] [*Polish*]
SZTI .... Szakfelugyeleti es Tovabbkepzesi Intezet [*Technical Supervision and Advanced Training Institute*] (HU)
SZTK........... Szakszervezeti Tarsadalombiztositasi Kozpont [*Trade Union Social Insurance Center*] (HU)
sztl .... Szamozatlan [*Unnumbered*] (HU)
SZU .... Self-Propelled Antiaircraft Gun (RU)
SZU .... Statni Zdravotni Ustav [*State Health Institute*] (CZ)
SZU .... Statni Zememericsky Ustav [*State Geodetic Institute*] (CZ)
SZU .... Statny Zemepisny Ustav [*State Geographical Institute*] (CZ)
SZU .... Strojirensky Zkusebni Ustav [*Testing Institute for Engineering*] (CZ)
SzU.............. Szovjetunio [*Soviet Union*] (HU)
SZUB........... Sluzba Zagraniczna Urzedu Bezpieczenstwa [*Foreign Service of the Security Administration*] (POL)
SZUGMS..... Northwestern Administration of the Hydrometeorological Service (RU)
SZUL .... Szuletett [*Born*] (HU)
SZUMT........ Szovjetunio Minisztertanacsa [*Council of Ministers of the Soviet Union*] (HU)
SZUTA .... Szovjetunio Tudomanyos Akademiaja [*USSR Academy of Sciences*] (HU)
SZUV........... Szamitastechnikai es Ugyvitelszervezesi Vallalat [*Computer Technology and Management Organization Enterprise*] (HU)
SZV .... Sdruzeni Zahranicnich Vojaku [*Association of Veterans of Foreign Wars*] (CZ)
SZV .... Svaz Zahranicnych Vojakov [*Association of Veterans of Foreign Wars*] (CZ)
szv.............. Szemelyvonat [*Local Train*] (HU)
szv.............. Szovetkezeti Vallalat [*Cooperative Enterprise*] (HU)
SZVD........... Slovensky Zvaz Vyrobnych Druzstiev [*Slovak Union of Production Cooperatives*] (CZ)
SZVI .... Saratov Zootechnical and Veterinary Institute (RU)
SzVK .... Szakszervezeti Vilagkongresszus [*World Congress of Trade Unions*] (HU)
SZVMKI....... Szerves Vegyipari es Muanyagipari Kutato Intezet [*Industrial Research Institute on Organic Chemistry and Plastics*] (HU)
SZVSZ......... Szakszervezeti Vilagszovetseg [*World Federation of Trade Unions*] (HU)
SZVT .... Szervezesi es Vezetesi Tudomanyos Tarsasag [*Scientific Society of Organization and Management*] (HU)
SZVU........... Sdruzeni Zapadoceskych Vytvarnych Umelcu [*Association of West Bohemian Creative Artists*] (CZ)
SZWI .... Stalinogrodskie Zjednoczenie Wodno-Inzynierskie [*Stalinogrod (now again Katowice) Hydraulic Engineering Association*] (POL)
SZWS.......... Szczecinskie Zaklady Wlokien Sztucznych [*Szczecin (Stettin) Synthetic Fiber Plant*] (POL)
SZZ .... Savez Zemljoradnickih Zadruga [*Union of Agricultural Cooperatives*] (YU)
SZZ .... Slovenska Zenska Zveza (v Ameriki) [*Slovenian Women's Union (in America)*] [*Chicago*] (YU)
SZZ .... Sreska Zanatska Zadruga [*District Artisan Cooperative*] (YU)
SZZ .... Svaz Zamestnancu v Zemedelstvi [*Union of Agricultural Workers*] (CZ)
SZZA........... Slovenska Zenska Zveza v Ameriki [*Slovenian Women's Union in America*] (YU)
SZZLS......... Statni Zkusebna Zemedelskych a Lesnickych Stroju [*State Testing Center for Agricultural and Forestry Machinery*] (CZ)
SZZPI.......... Northwestern Correspondence Polytechnic Institute (RU)
SZZTS......... Svaz Zamestnancu Zavodu Tezkeho Strojirenstvi [*Union of Workers in the Heavy Machine Industry*] (CZ)
SZZV .... Savez Zemljoradnickih Zadruga Vojvodine [*Union of Agricultural Cooperatives of Vojvodina*] (YU)

T

T .... A Tracteur [*Said of a battery*] [*Military*] [*French*] (MTD)
T° .... Absolute Temperature [*Absolute Temperature*] [*German*]
t° .... Celsiusgrad [*Centigrade*] [*German*]
t .... Comrade (RU)
T- .... Current Maintenance [*Motor vehicles*] (RU)
T .... Hard [*Nature of bottom of a ford*] [*Topography*] (RU)
t .... He, This (BU)
T .... Heavy Structures [*Military term*] (RU)
T .... Instrumental [*Case*] (RU)
t .... Point, Period (BU)
t .... Point, Spot, Period (RU)
t .... Printing [*Number of copies*] (RU)
T .... Rear, Service Area, Service Troops (RU)
T .... Tablazat [*Chart*] (HU)
T .... Tag [*Member*] (HU)
t .... Tai [*Or*] [*Finnish*] (GPO)
T .... Takhsis [*Academic degree*] [*Moroccan*]
T .... Tanacs [*Council*] (HU)
T- .... Tank (RU)
t .... Tarde [*Afternoon*] [*Spanish*]
T .... Tare [*French*]
T .... Tarih [*or Tarihli*] [*Date or Dated*] (TU)
T .... Tausend [*Thousand*] [*German*]
T .... Taxe a Percevoir [*French*]
T .... Taxi (RU)
T .... Technical (RU)
T .... Technisch [*German*]
T .... Teil [*or Teile*] [*Part or Parts*] [*German*] (GPO)
T .... Telefon [*Telephone*] (TU)
t .... Telephone (RU)
T .... Telgraf [*Telegraph*] (TU)
t .... Temperatura [*Temperature*] [*Polish*]
T .... Temperature (RU)
t .... Tempore [*In the Time Of*] [*Latin*] (GPO)
t .... Teos [*Former*] (GC)
T .... Tepe [*Hill, Peak*] (TU)
T .... Terkep [*Map*] (HU)
T .... Territorial [*Territorial*] [*French*] (MTD)
T .... Terulet [*Area*] (HU)
T .... Tervezet [*Plan, Schedule*] (HU)
t .... Thousand (RU)
t .... Tie [*Road*] [*Finnish*] (CED)
T .... Timbre [*On documents, indicates that they are to be stamped*] [*French*] (MTD)
T .... Tisztelt [*Honored*] (HU)
T .... Titer (RU)
t .... Tom [*Volume*] (POL)
t .... Tome [*Book, Volume*] [*French*]
t .... Tomo [*Book, Volume*] [*Spanish*]
T .... Tomos [*Volume*] (GC)
t .... Ton (BU)
t .... Ton (RU)
T .... Ton-Force (RU)
t .... Tona [*Ton*] [*Polish*]
t .... Tone (BU)
t .... Tonne [*Ton (Metric)*] (EG)
T .... Tonnen [*Tons*] [*German*]
t .... Tonni(a) [*Finnish*]
T .... Toplam [*Total*] (TU)
T .... Torrente [*Torrent*] [*Italian*] (NAU)
T- .... Tractor (RU)
T/ .... Traite [*Agreement*] [*French*]
T .... Transforme [*Transformed*] [*French*] (MTD)
T .... Transport, Transportation (RU)
T .... Transportni [*Transportation*] (CZ)
T .... Triebwagen [*Rail Motor Car*] (EG)
T .... Trotyl (RU)
T .... Tube, Fuze (RU)
T .... Turistik [*Touristic*] [*As a higher-class hotel*] (TU)
T .... Turkce [*Turkish*] (TU)
t .... Volume (BU)
t .... Volume (RU)
t-a .... Packing Materials (RU)
TA .... Tameion Arogis [*Assistance Fund*] (GC)
TA .... Tameion Asfaliseos [*Insurance Fund*] (GC)
TA .... Tananarive-Antsirabe (MAR)
TA .... Tank Army (BU)
TA .... Tank Army (RU)
TA .... Tankova Armada [*Tank Army*] (CZ)
TA .... Technical Archives (RU)
TA .... Tehnicka Akademija [*Technical Academy*] [*Zagreb*] [*Army*] (YU)
TA .... Telegraph (RU)
TA .... Telegraphie Acoustique [*Military*] [*French*] (MTD)
TA .... Telephone (RU)
TA .... Telepulesi Alap [*Resettlement Fund*] (HU)
TA .... Territorial Administrator (MAR)
TA .... Territorial Army (ML)
TA .... Tetarti Avgoustou [*Fourth of August*] [*Greek*] (GC)
TA .... Tierarzt [*German*]
TA .... Tirailleurs Algeriens (MAR)
TA .... Tramways Algeriens (MAR)
TA .... Transport Aviation (RU)
TA .... Trapeza Anaptyxeos [*Development Bank*] [*Cypriot*] (GC)
TA .... Turk Ajansi [*Turkish Agency*] (TU)
TAA .... Tameion Agrotikon Asfaliseon [*Agricultural Insurance Fund*] [*Greek*] (GC)
TAA .... Tanganyika African Association (MAR)
TAA .... Trans-Australia Airlines
TAA .... Transafricair (MAR)
TAA .... Transitional Administrative Authority [*South African*] (AF)
TAAA .... Tanzania Amateur Athletic Association (MAR)
TAAD .... Turk Atlantik Anlasmasi Dernegi [*Turkish Atlantic Agreement Organization*] (TU)
TAAG .... Transportes Aereos de Angola [*Air Transportation of Angola*] (AF)
TAAG .... Tropical Africa Advisory Group (MAR)
TAAKh .... Tameion Apallotrioseos Arkhaiologikon Khoron [*Fund for Expropriation of Archeological Areas*] [*Greek*] (GC)
TAAKh .... Tameion Arogis Axiomatikon Khorofylakis [*Gendarmerie Officers' Relief Fund*] [*Greek*] (GC)
TAAMM .... Tameion Asfaliseos Artergaton, Mylergaton, kai Makaronopoion [*Bakery and Mill Workers and Macaroni Makers Insurance Fund*] [*Greek*] (GC)
Taar .... Taaruz [*Attack, Assault*] (TU)
TAAS .... Tameion Allilovoitheias Axiomatikon (kai Anthypaspiston) Stratou [*Mutual Aid Fund for Army Officers (and Warrant Officers)*] [*Greek*] (GC)
TAAT .... Tanganyika Association Against Tuberculosis (MAR)
TAAThP .... Tameion Arogis Anapiron kai Thymaton Polemou [*War Victims and Disabled Assistance Fund*] [*Greek*] (GC)
TAB .... Aerial Thermite Bomb (RU)
tab .... Tabela [*Table*] [*Polish*]
Tab .... Tabelle [*Table*] [*German*]
tab .... Tabori [*Of the Field, Camping*] (HU)
TAB .... Tanacsi Allando Bizottsag [*Standing Committee of the Council*] (HU)
Tab .... Tobacco Factory [*Topography*] (RU)
tab .... Tobacco-Growing Sovkhoz [*Topography*] (RU)
tab .... Tobacco Plantation [*Topography*] (RU)
TAB .... Totalisator Agency Board (MAR)
TAB .... Transportoarele Amfibii Blindate [*Armored Amphibian Transports*] (RO)
TAB .... Turk-Arap Bankasi [*Turkish-Arabic Bank*] [*Established February 1977*] (TU)
TABA .... Tanzania Amateur Boxing Association (MAR)
TABACOL ... Tabacos Colombianos Ltda. [*Bogota*] (COL)
TABATCHAD ... Societe Agricole Tchadienne de Collecte et de Traitement des Tabacs (MAR)
TABEA .... Tanzania Beekeepers Association (MAR)

TABGIS....... Turkiye Akaryakit Acenta ve Bayileri ile Garaj Isletenler Sendikasi [*Turkish Liquid Fuel Agents', Dealers', and Garage Operators' Union*] (TU)
tabl............. Plate, Table (RU)
tabl............. Tablazat [*Chart*] (HU)
tabl............. Table (BU)
tabl............. Tablet (RU)
tabl............. Tablica [*Figure, Table*] (POL)
tab sar......... Tobacco Shed [*Topography*] (RU)
TAC............. Compagnie des Tramways et Autobus de Casablanca (MAR)
TAC............. Empresa de Transportes Aereao Catarinense [*Brazilian*]
TAC............. Soweto Teachers Action Committee [*South African*] (AF)
TAC............. Tanganyika Agricultural Corporation (MAR)
TAC............. Tanzania Railway Corporation (AF)
TAC............. Togo Amusement Corporation (MAR)
TAC............. Toplumsal Arastirma ve Calisma Kurumu [*Social Research and Labor Institute*] (TU)
TAC............. Transitos Adouanas y Consignaciones [*Moroccan*] (MAR)
TAC............. Transmeridian Air Cargo Limited (MAR)
TAC............. Transportes Aereos del Cesar [*Bogota*] (COL)
TAC............. Transvaal Automobile Club (MAR)
TACA.......... Transportes Aereos Centroamericanos, SA [*Central America Air Lines Transportation*] [*Salvadoran*]
TACATA...... Transportes Aereos del Caqueta [*Cucuta*] (COL)
TACC.......... Tribunal Anti-Imperialista Centroamericano y del Caribe [*Anti-Imperialist Tribunal of Central America and the Caribbean*] (LA1)
TACIP.......... Tripoli Anonima Commercio Industria Pelli (MAR)
TACO.......... Etablissements Togolais d'Activites Commerciales (MAR)
TACOLOMBIA ... Taller Colombia [*Girardot*] (COL)
TACONA..... Fabrica de Tacones de Aluminio [*Bogota*] (COL)
TACONAL... Fabrica de Tacones de Aluminio [*Bogota*] (COL)
TACORAL... Alfombras Cortinas y Tapetes [*Bogota*] (COL)
TACOSHILI ... Tanzania Coastal Shipping Line (MAR)
TACV.......... Transportes Aereos de Cabo Verde [*Cape Verde Airlines*] (AF)
tad............. Heavy Artillery Battalion (RU)
TAD............. Taktiki Aeroporiki Dynamis [*Tactical Air Force*] [*Cypriot*] (GC)
tad............. Tamadas [*Attack, Offensive*] (HU)
Tad............. Tausend [*Thousand*] [*German*]
TAD............. Teknik Arastirma Dairesi [*Technical Research Office*] [*Under Ministry of Forestry*] (TU)
TAD............. Turk-Amerikan Dernegi [*Turkish-American Society*] (TU)
TADAM....... Tanzanian Association of Development Administration and Management (MAR)
TADECO..... Tanga Development Corporation (MAR)
TADKY........ Tameion Asfaliseos Dimotikon kai Koinonikon Ypallilon [*Municipal and Communal Employees Insurance Fund*] [*Greek*] (GC)
TADSIS....... Turkiye Ayakkabi ve Deri Sanayi Iscileri Sendikasi [*Turkish Shoe and Leather Industry Workers Union*] (TU)
tadzh........... Tadzhik (RU)
Tadzhikgosizdat ... Tadzhik State Publishing House (RU)
TadzhikTA ... Tadzhik News Agency (RU)
Tadzhikuchpedgiz ... Tadzhik State Publishing House of Textbooks and Pedagogical Literature (RU)
TadzhNIIZhV ... Tadzhik Scientific Research Institute of Livestock Breeding and Veterinary Science (RU)
TadzhSSR... Tadzhik Soviet Socialist Republic (RU)
tae............. Air Transport Squadron (RU)
TAE............. Tadzhik Archaeological Expedition (RU)
TAE............. Tameion Asfaliseos Emboron [*Merchants Insurance Fund*] [*Greek*] (GC)
TAE............. Tmima Anikhnevseos Englimaton [*Criminal Investigation Department*] (GC)
taegl............ Taeglich [*Daily, Per Day*] (EG)
TAEK........... Turk Atom Enerjisi Komisyonu [*Turkish Atomic Energy Commission*] [*Under Office of Premier*] (TU)
TAES........... Tanzania Agricultural Economics Society (MAR)
TAETA......... Tameion Asfaliseos Ergaton Typou Athinon [*Athens Press Workers Insurance Fund*] (GC)
TAF............. Triammonium Phosphate (RU)
TAFCO........ Tanzania Finance Company Limited (MAR)
TAFGI.......... Tenyeszallatforgalmi Gazdasagi Iroda [*Economic Control Office - Livestock Trade*] (HU)
TAFICO....... Tanzanian Fisheries Corporation (MAR)
TAFORG...... Takarmanyforgalmi Vallalat [*Fodder Store*] (HU)
TAG............. News Agency (RU)
tag............. Tagozat [*Section, Branch*] (HU)
TAG............. Transports Aeriens du Gabon (MAR)
TAGB.......... Transportes Aereos de Guine-Bissau [*Guinea-Bissau Airlines*] (AF)
TAGSA........ Tanganyika African Government Servants Association (MAR)
TAH............. Trans-African Highway (MAR)
TAHA........... Tanzania Amateur Handball Association (MAR)
TAHI........... Tanzania Hotels Investments Limited (MAR)
TAI............. Transactions of the All-Union Arctic Institute (RU)
TAIC............ [*The*] Tokyo Atomic Industrial Consortium (SJT)
TAICH......... Technical Assistance Information Clearing House (MAR)
TAISYT....... Tameion Asfaliseos Idioktiton Syndakton kai Ypallilon Typou [*Insurance Fund of Press Owners, Editors, and Employees*] [*Greek*] (GC)
TAJA........... Tanzanian African Journalists Association (AF)
TAK............. Taal en Aktie Komitee [*Language Action Committee*] [*Belgian*] (WEN)
TAK............. Tactical Air Command [*United States*] (RU)
TAK............. Tactical Aviation Command Element (BU)
Tak............. Takriben [*Approximate, Approximately*] (TU)
Tak............. Taktik [*Tactics, Tactical*] (TU)
TAK............. Tameion Asfaliseos Kapnergaton [*Tobacco Workers Insurance Fund*] [*Greek*] (GC)
TA K............ Tankonyvkiado [*Textbook Publishing House*] (HU)
TAK............. Technisch-Allgemeine Kontrolle [*General and Technical Control*] (EG)
TAK............. Turk Ajansi Kibris [*Turkish News Agency Cyprus*] (GC)
TAKE........... Tameion Asfaliseos (Orthodoxou Efimeriakou) Klirou Ellados [*Greek (Orthodox Parish) Clergy Insurance Fund*] [*Greek*] (GC)
TAKE........... Termez Complex Archaeological Expedition (RU)
TAKhDIK..... Tameion Khrimatodotiseos Dikastikon Ktirion [*Court Building Construction Financing Fund*] [*Greek*] (GC)
TAKhMAYKhA ... Tameion Asfaliseos Khrimatiston, Mesiton, Antikryston, kai Ypallilon Khrimatistiriou Athinon [*Insurance Fund of Brokers, Account Executives, Specialists, and Employees of the Athens Stock Exchange*] (GC)
TAKI............ Tavkozlesi Kutato Intezet [*Telecommunication Research Institute*] (HU)
TAKKD........ Turk Amerikan Kadinlar Kultur Dernegi [*Turkish-American Women's Cultural Association*] (TU)
tak obr........ Thus, In Such a Manner (RU)
TAKRAF...... Transportausruestungen-Kraene Foerderanlagen [*Transportation Equipment, Conveying Equipment, and Cranes*] (EG)
taks............. Forest Valuation, Valuation Survey (RU)
TAKSAN..... Takim Tezgahlari Sanayii ve Ticaret AS [*Machinery Spare Parts Industry and Trade Corp.*] (TU)
TAL............. Societe Nationale des Tanneries Algeriennes (MAR)
tal............. Taloustieteet [*Economics*] [*Finnish*]
TALARCO... Larco-Laminados Metalicos y Aire Acondicionado SA [*Medellin*] (COL)
TALICOL..... Tarjetas Litografiadas Colombia [*Bogota*] (COL)
TALIKOM.... Talikomunikasi [*Telecommunications*] (ML)
tal'k........... Talc Quarry [*Topography*] (RU)
tal qual........ Talis Qualis [*Just as They Come*] [*Latin*] (GPO)
tam............. Customhouse [*Topography*] (RU)
TAM............. Societe des Travaux Aeriens de Madagascar (MAR)
Tam............. Tamirathane [*Repair Shop*] (TU)
TAM............. Tamtama [*Enlisted Man (Corporal and below)*] (IN)
TAM............. Tovarna Avtomobilov Maribor [*Maribor Automobile Factory*] (YU)
TAM............. Transportes Aereos Militares [*Military Air Transport*] [*Bolivian*] (LA)
TAM............. Transportes Aereos de Mocambique Lda. (MAR)
TAM............. Transports Automobiles et Manutention (MAR)
TAM............. Turkiye Amator Milli Takimi [*Turkish National Amateur Team*] (TU)
TAMALI....... Tanneries Maliennes (MAR)
TAMCO....... Societe de Transports, d'Automobiles, et de Mecanique au Congo (MAR)
TAMCO....... Tanzania-Madagascar Clove Organisation (MAR)
TAMDA....... Timber and Allied Materials Development Association (MAR)
TAME.......... Transportes Aereos Militares Ecuatorianos [*Ecuadorean Military Air Transport*] (LA)
TAMEMA.... Taller de Metales y Maderas Elaboradas Ltda. [*Medellin*] (COL)
TAMEPRE... Taller de Mecanica Alta Precision [*Bogota*] (COL)
TAMETAL... Talleres Metalicos Andina Ltda. [*Bogota*] (COL)
TAMISAS.... Tarim Makinalari Imalat Sanayii Anonim Sirketi [*Agricultural Machinery Manufacturing Industry Corporation*] (TU)
TAMS.......... Tippetts-Abbett-McCarthy-Stratton Agricultural Development Group (MAR)
TAMSA....... Tornilleria y Aplicaciones Mecanicas, Sociedad Anonima [*Bogota*] (COL)
TAMSAN..... Tomruk ve Agac Mamulleri Sanayii AS [*Log and Wood Products' Industry Corp.*] (TU)
TAMTAS..... Teknik Ambalaj ve Makina Sanayi ve Ticaret Anonim Sirketi [*Technical Packing and Mechanical Industry and Trade Corporation*] (TU)
TAMTU........ Tanzania Agricultural Machinery Testing Unit (MAR)
TAN............. Technisch Begruendete Arbeitsnorm [*Technically Established Work Norm*] (EG)
TANA.......... Tribunal Anti-Imperialista de Nuestra America [*Anti-Imperialist Tribunal of Our America*] (LA1)
TANAP........ Tatransky Narodny Park [*Tatra National Park*] (CZ)
tanars........... Tanarseged [*Assistant to a Professor*] (HU)
tanb............. Tank Battalion (RU)
TANC.......... Tanganyika African National Congress (MAR)
TANCUT...... Tanzania Diamond Cutting Company Limited (MAR)
TANDANOR ... Talleres Navales Darsena Norte [*North Basin Shipyards*] [*Argentine*] (LA)
TANESCO... Tanganyika Electric Supply Company [*Tanzanian*] (AF)
TANG.......... Tanganyika (MAR)
TANG.......... Tvornica Alata Nova Gradiska [*Nova Gradiska Tools Factory*] (YU)

TANIC .... Tabacalera Nicaraguense, SA [*Nicaraguan Tobacco Company, Inc.*] (LA1)
Tanie .... Tannerie [*Tannery*] [*Military map abbreviation*] [*World War I*] [*French*] (MTD)
TANII .... Transactions of the Arctic Scientific Research Institute (RU)
TANITA .... Tanzania Italia Company (MAR)
TANJUG ...... Telegrafska Agencija Nove Jugoslavije [*New Yugoslavia Telegraph Agency*] (YU)
tankr .... Tank Company (RU)
TANKS .... Tanganyika Concessions (MAR)
Tankvoj .... Tankove Vojsko [*Armored Corps*] (CZ)
TANNIMPEX ... TANNIMPEX Bor es Szorme Kulkereskedelmi Vallalat [*TANNIMPEX Foreign Trade Enterprise for Leather and Fur*] (HU)
TANPY .... Tameion Asfaliseos Navtikon Praktoron kai Ypallilon [*Shipping Agents' and Employees' Insurance Fund*] [*Greek*] (GC)
TANR .... Tank Reserve (RU)
TANSEED ... Tanzania Seed Company (MAR)
tansk .... Tanskaa [*or Tanskaksi*] [*Finnish*]
tansk .... Tanskalainen [*Finnish*]
TAN TadzhSSR ... Transactions of the Academy of Sciences of the Tadzhik SSR (RU)
TANU .... Tanganyika African National Union [*Tanzanian*] (AF)
TANZ .... Tanzania (MAR)
TANZAM ..... Tanzania-Zambia Highway (MAR)
TAO .... Tashkent Astronomical Observatory (RU)
TAO .... Taxi Aereo Opita [*Neiva*] (COL)
TAO .... Triacetyloleandomycin (RU)
TAO .... Turk Anonim Ortaklari [*Commercial Partnership*] (TU)
TAO .... Tuva Autonomous Oblast [*1944-1961*] (RU)
TAOA .... Tameion Arogis Organon Agrofylakis [*Rural Police Assistance Fund*] [*Greek*] (GC)
TAOKh .... Tameion Asfaliseos Opliton Khorofylakis [*Gendarmerie Officer Insurance Fund*] [*Greek*] (GC)
TAOK-Is ...... Turkiye Agac, Dograma, ve Kereste Sanayii Iscileri [*Turkish Wood, Carpentry, and Lumber Industry Workers' Union*] (TU)
TAON .... Special-Purpose Heavy Artillery (RU)
TAOs .... Tenkovski Staresina Kao Artiljeriski Osmatrac [*Tank Commander as Artillery Observer*] (YU)
TAP .... Air Transport Regiment (RU)
t ap .... Heat Exchange Apparatus (RU)
TAP .... Heavy Artillery Regiment (RU)
TAP .... Penetapan [*Decision, Directive*] (IN)
Tap .... Tapulamasi [*Registration*] (TU)
TAP .... Teatro de Arte Popular [*Bogota*] (COL)
TAP .... Training Air Regiment (RU)
TAP .... Transfer Analysis Trigger [*Computers*] (RU)
TAP .... Transportes Aereos Portuguesas [*Portuguese Air Transport*] (AF)
TAP .... Tunis-Afrique Presse [*Tunis-Africa Press Agency*] (AF)
TAP .... Turystyczna Agencja Prasowa [*Tourist Press Agency*] [*Polish*]
TAPA .... Tanganyika African Parents Association [*Tanzanian*] (AF)
TAPALTEX ... Fabrica de Alfombras y Tapetes [*Bogota*] (COL)
TAPAMETAL ... Fabrica de Tapas y Envases Metalicos Ltda. [*Bogota*] (COL)
TAPAP .... Tameion Andallaximou Periousias kai Apokatastaseos Prosfygon [*Exchangeable Property and Refugee Resettlement Fund*] [*Greek*] (GC)
TAPD .... Turkiye Aile Planlama Dernegi [*Turkish Family Planning Organization*] (TU)
TAPENSA ... Tapas y Envases, Sociedad Anonima [*Barranquilla*] (COL)
TAPET .... Tameion Asfaliseos Prosopikou Ethnikou Typografeiou [*National Printing Office Personnel Insurance Fund*] [*Greek*] (GC)
TAPL .... Trustul Alimentatiei Publice Locale [*Local Public Food Trust*] (RO)
TAPline .... Trans-Arabian Pipeline [*Saudi*] (ME)
TAPOL .... Tahanan Politik [*Political Prisoner*] (IN)
TAPOTE ...... Tameion Asfaliseos Prosopikou tou Organismou Tilepikoinonion Ellados [*Greek Telecommunications Organization Personnel Insurance Fund*] (GC)
TAPT .... Tameion Asfaliseos Prosopikou Trapezon [*Bank Personnel Insurance Fund*] [*Greek*] (GC)
TAPU .... Transistorized Field Beta and Gamma Counter (RU)
TAPV .... Three-Phase Automatic Reclosing (RU)
TAPVOS ...... Three-Phase Automatic Reclosing with Synchronism Expectation (RU)
TAPVUS ...... Three-Phase Automatic Reclosing with Synchronism Catching (RU)
TAR .... Current Repair Service (BU)
t ar .... Heavy Artillery (BU)
Tar .... Tarih [*History*] (TU)
TAR .... Transporte Aereo Rioplatense [*River Plate Air Transport*] [*Argentine*] (LA1)
TAR .... Tunis Air (MAR)
TARCA .... Taxi Aereo de Caldas Ltda. [*Manizales*] (COL)
TARENA ...... Talleres de Reparaciones Navales [*Ship Repair Yards*] [*Argentine*] (LA)
TARIM-Is ..... Turkiye Tarim ve Tarim Sanayii Iscileri Sendikasi [*Farm Workers Union of Turkey*] (TU)
Tarim-Sen .. Tarim Isciler Sendikasi [*Agricultural Workers Union*] (GC)
TARIS .... Tarim Isciler Sendikasi [*Agricultural Workers Union*] (TU)
tark .... Tarkastaja [*Finnish*]
tark .... Tarkastettu [*Finnish*]
tark .... Tarkoittaa [*Finnish*]
TARKIM ...... Tarim Araclari ve Kimya Sanayii AS [*Agricultural Equipment and Chemical Industry Corp.*] (TU)
TARKO .... Tarim Satis Kooperatifleri Birlikleri [*Agricultural Sales Cooperatives Unions*] (TU)
Tarkom .... Tariff Committee (RU)
Tar kv spr .... Tariff-Grade Reference Manual (BU)
TARMASAN ... Tarim Makine Sanayi ve Ticaret AS [*Agricultural Machinery Industry and Trade Corp.*] (TU)
TARO .... Tanzania Agricultural Research Organisation (MAR)
TAROM .... Transporturi Aeriene Romane [*Romanian Air Transport*] (RO)
TARR .... Tractor Army Repair Shop (BU)
tar ruk .... Tariff Regulations (RU)
TARS .... Transporturi Aeriene Romane-Sovietice [*Romanian-Soviet Air Transport*] (RO)
tart .... Tartalekos [*Reserves, Of the Reserves*] [*Military*] (HU)
tart .... Tartalom [*Contents*] (HU)
Tarz .... Tbilisi Automobile Repair Plant (RU)
TAS .... Secretariado Teleinformativo [*Bogota*] (COL)
TAS .... Tactical Air Force (BU)
TAS .... Tameion Asfaliseos Symvolaiografon [*Notaries Insurance Fund*] [*Greek*] (GC)
TAS .... Tankova a Automobilova Sprava [*Tank and Vehicle Directorate*] (CZ)
TAS .... Technische Aussenstelle [*Technical Field Office*] (EG)
TAS .... Torpedo Data Computer (RU)
TAS .... Turk Anonim Sirketi [*Turkish Joint-Stock Company*] (CED)
TASA .... Telecomunicacoes Aeronauticas, Sociedade Anonima [*Aeronautical Telecommunications, Incorporated*] [*Brazilian*] (LA)
TASA .... Tennis Association of South Africa (MAR)
TASAS .... Turk Ambalaj Sanayii Anonim Sirketi [*Turkish Packing Industry Corporation*] (TU)
TASE .... Tameion Anasyngrotiseos para to Symvoulion Evropis [*Council of Europe Reconstruction Fund*] (GC)
TASEL .... Turk Alkollu Icki ve Sarap Endustrisi Limited [*Turkish Alcoholic Beverage and Wine Industry Limited*] [*Turkish Cypriot*] (GC)
Tashavtomash ... Tashkent Machinery Plant for Assembling Automobiles and Trailers (RU)
TAShFEI ..... Tashkent Institute of Finance and Economics (RU)
TashGU .... Tashkent State University (RU)
TAShIIT .... Tashkent Institute of Railroad Transportation Engineers (RU)
TAShINYaZ ... Tashkent Pedagogical Institute of Foreign Languages (RU)
Tashirmash ... Tashkent Irrigation Machinery Plant (RU)
Tashkhlopkomash ... Tashkent Cotton Machinery Plant (RU)
TAShMI .... Tashkent Medical Institute (RU)
TashPI .... Tashkent Polytechnic Institute (RU)
Tashprodmash ... Tashkent Food-Processing and Cotton-Ginning Machinery Plant (RU)
Tashsel'mash ... Tashkent Agricultural Machinery Plant (RU)
TAShSKhI ... Tashkent Agricultural Institute (RU)
Tashtekstil'mash ... Tashkent Textile Machinery Plant (RU)
TASIS .... Turkiye Agac ve Agac Sanayii Iscileri Sendikasi [*Turkish Tree and Wood Industry Workers Union*] (TU)
TASIT .... Taller de Asistencia y Servicio de la Industria Tabacalera [*Tobacco Industry Service and Assistance Workshop*] [*Cuban*] (LA)
TASKOBIRLIK ... Tarim Satis Kooperatifleri Birligi [*Agricultural Sales Cooperatives' Union*] (TU)
TASMA .... Tanganyika Sisal Marketing Association (MAR)
TASO .... Transports Automobiles Subventionnes de l'Ouest (MAR)
TASS .... Tawao Assisted Settlers' Scheme (ML)
TASS .... Telegraphnoye Agentstvo Sovyetskovo Soyuza [*Telegraph Agency of the Soviet Union*] [*News agency*]
TASSR .... Tatar Autonomous Soviet Socialist Republic (RU)
TASSR .... Turkestan Autonomous Soviet Socialist Republic [*1918-1924*] (RU)
TASZI .... Termeloszovetkezetek Aruertekesiteset Szervezo Iroda [*Producer Cooperative Merchandise Sales Organizing Bureau*] (HU)
TAT .... Tanzania Tobacco Authority (MAR)
tat .... Tatar (BU)
tat .... Tatar, Tatarian (RU)
TAT .... Tobacco Authority of Tanzania (MAR)
TAT .... Transports Athane-Tual (MAR)
TAT .... Transports Automobiles Tual (MAR)
TATA .... Tanzania Agricultural Trainers Association (AF)
TATAS .... Turk-Alman Turizm Anonim Sirketi [*Turkish-German Tourism Corporation*] (TU)
TatASSR ..... Tatar Autonomous Soviet Socialist Republic (RU)
TATB .... Tarcakozi Ar- es Termekforgalmazasi Bizottsag [*Interministerial Price and Product Marketing Commission*] (HU)
TATE .... Tyumen' Automobile and Tractor Electrical Equipment Plant (RU)
Tatgosizdat ... Tatar State Publishing House (RU)
Tatknigoizdat ... Tatar Book Publishing House (RU)

TATMGT ..... Tameion Asfaliseos Typografon kai Misthoton Grafikon Tekhnon [*Insurance Fund of Typographers and Graphic Arts Employees*] [*Greek*] (GC)
Tatneft' .... Association of the Petroleum Industry of the Tatar ASSR (RU)
TatNII .... Tatar Scientific Research Petroleum Institute (RU)
TATO........... Tagestonnen [*Tons per Day*] [*German*]
TATs .... Sodium Trichloroacetate (RU)
TAU .... Peat-Ammonia Fertilizers (RU)
TAU .... Transvaal Agricultural Union (MAR)
TAV .... Tameion Asfaliseos Voulevton [*Deputies Insurance Fund*] [*Greek*] (GC)
tav .... Tavallinen [*Finnish*]
tav .... Tavallisesti [*Usually*] [*Finnish*]
TAV .... Tiszantuli Aramszolgaltato Vallalat [*Electric Power Enterprise of the Trans-Tisza Region*] (HU)
tavb .... Tavbeszelo [*Telephone*] (HU)
Tavkut......... Tavkozlesi Kutato Intezet [*Telecommunication Research Institute*] (HU)
TAVN.......... Tameion Allilovoitheias Vasilikou Navtikou [*Royal Navy Mutual Aid Fund*] [*Greek*] (GC)
TAWE.......... Trans-Africa Walk Expedition (MAR)
TAWICO...... Tanzania Wildlife Corporation (MAR)
TAWU.......... Technical and Allied Workers Union [*Grenadian*] (LA1)
TAWU.......... Transport and Allied Workers Union [*Kenyan*] (AF)
TAXY.......... Tameion Asfaliseos Xenodokho-Ypallilon [*Hotel Employees Insurance Fund*] [*Greek*] (GC)
TAYAP .... Tameion Arogis Ypallilon Astynomias Poleon [*Cities Police Employees Assistance Fund*] (GC)
TAYAYS...... Tameion Arogis Ypallilon Armodiotitos Ypourgeiou Syngoinonion [*Communications Ministry Employees Assistance Fund*] [*Greek*] (GC)
TAYeM........ Millimass Unit (RU)
TAYMIS....... Turkiye Agir Yapi Montaj Insaat Iscileri Sendikasi [*Turkish Heavy Structures Assembly and Construction Workers' Union*] (TU)
TAZ .... Fuel Automatic Starter (RU)
TAZ .... Trnavske Automobilove Zavody [*Trnava Automobile Works*] (CZ)
TAZ .... Truckers Association of Zambia (MAR)
TAZARA...... Tanzania Zambia Railway Authority (AF)
TB............... Drum Trigger (RU)
TB............... Heavy Bomber (RU)
TB............... Industrial Safety (BU)
TB............... Rear Area Base (RU)
TB............... Safety Engineering (RU)
tb................ Tablet (RU)
tb................ Tabulka [*Table, Chart*] (CZ)
Tb............... Tabur [*Battalion*] (TU)
tb................ Tank Battalion (BU)
Tb............... Tank Battalion (RU)
TB............... Tank Brigade (RU)
tb................ Targyaban [*Concerning*] (HU)
TB............... Technical Office (RU)
TB............... Tehnicki Bataljon [*Technical Battalion*] (YU)
TB............... Tenkovski Bataljon [*Tank Battalion*] (YU)
TB............... Teruleti Bizottsag [*Area Committee*] (HU)
TB............... Thermite Bomb (RU)
TB............... Thermostatic Bi-Metal (RU)
tb................ Tiszteletbeli [*Honorary*] (HU)
TB............... Toprak Bilimi [*Soil Science*] [*As of an agricultural faculty*] (TU)
TB............... Traktorova Brigada [*Tractor Brigade*] (CZ)
TB............... Trigger of Input-Blocking Circuit [*Computers*] (RU)
TB............... Tubercle Bacillus (RU)
TBA .... Tanzania Badminton Association (MAR)
TBA .... Tetrabutylammonium (RU)
TBA .... Tierkoerperbeseitigungsanstalt [*Carcass Disposal Plant*] (EG)
tbad............ Heavy Bombardment Division (BU)
tbae............ Heavy Bombardment Aviation Squadron (BU)
tbak............ Heavy Bombardment Aviation Corps (BU)
tbap............ Heavy Bombardment Air Regiment (BU)
TBAP.......... Heavy Bomber Regiment (RU)
tbatr .... Maintenance Battery (BU)
tbatr .... Technical Battery (RU)
TBB .... Transports Bernard Bismuth (MAR)
TBB .... Turkiye Barolar Birligi [*Turkish Bar Associations' Union*] (TU)
TBB .... Turkiye Basin Birligi [*Turkish Press Union*] (TU)
TBBI .... Technische Bezirksbergbauinspektion [*Bezirk Technical Mine Inspection Office*] (EG)
TBC .... Tanganyika Broadcasting Corporation (MAR)
tbc.............. Tuberkulozis [*Tuberculosis*] (HU)
TBCR.......... Times British Colonies Review [*London*] [*A publication*] (MAR)
TBD .... Tanganyika Pyrethrum Board (MAR)
TBD .... Turk Belediyecilik Dernegi [*Turkish Mayors' Association*] (TU)
TBDzRwP.... Towarzystwo Badan Dziejow Reformacji w Polsce [*Society for Research on the History of the Reformation in Poland*] (POL)
TBEPO .... Heavy Armored Train (RU)
TBES .... Excursion Trolleybus of the SVARZ (RU)
TBF............ Tributyl Phosphate (RU)
TBFT .... Test de Bon Fonctionnement [*Spacelab*]
TBI.............. Technische Bergbauinspektion [*Technical Mine Inspection Office*] (EG)
TBIA .... Transvaal British Indian Association (MAR)
TBIIZhT....... Tbilisi Institute of Railroad Transportation Engineers Imeni V. I. Lenin (RU)
TbilNIGMI ... Tbilisi Scientific Research Hydrometeorological Institute (RU)
TbilNIISh..... Tbilisi Scientific Research Institute of Sericulture (RU)
TBIOT.......... All-Union Scientific Research Institute of Work Safety of the VTsSPS [*Tbilisi*] (RU)
TBK .... Combined Casing Block (RU)
tbk .... Heavy Armored Car (BU)
tbk.............. Tabornok [*General*] [*Military*] (HU)
TBK .... Turk Baris Kuvvetleri [*Turkish Peace Forces*] [*Cypriot*] (TU)
TBKE.......... Tavkozlo es Biztositoberendezesi Kozponti Ellenorseg [*Central Supervisory Department of Telecommunication and Safety Equipment*] (HU)
tb/kh .... Turbine Ship (RU)
TBKI .... Togolandische Bau- und Kunststoff Industrie GmbH (MAR)
TBL............. (Abteilung) Textil, Bekleidung, Leder (der Staatlichen Plankommission) [*Textile, Clothing, and Leather Department (of the State Planning Commission)*] (EG)
TBL............. Tanzania Breweries Limited (MAR)
TBL............. Turk Bankasi Limited [*Turkish Bank Limited (of Nicosia)*] [*Turkish Cypriot*] (GC)
TBMM .... Turkiye Buyuk Millet Meclisi [*Turkish Grand National Assembly*] [*See also BMM*] (TU)
TBN .... Technisches Buero fuer Nachrichtenmittel [*Technical Office for Communications Equipment*] (EG)
TBND.......... Tartos Bekeert, Nepi Demokraciaert! [*For Lasting Peace, For People's Democracy*] (HU)
TBOS.......... Towarzystwo Budowy Osiedli Stolecznych [*Society for Construction of Settlements in Warsaw*] (POL)
Tbp.............. Tabiplik [*Medicine*] [*The practice of*] (TU)
TBP .... Turk Birligi Partisi [*Turkish Union Party*] [*Turkish Cypriot*] (PPE)
TBP .... Turkiye Birlik Partisi [*Turkish Unity Party*] [*See also BP*] (TU)
tbr .... Tank Brigade (BU)
TBR .... Tank Brigade (RU)
TBR .... Tiszafoldvari Buzatermelesi Rendszer [*Tiszafoldvar Wheat Growing System*] (HU)
t br.............. Tonne Brut [*French*]
TBS .... Tanzania Bureau of Standards (MAR)
TBS .... Technische Betriebsschule [*Enterprise Technical School*] (EG)
TBS .... Towarzystwo Burs i Stypendiow [*Society for Student Homes and Scholarships*] (POL)
TBS .... Warm White Light [*Fluorescent tube*] (RU)
TBSD.......... Turkiye Bagimsiz Sosyalist Dernegi [*Turkish Independent Socialist Association*] (TU)
TBTAK .... Turkiye Bilimsel ve Teknik Arastirma Kurumu [*Turkish Scientific and Technical Research Organization*] [*Under Office of Premier*] [*See also TUBITAK*] (TU)
TBTs........... Tuberculosis, Bacillus Tuberculosis (BU)
TBVA.......... Tactical Bomber Air Force (RU)
TBZ .... Tanvaldske Bavlnarske Zavody [*Tanvald Cotton Mills*] (CZ)
TBZ .... Tobacco Board of Zambia (MAR)
TC .... Tankova Ceta [*Tank Platoon*] (CZ)
tc .... Technicky Cisty [*Technically Pure (Industrial grade of raw materials)*] (CZ)
Tc .... Telecomunicatii [*Telecommunications*] (RO)
TC .... Telegramme avec Collationnement [*French*]
TC .... Tenkovska Ceta [*Tank Company*] (YU)
tc .... Tisztelt Cim [*Sir, Madam (In correspondence)*] (HU)
TC .... Togoland Congress (MAR)
tc .... Toho Casu [*At Present*] (CZ)
TC .... Torpedna Cijev [*Torpedo Tube*] (YU)
tc .... Torvenycikk [*Law Article*] [*Hungarian*] (GPO)
tc .... Toutes Coupures [*French*]
TC .... Train de Combat [*Military*] [*French*] (MTD)
TC .... Transmisora Caldas-Transmicentro [*Manizales*] (COL)
TC .... Tripartite Commission [*St. Lucian*] (LA1)
TC .... Trusteeship Council (MAR)
tc .... Tucet [*Dozen*] (CZ)
TC .... Turkiye Cumhuriyeti [*Republic of Turkey*] (TU)
TC .... Turks and Caicos Islands [*Two-letter standard code*] (CNC)
TCA............ Tanzania Cotton Authority (MAR)
TCA............ Tanzania Cricket Association (MAR)
TCA............ Tanzania Cycling Association (MAR)
TCA............ Taxe sur le Chiffre d'Affaires [*Business Turnover Tax*] [*French*] (WER)
TCA............ Telecommunications et Constructions Africaines (MAR)
TCA............ Territorial Census Area (MAR)
TCA............ Touring-Club d'Algerie (MAR)
TCA............ Turks and Caicos Islands [*Three-letter standard code*] (CNC)
TCAA .... Tropas Cohoteriles Antiaereas [*Antiaircraft Rocket Troops*] [*Cuban*] (LA1)
TCAE.......... Transports en Commun d'Afrique Equatoriale (MAR)
TCB .... Tanganyika Coffee Board (MAR)
TCB .... Turkiye Cumhuriyeti Bahriye [*Turkish Republic Navy*] (TU)
TCC............ Tanzania Cigarette Company Limited (MAR)
TCC............ Technology Consultancy Centre (MAR)

tcc .... Tone de Combustibil Conventional [*Tons of Conventional Fuel*] (RO)
TCC .... Transport and Communications Commission (MAR)
TCC .... Transports en Commun du Congo (MAR)
TCCB .... Touring-Club du Congo Belge (MAR)
TCD .... Chad [*Three-letter standard code*] (CNC)
TCD .... Tennis-Club Dakarois (MAR)
TCDC .... Technical Cooperation among Developing Countries (AF)
TCDD .... Turkiye Cumhuriyet Devlet Demiryollari [*Turkish State Railways*] (TU)
TCDPPA .... Trustul de Constructii Drumuri, Poduri, Posturi, si Aeroporturi [*Trust for the Construction of Roads, Bridges, Posts, and Airports*] (RO)
TCE .... Tananarive-Cote Est (MAR)
TCE .... Touring-Club d'Egypte (MAR)
TCE .... Travaux de Construction d'un Ensemble (MAR)
TCEK .... Turkiye Cocuk Esirgeme Kurumu [*Turkish Child Protection Association*] [*See also CEK*] (TU)
TCES .... Turkiye Cumhuriyeti Emekli Sandigi Genel Mudurlugu [*Turkish Retirement Fund Directorate General*] (TU)
TCF .... Touring-Club of France [*Touring Club of France*] (WER)
TCG .... Rurkiye Cumhuriyeti Gemisi [*Ship of Turkish Republic*] (TU)
TCGA .... Tanganyika Coffee Growers Association (MAR)
TCh .... Number Trigger [*Computer*] (RU)
tch .... Period, Point (RU)
Tch .... Techizat [*Equipment*] (TU)
TCh .... Technical Section, Technical Unit (RU)
t ch .... This Date (BU)
TCh .... Tone Frequency (RU)
TCH .... Trustul de Constructii Hidroenergetice [*Trust for Hydraulic Power Constructions*] (RO)
t/24 ch .... Tons per Twenty-Four Hours (BU)
TCHADIS .... Societe Tchadienne de Distribution et de Services (MAR)
TCHAMAG .... Societe Tchadienne de Grands Magasins (MAR)
TChD .... Division Tank Unit (RU)
TChK .... Extraordinary Transportation Commission for Combating Counterrevolution and Sabotage (RU)
tchk .... Period, Point (RU)
TChP .... Towarzystwo Chirurgow Polskich [*Association of Polish Surgeons*] [*Polish*]
TCI .... Technical College Ibadan (MAR)
TCI .... Trustul de Constructii Ilfov [*Ilfov Construction Trust*] (RO)
TCI .... Trustul de Constructii Industriale [*Industrial Constructions Trust*] (RO)
TCI .... Turks and Caicos Islands (LA1)
TCIB .... Trustul de Constructii Industriale Bucuresti [*Bucharest Industrial Construction Trust*] (RO)
TCIF .... Trustul de Constructii pentru Imbunatatiri Funciare [*Trust for Land Improvement Constructions*] (RO)
TCIP .... Trustul de Constructii Instalatii Petroliere [*Trust for Petroleum Constructions and Installations*] (RO)
TCK .... Turk Ceza Kanunu [*Turkish Criminal Law, Turkish Penal Code*] (TU)
TCK .... Turkiye Cografya Kurumu [*Turkish Geographic Society*] [*See also TUCK*] (TU)
TCKIB .... Turkiye Cumhuriyeti Koy Isleri Bakanligi [*Republic of Turkey Village Affairs Ministry*] (TU)
TCL .... Tanganyika Concessions Limited (MAR)
TCL .... Tanganyika Creameries Limited (MAR)
TCL .... Tanzania Cables Limited (MAR)
TCL .... Towarzystwo Czyteln Ludowych [*Society for Public Reading Rooms*] (POL)
TCL .... Transports Colonel Lotfi [*Algerian*] (MAR)
TCL .... Tsumeb Corporation Limited [*Namibian*] (AF)
TCM .... Kibris Turk Cemaat Meclisi [*Turkish Cypriot Communal Assembly*] (TU)
TCM .... Turk Cemaat Meclisi [*Turkish Cypriot Communal Assembly*] (GC)
TCMAIA .... Trustul de Constructii Montaj pentru Agricultura si Industria Alimentara [*Construction and Assembly Trust for Agriculture and the Food Industry*] (RO)
TCMB .... Turkiye Cumhuriyeti Merkez Bankasi [*The Central Bank of Turkey*] (TU)
TCME .... Trustul de Constructii Montaje Energetice [*Construction and Assembly Trust for Power Generation*] (RO)
TCMMS .... Turk Cemaat Meclisi Memurlari Sendikasi [*Turkish Communal Assembly Employees Union*] [*Turkish Cypriot*] (GC)
TCMRIC .... Trustul de Constructii, Montaje, si Reparatii in Industria Chimica [*Trust for Construction, Installation, and Repairs in the Chemical Industry*] (RO)
TCMS .... Kibris Turk Cemaat Meclisi Sendikasi [*Turkish Cypriot Communal Assembly Union*] (TU)
TCMS .... Total, Compagnie Miniere du Senegal (MAR)
TCMSB .... Turkiye Cumhuriyeti Milli Savunma Bakanligi [*Republic of Turkey National Defense Ministry*] [*See also MSB*] (TU)
TCMWU .... Textile and Clothes Manufacturing Workers Union [*Mauritian*] (AF)
TCO .... Tjanstemannens Centralorganisation [*Central Organization of Salaried Employees*] [*Swedish*] (WEN)
TCO .... Travel Control Officer (ML)
TCOA .... Transvaal Coal Owners Association (MAR)
TCOR .... Trusteeship Council Official Records (MAR)
TCOT .... Transit Congo-Oubangui-Tchad (MAR)
TCP .... Tropical Cyclone Programme (MAR)
TCR .... Taxe de Cooperation Regionale [*Regional Cooperation Tax*] (AF)
TCR .... Temoignages Chretiens de la Reunion [*Christian Witnesses of Reunion*] (AF)
TCRCB .... Touring-Club Royal du Congo Belge (MAR)
TCRS .... Tanganyika Christian Refugee Service [*Tanzanian*] (AF)
TCS .... Turkiye Cimento Sanayii [*Turkish Cement Industry*] (TU)
TCSD .... Tiskovy Referat CSD [*Press Department of the Czechoslovak Railroads*] (CZ)
TCT .... Tropas Coheteriles Terrestres [*Land Missile Troops*] [*Cuban*] (LA)
tct .... Tucat [*Dozen*] (HU)
TCTD .... Transport, Communications, and Tourism Division (MAR)
TCU .... Tribunal de Contas da Uniao [*National Accounting Office*] [*Brazilian*] (LA)
TCVN .... Tieu Chuan Viet Nam [*Vietnam Standards*] (TVP)
TCY .... Transports Charmy & Cie. (MAR)
TCY .... Turkiye Cumhuriyeti Yonetmelik [*Turkish Republic Regulation*] (TU)
tcz .... Tuna Cistych Zivin [*Ton of Pure Nutrients*] (CZ)
TCZB .... Turkiye Cumhuriyeti Ziraat Bankasi [*Agricultural Bank of Turkey (Branch in Nicosia)*] [*Turkish Cypriot*] (GC)
TD .... Chad [*Two-letter standard code*] (CNC)
TD .... Dispatcher's Track Indicator (RU)
TD .... Dynamic Flip-Flop (RU)
TD .... Heat Engine (RU)
TD .... Peat Industry (RU)
TD .... Rear Patrol (BU)
td .... So Forth (RU)
TD .... Tank-Borne (RU)
td .... Tank Division (BU)
TD .... Tank Division (RU)
TD .... Tank Range Finder (RU)
tD .... Technischer Dienst [*German*]
TD .... Tekhnitos Doryforos [*Artificial Satellite*] (GC)
TD .... Temperature Gauge Pickup (RU)
TD .... Temperature-Sensitive Element (RU)
TD .... Tentera Darat [*Army*] (ML)
TD .... Trgovinski Dukan [*Commercial Shop*] (YU)
Td .... Triebwagenschnellzug [*Multiple Unit Fast Express Train*] (EG)
TD .... Tripartite Declaration (MAR)
TD .... Tudomanyok Doktora [*Hungarian*]
TD .... Tunisian Dinar (MAR)
TD .... Tunnel Diode (RU)
TDA .... Tanzania Drivers Association (MAR)
TDA .... Tea Development Authority [*Mauritian*] (AF)
TDA .... Transport Airborne-Landing Aviation (RU)
TDAP .... Transport Airborne-Landing Aviation Regiment (RU)
TDC .... Tanganyika Development Corporation (MAR)
TDC .... Tarif Douanier Commun [*North African*] (MAR)
TDC .... Tema Development Corporation (MAR)
TDC .... Trankei Development Corporation (MAR)
TDC .... Travaux de Developpement Communautaire (MAR)
TDC .... Turk Donanma Cemiyeti [*Turkish Fleet Society*] (TU)
TDCI .... Turkiye Demir ve Celik Isletmesi [*Turkish Iron and Steel Works*] (TU)
TDCK .... Technisch Documentatie- en Informatiecentrum voor de Krijgsmacht [*'s-Gravenhage*]
TDCU .... Torit District Co-Operative Union (MAR)
TDD .... Long-Range Tank (RU)
TDDF .... Turk Demir Dokum Fabrikasi [*Turkish Iron Foundry*] (TU)
TDE .... Tribunal Departamental de Elecciones [*Departmental Court of Elections*] [*Honduran*] (LA1)
TDel .... Division Control Trigger [*Computers*] (RU)
TDF .... Talebe Dernekleri Federasyonu [*Federation of Student Societies*] [*See also TTF*] (TU)
TDF .... Thiamine Diphosphate (RU)
TDFL .... Tanganyika Development Finance Company Limited (MAR)
TDGF .... Turkiye Devrimci Genclik Federasyonu [*Turkish Revolutionary Youth Federation*] [*See also DEV GENC*] (TU)
TDIF .... Turkiye Demiryollari Iscileri Federasyonu [*Turkish Federation of Railway Worker Unions*] (TU)
TDIS .... Turkiye Deniz Iscileri Sendikasi [*Turkish Maritime Workers' Union*] (TU)
TDK .... Tarimsal Donatim Kurumu [*Agricultural Equipment Association*] [*Under the TFSC Ministry of Agriculture*] (TU)
TDK .... Technische Durchsicht und Kontrolle [*Technical Inspection and Control*] (EG)
TDK .... Turk Devrim Kurumu [*Turkish Revolution Society*] (TU)
TDK .... Turk Dil Kurumu [*Turkish Linguistic Organization (of Ankara)*] (GC)
TDK .... Tyden Detske Knihy [*Week for the Promotion of Children's Books*] (CZ)
TDKP .... Turkish Revolutionary Communist Party (PD)
TDM .... Tank Destroyer Armed with Missiles
tdn .... Maintenance Battalion (BU)
tdn .... Technical Battalion (RU)
TDO .... Training Development Officer (MAR)

TDO............ Turk Devrim Ocaklari [*Turkish Revolutionary Hearths*] [*Clubs*] (TU)
t dob........... Telephone Extension (RU)
TDOB......... Turkiye Devrimci Ogretmenler Birligi [*Turkish Revolutionary Teachers' Union*] (TU)
TDOD......... Turkiye Devrimci Ogretmenler Dernegi [*Turkish Revolutionary Teachers' Organization*] [*See also DOD*] (TU)
TDP............ Strain Gauge (RU)
TDPSK........ Turkiye Devlet Personeli Sendikalari Konfederasyonu [*Turkish State Personnel Unions' Confederation*] (TU)
TDR............ Tank-Borne Company (RU)
TDR............ Tropical Disease Research and Training Programme (MAR)
TDR............ Tvornica Duhana Rovinj [*Rovinj Tobacco Factory*] (YU)
TDR............ Tyden Detske Radosti [*Children's Week*] (CZ)
TDS............ Technicke Dokumentacni Stredisko [*Technical Documentation Center*] (CZ)
TDSG.......... Long-Distance Bare Telephone [*Cable*] (RU)
TDS-IS........ Tatvan Deniz Tasitmaciligi Iscileri Sendikasi [*Tatvan Marine Transport Workers' Union*] (TU)
TDSK.......... Technisch Documentatieen Informatiecentrum van de Krijgsmacht [*Armed Forces Technical Documentation and Information Center*] [*Dutch*] (WEN)
TDSNF........ Three-Valued Disjunctive Perfect Normal Form (RU)
TDT-............ Skidding Diesel Tractor (RU)
TDU............ Retropackage, Braking Engine (RU)
TDV............ Tovarny Detskych Vozidel [*Plants for Baby Carriages*] (CZ)
Tdv............ Triebwagenschnellzug [*Multiple Unit Fast Express Train*] (EG)
TDV............ Turk Donanma Vakfi [*Turkish Fleet Fund*] (TU)
Tdw............ Tonnen Deadweight, Tonnen Tragfaehigkeit [*Deadweight (Metric) Tons*] (EG)
TDZ............ Tvornica Duhana Zagreb [*Zagreb Tobacco Factory*] (YU)
TE............... Diesel Locomotive with Electric Drive (RU)
TE............... Electric Tachometer (RU)
TE............... La Telemecanique Electrique (MAR)
TE-.............. Peat Excavator (RU)
TE............... Rear Echelon (BU)
Te............... Take [*Hill, Mountain*] [*Japanese*] (NAU)
TE............... Technical Encyclopedia (RU)
TE............... Technische Entwicklung [*Technical Development Office*] (EG)
TE............... Technologiai Eloirasok [*Technological Instructions*] (HU)
Te............... Tepe [*or Tepesi*] [*Hill or Peak*] [*Turkish*] (NAU)
TE............... Termoelektrana [*Thermoelectric Power Plant*] (YU)
TE............... Tete d'Etapes [*Military*] [*French*] (MTD)
t e.............. That Is (BU)
te............... To Est [*That Is*] (YU)
TE............... Train des Equipages [*Army Service Corps*] [*French*] (MTD)
TE............... Trapeza tis Ellados [*Bank of Greece*] (GC1)
Te............... Triebwageneilzug [*Express Rail Motor Train*] (EG)
TE............... Tudomanyegyetem [*University*] (HU)
TE............... Turboelektricni Pogon [*Turboelectrical Power*] (YU)
TE............... Turk Edebiyatcilar [*Turkish Men of Letters*] (TU)
TEA............ Tagmata Ethnikis Asfaleias [*National Defense Battalions*] [*Greek*] (GC)
TEA............ Technische Entwicklung fuer Antennen [*(Laboratory for) Technical Development of Antennas*] (EG)
TEA............ Tekhniki Epopteia Alieias [*Fishing Control Service*] [*Greek*] (GC)
TEA............ Topikai Epitropai Ardevseos [*Local Irrigation Committees*] [*Greek*] (GC)
TEA............ Transportation and Forwarding Agency (RU)
TEA............ Triethanolamine (RU)
TEA............ Typografiki Enosis Athinon [*Athens Printers' Union*] (GC)
TEAEDX...... Tameion Epikourikis Asfaliseos Ergatotekhnikon Domikon kai Xylourgikon Ergasion [*Auxiliary Insurance Fund for Construction and Carpentry Workers and Technicians*] [*Greek*] (GC)
Teakinopechat' ... Theater and Motion-Picture Publishing House (RU)
TEAM.......... Training and Employment of Auto Mechanics (MAR)
TEAMK........ Tameion Epikourikis Asfaliseos Misthoton Klosto-Yfandourgias [*Auxiliary Insurance Fund for Salaried Textile Workers*] [*Greek*] (GC)
Teamontazh ... All-Union Office for the Installation of Mechanical and Electrical Equipment in Theater and Show Establishments (RU)
TEAPET...... Tameion Epikourikis Asfaliseos Prosopikou Etaireion Tsimendon [*Auxiliary Insurance Fund for Cement Company Employees*] [*Greek*] (GC)
TEAPOKA... Tameion Epikourikis Asfaliseos Prosopikou Organismon Koinonikis Asfaliseos [*Auxiliary Insurance Fund for Social Insurance Organization Personnel*] [*Greek*] (GC)
Teaproyektstroymontazh ... All-Union State Trust for the Planning of Construction and Installation of Electrical Equipment of the Art Committee at the Art Committee at the Council of Ministers, USSR (RU)
Teasvet....... Theater Lighting Equipment Plant (RU)
teatr............ Theater term (BU)
teatt............ Teatteri [*Theatre*] [*Finnish*]
teavuz......... Higher Educational Theatrical Institution (RU)
TEAYEK...... Tameion Epikourikis Asfaliseos Ypallilon Emborikon Katastimaton [*Auxiliary Insurance Fund of Commercial Establishment Employees*] [*Greek*] (GC)
TEAYEOK ... Tameion Epikourikis Asfaliseos Ypallilon Ethnikou Organismou Kapnou [*Auxiliary Insurance Fund of National Tobacco Organization Employees*] [*Greek*] (GC)
TEB............ Fuel and Power Balance (RU)
TEB............ Teruleti Egyezteto Bizottsag [*Territorial Arbitration Committee*] (HU)
TEB............ Turk Eczacilar Birligi [*Union of Turkish Pharmacists*] (TU)
TEB............ Wage Rate and Economics Office (RU)
TEBE.......... Takarekpenztarak es Bankok Egyesulete [*Association of Savings Institutions and Banks*] (HU)
TEC............ Tanganyika Episcopal Conference (MAR)
TEC............ Tanganyika European Council (MAR)
TEC............ Tarif Exterieur Commun [*North Africa*] (MAR)
TEC............ Teatro Escuela de Cali (COL)
Tec............ Techizat [*Equipment*] (TU)
Tec............ Tecnico [*Type of diploma*] [*Spanish*]
Tec............ Tecrube [*Experiment, Experimental*] (TU)
TEC............ Teritorijski Evakuaciski Centar [*Territorial Evacuation Center*] (YU)
TECBA........ Societe d'Etudes Techniques et de Realisation de Travaux Publics et de Batiments (MAR)
TECh.......... Maintenance-Operating Unit (BU)
TECh.......... Technical Maintenance Unit (RU)
TECHCOL... Techos Colombia [*Medellin*] (COL)
TECHKERAM ... Technische Keramik (VVB) [*Technical Ceramics (VVB)*] (EG)
TECHMINEMET ... Bureau Technique d'Etudes des Minerais et de Metaux (MAR)
techn.......... Technik [*Technician*] [*Polish*]
techn.......... Technikum [*Technical School*] (POL)
techn.......... Technisch [*Technical*] [*German*]
TECHNACO ... Societe Africaine des Techniques pour l'Amenagement et la Construction (MAR)
TECHNOIMPEX ... TECHNOIMPEX Gepipari Kulkereskedelmi Vallalat [*TECHNOIMPEX Foreign Trade Enterprise of the Machine Industry*] (HU)
TECHNOSPOL ... Akciova Spolecnost pro Zprostredkovani Vedeckotechnicke Pomoci [*Joint-Stock Company for Scientific and Technical Assistance*] (CZ)
Techn zbrojsl ... Technicka Zbrojni Sluzba [*Technical Weapons Service*] (CZ)
Tech r.......... Technicka Rota [*Technical Company*] [*Military*] (CZ)
TECHSOSA ... Technology Secondary School Old Students Association (MAR)
TECMECOL ... Tecnica Metalica Colombiana [*Medellin*] (COL)
Tecn........... Tecnologo [*Type of diploma*] [*Spanish*]
TECNICOLSA ... Tecnica Colombiana, Sociedad Anonima [*Bogota*] (COL)
TECNIGRAF ... Tecnicas Graficas [*Bogota*] (COL)
TECNOIMPORT ... Empresa Cubana Importadora de Productos Tecnicos [*Cuban Enterprise for the Import of Technical Products*] (LA)
TECO.......... Tanzania Extract Company (MAR)
TECO.......... Technical Committee of Experts (MAR)
TECON........ Theatre Council of Natal (MAR)
TECORIN.... Tecnicas de Organizacion Industrial [*Medellin*] (COL)
TECTRO...... Societe de Techniques Tropicales (MAR)
TED............ Technical and Economic Report (RU)
TED............ Tenis Eskrim Dagcilik Kulubu [*Tennis, Fencing, and Mountain Climbing Club*] [*Istanbul*] (TU)
TED............ Transvaal Electrical Department (MAR)
TED............ Turkiye Egitim Dernegi [*Turkish Education Association*] (TU)
TEDA.......... Tetekofe Development Association (MAR)
Ted Bsk....... Tedarik Baskanligi [*Procurement Chairman*] [*Military*] (TU)
TEDK.......... Tekhnikos Exoplismos Dimon kai Koinotiton [*Technical Equipment of Municipalities and Communities*] [*Greek*] (GC)
TEDKA........ Topiki Enosis Dimon kai Koinotiton Attikis [*Local Union of Municipalities and Communities of Attiki*] (GC)
TEDS.......... Thermoelectromotive Force, Thermoelectric Power (RU)
TEE............ Taxe Exceptionnelle d'Equipement [*Special Tax on Equipment*] (CL)
TEE............ Tekhnika kai Epangelmatiki Ekpaidevsis [*Technical and Vocational Education*] (GC1)
TEE............ Tekhnikon Epimelitirion Ellados [*Technical Chamber of Greece*] (GC)
TEE............ Trans-Europe-Express [*Continental High-Speed Train*] [*French*]
TEE............ Trapeza Exagogon-Eisagogon [*Export-Import Bank*] (GC)
TEEFAE...... Tameion Eispraxeos Esodon Forologias Anonymon Etaireion [*Joint Stock Companies Tax Revenues Collection Fund*] [*Greek*] (GC)
teesz.......... Termeloszovetkezet [*Producer Cooperative*] (HU)
TEETECO ... Tanganyika Transport Co-Operative Company (MAR)
TEF............ Division of Heat Power Engineering (RU)
TEF............ Triethylenephosphoramide (RU)
TEF............ Turkiye Emeklileri Federasyonu [*Turkish Retired Workers' Federation*] (TU)
TEFL........... Teaching English as a Foreign Language (MAR)
TEFRACO ... Societe Congo Francais Textile (MAR)
teft............ Account Book, Notebook (BU)
TEFU.......... Teherautofuvarozasi Kozpont [*Trucking Center*] (HU)
TEG............ Tete d'Etapes de Guerre [*Military*] [*French*] (MTD)
TEG............ Therapeutic Evacuation Hospital (RU)

TEG............ Thermal Electric Power Generator (RU)
TEGESAN... Trakya Gubre Sanayii Anonim Sirketi [*Thrace Fertilizer Industry Corporation*] [*Tekirdag*] (TU)
TEGU.......... Turbine-Electric Drive [*Ship propulsion*] (RU)
TEHAG........ Temperaltvizu Halszaporito Gazdasag [*Temperate Water Fish Breeding Farm*] (HU)
Tehazet....... Towarzystwo Handlu Zagranicznego i Hurtowego Artykulami Spozywczymi [*Foreign and Wholesale Food Trade Company*] (POL)
TEI.............. Institute of Power Engineering in Transportation (of the Siberian Department of the Academy of Sciences, USSR) (RU)
TEI.............. Institute of Transportation Economics (RU)
TEI.............. Technical Standard Isooctane (RU)
teilw........... Teilweise [*Partly*] [*German*] (GPO)
TEiM........... Trzaska, Evert, i Michalski [*Trzaska, Evert, and Michalski*] [*Publishing house*] (POL)
TEIS............ Turkiye Turizm Endustrisi Isverenleri Sendikasi [*Turkish Tourism Industry Employers Union*] [*Istanbul*] (TU)
TEJA........... Tutmonda Esperantista Jurnalista Asocio [*World Association of Esperanto Journalists - WAEJ*] (EA)
TEJICONDOR... Tejidos el Condor SA [*Medellin*] (COL)
TEJIDUNION... Compania Colombiana de Tejidos Union SA [*Medellin*] (COL)
TEJO........... Tutmonda Esperantista Junulara Organizo [*World Organization of Young Esperantists*] (EA)
TEJOMNES... Compania de Tejidos de Lana Omnes Ltda. [*Pereira*] (COL)
TEK............ Office of Transportation and Forwarding Operations (RU)
tek.............. Tekintetes [*Honorable*] (HU)
Tek............. Teknik [*Technical, Technician*] (TU)
tek.............. Tekuty [*Liquid*] (CZ)
TEK............ Termeloeszkoz Kereskedelmi Vallalat [*Capital Equipment Marketing Enterprise*] (HU)
TEK............ Terra Kiado [*Terra Publishing House*] (HU)
TEK............ Transportation and Shipping Office (BU)
TEK............ Turkiye Elektrik Kurumu Genel Mudurlugu [*Turkish Electric Power Enterprise Directorate General*] (TU)
TEKB........... Turkiye Emlak Kredi Bankasi [*Turkish Real Estate Credit Bank*] (TU)
Tek Der....... Teknisyenler Dernegi [*Technicians' Organization*] (TU)
TEKEKK...... Turk Esnaf ve Kucuk Endustri Kredi Kooperatifi [*Credit Cooperative for Turkish Tradesmen and Small Industry*] [*Turkish Cypriot*] (GC)
TEK-F.......... Technische Entwicklungskommission-Funk [*Technical Development Commission for Radio*] (EG)
Tek Gida-Is... Turkiye Tutun Muskirat Gida ve Yardimci Iscileri Sendikasi [*Turkish Tobacco, Intoxicants, Food and Ancillary Workers Union*] (TU)
tekh............ Engineering, Technical, Technology (RU)
tekh............ Technical, Technological, Engineering (BU)
Tek H.......... Teknik Hizmetleri [*Technical Duties*] (TU)
tekhekonomsovet... Technical and Economic Council (RU)
Tekhizdat... State Publishing House of Technical Literature (RU)
tekhkom..... Technical Committee (RU)
tekhn.......... Equipment, Technology, Technician (BU)
tekhn.......... Technical, Engineering (RU)
tekhn.......... Technicum [*Topography*] (RU)
tekhn-ekonom... Technical and Economic (RU)
tekhnol........ Technological, Engineering (RU)
Tekhn rukov... Technical Manager (BU)
Tekhn sbor... Technical Collection (RU)
tekhn shk.... Technical School (RU)
Tekhn tr...... Technical Requirements (RU)
Tekhpromfinplan... Technical Industrial Financial Plan (BU)
tekhr.......... Technical Company (RU)
tekhred....... Technical Editor (RU)
tekhsnab..... Technical Supply (RU)
TEKhSO...... Technical Council (RU)
Tekhstroyfinplan... Technical Construction-Finance Plan (BU)
Tekhteorizdat... State Publishing House of Technical Theoretical Literature (RU)
Tekhupr...... Technical Administration (RU)
Tekhzhirprom... Moscow Oblast Trust of Industrial Fats of the Rosglavmyaso of the Ministry of the Meat and Diary Products Industry, RSFSR (RU)
TEK-Is........ Turkish Energy Distribution and Establishment Workers Union (TU)
Tek-Iz.......... Teknik Izolasyon AS [*Technical Insulation Corp.*] [*A Koc subsidiary*] (TU)
Tek-Met-Is... Turkiye Metal Mamulleri ve Makine Sanayi Iscileri Sendikasi [*Composite Turkish Metal Products and Machine Industry Workers' Union*] (TU)
tekn............ Tekniikassa [*Finnish*]
tekn............ Tekniikka [*Engineering*]
tekn............ Teknillinen [*Finnish*]
tekn............ Tekninen [*Finnish*]
Teknik-Is..... Turkiye Cumhuriyeti PTT [*Posta, Telefon, Telgraf*] Teknik Servisleri Iscileri Sendikasi [*Republic of Turkey, PTT (Post, Telephone, Telegraph) Technical Services Workers' Union*] [*Also, TCPTTTSIS*] (TU)
TEKNIK-IS... Yuksek Muhendis, Yuksek Mimar, Muhendis, Mimar, Fen Memuru, Teknikler, Teknisyen Birligi [*Senior Engineers, Senior Architects, Engineers, Architects, Scientific Workers, and Technicians Union*] [*Ankara*] (TU)
teknlis......... Tekniikan Lisensiaatti [*Finnish*]
tekntri......... Tekniikan Tohtori [*Finnish*]
TEKOSZ...... Textilkereskedok Orszagos Szovetsege [*National Association of Textiie Merchants*] (HU)
TEKSA........ Tekstil Sanayi ve Ticaret AS [*Textile Industry and Trade Corp.*] [*Adana*] (TU)
TEKSEN...... Turk Elektrik Kurumu Teknik Iscileri Sendikasi [*Turkish Cypriot Electric Power Organization Technical Workers' Union*] (GC)
TEK-SIF...... Turkiye Tekstil, Orme, ve Giyim Sanayii Iscileri Federasyonu [*Federation of Turkish Textile, Weaving, and Wearing Apparel Industry Workers Unions*] (TU)
TEKSIS....... Turkiye Ticaret, Egitim, Kooperatif, ve Sigorta Iscileri Sendikasi [*Turkish Trade, Education, Cooperatives, and Insurance Workers Union*] (TU)
TEKSO........ Technical and Economic Card Index of Socialist Experience (RU)
tekst........... Textile (BU)
tekst........... Textile (RU)
Tekst........... Textile Kombinat, Textile Mill [*Topography*] (RU)
tekstil'mash... Textile Machinery Plant (RU)
Tekstil'mashdetal'... Republic Trust for the Manufacture of Parts and Spare Parts of the Ministry of the Textile Industry, RSFSR (RU)
tekstil'promsoyuz... Producers' Union of the Textile Industry (RU)
Tekstil'proyekt... State Trust for the Planning of Construction in the Textile Industry (RU)
tekushto zagl... Current Title (BU)
Tel.............. Telefon [*German*]
tel.............. Telefon [*Telephone*] (HU)
tel.............. Telefon [*Telephone*] (POL)
tel.............. Telefon [*Telephone*] (CZ)
Tel.............. Telegramm [*Telegram*] (EG)
tel.............. Telegraph (BU)
Tel.............. Telegraph [*German*]
Tel.............. Telephon [*Telephone*] (EG)
tel.............. Telephone (BU)
Tel.............. Telephone [*Telephone*] [*French*]
tel.............. Telephone (RU)
Tel.............. Tunnel [*Tunnel*] [*Military map abbreviation*] [*World War I*] [*French*] (MTD)
TELA........... Tovarna Elektricnih Aparatov [*Electric Apparatus Factory*] [*Ljubljana*] (YU)
TELA KHMER... Societe Cambodgienne de Distribution des Produits Petroliers [*Cambodian Petroleum Products Distribution Company*] (CL)
TELARANA... Telares Arana [*Medellin*] (COL)
TELCO........ Trinidad and Tobago Telephone Company (LA1)
TELCOR...... Telecomunicaciones y Correos de Nicaragua [*Nicaraguan Telecommunications and Postal Services*] (LA1)
TELEBRAS... Telecomunicacoes Brasileiras, SA [*Brazilian Telecommunications, Inc.*] (LA)
TELECOM... Empresa Nacional de Telecomunicaciones [*National Telecommunications Enterprise*] [*Colombian*] (LA)
Telege......... Telegraphe [*Telegraph*] [*Military map abbreviation*] [*World War I*] [*French*] (MTD)
telegr.......... Telegram [*Telegram*] [*Polish*]
TELEMALI... Telecommunications Internationales du Mali [*International Telecommunications of Mali*] (AF)
TELEP......... Societe Tele-Publicite Cote-d'Ivoire (MAR)
telepress..... Telegraph Information (BU)
TELESENEGAL... Societe de Telecommunications Internationales du Senegal [*Senegal International Telecommunications Company*] (AF)
TELETRANSCAM... Societe pour la Construction de Telecommunications du Transcamerounais (MAR)
Teletrest..... Moscow Television Trust (RU)
telev........... Television (BU)
Telf............. Telefon [*Telephone*] (TU)
TELK........... Labor Expert Medical Commission (BU)
TELMA........ Tele-Maroc (MAR)
Telpod......... Fabryka Podzespolow Telekomunikacyjnych [*Factory of Telecommunication Equipment*] [*Polish*]
Telra........... Televizyon Radyo Sanayii ve Ticaret AS [*Television and Radio Industry and Trade Corp.*] [*Istanbul*] (TU)
TELSA......... Tejidos Leticia Ltda. [*Medellin*] (COL)
TEL-SEN..... Kibris Turk Telekomunikasyon Mustahdemler Sendikasi [*Turkish Cypriot Telecommunications Employees' Union*] (GC)
TELVALL..... Televizios Vallalat [*Television Enterprise*] (HU)
TEM............ Switching Diesel-Electric Locomotive (RU)
TEM............ Talasi Electromagnetski [*Electromagnetic Waves*] (YU)
Tem............ Teminat [*Security, Deposit*] (TU)
TEM............ Tete d'Etapes de Manoeuvre [*Military*] [*French*] (MTD)
TEM............ Triethylenemelamine (RU)
TEM............ Trustul Electromontaj [*Electrical Assembly Trust*] (RO)

TEMAY........ Tum Emekli, Malul, ve Mustafi Assubaylar Yardimlasma Dernegi [*Retired, Disabled, and Resigned Noncommissioned Officers Assistance Association*] (TU)
TEMD.......... Thermoelectromagnetic Motor (RU)
TEMG.......... Thermoelectromagnetic Generator (RU)
TEMIIT........ Tomsk Electromechanical Institute of Railroad Transportation Engineers (RU)
TEMO.......... Tanganyika Elected Members Organization (MAR)
TEMOSA..... Tejar Moderno Ltda. [*Bucaramanga*] (COL)
Temp........... Temperatur [*Temperature*] [*German*]
temp........... Temperatura [*Temperature*] [*Polish*]
temp........... Temperature (RU)
Temp........... Temple [*Temple*] [*Military map abbreviation*] [*World War I*] [*French*] (MTD)
temp........... Tempore [*In the Time Of*] [*Latin*] (GPO)
temp abs..... Absolute Temperature (RU)
TEMPAS..... Tekel Mamulleri Pazarlama Subesi [*Monopolies Products' Marketing Branch*] [*A subsidiary of ETI in the TFSC*] [*Turkish Cypriot*] (TU)
temp isp...... Evaporation Temperature (RU)
temp kip..... Boiling Point (RU)
temp kond... Dew Point (RU)
temp krit..... Critical Temperature (RU)
tem pl.......... Plan of Subjects (RU)
temp otv..... Solidification Temperature (RU)
Tempp........ Temperaturer [*Temperatures*] [*German*]
temp pl........ Melting Point (RU)
temp razl.... Decomposition Temperature (RU)
temp razmyagch... Softening Temperature, Softening Point (RU)
temp stekl... Vitrification Temperature (RU)
temp vospl... Ignition Temperature (RU)
temp vozg... Sublimation Temperature (RU)
temp vsp..... Flash Point (RU)
temp zam.... Freezing Point (RU)
temp zast.... Solidification Point (RU)
TEMSA........ Telephone Manufacturers of South Africa (MAR)
TEMSA........ Termo Mekanik Sanayi ve Ticaret AS [*Thermo-Mechanical Industry and Trade Corp.*] [*Adana*] (TU)
TEMSAN..... Turkiye Elektromekanik Sanayi AS [*Turkish Electromechanical Industry Corp.*] (TU)
TEMSE-IS... Turkiye Muzik, Sahne, ve Edebi Guzel Sanatlari Sendikasi [*Turkish Music, Stage, and Literary Fine Arts Union*] [*Istanbul*] (TU)
TEN............ Thermoelectric Heater (RU)
TEN............ Tubular Electric Heater (RU)
TENG.......... Tengeri [*Naval, Marine*] (HU)
TenkovilCU... Tenkovi sa Infracrvenim Uredajem [*Tanks with Infrared Equipment*] (YU)
tenn............ Tennis [*Tennis*] [*Finnish*]
TENPT......... Tameion Esodon Nomikon Prosopon kai Triton [*Legal Persons and Third Parties Revenue Fund*] (GC)
tente........... Teniente [*Spanish*]
TEO............ Tameion Ethnikis Odopoiias [*National Road Construction Fund*] [*Greek*] (GC)
TEO............ Technical and Economic Substantiation (RU)
TEO............ Theater Department of the Narkompros (RU)
TEO............ Theater Department of the Political Education Administration (RU)
teol............ Teologia [*Theology*] [*Finnish*]
teolkand...... Teologian Kandidaatti [*Finnish*]
teollis.......... Teologian Lisensiaatti [*Finnish*]
teor............ Theoretical (RU)
TEP............ All-Union State Institute for the Planning of Electrical Equipment for Heat Engineering Installations (RU)
TEP............ Rear Echelon of the Trains (RU)
TEP............ Rear Evacuation Station (RU)
TEP............ Technical and Economic Indices (RU)
TEP............ Thermoelectric Pyrometer (RU)
TEP............ Thermoelectronic Converter (RU)
TEP............ Tonnes d'Equivalent Petrole [*Equal to _____ Tons of Oil*] (AF)
TEP............ Turkiye Emekci Partisi [*Workers' Party of Turkey*] (PPW)
TEP............ Tvornica Elektrotehnickih Proizvoda [*Electrical Engineering Works*] [*Zagreb*] (YU)
TEPCE........ Talleres de Evaluacion, Programacion, y Capacitacion Educativa [*Educational Evaluation, Programing, and Training Workshops*] [*Nicaraguan*] (LA1)
TEPCORN... Tobacco Export Promotion Council of Rhodesia and Nyasaland (MAR)
TEPERPU.... Team Pemeriksaan Pusat [*Central Investigation Team*] (IN)
TEPET......... Texas Petroleum Company SA [*Guamo-Tolima*] (COL)
Teploelektroproyekt... All-Union State Institute for the Planning of Electrical Equipment for Heat Engineering Structures (RU)
Teploproyekt... All-Union Scientific Research and Planning Institute for Heat Engineering Structures (RU)
Teploset'..... Moscow City Trust of Centralized Heat Supply Networks of the Mosenergo (RU)
TEPREC...... Technique et Precision (MAR)
TEPS........... Tiskova, Edicni, a Propagacni Sluzba Mistniho Hospodarstvi [*Press, Editorial, and Propaganda Service for Local Economy*] (CZ)
TER............ Tank Evacuation Company (BU)
TER............ Technical and Economic Calculation (RU)
TER............ Technische Entwicklung-Radar [*Technical Development (Laboratory) for Radar*] (EG)
Ter.............. Terim [*Term*] [*As a technical term*] (TU)
TER............ Tete d'Etapes de Route [*French*] (MTD)
ter.............. Waste Tip [*Topography*] (RU)
terarmiya.... Territorial Army (RU)
terc............. Tercume Eden [*Translated By*] (TU)
TEREVSAT... Theater of Revolutionary Satire (RU)
TERI........... Tata Energy Research Institute [*Indian*]
TERIMPEX... TERIMPEX Allat- es Termenyforgalmi Kulkereskedelmi Vallalat [*TERIMPEX Foreign Trade Enterprise for Livestock and Crops*] (HU)
term........... Termeszet [*or Termeszeti*] [*Nature or Natural*] (HU)
TerMb......... Teretni Motorni Brod [*Motor Freighter*] (YU)
TERMERT... Termenyertekesito es Raktarozasi Vallalat [*Store and Storage Enterprise for Farm Products*] (HU)
TERMIA....... Association Internationale de Terminologie [*International Association of Terminology*] (EA)
term issled... Thermal Research (RU)
termoeds.... Thermoelectromotive Force (RU)
Termoproyekt... State Planning Institute for Heat Engineering (RU)
TEROTO...... Tercuman Motorlu Araclar Sanayi ve Ticaret AS [*The Tercuman Motor Vehicles Industry and Trade Corp.*] (TU)
TerPb.......... Teretni Parabrod [*Steam Freighter*] (YU)
terr............. Terrasse [*Terrace*] [*Norwegian*] (CED)
terr............. Territory (RU)
terr-proizvod upr... Territorial Production Administration (RU)
tert............. Tertiaer [*Tertiary*] [*German*]
Tervgazd K... Tervgazdasagi Kiado [*Publishing House on Planned Economy*] (HU)
TERZ.......... Transformer Electric Repair Plant (RU)
TES............ Spot Electric Welding (RU)
TES............ Tagma Ekmetallevseos Sidirodromon [*Railroad Operating Battalion*] [*Greek*] (GC)
TES............ Tameion Ethnikou Stolou [*National Fleet Fund*] [*Greek*] (GC)
TES............ Tanzania Elimu Supplies (MAR)
TES............ Teatrul Evreiesc da Stat [*Jewish State Theater*] (RO)
TES............ Technische Entwicklung-Schiffsfunk [*Technical Development (Laboratory) for Marine Radio*] (EG)
TeS............. Tekhnikon Soma [*Technical Corps*] [*Army*] (GC)
TES............ Tetraethyllead (RU)
TES............ Thermal Electric Power Plant (RU)
TES............ Thermoelectric Supply (BU)
TES............ Tractor Electric Power Plant (RU)
TESA.......... Personal Tehnic, Economic, de Alta Specialitate, si Administrativ [*Technical, Economic, Specialized, and Administrative Personnel*] (RO)
TESA.......... Personal Tehnic, Stiintific, si Administrativ [*Technical, Scientific, and Administrative Personnel*] (RO)
TESAD........ Personal Tehnic, Economic, de Alta Specialitate, Administrativ, de Servire si de Paza [*Technical, Economic, Highly Specialized, Administrative, Service, and Guard Personnel*] (RO)
TESCO........ Muszaki Tudomanyos Egyutmukodesi Iroda [*Office of Technical-Scientific Cooperation*] (HU)
TESG.......... Thermal Electrostatic Generator (RU)
TES-IS........ Turkiye Enerji, Su, Gas, YSE, ve DSI Isci Sendikalari Federasyonu [*Federation of Turkish Energy, Water, and Gas Workers Unions*] (TU)
TESK.......... Topiki Epitropi Syndesmos Ellinikon Gymnastikon kai Athlitikon Somateion Kyprou [*Association of Greek Gymnastic and Athletic Clubs Local Committee in Cyprus*] (GC)
tesn............ Gorge [*Topography*] (RU)
testa........... Testamentaria [*Estate Of*] [*Business and trade*] [*Spanish*]
TESTAS...... Turkiye Elektronik Sanayi ve Ticaret Anonim Sirketi [*Turkish Electronic Industry and Trade Corporation*] (TU)
testmto....... Testamento [*Spanish*]
testo........... Testigo [*Witness*] [*Spanish*]
TeSTOS...... Terenowe Stacje Technicznej Obslugi Samochodow [*Local Auto Service Stations*] (POL)
TESTROJ.... Teplicka Strojirna [*Teplice Engineering Works*] (CZ)
TESZ.......... Termeszettudomanyi Egyesuletek Szovetsege [*Federation of Natural Sciences Associations*] (HU)
TESZI......... Termeloszovetkezetek Ertekesitest Szervezo Iroda [*Office for Organization of TSZ Sales*] (HU)
TET............ Topiki Epitropi Tourismou [*Local Tourism Committee*] [*Greek*] (GC)
TETOC........ Technical Education and Training Organisation for Overseas Countries (MAR)
tetr............. Notebook (BU)
tetraedr...... Tetrahedral (RU)
tetrag s........ Tetragonal Syngony (RU)
TETs........... Heat and Electric Power Plant (RU)
TETs........... Thermoelectric Power Plant (BU)
TETs-PAVETs... Thermoelectric Power Plant - Pump Storage Hydroelectric Power Plant (BU)
TEU............ Fuel and Power Engineering Administration (RU)
TEU............ Teatro Universitario de Popayan [*Cauca*] (COL)
TEU............ Thermal Electric Installation (RU)
TEU............ Tourist and Excursion Administration (RU)

Tev .... Triebwageneilzug [*Express Rail Motor Train*] (EG)
TEV .... Turk Egitim Vakfi [*Turkish Educational Fund*] (TU)
TEVA .... Tutmonda Esperantista Vegetara Asocio [*World Esperantist Vegetarian Association - WEVA*] (EA)
TEVD .... Tatranska Elektricka Vicinalni Draha [*Tatra Local Electric Railroads*] (CZ)
TEVE .... Tameion (Asfaliseos) Epangelmation kai Viotekhnon Ellados [*Greek Craftsmen's and Tradesmen's (Insurance) Fund*] (GC)
TEVI .... Tervezo Iroda [*Planning Office*] (HU)
Tev Muzek ... Tevkif Muzekkeresi [*Arrest Warrant*] (TU)
TEVT .... Technical Education and Vocational Training (MAR)
TEVUH .... Technicke-Ekonomicky Vyzkumny Ustav Hutniho Prumyslu [*Technical Economic Research Institute for Smelting*] (CZ)
TEVZ .... Tatranska Elektricka Vicinalna Zeleznica [*Tatra Local Electric Railroad*] (CZ)
TEVZ .... Tbilisi Electric Locomotive Plant (RU)
TEWA .... Technische Eisenwaren und Werkzeuge (VVB) [*Industrial Hardware and Tools (VVB)*] (EG)
t ex .... Till Exempel [*For Instance*] [*Swedish*] (GPO)
TEXAF .... Societe des Textiles d'Afrique (MAR)
TEXCO .... National Textile Corporation of Tanzania (MAR)
TEXCO .... Societe Textile de Confection (MAR)
TEXFA .... Textilipari Fakellektermelo Vallalat [*Manufacturing Enterprise of Wooden Tools for the Textile Industry*] (HU)
TEXIMEI ...... Textilipari Minosegellenorzo Intezet [*Quality Control Institute on Industrial Textiles*] (HU)
Texkut .... Textilipari Kutato Intezet [*Research Institute of the Textile Industry*] (HU)
TEXMAN ..... Manufacturas Textiles SA [*Manizales*] (COL)
TEXMERALDA ... Textiles la Esmeralda SA [*Cali*] (COL)
TEXNAL ...... Textiles Nacionales [*Cali*] (COL)
TEXTICAM ... Societe Textile du Cameroun (MAR)
TEXTIMA .... Textil- und Bekleidungsindustrie Maschinenbau [*Textile and Clothing Industry Machine Building*] (EG)
TEYPA .... Tameion Efimeridopolon kai Ypallilon Praktoreion Athinon [*Insurance Fund of Newspaper Dealers and Employees of Athens Newspaper Distribution Agencies*] (GC)
tez .... Thesis (RU)
TEZ .... Tvornica Elektricnih Zarulja [*Factory of Incandescent Lamps*] [*Zagreb*] (YU)
Tez Buro-Is ... Turkiye Ticaret, Banka, Sigorta, Kooperatif, Egitim, Tezgahtarlar ve Buro Iscileri Sendikasi [*Turkish Office and Clerical Employees Union*] (TU)
TEZhE .... State Trust of Fine Perfumery of the Fats and Bone-Processing Industry (RU)
TEZS .... Thermal Electric Charging Station (RU)
TEZSAN ...... Takim Tezgahlari Sanayi ve Ticaret AS [*Industrial Spare Parts Industry and Trade Corp.*] (TU)
TF .... Fixation of the Point of Burst (RU)
TF .... Pacific Fleet (RU)
tf .... Telegraph (RU)
TF- .... Telephotometer (RU)
TF .... Testnevelesi Foiskola [*College of Physical Education*] (HU)
TF .... Thomas-Fermi [*Potential*] (RU)
TF .... Thymolphthalein (RU)
TF .... Traegerfrequenz (System) [*Carrier Frequency (System)*] [*West German*] (WEN)
TF .... Triphosphate (RU)
TF .... Tropical Front [*Meteorology*] (RU)
TF .... Warm Front [*Meteorology*] (RU)
TFA .... Tanganyika Farmers Association Limited (MAR)
TFAI .... Territoire Francais des Afars et Issas [*French Territory of Afars and Issas*] [*Djibouti*] [*Use FTAI*] (AF)
TFAN .... Turkmen Branch of the Academy of Sciences, USSR (RU)
TFB .... Rear Base of a Front (RU)
TFB .... Tehnicki Fakultet, Beograd [*Faculty of Technology, Belgrade*] (YU)
TFC .... Tanzania Fertilizer Company Limited (MAR)
TFC .... Tanzania Film Company (MAR)
TFCA .... [*The*] Federation of Commodity Associations (EA)
TFD .... Thomas-Fermi-Dirac (RU)
TFDP .... Theory of Functions of a Real Variable (RU)
TFF .... Triphenyl Phosphate (RU)
TFH .... Traegerfrequenz-Nachrichtenanlage (auf Hochspannungsnetz) [*Carrier-Frequency Communications Facility (via Power Lines)*] [*Equipment*] (EG)
TFJ-Senegal ... Tableau Fiscal et Juridique Senegal (MAR)
TFK .... Tarsadalmi Felhasznalasnak Utat Nyito Kutatas [*Research Seeking the Application or Utility by Society of the Results of Basic Research*] (HU)
tfk .... Telephone Crew (BU)
TFKI .... Magyar Testnevelesi Foiskola Kutato Intezet [*Research Institute of the Hungarian College of Physical Education*] (HU)
TFKP .... Theory of Functions of a Complex Variable (RU)
Tfl .... Tafel [*Table*] [*German*]
TFL .... Tanganyika Federation of Labour (MAR)
TFM .... Triphenylmethyl (RU)
TFNC .... Tanzania Food and Nutrition Centre (MAR)
TFP .... Sociedad Argentina de Defensa de la Tradicion, Familia, y Propiedad [*Argentine Society for the Defense of Tradition, Family, and Property*] (LA)
TFP .... Sociedad Venezolana de Defensa de la Tradicion, Familia, y Propiedad [*Venezuelan Society for the Defense of Tradition, Family, and Property*] (LA)
TFP .... Tradicao, Familia, e Propriedade [*Tradition, Family, and Property*] [*Brazilian*] (LA1)
TFP .... Tradicion, Familia, y Propiedad [*Tradition, Family, and Property*] [*Colombian*] (LA)
TFR .... Heavy Manual Work (BU)
TFR .... Telefunken Fernseh und Rundfunk [*Home Electronics Subsidiary*]
TFR .... Total Fertility Rate (MAR)
TFS .... Tehnicki Fakultet, Sarajevo [*Faculty of Technology, Sarajevo*] (YU)
TFS .... Telephone Exchange (BU)
TFS .... Telephone Exchange (RU)
TFSC .... Turkish Federated State of Cyprus [*See also KTFD*] (TU)
TFSM .... Union of Malagasy Socialist Youth (AF)
TFSN .... Taxe Forfaitaire de Solidarite Nationale (MAR)
TFZ .... Tylova Frontava Zakladna [*Frontline Supply Base*] (CZ)
TG .... Diesel Locomotive with a Hydraulic Transmission (RU)
TG .... Gas Thyratron (RU)
tg .... Of the Current Year, In the Current Year (RU)
TG .... Solid Fuel (RU)
TG .... Tachometer Generator (RU)
Tg .... Tag [*Day*] [*Business and trade*] [*German*]
Tg .... Tandjong [*or Tandjung or Tanjong*] [*Cape*] [*Malay*] (NAU)
tg .... Tangente [*Tangent*] [*German*]
TG .... Tank Group (RU)
TG .... Technische Grundsaetze [*Technical Principles*] (EG)
tg .... Tekuce Godine [*Current Year*] (YU)
TG .... Tenkovsko Gadanje [*Tank Firing*] (YU)
TG .... Therapeutic Hospital (RU)
tg .... This Year (BU)
TG .... Togo [*Two-letter standard code*] (CNC)
T/G .... Ton/Gun [*Tons Per Day*] [*Capacity*] (TU)
t/g .... Tons/Year (BU)
TG .... Transportgemeinschaft [*Transportation Group*] (EG)
Tg .... Trapeang [*Often part of a place name*] [*Cambodian*] (CL)
TG .... Trotyl and Hexogen (RU)
TGA .... State Archives of the City of Tallin and the Khar'yuskiy Rayon (RU)
TGA .... Tameion Georgikon Asfaliseon [*Farm Insurance Fund*] [*Greek*] (GC)
TGA .... Technische Gebaeudeausruestung [*Technical Building Equipment*] (EG)
TGA .... Tissages Goujat Algerie (MAR)
TGA .... Tmima Georgikon Asfaliseon [*Farm Insurance Unit*] [*Greek*] (GC)
tgabr .... Heavy Howitzer Artillery Brigade (BU)
tgabr .... Heavy Howitzer Artillery Brigade (RU)
tgap .... Heavy Howitzer Artillery Regiment (RU)
TGAS .... Turkiye Gemi Adamlari Iscileri Sendikasi [*Turkish Seamen's Union*] (TU)
TGASA .... Tour Guides Association of South Africa (MAR)
TGE .... Tmima Georgikon Efarmogon [*Applied Agriculture Unit*] [*Greek*] (GC)
TGF .... Tropas Guardafronteras [*Border Guard Troops*] [*Cuban*] (LA)
TGFA .... Tropas de Guarda Fronteiras de Angola (MAR)
TGFO .... Tashkent Geophysical Observatory (RU)
TGGRU .... Transactions of the Main Administration of Geological Exploration (RU)
TGH .... Transportgemeinschaft des Handels [*Trade Transportation Group*] (EG)
TGHD .... Turkiye Genclik Hostelleri Dernegi [*Turkish Youth Hostels Organization*] (TU)
TGII .... Transactions of the Georgian Industrial Institute Imeni S. M. Kirov (RU)
TGIM .... Transactions of the State Historical Museum (RU)
TGK .... Hot-Cathode Thyratron (RU)
TGK .... Tehergepkocsi [*Truck*] (HU)
TGK .... Transactions of the Geological Committee (RU)
TGK .... Turk Genel Kurmayi [*Turkish General Staff*] (TU)
TGKD .... Tameion Georgias, Ktinotrofias kai Dason [*Farm, Animal Husbandry, and Forests Fund*] [*Greek*] (GC)
TGLP .... Tribal Grazing Land Policy (MAR)
TGM .... Shunting Diesel Locomotive with a Hydraulic [*or Hydromechanical*] Transmission (RU)
TGM .... Talab, Gasim, Mahmoud [*Sudanese*] (MAR)
TGM .... Technika i Gospodarka Morska [*Marine Engineering and Economics*] [*A periodical*] (POL)
Tgm .... Tegmen [*Lieutenant*] (TU)
TGM .... Transactions of the Geological Museum of the Academy of Sciences, USSR (RU)
TGM .... Tunis-La Goulette-La Marsa (MAR)
TGMI .... Tomsk State Medical Institute (RU)
TGNII .... Turkmen State Scientific Research Institute of History (RU)
tgo .... Telegraph Team (BU)
TGO .... Togo [*Three-letter standard code*] (CNC)

TGO............ Trafik AB Grangesberg-Oxelosund [*Grangesberg-Oxelosund Transport Co.*] [*Swedish*] (WEN)
TGPI........... Tomsk State Pedagogical Institute (RU)
tgr............. Telegram (RU)
tgr............. Telegraph (RU)
tgs............. Telegraph Station (BU)
TGS............ Telegraph Station (RU)
TGS............ Triglycine Sulfate (RU)
TGS............ Turkiye Gazeteciler Sendikasi [*Turkish Journalists Union*] (TU)
TGSSA........ Transactions of the Geological Society of South Africa [*A publication*] (MAR)
TGSYO........ Tatbiki Guzel Sanatlar Yuksek Okulu [*Advanced School of Applied Fine Arts*] (TU)
TGSYOKD... Tatbiki Guzel Sanatlar Yuksek Okulu Kultur Dernegi [*Cultural Association of the Istanbul Advanced School of Applied Fine Arts*] (TU)
TGTT.......... Turkiye Genclik Turizm Teskilati [*Turkish Youth Tourism Organization*] (TU)
TGU............ Tanzania Gulf Union (MAR)
TGU............ Tartu State University (RU)
TGU............ Tbilisi State University (RU)
TGU............ Tomsk State University Imeni V. V. Kuybyshev (RU)
TGV............ Tres Grande Vitesse [*Very Great Speed*] [*French high-speed train*]
TGWU......... Transport and General Workers Union [*Mauritian*] (AF)
TGZ............ Teminin Gucluk Zammi [*Job Security Premium*] (TU)
TGZ............ Tikhvin Alumina Plant (RU)
TH............... (Orszagos) Tervhivatal [*(National) Planning Office*] (HU)
t/h.............. Stundentonnen [*Tons per Hour*] [*German*]
TH............... Tanacsi Hivatal [*Office of the Council*] (HU)
TH............... Tapia House [*Trinidadian and Tobagan*] (LA1)
TH............... Tavirohivatal [*Telegraph Office*] (HU)
TH............... Technicko-Hospodarske (Planovani) [*Technical and Economic (Planning)*] (CZ)
TH............... Technika Haza [*House of Technology*] (HU)
TH............... Technische Hochschule [*Technical College, Advanced Technical School*] [*German*] (WEN)
th................ Teherpalyaudvar [*Freight Depot*] (HU)
TH............... Teknik Hizmetler [*Technical Duties*] (TU)
TH............... Thailand [*Two-letter standard code*] (CNC)
TH............... Tkalcovny Hedvabi [*Silk Weaving Mills*] (CZ)
THA............ Tanzania Harbors Authority (AF)
THA............ Tanzania Hockey Association (MAR)
THA............ Thailand [*Three-letter standard code*] (CNC)
THA............ Turk Haberler Ajansi [*Turkish News Agency*] (TU)
THB............ Tanzania Housing Bank (MAR)
THB............ Treuhandbetrieb [*Enterprise under Trusteeship*] (EG)
THB............ Turk Hamallar Birligi [*Turkish Porters Union*] [*Turkish Cypriot*] (GC)
THB............ Turkiye Halk Bankasi [*Peoples Bank of Turkey*] [*See also HB*] (TU)
THC............ Technische Hochschule fuer Chemie [*Advanced Technical School for Chemistry*] (EG)
THC............ Tourism and Hotels Corporation [*Sudanese*] (MAR)
THD............ Technische Hogeschool Delft
ThDr........... Doctor Theologiae [*Doctor of Divinity*] (CZ)
ThDr........... Doktor der Theologie [*German*]
THE............ Technische Hogeschool Eindhoven
theilw......... Teilweise [*Partly*] [*German*]
theol........... Theologisch [*German*]
Thes/niki.... Thessaloniki [*Salonica*] (GC)
ThETh......... Thalamos Endatikis Therapeias [*Intensive Care Unit*] (GC)
THI.............. Technische Hochschule Ilmenau [*Ilmenau Advanced Technical School*] (EG)
thj v............ Torvenyhatosagi Jogu Varos [*Municipal Borough*] (HU)
Thk............. Tahkimat [*Fortification*] (TU)
THK............ Turk Hava Kurumu [*Turkish Air League*] [*Similar to civil aeronautics*] (TU)
THKC.......... Turkiye Halk Kurtulus Cephesi [*Turkish People's Liberation Front*] (TU)
THKGV........ Turk Hava Kuvvetlerini Guclendirme Vakfi [*Fund to Strengthen Turkish Air Force*] (TU)
THKMS........ Technische Hochschule Karl-Marx-Stadt [*Karl Marx Stadt Advanced Technical School*] (EG)
THKO.......... Turkiye Halk Kurtulus Ordusu [*Turkish People's Liberation Army*] (TU)
THKP.......... Turkiye Halk Kurtulus Parti Cephesi [*Turkish People's Liberation Party Front*] (TU)
Thl.............. Thermal [*Thermal*] [*Military map abbreviation*] [*World War I*] [*French*] (MTD)
Thlr............ Thaler [*Dollar*] [*German*]
THM............ Technische Hochschule "Otto Von Guericke" Magdeburg [*"Otto Von Guericke" Advanced Technical School, Magdeburg*] (EG)
THMGC....... Turkiye Harp Malulu Gaziler, Sehit, Dul, ve Yetimler Cemiyeti [*Society for Turkish Wounded War Veterans, Martyrs, Widows, and Orphans*] (TU)
THN............ Technicko-Hospodarske Normy [*Technical and Economic Standards*] (CZ)
ThOA.......... Thalassia Oikonomiki Astynomia [*Sea Revenue Police*] [*Greek*] (GC)
ThOA.......... Theatrikos Organismos Athinon [*Athens Theatrical Organization*] (GC)
ThOI........... Thriskevtikon Orthodoxon Idryma [*Orthodox Religious Foundation*] [*Cypriot*] (GC)
ThOK.......... Theatrikos Organismos Kyprou [*Cyprus Theatrical Organization*] (GC)
Thr.............. Thaler [*Dollar*] [*German*]
THR............ Tundjangan Hari Raya [*Holiday Bonus*] (IN)
THS............ [*The*] Hydrographic Society (EA)
THS............ Tatranska Horska Sluzba [*Tatra Mountain Service*] (CZ)
THSG.......... Transactions of the Historical Society of Ghana [*A publication*] (MAR)
THT............ Technische Hogeschool Twente [*Enschede*]
thts............. Tiszthelyettes [*Senior Noncommissioned Officer*] (HU)
THY............ Turk Havayollari [*Turkish Airlines*] (TU)
TI-............... Current Indicator, Current Detector (RU)
TI................ Heat Detector (RU)
TI................ Information Theory (RU)
TI................ Instrument Transformer (RU)
TI................ Radiation Thermometer (RU)
TI................ Technical Information (RU)
TI................ Technische Intelligenz [*Technical Intelligentsia*] (EG)
TI................ Technological Institute (BU)
TI................ Tekstilna Industrija [*Textile Industry*] (YU)
TI................ Telemetering (RU)
TI................ Textile Institute (EA)
TI................ Thermal Radiation (RU)
ti................. Tiistai(na) [*Finnish*]
Ti................ Tirol [*or Tiroler*] [*German*]
ti................. Tiszt [*Officer*] (HU)
TI................ Transports Ivoiriennes (MAR)
TI................ Trzisni Inspektorat [*Market Inspectorate*] (YU)
ti................. Tudniillik [*Namely, That Is*] (HU)
T2000I......... Transport 2000 International (EA)
TIA.............. Torrefaction Industrielle Abidjanaise (MAR)
TIAAE.......... Transactions of the Institute of Anthropology, Archaeology, and Ethnography (RU)
TIAB............ Trustul de Instalatii si Automatizari Bucuresti [*Bucharest Trust for Installations and Automation*] (RO)
TIAFT.......... [*The*] International Association of Forensic Toxicologists (EA)
TIAR............ Tratado Interamericano de Asistencia Reciproca [*Inter-American Reciprocal Assistance Treaty*] (LA)
TIAVSC....... [*The*] International Assets Valuation Standards Committee (EA)
TIB.............. Tanzania Investment Bank (MAR)
TIB.............. Technical Information Bulletin (RU)
TIB.............. Technische Informatie Bibliotheek
TIB.............. Tezek Iscileri Birligi [*Solid Fuel (Cattle Dung) Workers Union*] (TU)
TIB.............. Transivoirienne des Bois (MAR)
TIB.............. Tum Iktisatcilar Dernegi [*Association of All Economists*] (TU)
TIB.............. Turkiye Is Bankasi [*Turkish Labor Bank*] (TU)
TIBAS.......... Turkiye Is Bankasi Anonim Sirketi [*Turkish Labor Bank Corporation*] (TU)
TIBAS Sendikasi... Turkiye Is Bankasi Anonim Sirketi Mensuplari Sendikasi [*Turkish Labor Bank Corporation Employees' Union*] (TU)
TIBE............ Travaux, Isolation, Batiment, Etancheite (MAR)
TIBEA.......... Societe Travaux, Isolation, Batiment, Etancheite Afrique (MAR)
TIBRAS....... Titanio do Brasil [*Brazilian Titanium*] (LA)
TIC.............. Tantalum Producers International Study Center (EA)
TIC.............. Taxe Interieure de Consommation [*Domestic Consumption Tax*] [*French*] (WER)
Tic............... Ticaret [*Trade, Commerce*] [*Turkish*] (CED)
TIC.............. Transvaal Indian Congress [*South African*] (PD)
TIC.............. Tripartite Industrial Co-Operation (MAR)
TIC.............. Tuberculosis Investigation Centre (MAR)
TICAF.......... Tororo Industrial Chemicals and Fertilisers Ltd. [*Ugandan*] (MAR)
TICB............ Ticaret Bakanligi [*Ministry of Commerce*] (TU)
TICOFIMA... Tissage de Coton et Fibranne Marocains [*Moroccan Cotton and Fiber Weaving*] (AF)
TID.............. Technical and Economic Report (BU)
TIDKON....... Turkiye Iktisadi Devlet Tesekkul ve Tesebbusleri Personel Sendikalari Konfederasyonu [*Confederation of Turkish Economic State Organization and Enterprises Personnel Unions*] (TU)
TIE.............. Trudy Instituta Etnografii ANSSSR (MAR)
Tie.............. Tuilerie [*Tilekiln*] [*Military map abbreviation*] [*World War I*] [*French*] (MTD)
Tierz........... Tierzucht [*German*]
tiet.............. Tieteellinen [*or Tieteessa*] [*Scientific, In Science*] [*Finnish*]
TIEx............ Einheitliches Reglement Betreffend des Internationalen Eisenbahn-Expressgutverkehrs [*Uniform Regulations on International Railway Express Freight Traffic*] (EG)
TIFC............ Towarzystwo Imienia Fryderyka Chopina [*Frederic Chopin Society*] [*Polish*]
TIFO............ Tiszai Koolajipari Vallalat [*Tisza Petroleum Industry Enterprise*] (HU)
TIG.............. Societe de Telecommunications Internationales Gabonaises [*Gabonese International Telecommunications Company*] (AF)

TIG .... Transactions of the Institute of Geography (of the Academy of Sciences, USSR) (RU)
TIGN .... Transactions of the Institute of Geological Sciences (of the Academy of Sciences, USSR) (RU)
TII .... Telecommunications Industries Incorporated (MAR)
TII .... Tentara Islam Indonesia [*Indonesian Islamic Army*] (IN)
TII .... Tomsk Industrial Institute Imeni S. M. Kirov (RU)
TIIET .... Transactions of the Institute of History, Natural Sciences, and Technology (RU)
TIIF .... Transactions of the Institute of History and Philosophy (RU)
TIIGM .... Toprak ve Iskan Isleri Genel Mudurlugu [*Soil and Settlement Affairs Directorate General*] [*Under Village Affairs Ministry*] (TU)
TIIMSKh ..... Tashkent Engineering Instiute of Irrigation and Mechanization of Agriculture (RU)
TIIKP .... Turkiye Ihtilalci Isci Koylu Partisi [*Turkish Revolutionary Worker Peasant Party*] [*A pro-Maoist illegal party*] (TU)
TIIMSKh ...... Tashkent Institute of Irrigation and Mechanization of Agriculture (RU)
TIIZhT .... Tashkent Institute of Railroad Transportation Engineers (RU)
TIK .... Turkiye Insaat Kalfalari Birligi [*Turkish Construction Foremen's Union*] (TU)
TIKA .... Technical Industrial Kalumbila Associate (MAR)
TIKh .... Technical School of Industrial Chemistry (BU)
TIKKO .... Turkiye Isci Koylu Kurtulus Ordusu ile Marksist-Leninist Genclik Birligi Illegal Orgutleri [*Turkish Worker Peasant Liberation Army and Marxist-Leninst Youth Union Illegal Organizations*] (TU)
TIKP .... Turkiye Isci Koylu Partisi [*Worker-Peasant Party of Turkey*] (PD)
TIL .... Taw International Leasing (MAR)
TIL .... Trustul pentru Industrializarea Lemnului [*Trust for the Industrializaton of Wood*] (RO)
TIL .... Trustul Industriei Lemnului [*Trust for the Wood Industry*] (RO)
tilastot .... Tilastotiede [*Statistics*] [*Finnish*]
TILCOR .... Tribal Trust Land Development Corporation (MAR)
TILIB .... Trustul de Izolatii pentru Lucrari Industriale Bucuresti [*Bucharest Insulation Trust for Industrial Projects*] (RO)
Til/nia .... Tilepikoinonia [*Telecommunications*] (GC)
TIM .... Plant of Heat Insulation Materials (RU)
TIM .... Theater Imeni V. E. Meyerkhol'd (RU)
TIM .... Trustul de Instalatii Montaj [*Installations and Assembly Trust*] (RO)
TIMB .... Timbalan [*Deputy*] (ML)
TIMB .... Trustul de Instalatii Montaj Bucuresti [*Bucharest Installations and Assembly Trust*] (RO)
TIMBOD ...... Timber Marketing Board (MAR)
TIMDER ...... Turkiye Ilkogretim Mufettisleri Dernegi [*Turkish Elementary Education Inspectors Association*] (TU)
TIMLO .... Turkiye Insaat ve Malzeme Limited Ortaklari [*Turkish Construction and Equipment Corp.*] [*Istanbul*] (TU)
TIMM .... Thermionic Micromodules (RU)
TIMMP .... Technological Institute of the Meat and Dairy Industry (RU)
TIMTAS ...... Tesisat Insaat Malzemeleri Ticaret Anonim Sirketi [*Installations Construction Equipment Corporation*] (TU)
TINRO .... Pacific Ocean Scientific Research Institute of Fisheries and Oceanography (RU)
TIOSF .... Turkiye Ilkokul Ogretmen Sendikalari Federasyonu [*Turkish Elementary School Teacher Unions' Federation*] (TU)
Tiotef .... Triethylenethiophosphoramide (RU)
tip .... Printing (RU)
tip .... Printing House (RU)
TIP .... Taxe Interieure a la Production (MAR)
TIP .... Techniczna Inspekcja Pracy [*Technical Inspection of the Labor Force*] (POL)
TIP .... Tekstilna Industrija "Pobjeda" [*"Pobjeda" Textile Industry*] [*Zagreb*] (YU)
tip .... Tipografia [*Printing Office*] [*Spanish*]
TIP .... Towarzystwo Internistow Polskich [*Society of Polish Physicians in Internal Medicine*] (POL)
TIP .... Turkiye Isci Partisi [*Turkish Labor Party*] (TU)
TIP .... Tutunski Institut vo Prilep [*Tobacco Institute in Prilep*] (YU)
Tip-Der .... Tibbiyeliler Kultur Dernegi [*Medical Faculty Alumni Cultural Association*] (TU)
TIPER .... Tanzanian and Italian Petroleum Refinery Company (MAR)
TIPICOL ...... Trabajos Tipicos Colombianos en Todos los Metales Preciosos [*Bogota*] (COL)
Tip-Is .... Tip Iscileri Sendikasi [*Medical Workers Union*] [*Turkish Cypriot*] (GC)
tipogr .... Printing, Typographic (BU)
tipolitogr ..... Printing and Lithographic Establishments (RU)
TIPPROYeKT ... Central Institute of Standard Designs (RU)
Tip-Tek ...... Tip Teknolog Kurulus [*Medical Technicians Organization (on Cyprus)*] [*Turkish Cypriot*] (GC)
tir .... Circulation, Number of Copies Printed (RU)
TiR .... Technika i Racjonalizacja (Klub) [*Engineering and Production Efficiency (Club)*] (POL)
Tir .... Tirol [*German*]
tir .... Total Printing, Circulation (BU)
TIR .... Transport International Routier [*International Highway Transport*] [*French*] (HU)
TIRAL .... Transports Ivoiriens RL (MAR)
TIRDO .... Tanzania Industrial Research and Development Organization (MAR)
TIRS .... Travaux de l'Institut des Recherches Sahariennes [*Algerian*] (MAR)
TIS .... Dark Izyum Glass (RU)
TIS .... Tarim Iscileri Sendikasi [*Agricultural Workers Union*] [*An affiliate of DISK*] (TU)
TIS .... Technical and Economic Councils (BU)
TIS .... Technologische Informations Systeme
TIS .... Turkiye Toprak-Su-Tarim Iscileri Sendikasi [*Turkish Union of Land, Water, and Agricultural Workers*] (TU)
TISA .... Tejidos Industriales, Sociedad Anonima [*Industrial Fabrics Corporation*] [*Salvadoran*]
TISA .... Transportadora International, Sociedad Anonima [*International Transport Company, Incorporated*] [*Nicaraguan*] (LA1)
TISCO .... Tanzania Industrial Studies [*or Service*] & Consulting Organisation (MAR)
Ti-Sen .... Turkiye Tiyatrocular Sendikasi [*Turkish Theatre Performers Union*] [*Istanbul*] (TU)
TIS-IS .... Turkiye Insaat Sanayii Iscileri Sendikasi [*Turkish Construction Industry Workers' Union*] (TU)
TISK .... Turkiye Isci Sendikalari Konfederasyonu [*Confederation of Turkish Worker Unions*] [*Turkish Cypriot*] (GC)
TISK .... Turkiye Isveren Sendikalari Konfederasyonu [*Turkish Confederation of Employer Unions*] (TU)
TIS na LVZ G Dimitrov ... Technical and Economic Council of the G. Dimitrov Locomotive Engines and Railroad Cars Plant (BU)
t isp .... Vaporization Temperature (RU)
TISS .... Tanzanian Intelligence and Security Service (AF)
TISSKh .... Pacific Institute of Socialist Agriculture (RU)
TISSS .... Institute of Earthquake-Proof Construction and Seismology (of the Academy of Sciences, Tadzhik SSR) (RU)
TISTR .... Thailand Institute of Scientific and Technological Research
TIT .... Experimental Television Screen (BU)
TIT .... Taxe Interieure sur les Transactions (MAR)
TIT .... Telecommunications Internationales du Tchad [*International Telecommunications of Chad*] (AF)
t i t .... Telegraph and Telephone (RU)
TIT .... Television Test Pattern (RU)
tit .... Titre [*Title*] [*French*] (GPO)
tit .... Tituliert [*German*]
tit .... Titulo [*Title*] [*Spanish*]
TIT .... Transactions on the History of Technology (RU)
TIT .... Tudomanyos Ismeretterjeszto Tarsulat [*Society for the Propagation of Scientific Knowledge*] (HU)
TITASZ V .... Tiszantuli Aramszolgaltato Vallalat [*Electricity Distribution Enterprise of the Trans-Tisza Region*] (HU)
TiTbP .... Wireless Telegraphy and Telephony (RU)
titk .... Titkos [*Secret*] (HU)
tit l .... Title Page (RU)
tito .... Titulo [*Spanish*]
TIWU .... Tea Industry Workers' Union [*Mauritian*] (AF)
Tiy .... Tiyatro [*Theatre*] (TU)
TIYa .... Transactions of the Institute of Linguistics (of the Academy of Sciences, USSR) (RU)
TIYC .... Transvaal Indian Youth Congress (MAR)
TIZ .... Recording Pulse Flip-Flop (RU)
tiz .... Tizedes [*Corporal*] (HU)
Tizpribor ..... Precision Measuring Instrument Plant (RU)
TJ .... Telocvicna Jednota [*Gymnastic Association*] (CZ)
tj .... To Je [*That Is*] (YU)
tj .... To Jest [*That Is*] (CZ)
tj .... To Jest [*That Is*] (YU)
tj .... To Jest [*That Is*] (POL)
tj .... Torvenyjavaslat [*Bill (In preparation)*] (HU)
TJ .... Tribuna de la Juventud [*Tribune of Youth*] [*Mexican*] (LA)
TJAPA .... Tjalon Perwira [*Officer Candidate*] (IN)
TJD .... Turkiye Jeofizikciler Dernegi [*Turkish Geophysicists Organization*] (TU)
TJK .... Turkiye Jeoloji Kurumu [*Turkish Geological Organization*] (TU)
TJK .... Turkiye Jokey Kulubu [*Turkish Jockey Club*] (TU)
tjs .... Tai Jotakin Sellaista [*Finnish*]
tk .... Boiling Point (BU)
TK- .... Contact Thermometer (RU)
TK- .... Contact Transformer (RU)
TK .... Customs Code of the USSR (RU)
TK .... Electric Logging Method (RU)
TK .... Fuel Channel [*Nuclear physics and engineering*] (RU)
TK .... Kenotron Transformer (RU)
TK .... Labor Cadre (BU)
TK .... Labor Card (BU)
TK .... Labor Code (RU)
TK .... Merchant Marine (BU)
TK .... Pacific Ocean Committee (of the Academy of Sciences, USSR) (RU)
TK .... Remote Control (RU)
TK .... Rockwell Conical Hardness Tester (RU)
tk .... Since, Because, As (RU)
TK .... Skin Graft (RU)
TK .... Small Intestine (RU)

TK .... Tajvedelmi Korzet [*Protected Conservation Area*] (HU)
Tk .... Takim [*or Takimlar*] [*Set or Sets*] [*As of equipment or instruments*] (TU)
tk .... Taman Kuun [*This Month*] [*Finnish*] (GPO)
TK .... Tancsics Kiado [*Publishing House*] (HU)
TK .... Tank Corps (RU)
TK .... Tank Shortwave [*Radio*] (RU)
tk .... Tata Kuuta [*Finnish*]
TK .... Technical Commission [*or Committee*] (RU)
TK .... Technical Control (RU)
TK .... Technicka Knihovna [*Technical Library*] (CZ)
TK .... Technicka Kontrola [*Technical Control*] (CZ)
TK .... Technische Konstruktion [*Technical Designing Office*] (EG)
TK .... Technologiai Kutatas [*Research Aiming at the Implementation for the Purpose of Mass Production the Results of Basic Research*] (HU)
Tk .... Telok [*Teluk*] [*Bay*] [*Indonesian*] (NAU)
Tk .... Telok [*Teluk*] [*Bay*] [*Malay*] (NAU)
TK .... Temperature Coefficient (RU)
TK .... Tenaga Kuda [*Horsepower*] (IN)
TK .... Teologian Kandidaatti [*Finnish*]
tk .... Teretna Kola [*Freight Car*] [*Railroads*] (YU)
TK .... Terminology Commission (RU)
tk .... Tezky Kulomet [*Heavy Machinegun*] (CZ)
TK .... Thermal Cracking (RU)
TK .... Thermostated Chamber (RU)
TK .... Ticaret Kanunu [*Commercial Law*] (TU)
TK .... Tokelau Islands [*Two-letter standard code*] (CNC)
TK .... Tolmac Kratic [*Explanation of Abbreviations*] (YU)
TK .... Tonnes Kilometriques (MAR)
TK .... Trgovinska Komora [*Chamber of Commerce*] (YU)
TK .... Turbocompressor (RU)
TK .... Tvornica Koza [*Leather Factory*] (YU)
TK- .... Wheeled Tractor (RU)
TKA .... Motor Torpedo Boat (RU)
TKA .... Tameion Koinonikon Asfaliseon [*Social Insurance Fund*] [*Greek*] (GC)
TKA .... Techniczna Komisja Awaryjna [*Technical Damage Commission*] (POL)
tk ad .... Takma Ad [*Nickname*] (TU)
TKAE .... Turk Kulturunu Arastirma Enstitusu [*Turkish Institute for Cultural Research*] (TU)
t kapl .... Drop Point (RU)
tkatsk .... Weaving Mill [*Topography*] (RU)
tkatsk pryad ... Weaving and Spinning Mill [*Topography*] (RU)
TKB .... Quick-Saturation Coil Transformer (RU)
TKB .... Technisch-Kommerzielles Buero [*Technical Commercial Office*] (EG)
TKBA .... Tierkoerperbeseitigungsanstalt [*Carcass Disposal Plant*] (EG)
TKCh .... Temperature Frequency Coefficient (RU)
TKC ZMS .... Tmyczasowy Komitet Centralny Zwiazku Mlodziezy Socjalistycznej [*Temporary Central Committee of the Socialist Youth Union*] (POL)
TKD .... Turkiye Kizilay Dernegi [*Turkish Red Crescent Organization*] (TU)
TKDP .... Temperature Coefficient of Dielectric Constant (RU)
t k dr .... Heavy Machine-Gun Detachment (BU)
TKE- .... Pipe-Laying Electric Crane (RU)
TKF .... Tetracalcium Phosphate (RU)
TKF .... Tricalcium Phosphate (RU)
TKF .... Tricresyl Phosphate (RU)
TKFN .... Terenowy Komitet Frontu Narodowego [*Local Committee of the People's Front*] (POL)
TKGM .... Tapu ve Kadastro Genel Mudurlugu [*Land Registration and Survey Directorate General*] [*Under Office of Premier*] (TU)
TKh .... Table of Characteristics [*Computers*] (RU)
TKh .... Tachometer Generator (RU)
TKH .... Trgovinska Komora Hrvatske [*Chamber of Commerce of Croatia*] (YU)
TKhA .... Chromel-Alumel Thermocouple (RU)
TKhA .... Sodium Trichloroacetate (RU)
TKhB .... Theater and Art Bureau (RU)
TKhE .... Trichloroethane (RU)
TKhFM .... Copper Trichlorophenolate (RU)
TKhK .... Chromel-Copel Thermocouple (RU)
TKhK .... Cold-Cathode Thyratron (RU)
TKhNB .... Tetrachloronitrobenzene (RU)
TKhP .... Device for Checking Gun Bore Sighting (RU)
TKhS .... Refrigerated Transportation Vessel (RU)
TKhTU .... Theatrical Applied Art School (RU)
TKhU .... Trichloroacetic Acid (RU)
TKI .... Tavkozlesi Kutato Intezet [*Telecommunication Research Institute*] (HU)
TKI .... Temperature Coefficient of Inductance (RU)
TKI .... Termeloszovetkezetek Kereskedelmi Irodaja [*Producing Cooperatives' Commercial Office*] (HU)
TKI .... Turkiye Kibris Idaresi [*Turkish Cypriot Administration*] (TU)
TKI .... Turkiye Komur Isletmesi Genel Mudurlugu [*Turkish Coal Works Directorate General*] (TU)
TKIChP .... Transactions of the Commission for the Study of the Quaternary Period (of the Academy of Sciences, USSR) (RU)
TKID .... Turk Kooperatif Isleri Dairesi [*Turkish Cooperative Affairs Office*] [*Turkish Cypriot*] (GC)
t kip .... Boiling Point (RU)
TKITPSF ..... Turkiye Kamu Iktisadi Tesebbusleri Personeli Sendikalari Federasyonu [*Federation of Turkish Public Economic Enterprises Personnel Unions*] (TU)
TKKD .... Turk Kadinlari Kultur Dernegi [*Turkish Women's Cultural Association*] (TU)
TKKF .... Towarzystwo Krzewienia Kultury Fizycznej [*Society for Promotion of Physical Culture*] (POL)
TkL .... Tekniikan Lisensiaatti [*Finnish*]
TKL .... Tokelau Islands [*Three-letter standard code*] (CNC)
TKM .... Tatrzanski Klub Motocyklowy [*Tatra Mountains Motorcycle Club*] (POL)
tkm .... Ton-Kilometer (RU)
tkm .... Tonnenkilometer [*Tons per Kilometer*] [*German*]
t/km .... Tons/Kilometer (BU)
TKMC-IS ..... Turkiye Yeralti Madenleri Komur, Metal, Cevherleri, ve Maden Arama Iscileri Sendikasi [*Turkish Subterranean Ores, Coal, Metal, and Mine Exploitation Workers' Union*] [*Ankara*] (TU)
TKMD .... Turk Komunist Mucadele Dernegi [*Turkish Association for Combating Communism*] (TU)
TKNL .... Tovarny Kobercu a Nabytkovych Latek [*Carpet and Upholstery Material Factories*] (CZ)
TKO .... Circular-Scope Tube (RU)
TKO .... Technische Kontrollorganisation [*Technical Control Organization*] (EG)
TKO .... Tvornica Koza Osijek [*Osijek Leather Factory*] (YU)
t komm .... Switchboard Telephone (RU)
t kond .... Dew Point (RU)
TKOOS .... Terek-Kuma Irrigation Canal System (RU)
TKOVM .... Transactions of the Commission for the Permafrost Study (RU)
TKP .... Crystal Field Theory (RU)
TKP .... Terenowa Koordynacja Przewozow [*Local Coordination of Transport*] (POL)
TKP .... Toplumcu Kurtulus Partisi [*Communal Liberation Party*] [*Turkish Cypriot*] (GC)
TKP .... Trikresylphosphat [*Tricresyl Phosphate*] (EG)
TKP .... Turk Komunist Partisi [*Turkish Communist Party*] [*Illegal*] (TU)
TKPD .... Thermal Efficiency Factor (RU)
TKP-ML .... People's Revolutionary Union - Marxist-Leninist [*Turkish*] (PD)
TKPO .... Ryazan' Heavy Forging-and-Pressing Equipment Plant (RU)
Tkr .... Tanskan Kruunu(a) [*Finnish*]
TKR .... Telephone Cable Laying Company (RU)
TKR .... Terenowa Komisja Rozjemcza [*Local Arbitration Commission*] (POL)
TKR .... Tons/Kilometers (AF)
Tkrb .... Takribi [*Approximate, Approximately*] (TU)
TKRD .... Turbojet Engine (RU)
t krist .... Crystallization Temperature (RU)
t krit .... Critical Temperature (RU)
TKRP .... Tymczasowy Komitet Rewolucyjny Polski [*Temporary Revolutionary Committee of Poland*] (POL)
TKS .... Tank Firing Course (RU)
TKS .... Technicke Kontrolni Stanoviste [*Technical Control Station*] (CZ)
TKS .... Temperature Coefficient of Resistance (RU)
TKS .... Temperature Resistance Coefficient (BU)
TKS .... Terenowy Klub Sportowy [*Country Sports and Athletics Club*] [*Polish*]
TKS .... Trgovinska Komora Split [*Chamber of Commerce of the Town of Split*] (YU)
TKS .... Wage Rates and Skills Handbook (RU)
TKS-IS .... Turkiye Kamu ve Saglik Adamlari Sendikasi [*Turkish Public and Health Workers Union*] [*Istanbul*] (TU)
TKSNF .... Three-Valued Conjunctive Perfect Normal Form (RU)
TkT .... Tekniikan Tohtori [*Finnish*]
TKT .... Tonnes Kilometriques Transportees (MAR)
TKT .... Tovarny Krajek a Tylu [*Lace and Tulle Factories*] (CZ)
tk-tsa .... Heavy Machine-Gun (BU)
TKU .... Tatar Communist University (RU)
TKU .... Tundjangan Kemahalan Umum [*Cost of Living Allowance*] (IN)
TKU .... Turbine and Boiler Set (RU)
TKV .... Temperature Coefficient of Viscosity (RU)
TKV .... Turk Kalp Vakfi [*Turkish Heart Fund*] (TU)
TKV .... Turk Kultur Vakfi [*Turkish Cultural Fund*] (TU)
TKV .... Water Boiling Point (RU)
TKVD .... High-Pressure Turbocompressor (RU)
Tkvkiad .... Tankonyvkiado Vallalat [*Textbook Publishing Enterprise*] (HU)
TKVRD .... Turbojet Engine (RU)
TKWP .... Towarzystwo Krzewienia Wiedzy Praktycznej [*Society for the Propagation of Practical Knowledge*] [*Polish*]
TKYe .... Temperature Coefficient of Capacitance (RU)
TKZ .... Short-Circuit Current (RU)
TKZ .... Taganrog Boiler Plant (RU)
TKZ .... Territorial Commission of Mineral Resources (RU)
TKZ .... Turbine and Boiler Plant (RU)

TKZS.......... Labor Cooperative Farm (BU)
TI.......... Gewichtsteil [*Part by Weight*] [*German*]
TL.......... Tape Flip-Flop (RU)
TL.......... Technische Leitung [*Technical Management*] (EG)
tl.......... Teelusikallinen [*Finnish*]
tl.......... Tega Leta [*Current Year, This Year*] (YU)
TI.......... Teil [*Part*] [*German*]
tl.......... Teilweise Loeslich [*Partly Soluble*] [*German*]
tl.......... Tekoce Leto [*Current Year, This Year*] (YU)
TL.......... Telescope Lens (RU)
TL.......... Tentera Laut [*Navy*] (ML)
TL.......... Teologian Lisensiaatti [*Finnish*]
tl.......... Tesla (RU)
tl.......... Title Page (RU)
TL.......... Turk Lira [*Turkish Lira*] (TU)
TL.......... Turnlehrer [*German*]
TI.......... Turun ja Porin Laani [*Finnish*]
TL.......... Tyzden Lesov [*Forest Week (A campaign)*] (CZ)
TLA.......... Tanzania Library Association (MAR)
TLA.......... Transkei Legislative Assembly (MAR)
TLB.......... Technische Leistungsbedingungen [*Technical Performance Specifications*] (EG)
TLB.......... Technische Lieferbedingungen [*Technical Delivery Terms*] (EG)
TLB.......... Transport Licensing Board (MAR)
TLB.......... Tres Large Bande (MAR)
TLC.......... Tanganyika Legislative Council (MAR)
TLC.......... Tanganyika Library Services Board (MAR)
TLC.......... Tanzania Legal Corporation (MAR)
TID.......... Rear Patrol (BU)
TID.......... Rear Point (RU)
TLDA.......... Groupe pour le Triomphe des Libertes Democratiques en Algerie (MAR)
TLDM.......... Tentera Laut Di-Raja Malaysia [*Royal Malaysian Navy*] (ML)
TLdP.......... Tiskarna Ljudske Pravice [*Ljudska Pravica Printers*] [*Ljubljana*] (YU)
Tle.......... Teile [*German*]
Tlf.......... Telefon [*Telephone*] (TU)
tlf.......... Telephone (RU)
TLF.......... Telephony (RU)
TLG.......... Telegraphy (RU)
TLGP.......... Tribal Land Grazing Policy (MAR)
tlgr.......... Telegraph (RU)
TLH.......... Trefileries et Laminoirs du Havre (MAR)
TLHS.......... Trustul de Lucrari Hidrotehnice Speciale [*Trust for Special Hydrotechnical Projects*] (RO)
TLI.......... Current-Distributing Final Selector (RU)
TLim AM.......... Towarzystwo Literackie Imienia Adama Mickiewicza [*Adam Mickiewicz Literary Society*] (POL)
TLim M.......... Towarzystwo Literackie Imienia Mickiewicza [*Mickiewicz Literary Society*] (POL)
TLK.......... Moscow Theater Imeni Lenin Young Communist League (RU)
tlk.......... Taman Lehden Konttoriin [*Finnish*]
TLP.......... Telefonistas de Lisboa e Porto [*Telephone Workers of Lisbon and Porto*] [*Portuguese*] (WER)
TLRS.......... Rayon Communications Telephone Line (RU)
TLS.......... Tanzania Library Services (MAR)
Tls.......... Telsiz [*Radio, Wireless*] (TU)
TLS.......... Trustul de Lucrari Speciale [*Special Projects Trust*] (RO)
TLSB.......... Trustul de Lucrari Speciale Bucuresti [*Bucharest Trust for Special Projects*] (RO)
TLT.......... Tanzania Labour Tribunal (MAR)
tlum.......... Tlumacz [*or Tlumaczenie or Tlumaczyl*] [*Translator or Translation or Translated By*] (POL)
TM.......... Antitank Mine (RU)
TM.......... Convoi de Transport de Materiel [*Military*] [*French*] (MTD)
TM.......... Front des Travailleurs [*Workers Front*] [*Malagasy*] (AF)
TM.......... Heat Engine (RU)
TM.......... Meteorological Table (RU)
tm.......... Of the Current Month, in the Current Month (RU)
tm.......... Quarterly (BU)
TM-.......... Sea Wind-Turbulence Meter (RU)
TM.......... Standard Machines (RU)
TM.......... Tajekoztatasi Miniszterium/Miniszter [*Ministry/Minister of Information*] (HU)
TM.......... Tausend Mark [*Thousand Marks*] (EG)
TM.......... Technology for the Youth (RU)
tm.......... Tego Miesiaca [*That Month*] [*Polish*]
tm.......... Tekoci Mesec [*Current Month*] (YU)
TM.......... Telegramme Multiple [*Multiple Telegram*] [*French*] (CL)
TM.......... Telegraphie Militaire [*Military*] [*French*] (MTD)
TM.......... Telemechanics (RU)
TM.......... Telemechanization (RU)
TM.......... Terre Malgache [*Tananarive*] (MAR)
tm.......... Teski Mitraljez [*Heavy Machine Gun*] (YU)
TM.......... Tetragonika Metra [*Square Meters*] (GC)
TM.......... Thay Mat [*On Behalf Of, In the Name Of, Representing*] (TVP)
tm.......... This Month (BU)
tm.......... Tohoto Mesice [*Of the Present Month*] (CZ)
tm.......... Ton-Meter (RU)
TM.......... Tone Manipulator (RU)
TM.......... Tour du Monde (MAR)
TM.......... Transformatur Merkezi [*Transformer Center, Transformer Vault*] (TU)
TM.......... Transversalni Magnetski [*Transversal Magnetic*] (YU)
TM.......... Trat Mladeze [*Youth Railroad Track (Built by Youth Brigades)*] (CZ)
TM.......... Travaux Municipaux [*Municipal Projects*] (CL)
tm.......... Trekhondos Minos [*Current Month*] (GC1)
TM.......... Turk Mali [*Made in Turkey*] (TU)
tM.......... Warm Air Mass (RU)
TMA.......... Tanzanian Military Academy (MAR)
TMA.......... Tierra Mar y Aire Ltda. [*Bogota*] (COL)
TMA.......... Track Motors Africa Ltd. (MAR)
TMA.......... Trans-Mediterranean Airways SAL [*Lebanese*] (ME)
TMAU.......... Peat-Mineral and Ammonia Fertilizers (RU)
TMB.......... Antitank Paper-Cased Mine (RU)
TMB.......... Tobacco Marketing Board (MAR)
TMB.......... Towarzystwo Milosnikow Bydgoszczy [*Society of Friends of Bydgoszcz*] (POL)
TMB.......... Tudomanyos Minosito Bizottsag [*Committee on Scientific Qualifications*] (HU)
TMC.......... Tanganyika Mennonite Church (MAR)
TMCN.......... Traditional Medical Council of Nigeria (MAR)
TMD.......... Antitank Wood-Cased Mine (RU)
TMD.......... Tiskovy Referat Ministerstva Dopravy [*Press Department of the Ministry of Transportation*] (CZ)
TMD.......... Turk Mukavemetciler Dernegi [*Turkish Cypriot Resistance Fighters Association*] (GC)
TMD.......... Turkiye Muharipler Dernegi [*Turkish Fighters Association*] (TU)
TMD-1.......... Protivtenkovska Mina-Drvena [*Wooden Antitank Mine*] (YU)
TMDB.......... Teruleti Munkaugyi Dontobizottsag [*Regional Labor Arbitration Committee*] (HU)
TMDB.......... Wood Briquette Antitank Mine (RU)
TMDN.......... Tausend Mark der Deutschen Notenbank [*Thousand Marks of the German Bank of Issue (Replaced DM as of 1 August 1964)*] (EG)
TME.......... Tudomanyos es Muszaki Egyuttmukodes [*Scientific and Technical Cooperation*] (HU)
tmet.......... Topovski Metak [*Gun Shell*] (YU)
TMF.......... Thiamine Monophosphate (RU)
TMF.......... Tiskovy Referat Ministerstva Financi [*Press Department of the Ministry of Finance*] (CZ)
TMG.......... Thermal Magnetic Hysteresis (RU)
TMGT.......... Turkiye Milli Genclik Teskilati [*Turkish National Youth Organization*] (TU)
TMH.......... Towarzystwo Milosnikow Historii [*Society of Friends of History*] (POL)
TMHiZ.......... Towarzystwo Milosnikow Historii i Zabytkow [*Society of Friends of History and Historical Relics*] (POL)
TMHiZK.......... Towarzystwo Milosnikow Historii i Zabytkow Krakowa [*Society of Friends of the History and Historical Relics of Krakow*] (POL)
TMI.......... Tiskovy Referat Ministerstva Informaci [*Press Department of the Ministry of Information*] (CZ)
tmi.......... Toiminimi [*Finnish*]
TMI.......... Tomsk Medical Institute (RU)
TMI.......... Tula Institute of Mechanics (RU)
TMIE.......... Travaux et Memoires de l'Institut d'Ethnologie [*Paris*] [*A publication*] (MAR)
tminbr.......... Heavy Mortar Artillery Brigade (RU)
tminbr.......... Heavy Mortar Brigade (BU)
TMJP.......... Towarzystwo Milosnikow Jezyka Polskiego [*Society of Friends of the Polish Language*] (POL)
TMK.......... Tarsadalmi Munka Kozpont [*Social Service Center*] (HU)
TMK.......... Tervszeru Megelozo Karbantartas [*Preventive Maintenance (Machinery)*] (HU)
TMK.......... Transactions of the Commission on Mongolia (RU)
TMK.......... Turk Maarif Koleji [*Turkish Teachers' College*] [*Turkish Cypriot*] (GC)
tmkh.......... Heavy Mortar (BU)
tmkh.......... Telemechanics (RU)
TMKh.......... Transformer-Oil Supply (RU)
TMKhB.......... Trust of Slaughterhouses and Cold Storage Plants (RU)
TMKKAB.......... Tudomanyos es Muszaki Kutatasokat Koordinalo Allando Bizottsaga (KGST) [*Permanent Commission for Coordinating Scientific and Technical Research (CEMA)*] (HU)
TMKKB.......... Tudomanyos es Muszaki Kutatasokat Koordinalo Bizottsag [*Commission for Coordinating Scientific and Technical Research*] (HU)
TMKV.......... Turkiye Milli Kultur Vakfi [*Turkish National Cultural Foundation*] (TU)
TMM.......... Technikum Mechaniczno-Morskie [*Marine Engineering Technical School*] (POL)
TMM.......... Theory of Mechanisms and Machines (RU)
TMM.......... Towarzystwo Milosnikow Muzyki [*Association of Music Lovers*] [*Polish*]
TMM-1.......... Protivtenkovska Mina-Metalna [*Metal Antitank Mine*] (YU)
TMMOB.......... Turkiye Mimar ve Muhendisler Odalari Birligi [*Turkish Union of Chambers of Architects and Engineers*] (TU)
TMNO.......... Tiskovy Referat Ministerstva Narodni Obrany [*Press Department of the Ministry of National Defense*] (CZ)

TMO .... Molecular Orbital Theory (RU)
TMO .... Technische Montageabteilung [*Technical Assembly Department*] (EG)
TMO .... Thermomechanical Working (RU)
TMO .... Toprak Mahsulleri Ofisi [*Soil Products Office*] (TU)
TMOA .... Tameion Monimon Odostromaton Athinon [*Athens Permanent Road Pavement Fund*] (GC)
TMOK .... Turkiye Milliyetci Ogretmenler Konfederasyonu [*Confederation of Turkish Nationalist Teachers*] (TU)
TMP- .... Device for the Thermomechanical Investigation of Polymers (RU)
TMP .... Heavy Bridge Train (RU)
TMP .... Tiskovy Referat Ministerstva Prumyslu [*Press Department of the Ministry of Industry*] (CZ)
tmp .... Tuna Merneho Paliva [*Ton of Standard Fuel*] (CZ)
TMP .... Turk Milli Polis [*Turkish National Police*] (TU)
TMPO .... Tiskovy Referat Ministerstva Post [*Press Department of the Ministry of Postal Service*] (CZ)
TMRP .... Technical School for the Mining and Ore Industry (BU)
TMS .... Societe de Tricotage Mecanique du Senegal (MAR)
tms .... Tai Muuta Sellaista [*Et Cetera*] [*Finnish*]
tms .... Tai Muuta Semmoista [*And So On*] [*Finnish*] (GPO)
TMS .... Tefari Makonnen School (MAR)
TMS .... Tetramethyllead (RU)
TMS .... Tezka Mostova Souprava [*Heavy Bridging Section*] (CZ)
TMS .... Tiskovy Referat Ministerstva Spravedlnosti [*Press Department of the Ministry of Justice*] (CZ)
TMS .... Tovarny Mlynskych Stroju [*Flour Mill Machinery Works*] [*Pardubice*] (CZ)
TMS .... Transport Management Services Ltd. (MAR)
TMS .... Transvaal Medical Society (MAR)
TMS .... Tvornica Mlinskih Strojeva [*Mill Machinery Factory*] [*Zagreb*] (YU)
TMSA .... Telephone Manufacturers of South Africa (MAR)
TMSI .... Grinding-Washing and Sorting Installation [*Quarry*] (BU)
TMSI .... Technical School for the Mechanization of Construction Products (BU)
TMSO .... Tiskovy Referat Ministerstva Skolstvi a Osvety [*Press Department of the Ministry of Education and Culture*] (CZ)
TMSP .... Tiskovy Referat Ministerstva Socialni Pece [*Press Department of the Ministry of Social Welfare*] (CZ)
TMSS .... Technical School for Agricultural Mechanization (BU)
TMSZ .... Tiskovy Referat Ministerstva pro Sjednoceni Zakonu [*Press Department of the Ministry for the Unification of Laws*] (CZ)
TMT .... Theoretical Molecular Plate (RU)
TMT .... Tiskovy Referat Ministerstva Techniky [*Press Department of the Ministry of Technology*] (CZ)
TMT .... Turk Mukavemet Teskilati [*Turkish Resistance Organization*] [*Cypriot*] (TU)
TMTD .... Tetramethylthiuram Disulfide (RU)
TMTE .... Textilipari Muszaki es Tudomanyos Egyesulet [*Technical and Scientific Association of the Textile Industry*] (HU)
TMTF .... Turk Milli Talebe Federasyonu [*Turkish National Student Federation*] (TU)
TMTM .... Tetramethylthiuram Monosulfide (RU)
TMTS .... Trapeza Metokhikou Tameiou Stratou [*Bank of the Army Pensioners Fund*] [*Greek*] (GC)
TMUCB .... Trustul de Montaj Utilaj Chimic Bucuresti [*Bucharest Trust for Chemical Equipment Assembly*] (RO)
TMUD .... Turkiye Muharipler Dernegi [*Turkish Veterans Association*] (TU)
TMUP .... Trust of Medical Education Visual Aids (RU)
TMV .... Tiskovy Referat Ministerstva Vnitra [*Press Department of the Ministry of Interior*] (CZ)
TMVO .... Tiskovy Referat Ministerstva Vnitrniho Obchodu [*Press Department of the Ministry of Domestic Trade*] (CZ)
TMVSZ .... Tudomanyos Munkasok Vilagszovetsege [*World Federation of Scientific Workers*] (HU)
TMVZ .... Tiskovy Referat Ministerstva Vyzivy [*Press Department of the Ministry of Food Supply*] (CZ)
TMW .... Teatr Mlodego Widza [*Theatre of the Young Spectator*] (POL)
TMZ .... Tiskovy Referat Ministerstva Zemedelstvi [*Press Department of the Ministry of Agriculture*] (CZ)
TMZ .... Tvornica Motora Zagreb [*Motor Works, Zagreb*] (YU)
TMZD .... Tiskovy Referat Ministerstva Zdravotnictvi [*Press Department of the Ministry of Public Health*] (CZ)
TMZO .... Tiskovy Referat Ministerstva Zahranicniho Obchodu [*Press Department of the Ministry of Foreign Trade*] (CZ)
TMZV .... Tiskovy Referat Ministerstva Zahranicnich Veci [*Press Department of the Ministry of Foreign Affairs*] (CZ)
TN .... Aiming Point (RU)
tn .... And So Forth (BU)
TN .... Filament Transformer (RU)
TN- .... Load Transformer (RU)
TN .... Observation Point (RU)
tn .... Payload (RU)
tn .... So-Called (RU)
tn .... Takanarecen [*So-Called*] (YU)
TN .... Tanker (RU)
Tn .... Taren [*Sunken Rock*] [*Norwegian*] (NAU)
TN .... Telovychovny Nacelnik [*Senior Physical Education Officer*] (CZ)
tn .... Tonni(a) [*Finnish*]
TN .... Towarzystwo Naukowe [*Scientific Society*] [*Polish*]
TN .... Tuan [*Sir, Mister*] (IN)
TN .... Tunisia [*Two-letter standard code*] (CNC)
TN .... Turbocharging (RU)
TN .... Voltage Transformer (RU)
TNA .... Theatre National Algerien [*Algerian National Theatre*] (AF)
TNA .... Turbine-Pump Assembly (RU)
t nar .... So-Called (BU)
TNB .... Technical Norm-Setting Office (RU)
TNB .... Transnational Bank (MAR)
TNB .... Turkiye Noterler Birligi [*Turkish Notaries' Union*] (TU)
TNB .... Wage Rate and Norm-Setting Office (RU)
tnch .... Low-Frequency Current (RU)
TND .... Low-Pressure Turbine (RU)
TNDPKh ...... Low-Pressure Ahead Turbine (RU)
TNDZKh ...... Low-Pressure Reverse Turbine (RU)
TNF .... Trinitrophenol (RU)
TNG .... Tangier Airport (MAR)
TNI .... Tentara Nasional Indonesia [*Indonesian National Army*] (IN)
TNIEI .... Tatar Scientific Research Institute of Economics (RU)
TNIETI .... Tbilisi Scientific Research Electrotechnical Institute (RU)
TNIGEI .... Tbilisi Water Power Engineering Scientific Research Institute (RU)
TNIGMI .... Tbilisi Scientific Research Hydrometeorological Institute (RU)
TNIISA .... Tbilisi Scientific Research Institute of Instrument Making and Automation Equipment (RU)
TNIISGEI ..... Tbilisi Scientific Research Institute of Structures and Water Power Engineering (RU)
TNIIYaK ...... Transactions of the Scientific Research Institute of Language and Culture at the SNK YaASSR (RU)
TNIIYaLI ...... Tuva Scientific Research Institute of Language, Literature, and History (RU)
TNIIZ .... Turkmen Scientific Research Institute of Agriculture (RU)
TNIKhFI ...... Tbilisi Scientific Research Chemical and Pharmaceutical Institute (RU)
TNIMA .... Tubman National Institute of Medical Arts (MAR)
TNIP .... Transkei National Independence Party [*South African*] (AF)
TNIRO .... Pacific Ocean Scientific Research Institute of Sea Fisheries and Oceanography (RU)
TNIS .... Tbilisi Scientific Research Institute of Structures (RU)
TNISGEI ...... Tbilisi Scientific Research Institute of Structures and Water Power Engineering (RU)
TNK .... Small Intestines (RU)
TNK .... Thymonucleic Acid (RU)
TNK .... Trestni Nalezaci Komise [*Board for the Determination of Criminal Offenses*] (CZ)
TNKU .... Tentara Nasional Kalimantan Utara [*North Kalimantan National Army*] (IN)
TN KUL .... Towarzystwo Naukowe Katolickiego Uniwersytetu Lubelskiego [*Learned Society of Lublin Catholic University*] (POL)
TNLDVN ...... Thanh Nien Lao Dong Viet Nam [*Lao Dong Youth Group*] (TVP)
TNM .... Initial Point of Maneuver (RU)
TNM .... Tentera Nasional Malaya [*Malayan National Army*] (ML)
TNN .... Low-Voltage Current (RU)
TNO .... Nederlands Centrale Organisatie voor Toegepast-Natuurwetenschappelijk Onderzoek [*Netherlands Central Organization for Applied Natural Scientific Research*] (WEN)
TNO .... Wage Rate and Norm-Setting Department (RU)
TNOiK .... Towarzystwo Naukowe Organizacji i Kierownictwa [*Scientific Society of Organization and Administration*] (POL)
TNP .... Tabor Nucenych Praci [*Forced Labor Camp*] (CZ)
TNP .... Theatre National Populaire [*National People's Theater*] [*French*] (WER)
TNPP .... Tank in Direct Support of Infantry (RU)
TNPP .... Transkei National Progressive Party [*South African*] (AF)
TNR .... Initial Point of Turn (RU)
TNR .... Tanganyika Notes and Records [*Dar Es Salaam*] [*A publication*] (MAR)
TNR .... Trinitroresorcinol (RU)
TNR .... Tuvinian People's Republic [*1921-1944*] (RU)
TNRP .... Tuvinian People's Revolutionary Party (RU)
TNRS .... Trinitroresorcinol Lead Complex (RU)
TNS .... Initial Point of Descent (RU)
TNS .... Tanganyika National Society (MAR)
TNSW .... Towarzystwo Nauczycieli Szkol Wyzszych [*Society of University and College Teachers*] (POL)
TNT .... Terror Against Terror [*Israeli clandestine organization*]
Tnt .... Torrent [*Torrent*] [*Military map abbreviation*] [*World War I*] [*French*] (MTD)
TNT .... Towarzystwo Naukowe w Toruniu [*Torun Learned Society*] (POL)
TNT .... Trinitrotoluene (RU)
TNTB .... Tanzania National Tourist Board (MAR)
TNTM .... Movement for Youth Technical and Scientific Creativity (BU)
TNW .... Towarzystwo Naukowe Warszawskie [*Warsaw Learned Society*] (POL)

TNwT .... Towarzystwo Naukowe w Toruniu [*Torun Learned Society*] (POL)
TNXPCMCN ... Thanh Nien Xung Phong Chong My Cuu Nuoc [*"Resist America for National Salvation" Assault Youth*] (TVP)
TNZ .... Initial Point of Deployment [*Aviation*] (BU)
to .... Fine Purification [*Of gases*] (RU)
TO .... Fire Plan [*Artillery*] (RU)
TO .... Heat Treatment (RU)
TO .... Precision Reading (RU)
TO .... Rear Detachment, Rear Guard (RU)
TO .... Rear Security (RU)
to .... So, In This Way (RU)
TO .... Tank Detachment (RU)
TO- .... Technical Automobile Service (RU)
TO .... Technical Department (RU)
TO .... Technical Description (RU)
TO .... Technological Department (RU)
TO .... Tehnicka Oprema [*Technical Equipment*] [*Military*] (YU)
TO .... Tehnicki Odbor [*Technical Committee*] (YU)
TO .... Telegramme Ordinaire [*Military*] [*French*] (MTD)
t/o .... Telegraph Office (RU)
to .... Tizedes Osztalyozas [*Decimal Classification (Dewey)*] (HU)
To .... Tohtori [*Finnish*]
to .... Tomo [*Tome*] [*Spanish*]
TO .... Tonga [*Two-letter standard code*] (CNC)
to .... Tonna [*Ton*] (HU)
TO .... Torpedo, Tvornica Motora [*The "Torpedo" Motor Factory*] [*Rijeka*] (YU)
to .... Torstai(na) [*Finnish*]
TO .... Transport Detachment (RU)
TO .... Transport Section, Transportation Department (RU)
TO .... Transvaalse Onderwijsersunie (MAR)
TO .... Transvaalse Onderwysersvereniging (MAR)
TO-1 .... Technical Automotive Service Number 1 (BU)
TOA .... Tameion Oikonomikis Anaptyxeos [*Economic Development Fund*] [*Greek*] (GC)
TOA .... Total Obligational Authority (MAR)
TOAME .... Transactions of the Antiquity Department of the State Ermitage Museum (RU)
TOB .... Tarcakozi Operative Bizottsag [*Interministerial Operating Committee*] (HU)
TOB .... Turkiye Ogretmenler Bankasi [*Turkish Teachers' Bank*] (TU)
TOB .... Turkiye Ticaret Odalari, Sanayi Odalari, ve Ticaret Borsalari Birligi [*Turkish Union of Chambers of Commerce, Industry, and Stock Exchanges*] [*See also TSBB*] (TU)
TOBANK ..... Turkiye Ogretmenler Bankasi [*Turkish Teachers' Bank*] [*See also TOB*] (TU)
TOBD .... Turkiye Ogretmenler Birligi Dernegi [*Turkish Teachers' Unions Organization*] (TU)
TOBDD .... Tum Ogretmenler Birlesme ve Dayanisma Dernegi [*Pan-Teachers' Unity and Mutual Solidarity Association*] (TU)
TOB-DER .... Turkiye Ogretmenler Birlesme ve Dayanisma Dernegi [*Turkish Teachers' Unity and Solidarity Organization*] (TU)
TOBETON ... Societe Togolaise de Beton (MAR)
t obr .... So, In This Way (RU)
TOC .... Tanzania Olympic Committee (MAR)
TOC .... Turkiye Ormancilar Cemiyeti [*Turkish Foresters' Society*] (TU)
Tochelektropribor ... Precision Electrical Instrument Plant (RU)
Tochizmeritel' ... Precision Measuring Instrument Plant (RU)
Tochmekh ... State Trust of Precision Mechanics (RU)
Tochpribor ... Precision Instrument Plant (RU)
ToD .... Technicko-Obchodni Dotazy [*Technical and Business Inquiries*] (CZ)
TOD .... Tum Ogretim Uyeleri Dernegi [*Comprehensive Teaching Members (Higher Educational Level) Organization*] (TU)
TODAIE .... Turkiye ve Orta Dogu Amne Idaresi Enstitusu [*Turkey and Middle East Public Administration Institute*] [*Under Middle East Technological University*] (TU)
TODELAR ... Tobon de la Roche, Jaime [*Bogota*] (COL)
TODIREP ..... Societe Togolaise de Diffusion et de Representation (MAR)
TODMF .... Turkiye Ogretmen Dernekleri Milli Federasyonu [*National Federation of Turkish Teachers Organizations*] (TU)
TODRL .... Transactions of the Department of Old Russian Literature (RU)
TOE .... Heat-Releasing Elements [*Nuclear energy*] (BU)
TOE .... Tubular Collecting Electrode (RU)
TOE .... Turk Otomobile Endustri [*Turkish Automobile Industry*] (TU)
TOEFL .... Test of English as a Foreign Language (MAR)
TOEV .... Topikos Organismos Engeion Veltioseon [*Local Organization for Land Reclamation*] [*Greek*] (GC)
TOF .... Fleet Technical Division (RU)
TOF .... Pacific Ocean Fleet (RU)
TOFAS .... Turk Otomobile Fabrikasi Anonim Sirketi [*Turkish Automobile Factory Corporation*] (TU)
TOG .... Transportordnung fuer Gefaehrliche Gueter [*Transport Regulation for Hazardous Goods*] (EG)
TOGOBUND ... Bund der Deutschen Togolaender (MAR)
TOGOFRUIT ... Societe Nationale de Developpement de la Culture Fruitiere [*Togolese*] (MAR)
TOGOGAZ ... Societe Togolaise des Gaz Industriels (MAR)
TOGO-KAIK ... Societe Togolaise pour l'Industrie de la Chaux (MAR)
TOGOPROM ... Societe Togolaise de Promotion Immobiliere (MAR)
TOGTO .... Turkiye Ogrenci ve Genclik Turizm Orgutu [*Turkish Student and Youth Tourism Organization*] (TU)
toht .... Tohtori [*Finnish*]
TOI .... Total Ocean Indien (MAR)
toim .... Toimittaja [*Finnish*]
toim .... Toimittanut [*Finnish*]
TOK .... Trestni Odvolaci Komise [*Criminal Appeals Board*] (CZ)
TOK .... Turystyczna Odznaka Kajakowa [*Canoe-Touring Badge*] (POL)
TOKO .... Tovarna Kovckov in Usnjenih Izdelkov [*Luggage and Leather Products Factory*] [*Domzale*] (YU)
TOKTEN ...... Transfer of Knowhow through Expatriate Nationals (MAR)
tol .... Roofing Paper Factory [*Topography*] (RU)
TOL .... Tanzania Oxygen Limited (MAR)
TOL .... Temporary Occupation License (MAR)
TOL .... Turk Ocagi Ligi [*Turkish Club (Hearth) League*] (TU)
TOLES-IVOIRE ... Societe de Galvanisation de Toles en Cote-d'Ivoire (MAR)
TOLEYIS ..... Turkiye Otel, Lokanta, ve Eglence Yerleri Isci Sendikasi [*Turkish Hotel, Restaurant, and Amusement Place Workers Union*] [*See also OLEYIS*] (TU)
TOLIMO ...... Togoland Liberation Movement (AF)
tolshch .... Thickness (RU)
TOM .... Tagma Oreinon Metaforon [*Mountain Transport Battalion*] [*Greek*] (GC)
TOM .... Technischorganisatorische Massnahmen [*Technical-Organizational Measures*] (EG)
TOM .... Territoires d'Outre-Mer [*Overseas Territories*] [*French*] (AF)
tom .... Till Och Med [*Even*] [*Swedish*] (GPO)
tom .... Tome [*Book*] [*French*]
tom .... Tomo [*Tome, Volume*] [*Spanish*]
TOM .... Tomsk Railroad (RU)
tomat .... Tomato Cannery [*Topography*] (RU)
Tomb .... Tombe [*or Tombeau*] [*Grave*] [*Military map abbreviation*] [*World War I*] [*French*] (MTD)
TOMI .... Tiskovy Odbor Ministerstva Informaci [*Press Department of the Ministry of Information*] (CZ)
TOMILENCO ... Togoland Mill and Engineering Co. Inc. (MAR)
TomNIIVS ... Tomsk Scientific Research Institute of Vaccines and Serums (RU)
TOMP .... All-Union Trust of the Optical Instrument Industry (RU)
TOM-Plan ... Plan der Technischorganisatorischen Massnahmen [*Plan for Technical-Organizational Measures*] (EG)
TOMS .... Turkiye Orman Memurlari Sendikasi [*Turkish Forestry Officials Union*] (TU)
TO-MSv .... Technicky Odbor Ministerstva Stavebnictvi [*Technical Department of the Ministry of Construction*] (CZ)
TON .... Peleton [*Platoon*] (IN)
TON .... Tonga [*Three-letter standard code*] (CNC)
TONAK .... Tovarny na Klobouky [*Hat Factories*] (CZ)
TONGE .... Transactions of the Numismatics Department of the State Ermitage Museum (RU)
TOnZ .... Towarzystwo Opieki nad Zwierzetami [*Society for the Prevention of Cruelty to Animals*] (POL)
TOO .... Technicko-Organisacni Opatreni [*Technical and Organizational Measures*] (CZ)
TOOL .... Teams of Our Lady [*See also END*] (EA)
top .... Fuel (RU)
Top .... Topcu [*Artillery*] (TU)
TOP .... Toplumcu Ozgurluk Partisi [*Socialist Freedom Party*] [*Established spring 1975*] [*Cypriot*] (TU)
top .... Topography (RU)
TOP .... Transports Omer Pressegue (MAR)
TOP .... Tribunal del Orden Publico [*Court of Public Order*] [*Spanish*] (WER)
TOP .... Tunisskie Obshchestva Popecheniia (MAR)
TOP .... Tvornica Olovnih Proizvoda [*Lead Products Factory*] [*Zagreb*] (YU)
topbatr .... Topographic Battery (BU)
topbatr .... Topographic Battery [*Military term*] (RU)
TOPCIM-IS ... Turkiye Toprak Porselen ve Cimento Sanayi Iscileri Sendikasi [*Turkish Earthenware, Porcelain, and Cement Industry Workers' Union*] (TU)
TOPL .... Terenowa Obrona Przeciwlotnicza [*Local Anti-Aircraft Defense*] (POL)
Toplomontazh ... Installation of Heating Equipment (BU)
Topo .... Topografic [*Topographic*] (TU)
TOPO .... Topograficka Sluzba [*Topographic Service*] (CZ)
topotd .... Topographic Department, Topographic Section (RU)
topprom .... Fuel Industry (RU)
TOPRAKSU ... Toprak Muhafaza ve Zirai Sulama Isleri Genel Mudurlugu [*Soil Conservation and Agricultural Irrigation Affairs Directorate General*] (TU)
TOPRAS ...... Toprak Pazarlama Sirketi [*Land (Real Estate) Marketing Corporation*] (TU)
TOPS .... Tovarna Pisalnih Strojev [*Typewriter Factory*] (YU)
TOPSUKOYTAR IS ... Toprak, Su, Koy, Tarim, ve Arastirma Iscileri Sendikasi [*Soil, Water, Village, Agriculture, and Research Workers Union*] (TU)
tor .... Heavy Gun (BU)
TOR .... Sektor [*Sector*] (IN)
TOR .... Techniczna Obsluga Rolnictwa [*Engineering Service for Agriculture*] (POL)

tor............... Torok [*Turkish*] (HU)
TOR............ Towarszystwo Osiedli Robotniczych [*Workers' Settlements Society*] (POL)
torf............ Peat (RU)
torf............ Peat Bank [*Topography*] (RU)
Torfrabsnab ... Moscow Oblast Office for the Peat Industry Workers' Supply (RU)
torg............ Trade (RU)
torg-fin........ Trade and Finance (RU)
Torgizdat.... State Publishing House of Literature on Trade (RU)
Torgposredkontora ... Republic Trade Exchange Office (RU)
Torgsin....... All-Union Association for the Trade with Foreigners (RU)
torguch....... School of Commercial Apprenticeship (RU)
TOR-IS........ Turistik Otel Restoran Iscileri Sendikasi [*Touristic Hotel and Restaurant Workers Union*] [*Izmir*] (TU)
torm........... Torszormester [*Staff Sergeant*] (HU)
TORSAN..... Trakya Orman Urunleri Sanayi ve Ticaret AS [*Thrace Forest Products Industry and Trade Corp.*] (TU)
TOS............ Current-Limiting Resistor (RU)
TOS............ Techniczna Obrobka Szkla [*Heat Processing of Glass*] (POL)
TOS............ Techniczna Obsluga Samochodow [*Automobile Technical Service*] (POL)
TOS............ Terenowy Oddzial Samoobrony [*Local Civil Defense Unit*] (POL)
TOS............ Three-Phase Deflecting System (RU)
TOS............ Tovarny na Obrabeci Stroje [*Machine Tool Factories*] (CZ)
TOS............ Turkiye Ogretmenler Sendikasi [*Turkish Teachers' Union*] (TU)
TOS............ Turkiye Otomotive Sanayii [*Turkish Automotive Industry*] [*See also TOE*] (TU)
TOS............ Tvornica Optickog Stakla [*Optical Glass Factory*] [*Zagreb*] (YU)
TOSD.......... Third Order of Saint Dominic (EA)
TOSLEY-IS ... Ege Bolgesi Turistik Otel Sinema Lokanta, Eglence Yerleri Iscileri Sendikasi [*Aegean Region Touristic, Hotel, Cinema, Restaurant and Amusement Places Workers' Union*] [*Izmir*] (TU)
TOst............ Stop Trigger [*Computers*] (RU)
TOST........... Turkiye Ogretmenler Sendikasi Tiyatrosu [*Turkish Teachers Union Theatre*] (TU)
TOSTA........ Tovarny Stavkoveho Zbozi [*Hosiery Mills*] (CZ)
TOSWL........ Techniczna Oficerska Szkola Wojsk Lotniczych [*Air Force Officers Technical School*] [*Olesnica*] (POL)
TOT............ Termeloszovetkezetek Orszagos Tanacsa [*National Council of Producer Cooperatives*] (HU)
TOT............ Three-Winding Transformer (RU)
TOTI........... Torzstiszt [*Staff Officer*] (HU)
TOTP.......... Transactions of the Department of Commercial Ports (RU)
TOTRA........ Tovarna Trakov [*Ribbon Factory*] [*Ljubljana*] (YU)
t otv........... Temperature of Solidification (RU)
TOURAC..... Association Internationale Auxiliaire des Touring Clubs de l'Afrique Centrale (MAR)
TOURDYK... Tourkiki Dynamis Kyprou [*Turkish Forces in Cyprus*] (GC)
TOURISMAD ... Societe Hoteliere et Touristique de Madagascar (MAR)
tov.............. Comrade (RU)
tov.............. Freight [*Train*] (RU)
TOVALL...... TSZ Onallo Epito es Szereloipari Vallalkozasok [*Producer Cooperative Independent Construction and Assembling Enterprises*] (HU)
TOVChK...... Transportation Department of the All-Russian Extraordinary Commission for Combating Counterrevolution and Sabotage (RU)
TOVE.......... Transactions of the Oriental Department of the State Ermitage Museum (RU)
TOVENCA... Topflight de Venezuela, Compania Anonima
tov st.......... Freight Station [*Topography*] (RU)
TOVU.......... Technicko-Organisacni Vyzkumny Ustav [*Technical and Organizational Research Institute*] (CZ)
TOVUS........ Technicko-Organisacni Vyzkumny Ustav Strojirensky [*Technical and Organizational Research Institute on Machine Building*] (CZ)
tow............. Towarzystwo [*Society, Company*] (POL)
tow............. Towarzysz [*Comrade*] (POL)
TOZ............ Association for Joint Cultivation of Land (RU)
TOZ............ Technischoekonomische Zielstellungen [*Technical-Economic Goals*] (EG)
TOZ............ Towarzystwo Ochrony Zdrowia [*Society of Health Protection*] (POL)
TOZ............ Towarzystwo Opieki nad Zwierzetami [*Society for the Prevention of Cruelty to Animals*] [*Polish*]
TOZ............ Tula Arms Plant (RU)
TOZ............ Tyrsuv Odznak Zdatnosti [*Tyrs Physical Fitness Medal*] (CZ)
TP.............. Aiming Point (RU)
tp............... (And) So On, (And) So Forth (RU)
TP-............. Calibration Furnace (RU)
TP.............. Commercial Port (RU)
TP.............. Current-Supplying Spring (RU)
TP.............. Freight Train (RU)
TP.............. Heat Flow (RU)
TP-............. Pneumatic Conveyor (RU)
TP.............. Point of Fall (RU)
TP.............. Point of Impact (RU)
TP.............. Safety Brake (RU)
TP.............. Tank Gun (RU)
tp............... Tank Regiment (BU)
TP.............. Tank Regiment (RU)
TP.............. Tank Support (RU)
TP.............. Technical Inspection (BU)
TP.............. Technical Paper (MAR)
TP.............. Technical Regulations (RU)
TP.............. Technicke Podminky [*Technical Requirements*] (CZ)
TP.............. Technische Planung [*Technical Planning Office*] (EG)
TP.............. Telegraph and Post (BU)
TP.............. Telephone Out of Order (BU)
TP.............. Telephone Tapping [*Military term*] (RU)
Tp.............. Tempiranje [*Fuse Setting*] [*Artillery*] (YU)
Tp.............. Tepe [*Peak*] [*of a mountain or hill*] (TU)
TP.............. Territorial Party [*Northern Marianas*] (PPW)
TP.............. Theodolite Point (RU)
Tp.............. Thermal [*Nuclear physics and engineering*] (RU)
tp............... Timbre-Poste [*Postage Stamp*] [*French*]
TP.............. Tir de Place [*Military*] [*French*] (MTD)
TP.............. Topografska Planseta [*Map Board*] (YU)
tp............... Tout Paye [*French*]
TP.............. Trade Enterprise (BU)
TP.............. Trajno Prisutni [*Permanently Present*] [*Census*] (YU)
TP.............. Transformer Substation (RU)
TP.............. Transportno Preduzece [*Transportation Establishment*] [*Railroads*] (YU)
TP.............. Trapeza Pisteos [*Credit Bank*] [*Greek*] (GC)
TP.............. Travaux Publics [*Public Works*] [*French*] (WER)
TP.............. Trgovinsko Poduzece [*Commercial Establishment*] (YU)
TP.............. Triangular Prism (RU)
TP.............. Trichlorophenoxypropionic Acid (RU)
Tp.............. Triebwagenzug [*Rail Motor Car Train*] (EG)
TP.............. Trigonometric Point (RU)
TP.............. Trihedral Prism (RU)
TP.............. Trust Podniku [*Trust of Enterprises*] (CZ)
TP.............. Turkiye Petrolleri [*Turkish Petroleum*] (TU)
TP.............. Warm Period (RU)
TPA............ Heavy Gun Artillery (RU)
TPA............ Tarolt Program Adatfeldolgozo (Rendszer) [*Stored Program Data Processing (System)*] (HU)
TPA............ Televisao Popular de Angola (MAR)
TPA............ Togo Pflanzungs-Aktien-Gesellschaft (MAR)
TPA............ Transports Populaires Blideens [*Algerian*] (MAR)
TPAEN........ Tameion Prostasias Axiomatikon Emborikou Navtikou [*Merchant Marine Officers Protection Fund*] [*Greek*] (GC)
TPAO.......... Turkiye Petrol Anonim Ortaklari [*Turkish Petroleum Corporation*] (TU)
tpb............. Pipeline Battalion (BU)
tpb............. Pipeline Battalion (RU)
TPB............ Tractor and Field Cropping Brigade (RU)
TPB............ Tudomanypolitikai Bizottsag [*Committee on Science Policy*] (HU)
tpbr........... Pipeline Brigade (BU)
tpbr........... Pipeline Brigade (RU)
TPC............ Tanganyika Planting Company (MAR)
TPC............ Transports Provost & Cie. (MAR)
TPCh.......... Commercial Frequency Current (RU)
TPD............ Tameion Parakatathikon kai Daneion [*Savings and Loan Fund*] [*Greek*] (GC)
TPD............ Tameion Pronoias Dikigoron [*Lawyers Welfare Fund*] [*Greek*] (GC)
TPD............ Towarzystwo Przyjaciol Dzieci [*Society of the Friends of Children*] (POL)
TPD............ Tribunal Populaire de District [*District People's Court*] [*Beninese*] (AF)
TPD............ Turkiye Proleter Devrimcileri [*Turkish Proletarian Revolutionaries*] (TU)
TPDC.......... Tanzania Petroleum Development Corporation (MAR)
TPDF.......... Tanzania People's Defense Forces (AF)
TPDUH........ Ministry of Public Works and Lands, Urbanism, and Housing (MAR)
TPDY.......... Tameion Pronoias Dimosion Ypallilon [*Civil Servants Welfare Fund*] [*Greek*] (GC)
TPE............ Heavy Industry and Electrification (BU)
TPE............ Travaux Publics de l'Etat [*State Public Works*] [*Tunisian*] (AF)
TPE Abteilung ... Typhus, Paratyphus, und Enteritis Abteilung [*Typhus, Paratyphus, and Enteritis Department*] (EG)
TPEK.......... Aeroporiki Etaireia Notiou Afrikis [*South African Air Line*] (GC)
TPEN.......... Tameion Pronoias Emborikou Navtikou [*Merchant Marine Welfare Fund*] [*Greek*] (GC)
t per........... Transition Temperature (RU)
TPF............ Tanzanian People's Front (AF)
TPF............ Technicko-Prumyslovy a Financni Plan [*Technical, Industrial, and Financial Plan*] (CZ)
TPF............ Thiamine Pyrophosphate (RU)
TPFLM........ Trano Printy Fiangonana Loterana Malagasy (MAR)
TPFP.......... Technicko-Prumyslovy a Financni Plan [*Technical, Industrial, and Financial Plan*] (CZ)
TPF Plan..... Techniczno-Przemyslowo-Finansowy Plan [*Technical, Industrial, and Financial Plan*] (POL)

TPG .... Rear Field Hospital (RU)
TPG .... Taiping [*Malaysia*] (ML)
TPGF .... Tropas Populares de Guarda-Fronteiras [*People's Border Guard Troops*] [*Angolan*] (AF)
TPH .... Tanzania Publishing House Limited (MAR)
TPI .... Flotation Equipment (BU)
TPI .... Tallinn Polytechnic Institute (RU)
TPI .... Tbilisi Polytechnic Institute (RU)
TPI .... Technischphysikalisches Institut [*Technical-Physical Institute (at Friedrich-Schiller University, Jena)*] (EG)
TPI .... Tomsk Polytechnic Institute Imeni S. M. Kirov (RU)
TPI .... Tropical Products Institute (MAR)
TPI .... Tvornica za Pamucnu Industriju [*Cotton Industrial Mill*] [*Zagreb*] (YU)
TPIIYa .... Tbilisi Pedagogical Institute of Foreign Languages (RU)
TPIM .... Tout pour l'Interieur de la Maison (MAR)
TPIS .... Tropical Pesticides Information Service (MAR)
TPK .... Commander's Tank Periscope (RU)
TPK .... Labor Productive Cooperative (BU)
TPK .... Torzsparancsnok [*Staff Commander (Usually in civil defense)*] (HU)
TPK .... Tvornica Parnih Kotlova [*Steam Boiler Factory*] [*Zagreb*] (YU)
TPKK .... Turk Parasi Kiymetini Koruma [*Protection of Turkish Monetary Value*] (TU)
TPKPEN .... Tameion Pronoias Katoteron Pliromaton Emborikou Navtikou [*Merchant Marine Welfare Fund for Lower-Ranking Seamen*] [*Greek*] (GC)
TPKSI .... Turkiye Petrol ve Kimya Sanayii Iscileri Sendikasi [*Turkish Petroleum and Chemical Industry Workers Union*] (TU)
t pl .... Melting Point (RU)
TPL .... Tanganyika Packers Limited (MAR)
TPL .... Tribunal Populaire Local [*Local People's Court*] [*Beninese*] (AF)
TPLA .... Turkish People's Liberation Army (PD)
TPLF .... Tigre People's Liberation Front [*Ethiopian*] (PD)
TPLP .... Turkish People's Liberation Party (PD)
TPM .... Taxe a la Production Majoree [*Tunisian*] (MAR)
TPM .... Towarzystwo Przyjaciol Nauk [*Society of Friends of Learning*] (POL)
TPMSW .... Towarzystwo Przyjaciol Mlodziezy Szkol Wyzszych [*Society of Friends of University and College Youth*] (POL)
TPN .... Tatrzanski Park Narodowy [*Tatra National Park*] [*Polish*]
TPN .... Towarzystwo Przyjaciol Nauk [*Society of the Friends of Science*] [*Polish*]
TPNiSz .... Towarzystwo Przyjaciol Nauki i Sztuki [*Society of Friends of Science and Art*] (POL)
TPNiSz w Gd ... Towarzystwo Przyjaciol Nauki i Sztuki w Gdansku [*Gdansk (Danzig) Society of Friends of Science and Art*] (POL)
TPO .... Heavy Infantry Flame-Thrower (RU)
TPO .... Industrial Design Organization (BU)
tpo .... Tiempo [*Time*] [*Spanish*]
TPO .... Turkiye Petrol Ofisi Genel Mudurlugu [*Turkish Petroleum Office Directorate General*] [*See also PO*] (TU)
TPOM .... Travail et Profession d'Outre-Mer (MAR)
TPP .... Freight and Passenger Train (RU)
TPP .... Heavy Bridge Train (RU)
TPP .... Platinum-Rhodium Alloy-Platinum Thermocouple (RU)
TPP .... Strength Loss Temperature (RU)
TPP .... Tanks in Support of Infantry (RU)
TPP .... Taxpayers and Producers Party [*Seychelles*] (AF)
TPP .... Textilni Pomocne Pripravky [*Auxiliary Materials for the Textile Industry*] (CZ)
TPP .... Timbalan Penguasa Polis [*Deputy Superintendent of Police*] (ML)
TPP .... Toledo Progressive Party [*Belizean*] (PPW)
TPP .... Towarzystwo Produkcji Przemyslowej [*Industrial Production Society*] (POL)
TPP .... Tribunal Populaire de Province [*People's Court of the Province*] [*Beninese*] (AF)
TPP .... Trust of Manufacturing Establishments (RU)
TPPB .... Mobile Therapeutical Field Hospital (BU)
TPPE .... Tmima Poleodomias kai Poleodomikon Efarmogon [*City Planning and City Planning Enforcement Department*] (GC1)
TPPG .... Mobile Therapeutical Field Hospital (BU)
TPPG .... Therapeutic Field Mobile Hospital (RU)
TPPN .... Towarzystwo Przyjazni Polsko-Norweskiej [*Society for Polish-Norwegian Friendship*] [*Polish*]
TPPR .... Towarzystwo Przyjazni Polsko-Radzieckiej [*Society for Polish-Soviet Friendship*] (POL)
TPPTT .... Tarifni Pravilnik Postansko-Telegrafsko-Telefonski [*Rate Regulations of the Postal, Telegraph, and Telephone Services*] (YU)
TPR .... Current Planned Repairs (BU)
tpr .... Pipeline Company (BU)
TPR .... Taxe a la Production Reduite [*Tunisian*] (MAR)
TPR .... Teatr Polskiego Radia [*The Theatre of the Polish Radio*] [*Polish*]
TPR .... Tendencia Proletaria Revolucionaria [*Revolutionary Proletarian Faction*] [*Mexican*] (LA1)
TPR .... Terga Preliminary Reports (MAR)
TPr .... Tyutyunov Pregled [*Tobacco Review*] [*A periodical*] (BU)
t prevr .... Transformation Temperature, Critical Point (RU)
TPRF .... Tropical Plant Research Foundation (MAR)
TPRI .... Tropical Pesticide Research Institute (MAR)
TPRI .... Tropical Pesticide Research Institute of Tanganyika (MAR)
TPriv .... Drive Flip-Flop (RU)
TPRP .... Towarzystwo Przyjazni Radziecko-Polskiej [*Society for Soviet-Polish Friendship*] (POL)
TPS .... Relay Transmitter (RU)
TPS .... Taxe sur les Prestations de Service [*French*]
TPS .... Taxe sur les Produits et les Services (MAR)
TPS .... Technical Manufacturing Council (RU)
TPS .... Telegraph and Post Office (BU)
TPS .... Telegraphie par le Sol [*Military*] [*French*] (MTD)
TPS .... Tempat Pemungutan Suara [*Polling Place*] (IN)
TPS .... Thermal Direction-Finding Station (RU)
TPS .... Tourism Promotion Services (MAR)
TPS .... Turnovo Court of Reconciliation (BU)
tpsl .... Telegraph and Post Service (BU)
TPSL .... Tyoevaeen ja Pienviljelijaein Sosialidemokraattinen Liitto [*Social Democratic League of Workers and Smallholders*] [*Finnish*] (PPE)
TPSM .... Transports Populaires Sahel Mitidja [*Algerian*] (MAR)
TPSP .... Towarzystwo Przyjaciol Sztuk Pieknych [*Society of Friends of the Fine Arts*] (POL)
TPT .... Alternating-Current Theory (RU)
TPT .... Totul pentru Tara [*"All for the Fatherland"*] [*Romanian*] (PPE)
TPT .... Travail pour Tous [*Work for All*] [*French*] (WER)
TPT .... Trestni Pracovni Tabor [*Penal Labor Camp*] (CZ)
TPTC .... Tanzania Posts and Telecommunications Corporation (MAR)
TPU .... Rear-Area Control Post (RU)
TPU .... Standardized Technological Process (RU)
TPU .... Tank Intercom (RU)
TPU .... Technical Production Administration (RU)
TPU .... Territorial Production Administration (RU)
TPU .... Tiv Progressive Union (MAR)
TPU .... Universal Pneumatic Midget Turbine (RU)
TPusk .... Start Trigger [*Computers*] (RU)
TPV .... Technicka Priprava Vyroby [*Technical Preparations for Production*] (CZ)
Tpv .... Triebwagenzug [*Rail Motor Car Train*] (EG)
TPV .... Withdrawable Soil Thermometer (RU)
TPVN .... Tameion Pronoias Vasilikou Navtikou [*Royal Navy Welfare Fund*] [*Greek*] (GC)
TPW .... Technischphysikalische Werkstaetten (VEB) [*Technical-Physical Workshops (VEB)*] (EG)
TPZ .... Rear March Security Patrol (BU)
TPZ .... Rear Security Detachment (RU)
TPZ .... Towarzystwo Przyjaciol Zolnierza [*Society of Soldier's Friends*] (POL)
TPZK .... Labor Productive Craftsmen's Cooperative (BU)
TQ .... Timbre de Quittance [*Receipt Stamp*] (CL)
TR .... Current Relay (RU)
TR .... Current Repair (RU)
tr .... Floor [*Swedish*] (CED)
TR .... Isolation Transformer (RU)
Tr- .... Mercury Thyratron (RU)
TR .... Severely Wounded (RU)
TR .... Single-Perforated Powder (RU)
TR .... Tactical Missile (RU)
TR .... Tactical Reconnaissance (RU)
tr .... Tank Company (BU)
TR .... Tank Company (RU)
TR .... Tecnicka Rada [*Technical Council*] (CZ)
TR .... Telephone Relay (RU)
TR- .... Teleradiometer (RU)
TR .... Temperature Relay (RU)
t-r .... Theater (RU)
TR .... Thermal Dissolution (RU)
TR .... Thermoregulator, Heat Controller (RU)
Tr .... Thousand Rubles (RU)
tR .... Tierische Rohstoffe [*Animal Raw Materials*] (EG)
TR .... Tir Rapide [*Military*] [*French*] (MTD)
tr .... Tohoto Roku [*Of This Year*] (CZ)
Tr .... Torni [*Tower*] [*Finnish*] (NAU)
Tr .... Tour [*Tower*] [*French*] (NAU)
TR .... Train Regimentaire [*Military*] [*French*] (MTD)
tr .... Traite [*Agreement*] [*French*]
tr .... Transactions (RU)
Tr .... Transforme [*Transformed*] [*French*] (MTD)
TR .... Transformer (RU)
tr .... Transitiiviverbi [*Verb Transitive*] [*Finnish*]
TR .... Transportation Company (RU)
Tr .... Tratte [*Draft*] [*Business and trade*] [*German*]
tr .... Travessa [*Cross*] [*Portuguese*] (CED)
TR .... Trgovinska Radnja [*Commercial Shop*] (YU)
TR .... Tribus (MAR)
tr .... Trida [*Class, Avenue*] (CZ)
Tr .... Trud [*Labor*] [*A newspaper*] (BU)
TR .... Turkey [*Two-letter standard code*] (CNC)
tr .... Tytar [*Finnish*]
Tr .... Works (BU)

t-ra .... Temperature (RU)
trab .... Transport Aviation Base (BU)
TRACTOIMPORT ... Empresa Cubana Importadora de Maquinarias y Equipos Agricolas [*Cuban Enterprise for the Import of Agricultural Machinery and Equipment*] (LA)
trad .... Transport Aviation Division (BU)
TRADEVCO ... Liberian Trading and Development Bank Ltd. (MAR)
TRAF .... Societe Transports Africains (MAR)
TRAFIPRO... Travail, Fidelite, Progres (MAR)
TRAFOSAN ... Transformator Sanayii Anonim Sirketi [*Transformer Industry Corporation*] (TU)
TRAGESOM ... Travaux Generaux Sous-Marins (MAR)
Tragk .... Tragkraft [*Load*] [*German*]
tragr .... Transport Aviation Group (BU)
trak............. Transport Aviation Wing (BU)
t-ra kip .... Boiling Point (RU)
Trakt .... Tractor Plant [*Topography*] (RU)
trakt brig..... Tractor Team (RU)
trakt st .... Tractor Station (RU)
tralbaza....... Trawler Base, Mine Sweeper Base (RU)
TRAM .... Theater of Young Workers (RU)
TRAM .... Transports Automobiles et Manutentions [*Dakar*] (MAR)
TRAMCO..... Tanzania Railway Manufacturing Company (MAR)
TRAMETALCO ... Compania de Trabajos Metalicos y Estructurales [*Bogota*] (COL)
TRAMO .... Tanzania Railway Wagon Manufacturing Company (MAR)
TRANCHE ... Travail Nucleaire Chef
Tranposektsiya ... All-Union Central Autonomous Section of Consumers' Cooperative Societies of Railroad and Water Transportation Workers at the Tsentrosoyuz (RU)
TRANSACO ... Compagnie Africaine de Transactions Internationales (MAR)
TRANSAFRIC ... Societe de Transit et de Transports en Afrique (MAR)
TRANSBALBOA ... Compania de Transportes Balboa Ltda. [*Bogota*] (COL)
TRANSCAM ... Chemin de Fer Trans-Camerounais [*Trans-Cameroonian Railroad*] (AF)
TRANSCAP-NIGER ... Societe Eurafricaine de Voyage, de Transit, et de Camionnage Portuaire (MAR)
TRANSCARTOL ... Cooperativa de Transportadores de Carga del Tolima [*Ibague*] (COL)
TRANSCOBOIS ... Societe de Transport et de Commercialisation des Bois en Provenance de Centrafrique, Cameroun, et Gabon (MAR)
TRANSCOGAZ ... Societe Transcontinentale des Gaz de Petrole BP (MAR)
TRANSCOM ... Societe Nationale de Transports en Commun (MAR)
TRANSCONGO SA ... Societe de Transports du Congo (MAR)
TRANSCRUZ ... Transportes Unidos Cruz [*Bogota*] (COL)
TRANSELEKTRO ... TRANSELEKTRO Villamossagi Kulkereskedelmi Vallalat [*TRANSELEKTRO Foreign Trade Enterprise for Electric Power*] (HU)
Transelektromontazh ... All-Union Specialized Installation Trust for Railroad Electrification (RU)
Transelektroproyekt ... State Planning and Surveying Institute of Railroad Electrification and Power Installations of the State Industrial Committee for Transportation Construction, USSR (RU)
TRANSEQUAT ... Societe de Transit Equatorial (MAR)
TRANSFEDERAL ... Transportes Federados Huila, Cauca, Caqueta Ltda. [*Bogota*] (COL)
TRANSFLUVIAL ... Transportes Fluviales Magdalena Ltda. [*Barranquilla*] (COL)
TRANSFRACHT ... Deutsche Transportgesellschaft [*German Transport Company*] [*West German*] (WEN)
TRANSFRIA ... Societe des Transports et des Installations Portuaires de Fria (MAR)
Transgidromekhanizatsiya ... Specialized Trust of Mechanized Hydraulic Operations of the Glavmorrechstroy (RU)
Transgidrostroy ... All-Union Trust for the Construction of Hydraulic Engineering Structures of the Glavrechstroy (RU)
Transgiz...... State Publishing House of Transportation and Railroad Literature (RU)
TRANSGRUM ... Societe Anonyme Exploitation et Transport de Grumes (MAR)
TRANSIMOL ... Sociedade Transitaria de Mocambique Lda. (MAR)
TRANSIMPORT ... Empresa Cubana Importadora de Transporte (Vehiculos y Equipos) [*Cuban Enterprise for the Import of Vehicles and Transportation Equipment*] (LA)
transl........... Translatiivi [*Finnish*]
TRANSLAG ... Transports Lagunaires (MAR)
Translesproyekt ... Planning Office of the Glavtransles (RU)
TRANSLITORAL ... Transportes el Litoral Ltda. [*Cali*] (COL)
TRANSLOBO ... Societe de Transports de la Lobo (MAR)
TRANSMAR ... Transportes el Mar SA [*Bogota*] (COL)
Transmash ... Ministry of Transportation Machinery Manufacture (RU)
TRANSMECA ... Transports Mecaniques (MAR)
Transmedsnabtorg ... Office for the Supply of Medical Equipment and Sale of Drugs on Railroads (RU)
TRANSMER ... Societe de Transformation des Produits de la Mer (MAR)
Transmostproyekt ... All-Union Specialized Office for the Planning and Surveying of Large Railroad Bridges (RU)
Transorgmashuchet ... State Trust for the Organization of Mechanized Accounting of the Ministry of Railroads, USSR (RU)
Transotdelstroy ... Trust for Architectural and Finishing Work of the Glavzheldorstroy of the Central and Western Regions (RU)
transp .... Transportation, Transport (RU)
Transpechat' ... Administration for the Distribution and Dispatch of Publications of Transzheldorizdat (RU)
TRANSPLAN ... Transportation Planning Commission (RU)
Transproekt ... Transport Design Institute (BU)
Transproyektkar'yer ... Office for the Surveying and Planning of Quarries for Transportation Needs (RU)
TRANSRAPID ... Les Transports Rapides du Cameroun (MAR)
Transremstroy ... Transportation Repair and Construction Office (RU)
Transsignalstroy ... All-Union Trust of the Glavtranselektromontazh of the Ministry of Transportation Construction, USSR (RU)
Transsnab... Transport Supplies Organization (BU)
Transspetsstroy ... Trust for Special and Road Work of the Ministry of Construction, USSR (RU)
Transstroyprom ... Trust of Industrial Establishments of the Glavstroymekhanizatsiya (RU)
Transstroypromkonstruktsiya ... Trust of the Glavstroyprom of the Ministry of Transportation Construction, USSR (RU)
Transsvyaz'stroy ... All-Union Trust of the Glavmontazhstroy of the Ministry of Transportation Construction, USSR (RU)
Transteiproyekt ... All-Union Planning Office for Technical and Economical Problems and for the Study of Scientific Methods in Railroad Transportation (RU)
Transtekhmontazh ... Trust of the Glavzheldorstroy of the Central and Western Regions of the Ministry of Transportation Construction, USSR (RU)
Transtekhproyekt ... State Planning Institute for the Design and Study of Technical Structures in Railroad Transportation (RU)
Transtorgsnab ... All-Union Office of the Glavurs of the Ministry of Railroads, USSR (RU)
TRANSUD ... Societe des Transports du Sud de Madagascar (MAR)
TRANSUNIS ... Societe des Transitaires Unis (MAR)
TRANSURBAINS ... Regie Autonome des Transports Urbains [*Autonomous Urban Transport Administration*] [*Cambodian*] (CL)
Transzavodproyekt ... State Institute for the Planning of Plants on Transportation Routes (RU)
Transzheldorizdat ... All-Union Publishing and Printing Association of the Ministry of Railroads, USSR (RU)
TRANSZVILL ... Transzformator es Villamoskeszulekgyar [*Factory for Transformers and Electric Appliances*] (HU)
tranz........... Transit, Transient (RU)
TRAP........... Air Transport Regiment (RU)
TRAP........... Transportni Avio Puk [*Air Transport Regiment*] (YU)
TRAPAG...... Societe Industrielle de Stockage et de Traitement de Produits Agricoles (MAR)
TRAPAL ...... Societe pour le Transport des Hydrocarbures Sahariens au Littoral Algerien (MAR)
TRAPES ...... Societe des Transports des Petroles de l'Est Saharien (MAR)
t-ra plavl ..... Melting Point (RU)
TRAPO .... Transportpolizei [*Transportation Police*] (EG)
TRAPSA...... Compagnie des Transports par Pipeline au Sahara [*Saharan Pipeline Transportation Company*] [*Algerian*] (AF)
TRATAM ..... Transportes Titiribi Amaga-Medellin Ltda. [*Medellin*] (COL)
TRAU........... Tanganyika Railway African Union (MAR)
TraV .... Transpress Verlag fuer Verkehrswesen [*"Transpress" Publishing House for Transportation Affairs*] (EG)
TRAVAUX ... Compagnie Congolaise de Travaux Publics Congo (MAR)
TRAVCAMAP ... Etudes et Travaux du Centre d'Archeologie Mediterraneenne de l'Academie Polonaise des Sciences [*Varsovie*] [*A publication*] (MAR)
TRAV IRS.... Travaux de l'Institut de Recherches Sahariennes [*Algerian*] [*A publication*] (MAR)
t ravn........... Equilibrium Temperature (RU)
t razl........... Decomposition Temperature (RU)
t razmyagch ... Softening Point (RU)
TRB .... Big Fishing Trawler (RU)
TRB-............ Thyratron Relay Unit (RU)
TRBR........... Tobacco Research Board of Rhodesia (MAR)
TRC .... Tanzania Railway Corporation (AF)
TRCL........... Trustul Regional de Constructii Locale [*Regional Trust for Local Constructions*] (RO)
TRCLB .... Trustul Regional de Constructii Locale Bucuresti [*Bucharest Regional Trust for Local Constructions*] (RO)
Tr Comb...... Train de Combat [*Military*] [*French*] (MTD)
TRD............ Liquid-Fuel Jet Engine (BU)
tr-d .... Pipeline (RU)
TRD .... Tehran Redevelopment Corporation (ME)
TRD .... Turbojet Engine (RU)
TRDA........... Tana River Development Authority (MAR)
TRDB........... Tanzania Rural Development Bank (MAR)
TRDF........... Turbojet Engine with Afterburner (RU)
TRDV........... Turboprop Engine (RU)
Tre............... Torre [*Tower*] [*Italian*] (NAU)
TRE .... Tribunal Regional Eleitoral [*Regional Electoral Court*] [*Brazilian*] (LA1)
TRED........... Work Report Unit (RU)
TREFILCO... Trefileria Colombiana SA [*Bucaramanga*] (COL)
t rekrist ...... Recrystallization Temperature (RU)
tremb .... Tank Repair Battalion (RU)

TRez .... Tank Reserve (RU)
TRF .... Tariff Clerk (RU)
TRFA .... Tanga Regional Football Association (MAR)
TRGK .... Tank Reserve of the High Command (RU)
TRGOPRED ... Trgovinsko Preduzece [*Commercial Establishment*] (YU)
TRGOTEKSTIL ... Trgovina Tekstilom [*Textile Trade*] (YU)
TRI .... Taganrog Radiotechnical Institute (RU)
Tri .... Tohtori [*Doctor*] [*Finnish*] (GPO)
TRIB .... Towarzystwo Robot Inzynierskich i Budowlanych [*Engineering and Construction Work Company*] (POL)
tribl .... Tribunal [*Spanish*]
TRIBOIS ...... Societe de Transformation Industrielle du Bois (MAR)
TRICO .... Training, Research, Isotope Production Reactor, Congo (MAR)
TRICOMAD ... Societe Industrielle des Tricotages de Madagascar (MAR)
TRIEA .... Tea Research Institute of East Africa (MAR)
trig .... Trigonometric, Trigonometry (RU)
TRIGAB .... Tricots Gabonais (MAR)
trik .... Knitting, Knit-Goods (RU)
TRIKORA .... Tri Komando Rakjat [*Three Commands of the People (Refers to West Irian campaign)*] (IN)
trim .... Trimestre [*Trimester*] [*French*]
TRIMECAF ... Societe de Tricotage Mecanique Africain (MAR)
TRIMETA .... Societe de Tricotage Mecanique de Tananarive (MAR)
TRINDELCI ... Travaux Industriels pour l'Electricite Cote-d'Ivoire (MAR)
TRINTOC .... Trinidad and Tobago Oil Company (LA1)
TRIP .... Transports Interregionaux de Personnes [*Interregional Personnel Transportation*] [*French*] (WER)
TRITURAF ... Societe Ivoirienne pour la Trituration des Graines Oleagineuses et le Raffinage d'Huiles Vegetales (MAR)
TriV .... Tribuene Verlag [*"Tribuene" Publishing House*] (EG)
TRJN .... Tymczasowy Rzad Jednosci Narodowej [*Provisional Government of National Unity (1945-1947)*] [*Polish*]
TRK .... Poorly Soluble Components (RU)
tr-k .... Triangle (RU)
Tr KMA .... Transactions of the Special Commission for the Research on the Kursk Magnetic Anomaly (RU)
Tr Knt Nok ... Trafik Kontrol Noktasi [*Traffic Control Point*] (TU)
TRL .... Telegraph Line Relay (RU)
Trl .... Treuil [*Windlass*] [*Military map abbreviation*] [*World War I*] [*French*] (MTD)
TRM .... Local Telegraph Relay (RU)
TRM .... Tank-Repair Shop (RU)
TRM .... Technikum Rybolowstwa Morskiego [*Sea Fishery Technical School*] (POL)
TRM .... Toutes Roues Motrices (MAR)
TRM .... Transport Regional Maritim [*Regional Maritime Transportation*] (RO)
trm .... Trekhondos Minos [*Current Month*] (GC1)
TRMA .... Tank-Repair Shop, Type A (RU)
TRMB .... Tank-Repair Shop, Type B (RU)
TRML .... Terenowa Rada Modelarstwa Lotniczego [*Local Council for Airplane Models*] (POL)
TRML .... Tropical Research Medical Laboratory (MAR)
TrN .... Storage Transformer (RU)
TRO .... Transformatorenwerk Oberschoeneweide (VEB) [*Berlin-Oberschoeneweide Transformer Works (VEB)*] (EG)
TRO .... Transportation Department, Transport Section (RU)
TRODECOL ... Troquelados de Colombia Ltda. [*Cali*] (COL)
TROMECAN ... Troqueleria Mecanica [*Medellin*] (COL)
trop .... Tropical (RU)
TROP .... Tropical Agriculture [*Guildford, Surrey*] [*A publication*] (MAR)
TROPIC .... Societe des Forges Tropicales (MAR)
TROPIC .... Societe Tropicale des Piles (MAR)
TROPM .... Tropical Man [*Leiden*] [*A publication*] (MAR)
TROPMED ... Regional Tropical Medicine and Public Health [*Center*] [*Subsidiary of SEAMEC*] (CL)
TROS .... Televisie Radio Omroep Stichting [*Television-Radio Broadcasting Corporation*] [*Dutch*] (WEN)
TROTRA ...... Societe Tropicale de Transports (MAR)
TRP .... Memory Configuration Table [*Computers*] (RU)
Tr p .... Trigonometric Point [*Topography*] (RU)
Trp .... Tropfpunkt [*Drip Point*] [*German*]
TrPrlzpD ..... Papers of the Society of Natural Science (BU)
TRPSh .... Transformer Regulated with Shunt Magnetization (RU)
TRPT-Nr ...... Transport-Genehmigungs Nummer [*Transportation Permit Number*] (EG)
TRR .... Tank Repair Shop (BU)
tr-r .... Transformer (RU)
Trr .... Trestni Rad [*Code of Criminal Procedure*] (CZ)
Trr .... Trestni Rizeni [*Criminal Procedure*] (CZ)
Tr Reg .... Train Regimentaire [*Military*] [*French*] (MTD)
TRS .... Spin-Stabilized Missile (RU)
TRS .... Television Relay Station (RU)
TRS .... Torunska Rektyfikacja Spirytusu [*Torun Alcohol Distillation Plant*] (POL)
Tr s .... Transport Facility (BU)
TRSp .... Coincidence Flip-Flop (RU)
Trsp .... Transportieren [*Transport*] [*German*] [*Business and trade*]
TRT .... Solid Rocket Propellant (RU)
TRT .... Telecommunications Radio-Electriques et Telephoniques [*North African*] (MAR)
TRT .... Telefongyar [*Telephone Factory*] (HU)
TRT .... Transportation for Severely Wounded (RU)
TrT .... Truppenteil [*Unit*] [*Military*] (EG)
TRT .... Turk Radyo ve Televisyon Idaresi [*Turkish Radio and Television Administration*] (TU)
TRTA .... Telecommunications Radio-Electriques Africaines [*Algerian*] (MAR)
TRT-DER ..... Tum Radyo Televizyon Calisanlari Dernegi [*Comprehensive Radio and Television Workers Organization*] (TU)
TRTG .... Tactical Radar Threat Generator (MAR)
TRTI .... Taganrog Radiotechnical Institute (RU)
TRTs .... Initial Point to the Target (RU)
TRU .... Tank Radio Set (BU)
TRU .... Taxa Rodoviaria Unica [*Single Road Tax*] [*Brazilian*] (LA)
trub .... Pipe-Rolling Mill [*Topography*] (RU)
trud .... Work, Labor (RU)
trudchast' ... Work Team, Military Work Team (RU)
Trud kol ...... Labor Colony (RU)
Trudrezervizdat ... All-Union Publishing House of Textbooks and Pedagogical Literature of the Main Administration of Labor Reserves at the Council of Ministers, USSR (RU)
TRUTAS ...... Truva Sanayi ve Ticaret Anonim Sirketi [*Truva Industry and Trade Corporation*] (TU)
TRUVA .... Truva Shipping Co. Ltd. [*Cypriot*] (TU)
TRV .... Thermal Timing Relay (RU)
TRV .... Thermoregulating Valve (RU)
TRV .... Tiszantuli Rostkikeszito Vallalat [*Fiber Processing Industry of the Trans-Tisza Region*] (HU)
TRVA .... Automatic Thermoregulating Valve (RU)
TRWC .... Tehran Regional Water Company (ME)
TRZ .... Diesel Locomotive Repair Plant (RU)
Trz .... Trestni Zaken [*Criminal Law*] (CZ)
TRZh .... Hydraulic Thermoregulator (RU)
TRZZ .... Terenowa Rada Zwiazkow Zawodowych [*Local Trade Union Council*] (POL)
TRZZ .... Towarzystwo Rozwoju Ziem Zachodnich [*Society for the Development of the Western Territories*] (POL)
°Ts .... Celsius Degree [*°C*] (RU)
Ts .... Cement (RU)
ts .... Center (BU)
ts .... Centner (RU)
TS .... Coupled Trolley Bus (RU)
t/s .... Current Account (RU)
Ts .... Cylindrical (RU)
TS .... Dark Glass (RU)
TS .... Dictionary of Commodities [*A publication*] (RU)
ts .... Digital, Number, Numerical (RU)
TS .... Grid Transformer (RU)
TS .... Power Transformer (RU)
ts .... Price (RU)
Ts .... Rate of Fire (RU)
TS .... Remote Signal System (RU)
TS .... Resistance Temperature (RU)
TS .... Resistance Thermometer (RU)
TS .... Restaurant Trust (RU)
TS .... Sectional Turbodrill (RU)
ts .... Shop (RU)
TS .... Signal Transformer (RU)
TS .... Solid Lubricant (RU)
TS .... Spin-Stabilized Missile (RU)
TS .... Stabilizing Transformer (RU)
ts .... Tanarseged [*Assistant to a Professor*] (HU)
TS .... Tanecni Soubor [*Dance Ensemble*] (CZ)
TS .... Tank Unit (RU)
Ts .... Target, Objective (RU)
TS .... Tarif Special [*French*]
TS .... Technical Specifications (RU)
TS .... Technicka Skupina [*Technical Group*] (CZ)
TS .... Technicka Sprava [*Technical Directorate*] (CZ)
TS .... Tehnicka Sredstva [*Technical Equipment*] [*Military*] (YU)
TS .... Telegrafska Stanica [*Telegraph Station*] [*Military*] (YU)
TS .... Telegraph Station (BU)
TS .... Telegraph Station (RU)
TS .... Telephone Exchange (RU)
ts .... Television Station (RU)
TS .... Thermistor (RU)
TS- .... Thermometric Signaler (RU)
TS- .... Thermostat (RU)
TS .... Thymol Blue [*Indicator*] (RU)
TS .... Tirailleurs Senegalais (MAR)
ts .... Tisztes [*Junior Noncommissioned Officer*] (HU)
TS .... Tmimatikon Symvoulion [*Branch Council*] (GC)
TS .... Toa Soan [*Editor*] (TVP)
ts .... Toisin Sanoen [*In Other Words*] [*Finnish*] (GPO)
TS .... Tolkien Society (EA)
ts .... Ton-Force (RU)
TS .... Topographic Service (RU)
TS .... Tragkraftspritze [*Portable Power Sprayer (Fire-fighting equipment)*] (EG)
TS .... Traitements, Salaries (MAR)
TS .... Transformatorska Stanica [*Transformer Station*] (YU)

TS........ Transportation Construction (RU)
TS........ Transportna Sluzba [*Transport Service*] [*Railroads*] (YU)
TS........ Trockensubstanz [*Dry Matter*] (EG)
TS........ Trotyl Sulfite (RU)
TS........ Turcianske Strojarne [*Engineering Works, Turciansky Svaty Martin*] (CZ)
TS........ Turk Standartlar [*Turkish Standards*] [*Referring to TSE-designated equipment*] (TU)
TS........ Turner Society (EA)
TsA........ Cementation Unit (RU)
TsA........ Central Operating Room, Central Manual Switchroom [*Telephony*] (RU)
TsA........ Digital Automation (RU)
TSA........ Etablissements Thivolle SA (MAR)
TSA........ Tameion Syndaxeon Avtokinitiston [*Drivers' Retirement Fund*] [*Greek*] (GC)
TSA........ Tanzania Sisal Authority (MAR)
tsa........ Tarsa [*Business Partner*] (HU)
TSA........ Tragkraftspritze Anhaenger [*Portable Power Sprayer Trailer (Fire-fighting equipment, used for transportation of the low-pressure pump)*] (EG)
TsAB........ Central Address Bureau (RU)
tsae........ Medical Air Transport Group (BU)
TsAF........ Central Aerial Surveying Film Library (RU)
TsAGE........ Central Aerogeological Expedition (RU)
TsAGI........ Central Institute of Aerohydrodynamics Imeni N. Ye. Zhukovskiy (RU)
TsAGRU........ Central Agricultural Administration (RU)
TSAGU........ Transactions of the Central Asia State University (RU)
tsai........ Tarsai [*Partners*] (HU)
TsAK........ Central Aviation Club (BU)
TsAK........ Central Aviation Club of the USSR Imeni V. P. Chkalov (RU)
TsAKA........ Central Archives of the Red Army (RU)
TsAL........ Central Laboratory of Batteries (RU)
TsAMA........ Central Model Aircraft Laboratory (BU)
TsAMK........ Central Automobile-Motorcycle Club (BU)
TsAMK........ Central Automobile and Motorcycle Club of the USSR (RU)
TsAML........ Central Model Aircraft Laboratory (BU)
TsAML........ Central Model Aircraft Laboratory (RU)
TsAMMF........ Central Archives of the Ministry of the Maritime Fleet (RU)
TsAMS........ Central Air Weather Station (RU)
TsAMSG........ Central Air Weather Station of the Civil Air Fleet (RU)
TsANII........ Central Pharmaceutical Scientific Research Institute (RU)
TsANII........ Central Scientific Research Institute of Automobile Operation (RU)
TsANIIP........ Central American Industrial Scientific Research Institute (RU)
TsANIL........ Central Pharmaceutical Scientific Research Laboratory [*1940-1944*] (RU)
TsANIS........ Central Pharmaceutical Scientific Research Station [*1931-1940*] (RU)
TsANKh........ Central Archives of the National Economy [*in Leningrad*] (RU)
TsANS........ Central Air Navigation Station (RU)
TsAO........ Central Aerological Observatory (RU)
TSAOA........ Tameion Syndaxeon kai Arogis Organon Agrofylakis [*Rural Police Pension and Assistance Fund*] [*Greek*] (GC)
TsAOR........ Central Archives of the October Revolution (RU)
TsAOS........ Central Pharmaceutical Experimental Station [*1928-1931*] (RU)
TsAP........ Central Artillery Post [*on shipboard*] (RU)
TsAP........ Digital-Analog Converter (RU)
tsap........ Medical Air Transport Regiment (BU)
TsAPO........ Central Architectural Design Organization (BU)
TsAR........ Central African Republic [*Oubangui-Chari*] (RU)
TsAR........ Tsentralnoafrikanskaia Respublika (MAR)
TsARM........ Central Automobile Repair Shops (RU)
TsARZ........ Central Automobile Repair Plant (RU)
TsAS........ Center Column Unit Machine Tool (RU)
TsAS........ Central Ammunition Depot (RU)
TsAS........ Central Artery of the Retina (RU)
TsAS........ Central Pharmaceutical Warehouse (RU)
TsAS........ Digital Automatic System (RU)
TsAS........ Fire Director [*on shipboard*] (RU)
TsATO........ Central Joint-Stock Trade Company (RU)
TsAU........ Central Administration of Archives (RU)
TsAU........ Central Administrative Office (RU)
TsAVP........ Central Foreign Policy Archives (RU)
TSAY........ Tameion Syndaxeos kai Avtasfaliseos Ygeionomikon [*Medical Personnel Pension and Self-Insurance Fund*] [*Greek*] (GC)
TsB........ Central Accounting Office (RU)
TsB........ Central Bank (RU)
TsB........ Central Base (BU)
TsB........ Central Base (RU)
TsB........ Central Battery (BU)
TsB........ Central Battery [*Communications*] (RU)
TsB........ Central Library (RU)
TsB........ Central Office (RU)
tsb........ Tank and Self-Propelled Gun Battalion (RU)
TSB........ Technical Service Bureau (BU)
TSB........ Turkiye Sanatcilar Birligi [*Turkish Artists Union*] (TU)
TsBAK........ Royal Bulgarian Automobile Club (BU)
TSBB........ Turkiye Ticaret Odalari, Sanayi Odalari ve Ticaret Borsalari Birligi [*Turkish Union of Chambers of Commerce, Industry, and Stock Exchanges*] [*See also TOB*] (TU)
TsBDKO........ Central Bureau of Children's Communist Organizations (RU)
TsBI........ Central Office of Information (RU)
TsBK........ Central Library Commission (RU)
TsBK........ Central Office of Regional Studies (RU)
TsBK........ Pulp and Paper Kombinat (RU)
TsBKM........ Central Planning and Design Office of the Forging-and-Pressing Machinery (RU)
TsBL........ Central Hospital Laboratory (BU)
TsBN........ Central Office of Standardization (RU)
TsBNSEV........ Central Office of Standardization of Electric Vacuum Equipment Components (RU)
TsBNTI........ Central Office of Scientific and Technical Information (RU)
TsBP........ Central Bureau of Weather Forecasts (RU)
TsBP........ Central Office for Checking (Hydrometeorological Instruments) (RU)
TsBP........ Central Party Bureau (RU)
TsBP........ Central Weather Bureau (RU)
TsBP........ Pulp and Paper Industry (RU)
TsBPM........ Central Office for Checking Meteorological Instruments (RU)
TsBPS........ Central Office of Proletarian Students (RU)
TsBS........ Center of Lateral Resistance [*Nautical term*] (RU)
TsBSKUP........ Central Office of Standardization of the Shale and Coal Industry (RU)
TsBSP........ Central Library of the Construction Industry (RU)
TsBTEIN........ Central Office of Technical and Economic Information (RU)
TsBTI........ Central Office of Technical Information (RU)
TsBTK........ Central Office of Technical Control (RU)
TsBTM........ Central Office of Heavy Machinery Manufacture (RU)
TsBTN........ Central Office of Work Standards (RU)
TsBTS........ Central Design Office of Heavy Machine Tool Manufacture (RU)
TsBVK........ Central Hydrological Register Office (RU)
TsBYuP........ Central Office of Young Pioneers (RU)
TsBZ........ Cement-Concrete Plant (RU)
TsBZG........ Central Bureau of Foreign Groups for Assisting the RSDRP [*1907-1916*] (RU)
TSC........ Tanzania Sisal Corporation (MAR)
TSC........ Teachers Service Commission (MAR)
TSC........ Tehnicki Skolski Centar [*Technical School Center*] [*Army*] [*Zagreb*] (YU)
TsCh........ Cetane Number (RU)
t/schet........ Current Account (RU)
TsChO........ Central Black Earth Region (RU)
Tschovodproyekt........ All-Union Office for Surveying and Planning of Irrigation Systems in the Central Black Earth Regions (RU)
TsChP........ Central Black Earth Belt (RU)
TsD........ Center of Pressure [*Nautical term*] (RU)
TsD........ Digital Discriminator (RU)
TSD........ Medium-Pressure Turbine (RU)
TSD........ Turk Sinematek Dernegi [*Turkish Cinematic Association*] (TU)
TsDA........ Central House of Actors (RU)
TsDA........ Central House of Architects (RU)
TsDA........ Central State Archives (BU)
TsDA........ Digital Differential Analyzer (RU)
TsDB........ Central Dispatcher's Office, Central Control Office (RU)
TsDDZh........ Central House of Railroad Workers' Children (RU)
TsDETS........ Central Children's Excursion and Tourist Station (RU)
TsDF........ Cytidine Diphosphate (RU)
TsDI........ Documentation and Information Center (RU)
TsDIA........ Central State Historical Archives (BU)
TsDK........ Central Commission for Children (RU)
TsDK........ Central House of Composers (RU)
TsDK........ Central House of Cooperatives (RU)
TsDK........ Central House of Culture (RU)
TsDK........ Central House of Motion Pictures (RU)
TsDK........ Central House of the Peasant (RU)
TsDKA........ Central House of the Red Army Imeni M. V. Frunze (RU)
TsDKhVD........ Central House of Children's Art Education (RU)
TsDKMR........ Central House of Culture of Medical Workers (RU)
TsDKZh........ Central House of Culture of Railroad Workers (RU)
TsDL........ Central House of Writers (RU)
TsDNA........ Central House of the People's Army (BU)
TsDNT........ Central Folklore Club (BU)
TsDNT........ Central House of Folk Art Imeni N. K. Krupskaya (RU)
TsDNV........ Central House of the People's Army (BU)
TsDORNII........ Central Scientific Research Institute of Truck and Cart Roads and Road Machinery (RU)
TsDP........ Central Dispatcher's Station, Central Control Post (RU)
TsDP........ Central House of Pioneers (RU)
TsDP........ Central Radiation-Monitoring Control Panel (RU)
TsDR........ Central Dispatcher Control (BU)
TsDRFK........ Central House of Workers in Physical Culture (RU)
TsDRI........ Central House of Workers in the Arts, USSR (RU)
TsDS........ Central Traffic Control Service (RU)
TSDS........ Long-Distance Telephone Exchange (RU)
TsDSA........ Central House of the Soviet Army Imeni M. V. Frunze (RU)
TsDT........ Central Children's Theater (RU)
TsDTS........ Central Children's Excursion and Tourist Station (RU)
TsDTS........ Central House of Communications Engineering (RU)

TsDU.......... Central Dispatching of the Integrated Power System of Socialist Countries (RU)
TsDZh......... Central House of Journalists (RU)
TsDZh......... Central Journalists' Club (BU)
TsDZht........ Central House of Technology of Railroad Transportation (RU)
TSE............ Technical Soviet Encyclopedia [*A publication*] (RU)
TSE............ Tehran Stock Exchange (ME)
TSE............ Tribunal Superior Eleitoral [*Superior Electoral Court*] [*Brazilian*] (LA1)
TSE............ Tribunal Supremo Electoral [*Supreme Electoral Court*] [*Ecuadorean*] (LA)
TSE............ Turk Standartlar Enstitusu [*Turkish Institute of Standards*] (TU)
TSE............ Turkiye Sap Enstitusu [*Turkish Foot and Mouth Institute*] [*Ankara*] (TU)
TsEDISK..... Central House of Amateur Performances (RU)
TsEGAZO.... Central State Anti-Aircraft Defense (RU)
TsEIL.......... Central Experimental Research Laboratory (RU)
TsEIM......... Digital Computers (BU)
TSEK.......... Turkiye Sut Endustri Kurumu Genel Mudurlugu [*Turkish Milk Industry Organization Directorate General*] (TU)
tseka.......... Central Committee (RU)
tsekhkom.... Shop Committee (RU)
Tsekombank ... Central Municipal Bank, USSR (RU)
Tsekomol.... Central Committee of the Russian Young Communist League (RU)
Tsekomrabsnab ... Central Commission for Workers' Supply (RU)
Tsekprofsozh ... Central Committee of the Trade Union of Railroad Workers (RU)
TsEKPROS ... Central Committee of the Trade Union of Education Workers (RU)
Tsekrabis.... Central Committee of the Trade Union of Workers in the Arts (RU)
Tsektran..... Central Committee of the United Trade Union of Railroad and Water Transportation Workers (RU)
TsEKUBU.... Central Commission for the Improvement of Scientists' Living Conditions (RU)
TsEKVOD.... Central Committee of the All-Russian Union of Water Transportation Workers (RU)
tsem........... Cement (RU)
tsem........... Cement Plant [*Topography*] (RU)
TsEM.......... Trust for Performing Electrical Installation Work in the Central Regions (RU)
TsEMM........ Central Electromechanical Shops (RU)
TsENII......... Central Scientific Research Institute of Economics (at the Gosplan RSFSR) (RU)
Tsenkomdezertir ... Central Commission for Combating Desertion (RU)
Tsenkompomgol ... Central Famine Relief Commission (RU)
Tsenkoopizdat ... Central Cooperative Publishing House (BU)
TsENTOEP ... Central Administration of the Scientific and Technical Society of the Power Industry (RU)
tsentr.......... Central (RU)
Tsentrakademsnab ... Central Supply Administration of the Academy of Sciences, USSR (RU)
Tsentrakademstroy ... Central Construction Administration of the Academy of Sciences, USSR (RU)
Tsentrarkhiv ... Central State Archives (RU)
TsENTRIZDAT ... Central Publishing House (RU)
Tsentr mlad kom ... Central Youth Commission (BU)
Tsentrobalt ... Central Committee of the Baltic Fleet [*1917-1918*] (RU)
Tsentrobelsoyuz ... Central Union of Consumers' Cooperatives of Belorussia (RU)
TsENTROBUMTREST ... Central Trust of the Pulp and Paper Industry (RU)
Tsentroelektromontazh ... Trust for Performing Electrical Installation Work in the Central Regions (RU)
Tsentroelektroset'stroy ... All-Union Trust of the Glavvostokelektroset'stroy of the Ministry of Construction of Electric Power Plants, USSR (RU)
Tsentroenergomontazh ... State All-Union Installation Trust of the Glavteploenergomontazh of the State Industrial Committee for Power Engineering and Electrification, USSR (RU)
Tsentroevak ... Central Evacuation Station (RU)
Tsentrogiproshakht ... All-Union Central State Institute for the Planning and Technical and Economic Prerequisites for the Development of the Coal Industry (RU)
Tsentrogiproshakhtostroy ... All-Union Central State Institute for the Planning of Mine Construction (RU)
Tsentrogosrybvod ... State Inspection for the Conservation of Fish Resources and Regulation of Fishing in the Central Regions (RU)
Tsentrokhimles ... All-Union Trust of the Wood-Chemistry Industry (RU)
Tsentrolak ... Main Committee of the Varnish and Paint Industry (RU)
Tsentronerud ... State All-Union Trust of the Glavnerud (RU)
Tsentropechat' ... Central Agency of the All-Russian Central Executive Committee for the Distribution of Publications [*1918-1922*] (RU)
Tsentroplen ... Central Committee for Prisoners of War (RU)
Tsentroplenbezh ... Central Committee for Prisoners of War and Refugees (RU)
Tsentroprofshkola ... Central Higher School of Trade Unionism (RU)
Tsentroprofsovet ... All-Russian Central Trade-Union Council (RU)
Tsentroprompoyekt ... Central Planning Institute (for the Planning of Industrial Structures) (RU)
Tsentropromsovet ... Central Council of Producers' Cooperatives of the USSR (RU)
Tsentroruda ... State Trust for the Iron Ore Industry of the Central Part of the USSR (RU)
Tsentrosantekhmontazh ... Central Sanitary Engineering Installation Trust of the Glavsantekhmontazh (RU)
Tsentrosnab ... Central Supply Administration of the VSNKh (RU)
Tsentrosovnatsmen ... Central Council of National Minorities (of the Narkompros RSFSR) (RU)
Tsentrosoyuz ... Central Union of Consumers' Societies, USSR (RU)
Tsentrostal' ... State All-Union Association of the Metallurgical Industry of the Central Part of the USSR (RU)
Tsentrostroymekhanizatsiya ... Trust for the Earthwork Mechanization on Roads of the Northern and Western Regions of the Glavzheldorstroy (RU)
Tsentrotop ... Central Fuel Administration (RU)
Tsentrotransstroy ... Construction and Installation Trust of the Glavzheldorstroy of the Northern and Western Regions of the State Industrial Committee for Transportation Construction, USSR (RU)
Tsentroupravkozh ... Central Administration of State Establishments of the Leather Industry (RU)
Tsentrovoyenzag ... Central Military Procurement Section (RU)
Tsentrozagotzerno ... Association for the Procurement and Marketing of Grain in the Central Regions (RU)
Tsentrozhilsoyuz ... Central Union of Housing Cooperatives (RU)
tsenz........... Censorship (RU)
Tsenz.......... Censured (BU)
TsEPAZ....... Central Directorate of Artillery Weapons Plants [*1919-1921*] (RU)
TsEPAZO.... Central Antiaircraft Defense Post (RU)
TsEPK......... Central Expert Verification Commission (RU)
TsERA......... Central Power Repairs and Automation (BU)
Tserabkom ... Central Workers' Committee (RU)
Tserabkoop ... Central Workers' Cooperative (RU)
tserk............ Church (RU)
tserk............ Ecclesiastical Word (RU)
Tseroz......... Central State Trust for the Mining and Processing of Ozokerite (RU)
TsES........... Central Electric Power Plant (RU)
TsES........... Central Electrotechnical Council (RU)
TsESS......... Aircraft Central Electric Power Unit (RU)
TsESZ......... Central Electric Power Plant of a Factory (RU)
TsETETIS.... Central Technicum of Theatrical Art [*1925-1931*] (RU)
TsF.............. Circular Milling (RU)
TSF............. Telegraphie sans Fil [*Wireless Telegraphy*] [*French*]
TSF............. Turkiye Seker Fabrikalari AS [*Turkish Sugar Factories Corporation*] (TU)
TsFDK......... Central Long-Term Credit Fund (RU)
TsFMU........ Central Machine Accounting and Computing Office (RU)
TsFSh.......... Centrifugal Pitch Arrester (RU)
TsFU........... Central Finance Administration (RU)
TSG............. Labor and Social Welfare (BU)
TsGA........... Central Group of Armies [*NATO*] (RU)
TsGA........... Central State Archives (RU)
TSGA........... Tanzania Sisal Growers Association (MAR)
TsGADA...... Central State Archives of Ancient Documents, USSR (RU)
TsGAKA...... Central State Archives of the Red Army, USSR (RU)
TsGAKFFD ... Central State Archives of Motion-Picture, Photographic, and Phonographic Records, USSR (RU)
TsGALI........ Central State Archives of Literature and Art, USSR (RU)
TsGANKh.... Central State Archives of the National Economy, USSR (RU)
TsGAOR...... Central State Archives of the October Revolution, High State Government Bodies, and State Administrative Bodies, USSR (RU)
TsGAOR i SS ... Central State Archives of the October Revolution and the Building of Socialism (RU)
TsGAORSS ... Central State Archives of the October Revolution and the Building of Socialism (RU)
TsGASA...... Central State Archives of the Soviet Army (RU)
TsGAVMF.... Central State Archives of the Navy, USSR (RU)
TsGB........... Central Geological Library (RU)
TsGFU......... Central Installation for Gas Fractionation (RU)
TsGIA.......... Central State Historical Archives (RU)
TsGIAG....... Central State Historical Archives of Georgia (RU)
TsGIAL........ Central State Historical Archives in Leningrad (RU)
TsGIAM....... Central State Historical Archives in Moscow (RU)
TsGII........... Central Forestry Research Institute (BU)
Tsgintsvetmet ... Central State Scientific Research Institute of Nonferrous Metals (RU)
TsGIRD........ Central Group for the Study of Jet Propulsion (RU)
TsGL........... Central Genetics Laboratory Imeni I. V. Michurin (RU)
TsGLA......... Central State Archives of Literature (RU)
TsGM.......... State Central Geographic Museum (RU)
TsGMB........ Central Hydrometeorological Office (RU)
TsGNKI....... Central State Scientific Control Institute (RU)
TsGNKI....... Central State Scientific Control Institute of Veterinary Preparations (RU)
TsGOI.......... Central State Institute of Smallpox (RU)

TsGOK .... Central Mining and Concentration Kombinat (RU)
TsGT .... Central Geophysical Trust (RU)
TsGTI .... Central State Institute of Traumatology (RU)
TsGU .... Central Hydrographic Administration (RU)
TsGU .... Tsimlyanskiy Hydroelectric Development (RU)
TsGV .... Master Vertical Gyro (RU)
TsGVIA .... Central State Archives of Military History, USSR (RU)
TsGVIAL ..... Branch of the Central State Archives of Military History in Leningrad (RU)
TsGVIALF ... Branch of the Central State Archives of Military History in Leningrad (RU)
TsGVMA ..... Central State Naval Archives (RU)
TSh .... Brinell Ball Hardness Tester (RU)
TSh .... Tank Hinge [*Sight*] (RU)
TSh .... Tanzanian Shilling (MAR)
TSh .... Telescopic Hinge [*Sight*] (RU)
t-shch .... Comrade (RU)
TShch .... Minesweeper (RU)
TsI .... Digital Indicator (RU)
TSI .... Tameion Syndaxeon Ithopoion [*Actors' Pensions Fund*] [*Greek*] (GC)
TSI .... Tovarna Steklenih Izdelkov [*Glass Products Factory*] [*Slovenska Bistrica*] (YU)
TsIA .... Central Historical Archives (RU)
TsIAG .... Central Institute of Obstetrics and Gynecology (RU)
TsIAM .... Central Scientific Research Institute of Aircraft Engines Imeni P. I. Baranov (RU)
TsIATIM ...... Central Scientific Research Institute of Aviation Fuel and Lubricants (RU)
TsIChM .... Central Scientific Research Institute of Ferrous Metallurgy (RU)
TsID .... Digital Diameter Gauge (RU)
TSID .... Turk Sanayici ve Is Adamlari Dernegi [*Turkish Industrialists and Businessmen's Organization*] (TU)
TsIEGM .... Central Institute of Experimental Hydrology and Meteorology (RU)
TsIEI .... Central Institute of Economic Research (RU)
TsIEM .... Central Institute of Epidemiology and Microbiology (RU)
TsIEM .... Central Institute of Experimental Medicine (RU)
TsIETIN .... Central Scientific Research Institute for Determination of Disability and Organization of Work for Disabled Persons (RU)
tsig .... Gypsy (BU)
TsII .... Central Information Institute (RU)
TsIIKhPROM ... All-Union Central Scientific Research Institute of the Cotton Industry (RU)
TsIIN .... Central Information Institute (RU)
TsIIN .... Central Testing Institute (BU)
TsIINChM .... Central Information Institute of Ferrous Metallurgy (RU)
TsIINS .... Central Institute of Information on Construction (RU)
TsIINTsvetmet ... Central Information Institute of Nonferrous Metallurgy (RU)
TsIIT .... Central Computer Equipment Institute (BU)
TsIITsvetmet ... Central Information Institute of Nonferrous Metallurgy (RU)
TsIK .... Central Executive Committee (BU)
TsIK .... Central Executive Committee (RU)
TsIK .... Central Executive Committee, USSR [*1924-1937*] (RU)
TsIK .... Central Institute of Health Resorts [*1926-1958*] (RU)
Tsikl izd ...... Mimeographed Edition (BU)
Tsiklopech ... Mimeographed (BU)
TsIL .... Central Measurement Laboratory (RU)
TsIM .... Central Institute of Metals (RU)
TsIM .... Central Scientific Research Institute of Materials (RU)
TsIM .... Digital Computer (BU)
TsIM .... Digital Integrating Computer (RU)
TsIM .... Macromolecular Research Center (RU)
TsIMTNeft' ... Central Scientific Research Institute for the Mechanization and Organization of Labor in the Petroleum Industry (RU)
TsINIS .... Central Institute of Scientific Information on Construction and Architecture (of the State Committee for Construction, USSR) (RU)
TsINISiA ...... Central Institute of Scientific Information on Construction and Architecture (RU)
tsinkogr ...... Zincography (RU)
TsINS .... Central Scientific Research Institute of the Sugar Industry (RU)
TsINTEI .... Central Institute of Scientific, Technical, and Economic Information (RU)
TsINTI .... Central Institute of Scientific and Technical Information (BU)
TsINTI .... Central Institute of Scientific and Technical Information (RU)
TsINTIAM .... Central Institute of Scientific and Technical Information on Automation and Machinery Manufacture (RU)
TsINTIElektroprom ... Central Institute of Scientific and Technical Information of the Electrotechnical Industry and Instrument Making (RU)
TsINTIEP ..... Central Institute of Scientific and Technical Information and Standardization of the Electrical Equipment Industry (RU)
TsINTIMASh ... Central Institute of Scientific and Technical Information of Machinery Manufacture (RU)
TsINTIPishcheprom ... Central Institute of Scientific and Technical Information of the Food Industry (RU)
TsINTIpriborelektroprom ... Central Institute of Scientific and Technical Information of Instrument Making, Electrical Equipment Industry, and Means of Automation (RU)
TsINUPMED ... Central Scientific Research Institute of Educational Visual Aids in Medicine, Biology, and Sanitation (RU)
TsIONP .... Central Institute of Organizers of Public Education (RU)
TsIP .... Central Institute of Psychiatry (RU)
TsIP .... Central Institute of Weather Forecasts (RU)
TSIP .... Turkiye Sosyalist Isciler Partisi [*Turkish Socialist Workers Party*] (TU)
TsIPK .... Central Institute of Blood Transfusion (RU)
TsIPKKNO .. Central Institute for Improving the Qualifications of Public Education Personnel (RU)
TsIPKNO ..... Central Institute for the Training of Public Education Personnel (RU)
TsIPKP .... Central Institute for Improving the Qualifications of Teachers (RU)
TsIPKRRNO ... Central Institute for Improving the Qualifications of Supervisory Personnel in Public Education (RU)
TsIPTK .... Central Institute for the Training of Transportation Personnel (RU)
TsIRIR .... Central Scientific Research Institute of Roentgenology and Radiology (RU)
TsIS .... Central Institute of Communications (RU)
TsIS .... Central Scientific Research Institute of Transportation Construction (RU)
TsIS .... Central Tool Warehouse (RU)
TsISON .... Central Institute for the Socialist Exchange of Experience in the Petroleum Industry of the USSR (RU)
TsISP .... Central Scientific Research Institute of Hygiene Education (RU)
tsist .... Cistern [*Topography*] (RU)
TsIT .... Central Institute of Labor (RU)
TsITEIN .... Central Institute of Technical and Economic Information (RU)
TsITI .... Central Institute of Technical Information (RU)
TsITIUglya ... Central Institute of Technical Information of the Coal Industry (RU)
tsit kn .... Quoted Book (BU)
TsITLegprom ... Central Scientific Research Institute of Labor in Light Industry (RU)
TsITM .... Central Institute for the Organization of Labor and Mechanization of Production (RU)
TsITO .... Central Scientific Research Institute of Traumatology and Orthopedics (RU)
TsITP .... Central Institute of Standard Designs (RU)
tsitrus .... Citrus [*Topography*] (RU)
tsit st .... Article Cited (BU)
tsit such ...... Quoted Work (BU)
TsIU .... Central Institute for the Advanced Training of Physicians (RU)
TsIUU .... Central Institute for the Advanced Training of Teachers (BU)
TsIVIM .... Central Historical Museum of Military Engineering (RU)
TsIZ .... Central Publishing House (RU)
TsIZAS .... Central Institute for the Study of Drought and Dry Winds in the RSFSR (RU)
TsIZhVYa .... Central Institute of Living Oriental Languages [*1920-1921*] (RU)
TsIZIO .... Central Industrial Correspondence Training Institute (RU)
TsIZMAE ..... Central Institute of Terrestrial Magnetism and Atmospheric Electricity (RU)
TsIZO .... Central Correspondence Training Institute (RU)
TsIZO .... Central Institute of Public Health (RU)
TsIZPO .... Central Pedagogical Correspondence Training Institute (RU)
TSJ .... Tanzania School of Journalism (MAR)
TsK .... Central Commission (BU)
TsK .... Central Committee (BU)
TsK .... Central Committee (RU)
TsK .... Central Committee of the KPSS (RU)
TSK .... Commodity Warehouse Office (RU)
TsK .... Crystallization Nucleus (RU)
TSK .... Heat-Resisting Suit (RU)
TSK .... Turk Satis Kooperatifleri [*Turkish Sales Cooperatives*] (TU)
TsKB .... Central Design Office (RU)
TsKB .... Central Municipal Bank, USSR (RU)
TSKB .... Tarim Satislari Kooperatifleri Birligi [*Agricultural Sales Cooperatives Union*] (TU)
TSKB .... Turkiye Sinai Kalkinma Bankasi [*Turkish Industrial Development Bank*] (TU)
TsKBA .... Central Design Office of Fittings (RU)
TsKBD .... Central Traffic Safety Commission (BU)
TsKBF .... Central Committee of the Baltic Fleet (RU)
TsKBGM ..... State Central Design Office of Hydraulic Machinery in Moscow (RU)
TsKBKhM ... Central Design Office of Chemical Machinery (RU)
TsKBKhM ... Central Design Office of Refrigeration Machinery (RU)
TsKBLO ...... Central Design Office for Foundry Equipment (RU)
TsKBMM ..... Central Design Office of Metallurgical Machinery (RU)
TsKBPP .... Central Design Office of the Bearing Industry (RU)
TsKBS .... Central Shipbuilding Design Office (RU)
TsKDM .... Central Committee of Democratic Youth (BU)
TsK na DSNM ... Central Committee of the Dimitrov People's Youth Union (BU)
TsKEB .... Central Design and Experimental Office (RU)
TsKGF .... Central Cartographic and Geodetic Fund (RU)

TsKGU .... Central Kazakhstan Geological Administration (RU)
TSKhA .... Timiryazev Agricultural Academy (RU)
TSKhI .... Turkmen Agricultural Institute (RU)
TsKhK .... Cellulose and Paper Combine (BU)
TsKhL .... Central Chemical Laboratory (BU)
TsKhL .... Central Chemical Laboratory (RU)
TsKhOL....... Central Chemical and Organoleptic Laboratory (RU)
TsKIB .... Central Design and Research Office of Hunting and Sporting Arms (RU)
TsKK .... Central Classification Committee of the MFD (RU)
TsKK .... Central Control Commission (BU)
TsKK .... Central Control Commission of the VKP(b) [*1921-1934*] (RU)
TsKK-NK RKI ... Central Control Commission and People's Commissariat of Workers' and Peasants' Inspection [*1923-1934*] (RU)
TsKKOV ...... Central Peasants' Public Mutual Aid Committee (RU)
TsKKPB ..... Central Committee of the Communist Party of Belorussia (RU)
TsKKP(b).... Central Committee of the Communist Party (of Bolsheviks) (RU)
TsKKP(b)U ... Central Committee of the Communist Party (of Bolsheviks) of the Ukraine (RU)
TsKKPCh.... Central Committee of the Communist Party of Czechoslovakia (RU)
TsKKPK ...... Central Committee of the Communist Party of China (RU)
TsK na KPSS ... Central Committee of the Communist Party of the Soviet Union (BU)
TsKKPSS.... Central Committee of the Communist Party of the Soviet Union (RU)
TsKKPU ...... Central Committee of the Communist Party of the Ukraine (RU)
TsKKPYa .... Central Committee of the Communist Party of Japan (RU)
TsKK-RKI.... Central Control Commission and Workers' and Peasants' Inspection [*1923-1934*] (RU)
TsKL............ Central Laboratory of Criminology (of the All-Union Institute of Jurisprudence) (RU)
TsKNA......... Central Committee on New Alphabet of the RSFSR (RU)
TsKNB......... Central Scientific Libraries Pool (RU)
TsKNII .... Central Confectionery Scientific Research Institute (RU)
TsKO .... "Target-Commander-Gun" Angle (RU)
TsKORPS.... CC of the General Workers' Trade Union (BU)
TsKOZ......... Central Office for the Processing of Journal and Newspaper Subscriptions (RU)
TsKP .... Central Command Post (RU)
TsKP .... Central Committee on Transportation (RU)
TsKP .... Central Control Post (BU)
TsKPM .... CC of the Mining Workers' Trade Union (BU)
TsKPOMGOL ... Central Famine Relief Commission (RU)
TsKPOSLEDGOL ... Central Commission for Combating the After-Effects of Famine (RU)
TsK na profsuyuzite ... CC of the Trade Unions (BU)
TsKPS......... CC of the Trade Unions (BU)
TsKRABIS... Central Committee of the Trade Union of Workers in the Arts (RU)
TsKRKP(b) ... Central Committee of the Russian Communist Party (of Bolsheviks) (RU)
TsKRMS...... CC of the Young Workers' League (BU)
TsKRRS ...... Central Courses for Supervisory Communications Personnel (RU)
TsKRSDRP(b) ... Central Committee of the Russian Social Democratic Workers' Party (of Bolsheviks) (RU)
TsKS .... Central Cooperative Union (BU)
TsKSh .... Central Komsomol School (BU)
TsKSh .... Central Komsomol School (RU)
TsKSKhS .... Central Cottonseed-Testing Station (RU)
TsKSL .... Central Seed-Testing Laboratory (RU)
TsK na SNM ... CC of the People's Youth Union (BU)
TsKSNM..... CC of the People's Youth Union (BU)
TsKTB......... Central Design Technical Office (RU)
TsKTEK....... Administration for Container Shipments and Transportation and Forwarding Operations (RU)
TsKTI .... Central Committee of Heavy Industry (RU)
TsKTI .... Central Scientific Research, Planning, and Design Boiler and Turbine Institute Imeni I. I. Polzunov (RU)
TsKVI .... Central Scientific Research Institute of Dermatology and Venereal Diseases (RU)
TsKVKP(b) ... Central Committee of the All-Union Communist Party (of Bolsheviks) (RU)
TsKVLKSM ... Central Committee of the All-Union Lenin Young Communist League (RU)
TsKZ .... Central Correspondence Courses (RU)
TSKZ.......... Towarzystwo Spoleczno-Kulturalne Zydow [*Jewish Social and Cultural Society*] (POL)
TSl.............. Addition Control Trigger [*Computers*] (RU)
TsL .... Central Laboratory (RU)
TSL............. Techniczna Szkola Lotnicza [*Aviation Engineering School*] (POL)
TSL............. Towarzystwo Szkoly Ludowej [*Society for Public Schools*] (POL)
TsLA........... Central Laboratory of Automation (RU)
TsLAM .... Central Laboratory of Automation and Mechanization (RU)
TsLAM .... Central Laboratory of Aviation Medicine (RU)
TsLAM .... Central Model Automobile Laboratory (RU)
TsLB........... Central Lecture Bureau (RU)
TsLEB .... Central Lumber Export Office (RU)
TsLEKhIT.... Central Laboratory for Electrochemical Sources of Electricity (BU)
TsLEM......... Central Laboratory and Experimental Workshops of the Mosenergo (RU)
TsLMM........ Central Laboratory of Ship Modeling (RU)
TsLOS .... Central Forest Experimental Station (RU)
TsLPS .... Central Laboratory of Wire Communications (RU)
TsLSI........... Central Laboratory of Sports Equipment (RU)
TsM .... Center of Mass (RU)
TsM .... Central Workshop (RU)
TsM .... Colorimeter (RU)
TSM............ Copper Resistance Thermometer (RU)
TsM .... Nonferrous Metallurgy (BU)
TsM .... Nonferrous Metallurgy (RU)
TSM............ Towarzystwo Swiadomego Macierzynstwa [*Society for Planned Parenthood*] (POL)
TsMB.......... Central Medical Library (BU)
TsMB.......... Central Medical Library (RU)
TsME.......... Digital Magnetic Element (RU)
TSMEDE ..... Tameion Syndaxeon Mikhanikon Ergolipton Dimosion Ergon [*Pension Fund for Public Works Engineer-Contractors*] [*Greek*] (GC)
TsMetl......... Central Meteorological Institute (BU)
TsMF.......... Cytidine Monophosphate (RU)
TsMI........... Central Meteorological Institute (BU)
TsMI........... Central Moscow Racetrack (RU)
TsMIS......... Central Machine-Testing Station (RU)
TsMK.......... Central Naval Club of the DOSAAF SSSR (RU)
TsMK.......... Central Youth Committee (BU)
TsMKA........ Central Museum of the Red Army (RU)
TsMKB........ Central Furniture Design Office (RU)
TsMM......... Central Machine Shop (RU)
TsMO .... Central Mobilization Section (RU)
TsMP.......... Central Museum of Soil Science (RU)
TsMS.......... Central Meteorological Station (BU)
TsMS.......... Central Warehouse (BU)
TsMSA........ Central Museum of the Soviet Army (RU)
TsMSh........ Central School of Music (RU)
TsMTMLP ... Central Model Textile Mill of the Ministry of Light Industry (BU)
TsMTS .... Central Long Distance Telephone Exchange, USSR (RU)
TsMTU .... Technical Specifications for Nonferrous Metallurgy (RU)
TsMV.......... All-Metal (Passenger) Car (RU)
tsn .... Centner (RU)
TsN............. Central Aiming [*Artillery*] (RU)
TsN............. Centrifugal Supercharger (RU)
TSN .... Tameion Syndaxeon Nomikon [*Judiciary Personnel Pension Fund*] [*Greek*] (GC)
TsNA IML.... Central People's Archives of the Institute of Marxism-Leninism at the TsK KPSS (RU)
TsND .... Low-Pressure Cylinder (RU)
TsNEL .... Central Scientific Experimental Laboratory (RU)
TsNELkozh ... Central Scientific Experimental Laboratory of Leather (RU)
TsNIAG .... Central Scientific Research Aviation Hospital (RU)
TsNIAGI ...... Central Scientific Research Institute of Obstetrics and Gynecology (RU)
TsNIAL........ Central Scientific Research Pharmaceutical Laboratory (RU)
TsNIB .... Central Office of Standards Research (RU)
Tsnib .... Central Scientific Research Center (RU)
TsNIB .... Central Scientific Research Office (RU)
Tsnibgrazhdanstroy ... Central Scientific Research Center of Civil Engineering Construction (RU)
TsNIDI .... Central Scientific Research Diesel Institute (RU)
TsNIDI .... Central Scientific Research Institute of Disinfection (RU)
TsNIEL .... Central Scientific Research Electrotechnical Laboratory (RU)
TsNIF .... Central Scientific Research Institute for Physical Culture (BU)
TsNIFK .... Central Scientific Institute of Physical Culture (BU)
TsNIGMA .... Central Hydrometeorological Scientific Research Archives (RU)
TsNIGRI ...... Central Scientific Research Institute for Geological Exploration [*Leningrad, 1931-1939*] (RU)
TsNIGRI ...... Central Scientific Research Institute of Prospecting for Nonferrous, Rare, and Noble Metals [*Moscow*] (RU)
TsNII........... Central Scientific Research Institute (RU)
TsNIIASh .... Central Scientific Research Institute of Abrasives and Grinding (RU)
TsNIIAT....... Central Scientific Research Institute of Automobile Transportation (RU)
TsNIIB .... Central Scientific Research Institute of the Pulp and Paper Industry (RU)
TsNIIBUMMASh ... All-Union Scientific Research Institute of Paper Machinery (RU)
TsNIIChERMET ... Central Scientific Research Institute of Ferrous Metallurgy Imeni I. P. Bardin (RU)
TsNII Chermetal ... Central Scientific Research Institute of Ferrous Metals (BU)
TsNIIChM.... Central Scientific Research Institute of Ferrous Metallurgy Imeni I. P. Bardin (RU)
TsNIID .... Central Scientific Research Institute of Lumber (RU)
TsNIIEP .... Central Scientific Research Institute of Experimental Planning (RU)

TsNIIEPZhilishcha ... Central Scientific Research and Planning Institute of Standard and Experimental Planning of Housing (RU)
TsNIIEVT..... Central Scientific Research Institute of Economics and Operation of Water Transportation (RU)
TsNIIFK....... Central Scientific Research Institute of Physical Culture (BU)
TsNIIFK....... Central Scientific Research Institute of Physical Culture (RU)
TsNIIFM ...... Central Scientific Research Institute of Plywood and Furniture (RU)
TsNIIGAiK... Central Scientific Research Institute of Geodesy, Aerial Surveying, and Cartography (RU)
TsNIIGS ...... Central Scientific Research Forestry Institute (BU)
TsNIIISA...... Central Scientific Research Institute of Communications Engineers of the Soviet Army (RU)
TsNIIKA ...... State All-Union Central Scientific Research Institute of Complex Automation (RU)
TsNIIKhP..... Central Scientific Research Institute of the Baking Industry (RU)
TsNIIKhProm ... Central Scientific Research Institute of the Cotton Industry (RU)
TsNIIKOP.... Central Scientific Research Institute of the Canning and Dehydrated Vegetables Industry (RU)
TsNIIKP....... Central Scientific Research Institute of the Leather and Footwear Industry (RU)
TsNIIKPP .... Central Scientific Research Institute of the Starch and Syrup Industry (RU)
TsNIIKZ....... Central Scientific Research Institute of Leather Substitutes (RU)
TsNIILesosplava ... Central Scientific Research Institute of Log Rafting (RU)
TsNIILKh..... Central Scientific Research Institute of Forestry (RU)
TsNIILV .... Central Scientific Research Institute of the Bast-Fiber Industry (RU)
TsNIIMAP.... Central Scientific Research Laboratory of the Macaroni Industry (RU)
TsNIIMASh ... Central Scientific Research Institute of Machinery Manufacture and Metalworking (RU)
TsNIIMashdetal' ... Central Scientific Research Institute of Accessories and Spare Parts for Textile Equipment (RU)
TsNIIME ...... Central Scientific Research Institute of Mechanization and Power Engineering in the Lumber Industry (RU)
TsNIIMESKh ... Central Scientific Research Institute of Rural Mechanization and Electrification of the Non-Black Earth Belt of the USSR (RU)
TsNIIMF ...... Central Scientific Research Institute of the Maritime Fleet (RU)
TsNIIMOD ... Central Scientific Research Institute for the Mechanical Processing of Lumber (RU)
TsNIIMP ...... Central Scientific Research Institute of the Fur Industry (RU)
TsNIIMPS.... All-Union Scientific Research Institute of Railroad Transportation (RU)
TsNIIMS ...... Central Scientific Research Institute of the Butter- and Cheese-Making Industry (RU)
TsNIINChM ... Central Scientific Research Institute of Information and Technical and Economic Research of Ferrous Metallurgy (RU)
TsNIINSh .... Central Scientific Research Institute of Elementary Schools (RU)
TsNIIOLOVO ... Central Scientific Research Institute of Tin, Antimony, and Mercury (RU)
TsNIIP .... Central Scientific Experimental Cotton Institute (BU)
TsNIIP .... Central Scientific Research Institute of Industrial Structures (RU)
TsNIIP .... Central Scientific Research Institute of Pedagogy (RU)
TsNIIP .... Central Scientific Research Institute of the Poultry-Processing Industry (RU)
TsNII po pamuka ... Central Scientific Research Institute on Cotton (BU)
TsNIIPBiVP ... Central Scientific Research Institute of the Beer, Soft Drink, and Wine Industry (RU)
TsNIIPI .... Central Scientific Research Institute of Patent Information and Technical and Economic Research (of the State Committee for Inventions and Discoveries, USSR) (RU)
TsNIIPO....... Central Scientific Research Institute on Fire Prevention (BU)
TsNIIPO....... Central Scientific Research Institute of Fire Protection (RU)
TsNIIPodzemshakhtostroy ... Central Scientific Research, Planning, and Design Institute of Underground Mine Construction (RU)
TsNIIPP .... Central Scientific Research Institute of the Poultry-Processing Industry (RU)
TsNIIPP .... Central Scientific Research Institute of Prosthetics and Orthopedic Appliances (RU)
TsNIIPromzdaniy ... Central Scientific Research, Planning, and Experimental Institute of Industrial Buildings and Structures (RU)
TsNIIPS....... Central Scientific Research Institute of Industrial Structures (RU)
TsNIIRF .... Central Scientific Research Institute of the River Fleet (RU)
TsNIIS .... All-Union Scientific Research Institute of Transportation Construction (RU)
TsNIIS .... Central Scientific Research Institute of Communications (RU)
TsNIISh .... Central Scientific Research Institute of the Silk Industry (RU)
TsNIIShelka ... Central Scientific Research Institute of the Silk Industry (RU)
TsNIIShersti ... Central Scientific Research Institute of the Wool Industry (RU)
TsNIIShP..... Central Scientific Research Institute of the Garment Industry (RU)
TsNIIShveyprom ... Central Scientific Research Institute of the Garment Industry (RU)
TsNIISK....... Central Scientific Research Institute of Structural Parts (RU)
TsNIISKT .... Central Scientific Research Institute of Soviet Cooperative Trade (RU)
TsNIISM...... Central Scientific Research Institute of Building Materials (RU)
TsNIISP....... Central Scientific Research Institute of the Alcohol, Liqueur, and Vodka Industry (RU)
TsNIISP....... Central Scientific Research Institute of Forensic Psychiatry Imeni Prof. V. P. Serbskiy (RU)
TsNIIST....... Central Scientific Research Institute of Soviet Trade (RU)
TsNIISTEF ... Central Scientific Research Institute of Construction and Technical Operation of the Maritime and River Fleets (RU)
TsNIITEI...... Central Scientific Research Institute of Information and Technical and Economic Research (RU)
TsNIITENeft' ... Central Scientific Research Institute of Technical Information and Economics of the Petroleum Industry (RU)
TsNIITLAMP ... Central Scientific Research Institute of Technical Vacuum Tubes (RU)
TsNIITMASh ... Central Scientific Research Institute of Heavy Machinery (RU)
TsNIITMASh ... Central Scientific Research Institute for Machine Building Technology (BU)
TsNIITMASh ... Central Scientific Research Institute of Machinery-Manufacturing Technology (RU)
TsNIITMASh ... Central Scientific Research Institute of Technology and Machinery Manufacture (RU)
TsNIITOP .... Central Scientific Research Institute of Technology and Organization of Production (RU)
TsNIITS....... Central Scientific Research Institute of Transportation Construction (RU)
TsNIITU....... Central Scientific Research Institute of Packing Materials and Packaging (RU)
TsNIIVT....... Central Scientific Research Institute of Water Transportation (RU)
TsNIIZH....... Central Scientific Research Institute of Animal Husbandry (BU)
TsNIIZhT..... Central Scientific Research Institute of Railroad Transportation (RU)
TsNIKhBI .... Central Scientific Research Institute of the Cotton Industry (RU)
TsNIKP........ Central Scientific Research Institute of the Leather and Footwear Industry (RU)
TsNIKZ........ Central Scientific Research Institute of Leather Substitutes (RU)
TsNIL........... Central Scientific Research Laboratory (RU)
TsNILASh ... Central Scientific Research Laboratory of Abrasives and Grinding (RU)
TsNILBP...... Central Scientific Research Laboratory of the Ferment Industry (RU)
TsNILELEKTROM ... Central Scientific Research Laboratory for Electrical Treatment of Materials (RU)
TsNILEPS ... Central Scientific Research Laboratory for the Electrification of Industry and Construction (RU)
TsNILGE ..... Central Scientific Research Laboratory of Hygiene and Epidemiology (RU)
TsNILGiVT ... Central Scientific Research Laboratory of Hygiene in Water Transportation (RU)
TsNILiSV..... Central Scientific Research Laboratory of Wine Making and Northern Viticulture (RU)
TsNILKhI..... Central Scientific Research and Planning Institute of the Wood-Chemistry Industry (RU)
TsNILKhimstroy ... Central Scientific Research Laboratory for the Anticorrosion Protection of Structural Parts (RU)
TsNILKIP..... Central Scientific Research Laboratory of Control and Measuring Instruments (RU)
TsNILKOMBIKORM ... Central Scientific Research Laboratory of the Combined-Fodder Industry (RU)
TsNILkozhsyr'ye ... Central Scientific Research Laboratory of Leather Raw Materials (RU)
TsNILKR...... All-Union Central Scientific Research Laboratory for Preservation and Restoration of Museum Art Treasures (RU)
TsNILLVP.... Central Scientific Research Laboratory of the Liqueur and Vodka Industry (RU)
TsNILP .... Central Scientific Research Laboratory of Fruits and Vegetables (RU)
TsNILPP...... Central Scientific Research Laboratory of the Brewing and Soft Drink Industry (RU)
TsNILS .... Central Scientific Research Laboratory of the Match Industry (RU)
TsNILsherst' ... Central Scientific Research Laboratory of the Wool Industry (RU)
TsNILShOR ... Central Scientific Research Laboratory of Harness, Saddle, and Leather Notions Industry (RU)
TsNILShora ... Central Scientific Research Laboratory of Harness, Saddle, and Leather Notions Industry (RU)
TsNILSP...... Central Scientific Research Laboratory of the Match Industry (RU)
TsNILSS...... Central Scientific Research Laboratory of Steel Structures (RU)

TsNILStroymaterialy ... Central Scientific Research Laboratory of Building Materials (RU)
TsNILTara ... Central Scientific Research Laboratory of Packing Materials (RU)
TsNILTGP ... Central Scientific Research Laboratory of the Textile and Notions Industry (RU)
TsNILU .... Central Scientific Research Laboratory of Weighting Compounds (RU)
TsNILV .... Central Scientific Research Laboratory of Wind-Power Installations and Wind-Driven Electric Power Plants (RU)
TsNILVP ...... Central Scientific Research Laboratory of the Vitamin Industry (RU)
TsNILVP ...... Central Scientific Research Laboratory of the Wine-Making Industry (RU)
TsNIMASh ... Central Scientific Research Institute of Machinery Manufacture and Metalworking (RU)
TsNIMB .... Central Scientific Research Office of Mine Surveying (RU)
TsNIMOTNP ... Central Scientific Research Institute for the Mechanization and Organization of Labor in the Petroleum Industry (RU)
Tsniotsvetmet ... Central Scientific Research Institute for the Processing of Nonferrous Metals (RU)
TsNIP .... Central Scientific Research Firing Range (RU)
TsNIPI .... Central Scientific Research Institute of Pedagogy (RU)
TsNIPI .... Central Scientific Research Institute of Pediatrics (RU)
TsNIPIA .... Central Scientific Research and Design Automation Institute (BU)
TsNIPO .... Central Scientific Research Institute of Fire Protection (RU)
TsNIPS .... Central Scientific Research Institute of Industrial Structures (RU)
TsNIRD .... Center for Scientific and Development Work (BU)
TsNIRKh ...... Central Scientific Research Institute of Fisheries (RU)
TsNIS .... Central Standards Research Station (RU)
TsNITA .... Central Scientific Research and Design Institute of Combustion Equipment for Automobile, Tractor, and Stationary Engines (RU)
TsNITI .... Central Scientific Research Institute of the Textile Industry (RU)
TsNITI .... Central Scientific Research Institute of Textiles (BU)
TsNN .... Low-Pressure Cylinder [*Nuclear energy*] (BU)
TsNOL .... Central Scientific Experimental Laboratory (RU)
TsNOPS .... Central Scientific Experimental Model Station (RU)
TsNPS .... Central People's Government Council [*Chinese People's Republic*] (RU)
TsNRM .... Central Scientific Restoration Shops (RU)
TsNS .... Central Nervous System (BU)
TsNS .... Central Nervous System (RU)
TsNSB .... Central Scientific Agricultural Library (RU)
TsNSKhB .... Central Scientific Agricultural Library (RU)
TsNTB .... Central Scientific and Technical Library (RU)
TsNTBS .... Central Scientific and Technical Construction Library (RU)
TsNTK .... Central Scientific and Technical Club (RU)
TsNTL .... Central Scientific and Technical Laboratory (RU)
TsNTO .... Central Administration of the Scientific and Technical Society of Railroad Transportation (RU)
TsNTO .... Central Scientific and Technical Society (RU)
TsO .... Central Department, Central Section (RU)
TsO .... Central Organ [*Newspaper, periodical*] (RU)
TSOB .... Teatrul de Stat si Opera Bucuresti [*Bucharest State Theater and Opera*] (RO)
TsOF .... Central Concentration Plant (RU)
TsOF .... Central Ore Dressing Factory (BU)
TsOI .... Central Scientific Research Institute of Oncology Imeni P. A. Gertsen (RU)
TsOI .... Information Processing Center (RU)
TsOKB .... Central Experimental Design Office of Sports Equipment (RU)
TsOLIPK ...... Central "Order of Lenin" Scientific Research Institute of Hematology and Blood Transfusion (RU)
TsON .... Central Department of Standardization (RU)
TsONII .... Central Scientific Research Institute on Fruit Growing (BU)
TsOP .... Central Heating Station (RU)
TsOPE .... Central Association of Postwar Emigres from USSR (RU)
TsOPF .... Central Trade-Union Association of Finland (RU)
TsOPI .... Central Trade-Union Association of Iceland (RU)
TsOPL .... Central Experimental Industrial Laboratory for Pest Control in Granaries (RU)
TsOPSh .... Central Trade-Union Association of Sweden (RU)
TsORS .... Central Department of Workers' Supply (RU)
TsOS .... Central Department of Statistics (RU)
TsOS .... Central Experimental Station (RU)
TsOSAB .... Colored Orientation and Signalling Aerial Bomb (RU)
TsOTShL ...... Central Experimental Technical Garment Laboratory (RU)
TsOVZ .... Central Military Procurement Section [*1919-1920*] (RU)
TsP .... Center of the Sail (RU)
TsP .... Central Administration (RU)
TsP .... Color Index (RU)
TsP .... Control Room (of a Ship) (RU)
TsP .... Digitizer (RU)
TSP .... Platinum Resistance Thermometer (RU)
TsP .... Power Supply Center (RU)
tsp .... Self-Propelled Tank Regiment (BU)
TsP .... Shop Substation (RU)
tsp .... Tank and Self-Propelled Gun Regiment (RU)
TSP .... Tanks in Support of Infantry (RU)
TSP .... Tehnicka Sekcija za Puteve [*Technical Section for Roads*] (YU)
TSP .... Thermistor (BU)
TSP .... Tovarny na Samety a Plys [*Velvet and Plush Factories*] (CZ)
TSP .... Tovarny na Stuhy a Prymky [*Ribbon and Braid Factories*] (CZ)
TsP .... Translation Center (RU)
TsPA .... Central Party Archives (BU)
TsPA .... Central Party Archives (of the Institute of Marxism-Leninism at the TsK KPSS) (RU)
TSPAE .... Tameion Syndaxeon Prosopikou Athinaikon Efimeridon [*Athens Newspaper Personnel Pension Fund*] (GC)
TsPAIML ..... Central Party Archives of the Institute of Marxism-Leninism (at the TsK KPSS) (RU)
TsPAS .... Central Industrial Acclimatization Station (RU)
TsPB .... Central Polytechnical Library (RU)
TsPD .... Central Dispatcher's Station, Central Control Post (RU)
TSPEATh .... Tameion Syndaxeon Prosopikou Efimeridon Athinon kai Thessalonikis [*Pension Fund of Athens and Salonica Newspaper Personnel*] (GC)
TsPEB .... Central Planning and Experimental Office (RU)
TsPEU .... Central Economic Planning Administration (RU)
TsPF .... Cyclopentylperhydrophenanthrene (RU)
TsPIL .... Central Industrial Research Laboratory (RU)
TsPKB .... Central Planning and Design Office (RU)
TsPKBKO .... Central Planning and Design Office of Cable Accessories (RU)
TsPKiO .... Central Park of Culture and Rest (RU)
TsPKP .... Central Administration of the Coal Industry of the Donets Basin (RU)
TsPKPDB .... Central Administration of the Coal Industry of the Donets Basin (RU)
TsPKTB .... Central Planning, Design, and Technological Office (RU)
TSPM .... Three-Self Patriotic Movement [*Chinese*]
TsP NTO NP ... Central Administration of the Scientific and Technical Society of the Petroleum Industry (RU)
TsPO .... Central Consumers' Society (RU)
TsPO .... Central Industrial Region (RU)
TSPor .... Tiskarna Slovenskega Porocevalca [*Slovenski Porocevalec Printers*] [*Ljubljana*] (YU)
TsPP .... Central Underground Substation [*Mining*] (RU)
TsPP .... Reception and Conversion Center [*Computers*] (RU)
TsPR .... Central Industrial Region (RU)
TsPR .... Central Port Radio Station (RU)
TSPS .... Turkmen Republic Council of Trade Unions (RU)
TsPTS .... Central Suburban Telephone Exchange (RU)
TsPU .... Central Control Panel, Central Console (RU)
TsPU .... Central Control Post [*Aviation*] (RU)
TsPU .... Digital Printer (RU)
TsPVSh .... Central Glider and Helicopter School (RU)
TsR .... Central Management (BU)
TsR .... Control Circuit (RU)
TsR .... Cyclic Machine Operating Mode [*Computers*] (RU)
TsR- .... Digital Regulator (RU)
TSR .... Telegraph-Constructing Company [*Military term*] (RU)
TsRA .... Central Workers' Archives (BU)
TSRA .... Tanzania Squash Rackets Association (MAR)
TsR na DZS ... Central State Farms Management (BU)
TsRK .... Central Auditing Commission (BU)
TsRK .... Central Clearing Commission (RU)
TsRK .... Central Inspection Commission (RU)
TsRK .... Central Radio Club (BU)
TsRK .... Central Retail Office "Soyuzpechat'" (RU)
TsRK .... Central Workers' Cooperative (RU)
TsRKMKSB ... Central Zoning Commission of the Ministry of Communal Economy (BU)
TsRL .... Central Radio Laboratory (RU)
TsRM .... Central Repair Shop (RU)
TsRMM .... Central Mechanical Repair Shop (RU)
TsRMP .... Open-Hearth Furnace Repair Shop (RU)
TsRMZ .... Central Mechanical Repair Plant (RU)
TsRP .... Central Distribution Point [*Electricity*] (RU)
TsRP .... Central Distribution Substation (RU)
TsRP .... Centrifugal Rotary Dust Separator (RU)
TSRPP .... Model Account Plan and Guide for Industrial Enterprise Accounting (BU)
TsRR .... Central Relay Distributor (RU)
TsRR .... Central Repair Shop (BU)
TsRR .... Radar Reconnaissance Center (RU)
TsRSB .... Central Bureau of Compensation of the International Union of Railways (RU)
TsRTs .... Central Repair Shop (RU)
TsRU .... Central Distribution System [*Aviation*] (RU)
TsRU .... Central Intelligence Agency [*CIA*] (RU)
TsRV .... Centrifugal Mercury Switch (RU)
TSRV .... Rayon Broadcasting Repeater Station (RU)
TsRYa .... Main Junction Box [*Artillery*] (RU)
TsRZ .... Central Repair Plant (RU)
TsS .... Central Council (BU)
TsS .... Central Council (RU)
TsS .... Central Stadium (RU)
TsS .... Central Union (BU)

TsS............. Central Warehouse (RU)
TsS............. Centrifugal Scrubber (RU)
TsS............. Resistance Center [*Military term*] (RU)
TSS............. Tehnicka Srednja Skola [*Secondary Technical School*] (YU)
TSS............. Thermoelectric Power System (BU)
TSS............. Towarzystwo Szkoly Swieckiej [*Society for Secular Schools*] (POL)
TSS............. Trust Statnich Statku [*State Farm Trust*] (CZ)
TSS............. Turkiye Soforler Sendikasi [*Turkish Chauffeurs Union*] [*Istanbul*] (TU)
TsSA........... Central Reference Service [*Library*] (RU)
TsSB........... Central Construction Library (RU)
TsS na BChK... Central Council of the Bulgarian Red Cross (BU)
TsSBS......... Central Botanical Garden of Siberia (RU)
TsSD........... Medium-Pressure Cylinder (RU)
TsSDF......... Central Documentary Film Studio (RU)
TsS na DSO... Central Council of the Voluntary Sports Organization (BU)
TsSE........... Central Council of Experts (RU)
TsSE........... Centralized Electric Power Supply (RU)
TsSGD......... Central Warehouse of Finished Parts (RU)
TsSGP......... Central Warehouse of Finished Products (RU)
TsShK......... Central Chess Club (RU)
TsShO......... Central Cryptographic Section (RU)
TsShPD....... Central Headquarters of the Partisan Movement (at the Supreme Command Headquarters) [*1942-1945*] (RU)
TsSI............ Central Council on Measurements (BU)
TsSK........... Central Department of Statistics and Cartography (RU)
TsSK........... Central Savings Bank (RU)
TsSK........... Central Scholarship Commission (RU)
TsSK........... Central Sports Club (RU)
TsSKA......... Central Army Sports Club (RU)
TsSKhB....... Central Agricultural Bank, USSR (RU)
TsSKhI........ Central Medico-Chemical Institute (RU)
TsSK MO..... Central Sports Club of the Ministry of Defense, USSR (RU)
TsSL........... Central Construction Laboratory (RU)
TsSL........... Central Welding Laboratory (RU)
tssl............ Church Slavonic (BU)
ts -sl........... Church Slavonic (RU)
TsSNKh....... Central Council of the National Economy (RU)
TsSNM........ Central Council of National Minorities (RU)
TsSO........... Central Council of a Society (RU)
TsSO........... Central Heating System (RU)
TsS na ORPS... Central Council of the General Workers' Trade Union (BU)
TsSP........... Central Trade-Union Council (RU)
TsSPS......... Central Council of the Bulgarian Trade Unions (BU)
TsS na PS... Central Trade Union Council (BU)
TsSPS......... Central Trade-Union Council [*Romanian People's Republic*] (RU)
TsS na PSB... Central Council of the Bulgarian Trade Unions (BU)
TSSR........... Turkmen Soviet Socialist Republic (RU)
TsSRV......... Rayon Central Broadcasting Station (RU)
TsSS........... Central Selection Station (RU)
TsSSK......... Central Shooting Sport Club of the DOSAAF SSSR (RU)
TsSSMSh.... Central Secondary Special School of Music (RU)
TsSSNCh.... Central Council of the Union of Public Libraries (BU)
TsSSSh....... Central Shooting Sport School (RU)
TsST........... Central Television Studio (RU)
TsS na TPK... Central Council of Labor Productive Cooperatives (BU)
TsSTPK....... Central Union of Labor Productive Cooperatives (BU)
TsSU........... Central Statistical Administration (BU)
TsSU........... Central Statistical Administration (RU)
TsSUA......... Central Station of Fertilizers and Soil Science (RU)
TsSUMS...... Central Statistical Administration of the Council of Ministers (BU)
TsSYuN....... Central Station of Young Naturalists and Agricultural Experimenters (RU)
TsSYuT....... Central Station of Young Technicians (RU)
TsT............. Center of Gravity (BU)
TsT............. Center of Gravity (RU)
TsT............. Central Telegraph Office (RU)
TsT............. Color Television (RU)
TST............. Testnevelesi es Sport Tanacs [*Council for Physical Education and Sports*] (HU)
TSt............. Thomas Steel (RU)
TST............. Tovarny Strojirenske Techniky [*Plants for Engineering Machinery*] (CZ)
TST-............ Transport Dump Tractor (RU)
TST............. Transportation Worker's Technical Handbook [*A publication*] (RU)
TsTA........... Central Technical Archives (RU)
TsTA........... Combustion Equipment Shop (RU)
TsTAK......... Central News Agency of Korea [*North Korean*] (RU)
TsTEA......... Central Transportation and Forwarding Agency (RU)
t stekl.......... Vitrification Temperature (RU)
TsTEU......... Central Tourist and Excursion Administration (RU)
TsTF........... Cytidine Triphosphate (RU)
TsTI............ Central Scientific Research Institute of Tuberculosis (RU)
TsTI............ Technical Information Center (RU)
TsTK........... Central Puppet Theater (RU)
TsTK........... Central Theater Ticket Office (RU)
TsTK........... Tricarboxylic Acid Cycle (RU)
TsTKA......... Central Theater of the Red Army (RU)
TsTKB......... Central Technical Design Office (RU)
TsTL........... Central Textile Laboratory (RU)
TsTML......... Central Tobacco and Makhorka Laboratory (RU)
TsTNB......... Central Wage Rate and Norm-Setting Office (RU)
TsTO........... Central Trade Department (RU)
TsTO........... Cyclic Heat Treatment (of Uranium) (RU)
TsTO........... Technical Service Shop (RU)
tsto............. Toimisto [*Finnish*]
TsTOS......... Central Experimental Peat Station (RU)
TsTRK......... Radio Technical Control Center (RU)
TsTS........... Central Telephone Exchange (RU)
TsTSA......... Central Theater of the Soviet Army (BU)
TsTSA......... Central Theater of the Soviet Army (RU)
TsTShch..... Central Heat Control Panel (RU)
TsTU........... Central Telephone Administration (RU)
TsTV........... Color Television (RU)
TsTVR......... Main Administration for the Repair of Rolling Stock and the Production of Spare Parts (RU)
TsTYuZ....... Young Spectator's Theater of the Central House of Art Education (RU)
TSU............ Area Construction Administration (RU)
TsU............. Central Administration (BU)
TsU............. Central Administration (RU)
TsU............. Central Control [*Computers*] (RU)
TsU............. Central Department Store (RU)
TsU............. Digital Printer (RU)
TSU............ Textilni Synteticky Ustav [*Artificial Fiber Institute*] (CZ)
Tsuardel...... Central Administration of Archives (RU)
TsU na BNB... Central Administration of the Bulgarian National Bank (BU)
Tsudortrans... Central Administration of Highways, Dirt Roads, and Automobile Transportation (RU)
TsUGAZ...... Central Administration of the State Automobile Plants (RU)
TSUGM....... Toprak ve Su Genel Mudurlugu [*Soil and Water Directorate General*] [*Under Village Affairs Ministry*] (TU)
TsUGTO..... Central Administration of State Tractor Brigades (RU)
TsUGTs...... Central Administration of State Circuses (RU)
TsUIZUL...... Central Administration for Inventions and Technical Improvements in Transportation (RU)
TsUK........... Central Command Control [*Computers*] (RU)
TsUKADR.... Central Personnel Administration (RU)
TsUKS......... Central Administration of Capital Construction (of the Academy of Sciences, USSR) (RU)
TsULP......... Central Administration of the Lumber Industry (RU)
TsUM.......... Central Department Store (BU)
TsUM.......... Central Department Store (RU)
TsUMOR..... Central Administration of Maritime Transportation (RU)
TsUMS........ Central Administration of Trunk-Line Communications (RU)
TsUMT........ Central Administration of Local Transportation (RU)
TsUMT........ Central Local Trade Administration (BU)
TsUMTSDR... Central Administration of Material and Technical Supply and State Reserves (BU)
TsUMV........ Central Administration of Measures and Scales (RU)
TsUMZ........ Central Administration of Machinery Plants (RU)
TsUNKhU.... Central Administration of the Statistical Survey of the National Economy (RU)
TsUNP......... Central Administration of the Petroleum Industry (RU)
Tsup........... Technicien Superieur [*French*]
TsUPI.......... Central Information Processing Device (RU)
TsUPVOSO... Central Directorate of Military Communications (RU)
TsUPVOZ.... Central Directorate of Military Procurement (RU)
Tsurek......... Central Administration of Inland Waterways (RU)
Tsurek......... Central Administration of River Transportation (RU)
TsURF......... Central Administration for the Development of Radio Facilities (RU)
TsURIR........ Central Administration for the Development of Radio Facilities and for Radio Broadcasting (RU)
TsURK......... Central Stocktaking and Distribution Commission (RU)
tsurk........... Clerical Term (BU)
TsURREK.... Central Administration of the River Register of the USSR (RU)
TsUS........... Central Repeater Station (RU)
TsUS........... Central Supply Administration (RU)
TsUS........... Digital Controlled Resistor (RU)
TSUS.......... Technicky a Skusobny Ustav Stavebny [*Institute for Technology and Testing in Construction*] (CZ)
Tsusstrakh... Central Administration of Social Insurance (RU)
TsUSTRAKh... Central Administration of Social Insurance (RU)
Tsutorf........ Central Administration for Peat Extraction (RU)
Tsutranpros... Central Administration for Education of Transportation Workers (RU)
Tsutrans..... Central Administration of Transportation (RU)
TsUU........... Central Control Device [*Data processing*] (RU)
TsUU........... Central Control System [*Data processing*] (BU)
TsUVODPUT'... Central Administration of Inland Waterways (RU)
TsUVS......... Central Directorate of Military Communications (RU)
TsUYeGMS... Central Administration of the United Hydrometeorological Service (RU)
TsUZhEL..... Central Administration of Railroad Transportation (RU)
TSUZHELDORSTROY... Central Administration of Railroad Construction (RU)
Ts/V........... Cement-Water Ratio (RU)

TsV .... Center of Buoyancy [*Nautical term*] (RU)
tsv .... Color, Colored (RU)
Tsv .... In Color (BU)
TSv .... Tehnicko-Snabdevacki Vod [*Technical Supply Platoon*] [*Military*] (YU)
TsV .... Tsurkoven Vestnik [*Church Gazette*] [*A newspaper*] (BU)
TsVD .... Central Army Club (BU)
TsVD .... High-Pressure Cylinder (RU)
TsVEI .... Central Scientific Research Institute of Wind Power (RU)
TsVEK .... Central Commission of Medical Experts (RU)
tsvet .... Colored (RU)
tsvet .... Nonferrous Metallurgy Plant [*Topography*] (RU)
TsVetBaktI ... Central Veterinary Bacteriological Institute (BU)
Tsvetmetavtomatika ... Automation in Nonferrous Industry (RU)
Tsvetmetizdat ... State Scientific and Technical Publishing House of Nonferrous Metallurgy and Gold and Platinum Industry (RU)
Tsvetmetprom ... Nonferrous Metals Industry (BU)
Tsvetmetproyekt ... State Institute for the Planning of Establishments of Nonferrous Metallurgy (RU)
Tsvetmetzoloto ... All-Union Association for the Mining, Processing, and Sale of Nonferrous Metals, Gold, and Platinum (RU)
TsVFU .... Central Military Finance Directorate (RU)
TsVIA .... Central Archives of Military History (RU)
tsv il .... Colored Illustration (BU)
TsVL .... Central Military Laboratory (RU)
TsVLK .... Central Medical Commission for Determination of Flight Fitness (RU)
TsVM .... Digital Computer (RU)
TsVMB .... Central Naval Library (RU)
TsVMK .... Central Motorboat Club Imeni P. I. Baranov (RU)
TsVMK .... Central Naval Club (RU)
TsVMM .... Central Naval Museum (RU)
TsVMU .... Central Military Medical Directorate (RU)
TsVMU .... Central Naval Directorate (RU)
TsVN .... High-Pressure Cylinder [*Nuclear energy*] (BU)
tsvp .... Tournez, S'il Vous Plait [*Please Turn*] [*French*] (GPO)
TsVPK .... Central War Industry Committee [*1915-1918*] (RU)
TsVS .... Central Exhibition Hall (RU)
TsVSK .... Central Water Sports Club of the VMF (RU)
TsVTs .... Central Military Censorship (RU)
TsVU .... Digital Computer (RU)
TsVVK .... Central Military Medical Commission (RU)
TsVZ .... Central Air Charger (RU)
TSWL .... Techniczna Szkola Wojsk Lotniczych [*Air Force Technical School*] (POL)
TSYD .... Turkiye Spor Yazarlari Dernegi [*Turkish Sports Writers Association*] (TU)
TSYK .... Turkiye Spor Yazarlari Kulubu [*Turkish Sports Writers Club*] (TU)
TsZ .... Cement Plant (BU)
TsZ- .... Refueling Unit (RU)
tsz .... Termeloszovetkezet [*Producer Cooperative*] (HU)
tsz .... Tobbesszam [*Plural*] (HU)
tsz .... Tovabbszolgalo [*Reenlisted*] (HU)
TSZ .... Tovarny Stavkeveho Zbozi [*Hosiery Mills*] (CZ)
TsZAI .... Central Correspondence Antireligious Institute (RU)
TsZB .... Central Purchasing Office (RU)
t szh .... Liquefaction Temperature (RU)
TSZh .... Railroad Worker's Technical Handbook [*A publication*] (RU)
TsZhIZUL ... Central Railroad Office for Inventions and Improvements (RU)
TsZhO .... Central Housing Department of the Mossovet (RU)
TsZII .... Central Agricultural Research Institute (BU)
TsZII .... Central Correspondence Industrial Institute (RU)
TsZIPP .... Central Correspondence Institute of the Food Industry (RU)
TsZIRP .... Central Correspondence Institute of the Fish Industry (RU)
TsZIS .... Central Correspondence Institute of Communications (RU)
TsZIS .... Central Correspondence Institute of the Sugar Industry (RU)
TsZISS .... Central Correspondence Institute of the Sugar and Alcohol Industry (RU)
TsZIzsII .... Central Agricultural Research and Control Institute (BU)
tszk .... Tanszek [*Department, Chair (of a given discipline at a college or university)*] (HU)
TsZKTI .... Central Correspondence Boiler and Turbine Institute (RU)
TsZL .... Central Laboratory of a Plant (RU)
TsZLT .... Central Correspondence Forestry-Engineering Technicum (RU)
TsZM .... Central Intermediate Production Shop (RU)
TsZMetl .... Central Correspondence Institute of Metallurgy (RU)
TsZMMI .... Central Correspondence Institute of Mechanics and Mechanical Engineering (RU)
TT .... Body Temperature (RU)
TT .... Carrier Telegraphy (RU)
tt .... Comrades (RU)
TT .... Current Transformer (RU)
tt .... Melting Point (BU)
TT- .... Skidding Tractor (RU)
TT .... Takhydromiki Thyris [*Post Office Box*] (GC)
TT .... Takhydromikos Tomevs [*Postal Zone*] [*Greek*] (GC)
TT .... Technical School of Transportation (BU)
TT .... Tekstilna Tovarna [*Textile Factory*] (YU)
Tt .... Telegrafsko-Telefonski [*Telegraphic and Telephonic*] (YU)
TT .... Telegraph and Telephone (BU)
T/T .... Telegraph-Telephone [*Communications*] (RU)
TT .... Telluric Current (RU)
TT .... Theodolite-Tachometer (RU)
TT .... Theoretical Plate (RU)
TT .... Tidningarnas Telegrambyra [*Press Wire Service, Incorporated*] [*Swedish*] (WEN)
TT .... Tirailleurs Tunisiens (MAR)
Tt .... Tone Tereta [*Freight Tons*] (YU)
tt .... Tornaterem [*Gymnasium, Drill Hall*] (HU)
TT .... Trinidad and Tobago [*Two-letter standard code*] (CNC)
TT .... Tula Tokarev [*Pistol*] (RU)
TT .... Tutkintatoimisto [*Investigation Bureau, General Staff*] [*Finnish*] (WEN)
tt .... Volumes (BU)
tt .... Volumes (RU)
TTA .... Tanzania Tea Authority (MAR)
TTA .... Transkei Territorial Assembly (MAR)
TTA .... Transvaal Teachers' Association (MAR)
TTACSA ...... Tanganyika Territory Civil Service Association (MAR)
ttb .... Heavy Tank Battalion (BU)
ttb .... Heavy Tank Battalion (RU)
TTB .... Tanzania Tea Blenders (MAR)
TTB .... Turizm ve Tanitma Bakanligi [*Ministry of Tourism and Orientation*] (TU)
TTB .... Turk Tabibler Birligi [*Turkish Physicians Union*] (TU)
TTC .... Tanzania Tourist Corporation (AF)
TTC .... Teachers Training College [*Namibian*] (AF)
TTC .... Tewfikieh Tennis Club [*Egyptian*] (MAR)
TTC .... Toutes Taxes Comprises [*French*]
TTC .... Transit Transports Camerounais (MAR)
TTCI .... Transit et Transports de Cote-d'Ivoire (MAR)
ttd .... Heavy Tank Division (BU)
ttd .... Heavy Tank Division (RU)
TTD .... Tactical and Technical Data (RU)
TTDE .... Typopoiimeni Taxinomisis Diethnous Emboriou [*Standard International Trade Classification*] (GC)
TTE .... Termeszetbaratok Turista Egyesulete [*Tourist Association of Nature Lovers*] (HU)
Tte .... Torrente [*Torrent*] [*See also T*] [*Italian*] (NAU)
TTE .... Tropical Testing Establishment (MAR)
TTE .... Turk Telekomunikasyon Endustrisi AS [*Turkish Telecommunication Industry Corp.*] (TU)
TTEC .... Trinidad and Tobago Electricity Commission (LA1)
TTED .... Tum Teknik Elemanlar Dernegi [*The United Technicians Association*] (TU)
TTF .... Talebe Teskilatlari Federasyonu [*Federation of Student Organizations*] (TU)
TTF .... Thymidine Triphosphate (RU)
TTF .... Tudomanyos Technikai Forradalom [*Scientific-Technical Revolution*] (HU)
TTF .... Turk Traktor Fabrikasi [*Turkish Tractor Factory*] (TU)
TTFA .... Trinidad and Tobago Farmers Association (LA1)
TTG .... Thyrotropic Hormone (RU)
TTGA .... Tanganyika Tea Growers' Association (MAR)
TTGFO .... Transactions of the Tashkent Geophysical Observatory (RU)
TTGU .... Tyumen' Territorial Geological Administration (RU)
TTH .... Tieftemperatur Hydrierung [*Low Temperature Hydrogenation*] (EG)
TTH .... TransTurk Holding [*Trans-Turk Holding Corporation*] (TU)
TTI .... Tashkent Textile Institute (RU)
TTI .... Tehnica Tensiunilor Inalte [*High Voltage Technology*] (RO)
TTI .... Transvaal Technical Institute (MAR)
TTIP .... Tvornica Turpija i Pila [*Files and Saws Factory*] [*Zagreb-Podsused*] (YU)
TTIS .... Turkiye Toprak Tarim Iscileri Sendikasi [*Turkish Soil and Agricultural Workers Union*] (TU)
ttisspostrojenja ... Telegrafsko-Telefonska i Signalno-Sigurnosna Postrojenja [*Telegraph, Telephone, and Signal Safety Appliances*] (YU)
TTIT .... Tarsadalom- es Termeszettudomanyi Ismeretterjeszto Tarsulat [*Popular Educational Association for the Social and Natural Sciences*] (HU)
TTK .... Heat Engineering Control (RU)
TTK .... Teknillisen Tuonnin Keskusliitto [*Confederation of Technical Importers*] [*Finnish*] (WEN)
TTK .... Turk Tarih Kurumu [*Turkish Historic Society*] (TU)
TTK .... Turk Teskilatlari Kanunu [*Law on Turkish Organizations*] (TU)
TTK .... Turk Ticaret Kanunu [*Turkish Commercial Law*] (TU)
TTK .... Turkiye Turizm Kurumu [*Turkish Tourism Organization*] (TU)
TTKI .... Testnevelesi Tudomanyos Kutato Intezet [*Scientific Research Institute of Physical Education*] (HU)
TTKOC .... Turkiye Trafik Kazalarini Onleme Cemiyeti [*Turkish Society for Prevention of Traffic Accidents*] (TU)
TTKR .... Boiling Heavy-Water Reactor (RU)
TTKR-Up ..... Boiling Heavy-Water Natural-Uranium Reactor (RU)
TTL .... Tanzania Tours Limited (MAR)
TTL .... Telephone-Telegraph Line (BU)
TTL .... Tema Textiles Limited (MAR)
TTL .... Transistor-Transistor-Logik [*Transistor-Transistor-Logic*] (EG)
TTL .... Tribal Trust Land [*Rhodesian*] (AF)

TTLC .... Trinidad and Tobago Labor Council (LA1)
TTM .... Maghrebine de Telephone et de Telematique (MAR)
TTMS .... Telekomunikasyon Turk Mustahdemler Sendikasi [*Turkish Telecommunications Employees' Union*] (TU)
TTN .... Tatrzanskie Towarzystwo Narciarskie [*Tatra Mountain Ski Society*] (POL)
TTO .... Technical Tank Support (RU)
TTO .... Trinidad and Tobago [*Three-letter standard code*] (CNC)
TTOK .... Turkiye Turing ve Otomobil Kurumu [*Turkish Touring and Automobile Association*] (TU)
TTOSOTB ... Turkiye Ticaret Odalari Sanayi Odalari, ve Ticaret Borsalari Birligi [*Union of Turkish Chambers of Commerce, Industry, and Stock Exchanges*] (TU)
TTOSZ .... Tejtermelok es Tejszovetkezetek Orszagos Szovetsege [*National Association of Milk Producers and Milk Producers' Cooperatives*] (HU)
ttp .... Heavy Tank Regiment (BU)
TTP .... Heavy Tank Regiment (RU)
TTP .... Tekstilna Tovarna Prebold [*Prebold Textile Factory*] (YU)
TTP .... Theater Pickup Station [*Television*] (RU)
TTP .... Typifying of Technological Processes (RU)
TTPC .... Trans-Tunisia Pipeline Company (MAR)
TTPS .... Tum Tek Personel Sendikasi [*Comprehensive Technical Personnel Union*] (TU)
TTR .... Glow-Discharge Thyratron (RU)
ttr .... Heavy Tank Company (BU)
ttr .... Heavy Tank Company (RU)
TTR .... Heavy-Water Cooled and Moderated Reactor (RU)
TTR .... Standard Television Station (RU)
TTRM .... Toprak ve Tarim Reformu Mustesarligi [*Undersecretariat of Land and Agricultural Reform*] (TU)
TTS .... Tekstilstroj [*Textile Machinery Factory*] [*Zagreb*] (YU)
TTS .... Telegraph and Telephone Exchange (RU)
TTs .... Television Center (RU)
tts .... Tiszthelyettes [*Senior Noncommissioned Officer*] (HU)
TTsK .... Secret Central Committee (BU)
ttsp .... Heavy Tank and Self-Propelled Gun Regiment (RU)
ttsp .... Self-Propelled Heavy Tank Regiment (BU)
TTSZ .... Takticko-Tehnicka Sredstva za Zaprecavanje [*Tactical and Technical Means for Obstruction*] [*Military*] (YU)
TTSZ .... Toxikologiai Tajekoztato Szolgalat [*Toxicological Information Service*] (HU)
TTT .... Streetcar and Trolleybus Trust (RU)
TTT .... Tactical and Technical Requirements [*Military term*] (RU)
TTT .... Takhydromeia-Tilegrafoi-Tilefona [*Posts, Telegraph, and Telephone (Administration)*] [*Greek*] (GC)
TTT .... Taloudellisen, Teknisen, ja Teollisen Yhteistoiminta [*Economic, Technical, and Industrial Cooperation*] [*Finnish*] (WEN)
TTT .... Termeszettudomanyi Tarsulat [*Natural Sciences Association*] (HU)
TTT .... Testnevelesi Tudomanyos Tanacs [*Scientific Council of Physical Education*] (HU)
TTT .... Trinidad and Tobago Television (LA1)
TTT .... Tudomanyos Testuleti Titkarsag [*Scientific Corporate Secretariat*] (HU)
TTTA .... Tanzania Table Tennis Association (MAR)
TTTNR .... Tarsadalomtudomanyi Tajekoztato Nemzetkozi Rendszere [*International System for Information on the Social Sciences*] (HU)
TTTS .... Telegrafsko-Telefonska Tehnicka Sekcija [*Telegraph and Telephone Technical Section*] (YU)
TTU .... Area Technical Section (RU)
TTU .... Freight Transportation Administration (RU)
TTU .... Telephone and Telegraph Administration (RU)
TTU .... Tetouan Airport (MAR)
TTUB .... Textilni Tiskarny, Upravny, a Barvirny [*Textile Printing, Dressing, and Dyeing Plants*] (CZ)
TTUTA .... Trinidad and Tobago Unified Teachers Association (LA1)
ttv .... Heavy Tank Platoon (BU)
TTV .... Tarifsko-Transportni Vesnik [*Transport Tariff Review*] [*A periodical*] (YU)
TTVK .... Telephone and Telegraph Lead-In Cable (RU)
TTVP .... Trentiner Tiroler Volkspartei [*Trentino Tirol People's Party*] [*Italian*] (PPE)
TTW .... Taegliche Technische Wartung [*Daily Technical Maintenance*] (EG)
TTWA .... Trinidad and Tobago Workers Association (LA1)
TTXGP .... Thong Tan Xa Giai Phong [*Liberation Press Agency*] (TVP)
TTZ .... Takticko-Tehnicki Zahtevi [*Tactical-Technical Requirements*] [*Military*] (YU)
TU .... Aircraft Designed by A. N. Tupolev (RU)
TU .... Control Transformer (RU)
TU .... Control Trigger (RU)
TU .... Narrow-Gauge Diesel Locomotive (RU)
TU .... Packing Materials and Packaging (RU)
TU .... Radio Rediffusion Station (RU)
TU .... Remote Control (RU)
TU .... Repeater (RU)
TU .... Taxe Unique (MAR)
TU .... Technical Administration (RU)
TU .... Technical Conditions (BU)
TU .... Technical School (BU)
TU .... Technical School (RU)
TU .... Technical Specifications (RU)
TU .... Technische Universitaet [*Technical University*] [*German*] (WEN)
TU .... Tehnicka Uprava [*Technical Administration*] [*Military*] (YU)
TU .... Telefonni Ustredna [*Telephone Central*] (CZ)
TU .... Telegrafni Ustredna [*Telegraph Cable Center*] (CZ)
TU .... Telegramme Tres Urgent [*Military*] [*French*] (MTD)
TU .... Temps Universel (MAR)
TU .... Tovarna Usnja [*Leather Factory*] (YU)
TU .... Transit Junction (RU)
TU .... Transportation Administration (RU)
TU .... Trichlorophenoxyacetic Acid (RU)
Tu .... Tunel [*Tunnel*] (TU)
TU .... Tunezja [*Tunisia*] [*Polish*]
tu .... Tuzer [*Artilleryman, Gunner*] (HU)
TUA .... Ketua [*Chairman, Chief*] (IN)
TUACC .... Trade Union Advisory and Coordinating Council (MAR)
TUAC OECD ... Trade Union Advisory Committee to the Organization for Economic Cooperation and Development (EA)
TUB .... Technische Universitaet Berlin [*Berlin Technical University*] [*West German*] (WEN)
TUB .... Transports Urbains de Bamako (MAR)
tub .... Tubercular, Tuberculosis (RU)
TUBA .... Turkiye Basin Ajansi [*Turkish Press Agency*] (TU)
TUBITAK ..... Turkiye Bilimsel ve Teknik Arastirma Kurumu [*Turkish Scientific and Technical Research Organization*] [*Under Office of Premier*] [*See also TBTAK*] (TU)
Tubsanatorium ... Tuberculosis Sanatorium (BU)
TUC .... Trade Union Conference [*Grenadian*] (LA1)
TUC .... Trade Union Congress [*Guyanese*] (LA)
TUC .... Trades Union Congress [*Ghanaian*] (AF)
TUC .... Trades Union Congress [*Jamaican*] (LA1)
TUC .... Transport Urbain de Conakry (MAR)
TUC .... Transvaal University College (MAR)
TUCK .... Turkiye Cografya Kurumu [*Turkish Geographic Society*] [*See also TCK*] (TU)
TUCM .... Trade Union Congress of Malawi (MAR)
TUCN .... Trades Union Congress of Nigeria (AF)
TUCR .... Trade Union Congress of Rhodesia (AF)
TUCSA .... Trade Union Council of South Africa (AF)
TUD .... Technische Universitat Dresden [*Dresden Technical University*] (EG)
TUD EGY ..... Tudomanyegyetem [*University*] (HU)
TUDM .... Tentera Udara Di-Raja Malaysia [*Royal Malaysian Air Force*] (ML)
TUe .... Technische Ueberwachung [*Technical Supervision*] (EG)
TUE .... Universal Electric Thermometer (RU)
TUeV .... Technische Ueberwachungsverwaltung [*West German Automobile Inspection*] (EG)
TUF .... Cloth-Coal Filter (RU)
TUF .... Turnhalle United Front [*Namibian*] (AF)
TUFEM .... Turizm ve Folklor Egitim Merkezi [*Tourism and Folklore Training Center*] [*Ankara*] (TU)
TUFMAC ..... [*The*] Uganda Fish Marketing Corporation Ltd. (MAR)
TUG .... Trustul de Utilaj Greu [*Heavy Equipment Trust*] (RO)
Tuga .... Tugamiral [*Rear Admiral*] (TU)
Tugg .... Tuggeneral [*Brigadier General*] (TU)
TUGP .... Taxe Unique Globale a la Production [*Single Total Production Tax*] [*Algerian*] (AF)
TUH .... Teljesulesi Hatarozat [*Decision of the Full Bench (of the Royal Curia)*] (HU)
TUHUM .... Turkish Harita Umum Mudurlugu [*Turkish Directorate General of Cartography*] (TU)
TUIAFPW .... Trade Unions International of Agriculture, Forestry, and Plantation Workers [*See also UISTAFP*] (EA)
TUiN .... Technical Specifications and Norms (RU)
TUIPAE .... Trade Unions International of Public and Allied Employees (EA)
TUIS .... Turkiye Ulastirma Iscileri Sendikasi [*Turkish Communications Workers Union*] [*Ankara*] (TU)
TUIWC .... Trade Unions International of Workers in Commerce (EA)
TUJL .... Tkalcovny a Upravny Jemneho Lnu [*Fine Linen Weaving and Finishing Mills*] (CZ)
TUJNA .... Tehnicka Uprava Jugoslovenske Narodne Armije [*Technical Administration of the Yugoslav People's Army*] (YU)
TUK .... Technical Specifications for Cables (RU)
TUK .... Toprak Urunleri Kurumu [*Soil Products Organization*] [*Turkish Cypriot*] (GC)
TUK .... Trgovinsko-Ugostiteljska Komora [*Chamber of Commerce and Hotel and Catering Trade*] (YU)
TUKAS .... Turgutlu Konserve Anonim Sirketi [*Turgutlu Canning Corporation*] [*With backing of OYAK*] (TU)
TUKER .... Tuzeloanyagkereskedelmi Vallalat [*Fuel Trade Enterprise*] (HU)
TUKERT .... Tuzifa Kereskedelmi Reszvenytarsasag [*Firewood Trade Company Limited*] (HU)
TUKO .... Turkiye Ulusal Kurtulus Ordusu [*Turkish National Liberation Army*] (TU)
TUKP .... Turkiye Ulusal Kadinlar Partisi [*Turkish National Women's Party*] (TU)
TUL .... Towarzystwo Uniwersytetow Ludowych [*Society of People's Universities (Extension courses)*] (POL)

TUL .... Tyovaen Urheiluliitto [*Workers' Sports League*] [*Finnish*] (WEN)
TULESTAL ... Societe des Tuileries de l'Est-Algerien (MAR)
TULF .... Tamil United Liberation Front [*Sri Lankan*] (PD)
TUL IS .... Turkiye Liman Iscileri Sendikasi [*Turkish Harbor Workers' Union*] (TU)
tum .... Fog (RU)
tum .... Nebula (RU)
TUM .... Peat Removal Machine (RU)
TUMAD DER ... Tutuklu ve Mahkumlarla Dayanisma Dernegi [*Detainees and Prisoners Mutual Solidarity Organization*] (TU)
TUMAS .... Tum Universite, Akademi, ve Yuksek Okulu Asistanlari Birligi [*Comprehensive University, Academy, and College Teaching Assistants' Union*] (TU)
TUMAS .... Turk Muhendislik, Musavirlik, ve Muteahhitlik Anonim Sirketi [*Turkish Engineering, Consulting, and Contracting Corporation*] (TU)
TUMAS .... Turkiye Muhendislik Anonim Sirketi [*Turkish Engineering Corporation*] [*A subsidiary of ASTAS*] (TU)
TUMATA ..... Turk Musikisini Arastirma ve Tanitma Grubu [*Turkish Musical Research and Orientation Group*] (TU)
TUM-DER.... Tum Memurlar Birlesme ve Dayanisma Dernegi [*Comprehensive (Government) Officials' Unity and Mutual Solidarity Association*] (TU)
Tumg........... Tumgeneral [*Major General*] (TU)
TUMHAK..... Turkiye Memur ve Emekli Haklarini Koruma Dernegi [*Society for the Protection of Turkish Employee and Retiree Rights*] (TU)
TUMKA-Is ... [*The*] Mamara District Paper and Cellulose Industries Workers Union (TU)
TUM KULTUR-IS ... Turkiye Milli Egitim, Fikir, ve Beden Iscileri Sendikasi [*Turkish National Education, Intellectual, and Physical Workers Union*] [*Ankara*] (TU)
TUmn .... Multiplication Control Trigger [*Computers*] (RU)
TUMOD .... Tum Ogretim Uyeleri Dernegi [*Comprehensive Educators' Association*] (TU)
TUMOSAN ... Turk Motor Sanayii ve Ticaret AS [*Turkish Motor Industry and Trade Corporation*] (TU)
TUMPECO ... [*The*] Uganda Metal Products and Enamelling Company Ltd. (MAR)
Tum-Person-Kon ... Tum Kamu Personeli Haklarini Koruma Kuruluslari Konfederasyonu [*Confederation of Organizations for the Protection of Rights of All Public Service Personnel*] (TU)
TUM-PTT-DER ... Tum PTT [*Posta, Telefon, Telegraf*] Dernekleri Iscileri Sendikalar [*National PTT (Post, Telephone, and Telegraph) Organizations' Workers' Unions*] (TU)
Tumsit......... Turkiye Belediyeleri Temizlik Iscileri Sendikasi [*Turkish Municipalities Sanitations Workers Union*] [*Istanbul*] (TU)
TUM-TEK.... Tum Teknik Elemanlari Sendikasi [*Comprehensive Technical Workers' Union*] (TU)
TUMTIS....... Turkiye Motorlu Tasit Iscileri Sendikasi [*Turkish Motorized Transport Workers Union*] (TU)
TUN .... Tunis-Carthage Airport (MAR)
TUN .... Tunisia [*Three-letter standard code*] (CNC)
tun .... Tunnel [*Topography*] (RU)
Tun-Is.......... Turkiye Tutun Iscileri Sendikasi [*Turkish Tobacco Workers' Union*] (TU)
TUNISAIR.... Societe Tunisienne de l'Air [*Tunisian airline*]
tunzhpb ...... Railway Tunnel Battalion (BU)
Tuom........... Tuomari [*Judge*] [*Finnish*] (GPO)
tup.............. Blind Alley, Dead End (RU)
TUP .... Rear Fortified Zone (RU)
TUP .... Remote-Control Instrument (RU)
TUP .... Technical Planning Specifications (RU)
TUP .... Tovarystvo Ukrainskykh Progresystiv [*Ukrainian Progressive Association*] [*Russian*] (PPE)
TUP .... Towarzystwo Urbanistow Polskich [*Society of Polish City Planners*] (POL)
TUP .... Turkish Unity Party [*See also TBP*] (TU)
TUP .... Tvornica Ugljenografitnih Proizvoda [*Carbon and Graphite Products Factory*] [*Dubrovnik*] (YU)
TUPE........... Tanganyika Union of Public Employees (MAR)
TUPE........... Technical Specifications for Planning Train Traction Electrification (RU)
TUPM.......... Technical Specifications for Bridge Designing (RU)
TUpr........... Control Trigger [*Computers*] (RU)
TUPS........... Technical Specifications for the Planning of Railroad Stations and Junctions (RU)
TUR .... Towarzystwo Uniwersytetow Robotniczych [*Society of Workers' Universities (Extension courses) (1922-1948)*] (POL)
TuR............. Transformatoren- und Roentgenwerk Dresden (VEB) [*Dresden Transformer and X-Ray Equipment Works (VEB)*] (EG)
TUR .... Turkey [*Three-letter standard code*] (CNC)
tur.............. Turkish (BU)
tur.............. Turkish (RU)
TURBANK ... Turkiye Cumhuriyeti Turizm Bankasi AS [*Turkish Republic Tourism Bank, Inc.*] (TU)
TuRD........... Turbojet Engine (BU)
TURDC........ Trade Union Research and Development Center [*Jamaican*] (LA1)
TURDOK ..... Turkiye Bilimsel ve Teknik Arastirma Kurumu Dokumantasyon Merkezi [*Documentation Center for the Turkish Scientific and Technical Research Organization*] (TU)
tur ez.......... Turkish Language (BU)
turg .... Commercial, Trade (BU)
TURiL .... Towarzystwo Uniwersytetow Robotniczych i Ludowych [*Society of Workers' and Peasants' Universities (Extension courses) (1948-1950)*] (POL)
TURIMPEX ... Empresa Cubana Importadora y Exportador para el Turismo [*Cuban Enterprise for the Import and Export of Tourism*] (LA)
TURISVALLE ... Turismo del Valle del Cauca Ltda. [*Tulua-Valle*] (COL)
TURIZK .... Turkiye Turizm Kurumu [*Turkish Tourism Organization*] (TU)
turk .... Turkestan (RU)
TURKAR-IS ... Turkiye Petrol Kimya Atom, Azot, ve Rafiner Iscileri Sendikasi [*Turkish Petroleum, Chemical, Atomic, Nitrogen, and Refinery Workers Union*] (TU)
TURKAY...... Turkiye Kibrit Sanayii Iscileri Sendikasi [*Turkish Match Industry Workers' Union*] (TU)
Turk Deniz-Ulas-Is ... Turkiye Deniz Tasitmaciligi Isci Sendikalari Federasyonu [*Federation of Turkish Maritime Transport Worker Unions*] (TU)
Turk Dev-Sen ... Turkiye Iktisadi Devlet Tesekkuleri Memur ve Hizmetlileri Sendikasi [*Turkish Union of Economic State Organization Officials and Workers*] (TU)
Turkimya .... Turk Kimya Sanayi Iscileri Sendikasi [*Turkish Chemical Industry Workers Union*] [*See also Kimya-Is*] (TU)
Turk-Is .... Turkiye Isci Sendikalari Konfederasyonu [*Turkish Confederation of Labor*] (TU)
TURKKABLO ... Turk Kablo Anonim Ortaklari [*Turkish Cable Manufacturing Corporation*] (TU)
turkkil .... Turkkilainen [*Finnish*]
TURKKUSU ... Turkish Aviation Association (TU)
turkm .... Turkmen (RU)
Turkmengosizdat ... State Publishing House of the Turkmen SSR (RU)
TurkmenTAG ... Turkmen News Agency (RU)
Turkmenuchpedgiz ... Turkmen State Publishing House of Textbooks and Pedagogical Literature (RU)
TurkmSSR ... Turkmen Soviet Socialist Republic (RU)
TurkNIIGiM ... Turkmen Scientific Research Institute of Hydraulic Engineering and Reclamation (RU)
Turkombyuro ... Bureau of the VTsIK and SNK RSFSR Commission on Turkestan Affairs [*Archives*] (RU)
TURK OTOSAN ... Turkish Auto Industry Workers Union (TU)
Turk-Persen ... Turkiye Kamu Personeli Sendikalari Konfederasyonu [*Confederation of Turkish Public Service Personnel Unions*] (TU)
TURK PERSON-KON ... Turk Kamu Personel Haklarini Koruma Dernekleri Konfederasyonu [*Confederation of Organizations for the Protection of Rights of Turkish Public Service Personnel*] (TU)
Turk-Sag-Kur ... Turkiye Saglik Kurumlari Sendikasi [*Union of Turkish Health Associations*] (TU)
Turk-Sen..... Kibris Turk Isci Sendikalari Federasyonu [*Turkish Cypriot Federation of Labor Unions*] (TU)
Turksib .... Turkestan-Siberian Railroad (RU)
TurkSSR ..... Turkmen Soviet Socialist Republic (RU)
TurkVO .... Turkestan Military District (RU)
TURSAB...... Turkiye Seyahat Ajanlari Birligi [*Turkish Travel Agents' Union*] (TU)
TURSAN...... Kibris Turk Turizm Sanayii [*Turkish Cypriot Tourism Industry*] (GC)
TURSOCIAL ... Turismo Social [*Bogota*] (COL)
TurTsIK....... Turkestan Central Executive Committee (RU)
TURYAG...... Turkiye Sebze Yaglar Sanayii [*Turkish Vegetable Oil Processing Industry*] (TU)
TURYAG...... Turkiye Yag ve Mamulati Anonim Sirketi [*Turkish Oil and Oil Products Corporation*] (TU)
TUS .... Equalizing Coupling Transformer (RU)
TUS .... Technicka Ustredna Spoju [*Technical Center for Communications*] (CZ)
TUS .... Telegraph Communications Regulations (RU)
TUS .... Tenants Union of the Sudan (MAR)
TUS .... Trybunal Ubezpieczen Spolecznych [*Social Security Court*] (POL)
tus .... Tusina(a) [*Finnish*]
TUS .... Tyden Udernichych Smen [*Week of Shock Workers' Shifts*] (CZ)
TUSAS .... Turk Ucak Sanayii Anonim Sirketi [*Turkish Aircraft Industry Corporation*] (TU)
TUS-DER .... Tum Saglik Personeli Birlesme ve Dayanisma Dernegi [*Comprehensive Health Personnel Unity and Solidarity Association*] (TU)
TUSh........... Teater Un Shpil (MAR)
TUSIAD .... Turk Sanayicileri ve Is Adamlari Dernegi [*Turkish Industrialists' and Businessmen's Association*] (TU)
TUSN........... Heat Wave Homing Device, Heat Seeker (RU)
TUSPED ...... Tuzeloanyag Szallitasi Vallalat [*Fuel Transportation Enterprise*] (HU)
TUT .... Taxe Unique sur les Transactions [*Single Tax on Transactions*] (AF)

TUTAS .... Turizm ve Ticaret Anonim Sirketi [*Tourism and Trade Corporation*] (TU)
TUTED .... Tum Teknik Elemanlar Dernegi [*Universal Technical Workers Organization*] (TU)
TUTIS .... Turkiye Tasit Isverenleri Sendikasi [*Union of Turkish Transit Workers Employers*] (TU)
TUTOS .... Turkiye Teknik Ogretmenler Sendikasi [*Turkish Technical Teachers' Union*] (TU)
TU-TS .... Relay Device for Remote Control and Remote Signaling (RU)
TUTVS .... Tyrsuv Ustav pro Telesnou Vychovu a Sport [*Tyrs Institute for Physical Education and Sports*] (CZ)
TUV .... Tarifni Umluva Vojenska [*Military Tariff Agreement*] (CZ)
TUV .... Teatro Universitario. Universidad del Valle [*Cali*] (COL)
TUV .... Trabalhadores Unidos Vencerao [*Workers United Will Win*] [*Portuguese*] (WER)
TUV .... Tuvalu [*Three-letter standard code*] (CNC)
tuv .... Tuvinian (RU)
TUVESAD ... Turkiye Ulusal Verem Savas Dernegi [*Turkish National Society for the Prevention of Tuberculosis*] (TU)
Tuvknigoizdat ... Tuvinian Book Publishing House (RU)
TUYM .... Trade Union Youth Movement [*Guyanese*] (LA)
tuy nar .... So-Called (BU)
TUZ .... Technical Educational Institution (RU)
TUZEP .... Tuzeloszer es Epitoanyag Ertekesito Vallalat [*Fuel and Building Material Trade Enterprise*] (HU)
TUZMAS ..... Tuz ve Mamulleri Kimya Sanayii Anonim Sirketi [*Salt and By-Products Chemical Industry Corporation*] (TU)
TV .... Construction Troops (BU)
TV .... Drop Point (RU)
Tv .... Freight Car (RU)
tv .... Hard, Hardness, Solid, Solidity (RU)
TV .... Heavy-Water [*Nuclear physics and engineering*] (RU)
TV .... Input Transformer (RU)
tv .... Instrumental [*Case*] (RU)
TV .... Output Transformer (RU)
TV .... Pipe Air Preheater (RU)
TV .... Rectifying Transformer (RU)
TV .... Remote Control Switch (RU)
TV .... Slow-Speed Wind Motor (RU)
TV .... Tacno Vreme [*Correct Time*] (YU)
tv .... Tana Vuonna [*This Year*] [*Finnish*] (GPO)
tv .... Tank Platoon (BU)
TV .... Tank Platoon (RU)
TV .... Tarifvertrag [*Collective Bargaining Agreement, Trade Agreement*] (EG)
TV .... Technicke-Vedecke Vydavatelstvi [*Technical and Scientific Publishing House*] [*Prague*] (CZ)
tv .... Tehervonat [*Freight Train*] (HU)
TV .... Telesno Vezbanje [*Physical Exercise*] (YU)
TV .... Televisio [*Television*] [*Finnish*]
TV .... Telewizja [*Television*] [*Polish*]
TV .... Terak Vithei [*Boulevard*] [*Literally, Esplanade or Road Along the Shore*] [*Cambodian*] (CL)
tv .... Terv [*Plan*] (HU)
tv .... Torveny [*Law (Legal)*] (HU)
TV .... Tratove Velitelstvi [*Railroad Command*] (CZ)
tv .... Travessa [*Cross*] [*Portuguese*] (CED)
TV- .... Trolley Pusher (RU)
TV .... Tropical Air (RU)
TV .... Tuvalu [*Two-letter standard code*] (CNC)
tv .... Tyovaenyhdistys [*Finnish*]
TVA .... External Address Table [*Computers*] (RU)
TVA .... Tables of Altitudes and Azimuths (RU)
TVA .... Tactical Air Force (RU)
TVA .... Tanzania Volleyball Association (MAR)
TVA .... Tarif- und Verkehrsanzeiger [*Rate and Traffic Schedule*] (EG)
TVA .... Taxa pe Valoarea Adaugata [*Value-Added Tax*] (RO)
TVA .... Taxe sur la Valeur Ajoutee [*Value-Added Tax*] [*French*] (WER)
TVA .... Tourisme et Voyages en Afrique (MAR)
TVA .... Turbofan Assembly (RU)
TVAZ .... Tables of Altitudes and Azimuths of Stars (RU)
TVBTAO ...... Turkiye Vakiflar Bankasi Turk Anonim Ortaklari [*Turkish Religious Trusts/Bank Corporation*] (TU)
tvc .... Torvenycikk [*Article of Law*] (HU)
TVCh .... High-Frequency Current (BU)
TVCh .... High-Frequency Current (RU)
TVD .... High-Pressure Turbine (RU)
TVD .... Telesno Vzgojno Drustvo [*Physical Education Society*] (YU)
tvd .... Television (RU)
TVD .... Theater of Operations (RU)
TVD .... Turboprop Engine (RU)
TVDPKh ...... High-Pressure Ahead Turbine (RU)
TVDZKh ...... High-Pressure Astern Turbine (RU)
TVE .... Fuel Element [*Nuclear physics and engineering*] (RU)
TVE .... Televisao Experimental (MAR)
TVE .... Television Espanola [*Spanish Television*] (WER)
TVEL .... Fuel Element [*Nuclear physics and engineering*] (RU)
TVEO .... Transactions of the Free Economic Society [*A publication*] (RU)
TVF .... Air Fleet Engineering (RU)
TVG- .... Exhaust Gas Temperature Gauge (RU)
TVGRO .... Transactions of the All-Union Geological Exploration Association [*A publication*] (RU)
TVHB .... Turk Veteriner Hekimler Birligi [*Turkish Veterinary Doctors Union*] (TU)
TVID .... Turbofan Engine (RU)
TVK .... Tiszai Vegyikombinat [*Tisza Chemical Combine*] (HU)
TVK .... Toimihenkilo- ja Virkamiesjarjestojen-Keskusliitto [*Confederation of Salaried Employees*] [*Finnish*] (WEN)
TVL .... Transvaal (MAR)
TVLC .... Takoradi Veneer and Lumber Company Ltd. (MAR)
TVM .... Heavy Suspension Bridge (RU)
TVM .... Telesna Vychova Mladeze [*Physical Education for Young People*] (CZ)
TVM .... Tiszai Vegyi Muvek [*Tisza Chemical Works*] (HU)
TVM .... Tiszamenti Vegyimuvek [*Tisza Bank Chemical Works*] [*Later, Tiszai Vegyi Muvek*] (HU)
TVM .... Tropical Veterinary Medicine (MAR)
TVN .... High-Voltage Current (RU)
TVN .... High-Voltage Engineering (RU)
TVN .... High-Voltage Transformer (RU)
TVNK .... Television Nationale Khmere [*Cambodian National Television*] (CL)
t-vo .... Association, Company (RU)
TVO .... Educational Labor Camp (BU)
TVO .... Transportverordnung [*Transportation Ordinance*] (EG)
tvor .... Instrumental [*Case*] (RU)
t vospl .... Ignition Temperature (RU)
t vozg .... Sublimation Temperature (RU)
TVP .... Tamil Vimukhti Peramena [*Sri Lankan*] (PPW)
TVP .... Technische Vorplanung [*Advance Technical Planning*] (EG)
TVR .... Heavy-Water Reactor (RU)
tvr .... Torvenyereju Rendelet [*Law Decree*] (HU)
TVRD .... Turbofan Engine (RU)
TVRD .... Turbojet Engine (BU)
TVRD .... Turboprop Engine (RU)
TVREK .... Television de la Republique Khmere [*Television of the Khmer Republic*] [*Cambodian*] (CL)
TVRF .... Terrorist Victims Relief Fund (MAR)
TVRO .... Transports Voyageurs de la Region d'Oran [*Algerian*] (MAR)
tv r-r .... Solid Solution (RU)
TVR-Up .... Water-Cooled Heavy-Water-Moderated Natural Uranium Reactor (RU)
TVRZ .... Tambov Railroad Car Repair Plant (RU)
TVS .... Tehnicka Visa Skola [*Advanced Technical School*] (YU)
TVS .... Telesna Vychova a Sport [*Physical Education and Sports*] (CZ)
TVS .... Telovychovne Slavnosti Skol [*School Physical Education Festival*] (CZ)
TVS .... Tylove Velitelske Stanoviste [*Rear Area Command Post*] (CZ)
TVSORGO ... Transactions of the East Siberian Branch of the Russian Geographical Society [*A publication*] (RU)
t vsp .... Flash Point (RU)
TVT .... Trans-Volta Togoland (MAR)
TVT .... Troupe de la Ville de Tunis (MAR)
TVV .... Technicko-Vedecke Vydavatelstvi [*Technical and Scientific Publishing House*] [*Prague*] (CZ)
TVV .... Topographic Computing Platoon (RU)
TVZ .... Television Zambias (MAR)
TW .... Taiwan [*Two-letter standard code*] (CNC)
TW .... Teatr Wielki [*Grand Theatre*] (POL)
TW .... Technische Wartung [*Technical Maintenance*] (EG)
TW .... Trung Uong [*Central, Central Committee*] (TVP)
tw .... Twardosc [*Hardness*] [*Polish*]
TWAU .... Transvaal Women's Agricultural Union (MAR)
TWD .... Tanganyika Wildlife Development (MAR)
TWF .... Third World Forum (EA)
TWF .... Third World Foundation (EA)
Twg .... Topfwagen [*Container Car*] (EG)
Twgf .... Triebwagenfuehrer [*Rail Motor Car Engineer*] (EG)
Twgsch .... Triebwagenschaffner [*Rail Motor Car Conductor*] (EG)
TWI .... Training within Industry (MAR)
TWICO .... Tanzania Wood Industry Corporation (AF)
TWIU .... Textile Workers' Industrial Union (MAR)
TWK .... Technischwirtschaftliche Kennziffer [*Industrial-Economic Index*] (EG)
TWLF .... Third World Liberation Force (MAR)
TWLS .... Tanzania Wildlife Safaris Limited (MAR)
TW-MAE-W ... Third World Movement Against the Exploitation of Women (EA)
TWMP .... Towarzystwo Wydawnicze Muzyki Polskiej [*Society for Publication of Polish Music*] (POL)
TWN .... Taiwan [*Three-letter standard code*] (CNC)
TWN .... Taylor Woodrow of Nigeria (MAR)
TWP .... Teatr Wojska Polskiego [*Polish Army Theater*] (POL)
TWP .... Towarzystwo Wiedzy Powszechnej [*Society for Popularization of Knowledge*] (POL)
TWP .... True Whig Party [*Liberian*] (AF)
TWP .... Turkish Workers' Party [*See also TEP*] (TU)
tw szt .... Tworzywo Sztuczne [*Plastic*] [*Polish*]
TWT .... Tanzania Wildlife Tour (MAR)
TWU .... Telecommunications Workers Union [*Mauritian*] (AF)
TWU .... Transport Workers' Union (ML)

TWZ............ Technischwissenschaftliches Zentrum [*Technical and Scientific Center (Production development)*] (EG)
t/x............... Motor Ship (RU)
tx................ Tonneaux [*French*]
Tx................ Wytwornia Telekomunikacyjnego Sprzetu Numer X [*Number X Telecommunications Equipment Plant*] (POL)
TY................ Tagma Ygeionomikou [*Medical Battalion*] (GC)
ty................ Tarih Yok [*Undated*] (TU)
Ty................ Tayyare [*Airplane*] (TU)
TY................ Teyateyaneng (MAR)
T/Y.............. Ton/Yil [*Tons per Year*] (TU)
TYaD............ Thermonuclear Engine (RU)
TYaEG.......... Thermonuclear Electric Generator (RU)
TYaES.......... Thermonuclear Electric Power Plant (RU)
TYaTG.......... Thermonuclear Heat Generator (RU)
tyazhmash ... Heavy Machinery Manufacture, Heavy Machinery (RU)
tyazhprom ... Heavy Industry (RU)
tyazhpromelektroproyekt ... State Planning Institute for the Planning of Electrical Equipment for Heavy Industry (RU)
Tyazhstankogidropress ... Heavy Machine Tool and Hydraulic Press Plant (RU)
TYB............. Turkiye Yazarlar Birligi [*Turkish Writers' Union*] (TU)
TYC............. Turkiye Yesilay Cemiyeti [*Turkish Red Crescent Society*] (TU)
TYDK........... Tekhniki Ypiresia Dimon kai Koinotiton [*Technical Service of the Municipalities and Communes*] [*Greek*] (GC)
TYE............. Tekhniki Ypiresia tis Ekklisias [*Church Technical Service*] [*Greek*] (GC)
tye.............. That Is (RU)
TYeM........... Technical Unit of Mass (RU)
tyg.............. Tygodnik [*Weekly*] (POL)
TYH-Is......... Turkiye Yeni Haber-Is [*New Turkish Information Union*] (TU)
TYL............. TANU [*Tanganyika African National Union*] Youth League [*Tanzanian*] (AF)
TYOSKK..... Turkiye Yusek Ogretim Spor Koordinasyon Kurulu [*Turkish Higher Education Sports Coordination Committee*] (TU)
TYS............. Takhydromiki Ypiresia Stratou [*Army Postal Service*] [*Greek*] (GC)
TYS............. Tameiaki Ypiresia Stratou [*Army Finance Service*] [*Greek*] (GC)
tys.............. Thousand (RU)
TYS............. Turkiye Yazarlar Sendikasi [*Turkish Writers' Union*] (TU)
tys.............. Tysiac [*Thousand*] [*Polish*]
TYSD........... Turkiye Yardim Sevenler Dernegi [*Turkish Philanthropic Society*] [*See also YSD*] (TU)
TYSE........... Turk Yapi Sanat Enstitusu [*Turkish Construction Trades Institute*] [*Cypriot*] (TU)
tyt............... Tytul [*Title*] (POL)
Tyumen'sel'mash ... Tyumen' Plant of Agricultural Machinery (RU)
tyurk............ Turkic (RU)
TYuTAKE.... Transactions of the South Turkmenistan Complex Archaeological Expedition [*A publication*] (RU)
TYuZ........... Young Spectator's Theater, Children's Theater (RU)
TYYK........... Turk Yoksullara Yardim Kurumu [*Society for Aid to Turkish Orphans*] [*Turkish Cypriot*] (GC)
TYYK........... Turk Yonetimi Yurutme Kurulu [*Turkish (Cypriot) Administration Executive Council*] (GC)
TZ............... Commercial Law (BU)
TZ............... Fueling Truck (RU)
TZ............... Technical Task (RU)
TZ............... Times of Zambia (MAR)
TZ............... Trgovska Zbornica [*Chamber of Commerce*] (YU)
TZ............... Trinecke Zelezarny Velke Rijnove Socialisticke Revoluce [*Trinec Iron Works of the Great October Socialist Revolution*] (CZ)
TZ............... Turgoviya i Zemedelie [*Commerce and Agriculture*] [*A periodical*] (BU)
TZ............... United Republic of Tanzania [*Two-letter standard code*] (CNC)
TZA............. Heavy Antiaircraft Artillery (RU)
TZA............. Technisches Zentralamt [*Central Technical Office*] (EG)
TZA............. Turbogear Assembly (RU)
TZA............. United Republic of Tanzania [*Three-letter standard code*] (CNC)
t zam.......... Freezing Point (RU)
t zast.......... Solidification Point (RU)
t zatv.......... Solidification Temperature (RU)
TZC............. Turkiye Ziraatciler Cemiyeti [*Turkish Agriculturalists Society*] (TU)
TZCh........... Tractor Spare-Part Plant (RU)
TZDK........... Turkiye Zirai Donatim Kurumu [*Turkish Agricultural Equipment Board*] (TU)
TZGT........... Tula Correspondence Mining Technicum (RU)
t:zh............. Solid-to-Liquid Ratio (RU)
t zh............. Thousand Inhabitants (RU)
TZhMat....... Journal of Abstracts: Mathematics [*A publication*] (RU)
tzhpb........... Railway Maintenance Battalion (BU)
TZhRU......... Tula Iron Mine Administration (RU)
TZhS........... Railroad Technical Dictionary (RU)
TZI............. Floating River-Crossing Equipment [*Military term*] (RU)
Tz Ist.......... Telsiz Istasyonu [*Wireless Station*] (TU)
TZK............. Commander's Zenith Telescope (RU)
TZK............. Taganrog Combine Plant (RU)
TZK............. Technicka Zavodni Knihovna [*Factory Technical Library*] (CZ)
TZKh........... Reverse Turbine (RU)
TZM............ Floating River-Crossing Material [*Military term*] (RU)
tzn.............. To Znaczy [*That Is*] (POL)
TZOB........... Turkiye Ziraat Odalari Birligi [*Turkish Union of Chambers of Agriculture*] (TU)
TZp............. Recording Flip-Flop (RU)
TZP............. Technical School for Grain Storage and Processing (BU)
TZP............. Tymczasowy Zarzad Panstwowy [*Provisional State Administration*] (POL)
TZP............. Unsinkable Float [*Military term*] (RU)
TZS............. Technicum of Landscaping (RU)
TZS............. Titulni Zarizeni Staveniste [*Specified Building Equipment*] (CZ)
TZU............. Technical Establishments and Systems (BU)
TZUS........... Technicky a Zkusebni Ustav Stavebni [*Institute for Technology and Testing in Construction*] (CZ)
tzv.............. Takozvani [*So-Called*] (YU)
tzv.............. Tuna Zive Vahy [*Ton of Live Weight*] (CZ)
tzw.............. Tak Zwany [*So-Called*] (POL)
TZWS.......... Tomaszowskie Zaklady Wlokien Sztucznych [*Tomaszow Artificial Fiber Plant*] (POL)
TZZ............. Barely Perceptible Obstacle (BU)
TZZ............. Hall Darkener (RU)

U

U- .... Amplifier (RU)
u .... Ante Meridiem [*Before Noon*] (RU)
U- .... Instruction [*Standardization document*] (RU)
U .... Regulations, Manual (RU)
U- .... Trainer [*Aircraft*] (RU)
U .... Uafhaengige Parti [*Independent Party*] [*Danish*] (PPE)
U .... Uhr [*Hour*] [*German*]
U .... Umdrehung [*Revolution*] [*German*]
U .... Umgangssprache [*German*]
U .... Unbesetzt [*Unoccupied, No One on Duty*] (EG)
u .... Und [*And*] [*German*] (GPO)
u .... Under [*Under*] [*Norwegian*] (GPO)
U .... Universal (RU)
u .... Unser [*Our*] [*Business and trade*] [*German*]
u .... Unten [*Below*] [*German*]
u .... Unter [*Under, Among*] [*German*]
U .... Unterkunft [*Billet, Accommodation, Shelter*] (EG)
U .... Unverseifbares [*Unsaponifiable*] [*German*]
U .... Urania Verlag [*Urania Publishing House*] (EG)
U .... Urugwaj [*Uruguay*] [*Polish*]
U .... Usted [*You (Singular, formal)*] [*Spanish*]
u .... Utan [*or Utani*] [*After*] (HU)
U .... Utara [*North*] (ML)
u .... Utasz [*Combat Engineer*] (HU)
u .... Utca [*Street*] (HU)
u .... Uteg [*Battery*] (HU)
U .... Uvala [*or Uvalica*] [*Inlet*] [*Yugoslav*] (NAU)
u .... Uyezd [*District, 1775-1929*] (RU)
u .... Uzem [*Industrial Plant*] (HU)
u .... Uzlet [*Store*] (HU)
UA .... Bar Ukase (BU)
UA .... Specific Activity (RU)
ua .... Ueber Alle [*Over All*] [*German*]
ua .... Ugyanakkor [*At the Same Time, Simultaneously*] (HU)
ua .... Ugyanaz [*Same As*] [*Hungarian*] (GPO)
ua .... Und Aehnlich [*And So On*] [*German*]
ua .... Und Andere [*And Others*] [*German*] (GPO)
UA .... Underwater Association for Scientific Research (EA)
UA .... Universal Algorithm (RU)
U de A .... Universidad de Antioquia [*Medellin*] (COL)
ua .... Unter Anderem [*Among Other Things*] [*German*] (GPO)
ua .... Unter Andern [*Among Others*] [*German*] (GPO)
UAA .... Administration of Arctic Aviation (RU)
uaa .... Und An Anderen Orten [*And Elsewhere*] [*German*]
UAA .... Union des Avocats Arabes [*Arab Lawyers Union - ALU*] (EA)
UAA .... United Arab Airlines [*Egyptian*] (MAR)
UAAEE .... United Arab Atomic Energy Establishment (MAR)
UAAI .... Union Africaine Agricole et Industrielle [*African Agricultural and Industrial Union*] [*Senegalese*] (AF)
UAAJ .... Union Arabe des Auberges de la Jeunesse (MAR)
UAB .... Guided Bomb (RU)
UABB .... Union Arabe de Basketball (MAR)
U-Abt .... Unterabteilung [*Subdivision, Branch*] (EG)
UAC .... Uganda Action Convention (AF)
UAC .... Unified Arab Command (ME)
UAC .... Union Arabe de Cyclisme (MAR)
UAC .... United Africa Company [*Nigerian*] (AF)
UACAS .... Unidades de Abastecimiento para las Comunas Agricolas Sandinistas [*Supply Units for the Sandinist Agricultural Communes*] [*Nicaraguan*] (LA)
UACF .... Union Africaine des Chemins de Fer (MAR)
UACHP .... Ustav pro Automatizaci Chemickeho Prumyslu [*Institute for Automation of Chemical Industry*] (CZ)
UAChR .... Automatic Frequency-Controlled Unloading Device of Power Systems (RU)
UACPB .... Union Apostolique et Culturelle de Pretres Burundais (MAR)
UAD .... Union des Anciens du Dahomey (MAR)
UADA .... Union Argentina de Aseguradores [*Insurers Union of Argentina*] (LA)
UADD .... Directorate of Long-Range Aviation (RU)
UADE .... Universidad Argentina de la Empresa [*Argentine Business University*] (LA)
UADW .... Universal Alliance of Diamond Workers [*See also AUOD*] (EA)
uae .... Und Aehnliche [*And the Like*] (EG)
UAE .... United Arab Emirates (ME)
UAFA .... Union Arabe de Football Association [*Union Arab Football Association*] (EA)
UAFT .... Union Africaine des Telecommunications [*African Telecommunications Union*] (AF)
UAG .... Air Attack Group (RU)
UAG .... Ugandan Action Group (AF)
UAG .... Universidad Autonoma de Guadalajara
UAGT .... Administration of the City Automobile Transportation (RU)
UAI .... Ufa Aviation Institute Imeni Sergo Ordzhonikidze (RU)
UAI .... Union des Associations Internationales [*Union of International Associations - UIA*] (EA)
UAIA .... Union des Agences d'Information Africaines [*Union of African News Agencies*] (AF)
UAJ .... Union of Arab Jurists (EA)
UAK .... United Arab Kingdom [*Jordanian*] (ME)
UALE .... Universal Artist League of Esperantists (EA)
uam .... Und Aehnliches Mehr [*And the Like, And So On*] [*German*]
uam .... Und Andere [*or Anderes*] Mehr [*And So Forth, And So On*] [*German*]
UAM .... Unia Afrykansko-Malgaska [*African-Malagasy Union*] [*Polish*]
UAM .... Union Africaine et Malgache [*African and Malagasy Union*] (AF)
UAM .... Union des Artisans du Meuble (MAR)
UAM .... Universidad Autonoma Metropolitana [*Metropolitan Autonomous University*] [*Mexican*] (LA1)
UAM .... Uniwersytet Adama Mickiewicza [*Adam Mickiewicz University*] [*Poznan*] (POL)
UAMBD .... Union Africaine et Malgache des Banques pour le Developpement [*African and Malagasy Union of Banks for Development*] (AF)
UAMBD .... Union Africaine et Mauricienne de Banques pour le Developpement [*African and Mauritian Union of Banks for Development*] (AF)
UAMCE .... Union Africaine et Malgache de Cooperation Economique [*Afro-Malagasy Union for Economic Cooperation*] (AF)
UAMD .... Union Africaine et Malgache de Defense [*Afro-Malagasy Defense Union*] (AF)
UAMPT .... Union Africaine et Malgache des Postes et Telecommunications (MAR)
UAMV .... Ustredni Archiv Ministerstva Vnitra [*Central Archives of the Ministry of the Interior*] (CZ)
UAN .... Progress of Astronomical Sciences (RU)
UAN .... Ukrainian Academy of Sciences (RU)
UAN .... Union Autonomista Navarra [*Navarra Autonomist Union*] [*Spanish*] (WER)
UAN .... United Animal Nations (EA)
UANA .... Union of African News Agencies (AF)
UANA .... Union of Arab News Agencies (MAR)
UANC .... United African National Council [*Zimbabwean*] (PPW)
UANM .... Universal African Nationalist Movement (MAR)
uaO .... Und Andere Orte [*And Elsewhere*] [*German*]
uaO .... Unter Anderen Orten [*Among Other Places*] [*German*]
UAP .... Directorate of the Aircraft Industry (RU)
UAP .... Unabhaengige Arbeiterpartei [*Independent Labor Party*] [*West German*] (PPE)
UAP .... Unabhaengige Arbeiterpartei - Deutsche Sozialisten [*Independent Labor Party - German Socialists*] [*West German*] (PPW)
UAP .... Union Assurances de Paris (MAR)
UAP .... Uniunea Artistilor Plastici [*Union of Plastic Artists*] (RO)
UAPA .... Union des Agences de Presse Africaines [*Union of African Press Agencies*] (AF)
UAPP .... Automatic Reclosing (RU)
UAPP .... Training Glider Regiment (RU)
UAPT .... Union Africaine des Postes et des Telecommunications [*African Postal and Telecommunications Union*] [*Use APTU*] (AF)

UAPV.......... Automatic Recloser (RU)
UAR.......... Ujedinjena Arapska Republika [*United Arab Republic*] (YU)
UARAEE...... United Arab Republic Atomic Energy Establishment (MAR)
UARAF........ United Arab Republic Air Force (MAR)
UARBC........ United Arab Republic Broadcasting Corporation (MAR)
UARBS........ United Arab Republic Broadcasting Service (MAR)
UARS.......... Guided Air-Launched Missile (RU)
UARTO........ United Arab Republic Telecommunication Organization (MAR)
UARV.......... Device for Automatic Control of Synchronous Machine Excitation (RU)
UARZ.......... Administration of Automobile Repair Plants and of Technical Supply of Automobile Transportation (of the Mosgorispolkom) (RU)
UAS.......... Uganda Air Services Ltd. (MAR)
UAS.......... Uluslararasi Anonim Sirketi [*International Corporation*] (TU)
uas.......... Und Andere Solche [*And Others*] [*German*]
UAS.......... Union of African States (MAR)
UAS.......... United Arab States (MAR)
UAS.......... Uniunea Asociatilor Studentesti [*Union of Student Associations*] (RO)
UASC.......... Union of African Sports Confederations (MAR)
UASC.......... United Arab Shipping Company (ME)
UASCR........ Uniunea Asociatilor Studentilor Comunisti din Romania [*Union of Communist Student Associations in Romania*] (RO)
UASD.......... Universidad Autonoma de Santo Domingo [*Autonomous University of Santo Domingo*] [*Dominican Republic*] (LA)
UASE.......... Union of African Students in Europe (MAR)
UASI.......... Union of Artisans of the Sugar Industry [*Mauritian*] (AF)
UASKhN....... Ukrainian Academy of Agricultural Sciences (RU)
UASP i VS... Administration of Special Purpose Aviation and Aerial Photography [*Civil aviation*] (RU)
UASS.......... Guided Air-Launched Cruise Missile (RU)
UASSR........ Udmurt Autonomous Soviet Socialist Republic (RU)
UASSU........ Union des Associations Sportives, Scolaires, et Universitaires (MAR)
UAT.......... Adjusting Autotransformer (RU)
UAT.......... Administration of Automobile Transportation (RU)
UAT.......... Motor Vehicle Transport Administration (BU)
UAT.......... Public Motor Vehicle Transport Statutes (BU)
UAT.......... Union Aeromaritime des Transports (MAR)
UATA.......... Uganda African Teachers' Association (MAR)
UATI.......... Union des Associations Techniques Internationales [*Union of International Technical Associations - UITA*] (EA)
UATS.......... Agency Automatic Telephone Exchange (RU)
UAU.......... Universal Arithmetic Unit [*Computers*] (RU)
UAUP.......... Ustav Architektury a Uzemniho Planovani [*Institute of Architecture and Regional Planning*] (CZ)
UAV.......... Attack Aircraft Carrier (RU)
UAV.......... Unidad de Accion Vallecaucana [*Cali*] (COL)
UAV.......... Ustredni Akcni Vybor [*Central Action Committee*] (CZ)
UAVR.......... Device for Automatic Switching of Reserve Power Supply (RU)
UAVT.......... Heavy Attack Aircraft Carrier (RU)
UAwg.......... Um Antwort Wird Gebeten [*An Answer Is Requested*] (EG)
UAWU.......... University and Allied Workers Union [*Jamaican*] (LA1)
UAZ.......... Automobile Made by the Ul'yanovsk Automobile Plant (RU)
UAZ.......... Emergency Protection Device (RU)
UAZ.......... Ul'yanovsk Automobile Plant (RU)
UAZ.......... Ural Aluminum Plant (RU)
UAZ.......... Ural Automobile Plant (RU)
UB.......... Amplification Unit (RU)
UB.......... Shock Brigade (RU)
ub.......... Ubiegly [*Last*] [*Polish*]
ub.......... Ubiegly Rok [*Last Year*] (POL)
UB.......... Udarna Brigada [*Shock Brigade*] (YU)
UB.......... Umelecka Beseda [*Artists' Club*] (CZ)
UB.......... Universitaetsbibliothek [*University Library*] (EG)
UB.......... Universite du Benin [*University of Benin*] [*Togolese*] (AF)
UB.......... Universiteits-Bibliotheek
UB.......... University Library (BU)
UB.......... Univerzitetska Biblioteka [*University Library*] (YU)
UB.......... Urzad Bezpieczenstwa [*Security Administration*] (POL)
UB.......... Uzemi Bizottsag [*Factory Shop Committee*] (HU)
UBA.......... Uniao Brasileira dos Avicultores [*Brazilian Poultrymen's Union*] (LA)
UBA.......... United Bank for Africa Ltd. (MAR)
UBA.......... Universite des Beaux-Arts [*Fine Arts University*] [*Replaced URBA*] [*Cambodian*] (CL)
UBAC.......... Union Bancaire en Afrique Centrale [*Banking Union in Central Africa*] (AF)
UBAF.......... Union de Banques Arabes et Francaises (MAR)
UBAN.......... Statutes of the Bulgarian Academy of Sciences (BU)
UBB.......... Uniwersytet Boleslawa Bieruta [*Boleslaw Bierut University*] (POL)
UBBS.......... University of Basutoland, Bechuanaland Protectorate, and Swaziland (MAR)
UBC.......... United Brethren Church (MAR)
UBC.......... Universal Bibliographic Control [*IFLA*] [*'s-Gravenhage*]
UBC.......... Urban Bantu Council (MAR)
UBCI.......... Union Bancaire pour le Commerce et l'Industrie [*Banking Union for Commerce and Industry*] [*Tunisian*] (AF)
UBD.......... Union Blanca Democratica [*Blanco Democratic Union*] [*Uruguayan*] (LA)
UBD.......... Ustredni Banka Druzstev [*Central Bank of Cooperatives*] (CZ)
UBDKh........ Ukase on Fight Against Petty Hooliganism (BU)
UBDP.......... Union Belge pour la Defense de la Paix [*Belgian Union for the Defense of Peace*] (WER)
UBE.......... Uniao Brasileira de Escritores [*Brazilian Writers Union*] (LA)
UBEC.......... Union of Banana-Exporting Countries [*See also UPEB*] (EA)
ubers.......... Uebersetzt [*Translated*] [*German*]
ubert.......... Uebertragen [*Translated*] [*German*]
UBES.......... Uniao Brasileira de Estudantes Secundarios [*Brazilian Union of Secondary Students*] (LA)
UBF.......... Device for High-Speed Excitation Forcing (RU)
UBFU.......... Administration of Balneologic and Physiatric Institutions (RU)
UBHC.......... Uy Ban Hanh Chinh [*Administrative Committee*] (TVP)
UBIB.......... Charter of the Bulgarian Investment Bank (BU)
UBiKO........ Administration of Personal and Municipal Services (RU)
UBIMAT...... Universal-Drahtbiege-Automat [*Universal Automatic Wire-Bending Machine*] (EG)
UBIW.......... Union of Bus Industry Workers [*Mauritian*] (AF)
UBJ.......... Union of Black Journalists (MAR)
UBK.......... Berezin Universal Wing [*Machine gun*] (RU)
UBK-.......... Universal Tower Crane (RU)
UBK.......... Ustredni Bytova Komise [*Central Housing Committee*] (CZ)
UBKhSS...... Administration for Combating the Embezzlement of Socialist Property and Speculation (RU)
UBKJVDM... Udruzenje Boraca Kraljevske Jugoslovenske Vojske "Draza Mihailovic" [*Draza Mihailovic Association of Veterans of the Royal Yugoslav Armed Forces*] [*World War II*] (YU)
UBKK.......... Ustredni Branna Koordinacni Komise [*Central Defense Coordinating Committee*] (CZ)
UBKO.......... Administration of Personal and Municipal Services (RU)
UBKS.......... Universal Construction Tower Crane (RU)
ubl.......... Ublich [*Usual*] [*Business and trade*] [*German*]
UBLS.......... University of Botswana, Lesotho, and Swaziland (AF)
UBN.......... Pipeless Pump Unit (RU)
UBNB.......... Charter of the Bulgarian National Bank (BU)
UBO.......... Coast Defense Directorate (RU)
UBO.......... Coast Defense School (RU)
UBO.......... Coastal Defense Administration (BU)
UBOK.......... Ustav Bytove a Odevni Kultury [*Institute for Apartment and Clothing Improvement*] (CZ)
UBP.......... Combat Training (RU)
UBP.......... Directorate of Combat Training (RU)
UBP.......... Ulusal Birlik Partisi [*National Unity Party*] [*See also MBP*] [*Cypriot*] (TU)
UBP.......... United Bahamian Party (PPW)
UBP.......... United Bermuda Party (PPW)
UBP.......... Urzad Bezpieczenstwa Publicznego [*Public Security Administration*] (POL)
UBP.......... Usines Beninoises de Prefabrication (MAR)
UBP.......... Ustav Bezpecnosti Prace [*Institute for Labor Safety*] (CZ)
UBPTs........ Statute of the Bulgarian Eastern Orthodox Church (BU)
UBR.......... Device for High-Speed Excitation Damping (RU)
UBR.......... Guided Ballistic Missile (RU)
UBS.......... Berezin Universal Synchronized [*Machine gun*] (RU)
UBS.......... Control, Blocking, and Signaling (RU)
UBS.......... Umelecka Beseda Slovenska [*Slovak Artists' Association*] (CZ)
UBS.......... United Building Society (MAR)
UBS.......... University of Botswana and Swaziland (MAR)
UBS.......... Uredba o Bankama i Stedionicama [*Decree on Banks and Savings Banks*] (YU)
ubsch.......... Ueberschuessig [*In Excess*] [*German*]
UB St.......... University Library in Stalin [*Varna*] (BU)
UB ST-IPIS... University Library in Stalin - Institute of the Planned Economy (BU)
UBT.......... Berezin Universal Flexible [*Machine gun*] (RU)
UBT.......... Extra-Strong Drilling Pipe (RU)
UBTH.......... University of Benin Teaching Hospital (MAR)
UBU.......... Usredni Biologicky Ustav [*Central Biological Institute (of the Czechoslovak Academy of Sciences)*] (CZ)
UBU.......... Ustredni Bansky Urad [*Central Office for Mining*] (CZ)
UBUR.......... Union de Bancos del Uruguay [*Union of Banks of Uruguay*] (LA)
UBV.......... Device for High-Speed Excitation Forcing (RU)
UBV.......... Traveling-Wave Amplifier (RU)
UBW.......... Uniwersytet Imienia Boleslawa Bieruta we Wroclawiu [*Boleslaw Bierut University at Wroclaw (Breslau)*] (POL)
UBYKP........ Ucuncu Bes Yil Kalkinma Plan [*Third Five-Year Development Plan*] [*See also UBYP*] (TU)
UBYP.......... Ucuncu Bes Yillik Plani [*Third Five-Year Plan*] [*See also IBYKP, UBYKP*] (TU)
UBZ.......... United Bus Company of Zambia (MAR)
UBz.......... Unser Bild Zeigt [*Our Photo Shows*] (EG)
UC.......... Union Camerounaise [*Cameroonian Union*] (AF)
UC.......... Union Congolaise (MAR)
UC.......... Unite Commerciale [*Tunisian*] (MAR)
UC.......... Unite de Compte [*Unit of Account*] [*Currency unit formerly used by the EEC, equal to approximately one dollar*] (AF)
UC.......... Uniunea Compozitorilor [*Composers' Union*] (RO)
UC.......... Uprava Carina [*Customs Administration*] (YU)

UC .... Ured za Cene [*Price Office*] (YU)
UCA .... Unie Ceskoslovenskych Architektu [*Union of Czechoslovak Architects*] (CZ)
UCA .... Union de Campesinos Asturianos [*Union of Asturian Rural Workers*] [*Spanish*] (WER)
UCA .... Union Chimique Africaine [*African Chemical Union*] [*Congolese*] (AF)
UCA .... Union Commerciale Africaine (MAR)
UCA .... Universidad Catolica Argentina [*Argentine Catholic University*] (LA)
UCA .... Universidad Centro Americana (Jose Simeon Canas) [*Central American University (Jose Simeon Canas Catholic University)*] [*Salvadoran*] (LA1)
UCA .... Universidad Centroamericana [*Central American University*] [*Nicaraguan*] (LA1)
UCAA .... United Central Africa Association (MAR)
UCAA .... University College of Addis Ababa (MAR)
UCAB .... Universidad Catolica Andres Bello [*Andres Bello Catholic University*] [*Venezuelan*] (LA)
UCAC .... Union Commerciale et Agricole du Cameroun (MAR)
UCAMAIMA ... Universidad Catolica "Madre y Maestra" [*"Madre y Maestra" Catholic University*] [*Dominican Republic*] (LA)
UCAPO .... Union de Campesinos Pobres [*Union of Poor Peasants*] [*Bolivian*] (LA)
UCB .... Union Camerounaise des Brasseries (MAR)
UCB .... Union Colorado y Batllista [*Colorado and Batllista Union*] [*Uruguayan*] (LA)
UCB .... Union Congolaise de Banques (MAR)
UCB .... University College of Botswana (MAR)
UCBWM ...... United Church Board for World Missions (MAR)
UCC .... Union de Campesinos Cristianos [*Union of Christian Peasants*] [*Chilean*] (LA)
UCC .... Union de Ciudadanas de Colombia [*Union of Colombian Women*] [*Medellin*] (LA)
UCC .... University of the Cape Coast (MAR)
UCCA .... Union des Chambres de Commerce Arabes (MAR)
UCCA .... Union Cotonniere Centrafricaine [*Central African Cotton Union*] (AF)
UCCA .... Union Council for Coloured Affairs (MAR)
UCCAO .... Union Centrale des Cooperatives Agricoles de l'Ouest [*Central Union of Agricultural Cooperatives of the West*] [*Formerly, Union of Arabica Coffee Cooperatives of the West*] [*Cameroonian*] (AF)
UCCAO .... Union des Cooperatives de Cafe Arabica de l'Ouest [*Union of Arabica Coffee Cooperatives of the West*] [*Later, Central Union of Agricultural Cooperatives of the West*] [*Cameroonian*] (AF)
UCCC .... Uniunea Centrala a Cooperativelor de Consum [*Central Union of Consumer Cooperatives*] (RO)
UCCE .... Union Centrale des Cooperatives d'Elevage [*Central Union of Livestock Cooperatives*] [*Tunisian*] (AF)
UCCLO .... United Committee of Central Labor Organizations [*Nigerian*] (AF)
UCCN .... Unidad y Convivencia Civica Nacional [*National Civic Unity and Coexistence*] [*Spanish*] (WER)
UCCO .... Union Centrale des Cooperatives Oleicoles [*Central Olive Products Cooperatives Union*] [*Tunisian*] (AF)
UCCSA .... United Congregational Church of Southern Africa (MAR)
UCD .... Union du Centre Democratique (MAR)
UCD .... Union de Centro Democratico [*Union of the Democratic Center*] [*Spanish*] (PPE)
UCDC .... Uniado do Centro Democrata Cristao [*Union of the Christian Democratic Center*] [*Portuguese*] (PPE)
UCDCC .... Union Centro y Democratica Cristiana de Catalunya [*Union of the Center and Christian Democrats of Catalonia*] [*Spanish*] (PPE)
UCE .... Union Culturelle Egyptienne (MAR)
UCE .... Unite de Compte Europeenne [*European Currency Unit*] [*Use ECU*] (AF)
UCE .... Universidad Central del Este [*Central University of the East*] [*Dominican Republic*] (LA1)
UCECOM .... Uniunea Centrala a Cooperativelor Mestesugaresti [*Central Union of Artisan Cooperatives*] (RO)
UCEMA .... Usine Ceramique du Mali (MAR)
UCEP .... Union Colombiana de Empresas Publicitarias [*Colombian Union of Advertising Companies*] (LA)
UCESA .... University College Education Students Association (MAR)
UCF .... Union Civica Femenina [*Women's Civic Union*] [*Guatemalan*] (LA)
UCFA .... Union pour la Communaute Franco-Africaine (MAR)
UCFB .... Union Culturelle de la Femme au Burundi (MAR)
UCFC .... United Christian Fellowship Conference (MAR)
UCFML .... Union des Communistes de France Marxiste-Leniniste [*Marxist-Leninist Union of Communists of France*] (PPW)
UCFS .... Uniunea de Cultura Fizica si Sport [*Union of Physical Culture and Sports*] (RO)
UCh .... Control Element [*Computers*] (RU)
uch .... Educational, Training (RU)
UCh .... Frequency Equalizer (RU)
uch .... Scientist, Scientific (RU)
uch .... Section, Zone, Lot (RU)
uch .... Training, Teaching (BU)
UCH .... Unie Ceskych Hudebniku [*Union of Czech Musicians*] (CZ)
UCH .... University College Hospital (MAR)
UCH .... Ustredi Ceskoslovenskych Hospodyn [*Center for Czechoslovak Housewives*] (CZ)
uchabr .... Training Artillery Brigade (BU)
uchap .... Training Artillery Regiment (BU)
UchB .... Uchitelska Borba [*Teachers' Struggle*] [*A newspaper*] (BU)
uchbat .... Training Battalion (RU)
ucheb .... Educational, Training (RU)
uchebn .... Educational, Training (RU)
uchen .... Scientific (RU)
uchen sek ... Scientific Secretary (RU)
uch g .... School Year (RU)
Uchgiz .... State Publishing House of Textbooks and Pedagogical Literature (RU)
Uch god ...... School Year (BU)
uchil .... School (BU)
uch-izd l ...... Publisher's Record Sheet (RU)
uch-k .... Section, Zone, Lot (RU)
uch khranit ... Scientific Custodian (RU)
uchkom .... Student Committee (RU)
Uchkom ...... Students' Committee (BU)
Uchkor .... Students' Correspondent (BU)
uchlet .... Student Pilot (RU)
uchpbr .... Training Infantry Brigade (BU)
uchpd .... Training Infantry Division (BU)
uchpedgiz ... Educational Books Publishing House (BU)
Uchpedgiz ... State Publishing House of Textbooks and Pedagogical Literature (RU)
UchPr .... Uchilisten Pregled [*School Review*] [*A periodical*] (BU)
Uchraspred ... Stocktaking and Distribution Department (RU)
Uchrasprot ... Administration for the Stocktaking and Distribution of Industrial Waste Products (RU)
uch-shche ... School (RU)
uch sotr .... Scientific Worker (RU)
uch spets .... Scientific Specialist (RU)
uchstat .... Accounting and Statistical Department (RU)
UChSU .... Training Ship (RU)
uch-sya .... Student (RU)
uchtd .... Training Tank Division (BU)
Uchtekhprom ... School Equipment Industry (BU)
UChTOL ...... Ustav Chemickej Technologie Organickych Latok [*Technological Institute of Organic Chemistry (of the Slovak Academy of Sciences)*] (CZ)
Uch zap .... Scientific Notes (RU)
UCI .... Union Campesina Independiente [*Independent Peasant Union*] [*Mexican*] (LA)
UCI .... Unione dei Comunisti Italiani [*Union of Italian Communists*] (WER)
UCI .... University College of Ibadan (MAR)
UCI .... Ustredni Cejchovni Inspektorat [*Central Inspectorate of Weights and Measures*] (CZ)
UCIA .... Union Commerciale Indochinoise et Africaine (MAR)
UCIA .... Union Commerciale Industrielle Africaine (MAR)
UCID .... Independent Democratic Union of Cape Verde (PD)
UCIG .... Unions Chretiennes de Jeunes Gens [*Young Men's Christian Association*] [*Use YMCA*] (AF)
UCINA .... Union Cinematographique Africaine (MAR)
UCIPI .... Unione Coloniale Italiana Pubblicita e Informazioni (MAR)
UCISS .... Union Catholique Internationale de Service Social [*Catholic International Union for Social Service*] (EA)
UCIT .... Union Caneros Independientes de Tucuman [*Independent Cane Workers Union of Tucuman*] [*Argentine*] (LA)
UCITRA .... Union Civica del Trabajo [*Civic Labor Union*] [*Chilean*] (LA)
UCK .... Uradovna Cenove Kontroly [*Office of Price Control*] (CZ)
UCK .... Ustredni Cvicitelska Komise [*Central Commission for Physical Training*] (CZ)
UCL .... Uganda Creameries Limited (MAR)
UCL .... Union Comunista de Liberacion [*Communist Liberation Union*] [*Spanish*] (WER)
UCL .... Universite Catholique de Louvain [*Catholic University of Louvain*] [*Belgian*] (WER)
UCL .... Ustav pro Ceskou Literaturu [*Institute of Czech Literature (of the Czechoslovak Academy of Sciences)*] (CZ)
UCLA .... Uniao Congolesa para a Libertacao de Angola (MAR)
UCM .... Union des Croyants Malgaches [*Union of Malagasy Believers*] (AF)
UCM .... Union Culturelle Musulmane (MAR)
UCM .... Uniunea de Cooperative Mestesugaresti [*Union of Artisan Cooperatives*] (RO)
UCM .... University Christian Movement of Southern Africa (MAR)
UCMCIPN ... Uniunea Cooperativelor Mestesugaresti Confectii, Incaltaminte, Prestatii Neindustriale Bucuresti [*Bucharest Union of Artisan Cooperatives for Clothing, Footwear, and Nonindustrial Services*] (RO)
UCMLB .... Union des Communistes Marxistes-Leninistes Belges [*Union of Belgian Marxist-Leninist Communists*] (WER)
UCMM .... Universidad Catolica Madre y Maria [*Madre and Maria Catholic University*] [*Dominican Republic*] (LA1)

UCMMBMCHLC ... Uniunea Cooperativelor Mestesugaresti Metal, Chimie, Lemn, Constructii, din Municipiul Bucuresti [*Bucharest Municipality Union of Artisan Cooperatives for Metals, Chemistry, Wood, and Constructions*] (RO)
UCN............ Union de Campesinos Nicaraguenses [*Nicaraguan Peasants Union*] (LA1)
UCN............ Union Civica Nacional [*National Civic Union*] [*Dominican Republic*] (PPW)
UCN............ Union Civica Nacional [*National Civic Union*] [*Bolivian*] (LA)
UCN............ Union Civica Nacionalista [*Nationalist Civic Union*] [*Argentine*] (LA)
UCN............ Union Commerciale du Niger (MAR)
UCN............ Union Congolaise Nationale (MAR)
UCN............ University College, Nairobi (MAR)
UCN............ Ustredni Cirkevni Nakladatelstvi [*Central Church Publishing House*] (CZ)
UCOA.......... Union Chimique de l'Ouest Africain (MAR)
UCODEF ..... Union Commerciale d'Exploitation Forestiere (MAR)
UCODIMA ... Union Commerciale de Diffusion de Marques (MAR)
UCODIS ...... Union pour le Commerce et la Distribution des Grandes Marques (MAR)
UCOKA .... Union des Petits Commercants de Kaolack (MAR)
UCOL .... Union pour la Colonisation (MAR)
UCOM .... Union Commerciale du Diognikg (MAR)
UCOMA........ Union des Commercants Maliens (MAR)
UCOMAF..... Union Commerciale Africaine (MAR)
UCOMO....... Union Commerciale de l'Oubangui (MAR)
UCOMPDA ... Union Cooperative des Maraichers Pecheurs du Dahomey (MAR)
UCONAL..... Union Cooperativa Nacional [*National Cooperative Union*] [*Colombian*] (LA)
UCOPAN..... Union Cooperativa Agraria Nacional [*Bogota*] (COL)
UCOR .... Uranium Enrichment Corporation [*South African*] (AF)
UCOSA .... Union Commerciale des Sarakoles Bamakois (MAR)
UCOSAB..... Union Commerciale de Saboya (MAR)
UCOT .... Union Cooperativa de Obreros del Transporte [*Cooperative Union of Transport Workers*] [*Uruguayan*] (LA)
UCOVAL ..... Union Commerciale du Valo (MAR)
UCP............ Union Comorienne pour le Progres [*Comorian Union for Progress*] (PD)
UCP............ Unite Cooperative de Production [*Tunisian*] (MAR)
UCP............ United Congress Party (MAR)
UCP............ United Conservative Party (MAR)
UCPB .... United Coconut Planters Bank [*Philippine*]
UCPL........... Unites de Combat de Pathet Lao [*Pathet Lao Combat Units*] (CL)
UCPN .... Union des Chefs et des Populations du Nord (MAR)
UCPTE .... Union pour la Coordination de la Production et du Transport de l'Electricite [*Union for the Coordination of the Production and Transport of Electric Power*] (EA)
UCR............ Union de Campesinos Revolucionarios [*Revolutionary Peasants Union*] [*Salvadoran*] (LA1)
UCR............ Union Civica Radical [*Radical Civic Union*] [*Argentine*] (PD)
UCR............ Union Civica Radical [*Radical Civic Union*] [*Colombian*] (LA1)
UCR............ Union Civica Revolucionaria [*Revolutionary Civic Union*] [*Costa Rican*] (LA)
UCR............ University College of Rhodesia (MAR)
UCR............ Uzinele Chimice Romane [*Romanian Chemical Plants*] (RO)
UCRG.......... Union des Clubs pour le Renouveau de la Gauche [*Union of Clubs for the Renovation of the Left*] [*French*] (PPE)
UCRI........... Union Civica Radical Intransigente [*Intransigent Radical Civic Union*] [*Argentine*] (LA)
UCRM.......... University College of Rhodesia and Malawi (MAR)
UCRN .... University College of Rhodesia and Nyasaland (MAR)
UCRP .... Union Civica Radical del Pueblo [*People's Radical Civic Union*] [*Argentine*] (LA)
UCRP(ML) ... Uniao Comunista para a Reconstrucao do Partido Marxista-Leninista [*Communist Union for the Reconstruction of the Marxist-Leninist Party*] [*Portuguese*] (WER)
UCRSU........ United Copperbelt Regional Students Union [*Zambian*] (AF)
UCRU .... Uzinal de Constructii si Reparatii Utilaje [*Factory for Equipment Construction and Repairs*] (RO)
UCS............ Unified Co-Operative Services (MAR)
UCS............ Union Comunal Salvadorena [*Salvadoran Communal Union*] (LA)
UCS............ Ustredni Celni Spraya [*Central Customs Administration*] (CZ)
UCSA .... Ustredi Ceskoslovenske Advokacie [*Czechoslovak Lawyers Center*] (CZ)
UCsC........... Ustredi Ceskoslovenskych Cyklistu [*Center of Czechoslovak Cyclists*] (CZ)
UCSL........... Union Congolais des Syndicats Libres (MAR)
UCSV .... Ucaksavar [*Antiaircraft*] (TU)
UCT............ Union Commerciale de Transports [*Moroccan*] (MAR)
UCT............ University of Cape Town (MAR)
UCTAT .... Union des Co-Operatives de Travaux Agricoles de Tunisie (MAR)
UCTC .... Union Camerounaise des Travailleurs Croyants [*Cameroonian Union of Believing Workers*] (AF)
UCTPIC....... Unitatea de Colectare si Transportul Paielor pentru Industria de Celuloza [*Unit for the Collection and Transportation of Straw for the Cellulose Industry*] (RO)
UCU............ Union Cultural Universitaria [*University Cultural Union*] [*Guatemalan*] (LA)
UCV............ Universidad Central de Venezuela [*Central University of Venezuela*] (LA)
UCV............ Uprava Civilnog Vazduhoplovstva [*Civil Aeronautics Administration*] (YU)
Ucvs .... Uscavus [*Master Sergeant*] (TU)
ucz .... Uczen [*or Uczennica*] [*Pupil*] [*Polish*]
UCZ............ United Church of Zambia (MAR)
UD .... Administration, Management (RU)
UD .... Controlled Diode (RU)
UD .... Impact Effect (RU)
ud .... Satisfactory [*Mark in school*] (RU)
UD .... Uranove Doly [*Uranium Mines*] (CZ)
UD .... Usekovy Duvernik [*Shop Steward*] (CZ)
Ud.............. Usted [*You (Singular, formal)*] [*Spanish*]
UD .... Ustredni Dilny [*Central Workshops*] (CZ)
UD .... Utrikesdepartment [*Ministry of Foreign Affairs*] [*Swedish*] (WEN)
UD .... Uzun Dalga [*Long Wave*] (TU)
UDA............ Shirika la Usafiri Dar Es Salaam Limited (MAR)
UDA............ Union Democratique Afar (MAR)
UDA............ Union Democratique Africaine (MAR)
UDA............ Urban Development Association [*Malaysian*] (ML)
UDA............ Ustredni Dum Armady [*Central Army Building*] (CZ)
UDAC .... Union de Actores Costarricenses [*Costa Rican Actors Union*] (LA1)
UDAE .... Union Douaniere d'Afrique Equatoriale [*Equatorial Africa Customs Union*] (AF)
ud akt.......... Specific Activity (RU)
UDAP .... Licensed State Motor Vehicle Carriers (BU)
udar............ Accent (RU)
UDA-RDA.... Union Democratique Africaine-Rassemblement Democratique Africain [*African Democratic Union-African Democratic Rally*] [*Upper Voltan*] (AF)
UDB............ Union Democratique Bretonne - Unvaniezh Demokratel Breizh [*Breton Democratic Union*] [*French*] (PPW)
UDB............ Union pour le Developpement de Beoumi (MAR)
UDB............ Universite du Burundi (MAR)
UDBA .... Uprava Drzavne Bezbednosti [*State Security Administration*] (YU)
UDC............ Uganda Development Company (AF)
UDC............ Uniao Democratica Caboverdeana (MAR)
UDC............ Union of the Democratic Centre [*Saharan*] (PPW)
UDC............ Union Democratica de Campesinos [*Peasants Democratic Union*] [*Ecuadorean*] (LA)
UDC............ Union Democratica de Cataluna [*Catalan: Unio Democratica de Catalunya*] [*Democratic Union of Catalonia*] [*Spanish*] (WER)
UDC............ Union Democratica Cristiana [*Christian Democratic Union*] [*Spanish*] (WER)
UDC............ Union Democratica Cristiana [*Christian Democratic Union*] [*Bolivian*] (PPW)
UDC............ Union Democratique Centrafricaine [*Central African Democratic Union*] (PPW)
UDC............ Union Democratique du Centre [*Democratic Union of the Center*] [*Swiss*] (PPE)
UDC............ Union Democratique Comorienne [*Comorian Democratic Union*] (AF)
UDC............ Universele Decimale Classificatie [*FID*] [*'s-Gravenhage*]
UDCA .... Union pour la Defense des Commercants et des Artisans [*Union for the Defense of Traders and Artisans*] [*French*] (PPE)
UDC BME.... Universele Decimale Classificatie Basic Medium Edition [*FID*] [*'s-Gravenhage*]
UDCCA .... Union Democratica Cristiana de Centroamerica [*Christian Democratic Union of Central America*] (LA)
UDCH .... Ustredny Dom Cervenej Hviezdy [*Red Star Center (Building)*] (CZ)
UDCV .... Uniao Democratica de Cabo Verde (MAR)
UDD............ Association pour l'Utilisation et la Diffusion de la Documentation [*French*]
UDD............ Union Democratique Dahomeenne (MAR)
UDDIA .... Union Democratique de Defense des Interets Africains (MAR)
UDDT .... Ustredni Dum Dopravni Techniky [*Center for Management of Transport Organizations*] (CZ)
UDE............ Union Democratica Espanola [*Spanish Democratic Union*] (WER)
UDE............ Union Democratica de Estudiantes [*Democratic Students Union*] [*Ecuadorean*] (LA)
UDE............ Union Democratique Ethiopienne [*Ethiopian Democratic Union*] [*Use EDU*] (AF)
UDE............ Union Douaniere Equatoriale [*Equatorial Customs Union*] (AF)
UDE............ Ustredi Demokratickeho Exilu z CSR [*Center of Democratic Exiles from Czechoslovakia*] (CZ)
UDEA .... Union Democratica de Entidades Argentinas [*Democratic Union of Argentine Organizations*] (LA)
UDEA .... Union Democratique des Etats Africains [*Democratic Union of African States*] (AF)
UDEAC........ Union Douaniere et Economique d'Afrique Centrale [*Customs and Economic Union of Central Africa*] (AF)

UDEAO........ Union Douaniere des Etats de l'Afrique de l'Ouest [*Customs Union of the West African States*] (AF)
UDEBOP..... Union pour le Developpement du Bopri (MAR)
UDEC......... Union d'Entreprises de Constructions [*Building Enterprises Union*] [*Chadian*] (AF)
UDECMA..... Union Democratique Chretienne Malgache [*Malagasy Christian Democratic Union*] (AF)
UDECMA-KMPT... Parti Democratique Chretien Malgache [*Malagasy Christian Democratic Party*] (PPW)
UDECO........ Union Democratique Comorienne [*Comorian Democratic Union*] (AF)
UDECO........ Union Democratique Congolaise (MAR)
UDECTO..... Union d'Entreprise de Construction au Togo (MAR)
UDEEM....... Union Democratica de Estudiantes de Ensenanza Media [*Democratic Union of Secondary Education Students*] [*Spanish*] (WER)
UDEF.......... Union des Exploitants Familiaux [*Union of Family Farmers*] [*Belgian*] (WER)
UDEFA........ Union de Entidades Economicas-Financieras Argentinas [*Union of Argentine Economic and Financial Organizations*] (LA)
UDEL.......... Union Democratica de Liberacion [*Democratic Liberation Union*] [*Nicaraguan*] (LA)
UDELPA...... Union del Pueblo Argentino [*Argentine People's Union*] (LA)
UDEM.......... Universidad de Medellin (COL)
UDEMU....... Uniao Democratica das Mulheres da Guine e Cabo Verde (MAR)
UDENAMO... Uniao Democratica Nacional de Mocambique (MAR)
UDEPA........ Union de Empresas Petroquimicas Argentinas [*Union of Argentine Petrochemical Enterprises*] (LA)
UDEPRU...... Unidad de Estudios de Planeamiento Regional y Urbano. Universidad del Valle [*Cali*] (COL)
UDERMA..... Union pour le Developpement de la Region Mayo (MAR)
UDES.......... Union Democratique des Etudiants Senegalais [*Democratic Union of Senegalese Students*] (AF)
UDETD........ Union Democratica Ecuatoriana de Trabajadores de Derecha [*Democratic Union of Right Wing Workers*] [*Ecuadorean*] (LA)
udf............... Und Die Folgende [*And Those Following*] [*German*]
UDF............ Union Defence Force (MAR)
UDF............ Union pour la Defense de la Republique [*Union for the Defense of the Republic*] [*French*] (AF)
UDF............ Union Democratica Fernandina (MAR)
UDF............ Union pour la Democratie Francaise [*Union for French Democracy*] [*French Guiana*] (PPW)
UDF............ Union pour la Democratie Francaise [*Union for French Democracy*] [*French*] (PPW)
UDF............ Union pour la Democratie Francaise [*Union for French Democracy*] [*New Caledonian*] (PPW)
UDF............ Union Democratique Francaise [*French Democratic Union*] (WER)
UDF............ United Democratic Front [*Indian*] (PPW)
UDF............ Uridine Diphosphate (RU)
UDFC.......... Union Democratique des Femmes du Congo (MAR)
UDFG.......... Uridine Diphosphate Glucose (RU)
UDFGal....... Uridine Diphosphate Galactose (RU)
UDFI............ Union Defence Forces Institute (MAR)
UDFT........... Union Democratique des Femmes Tunisiennes [*Democratic Union of Tunisian Women*] (AF)
UDG............ Unabhaengige Deutsche Gemeinschaft [*Independent German Society*] (EG)
UDG............ Uniao Democratica da Guine (MAR)
UDG............ Union Democratica Galega [*Galician Democratic Union*] [*Spanish*] (WER)
UDGE.......... Union Democratica de Guinea Ecuatorial [*Democratic Union of Equatorial Guinea*] (AF)
Udgiz........... Udmurt State Publishing House (RU)
u dgl........... Und Dergleichen [*And the Like*] [*German*]
u dgl m....... Und Dergleichen Mehr [*And the Like*] [*German*]
UDHS.......... Ururka Demograadiga Haweenka Soomaaliyeed (MAR)
UDI............. Unilateral Declaration of Independence [*Rhodesian*] (AF)
UDI............. Unilateral Declaration of Independence [*Cypriot Turks*] (TU)
UDI............. Union Democratica Independiente [*Independent Democratic Union*] [*Venezuelan*] (LA)
UDI............. Union Democratica de Izquierda [*Leftist Democratic Union*] [*Colombian*] (LA1)
UDI............. Union Democratique des Independants [*Democratic Union of Independents*] [*French*] (PPE)
UDI............. Union Dominicana de Independientes [*Dominican Union of Independents*] [*Dominican Republic*] (LA1)
UDI............. Union de Izquierda [*Leftist Union*] [*Peruvian*] (LA)
UDI............. Unione delle Donne Italiane [*Union of Italian Women*] (WER)
UDIR........... Union pour la Diffusion Reunionnaise (MAR)
UDIT........... Union de Defense des Interets Tchadiens (MAR)
UDIT........... Union Democratique et Independante du Tchad (MAR)
UDJ............ Union Deutscher Jazzmusiker [*Union of German Jazz Musicians*] [*West German*] (EG)
UDJM......... Union Democratique de la Jeunesse Marocaine [*Democratic Union of Moroccan Youth*] (AF)
UDJUNH...... Union Democratica de la Juventud Nacionalista Hondurena [*Honduran Nationalist Youth Democratic Union*] (LA)
UDK............ Universal Decimal Classification (RU)
UDK............ Univerzalna Decimalna Klasifikacija [*Universal Decimal Classification*] (YU)
UDK............ Ustredni Dopravni Komise [*Central Transportation Commission*] (CZ)
UD KSC....... Ustav Dejin Komunisticke Strany Ceskoslovenska [*Institute of History of the Communist Party of Czechoslovakia*] (CZ)
UD KSS....... Ustav Dejin Komunistickej Strany Slovenska [*Institute of History of the Communist Party of Slovakia*] (CZ)
UDLP.......... United Democratic Labour Party [*Trinidadian and Tobagan*] (PPW)
UDLUT........ Ustredni Dum Lidove Umelecke Tvorivosti [*Folk Arts Center*] (CZ)
udm............ Udmurt (RU)
UDM........... Union Democratica de Mujeres [*Women's Democratic Union*] [*Ecuadorean*] (LA)
UDM........... Union Democratique Mauricienne [*Mauritian Democratic Union*] (AF)
UDM........... Union Democratique Mauritanienne [*Mauritanian Democratic Union*] (PD)
udM............ Unter dem Meeresspiegel [*Below Sea Level*] (EG)
UDM........... Ustav Dulni Mechanisace [*Institute for the Mechanization of Mining*] (CZ)
UDMA.......... Union Democratique de Manifeste Algerienne (MAR)
UdmASSR... Udmurt Autonomous Soviet Socialist Republic (RU)
Udmurtgosizdat... Udmurt State Publishing House (RU)
UDN............ Detailed Observations Sector (RU)
UDN............ Uniao Democratica Nacional [*National Democratic Union*] [*Brazilian*] (LA)
UDN............ Union Democrata Nacional [*National Democratic Union*] [*Salvadoran*] (PPW)
UDN............ Union Democratica Nicaraguense [*Nicaraguan Democratic Union*] (PD)
UDN............ Union Democratique Nigerienne (MAR)
UDNA.......... Unidad Democratica Nacional Anticonservadora [*National Anti-Conservative Democratic Union*] [*Ecuadorean*] (LA)
UDN-FARN... Union Democratica Nicaraguense - Fuerzas Armadas Revolucionarias [*Nicaraguan Democratic Union - Revolutionary Armed Forces*] (LA1)
UDNR.......... Unione Democratico per la Nuova Repubblica [*Democratic Union for the New Republic*] [*Italian*] (WER)
udo............. Shock Squad (BU)
UDO............ Universidad de Oriente [*Eastern University*] [*Venezuelan*] (LA)
UDOA.......... Union Douaniere Ouest-Africaine [*West African Customs Union*] (AF)
ud ob.......... Specific Volume (RU)
udobr.......... Fertilizer (RU)
UDOO.......... State Social Insurance Administration (BU)
UDP............ L'Union des Progressistes [*Union of Progressives*] [*Belgian*] (WER)
UDP............ Statutes of State Enterprises (BU)
UDP............ Submarine Training Division (RU)
UDP............ Supplementary High-Calorie Diet (RU)
UDP............ Ukase on State Enterprises (BU)
UDP............ Ukase on State Pensions (BU)
UDP............ Umelecky Drevoprumysl [*Woodcraft Industry*] (CZ)
UDP............ Uniao Democratica Popular [*Popular Democratic Union*] [*Portuguese*] (WER)
UDP............ Unidad Democratica Popular [*Democratic Popular Unity*] [*Bolivian*] (PPW)
UDP............ Unidad Democratica Popular [*Popular Democratic Unity*] [*Peruvian*] (PPW)
UDP............ Union Democrate Paysanne (MAR)
UDP............ Union Democratica Popular [*Popular Democratic Union*] [*Ecuadorean*] (LA)
UDP............ Union Democratica Popular [*Popular Democratic Union*] [*Peruvian*] (LA)
UDP............ Union Democratica del Pueblo [*People's Democratic Union*] [*Bolivian*] (LA)
UDP............ Union Democratica del Pueblo [*People's Democratic Union*] [*Ecuadorean*] (LA)
UDP............ United Democratic Party [*Belizean*] (PD)
UDP............ United Democratic Party [*Basotho*] (PPW)
UDP............ United Democratic Party (ML)
UDP............ United Democratic Party [*Bermudian*] (LA1)
UDP............ Uredba o Deviznom Poslovanju [*Decree on Foreign Exchange Operations*] (YU)
UDP............ Usines Dahomeennes de Prefabrication (MAR)
UDP............ Ustredni Delnicke Podniky [*Central Workers' Enterprises*] (CZ)
UDPD.......... Ustredi Delnickych Potravnich Druzstev [*Central Office of the Workers' Food Cooperatives*] (CZ)
UDPE.......... Union del Pueblo Espanol [*Union of the Spanish People*] (WER)
UDPM......... Union Democratique du Peuple Malien [*Mali People's Democratic Union*] (PPW)
UDPT.......... Union Democratique des Populations Togolaises (MAR)
UDPV.......... Union Democratica del Pais Valenciano [*Democratic Union of the Valencian Country*] [*Spanish*] (WER)
ud r............ Specific Reactivity (RU)
UDR............ State Management Ukase (BU)
UDR............ Union pour la Defense de la Republique [*Union for the Defense of the Republic*] [*French*] (PPE)

UDR............ Union des Democrates pour la Republique [*Union of Democrats for the Republic (Gaullist party)*] [*French*] (WER)
UDROCOL... Union de Droguistas Colombianos Ltda. [*Cali*] (COL)
UDRT/RAD ... Union Democratique pour le Respect du Travail - Respect voor Arbeid en Democratie [*Democratic Union for the Respect of Labor*] [*Belgian*] (PPW)
UDS............ Road Construction Administration (RU)
UDS............ Union Democratique Senegalaise (MAR)
Uds............ Ustedes [*You (Plural, formal)*] [*Spanish*]
UDS............ Ustredni Delnicka Skola [*Central Workers' School*] (CZ)
UDSDR........ State Supplies and Reserves Administration (BU)
UDSG......... Union Democratique et Sociale Gabonaise [*Gabonese Democratic and Social Union*] (AF)
UDSIP......... Uprava Drzavnih Sumsko-Industriskih Preduzeca [*Administration of State Forest Industrial Enterprises*] (YU)
UDSK......... Charter of the State Savings Bank (BU)
UDSM......... Union Democratique et Socialiste de Madagascar [*Democratic and Socialist Union of Madagascar*] (AF)
UDSR......... Union Democratique et Socialiste de la Resistance [*Democratic and Socialist Union of the Resistance*] [*French*] (PPE)
UdSSR........ Union der Sozialistischen Sowjet-Republiken [*Union of Soviet Socialist Republics, USSR*] (EG)
UDT............ Union Democratica de Trabajadores [*Democratic Union of Workers*] [*Ecuadorean*] (LA)
UDT............ Union Democratica de Trabajadores [*Democratic Union of Workers*] [*Chilean*] (LA1)
UDT............ Union Democratique de Timor (MAR)
UDT............ Union Democratique de Travail [*Democratic Union of Labor*] [*French*] (WER)
UDT............ Wood Production and Transportation Administration (BU)
UDU............ Remote Level Indicator (HU)
UDU............ Uganda Democratic Union (AF)
UDU............ Unabhaengige Demokratische Union [*Independent Democratic Union*] [*Austrian*] (PPE)
ud v............ Specific Gravity (RU)
UDV............ Union Democratique Voltaique [*Voltan Democratic Union*] (AF)
UDV............ Uprava Drzavne Varnosti [*State Security Administration*] (YU)
UD-Ve......... Union Democratique pour la Cinquieme Republique [*Democratic Union for the Fifth Republic*] [*French*] (PPE)
ud vl........... Specific Humidity (RU)
UD/VR......... Union Democratique pour la Cinquieme Republique [*Democratic Union for the Fifth Republic*] [*French*] (WER)
UDZI........... Statute of the State Insurance Institute (BU)
UE.............. Holding Electromagnet (RU)
UE.............. Union Espanola [*Spanish Union*] (WER)
uE.............. Unseres Erachtens [*In Our Opinion*] (EG)
ue.............. Uzemegyseg [*Factory Working Unit*] (HU)
UEA............ General-Purpose Artificial Aerial (RU)
uea............ Und Einige Andere [*And Some Others*] [*German*]
UEA............ Uniao dos Estudantes Angolanos (MAR)
UEA............ Union des Ecrivains Algeriens [*Union of Algerian Writers*] (AF)
UEA............ Union des Etats Africaine (MAR)
UEA............ Uralelektroapparat [*Plant*] (RU)
UEAC.......... Union des Etats de l'Afrique Centrale [*Union of Central African States*] (AF)
UEASSC..... University of East Africa Social Science Conference (MAR)
UEB............ Uganda Electricity Board (MAR)
UEB............ Unite d'Exploitation du Bois de Betou (MAR)
UEBL.......... Union Economique Belgo-Luxembourgeoise [*Belgium-Luxembourg Economic Union*] (WER)
Uebsch........ Ueberschuss [*Excess*] [*German*]
UEC............ Uniao de Estudantes Comunistas [*Union of Communist Students*] [*Portuguese*] (WER)
UEC............ Union des Etudiants Cambodgiens en URSS [*Union of Cambodian Students in the USSR*] (CL)
UEC............ Union des Etudiants Communistes [*Union of Communist Students*] [*French*] (WER)
UECEB........ Union of Employees of Central Electricity Board [*Mauritian*] (AF)
UECU.......... Union de Empleados Cinematograficos del Uruguay [*Movie Theater Employees Union of Uruguay*] (LA)
UED............ Union de Estudiantes Democraticos [*Democratic Students Union*] [*Spanish*] (WER)
UED............ Union des Etudiants de Dakar [*Dakar Students Union*] [*Senegalese*] (AF)
uedM.......... Ueber dem Meeresspiegel [*Above Sea Level*] (EG)
UEDS.......... Uniao de Esquerda para a Democracia Social [*Left Union for Social Democracy*] [*Portuguese*] (PPE)
UEE............ Uniao Estadual dos Estudantes [*State Students Union*] [*Brazilian*] (LA)
UEF............ Ustav pro Etnografii a Folkloristiku [*Institute of Ethnology and Folklore (of the Czechoslovak Academy of Sciences)*] (CZ)
UEI............ Union de Estudiantes Independientes [*Independent Students Union*] [*Guatemalan*] (LA)
UEIA........... Union des Etats Independants d'Afrique (MAR)
UEIF........... Union Europeenne Industrielles et Financiere (MAR)
UEK............ Uluslararasi Ekonomik Kuruluslar Genel Mudurlugu [*International Economic Organizations Directorate General*] [*of Foreign Affairs Ministry*] (TU)
UEK............ Union des Etudiants Khmers [*Union of Cambodian Students*] (CL)
UEM............ Union des Ecrivains du Maroc [*Writers Union of Morocco*] (AF)
UEM............ Universal Electron Microscope (RU)
UEO............ Union de l'Europe Occidentale [*Western European Union*] [*Use WEU*] [*French*] (CL)
UEO............ Unione Europa Occidentale [*Western European Union*] [*Use WEU*] [*Italian*] (WER)
UEOA.......... Union des Etudiants Ouest-Africains [*Union of West African Students*] (AF)
UEOS.......... Ustav Ekonomiky a Organizacie Stavebnictva [*Institute of Economy and Organization in Construction*] (CZ)
UEP............ Electric Power Industry Administration (BU)
UEP............ Uniao dos Estudantes de Pernambuco [*Pernambuco Students Union*] [*Brazilian*] (LA)
UEP............ Union Europeenne des Paiements [*European Payments Union*] [*Use EPU*] [*French*]
UEP............ Unione Europea dei Pagamenti [*European Payments Union*] [*Use EPU*] [*Italian*] (WER)
UEPP.......... Union de Empresarios Privados del Peru [*Peruvian Private Enterprise Union*] (LA)
UER............ Union de Estudiantes Revolucionarios [*Revolutionary Students Union*] [*Dominican Republic*] (LA1)
UER............ Union Estudiantil Revolucionaria [*Revolutionary Student Union*] [*Mexican*] (LA1)
UER............ Unione Europea di Radiodiffusione [*European Broadcasting Union*] [*Use EBU*] [*Italian*] (WER)
UER............ Unite d'Enseignement et de Recherche [*Teaching and Research Unit*] [*French*] (WER)
UES............ Specific Electrical Resistance (RU)
UES............ Union des Etudiants Socialistes [*Union of Socialist Students*] [*Malagasy*] (AF)
UES............ Universidad de El Salvador [*University of El Salvador*] (LA1)
UESD.......... Uniao da Esquerda Socialista Democratica [*Union of the Socialist and Democratic Left*] [*Portuguese*] (PPW)
UESM.......... Union des Etudiants Socialistes Malgaches [*Union of Malagasy Socialist Students*] (AF)
UETB.......... Union des Etudiants Tchadiens dans le BENELUX [*Union of Chadian Students in BENELUX*] (AF)
UETP.......... Uprava za Ekonomsku i Tehnicku Pomoc [*Administration of Economic and Technical Aid*] (YU)
UETPF......... Union des Entrepreneurs des Travaux Publics du Fleuve (MAR)
UEZa.......... Union des Ecrivains Zairois [*Union of Zairian Writers*] (AF)
UF.............. Moderate Front [*Meteorology*] (RU)
UF.............. Narrow-Band Filter (RU)
UF.............. Photocurrent Amplifier (RU)
UF.............. Shaping Amplifier (RU)
uf.............. Uj Folyam [*New Series*] (HU)
UF.............. Ultraviolet (RU)
Uf.............. Und Folgende [*And the Following*] (EG)
UF.............. Union Ferroviaria [*National Railway Union*] [*Argentine*] (LA)
UF.............. Union de Fribourg: Institut International des Sciences Sociales et Politiques [*Union de Fribourg: International Institute of Social and Political Sciences*] (EA)
UF.............. United Force [*Guyanese*] (PD)
UF.............. Unterfamilie [*Subfamily*] [*German*]
UFA............ Union des Femmes Angolaises (MAR)
UFA............ Union Fonciere Africaine (MAR)
UFAC.......... Union Federative d'Anciens Combattants (MAR)
UFAC.......... Union Francaise des Associations de Combattants et de Victimes de la Guerre (MAR)
UFAC.......... United French Africa Committee (MAR)
UFACFM..... Union Fraternelle des Anciens Combattants Francophones et de Madagascar [*Fraternal Union of French-Speaking and Malagasy Veterans*] (AF)
UFAG.......... Union des Femmes Africaine de Guinee (MAR)
UFAN.......... Ural Branch of the Academy of Sciences, USSR (RU)
UFB............ Union des Femmes Burundi [*Union of Burundi Women*] (AF)
UFBR.......... Ustav Fyziologie a Biologie Rastlin [*Institute of Physiology and Plant Biology*] (CZ)
UFBS.......... Union des Francais de Bon Sens [*Union of Frenchmen of Good Sense*] (PPW)
UFC............ Federal University of Ceara [*Brazilian*]
UFC............ Uganda Freedom Convention (MAR)
UFC............ Union des Femmes Congolaises [*Union of Congolese Women*] (AF)
UFC............ Union Fraternelle des Croyants (MAR)
UFC............ Universite Federale du Cameroun (MAR)
UFCA.......... Union pour la Communaute Franco-Africaine (MAR)
UFCA.......... Union Feminine Centrafricaine [*Central African Women's Union*] (AF)
UFCSM....... United Free Church of Scotland Mission (MAR)
UFD............ Union des Forces Democratiques [*Union of Democratic Forces*] [*French*] (PPE)
UFD............ Union de Fuerzas Democraticas [*Democratic Forces Union*] [*Spanish*] (WER)
UFDC.......... Union Femenina Democrata Cristiana [*Christian Democratic Women's Union*] [*Salvadoran*] (LA1)
UFDR.......... Uniunea Femeilor Democrate Romane [*Union of Romanian Democratic Women*] (RO)
UFDS.......... Union des Forces Democratiques du Senegal [*Union of the Democratic Forces of Senegal*] (AF)

UFE .... Uniao Federal dos Estudantes [*Federal Students Union*] [*Brazilian*] (LA)
UFE .... Uniao dos Federalistas Europeos [*European Federalists Union*] [*Portuguese*] (WER)
UFE .... Union Forestiere de l'Estuaire (MAR)
UFEA........... Union Financiere pour l'Europe et l'Afrique [*Financial Union for Europe and Africa*] [*French*] (AF)
UFEMTO ..... Union des Femmes du Togo [*Union of Togolese Women*] (AF)
uff............... Und Folgende [*And the Following*] (EG)
UFF............. Union des Femmes Francaises [*Union of French Women*] (WER)
UFF............. Union et Fraternite Francaise [*French Union and Fraternity*] (PPE)
UFG............. Union Forestiere du Gabon (MAR)
UFG............. Union Franco-Guineenne (MAR)
UFG............. Union Fraternelle Guineenne [*Guinean Fraternal Union*] (AF)
UFI............... Pulse Shaping Amplifier (RU)
UFI............... Ubungo Farm Implements (MAR)
UFI............... Union Francaise d'Informations [*French News Union*] (WER)
UFI............... Union of International Fairs (EA)
UFIDA.......... Union Financiere Internationale pour le Developpement de l'Afrique [*International Financial Association for the Development of Africa*] (AF)
UFK .... Ukase on Financial Control (BU)
UFK .... Union Franco-Kanembou (MAR)
UFL............. Uganda Federation of Labour (MAR)
UFL............. Ultraviolet Rays (RU)
UFL............. Union des Femmes Luxembourgeoises [*Union of Women of Luxembourg*] (WER)
UFM............. Uganda Freedom Movement (PD)
UFM............. Ultraviolet Meter (RU)
UFM............. Ultraviolet Microirradiation [*Biology*] (RU)
UFM............. Unevangelized Fields Missions (MAR)
UFM............. Union des Femmes du Mali (MAR)
UFM............. Union Franco-Musulmane (MAR)
UFMAC .... Uganda Fish Marketing Association (MAR)
UFMG.......... Universidade Federal de Minas Gerais [*Federal University of Minas Gerais*] [*Brazilian*] (LA1)
UFN .... Progress of Physical Sciences (RU)
UFN .... Union des Femmes Nigeriennes [*Nigerien Women's Union*] [*Niger*] (AF)
UFNA........... Union Francaise Nord-Africaine (MAR)
UFNI............ Ufa Petroleum Institute (RU)
UFNII........... Ufa Petroleum Scientific Research Institute (RU)
UFO............. Ultraviolet Illumination (RU)
UFO............. Ultraviolet Irradiation (RU)
UFO............. Union Forestiere de l'Ogooue (MAR)
UFOA .... Union des Femmes de l'Ouest Africaine (MAR)
UFOCA........ Union Forestiere Camerounaise (MAR)
UFOD .... Union Francaise des Organismes de Documentation
UFOM.......... Union Francaise d'Outre-Mer (MAR)
UFOR........... Union Forestiere (MAR)
UFOSZ .... Ujgazdak es Foldhozjuttatottak Orszagos Szovetsege [*National Association of New Farmers and Recipients of Land*] (HU)
UFOV........... Union des Forces Ouvrieres Voltaiques (MAR)
UFP .... United Federal Party [*Zambian*] (AF)
UFP .... United Force Party [*Guyanese*] (LA)
UFP .... Universidade Federal do Parana [*Federal University of Parana*] [*Brazilian*] (LA1)
UFPC........... Union des Forces Populaires Congolaises (MAR)
UFPDG .... Union des Femmes du Parti Democratique Gabonais [*Women's Union of the Gabonese Democratic Party*] (AF)
UFPN........... United Federal Party of Nyasaland (MAR)
UFPV........... Union des Forces Progressistes Voltaiques [*Union of Voltan Progressive Forces*] (AF)
UFR .... Ultraviolet Radiation (RU)
UFR .... Union des Femmes de la Reunion [*Women's Union of Reunion*] (AF)
UFRC........... University Famine Relief Committee (MAR)
UFRGS .... Universidade Federal do Rio Grande Do Sul [*Federal University of Rio Grande Do Sul*] [*Brazilian*] (LA1)
UFRM .... Union des Forces Revolutionnaires Marocaines [*Union of Moroccan Revolutionary Forces*] (AF)
UFRN........... Universidade Federal do Rio Grande Do Norte [*Federal University of Rio Grande Do Norte*] [*Brazilian*] (LA1)
UFRRO .... University Famine Relief and Rehabilitation Organization (MAR)
UFS .... Ultraviolet Glass (RU)
UFSIA........... Universitaire Faculteiten Sint Ignatius Antwerpen
UFSICA .... Union Federale des Syndicats Industriels, Commercants, et Artisanaux (MAR)
UFSO........... UNESCO Field Science Office [*Egyptian*] (MAR)
UFT .... Unified Phonetic Transcription (RU)
UFTAA .... Universal Federation of Travel Agents' Associations [*See also FUAAV*] (EA)
UFTI .... Ukrainian Scientific Research Physicotechnical Institute (RU)
UFU .... Uganda Freedom Union (MAR)
UFUS........... Udruzenje Filmskih Umetnika Srbije [*Association of Motion Picture Artists of Serbia*] (YU)
UFVF .... Ustav pro Fotochemii a Vedeckou Fotografii [*Institute of Photochemistry and Science Photography*] (CZ)
UFVR........... Union des Femmes Volontaires de la Republique [*Union of Women Volunteers of the Republic*] [*Zairian*] (AF)
UFZ .... Feeder Protective Device (RU)
ug .... Angle, Corner (RU)
ug .... Conventional Fuel (BU)
Ug............... Udjung [*Cape*] [*Indonesian*] (NAU)
UG............... Uganda [*Two-letter standard code*] (CNC)
UG .... Uganda Growers (MAR)
UG .... Union Government (MAR)
UG .... Unite Guyanaise [*Guyanese Unity*] (PPW)
UG .... Universal Gas Analyzer (RU)
UG .... Uprava za Gozdarstvo [*Forestry Administration*] (YU)
UGA............. Office of the City Architect (RU)
UGA............. Uganda [*Three-letter standard code*] (CNC)
UGA............. Universite de Grenoble. Annales [*A publication*] (MAR)
UGAASAL... Union General de Artistas y Autores Salvadorenos [*General Union of Salvadoran Artists and Authors*] (LA1)
UGAIP .... Union Generale de l'Artisanat, de l'Industrie, et des Peches (MAR)
UGAL .... Union des Groupements d'Achat de l'Alimentation [*Association of Retailer-Owned Wholesalers in Foodstuffs - AROWF*] (EA)
UGAT .... Union Generale de l'Agriculture Tunisienne (MAR)
UGB............. State Security Administration (RU)
UGB............. Union Gabonaise de Banque [*Gabonese Banking Union*] (AF)
UGB............. Union de Guerreros Blancos [*White Warriors' Union*] [*Salvadoran*] (PD)
UGC .... University Grants Commission [*Bangladesh*]
UGCA........... Union Generale des Commercants Algeriens [*General Association of Algerian Merchants*] (AF)
UGCB .... Uniforme Grondslagen en Cooerdinatie van Informatieverzorging in het Bouwwezen [*Rijswijk*]
UGCC........... United Gold Coast Convention (MAR)
UGCI/ML..... Unione della Gioventu Comunista d'Italia/Marxista-Leninista [*Union of Communist Youth of Italy/Marxist-Leninist*] (WER)
UGEA .... Union des Groupements pour l'Explotation Agricole [*Union of Farming Groups*] [*Guadeloupe*] (LA1)
UGEAA........ Union Generale des Etudiants Africains en Algerie [*General Union of African Students in Algeria*] (AF)
UGEAN........ Union Generale d'Etudiants de l'Afrique Noire [*General Union of Students of Black Africa*] (AF)
UGEAO........ Union Generale des Etudiants de l'Afrique Occidentale [*General Union of West African Students*] (AF)
UGEC .... Union Generale des Etudiants Congolais (MAR)
UGECI .... Union Generale des Etudiants de Cote-d'Ivoire [*General Union of Students of the Ivory Coast*] (AF)
UGECOBA ... Union Generale des Cooperatives Bananieres du Mungo (MAR)
UGECOBAM ... Union Generale des Cooperatives Bananieres du Mungo (MAR)
UGECR........ Union Generale des Etudiants Creoles de la Reunion [*General Union of Creole Students of Reunion*] (AF)
UGED .... Union Generale des Etudiants Dahomeens (MAR)
UGEDA........ Union Generale des Etudiants Democratiques Algeriens [*General Union of Algerian Democratic Students*] (AF)
UGEEC........ Union Generale des Eleves et Etudiants Congolais [*General Union of Congolese Pupils and Students*] (AF)
UGEED........ Union Generale des Etudiants et Eleves Dahomeens (MAR)
UGEFCO ..... Union Generale pour la Promotion et l'Emancipation de la Femme Congolais (MAR)
UGEL........... Union Generale des Etudiants Lybiens (MAR)
UGEM.......... Union Generale des Etudiants du Maroc [*General Union of Moroccan Students*] (AF)
UGEMA .... Union Generale des Etudiants Musulmans d'Algerie [*General Union of Moslem Students of Algeria*] (AF)
UGES .... Uniao Geral de Estudantes Secundarios [*General Secondary Students Union*] [*Brazilian*] (LA)
UGES .... Union Generale des Etudiants Senegalais [*General Union of Senegalese Students*] (AF)
UGET........... Union Generale des Etudiants Tunisiens [*General Union of Tunisian Students*] (AF)
UGEV .... Union Generale des Etudiants Voltaiques [*General Union of Voltan Students*] (AF)
UGFC .... United Ghana Farmers' Council (MAR)
UGFCC........ United Ghana Farmers' Cooperative Council (MAR)
UGFT........... Union Generale des Fils du Tchad (MAR)
UGGF .... Union Generale des Guineens en France (MAR)
UGGI .... Union Geodesique et Geophysique Internationale [*International Union of Geodesy and Geophysics*] [*Use IUGG*] [*French*] (WER)
UGI............. Union General de Inversiones [*Bogota*] (COL)
UGI............. Unione Goliardica Italiana [*Italian Student Union*] (WER)
UGICT .... Union Generale des Ingenieurs, des Cadres, et des Techniciens [*General Union of Engineers, Administrative Personnel, and Technicians*] [*French*] (WER)
UGID .... Union Generale Immobiliere de Douala (MAR)
UGIK .... Administration of the State Quality Inspection (RU)
UGiKS .... Garrison and Guard Duty Regulations (RU)
UGINA......... Union Generale Industrielle Africaine [*African General Industrial Union*] [*Moroccan*] (AF)
UgJ.............. Uganda Journal [*A publication*] (MAR)

Ug K .... Criminal Code (RU)
UGK .... Ustav Geodezie a Kartografie [*Institute of Geodesy and Cartography*] (CZ)
UGKh .... Gas Service Administration (RU)
Ug kod .... Criminal Code (RU)
UGKS .... Interior Garrison and Guard Duty Regulations (BU)
UGL .... Universitaetsgewerkschaftsleitung [*University Labor Union Management*] (EG)
uglemash .... Coal Machinery Plant (RU)
Ugletekhizdat ... State Scientific and Technical Publishing House of Literature on the Coal Industry (RU)
UGLJ .... University of Ghana Law Journal [*A publication*] (MAR)
ugl korr .... Angular Correlation (RU)
UGLT .... Union Generale Libyenne du Travail (MAR)
UGM .... General-Purpose Horizontal Camouflage Net (RU)
UGM .... Universitas Gadjah Mada [*Gadjah Mada University*] (IN)
UGMS .... Administration of Hydrometeorological Service (RU)
UGO .... Unabhaengige Gewerkschaftsorganisation [*Independent Trade Union Organization*] (EG)
UGOCM .... Union General de Obreros y Campesinos de Mexico [*General Union of Workers and Peasants of Mexico*] (LA)
UGP .... Udruzenje Grafickih Preduzeca [*Association of Graphic Establishments*] (YU)
UGP .... Union des Gaullistes de Progres [*Union of Progressive Gaullists*] [*French*] (PPE)
UGP .... Union Generale des Petroles [*North African*] (MAR)
UGP .... Uredba o Gradevinskim Preduzecima [*Decree on Building Enterprises*] (YU)
UGPFNRJ .... Udruzenje Gradevinskih Preduzeca Federativna Narodna Republika Jugoslavija [*Association of Building Enterprises of Yugoslavia*] (YU)
UGPI .... Ul'yanovsk State Pedagogical Institute (RU)
UGPROM ..... State Industry Administration (RU)
Ug-prots kod ... Code of Criminal Procedure (RU)
UGRI .... Geological Coal Exploration Institute (RU)
UGRS .... Unione dei Giovani Rivoluzionari Somali (MAR)
UGRU .... Ural Administration of Geological Exploration (RU)
UGS .... Forest Resources Administration (BU)
UGS .... State Insurance Administration (RU)
UGS .... Union de la Gauche Socialiste [*Leftist Socialist Union*] [*Belgian*] (WER)
UGS .... Union des Guineens au Senegal [*Union of Guineans in Senegal*] (PD)
UGS .... Uniunea Generala a Sindicatelor [*General Union of Trade Unions*] (RO)
UGSA .... Union Generale Siderurgique Arabe (MAR)
UGSA .... Union Generale des Syndicats Algeriens (MAR)
UGSCM .... Union Generale des Syndicats Confederes du Maroc [*Moroccan*] (MAR)
UGSD .... Union Generale des Syndicats du Dahomey (MAR)
UGSR .... Uniunea Generala a Sindicatelor din Romania [*General Union of Romanian Trade Unions*] (RO)
UGT .... Union General de Trabajadores [*General Union of Workers*] [*Spanish*] (WER)
UGT .... Universal Nose Tetryl Fuze (RU)
UGT .... Urbaine Gabonaise de Travaux (MAR)
UGTA .... Union Generale des Travailleurs Algeriens [*General Union of Algerian Workers*] (AF)
UGTAN .... Union Generale des Travailleurs de l'Afrique Noire [*General Union of Workers of Black Africa*] (AF)
UGTC .... Union Generale des Travailleurs Camerounais [*General Union of Cameroonian Workers*] (AF)
UGTC .... Union Generale des Travailleurs Centrafricains [*General Union of Central African Workers*] (AF)
UGTC .... Union Generale des Travailleurs Congolais [*General Union of Congolese Workers*] (AF)
UGTCI .... Union Generale des Travailleurs de la Cote-d'Ivoire [*General Union of Ivory Coast Workers*] (AF)
UGTD .... Union General de Trabajadores Dominicanos [*General Union of Dominican Workers*] [*Dominican Republic*] (LA)
UGTD .... Union Generale des Travailleurs Dahomeens (MAR)
UGTE .... Union General de Trabajadores Ecuatorianos [*General Union of Ecuadorean Workers*] (LA1)
UGTG .... Union Generale des Travailleurs de la Guadeloupe (PD)
UGTG .... Union Generale des Travailleurs de Guinee [*General Union of Workers of Guinea*] (AF)
UGTGB .... Uniao Geral dos Trabalhadores da Guine-Bissau (MAR)
UGTGE .... Union General de Trabajadores de Guinea Ecuatorial (MAR)
UGTM .... Union Generale des Travailleurs Marocains [*General Union of Moroccan Workers*] (AF)
UGTRF .... Union Generale des Travailleurs Reunionnais en France [*General Union of Reunionese Workers in France*] (AF)
UGTRP .... Union General de Trabajadores de la Republica de Panama [*General Union of Workers of the Republic of Panama*] (LA)
UGTS .... Union Generale des Travailleurs du Senegal [*General Union of Workers of Senegal*] (AF)
UGTSF .... Union Generale des Travailleurs Senegalais en France (MAR)
UGTT .... Union Generale Tunisienne du Travail [*Tunisian General Federation of Labor*] (AF)
UGTU .... Ural Territorial Geological Administration (RU)
UGU .... Ural State University (RU)
UGU .... Ustredni Geologicky Urad, Praha [*Central Geological Office, Prague*] (CZ)
UGWU .... United General Workers Union [*Bermudian*] (LA1)
ugyn .... Ugynevezett [*So-Called*] (HU)
ugyoszt .... Ugyosztaly [*Department, Section*] (HU)
ugyv .... Ugyvivo [*Charge d'Affaires*] (HU)
UGZ .... Main Contamination Area [*Military term*] (RU)
UGZhD .... Administration of City Railroads (RU)
UHA .... Untersuchungshaftanstalt [*House for Investigative Detention*] (EG)
UHACI .... Union Harriste de Cote-d'Ivoire (MAR)
UHCP .... Uganda Hereditary Chieftainship Party (MAR)
UHKS .... Urad Hospodarske Kontrolni Sluzby [*Office of Economic Control*] (CZ)
UHO .... Ceskoslovensky Urad pro Hospodarskou Pomoc a Obnovu [*Czechoslovak Office of the United Nations Relief and Rehabilitation Administration*] (CZ)
UHP .... Ustav Hospodarskeho Prava Statni Arbitraze CSSR [*Economic Law Institute of State Arbitration Office of Czechoslovakia*] (CZ)
UHP .... Ustav Hygieny Prace [*Industrial Health Institute*] (CZ)
UHP .... Ustredi Hospodarskych Poradcu [*Center of Economic Advisers*] (CZ)
UHR .... Ustredni Hospodarska Rada [*Central Economic Council*] (CZ)
UHSV .... Ustav pro Hospodarsky a Socialni Vyzkum [*Institute for Economic and Social Research*] (CZ)
UHTTB .... Union des Hutu, Tutsi, Twa du Burundi (MAR)
UHZ .... Ustredna Hmotneho Zasobovani [*Materiel Supply Center*] (CZ)
UHZV .... Ustredi pro Hospodareni Zemedelskymi Vyrobky [*Agricultural Produce Center*] (CZ)
UI .... Control Pulse (RU)
UI .... Pulse Amplifier (RU)
UI .... Teachers' Institute (BU)
ui .... Ugyanigy [*In the Same Way*] (HU)
ui .... Ugyanis [*Namely, That Is*] (HU)
ui .... Ugyintezo [*Official in Charge, Manager*] (HU)
UI .... Ujitasi Iroda [*Office of Innovations (For submission of new ideas)*] (HU)
UI .... Unidad de la Izquierda [*Unity of the Left*] [*Peruvian*] (LA)
UI .... Unidades de Instruccion [*Educational Centers*] [*Peruvian*] (LA)
UI .... United Left [*Peruvian*] (PD)
UI .... Universitas Indonesia [*University of Indonesia*] (IN)
UI .... Uprava za Investicije [*Investments Administration*] (YU)
UI .... Uprava Inzenjerije [*Engineer Corps Administration*] [*Military*] (YU)
UI .... Uranium Institute (EA)
ui .... Utoirat [*Postcript*] (HU)
ui .... Uzletigazgato [*Shop Manager*] (HU)
UIA .... Union Immobiliere Africaine (MAR)
UIA .... Union Industrial Argentina [*Argentine Industrial Union*] (LA)
UIA .... Union Industrielle Africaine [*African Industrial Union*] [*Algerian*] (AF)
UIA .... Union des Ingenieurs Algeriens [*Union of Algerian Engineers*] (AF)
UIA .... Union des Ingenieurs Arabes [*Moroccan*] (MAR)
UIA .... Union of International Associations [*See also UAI*] (EA)
UIA .... Union Internationale des Architectes [*International Union of Architects*] (EA)
UIAA .... Union Internationale des Associations d'Alpinisme [*Mountaineering association*]
UIAC .... Unite d'Afforestation Industrielle du Congo (MAR)
UIAE .... Union Industrielle pour l'Afrique Equatoriale [*Industrial Union for Equatorial Africa*] [*Gabonese*] (AF)
UIAOM .... Union Internationale des Agriculteurs de l'Outre-Mer [*International Union of Overseas Farmers*] [*French*] (AF)
UIAS .... Directorate of Engineer Aviation Services (RU)
UIC .... Unidad de Izquierda Comunista [*Unity of the Communist Left*] [*Mexican*] (PPW)
UIC .... Union Industrielle pour le Cameroun (MAR)
UIC .... Union Internationale des Chemins de Fer [*International Union of Railways*] (EA)
UICC .... Union des Industries et Commerce au Congo (MAR)
UIChM .... Ural Institute of Ferrous Metals (RU)
UICN .... Union Internationale pour la Conservation de la Nature et des Ressources (MAR)
UICR .... Union Internationale des Chauffeurs Routiers (EA)
UICT .... Union Internationale Contre la Tuberculose [*International Union Against Tuberculosis - IUAT*] (EA)
UIDIC .... Union Independante pour la Defense des Interets Communaux (MAR)
UIE .... Union des Industries et Entreprises [*Industrial and Business Union*] [*Tunisian*] (AF)
UIE .... Union Internacional de Estudiantes [*International Union of Students*] [*Use IUS*] (LA)
UIE .... Union Internationale d'Editeurs [*International Publishers Association - IPA*] (EA)
UIE .... Union Internationale d'Electrothermie [*International Union for Electroheat*] (EA)
UIE .... Union Internationale des Etudiants [*International Union of Students - IUS*] (EA)

UIEC........... Union Industrielle et d'Entreprise pour le Congo (MAR)
UIEC........... Union Internationale de l'Exploitation Cinematographique [*International Union of Cinematographic Exhibitors*] (EA)
UIEE........... Ukrainian Institute of Experimental Endocrinology (RU)
UIES........... Union Internationale d'Education pour la Sante [*International Union of Health Education - IUHE*] (EA)
UIESP.......... Union Internationale pour l'Etude Scientifique de la Population (MAR)
UIEV........... Ukrainian Institute of Experimental Veterinary Science (RU)
UIFA........... Union Internationale des Femmes Architectes [*International Union of Women Architects - IUWA*] (EA)
UIGSE......... Union Internationale des Guides et Scouts d'Europe [*International Union of European Guides and Scouts - IUEGS*] (EA)
UIHMSU...... Union Internationale d'Hygiene et de Medecine Scolaires et Universitaires [*International Union of School and University Health and Medicine - IUSUHM*] (EA)
UII................ Ural Industrial Institute Imeni S. M. Kirov (RU)
UIIG............ Union Internationale de l'Industrie du Gaz [*International Gas Union - IGU*] (EA)
UIIOM.......... Union Intersyndicale de l'Industrie d'Outre-Mer (MAR)
UIJA............ Union Internationale des Journalistes Africains (MAR)
UIJPLF........ Union Internationale des Journalistes et de la Presse de Langue Francaise [*International Union of French-Language Journalists and Press - IUFLJP*] (EA)
UIJS............ Union Internacional de Juventudes Socialistas [*International Union of Socialist Youth*] [*Use IUSY*] (LA)
UIJS............ Union Internationale de la Jeunesse Socialiste [*International Union of Socialist Youth*] [*Use IUSY*] (AF)
UIK.............. Air Conditioner (RU)
UIL............... Unione Italiana del Lavoro [*Italian Union of Labor*] (WER)
UILI.............. Union Internationale des Laboratoires Independents (EA)
UIL-MD........ Unione Italiana del Lavoro - Metalmeccanici Democratici [*Italian Union of Labor - Democratic Metalworkers*] (WER)
UIM.............. Union Internationale Monarchiste (EA)
UIM.............. Union Internationale Motonautique [*Union of International Motorboating*] (EA)
UIM.............. Universal Measuring Microscope (RU)
UIM.............. Ural Scientific Research Institute of Ferrous Metals (RU)
UIML............ Ukrainian Institute of Marxism-Leninism (RU)
UIMM........... Union des Industries Metallurgiques et Minieres [*Union of Metal and Mining Industries*] [*French*] (WER)
UIM-NATI.... NATI Oil-Testing Unit (RU)
UIM-NRS..... Udruzenje Industrije Gradevinskog Materijala Narodna Republika Srbije [*Association of Building Materials Industries of Serbia*] (YU)
UIMS........... Ukrainian Scientific Research Institute of Metrology and Standardization (RU)
UINO........... Administration of Foreign Transactions of the State Bank of the USSR (RU)
UINRM......... Ured za Informacii na Narodnata Republika Makedonija [*Information Office of Macedonia*] (YU)
UIO.............. Termination Control Pulse (RU)
UIOF............ Union Internationale des Organismes Familiaux [*International Union of Family Organizations*] [*Use IUFO*] (AF)
UIOOT......... Union Internationale des Organismes Officiels de Tourisme [*International Union of Official Travel Organizations*] [*Use IUOTO*] (CL)
UIOSRZ....... Uredba o Imovinskim Odnosima i Reorganizaciji Seljackih Radnih Zadruga [*Decree on Property Relations and the Reorganization of Peasant Work Cooperative*] (YU)
UIOV............ Ukase on the Property Liability of Military Personnel (BU)
UIP.............. General-Purpose Power Supply (RU)
UIP.............. Union Industrial Paraguaya [*Paraguayan Industrial Union*] (LA)
UIP.............. Union Industrielle des Petroles (MAR)
UIP.............. Union Internationale d'Associations de Proprietaires de Wagons de Particuliers [*International Union of Private Railway Truck Owners' Associations*] (EA)
UIP.............. Union Internationale de Patinage [*International Skating Union - ISU*] (EA)
UIP.............. Union Interparlementaire Mondiale [*Interparliamentary Union*] [*Use IPU*] (CL)
UIPA............ Union Industrielle des Petroles Algerie (MAR)
UIPE............ Ukrainian Scientific Research Institute of Industrial Power Engineering (RU)
UIPF............ Ukrainian Scientific Research Institute of Applied Physics (RU)
UIPFKh........ Ukrainian Scientific Research Institute of Applied Physical Chemistry (RU)
UIPFNRJ...... Udruzenje Izdavackih Preduzeca Federativna Narodna Republika Jugoslavija [*Association of Yugoslav Publishing Establishments*] (YU)
UIPI............. Union Internationale de la Propriete Immobiliere [*International Union of Property Owners*] (EA)
UIPKKh....... Ural Institute for Improving Qualifications of the Managerial Personnel (RU)
UIPNRH....... Udruzenje Izdavackih Poduzeca Narodne Republike Hrvatske [*Association of Publishing Houses of Croatia*] (YU)
UIPNRSrbije... Udruzenje Izdavackih Preduzeca Narodne Republike Srbije [*Association of Publishing Houses of Serbia*] (YU)
UIPRE.......... Union Internationale de la Presse Radiotechnique et Electronique (EA)
UIR.............. Educational Research Work (RU)
UIR.............. Engineer Work Directorate (RU)
UIR.............. Training-Research Work (BU)
UIR.............. Udruzenje Invalida Rada [*Association of Disabled Workers*] (YU)
UIRD............ Union Internationale de la Resistance et de la Deportation (MAR)
UIRS............ Udruzenje Invalida Rada Srbije [*Association of Disabled Workers of Serbia*] (YU)
UIS.............. Union Internationale de Speleologie [*International Union of Speleology - IUS*] (EA)
UIS.............. Unione Internazionale degli Studenti [*International Union of Students*] [*Use IUS*] [*Italian*] (WER)
UIS.............. Uniunea Internatonala a Studentiilor [*International Union of Students*] (RO)
UIS.............. Universidad Industrial de Santander [*Bucaramanga*] (COL)
UIS.............. Ural Complex Institute of Structures (RU)
UIS.............. Ustredni Informacni Sluzba [*Central Information Service*] (CZ)
UISAE......... Union Internationale des Sciences Anthropologiques et Ethnologiques [*International Union of Anthropological and Ethnological Sciences - IUAES*] (EA)
UISG............ Union Internationale des Superieures Majeures [*International Union of Superiors General*] (EA)
UISIF........... Union Internationale des Societies d'Ingenieurs Forestiers [*International Union of Societies of Foresters - IUSF*] (EA)
UISP............ Union Internationale des Syndicats de Police [*International Union of Police Syndicates*] (EA)
UIST............ Ukrainian Institute of Soviet Trade (RU)
UISTAFP..... Union Internationale des Syndicats des Travailleurs de l'Agriculture, des Forets, et des Plantations [*Trade Unions International of Agriculture, Forestry, and Plantation Workers - TUIAFPW*] (EA)
UISTAV....... Union Internationale pour la Science, la Technique, et les Applications du Vide [*International Union for Vacuum Science, Technique, and Applications - IUVSTA*] (EA)
UIT.............. Union de Industrias Textiles [*Union of Textile Industries*] [*Salvadoran*] (LA1)
UIT.............. Union Internationale des Telecommunications [*International Telecommunications Union*] [*Use ITU*] [*French*] (CL)
UIT.............. Union Internationale de Tir [*International Shooting Union*] (EA)
UIT.............. Unione Internazionale Telecomunicazioni [*International Telecommunications Union*] [*Use ITU*] [*Italian*] (WER)
UITA............ Union of International Technical Associations [*See also UATI*] (EA)
UITLK.......... Administration of Corrective Labor Camps and Colonies (RU)
UITR............ Ukase on Inventions, Technical Improvements, and Rationalization Suggestions (BU)
UITU............ Administration of Corrective Labor Establishments (RU)
UIYuN.......... Ukrainian Scientific Research Institute of Jurisprudence (RU)
UIZh............ Ukrainian Scientific Research Institute of Livestock Breeding (RU)
UJ................ Uganda Journal [*A publication*] (MAR)
UJ................ Uniwersytet Jagiellonski [*Jagiellonian University*] (POL)
UJA............. Union des Journalistes Africains (MAR)
UJA............. Union des Journalistes Algeriens [*Algerian Journalists Union*] (AF)
UJA............. United Jewish Appeal (ME)
UJARF......... Union de la Jeunesse Agricole et Rurale de France [*Union of French Agricultural and Rural Youth*] (WER)
UJC............. Uniao da Juventude Comunista [*Union of Communist Youth*] [*Portuguese*] (WER)
UJC............. Union de la Jeunesse Congolaise (MAR)
UJC............. Union de Jovenes Comunistas [*Union of Young Communists*] [*Nicaraguan*] (LA1)
UJC............. Union de Jovenes Comunistas [*Union of Young Communists*] [*Cuban*] (LA)
UJC............. Union de Jovenes Comunistas [*Union of Young Communists*] [*Uruguayan*] (LA)
UJC............. Ustav pro Jazyk Cesky [*Czech Language Institute (of the Czechoslovak Academy of Sciences)*] (CZ)
UJCAZ......... Ustredni Jednota Cesko-Americkych Zen [*Central Organization of Czech-American Women*] (CZ)
UJCC........... Uniunea Judeteana a Cooperativelor de Consum [*County Union of Consumer Cooperatives*] (RO)
UJCDE......... Union de la Juventud Comunista Democratica Espanol [*Spanish Democratic Communist Youth Union*] (WER)
UJCF........... Union des Jeunesses Communistes de France [*Union of Communist Youth of France*] (WER)
UJCL........... Ustredni Jednota Ceskoslovenskych Lekaru [*Central Organization of Czechoslovak Physicians*] (CZ)
UJCM.......... Uniunea Judeteana a Cooperativelor Mestesugaresti [*County Union of Artisan Cooperatives*] (RO)
UJCML........ Union des Jeunesses Communistes Marxistes-Leninistes [*Union of Young Marxist-Leninist Communists*] [*French*] (PPE)
UJCS........... Ustredni Jednota Ceskoslovenskych Sachistu [*Central Organization of Czechoslovak Chess Players*] (CZ)
UJCsL......... Ustredni Jednota Ceskoslovenske Obce Legionarske [*Czechoslovak Legion Headquarters*] (CZ)
UJD............. Utriusque Juris Doctor [*Doctor of Both Civil and Canon Law*] [*Latin*] (GPO)

UJECML...... Uniao da Juventude Estudantil Comunista Marxista-Leninista [*Union of Communist Student Youth/Marxist-Leninist*] [*Portuguese*] (WER)
UJEP........... Universita Jana Evangelisty Purkyne [*University of Jan Evangelista Purkyne*] (CZ)
UJHD........... Ustredni Jednota Hospodarskych Druzstev [*Central Organization of Economic Cooperatives*] (CZ)
UJI............... Ustredni Jednota Invalidu [*Central Association of Disabled Persons*] (CZ)
UJK............. Union de la Jeunesse Khmere [*en RDA*] [*Cambodian Youth Union (in the GDR)*] (CL)
UJKI........... Union de la Jeunesse Kimbanguiste (MAR)
UJM............. Union de la Jeunesse Marocaine [*Moroccan Youth Union*] (AF)
Uj M Kk....... Uj Magyar Konyvkiado [*New Hungarian Book Publishing Enterprise*] (HU)
UJP............. Udruzenje Jugoslovenskih Pronalazaca [*Association of Yugoslav Inventors*] (YU)
UJP............. Union des Jeunes pour le Progres [*Union of Youth for Progress*] [*Youth group of the UDR*] [*French*] (WER)
UJP............. Union de la Jeunesse pour la Patrie [*Union of Youth for the Nation*] [*French*] (WER)
UJP............. Uredba o Organizaciji, Poslovanju, i Upravljanju Jugoslovenskim Postama, Telegrafima, i Telefonima [*Decree on the Organization, Operation, and Management of Yugoslav Post, Telegraph, and Telephone*] (YU)
UJPC........... Union des Journalistes Professionnels du Congo (MAR)
UJPDC........ Union des Jeunes du Parti Democratique Gabonais (MAR)
UJPM.......... Union des Jeunes pour le Progres de Mayotte [*Union of Youth for the Progress of Mayotte*] [*Comoran*] (AF)
UJRB........... Union de la Jeunesse Revolutionnaire Burundaise (MAR)
UJS............. Union de Juventudes Socialistas [*Socialist Youth Union*] [*Argentine*] (LA)
UJSC........... Union de la Jeunesse Socialiste Congolaise [*Union of Congolese Socialist Youth*] (AF)
UJT............. Union de la Jeunesse Tunisienne [*Tunisian Youth Union*] (AF)
UJU............. Udruzenje Jugoslovenskog Uciteljstva [*Association of Yugoslav Teachers*] (YU)
UJV CSAV... Ustav Jaderneho Vyzkumu CSAV [*Nuclear Research Institute of the Czechoslovak Science Academy*] (CZ)
UJWF.......... United Jewish Welfare Fund (MAR)
UJZ............. Uredba o Organizaciji, Poslovanju, i Upravljanju Jugoslovenskim Zeljeznicama [*Decree on the Organization, Operation, and Management of Yugoslav Railroads*] (YU)
UK............... Acetic Acid (RU)
UK............... Administrative Committee (BU)
UK............... Command Control [*Computers*] (RU)
UK............... Compounding Device (RU)
UK............... Criminal Code (RU)
UK............... Institution's Trade Union Committee (BU)
UK............... Percussive Contact (RU)
UK............... Personnel Administration (RU)
UK-.............. Stowing Crane, Stacking Crane (RU)
UK............... Training Center (RU)
UK............... Training Ship (RU)
UK............... Ugostiteljska Komora [*Chamber of Hotel and Catering Trade*] (YU)
uk............... Ukonczono [*Finished*] (POL)
UK............... United Kingdom
UK............... Universita Karlova [*Charles University*] (CZ)
UK............... Universiti Kebangsaan [*National University*] [*Malaysian*] (ML)
UK............... Universitni Knihovna [*University Library*] [*Prague*] (CZ)
UK............... Univerzalna Klasifikacija [*Universal Classification*] (YU)
UK............... Univerzitetni Komite [*University Committee*] (YU)
UK............... Urzad Konserwatorski [*Administration for Preservation*] [*Of monuments, works of art, etc.*] (POL)
UK............... Ustredni Knihovna [*Central Library*] (CZ)
uk............... Uzletszeru Kejelges [*Prostitution*] (HU)
UKA............. Training Set of Aerial Photographs (RU)
UKA............. United Khmer Airlines [*Cambodian*] (CL)
UKAC........... United Kingdom Automation Council
UKAI........... Kenya Agriculture Institute (MAR)
UKAI........... Ukambani Agricultural Institute (MAR)
UKB-........... Core Drilling Unit (RU)
UKB............. Universitni Knihovna v Brne [*University Library in Brno*] (CZ)
UKB............. Urkutatasi Kormanybizottsag [*Government Committee on Space Research*] (HU)
UKCG.......... Udruzenje Knjizevnika Crne Gore [*Association of Writers of Montenegro*] (YU)
UKCh.......... Pure Acetic Acid (RU)
UKChV........ Ustav Kozeluzstva a Chemie Vody [*Institute of Tanning and Hydrochemistry*] (CZ)
UKCIS......... United Kingdom Chemical Information Service
UKCOSA...... United Kingdom Council for Overseas Student Affairs (MAR)
UKCS.......... Union of Kenya Civil Servants (MAR)
UKD............ Universiteli Kadinlar Dernegi [*University Women's Association*] (TU)
UkDP.......... Ukase on State Enterprises (BU)
UKEC.......... Usines Khmeres de Confection et de Tissage [*Cambodian Mills for Ready-to-Wear Clothing and Woven Textiles*] (CL)
UKF............ Ultrakrotkie Fale [*Ultra-Short Waves*] [*Polish*]
UKGB.......... Administration of the State Security Committee (RU)
UKGB.......... Plenipotentiary of the State Security Committee (RU)
UKGVF........ Training Center of the Civil Air Fleet (RU)
UKh............ Ubiquinone (RU)
UKH............ Ugostiteljska Komora Hrvatske [*Chamber of Hotel and Catering Trade of Croatia*] (YU)
UKh............ Universal Chromathermograph (RU)
UKhIN......... Scientific Research Institute of Coal Chemistry (RU)
UK Hlm Prahy... Ustredni Knihovna Hlavniho Mesta Prahy [*Central Library of the Capital Prague*] (CZ)
UKhLU........ Administration of Self-Supporting Medical Institutions (RU)
UKhR.......... Chemical Equilibrium Equation (RU)
Ukhtizhemlag... Ukhta-Izhma Corrective Labor Camp (RU)
UKI............ Ulastirma Koordinasyonu Idaresi [*Communications Coordination Administration*] [*of Communications Ministry*] (TU)
UKID.......... Angular Ion Diffusion Coefficient (RU)
UKIS.......... Ukrainian Complex Scientific Research Institute of Structures (RU)
UKIZh......... Ukrainian Communist Institute of Journalism (RU)
UKK............ Criminal Cassation Collegium of the Supreme Court (RU)
UKK............ Ulastirma Koordinasyon Kurulu [*Communications Coordination Committee*] [*In Public Works Ministry*] (TU)
UKK............ Ural-Kuznetsk Kombinat (RU)
UKK............ Ustredna Katolicka Kancelaria [*Central Catholic Bureau*] (CZ)
UKK............ Ustredni Kulturni Komise [*Central Cultural Commission*] (CZ)
UKKh.......... Open-Pit Administration (RU)
UKLK.......... Ustredni Komise Lidove Kontroly [*Central Commission of People's Control*] (CZ)
UKLKS........ Ustredni Komise Lidove Kontroly a Statistiky [*Central Commission of People's Control and Statistics*] (CZ)
UKM........... Administration of Cable Trunk Lines (RU)
UKM........... General-Purpose Kitchen Machine (RU)
UKM........... Ukrainian Crystalline Massif (RU)
UKm........... Umni Kmetovalec [*Prudent Farmer*] [*A periodical*] (YU)
UKM........... Ustredni Komise Mladeze [*Central Youth Commission*] (CZ)
UKN............ Consolidated Structural Norms (RU)
UKN............ Ustrzyckie Kopalnictwo Naftowe [*Ustrzyki Oil Wells*] (POL)
UKNIALMI... Ukrainian Scientific Research Institute of Conservational Afforestation (RU)
UKNS.......... Ustredni Komise Narodni Souteze [*Central Committee for National Competition*] (CZ)
U Ko........... Univerzita Komenskeho [*Comenius University*] [*Bratislava*] (CZ)
UKOB.......... Ugyvedi Kamarak Orszagos Bizottsaga [*National Board of the Bar Association*] (HU)
UKOL.......... Universitni Knihovna, Olomouc [*Olomouc University Library*] (CZ)
ukoncz........ Ukonczono [*Finished*] (POL)
UKOS.......... Uredba o Kreditima za Obrtna Sredstva i Drugim Kratkorocnim Kreditima [*Decree on Credits for Current Assets and Other Short-Term Credits*] (YU)
UKP............ Administration of Municipal Establishments (RU)
UKP............ Edible Acetic Acid (RU)
UKP............ Training and Consultation Post [*Civil aviation*] (RU)
UKP............ Ukrainian Communist Party (RU)
UKP............ Ukrajna Kommunista Partja [*Communist Party of the Ukraine*] (HU)
UKPK.......... Ustredni Kulturne-Propagacni Komise [*Central Commission of Culture and Propaganda*] (CZ)
UKPL.......... Ustredni Knihovna Patentove Literatury [*Central Library of Literature on Patents*] (CZ)
UKPM.......... Ulastirma Koordinasyon Proje Merkezi [*Communications Coordination Plans Center*] [*In Public Works Ministry*] (TU)
UKPO.......... Ustredni Kulturne-Propagacni Oddeleni [*Central Department of Culture and Propaganda (of the Revolutionary Trade Union Movement)*] (CZ)
Ukr............. Fortification [*Topography*] (RU)
ukr............. Ukrainian (BU)
Ukr............. Ukrainian (RU)
UKR............ Ustredna Kupelna Rada [*Central Council of Health Resorts*] (CZ)
UKR............ Ustredni Knihovnicka Rada [*Central Library Council*] (CZ)
UKRDORTRANSNII... Ukrainian Road Transportation Scientific Research Institute (RU)
ukrepl......... Fortification [*Topography*] (RU)
Ukr fiz zh.... Ukrainian Journal of Physics [*A publication*] (RU)
UKRGEOMIN... Ukrainian Branch of the Scientific Research Institute of Geology and Mineralogy (RU)
UkrGIDEP... Ukrainian Branch of the All-Union State Planning Institute Gidroenergoproyekt [*Planning hydroelectric power plants*] (RU)
UkrGIPKh.... Ukrainian State Institute of Applied Chemistry (RU)
Ukrgiprodortrans... Ukrainian State Institute for the Planning of Roads and Transportation (RU)
Ukrgipromash... Ukrainian State Planning and Design Institute of Machinery Manufacture (RU)
Ukrgipromesttoplivprom... Ukrainian Institute for the Planning of Local and Fuel Industries (RU)
Ukrgiproprod... Ukrainian State Institute for the Planning of Food Establishments (RU)

Ukrgiproprom ... Ukrainian Institute for the Planning of Industry (RU)
Ukrgiprosel'elektro ... Ukrainian State Institute for the Planning of Rural Electrification (RU)
Ukrgiprosel'khoz ... Ukrainian State Planning Institute of Rural and Agricultural Construction (RU)
Ukrgiprosel'stroy ... Ukrainian State Institute for the Planning of Rural and Kolkhoz Construction (RU)
Ukrgiprostanok ... Ukrainian State Planning Institute of the Machine Tool Industry (RU)
Ukrgiprostroymaterialy ... Ukrainian Institute for the Planning of Production of Building Materials (RU)
Ukrgiprotsvetmet ... Ukrainian State Planning Institute of Nonferrous Metallurgy (RU)
Ukrgiprovodkhoz ... Ukrainian State Institute for the Planning of Water Management Structures and Rural Electric Power Plants (RU)
Ukrglavneftesbyt ... Ukrainian Branch of the Main Administration for the Marketing of Petroleum (RU)
Ukrgostekhizdat ... Ukrainian State Publishing House of Technical Literature (RU)
UkrIEV......... Ukrainian Scientific Research Institute of Experimental Veterinary Science (RU)
Ukrinstoplivo ... Ukrainian Scientific Research Institute of Local Fuels (RU)
UKRIOK....... Ukrainian Scientific Research Institute of Refractory and Acid-Resistant Materials (RU)
UKRIPKh..... Ukrainian Institute of Applied Chemistry (RU)
UKRK .... Ustredni Kontrolni a Revisni Komise [*Central Control and Audit Commission (of the Communist Party of Czechoslovakia)*] (CZ)
Ukrkabel'.... Ukrainian Cable Plant (RU)
Ukrkhimprom ... Main Administration of the Chemical Industry of the UkrSSR (RU)
Ukr khim zh ... Ukrainian Chemical Journal [*A publication*] (RU)
Ukr matem zh ... Ukrainian Mathematical Journal [*A publication*] (RU)
Ukrmedgiz ... State Medical Publishing House of the Ukrainian SSR (RU)
UKRMEKhANOBR ... Ukrainian Branch of the Scientific Research Institute for the Mechanical Processing of Minerals (RU)
Ukrmuzradioprom ... Main Administration of the Music and Radio Industries of the UkrSSR (RU)
Ukrneft'....... Association of the Ukrainian Petroleum Industry (RU)
UkrNIGMI.... Ukrainian Scientific Research Hydrometeorological Institute (RU)
UkrNIGRI..... Ukrainian Scientific Research Institute of Geological Exploration (RU)
UkrNII.......... Ukrainian Scientific Research Institute (RU)
UkrNIIB .... Ukrainian Scientific Research Institute of Paper (RU)
UkrNIIGiM... Ukrainian Scientific Research Institute of Hydraulic Engineering and Reclamation (RU)
UkrNIIKP..... Ukrainian Scientific Research Institute of the Leather and Footwear Industry (RU)
UKRNIIMASh ... Ukrainian Scientific Research Institute of Metalworking and Chemical Machinery Manufacture (RU)
UkrNIImesttopprom ... Ukrainian Scientific Research Institute of Local and Fuel Industries (RU)
UkrNIIMOD ... Ukrainian Scientific Research Institute for the Mechanical Processing of Lumber (RU)
UkrNIIMP .... Ukrainian Scientific Research Institute of the Oil and Fats Industries (RU)
UkrNIImyasomolprom ... Ukrainian Scientific Research Institute of the Meat and Dairy Industry (RU)
UkrNIIO....... Ukrainian Scientific Research Institute of Refractories (RU)
UkrNIIOMShS ... Ukrainian Scientific Research Institute for the Organization and Mechanization of Mine Construction (RU)
UkrNIIPlastmass ... Ukrainian Scientific Research Institute of Plastics (RU)
UkrNIIProyekt ... State Scientific Research and Planning Institute of Coal, Ore, Petroleum, and Gas Industries of the Ukrainian SSR (RU)
UkrNIIS .... Ukrainian Scientific Research Institute of Construction (RU)
UkrNIIS .... Ukrainian Scientific Research Institute of Structures (RU)
UkrNIISKhOM ... Ukrainian Scientific Research Institute of Agricultural Machinery (RU)
UkrNIISol' ... Ukrainian Scientific Research Institute of the Salt Industry (RU)
UkrNIITP..... Ukrainian Scientific Research Institute of the Textile Industry (RU)
UkrNIIZh ..... Ukrainian Scientific Research Institute of Livestock Breeding (RU)
UkrNIKhI..... Ukrainian Scientific Research Institute of Cotton Growing and Irrigation Farming (RU)
UKRNIKhIM ... Ukrainian Scientific Research Chemical Institute (RU)
UkrNITI .... Ukrainian Scientific Research Institute of Pipes (RU)
UKRNITI...... Ukrainian Scientific Research Textile Institute (RU)
UkrNITO...... Ukrainian Branch of the All-Union Scientific, Engineering, and Technical Society (RU)
UkrNITO...... Ukrainian Scientific, Engineering, and Technical Society (RU)
UkrNIZ .... Ukrainian Scientific Research Institute of Grain and Grain Products (RU)
UkrNTO....... Ukrainian Republic Administration of the Scientific and Technical Society (RU)
UKROP........ Ukrainian Society of Pathologists (RU)
Ukrpromsovet ... Ukrainian Council of Producers' Cooperatives (RU)
UkrROSTA ... Ukrainian Branch of the Russian News Agency (RU)
Ukrsel'mash ... Main Administration of Agricultural Machinery Manufacture of the UkrSSR (RU)
Ukrtrestsel'mash ... Ukrainian Trust of Agricultural Machinery (RU)
Ukrtsentrarkhiv ... Central Administration of Archives of the Ukrainian SSR (RU)
UkrTsIETIN ... Ukrainian Central Scientific Research Institute for Determination of Disability and Organization of Work for Disabled Persons (RU)
UkrVODGEO ... Ukrainian Scientific Research Institute of Water Supply, Sewer Systems, Hydraulic Engineering Structures, and Engineering Hydrogeology (RU)
Ukrvozdukhput' ... Ukrainian Voluntary Society of the Air Fleet (RU)
UKS............ Administration of Capital Construction (RU)
UKS............ Guard Duty Regulations (RU)
UKS............ Udruzenje Knjizevnika Srbije [*Association of Writers of Serbia*] (YU)
UKS............ Ustredna Karita na Slovensku [*Central Office of the Charity Society in Slovakia*] (CZ)
UKSATA ..... United Kingdom-South Africa Trade Association (MAR)
UKSBiH....... Udruzenje Katolickih Svecenika Bosne i Hercegovine [*Association of Catholic Priests of Bosnia and Hercegovina*] (YU)
UKShch....... Ukrainian Crystalline Shield (RU)
uks k .... Acetic Acid (RU)
UKSKhU...... Ukrainian Communist Agricultural University Imeni Artem (RU)
UKSS-......... Universal Switchboard for Station's Service Traffic (RU)
UKT............ Ultrakratki Talasi [*Ultrashort Wave*] (YU)
UKTA .... United Kingdom Trade Agency (MAR)
UKTEK .... Junction Office for Container Shipments and Transportation and Forwarding Operations (RU)
UKTS........... United Kingdom Treaty Series [*A publication*] (MAR)
UKTZ........... Ustredni Klub Techniku a Zlepsovatelu [*Central Club of Technicians and Innovators*] (CZ)
UKU............ Coding and Controlling Device (RU)
UK-U .... Improved Compounding Device (RU)
UKU............ Ural Communist University Imeni V. I. Lenin (RU)
UKUTA........ Chama cha Usanyu wa Kiswahili na Ushairi [*Organization for the Writing of Swahili and Poetry*] [*Tanzanian*] (AF)
UKUZ .... Administration of Personnel and Educational Institutions (RU)
UKV............ Ultrakratka Vlna [*Ultrashort Wave*] (CZ)
UKV............ Ultrashort-Wave (RU)
UKV............ Ultrashort-Wave Radio Station (RU)
UKV............ Ultrashort Waves (BU)
UKV-ChM.... Ultrashort Waves with Frequency Modulation (RU)
UKVT........... Statutes of the Coastal Water Transportation System (BU)
UKW............ Ultrakurzwelle [*Ultrashort Wave, Very High Frequency*] [*German*] (WEN)
UKW............ Ultrakurzwellenfunk [*Ultrashort-Wave Radio*] (EG)
UKWAL .... United Kingdom/West Africa Lines (AF)
UKW Vorsatzgeraet ... Ultrakurzwellenvorsatzgeraet [*Ultrashort-Wave Converter*] (EG)
UKZhD .... Narrow-Gauge Railway (RU)
UKZKO........ Correspondence Training Center of Municipal Education (RU)
UKZUZ........ Ustredni Kontrolni a Zkusebni Ustav Zemedelsky [*Central Agricultural Control and Testing Institute*] (CZ)
u-l............... Teacher (BU)
ul .... Ulica [*Street*] (POL)
ul .... Ulica [*Street*] [*Slovak*]
ul .... Ulica [*Street*] [*Yugoslav*] (CED)
ul .... Ulice [*Street*] (CZ)
ul .... Ulita [*Street*] [*Romanian*]
ul .... Ulitsa [*Street*] [*Bulgarian*]
ul .... Ulitsa [*Street*] [*Russian*]
UL................ Universal League (EA)
UL................ Uniwersytet Lodzki [*Lodz University*] (POL)
UL................ Uniwersytet Lubelski [*Lublin University*] (POL)
ul .... Unloeslich [*Insoluble*] [*German*]
UL................ Uprava za Lov [*Administration for Hunting*] (YU)
Ul................. Uredni List Republiky Ceskoslovenske [*Official Gazette of the Czechoslovak Republic*] (CZ)
Ul................. Uudenmaan Laani [*Finnish*]
ul .... Uutta Lukua [*Finnish*]
ula .... Ultralyhytaalto [*Finnish*]
ULA .... Union der Leitenden Angestellten [*Union of Management Personnel*] (EG)
ULA .... Universidad de Los Andes [*Los Andes University*] [*Venezuelan*] (LA)
ULAPC .... Union Latinoamericana de Prensa Catolica [*Latin American Catholic Press Union*] (LA)
ULAS........... Ulastirma ve Nakliye Subesi [*Communications and Transport Branch*] [*A subsidiary of ETI in the TFSC*] [*Turkish Cypriot*] (TU)
Ulas-Is......... Turkiye Deniz Tasitmacligi Isci Sendikalari Federasyonu [*Turkish Seamen's Federation*] (TU)
Ulas-Is......... Turkiye Ulastirma Iscileri Sendikasi [*Turkish Communications Workers Union*] (TU)
ULB .... Union Laitiere de Bamako (MAR)
ULB .... Universite Libre de Bruxelles [*Free University of Brussels*] [*Belgian*] (WER)
ULBA........... Universal Love and Brotherhood Association (EA)
ULC .... Philippines Civil Liberties Union (PD)

ULC .... Uganda Labour Congress (MAR)
ULC .... United Labor Congress [*Nigerian*] (AF)
ULC .... Universite Libre du Congo (MAR)
ULCN .... United Labor Congress of Nigeria (MAR)
ULD .... Ustredni Loutkove Divadlo [*Central Puppet Theater*] (CZ)
ULDF .... United Left Democratic Front [*Indian*] (PPW)
ULDS .... Union Liberale-Democratique Suisse [*Liberal Democratic Union of Switzerland*] (PPE)
ULDS .... Ustredni Letecka Dopravni Sprava [*Central Air Transport Directorate*] (CZ)
ULF .... United Labour Front [*Trinidadian and Tobagan*] (PD)
ULFLRJ .... Uradni List Federativne Ljudske Republike Jugoslavije [*Yugoslav Official Gazette*] [*A publication*] (YU)
ULFWS .... United Liberation Front for Western Somalia [*Ethiopian*] (AF)
ULGS .... Unified Local Government Service (MAR)
ULGTS .... Administration of the Leningrad City Telephone Network (RU)
ULI .... Ural Forestry-Engineering Institute (RU)
ULI .... Varnished Measuring Carbon [*Resistor*] (RU)
ULK .... Ustredna Lekarska Kniznica [*Central Medical Library*] [*Bratislava*] (CZ)
ULK .... Ustredni Lidova Knihovna [*Central People's Library*] (CZ)
ULKU ES ..... Ulkucu Esnaf Dernegi [*Idealist Tradesmen's Association*] (TU)
ULKUM .... Ulkucu Memurlar Dernegi [*Idealist Employees (Officials) Organization*] [*Ankara*] (TU)
Ulku-Tek ..... Ulkucu Teknik Elemanlar Dernegi [*Idealist Technical Elements (Workers) Organization*] (TU)
ULLRS .... Uradni List Ljudska Republika Slovenija [*Slovenian Official Gazette*] [*Ljubljana*] [*A publication*] (YU)
ULMLT .... Union pour la Lutte Marxiste-Leniniste Tunisien [*Union for the Tunisian Marxist-Leninist Struggle*] (AF)
ULO .... United Left Opposition [*Trinidadian and Tobagan*] (LA1)
ULPAR .... Ukase on Internal Passports and Address Registration of Citizens of the Bulgarian People's Republic (BU)
ULRC .... United Liberia Rubber Corporation (MAR)
ULS .... False Signal Level (RU)
ULS .... Ustredni Letecky Sklad [*Central Aviation Depot*] (CZ)
UlsB .... Ulastirma Bakanligi [*Ministry of Communications*] (TU)
ULSMSv ...... Uredni Likvidacni Sprava pri Ministerstvu Stavebnictvi [*Administrative Liquidation Office of the Ministry of Construction*] (CZ)
ULSU .... University of Liberia Student Union (MAR)
ult .... Ultimo [*Last Month*] [*Latin*] (GPO)
ult .... Ultimo [*Last*] [*Spanish*]
ULT .... Ustredi Lidove Tvorivosti [*Folk Arts Center*] (CZ)
ULTAB .... Uniao dos Lavradores e Trabalhadores Agricolas do Brasil [*Union of Farmers and Farm Workers of Brazil*] (LA)
ULTI .... Ural Forestry-Engineering Institute (RU)
ULTRAHUILCA ... Union de Trabajadores del Huila y Caqueta [*Neiva*] (COL)
ULUBiH .... Udruzenje Likovnih Umjetnika Bosne i Hercegovine [*Representational Artists' Association of Bosnia and Hercegovina*] (YU)
ULUCG .... Udruzenje Likovnih Umjetnika Crne Gore [*Representational Artists' Association of Montenegro*] (YU)
uluchsh .... Improved (RU)
ULUH .... Udruzenje Likovnih Umjetnika Hrvatske [*Representational Artists' Association of Croatia*] (YU)
ULUS .... Udruzenje Likovnih Umetnika Srbije [*Representational Artists' Association of Serbia*] (YU)
ULUV .... Ustredi Lidove Umelecke Vyroby [*Center for Folk Art*] (CZ)
ULUV .... Ustredi Lidoveho Umeni Vytvarneho [*Creative Folk Arts Center*] (CZ)
ULZ .... Ultrasonic Delay Line (RU)
ULZ .... Ustav Leteckeho Zdravotnictvi [*Air Force Medical Institute*] (CZ)
UM .... Controlling Device, Controller (RU)
um .... Deceased (RU)
UM .... Mauritanian Ouguiya (AF)
UM .... Microphone Amplifier (RU)
UM .... Militia Administration (RU)
UM .... Power Amplifier (RU)
um .... Sea Level (RU)
UM .... Uchitelska Misul [*Teacher's Thought*] [*A periodical*] (BU)
um .... Ugymint [*Namely, That Is*] (HU)
UM .... Ujjaepitesi Miniszterium/Miniszter [*Ministry/Minister of Reconstruction*] (HU)
U/M .... Umlaufungen pro Minute [*Revolutions per Minute*] [*German*]
UM .... Unidad Militar [*Military Unit*] [*Cuban*] (LA)
UM .... Uttoro Mozgalom [*Pioneer Movement*] (HU)
UMA .... Mechanization and Motor Transportation Administration (BU)
UMA .... Uniao das Mulheres da Angola (MAR)
UMA .... Union Marocaine de l'Agriculture (MAR)
UMA .... Union Medicale Algerienne [*Algerian Medical Union*] (AF)
UMA .... Union de Mujeres Americanas [*Union of American Women*] [*Ecuadorean*] (LA)
UMA .... Union de Mujeres de la Argentina [*Union of Argentine Women*] (LA)
UMAC .... Union Marocaine des Associations de Chantiers (MAR)
UMAC .... Union Mediterraneenne Anticommuniste (MAR)
UMAEC .... Union Monetaire de l'Afrique Equatoriale et du Cameroun (MAR)
UMAH .... Uyusmazlik Mahkemesi [*Court of Disagreement (Discord)*] (TU)
UMAIA .... Uzina Mecanica a Agriculturii si Industriei Alimentare [*Mechanical Plant for Agriculture and the Food Industry*] (RO)
UMATI .... Tanzania Family Planning Association (MAR)
UMAVALCA ... Union de Maestros del Valle del Cauca [*Cali*] (COL)
UMB .... Union Marocaine de Banques (MAR)
UMBC .... United Middle Belt Congress (MAR)
UMC .... Union Malienne de Constructions (MAR)
UMC .... Union de Mineros de Colombia [*Union of Miners of Colombia*] (LA)
UMC .... Uniwersytet Marii Curie-Sklodowskiej (w Lublinie) [*Maria Curie-Sklodowska University (in Lublin)*] [*Polish*]
UMCA .... Universities Mission to Central Africa (MAR)
UMCB .... United Missions in the Copperbelt (MAR)
UMCh .... Intermediate Frequency Amplifier (BU)
UMCh .... Union de Mujeres de Chile [*Women's Union of Chile*] (LA)
UMCIA .... Union Marocaine de l'Industrie, du Commerce, et de l'Artisanat (MAR)
UMCO .... Manufacturas Metalicas Umco e Ica SA [*Medellin*] (COL)
UMCS .... Uniwersytet Marii Curie-Sklodowskiej [*Maria Curie-Sklodowska University*] (POL)
UMD .... Motherhood and Childhood Administration (BU)
UMD .... Training Mine Detonator (RU)
U Md .... Umumi Mudur [*Director General*] (TU)
UMD .... Union Militar Democratica [*Military Democratic Union*] [*Spanish*] (WER)
UMD .... Union de Mujeres Democratas [*Union of Democratic Women*] [*Colombian*] (LA)
UMD .... Universidad Mundial Dominicana [*Dominican World University*] [*Dominican Republic*] (LA1)
UMD .... Ustav pro Mechanisaci Dolu [*Institute for the Mechanization of Mining*] (CZ)
UMDOC .... Ustredni Matice Divadelnich Ochotniku Ceskych [*Federation of Czech Amateur Actors*] (CZ)
UMDr .... Doktor der Gesamten Heilkunde [*German*]
UME .... Uniao Metropolitana de Estudantes [*Metropolitan Union of Students*] [*Brazilian*] (LA)
UME .... United Medical Enterprises (MAR)
UME .... Ustredna Mechanisovane Evidence [*Machine Records Center*] [*Prague*] (CZ)
UMEA .... Universal Medical Esperanto Association (EA)
UMEAC .... Union Monetaire de l'Afrique Equatoriale et du Cameroun (MAR)
UMEB .... Uzina de Masini Electrice Bucuresti [*Bucharest Electrical Machines Plant*] (RO)
UMECO .... Union Mediatrice Congolaise (MAR)
UMEP .... Administration of Local Evacuation Stations (RU)
UMEWU ...... United Malayan Estate Workers Union (ML)
UMEZ .... Ustredi pro Mechanisaci Zemedelstvi [*Center for the Mechanization of Agriculture*] (CZ)
UMF .... Uridine Monophosphate (RU)
UMFCM .... United Methodist Free Churches' Mission (MAR)
UMGB .... Administration of the Ministry of State Security (RU)
UMGSB .... Ukrainian Local Geodetic Information Office (RU)
UMGTS .... Administration of the Moscow City Telephone Network (RU)
UMH .... Union de Mujeres Hondurenas [*Union of Honduran Women*] (LA)
UMHK .... Union Miniere du Haut Katanga (MAR)
UMI .... Union Mathematique Internationale [*International Mathematical Union - IMU*] (EA)
UMIF .... Uluslararasi Gida ve Muskirat Iscileri Birlikleri Federasyonu [*International Federation of Food and Intoxicants Workers Union*] (TU)
UMIMA .... Union Malienne d'Industries Maritimes (MAR)
UMIMA .... Union Mauritanienne d'Industries Maritimes (MAR)
U/min .... Umdrehungen in der Minute [*Revolutions per Minute*] [*German*] (WEN)
UMK .... Amplification of Modulated Oscillations (RU)
UMK .... Ugyvedi Munkakozosseg [*Working Association of Lawyers*] (HU)
UMK .... Uniwersytet Imienia Mikolaja Kopernika (w Toruniu) [*Nicholas Copernicus University (in Torun)*] [*Polish*]
UMKAD .... Administration of the Moscow Belt Highway (RU)
umkr .... Umkristallisieren [*Recrystallize*] [*German*]
UMKS .... Administration of Trunk Cable Network (RU)
Uml/Min ..... Umlaufungen pro Minute [*Revolutions per Minute*] [*German*]
UMM .... Directorate for the Mechanization and Motorization of the RKKA (RU)
UMM .... Union del Magisterio de Montevideo [*Montevideo Teachers Union*] [*Uruguayan*] (LA)
UMM .... Unione Medica Mediterranea (MAR)
UMM .... United Methodist Mission (MAR)
UMMKS .... Administration of the Moscow Trunk Cable Network (RU)
UMML .... Unione Medicale Mediterranea Latina [*Latin Mediterranean Medical Union - LMMU*] (EA)
UMMP .... Local Metallurgical Industry Administration (RU)
UMMR .... Uzina Mecanica de Material Rulant [*Mechanical Plant for Rolling Stock*] (RO)
UMN .... Progress of Mathematical Sciences (RU)
UMN .... Union pour la Majorite Nouvelle [*Union for the New Majority*] [*French*] (PPE)

UMNiR......... Unified Local Norms and Wages, Unified Local Standards and Costs (RU)
UMNO......... United Malays National Organization (ML)
UMOA......... Union Monetaire Ouest-Africaine [*West African Monetary Union*] (AF)
UMOF......... Union Maghrebine des Organismes Familiaux [*North African*] (MAR)
UMOFC....... Union Mondiale des Organisations Feminines Catholiques [*World Union of Catholic Women's Organizations*] [*Use WUCWO*] (AF)
UMOSEA..... Union Mondiale des Organismes pour la Sauvegarde de l'Enfance et de l'Adolescence (MAR)
UMOTAP..... Union de Motoristas, Obreros, Tecnicos, y Administrativos Portuarios [*Union of Port Crane Operators, Longshoremen, Technicians, and Managers*] [*Uruguayan*] (LA)
UMP........... Controlled Minefield (RU)
UMP........... Local Industry Administration (RU)
UMP........... Uganda Meat Packers Ltd. (MAR)
UMP........... Uniao de Mulheres Portuguesas [*Union of Portuguese Women*] (MAR)
UMPA......... Union de Mujeres Paraguayas [*Union of Paraguayan Women*] (LA1)
UMPG......... United Malayan Pineapple Growers (ML)
UMPVJNA... Uprava za Moralno-Politicko Vaspitanje, Jugoslovenska Narodna Armija [*Administration for Moral and Political Education, Yugoslav People's Army*] (YU)
umr............. Deceased (BU)
UMRJ......... Udruzenje Morskog Ribarstva Jugoslavije [*Association of Marine Fisheries of Yugoslavia*] (YU)
UMS........... Council on Educational Methods (BU)
UMS........... Educational Methodological Council (RU)
UMS........... Ucus Malumat Sahrasi [*Flight Information Region*] (TU)
UMS........... United Missionary Society (MAR)
UMS........... Ustav Montovanych Staveb [*Institute of Prefabricated Building Construction*] (CZ)
UMS........... Ustredni Matice Skolska [*Central School Aid Association*] (CZ)
UMSA......... Unity Movement of South Africa (MAR)
UMSA......... Universidad Mayor de San Andres [*Greater University of San Andres*] [*Bolivian*] (LA)
UMSA......... Uzmanlar Mali Musavirlik ve Sanai Arastirmalar Ltd. Sti. [*Specialists' Financial Counseling and Industrial Research Corp.*] (TU)
UMShN........ General-Purpose Control Computer (RU)
UMSKh........ School of Agricultural Mechanization (RU)
UmSKhI...... Uman' Agricultural Institute (RU)
UMSN......... Union Mondiale de Ski Nautique [*World Water Ski Union - WWSU*] (EA)
UMSS......... Universidad Mayor de San Simon [*Greater University of San Simon*] [*Bolivian*] (LA)
UMSU......... University of Malaya Students Union (ML)
UMSWU...... Uganda Mines and Smelter Workers Union (AF)
UMT........... Bridge Amplifier (RU)
UMT........... Union Marocaine du Travail [*Moroccan Labor Federation*] (AF)
UMT........... Union Musulmans Togolaise [*Togolese Moslem Union*] (AF)
UMT........... Unutarnja Mrtva Tacka [*Inner Dead Center*] (YU)
UMTA......... Union Marocaine du Travail (Autonome) [*Moroccan Labor Union (Autonomous)*] (AF)
UMTEO....... Administration for the Installation of Heat and Electric Power Equipment (RU)
UMTI......... Uprava za Mornaricko Tehnicka Istrazivanja [*Administration of Naval Technical Research*] (YU)
UMTS......... Administration of Materials and Equipment Supply (RU)
UMTS......... Machine-Tractor Stations Administration (BU)
UMTS......... Material and Technical Supplies Administration (BU)
UMTSS....... Administration of Materials and Equipment Supply and Marketing (RU)
UMTU......... Uganda Monarch Traditionalist Unity (AF)
UMU........... United Mineworkers' Union (MAR)
UMUR......... Administration of the Moscow Office of Criminal Investigation (RU)
UMV........... Umleitungswege-Verzeichnis [*Index of Detours*] (EG)
UMV........... Union de Mujeres de Vanguardia [*Vanguard Women's Union*] [*Nicaraguan*] (LA1)
UMV........... Universal Wheatstone Bridge (RU)
UMVD......... Administration of the Ministry of Internal Affairs (RU)
UMVL......... Administration of International Airlines (RU)
Umwandl.... Umwandlung [*Conversion*] [*German*]
UMYu......... Administration of the Ministry of Justice (RU)
UMZ........... Ustredi pro Mechanisaci Zemedelstvi [*Center for the Mechanization of Agriculture*] (CZ)
UMZ........... Uzbek Metallurgical Plant (RU)
UMZh......... Ukrainian Mathematical Journal [*A publication*] (RU)
UMZUB....... Magnetic Drum Storage Control (RU)
UMZUL....... Magnetic Tape Storage Control (RU)
UN............. Leveling Goniometer (RU)
un............... Ugy-Nevezett [*So-Called*] (HU)
UN............. Ujedinjene Nacije [*United Nations*] (YU)
UN............. Uniao Nacional [*National Union*] [*Portuguese*] (WER)
UN............. Union Nacional [*National Union*] [*Spanish*] (PPE)
UN............. Union Navarra [*Union of Navarra*] [*Spanish*] (WER)
UN............. United Nations
UN............. Urad pro Normalizaci [*Bureau of Standards*] (CZ)
UN............. Voltage Amplifier (RU)
UNA........... Standard Telephone (RU)
UNA........... Uganda News Agency (AF)
UNA........... Uniao Nacional Angolana [*Angolan National Union*] (AF)
UNA........... Union Nacionalista Argentina [*Argentine Nationalist Union*] (LA1)
UNA........... Union Nationale des Agriculteurs [*National Farmers Union*] [*Tunisian*] (AF)
UNA........... Unite Nationale Africaine (MAR)
UNA........... Universidad Nacional Agraria [*National Agrarian University*] [*Peruvian*] (LA)
UNAC......... Union Nationale des Artistes Congolais [*National Union of Congolese Artists*] (AF)
UNAC......... United Native African Church (MAR)
UNACAP..... Union des Anciens Eleves des Peres Capucins de l'Ubangi (MAR)
UNACAST... United Nations Advisory Committee on the Application of Science and Technology to Development (MAR)
UNACh....... Union Nacional Arabe de Chile [*Arab National Union of Chile*] (LA)
UNACHOSIN... Union Nacional de Choferes Sindicados Independientes [*National Union of Independent Syndicated Drivers*] [*Dominican Republic*] (LA1)
UNACI......... Union Africaine pour le Commerce et l'Industrie en Cote-d'Ivoire (MAR)
UNACO....... Union Nationale Congolaise (MAR)
UNACOOP... Union Nationale de Cooperatives [*National Cooperatives Union*] [*Cambodian*] (CL)
UNACOOPH... Union Nacional de Cooperativas Populares de Honduras [*National Union of People's Cooperatives of Honduras*] (LA1)
UNADE....... Union Nacional Democratica [*National Democratic Union*] [*Ecuadorean*] (PPW)
UNADECO... Union Nacional de Asociaciones de Desarrollo Comunal [*National Union of Community Development Associations*] [*Costa Rican*] (LA1)
UNAF......... Union des Anciens Eleves des Ecoles de l'AEF (MAR)
UNAF......... Union Nacional de Asociaciones Familiares [*National Union of Family Associations*] [*Spanish*] (WER)
UNAFCO..... Union Africaine Compagnie (MAR)
UNAH......... Universidad Nacional Autonoma de Honduras [*National Autonomous University of Honduras*] (LA)
UNAHM....... Union Nationale d'Aide aux Handicapes de Madagascar (MAR)
UNAIEDP.... United Nations African Institute for Economic Development and Planning (MAR)
UNALOR..... Union Allumettiere Equatoriale (MAR)
UNAM......... Union Nationale des Anciens Moudjahidines (MAR)
UNAM......... Universidad Nacional Autonoma de Mexico [*National Autonomous University of Mexico*] (LA)
UNAMAT..... Union Algerienne de l'Industrie et du Commerce des Materiaux de Construction [*Algerian Association of Producers and Marketers of Construction Materials*] (AF)
UNAMI......... Uniao Nacional Africana de Mocambique Independente (MAR)
UNAMILE.... Union des Anciens Eleves de la Mission de Leverville (MAR)
UNAMO....... Uniao Nacional Africana de Mocambique (MAR)
UNAN......... Universidad Nacional Autonoma de Nicaragua [*National Autonomous University of Nicaragua*] (LA)
UNAP......... Union Nationale des Arts Populaires [*Algerian*] (MAR)
UNAP......... Ustredni Nakupna a Prodejna Vytvarnych Del [*Central Purchase and Sales Office of Art Objects*] (CZ)
UNAR......... Union Nationale Rwandaise [*Rwandan National Union Party*] (AF)
UNARU....... Union Nationale Africaine du Ruanda-Urundi (MAR)
UNAT......... Union Nationale des Agriculteurs Tunisiens [*National Union of Tunisian Farmers*] (AF)
UNAT......... Union Nationale des Aveugles de Tunisie (MAR)
UNATA....... Uniao dos Naturais de Angola (MAR)
UNATAC..... Union d'Assistance Technique pour l'Automobile et la Circulation Routiere [*Union of Technical Assistance for Motor Vehicle and Road Traffic*] (EA)
UNATI......... Union Nationale des Travailleurs Independants [*National Union of Self-Employed Workers*] [*French*] (WER)
UNATOM..... Atomic Unity Organization (WEN)
UNATRAT... Union Nationale des Travailleurs du Tchad [*National Union of Workers of Chad*] (AF)
UNAULA...... Universidad Autonoma Latinoamericana [*Medellin*] (COL)
UNAZA....... Universite Nationale du Zaire [*National University of Zaire*] (AF)
UNB........... Union Nacional Blanca [*Blanco National Union*] [*Uruguayan*] (LA)
UNB........... Union Nationale du Burundi-Abadahemuka (MAR)
UNB........... Universite Nationale du Benin [*Benin National University*] (AF)
UNB........... Urad Narodni Bezpecnosti [*National Security Office*] (CZ)
UNBA......... Universidad Nacional de Buenos Aires [*National University of Buenos Aires*] [*Argentine*] (LA)
unbest......... Unbestimmt [*Indefinite*] [*German*]
unbest Fw.... Unbestimmtes Fuerwort [*German*]
UNBT......... United Nations "Blue Top" (MAR)
UNC........... Uganda National Congress (MAR)
UNC........... Uniao Nacional dos Cabindas (MAR)

UNC............ Union Nacional de Campesinos [*National Union of Peasants*] [*Honduran*] (LA)
UNC............ Union National Congolaise (MAR)
UNC............ Union Nationale Camerounaise [*Cameroonian National Union*] (AF)
UNC............ Union Nationale de la Cooperation [*National Cooperation Union*] [*Tunisian*] (AF)
UNC............ United National Convention [*Ghanaian*] (PPW)
UNC............ Universidad Nacional de Colombia [*Bogota*] (COL)
UNCAC....... Union Nationale des Cooperatives Agricoles de Commercialisation [*National Agricultural Marketing Cooperatives Union*] [*Algerian*] (AF)
UNCAF....... Union Nationale des Caisses d'Allocations Familiales (MAR)
UNCAFENIC ... Union Nacional de Caficultores de Nicaragua [*National Union of Nicaraguan Coffee Growers*] (LA1)
UNCAH....... National Union of Authentic Peasants of Honduras (PD)
UNCAL....... Union Nationale des Comites d'Action Lyceens [*National Union of Lycee Action Committees*] [*French*] (WER)
UNCAP....... Uniunea Nationala a Cooperativelor Agricole de Productie [*National Union of Agricultural Production Cooperatives*] (RO)
UNCC......... Union Nationale des Cheminots du Cameroun [*National Union of Railroad Employees of Cameroon*] (AF)
UNCC......... Union Nationale des Cooperatives de Construction (MAR)
UNCC......... Union Nigerienne de Credit et de Cooperation [*Niger Credit and Cooperation Union*] (AF)
UNCDF....... United Nations Capital Development Fund (MAR)
UNCEA....... Union Commerciale pour l'Europe et l'Afrique (MAR)
UNCEACI.... Union Nationale des Educateurs, Conseillers d'Education, et Assimiles de Cote-d'Ivoire (MAR)
UNCh......... Low-Frequency Amplifier (BU)
UNCh......... Low-Frequency Amplifier (RU)
UNCh......... Very Low Frequency (RU)
UNCHS....... United Nations Centre for Human Settlements (Habitat) (MAR)
UNCI.......... Universite Nationale de Cote-d'Ivoire (MAR)
UNCIVPOL ... United Nations Civil Police (MAR)
UNCL.......... United Nations Commissioner for Libya (MAR)
UNCLOS..... United Nations Conference on the Law of the Sea (MAR)
UNCO......... Union des Nationalistes Congolais (MAR)
UNCO......... United Nations Civilian Operations Mission (MAR)
UNCOD....... United Nations Conference on Desertification (AF)
UNCORS..... United Nations Commission on the Racial Situation in the Union of South Africa (MAR)
UNCSTD..... United Nations Conference on Science and Technology for Development [*Vienna, Austria, August, 1979*]
UNCTAD..... United Nations Conference on Trade and Development (WER)
UNCTT........ Union Nationale des Chefs Traditionnels du Togo [*National Union of Traditional Chiefs of Togo*] (AF)
UNCU......... Union Nacional del Cooperativismo Uruguayo [*National Union of Uruguayan Cooperatives*] (LA)
UNCULTA... Union Nacional de Cultivadores de Tabaco [*National Tobacco Growers Union*] [*Venezuelan*] (LA)
UND............ Ukrajinske Narodni Divadlo [*Ukrainian National Theater*] (CZ)
und............ Undantag [*Exception*] [*Swedish*] (GPO)
UND............ Union Nationale et Democratique [*National and Democratic Union*] [*Monegasque*] (PPW)
UND............ Union Nationale et Democratique [*National Democratic Union*] [*Chadian*] (AF)
UNDAL....... Union de Arroceros Ltda. [*Ibague*] (COL)
UNDAT....... United Nations Development Advisory Team (MAR)
UNDATS..... United Nations Multidisciplinary Development Advisory Team (MAR)
UNDD......... Union Nationale pour la Defense de la Democratie [*National Union for the Defense of Democracy*] [*Upper Voltan*] (AF)
UNDECA..... Union de Empleados de la Caja [*Social Security Employees Union*] [*Costa Rican*] (LA)
UNDEMO..... Union Democratica Fernandina (MAR)
UNDERMA ... Union pour le Developpement de la Region Mavo (MAR)
UNDETOC... Union de Toreros Colombianos [*Bogota*] (COL)
UNDL.......... Union des Nationalistes pour la Democratie Liberale [*Union of Nationalists for Liberal Democracy*] [*Laotian*] (CL)
UNDOF/C ... United Nations Disengagement Observer Force/Command [*Israeli, Syrian*] (ME)
UNDP......... Programa de las Naciones Unides para el Desarrollo [*United Nations Development Program*] (LA)
UNDP......... United Nations Development Program (AF)
UNDPG....... United Nations Development Program in Ghana (MAR)
UNDPR....... United Nations Development Program in Rwanda (MAR)
UNDPS....... United Nations Development Program in the Sudan (MAR)
UNDP/SF.... United National Development Plan/Special Fund [*Malaysian*] (ML)
UNDRO....... United Nations Disaster Relief Organisation (MAR)
UNE............ Uniao Nacional dos Estudantes [*National Students Union*] [*Brazilian*] (LA)
UNE............ Union Nacional de Educadores [*National Union of Teachers*] [*Ecuadorean*] (LA)
UNE............ Union Nacional de Empleados [*National Union of Employees*] [*Nicaraguan*] (LA1)
UNE............ Union Nacional Espanola [*Spanish National Union*] (WER)
UNE............ Union Nacional de Estudiantes [*National Students Union*] [*Argentine*] (LA)
UNE............ Union Nacional de Estudiantes [*National Students Union*] [*Ecuadorean*] (LA)
UNEA......... Union Nationale des Etudiants Algeriens [*National Union of Algerian Students*] (AF)
UNEA......... Union Nationale des Etudiants Angolais [*National Union of Angolan Students*] (AF)
UNEAC....... Uniao Nacional des Escritores et Artistas Congoleses (MAR)
UNEAC....... Union Nacional de Escritores y Artistas de Cuba [*National Union of Cuban Writers and Artists*] (LA)
UNEB......... Union Nacional de Empleados Bancarios [*National Union of Bank Employees*] [*Colombian*] (LA)
UNEBA....... Union Nationale des Etudiants Burundi [*National Union of Burundi Students*] (AF)
UNEC......... Union de Empresas de Publicidad de Colombia [*Colombian Advertising Companies Union*] (LA)
UNEC......... Union pour l'Exportation du Cacao (MAR)
UNEC......... Union Nacional de Escuelas Catolicas [*National Union of Catholic Schools*] [*Dominican Republic*] (LA1)
UNEC......... Union Nacional de Estudiantes Catolicos [*National Union of Catholic Students*] [*Peruvian*] (LA)
UNEC......... Union Nacional de Estudiantes Colombianos [*National Union of Colombian Students*] (LA)
UNECA....... Union de Empresas de Construccion del Caribe [*Union of Caribbean Construction Enterprises*] [*Cuban*] (LA)
UNECA....... United Nations Economic Commission for Africa
UNECE....... United Nations Economic Commission for Europe
UNECh....... Union Nacional de Estudiantes Chilenos [*National Union of Chilean Students*] (LA)
UNECI......... Union Nationale des Etudiants de la Cote-d'Ivoire [*National Union of Ivory Coast Students*] (AF)
UNECO....... Union Nationale des Enseignants du Congo (MAR)
UNECO....... Union Nationale des Etudiants du Congo (MAR)
UNED......... State Distance University [*Costa Rican*]
UNED......... Union Nacional de Estudiantes Democraticos [*National Union of Democratic Students*] [*Chilean*] (LA1)
UNEDAMO ... Uniao Democratica Nacional de Mócambique (MAR)
UNEDIC....... Union Nationale des ASSEDIC [*Association pour l'Emploidans l'Industrie et le Commerce*] [*French*]
UNEECI....... Union Nationale des Etudiants et Eleves de Cote-d'Ivoire (MAR)
UNEED....... Union Nationale des Etudiants et Eleves Dahomeens (MAR)
UNEEG....... Union Nationale des Eleves et Etudiants de la Guadeloupe (PD)
UNEEM....... Union Nationale des Eleves et Etudiants du Mali [*National Union of Pupils and Students of Mali*] (PD)
UNEF.......... Union Nationale des Etudiants de France [*National Union of French Students*] (WER)
UNEF.......... United Nations Emergency Force (MAR)
UNEF/Renouveau ... Union Nationale des Etudiants de France [*National Union of French Students for Renewal*] (WER)
UNEK.......... Union Nationale des Etudiants du Kamerun [*National Union of Cameroon Students*] (AF)
UNEL.......... Union Nationale des Etudiants de Luxembourg [*National Union of Students of Luxembourg*] (WER)
UNELCO..... Union Electrique d'Outre-Mer (MAR)
UNELMA..... Union des Eleves des Freres Maristes (MAR)
UNEM......... Union Nationale des Etudiants du Maroc [*National Union of Moroccan Students*] (PD)
UNEMAF..... Union des Employeurs Agricoles et Forestiers (MAR)
UNEMEPHARCO ... Union Nationale des Etudiants en Medecine et Pharmacie du Congo (MAR)
UNEMO....... Uniao Nacional dos Estudiantes de Mocambique [*National Union of Mozambique Students*] [*Portuguese*] (AF)
UNEMO....... Union Nationale des Etudiants du Mocambique [*National Union of Mozambique Students*] [*French*] (MAR)
UNEMOP..... Union de Empleados del Ministerio de Obras Publicas [*Union of White Collar Workers of the Ministry of Public Works*] [*Costa Rican*] (LA)
UNEP.......... Uniao Nacional de Estudantes Portugueses [*National Union of Portuguese Students*] (WER)
UNEP.......... Union Nacional de Empleados Publicos [*National Union of Public Employees*] [*Venezuelan*] (LA)
UNEP.......... United Nations Environment Program (AF)
UNEPAR...... Unidad Ejecutoria de Acueductos Rurales [*Executive Unit of Rural Aqueducts*] [*Guatemalan*] (LA1)
UNEPREC ... Union Nacional de Ex-Presos Constitucionalistas [*National Union of Constitutionalist Former Prisoners*] [*Dominican Republic*] (LA1)
UNEPTA...... United Nations Expanded Program of Technical Assistance (MAR)
UNES......... Uniao Nacional de Estudantes Secundarios [*National Secondary Students Union*] [*Brazilian*] (LA)
UNES......... Union Nacional de Estudiantes de Secundaria [*National Union of High School Students*] [*Colombian*] (LA)
UNES......... Union Nationale des Etudiants Senegalais [*National Union of Senegalese Students*] (AF)
UNESCAPVERT ... Union des Entrepreneurs Senegalais de la Region du Cap-Vert (MAR)
UNESCO..... United Nations Educational, Scientific, and Cultural Organization
UNETE........ Union Electoral Independiente [*Independent Electoral Union*] [*Venezuelan*] (LA)

UNETI.......... Uniao Nacional dos Estudantes Tecnicos Industriais [*National Union of Industrial and Technical Students*] [*Brazilian*] (LA)
UNETO........ Union Nationale des Etudiants Togolais [*National Union of Togolese Students*] (AF)
UNEU.......... Union Nacional de Estudiantes Universitarios [*National Union of University Students*] [*Colombian*] (LA)
UNE-UNED ... Union de Empleados de la Universidad Estatal a Distancia [*State Correspondence University Employees Union*] [*Costa Rican*] (LA1)
UNF............. United National Front [*Sudanese*] (MAR)
UNFA........... Union Nationale des Femmes Algeriennes [*National Union of Algerian Women*] (AF)
UNFACH..... Union de Farmacias de Chile [*Union of Chilean Pharmacies*] (LA)
UNFC.......... Union Nationale des Femmes Congolaises [*National Union of Congolese Women*] (AF)
UNFDAC..... United Nations Fund for Drug Abuse Control [*Appears thus in Turkish Newspapers*] (TU)
UNFE........... United Nations Fund for Equipment (MAR)
UNFM.......... Union Nationale des Femmes du Mali (MAR)
UNFM.......... Union Nationale des Femmes Marocaines (MAR)
UNFP........... Union Nationale des Forces Populaires [*National Union of Popular Forces*] [*Moroccan*] (AF)
UNFP........... United National Federal Party [*Zimbabwean*] (PPW)
UNFPA........ United Nations Fund for Population Activities (AF)
UNFPO........ United National Front Political Organisation (MAR)
UNFT........... Union Nationale des Femmes Togolaises [*National Union of Togolese Women*] (AF)
UNFT........... Union Nationale des Femmes de Tunisie [*National Union of Tunisian Women*] (AF)
UNG............. Hexahydrate of Uranyl Nitrate (RU)
ung.............. Hungarian (BU)
ung.............. Ungefaehr [*About, Approximately*] [*German*]
ung.............. Unguentum [*Ointment*] [*Latin*] (GPO)
UNGA.......... United Nations General Assembly (MAR)
UNG bolesti ... Otorhinolaryngological Diseases (BU)
ungeb.......... Ungebunden [*Unbound*] [*German*]
ungel........... Ungeloest [*Undissolved*] [*German*]
unges.......... Ungesaettigt [*Unsaturated*] [*German*]
UNGP.......... Uniao dos Naturais da Guine Portuguesa (MAR)
UNGS VMS ... Office of the Chief of the Hydrographic Service of the Navy, USSR (RU)
UNHCR........ United Nations High Commissioner for Refugees (MAR)
UNHHSF...... United Nations Habitat and Human Settlements Foundation (MAR)
UNHS.......... Uganda Natural History Society (MAR)
UNI.............. Union Nacional Independiente [*Independent National Union*] [*Guatemalan*] (LA)
UNI.............. Union Nationale pour l'Independance [*Djibouti*] (PPW)
UNI.............. Union Nationale des Independants [*National Union of Independents*] [*Upper Voltan*] (AF)
UNI.............. Union Nationale pour l'Independence [*National Union for Independence*] [*Djibouti*] (AF)
UNI.............. Union Nationale des Independents [*National Union of Independents*] [*Monegasque*] (PPE)
UNI.............. Union Nationale des Ingenieurs [*National Engineers Union*] [*Tunisian*] (AF)
UNI.............. Universidad Nacional de Ingenieria [*National Engineering University*] [*Peruvian*] (LA)
UNIA............ Universal Negro Improvement Association (MAR)
UNIAL.......... Union Industrial de Astilleros Barranquilla SA (COL)
UNIANDES ... Universidad de los Andes [*Bogota*] (COL)
UNIAPAC.... Union Internationale Chretienne des Dirigeants d'Entreprise [*International Christian Union of Business Executives*] (EA)
UNIATEC.... Union Internationale des Associations Techniques Cinematographiques [*International Union of Technical Cinematograph Associations - IUTCA*] (EA)
UNIBACAM ... Union Bananiere du Cameroun (MAR)
UNIBAN....... Union de Bananeros de Uraba [*Uraba Banana Growers Union*] [*Colombian*] (LA1)
UNIBAN....... Union Bancaire Hispano-Marocaine (MAR)
UNIBAT....... Union des Bateke (MAR)
UNIBEN....... University of Benin (MAR)
UNIBID........ UNISIST International Centre for Bibliographic Descriptions [*London, England*]
UNIC............ United Nations Information Centre (MAR)
UNICA......... Union Internationale du Cinema d'Amateurs [*North African*] (MAR)
UNICA......... Union Internationale du Cinema Non Professionnel [*International Union of Amateur Cinema*] (EA)
UNICA......... Universidad e Institutos del Caribe [*Barranquilla*] (COL)
UNICAF....... Union d'Importations Industrielles et Commerciales Africaines [*African Industrial and Commercial Imports Union*] [*French*] (AF)
UNICAFRA ... Union Camerounaise Francaise (MAR)
UNICAMP.... Universidade Estadual de Campinas [*Campinas State University*] [*Brazilian*] (LA)
UNICAUCA ... Universidad del Cauca [*Popayan*] (COL)
UNICE......... European Community Industrial Union (WEN)
UNICEF....... United Nations International Children's Emergency Fund (MAR)
UNICEMA.... Union Nationale des Industriels, Commercants, et Entrepreneurs de Mauritanie [*National Union of Industrialists, Merchants, and Entrepreneurs of Mauritania*] (AF)
UNICHAD.... Union Interprofessionnelle du Tchad [*Chad Interoccupational Union*] (AF)
UNICHAL.... Union Internationale des Distributeurs de Chaleur [*International Union of Heat Distributors*] (EA)
UNICO......... Union Congolaise (MAR)
UNICO......... Union Industrielle and Commerciale de l'Ouest de la Cote-d'Ivoire (MAR)
UNICO......... United Construction Company (MAR)
UNICOBAT ... Union de Cooperatives de Battambang [*Battambang Cooperative Union*] [*Cambodian*] (CL)
UNICOCAM ... Union des Commercants Camerounais (MAR)
UNICOCYM ... International Association of Bicycle and Motorcycle Trade and Repair (EA)
UNICOL....... Unidad Colombiana de Comercio [*Bogota*] (COL)
UNICOL-HV ... Union Industrielle et Commerciale des Oleagineux de Haute-Volta (MAR)
UNICOM...... Union Commerciale Africaine de Kaolack (MAR)
UNICOMA... Union des Cooperatives Maritimes (MAR)
UNICOMA... Union des Cooperatives du Morbihan et de Loire-Atlantique (MAR)
UNICOMER ... Union des Comptoirs d'Outre-Mer (MAR)
UNICONGO ... Union Patronale et Interprofessionnelle du Congo (MAR)
UNICOOKA ... Union de Cooperatives de Kandal [*Kandal Cooperative Union*] [*Cambodian*] (CL)
UNICOOP.... Union des Cooperatives de Klouts (MAR)
UNICOOP.... Union des Cooperatives des Planteurs Malagasy (MAR)
UNICOOP.... Unions Provinciales de Cooperatives [*Provincial Cooperative Unions*] [*Cambodian*] (CL)
UNICOP....... Union de Cooperatives Nationales du Mali [*Union of Malian National Cooperatives*] (AF)
UNICOPRE ... Union de Cooperatives de Prey Veng [*Prey Veng Cooperative Union*] [*Cambodian*] (CL)
UNICOS...... Union Commerciale Senegalaise (MAR)
UNICOTA.... Union de Cooperatives de Takeo [*Takeo Cooperative Union*] [*Cambodian*] (CL)
UNICOTRAL ... Union Commerciale et de Transports du Littoral (MAR)
UNID........... Union Nacional de Integracion y Desarrollo [*National Union of Integration and Development*] [*Bolivian*] (LA)
UNIDAS....... Uniao Democratica Assistencial [*Democratic Welfare Union*] [*Brazilian*] (LA)
UNIDO......... United Nationalist Democratic Opposition [*Philippine*]
UNIDO......... United Nations Industrial Development Organization (WEN)
UNIDROIT ... Institut International pour l'Unification du Droit Prive [*International Institute for the Unification of Private Law*] (EA)
U-nie........... Administration (BU)
UNIEMA...... Union des Industries de Mauritanie (MAR)
UNIEP.......... Union Internationale des Entrepreneurs de Peinture [*International Union of Master Painters - IUMP*] (EA)
UNIET.......... Ecole Normale d'Instituteurs d'Enseignement Technique (MAR)
UNIFACO.... Union Industrielle Forestiere et Agricole Congo Ocean (MAR)
UNIFAC-SIMCOFA ... Union Fluviale de l'Afrique Centrale. Societe Immobiliere et Commerciale Francaise (MAR)
UNIFAR....... Uniao Fabril de Refrigerantes Lda. (MAR)
UNIFAR....... Union de Farmacias Ltda. [*Barranquilla*] (COL)
UNIFE.......... University of Ife [*Nigeria*] (MAR)
UNIFSTD..... United Nations Interim Fund for Science and Technology (MAR)
UNIGABON ... Union Interprofessionnelle du Gabon [*Interoccupational Union of Gabon*] (AF)
UNIGES....... Union des Groupements Economiques du Senegal [*Union of Economic Groups of Senegal*] (AF)
UNIGRI........ Ukrainian Scientific Research Institute of Geological Exploration (RU)
UNII AKKh .. Ukrainian Scientific Research Institute of the Academy of Municipal Services Imeni K. D. Pamfilov (RU)
UNIIFR......... Ukrainian Scientific Research Institute of Plant Physiology (RU)
UNIIM.......... Ukrainian Scientific Research Institute of Agricultural Mechanization (RU)
UNIIM.......... Ukrainian Scientific Research Institute of Metals (RU)
UNIIMESKh ... Ukrainian Scientific Research Institute of Rural Mechanization and Electrification (RU)
UNIIO.......... Ukrainian Scientific Research Institute of Production Organization and Industrial Management (RU)
UNIIO i K..... Ukrainian Scientific Research Institute of Vegetables and Potatoes (RU)
UNIIP........... Ukrainian Scientific Research Institute of Pedagogy (RU)
UNIIP........... Ukrainian Scientific Research Institute of Poultry Raising (RU)
UNIIPP......... Ukrainian Scientific Research Institute of the Food Industry (RU)
UNIIPP......... Ukrainian Scientific Research Institute of the Printing Industry (RU)
UNIIS........... Ukrainian Scientific Research Institute of Horticulture (RU)
UNIISOZ...... Ukrainian Scientific Research Institute of Socialist Agriculture (RU)
UNIIZh......... Ukrainian Scientific Research Institute of Livestock Breeding (RU)

UNIIZKh ...... Ukrainian Scientific Research Institute of Grain Farming Imeni V. V. Kuybyshev (RU)
UNIKA .... Universal Kablo Sanayi ve Ticaret AS [*Universal Cable Industry and Trade Corp.*] (TU)
UNIKhIM ..... Ural Scientific Research Chemical Institute (RU)
Unikhimmash ... Ural Scientific Research Institute of Chemical Machinery (RU)
UNILAG .... University of Lagos (MAR)
UNILI .... Ural Scientific Research Institute of the Lumber Industry (RU)
UNIM .... Union Nationale des Ingenieurs Marocains (MAR)
UNIMAP ...... Union des Industriels des Matieres Plastiques [*North African*] (MAR)
UNIMAROC ... Union Commerciale Marocaine [*Moroccan Commercial Union*] (AF)
UNIMES ...... Union des Importateurs-Exportateurs Senegalais (MAR)
UNIMES ...... Union des Industries Metallurgiques et Electriques Socialistes [*Socialist Metallurgical and Electric Industries Association*] (AF)
UNIMES ...... Union Nationale des Industries Mecaniques et Electriques Socialistes [*North African*] (MAR)
UNIMO .... Union des Mongo (MAR)
UNIN .... United Nations Institute for Namibia (MAR)
UNINCCA .... Universidad Incca de Colombia [*Bogota*] (COL)
UNIOK .... Ukrainian Scientific Research Institute of Refractory and Acid-Resistant Materials (RU)
UNIOM .... Union Interprofessionnelle des Industries d'Outre-Mer (MAR)
UNIP .... United National Independence Party [*Zambian*] (PD)
UNIP .... United National Independence Party [*Trinidadian and Tobagan*] (PPW)
UNIPA .... Union de Participation de France et d'Outre-Mer (MAR)
UNIPESCA ... Uniao Brasileira de Pesca [*Brazilian Fishing Union*] (LA)
UNIPETROL ... Union pour la Recherche et l'Exploitation Petrolieres Sahariennes (MAR)
UNIPOL .... Union des Industries de Produits Oleagineux (MAR)
UNIPOMO ... Uniao das Populacoes de Mocambique (MAR)
UNIPRESSE ... Union pour l'Expansion de la Presse Francaise dans le Monde [*Union for the Expansion of the French Press in the World*] (AF)
Unipromed' ... Ural Scientific Research and Planning Institute of the Copper Industry (RU)
UNIR .... Union Nacional de Innovadores y Racionalizadores [*National Union of Innovators and Efficiency Experts*] [*Cuban*] (LA)
UNIR .... Union Nacionalista Independiente Regional [*Regional Nationalist Independent Union*] [*Venezuelan*] (LA)
UNIREP .... Union Francaise et Africaine de Prospections Minieres et de Recherches Petrolieres (MAR)
UNIROUTE ... Union Routiere du Logone-Benoue (MAR)
UNIS .... Ukrainian Scientific Research Institute of the Sugar Industry (RU)
UNIS .... Union Nigerienne des Independants et Sympathisants (MAR)
UNISA .... University of South Africa (MAR)
UNISCO ...... Union des Interets Sociaux Congolais (MAR)
UNISIST ...... Universal System for Information in Science and Technology [*UNESCO*]
UNISkhOM ... Ukrainian Scientific Research Institute of Agricultural Machinery (RU)
UNISM .... Nonmetallic Minerals and Construction Materials Administration (BU)
UNISYNDI ... Union Intersyndicale d'Entreprises et d'Industries de l'Ouest Africain (MAR)
UNIT .... Union Nationale des Interpretes-Traducteurs (MAR)
UNIT .... Unitarius [*Unitarian*] (HU)
UNITA .... Uniao Nacional para a Independencia Total de Angola [*National Union for the Total Independence of Angola*] (AF)
UNITAR .... United Nations Institute for Training and Research (CL)
UNITCHAD ... Union Interprofessionnelle du Tchad (MAR)
UNITCHADIENNE ... Union Tchadienne de Transports [*Chad Transportation Union*] (AF)
UNITEC .... Union Distribuidora Tecnica [*Medellin*] (COL)
UNITEC .... Union Togolaise de Commerce (MAR)
UNITEGUA ... Union de Transportistas Terrestres de Guatemala [*Union of Land Transport Workers of Guatemala*] (LA)
UNITEXTIL ... Union of Textile Industries [*Syrian*] (MAR)
UNITRA .... Union pour l'Industrie et les Travaux Publics [*Union for Industry and Public Works*] [*Senegalese*] (AF)
UNITRA .... Zjednoczenie Przemyslu Elektronicznego i Teletechnicznego [*Electronics and Telecommunications Industry Union*] (POL)
UNIUM .... Union des Intellectuels et Universitaires Malgaches (MAR)
Univ .... Universitaet [*German*]
univ .... University (BU)
univ .... University (RU)
UNIVALLE ... Universidad del Valle [*Cali*] (COL)
Univermag ... Department Store (BU)
UNIVEX .... Universal Exports (MAR)
UNIVIA .... Universal de Viajes [*Medellin*] (COL)
UNIVIR .... Union Industrial Vidriera Ltda. [*Medellin*] (COL)
Univ pech .... University Press (BU)
UNIWARRANT ... Mutuelle Universelle de Garantie (MAR)
UNJ .... Union Nacional Jornalera [*National Union of Laborers*] [*Salvadoran*] (LA1)
UNJA .... Union Nationale de la Jeunesse Algerienne [*National Union of Algerian Youth*] (AF)
UNJC .... Union Nacional de Juristas Cubanos [*National Union of Cuban Lawyers*] (LA1)
UNJD .... Union Nationale de la Jeunesse du Dahomey (MAR)
UNJM .... Union Nationale de la Jeunesse du Mali (MAR)
UNJS .... Union Nationale de la Jeunesse du Senegal [*National Union of Senegalese Youth*] (AF)
UNK .... Undelayed Channel Amplifier (RU)
unk .... Unkariksi [*Finnish*]
unk .... Unkarilainen [*Finnish*]
UNKF .... Administration of the People's Commissariat of Finance (RU)
UNKGB .... Administration of the People's Commissariat of State Security (RU)
UNKhU .... Administration of the Statistical Survey of the National Economy (RU)
UNKO .... United National Kadazan Organization [*Sabah*] (ML)
UNKVD .... Administration of the People's Commissariat of Internal Affairs (RU)
unl .... Unloeslich [*Insoluble*] [*German*]
UNLA .... Uganda National Liberation Army (AF)
UNLA .... Uniao Nacional Luso-Angolana (MAR)
UNLF .... Uganda National Liberation Forces (AF)
UNLF .... Ugandan National Liberation Front (PD)
unlosl .... Unloeslich [*Insoluble*] [*German*]
UNLP .... Universidad Nacional de La Plata [*National University of La Plata*] [*Argentine*] (LA)
UNM .... Ugandan National Movement (AF)
UNM .... Ukase on the People's Militia (BU)
UNM .... Union Nationale Malgache [*Malagasy National Union*] (AF)
UNM .... Union Nationale Mauritanienne [*Mauritanian National Union*] (AF)
UNM .... Urad pro Normalizaci a Mereni [*Office for Standardization and Measurements*] (CZ)
UNMAC .... Mixed Armistice Commission (MAR)
UNMC .... United Nations Mediterranean Commission (MAR)
UNML .... United Nations Mission in Libya (MAR)
UNMOCO .... Union Morale Congolaise (MAR)
UNN .... Low-Voltage Indicator (RU)
UNNE .... Universidad Nordestana [*Dominican Republic*]
UNNRRF ..... United Nations Natural Resources Revolving Fund (MAR)
UNO .... Administration of Street Lighting (RU)
UNO .... Ugandan Nationalist Organization (AF)
UNO .... Union Nacional Odriista [*National Odriista Union*] [*Peruvian*] (LA)
UNO .... Union Nacional de Oposicion [*National Opposition Union*] [*Colombian*] (LA)
UNO .... Union Nacional de Oposicion [*National Opposition Union*] [*Salvadoran*] (LA)
UNO .... Union Nacional Opositora [*National Union of Opposition*] [*Nicaraguan*] (LA)
UNO .... United Nations Organization (MAR)
UNOC .... Union Nacional de Obreros Cristianos [*National Union of Christian Workers*] [*Salvadoran*] (LA)
UNOC .... United Nations Operation in the Congo (MAR)
UNOCIC ...... Union Nacional de Organizaciones Sindicales Campesinos [*National Union of Peasant Trade Union Organizations*] [*Chilean*] (LA)
UNOPI .... United Nations Office of Public Information (MAR)
UNOTC .... United Nations Office for Technical Co-Operation (MAR)
UNP .... Statics Indicator (RU)
UNP .... Uganda National Party (MAR)
UNP .... Union Nacional Paraguaya [*Paraguayan National Union*] (LA)
UNP .... Union Nacional de Periodistas [*National Union of Journalists*] [*Ecuadorean*] (LA)
UNP .... Union Nacionalista del Pueblo [*People's Nationalist Union*] [*Bolivian*] (LA)
UNP .... Union Nationale du Peuple (MAR)
UNP .... United National Party [*Sri Lankan*] (PPW)
UNP .... United Nationalist Party [*Ghanaian*] (AF)
UNP .... Universal Adjusting Device (RU)
UNP .... Ustredni Narodni Pojisteni [*Central Social Insurance Agency*] (CZ)
UNPA .... Union Nationale des Paysans Algeriens [*National Union of Algerian Peasants*] (AF)
UNPAZA ..... Union Nationale des Producteurs Agricoles et Artisans du Zaire [*National Agricultural Producers and Craftsmen's Union of Zaire*] (AF)
UNPC .... Union Nacional de Pequenos Caneros [*National Union of Small Cane Plantation Owners*] [*Mexican*] (LA)
UNPC .... Union Nationale des Professionnels de la Comptabilite (MAR)
UNPDAC ..... United Nations Program for Drug Abuse Control (AF)
UNPHU .... Universidad Nacional "Pedro Henriquez Urena" [*Pedro Henriquez Urena National University*] [*Dominican Republic*] (LA)
UNPM .... United National Pasok Momogun [*Kadazan organization in Sabah*] [*Also known as UPKO*] (ML)
UNPO .... Ukase on Naming and Renaming Sites of National and Local Importance (BU)
UNPOC .... United Nations Peace Observation Commission (MAR)
UNPS .... Controlled Nonlinear Semiconductor Resistance (RU)

UNPZ........... Ufa Petroleum-Processing Plant (RU)
UNPZA........ Union Nationale de la Presse du Zaire (MAR)
UNR............ Hungarian People's Republic (BU)
UNR............ Office of the Work Supervisor (RU)
UNR............ Ukase on Encouraging the Birthrate (BU)
UNR............ Ukrajinska Narodni Rada [*Ukrainian National Council*] (CZ)
UNR............ Uniao Nacional Republicana [*National Republican Union*] [*Portuguese*] (PPE)
UNR............ Union pour la Nouvelle Republique [*Union for the New Republic*] [*French*] (WER)
UNR............ Union pour la Nouvelle Republique [*Union for the New Republic*] [*Upper Voltan*] (AF)
UNR............ Universite Nationale du Rwanda [*National University of Rwanda*] (AF)
UNREF........ United Nations Refugee Fund (MAR)
UNRF.......... Uganda National Rescue Front (PD)
UNRISD....... United Nations Research Institute for Social Development (MAR)
UNRM.......... Ukase on Encouraging Births and Large Families (BU)
UNRP........... Ukrajinska Narodna Rada Presovsciny [*Ukrainian National Council of the Presov Region*] (CZ)
UNRS.......... Continuous Steel Pouring Unit (RU)
UNRV.......... Union pour la Nouvelle Republique Voltaique (MAR)
UNRWA....... United Nations Relief and Works Agency for Palestine Refugees in the Near East (PD)
UNRWAPR... United Nations Relief and Works Agency for Palestine Refugees (ME)
UNS............ Barrel Inclination Angle (RU)
UNS............ Office of the Chief of Supply (RU)
UNS............ Optimum Speed Indicator (RU)
UNS............ Udruzenje Novinara Srbije [*Association of Journalists of Serbia*] (YU)
UNS............ Union Nacional Sinarquista [*National Sinarchist Union*] [*Mexican*] (LA)
UNS............ Union Nationale Somalo [*Somali National Union*] (AF)
uns............. Unsymmetrisch [*Unsymmetric*] [*German*]
UNS............ Ustaska Narodna Straza [*Ustashi National Guard*] [*Croatia*] [*World War II*] (YU)
UNS............ Ustav Nerostnych Surovin [*Mineral Raw Material Research Institute*] (CZ)
UNS............ Ustavodarne Narodni Shromazdeni [*Constituent National Assembly*] (CZ)
UNS............ Ustredni Normativni Komise [*Central Standards Committee (of the Research Institute of Construction Economy)*] (CZ)
UNSC.......... United Nations Security Council (MAR)
UNSF........... United Nations Special Fund (MAR)
UNSO.......... United Nations Sahelian Office (MAR)
UNSP........... Uniao Nacional dos Servidores Publicos [*National Union of Public Employees*] [*Brazilian*] (LA)
UNSSFNRJ... Udruzenje Nastavnika Strucnih Skola Federativna Narodna Republika Jugoslavija [*Association of Vocational School Teachers of Yugoslavia*] (YU)
UNSTB........ Union Nationale des Syndicats des Travailleurs du Benin [*National Federation of Workers Unions of Benin*] (AF)
UNSTD........ Union Nationale des Syndicats des Travailleurs du Dahomey (MAR)
UNSTHV...... Union Nationale des Travailleurs de la Haute-Volta (MAR)
UNSWP....... United National South-West Party [*Namibian*] (AF)
UNT............ Union Nationale Tchadienne (MAR)
UNT............ Union Nationale des Travailleurs (MAR)
u-nt............ University (BU)
un-t............ University (RU)
UNTA.......... Uniao Nacional dos Trabalhadores de Angola [*National Union of Workers of Angola*] (AF)
UNTA.......... Union Nacional de Trabajadores Agricolas [*National Union of Agricultural Workers*] [*Mexican*] (LA1)
UNTA.......... United Nations Technical Assistance (MAR)
UNTAA........ United Nations Technical Assistance Administration (MAR)
UNTAB........ United Nations Technical Assistance Board (MAR)
UNTAC........ United Nations Technical Assistance Committee (MAR)
UNTAG........ United Nations Transition Assistance Group [*Namibian*] (AF)
UNTAM....... United Nations Technical Assistance Mission (MAR)
UNTAP........ United Nations Technical Assistance Programme (MAR)
UNTC.......... Union Nationale des Travailleurs Camerounais [*National Union of Cameroonian Workers*] (AF)
UNTC.......... Union Nationale des Travailleurs Congolais (MAR)
UNTC.......... United Nations Trusteeship Council (MAR)
UNTCI......... Union Nationale des Travailleurs de Cote-d'Ivoire [*National Union of Ivory Coast Workers*] (AF)
UNTEA........ United Nations Temporary Executive Authority [*Supervised transfer of Netherlands New Guinea to Indonesia*] (IN)
Unters......... Untersuchung [*Examination, Investigation*] [*German*]
Untertit....... Untertitel [*Subtitle*] [*German*]
UNTFAD....... United Nations Trust Fund for African Development (MAR)
UNTG.......... Uniao Nacional de Trabalhadores da Guine [*National Union of Guinea-Bissau Workers*] (AF)
UNTGB........ Union Nationale des Travailleurs de Guinee-Bissau (MAR)
UNTHV........ Union Nationale des Travailleurs de Haute-Volta [*National Union of Upper Volta Workers*] (AF)
UNTM.......... Union Nationale des Travailleurs du Mali [*National Union of Mali Workers*] (AF)
UNTMRA..... Union Nacional de Trabajadores del Metal y Ramas Afines [*National Union of Metalworkers and Related Industries Workers*] [*Uruguayan*] (LA)
UNTN.......... Union Nationale des Travailleurs Nigeriens [*National Union of Nigerien Workers*] [*Niger*] (AF)
UNTRA........ Radio and Television Organisations of Africa (MAR)
UNTRAD..... United Nations Conference on Trade and Development (CL)
UNTRAHUILA... Union de Trabajadores del Huila [*Neiva*] (COL)
UNTS........... Union Nationale des Travailleurs du Senegal [*National Union of Workers of Senegal*] (AF)
UNTS........... Union Nationale des Travailleurs du Soudan (MAR)
UNTS........... United Nations Treaty Series [*A publication*] (MAR)
UNTSO........ United Nations Truce Supervision Organization (ME)
UNTT........... Union Nationale des Travailleurs Tchadiens [*National Union of Workers of Chad*] (MAR)
UNTT........... Union Nationale des Travailleurs du Togo [*National Union of Workers of Togo*] (AF)
UNTZa......... Union Nationale des Travailleurs du Zaire [*National Union of Workers of Zaire*] (AF)
UNU............ Universidad de las Naciones Unidas [*United Nations University*] [*Mexican*] (LA)
UNU............ Unprotected Ultrahigh-Frequency Carbon (Resistor) (RU)
UNURI......... Unione Nazionale Universitaria Rappresentativa Italiana [*National Union of Italian University Representatives*] (WER)
UNV............ Ujpesti Novenyolajipari Vallalat [*Vegetable Oil Industrial Enterprise of Ujpest*] (HU)
UNV............ Ustredni Narodni Vybor [*Central People's Committee*] (CZ)
UNVDA........ Upper Noun Valley Development Authority (MAR)
unverand.... Unveraenderlich [*Unchangeable, Invariable, Constant*] [*German*]
UNViR......... Consolidated Time Norms and Wages (RU)
UNWFP........ United Nations World Food Programme (MAR)
UNYEK........ Universite Yemek Kurulu [*University Food Association*] (TU)
UNZ............ Ustav Narodniho Zdravi [*National Health Institute*] (CZ)
UNZA.......... University of Zambia (MAR)
UNZAAWU... University of Zambia and Allied Workers Union (MAR)
UNZABECA... University of Zambia Business and Economic Association (MAR)
UNZAGA..... University of Zambia Geographical Association (MAR)
Unzhlag....... Unzha Corrective Labor Camp (RU)
UNZhS......... Ukase on Encouraging and Assisting Cooperative and Individual Housing Construction (BU)
UO.............. Limiting Amplifier (RU)
UO.............. Optical Goniometer (RU)
UO.............. Strongpoint, Center of Resistance (RU)
UO.............. Training Detachment (RU)
uo............... Ugyanott [*In the Same Place*] (HU)
uo............... Ugyosztaly [*Department*] (HU)
UO.............. Ulku Ocaklari [*Idealist Clubs*] (TU)
UO.............. Union Observatory (MAR)
UO.............. Unterordnung [*Suborder*] [*German*]
UO.............. Upravni Odbor [*Administrative Committee*] (YU)
UO.............. Uredni Oznamovatel [*Official Bulletin*] [*A publication*] (CZ)
UO.............. Ustredni Opravny [*Central Repair Shops (of the State Tractor Stations)*] (CZ)
UO.............. Utvorova Organisace [*Communist Party Organization within a Military Unit*] (CZ)
UOAPV........ Single-Phase Automatic Recloser (RU)
UOB............ Universite Officielle de Bujumbura [*Burundi*]
UOC............ Union Obrera Catolica [*Catholic Trade Union*] [*Bolivian*] (LA)
UOC............ Union Obrera de la Construccion [*Union of Construction Workers*] [*Argentine*] (LA)
UOC............ Universite Officielle du Congo (MAR)
UOCh.......... Ustav Organicke Chemie [*Institute of Organic Chemistry (of the Czechoslovak Academy of Sciences)*] (CZ)
UOCRA........ Union Obrera de la Construccion de la Republica Argentina [*Construction Workers Union of the Argentine Republic*] (LA)
UOD............ Ulku Ocaklari Dernegi [*Idealist Hearths (Clubs) Organization*] (TU)
UOEM.......... Union de Obreros y Empleados Municipales [*Municipal Workers and Employees Union*] [*Argentine*] (LA)
UOGK.......... Ukrainian Branch of the Geological Committee (RU)
UOI............. Union de Obreros Independientes [*Union of Independent Workers*] [*Mexican*] (LA1)
UOK............ Ustredna Obchodnich Komor [*Central Bureau of the Chambers of Commerce*] (CZ)
UOK............ Ustredni Organisacni Komise [*Central Organizational Commission*] (CZ)
UOKh.......... Training and Experimental Farm (RU)
UOM............ Union Obrera Metalurgica [*Metalworkers Union*] [*Argentine*] (LA)
UoM............ University of Malaya (ML)
UOM............ Uradovna Ochrany Mladeze [*Office for the Protection of Youth*] (CZ)
UOMA.......... Union Obrera Molinera Argentina [*Argentina Flour Mill Workers Union*] (LA)
UOMPZ........ Ukase on Orders, Medals, and Honorary Titles (BU)
UON............ Charter of the League of Nations (BU)
UON............ Reference Voltage Amplifier (RU)

UON............ University of Nairobi [*Kenyan*] (AF)
UOO............ Uredba o Obaveznom Osiguranju [*Decree on Compulsory Insurance*] [*Railroads*] (YU)
UOOP.......... Administration for the Protection of Public Order (RU)
UOp............ Operation Control (RU)
UOP............ Unidade Operativa de Proteccao [*Unit for Protective Operations*] [*Angolan*] (AF)
UOP............ Urad Ochrany Prace [*Office for the Protection of Labor*] (CZ)
UOP............ Uredba o Osnivanju Preduzeca i Radnji [*Decree on the Foundation of Enterprises and Shops*] (YU)
UOPDK........ Ukase on Insurance and Pensions of Cultural Workers (BU)
UOPDP........ Union Ouvriere et Paysanne pour la Democratie Proletarienne [*Peasant and Worker Union for Proletarian Democracy*] [*French*] (PPE)
UOR............ Administration of Finishing Work (RU)
UORU.......... Ustredni Odborova Rada Ucitelska [*Central Council of Teachers' Unions*] (CZ)
UOS............ Defense Construction Directorate (RU)
UOS............ Feedback Amplifier (RU)
UOS............ Irrigation System Administration (RU)
UOS............ Uredba o Upravljanju Osnovnim Sredstvima Privrednih Organizacija [*Decree on the Management of Basic Resources of Economic Organizations*] (YU)
UOS............ Ustredie Odborovych Svazov [*Trade-Union Headquarters*] (CZ)
UOSS.......... Ukase on the Protection of Agriculture (BU)
UOT............ Labor Safety Administration (BU)
UOT............ Union Obrera Textil [*Textile Workers Union*] [*Uruguayan*] (LA)
UOV............ Chocking Agent (RU)
UOV............ Persistent Chemical Agent (BU)
UOVS.......... Universiteit van die Oranje Vrijstaat (MAR)
UOVTI......... Ural Branch of the All-Union Institute of Heat Engineering Imeni F. E. Dzerzhinskiy (RU)
UOW............ Ukrainska Organizacja Wojskowa [*Ukrainian Military Organization*] (POL)
UOZK.......... Ustredna Obchodnich a Zivnostenskych Komor [*Central Bureau of the Chambers of Commerce and Trade*] (CZ)
UOZTVPSNVN... Ukase Repealing the Law on Foreign Exchange Transactions and Penalties for Currency Violations (BU)
UP............... Angle of Approach (RU)
UP............... Conditional Jump [*Computers*] (RU)
UP............... Consolidated Index (RU)
UP............... Emergency Situation [*Civil defense*] (RU)
UP............... Fortified Zone (RU)
UP............... General-Purpose Switch (RU)
UP............... Intermediate Repeater (RU)
UP............... Pension Administration (BU)
UP............... Position Indicator (RU)
UP............... Repeater Station (RU)
UP............... Repeater Substation (RU)
UP............... Slaughterhouse (RU)
UP............... Street Loudspeaker (RU)
UP............... Turn Indicator (RU)
UP............... Ubrzani-Putnicki [*Express Passenger*] [*Railroads*] (YU)
UP............... Ugostiteljsko Poduzece [*Hotel and Catering Trade Establishment*] (YU)
UP............... Unidad Popular [*Popular Unity*] [*Chilean*] (LA)
UP............... Union Patriotica [*Patriotic Union*] [*Spanish*] (PPE)
UP............... Union Popular [*Popular Union*] [*Uruguayan*] (PD)
UP............... Union Popular [*Popular Union*] [*Argentine*] (LA)
UP............... Union del Pueblo [*Union of the People*] [*Mexican*] (PD)
UP............... Unita Popolare [*Popular Unity*] [*Italian*] (WER)
UP............... United Party [*Gambian*] (PPW)
UP............... United Party [*Ghanaian*] (AF)
UP............... United Party [*Jamaican*] (LA1)
UP............... United Party [*Papua New Guinean*] (PPW)
UP............... United Party [*South African*] (AF)
UP............... United Party [*Virgin Islands*] (LA1)
UP............... United Party [*Zambian*] (AF)
UP............... Unites de Production (MAR)
UP............... Unity Party [*Nigerian*] (AF)
UP-.............. Universal Device (RU)
UP............... Universita Palackeho [*Palacky University*] [*Olomouc*] (CZ)
UP............... Uniwersytet Powszechny [*Popular University*] [*Polish*]
UP............... Uniwersytet Poznanski [*Poznan University*] (POL)
UP............... Unterpulver-Schweissverfahren [*Flux Powder Welding*] (EG)
UP............... Uprava Prihoda [*Revenue Administration*] (YU)
UP............... Urazova Pojistovna [*Accident Insurance Agency*] (CZ)
UP............... Urzad Patentowy [*Patent Office*] (POL)
UP............... Urzad Pocztowy [*Post Office*] (POL)
UP............... Ustav Prefabrikace [*Institute of Prefabricated Building*] (CZ)
UP............... Ustredni Prodejna [*Central Sales Office*] (CZ)
UP............... Uzemni Planovani [*Regional Planning*] (CZ)
UPA............ Ucuz Emtia Pazarlama, Sanayii, ve Ticaret TAS [*Low Priced Commodities Marketing, Industry, and Commerce Corporation*] (TU)
UPA............ Uganda People's Alliance (AF)
UPA............ Ukrainska Powstancza Armia [*Ukrainian Guerrilla Army*] (POL)
UPA............ Unia Poludniowoafrykanska [*South African Union*] [*Polish*]
UPA............ Uniao dos Povos Angolanos [*Union of Angolan Peoples*] (AF)
UPA............ Unidad para Avanzar [*Unity for Advancement*] [*Costa Rican*] (LA)
UPA............ Union para Avanzar [*Union for Advancement*] [*Venezuelan*] (LA)
UPA............ Union Panafricaine des Agriculteurs (MAR)
UPA............ Union des Parlements Africains [*African Parliaments Union*] (AF)
UPA............ Union Patriotica Anti-Imperialista [*Anti-Imperialist Patriotic Union*] [*Dominican Republic*] (LA)
UPA............ Union Populaire Africaine [*African People's Union*] [*Djibouti*] (AF)
UPA............ Union Populaire Algerienne (MAR)
UPA............ Union Popular de Artistas [*Peoples' Artist Union*] [*Spanish*] (WER)
UPA............ Union Postale Arabe [*North African*] (MAR)
UPAC.......... Unidad de Poder Adquisitivo Constante [*Savings Certificates with Constant Purchasing Power*] [*Colombian*] (LA)
UPAC.......... Unificacion y Progreso [*Unification and Progress*] [*Mexican*] (PPW)
UPACH........ Union de Periodistas Antifascistas de Chile [*Union of Antifascist Chilean Journalists*] (LA)
UPAE.......... Union Postal de las Americas y Espana [*Postal Union of the Americas and Spain - PUAS*] (EA)
UPAF.......... Union Postale Africaine [*African Postal Union*] [*Use APU*] (AF)
UPAJ.......... Union Panafricaine des Journalistes (MAR)
UPAM.......... United People's Association of Matabeleland [*Zimbabwean*] (PPW)
UPAM.......... United Planting Association of Malaya (ML)
UPAN.......... United Pools Agents Association (MAR)
UPANIC....... Union de Productores Agropecuarios de Nicaragua [*Agriculture and Livestock Producers Union of Nicaragua*] (LA1)
UPARA........ Union de Productores Agropecuarios de la Republica Argentina [*Union of Agriculture and Livestock Producers of the Argentine Republic*] (LA)
UPAS.......... Usak Elektro Porselen Anonim Sirketi [*Usak Electro-Porcelain Manufacturing Corporation*] (TU)
UPB............ Amplifying-Converting Unit (RU)
UPB............ Uniao dos Portuarios do Brasil [*Brazilian Longshoremen's Union*] (LA)
UPB............ Union Patriotica Bonairiana [*Bonaire Patriotic Union*] [*Netherlands Antillean*] (PPW)
UPB............ Union Populaire du Burundi (MAR)
UPB............ Universidad Pontificia Bolivariana [*Medellin*] (COL)
UPC............ Uganda People's Congress (AF)
UPC............ Unidade Padrao de Capital [*Standard Unit of Capital*] [*Brazilian*] (LA)
UPC............ Union de Pioneros Cubanos [*Union of Cuban Pioneers*] (LA)
UPC............ Union des Populations Camerounaises [*Union of Cameroonian Peoples*] (PD)
UPC............ Union del Pueblo Canario [*Union of the Canarian People*] [*Spanish*] (PPE)
UPC............ Unione di u Populu Corsu [*Union of the Corsican People*] [*French*] (PPE)
UPC............ Unions Paysannes Communales [*Communal Peasant Unions*] [*Algerian*] (AF)
UPC............ Universidad Pedagogica de Colombia [*Bogota*] (COL)
UPCC.......... Union Popular del Campo de Cataluna [*Popular Union of the Catalonian Countryside*] [*Spanish*] (WER)
UPCh.......... Intermediate-Frequency Amplifier (RU)
UPCh.......... Union de Profesores de Chile [*Chilean Teachers Union*] (LA)
UPCN.......... Union del Personal Civil de la Nacion [*National Civil Service Personnel Union*] [*Argentine*] (LA)
UPCPV........ Union Popular de Campesinos del Pais Valenciano [*People's Union of Valencia Country Farmers*] [*Spanish*] (WER)
UPCSM........ United Presbyterian Church of Scotland Mission (MAR)
UPD............ Unidad Preventiva del Delito [*Crime Prevention Unit*] [*Costa Rican*] (LA1)
UPD............ Union Popular Democratica [*People's Democratic Union*] [*Spanish*] (WER)
UPD............ Union Progressiste Dahomeenne (MAR)
UPD............ Uredba o Porezu na Dobit iz Deviznog Poslovanja [*Decree on the Tax on Profit in Foreign Exchange Operations*] (YU)
UPD............ Urusan Perumahan Djakarta [*Djakarta Housing Authority*] (IN)
UPDC.......... Union Popular Democratica Cristiana [*Christian Democratic Popular Union*] [*Bolivian*] (LA)
UPDEA........ Union of Producers and Distributors of Electricity in Africa (MAR)
UPDED........ Unidad Progresista de Diplomacia [*Progressive Unity of Diplomacy*] [*Panamanian*] (LA)
UPDK.......... Upravleniye po Obsluzhivaniyu Diplomaticheskogo Korpusa [*Administration for Servicing the Diplomatic Corps*] [*Russian*]
UPE............ Uniao Paranaense dos Estudantes [*Parana Students Union*] [*Brazilian*] (LA)
UPE............ Unidades de Produccion Estatal [*State Production Units*] [*Nicaraguan*] (LA1)
UPE............ Union del Pueblo Espanol [*Spanish People's Union*] (WER)
UPE............ Universal Primary Education Programme (MAR)
UPE............ Ustav Prumyslove Ekonomiky [*Institute of Industrial Economics*] [*Prague*] (CZ)

UPEB........... Union de Paises Exportadores de Banano [*Union of Banana-Exporting Countries - UBEC*] (EA)
UPEB........... Union des Pays Exportateurs de Bananes [*Union of Banana Exporting Countries - UBEC*] (MAR)
UPEC........... Union de Periodistas Cubanos [*Union of Cuban Journalists*] (LA)
UPECO........ Union Progressiste Congolaise (MAR)
UPEF........... Union et Progres dans l'Ensemblement Francaise (MAR)
UPEL........... Union de Periodistas Escolares de Lima [*Union of Student Journalists of Lima*] [*Peruvian*] (LA)
UPEL........... Uprava za Elektroprivredu [*Administration of Electric Industries*] (YU)
UPEM.......... Union Progressive des Femmes Marocaines [*Progressive Union of Moroccan Women*] (AF)
UPENCOL... Union de Pensionados Oficiales y Particulares de Colombia [*Colombian Government and Private Industry Pensioners Union*] (LA)
UPES........... Unidades de Produccion Estatal Sandinista [*Sandinist State Production Units*] [*Nicaraguan*] (LA)
UPESUNA... United Progressive Ethiopian Students' Union in North America [*Bolshevik*] (AF)
UPEU........... Uganda Public Employees Union (AF)
UPF............. Primary Clamping Device (RU)
UPF............. Uganda Popular Front (PD)
UPF............. United People's Front [*Singapore*] (PPW)
UPF............. Ustav pro Prakticku Fotografii [*Institute of Practical Photography*] (CZ)
UPF............. Ustredni Pujcovna Filmu [*Central Film Lending Library*] (CZ)
UPFSI.......... Porcelain-Faience and Glassware Administration (BU)
UPFT........... Uluslararasi Para Fonu Teskilati [*International Monetary Fund Organization*] (TU)
UPFT........... Union Progressiste Franco-Tchadienne (MAR)
UPG............. Uniao das Populacoes da Guine (MAR)
UPG............. Union Patriotica Guatemalteca [*Guatemalan Patriotic Union*] (LA)
UPG............. Union des Populations de Guinee [*Guinea People's Union*] (PD)
UPG............. Union Progressiste Guineenne (MAR)
UPG............. Union del Pueblo Gallego [*Galician People's Union*] [*Spanish*] (WER)
UPGA.......... United Progressive Grand Alliance (MAR)
UPGS.......... Unione Progressista della Gioventu Somala (MAR)
UPH............ Udruzenje Pravnika Hrvatske [*Croatian Lawyers' Association*] (YU)
UPHA.......... Union Phosphatiere Africaine (MAR)
UPHILBAFUMA... Union Philanthropique des Bantandu de Nfuma de Leopoldville-Ouest (MAR)
UPI.............. Simplified Indicator (of Toxic Agents) (RU)
UPI.............. Union Popular Izquierdista [*Popular Leftist Union*] [*Venezuelan*] (LA)
UPI.............. United Press International (MAR)
UPI.............. Ural Polytechnic Institute Imeni S. M. Kirov (RU)
UPIA............ Union Pharmaceutique Inter-Africaine (MAR)
UPICV......... Union du Peuple des Iles du Cap Vert (MAR)
UPINCh....... General-Purpose Device of Infrasonic Frequencies (RU)
UPJNA......... Uredba o Privrednim Preduzecima Koja Proizvode za Potrebe Jugoslovenske Narodne Armije [*Decree on Economic Enterprises Producing for the Yugoslav People's Army*] (YU)
UPJU........... Uganda Vernacular, Primary, and Junior Secondary Teachers Union (AF)
UPK............. Code of Criminal Procedure (RU)
UPK............. Equation for the Concentration of Predominant Components (RU)
UPK............. Industrial Training Center (RU)
UPK............. Personnel Training Administration (RU)
UPK............. Series Capacitor Battery Installation (RU)
UPK............. Ustredna Podohospodarska Kniznica, Kosice [*Central Agricultural Library in Kosice*] (CZ)
UPK............. Ustredni Pedagogicka Knihovna [*Central Pedagogical Library*] (CZ)
UPK............. Ustredni Planovaci Komise [*Central Planning Commission*] (CZ)
UPK............. Ustredni Politicka Kancelar [*Central Political Bureau*] (CZ)
UPK............. Ustredni Povodnova Komise Zemskeho Narodniho Vyboru [*Central Flood Prevention Commission of the Provincial People's Committee*] (CZ)
UPK............. Ustredni Proverovaci Komise Svazu Narodni Revoluce [*Central Investigating Commission (of the National Revolution League)*] (CZ)
UPKO.......... Administration of Municipal Services Establishments (RU)
UPKO.......... United Pasokmomogun [*United Sons of the Soil*] [*Kadazan organization in Sabah*] [*Also known as UNPM*] (ML)
UPL............. Universitaetsparteileitung [*University Party Management*] (EG)
UPL............. Uredba o Postupku Likvidacije Preduzeca [*Decree on the Procedure of Liquidation of Establishments*] (YU)
UPL............. Ustav Pracovniho Lekarstvi [*Institute of Industrial Medicine*] (CZ)
UPLG........... Uniao Popular para e Libertacao da Guine (MAR)
UPLG........... Union Populaire pour la Liberation de la Guadeloupe [*Popular Union for the Liberation of Guadeloupe*] (PD)
UPLG........... Union Populaire de Liberation de la Guinee Portugaise (MAR)
UPLGE......... Union Populaire de la Liberation de la Guinee Equatoriale (MAR)
UPM............ Industrial Training Shop (RU)
UPM............ Uganda Patriotic Movement (PD)
UPM............ Umelecko-Prumyslove Museum [*Industrial Arts Museum*] (CZ)
UpM............ Umlanfungen pro Minute [*Revolutions per Minute*] [*German*]
UPM............ Uniao Progressiva de Mocambique (MAR)
UPM............ Union Popular de Mujeres [*Women's Popular Union*] [*Spanish*] (WER)
UPM............ Union Progressiste Mauritanienne [*Mauritanian Progressive Union*] (AF)
UPM............ Unione Politica Maltese [*Maltese Political Union*] (PPE)
UPM............ United People's Movement [*St. Vincentian*] (PPW)
UPM............ United Presbyterian Mission (MAR)
UPM............ Universal Pneumatic Machine (RU)
UPM............ University Pertanian Malaysia
UPM............ University of Petroleum and Minerals [*Saudi*] (ME)
UPMI........... Union Progressiste Melanesienne [*Progressive Melanesian Union*] [*New Caledonian*] (PPW)
Up MPS....... Administration of International Traffic of the Ministry of Railroads (RU)
UPMTC....... Union Panafricaine et Malgache des Travailleurs Croyants (MAR)
UPMUPE..... Union Popular de Mujeres Peruanas [*Popular Union of Peruvian Women*] (LA)
UPN............ Union de Periodistas de Nicaragua [*Union of Nicaraguan Journalists*] (LA)
UPN............ Union Progressiste Nigerienne (MAR)
UPN............ Union del Pueblo Navarrese [*Union of the Navarrese People*] [*Spanish*] (PPW)
UPN............ Unity Party of Nigeria (AF)
UPN............ Ustredni Narodni Pojistovna [*Central Insurance Agency*] (CZ)
UPNA.......... Uniao das Populacoes do Norte de Angola [*Union of the Populations of North Angola*] (MAR)
Upnachvoso... Office of the Chief of Military Transport (RU)
UPNI........... Ukrainian Institute of Neuropsychiatry (RU)
UPNI........... Unionist Party of Northern Ireland (PPW)
up-niye........ Directorate [*Military term*], Administration, Office (RU)
UPO............ Administration of Fire Prevention (RU)
UPO............ Ukase on Fire Prevention in the Bulgarian People's Republic (BU)
UPO............ Universite Populaire [*People's University*] [*Cambodian*] (CL)
upol............ Plenipotentiary, Authorized Representative (RU)
UPOLI......... Universidad Politecnica de Nicaragua [*Nicaraguan Polytechnical University*] (LA1)
upolkomzag... Plenipotentiary of the Committee for Procurement of Agricultural Products (RU)
upolminzag... Plenipotentiary of the Ministry of Procurement (RU)
Upolsto....... Plenipotentiary of the Council of Labor and Defense (RU)
UPOMZ....... Training Antipersonnel Fragmentation Mine (RU)
UPONA........ Uniao das Populacoes do Norte de Angola (MAR)
UPONF........ Unified Political Organization, The National Front [*Yemeni*] (ME)
UPOV.......... Union for the Protection of New Varieties of Plants (MAR)
UPOWU....... Uganda Petroleum Oil and Chemical Workers Union (AF)
UPP............ Administration of the Food Industry (RU)
UPP............ Administration of Industrial Establishments (RU)
UPP............ Administration of the Printing Industry (RU)
UPP............ Conditional Jump to Subroutine [*Computers*] (RU)
UPP............ Industrial Training Establisment (RU)
UPP-........... Intermediate Semiconductor Repeater (RU)
UPP-........... Stand for Checking Parameters [*Aviation*] (RU)
UPP............ Union des Partis Populaires (MAR)
UPP............ Union del Pueblo Peruano [*Union of the Peruvian People*] (LA)
UPP............ United Peasants' Party [*Polish*] (PD)
UPP............ United People's Party [*Botswana*] (AF)
UPP............ United People's Party [*Grenadian*] (PPW)
UPP............ United People's Party [*Sierra Leonean*] (AF)
UPP............ United People's Party [*Singapore*] (ML)
UPP............ United People's Party [*Zambian*] (AF)
UPP............ United Progressive Party [*Trinidadian and Tobagan*] (PPW)
UPP............ United Sierra Leone Progressive Party (MAR)
UPP............ Unveraenderte Planpreise [*Fixed Plan Prices*] (EG)
UPP............ Uredba o Prestanku Preduzeca i Radnji [*Decree on the Suspension of Establishments and Shops*] (YU)
UPPA.......... United People's Party of Arunachal [*Indian*] (PPW)
UPPBCB...... Union Professionnelle des Producteurs de Bois du Congo Belge (MAR)
UPPD.......... Union Popular de Profesores Democratas [*Popular Union of Democratic Teachers*] [*Spanish*] (WER)
UPPenh....... Universite de Phnom Penh [*University of Phnom Penh*] [*Cambodian*] (CL)
UPPG.......... Union des Paysans Pauvres de la Guadeloupe (PD)
UPPN.......... United People's Party of Nigeria (AF)
UPPO.......... Uredba o Ukupnom Prihodu Privredne Organizacije i Njegove Raspodele [*Decree on the Gross Income of Economic Organizations and Its Distributions*] (YU)
UPPZ.......... Fire Protection Administration (BU)
UPR............ Administration of Planning Work (RU)
upr............. Administrator, Manager (RU)

Upr .... Directorate [*Military term*], Administrations, Office (RU)
UPr .... Uchilishten Pregled [*School Review*] [*A periodical*] (BU)
UPR .... Universal Field Radiation Counter Analyzer (RU)
UPRA .... Uniao das Populacoes Revolucionarias Angolanas (MAR)
upravl .... Administration (BU)
uprazdn .... Abolished (RU)
uprazh .... Exercise (BU)
UPRBiH .... Udruzenje Prosvjetnih Radnika Bosne i Hercegovine [*Association of Educators of Bosnia and Hercegovina*] (YU)
upriye .... Directorate [*Military term*], Administration, Office (RU)
UPROCA .... Union Professionnelle des Producteurs du Caoutchouc du Congo Belge (MAR)
Uprochmashdetal' ... Industrial-Experimental Establishment for the Reconditioning and Strengthening of Machine Parts (RU)
uprodor .... Administration of Roads (RU)
UPROHUTU ... Union pour la Promotion Hutu (MAR)
UPRONA .... Union pour le Progres National [*Union for National Progress*] [*Burundi*] (PPW)
UPRONA .... Union Progressiste Nationale de l'Angola (MAR)
UPRP .... Ujedinjena Poljska Radnicka Partija [*United Polish Workers Party*] (YU)
UPRP .... Urzad Patentowy Rzeczypospolitej Polskiej [*Patent Office of the Polish Republic*] (POL)
uprpishcheprom ... Administration of the Food Industry (RU)
UPRS .... Uprava Pomorstva i Recnog Saobracaja [*Sea and River Navigation Administration*] (YU)
Uprspetsdor ... Administration of Special Roads (RU)
UPS .... Boundary Layer Control (RU)
UPS .... Food Supply Administration (RU)
UPS .... Udruzenje Pravnika Srbije [*Serbian Lawyers' Association*] (YU)
UPS .... Udruzenje Pravoslavnog Svestenstva [*Association of Orthodox Clergy*] [*Serbian Orthodox Church*] (YU)
UPS .... Union des Producteurs Suisses [*Union of Swiss Producers*] (WER)
UPS .... Union Progressiste Senegalaise [*Senegalese Progressive Union*] (AF)
UPS .... Unutrasnja Pismonosna Sluzba [*Domestic Mail Service*] (YU)
UPS .... Uprava Pomorskog Saobracaja [*Sea Navigation Administration*] (YU)
UPS .... Upustvo za Vrsenje Postanske Sluzbe [*Directives for Postal Service Operation*] (YU)
UPS .... Uputstva za Vrsenje Unutrasnje Pismonosne Sluzbe [*Directives for Domestic Mail Service*] (YU)
UPS .... Ustredni Politicka Skola [*Central Political School*] (CZ)
UPSET .... Union of Private Secondary Education Teachers [*Mauritian*] (AF)
UPSG .... Pensions and Social Welfare Administration (BU)
UPSM .... Administration of the Building Materials Industry (RU)
UPSNR .... Urad Predsednictva Slovenskej Narodnej Rady [*Office of the Presidium of the Slovak National Council*] (CZ)
UPSOB .... Union Professionnelle des Sousofficiers Belges [*Professional Union of Belgian Non-Commissioned Officers*] (WER)
UPSP .... Union Progressive Socialist Party [*Egyptian*] (MAR)
UPSP .... Urad Predsednictva Sboru Poverenikov [*Office of the Presidium of the Board of Commissioners*] (CZ)
UPSS .... Ukrainska Partiia Samostiinykiv-Sotsiialistiv [*Ukrainian Party of Socialist-Independentists*] [*Russian*] (PPE)
UPST .... Union of Primary School Teachers [*Mauritian*] (AF)
UPT .... Administration of Public Transportation [*Of the Mosgorispolkom*] (RU)
UPT .... Direct-Current Amplifier (RU)
UPT .... Television Amplifier Attachment (RU)
UPT .... Union de Pobladores de Tugurio [*Union of Slum Dwellers*] [*Salvadoran*] (LA1)
UPT .... Union pour le Progres du Tchad (MAR)
UPT .... Urzad Pocztowo-Telekomunikacyjny [*Post and Telecommunication Office*] [*Polish*]
UPTC .... Union Pan-Africaine et Malgache des Travailleurs Croyants [*Pan-African Workers Congress*] [*Use PAWC*] (AF)
UPTC .... Universidad Pedagogica y Tecnologica de Colombia [*Tunja*] (COL)
UPTE .... Union of Posts and Telecommunications Employees (MAR)
UPTEU .... Uganda Posts and Telecommunications Employees Union (AF)
UPTIFNRJ ... Udruzenje Preduzeca Tekstilne Industrije Federativna Narodna Republika Jugoslavija [*Association of Establishments of the Textile Industry of Yugoslavia*] (YU)
UPTM .... Administration of Public Transportation of the Mosgorispolkom (RU)
UPTR .... Administration of Underwater Technical Operations (RU)
UPTs .... Impact Pneumatic Cylinder (RU)
UPTS .... Semiautomatic Telephone Communication System (RU)
UPTU .... Uredba o Privrednim Organizacijama za Trgovinske Usluge [*Decree on Economic Organizations for Commercial Service*] (YU)
UPU .... Amplifying-Converting Device (RU)
UPU .... Uganda People's Union (MAR)
UPU .... Union Postale Universelle [*Universal Postal Union*] [*French*]
UPU-Automat ... Unter-Pulver-Universal-Automat [*Automatic Flux Powder Welding Machine*] (EG)
UPUP .... Ulster Progressive Unionist Party [*Northern Ireland*] (PPW)
UPV .... Directorate of Border Troops (RU)
UPV .... Union Progressiste Voltaique [*Voltan Progressive Union*] (AF)
UPV .... Urad pro Patenty a Vynalezy [*Patents and Inventions Office*] (CZ)
UPV .... Urad Predsednictva Vlady [*Office of the Government Presidium*] (CZ)
UPV CSAV ... Ustav Planovani Vedy CSAV [*Science Planning Institute of the Czechoslovak Science Academy*] (CZ)
UPVO .... Directorate of Air Defense (RU)
UPVO .... Uciliste Protivzdusne Obrany [*Air Defense Training Center*] (CZ)
UPW .... Unions Paysannes des Wilaya [*Governorate Peasant Unions*] [*Algerian*] (AF)
UPWU .... Uganda Plantation Workers Union (MAR)
UPZ .... Sonic Dust Collector (RU)
UPZ .... Uredba o Prevozu (Putnika, Prtljaga, i Robe na) Zeljeznicama [*Decree on Rail Transport (of Passengers, Parcels, and Goods)*] (YU)
UPZNA .... Ukase on the Application of the Law on Legal Acts (BU)
UPZT .... Ustredni Podnik Zemedelske Techniky [*Central Enterprise of Agricultural Equipment*] (CZ)
UQ .... Fronte dell'Uomo Qualunque; Uomo Qualunque [*Common Man Front*] [*Italian*] (PPE)
UR .... Adjusting Rheostat (RU)
ur .... Administrator, Curator (BU)
UR .... Angle of Turn (RU)
ur .... Area, Tract [*Topography*] (RU)
UR .... Control Relay (RU)
ur .... Equation (RU)
UR .... Fortified Area (BU)
UR .... Fortified Area (RU)
UR .... Guided Missile (BU)
UR .... Guided Missile (RU)
UR .... Holding Relay (RU)
ur .... Level (RU)
UR .... Office of Criminal Investigation (RU)
UR .... Recording Control (RU)
UR .... Specific Radioactivity (RU)
UR .... Ugostiteljska Radnja [*Hotel and Catering Trade Shop*] (YU)
UR .... Uniao Republicana [*Republican Union*] [*Portuguese*] (PPE)
UR .... Union Republicana [*Republican Union*] [*Spanish*] (WER)
UR .... University of Rhodesia (MAR)
UR .... Uniwersytet Robotniczy [*Workers' University*] [*Polish*]
ur .... Urad [*Office*] (CZ)
Ur .... Uretim [*Production*] [*See also Istih*] (TU)
ur .... Urodzony [*Born*] [*Polish*]
UR .... Ustredni Rada [*Central Council*] (CZ)
UR .... Ustredni Reditelstvi [*Central Directorate*] (CZ)
UR-19 .... Universitarios Revolucionarios 19 de Julio [*19 July Revolutionary University Students*] [*Salvadoran*] (LA)
URA .... Union Regionale des Agriculteurs [*Tunisian*] (MAR)
URA .... Union des Remorqueurs d'Abidjan (MAR)
URA .... Union des Republiques Arabes (MAR)
URA .... United Red Army [*Japanese*] (PD)
URA .... Uzina de Reparatii Auto [*Automotive Repair Plant*] (RO)
URAC .... Union des Republiques d'Afrique Centrale (MAR)
URADEP .... Upper Regional Agricultural Development Programme (MAR)
URAI .... Union des Representations Automobiles et Industrielles (MAR)
Uralelektroapparat ... Ural Electrical Equipment Plant (RU)
Uralenergo ... Ural Power System (RU)
URALFIZKhIM ... Ural Scientific Research Physicochemical Institute (RU)
URALFTI .... Ural Physicotechnical Institute (RU)
URALGINTsVETMET ... Ural State Scientific Research Institute of Nonferrous Metals (RU)
Uralgiprolesdrev ... Ural State Institute for the Planning of Establishments of the Lumber, Woodworking, Wood-Chemistry, and Paper Industry (RU)
Uralgipromez ... Ural State Institute for the Planning of Metallurgical Plants (RU)
Uralgiproshakht ... Ural State Institute for the Planning of Mines (RU)
Uralkhimmash ... Ural Heavy Chemical Machinery Plant (RU)
Uralmash .... Ural Heavy Machinery Plant Imeni Sergo Ordzhonikidze (RU)
URALMEKhANOBR ... Ural Scientific Research and Planning Institute of Concentration and Mechanical Processing of Minerals (RU)
URALNIGRI ... Ural Scientific Research Institute of Geological Exploration (RU)
UralNIISKhOZ ... Ural Scientific Research Institute of Agriculture (RU)
UralNILKhI ... Ural Scientific Research Institute of Wood Chemistry (RU)
URALNITOMASh ... Ural Branch of the All-Union Scientific, Engineering, and Technical Society of Machine Builders (RU)
Uralsel'mash ... Ural Agricultural Machinery Plant (RU)
Uraltyazhkhimmash ... Ural Heavy Chemical Machinery Plant (RU)
Uraltyazhmash ... Ural Heavy Machinery Plant (RU)
URALUGLEKOKS ... Ural Scientific Research Institute of Coal and Coke (RU)
Uralvagon ... Ural Railroad Car Plant (RU)
Uralvagonzavod ... Ural Railroad Car Plant (RU)
UralVO .... Ural Military District (RU)
URAMEX .... Uranio Mexicano [*Mexican Uranium*] (LA1)
URAN .... Active Load Distribution System (RU)

URAS .... Union des Republicains d'Action Sociale [*Union of Republicans of Social Action*] [*French*] (PPE)
uraut .... Uredne Autorisovany [*Officially Authorized*] (CZ)
URB .... Battalion Fortified Area (RU)
URBA .... Compagnie des Mines d'Uranium de Bakouma [*Bakouma Uranium Mines Company*] [*Central African*] (AF)
URBA .... Universite Royale des Beaux-Arts [*Royal Fine Arts University*] [*Replaced by UBA*] [*Cambodian*] (CL)
URBANAL ... Urbanizadora Nacional [*Medellin*] (COL)
URBANICOM ... Association Internationale Urbanisme et Commerce [*International Association for Town Planning and Distribution*] (EA)
URBAT .... Societe d'Etudes pour l'Urbanisme et le Batiment (MAR)
URC .... Union Routiere et Commerciale (MAR)
URCA .... Societe d'Uranium Centrafricaine (MAR)
URCC .... Uniunea Raion de Cooperative de Consum [*Raion Union of Consumer Cooperatives*] (RO)
URCDPC ..... Union des Ressortissants du Congo pour la Defense et la Promotion du Congo (MAR)
URCh .... Narrow-Band Frequency Relay (RU)
URCh .... Radio-Frequency Amplifier (RU)
URCM .... Uniunea Raion de Cooperative Mestesugaresti [*Raion Union of Artisan Cooperatives*] (RO)
URCO .... Union Regionale des Cooperatives Oleicoles [*Regional Olive Products Cooperatives Union*] [*Algerian*] (AF)
URCO .... Universidad Regional Centro-Occidental [*Midwestern Regional University*] [*Venezuelan*] (LA)
URCO .... Ustredni Rada Ceskoslovenskeho Obchodnictva [*Central Council of Czechoslovak Businessmen*] (CZ)
UR CSF .... Ustredni Reditelstvi Ceskoslovenskeho Filmu [*Central Directorate of Czechoslovak Films*] (CZ)
URD .... General-Purpose Pressure Governor (RU)
URD .... Union des Remorqueurs de Dakar (MAR)
URD .... Union pour le Renouveau du Dahomey (MAR)
URD .... Union Republicana Democratica [*Democratic Republican Union*] [*Venezuelan*] (LA)
URD .... Union Revolucionaria Democratica [*Democratic Revolutionary Union*] [*Guatemalan*] (LA)
URD .... Upper River Division (MAR)
URD .... Uredba o Raspodeli Dobitka i Porezu na Dobit Privrednih Organizacija [*Decree on the Distribution of Profit and the Tax on Profit of Economic Corporations*] (YU)
URD .... Ustredni Rada Druzstev [*Central Council of Cooperatives*] (CZ)
URD .... X-Ray Diagnostic Unit (RU)
URDEC .... Universitarios Revolucionarios Democrata Cristianos [*Christian Democratic Revolutionary University Students*] [*Costa Rican*] (LA)
URDECO ..... Upper Regional Development Corporation (MAR)
URDO .... Union des Remorqueurs de Douala (MAR)
URE .... Union Revolucionaria Estudiantil [*Revolutionary Student Union*] [*Ecuadorean*] (LA)
URE CSAV ... Ustav Radiotechniky a Elektroniky CSAV [*Institute of Radiotechnology and Electronics of the Czechoslovak Science Academy*] (CZ)
Ured .... Administrator, Curator (BU)
UrEMIIT .... Ural Electromechanical Institute of Railroad Transportation Engineers (RU)
UREMOAS ... Uzina de Radiatoare, Echipament Metalic, Objecte si Armature Sanitare [*Factory for Radiators, Metal Equipment, and Sanitary Articles and Fittings*] (RO)
URER .... Union Regionale d'Expansion Rurale [*Regional Union for Rural Expansion*] [*Malagasy*] (AF)
URES .... Administration for the Development of Radio Facilities and Intrarayon Telecommunications (RU)
URF .... Union des Femmes de la Reunion (MAR)
URFC .... Union Revolutionnaire des Femmes Congolaises [*Revolutionary Union of Congolese Women*] (AF)
URFG .... Union Revolutionnaire des Femmes Guineennes (MAR)
URG .... Union de Radioperiodicos de Guatemala [*Union of Radio Newsmen of Guatemala*] (LA)
URGE .... Union Revolucionaria de la Guinea Ecuatorial [*Revolutionary Union of Equatorial Guinea*] [*Spanish*] (AF)
URGE .... Union Revolutionnaire de la Guinea Equatoriale [*Revolutionary Union of Equatorial Guinea*] [*French*] (AF)
Urgiz .... Ural State Publishing House (RU)
URGP .... Union des Ressortissants de la Guinee Portugaise (MAR)
URGS .... Universidade do Rio Grande Do Sul [*University of Rio Grande Do Sul*] [*Brazilian*] (LA)
UrGU .... Ural State University Imeni A. M. Gor'kiy (RU)
Ur g v .... Ground-Water Level (RU)
urh .... Ultra Rovid Hullamu [*Ultra Short Wave*] (HU)
urh .... Urheilu [*Sports*] [*Finnish*]
URI .... Pulse Distribution Amplifier (RU)
URI .... Union Revolucionaria Independiente [*Independent Revolutionary Union*] [*Mexican*] (LA1)
URJC .... Union Revolucionaria de Jovenes Comunistas [*Revolutionary Union of Young Communists*] [*Colombian*] (LA)
URJE .... Union Revolucionaria de la Juventud del Ecuador [*Revolutionary Union of Ecuadorean Youth*] (LA)
urk .... Urkundlich [*German*]
URK .... Ustredna Rozhodcia Komisia [*Central Arbitration Commission*] (CZ)
URK .... Ustredni Revisni Komise [*Central Auditing Commission*] (CZ)
URKM .... Administration of Workers' and Peasants' Militia (RU)
URL .... Union Radical del Liberalismo [*Radical Union of Liberalism*] [*Ecuadorean*] (LA)
UrLFLRJst ... Uradni List Federativne Ljudske Republike Jugoslavije Stevilka [*Official Gazette of Yugoslavia Number*] (YU)
ur m .... Sea Level (RU)
URM .... Urzad Rady Ministrow [*Office of the Council of Ministers*] (POL)
UR M-L .... Uniao Revolucionaria, Marxista-Leninista [*Marxist-Leninist Revolutionary Union*] [*Portuguese*] (PPE)
URN .... Carbon Voltage Regulator (RU)
URN .... High-Voltage Current Unit for Splitting of Large Rocks (RU)
URNG .... Unidad Revolucionaria Nacional Guatemalteca [*Guatemalan National Revolutionary Unity*] (PD)
ur-niye .... Equation (RU)
URO .... Guided-Missile Weapon (RU)
URO .... Stocktaking and Distribution Department (RU)
URO .... Udruzenje Rezervnih Oficira [*Association of Reserve Officers*] (YU)
URO .... Union des Remorqueurs de l'Ocean (MAR)
URO .... Ustredni Rada Odboru [*Central Council of Trade Unions*] (CZ)
uroch .... Area, Tract [*Topography*] (RU)
UROJ .... Udruzenje Rezervnih Oficira Jugoslavije [*Association of Reserve Officers of Yugoslavia*] (YU)
urol .... Urologist, Urology (BU)
UROM .... Union Regionale de l'Ogooue Maritime (MAR)
URP .... Administration for the Distribution of Publications (RU)
URP .... General-Purpose Borer (RU)
URP .... Radioactive Position Level Gauge (RU)
URP .... Union Revolucionaria Popular [*People's Revolutionary Union*] [*Honduran*] (LA1)
URP .... United Rhodesian Party (MAR)
URPT .... Union Republicaine et Progressiste du Tchad (MAR)
URR .... Scanning Turn Angle (RU)
URRU- .... General-Purpose Radioactive Level Regulator (RU)
URS .... Administration of Workers' Supply (RU)
URS .... Guided Missile (RU)
URS .... Self-Propelled Guided Projectile (BU)
URS .... Ujedinjeni Radnicki Sindikati [*United Workers Trade-Unions*] (YU)
URS .... Union Revolucionaria Socialista [*Socialist Revolutionary Union*] [*Colombian*] (LA)
URS .... Universal Speed Regulator (RU)
URS .... Uprava Recnog Saobracaja [*River Transportation Administration*] (YU)
URS .... Ustav Racionalizace ve Stavebnictvi [*Institute for Rationalization in Construction*] (CZ)
URSA .... Universite Royale des Sciences Agronomiques [*Royal University of Agronomical Sciences*] [*Replaced by USCA*] [*Cambodian*] (CL)
URSFNRJ .... Udruzenje Radio Stanica Federativna Narodna Republika Jugoslavija - Jugoslovenska Radio-Difuzija [*Radio Stations Association of Yugoslavia - Yugoslav Radio Broadcasting*] [*Belgrade*] (YU)
URSPA .... Ustredni Rozvojove Stredisko Prumyslu Armatur [*Main Development Center of the Armature Industry*] (CZ)
urspr .... Urspruenglich [*Original, Originally*] (EG)
URSPS .... Ukrainian Republic Trade-Union Council (RU)
URSS .... Union des Republiques Socialistes Sovietiques [*Union of Soviet Socialist Republics - USSR*] [*French*] (MAR)
URSS .... Uniunea Republicilor Sovietice Socialiste [*Union of Soviet Socialist Republics*] (RO)
URSSAF ...... Union pour le Recouvrement des Cotisations de la Securite Sociale et des Allocations Familiales [*Union for Collection of Social Security Contributions and Family Allotments*] [*French*] (WER)
URSSJ .... Ujedinjeni Radnicki Sidikalni Savez Jugoslavije [*United Workers Trade-Union of Yugoslavia*] (YU)
urstorg .... Administration of Workers' Supply and Trade (RU)
URT .... Union Republicaine du Tchad (MAR)
URT .... United Republic of Tanzania (MAR)
URTK .... Universite Royale Takeo-Kampot [*Royal Takeo-Kampot University*] [*Cambodian*] (CL)
URTNA .... Union des Radio-Televisions Nationales Africaines [*African National Radio-Television Union*] (AF)
URTS .... Agency Manual Exchange (RU)
URU .... Ustredni Rozdelovny Uhli [*Central Coal Distribution Enterprises*] (CZ)
URUKhIN ..... Ural Institute of Coal Chemistry (RU)
URUPABOL ... Comision Mixta Permanente de Uruguay, Paraguay, y Bolivia [*Permanent Joint Commission of Uruguay, Paraguay, and Bolivia*] (LA)
URV .... Controlled Mercury-Arc Rectifier (RU)
URV .... Video Distribution Amplifier (RU)
URV-D .... Controlled Mercury-Arc Rectifier-Motor (RU)
URVL .... Ustav pro Racionalizaciu Vyroby Lozisk ZVL [*Institute for Rationalization of Production of Ball Bearings*] (CZ)
UrVO .... Ural Military District (RU)

URVR.......... Ustredni Redakcne-Vydavatelska Rada [*Central Editorial and Publishing Council (of the Czechoslovak Academy of Sciences)*] (CZ)
URY............ Uruguay [*Three-letter standard code*] (CNC)
URZ............ Threat of Radioactive Contamination [*Warning*] (RU)
urz.............. Urzad [*Administration, Office*] (POL)
US.............. Administrative Council (BU)
US.............. Amplifier-Mixer (RU)
US.............. Carbon Column (RU)
US.............. Communications Center (RU)
US.............. Construction Administration (RU)
US.............. Drift Angle [*Aviation*] (RU)
us.............. Farmstead, Homestead [*Topography*] (RU)
US.............. Fortified Sector (RU)
US.............. Guided Missile (RU)
US.............. Scientific Council (RU)
US.............. Signal Amplifier (RU)
US.............. Speed Indicator [*Aviation*] (RU)
US.............. Trainer Aircraft (RU)
US.............. Training Ship (RU)
US.............. Transmission Device [*Automation*] (RU)
US.............. Ubezpieczalnia Spoleczna [*Social Security and Health Service*] (POL)
us.............. Ubi Supra [*In the Place Above Mentioned*] [*Latin*] (GPO)
U/S............ Ukrcne Stanice [*Embarkment Stations*] (YU)
US.............. Uni Sovjet [*Soviet Union*] (IN)
US.............. Union Senegalaise [*Senegalese Union*] (AF)
US.............. Union Soudanaise (MAR)
US.............. Uniunea Scriitorilor [*Writers' Union*] (RO)
us.............. Usea [*Finnish*]
us.............. Usein [*Often*] [*Finnish*]
US.............. Ustredni Sekretariat [*Central Secretariat*] (CZ)
Us.............. Ustrem [*Drive*] [*A journal*] (BU)
US.............. Uza Srbija [*Serbia Proper (Without Vojvodina and Kosovo-Metohija)*] (YU)
USA............ General-Purpose Welder (RU)
USA............ Union Socialiste Arabe [*North African*] (MAR)
USA............ Union des Syndicats Agricoles [*Moroccan*] (MAR)
USA............ United Swaziland Association (AF)
USA............ Uniunea Sud Africana [*South African Union*] (RO)
USAC.......... Union des Syndicats Autonomes Camerounais [*Federation of Cameroonian Autonomous Trade Unions*] (AF)
USACA........ Universidad Santiago de Cali (COL)
USAEA........ University Students Association of East Africa (MAR)
USAFICA..... United States Army Forces in Central Africa (MAR)
USAID......... United States Agency for International Development (MAR)
USAK.......... General-Purpose System for Automated Control of Agricultural Transportation Facilities (BU)
USAM.......... Union des Syndicats Autonomes de Madagascar [*Federation of Malagasy Autonomous Trade Unions*] (AF)
USAM.......... United States Aid Mission (MAR)
USANP........ United South African National Party (MAR)
USAO.......... United Sabah Action Organization (ML)
USAOBiH.... Ujedinjeni Savez Antifasisticke Omladine Bosne i Hercegovine [*United Federation of Anti-Fascist Youth of Bosnia and Hercegovina*] (YU)
USAOH........ Ujedinjeni Savez Antifasisticke Omladine Hrvatske [*United Federation of Anti-Fascist Youth of Croatia*] (YU)
USAOJ........ Ujedinjeni Savez Antifasisticke Omladine Jugoslavije [*United Federation of Anti-Fascist Youth of Yugoslavia*] (YU)
USAP.......... Union of Sabah People's Party (ML)
USAS.......... Unione Sindicale Africana della Somalia [*Organization of African Unions of Somalia*] (AF)
USB............ Drift Angle on Bomb Run (RU)
USB............ High-Speed Trainer Bomber (RU)
USB............ Standardized Medical Barrack Tent (RU)
USB............ Union Senegalaise de Banque [*Senegalese Banking Union*] (AF)
USB............ Ustredi Svazu Brannosti [*Headquarters of the Union for Military Preparedness*] (CZ)
USB............ Ustredna Statnej Bezpecnosti [*State Security Headquarters*] (CZ)
USBE.......... Universal Serials & Book Exchange
USBN.......... Universal Standard Book Number
USBO.......... Fortified Sector of Coast Defense (RU)
USC............ Union Sociale Camerounaise (MAR)
USC............ Union Socialista de Cataluna [*Socialist Union of Catalonia*] [*Spanish*] (WER)
USC............ Union Suisse des Cooperatives de Consommation (MAR)
USC............ Urzad Stanu Cywilnego [*Office of Registration of Births, Marriages, and Deaths*] (POL)
USC............ Ustredna Slovenskych Celuloziek [*Central Bureau of Slovak Cellulose Factories*] (CZ)
USCA.......... United Chinese Schoolteachers' Association (ML)
USCA.......... Universite des Sciences Agronomiques [*University of Agronomical Sciences*] [*Replaced URSA*] [*Cambodian*] (CL)
USCC.......... Union des Syndicats Croyants du Cameroun [*Federation of Cameroonian Believers Trade Unions*] (AF)
USCD.......... Ustredni Svaz Ceskoslovenske Dopravy [*Czechoslovak Central Transport Union*] (CZ)
USCI............ Union Syndicale des Commercants Independants (MAR)
USCL........... United Society for Christian Literature (MAR)
USCM.......... Ustredi Svazu Ceske Mladeze [*Headquarters of the Union of Czech Youth*] (CZ)
USCN.......... Ustredni Svaz Ceskoslovenskych Novinaru [*Central Union of Czechoslovak Journalists*] (CZ)
USCO.......... Union Steel Corporation (MAR)
USCOA........ Union Senegalaise pour le Commerce et l'Agriculture (MAR)
USCP.......... Union des Syndicats Categerials de Police [*French*]
USCP.......... Ustredni Svaz Ceskoslovenskeho Prumyslu [*Central Union of Czechoslovak Industry*] (CZ)
USCR.......... Ustredni Svaz Ceskoslovenskeho Remesla [*Central Union of Czechoslovak Artisans*] (CZ)
USCR.......... Ustredni Svaz pro Cizinecky Ruch [*Central Organization for Tourist Trade*] (CZ)
USCS.......... Union des Syndicats Confederes du Senegal (MAR)
USCSN........ Ustredni Svaz Ceskoslovenskych Novinaru [*Central Union of Czechoslovak Journalists*] (CZ)
USCSP........ Ustredni Svaz Ceskoslovenskeho Prumyslu [*Central Union of the Czechoslovak Industry*] (CZ)
USCsS........ Ustredni Svaz Ceskoslovenskeho Studentstva [*Central Union of Czechoslovak Students*] (CZ)
USCSVU..... Ustredni Spolek Ceskoslovenskych Vytvarnych Umelcu [*Central Association of Czechoslovak Creative Artists*] (CZ)
USCSVU..... Ustredni Svaz Ceskoslovenskych Vytvarnych Umelcu [*Central Association of Czechoslovak Creative Artists*] (CZ)
USD............ Uniao Social Democratico [*Social Democratic Union*] [*Portuguese*] (PPE)
USD............ Ustredni Skola Delnicka [*Central Training School for Workers*] (CZ)
USD............ Ustredni Svaz Druzstev [*Central Union of Cooperatives*] (CZ)
USDE.......... Union Social-Democrata Espanola [*Spanish Social Democratic Union*] (WER)
USDECO..... Union Sindical Departamental de los Empleados, Campesinos, y Obreros (del Cuzco) [*Departmental Trade Union of Employees, Peasants, and Workers (of Cuzco)*] [*Peruvian*] (LA)
USDTP........ Ukrainska Sotsial Demokraticheskaia Truda Partiia [*Ukrainian Social Democratic Labor Party*] [*Russian*] (PPE)
USE............ Unidad de Servicios Especiales [*Special Services Unit*] [*Peruvian*] (LA)
USE............ Union Socialista Espanola [*Spanish Socialist Union*] (WER)
USE............ Ural Soviet Encyclopedia (RU)
Use............ Usine [*Works*] [*Military map abbreviation*] [*World War I*] [*French*] (MTD)
USE............ Ustav Stavebni Ekonomie [*Institute of Construction Economics*] (CZ)
USE............ Ustredni Sprava Energetiky [*Central Administration Office for Electric Power*] (CZ)
USEC.......... Union Social de Empresarios Cristianos [*Social Union of Christian Businessmen*] [*Chilean*] (LA)
USECOT..... Usine d'Egrenage du Coton [*Cotton Ginning Plant*] [*Cambodian*] (CL)
USEFMC..... Uniunea Sindicatelor din Economia Forestiera si Materiale de Constructii [*Union of Trade Unions in the Forestry Economy and Construction Materials*] (RO)
USEG.......... Union Syndicale de l'Est Gabon (MAR)
USEK.......... Ustredie Evanjelickych Knazov [*Central Association of Protestant Ministers*] (CZ)
USEK.......... Ustredni Svaz Evangelickych Knezi [*Central Association of Protestant Ministers*] (CZ)
USEM.......... Union Social de Empresarios Mexicanos [*Social Union of Mexican Businessmen*] (LA)
USEMA....... Union des Syndicats des Employeurs de Mauritanie (MAR)
USEPA........ Union Sportive de l'Enseignement Primaire en Algerie (MAR)
USEPPA...... Universal System of Elements of Industrial Pneumoautomation (RU)
USETRAM... Union Senegalaise de Transit, Transport, et Manutention (MAR)
usf.............. Und So Fort [*And So Forth*] (EG)
USF............ United Socialist Front [*Thai*] (PD)
USFP.......... Union Socialiste des Forces Populaires [*Socialist Union of Popular Forces*] [*Moroccan*] (PPW)
USG............ Fuel Supply Administration (RU)
USG............ Ustav Stavebni Geologie [*Institute of Construction Geology*] (CZ)
USGaK........ Ustredni Sprava Geodesie a Kartografie [*Central Geodetic and Cartographic Administration*] (CZ)
USh............ Navigator's Indicator [*Aviation*] (RU)
USh............ Uganda Shilling (MAR)
USH............ Ustav Skladoveho Hospodarstvi [*Institute of Storage Economy*] (CZ)
USh............ Wide-Band Amplifier (RU)
UShB-......... Auger Drill Unit (RU)
ushch.......... Gorge, Canyon [*Topography*] (RU)
u-shche....... School (RU)
USHK.......... Ustav Stavebnich Hmot a Konstrukci [*Institute of Building Materials and Construction Engineering*] [*Prague*] (CZ)
ushosdor..... Administration of Highways (RU)
u-shte......... School (BU)
USI............ United Schools International (EA)

USI .... Video Amplifier (RU)
USIA .... Administration of Soviet Property in Austria (RU)
USIA .... Uprava Sovjetske Imovine u Austriji [*Administration of Soviet Property in Austria*] (YU)
USIBA .... Usina Siderurgica da Bahia [*Bahia Iron and Steel Mill*] [*Brazilian*] (LA)
USICA .... United States International Communications Agency (MAR)
USID .... Signaling Dosimeter System (RU)
USIEM .... Union des Syndicats d'Interet Economique de Madagascar [*Malagasy Federation of Unions of Economic Interest*] (AF)
USIM .... Union de Sindicatos de la Industria Maderera [*Lumber Workers Union*] [*Argentine*] (LA)
USIMA .... Union Senegalaise d'Industries Maritimes [*Senegalese Maritime Industries Union*] (AF)
USIMA .... Union Soudanaise d'Industries Maritimes (MAR)
USIMETAL ... Societe Industrielle de Ets. Roland Guiol (MAR)
USIMINAS ... Usinas Siderurgicas de Minas Gerais, SA [*Minas Gerais Iron and Steel Mills, Inc.*] [*Brazilian*] (LA)
USINDO .... Usaha Industri Indonesia [*Indonesian Industrial Concern*] (IN)
USINEN .... Societe Ivoirienne d'Usinage (MAR)
USINEX .... Usine d'Extraction de Pyrethrine et pour l'Assimilation de l'Industrialisation (MAR)
USINOR .... Union Siderurgique du Nord de la France (MAR)
USIP .... United Solomon Islands Party (PPW)
USIS .... United States Information Service (MAR)
USITT .... Uniunea Sindicatelor din Intreprinderile de Transporturi si Telecomunicatii [*Union of Trade Unions in Transportation and Telecommunications Enterprises*] (RO)
USJ .... Ustav Slovenskeho Jazyka [*Slovak Language Institute (of the Slovak Academy of Sciences)*] (CZ)
USJC .... Union Socialiste de la Jeunesse Congolaise (MAR)
usk .... Acceleration (RU)
USK .... Court Criminal Collegium (RU)
USK .... Union Sportive de Sidi Kacem [*Moroccan*] (MAR)
USK .... University Sports Club (RU)
usk .... Uskonto [*Religion*] [*Finnish*]
USKh .... Administration of Agriculture (RU)
USKh .... Administration of Warehouses and Cold Storage Plants (RU)
USKhI .... Ul'yanovsk Agricultural Institute (RU)
usl .... Conventional (RU)
usl .... Conventional Designation (RU)
USL .... Universal Slide Rule (RU)
USL .... Ustav Slovenskej Literatury [*Institute of Slovak Literature*] (CZ)
USL .... Ustredni Svaz Lekarniku [*Central Union of Pharmacists*] (CZ)
USLC .... Union des Syndicats Libres du Cameroun (MAR)
Us lesn .... Forest Homestead [*Topography*] (RU)
USLG .... Union des Societes Luxembourgeoises de Gymnastique [*Union of Luxembourg Gymnastic Societies*] (WER)
USLSZ .... Ustredni Sprava Lazni, Sanatorii, a Zotaven [*Central Administration of Spas, Sanatoriums, and Rest Homes*] (CZ)
usl yed .... Conventional Unit (RU)
USM .... General-Purpose Washing Machine (RU)
USM .... Union Socialiste Malgache [*Malagasy Socialist Union*] (AF)
USM .... Universal Welding Manipulator (RU)
USMM .... Union Socialiste des Musulmans Mauritaniens [*Socialist Union of Mauritanian Muslims*] (AF)
USMO .... Communications Administration of the Moscow Oblast (RU)
USMSKhI .... Administration of Medical and Sanitary Equipment Supply (RU)
USN .... Consolidated Norms Used in Estimates (RU)
USn .... Guided Missile (RU)
USN .... Union Scolaire Nigerienne [*Nigerien School Union*] [*Niger*] (AF)
USN .... Union Syndicale de la Ngounie (MAR)
USN .... Union Syndicale de la Nyanga (MAR)
USN .... Universal Voltage Stabilizer (RU)
USN .... Ustredni Sklad Naradi [*Central Equipment Depot*] (CZ)
USNKh .... Ukrainian Council of the National Economy (RU)
USNO .... United Sabah National Organization [*Malaysian*] (PPW)
USNP .... Ustav Slovenskeho Narodneho Povstania [*Institute of the Slovak National Uprising*] (CZ)
USNP .... Ustredni Svaz Nemocenskych Pojistoven [*Central Union of Health Insurance Agencies*] (CZ)
USNZV .... Ustredni Sprava Nakupu Zemedelskych Vyrobku [*Central Administration Office for Purchase of Agricultural Products*] (CZ)
USO .... Administration of Judicial Bodies (of the Ministry of Justice, RSFSR) (RU)
USO .... Contact Arrangement with an Object (RU)
USO .... Union Sindical Obrera [*Workers Union*] [*Colombian*] (LA)
USO .... Union Sindical Obrero [*Workers' Trade Union*] [*Spanish*] (WER)
USO .... Ural-Siberian Branch (RU)
USO .... Ustredni Svaz Obchodu [*Central Commerce Union*] (CZ)
USOD .... Ustredie Slovenskych Ochotnickych Divadiel [*Center of Slovak Amateur Theaters*] (CZ)
USOI .... Union des Syndicats de l'Ogooue Ivindo (MAR)
usokr .... Directorate of Communications of a Military District (RU)
Usol'lag .... Usol'ye Corrective Labor Camp (RU)
USOM .... United States Operations Mission (CL)
USOMS .... Uniao dos Sindicatos da Orla Maritima de Santos [*Union Confederation of the Santos Coast*] [*Brazilian*] (LA)
USOP .... Union Solidaria de Obreros Portuarios [*Common Union of Port Workers*] [*Uruguayan*] (LA)
USOPD .... Ustredni Svaz Obchodu, Pohostinstvi, a Dopravy [*Central Union of Commerce, Hotel and Restaurant Trade, and Transportation*] (CZ)
USP .... Uniao de Sindicatos do Porto [*Porto Union Federation*] [*Portuguese*] (WER)
USP .... Unidad de Servicio y Produccion [*Service and Production Unity*] [*Cuban*] (LA)
USP .... Union des Services Publics d'Afrique (MAR)
USP .... United Socialist Party [*Tongsa Dang*] [*South Korean*] (PPW)
USP .... United Somali Party (MAR)
USP .... Universal Assembly Device (RU)
USP .... Universidade de Sao Paulo [*Sao Paulo University*] [*Brazilian*] (LA)
USP .... University of the South Pacific [*Fijian*]
USP .... Uniwersyteckie Studium Przygotowawcze [*University Preparation Course*] (POL)
USP .... Ustredni Socialni Pojistovna [*Central Social Insurance Agency*] (CZ)
USP .... Ustredni Statni Pokladna [*Central State Treasury*] (CZ)
USP .... Ustredni Svaz Prumyslu [*Central Union of Industry*] (CZ)
USPA .... Union de Services Publics-Abidjan (MAR)
USPA .... Union Syndicale Panafricaine [*All-African Trade Union Federation*] [*Use AATUF*] (AF)
USPAC .... Union des Syndicats Professionnels Agricoles et Activites Connexes (MAR)
USPAC .... Union des Syndicats Professionnels Agricoles du Cameroun (MAR)
USPC .... Union Syndicale des Planteurs du Cameroun (MAR)
USPC .... Union des Syndicats Professionnels du Cameroun (MAR)
USPD .... Unabhaengige Sozialdemokratische Partei Deutschlands [*Independent Social Democratic Party of Germany*] (PPE)
USPM .... Union des Syndicats Patronaux de Madagascar (MAR)
USR .... Administration of Construction Operations (RU)
USR .... Administration of Specialized Operations (RU)
USR .... Ukrainska Partiia Sotsialistov Revolyutsionerov [*Ukrainian Socialist Revolutionary Party*] [*Russian*] (PPE)
USR .... Universidad Simon Rodriguez [*Venezuelan*]
USR .... Ustredni Svaz Remesel [*Central Union of Crafts*] (CZ)
USRA .... Union des Syndicats Revolutionnaires Angolais (MAR)
USRAF .... Union pour le Salut et le Renouveau de l'Algerie Francaise (MAR)
USR-Borotbists ... Ukrainska Partiia Sotsialistov Revolyutsionerov-Borotbists [*Ukrainian Socialist Revolutionary Party-Fighters*] [*Russian*] (PPE)
US-RDA .... Union Soudanaise-Rassemblement Democratique Africain [*Sudanese Union-African Democratic Rally*] [*Malian*] (AF)
USRO .... UNESCO Sub-Regional Office (MAR)
USRP .... Administration of Workers' Settlements Construction (RU)
USRP .... Hungarian Socialist Workers Party (BU)
USRR .... Ukrainska Socjalistyczna Republika Radziecka [*Ukrainian Soviet Socialist Republic*] (POL)
USRV .... Rayon Junction Broadcasting Station (RU)
USS .... Strategic Services Administration (BU)
USS .... Ucena Spolecnost Safarikova [*Safarik Learned Society*] (CZ)
USS .... Universitelararasi Secme Sinavina [*Inter-University Proficiency Examination*] (TU)
USS .... Universiteler Arasi Secme Sinavinda Basari [*Inter-University Entrance Examination*] [*Turkish*]
USS .... Ustredi Stredoskolskeho Studentstva [*Center of Secondary School Students*] (CZ)
USS .... Ustredna Sprava Spojov [*Central Communications Administration*] (CZ)
USS .... Ustredna Stavebna Sprava [*Central Construction Administration (of the State Railroads)*] (CZ)
USS .... Ustredni Svazova Skola [*Central Trade Union School*] (CZ)
USSALEP .... United States-South Africa Leadership Exchange Program (AF)
USSC .... Universities Social Science Council (MAR)
USSCC .... University Social Sciences Council Conference (MAR)
USSD .... Ustredni Svaz Spotrebnich Druzstev [*Central Union of Consumer Cooperatives*] (CZ)
USSL .... Uganda School Supply Limited (MAR)
USSM .... Uniunea Societatilor de Stiinte Medicale [*Union of Medical Sciences Societies*] (RO)
USSM .... Ustredie Svazu Slovenskej Mladeze [*Center of the Union of Slovak Youth*] (CZ)
USSP .... Universal Assembly Welding Device (RU)
USSP .... Ustredne Sdruzenie Slovenskeho Priemyslu [*Central Association of Slovak Industry*] (CZ)
USSPC .... Ustredi Stredoskolske Socialni Pece pro Cechy [*Central Social Welfare Bureau for Students of Secondary Schools in Bohemia*] (CZ)
USSPEI .... Union des Syndicats des Services Publics Europeens et Internationaux [*European and International Public Services Union*] (EA)
USSPM .... Ustredi Stredoskolske Socialni Pece pro Zemi Moravskoslezskou [*Central Social Welfare Bureau for Students of Secondary Schools in Moravia and Silesia*] (CZ)

USSR........... Ukrainian Soviet Socialist Republic (BU)
USSR........... Ukrainian Soviet Socialist Republic (RU)
USSR........... Ukrajinska Sovjetska Socijalisticka Republika [*Ukrainian Soviet Socialist Republic*] (YU)
USSR........... Union of Soviet Socialist Republics [*See also SSSR, CCCP*]
ust............... Obsolete [*Lexicography*] (RU)
ust............... Stability (RU)
UST............. Standardized Medical (Tent) (RU)
UST............. Transportation Construction Administration (BU)
UST............. Union Senegalaise du Travail [*Senegalese Labor Union*] (AF)
UST............. Union Socialiste Tchadienne (MAR)
UST............. University of Science and Technology (MAR)
UST............. Uredba o Spoljnotrgovinskom Poslovanju [*Decree on Foreign Trade Operations*] (YU)
ust............... Ustawa [*Act, Law*] (POL)
ust............... Ustep [*Paragraph*] (POL)
USTA........... Union Sindical de Trabajadores de Arequipa [*Arequipa Labor Union Group*] [*Peruvian*] (LA)
USTA........... Union Syndicale des Travailleurs Algeriens (MAR)
USTA........... Universities of Science and Technology of Algiers
ustar........... Obsolete [*Lexicography*] (RU)
USTARCH SAV ... Ustav Stavebnictva a Architektury SAV [*Construction and Architecture Institute of the Slovak Science Academy*] (CZ)
USTB........... Union Syndicale des Travailleurs du Burundi (MAR)
Ust BIB........ Charter of the Bulgarian Investment Bank (BU)
USTC........... Unitatea de Supraveghere si Terapie Intensiva a Coronarienilor [*Unit for Observation and Intensive Therapy of Coronary Patients*] (RO)
USTC........... United States Trading Company (MAR)
USTD........... Union Sportive des Tireurs de Dakar (MAR)
UStDB......... Umsatzsteuerdurchfuehrungsbestimmung [*Implementing Regulation for Turnover Tax*] (EG)
UStG........... Umsatzsteuergesetz [*Turnover Tax Law*] [*German*] (WEN)
USTIA.......... Union de Sindicatos de Trabajadores de Industrias Alimenticias [*Food Industry Labor Union Group*] [*Uruguayan*] (LA)
USTL........... Union Syndicale des Travailleurs Libres [*Trade Union of Free Workers*] [*Moroccan*] (AF)
USTM.......... Union Senegalaise de Transports Maritimes (MAR)
USTN........... Union des Syndicats des Travailleurs du Niger [*Federation of Labor Unions of Niger*] (AF)
USTO........... Universities of Science and Technology of Oran [*Algerian*]
USTOC........ Unitatea de Servicii Tehnice pentru Obiective in Constructie [*Technical Services Unit for Projects under Construction*] (RO)
USTOM....... Union Syndicale des Transport d'Outre-Mer (MAR)
USTPM........ Union Syndicale des Travailleurs et Paysans Malgaches (MAR)
USTSTP...... Union Syndicale des Travailleurs de Sao Tome et Principe (MAR)
USTT........... Union Syndicale des Travailleurs Tunisiens (MAR)
USTV........... Union Syndicale des Travailleurs Voltaiques [*Voltan Workers Trade Union Federation*] (AF)
Ust'-Vymlag ... Ust'-Vym' Corrective Labor Camp (RU)
USU............. Percussion Drilling Device (RU)
USU............. Union Sindical del Uruguay [*Union Association of Uruguay*] (LA)
USU............. Uplne Strediskove Ucetnictvi [*Complete Central Accounting*] (CZ)
USU............. Ustredni Socialni Ustav [*Central Social Welfare Institute*] (CZ)
USUAA........ University Students Union of Addis Ababa [*Ethiopian*] (AF)
USUCA........ United Steelworkers Union of Central Africa [*Rhodesian*] (AF)
USUD.......... University Students' Union of Dar Es Salaam [*Tanzanian*] (AF)
USUMA....... Union des Superieures Majeures du Burundi (MAR)
USUS........... Uniunea Sindicatelor din Unitatile Sanitare [*Union of Trade Unions in Health Units*] (RO)
USV............. Ustredni Spravni Vybor [*Central Administrative Committee*] (CZ)
USVA........... Directorate of the Soviet Military Administration (RU)
USVAB........ Ustredni Svaz Ceskoslovenskych Vynalezcu a Badatelu [*Central Union of Czechoslovak Investors and Researchers*] (CZ)
USVAG........ Directorate of the Soviet Military Administration in Germany (RU)
USVCh........ Superhigh-Frequency Amplifier (RU)
USVH........... Ustredni Sprava Vodniho Hospodarstvi [*Central Administration for Water Utilization*] (CZ)
USVO........... Statute of the Council for the Mutual Insurance of Members of Labor Productive Cooperatives (BU)
USVPS........ Administration of Through Sleeping Cars (RU)
USVR........... Administration of Construction and Reconstruction Work (RU)
USVU........... Ustredni Statni Veterinarni Ustav [*State Central Veterinary Institute*] (CZ)
usw............. Und So Weiter [*And So Forth*] [*German*] (GPO)
USW............. Urzad do Spraw Wyznan [*Office of Religious Denominational Affairs*] (POL)
USWAP....... United South West Africa Party (MAR)
USWU.......... Uganda Sugar Workers Union (AF)
USYM.......... Universitelerarasi Ogrenci Secme ve Yerlestirme Merkezi [*Inter-University Student Selection and Placement Center*] (TU)
USZ............. Ucnovske Skoly Zemedelske [*Agricultural Apprentice Schools*] (CZ)
USZD........... Ustredni Svaz Zemedelskych Druzstev [*Central Union of Agricultural Cooperatives*] (CZ)
USZH........... Ustredni Svaz Zamestnancu v Hornictvi [*Central Union of Employees in the Mining Industry*] (CZ)
USZNO........ Ustredni Svaz Zidovskych Nabozenskych Obci [*Central Union of Jewish Religious Congregations*] (CZ)
USZO........... Ustredni Socialni a Zamestnanecke Oddeleni [*Central Department for Social and Employee Relations*] (CZ)
USZRP........ Administration of Shipyards of River Steamship Lines (RU)
UT............... General-Purpose Refractory (Lubricant) (RU)
UT............... Percussion Primer (RU)
ut................ Specific Heat (RU)
UT-.............. Trainer (Aircraft) (RU)
UT............... Uciteljska Tiskarna [*Teachers' Printing House*] [*Ljubljana*] (YU)
UT............... Union Tchadienne (MAR)
UT............... Union Tradicionalista [*Traditionalist Union*] [*Spanish*] (WER)
UT............... Unite Togolaise [*Togolese Unity Party*] (AF)
UT............... Unite de Traffic (MAR)
UT............... Universidad del Tolima [*Ibague*] (COL)
UT............... Universite Technique [*Technical University*] [*Replaced UTRK*] [*Cambodian*] (CL)
UT............... Uniwersytet w Toruniu [*Torun University*] (POL)
UT............... Urzad Telekomunikacyjny [*Telecommunications Office*] (POL)
ut................ Utalvany [*Sent by Postal Order*] (HU)
ut................ Utasitas [*Directive*] (HU)
ut................ Utca [*Street*] [*Hungarian*] (CED)
UT............... Uusi Testamentti [*Finnish*]
UTA............. Ukrainian News Agency (RU)
UTA............. Union Trading Afrique (MAR)
UTA............. Union de Transports Aeriens [*Air Transport Union*] [*French*] (WER)
UTA............. Union Transviarios Automotor [*Motor Transport Workers Union*] [*Argentine*] (LA)
UTAA........... Union de Trabajadores Azucareros de Artigas [*Artigas Sugar Workers Union*] [*Uruguayan*] (LA)
UTAC........... Union de Transporteurs Agrees de Casablanca et de Sa Region (MAR)
UTAC........... Union Tunisienne de l'Artisanat et du Commerce [*Tunisian Artisans and Merchants Association*] (AF)
UTAE........... Union de Trabajadores Arroceros del Este [*Uruguayan Rice Workers Union*] (LA)
UTAF........... Union des Travailleurs Algeriens en France (MAR)
UTAG........... University Teachers Association of Ghana (MAR)
UTAIM......... Union Tunisienne d'Aide aux Insuffisants Mentaux (MAR)
UTAM.......... Ustav Teoreticke a Aplikovane Mechaniky [*Institute of Theoretical and Applied Mechanics (of the Czechoslovak Academy of Sciences)*] (CZ)
utanny......... Utannyomas [*Reprint*] (HU)
UTAP........... Air Training Regiment (RU)
UTAPITI...... Baraza la Taipa la Utapiti wa Sayansi [*Tanzanian*]
UTAPV........ Three-Phase Automatic Recloser (RU)
UTB............. Union Togolaise de Banque [*Togolese Banking Union*] (AF)
UTB............. Union de Trabajadores de Bauca [*Union of Bauca Workers*] [*Spanish*] (WER)
UTB............. Union des Travailleurs du Burundi [*Burundi Workers Union*] (AF)
UTB............. Uzina Tractorul Brasov [*Brasov Tractorul Enterprise*] (RO)
UTC............. Uganda Transport Company (MAR)
UTC............. Unidad Tactica de Combate [*Tactical Combat Unit*] [*Venezuelan*] (LA)
UTC............. Union Technique et Commerciale (MAR)
UTC............. Union Tennis-Club (MAR)
UTC............. Union Togolaise de Constructions et de Travaux Publics (MAR)
UTC............. Union de Trabajadores Campesinos [*Agricultural Workers' Union*] [*Salvadoran*] (PD)
UTC............. Union de Trabajadores de Colombia [*Colombia Workers Union*] (LA)
UTC............. Union Trading Cameroun SA (MAR)
UTC............. Union Trading Company Ltd. (MAR)
UTC............. Union des Travailleurs des Comores (MAR)
UTC............. Union des Travailleurs Congolais (MAR)
UTC............. United Touring Company (MAR)
UTC............. Uniunea Tineretului Comunist [*Union of Communist Youth*] (RO)
UTCAP........ Union de Trabajadores del Cemento y Afines de Panama [*Panamanian Union of Cement and Related Workers*] (LA)
UTCC........... Unio de Treballadors Cristians de Cataluna [*Christian Workers Union of Catalonia*] [*Spanish*] (WER)
UTCGA........ Union Tunisienne de la Confederation Generale de l'Agriculture (MAR)
UTCh........... Ustav Technicke Chemie [*Institute of Applied Chemistry*] [*Usti Nad Labem*] (CZ)
UTCL........... Union des Travailleurs Communistes Libertaires [*Union of Libertarian Communist Workers*] [*French*] (PPW)
UTCPR........ Union de Trabajadores de la Corporacion Panamena de Radiodifusion [*Workers Union of the Panamanian Radiobroadcasting Corporation*] (LA)
UTD............. Uredba o Trgovinskoj Delatnosti i Trgovinskim Preduzecima i Radnjama [*Decree on Commercial Operations Establishments and Shops*] (YU)
UTD............. Ustav Technickeho Dozoru [*Technical Control Institute*] (CZ)

ut dict .... Ut Dictum [*As Directed*] [*Latin*] (GPO)
UTDN .... Union des Transitaires du Dakar-Niger (MAR)
UTE .... Administracion General de las Usinas Electricas y los Telefonos del Estado [*General Administration of State Electric Power and Telephones*] [*Uruguayan*] (LA)
UTE .... Union de Trabajadores del Este [*Uruguayan Workers Union*] (LA)
UTE .... Universidad Tecnica del Estado [*State Technical University*] [*Chilean*] (LA)
UTEG .... Union de Trabajadores de la Ensenanza Gallega [*Union of Galician Educational Workers*] [*Spanish*] (WER)
UTEIN .... Ustav pro Technickou a Ekonomickou Informace [*Institute for Technical and Economic Information*] [*Prague*] (CZ)
UTEK .... Junction Office for Transportation and Forwarding Operations (RU)
UTEKh .... Administration of Fuel and Power System Managment (RU)
UTERPRA .... Urusan Teritoriil dan Perlawanan Rakjat [*Territorial Affairs and People's Resistance*] (IN)
UTESA .... Universidad Tecnologica de Santiago [*Technological University of Santiago*] [*Dominican Republic*] (LA1)
UTEX .... Union Textile Marocaine (MAR)
UTEX .... Union Transafricaine d'Expansion Industrielle et Commerciale (MAR)
UTEX .... Ustecky Textilni Zavod [*Textile Mills in Usti Nad Labem*] (CZ)
UTEXI .... Union Textile Industrielle de Cote-d'Ivoire [*Ivory Coast Textile Industry Union*] (AF)
UTF .... Union de Trabajadores Ferrocarrileros [*Railroad Workers Union*] [*Salvadoran*] (LA)
UTF .... Union des Transporteurs de Ferkessedougou (MAR)
UTF .... Uridine Triphosphate (RU)
UTF .... Ustav Technicke Fysiky [*Institute of Applied Physics (of the Czechoslovak Academy of Sciences)*] (CZ)
UTG .... Mining Goniometer-Tachometer (RU)
UTG .... Union de Trabajadores de Golfito [*Golfito Workers Union*] [*Costa Rican*] (LA)
UTGU .... Ukhta Territorial Geological Administration (RU)
UTH .... Union Touristique et Hoteliere [*Hotel and Tourist Union*] (CL)
UTH .... University Teaching Hospital (MAR)
UTHD .... Ustav Technicke a Hospodarske Dokumentace [*Institute for Technical and Economic Documentation*] (CZ)
UTHK .... Ustav pro Technologii Hrube Keramiky [*Technical Institute for Industrial Ceramics*] (CZ)
UTI .... Trainer Fighter Aircraft (RU)
UTI .... Union Technique Interfederale (MAR)
UTIA CSAV ... Ustav Teorie Informace a Automatizace CSAV [*Institute of Information Theory and Automation of the Czechoslovak Science Academy*] (CZ)
UTIC .... Union Tunisienne de l'Industrie et du Commerce [*North African*] (MAR)
UTICA .... Union Tunisienne de l'Industrie, du Commerce, et de l'Artisanat [*Tunisian Union for Industry, Trade, and Crafts*] (AF)
UTIM .... Trade Administration of the Executive Committee of the Mosoblsovet (RU)
UTIMACO ... Centrale Mecanographique [*Moroccan*] (MAR)
UTINA .... Union Technique Nord-Africaine [*Moroccan*] (MAR)
UTIP .... Unidades de Terapia Intensiva Pediatrica [*Pediatric Intensive Care Units*] [*Cuban*] (LA1)
UTJ .... Union Tunisienne de la Jeunesse [*Tunisian Youth Union*] (AF)
UTK .... Ugostiteljsko-Turisticka Komora [*Chamber of Hotel and Catering and Tourist Trade*] (YU)
UTK .... Ukase on the Merchant Marine in the Bulgarian People's Republic (BU)
UTK .... "Unitas" Tvornica Konca [*"Unitas" Thread Factory*] [*Zagreb*] (YU)
UTK .... University of the Workers of China Imeni Sun Yat-Sen (RU)
UTK .... Ustredna Technicka Kniznica [*Central Technical Library*] [*Bratislava*] (CZ)
UTK .... Ustredni Technicka Knihovna [*Central Technical Library*] [*Prague*] (CZ)
UTK .... Ustredni Technicka Komise [*Central Technical Commission*] (CZ)
UTL .... Ustav Telovychovneho Lekarstvi [*Institute for the Study of Medicine (with regard to physical education)*] (CZ)
UTLS .... Union des Travailleurs Libres du Senegal (MAR)
UTM .... General-Purpose Refractory Frost-Resistant (Lubricant) (RU)
UTM .... Unevangelized Tribes Mission (MAR)
UTM .... Union Trading Monaco (MAR)
UTM .... Union des Travailleurs Marocains [*Union of Moroccan Workers*] (AF)
UTM .... Union des Travailleurs de Mauritanie [*Workers Union of Mauritania*] (AF)
UTM .... Union des Travailleurs de Mayotte [*Comoran*] (PD)
UTM .... Uniunea Tineretului Muncitor [*Union of Working Youth*] (RO)
UTMD .... Training Antitank Wooden Mine (RU)
UTMDB .... Training Antitank Wooden Briquette Mine (RU)
UTMZ .... Ural Turbomotor Plant (RU)
UTN .... Adjusting Voltage Transformer (RU)
UTN .... Universal Voltage Transformer (RU)
UTN .... Universidad Tecnica Nacional [*National Technical University*] [*Argentine*] (LA)
UTO .... United Towns Organisation [*See also FMVJ*] (EA)
UTO .... Universidad Tecnica de Oruro [*Technical University of Oruro*] [*Bolivian*] (LA)
UTOK CSAV ... Ustav pro Tvorbu a Ochranu Krajiny CSAV [*Institute for Care and Protection of Natural Environment, Czechoslovak Science Academy*] (CZ)
UTONA .... Uniao dos Trabalhadores e Operarios Negros de Angola (MAR)
utosz .... Utoszo [*Postscript, Epilogue, Conclusion*] (HU)
UTP .... Fuel Industry Administration (RU)
UTP .... Ucilista Telesne Pripravy [*Physical Education School*] (CZ)
UTP .... Union de Titres et de Participants (MAR)
UTP .... Union Togolaise Parti (MAR)
UTP .... United Tanganyika Party (MAR)
UTP .... Universite Technique et Populaire [*People's Technical University*] [*Cambodian*] (CL)
UTP-France ... Materiaux de Soudure (MAR)
UTR .... Labor Reserves Administration (BU)
UTR .... Union des Travailleurs du Rwanda (MAR)
UTR .... Universite Technique Royale Khmere [*Cambodian Royal Technical University*] [*Use UTRK*] (CL)
UTRABO ..... Union de Trabajadores Boyacenses [*Boyaca Workers Union*] [*Colombian*] (LA)
UTRACAL ... Union de Trabajadores Caldenses [*Manizales*] (COL)
UTRACh ...... Union de Trabajadores de Chile [*Union of Chilean Workers*] (LA)
UTRACO ..... Union des Transporteurs Routiers et Camionneurs de l'Oubangui-Chari (MAR)
UTRACUN ... Union de Trabajadores de Cundinamarca [*Cundinamarca Workers Union*] [*Colombian*] (LA)
UTRAL .... Union de Trabajadores Agricolas de Limon [*Union of Limon Agricultural Workers*] [*Costa Rican*] (LA)
UTRAL .... Union de Trabajadores del Atlantico [*Atlantico Workers Union*] [*Colombian*] (LA)
UTRALLANO ... Union de Trabajadores de Llano [*Villavicencio*] (COL)
UTRAM .... Union des Transitaires et Agents Maritimes du Sine Saloum (MAR)
UTRAMIG .... Universidade do Trabalho de Minas Gerais [*Minas Gerais Labor University*] [*Brazilian*] (LA)
UTRAMMICOL ... Union de Trabajadores Metalurgicos y Mineros de Colombia [*Union of Metalworkers and Miners of Colombia*] (LA)
UTRAN .... Union de Trabajadores Antioquenos [*Antioquia Workers Union*] [*Colombian*] (LA)
UTRANCO ... Union Transports Cameroun-Oubangui (MAR)
UTRAQUINDIO ... Union de Trabajadores del Quindio [*Armenia*] (COL)
UTRASAN ... Union de Trabajadores de Santander [*Santander Workers Union*] [*Colombian*] (LA)
UTRATEXCO ... Union de Trabajadores Textiles de Colombia [*Textile Workers Union of Colombia*] (LA)
UTRATOL .... Union de Trabajadores del Tolima [*Ibague*] (COL)
UTRAVAL .... Union de Trabajadores del Valle [*Valle Workers Union*] [*Colombian*] (LA)
UTRK .... Universite Technique Royale Khmere [*Cambodian Royal Technical University*] [*Replaced by UT*] (CL)
UTS .... Agency Telephone Exchange (RU)
UTS .... General-Purpose Refractory Synthetic (Lubricant) (RU)
UTS .... Telephone Network Administration (RU)
UTS- .... Temperature Signaling Device (RU)
UTS .... Unified Teaching Service (MAR)
UTS .... Union Thoniere Senegalaise (MAR)
UTS .... Union Togolaise de Scierie (MAR)
UTS .... Union de Trabajo Sindical [*Labor Trade Union*] [*Spanish*] (WER)
UTS .... Union des Travailleurs Scientifiques [*Union of Scientific Workers*] [*French*] (WER)
UTS .... Union des Travailleurs du Senegal (MAR)
UTS .... Unit of Tropical Silviculture (MAR)
UTS .... Uprava Transportne Sluzbe [*Transport Service Administration*] (YU)
UTS .... Uredni Telefonni Seznam [*Official Telephone Directory*] (CZ)
UTS .... Usine des Tissus Synthetiques (MAR)
UTS .... Ustredni Televisni Studio [*Central Television Studio*] (CZ)
UTsBiPP ...... Administration of the Pulp, Paper, and Printing Industry (RU)
UTsGAL ...... Administration of the Central State Archives of Leningrad (RU)
UTSK .... Ustav Typisace Stavebnich Konstrukci [*Institute for Standardization of Structural Elements*] (CZ)
UTsM .... Control Digital Computer (RU)
UTsM .... Simplified Digital Computer (RU)
UTSM .... Ukrainian Trust of Agricultural Machinery (RU)
ut sup .... Ut Supra [*As Above*] [*Latin*] (GPO)
UTsVM .... General-Purpose Digital Computer (RU)
UTT .... Union de Tecnicos y Trabajadores del Metal [*Union of Technicians and Metalworkers*] [*Spanish*] (WER)
UTT .... Union des Travailleurs Tchadiens (MAR)
UTT .... Universal Current Transformer (RU)
UTTA .... United Taxis and Transport Association (MAR)
UTTC .... United Togo Trading Company (MAR)
UTTE .... Junta de los Usuarios del Telefono y la Telecomunicacion [*Union of Users of the Telephone and Telecommunications*] [*Spanish*] (WER)
UTTEFU ...... Utfenntarto Teherautofuvarozasi Vallalat [*Road Maintenance Truck Transportation Enterprise*] (HU)

UTU .... Office of Technical Services [*OTS*] (RU)
UTU .... Universal Telephone Repeater (RU)
UTU .... Universidad del Trabajo del Uruguay [*Labor University of Uruguay*] (LA)
UTUC .... Uganda Trade Union Congress (AF)
UTUC .... United Trade Union Congress (MAR)
UTUZ .... United Trade Unions of Zimbabwe (AF)
utv .... Approved (RU)
UTV .... Armored Troops Regulations (RU)
UTV .... General-Purpose Refractory Water-Resistant (Lubricant) (RU)
UTV .... Universal Slow-Speed Wind Motor (RU)
UTV .... Ustredni Technicky Vybor [*Central Technical Committee*] (CZ)
UTWU .... Uganda Textile Workers Union (AF)
UTWU .... United Textile Workers Union [*Rhodesian*] (AF)
UTZ .... Union Nationale des Travailleurs Zairois (MAR)
UTZ .... Union de Trabajadores del Zulia [*Zulia Workers Union*] [*Venezuelan*] (LA)
UU .... Control Unit [*Computers*] (RU)
UU .... Enlarger (RU)
UU .... Multiplexing Device (RU)
UU .... Undang-Undang [*Law*] (IN)
uU .... Unter Umstaenden [*Circumstances Permitting, Possibly, Perhaps*] [*German*] (WEN)
UU .... Uzlova Telefonni Ustredna [*Main Telephone Exchange*] (CZ)
UUA .... Ustredni Ustav Astronomicky [*Central Institute of Astronomy*] [*Prague*] (CZ)
UUAL .... Union de Universidades de America Latina [*Union of Latin American Universities*] (LA)
UUD .... Undang-Undang Dasar [*Constitution (National)*] (IN)
uud .... Uudismuodoste [*Finnish*]
UUDN .... Ukase on Awarding Dimitrov Prizes (BU)
uueV .... Unter Ueblichem Vorbehalt [*With the Usual Reservation*] (EG)
UUG .... Ustredni Ustav Geologicky [*Central Geological Institute*] [*Prague*] (CZ)
UUKI .... Utugyi Kutato Intezet [*Road Research Institute*] (HU)
UUM .... Standardized Controlling Device, Standardized Controller (RU)
UUMR .... Uzina de Utilaj Minier si Reparatii [*Plant for Mining Equipment and Repairs*] (RO)
UUN .... Ustredni Ucitelske Nakladatelstvi [*Central Teachers' Publishing House*] (CZ)
UUNZ .... Ustredni Ustav Narodniho Zdravi [*Central Public Health Institute*] (CZ)
UUP .... Uredba o Ugostiteljskim Preduzecima i Radnjama [*Decree on Hotel and Catering Enterprises and Shops*] (YU)
UUP .... Ustav Uzemniho Planovani [*Institute of Area Planning*] [*Brno*] (CZ)
UUP .... Ustredni Ustav Polarograficky [*Central Polarographic Institute*] [*Prague*] (CZ)
UUPO .... Uredba o Udruzivanju Privrednih Organizacija [*Decree on the Merger of Economic Organizations*] (YU)
UUPSMB ..... Uzina de Utilaje si Piese de Schimb Municipiul Bucuresti [*Bucharest Municipality Factory for Equipment and Spare Parts*] (RO)
UUR .... Register Control (RU)
UUR .... Turn Lead Angle (RU)
UUS .... Regulations on Criminal Legal Procedure (RU)
UUSF .... Uredba o Ustanovama sa Samostalnim Finansiranjem [*Decree on Self-Financing Institutions*] (YU)
UUTS .... Ukase on Establishing Length of Labor Service (BU)
UUUP .... United Ulster Unionist Party [*Northern Ireland*] (PPW)
uuV .... Unter Ueblicher Vorbehalt [*Errors and Omissions Excepted*] [*Business and trade*] [*German*]
UUVT .... Ukase on the Regulation of Internal Trade (BU)
UUZ .... Administration of Educational Institutions (RU)
UUZZ .... Ustredni Ustav Zeleznicniho Zdravotnictvi [*Central Institute of Railroads Health Services*] (CZ)
UV .... All-Purpose Fuze (RU)
UV .... Level Variometer (RU)
UV .... Moderate Air (RU)
UV .... Specific Gravity (RU)
UV .... Subtracter (RU)
UV .... Ultravioletni [*Ultraviolet*] (YU)
UV .... Ultraviolett [*Ultraviolet*] (EG)
UV .... Unione di Valdotaine [*Aostan Union*] [*Italian*] (WER)
UV .... Unite de Valeur [*Teaching Unit*] [*French*]
UV .... Universidad del Valle [*Cali*] (COL)
UV .... Uprava za Vodoprivredu [*Water Power Administration*] (YU)
Uv .... Uradny Vestnik [*Official Gazette (for Slovakia)*] [*A publication*] (CZ)
UV .... Ustredni Vybor [*Central Committee*] (CZ)
UV .... Utocna Vozba [*Assault Vehicles*] (CZ)
uv .... Uvod [*or Uvodni*] [*Introduction or Introductory*] (CZ)
UV .... Uzemi Vallalat [*Plant Marketing Department*] (HU)
UV .... Wind Angle (RU)
uva .... Und Viele Andere [*And Many Others*] [*German*]
UVA .... Ustredni Vojenska Akademie [*Central Military Academy*] (CZ)
UVA .... Uzina de Vagoane Arad [*Arad Railway Car Factory*] (RO)
UV-Anlage ... Ultrakurzwellen-Verkehrsfunkanlage [*VHF Two-Way Voice Communications System (Dispatcher Unit)*] (EG)
UVATERV .... Ut-Vasuttervezo Vallalat [*Road and Railroad Planning Enterprise*] (HU)
UVCh .... High-Frequency Amplifier (BU)
UVCh .... High-Frequency Amplifier (RU)
UVCh .... Ultrahigh Frequency (RU)
UVD .... Administration of Internal Affairs (RU)
UVD .... Flight Control (RU)
UVDP .... Improved Mobile Decontamination Apparatus (RU)
UVG .... Uprava za Vodno Gospodarstvo [*Water Power Administration*] (YU)
UVI .... Administration of the Military Publishing House (RU)
UVICAR .... Union des Villes de la Caraibe [*Union of Caribbean Towns*] (LA1)
UVKES .... Ustav pro Dalsi Vzdelavani v Kontrole, Evidenci, a Statistice [*Institute of Advance Education in Control, Reporting, and Statistics*] (CZ)
UVKh .... Administration of Water Management (RU)
UVKh- .... Chromatograph Computer Device (RU)
UVKI .... Wool and Silk Industry Administration (BU)
UVKSKhSH ... Ural Higher Communist Agricultural School (RU)
UVKU .... Ural Evening Communist University Imeni V. I. Lenin (RU)
UVM .... General-Purpose Computer (RU)
UVM .... Ustav Vyzkumu Materialu [*Materials Research Institute*] [*Prague*] (CZ)
UVMS .... Directorate of the Navy (RU)
UVMUZ .... Directorate of Naval Educational Institutions (RU)
UVMV .... Ustav pro Vyzkum Motorovych Vozidel [*Automotive Research Institute*] (CZ)
UVMV .... Ustav Vyzkumu Mechanisace Vyroby [*Research Institute for the Mechanization of Production*] (CZ)
UVN- .... High-Voltage Indicator (RU)
u-vo .... Device, Apparatus, Arrangement (RU)
UVO .... Ukrainian Military District (RU)
UVO .... Ural Military District (RU)
UVOCAM .... Union Voltaique des Cooperatives Agricoles et Maraicheres [*Voltan Union of Agricultural and Market-Gardening Cooperatives*] (AF)
UVOChTPK ... Ukase on Mutual Insurance of Members of Labor Productive Cooperatives (BU)
UVOD .... Ustredni Vedeni Domaciho Odboje [*Headquarters of the Domestic Resistance Movement*] (CZ)
UVOJM .... Ustav pro Vyzkum Optiky a Jemne Mechaniky [*Institute for Research in Optics and Precision Mechanics*] (CZ)
UVP .... Airport Administration (RU)
UVP .... Union pour la Vente des Produits [*Union for the Sale of Products*] [*French*] (WER)
UVP .... Unvollendete Produktion [*Unfinished Production*] (EG)
UVP .... Uprava Vazdusne Plovidbe [*Air Transport Administration*] (YU)
UVP .... Ustav pro Vyzkum a Vyuziti Paliv [*Institute for Research and Utilization of Fuels*] (CZ)
UVP .... Ustredni Vybor Propagacni [*Central Committee for Propaganda*] (CZ)
UVPD .... Altitude and Pressure Difference Indicator (RU)
UVPI .... Ul'yanovsk Evening Polytechnic Institute (RU)
UVPK .... Ustav pro Vyzkum a Pouziti Kovu [*Metal Research and Utilization Institute*] [*Prague*] (CZ)
UVPS .... Directorate of Wartime Military Construction (RU)
UVPS .... Ustav Vzdelavani Pracovniku ve Stavebnictvi [*Institute for Specialist Schooling in Construction*] (CZ)
UVPUFNRJ ... Udruzenje Vaspitaca Pretskolskih Ustanova Federativna Narodna Republika Jugoslavija [*Association of Teachers in Preschool Institutions of Yugoslavia*] (YU)
UVR .... Ungarische Volksrepublik [*Hungarian People's Republic*] (EG)
UVR .... Unit for Vacuum Dispersion (RU)
UVR .... Ustav pro Vyzkum Radiotechniky [*Research Institute for Radio Engineering*] (CZ)
UVR .... Ustav pro Vyzkum Rud [*Ore Research Institute*] [*Prague*] (CZ)
UVS .... Interior Service Regulations [*Military term*] (RU)
UVS .... Internal Service Regulations (BU)
UVS .... Umelecky Vojensky Soubor [*Military Artistic Ensemble*] (CZ)
UVS .... Ustav pro Vyzkum Stroju [*Machine Research Institute (of the Czechoslovak Academy of Sciences)*] (CZ)
UVS .... Ustredni Velitelske Stanoviste [*Central Command Post*] (CZ)
UVSB .... Ustredni Vybor Svazu Brannosti [*Central Committee of the Union for Military Preparedness*] (CZ)
uvsf .... Unverseifbar [*Nonsaponifiable*] [*German*]
UVSS .... Military Medical Service Regulations (RU)
UVT .... Coastal Water Transportation Statutes (BU)
UVT .... Uciliste Vojenske Telovychovy [*School of Military Physical Education*] (CZ)
UVT .... Ukopane Vatrene Tacke [*Intrenched Firing Points*] (YU)
UVT .... Umoja wa Vijana wa TANU [*TANU Youth League*] [*Tanzanian*] [*Use YL*] (AF)
UVT .... Union Voltaique de Transit (MAR)
UVT .... Water Transportation Administration (BU)
UVTA .... Ustav Vypocetni Techniky a Automatizace [*Institute for Measurement Techniques and Automation*] (CZ)
UVTBM .... Administration of Water Transportation of the Baltic Sea (RU)
UVTEI .... Ustredi Vedeckych, Technickych, a Ekonomickych Informaci [*Information Center for Science, Technology, and Economy*] (CZ)
UVTI .... Uprava za Vojno Tehnicka Istrazivanja [*Administration of Military Technical Research*] (YU)

UVTR.......... Ustredi Vyzkumu a Technickeho Rozvoje [*Research and Technological Development Center*] (CZ)
UVUMZ........ Administration of Higher Educational Institutions of the Ministry of Public Health, USSR (RU)
UVUPP........ Ustredni Vyzkumny Ustav Potravinarskeho Prumyslu [*Central Research Institute for Food Industry*] (CZ)
UVUZ.......... Directorate of Military Educational Institutions (RU)
UVV............ Input-Output Device (RU)
UVV............ Unfallverhuetungs-Vorschriften [*Accident Prevention Regulations*] (EG)
UVV............ Ustredie Vedeckeho Vyskumu [*Scientific Research Center*] (CZ)
UVV............ Ustredni Vykonny Vybor [*Central Executive Committee*] (CZ)
UVV............ Wartime Record [*Of military service*] (RU)
UVVL.......... Ustav pro Vyzkum Vyzivy Lidu [*Nutrition Research Institute*] (CZ)
UVVO.......... Ustav pro Vyzkum Vnitrniho Obchodu [*Domestic Trade Research Institute*] (CZ)
UVVP.......... Ustav pro Vedecky Vyzkum Paliv [*Fuel Research Institute*] (CZ)
UVVP.......... Ustav pro Vyzkum a Vyuziti Paliv [*Institute for Fuel Research and Utilization*] (CZ)
UVVS.......... Directorate of the Air Force (RU)
UVVT.......... Regulations on Inland Water Transportation of the USSR (RU)
UVVTR........ Ustredie Vedeckeho Vyskumu a Technickeho Rozvoja [*Science Research and Technological Development Center*] (CZ)
UVVUZ........ Directorate of Higher Military Educational Institutions (RU)
UVVVJNA.... Uprava za Vanarmisko Vojno Vaspitanje, Jugoslavenska Narodna Armija [*Administration for Military Training Outside the Army, Yugoslav People's Army*] (YU)
UVVVR........ Ustav pro Vyrobu, Vyzkum, a Vyuziti Radioizotopu [*Institute for Production, Research, and Use of Radioisotopes*] [*Prague*] (CZ)
UVZ............ Ural Railroad Car Plant (RU)
UVZ............ Ustredi Verejnych Zamestnancu [*Center of Public Employees*] (CZ)
UVZK.......... Ustredni Vybor Svazu Zamestnancu v Kovoprumyslu [*Central Committee of the Union of Employees in Metalworking Industries*] (CZ)
UVZN.......... Urad pro Vynalezy a Zlepsovaci Navrhy [*Office for Inventions and Improvement Suggestions*] (CZ)
UVZSO........ Ustredni Vybor Zamestnancu Skolstvi a Osvety [*Central Committee of Employees in Educational and Cultural Establishments*] (CZ)
UVZSS........ Ustredni Vybor Zamestnancu Skolske Sluzby [*Central Committee of Employees in Education*] (CZ)
UW.............. Uklad Warszawski [*Warsaw Treaty Organization*] [*Polish*]
Uw.............. Umstandswort [*German*]
UW.............. Uniwersytet Warszawski [*Warsaw University*] (POL)
UW.............. Uniwersytet Wroclawski [*Wroclaw University*] [*Polish*]
UW.............. Unterwerk [*Substation*] [*Electric power*] (EG)
uw.............. Uwaga [*Note*] (POL)
UWC............ Ukwashi Wa Chokwe (MAR)
UWC............ United Worker Congress [*Liberian*] (AF)
UWCL.......... United Worker Congress - Liberia (MAR)
UWD............ Urzedowy Wykaz Drukow [*Official Register of Publications*] (POL)
UWFPC........ Union Wallisienne et Futunienne pour la Caledonie [*Wallisian and Futunian Union for Caledonia*] (PPW)
UWI............ University of the West Indies (LA1)
UWK............ University of West Cape Province [*South African*] (AF)
UWO............ Ukrainska Wojskowa Organizacja [*Ukrainian Military Organization*] (POL)
UWP............ United Workers' Party [*St. Lucian*] (PPW)
UWP............ United Workers' Party [*Hungarian*] (PPW)
UWPF.......... Union of Working People's Forces (MAR)
UWR............ Upowszechnienie Wiedzy Rolniczej [*Popularization of Agricultural Science*] (POL)
UWSLF........ United Western Somali Liberation Front (AF)
UWT............ Umoja wa Wanawake wa Tanzania [*Women's Union of Tanzania*] (AF)
UWV............ Umleitungswege-Verzeichnis [*Index of Detours*] (EG)
ux.............. Uxor [*Wife*] [*Latin*] (GPO)
UY.............. Uruguay [*Two-letter standard code*] (CNC)
Uyg............ Uygulamali [*Applied*] (TU)
UZ.............. Contaminated Area (RU)
UZ.............. Delay System (RU)
UZ.............. Distributed Charge (RU)
UZ.............. Flood Danger [*Warning*] (RU)
UZ.............. Scientific Notes (RU)
UZ.............. Tender [*Maritime term*] (RU)
UZ.............. Ultrasonic (RU)
UZ.............. Ultrasound (RU)
UZ.............. Universitaet Zurich [*University of Zurich*] [*Swiss*]
uZ.............. Unter Zersetzung [*With Decomposition*] [*German*]
UZ.............. Uredba o Zemljarini [*Decree on Land Tax*] (YU)
UZ.............. Urxovy Zavody [*Urxa Plants*] (CZ)
UZ.............. Urzad Ziemski [*Polish*]
UZ.............. Ustavni Zakon [*Constitutional Law*] (YU)
Uz.............. Uzbek (RU)
UZA............ Antiaircraft Artillery Azimuth Circle (RU)
UZA............ Ultrasonic Unit (RU)
uza............ Uzemanyag [*Fuel*] (HU)
UZAP.......... Administration of the Protection of Authors' Rights (RU)
UZB............ Union Zairoise de Banques [*Zairian Banking Union*] (AF)
uzb............ Uzbek (RU)
Uzbeksel'mash... Uzbek Agricultural Machinery Plant (RU)
UZBER........ Uzletepitesi es Berendezo Vallalat [*Store Construction and Equipment Enterprise*] (HU)
UzbGU........ Uzbek State University Imeni Alisher Navoi (RU)
UzbSSR...... Uzbek Soviet Socialist Republic (RU)
UZCh.......... Audio Frequency Accelerator (RU)
UZD............ Dalton Law Equation (RU)
UZD............ Ultrasonic Diagnostic Apparatus (RU)
UZD............ Ultrasonic Flaw Detector (RU)
UZD............ Umetnostno Zgodovinsko Drustvo [*Society of Art History*] (YU)
UZDM.......... Equation of the Law of Mass Action (RU)
UZE............ Unia Zachodnio-Europejska [*West European Union*] (POL)
UZEMP........ Usluzno Zemjodelsko Masinsko Pretprijatie [*Agricultural Machinery Service Establishment*] (YU)
uzemvez..... Uzemvezeto [*Factory Manager*] (HU)
uZers.......... Unter Zersetzung [*With Decomposition*] [*German*]
UzFAN.......... Uzbekistan Branch of the Academy of Sciences, USSR (RU)
UZG............ Ultrasonic Generator (RU)
UzGIMEIN... Uzbekistan Hydrometeorological Institute (RU)
Uzgiz.......... Uzbek State Publishing House (RU)
UZGN.......... Rated Load Master Device (RU)
Uzgosizdat... Uzbek State Publishing House (RU)
Uzgosproyekt... Uzbek State Planning Institute (RU)
UZh............ Railroads Statutes (BU)
UZhD.......... Narrow-Gauge Railway (RU)
UZhGU........ Uzhgorod State University (RU)
UZhKh........ Housing Administration (RU)
uzhog.......... Neutralization Fire (BU)
UZhSP........ Ukase on Complaints, Signals, and Suggestions (BU)
UZII............ Ukrainian Correspondence Industrial Institute (RU)
UZIMO........ Uchenye Zapiski Instituta Mezhdunarodnykh Otnoshenii (MAR)
UZIP............ Uredba o Zajmovima za Investicije u Privredi [*Decree on Loans for Economic Investments*] (YU)
UZIV............ Scientific Notes of the Institute of Oriental Studies (of the Academy of Sciences, USSR) (RU)
UZJII............ Ured za Zastitu Jugoslovenske Imovine u Inostranstvu [*Office for the Protection of Yugoslav Property Abroad*] (YU)
UZK............ Delayed Channel Amplifier (RU)
UZK............ Ultrasonic Logging (RU)
UZK............ Ultrasonic Vibrations (RU)
UZK............ Ustredni Zemedelska Knihovna [*Central Agricultural Library (of the Czechoslovak Academy of Agricultural Sciences)*] (CZ)
UZK............ Ustredni Zemedelska Komise [*Central Agricultural Commission*] (CZ)
UZKhM........ Ural Heavy Chemical Machinery Plant (RU)
UZKU.......... Scientific Notes of the Kazan' University [*A publication*] (RU)
UzL.............. Ultrasonic Delay Line (RU)
UZLGU........ Scientific Notes of the Leningrad State University [*A publication*] (RU)
Uzm............ Uzman [*Specialist*] (TU)
UZMD.......... Ul'yanovsk Small Engine Plant (RU)
Uzmedgiz... State Medical Publishing House of the Uzbek SSR (RU)
UZMGPI...... Scientific Notes of the Moscow State Pedagogical Institute [*A publication*] (RU)
UZMGU........ Scientific Notes of the Moscow State University [*A publication*] (RU)
UZmolGU.... Scientific Notes of the Molotov State University [*A publication*] (RU)
UZMOPI...... Scientific Notes of the Moscow Oblast Pedagogical Institute [*A publication*] (RU)
UzNIIL.......... Uzbekistan Scientific Research Forest Institute (RU)
UzNIIPN...... Uzbek Scientific Research Institute of Pedagogical Sciences (RU)
UzNIIShP.... Uzbek Scientific Research Institute of the Silk Industry (RU)
UzNIIYaL..... Uzbekistan Scientific Research Institute of Language and Literature (RU)
UzNIIZh....... Uzbek Scientific Research Institute of Animal Husbandry (RU)
UzNIPI.......... Uzbek Scientific Research Pedagogical Institute (RU)
UzNIVI.......... Uzbek Scientific Research Veterinary Institute (RU)
UZNRBiH..... Ustavni Zakon Narodne Republike Bosne i Hercegovine [*The Constitution of Bosnia and Hercegovina*] (YU)
UZO............ United Zimbabwe Organization (AF)
UZOKh........ Reservations and Hunting Grounds Administration (RU)
UZpB.......... Amplifier of Pulses Recorded on a Magnetic Drum (RU)
UZPI............ Ukrainian Correspondence Polytechnic Institute (RU)
UZpL............ Amplifier of Pulses Recorded on a Magnetic Tape (RU)
UZR............ Uredba o Zanatskim Radnjama i Zanatskim Preduzecima [*Decree on Artisans' Shops and Enterprises*] (YU)
UZRG.......... Standardized Handgrenade Igniter (RU)
UZRT.......... Ultrasonic Resonance Thickness Gage (RU)
UZS-.......... Ultrasonic Seismograph (RU)
UZS............ Universal Tool Grinder (RU)
UZS............ Ustredni Zdravotnicka Sprava [*Central Health Administration*] (CZ)
UZSGU........ Scientific Notes of the Saratov State University (RU)
UZSS.......... Ufa Synthetic Alcohol Plant (RU)
UzSSR........ Uzbek Soviet Socialist Republic (RU)

UZT .... Ultrasonic Thickness Gauge (RU)
UzTAG .... Uzbek News Agency (RU)
UZTGPI .... Scientific Notes of the Tomsk State Pedagogical Institute [*A publication*] (RU)
UZTM .... Ural Heavy Machinery Plant Imeni Sergo Ordzhonikidze (RU)
UZTS .... Ul'yanovsk Plant of Heavy and Unique Machine Tools (RU)
UZTuvIYaLI ... Scientific Notes of the Tuvinian Institute of Language, Literature, and History [*A publication*] (RU)
UZU .... Storage Control, Memory Control (RU)
UZU .... Ustredni Zdravotnicky Ustav [*Central Medical Institute*] (CZ)
UZUS .... Guided-Missile Launcher (RU)
UZV .... Ustredi Zdravotnickeho Vyzkumu [*Health Research Center*] (CZ)
u zw .... Und Zwar [*That Is, Namely*] [*German*]
UZZ .... Uredba o Zemljoradnickim Zadrugama [*Decree on Agricultural Cooperatives*] (YU)
UZZPP .... Ukase on the Mandatory Insurance of Railway, Motor Vehicle, Water, and Air Transportation of Passengers and Personnel (BU)

V

V .... Accusative [*Case*] (RU)
V .... Calculation, Computation (RU)
v .... Century (BU)
v .... Century (RU)
V .... East, Eastern (RU)
V .... Great [*Toponymy*] (RU)
V .... High [*Bearing precision class*] (RU)
v .... Issue (RU)
V .... Miry [*Nature of bottom of a ford*] [*Topography*] (RU)
v .... Newspaper (BU)
v .... Peak (BU)
v .... Post Meridiem [*After Noon*] (RU)
V .... Quinque [*Five*] [*Latin*]
V .... Rectifier (RU)
v .... Sunrise (RU)
V .... Supreme (RU)
V .... Switch (RU)
V .... Upper [*Toponymy*] (RU)
V .... Usted [*You (Singular, formal)*] [*Spanish*]
v .... Vaegen [*Way*] [*Swedish*] (CED)
v .... Vagy [*Or*] (HU)
V .... Vale [*Bond, Promissory Note*] [*Spanish*]
V/ .... Valeur [*Value*] [*French*]
V .... Vallalat [*Enterprise*] [*Hungarian*] (CED)
v .... Valtozas [*Change, Changing*] (HU)
v .... Vease [*See*] [*Spanish*]
v .... Vedi [*See*] [*Italian*]
v .... Vegyes [*Mixed*] (HU)
v .... Vei [*Way*] [*Norwegian*] (CED)
v .... Vendeur [*Vendor*] [*French*]
V .... Venstre [*Liberal Party*] [*Norwegian*] (PPE)
V .... Venstre (Liberale Parti) [*Liberal Party*] [*Danish*] (PPE)
V .... Verbrennungslokomotive [*Internal Combustion Locomotive (Mainly diesel locomotives)*] (EG)
V .... Vergangenheit [*German*]
V .... Verkehr [*Traffic, Transportation*] (EG)
V .... Verlag [*Publisher*] [*German*]
V .... Vers [*Line, Verse*] (EG)
V .... Verse [*Verse*] [*German*]
v .... Versiculo [*Verse*] [*Spanish*]
v .... verso [*Left-Hand Page*] [*Latin*]
v .... Verst (RU)
v .... Versus [*Against*] [*Latin*] (GPO)
V .... Vertrag [*German*]
v .... Vezetek [*Line, Pipe*] (HU)
v .... Via [*Way*] [*Italian*] (CED)
v .... Vide [*See*] [*Latin*] (GPO)
V .... Viehzug [*Cattle Train*] (EG)
v .... Viz [*See*] (CZ)
V .... Vize- [*German*]
v .... Voce [*Voice*] [*Latin*] (GPO)
v .... Voir [*To See*] [*French*]
v .... Volt (BU)
v .... Volt [*Former, Formerly*] (HU)
V .... Volt [*Volt*] (EG)
v .... Volt (RU)
V .... Voltti [*or Volttia*] [*Finnish*]
V .... Volumen [*Volume*] (EG)
v .... Vom [*Of The, From The, By The*] (EG)
v .... Von [*Of, From, By*] [*German*] (GPO)
V .... Vorkommen [*Presence, Occurrence*] [*German*]
V .... Vormals [*Formerly*] [*German*]
V .... Vormittags [*In the Forenoon*] [*German*]
V .... Vorsitzender [*Chairman*] (EG)
v/ .... Vostra [*Your*] [*Italian*]
v/ .... Votre [*Your*] [*Correspondence*] [*French*]
v .... Vuonna [*Finnish*]
v .... Vuosi [*or Vuotta*] [*Year*] [*Finnish*] (GPO)
v .... Vuosina [*Finnish*]
v .... Vychod [*East*] (CZ)
v .... Watt (BU)
V .... Watykan [*Vatican City*] [*Polish*]
V .... Wolt [*Volt*] [*Polish*]
V .... Your, Yours (RU)
VA .... Air Army (RU)
VA .... Air Attack (RU)
VA .... Air Force, Air Army (BU)
VA .... Army Aviation (RU)
VA .... Automatic Altimeter (RU)
VA .... Enlightened Action [*South African*] (AF)
VA .... Herald of Asia [*A publication*] (RU)
VA .... Military Academy (BU)
VA .... Military Academy (RU)
VA .... Vacuum Unit (RU)
va .... Valiaikainen [*Finnish*]
Va .... Valuta [*Exchange Equivalent*] [*Banking*] [*German*]
va .... Vasutallomas [*Railroad Station*] (HU)
VA .... Vatican City [*Two-letter standard code*] (CNC)
VA .... Verlagsanstalt [*Publishing House*] [*German*]
VA .... Veterinarska Ambulanta [*Veterinary Ambulance*] (YU)
Va .... Vila [*Village*] [*Portuguese*] (NAU)
Va .... Villa [*Villa, Small Town*] [*Spanish*] (NAU)
Va .... Villa [*Villa*] [*Italian*] (NAU)
VA .... Vinylacetylene (RU)
va .... Vista [*Sight*] [*Banking*] [*Spanish*]
VA .... Vojenska Akademie [*Military Academy*] (CZ)
VA .... Vojna Akademija [*Military Academy*] (YU)
VA .... Volt-Ammeter (RU)
va .... Volt-Ampere (BU)
va .... Volt-Ampere (RU)
VA .... Voltampere [*Volt-Ampere*] (EG)
VA .... Voluntary Agency (MAR)
VA .... Vuestra Alteza [*Your Highness*] [*Spanish*]
VA .... Woltamper [*Volt-Ampere*] [*Polish*]
VAAC .... Verbond van Ambtenaren en Agenten in Congo (MAR)
vaap .... Vaapeli [*Finnish*]
VAAZ .... Vojenska Akademie Antonina Zapotockeho [*Antonin Zapotocky Military Academy*] (CZ)
VAB .... High-Speed Automatic Switch (RU)
VAB .... Versicherungsanstalt Berlin [*Berlin Insurance Company*] (EG)
VAB .... Voluntary Agencies' Bureau (MAR)
VABMV .... Military Academy of Armored and Mechanized Troops (RU)
VABTV .... Military Academy of Armored Troops (RU)
VACAP .... Vacances Cap-Skirring (MAR)
Vacie .... Vacherie [*Cow House*] [*Military map abbreviation*] [*World War I*] [*French*] (MTD)
VACOMBY ... Societe pour la Mise en Valeur et la Commercialisation du Betail Malgache (MAR)
VAD .... Military Highway (RU)
VAD .... Pressure Accumulator [*Jet engine*] (RU)
VAD .... Vadaszzaszloalj [*Rifle Battalion (Army), Fighter Battalion (Air Force)*] (HU)
VAD .... Vereinigte Arbeitnehmerpartei Deutschland [*United Employees' Party of Germany*] [*West German*] (PPW)
VAD .... Vereinigung der Afrikanisten in Deutschland (MAR)
VAD .... Vermogensaanwasdeling [*Excess Profits Sharing Bill*] [*Dutch*] (WEN)
v ad .... Vice Admiral (BU)
VADIZO .... All-Union Highway Correspondence Training Institute (RU)
VADZI .... All-Union Highway Correspondence Institute (RU)
vae .... Helicopter Aviation Squadron (BU)
VAF .... Military Academy Imeni Frunze (RU)
VAFOSZ ...... Vallalati Alkalmazottak Fogyasztasi Szovetkezete [*Consumers' Cooperative of Business Employees*] (HU)
VAFP .... All-African Trade-Union Federation [*AATUF*] (RU)
VAFP .... Vseafrikanskaia Federatsiia Profsoiuzov (MAR)
vag .... Railroad Car Plant [*Topography*] (RU)
Vag .... Vagon [*Railway Car*] (TU)
Vage .... Village [*Village*] [*Military map abbreviation*] [*World War I*] [*French*] (MTD)
VAGO .... All-Union Astronomical and Geodetic Society (RU)
VAGT .... All-Union Aerogeological Trust (RU)

VAGVF .... All-Union Academy of the Civil Air Fleet (RU)
VAh .... Woltamperogodzina [*Volt-Ampere-Hour*] [*Polish*]
VAI .... All-Russian Association of Engineers [*1919-1926*] (RU)
VAI .... All-Union Arctic Institute (RU)
VAI .... All-Union Association of Engineers [*1926-1929*] (RU)
VAI .... Herald of Archaeology and History [*A publication*] (RU)
VAI .... Military Motor Vehicle Inspection (RU)
VAI .... Military Motor Vehicle Inspectorate (BU)
VAI .... Vakok Allami Intezete [*State Institute for the Blind*] (HU)
VAIZ .... All-Russian Association of Inventors (RU)
VAJNA .... Vojna Akademija Jugoslovenske Narodne Armije [*Military Academy of the Yugoslav People's Army*] (YU)
VAK .... High Arbitration Commission (RU)
VAK .... High Degree Commission (RU)
VAK .... Higher Academic Courses (RU)
VAK .... Higher Certification Commission (BU)
VAK .... Military Administrative Committee [*Chinese People's Republic, 1949-1952*] (RU)
vak .... Vakinainen [*Finnish*]
Vak .... Vakuum [*Vacuum*] [*German*]
vak .... Vakuutustoiminta [*Insurance*] [*Finnish*]
VAK .... Volkhov Aluminum Kombinat (RU)
Vak Exs ...... Vakuumexsikkatur [*Vacuum Desiccator*] [*German*]
VAKh .... All-Russian Academy of Arts (RU)
VAKh .... Volt-Ampere Characteristic (RU)
VAKhZ .... Military Academy of Chemical Defense (RU)
VAKK .... Intrapharmaceutical Quality Control (BU)
VAKL .... International Confederation of Free Trade Unions - ICFTU [*Finnish*] (WEN)
VAKOT .... All-Ukrainian Joint-Stock Trading Company (RU)
VAKSA .... Vakbondraad van Suid-Afrika [*Trade Union Council of South Africa*] [*Use TUCSA*] (AF)
VAKSTO ..... High Arbitration Commission at the Council of Labor and Defense (RU)
VAKT .... All-Union Battery and Cell Industry Trust (RU)
VAKUS .... Vypocetni a Kontrolni Ustredna Spoju (Prague) [*Communications Computation and Control Center established 21 March 1963*] [*Branch in Bratislava*] (CZ)
Val .... Vaasan Laani [*or Vaasan Laania*] [*Finnish*]
val .... Valeur [*Value*] [*French*]
val .... Valine (RU)
Val .... Valuta [*Exchange Equivalent*] [*Banking*] [*German*]
VAL .... Viomikhania Azotoukhon Lipasmaton [*Nitrogenous Fertilizers Company*] [*Greek*] (GC)
VALCO .... Volta Aluminium Company Ltd. (MAR)
VALDIRIDA ... Confecciones Valdiri Ltda. [*Bogota*] (COL)
valiotkand ... Valtiotieteen Kandidaatti [*Finnish*]
ValK .... Valtiotieteen Kandidaatti [*Finnish*]
valok .... Valokuvaus [*Photography*] [*Finnish*]
VALOR .... Societe de Vente d'Aciers Lorrains (MAR)
Valpo .... Valtiollinen Poliisi [*State Police*] [*Finnish*] (WEN)
valtiotKand ... Master's Degree in Social Sciences [*Finnish*]
valtiotlis ...... Valtiotieteen Lisensiaatti [*Finnish*]
valtiotmaist ... Valtiotieteen Maisteri [*Finnish*]
valtiottri ...... Valtiotieteen Tohtori [*Finnish*]
VAM .... Verwaltung des Vermoegens der Auslaendischen Mineraloelgesellschaften [*Administration of the Assets of Foreign Petroleum Companies*] (EG)
VAM .... World Assembly of Youth [*WAY*] (RU)
VAMI .... All-Union Institute of Aluminum and Magnesium (RU)
VAMM .... Military Academy of Mechanization and Motorization (RU)
VAMU .... Higher School of Aeromechanics (RU)
VAN .... All-Union Association of Naturalists (RU)
VAN .... Artesian Screw Pump (RU)
VAN .... Herald of the Academy of Sciences, USSR [*A publication*] (RU)
VAN .... Vereniging van Archivarissen in Nederland
VAN .... Vorlaeufige Arbeitsnorm [*Tentative Work Norm*] (EG)
vanh .... Vanhahtava [*Finnish*]
vanh .... Vanhempi [*Finnish*]
vanh .... Vanhentunut [*Archaic, Obsolete*] [*Finnish*]
VANO .... All-Union Scientific Architectural Society [*1930-1932*] (RU)
vanr .... Vanrikki [*Finnish*]
VAO .... All-Union Joint-Stock Company (RU)
vao .... Helicopter Aviation Detachment (BU)
VAO .... State All-Union Association of the Aircraft Industry (RU)
VAOSZ .... Varosi, Varmegyei, es Kozsegi Alkalmazottak Orszagos Szovetsege [*National Association of City, County, and Village Employees*] (HU)
VAP .... Aircraft Spray Tank, Aircraft Spray Apparatus (RU)
vap .... Helicopter Aviation Regiment (BU)
VAP .... Vysotnaia Asuanskaia Plotina (MAR)
VAPI .... All-Union Agricultural Pedagogical Institute (RU)
VAPM .... All-Russian Association of Proletarian Musicians (RU)
VAPP .... All-Russian Association of Proletarian Writers (RU)
VAPP .... All-Union Association of Proletarian Writers (RU)
VAPSIE .... Volunteers' Association for the Promotion of Small-Scale Industries in Ethiopia (MAR)
VAR .... Vanguarda Armada Revolucionaria [*Armed Revolutionary Vanguard*] [*Brazilian*] (LA)
VAR .... Vanguardia Armada Revolucionaria [*Armed Revolutionary Vanguard*] [*Chilean*] (LA)
VAR .... Vereinigte Arabische Republik [*United Arab Republic (UAR)*] (EG)
VAR .... Vintage Austin Register (EA)
VAR .... Vrij Anti-Revolutionaire Partij [*Free Anti-Revolutionary Party*] [*Dutch*] (PPE)
VAR .... Vuestra Alteza Real [*Spanish*]
VARA .... Vereniging van Arbeiders Radio Amateurs [*Workers Radio Amateurs Association*] [*Dutch*] (WEN)
VARA .... Villages Agricoles de la Revolution Agraire (MAR)
VARAT .... All-Union Association of Workers--Authors of Technical Literature (RU)
varat .... Varatuomari [*Finnish*]
VAREM .... Military Mobile Repair and Maintenance Shop (RU)
VArh .... Warogodzina [*Varhour*] [*Polish*]
variats .... Variation (RU)
VARIG .... Viacao Aerea Rio-Grandense [*Brazilian airline*]
VARNITSO ... All-Union Association of Workers of Science and Technology for Assistance to the Building of Socialism (RU)
vars .... Varsinainen [*Finnish*]
vars .... Varsinkin [*Especially*] [*Finnish*]
VARTEKS ... Varazdinska Tekstilna Industrija [*Varazdin Textile Industry*] (YU)
VARU .... Automatic Time Gain Control (RU)
VARZ .... Railroad Car Repair Plant (RU)
VARZ .... Second Automobile Repair Plant (RU)
VAS .... All-Russian Astronomical Union (RU)
VAS .... Departmental Automated System (BU)
VAS .... High Lawyers' Council (BU)
VAS .... Supreme Administrative Court (BU)
vas .... Vasarnap [*Sunday*] (HU)
vas .... Vasemmalla [*Finnish*]
VAS .... Voreio-Atlandiki Symfonia [*North Atlantic Treaty Organization*] (GC)
VASERT ...... Vastomegcikk Ertekesito Vallalat [*Trade Enterprise for Mass-Produced Ironware*] (HU)
VASh .... Military Aviation School (RU)
VAShL .... Military Aviation School for Pilots (RU)
VASI .... Higher Architectural and Construction Institute (RU)
VASKhNIL ... All-Union Academy of Agricultural Sciences Imeni V. I. Lenin (RU)
VASKUT ...... Vasipari Kutato Intezet [*Iron Industry Research Institute*] (HU)
Vasm Ei Es ... Vasmegyei Epitoipari Egyesules [*Building Industry Association of Vas County*] (HU)
VASNIC .... Vassiliadis-Nicolaidis (MAR)
VASNOS ..... Velika Antifasisticka Skupstina Narodnog Oslobodenja Srbije [*Great Anti-Fascist Assembly of the National Liberation of Serbia*] (YU)
VASO .... Motorized Medical Detachment (RU)
VASP .... Viacao Aerea Sao Paulo, SA [*Brazilian airline*]
vast .... Vastaavasti [*Finnish*]
vast .... Vastaus [*Finnish*]
vastak .... Vastakohta [*The Opposite Of*] [*Finnish*]
VAT .... All-Union Gas-Welding Trust (RU)
VAT .... Military Motor Transport (RU)
VAT- .... Tensometric Truck Scales (RU)
VAT .... Value-Added Tax [*Dutch*] (WEN)
VAT .... Vatican City [*Three-letter standard code*] (CNC)
VAT .... Volontaires de l'Aide Technique [*Technical Aid Volunteers*] [*French*] (AF)
VAT .... Voronezh Aviation Technicum (RU)
VATA .... World Association of Travel Agencies [*WATA*] (RU)
VATEKISZ ... Vasipari Tervezo es Kivitelezo KSZ [*Cooperative Enterprise for Planning and Production in the Iron Industry*] (HU)
VATI .... Military Motor Vehicle and Tractor Inspection (RU)
VATI .... Varostervezo Intezet [*City Planning Institute*] (HU)
VATO .... All-Union Association of the Automobile and Tractor Industry (RU)
Vatozapchast' ... All-Union State Association for the Production and Marketing of Automobile and Tractor Spare Parts and Components (RU)
VATS .... Military Air Transport Service [*MATS*] (RU)
VATU .... Military Aviation Technical School (RU)
VATUKI .... Vasuti Tudomanyos Kutato Intezet [*Railway Scientific Research Institute*] (HU)
VAU .... All-Ukrainian Pharmaceutical Administration (RU)
VAU .... All-Union Administration of Archives (RU)
VAU .... Higher Aviation School (RU)
VAU .... Military Aviation School (RU)
VAU .... Mobile Water Purifier (RU)
VAU .... Veterinarni Asanacni Ustav [*Veterinary Sanitation Institute*] (CZ)
VAV .... Verordnung ueber die Arbeitslosenversicherung [*Regulation Concerning Unemployment Insurance*] (EG)
VAV .... Villamos Allomasszerelo Vallalat [*Electric Power Station Engineering Enterprise*] (HU)
VAVT .... All-Union Academy of Foreign Trade (RU)
VAW .... Versuchsanstalt fuer Wasserbau, Hydrologie, und Glaziologie [*Laboratory of Hydraulics, Hydrology, and Glaciology*] [*Swiss*]
vaz .... Vazany [*Bound*] (CZ)
VAZ .... Venyukovskiy Fittings Plant (RU)

VAZ .... Volkhov Aluminum Plant (RU)
VB .... Diving Boat (RU)
VB .... Drum Switch (RU)
VB .... Head Water (RU)
VB .... Hydrologic Balance (RU)
Vb .... Mean Deflection (Probable) Error (RU)
VB .... Turkiye Vakiflar Bankasi [*Turkish Religious Trusts Bank*] (TU)
vb .... Ve Baskalar [*And Others*] [*Turkish*] (GPO)
vb .... Ve Benzeri [*And Similar, equivalent of Et Cetera*] (TU)
VB .... Vegrehajto Bizottsag [*Executive Committee*] (HU)
VB .... Velke Brno [*Greater Brno*] (CZ)
vb .... Verbessert [*Revised*] [*German*]
vb .... Verbi [*Verb*] [*Finnish*]
VB .... Verejna Bezpecnost [*Public Security (Police)*] (CZ)
VB .... Verlag fuer Bauwesen Berlin (VEB) [*Berlin Architectural Publishing House (VEB)*] (EG)
VB .... Verlagsbuchhandlung [*Publishing House*] [*German*]
VB .... Vertragsbediensteter [*German*]
VB .... Verwalteter Betrieb [*Administered Enterprise*] (EG)
VB .... Vilagbajnoksag [*World Championship*] (HU)
VB .... Viven Bessieres [*Type of grenade*] [*Military*] [*French*] (MTD)
VB .... Voelkischer Beobachter (MAR)
vb .... Weber (RU)
Vbb .... Verbindungen [*Compounds*] [*German*]
VBB .... Verlag fuer Buch- und Bibliothekswesen (VEB) [*Book and Library Publishing House (VEB)*] (EG)
VBC .... Vlaamse Bibliotheek Centrale
V Bd .... Vuestra Beatitud [*Spanish*]
VbE .... Vollbeschaeftigteneinheit [*Full Employment Unit*] (EG)
Vbf .... Verschiebebahnhof [*Classification Yard*] (EG)
Vbg .... Vorarlberg [*or Vorarlberger*] [*German*]
VBGO .... All-Union Grocery and Delicatessen Association (RU)
vb h .... Vegyesbizottsagi Hatarozat (A Magyarcsehszlovak Lakossagcsere Vegrehajtasara Alakult Vegyesbizottsag Hatarozata) [*Resolution of the Joint Commission (for the Implementation of the Hungarian-Czechoslovak Exchange of Population)*] (HU)
VBKD .... Verband Bildender Kuenstler Deutschlands [*League of Graphic Artists in Germany*] (EG)
VBKM .... Villamosberendezes es Keszulek Muvek [*Electrical Equipment and Appliance Works*] (HU)
VBL .... Dienstvorschrift fuer die Ermittlung der Betriebsleistungen [*Service Regulation for Determining Operational Performance*] (EG)
VBL .... Veterinary Bacteriological Laboratory (RU)
VBN .... Vereniging van de Belgische Nijverheid [*Federation of Belgian Industries*] (WEN)
VBO .... All-Union Botanical Society (RU)
VBogU .... Higher School of Theology (BU)
VBP .... Ammunition Supply Platoon (RU)
VBP .... Upper Sideband (RU)
VBPDCh .... Upper Sideband of Doppler Frequencies (RU)
vbrtr .... Armored Carrier Platoon (RU)
VBS .... Hungarian Bureau of Standardization (RU)
vbtr .... Armored Carrier Platoon (RU)
VBTs .... Waterproof, Shrinkproof Cement (RU)
VBV .... Verwaltung Banken und Versicherungen [*Administration of Banks and Insurance*] (EG)
VBVP .... Volga-Baltic Waterway (RU)
VBZ .... Verejna Bezpecnost na Zeleznici [*Railroad Police*] (CZ)
VBZ .... Vychodoceske Bavlnarske Zavody, Narodni Podnik [*East Bohemian Cotton Mills, National Enterprise*] (CZ)
VC .... St. Vincent [*Two-letter standard code*] (CNC)
v en c .... Valor en Cuenta [*Value Accounted For*] [*Business and trade*] [*Spanish*]
VC .... Vanguardia Comunista [*Communist Vanguard Party*] [*Venezuelan*] (LA)
VC .... Vatan Cephesi [*Fatherland Front*] (TU)
VC .... Vice-Consul [*Vice-Consul*] [*French*] (MTD)
vc .... Vicolo [*Lane*] [*Italian*] (CED)
VC .... Viet Cong (CL)
v/c .... Votre Compte [*French*]
v/c .... Vuelta de Correo [*Return Mail*] [*Spanish*]
VC .... Vyrobni Cislo [*Production Number, Serial Number*] (CZ)
VCA .... Vestnik Ceske Akademie Ved a Umeni [*Bulletin of the Czech Academy of Sciences and Arts*] [*A publication*] (CZ)
VCAC .... Vehicule de Combat Anti-Chars (MAR)
VCC .... Vychodoceske Cihelny [*East Bohemian Brick Works*] (CZ)
VCE .... Vychodoceske Elektrarny, Narodni Podnik [*East Bohemian Electric Power Works, National Enterprise*] (CZ)
VCG .... Societe Voltaique des Corps Gras (MAR)
VCG .... Vice Consul General [*French*] (MTD)
VCh .... High Frequency (BU)
VCh .... High Frequency (RU)
VCh .... High-Sensitive (Motion-Picture Film) (RU)
VCh .... Military Unit (RU)
v ch .... Part by Weight (RU)
VChIM .... High-Frequency Pulse Modulation (RU)
VChK .... All-Russian Extraordinary Commission for Combating Counterrevolution and Sabotage [*1917-1922*] (RU)
VChKLB .... All-Russian Extraordinary Commission for the Liquidation of Illiteracy (RU)
VChKLN .... All-Russian Extraordinary Commission for the Liquidation of Illiteracy (RU)
v Chr .... Vor Christus [*Before Christ (BC)*] [*German*] (GPO)
VChS .... High-Frequency Communications (RU)
VChS .... High-Frequency Seismic Exploration (RU)
VChS .... Supreme Union of Libraries (BU)
VChSS .... High-Frequency Seismic Station (RU)
VChV .... Velitelstvi Chemickeho Vojska [*Chemical Troops Headquarters*] (CZ)
VChZ .... Vychodoceske Chemicke Zavody Synthesia [*East Bohemian Chemical Factories*] (CZ)
VCI .... Vehicule de Combat de l'Infanterie (MAR)
Vclbr .... Vidi Clan Broj [*See Article Number*] (YU)
VCNO .... Vybor Ceskoslovenskeho Narodniho Odboje [*Committee of the Czechoslovak National Resistance Movement*] (CZ)
VCP .... Vetements et Chemiserie de Paris (MAR)
VCPOR .... Vanguardia Comunista del Partido Obrero Revolucionario [*Bolivian*] (PPW)
VCST .... Voros Csillag Traktorgyar [*Red Star Tractor Factory*] (HU)
VCSZ .... Vybor Ceskoslovenskych Zen [*Czechoslovak Women's Committee*] (CZ)
VCT .... St. Vincent [*Three-letter standard code*] (CNC)
VCT .... Vychodoceske Tiskarny [*East Bohemian Printing Works*] (CZ)
Vcte .... Vicomte [*Viscount*] [*French*] (MTD)
v/cte .... Votre Compte [*Your Account*] [*Business and trade*] [*French*]
VCU .... Association for Cultural Exchange [*Pro-Moscow*] [*Dutch*] (WEN)
VCZ .... Vybor Ceskych Zen [*or Vybor Ceskoslovenskych Zen*] [*Czech Women's Committee or Czechoslovak Women's Committee*] (CZ)
VD .... Air Depolarization (RU)
VD .... Airborne Force (RU)
vd .... East Longitude (RU)
Vd .... High Pressure (RU)
Vd .... Mean Range (Probable) Error (RU)
VD .... Military Road (RU)
Vd .... Usted [*You (Singular, formal)*] [*Spanish*]
Vd .... Vand [*Lake*] [*Norwegian*] (NAU)
VD .... Vasilevomeni Dimokratia [*Royalist Republic*] [*Greek*] (GC)
VD .... Vasilikon Diatagma [*Royal Decree*] (GC)
VD .... Vatrogasno Drustvo [*Firemen's Society*] (YU)
VD .... Vazduhoplovna Divizija [*Air Force Division*] (YU)
VD .... Velitelstvi Delostrelectva [*Artillery Headquarters*] (CZ)
VD .... Venous Pressure (RU)
VD .... Vertrauliche Dienstsache [*Confidential Matter*] (EG)
VD .... Vesnicke Divadlo [*Village Theater*] (CZ)
vd .... Von Der [*In Names*] [*German*]
VD .... Voreiodytikos (Anemos) [*Northwesterly (Wind)*] (GC)
Vd .... Vrsi Duznost [*Acting As*] (YU)
VD .... Vysadkova Divize [*Airborne Division*] (CZ)
vd .... Vzhodna Dolzina [*Eastern Longitude*] (YU)
vda .... Viuda [*Widow*] [*Spanish*]
VDA .... Volksbund fuer das Deutschtum im Ausland [*NAZI Germany*]
vdb .... Airborne Battalion (RU)
VDB .... Airborne Brigade (RU)
VDB .... Military Road Battalion (RU)
VDB .... Vrij Democratisch Bond [*Liberal Democratic Union*] [*Dutch*] (WEN)
VDB .... Vrijzinnige-Democratische Bond [*Radical Democratic League*] [*Dutch*] (PPE)
vdbr .... Airborne Brigade (BU)
VD Brno .... Vyvojove Dilny, Brno [*Development Workshops in Brno (of the Czechoslovak Academy of Sciences)*] (CZ)
VDC .... Village Development Committee (MAR)
VDCH .... Verein Deutscher Chemiker [*Association of German Chemists*] [*German*]
VDCK .... Volksverein Deutsch Canadischer Katholiken [*Association of German Canadian Catholics*]
VDD .... Airborne Division (RU)
vdd .... Vadaszdandar [*Fighter Plane Command (Two wings)*] (HU)
VDD .... Verein Deutscher Dokumentare
VDE .... Verband Deutscher Elektrotechniker [*Association of German Electrical Engineers*] (EG)
VDF .... Danube Navy Fleet (BU)
VDFZh .... All-Chinese Democratic Federation of Women (RU)
VDG- .... Glubshev Differential Water Gauge (RU)
VdgB .... Vereinigung der Gegenseitigen Bauernhilfe [*Peasant's Mutual Aid Association*] (EG)
VdgB(BHG) ... Vereinigung der Gegenseitigen Bauernhilfe (Baeuerliche Handelsgenossenschaft) [*Peasant's Mutual Aid Association (Peasant's Trade Cooperative)*] (EG)
VDI .... Herald of Ancient History [*A publication*] (RU)
VDI .... Verein Deutscher Ingenieure [*Association of German Engineers*] (WEN)
VDI .... Vestnik Drevnei Istorii [*A publication*] (MAR)
VDJ .... Verband der Deutschen Journalisten [*German Journalists' Association*] [*West German*] (WEN)
VDJD .... Vereinigung Demokratischer Juristen Deutschlands [*Union of Democratic Jurists of Germany*] (EG)

vdk .... Airborne Corps (RU)
vdk .... Airborne Corps (BU)
VDK .... Verband Deutscher Konsumgenossenschaften [*Association of German Consumer Cooperatives*] (EG)
VDK .... Vietnami Demokratikus Koztarsasag [*Democratic Republic of Vietnam*] (HU)
VDK .... Volga-Don Canal (RU)
VDK .... Vsegambiiskii Demokraticheskii Kongress (MAR)
VDK .... Vyrobne-Dispecerske Kancelare [*Production and Management Control Offices*] (CZ)
vdkch .... Water-Pumping Station [*Topography*] (RU)
vdkhr .... Reservoir (RU)
VDL .... Vojenske Dopravni Letectvo [*Military Transport Airforce*] (CZ)
vdm .... Ground Decontamination Platoon (RU)
VDM .... World Movement of Mothers [*WMM*] (RU)
VDNKh .... Exhibition of Achievements of the National Economy of the USSR (RU)
VDNT .... All-Union House of Folk Art Imeni N. K. Krupskaya (RU)
VDO .... Airborne Detachment (RU)
VDO .... Military Road Detachment (RU)
VDO .... Military Road Section (RU)
VDO .... Velkonakupni Druzstvo Obchodniku [*Merchants' Cooperative for Wholesale Buying*] (CZ)
VDO .... Vyrobne-Dispecersky Odbor [*Production and Management Control Department*] (CZ)
VDP .... Airborne Regiment (RU)
VDP .... High-Altitude Deformation Field (RU)
VDP .... Military Preinduction Training (RU)
VDP .... Mobile Decontamination Apparatus (RU)
VDP .... Portable Decontamination Equipment (BU)
VDP .... United Democratic Parties [*Surinamese*] (PD)
VDP .... Velkodistribucni Podnik [*Wholesale Distribution Enterprise*] (CZ)
VDP .... Velkodruzstevni Prodejny [*Wholesale Cooperative Sales Outlets*] (CZ)
VDP .... Velkonakupni Druzstevni Podniky [*Cooperative Enterprises for Wholesale Buying*] (CZ)
VDP .... Verband der Deutschen Presse [*German Press Association*] (EG)
VDP .... Verenigde Democratische Partijen [*United Democratic Parties*] [*Surinamese*] (PPW)
VDP .... Volga-Don Steamship Line (RU)
vdp .... Waterfall [*Topography*] (RU)
VDQS .... Vins Delimites de Qualite Superieure [*Tunisian*] (MAR)
vdr .... Airborne Company (RU)
VDR .... Vietnamska Demokraticka Republika [*People's Republic of Vietnam*] (CZ)
VdrevNITO ... All-Union Scientific, Engineering, and Technical Society of the Woodworking Industry (RU)
VDRO .... Internal Dobrudzha Revolutionary Organization (BU)
VDS .... Airborne Forces (RU)
Vds .... Ustedes [*You (Plural, formal)*] [*Spanish*]
VDS .... Verband Demokratischer Studenten [*Union of Democratic Students (Communist)*] [*Austrian*] (WEN)
VDS .... Verband Deutscher Studentenschaften [*Association of German University Student Organizations*] [*West German*] (EG)
VDS .... Vodohospodarska Sluzba [*Water Conservation Service*] [*Civil defense*] (CZ)
VDS .... Vseobecny Druzstevni Svaz [*General Cooperative Union*] (CZ)
VDSh .... Higher School of Diplomacy (RU)
VDSM .... Internationaler Verband der Stadt-, Sport-, und Mehrzweckhallen [*International Federation of City, Sport, and Multi-Purpose Halls*] (EA)
VDSO .... All-Union Voluntary Sports Society (RU)
VDU .... Verband Deutschsprachiger Uebersetzer Literarischer und Wissenschaftlicher Werke [*Association of German-Speaking Translators of Literary and Scientific Works*] [*West German*]
VdU .... Verband der Unabhaengigen [*League of Independents*] [*Dissolved, 1956*] [*Austrian*] (PPE)
Vduc .... Viaduc [*Viaduct*] [*Military map abbreviation*] [*World War I*] [*French*] (MTD)
VDV .... Airborne Troops (RU)
VDV .... Vojska Drzavne Varnosti [*State Security Army*] (YU)
VE .... Electric Fan (RU)
ve .... Helicopter Squadron (RU)
VE .... Vasiliki Enosis [*Royalist Union*] [*Greek*] (GC)
VE .... Venezuela [*Two-letter standard code*] (CNC)
VE .... Verrechnungseinheit [*Accounting Unit (Used in inner-German trade)*] (WEN)
VE .... Vodni Elektrarny [*Hydroelectric Plants*] (CZ)
VE .... Vojna Enciklopedija [*Military Encyclopedia*] (YU)
VE .... Vuestra Excelencia [*Your Excellency*] [*Spanish*]
VE .... Wind-Driven Electric Power Unit (RU)
VEA .... Viotekhnikon Epimelitirion Athinon [*Athens Chamber of Craftsmen*] (GC)
VEAB .... Volkseigener Erfassungs- und Aufkaufvertrieb [*State Procurement and Purchase Enterprise for Agricultural Products*] (EG)
VEAP .... Viomikhaniki Etaireia Ambelourgon Pafou [*Paphos Vinegrowers Industrial Company*] (GC)
VEB .... Volkseigener Betrieb [*State Enterprise*] (EG)
VEBA .... Vereinigte Elektrizitaets- und Bergwerks-AG [*United Electricity and Mining Corporation*] (EG)
vech .... PM [*in designation of time*] (RU)
VECh .... Secondary Frequency Standard (RU)
Vecheka .... All-Russian Extraordinary Commission for Combating Counterrevolution and Sabotage (RU)
VECOL .... Empresa Colombiana de Productos Veterinarios [*Colombian Veterinary Products Enterprise*] (LA)
VECOR .... Vanderbijl Engineering Corporation (MAR)
ved .... Vedelem [*Defense*] (HU)
vedr .... Vedrorende [*Concerning*] [*Danish*] (GPO)
Vee .... Vallee [*Valley*] [*Military map abbreviation*] [*World War I*] [*French*] (MTD)
VEETh .... Vasiliki Ethniki Enosis Thessalonikis [*National Royalist Union of Salonica*] (GC)
VEFRPA .... Vie Economique de la RAU et des Pays Arabes (MAR)
VEG .... Voithos Eparkhiakos Grammatevs [*Deputy District Secretary*] [*Cypriot*] (GC)
VEG .... Volkseigenes Gut [*State Farm*] (EG)
VEGEPHA ... Bureau d'Etudes et de Recherches sur les Matieres Premieres Vegetales (MAR)
Vegr ut .... Vegrehajtasi Utasitas [*Implementing Instruction*] (HU)
vegy .... Vegyes [*Mixed*] (HU)
vegz .... Vegzes [*Order*] (HU)
VEHIDELPA ... Vehiculos del Pacifico (COL)
VEI .... All-Union Electrotechnical Institute Imeni V. I. Lenin (RU)
VEI .... Vasilikon Ethnikon Idryma [*Royal National Foundation*] [*See also EI-VP*] (GC)
VEIKI .... Villamosenergiaipari Kutato Intezet [*Electric Power Industry Research Institute*] (HU)
VEK .... All-Union Power Engineering Committee (RU)
VEK .... Veterana Esperantista Klubo [*Esperantist Club of Veterans - ECV*] (EA)
VEK .... Volkseigenes Kombinat [*State Combine*] (EG)
VEKA .... Viomikhaniki Etaireia Kapnon Agriniou [*Agrinion Tobacco Industry Company*] [*Greek*] (GC)
VEKS .... Vectorcardioscope (RU)
Vel .... Great [*Toponymy*] (RU)
VELAZ .... Velkochov Laboratornich Zvirat [*Wholesale Breeding of Laboratory Animals*] (CZ)
VELDLS .... All-Union Experimental Laboratory of Dispersion Drugs (RU)
VELK .... Vereinigte Evangelisch-Lutherische Kirche [*United Evangelical-Lutheran Church*] (EG)
VELKD .... Vereinigte Evangelisch-Lutherische Kirche Deutschlands [*United Evangelical-Lutheran Church of Germany*] [*West German*] (WEN)
VELKSWA... Vereinigung Evangelisch-Lutherischer Kirchen Suedwestafrika [*Associated Evangelical Lutheran Church of South-West Africa*] [*Namibian*] (AF)
Vel MSD .... Velitelstvi Motostrelecke Divize [*Motorized Rifle Division Headquarters*] (CZ)
VELO-MOTO zavod ... Bicycle and Motorcycle Plant (BU)
Vel SR .... Velitelstvi Strelecke Roty [*Rifle Company Headquarters*] (CZ)
Vel TPR .... Velitelstvi Tankoveho Praperu [*Tank Headquarters Battalion*] (CZ)
VEM .... Elektromaschinenbau [*Electrical-Machine Construction (VVB)*] (EG)
VEM .... Vereinigte Evangelische Mission (MAR)
VEM .... Vjesnik Etnografskog Muzeja u Zagrebu [*Review of the Ethnographic Museum in Zagreb*] [*A publication*] (YU)
VEM-Betrieb ... Volkseigener Elektromaschinenbau Betrieb [*State Electrical Machine Building Enterprise*] (EG)
ven .... Venajaa [*or Venajaksi*] [*Finnish*]
ven .... Venalainen [*Finnish*]
VEN .... Venezuela [*Three-letter standard code*] (CNC)
VENALUM... Venezolana de Aluminios, CA [*Aluminum Company of Venezuela*] (LA)
VENFERCA ... Venezolana de Fertilizantes, CA [*Fertilizer Company of Venezuela*] (LA)
veng .... Hungarian (RU)
VenPK .... Venizelikon Phileleftheron Komma [*Venizelist Liberal Party*] [*Greek*] (PPE)
VENUS .... Viseur Ecartometrique de Nuit Stabilise (MAR)
VEO .... All-Union Electrotechnical Association (RU)
VEO .... All-Union Entomological Society (RU)
VEO .... All-Union Export Association (RU)
VEO .... Free Economics Society (RU)
VEO .... Supreme Economic Council (RU)
VEO .... Vasiliki Ethniki Organosi [*Royalist National Organization*] [*Greek*] (GC)
VEO .... Village Executive Officer (MAR)
VEO .... Vyzantini Ethniki Organosis [*Byzantine National Organization*] [*Greek*] (GC)
VEP .... Herald of the Electrical Equipment Industry [*A publication*] (RU)
VEP .... Military Evacuation Station (RU)
VEP .... Vasiliki Ethniki Parataxis [*National Faction of Royalists*] [*Greek*] (GC)
VEP .... Verbrauchsendpreis [*Retail Sales Price*] (EG)

VEP .... Vojno-Ekonomski Pregled [*Military Economic Review*] [*A periodical*] (YU)
VEPUAZO ... Vector Electrical Anti-Aircraft Fire Director (RU)
VER .... Vanguardia Estudiantil Revolucionaria [*Revolutionary Student Vanguard*] [*Peruvian*] (LA)
ver .... Verbessert [*Revised*] [*German*]
Ver .... Verein [*German*]
ver .... Vereinigt [*United*] [*German*]
Ver .... Verger [*Orchard*] [*Military map abbreviation*] [*World War I*] [*French*] (MTD)
Ver .... Verici [*Sending, Broadcasting*] (TU)
verachtl ...... Veraechtlich [*German*]
Verb .... Verband [*German*]
verb .... Verbessert [*Improved, Revised*] [*German*]
Verb .... Verbindung [*Compound*] [*German*]
Verbb .... Verbindungen [*Compounds*] [*German*]
verbr .... Verbraucht [*Consumed*] [*German*]
verb sap ...... Verbum (Satis) Sapienti [*A Word to the Wise Suffices*] [*Latin*] (GPO)
verd .... Verdeutscht [*Translated into German*] [*German*]
verd .... Verduennt [*Dilute, Diluted*] [*German*]
Verd .... Verduennung [*Dilution*] [*German*]
Verf .... Verfahren [*Process*] [*German*]
Verf .... Verfasser [*Author*] [*German*] (GPO)
Verfahr .... Verfahren [*Process*] [*German*]
Verff .... Verfahren [*Methods*] [*German*]
verg .... Vergoldet [*Gilt*] [*German*]
verg .... Vergriffen [*Suppressed*] [*German*]
Vergl .... Vergleich [*Compare, Confer, See, Refer*] [*German*]
vergr .... Vergroessert [*Enlarged, Magnified*] [*German*]
Vergr .... Vergroesserung [*Magnification*] [*German*]
Verh .... Verhaeltnis [*Proportion*] [*German*]
Verh .... Verhalten [*Behavior*] [*German*]
verif .... Verification [*Verification*] [*Business and trade*] [*French*]
verk .... Verkuerzt [*Abbreviated*] [*German*]
verkh .... Upper (RU)
verkl .... Verkleinert [*Reduced*] [*German*]
Verl .... Verlag [*Publication, Publishing House*] [*German*]
Verl .... Verleger [*Publisher*] [*German*] (GPO)
verm .... Vermehrt [*Augmented*] [*German*]
Verm .... Vermessung [*German*]
Verma .... Vermessungsamt [*Surveying Office*] (EG)
VERRETAT ... Verrerie d'Etat [*State Glass Factory*] [*Cambodian*] (CL)
Vers .... Versammlung [*Meeting*] [*German*]
vers .... Versiculo [*Spanish*]
Vers .... Versuch [*Assay, Test*] [*German*]
verso .... Versiculo [*Verse*] [*Spanish*]
Verss .... Versuche [*Experiments, Tests*] [*German*]
VerSt .... Vereinigten Staaten [*United States*] [*German*]
VerSt .... Verladestelle [*Entraining Point, Loading Point, Point of Embarkation, Entrucking Point*] (EG)
vert .... Vertaa [*Compare*] [*Finnish*] (GPO)
VERTESZ .... Villamos Eromu Tervezo es Szerelo Vallalat [*Planning and Engineering Enterprise of Electric Power Plants*] (HU)
verw .... Verwandt [*Related*] [*German*]
VES .... All-Union Electrotechnical Handbook [*A publication*] (RU)
VES .... Vasiliki Enosi Salaminas [*Royalist Union of Salamis*] (GC)
VES .... Versuchs- und Entwicklungsstellen der DR [*GDR Railroad Experimental and Development Offices*] (EG)
VES .... Veterinary Encyclopedic Dictionary [*A publication*] (RU)
Ves .... Vrakhonisides [*Rocky Islets*] [*Greek*] (NAU)
ves .... Weight, Gravimetric (RU)
VES .... Wind-Driven Electric Power Plant (RU)
ves ch .... Part by Weight (RU)
VESchG ...... Volkseigentumschutzgesetz [*Law for the Protection of State Property*] (EG)
VESh .... Military Electrotechnical School (RU)
veshch .... Substance, Material, Matter (RU)
vesi .... Vesirakennus [*Hydraulic Engineering*] [*Finnish*]
VESO .... All-Union Electrical Communications Association (RU)
VEST .... Departmental Standard, Institutional Standard (RU)
vestn .... Herald (RU)
VestnikGSZ ... Vestnik Glasilo Slovenskih Zeleznicarjev [*Review Organ of the Slovenian Railroad Workers*] (YU)
Vestn vozd flota ... Herald of the Air Force [*A publication*] (RU)
VET .... All-Union Electrotechnical Trust (RU)
vet .... Siding [*Railroads*] (RU)
Vet .... Veterinaer [*German*]
vet .... Veterinary (BU)
vet .... Veterinary, Veterinary Science (RU)
Vet .... Veteriner [*Veterinary*] (TU)
VETB .... Turk Veteriner Hekimleri Birligi [*Turkish Union of Doctors of Veterinary Medicine*] [*See also VHB*] (TU)
veter .... Veterinary (RU)
veter .... Veterinary, Veterinary Medicine (BU)
Veter-med fak ... School of Veterinary Medicine (BU)
Veter sl .... Veterinarska Sluzba [*Veterinary Service*] (CZ)
VETh .... Vasiliki Ethniki Enosis Thessalonikis [*National Royalist Union of Salonica*] [*See also VEETh*] (GC1)
VetIProizvSerVaks ... Veterinary Institute for the Production of Serums and Vaccines (BU)
Vetpromsnab ... Veterinary Supplies Enterprise (BU)
vetr mln ...... Windmill [*Topography*] (RU)
VETROM ..... Preduzece za Promet Veterinarskim Materijalom [*Trade Establishment in Veterinary Supplies*] (YU)
VETS .... Height of Equivalent Theoretical Separation Phase (RU)
VETs .... Hydroelectric Power Plant (BU)
VetSb .... Veterinarna Sbirka [*Veterinary Collection*] [*A periodical*] (BU)
VETT .... Height Equivalent to a Theoretical Plate (RU)
VETTEX ...... Vetements et Textiles (MAR)
vetupr .... Veterinary Administration (RU)
VETZ .... Vyaz'ma Electrical Equipment Plant (RU)
VEU .... Secondary Electron Multiplier (RU)
VEV .... Vetomagtermelteto es Ertekesito Vallalat [*Seed Producer and Sales Enterprise*] (HU)
VEV .... Vlaams Ekonomisch Verbond [*Flemish Economic Association*] [*Belgian*] (WEN)
VEV .... Volkseigener Verlag [*State-Owned Publishing House*] (EG)
VEV Exa ...... Vossa Excelencia [*or Vossa Excellencia*] [*Your Excellency*] [*Portuguese*] (GPO)
VEW .... Volkseigene Werft [*State-Owned Shipyard*] (EG)
VEW .... Volkseigene Wirtschaft [*State Sector of the Economy*] (EG)
VExa .... Vuestras Excelencias [*Your Excellencies*] [*Portuguese*]
VEXPORT .... Vojvodina Export-Import, Novi Sad (YU)
VEZ .... Vertical Electric Logging (RU)
vez .... Vezenyel [*Conductor (Music)*] (HU)
vez .... Vezeto [*Leader*] (HU)
VEZ .... Voronezh Excavator Plant (RU)
VEZ .... Vystavba Energetickych Zavodu [*Construction of Electric Power Plants*] (CZ)
VEZ .... Vyvojovy Elektrokeramicky Zavod [*Electroceramic Development Plant*] (CZ)
vezerig .... Vezerigazgato [*Director General*] (HU)
vezrad .... Vezetekes Radio [*Closed Circuit Transmission*] (HU)
vez radio ..... Vezetekes Radio [*Closed Circuit Transmission*] (HU)
VF .... Air Force (RU)
VF .... Naval Flotilla (RU)
VF .... Problems of Philosophy [*A publication*] (RU)
Vf .... Verfasser [*Author*] [*German*]
VF .... Verlag fuer die Frau [*Publishing House for the Woman*] (EG)
VF .... Veterinarski Fakultet [*Faculty of Veterinary Medicine*] (YU)
VF .... Visokofrekventni [*High-Frequency*] (YU)
VFASOON ... World Federation of United Nations Associations (RU)
VFCDC .... Virginia Frank Child Development Center (MAR)
VFCU .... Victoria Federation of Co-Operative Unions (MAR)
VFD .... Military Photographer-Correspondent (BU)
VFDC .... United Nations Voluntary Fund for the Decade of Women (MAR)
VFDM .... World Federation of Democratic Youth [*WFDY*] (RU)
vfelv .... Vonalfelvigyazo [*Line Inspector (Railroad)*] (HU)
VfG .... Verfuegung [*Disposition, Directive*] (EG)
VfGerH .... Verfassungsgerichtshof [*German*]
VfGH .... Verfassungsgerichtshof [*German*]
VFI .... Higher Institute of Finance (BU)
VfI .... Verwaltung fuer Industriebedarf [*Administration for Industrial Demand*] (EG)
VFM .... All-Chinese Youth Federation (RU)
Vfm .... Vorratsfestmeter [*Storage Cubic Meter*] (EG)
VFNR .... World Federation of Scientific Workers [*WFSW*] (RU)
VFO .... Military Finance Section (RU)
VFP .... All-Chinese Federation of Trade Unions (RU)
VFP .... Problems of Philosophy and Psychology (RU)
VFP .... World Federation of Trade Unions [*WFTU*] (RU)
VFPS .... Postal Courier Communications Center (BU)
VFSh .... Adjustable-Pitch Propeller (RU)
VFSI .... Higher Institute of Finance and Economics (BU)
VFSKh .... World's Student Christian Federation [*WSCF*] (RU)
VF-Stelle ..... Verrechnungsstelle fuer Forderungen [*Clearing House for Claims*] (EG)
VFTB .... General Federation of Labor of Belgium (RU)
VF-Verfahren ... Verrechnungsverfahren fuer Forderungen [*Debiting Procedure for Claims*] (EG)
VFVV .... World Veterans Federation (RU)
VFW .... Vereinigte Flugtechnische Werke [*United Aeronautical Works*] (EG)
VFW-Fokker ... Vereinigte Flugtechnische Werke-Fokker [*Fokker United Aeronautical Works*] [*West German*] (WEN)
VFZ .... Upper Front (RU)
vfzo .... Vonalfelvigyazo [*Line Supervisor*] (HU)
VfzV .... Verordnung ueber die Freiwillige und Zusaetzliche Versicherung [*Regulation Concerning Voluntary and Supplementary Insurance*] (EG)
VG .... Auxiliary Generator (RU)
VG .... British Virgin Islands [*Two-letter standard code*] (CNC)
VG .... Generator Switch (RU)
VG .... Horizontal Dipole (RU)
VG .... Military Hospital (RU)
VG .... Military Personnel Settlement (RU)
VG .... Supreme Command (RU)
Vg .... Vag [*or Vagen*] [*Bay, Cove*] [*Norwegian*] (NAU)
vg .... Vagon [*Freight Car, Carload*] (CZ)
VG .... Vatrena Grupa [*Fire Group*] [*Military*] (YU)

vg .... Verbi Gratia [*For Example*] [*Latin*] (GPO)
vg .... Verbigracia [*For Example*] [*Spanish*]
VG .... Vertragsgesetz [*Contract Law*] (EG)
vg .... Virgen [*Virgin*] [*Spanish*]
VGAS .... High-Altitude Geophysical Automatic Station (RU)
VGB .... All-Union Geological Library (RU)
VGB .... British Virgin Islands [*Three-letter standard code*] (CNC)
VGBIL .... All-Union State Library of Foreign Literature (RU)
VGBO .... All-Union Hydrobiological Society (RU)
VGD .... Band Horizontal Dipole (RU)
VGD .... D'yakonov Rifle Grenade (RU)
VGD .... Intraocular Pressure (RU)
VGE .... Vereinigte Gesundheitseinrichtungen [*United Public Health Facilities*] (EG)
Vge .... Vierge [*Virgin*] [*Military map abbreviation*] [*World War I*] [*French*] (MTD)
VGE .... Vollbeschaeftigteneinheit [*Full Employment Unit*] (EG)
VGF .... All-Union Geological Fund (RU)
VGF .... Vieja Guardia de Franco [*Old Guard of Franco*] [*Spanish*] (WER)
VGG .... Voithos Genikos Grammatevs [*Deputy Secretary General*] (GC)
VGGRU .... Herald of the Main Administration of Geological Exploration [*A publication*] (RU)
VGI .... Vojni Geografski Institut [*Institute of Military Geography*] (YU)
VGIJ .... Vestnik Geoloskog Instituta Jugoslavije [*Review of the Geological Institute of Yugoslavia*] [*Belgrade*] [*A publication*] (YU)
VGIK .... All-Union State Institute of Cinematography (RU)
VGIK .... High State Quality Inspection of Industrial Production (RU)
VGITIS .... All-Union State Institute of Remote Control and Communications (RU)
VGK .... Herald of the Geological Committee [*A publication*] (RU)
VGK .... Supreme Command (RU)
VGKO .... All-Russian Concert Tour Association (RU)
vgl .... Vergelijk [*Compare*] [*Dutch*] (GPO)
VGL .... Vergleich [*Compare, Confer, See, Refer*] [*German*]
vgl a .... Vergleiche Auch [*See Also*] [*German*]
VGLK .... State Higher Courses in Literature (RU)
vglk .... Supreme Commander in Chief (BU)
VGM .... Vakiflar Genel Mudurlugu [*Director General of Religious Foundations*] [*Under Office of Premier*] (TU)
VGMG .... Herald of the State Museum of Georgia [*A publication*] (RU)
VGMI .... Voronezh State Medical Institute (RU)
VGO .... All-Union Geographic Society (RU)
VGO .... All-Union Hydrobiological Society (RU)
VGO .... Military Geological Detachment (RU)
VGOLPITEP ... All-Union State "Order of Lenin" Planning Institute Teploelektroproyekt (RU)
VGP .... Vojno-Gradevinsko Preduzece [*Military Building Establishment*] (YU)
VGPI .... All-Union State Planning Institute (RU)
VGPI .... Vilnius State Pedagogical Institute (RU)
VGPI .... Vladimir State Pedagogical Institute Imeni P. I. Lebedev (RU)
VGPI .... Voronezh State Pedagogical Institute (RU)
VGPO .... All-Union Notions and Perfumery Association (RU)
vgr .... Verbigracia [*For Example*] [*Spanish*]
Vgr .... Vidi Grupu [*See Group*] (YU)
VGRO .... All-Union Geological Exploration Association (RU)
VGRP .... Volga River Cargo Steamship Line (RU)
VGRS .... General German Workers' Union (RU)
VGS .... Higher City Planning Council (BU)
VGS .... Vertical Synchronous Hydraulic Generator (RU)
VGSB .... All-Union Geodetic Information Office (RU)
VGSCh .... Militarized Mine Rescue Unit (RU)
VGSI .... All-Union State Sanitary Inspection (RU)
VGSO .... Militarized Mine Rescue Detachment (RU)
VGSV .... Militarized Mine Rescue Platoon (RU)
VGTL .... Rope-Pulled Rubber Conveyor Belt (BU)
VGTVRZ .... All-Union State Trust of Railroad Car Repair Plants (RU)
VgTZ .... Volgograd Tractor Plant (RU)
VGU .... High Geodetic Administration (RU)
VGU .... Military Geographic Directorate (RU)
VGU .... Vilnius State University Imeni V. Kapsukas (RU)
vgu .... Vorgelesen, Genehmigt, Unterschrieben [*Read, Confirmed, and Signed (Legal documents)*] (EG)
VGU .... Voronezh State University (RU)
VGV .... High-Water Level (RU)
VGZ .... Vjestnik Geoloskog Zavoda [*Review of the Geological Institute*] [*Zagreb*] [*A publication*] (YU)
VH .... Volkseigener Handel [*State Trade Enterprise*] (EG)
vH .... Vom Hundert [*Percent*] [*German*] (GPO)
v/h .... Voorheen [*Formerly*] [*Dutch*] (CED)
VHAD .... Vjesnik Hrvatskog Arheoloskog Drustva [*Review of the Croatian Archaeological Society*] (YU)
VHB .... Turk Veteriner Hekimleri Birligi [*Turkish Union of Doctors of Veterinary Medicine*] [*See also VETB*] (TU)
Vhdl .... Verhandlungen [*Transactions*] [*German*]
VHI .... Veterinaerhygiene-Inspektion [*Veterinary Hygiene Inspection*] (EG)
VHJ .... Vyrobni Hospodarska Jednotka [*Economic Production Unit*] (CZ)
vhk .... Vihko [*Finnish*]
VHM .... Vojenske Historicke Museum [*Museum of Military History*] (CZ)
VHMP .... Vestnik Hlavniho Mesta Prahy [*Bulletin of the Capital Prague*] [*A publication*] (CZ)
VHP .... Vooruitstrewende Hervormings Partij [*Progressive Reform Party*] [*Surinamese*] (PPW)
vhr .... Vegrehajtasi Rendelet [*Implementing Decree*] (HU)
VHS .... Vojenska Hudebni Skola [*Military Music School*] (CZ)
VHS .... Volkshochschule [*German*]
VHSD .... Vyssia Hospodarska Skola Druzstevna [*Higher School of Cooperative Management*] (CZ)
VHSZ .... Villamos Halozati Szolgalat [*Electric Network Service*] (HU)
vht .... Veghatarozat [*Final Decision*] (HU)
VHU .... Vojensky Historicky Ustav [*Institute of Military History*] (CZ)
Vh Z .... Verhaeltniszahl [*Proportional Number*] [*German*]
VHZ .... Volkseigene Handelszentrale [*State Trade Center*] (EG)
VI .... Herald of Engineers [*A publication*] (RU)
VI- .... Ionization Gauge (RU)
VI .... Military Inspection (RU)
VI .... Problems of History [*A publication*] (RU)
VI .... Veterinarski Inspektorat [*Veterinary Inspectorate*] (YU)
VI .... Victoria Institution (ML)
VI .... Video Amplifier (RU)
VI .... Virgin Islands of the US [*Two-letter standard code*] [*Postal code*] (CNC)
VI .... Viskositaetsindex [*Viscosity Index*] (EG)
VIA .... Archives of Military History [*A publication*] (RU)
VIA .... Military Engineering Academy (RU)
VIA .... Military History Archives (BU)
VIA .... Vietnamese Information Agency [*North Vietnam*] (RU)
VIAA .... Comite des Volontaires Internationales d'Aide et d'Assistance aux Refugies [*Committee of International Women Volunteers for Aid and Relief to Refugees*] [*Use CVIAA*] [*Cambodian*] (CL)
VIAAR .... Comite des Volontaires Internationales d'Aide et d'Assistance aux Refugies [*Committee of International Women Volunteers for Aid and Relief to Refugees*] [*Use CVIAA*] [*Cambodian*] (CL)
VIAKO .... All-Union Institute of Variety Goods of Light Industry and Fashion (RU)
VIALEGPROM ... All-Union Institute of Variety Goods of Light Industry and Fashion (RU)
VIAM .... All-Union Scientific Research Institute of Aviation Materials (RU)
VIAP .... All-Union Institute of Soil Science (RU)
VIARKKA .... Military Engineering Academy of the RKKA (RU)
VIASA .... Venezolana Internacional de Aviacion, Sociedad Anonima [*Venezuelan airline*]
VIAVER .... Hotel de Viajes Veracruz [*Medellin*] (COL)
VIAVU .... Higher Military Engineering Aviation School (RU)
VIBEG .... Vendeglatoipari Berendezes es Felszereles Javito Vallalat [*Repair Enterprise for Hotel and Catering Trade Equipment*] (HU)
VICICONGO ... Societe des Chemins de Fer Vicinaux du Congo (MAR)
VID .... Vienna Institute for Development (EA)
VIDRIOCAL ... Vidriera de Caldas [*Pereira*] (COL)
VIDRIOVAL ... Vidriera del Valle [*Cali*] (COL)
VIDUS .... Tatabanyai Szenbanyak Viztisztito es Dusito Berendezesek Gyara [*Tatabanya Coal Mines Water Purification and Dressing Equipment Factory*] (HU)
VIE .... Vasilikon Idryma Erevnon [*Royal Research Foundation*] [*See also EIE*] (GC)
VIEE .... All-Union Scientific Research Institute of Experimental Endocrinology (RU)
VIEM .... All-Union Institute of Experimental Medicine Imeni A. M. Gor'kiy (RU)
VIEMP .... All-Union Scientific Research Institute of Essential-Oil Industry (RU)
VIEMR .... All-Union Scientific Research Institute of Essential-Oil Plants [*1947-1954*] (RU)
VIEMS .... All-Union Scientific Research Institute of Economics of Mineral Raw Materials and Geological Exploration (RU)
vier .... Viernes [*Friday*] [*Spanish*]
VIESKh .... All-Union Scientific Research Institute of Rural Electrification (RU)
VIETSEL ..... Vietnam Selatan [*South Vietnam*] (IN)
VIETUT .... Vietnam Utara [*North Vietnam*] (IN)
VIEV .... All-Union Institute of Experimental Veterinary Science (RU)
VIF .... Higher Physical Education Institute (BU)
VIFK .... Higher Physical Education Institute (BU)
VIFKA .... Vereniging van Importeurs en Fabrikanten van Kantoormachines
VIFS .... All-Union Information Fund of Standards and Technical Specifications (RU)
VIG .... Vojnoistoriski Glasnik [*Bulletin of Military History*] [*A publication*] (YU)
VIGE .... Vasilikon Institouton Geoponikon Epistimon [*Royal Institute of Agricultural Sciences*] [*See also IGE*] (GC)
VIGIS .... All-Union Institute of Helminthology Imeni Academician K. I. Skryabin (RU)

VIGM .... All-Union Scientific Research Institute of Hydraulic Machinery (RU)
VIGM .... Veteriner Isleri Genel Mudurlugu [*Veterinary Affairs Directorate General*] (TU)
Vigne .... Vignoble [*Vineyards*] [*Military map abbreviation*] [*World War I*] [*French*] (MTD)
VII .... Higher Institute of Economics (BU)
VII .... Military Engineering Inspection (RU)
VIIbre .... Septembre [*September*] [*French*]
VIIbre .... Septiembre [*September*] [*Spanish*]
VIII .... Higher Institute of Representational Art (BU)
VIIIbre .... Octobre [*October*] [*French*]
VIIIbre .... Octubre [*October*] [*Spanish*]
VIIJA .... Vojnoistoriski Institut Jugoslovenske Armije [*Institute of Military History of the Yugoslav Army*] [*Belgrade*] (YU)
VII Karl Marks ... [*The*] Karl Marx Higher Institute of Economics (BU)
viim .... Viimeinen [*Finnish*]
viim .... Viimeksi [*Finnish*]
VIIYa .... Military Institute of Foreign Languages (RU)
VIK .... All-Union Scientific Research Institute of Fodder (RU)
VIK .... Higher Engineering Courses (RU)
VIK .... Military History Commission (RU)
VIK .... Provisional Executive Committee (RU)
VIK .... Vereinigung Internationaler Kulturaustausch (MAR)
VIK .... Vrhovna Invalidska Komisija [*Supreme Commission for Disabled Veterans*] (YU)
ViK .... Water Supply and Sewers (BU)
VIKER .... Vegyipari es Kereskedelmi Korlatolt Felelossegu Tarsasag [*Chemical Manufacturing and Trade Co. Ltd.*] (HU)
VIKhVP .... Higher Food Industry Institute (BU)
VIKP .... All-Indian Congress of Trade Unions (RU)
VIKT .... General Confederation of Labor of Italy (RU)
VIKZhEDOR ... All-Russian Executive Committee of Railroad Workers [*1918-1919*] (RU)
VIKZhEL' .... All-Russian Executive Committee of the Railroad Trade Union (RU)
VIL .... Herald of Foreign Literature [*1928-1930*] [*A publication*] (RU)
VILAR .... All-Union Scientific Research Institute of Medicinal and Aromatic Plants (RU)
VILATI .... Villamos Automatika Intezet [*Institute of Electrical Automation*] (HU)
VILLA .... Ventes Immobilieres de Logements et Lotissements en Afrique (MAR)
VILLENKI .... Villamos Energetikai Kutato Intezet [*Electric Power Research Institute*] (HU)
VILLERT .... Villamossagi es Szerelesi Cikkeket Ertekesito Vallalat [*Marketing Enterprise for Electrical Items and Equipment*] (HU)
VILLESZ .... Villanyszerelo Segedipari Vallalat [*Subsidiary Industrial Enterprise for Electric Engineering Equipment*] (HU)
VILLTESZ ... Autovillamossagi es Muszeresz KSZ [*Cooperative Enterprise for Automotive Electrical Equipment and Machine Parts*] (HU)
VIM .... All-Union Scientific Research Institute of Agricultural Mechanization (RU)
VIM .... Pulse-Time Modulation (RU)
VI M .... Vegyipari Miniszter [*or A Vegyipari Miniszter Rendelete*] [*Minister of the Chemical Industry or Decree of the Minister of the Chemical Industry*] (HU)
VIM .... Water Installation Works (BU)
VIME .... All-Union Scientific Research Institute of Rural Mechanization and Electrification [*1937-1948*] (RU)
VIMEDA .... Vice Ministerio de Educacion para Adultos [*Vice Ministry of Adult Education*] [*Nicaraguan*] (LA1)
VIMESS .... Higher Institute for the Mechanization and Electrification of Agriculture (BU)
VIMK .... Herald of the History of World Culture [*1957-1961*] [*A publication*] (RU)
VIMME .... Viomikhania Metallon kai Metallevtikon Epikheiriseon [*Metals and Mining Enterprises Industry*] [*Greek*] (GC)
VIMMESS .... Higher Institute for Agricultural Machinebuilding and Mechanization and Electrification of Agriculture (BU)
VIMP .... All-Union Institute of the Makhorka Industry (RU)
VIMS .... All-Union Institute of Metrology and Standardization [*1931-1934*] (RU)
VIMS .... All-Union Scientific Research Institute of Mineral Raw Materials (RU)
VIMT .... All-Union Scientific Research Institute of Mechanization in the Peat Industry (RU)
vin .... Accusative [*Case*] (BU)
vin .... Accusative [*Case*] (RU)
Vin .... Distillery [*Topography*] (RU)
VIN .... Value of Direction Change (RU)
vin .... Vineyard [*Topography*] (RU)
VINAFRANCE ... Societe d'Importation de Vins en Afrique Francaise [*Abidjan*] (MAR)
VINALKO .... Poduzece za Promet Vinom i Alkoholnim Picima [*Trade Enterprise in Wine and Alcoholic Beverages*] (YU)
VINITI .... All-Union Institute of Scientific and Technical Information (of the State Committee of the Council of Ministers, USSR, for Science and Technology and of the Academy of Sciences, USSR) (RU)
VINITI .... Vsesojuznij Institut Naucnoj i Tekniceskoj Informacij [*USSR*]
VINK .... Military History Scientific Commission (RU)
VINLEC .... St. Vincent Electricity Services (LA1)
vinogr .... Vineyard (RU)
vinogr .... Viticulture (RU)
Vinprom .... Wine Industry (BU)
VINS .... Higher Institute for the National Economy (BU)
Vinsindikat ... State Grape-Growing and Wine-Making Syndicate (RU)
VINTI .... All-Union Institute of Scientific and Technical Information on Agriculture (of the Ministry of Agriculture, USSR) (RU)
VIO .... Military History Society (RU)
VIO .... Varazdinska Industrija Obuce [*Varazdin Shoe Industry*] (YU)
VIOK .... All-Union Scientific Research Institute of Refractory and Acid-Resistant Materials (RU)
VIOS .... All-Union Scientific Research Institute for the Study of Foundations and Substructures of Engineering Installations (RU)
VIOZKh .... All-Union Institute of Irrigation Grain Farming (RU)
VIP .... Auxiliary Power Supply Unit (RU)
VIP .... Bearing Change (RU)
vip .... Issue (BU)
VIP .... Venda Independence Party [*South African*] (AF)
VIP .... Virgin Islands Party (LA1)
VIPASA .... Vivienda Panamericana Colombiana Ltda. [*Cali*] (COL)
VIPB .... All-Union Institute of Applied Botany and New Crops (RU)
VIPBiNK .... All-Union Institute of Applied Botany and New Crops (RU)
VIPCOR .... Viphya Pulp and Paper Corporation (MAR)
VIPK .... Visja Invalidsko-Pokojninska Komisija [*Higher Invalid Retirement Commission*] (YU)
VIPKIZO .... All-Union Institute for Improvement of Qualifications and for Correspondence Training of Agricultural Specialists (RU)
VIPP .... Venda Independent People's Party (PPW)
VIPT .... All-Union Scientific Research Institute of Industrial Transportation (RU)
VIR .... All-Union Scientific Research Institute of Plant Growing (RU)
VIR .... Mobile Incubator "Record" (RU)
VIR .... Probable Range Rate [*Artillery*] (RU)
VIR .... Range Rate [*Artillery*] (RU)
VIR .... Virgin Islands of the US [*Three-letter standard code*] (CNC)
vir .... Viroksi [*Finnish*]
vir .... Virolainen [*Finnish*]
VIRG .... All-Union Scientific Research Institute of Exploration Geophysics (RU)
VIRG .... Institute of Mining Geophysics (RU)
virg .... Virgen [*Spanish*]
virh .... Virheellisesti [*Erroneously*] [*Finnish*]
virt .... Virement [*French*]
VIRts .... Range Rate Due to Target Motion (RU)
virusol .... Virological, Virology (RU)
VIS .... All-Union Institute of Structures (RU)
VIS .... Army Engineering Signal Apparatus Factory (BU)
VIS .... Eastern Scientific Research Institute of Structures [*Sverdlovsk*] (RU)
vis .... Height, Altitude, Elevation, Hill (BU)
VIS .... Inertial System Computer (RU)
VIS .... Varazdinska Industrija Svile [*Varazdin Silk Industry*] (YU)
Vis .... Vrakhonisis [*Rocky Islet*] [*Greek*] (NAU)
VIS .... Vrhovno Islamsko Starjesinstvo [*Supreme Islamic Authority*] [*Sarajevo*] (YU)
VISACAM .... Societe des Viandes et Salaisons du Cameroun (MAR)
VISAN .... Vida Sanayi ve Ticaret AS [*Sheet Metal Screw Industry and Trade Corp.*] (TU)
VISb .... Military History Collection [*Series*] (BU)
VISF .... Army Engineering Signal Apparatus Factory (BU)
VISh .... Controllable-Pitch Propeller (RU)
VIShKhIMZ ... Vishera Chemical Plant (RU)
VISI .... Higher Construction Engineering Institute (BU)
VISI .... Voronezh Construction Engineering Institute (RU)
VISK .... Military History Commission (RU)
VISKhM .... All-Union Institute of Agricultural Microbiology (RU)
VISKhOM .... All-Union Scientific Research Institute of Agricultural Machinery (RU)
VISM .... All-Union Institute of Building Materials (RU)
VISP .... All-Union Institute of the Soda Industry (RU)
Vissh ikon inst ... Higher Institute of Economics (BU)
VISU .... Higher School of Construction Engineering (RU)
VISZ .... Vegyipari Szakszervezet [*Chemical Industry Trade Union*] (HU)
VIT .... All-Union Institute of Peat (RU)
VIT .... Antitank Fighter Aircraft (RU)
VIT- .... V. I. Tyzhnov [*in combination: VIT-iron*] (RU)
VIT .... Valeur Immobiliere Totale [*Moroccan*] (MAR)
VIT .... Vilag Ifjusagi Talalkozo [*World Youth Meeting*] (HU)
VITA .... Volunteers in Technical Assistance, Inc. (MAR)
VITECO .... Vidrio Tecnico de Colombia [*Bogota*] (COL)
VITEO .... All-Union Scientific Research Institute of Heat and Water Power Engineering Equipment (RU)
VITGEO .... All-Union Scientific Research Institute of Heat and Water Power Engineering Equipment (RU)
VITI .... Higher Institute of Theatrical Art (BU)
VITIM .... All-Union Scientific Research Institute of Tobacco and Makhorka Imeni A. I. Mikoyan (RU)

VITIZ .... [*The*] Krust'o Sarafov Higher Institute of Theatrical Art (BU)
VITMP .... All-Union Scientific Research Institute of the Tobacco and Makhorka Industry Imeni A. I. Mikoyan (RU)
VITP .... All-Union Institute of the Tobacco Industry (RU)
VITR .... All-Union Scientific Research Institute of Methods and Techniques of Exploration (of the State Geological Committee, USSR) (RU)
VITU .... Higher Engineering and Technical School (of the Navy, USSR) (RU)
VITUKI......... Vizgazdalkodasi Tudomanyos Kutato Intezet [*Scientific Research Institute on Water Resources*] (HU)
VIU .... Military Engineering Directorate (RU)
VIU .... Military Engineering School (RU)
VIUA............ All-Union Scientific Research Institute of Fertilizers and Soil Science (RU)
VIUAA .... All-Union Scientific Research Institute of Fertilizers, Agricultural Engineering, and Soil Science (RU)
VIUZ............ Higher Schools of Economics (BU)
VIV.............. All-Union Synthetic Fiber Trust (RU)
VIV.............. Altitude Change [*of an aerial target*] (RU)
VIVA............ Visa Intendantska Vojna Akademija [*Higher Quartermaster Service Academy*] (YU)
VIVG............ Sudden Coal and Gas Ejection (BU)
VIYuN.......... All-Union Institute of Jurisprudence (RU)
viz............... Byzantine (BU)
VIZ.............. Verkh-Isetskiy Plant [*Sverdlovsk*] (RU)
viz............... Videlicet [*Namely*] [*Latin*] (GPO)
VIZ.............. Vojni Izdavacki Zavod [*Military Publishing Institute*] (YU)
VIZEP.......... Vizugyi Epito Vallalat [*Hydraulic Engineering Enterprise*] (HU)
VIZh............ All-Union Scientific Research Institute of Livestock Breeding (RU)
VIZh............ Military Engineering Journal [*A publication*] (RU)
VIZITERV .... Vizugyi Tervezo Iroda [*Water Resources Planning Office*] (HU)
VIZKh.......... All-Union Institute of Grain Farming (RU)
VIZMAE....... All-Union Institute of Terrestrial Magnetism and Atmospheric Electricity (RU)
VIZO............ All-Union Correspondence Training Institute (RU)
VIZR .... All-Union Institute for the Protection of Plants (RU)
vizv............. Vizvezetek [*Water Conduit*] (HU)
vJ................ Vom Jahre [*Of the Year*] [*German*]
vJ................ Vorigen Jahres [*Of Last Year*] [*German*] (GPO)
VJD............. Vanguardia de la Juventud Dominicana [*Vanguard of Dominican Youth*] [*Dominican Republic*] (LA1)
VK .... Air Code (RU)
VK .... Aircraft Engine Designed by V. Ya. Klimov (RU)
VK .... All-Chinese Committee (of the People's Political Advisory Council of China) (RU)
V/k .... All-Union Office (RU)
VK .... Auxiliary Team (RU)
VK .... Calling Drop (RU)
VK .... End Switch (RU)
VK .... Highly Durable Glue (RU)
VK .... Internal Conversion (RU)
VK .... Medical Commission (RU)
VK .... Military Collegium (BU)
VK .... Military Commandant (RU)
VK .... Military Commissar, Military Commissariat (RU)
VK .... Military Guard (BU)
v-k .... Newspaper (BU)
VK .... Of Highest Quality (RU)
VK .... Officers' Club (BU)
VK .... Output Stage (RU)
VK .... Vacuum Valve (RU)
vk .... Valasz Keretik [*Reply Requested*] (HU)
VK .... Vazduhoplovni Korpus [*Air Corps*] (YU)
VK .... Vergaserkraftstoff [*Carburetor Fuel (Gasoline)*] (EG)
VK .... Verkehrskontrolle [*Traffic Control*] (EG)
VK .... Versorgungskontor [*Supply Office*] (EG)
vk .... Vezerkar [*or Vezerkari*] (Tiszt) [*General Staff or General Staff Officer*] (HU)
vk .... Viime Kuun [*Finnish*]
vk .... Viime Kuuta [*Last Month*] [*Finnish*] (GPO)
Vk .... Vik [*or Vika or Viken*] [*Bay, Inlet*] [*Norwegian*] (NAU)
VK .... Villamosgep- es Kabelgyar [*Electrical Machine and Cable Factory*] (HU)
vk .... Virkaa Tekeva [*Acting*] [*Finnish*] (GPO)
VK .... Vojenska Kuchyne [*Military Field Kitchen*] (CZ)
VK .... Voyageurs/Kilometres (MAR)
V/K.............. Vsesojuznaya Kontora [*All-Union Office*] [*Russian*] (CED)
VKAS .... "Red Banner" Military Academy of Communications (RU)
VKB............. Higher Courses in Library Science (RU)
VKB............. Veliko Krizarsko Bratstvo [*Great Brotherhood of Crusaders*] [*Croatian*] (YU)
vkb .... Vezerkarhoz Beosztott [*Assigned to the General Staff*] (HU)
VKB............. Villamositasi Kutatasi Bizottsag [*Research Committee on Electrification*] (HU)
VKB............. Wentzel-Kramers-Brillouin [*Approximation, method*] (RU)
VKD............. Military Cableway (RU)
VKE............. Vasilikon Komma Ellados [*Royalist Party of Greece*] [*Greek*] (GC)
VKE............. Voroskereszt Egylet [*Red Cross Association*] (HU)
vk f .... Vezerkari Fonok [*or Vezerkari Fonokseg*] [*Chief of Staff or Office of the Chief of Staff*] (HU)
VKF .... Vietnami Kommunista Part [*Vietnamese Communist Party*] (HU)
VKF .... Volga-Kama Branch (RU)
VKFKiS .... All-Union Committee for Physical Culture and Sport (RU)
VKFKSMS... Higher Committee for Physical Culture and Sports of the Council of Ministers (BU)
VKFM .... All-Chinese Youth Federation (RU)
VKFP........... All-Chinese Trade-Union Federation (RU)
VKFPS......... All-Chinese Trade-Union Federation (RU)
VKFS........... All-Chinese Student Federation (RU)
VKFS........... Higher Committee for Physical Culture and Sports (BU)
VKG............. Vectorcardiogram (RU)
vkgr............ Air Movement Control Team (BU)
vkh .... Entrance (BU)
vkh .... Input (BU)
VKh .... Logistics (RU)
VKh .... Vinyl Chloride (RU)
VKh .... Vinylidene Chloride (RU)
VKhA........... Chemical Warfare Academy (RU)
VKhI .... All-Union Grain Inspection (RU)
VKhK........... Multipurpose Water Development Project (RU)
VKhK........... Voskresensk Chemical Kombinat Imeni V. V. Kuybyshev (RU)
VKhO........... All-Russian Choral Society (RU)
VKhO........... All-Union Chemical Society Imeni D. I. Mendeleyev (RU)
VKhO........... Logistics Section (RU)
VKhR........... Chemical Reconnaissance (RU)
vkhrr .... Chemical and Radiation Reconnaissance Platoon (BU)
vkhrr .... Chemical and Radiation Reconnaissance Platoon (RU)
VKhTU .... Higher School of Chemical Engineering (RU)
VKhU........... Directorate of Logistics (RU)
VkhU .... Input Device (RU)
VKhUP .... Chemical Warfare Training Post (RU)
VKhUTEIN... Higher State Art and Craft Institute [*1926-1930*] (RU)
VKhUTEMAS ... Higher State Art and Craft Shops [*1921-1926*] (RU)
vkhz .... Chemical Defense Platoon (BU)
vkhz .... Chemical Defense Platoon (RU)
VKI .... Tartrate of Lime (RU)
vki .... Valaki [*Someone*] (HU)
VKIP .... Higher Communist Institute of Education [*1931-1938*] (RU)
VKIZh.......... All-Union Communist Institute of Journalism Imeni "Pravda" (RU)
VKK............. Evening Courses for Peasants (RU)
VKK............. Medical Consultation Commission (RU)
VKK............. Medical Control Commission (RU)
VKK............. Military Control Committee [*Chinese People's Republic; 1946-1949*] (RU)
VKK............. Pressure Suit (RU)
VKK............. Tartaric Acid (RU)
VKK............. Temporary Control Commission (RU)
VKKL........... Villamosipari Kozponti Kutato Laboratorium [*Central Research Laboratory for the Electrical Engineering Industry*] (HU)
VKKMTS ..... Interim Coordinating Committee for International Commodity Arrangements [*ICCICA*] (RU)
vkl .... Enclosure, Insertion, Insert, Inset (RU)
vkl .... Including (BU)
vkl .... Inclusive, Including (RU)
VKL-........... Switch (RU)
VKL .... Volkseigener Kreislichtspielbetrieb [*State Kreis Movie Theater*] (EG)
vklyuch .... Inclusive, Including (RU)
VKM .... Vallas- es Kozoktatasugyi Miniszterium/Miniszter [*Ministry/Minister of Religious and Educational Affairs*] (HU)
VKM .... Varos- es Kozseggazdalkodasi Miniszterium/Miniszter [*Ministry/Minister of City and Community Management*] (HU)
VKM .... Versorgungskontor fuer Maschinenbauerzeugnisse [*Supply Office for Machine Building Products*] (EG)
VKM .... Vertical Forging Machine (RU)
VKM .... Villamos Kismotorgyar [*Factory for Small Electric Motors*] (HU)
v kn .... In the Book (RU)
VKNII.......... All-Union Scientific Research Institute of the Confectionery Industry (RU)
VKO............. All-Union Leather Association (RU)
VKO............. Military Cartographic Section (RU)
vko .... Vihko [*Finnish*]
VKO............. Vojenska Komise Obrany [*Military Defense Commission*] (CZ)
VKOShO ..... All-Union Leather, Footwear, and Garment Association (RU)
VKOUP........ World Confederation of Organizations of the Teaching Profession (RU)
VKP .... All-Union Book Chamber (RU)
VKP .... All-Union Communist Party (of Bolsheviks) (RU)
VKP .... Hungarian Communist Party [*1918-1948*] (RU)
VKP .... Mobile Command Post (RU)
VKP .... Verkaufspreis [*Selling Price*] (EG)
VKP .... Vsezvezna Komunisticna Partija (Boljsevikov) [*All-Union Communist Party (Bolsheviks)*] (YU)
VKP(b) .... All-Union Communist Party (of Bolsheviks) [*1925-1952*] (RU)
VKPG .... All-Russian Famine Relief Commission (RU)

VKPL .... Velkorazne Kulomety Proti Letadlum [*Heavy Caliber Antiaircraft Machine Guns*] (CZ)
VKPR .... Vojenska Kancelar Presidenta Republiky [*Military Office of the President of the Republic*] (CZ)
VKPT .... Tobacco Ring Spot Virus (RU)
VKR .... Auxiliary Cruiser (RU)
VKR .... Congress of Representatives for the Colored [*South African*] (AF)
VKR .... Velitel Vojenske Kontrarozvedky [*Commander of Military Counterintelligence*] (CZ)
VKRS .... Military Commandant of an Unloading Area (BU)
VKS .... All-Union Committee for Standardization (RU)
VKS .... Higher Committee for Standardization (BU)
VKS .... Leading-In Cable Rack (RU)
vks .... Military Court of Appeals (BU)
VKS .... Veliko Krizarsko Sestrinstvo [*Great Sisterhood of Crusaders*] [*Croatian*] (YU)
VKS .... Visa Komercijalna Skola [*Advanced Business School*] (YU)
VKS(b) .... Vsesvazova Komunisticka Strana [*All-Union Communist Party (Bolshevik)*] [*USSR*] (CZ)
VKSh .... Higher Cooperative School (RU)
VKSK .... Verband der Kleingaertner, Siedler, und Kleintierzuechter [*Union of Small Gardeners, Settlers, and Small Livestock Breeders*] (EG)
VKSKhSh .... Higher Communist Agricultural School (RU)
VKSM .... Hungarian Young Communist League (RU)
VKSt .... Verkaufsstelle [*Sales Outlet*] (EG)
VKSZ .... Vybor pro Kulturni Styky se Zahranicim [*Committee for Cultural Relations with Foreign Countries*] (CZ)
VKT .... All-Union State Cartographic Trust (RU)
VKT .... General Confederation of Labor (RU)
vkt .... Higher Critical Temperature (RU)
VKT .... Vrlo Kratki Talasi [*Ultrashort Waves*] (YU)
VKTI .... All-Union Boiler and Turbine Institute (RU)
VKTK .... General Confederation of Labor of Cameroun (RU)
VKTO .... All-Union Association of the Boiler and Turbine Industry (RU)
VKTR .... General Confederation of Labor of Romania (RU)
VKTV .... General Confederation of Labor of Vietnam (RU)
VKU .... All-Union Communist University (RU)
VKU .... Military Commandant of a Railroad Section (BU)
VKU .... Video Control Unit (RU)
VKV .... Vaskohaszati Kemenceepito Vallalat, Szekesfehervar [*Metallurgical Furnace, Building Enterprise Szekesfehervar*] (HU)
VKV .... Velmi Kratke Vlny [*Ultrashort Wave (Ultrahigh Frequency)*] (CZ)
VKVS .... Vojenske Katedry Vysokoskolske [*Military Departments at Universities*] (CZ)
VKVSh .... All-Union Committee on Higher Education (RU)
VKVTO .... All-Union Committee on Higher Technical Education (RU)
VKZ .... All-Union Commission for Mineral Resources (RU)
vkz .... Railroad Station [*Topography*] (RU)
VKZO .... All-Union Correspondence Training Center for Communications Personnel (RU)
VL .... Calling Lamp (RU)
VL- .... Electron Tube Voltmeter, Tube Voltmeter (RU)
vl .... Humidity (RU)
VL .... Military Infirmary (RU)
VL .... Overhead Line (RU)
VL .... Problems of Literature [*A publication*] (RU)
VL- .... Ribbon-Type Weighing Device (RU)
Vl .... Vaasan Laani [*or Vaasan Laania*] [*Finnish*]
vl .... Vanhaa Lukua [*Finnish*]
vl .... Varia Lecto [*A Variant Reading*] [*Latin*]
VL .... Velitelstvi Letectva [*Air Force Headquarters*] (CZ)
VL .... Vereinigte Linke [*United Left*] [*West German*] (PPW)
VL .... Veterinary Hospital (RU)
vl .... Viale [*Avenue*] [*Italian*] (CED)
vl .... Vialetto [*Avenue*] [*Italian*] (CED)
Vl .... Vitesse du Vent dans la Direction de la Ligne de Tir [*French*] (MTD)
VL .... Vladimir Lenin [*Electric locomotive type*] (RU)
VL .... Waterline (RU)
Vla .... Villa [*Small Town*] [*See also VA*] [*Spanish*] (NAU)
VLA .... Vojenska Lekarska Akademie [*Military Medical Academy*] [*Hradec-Kralove*] (CZ)
Vladoblgosarkhiv ... State Archives of the Vladimir Oblast (RU)
VLCC .... Very Large Crude Carriers (LA1)
VLE .... Medical Determination of Flight Fitness (RU)
VLET .... All-Union Lumber Export Technicum (RU)
VLGU .... Herald of the Leningrad State University [*A publication*] (RU)
VLI .... Higher Institute of Forestry Engineering (BU)
VLI .... Incoming Final Selector (RU)
VLI .... Voronezh Forestry Institute (RU)
VLK .... Medical Commission for Determination of Flight Fitness (RU)
VLK .... VE - Versorgungs- und Lagerungskontor [*State Supply and Stockpiling Agency*] (EG)
vlk .... Volcano (RU)
VLKhI .... Higher Institute of Literature and Art Imeni Valeriy Bryusov (RU)
VLKhI .... Voronezh Forestry Institute (RU)
vlkm .... Vlakovy Kilometr [*Railroad-Kilometer*] (CZ)
VLKSM .... All-Union Lenin Young Communist League (RU)
Vlle .... Vieille [*Old*] [*Military map abbreviation*] [*World War I*] [*French*] (MTD)
vlnar .... Vladni Narizeni [*Government Decree*] (CZ)
VLR .... Vive la Revolution [*Long Live the Revolution (Name of leftwing group no longer extant since July 1971)*] [*French*] (WER)
VLR .... Vocno Lozni Rasadnik [*Fruit and Viticulture Nursery*] (YU)
VLRA .... Vehicule Leger de Reconnaissance et d'Appui (MAR)
VLRO .... Military Hunting and Fishing Organization (BU)
VLRZ .... Vojenska Lazenska a Rekreacni Zarizeni [*Military Health and Recreation Resorts*] (CZ)
VLS .... Valstieciu Liaudininku Sajunga [*Peasant Populist Union*] [*Lithuanian*] (PPE)
VLT .... High-Frequency Beam Tetrode (RU)
VLTI .... Higher Institute of Forestry Engineering (BU)
VLTI .... Voronezh Forestry-Engineering Institute (RU)
VLU .... Herald of the Leningrad University [*A publication*] (RU)
VLU .... Vedecky Letecky Ustav [*Scientific Institute of Aeronautics*] (CZ)
VLU .... Vojensky Letecky Ustav [*Military Institute of Aeronautics*] (CZ)
VM .... Air-Manganese (RU)
VM .... Air Mass (RU)
VM- .... Beater (RU)
vm .... Capacity (BU)
VM .... Computer (RU)
VM .... Drawing Machine (RU)
VM .... Explosive Material (RU)
VM .... Explosives (BU)
vm .... In Place Of (BU)
vm .... Instead Of, In Place Of, For (RU)
V/m .... Intramuscular (RU)
VM .... Microswitch (RU)
vm .... Minister of War (BU)
VM .... Oil Circuit Breaker (RU)
VM .... Suspension Bridge (RU)
vm .... Valogatott Muvek [*Selected Works*] (HU)
VM .... Valuta Mark [*West German*] (WEN)
vm .... Varmegye [*County*] [*Hungarian*] (GPO)
VM .... Vertrauensmann [*Union Shop Steward, Spokesman of a Union Group*] (EG)
VM .... Vieille-Montagne (MAR)
VM .... Viet Minh [*An underground organization set up in Vietnam to overthrow the French*] [*Defunct since 1954*] [*Now popularly used to refer to communists or leftists, especially Vietnamese communists*] (CL)
vm .... Voormiddag [*Before Noon*] [*Dutch*] (GPO)
vM .... Vorigen Monats [*Of Last Month*] [*German*] (GPO)
Vm .... Vormittags [*In the Forenoon*] [*German*]
V M .... Vossa Merce [*Your Grace*] [*Portuguese*] (GPO)
VM .... Vuestra Majestad [*Your Majesty*] [*Spanish*]
Vm .... Vuestra Merced [*Your Worship*] [*Spanish*]
VM .... War Ministry (RU)
VMA .... Military Medical Academy (RU)
VMA .... Naval Academy (RU)
VMA .... Vojnomedicinska Akademija [*Academy of Military Medicine*] (YU)
VMAK .... Naval Academic Courses (RU)
VMAKV .... Naval Shipbuilding and Armament Academy (RU)
VMAU .... Naval Artillery School (RU)
VMB .... Naval Base (RU)
VMBI .... Vereniging Medische en Biologische Informatieverwerking
VMBIT .... All-Union Intersectional Office of Engineers and Technicians (RU)
Vmce .... Vossa Merce [*Your Grace*] [*Portuguese*] (GPO)
VMD .... Vanguarda Militar Democratica [*Democratic Military Vanguard*] [*Brazilian*] (LA)
Vmd .... Vuestra Merced [*Your Worship*] [*Spanish*]
VME .... Vychodomoravske Elektrarny [*East Moravian Electric Power Plants*] (CZ)
VMEI .... Higher Machine - Electrical Institute (BU)
VMF .... Navy (RU)
VMFU .... Naval School for Medical Assistants (RU)
VMG .... Engine-Propeller Unit [*Aviation*] (RU)
VMG .... Herald of the Museum of Georgia [*A publication*] (RU)
VMG .... Naval Hospital (RU)
VMG .... Power Plant Aircraft, Turbine Aggregate (BU)
VMGA .... Herald of the Moscow Mining Academy [*A publication*] (RU)
VMGI .... Higher Mining Geological Institute (BU)
VMGU .... Herald of the Moscow State University [*A publication*] (RU)
VMGU .... Naval Hydrographic School (RU)
VMI .... Higher Medical Institute (BU)
VMI .... Institute of Veterinary Medicine (BU)
VMI .... Naval Inspection (RU)
VMI .... Vazduhoplovni Modelarski Institut [*Air Force Modeling Institute*] (YU)
VMI .... Vitebsk Medical Institute (RU)
VMICh .... Naval Engineering Unit (RU)
VMIG .... Naval Hospital for Contagious Diseases (RU)
VMIU .... Naval Engineering School (RU)
VMK .... High-Molecular Weight Component (RU)
VMK .... High Naval Command (RU)

VMK .... Naval Club (RU)
VMK .... Temporary International Collective (BU)
VMKhl .... Vologda Institute of Dairying (RU)
VML............. Veroeffentlichungen des Museums fuer Voelkerkunde zu Leipzig (MAR)
VMM............ Military Medical Museum (RU)
VMM............ Volunteer Missionary Movement (EA)
VMMA .... Naval Medical Academy (RU)
VMN .... Capital Punishment (RU)
VMNO.......... Naval Scientific Society (RU)
VMNO.......... People's Military Youth Organization (BU)
VMNU.......... People's Naval Military Academy (BU)
VMO .... All-Union Microbiological Society (RU)
VMO .... All-Union Mineralogical Society (RU)
VMO .... Vlaamse Militantenorde [*Flemish Militant Order*] [*Belgian*] (WEN)
VMO .... World Meteorological Organization [*WMO*] (RU)
VMOIDR ...... Annals of the Moscow Society of Russian History and Antiquities [*A publication*] (RU)
VMOLA .... Military Medical "Order of Lenin" Academy Imeni S. M. Kirov (RU)
VMOLA .... Naval "Order of Lenin" Academy (RU)
VMORO....... Internal Macedonian-Odrin Revolutionary Organization (BU)
VMORO....... Internal Macedonian Okrug Revolutionary Organizations (BU)
VMORO....... Vnatresna Makedono-Odrinska Revolucionerna Organizacija [*Internal Macedonian Odrin Revolutionary Organization*] (YU)
VMP............. All-Union A. S. Pushkin Museum (RU)
VMP............. Temporary Medical Station (RU)
VMP............. Vestnik Ministarstva za Prosveto [*Review of the Ministry of Education*] [*A publication*] (YU)
VMPU .... Naval Political School (RU)
VMPU .... Naval Preparatory School (RU)
VMR .... Naval District (RU)
VMR .... Voice of Malayan Revolution (ML)
VMRO.......... Internal Macedonian Revolutionary Organization (RU)
VMRO.......... Vnatresna Makedonska Revolucionerna Organizacija [*Internal Macedonian Revolutionary Organization (Known popularly among English-speaking nations as the IMRO)*] [*Yugoslav*] (PPE)
VMRO.......... Vutreshna Makidoniski Revoliutsionna Organizatsiia [*Internal Macedonian Revolutionary Organization*] [*Bulgarian*] (PPE)
VMRO(U) .... Vnatresna Makedonska Revolucionerna Organizacija (Udruzena) [*Internal Macedonian Revolutionary Organization (United)*] [*Yugoslav*] (PPE)
VMS .... Naval Court (RU)
VMS .... Naval Forces, Navy (BU)
VMS .... Navy, Naval Forces (RU)
VMS .... Propeller-Driven Sled (RU)
VMSh .... Higher School of Music (RU)
VMSh .... Naval School (RU)
VMT............. Upper Dead Center (RU)
VMTP .... Village Management Training Programme (MAR)
VMTs........... Digital Computer (RU)
VMTs........... Meteorological Computation Center (RU)
VMTV .... Vegyimuveket Tervezo Vallalat [*Designing Enterprise for Chemical Plants*] (HU)
VMTVV........ Veleni Motostreleckemu Tankovemu a Vysadkovemu Vojsku [*Motorized Rifle, Tank, and Airborne Command*] (CZ)
VMU .... Engine-Propeller Unit [*Aviation*] (RU)
VMU .... Herald of the Moscow University [*A publication*] (RU)
VMU .... Military Medical Directorate (RU)
VMU .... Military Medical Establishment (RU)
VMU .... Naval School (RU)
VMUK.......... Naval Training Center (RU)
VMUZ.......... Naval Educational Institution (RU)
VMV-........... High-Voltage Oil Circuit Breaker (RU)
VMV .... Higher Low Water (RU)
VMW............ Vereinigte Metallgusswerke (VEB) [*United Metal Foundry (VEB)*] (EG)
VMYa .... Auxiliary International Language (RU)
VMZ............ Vyksa Metallurgical Plants (RU)
VMZ............ Water and Oil Servicing Truck (RU)
VMZh .... Military Medical Journal [*A publication*] (RU)
VMZhK........ Macromolecular Fatty Acids (RU)
VN .... Civilian Employee [*Military institutions or labor camps*] (RU)
VN .... Departmental Standard, Institutional Standard (RU)
VN .... High Tension (BU)
VN .... High Voltage, High Tension (RU)
vn .... Inner, Internal, Inside (RU)
VN .... Load Equalizer (RU)
VN-............. Table Fan (RU)
VN .... Vacuum Pump (RU)
VN .... Valtioneuvosto [*Council of State*] [*Finnish*] (WEN)
Vn............... Vann [*or Vatn*] [*Lake*] [*Norwegian*] (NAU)
VN .... Vasilikon Navtikon [*Royal Navy*] [*Greek*] (GC)
VN .... Vatreni Nalet [*Firing Assault*] [*Military*] (YU)
vn .... Veien [*Way*] [*Norwegian*] (CED)
vn .... Vellon [*Spanish*]
VN .... Vietnam [*Two-letter standard code*] (CNC)
Vn............... Vorname [*German*]
VN .... Vychovny Nacelnik [*Training Officer*] (CZ)
VN .... Vyrobni Normy [*Production Standards*] (CZ)
vn .... Vysoke Napeti [*High Voltage*] (CZ)
VN .... Vystrojni Nacelnik [*Equipment Chief*] (CZ)
VN .... Water Pump (RU)
VN .... Wietnam [*Vietnam*] [*Polish*]
VNA............. Hungarian People's Army (RU)
VNA............. Rotating Guide Vane (RU)
VNA............. Valores Nacionales Ajustables [*National Adjustable Securities*] [*Argentine*] (LA)
VNA............. Vietnamese People's Army [*North Vietnamese*] (RU)
vnab .... Air Observation (RU)
VNAIZ.......... All-Union Scientific Research Institute of Sound Recording (RU)
VNAR .... Air Observation and Reconnaissance (RU)
VNAV .... All-Russian Scientific Association of Oriental Studies (RU)
VNB............. Household Table Scales (RU)
VND............. Higher Nervous Activity (RU)
VND............. Low-Pressure Air (RU)
VND............. Vprasanje Nasih Dni [*Questions of Our Times*] [*Supplement to the newspaper Ljudska Pravica*] [*A publication*] (YU)
VND............. Vychodoceske Narodni Divadlo [*East Bohemian National Theater*] (CZ)
Vneshtorg... Ministry of Foreign Trade, USSR (RU)
Vneshtorgbank ... Foreign Trade Bank, USSR (RU)
Vneshtorgizdat ... State Publishing House of the Ministry of Foreign Trade, USSR (RU)
VNG............. Vereniging van Nederlandse Gemeenten
VNIALMI...... All-Union Scientific Research Institute of Conservational Afforestation (RU)
VNIEKIPRODMASh ... All-Union Scientific Research and Experimental Design Institute of Food Machinery (RU)
VNIEMK ...... All-Union Scientific Research Institute of Essential-Oil Crops (RU)
VNIEMS ...... All-Union Scientific Research Institute of Veterinary Ectoparasitology, Mycology, and Sanitation (RU)
VNIESKh..... All-Union Scientific Research Institute of Agricultural Economics (RU)
VNIFS.......... All-Union Scientific Research Antiphylloxera Station (RU)
VNIFTRI....... All-Union Scientific Research Institute of Physicotechnical and Radiotechnical Measurements (RU)
VNIGI........... All-Union Scientific Research Institute of Gas and Synthetic Liquid Fuel (RU)
VNIGL.......... Valday Scientific Research Hydrological Laboratory (RU)
VNIGMI .... All-Union Scientific Research Institute of Hydraulic Machinery (RU)
VNIGNI........ All-Union Petroleum Scientific Research Institute of Geological Exploration [*Moscow*] (RU)
VNIGRI .... All-Union Petroleum Scientific Research Institute of Geological Exploration [*Leningrad*] (RU)
VNII .... All-Union Petroleum Scientific Research Institute [*1943-1945*] (RU)
VNII .... All-Union Scientific Research Institute (RU)
VNII .... All-Union Scientific Research Institute of Petroleum and Gas (RU)
VNII .... All-Union Scientific Research Institute of Tools (RU)
VNII .... Veterinary Scientific Research Institute of the RKKA (RU)
VNII-1 .... All-Union Scientific Research Institute of Gold and Rare Metals (RU)
VNIIA........... All-Union Scientific Research Institute of Antibiotics (RU)
VNIIASBEST ... All-Union Scientific Research Institute of the Asbestos-Processing Industry (RU)
VNIIAsbesttsement ... All-Union Scientific Research Institute for Asbestos, Mica, Asbestos Cement Products, and for the Planning of Mica Industry Establishments (RU)
VNIIASh ...... All-Union Scientific Research Institute of Abrasives and Grinding (RU)
VNIIAT......... All-Union Scientific Research Institute of Automobile Transportation (RU)
VNIIATI .... All-Union Scientific Research, Design, and Technological Institute of Industrial Asbestos Products (RU)
VNIIAVTOGEN ... All-Union Scientific Research Institute of Gas Welding and Cutting of Metals (RU)
VNIIB i TsP ... All-Union Scientific Research Institute of the Pulp and Paper Industry (RU)
VNIIBT......... All-Union Scientific Research Institute for Drilling Techniques (RU)
VNIIBurtekhnika ... All-Union Scientific Research Institute for Drilling Techniques (RU)
VNIIChISK ... All-Union Scientific Research Institute of Tea and Subtropical Crops (RU)
VNIIChKh.... All-Union Scientific Research Institute of the Tea Cultivation (RU)
VNIIChP ...... All-Union Scientific Research Institute of the Tea Industry (RU)
VNIID........... All-Union Scientific Research Institute of Lumber (RU)
VNIIDMASh ... All-Union Scientific Research and Design Institute of Woodworking Machinery (RU)
VNIIDrev ..... All-Union Scientific Research Institute of the Woodworking Industry (RU)

VNIIE .... All-Union Scientific Research Institute of Electric Power Engineering (RU)
VNIIEE .... All-Union Scientific Research Institute of Power Engineering and Electrification (RU)
VNIIEKIProdmash ... All-Union Scientific Research and Experimental Institute of Food Machinery (RU)
VNIIElektromash ... All-Union Scientific Research Institute of the Technology of Electric Machinery and Equipment Manufacture (RU)
VNIIElektroprivod ... All-Union Scientific Research, Planning, and Design Institute for Automatic Electric Drive in Industry, Agriculture, and Transportation (RU)
VNIIEM .... All-Union Scientific Research Institute of Electromechanics (RU)
VNIIEP .... All-Union Scientific Research Institute of Electrical Measuring Instruments (RU)
VNIIESKh .... All-Union Scientific Research Institute of Agricultural Economics (RU)
VNIIESKh .... All-Union Scientific Research Institute of Rural Electrification (RU)
VNIIESO ...... All-Union Scientific Research Institute of Electric Welding Equipment (RU)
VNIIETO ...... All-Union Scientific Research Institute of Electrothermal Equipment (RU)
VNIIF .... All-Union Scientific Research Institute of Phytopathology (RU)
VNIIFIB .... All-Union Scientific Research Institute of Physiology and Biochemistry of Farm Animals (RU)
VNIIFS .... All-Union Scientific Research Institute of the Ferment and Alcohol Industry (RU)
VNIIFTRI ..... All-Union Scientific Research Institute of Physicotechnical and Radiotechnical Measurements (RU)
VNIIG .... All-Union Scientific Research Institute of the Goznak (RU)
VNIIG .... All-Union Scientific Research Institute of Halurgy (RU)
VNIIG .... All-Union Scientific Research Institute of Hydraulic Engineering Imeni B. Ye. Vedeneyev (RU)
VNIIGAZ ...... All-Union Scientific Research Institute of Natural Gas (RU)
VNIIGEOFIZIKA ... All-Union Scientific Research Institute of Geophysical Exploration Methods (RU)
VNIIGI .... All-Union Scientific Research Institute of Gas and Synthetic Liquid Fuel (RU)
VNIIGidromash ... All-Union Scientific Research, Design, and Technological Institute of Hydraulic Machinery (RU)
VNIIGidrougol' ... All-Union Scientific Research, Planning, and Design Institute of Hydraulic Coal Mining (RU)
VNIIGIM ...... All-Union Scientific Research Institute of Hydraulic Engineering and Reclamation Imeni A. N. Kostyakov (RU)
VNIIGIPS ..... All-Union Scientific Research Institute of Gypsum and Lime (RU)
VNIIGL .... All-Union Hydrometeorological Scientific Research Laboratory (RU)
VNIIGORMash ... All-Union Scientific Research and Planning Institute of Mining Machinery (RU)
VNIIgoznaka ... All-Union Scientific Research Institute of the Goznak (RU)
VNIIGPE ...... All-Union Scientific Research Institute of the State Patent Examination (RU)
VNIIGS .... All-Union Scientific Research Institute of Hydraulic Engineering and Sanitation (RU)
VNIIGS .... All-Union Scientific Research Institute of the Hydrolysis and Sulfite Liquor Industry (RU)
VNIIGShveyprom ... All-Union State Scientific Research Institute of the Garment Industry (RU)
VNIIK .... All-Union Scientific Research Institute of Artificial Leather (RU)
VNIIK .... All-Union Scientific Research Institute of Ceramics (RU)
VNIIK .... All-Union Scientific Research Institute of the Committee of Standards, Measures, and Measuring Instruments (RU)
VNIIK .... All-Union Scientific Research Institute of Criminology (RU)
VNIIK .... All-Union Scientific Research Institute of Fodder (RU)
VNIIK .... All-Union Scientific Research Institute of Horse Breeding (RU)
VNIIK .... All-Union Scientific Research Institute of Rubber-Yielding Plants (RU)
VNIIKANeftegaz ... All-Union Scientific Research, Planning, and Design Institute of Complex Automation in the Petroleum and Gas Industry (RU)
VNIIKh .... All-Union Scientific Research Institute of the Baking Industry (RU)
VNIIKh .... All-Union Scientific Research Institute of Cotton Growing (RU)
VNIIKhimmash ... All-Union Scientific Research and Experimental Institute of Chemical Machinery (RU)
VNIIKhP ...... All-Union Scientific Research Institute of the Baking Industry (RU)
VNIIKhSZR ... All-Union Scientific Research Institute of Chemicals Used for Plant Protection (RU)
VNIIKI .... All-Union Scientific Research Institute of Technical Information, Classification, and Coding (of the State Committee of Standards, Measures, and Measuring Instruments, USSR) (RU)
VNIIKiG .... All-Union Scientific Research Institute of Rubber and Gutta-Percha (RU)
VNIIKIMASh ... All-Union Scientific Research Institute of Oxygen Machinery (RU)
VNIIKKh ...... All-Union Scientific Research Institute of Potato Growing (RU)
VNIIKOP ...... All-Union Scientific Research Institute of the Canning and Dehydrated Vegetables Industry (RU)
VNIIKorm .... All-Union Scientific Research Institute of Fodder Imeni V. R. Vil'yams (RU)
VNIIKP .... All-Union Scientific Research Institute of the Canning Industry (RU)
VNIIKS .... All-Union Scientific Research Institute of Municipal Sanitation (RU)
VNIIKSMIP ... All-Union Scientific Research Institute of the Committee of Standards, Measures, and Measuring Instruments (RU)
VNIIL .... All-Union Scientific Research Institute of Flax (RU)
VNIILK .... All-Union Scientific Research Institute of Bast Cultures (RU)
VNIILKh ...... All-Union Scientific Research Institute of Forestry [*1938-1956*] (RU)
VNIILM .... All-Union Scientific Research Institute of Silviculture and Forestry Mechanization (RU)
VNIILTEKMASh ... All-Union Scientific Research Institute of Textile and Light Machinery (RU)
VNIILV .... All-Union Scientific Research Institute of the Bast-Fiber Industry (RU)
VNIIM .... All-Union Scientific Research Institute of Metrology Imeni D. I. Mendeleyev (RU)
VNIIMEMK ... All-Union Scientific Research Institute of Oil-Bearing and Essential-Oil Crops (RU)
VNIIMES ..... All-Union Scientific Research Institute of Mechanization and Electrification of Sovkhozes (RU)
VNIIMESKh ... All-Russian Scientific Research Institute of Rural Mechanization and Electrification (RU)
VNIIMETMASh ... All-Union Scientific Research, Planning, and Design Institute of Metallurgical Machinery (RU)
VNIIMI .... All-Union Scientific Research Institute of Heat Engineering in Metallurgy (RU)
VNIIMI .... All-Union Scientific Research Institute of Medical and Medicotechnical Information (of the Academy of Medical Sciences, USSR) (RU)
VNIIMIO ...... All-Union Scientific Research Institute of Medical Instruments and Equipment (RU)
VNIIMK .... All-Union Scientific Research Institute of Oil-Bearing Crops (RU)
VNIIMP .... All-Union Scientific Research Institute of the Meat Industry (RU)
VNIIMS .... All-Union Scientific Research Institute of the Butter- and Cheese-Making Industry (RU)
VNIINeft' ..... All-Union Scientific Research Institute of Petroleum and Gas (RU)
VNIINEFTEKhIM ... All-Union Scientific Research Institute of Petrochemical Processes (RU)
VNIINERUD ... All-Union Scientific Research Institute of Nonmetallic Building Materials and Hydraulic Mechanization (of the Academy of Construction and Architecture, USSR) (RU)
VNIING .... Volgograd Scientific Research Institute of the Petroleum and Gas Industry (RU)
VNIINMASh ... All-Union Scientific Research Institute of Standardization in Machinery Manufacture (RU)
VNIINP .... All-Union Scientific Research Institute of Petroleum and Gas Processing and the Production of Synthetic Liquid Fuel (RU)
VNIINP .... All-Union Scientific Research Institute of the Petroleum Industry (RU)
VNIINSM ..... All-Union Scientific Research Institute of New Building Materials (RU)
VNIINTM ..... All-Union Scientific Research Institute of Nonwoven Fabrics (RU)
VNIIO .... All-Union Scientific Research Institute of Refractories (RU)
VNIIOChERMET ... All-Union Scientific Research Institute for the Organization of Production and Labor in Ferrous Metallurgy (RU)
VNIIOK .... All-Union Scientific Research Institute of Sheep and Goat Breeding (RU)
VNIIOKh ...... All-Union Scientific Research Institute of Vegetable Growing (RU)
VNIIOMPROMZhILSTROY ... All-Union Scientific Research Institute for the Organization and Mechanization of Industrial and Housing Construction (RU)
VNIIOMS ..... All-Union Scientific Research Institute for the Organization and Mechanization of Construction (RU)
VNIIOMShS ... All-Union Scientific Research Institute for the Organization and Mechanization of Mine Construction (RU)
VNIIOT .... All-Union Scientific Research Institute of Work Safety of the VTsSPS (RU)
VNIIP .... All-Union Scientific Research Institute of Penicillin and Other Antibiotics (RU)
VNIIP .... All-Union Scientific Research Institute of the Poultry-Processing Industry (RU)
VNIIP .... All-Union Scientific Research Institute of Poultry Raising (RU)
VNIIP .... All-Union Scientific Research and Planning Institute for Underground Gasification of Fuels (RU)
VNIIPBiVP ... All-Union Scientific Research Institute of the Beer, Soft Drink, and Wine-Making Industry (RU)
VNIIPIK .... All-Union Scientific Research Institute of Film Materials and Artificial Leather (RU)

VNIIPIT........ All-Union Scientific Research Institute of the Printing Industry and Technology (RU)
VNIIPKhV.... All-Union Scientific Research Institute for the Processing of Synthetic Fibers (RU)
VNIIPN .... All-Union Scientific Research Institute of Petroleum Processing (RU)
VNIIPODZEMGAZ ... All-Union Scientific Research Institute of the Underground Gasification of Coal (RU)
VNIIPP......... All-Union Scientific Research, Design, and Technological Institute of the Bearing Industry (RU)
VNIIPP......... All-Union Scientific Research Institute of the Brewing Industry (RU)
VNIIPP......... All-Union Scientific Research Institute of Fruit and Vegetable Processing Industry (RU)
VNIIPP......... All-Union Scientific Research Institute of the Printing Industry (RU)
VNIIPPIT ..... All-Union Scientific Research Institute of the Printing Industry and Technology (RU)
VNIIPRKh.... All-Russian Scientific Research Institute of Pond Fisheries (RU)
VNIIProdmash ... All-Union Scientific Research Institute of Food Machinery (RU)
VNIIPromgaz ... All-Union Scientific Research Institute of Gas Utilization in the National Economy and of Underground Storage of Petroleum, Petroleum Products, and Liquefied Gas (RU)
VNIIPromzhilstroy ... All-Union Scientific Research Institute for the Organization and Mechanization of Industrial and Housing Construction (RU)
VNIIPS......... All-Union Scientific Research Institute of Beet Growing (RU)
VNIIPS......... All-Union Scientific Research Institute for Shale Processing (RU)
VNIIPT......... All-Union Scientific Research Institute of Industrial Transportation (RU)
VNIIPTMash ... All-Union Scientific Research, Planning, and Design Institute of Hoisting and Conveying Machinery, Loading, Unloading, and Warehouse Equipment and Containers (RU)
VNIIPTO...... All-Union Scientific Research Institute of Hoisting and Conveying Equipment (RU)
VNIIPTUGLEMASh ... All-Union Scientific Research, Planning, and Technological Institute of Coal Machinery (RU)
VNIIRT......... All-Union Scientific Research Institute of Magnetic Sound Recording and the Technology of Radio Broadcasting and Television (RU)
VNIIRTMash ... All-Union Scientific Research and Design Institute of Industrial Rubber Machinery (RU)
VNIIS........... All-Union Scientific Research Institute of Cheese-Making Industry (RU)
VNIIS........... All-Union Scientific Research Institute of Glass (RU)
VNIIS........... All-Union Scientific Research Institute of Standardization (RU)
VNIISel'khozmikrobiologii ... All-Union Scientific Research Institute of Agricultural Microbiology (RU)
VNIIShP ...... All-Union Scientific Research Institute of the Garment Industry (RU)
VNIIShveyprom ... All-Union Scientific Research Institute of the Garment Industry (RU)
VNIISI.......... All-Union Scientific Research Institute of Sanitary Testing (RU)
VNIISINZh... All-Union Scientific Research and Planning Institute of Synthetic Fat Substitutes (RU)
VNIISK .... All-Union Scientific Research Institute of Soybean and Castor-Oil Plants (RU)
VNIISK .... All-Union Scientific Research Institute of Synthetic Rubber Imeni S. V. Lebedev (RU)
VNIISKhA.... All-Union Scientific Research Institute of Agricultural and Forestry Aviation (RU)
VNIISKhM... All-Union Scientific Research Institute of Agricultural Microbiology (RU)
VNIISLVP.... All-Union Scientific Research Institute of the Alcohol, Liqueur, and Vodka Industry (RU)
VNIISM........ All-Union Scientific Research Institute of Building Materials (RU)
VNIISNDV ... All-Union Scientific Research Institute of Synthetic and Natural Fragrant Substances (RU)
VNIISP......... All-Union Scientific Research Institute of the Alcohol, Liqueur, and Vodka Industry (RU)
VNIISP......... All-Union Scientific Research Institute of Beet Growing (RU)
VNIISS .... All-Russian Scientific Research Institute of Sugar Beets and Sugar (RU)
VNIISS .... All-Union Scientific Research Institute of Arid Subtropics (RU)
VNIISSV...... All-Union Scientific Research Institute of Glass Plastics and Glass Fibers (RU)
VNIIST......... All-Union Scientific Research Institute for the Construction of Trunk Pipelines (RU)
VNIIST......... All-Union Scientific Research Institute of Hard Alloys (RU)
VNIISteklo ... All-Union Scientific Research Institute of Glass (RU)
VNIISTO...... All-Union Scientific Research Institute of Sanitary Engineering Equipment (RU)
VNIIStrom... All-Union Scientific Research Institute of Building Materials and Structural Parts (RU)
VNIISTROMMASh ... All-Union Scientific Research Institute of Machinery for the Building Materials Industry (RU)
VNIISTROYDORMASh ... All-Union Scientific Research Institute of Construction and Road Machinery (RU)
VNIIStroyneft' ... All-Union Scientific Research Institute for the Construction of Petroleum Industry Establishments (RU)
VNIISV .... All-Union Scientific Research Institute of Glass Fibers (RU)
VNIISZ......... All-Union Scientific Research Institute of the Soviet Legislation (RU)
VNIIT........... All-Union Scientific Research Institute of Fuel Processing and Utilization (RU)
VNIIT........... All-Union Scientific Research Institute of Fuel Utilization (RU)
VNIIT........... All-Union Scientific Research Institute of Sources of Current (RU)
VNIIT........... All-Union Scientific Research Institute of Television (RU)
VNIITB......... All-Union Scientific Research Institute of Safety Engineering in the Petroleum Industry (RU)
VNIITE......... All-Union Scientific Research Institute for Aesthetic Styling in Engineering (RU)
VNIITGP...... All-Union Scientific Research Institute of the Textile and Notions Industry (RU)
VNIITIPribor ... All-Union Scientific Research Technological Institute of Instrument Making (RU)
VNIITISM .... All-Union Scientific Research Institute of Fine Grinding of Building Materials (RU)
VNIITMash ... All-Union Scientific Research Institute of Machinery-Manufacturing Technology (RU)
VNIITMASh ... Volgograd Scientific Research Institute of Machinery-Manufacturing Technology (RU)
VNIITNeft' ... All-Union Scientific Research Institute of Petroleum-Processing Technology (RU)
VNIITneft'.... All-Union Scientific Research Institute for Transportation, Storage, and Use of Petroleum Products (RU)
VNIITORGmash ... All-Union Scientific Research and Experimental Design Institute of Commercial Machinery (RU)
VNIITP......... All-Union Scientific Research Institute of Knit Goods Industry (RU)
VNIITP......... All-Union Scientific Research Institute of the Peat Industry (RU)
VNIITS......... All-Union Scientific Research Institute of Hard Alloys (RU)
VNIITsvetmet ... All-Union Scientific Research Institute of Nonferrous Metallurgy (RU)
VNIIUgleobogashcheniye ... All-Union Planning, Design, and Scientific Research Institute of Coal Enrichment and Briquetting (RU)
VNIIV........... All-Union Scientific Research Institute of Railroad Car Building (RU)
VNIIV........... All-Union Scientific Research Institute of Synthetic Fibers (RU)
VNIIVESPROM ... All-Union Scientific Research Institute of Scales and Instruments (RU)
VNIIVIV .... All-Union Scientific Research Institute of Wine Making and Viticulture (RU)
VNIIVODGEO ... All-Union Scientific Research Institute of Water Supply, Sewer Systems, Hydraulic Engineering Structures, and Engineering Hydrogeology (RU)
VNIIVS .... All-Union Scientific Research Institute of Humid Subtropics (RU)
VNIIVS .... All-Union Scientific Research Institute of Veterinary Sanitation (RU)
VNIIVSE .... All-Union Scientific Research Institute of Veterinary Sanitation and Ectoparasitology (RU)
VNIIVViM .... All-Union Scientific Research Institute of Veterinary Virology and Microbiology (RU)
VNIIYaGG.... All-Union Scientific Research Institute of Nuclear Geophysics and Geochemistry (RU)
VNIIZ........... All-Union Scientific Research Institute of Grain and Grain Products (RU)
VNIIZ........... All-Union Scientific Research Institute of Sound Recording (RU)
VNIIZh......... All-Union Scientific Research Institute of Fats (RU)
VNIIZh......... All-Union Scientific Research Institute of Livestock Breeding (RU)
VNIIZhelezobeton ... All-Union Scientific Research Institute of Industrial Technology of Precast Reinforced Concrete Structural Parts and Products (RU)
VNIIZhG...... All-Union Scientific Research Institute of Railroad Hygiene (RU)
VNIIZhP....... All-Union Scientific Research Institute of Animal Raw Materials and Furs (RU)
VNIIZhS ...... All-Union Scientific Research Institute for the Industrialization of Housing Construction (RU)
VNIIZhT....... All-Union Scientific Research Institute of Railroad Transportation (RU)
VNIIZKh ...... All-Union Scientific Research Institute of Grain Farming (RU)
VNIK............ All-Union Scientific Research Institute of Rubber-Yielding Plants (RU)
VNIKhFI ...... All-Union Scientific Research, Chemical, and Pharmaceutical Institute Imeni Sergo Ordzhonikidze (RU)
VNIKhI......... All-Union Scientific Research Institute of the Refrigeration Industry (RU)
VNIKhT .... All-Union Scientific Research Institute of the Solid Fuel Chemistry (RU)
VNIKO......... All-Union Scientific Research Institute of Hemp (RU)
VNIL............ All-Union Scientific Research Laboratory (RU)
VNILALMAZ ... All-Union Scientific Research Laboratory of Diamond Tools and Diamond Substitutes (RU)

VNILAMI...... All-Union Scientific Research Institute of Silviculture and Conservational Afforestation (RU)
VNILAR....... All-Union Scientific Research Institute of Medicinal and Aromatic Plants (RU)
VNILDILS.... All-Union Scientific Research Laboratory of Dispersion Medicinal Herbs (RU)
VNILP.......... All-Union Scientific Research Laboratory of the Brewing Industry (RU)
VNILRO....... All-Union Scientific Research Laboratory for the Chemical Processing of Vegetable Wastes (RU)
VNILTARA... All-Union Scientific Research Laboratory of Packing Materials (RU)
VNILZO....... All-Union Scientific Research Laboratory of Fur Farming and Antlered Reindeer Breeding (RU)
VNIMI.......... All-Union Scientific Research Institute of the Dairy Industry (RU)
VNIMI.......... All-Union Scientific Research Institute of Mine Surveying (RU)
VNIMS......... Vorkuta Permafrost Scientific Research Station (RU)
VNIO........... All-Union Scientific Research Institute of Hunting (RU)
VNIOChERMET... All-Union Scientific Research Institute for the Organization of Production and Labor in Ferrous Metallurgy (RU)
VNIOK......... All-Union Scientific Research Institute of Sheep and Goat Breeding (RU)
VNIOMS...... All-Union Scientific Research Institute for the Organization and Mechanization of Construction (RU)
VNIORKh..... All-Union Scientific Research Institute of Lake and River Fisheries (RU)
VNIOSP....... All-Union Scientific Research Institute of the Dehydrated Vegetables Industry (RU)
VNIOT......... All-Union Scientific Research Institute of Work Safety (RU)
VNIPI........... All-Union Scientific Research and Planning Institute (RU)
VNIPISel'elektro... All-Union Scientific Research and Planning Institute for the Supply of Electric Power to Agricultural and Other Users in Rural Areas (RU)
VNIPO......... All-Union Scientific Research Institute of Fur, Peltry, and Hunting (RU)
VNIPP.......... All-Union Scientific Research, Design, and Technological Institute of the Bearing Industry (RU)
VNIPRKh..... All-Russian Scientific Research Institute of Pond Fisheries (RU)
VNIPTI......... All-Union Scientific Research, Planning, and Technological Institute of Crane and Traction Electrical Equipment (RU)
VNiR............ Departmental Norms and Wages, Departmental Standards and Costs (RU)
VNIRO......... All-Union Scientific Research Institute of Sea Fisheries and Oceanography (RU)
VNIS............ All-Union Scientific Research Institute of Sugar Beets (RU)
VNIS............ All-Union Scientific Research Institute of the Sugar Industry (RU)
VNISI........... All-Union Scientific Research Institute of Illuminating Engineering (RU)
VNISK......... All-Union Scientific Research Institute of Subtropical Crops (RU)
VNISP.......... All-Union Scientific Research Institute of the Salt Industry (RU)
VNISS......... All-Russian Scientific Research Institute of Sugar Beets and Sugar (RU)
VNITB.......... All-Union Scientific Research Institute of Safety Engineering in the Petroleum Industry (RU)
VNITI........... All-Union Scientific Research Diesel Locomotive Institute (RU)
VNITI........... All-Union Scientific Research Institute of Pipes (RU)
VNITIMashpribor... All-Union Scientific Research Technological Institute of Machinery Manufacture and Instrument Making (RU)
VNITIPRIBOR... All-Union Scientific Research Technological Institute of Instrument Making (RU)
VNITO......... All-Union Scientific, Engineering, and Technical Society (RU)
VNITOE....... All-Union Scientific, Engineering, and Technical Society of Power Engineers (RU)
VNITOEP..... All-Union Scientific, Engineering, and Technical Society of the Power Industry (RU)
VNITOGET... All-Union Scientific, Engineering, and Technical Society of the City Electric Transportation Systems (RU)
VNITOKF..... All-Union Scientific, Engineering, and Technical Society of the Motion Picture and Photo Industry (RU)
VNITOKhim... All-Union Scientific, Engineering, and Technical Society of Chemists (RU)
VNITOKozhobuvmekh... All-Union Scientific, Engineering, and Technical Society of the Leather, Footwear, Fur, and Leather Substitute Industries (RU)
VNITOKSh... All-Union Scientific, Engineering, and Technical Society of the Forging and Stamping Industry Workers (RU)
VNITOL....... All-Union Scientific, Engineering, and Technical Society of Foundry Workers (RU)
VNITOLegprom... All-Union Scientific, Engineering, and Technical Society of Light Industry (RU)
VNITOLES... All-Union Scientific, Engineering, and Technical Society of the Lumber Industry and Forestry (RU)
VNITOLKh... All-Union Scientific, Engineering, and Technical Society of Forestry (RU)
VNITOM...... All-Union Scientific, Engineering, and Technical Society of Metallurgists (RU)
VNITOMASh... All-Union Scientific, Engineering, and Technical Society of Machine Builders (RU)
VNITOMASh... All-Union Scientific Research Institute of Machinery-Manufacturing Technology (RU)
VNITO MKhKP... All-Union Scientific, Engineering, and Technical Society of Flour-Milling, Baking, and Groats Industry (RU)
VNITO-NEFT'... All-Union Scientific, Engineering, and Technical Society of Petroleum Workers (RU)
VNITOPribor... All-Union Scientific, Engineering, and Technical Society of Instrument Making (RU)
VNITOS....... All-Union Scientific, Engineering, and Technical Society of Welders (RU)
VNITOSS..... All-Union Scientific, Engineering, and Technical Society of Shipbuilding (RU)
VNITO tsemkeramikov... All-Union Scientific, Engineering, and Technical Society of the Cement and Ceramics Industry (RU)
VNITO tsvetnikov... All-Union Scientific, Engineering, and Technical Society of Workers of Nonferrous Metallurgy (RU)
VNITOVT..... All-Union Scientific, Engineering, and Technical Society of Water Transportation (RU)
VNITs.......... All-Union Scientific Research Institute of Cements (RU)
VNITs SSD... All-Union Scientific Research Center of Standard and Reference Data (RU)
VNIVI........... All-Union Scientific Research Institute of Vitamins (RU)
VNIZhP........ All-Union Scientific Research Institute of Animal Raw Materials and Furs (RU)
VNK............. Water-Oil Contact (RU)
VNKh........... Great People's Assembly [*Mongolian People's Republic*] (RU)
VNKK.......... Provisional People's Advisory Congress [*Indonesian*] (RU)
VNKSK........ North Korean Provisional National Committee (BU)
VNKSK........ Provisional People's Committee of North Korea (RU)
VNM............ Verlag Neue Musik [*Neue Musik Publishing House*] (EG)
VNM............ Vietnam [*Three-letter standard code*] (CNC)
VNIIBurneft'... All-Union Scientific Research and Planning Institute for Drilling Oil and Gas Wells (RU)
VNO............. Military Scientific Society (RU)
VNO............. Verbond van Nederlandse Ondernemingen [*Federation of Netherlands Enterprises*] (WEN)
VNOAGE..... All-Union Scientific Society of Anatomists, Histologists, and Embryologists (RU)
VNOE.......... Vasilikos Navtikos Omilos Ellados [*Royal Yacht Club of Greece*] (GC)
VNOLO........ All-Union Scientific Society of Otolaryngologists (RU)
VNORiE....... All-Union Scientific Society of Radio Engineering and Telecommunications Imeni A. S. Popov (RU)
VNOS.......... Air Warning and Communications Service (BU)
VNOS.......... Aircraft-Warning Service (RU)
VNP............. Auxiliary Observation Post (RU)
VNP............. Gross National Product (RU)
VNP............. Temporary Observation Post (RU)
VNP............. Vanguardia Nacionalista Popular [*Nationalist Popular Vanguard*] [*Colombian*] (LA)
VNP............. Venda National Party (PPW)
VNP............. Vlaamse Nationaale Partij (Volksunie) [*Flemish National Party (People's Union)*] [*Belgian*] (WEN)
VNPK........... Higher Scientific Pedagogical Courses (RU)
VNPO.......... Vsenarodni Priprava Obyvatelstva [*National Training Program*] [*Civil defense*] (CZ)
VNR............. Hungarian People's Republic (RU)
VNS............. Grand National Assembly (BU)
VNS............. Heterologous Serum (RU)
VNS............. Supreme People's Assembly [*North Korean*] (RU)
VNTO.......... All-Union Scientific and Technical Society (RU)
VNTOE........ All-Union Scientific, Engineering, and Technical Society of Power Engineers (RU)
VNTS........... All-Union Petroleum Technical Station (RU)
VNTTX......... Viet Nam Thong Tan Xa [*Vietnam News Agency*] (TVP)
VNUS.......... Service Troops (RU)
vnutr.......... Interior, Inner, Internal (RU)
VNV............. Vlaamsch Nationaal Verbond [*Flemish National League*] [*Dissolved*] [*Belgian*] (PPE)
v n vr.......... Now, At Present, At the Present Time (RU)
VNVSU........ Higher People's Military Construction Academy (BU)
VNVSU........ Higher People's Military Signals Academy (BU)
VNVU.......... Higher People's Military Academy (BU)
VNW............ Verbond van Nederlandse Werkgevers [*Federation of Netherlands Employers*] [*Defunct*] (WEN)
VNZ............. Military Criminal Law (BU)
VNZ............. Verlag Neue Zeit [*Neue Zeit Publishing House*] (EG)
vn zak.......... Military Criminal Law (BU)
VO............... Air Cooler (RU)
VO............... Air Raid Danger (BU)
VO............... All-Union Association (RU)
VO............... Armed Guards (RU)
VO............... Deviation Detector (RU)
VO............... Dump Car (RU)
vo................ Helicopter Detachment (RU)
VO............... Light Switch (RU)
vo................ Military Detachment (BU)
VO............... Military District (RU)
VO............... Obzor, Vydavatelstvo Knih a Casopisov [*Obzor, Publishing House for Books and Magazines*] (CZ)
VO............... Probable Error (RU)

vo .... Vaimo [*Finnish*]
VO .... Vanguardia Obrera [*Workers' Vanguard Party*] [*Bolivian*] (LA)
VO .... Vasil'yevskiy Ostrov [*Leningrad*] (RU)
VO .... Vatreno Osmatranje [*Fire Observation*] [*Military*] (YU)
VO .... Vazdusna Odbrana [*Air Defense*] (YU)
VO .... Velitelstvi Oblasti [*Regional Military Headquarters*] (CZ)
VO .... Velitelstvi Oddilu [*Detachment Headquarters (Security Police)*] (CZ)
VO .... Velkoodberatelia [*Bulk Consumers*] (CZ)
VO .... Verordnung [*Decree, Ordinance*] [*German*] (WEN)
vo .... Vesd Ossze [*Compare*] (HU)
VO .... Voimistelunopettaja [*Finnish*]
VO .... Vojenska Osveta [*Military Cultural Activities*] (CZ)
VO .... Vojenske Oddeleni [*Military Department*] (CZ)
VO .... Vojensky Okruh [*Military District*] (CZ)
vo .... Von Oben [*From Above*] [*German*]
V/O .... Vsesojuznoje Objedinenije [*All-Union Association*] [*Russian*]
VO .... Vycvikovy Odbor [*Training Branch*] (CZ)
VO .... Vydavatelstvi Obchodu [*Trade Literature Publishing House*] (CZ)
VO .... Vydavatelstvi Osveta [*Cultural Publishing House (in Martin)*] (CZ)
VO .... Vyrobna Oblast [*Production Area*] (CZ)
VOAPP .... All-Union Society of Associations of Proletarian Writers (RU)
VOB .... Battery Computation Section [*Artillery*] (RU)
VOB .... Vereinigung Organisationseigener Betriebe [*Association of Organization-Owned Enterprises*] (EG)
VOBL .... Verordnungsblatt [*Decree Gazette*] (EG)
VoBo .... Visto Bueno [*All Right*] [*Spanish*]
VOC .... Vanguardia Obrero Catolica [*Catholic Workers Vanguard*] [*Spanish*] (WER)
VOC .... Vereenigde Nederlandsche Ge-Octroeerde Oost-Indische Compagnie (MAR)
VOC .... Verenigde Oost Indische Compagnie [*United East Indies Company*] (IN)
VOCAST ..... Vocational College of Arts (MAR)
vod .... Aqueous, Hydrous, Water (RU)
VOD .... Battalion Computation Section [*Artillery*] (RU)
vod .... Water Tower [*Topography*] (RU)
VODGEO ..... All-Union Scientific Research Institute of Water Supply, Sewer Systems, Hydraulic Engineering Structures, and Engineering Hydrogeology (RU)
VODK .... [*The*] Voice of Democratic Kampuchea [*Radio station of the Red Khmers*] (PD)
vodn .... Aqueous, Hydrous, Water (RU)
Vodokanal ... Water Supply and Sewer System Administration (RU)
Vodokanalproekt ... Water Supply and Sewage Planning Service (BU)
VODOKANALPROYeKT ... State Planning Institute for the Surveying and Planning of Outdoor Water Supply, Sewer Systems, and Hydraulic Engineering Structures (RU)
VODOPLIN ... Poduzece za Plin i Vodovod [*Enterprise for Transmission of Gas and Water*] (YU)
Vodoprojekt ... Statni Ustav pro Projektovani Zdravotne Hospodarskych Staveb [*State Institute for the Design of Sanitation Installations*] (CZ)
Vodostroy ... Water Works Enterprise (BU)
Vodproekt ... Water Works Designing Enterprise (BU)
VODSANTEKh ... State Institute of Water Supply and Sanitary Engineering (RU)
vod st .... Water Column [*In units of pressure*] (RU)
Vodstroy ..... Hydraulic Engineering (BU)
Vodtransizdat ... State Publishing House of Water Transportation (RU)
VOeEST ...... Vereinigte Oesterreichische Eisen- und Stahlwerke AG [*United Austrian Iron and Steel Works, Inc.*] (WEN)
VOeI .... Vereinigung Oesterreichischer Industrieller [*Association of Austrian Industrialists*] (WEN)
Voen .... Military (BU)
Voenkom .... Military Commandant (BU)
Voenkor ..... Military Correspondent (BU)
Voenna A .... Military Academy (BU)
VOEST .... Vereinigte Oesterreichische Edelstahlwerke AG
VOF .... All-Russian Philatelic Society (RU)
VOFU .... Military Finance Directorate (RU)
VOFVTI .... Eastern Branch of the All-Union Institute of Heat Engineering (RU)
VOG .... All-Russian Society of Deaf-Mutes (RU)
VOG .... All-Union Society of Helminthologists (RU)
VOGA .... Vologda Oblast State Archives (RU)
VOGES .... All-Union Association of Hydroelectric Power Plants (RU)
VOGI .... All-Russian Society of Civil Engineers (RU)
VOGRES ..... Voronezh State Regional Electric Power Plant (RU)
VOGVF .... All-Union Association of the Civil Air Fleet [*1930-1932*] (RU)
Voi .... Vrakhoi [*Rocks*] [*See also Vos*] [*Greek*] (NAU)
voim .... Voimistelu [*Gymnastics*] [*Finnish*]
voimop .... Voimistelunopettaja [*Finnish*]
VOINZhAK ... Military Engineering Academy (RU)
VOIP .... All-Union Association of the Tool Industry (RU)
VOIR .... All-Union Society of Inventors and Efficiency Experts (RU)
VOIUU .... Voronezh Oblast Institute for the Advanced Training of Teachers (RU)
VOIV .... All-Union Association of the Synthetic Fiber Industry (RU)
VOIZ .... All-Union Society of Inventors (RU)
VOJ .... Vazduhoplovno Osmatranje, Obavestavanje, i Javljanje [*Air Force Observation, Information, and Reporting*] (YU)
Vojno-medB ... Vojno-Medicinski Bilten Garnizona Vojne Bolnice [*Medical Bulletin of the Military Hospital Garrison*] [*Ljubljana*] [*A publication*] (YU)
Vojv .... Vojvodina (Novi Sad) [*A periodical*] (YU)
Voj z sl .... Vojin Zakladni Sluzby [*Private Serving His Basic Conscription Term*] (CZ)
VOK .... All-Russian Association of Health Resorts (RU)
VOK .... Verejna Obecni Knihovna [*Municipal Public Library*] (CZ)
VOK .... Voice of Kenya (MAR)
VOKD .... Vystavba Ostravsko-Karvinskych Dolu [*Development of the Ostrava Karvina Mines*] (CZ)
VOKhIMFARM ... All-Union Association of Chemical and Pharmaceutical Industry (RU)
VOKhIMU .... Chemical Warfare Directorate (RU)
VOKhR .... Internal Security Troops of the Republic (RU)
VOKhR .... Militarized Guard [*At airfields and warehouses*] (RU)
VOKK .... All-Union Society of the Red Cross and Red Crescent (RU)
VOKO .... All-Union State Association for the Production of Municipal Equipment (RU)
VOKP .... All-Union Society of Peasant Writers (RU)
VOKS .... All-Union Society for Cultural Relations with Foreign Countries [*1925-1958*] (RU)
VO KSC .... Vesnicka Organizace KSC [*Village Organization of the Czechoslovak Communist Party*] (CZ)
VOKT .... All-Union Association for Goods for Cultural Purposes (RU)
VOKU .... Higher Joint Command School (RU)
VOL .... Voice of Lebanon (MAR)
vol .... Volost (RU)
Vol .... Volum [*Volume*] [*German*]
vol .... Volume [*Volume*] [*French*]
vol .... Volumen [*Spanish*]
Vol-% .... Volumenprozent [*Percent by Volume*] (EG)
vol .... Voluntad [*Spanish*]
VO-LA .... Vazdusna Odbrana - Lovacka Avijacija [*Air Defense - Fighter Aviation*] (YU)
VOLBRICERAM ... Societe Voltaique de Briqueterie et de Ceramique (MAR)
Vol-Gew ...... Volumetrisches Gewicht [*Volumetric Weight*] [*German*]
Volgo-Balt ... Volga-Baltic Waterway (RU)
VolgogradNII NG ... Volgograd Scientific Research Institute of the Petroleum and Gas Industry (RU)
Volkhovges ... Volkhov Hydroelectric Power Plant Imeni V. I. Lenin (RU)
volkstuml .... Volkstuemlich [*German*]
voln .... Wave (RU)
VOLT .... All-Union Association of the Lumber and Woodworking Industry in Transportation (RU)
Vol T .... Volumenteil [*Part by Volume*] [*German*]
VOLTAICA ... Societe Voltaique pour l'Avancement de l'Industrie, du Commerce, et de l'Agriculture (MAR)
VOLTAP ...... Societe Voltaique de Diffusion d'Appareils Eletriques (MAR)
VOLTAPAT ... Societe Voltaique de Pates Alimentaires (MAR)
VOLTAVIN ... Societe des Vins de la Haute-Volta (MAR)
VOLTELEC ... Societe Voltaique d'Electricite [*Voltan Electric Company*] (AF)
VOLTEMA ... Volta Emaillerie (MAR)
VOLTEX ...... Societe Voltaique du Textile (MAR)
VOLTOA ...... Societe Voltaique d'Oxygene et d'Acetylene (MAR)
VOM .... All-Russian Society of Motorcyclists (RU)
VOM .... Power Takeoff Shaft (RU)
VOM .... Vybor Obrancu Miru [*Committee of the Defenders of Peace*] (CZ)
VOMEDAK ... Military Medical Academy (RU)
VOMI .... Volksdeutsche Mittelstelle [*NAZI Germany*]
VOMT .... All-Union Heavy Machinery-Manufacturing Association (RU)
VON .... Reference-Voltage Rectifier (RU)
VON .... Reivers Vegetable Oils Nigeria Limited (MAR)
Von .... Vallon [*Vale*] [*Military map abbreviation*] [*World War I*] [*French*] (MTD)
VON .... Vasiliki Organosis Neolaias [*Greek Royalist Youth*] (GC)
VON .... Voice of Nigeria (MAR)
von .... Vonal [*Line (In transportation, communication)*] (HU)
von .... Vonat [*Train*] (HU)
vonalm .... Vonalmester [*Line Supervisor*] (HU)
VONJY .... Elan Populaire pour l'Unite Nationale [*Popular Impulse for National Unity*] [*Malagasy*] (PPW)
VONS .... Committee for the Defense of Persons Unjustly Persecuted [*Czechoslovak*] (PD)
VOO .... Military Hunting Society (RU)
VOO .... Military Operations Section (RU)
VOOMP .... All-Union Optical Instrument Industry Association (RU)
VOOP .... All-Russian Society for the Conservation of Natural Resources (RU)
voorh .... Voorheen [*Formerly*] [*Dutch*]
VOOV .... Vazdusno Osmatranje, Obavestavanje, i Veza [*Air Observation, Information, and Communication*] [*Military*] (YU)
VOP .... All-Union Society of Soil Scientists (RU)
VOP .... Explosive Item (RU)
VOP .... Vallalati Optimalis Program [*Optimal Enterprise Plan*] (HU)
VOP .... Vanguardia Organizada del Pueblo [*People's Organized Vanguard*] [*Chilean*] (LA)

VOP............ Voice of Palestine (ME)
VOPA.......... General Association of Trade Unions of Algeria (RU)
VOPB........... Voice of the People of Burma [*Radio station of the Burma Communist Party*] (PD)
Vopedak..... Military Pedagogical Academy (RU)
VOPKP........ All-Russian Organization of Proletarian and Kolkhoz Writers (RU)
VOPO.......... Volkspolizei [*People's Police*] (EG)
VOPP........... All-Union Society of Proletarian Writers (RU)
VOPRA........ All-Union Association of Proletarian Architects [*1929-1932*] (RU)
VOPRD........ Vin de Qualite Produit dans Une Region Determinee (MAR)
Vopr raketn tekhn Sb perev i obz in period lit ... Problems of Rocketry. Collections of Translations and Reviews of Foreign Periodical Literature [*A publication*] (RU)
VOPT........... Voice of the People of Thailand [*Radio station of the Communist Party of Thailand*] (PD)
VOR............ Vegetable Oil Refiners (MAR)
vor.............. Vorig [*Preceding*] [*German*]
VORAO........ Eastern Branch of the Russian Archaeological Society (RU)
vorgy........... Vezerornagy [*Major General*] (HU)
vorh............. Vorhanden [*In Stock*] [*German*]
VORI............ General Association of Workers of Spain (RU)
Vork............. Vorkommen [*Occurrence*] [*German*]
VORKM....... General Association of Workers and Peasants of Mexico (RU)
vorm............ Vormals [*Formerly, Previously*] (EG)
vorm............ Vormittags [*In the Morning*] [*German*] (GPO)
Voronezhsel'mash ... Voronezh Agricultural Machinery Plant (RU)
VORP........... Volga United River Steamship Line (RU)
VORS.......... All-Union Society of Construction Efficiency Experts [*1932-1934*] (RU)
VORS.......... All-Union Society of Efficiency Experts of Construction and the Building Materials Industry [*1929-1932*] (RU)
Vors............. Vorsitzender [*Chairman*] [*German*] (GPO)
Vorst........... Vorstand [*German*]
Vorst........... Vorsteher [*German*]
Vorst........... Vorstehung [*German*]
VORT........... All-Union River Transportation Association (RU)
Vortr............ Vortragender [*German*]
VORZ........... All-Union Association of Repair Plants of the NKPS (RU)
VOS............. All-Russian Society of the Blind (RU)
VOS............. High-Altitude Optical Station (RU)
VOS............. Varna Oblast Court (BU)
VOS............. Varnostna Obvescevalna Sluzba [*Security Information Service*] (YU)
VOS............. Veterinary Experimental Station (RU)
VOS............. Vojenska Odborna Skola [*Military Career Specialist School (NCO)*] (CZ)
VOS............. Vojno-Obavestajna Sluzba [*Military Information Service*] (YU)
Vos.............. Vrakhos [*Rock*] [*See also Voi*] [*Greek*] (NAU)
VoSam........ Soldiers' Amateur Art Activities (BU)
VoSand....... Voenno-Sanitarno Delo [*Military Medical Affairs*] [*A periodical*] (BU)
VOSB.......... All-Union Society of Old Bolsheviks (RU)
vosk............ Wax Refinery [*Topography*] (RU)
VOSKhIM.... All-Union State Association of Sugar and Chemical Machinery Manufacture (RU)
VOSM.......... All-Russian Society of Modern Music (RU)
VOSO.......... Military Communications Service (RU)
VOSOF........ Varnostnoobvescevalna Sluzba Osvobodilne Fronte [*Security Information Service of the Liberation Front*] [*Slovenia*] [*World War II*] (YU)
VOSOP........ All-Russian Society for Assisting the Conservation of Natural Resources and the Landscaping of Populated Places (RU)
vosp............ Education, Educational, Memoirs, Training, Upbringing (RU)
VOSR.......... [*The*] Great October Socialist Revolution (BU)
vosst pl....... Reducing Flame (RU)
vost............. Eastern (RU)
VOSt............ Vizuelna Osmatracka Stanica [*Visual Observation Station*] [*Army*] (YU)
VOSTGOSTORG ... All-Union Association for Trade with the Countries of the East (RU)
VOSTKIS..... Eastern Complex Scientific Research Institute of Structures (RU)
VostNIGRI... Eastern Scientific Research Ore-Mining Institute (RU)
VOSTNII...... Eastern Scientific Research Institute of Work Safety in Mining (RU)
Vostokintorg ... All-Union Import-Export Association (of the Ministry of Foreign Trade, USSR) (RU)
Vostokostal' ... All-Union Association of the Metallurgical, Iron Ore, and Manganese Industry of the Eastern Part of the USSR [*1927-1933*] (RU)
VOSU.......... All-Union Society of Social Census (RU)
VOSZ........... Vakok Orszagos Szovetsege [*National Association of the Blind*] (HU)
VOSZK........ "VOSZK" Kereskedelmi, Ipari es Szolgaltato Szovetkezeti Vallalat [*"VOSZK" Servicing Cooperative Enterprise of Trade and Industry*] (HU)
VOT............. Venerable Orden Tercera [*Spanish*]
VOTA.......... General Association of Workers of Algeria (RU)
VOTChA...... General Association of Workers of Black Africa (RU)
VOTChA...... Vseobshchee Ob'edinenie Trudiashchikhsia Chernoi Afriki (MAR)
VOTI............ All-Union Precision Industry Association (RU)
VOTI............ State All-Union Precision Industry Trust (RU)
VOU............. Vyzkumny Osvetovy Ustav [*Cultural Research Institute*] (CZ)
VOVAT........ All-Union Association of Railroad Car and Streetcar Manufacture (RU)
VOVG.......... All-Russian Society of Homeopathists (RU)
VOVI............ Vlaams Opleidingsinstituut voor Informatie
VOW............ Voice of Women (MAR)
voy............... Voyez [*See*] [*French*] (GPO)
voyen........... Military, Military Term (RU)
Voyengiz..... State Military Publishing House (RU)
Voyenizdat ... Military Publishing House of the Ministry of Defense, USSR (RU)
voyenkhozupr ... Directorate of Logistics (RU)
voyen kom ... Military Commissar (RU)
voyenkor..... Military Correspondent (RU)
voyenlet...... Military Pilot (RU)
voyen-med ... Military Medical (RU)
Voyen-med zh ... Military Medical Journal [*A publication*] (RU)
voyen-mor ... Naval (RU)
voyenmor.... Naval Serviceman (RU)
Voyenmorizdat ... Naval Publishing House (RU)
Voyenokhot ... Factory of the All-Army Hunting Society (RU)
Voyensanupr ... Military Medical Directorate (RU)
Voyensov.... Military Council (RU)
Voyenspets ... Military Specialist (RU)
Voyenstrupr ... Military Construction Directorate (RU)
voyentekhupr ... Military Technical Directorate (RU)
voyentorg ... Directorate of Trade Establishments for Military Personnel (RU)
voyentorg ... Trade Establishment for Military Personnel (RU)
voyenved.... Military Department (RU)
Voyen vestn ... Military Herald [*A publication*] (RU)
Voyenvetupr ... Military Veterinary Directorate (RU)
voyenzag.... Military Procurement Section [*1918-1920*] (RU)
VOZ............. Military Defense Zone (BU)
VOZ............. Military Zone of Operations (BU)
VOZ............. Vojenske Opravarenske Zavody [*Military Repair Shops*] (CZ)
VOZ............. Vojensky Odznak Zdatnosti [*Military Emblem of Bravery*] (CZ)
VOZ............. Vsemirnaia Organizatsiia Zdravookhraneniia (MAR)
VOZ............. World Health Organization [*WHO*] (RU)
vozdush...... Air, Aerial (RU)
VOZOT........ All-Union Society "For the Mastering of Technology" (RU)
vozv............. Elevation (RU)
VP................ Air Mail (RU)
vp................ Army Postal Service (BU)
VP................ Auxiliary Device, Auxiliary Instrument (RU)
v/p............... Bound (RU)
VP................ Drinking Water (RU)
vp................ Helicopter Regiment (RU)
vp................ Judge Advocate (BU)
VP................ Military Prosecutor (RU)
VP................ Military Subunit (BU)
VP................ Naval Port (RU)
V/P.............. Prisoner of War (RU)
VP................ Range of Tide (RU)
VP................ Starting Switch (RU)
VP................ Telephone Line Out of Order (BU)
VP................ Troop Train (RU)
VP................ Vanguardia Popular [*Popular Vanguard*] [*Argentine*] (LA)
VP................ Vanguardia Proletaria [*Proletarian Vanguard*] [*Salvadoran*] (LA1)
VP................ Vanparnicni Postupak [*Nonadversary Procedure*] (YU)
VP................ Vanuatu Pati (PD)
VP................ Vasiliki Pronoia [*Royal Welfare Fund*] [*See also EOP*] (GC)
VP................ Vasilikon Ploion [*His Hellenic Majesty's Ship*] (GC)
Vp................ Vastausta Pyydetaan [*Finnish*]
VP................ Vatreni Polozaj [*Firing Position*] [*Military*] (YU)
VP................ Vazdusni Pravac [*Aerial Direction Indicator*] (YU)
VP................ Vece Proizvodaca [*Council of Producers*] (YU)
VP................ Velka Praha [*Greater Prague*] (CZ)
VP................ Vereenigde Partij (MAR)
Vp................ Versuchsperson [*Experimental Person*] [*German*]
VP................ Veterinary Station (RU)
VP................ Vojenska Policie [*Military Police*] (CZ)
VP................ Vojensky Prukaz [*Military Identity Card*] (CZ)
VP................ Vojna Posta [*Military Mail*] (YU)
VP................ Volkspartie [*People's Party*] [*Liechtenstein*] (PPE)
VP................ Vratimovske Papirny [*Vratimov Paper Works*] (CZ)
VP................ Vuestra Paternidad [*Spanish*]
VP................ Vylucny Prodej [*Franchise Sale*] (CZ)
V/p............... Your Letter (RU)
VPA.............. All-Union Industrial Academy (RU)
VPA.............. Military Political Academy Imeni V. I. Lenin (RU)
VPA.............. Vietnam People's Army [*North Vietnamese*] (CL)
VPA.............. Vojenska Politicka Akademie [*Military Political Academy*] (CZ)
VPA.............. Vojno-Pomorska Akademija [*Naval Academy*] (YU)
VPA(B)......... Volkspolizeiabteilung (Betrieb) [*Special Factory Police Detachment*] (EG)

vpad .... Hollow, Depression [*Topography*] (RU)
VPAK .... Military Political Academic Courses (RU)
VPAP .... V Pomosht na Agitatora i Propagandista [*Agitator's and Propagandist's Aid*] [*A periodical*] (BU)
VPAR .... Vremennoe Pravitel'stvo Alzhirskoi Respubliki (MAR)
VPb .... Vatreni Polozaj Baterije [*Battery Firing Position*] (YU)
VPB .... Vojno-Partizanska Bolnica [*Partisan Military Hospital*] (YU)
VPB .... Vojnopomorska Baza [*Naval Base*] (YU)
VPB .... Voortrekkerpers Beperk (MAR)
VPC .... Vardepapperscentralen [*Swedish*]
VPCW .... Verbond van Protestant-Christelijke Werkgevers in Nederland [*Association of Protestant Employers in the Netherlands*] (WEN)
VPD .... Vierte Partei Deutschlands [*Fourth Party of Germany*] [*West German*] (PPW)
VPD .... Volkspolizeidienststelle [*People's Police Post*] (EG)
VPDT .... Temporary Site for Transportation Decontamination (RU)
VPE .... Vojvodanski Pokret u Emigraciji [*Vojvodina Movement in Exile*] (YU)
VPF .... Land Mine Fuze (RU)
VPFEI .... Higher Pedagogical Institute of Finance and Economics (RU)
VPFZ .... High-Altitude Planetary Frontal Zone (RU)
VPG .... Antitank Rifle Grenade (RU)
VPG .... Military Field Hospital (RU)
VPG .... Military Mobile Hospital (RU)
VPI .... Higher Pedagogical Institute of Applied Economics and Science of Commodities (RU)
VPI .... Moscow Higher Pedagogical Institute of the Tsentrosoyuz (RU)
VPI .... Water Preparation Installation [*Nuclear energy*] (BU)
VPJ .... Velitel Vojenskych Pracovnich Jednotek [*Commander of Military Labor Units*] (CZ)
VPK .... All-Union Industrial Office (RU)
VPK .... All-Union Resettlement Committee (RU)
VPK .... Auxiliary Fire Brigade (RU)
VPK .... Higher Pedagogical Courses (RU)
VPK .... Junction Party Committee (BU)
VPK .... Militarized Fire Brigade (RU)
VPK .... Vaensterpartiet Kommunisterna [*Left-Wing Communist Party*] [*Swedish*] (WEN)
VPK .... Vapaahetoinen Palokunta [*Finnish*]
VPKA .... Volkspolizeikreisamt [*Kreis Office of the People's Police*] (EG)
VPKITIM .... All-Union Planning, Design, and Technological Institute of Furniture (RU)
VPL .... Vydavatelstvo Politickej Literatury [*Political Literature Publishing House*] (CZ)
VPLD .... Velkorazni Protiletadlove Delostrlectvo [*Large Caliber AAA*] (CZ)
vplvs .... Drumhead Court Martial (BU)
VPM .... Auxiliary Medical Aid Station (RU)
VPM .... La Voix du Peuple Murundi (MAR)
VPN .... Vanguardia Popular Nacionalista [*Nationalist Popular Vanguard*] [*Venezuelan*] (LA)
VPO .... All-Russian Printing Association (RU)
VPO .... All-Union Paleontological Society (RU)
VPO .... Militarized Fire Prevention (RU)
VPO .... Military Consumers' Society (RU)
VPOD .... Verband des Personals Oeffentlicher Dienste [*Union of Public Service Personnel*] [*Swiss*] (WEN)
VPOO .... Vojna Preduzeca za Izradu Oficirske Odece i Opreme [*Military Establishments for Preparation of Officers' Uniforms and Equipment*] (YU)
VPOP .... Vam es Penzugyorseg Orszagos Parancsnoksaga [*National Command of the Customs and Internal Revenue Police*] (HU)
VPOS .... Visa Pomorska Skola [*Advanced Naval Academy*] (YU)
VPP .... Military Food Supply Station (RU)
VPP .... Platoon Small-Arms Ammunition Supply Point (RU)
VPP .... Runway (RU)
VPR .... Boiling-Water Reactor with Nuclear Superheat (RU)
VPr .... Herald of Industry [*A publication*] (RU)
VPR .... Temporary Transshipment Area (BU)
VPR .... Vanguarda Popular Revolucionaria [*Popular Revolutionary Vanguard*] [*Brazilian*] (LA)
VPrM .... Voenno-Pravna Misul [*Military Law Review*] [*A periodical*] (BU)
VPRO .... Vrijzinnig Protestante Radio Omroep [*Liberal Protestant Broadcasting Association*] [*Dutch*] (WEN)
VPS .... All-Union Fur Syndicate (RU)
VPS .... All-Union Trade Union (RU)
VPS .... Military Lines of Communication (RU)
VPS .... Military Post Office Station (RU)
VPS .... Military Postal Station (BU)
VPS .... Universal Postal Union (RU)
VPS .... Visa Pedagoska Skola [*Advanced Pedagogical School*] (YU)
VPS .... Visi Privredni Sud [*Higher Economic Court*] (YU)
VPS .... Vojensky Pevecky Soubor [*Military Choral Ensemble*] (CZ)
VPS .... Vyssi Pedagogicka Skola [*Higher School of Education*] (CZ)
VPS .... Vyssi Prumyslova Skola [*Higher Industrial School*] (CZ)
VPSB .... Vyssia Priemyselna Skola Banicka [*Higher Industrial School of Mining*] (CZ)
VPSFNRJ .... Vrhovni Privredni Sud Federativna Narodna Republika Jugoslavija [*Supreme Economic Court of Yugoslavia*] (YU)
VPSh .... Fixed-Pitch Propeller (RU)
VPSh .... Higher Party School (BU)
VPSh .... Higher Party School (RU)
VPSh .... Military Political School (RU)
VPSO .... All-Russian Producers' Union of Hunters (RU)
VPSP .... Stimulating Postsynaptic Potential (RU)
VPSRPP ...... All-Russian Trade Union of Workers of the Printing Industry (RU)
VPST .... All-Russian Trade Union of Textile Workers (RU)
VPT .... Hungarian Workers' Party (RU)
VPT .... Vertically Movable Pipe [*Underwater concrete laying*] (RU)
VPT .... Vietnam Lao Dong Party (BU)
VPTI .... All-Union Planning and Technological Institute (RU)
VPTISTROYDORMASh ... All-Union Planning and Technological Institute of Construction and Road Machinery Manufacture (RU)
VPTITYaZhMASh ... All-Union Planning and Technological Institute of Heavy Machinery Manufacture (RU)
VPTO .... Antitank Platoon (RU)
vptr .... Troop Mobile Repair Workshop (BU)
VPU .... Auxiliary Control Post (RU)
VPU .... Extension Control Panel (RU)
VPU .... Intercommunication, Intercom (RU)
VPU .... Military Political School (RU)
VPU- .... Reproducing Sequence Apparatus (RU)
VPU .... Video Control Board (RU)
VPU .... Visa Privredna Udruzenja [*Higher Economic Associations*] (YU)
VPU .... Vojensky Projektovy Ustav [*Military Design Institute*] (CZ)
VPU .... Vojnopomorsko Uporiste [*Naval Stronghold*] (YU)
VPU .... Vseobecny Pensijni Ustav [*General Pension Institute*] (CZ)
VPV .... All-Union Industrial Exhibition (RU)
VPV .... Higher High Water (RU)
VPV .... Velitelstvo Pozemneho Vojska [*Ground Forces Command*] (CZ)
VPV .... Vidam Park Vallalat [*Amusement Park Enterprise*] (HU)
VPVS .... Velitelstvi Pohranicni a Vnitrni Straze [*Border and Interior Guard Headquarters*] (CZ)
VPZ .... Velkoobchod Potravinarskym Zbozim [*Wholesale Food Store*] (CZ)
VPZh .... Plastic-Viscous Liquid (RU)
VQPRD .... Vin de Qualite Produit dans des Regions Determinees [*French*]
VR .... Aerial Reconnaissance (RU)
VR .... Calling Relay (RU)
VR .... Connection for Radio Broadcasting (BU)
VR .... Dining Car (RU)
VR .... Military Reconnaissance (BU)
vr .... Peak (BU)
vr .... Physician (RU)
vr .... Reconnaissance Platoon (RU)
Vr .... Temporary (BU)
Vr .... Time (BU)
VR .... Valtion Rautatiet [*State Railways*] [*Finnish*] (WEN)
VR .... Vanguardia Revolucionaria [*Revolutionary Vanguard*] [*Peruvian*] (PPW)
VR .... Vapaudenristi [*Finnish*]
VR .... Vedecka Rada [*Science Council*] (CZ)
Vr .... Vedouci Reditel [*Managing Director*] (CZ)
VR .... Verlagsrichtlinien [*Guidelines for Publishing Houses*] (EG)
Vr .... Vitesse Totale du Vent [*French*] (MTD)
vr .... Vlastnorucne, Vlastni Rukou [*Signed by Hand*] (CZ)
vr .... Vlastorucan [*By One's Own Hand*] (YU)
VR .... Volksrepublik [*People's Republic*] (EG)
vr .... Vrchni Rada [*Senior Counselor (Title of government official)*] (CZ)
VR .... Vuestra Reverencia [*Your Reverence*] [*Spanish*]
VRA .... Volta River Authority (AF)
vra .... Vuestra [*Your*] [*Spanish*]
vras .... Vuestras [*Your (Plural)*] [*Spanish*]
VRB .... Probable Bomb Release Line (BU)
VRB .... Vereniging Religieuze Bibliotheken
VRB .... Volksrepublik Bulgarien [*People's Republic of Bulgaria*] (EG)
VRC .... Ventas Remates Consignaciones [*Bogota*] (COL)
Vrch strzm ... Vrchni Strazmistr [*First Sergeant*] (CZ)
VRD .... Air Jet Engines (BU)
VRD .... Jet Engine, Air-Breathing Jet Engine (RU)
VRD .... Vanguardia Revolucionaria Dominicana [*Dominican Revolutionary Vanguard*] [*Dominican Republic*] (LA)
VRD .... Voierie-Resaux Divers (MAR)
VRE .... Air Reconnaissance Squadron (RU)
Vrem oz ...... Temporary Lake [*Topography*] (RU)
VRF .... Naval River Flotilla (RU)
VRGO .... Herald of the Russian Geographic Society [*A publication*] (RU)
VRI .... Virus Research Institute (MAR)
vrid .... Acting (RU)
Vrie .... Verrerie [*Glass Works*] [*Military map abbreviation*] [*World War I*] [*French*] (MTD)
vrio .... Acting (RU)
VRK .... All-Union Radio Committee (RU)
VRK .... Military Revolutionary Committee (RU)
VRK .... Radio Comparison Circuit for All Wavelengths (RU)
vrk .... Vuorokausi [*or Vuorokautta*] [*Finnish*]
VRKhBI .... Quality Baked Goods Kombinat (RU)

VRKSS........ All-Union Service-Dog Studbook (RU)
VRO............ Air Reconnaissance Detachment (RU)
VRO............ Verbond Recht en Orde [*League of Law and Order*] [*Dutch*] (WEN)
VRO............ Veterinary Research Organisation (MAR)
vro.............. Vuestro [*Your*] [*Spanish*]
VROS.......... All-Union Rice Experimental Station (RU)
VrOS.......... Vratsa Oblast Court (BU)
vros............ Vuestros [*Your (Plural)*] [*Spanish*]
VRP............ Railroad Car Repair Station (RU)
VRP............ Volksrepublik Polen [*Polish People's Republic*] (EG)
VRP............ Volta River Project (MAR)
VRP............ Voyageurs de Commerce, Representants et Placiers [*French*]
VRP............ Vyatka River Steamship Line (RU)
VRPK.......... Verdauliche Rohproteinkonzentration [*Digestible Raw Protein Concentration*] (EG)
VRPM.......... Vanguardia Revolucionaria Politico-Militar [*Political-Military Revolutionary Vanguard*] [*Peruvian*] (LA)
VRS............ Intrarayon Communications (RU)
VRS............ Military Editorial Council [*1921*] (RU)
VRS............ Vodohospodarske Rozvojove Stredisko [*Central Office for Development of Water Resources*] (CZ)
VRSh.......... Adjustable-Pitch Propeller (RU)
VRSh.......... Workers' Evening School (RU)
Vrstd.......... Vorstand [*German*]
VRT............ Military Revolutionary Tribunal (RU)
vrt.............. Vertaa [*Compare, Confer*] [*Finnish*] (GPO)
VRT............ Workers' Evening Technicum (RU)
vrto............ Missile Support Platoon (BU)
VRTS.......... Intrarayon Telephone Exchange (RU)
VRTs.......... Waterproof Expanding Cement (RU)
VRU............ Time Gain Control (RU)
VRU............ Verfassung und Recht in Uebersee [*Hamburg*] [*A publication*] (MAR)
VRV............ Water-Regulating Valve (RU)
VRVD.......... Velitelstvi Raketovych Vojsk a Delostrolectva [*Rocket and Artillery Troop Headquarters*] (CZ)
VRZ............ Protective Output Line Relay (RU)
VRZ............ Railroad Car Repair Plant (RU)
VS.............. Armed Forces (of the USSR) (RU)
VS.............. Auxiliary Vessel (RU)
VS.............. Detraining Station, Unloading Station (RU)
VS.............. Herald of Standardization [*A publication*] (RU)
VS.............. Leading-In Rack (RU)
VS.............. Military Communications (RU)
VS.............. Military Council (RU)
VS.............. Of Service Troops (RU)
VS.............. Selenium Rectifier (RU)
VS.............. Signal Platoon (RU)
vs.............. Sunday (RU)
VS.............. Supreme Court (BU)
VS.............. Supreme Court of the USSR (RU)
VS.............. Supreme Soviet of the USSR (RU)
v/s.............. Top Grade (RU)
vS.............. Train Operates Only on Weekdays Preceding Sundays and Holidays (EG)
VS.............. Valence Bond (Method) (RU)
VS.............. Varnostni Svet [*Security Council*] (YU)
vs.............. Vatrena Sredstva [*Firing Equipment*] (YU)
vs.............. Ve Saire [*Et Cetera*] [*Turkish*] (GPO)
VS.............. Vegan Society (EA)
VS.............. Velitel Smeny [*Shift Commander*] (CZ)
VS.............. Velitel Stanice [*Station Commander*] (CZ)
VS.............. Velitelske Stanoviste [*Command Post*] (CZ)
VS.............. Venstresocialisterne [*Left Socialists Party*] [*Danish*] (PPE)
VS.............. Ventilation Shaft [*Mining*] (RU)
VS.............. Verband Deutscher Schriftsteller [*Association of German Writers*] [*West German*]
VS.............. Verschlusssache [*Classified Material (To be secured in safe)*] (EG)
Vs.............. Versorgung [*Provisions, Supply, Making Provisions For*] (EG)
vs.............. Versus [*Against*] [*Latin*]
VS.............. Vertical Drilling Machine (RU)
VS.............. Veterinarska Stanica [*Veterinary Station*] (YU)
VS.............. Veterinary Service (RU)
vs.............. Vide Supra [*See Above*] [*Latin*] (GPO)
VS.............. Vodni Stavby [*Water Construction*] (CZ)
VS.............. Volksschule [*German*]
(VS)............ Volksschulexpositur [*German*]
v-s.............. Volt-Second (RU)
VS.............. Vostra Signoria [*Your Honor*] [*Italian*]
VS.............. Vrhovni Stab [*Supreme Headquarters*] (YU)
VS.............. Vrhovni Sud [*Supreme Court*] (YU)
VS.............. Vuesenoria Ilustrisima [*or Usia Ilustrisima*] [*Spanish*]
VS.............. Vystrojovaci Stredisko [*Equipment Center*] (CZ)
VS.............. Vyvojove Stredisko [*Development Center*] (CZ)
VS.............. Vzorove Stanovy [*Model Statutes*] (CZ)
VSA............ Verkehrssicherheitsaktiv [*Traffic Safety Aktiv*] (EG)
VSA............ Vysoka Skola Architektury [*College of Architecture*] (CZ)
VSAT.......... General Union of Algerian Workers (RU)
vsau............ Platoon of Self-Propelled Guns (RU)
vsb.............. Military Construction Battalion (RU)
VSB............ Vereinigter Schienenfahrzeugbau der DDR [*GDR United Rolling Stock Construction Combine*] (EG)
VSB............ Vysoka Skola Banska [*Mining College*] [*Ostrava*] (CZ)
VSBD-PdA... Volkssozialistische Bewegung Deutschlands - Partei der Arbeit [*People's Socialist Movement of Germany - Party of Labor*] [*West German*] (PD)
VSBH.......... Vysoka Skola Banska a Hutni [*College of Mining and Metallurgy*] (CZ)
VSCh.......... Vysoka Skola Chemicka [*College of Chemistry*] (CZ)
V/sch.......... Your Account (RU)
VSChP........ Vyzkumny Ustav Stroju Chladicich a Potravinarskych [*Research Institute for Refrigeration and Food Industry Machinery*] (CZ)
VSChT........ Vysoka Skola Chemicke-Technologicka [*College of Chemical Technology in Prague*] (CZ)
VSCP.......... Vychodoslovenske Celulozky a Papierne [*East Slovak Cellulose and Paper Works*] (CZ)
VSD............ Computational Dispatching System (RU)
VSD............ Vesnicke Spotrebni Druzstvo [*Village Consumer Cooperative*] (CZ)
VSD............ Vysoka Skola Dopravni [*College of Transportation*] (CZ)
VSD............ Vyssi Skola Dustojniku [*Higher School for Officers*] (CZ)
VSE............ Vychodoslovenske Elektrarne [*Electric Power Plants for Eastern Slovakia*] [*Presov*] (CZ)
VSE............ Vysoka Skola Ekonomicka [*College of Economics*] [*Prague*] (CZ)
Vsechrezkom... All-Russian Extraordinary Commission for Combating Counterrevolution and Sabotage (RU)
VSEGEI....... All-Union Scientific Research Institute of Geology (RU)
VSEGINGEO... All-Union Scientific Research Institute of Hydrogeology and Engineering Geology (RU)
Vseispros.... All-Russian Union of Workers in Education and Arts (RU)
Vsekhimprom... All-Union Association of the Chemical Industry (RU)
Vsekokhudozhnik... All-Russian Cooperative Association "Artist" [*1931*] (RU)
Vsekokhudozhnik... All-Russian Cooperative Union of Artists [*1932*] (RU)
Vsekokhudozhnik... All-Russian Cooperative Union of Workers in the Fine Arts (RU)
Vsekoopinsovet... All-Union Council of Disabled Persons' Cooperatives (RU)
Vsekoopinsoyuz... All-Russian Union of Disabled Persons' Cooperative Associations (RU)
Vsekoopit... All-Union Autonomous Section for Public Eating Facilities of the Tsentrosoyuz (RU)
Vsekooptorg... All-Union Association for Cooperative Trade in Cities and Settlements (RU)
Vsekopromsovet... All-Union Council of Producers' Cooperatives (RU)
VSEKZO...... All-Union Cooperative Correspondence Training Center (RU)
Vsemediksantrud... All-Russian Union of Medical and Sanitary Personnel [*1919-1923*] (RU)
vseobuch.... Universal Education (RU)
Vserabis...... All-Union Trade Union of Workers in the Arts (RU)
VSERABOTPROS... All-Russian Trade Union of Education Workers (RU)
Vserabotzem... All-Russian Producers' Union of Agricultural Workers (RU)
Vserabotzemles... All-Russian Trade Union of Agricultural and Forest Workers (RU)
Vserabpros... Union of Education Workers of the USSR (RU)
Vserokompom... All-Russian Committee for Assistance to Sick and Wounded Red Army Soldiers and Disabled Veterans (at the VTsIK) (RU)
Vserokpom... All-Russian Committee for Assistance to Sick and Wounded Red Army Soldiers and Disabled Veterans (at the VTsIK) (RU)
vseros......... All-Russian (RU)
Vserosskomdram... All-Russian Society of Playwrights and Composers (RU)
vses............ All-Union (RU)
Vsesovfizkul't... All-Union Council of Physical Culture (at the TsIK SSSR) (RU)
vsesoyuz..... All-Union (RU)
Vsespichprom... All-Union Association of the Match Industry (RU)
VseTsIK...... All-Russian Central Executive Committee (RU)
Vseukrevkom... All-Ukrainian Revolutionary Committee (RU)
vsevobuch... Universal Military Training (RU)
VSFK.......... All-Union Council of Physical Culture (RU)
VSFK.......... Supreme Council of Physical Culture [*Until 1933*] (RU)
VSFL.......... Veroeffentlichungen des Staatlich-Saechsischen Forschungsinstitut fuer Voelkerkunde in Leipzig (MAR)
VSFV.......... Visa Skola za Fizicko Vaspitanje [*Advanced School of Physical Education*] (YU)
VSFVU........ Vydavatelstvo Slovenskeho Fondu Vytvarnych Umeni [*Publishing House of the Slovak Fund of Creative Art*] (CZ)
VSG............ All-Union Miners' Union (RU)
vsg.............. Upper Horizontal Base Line (RU)
VSGI.......... All-Union Institute of Selection and Genetics (RU)
VSGRU........ East Siberian Administration of Geological Exploration (RU)
VSGU.......... Vestnik Statneho Ustavu Geologickeho [*Bulletin of the State Geological Institute*] [*A publication*] (CZ)
VSh............ Drag Hinge (RU)
VSh............ Fuze Igniter (RU)
VSh............ Higher School (RU)

VSh .... Mine Car (RU)
v-shche .... Reservoir (RU)
VShK .... Incoming Cord Assembly (RU)
VShOMO ..... Evening School of General Music Education (RU)
VShPD .... Higher School of Trade Unionism of the VTsSPS (RU)
vshtsk .... Supply Room (BU)
VSHV .... Vysoka Skola Hospodarskych Ved [*College of Economic Sciences*] (CZ)
VShZ .... Voronezh Tire Plant (RU)
VSI .... Higher Agricultural Institute (BU)
VSIB .... East Siberian Railroad (RU)
VSIS .... Vysoka Skola Inzenyrskeho Stavitelstva [*Technical Institute of Construction Engineering*] (CZ)
VSJ .... Vazduhoplovni Savez Jugoslavije [*Yugoslav Air Force Association*] (YU)
VSJ .... Vojenska Sokolska Jednota [*Sokol (Athletic Organization) Military Unit*] (CZ)
VSK .... Higher Chamber of Commerce (BU)
VSK .... Vietnami Szocialista Koztarsasag [*Socialist Republic of Vietnam*] (HU)
vsk .... Vuosikerta [*Finnish*]
VSKD .... All-Russian Congress of Peasants' Deputies (RU)
VSKh .... Kharin Vertical Seismograph (RU)
VSKhI .... Voronezh Agricultural Institute (RU)
VSKhIZO ..... All-Union Agricultural Correspondence Training Institute (RU)
VSKhO .... All-Union Agricultural Society (RU)
VSKhV .... All-Union Agricultural Exhibition (RU)
VSKIUTU ..... East Siberian Regional Administration of Corrective Labor Institutions (RU)
VSKKh .... All-Union Council of Municipal Services (at the TsIK SSSR) (RU)
VSKP .... Auxiliary Flight Command Post (RU)
vsl .... Military Investigating Magistrate (BU)
vsl .... Military Service (BU)
VSL .... Vychodni Slovensko [*East Slovakia*] (CZ)
VSLD .... Vysoka Skola Lesnicka a Drevarska [*Forestry and Lumbering College*] (CZ)
VSLU .... Vyskumny a Skusobny Letecky Ustav [*Research and Testing Air Force Institute*] (CZ)
VSM .... High-Molecular Weight Compound (RU)
VSM .... Verband Sozialistischer Mittelschueler [*Union of Socialist Secondary School Students*] [*Austrian*] (WEN)
VSM .... Vondrona Socialiste MONIMA [*Mouvement National pour l'Independence de Madagascar*] [*Socialist Group MONIMA*] [*Malagasy*] (MAR)
VSM .... World Council of Peace (RU)
VSMU .... Vysoka Skola Musickych Umeni [*College of the Fine Arts*] (CZ)
VSN .... Verband Schweizerischer Nachrichtenoffiziere [*Association of Swiss Intelligence Officers*] (WEN)
VSN .... Volontaires de la Securite Nationale (MAR)
VSNA .... Volontaires du Service National Actif [*Active National Service Volunteers*] [*French*] (AF)
VSNB .... Velitelstvi Sboru Narodni Bezpecnosti [*Headquarters of the National Security Corps*] (CZ)
VSNII .... All-Union Scientific Research Institute of the Salt Industry (RU)
VSNIPILesdrev ... East Siberian Scientific Research and Planning Institute of the Lumber and Woodworking Industry (RU)
VSNITO .... All-Union Council of Scientific, Engineering, and Technical Societies (RU)
VSNKh .... All-Russian Council of the National Economy [*RSFSR*] (RU)
VSNKh .... Supreme Council of the National Economy [*1917-1932*] (RU)
VSNKh .... Supreme Council of the National Economy, USSR (of the Council of Ministers, USSR) (RU)
VSNOViPOJ ... Vrhovni Stab Narodnooslobodilacke Vojske i Partizanskih Odreda Jugoslavije [*Supreme Headquarters of the National Liberation Army and Partisan Units of Yugoslavia*] (YU)
VSNP .... All-Chinese Assembly of National Representatives (RU)
VSNR .... Supreme Court of the People's Republic (BU)
VSNRB .... Supreme Court of the Bulgarian People's Republic (BU)
VSNTO .... All-Union Council of Scientific and Technical Societies (RU)
VSO .... All-Union Sports Society (RU)
VSO .... British Volunteers Service Overseas (MAR)
VSO .... District Military Council (RU)
VSO .... Military Construction Section (RU)
VSO .... Military Medical Section (RU)
VSO .... Voluntary Service Overseas (MAR)
VSO .... Vysoka Skola Obchodni [*College of Business Administration*] (CZ)
VSOH .... Vyzkumne Stredisko Odpadovych Hmot [*Research Center for Waste Materials*] (CZ)
VSON .... Special-Purpose Auxiliary Vessel (RU)
VSOPM .... Vseobshchii Soiuz Ob'edinennykh Profsoiuzov Marokko (MAR)
VSORGO ..... East Siberian Branch of the Russian Geographic Society (RU)
vsotob .... Ammunition Train (BU)
VSOZOT ...... All-Union Society "For the Mastering of Technology" (RU)
VSP .... Air Gunnery Training (RU)
VSP .... All-Russian Union of Writers (RU)
VSP .... All-Union Freight Transportation Council (RU)
VSP .... Hydroelectric Power Line (BU)
VSP .... Liaison Platoon with Infantry [*Artillery*] (RU)
VSP .... Military Hospital Train (RU)
VSP .... Supreme Audit Office (BU)
VSP .... Temporary Hospital Train (RU)
VSP .... Tracked Amphibious Ferry (BU)
VSP .... Vertical Seismic Profiling (RU)
VSP .... Vojno-Sanitetski Pregled [*Military Medicine Review*] [*A periodical*] (YU)
VSP .... Vysoka Skola Pedagogicka [*College of Education*] (CZ)
VSP .... Vysoka Skola Polnohospodarska [*Agricultural College*] [*Nitra*] (CZ)
VSPEO .... Military Epidemic Control Detachment (RU)
VSPHN .... Vysoka Skola Politickych a Hospodarskych Nauk [*College of Political and Economic Sciences*] [*Prague*] (CZ)
VSPHV .... Vysoka Skola Politickych a Hospodarskych Ved [*College of Political and Economic Sciences*] [*Prague*] (CZ)
VSPK .... All-Union Council of Producers' Cooperatives (RU)
VSPLI .... Vysoka Skola Polnohospodarskeho a Lesnickeho Inzinierstva [*College of Agriculture and Forestry*] [*Kosice*] (CZ)
VSPOV .... All-Russian Union of Physicians' Professional Associations (RU)
VSPS .... All-Russian Trade-Union Council (RU)
VSPS .... Auxiliary Forces (RU)
VSPS .... Vysoka Skola Politicka a Socialni [*College of Political and Social Sciences*] (CZ)
VSR .... Military Construction Area (RU)
VSRD .... All-Union Woodworkers' Union (RU)
VSRJL .... Vysoka Skola Ruskeho Jazyka a Literatury [*College of Russian Language and Literature*] (CZ)
VSRK .... Supreme Council of Workers' Control (RU)
VSRKh .... All-Russian Union of Workers of the Chemical Industry (RU)
VSRKh .... All-Union Union of Workers of the Chemical Industry (RU)
VSRKM .... General Union of Workers and Peasants of Mexico (RU)
VSRM .... All-Russian Metal Workers' Union (RU)
VSRM .... All-Union Metal Workers' Union (RU)
VSRP .... Hungarian Socialist Workers' Party (RU)
VSRP .... Vychodoslovensky Rudny Pruzkum [*Ore Prospecting for Eastern Slovakia*] (CZ)
VSRPD .... All-Russian Union of Printing Trade Workers (RU)
VSRPP .... All-Russian Union of Workers of the Printing Industry (RU)
VSRPVP ...... All-Russian Union of Workers of the Food and Flavoring Industry (RU)
VSRPVP ...... All-Union Union of Workers of the Food and Flavoring Industry (RU)
VSRTM .... All-Union Union of Transportation Machinery Workers (RU)
VSRVT .... All-Union Union of Water Transportation Workers (RU)
VSRZL .... All-Russian Union of Agricultural and Forest Workers (RU)
VSS .... Medical and Sanitary Service (RU)
VSS .... Military Medical Service (RU)
VSS .... Supreme Economic Council (BU)
VSS .... Supreme Union Council [*Bulgarian National Agrarian Union*] (BU)
vss .... Vaestonsuojelu [*Finnish*]
VSS .... Vazduhoplovna Sekcija Sadejstva [*Air Force Section for Support and Coordination*] (YU)
VSS .... Verband Schweizerischer Studentenschaften [*Union of Swiss Students*] (WEN)
VSS .... Vychodoslovenske Strojarne [*East Slovakia Machine Building Plants*] (CZ)
VSS .... Vysoka Skola Socialni [*College of Social Work*] [*Brno*] (CZ)
VSS .... Vysoka Skola Strojirenska [*Technical Institute of Machine Building*] [*Brno*] (CZ)
VSS .... Vysoka Stranicka Skola [*Communist Party College*] (CZ)
VSS .... World Student Union (RU)
VSSI .... Higher Agricultural Institute (BU)
VSSIPd .... Higher Agricultural Institute in Plovdiv (BU)
VSSMA .... General Union of Muslim Students of Algeria (RU)
VSSMOR ..... Military Secondary Specialized School for Sea and Ocean Fishing (BU)
VSSN .... Vysoka Skola Specialnich Nauk [*College of Special Sciences (Statistics, insurance, higher mathematics, etc.)*] (CZ)
VSSP .... All-Russian Union of Soviet Writers (RU)
VSSR .... All-Russian Construction Workers' Union (RU)
VSSR .... All-Union Construction Workers' Trade Union (RU)
VSSTOe ...... Verband Sozialistischer Studenten Oesterreichs [*Socialist Students Association of Austria*] (WEN)
VSSZh .... All-Russian Union of Soviet Journalists (RU)
VST .... Departmental Standard, Institutional Standard (RU)
VST .... General Workers' Union (RU)
VSt .... Vorstadt [*German*]
VST .... Vysoka Skola Technicka [*Institute of Technology*] [*Kosice*] (CZ)
V St A .... Vereinigte Staaten von Amerika [*United States of America*] [*German*]
VStA .... Volksstaatsanwalt [*People's Prosecutor (A state prosecutor with abbreviated training)*] (EG)
VStFB .... Verwaltung Staatlicher Forstwirtschaftsbetriebe [*Administration of State Forestry Enterprises*] (EG)
VstG .... Vermoegensteuergesetz [*Property Tax Law*] [*German*] (WEN)
VSTM .... General Union of Moroccan Workers (RU)
VSTM .... Vseobshchii Soiuz Trudiashchikhsia Marokko (MAR)
VSTP .... Vysoka Skola Textilna a Papiernicka [*Technical Institute of Textile and Paper Technology*] [*Ruzomberok*] (CZ)
VStr .... Vycvikove Stredisko [*Training Center*] (CZ)

VSTT .... General Union of Tunisian Workers (RU)
VSTT .... Vseobshchii Soiuz Tunisskikh Trudiashchikhsia (MAR)
vstup .... Entrance (BU)
vstup .... Introductory (BU)
vstup .... Introductory (RU)
VStw .... Vermittlungsstellenwesen [*Telephone Exchange System*] (EG)
VSU .... Auxiliary Power Plant (RU)
vsu .... Auxiliary Vessel (RU)
VSU .... Military Construction Directorate (RU)
VSU .... Military Construction Site (RU)
VSU .... Military Medical Directorate [*1929-1935*] (RU)
VSU .... Volksunie Student Union [*Volksunie Student Association*] [*Belgian*] (WEN)
VSU .... Wind-Power Installation (RU)
VSV .... Velitelstvi Spojovaciho Vojska [*Communications Troops Headquarters*] (CZ)
VSV .... Verordnung fuer Sozialpflichtversicherung [*Regulations Concerning Compulsory Social Insurance*] (EG)
VSV .... Vysoka Skola Valecna [*War College*] (CZ)
VSV .... Vysoka Skola Veterinarska [*College of Veterinary Medicine*] (CZ)
VSVF .... Veroeffentlichungen aus den Staedtischen Voelkermuseum Frankfurt/Main (MAR)
VSVO .... East Siberian Military District (RU)
VSVZ .... Vysoka Skola Ved Zemedelskych [*College of Agricultural Sciences*] (CZ)
VSW .... Vierteljahrschrift fuer Social- und Wirtschaftsgeschichte (MAR)
VSYa .... Problems of Slavic Linguistics (RU)
VSYuR .... Armed Forces of Southern Russia (RU)
VsZ .... Vsevojskova Zaloha [*All-Army Reserve*] (CZ)
VSZ .... Vysoka Skola Zeleznicni [*Railroad College*] (CZ)
VSZ .... Vysoka Skola Zemedelska [*Agricultural College*] (CZ)
VSZ .... Vyssi Skola Zememericska [*College of Geodesy*] (CZ)
VSZI .... Vysoka Skola Zemedelskeho Inzenyrstvi [*College of Agricultural Engineering*] (CZ)
VSZK .... Vietnami Szocialista Koztarsasag [*Socialist Republic of Vietnam*] (HU)
V Sz Sz .... Vasuti Szemelyfuvarozas Szabalyzata [*Regulations for Railroad Passenger Transportation*] (HU)
VSZT .... Vallalati Szakszervezeti Tanacs [*Factory Trade Union Committee*] (HU)
VSZV .... Vegyimuveket Szerelo Vallalat [*Chemical Works Equipping Enterprise*] (HU)
VT .... Air Alert, Air-Raid Alarm (RU)
VT .... Air Raid Alert (BU)
VT .... Auxiliary Aiming Point [*Artillery*] (RU)
VT .... Auxiliary Transformer (RU)
VT .... Computer Engineering (RU)
VT .... High-Temperature (RU)
VT .... Internal Friction (RU)
VT .... Military Tribunal (RU)
VT .... Output Transformer (RU)
Vt .... Tuesday (RU)
vt .... Valamint [*As Well As*] (HU)
VT .... Vanha Testamentti [*Finnish*]
VT .... Varatuomari [*Finnish*]
VT .... Varilna Tehnika [*Welding Technology*] [*Ljubljana*] [*A periodical*] (YU)
VT .... Varosi Tanacs [*City Council*] (HU)
VT .... Verlag Technik Berlin (VEB) [*Technik Publishing House, Berlin*] (EG)
Vt .... Veterinaer [*German*]
vt .... Viikkotunti [*or Viikkotuntia*] [*Finnish*]
vt .... Virkaa Toimittava [*Finnish*]
vt .... Virkaatekeva [*Finnish*]
VT .... Visoka Temperatura [*High Temperature*] (YU)
Vt .... Vitesse du Vent dans la Direction Perpendiculaire a la Ligne de Tir [*French*] (MTD)
vT .... Von Tausend [*Per Thousand*] [*German*]
VT .... Water Transportation (RU)
vt .... Watt (BU)
vt .... Watt (RU)
VTA .... Military Technical Academy (RU)
VTA .... Military Technical Academy (BU)
VTA .... Military Transport Aviation (RU)
VTA .... Vojenska Technicka Akademie [*Military Academy of Technology*] (CZ)
VTA .... Vojnotehnicka Akademija [*Technical Military Academy*] [*Zagreb*] (YU)
vta .... Vuelta [*Return*] [*Spanish*]
VTAB .... All-Union Streetcar and Bus Office (RU)
vtac .... Vidi Tacku [*See Paragraph*] (YU)
vtad .... Military Transport Aviation Division (BU)
vtae .... Military Transport Air Squadron (RU)
vtae .... Military Transport Aviation Squadron (BU)
VTAK .... Foreign Trade Arbitration Commission (BU)
VTAK .... Foreign Trade Arbitration Commission (at the All-Union Chamber of Commerce) (RU)
vtap .... Military Transport Aviation Regiment (BU)
VTAZ .... Vojenska Technicka Akademie Antonina Zapotockeho [*Antonin Zapotocky Military Academy of Technology*] (CZ)
VTB .... Foreign Trade Bank (BU)
VTB .... Vazduhoplovno-Tehnicki Bataljon [*Air Technical Battalion*] (YU)
VTB .... Vereniging voor het Theologisch Bibliothecariaat
vtch .... Including (BU)
v t ch .... Including (RU)
vtch .... Watt-Hour (RU)
VTD .... Foreign Trade Directorate (BU)
VTD .... Military Topographic Depot (RU)
VTE .... Medical Determination of Disability (RU)
vte .... Vente [*Sale*] [*Business and trade*] [*French*]
Vte .... Vicomte [*Viscount*] [*French*] (MTD)
VTEIP .... Vedeckotechnicke a Ekonomicke Informace a Propaganda [*Scientific, Technical, and Economic Information and Propaganda*] (CZ)
VTEK .... Medical Commission for Determination of Disability (RU)
VTERU .... Vojensko-Technicko-Ekonomicky Rozborovy Ustav [*Military-Technical-Economic Analysis Institute*] (CZ)
Vtesse .... Vicomtesse [*Viscountess*] [*French*] (MTD)
VTEZ .... All-Union State Trust of Experimental Plants (RU)
VTF .... Technical Committee for Education [*Malagasy*] (AF)
VTF .... Vilnius Tobacco Factory Imeni F. E. Dzerzhinskiy (RU)
VTG .... Vojno-Tehnicki Glasnik [*Military Technical Journal*] [*A publication*] (YU)
VTGOkhR .... High-Temperature Gas-Cooled Reactor (RU)
VTI .... All-Union Institute of Heat Engineering Imeni F. E. Dzerzhinskiy (RU)
VTI .... Materiel (RU)
VTIJNA .... Vojno Tehnicka Istrazivanja Jugoslovenske Narodne Armije [*Military Technical Research of the Yugoslav People's Army*] (YU)
VTIV .... All-Union Synthetic Fiber Trust (RU)
VTIZ .... All-Union Trust of Construction Engineering Surveying (RU)
VTJ .... Vojenska Telocvicna Jednota [*Military Athletic Unit*] (CZ)
VTK .... High Technical Committee (RU)
VTK .... Military Technical Commission (RU)
VTK .... Upper Large Intestine (RU)
VTK .... Valtiotieteen Kandidaatti [*Finnish*]
VTK .... Vazduhoplovna Takticka Komanda [*Air Force Tactical Command*] (YU)
VTK .... Vyrobni Technicka Komise [*Technical Production Commission*] (CZ)
VTK .... Water Transportation Collegium (RU)
VTKh .... Viscosity Index (RU)
VTKI .... Vasuti Tudomanyos Kutato Intezet [*Scientific Research Institute of the Railroads*] (HU)
VTL .... Valtiotieteen Lisensiaatti [*Finnish*]
vtl .... Veterinarian (BU)
vtlch .... Veterinary Hospital (BU)
VTM .... Tobacco Mosaic Virus (RU)
VTM .... Valtiotieteen Maisteri [*Finnish*]
VtMDr .... Doktor der Tierheilkunde [*German*]
VTN .... Auxiliary Aiming Point [*Artillery*] (RU)
VTO .... All-Russian Theatrical Society (RU)
VTO .... All-Union Textile Association [*1929-1931*] (RU)
VTO .... All-Union Theatrical Society (RU)
VTO .... Departmental Technical Organization (BU)
VTO .... Military Topographic Section (RU)
VTO .... Technical Support Platoon (RU)
VTO .... Vazduhoplovno Takticko Osmatranje [*Air Tactical Observation*] (YU)
vto .... Vuelto [*Verso*] [*Spanish*]
Vtorchermet ... Plant for the Processing of Secondary Ferrous Metals (RU)
Vtorchermet ... State Trust for the Procurement and Processing of Secondary Ferrous Metals (RU)
Vtorgrafit .... All-Union Office for Collection and Utilization of Graphite-Containing Waste (RU)
vtorsyr'yepromsoyuz ... Producers' Union for the Procurement and Processing of Secondary Raw Materials (RU)
Vtortsvetmet ... Plant for the Processing of Secondary Nonferrous Metals (RU)
Vtortsvetmet ... State Trust for the Procurement and Processing of Secondary Nonferrous Metals (RU)
VTOS .... Visa Tehnicka Oficirska Skola [*Advanced Officers' Technical School*] [*Zagreb*] (YU)
VTOSh .... Herald of the Tashkent Officers' School of Oriental Languages [*A publication*] (RU)
VTP .... All-Union Chamber of Commerce (RU)
VTP .... Auxiliary Aiming Point [*Artillery*] (RU)
VTP .... Foreign Trade Enterprise (BU)
vtp .... Villanytelep [*Electric Power Station*] (HU)
VTP .... Vise Tehnicko Preduzece [*Higher Technical Establishment*] (YU)
VTR .... Topographic Reconnaissance Platoon (RU)
VTR .... Vedecko-Technicka Rada [*Council for Science and Technology*] (CZ)
VTR .... Vedeckotechnicky Rozvoj [*Scientific and Technical Development*] (CZ)
vtr sl .... Garrison Duty (BU)
VTS .... All-Russian Textile Syndicate [*1922-1929*] (RU)

VTS .... Ceskoslovenska Vedecka Technicka Spolecnost pro (Energetiku a) Elektrotechniku [*Czechoslovak Scientific Society of (Power and) Electrical Engineering*] (CZ)
VTs .... Computation Center (RU)
VTS .... Materiel Depot (RU)
VTS .... Materiel Supply (RU)
VTS .... Military Topographic Service (RU)
VTS .... Vedecka Technicka Spolecnost [*Society for Scientific Technology*] (CZ)
VTS .... Visa Tehnicka Skola [*Advanced Technical School*] (YU)
V/Ts .... Water-Cement Ratio (RU)
VTSB .... Varosi Tarsadalmi Sport Bizottsag [*City Mass Sport Committee*] (HU)
vt-sek .... Watt-Second (RU)
VTsGADA ... Vilnius Central State Archives of the Lithuanian SSR. Division of Ancient Documents (RU)
VTSh .... Evening Technical School (RU)
VTSh .... Higher Trade School (RU)
VTsIK .... All-Russian Central Executive Committee [*1917-1936*] (RU)
VTsIPK .... All-Union Central Institute for Improving the Qualifications of Engineering and Technical Personnel (RU)
VTsK NA ..... All-Union Central Committee on the New Alphabet (RU)
VTsK NTA ... All-Union Central Committee on the New Turkic Alphabet (RU)
VTsKS .... Higher Central Stenography Courses (RU)
vt sl .... Veterinary Service (BU)
VTsLK .... All-Russian Central Liquidation Commission (RU)
vtsm .... In the Narrow Sense (BU)
VTsN .... Central Aiming Sight (RU)
VTsNIB .... All-Union Central Office of Standards Research (RU)
VTsNIB .... All-Union Central Scientific Research Office (RU)
VTsNIIOT .... All-Union Scientific Research Institute of Work Safety (RU)
VTsNILKR ... All-Union Central Scientific Research Laboratory for Preservation and Restoration of Museum Art Treasures (RU)
VTSO .... Departmental Technical Construction Organization of the Holy Synod (BU)
VTsRK .... All-Russian Central Workers' Cooperative (RU)
VTsSPO ...... All-Russian Central Union of Consumers' Societies (RU)
VTsSPS .... All-Union Central Trade-Union Council (RU)
VTsU .... Slewing Sight [*Artillery*] (RU)
VTT .... Technical Research Centre of Finland
VTT .... Valtiotieteen Tohtori [*Finnish*]
VTTH .... Vo Tuyen Truyen Hinh [*Television*] (TVP)
VTTI .... All-Union Precision Industry Trust (RU)
VTU .... Departmental Technical Specifications (RU)
VTU .... Higher School of Commerce (BU)
VTU .... Higher School of Technology (BU)
VTU .... Higher Technical School (RU)
VTU .... Military Technical Directorate (RU)
VTU .... Military Topographic Directorate (RU)
VTU .... Provisional Technical Specifications (RU)
VTU .... Vojensky Technicky Ustav [*Institute of Military Technology*] (CZ)
VTUE .... Provisional Technical Specifications of Operation (RU)
VTUZ .... Higher Technical Educational Institution (RU)
VTUZ .... Higher Technical School (BU)
VTV .... Varosepitesi Tervezo Vallalat [*Planning Enterprise for Urban Construction*] (HU)
VTV .... Vazduhoplovne Tekticke Vezbe [*Air Force Exercises*] (YU)
VTV .... Videki Tejipari Vallalatok [*Provincial Dairy Enterprises*] (HU)
VTZ .... Vladimir Tractor Plant Imeni A. A. Zhdanov (RU)
VTZ .... Vojno-Tehnicki Zavod [*Military Technology Institute*] [*Kragujevac*] (YU)
VU .... Computer (RU)
VU .... Conventional Viscosity (RU)
VU .... Headquarters Platoon (RU)
Vu .... Military School, Military Academy (BU)
VU .... Rectifier (RU)
VU .... Upper Level (RU)
VU .... Vaeterlandische Union [*Patriotic Union*] [*Liechtenstein*] (PPE)
VU .... Valve Installation (RU)
VU .... Verkstallande Utskott [*Executive Committee*] [*Swedish*] (WEN)
VU .... Vertical Angle (RU)
VU .... Video Amplifier (RU)
VU .... Virologicky Ustav [*Institute of Virology (of the Czechoslovak Academy of Sciences)*] (CZ)
VU .... Voice of Uganda (MAR)
vu .... Vojensky Utvar [*Military Unit*] (CZ)
VU .... Volksunie [*People's Union*] [*Belgian*] (WEN)
vu .... Von-Unten [*From Beneath, From Below*] [*German*]
VU .... [*De*] Vrije Universiteit [*(The) Free University*] [*Dutch*] (WEN)
VUA .... Military Registration Archives (RU)
VUA .... Military Science Archives (RU)
VUA .... Vojensky Ustredni Archiv [*Central Military Archives (of the Ministry of National Defense or of the Military Office of the President of the Republic)*] (CZ)
VUA .... Vyzkumny Ustav Antibiotik [*Antibiotics Research Institute*] (CZ)
VUAcCh ...... Vyzkumny Ustav Acetylenove Chemie [*Research Institute of Acetylene Chemistry*] (CZ)
VUACh .... Vyzkumny Ustav Anorganicke Chemie [*Research Institute for Inorganic Chemistry*] (CZ)
VUAgT .... Vyzkumny Ustav Agrochemicke Technologie [*Research Institute of Agrochemical Technology*] [*Bratislava*] (CZ)
VUAK .... All-Ukrainian Archaeological Committee (RU)
VUAMLIN .... All-Ukrainian Association of Marxist-Leninist Scientific Research Institutes (RU)
VUAN .... All-Ukrainian Academy of Sciences (RU)
VUAnCh ...... Vyzkumny Ustav Anorganicke Chemie [*Research Institute of Inorganic Chemistry*] [*Usti Nad Labem*] (CZ)
VUAP .... Vyzkumny Ustav Automatizacnich Prostredku [*Institute of Research in Automation Means*] (CZ)
VUAT .... Vyskumny Ustav Agrochemickej Technologie [*Research Institute of Agrochemical Technology*] [*Bratislava*] (CZ)
vub .... Battery Headquarters Platoon (RU)
Vub .... Vorname Unbekannt [*First Name Unknown (FNU)*] [*West German*] (WEN)
VUB .... Vyzkumny Ustav Bavlnarsky [*Cotton Research Institute*] [*Usti Nad Orlici*] (CZ)
VUB .... Vyzkumny Ustav Bramborarsky [*Potato Research Institute*] [*Havlickuv Brod*] (CZ)
VUBH .... Vyzkumny Ustav Bavlnarsky a Hedvabnicky [*Cotton and Silk Research Institute*] [*Usti Nad Orlici*] (CZ)
VUBP .... Vyzkumny Ustav Bezpecnosti Prace [*Research Institute of Industrial Safety*] [*Prague*] (CZ)
VUC .... Vanguardia Unitaria Comunista [*Communist Unitary Vanguard*] [*Venezuelan*] (LA)
VUC .... Vyzkumny Ustav Cukrovarnicky [*Research Institute of the Sugar Refining Industry*] [*Prague*] (CZ)
VUChK .... All-Ukrainian Extraordinary Commission for Combating Counterrevolution and Sabotage (RU)
VUCHV .... Vyskumny Ustav Chemickych Vlakien [*Institute for Research in Chemical Fibers*] (CZ)
VUCHZ .... Vyzkumny Ustav Chemickych Zarizeni [*Institute for Research in Chemical Equipment*] (CZ)
VUCKD .... Vyzkumny Ustav CKD Praha [*Research Institute CKD Prague*] (CZ)
VUCSKZ ..... Vyzkumny Ustav Cs. Keramickych Zavodu [*Research Institute of the Czechoslovak Ceramics Plants*] (CZ)
VUCSSZ ...... Vyzkumny Ustav Ceskoslovenskych Zavodu [*Research Institute of Czechoslovak Construction Enterprises*] (CZ)
VUD .... Battalion Headquarters Platoon (RU)
VUD .... Vychodoceske Uhelne Doly [*East Bohemian Coal Mines*] (CZ)
VUD .... Vyzkumny Ustav Dopravni [*Transportation Research Institute*] (CZ)
VUE .... Vyzkumny Ustav Energeticky [*Power Research Institute*] [*Brno*] (CZ)
VUEH .... Vyzkumny Ustav Ekonomiky Hornictvi [*Institute of Research in Mining Economy*] (CZ)
VUEK .... All-Union Accounting and Economic Courses (RU)
VUEK .... Vyzkumny Ustav Elektrokeramiky [*Institute of Research in Ceramics for Use in Electronics*] (CZ)
VUEP .... Vyzkumny a Vyvojovy Ustav Elektrickych Pristroju a Rozvadecu [*Institute for Research and Development of Electrical Machinery and Distributors*] (CZ)
VUEPS .... Vyzkumny Ustav Ekonomiky Prumyslu a Stavebnictvi [*Institute of Research in Industry and Construction Economy*] (CZ)
VUES .... Vyzkumny Ustav Elektrickych Stroju Tocivych [*Institute for Research in Electrical Rotary Machines*] (CZ)
VUEZ .... Vyzkumny Ustav Energetickych Zarizeni [*Institute for Research in Electric Power Equipment*] (CZ)
VUF .... Higher School of Physical Education (BU)
VUF .... Vanster Ungdoms Forbund [*Leftist Youth League*] [*Swedish*] (WEN)
VUF .... Vyzkumny Ustav Financi [*Finance Research Institute*] (CZ)
VUFB .... Vyzkumny Ustav pro Farmacii a Biochemii [*Research Institute for Pharmacology and Biochemistry*] (CZ)
VUFCh .... Vyzkumny Ustav pro Fotografickou Chemii [*Research Institute of Photographic Chemistry*] [*Prague*] (CZ)
VUFKU .... All-Ukrainian Photography and Motion Picture Administration (RU)
VUFVNIIGeofizika ... Volga-Ural Branch of the VNIIGeofizika (RU)
VuG .... Verlag Volk und Gesundheit (VEB) [*"Volk und Gesundheit" Publishing House (VEB)*] (EG)
VUGI .... All-Union Scientific Research Institute of Coal (RU)
VUGPT .... Vyzkumny Ustav Gumarenske a Plastikarske Techniky [*Research Institute of Rubber and Plastics Technology*] (CZ)
VUGTK .... Vyzkumny Ustav Geodeticky, Topograficky, a Kartograficky [*Research Institute of Geodesy, Topography, and Cartography*] (CZ)
VUHK .... Vyskumny Ustav Hutnickej Keramiky [*Metallurgical Research Institute for Refractory Materials*] (CZ)
VUHP .... Vyskumny Ustav Hydinarskeho Priemyslu [*Research Institute of the Poultry Industry*] (CZ)
VUHU .... Vyzkumny Ustav Hnedeho Uhli, Severocesky Hnedouhelny Revir [*Soft Coal Research Institute, North Bohemian Soft Coal Region*] (CZ)
VUHZ .... Vyzkumny Ustav Hutnictvi Zeleza [*Institute for Research in Ferrous Metallurgy*] (CZ)
VUIEM .... All-Ukrainian Institute of Experimental Medicine (RU)

VUIS............ Vyskumny Ustav Inzinierskych Stavieb [*Institute for Research in Engineering Construction*] (CZ)
VUJAK........ Vyzkumny Ustav Pedagogicky Jana Amose Komenskeho [*J. A. Comenius Pedagogical Research Institute*] (CZ)
VUJASTO.... Vojna Uprava Jugoslovenske Armije Svobodno Trzasko Ozemlje [*Yugoslav Army's Military Administration for Zone B of the Free Territory of Trieste*] (YU)
VUJK........... Vyzkumny Ustav Jemne Keramiky [*Institute for Research in Fine Ceramics*] (CZ)
VUK............. All-Union Training Center (of the Ministry of Construction, RSFSR) (RU)
VUK............. Vyzkumny Ustav Kovu [*Metallurgical Research Institute*] (CZ)
VUK............. Vyzkumny Ustav Kozedelny [*Leather Industry Research Institute*] (CZ)
VUK............. Vyzkumny Ustav Krmivarsky [*Animal Feeding Research Institute (of the Czechoslovak Academy of Agricultural Sciences)*] (CZ)
VUKAI......... All-Ukrainian Association of Engineers (RU)
VUKhIN....... Eastern Scientific Research Institute of Coal Chemistry (RU)
VUKI............ Vyskumny Ustav Kabelov a Izolantov [*Research Institute of Cables and Insulators*] [*Bratislava*] (CZ)
VUKS.......... Vyzkumny Ustav Krmivarskeho Prumyslu a Sluzeb, Pecky [*Institute for Research in the Feed Industry and Services, Pecky*] (CZ)
Vuktekstil'... All-Union Training Center of the Ministry of the Textile Industry, USSR (RU)
VUKV.......... Vyzkumny Ustav Kolejovych Vozidel [*Institute for Research on Railroad Cars*] (CZ)
VUKZO........ Correspondence Training Center (RU)
VUL............. Vyzkumny Ustav Lazensky [*Balneological Research Institute*] [*Marianske Lazne*] (CZ)
vulg............. Vulgar (BU)
VULHM........ Vyskumny Ustav Lesneho Hospodarstva a Myslivosti [*Forest and Wildlife Management Research Institute*] (CZ)
Vulk............. Volcano [*Topography*] (RU)
VULK........... Vyskumny Ustav Liehovarov a Konzervarni [*Research Institute of Distilleries and Canneries*] (CZ)
vulkmast..... Recapping Workshop (RU)
VULV........... Vyzkumny Ustav Lykovych Vlaken [*Research Institute of Bast Fibers*] [*Sumperk*] (CZ)
VuM............. Verfuegungen und Mitteilungen [*Directives and Information*] (EG)
VUM............ Vilnius Department Store (RU)
VUM............ Volo Umano Moscolare [*Italian*]
VUM............ Vyzkumny Ustav Mlekarensky [*Dairy Research Institute*] (CZ)
VUM............ Vyzkumny Ustav Mrazirensky [*Research Institute for Refrigeration*] [*Olomouc*] (CZ)
VUMA.......... Vyskumny Ustav pro Mechanizaciu a Automatizaciu [*Research Institute of Mechanization and Automatization*] (CZ)
VUMACh..... Vyzkumny Ustav Makromolekularni Chemie [*Institute for Research in Macromolecular Chemistry*] (CZ)
VUMAT........ Vyzkumny Ustav Mechanizace, Automatizace, a Technologie [*Institute for Research in Mechanization, Automation, and Technology*] (CZ)
VUMEPP..... Vyzkumny Ustav pro Mechanisaci a Ekonomiku Potravinarskeho Prumyslu [*Research Institute for Mechanization and Efficiency in the Food Industry*] (CZ)
VUMEZ........ Vyzkumny Ustav Mechanisace a Elektrifikace Zemedelstvi [*Research Institute for the Mechanization and Electrification of Agriculture*] [*Prague-Vokovice*] (CZ)
VUML.......... Evening University of Marxism-Leninism (RU)
VUML.......... Vecerni Universita Marx-Leninismu [*University Night Classes on Marxism and Leninism*] (CZ)
VUMLP........ Vyskumny Ustav Mechanizacie Lesneho Priemyslu [*Research Institute for Mechanization of the Lumber Industry*] [*Oravsky Podzamok*] (CZ)
VUMLZ........ Vyzkumny Ustav pro Myslivest a Lesni Zoologii, Abraslav [*Zoological Research Institute of Wild Animal Life, in Zbraslav*] (CZ)
VUMM......... Vyzkumny Ustav Manipulace s Materialem [*Materials Handling Research Institute*] (CZ)
VUMO.......... Vyzkumny Ustav Mechaniky a Optiky [*Research Institute of Mechanics and Optics*] (CZ)
VUMP.......... Vyzkumny Ustav Masneho Prumyslu [*Research Institute of the Meat Industry*] [*Brno*] (CZ)
VUMPJK...... Vyzkumny Ustav pro Mechanisaci Prumyslu Jemne Keramiky [*Research Institute for the Mechanization of the Fine Ceramics Industry*] (CZ)
VUMPP........ Vyzkumny Ustav Mlynskeho a Pekarenskeho Prumyslu [*Miller and Bakery Industry Research Institute*] (CZ)
VUMS.......... Vyzkumny Ustav Matematickych Stroju [*Mathematical Machines Research Institute*] (CZ)
VUMSK....... Vyzkumny Ustav pro Mechanisaci Prumyslu Skla a Jemne Keramiky [*Research Institute for the Mechanization of the Glass and Fine Ceramics Industries*] (CZ)
VUMT.......... Vyzkumny Ustav Materialu a Technologie [*Research Institute of Materiel and Technological Processes*] (CZ)
VUMV.......... Vyzkumny Ustav Motorovych Vozidel [*Research Institute of Motor Vehicles*] (CZ)
VUMZ.......... Vyzkumny Ustav pro Mechanisaci Zemedelstvi [*Research Institute for the Mechanization of Agriculture*] [*Prague*] (CZ)
VUN............. Auxiliary Aiming Angle (RU)
VUN............. Provisional Consolidated Norms (RU)
VUN............. Vyzkumny Ustav Nafty [*Petroleum Research Institute*] [*Brno*] (CZ)
VUNBrn....... Vestnik Ustredniho Narodniho Vyboru, Brno [*Bulletin of the Central National People's Committee in Brno*] [*A publication*] (CZ)
VUNH.......... Vyzkumny Ustav Naterovych Hmot [*Institute of Dye Paint Research*] (CZ)
VUNM.......... Vyzkumny Ustav Naftovych Motoru [*Diesel Engines Research Institute*] (CZ)
VUNP.......... Vyzkumny Ustav Narodohospodarskeho Planovani [*National Economy Planning Research Institute*] (CZ)
VUO............. Vyzkumny Ustav Obalovy [*Research Institute of Packaging*] (CZ)
VUO............. Vyzkumny Ustav Obchodu [*Trade Research Institute*] (CZ)
VUO............. Vyzkumny Ustav Odevnictvi [*Research Institute of the Garment Industry*] (CZ)
VUOAP........ All-Union Administration for the Protection of Copyrights (RU)
VUOM.......... Vyzkumny Ustav Ochrany Materialu [*Research Institute for Protection of Materiel*] [*Prague*] (CZ)
VUOS.......... Vyzkumny Ustav Odborneho Skolstvi [*Professional Schooling Research Institute*] (CZ)
VUOS.......... Vyzkumny Ustav Organickych Synthes [*Research Institute of Organic Compounds*] [*Pardubice*] (CZ)
VUOSO........ Vyzkumny Ustav Obrabecich Stroju a Obrabeni [*Machine Tools Research Institute*] [*Praha-Zabehlice*] (CZ)
VUOZ.......... Vyzkumny Ustav Organisace Zdravotnictvi [*Research Institute for the Organization of Health Services*] [*Prague*] (CZ)
VUP............. Military Training Installation (RU)
VUP............. Vyzkumny Ustav pro Petrochemiu [*Petrochemistry Research Institute*] (CZ)
VUP............. Vyzkumny Ustav Pedagogicky [*Pedagogical Research Institute*] (CZ)
VUP............. Vyzkumny Ustav Pletarsky [*Knitwear Research Institute*] [*Brno*] (CZ)
VUP............. Vyzkumny Ustav Polygraficky [*Polygraphy Research Institute*] (CZ)
VUPC.......... Vyskumny Ustav Papieru a Celulozy [*Paper and Cellulose Research Institute*] [*Bratislava*] (CZ)
VUPChS...... Vyzkumny Ustav Potravinarskych a Chladicich Stroju [*Food and Refrigeration Machines Research Institute*] (CZ)
VUPE........... Vyskumny Ustav Polnohospodarskej Ekonomiky [*Research Institute of Agricultural Economics*] (CZ)
VUPEF......... Vyzkumny Ustav pro Elektrotechnickou Fysiku [*Research Institute of Electrophysics*] [*Prague*] (CZ)
VUPM.......... Vyzkumny Ustav Praskove Metalurgie [*Research Institute of Powder Metallurgy*] [*Vestec near Prague*] (CZ)
VUPP........... Vyzkumny Ustav Papirenskeho Prumyslu [*Research Institute of the Paper Industry*] [*Prague*] (CZ)
VUPP........... Vyskumny Ustav Potravinarskeho Priemyslu [*Institute of the Food Industry*] [*Bratislava*] (CZ)
Vupros........ Interrogative [*Grammar*] (BU)
VUPS........... Vyzkumny Ustav Pozemnich Staveb [*Ground Construction Research Institute*] (CZ)
VUPT........... Vyzkumny Ustav Potravinarske Techniky [*Food Research Institute*] [*Prague*] (CZ)
VURK.......... Vyzkumny Ustav Radiokomunikaci [*Research Institute of Radio Communications*] (CZ)
Vurkh stop suv... Supreme Economic Council (BU)
VURT........... Vyzkumny Ustav Rozhlasu a Televize [*Broadcasting and Television Research Institute*] (CZ)
vurt/min...... Revolutions per Minute (BU)
VURUP........ Vyskumny Ustav pre Ropu a Uhlovodikove Plyny [*Crude Oil and Hydrocarbon Gases Research Institute*] [*Bratislava*] (CZ)
VURV........... Vyzkumny Ustav Rostlinne Vyroby [*Institute for the Research of Vegetable Produce*] (CZ)
VUS............. All-Russian Coal Syndicate (RU)
VUS............. All-Russian Teachers' Union [*1917-1918*] (RU)
VUS............. Auxiliary Communications Center (RU)
VUS............. Auxiliary Repeater Station (RU)
VUS............. Higher Council on Education (BU)
VUS............. Military Occupational Specialty (RU)
VUS............. Military School of Communications (RU)
VUS............. Video Amplifier (RU)
VUS............. Vojensky Umelecky Soubor [*Armed Forces Artistic Ensemble*] (CZ)
VUS............. Vyskumny Ustav Svaracsky [*Research Institute of Welding*] [*Bratislava*] (CZ)
VUS............. Vyzkumny Ustav Sklarsky [*Research Institute of the Glass Industry*] (CZ)
VUS............. Vyzkumny Ustav Spoju [*Communications Research Institute*] (CZ)
VUS............. World University Service [*WUS*] (RU)
VUSA.......... Vyzkumnu Ustav pro Stavebnictvi a Architekturu [*Research Institute of Building and Architecture*] (CZ)
VUSB........... Vyzkumny Ustav Skla a Bizuterie [*Glass and Costume Jewelry Research Institute*] (CZ)

VUSChP...... Vyzkumny Ustav Stroju Chladicich a Potravinarskych [*Research Institute for Refrigeration and Food Machinery*] [*Prague*] (CZ)
VUSE.......... Vyzkumny Ustav Silnoproude Elektrotechniky [*Research Institute for High Voltage Electrical Engineering*] [*Bechovice near Prague*] (CZ)
VUSE.......... Vyzkumny Ustav Stavebni Ekonomiky [*Research Institute of Construction Economics*] (CZ)
VUSH.......... Vyzkumny Ustav Stavebnich Hmot [*Building Materials Research Institute*] (CZ)
VUSK.......... Vyzkumny Ustav Stavebnich a Keramickych Stroju [*Research Institute of Construction and Ceramic Machinery*] (CZ)
VUSK.......... Vyzkumny Ustav Synthetickeho Kaucuku [*Synthetic Rubber Research Institute*] (CZ)
VUSKM....... Vyzkumny Ustav Stavebnich Konstruckci a Montazi [*Construction and Assembly Research Institute*] (CZ)
VUSNITO.... All-Ukrainian Council of Scientific, Engineering, and Technical Societies (RU)
VUSPL......... Vyzkumny Ustav Synthetickych Prayskyric a Laku [*Research Institute for Synthetic Resins*] [*Pardubice*] (CZ)
VUSPP........ All-Ukrainian Union of Proletarian Writers (RU)
VUSPS........ All-Ukrainian Trade-Union Council (RU)
VUSS........... Vyzkumny Ustav pro Strojni Sklo [*Structural Glass Research Institute*] (CZ)
VUSSN........ Higher School of Economic and Social Sciences (BU)
VUSSN Sv... Higher School of Economic and Social Sciences in Svishtov (BU)
VUSSTS...... Vyzkumny Ustav Svarovacich Stroju a Technologie Svarovani [*Research Institute for Welding Machines and Welding Technology*] [*Branch in Chotebor*] (CZ)
VUST........... Vyzkumny Ustav pro Sdelovaci Techniku A. S. Popova [*A. S. Popov Research Institute for Communications Techniques*] (CZ)
VUSTE........ Vyzkumny Ustav Strojirenske Technologie a Ekonomiky [*Engineering Technology and Economy Research Institute*] (CZ)
V U SZ......... Vasuti Uzletszabalyzat [*Railroad Regulations*] (HU)
VUSZ........... Vyzkumny Ustav Socialniho Zabezpeceni [*Social Security Research Institute*] (CZ)
VUSZS........ Vyzkumny Ustav Stavebnich a Zemnich Stroju [*Heavy Construction Machinery Research Institute*] (CZ)
vut.............. Vegrehajtasi Utasitas [*Implementing Instruction*] (HU)
VUT............ Vojensky Technicky Ustav [*Military Institute of Technology*] [*Decin-Podmokly*] (CZ)
VUT............ Vysoke Uceni Technicke [*Technical Institute*] (CZ)
VUT............ Vyzkumny Ustav Telekomunikaci [*Telecommunication Research Institute*] [*Prague*] (CZ)
VUT............ Vyzkumny Ustav Telovychovny [*Research Institute on Physical Education*] (CZ)
VUT............ Vyzkumny Ustav Tuberkulosy [*Tuberculosis Research Institute*] [*Prague*] (CZ)
VUTD.......... Vyzkumny Ustav Technickeho Drevoprumyslu [*Research Institute of the Lumber (or Wood Working) Industry*] [*Prague-Nusle*] (CZ)
VUTEChP.... Vyzkumny Ustav Technicko-Ekonomicky Chemickeho Prumyslu [*Technical Economic Research Institute of the Chemical Industry*] (CZ)
VUTMS........ Vyzkumny Ustav Technologie a Mechanisace Stavebnictvi [*Research Institute of Construction Technology and Mechanization*] (CZ)
VUTO.......... Vyzkumny Ustav Technicko-Organisacni [*Research Institute of Management Efficiency*] (CZ)
VUTP.......... Oborovy Vyzkumny Ustav Tukoveho Prumyslu [*Sectoral Research Institute of the Fats Industry*] (CZ)
VUTP.......... Vyskumny Ustav Tabakoveho Priemyslu [*Tobacco Industry Research Institute*] (CZ)
VUTRIZ....... All-Ukrainian Scientific and Industrial Trust for Testing and Application of Inventions (RU)
VUTS.......... Vyzkumny Ustav Textilniho Strojirenstvi [*Textile Engineering Research Institute*] (CZ)
VUTS.......... Vyzkumny Ustav Tezkeho Strojirenstvi [*Research Institute of the Heavy Machine Industry*] (CZ)
VUTS.......... Vyzkumny Ustav pro Travopolni Soustavu [*Research Institute for the Grass-Clover System*] [*Pohorelice*] (CZ)
VUTS.......... Vyzkumny Ustav Tvarecich Stroju a Technologie Tvareni [*Research Institute on Moulding Machines and the Technology of Moulding*] (CZ)
VUTsIK........ All-Ukrainian Central Executive Committee [*1920-1936*] (RU)
VUTT.......... Vyzkumny Ustav Tepelne Techniky [*Research Institute of Thermodynamics*] (CZ)
VUTT.......... Vyzkumny Ustav Textilni Technologie [*Research Institute of Textile Technology*] [*Liberec*] (CZ)
VUTV.......... Higher School of Physical Education (BU)
VUUPV........ Vyzkumny Ustav Upravy Prumyslovych Vod [*Research Institute for Treatment of Industrial Water*] (CZ)
VUUS.......... Vyzkumny Ustav Uzitkoveho Skla [*Utility Glass Research Institute*] (CZ)
VUUV.......... Vyzkumny Ustav Umelych Vlaken [*Research Institute of Synthetic Fibers*] [*Svit*] (CZ)
VUV............ Vyzkumny Ustav Vlnarsky [*Wool Research Institute*] [*Brno*] (CZ)
VUV............ Vyzkumny Ustav Vodohospodarsky [*Water Utilization Research Institute*] [*Prague*] (CZ)
VUV............ Vyzkumny Ustav Vzduchotechniky [*Air Technology Research Institute*] (CZ)
VUVA.......... Vyzkumny Ustav Vystavby a Architektury [*Research Institute of Construction and Architecture*] (CZ)
Vuved.......... Preface, Introduction (BU)
VUVET........ Vyzkumny Ustav Vakuove Elektrotechniky [*Vacuum Electro-Technology Research Institute*] (CZ)
VUVL.......... Vyzkumny Ustav pro Valiva Loziska [*Research Institute of Roller Bearing*] (CZ)
VUVPH........ Vyzkumny Ustav pro Vyuziti Plastickych Hmot [*Research Institute for the Utilization of Plastic Materials*] [*Gottwaldov*] (CZ)
VUVT.......... Vyzkumny Ustav Vodnich Turbin [*Water Turbine Research Institute*] (CZ)
VUVU.......... Vyzkumny Ustav pro Vinohradnictvi a Vinarstvi [*Research Institute of Viticulture and the Wine Industry*] (CZ)
VuW............ Verlag Volk und Welt [*"Volk und Welt" Publishing House*] (EG)
VuW............ Verlag Volk und Wissen [*"Volk und Wissen" Publishing House*] (EG)
VUZ............ Higher Education Institution (BU)
VUZ............ Higher Educational Institution (RU)
VUZ............ Military Educational Institution (RU)
VUZ............ Vyzkumny Ustav Zeleznicni [*Railroad Research Institute*] (CZ)
VUZ............ Vyzkumny Ustav Zemedelsky [*Agricultural Research Institute*] [*Prague*] (CZ)
VUZ............ Vyzkumny Ustav Zuslechtovaci [*Research Institute for (Textile) Processing*] [*Dvur Kralove n.L.*] (CZ)
VUZ............ Vyzkumny Ustav Zvaracsky [*Research Institute of Welding*] (CZ)
VUZE.......... Vyzkumny Ustav Zemedelske Ekonomiky [*Research Institute for Agricultural Economics*] (CZ)
VUZLM........ Vyzkumny Ustav Zemedelske a Lesnicke Mechanisace [*Research Institute for Mechanization in Agriculture and Forestry (of Agricultural Sciences)*] (CZ)
VUZO.......... Vyzkumny Ustav pro Zahranicni Obchod [*Foreign Trade Research Institute*] (CZ)
VUZO.......... Vyzkumny Ustav Zdravotnicke Osvety [*Research Institute of Health Education*] (CZ)
VUZORT...... Vyzkumny Ustav Zvukove, Obrazove, a Reprodukcni Techniky [*Research Institute of Audio, Video, and Reproduction Technology*] [*Prague*] (CZ)
VUZS.......... Vyzkumny Ustav Zemedelskych Stroju [*Research Institute of Agricultural Machinery*] (CZ)
VUZT.......... Vyzkumny Ustav Zdravotnicke Techniky [*Health Care Research Institute*] (CZ)
VUZV.......... Vyzkumny Ustav Zivocisne Vyroby [*Research Institute for Animal Husbandry*] [*Uhrineves*] (CZ)
v-v.............. Air-to-Air [*Missile*] (RU)
VV............... Air-Break Switch (RU)
VV............... Air Force, Military Aviation (BU)
VV............... Byzantine Annals [*A publication*] (RU)
vv............... Centuries (RU)
VV............... Delay (RU)
VV............... Explosive (RU)
VV............... Explosives (BU)
VV............... High-Voltage, High-Tension (RU)
VV............... High-Voltage Rectifier (RU)
VV............... High-Voltage Switch (RU)
V/v............. Intravenous (RU)
Vv............... Mean Vertical (Probable) Error (RU)
VV............... Military Herald (RU)
VV............... Propeller (RU)
VV............... Transpress VEB Verlag fuer Verkehrswesen Berlin [*"Transpress" Publishing House for Transportation Affairs, Berlin*] (EG)
VV............... Upper Volga (RU)
VV............... Ustedes [*You (Plural, formal)*] [*Spanish*]
VV............... Vasiliko Velos [*Royalist Arrow*] [*Greek*] (GC)
VV............... Vatreni Val [*Firing Wave*] (YU)
vv............... Ve Vysluzbe [*Retired*] (CZ)
VV............... Vecny Vestnik [*Gazette (of the Ministry of National Defense)*] [*A publication*] (CZ)
VV............... Velike Vode [*High Tides*] (YU)
VV............... Verenigd Verzet 1940-45 [*United Resistance 1940-45*] [*Dutch*] (WEN)
VV............... Vildmarkens Var, Stockholm 1928 (MAR)
VV............... Vivres-Viande [*On earmark or button of cattle*] [*Military*] [*French*] (MTD)
VV............... Vizantiyski Vremennik [*Byzantine Chronicle*] [*A periodical*] (BU)
Vv............... Vodovod [*Water Pipes, Aqueduct*] (YU)
v/v.............. Votre Ville [*Your City*] [*Business and trade*] [*French*]
vv............... Vseobecna Verejna (Nemocnice) [*Public General (Hospital)*] (CZ)
vv............... Vuodet [*Finnish*]
VV............... Vzorny Vojak [*Exemplary Soldier*] (CZ)
VVA............. Air Force Academy (RU)
VVA............. High-Voltage Equipment (RU)
VVA............. Military Veterinary Academy (RU)

VVA............ Visa Vojna Akademija [*Advanced Military Academy*] (YU)
Vva............ Viuva [*Widow*] [*Business and trade*] [*Portuguese*]
VVAP............ Mouvement Socialiste Occitan - Volem Viure al Pais [*Occitanian Socialist Movement*] [*French*] (PPW)
vvar............ Vapaasti Varastossa [*Finnish*]
VVAU............ Higher Military Aviation School (RU)
VVAUL............ Higher Military Aviation School for Pilots (RU)
vvaun............ Vapaasti Vaunussa [*Finnish*]
VVAUSh............ Higher Military Aviation School for Navigators (RU)
VVB............ Vereinigung Volkseigener Betriebe [*Association of State Enterprises*] [*Formerly known as Verwaltung Volkseigener Betriebe, Administration of State Enterprises*] (EG)
VVB............ Vlaamse Volksbeweging [*Flemish Popular Movement*] [*Belgian*] (WEN)
VVBADP............ Vlaamse Vereniging van Bibliotheek, Archief en Documentatie Personeel
vvd............ Airborne Division (BU)
VVD............ Extremely High Pressure (RU)
VVD............ High-Pressure Air (RU)
VVD............ Volkspartij voor Vrijheid en Democratie [*People's Party for Freedom and Democracy*] [*Dutch*] (WEN)
VVD............ Voreio-Voreio-Dytikos [*North-Northwest*] (GC)
VVDM............ Vereniging voor Dienstplichtige Militairen [*Union of Conscripts*] [*Dutch*] (WEN)
VVE............ Medical Determination of Fitness for Military Service (RU)
VVE............ Veszpremi Vegyipari Egyetem [*Chemical Industry University of Veszprem*] (HU)
Vve............ Veuve [*Widow*] [*French*] (GPO)
VVEAB............ Vereinigung Volkseigener Erfassungs- und Aufkaufbetriebe [*Association of State Procurement and Purchase Enterprises*] (EG)
vved............ Introduction (RU)
VVEG............ Vereinigung Volkseigener Gueter [*Association of State Farms*] [*See VVG*] (EG)
VVER............ Water-Cooled Nuclear Power Reactor (BU)
VVER............ Water-Moderated Water-Cooled Power Reactor (RU)
VVF............ Air Force (RU)
VVF............ Herald of the Air Force [*A publication*] (RU)
VVF............ High-Voltage Feeder (RU)
VVF............ Volga Naval Flotilla (RU)
VVFK............ Intradepartmental Financial Control (BU)
VVFSh............ Military School for Veterinary Assistants (RU)
VVG............ Vereinigung Volkseigener Gueter [*Association of State Farms*] [*See VVEG*] (EG)
VVGMI............ Higher Military Hydrometeorological Institute [*1941-1945*] (RU)
VVH............ Vereinigung Volkseigener Handelsbetriebe [*Association of State Trade Enterprises*] (EG)
VVHB............ Vereinigung Volkseigener Handelsbetriebe [*Association of State Trade Enterprises*] (EG)
VVI............ Herald of World History [*A publication*] (RU)
VVI............ High Military Inspection (RU)
VVI............ Vojaski Vojni Invalidi [*Disabled Veterans*] (YU)
VVIA............ Air Force Engineering Academy (RU)
VVIL............ Herald of Foreign Military Literature [*A publication*] (RU)
VVIMU............ Vladivostok Higher Engineering Nautical School (RU)
VVK............ High-Voltage Cable (RU)
VVK............ Military Medical Commission (RU)
VVK............ Verwaltung Vermessungs- und Kartenwesen [*Administration for Surveying and Mapping (Civilian agency in GDR subordinate to the Ministry of the Interior)*] (EG)
VVK............ Viscosity-Gravity Constant (RU)
VVKB............ Code Input-Output Unit on Magnetic Storage Drum (RU)
VVKFEP............ Military Medical Commission of a Frontline Evacuation Station (RU)
VVKhKI............ Higher Institute of Veterinary Hygiene and Control (BU)
VVKL............ Code Input-Output Unit on Magnetic Storage Tape (RU)
VVKR............ Boiling-Water Reactor (RU)
VVL............ High-Voltage Laboratory (RU)
VVL............ Military Veterinary Hospital (RU)
VVMGU............ Higher Naval Hydrographic School (RU)
VVMI............ Higher Institute of Veterinary Medicine (BU)
VVMIU............ Higher Naval Engineering School (RU)
VVMMU............ Higher Naval Medical School (RU)
VVMTS............ Verwaltung Volkseigener Maschinen- und Traktorenstationen [*Administration of State Machine and Tractor Stations*] (EG)
VVMUPP............ Higher Naval Submarine School Imeni Lenin Komsomol (RU)
VVN............ Rotary Vacuum Pump (RU)
vvn............ Velmi Vysoke Napeti [*Very High Voltage*] (CZ)
VVN............ Vereinigung der Verfolgten des Naziregimes [*Association of Persecutees of the NAZI Regime*] (EG)
VVO............ High-Voltage Equipment (RU)
VVO............ Most Urgent, Top Priority (RU)
v-vo............ Substance, Matter (RU)
VVO............ Vaterlaendischer Verdienstorden [*Patriotic Order of Merit*] (EG)
VVO............ Verenigde Volke-Organisasie [*United Nations Organization*] [*Use UN*] (AF)
VVO............ Verordnung ueber die Verfolgung von Verfehlungen [*Decree on Prosecution of Violations*] (EG)
VVO............ Vybor Vesnicke Organizace (KSC) [*Committee of the Village Organization (Czechoslovak Communist Party)*] (CZ)
VVO............ Vychodni Vojensky Okruh [*Eastern Military District*] (CZ)
v-vod............ Wave Guide (RU)
vvod sl............ Parenthetic Word (RU)
VVOO............ All-Army Hunting Society (RU)
VVP............ High-Voltage Cable (RU)
VVP............ Universal Military Training (RU)
VVP............ Vertical Takeoff and Landing (RU)
VVP............ Vojensky Vycvikovy Prapor [*Military Training Battalion*] (CZ)
VVP............ Vojensky Vycvikovy Prostor [*Military Training Area*] (CZ)
VVPI............ Higher Military Pedagogical Institute Imeni M. I. Kalinin (RU)
VVPJ............ Velitelstvi Vojenskych Pracovnich Jednotek [*Headquarters of Military Labor Units*] (CZ)
VVPVO............ Velitelstvi Vojsk PVO [*PVO Troop Headquarters*] (CZ)
VVR............ Vereinigung Volkseigener Reparatur Werften [*Association of State Repair Shipyards*] (EG)
VVr............ Vizantiyski Vremennik [*Byzantine Chronicle*] [*A periodical*] (BU)
VVR............ Water-Moderated Water-Cooled Reactor (RU)
VVRD............ Pressurized Water Reactor (RU)
VVRK............ Boiling-Water Reactor (RU)
VVRK-P............ Boiling-Water Reactor with Nuclear Superheat (RU)
VVRP............ Upper Volga River Steamship Line (RU)
VVRS............ Supreme Military Editorial Council [*1921-1926*] (RU)
VVR-Uvo............ Water-Moderated Water-Cooled Reactor Using Highly Enriched Uranium (RU)
VVRW............ Vereinigung Volkseigener Reparatur Werften [*Association of State Repair Ship Yards*] (EG)
VVS............ Air Force (BU)
VVS............ Air Force (RU)
VVS............ Gazette of the Supreme Soviet [*A publication*] (RU)
VVS............ High-Voltage Network (RU)
VVS............ High-Voltage Selenium Rectifier (RU)
VVS............ Military Veterinary Service (RU)
VVS............ Service Troops (RU)
VVS............ Supreme Military Council (RU)
VVS............ Vereniging der Vlaamse Studenten [*Association of Flemish Students*] [*Belgian, Dutch*] (WEN)
VVS............ Verkehrsversicherungsschein [*Transportation Insurance Policy*] (EG)
VVS............ Vertical Glass Drawing (RU)
VVS............ Vertrauliche Verschluss-Sache [*Confidential Classified Material (Requiring custody in safe)*] [*German*] (WEN)
VVS............ Vojenske Vycvikove Stredisko [*Military Training Center*] (CZ)
VVS............ Vy, Vato, Sakelika (MAR)
VVSBM............ Baltic Sea Air Force (RU)
VVSh............ Herald of Higher Education [*A publication*] (RU)
VVSP............ Temporary Military Hospital Train (RU)
VVSSA............ Soviet Army Air Force (RU)
VVT............ Inland Water Transportation (RU)
VVT............ Vojensky Vycvikovy Tabor [*Military Training Camp*] (CZ)
VVU............ Input-Output Device (RU)
VVU............ Military Veterinary Directorate (RU)
VVU............ Vojensky Vedecky Ustav [*Institute of Military Science*] (CZ)
VVU............ Vojensky Vyzkumny Ustav [*Military Research Institute*] (CZ)
VVU............ Vojno Vazduhoplovno Uciliste [*Air Force School*] (YU)
VVU............ Vyssi Vojenske Uciliste [*Higher Military Training Center*] (CZ)
VVUD............ Vedecko-Vyzkumny Ustav Dopravni [*Transportation Research Institute*] (CZ)
VVUD............ Vyzkumny a Vyvojovy Ustav Drevarsky [*Institute for Research and Development of the Wood Industry*] (CZ)
VVUMH............ Vyzkumny a Vyvojovy Ustav Mistniho Hospodarstvi [*Institute for Research and Development of Local Economy*] (CZ)
VVUTS............ Vyzkumny a Vyvojovy Ustav Technickeho Skla [*Institute for Research and Development of Industrial Glass*] (CZ)
VVUU............ Vedecko-Vyzkumny Uhelny Ustav [*Coal Research Institute*] [*Ostrava*] (CZ)
VVUZ............ Higher Military Educational Institution (RU)
VVUZVS............ Vyzkumny a Vyvojovy Ustav Zavodu Vseobecneho Strojirenstvi [*Institute for Research and Development of the General Engineering Plants*] (CZ)
VVV............ Vereinigung Volkseigener Verlage [*Association of State-Owned Publishing Houses*] (EG)
VVV............ Vladni Vybor pre Vystavbu [*Government Committee on Building*] (CZ)
VVVA............ Visa Vazduhoplovna Vojna Akademija [*Advanced Air Force Academy*] [*Equivalent to command and staff school*] (YU)
VVW............ Vereinigung Volkseigener Warenhaeuser [*Association of State Department Stores*] (EG)
VVW............ Vereinigung Volkseigener Werften [*Association of State-Owned Shipyards*] (EG)
VVZ............ Vedecko-Vyzkumna Zakladna [*Scientific-Research Base*] (CZ)
VVZ............ Velikomoravska Vodna Zajednica [*Greater Morava Water Resources Group*] (YU)
VVZ............ Vocarsko-Vinogradarska Zadruga [*Fruit and Viticulture Cooperative*] (YU)
VVZ............ Vyzkumna a Vyvojova Zakladna [*Research and Development Base*] (CZ)
VW............ Verlag Die Wirtschaft [*Die Wirtschaft Publishing House*] (EG)
VW............ Verlag Weltbuehne [*Weltbuehne Publishing House*] (EG)

VW............ Verrechnungswaehrungen [*Clearing Currencies*] (EG)
Vw............ Verwaltung [*German*]
VW............ Volkswagen [*Volkswagen*] (EG)
Vw............ Vorwort [*German*]
VWB............ Volkswagen do Brasil [*Brazilian*]
Vwbz............ Verwaltungsbezirk [*Administrative District*] (EG)
VwGerH....... Verwaltungsgerichtshof [*German*]
VwGH............ Verwaltungsgerichtshof [*German*]
Vwltg............ Verwaltung [*German*]
Vwltr............ Verwalter [*German*]
VWO............ Verbond van Wetenschappelijke Onderzoekers [*Utrecht*]
VWP............ Vietnam Workers' Party (PPW)
VWP............ Volkswirtschaftsplan [*Economic Plan*] (EG)
Vwr............ Verwalter [*German*]
VWR............ Volkswirtschaftsrat [*Economic Council*] (EG)
Vx............ Vieux [*Old*] [*Military map abbreviation*] [*World War I*] [*French*] (MTD)
VY............ Virkamiesten Yhteisjarjesto [*Government Employees' Confederation*] [*Finnish*] (WEN)
VYa............ Problems of Linguistics [*A publication*] (RU)
Vyatlag........ Vyatka Corrective Labor Camp (RU)
Vybor ZLV... Vybor pro Zvelebeni Zemedelskeho, Lesniho, a Vodniho Hospodarstvi [*Committee for Management Efficiency in Agriculture, Forestry, and Water Utilization*] (CZ)
vychisl......... Calculated, Computed (RU)
VYe............ Herald of Europe [*A publication*] (RU)
VYeP............ Height of Transfer Unit (RU)
V'yetn.......... Vietnamese (RU)
VykhU.......... Output Device (RU)
vyn............ Vynos [*Decree*] (CZ)
vyp............ Issue (RU)
vyp dan....... Imprint (RU)
vyrez............ Clipping (RU)
vys............ Height, Elevation, Altitude (RU)
vys............ Settlement [*Topography*] (RU)
VysC............ Vysadkova Ceta [*Airborne Platoon*] (CZ)
Vysofizkul't ... Supreme Council of Physical Culture (at the VTsIK) (RU)
Vysovfizkul't ... Supreme Council of Physical Culture (at the VTsIK) (RU)
vyssh............ Supreme, Highest, Higher (RU)
Vystrel.......... Higher Marksmanship Courses (RU)
VYuK............ Higher Law Courses (RU)
VYuZI.......... All-Union Correspondence Law Institute (RU)
v-z............ Air-to-Surface [*Missile*] (RU)
VZ............ Oscillating Switch (RU)
vz............ Platoon (BU)
VZ............ Platoon (RU)
VZ............ Railway Cars Building Plant (BU)
VZ............ Railway Cars Repair Plant (BU)
vz............ V Zaloze [*In Reserve*] (CZ)
VZ............ Verseifungszahl [*Saponification Value*] [*German*]
VZ............ Vetrinarski Zavod [*Veterinary Institute*] (YU)
VZ............ Vinarska Zadruga [*Wine Cooperative*] (YU)
VZ............ Vitkovicke Zelezarny [*Vitkovice Iron Works*] (CZ)
VZ............ Vodna Zajednica [*Water Resources Group*] (YU)
VZ............ Vodni Zdroje [*Water Resources (A budgetary organization)*] (CZ)
VZ............ Vojenske Zatisi [*Military Recreation Center*] (CZ)
Vz............ Vorzug [*First Section of a Train (Operated separately)*] (EG)
VZ............ Vybor Zen [*Women's Committee*] (CZ)
VZ............ Vykupni Zavod [*Purchasing Enterprise (for agricultural products)*] (CZ)
vz............ Vzor [*Sample, Example, Type*] (CZ)
VZA............ Organic Antiaircraft Artillery (RU)
VZADT........ All-Union Correspondence Highway Technicum (RU)
vzbe............ Combat Squadron [*Aviation*] (BU)
VZD............ Delayed-Action Fuze, Delayed-Action Detonator (RU)
VZEI............ All-Union Correspondence Institute of Economics (RU)
VZEI............ All-Union Correspondence Power Engineering Institute (RU)
VZEIS.......... All-Union Correspondence Electrotechnical Institute of Communications (RU)
VZEMT........ All-Union Correspondence Electromechanical Technicum (RU)
VZESO........ Vilnius Electric Welding Equipment Plant (RU)
VZET............ All-Union Correspondence Power Engineering Technicum (RU)
VZF............ Vlnarske Zavody a Fezarny [*Woolen Mills and Fez Factories*] (CZ)
VZFEI.......... All-Union Correspondence Institute of Finance and Economics (RU)
VZFI............ All-Union Correspondence Institute of Finance (RU)
VZFKT.......... All-Union Correspondence Technicum of Finance and Credit (RU)
VZFT............ All-Union Correspondence Technicum of Finance (RU)
VZGMT.......... All-Union Correspondence Hydrometeorological Technicum (RU)
VZGRU.......... Herald of the West Siberian Administration of Geological Exploration [*A publication*] (RU)
VZh............ Logbook (RU)
vzh............ See (BU)
VZh chl....... See Article [*Law*] (BU)
VZhDB.......... Railroad Reconstruction Battalion (RU)
VZhMT.......... Turnip Yellow Mosaic Virus (RU)
VZhPP.......... Railroad Military Ration-Distributing Point (RU)
VZI............ All-Union Correspondence Institute (RU)
VZIF............ All-Union Correspondence Institute of Finance (RU)
VZII............ All-Union Correspondence Industrial Institute (RU)
VZIIT............ All-Union Correspondence Institute of Railroad Transportation Engineers (RU)
VZIIZhT....... All-Union Correspondence Institute of Railroad Transportation Engineers (RU)
VZIMP.......... All-Ukrainian Correspondence Institute of Mass Education of Party Activists at the TsK KP(b)U (RU)
VZINO.......... All-Union Correspondence Institute of Finance, Economics, and Accountancy (RU)
VZIPP.......... All-Union Correspondence Institute of the Food Industry (RU)
VZIPSKh..... All-Union Zootechnical Institute of Fur and Peltry (RU)
VZIPSM....... All-Union Correspondence Institute of the Building Materials Industry (RU)
VZIPT.......... All-Union Correspondence Institute of the Textile Industry (RU)
VZIS............ All-Union Correspondence Institute of Communications (RU)
VZISI............ All-Union Correspondence Construction Engineering Institute (RU)
VZIST.......... All-Union Correspondence Institute of Soviet Trade (RU)
VZIT............ All-Union Correspondence Industrial Technicum (RU)
VZIT............ All-Union Correspondence Institute of Railroad Transportation Engineers (RU)
VZIT............ All-Union Correspondence Institute of Trade (RU)
VZITLP........ All-Union Correspondence Institute of Textile and Light Industries (RU)
VZITO.......... All-Union Correspondence Institute of Technical Education (RU)
VZITP.......... All-Union Correspondence Institute of the Textile Industry (RU)
VZK............ Vojensky Zdokonalovaci Kurs [*Military Advance Course*] (CZ)
VZKG............ Vitkovicke Zelezarny Klementa Gottwalda [*Klement Gottwald Iron Works in Vitkovice*] (CZ)
VZKhTT....... All-Union Correspondence Technicum of Chemical Technology (RU)
VZKT............ All-Union Correspondence Cooperative Technicum (RU)
VZLT............ All-Union Correspondence Forestry-Engineering Technicum (RU)
VZLTI.......... All-Union Correspondence Forestry-Engineering Institute (RU)
VZLU............ Vyzkumny a Zkusebny Letecky Ustav [*Aeronautical Research and Testing Institute*] (CZ)
VZMI............ All-Union Correspondence Institute of Mechanical Engineering (RU)
vznb............ Air Observation (BU)
vznbe.......... Observation Squadron [*Aviation*] (BU)
VZO............ Vojensky Zemepisny Ustav [*Military Geographical Institute*] (CZ)
VzOR............ Flash-Ranging Platoon (RU)
VZOS............ All-Union Stenography Correspondence Courses (RU)
VZP............ Antiaircraft Machine-Gun Platoon (RU)
VZP............ Vatra za Zaprecavanje Pesadije [*Barrage Fire Against Infantry*] (YU)
VZPI............ All-Union Correspondence Polytechnic Institute (RU)
VZPSh.......... Higher Correspondence Party School at the TsK KPSS (RU)
VZR............ Fuze, Detonator (RU)
VZR............ Sound-Ranging Platoon (RU)
VZR............ Voice of Zimbabwe Rhodesia (AF)
VZRO............ Vestnik Zemske Rady Osvetove [*Bulletin of the Provincial Cultural Council*] [*A publication*] (CZ)
Vzryvsel'prom ... Administration of Blasting Operations in Agriculture, Forestry, Industry, and Construction of the Main Military Engineering Directorate [*1922*] (RU)
Vzryvsel'prom ... Central Administration of Agricultural and Industrial Blasting Operations [*1931*] (RU)
Vzryvsel'prom ... Office of Agricultural and Industrial Blasting Operations [*1928-1930*] (RU)
Vzryvsel'prom ... Office of Blasting Operations in Agriculture and Industry at the Military Technical Directorate of the RKKA [*1926-1927*] (RU)
VzS............ Compressed Air (RU)
VZShPD....... Higher Correspondence School of Trade Unionism of the VTsSPS (RU)
VZSIT.......... All-Union Correspondence Technicum of Machine Tools and Tools (RU)
VZSKhT....... All-Union Correspondence Agricultural Technicum (RU)
VZST............ All-Union Correspondence Construction Technicum (RU)
VZT............ All-Union Correspondence Technicum (RU)
VZT............ Vatra za Zaprecavanje Tenkova [*Barrage Fire Against Tanks*] (YU)
VZTI............ All-Union Correspondence Technicum of Measurements (RU)
VZTLP.......... All-Union Correspondence Technicum of Light Industry (RU)
VZTMiMP.... All-Union Correspondence Technicum of the Meat and Dairy Industry (RU)
VZTPK.......... All-Union Correspondence Technicum of Producer's Cooperatives (RU)
VZTPP.......... All-Union Correspondence Technicum of the Food Industry (RU)
VZTRT.......... All-Union Correspondence Technicum of River Transportation (RU)
VZTS............ All-Union Correspondence Technicum of Communications (RU)
VZTST.......... All-Union Correspondence Technicum of Soviet Trade (RU)

VZTTM........ All-Union Correspondence Technicum of Heavy Engineering (RU)

VZU............. External Memory Systems (BU)

VZU............. External Storage, External Memory (RU)

VZUK........... All-Union Correspondence Accounting Courses (RU)

VZUKT........ All-Union Correspondence Accounting and Credit Technicum (RU)

VZUP........... Vyvojovy Zavod Uranovehe Prumyslu [*Development Center of the Uranium Industry*] (CZ)

vzv............... Platoon (BU)

VZV............. Platoon (RU)

VZVI............ Voronezh Zootechnical and Veterinary Institute (RU)

vzv SAU...... Platoon of Self-Propelled Guns (RU)

VZW............ Vereniging Zonder Winstoogmerk [*Non-Profit Society*] [*Dutch*]

VZZhT......... All-Union Correspondence Railroad Technicum (RU)

W

W: .... Die Wichtigsten Werke [*German*]
W .... Ouest [*West*] [*French*] (MTD)
W .... Train Operates Only on Weekdays (EG)
W/ .... Valued [*Correspondence*] [*German*]
W .... Wache [*German*]
W .... Wad [*or Wadi or Wed*] [*Valley, River, River Bed*] [*Arab*] (NAU)
W .... Wai [*River*] [*Indonesian*] (NAU)
W .... Wappen [*Coat of Arms*] [*German*]
w .... Warm [*Warm*] [*German*]
W .... Wasser [*Water*] [*German*]
W .... Wat [*Watt*] [*Polish*]
W .... Watt [*Watt, Watts*] (EG)
W .... Watti [*or Wattia*] [*Finnish*]
w .... Weg [*Way*] [*Dutch*]
W .... Weiler [*3 bis 9 Haeuser*] [*German*]
w .... Weiss [*White*] [*German*]
W .... Westen [*West*] (EG)
W .... Wetteren [*Powder*] [*German*] (MTD)
W .... Widerstand [*Electrical Resistance*] [*German*]
w .... Wiek [*Century*] (POL)
W .... Wielmozny [*Esquire*] [*Polish*]
w .... Wies [*Village*] (POL)
W .... Wirklicher [*German*]
W .... Wirtschaft [*German*]
W .... Witwe [*Widow*] [*Business and trade*] [*German*]
W .... Wolfram [*Tungsten*] [*German*]
W .... Word (MAR)
w .... Wyspa [*Island*] [*Polish*]
WA .... (Abteilung) Werkzeugmaschinen und Automatisierung (der Staatlichen Plankommission) [*Machine-Tool and Automation Department (of the State Planning Commission)*] (EG)
WA .... West Africa (MAR)
WA .... World Archaeology [*Londres*] [*A publication*] (MAR)
Wa .... Wyspa [*Island*] [*Polish*] (NAU)
WAA .... West African Army [*Artillery*] (MAR)
WAA .... Workers Affairs Association (AF)
WAAC .... West African Agricultural Corporation (MAR)
WAAC .... West African Airways Corporation (MAR)
WAAN .... West African Archaeological Newsletter [*Ibadan*] [*A publication*] (MAR)
WAAP .... World Association for Animal Production (EA)
WAAPHI .... West African Association of Public Health Inspectors (MAR)
WAAS .... Wakil Asisten (IN)
WAAVP .... World Association for the Advancement of Veterinary Parasitology (EA)
WAB .... World Association for Buiatrics (EA)
WABA .... West African Bankers' Association (MAR)
WABO .... Writers Association of Botswana (MAR)
WAC .... West Africa Company (MAR)
WAC .... West African Conference (MAR)
WAC .... Women's Affairs Committee [*Nigerian*] (AF)
WAC .... World Assistance Corps (EA)
WACA .... West African Court of Appeal (MAR)
WACA .... World Airlines Clubs Association (EA)
WACB .... West African Currency Board (MAR)
WACC .... World Association of Christian Communications (MAR)
wach .... Wachmistrz [*Sergeant-Major (Cavalry)*] [*Polish*]
WACH .... West African Clearing House (MAR)
WACL .... World Anti-Communist League (EA)
WACMR .... West African Council for Medical Research (MAR)
WACRAL .... World Association of Christian Radio Amateurs and Listeners (EA)
WACRI .... West African Cocoa Research Institute (MAR)
WACU .... West African Customs Union (MAR)
WADA .... West African Development Association (MAR)
WADA .... Wum Area Development Authority (MAR)
WADB .... West African Development Bank (AF)
WADU .... Wollamo Agricultural Development Unit (MAR)
WAEC .... West African Episcopal Church (MAR)
WAEC .... West African Examinations Council [*Nigerian*] (AF)
WAEJ .... World Association of Esperanto Journalists [*See also TEJA*] (EA)
WAEP .... World Association for Element Building and Prefabrication (EA)
WAER .... World Association for Educational Research [*See also AMSE*] (EA)
WAERSA .... World Agricultural Economics and Rural Sociology Abstracts [*United Kingdom*]
WAES .... Workshop on Alternative Energy Strategies (MAR)
WAF .... Wojskowa Agencja Fotograficzna [*Military Photographic Agency*] (POL)
WAFA .... Palestine News Agency (ME)
WAFC .... West African Fisheries Commission (MAR)
WAFD .... West African Fisheries Development Company (MAR)
WAFF .... West African Frontier Force (MAR)
WAFRI .... West African Fisheries Research Institute (MAR)
WAFRU .... West African Fungicide Research Unit (MAR)
WAFS .... West African Ferrying Squadron (MAR)
WAFU .... West African Football Union (MAR)
WAG .... Wydawnictwo Artystyczno-Graficzne [*Fine Printing Publishing House*] (POL)
WAG .... Wytwornia Artykulow Gumowych [*Rubber Goods Plant*] (POL)
WAGFEI .... Women's Action Group on Excision and Infibulation (EA)
WAGGGS .... World Association of Girl Guides and Girl Scouts [*See also AMGE*] (EA)
Wagum .... Wytwornia Artykulow Gumowych [*Rubber Goods Plant*] (POL)
WAHO .... World Arabian Horse Organization (EA)
WAHS .... West African Health Secretariat (MAR)
WAHSC .... West African High School Certificate (MAR)
WAHVM .... World Association for the History of Veterinary Medicine (EA)
WAIA .... Wojewodzka Agencja Imprez Artystycznych [*Voivodship Art Show Agency*] (POL)
WAICA .... West African Insurance Consultative Association (MAR)
WAIFOR .... West African Institute for Oil Palm Research (MAR)
WAII .... Wester State Agricultural and Industrial Investment Company (MAR)
WAISER .... West African Institute of Social and Economic Research (MAR)
WAITR .... West African Institute for Trypanosomiasis Research (MAR)
WAITRO .... World Association of Industrial and Technological Research Organizations
WAJA .... West African Journal of Archaeology [*Ibadan*] [*A publication*] (MAR)
WAJAL .... West African Joint Agency Limited (MAR)
WAK .... Wake Island [*Three-letter standard code*] (CNC)
WAŁ .... West African Pound (MAR)
WALA .... West African Library Association (MAR)
WALCON .... West African Lines Conference (MAR)
WALL .... Warszawski Aeroklub Ligi Lotniczej [*Warsaw Aeroclub of the Aeronautical League*] (POL)
Wallf .... Wallfahrtsort [*German*]
WAM .... Wojskowa Akademia Medyczna [*Military Medical Academy*] (POL)
WAM .... Wytwornia Aparatow i Maszyn [*Apparatus and Machine Plant*] (POL)
WAMEX .... West African Monsoon Experiment (AF)
WAMILDA .... Wadjib Militer Darurat [*Emergency Military Obligation (Conscription)*] (IN)
WAMRU .... West African Maize Research Unit (MAR)
WAMU .... West African Monetary Union (AF)
WAMY .... World Assembly of Muslim Youth (EA)
WAN .... Nigeria [*Polish*]
WAN .... Warszawska Administracja Nieruchomosci [*Warsaw Real Estate Administration*] (POL)
WAN .... Wegierska Akademia Nauk [*Hungarian Academy of Sciences*] (POL)
WANHAT .... Dewan Penasehat [*Council of Advisers*] (IN)
WANS .... West African News Service [*Nigerian*] (AF)
WAO .... Wet op de Arbeidsongeschiktheid [*Law on Labor Disability*] [*Dutch*] (WEN)
WAO .... Wissenschaftliche Arbeitsorganisation [*Scientific Labor Organization*] (EG)

WAP .... Werkabgabepreis [*Plant Delivered Price*] (EG)
WAP .... Wojewodzkie Archiwum Panstwowe [*Voivodship State Archives*] (POL)
WAP .... Wojskowa Akademia Polityczna [*Military Political Academy*] (POL)
WAPCC .... West African Portland Cement Company (MAR)
WAPKr .... Wojewodzkie Archiwum Panstwowe w Krakowie [*Voivodship State Archives in Cracow*] (POL)
WAPLub ...... Wojewodzkie Archiwum Panstwowe w Lublinie [*Voivodship State Archives in Lublin*] (POL)
WAPMC ...... West African Postgraduate Medical College (MAR)
WAPPoz ...... Wojewodzkie Archiwum Panstwowe w Poznaniu [*Voivodship State Archives in Poznan*] (POL)
WAR .... West African Regiment (MAR)
WAR .... West African Review [*Londres*] [*A publication*] (MAR)
WARA .... Wanita Angkatan Udara [*Women's Air Force Corps*] (IN)
WARC .... World Alliance of Reformed Churches [*See also ARM*] (EA)
WARDA .... West Africa Rice Development Association (AF)
WARG .... West Africa Regional Group (AF)
WARP .... West African Replenishment Plan (AF)
WARRS .... West African Rice Research Station (MAR)
WAS .... Pengawas [*or Pengawasan*] [*Supervisor or Supervision*] (IN)
WAS .... Waggonabnahmestelle [*Railroad Car Acceptance Office*] (EG)
WAS .... Witwatersrand Agricultural Society (MAR)
WASA .... Water and Sewerage Authority [*Trinidadian and Tobagan*] (LA1)
WASA .... West African Science Association (AF)
WASA .... Writers Association of South Africa (AF)
WASC .... West African School Certificate (MAR)
WASC .... West African Students Confederation (AF)
WASMAR .... Kawasan Maritim [*Maritime District*] (IN)
WASMO ...... West African Schools Mathematics Programme (MAR)
WASPRU ..... West African Stored Products Research Unit (MAR)
wassr .... Waesserig [*Aqueous, Hydrous*] [*German*]
WASU .... West African Students Union (AF)
WAT .... Wojskowa Akademia Techniczna [*Military Technical Academy*] (POL)
WAT .... Woordeboek van die Afrikaanse Taal (MAR)
WAT .... Wytwornia Artykulow Technicznych [*Technical Goods Plant*] (POL)
WATBRU ..... West African Timber Borer Research Unit (MAR)
WATTE .... West African Tropical Testing Establishment (MAR)
WATWF ...... West African Transport Workers Federation (MAR)
WAV .... Wirtschaftliche Aufbau Vereinigung [*Economic Reconstruction Union*] [*West German*] (PPE)
WAVFH .... World Association of Veterinary Food-Hygienists [*See also AMVHA*] (EA)
WAVMI .... World Association of Veterinary Microbiologists, Immunologists, and Specialists in Infectious Diseases [*See also AMVMI*] (EA)
WAWA .... West Africa Wins Again (MAR)
WAWF .... World Association of World Federalists (AF)
WAWU .... Waterfront and Allied Workers Union [*Barbadian*] (LA1)
WAY .... World Assembly of Youth (EA)
WAYL .... West African Youth League (MAR)
WAYMCA .... World Alliance of Young Men's Christian Associations (EA)
Wb .... Weber [*Weber*] [*Polish*]
WB .... Wetenschappelijke Bibliotheken
Wb .... Wirtschaftsbesitzer [*German*]
WB .... Wohnbezirk [*Residential District*] (EG)
WBA .... Wohnbezirksausschuss [*Residential District Committee*] (EG)
WBA .... World Boxing Association
WBC .... World Boxing Council (EA)
WBDJ .... Weltbund der Demokratischen Jugend [*World Federation of Democratic Youth (WFDY)*] [*German*] (WEN)
WBK .... Wohnungsbaukombinat [*Housing Construction Combine*] (EG)
WBK .... Wytwornia Biletow Kolejowych [*Railroad Ticket Printing Plant*] (POL)
WBMS .... World Bureau of Metal Statistics (EA)
WBP .... Wojewodzka Biblioteka Publiczna [*Voivodship Public Library*] (POL)
WBP .... Wojewodzkie Biuro Projektow [*Voivodship Office of Plans*] (POL)
WBR .... Wet op de Bibliotheekraad
W Br .... Wielka Brytania [*Great Britain*] (POL)
WBR .... Wohnungsbaureihe [*Housing Construction Series*] (EG)
W Bryt .... Wielka Brytania [*Great Britain*] [*Polish*]
WBS .... Warenbegleitschein [*Bill of Lading*] (EG)
WBS .... Wojewodzkie Biuro Skierowan [*Voivodship Office for Vacation Assignment*] (POL)
WBV .... Wagenbehandlungsvorschriften [*Car Handling Regulations*] (EG)
WCARRD .... World Conference on Agrarian Reform and Rural Development (MAR)
WCC .... War Claims Commission (MAR)
WCC .... War Crimes Commission (MAR)
WCC .... World Council of Churches
WCCL .... World Council for Colonial Liberation (MAR)
WCDA .... West Cameroons Development Agency (MAR)
WCEC .... West Cameroon Electricity Company (MAR)
WCF .... World Congress of Faiths (EA)
WCFBA .... World Catholic Federation for the Biblical Apostolate (EA)
WCH .... Wojskowa Centrala Handlowa [*Military Trade Center*] (POL)
WCIP .... World Council of Indigenous Peoples (EA)
WCKS .... Wojskowy Centralny Klub Sportowy [*Military Central Sports and Athletics Club*] [*Polish*]
WCL .... World Confederation of Labour [*See also CMT*] (EA)
WCNU .... Women's Wing of the Cameroon National Union (MAR)
WCOTP .... World Confederation of Organizations of the Teaching Profession (AF)
WCPPG .... Wojewodzkie Centralne Poradnie Przeciwgruzlicze [*Voivodship Central Anti-Tubercular Stations*] (POL)
WCRZZ .... Wszechzwiazkowa Centralna Rada Zwiazkow Zawodowych [*All-Union Central Council of Trade Unions*] [*Polish*]
WCSPS .... Wszechrosyjski Centralny Sojusz Profesjonalnych Sojuszow [*All-Russian Central Trade Union Organization*] (POL)
WCT .... World Confederation of Teachers [*See also CSME*] (EA)
WCT .... Wydawnictwo Czasopism Technicznych [*Technical Periodicals Publishing House*] (POL)
WCTA .... World Committee for Trade Action [*See also CMAP*] (EA)
WCTUC .... West Cameroon Trade Union Congress (AF)
WCWB .... World Council for the Welfare of the Blind [*See also OMPSA*] (EA)
wd .... Wdowa [*Widow*] [*Polish*]
WD .... Wettelijk Depot
WDC .... Workers' Defence Committee [*Polish*] (PD)
WDC .... World Data Centre
WDD .... Water Development Department (MAR)
WDF .... Western Desert Force (MAR)
WDF .... World Draughts (Checkers) Federation [*See also FMJD*] (EA)
WDK .... Wiejski Dom Kultury [*Rural House of Culture*] (POL)
WDK .... Wojewodzki Dom Kultury [*Voivodship House of Culture*] (POL)
WDK .... Wojskowy Dom Kultury [*Military House of Culture*] (POL)
WDN .... Warszawska Dzielnica Naukowa [*Warsaw Academic Quarter*] (POL)
WDO .... Warszawska Dyrekcja Odbudowy [*Warsaw Reconstruction Administration*] (POL)
WDT .... Wiejski Dom Towarowy [*Rural Department Store*] (POL)
WDU .... Wahlblock der Unabhaengigen [*German*]
WdU .... Wahlpartei der Unabhaengigen [*Electoral Party of Independents*] [*Austrian*] (PPE)
WDW .... Wojskowy Dom Wypoczynkowy [*Military Rest Home*] (POL)
WDZ .... Wydzial Drog i Zielencow [*Department of Roads and Verdure*] (POL)
WE .... Waermeeinheit [*Thermal Unit*] (EG)
WE .... Wohnungseinheit [*Dwelling Unit*] [*German*] (WEN)
WEAL .... West End Limited (MAR)
WEBE .... Werkgroep Beleidsplan [*NOBIN*] [*'s-Gravenhage*]
WEC .... World Energy Conference [*See also CME*] (EA)
WEC .... Worldwide Evangelization Crusade (MAR)
WED .... World Energy Development (MAR)
WEDC .... Water and Waste Engineering for Developing Countries (MAR)
weibl .... Weiblich [*German*]
WEk .... Elektrizitatswerk [*German*]
WENELA ...... Witwatersrand Native Labour Association (MAR)
WEPCO .... Western Desert Petroleum Company [*Egyptian*] (MAR)
WERC .... World Environment and Resources Council (EA)
WEREDEC ... Western Regional Development Corporation (MAR)
WEREDI ...... Union of Dutch Working Communities (WEN)
westl .... Westlich [*German*]
WEU .... Western European Union (WER)
WEVA .... World Esperantist Vegetarian Association [*See also TEVA*] (EA)
Wewa .... Wetterwarte [*Meteorological Observatory*] [*German*]
wewn .... Wewnetrzny [*Interior*] (POL)
WEZ .... Westeuropaische Zeit [*Western European Time (Greenwich Time)*] [*German*] (WEN)
WF .... Waehrungsfaktura [*Foreign Exchange Invoice*] (EG)
WF .... Wallis and Futuna [*Two-letter standard code*] (CNC)
wf .... Wasserfrei [*Anhydrous*] [*German*]
WF .... Werk fuer Fernmeldewesen, Berlin-Oberschoeneweide (VEB) [*Berlin-Oberschoeneweide Telecommunications Equipment Plant (VEB)*] (EG)
WF .... White Fathers [*Roman Catholic men's religious order*] (MAR)
WF .... Wychowanie Fizyczne [*Physical Education*] (POL)
WFA .... White Fish Authority (MAR)
WFAC .... World Federal Authority Committee (EA)
WFALW .... Weltbund Freiheitlicher Arbeitnehmerverbande auf Liberaler Wirtschaftsgrundlage [*World Union of Liberal Trade Union Organisations - WULTUO*] (EA)
WFAPS .... World Federation of Associations of Pediatric Surgeons (EA)
WFAW .... World Federation of Agricultural Workers [*See also FMTA*] (EA)
WFB .... World Fellowship of Buddhists (EA)
WFBY .... World Fellowship of Buddhist Youth (EA)
WFC .... World Food Council (MAR)
WFCC .... World Federation for Cancer Care (EA)
WFCLC .... World Federation of Christian Life Communities [*See also FMCVC*] (EA)
WFD .... Warszawska Fabryka Dzwigow [*Warsaw Hoisting Machinery Factory*] (POL)
WFD .... World Federation of the Deaf (MAR)

WFD .... Wytwornia Filmow Dokumentalnych [*Documentary Motion Picture Studio*] (POL)
WFDFI .... World Federation of Development Financing Institutions [*See also FEMIDE*] (EA)
WFDWRHL ... World Federation of Doctors Who Respect Human Life (EA)
WFDY .... World Federation of Democratic Youth [*See also FMJD*] (EA)
WFEO .... World Federation of Engineering Organizations [*United Kingdom*]
WFF .... Wytwornia Filmow Fabularnych [*Dramatic Motion Picture Studio*] (POL)
WFFM .... World Federation of Friends of Museums [*See also FMAM*] (EA)
WFFTH .... World Federation of Workers in Food, Tobacco, and Hotel Industries [*See also FMATH*] (EA)
WFIM .... World Federation of Islamic Missions (EA)
WFiPW .... Wychowanie Fizyczne i Przysposobienie Wojskowe [*Physical and Military Training*] [*Polish*]
WFIS .... Wytwornia Filmow Instruktorsko-Szkoleniowych [*Instructional and Educational Motion Picture Studio*] (POL)
WFJJ .... World Federation of Jewish Journalists (EA)
WFM .... Warszawska Fabryka Motocykli [*Warsaw Motorcycle Plant*] (POL)
WFMH .... World Federation of Mental Health (MAR)
WFMW .... World Federation of Methodist Women (EA)
WFNMW ...... World Federation of Trade Unions of Non-Manual Workers [*See also FMTNM*] (EA)
WFO .... Wytwornia Filmow Oswiatowych [*Educational Motion Picture Studio*] (POL)
WFOiP .... Wytwornia Filmow Oswiatowych i Przezroczy [*Educational Motion Picture and Filmstrip Studio*] (POL)
WFOT .... World Federation of Occupational Therapists (EA)
WFP .... Warszawska Fabryka Platerow [*Warsaw Flatware Factory*] (POL)
WFP .... Workers and Farmers Party [*Trinidadian and Tobagan*] (LA)
WFP .... World Federation of Parasitologists (EA)
WFP .... World Food Programme [*United Nations*] [*United Nations*] (MAR)
WFPiU .... Warszawska Fabryka Przyrzadow i Uchwytow [*Warsaw Instrument and Fixture Factory*] (POL)
WFR .... Weltfriedensrat [*World Peace Council (WPC)*] (EG)
WFRS .... World Federation of Rose Societies (EA)
WFS .... Wasserfilterstation [*Water Purification Station*] (EG)
WFS .... World Fertility Survey (MAR)
WFSA .... World Federation of Societies of Anaesthesiologists (EA)
WFSW .... World Federation of Scientific Workers [*See also FMTS*] (EA)
WFTiW .... Wojewodzki Fundusz Turystyki i Wypoczynku [*Provincial Fund for the Organization of Tourism and Recreation*] [*Polish*]
WFTU .... World Federation of Trade Unions [*See also FSM*] (EA)
WFUM .... Wielkopolska Fabryka Urzadzen Mechanicznych [*Greater Poland (Wielkoposka) Mechanical Equipment Factory*] (POL)
WFUM .... Wroclawska Fabryka Urzadzen Mechanicznych [*Wroclaw (Breslau) Mechanical Equipment Factory*] (POL)
WFW .... Weltfoederation der Wissenschaftler [*World Federation of Scientists*] (EG)
WFY/NIO ..... World Federalist Youth - Youth Movement for a New International Order (EA)
Wg .... Wagen [*Railroad Car*] (EG)
Wg .... Wagenreinigung [*Railroad Car Cleaning Department*] (EG)
wg .... Wedlug [*According To*] (POL)
WG .... Working Group on the Constitution and Electoral Law (MAR)
WG .... Wydawnictwo Geologiczne [*Geology Publishing House*] (POL)
WGB .... Weltgewerkschaftsbund [*World Federation of Trade Unions - WFTU*] [*West German*] (WEN)
WGC .... World Games Council (EA)
WGH .... Wydawnictwo Gorniczo-Hutnicze [*Mining and Metallurgy Publishing House*] (POL)
Wgm .... Wagenmeister [*Car Master*] (EG)
Wgnr .... Wagennummer [*Railroad Car Number*] (EG)
Wh .... Watogodzina [*Watt-Hour*] [*Polish*]
WHA .... World Health Assembly (MAR)
WHL .... Wissenschaftliche Hauptleitung [*Scientific Main Directorate*] (EG)
WHO .... World Health Organization (WEN)
WHT .... Wojewodzka Hurtownia Tekstylna [*Provincial Center for the Wholesale Textile Trade*] [*Polish*]
WHW .... Warszawska Hurtownia Wlokiennicza [*Warsaw Textile Wholesale House*] (POL)
WHWM .... Wojewodzka Hurtownia Wod Mineralnych [*Voivodship Wholesale Mineral Water Warehouse*] (POL)
Whz .... Warmwasserheizung [*Warm Water Heating*] (EG)
WIADOK ...... Wirtschafts-Archiv mit Dokumentation
WIAS .... West Indies Associated States (LA1)
WIB .... Waktu Indonesia Barat [*West Indonesia Time*] (IN)
WIB .... Werkgroep Internationale Betrekkingen [*NOBIN/CIIB*]
WIC .... Wayfarer International Committee (EA)
WIC .... West India Committee (LA1)
WICBE .... World Information Centre for Bilingual Education [*See also CMIEB*] (EA)
wicemin ...... Wiceminister [*Vice-Minister*] [*Polish*]
WID .... Women in Development (MAR)
WIDF .... Women's International Democratic Federation [*See also FDIF*] (EA)
Widm .... Widmung [*Dedication (of a book)*] [*German*]
Wi-Fa-Ma .... Widzewska Fabryka Maszyn [*Widzew Machine Factory*] (POL)
WIFO .... Oesterreichisches Institut fuer Wirtschaftsforschung [*Austrian Institute for Economic Research*] (WEN)
WIG .... Wojskowy Instytut Geograficzny [*Military Geographic Institute*] (POL)
WIGMO .... Western International Ground Maintenance Organization (MAR)
WIH .... Wojskowy Instytut Historyczny [*Military Institute of History*] (POL)
WIIP .... West Indian Independence Party [*Trinidadian and Tobagan*] (LA)
WIL .... Wilajah [*Territory, Region*] (IN)
WIM .... Women's Institutes of Malaya (ML)
WIML .... Wojskowy Instytut Medycyny Lotniczej [*Military Institute of Aviation Medicine*] (POL)
WiN .... Wolnosc i Niepodleglosc [*Freedom and Independence*] [*Underground political organization*] [*World War II*] (POL)
WINB .... Wojskowy Instytut Naukowo-Badawczy [*Military Scientific Research Institute*] (POL)
WINBAN ...... Windward Islands Banana Association (LA1)
WINP .... West Indian National Party [*Trinidadian and Tobagan*] (LA)
WIPO .... World Intellectual Property Organization (MAR)
WIPTC .... Women's International Professional Tennis Council (EA)
WiR .... Wynalazczosc i Racjonalizacja [*Inventiveness and Rationalization*] (POL)
WIRFMD ...... Wellcome Institute for Research into Foot and Mouth Disease (MAR)
Wirk .... Wirkung [*Action, Effect*] [*German*]
WISAREP .... Wintershall Saharienne Societe Anonyme pour la Recherche et l'Exploitation Petrolieres (MAR)
WISE .... World Information Systems Exchange
wiss .... Wissenschaftlich [*Scientific*] [*German*]
WIT .... Waktu Indonesia Timur [*East Indonesia Time*] (IN)
WITA .... Waktu Indonesia Tengah [*Central Indonesia Time*] (IN)
WITS .... Worldwide Information and Trade System (MAR)
WIVR .... West Irian Volunteer Returnees (ML)
WIW .... Weterynaryjny Instytut Wydawniczy [*Veterinary Publishing Institute*] (POL)
WIYS .... World Islamic Youth Seminar (ME)
WK .... Wake Island [*Two-letter standard code*] (CNC)
Wk .... Werk [*German*]
WK .... Wissenschaftliche Konzeptionen [*Scientific Concepts*] (EG)
WK .... Wydawnictwo Komunikacyjne [*Transportation Publishing House*] (POL)
WKAU .... Wojewodzka Komisja Architektoniczno-Urbanistyczna [*Voivodship Commission on Urban Architecture*] (POL)
WKBA .... Wojewodzka Komisja Brakowania Akt [*Voivodship Commission for the Destruction of Records*] (POL)
WKC .... Wojewodzka Komisja Cen [*Voivodship Price Commission*] (POL)
WKD .... Warszawskie Koleje Dojazdowe [*Warsaw Suburban Railroads*] (POL)
WKD .... Wyzsza Komisja Dyscyplinarna [*Higher Disciplinary Commission*] (POL)
WK FJN .... Wojewodzki Komitet Frontu Jednosci Narodu [*National Unity Front Voivodship Committee*] (POL)
WKFN .... Wojewodzki Komitet Frontu Narodowego [*Voivodship Committee of the People's Front*] (POL)
WKK .... Wehrkreiskommando [*Kreis Military Command*] (EG)
WKKF .... Wojewodzki Komitet Kultury Fizycznej [*Voivodship Committee on Physical Culture*] (POL)
WKKFiT .... Wojewodzki Komitet Kultury Fizycznej i Turystyki [*Voivodship Committee on Physical Culture and Tourism*] (POL)
WKKP .... Wojewodzki Komitet Kontroli Partyjnej [*Voivodship Party Control Committee*] (POL)
WKL .... Wojewodzka Komisja Lokalowa [*Provincial Housing Board*] [*Polish*]
WKN .... Wyzsze Kursy Nauczycielskie [*Higher Courses for Teachers*] (POL)
WKO .... Wojewodzka Komisja Organizacyjna [*Voivodship Organization Commission*] (POL)
WKOP .... Wojewodzki Komitet Obroncow Pokoju [*Voivodship Committee of Partisans of Peace*] (POL)
WKOPI .... Wojewodzka Komisja Oceny Projektow Inwestycyjnych [*Voivodship Commission on the Evaluation of Investment Plans*] (POL)
WKP .... Weibliche Kriminalpolizei [*Women Detectives or Women's Detective Force*] [*West German*] (WEN)
WKP(b) .... Wszechzwiazkowa Komunistyczna Partia (Bolszewikow) [*All-Union Communist Party (Bolsheviks)*] (POL)
WKPG .... Wojewodzka Komisja Planowania Gospodarczego [*Voivodship Commission on Economic Planning*] (POL)
WKR .... Wojskowa Komenda Rejonowa [*District Military Headquarters*] (POL)
WKS .... Warsztat Konstrukcji Stalowych [*Steel Construction Shop*] (POL)
WKS .... Wojskowe Kolo Sportowe [*Military Sports Circle*] (POL)

WTID .... Wissenschaftliche und Technische Information und Dokumentation
WTK .... Waermetechnische Kommission [*Heat-Engineering Commission*] (EG)
WTK .... Wissenschaftlich-Technische Konzeption [*Scientific-Technical Concept*] (EG)
WTM .... Warszawskie Towarzystwo Muzyczne [*Warsaw Music Society*] (POL)
WTMH .... Wroclawskie Towarzystwo Milosnikow Historii [*Wroclaw (Breslau) Society of Friends of History*] (POL)
WTMK .... Wydawnictwa Techniczne Ministerstwa Komunikacji [*Technical Publishing House of the Ministry of Transportation*] (POL)
WTN .... Wroclawskie Towarzystwo Naukowe [*Wroclaw (Breslau) Learned Society*] (POL)
WTO .... World Tourism Organization (MAR)
WTO .... Wszechzwiazkowe Towarzystwo Teatralne [*All-Union Theatrical Society (Soviet)*] (POL)
WTRD .... Water Treatment Research Division (MAR)
WTS .... Wydzial Transportu Samochodowego [*Department of Automobile Transportation*] (POL)
WTYF .... World Theosophical Youth Federation (EA)
WTZ .... Wissenschaftlich-Technisches Zentrum [*Scientific-Technical Center*] (EG)
Wu .... Werturteil [*Evaluation*] [*German*]
WUA .... Workers' Unions' Association [*Sudanese*] (MAR)
WUB .... Wet Universitaire Bestuurshervorming
WUB .... Wojewodzki Urzad Bezpieczenstwa [*Voivodship Security Administration*] (POL)
WUCWO .... World Union of Catholic Women's Organizations (EA)
WUeV .... Dienstvorschrift fuer die Aufstellung von Wagenuebergangs- und Bahnhofsbedienungsplaenen und fuer die Ueberwachung des Wagenuebergangs [*Service Regulations for Formulating Car Transfer and Station Service Plans and for the Supervision of Car Transfers*] (EG)
WUKF .... Wojewodzki Urzad Kultury Fizycznej [*Voivodship Administration of Physical Culture*] (POL)
WUKO .... World Union of Karatedo Organizations (EA)
WULTUO .... World Union of Liberal Trade Union Organisations [*See also WFALW*] (EA)
WUML .... Wieczorowy Uniwersytet Marksizmu-Leninizmu [*Evening University of Marxism-Leninism*] (POL)
WUPO .... World Union of Pythagorean Organizations (EA)
WUS .... Wojewodzki Urzad Statystyczny [*Voivodship Office of Statistics*] (POL)
WUS .... World University Service [*See also EUM*] (EA)
WUSG .... World Union Saint Gabriel (EA)
WUTHH .... World Union of Tnuat Haherut Hatzorar (EA)
WVA .... Wissenschaftliche Vereinigung der Augenoptiker [*Scientific Society of Opticians*] (EG)
WVA .... World Veterinary Association [*See also AMV*] (EA)
WVF .... World Veterans Federation [*See also FMAC*] (EA)
WVPA .... World Veterinary Poultry Association [*See also AMVA*] (EA)
WVRD .... World Vision Relief Organization, Inc. (MAR)
Wvst .... Wagenverteilungsstelle [*Railroad Car Distribution Office*] (EG)
Ww .... Weichenwaerter [*Switch Operator*] (EG)
WW .... Werklos Wet [*Unemployment Law*] [*Dutch*] (WEN)
WW .... Wojska Wewnetrzne [*Internal Forces*] (POL)
ww .... Wyzej Wymieniony [*Above Mentioned*] [*Polish*]
W-wa .... Warszawa [*Warsaw*] (POL)
WWB .... Wit Weerstandsbeweging [*White Resistance Movement*] [*Namibian*] [*Use WRM*] (AF)
WWCS .... Warszawska Wytwornia Czesci Samochodowych [*Warsaw Automobile Parts Plant*] (POL)
WWCTU .... World's Woman's Christian Temperance Union (EA)
WWD .... Wasserwirtschaftsdirektion [*Directorate of Water Management*] (EG)
Wwe .... Witwe [*Widow*] [*German*] (GPO)
WWFI .... World Wildlife Fund International (EA)
WWI .... Institut fuer Weltwirtschaft (MAR)
WWO .... Wet op het Wetenschappelijk Onderwijs
WWO .... Wojewodzki Wydzial Odbudowy [*Voivodship Branch for Reconstruction*] (POL)
WWO .... Wydzial Wyposazenia Okretow [*Department of Ship Equipment*] (POL)
WWSU .... World Water Ski Union [*See also UMSN*] (EA)
WWTB .... Werkgroep Wetenschappelijke Theologische Bibliotheken
WYA .... World Youth Assembly (WEN)
wyd .... Wydanie [*Edition*] (POL)
wyd .... Wydany [*Edited, Published*] (POL)
wydawn .... Wydawnictwo [*Publication*] (POL)
wydz .... Wydzial [*Department (of a university or learned society)*] (POL)
wyj .... Wyjasnienie [*Explanation*] (POL)
WYK .... Wykonal [*Made By, Performed By, Taken By (Photograph)*] (POL)
wym .... Wymawiaj [*Pronounce*] [*Polish*]
wym .... Wymiar [*Dimension*] [*Polish*]
wys .... Wysokosc [*Height*] [*Polish*]
Wyz .... Wyzyna [*Eminence*] [*Polish*]
W-Z .... (Trasa) Wschod-Zachod [*East-West (Thoroughfare)*] [*Warsaw*] (POL)
w z .... W Zastepstwie [*In Place Of*] (POL)
W-Z .... Wschod-Zachod [*East-West*] [*Polish*]
WZ .... Wydawnictwo Zachodnie [*Western Territories Publishing House*] (POL)
WZAB .... Wojewodzki Zarzad Architektoniczno-Budowlany [*Voivodship Administration of Architecture and Construction*] (POL)
WZBM .... Wojewodzki Zarzad Budynkow Mieszkalnych [*Voivodship Administration for Residential Buildings*] (POL)
WZBUP .... Warszawskie Zaklady Budowy Urzadzen Przemyslowych [*Warsaw Industrial Equipment Plant*] (POL)
WZBW .... Wojewodzkie Zjednoczenie Budownictwa Wiejskiego [*Voivodship Association of Rural Construction*] (POL)
WZBZ .... Wroclawskie Zaklady Betoniarsko-Zelbetowe [*Wroclaw (Breslau) Concrete and Reinforced Concrete Plant*] (POL)
WZC .... Warszawskie Zaklady Ciastkarskie [*Warsaw Pastry Bakeries*] (POL)
WZDP .... Wojewodzki Zarzad Drog Publicznych [*Voivodship Administration of Public Roads*] (POL)
WZF .... Warszawskie Zaklady Farmaceutyczne [*Warsaw Pharmaceutical Establishments*] (POL)
WZF .... Warszawskie Zaklady Fotochemiczne [*Warsaw Photochemical Plant*] (POL)
WZG .... Warenzeichengesetz [*Trade Mark Law*] (EG)
WZG .... Warszawskie Zaklady Garbarskie [*Warsaw Tanneries*] (POL)
WZG .... Warszawskie Zaklady Gastronomiczne [*Warsaw Restaurant Enterprises*] (POL)
WZG .... Wroclawskie Zaklady Gastronomiczne [*Wroclaw Catering Establishments*] [*Polish*]
WZGS .... Wojewodzki Zarzad Gminnych Spoldzielni [*Voivodship Administration of Communal Cooperatives*] (POL)
WZGS .... Wojewodzki Zwiazek Gminnych Spoldzielni [*Polish*]
WZGS .... Wojewodzkie Zjednoczenie Gminnych Spoldzielni [*Voivodship Association of Rural Communal Cooperatives*] (POL)
WZH .... Wojewodzki Zarzad Handlu [*Voivodship Trade Administration*] (POL)
WZHW .... Wojewodzki Zarzad Higieny Weterynaryjnej [*Voivodship Administration of Veterinary Hygiene*] (POL)
WZIP .... Warszawskie Zjednoczenie Instalcji Przemyslowych [*Warsaw Association of Industrial Installations*] (POL)
WZL .... Wojewodzki Zarzad Lacznosci [*Voivodship Communications Administration*] (POL)
WZL .... Wojskowy Zwiazek Lowiecki [*Military Hunting Union*] (POL)
WZLK .... Wirtschaftszweiglohngruppenkatalog [*Economic Branch Wage-Group Catalog*] (EG)
WZMO .... Wroclawskie Zaklady Materialow Ogniotrwalych [*Wroclaw (Breslau) Fireproof Material Plant*] (POL)
WZO .... World Zionist Organization [*Israeli*] (ME)
WZO .... Wystawa Ziem Odzyskanych [*Exhibition of the Recovered Territories*] (POL)
WZP .... Warszawskie Zaklady Papiernicze [*Warsaw Paper Plants*] (POL)
WZP .... Warszawskie Zaklady Piekarnicze [*Warsaw Bakeries*] (POL)
WZPB .... Warszawskie Zaklady Przemyslu Budowlanego [*Warsaw Construction Industry Plants*] (POL)
WZPG .... Warszawskie Zaklady Przemyslu Gastronomicznego [*Warsaw Restaurant Establishments*] (POL)
WZPG .... Warszawskie Zaklady Przemyslu Gumowego [*Warsaw Rubber Works*] (POL)
WZPMR .... Wojewodzkie Zjednoczenie Przedsiebiorstw Mechanizacji Rolnictwa [*Voivodship Association of Agricultural Mechanization Enterprises*] (POL)
WZPO .... Warszawskie Zaklady Przemyslu Odziezowego [*Warsaw Clothing Factory*] (POL)
WZPS .... Warszawskie Zaklady Piwowarsko-Slodownicze [*Warsaw Breweries*] (POL)
WZPT .... Wadowickie Zaklady Przemyslu Terenowego [*Wadowice Local Industry Plant*] (POL)
WZPT .... Warszawskie Zaklady Przemyslu Tluszczowego [*Warsaw Oleaginous Industries*] (POL)
WZPT .... Wojewodzki Zarzad Przemyslu Terenowego [*Voivodship Administration of Local Industry*] (POL)
WZPT .... Wojewodzkie Zaklady Przemyslu Terenowego [*Voivodship Local Industry Plants*] (POL)
WZPTMB .... Wojewodzki Zarzad Przemyslu Terenowego Materialow Budowlanych [*Voivodship Administration of the Local Building Materials Industry*] (POL)
WZPUK .... Wojewodzki Zarzad Przedsiebiorstw i Urzadzen Komunalnych [*Voivodship Administration of Communal Enterprises and Installations*] (POL)
WZPW .... Wschodnie Zaklady Przemyslu Welnianego [*Eastern Wool Plants*] (POL)
WZRLI .... Wroclawskie Zjednoczenie Robot Ladowo-Inzynieryjnych [*Wroclaw (Breslau) Association of Civil Engineering Work*] (POL)
WZRSB .... Warszawskie Zaklady Remontu Sprzetu Budowlanego [*Warsaw Repair Establishments for Building Equipment*] (POL)
WZRSP .... Wojewodzki Zwiazek Rolniczych Spoldzielni Produkcyjnych [*Voivodship Union of Farm Producer Cooperatives (Collective farms)*] (POL)
WZT .... Warszawskie Zaklady Telewizyjne [*Warsaw Television Establishments*] (POL)

WZT............ Warszawskie Zaklady Transportowe [*Warsaw Transportation Establishments*] (POL)

WZTBP........ Warszawskie Zjednoczenie Terenowe Budownictwa Przemyslowego [*Warsaw Association of the Local Construction Industry*] (POL)

WZTBP........ Wroclawskie Zjednoczenie Transportowego Budownictwa Przemyslowego [*Wroclaw (Breslau) Association of the Transportation Construction Industry*] (POL)

WZUR.......... Wojewodzki Zarzad Urzadzen Rolnych [*Voivodship Farm Equipment Administration*] (POL)

WZUS.......... Wojewodzki Zarzad Ubezpieczen Spolecznych [*Voivodship Social Security Administration*] (POL)

WZW............ Wojewodzki Zarzad Weterynarii [*Voivodship Veterinary Science Administration*] (POL)

WZWM........ Wojewodzkie Zarzady Wodno-Melioracyjne [*Voivodship Administrations for Irrigation and Land Reclamation*] (POL)

WZWS......... Wroclawskie Zaklady Wlokien Sztucznych [*Wroclaw (Breslau) Artificial Fiber Plant*] (POL)

WZZ............ Wojewodzki Zarzad Zbytu [*Voivodship Sales Board*] (POL)

WZZ............ Wojewodzkie Zaklady Zbozowe [*Voivodship Grain Elevators*] (POL)

YDN............ Ypiresia Dioxeos Narkotikon [*Anti-Narcotics Service*] (GC1)
YDO............ Yuksek Denizcilik Okulu [*Higher (Advanced) Maritime School*] (TU)
Yd Sb......... Yedek Subay [*Reserve Officer*] (TU)
YDYF.......... Yemeni Democratic Youth Federation (ME)
Ye............... Spruce (RU)
ye............... United, Only, Single (RU)
YE............... Yemen (Sana) [*Two-letter standard code*] (CNC)
YEA............ Ypopsifios Efedros Axiomatikos [*Reserve Officer Candidate*] [*Greek*] (GC)
YEA............ Ypourgeion Ethnikis Amynis [*Ministry of National Defense*] (GC)
YeAO.......... Yerevan Astronomical Observatory (RU)
YeAP.......... European Productivity Agency [*EPA*] (RU)
YeASS........ Unified Automated Network of the Soviet Union [*Telecommunications*] (RU)
YeAST........ European Free Trade Association [*EFTA*] (RU)
yed............ Singular, Unit (RU)
YeDA.......... United Democratic Left Party [*Greek*] (RU)
yed izm....... Unit of Measurement (RU)
YeDK.......... European Danube Commission (RU)
yed khr....... Unit of Storage (RU)
YeDNF........ United Democratic National Front [*North Korean*] (RU)
YeDOF........ United Democratic Fatherland Front [*North Korean*] (RU)
YEDSAN...... Yedek Parca Sanayii ve Ticaret AS [*Spare Parts Industry and Trade Corp.*] (TU)
YEE............ Ypiresia Endellomenon Exodon [*Authorized Expenses Service*] [*Greek*] (GC)
YEEA.......... Ypiresia Epistimonikis Erevnis kai Anaptyxeos [*Scientific Research and Development Service*] [*Greek*] (GC)
YEED.......... Ypiresia Enimeroseos Enoplon Dynameon [*Armed Forces Information Service*] [*Greek*] (GC)
YEEEthA..... Ypiresia Epeigondon Ergon Ethnikis Amynis [*Service for Urgent National Defense Projects*] [*Greek*] (GC)
YeEK.......... European Economic Commission of the United Nations Organization (RU)
YEEPP........ Ypiresia Exypiretiseos kai Erevnis Paraponon ton Politon [*Citizen Complaints Investigation Service*] [*Greek*] (GC)
YeES.......... European Economic Community [*EEC*] (RU)
YeES.......... Unified Power System (RU)
YEET.......... Ypiresia Epistimonikis Erevnis kai Tekhnologias [*Scientific Research and Technology Service*] (GC1)
YEFA.......... Ypiresia Elengkhou Fortotikon Avtokiniton [*Truck Control Service*] [*Greek*] (GC)
yefr............ Private First Class (RU)
YeFT........... Unified Physical Theory (RU)
YeG............ Natural Science and Geography (RU)
YeGAF......... United State Archives Fund (RU)
yegip.......... Egyptian (RU)
YeGMS........ United Hydrometeorological Service [*1929-1936*] (RU)
YeGSVTs.... Unified State Network of Computation Centers (RU)
YeGU.......... Yerevan State University (RU)
Yek............. Yekun [*Total*] (TU)
YEK............ Ypiresia Enaeriou Kykloforias [*Air Traffic Service*] (GC1)
YEKDP........ Ypiresia Elengkhou Kratikou Diylistiriou Petrelaiou [*National Oil Refinery Control Service*] [*Greek*] (GC)
YeKGR........ European Goods Timetable Conference (RU)
YeKGT........ United Labor Confederation of Guatemala (RU)
YeKK........... European Advisory Commission [*1943-1945*] (RU)
YeKK........... European Committee for Boilermaking and Kindred Steel Structures (RU)
YEKMO....... Ypiresia Elengkhou Kataskevis Monimon Odostromaton [*Permanent Road Construction Inspection Service*] [*Greek*] (GC)
YeKMT........ European Conference of Ministers of Transport [*ECMT*] (RU)
YeKO.......... Jewish Colonization Society (RU)
YeKOPO...... Jewish Committee for Assistance to Refugees (RU)
YeKP.......... Egyptian Communist Party (RU)
YeKP.......... Jewish Communist Party (RU)
YeKPR........ European Passenger Timetable Conference (RU)
YeKS.......... Jewish Communist League (RU)
YeKUP........ Standard Set of Universal Devices [*for a repair shop*] (RU)
YEKY.......... Ypiresia Elengkhou Kataskevis Yponomon [*Sewer Construction Control Service*] [*Greek*] (GC)
YeLES......... European League for Economic Cooperation [*ELEC*] (RU)
Yelgavsel'mash... Jelgava Agricultural Machinery Plant (RU)
YeLM........... Liberal European Youth [*LEY*] (RU)
YEM............ Yemen (Sana) [*Three-letter standard code*] (CNC)
YeMI........... Yerevan Medical Institute (RU)
yemk........... Capacity (RU)
YeMK.......... European Youth Campaign [*EYC*] (RU)
YeMS.......... Unified Modular Reference System (RU)
YEMSANAYII... Yem Sanayii Turk Anonim Sirketi [*Turkish Fodder Industry Corporation*] (TU)
YEMTA........ Izmir Yem Fabrikasi [*Izmir Fodder Factory*] (TU)
YEN............ Ypourgeion Emborikis Navtilias [*Ministry of Merchant Marine*] [*Also used for automobile license plate designation*] [*Greek*] (GC)
YeNDF........ United Popular Democratic Front [*Chinese*] (RU)
YENED........ Ypiresia Enimeroseos Enoplon Dynameon [*Armed Forces Information Service*] [*Greek*] (GC)
YeNIL.......... State Natural Science Institute Imeni P. F. Lesgaft (RU)
YeNIR.......... Unified Norms and Wages, Unified Standards and Costs (RU)
Yeniseyzoloto... State Yenisey Gold-Mining Trust (RU)
YeNRP........ Jewish Independent Workers' Party (RU)
YENTAS...... Yapi Endustri ve Ticaret Anonim Sirketi [*Construction Industry and Trade Corporation*] (TU)
YeNV.......... Unified Output Norms (RU)
YeNViR........ Unified Output and Wage Norms, Unified Output and Cost Standards (RU)
YeO............ Daily Inspection [*of automobiles*] (RU)
YeO............ Daily Servicing [*of automobiles*] (RU)
YeOEGV...... European Railway Wagon Pool (RU)
YeOES........ Organization for European Economic Cooperation [*OEEC*] (RU)
YeOS.......... Egyptian Organization for Standardization and Calibration (RU)
YeOS.......... European Defense Community (RU)
YeOUS........ European Coal and Steel Community (RU)
YeOYal........ European Organization for Nuclear Research (RU)
YeOZR........ European and Mediterranean Plant Protection Organization [*EPPO*] (RU)
YePChT....... United Trade-Union Center of Chilean Workers (RU)
YePO.......... United Consumers' Society (RU)
YePS.......... European Payment Union (RU)
YePSR........ United Party of the Socialist Revolution (RU)
YEPTh........ Ypourgeion Ethnikis Paideias kai Thriskevmaton [*Ministry of National Education and Religions*] [*See also YPEPTh*] (GC1)
YePTs......... United Trade-Union Center [*Dutch*] (RU)
YePTsN....... United Trade-Union Center of the Netherlands (RU)
YePTsTCh.. United Trade-Union Center of Chilean Workers (RU)
yer.............. Split Stream, Channel, Braided Stream [*Topography*] (RU)
YeRF.......... United Workers' Front [*Romanian*] (RU)
YeRO.......... European Regional Organization [*of the International Confederation of Free Trade Unions*] (RU)
YerPI.......... Yerevan Polytechnic Institute Imeni K. Marx (RU)
YeRYeR....... Regional Unified Unit Cost Rates, Regional Unified Unit Wage Rates (RU)
YeS............. Jewish Socialists (RU)
YESCE........ Turkiye Yesilay Cemiyeti [*Turkish Green Crescent Society*] [*Turkish temperance society*] (TU)
YeSDRP...... Jewish Social Democratic Workers' Party (RU)
YeShB......... Unified Scale of Drillability (RU)
YeSK........... European Seismological Commission (RU)
YeSKhK...... United Agricultural Cooperative [*Czechoslovak*] (RU)
YeSKhN...... Unified Agricultural Tax (RU)
YeSP........... European Community of Writers (RU)
YeSP........... Natural Synoptic Period (RU)
YeSR........... European Broadcasting Union [*EBU*] (RU)
YeSR........... Natural Synoptic Region (RU)
YeSS........... Unified Seismic Service of the USSR (RU)
YeSSN......... Unified System of Seismic Observations (RU)
yestestv...... Natural (RU)
yestfak........ Natural Science Division (RU)
YeSYu......... Yearbook of Soviet Justice [*A publication*] (RU)
YEthA.......... Ypourgeion Ethnikis Amynis [*Ministry of National Defense*] (GC)
YETIS.......... Yesilada Eczacilari Turk Ithalat Sirketi [*Green Island Pharmacists' Turkish Import Corporation*] [*Cypriot*] (TU)
YeTK........... European Travel Commission [*ETC*] (RU)
YeTKS......... Unified Wage Rates and Qualifications Guide (RU)
YeTP........... Unified Technological Process (RU)
YeTS........... European Territory of the Soviet Union (RU)
YeTSh......... United Labor School (RU)
YeTsIN........ European Center for Population Studies (RU)
YeTsP......... European Translation Center [*ETC*] (RU)
YeTT........... Unified Transit Tariff [*Railroads*] (RU)
YeU............ Daily Servicing [*of automobiles*] (RU)
YEV............ Ypiresia Engeion Veltioseon [*Land Reclamation Service*] [*Greek*] (GC)
YeVKOM..... Jewish Commissariat on Nationality Problems [*1918-1920*] (RU)
Yevkombed... Committee for Assistance to Indigent Jews (RU)
Yevkomol.... Jewish Young Communist League (RU)
Yevobshchestkom... Jewish Public Committee for Assistance to Victims of War and Pogroms [*1920-1924*] (RU)
yevr............ European (RU)
yevr............ Jewish (RU)
Yevratom.... European Atomic Energy Community [*EURATOM*] (RU)
YeVROFIMA... European Company for the Financing of Railway Rolling Stock [*EUROFIMA*] (RU)
YeVS.......... European Monetary Agreement (RU)
YeVS.......... Unified High-Voltage Network, Unified High-Voltage System (RU)
Yevsektsiya... Jewish Communist Section at the TsK VKP(b) [*1918-1930*] (RU)
YeVSK........ All-Union Unified Sports Qualification (RU)
Yevtsib........ Jewish Central Information Office (RU)
yezhednev... Daily, Diurnal (RU)
yezhegod.... Annual (RU)
yezhemes... Monthly (RU)

yezhened .... Weekly (RU)
YeZMO .... Yelets Medical Equipment Plant (RU)
YFC .... Young Farmers' Clubs (MAR)
YFC .... Youth for Conservation (MAR)
YFCI .... Youth for Christ International [*See also JPC*] (EA)
Yfyp .... Yfypourgos [*Deputy Minister*] (GC)
YG .... Ysterografon [*Post Script*] (GC)
YG .... Yuksek Gerilim [*High Tension*] (TU)
YGD .... Yurtsever Genclik Dernegi [*Patriotic Youth Society*] (TU)
YGKTIL .... Ypalliloi Grafeion Koinon Tameion Idiotikon Leoforeion [*Office Employees of Joint Private Bus Funds*] [*Greek*] (GC)
YGO .... Yurtsever Genclik Orgutu [*Patriotic Youth Organization*] (TU)
YGS .... Youth Guidance Service (MAR)
YGT .... Yargitay [*Court of Cassation*] (TU)
YH .... Yrkesorganisasjonenes Hovedsammenslutning [*Central Association of Professional Organizations*] [*Norwegian*] (WEN)
YHB .... Yurtsever Hanimlar Birligi [*Patriotic Women's Association*] [*Turkish Cypriot*] (GC)
yhdyss .... Yhdyssanoissa [*or Yhdyssana*] [*Compound Word*] [*Finnish*]
YHK .... Yuksek Hakimler Kurulu [*Supreme Juridical Council*] (TU)
YHS .... Yurt Haberler Servisi [*Homeland News Service*] (TU)
yht .... Yhteensa [*Finnish*]
yht .... Yhteinen [*Finnish*]
yhteiskuntatkand ... Yhteiskuntatieteiden Kandidaatti [*Finnish*]
YIBITAS ...... Yozgat Isci Birligi Ins Malz ve San Anonim Sirketi [*Yozgat Worker Union Construction Equipment and Industry Corporation*] (TU)
YICAM .... Societe Yoo-Hoo Industrie of Cameroun (MAR)
Yill .... Yilligi [*Annual*] (TU)
YIM .... Yapi Isleri Mudurlugu [*Construction Affairs Directorate*] [*Under Public Works Ministry*] (TU)
YIS .... Yapi Iscileri Sendikasi [*Construction Workers Union*] (TU)
YIS .... Ydroilektrikos Stathmos [*Hydroelectric Station*] [*Greek*] (GC)
YJ .... Young Jamaicans (LA1)
YK .... Yhdistyneet Kansakunnat [*Finnish*]
YK .... Yhteiskuntatieteiden Kandidaatti [*Finnish*]
YK .... Yonetim Kurulu [*Administrative Council*] [*Of a political party or other organization*] (TU)
YK .... Ypiresia Kostologiseos [*Cost Evaluation Service*] (GC1)
Yk .... Yukari [*Upper, Superior*] (TU)
YKB .... Yonetim Kurulu Baskani [*Administrative Board Chairman*] (TU)
YKB .... Yurtsever Hanimlar Birligi [*Patriotic Women's Association*] [*Turkish Cypriot*] (TU)
YKE .... Ypiresia Koinonikis Evimerias [*Social Welfare Service*] (GC1)
YKhK .... Ypiresia Khartografiseos kai Ktimatologiou [*Cartography and Land Registry Service*] (GC1)
YKhOP .... Ypourgeion Khorotaxias, Oikismou, kai Perivallondos [*Ministry of Zoning, Housing, and Environment*] (GC1)
YKP .... Ypiresia Kratikon Promitheion [*State Supplies Service*] [*See also AEKP*] [*Greek*] (GC)
YKP .... Ypourgeion Kyvernitikis Politikis [*Ministry of Government Policy*] [*Greek*] (GC)
yks .... Yksikko [*Finnish*]
yks .... Yksikon [*Finnish*]
YKU .... Yonetim Kurulu Uyesi [*Administrative Board Member*] (TU)
YKU .... Yuksek Kimya Uzmani [*Senior Chemical Specialist*] (TU)
YKY .... Ypourgeion Koinonikon Ypiresion [*Ministry of Social Services*] (GC1)
Yl .... Yil [*Year*] (TU)
yl .... Yleensa [*Generally, Mostly*] [*Finnish*]
yl .... Yleinen [*Finnish*]
yl .... Yleisesti [*Finnish*]
YL .... Youth League (MAR)
ylapm .... Ylapuolella Merenpinnan [*Finnish*]
Yld .... Yuksek Lisans Diplomasi [*Turkish*]
ylik .... Ylikersantti [*Finnish*]
yliltn .... Yliluutnantti [*Finnish*]
yliluutn .... Yliluutnantti [*Finnish*]
ylim .... Ylimaarainen [*Finnish*]
yliop .... Yliopettaja [*Finnish*]
yliop .... Yliopisto [*University*] [*Finnish*]
yliopp .... Ylioppilas [*Finnish*]
yliv .... Ylivaapeli [*Finnish*]
ym .... Ynna Muuta [*And So Forth, Et Cetera*] [*Finnish*] (GPO)
YMCA .... Young Men's Christian Association (MAR)
YMD .... Yemen (Aden) [*Three-letter standard code*] (CNC)
Ymd .... Yuksek Muhendis Diplomasi [*Turkish*]
YMK .... Ypiresia Mikhanikis Kalliergeias [*Machine Cultivation Service*] [*Greek*] (GC)
YMMA .... Young Men's Moslem Association (MAR)
yms .... Ynna Muuta Sellaista [*And So On*] [*Finnish*]
yms .... Ynna Muuta Semmoista [*Finnish*]
Y Muh .... Yuksek Muhendis [*Senior Engineer*] (TU)
Yng Son .... Yangin Sondurme [*Fire Fighting*] (TU)
YNJM .... Youth of the New JEWEL Movement [*Grenadian*] (LA1)
YNME .... Ypourgeion Navtilias Metaforon kai Epikoinonion [*Ministry of Shipping, Transport, and Communications*] (GC)
yo .... Ylioppilas [*Finnish*]
YO .... Ypiresia Oikismou [*Housing Service*] (GC1)
YO .... Yuksek Okul [*Advanced School*] [*As a college*] (TU)
YOAK .... Yuksek Ogretim Adaylari Komitesi [*Higher Education Candidates' Committee*] [*Turkish Cypriot*] (GC)
YOG .... Yuksek Ogretim Genclik [*Higher Educated Youth*] [*Cypriot*] (TU)
YOGM .... Yuksek Ogretim Genel Mudurlugu [*Higher Education Directorate General*] (TU)
YOK .... Yuksek Ogretim Kurulu [*Higher Education Council*] (TU)
Yo Kvs .... Yol Kavsagi [*Crossroads, Road Confluence*] (TU)
YOKYK .... Yuksek Ogrenim Kredi ve Yurtlar Koruma Genel Mudurlugu [*Higher Education Credit and Dormitories Organization Directorate General*] (TU)
YOL .... Yleinen Osuuskauppojen Liitto [*Central Cooperative Union*] [*Finnish*] (WEN)
YOL IS .... Kibris Turk Karayollari Iscileri Sendikasi [*Turkish Cypriot Highway Workers Union*] (TU)
Yol Is .... Turkiye Karayolu, Yapim, Bakim, ve Onarim Isci Sendikalari Federasyonu [*Turkish State Higher Workers Federation*] (TU)
Yon-Sen .... Kibris Turk Federe Devleti Iscileri Sendikasi [*Turkish Cypriot Federated State Workers' Union*] (TU)
YOO .... Yuksek Ogretmen Okulu [*Advanced Teachers School*] [*Ankara*] (TU)
YOPAM .... Yatirim, Organizasyon, Pazarlama, ve Arastirma Merkezi Ltd. Sti. [*Investment, Organization, Marketing, and Research Center Incorporated*] (TU)
YOSS .... Yesilada Ortakoy Sonmez Spor [*Green Island Ortakoy Sonmez Sports' Club*] [*Cypriot*] (TU)
YP .... Malawi Young Pioneers (MAR)
yp .... Ylempi Palkkausluokka [*Finnish*]
YP .... Ypsili Piesis [*High Pressure*] (GC)
YPA .... Ypiresia Politikis Aeroporias [*Civil Aviation Service*] [*Greek*] (GC)
YPAAA .... Ypiresia Perifereiakis Anaptyxeos (Nison) Anatolikou Aigaiou [*Service for the Regional Development of the Eastern Aegean (Islands)*] (GC1)
YPAASE .... Ypiresia Perifereiakis Anaptyxeos Anatolikis Stereas Ellados [*Regional Development Service for Eastern Mainland Greece*] (GC)
YPATh .... Ypiresia Perifereiakis Anaptyxeos Thessalonikis [*Salonica Area Development Service*] (GC)
YPAVE .... Ypiresia Perifereiakis Anaptyxeos Voreiou Ellados [*Service for the Regional Development of Northern Greece*] (GC)
YPDYS .... Ypiresia Perithalpseos Dimosion Ypallilon kai Syndaxioukhon [*Aid Service for Civil Servants and Pensioners*] [*Greek*] (GC)
YPEA .... Ypiresia Ethnikis Asfaleias [*National Security Service*] [*Replaced GDEA*] [*Greek*] (GC)
YPEDA .... Ypiresia Elenkhou Diakiniseos Agathon [*Service for Goods Movement Control*] (GC1)
YPEM .... Ypiresia Paragogikon Ergon Makedonias [*Productive Works Service of Macedonia*] (GC)
YPEN .... Ypiresia Prostasias Ethnikou Nomismatos [*National Currency Protection Service*] [*Greek*] (GC)
YPEP .... Ypiresia Provolis Ellinikon Proiondon [*Greek Products Promotion Service*] [*Greek*] (GC)
YPEPTh .... Ypourgeion Ethnikis Paideias kai Thriskevmaton [*Ministry of National Education and Religions*] (GC1)
YPF .... Yacimientos Petroliferos Fiscales [*Government Oil Deposits*] [*Argentine*] (LA)
YPFB .... Yacimientos Petroliferos Fiscales Bolivianos [*Bolivian Government Oil Deposits*] (LA)
YPGP .... Ypiresia Prostasias Georgikon Proiondon [*Farm Products Protection Service*] [*Greek*] (GC)
YPK .... Yigitbas Parca Kollektif [*Yigitbas Parts Collective*] [*Turkish Cypriot*] (GC)
YPK .... Ypiresia Politikis Kinitopoiiseos [*Civilian Mobilization Service*] [*Greek*] (GC)
YPK .... Yuksek Planlama Kurulu [*Supreme Planning Organization*] (TU)
YPM .... Young Pioneer Movement (MAR)
YPP .... Udostoverenie za Praktika Pedagogiceska [*Bulgarian*]
YPP .... Young Professional Program (MAR)
YPPAXE .... Ypiresia Prosanatolismou, Pliroforion, kai Axiologiseos Xenon Ependyseon [*Agency for Orientation, Information, and Development of Foreign Investments*] (GC1)
YPPK .... Ypourgeion Proedrias Kyverniseos [*Ministry to the Premier*] (GC)
yr .... Den Yngre [*Junior*] [*Norwegian*] (GPO)
Yrb .... Yarbay [*Lieutenant Colonel (Army), Commander (Navy)*] (TU)
YS .... Ypourgikon Symvoulion [*Council of Ministers*] (GC)
YS .... Ypsili Sykhnotis [*High Frequency*] (GC)
YSAE .... Ypiresiakon Symvoulion Anoteras Ekpaidevseos [*Service Council for Secondary Education*] [*Greek*] (GC)
YSAP .... Ypiresia Syndonismou Anaptyxeos Perifereias [*Area Development Coordinating Service*] [*Greek*] (GC)
YSD .... Turkiye Yardim Sevenler Dernegi [*Turkish Philanthropic Organization*] [*See also TYSD*] (TU)
YSE .... Yol-Su ve Elektrik Isler Genel Mudurlugu [*Highways, Water, and Electric Affairs Directorate General*] [*Under Ministry of Village Affairs*] (TU)

ZakOIIVKh ... Transcaucasian Experimental Research Institute of Water Management (RU)
Zak prok ..... Law on the Procuracy (BU)
ZakVO .... Transcaucasus Military District (RU)
zal .... Bay, Gulf [*Topography*] (RU)
zal .... Deposit, Bed, Seam [*Topography*] (RU)
zal .... Zalacznik [*Enclosure*] (POL)
zal .... Zalozeno [*Founded*] (CZ)
zal .... Zalozony [*or Zalozyl*] [*Founded or Founded By*] [*Polish*]
ZAL .... Zamrud Air Lines (IN)
ZAL .... Zeitschrift fuer Auslaendische Landwirtschaft [*Frankfurt*] [*A publication*] (MAR)
Zam .... Castle [*Topography*] (RU)
zam .... Contactor [*Electricity*], Lock, Closer (RU)
zam .... Deputy, Substitute (RU)
zam .... Substitute, Deputy (BU)
ZAM .... Zambia Association of Marketing (MAR)
zam .... Zamiast [*Instead*] [*Polish*]
zam .... Zamieszkaly [*Living At*] (POL)
zam .... Zamowienie [*Order*] (POL)
ZAMANGLO ... Zambia Anglo-American Corporation (MAR)
ZAMBECO ... Companhia de Desenvolviments Agro-Pecuario e Comercial do Vale do Zambeze Lda. (MAR)
ZAMCO .... Zambesi Consorsio Hidra-Elettrico (MAR)
zamdir .... Deputy Director (RU)
ZAMEFA ..... Metal Fabricators of Zambia Limited (MAR)
ZAMINI .... Ministerstvo Zahranicnich Veci [*Ministry of Foreign Affairs*] (CZ)
zamkom ...... Deputy Commandant (RU)
zamkom ...... Deputy Commander, Second-in-Command (RU)
zamkom ...... Deputy Commissar (RU)
zamnach ..... Acting Head, Deputy Chief (RU)
zam n-k .... Deputy Chief (BU)
zam n-k u-nie ... Deputy Chief of Administration (BU)
ZAMP .... Antiaircraft Artillery Meteorological Post (RU)
ZAMP .... Zavod za Mala Prava [*Institute for (Authors') Minor Rights*] (YU)
ZAMP .... Zwiazek Akademickiej Mlodziezy Polskiej [*Union of Polish Student Youth*] (POL)
zampolit ...... Deputy Commander for Political Affairs (RU)
zampotekh ... Deputy Commander for Technical Matters (RU)
ZAMS .... Antiaircraft Artillery Meteorological Station (RU)
ZAMS .... Zimowe Akademickie Mistrzostwa Swiata [*World Winter Sports Student Championship*] (POL)
ZAMTs .... Zonal Air Weather Center (RU)
zamzav .... Acting Manager, Deputy Chief (RU)
zamzavbib ... Acting Head Librarian, Deputy Librarian (RU)
zan .... Artisan's (BU)
ZAN .... Notes of the Academy of Sciences, USSR [*A publication*] (RU)
ZANA .... Zambia News Agency (AF)
ZANC .... Zambia African National Congress (MAR)
ZanD .... Zanayatchiyska Duma [*Artisan's Word*] [*A periodical*] (BU)
ZANDU .... Zambia National Democratic Union (MAR)
ZANEWS ..... Zanzibar News Service [*Tanzanian*] (AF)
Zankombinat ... Artisans' Combine (BU)
ZANLA .... Zimbabwe African National Liberation Army (PD)
ZANN .... Law on Administrative Violations and Penalties (BU)
ZANTAA ...... Zambia National Theatre Arts Association (MAR)
ZANU .... Zimbabwe African National Union (PPW)
ZANU-PF ..... Zimbabwe African National Union - Patriotic Front (PD)
ZAO .... Antiaircraft Artillery Detachment (BU)
ZAO .... Zagrebacka Armijska Oblast [*Zagreb Army District*] (YU)
ZAOb .... Law on Turnover Tax (BU)
ZAOMK .... Notes of the Amur Oblast Regional Museum and the Society of Regional Studies [*A publication*] (RU)
ZAOR .... For Active Defense Work [*Badge*] (RU)
ZAOU .... Zuid Afrikaansche Onderwijzers Unie (MAR)
ZAP .... Lag [*Electrical equipment*] (RU)
ZAP .... Law on Administrative Proceedings (BU)
ZAP .... Law on Copyright (BU)
ZAP .... Law on Motor Vehicle Transport (BU)
zap .... Notes, Records (RU)
ZAP .... Reserve Air Regiment (RU)
ZAP .... Reserve Artillery Regiment (RU)
zap .... West, Western (BU)
Zap .... West, Western (RU)
Zap .... Western Railroad (RU)
ZAP .... Zachodnia Agencja Prasowa [*Western Press Agency*] (POL)
ZAP .... Zaklad Architektury Polskiej [*Institute of Polish Architecture*] (POL)
ZAP .... Zakon o Autorskom Pravu [*Copyright Law*] (YU)
ZAPASA ...... Zambia Police Sports Association (MAR)
ZAPEK .... Zadruzna Pekarna Pekarskih Radnika [*Bakery Cooperative*] (YU)
ZAPI .... Zones d'Action Prioritaires Integrees [*Areas of Combined Priority Action*] [*Cameroonian*] (AF)
ZAPI de l'EST ... Societe Regionale des Zones d'Actions Prioritaires Integrees de l'Est (MAR)
Zap Maked ... Western Macedonia (BU)
ZAPOR .... Zapovjednistvo Oruznistva [*Military Supreme Command*] [*Croatia*] [*World War II*] (YU)
Zaporozhstal' ... Zaporozh'ye Metallurical Plant (RU)
ZAPORUK ... Zapovjednistvo Oruznickog Krila [*Military Wing Command*] [*Croatia*] [*World War II*] (YU)
Zapov .... Reservation, Sanctuary [*Topography*] (RU)
ZapOVO ...... Western Special Military District (RU)
ZAPP .... Transcaucasian Association of Proletarian Writers (RU)
ZAPP .... Zambia Pork Products (MAR)
zapr .... Fueling, Servicing (BU)
zapr .... Refueling Point (RU)
ZAPU .... Zimbabwe African People's Union (AF)
ZapVO .... Western Military District (RU)
zar .... Charge, Load (RU)
zar .... Earnings (RU)
zar .... Honored Artist of the Republic (RU)
ZAR .... Zaire [*Three-letter standard code*] (CNC)
ZAR .... Zentralafrikanische Republik (MAR)
ZAR .... Zuid Afrikaansche Republik (MAR)
ZARAT .... Zaklady Zjednoczenia Stacji Radiowych i Telewizyjnych [*Agencies of the Union of Radio and Television Transmitters*] (POL)
ZARIK .... Zakon o Agrarnoj Reformi i Kolonizaciji [*Law on Agrarian Reform and Colonization*] (YU)
zaryashch ... Caisson (RU)
zarz .... Zarzad [*Administration*] (POL)
zarz .... Zarzadzenie [*Administrative Order*] (POL)
zarz Gl .... Zarzad Glowny [*Headquarters*] [*Polish*]
ZAS .... Glass Containers Plant (BU)
zas .... Meeting, Conference (RU)
ZAS .... Zpravodajska Agentura Slovenska [*Slovak Press Agency*] (CZ)
ZASE .... Zambia Association for Science Education (MAR)
zashch .... Defense, Defensive, Protective (RU)
Zasl .... Honored [*Title*] (BU)
zasl .... Honored (RU)
zasl art resp ... Honored Artist of the Republic (RU)
zasl d .... Honored Worker [*In art, science, etc.*] (RU)
zasl deyat n ... Honored Worker in the Sciences (RU)
zasl deyat n i t ... Honored Worker in Science and Technology (RU)
zasl m sp .... Honored Master of Sports (RU)
ZASP .... Zwiazek Artystow Scen Polskich [*Union of Polish Actors*] (POL)
zast .... Freezing, Solidification (RU)
Zast .... Outpost, Gate, Barrier [*Topography*] (RU)
zast .... Zastepczy [*Substitute*] (POL)
zast .... Zastupce [*Deputy, Representative, Agent*] (CZ)
zast .... Zastupitelsky [*Representative*] (CZ)
ZASTAL ...... Zaodrzanskie Zaklady Konstrukcji Stalowej [*Trans-Odra (Oder) Steel Construction Plant*] (POL)
ZASTI .... Zambia Air Services Training Institute (MAR)
zat .... Creek, Backwater [*Topography*] (RU)
ZAT .... Law on Automotive Transportation (BU)
ZAT .... Zakon o Administrativnim Taksama [*Law on Administrative Fees*] (YU)
zat .... Zatimni [*Temporary*] (CZ)
Zat .... Zatoka [*Gulf, Bay*] [*Polish*] (NAU)
ZATE .... Automobile and Tractor Electrical Equipment Plant (RU)
ZATI .... Automobile and Tractor Parts Plant (RU)
zatv .... Solidification, Hardening, Congealing (RU)
zatw .... Zatwierdzony [*Approved*] (POL)
zav .... Attestation (BU)
zav .... Manager, Chief, Head (RU)
zav .... Ovary [*Botany*] (RU)
zav .... Plant (BU)
Zav .... Plant, Factory (RU)
ZAVA .... Zambia Amateur Volleyball Association (MAR)
zavbib .... Library Chief, Head Librarian (RU)
zavdel .... Chief Clerk, Office Supervisor (RU)
zavgar .... Garage Manager (RU)
ZAVK .... Zentrales Absatz- und Vermittlungskontor [*Central Sales and Brokerage Office*] (EG)
zavkants ..... Office Manager (RU)
zavkhim .... Chemical Section Chief, Head of Chemical Unit (RU)
zavkhoz ...... Business Manager, Manager (RU)
zavkom .... Plant Committee (BU)
zavkont .... Office Manager (RU)
zav lab .... Laboratory Chief (RU)
zav lab .... Plant Laboratory, Factory Laboratory (RU)
zavmag .... Store Manager (RU)
ZAVNO .... Zemaljsko Antifasisticko Vece Narodnog Oslobodenja [*Territorial Anti-Fascist Council of National Liberation*] (YU)
ZAVNOBiH ... Zemaljsko Antifasisticko Vijece Narodnog Oslobodenja Bosne i Hercegovine [*Territorial Anti-Fascist Council of National Liberation of Bosnia and Hercegovina*] (YU)
ZAVNOH ..... Zemaljsko Antifasisticko Vijece Narodnog Oslobodenja Hrvatske [*Territorial Anti-Fascist Council of National Liberation of Croatia*] (YU)
Zavodstal'konstruktsiya ... State All-Union Trust for the Manufacture of Steel Structures (RU)
zavorgot ...... Organization Department Chief (RU)
zav pos .... Factory Settlement (RU)
zavprod .... Food Supply Manager (RU)
zavradio ...... Radio Station Manager (RU)
zavrayfo ...... Chief of the Rayon Finance Department (RU)

zavrono .... Chief of the Rayon Department of Public Education (RU)
Zavstol .... Canteen Manager (BU)
ZAvtP .... Law on Authorship Copyright (BU)
Zavuch .... Chief of the Educational Section (BU)
zavuch .... Director of Studies (RU)
Zav u-t .... Section Chief (BU)
ZavVO .... Trans-Volga Military District (RU)
zavvod .... Chief of Water Transportation (RU)
zaw .... Zawodowy [*Professional, Vocational*] (POL)
ZAWI .... Zambia Association of Women's Institutes (MAR)
zawod .... Zawodowy [*Professional, Vocational*] (POL)
ZAWU .... Zimbabwe African Women's Union (AF)
ZAZ .... Automobile Made by the Zaporozh'ye Automobile Plant (RU)
ZAZ .... Zaporozh'ye Automobile Plant (RU)
ZAZ .... Zatrovano Zemljiste [*Contaminated (by Poison) Area*] (YU)
ZAZ .... Zavody Antonina Zapotockeho [*Antonin Zapotocky Works*] (CZ)
ZAZ .... Zelezarny Antonina Zapotockeho [*Antonin Zapotocky Iron Works*] [*Vamberk*] (CZ)
ZB .... Antiaircraft Battery (RU)
zb .... Barrage Battery (RU)
ZB .... Earth Auger (RU)
ZB .... Foreign Bureau (BU)
ZB .... Foreign Office (RU)
ZB .... Incendiary Tanks [*Containers*] (RU)
ZB .... Law on Banks (BU)
ZB .... Law on the Budget (BU)
ZB .... Law on Marriage (BU)
ZB .... Mirror Drum, Mirror Wheel (RU)
ZB .... Retreat-Blocking Battalion (RU)
ZB .... Zakon o Braku [*Marriage Law*] (YU)
ZB .... Zaprecni Baloni [*Barrage Balloons*] (YU)
zb .... Zbierka [*Collection*] (CZ)
Zb .... Zbierka Zakonov CSSR [*Collection of Laws of the Czechoslovak Socialist Republic*] (CZ)
ZB .... Zeleznorudne Bane [*Iron Ore Mines*] (CZ)
ZB .... Ziraat Bank [*Agricultural Bank*] (TU)
ZB .... Zivnostenska Banka [*Bank of Commerce*] (CZ)
zB .... Zum Beispiel [*For Example, For Instance*] [*German*] (GPO)
ZB .... Zveza Borcev [*Union of Veterans*] (YU)
ZBA .... Zambia Badminton Association (MAR)
ZbA .... Zusammenstellung Betrieblicher Anordnungen [*Compilation of Operational Instructions*] (EG)
ZBBS .... Protein and Bioconcentrate Mixes Plant (BU)
ZBC .... Zimbabwe Broadcasting Corporation (MAR)
ZBE .... Zwischenbetriebliche Einrichtungen [*Interplant Facilities*] (EG)
ZbFF .... Zbornik Radova Filozofskog Fakulteta [*Collected Papers of the Faculty of Philosophy*] [*Zagreb*] [*A publication*] (YU)
ZBG .... Law on Bulgarian Citizenship (BU)
ZBHD .... Zambia Broken Hill Development Co. (MAR)
ZBiAP .... Zwiazek Bibliotekarzy i Archiwistow Polskich [*Union of Polish Librarians and Archivists*] (POL)
ZBIM .... Zjednoczone Budownictwo Inzynieryjno-Morskie [*Maritime Engineering Construction Association*] (POL)
ZBK .... Zentrale Begutachtungskommission [*Central Evaluation Commission*] (EG)
ZBK .... Zjednoczenie Budownictwa Komunalnego [*Communal Construction Association*] (POL)
ZBKiC .... Zaklad Badan Konjunktur i Cen [*Price and Market Research Institute*] (POL)
ZBL .... Zambia Breweries Limited (MAR)
ZBl .... Zentralblatt [*Central Gazette*] (EG)
ZBM .... Zarzad Budynkow Mieszkalnych [*Administration of Apartment Houses*] (POL)
ZBM .... Zjednoczenie Budownictwa Miejskiego [*Association for Urban Construction*] (POL)
ZBM .... Zjednoczenie Budownictwa Mieszkaniowego [*Association for Housing Construction*] (POL)
ZBM .... Zjednoczenie Budowniczych Miejskich [*Association of Urban Builders*] (POL)
ZBMA .... Zaklady Budowy Maszyn i Aparatury [*Machine and Appliance Plant*] (POL)
ZBMiA .... Zaklady Budowy Maszyn i Aparatury [*Machine and Appliance Plant*] (POL)
ZBMIK .... Notes of the Buryat-Mongolian Scientific Research Institute of Culture [*A publication*] (RU)
ZBMNH .... Zjednoczenie Budownictwa Miejskiego Nowa Huta [*Nowa Huta Urban Construction Association*] (POL)
ZBMO .... Zjednoczenie Budownictwa Miast i Osiedli [*Association for Urban and Settlement Construction*] (POL)
ZbMS .... Zbornik Matice Srpske [*Collected Papers of Matica Srpska (Serbian cultural society)*] [*Novi Sad*] [*A publication*] (YU)
ZBMW-1 .... Zjednoczenie Budownictwa Mieszkaniowego Warszawy-1 [*Association for Housing Construction in the First District of Warsaw*] (POL)
ZBNOVS .... Zveza Borcev Narodnoosvobodilne Vojne Slovenije [*Union of Veterans of the National Liberation War of Slovenia*] (YU)
ZbNZO .... Zbornik za Narodni Zivot i Obicaje Juznih Slavena Jugoslavenske Akademije Znanosti i Umjetnosti [*Collected Papers of the National Life and Customs of the South Slavs, Yugoslav Academy of Sciences and Arts*] [*Zagreb*] [*A periodical*] (YU)
ZBO .... Zwischengenossenschaftliche Bauorganisation [*Intercooperative Construction Organization*] (EG)
ZBOB .... Law on the Budget and Budget Accountability (BU)
ZBOP .... Law on the Budget of Public Enterprises (BU)
ZBoWiD .... Zwiazek Bojownikow o Wolnosc i Demokracje [*Union of Fighters for Freedom and Democracy*] (POL)
ZBP .... Law on Cashless Payments (BU)
ZBP .... Zaklad Badan Prasoznawczych [*Press Research Institute*] (POL)
ZBP .... Zarzad Bibliotek Polskich [*Administration of Polish Libraries*] (POL)
ZBP .... Zjednoczenie Budownictwa Przemyslowego [*Industrial Construction Association*] (POL)
ZBP .... Zvlastni Bojove Prostredky [*Special Warfare Agents*] (CZ)
ZBPP .... Zjednoczenie Budowy Piecow Przemyslowych [*Association for Industrial Furnace Construction*] (POL)
ZBPPMN .... Law on the Struggle Against Antisocial Actions of Minors and Juveniles (BU)
ZBPPV .... Law on Cashless Payments and Use of Deposits (BU)
ZBRol .... Zjednoczenie Budownictwa Rolnego [*Rural Construction Association*] (POL)
ZBS .... Coastal Sound-Locator Station (RU)
ZBS .... Zambia Broadcasting Service (AF)
ZBSM-Ch .... Zwiazek Branzowy Spoldzielni Mineralno-Chemicznych [*Professional Association of Mineral and Chemical Cooperatives*] (POL)
ZBTsK .... Foreign Office of the Central Committee of the RSDRP (RU)
ZBUT .... Zaklady Budowy Urzadzen Technicznych [*Technical Equipment Construction Plants*] (POL)
ZBUT .... Zjednoczenie Budowy Urzadzen Technicznych [*Association for the Construction of Technical Equipment*] (POL)
zbV .... Zur Besonderen Verwendung [*For Special Use*] [*German*]
ZBVB .... Law on the Fight Against Venereal Diseases (BU)
ZBW .... Zjednoczenie Budownictwa Wojskowego [*Association for Military Construction*] (POL)
ZBWP .... Zwiazek Bylych Wiezniow Politycznych [*Union of Former Political Prisoners*] (POL)
ZByud .... Law on the State Budget (BU)
Z byudzh .... Law on the State Budget (BU)
ZBZ .... Bacterial Contamination Zone (BU)
ZBZ .... Bacteriological Contamination Zone (RU)
ZC .... Zarzad Celny [*Customs Administration*] (POL)
ZC .... Zenijni Ceta [*Engineer Platoon*] (CZ)
ZC .... Zgodovinski Casopis [*Historical Journal*] [*Ljubljana*] (YU)
ZC .... Zimni Cviceni [*Winter Maneuvers*] (CZ)
ZC .... Zinfandel Club (EA)
z-ca .... Zastepca [*Deputy, Substitute*] (POL)
ZCBC .... Zambia Consumer Buying Corporation (MAR)
ZCC .... Zapodoceske Cihelny [*West Bohemian Brick Works*] (CZ)
ZCCM .... Zambia Consolidated Copper Mines (MAR)
ZCE .... Zapodoceske Elektrarny, Narodni Podnik [*West Bohemian Electric Power Works, National Enterprise*] (CZ)
ZCF .... Zambia Cooperative Federation (MAR)
ZCh .... Audio Frequency (RU)
ZCh- .... Spiegeleisen, Mirror Iron (RU)
ZChO .... Cast Iron Foundry (BU)
ZChOB .... Law on Private and Public Security (BU)
ZChV .... Zavod pro Chemickou Vyrobu [*Chemical Factories*] (CZ)
ZCI .... Zambia Copper Investments Limited (MAR)
ZCN .... Zaklady Czyszczenia Nasion [*Seed Cleaning Establishments*] (POL)
ZCPK .... Zapodocesky Prumysl Kamenny [*West Bohemian Stone Industry*] (CZ)
ZCRP .... Zapadocesky Rudny Pruzkum [*West Bohemian Mineral Prospecting*] (CZ)
ZCS .... Zapadoceske Sklarny, Narodni Podnik [*West Bohemian Glass Factories, National Enterprise*] (CZ)
ZCSD .... Zambia Council for Social Development (MAR)
ZCT .... Zapadoceske Tiskarny [*West Bohemian Printing Plants*] (CZ)
ZCTU .... Zambia Congress of Trade Unions (AF)
ZCTU .... Zimbabwe Congress of Trade Unions (MAR)
ZCU .... Zambia Cricket Union (MAR)
ZD .... Antiaircraft Range Finder (RU)
Zd .... Building [*Topography*] (RU)
ZD .... Law on Prescription (BU)
Z-d .... Plant, Factory (RU)
zd .... West Longitude (RU)
zd .... Zahodna Dolzina [*Western Longitude*] (YU)
ZD .... Zbrano Delo [*Collected Works*] (YU)
ZD .... Zemske Divadlo [*Province Theater*] (CZ)
ZDA .... Law on State Arbitration (BU)
ZDA .... Zakon o Drzavnoj Arbitrazi [*Law on State Arbitration*] (YU)
ZDA .... Zedinjene Drzave Amerike [*United States of America*] (YU)
ZDA .... Zinc Development Association (EA)
ZDAS .... Zdarske Strojirny a Slevarny [*Zdar Engineering Plants and Foundries*] (CZ)

ZhDCh......... Railroad Unit (RU)
ZhDIZ......... State Railroad Transportation Publishing House (RU)
ZhDK......... Railroad Collegium (RU)
ZhDO......... Railroad Department of Transportation (RU)
zhdp......... Railroad Regiment (RU)
zh d pos...... Railroad Settlement [*Topography*] (RU)
zhdr......... Railway Battalion (BU)
zh d st......... Railroad Station [*Topography*] (RU)
zhdstroyb... Railroad Construction Battalion (RU)
ZhDV......... Railroad Troops (RU)
ZhEK......... Housing Operation Office (RU)
Zh eksp i teor fiz... Journal of Experimental and Theoretical Physics [*A publication*] (RU)
zhel......... Ferruginous Spring [*Topography*] (RU)
zhel......... Iron Concentration Plant (RU)
Zhel......... Iron Mine, Iron Works [*Topography*] (RU)
zhel bet....... Reinforced Concrete [*Material for dams and bridges*] [*Topography*] (RU)
Zheldorizdat... State Publishing House of Literature on Railroad Transportation (RU)
Zheldorvzryvprom... All-Union Trust for Drilling and Blasting Operations of the Glavzheldorstroy of the Urals and Siberia (RU)
Zheleskom... Committee for Logging and Equipment for Railroads (RU)
zhelez......... Railroad (BU)
zhel ist........ Ferruginous Spring [*Topography*] (RU)
zhel kisl....... Ferruginous Spring [*Topography*] (RU)
zhenkor....... Woman Correspondent (RU)
zhensk........ Feminine, Woman's, Women's (RU)
ZhES......... Railroad Electric Power Plant (RU)
ZhETF......... Journal of Experimental and Theoretical Physics [*A publication*] (RU)
ZhFKh......... Journal of Physical Chemistry [*A publication*] (RU)
ZhG......... Gordeyev's Solution (RU)
ZhGUP......... Journal of Civil and Criminal Law [*A publication*] (RU)
Zh i......... Ooze, Liquid Silt [*Topography*] (RU)
zhil......... Housing (RU)
Zhilfond...... State Housing Resources. State Real Estate Management Administration (BU)
Zhilkom....... Housing Committee (BU)
zhilkommunotdel... Housing Department of the Municipal Administration (RU)
Zhilstroy..... Housing Construction Administration (BU)
Zhilstroy..... Industrial Housing Construction Trust (RU)
zhilupr......... Housing Administration (RU)
zhir......... Fats Kombinat [*Topography*] (RU)
Zhirkost'..... Association of Moscow State Plants of the Fats and Bone-Processing Industry (RU)
ZHISA......... Zambia Higher Institutions Sports Association (MAR)
zhit......... Inhabitants (RU)
zhiv......... Livestock Breeding, Animal Husbandry (RU)
zhiv......... Painting (RU)
Zhivkontora... State Office for the Procurement and Marketing of Pedigree Livestock (RU)
zhivop......... Painting (RU)
zhivop......... Painting, Pictorial Art (BU)
zhivotn........ Livestock-Breeding Farm, Livestock-Breeding Sovkhoz [*Topography*] (RU)
ZhIVSNAB... State Commercial Enterprise for Supplying Livestock (BU)
zhiv-vo........ Livestock Breeding, Animal Husbandry (RU)
ZhK......... Fats Kombinat (RU)
ZhK......... Fatty Acids (RU)
ZHK......... Zentrale Hochwasserkommission [*Central Flood Control Commission*] (EG)
Zh khim pr... Journal of the Chemical Industry [*A publication*] (RU)
ZhKK......... Municipal Housing Office (RU)
ZhKKh......... Journal of Colloid Chemistry [*A publication*] (RU)
ZhKO......... Communal Housing Department (RU)
ZhKP......... Liquid-Oxygen Apparatus (RU)
ZhLP......... Journal of Light Industry [*A publication*] (RU)
ZhM......... Iron Bridge (RU)
ZhMEI......... Journal of Microbiology, Epidemiology, and Immunobiology [*A publication*] (RU)
ZhMG......... Liquid-Metal Fuel (RU)
ZhMGR......... Liquid-Metal Fuel Reactor (RU)
ZhMI......... Zhdanov Metallurgical Institute (RU)
ZhMPS......... Journal of the Ministry of Railroads [*A publication*] (RU)
ZhMVD......... Journal of the Ministry of Internal Affairs [*A publication*] (RU)
ZhMYu......... Journal of the Ministry of Justice [*A publication*] (RU)
ZHN......... Zbrane Hromadneho Niceni [*Weapons of Mass Destruction*] (CZ)
zhn dr......... Gendarme Battalion (BU)
ZhNKh......... Journal of Inorganic Chemistry [*A publication*] (RU)
zh-noye....... Animal (RU)
ZhNPFK...... Journal of Scientific and Applied Photography and Cinematography [*A publication*] (RU)
zhn sl......... Gendarmery (BU)
ZhO......... Railroad Section (RU)
ZhOB......... Journal of General Biology [*A publication*] (RU)
ZhOKh......... Journal of General Chemistry [*A publication*] (RU)
Zhp......... Constant Hardness [*Chemistry*] (RU)
zhp......... Female Sex (RU)
zhp......... Gendarme Regiment (BU)
zhp......... Railroad (BU)
ZHP......... Zwiazek Harcerstwa Polskiego [*Polish Scout Union*] (POL)
zhpbm......... Railway Mechanization Battalion (BU)
zhpbr......... Railway Brigade (BU)
ZhPF......... Journal of Applied Physics [*A publication*] (RU)
zhpk......... Railway Corps (BU)
ZhPKh......... Journal of Applied Chemistry [*A publication*] (RU)
ZhPR......... Railroad Workshop (BU)
zhpsvb........ Railway Signal Battalion (BU)
zhpsvr......... Railway Signal Company (BU)
ZhPT......... Railway Transportation (BU)
ZhPU......... Railway School (BU)
ZhPZ......... Railroad Plant (BU)
zh r......... Feminine Gender (BU)
zhr......... Feminine Gender (RU)
ZhR......... Railroad Radio Station (RU)
zhr......... Railway Company (BU)
ZHR......... Zemska Hospodarska Rada [*Provincial Economic Council*] (CZ)
ZhRD......... Liquid Propellant Rocket Engine (RU)
ZhRFKhO.... Journal of the Russian Physicochemical Society [*1879-1930*] [*A publication*] (RU)
ZhRFO......... Journal of the Russian Physical Society [*1873-1930*] [*A publication*] (RU)
ZHRiN......... Zjednoczenie Hodowli Roslin i Nasiennictwa [*Plant Cultivation and Seed Union*] (POL)
ZhRKhO...... Journal of the Russian Chemical Society [*1869-1930*] [*A publication*] (RU)
ZhRMO........ Journal of the Russian Metallurgical Society [*A publication*] (RU)
ZhS......... Aliphatic Alcohols (RU)
ZhS......... Hard Seats [*Railroads*] (RU)
ZhS......... Kinetic Energy (RU)
ZhS......... Yellow Glass (RU)
ZHS......... Zambia Horse Society (MAR)
ZhSK......... Housing Construction Cooperative (BU)
ZhSK......... Housing Construction Cooperative (RU)
ZhSKh......... Journal of Structural Chemistry [*A publication*] (RU)
ZhSKT......... Housing Construction Cooperative Association (RU)
ZhT......... Railroad Transportation (RU)
ZhTF......... Journal of Technical Physics [*A publication*] (RU)
ZhTU......... Railroad Television Apparatus (RU)
ZhTV......... Live Tularemia Vaccines (RU)
ZhU......... Railroad School (RU)
ZHU......... Zentrales Handelsunternehmen [*Central Trade Enterprise*] (EG)
ZhUB......... Refractory Concrete (RU)
Zhurgaz...... Periodical and Newspaper Association (RU)
zhurn......... Journal, Periodical (RU)
zhurn......... Journalism, Journalistic (BU)
ZhUVR......... Completed Operations Record [*Construction*] (RU)
ZhVKhO...... Journal of the All-Union Chemical Society Imeni D. I. Mendeleyev [*A publication*] (RU)
ZhVND........ Journal of Higher Nervous Activity Imeni I. P. Pavlov [*A publication*] (RU)
Zhvr......... Temporary Hardness [*Chemistry*] (RU)
ZhVS......... Liquid Explosive Mixture (RU)
ZhVZ......... Zhukovka Bicycle Plant (RU)
ZhYeL......... Vital Capacity (RU)
ZhZL......... Lives of Outstanding People [*Book series*] (RU)
ZhZS......... Yellow-Green Glass (RU)
ZI......... "For Industrialization" [*Publishing house*] [*Newspaper*] (RU)
ZI......... Ionization Zone (RU)
ZI......... Quenching Inductor, Hardening Inductor (RU)
Zi......... Zaki [*Cape, Point*] [*See also Si*] [*Japanese*] (NAU)
Z-I......... Zapad-Istok [*West-East*] (YU)
ZI......... Zonal Index [*Meteorology*] (RU)
ZIA......... Central Institute for Automation [*Jena*] (EG)
ZIAD......... Zeni Angkatan Darat [*Army Engineers*] (IN)
ZIAN......... Zoological Institute of the Academy of Sciences, USSR (RU)
ZIANA......... Zimbabwe Inter-African News Agency (MAR)
ZIBANG....... Zeni Pembangunan [*Construction Engineers*] (IN)
ZICEG......... Zona Industrial e Comercial de Exportacao da Guanabara [*Guanabara Industrial and Commercial Export Zone*] [*Brazilian*] (LA)
ZID......... Plant Imeni F. E. Dzerzhinskiy (RU)
ZID......... Zentralinstitut fuer Information und Dokumentation [*Central Institute for Information and Documentation*] (EG)
Zid......... Zidovsky [*Jewish*] (CZ)
ZID......... Zone d'Industrialisation Decentralisee [*Algerian*] (MAR)
ZIDA......... Zentrum fuer Information und Dokumentation des Aussenhandels [*Center for Foreign Trade Information and Documentation*] (EG)
ZIDKT......... Law on Amendments and Supplements to the Labor Code (BU)
ZIE......... Zjednoczenie Instalacji Elektrycznych [*Association for Electrical Installation*] (POL)
ZIENO......... Instruments and Nonstandard Equipment Plant (BU)
ZIF......... "Land and Factory" [*Publishing house*] [*Almanac*] [*1922-1930*] (RU)
ZIF......... Plant Imeni M. V. Frunze (RU)

ZIF.............. Zentralinstitut fuer Fertigungstechnik [*Central Institute for Production Technology*] (EG)
ZIF.............. Zentralinstitut fuer Funktechnik [*Central Institute for Radio Engineering*] (EG)
ZIFA............ Zambia India Friendship Association (MAR)
ZIFA............ Zimbabwe Football Association (MAR)
Ziff.............. Ziffer [*Number, Figure*] (EG)
ZIG.............. Zentralinstitut fuer Giessereitechnik [*Central Institute for Foundry Technology*] (EG)
ZIGDJZ........ Zeleznicki Institut Glavne Direkcije Jugoslavenskih Zeleznica [*Railroad Institute of the General Administration of Yugoslav Railroads*] (YU)
ZIGM............ Ziraat Isleri Genel Mudurlugu [*Agricultural Affairs Directorate General*] (TU)
ZIH.............. Zydowski Instytut Historyczny [*Jewish Historical Institute*] (POL)
ZII................ Agricultural Experimental Institute (BU)
ZII................ Zemjodelsko-Ispitalen Institut [*Agricultural Research Institute*] (YU)
ZIID.............. Zentralinstitut fuer Information und Dokumentation [*East German*]
ZIISSP......... Correspondence Institute of Engineers of the Silicate and Construction Industries (RU)
ZIK.............. Zakon o Izvrsenju Kazni [*Law on the Enforcement of Penalties*] (YU)
ZIK.............. Zemjodelsko-Industriski Kombinat [*Agricultural Industrial Combine*] [*Belje*] (YU)
ZIL............... Automobile Made by the Moscow Automobile Plant Imeni I. A. Likhachev (RU)
ZIL............... Moscow Automobile Plant Imeni I. A. Likhachev (RU)
ZIL............... Plant Imeni V. I. Lenin (RU)
ZIM.............. Automobile Made by the Gor'kiy Automobile Plant Imeni Molotov (RU)
ZIM.............. Gor'kiy Automobile Plant Imeni Molotov [*1932-1958*] (RU)
ZIM.............. National Shipping Line [*Israeli*] (ME)
zim............... Winter Dwelling, Winter Camp [*Topography*] (RU)
zim............... Winter Road [*Topography*] (RU)
ZIM.............. Zambezi Industrial Mission (MAR)
ZIM.............. Zentralinstitut der Metallurgie [*Central Institute of Metallurgy*] (EG)
ZIM.............. Zomancipari Muvek [*Enamel Industry Works*] (HU)
ZIMCO......... Zambia Industrial and Mining Corporation (AF)
ZIMCORD.... Zimbabwe Conference on Reconstruction and Development (MAR)
zimn............ Winter (RU)
ZIMP........... Correspondence Institute of the Metal-Working Industry (RU)
ZIN.............. Law on Execution of Penalties (BU)
ZIN.............. Zoological Institute (of the Academy of Sciences, USSR) (RU)
ZINAN......... Zoological Institute of the Academy of Sciences, USSR (RU)
ZINC........... Zim Israel Navigation Company (MAR)
ZINCO......... Zim Israel Navigation Company (MAR)
ZINCOM...... Zambia Industrial and Commercial Association (MAR)
Z-Industrie... Zentralgeleitete Industrie [*Centrally Administered Industry*] (EG)
ZINPONS.... Law on the Election of People's Representatives to the Ordinary National Assembly (BU)
ZINS............ Law on the Election of People's Councils (BU)
ZINSDT....... Law on the Election of People's Councils of Deputies of the Working People (BU)
ZINSNRB..... Law on the Election of People's Councils of Deputies of the Working People in the Bulgarian People's Republic (BU)
ZINSSZ....... Law on the Election of Judges and Juries of People's Courts (BU)
ZIO.............. Podol'sk Machinery Plant Imeni Ordzhonikidze (RU)
ZIO.............. Zaklad Imienia Ossolinskich [*The Ossolinski Institute*] (POL)
ZIP.............. Kit of Spare Parts, Tools, and Accessories (RU)
ZIP.............. Measuring Instruments Plant (RU)
ZIP.............. Spare Parts, Instruments, and Accessories (BU)
ZIP.............. Zjednoczenie Instalacji Przemyslowych [*Association for Industrial Installations*] (POL)
ZIP.............. Zonas de Influencia Pedagogica [*Zones of Educational Influence*] [*Mozambican*] (AF)
ZIPA............ Zimbabwe People's Army (MAR)
ZIPRA......... Zimbabwe People's Revolutionary Army (PD)
ZIPU........... Given True Track Angle (RU)
ZIPUR......... Zeni Pertempuran [*Combat Engineers*] (IN)
ZIR.............. Law on Inventions and Rationalizations (BU)
Zir............... Ziraat [*Agriculture*] (TU)
ZIR.............. Zwiazek Izb Rzemieslniczych [*Union of Crafts Chambers*] (POL)
ZIRC............ Turkiye Ziraatcilar Cemiyeti [*Turkish Agriculturalists' Society*] (TU)
ZIS.............. Automobile Made by the Moscow Automobile Plant Imeni Stalin (RU)
ZIS.............. Moscow Automobile Plant Imeni Stalin [*1934-1956*] (RU)
ZIS.............. Transcaucasian Scientific Research Institute of Structures (RU)
ZIS.............. Zaklad Instalacji Sanitarnych [*Enterprise for Sanitary Installations*] (POL)
ZIS.............. Zambia Information Service (MAR)
ZIS.............. Zarzad Instalacji Sanitarnych [*Administration of Sanitary Installations*] (POL)
ZIS.............. Zentralinstitut fuer Schweisstechnik [*Central Institute for Welding Technology*] (EG)
ZIS.............. Ziekenhuis Informatie-Systeem
ZIS.............. Zjednoczenie Instalacji Sanitarnych [*Association for Sanitary Installations*] (POL)
ZIS.............. Zvezni Izvrsni Svet [*Federal Executive Council*] (YU)
ZIS/AZL...... Ziekenhuis Informatie-Systeem/Academisch Ziekenhuis Leiden
ZIS/BC........ Ziekenhuis Informatie-Systeem/Begeleidingscommissie [*NOBIN*] [*'s-Gravenhage*]
ZISE............ Zjednoczenie Instalacji Sanitarno-Elektrycznych [*Electrotherapy Equipment Association*] (POL)
ZISPO......... Zaklady Imienia Stalina w Poznaniu (Przemyslu Metalowego) [*Stalin (Metal) Plant in Poznan*] (POL)
ZISS............ Law on Property Ownership and Easements (BU)
ZISS............ Zambian Intelligence and Security Service (AF)
ZISSP......... Correspondence Institute of the Silicate and Construction Industries (RU)
ZIST............ Correspondence Institute of Soviet Trade (RU)
ZIT.............. Zambia Institute of Technology (MAR)
ZiT.............. Zivljenje in Tehnika [*Life and Technology*] [*Ljubljana*] [*A periodical*] (YU)
ZIU.............. Correspondence Institute for Advanced Training (RU)
ZIU.............. Motor Coach or Trolley-Bus Made by the Plant Imeni M. S. Uritskiy (RU)
ZIU.............. Plant Imeni M. S. Uritskiy (RU)
ZIUITR......... Correspondence Institute for the Advanced Training of Engineering and Technical Personnel (RU)
ZIV.............. Plant Imeni V. V. Vorovskiy (RU)
ZIV.............. Zentrale Informationsstelle fuer Verkehr
ZIVAN.......... Notes of the Institute of Oriental Studies of the Academy of Sciences, USSR (RU)
ZIVT............ Zagorska Industrija Vunenih Tkanina [*Zagorje Woolen Textile Industry*] (YU)
ZIW.............. Zwiazek Inwalidow Wojennych [*Union of Disabled Veterans*] (POL)
ZJ................ Zavodni Jidelna [*Factory Dining Hall*] (CZ)
ZJA.............. Zambia Judo Association (MAR)
ZJE.............. Zajednica Jugoslovenske Elektroprivrede [*Federation of Yugoslav Electric Industries*] (YU)
ZJNA........... Zakon o Jugoslovenskoj Narodnoj Armiji [*Law on the Yugoslav People's Army*] (YU)
ZJP.............. Zakon o Javnom Pravobraniostvu [*Law on the Body of Government Attorneys*] (YU)
ZJS.............. Zakon o Javnim Sluzbenicima [*Law on Public Employees*] (YU)
ZJS.............. Zavod Jana Svermy [*Jan Sverma Plant*] [*Brno*] (CZ)
ZJT.............. Zakon o Javnom Tuziostvu [*Law on Public Prosecutors*] (YU)
ZJU.............. Zambia Judo Union (MAR)
ZJVS............ Zavod J. V. Stalina [*J. V. Stalin Works*] (CZ)
ZJZ.............. Zapad Jugo-Zapad [*West Southwest*] (YU)
ZK............... Course Setter, Course Selector (RU)
z/k............... Imprisoned (RU)
ZK............... Land Code (RU)
ZK............... Law on Cooperatives (BU)
ZK............... Plant Committee (BU)
ZK............... Plant Committee, Factory Committee (RU)
ZK............... Sound Coagulation, Acoustic Coagulation (RU)
ZK............... Zadruzno Kmetijstvo [*Cooperative Agriculture*] (YU)
ZK............... Zakladni Knihovna [*Fundamental Library (of the Czechoslovak Academy of Sciences)*] (CZ)
ZK............... Zambia Kwache (MAR)
ZK............... Zanatska Komora [*Chamber of Artisans*] (YU)
ZK............... Zarzad Kina [*Motion Picture Administration*] (POL)
ZK............... Zavodni Klub [*Factory Club*] (CZ)
ZK............... Zavodni Krouzek [*Factory Circle*] (CZ)
ZK............... Zdokonalovaci Kurs [*Advance Course*] (CZ)
ZK............... Zemedelska Komise [*Agricultural Commission*] (CZ)
Z K.............. Zenekiado [*Music Publishing House*] (HU)
ZK............... Zentralkomitee [*Central Committee*] (EG)
ZK............... Zilinsky Kraj [*Zilina Region*] (CZ)
ZKB............. Zentrales Konstruktionsbuero [*Central Designing Office*] (EG)
ZKD............. Ship Engines Plant (BU)
ZKd............. Zamenik Komandanta Diviziona [*Deputy Commander of an Artillery Battalion*] (YU)
ZKD............. Zapadoceske Konsumni Druzstvo [*West Bohemian Consumer Cooperative*] (CZ)
ZKD............. Zentraler Kurierdienst [*Central Courier Service*] (EG)
ZKD............. Zentrales Konstruktions- und Technologisches Buero [*Central Designing and Technological Bureau*] (EG)
ZKE............. Ship Electrical Appliances Plant (BU)
ZKE............. Zugkrafteinheit [*Tractive Unit*] (EG)
ZKF............. Zentrale Kommission der Fotografie [*Central Photography Commission*] (EG)
ZKFF........... Zentraler Kraftfutterfonds [*Central Supply of High-Concentrate Feeds*] (EG)
ZKG............. Prvni Brnenska a Kralovopolska Strojirna, Gottwaldovy Zavody, Narodni Podnik [*First Machine Factory at Brno and Kralovo Pole, Gottwald Plants, National Enterprise*] (CZ)
ZKG............. Zadruzno Kmetijsko Gospodarstvo [*Cooperative Agriculture Economy*] (YU)
ZKG............. Zavod Klementa Gottwalda [*Klement Gottwald Factory*] [*Povazska Bystrica*] (CZ)

ZOJS .... Zakon o Javnim Sluzbenicima [*Law on Public Employees*] (YU)
ZOK .... Experimental Structures Plant (RU)
ZOK .... Foreign Organization Commission of the TsK RSDRP (RU)
ZOK .... Zavodni Odborna Knihovna [*Factory Technical Library*] (CZ)
ZOKP .... Zakon o Krivicnom Postupku [*Law on Criminal Procedure*] (YU)
ZOKS .... Transcaucasian Society for Cultural Relations with Foreign Countries (RU)
ZO KSS .... Zavodna Organizacia Komunistickej Strany Slovenska [*Factory Organization of the Communist Party of Slovakia*] (CZ)
ZOKZ .... Zakon o Komasaciji Zemljista [*Law on the Consolidation of Lands*] (YU)
ZOKZ .... Zwiazek Obrony Kresow Zachodnich [*Union for the Defense of the Western Borders (Prewar)*] (POL)
zol .... Gold (RU)
zol .... Zolotnik [*Measures*], Slide, Valve (RU)
ZOLDEX .... Zoldseg-Gyumolcs Exportra Termelteto es Felvasarlo Szovetkezeti Vallalat [*Producers' and Buyers' Cooperative Enterprise for the Export of Vegetables and Fruit*] (HU)
ZOLDKER ... Zoldseg- es Gyumolcskereskedelmi Vallalat [*Trade Enterprise for Vegetables and Fruit*] (HU)
ZOLDSZOV ... Zoldseg- es Gyumolcs Termelteto es Felvasarlo Szovetkezet [*Producers' and Buyers' Cooperative for Vegetables and Fruit*] (HU)
ZOLL .... Zarzad Okregu Ligi Lotniczej [*District Administration of the Aeronautical League*] (POL)
Zol-pl .... Gold and Platinum Mines [*Topography*] (RU)
zol rub .... Gold Ruble (RU)
ZOM .... Finishing Machine Plant (RU)
ZOM .... Refractory Materials Plant (BU)
ZOM .... Zaklad Oczyszczania Miasta [*Municipal Sanitation Department*] (POL)
ZOMGBT .... Correspondence Department of the Moscow City Library Technicum (RU)
ZOMLTI .... Correspondence Department of the Moscow Forestry Engineering Institute (RU)
ZOMM .... Metal Cutting Machine Attachments Plant (BU)
ZOMNI .... Correspondence Department of the Moscow Petroleum Institute Imeni I. M. Gubkin (RU)
ZOMO .... Riot Police [*Polish*]
ZOMOPI .... Correspondence Department of the Moscow Oblast Pedagogical Institute (RU)
ZOMP .... Defense Against Mass-Destruction Weapons (RU)
ZOMP .... Protection Against Mass-Destruction Weapons (BU)
ZOMS .... Zonal Experimental Reclamation Station (RU)
ZOMTI .... Correspondence Department of the Moscow Peat Institute (RU)
ZOMZ .... Zagorsk Optical Instrument Plant (RU)
ZON .... Zakon o Nasledivanju [*Law on Inheritance*] (YU)
ZON .... Zonal Experimental Station (RU)
Zon DMMA ... Zonguldak Devlet Mimarlik ve Muhendislik Akademisi [*Zonguldak State Academy of Architecture and Engineering*] (TU)
ZONFM .... Zemski Odbor na Narodniot Front na Makedonija [*Territorial Committee of the People's Front of Macedonia*] (YU)
ZONI .... Western Oblast Scientific Research Institute for Comprehensive Studies (RU)
ZONIODOP ... Law on the Appraisal of Real Estate Expropriated for State or Public Use (BU)
ZONIPBN .... Law on the Expropriation of Unpurchased Real Estate (BU)
ZOO .... Law on Social Insurance (BU)
Z oo .... Z Ograniczona Odpowiedzialnoscia [*Limited*] [*Polish*]
ZOO .... Zakon o Osiguranju [*Insurance Law*] (YU)
zoofak .... Zootechnical Division (RU)
ZOOID .... Notes of the Odessa Society of History and Antiquities [*A publication*] (RU)
zookhim .... Zoochemistry (RU)
zool .... Zoological, Zoology (RU)
zool .... Zoology, Zoological (BU)
zootekh .... Zootechnician, Zootechny (RU)
zootekh st ... Zootechnical Station [*Topography*] (RU)
ZOOUP .... Zakon o Opcem Upravnom Postupniku [*Law on General Administrative Procedure*] (YU)
zoovettekhnikum ... Zootechnical and Veterinary Technicum (RU)
ZOOZP .... Law on the Protection of the Arable Land and Pastures (BU)
ZOP .... Alternate Firing Position (RU)
ZOP .... Concealed Firing Positions (BU)
ZOP .... Law on Protection Against Crime (BU)
ZOP .... Sekcija za Odrzavanje Pruge [*Railroad Track Maintenance Section*] (YU)
ZOP .... Zaklad Ochrony Przyrody [*Institute for the Conservation of Nature*] (POL)
ZOPGR .... Zarzad Okregowy Panstwowych Gospodarstw Rolnych [*District Administration of State Farms*] (POL)
ZOPI .... Zone de Pre-Industrialisation [*Algerian*] (MAR)
ZO PKS .... Zarzad Okregowy Panstwowej Komunikacji Samochodowej [*District Administration of State Motor Transport*] (POL)
ZOPZF .... Zakon o Poljoprivrednom Zemljisnom Fondu [*Law on the Agricultural Land Fund*] (YU)
ZOPZIP .... Zakon o Poslovnim Zgradama i Prostorijama [*Law on Office Buildings and Apartments*] (YU)
ZOR .... Plant Imeni October Revolution (RU)
ZOR .... Zabiegi Ochrony Roslin [*Plant Protection Measures*] (POL)
ZOR .... Zaklad Osiedli Robotniczych [*Polish*]
ZOR .... Zarzad Osiedli Robotniczych [*Administration of Workers' Settlements*] (POL)
ZORK .... Zarzad Okregowy Radiofonizacji Kraju [*District Administration of Country-Wide Radio Installation*] (POL)
ZORSA .... Records of the Department of Russian and Slavic Archaeology (of the Russian Archaeological Society) [*A publication*] (RU)
ZORSARAO ... Records of the Department of Russian and Slavic Archaeology of the Russian Archaeological Society [*A publication*] (RU)
ZORU .... All-Union Correspondence Training Center for Accounting and Statistical Personnel (RU)
ZORU .... Correspondence Training of Accounting and Statistical Personnel (RU)
zos .... Antiaircraft Illuminating Service (RU)
ZOS .... Ground Aids to Navigation [*Aviation*] (BU)
ZOS .... Ground Aids to Navigation [*Aviation*] (RU)
ZOS .... Zakladowy Oddzial Samoobrony [*Plant Civil Defense Unit*] (POL)
ZOS .... Zakon o Sudovima [*Law on Courts of Law*] (YU)
ZOS .... Zavodni Odborova Skupina [*Factory Trade-Union Group*] (CZ)
ZOS .... Zonal Experimental Station (RU)
ZOS .... Zootechnical Experimental Station (RU)
ZOSBNOBM ... Zemski Odbor na Sojuzot na Borcite od Narodnooslobodителnata Borba na Makedonija [*Territorial Committee of the Union of Veterans of the National Liberation Struggle of Macedonia*] (YU)
ZOSBNOV ... Zemski Odbor na Sojuzot na Borcite od Narodnoosloboditelnata Vojna [*Territorial Committee of the Union of Veterans of the National Liberation War*] [*World War II*] (YU)
ZOSO .... Zakon o Stanbenim Odnosima [*Law on Housing Relations*] (YU)
ZOSP .... Zwiazek Ochotniczych Strazy Pozarnych [*Union of Voluntary Fire-Brigades*] [*Polish*]
ZOSRTs .... Law on Insuring Supplies and Price Control (BU)
ZOSZS .... Zarzad Okregowy Szkolnego Zwiazku Sportowego [*District Authority of School Sports Union*] (POL)
ZOT .... All-Union Society "For the Mastering of Technology" (RU)
ZOT .... Zakon o Taksama [*Tax Law*] (YU)
ZOT .... Zeglarska Odznaka Turystyczna [*Sailor's Touring Badge*] [*Polish*]
ZOT .... Zespol Opracowan Technicznych [*Technical Designing Unit*] (POL)
ZOTS .... Zonal Experimental Tobacco Growing Station (BU)
ZOTS .... Zonal Experimental Tobacco Growing Station (RU)
ZOUP .... Zakon o Opstem Upravnom Postupku [*Law on General Administrative Procedure*] (YU)
ZOUP .... Zakon o Organima Unutrasnjih Poslova [*Law on the Organs of Internal Affairs*] (YU)
ZOUS .... Zakon o Upravnim Sudovima [*Law on Administrative Courts*] (YU)
ZOV .... Zakon o Ovjeravanju Potpisa, Rukopisa, i Prijepisa [*Law on Certification of Signatures, Manuscripts, and Copies*] (YU)
ZOVB .... Zeleznicni Oddeleni Verejne Bezpecnosti [*Railroad Department of Public Security*] (CZ)
ZOVPSh .... Correspondence Department of the Higher Party School (RU)
ZOVVPZ .... Law on the Protection of the Air, Water, and Soil from Pollution (BU)
ZOW .... Zwiazek Osadnikow Wojskowych [*Association of Military Settlers*] (POL)
ZOW .... Zydowska Organizacja Wojskowa (MAR)
ZOWO .... Zaklady Obrotu Warzywami i Owocami [*Vegetable and Fruit Marketing Establishments*] (POL)
ZOZ .... Zakladowa Organizacja Zwiazkowa [*Labor Union Local*] (POL)
ZOZK .... Zakon o Zemljisnim Knjigma [*Law on Land Title Records*] (YU)
ZO ZMS .... Zarzad Okregu Zwiazku Mlodziezy Socjalistycznej [*Socialist Youth Union District Authority*] (POL)
ZO ZMW .... Zarzad Okregu Zwiazku Mlodziezy Wiejskiej [*Rural Youth Union District Authority*] (POL)
ZO ZZM .... Zarzad Okregowy Zwiazku Zawodowego Metalowcow [*District Administration of the Trade Union of Metal Workers*] (POL)
ZP .... Alternate Command Post (RU)
ZP .... Antiaircraft Gun (RU)
ZP .... Antiaircraft Machine Gun (RU)
ZP .... Antiaircraft Searchlight (RU)
z/p .... Dispensary, First Aid Station, Public Health Station (RU)
ZP .... Field Sound Locator (RU)
ZP .... Foreign Representation, Foreign Mission (BU)
zp .... Lag (RU)
ZP .... Law on Pensions (BU)
Zp .... Record, Recording [*Computers*] (RU)
ZP .... Replacement Regiment (RU)
ZP .... Sound-Locator Post (RU)
ZP .... Sound Ranging Station (RU)
ZP .... Threatened Position (BU)
ZP .... Zadruzno Posestvo [*Cooperative Property*] (YU)
ZP .... Zamoreny Prostor [*Contaminated Area*] (CZ)
ZP .... Zapadoceske Plynarny [*West Bohemian Gasworks*] (CZ)

ZP .... Zarzad Polityczny [*Political Administration*] [*Military*] (POL)
ZP .... Zarzad Powiatowy [*County Administration*] (POL)
ZP .... Zegluga Polska [*Polish Navigation*] [*Polish*]
Zp .... Zersetzungspunkt [*Decomposition Point*] [*German*]
Zp .... Zugbildungsplaene [*Train Assembly Plans (For passenger trains)*] (EG)
ZPA .... Zaklady Przemyslu Azotowego [*Nitrogen Plant*] (POL)
ZPA .... Zavody Pristroju a Automatizace [*Machinery and Automation Plants*] (CZ)
ZPAF .... Zwiazek Polskich Artystow Fotografiki [*Union of Polish Art Photographers*] (POL)
ZPANV .... Polyacrylonitryl Fibers Plant (BU)
ZPAP .... Zwiazek Polskich Artystow Plastykow [*Union of Polish Artists in the Plastic Arts*] (POL)
ZPARK .... Zakon o Provodenju Agrarne Reforme i Kolonizacije [*Law on the Enforcement of Agrarian Reform and Colonization*] (YU)
ZPB .... Zaklady Przemyslu Bawelnianego [*Cotton Plants*] (POL)
ZPB .... Zarazna Poljska Bolnica [*Field Hospital for Contagious Disease*] (YU)
ZPB .... Zjednoczenie Przemyslu Bawelnianego [*Cotton Industry Association*] (POL)
ZPBH .... Zjednoczenie Przemyslowe Budowy Huty [*Industrial Association for Metallurgical Plant Construction*] (POL)
ZPBNH .... Zjednoczenie Przemyslowe Budowy Nowej Huty [*Industrial Association for Construction in Nowa Huta (Metallurgical center)*] (POL)
ZPBS .... Zentrales Projektierungsbuero Schwermaschinenbau [*Central Project-Planning Office for Heavy Machine Building*] (EG)
ZPBSE .... Zarzad Przedsiebiorstw Budowy Sieci Elektrycznych [*Administration of Electrical Network Construction Companies*] (POL)
ZPC .... Zaklady Przemyslu Cukierniczego [*Sugar Plants*] (POL)
ZPC .... Zambia Printing Company Ltd. (MAR)
ZPC .... Zimbabwe Promotion Council (MAR)
ZPC .... Zjednoczenie Przemyslu Cukierniczego [*Association of the Sugar Industry*] (POL)
ZPCh .... Zavody Prumyslove Chemie [*Industrial Chemistry Plants*] (CZ)
ZPChNRB .... Law on the Stay of Foreigners in the Bulgarian People's Republic (BU)
ZPD .... Zadruzno Poljoprivredno Dobro [*Agricultural Cooperative Farm*] (YU)
ZPD .... Zakladowe Punkty Dokumentacji [*Factory Documentation Points*] (POL)
ZPD .... Zaklady Przemyslu Drzewnego [*Lumber Plants*] (POL)
ZPD .... Zaklady Przemyslu Dziewiarskiego [*Knitwear Goods Plant*] (POL)
ZPD .... Zentralstelle fuer Primaerdokumentation [*Central Office for Primary Documentation*] (EG)
ZPD .... Zrzeszenie Prawnikow Demokratow [*Democratic Lawyers' Association*] (POL)
ZPDS .... Zdruzenje Prosvetnih Delavcev Slovenije [*Association of Educators of Slovenia*] (YU)
ZPDS .... Zveza Pedagoskih Drustev Slovenije [*Union of Pedagogical Societies of Slovenia*] (YU)
ZPDz .... Zaklady Przemyslu Dziewiarskiego [*Knitwear Goods Plant*] (POL)
ZPEV .... Zentrale Pruef- und Entwicklungsstelle fuer das Verkehrswesen [*Central Testing and Development Station for Transportation*] (EG)
ZPF .... Zaklady Przemyslu Farmaceutycznego [*Pharmaceutical Plants*] (POL)
ZPF .... Zambia Police Force (MAR)
ZPFL .... Zanzibar and Pemba Federation of Labor [*Tanzanian*] (AF)
ZPG .... Pneumatic Tires Plant (BU)
ZPG .... Zarzad Przemyslu Gastronomicznego [*Administration of the Restaurant Industry*] (POL)
ZPG .... Zentrale Projektierung Giessereien [*Central Project Planning Office for Foundries*] (EG)
ZPGG .... Zarzad Portu Gdansk-Gdynia [*Administration of the Gdansk (Danzig)-Gdynia Port*] (POL)
ZPGUP .... Zarzad Projektowania Gmachow Uzytecznosci Publicznej [*Administration for Planning of Public Buildings*] (POL)
ZPI .... Correspondence Pedagogical Institute (RU)
ZPI .... For the Food Industry [*Newspaper*] (RU)
ZPI .... Law on Privileges and Mortgages (BU)
ZPiER .... Zespol Planowanie i Ekonomiki Rolnictwa [*Agricultural Planning and Economics Team*] (POL)
ZPINM .... Law and Regulation on the Planned Building of Settlements (BU)
ZPJ .... Zaklad Przemyslu Jedwabniczego [*Silk Plant*] (POL)
ZPK .... Plant Party Committee, Factory Party Committee (RU)
ZPK .... Zarzad Przemyslu Kosmetycznego [*Administration of the Cosmetics Industry*] (POL)
ZPK .... Zentrale Planungskommission [*Central Planning Commission*] (EG)
ZPKK .... Zentrale Parteikontrollkommission [*Central Party Control Commission*] (EG)
ZPKM .... Law on Cultural Monuments and Museums (BU)
ZPL .... Antiaircraft Machine Gun (RU)
ZPL .... Zaklad Przemyslu Lniarskiego [*Linen Plant*] (POL)
ZPLL .... Zarzad Powiatowy Ligi Lotniczej [*County Administration of the Aeronautical League*] (POL)
ZPM .... Zaklad Przedsiebiorstw Morskich [*Marine Enterprise Establishment*] (POL)
ZPMiUM ...... Zarzad Przemyslu Maszyn i Urzadzen Mlynskich [*Administration of the Flour Mill Machinery and Equipment Industry*] (POL)
ZPMiW .... Zwiazek Proletariatu Miast i Wsi [*Union of the Urban and Rural Proletariat*] (POL)
ZPMot .... Zjednoczenie Przemyslu Motoryzacyjnego [*Association of the Automotive Industry*] (POL)
ZPNRB .... Law on the Procuracy in the Bulgarian People's Republic (BU)
ZPO .... Zakladni Podnimky Odberu [*Basic Conditions for Procurement*] (CZ)
ZPO .... Zaklady Przemyslu Odziezowego [*Clothing Plants*] (POL)
ZPO .... Zakon o Penziskom Osiguranju [*Law on Pension Insurance*] (YU)
ZPO .... Zavodni Politicka Organisace [*Factory Political Organization*] (CZ)
ZPO .... Zavodni Protiletecka Obrana [*Factory Antiaircraft Defense*] (CZ)
ZPO .... Zivilprozessordnung [*Code of Civil Procedure*] [*German*] (WEN)
ZPO .... Zjednoczenie Przemyslu Okretowego [*Shipbuilding Industry Union*] (POL)
ZPP .... Semiconductors Plant (BU)
ZPP .... Zadruzno Poljoprivredno Preduzece [*Agricultural Cooperative Establishment*] (YU)
ZPP .... Zaklady Przemyslu Ponczoszniczego [*Hosiery Plants*] (POL)
ZPP .... Zakon o Parnicnom Postupku [*Law on Civil Procedure*] (YU)
ZPP .... Zavod za Privredno Planiranje [*Economic Planning Institute*] (YU)
ZPP .... Zeleznicny Prepravny Poriadok [*Railroad Transportation Regulations*] (CZ)
ZPP .... Zrzeszenie Prawnikow Polskich [*Association of Polish Lawyers*] (POL)
ZPP .... Zwiazek Patriotow Polskich [*Union of Polish Patriots (1943-1946)*] (POL)
ZPP .... Zwiazek Przemyslu Piekarniczego [*Union of the Baking Industry*] (POL)
ZPPB .... Zarazna Pukovska Poljska Bolnica [*Regimental Field Hospital for Contagious Diseases*] (YU)
ZPPiS .... Zjednoczenie Pracownikow Panstwowych i Spolecznych [*Union of Government and Social Institution Employees*] (POL)
ZPPO .... Creeping Antitank Barrage, Rolling Antitank Barrage (RU)
ZPPP .... Zanzibar and Pemba People's Party (MAR)
ZPR .... Antiaircraft Machine-Gun Company (RU)
ZPr .... Antiaircraft Searchlight (RU)
ZPr .... Law on the Procuracy in the Bulgarian People's Republic (BU)
z pr .... Subsistence Officer (BU)
ZPR .... Zeleznicni Prepravni Rad [*Railroad Transportation Regulations*] (CZ)
ZPr .... Zenijni Prapor [*Engineer Battalion*] (CZ)
ZPR .... Zjednoczenie Przedsiebiorstw Rozrywkowych [*Association of Entertainment Enterprises*] (POL)
ZPRA .... Zimbabwe People's Revolutionary Army (MAR)
zprb .... Antiaircraft Searchlight Battalion (BU)
zprb .... Antiaircraft Searchlight Battalion (RU)
ZPRN .... Zarzad Przemyslu Rafinerii Nafty [*Administration of the Oil Refinery Industry*] (POL)
zprp .... Antiaircraft Searchlight Regiment (BU)
zprp .... Antiaircraft Searchlight Regiment (RU)
ZPRW .... Zrzeszenie Plantatorow Roslin Wloknistych [*Association of Fiber Planters*] (POL)
ZPS .... Low Velocity Layer (RU)
ZPS .... Underwater Sound Communication Station (RU)
ZPS .... Underwater Sound Communication, Underwater Acoustic Communication (RU)
ZPS .... Underwater Sound-Signaling Station (RU)
ZPS .... Zaklady Piwowarsko-Slodownicze [*Breweries*] (POL)
ZPS .... Zakon o Izboru Povremenih Sudija Okruznih Privrednih Sudova [*Law on Electing Temporary Judges of District Economic Courts*] (YU)
ZPS .... Zakon o Privrednim Sudovima [*Law on Economic Courts*] (YU)
ZPS .... Zarzad Portu w Szczecinie [*Administration of the Szczecin (Stettin) Port*] (POL)
ZPS .... Zavody Presneho Strojirenstvi [*Precision Machine Plants*] (CZ)
ZPS .... Zveza Pionirjev Slovenije [*Union of Pioneers of Slovenia*] (YU)
ZPT .... Comma (RU)
ZPTM .... DC Motors Plant (BU)
ZPTMB .... Zarzad Przemyslu Terenowego Materialow Budowlanych [*Administration of the Local Building Materials Industry*] (POL)
ZPTO .... Hoisting and Conveying Equipment Plant Imeni S. M. Kirov (RU)
ZPTS .... Zaklady Przemyslu Tworzyw Sztucznych [*Synthetic Products Plants*] (POL)
ZPU .... Antiaircraft Machine-Gun Mount (RU)
ZPU .... Given Track Angle (RU)
ZPU .... Zabezpeceni Pohranicniho Uzemi [*Border Area Defense*] (CZ)
ZPU .... Zjednoczenie Polskich Uchodzcow [*Association of Polish Refugees*] (POL)
zpv .... Antiaircraft Machine-Gun Platoon (RU)

ZU............ Storage, Memory (RU)
ZU............ Zahranicni Ustav [*Foreign Institute*] (CZ)
ZU............ Zamoreny Usek [*Contaminated Sector*] (CZ)
ZU............ Zarzad Uczelniany [*School Administration (of the Polish Youth League)*] (POL)
ZU............ Zastupitelsky Urad [*Representative Office or Mission*] (CZ)
ZU............ Zememericsky Ustav [*Geodetic Institute*] (CZ)
ZU............ Zemepisny Ustav [*Geographical Institute*] (CZ)
ZU............ Zemsky Urad [*Provincial Administration Office*] (CZ)
ZU............ Zpravodajska Ustredna [*Information Center*] (CZ)
zub............ Dental (RU)
Zub............ Zugbegleitpersonal [*Train Personnel (Excluding locomotive personnel)*] (EG)
ZubPr......... Zubolekarski Pregled [*Dentists' Review*] [*A periodical*] (BU)
ZUBRI......... Nondestructive Storage, Nondestructive Memory [*Computers*] (RU)
ZUC............ Zvezna Uprava za Ceste [*Federal Administration of Roads*] (YU)
ZUD............ Zapadoceske Uhelne Doly [*West Bohemian Coal Mines*] (CZ)
ZUD............ Zjednoczenie Urzadzen Dzwigowych [*Association for Hoisting Equipment*] (POL)
Zue............ Zugueberwachungsanlagen [*Train Control Installations*] (EG)
ZUES.......... Zimbabwe University Economic Society (MAR)
ZUFI........... Zambia Union of Financial Institutions (MAR)
zug............ Zugeteilt [*German*]
Zugres........ Zuyevka State Regional Electric Power Plant (RU)
ZUI............ Correspondence University of the Arts (RU)
ZUI............ Zaklad Uslug Inwestycyjnych [*Investment Service Enterprise*] (POL)
ZUK............ Astrocompass (RU)
ZUK............ Zavody Umelecke Kovovyroby [*Decorative Metalwork Plants*] (CZ)
ZUKiW......... Zjednoczenie Urzadzen Klimatyzacyjnych, i Wentylacyjnych [*Association for Heating, Air-Conditioning, and Ventilating Equipment*] (POL)
ZUKVRS....... Ultrashort Wave Radio Stations Plant (BU)
ZUL............ Zeitschrift fuer Lebensmitteluntersuchung und Forschung
ZULAWU...... Zambia United Local Authorities Workers Union (MAR)
ZUM............ Contaminated Area (RU)
ZUM............ Zaklady Urzadzen Mechanicznych [*Mechanical Appliance Factory*] (POL)
ZUM............ Zambia Union of Musicians (MAR)
ZUMA.......... Zambia Union of Musicians and Artists (MAR)
ZUMK.......... Taped Memory System (BU)
ZUNOO........ Zavod za Unapredenje Nastave i Opsteg Obrazovanja [*Institute for the Improvement of Teaching and General Culture*] (YU)
ZUNS.......... Zakon o Uredenju Narodnih Sudova [*Law on the Organization of People's Courts*] (YU)
ZUNVP........ Law on the Settlement of Some Questions of Pensions (BU)
ZUNZ.......... Zavodni Ustav Narodniho Zdravi [*Factory Public Health Institute (Attached to an industrial enterprise)*] (CZ)
ZUO............ Law on Suspended Sentences (BU)
ZUO............ Zakon o Upravnih Organih [*Law on Administrative Organs*] (YU)
ZUO............ Zboziznalecky Ustav Obchodu [*Commodity Study Institute of Trade*] (CZ)
ZUOLRS....... Zakon o Upravnih Organih v Ljudski Republiki Sloveniji [*Law on Administrative Organs in Slovenia*] (YU)
ZUP............ Law on Conditional Pardon (BU)
ZUP............ Zadanka a Uverenou Prepravu [*Request for Authorized Transportation*] (CZ)
ZUP............ Zakon o Opstem Upravnom Postupku [*Law on General Administrative Procedure*] (YU)
ZUP............ Zemsky Urad Ochrany Prace [*Provincial Office for Labor Protection*] (CZ)
ZUP............ Zone a Urbaniser en Priorite [*Priority Urbanization Zone*] [*French*]
ZUPO.......... Zimbabwe United People's Organization (PPW)
ZUPRO........ Zwiazek Uczestnikow Polskiego Ruchu Oporu [*Union of Participants in the Polish Resistance Movement*] (POL)
ZUPU.......... Zaklad Ubezpieczen Pracownikow Umyslowych [*Polish*]
ZUR............ Antiaircraft Guided Missile (BU)
ZUR............ Antiaircraft Guided Missile (RU)
zur............ Honored Teacher of the Republic (RU)
ZUR............ Zapadocesky Uhelny Revir [*West Bohemian Coal Basin*] (CZ)
ZUR............ Zarzad Urzadzen Rolnych [*Administration of Agricultural Establishments*] (POL)
Zurges......... Zurnabad Hydroelectric Power Plant (RU)
ZURS.......... Antiaircraft Guided Missile (BU)
ZURS.......... Antiaircraft Guided Missile (RU)
ZUS............ Alternate Communications Center, Alternate Signal Center (RU)
ZUS............ Law on Court Structure (BU)
ZUS............ Zaklad Ubezpieczen Spolecznych [*Social Security Agency*] (POL)
ZUS............ Zakon o Upravnim Sporovima [*Law on Administrative Disputes*] (YU)
ZUS............ Zavodni Ucnovska Skola [*Factory Apprentice School*] (CZ)
zus............ Zusammen [*Together, Totaling*] [*German*] (GPO)
Zus............ Zusammensetzung [*Composition*] [*German*]
Zus............ Zusatz [*Addition*] [*German*]
Zus-P......... Zusatspatent [*Addition to a Patent*] [*German*]
ZUstb......... Zemska Uradovna Statni Bezpecnosti [*Provincial Headquarters of the State Security Police*] (CZ)
ZUT............ Zaklad Uprawy Tytoniu [*Tobacco Cultivation Establishment*] (POL)
ZUT............ Zaklad Urzadzen Technicznych [*Engineering Equipment Plant*] (POL)
ZUUS.......... Zemedelsky Ustav Ucetnickospravovedny [*Agricultural Institute for Accounting and Administration*] (CZ)
ZUWZ(ND)... Zwiazek Uczestnikow Walki Zbrojnej o Niepodleglosc i Demokracje [*Union of Participants in the Armed Struggle for Independence and Democracy*] (POL)
ZUZ............ Zbornik za Umetnostno Zgodovino [*Collected Papers on the History of Art*] [*Ljubljana*] (YU)
ZUZ............ Zrzeszenie Uprawy Ziemi [*Association for Soil Cultivation*] (POL)
zv............ Bell (RU)
ZV............ Blanket Region [*Nuclear physics and engineering*] (RU)
zv............ Explosives Factory (RU)
ZV............ Incendiary Agent, Incendiary (RU)
ZV............ Incendiary Materials (BU)
zv............ Star (RU)
z-v............ Surface-to-Air [*Missile*] (RU)
zv............ Vocative [*Case*] (RU)
ZV............ Zagrebacki Velesajm [*Zagreb International Fair*] (YU)
ZV............ Zaprecna Vatra [*Barrage Fire*] [*Military*] (YU)
ZV............ Zastupce Velitele [*Deputy Commander*] (CZ)
ZV............ Zavodni Vybor [*Factory Committee, Establishment Committee*] (CZ)
ZV............ Zemske Velitelstvi [*Provincial Military Headquarters*] (CZ)
ZV............ Zemsky Vybor [*Provincial Committee*] (CZ)
ZV............ Zentralverwaltung [*Central Administration*] (EG)
ZV............ Zentralvorstand [*Central Executive*] (EG)
zv............ Ziva Vaha [*Live Weight*] (CZ)
zV............ Zur Verfugung [*At Disposal*] [*Business and trade*] [*German*]
ZV............ Zwischenverstaerker [*Intermediate Amplifier, Repeater*] (EG)
ZVA............ Zeitungsvertriebsamt [*Newspaper Distribution Office*] (EG)
ZVAK.......... Sprava Zasobovani Vodou a Kanalisace [*Water Supply and Sewage Management*] (CZ)
zvat............ Vocative [*Case*] (RU)
ZVD............ Zbrinjavanje i Vaspitanje Dece [*Care and Protection of Children*] (YU)
ZVD............ Zemedelske Vyrobni Druzstvo [*Agricultural Producer Cooperative*] (CZ)
ZVdbB(BHG)... Zentralvereinigung der Gegenseitigen Bauernhilfe (Baeuerliche Handelsgenossenschaft) [*Central Association of the Peasants Mutual Aid Association (Peasants Trade Cooperative)*] (EG)
zver............ Fur-Bearing Animal Breeding Farm [*Topography*] (RU)
zver............ Fur-Bearing Animal Sovkhoz, State Fur Farm [*Topography*] (RU)
ZVI............ Electromechanical Plant Imeni Vladimir Il'ich (RU)
ZVIL........... Zavody V. I. Lenina [*V. I. Lenin Works (Skoda Works in Plzen)*] (CZ)
ZVK............ Closed Military Cooperative (RU)
ZVL............ Law on Military Personnel (BU)
ZVL............ Reserve Veterinary Hospital (RU)
zvl............ Zvlastni [*Special*] (CZ)
ZVM............ Zvaz Vojenskej Mladeze [*Military Youth Alliance*] (CZ)
ZVMM.......... Zelezarny V. M. Molotova [*V. M. Molotov Iron Works*] [*Trinec*] (CZ)
ZVMO.......... Notes of the All-Russian Mineralogical Society [*A publication*] (RU)
ZVMT.......... Zelezarny V. M. Molotova v Trinci [*V. M. Molotov Ironworks in Trinec*] (CZ)
ZVNB.......... Zemliachestvo Vykhodtsev uz Naroda Bazombo (MAR)
ZVNMM........ Zemskoto Veke na Narodnata Mladina na Makedonija [*Territorial Council of the People's Youth of Macedonia*] (YU)
ZVO............ Law on Higher Education (BU)
ZVO............ Notes of the Eastern Branch of the Russian Archaeological Society [*A publication*] (RU)
ZVO............ Trans-Volga Military District (RU)
ZVO............ Zagrebacka Vojna Oblast [*Zagreb Military District*] (YU)
ZVO............ Zapadni Vojensky Okruh [*Western Military District*] (CZ)
ZVOBl.......... Zentralverordnungsblatt [*Central Decree Bulletin*] (EG)
zvod............ Chief of Water Transportation (RU)
ZVORAO...... Notes of the Eastern Branch of the Russian Archaeological Society [*A publication*] (RU)
ZVP............ Zastupce Velitele pro Veci Politicke [*Deputy Commander for Political Affairs*] (CZ)
ZVPP.......... Chief of Military Ration-Distributing Point (RU)
ZVPS.......... Zahranicni Vybor Poslanecke Snemovny [*Foreign Affairs Committee of the National Assembly*] (CZ)
ZVPSh......... Correspondence Higher Party School (RU)
ZVRPzS....... Zastupce Velitele pro Radiovy Pruzkum a Spojeni [*Deputy Commander for Radio Reconnaissance and Communications*] (CZ)
ZVS............ Sound-Locator Station (RU)
ZVS............ Zakon o Vojnim Sudovima [*Law on Military Courts*] (YU)

ZVS .... Zalozni Velitelske Stanoviste [*Reserve Command Post*] (CZ)
ZVS .... Zastupce Vojenske Spravy [*Military Directorate Representative*] (CZ)
ZVS .... Zavody Verejneho Skladovani [*Public Storage Enterprises*] (CZ)
ZVS .... Zavody Vseobecneho Strojirenstvi [*General Engineering Plants*] (CZ)
ZVS .... Zvezno Vrhovno Sodisce [*Federal Supreme Court*] (YU)
ZVShS......... Moscow Internal Grinding Machine Plant (RU)
ZVSNB .... Zemske Velitelstvi Sboru Narodni Bezpecnosti [*Provincial Command of the National Security Corps*] (CZ)
ZVSORGO... Notes of the East Siberian Branch of the Russian Geographical Society [*A publication*] (RU)
ZVST .... Zpravy Verejne Sluzby Technicke [*Reports of the Public Technical Service*] (CZ)
ZVT .... Law on Foreign Trade (BU)
ZVT .... Zakon o Vojnom Tuziostvu [*Law on Military Prosecutors*] (YU)
ZVT .... Zastupce Velitele pro Technicke Veci [*Deputy Chief for Technical Affairs*] (CZ)
ZVU .... Zavody Vitezneho Unora, Narodni Podnik [*"Victorious February" Plant, National Enterprise*] [*Hradec Kralove*] (CZ)
zvukobaza ... Sound-Ranging Base (RU)
zvukomaskirovka ... Sound Camouflage, Sound Concealment, and Deception (RU)
zvukopodrazh ... Onomatopoeic (RU)
zvukopost... Sound-Ranging Station (RU)
ZVV .... Zemske Vojenske Velitelstvi [*Provincial Military Command*] (CZ)
ZVVI .... Zveza Vojaskih Vojnih Invalidov [*Union of Disabled Veterans*] (YU)
ZVVS.......... Law on Universal Military Service (BU)
ZVVZ.......... Zavody na Vyrobu Vzduchotechnickeho Zarizeni [*Plants for Production of Air Technology Equipment*] (CZ)
ZVZ .... Zastupce Velitele pro Veci Zasobovani [*Deputy Commander for Supplies*] (CZ)
ZVZhPP....... Chief of Military Railroad Ration-Distributing Point (RU)
ZW.............. Zarzad Wojewodzki [*Voivodship Administration*] (POL)
Zw .... Zeitwort [*German*]
Zw .... Zellwolle [*Wool Rayon, Synthetic Wool, Rayon Staple Fiber*] (EG)
zw............... Zwany [*Called*] [*Polish*]
zw............... Zwar [*No Doubt*] [*German*]
Zw .... Zwiazek [*Association, Union*] (POL)
zw............... Zwischen [*Between, Among*] [*German*]
zw............... Zwykle [*Usually*] [*Polish*]
ZWAM .... Zatovo Western Friendship Society of Madagascar (AF)
ZWANN .... Zaklady Wytworcze Aparatury Niskiego Napiecia [*Low-Tension Equipment Plant*] (POL)
ZWAO.......... Zaklady Wytworcze Aparatury Oswietleniowej [*Lighting Equipment Plant*] (POL)
ZWAP.......... Zaklady Wytworcze Aparatury Precyzyjnej [*Precision Equipment Plant*] (POL)
ZWAWN ...... Zaklady Wytworcze Aparatury Wysokiego Napiecia [*High-Tension Apparatus Plant*] (POL)
ZWBK.......... Zentrale Werbekommission [*Central Recruitment Commission, Central Advertising Commission*] (EG)
Zwg .... Zweig [*Branch*] (EG)
ZWHA.......... Zambia Women's Hockey Association (MAR)
ZWK .... Zentrales Warenkontor [*Central Commodities Office*] (EG)
ZWL............. Zentralstelle fuer Wissenschaftliche Literatur [*Headquarters for Scientific Literature*] (EG)
zwl.............. Ziemlich Wenig Loeslich [*Only Slightly Soluble*] [*German*]
ZWLE .... Zaklady Wytworcze Lamp Elektrycznych [*Electric Bulb Plant*] (POL)
ZWM............ Zarzady Wodnych Melioracji [*Administration for Land Irrigation*] (POL)
ZWM............ Zwiazek Walki Mlodych [*Union of Young Fighters (1943-1948)*] (POL)
ZWME .... Zaklady Wytworcze Materialow Elektro-Technicznych [*Electrical Materials Plants*] (POL)
ZWMS .... Zwiazek Wiejskiej Mlodziezy Socjalistycznej [*Union of Peasant Socialist Youth*] (POL)
ZWO .... Nederlands Organisatie voor Zuiver-Wetenschappelijk Onderzoek [*Netherlands Organization for Pure Scientific Research*] (WEN)
ZWO .... Zuiver Wetenschappelijk Onderzoek [*'s-Gravenhage*]
ZWPP .... Zaklady Wytworcze Przyrzadow Pomiarowych [*Measuring Instrument Plants*] (POL)
ZWPPB........ Zjednoczenie Warszawskie Panstwowych Przedsiebiorstw Budowlanych [*Warsaw Association of State Construction Enterprises*] (POL)
ZWPT .... Zaklady Wytworcze Przedsiebiorstw Teletechnicznych [*Production Plants of the Telecommunications Equipment Enterprises*] (POL)
Zw Radz...... Zwiazek Radziecki [*Soviet Union*] [*Polish*]
ZWS .... Zaklady Wlokien Sztucznych [*Artificial Fiber Plants*] (POL)
ZWS-Chodakow ... Chodakowskie Zaklady Wlokien Sztucznych [*Chodakow Artificial Fiber Plant*] (POL)
ZWSI .... Zaklady Wytworcze Sprzetu Instalacyjnego [*Installation Equipment Plant*] (POL)
ZWT............ Zaklady Wytworcze Transformatorow [*Transformer Plant*] (POL)
ZWUT .... Zaklady Wytworcze Urzadzen Telefonicznych [*Telephone Equipment Plant*] (POL)
ZWUT .... Zaklady Wytworcze Urzadzen Teletechnicznych [*Telecommunications Equipment Plant*] (POL)
ZWV .... Zentrale Wagenverwaltung [*Central Railroad Car Administration*] (EG)
ZwV .... Zentrale Wagenwirtschaftsverwaltung [*Central Railroad Car Management Administration*] (EG)
ZWWWN...... Zaklady Wytworcze Wylacznikow Wysokiego Napiecia [*High-Tension Switch Plant*] (POL)
ZWZ............ Zwiazek Walki Zbrojnej [*Union of Armed Struggle*] (POL)
ZWZMP .... Zarzad Wojewodzki Zwiazku Mlodziezy Polskiej [*Voivodship Administration of the Polish Youth Union*] (POL)
ZYa............. Caisson (RU)
ZYa............. Storage Cell, Memory Cell (RU)
ZYaKOGO ... Notes of the Yakut Kray Branch of the Geographic Society [*A publication*] (RU)
ZYaP .... Nuclear Instruments Plant (BU)
ZYeS .... West European Union (RU)
z-yevrop..... West European (RU)
ZYFA........... Zambia Youth Football Association (MAR)
Zyl .... Zylinder [*Cylinder*] [*German*]
ZYS .... Zambia Youth Service (MAR)
ZYuZ .... West-Southwest (RU)
ZZ............... Restricted Area, Prohibited Area (RU)
ZZ............... Sugar Refinery (BU)
z-z .... Surface-to-Surface [*Missile*] (RU)
zz............... Zakladni Zavod [*Base Enterprise*] (CZ)
ZZ............... Zemedelske Zpravodajstvi [*Agricultural Information Service*] (CZ)
ZZ............... Zemljoradnicke Zadruge [*Agricultural Cooperatives*] (YU)
ZZ............... Zenijni Zaloha [*Engineer Reserve*] (CZ)
zZ .... Zur Zeit [*At the Time, At Present, Acting, Temporary*] [*German*] (GPO)
ZZ............... Zvezni Zavod [*Federal Institute*] (YU)
ZZ............... Zwiazek Zawodowy [*Trade-Union*] (POL)
ZZB .... Zwiazek Zawodowy Budowlanych [*Trade-Union of Construction Workers*] (POL)
ZzBuvo........ Zusatzbestimmungen zur Betriebsunfallvorschrift [*Regulations Supplementary to the Industrial Accident Regulations*] (EG)
ZZD .... Law on Obligations and Contracts (BU)
ZZD .... Law on the Protection of the State (BU)
ZZD .... Zveza Zenskih Drustev [*Federation of Women's Clubs*] (YU)
ZZDKSS...... Law on the Protection of State and Cooperative Socialist Property (BU)
ZZDS .... Zveza Zenskih Drustev Slovenije [*Federation of Women's Clubs of Slovenia*] (YU)
ZZE............. Zaklady Zbytu Energii [*Power Distribution Plants*] (POL)
ZZEE .... Zaklady Zbytu Energii Elektrycznej [*Electric Power Distribution Plants*] (POL)
ZZG .... Zwiazek Zawodowy Gornikow [*Trade-Union of Miners*] (POL)
ZZG .... Zyrardowskie Zaklady Garbarskie [*Zyrardow Tanneries*] (POL)
ZZh............. Agricultural Journal [*A publication*] (RU)
ZZH .... Zwiazek Zawodowy Hutnikow [*Trade-Union of Metallurgical Workers*] (POL)
ZZhBI .... Reinforced Concrete and Concrete Products Plant (RU)
ZZhBK......... Reinforced Concrete Structural Parts Plant (RU)
ZZI.............. Law on Obligations and Support (BU)
ZZI.............. Law on Property Insurance (BU)
ZZK .... Zakon o Zemljisnim Knjigama [*Law on Land Title Records*] (YU)
ZZK .... Zavodni Zamestnanecka Komise [*Factory Employment Commission*] (CZ)
ZZK .... Zwiazek Zawodowy Kolejarzy [*Trade-Union of Railroad Workers*] (POL)
ZZK .... Zwiazek Zrzeszen Kupieckich [*Union of Merchants' Associations*] (POL)
ZZLP .... Zwiazek Zawodowy Literatow Polskich [*Trade-Union of Polish Writers*] (POL)
ZZM............ Zarzad Zieleni Miejskiej [*City Administration of Parks and Gardens*] (POL)
ZZM............ Zwiazek Zawodowy Metalowcow [*Trade-Union of Metal Workers*] (POL)
ZZM............ Zwiazek Zawodowy Muzykow [*Trade-Union of Musicians*] (POL)
ZZMiP .... Zwiazek Zawodowy Marynarzy i Portowcow [*Seamen's and Longshoremen's Trade Union*] (POL)
ZZN .... Zavod Zdenka Nejedleho [*Zdenek Nejedly Plant*] [*Nachod*] (CZ)
ZZn............. Zemedelsko Zname [*Agrarian Banner*] [*A periodical*] (BU)
ZZNP .... Zwiazek Zawodowy Nauczycielstwa Polskiego [*Trade-Union of Polish Teachers*] (POL)
ZZNRM........ Zdruzenieto na Zurnalistite na Narodnata Republika Makedonija [*Association of Journalists of Macedonia*] (YU)
ZZNS .... Zeranskie Zaklady Napraw Samochodowych [*Zeran Automobile Repair Shop*] (POL)
ZZNV .... Law on the Defense of the People's Government (BU)